Who'sWho in America

Biographical Reference Works Published by Marquis Who's Who

Who's Who in America

Who Was Who in America

Historical Volume (1607-1896)

Volume I (1897-1942)

Volume II (1943-1950)

Volume III (1951-1960)

Volume IV (1961-1968)

Volume V (1969-1973)

Who Was Who in American History—Arts and Letters

Who Was Who in American History—The Military

Who Was Who in American History—Science and Technology

Who's Who in the Midwest

Who's Who in the East

Who's Who in the South and Southwest

Who's Who in the West

Who's Who of American Women

Who's Who in Government

Who's Who in Finance and Industry

Who's Who in Religion

Who's Who in American Law

Who's Who in the World

Who's Who Biographical Record—Child Development Professionals

Who's Who Biographical Record—School District Officials

World Who's Who in Science

Directory of Medical Specialists

Marquis Who's Who Publications/Index to All Books

Travelers' Guide to U.S. Certified Doctors Abroad

Who's Who in America®

41st edition
1980–1981
Volume 2

MARQUIS
Who's Who

Marquis Who's Who, Inc.
200 East Ohio Street
Chicago, Illinois 60611 U.S.A.

Library of Congress Catalog Card Number 4-16934
International Standard Book Number 0-8379-0141-3
Product Code Number 030236

Distributed in the United Kingdom by
George Prior Associated Publishers
37-41 Bedford Row
London WC1, England

Manufactured in the United States of America

Table of Contents

Standards of Admission

The foremost consideration in determining who will be admitted to the pages of *Who's Who in America* is the extent of an individual's reference interest. Reference value is judged on one or more of three factors: 1) the position of responsibility held, 2) the level of significant achievement attained in a career of meritorious activity, or 3) public interest.

Admissions based on the factor of position include the following:

- High-ranking members of the executive, legislative and judicial branches of the U.S government
- Officers on active duty beginning with the rank of major general in the Army, Air Force, and Marine Corps; and with rear admiral in the Navy
- Governors and selected cabinet officials of U.S. states, island possessions, and territories
- Judges of state and territorial courts of highest appellate jurisdiction
- Mayors of the larger U.S. cities
- Leading government officials of Canada and Mexico
- Principal officers of national and international businesses capitalized at or above a certain figure, or of the highest commercial "rating"
- Heads of the major universities and colleges
- Heads of leading philanthropic, cultural, educational, professional, and scientific institutions and associations
- Selected members of the National Academy of Sciences, the National Academy of Design, the American Academy and Institute of Arts and Letters
- Chief ecclesiastics of the principal religious denominations
- Recipients of major national and international awards
- Others chosen because of incumbency, authorship, or membership

Admissions based on individual achievement or public interest must be decided by a judicious process of evaluating qualitative factors. To be selected on this basis, a person must have accomplished some conspicuous achievement—something that distinguishes him or her from the vast majority of contemporaries.

Key to Information in this Directory

❶ **WELLINGTON, STANLEY ROBINSON,** ❷ advt. agy. exec.; ❸ b. Cleve., Feb. 22, 1921; ❹ s. Walter and Louise (Robinson) W.; ❺ B.A., Ohio State U., 1943, M.B.A., 1947; ❻ m. Anita Howland, Aug. 3, 1943; ❼ children—Mary Ellen Wellington Penrose, Susan Louise Wellington Jackson. ❽ Account exec. Clarke, Latham & Pease, Cleve., 1947-53, account supr., 1953-55; sr. v.p. mktg. services Bowman & Crowell, Cleve., 1955-57, pres., 1957-74, chmn. bd., 1974—; lectr. advt. Cleve. Coll. Liberal Arts, 1956-60. ❾ Active Boy Scouts Am.; mem. Cleve. Dist. Park Bd., 1963-65; trustee Wrightwood Jr. Coll. ❿ Served to maj. U.S. Army, 1943-46; PTO. ⓫ Named Man of Year, Cleve. Assn. Indsl. Advertisers, 1965; recipient Distinguished Public Service award Cleve. C. of C., 1975. ⓬ Mem. Am. Assn. Advt. Agencies, Am. Mktg. Assn. ⓭ Republican. ⓮ Methodist. ⓯ Clubs: Shady Knoll Country (Cleve.); Masons. ⓰ Contbr. articles to profl. publs. ⓱ Home: 220 Bluff Hills Rd Cleveland OH 44123 ⓲ Office: 11 Main St Cleveland OH 44102

Key

❶ Name
❷ Occupation
❸ Vital statistics
❹ Parents
❺ Education
❻ Marriage
❼ Children
❽ Career
❾ Civic and political activities
❿ Military record
⓫ Awards and certifications
⓬ Professional and association memberships
⓭ Political affiliation
⓮ Religion
⓯ Clubs (including lodges)
⓰ Writings and special achievements
⓱ Home address
⓲ Office address

The biographical listings in *Who's Who in America* are arranged in alphabetical order according to the first letter of the last name of the biographee. Each sketch is presented in a uniform order as in the sample sketch above. The many abbreviations used in the sketches are explained in the Table of Abbreviations.

Table of Abbreviations

The following abbreviations and symbols are frequently used in this Directory

***** (An asterisk) following a sketch indicates that it was researched by the Marquis Who's Who editorial staff and has not been verified by the biographee.

A.A. Associate in Arts
AAAL American Academy of Arts and Letters
AAAS American Association for the Advancement of Science
AAHPER Alliance for Health, Physical Education and Recreation
A. and M. Agricultural and Mechanical
AAU Amateur Athletic Union
AAUP American Association of University Professors
AAUW American Association of University Women
A.B. Arts, Bachelor of
AB Alberta
ABC American Broadcasting Company
AC Air Corps
acad. academy, academic
acct. accountant
acctg. accounting
ACDA Arms Control and Disarmament Agency
ACLU American Civil Liberties Union
A.C.P. American College of Physicians
A.C.S. American College of Surgeons
ADA American Dental Association
a.d.c. aide-de-camp
adj. adjunct, adjutant
adj. gen. adjutant general
adm. admiral
adminstr. administrator
adminstrn. administration
adminstrv. administrative
adv. advocate, advisory, adviser
advt. advertising
A.E. Agricultural Engineeer
A.E. and P., AEP Ambassador Extraordinary and Plenipotentiary
AEC Atomic Energy Commission
aero. aeronautical, aeronautic
aerodyn. aerodynamic
AFB Air Force Base
AFL-CIO American Federation of Labor and Congress of Industrial Organizations
AFTRA American Federation TV and Radio Artists
agr. agriculture
agrl. agricultural
agt. agent
AGVA American Guild of Variety Artists
agy. agency
A&I Agricultural and Industrial
AIA American Institute of Architects
AIAA American Institute of Aeronautics Astronautics
AID Agency for International Development
AIEE American Institute of Electrical Engineers
AIM American Institute of Management
AIME American Institute of Mining, Metallurgy, and Petroleum Engineers
AK Alaska
AL Alabama
ALA American Library Association
Ala. Alabama
alt. alternate
Alta. Alberta
A&M Agricultural and Mechanical
A.M. Arts, Master of
Am. American, America
AMA American Medical Association
A.M.E. African Methodist Episcopal
Amtrak National Railroad Passenger Corporation
AMVETS American Veterans of World War II, Korea, Vietnam
anat. anatomical
ann. annual
ANTA American National Theatre and Academy
anthrop. anthropological
AP Associated Press
APO Army Post Office
apptd. appointed
apt. apartment
AR Arkansas
ARC American Red Cross
archeol. archeological
archtl. architectural
Ariz. Arizona
Ark. Arkansas
Arts D. Arts, Doctor of
arty. artillery
ASCAP American Society of Composers, Authors and Publishers
ASCE American Society of Civil Engineers
ASHRAE American Society of Heating, Refrigeration, and Air Conditioning Engineers
ASME American Society of Mechanical Engineers
assn. association
asso. associate
asst. assistant
ASTM American Society for Testing and Materials
astron. astronomical
astrophys. astrophysical
ATSC Air Technical Service Command
AT&T American Telephone & Telegraph Company
atty. attorney
AUS Army of the United States
aux. auxiliary
Ave. Avenue
AVMA American Veterinary Medical Association
AZ Arizona

B. Bachelor
b. born
B.A. Bachelor of Arts
B. Agr. Bachelor of Agriculture
Balt. Baltimore
Bapt. Baptist
B.Arch. Bachelor of Architecture
B.A.S. Bachelor of Agricultural Science
B.B.A. Bachelor of Business Administration
BBC British Broadcasting Corporation
B.C.,BC British Columbia
B.C.E. Bachelor of Civil Engineering
B.Chir. Bachelor of Surgery
B.C.L. Bachelor of Civil Law
B.C.S. Bachelor of Commerical Science
B.D. Bachelor of Divinity
bd. board
B.E. Bachelor of Education
B.E.E. Bachelor of Electrical Engineering
B.F.A. Bachelor of Fine Arts
bibl. biblical
bibliog. bibliographical
biog. biographical
biol. biological
B.J. Bachelor of Journalism
Bklyn. Brooklyn
B.L. Bachelor of Letters
bldg. building
B.L.S. Bachelor of Library Science
Blvd. Boulevard
bn. battalion
B.&O.R.R. Baltimore & Ohio Railroad
bot. botanical
B.P.E. Bachelor of Physical Education
br. branch
B.R.E. Bachelor of Religious Education
brig. gen. brigadier general
Brit. British, Britannica
Bros. Brothers
B.S. Bachelor of Science
B.S.A. Bachelor of Agricultural Science
B.S.D. Bachelor of Didactic Science
B.S.T. Bachelor of Sacred Theology
B.Th. Bachelor of Theology
bull. bulletin
bur. bureau
bus. business
B.W.I. British West Indies

CA California
CAA Civil Aeronautics Administration
CAB Civil Aeronautics Board
Calif. California
C.Am. Central America
Can. Canada, Canadian
CAP Civil Air Patrol
capt. captain
CARE Cooperative American Relief Everywhere
Cath. Catholic
cav. cavalry
CBC Canadian Broadcasting Company
CBI China, Burma, India Theatre of Operations
CBS Columbia Broadcasting System
CCC Commodity Credit Corporation
CCNY City College of New York
CCU Cardiac Care Unit
CD Civil Defense
C.E. Corps of Engineers, Civil Engineer
CENTO Central Treaty Organization
CERN European Organization of Nuclear Research
cert. certificate, certification, certified
CETA Comprehensive Employment Training Act
CFL Canadian Football League
ch. church
Ch.D. Doctor of Chemistry
chem. chemical
Chem. E. Chemical Engineer
Chgo. Chicago
chirurg. chirurgical
chmn. chairman
chpt. chapter
CIA Central Intelligence Agency
CIC Counter Intelligence Corps
Cin. Cincinnati
Cleve. Cleveland
climatol. climatological
clin. clinical
clk. clerk
C.L.U. Chartered Life Underwriter
C.M. Master in Surgery
C.& N.W.Ry. Chicago & Northwestern Railway
CO Colorado
Co. Company
COF Catholic Order of Foresters
C. of C. Chamber of Commerce
col. colonel
coll. college
Colo. Colorado
com. committee
comd. commanded
comdg. commanding

comdr. commander
comdt. commandant
commd. commissioned
comml. commercial
commn. commission
commr. commissioner
condr. conductor
Conf. Conference
Congl. Congregational
Conglist. Congregationalist
Conn. Connecticut
cons. consultant, consulting
consol. consolidated
constl. constitutional
constn. constitution
constrn. construction
contbd. contributed
contbg. contributing
contbn. contribution
contbr. contributor
Conv. Convention
coop., co-op. cooperative
CORDS Civil Operations and Revolutionary Development Support
CORE Congress of Racial Equality
corp. corporation, corporate
corr. correspondent, corresponding, correspondence
C.&O.Ry. Chesapeake & Ohio Railway
C.P.A. Certified Public Accountant
C.P.C.U. Chartered property and casualty underwriter
C.P.H. Certificate of Public Health
cpl. corporal
CPR Cardiac Pulmonary Resuscitation
C.P.Ry. Canadian Pacific Railway
C.S. Christian Science
C.S.B. Bachelor of Christian Science
CSC Civil Service Commission
C.S.D. Doctor of Christian Science
CT Connecticut
ct. Court
CWS Chemical Warfare Service
C.Z. Canal Zone

d. daughter
D. Doctor
D.Agr. Doctor of Agriculture
DAR Daughters of the American Revolution
dau. daughter
DAV Disabled American Veterans
D.C., DC District of Columbia
D.C.L. Doctor of Civil Law
D.C.S. Doctor of Commercial Science
D.D. Doctor of Divinity
D.D.S. Doctor of Dental Surgery
DE Delaware
dec. deceased
def. defense
Del. Delaware
del. delegate, delegation
Dem. Democrat, Democratic
D.Eng. Doctor of Engineering
denom. denomination, denominational
dep. deputy
dept. department
dermatol. dermatological
desc. descendant
devel. development, developmental
D.F.A. Doctor of Fine Arts
D.F.C. Distinguished Flying Cross
D.H.L. Doctor of Hebrew Literature
dir. director
dist. district
distbg. distributing
distbn. distribution
distbr. distributor
disting. distinguished
div. division, divinity, divorce
D.Litt. Doctor of Literature
D.M.D. Doctor of Medical Dentistry
D.M.S. Doctor of Medical Science
D.O. Doctor of Osteopathy
D.P.H. Diploma in Public Health
D.R. Daughters of the Revolution
Dr. Drive
D.R.E. Doctor of Religious Education
Dr.P.H. Doctor of Public Health, Doctor of Public Hygiene
D.S.C. Distinguished Service Cross
D.Sc. Doctor of Science
D.S.M. Distinguished Service Medal
D.S.T. Doctor of Sacred Theology
D.T.M. Doctor of Tropical Medicine
D.V.M. Doctor of Veterinary Medicine
D.V.S. Doctor of Veterinary Surgery

E. East
E. and P. Extraordinary and Plenipotentiary
Eccles. Ecclesiastical
ecol. ecology, ecological
econ. economic
ECOSOC Economic and Social Council (of the UN)
E.D. Doctor of Engineering
ed. educated
Ed.B. Bachelor of Education
Ed.D. Doctor of Education
edit. edition
Ed.M. Master of Education
edn. education
ednl. educational
EDP electronic data processing
Ed.S. Specialist in Education
E.E. Electrical Engineer
E.E. and M.P. Envoy Extraordinary and Minister Plenipotentiary
EEC European Economic Community
EEG electroencephalogram
EEO Equal Employment Opportunity
EKG electrocardiogram
E.Ger. German Democratic Republic
elec. electrical
electrochem. electrochemical
electrophys. electrophysical
elem. elementary
E.M. Engineer of Mines
ency. encyclopedia
Eng. England
engr. engineer
engring. engineering
entomol. entomological
environ. environmental, environment
EPA Environmental Protection Agency
epidemiol. epidemiological
Episc. Episcopalian
ERA Equal Rights Amendment
ERDA Energy Research and Development Administration
ESEA Elementary and Secondary Education Act
ESSA Environmental Science Services Administration
ethnol. ethnological
ETO European Theatre of Operations
Evang. Evangelical
exam. examination, examining
exec. executive
exhbn. exhibition
expdn. expedition
expn. exposition
expt. experiment
exptl. experimental

F.A. Field Artillery
FAA Federal Aviation Administration
FAO Food and Agriculture Organization (of the UN)
FBI Federal Bureau of Investigation
FCA Farm Credit Administration
FCC Federal Communication Commission
FCDA Federal Civil Defense Administration
FDA Food and Drug Administration
FDIA Federal Deposit Insurance Administration
FDIC Federal Deposit Insurance Corporation
F.E. Forest Engineer
FEA Federal Energy Administration
fed. federal
fedn. federation
fgn. foreign
FHA Federal Housing Administration
fin. financial, finance
FL Florida
Fla. Florida
FMC Federal Maritime Commission
FOA Foreign Operations Administration
found. foundation
FPC Federal Power Commission
FPO Fleet Post Office
frat. fraternity
FRS Federal Reserve System
FSA Federal Security Agency
Ft. Fort
FTC Federal Trade Commission

G-1 (or other number) Division of General Staff
Ga., GA Georgia
GAO General Accounting Office
gastroent. gastroenterological
GATT General Agreement of Tariff and Trades
gen. general
geneal. genealogical
geod. geodetic
geog. geographic, geographical
geol. geological
geophys. geophysical
gerontol. gerontological
G.H.Q. General Headquarters
G.N.Ry. Great Northern Railway
gov. governor
govt. government
govtl. governmental
GPO Government Printing Office
grad. graduate, graduated
GSA General Services Administration
Gt. Great
GU Guam
gynecol. gynecological

hdqrs. headquarters
HEW Department of Health, Education and Welfare
H.H.D. Doctor of Humanities
HHFA Housing and Home Finance Agency
HI Hawaii
hist. historical, historic
H.M. Master of Humanics
homeo. homeopathic
hon. honorary, honorable
Ho. of Dels. House of Delegates
Ho. of Reps. House of Representatives
hort. horticultural
hosp. hospital
HUD Department of Housing and Urban Development
Hwy. Highway
hydrog. hydrographic

IA Iowa
IAEA International Atomic Energy Agency
IBM International Business Machines Corporation
IBRD International Bank for Reconstruction and Development
ICA International Cooperation Administration
ICC Interstate Commerce Commission
ICU Intensive Care Unit
ID Idaho
IEEE Institute of Electrical and Electronics Engineers
IFC International Finance Corporation
IGY International Geophysical Year
IL Illinois
Ill. Illinois
illus. illustrated
ILO International Labor Organization
IMF International Monetary Fund
IN Indiana
Inc. Incorporated
ind. independent
Ind. Indiana
Indpls. Indianapolis
indsl. industrial
inf. infantry
info. information
ins. insurance
insp. inspector
insp. gen. inspector general
inst. institute
instl. institutional
instn. institution
instr. instructor
instrn. instruction
internat. international
intro. introduction
IRE Institute of Radio Engineers
IRS Internal Revenue Service
ITT International Telephone & Telegraph Corporation

J.B. Jurum Baccolaureus
J.C.B. Juris Canonici Bachelor
J.C.L. Juris Canonici Lector
J.D. Juris Doctor
j.g. junior grade
jour. journal
jr. junior
J.S.D. Jurum Scientiae Doctor
J.U.D. Juris Utriusque Doctor
Judge Adv. Gen. Judge Advocate General

Kans. Kansas
K.C. Knights of Columbus
K.P. Knights of Pythias
KS Kansas
K.T. Knight Templar
Ky., KY Kentucky

La., LA Louisiana
lab. laboratory
lang. language
laryngol. laryngological
LB Labrador
lectr. lecturer
legis. legislation, legislative
L.H.D. Doctor of Humane Letters
L.I. Long Island
lic. licensed, license
L.I.R.R. Long Island Railroad
lit. literary, literature
Litt. B. Bachelor of Letters
Litt. D. Doctor of Letters
LL.B. Bachelor of Laws
LL.D. Doctor of Laws
LL.M. Master of Laws
Ln. Lane
L.&N.R.R. Louisville & Nashville Railroad
L.S. Library Science (in degree)
lt. lieutenant
Ltd. Limited
Luth. Lutheran
LWV League of Women Voters

m. married
M. Master
M.A. Master of Arts
MA Massachusetts
mag. magazine
M.Agr. Master of Agriculture
maj. major
Man. Manitoba
M.Arch. Master in Architecture
Mass. Massachusetts
math. mathematics, mathematical
MATS Military Air Transport Service
M.B. Bachelor of Medicine
MB Manitoba
M.B.A. Master of Business Administration
MBS Mutual Broadcasting System
M.C. Medical Corps
M.C.E. Master of Civil Engineering
mcht. merchant
mcpl. municipal
M.C.S. Master of Commercial Science
M.D. Doctor of Medicine
Md., MD Maryland
M.Dip. Master in Diplomacy
mdse. merchandise
M.D.V. Doctor of Veterinary Medicine
M.E. Mechanical Engineer
ME Maine
M.E. Ch. Methodist Episcopal Church
mech. mechanical
M.Ed. Master of Education
med. medical
M.E.E. Master of Electrical Engineering
mem. member
meml. memorial
merc. mercantile
met. metropolitan
metall. metallurgical
Met. E. Metallurgical Engineer
meteorol. meteorological
Meth. Methodist
Mex. Mexico
M.F. Master of Forestry
M.F.A. Master of Fine Arts
mfg. manufacturing
mfr. manufacturer
mgmt. management
mgr. manager
M.H.A. Master of Hospital Administration
M.I. Military Intelligence
MI Michigan
Mich. Michigan
micros. microscopic, microscopical
mil. military
Milw. Milwaukee
mineral. mineralogical
Minn. Minnesota
Miss. Mississippi
M.I.T. Massachusetts Institute of Technology
mktg. marketing
M.L. Master of Laws
MLA Modern Language Association
M.L.D. Magister Legnum Diplomatic
M.Litt. Master of Literature
M.L.S. Master of Library Science
M.M.E. Master of Mechanical Engineering
MN Minnesota
mng. managing
Mo., MO Missouri
moblzn. mobilization
Mont. Montana
M.P. Member of Parliament
M.P.E. Master of Physical Education
M.P.H. Master of Public Health
M.P.L. Master of Patent Law
Mpls. Minneapolis
M.R.E. Master of Religious Education
M.S. Master of Science
MS Mississippi
M.Sc. Master of Science
M.S.F. Master of Science of Forestry
M.S.T. Master of Sacred Theology
M.S.W. Master of Social Work
MT Montana
Mt. Mount
MTO Mediterranean Theatre of Operations
mus. museum, musical
Mus.B. Bachelor of Music
Mus.D. Doctor of Music
Mus.M. Master of Music
mut. mutual
mycol. mycological

N. North
NAACP National Association for the Advancement of Colored People
NACA National Advisory Committee for Aeronautics
NAD National Academy of Design
N.Am. North America
NAM National Association of Manufacturers
NAPA National Association of Performing Artists
NAREB National Association of Real Estate Boards
NARS National Archives and Record Service
NASA National Aeronautics and Space Administration
nat. national
NATO North Atlantic Treaty Organization
NATOUSA North African Theatre of Operations
nav. navigation
N.B., NB New Brunswick
NBC National Broadcasting Company
N.C., NC North Carolina
NCCJ National Conference of Christians and Jews
N.D., ND North Dakota
NDEA National Defense Education Act
NE Nebraska
N.E. Northeast
NEA National Education Association
Nebr. Nebraska
neurol. neurological
Nev. Nevada
NF Newfoundland
NFL National Football League
Nfld. Newfoundland
N.G. National Guard
N.H., NH New Hampshire
NHL National Hockey League
NIH National Institutes of Health
NIMH National Institute of Mental Health
N.J., NJ New Jersey
NLRB National Labor Relations Board
NM New Mexico
N.Mex. New Mexico
No. Northern

NOAA National Oceanographic and Atmospheric Administration
NORAD North American Air Defense
NOW National Organization for Women
N.P. Ry. Northern Pacific Railway
nr. near
NRC National Research Council
N.S., NS Nova Scotia
NSC National Security Council
NSF National Science Foundation
N.T. New Testament
NT Northwest Territories
numis. numismatic
NV Nevada
NW Northwest
N.W.T. Northwest Territories
N.Y., NY New York
N.Y.C. New York City
N.Z. New Zealand

OAS Organization of American States
Ob-Gyn obstetrics-gynecology
obs. observatory
O.D. Doctor of Optometry
OECD Organization of European Cooperation and Development
OEEC Organization of European Economic Cooperation
OEO Office of Economic Opportunity
ofcl. official
OH Ohio
OK Oklahoma
Okla. Oklahoma
ON Ontario
Ont. Ontario
ophthal. ophthalmological
ops. operations
OR Oregon
orch. orchestra
Oreg. Oregon
orgn. organization
ornithol. ornithological
OSRD Office of Scientific Research and Development
OSS Office of Strategic Services
osteo. osteopathic
otol. otological
otolaryn. otolaryngological

Pa., PA Pennsylvania
P.A. Professional Association
paleontol. paleontological
path. pathological
P.C. Professional Corporation
PE Prince Edward Island
P.E. Professional Engineer
P.E.I. Prince Edward Island
PEN Poets, Playwrights, Editors, Essayists and Novelists (international association)
penol. penological
P.E.O. women's organization (full name not disclosed)
pfc. private first class
PHA Public Housing Administration
pharm. Pharmaceutical
Pharm.D. Doctor of Pharmacy
Pharm.M. Master of Pharmacy
Ph.B. Bachelor of Philosophy
Ph.D. Doctor of Philosophy
Phila. Philadelphia
philharm. philharmonic
philol. philological
philos. philosophical
photog. photographic
phys. physical
physiol. physiological
Pitts. Pittsburgh
Pkwy. Parkway
Pl. Place
P.&L.E.R.R. Pittsburgh & Lake Erie Railroad
P.O. Post Office
PO Box Post Office Box
polit. political
poly. polytechnic, polytechnical
P.Q. Province of Quebec
P.R., PR Puerto Rico
prep. preparatory
pres. president
Presbyn. Presbyterian
presdl. presidential
prin. principal
proc. proceedings
prod. produced (play production)
prof. professor
profl. professional
prog. progressive
propr. proprietor
pros. atty. prosecuting attorney
pro tem pro tempore
PSRO Professional Services Review Organization
psychiat. psychiatric
psychol. psychological
PTA Parent-Teachers Association
PTO Pacific Theatre of Operations
pub. publisher, publishing, published
publ. publication
pvt. private

quar. quarterly
q.m. quartermaster
Q.M.C. Quartermaster Corps
Que. Quebec

radiol. radiological
RAF Royal Air Force
RCA Radio Corporation of America
RCAF Royal Canadian Air Force
R.D. Rural Delivery
Rd. Road
REA Rural Electrification Administration
rec. recording
ref. reformed
regt. regiment
regtl. regimental
rehab. rehabilitation
rep. representative
Rep. Republican
Res. Reserve
ret. retired
rev. review, revised
RFC Reconstruction Finance Corporation
R.F.D. Rural Free Delivery
rhinol. rhinological
R.I., RI Rhode Island
R.N. Registered Nurse
roentgenol. roentgenological
ROTC Reserve Officers Training Corps
R.R. Railroad
Ry. Railway

s. son
S. South
SAC Strategic Air Command
SALT Strategic Arms Limitation Talks
S.Am. South America
san sanitary
SAR Sons of the American Revolution
Sask. Saskatchewan
savs. savings
S.B. Bachelor of Science
SBA Small Business Administration
S.C., SC South Carolina
SCAP Supreme Command Allies Pacific
Sc.B. Bachelor of Science
S.C.D. Doctor of Commercial Science
Sc.D. Doctor of Science
sch. school
sci. science, scientific
SCLC Southern Christian Leadership Conference
SCV Sons of Confederate Veterans
S.D., SD South Dakota
SE Southeast
SEATO Southeast Asia Treaty Organization
sec. secretary
SEC Securities and Exchange Commission
sect. section
seismol. seismological
sem. seminary
sgt. sergeant
SHAEF Supreme Headquarters Allied Expeditionary Forces
SHAPE Supreme Headquarters Allied Powers in Europe
S.I. Staten Island
S.J. Society of Jesus (Jesuit)
S.J.D. Scientiae Juridicae Doctor
SK Saskatchewan
S.M. Master of Science
So. Southern
soc. society
sociol. sociological
S.P. Co. Southern Pacific Company
spl. special
splty. specialty
Sq. Square
sr. senior
S.R. Sons of the Revolution
S.S. Steamship
SSS Selective Service System
St. Saint
St. Street
sta. station
statis. statistical
stats. statistics
S.T.B. Bachelor of Sacred Theology
stblzn. stabilization
S.T.D. Doctor of Sacred Theology
subs. subsidiary
SUNY State University of New York
supr. supervisor
supt. superintendent
surg. surgical
SW Southwest

TAPPI Technical Association of Pulp and Paper Industry
Tb Tuberculosis
tchr. teacher
tech. technical, technology
technol. technological
Tel.&Tel. Telephone & Telegraph
temp. temporary
Tenn. Tennessee
Ter. Territory
Terr. Terrace
TESL Teaching English as a Second Language
Tex. Texas
Th.D. Doctor of Theology
theol. theological
Th.M. Master of Theology
TN Tennessee
tng. training

topog. topographical
trans. transaction, transferred
transl. translation, translated
transp. transportation
treas. treasurer
TV television
TVA Tennessee Valley Authority
twp. township
TX Texas
typog. typographical

U. University
UAW United Auto Workers
UCLA University of California at Los Angeles
UDC United Daughters of the Confederacy
U.K. United Kingdom
UN United Nations
UNESCO United Nations Educational, Scientific and Cultural Organization
UNICEF United Nations International Children's Emergency Fund
univ. university
UNRRA United Nations Relief and Rehabilitation Administration
UPI United Press International
U.P.R.R. Union Pacific Railroad
urol. urological
U.S. United States
U.S.A. United States of America
USAAF United States Army Air Force
USAF United States Air Force
USAFR United States Air Force Reserve
USAR United States Army Reserve
USCG United States Coast Guard
USCGR United States Coast Guard Reserve
USES United States Employment Service
USIA United States Information Agency
USIS United States Information Service
USMC United States Marine Corps
USMCR United States Marine Corps Reserve
USN United States Navy
USNG United States National Guard
USNR United States Naval Reserve
USO United Service Organizations
USPHS United States Public Health Service
U.S.S. United States Ship
USSR Union of the Soviet Socialist Republics
USV United States Volunteers
UT Utah

VA Veterans' Administration
Va., VA Virginia
vet. veteran, veterinary
VFW Veterans of Foreign Wars
V.I., VI Virgin Islands
vice pres. vice president
vis. visiting
VISTA Volunteers in Service to America
VITA Volunteers in Technical Service
vocat. vocational
vol. volunteer, volume
v.p. vice president
vs. versus
VT., VT Vermont

W. West
WA Washington
WAC Women's Army Corps
Wash. Washington
WAVES Women's Reserve, U.S. Naval Reserve
WCTU Women's Christian Temperance Union
W. Ger. Germany, Federal Republic of
WHO World Health Organization
WI Wisconsin
Wis. Wisconsin
WSB Wage Stabilization Board
WV West Virginia
W. VA. West Virginia
WY Wyoming
Wyo. Wyoming

YK Yukon
YMCA Young Men's Christian Association
YMHA Young Men's Hebrew Association
YM & YWHA Young Men's and Young Women's Hebrew Association
YWCA Young Women's Christian Association
yr. year

zool. zoological

Alphabetical Practices

Names are arranged alphabetically according to the surnames, and under identical surnames according to the first given name. If both surname and first given name are identical, names are arranged alphabetically according to the second given name. Where full names are identical, they are arranged in order of age — those of the elder being put first.

Surnames, beginning with De, Des, Du, etc., however capitalized or spaced, are recorded with the prefix preceding the surname and arranged alphabetically, under the letter D.

Surnames beginning with Mac are arranged alphabetically under M. This likewise holds for names beginning with Mc ; that is, all names beginning Mc will be found in alphabetical order after those beginning Mac.

Surnames beginning with Saint or St. all appear after names that would begin Sains, and such surnames are arranged according to the second part of the name, e.g., St. Clair would come before Saint Dennis.

Surnames beginning with prefix Van are arranged alphabetically under letter V.

Surnames containing the prefix Von or von are usually arranged alphabetically under letter V; any exceptions are noted by cross references (Von Kleinsmid, Rufus Bernhard; see Kleinsmid, Rufus Bernhard von).

Compound hyphenated surnames are arranged according to the first member of the compound.

Compound unhyphenated surnames common in Spanish are not rearranged but are treated as hyphenated names.

Since Chinese names have the family name first, they are so arranged, but without comma between family name and given name (as Lin Yutang).

Parentheses used in connection with a name indicate which part of the full name is usually deleted in common usage. Hence Abbott, W(illiam) Lewis indicates that the usual form of the given name is W. Lewis. In alphabetizing this type name, the parentheses are not considered. However if the namc is recorded Abbott, (William) Lewis, signifying that the entire name William is not commonly used, the alphabetizing would be arranged as though the name were Abbott, Lewis.

Who'sWho in America

LAARTZ, ESTHER ELIZABETH, interior designer; b. Adair, Iowa, May 28, 1913; d. Christian Henry and Pearl Ethel (Hardenbrook) L.; B.A., Riverside Jr. Coll., 1933; grad. Parsons Sch. Design, N.Y. Sch. of Design, 1943. Designer, mgr. studio interior design Bloomingdales, N.Y.C., 1944-51; mgr. studio interior design Gimbel Bros., Pitts., 1951-61; pvt. practice interior design, Los Angeles, 1963-70; interior designer Ross Thiele & Son, La Jolla, Calif., 1970-74, Wiseman & Gale, Scottsdale, Ariz., 1977—; mem. faculty Scottsdale Coll. Fellow Am. Inst. Interior Designers (pres. Western Pa. chpt. 1955-59, N.E. regional v.p. 1958, pres. Los Angeles chpt. 1967-69, nat. sec. 1959, regional v.p. Calif. South 1968-70). Republican. Home: 4129 E Indian School Rd Phoenix AZ 85018 Office: 7120 E Indian School Rd Phoenix AZ 85018. *Because of the special people with whom I have worked, I have never had the feeling of being a woman in a man's world, but that hard work, initiative, and talent can surmount any and all obstacles.*

LABARGE, MARY JANE, business exec.; b. Ticonderoga, N.Y., Nov. 30, 1930; d. Albert J. and Marguerite D. LaB.; student Katharine Gibbs Sch., N.Y.C. Corp. sec. Martin Marietta Corp., Bethesda, Md., 1977—, Martin Marietta Aluminum Inc., Bethesda, 1977—. Mem. Am. Soc. Corp. Secs Inc. Home: 7727 Heatherton Ln Potomac MD 20854 Office: 6801 Rockledge Dr Bethesda MD 20034

LA BARGE, PIERRE LAUCK, JR., mfg. co. exec.; b. May 29, 1925; s. Pierre Lauck and Elsie (Warnhoff) La B.; B.B.A., Washington U., St. Louis, 1948; m. Mary Ann Miller, 1948 (div. 1978); children—Pierre Lauck, Craig, Mark, Denise, Jon, Marie; m. 2d, Pauline C. Tostenson, 1979. With Valley Industries, St. Louis, 1948-52, v.p. sales, 1951, exec. v.p., 1952; founder, owner, mgr. LaBarge Pipe & Steel Co. and associated cos. (merger with Dorsett Electronics, Inc. 1967; name changed to LaBarge, Inc. 1968), St. Louis, 1953-67, chmn., chief exec. officer, 1967—; founder, dir., mem. exec. com. South County Bank, St. Louis. Bd. dirs. St. Louis U. High Sch., Downtown St. Louis, Inc.; mem. pres's. council St. Louis U. Served to 1st lt. USAAF, 1943-45. Mem. Met. St. Louis C. of C., Am. Petroleum Inst., Steel Service Center Inst. Clubs: Mo. Athletic, Sunset Country, Media, Washington U. (St. Louis). Office: 500 Broadway Bldg Saint Louis MO 63102

LABARRE, CARL ANTHONY, govt. adminstr.; b. Sherwood, N.D., July 16, 1918; s. William Paul and Josephine K. LaB.; student U. Mont., 1936-40; postgrad. Naval Acad. Postgrad. Sch., 1945-46; grad. Naval War Coll., 1958-59; grad. Advanced Mgmt. Program, Harvard U.; m. Persis Wester, Sept. 9, 1941; 1 son, William Paul, II. Commd. ensign U.S. Navy, 1941, advanced through grades to capt., 1971; served in various fin., inventory control systems and purchasing assignments, to 1971, insp. gen. Naval Supply Systems Command, to 1971; ret., 1971; dep. dir. materials mgmt. service Govt. Printing Office, Washington, 1971-75, dir. materials mgmt. service, 1975, asst. public printer, supt. documents, 1975—. Decorated Navy Commendation medal with V, Joint Service commendation medal, Legion of Merit with gold star. Club: Harvard Bus. Sch. (Washington). Office: 941 N Capitol St NE Washington DC 20402

LABELLE, DAVID MAURICE, photographer; b. Orange, Calif., June 7, 1951; s. Charles D. and Jeanetta Ruth (Miller) LeB.; grad. high sch.; m. Joyce Lynn French, Dec. 5, 1972; children—Charbonee Renée, Bergen David. Photographer, Star Free Press, Ventura, Calif., 1969-70, San Bernardino (Calif.) Sun Telegram, 1971-72; photog. chief Simi Valley (Calif.) Enterprise, 1973-74; photographer Ojai Valley News, Ojai, Calif., 1975-76; staff photographer Anchorage Daily Times, 1976; chief photographer Goleta (Calif.) Valley Today, 1976-77; photog. dir. Chanute (Kans.) Tribune, 1977—. Mem. Nat. (Named west coast Photographer of the Year 1970-72, runner-up Calif. press photographers. Mem. Ch. of Christ. Home: 1310 S Highland St Chanute KS 66720 Office: 15 N Evergreen St Chanute KS 66720. *I feel one can accomplish almost anything in this life. I have found that the achievement of any goal demands a sacrifice. Regardless of the field of endeavor, the price of success is always high. I have in the past sacrificed so much, for so little. I believe in success, but not at the expense of denying the Creator.*

LA BERGE, WALTER BARBER, govt. ofcl.; b. Chgo., Mar. 29, 1924; s. Walter C. and Marie J. (Barber) LaB.; B.S. in Naval Sci., U. Notre Dame, 1944, B.S. in Physics, 1947, Ph.D. in Physics, 1950; m. Patricia Anne Sammon, Sept. 5, 1949; children—Peter Robert, Steven Michael, Jeanne Marie, Philip Charles, Jacqueline Anne. Program engr. Sidewinder missile Naval Ordnance Test Sta., China Lake, Calif., 1950-55, program mgr., 1955-57; dir. engring. Western Devel. Labs., Philco-Ford Corp., Palo Alto, Calif., 1957-63, dir. Philco Houston ops., 1963-65, v.p. research and devel. corporate staff, Phila., 1965-66, v.p. Western Devel. Labs., 1966-67, v.p. electronics group, Palo Alto, 1967-71; dep. tech. dir. Naval Weapons Center, China Lake, Calif., 1971-73, tech. dir., 1973; asst. sec. for research and devel. U.S. Dept. Air Force, Washington, 1973-76; asst. sec. gen. def. support NATO, 1976-77; undersec. army, Washington, 1977—. Mem. panel on remotely piloted vehicles Def. Sci. Bd., 1971-72; mem. industry adv. com. on telecommunications Chief Naval Ops., 1972. Mem. adv. council Coll. Sci., U. Notre Dame. Served with USN, 1943-46. Recipient Centennial award U. Notre Dame, 1967; Superior Civilian Service award Navy Dept., 1972, Exceptional Civilian Service award Air Force, 1975. Office: Dept Army The Pentagon Washington DC 20310

LABES, LEON MARTIN, lawyer; b. N.Y.C., Aug. 7, 1913; s. Hyman and Anna Ethel (Rubel) L.; B.A., Bklyn. Coll., 1933; LL.B., Bklyn. Law Sch., 1936, J.S.D. cum laude, 1937; m. Peggy Karr, June 15, 1938; children—Barbara (Mrs. Howard R. Harrison), Steven Hugh. Admitted to N.Y. bar, 1937; mem. law firm Bainbridge Colby, Brown & Pollack, N.Y.C., 1938-42, Hartman, Sheridan, Tekulsky & Pecora, N.Y.C., 1942-52, Alderman & Labes, N.Y.C., 1952-55; pvt. practice, N.Y.C., 1955-70; mem. firm Auerbach & Labes, N.Y.C., 1970—. Cons. U.S. War Prodn. Bd., 1942-45; treas. dir. Lewisohn Copper Corp., 1959-66; exec. dir. Electronics Mfrs. Assn., N.Y.C., 1962-74; moderator Labor Relations Forum, Radio Sta. WEVD, N.Y.C., 1962-65; lectr. labor law Columbia, Coll. City N.Y., N.Y. U.; mem. Supreme Ct. Panel for Mediation of Med. Malpractice litigation, spl. master apptd. by appellate div. Supreme Ct. N.Y. County. Bd. dirs. Manpower Edn. Inst. Mem. Am. Bar Assn. (labor arbitration com.), N.Y. County Lawyers Assn. (labor com.), N.Y. State Bar Assn., N.Y. State Trial Lawyers Assn., N.Y. Urban League (dir.). Author: A Fresh Approach to the Problem of Strikes, 1967. Contbr. numerous articles to profl. jours. Home: 1010 Fifth Ave New York City NY 10028 Office: 605 3d Ave New York City NY 10016. *I have always emphasized the fact that nothing can be good for labor if it is not good for management and that nothing can be good for management unless it is good for labor. The two parties cannot exist without each other. A fairly paid worker requires a financially successful employer. An employer cannot become financially successful without satisfied workers. This concept has been of great help in my dealings with labor and management over the years.*

LABLANC, CHARLES WESLEY, JR., corp. exec.; b. Bayshore, L.I., N.Y., June 4, 1925; s. Charles Wesley and Anne (Dobson) LaB.; B.S., Tufts Coll., 1949; M.B.A., N.Y.U., 1952, Ph.D., 1956; m. Marie Dolan, Oct. 26, 1963; children—Charles Wesley III, Gregory, Suzanne. Securities portfolio mgr. Manhattan Life Ins. Co., N.Y.C., 1952-57; asst. to pres. Magnavox Co., Ft. Wayne, Ind., 1957-60; security analyst C.W. LaBlanc & Assos., N.Y.C., 1960-62; treas. Macke Co., Cheverly, Md., 1962-72, dir., 1974—; v.p., treas., dir. After Six, Inc., Phila., 1972—, pres. Bert Paley Ltd., Inc. subs., 1976-77; dir. Century Mgmt. Corp. Pres. Queens County Young Reps., 1955-57; bd. dirs. Temple U. Music Festival. Served with AC, USNR, 1943-46. Mem. Washington Soc. Investment Analysts, N.Y. Soc. Security Analysts, Financial Analysts Phila., Financial Execs. Inst., Am. Accounting Assn., Am. Soc. Ins. Mgmt., Pub. Relations Soc. Am., Nat. Assn. Bus. Economists, Nat. Investor Relations Inst. Home: 370 Aubrey Rd Wynnewood PA 19096 also 11 N Pompano Beach Blvd Pompano Beach FL 33062 Office: 2137 Market St Philadelphia PA 19103

LA BLANC, ROBERT EDMUND, utility exec.; b. N.Y.C., Mar. 21, 1934; s. Charles Wesley and Anne R. (Dobson) La B.; B.E.E., Manhattan Coll., 1956; M.B.A., N.Y. U., 1962; m. Elizabeth Lammers, 1962; children—Beth, Robert, Jeanne Marie, Paul, Michelle. With Bell System, 1956-69, seminar leader AT&T Long Lines, Cooperstown, N.Y., 1965-67, mktg. supr. AT&T Hdqrs., N.Y.C., 1967-68, planning engr. N.Y. Telephone, 1968-69; mgr. Salomon Bros., N.Y.C., 1969-73, v.p., 1973-75, gen. partner, 1975-79; vice chmn. Continental Telephone Corp., N.Y.C., 1979—; mem. space applications bd. Nat. Acad. Scis.; dir. Storage Tech. Corp., M/A-COM Inc. Served to 1st lt. USAF, 1956-59. Named Wall St. Leading Analyst, Instl. Investor Mag., 1973-78. Fellow Fin. Analyst Fedn.; mem. N.Y. Soc. Security Analysts (sr. analyst), Assn. Computing Machinery, Nat. Soc. Rate of Return Cons. Republican. Roman Catholic. Clubs: Univ., N.Y. U. Office: 405 Park Ave New York NY 10022

LABONTÉ, C(LARENCE) JOSEPH, entertainment co. exec.; b. Salem, Mass., Sept. 23, 1939; s. Arthur and Alice Bella (Lecombe) LaB.; B.S., Northeastern U., 1966; M.B.A. with distinction (Baker scholar), Harvard U., 1969; m. Donna Marie Chiaradonna, Aug. 2, 1959; children—Linda Jean, Joseph Michael. With H.P. Hood & Sons, Boston, 1958-63; project engr., mktg. coordinator Market Forge Co., Everett, Mass., 1963-67; with ARA Services, Inc., Phila., 1969-79, v.p. Food Services Co., 1971-72, pres. Western Co., Los Angeles, 1972-76, exec. v.p. ARA, Phila., 1976-79; pres.Twentieth Century-Fox Film Corp., Beverly Hills, Calif., 1979—. Nat. bd. dirs. Big Bros. Am., 1970-74; vis. bd. dirs. Northeastern U., 1974—; mem. Harvard Bus. Sch. Fund, 1971—. Recipient Brown award Harvard Bus. Sch. Mem. Harvard Bus. Sch. Assn. (dir. So. Calif. chpt.), Husky Assos. Northeastern U. Clubs: Philadelphia Country, Down Town, Vesper; Bankers (San Francisco). Home: 511 Hillbrook Rd Bryn Mawr PA 19010 Office: Box 900 Beverly Hills CA 90213

LABORDE, ALDEN JAMES, oil co. exec.; b. Vinton, La., Dec. 18, 1915; s. Cliffe E. and Hilda (Moreau) L.; student La. State U., 1932-34; B.S., U.S. Naval Acad., 1938; m. Margaret Bienuenu, Mar. 11, 1943; children—Susan, J. Monroe, John P., Stephanie, Jane. Engr., S.W. Richardson Oil Co., 1946-48; marine supt. Kerr McGee Oil Industries, 1948-52; pres. Ocean Drilling & Expdn. Co., 1953-74, chmn. bd., chief exec. officer, 1974—, also dir.; dir. Ocean Oil & Gas Co., Central La. Energy Co. Inc., Whitney Nat. Bank, Tidewater Inc., Raymond Internat. Inc., H.J. Wilson Co. Inc. Bd. adminstrs. Tulane U., 1973—; bd. regents Loyola U. South, 1967—; trustee Catholic U. Am., U.S. Naval Acad. Found. Served from ensign to comdr. USNR, 1938-46. Decorated knight St. Gregory the Great (Vatican); recipient Order St. Louis medal, 1976; Disting. Achievement award Offshore Tech. Conf., 1977; St. Mary's Dominican Coll. medal, 1978. Mem. Internat. Assn. Oilwell Drilling Contractors. (pres. 1973), Midcontinent Oil and Gas Assn. (pres. 1970-71), Nat. Petroleum Council, St. Vincent de Paul Soc. Home: 63 Oriole St New Orleans LA 70124 Office: 1600 Canal St New Orleans LA 70119

LABOUISSE, HENRY RICHARDSON, cons., former orgn. exec., former U.S. ambassador; b. New Orleans, Feb. 11, 1904; s. Henry Richardson and Frances Devereux (Huger) L.; A.B., Princeton, 1926; LL.B., Harvard, 1929; LL.D., U. Bridgeport, Princeton, Lafayette Coll., Tulane U.; m. Elizabeth Scriven Clark, June 29, 1935 (dec. 1945); 1 dau., Anne (Mrs. Martin Peretz); m. 2d, Eve Curie, Nov. 19, 1954. Admitted to N.Y. bar, 1930; practice with firm of Taylor, Blanc, Capron and Marsh, and successor, N.Y.C., 1929-40; mem. firm Mitchell, Taylor, Capron and Marsh, 1940-41; with State Dept., 1941-51, chief div. def. materials, 1943, chief Eastern Hemisphere div., 1944; minister econ. affairs Am. embassy, Paris, 1944-45; spl. rep. in France for FEA, 1944-45; spl. asst. to under sec. for econ. affairs, Washington, 1945-46; spl. asst. and econ. advisor to dir. Office European Affairs, 1946-48; head U.S. del. Econ. Commn. Europe, 1948; coordinator fgn. aid and assistance, 1948-49; dir. Office Brit. Commonwealth and No. European Affairs, 1949-51; chief ECA mission to France, 1951-52; chief MSA spl. mission to France, 1953-54; dir. UN Relief and Works Agy. for Palestine Refugees, 1954-58; cons. IBRD. 1959-61; dir. ICA, 1961; U.S. ambassador to Greece, 1962-65; exec. dir. UN Children's Fund (orgn. won Nobel Peace prize 1965), 1965-79. Bd. dirs. Farmers' Museum, Bassett Hosp., Cooperstown, N.Y.; trustee Clark Found., N.Y., Am. Farm Sch., Thessoloniki, Greece. Mem. N.Y. State Hist. Assn. (dir.), Council Fgn. Relations. Episcopalian. Clubs: Metropolitan, Chevy Chase (Washington); Century Assn., University (N.Y.C.). Home: 1 Sutton Pl S New York NY 10022

LA BOUNTY, HUGH ORVICE, JR., univ. adminstr.; b. Chgo., Sept. 22, 1927; s. Hugh Orvice and Dorothy (Cooper) La B.; B.A., U. Redlands, 1950, M.A., 1951; Ed.D., UCLA, 1961; m. Gwen Evans, Sept. 5, 1950; children—Brian, Mark, Kim, Paul, Eric. Mem. faculty Citrus Coll., Azusa, Calif., 1950-53; mem. faculty dept. social scis. and history Calif. State Poly. U., Pomona, 1953—, v.p. acad. affairs 1967-77, pres., 1977—; cons. in field. Chmn. univ. div. United Way, Region II, 1978-79. Served with USNR, 1945-46. Mem. Inland Valley World Affairs Council (dir.), Am. Assn. Higher Edn., Pomona C. of C. (dir. 1979—). Club: Commonwealth of Calif. Author: Government of California, 1957. Home: 1011 E Coronet Glendora CA 91740 Office: Calif State Polytechnic Univ 3801 W Temple Ave Pomona CA 91768

LABOV, WILLIAM, linguist; b. Passaic, N.J., Dec. 4, 1927; s. Benjamin and Rhea (White) L.; B.A., Harvard U., 1948; M.A., Columbia U., 1963, Ph.D., 1964; m. Teresa Gnasso, June 26, 1949; children—Susannah, Sarah, Simon, Joanna, Jessie. Indsl. chemist Union Ink Co., Ridgefield, N.J., 1949-61; asst. prof. dept. linguistics Columbia U., 1964-70; prof. linguistics and psychology U. Pa., Phila., 1971—. Served with USMC, 1952-54. Guggenheim fellow, 1970. Mem. Linguistics Soc. Am. (pres. 1979), Am. Acad. Arts and Scis. Author: The Social Stratification of English in New York City, 1966; Sociolinguistic Patters, 1972; Language in the Inner City, 1972. Asso. editor Language in Society, 1975—. Home: 204 N 35th St Philadelphia PA 19104 Office: 3733 Locust Walk Philadelphia PA 19104

LA BREE, JOHN WILLIAM, physician, univ. dean; b. Duluth, Minn., May 8, 1917; s. Herman J. and Lulu Edna (Kleis) LaB.; B.S., U. Minn., 1938, M.D., 1940; m. G. Anne Johnson, May 10, 1976. Intern, Ancker Hosp., St. Paul, 1940-41; resident internal medicine Cleve. Clinic, 1941-42; med. fellow U. Minn., Duluth, 1946-47, instr. medicine, 1947-51, clin. prof., 1960-75, prof. clin. scis., 1975—, dean Sch. Medicine, 1975—; pvt. practice medicine, specializing in cardiology and internal medicine, Duluth, 1951-70; co-founder St. Louis Park Med. Center, 1951; dir. med. edn. St. Marys Hosp., Mpls., 1970-75; vice chmn. Duluth Grad. Med. Edn. Council, Inc., 1975-79; chmn. hosp. staff adv. com. Found. for Health Care Evaluation, 1975; bd. dirs. Western Lake Superior Health Systems Agy. Bd. dirs. United Way of Duluth. Served with USAAF, 1942-46. Decorated Bronze Star medal. Diplomate Am. Bd. Internal Medicine. Fellow Am. Coll. Cardiology; mem. AMA, Am. Heart Assn., Minn. Heart Assn. (pres. 1970-71), Minn. Soc. Internal Medicine, Minn. Soc. for Study Diseases of Heart and Circulation, Hennepin County Med. Soc. (pres. 1972-73, chmn. bd. 1973-74), Twin Cities Diabetes Assn., Alpha Omega Alpha. Contbr. articles to med. jours. Home: 3121 E 1st St Duluth MN 55812 Office: U Minn-Duluth Sch Medicine Duluth MN 55812

LABREQUE, ALEXANDER A., pulp and paper co. exec.; b. Quebec City, Can., Oct. 20, 1914; s. Ernest and Ivy (Langlois) L.; LL.L., Laval U., 1936; m. Monique Paquet, June 5, 1942 children—Michel, Alice, Ernest, Suzanne. Called to Que. bar, 1936, created Queen's counsel, 1948; pvt. practice of law, Quebec City, 1936-60; chmn. bd., dir. Price Co., Ltd., Quebec City, 1960—, Que. Assurance Co., Gaspersia Pulp & Paper Co. Ltd.; dir. Terra Nova Properties, Ltd., Western Assurance Co., Royal Ins. Co. of Can., Roins Holding Ltd. Served to lt. comdr. Canadian Navy, 1941-45. Mem. Que. Bd. Trade (past pres.). Home: 600 Laurier Ave Quebec City PQ Canada Office: 65 Ann St Quebec City PQ Canada

LABROSSE, GUY, pharm. co. exec.; b. Montreal, Que., Can., Nov. 28, 1922; s. Eddy and Hortense (Crevier) LaB.; student Sir George Williams U.; m. Lucile Guay, June 21, 1947; children—Francine, Diane, Louise, Guy. With G. D. Searle & Co., 1951—, dir. v.p., dir. mktg., 1972-76, exec. v.p., gen. mgr. worldwide pharm./consumer products group U.S. ops., Chgo., 1976—. Mem. Pharm. Mfrs. Assn., Nat. Pharm. Council. Home: 541 Turilum Rd Lake Forest IL 60045 Office: Searle Pharmaceuticals Inc Box 5110 Chicago IL 60680

LABROSSE, GUY, pharm. co. exec.; b. Montreal, Que., Can., Nov. 28, 1922; s. Eddy and Hortense (Cravier) LaB.; student Sir George Williams U.; m. Lucile Guey, June 21, 1947; children—Francine, Diane, Louise, Guy. With G. D. Searle & Co., 1951—, dir. v.p., dir. mktg., 1972-76, exec. v.p., gen. mgr. worldwide pharm./consumer products group U.S. ops., Chgo., 1976—. Mem. Pharm. Mfrs. Assn., Nat. Pharm. Council. Home: 541 Turicum Rd Lake Forest IL 60045 Office: Searle Labs Div GD Searle & Co Box 5110 Chicago IL 60680

LA BUDDE, KENNETH JAMES, librarian; b. Sheboygan Falls, Wis., Jan. 20, 1920; s. Arno Peter and Claire (DeVoy) LaB.; A.B., U. Wis., 1941, B.L.S., 1942; student U. Chgo., 1943-44; M.A., U. Minn., 1948 Ph.D., 1954. Student asst. U. Wis. Library, 1939-42; sr. library asst. Milw. Pub. Library, 1942; librarian Sheboygan (Wis.) Press, 1944-46; instr. English, Milton (Wis.) Coll., 1946-47; dir. libraries U. Mo. at Kansas City, 1950—, asst. prof. history, 1958-61, asso. prof., 1961, prof., 1962—. Served with AUS, 1942-44. Mem. A.L.A., Am. Studies Assn., Bibliog. Soc. Am., Mo. Library Assn. (chmn. coll. and univ. div. 1954-55), Kansas City Posse of Westerners, Joseph H. Tedrow Library Assn. (adviser), Wis. Meml. Union, Mid-Continent Am. Studies Assn. (pres. 1963-64, arts editor jour. 1959-63), Orgn. Am. Historians, Soc. Archtl. Historians, Beta Phi Mu, Phi Kappa Phi, Phi Alpha Theta. Contbr. articles profl. jours. Home: 311 Brush Creek Blvd Kansas City MO 64112

LABUE, ANTHONY CHARLES, univ. dean; b. Rochester, N.Y., Jan. 1, 1918; s. John and Rose (LoVullo) LaB.; B.S., State Tchrs. Coll., Buffalo, 1940; Ed.M., U. Rochester, 1951; Ed.D., Syracuse U., 1954; m. Elizabeth Sutkins, June 26, 1937; 1 son, Anthony Charles. Elementary sch. tchr., Washington, 1941-43, Monroe County, N.Y., 1946-51; dir. student teaching Syracuse U., 1952-54; asso. prof., then prof. edn. George Washington U., 1954-62, asst. dean Sch. Edn., 1960-62; prof., dean Sch. Edn., Calif. State U., Northridge, 1962—; vis. prof. U. Calif. at Los Angeles, summers 1963-67. Mem. ednl. adv. bd. Epilepsy Found., 1960-63. Served to lt. USNR, 1943-46. Mem. Calif. Tchrs. Assn., Calif. Employees Assn., Am. Ednl. Research Assn., Calif. Coll. and Univ. Faculty Assn., Assn. Higher Edn., Council Exceptional Children. Contbr. articles to profl. jours. Home: 9321 Wystone Ave Northridge CA 91324

LABUNSKI, STEPHEN BRONISLAW, assn. exec.; b. Jordanow, Poland, Sept. 24, 1924; s. Wiktor and Wanda (Mynarski) L.; came to U.S., 1928, naturalized, 1943; student U. Kansas City (Mo.), 1946-49, George Washington U., 1950; m. Betty E. Marley, Oct. 2, 1947 (div. June 1963); children—Linda, Richard, Roger; m. 2d, Jeralyn LeBrun, Aug. 28, 1967. Adminstrv. asst. to U.S. Congressman Richard W. Bolling, 1949-51; with Storz Broadcasting Co., 1954-57, v.p., gen. mgr. outlet radio sta. WDGY, Mpls., 1955-57; v.p. ABC radio network, 1957; head broadcast div. Crowell Collier Pub. Co., 1958; v.p., gen. mgr. WMCA Radio/Straus Broadcasting Group, N.Y.C., 1958-65; pres. radio div. NBC, 1965-69; mng. dir. WMCA Radio, 1969-71; v.p., partner Chuck Blore Creative Services, 1971-75; exec. v.p. Merv Griffin Group Radio, 1975-77; exec. dir. Internat. Radio and TV Soc., N.Y.C., 1978—. Bd. dirs. Radio Advt. Bur., 1965-69, Nat. Assn. Broadcasters, 1965-67. Democratic candidate for Mo. Legislature, 1948. Served with AUS and USAAF, 1943-46. Mem. Advt. Council. Address: 30 E 37th St New York NY 10016 Office: 420 Lexington Ave New York NY 10017

LACAGNINA, MICHAEL ANTHONY, lawyer; b. Rochester, N.Y., July 6, 1932; s. Frank and Josephine (LoMaglio) L.; B.S. in Bus. Adminstrn., U. Ariz., 1955, LL.B., 1957; m. Mary Laura Mantle, June 8, 1952; children—John Michael, Gina Laura, Frank Anthony. Admitted to Ariz. bar, 1957; asst. U.S. atty., Tucson, 1958-60; partner firm Bilby, Shoenhair, Warnock & Dolph, Tucson, 1960—; dir. Dick Delfs Constrn. Co., Walker Lithograph Co. Served with USMCR, 1950-52. Fellow Am. Coll. Trial Attys.; mem. Am., Ariz., Pima County (exec. com.) bar assns., Nat. Assn. R.R. Trial Attys., Am. Bd. Trial Advs. (nat. exec. com.), Tucson Def. Attys. (pres.), Phi Delta Phi, Alpha Kappa Psi. Republican. Episcopalian. Home: 6960 E Taos Pl Tucson AZ 85715 Office: Valley Nat Bank Bldg Tucson AZ 85701

LACAYO, CARMELA GLORIA, corp. exec., polit. party ofcl.; b. Chihuahua, Mexico, June 28, 1943; d. Enrique Luis and Maria Louisa (Velazquez) Lacayo; came to U.S., 1944, naturalized, 1968; B.A., Immaculate Heart Coll., 1974; B.A., Regina Mundi Internat. U., Rome, Italy, 1971. Dir., Regis House Community Center, Los Angeles, 1965-67; dir. St. Andrews Center, Oakland, Calif., 1968-70; dir. govt. projects Am. Med. Mgmt. Corp., Los Angeles, 1971-72; adminstrv. coordinator Mayor's Office, City of Los Angeles, 1974-75; founder, exec. dir. Asociacion Nacional Pro Personas Mayores, Los Angeles, 1975—; 1st vice chairperson Democratic Nat. Com., 1977—; vis. prof. urban planning U. de San Buenaventura, Medellin, Colombia, 1972-74. Pres., founder Nat. Hispanic Inst. Public Policy, 1978—; bd. dirs. Nat. Council on Aging, 1978. Recipient Outstanding Community Service award Calif. State Assembly, 1977; named Latin Am. Woman of Year, Latino Media, 1977; hon. mayor, San Antonio, 1977. Mem. Nat. Assn. Pro Spanish Speaking (pres., founder), Nat. Assn. Hispanic Ams. (founder). Roman Catholic. Office: 3875 Wilshire Blvd Suite 401 Los Angeles CA 90010 also Democratic Nat Com 1625 Massachusetts Ave NW Washington DC 20036

LA CELLE, PAUL LOUIS, physician; b. Syracuse, N.Y., July 4, 1929; s. George Clarke and Marguerite Ellen (Waggoner) La C.; A.B., Houghton Coll., 1951; M.D., U. Rochester, 1959; m. June Dukeshire, May 23, 1953; children—Andrea Jean, Peter Theodore, Kristina Marie, Erik Clarke. Intern, U. Rochester Med. Center-Strong Meml. Hosp., 1959-60, resident, 1960-62; asst. prof. medicine U. Rochester, 1967-70, asso. prof., 1970-74, prof., 1974—, chmn. dept. radiation biology and biophysics, 1977—; cons. to govt. Mem. Gates-Chili Sch. Bd., Rochester, 1964-72; trustee Houghton Coll., 1976—. Served to lt. (j.g.), USNR, 1952-55. NIH spl. fellow, 1965-66. Mem. Biophys. Soc., Microcirculation Soc., European Microcirculation Soc., Am. Soc. Hematology, AAAS, Sigma Xi, Alpha Omega Alpha. Research in biophysics of blood cells, physiology of microcirculation. Office: Box RBB Med Center 601 Elmwood Ave Rochester NY 14642

LACEY, BEATRICE CATES, psychophysiologist; b. N.Y.C., July 22, 1919; d. Louis H. and Mollie S. (Libowitz) Cates; student Columbia U., 1935-38; A.B. with distinction, Cornell U., 1940; M.A., Antioch Coll., 1958; m. John I. Lacey, Apr. 16, 1938; children—Robert A., Carolyn E. Mem. staff Fels Research Inst., Yellow Springs, Ohio, 1953—, sr. investigator, 1966-72, sr. scientist, 1972—; instr. Antioch Coll., Yellow Springs, 1956-73, asst. prof., 1963-68, asso. prof., 1968-73, prof., 1973—; Fels prof. psychiatry Wright State U. Sch. Medicine, 1977—, acting sci. dir. Fels Research Inst., 1979—. Recipient Distinguished Sci. Contbn. award Am. Psychol. Assn., 1976. Fellow Acad. Behavioral Medicine Research, Soc. Exptl. Psychologists; mem. Soc. Psychophysiol. Research (dir. 1972-75, pres. 1978-79), Soc. for Neurosci., Phi Kappa Phi. Asso. editor: Psychophysiology, 1975-78. Research and publs. in psychophysiology of the autonomic nervous system. Home: 1425 Meadow Ln Yellow Springs OH 45387 Office: Fels Research Inst Wright State U Sch Medicine 800 Livermore St Yellow Springs OH 45387

LACEY, FREDERICK BERNARD, judge; b. Newark, Sept. 9, 1920; s. Frederick Robert and Mary Agnes (Armstrong) L.; A.B., Rutgers U., 1941; J.D., Cornell U., 1948; LL.D. (hon.), Montclair State Coll., 1971, Seton Hall U., 1973; m. Mary C. Stoneham, May 20, 1944; children—Frederick Bernard, James, Virginia, Robert, Mary, Kathleen, John. Admitted to N.Y. State bar, 1948, N.J. bar, 1952; asso. firm Whitman & Ransom, N.Y.C., 1948-53; asst. U.S. atty. for N.J., 1953-55, U.S. atty., 1969-71; practiced in Newark, 1955-69; partner firm Shanley & Fisher, Newark, 1955-69; U.S. dist. judge for N.J., 1971—. Served to lt. comdr. USNR, 1942-46. Mem. Order of Coif, Phi Beta Kappa. Office: US Dist Ct Dist NJ US Ct House Newark NJ 07102

LACEY, HOWARD ELTON, mathematician; b. Leakey, Tex., Feb. 9, 1937; s. J. D. and Lona Belle (Brice) L.; B.A., Abilene Christian Coll., 1959, M.A., 1961; Ph.D., N.Mex. State U., 1963; m. Bonnielie Brown, Aug. 16, 1958; children—Michael Thoreau, Christopher Brown, James David, Lie Scott. Asst. prof. math. Abilene Christian Coll., 1963-64; mem. faculty dept. math. U. Tex., Austin, 1964—, prof., 1974—. Nat. Acad. Scis. grantee, 1968-69, 72-73; NSF grantee, 1975-78. Mem. Am. Meth. Soc., Math. Assn. Am. Author: The Isometric Theory of Classical Barach Spaces, 1973. Home: 1805 Basin Ledge Austin TX 78746 Office: Dept Math Univ of Texas Austin TX 78712

LACEY, J.W., data processing and fin. co. exec.; b. London, Eng., May 1, 1930; s. William J. and Florence (Farbus) L.; B.A. with honors in physics, Oxford (Eng.) U., 1952, M.A. with honors, 1956; m. Edna Winifred Burns, July 28, 1951; children—Jonathan Charles, Erika Jane. Sr. sci. officer Govt. of U.K., 1952-60; U.S. liaison officer Brit. embassy, Washington, 1956-60; mgr. research and devel., spl. systems Control Data Corp., Bloomington, Minn., 1960-63, dir. ops., 1963, pres. Control Corp. subs., 1964-65, gen. mgr. Devel. and Standard Systems div., 1965, v.p. computer equipment group, 1966-67, v.p. corp. devel., 1967-71, v.p., sr. staff officer corp. plans and controls, 1971-73, sr. v.p. corp. plans and controls, chmn. mgmt. com., 1973-77; pres. Control Data Edn. Co., 1977-79, Control Data Info. & Edn. Systems Co., 1979—; dir. Computer Peripherals, Inc., GRACO, Inc.; chmn. bd. Control Corp., Adcomp Corp., 1963-65. Bd. dirs. Jr. Achievement Greater Mpls., 1966-77, Mpls. Acquatennial, 1975—. Served with Brit. Royal Navy, 1948-49. Mem. Greater Mpls. C. of C. (dir. 1975-79). Home: 7141 Gleason Rd Edina MN 55435 Office: Control Data Corp 8100 34th Ave S Minneapolis MN 55440

LACEY, JOHN IRVING, psychologist, physiologist; b. Chgo., Apr. 11, 1915; s. David and Cecelia (Burnstein) L.; A.B., Cornell U., 1937, Ph.D., 1941; m. Beatrice Lucile Cates, Apr. 16, 1938; children—Robert Arnold, Carolyn Ellen. Instr., Queen's Coll., Flushing, N.Y., 1941-42; faculty Antioch Coll., 1946-77, prof. psychophysiology, 1956-77; mem. staff Fels Research Inst., Yellow Springs, Ohio, 1946—; chief sect. behavioral physiology, 1946—; Fels prof. psychiatry Sch. Medicine, Wright State U., 1977—; cons. USPHS, 1957—, FDA, 1977—; Mem. bd. sci. counselors Nat. Inst. Aging NIH, 1977-80. Centennial scholar Johns Hopkins U., 1976. Served to capt. USAAF, 1942-46. Mem. Soc. Psychophysiol. Research (award for distinguished contbns. 1970, pres. 1961-62, dir. 1965-68), Am. Psychosomatic Soc. (dir. 1959-62), Soc. Exptl. Psychologists, Am. Psychol. Assn. (pres. div. physiology and comparative psychology 1969-70, mem. council 1964-68, 70-73, 78-79 dir. 1974-77, Distinguished Sci. Contbn. award 1976), AAAS, Psychonomic Soc., Soc. for Neurosci., Acad. Behavioral Medicine Research, IEEE, Internat. Brain Research Orgn., Sigma Xi, Phi Kappa Phi. Cons. editor Jour. Comparative and Physiol. Psychology, 1953-69, Jour. Psychosomatic Medicine, 1962-65, Jour. Psychophysiology, 1964-69, Jour. Physiol. Psychology. Contbr. articles to profl. jours. Home: 1425 Meadow Ln Yellow Springs OH 45387

LACH, ALMA, food editor, author; b. Petersburg, Ill.; d. John H. and Clara E. (Boeker) Satorius; Diplome de Cordon Bleu (Paris), 1956; Chevalier du Tastevin (Dijon), 1962; Confrerie de la Chaine des Rotisseurs, 1964; m. Donald F. Lach, Mar. 18, 1939; 1 dau., Sandra Judith. Feature writer Children's Activities mag., 1954-55; creator, performer TV show Let's Cook, children's cooking show, 1955; food editor Chgo. Daily Sun-Times, 1957-66; CBS-TV Food Show, 1962-66; appears with Hugh Downes Over Easy, Sta. KQED-TV; pres. Alma Lach Kitchens, Inc., 1966—, Alma Lach Cooking Sch., 1976—; lectr. U. Chgo., Downtown Coll., U. Md., 1962, Chgo. Alliance Française Cooking Sch., 1968-72, Detroit Kitchen Glamor Cooking Sch., 1972, Modesto Coll., 1978; resident master U. Chgo., 1978—. Recipient Pillsbury award, 1958; Grocery Mfrs. Am. Trophy award and Certificate of Honor award, 1959, 61. Mem. U. Chgo. Settlement League, Internat. Platform Assn. Clubs: Tavern, Quadrangle. Author: A Child's First Cookbook, 1950; The Campbell Kids Have a Party, 1953; The Campbell Kids at Home, 1953; Let's Cook, 1956; Candlelight Cookbook, 1959; Cooking ala Cordon Bleu, 1970; Alma's Almanac, 1972; Hows and Whys of French Cooking, 1975. Contbr. to World Book Yearbook, 1962-75, Grolier Soc. Yearbook, 1962. Food cons. to Food Bud. Mag.; columnist Modern Packaging, 1967-68, Lettuce Entertain You Enterprises, The Pump Room, Bitter End Yacht Club (V.I.). Home: 5750 Kenwood Ave Chicago IL 60637 Office: 710 N Rush St Chicago IL 60611. *The art of cooking rests upon one's ability to taste, to reproduce taste, and to create taste. To achieve distinction the cook must taste everything, study cookbooks of all kinds, and experiment constantly in the kitchen. I stress in my writing and teaching the logic of food preparation, for the cook who possesses logic, needs to know how to create dishes rather than being content merely to duplicate the recipes of others.*

LACH, DONALD F., educator, author; b. Pitts., Sept. 24, 1917; s. Frederick Carl and Bertha (Hilberer) L.; A.B., W.Va. U., 1937; Ph.D., U. Chgo., 1941; m. Alma E. Satorius, Mar. 18, 1939; 1 dau., Sandra Judith. Mem. faculty Elmira Coll., 1941-48; mem. faculty U. Chgo., 1948—, now Bernadotte E. Schmitt prof. modern history; vis. prof. Cornell U., summers 1945, 52, 63; Distinguished vis. prof. Kent State U., summer 1965; Rockefeller prof. history U. Delhi (India), 1967-68. Recipient Gordon J. Laing prize, 1967. Fulbright fellow to France, 1949-50; Social Sci. fellow to Europe, 1952-53; Smith-Mundt fellow to Formosa and Eastern Asia, 1955-56; Am. Council Learned Socs. fellow to Portugal, 1960; Doner fellow, Italy, 1965. Mem. Am. Hist. Assn., Soc. History Discoveries, Hakluyt Soc., AAUP, Assn. Asian Studies, Phi Beta Kappa. Author: Modern Far Eastern International Relations, 2d edit., 1954, reprinted 1975; Europe and the Modern World, 1952-54; The Preface to Leibniz Novissima Sinica, 1957; Asia in the Making of Europe, Vol. I, 1965, Vol. II, Part I, 1970, Parts 2 and 3, 1977; Asia on the Eve of Europe's Expansion, 1965; (with L. Gottschalk) Toward the French Revolution, 1973; (with E. Wehrle) International Politics in East Asia since World War II, 1975; also articles and revs. in field. Editor Judge Dee Detective Stories, 1977. Contbr. to Ency. Brit., Dict. History Ideas, Hakluyt Handbook, Dictionary Am. Biography. Clubs: Quadrangle, Tavern, Wine and Food Soc. (Chgo.); Resident Master (Shoreland). Home: 5750 Kenwood Ave Chicago IL 60637

LACHANCE, PAUL ALBERT, educator, clergyman; b. St. Johnsbury, Vt., June 5, 1933; s. Raymond John and Lucienne (Landry) L.; B.S., St. Michael's Coll., 1955; postgrad. U. Vt., 1955-57; Ph.D., U. Ottawa, 1960; m. Therese Cecile Cote, Aug. 6, 1955; children—Michael P., Peter A., M.-Andre, Susan A. Aerospace biologist Aeromed. Research Labs., Wright-Patterson AFB, Ohio, 1960-63; lectr. dept. biology U. Dayton (Ohio), 1963; flight food and nutrition coordinator NASA Manned Spacecraft Center, Houston, 1963-67; asso. prof. dept. food sci. Rutgers U., New Brunswick, N.J., 1967-72, prof., 1972—, dir. Sch. Feeding effectiveness research project, 1969-72; cons. nutritional aspects of food processing, food service nutrition; mem. vitamin adv. bd. Roche Chem. div. Hoffmann LaRoche Co.; ordained deacon Roman Catholic Ch., 1977. Served to capt. USAF, 1960-63. Mem. Am. Assn. Cereal Chemists, AAAS, Inst. Food Technologists, Am. Inst. Nutrition, N.Y. Inst. Food Technologists (chmn. 1977-78), Am. Soc. Clin. Nutrition, N.Y. Acad. Sci., Am. Dietetic Assn., Soc. Nutrition Edn., Am. Public Health Assn., Soc. for Advancement Food Service Research, Nat. Assn. Cath. Chaplains, Sociedad Latino Americano de Nutricion, Sigma Xi, Delta Epsilon Sigma. Mem. editorial adv. bd. Sch. Food Service Research Rev., AVI Pub. Co., Inc., Nutrition Reports Internat., Profl. Nutritionist; contbr. articles to profl. jours. Home: 34 Taylor Rd RD 4 Princeton NJ 08540 Office: Rutgers U PO Box 231 New Brunswick NJ 08903

LACHENBRUCH, DAVID, editor; b. New Rochelle, N.Y., Feb. 11, 1921; s. Milton Cleveland and Leah Judith (Herold) L.; B.A., U. Mich., 1942; m. Gladys Kidwell, Dec. 12, 1941; 1 dau., Ann Leah (Mrs. Daniel J. Zulawski). Corr., Variety, also Detroit Times, 1940-42; reporter, asst. city editor, then wire editor Gazette & Daily, York, Pa., 1946-50; asso. editor TV Digest with Consumer Electronics, Washington, 1950-58, mng. editor, 1959-68, editorial dir., N.Y.C., 1968—; v.p. TV Digest, Inc., Washington, 1962—; columnist TV Guide, House & Garden, Panorama, Radio-Electronics mag.; contbr. articles to consumer mags. Served with AUS, 1942-45. Mem. White House Corrs. Assn., Union Internat. de la Presse Radiotechnique et Electronique. Contbg. editor N.Y. Times Ency. of TV; author: Videocassette Recorders—The Complete Home Guide, 1978; Color Television-How It Works, 1980. Home: 77 7th Ave New York NY 10011 Office: 510 Madison Ave New York NY 10022 also Cross Brook Rd Roxbury CT 06843

LACHMAN, LAWRENCE, bus. cons., former dept. store exec.; b. N.Y.C., Jan. 9, 1916; s. Charles and Dorothy (Rubin) L.; B.S. summa cum laude, N.Y. U., 1936; m. Judith Lehman, Apr. 8, 1945; children—Robert Ian, Charles Scott. Controller, James McCreery & Co., N.Y.C., 1938-46; treas., dir. Citizens Utilities Co., Stamford, Conn., 1946-47; treas. Bloomingdale's, N.Y.C., 1947-53, v.p. personnel and operations, 1953-58, exec. v.p. adminstrn. and personnel, 1958-64, pres., chief exec. officer, 1964-69, chmn. bd., chief exec. officer, 1969-78; chmn. bd., chief exec. officer Bus. Mktg. Corp., 1978—; dir. Am. Can Co., Cole Nat. Corp., Bank of N.Y., Barbizon Corp., Frances Denney, United Mchts. and Mfrs., Bank of N.Y. Co.; trustee Dry Dock Savs. Bank. Mem. Mayor's Mgmt. Adv. Bd., N.Y.C. Trustee N.Y. U., 1974—; bd. dirs., mem. exec. com. N.Y. Visitors Bur.; trustee Citizens Budget Commn.; mem. pres.'s adv. council N.Y. U. Sch. Bus. Served to maj. USAAF, 1942-46. Decorated Bronze Star; French Legion of Honor; recipient Madden award N.Y. U., 1969. Home: 104 E 68th St New York NY 10021 Office: 450 Park Ave New York NY 10022

LACHMAN, MARGUERITE LEANNE, econ. and real estate cons.; b. Vancouver, B.C., Can., Mar. 16, 1943; came to U.S., 1955; d. Wilfred Harry and Claire Elisha (Silverthorn) L.; B.A., U. So. Calif., 1964; M.A., Claremont Grad. Sch., 1966. With Real Estate Research Corp. subs. First Chgo. Corp., 1965—, sr. v.p., 1977-79, pres., chief exec. officer, 1979—, also dir. Author: (with Al Smith and Anthony Downs) Achieving Effective Desegregation, 1973; (with Susan Olson) Tax Delinquency in the Inner City, 1976; contbr. articles to periodicals. Office: 72 W Adams St Chicago IL 60603

LACHMAN, MORTON, writer, dir., producer; b. Seattle, Mar. 20, 1918; s. Sol and Rose (Bloom) L.; B.A., U. Wash., Seattle, 1939; m. Elaine, June 23, 1940; children—Joanne Lachman Culbert, Dianne Lachman Bishop, Robert. Producer, dir., head writer for Bob Hope TV spls., Flip Wilson shows, Emmy Award shows, Oscar Award shows; exec. producer TV series All in the Family, One Day At a Time; co-writer feature movies Yours, Mine and Ours, Mixed Company. Served with AUS, 1942-45. Recipient Emmy award for directing The Girl Who Couldn't Lose. Clubs: El Caballero, Queens, Marina City, Rangoon Racquet. Address: 4115 B Warner Blvd Burbank CA 91505*

LACHNER, BERNARD JOSEPH, hosp. adminstr.; b. Rock Island, Ill., Oct. 13, 1927; s. Bernard Joseph and Anne Lenore (Canty) L.; student U. Notre Dame, 1945-46, 47-48; B.S., Creighton U., 1950; M.B.A., U. Chgo., 1952; m. Berneice Groen, Aug. 16, 1952; children—Bernard Joseph, Thomas Frederick, James Timothy. From adminstrv. intern to adminstrv. asst. Iowa Meth. Hosp., Des Moines, 1950-54, asst. adminstr., 1954-58; asso. adminstr. Ohio State Univ. Hosps., Columbus, 1958-62, adminstr., 1962-71; asst. dean Ohio State U. Coll. Medicine, 1961-71, asst. v.p. med. affairs, 1971, v.p. administrv. operations, 1971-72, prof. grad. program hosp. and health services adminstrn., 1967-72; pres., chief exec. officer Evanston (Ill.) Hosp. Corp., 1972—; prof. Grad. Sch. Mgmt., Northwestern U., 1972—. Chmn. hosp. adv. com. Blue Cross Plan, 1965-71; vice chmn. adminstrs. council Mid-Ohio Health Planning Fedn., 1968-71; mem. commn. goals, adv. body to bd. dirs. Am. Soc. Hosp. Pharmacists, 1975-76; rep. Coordinating Council on Med. Edn., 1977—; mem. health services research tng. com. Nat. Center for Health Services Research and Devel., HEW, 1970-71. Chmn. Northbrook (Ill.) Heart Fund, 1974. Bd. dirs. Ohio League Nursing, 1969-70; bd. dirs. McGaw Med. Center, Northwestern U., 1972—, chmn. adminstrv. com., 1974-77; nat. adv. com. Sangamon State U., Springfield, Ill., 1973—; citizens com. U. Ill., 1973—. Served with AUS, 1946-47. Recipient Creighton U. Alumni Merit award, 1977; Disting. Service award Ohio State U. Hosp. and Health Service Adminstrn., 1978. Fellow Am. Coll. Hosp. Adminstrs. (regent 1970-71, gov. 1976-80); mem. Am. (ho. of dels. 1969-71, 75-78, council on legislation 1971-73, trustee 1978—), Ill. (trustee 1973-78, exec. com. 1975-78, chmn. 1976-77, chmn.-elect 1979), Ohio (pres. 1969-70) hosp. assns., Assn. Am. Med. Colls. (exec. com. Council Teaching Hosps.), Assn. Univs. for Research and Astronomy (dir. 1971-72), U. Chgo. Hosp. Adminstrn. Alumni Assn. (pres. 1967-68), Chgo. Council Fgn. Relations. Kiwanian (trustee 1969-70). Contbr. articles to profl. Jours. Address: Evanston Hospital 2650 Ridge Ave Evanston IL 60201

LACHNER, MARSHALL SMITH, mgmt. service exec.; b. Anna, Ill., May 15, 1914; s. Ernest George and Margaret (Newcomb) C.; student Northwestern U., 1933-34; grad. Wharton Sch. Bus., U. Pa., 1936; m. Eleanor Blochwitz, Dec. 30, 1935; children—Melody, Marshall, Geoffrey, Crispin, Brandon. With R.H. Macy & Co., 1936-38; with Colgate Palmolive Co., Jersey City, 1938-56, successively displayman, salesman, supr., sales mgr. Jersey City dist. and Chgo. dist., div. sales mgr., Berkeley, Calif., gen. sales mgr., v.p. soap sales, 1954-56; pres. Pabst Brewing Co., Chgo., 1956-57; pres., chief exec. officer B.T. Babbitt, Inc., N.Y.C., 1957-60; sr. v.p. cosmetics Revlon, Inc., 1960-62; pres. Lachner Assos., Inc., creative services to mgmt., Summit, N.J., 1962—; dir. C.W. Carnrick. Mem. exec. com. Nat. Football Found. and Hall of Fame; dir. Parkingston Found. Recipient award Poor Richard Club Phila., 1958; Applause award Sales Exec. Club N.Y., 1958; award Adcraft Club Detroit, 1958. Mem. Phi Kappa Psi. Presbyn. (elder). Club: Wis. Boat. Home: Thunder-Ridge Lodi WI 53555 also 1111 S Ocean Blvd Boca Raton FL 33432

LACHS, JOHN, philosopher, educator; b. Budapest, Hungary, July 17, 1934; s. Julius and Magda (Brod) L.; B.A., McGill U., 1956, M.A., 1957; Ph.D., Yale, 1961; m. Shirley Marie Mellow, June 3, 1967; children—Sheila Marie, James Richard. From asst. prof. to prof. philosophy Coll. William and Mary, 1959-67; prof. philosophy Vanderbilt U., 1967—. Past chmn. Tenn. Com. for Humanities. Recipient Phi Beta Kappa award for advancement scholarship, 1962; E. Harris Harbison award for distinguished teaching Danforth Found., 1967; Chancellor's cup Vanderbilt U., 1970, Madison Sarratt prize excellence undergrad. teaching, 1972. Mem. Am. Philos. Assn., Mind Assn., Royal Inst. Philosophy, Soc. Advancement Am. Philosophy (past pres.). Episcopalian. Author: Marxist Philosophy: A Bibliographical Guide, 1967; The Ties of Time, 1970; also articles. Editor: Animal Faith and Spiritual Life, 1967; Physical Order and Moral Liberty, 1969. Co-translator: Fichte, Science of Knowledge, 1970. Home: 2005 Maplemere Dr Nashville TN 37215

LACITIS, ERIK, journalist; b. Buenos Aires, Argentina, Dec. 10, 1949; s. Erik and Irene Z. L.; came to U.S., 1960, naturalized, 1965; student Coll. Forest Resources, U. Wash., 1967-71; m. Malorie Nelson, Aug. 30, 1976. Editor, U. Wash. Daily, 1970; pub. New Times Jour., 1970-71; reporter, pop-music cons. Seattle Post Intelligencer, 1972—; reporter, columnist Seattle Times, 1972. Recipient numerous awards from Wash. State chpt. Sigma Delta Chi; Nat. Headliners Club award, 1978. Lutheran. Office: PO Box 70 Seattle WA 98111

LACK, FREDELL, concert violinist; b. Tulsa, Feb. 19, 1922; d. Abram I. and Sarah (Stillman) L.; grad. Juilliard Grad. Sch. Music, 1943; m. Ralph David Eichhorn, July 10, 1947; children—Ardis, Eric Joel. Made debut as soloist with St. Louis Symphony, 1939; Town Hall debut recital, 1943; numerous recitals subsequently, at Town Hall, Carnegie Hall, Philharmonic Hall, Tully Hall (All N.Y.C.); tours in U.S., Can., Central Am., Hawaii, 1943—; featured soloist coast to coast Mut. Network radio program, 1946-47; concertmistress Little

Orch. Sch., N.Y.C., 1947-49; founder, 1st violin Lyric Art Quintet, Houston, 1956; rec. for Allegro, Mus. Appreciations, C.R.I.; artist in residence, prof. U. Houston, 1961—; ann. concert tour, Europe, 1959—; has appeared with Orchs. including Pitts., Portland, Salt Lake City, Kansas City, Houston, San Antonio, Albuquerque, Alaska, Tulsa, Oklahoma City, Baton Rouge, also BBC, Royal Philharmonic (London, Eng.), Rias (Berlin, Germany), Oslo, Stockholm Philaharmonics, Concertgebouw (Amsterdam), Rotterdam, Munich. Bd. dirs. Houston Humane Soc.; founder Young Audiences Chamber Music concerts, Houston. Recipient MacDowell Club Young Artists' Award, 1942, Nat. Fed. Mus. Clubs Young Artists award, 1943, Bklyn. Acad. Mus. Young Artists award, 1945; one of 12 laureates of Queen Elizabeth of Belgium Internat. Competition, 1951. Home: 4202 S MacGregor Way Houston TX 77021

LACK, LEON, biochemist, pharmacologist; b. Bklyn, Jan. 7, 1922; s. Jacob and Yetta (Wolf) L.; B.A., Bklyn. Coll., 1943; M.S., Mich. Stae Coll., 1948; Ph.D., Columbia U., 1953; postgrad. (Univ. postdoctoral fellow) Duke U., 1954-55; m. Pauline Kaplan, Feb. 14, 1948; children—Elias David, Joshua Morris, Johanna Elaine, Adina Roberta, Evonne Clara. Instr. in pharmacology end exptl. therapeutics Johns Hopkins U. Sch. Medicine, 1955-59, asst. prof. pharmacology and exptl. therapeutics, 1959-63; asst. prof. physiology and pharmacology Duke U. Med. Center, 1964-66, prof. pharmacology, 1966—, chief biochemist to clin. research, 1966-70. Served with USAAF, 1943-46; PTO. NIH grantee, 1960—. Mem. Am. Soc. Biol. Chemists, Am. Soc. Pharmacology and Exptl. Therapeutics. Jewish. Contbr. numerous articles to profl. publs.; research in pharmacology of cholesterol and lipids, pharmacology of intestinal bile salt transport. Home: 2936 Welcome Dr Durham NC 27705 Office: Box 3185 Duke U Med Center Durham NC 27710

LACKAS, JOHN CHRISTOPHER, educator; b. N.Y.C., Oct. 15, 1904; s. John William and Caroline (Mildenberger) L.; B.S., N.Y.U., 1930, M.A., 1931, Ph.D., 1938; J.S.D., St. John's U., 1938; LL.B., Rutgers U., 1929, LL.M., 1935; M.S.S., New Sch. Social Research, 1936; m. Genevieve Mary Meekins, June 29, 1935. Dir. Sch. Bus., Seton Hall U., 1938-42; commd. 1st lt. U.S. Army, 1942, advanced through grades to col., 1950; from asst. comdt. to comdt. U.S. Army Finance Sch., 1948-52; asst. comptroller for internat. affairs Army Gen. Staff, 1952-56; mem. faculty Indsl. Coll. Armed Forces, 1956-60; ret., 1960; prof. bus. Queensborough Community Coll., 1960-74, prof. emeritus, 1974—, dean adminstrn., 1960-68, acting pres., 1961-63; Coe fellow Inst. Am. Studies, 1960. Pres., Queensboro Council Social Welfare Agys.; bd. dirs. L.I. Ednl. TV Council. Decorated Legion of Merit; recipient Excellence in Teaching award Bd. Higher Edn., City U. N.Y. Mem. Acad. Polit. Sci., AAAS, Am. Econs. Assn., Am. Polit. and Social Sci. Assn., AAUP, Phi Delta Kappa. Author: (with Col. Seeds) Military Supply Management, 1957; also articles. Home: 41 Hicks Ave Syosset NY 11791 Office: Queensborough Community Coll Bayside NY 11364. *As I assess the past, it seems to me that I have always been concerned with people and in participating in causes. My concern for people apparently spurred me to inquiry which resulted in my educating myself and thereby maximizing whatever capabilities I may have. Then, too, I have been fortunate in having been provided the opportunity to become associated with activities which have given me the chance to perform tasks which I, apparently, was fitted to do. But, really, it appears to me, that much that has happened in my life was fortuitous or by the Grace of God.*

LACKEY, ROBERT (SHIELDS), ins. co. exec.; b. Bryn Mawr, Pa., Nov. 4, 1936; s. Homer C. and Elizabeth L. Lackey; B.S., U.S. Naval Acad., 1958; M.B.A., Harvard U., 1964; m. Sandra Frerichs, June 4, 1960; children—Courtney, Elise, Sara. Cons., McKinsey & Co., Inc., San Francisco, 1964-66, London, 1966-68; pres., chief exec. officer Atlantic Microfilm Corp., Spring Valley, N.Y., 1968-72; pres., chief exec. officer Mohwak Recreation Products, Ramsey, N.J., 1972-74; exec. v.p. Fidelity Union Life Ins. Co., Dallas, 1975—. Served with USAF, 1958-62. Clubs: Bent Tree Country, Lancers. Home: 5320 Bent Tree Dr Dallas TX 75248 Office: Fidelity Union Life Tower PO Box 500 Dallas TX 75221

LACKS, STANLEY BERNARD, banker; b. Weymouth, Mass., Sept. 11, 1916; s. Samuel and Emma (Lyons) L.; student Duke U., 1934-38; grad. Sch. Bank Adminstrn., U. Wis., 1956, Stonier Grad. Sch. Banking, Rutgers U., 1960; m. Kathryn Dorothy Ash, June 7, 1941; children—Stanley Bernard, Stephen Ash, Kathryn Dorothy. Asst. br. mgr. Weymouth Trust Co., 1939-43; with Fed. Res. Bank Boston, 1947—, gen. auditor, 1960-73, asst. v.p., asst. fed. res. agt., 1973—. Chmn. standing com. gen. auditors Fed. Res. Banks, 1968-69. Served with AUS, 1943-46. Mem. Bank Adminstrn. Inst. (pres. Boston conf. 1956-57), Boston Bank Officers Assn., Am. Inst. Banking. Home: 47 Alroy Rd South Weymouth MA 02190 Office: 600 Atlantic Ave Boston MA 02106

LACOSTE, PAUL, lawyer, univ. adminstr.; b. Montreal, Que., Can., Apr. 24, 1923; s. Emile and Juliette (Boucher) L.; B.A., U. Montreal, 1943, M.A., 1944, Licenciate in Philosophy, 1946, Licenciate in Law, 1960; postgrad. U. Chgo., 1946-47; Docteur de l'Universite, U. Paris, 1948; LL.D. (hon.), McGill U., 1975, U. Toronto, 1978; m. Louise Marcil, Aug. 31, 1973; 1 dau., Helene. Admitted to practice, 1960; prof. philosophy U. Montreal, 1946—, prof. law, 1960—, vice rector, 1966-68, exec. vice rector, 1968-75, rector, 1975—; moderator, commentator Canadian Broadcasting Corp., 1956-63; mem. firm Lalande, Brière, Reeves, LaCoste et Paquette, Montreal, 1964-66; mem. Royal Commn. on Bilingualism and Biculturalism, 1963-71, Que. Superior Council Edn., 1964-68, Que. Council Univs., 1969-77. Mem. Corp. de l'Ecole des Hautes Etudes Commerciales, 1968-75, Ecole Polytechnique, 1975—, Corp. du Coll. Marie de France; bd. dirs. Inst. Diagnostic and Research Clinics, 1975—; bd. dirs. Assn. des universités partiellement ou entièrement de langue française, 1975—, pres., 1978—. Mem. Assn. Univs. and Colls. of Can. (mem. com. of pres. 1975—, v.p. 1977, pres. 1978-79), Conf. Rectors and Prins. Que. Univs. (pres. 1977-79), Canadian Bar Assn., Assn. Canadienne des Professeurs d'Universite, Assn. Commonwealth Univs. (dir. 1977—). Author: (with others) La crise de l'enseignement au Canada Francais, 1961, Justice et Paix scolaire, 1962, A Place of Liberty, 1964, Le Canada au seuil du siecle de l'abondance, 1969. Contbr. articles to profl. jours. Home: 356 Woodlea Ville Mont Royal PQ Canada Office: University of Montreal PO Box 6128 Montreal PQ H3C 3J7 Canada

LACOUTURE, FELIPE ERNESTO, museum adminstr.; b. Mexico City, Feb. 25, 1928; s. Juan and Guadalupe (Fornelli) L.; architect's degree Universidad Nacional Autónoma de México, 1952; postgrad. Ecole du Louvre, Paris, 1952-53, Inst. de Cultura Hispánica, Universidad de Madrid (Spain), 1953-54; m. Josefina Dahl Cortés, Nov. 21, 1959; children—Yvonne Josefina, Jacqueline, Geraldine, Verónica, Juan Felipe. Dir. Mus. Art and History in Ciudad Juárez, 1964-70; head dept. regional museums Nat. Inst. Anthropology and History, 1970-73; dir. San Carlos Mus., 1973-77; head dept. plastic arts Nat. Inst. Fine Arts, 1974-77; dir. Nat. Mus. History, Mexico City, 1977—; prof. museology Churubusco Sch.; adviser in museology UNESCO. Decorated comendador Orden de Rio Banco (Brazil). Mem. Internat. Council Museums (sec. Mexican nat. com.), Internat. Council Monuments and Sites, Colegio de Arquitectos de México, Sociedad de Arquitectos Mexicanos. Club: France. Home: Alborada 180 Parques del Pedregal Mexico 22 DF Mexico Office: Museo Nacional de Historia Castillo de Chapultepec Mexico 5 DF Mexico

LACOUTURE, PAUL EDGAR, lawyer; b. Boston, Apr. 9, 1920; s. Edgar R. and Edith Gretchen (Vroom) L.; A.B. magna cum laude, Yale, 1942, LL.B., 1947; m. Jeannette Kittredge, Oct. 23, 1943; children—Peter V., Paul M., Linda, Helen, Anne. Admitted to Ohio bar, 1948, since practiced in Dayton; partner firm Smith & Schnacke, 1957—. Pres. bd. Dayton Sr. Citizens Center, 1961-63; v.p. Vol. Service Bur., Dayton, 1960-61. Served to lt. USNR, 1942-45. Mem. Am., Ohio (bd. govs. real property sect. 1953—, chmn. 1973-75), Dayton bar assns., Dayton Lawyers Club. Clubs: Miami Valley Hunt and Polo, Buz Fuz (Dayton); Hyannis Port (Mass.) Yacht. Home: 240 W Dixon Ave Dayton OH 45419 Office: 2000 Courthouse Plaza NE PO Box 1817 Dayton OH 45401

LACOVARA, PHILIP ALLEN, lawyer; b. N.Y.C., July 11, 1943: s. P. Philip and Elvira L.; A.B. magna cum laude, Georgetown U., 1963; J.D. summa cum laude Columbia U., 1966; m. Madeline E. Papio, Oct. 14, 1961; children—Philip, Michael, Christopher, Elizabeth, Karen, Daniel, Andrew. Admitted to N.Y. bar, 1967, D.C. bar, 1974, U.S. Supreme Ct. bar, 1970; law clk. to Circuit Judge Harold Leventhal, U.S. Ct. Appeals, D.C. Circuit, 1966-67; asst. to solicitor gen. U.S., Washington, 1967-69; asso. firm Hughes, Hubbard & Reed, N.Y.C., 1969-71, partner, N.Y.C. and Washington, 1974—; spl. counsel to N.Y.C. Police Commr., 1971-72; dep. solicitor gen. U.S. Dept. Justice, Washington, 1972-73; counsel to spl. prosecutor Watergate Spl. Prosecution Force, 1973-74; lectr. law Columbia U.; adj. prof. Georgetown U. Law Center; vis. lectr. various colls., univs.; mem. legal ethics com. D.C. Bar, 1976—, chmn. code subcom., 1977—; mem. Jud. Conf. D.C. Circuit, 1973—; spl. counsel U.S. Ho. of Reps. Com. on Standards Ofcl. Conduct, 1976-77; chmn. bd. trustees Public Defender Service for D.C., 1976—; sec. exec. com. bd. visitors Columbia U. Sch. Law. Mem. Am. Bar Assn. (ho. of dels. 1978—), Am. Law Inst. Roman Catholic. Clubs: Fed. City, Nineteen Twenty Five F St. Contbr. articles to profl. jours. Home: 4819 V St NW Washington DC 20007 Office: 1660 L St NW Washington DC 20036

LACROIX, FERNAND, bishop; b. Quebec City, Que., Can., Oct. 16, 1919; s. Jean-Charles and Cecile (Dore) L.; B.A., Sacred Heart Coll., Bathurst, N.B., 1937; licenciate in canon law, Angelicum U., Rome, 1949; Ph.D. (hon.), U. Moncton, 1971. Ordained priest Roman Catholic Ch., 1946; tchr. Holy Heart Sem., Halifax, N.S., Can., 1953-61; dir. Eudist students in Rome, 1950-53; superior Eudist Sem., Limbour, Que., 1961-66; superior gen. Eudist Fathers, Rome, 1966-70; bishop of Edmundston, N.B., Can., 1970—. Address: Centre Diocesain Edmundston NB E3V 3K1 Canada

LACY, ALEXANDER SHELTON, lawyer, utility co. exec.; b. South Boston, Va., Aug. 18, 1921; s. Cecil Baker and Lura Elizabeth (Byram) L.; B.S. in Chemistry, U. Ala., 1943; LL.B., U. Va., 1949; m. Carol Jemison, Aug. 8, 1952; children—John Blakeway, Joan Elizabeth, Alexander Shelton. Admitted to Ala. bar, 1949; asso. firm Bradley, Arant, Rose & White, Birmingham, Ala., 1949-54; with Ala. Gas Corp., Birmingham, 1954—, v.p., asst. sec., atty., 1969-74, v.p., sec., atty., 1974—. Pres., chmn. bd. Birmingham Symphony Assn., 1964-67; chmn. Birmingham-Jefferson Civic Center Authority, 1965-71. Served with USN, 1943-46. Mem. Am. Bar Assn., Ala. Bar Assn., Birmingham Bar Assn., Council Fgn. Relations, Am. Gas Assn., So. Gas Assn., Phi Gamma Delta, Phi Delta Phi. Democrat. Episcopalian. Clubs: Relay House, Downtown, The Club, Montgomery Country. Home: 3730 Montrose Rd Birmingham AL 35213 Office: 1918 1st Ave N Birmingham AL 35295

LACY, BILL N., architect; b. Madill, Okla., Apr. 16, 1933; s. Leon and Eunice L.; B. Arch., Okla. State U., 1955, M. Arch., 1958; m. Susan E. Wagner, Apr. 16, 1977; children—Jan, Kate, Shawn, Ross, Jessica. Design architect Caudill, Rowlett, Scott, Houston, 1958-61; prof., asso. chmn. dept. architecture Rice U., Houston, 1961-65; prof., dean sch. architecture U. Tenn. at Knoxville, 1965-70; v.p. Omniplan, Dallas, 1970-71; dir. architecture and environ. arts Nat. Endowment for the Arts, Washington, 1971-77; coordinator Fed. Design program, 1972-77; pres. Am. Acad. in Rome, N.Y.C., 1977-80, The Cooper Union, N.Y.C., 1980—. Bd. advisers Internat. Design Conf., Aspen, 1973—; mem. vis. com. visual and environ. studies Harvard U., 1980—. Served with C.E., U.S. Army, 1955-57. LeBrun Traveling fellow, 1958; Loeb fellow Harvard, 1973. Fellow AIA (corporate mem.; honor awards 1968). Contbr. articles, designs to profl. jours. Office: The Cooper Union Cooper Sq New York NY 10003

LACY, DAN MABRY, pub. co. exec.; b. Newport News, Va., Feb. 28, 1914; s. Tolbert Hardy and Ann Electa (Boatwright) L.; A.B. with honor, U. N.C., 1933, A.M. with distinction, 1935, Litt.D., 1968; m. Hope Lenore Leiken, Dec. 14, 1946; children—Philip Tolbert, Dudley Boatwright, Elizabeth Hardy. Instr. history U. N.C., 1935; asst. state supr. Hist. Records Sur., WPA, 1936-37, state supr., 1937-39, regional supr., 1939-40, asst. nat. dir., 1940-41; exec. sec. Com. Conservation of Cultural Resources, Nat. Resources Planning Bd., 1941- 42; asst. to archivist Nat. Archives, 1942-43, dir. operations, 1943-46, asst. archivist of U.S., 1947; asst. dir. processing dept. Library of Congress, 1947-50, dep. chief asst. librarian, 1950-51; asst. adminstr. Internat. Info. Adminstrn., Dept. State 1951-53; mng. dir. Am. Book Pubs. Council, 1953-66; sr. v.p. McGraw Hill Book Co., N.Y.C., 1966-74; sr. v.p., exec. asst. to pres. McGraw-Hill, Inc., 1974—. Mem. Pres.'s Nat. Adv. Commn. on Libraries, 1967-69, Nat. Commn. on New Technol. Uses of Copyrighted Works, 1975-78. Trustee, Nat. Humanities Center. Recipient Superior service medal Dept. State, 1952. Mem. Phi Beta Kappa, Tau Kappa Alpha. Club: Century Assn. (N.Y.C.). Author: The Library of Congress, a Sesquicentenary Review, 1950; Books and the Future—A Speculation, 1956; Freedom and Communications, 1961; Meaning of the American Revolution, 1964; White Use of Blacks in America, 1972; Birth of America, 1975. Editor: (with C.C. Crittenden) The Historical Records of North Carolina, 3 vols., 1938-40. Home: 52 W Clinton Ave Irvington NY 10533 Office: 1221 Ave of Americas New York City NY 10020

LACY, EDNA BALZ, mfg. co. exec.; b. Indpls., Sept. 21, 1906; d. Peter Fred and Lydia (Jose) Balz; B.A., U. Mich., 1928; LL.D., Franklin Coll., 1968; m. Howard John Lacy II, Nov. 29, 1934 (dec. Mar. 29, 1959); children—Margot Diane (Mrs. Robert Eccles), Howard John III, Andre Balz, Stanley Kermit (dec. Apr. 1973). Sec., asst. treas. U.S. Corrugated-Fibre Box Co., Indpls., 1952-58, pres., treas., chmn. bd., 1959—; pres. Speedway, Inc., also treas., chmn. bd., 1959-64; chmn. bd. U.S. Corrugated-Fibre Box Co. Ala., 1969—, Lacy Diversified Industries, Inc., 1972—; pres. Jessup Door Co., Inc., 1973-77, treas., 1977—, dir., 1973—; dir. Acme Paper Stock Co., Inc. Bd. dirs. Starlight Musical, 1959—, Community Hosp. of Indpls., 1975—, Citizens Forum, 1976-79, Indpls. Goodwill Industries, 1974—, Goodwill Industries Found. Central Ind., Inc., 1978—, Indpls. Center for Advanced Research, 1977—; mem. Pres.'s Club of U. Mich.; bd. dirs., mem. exec. com. YMCA Greater Indpls., 1963-72; del. Nat. Council of YMCA, 1967-72; mem. nat. council Met. Opera Assn., N.Y.C., 1965-70; bd. dirs. Ind. Symphony Soc., 1968-78, sec., 1972-78; exec. com. Marion County chpt. Nat. Found. March of Dimes; trustee Winona Meml. Hosp., 1965-76, YMCA Found. of Greater Indpls., 1975—; trustee, vice chmn. exec. com., chmn. devel. com. Franklin Coll., 1965—; gen. campaign chmn. Franklin Coll. Devel. Fund, 1966, 67, heart fund dr. Marion County Heart Assn., 1968; bd. dirs. United Fund Greater Indpls., 1967—, mem. exec. com., also mem. corp. div.; life mem. Winona Meml. Hosp. Aux., Winona Meml. Found.; chmn. Christmas campaign Salvation Army, 1976—; adv. bd. Ind. U.-Purdue U., Indpls., 1975—; mem. Roscoe Turner Aviation Found., 1970-74; mem. Confederacy Ind. Sachems, 1971—; bd. govs. Asso. Colls. Ind.; bd. dirs. Wright Inst. Otology, 1974—, Ind. Vocational Tech. Coll. Found. Named Sagamore of Wabash by Gov. Handley, 1960; Woman of Yr. award Indpls. chpt. Women in Communications, 1976, Ind. Republican Mayor Assn., 1976. Mem. Ind. Acad., Indpls. Women's Symphony Assn., Indpls. C. of C. (dir. 1973—), Athenaeum-Turners, Beta Gamma Sigma, Kappa Alpha Theta. Clubs: Lambs, Contemporary, Players (Indpls.); Maxinkuckee Yacht (Culver, Ind.); Capitol Hill (Washington); Union League (Chgo.). Home: 7030 W 79th St Indianapolis IN 46278 Office: 3200 One Indiana Sq Indianapolis IN 46204

LACY, JACK, former govt. ofcl.; b. Rocky Ford, Colo., Feb. 14, 1914; s. John B. and Mayme (Etzel) L.; student U. Colo. Sch. Journalism, 1934-35; m. Madeline Ann Lane, May 16, 1936; 1 son, Jack. City editor World-Ind., Walsenburg, Colo., 1936-40; mgr. La Junta (Colo.) C. of C., 1940-45, St. Joseph (Mo.) C. of C., 1945-47, Pueblo (Colo.) C. of C., 1947-57, Amarillo (Tex.) C. of C., 1957-61; dept. dir. dept. devel. State of N.Mex., Santa Fe, 1961-64; dir. Econ. Devel. Commn. Kans., Topeka, 1964-72; dir. Junction City (Kans.)-Geary County Econ. Devel. Commn., 1972-79; mem. faculty Southwestern Inst. for C. of C. Mgrs., U. Houston, 1947-61, pres., dean faculty, 1956-60; Mem. civic devel. com., govt. expenditures com. U.S. C. of C., 1957-61; assigned to AID Mission to Ecuador, 1969. Fellow Am. Indsl. Devel. Council; mem. Colo. Jr. C. of C. (life). Roman Catholic. Clubs: K.C. (4 deg.), Rotary, Elks. Home: 704 La Casa de Prasa Rio Rancho NM 87124

LACY, JERRY (GERALD LEROY), actor; b. Sioux City, Iowa, Mar. 27, 1936; s. Francis John and Mary Ann (Faligo) L.; student theatre arts Los Angeles City Coll., 1959-61. First profl. stage appearance Circle In The Square, N.Y.C., 1963; mem. summer stock companies in Mass., Va. and Pa., 1965-67; Broadway appearance in Play It Again, Sam, 1969-70; TV appearances include Dark Shadows, 1967-70, As The World Turns, 1971, Love of Life, 1972-77; film appearance in Play It Again, Sam, 1971; pres. Oak Leaf Prodns., Inc. Served with USMC, 1954-57.

LACY, JOSEPH NEWTON, architect; b. Kansas City, Mo. Oct. 6, 1905; s. John James and Theresa (Conboy) L.; B.Arch., U. Pa., 1927; m. Mary Duncan, Oct. 6, 1927 (dec. Aug. 1978); children—Mary-Louise, John Duncan, William Duncan. Asso. several archtl. firms in Phila. 1927-45, including Paul P. Cret, 1941-43, Louis I. Kahn, 1943-45; asso. Eliel and Eero Saarinen, Bloomfield Hills, Mich., 1945-51; partner Eero Saarinen & Assos., Bloomfield Hills, 1951-66, ret., 1966. Mem. Coll. Fellows of AIA, Hon. Order Ky. Cols. Specialized in devel. of new bldg. materials.

LACY, PAUL ESTON, pathologist, educator; b. Trinway, Ohio, Feb. 7, 1924; s. Benjamin Lemert and Amy (Cass) L.; B.A. cum laude, Ohio State U., 1945, M.D. cum laude, 1948, M.Sc. in Anatomy, 1948; Ph.D. in Pathology, Mayo Found., 1955; D.Med. (honoris causa), 5th Centenary, Uppsala, Sweden, 1977; m. Emelyn Ellen Talbot, June 7, 1945; children—Paul Eston, Steven Talbot. Asst. instr. anatomy Ohio State U., 1944-48; intern White Cross Hosp., Columbus, Ohio, 1948-49; fellow pathology Mayo Clinic, 1951-55; postgrad. fellow Nat. Cancer Inst., dept. anatomy Washington U. Med. Sch., St. Louis, 1955-56, mem. faculty, 1956—, Mallinckrodt prof. pathology, chmn. dept. 1961—; pathologist-in-chief Barnes and Allied Hosps., also St. Louis Children's Hosp., 1961—; Eliott Proctor Joslin Meml. lectr., Boston, 1966; Banting Meml. lectr. Brit. Diabetes Assn., 1963; Richard M. Jaffe lectr., 1969; Rollin Turner Woodyatt Meml. lectr., 1970. Mem. pathology B study sect. NIH, 1961-66, chmn., 1966-67, chmn. diabetes and tng. grants com., 1969-70, mem. Nat. Commn. Diabetes, 1974-76, also mem. Nat. Arthritis, Metabolism and Digestive Disease Adv. council, mem. Nat. Adv. Environ. Health Scis. Council; adv. com. research personnel Am. Cancer Soc., 1966-70; basic sci. adv. com. Nat. Cystic Fibrosis Found., 1967-69; com. on pathology Nat. Acad. Scis.; lifetime founding mem., med. adv. bd. Juvenile Diabetes Found. Served as officer M.C., U.S. Army, 1949-51. Recipient Outstanding Achievement award Mayo Found., 1964; Centennial Achievement award Ohio State U., 1970; Alumni citation Washington U.; Sci. award Juvenile Diabetes Found., 1973, David Rumbough Meml. award, 1979. Mem. Am. Assn. Exptl. Pathologists, Am. Diabetes Assn. (dir. 1975—, Banting award, Banting Meml. lectr. 1970), St. Louis Pathol. Soc., Internat. Acad. Pathology (council 1964-67), N.Y. Acad. Scis., Am. Assn. Pathologists and Bacteriologists, Am. Assn. Anatomists, Fedn. Soc. Exptl. Biology; asso. mem. Royal Soc. Medicine. Mem. editorial bd. Diabetes, 1963—, Archives of Pathology, 1965-75, Lab. Investigation, 1967-73; asso. editor Diabetes. Home: 63 Marshall Pl Webster Groves MO 63119 Office: 660 S Euclid Ave St Louis MO 63110

LACY, WILLARD CARLETON, educator; b. Waterville, Ohio, July 17, 1916; s. William Irving and Grace (Farnsworth) L.; A.B., Depauw U., 1938; M.S., U. Ill., 1940; Ph.D., Harvard, 1950; m. Josephine Wipior, Aug. 31, 1940; children—John Carleton, Carol Sue, Marian Louise, Barbara Jo, Linda Alice, Martha Anne. Geologist, Titanium Alloy Mfg. Co., Niagara Falls, N.Y., 1942-44; petrologist to chief geologist Cerro de Pasco Corp., Peru, S.Am., 1946-55; prof. geology U. Ariz., Tucson, 1955-61, prof., head dept. mining and geol. engring., 1961-72; prof. geology James Cook U., Townsville, Australia, 1972—; vis. lectr. econ. geology Harvard, 1952; Fulbright lectr. geol. engring. U. Queensland (Australia), 1967—. Served to lt. (j.g.) USNR, 1944-46. Fellow Geol. Soc. Am.; mem. Am. Soc. Photogrammetry, Soc. Econ. Geology, Am. Inst. Mining, Metall. and Petroleum Engrs., Australian Inst. Mining and Metallurgy, Geol. Soc. Australia. Methodist. Home: 14/43 The Strand Townsville Queensland Australia. *1) A sincere belief that people are more important than things or regulations and 2) the belief that there is always a way to accomplish a worthwhile objective.*

LADAR, SAMUEL ABRAHAM, lawyer; b. Jackson, Calif., Oct. 4, 1903; s. Max and Dora (Axelrod) L.; A.B., U. Calif. at Berkeley, 1925; J.D., U. Calif., 1928; m. Sylvia Favorman, Jan. 1, 1927; 1 son, Jerrold M. Admitted to Calif. bar, 1928; with Jesse H. Steinhart, lawyer, San Francisco, 1928-46; mem. firm Steinhart, Goldberg, Feigenbaum & Ladar, San Francisco, 1946—; vis. lectr. Boalt Hall, U. Calif. Law Sch., 1951—. Pres. San Francisco Bd. Edn., 1962, San Francisco Police Commn., 1965, Jewish Welfare Fedn. San Francisco, Marin County and Peninsula, 1965-66; mem. San Francisco Crime Commn., 1970-71. Bd. dirs. Mt. Zion Hosp. and Med. Center, San Francisco, San Francisco chpt. Am. Jewish Com.; nat. bd. dels. Am. Jewish Com. Mem. Am. Bar Assn., State Bar Calif., Bar Assn. San Francisco, U. Calif. Law Sch. Alumni Assn. (pres. 1967-68). Home: 1918 Vallejo St San Francisco CA 94123 Office: 600 Market St Suite 3400 San Francisco CA 94104

LADD, ALAN WALBRIDGE, JR., motion picture exec.; b. Los Angeles, Oct. 22, 1937; s. Alan Walbridge and Marjorie Jane (Harrold) L.; m. Patricia Ann Beazley, Aug. 30, 1959;

children—Kelliann, Tracy Elizabeth, Amanda Sue. Motion picture agt. Creative Mgmt., Los Angeles, 1963-69; producer films Walking Stick, 1969, A Severed Head, 1969, TamLin, 1970, Villian Zee and Co., 1971; exec. producer Nightcomers, 1971; producer Fear is the Key, 1973; v.p. prodn. 20th Century Fox Film Corp., Los Angeles, 1973-74, sr. v.p. Worldwide Prodns. div., Beverly Hills, Calif., 1974-76, pres. Twentieth Century-Fox Pictures, 1976—. Served with USAF, 1961-63. Office: 20th Century Fox Box 900 Beverly Hills CA 90213

LADD, CHARLES CUSHING, III, educator; b. Bklyn., Nov. 23, 1932; s. Charles Cushing and Elizabeth (Swan) L.; A.B., Bowdoin Coll., 1955; S.B., Mass. Inst. Tech., 1955, S.M., 1957, Sc.D., 1961; m. Carol Lee Ballou, June 11, 1954; children—Melissa, Charles IV, Ruth, Matthew. Asst. prof. civil engring. Mass. Inst. Tech., 1961-64, asso. prof., 1964-70, prof., 1970—; gen. reporter 9th Internat. Conf. Soil Mechanics and Found. Engring., Tokyo, 1977. Mem. Concord (Mass.) Republican Town Com., 1968—; commr. Concord Dept. Pub. Works, 1965-78, chmn., 1972-74. Fellow ASCE (research prize 1969 Croes medal 1973, Norman medal 1976); mem. Boston Soc. C.E. (bd. govt. 1972—, pres. 1977-78), ASTM, Transp. Research Bd. Contbr. articles to profl. jours. Home: 46 Tarbell Spring Rd Concord MA 01742 Office: Dept Civil Engring Mass Inst Tech Cambridge MA 02139

LADD, CHERYL (CHERYL STOPPELMOOR), actress; b. Huron, S.D., July 12, 1951; d. Marion and Dolores (Katz) Stoppelmoor; ed. pub. schs.; m. David Alan Ladd, May 24, 1973; 1 dau., Jordan Elizabeth. Toured with singing group The Music Shop, 1968-70; singing voice on TV cartoon series Josie and the Pussycats, 1970-72; appeared over 100 commls.; TV appearances include: The Rookies, Code R, The Tonight Show, Switch, Ironside, Happy Days, The Partridge Family, Police Woman; regular on TV series Charlie's Angels, 1977—; TV movie Satan's School for Girls, When She Was Bad, 1979; films include: Jamaica Reef, Marriage of a Young Stockbroker; rec. artist for Capitol Records. Recipient Photoplay award, 1978. Mem. AFTRA, AGVA, Screen Actors Guild. Office: care R Grant 8489 W 3d St Los Angeles CA 90048

LADD, DAVID LOWELL, lawyer, educator; b. Nauvoo, Ill., Sept. 18, 1926; s. David Mills and Anna Laura (Lowe) L.; student Kenyon Coll., 1944; B.A., U. Chgo., 1949, J.D., 1953; m. Carol Ann Weaver, 1966. Admitted to Ill. bar, 1953, Ohio bar, 1970; practice in Chgo., 1953-61, 63-69, Dayton, 1969—; counsel firm Biebel, French & Nauman; U.S. commr. patents, 1961-63; adj. prof. law Ohio State U., 1971-77; adj. prof. law U. Miami (Fla.), 1974-77, vis. prof., 1977-78, research prof. law, 1978-79, prof. law, 1979—, co-dir. Olin Found. program in law and econs. Law and Econs. Center, 1978—. Served with AUS, 1945-46. Mem. Am. Bar Assn., Am., Chgo. patent law assns. Democrat. Episcopalian. Clubs: Quadrangle (Chgo.); Dayton Racquet. Home: 6111 Granada Blvd Coral Gables FL 33146 Office: LEC PO Box 248000 Coral Gables FL 33124

LADD, ERNEST FLEETWOOD, JR., banker; b. Mobile, Ala., Aug. 27, 1911; student U. Ala., 1929-33; postgrad. Rutgers U., 1951, Dartmouth Coll., 1959; m. Fanny Knight Gaillard, Apr. 27, 1938; children—Ernest Fleetwood, III, Sam Gaillard, Milton Aldridge, Marshall McRae. With Merchants Nat. Bank, Mobile, 1935-76, exec. v.p., 1967-69, pres., 1969-72, chmn. bd., chief exec. officer, 1972-76; chmn., chief exec. officer Southland Bancorporation, Mobile, 1974-76, chmn., pres., chief exec. officer, 1976—; dir. New Orleans br. Fed. Res. Bank of Atlanta, 1973-75, Ala. Dry Dock & Shipbuilding Co., Mobile, Ala. Power Co.; hon. coach girls basketball team U. Ala.; mem. nat. adv. com. on banking politics and practices U.S. Comptroller of Currency, 1974-75. Mem. vestry St. Pauls Episcopal Ch., 1955-57; mem. S.W. Ala. Health Planning Council, Gov. Wallace's Ameraport Task Force Com., S.Ala. Regional Planning Commn.. Mobile County Found. for Pub. Higher Edn.. Mobile United, U. Ala. Pres.'s Cabinet; mem. nominating com. Ala. Bus. Hall of Fame, spl. com. Ala. Hist. Commn.; mem. Gov.'s Mansion Adv. Bd.; chmn. United Fund of Mobile County campaign. 1961. also dir.. chmn. bd. trustees, co-chmn. U.S.S. Ala. Campaign, 1964; campaign treas. Mobile chpt. ARC, 1943-44, bd. dirs., 1945-46; treas., trustee, mem. exec. com. 6th Dist. Tb. Hosp.. 1958-66; pres.. bd. dirs. Ala. Safety Council; bd. dirs. Ala. Council Econ. Edn.; pres., trustee Ernest F. Ladd Meml. Stadium Corp.; trustee, chmn. fin. com. Mobile Infirmary; trustee Mobile Arts and Sports Assn.. Univ. Mil. Sch. of Mobile, Mobile Opera Guild; trustee Coast Guard Acad. Found.; bd. visitors U. Ala. Coll. Bus. Adminstrn. Mem. Am. (governing council 1975, v.p. for Ala.), Ala. (pres. 1974-75, exec. mgmt. com., dir. edn. found. 1971-74) bankers assns., Nat. Alliance Businessmen (adv. bd.), U.S. (monetary and fiscal affairs com. 1972-75), Mobile Area (dir.) chambers commerce, Ala. Assn. Ind. Colls. and Univs. (trustee 1976, dist. bd. govs. 1976), Beta Gamma Sigma. Clubs: Rotary of Mobile (dir., past pres.), Mobile Country (past dir.), Athelstan (Mobile); Lakewood Golf (Point Clear, Ala.). Address: 106 Saint Francis St Mobile AL 36622

LADD, EVERETT CARLL, JR., data center dir., educator; b. Saco, Maine, Sept. 24, 1937; s. Everett Carll and Agnes Mary (MacMillan) L.; A.B. magna cum laude, Bates Coll., 1959; Ph.D. (Woodrow Wilson fellow Social Sci. Research Council fellow), Cornell U., 1964; m. Cynthia Louise Northway, June 13, 1959; children—Everett Carll, III, Corina Ruth, Melissa Ann, Benjamin Elliot. Asst. dean students for public affairs Cornell U., 1963-64; asst. prof. U. Conn., Storrs, 1964-67, asso. prof., 1967-69, prof. polit. sci., 1969—, dir. Social Sci. Data Center, 1968-77, co-exec. dir. Roper Center, 1977-79, exec. dir., 1979—, also trustee research fellow Center for Internat. Studies Harvard U., 1969-75; mem. exec. council Inter-Univ. Consortium for Polit. and Social Research, 1975-77; mem. council Project on Am. Democratic Instns., Yale U.; adj. scholar Am. Enterprise Inst. Public Policy Research, 1978—. spl. cons. for legis. reapportionment Conn. Gen. Assembly, 1970-71; spl. cons. to Conn. state and mcpl. agys., to Carnegie Commn. on Higher Edn., 1969-73. Ford Found. fellow, 1969-70; Guggenheim fellow, 1971-72; Rockefeller Found. fellow, 1976-77; Center Advanced Study in Behavioral Scis., 1979. Mem. AAAS, Am. Polit. Sci. Assn., Am. Sociol. Assn., Am. Assn. Public Opinion Research, Acad. Polit. Sci., Phi Beta Kappa, Delta Sigma Rho. Author: Negro Political Leadership in the South, 1966; Ideology in America: Charge and Response in a City, a Suburb, and a Small Town, 1969; American Political Parties: Social Change and Political Response, 1970; (with S.M. Lipset) Professors, Unions, and American Education, 1973, Academics, Politics, and the 1972 Election, 1973, The Divided Academy: Professors and Politics, 1975; (with C. D. Hadley) Political Parties and Political Issues: Patterns in Differentiation Since the New Deal, 1973, Transformations of the American Party System: Political Coalitions from the New Deal to the 1970's, 1975. Editorial bd. Public Opinion Quar., 1976—, Polit. Behavior, 1978—; cons. editor, mem. editorial bd. Public Opinion, 1977—. Home: 86 Ball Hill Rd Storrs CT 06268 Office: Roper Center U Conn Box U-164 Storrs CT 06268

LADD, JOHN, educator; b. Middletown, Conn., June 24, 1917; s. William P. and Ailsie (Taylor) L.; grad. Choate Sch., 1933; A.B. magna cum laude, Harvard U., 1937, A.M., 1941, Ph.D., 1948; M.A., Brown U., 1957, U. Va., 1941; m. Hylda Higginson, Jan. 1943 (div. 1959); 1 dau., Mary Madeleine; m. 2d, Rosalind Ekman, July 8, 1963; children—Sarah, Deborah. Gast-dozent U. Gottingen (Germany), 1948-49; instr. Harvard, 1949-50; mem. faculty Brown U., 1950—, prof. philosophy, 1962—; vis. prof. Harvard U., spring 1961; vis. lectr. Smith Coll., 1961-62. Served to lt. USNR, 1942-46. Rockefeller fellow, 1948-49; Guggenheim fellow, 1958-59. Mem. Am. Soc. Polit. and Legal Philosophy (sec.-treas. 1956-69, pres. 1976-78), Am. Philos. Assn. (exec. com. 1962-64, chmn. com. on philosophy and medicine, 1975—). Author: The Structure of a Moral Code, 1957; also articles. Editor with introduction: Ethical Relativism, 1973. Translator with Introduction: (Kant) Metaphysical Elements of Justice, 1965; Ethical Issues Relating to Life and Death, 1979. Home: 72 Taber Ave Providence RI 02906

LADD, JOSEPH CARROLL, ins. co. exec.; b. Chgo., Jan. 26, 1927; s. Stephen C. and Laura (McBride) L.; B.A., Ohio Wesleyan U., 1950; m. Barbara Virginia Carter, June 5, 1965; children—Carroll, Joseph Carroll, Barbara, Virginia, William. Agt., Conn. Gen. Life Ins. Co., Chgo., 1950-3, staff asst., 1953-54, mgr. Evanston (Ill.) br. office, 1954-60, dir. agys., 1960-62, mgr. Los Angeles br. office, 1963; v.p. sales Fidelity Mut. Life Ins. Co., Phila., 1964-67, sr. v.p. sales, 1968, exec. v.p., 1969-71, pres., chief exec. officer, dir., 1971—; dir. Rorer Group Inc., First Pa. Corp., Western Sav. Fund Soc., Phila. Electric Co., First Pa. Bank. Bd. dirs. Children's Hosp., Phila., Phila. YMCA, Greater Phila. Partnership; trustee Phila. United Way, also gen. chmn. 1978 campaign; trustee Phila. Mus. Art. Served with USNR, 1945-46. Mem. Am. Coll. Life Underwriters (trustee), Greater Phila. C. of C. (dir., chmn. 1979). Clubs: Philadelphia Country, Sunday Breakfast, Union League (Phila.). Home: 1111 Beech Rd Rosemont PA 19010 Office: Fidelity Mutual Life Ins Co Fidelity Mutual Life Bldg Philadelphia PA 19101

LADEN, KARL, toiletries co. exec.; b. Bklyn., Aug. 10, 1932; s. Judah and Anna (Bernstein) L.; B.S., U. Akron (Ohio), 1954; Ph.D., Northwestern U., 1957; m. July Talisman, June 24, 1956; children—Ben, Ethan, Adam, Noam, Zev. Cons., Indsl. Bio-Test Labs., Northbrook, Ill., 1955-57; research chemist William Wrigley Jr. Co., Chgo., 1957-58; research mgr. Toni Co., Chgo., 1959-64; with Gillette Research Inst., Washington, 1964-76, v.p. biomed. scis., 1968-71, pres., 1971-76; v.p. research and devel. Carter Products Co., Cranbury, N.J., 1976—. Recipient award Internat. Flavors and Fragrances, 1963, 67. Fellow Soc. Cosmetic Chemists (pres. 1977, chmn. bd. 1978, editor jour. 1967-72, Mid-West chpt. award 1964, Lit. award 1969, Merit award 1972; Medal award 1979); mem. Am. Chem. Soc., Soc. Investigative Dermatology, AAAS, ADA, Indsl. Research Inst. (bd. editors Research Mgmt.), Internat. Assn. Dental Research, Sigma Xi. Contbr. articlgs to profl. jours. Contbg. editor Nat. Beauty Sch. Jour., 1970—. Home: 704 River Rd Ewing NJ 08628 Office: Carter Products Co Half Acre Rd Cranbury NJ 08512

LADENSON, ALEX, librarian; b. Kiev, Russia, Sept. 25, 1907; s. Nathan and Bertha (Schonheit) L.; came to U.S., 1913, naturalized, 1922; B.S. in Law, Northwestern U., 1929, J.D., 1932; M.A., U. Chgo. 1935, Ph.D., 1938; Litt.D., Rosary Coll., 1968; m. Inez Sher, Aug. 14, 1938; children—Mark Lawrence, Robert Franklin. Admitted to Ill. bar, 1931; project supr. WPA Library Omnibus Project, Chgo., 1938-43; asst. librarian Chgo. Pub. Library, 1943-67, acting librarian, 1967-70, chief librarian, 1970-74, spl. exec. asst. to bd. dirs., 1975-78, cons., 1978—; asst. dean Schurz Eve. Jr. Coll., Chgo., 1938-48; lectr. grad. dept. library sci. Rosary Coll., River Forest Ill., 1965-69; legal counsel Soc. Am. Archivists, 1975—, Urban Libraries Council, 1978—. Pres. Northtown Civic League, Chgo., 1958-60. Mem. Am., Ill. (pres. 1959-60, Librarian Citation award 1965) library assns. Clubs: Chicago Literary, Chicago Press. Editor: American Library Laws, 1964, 1st supplement, 1965, 2d supplement, 1967, 3d supplement, 1969, 4th supplement, 1971, 4th edit, 1973, 1st supplement, 1974, 2d supplement, 1977. Home: 6517 N Artesian Ave Chicago IL 60645 Office: 425 N Michigan Ave Chicago IL 60611

LADER, LAWRENCE, writer; b. N.Y.C., Aug. 6, 1919; s. Ludwig and Myrtle (Powell) L.; A.B., Harvard U., 1941; m. Jean MacInnis, Aug. 24, 1942 (div. Jan. 1946); m. 2d, Joan Summers, Sept. 27, 1961; 1 dau., Wendy Summers. With press dept. ABC, 1941-42; contbg. editor Coronet mag., 1946; feature editor Glamour mag., 1953; lectr. N.Y.U., 1957-59, Philips Brooks Assn., Harvard, 1962—; regular contbr. Am. Heritage, Reader's Digest, McCall's mags., others, 1941—; exec. dir. Hugh Moore Fund, 1966-67; fgn. corr. Arab-Israel War, 1948, other overseas assignments, 1951, 55, 57; adj. asso. prof. journalism N.Y. U., 1967-72. Chmn. exec. com. Nat. Abortion Rights Action League, 1969-72, chmn. bd., 1972-76; pres. Abortion Rights Mobilization, 1976—. Served to lt. AUS, 1942-46; officer-in-charge N.Y. Troop Information, Armed Forces Radio Service. Mem. Am. Soc. Authors and Journalists (pres. 1958). Club: Harvard (N.Y.C.). Author: Margaret Sanger, 1955; The Bold Brahmins, New England's War Against Slavery, 1961; Abortion, 1966; (juvenile) Margaret Sanger, 1969; Breeding Ourselves to Death, 1971; Foolproof Birth Control, 1972; Abortion II: Making the Revolution, 1973; Power on the Left: American Radical Movements since 1946, 1979. Home: 51 Fifth Ave New York NY 10003

LADERMAN, EZRA, composer, educator; b. Bklyn., June 29, 1924; s. Isidor and Leah (Stock) L.; B.A., Bklyn. Coll., 1949, M.A., Columbia, 1951; m. Aimlee H. Davis, Dec. 9, 1951; children—Isaiah, Jacob, Rachel. Prof. composition State U. N.Y., Binghamton; pres. Am. Music Center, 1973-76; chmn. composer, librettist program Nat. Endowment for Arts, dir. music program, 1979—. Served with AUS, 1942-46. Guggenheim fellow, 1955, 59, 64; recipient Prix d'Rome, 1963; Rockefeller Found. grantee; Ford Found. grantee; Nat. Endowment for Arts grantee. Mem. Composer's Forum (dir.), A.S.C.A.P. (adv. bd.) Composer numerous works, including operas, cantatas, oratorio, symphonies, string quartets, chamber works, song cycles, dance works, works for large orchs. and for solo instruments, and film scores. Home: Box 689 Teaneck NJ 07666 Office: Music Dept State U NY Binghampton NY 13901

LADERMAN, GABRIEL, artist; b. Bklyn., Dec. 26, 1929; s. Isidore and Leah (Stock) L.; B.A., Bklyn. Coll., 1952; M.F.A., Cornell U., 1957; m. Carol Ciavati, Feb. 12, 1953; children—Raphael, Michael. Faculty, State U. N.Y., New Paltz, 1957-59, Pratt Inst., 1959-66; faculty Queens Coll., Flushing, N.Y., 1966—, chmn., 1979—; vis. prof. La. State U., Baton Rouge, 1966-67, Yale U., 1968, Viterbo Coll., 1969, 80, Art Students League, 1972—, Boston U., 1973, N.Y. Studio Sch.; vis. critic, lectr. Yale U., Syracuse U., Bennington Coll., Rutgers U., Princeton, Cooper-Union, Phila. Coll. Art, Md. Inst. Art, Swain Sch., Boston U., Boston Mus. Sch., Ind. U., Bard Coll., Kansas City Art Inst., Fla. State U., State U. N.Y., New Paltz, Amherst Coll., Skowhegan Sch., Yale-Norfolk Sch., New York Studio Sch., Pratt Inst., N.Y. Inst. Tech., Boston Mus., Tyler Sch. of Temple U., U. R.I., U. N.H., Artists for Environment, Iowa State U., Hobart Coll., U. Wis., 1980, numerous others; one man shows at Schoelkopf Gallery, 1964, 67, 70, 72, 74, 77, Hobart Coll., 1968, R.I. U., 1969, Temple U., 1971, La. State U., 1967, Bennington Coll., Ithaca Coll., R.I. U., So. U., Dart Gallery, Chgo., 1977; exhibited in group shows at Whitney Mus., 1971, Mus. Modern Art, 1974, Corcoran Gallery, 1972, 76, Boston Mus., 1974, 75, Bklyn. Mus., 1952, 57, 59, 61, Library of Congress, 1957, 59, Gallery of Modern Art, 1972, N.Y. Cultural Center, 1972, Phila. Mus., 1970, Wadsworth Atheneum, 1976, Fogg Mus., 1976, Mpls. Inst. Arts, 1976, Milw. Art Center, 1977, Ft. Worth Art Mus., 1977, High Mus., 1977, San Francisco Mus. Modern Art, 1977; traveling shows sponsored by A.F.A., Smithsonian Instn., Library of Congress; represented in permanent collection Witherspoon Mus., Cleve. Mus., Mus. Fine Arts, Boston; lectr., vis. critic Royal Sch. Art, Bangkok, Thailand, 1976, Nat. Art Sch., Jakarta, Indonesia, 1975, Art Sch., Surabaya, Indonesia, 1975, Victorian Coll. Art, Melbourne, Australia, 1975, Coll. Art, Ballarat, Australia, 1975, Prahran Coll., Melbourne, 1975; USIS lectr., Japan, 1975. Recipient Research award City U. N.Y., 1971; Fed. Govt. Commn. through Interior Dept. for Bicentennial, 1974; asst. Cornell U., 1955-57; L.C. Tiffany grantee, 1959, Fulbright fellow to Italy, 1962-63, Yaddo fellow, 1960, 62; Ingram Merrill fellow, 1975-76; recipient City U. N.Y. research award, 1970-71, 75-76. Contbr. articles to profl. jours. Home: 760 West End Ave New York NY 10025 Office: Queens Coll Flushing NY 11367

LADIN, EUGENE, communications co. exec.; b. N.Y.C., Oct. 26, 1927; s. Nat and Mae (Cohen) L.; B.B.A., Pace U., 1956, M.B.A., Air Force Inst. Tech., 1959; postgrad. George Washington U., 1966-69; m. Millicent Dolly Frankel, June 27, 1948; children—Leslie Hope, Stephanie Joy. Cost engr. Rand Corp., Santa Monica, Calif., 1960-62; mgr. cost and econ. analysis Northrop Corp., Hawthorne, Calif., 1962-66; dir. financial planning Communications Satellite Corp., Washington, 1966-70; treas., chief fin. and adminstrv. officer Landis & Gyr, Inc., Elmsford, N.Y., 1970-76; v.p., treas., comptroller P.R. Telephone Co., San Juan, 1976-77; v.p. fin. Comtech Telecommunications Corp., Smithtown, N.Y., 1977—; acting pres. Comtech Antenna Corp., St. Cloud, Fla., 1978—; asso. prof. accounting So. Ill. U., East St. Louis, 1960; asso. prof. bus. U. Md., 1969-70; adj. prof. George Washington U., 1969-70; vis. prof. accounting Pace U., 1970. Served to capt. USAF, 1951-60. Decorated Air Force Commendation medal. Mem. Nat. Assn. Accountants. Clubs: Sheldrake Yacht (Mamaroneck, N.Y.); Dorado Golf and Beach (Dorado Beach, P.R.). Home: 170 Spring Lake Hills Dr Maitland FL 32751 Office: 3100 Communications Rd Saint Cloud FL 32769 also 135 Engineers Rd Smithtown NY 11787. *We must recognize that the individual, business and government must function in an atmosphere of mutual respect and consideration to achieve our national goals on a compatible basis.*

LADMAN, A(ARON) J(ULIUS), anatomist, educator; b. Jamaica, N.Y., July 3, 1925; s. Thomas and Ida (Sobin) L.; student Miami U., Oxford, Ohio, 1942-43; A.B., N.Y. U., 1947; postgrad. U. Cin., 1948-49; Ph.D., Ind. U., 1952; m. Barbara Powers, Dec. 26, 1948; children—Susan Elizabeth, Thomas Frederick. Teaching fellow anatomy U. Cin., 1948-49, Ind. U., 1949-52; with Harvard Med. Sch., 1952-61, asso., 1955-61; asso. prof. U. Tenn. Med. Units, 1961-64; vis. asso. prof. Yale, 1964; prof., chmn. dept. anatomy U. N.Mex. Sch. Medicine, Albuquerque, 1964—; research fellow Am. Cancer Soc., 1952-55; USPHS Spl. Research fellow, 1955-57, 71-72; recipient Research Career Devel. award USPHS, 1962-64. Mem. Soc. for Exptl. Biology and Medicine, Am. Assn. Anatomists (exec. com. 1972-76), Am. Soc. for Cell Biology, Nat. Inst. Gen. Med. Scis. (research career awards com. 1967-71), Electron Microscope Soc. Am. (exec. council 1974-76), Endocrine Soc., Council Biol. Editors (sec. 1977—), Histochem. Soc., Am. Soc. Zoologists, AAAS, Sigma Xi. Asso. editor Anatomical Record, 1967-68, mng. editor, 1968—. Contbr. articles to profl. jours. Home: 2617 Cutler Ave NE Albuquerque NM 87106

LADNER, HEBER A., former sec. state Miss.; b. Lumberton, Miss., Oct. 4, 1902; s. Webster L. and Velena (Beall) L.; A.B., Millsaps Coll., 1929; A.M., Duke U., 1938; student Nat. Inst. Pub. Affairs, Washington; m. Daisy Bowles, Dec. 22, 1935; children—Mary Eloise, Heber. Mem. Miss. Ho. of Reps., 1936-40, clk., 1942-48; sec. Miss. Budget Commn., 1940-42; sec. state Miss., 1948-80. Mem. Nat. Assn. Secs. State (past pres.), Kappa Sigma. Democrat. Baptist. Clubs: Lions, Masons. Office: New Capitol Bldg Jackson MS 39205*

LADNER, THOMAS E., lawyer; b. Vancouver, B.C., Can., Dec. 8, 1916; B.A., U. B.C., 1937; grad. Osgoode Hall. Admitted to B.C. bar, 1940; now partner firm Ladner Downs, Vancouver. Mem. Canadian, Vancouver bar assns., Law Soc. B.C. Office: PO Box 10021 2100 Pacific Centre Vancouver 1 BC Canada

LA DOW, C. STUART, finance co. exec.; b. Warren, Pa., Apr. 21, 1925; s. Clyde and Glendine (Bentley) LaD.; B.A., Cornell U., 1947; m. Gayle Carol Koenig, July 11, 1953; 1 son, Paul Stuart. With Gen. Electric Co., 1947—, mgr. N.Y. region Gen. Electric Credit Corp., N.Y.C., 1965-67, v.p., Stamford, Conn., 1971—; pres. Homemakers Finance Service, Inc., 1970-78; dir. Puritan Life Ins. Co., Providence. Vice pres., bd. dirs. Jr. Achievement of Stamford, Inc., 1973—; mem. exec. budget com., chmn. budget panel United Way of Stamford, 1973—; chmn. Stamford chpt. Am. Cancer Soc., 1977. Served with USN, 1944-46; ETO. Recipient Community Service award Gen. Electric Credit Corp., 1976. Mem. Nat. Second Mortgage Assn. (dir., mem. exec. com., Outstanding Service award), Nat. Consumer Finance Assn. (certificate of appreciation). Republican. Baptist. Clubs: Masons, Shriners, Cornell of Fairfield County. Home: 84 W Bank Ln Stamford CT 06902 Office: 260 Long Ridge Rd Stamford CT 06904

LA DU, BERT NICHOLS, JR., physician, educator; b. Lansing, Mich., Nov. 13, 1920; s. Bert Nichols and Natalie (Kerr) L.; B.S., Mich. State Coll., 1943; M.D., U. Mich., 1945; Ph.D. in Biochemistry, U. Calif.; Berkeley, 1952; m. Catherine Shilson, June 14, 1947; children—Elizabeth, Mary, Anne, Jane. Intern Rochester (N.Y.) Gen. Hosp., 1945-46; research asso. N.Y.U. Research Service, Goldwater Meml. Hosp., N.Y.C., 1950-53; sr. asst. surgeon USPHS, Nat. Heart Inst., 1954-57; surgeon, later sr. surgeon, med. dir. Nat. Inst. Arthritis and Metabolic Disease, 1957-63; prof., chmn. dept. pharmacology N.Y.U. Med. Sch., 1963-74; chmn. dept. pharmacology U. Mich. Med. Sch., Ann Arbor, 1974—. Served with AUS, 1943-45. Mem. A.A.A.S., Am. Chem. Soc., N.Y. Acad. Sci. (pres.), Am. Soc. Biol. Chemistry, Am. Soc. Pharmacol. Therapeutics, Am. Soc. Human Genetics, Biochem. Soc. (Gt. Britain). Contbr. articles to profl. jours. Home: 817 Berkshire Rd Ann Arbor MI 48104 Office: 6322 Med Sci I U Mich Med Sch Ann Arbor MI 48109

LA DUE, JOHN SAMUEL, physician; b. Minot, N.D., Sept. 6, 1911; s. Samuel and Edith Woodsworth (Mann) La.D.; A.B., U. Minn., 1932, S.M. in Medicine, 1940, Ph.D. in Medicine, 1941; M.D., Harvard, 1936; m. Margaret Ruth Stokes, Apr. 24, 1937. Intern L.I. Hosp., 1936-37; resident Mpls. Gen. Hosp., 1937-40, adj. staff physician, 1940-41; asst. vis. physician Charity Hosp., New Orleans, 1941-43, vis. physician, 1943-45, dir. lung sta., 1943-45; clin. asst. Meml. Hosp., N.Y.C., 1945-46, asst. attending physician, 1946-48, asso. attending physician, 1948—; physician to outpatient dept. N.Y. Hosp., 1946-47, asst. attending physician, 1948—; tchr. fellow U. Minn. Med. Sch., 1937-40, instr. medicine, 1940-41; instr. La. State U. Sch. Medicine, 1941-43, asst. prof. medicine, 1943-44, asso. prof. clin. medicine, 1944-45; clin. asst. Cornell U. Med. Coll., 1945-46, faculty, 1946—, asso. prof. clin. medicine, 1958—; dir. heart sta. Meml. Center, N.Y.C., 1955-57; dir. cardiovascular sect. Meml. Center and Sloan Kettering Inst., 1957-66; sr. attending cardiologist St. Barnabas Hosp. Chronic Diseases. Bd. dirs., sec., past pres. med. staff Doctors Hosp., N.Y.C. Recipient Hektoen medal A.M.A., 1955; Alfred P. Sloan award clin. investigation, 1955; Cummings Humanitarian award, 1963, 64. Diplomate Nat. Bd. Med. Examiners,

Am. Bd. Internal Medicine. Mem. Am. Coll. Cardiology (pres. 1962-63), Academia Nacional de Medicina do Brazil, Am. Fedn. Clin. Research (past pres.), A.M.A., A.C.P., Am. Coll. Chest Physicians, Harvey Soc., Soc. Exptl. Biology and Medicine, Am., N.Y. heart assns., N.Y. Acad. Med., N.Y. Acad. Sci., James Ewing Soc., N.Y. Cardiological Soc. (past pres.), N.Y. State Soc. Internal Medicine (past pres.), Harvard Med. Soc. N.Y., Academia Nacional de Medicina de Peru (hon.), Sigma Xi, Sigma Chi. Episcopalian. Contbr. articles to profl. jours., sects. several med. text books. Home: 1185 Park Ave New York City NY 10028 Office: 34 E 67th St New York City NY 10021

LADUE, WENDELL RICHARD, civil engr.; b. Mt. Pleasant, Ohio, Oct. 1, 1894; s. Charles Garrison and Clara Elizabeth (Duncan) LaD.; B.S. in C.E., U. So. Calif., 1918; D.Eng., U. Akron, 1963; m. Carrie Tina Bachmann, Apr. 5, 1920 (dec. Apr. 1957); m. 2d, Dorothy Kline Courtney, Sept. 18, 1959 (dec. Sept. 1978). With Nat. Tube Co. and Wheeling Corrugating Co., Wheeling, W.Va., 1912-14; draftsman to design engr. and engr. Bur. Waterworks Improvement, Akron, Ohio, 1919-33; engr. to supt. and chief engr., Bur. Water Supply, Akron, 1933-42; supt. and chief engr., Bur. Water and Sewerage, Akron, 1942-53; supt. and chief engr. Bur. of Water Supply, 1954-63; now cons. san. engr. Akron; chmn. water and sewerage devel. com. Nat. Safety Council, 1950—; mem. 5 man adv. panel on water facilities FCDA, 1950, spl. cons. on water supply, 1951-53; mem. water and sewerage industry and com., mem. engrs. joint council com. on Nat. Water Policy, 1950; mem. adv. com. Ohio Water Resources Bd., 1958-60; chmn. municipal water supplies sub-com. Govs. Adv. Com. on Ohio's Water Resources, 1954-60; mem. Ohio Water Commn., 1962-70, pres., 1962, 64, 67, 70; dir. Cuyahoga Watershed Council, 1955-63; mem. adv. com. Coll. Engring., U. Akron, 1954—, organizer, condr. course on engring. mgmt. of water utilities, 1963-70; mem. Nat. Def. Exec. Res., 1958—; mem. task group continuity prodn. planning for water and sewerage facilities U.S. Dept. Commerce; cons. water utility mgmt. AID; chmn. bd. dirs. 3-Rivers Watershed Dist., 1966—; mem. Ohio Recreation Resources Commn., 1966-72; mem. water supply works group Great Lakes Basin Commn., 1968; chmn. N.E. Ohio Water Plan Adv. Com., 1970-72; mem. adv. com. Akron Children's Zoo, 1972—; trustee Am. San. Engring. Inter-Soc. Bd., Inc., 1955-59, Summit County Mus. Nat. History, 1974—. Served in USN bur. of constrn. and repair, 1917-19. Mem. war ration board, citizens Navy com., 1942-45. Recipient George Warren Fuller Meml. award, 1939, (honoree) Wendell R. LaDue Safety award, 1957, John M. Diven Meml. medal, 1951, all of Am. Water Works Assn.; Samuel A. Greeley Service award Am. Pub. Works Assn., 1951; award, 1950 of Ohio Forestry Assn.; Wendell R. La Due Reservoir named by City of Akron, 1961; citation, Distinguished Pub. Service award, Ohio Soc. Profl. Engrs., 1963; named to Hall of Fame, Ohio Water Mgmt. Assn., 1975. Diplomate Am. Acad. San. Engrs. (organizing com.). Mem. Am. Water Works Assn. (life mem., hon. mem., trustee Central States sect. 1934-37, organizer Ohio sect. 1937, nat. dir. 1940-42, 45-50, 49-63, v.p., 1945-46, pres., 1946-47; chmn. com. water works adminstrn., 1947-63; Distinguished Pub. Service award 1969; rep. on President's Com. Indsl. Safety, 1950-56; rep. on engrs. joint council for advancement of san. engring. Ohio and Am. Forestry Assn.), ASCE (life mem., trustee Cleve. sect.; founder and pres. Akron sect., 1947-48), Nat. Soc. Profl. Engrs. (chmn. Municipal div., Ohio sect., 1946-47), Am. Pub. Works Assn. (chmn. water works com. 1947), Akron Council Engring. and Sci. Socs. (co-founder, v.p. 1946-47, Distinguished Service award 1962), Water Pollution Control Fedn., Inter Am. Assn. San. Engrs., Sigma Alpha Epsilon. Republican. Presbyterian. Mason (32 deg., Shriner, K.T.), Rotarian (pres. Akron 1942-43). Clubs: Internat. Torch (pres. Akron chpt. 1941); Congress Lake Country, Akron City; Portage County (mem. greens and grounds com. 1972—). Author: Geology of Akron District (monograph), 1920. Contbr. numerous articles to profl. jours. Address: 2344 Amesbury Rd Akron OH 44313

LADY, WENDELL, state legislator; b. Abilene, Kans.; B.S. in Engring., Kans. State U.; m. Mary Jean Robbins; children—Jan Lady Beam, Jill, Dave. Project engr. Black and Veatch, Cons. Engrs.; former mem., then pres. Overland Park (Kans.) City Council; now mem. Kans. Ho. of Reps. from 19th dist., former house minority leader, now speaker of house, chmn. interstate coop. commn., chmn. legis. budget. Mem. ASCE, Am. Water Works Assn., Johnson County Mental Health Assn., Overland Park C. of C., State-Fed. Assembly of Nat. Conf. of State Legislatures (chmn.), Phi Kappa Phi, Sigma Tau, Delta Tau Delta. Methodist. Home: 8732 Mackey Overland Park KS 66212

LAERI, JOHN HOWARD, company dir.; b. Youngstown, Ohio, Mar. 22, 1906; s. Anton John and Lillian (Resch) L.; A.B., Williams Coll., 1928; m. Betty Cochrane, Dec. 7, 1929; children—Suzanne (Mrs. Lee Plein), John Howard. Past vice chmn. Citicorp, Citibank N.A.; now dir. F & M Schaeffer Corp., St. Regis Paper Co., First Boston Corp., Firemans Fund Ins. Co. Mem. Am. Bankers Assn. (pres. 1967). Methodist. Clubs: Augusta (Ga.) Nat. Golf; Blind Brook (Purchase, N.Y.). Home: 31 Meadowcroft Ln Greenwich CT 06830 Office: 399 Park Ave New York City NY 10022

LA FALCE, JOHN JOSEPH, congressman, lawyer; b. Buffalo, Oct. 6, 1939; s. Dominic E. and Catherine M. (Stasio) La F.; B.S., Canisius Coll., 1961; J.D., Villanova U., 1964; LL.D. (hon.), Niagara U., 1979; m. Patricia Fisher, 1979. Admitted to N.Y. State bar, 1964; mem. N.Y. State Legislature, 1971-74; mem. 94th-96th congresses 36th Dist. N.Y., mem. Banking Com., Small Bus. Com., chmn. subcom. gen. oversight. Lectr. law George Washington U., 1965-66. Served as capt., Adj. Gen. Corps, AUS, 1965-67. Recipient Distinguished Service award U.S. Jaycees, 1971, All-Am. Columbus award Fedn. Italian Am.-Dem. Orgns., 1974; awards N.Y. State Cath. War Vets, 1976, Niagara Frontier chpt. Nat. Assn. Homebuilders, 1976; Man of Year awards N.Y. State chpt. Asso. Gen. Contractors Am., 1975, Niagara-Orleans Labor Council AFL-CIO, 1975, Tonawanda (N.Y.) Labor Council, 1975, Cystic Fibrosis Found., 1975, Fedn. Italian-Am. Socs. Western N.Y., 1976. Mem. Erie County N.Y.) Bar Assn. Home: 800 Starin Ave Buffalo NY 14223 Office: Cannon House Office Bldg Room 225 Washington DC 20515

LAFARGE, LOUIS BANCEL, architect; b. Boston, May 17, 1900; s. Bancel and Mabel (Hooper) LaF.; grad. Choate Sch., 1918; A.B., Harvard, 1922; B.F.A., Yale, 1925; m. Hester Emmet, July 28, 1928 (div. 1962); children—Timothy, Benjamin, Celestine; m. 2d, Margaret Hockaday, Apr. 12, 1962. Apprentice, Delano & Aldrich, Peabody, Wilson & Brown, N.Y.C., 1925-32; practice architecture, N.Y.C., 1932-38; partner LaFarge & Knox, 1938-42, LaFarge, Knox & Murphy, N.Y.C., 1947-60, LaFarge and Morey, N.Y.C., 1961-66. Mem. N.Y.C. Landmarks Preservation Commn., 1965-70; chmn. Historic Dist. Commn. for Nantucket, Mass., 1971-76; mem. adv. council Cooper Union Sch. Art and Architecture, 1959-61. Served from capt. to maj., USAAF, 1942-45, Gen. Staff Corps., 1945-46; chief monuments, fine arts and archives Hdqrs. SHAEF, 1945, Office Mil. Govt. for Germany, 1945-46. Decorated Legion of Merit, Bronze Star (U.S.); chevalier Legion of Honor, Croix de Guerre, Medaille de la Reconnaissance (France); officer Ordre de la Couronne (Belgium); officer Order Orange-Nassau (Netherlands); Order of Merit 1st class (Czechoslovakia). A.N.A. Fellow A.I.A. (pres. N.Y. 1958-60, sec., dir. 1952-54, 56-60, chmn. fine arts com. 1960-63); mem. Beaux Arts Inst. Design (past trustee), Municipal Art Soc. N.Y. (pres. 1954-56, dir. 1956-59), Yale Arts Assn. (exec. com. 1959-61), Liturgical Art Soc. (pres., dir. 1949-51), Am. Arbitration Assn. (dir., exec. com. 1961-69), Archtl. League N.Y. Club: Century Assn. (N.Y.C.). Home: Head of the Plains Nantucket MA 02554

LAFAUCI, HORATIO MICHAEL, educator; b. Providence, Aug. 12, 1917; s. Horatio Domenico and Virginia (Camardo) LaF.; A.B., Brown U., 1938, M.A., 1949; Ed.D., Harvard U., 1957; m. Bertha Beatrice Lukas, June 29, 1946; children—Roger John, David Michael. Tchr. Latin, Mt. Pleasant High Sch., Providence, 1939-40; head history dept. East Greenwich Acad., 1940-41; tchr. econs. and accounting, head dept. accounting, bus. mgr. athletics Becker Jr. Coll., Worcester, Mass., 1946-50; registrar Coll. Gen. Edn., Boston U., 1951-52, Coll. Gen. Edn. and Jr. Coll., 1952-53, asst. dean and registrar Jr. Coll., 1953-56, asst. dean, asso. prof. psychology and guidance Jr. Coll., 1957-58, asst. to dean of univ., 1958, dir. univ. budget, 1958, exec. asst. to pres., dir. budget, 1959-61, dean Coll. Basic Studies, 1961-75, prof. edn., 1961—. Served to 1st lt. AUS, 1941-46. Mem. Assn. Higher Edn., Nat. Soc. Study Edn., Assn. Gen. and Liberal Studies (pres. 1970). Episcopalian. Co-author: Team Teaching at the College Level, 1970. Home: 238 Park Ave Arlington MA 02174 Office: 718 Commonwealth Ave Boston MA 02215

LAFEBER, WALTER FREDERICK, educator; b. Walkerton, Ind., Aug. 30, 1933; s. Ralph N. and Helen (Lidecker) LaF.; B.A., Hanover Coll., 1955; M.A., Stanford, 1956; Ph.D., U. Wis., 1959; m. Sandra Gould, Sept. 11, 1955; children—Scott Nichols, Suzanne Margaret. Asst. prof. history Cornell U., 1959-63, asso. prof., 1963-67, prof., 1967-68, Noll prof. history, 1968—; Commonwealth lectr. U. London (Eng.), 1973. Mem. adv. com. hist. div. State Dept., 1971-75; asso. Lehrman Inst.; mem. Eleanor Roosevelt Fellowship Found. Mem. Orgn. Am. Historians, Am. Hist. Assn. (Albert Beveridge prize 1962), Soc. Historians of Am. Fgn. Policy. Author: The New Empire . . . 1860-1898, 1963; America, Russia and the Cold War, 4th edit., 1980; The Panama Canal, The Crisis in Historical Perspective, 1978, expanded edit., 1979; co-author: Creation of the American Empire; The American Century, 2d edit., 1979. Editor: John Quincy Adams and American Continental Empire, 1965; America in the Cold War, 1969; American Issues Forum, Vol. 2, 1976, also others; mem. editorial adv. bd. Polit. Sci. Quar., Jour. Am. History, Internat. History Rev. Home: 24 Cornell St Ithaca NY 14850

LAFERRIERE, ROLAND PAUL, ins. co. exec.; b. Chicopee, Mass., Mar. 19, 1925; s. August and Yvonne (Hamel) L.; B.A., Boston U., 1951; m. Doris Rita Gamache, May 3, 1947; children—Lee Ann, Suzanne. With Mass. Mut. Life Ins. Co., Springfield, 1951—, asst. group sec., 1960-65, asso. dir. group life and health adminstrn., 1965-68, asso. dir. policyholder service, then dir., 1968, 2d v.p., 1969, v.p., exec. officer, 1970-76, sr. v.p., 1976—. Bd. dirs. Jr. Achievement of Western Mass., Community Council Greater Springfield, Stage/West Theatre; corporator Med. Center Western Mass. Served with USAF, 1943-46. Decorated Air medal with three oak leaf clusters; Croix de Guerre (France). Mem. Life Office Mgmt. Assn., Planning Execs. Inst., Health Ins. Assn. Am. Clubs: Longmeadow (Mass.) Country; Colony (Springfield); Elks. Home: 15 Highridge Rd Wilbraham MA 01095 Office: 1295 State St Springfield MA 01111

LAFFER, ARTHUR, economist; B.A., Yale U.; M.B.A., Ph.D., Stanford U. Former faculty mem. Stanford U., U. Chgo.; former chief economist Office of Mgmt. and Budget, Exec. Office of the Pres., Washington; prof. fin. and bus. econs. U. So. Calif., Los Angeles, 1976—. Office: Sch Business Adminstrn Univ of So Calif University Park Los Angeles CA 90007

LAFFERTY, JAMES MARTIN, physicist; b. Battle Creek, Mich., Apr. 27, 1916; s. James V. and Ida M. (Martin) L.; student Western Mich. U., 1934-37; B.S. in Engring. Physics, U. Mich., 1939, M.S. in Physics, 1940, Ph.D. in Elec. Engring., 1946; m. Eleanor J. Currie, June 27, 1942; children—Martin C., Ronald J., Douglas J., Lawrence E. Physicist, Eastman Kodak Research Lab., Rochester, N.Y., 1939; physicist Gen. Electric Research Lab., Schenectady, 1940, 42—, mgr. physics and elec. engring. lab., 1972—; with Carnegie Instn., Washington, 1941-42. Pres.-elect exec. council Internat. Union Vacuum Sci., Technique and Applications, 1977—. Mem. greater consistory Ref. Ch.; trustee Schenectady Museum, 1967-73, sec., 1971-72, pres., 1972-73. Recipient Devel. award Bur. Naval Ordnance, 1946; Distinguished Alumnus citation U. Mich., 1953; IR-100 award, 1968. Fellow Am. Phys. Soc., IEEE (Lamme medal 1979), AAAS, mem. Am. Vacuum Soc. (hon. life, dir. 1962-70, sec. 1965-67, pres., 1968-69), U.S. Power Squadrons (past comdr. Lake George squadron), Sigma Xi, Phi Kappa Phi, Iota Sigma, Tau Beta Pi. Editor, contbg. author: Scientific Foundations of Vacuum Technique (Dushman), 1962; asso. editor Jour. Vacuum Sci. and Tech., 1966-69. Editorial bd. Internat. Jour. Electronics, 1968—. Contbr. articles to profl. jours. Patentee in field; inventor lanthanum boride cathode, 1950, hot cathode magnetron ionization gauge, 1961, triggered vacuum gap, 1966. Home: 1202 Hedgewood Ln Schenectady NY 12309 Office: PO Box 8 Schenectady NY 12301

LAFFERTY, RALPH FREDRICK, recreational equipment mfg. co. exec.; b. Portland, Oreg., Dec. 13, 1918; s. Raymond Edward and Florence (Harvey) L.; B.B.S., U. Oreg., 1940; m. Barbara Sumers, Oct. 2, 1943 (div. Jan. 31, 1977); children—Georgette S., Ralph Fredrick, John R., Lucille, Robert, Paul Gregory, Barbara Antonia; m. 2d, Traudl Heinrich, Dec. 31, 1977. Partner, R.F. Lafferty & Co., mem. Am. Stock Exchange, N.Y.C., 1946-56, ltd. partner, 1956-77; exec. v.p., gen. mgr. Zero Hour Bomb Co., Tulsa, 1956-59; pres. Zebco Co., Tulsa, 1959-61; pres. Zebco div. Brunswick Corp., Tulsa, 1961-67, 71-77, pres. consumer div., 1967-71, v.p. corp., Chgo., 1967-77; pres., chief exec. officer Garcia Corp., Teaneck, N.J., 1977-78; pres. Garcia Tackle Co., Teaneck, 1978; pres. Fenwick div. Woodstream Corp., Lititz, Pa., 1979—. Chmn. bd. Tulsa YMCA, 1972; bd. dirs. Indian Nations council Boy Scouts Am., Tulsa, Tulsa chpt. NCCJ, St. John's Hosp., Tulsa. Served to capt. U.S. Army, 1941-45. Decorated Purple Heart with oak leaf cluster, Silver Star. Mem. Tulsa C. of C. (dir. 1967-71). Clubs: Tulsa Polo and Hunt, Tulsa Ski (Tulsa); Amateur Ski (N.Y.); Smoke Rise (N.J.); Sun Valley (Idaho) Ski; Am. Alpine (N.Y.C.); Chgo. Office: Fenwick 14799 Chestnut St Westminster CA 92683

LAFFOON, CARTHRAE MERRETTE, mgmt. cons.; b. Wilkinsburg, Pa., Jan. 1, 1920; s. Carthrae Merrette and Kittie (Painter) L.; B.S., Mass. Inst. Tech., 1942; m. Helen Elizabeth Frisk, July 3, 1943; children—Judith Karin (Mrs. Wright), Catharine Elizabeth, Carthrae Merrette III (dec.), Barbara Louise. Jr. engr. research lab. Westinghouse Electric Corp., Pitts., 1942-45, asst. project engr. aviation gas turbine div., South Phila., 1945-47; asst. project engr. Ryan Aero. Co., San Diego, 1947-48, power plant group leader, 1948-49; jr. engr. San Diego Gas & Electric Co., 1950-53, asst. efficiency engr., 1953-58, asst. sta. chief, 1958-60, mech. engr., 1960-63, chief mech. engr., 1963, v.p. prodn., transmission, 1963-65, v.p. electric, 1965-70, sr. v.p., 1971-76; pres. C.M. Laffoon Cons., 1976—; pres., dir. Geothermal Generation, Inc., 1976—; dir. Kay Labs. Registered prof. engr., Calif. Mem. Pacific Coast Electric Assn., Pacific Coast Gas Assn., ASME, Am. Nuclear Soc., Sigma Xi, Tau Beta Pi. Republican. Presbyterian (elder). Club: Kiwanis. Home: 1109 Merritt Ln El Cajon CA 92020 Office: PO Box 1892 El Cajon CA 92022

LAFLEUR, GUY, profl. hockey player; b. Thurso, Que., Can., Sept. 20, 1951; s. Rejean and Pierrette Lafleur; student pub. schs.; m. Lise Barre, June 16, 1973; 1 son, Martin. Mem. jr. hockey team Que. Remparts; now player Montreal Canadiens Profl. Hockey Team. Recipient Art Ross trophy, 1976, 77; Conny Smythe trophy, 1977; Hart trophy, 1977. Home: 15 Magnolia Rd Baie Durphe PQ Canada Office: 2313 St Catherine St W Montreal PQ H3H 1N2 Canada

LAFLEUR, HENRI GRIER, lawyer; b. Montreal, Que., Can., June 17, 1908; s. Henri Amédée and Olive Masson (Grier) L.; B.A., McGill U., 1929; B.A., Oxford (Eng.) U., 1931, B.C.L., 1932; m. Celia Frances Cantlie; 2 sons by previous marriage. Admitted to Que. bar, 1933; counsel to firm Lafleur, Brown, de Grandpré, Montreal. Mem. Canadian Bar Assn., Zeta Psi. Clubs: Mount Royal, Montreal, Montreal Racket; Orleans Fish and Game; Canadian (N.Y.C.). Office: Box 214 Stock Exchange Tower 800 Victoria Sq Montreal PQ H4Z 1E4 Canada

LAFLEY, ALAN FREDERICK, banker; b. Stamford, Conn., Aug. 26, 1922; s. Alan George and Clara (Petersen) L.; B.B.A., Clarkson Coll., Potsdam, N.Y., 1946; M.B.A., U. Mich., 1948; m. Kathryn Margaret Irwin, Mar. 1, 1946; children—Alan George, Nora Kathryn, Jo Anne, Mary Patricia. Asst. prof. Sch. Mgmt., placement dir. Clarkson Coll., 1948-50; placement dir. Sch. Bus., Ind. U., Bloomington, 1950-51; with Gen. Electric Co., 1951-73, mgr. exec. personnel and compensation, N.Y.C., 1968-73; v.p. personnel Clark Equipment Co., Buchanan, Mich., 1973-75; exec. v.p. human resources Chase Manhattan Bank, N.Y.C., 1975—; mem. Personnel Round Table. Served to 1st lt. U.S. Army and USAAF, 1942-46. Decorated Air medal with oak leaf cluster. Office: 1 Chase Manhattan Plaza New York NY 10015

LA FOLLETTE, BRONSON CUTTING, atty. gen. Wis.; b. Washington, Feb. 2, 1936; s. Robert Marion, Jr. and Rachel Wilson (Young) LaF.; B.A. in Polit. Sci., U. Wis., 1958, J.D., 1960; children—Robert M., Deborah C. Admitted to Wis. bar, 1960; asst. U.S. atty. Western Dist. Wis., 1962-64; atty. gen. State of Wis., 1965-69, 74—; Am. specialist abroad for State Dept. in India and Ceylon, 1965; Democratic nominee for gov. Wis., 1968; pres. Wis. Consumers League, 1969; chmn. Pres.'s Consumer Adv. Council, 1967-69; bd. dirs. Consumers Union, 1968-77. Home: 733 Lakewood Blvd Madison WI 53704 Office: 114E State Capitol Bldg Madison WI 53702

LAFOLLETTE, CHARLES SANBORN, paper co. exec.; b. Indpls., Sept. 3, 1929; s. Charles D. and Elizabeth (Sanborn) LaF.; A.B. cum laude, Harvard U., 1951, M.B.A., 1953; m. Ellen Unwin McHugh, Apr. 24, 1954; children—Laetitia Amelia, Lizellen, Anne Unwin, Charles McHugh. With Corning Glass Works (N.Y.), 1955-70, asst. comptroller, 1961-64, asst. treas., financial v.p. internat., 1964-66; financial dir. Europe of Corning Glass Internat., Brussels, 1966-68; financial v.p. Corning Glass subs. Sovirel, Paris, 1968-70; exec. v.p. finance, dir., mem. exec. com. Crown Zellerbach Corp., San Francisco, 1970—; dir. Bunker Hill Income Securities, Inc., Impell, New Eng. Nuclear Co., Allendale Ins., U.S. Leasing. Treas. European Rep. Nat. Com., 1970. Dir. Arnot Art Gallery, Elmira, N.Y., 1963-67; bd. dirs. de Young Mus., Sta. KQED-TV, San Francisco Symphony. Served with AUS, 1953-55. Mem. Bankers Club San Francisco, Circle Interalliee (Paris), Circle Gauloise (Brussels). Clubs: University (N.Y.C. and San Francisco); St. Francis Yacht, Pacific Union, Vintners (San Francisco). Home: 2620 Larkin St San Francisco CA 94109 Office: 1 Bush St San Francisco CA 94104

LA FOLLETTE, DOUGLAS J., former sec. state Wis.; b. Des Moines, June 6, 1940; s. Joseph Henry and Frances (Van der Wilt) La F.; B.S., Marietta Coll., 1963; M.S., Stanford U., 1964; Ph.D., Columbia U., 1967. Asst. prof. chemistry and ecology U. Wis., Parkside, 1969-72; mem. Wis. Senate, 1973-75; sec. state Wis., 1975-79; mem. Council Econ. Priorities, Lake Mich. Fedn., Wis. Environ. Decade, S.E. Wis. Coalition for Clean Air. Democratic candidate for U.S. Congress, 1970, for Wis. lt. gov., 1978. Recipient Environ. Quality award EPA. Mem. Am. Fedn. Tchrs., Fedn. Am. Scientists, Phi Beta Kappa. Author: Wisconsin's Survival Handbook, 1971. Home: 705 Orton Ct Madison WI 53703 Office: 13 W State Capitol Bldg Madison WI 53702

LAFONTAINE, JEAN-MARIE, clergyman; b. Montreal, Can., Apr. 4, 1923; s. Georges Albert and Emmeline (Martel) L.; Licence in Theology, U. Montreal, 1948; Doctorate in Social, Polit. and Econ. Scis., U. Lille (France), 1951. Ordained priest Roman Catholic Ch., 1948; adviser Confedn. Nat. Trades Union, Can., 1951-66; prof. social scis. U. Montreal, 1953-67; exec. sec. Que. Conf. Cath. Bishops, 1966-68; vicar gen. Cath. Diocese Montreal, 1968-79, aux. bishop, 1979—. Vice pres. United Council for Human Rights, 1965-68. Mem. Theologians Assn. Am. Home: 1450 Blvd Saint-Joseph East Montreal PQ H2J 1M5 Canada Office: 2000 Sherbrooke St West Montreal PQ H3H 1G4 Canada

LAFONTANT, JEWEL STRADFORD, lawyer; b. Chgo., Apr. 28, 1922; d. Cornelius Francis and Aida Arabella (Carter) Stradford; A.B., Oberlin Coll., 1943; LL.D., U. Chgo., 1946; 1 son, John W. Rogers III. Admitted to Ill. bar, 1947; asst. U.S. atty., 1955-58; partner firm Lafontant, Wilkins & Butler, Chgo.; dep. solicitor gen. U.S., Washington, 1972-75; dir. Trans World Airlines, Continental Bank, Foote, Cone & Belding, Bendix Corp., Equitable Life Assurance Soc. U.S. Mem. U.S. Adv. Commn. Internat. Edn. and Cultural Affairs, Nat. Council Minority Bus. Enterprises, Nat. Council on Ednl. Research; chmn. adv. bd. Civil Rights Commn. Trustee Lake Forest (Ill.) Coll., Howard U., Tuskegee Inst. Mem. Chgo. Bar Assn. (bd. govs.). Bd. editors Am. Bar Assn. Jour. Home: 180 E Pearson St Chicago IL 60611 Office: 69 W Washington St Chicago IL

LAFORCE, ARNOLD ROBERTSON, investment cons.; b. Newark, Aug. 4, 1913; s. Harry Camp and Effie (Robertson) LaF.; B.S., Middlebury Coll., 1935; M.B.A., N.Y. U., 1938; m. Isobel Drummond, Aug. 1939; 1 dau., Susanne. Security analyst Granbery, Marache & Co., 1935-39; prof. finance N.Y. U. Grad. Sch. Bus., 1940-42; v.p. Met. Life Ins. Co., 1942-56; exec. v.p., dir. El Paso Natural Gas Co., 1956-62; pres., dir. Central Securities Corp., N.Y.C., 1962-72; financial and investment cons., 1972—; dir. Am. Natural Resources Co., Purolator, Inc., Guardian Life Ins. Co. Am., ASA Ltd., Wolverine Worldwide. Chmn. bd. trustees Middlebury (Vt.) Coll. Mem. Kappa Delta Rho. Clubs: Mendham Golf and Tennis; Baltusrol Golf; University (N.Y.C.). Author: (with J.I. Bogen) Financial Handbook, 1948; (with D. McCahon) Investment of Life Insurance Funds, 1952. Home: Green Hills Rd Mendham NJ 07945 Office: PO Box 351 Gladstone NJ 07934

LA FORCE, JAMES CLAYBURN, JR., economist, educator; b. San Diego, Dec. 28, 1928; s. James Clayburn and Beatrice Maureen (Boyd) La F.; B.A., San Diego State Coll., 1951; M.A., U. Calif. at Los Angeles, 1958, Ph.D., 1962; m. Barbara Lea Latham, Sept. 23, 1952; children—Jessica, Allison, Joseph. Asst. prof. econs. U. Calif. at Los Angeles, 1962-66, asso. prof., 1967-70, prof., 1971—, chmn. dept.

econs., 1969-78, dean Grad. Sch. Mgmt., 1978—; dir. Transport Indemnity, Inc., Cypress Mines. Chmn. adv. com. Calif. Workmen's Compensation, 1974-75. Bd. dirs. Nat. Bur. Econ. Research, 1975—; trustee Inst. Contemporary Studies, 1974—; trustee Found. for Research in Econs. and Edn., 1970—, chmn., 1977—. Social Sci. Research Council research tng. fellow, 1958-60; Fulbright sr. research grantee, 1965-66, Am. Philos. Soc. grantee, 1965-66. Mem. Econ. History Assn., Mont Pelerin Soc., Western Econ. Assn. Author: The Development of the Spanish Textile Industry 1750-1800, 1965; (with Warren C. Scoville) The Economic Development of Western Europe, vols. 1-5, 1969-70. Home: 10581 Wyton Dr Los Angeles CA 90024

LAFORE, LAURENCE DAVIS, educator, author; b. Narberth, Pa., Sept. 15, 1917; s. John Armand and Anne (Shearer) L.; B.A., Swarthmore Coll., 1938; M.A., Fletcher Sch. Law and Diplomacy, 1939, Ph.D., 1950. Mem. faculty Trinity Coll., Hartford, Conn., 1940-42; with State Dept. 1942-43, OWI, 1943-44; asst. press attache Am. embassy, Paris, France, 1944-46; research asso. ECA, 1948; mem. faculty Swarthmore Coll., 1946-67, prof. history, 1960-67; vis. prof. U. Iowa, 1967-68, prof. history, 1969—, chmn. dept., 1974-77. Mem. Am. Hist. Soc., Conf. Brit. Studies, Phi Beta Kappa, Delta Upsilon. Author: (with Paul Beik) Modern Europe, 1958; (novel) Learner's Permit, 1962; (novel) The Devil's Chapel, 1964; The Long Fuse, 1965; (with Sarah L. Lippincott) Philadelphia, The Unexpected City, 1965; (novel) Stephen's Bridge, 1968; (novel) Nine Seven Juliet, 1969; The End of Glory, 1970; The Days of Emperor and Clown, 1973; American Classic, 1975. Home: 9 Parsons St Iowa City IA 52240

LA FOREST, GERARD VINCENT, Can. govt. ofcl.; b. Grand Falls, N.B., Can., 1926; s. Alfred and Philomene (Lajoie) La F.; student in art St. Francis Xavier U., Antigonish, N.S., 1944-46; B.C.L., U. N.B., 1949; B.A. in Jurisprudence (Rhodes scholar), Oxford (Eng.) U., 1951, M.A., 1956; LL.M. (Univ. fellow), Yale U., 1965, J.S.D., 1966; m. Marie Warner, Dec. 27, 1952; children—Marie, Kathleen, Anne, Elizabeth, Sarah. Called to N.B. bar, 1949, created queen's counsel, 1968; practiced law, Grand Falls, 1951-52; adv. counsel legal br. Can. Dept. Justice, Ottawa, Ont., 1952-55; legal adv. Irving Oil and Asso. Cos., St. John, N.B., 1955-56; asso. prof. law U. N.B., 1956-63, prof., 1963-68; dean law U. Alta. (Can.), 1968-70; asst. dept. atty. gen. Can. Research and Planning, Ottawa, 1970-74; mem. Law Reform Commn. of Can., Ottawa, 1974—; on leave as exec. vice chmn. Can. Bar Assn. Com. on Constn., 1977-78; cons. to fed. and provincial govts., including appearances in constl. law cases before Supreme Ct. Can.; adv. to spl. counsel on const. to Minister of Justice and Prime Minister Can., 1967-70; mem. exec. com. Task Force on Computers and Privacy, 1971-72; vis. prof. U. Montreal, 1962-63; professeur a la lecon U. Ottawa, 1971—; lectr. in law McGill U., 1973, 77-78. Fellow Royal Soc. Can., World Acad. Art and Sci.; mem. Can. Bar Assn., Assn. Can. Law Tchrs., Internat. Law Assn. (v.p. Can. br.). Roman Catholic. Author: Disallowance and Reservation of Provincial Legislation, 1955; Extradition to and from Canada, 1961, 2d rev. edit., 1977; The Allocation of Taxing Power Under the Canadian Constitution, 1967; Natural Resources and Public Property Under the Canadian Constitution, 1969; (with others) Le Territoire Quebecois, 1970; (with assos.) Water Law in Canada—The Atlantic Provinces, 1973; contbr. numerous articles, revs. to profl. publs. Office: 130 Albert St Ottawa ON K1A 0L6 Canada

LAFRANCE, FRANCIS X., lawyer; b. Fall River, Mass., Mar. 15, 1902; s. Peter P. and Anna M. (Vaillancourt) LaF.; B.S., Nat. U., 1926; J.D., George Washington U., 1926; LL.D., Providence Coll., 1970; m. Marguerite Jean Cote, Sept. 4, 1931; children—Richard C., Robert H. Admitted to R.I. bar; former sr. partner firm Swan, Kenney, Jenckes & Asquith, Providence, 1935—. Founder, Woodlawn Credit Union, Pawtucket, R.I.; sec., dir. Cheever, Tweedy & Co., Inc., North Attleboro, Mass.; former dir. Rayhill & Greene Supply Co., Oceanside Holdings, Newport, R.I., Indsl. Paper & Cordage Co., J.C. Campbell Paper Co., Pawtucket, also Worcester and Brockton, Mass. Mem. R.I. Commn. to Study Orgn. and Operation of State Govt., 1962; sec. Commn. for Reorgn. of State Jud. System; chmn., mem. Selective Service System, 30 yrs.; former dist. commr. Blackstone Valley council Boy Scouts Am.; former chmn. speakers bur. ARC; mem. adv. bd. Salve Regina Coll., Newport. Mem. Am., R.I. (chmn. exec. com., treas.) bar assns., Town Criers for R.I., Georgetown U., George Washington U., Providence Coll. alumni assns. Kiwanian. Club: Turks Head. Home: 17 Cathedral Ave Providence RI 02908

LAGANO, SANTO ROCCO, banker; b. Port Chester, N.Y., Oct. 1, 1928; s. Rocco and Santa (Morabito) L.; grad. Am. Inst. Banking, 1950, Stonier Grad. Sch. Banking, Rutgers U., 1970; m. Antoinette Pugliese, May 9, 1954; children—Daniel, Stephen. Messenger, teller Peoples Nat. Bank & Trust Co., White Plains, N.Y., 1946-50; asst. nat. bank examiner, comptroller of currency, Washington, 1953-63, nat. bank examiner, comptroller of currency, 1963-66; v.p. Marine Midland Bank, Poughkeepsie, N.Y., 1966-71, sr. vp., 1971—. Bd. dirs., mem. exec. com. Dutchess County chpt. ARC, Mid-Hudson Pattern, Inc.; bd. dirs. United Way Dutchess County; trustee Poughkeepsie Area Fund, Inc., St. Francis Hosp. Mem. Council of Industry of S.E. N.Y., Poughkeepsie Area C. of C., Robert Morris Assos., Dutchess-Putnam Bankers Assn., Poughkeepsie Area C. of C. (dir.). Rotarian. Club: Amrita (Poughkeepsie). Home: 27 Putnam Rd Hyde Park NY 12538 Office: 347 Main St Poughkeepsie NY 12601

LAGARIAS, JOHN SAMUEL, engring. co. exec.; b. Rochester, N.Y., July 4, 1921; s. Soterios Nicholas and Aspacia (Basil) L.; B.S. in Physics, Rensselaer Poly. Inst., 1948; postgrad. Oak Ridge Sch. Reactor Tech., 1955-56; m. Virginia Jane Clark, June 16, 1947; children—Jeffrey, Peter, Clark. Research engr. Westinghouse Electric Research Labs., Pitts., 1948-51; mgr. metal products research Koppers Co., Inc., Pitts., 1951-63; mgr. research and devel. Am. Instrument Co., Silver Spring, Md., 1963-64; pres. Resources Research, Inc., Reston, Va., 1964-71; dir. environ. quality Kaiser Engrs., Oakland, Calif., 1971—; lectr. civil engring. dept. on environment U. Md., 1970-71; mem. tech. adv. com. Commonwealth of Va., 1969-71, Washington Council of Govts., 1968-70; conf. chmn. 2d Internat. Clean Air Congress, Washington, 1970; planning commr. City of Moraga (Calif.), 1975-78. Served with AUS, 1943-46. Registered prof. engr., Md. Diplomate Am. Acad. Environ. Engrs. Mem. Air Pollution Control Assn. (pres. 1968-69), Nat. Engring. Council on Air Resources (commr. 1970-77), IEEE, Am. Phys. Soc., Water Pollution Control Fedn., Am. Inst. Metall. Engrs. Club: Cosmos (Washington). Contbr. articles to tech. jours. Patentee electrostatic precipitators, analytical instruments and indsl. gas cleaning equipment. Home: 276 Donald Dr Moraga CA 94556 Office: Kaiser Engrs PO Box 23210 Oakland CA 94623

LAGATHER, ROBERT B., govt. ofcl.; b. Chisholm, Minn., Dec. 8, 1925; LL.B., George Washington U., 1951. Clk., night shift supr. welfare and retirement fund United Mine Workers, 1951-62; practiced in Washington, 1953-62; with Dept. Labor, 1962—, dep. asst. sec. Labor Mgmt. Relations Adminstrn., 1973-75, dep. solicitor for regional ops., 1975-78, asst. sec. mine safety and health, 1978—. Office: Dept Labor 4015 Wilson Blvd Arlington VA 22203

LAGERSTROM, PACO AXEL, scientist; b. Oskarshamm, Sweden, Feb. 24, 1914; s. Paco Harald and Karin (Wiedemann) L.; Filosofie Kandidat, U. Stockholm, 1935, Filosofie Licenciat, 1939; postgrad. U. Munster, Germany, 1938, Ph.D. in Math., U. Princeton, 1942. Instr. math. Princeton, 1941-44; flight test engr. Bell Aircraft, 1944-45; aerodynamicist Douglas Aircraft, 1945-46, cons., 1946-66; research asso. in aeros., staff engr. Calif. Inst. Tech., 1946-47, asst. prof. aero., 1947-49, asso. prof., 1949-52, prof., 1952-67, prof. applied math., 1967—; cons. TRW, 1966-68; vis. prof. U. Paris, 1960-61. Mem. bd. Coleman Chamber Music, Pasadena, 1950—, pres., 1958-60. Decorated Palmes Académiques (France); recipient Patron of Arts award Pasadena Arts Council, 1973. Guggenheim fellow, 1960-61. Mem. Am. Math. Soc., Soc. Indsl. and Applied Math. Clubs: The Travellers (Paris, France); Coral Casino (Santa Barbara); Brook, Knickerbocker (N.Y.C.); (N.Y.C.). Contbr. articles to profl. jours. and handbooks. Home: 57 San Miguel Rd Pasadena CA 91105 Office: Calif Inst Tech Pasadena CA 91125

LAGOMARSINO, ROBERT JOHN, congressman; b. Ventura, Calif., Sept. 4, 1926; s. Emilo J. and Marjorie (Gates) L.; B.A., U. Calif., Santa Barbara, 1953; J.D., U. Santa Clara (Calif.), 1954; m. Norma Jean Mabrey, Nov. 10, 1961; children—Dexter, Karen, Dana. Admitted to Calif. bar, 1954; individual practice law, Ventura, 1954; mem. Ojai (Calif.) City Council, 1958-60, mayor, 1958-61; mem. Calif. Senate, 1961-74; mem. 93d-96th Congresses from 19th Calif. Dist. Served with USNR, 1944-46. Named one of 5 outstanding young men Calif. Jaycees, 1961; recipient Pearl Chase Conservation Edn. award, 1970, Legislator Conservationist of Year award Calif. Wildlife Fedn., 1965, Honor award Calif. Conservation Council, 1967, Peace Officers Research Assn. award, 1966. Mem. Calif., Ventura County bar assns. Republican. Roman Catholic. Clubs: Elks, Moose, Eagles, Rotary. Office: 1117 Longworth House Office Bldg Washington DC 20515*

LAGOWSKI, J(OSEPH) J(OHN), chemist; b. Chgo., June 8, 1930; s. Joseph Thomas and Helen (Kasprzycski) L.; B.S., U. Ill., 1952; M.S., U. Mich., 1954; Ph.D., Mich. State U., 1957; Ph.D. (Marshall scholar), Cambridge (Eng.) U., 1959; m. Jeanne Wecker Mund, Feb. 13, 1954. Asst. demonstrator and supr. in inorganic chemistry Cambridge U., 1958-59; asst. prof. chemistry U. Tex., Austin, 1959-63, asso. prof., 1963-67, prof. chemistry and edn., 1967—. Mem. Am. Chem. Soc., Chem. Soc. (London), AAAS, Sigma Xi, Phi Lambda Upsilon. Author: (with G.W. Watt and L.F. Hatch) Chemistry, 1974, Chemistry in the Laboratory, 1964; The Structure of Atoms, 1964; The Chemical Bond, 1966; Modern Inorganic Chemistry, 1973; editor Jour. Chem. Edn., 1979—. Office: Dept Chemistry U Tex Austin TX 78712

LAGRONE, ALFRED HALL, educator; b. DeBerry, Tex., Sept. 25, 1912; s. William Taylor and Lena Enola (Westmoreland) LaG.; B.S. in Elec. Engring., U. Tex., Austin, 1938, M.S., 1948, Ph.D.. 1954; m. Dixie Louise Ballard, Sept. 8, 1955; children—Carrie Sue, Howard, Tracy, Kimberly. Distbn. engr. San Antonio Pub. Service Co., 1938-42; research engr. U. Tex., Austin, 1946-54, asso. prof., 1954-60, prof., 1960—, dir. antennas and propagation lab., 1966—. Cons., ABC, Collins Radio Co., Honeywell, Inc., Tex. Nuclear Co.; chmn. U.S. Commn. F of Union Radio-Scientifique Internationale, 1975—. Served to capt. USNR, 1942-46. Recipient Scott Helt Meml. award I.R.E., 1960. Fellow I.E.E.E. (nat. chmn. fellow com.); mem. Sigma Xi, Eta Kappa Nu, Tau Beta Pi. Home: 3925 Sierra Dr Austin TX 78731

LAGRONE, CYRUS WILSON, JR., psychologist, educator; b. Paint Rock, Tex., Jan. 8, 1911; s. Cyrus Wilson and Truda (Gough) LaG.; B.A., East Tex. State U., 1930; M.A., U. Tex., 1932, Ph.D., 1942; Ford fellow, vis. scholar, Columbia, 1954-55; m. Bessie Frances Shipley, July 29, 1968. Instr. psychology Lee Jr. Coll., Baytown, Tex., 1934-40, U. Tex., 1940-42; asst. prof. U. So. Calif., 1946-47; prof. psychology Tex. Christian U., 1947—, chmn. dept., 1947-67. Served to lt. col. AUS, 1942-46. Certified in clin. psychology Am. Bd. Examiners Profl. Psychology. Fellow Am. Psychol. Assn.; mem. Southwestern, Tex. (past pres.) psychol. assns., AAUP, Sigma Xi, Alpha Chi, Phi Delta Kappa. Contbr. articles to profl. jours. Home: 3200 Spanish Oak Dr Fort Worth TX 76109

LAGUE, RICHARD PAUL, magazine publisher; b. Providence, Apr. 26, 1944; s. Maurice Euclide and Elizabeth Copeland (Laurence) L.; B.A. in English, Coll. Holy Cross, Worcester, Mass., 1966; postgrad. Purdue U., 1970, U. Calif., 1971; m. Mary Ann Stark, Mar. 14, 1970; children—Mary Kathryn, Andrea Jean. Sales mgr., then product mgr. Yankee Motor Co., motorcycle mfg. and importing, Schenectady, 1972-73; dir. mktg. Cam Am. Motorcycles, Bombardier Ltd., Valcourt, Que., Can., 1973-76; publisher Motorcyclist mag., Los Angeles, 1976—. Served to capt. USAF, 1966-71. Mem. Mag. Pub.s Assn., Motorcycle Industry Council (dir.), Motorcycle Trades Assn., Am. Motorcycle Assn. Roman Catholic. Club: Holy Cross Coll. Varsity. Home: 18434 Bermuda St Northridge CA 91326 Office: 8490 Sunset Blvd Los Angeles CA 90069

LAHA, RADHA GOVINDA, educator; b. Calcutta, India, Oct. 1, 1930; s. Narayan Chandra and Savitri (Seal) L.; B.Sc., Presidency Coll., 1949, M.Sc., 1951; Ph.D., Calcutta U., 1957. Came to U.S., 1962, naturalized, 1971. Research asso. div. theoret. research Indian Statist. Inst., Calcutta, 1952-57; vis. research fellow dept. math. Catholic U., 1957-60; vis. research fellow Inst. Statistique, U. Paris, France, 1961-62, also Swiss Fed. Inst. Tech., Zurich, 1961-62; prof. math. statist. lab. Catholic U., 1967-72; prof. math. Bowling Green State U., 1972—; vis. research fellow Mass. Inst. Tech., 1968-69; vis. mem. Sch. Math., Inst. for Advanced Study, 1974. Recipient Saradaprasad prize; Smith-Mundt fellow, 1957; Fulbright fellow, 1957. Mem. Am. Math. Soc., Internat. Statis. Inst., Inst. Math. Statistics. Author (with E. Lukacs) Applications of Characteristic Functions, 1964; (with I. M. Chakravarti, J. Roy) Handbook of Methods of Applied Statistics, Vol. I and II, 1967; (with V.K. Rohatgi) Probability Theory, 1979. Home: 820 4th St Bowling Green OH 43402

LAHAUG, HENRY ALFRED, hosp. adminstr.; b. Skedsmo, Norway, Sept. 1, 1913; s. Hans Petter and Agnes (Halvorsen) L.; grad. Mil. Acad. Norway, 1935, Econ. Gymnas. Oslo, Norway, 1948; m. Andrea Omberg, Aug. 7, 1937; children—Lisbeth (Mrs. Mark Johnson), Anne Berit, Karen Lynn. Came to U.S., 1949, naturalized, 1955. Served from lt. to maj. Norwegian Army and Police, 1935-46; self-employed as accountant, 1946-48; accountant, Watertown, S.D., 1949-50; bus. mgr. Meml. Hosp., Watertown, 1950-51; office mgr., chief accountant R. E. Hubbard Co., Watertown, 1951-52; bus. mgr. Trinity Hosp., Minot, N.D., 1952-53, adminstr., 1953-59; supt. Jamestown (N.D.) State Hosp., 1959-61, adminstr., 1961—. Bd. dirs. N.D. Employees Retirement Plan; bd. dirs. N.D. Employees Assn., 1968-72, pres., 1971-72; trustee, 2d v.p. N.D. Blue Cross, 1955-72; pres. N.D. Hosp. Assn., 1957-59, trustee, 1955-72. Past dir., v.p. Jamestown United Fund. Recipient Minot Civic award, 1959. Fellow Am. Coll. Hosp. Adminstrs. (council regents 1966-72, 75—); mem. Am. Soc. Mental Hosp. Bus. Adminstrs., Am. Hosp. Assn. Lutheran (trustee, past pres.). Rotarian (pres. Jamestown 1963-64). Address: State Hospital Jamestown ND 58401

LA HAY, WAUHILLAU, writer; b. Claremore, Okla., July 14, 1909; d. Joseph Martin and Anne (Russell) La Hay; student Okla. State U., 1927-28; m. Philip M. Lohman, Jr., Feb. 9, 1929 (div. 1932); 1 son, Philip Merriman III; m. 2d, J. LeRoy Long, Dec. 30, 1953 (div. 1963). With Okla. Pub. Co., 1928-41; entertainment editor Chgo. Sun, 1941-43; dir. radio and TV publicity N.W. Ayer & Son, 1943-53; women's promotion dir. Kenyon & Eckhardt Advt., 1953-61; staff writer Scripps-Howard Newspaper Alliance, 1963-74; dir. Scripps-Howard Broadcasting Co. Mem. Kappa Alpha Theta. Democrat. Presbyn. Club: Press (past pres. Washington). Author mag. articles. Home: 10 Cherokee Rd Manitou Springs CO 80829

LAHEY, EDWARD VINCENT, JR., soft drink co. exec.; b. Boston, Mar. 11, 1939; s. Edward Vincent and Margery Tharsilla (Mehegan) L.; A.B., Holy Cross Coll., 1960; J.D., Georgetown U., 1964; postgrad. Bus. Sch. Columbia, 1969-70; m. Joan M. McCafferty, Sept. 26, 1964; children—Sheila, Edward Vincent III, Matthew. Admitted to D.C. bar, 1964, N.Y. bar, 1966; mem. firm Hester, Owen & Crowder, Washington, 1964-65; atty. PepsiCo, Inc., Purchase, N.Y., 1965-68, asst. gen. counsel, 1969-73, sec., 1970—, v.p., gen. counsel, 1973—. Trustee Village of Tuckahoe, N.Y., 1970. Served to lt. USNR, 1960-62. Mem. Am., D.C. bar assns., Am. Soc. Corporate Secs. Office: PepsiCo Inc Purchase NY 10577

LAHEY, MARION EUGENE, physician, educator; b. Ft. Worth, Dec. 28, 1917; s. Michael James and Mary Margaret (Kane) L.; A.B., U. Tex., 1939; M.D., St. Louis U., 1943; m. Edna M. Boyd, June 5, 1942; children—Gene, Michael, Kelly, Maureen, Kathleen, Patrick. Intern U.S. Naval Hosp., Great Lakes, Ill., 1943-44; resident pediatrics Hermann Hosp., Houston, 1946-47; resident pediatrics Children's Hosp., Cin., 1947-48, chief pediatric resident, 1948-49; NBC fellow med. scis. U. Utah Med. Sch., 1949-51, mem. faculty, 1951-52, 58—, prof., head dept. pediatrics, 1965—; asst. prof., then asso. prof. pediatrics U. Cin., 1952-58; dir. research Bruce Lyon Meml. Research Lab., Children's Hosp. East Bay, Oakland, Calif., 1964-65. Mem. fellowship com. Leukemia Soc., 1958—; hematology tng. grant com. NIH, 1959—. Mem. Soc. Pediatric Research (v.p. 1963), Am., Intermountain pediatric socs., Am. Acad. Pediatrics, Am. Soc. Clin. Oncology, Am. Hematology Soc., A.M.A., Western Soc. Pediatric Research, Western Soc. Clin. Research, Utah, Salt Lake County med. socs., Phi Beta Kappa, Alpha Omega Alpha, Alpha Sigma Nu. Home: 2114 Fardown Ave Salt Lake City UT 84121

LAHOOD, CHARLES GEORGE, JR., librarian; b. Omaha, Aug. 29, 1922; s. Charles George and Madeline Teresa (Raven) LaH.; B.S., Cath. U. Am., 1942, M.A., 1943, M.S. in L.S., 1952; m. Susanne Bracken, Aug. 28, 1948; children—Charles John, Daniel Edward, Patricia Anne, William David, Thomas George, Robert, Catherine. Mem. staff Library Congress, 1947—, head serial record sect., 1952-53, asst. chief photoduplication service, 1953-61, chief serial div., 1961—, chief photoduplication service, 1968—; adj. lectr. U. Md. Sch. Library and Info. Services. Library of Congress com. rep. Am. Nat. Standards Inst.; del. tech. com. Internat. Standards Inst. Mem. ALA (chmn. copy methods sect., resources and tech. services div., chmn. serial sect. RTSD 1968-69), Am. Documentation Inst. (council 1960-62), Saint Vincent de Paul Soc. Roman Catholic. Author: A Survey of Bibliographies and Checkists of Early American Imprints, 1956. Editor: Pictorial Americana, rev. edit., 1955; A Descriptive Checklist of Selected Manuscripts in the Monasteries of Mt. Athos, 1957. Home: 201 Port Tobacco Rd PO Box 273 LaPlata MD 20646 Office: Library of Congress Washington DC 20540

LAHR, JOHN, author; b. Los Angeles, July 12, 1941; s. Bert and Mildred (Schroeder) L.; B.A., Yale, 1963; B.A., Worcester Coll., Oxford, 1965, M.A.; m. Anthea Mander, Aug. 12, 1965; 1 son, Christopher David. Drama critic Manhattan East, 1966-68, New York Free Press, 1968-70, Evergreen Rev., 1968-71, Village Voice, 1969—; lit. adviser Tyrone Guthrie Theatre, Mpls., 1968; lit. mgr. Repertory Theatre of Lincoln Center, 1969-71. Mem. Rockefeller Theatre panel, 1969-73, Nat. Endowment for the Arts, 1969-73, Theatre Devel. Fund, 1970-73. Bd. dirs. Choreoconcerts, 1966—. Recipient George Jean Nathan award for drama criticism, 1969. Mem. P.E.N. (dir.). Author: Notes on a Cowardly Lion: The Biography of Bert Lahr, 1969; Up Against the Fourth Wall, 1970; The Autograph Hound, 1973; Astonish Me, 1973; (with Jonathan Price) Life-Show, 1973; Hot to Trot, 1974; Prick Up Your Ears: The Biography of Joe Orton (Gay News lit. prize 1979), 1978. Editor: (with Anthea Lahr) Casebook on Harold Pinter's The Homecoming, 1969; The Complete Plays of Joe Orton, 1976. Address: care Alfred A Knopf 201 E 50th St New York NY 10022

LAIDLAW, ROBERT RICHARD, pub. co. exec.; b. Berwyn, Ill., Mar. 25, 1923; s. John and Mabel Josephine (Howard) L.; student Dartmouth Coll., 1941-42; A.B., U. N.C., 1947, J.D., 1950; m. Evangeline Rene Harrelson, Aug. 12, 1944; children—Andrew Robert, Kimberly, Lisa. Sales rep. Laidlaw Bros., textbook pubs., River Forest, Ill., 1950-58, sales mgr., 1958-60, exec. v.p., 1960-68, pres., 1968—. Served with USNR, 1942-45. Congregationalist. Office: Laidlaw Bros Thatcher and Madison River Forest IL 60305

LAIDLER, KEITH JAMES, educator; b. Liverpool, Eng., Jan. 3, 1916; s. George James and Hilda (Findon) L.; came to Can., 1955, naturalized, 1960; student Liverpool Coll., 1929-34; B.A., Trinity Coll., Oxford, 1937, M.A., 1955, D.Sc., 1956; Ph.D., Princeton U., 1940; m. Mary Cabell Auchincloss, June 22, 1943; children—Margaret C., Audrey A., James R. Prof. chemistry U. Ottawa (Ont., Can.), 1955—; Commonwealth vis. prof. U. Sussex, U. Kent, U. London, 1966-67; Boomer lectr. U. Alta. (Can.), 1978. Decorated Queen's Jubilee medal; recipient Chemistry Tchr. award Mfg. Chemists Assn., 1975. Fellow Royal Soc. Can. (chmn. com. on symposia), Chem. Inst. Can. (medal 1971, Edn. award 1974), Chem. Soc. (London); mem. AAAS, Internat. Union Pure and Applied Chemistry (chmn. sub.-com. on chem. Kinetics). Clubs: Oxford Soc., Sherlock Holmes Soc. London. Author: Chemical Kinetics, 2d edit., 1965; Chemical Kinetics of Enzyme Action, 2d. edit., 1973; Reaction Kinetics, 1963; Principles of Chemistry, 1966; The Chemical Elements, 1970; Physical Chemistry with Biological Applications, 1978, others; contbr. articles to sci. jours. Home: 551 Mariposa Ave Rockcliffe Park ON K1M 0S5 Canada Office: Dept Chemistry U Ottawa Ottawa ON Canada

LAING, CHARLES BURNETT, company dir.; b. Winnipeg, Man., Can., June 15, 1910; s. George Stanley and Florence M. (Bradshaw) L.; B.A., U. Man., 1929; m. Aileen R. Thompson, Aug. 18, 1935; children—David Duncan Burnett, Rosalie Laing Lichtenfeld. With registrar's office U. Man., 1929-30; with Prudential Ins. Co. Am., 1930-70, actuarial student, mgr., supr., dir. orgn. and methods, 2d v.p., sr. v.p., 1954-70; dir. Sperry and Hutchinson Co., N.Y.C. Home: Post Kennel Rd Bernardsville NJ 07924

LAING, GERTRUDE MARY, assn. exec., civic worker; b. Tunbridge Wells, Eng., Feb. 13, 1905; d. Arthur George and Mary (Williams) Amies; came to Can., 1905; B.A., U. Man., 1925; postgrad. (French Govt. award) U. Paris, 1927; D. (hon.), U. Calgary, 1973, U. Ottawa, 1978; LL.D. (hon.), U. B.C., 1977; m. Stanley Bradshaw, June 16, 1930; children—Colin Douglas, Alan Richardson. Tchr. French, U. Man., Winnipeg, 1930-31, 43-46; exec. sec. Co-ordinating Council

War Services, Winnipeg, World War II; past pres. Winnipeg YWCA, Central Vol. Bur., Calgary (Alta., Can.) Social Planning Council; past v.p. Calgary Allied Arts Council, Western region Canadian Council Social Devel., Can.-World Youth; mem. Canadian Royal Commn. on Bilingualism and Biculturalism, 1963-70; part-time mem. Canadian Radio-TV Commn., 1968-73; mem. Canada Council, Ottawa, Ont., 1974—, chmn., 1975-78. Decorated officer Order of Can. Clubs: Ranchmen's (Calgary), Calgary Country. Co-author: Face to Face, 1972. Home: 1223 38th Ave SW Calgary AB T2T 2J3 Canada

LAING, JAMES TAMPLIN, educator; b. Montgomery, W.Va., Aug. 26, 1899; s. James McAlpin and Annie (Tamplin) L.; A.B., W.Va. U., 1924; M.A., Ohio State U., 1929, Ph.D., 1933; m. Claire Lenila Thomas, Aug. 2, 1927; 1 son, James Thomas. Instr., Dunbar (W.Va.) High Sch., 1924-25, Charleston, W.Va., 1926-28; asst. instr. Ohio State U., 1929-33; prof. sociology Holbrook Coll., 1933-34; asso. prof. W.Va. Inst. Tech., 1934-35; asso. prof. sociology Kent (Ohio) State U., 1935-37, prof., head dept., 1937-59, chmn. dept. sociology and anthropology, 1937-67, prof. sociology, 1967-69, prof. emeritus, 1969—; vis. prof. various summer assignments. Pres. Kent Welfare Bd., 1944-45, 45-46. Mem. Am., Ohio Valley (past pres.) sociol. socs., W.Va. Acad. Sci., AAUP, Alpha Kappa Delta, Pi Gamma Mu, Phi Sigma Kappa (dep. regional dir. region IV). Methodist. Rotarian (past pres.). Club: Wranglers. Co-author: Sociological Foundatios of Education, 1942; also articles, monographs. Home: 129 Sherman St Kent OH 44240 summer: Lansing WV 25862

LAING, PETER MARSHALL, lawyer; b. Montreal, Que., Can., Mar. 24, 1916; s. Campbell and Hazel (Marshall) L.; B.A., McGill U., 1935; B.A., Oxford (Eng.) U., 1938; m. Kathleen McConnell, May 12, 1945; children—Murdoch, David. Called to bar, Eng., 1939, Que., 1944, created Queen's counsel, 1959; practice in Montreal, 1944—; mem. firm Courtois, Clarkson, Parsons & Tetrault. Dir. Starlaw Investments; chmn. Comml. Trust Co., Ltd. Bd. govs. McGill U. Served with 9th Queen's Royal Lancers, 1939-43. Mem. Am. Coll. Trial Lawyers. Clubs: Mt. Royal, St. James, University. Home: 1291 Redpath Crescent Montreal PQ H3G 1A1 Canada Office: 630 Dorchester Blvd W Montreal PQ H3B 1V7 Canada

LAING, ROBERT STANLEY, company dir.; b. Seattle, Nov. 1, 1918; s. Robert Vardy and Marie Geddes (Scott) L.; B.S. in Mech. Engring., U. Wash., 1940; M.B.A., Harvard, 1947; m. Janet Emmott Orr, Aug. 26, 1947; children—Robert, Patricia, Cynthia, Martha, Elizabeth. With Nat. Cash Register Co., Dayton, Ohio, 1947-72, exec. asst., asst. comptroller, gen. auditor, asst. comptroller, comptroller, 1954-60, v.p. finance, 1960-62, exec. v.p., 1962-64, pres., 1964-72, dir., 1961-72; dir. Cin. Milacron, Inc., Armco Steel Corp., B.F. Goodrich Co.; past dir. Mead Corp., Gen. Mills. Bd. dirs. Sinclair Community Coll. Found., Dayton; past pres. United Fund, Dayton; trustee U. Dayton; chmn. bd. trustees Denison U., Granville, Ohio. Served to lt. comdr. USNR, 1941-46; PTO. Decorated Order Lateran Cross (Vatican). Mem. Bus. Equipment Mfg. Assn. (past chmn.). Clubs: Wequetonsing (Harbor Springs, Mich.); Moraine Country (Dayton); Cotton Bay (Bahamas); St. Andrews (Scotland); Cypress Lakes (Ft. Myers, Fla.). Home: 245 W Thruston Blvd Dayton OH 45419 Office: Suite 2850 Winters Bank Tower Dayton OH 45402

LAING, RONALD DAVID, psychiatrist; b. Glasgow, Scotland, 1927; M.D., U. Glasgow, 1951; m. Jutta; children—Adam, Natasha, Max. Intern, 1951; conscript psychiatrist Brit. Army, 1951-53; psychiatrist Glasgow Royal Med. Hosp.; tchr. dept. psychol. medicine U. Glasgow, 1953-56; clin. research Tavistock Inst. Human Relations, London, 1956-62; dir. Langham Clinic, London, 1962-65; co-founder Phila. assn. Kingsley Hall, London, 1965; speaker various colls. in U.S., 1970—. Author: The Divided Self, 1960; The Self and Others, 1961; Sanity, Madness and the Family, 1964; (with David G. Cooper) Reason and Violence: A Decade of Sartre's Philosophy, 1950-60, 1964; (with others) Interpersonal Perception, 1966; The Politics of Experience, 1967; The Politics of the Family, 1969, rev. edit., 1971; Knots, 1970; Self and Others, 1970; The Facts of Life, 1976; Do You Love Me?, 1976; Conversations with Adam and Natasha, 1977; Sonnets, 1979. Address: care Pantheon Books 201 E 50th St New York NY 10022

LAING, WILLIAM SCOTT, mktg. cons.; b. Leith, Scotland, Apr. 14, 1914; s. William Irvine and Jessie Mailer (Scott) L.; student George Watson's Coll., Edinburgh, 1921-31; M.A. (hons.), Edinburgh U., 1935; postgrad. U. Besançon, 1935-36; 1 son, John. Mem. Brit. Fgn. Service, Buenos Aires, 1938-47, Helsinki, 1947-50; consul to consul gen. Brit. Fgn. Service, N.Y.C., 1950-55; comml. counsellor, Brussels and Luxemburg, 1955-57; with UN Secretariat, 1961-76, chief sales sect. pub. service, 1969-76; internat. trade and mktg. cons. automotive and related fields, N.Y.C., 1977—. Club: Caledonian (London). Contbr. articles and studies profl. jours. Office: PO Box 4207 Grand Central Post Office New York NY 10017

LAINGEN, LOWELL BRUCE, ambassador; b. Odin Twp., Minn., Aug. 6, 1922; s. Palmer K. and Ida Mabel (Eng) L.; B.A. cum laude, St. Olaf Coll., 1947; M.A. in Internat. Relations, U. Minn., 1949; m. Penelope Babcock, June 1, 1957; children—William Bruce, Charles Winslow, James Palmer. Internat. relations officer State Dept., 1949-50; joined U.S. Fgn. Service, 1950; vice consul, Hamburg, Germany, 1951-53; 3d sec. embassy, Teheran, Iran, 1953-54; consul, Meshed, Iran, 1954-55; asst., then officer charge Greek affairs State Dept., 1956-60; 2d sec., then 1st sec. embassy, Karachi, Pakistan, 1960-64; with Pakistan/Afghanistan affairs bur. State Dept., 1964-67; assigned Nat. War Coll., 1967-68; dep. chief mission to Afghanistan, Kabul, 1968-71; country dir. Pakistan, Afghanistan and Bangladesh, State Dept., 1971-73, India, Nepal, Sri Lanka and the Maldives, 1973-74, acting dep. asst. sec. state for Near Eastern and South Asian affairs, 1974-75, dep. asst. sec. state for European affairs, 1975-76; ambassador to Malta, 1976—. Office: Dept State Washington DC 20520*

LAIR, FRANCIS LEO, coop. exec.; b. Albert Lea, Minn., Oct. 12, 1919; s. Frank and Gertrude Mary (Carey) L.; student Hamilton Sch. Bus., 1938-40; m. Dorothy Mary Sullivan, May 14, 1948; children—Kathleen M., Mary E., Jeanne D., Patrick J. Accountant, gen. mgmt. exec., local coops., 1941-42, 45-49; various positions mfg. and purchasing Nat. Coops., Inc., 1949-61; gen. mgr. Nat. Coops., Inc., Albert Lea, 1961-72, gen. mgr., exec. v.p. Universal Coops. Inc., Mpls., 1972—; dir. Agrl. Coop. Devel. Internat., Mut. Life Ins. Co. Served with USAAF, 1942-45. Mem. Am. Legion, Minn. State Automobile Assn. (dir.), Coop. League U.S. Roman Catholic. Elk, K.C. (4 deg.). Club: Decathlon. Home: 8295 131st St Apple Valley MN 55124 Office: 3001 Metro Dr Suite 500 Minneapolis MN 55420

LAIR, JESSE KAY, educator, author, advt. cons.; b. Bricelyn, Minn., Oct. 11, 1926; s. Merle Thomas and Bertha Christina (Evgen) L.; B.A., U. Minn., 1948, M.A., 1964, Ph.D., 1965; m. Jacqueline Patricia Carey, July 7, 1949; children—Janet Mary, Barbara Ann (Mrs. Robert Parker Dixon), Jesse Howard, Joseph Thomas, Michael Thaddeus. Copywriter, Bruce B. Brewer, Mpls., 1952-56, Leo Burnett Advt., Chgo., 1956-57; mktg. cons. Jesse Lair Co., Mpls., 1957-62; asso. prof. U. Minn., Mpls., 1963-67; asso. prof. ednl. psychology Mont. State U., Bozeman, 1967-77. Served with USAAF, 1944-45. Mem. Am., Mont. psychol. assns. Author: I Ain't Much Baby—But I'm All I've Got, 1972; (with Jacqueline C. Lair) Hey God, What Should I do Now?, 1973; I Ain't Well, But I Sure Am Better, 1975; Ain't I a Wonder, And Ain't You a Wonder Too, 1977; Sex-If I Didn't Laugh, I'd Cry, 1979. Home: PO Box 249 Bozeman MT 59715. *What I am most struck by in my life is how slowly I learn. Facts I learn easily and quickly, but learning how to live comes very slowly. The nice part, though, is that once I finally get beaten on hard enough by life to have the humility to be taught, there are always lovely teachers waiting right at my elbow ready to teach me gently what I need to learn.*

LAIR, ROBERT LOUIS, aircraft co. exec.; b. Albuquerque, Aug. 13, 1921; s. Louis E. and Inez B. (Mudd) L.; m. June Marie Moran, Aug. 9, 1941; children—Christopher Louis, Catherine Ann, Cynthia Susan. With Cessna Aircraft Co., Wichita, Kans., 1953—, sr. v.p., 1969—, also dir.; dir. Cessna Fin. Co., Cessna Internat. Fin. Co., Reims Aviation (France). Mem. AIAA, Am. Mgmt. Assn., Army Aviation Assn., Nat. Indsl. Conf. Bd., Kan., Wichita chambers commerce, Nat. Aero. Assn. Home: 105 Woodlawn Ct Wichita KS 67218 Office: Cessna PO Box 1521 Wichita KS 67201

LAIRD, ALAN DOUGLAS KENNETH, educator; b. Victoria, Can., Aug. 8, 1914; s. George Alexander and Edna A (Foy) L.; came to U.S., 1946, naturalized, 1955; B.A.Sc. in Mech. Engring., U. B.C., 1940; M.S., U. Calif. at Berkeley, 1949, Ph.D., 1951; m. Joyce Kathleen Morris, Nov. 3, 1941; children—William George, John Douglas, Linda Margaret. Engr., Def. Industries Ltd., Montreal, 1941-45, Leek and Co., Vancouver, Can., 1945-46; mem. faculty U. Calif. at Berkeley, 1948—, prof. mech. engring., 1964—, dir. Sea Water Conversion Lab., 1968—; cons. in field. Mem. ASME, Sigma Xi, Pi Tau Sigma. Home: 860 Sibert Ct Lafayette CA 94549 Office: Mech Engring Dept Univ Calif Berkeley CA 94720

LAIRD, CAMPBELL, metallurgist; b. Ardrishaig, Scotland, June 17, 1936; s. Albert and Janet Jackson (Grinlaw) L.; B.A., U. Cambridge, 1959, M.A., 1962, Ph.D., 1963; m. Frances Anne Beckwith, June 20, 1964; children—Katherine Flora, Andrew Kennedy, Lucy Margarette. Fellow, Christs Coll., Cambridge U., 1961-65; sr. scientist Ford Motor Co., Dearborn, Mich., 1963-68; vis. prof. Ohio State U., 1968-69; faculty U. Pa., Phila., 1969—, prof., chmn. dept. metallurgy and materials sci., 1974—. Served with Royal Engrs., U.K., 1954-56. Recipient Darwin and Haddon prizes Christs Coll., 1959; NSF grantee, 1973—, Army Research Office grantee, 1972—, Office Naval Research grantee, 1974-77, Alcoa Found. grantee, 1977-78. Mem. Am. Inst. Mining and Metall. Engrs. (past chmn. phys. metallurgy com., past chmn. program com.), Metall. Soc., Am. Soc. Metals, Electron Microscopy Soc. Am., Royal Instn., Inst. Metallurgists (U.K.). Asso. editor: Jour. Materials Sci. and Engring., 1970—. Contbr. engring. articles to sci. jours. Home: 951 Weadley Rd Radnor PA 19087 Office: U Pa Dept Metallurgy and Materials Sci Philadelphia PA 19104

LAIRD, DAVID, educator; b. Marshfield, Wis., Oct. 17, 1927; s. Melvin Robert and Helen Melissa (Connor) L.; Ph.B., U. Chgo., 1947; B.A. with highest honor, U. Wis., 1950, M.A., 1951, Ph.D., 1955; student Courtauld Inst., 1953; m. Helen Astrid Lauritzen, Sept. 10, 1955; 1 dau., Vanessa Ann. From instr. to asst. prof. Oberlin Coll., 1955-58; mem. faculty Calif. State U., Los Angeles, 1958—, chmn. dept. English, 1969-73, chmn. dept. Am. studies, 1977—; Nat. Humanities Inst. fellow U. Chgo., 1978-79. Mem. Western Shakespeare Seminar, Friends of Huntington Library; cons. to Choice. Uhrig Found. grantee, 1964-65; Fulbright fellow, 1953-54. Mem. Malone Soc., Am. Studies Assn., Modern Lang. and Lit. Assn., Phi Beta Kappa. Contbr. articles on Shakespeare, Am. lit. and cultural history to profl. jours. Home: 565 Milton Dr San Gabriel CA 91775 Office: California State U Los Angeles CA 90032

LAIRD, E. RUTH, artist; b. Houston, Mar. 21, 1921; d. James Irl and Beulah Laird; student U. Tex. at Austin, 1941-42, Cranbrook Acad. Art, 1953-55. Sec.-treas. Laird Lumber Co., Houston, 1945-53; instr. Art. U. Houston, 1955-58, U. St. Thomas, Houston, 1956-58; asst. dean Mus. Fine Arts, Houston, 1958-68; one woman shows include Elizabeth Ney Mus., Austin, 1970, Cranbrook Mus., Bloomfield Hills, Mich., 1954, Beaumont (Tex.) Mus., 1958, Rice U. Gallery, 1960, U. Houston, 1957; group shows include Everson Mus., Syracuse, N.Y., Met. Mus., Boston Mus., Bklyn. Mus., Contemporary Craft Mus., N.Y.C.; represented in permanent collections Everson Mus., Contemporary Crafts Mus., Children's Mus., Detroit, Cranbrook Mus.; executed fountain, New Harmony, Ind., 1960, baptismal font St. Basil's Ch., Angelton, Tex., 1962, altar pieces Chapel Rice U., 1962-73. Travel study grantee Tex. Swedish Cultural Found., 1955. Recipient Purchase award Internat. Invitational Exhbn., Syracuse Mus., 1957; named Woman of Yr., Houston chpt. Theta Sigma Phi, 1968, Woman of Press for outstanding contbn. to field fine art, 1968. Address: 1618 Cherryhurst St Houston TX 77006

LAIRD, JACK, film and TV producer, writer, dir.; b. Bombay, India, May 8, 1923; s. Leonard Von and Thelma (Laird) Schultheis; student dramatic workshop New Sch. Social Research, 1945-46, Actor's Lab, 1948-49; children—Sean, Persephone. Made profl. film debut, 1926, theatre debut in East Lynne, 1928; appeared on Broadway, 1946-48; appeared in summer stock, 1946-48, journalist N.Y. Times, N.Y.C., spring, 1948; freelance actor in West Coast theatre, films, radio and TV, 1948-61; producer with Bing Crosby Prodns., 1961-63; with Universal Studios, 1963; writer numerous plays; writer numerous films; writer TV films and shows, also radio dramas; producer films, including: Dark Intruder, Standig In Angst, Destiny of A Spy, Intrigo At Montecarlo, Perilous Voyage; producer numerous episodes for TV series, including: Ben Casey, Kraft Suspense Theatre, The Bold Ones, Night Gallery, Doctors Hospital, Kojak, Whatever Happened to the Class of '65?, Taylor Caldwell's Testimony of Two Men for Operation Primetime, The Dark Secret of Harvest Home, Beggarman, Thief; co-founder, mem. Stage Soc., Hollywood, Calif., 1951—. Served with USAAF, 1943-45; ETO. Recipient Grand prize for The Golden Asteroid 9th Internat. Festival Sci. Fiction Films, Trieste, Italy, 1971, 40th Annual Fame award, 1971, award for patriotic pub. service U.S. Treasury Dept., 1975, three Emmy nominations, two Writers Guild awards. Mem. Writers Guild Am., Dirs. Guild Am., Screen Actors Guild, Nat. Acad. TV Arts and Scis., ACLU, Am. Film Inst., Filmex, Los Angeles County Mus. Art. Democrat. Contbr. short stories to lit. jours. and popular mags. Office: Universal Studios Universal City CA 91608

LAIRD, MELVIN R., former sec. of def.; b. Omaha, Sept. 1, 1922; s. Melvin R. and Helen (Connor) L.; B.A., Carleton Coll., 1942; m. Barbara Masters; children—John, Alison, David. Mem. Wis. Senate, 1946-52, chmn. Wis. Legis. Council; mem. 83d-90th Congresses, chmn. Rep. Conf., mem. Appropriations com., chmn. House Rep. Minority, mem. Rep. Coordinating com.; sec. of def., 1969-72; domestic adviser to Pres. Nixon, 1973-74; sr. counsellor nat. and internat. affairs Reader's Digest Assn., 1974—; dir. Chgo. Pneumatic Tool Co., Met. Life Ins. Co., Northwest Airlines, Communications Satellite Corp., Purolator Inc., Investors Group of Cos., Phillips Petroleum Co. Bd. dirs. Thomas Jefferson Found. U. Va., World Rehab. Fund, Boys Clubs Am., Am. Film Inst., George Washington U., Wolf Trap Found. Performing Arts; trustee Kennedy Center; chmn. nat. def. project Am. Enterprise Inst., vice chmn. platform com. Rep. Nat. Conv., 1960, chmn., 1964. Decorated Order of Merit 1st class (Fed. Republic Germany); comdr. Nat. Order Legion of Honor (France); recipient 15th Ann. Albert Lasker med. award; Man of Year award Am. Cancer Soc.-Nat. Assn. Mental Health; Humanitarian award John E. Fogarty Found. for Mentally Retarded, 1974; Presdl. Medal of Freedom, 1974. Mem. Disabled Am. Vets., Mil. Order Purple Heart, 40 and 8, Am. Legion, VFW. Author: A House Divided: America's Strategy Gap, 1962. Editor: The Conservative Papers, 1964; Republican Papers, 1968. Office: 1730 Rhode Island Ave NW Washington DC 20036

LAIRD, STEPHEN, fgn. corr.; b. Emmaus, Pa., Aug. 1, 1915; s. Fred R. (D.D.S.) and Mary (Laird) Lichtenwalner; A.B., Swarthmore Coll., 1936; m. Lael Tucker, Mar. 1, 1940 (div. Sept. 1942); m. 2d, Jacqueline Cummins, Jan. 8, 1949; children—Maxime, Christopher. Reporter, Chester (Pa.) Times, 1936; staff writer Fortune mag. until 1939; with Time and Life mags., Washington; Japan, Russia, Germany for Time, Inc., 1940-41; chief Time, Inc. London bur., 1942; sr. fgn. news writer Time mag., 1943; war corr. Time, Inc., 1943-44; producer motion pictures R.K.O., 1944-45; producer-writer motion pictures Columbia Pictures, 1945; UN editor, Newsweek mag., 1946; fgn. corr. CBS in Paris, Berlin, Nuremberg, Warsaw, London, Washington, Geneva, 1946-51; chief information officer tech. assistance program FAO, Rome, 1951-52; chief Office Pub. Information, Intergovtl. Com. European Migration, Geneva, 1952; pub. relations counsellor, London, 1953; corr., editor France Actuelle, Paris, 1954-72; European reporter-counselor Japan Auto Mfrs. Assn., 1973—; European corr. Japan Auto Mfrs. Assn. Report, Automobile Industry; corr., commentator U.S. radio-TV, Paris, 1959—; corr. Fortune mag., Paris, 1966-68; chief Paris corr. Metromedia Radio, 1968-71. Mem. Soc. Friends. Clubs: Nat. Press (Washington); American (Paris). Author: Hitler's Reich and Churchill's Britain; Conversation In London; contbg. author Time, Inc. (books)—History In the Making; December 7—When War Came. Home: Soulaires 28130 Maintenon France Office: 33 rue de Ponthieu 75008 Paris France. *Above all, a man has to continue to grow and contribute and, in constant review of his life and work and outlook, change course if necessary so as to be able to live with himself in peace and, hopefully, pride and good usefulness to family, friends and community.*

LAIRD, WILBUR DAVID, JR., librarian; b. Kansas City, Mo., Mar. 15, 1937; s. Wilbur David and Alma Blanche (Turner) L.; student U. Wichita, 1959-60; B.A., U. Calif., Los Angeles, 1965, M.L.S., 1966; m. Linda Sue Tusler, Dec. 28, 1960; children—Wendy, Cynthia, Brian Andrew, David Alexander. Reference librarian U. Calif., Davis, 1966-67; acquisitions librarian U. Utah, 1967-70, asst. dir. for tech. services, 1970-71, asso. dir., 1971-72; univ. librarian U. Ariz., Tucson, 1972—. Bd. dirs. Tucson Civic Ballet, 1975-76. Served with U.S. Navy, 1955-59. Mem. ALA, Ariz. State (pres. 1978-79), Southwestern library assns., AAUP, Western History Assn. Author: The Hopi Indians, A Comprehensive Bibliography, 1977. Editor: Books of the Southwest, 1977—. Home: 4800 E San Francisco Tucson AZ 87512 Office: Main Library U Ariz Tucson AZ 85721. *Adaptability has been the key word in my life. I learned early that life requires constant adjustment. My mother attended college, but my father quit school in the fifth grade to help his family earn a living. We lived in a trailer house (no one had yet told us it was a mobile home) and followed the highway building boom of the 1930, 40s, and 50s. I attended more than 20 different grade schools, including one school year in six different schools, Living in cramped quarters and constantly on the move one must be flexible to survive.*

LAIRD, WILLIAM FREDERICK, utilities exec.; b. London, Ohio, July 15, 1919; s. Walter B. and Mary (Bostwick) L.; A.B., Capital U., 1941; LL.B., Columbia, 1943; m. Jane L. Buchman, Oct. 3, 1943; children—Frederick W., John W. Admitted to Ohio bar, 1945; practice in Columbus, 1945-51, pvt. practice, 1946-51; sec., gen. counsel Ohio Fuel Gas Co., 1951-63, sr. v.p., 1963-67, pres., 1967—; sr. v.p. Columbia Gas of Ohio, Ohio Valley Gas Co., 1963-67, pres., 73-74, chmn. bd., 1974—; exec. v.p., dir. Columbia Gas System, Inc., 1974-77, pres., 1977—. Served with U.S. Army, 1943-46. Mem. Am. Gas Assn., Columbus C. of C. (past chmn.). Home: 106 Brookmeadow Rd Wilmington DE 19807 Office: 20 Montchanin Rd Wilmington DE 19807

LAISE, FREDERIC STEVENS, coll. ofcl., former orgn. exec.; b. Ridgewood, N.J., Mar. 30, 1914; s. J. Fred and Elizabeth (Stevens) L.; student Deep Springs Coll., 1931-34, George Washington U., 1935; m. Helen Burdette Hunt, Feb. 20, 1937; children—Carl Stevens, Mary Burdette. Asso., Alexander Brown & Sons, investment bankers, Washington, 1935-42; field rep., later asst. mgr. Eastern area hdqrs. A.R.C., 1942-48, asso. nat. dir. fund raising, 1949-50, nat. dir. fund raising, 1949-51, dep. mgr. Midwestern area hdgrs., 1951-55, mgr. Midwestern area, 1955-62, nat. v.p., 1962-74, sr. v.p., 1974-78; dir. fund raising Deep Springs (Calif.) Coll., 1978—. Trustee Deep Springs Coll. Served as lt. USNR, 1944. Home: 3317 N Vermont St Arlington VA 22207

LAITIN, JOSEPH, govt. ofcl.; b. Bklyn., Oct. 2, 1914; s. Harry and Irene (Lubetkin) L.; m. Christine Henriette Houdayer, Apr. 26, 1961; children—Sigrid, Peter. Corr., UPI, Washington, 1941-45; fgn. corr. Reuters, Ltd., Far East, Europe, Latin Am., 1945-50; chief corr. Research Inst. Am., Washington, 1950-52; free lance writer, 1952-63; asst. to dir. Bur. of Budget, Washington, 1963-64; dep. press sec. to Pres., 1965-66; asst. to dir. for pub. affairs Office Mgmt. and Budget, 1966-74; asst. sec. pub. affairs Dept. Def., Washington, 1975-76; asst. adminstr. FAA, 1976-77; asst. sec. treasury, 1977—; cons. Commn. on Selective Service, 1966-67, Nat. Commn. on Causes and Prevention of Violence, 1968-70, Presdl. Commn. on Campus Unrest, 1970. Recipient Calif. State Fair award for best radio documentary The Changing Face of Hollywood, 1957; Disting. Public Service medal Dept. Def., 1975; Communicator of Year/Pub. Affairs award Nat. Assn. Government Communicators, 1977. Clubs: Nat. Press, Federal City (Washington). Home: 7204 Exfair Rd Bethesda MD 20014 Office: Dept Treasury 15th St and Pennsylvania Ave NW Washington DC 20220

LAITINEN, HERBERT AUGUST, educator; b. nr. Wadena, Minn., Jan. 17, 1915; s. Nestor Alfred and Minnie (Nikkari) L.; B. Chemistry, U. Minn., 1936, Ph.D., 1940; m. Marjorie Violet Gorans, June 15, 1940; children—Kenneth, Richard, Roger. Asst. in chemistry U. Minn., 1936-39, Shevlin fellow, 1939-40; chemist Russell-Miller Milling Co., Mpls., summers 1939-40; mem. faculty U. Ill., 1940-74, successively instr., asso. chemistry, asst. and asso. prof., prof., 1947-74, prof. emeritus, 1974—, head div. analytical chemistry, 1953-67; grad. research prof. U. Fla., Gainesville, 1974—; chemist Grasselli chem. div. E.I. du Pont de Nemours & Co., summer 1941; vis. prof. U. Calif. at Los Angeles, summer 1956. Mem. chemistry adv. com. USAF Office Sci. Research, 1957, chemistry adv. panel NSF, 1966-68, com. analytical chemistry NCR, 1948-55, 61—. Recipient Fisher award analytical chemistry, 1961; Synthetic Organic Chem. Mfrs. Assn. award in environ. chemistry, 1975. Guggenheim fellow, 1953, 62. Mem. Am. Chem. Soc. (chmn. div. analytical chemistry 1953, councilor), A.A.A.S., Finnish Chem. Soc. (corr.), Electrochem. Soc., N.Y. Acad. Scis., Internat. Union Pure and Applied Chemistry (sec. commn. electrochem. data), Sigma Xi, Phi Lambda Upsilon, Alpha Chi Sigma. Author: (with I.M. Kolthoff) pH and Electro-Titrations, 1941; Chemical Analysis, 1960, 2d edit. (with

W.E. Harris), 1975. Adv. bd. Analytical Chemistry, 1949-52. Editor monographs and spl. publs., Electrochem. Soc., 1959-67; asst. editor Analytica Chimica Acta, 1961-65; editor Analytical Chemistry, 1966-80. Home: 1729 NW 8th Ave Gainesville FL 32603. *Never take yourself too seriously; never fail to take others seriously enough.*

LAKE, CHARLES WILLIAM, JR., printing co. exec.; b. LaPorte, Ind., June 21, 1918; s. Charles William and Jessie Mae (Lyon) L.; student U. Wis., 1936-37; B.S., Cornell U., 1941; M.B.A., U. Chgo., 1949; m. Louise Safford Sprague, July 4, 1946; children—Charles William III, Elizabeth Sprague. With R.R. Donnelley & Sons Co., Chgo., 1946—, successively asst. to treas., mgr. mgmt. studies, dir. indsl. engring., 1947-56, dir. engring. research and devel., 1956-58, dir. operating, 1958-59, dir. Chgo. mfg. div., 1959-63, dir. sales div., 1963-64, v.p. co., 1953-63, sr. v.p., 1963-64, pres., 1964—, chmn. bd., 1975—, also dir.; dir. No. Trust Co., Inland Steel Co., Am. Hosp. Supply Corp., Chgo. Bridge and Iron Co. Mem. Adv. Com. for Arthritis in Industry; sr. mem. The Conf. Bd.; mem. Chgo. Com. Mem. vis. com. Div. Sch., also citizens bd. U. Chgo.; emeritus trustee, mem. emeritus engring. council, univ. council Cornell U.; bd. dirs. Protestant Found. Greater Chgo., John Crerar Library; mem. Northwestern U. Assos. Served from 2d lt. to capt., ordnance, AUS, 1941-46. Mem. Am. Inst. Indsl. Engrs., Tau Beta Pi, Beta Gamma Sigma. Congregationalist. Clubs: Masons; Univ., Economic, Chgo. Sunday Evening (trustee), Comml., Chgo., Cornell (Chgo.); Hinsdale (Ill.) Golf; Old Elm Golf, Sky, Links, Hemisphere (N.Y.C.); Coleman Lake (Wis.); Blind Brook (N.Y.) Golf; Lancaster (Pa.) Country; Royal Poinciana Golf, Hole in the Wall Golf (Naples, Fla.). Home: 222 E 4th St Hinsdale IL 60521 Office: 2223 Dr Martin Luther King Jr Dr Chicago IL 60616

LAKE, CLARENCE RICHARD, ry. exec.; b. Topeka, Sept. 30, 1914; s. Clarence Tryon and Esther (Root) L.; student U. Kan., 1932-35, Inst. Bus. Econs., U. So. Cal., 1952; m. Margaret McKenna, July 23, 1938; children—John R., Daniel E., Mary L. With A.T. & S.F. Ry., Topeka, 1936—, asst. paymaster, 1947-53, paymaster, 1953-60, asst. treas., 1960-66, sec., treas., 1966—; sec., treas., dir. Clinton, Okla. Western R.R. Co., Dodge City & Cimarron Valley Ry. Co., Garden City, Gulf & No. R.R. Co., Santa Fe Pacific R.R. Co., Kans. Southwestern Ry. Co., N.M. Central Ry. Co.; sec., treas. Produce Bldg. Corp. of Houston, St. Joseph Terminal R.R. Co., Wichita Union Terminal Ry. Co., Cherokee & Pitts. Coal & Mining Co., Coline Oil Corp., Haystack Mountain Devel. Co., Ill. No. Ry., Oil Devel. Co. Tex., Santa Fe Forwarding Co., Santa Fe Land Improvement Co., Southwestern Improvement Co.; asst. sec., asst. treas., dir. Rio Grande, El Paso and Santa Fe R.R. Co.; asst. sec., asst. treas. Gulf & Interstate Ry. Co.; asst. treas. Gulf Central Pipeline Co., Santa Fe Pipeline Co., S.W. Pipeline Co.; dir. Shawnee Fed. Savs. & Loan Assn. Trustee Topeka Pub. Library. Served to 1st lt. AUS, 1943-46. Decorated Purple Heart. Mem. Kans., Topeka chambers commerce, Am. Legion. Republican. Roman Catholic. Home: 3635 W 15th St Topeka KS 66604 Office: 920 Jackson St Topeka KS 66612

LAKE, DAVID S., lawyer, publisher; b. Youngstown, Ohio, July 17, 1938; s. Frank and Charlotte (Stahl) L.; B.A. in Mathematics, Youngstown State U., 1960; J.D. cum laude, Cleve. State U., 1965; m. Sandra J. Levin, Dec. 18, 1960; children—Joshua Seth, Jonathan Daniel. Admitted to Ohio bar, 1965, D.C. bar, 1970, U.S. Supreme Ct. bar, 1969; gen. counsel World Pub. Co., Cleve., 1965-68; dir. devel. Catholic U. Am., Washington, 1968-69; v.p., gen. counsel Microform Pub. Corp., Washington, 1969-70; dir. spl. projects Library Resources, Inc., Chgo., 1970-72; gen. mgr., partner Nat. Textbook Co., Skokie, Ill., 1972-76; pres. Fearon-Pitman Pubs., Inc., Belmont, Calif., 1976—. Served with USMC, 1960-62. Jewish. Contbr. to Cleve. Marshall Law Rev., 1964. Office: 6 Davis Dr Belmont CA 94002

LAKE, (FINLEY) EDWARD, transp. co. exec.; b. Newark, June 24, 1934; s. Finley S. and Dorothy R. (Davis) L.; B.A., Mich. State U., 1956; M.B.A., U. Chgo., 1970; m. Carol June Freeberg, Sept. 20, 1958; children—David, Jeffrey. With Harris Reames & Ambrose, C.P.A.'s, Lansing, Mich., 1956-60; with Mut. Trust Life Ins. Co., Chgo., 1960-63, asst. treas., 1962-63; with Greyhound Corp., Chgo. and Phoenix, 1963—, treas., 1968—, also v.p., 1975—. Served with AUS, 1957. C.P.A., Mich. Mem. Am. Inst. C.P.A.'s. Lutheran. Office: Greyhound Tower Phoenix AZ 85077

LAKE, FREDRIC DAVID, radiologist, physician; b. Perth Amboy, N.J., May 28, 1913; s. Earl and Jessie (Hanslip) L.; B.A., Amherst Coll., 1934; M.D., Harvard U., 1938; m. Harriet Avery, Jan. 3, 1942; children—Fredric David, Gordon, Susan, Arthur. Intern, Springfield (Mass.) Hosp., 1938-40; gen. practice medicine, Springfield, 1940-41; fellow, resident in radiology U. Chgo. Clinics, 1947-50; radiologist, chmn. dept. Columbus Hosp., Chgo., 1950—; mem. adv. hosp. council State of Ill., 1975—. Pres. bd. edn. Evanston (Ill.) Twp. High Sch., 1964-68. Served with M.C., AUS, 1941-46. Decorated Bronze Star. Diplomate Am. Bd. Radiology. Mem. Am. Coll. Radiology (chmn. bd. chancellors 1976-77, pres. 1977-78), Am. Roentgen Ray Soc., Radiol. Soc. N.Am., AMA (del. 1978-80), Ill. Med. Soc. (pres. 1974-75), Chgo. Med. Soc. (chmn. council 1970-72, sec. 1972-73), Ill. Radiol. Soc. (pres.), Chgo. Radiol. Soc. (pres.), Inst. Medicine Chgo. Republican. Congregationalist. Home: 999 Michigan Ave Evanston IL 60202 Office: Columbus Hosp 2520 N Lakeview Ave Chicago IL 60614

LAKE, I. BEVERLY, former state justice; b. Wake Forest, N.C., Aug. 29, 1906; s. James L. and Lula (Caldwell) L.; B.S., Wake Forest Coll., 1925; LL.B., Harvard, 1929; LL.M., Columbia, 1940, S.J.D., 1947; m. Gertrude Bell; 1 son, I. Beverly. Admitted to N.C. bar, 1928; prof. law Wake Forest Coll. Law Sch., 1932-51; asst. atty. gen. N.C., 1952-55; mem. firm Lake, Boyce & Lake, Raleigh, N.C.; now ret. asso. justice N.C. Supreme Ct., Raleigh; counsel firm Lake & Nelson, Raleigh. Mem. Am., N.C., Wake County bar assns., N.C. State Bar, Phi Alpha Delta. Author: Discrimination by Railroads and Other Public Utilities, 1947; North Carolina Practice Methods, 1952. Home: 403 N Main St Wake Forest NC 27587 Office: 310 Raleigh Bldg Raleigh NC 27602

LAKE, JOHN BYRON, publishing co. exec.; b. Follansbee, W.Va., Nov. 30, 1920; s. William Henry and Helen (Sanders) L.; student Ohio State U., 1938-40, U. Ala., 1940-41, Notre Dame U., 1943-44; m. Katharine Ann Kerr, June 28, 1947; children—Charlotte, Cynthia, Diane. Salesman advt. dept. Eagle-Gazette newspaper, Lancaster, Ohio, 1947-56; dir. advt. Elizabeth (N.J.) Daily Jour., 1956-60; with St. Petersburg (Fla.), Times and Evening Independent, 1960—, exec. v.p., 1968-71, publisher, 1971—; 1st v.p. Times Pub. Co., St. Petersburg, 1966—, also dir.; dir., v.p. Congl. Quar., Inc., Washington, 1966—; dir., pres. Semit Corp., St. Petersburg, 1971—. Mem. Fla. Council of 100, 1972—. Bd. dirs. Found. U. So. Fla., Tampa; trustee Poynter Fund. Served with USNR, 1941-45, USAF, 1951-53; ETO, Korea. Mem. Fla. C. of C., Fla. Press Assn. Home: 1105 Brightwaters Blvd NE Saint Petersburg FL 33704 Office: PO Box 1121 Saint Petersburg FL 33731

LAKE, MENO TRUMAN, ins. co. exec.; b. Esterhazy, Sask., Can., Aug. 19, 1919; s. Truman Thomas and Marguerite Elizabeth (White) L.; B.Comm., U. Man., 1940; m. Jean Ivy Hancock, Sept. 6, 1940; children—Bruce Meno, William Truman, Ralph Robert, Rex, Nora. With Occidental Life Ins. Co. Calif., Los Angeles, 1940-42, 46—, actuarial student, underwriter, controller's dept., supr. research actuarial dept., asst. actuary, asso. actuary, chief actuary, 1954—, pres., chief adminstrv. officer, 1971-77, pres., chief exec. officer, 1977—, also dir.; prin. cost accountant Basic Magnesium Co., Las Vegas, 1942-44; dir. Am. Life Ins. Co. N.Y., Transam. Ins. Co., Transam. Investment Mgmt. Co., Countrywide Life Ins. Co., Transam. Ins. Corp., Occidental Life Ins. Co. Cal., Transamerica Life Ins. & Annuity Co. Served with USNR, 1944-46. Fellow Soc. Actuaries; mem. Actuarial Club Pacific States (past pres.), Los Angeles Actuarial Club (past pres.). Methodist. Club: California. Office: Occidental Center Los Angeles CA 90015

LAKE, RICHARD HARRINGTON, internat. trade and pub. affairs cons.; b. Carlisle, Pa., Oct. 15, 1919; s. William Harrington and Diana C. (Strube) L.; grad. Strategic Intelligence Sch., 1951, Command and Gen. Staff Coll., 1954; B.S. in Commerce, Roosevelt U., 1958, M.A. in Econs. and Bus., 1961; postgrad. Fgn. Service Inst., 1965, Indsl. Coll. Armed Forces, 1972; m. Blair Moody, July 17, 1954; children—Richard Moody, Mary Anne (dec.), William Moody, Sara Blair. Free-lance writer, 1937-38; underwriter's asst. Guardian Life Ins. Co., 1938-40; cons. mktg. fgn. motion pictures in U.S., 1940; commd. 2d lt. U.S. Army, 1940, advanced through grades to lt. col., 1956; comdr. inf. and mil. police units U.S. and overseas, 1941-46; chief agt. Criminal Investigations Div., Europe, 1947; chief U.S. liaison to USSR Forces, Berlin, 1947-48; pub. relations and protocol officer to Mil. Gov. and High Commr. for Germany, 1948-50; staff officer 2d Army Hdqrs., Ft. Meade, Md., 5th Army Hdqrs., Chgo., 1951-53; sr. adviser to Royal Thai Army, Bangkok, 1954-56; dir. indsl. security, law enforcement and criminal investigations U.S. Army, 1957-61; mem. faculty Roosevelt U. Coll. Bus. Adminstrn., Chgo., 1958-60; cons. internat. affairs, alternate for sec. commerce to 1st White House Food for Peace Conf., Dept. Commerce, 1961, exec. sec. Fgn. Trade Zones Bd. U.S., 1961-69; dir. fgn. trade zones staff Bur. Internat. Bus. Operations, 1961-62, Bur. Internat. Commerce, 1963-69; owner Richard H. Lake Assos., 1970—; mem. Bangkok-Sattahip port study group, Thailand, 1972; head econ. devel. mission UN Indsl. Devel. Orgn., Belize, Brit. Honduras, 1973, Trinidad and Tobago, 1974. Mem. Res. Officers Assn., Ret. Officers Assn., D.A.V., Ill. Assn. Chiefs Police, Marquis Biog. Library Soc., Policia Secreta Nacional de Panama (hon.). Episcopalian. Contbr. articles to govt. and bus. publs. Office: PO Box 385 Annandale VA 22003. *A true measure of success may well be the ability to cope with one's limitations. To that extent, I have succeeded.*

LAKE, W(ILLIAM) ANTHONY KIRSOPP, fed. govt. ofcl.; b. N.Y.C., Apr. 2, 1939; s. Gerard K. and Eleanor (Hard) L.; A.B., Harvard U., 1961; postgrad. (Fiske scholar), Trinity Coll., Cambridge (Eng.) U., 1961-62; M.P.A., Princeton U., 1969, Ph.D., 1974; m. Antonia Plehn, June 16, 1962; children—Timothy K., Eleanor P., Eliza B. With fgn. service Dept. State, Washington, 1962-70, dir. policy planning staff, 1977—; fgn. policy coordinator Muskie Election Com., 1970-72; project dir. Carnegie Endowment for Internat. Peace, Washington and Council on Fgn. Relations, N.Y.C., 1972-74; exec. dir. Internat. Vol. Services, Inc., Washington, 1974-76. Mem. Council on Fgn. Relations, Internat. Inst. for Strategic Studies. Author: The Tar Baby Option, 1976. Editor, co-contbr. Legacy of Vietnam, 1976. Office: Office Policy Planning Dept State 2201 C St N W Washington DC 20520

LAKE, WALTER BENJAMIN, broadcasting exec.; b. Lincoln, Nebr., Oct. 4, 1918; s. Walter Benjamin and Zelma Elizabeth L.; student U. Nebr., 1937-39; B.A., San Diego State U., 1948; postgrad. Pasadena Inst. for Radio, 1949-50; m. Dorothy Elsie Brabec, Dec. 24, 1947. Sales mgr. Inland Broadcasting Co., Weiser, Idaho, 1950-52; regional mgr. San Diego Broadcasting, Inc., Los Angeles, 1953-56; gen. mgr. McGavren-Quinn, Los Angeles, 1957-60; exec. v.p. McGavren-Guild, Los Angeles, 1961-70; pres. North Sacramento Valley Broadcasting Co., Red Bluff, Calif., 1962-68; partner KSLY Broadcasting Co., San Luis Obispo, Calif., 1962-68; pres. KFRE Broadcasting Inc., Stas.-KFRE-AM-FM, Fresno, Calif., 1971—, also dir.; pres. Lake Enterprises, Inc., Fresno, 1975-77, also dir.; dir. Cali-Block, Inc. Served with USAAF, 1942-46; NATOUSA. Mem. Nat. Assn. Broadcasters, Calif. Broadcasters Assn. (dir. 1979-80), San Joaquin Valley Broadcasters Assn. (dir. 1973-74), Broadcast Fin. Mgmt. Assn., Am. Legion, VFW, Sigma Chi. Republican. Methodist. Clubs: Lions, Elks, Masons, Shriners, Sunnyside Country, San Joaquin Country. Home: 5205 N Pleasant Ave Fresno CA 93711 Office: 999 N Van Ness Ave Fresno CA 93728

LAKE, WILLIAM THOMAS, financial cons.; b. Ocean City, N.J., June 14, 1910; s. William Carson and Marie Cecelia (Kaiser) L.; grad. Rider Coll., Trenton, N.J., 1930; m. V. Blair Torbert, Nov. 25, 1933 (div.); children—Donna Blair Lake Wright, Deborah Caren Lake Coates, Darelle Dee, Carson Thomas; m. 2d, Dorothy Howell Caddelle, Mar. 1, 1968; 1 stepdau., Lynne E. Caddelle (Mrs. W. Dean Boecher). Pub. accountant Lybrand Ross Bros. and Montgomery, Phila., 1932-39; controller Keystone Portland Cement Co., Phila., 1939-42; controller, treas. narrow fabric div. Burlington Mills, Allentown, Pa., 1946-48; controller Rouge plants Ford Motor Co., 1948-53; comptroller Curtiss Wright Corp., Wood Ridge, 1953-61, Gen. Dynamics Corp., 1961-68; v.p. finance aerospace and systems group Rockwell Internat., 1968-70; financial cons., 1970—; pres. Talmud Internat. Mgmt. Co., Peripheral Engring. Inc.; treas. Talmud Internat. Ltd. Served to comdr. USNR, World War II; supply officer 4th Naval Dist., Naval Ordnance Plant, York, Pa. C.P.A., N.J., Pa., Mich., Calif., Colo., N.Y. Mem. Am. Inst. Profl. Cons.'s (charter), Fin. Execs. Inst. (life), Am. Inst. C.P.A.'s (40 year hon. mem. award), N.J., Calif., Colo., N.Y. socs. C.P.A.'s, Am. Ornance Assn., Navy League U.S. Presbyterian. Mason (32 deg., Shriner). Clubs: Economic, Engineers (N.Y.C.); Pinehurst Country. Home: 9 Oakwood Dr Glens Falls NY 12801

LAL, JOGINDER, chemist; b. Amritsar, India, July 2, 1923; s. Khem Singh and Champa Devi Mahajan; came to U.S., 1947, naturalized, 1957; B.Sc. with honors, Govt. Coll., Lahore, India (now Pakistan), 1944, M.Sc. in Chem. Tech., 1946; M.S. (Indian Govt. Merit scholar), Poly. Inst. Bklyn., 1949, Ph.D. in Polymer Chemistry, 1951; m. Ardyce M. Lundenburg, Mar. 24, 1951; children—Anjana K., Rajinder K. Sr. research chemist Polaroid Corp., Cambridge, Mass., 1950-51; prof. chemistry Hindu Coll., Amritsar, 1951-52; head polymer research H.D. Justi & Son., Inc., Phila., 1952-56; research scientist Goodyear Tire & Rubber Co., Akron, Ohio, 1956-66, sect. head, 1967-75, mgr. exploratory polymers, 1975—; chmn. Akron Polymer Lecture Group, 1961-62, Akron Summit Polymer Conf., 1976. Recipient Gold medal Hindu Coll., 1941, Akron Summit Polymer Conf. award, 1976. Mem. Am. Chem. Soc. (chmn. Akron sect. 1971, sect. Disting. Service award 1976, A.C.S. sci. counselor to Congressman John F. Seiberling 1974—, councilor 1965-67, 73-75, 79—, active polymer div. and nat. coms.). Contbr. numerous articles to profl. jours.; patentee in field; inventor Hexsyn rubber (IR-100 award Indsl. Research/Devel. mag.), 1976. Office: Goodyear Tire & Rubber Co 142 Goodyear Blvd Akron OH 44316

LALA, DOMINICK J., mfg. co. exec.; b. N.Y.C., June 2, 1928; s. Joseph and Mary (Billera) L.; B.S., N.Y.U., 1951; m. Nancy Bosco, Nov. 30, 1957; children—John, Steven, James, Thomas, Patrice. Mem. staff Siedman & Seidman, C.P.A.'s, N.Y.C., 1951-62; v.p., controller Universal Am. Corp., N.Y.C., 1962-68; sr. v.p. finance Paramount Pictures Corp., 1968-70; exec. v.p. Gould Paper Corp., 1970—. Served with AUS, 1946-47. Mem. Am. Inst. C.P.A.'s, N.Y. State Soc. C.P.A.'s, Financial Execs. Inst. Home: 10 Burnham Pl Manhassett NY 11030 Office: 145 E 32d St New York City NY 10016

LALANDE, GILLES, Can. diplomat; b. Montreal, Que., Can., May 10, 1927; s. Ernest and Azilda (Charette) L.; M.Com., U. Montreal, 1949; Docteur d'universite, Institut de Geographie Alpine, U. Grenoble (France), 1953; m. Simone Lavigne, June 11, 1951; children—Michele, Pierre, Dominique. Fgn. service officer Dept. External Affairs of Can., Ottawa, Ont., 1954-62; asst. prof. internat. relations U. Montreal, 1962-65, asso. prof., 1965-71, prof., 1971-76; v.p. multilateral programs Can. Internat. Devel. Agy., 1976-78; Can. ambassador to Ivory Coast, Mali, Upper Volta and Nigeria, Abidjan, Ivory Coast, 1978—; co-sec. Royal Commn. on Bilinqualism and Biculturalism, 1966-70. Mem. Royal Soc. Can., Canadian Polit. Sci. Assn. (pres. 1970-71). Roman Catholic. Author: The Department of External Affairs and Biculturalism, 1970; In Defence of Federalism—The View from Quebec, 1978. Office: B P 4104 Abidjan 01 Ivory Coast

LALANDE, WILLIAM ALFRED, JR., consultant; b. Phila., June 19, 1905; s. William Alfred and Agnes J. (Small) LaL.; B.S., U. Pa., 1927, M.S., 1928, Ph.D., 1931; George Leib Harrison fellow chemistry, Swiss Fed. Poly. Inst., 1937-38; m. Virginia C. Glover, Dec. 24, 1930; 1 dau., Virginia Helen (Mrs. William O. Holmes). Asst. instr. chemistry, then instr. and asst. prof. U. Pa., 1927-37; dir. research and devel. Attapulgus Clay Co., Phila., 1938-44; with Pennwalt Corp. (formerly Pennsalt Chems. Corp.), Phila., 1944-72, v.p., mgr. research and devel., 1954-55, v.p., tech. dir., dir., 1955-69, group v.p. health ops., 1970-72. Mem. Am. Chem. Soc., Am. Inst. Chem. Engrs. Home: 201 W Evergreen Ave Philadelphia PA 19118 Office: Chemistry Dept Univ Pa Philadelphia PA 19104

LA LEIKE, PHILIP DENYS, publishing co. exec.; b. Stoughton, Wis., May 17, 1934; s. Frederick Herman and Louise Freda (Wollenzien) LaL.; B.A., U. Wis., 1952-52; postgrad. Northwestern U., 1956-57; m. Judith Marie Johnson, Aug. 11, 1956; children—Mark, David. Tchr. English, public high sch., Downers Grove, Ill., 1956, Arlington Heights, Ill., 1957-60; sales rep. King Co., printing co., Chgo., 1960-62; with Houghton Mifflin Pub. Co., 1963-76, regional dir. sales, Geneva, Ill., 1968-72, v.p., gen. mgr., Geneva, 1973-76; sr. v.p. Scott, Foresman Pub. Co., Glenview, Ill., 1977-78; pres. Follett Pub. Co., Chgo., 1978—. Mem. Am. Assn. Pubs. (exec. com.), Nat. Council Tchrs. English, Am. Mgmt. Assn. Clubs: Chgo. Met.; Racquet (Lake Bluff, Ill.). Home: 1309 Inverlieth St Lake Forest IL 60045 Office: 1010 Washington Blvd Chicago IL 60607

LALL, ARTHUR SAMUEL, educator, diplomat; b. Lahore, India, July 14, 1911; s. Parmanand S. and Zoe (Lewis) L.; B.A., Punjab U., 1930, M.A., 1932; postgrad. Oxford (Eng.) U., 1932-34; m. Betty Goetz, Aug. 15, 1963; 1 dau., Kiren. Trade commr. for India in U.K., 1947-49; joint sec. Govt. India, 1949-51; consul gen., N.Y.C., 1951-54; permanent rep., ambassador to UN, N.Y.C., 1954-59; ambassador, gov. IAEA, Vienna, Austria, 1959-62; del. Disarmament Conf., 1962-63; prof. Columbia, 1965—. Chmn. Common Heritage Internat., 1978-79. Author: The House at Adampur, 1956; Seasons of Jupiter, 1958; Negotiating Disarmament, 1964; Modern International Negotiations, 1966; How Communist China Negotiates, 1967; The U.N. and the Middle East Crisis, 1968; The Security Council In A Universal United Nations, 1971. Home: 230 E 81st St New York City NY 10028. *Not only to love life, but to respect everyone's rights in life. To stretch myself—all my capacities—to the utmost, without diminishing my respect for life. To question, to sharpen, to quicken, to explore myself. I find these pursuits are invigorated by the practice of yoga, which helps me also to use my body as the grand instrument that it is meant to be. Yoga also opens me to the fulness of each moment. . . . Such, in brief, are my strivings; my achievements do not match my goals!*

LALLEY, JOHN SPALDING, internat. bus. sers. co. exec.; b. Balt., Nov. 5, 1926; s. Joseph Michael and Margaret Spalding (Parker) L.; B.S., Mt. St. Mary's Coll., Emmitsburg, Md., 1948; LL.B., J.D., U. Md., 1957; m. Ann Dudley Field, Apr. 20, 1950; children—John Spalding, Nancy P., Thomas B. With PHH Group, Inc., Hunt Valley, Md., 1952—, dir., 1966—, pres., 1966-79, chief exec. officer, 1969-79, chmn., 1974-79, chmn. bd., 1979—; chmn. PHH Services Ltd., Gt. Britain, PHH Services (Pty.) Ltd., S. Africa; pres. PHH (Can.) Ltd., 1967-72, dir., 1967—; dir. PHHBoston Ltda., Brazil; dir. Balt. Life Ins. Co., Md. Nat. Bank, Balt., corporator Savs. Bank Balt. Chmn. Assn. Ind. Colls. Md., 1979—; trustee Johns Hopkins Hosp., Johns Hopkins U.; adv. council Sch. Advanced Internat. Studies, Washington. Served with USNR, 1944-46. Mem. Newcomen Soc. N. Am. Republican. Episcopalian. Clubs: Balt. Country, Green Spring Valley Hunt, Maryland; Mt. Royal (Montreal, Can.); Princess Anne (Virginia Beach, Va.). Home: 2803 Caves Rd Owings Mills MD 21117 Office: PHH Group Inc 11333 McCormick Rd Hunt Valley MD 21031

LALLINGER, E. MICHAEL, savs. and loan assn. exec.; b. St. Louis, Aug. 17, 1915; s. Michael N. and Clara (Neiderhoff) L.; student Jefferson Coll., St. Louis, 1937; m. Johnetta Claire Ward, Jan, 14, 1948; children—Michael John, John Ward, Mary Jeanne. With RFC, 1941-51, asst. mgr. Dallas office, 1950-51; asst. regional commr. Internal Revenue Service, Dallas, 1952-56; exec. v.p. Gibraltar Savs. Assn., Houston, 1956-63, pres., 1963—; pres., dir. Houston Imperial Corp.; dir. First Internat. Bank, Houston, Gibraltar Savs. Assn., Imperial Corp. Am., Fed. Home Loan Mortgage Corp., Washington; tchr. individual and corp. tax accounting Jefferson Coll., 1939-40. Chmn. bd. equalization, Bunker Hill Village, Tex. Served to capt., inf., AUS, 1942-46; ETO. Decorated Silver Star, Bronze Star, Purple Heart; Order Leopold (Belgium); Croix de Guerre (France). Mem. Nat. League Insured Savs. Assn., U.S. Savs. and Loan League, U.S. C. of C., Houston C. of C. Clubs: Rotary, Houston. Home: 21 Briar Hollow Ln 802 Houston TX 77027 Office: 2302 Fannin St Houston TX 77002

LALLY, FRANCIS JOSEPH, clergyman, editor; b. Swampscott, Mass., June 11, 1918; s. Frank and Catherine (Farragher) L.; A.B., Boston Coll., 1940; grad. St. John's Sem., 1944; licentiate of social sci. Laval U., 1948; LL.D., Stonehill Coll., 1958, Marquette U., 1960, Manhattan Coll., 1961, Boston Coll., 1962, Northeastern U., 1966, Rivier Coll., Nashua, N.H., 1969. Ordained priest Roman Cath. Ch., 1944, privy chamberlain to Pope Pius XII, 1952, named domestic prelate, 1959; parish priest Sacred Heart Parish, Roslindale, 1971-75; asso. editor The Pilot, Boston, 1948-52, editor, 1952-72; spiritual dir. League Cath. Women, Boston, 1950-75. Dir. Tufts Civic Edn. Found., 1958—; mem. U.S. nat. commn. for UNESCO, 1957-62; mem. exec. com. Action for Boston Community Devel., 1962-69, v.p., 1964-66; mem. U.S. com. for UNICEF; mem. Boston Redevel. Authority, 1957-70, chmn., 1961-70; dir. Archbishop's Stewardship Appeal, 1971-75; sec. dept. social devel. and world peace U.S. Cath. Conf., 1975—. Trustee Opera Co. Boston, mem. com. for permanent charity fund, 1970—; bd. dirs. Boston Council for Internat. Vistors, 1962—; bd. dirs. Fund for Republic, 1957-77 Urban League Greater Boston;

trustee Ednl. Devel. Centre, 1967-73, St. Elizabeth Hosp., Brighton, French Library, Boston, 1956-69; bd. consultors Archdiocese Boston, 1968-70; mem. vis. com. Harvard-Radcliffe Coll.; mem. corp. Retina Found., 1972—; chmn. Cath. com. White House Conf. on Families, 1978—. Recipient Boston Coll. medal, 1953. Decorated chevalier Legion of Honor, 1955. Fellow Am. Acad. Arts and Scis. (v.p. 1964-66); mem. Internat. Friendship League (dir. 1958—), Catholic Press Assn., Boston Com. Fgn. Relations. Clubs: Tavern, Examiner (Boston); Federal City (Washington). Author: The Catholic Church in a Changing America, 1962. Address: U S Cath Conf 1312 Massachusetts Ave NW Washington DC 20005

LALLY, RICHARD FRANCIS, govt. ofcl.; b. Newark, Nov. 23, 1925; s. Francis J. and Helen (Fennesy) L.; B.S., Upsala Coll., 1950; m. Doris P. Yasko, Sept. 10, 1949; children—Barbara J. Lally-Dittler, Joan E. Lally Stalder. Spl. agt. FBI, Atlanta, Cin. and Washington, 1951-60; area dir., chief gen. investigations Dept. Labor, Newark and Washington, 1960-63; dep. dir. compliance and security FAA, Washington, 1963-65, dir. compliance and security, 1965-67; dir. investigations and security Dept. Transp., Washington, 1967-70, dir. equal opportunity, 1967-70, dir. civil rights, 1970-72, dir. transp. security, 1972-74, dir. civil aviation security service FAA, 1974—. Served with AC, U.S. Army, 1944-46. Recipient Exceptional Service citation Dept. Transp., 1969, Meritorious Achievement award, 1970, Sec.'s award, 1973, Superior Achievement award, 1973, 76, Superior Achievement in Equal Opportunity award, 1977. Mem. Am. Soc. Pub. Adminstrn., Am. Soc. Indsl. Security Soc. Former Spl. Agts. FBI. Home: 6303 Massachusetts Ave Wood Acres MD 20016 Office: FAA Dept Transp 800 Independence Ave SW Washington DC 20591

LALONDE, BERNARD JOSEPH, educator; b. Detroit, June 3, 1933; s. John Bernard and Fannie (Napier) LaL.; A.B., U. Notre Dame, 1955; M.B.A., U. Detroit, 1957; Ph.D., Mich. State U., 1961; m. Barbara Elaine Eggenberger, Sept. 6, 1958; children—Lisa Renee, Michell Ann, Christopher John. Asst. prof. marketing U. Colo., Boulder, 1961-65; asso. prof. Mich. State U., East Lansing, 1965-69; James R. Riley prof. marketing and logistics Ohio State U., Columbus, 1969—. Pres. Transp. Research Found. Recipient John Drury Sheehan award, 1976. Formerly Ford scholar, Gen. Electric fellow. Mem. Am. Marketing Assn., Regional Sci. Assn., Nat. Council Phys. Distbn. Mgmt., Soc. Logistics Engrs., Beta Gamma Sigma, Alpha Kappa Psi. Roman Catholic. Author: Physical Distribution Management, 2d edit. 1968; Customer Service: Meaning and Measurement, 1976. Editor: Jour. Bus. Logistics; Jour. book and monographs editor Am. Mktg. Assn. Contbr. articles to profl. jours. Home: 2355 Onandaga Dr Columbus OH 43221

LALONDE, MARC, Canadian govt. ofcl.; b. Ile Perrot, Que., Can., July 26, 1929; s. J. Albert and Nora (St-Aubin) L.; B.A., Coll. St. Laurent, Montreal, 1950; LL.B., U. Montreal, 1964, LL.M., 1955; M.Econs. and Polit. Sci., Oxford (Eng.) U., 1957; m. Claire Tetreau, Sept. 8, 1955; children—Marie, Luc, Paul, Catherine. Called to bar, Que., 1955; prof. bus. law and econs. U. Montreal, 1957-59; spl. asst. to Minister of Justice, Ottawa, Ont., Can., 1959-60; partner firm Gelinas, Bourque, Lalonde & Benoit, Montreal, 1960-68; policy adviser to Prime Minister Lester B. Pearson, Ottawa, 1967-68; prin. sec. to Prime Minister Pierre E. Trudeau, Ottawa, 1968-72; minister of nat. health and welfare, Ottawa, 1972-77; minister of state for fed.-provincial relations, Ottawa, 1977-78; minister responsible for status of women, Ottawa, 1975-78, minister of justice and atty. gen. Can., 1978-79. Recipient Dana award Am. Pub. Health Assn., 1978. Mem. Liberal Party. Author: The Changing Role of the Prime Minister's Office, 1971. Home: 5440 Legare Montreal PQ H3T 1Z4 Canada Office: House of Commons Ottawa ON K1A 0A6 Canada

LALONDE, WILLIAM SALEM, 3D, utility exec.; b. E. Orange, N.J., Dec. 24, 1932; s. William Salem, Jr. and Marion (Howard) LaL.; B.Civil Engring., Cornell U., 1955, M.B.A., 1956; m. Susanne R. Stewart, June 25, 1960; children—Bruce G., Scott W., Todd J. With Public Ser. Electric & Gas Co. N.J., 1956-68, dist. supt., 1965-68; with Elizabethtown Gas Co. (N.J.), 1968-78, v.p. ops. and engring. services, 1976-78; pres., chief exec. officer, dir. Gas Ser. Co., Kansas City, Mo., 1978—. Bd. dirs. United Way Greater Kansas City, Heart of Am. council Boy Scouts Am.; bd. regents Rockhurst Coll., Kansas City, Mo. Registered profl. engr. Fellow ASCE (past pres. N.J. sect.); mem. Nat. Soc. Profl. Engrs., Am. Gas Assn., Kans. Soc. Engrs., Cornell Soc. Engrs., Kans. Assn. Commerce and Industry (dir.). Episcopalian. Club: Kansas City. Home: 6600 Indian Ln Mission Hills KS 66208 Office: 2460 Pershing Rd Kansas City MO 64108

LAM, SAU-HAI, educator; b. Macao, Dec. 18, 1930; B.Aero. Engring., Rensselaer Poly. Inst., 1954; Ph.D. (Guggenheim fellow), Princeton, 1958; m. 1959. Asst., Princeton, 1956-58, research asso., 1958-59, asso. prof., 1963-68, prof. aerospace scis., 1968—; asst. prof. aero. engring. Cornell U., 1959-60. Mem. Am. Inst. Aeros. and Astronautics. Office: Sch Engring Princeton U Princeton NJ 08540

LAMAR, HOWARD ROBERTS, ednl. adminstr., historian; b. Tuskegee, Ala., Nov. 18, 1923; s. John Howard and Elma (Roberts) L.; B.A., Emory U., 1944; M.A., Yale, 1945, Ph.D., 1951; m. Doris Shirley White, Sept. 3, 1959; children—Susan Kent, Sarah Howard. Instr. U. Mass., 1945-46, Wesleyan U., Middletown, Conn., 1948-49; mem. faculty Yale, 1949—, prof. Am. History and history Am. West, 1964—, W.R. Coe prof. Am. history, 1970—, chmn. history dept., 1962-63, 67-70, dir. history grad. studies, 1964-67, fellow Ezra Stiles Coll., 1961—, dean Coll., 1979—. Alderman, New Haven, 1951-53. Mem. Orgn. Am. Historians, Western History Assn. (v.p. 1970-71), New Haven Colony Hist. Soc., Elihu Soc., Phi Beta Kappa. Democrat. Author: Dakota Territory, 1861-1889, 1956; The Far Southwest, 1846-1912, A Territorial History, 1966; also articles, reviews. Editor: (Joseph Downey) Cruise of the Portsmouth, 1958; Western Americana Series, 1961—; Reader's Encyclopedia of the American West, 1977. Home: 1747 Hartford Turnpike North Haven CT 06473 Office: Dept History Yale Univ New Haven CT 06520

LAMARCHINA, ROBERT ANTONIO, condr.; b. N.Y.C., 1929; s. Antonio and Dora (Barros) LaM.; ed. Curtis Inst. Music, Paris Conservatoire. Formerly solo cellist NBC Symphony Orch., Los Angeles Philharm., Chgo. Symphony Orch.; music dir. Met. Opera Nat. Co., N.Y.C., 1963-66, condr., 1964-65; dir. Spoletto Festival; now condr. Honolulu Symphony Orch.; guest condr. various orchs. Address: Honolulu Symphony 1000 Bishop St Bishop Trust Bldg Honolulu HI 96813*

LAMARR, HEDY (BORN HEDWIG KEISLER), motion picture actress; b. Vienna, Austria, Sept. 11, 1915; d. Emil and Gertrude Keisler; ed. by tutors and in pvt. schs., Vienna; m. Fritz Mandl; m. 2d, Gene Markey, 1939 (div. 1940); m. 3d, John Loder, May 1943 (div. 1947); m. 4th, Ernest Stauffer; m. 5th, Howard Lee; m. 6th, Lewis W. Bowles, Jr.; 1 adopted son, James. Came to U.S., 1937. Appeared on stage, Vienna, in The Weaker Sex, Private Lives, and on screen in Storm in a Water Glass (1930), One Doesn't Need Money; starred in Ecstasy at age of 16 yrs.; on screen in U.S., in Algiers, 1938; Lady of the Tropics, 1939; Boom Town, 1940, Ziegfeld Girl, 1941, Crossroads, 1942, H. M. Pulham, Esq., 1941; White Cargo, 1942; The Conspirators, 1944; Her Highness and the Bellboy, 1945; Experiment Perilous, 1944, Dishonoured Lady, 1947, Samson and Delilah, 1949, A Lady Without Passport, 1950, My Favorite Spy, 1951, The Story of Mankind, 1957, The Female Animal, 1957, others. Author: Ecstasy and Me, 1967. Address: care Paul J Sherman 410 Park Ave New York NY 10022*

LAMARSH, JOHN RAYMOND, educator; b. Hartford, Conn., Mar. 12, 1928; s. Euclid Wilfred and Lillian (Brogan) L.; B.S., Mass. Inst. Tech., 1948, Ph.D., 1952; m. Barbara Arden Glaser, Oct. 11, 1958; 1 dau., Michele. Group leader United Aircraft Corp., 1952-53; asst. prof. physics U. Ky., 1953-54; asso. physicist Brookhaven Nat. Lab., 1954-56; asst. prof. N.Y.U., 1956-57, Cornell U., 1957-62; mem. faculty N.Y.U., 1962-73, prof. nuclear engring., chmn. dept., 1966-73, adj. prof. environ. medicine, 1973—; prof., chmn. dept. nuclear engring. Poly. Inst. N.Y., Bklyn., 1973—; mem. adv. com. engring. sci. N.J. Inst. Tech., 1976—; cons. in field. Mem. Environ. Task Force, Mamaroneck, N.Y., 1970-73; mem. Mayor's Tech. Adv. Com. on Radiation, N.Y.C. Mem. Am. Nuclear Soc. (chmn. N.Y. Met. sect. 1977-78, chmn. edn. div. 1978-79). Author: Nuclear Reactor Theory, 1966; Introduction to Nuclear Engineering, 1975. Home: 68 N Chatsworth Ave Larchmont NY 10538 Office: Dept Nuclear Engring Poly Inst NY Brooklyn NY 11201

LAMAS, FERNANDO, actor, dir., writer; b. Buenos Aires, Argentina, Jan. 9, 1925; came to U.S., 1950, naturalized, 1955; ed. schs. Argentina, Europe; m. Esther Williams, Dec. 31, 1969. Star numerous motion pictures, Hollywood, Calif., Europe, S.Am.; dir. several films, numerous TV shows; actor, dir. several stage plays. Recipient Tony award, 1957, Drama Critics award, 1959, numerous other awards. Mem. Acad. Motion Picture Arts and Scis., Dirs. Guild, Screen Actors Guild, AFTRA, Actors Equity. Office: Suite 5 2080 Century Park E Los Angeles CA 90067*

LAMAS, JOSE RAMON, banker; b. Santurce, P.R., June 24, 1941; s. Ventura Lamas and Georgina (Martinez) L.; B.S., Fordham U., 1962; grad. Comml. Lending Sch., Am. Bankers Assn.-U. Okla., 1974, Nat. Comml. Lending Grad. Sch., 1975; m. Hilda Seda, June 30, 1962; children—Jose R., Jocelyn, Jessica, Javier. Officer trainee Banco Credito, San Juan, P.R., 1962-64, asst. to personnel dir., 1965-65, asst. v.p. constrn. dept., 1965-67, asst. v.p., mgr. airport br., 1967-71, asst. v.p. and mgr., San Patricio br., 1971, asst. v.p., mgr. Stop 17 br., 1972-76, v.p., area supr. Central Office, 1976-77; v.p. Banco Popular de P.R., 1978—, v.p., mgr. Stop 17-Condado br., 1978—. Treas. Airport Facilitation Com., San Juan, 1970—; pres. athletic soc. Providence Acad., 1971—. Mem. Phi Eta Mu (treas. 1972-74). Home: 364 San Genaro St Sagrado Corazon PR 00926 Office: GPO Box 2589 San Juan PR 00936

LAMB, ANDREW, investment banker; b. Sheffield, Eng., Oct. 15, 1917; s. George W. and Frances (Glossop) L.; came to U.S., 1921, naturalized, 1938; B.B.A., Pace Coll., 1939; m. Evelyn C. Behning, Sept. 7, 1941; children—Jeffrey, Andrée. With S.D. Leidesdorf & Co., C.P.A.'s, 1939-42, Sperry Gyroscope Co., 1942-43, Am. Airlines, 1946-48, Port of N.Y. Authority, 1948-57; asst. to financial v.p. Montgomery Ward & Co., Chgo., 1957-58, treas., 1958-65, financial v.p., 1965-67, chmn. finance com., 1965-67; pres., dir., treas. Montgomery Ward Credit Corp., 1960-67; pres. Montgomery Ward Realty Corp., 1963-67; pres., dir. Montgomery Ward Life Ins. Co., 1966-67; sr. v.p., dir. Chgo. Corp., 1967-69; treas., dir. Paddock Corp., 1971-76; pres. Astor Securities Corp., 1978—; mem. Chgo. Bd. Options Exchange, 1973—. Trustee Montgomery Ward Pension Fund, 1962-67. Club: Union League (N.Y.C.). Home: 1350 N Astor St Chicago IL 60610 Office: 217 W Campbell St Arlington Heights IL 60006

LAMB, EDWARD, lawyer, business exec.; b. Toledo, Apr. 23, 1902; s. Clarence M. and Mary (Gross) L.; student Dartmouth, 1920-24; A.B., Harvard, 1925; LL.B., Western Res. U., 1927; m. Prudence Hutchinson, June 15, 1931; children—Edward Hutchinson, Priscilla Prudence. Admitted to Ohio bar, 1927; asst. law dir. City of Toledo, 1928; ind. law practice, Toledo, 1928—. Pres., chmn. bd. Lamb Enterprises, Inc.; pres. Bancorp. Leasing Co.; chmn. bd. Seilon; past pres., chmn. bd. Lamb Enterprises, Inc.; chmn. Nev. Nat. Bank, Reno; chmn. bd., dir. Thomson Internat. Co.; chmn. exec. com. Seilon, Inc.; treas., dir. Gt. Lakes Communications, Inc.; licensee TV sta. WICU, Erie, Pa.; chmn. bd. Nev. Nat. Bancorp.; chmn. exec. com., dir. Nev. Nat. Bank; dir. Wyneco, Inc., Cheyenne, Wyo. Mem. Nat. Emergency Civil Liberties Com. Bd. dirs. Center Study Democratic Instns., Santa Barbara; trustee Wilberforce U.; gov. UN Assn.-U.S.A. Mem. Am., Ohio, Toledo, FCC bar assns., Am. Newspaper Pubs. Assn. Episcopalian. Clubs: Toledo; Kahkwa; Nat. Press (Washington); Overseas Press (N.Y.C.). Author: No Lamb for Slaughter; Planned Economy of Soviet Russia; Trial by Battle. Home: Sentinel Point Maumee OH 43537 Office: Edward Lamb Bldg Toledo OH 43604

LAMB, FLOYD ALVIN, investment co. exec.; b. North Platte, Nebr., Feb. 18, 1921; s. Everett and Esther A. (Anderson) L.; grad. high sch.; m. Margaret W. Milne, June 26, 1943; children—Margaret D., Douglas A. With John Hancock Mut. Life Ins. Co., Boston, 1946—, sr. v.p., 1973—; chmn. bd. John Hancock Advisers, Inc., John Hancock Investors, Inc., John Hancock Income Securities Corp., John Hancock Growth Fund, Inc., John Hancock Balanced Fund, Inc., John Hancock Bond Fund, Inc., John Hancock Tax Exempt Income Trust, John Hancock Money Market Trust; dir. John Hancock Distbrs., Inc., Manchester Electric Co., Gas Service, Inc. Home: 4 Loring Ave Kingston MA 02364 Office: 200 Berkeley St Boston MA 02117

LAMB, GEORGE A., univ. ofcl.; b. Pocatello, Idaho, Apr. 3, 1906; s. Luke F. and Mary (Burnell) L.; A.B., U. Portland, 1929, LL.D., 1970; M.S. (Strathcona fellow 1931-32), Yale, 1932; postgrad. U. Mich., 1932-33; m. Mary Mellefont, June 25, 1932; children—Mary Anthia (Mrs. Steve Dorenda), Rose Mary (Mrs. Steve Malay), Jacqueline (Mrs. R. O'Donnell), George Joseph. Transp. economist Dept. Agr., 1930-31, 34; teaching fellow U. Mich., 1932-33; mineral economist NRA, 1934-36; transp. economist ICC, 1936-38; economist bituminous coal div. Dept. Interior, 1938-40, chief econs. br., 1940-43, asst. dir. bur. mines, 1944-46, dir. Office Coal Research, 1961-63; chief econs. and statistics div. Solid Fuels Adminstrn. War, 1943-44; mgr. bus. surveys Pitts. Consol. Coal Co., 1946-61; dir. econ. studies Consol. Coal Co., Pitts., 1963-67; now dir. law enforcement edn., dir. research adminstrn. U. Portland; cons. Nat. Mediation Bd., 1941. Mem. Am. Coal Mission to Gt. Britain, 1944; cons. sec. interior, 1950, OPS, 1951-52, cabinet energy study, 1954-56; mem. Am. Coal Team vis. Poland, 1957; U.S. del. ECA Coal Comm., 1959, 60. Mem. Am. Statis. Assn., Am. Econ. Assn., Am. Inst. Mining and Metall. Engrs., Tau Kappa Epsilon, Beta Gamma Sigma. Roman Catholic. K.C. Contbr. articles to tech. publs. Home: 7908 NE 12th St Vancouver WA 98664 Office: U Portland Portland OR 97203

LAMB, GEORGE THOMAS, trust co. exec.; b. Atlanta, Mar. 14, 1921; s. George Thomas and Esther (Bandy) L.; ed. Ga. State Coll., Emory U., Stonier Grad. Sch. Banking Rutgers U.; LL.B., Atlanta Law Sch.; m. Frances Brown, Sept. 9, 1976; children—George Thomas, Martin Holmes. With Trust Co. Ga., Atlanta, 1939—, sr. v.p., sec., 1963—. Served with AUS. Mem. Am. Soc. Corporate Secs., Am. Inst. Banking (pres. chpt. 1959-60), Bank Adminstrn. Inst. (pres. chpt. 1965-66, Ga. bd. dirs. 1970-71), Nat. Assn. Accts. Club: Atlanta Athletic. Home: 260 Manning Dr #18 Marietta GA 30064 Office: Trust Co Ga PO Box 4418 Atlanta GA 30302

LAMB, JAMIE PARKER, JR., mech. engr., educator; b. Boligee, Ala., Sept. 21, 1933; s. Jamie Parker and Cletus (Hixson) L.; B.S., Auburn U., 1954; M.S., U. Ill., 1958, Ph.D., 1961; m. Nancy Catherine Flaherty, June 11, 1955; children—David Parker, Stephen Patrick. Asst. prof. engring. mechanics N.C. State U., Raleigh, 1961-63; faculty mech. engring. U. Tex., Austin, 1963—, prof., 1970—, chmn. dept., 1970-76, asso. dean engring., 1976—; cons. LTV Aerospace Corp., Dallas, Marshall Space Flight Center, Huntsville, Ala., Tracor, Inc., Austin, Rocketdyne, McGregor, Tex., ARO, Inc., Tullahoma, Tenn., Tex. Gas Transport Co., Austin; spl. cons. U. São Paulo, Brazil, 1974; cons. Mobil Oil Corp., Dallas, 1977. Mem. bd. boiler rules Tex. Dept. Labor and Standards, 1977—. Served to 1st lt. USAF, 1955-57. Mem. ASME (Founder's award Central Tex. sect. 1975, Leadership award 1976), Am. Inst. Aeros. and Astronautics, Am. Soc. Engring. Edn. (chmn. summer faculty programs com. 1978—, chmn. mech. engring. div. 1979-80), Sigma Xi, Pi Tau Sigma, Tau Beta Pi. Baptist. Asso. tech. editor: Jour. Fluids Engineering, 1976-79. Contbr. articles to profl. jours. Home: 2605 Pinewood Terr Austin TX 78757

LAMB, JOHN G., apparel mfg. co. exec.; b. Cleve., May 31, 1915; s. Paul and Mildred (Honecker) L.; A.B., Amherst Coll., 1937; m. Dorothy Cole, June 30, 1939; children—Nancy H. (Mrs. Arthur G. Fitsgerald), John G., Richard H. Chief accountant Union Carbide Corp. subsidiaries, Cleve., 1943-46; accountant Ernst & Ernst, Cleve., 1946-49; asst. to v.p., treas. Affiliated Gas Equipment, Cleve., 1949-51; chief internal auditor, gen. auditor, asst. treas. C. & C. Ry., 1951-61; treas. Work Wear Corp. and subsidiary cos., Cleve., 1962—. Mem. Cleve. Treas.'s Club, Am. Inst. C.P.A.'s, Ohio Soc. C.P.A.'s, Nat. Accounting Assn., Cleve. Soc. Security Analysts, Delta Kappa Epsilon. Republican. Episcopalian. Club: Mayfield Country (South Euclid, Ohio). Author: Cash Management, 1960. Home: 24449 Cedar Rd Lyndhurst OH 44122 Office: 1768 E 25th St Cleveland OH 44114

LAMB, LAWRENCE EDWARD, cardiologist; b. Fredonia, Kans., Oct. 13, 1926; s. John Robert and Dell M. (Ross) L.; M.D. (Battenfeld Hall scholar), U. Kans., 1949. Intern, U. Kans., Med. Center, 1950, resident, 1950-51, Am. Heart Assn. fellow cardiology, 1954; instr. medicine, fellow cardiology Emory U., 1953-54; fellow cardiology U. Geneva, Switzerland, 1954-55; dir. cardiology dept. internal medicine Sch. Aviation Medicine, Randolph AFB, Tex., 1955-57, chief dept. internal medicine, 1957-62; chief aerospace med. scis. div. USAF Sch. Aerospace Medicine, Brooks AFB, Tex., 1962-66; prof. medicine Baylor U. Coll. Medicine, Houston, 1965-71; cons. cardiology Project Mercury, NASA, 1960, cons. dir. life scis., 1965; cons. President's Council on Phys. Fitness and Sports, 1965—. Adv. bd. dirs. Houston Heart Assn. Recipient Distinguished Civilian Service medal Dept. Def., 1962; Meritorious Civilian Service award Dept. Air Force, 1955-66. Diplomate Am. Bd. Internal Medicine. Fellow Am. Coll. Cardiology, A.C.P., Am. Coll. Chest Physicians, Aerospace Med. Assn. (Arnold D. Tuttle award 1959), Am. Coll. Clin. Pharmacology and Chemotherapy, Am. Heart Assn. (council on epidemiology). Author: Fundamentals of Electrocardiography and Vector-cardiography, 1957; Electrocardiography and Vectorcardiography Instrumentation, Fundamentals and Clinical Applications, 1965; Your Heart and How to Live With It, 1969; What You Need to Know About Food and Cooking for Health, 1973; Dear Doctor: It's About Sex, 1973; Stay Youthful and Fit, 1974; Metabolics: Putting Your Food Energy to Work, 1974; also numerous articles, monographs, chpts. in books; editor Health Letter; producer, participant TV series Health Talk; syndicated columnist. Home: 135 Downing Dr San Antonio TX 78209

LAMB, WILLIS EUGENE, JR., physicist, educator; b. Los Angeles, July 12, 1913; s. Willis Eugene and Marie Helen (Metcalf) L.; B.S., U. Calif., 1934, Ph.D., 1938; D.Sc., U. Pa., 1953, Gustavus Adolphus Coll., 1975; M.A., Oxford (Eng.) U., 1956; M.A., Yale, 1961; L.H.D., Yeshiva U., 1965; m. Ursula Schaefer, June 5, 1939. Mem. faculty Columbia, 1938-52, prof. physics, 1948-52; prof. physics Stanford, 1951-56; Wykeham prof. physics and fellow New Coll., Oxford U., 1956-62; Henry Ford 2d prof. physics Yale, 1962-72, J. Willard Gibbs prof. physics, 1972-74; prof. physics and optical scis. U. Ariz., Tucson, 1974—; Morris Loeb lectr. Harvard, 1953-54; cons. Philips Labs., Bell Telephone Labs., Perkin-Elmer, NASA. Vis. com. Brookhaven Nat. Lab. Recipient (with Dr. Polycarp Kusch) Nobel prize in physics, 1955; Rumford premium Am. Acad. Arts and Scis., 1953; Research Corp. award, 1955; Guggenheim fellow, 1960-61; recipient Yeshiva award, 1962. Fellow Am. Phys. Soc., N.Y. Acad. Scis.; hon. fellow Inst. Physics and Phys. Soc. (Guthrie lectr. 1958); mem. Nat. Acad. Scis., Phi Beta Kappa, Sigma Xi. Office: Dept of Physics U Ariz Tucson AZ 85721

LAMBDIN, THOMAS ODEN, educator; b. Frederick, Md., Oct. 31, 1927; s. William Stewart and Mary (Seeger) L.; A.B., Franklin and Marshall Coll., 1948; Ph.D., Johns Hopkins, 1952; A.M., Harvard, 1964. Asst. prof. Johns Hopkins, 1956-60; asst. prof. Harvard, 1960-64, asso. prof., 1964-69, prof. semitic philology, 1969—. Mem. Am. Oriental Soc. Home: 20 Fernald Dr Cambridge MA 02138

LAMBE, THOMAS WILLIAM, civil engr., educator; b. Raleigh, N.C., Nov. 28, 1920; s. Claude Milton and Mary (Habel) L.; B.S., N.C. State Coll., 1942; S.M., Mass. Inst. Tech., 1944, Sc.D., 1948; m. Catharine Canby Cadbury, Sept. 13, 1947; children Philip Cadbury, Virginia Habel, Richard Lee, Robert Henry, Susan Elizabeth. With Standard Oil Co. Calif., 1944, Dames & Moore, 1945; mem. faculty Mass. Inst. Tech., 1945—, prof. civil engring., 1958-69, Edmund K. Turner prof., 1969—, head soil mechanics div., 1958-69, 72—, head geotech. div., 1972—; cons. geotech. engring., 1945—, NASA, 1965—. Rankine lectr., 1973. Recipient Desmond Fitzgerald medal Boston Soc. Civil Engring., 1954, 56. Fellow ASCE (Collingswood prize 1951, Wellington prize 1961, Norman medal 1964, Terzaghi lectr. 1970, Terzaghi award 1975); mem. Internat. Soc. Soil Mechanics and Found. Engring., Nat. Acad. Engring. Author books, numerous articles. Home: PO Box 37 South Pomfret VT 05067 Office: 77 Massachusetts Ave Cambridge MA 02139

LAMBERG-KARLOVSKY, CLIFFORD CHARLES, anthropologist, archaeologist; b. Prague, Czechoslovakia, Oct. 2, 1937; s. Carl Othmar von Lamberg and Bellina Karlovsky; came to U.S., 1939; A.B., Dartmouth Coll., 1959; M.A. (Wenner-Gren fellow), U. Pa., 1964, Ph.D., 1965; M.A. (hon.), Harvard U., 1970; m. Martha Louise Veale, Sept. 12, 1959; children—Karl Emil Othmar, Christopher William. Asst. prof. sociology and anthropology Franklin and Marshall Coll., 1964-65; asst. prof. anthropology Harvard U., 1965-69, prof., 1969—, curator Near Eastern archaeology Peabody Museum Archaeology and Ethnology, 1969—, mus. dir., 1977—; asso. Columbia U., 1969—; trustee Am. Inst. Iranian Studies, 1968—, Am. Inst. Yemeni Studies, 1976—; dir. research Am. Sch. Prehist. Research, 1974—; trustee Am. Sch. Oriental Research, 1969-71; cons. archaeology; Reckitt archaeol. lectr. Brit. Acad., 1973. Recipient medal Iran-Am. Soc., 1972. NSF grantee, 1966-75, 78-80; Nat. Endowment for Arts grantee, 1977—; Nat. Endowment for Humanities grantee, 1977—. Fellow Soc. Antiquaries Gt. Brit. and Ireland, Am. Anthrop. Assn., Am. Acad., N.Y. Acad. Sci., Prehist.

Soc., Soc. Am. Archaeology, Archeol. Inst. Am.; mem. German Archaeol. Inst., Danish Archaeol. Inst., Brit. Archaeol. Inst., Italian Archeol. Inst. Clubs: Explorers (N.Y.C.); Somerset, Tavern (Boston). Author: (with J. Sabloff) Ancient Civilizations: The Near East and Mesoamerica, 1979; editor: The Rise and Fall of Civilizations, 1973; Ancient Civilizations and Trade, 1975; Hunters, Farmers and Civilization, 1979; dir. archaeol. surveys in Syria, 1965, excavations at Tepe Yahya, Iran, 1967-75, archaeol. surveys in Saudia Arabia, 1977-79. Office: Peabody Mus Harvard U Cambridge MA 02138

LAMBERT, ALLEN THOMAS, banker; b. Regina, Sask., Can., Dec. 28, 1911; s. Willison Andrew and Sarah (Barber) L.; ed. Victoria pub. high schs.; m. Marion Grace Kotchapaw, May 20, 1950; children—William Allen, Anne Barbara. With Toronto Dominion Bank, 1927—, asst. gen. mgr., Toronto, 1953-56, gen. mgr., 1956, v.p., dir., 1956-60, pres., 1960-72, chmn. bd., 1961-72, chmn. bd., chief exec. officer, 1972-78, now dir.; dir. Continental Corp., R. Angus Alta. Ltd., Lonvest Corp., Royal Gen. Ins. Co. Can., Cyprus Anvil Mining Corp., Hudson Bay Mining & Smelting Co., Ltd., Canadian Internat. Paper Co., Raritan River Steel Co., IBM (Can.), Ltd., Westinghouse Can. Ltd., Dome Mines, Ltd., Western Broadcasting Co. Ltd., Dominion Ins. Corp., London Life Ins. Co., Inco, Ltd., Ont. Hydro, Hiram Walker-Gooderham & Worts Ltd., Rolls-Royce Holdings N.Am. Ltd., Pvt. Investment Corp. for Asia. Bd. dirs. Can. World Wildlife Fund; bd. govs. York U. Served with Royal Canadian Navy, 1943-45. Mem. United Ch. Can. Clubs: Toronto, Toronto Golf, Toronto Hunt, Rosedale Golf, Granite, York (Toronto). Office: PO Box 1 Toronto Dominion Centre Toronto ON M5K 1A2 Canada

LAMBERT, BYRON CECIL, educator; b. Delta, Ohio, Apr. 19, 1923; s. Adrian Clifton and Laverne Mae (Miley) L.; B.A., U. Buffalo, 1945, M.A., 1946; B.D., Butler U., 1950; Ph.D., U. Chgo., 1957; m. Phyllis June Wamsley, Aug. 14, 1949; 1 dau., Sharon Kay. Ordained to ministry Christian Ch., 1940; asso. prof. English, Milligan (Tenn.) Coll., 1957-60; dean, asso. prof. English, Simpson Coll., Indianola, Iowa, 1960-62; dean evening div. Fairleigh Dickinson U., 1962-65, campus dean, 1965-71, prof. edn., 1971—, acting provost, 1975, acting dean arts and scis., 1976-77, dir. Coll. Edn., 1977—; pastor in Buffalo, 1942-46, Indpls., 1946-51, Chgo., 1951- 57, Sullivan County, Tenn., 1957-60. Mem. exec. com. Tercentenary Commn., Hackensack, N.J., 1963-64; chmn. Bergen County (N.J.) Com. Arts, 1964-66; mem. Employees Legislative Com. Bergen County, 1965-69. Bd. dirs. Bergen Community Mus., 1965-67. Mem. Philosophy of Edn. Soc., Am. Philos. Assn., Eastern Pa. Philos. Assn., N.J. Regional Philos. Assn., Theol. Students Fellowship, N.J. Edn. Assn., Council for Basic Edn., Disciples of Christ Hist. Soc., N.Y. C.S. Lewis Soc. (co-founder), N.J. Council Edn., Am. Conservative Union. Mem. Christian Ch. Mason, Kiwanian. Author: The Essential Paul Elmer More, 1972; also articles, revs. Home: Box 163-D RD1 Hackettstown NJ 07840

LAMBERT, EDWARD CHARLES, educator, broadcaster; b. What Cheer, Iowa, Jan. 29, 1910; s. Edward Gray and Elsie May (King).; student Wichita U., 1931; B.A., Iowa State Tchrs. Coll., 1933; M.A., U. Iowa, 1938; Ph.D., U. Mo., 1952; m. Ella Cole, May 30, 1936; children—Pamela (Mrs. Richard Kaegel), Barbara (Mrs. Norris Reichel). Reporter, Cedar Falls (Iowa) Daily Record, 1933-35; tchr. Cedar Falls High Sch., 1935-37; instr. journalism, dir. publicity and radio activities East High Sch., Aurora, Ill., 1937-40; announcer, news editor radio sta. WMRO, Aurora, 1940-43; dir. journalism Stephens Coll., Columbia, Mo., 1946; news dir. radio sta. KFRU, Columbia, 1947-53; gen. mgr. sta. KOMU-TV, Columbia, 1955-58; mem. faculty U. Mo., 1946—, prof. journalism, 1953—, chmn. broadcasting dept., 1972-74; producer, moderator Missouri Forum, U. Mo. Tape Network, 1959—, asst. to pres. charge TV, 1953-66, asst. to chancellor charge TV, 1966-71; cons. sta. KMOX, St. Louis, also CBS-Radio, 1960-67. Mem. publicity div. Mo. chpt. Am. Cancer Soc., 1962-65; mem. NBC Affiliates Spl. Network Com., 1958, Gov. Mo. Ednl. TV Com., 1963-64. Served with USNR, 1943-45. Recipient citation Broadcasting mag., 1954; award Nat. Project Agrl. Communications, 1955; Nathan Stubblefield Excellence in Broadcast Edn. award, 1971. Mem. Nat. Assn. Ednl. Broadcasters, Nat. Assn. Broadcasters, Assn. Profl. Broadcast Edn., Mo. Broadcasters Assn. (life; award outstanding service 1975), Tabard Inn, Sigma Delta Chi, Kappa Tau Alpha, Pi Gamma Mu, Alpha Gamma Gamma, Alpha Delta Alpha. Rotarian (bd. dirs. Columbia 1963-64). Author: Television Newsroom Practices, 1950; Educational Television in the United States, 1953. Home: 4112 Faurot Dr Columbia MO 65201

LAMBERT, EDWARD HOWARD, physiologist, educator; b. Mpls., Aug. 30, 1915; s. Harry Edward and Ida Carine (Peterson) L.; B.S., U. Ill., 1936, M.S., 1938, M.D., 1939, Ph.D. in Physiology, 1944; m. Louise Augusta Rueckheim, Oct. 12, 1940 (dec. Nov. 1972); m. 2d, Vanda Alice Lennon, Dec. 23, 1975. Intern, Michael Reese Hosp., Chgo., 1938-39; fellow physiology U. Ill. Coll. Medicine, 1940-41; instr. med. tech. and biol. scis. Herzl Jr. Coll., Chgo., 1941-42; asso. medicine, research physiologist on OSRD project U. Ill. Coll. Medicine, 1942-43; research asst. acceleration lab. Mayo Aeromed. Unit, 1943-45; cons. physiology Mayo Clinic, 1945—; faculty Mayo Grad. Sch. Medicine, U. Minn., 1945-73, prof. physiology, 1958-73, faculty Mayo Med. Sch., 1973—, prof. physiology and neurology, 1973—. Cons. U.S. Navy, 1948, 52-53, USPHS, 1955; adv. bd. Myasthenia Gravis Found., 1959— (chmn. 1973-75); mem. pub. adv. group USPHS, 1963-71, 73-77. Recipient Presdl. Certificate of Merit, 1947. Mem. World Fedn. Neurology (mem. research group neuromuscular disease), Am. Electroencephalographic Soc., Am. Physiol. Soc., Am. Assn. Electromyography and Electrodiagnosis (pres. 1957-58; council 1954-67), Am. Neurol. Assn., Am. Acad. Neurology, Aerospace Med. Assn. (Arnold D. Tuttle award 1952), Soc. for Neuroscis., Soc. Exptl. Biology and Medicine, A.A.A.S., Minn. Acad. Sci., Amyotrophic Sclerosis Soc. Am. (sci. adv. com. 1976—), Walter Reed Soc., Rochester C. of C., Sigma Xi, Phi Chi, Alpha Omega Alpha, Phi Kappa Phi. Contbr. articles on physiology, effects of acceleration and neuromuscular disorders to profl. jours. Home: 202 14th St NE Rochester MN 55901 Office: Mayo Clinic Rochester MN 55901

LAMBERT, EDWARD MARK, record co. exec.; b. Bklyn., Dec. 28, 1942; s. Melvin and Betty (Levine) L.; student Coll. City N.Y., 1960-62; m. Marcia Ellen Lambert, Mar. 21, 1965; children—Brian Drew, Jennifer Mindy. Record producer Capitol Records, N.Y.C., 1969-70; gen. mgr. ABC/Dunhill Music, Inc., Los Angeles, 1970-73; v.p., gen. mgr. Haven Records, Inc., Hollywood, Calif., 1974-77; gen. mgr. Interworld Music Group, Hollywood, 1977—. Served with U.S. Army, 1964. Mem. Nat. Assn. Recording Arts and Scis. (nat. trustee). Democrat. Jewish. Home: 23445 Los Encinos Way Woodland Hills CA 91367 Office: 6255 Sunset Blvd Hollywood CA 90028

LAMBERT, ELEANOR (MRS. SEYMOUR BERKSON), fashion, pub. relations exec., journalist; b. Crawfordsville, Ind.; d. Henry Clay and Helen Houghton (Craig) Lambert; student John Herron Art Inst., Chgo. Art Inst.; 1 m. Seymour Berkson, 1936 (dec.); 1 son, William Craig. Pioneer publicist for Am. art and artists and later for creative talents in Am. fashion; originator, coordinator Coty Am. Fashion Critics Award and Cotton Fashion Awards; originator N.Y. Couture Groups Nat. Press weeks and ann. Internat. Best Dressed polls; author Field Enterprises syndicated column She; bd. dirs., hon. mem. Council Fashion Designers of Am.; original dir. ILGWU's consumer service program; producer large fashion shows; spl. cons. on uniforms WAC and U.S. Army Nurse Corps, 1943-45; mem. NRC advisory com. to Q.M. on Women's Mil Clothing; mem. advisory com. Costume Inst., Met. Mus. Art; apptd. by Pres. Johnson as mem. Nat. Council on Arts, 1965-66; mem. N.Y. Mayor's Com. World Fashion Center, Mayor's Hospitality Com., N.Y.; bd. dirs. N.Y. World's Fair, 1964, Ednl. Found. for Fashion Industries; coordinator, dir. Am. Designer Showings, Fashion Press Weeks. Recipient N.Y. Bd. of Trade gold medal award for exceptional contbns. to Am. fashion industries, 1960; Honor award Girls Clubs Am. Mem. Am. Women in Radio and TV, N.Y. Fashion Group (v.p. 1961-63). Presbyterian. Home: 1060 Fifth Ave New York NY 10028 Office: 32 E 57th St New York NY 10022

LAMBERT, EUGENE RAYMOND, newspaper publisher, found. exec.; b. Cloquet, Minn., Nov. 5, 1915; s. Joseph Eugene and Mathilda (Bodway) L.; student U. Minn.; m. June Dorothy Jensen, June 3, 1941; children—Judith, Eugene L., Laurence, Mary Lynn. Personnel mgr. Am. Hoist & Derrick Co., St. Paul, 1940-43; field rep. Dept. Labor, St. Paul, 1946-47; asst. mgr. Asso. Gen. Contractors Minn., Mpls., 1947-52; mgr. Builders Exchange, Duluth, Minn., 1952-56; mayor of Duluth, 1956-59; dir. employee relations Dispatch & Pioneer Press, St. Paul, also personnel dir. Ridder Publs., Inc., 1959-71; publisher Herald and News Tribune, Duluth, 1971-75, Eagle and Beacon, Wichita, Kans., 1975-79; pres., chief exec. officer Found. Wichita Devel., 1979—; past dir. N.W. Publs., First Nat. Bank Duluth. Chmn. St. Paul Housing and Redevl. Authority, 1962-67; v.p., dir. Duluth Area C. of C., 1971-75, Wichita Greater Downtown Devel. Assn., 1976—; pres., dir. N.E. Minn. Devel. Assn., 1971-75; v.p. Duluth Downtown Devel. Assn., 1972-75. Served with AUS, 1943-46. Recipient spl. citations Minn. Soc. Architects, City of Duluth, City of St. Paul, Air Def. Command, Air NG. Former mem. Am. Newspaper Pubs. Assn., Inland Daily Newspaper Assn., Newspaper Personnel Relations Assn.; mem. Wichita Area C. of C. (dir. 1976-79). Roman Catholic. Clubs: Wichita Country, Wichita, Crestview Country. Office: 1435 Kansas State Bank Bldg Wichita KS 67201

LAMBERT, GEORGE ROBERT, ins. co. exec.; b. Muncie, Ind., Feb. 21, 1933; s. George Russell and Velma Lou (Jones) L.; B.S., Ind. U., 1955; J.D., Chgo.-Kent Coll. Law, 1962; m. Mary Virginia Alling, June 16, 1956; children—Robert Allen, Ann Holt, James William. Admitted to Ill. bar, 1962; with Washington Nat. Ins. Co., Evanston, Ill., 1958—, now v.p., gen. counsel and sec., also v.p., gen. counsel Washington Nat. Corp. Mgr. Little League Baseball, 1965; chmn. Lake Bluff Sch. Caucus, 1968-69. Bd. dirs. Lake Bluff Elementary Sch. Dist., 1970-71; mem. adv. council Evanston Twp. High Sch.; mem. exec. com., chmn. 1st Ward, Evanston Regular Republican Orgn. Served to capt. USAF, 1955-57. Named Distinguished Air Force ROTC Grad., 1955. Mem. Am., Ill., Chgo. bar assns., Health Ins. Assn. Am. (govt. relations com.), Am. Judicature Soc., Assn. Life Ins. Counsel (chmn. punitive damages task force), Am. Council Life Ins., Chgo. Estate Planning Council, Chgo.-Kent (dir.), Ill. Inst. Tech. (dir.), Ind. U. alumni assns., Evanston Taxpayers Assn., Touhy Tennis Club, Delta Upsilon. Roman Catholic. Clubs: Kiwanis (dir.) (Evanston); Y Exec. Home: 1525 Judson Ave Evanston IL 60201 Office: 1630 Chicago Ave Evanston IL 60201

LAMBERT, JEREMIAH DANIEL, lawyer; b. N.Y.C., Sept. 11, 1934; s. Noah D. and Clara (Ravage) L.; A.B., Princeton U., 1955; postgrad. (Fulbright scholar) U. Copenhagen, 1955-56; LL.B., Yale U., 1959; m. Vicki Anne Asher, July 25, 1959; children—Nicole Stirling, Alix Stewart, Leigh Asher. Admitted to N.Y. State bar, 1960, D.C. bar, 1964; asso. firm Cravath, Swaine & Moore, N.Y.C., 1959-63; pvt. practice law, Washington, 1963-66; partner firm Drew & Lambert, Washington, 1966-69; sr. partner firm Peabody, Rivlin, Lambert & Meyers, Washington, 1969—; adj. prof. law Georgetown U., Washington, 1978—. Treas., Gas Employees Polit. Action Com., 1978—. Served to 1st lt. JAGC, U.S. Army Res., 1963-65. Mem. Am. Bar Assn., Fed. Bar Assn., N.Y.C. Bar Assn., D.C. Bar Assn., Am. Soc. Internat. Law. Clubs: Univ., Yale (Washington); Princeton (N.Y.C. and Washington); Cleve. Park. Contbr. articles to legal publs. Home: 3400 Newark St NW Washington DC 20016 Office: Peabody Rivlin Lambert & Meyers 1150 Connecticut Ave NW Washington DC 20036. *Some glide over the surface of life; others climb the sheer face of the precipice, piton by piton. I count myself in the latter category. Consistent effort, intelligently applied, does yield results. The intangibles, however, involve one's good relations with the people one lives and works with, and such things are elusive and non-linear. One should strive, I believe, to grasp the totality, to achieve balance.*

LAMBERT, JOHN HAROLD (JACK), football player; b. Mantua, Ohio, July 8, 1952; sutdent Kent State U. Linebacker with Pitts. Steelers, 1974—; played in Pro Bowl, 1975-78. Named to Sporting News AFC All-Star Team, 1975, 76, 78. Office: care Pitts Steelers 300 Stadium Circle Pittsburgh PA 15212*

LAMBERT, JOSEPH BUCKLEY, chemist; b. Ft. Sheridan, Ill., July 4, 1940; s. Joseph Idus and Elizabeth Dorothy (Kirwan) L.; B.S., Yale U., 1962; Ph.D. (Woodrow Wilson fellow 1962-63, NSF fellow 1962-65), Calif. Inst. Tech., 1965; m. Mary Wakefield Pulliam, June 27, 1967; children—Laura Kirwan, Alice Pulliam, Joseph Cannon. Asst. prof. chemistry Northwestern U., Evanston, Ill., 1965-69, asso. prof., 1969-74, prof. chemistry, 1974—; vis. asso. Brit. Mus., 1973. Recipient Nat. Fresenius award, 1976. Alfred P. Sloan fellow, 1968-70, Guggenheim fellow, 1973. Fellow Japan Soc. for Promotion of Sci., Brit. Interplanetary Soc.; mem. Ill. Acad. Sci. (life), AAAS, Am. Chem. Soc., Chem. Soc. (London), Phi Beta Kappa, Sigma Xi. Author: Organic Structural Analysis, 1976; Physical Organic Chemistry through Solved Problems, 1978; (audio course) Intermediate NMR Spectroscopy, 1973. Contbr. articles to sci. jours. Home: 1956 Linneman St Glenview IL 60025 Office: Dept Chemistry Northwestern U Evanston IL 60201

LAMBERT, MARVIN JOSEPH, food co. exec.; b. Altapass, N.C., Jan. 20, 1923; s. Fred Critz and Clara Augusta (Bird) L.; B.S., U. Md., 1943; M.B.A., Northwestern U., 1947; postgrad. Advanced Mgmt. Program, Harvard U., 1970; m. Jean Geissler, July 5, 1944; children—Judith Ann, Jana. With Kraft, Inc., N.Y.C., 1948—, v.p. devel. and long range planning, 1967-71, sr. v.p. corp., 1971—. Served to capt., AUS, 1943-46. Decorated Purple Heart. Club: Union League (N.Y.C.). Office: Kraft Inc Kraft Ct Glenview IL 60025

LAMBERT, NADINE MURPHY, educator; b. Ephraim, Utah; Ph.D. in Psychology, U. So. Calif., 1965; m. Robert E. Lambert, 1956; children—Laura Allan, Jeffrey. Sch. psychologist Los Nietos Sch. Dist., Whittier, Calif., 1952-53, Bellflower (Calif.) Unified Sch. Dist., 1953-58; research cons. Calif. Dept. Edn., Los Angeles, 1958-64; dir. sch. psychology tng. program U. Calif., Berkeley, 1964—, asst. prof. edn., 1964-70, asso. prof., 1970-76, prof., 1976—; mem. Joint Com. Mental Health of Children, 1967-68; cons. state depts. edn. Calif., Ga., Fla.; cons. Calif. Dept. Justice. NIMH grantee, 1965—; Calif. State Dept. Edn. grantee, 1971-72, 76-78. Fellow Am. Psychol. Assn. (council reps.), Am. Orthopsychiat. Assn.; mem. Calif. Assn. Sch. Psychologists and Psychometrists (pres. 1962-63), Am. Ednl. Research Assn., NEA, Am. Bd. Profl. Psychology (diplomate in sch. psychology). Author: (with Windmiller and Cole) School Version of the AAMD Adaptive Behavior Scale, 1974; (with Wilcox and Gleason) Educationally retarded child: Comprehensive assessment and planning for the EMR and slow-learning child, 1974; (with Windmiller and Turiel) Moral Development and Socialization—Three Perspectives, 1979; asso. editor Am. Jour. Orthopsychiatry, 1975—, Am. Jour. Mental Deficiency, 1977—; cons. editor to jours. Office: Dept Edn U Calif Berkeley CA 94720

LAMBERT, OLAF CECIL, hotel mgr.; b. Sherfield-on-London, Hampshire, Eng., Sept. 4, 1920; s. Stanislas and Jeanne Claire (Helsen) Lubienski; grad. Ecole Hoteliere, Nice, France, 1937; m. Erla Sunders, Aug. 19, 1950. Came to U.S., 1946, naturalized, 1958. Gen. mgr. Queensbury Hotel, Glens Falls, N.Y., 1956- 57; resident mgr. Istanbul (Turkey) Hilton, 1957-58; resident mgr., asst. project mgr. Berlin (Germany) Hilton, 1958-59; v.p., gen. mgr. Royal Orleans, New Orleans, 1959-65, Americana of N.Y., N.Y.C., 1965-66; gen. mgr. Chateau Louisianne, New Orleans, 1966—; treas. So. Motor Lodge, 1964—; pres. Dauphine Orleans Hotel Corp., Assos. Purchasing Co., Olaf Lambert and Assos., Inc., New Orleans, So. Scottish Inns, Inc.; pres., dir. Tamacor, Inc., New Orleans. Served to flight lt. RAF, 1939-45; prisoner of war, 1942-45. Recipient Instns. Nat. Merit award Hotel Mgmt. Rev., 1958; Golden Host Merit award, 1964. Mem. Chaine des Rotisseurs, New Orleans Hotel Assn. (dir.), Hotel Sales Mgmt. Assn., So. Motor Lodges La. (dir.). Mason (Shriner, Jester). Address: 2100 St Charles Ave New Orleans LA 70130

LAMBERT, PHILIP, educator; b. Piedmont, Calif., May 14, 1925; s. Peter Joseph and Fay (Franklin) L.; A.B., U. Calif., Berkeley, 1949, M.A., 1950, Ph.D. (Sheaff scholar), 1955; m. Sue Hensley Edwards, Dec. 15, 1949; children—Elizabeth, Paul, Peter. Tchr. Orinda (Calif.) public schs., 1950, vice prin., 1951, prin., 1952, curriculum coordinator, 1953, asst. supt., 1954, asso. supt., 1955-57; lectr. ednl. adminstrn. U. Calif., Berkeley, 1955-57; dir. UCLA Exptl. Sch., 1957-59, asst. prof., 1957-59; asso. prof. U. Wis., Madison, 1959-62, prof., 1962-72, Bassett research prof., 1972—, chmn. dept. ednl. psychology, 1963-65, 70-72, dir. Instructional Research Labs., 1964-69, chmn. Learning Area, 1979—; cons. to English Govt., 1952, Selection Bd., Sch. Medicine, UCLA, 1957-59, Japanese Ministry of Edn., 1958, Bank Street Sch., 1959-63, Groton Pre-Collegiate Sch., 1961-65, Nat. Adv. Council, NEA on Team Teaching Research, 1961-65, IBM Corp., 1961-63, Prime Minister on edn., Iran, 1975-76; dir. Nat. Conf. on World Tensions and Edn. for Dept. Elem. Sch. Prins.-NEA, 1961-62. Bd. dirs. Madison (Wis.) Art Assn., 1962-65. Teaching Styles grantee, 1961-64; lic. psychologist, Wis. Fellow Am. Psychol. Assn.; mem. Lab. Sch. Adminstrs. Assn. (v.p. 1958-59, pres. 1959-60), Alpha Tau Omega. Club: Maple Bluff Country. Contbr. articles to jours. on psychology and edn.; exec. editor Jour. Exptl. Edn., 1964-74, Jour. Ednl. Research, 1964-70. Home: 1050 Sherman Ave Madison WI 53703 Office: 1025 W Johnson St Madison WI 53706. *If man is to speak, he must abhor security and take risks.*

LAMBERT, ROBERT FRANK, elec. engr., educator; b. Warroad, Minn., Mar. 14, 1924; s. Fred Joseph and Nutah (Gibson) L.; B.E.E., U. Minn., 1948, M.S. in Elec. Engring., 1949, Ph.D., 1953; m. June Darlene Flatten, June 30, 1951; children—Cynthia Marie, Susan Ann, Katherine Cheryl. Asst. prof. U. Minn. Inst. Tech., Mpls., 1953-54, asso. prof., 1955-59, prof. elec. engring., 1959—, dir. propagation research lab. U. Minn., 1958—, asso. dean Inst. Tech., 1967-68; asst. prof. Mass. Inst. Tech., 1954-55; cons. elec. engr., also in acoustics, 1953—; guest scientist Third Phys. Inst., Göttingen, Germany, 1964; vis. scientist NASA, Hampton, Va., 1979; dir. Inst. Noise Control Engring., Washington, 1972-75. Served with USNR, 1943-46. Fellow IEEE, Acoustical Soc. Am.; mem. Am. Soc. Engring. Edn., Am. Soc. Engring. Sci., Inst. Noise Control Engrng. (dir.), Sigma Xi, Tau Beta Pi, Eta Kappa Nu, Gamma Alpha. Lutheran. Contbr. numerous articles to tech. jours. Research in acoustics, communication tech. random vibrations. Home: 2503 Snelling Curve Saint Paul MN 55113 Office: U Minn Inst Tech Dept Elec Engring Minneapolis MN 55455

LAMBERT, ROBERT GILBERT, aircraft service co. exec.; b. Ripon, Wis., May 3, 1930; s. Gilbert W. and Dorothy (Brunner) L.; B.A., Ripon Coll., 1952; M.B.A., Harvard, 1956; m. Margaret Meade, Apr. 8, 1961; children—John, Thomas, Jane. Budget supr. to coordinator prodn. control Jones & Laughlin Steel Corp., Pitts., 1956-64; with Cooper Industries, Inc., 1964—, div. controller, Mt. Vernon, Ohio, 1964-68, v.p., Houston, 1968-70, exec. v.p. div., Mt. Vernon, 1971-73; div. pres. Cooper Airmotive, Dallas, 1973—. Trustee, Ripon Coll.; mem. adv. bd. Jesuit Coll. Prep. Sch. Served to 1st lt., Fin. Corps, AUS, 1952-54. Mem. Financial Execs. Inst. Roman Catholic. Clubs: Dallas, Northwood Country. Home: 3940 Hockaday Dr Dallas TX 75229 Office: Cooper Airmotive Dallas TX 75209

LAMBERT, ROBERT JOE, educator; b. Dubuque, Iowa, Dec. 23, 1921; s. Joe Edwin and Mahala (Wirkler) L.; B.A., Drake U., 1943; M.S., Iowa State U., 1948, Ph.D., 1951; m. Marion Elizabeth Kochheiser, Dec. 20, 1942; children—Tracey Robert, Daniel Joe. Instr., Drake U., Des Moines, 1943-44, Iowa State U., Ames, 1946-51; mathematician Nat. Security Agy., Washington, 1951-53; mem. faculty Iowa State U., 1953—, asso. prof. math., 1959-64, prof., 1964—, asso. dir. computation center, 1979—; sr. mathematician Ames Lab., AEC, 1966—; cons. Zenith Radio Corp. and Collins Radio Co., 1955-65. Served with USNR, 1944-46. Mem. Des Moines Philatelic Soc. (pres. 1970-71), Soc. Indsl. and Applied Math (pres. Iowa 1969-70), Am. Math. Soc., Assn. Computing Machinery, Math. Assn. Am., Sigma Xi, Phi Beta Kappa. Contbr. articles to profl. jours. Home: 3301 Ross Rd Ames IA 50010

LAMBERT, ROBERT LOWELL, corp. exec.; b. Mpls., Jan. 3, 1923; s. Luell E. and Amy (Schwerin) L.; student U. Utah, 1941-42, Tex. A. and M. Coll., 1943-44, Biarritz (France) Am. U., 1945; B.S., U. Calif. at Los Angeles, 1947, M.B.A., 1948; grad. student U. Minn., 1948-50; m. Jean Louise Zavodney, Mar. 19, 1949; children—Thomas R., John N. Instr. bus. adminstrn. U. Minn., 1948-50; with Budget Pack, Inc., Los Angeles, 1950-55, v.p., 1954-55; with Riverside Cement Co. div. Amcord, Inc., Los Angeles, 1955-61, treas., 1960- 61, finance dir. Amcord, Inc., 1961-72, treas., 1965-72, 75—, v.p., 1967-72, sec., 1972-74, sr. v.p., 1972—; dir., officer various subsidiaries Amcord, Inc. Vice pres. Amcord Found., 1958—. Served with inf. AUS, World War II; ETO. Decorated Combat Inf. badge, Bronze Star, Belgian Fourragere. Mem. Financial Execs. Inst., Am. Mgmt. Assn., Calif. Soc. Accountants, Town Hall Calif., Tau Kappa Epsilon, Beta Gamma Sigma, Alpha Kappa Psi. Lutheran. Club: Jonathan (Los Angeles); Big Canyon Country (Newport Beach, Calif.), Contbr. articles to profl. jours. Home: 13 Cool Brook Irvine CA 92715 Office: 610 Newport Center Dr Newport Beach CA 92660

LAMBERT, ROBERT STANSBURY, educator; b. N.Y.C., Feb. 7, 1920; s. Robert Brightwell and Dorothy (Stansbury) L.; B.A., U. N.C., 1942, M.A., 1948, Ph.D., 1951; m. Edythe Rutherford, Mar. 7, 1946; children—Margaret Anne (Mrs. Peter Barton), Dorothy Lee (Mrs. Thomas Whisnant) (dec). Instr., asst. prof. history Clemson Coll., 1949-52; prof. history Vincennes U., 1952-53; asso. prof. Ga. Tchrs. Coll., 1953-54; asso. prof., then prof. history Shorter Coll., 1954-56; prof. history Clemson U., 1956—, head dept., 1963-74. Mem. S.C. Archives and History Commn., 1963-74, S.C. Hist. Records Adv. Bd., 1977—. Served to 1st lt., inf. AUS, 1942-46. Decorated Purple Heart;

So. Fellowships Fund grantee, 1956; Am. Assn. State and Local History grantee, 1963; Nat. Endowment Humanities bicentennial grantee, 1970-71. Mem. S.C. (pres. 1965), Am., So. hist. assns., Orgn. Am. Historians, S.C. Hist. Soc. Home: PO Box 1091 Clemson SC 29631

LAMBERT, WALLACE EARL, psychologist, educator; b. Amherst, N.S., Can., Dec. 31, 1922; s. Harry Brown and Alice Grace (Babcock) L.; ed. Brown U., Colgate U., U. N.C.; m. Janine Fraissinet, June, 1978; children—Sylvie M., Philippe H. Mem. faculty dept. psychology McGill U., Montreal, now prof. psychology; vis. prof. various univs., U.S., France, Philippines, Thailand. Served with U.S. Army, World War II. Fellow Royal Soc. Can.; mem. Nat. Acad. Edn. Author numerous books in field including: (with W.W. Lambert) Social Psychology; (with O. Klineberg) Bilingual Education of Children: The St. Lambert Experiment; Language, Psychology and Culture. Home: 4600 Michel Bibaud Montreal PQ H3W 2EZ Canada Office: 1205 Dr Penfield Ave Montreal PQ Canada

LAMBERT, WILLIAM G., journalist; b. Langford, S.D., Feb. 2, 1920; s. William G. and Blanche (Townsend) L.; Nieman fellow journalism Harvard U., 1959-60; m. Jean Kenway Mead, July 7, 1945; children—Kathryn (Mrs. R. Elliott), Mary H.V. (Mrs. K. Oxberry). News editor Enterprise-Courier, Oregon City, Oreg., 1945-50; reporter The Oregonian, Portland, 1950-59; news dir. KPTV, Oreg. Television, Inc., Portland, 1961-62; corr. Time mag., 1962-63; asso. editor, staffwriter Life mag., N.Y.C., 1963-71; staff corr. Time-Life News Service, 1971-73; freelance journalist, 1973; staff writer Phila. Inquirer, 1974—. Cons., U.S. commr. edn. Office of Edn., Washington, 1962. Served to 1st lt. AUS, World War II; PTO; maj. Res. (ret.). Recipient Pulitzer prize for local reporting, 1957; Heywood Broun award, 1957; award for mag. reporting Sigma Delta Chi, 1967; Worth Bingham prize for distinguished reporting, 1967; George Polk award for mag. reporting Abe Fortas articles, 1970, also Heywood Broun award, Sigma Delta Chi award, Nat. Headliners Club award, Page One award. Home: 529 Chandler Ln Villanova PA 19085

LAMBERT, WILLIAM WILSON, univ. dean; b. Amherst, N.S., Can., May 10, 1919; s. Harry Brown and Alice Grace (Babcock) L.; A.B., Brown U., 1942; M.S., U. Nebr., 1943; Ph.D., Harvard, 1951; m. Elisabeth Bird Carr, June 17, 1950; children—Hilary (Mrs. William Renwick), Holly Lee Alison. Tech. aide Nat. Def. Research Council, Washington, 1942-43; lectr. Harvard, Cambridge, Mass., 1950-51; asst. prof. Brown U., Providence, R.I., 1951-52; asst. prof. psychology, sociology and anthropology Cornell U., Ithaca, N.Y., 1952-55, asso. prof., 1955-60, prof., 1960—, dean Grad. Sch., 1974—. Cons. Fulbright Program, 1974—; fellow Center for Advanced Study, Palo Alto, Calif., 1954-55; Fulbright lectr. Oslo (Norway) U., 1957-58, U. Padua (Italy), 1973; Rockefeller exchange prof. U. Philippines, Quezon City, 1968-69. Served with USNR, 1943-46. NIH fellow, 1966-67, Guggenheim fellow, 1973. Fellow Am. Psychol. Assn. (mem. bd. sci. affairs 1970-73); mem. Am. Sociol. Assn., Soc. for Cross-Cultural Research (pres.-elect 1974-75), Phi Beta Kappa, Sigma Xi. Author: (with W.E. Lambert) Social Psychology, 1964, rev. edit., 1973; (with L. Minturn) Mothers of Six Cultures, 1963; (with G. Lindsey and others) Handbook of Social Psychology, 1969; (with R. Weisbrod) Comparative Perspectives in Social Psychology, 1971. Editor: (with E. Borgatta) Handbook Personality Theory and Research, 1968; (with H. Triandis) Handbook of Cross-Cultural Psychology, Vol. I, 1979. Home: 1676 Hanshaw Rd Ithaca NY 14850

LAMBERTI, N.A., operations mgmt. cons.; b. Ankeny, Iowa, Aug. 25, 1920; s. Frank and Caroline (Vignaroli) L.; B.S. in Indsl. Engring., Iowa State U., 1943; M.B.A., U. So. Calif., 1950, M.S. in Indsl. Engring., 1960, D.Bus. Adminstrn., 1961; m. Joan Schneider, Sept. 13, 1952; children—Catherine Marie, Linda Carol, Michael Joseph. Mech. engr. Northrop Aircraft Corp., 1947-49; chief indsl. engr., dir. materials, asst. v.p. mfg. McCulloch Motors, Los Angeles, 1950-54; v.p., gen. mgr., dir. Ryder-Elliott, Inc., Los Angeles, 1954-58; cons. Lamberti & Assos., 1958-61; asso. prof. U. So. Calif., 1961-64; v.p. ops., exec. asst. to pres. Studebaker Corp., South Bend, Ind., 1964-69; sr. v.p., dir. ops. Universal Am. Corp.; pres. Lamberti & Assos., mgmt. cons., 1970—; chmn. bd. Lamberti Industries, 1976—; dir. Franklin Electric Corp., Bluffton, Ind. Bd. dirs. San Gabriel Valley council Boy Scouts Am.; bd. councilors engring. sch. Calif. State Poly. U., Pomona; trustee Mayfield Sch., Pasadena, Calif.; bd. regents La Salle Sch., Pasadena. Served to lt. (j.g.) USNR, 1944-46. Registered profl. engr., Calif. Mem. Soc. Advancement Mgmt., Am. Inst. Indsl. Engrs. Republican. Clubs: Annandale Country (Pasadena); Jonathan (Los Angeles); Lake Arrowhead Country. Home: 195 Mt Olive Dr Bradbury CA 91010 also 26671 Thunderbird Dr Lake Arrowhead CA 92352

LAMBERTON, JAMES KIRKLAND, JR., banker; b. Bklyn., Jan. 10, 1919; s. James Kirkland and Ada Ethel (Dover) L.; student Hofstra U., 1947-48, Stonier Grad. Sch. Banking, Rutgers U., 1956; m. Alma D. Farr, Nov. 26, 1942; children—Roy S., Thomas J. With Franklin Nat. Bank, N.Y.C., 1946-67, v.p., 1961-67; with Security Nat. Bank (acquired by Chem. Bank N.Y., 1975), Hempstead, N.Y., 1967-75, sr. v.p. operations, 1971-73, sr. v.p., cashier, 1973-75; v.p. Chem. Bank N.Y., 1975; v.p., sr. operating officer Nat. State Bank, Elizabeth, N.J., 1975—. Served with USAAF, 1942-45. Mem. Bank Adminstrn. Inst. (com. mem. N.Y. chpt. 1954—), Middlesex, Somerset Union Bankers Assn. (pres. 1979-80). Lutheran (pres.). Home: 6 Joanna Way Chatham NJ 07928 Office: 68 Broad St Elizabeth NJ 07207

LAMBING, MALCOLM ELWYN, JR., banker; b. Pitts., Feb. 23, 1934; s. Malcolm Elwyn and Clara (Tremain) L.; student Dartmouth, U. Pitts.; m. Nancy Jane Hamilton, Nov. 30, 1957; children—Charles M., James E., Elizabeth A. With Thomas & Co., Pitts.; with First Nat. Bank of Pa., Erie, 1966—, sr. v.p., investment officer, 1969-72, pres., chief adminstrv. officer, dir., 1972-73, pres., chief exec. officer, dir., 1973—; dir. Pitts. br. Fed. Res. Bank Cleve., Eidco, Inc. Bd. dirs. Arts Council, Boys Club Erie, Erie chpt. A.R.C., Erie Conf., Erie Civic Theatre, YMCA; corporator Hamot Hosp.; trustee Mercyhurst Coll., St. Vincent Hosp. Mem. Young Pres.'s Orgn., Am. Inst. Banking. Clubs: Dartmouth of Western Pa., Rotary, Aviation, Kahkwa, Erie. Office: 717 State St Erie PA 16501*

LAMBOOY, JOHN PETER, chemist, educator; b. Kalamazoo, Dec. 6, 1914; s. Karl Willem and Janna (Bouman) L.; B.A., Kalamazoo Coll., 1937, M.S., 1938; M.A., U. Ill., 1939; Ph.D., U. Rochester, 1942; postdoctoral U. Chgo., 1946; m. Irene Thelma Slattery, Sept. 19, 1942; children—John Patrick, Kathleen Ann, Peter Karl, Philip John. Instr. to asso. prof. U. Rochester, 1946-56; prof. biochemistry, head biochemical pharmacology Eppley Research Inst., U. Nebr., 1963-69; prof. biochemistry, dean grad. studies U. Md., Balt., 1969-74, chmn. dept. biochemistry Sch. Dentistry, 1974—. Served to capt. AUS, 1942-46. Fellow A.A.A.S.; mem. Am. Chem. Soc., Am. Soc. Biol. Chemists, Am. Inst. Nutrition, Am. Physiol. Soc., Soc. Exptl. Biology and Medicine, Sigma Xi. (award for sci. achievement 1974). Sect. editor Biological Abstracts, 1956-73. Contbr. articles to profl. jours. Home: 904 Huntsman Rd Towson MD 21204 Office: 660 W Redwood St Baltimore MD 21201

LAMBORN, GEORGE DANIEL FLYNN, fin. services co. exec.; b. Montclair, N.J., Aug. 17, 1935; s. John Warren and Anna Elizabeth (Flynn) L.; student Brown U., 1954-57; m. Betty Burns Harris, Nov. 21, 1959; children—Elizabeth Flynn, Shelly Louis. Vice pres. Lamborn & Co. Inc., N.Y.C., 1957-64; v.p., co-mgr. commodity dept. Hornblower & Weeks, N.Y.C., 1964-72; v.p. H. Hentz Co., N.Y.C., 1972, CBWL-Hayden Stone Co. (merger H. Hentz and CBWL-Hayden Stone), N.Y.C., 1973; sr. exec. v.p., dir. commodities and internat. div. Shearson Hayden Stone Inc. (merger CBWL-Hayden Stone with Shearson Hammil), N.Y.C., 1974—, also dir.; chmn. Shearson Hayden Stone Ltd., London, Shearson-CLAL, Israel. Mem. Chgo. Bd. Trade, United Terminal Sugar Assn. London, N.Y. Coffee and Sugar Exchange (chmn. 1974), London Cocoa Exchange, Amex Commodities Exchange (chmn. 1979), Nat. Futures Assn. (founding), Future Industry Assn. (pres. 1976), Sugar Club (pres. 1972), Sugar Trade Golf Assn., Commodity Club. Republican. Clubs: Montclair Golf, Downtown Athletic. Office: I Western Union Internat Plaza New York NY 10004

LAMBORN, LEROY LESLIE, lawyer, educator; b. Marion, Ohio, May 12, 1937; s. LeRoy Leslie and Lola Fern (Grant) L.; A.B., Oberlin Coll., 1959; LL.B., Western Res. U., 1962; LL.M., Yale U., 1963; J.S.D., Columbia U., 1973. Admitted to N.Y. State bar, 1965, Mich. bar, 1974; asst. prof. law U. Fla., 1965-69; prof. Wayne State U., 1970—; bd. dirs. Nat. Orgn. Victim Assistance, 1978—. Mem. Am. Law Inst., Order of Coif. Club: Inland Whalers. Author: Legal Ethics and Professional Responsibility, 1963; asso. editor Victimology: An Internat. Jour., 1975—. Home: 630 Merrick St Detroit MI 48202 Office: Wayne State U Law Sch Detroit MI 48202

LAMBORN, ROBERT LOUIS, assn. exec.; b. Carlisle, Pa., July 30, 1918; s. Louis Emmor and F. Jean (Wagner) L.; A.B., Stanford, 1938; Ed.M., Harvard, 1941; Ed.D., Johns Hopkins, 1951; m. Dorothy Belle Rundle, Sept. 20, 1939; children—Kathleen R., Alan C., Jeffrey B. Dir., Camp Red Cloud for Boys and Camp Red Wing for Girls, Lake Champlain, Plattsburgh, N.Y., 1936-51; mem. faculty McDonogh (Md.) Sch., 1941-73, asso. headmaster, prin., 1941-43, 46-52, headmaster, 1952-73; exec. dir. Council for Am. Pvt. Edn., Washington, 1973—; vis. instr. U. Va., 1967; adj. prof. Cath. U.; past chmn. Md. Council Edn.; past commr. Middle States Assn. Colls. and Secondary Schs.; mem. Edn. Commn. of States. Served to 1st lt. AUS, 1943-46. Mem. Headmasters Assn., Nat. Assn. Ind. Schs. (past dir., sec.), Assn. Ind. Md. Schs. (past pres.), Country Day Sch. Headmasters Assn. (past v.p.), Am. Assn. Sch. Adminstrs., Assn. for Supervision and Curriculum Devel., Am. Ednl. Research Assn., Phi Beta Kappa, Phi Delta Kappa (past pres. Johns Hopkins chpt.). Contbr. articles to lay and profl. jours. Home: 11809 Greenleaf Ave Potomac MD 20854 Office: Council for Am Pvt Edn 1625 I St NW Suite 1010 Washington DC 20006

LAMBRO, PHILLIP, composer, condr., pianist; b. Wellesley Hills, Mass., Sept. 2, 1935; s. Pascal and Mary (Lapery) L.; student (scholar) Music Acad. of the West, 1955. Made piano debut in Pianist's Fair at Symphony Hall, Boston, 1952; composer: Miraflores for string orch., Dance Barbaro for percussion, Two Pictures for solo percussionist and orch., Four Songs for soprano and orch., Toccata for piano, Toccata for guitar, Parallelograms for flute quartet and jazz ensemble, Music for Wind, Brass and Percussion, Obelisk for oboist and percussionist, Structures for string orch., Fanfare and Tower Music for brass quintet, Night Pieces for piano, Biospheres for six percussionists; composer, condr. for films, including documentaries: Energy On The Move, Mineral King. Active in population control, conservation, protection of animals. Served with inf. AUS; NATO tennis team, 1958-59. Recipient award for Best Music for Mineral King, Nat. Bd. Rev., 1972. Mem. A.S.C.A.P., U.S. Tennis Assn., Composers and Lyricists Guild Am., Nat. Wildlife Fedn., Tau Kappa Epsilon. Compositions performed by Leopold Stokowski, Phila. Orch., Rochester Philharmonic, Balt., Indpls., Miami and Oklahoma City symphonies and others in U.S., Europe, S.Am., Orient; condr. debut rec. of U.S. Internat. Orch. Office: 1888 Century Park E (10) Century City CA 90067. *I am just a humble artist in this overcrowded world who uses music as a form of communication. My main goal is to live in harmony with my environment.*

LAMBROS, LAMBROS JOHN, petroleum co. exec.; b. Sharon, Pa., 1935; s. John and Niki (George) L.; A.B. magna cum laude in History and Lit., Harvard U., 1957, J.D., 1960; m. Cynthia Ryan, 1965; children—John F., Olivia W. Admitted to N.Y. bar, 1961; asso. firm White & Case, N.Y.C., 1961-64; counsel W.R. Grace & Co., N.Y.C., 1964-74, chief internat. counsel, 1970-74; v.p., gen. counsel Amerada Hess Corp., N.Y.C., 1974-76, sr. v.p., gen. counsel, 1976—; dir. Kaysam Corp. Am. Home: 520 E 86th St New York City NY 10028 Office: Amerada Hess Corp 1185 Ave of Americas New York NY 10036

LAMBROS, THOMAS DEMETRIOS, U.S. judge; b. Ashtabula, O., Feb. 4, 1930; s. Demetrios P. and Panagoula (Bellios) L.; student Fairmount (W.Va.) State Coll., 1948-49; LL.B., Cleveland-Marshall Law Sch., 1952; m. Shirley R. Kresin, June 20, 1953; children—Lesley P., Todd T. Admitted to Ohio bar, 1952; partner firm Lambros and Lambros, Ashtabula, 1952-60; judge Ct. Common Pleas, Jefferson, O., 1960-67; judge U.S. Dist. Ct., No. Dist. Ohio, Cleve., 1967—. Mem. exec. bd. N.E. Ohio council Boy Scouts Am.; pres. Ashtabula county chpt. National Found. Served with U.S. Army, 1954-56. Recipient Distinguished Service award Ashtabula Jr. C. of C., 1962, Outstanding Young Man of Ohio award Ohio Jaycees, 1963. Fellow Internat. Acad. Law and Sci.; mem. Am., Ohio, Ashtabula County (past pres.) bar assns., Nat. Conf. State Trial Judges, Ohio Common Pleas Judges Assn. Contbr. articles legal publs. Office: US Dist Ct 106 US Courthouse Cleveland OH 44114*

LAMEY, WILLIAM LAWRENCE, JR., mfg. co. exec.; b. Evanston, Ill., June 19, 1938; s. William Lawrence and Dorothy Matilda (Mann) L.; B.S. in Bus. Adminstrn., Xavier U., 1960; m. Barbara Mary Matulewicz, Oct. 7, 1961; children—William Lawrence III, Patricia, Elizabeth. Staff auditor Haskins & Sells, Chgo., 1960, 62-63, Celanese Corp., Charlotte, N.C., 1963-64; with DeSoto, Inc., Des Plaines, Ill., 1964—, treas., 1970-71, controller, 1971-73, asst. v.p. finance, 1973-74, v.p. fin., 1975—, dir., 1976—. Served with AUS, 1961-62. C.P.A., Ill. Mem. Am. Inst. C.P.A.'s, Ill. Soc. C.P.A.'s, Financial Execs. Inst., Chgo. Zool. Soc., Chgo. Ednl. TV Assn. Home: 1520 Chapel Ct Deerfield IL 60015 Office: 1700 S Mount Prospect Rd Des Plaines IL 60018

LAMIS, LEROY, artist; b. Eddyville, Iowa, Sept. 27, 1925; s. Leo and Blanche (Bennett) L.; B.A., N.Mex. Highlands U., 1953; M.A., Columbia U., 1956; m. Esther Sackler, Aug. 13, 1954; children—Alexander, Jonas. One-man sculpture exhbns. include: Staempli Gallery, N.Y.C., 1966, 69, 73, Gillman Gallery, Chgo., 1967, Tacoma Mus., 1970, Fort Wayne Art Mus., 1968, Des Moines Art Center, 1970, La Jolla Mus., 1970, Ind. State U., 1976, Sheldon Swope Gallery, Terre Haute, Ind., 1979; represented in permanent collections: Albright-Knox Mus., Des Moines Art Center, Whitney Mus. Am. Art, Joseph H. Hirshhorn Collection, Washington, Indpls. Mus., J.B. Speed Mus., Louisville; mem. faculty dept. art Ind. State U., 1961—, prof., 1972—; artist in residence Dartmouth Coll., 1970. Served with AUS, 1943. Mem. Am. Abstract Artists. Address: 3101 Oak Terre Haute IN 47803

LAMKIN, WILLIAM PIERCE, editor; b. Ansley, La., Oct. 17, 1919; s. John Mays and Carrie Ellen (Posey) L.; A.B., U. N.C., 1948; m. Irma Hazel Page, Dec. 30, 1948 (div.); children—John Page, Mary Jean, Carol Ellen; m. 2d, Jane Eagar Mills, Mar. 17, 1973. Reporter, Alexandria (La.) Daily Town Talk, 1941-43; copyreader Charlotte (N.C.) Observer, 1948-49, asst. city editor, then night city editor, 1950-58, city editor, then religion editor, 1958-61; news dir. Presbyn. Ch. U.S., 1961-78; editor Presbyn. Survey, Atlanta, 1978—; mem. news and info. com., ecumedia news com. Nat. Council Chs.; mem. com. advisers Templeton Prize Progress in Religion. Served with USAAF, 1943-45. Decorated D.F.C. (4), Air medal (5). Democrat. Home: 640 Royervista Dr NE Atlanta GA 30342 Office: 341 Ponce de Leon Ave NE Atlanta GA 30308

LAMM, DONALD STEPHEN, publishing co. exec.; b. N.Y.C., May 31, 1931; s. Lawrence William and Aleen Antonia (Lassner) L.; B.A. with high honors, Yale, 1953; postgrad. Oxford (Eng.) U., 1956; m. Jean Stewart Nicol, Sept. 27, 1958; children—Douglas William, Robert Lawrence, Wendy Nicol. With W.W. Norton & Co., Inc., N.Y.C., 1956—, v.p., 1968-76, pres., 1976—, also dir.; dir. Liveright Pub. Corp., Nat. Book Co., Scranton, Pa.; mem. Press Council, Rutgers U. Press. Chmn. curriculum council Bedford Central Sch. Dist., 1972; mem. council Inst. Early Am. History and Culture, Williamsburg, Va.; bd. dirs. Pound Ridge Assn.; chmn. Town of Pound Ridge Bd. Ethics, 1976—; trustee Hiram Halle Meml. Library. Served with AUS, 1953-55. Mem. Manuscript Soc., Phi Beta Kappa. Clubs: Elizabethan (New Haven); Century Assn., Publishers Lunch, Yale (mem. council) (N.Y.C.). Home: Trinity Pass RD 3 Box 264 Pound Ridge NY 10576 Office: 500 Fifth Ave New York NY 10036

LAMM, LESTER PAUL, civil engr.; b. Cohasset, Mass., Jan. 18, 1934; s. Lester Paul and Mary E. Lamm; B.S.C.E., Norwich U., 1955; postgrad. M.I.T., 1964-65, U. Md., 1966-67; m. Mary Elizabeth Briden, Sept. 17, 1960; children—Diana, Deborah, Michael. With Fed. Hwy. Adminstrn., 1955—, exec. dir., 1973—. Served with U.S. Army, 1955-57. Mem. Am. Public Works Assn. (bd. dirs.). Home: 1243 Titania Ln McLean VA 22101 Office: 400 7th St SW Washington DC 20590

LAMM, MICHAEL, journalist, editor; b. London, Eng., Feb. 11, 1936; s. Heinrich and Annie (Hirschel) L.; came to U.S., 1938, naturalized, 1945; student Reed Coll., 1954-57; B.S., Columbia, 1958-59; m. Joanne Carol Sills, Aug. 15, 1959; children—Robert, Charles, John. Mng. editor Motor Trend, Los Angeles, 1962-65, columnist, 1968—; newspaper columnist AP, Stockton, Calif., 1965-76; ind. newspaper columnist, 1976—; founder, editor Spl.-Interest Autos Mag., Stockton, 1970-74, 76-78; West Coast editor Popular Mechanics, Stockton, 1970—; owner, operator Lamm-Morada Pub. Co., Stockton, 1978—. Mem. Soc. Automotive Historians (Cugnot award 1974, pres. 1975-76, v.p. 1977), Audubon Soc., Sierra Club. Office: PO Box 7607 Stockton CA 95207

LAMM, NORMAN, univ. pres.; b. Bklyn., Dec. 19, 1927; s. Samuel and Pearl (Baumol) L.; B.A. summa cum laude, Yeshiva Coll., 1949, Ph.D., Bernard Revel Grad. Sch., 1966; m. Mindella Mehler, Feb. 23, 1954; children—Chaye (Mrs. David Warburg), Joshua B., Shalom E., Sara Rebecca. Ordained Rabbi, 1951; asst. rabbi Congregation Kehilath Jeshurun, N.Y.C., 1952-53; rabbi Congregation Kodimoh, Springfield, Mass., 1954-58, Jewish Center, N.Y.C., 1958-76; Erna and Jakob Michael prof. Jewish philosophy Yeshiva U., N.Y.C., 1966—, pres., univ., 1976—; pres. Rabbi Isaac Elchanan Theol. Sem., N.Y.C., 1976—; vis. prof. Judaic studies Bklyn. Coll., 1974-75; dir. Union Orthodox Jewish Congregations Am. Trustee-at-large Fedn. Jewish Philanthropies, N.Y.; bd. dirs. Am. Friends-Alliance Israelite Universelle; mem. Pres.'s Commn. Holocaust, 1978—. Chmn., N.Y. Conf. on Soviet Jewry, 1970; mem. Halakhah Commn., Rabbinical Council Am. Recipient Abramowitz Zeitlin Found. award, 1972. Mem. Assn. Orthodox Jewish Scientists (bd. govs.). Author: A Hedge of Roses, 1966; The Royal Reach, 1970; Faith and Doubt, 1971; Torah Lishmah, 1972; The Good Society, 1974. Co-editor: The Leo Jung Jubilee Volume, 1962; A Treasury of Tradition, 1967. Home: 101 Central Park W New York NY 10023 Office: Yeshiva U 500 W 185th St New York NY 10003

LAMM, RICHARD CARL, textile co. exec.; b. Reading, Pa., Oct. 30, 1926; s. Earl Fredrick and Carrie Amenda (Miller) L.; student Wharton Sch., U. Pa.; m. Dora Ann Berkley, Jan. 30, 1948; children—Suzanne, Karen, Joanne. With Vanity Fair Mills and subs.'s, 1944—, budget mgr., 1967-70, treas. and controller Berkshire Internat., 1971-73, controller, dir. Lee Co. Inc., Merriam, Kans., 1973—. Served with U.S. Army, 1945-46. Democrat. Club: Leawood South Country. Office: 9001 W 67th St Merriam KS 66202

LAMM, RICHARD DOUGLAS, gov. of Colo.; b. Madison, Wis., Aug. 3, 1935; s. Arnold E. and Mary (Townsend) L.; B.B.A., U. Wis., 1957; LL.B., U. Calif., Berkeley, 1961; m. Dorothy Vennard, May 11, 1963; children—Scott Hunter, Heather Susan. Accountant, Salt Lake City, 1958; tax clk. Calif. Franchise Tax Bd., San Francisco, summer 1959; law clk. firm Michael, Best & Friedrich, San Francisco, summer 1960; accountant Ernst & Ernst, Denver, 1961-62; admitted to Colo. bar, 1962; atty. Colo. Anti-Discrimination Commn., Denver, 1962-63; atty. Jones, Meiklejohn, Kilroy, Kehl & Lyons, Denver, 1963-65; individual practice law, 1965-74; mem. Colo. Ho. of Reps., 1966-74, asst. minority leader, 1971-74; gov. Colo., 1975—; asso. prof. law U. Denver, 1969—; chmn. natural resource and environ. mgmt. com. Nat. Gov.'s Conf. Pres., Denver Young Democrats, 1963; v.p. Colo. Young Democrats, 1964; mem. Conservation Found., Denver Center Performing Arts Center for Growth Alternatives, Central City Opera House Assn. Served as 1st lt. U.S. Army, 1957-58. C.P.A., Colo. Home: 400 E 8th Ave Denver CO 80203 Office: 136 State Capitol Denver CO 80203

LAMM, ROBERT WILLIAM, pianist; b. Bklyn., Oct. 13, 1944; s. Herbert James and Yvonne Katharine (Hyland) L.; student Roosevelt U., Chgo., 1966-68; m. Julie Nini, Jan. 23, 1976. Mem. musical group Chicago, 1967—; v.p., partner Chgo. Music, Inc.; pres. Nini-Lamm, Inc., Lamm Prodns., Lamminations Music, Inc.; partner Tenderness, Inc. Active campaigner Senator George McGovern for President, 1972. Hon. fellow Harry Truman Library Inst.; founder-patron Huntington Hartford Theatre. Recipient keys to cities of Reno and New Orleans; civic awards Southfield, Mich. and Des Moines, medal of merit City of Chgo., 1976. Mem. AFTRA, ASCAP, AGVA (Entertainer of Yr. award 1974). Club: Century (Los Angeles). Composer over 100 songs including: Questions 67 & 68, 1969; Beginnings, 1969; Does Anybody Really Know What Time it Is?, 1969; 25 Or 6 to 4, 1970; Free, 1972; Saturday in the Park, 1973; Dialogue, 1973; Harry Truman, 1975. Address: 9356 Santa Monica Blvd Beverly Hills CA 90210*

LAMMEL, JEANETTE OSBORN, interior designer; b. Pawnee City, Nebr., Jan. 1, 1917; d. David William and Emma Maude (Waddell) L.; B.A., U. Nebr., 1938; postgrad. Art Inst. Chgo., 1940; m. Harry George Lammel, Mar. 28, 1942; children—Claudia Jean Lammel Fenner, David George. Engring. draftsman, 1941-45; partner

Perdue & Lammel, interior designers, Vallejo, Calif., 1956-58; prin. Jeanette O. Lammel, Vallejo, 1958—; pres. Design Found., Inc., 1974-78. Chmn. 1st City Beautification Com., 1963; mem. design and ops. com. Vallejo Hist. Mus., 1973—; trustee 1st Presby. Ch., 1955-57; bd. dirs. Sem Yeta council Camp Fire Girls, 1954-55. Fellow Am. Inst. Interior Designers (v.p. 1970-72, exec. com. 1970-72, bd. govs. 1967-72, past pres. No. Calif. chpt.), Am. Soc. Interior Designers (bd. dirs.); mem. Nat. Home Fashions League, Internat. Farkleberry Growers Assn. (a founder), Museum Soc., Decorative Arts Trust, Nat. Trust for Hist. Preservation, Vallejo Ind. Press, Delta Phi Delta. Republican. Club: Commonwealth of Calif. Home: 258 Viewmont Ave Vallejo CA 94590

LAMMONS, AUBREY OWEN, lawyer; b. Hartford, Ala., Feb. 24, 1933; s. Milan D. and Lois (Dorrothy) L.; B.S., U. Ala., 1958, J.D., 1961; m. Margaret Ann Jackson, Oct. 17, 1954; children—Karen Alison, Keith Milan, Kevin Duncan, Kelli Lynne, Kerry Owen. Admitted to Ala. bar, 1961, since practiced in Huntsville; partner Archer & Lammons, 1961; asst. U.S. atty. No. Dist. Ala., 1961-62; partner Camp, Smith & Lammons, 1962-67, partner Smith, Lammons & Weaver, 1967-69, Lammons, Bell & Sneed and predecessor, 1969—; dist. atty. pro-tem 23d Jud. Circuit Ala., 1968-69; commr. Madison County Jud. Commn., 1974-75. Mem. Huntsville Planning Commn., 1966-74, sec., 1971; vice chmn. N. Ala. chpt. Nat. Multiple Sclerosis Soc., 1970-71; mem. dist. com. Boy Scouts Am., 1969-71; mem. budget and admissions com. United Givers Fund, 1967-70. Served with USAF, 1952-56. Recipient Distinguished Service citation Nat. Multiple Sclerosis Soc., 1969. Mem. Am., Ala., Huntsville-Madison County (v.p. 1975-76, pres. 1976—) bar assns., Huntsville-Madison County C. of C. (dir. 1974—), Sigma Delta Kappa. Methodist. Mason (32 deg., Shriner) Home: 2712 Westminister Way Huntsville AL 35801 Office: 132 W Holmes Ave Huntsville AL 35801

LAMON, HARRY VINCENT, JR., lawyer; b. Macon, Ga., Sept. 29, 1932; s. Harry Vincent and Helen (Bewley) L.; B.S. cum laude, Davidson Coll., 1954; J.D. magna cum laude, Emory U., 1958; m. Ada Healey Morris, June 17, 1954; children—Hollis Morris, Helen Kathryn. Admitted to Ga. bar, 1958, D.C. bar, 1965; practice in Atlanta, 1958—; mem. firm Crenshaw, Hansell, Ware & Brandon, 1958-62, Hansell, Post, Brandon & Dorsey, 1962-73, Henkel & Lamon, 1973—; dir. Sockwell Enterprises Inc., Leaselite Inc., Fulton Bros. Electric Co. (all Atlanta), Meidinger & Assos. Inc. (Louisville). Adj. prof. law Emory U., 1960—. Mem. adv. bd. Salvation Army, 1963—, chmn., 1975-79, mem. nat. adv. council, 1976—; mem. Adv. Council on Employee Welfare and Pension Benefit Plans, 1975-79. Trustee, past pres. So. Fed. Tax Inst. Inc.; trustee Inst. for Continuing Legal Edn. in Ga., 1976—. Served to 1st lt. AUS, 1954-56. Recipient Others award Salvation Army, 1979. Fellow Am. Coll. Probate Counsel, Internat. Acad. Estate and Trust Law; mem. Am., Fed., Atlanta bar assns., Am. Law Inst., Am., So. (pres. 1972) pension confs., State Bar Ga. (chmn. sect. taxation 1969-70), Am. Judicature Soc., Atlanta Tax Forum, Lawyers Club Atlanta, Nat. Emory U. Law Sch. Alumni Assn. (pres. 1967), Practicing Law Inst., ALI-ABA Inst., C.L.U.'s Inst., Phi Beta Kappa, Omicron Delta Kappa, Phi Delta Phi, Phi Delta Theta (chmn. community service day 1969-72, legal commr. 1973-76). Episcopalian (vestryman). Mason (Shriner), Kiwanian (pres. 1973-74, Atlanta). Clubs: Breakfast, Capital City, Commerce, Cherokee Town and Country (Atlanta); University (Washington). Contbr. articles to profl. jours. Home: 3375 Valley Rd NW Atlanta GA 30305 Office: 2500 Peachtree Center-Cain Tower 229 Peachtree St NE Atlanta GA 30303 also 702 Longfellow Bldg 1201 Connecticut Ave NW Washington DC 20036

LAMOND, GAYLORD MARVIN, retail food exec.; b. Chgo., Feb. 16, 1923; s. Herbert M. and Lottie (Glouser) LaM.; student U. Colo., 1943; certificate Wayne State U., 1947; m. Jean Elizabeth Carl, Sept. 20, 1947; children—Michele Jeanne, Gary Gaylord. With Campbell Soup Co., 1947-66; pres. Chock Full o'Nuts, N.Y.C., 1966-68; pres. New Dimensions Food Service div. Federated Dept. Stores, Inc., Cin., 1968-72; pres., chief exec. officer Isaly Co., Pitts., 1972—; pres. C-W Holdings Co., 1972—; chmn. Clabin Food Service Div. Office, Pitts.; dir. Clabin Corp., Old Greenwich, Conn. Home: 121 Pheasant Dr Pittsburgh PA 15238 Office: 3380 Blvd of Allies Pittsburgh PA 15213

LAMONE, RUDOLPH PHILIP, coll. dean; b. Wellsburg, W.Va., Dec. 20, 1931; s. Dominic and Maria (Branch) L.; B.S., U. N.C., Chapel Hill, 1960, Ph.D., 1966; m. Linda A. Hefler, Jan. 29, 1970. Instr., U. N.C., 1963-66; mem. faculty U. Md., 1966—, prof. mgmt. sci. 1971—, dean Coll. Bus. and Mgmt., 1973—; bd. dirs. Md. Center Productivity and Quality of Working Life; chmn. govtl. relations com. Am. Assembly Collegiate Schs. Bus., 1977-78; cons. Tatung Co., Taiwan; mem. adv. com. Md. Dept. Econ. and Community Devel. Served with AUS, 1952-55. Mem. Acad. Mgmt., Inst. Mgmt. Scis., Am. Inst. Decision Scis., Md. C. of C. (dir.), Phi Beta Kappa, Beta Gamma Sigma. Democrat. Roman Catholic. Club: Annapolis Yacht. Co-author: Linear Programming for Management Decisions, 1969; Marketing Management and the Decision Sciences, 1971; Production-Operations Management, 1972. Home: 1842 Lindamoor Dr Annapolis MD 21401 Office: Coll Bus and Mgmt U Md College Park MD 20742

LAMONT, BARBARA GIBSON, libarian; b. Huntington, Ind., Nov. 8, 1925; d. Herbert Donald and Edith (VanAntwerp) LaMont; A.B., Coll. William and Mary, 1947; M.A., Radcliffe Coll., 1952; M.S. in L.S., Simmons Coll., 1954. With Harvard Library, 1951-64; head librarian Douglass Coll., Rutgers U., 1964-67, Vassar Coll., 1967—. Trustee Southeastern (N.Y.) Library Resources Council, 1967-73. Home: Andrews Rd LaGrangeville NY 12540 Office: Vassar Coll Poughkeepsie NY 12601

LAMONT, CORLISS, author, educator; b. Englewood, N.J., Mar. 28, 1902; s. Thomas William and Florence Haskell (Corliss) L.; grad. Phillips Exeter Acad., 1920; A.B. magna cum laude, Harvard, 1924; postgrad. New Coll., Oxford (Eng.) U., 1924-25; Ph.D., Columbia, 1932; m. Margaret H. Irish, June 8, 1928 (div.); children—Margaret Hayes (Mrs. J. David Heap), Florence Parmelee (Mrs. Ralph Antonides), Hayes Corliss, Anne Sterling (Mrs. George Jafferis); m. 2d, Helen Boyden Lamb, 1962 (dec. July 1975). Instr. philosophy Columbia, 1928-32, New Sch. Social Research, 1940-42; lectr. intensive study contemporary Russian civilization Cornell U., 1943, Social Studies Workshop on Soviet Russia, Harvard Grad. Sch. Edn., 1944, Columbia Sch. Gen. Studies, 1947-59, Columbia seminar asso., 1971—. Bd. dirs. A.C.L.U., 1932-54; pres. Bill of Rights Fund, 1954-69; chmn. Nat. Emergency Civil Liberties Com.; chmn. Nat. Council American-Soviet Friendship, 1943-46. Candidate for U.S. Senate, Am. Labor Party, N.Y., 1952, Independent-Socialist Party, 1958; indictment for contempt of the Congress effected by Sen. Joseph McCarthy dismissed by U.S. Appeals Ct., 1956. Vice pres., mem. exec. bd. Poetry Soc. Am., 1971-74. Recipient of N.Y. City Tchrs. Union Ann. award, 1955; Mem. A.A.A.S., Acad. Polit. Sci., N.A.A.C.P., Am. Humanist Assn. (hon. pres. 1974—, John Dewey Humanist award 1972, Humanist of Yr. award 1977), P.E.N., Am. Philos. Assn., UN Assn., Phi Beta Kappa. Clubs: Columbia Faculty, Harvard (N.Y.C.). Editor: Man Answers Death: An Anthology of Poetry, rev. edit., 1952; Dialogue on John Dewey, 1959; Dialogue on George Santayana, 1959; A Humanist Symposium on Metaphysics, 1960; Albert Rhys Williams— In Memoriam, 1962; The Trial of Elizabeth Gurley Flynn by the American Civil Liberties Union, 1968; The Thomas Lamonts in America, 1971; (with Lansing Lamont) Letters of John Masefield to Florence Lamont, 1979; author: Issues of Immortality, 1932; The Illusion of Immortality, rev. edit., 1965; You Might Like Socialism: A Way of Life for Modern Man, 1939; The Peoples of the Soviet Union, 1946; A Humanist Funeral Service, 1947; Humanism as a Philosophy, 1949; The Independent Mind, 1951; Soviet Civilization, 1952; Freedom Is As Freedom Does: Civil Liberties Today, 1956; The Philosophy of Humanism, rev. edit., 1965; Freedom of Choice Affirmed, 1967; A Humanist Wedding Service, 1970; Remembering John Masefield, 1971; Lover's Credo, 1972; Voice in the Wilderness: Collected Essays of Fifty Years, 1974; Basic Pamphlet Series, 1952—; co-author: Introduction to Contemporary Problems in U.S. (syllabus), 1929; Russia Day by Day (with Margaret I. Lamont), 1933. Frequent contbr. to periodicals, speaker radio, TV; sec. Jour. Philosophy. Address: 315 W 106th St New York NY 10025

LAMONT, ELIZABETH CARRINGTON BROWN, civic worker; b. Stamford, Conn., Jan. 18, 1904; d. George Lockwood and Mabel Carrington (King) Brown; ed. Low and Heywood Sch., Stamford; m. John Lester Newland, May 1, 1926 (dec. 1927); 1 dau., Joan Carrington (dec.); m. 2d, Gordon Lamont, Dec. 7, 1938 (dec. Sept. 1977); 1 stepson, Richard. Chmn. Darien (Conn.) United Cancer Fund, 1946-58; founder Darien Book Aid Plan, 1949, hon. chmn., 1952—; founder Book and Mag. Aid Plans Am., 1956, Jupiter Island Book Aid Plan, 1959; founder Nat. Vols. in Action, 1974; mem. Com. 100, N.Y.C. Hon. vice chmn. Darien Republican campaign, 1956; pres. Darien Women's Rep. Assn., 1954-57, mem.-at-large, 1979—; dir. Fairfield County Rep. Women's Assn., 1954-62; vice chmn. Darien Ref. Fin. Campaigns, 1958, 60, 62, 64; chmn. nat. council, bd. govs. Women's Nat. Rep. Club, 1965—; bd. dirs. Nat. Fedn. Rep. Women, 1971—, also fin. chmn., vice chmn. ways and means; mem. Palm Beach Rep. Exec. bd., 1970—. Mem. D.A.R., Nat. Soc. New Eng. Women. Episcopalian. Clubs: Jupiter Island Garden (treas. 1962-64), Jupiter Island (Hobe Sound); Everglades, Four Arts (Palm Beach, Fla.); Colony (N.Y.C.). Home: Box 394 Hobe Sound FL 33455. *Because of the impact of government on the lives of all our people, for good or for bad, I have for years taken an active interest in politics—not as a candidate, but to interest all the people I can reach in voting for and supporting good candidates in the best interest of our country. I have little patience with those who say they will not take part because politics is an "unscrupulous" business.*

LAMONT, LANSING, journalist; b. N.Y.C., Mar. 13, 1930; s. Thomas Stilwell and Elinor (Miner) L.; grad. Milton (Mass.) Acad., 1948; A.B., Harvard, 1952; M.S. in Journalism with honors, Columbia, 1958; m. Ada Jung, Sept. 18, 1954; children—Douglas Ranlet, Elisabeth Jung, Virginia Alden, Thomas Stilwell II. Reporter, Washington Star, 1958-59; Washington corr. Worcester (Mass.) Gazette, also other New Eng. papers, 1959-60; sci. reporter Washington bur. Time mag., 1961-63, polit. reporter, 1964-68, corr., dep. chief London (Eng.) bur., 1969-71, chief Can. corr., chief Ottawa bur., 1971-73, chief corr. UN, N.Y.C., 1973-74. Alumni bd. dirs. Harvard U., also chmn. nominating com. for overseers; trustee Milton Acad., Am. Mus. Natural History, N.Y.C. Served to 1st lt., inf., U.S. Army, 1954-57. Clubs: Century Assn., Harvard (N.Y.C.); Coffee House, Metropolitan (Washington). Episcopalian. Author: Day of Trinity (alternate selection Lit. Guild Am.), 1965; Campus Shock, 1979; co-editor: Private Letters of John Masefield, 1979. Home: 133 E 80th St New York NY 10021 Office: 515 Madison Ave New York NY 10022

LAMONT, ROSETTE CLEMENTINE, educator, writer, translator; b. Paris, France; d. Alexandre and Loudmilla (Lamont) L.; came to U.S., 1941, naturalized, 1946; B.A., Hunter Coll., 1947; M.A., Yale U., 1948, Ph.D., 1954; m. Frederick Hyde Farmer, Aug. 9, 1969. Tutor romance langs. Queens Coll., City U. N.Y., 1950-54, instr., 1954-61, asst. prof., 1961-64, asso. prof., 1965-67, prof., 1967—; mem. doctoral faculty French and comparative lit. City U. N.Y., 1968—; State Dept. envoy Scholar Exchange Program, USSR, 1974; research fellow, 1976; lectr. Alliance Française, Maison Française of N.Y. U. Decorated Chevalier, then officier des Palmes Academiques (France). Guggenheim fellow, 1973-74. Mem. Modern Lang. Assn. Am., Am. Soc. Theatre Research, Internat. Brecht Soc., P.E.N., Phi Beta Kappa, Sigma Tau Delta, Pi Delta Phi. Club: Yale. Author: The Life and Works of Boris Pasternak, 1964; De Vive Voix, 1971; Ionesco, 1973; The Two Faces of Ionesco, 1978; also contbr. to various books. Mem. editorial bd. Performing Arts Jour., Centerpoint; contbr. articles to profl. jours., Columbia Dictionary of Modern European Literature. Home: 260 W 72d St New York NY 10023 also 51 W Chester St Nantucket MA 02554 Office: Dept Romance Languages Queens College City Univ New York Flushing NY 11367 also Grad Center CUNY 33 W 42 St New York NY 10036

LAMONTAGNE, JOSEPH GILLES, Can. govt. ofcl.; b. Montreal, Que., Can., Apr. 17, 1919; degree Jean de Brebeuf Coll., Ecole des Hautes Etudes commerciales; m. Mary Schaefer, Apr. 23, 1949; children—Michel, Pierre, Andre, Marie. Owner import bus., Quebec, 1946-66; mem. Quebec City Council, 1962-65, mayor, 1965-77; mem. Parliament (Liberal) for Langelier, 1977—; minister without portfolio, 1978; postmaster gen. Can., 1978—. Served with RCAF, 1940-45; ETO. Mem. Union des Municipalités du Que. (past pres.), Canadian Fedn. Municipalities (past v.p.), Port Quebec Authority, Conseil de Planification et de Devel. Quebec, Econ. Council Can. (dir.). Roman Catholic. Club: Que. Rotary (past pres.). Home: 1040 Moncton PQ G1S 2Y8 Canada Office: House of Commons Ottawa ON K1A 0A6 Canada

LAMONT-HAVERS, RONALD WILLIAM, physician, hosp. adminstr.; b. Wymondham, Norfolk, Eng., Mar. 6, 1920; s. William Fredrick L.-H.; came to U.S., 1955, naturalized, 1964; B.A., U. B.C., 1942; M.D., U. Toronto, 1946; diploma in internal medicine McGill U., 1953; m. Gabrielson, Oct. 16, 1965; children—Wendy, Melinda, Ian. Intern, Vancouver (B.C., Can.) Gen. Hosp., 1946-48; resident in internal medicine Queen Mary Vets. Hosp., Montreal, Que., Can., 1949-51; Canadian Arthritis and Rheumatism Soc. fellow Columbia Presbyterian Hosp., Coll. Physicians and Surgeons, Columbia U., N.Y.C., 1951-53; med. dir. Canadian Arthritis and Rheumatism Soc., B.C. div., Vancouver, 1953-55, The Arthritis Found., N.Y.C., 1955-64; instr. in medicine Coll. Physicians and Surgeons, Columbia U., 1955-64; asso. dir. for extramural programs Nat. Inst. Arthritis and Metabolic Diseases, NIH, Bethesda, Md., 1964-68, asso. dir. extramural programs, 1968-72, dep. dir. Nat. Inst. Arthritis, Metabolism, and Digestive Diseases, 1972-74, acting dep. dir. NIH, 1974, acting dir., 1975, dep. dir., 1974-76; dep. to gen. dir. for research policy and adminstrn. Mass. Gen. Hosp., Boston, 1976—; cons. Grayson Found., Inc., Lexington, Ky., 1965—; del. USSR-Arthritis Exchange Program, 1964; U.S. coordinator U.S.-USSR Coop. Program in Arthritis, 1973-75; chmn. HEW Study Group on Protection of Human Subjects in Biomed. and Behavioral Research, 1973—. Served with M.C., Royal Canadian Army, 1944-46. Recipient Golden Pen award Jour. Am. Phys. Therapy Assn., 1965; Superior Service award HEW, 1973; Spl. citation Sec. HEW, 1975. Fellow Royal Coll. Physicians (Can.); mem. Canadian, D.C. (pres. 1971) rheumatism socs., Am. (dir. Met. Washington sect. 1964—), N.Y. (pres. 1960) rheumatism assns., Dermatology Found. (med. adv. com., exec. com. 1967—), Arthritis Found. (dir., governing mem. 1966—), Am. Acad. Orthopaedic Surgeons (hon.), Am. Gastroent. Assn. (affiliate), Alpha Omega Alpha. Editor Bull. Rheumatic Diseases, 1964-66; contbr. articles in field to books, profl. jours. Office: Mass Gen Hosp Fruit St Boston MA 02114

LAMORE, GEORGE EDWARD, JR., clergyman, educator; b. North Adams, Mass., June 17, 1930; s. George Edward and Victoria Mary (Bird) LaM.; B.A., Williams Coll., 1953; M.Div. magna cum laude, Boston U., 1956, Th.D., 1959; honors citation Iowa Wesleyan Coll., 1965; m. Jane Esther Blackburn, June 27, 1953; children—Christian John, Wesley Paul. Ordained to ministry Methodist Ch., 1956; pastor Meth. Ch., Adams, Mass., 1951-58; dir. religious life, prof. religion and philosophy Iowa Wesleyan Coll., Mt. Pleasant, 1959-69, head dept. religion and philosophy, 1969—, chmn. div. humanities, 1970-76; lectr. in field; violinist S.E. Iowa Symphony Orch., 1959—. Chmn. edn. com. Midwest Old Threshers Reunion, 1970—; founder, dir. The Minister and Mental Health. Roswell R. Robinson fellow Boston U., 1956-57. Mem. Am. Acad. Religion, Am. Philos. Assn. Contbr. articles to profl. jours. Home: 307 W Pearl St Mount Pleasant IA 52641. *The basic mandates of life to me are not ten but two in number-Relate and Grow! By relating to others and the world at large I outgrow myself-and that is the most basic urge within me.*

LAMOREUX, FREDERICK HOLMES, financial exec.; b. Montreal, Que., Can., Dec. 10, 1941; s. Frederick Silas and Marie Paule (Dubuc) L.; B.C., McGill U., 1964; M.B.A., Columbia, 1966; m. Jill Adelle Reed, Dec. 21, 1963; children—David, John, Jenny. Fin. planning mgr. Cummins Engine Co., Columbus, Ind., 1966-67; mgr. acquisition analysis Am. Standard, N.Y.C., 1967-69, asst. to exec. v.p., 1970-71; asst. treas. Fairchild Industries, Germantown, Md., 1971-72; v.p. fin. and adminstrn. Fairchild, Space and Electronics div. Fairchild Industries, 1972-74; v.p., treas. Arvin Industries, Inc., Columbus, 1974-76, v.p., treas., chief fin. officer, 1976—, chmn. fin. com., dir., 1977—. Talcott fellow, 1965. Mem. Fin. Council, Machinery and Allied Products Inst., Phi Gamma Delta, Beta Gamma Sigma. Home: 1331 Crescent Dr Columbus IN 47201 Office: 1531 13th St Columbus IN 47201

LA MOTTE, CLYDE WILSON, pub. relations exec.; b. Quannah, Tex., July 18, 1916; s. Alfred and Herma Ona (Butler) La M.; student Abilene Christian Coll., 1933-35; B.J., U. Tex., 1940; m. Mary Louise Reynolds, June 14, 1941; children—Larry, LaLinda (Mrs. Lee Egerstrom), Michele, Kay, Gregory. Reporter, Austin (Tex.) Tribune, 1940-41; with Houston Post, 1941-51, successively reporter, night city editor, asst. city editor, sports editor; reporter Washington bur. McGraw-Hill, 1951-55, news editor Petroleum Week, N.Y.C., 1955-59; Washington editor Oil & Gas Jour., Tulsa, 1959-64; reporter, columnist LaMotte News Bur., Washington, 1964-79; exec. v.p. Pub. Relations Internat., Ltd., Tulsa, 1979—. Served with AUS, 1943-45. Mem. Nat. Assn. Petroleum Writers (pres. 1967-68), Environ. Writers Assn. Am. (chmn. bd. 1973), Ind. Newsletter Assn. (pres. 1972), Nat. Press Club (pres. 1974), Sigma Delta Chi. Home: 7137 S Darlington Ave Tulsa OK 74103 Office: 800 Franklin Bldg Tulsa OK 74103

L'AMOUR, LOUIS DEARBORN, author; b. Jamestown, N.D.; s. Louis Charles and Emily (Dearborn) LaMoore; self ed.; LL.D. (hon.) Jamestown Coll., 1972; m. Katherine Elizabeth Adams, Feb. 19, 1956; children—Beau Dearborn, Angelique Gabrielle. Lectr., U. Okla., Tulsa U., Baylor U., E. Tex. State Tchrs. Coll., Our Lady of Lake Coll., U. So. Calif., Claremont Coll., U. Redlands, LaCrosse Tchrs. Coll., Central Okla. State Coll.; appearances on Great Tchrs. TV program. Served to 1st lt. AUS, 1942-46. Named Theodore Roosevelt Rough Rider by N.D., 1972. Mem. Acad. Motion Picture Arts and Scis., Calif. Acad. Scis. Author: Smoke From This Altar (poems), 1939; Hondo, 1953; The Burning Hills, 1956; Sitka, 1957; The Daybreakers, 1960; Kid Rodelo, Mustang Man, Kilrone, 1966; The Sky-Liners, 1967; The Broken Gun; Matagorda, 1967; Brionne, 1968; Chancy, 1968; Down the Long Hills (Golden Spur awards Western Writers Assn.), 1968; The Empty Land, 1969; The Lonely Men, 1969; Conagher, 1969; A Man Called Noon, 1970; Reilly's Luck, 1970; Galloway, 1970; North to the Rails, 1971; Under the Sweet-Water Rim, 1971; Tucker, 1971; Callaghen, 1972; Ride the Dark Trail, 1972; Treasure Mountain, 1972; The Ferguson Rifle, 1973; The Man from Skibbereen, 1973; The Quick and the Dead, 1973; The Californios, 1974; Sackett's Land, 1974; War Party, 1975; Rivers West, 1975; Over on the Dry Side, 1975; Rider of Lost Creek, 1976; Where the Long Grass Blows, 1976; To the Far Blue Mountains, 1976; Borden Chantry, 1977; Fair Blows the Wind, 1978; The Mountain Valley War, 1978; Bendigo Shafter, 1979; The Proving Trail, 1979; The Iron Marshal (Golden Plate award), 1979; The Strong Shall Live, 1980. Address: care Bantam Books 666 Fifth Ave New York NY 10019

LAMPARD, ERIC EDWIN, econ. historian, educator; b. Southampton, Eng., Sept. 26, 1922; s. Edwin William and Nellie (James) L.; B.Sc. in Econs., London (Eng.) Sch. Econs., 1948; Ph.D., U. Wis., 1954; m. Marie Vera Turbow, Sept. 22, 1951; 1 dau., Sophie Alice. Came to U.S., 1948. Lectr. history Columbia, 1952-53; research fellow econ. history U. Pa., 1953-54; lectr., then asso. prof. econ. history Smith Coll., 1954-59; mem. faculty U. Wis., 1959-69, prof. history, 1962-69, adj. prof. urban and regional planning, 1962-69; prof. history State U. N.Y. at Stony Brook, 1969—. Mem. staff Resources for the Future, 1957-58, mem. com. urban econs., 1964—; mem. com. urbanization Social Sci. Research Council, 1958-64; mem. nat. research adv. panel HUD, 1970-72. Prothero lectr. Royal Hist. Soc. (U.K.), 1972. Served with Royal Marines, 1941-46. Recipient David Clark Everest prize in econ. history Wis. Hist. Soc., 1955. Mem. Econ. History Assn., Econ. History Soc. (U.K.), Am. Hist. Assn., Am. Econ. Assn. Author: Industrial Revolution, 1957; (with others) Regions, Resources and Economic Growth, 1960; Rise of the Dairy Industry, 1963; also articles. U.S. rev. editor Econ. History Rev., 1965-76. Home: 112 Jones Ave Port Jefferson NY 11777

LAMPARSKI, RICHARD, author; b. Grosse Pointe Farms, Mich., Oct. 5; s. Benjamin Walter and Virginia (Downey) Lynch; grad. high sch. Haberdashery salesman Saks Fifth Ave., Detroit, Beverly Hills, Calif., 1950-52; clk. CBS Radio, 1952-54; press agt. Ice Capades, 1954-57; asst. promotion dir. KTLA Channel 5, Los Angeles, 1957-60; press agt. Allen, Foster, Ingersoll, N.Y.C., 1964; producer, host Whatever Became of . . . ? radio series WBAI, N.Y.C., 1965-73. Author: Whatever Became of . . . ?, 1967, Vol. II, 1968, Vol. III, 1970, Vol. IV, 1973, Vol. V, 1975, Vol. VI, 1976, Vol. VII, 1977; Low Life, 1979. Home: 3289 Carse Canyon Dr Hollywood CA 90068

LAMPEN, SISTER MARY JOEL, coll. pres.; b. Carlyle, Ill.; d. Joseph Conrad and Mary Johanna (Hitpas) Lampen; student Ancilla Coll., 1939-41, DePaul U., 1948; Ph.B., Loyola U., Chgo., 1949, Ed.D., 1964; M.A., St. Mary's Coll., 1956. Tchr. elementary schs., 1941-47; tchr. Angel Guardian High Sch., 1948-52, St. Augustine's High Sch., 1952-60; tchr., dir. guidance Ancilla Domini High Sch., Donaldson, Ind., 1960-64; pres. Ancilla Coll., Donaldson, 1964—; commr. North Central Assn. Colls. and Schs., 1977—; mem. adv. council Ancilla Domini Sisters, 1966-79; mem. planning com. Marshall County (Ind.) Community Leaders Seminar, 1970. Mem. Constnl. Rev. Commn. Ind., 1972; sec. Marshall County Devel. Study Com., 1972-75; mem. Marshall County Econ. Devel. Com., 1976—;

mem. Plymouth Arts Commn., 1976—; v.p. bd. dirs. St. Catherine's Hosp., East Chicago, Ind., 1967-72, pres. bd. dirs., 1972—. Recipient Sagamore of Wabash citation Gov. of Ind., 1975. Mem. Am. Assn. Higher Edn., Nat. Cath. Ednl. Assn., Coll. Theology Soc., Assn. Curriculum Devel. and Supervision. Office: Ancilla College Donaldson IN 46513

LAMPERTI, JOHN WILLIAMS, mathematician, educator; b. Montclair, N.J., Dec. 20, 1932; s. Frank A. and Louise (Williams) L.; B.S., Haverford Coll., 1953; Ph.D., Calif. Inst. Tech., 1957; m. Claudia Jane McKay, Aug. 17, 1957; children—Matthew, Steven, Aaron, Noelle. Instr., then asst. prof. math. Stanford, 1957-62; research asso. Rockefeller Inst., 1962-63; faculty Dartmouth, 1963—, prof. math., 1968—. Sci. exchange visitor to USSR, 1970; vis. prof. U. Aarhus (Denmark), 1972-73. Active ACLU. Fellow Inst. Math. Statistics; mem. War Resisters League, SANE, Amnesty Internat., Fedn. Am. Scientists. Author: Probability: A Survey of the Mathematical Theory, 1966; Stochastic Processes: A Survey of the Mathematical Theory, 1977. Home: Loveland Rd Norwich VT 05055 Office: Dartmouth Coll Hanover NH 03755

LAMPHERE, ROBERT JOSEPH, ins. co. exec.; b. Wardner, Idaho, Feb. 14, 1918; s. Joseph Sherman and Lily L. (Valentine); student U. Idaho, 1936-40; LL.B., Nat. Law Sch., Washington, 1941; postgrad. Harvard Bus. Sch., 1962, Aspen Inst., 1967; 1 son, George E. Admitted to D.C. bar, 1941; with Dept. Treasury, 1940-41, FBI, 1941-55; with VA, Washington, 1955-61, dep. adminstr., 1960-61; with John Hancock Mut. Life Ins. Co., Boston, 1961—, 2d v.p. corporate planning, 1965-66, v.p. corporate planning, 1966-73, v.p. policyholders service adminstrn., 1973-76, sr. v.p., 1976—. Chmn. Boston Mayor's Com. for Employment of Handicapped, 1964, 66; chmn. ho. of dels. Nat. Easter Seal Soc., 1972-73; pres. Mass. Easter Seal Soc., 1974; trustee St. Margaret's Hosp., 1968—; bd. dirs. Tri-Lateral Council for Quality Edn., Boston, 1974—, Urban League Eastern Mass., 1975—; mem. exec. com. Mass. Adv. Council for Vocat.-Tech. Edn., 1975-78. Recipient Merit citation Nat. Civil Service League, 1959. Mem. Delta Chi. Republican. Clubs: Algonquin, Charles River Country. Office: John Hancock Mut Life Ins Co PO Box 111 Boston MA 02117

LAMPHIER, THOMAS JOSEPH, ry. exec.; b. Rochester, N.Y., May 2, 1924; s. John Francis and Anna Marie (Cromey) L.; B.S. in Civil Engring., Mass. Inst. Tech., 1949; postgrad. Harvard, 1968; m. Mallean G. Thidemann, Oct. 27, 1953; children—Jon F., Christine M. Chainman. Rodman, Gt. No. Ry., Superior, Wis., 1949-50, asst. to div. roadmaster, Grand Forks, N.D., 1950-51, dist. roadmaster, Watertown, S.D., 1952, transp. insp., St. Paul, 1952-54, asst. trainmaster, Mpls., 1954-55, co-chmn. computer research com., St. Paul, 1955-56, dir. systems and programming, 1956-57, asst. to v.p., 1957-58, dir. div. econ. research, 1958-62, div. supt., Klamath Falls, Oreg., 1962-63, asst. to v.p. ops., 1963-67, v.p. adminstrn., 1967-70; v.p. planning Burlington No., Inc., St. Paul, 1970, v.p. mgmt. services and planning, 1971-72, v.p. exec. dept., 1972, exec. v.p., 1973-76, pres. transp. div., 1977—; pres. Western Fruit Express Co., 1975; exec. v.p., dir. Colo. & So. Ry., Ft. Worth and Denver Ry.; dir. Burlington No. Dock Corp., Burlington No. Air Freight Inc., BN Transport Inc., Nat. R.R. Passenger Corp. (Amtrak), First Nat. Bank St. Paul, Pioneer Mut. Life Ins. Co. Bd. dirs., pres. Lake Superior Mus. Transp., Duluth, Minn. Served with USNR, 1943-46. Mem. Am. Ry. Engring. Assn., Transp. Research Bd. (exec. com.), N.Am. Soc. Corp. Planning. Clubs: St. Paul Athletic; Union League, Minn. Home: 8169 80th St N Stillwater MN 55082 Office: 176 E 5th St Saint Paul MN 55101

LAMPL, JACK WILLARD, JR., finance co. exec.; b. Cleve., Mar. 20, 1921; s. Jack Willard and Nelle M. (Engel) L.; B.S. in Fine Arts, Harvard, 1942; m. Carolyn Joan Cosel, Mar. 6, 1949: children—Jack Willard III, Joshua C. Pres. Arden Co., Miami, Fla., 1960—; chmn. bd., chief exec. officer Sunamerica Corp., 1976—; dir. Cleve. Trust Co. Dir. Nat. Consumer Finance Assn., Washington, 1967-74. Mem. Group '66 Cleve.; chmn. Arden House Consumer Credit Com., Columbia Grad. Sch. Bus., 1965-68; adv. council Cleve. Mus. Art, 1977—; mem. Cleve. Soc. Contemporary Art, 1962—; guarantor Cleve. Met. Opera, 1965—; trustee Cleve. Play House Found., Univ. Hosps. of Cleve., 1968—; Mem. Am. Indsl. Bankers Assn. (chmn. 1965, dir., mem. exec. com. 1965—), Am. Finance Conf. (pres., dir., mem. exec. com. 1965—), World Bus. Council, Western Res. Hist. Soc. (trustee). Rotarian. Clubs: Clevelander, Commerce, Harvard, Mid-Day, Oakwood Country, Cleve. Racquet, Union (Cleve.); Harvard, Metropolitan (N.Y.C.); Sandusky (Ohio) Sailing. Home: 18400 S Park Blvd Shaker Heights OH 44120 Office: Sunamerica Bldg 1015 Euclid Ave Cleveland OH 44115

LAMPL, PEGGY ANN, govt. ofcl.; b. N.Y.C., Dec. 12, 1930; d. Joseph and Alice L.; B.A., Bennington Coll., 1952. Dir. program devel. dept. mental health AMA, Chgo., 1962-66; spl. asst. NIMH, HEW, Washington, 1967-69; public relations dir. League Women Voters of U.S., Washington, 1969-73, exec. dir., 1973-78; dep. asst. Sec. of State for congressional relations, Dept. State, Washington, 1978—. Club: Federal City. Home: 1541 33d St NW Washington DC 20007 Office: Dept State Washington DC 20520

LAMPMAN, ROBERT JAMES, economist, educator; b. Plover, Wis., Sept. 25, 1920; s. Harry Gordon and Bernice (Pierce) L.; B.A., U. Wis., 1942, Ph.D., 1950; postgrad. U. Calif. at Berkeley, 1947-48; m. JoAnn Cockrell, June 27, 1943; children—Jonathan William, James Henry, Rebecca Jo, Thomas Robert. Asst., then asso. prof. econs. U. Wash., 1948-58; vis. prof. U. Wis., Madison, 1955-56, prof. econs., 1958—, chmn. dept., 1961-62, 74-75. Vis. asso. prof. Am. U. of Beirut, 1951-52; research asso. Nat. Bur. Econ. Research, 1957-58; staff Council Econ. Advisers, 1962-63; vis. prof. U. Philippines, 1966-67, Cornell U., 1973-74. Ford Faculty fellow, 1960-61. Served to lt. (j.g.) USNR, 1942-46. Mem. Am. Econ. Assn., Indsl. Relations Research Assn., A.A.U.P., Phi Beta Kappa, Phi Kappa Phi. Author: Re Low Income Population and Economic Growth, 1959; Top Wealth-Holders Share of National Wealth, 1962; Administration of Washington Medical Service Corporations, 1962; Ends and Means of Reducing Income Poverty, 1971; also numerous articles. Home: 729 Oneida Pl Madison WI 53711

LAMPORT, FELICIA (MRS. BENJAMIN KAPLAN), writer; b. N.Y.C., Jan. 4, 1916; d. Samuel C. and Miriam (Dworsky) Lamport; B.A., Vassar Coll., 1937; m. Benjamin Kaplan, Apr. 16, 1942; children—James, Nancy Mansbach. Reporter, N.Y. Jour., N.Y.C., 1935-36; dialogue sub-title writer MGM, N.Y.C., 1937-49; free lance writer various mags., newspapers including Harper's, Atlantic, Sat. Rev., New Yorker, N.Y. Times, 1949—. Bd. dirs. MacDowell Colony, Am. Chess Found. Mem. Writer's Guild, P.E.N. Author: Mink on Weekdays, 1950; Scrap Irony, 1961; Cultural Slag, 1966. Home: 2 Bond St Cambridge MA 02138

LAMPRON, EDWARD JOHN, state justice; b. Nashua, N.H., Aug. 23, 1909; s. John P. and Helene (Deschenes) L.; A.B., Assumption Coll., 1931, LL.D., 1954; J.D., Harvard, 1934; m. Laurette L. Loiselle, Sept. 22, 1938; children—Norman E., J. Gerard. Admitted to N.H. bar, 1935; practice in Nashua, 1935-47; city solicitor, Nashua, 1936-46; justice N.H. Superior Ct., 1947-49, N.H. Supreme Ct., 1949—, now chief justice. Mem. adv. bd. St. Joseph's Hosp., Nashua; trustee Nashua Pub. Library. Mem. Am., Nashua (past pres.) bar assns., Assn. Canado-Americaine (v.p., dir.). Clubs: Exchange (hon.), Serra (past pres.) (Nashua). Office: 115 Main St Nashua NH 03060*

LAMPRON, JOHN JOSEPH, utility exec.; b. Bklyn., Apr. 4, 1944; s. Joseph Felix and Margaret Ann Lampron; B.A., U. N.H., 1966, M.B.A., 1971; m. Elaine C. Bourgeois, Aug. 31, 1968; children—Stephanie Frances, Katherine Quinn. With Public Service Co. N.H., Manchester, 1971—, econ. analyst, then asst. treas., 1975-78, treas., 1978—; corporator Amoskeag Savs. Bank, Manchester. Bd. dirs. Manchester Boys Club, 1977—; mem. exec. bd. N.H. chpt. March of Dimes, 1979—. Served with USAR, 1967-69. Office: PO Box 330 Manchester NH 03105

LAMPTON, ROBERT BENJAMIN, banker; b. Magnolia, Miss., Oct. 26, 1920; s. Robert Benjamin and Gertrude (Thompson) L.; B.S. in Engring., Princeton, 1942; m. Katherine Anderson Bryan, Aug. 17, 1950; children—Kathy, Mary, Bob, Bryan, Jim. Instr. math. McCallie Sch., Chattanooga, 1946-49; with First Nat. Bank Jackson (Miss.), 1949—, exec. v.p., 1967-69, pres., 1969-76, vice chmn. bd., 1976—, also dir.; vice chmn. bd., dir. 1st Capital Corp., 1976—; dir. Entex, Inc.; lectr. Sch. Banking, La. State U., 1966—. Campaign chmn. United Givers Fund Jackson, 1962, v.p., 1963, pres., 1964; Miss. chmn. Radio Free Europe Fund, 1970; chmn. Miss. Arts Commn., 1967-70, Jackson City Planning Bd. Pres., bd. dirs. Pearl River Valley Water Supply Dist. Trustee Piney Woods (Miss.) Country Life Sch.; mem. lay adv. bd. St. Dominics Jackson Meml. Hosp. Served to lt. USNR, 1942-46. Mem. Newcomen Soc. N.Am. (treas. Miss.), Am. Bankers Assn. (governing council 1978), Miss. Bankers Assn. (pres. 1974-75), Jackson C. of C. (pres. 1973), Phi Beta Kappa. Kiwanian (pres. 1962). Club: River Hills (pres. 1967) (Jackson). Home: 125 Woodland Circle Jackson MS 39216 Office: PO Box 291 Jackson MS 39205

LAMSON, BALDWIN GAYLORD, physician, univ. adminstr.; b. Berkeley, Calif., May 20, 1916; s. Joseph Sterry and Eleanor Josephine (Baldwin) L.; B.A., U. Calif., Berkeley, 1938; M.D., U. Rochester, 1944; m. Ormond Ruth Snook, Dec. 5, 1942; children—Ann Gaylord, Baldwin Gaylord, Wade Sterry, Stephen Berry. Intern, Strong Meml. Hosp., Rochester, N.Y., 1944-45, resident, 1949-50; resident Emory U. Hosp., Atlanta, 1945-46; prof. pathology UCLA Sch. Medicine, 1962—, asso. dean, 1965-66, 74-76, asst. chancellor for health scis., 1977—, dir. hosps. and clinics UCLA, 1966—. Served with USNR, 1946-47, 50-51. Home: 4706 Balboa Ave Encino CA 91316 Office: 10833 Le Conte Ave Los Angeles CA 90024

LAMY, ANDRÉ, Canadian govt. ofcl.; b. Montreal, July 19, 1932; s. J. Adelard and Marie-Antoinette (Crepeau) L.; student U. Montreal, 1955, McGill U., Montreal, 1957; m. Françoise Martin, July 19, 1958; children—Mathieu, Marc, Philippe. Pharm. products rep. Upjohn Co. Can., 1957-62; dir. sales, producer Niagara Films, Montreal, 1962-64; founding v.p., dir., producer, adminstr. Onyx Films, Montreal, 1964-70; asst. govt. film commr. Nat. Film Bd. Can., Montreal, 1970-75, govt. film commr., chmn. film bd., 1975-79; v.p. Société Radio-Can./CBC, Ottawa, Ont., 1979—; bd. govs. CBC, Nat. Arts Centre, Canadian Film Devel. Corp. Home: 245 Outremont St Outremont PQ Canada Office: 1500 Ave Bronson Ottawa ON Canada*

LAMY, PETER PAUL, gerontologist, educator; b. Breslau, Germany, Dec. 14, 1925; s. Rudolf and Luise (Bettinger) L.; B.S. in Pharmacy, Phila. Coll. Pharmacy and Sci., 1956, M.S., 1958, Ph.D. in Biopharmaceutics, 1964; m. Angela Pogorilich, Nov. 27, 1952; children—Rudolf, Margaret, Carl. Instr. pharmacy Phila. Coll. Pharmacy and Sci., 1956-63; instr. pharmacology Woman's Hosp., Phila., 1960-62; asst. prof. pharmacy U. Md., 1963-67, asso. prof., 1967-72, prof., 1972—, dir. instnl. pharmacy programs, 1968—, co-dir. profl. experience program, 1970—, mem. faculty Med. Sch., 1974—; dir. dept. instnl. pharmacy practice U. Md. Hosp., Balt., 1970-77; cons. Yager Drug Co., Balt., Levindale Hebrew Geriatric Center and Hosp., Balt., 1972—, VA Hosp., Balt., 1972—, John L. Deaton Med. Center, 1973—, VA Med. Center, Washington, 1975—, VA Med. Center, Ft. Howard, Md., 1978—; lectr. psychopharmacology Sch. Nursing, Catholic U. Am., 1973. Vice pres. Catonsville (Md.) Elem. PTA, 1973-74, pres., 1974-75. Served with U.S. Army, 1948-51. Fellow AAAS, Am. Coll. Apothecaries, Am. Coll. Clin. Pharmacology; mem. Am. Geriatric Soc., Am. Soc. Hosp. Pharmacy, Acad. Pharm. Sci., Am. Pharm. Assn., Sigma Xi, Rho Chi. Reviewer Jour. Pharm. Scis., 1968-78, Jour. Am. Pharm. Assn., 1968-78, Am. Jour. Hosp. Pharmacy, 1972—; instnl. pharmacy editor Md. Pharmacist, 1974-76; mem. editorial bd. Hosp. Pharmacy, 1968-79, Drug Intelligence and Clin. Pharmacy, 1978—, Hosp. Formulary, 1978-79; editor Contemporary Pharmacy Practice, 1978; contbr. articles to sci. jours. Home: 110 Glenwood Ave Baltimore MD 21228 Office: 636 W Lombard St Baltimore MD 21201

LAN, DONALD, state ofcl.; b. Newark, Dec. 19, 1930; s. Samuel and Mary (Kufferman) L.; student Seton Hall U., 1948-51; m. Hannah Resnik, July 15, 1951; children—Donald Paul, Richard Allen, Barbara Susan. Officer, Dell Products Corp., Hillside, N.J., 1952-74, 75-76; exec. sec. to Gov., State of N.J., 1974-75; sec. of state, 1977—. Chmn., Union County Democratic Com., 1975-77; mem. N.J. Dem. Com., 1973-75, Dem. Nat. Com., 1974-76; Dem. municipal chmn. Springfield, N.J., 1968-71; v.p. Temple Sharey Shalom, Springfield; civic affairs chmn. Springfield B'nai Brith; asst. campaign mgr. Gov. Brendan Byrne, 1973; co-founder Springfield Instructional Football League; co-dir., coach Springfield Youth Baseball League; mem. employee relations policy council N.J. Bi-Centennial Commn.; trustee Support of Free Pub. Schs., 1977—; mem. State Bd. Canvassers and Electoral Coll., 1977—. Democrat. Jewish. Served with USAF, 1951-52. Home: 34 Cypress St Springfield NJ 07081 Office: Box 1330 State House Trenton NJ 08625

LANA, ROBERT EDWARD, psychologist, educator; b. Hoboken, N.J., Aug. 9, 1932; s. Edward Vincent and Daisy (Taborelli) L.; B.A., Rutgers U., 1954; M.A., U. Md., 1956, Ph.D., 1958; m. Mary Jean Harris, June 16, 1965. Asst. prof. Am. U., 1958-61; asso. prof. Alfred (N.Y.) U., 1962-65; sr. Fulbright lectr. U. Rome (Italy), 1965-66; mem. faculty Temple U., 1966—, prof. psychology, chmn. dept., 1969—; cons. NSF, 1966-67. Fellow Am. Psychol. Assn. Author: Assumptions of Social Psychology, 1969. Home: 233 Righters Mill Rd Narberth PA 19072

LANAHAN, JOHN STEVENSON, hotel exec.; b. Pitts., June 13, 1922; s. James S. and Katharine L. (Lauck) L.; B.A., Duke U., 1947; M.B.A., Harvard U., 1949; m. Rosemary Lourdes Ford, Feb. 20, 1954; children—Margaret Kayne, Brian James, Ellen Ford. Sales mgr. Mid-Atlantic region Allen B. Dumont Labs., E. Paterson, N.J., 1950-53; sr. asso. Booz, Allen & Hamilton, Inc., N.Y.C., 1954-59; pres. Richmond Hotels, Inc. (Va.), 1959-69, Flagler System, Inc., Palm Beach, Fla., 1969-71, Carlton House Resort Inns, Inc., Richmond, 1971-73; exec. v.p. Braniff Internat. Hotels, Dallas, 1973-74; pres., chief exec. officer The Greenbrier, White Sulphur Springs, W.Va., 1975—; sr. v.p. Chessie System, Inc., 1979—; dir. White Sulphur Springs Co. Bd. dirs. W.Va. Found. Ind. Colls.; chmn. bd. Richmond Forward, 1968. Served to lt. (j.g.) USNR, World War II. Named to Hotel Industry Hall of Fame, 1971. Mem. So. Innkeepers Assn., W.Va. Hotel and Motel Assn., Am. Hotel and Motel Assn., Beta Theta Pi, Omicron Delta Kappa. Republican. Roman Catholic. Clubs: Commonwealth (Richmond); Rotary. Address: The Greenbrier White Sulphur Springs WV 24986

LANCASTER, BILLY JACK, oil co. exec.; b. Cross Plains, Tex., Apr. 29, 1924; s. Benton Hale and Allie Frances (Gee) L.; B.S., U. Tex., 1948; m. Jeanne Marie Murphy, Oct. 28, 1944; children—Lynda (Mrs. Laurence K. Gustafson), Deborah. Mgr. engring. Atlantic Richfield Co., Dallas, 1963-68, v.p. research and engring., 1968-73, sr. v.p., 1973-78; pres. ARCO Oil and Gas Co., 1978—. Served to 1st lt. USAF, 1943-45. Decorated Purple Heart, Air medal. Mem. Am. Petroleum Inst., Mid Continent Oil and Gas Assn., Soc. Profl. Engrs., Dallas Petroleum Club. Club: Brook Hollow Golf. Home: 5322 Kelsey Rd Dallas TX 75229 Office: PO Box 2819 Dallas TX 75221

LANCASTER, BRUCE MORGAN, investment adv., lectr., ret. diplomat; b. Meridian, Miss., Oct. 5, 1923; s. Reuben MacDowell and Margaret (Morgan) L.; B.S. with highest honors, Miss. State U., 1943; grad. student Duke, 1946-47; Ph.D., Am. U., 1974; m. Mary Elinor Bickham, Nov. 1, 1947; 1 son, Bruce Morgan II. Instr. math. Miss. State U., 1943; joined U.S. Fgn Service, 1947; 3d sec. embassy, Nanking, Canton, Hong Kong, 1947-49; vice consul, Hamburg, Germany, 1950-53, consul, 1954; Dutch and Swiss desk officer State Dept., 1955-57, pub. affairs officer European bur., 1958; consul in charge, Medellin, Colombia, 1959-61; Colombia and Argentine desk officer State Dept., 1961-63, dep. dir. East Coast of Latin Am., 1963-65; dir. operations center, also dep. exec. sec. to sec. of state, 1965-67; consul gen., Stuttgart, Germany, 1967-69; fellow Imperial Defence Coll., London, 1970; country dir. Peru and Ecuador, Dept. State, 1971-72; detailed S.E. Fed. Regional Council, Atlanta, 1973-74; sr. research asso., lectr. Emory U., 1973-76; lectr. Johns Hopkins, 1977—. Campaign mgr. for Jimmy Carter in N.W. La., 1975-76. Served to capt. USMCR, 1943-46; col. Res. Hoover fellow Yale, 1963. Mem. Sigma Chi, Phi Kappa Phi. Episcopalian. Contbr. articles to profl. jours., also chpts. to books. Home: 3611 Tupelo Pl Alexandria VA 22304 Office: care Fgn Service Mail Room Dept State Washington DC 20520 also 815 Connecticut Ave NW 2d Floor Washington DC 20006

LANCASTER, BURT(ON) (STEPHEN), motion picture actor; b. N.Y.C., Nov. 2, 1913; s. James Lancaster; student N.Y. U.; m. Norma Anderson, Dec. 26, 1946 (div. 1969); children—James Steven, William Henry, Susan Elizabeth, Joanne Mari. Formed acrobatic team Lang & Cravat (with Nick Cravat), 1932, performed circuses, carnivals, vaudeville, 1932-39; floor walker lingerie dept. Marshall Field & Co., Chgo., 1939, then salesman haberdashery dept.; appeared in play A Sound of Hunting, N.Y.C., 1945; films include The Killers, 1946, I Walk Alone, 1947, Desert Fury, 1947, Brute Force, All My Sons, 1948, Sorry, Wrong Number, 1948, Kiss the Blood Off My Hands, 1948, Criss-Cross, 1949, Rope of Sand, 1949, Mister 880, 1950, Flame and the Arrow, 1950, Vengeance Valley, 1951, Jim Thorpe—All American, 1951, Ten Tall Men, 1951, The Crimson Pirate, 1952, Come Back Little Sheba, 1953, South Sea Woman, 1953, From Here to Eternity, 1953, The Big Top, His Majesty O'Keefe, 1954, The Rose Tattoo, 1955, The Kentuckian (also dir.), 1954, Trapeze, 1956, The Rainmaker, 1957, Gunfight at OK Corral, 1957, Sweet Smell of Success, 1957, Run Silent, Run Deep, 1958, Separate Tables, 1958, The Devil's Disciple, 1959, The Unforgiven, 1960, Elmer Gantry (Acad. award as best actor), 1960, The Young Savages, 1961, Judgement at Nuremberg, 1961, Bird Man of Alcatraz (Venice Film award for best actor), 1962, A Child is Waiting, 1963, The Leopard, 1963, Seven Days in May, 1964, The Train, 1965, The Hallelujah Trail, 1965, The Professionals, 1966, The Swimmer, 1968, The Scalphunters, 1968, Castle Keep, 1969, The Gypsy Moths, 1969, Airport, 1970, Lawman, 1971, Valdez is Coming, 1971, Ulzana's Raid, 1972, Executive Action, 1973, Scorpio, 1973, The Midnight Man, 1974, Buffalo Bill and The Indians, 1976, The Cassandra Crossing, 1977, "1900", 1977, The Island of Dr. Moreau, 1977, Twilight's Last Gleaming, 1977, Go Tell the Spartans, 1978. Served with spl. services div. Fifth Army, AUS, 1942-45.*

LANCASTER, EDWIN BEATTIE, ins. co. exec.; b. LeMars, Iowa, Aug. 1, 1916; s. Middleton John and Rosabelle (Beattie) L.; B.A., U. Iowa, 1938, postgrad., 1938-39; m. Marjorie Forshey, Sept. 1, 1951; children—Craig, Susan. With Met. Life Ins. Co., N.Y.C., 1939—, actuary, 1964-65, v.p., 1965-69, sr. v.p., 1969-71, sr. v.p., chief actuary, 1971-73, exec. v.p., 1973—. Chmn. Mt. Kisco (N.Y.) Planning Bd., 1962-69. Mem. Mt. Kisco Village Bd., 1959-61; mem. Mt. Kisco (N.Y.) Planning Bd., 1957-59, 61-69. Bd. dirs. U. Iowa Found., 1971—; trustee No. Westchester Hosp., 1976—. Served with AUS, 1941; from pvt. to lt. col., USAAF, 1941-46. Fellow Soc. Actuaries (pres. 1970-71, bd. govs. 1963-73), Phi Beta Kappa. Methodist (trustee). Home: 33 Meadow Brook Ln Mount Kisco NY 10549 Office: 1 Madison Ave New York City NY 10010

LANCASTER, JOHN HOWARD, civil engr.; b. Bklyn., July 3, 1917; s. George York and Alice Eliot (Littlejohn) L.; B.S., Worcester (Mass.) Poly. Inst., 1939; m. Phyllis Elaine Metcalf, June 1, 1938; children—Judith Ann, Barbara Jean, Marylin Sharon, Kathryn Joy, Debra Elizabeth. Engr., Austin Co., N.Y.C., 1939-40; engr. C.E., 1940-42, asst. to div. engr., N.Y.C., 1942-43; chief engring. and constrn. AEC, Upton, N.Y., 1946-54; chief project engr. Brookhaven Nat. Lab., Upton, 1954-72; asst. dir. Nat. Radio Astronomy Obs. and program mgr. very large array radio telescope program, Socorro, N.Mex., 1972—; propr. John H. Lancaster & Assos., cons. engrs., 1950-72; cons. in field, 1970—; mem. comml. panel Am. Arbitration Assn. Served with USNR, 1943-46. Recipient Meritorious Service award NSF, 1976; registered profl. engr., N.Y., N.Mex. Mem. Nat., N.Y., N.Mex. socs. profl. engrs. Club: Masons. Home: 1400 Hilton Pl PO Box 981 Socorro NM 87801 Office: 1000 Bullock Blvd PO Box O Socorro NM 87801

LANCASTER, JOSEPH LAWRENCE, JR., elec. utility exec.; b. Dunn, N.C., Oct. 11, 1925; s. Joseph Lawrence and Bessie (Garris) L.; grad. accounting, Kings Bus. Coll., Raleigh, N.C., 1948; m. Harriet Elizabeth Daniel; children—Debra Ann, Joseph Lawrence III. With Wachovia Bank & Trust Co., Raleigh, 1948-61; with Carolina Power and Light Co., Raleigh, 1961—, asst. sec., 1964-71, sec., 1971—; alternate dir. Utilities Services Ltd.; mem. ins. com. Nuclear Mut. Ltd., Edison Electric Inst., N.Y.C., 1966—. Chmn. troop com. Occoneeche council Boy Scouts Am., 1970—. Served with USNR, 1943-46. Mem. Am. Mgmt. Assn., Risk Ins. Mgrs. Soc. Am. Soc. Corporate Secs. (v.p., sec. Southeastern region). Methodist (past chmn. ofcl. bd.). Lion (past dep. dist. gov.). Home: 906 Brooks Ave Garner NC 27529 Office: 15A5 Center Plaza Bldg Raleigh NC 27602

LANCASTER, KELVIN JOHN, economist; b. Sydney, Australia, Dec. 10, 1924; s. John Kelvin and Margaret Louise (Gray) L.; B.Sc., Sydney U., 1948, B.A., 1949, M.A., 1953; B.Sc. in Economics, London U., 1953, Ph.D. (Leon fellow), 1958; m. Deborah Grunfeld, June 10, 1963; children—Clifton John, Gilead. Asst. lectr., lectr. London Sch. Economics, 1954-59; reader economics U. London, 1959-62; prof. polit. economy Johns Hopkins U., 1962-66; prof. econs. 1966-78, John Bates Clark prof. econs., 1978—, Columbia U., N.Y.C. Ford faculty fellow, 1968-69, chmn. dept. econs., 1970-73, Wesley

Clair Mitchell research prof., 1973-74; vis. prof. U. Birmingham, Brown U., 1961-62, City U. N.Y., 1965-66, N.Y. U., Australian Nat. U., 1969-77, Ottawa U., 1972; fellow Inst. Advanced Studies. Hebrew U. Jerusalem, 1976-77; dir. Nat. Bur. Economic Research, 1971-73. Served with Royal Australian Air Force, 1943-45. Fellow Econometric Soc.; mem. Am., N.Y. State (pres. 1974-75) economic assns., AAAS, AAUP. Author: Mathematical Economics, 1968; Introduction to Modern Microeconomics, 1969; Consumer Demand: A New Approach, 1971; Modern Economics: Principles and Policy. 1973; Variety, Equity and Efficiency, 1979; contbr. articles in economics to profl. jours. Home: 35 Claremont Ave New York City NY 10027 Office: Dept Econs Columbia Univ New York City NY 10027

LANCASTER, PETER, educator; b. Appleby, Westmorland, Eng., Nov. 14, 1929; s. John Thomas and Emily (Kellett) L.; B. Sc., U. Liverpool (Eng.), 1952, M.Sc., 1956; Ph.D., U. Singapore, 1964; m. Edna Lavinia Hutchinson, Sept. 3, 1951; children—Jane, Jill, Joy. Aerodynamicist, English Electric Co., Preston, Eng., 1952-57; sr. lectr. U. Singapore, 1957-62; asso. prof. U. Calgary (Alta., Can.), 1962-67, prof. math., 1967—; vis. asso. prof. Calif. Inst. Tech., 1965-66. Mem. Can. Math. Soc. (pres. 1979—). Author: Theory of Matrices, 1969; Lambda Matrices and Vibrating Systems, 1966; Mathematics: Models of the Real World, 1975. Contbr. articles to profl. jours. Home: 3052 Conrad Dr Calgary AB T2L 1B4 Canada

LANCASTER, ROBERT SAMUEL, lawyer, educator; b. Floyd, Va., July 9, 1909; s. Robert Tazwell and Rachel Elma (Barnard) L.; B.A., Hampden-Sydney Coll., 1929; M.A., U. South, 1934, D.C.L., 1979; student Andrew Jackson Law U., Nashville, 1937; Ph.D., U. Mich., 1952; m. Ernestine Martha DeSporte, June 21, 1931; children—Ulysse (Mrs. Andrew P. Butler), Evelyn Rachel (Mrs. David Tyrell). Instr. Gulf Coast Mil. Acad., Gulfport, Miss., 1929-31; instr. Sewanee (Tenn.) Mil. Acad., 1931-38, 46-49, comdt. cadets, 1941-43; admitted to Va. bar, 1937; pvt. practice, Pulaski, Va., 1938-41; mem. faculty U. of South, 1949—, acting dir. devel., 1965-66, prof. polit. sci., 1953—, dean men, 1951-56, dean Coll. Arts and Scis., 1957-69; Fulbright lectr. Coll. Arts and Scis., Baghdad, Iraq, 1955-56, Coll. Arts and Scis. and Coll. of Law, Seoul (Korea) Nat. U., 1964-65. Trustee Duck River Electric Membership Corp. Mem. Sewanee Civic Assn. Mem. acad. adv. bd. U.S. Naval Acad., 1970-75. Served to lt. (s.g.) USNR, 1943-46. Fellow Internat. Inst. Arts and Letters; mem. Va., Tenn. bar assns., So. Polit. Sci. Assn., Newcomen Soc., Phi Beta Kappa, Chi Phi, Phi Kappa Phi, Sigma Upsilon, Tau Kappa Alpha, Pi Gamma Mu, Pi Sigma Alpha, Blue Key. Republican. Episcopalian. Co-author: An Introduction to American Government, 1954. Contbr. articles to legal jours. Address: Univ of the South Sewanee TN 37375

LANCE, DOWE JEFFERSON, lawyer; b. Oregon County, Mo., May 25, 1916; s. Henry Luther and Attie (Jenkins) L.; student S.E. Mo. State Coll., 1938-41; J.D., U. Mo., 1945-48: m. Marguerite Coffman, July 26, 1943; 1 dau., Marguerite Susan. Supt. farms Three Way Land Co., Catron, Mo., 1940-42; admitted to Mo. bar, 1948; mem. firm Maus & Lance, Monett, 1948-49; examiner Pub. Service Commn. Mo., 1949-50; legal sec. to gov. Mo., 1950-52; atty. legal dept. Southwestern Bell Telephone Co., 1952-56; asst. compaign mgr. Blair for Gov. Mo., 1956-57; partner firm Cook, Murphy, Lance & English, St. Louis, 1957-61, Cook, Murphy, Lance & Mayer, St. Louis, 1963-76, Armstrong, Teasdale, Kramer & Vaughan, 1977—; U.S. atty. Eastern Dist. Mo., 1961-62. Mem. Bd. Police Commrs. St. Louis County, 1972-76. Mem. Law Sch. Found., U. Mo., 1966-70. Served to lt., aviator, USNR, 1942-45; PTO. Fellow Am. Coll. Trial Lawyers, Am. Bar Found.; mem. Am. Bar Assn., Mo. Bar (bd. govs. 1964-66), Bar Assn. St. Louis, U. Mo. Law Alumni (pres. 1970—, Distinguished Alumni award 1975), Am. Arbitration Assn., Order of Coif. Club: Masons (32 deg.). Home: 450 W Adams Ave Kirkwood MO 63122 Office: 611 Olive Saint Louis MO 63101

LANCE, THOMAS BERTRAM, TV commentator, former govt. ofcl.; b. Gainesville, Ga., June 3, 1931; s. Thomas Jackson and Annie Rose (Erwin) L.; student Emory U., 1948-50, U. Ga., 1951; Grad. Sch. Banking of South, La. State U., 1956; grad. Grad. Sch. Banking, Rutgers U., 1963; m. Lethia Belle David, Sept. 9, 1950; children—Thomas Bertram, David Jackson, Stuart Austin, Claude Beverly. Exec. v.p. Calhoun (Ga.) 1st Nat. Bank, 1958-63, pres., chief exec. officer, 1963-74, chmn. bd., 1974-77, dir., 1958-77; hwy. dir. State of Ga., 1970-73; dir. Office Mgmt. and Budget, Washington, 1977; TV commentator Sta. WXIA-TV, Atlanta, 1978—; Active various community drives; trustee Ga. Found. for Ind. Colls., Cherokee Boys Estate, Emory U.; chmn. bd. trustees Reinhardt Coll.; bd. counselors Oxford Coll. of Emory U.; adv. council Ga. State U.; mem. com. of 100, Emory U. Mem. Gridiron Secret Soc., Sigma Chi. Methodist (dist. lay leader, mem. Ga. commn. on higher edn.). Address: PO Box 637 Calhoun GA 20701

LANCEFIELD, REBECCA CRAIGHILL, microbiologist; b. Ft. Wadsworth, N.Y., Jan. 5, 1895; d. William Edward and Mary Wortley Montague (Byram) Craighill; A.B., Wellesley Coll., 1916, D.Sc. (hon.), 1976; A.M., Columbia U., 1918, Ph.D., 1925; D.Sc. (hon.), Rockefeller U., 1973; m. Donald E. Lancefield, May 27, 1918; 1 dau., Jane Lancefield Hersey. Tech. asst. Rockefeller U., N.Y.C., 1922-25, asst., 1925-29, asso., 1929-42, asso. mem., 1942-58, mem., prof., 1958-65, prof. emeritus bacteriology and immunology dept., 1965—. Recipient T. Duckett Jones Meml. award Helen Hay Whitney Fund, 1960; Achievement award Am. Heart Assn., 1964; medal N.Y. Acad. Medicine, 1973. Hon. fellow Royal Coll. Pathologists; mem. Nat. Acad. Scis. Home: 203 Arleigh Rd Douglaston NY 11363 Office: Rockefeller Univ 1230 York Ave New York NY 10021

LANCHESTER, ELSA, actress; b. Lewisham, London, Eng., Oct. 28, 1902; d. James and Edith (Lanchester) Sullivan; ed. pvt. sch.; studied dancing with Raymond Duncan, Chelsea and Isadora Duncan (scholarship); m. Charles Laughton, Feb. 10, 1929. Came to U.S., naturalized, 1950. Condr. free class which later became Children's Theatre, London, 1918; made debut legitimate stage in Thirty Minutes in a Street, 1922; appeared in The Way of the World and The Duenna, 1924; Riverside Nights, 1926; also engagements as singer; screen debut (Eng.) in The Constant Nymph; first appearance on N.Y. stage in Payment Deferred, 1931; motion picture role Anne of Cleves in The Private Life of Henry VIII, Eng., 1933; in repertory Old Vic-Sadler's Wells Co., 1933; various stage roles, Eng., 1935-37; role of Martha Jones in Vessel of Wrath (picture produced by Laughton and Pommer), The Beachcomber (in U.S.), 1937; on N.Y. stage in They Walk Alone, 1941; starring with Turnabout Theatre, Los Angeles, appearing nightly during 11 months each year, 1941-56; film appearances include: David Copperfield, Ladies in Retirement, 1941; Son of Fury, 1942; Tales of Manhattan, 1942; Forever and a Day, 1943; Lassie Come Home, 1943; Passport to Adventure, 1944; The Spiral Staircase, 1946; The Razor's Edge, 1946; Northwest Outpost, 1947; The Bishop's Wife, 1947; The Secret Garden, 1949; Come to the Stable, 1949 (nominated for Best Supporting Actress by Acad. 1949); The Inspector General, 1949; Mystery Street, 1950; Witness for the Prosecution, 1958 (nominated for Best Supporting Actress by Acad. 1958); Bell, Book and Candle, 1958; Mary Poppins, Honeymoon Hotel, 1963; That Darn Cat, 1964; Blackbeard's Ghost, 1966; Murder By Death, 1976. others. Author: Charles Laughton and I, 1938. Office: care Harold R Williams 9405 Brighton Way Beverly Hills CA 90210

LANCHNER, BERTRAND MARTIN, lawyer, advt. agy. exec.; b. Boston, Oct. 3, 1929; s. Abraham Joseph and Mina (Grossman) L.; B.A., Stanford U., 1951; postgrad. Columbia U. Grad. Sch. Bus., 1951-52, U. Vienna (Austria), summer 1955; J.D., Harvard U., 1955; m. Nancy Nelson, Apr. 26, 1979; 1 son by previous marriage, David; 1 stepdau., Renate. Admitted to N.Y. bar, 1956; asso. firm Sage, Gray, Todd & Sims, N.Y.C., 1955-57; atty. Warner Bros. Pictures, N.Y.C., 1957-59; asst. gen. counsel Dancer-Fitzgerald-Sample, N.Y.C., 1959-62; gen. counsel Lawrence C. Gumbinner Advt. Agy., N.Y.C., 1962-63; dir. bus. affairs and sports contract negotiations CBS-TV, N.Y.C., 1963-69; gen. counsel, exec. v.p. Videorecord Corp. Am., Westport, Conn., 1969-73, also dir.; v.p., sec., gen. counsel N.W. Ayer ABH Internat., N.Y.C., 1973—; dir. 170 E. 79th St. Corp.; guest lectr. Yale U. Law Sch. Mem. Am. Bar Assn., N.Y. State Bar Assn., Assn. Bar City N.Y., Copyright Soc. U.S., Am. Assn. Advt. Agys. Clubs: Harvard of N.Y.C., Bridgehampton Racquet and Surf, Tennisport, Uptown Racquet. Office: care NW Ayer ABH Internat 1345 Ave of Americas New York NY 10019

LANCTÔT, LÉOPOLD LAURENT, clergyman, publisher; b. Montreal, Que., Can., May 30, 1911; s. Roland Laurent and Marie Louise (Perreault) L.; B.A., U. Ottawa, 1932, Ph.L., 1932, Th.L., 1936, J.C.L., 1938. Joined Oblates of Mary Immaculate, 1930, ordained priest Roman Catholic Ch., 1935; asst. dir. U. Ottawa Press, 1936-46, dir., 1946—. Mem. Internat. Assn. Scholarly Pubs., Assn. Canadian U. Presses, Assocation des Editeurs Canadiens. Home: 305 Nelson St Ottawa ON K1N 7S5 Canada Office: 65 Hastey Ave Ottawa ON K1N 6N5 Canada

LAND, AUBREY CHRISTIAN, educator; b. Panola County, Miss., Sept. 2, 1912; s. William Alexander and Lois (Christian) L.; B.E., So. Ill. U., 1934; M.A., State U. Iowa, 1938, Ph.D., 1948; m. Helen Larrabee, Dec. 21, 1940 (dec. 1947); m. 2d, Anne Wolfshohl, Jan. 31, 1949; children—Alison Christian, Alexandra Anne. Prin., Mound City (Ill.) Jr. High Sch., 1935-37; asst. prof. history Carnegie Inst. Tech., 1946-49, Princeton, 1949; asso. prof. Vanderbilt U., 1950-55; prof. U. Nebr., 1955-57; Fulbright scholar London (Eng.) Sch. Econs., 1957-58; prof. history, head dept. U. Md., 1958-68; research prof. U. Ga., Athens, 1968—. Adv. bd. Am. Bibliog. Center, 1968—; Library of Congress adv. bd. on Bicentennial Am. Revolution, 1969—; bd. advisers Historic Annapolis, Inc., 1976—. Bd. dirs. Program for Loyalist Studies and Publs., 1974—. Served to capt. AUS, 1942-46. Guggenheim fellow, 1957-58; Huntington Library fellow, 1970. Mem. Am. (chmn. program com., dir. survey bibliog. service 1966-67), So. (chmn. Charles S. Sydnor prize com., council 1970—), Miss. Valley hist. assns., Md. Hist. Soc. Democrat. Episcopalian (vestry). Author: The Dulanys of Maryland, 1955; (with others) The Old Line State, 1956; Bases of the Plantation Society, 1969; Eddis, Letters From America, 1969. Editor: Archives of Maryland, LXXI, 1970; Law, Politics and Society, 1977. Editorial bd. Ga. Review, 1974—. Contbr. articles to hist. jours. Home: 175 Homestead Dr Athens GA 30605

LAND, EDWIN HERBERT, physicist, inventor; b. Bridgeport, Conn., May 7, 1909; s. Harry M. and Martha F. Land; ed. Norwich Acad.; student Harvard, Sc.D. (hon.), 1957; Sc.D. (hon.), Tufts Coll., 1947, Poly. Inst. Bklyn., 1952, Colby Coll., 1955, Northeastern U., 1959, Carnegie Inst. Tech., 1964, Yale U., 1966, Columbia U., 1967, Loyola U., 1970, N.Y. U., 1973; LL.D., Bates Coll., 1953, Wash. U., 1966, U. Mass., 1967; L.H.D., Williams Coll., 1968; m. Helen Maislen, 1929; children—Jennifer, Valerie. During coll. years invented 1st light-polarizer in form of an extensive synthetic sheet; developed a sequence of subsequent polarizers, theories and applications of polarized light, including automobile headlight system, 3 dimensional pictures, camera filters; during World War II developed optical, other systems for mil. use; founder Polaroid Corp., Cambridge, Mass., 1937, now chmn. bd., dir. research; created cameras, films that give instantaneous dry photographs in black and white and color; proposed Retinex Theory for mechanism of color perception and designed series of supporting expts. William James lectr. psychology Harvard, 1966-67, Morris Loeb lectr. physics, 1974; vis. Inst. prof. Mass. Inst. Tech., 1956—. Mem. Pres.'s Sci. Adv. Com., 1957-59, cons.-at-large, 1960-73; mem. Pres.'s Com. Nat. Medal of Sci., 1969-72, Carnegie Commn. on Ednl. TV, 1966-67, Nat. Commn. on Tech., Automation and Econ. Progress, 1964-66. Trustee Ford Found. Recipient numerous awards including Presdl. Medal of Freedom, 1963; Nat. Medal of Sci., 1967; Hood medal Royal Photog. Soc., 1935, Cresson medal, 1937, Potts medal, 1956, Vermilye medal Franklin Inst., Phila., 1974; John Scott medal and award, 1966; Rumford medal Am. Acad. Arts and Scis., 1945; Holley medal Am. Soc. M.E., 1948; Duddell medal Brit. Phys. Soc., 1949; Progress medal Soc. Photog. Engrs., 1955; Albert A. Michelson award Case Inst. Tech., 1966; Kulturpreis, Photog. Soc. Germany, 1967; Perkin medal Soc. Chem. Industry, 1974; Proctor award, 1963; Photographic Sci. and Engring. Jour. award, 1971; Progress medal Photog. Soc. Am., 1960; Kosar Meml. award, 1973; Golden Soc. medal Photog. Soc. Vienna, 1961; Interkamera award, 1973; Cosmos Club award, 1970; NAM award, 1940, 66; Jefferson medal N.J. Patent Law Assn., 1960; Indsl. Research medal, 1965; Diesel medal in gold, 1966. Named to Nat. Inventors Hall of Fame, 1977. Fellow Nat. Acad. Scis., Photog. Soc. Am., Am. Acad. Arts and Scis. (pres. 1951-53), Royal Photog. Soc. Gt. Britain (Progress medal 1967), Royal Micros. Soc. (hon.), Soc. Photog. Scientists and Engrs. (hon.; Lieven-Gevaert medal 1976); mem. N.Y. Acad. Scis., Nat. Acad. Engring. (Founders medal 1972), Optical Soc. Am. (hon. mem. 1972; dir. 1950-51; Frederick Ives medal 1967), Royal Instn. Gt. Britain (hon.), Am. Philos. Soc., German Photog. Soc. (hon.), Soc. Photog. Sci. and Tech. Japan (hon.), Sigma Xi. Home: 163 Brattle St Cambridge MA 02138 Office: 730 Main St Cambridge MA 02139

LAND, FRANCIS LAVERNE, physician, educator; b. Carrington, N.D., June 24, 1920; s. Harold L. and Lena (White) L.; student Ball State U., 1938-41; A.B., Ohio State U., 1946; M.D., Ind. U., 1950; m. Dorothy Julia Andrews, Sept. 1, 1946; children—Judith Ruth, Cynthia Andrews, Wendolyn White. Intern Milw. County Hosp., 1950-51; individual practice medicine, Fort Wayne, Ind., 1952-66; cons. to commn. of welfare HEW, 1966-67, commr. med. service adminstrn. social and rehab. services, 1967-69; chmn. dept. family practice U. Nebr. Med. Sch., 1969-74, asso. dean clin. affairs Coll. Medicine, 1972-74; asso. dean clin. affairs, med. dir. Bernallio County Med. Center, U. N.Mex. Coll. Medicine, Albuquerque, 1974-77, prof. family and community medicine, 1974-77, dir. continuing med. edn., 1976-77; prof., dir. div. family practice Georgetown U. Sch. Medicine, Washington, 1977—; cons. surgeon gen. USAF, 1962—, surgeon gen. USPHS, 1960-65. Bd. dirs. Fine Arts Planning Center, United Chest Council, Retarded Childrens Soc., Cancer Soc. Served with USAAF, 1941-46, USAF, 1950-52. Mem. A.M.A., Allen County Med. Soc. (pres. 1963-64), Am. (v.p. 1965-66), Ind. (pres. 1960) acads. gen. practice. Home: 1102 McLean House McLean VA 22101

LAND, GEORGE THOMAS LOCK. see Ainsworth-Land, George Thomas

LAND, MALCOLM LOUIS, cons. engr.; b. New Haven, June 21, 1916; s. Benjamin Daniel and Rachel Mary (Scheanblum) L.; B.S., N.Y. U., 1938; M.S., N.Y. U., 1943; m. Mabel Crystal, May 30, 1942; children—Cynthia, Kenneth, Richard. Mech. engr. U.S. Navy, 1939-45; chief engr. Elliott Co., Jeannette, Pa., 1946-53; mgr. engring. Air Products & Chems., Allentown, Pa., 1955-60, Worth Corp., Buffalo, 1960-68; v.p. tech. Studebaker Worthington, Inc., N.Y.C., 1969-77; v.p. tech. STP Corp., Fort Lauderdale, Fla., 1974-78; cons. engr., 1978—. Fellow ASME. Contbr. articles to profl. jours. Patentee in field. Address: 5400 N Ocean Blvd Fort Lauderdale FL 33308

LAND, REGINALD BRIAN, library adminstr.; b. Niagara Falls, Ont., Can., July 29, 1927; s. Allan Reginald and Beatrice Beryl (Boyle) L.; B.A., U. Toronto (Ont.), 1949, B.L.S., 1953, M.L.S., 1956, M.A., 1963; m. Edith Wyndham Eddis, Aug. 29, 1953; children—Mary Beatrice, John Robert Eddis. Catalogue copy editor T. Eaton Co. Ltd., Toronto, 1950-51; reference librarian Toronto Pub. Library, 1953-55; cataloguer U. Toronto Library, 1955-56, asst. librarian, 1959-63, asso. librarian, 1963; head div. bus. and industry Windsor (Ont.) Pub. Library, 1956-57; asst. editor Canadian Bus. mag., Montreal, Que., 1957-58, asso. editor, 1958-59; exec. asst. to Minister Finance of Can., Ottawa, Ont., 1963-64; prof. library sci. U. Toronto, 1964-78, part-time, 1978—, dean Faculty of Library Sci., 1964-72; dir. Research and Info. Services, Ont. Legis. Library, Toronto, 1978—. Mem. Canadian Radio-TV and Telecommunications Commn., 1973-78. Recipient Kenneth R. Wilson Meml. award Bus. Newspapers Assn. of Can., 1959, Distinguished Achievement award Ont. Library Trustees Assn., 1968, Queen's Silver Jubilee medal, 1977. Mem. Am. (chmn. com. on accreditation 1973-74), Canadian (pres. 1975-76), Ont. (1st v.p. 1962-63) library assns., Assn. Am. Library Schs. (pres. 1973-74), Bibliog. Soc. Can., Canadian Assn. Library Schs. (pres. 1966-67), Canadian Assn. Univ. Tchrs., Canadian Council Library Schs. (chmn. 1971-72), Inst. Profl. Librarians Ont. (pres. 1961-62), Ont. Council Library Schs. (chmn. 1968-72), Spl. Libraries Assn., Ont. Geneal. Soc. Anglican. Author: Eglinton: The Election Study of a Federal Constituency, 1965; Sources of Information for Canadian Business, 1962, 3d rev. edit., 1978; editor Directory of Associations in Canada, 1974, 3d rev. edit., 1978. Home: 18 Kirkton Rd Downsview ON M3H 1K7 Canada Office: Legislative Library Legislative Bldg Queen's Park Toronto ON M7A 1A2 Canada

LANDA, ALFONSO, lawyer, bus. exec.; b. Chgo., Dec. 14, 1897; s. Alfonso and Frances (Claes) L.; student Georgetown U., 1922; LL.B., George Washington U., 1925; student Oxford (Eng.) U., 1925; m. Alexandra Francesca; 1 son, Alfonso. Began with law firm of Joseph E. Davies, 1926, partner firm, 1935; now sr. mem. Davies, Richberg, Tydings, Landa & Duff. Pres. Detroit & Cleve. Nav. Co., 1954, Colonial Airlines, N.Y.C., 1951; dir., chmn. exec. com. Fairbanks Whitney Corp., 1959-62; chmn. bd. Fairbanks, Morse & Co., Chgo., 1958-62, Baruch-Foster Corp., 1955-62; pres., dir. Marquis Who's Who, Inc., 1969; v.p., dir. Walker & Dunlop, Inc.; dir. Pratt & Whitney, 1959-62, Crane Co., 1959-62, Gen. Fireproofing Co., 1964, Doehla Greeting Cards, 1964, Fla. Capital Corp., 1971, Fruehauf Trailer Co., Detroit, 1971. Enlisted with 132d Ill. Inf., 1917; served World War I. Decorated chevalier de l'Ordre du Saint Sepulchre. Mem. A.I.M. (dir.). Clubs: Racquet and Tennis, Brook (N.Y.C.); Travellers (Paris); Everglades, Bath and Tennis, Seminole (Palm Beach). Home: 340 S Ocean Blvd Palm Beach FL 33480 Office: 450 Royal Palm Beach Palm Beach FL 33480

LANDA, WILLIAM ROBERT, textile mfg. exec.; b. Jersey City, Dec. 4, 1919; s. G.B. and Henrietta (Elder) L.; student Ohio U., 1937-39; m. Anne E. Longley, June 24, 1939; children—Susanne (Mrs. L.H. Sprouse, Jr.), Stephen R., Scott W., Richard W. Salesman, Sterling Drug, Inc., 1942-44; asst. export mgr. Taylor, Pinkham & Co., Inc., 1944-52; export mgr. Bates Fabrics, Inc., 1952-55; pres. Burlington Export Co., N.Y.C., 1955-62; v.p. Burlington Mills Corp., 1957-62, Burlington Industries, Inc., Greensboro, N.C., 1959-62; v.p. Warner Bros. Co., Bridgeport, Conn., 1962-66, pres. Warner Bros. Intenat., 1962-66; exec. v.p. Turner Jones & Co., 1966-67, pres., 1967-68; group v.p. internat. Genesco, Inc., N.Y.C., 1968-70; v.p. Farah Mfg. Co., 1970-74; pres., dir. Holguin & Assos. Inc., El Paso, Tex.; dir. Affiliated Mfrs., Inc., North Branch, N.J., AMI-PRESCO. Mem. Gen. Arbitration Council Textile Industry; mem. Nat. Export Council, 1965-66. Decorated chevalier Order of Crown (Belgium). Mem. Commerce and Industry Assn. N.Y., Internat. Execs. Assn., U.S. C. of C. (spl. adv. com. on internat. trade), Am. Arbitration Assn., Beta Theta Pi. Presbyn. Clubs: Union League (N.Y.C.); Coronado Country, Rotary, Internat., Lancers (El Paso). Home: 5824 Mira Serena Dr El Paso TX 79912 Office: Holguin and Assos Inc Inc 5822 Cromo Dr El Paso TX 79912

LANDAU, BROOKSLEY ELIZABETH, lawyer; b. San Francisco, Aug. 27, 1940; d. Ronald Henry and Mary Ellen (Bortner) Born; A.B., Stanford U., 1961, J.D., 1964; m. Jacob Charles Landau, Aug. 15, 1965; children—Nicholas Jacob, Ariel Elizabeth. Admitted to Calif. bar, 1965, D.C. bar, 1966; law clk. U.S. Ct. Appeals, Washington, 1964-65; legal researcher Harvard Law Sch., 1967-68; asso. firm Arnold and Porter, Washington, 1965-67, 68-73, partner, 1974—; lectr. law Columbus Sch. Law, Cath. U. Am., 1972-74; adj. prof. Georgetown U. Law Center, Washington, 1972-73. Bd. visitors Stanford Law Sch., 1977-79; bd. dirs. Nat. Legal Aid and Defenders Assn., 1972-79; trustee Center for Law and Social Policy, Washington, 1977—. Mem. Am. Bar Assn. (chairperson sect. individual rights and responsibilities 1977-78, mem. fed. judiciary com.), D.C. Bar (sec. 1975-76, bd. govs. 1976-79), Am. Law Inst., Lawyers' Com. for Civil Rights Under Law (trustee 1978—), Order of Coif. Pres. Stanford Law Rev., 1963-64. Office: 1229 19th St NW Washington DC 20036

LANDAU, ELY, motion picture producer; b. N.Y.C., Jan. 20, 1920; ed. high sch.; m. Edythe Rein, Mar. 13, 1959; children—Neil Cary, Lester Michael, Jon P., Tina R., Kathy. Organizer, Nat. Telefilm Assos., Inc., N.Y.C., 1953, pres., chmn. bd., 1953-61; formed Am. Film Theatre also Ely Landau Orgn., 1972, now pres.; producer films Long Day's Journey into Night, 1962, The Pawnbroker, 1964, The Fool Killer, A Face of War, 1968, The Madwoman of Challiot, 1969, KING: A Filmed Record—Montgomery to Memphis, 1970; The Iceman Cometh, 1973, Butley, 1973, Lost in the Stars, 1974, Rhinoceros, 1974, The Homecoming, 1973, A Delicate Balance, 1973, Luther, 1974, Galileo, 1975, Man in the Glass Booth, 1975, In Celebration, 1975; The Greek Tycoon, 1977. Recipient George Foster Peabody award for Play of Week, Sidney Hillman Found. award, 1960; So. Christian Leadership spl. Man of Year award, 1970, Image award NAACP, 1970. Served with USAAF, World War II. Mem. Acad. Television Arts and Scis., Radio and Television Execs. Soc. Office: Edie and Ely Landau Inc 2029 Century Park E Los Angeles CA 90067

LANDAU, GENEVIEVE MILLET (MRS. SIDNEY LANDAU), writer, editor; b. Dallas, June 17, 1927; d. Harry and Elsie (Lazarus) Hershson; B.A. summa cum laude, William Smith Coll., 1954; postgrad. Columbia U., 1954-55; m. Sidney Landau, Mar. 21, 1967; children—Elizabeth Millet, Jessica Millet. Asso. editor Parents' mag., 1958-60, articles editor, 1960-65, exec. editor, 1965-70, editor-in-chief, 1970—; v.p. Parents' Mag. Enterprises. Bd. dirs.

Hasbro Center for Child Edn. and Devel., 1978—. Mem. Am. Soc. Mag. Editors, Phi Beta Kappa. Author, editor several books, articles. Home: 17 Bank St New York NY 10014 Office: 41 Madison Ave New York NY 10017

LANDAU, GEORGE WALTER, ambassador; b. Mar. 4, 1920; s. J.A. and Jeannette (Klausner) L.; A.A., George Washington U., 1969; grad. Canadian Nat. Def. Coll., 1966; m. Maria A. Jobst, July 15, 1947; children—Robert W., Christopher T. Fgn. service officer, 1st sec. in Uruguay, 1957-62; polit. officer, Madrid, 1962-65; dir. Office Spanish and Portuguese Affairs, Dept. State, 1966-72; ambassador A.E. and P. to Paraguay, 1972-77, to Chile, 1977—. Asst. v.p. Intra-Mar Shipping Corp., N.Y.C., 1947-54. Served to capt. AUS, 1942-47. Decorated Commendation medal, Meritorious Service medal; recipient Superior Honor award Dept. State, 1970. Mem. Fgn. Service Assn. Washington. Club: Federal City (Washington). Home: 5006 Nahant St Washington DC 20016 Office: Am Embassy APO Miami 34033

LANDAU, JACOB, artist; b. Phila., Dec. 17, 1917; s. Samuel and Deana (Kitaynick) L.; student Phila. Coll. Art, 1936-39, New Sch., N.Y.C., 1948-49, 52-53, Acad. de la Grande Chaumiere, Paris, France, 1950-52; m. Frances Paul, May 5, 1949; children—Stephen Paul, Jonas Michael. One-man shows include Galerie LeBar, Paris, 1952, Art Alliance, Phila., 1954, 75, Art Center, New Brunswick, N.J., 1957, Samuel Fleisher Meml. Gallery, Phila., 1959, Asso. Am. Artists Gallery, N.Y.C., 1960, 70, U. Maine, 1961, 71, Cober Gallery, N.Y.C., 1961, 63, Zora Gallery, Los Angeles, 1964, Original Prints Gallery, San Francisco, 1965, Gallery 100, Princeton, N.J., 1966, Art Gallery, U. Notre Dame, 1969, Print Club, Phila., 1970, Giraffe Gallery, Los Angeles, 1970, Van Straaten Gallery, Chgo., 1970, Lunn Gallery, Washington, 1970, Jorgensen Auditorium, U. Conn. at Storrs, 1971, Bloomfield (N.J.) Coll., 1971, 72, Orpheus Ascending Gallery, Stockbridge, Mass., 1972, Galeria Pecanins, Mexico City, 1972, Imprint Gallery, San Francisco, 1973, Congregation Keneseth Israel, Elkins Park, Pa., 1974, ACA Galleries, N.Y.C., 1976, Woodbridge (N.J.) Cultural Arts Commn., Schneder-Sato Gallery, Karlsruhe, Germany, 1977; numerous group shows, 1955—, latest include Four Painters, Art Alliance Phila., 1961, New Humanism, Nat. Sch. Plastics Arts, U. Mexico, 1963, regional exhbn. Pa. Acad. Fine Arts, 1964, N.J. and the Artist, N.J. State Mus., Trenton, 1965, Drawing Soc. Eastern Central Region, Phila. Mus. Art, 1965, N.J. Tercentenary Show, 1965, Contemporary N.J. Art, Newark Mus., 1965, Prize-Winning Am. Prints, circulating show N.Y. State Council on Arts, 1967, Drawings U.S.A., St. Paul Art Center, 1968, Am. Prints Today, Mus. Art, Munson-Williams-Proctor Inst., Utica, N.Y., 1968, Selections from 50th Ann., Soc. Am. Graphic Artists, USIA Nr. East Traveling Show, 1970, Tamarind: A Renaissance of Lithography, circulating show Internat. Exhbns. Found., 1971, State U. N.Y. Coll. at Brockport, 1972, Iowa State U., 1972, N.J. Arts Council, 1972, Art. Mus., Sao Paulo, Brazil, 1972, Am. Acad. Arts and Letters, 1973, 74, NAD, 1974, Washinton Club, 1976, Soc. Am. Graphic Artists Show, 1976, 77, Am. Color Print Soc. 35th Exhbn., Phila., 1976, 1st Biennial N.J. Artists, 1977; numerous nat. and internat. shows, 1953—, latest include woodcut annuals Print Club Phila., 1955, 59, 92d, 95th, 97th Am. Watercolor Soc. anns. NAD, 1954, 62, 64, 12th-17th print biennials Bklyn. Mus., 1960, 62, 64, 66, 68, 70, Xylon Internats., 1962, 65, Recent Paintings, U.S.A-The Figure, Mus. Modern Art, 1962, nominee exhbn. Nat. Inst. Arts and Letters, 1962, 65, 156th, 158th, 160th, 162d anns. Pa. Acad. Fine Arts, 1961, 63, 65, 67, graphics U.S.A., USIA traveling exhbn., 1963—, 19th, 20th print exhbns. Library of Congress, 1963, 66, 30th ann. Butler Art Inst., Youngstown, Ohio, 1965, Smithsonian invitational exhbn. White House, 1966, Nat. Drawing Exhbn., Rutgers U., 1975, Hawaii Nat. Print Exhbn., Honolulu Acad. Arts, 1975, Nat. Coll. Fine Arts, Miami Graphics, Bienneal Met. Mus., Coral Gables, Fla., Boston Printmakers, De Cordova Mus., Lincoln, Mass., Hunterdon (N.J.) Art Center, 1977; also exhibited at Mus. Modern Art, N.Y.C., 1969, Whitney Mus., N.Y.C. 1969, Mus. Art, Phila., 1970; represented in permanent collections Whitney Mus. Am. Art, Mus. Modern Art, Met. Mus., Pa. Acad. Fine Arts, art museums in Balt., Atlanta, New Orleans, Phila., Bklyn., Norfolk, Va., Montclair, N.J., San Antonio, Tucson, Ariz., Malmo, Sweden, Nuremberg, W.Ger., Slater Mus., Norwich, Conn., Library of Congress, Joseph J. Hirschhorn collection, also univs. Princeton, Rutgers, Maine, Minn., Syracuse, Yale, Ky., U. Calif. at Berkeley, U. Mass., U.S. Fla., Columbia, Butler Inst., Youngstown, Ohio, M.H. DeYoung Mus., San Francisco, N.J. State Mus., Trenton, Bibliotheque Nationale, Paris, Lessing Rosenwald Collection, also pvt. collections; commns. include sketches of participants at Pacem In Terris II, 1967; print of Peace, Internat. Art Program, Nat. Collection Fine Arts, Smithsonian Instn., 1967; cycle of ten stained glass windows The Prophetic Quest, Keneseth Israel Congregation, Elkins Park, 1970; lithograph Behold Jewish Center, Trenton, 1973; lithograph But if the Cause, Roten Galleries, Balt., 1976; now prof. graphic art Pratt Inst., Bklyn., founder, learning coordinator integrative studies program; vis. scholar Memphis Acad. Arts, 1969, U. Notre Dame (Ind.), 1969; graphic arts panelist N.J. Arts Council, 1969-73; vis. artist Skidmore Coll., Saratoga Springs, N.Y., 1971, Brookdale Coll., Lincroft, N.J., 1976; panelist N.J. State Mus., Trenton, 1973, N.Y. U., 1974, Rutgers U., New Brunswick, N.J., 1976; artist-in-residence U. No. Iowa; tchr. Artist/Tchr. Inst., N.J. State Council on Arts, 1978; cons. N.J. Dept. Higher Edn., 1974. Served with USAAF, 1943-46; MTO. Recipient Lessing Rosenwald Purchase award Print Club Phila., 1955, 59; Woodcut prize Print Fair of Phila. Free library, 1960; Louis Comfort Tiffany award, 1962; hon. mention Am. Water Color Soc., 1962; Paul F. Norton and Asso. Am. Artists awards Soc. Am. Graphic Artists, 1962; hon. mention Audubon Artists, 1965; named One of New Jersey's Five Finest, Com. Curators and Critics, 1962; recipient Phila. Watercolor prize Pa. Acad. Fine Arts, 1963; First award N.J. Tercentenary Art Festival, 1963; fellow Tamarind Lithography Workshop, Los Angeles, 1965; Edna Pennypacker Stauffer prize Soc. Am. Graphic Artists, 1965; purchase awards Asso. Am. Artists, 1967, Dulin Gallery Art, Knoxville, Tenn., Drawing U.S.A. '68, St. Paul Art Center, Contemporary Graphic Art on Contemporary Law and Justice, Assn. Bar City N.Y.; Vera List purchase prize Soc. Am. Graphic Artists, 1972; Childe Hassam purchase award Am. Acad. Arts and Letters, 1973-74; purchase prize Nat. Drawing Exhbn., Rutgers U., 1975; Purchase prize Nat. Print Exhbn., Hunterdon; Purchase prize AAA Gallery, N.Y.C., 1977. Grantee Nat. Arts Council, 1966, N.J. State Arts Council, 1974, Ford Found., 1975; Guggenheim Found. fellow, 1968-69. Mem. Internat. Assn. Art UNESCO, Soc. Am. Graphic Artists, Am. Color Print Soc. Home: 2 Pine Dr Roosevelt NJ 08555 Office: Pratt Inst Brooklyn NY 11205. *For me, art is more than formal exploration or exploitation. Without it, we are an endangered and endangering species.*

LANDAU, MARTIN, actor; b. Bklyn., 1934; student Art Students League, Actors Studio; m. Barbara Bain. Staff artist, cartoonist N.Y. Daily News; star TV series Mission Impossible, 1966-69, Space 1999; TV appearances include Omnibus, Playhouse 90, G.E. Theatre, Outer Limits, Twilight Zone, Gunsmoke, others; also TV movies; films include North by Northwest, 1959; Cleopatra, 1962; The Greatest Story Ever Told, 1965; Nevada Smith, 1966; They Call Me Mr. Tibbs, 1970; A Town Called Hell, 1971; Black Gunn, 1972; Strange Shadows in an Empty Room, 1977; Meteor, 1979; stage appearances include Middle of the Night, Uncle Vanya, Stalag 17, Wedding Breakfast, First Love, The Goat Song. Mem. Acad. Motion Picture Arts and Scis.*

LANDAU, MARTIN, educator; b. N.Y.C., July 12, 1921; s. User Noah and Clara (Markowitz) L.; A.B., Bklyn. Coll., 1947; M.A. in Pub. Adminstrn., N.Y. U., 1948; Ph.D., 1952; m. Bernice Feldman, July 11, 1943; children—Madeline, Claudia. Vis. research prof. U. Calif. at Berkeley, 1969-71, prof. polit. sci., 1972—; Distinguished prof. City U. N.Y., Bklyn., 1970-72; lectr. orgn. and decision theory Fgn. Service Inst., U.S. Dept. State, Washington, 1969-72; cons. in field; chancellor Grad. Sch. Pub. Adminstrn., U. P.R., San Juan, 1970-71. Served with Signal Corps, AUS, 1941-45. Recipient Distinguished Teaching award Bklyn. Coll., 1963, E. Harris Harbison award gifted teaching Danforth Found., 1969-70, William E. Mosher award distinguished scholarship Soc. Pub. Adminstrn., 1970; John Simon Guggenheim fellow, 1976-77; fellow Center Advanced Study in Behavioral Sci., 1976-77. Fellow Nat. Acad. Public Adminstrn.; mem. Am. Polit. Sci. Assn., Philosophy of Sci. Assn. Author: Political Theory and Political Science; Studies in the Methodology of Political Inquiry, 1972. Chmn. editorial bd. Polit. Sci., 1971—; mem. editorial bd. Jour. Comparative Adminstrv. Studies, 1969—, Comparative Politics, 1970—. Home: 1410 Summit Rd Berkeley CA 94708 Mailing Address: Dept Polit Sci U Calif Berkeley CA 94720

LANDAU, PETER EDWARD, editor; b. N.Y.C., July 16, 1933; s. Edward and Charlotte (Schmidt) L.; A.B., Duke, 1955; M.S. in Econs., Columbia, 1959. Editorial asst. Newsweek mag., N.Y.C., 1955-57, asst. editor, 1958-61, asso. editor, 1962-67; v.p. Tiderock Corp., 1967; sr. editor Instl. Investor, N.Y.C., 1968, mng. editor, 1968-70, editor, 1971—. Home: 300 E 51st St New York City NY 10022 Office: 488 Madison Ave New York City NY 10022

LANDAU, RICHARD L., physician, educator; b. St. Louis, Aug. 8, 1916; s. Milton S. and Amelia (Rich) L.; B.S., M.D., Washington U., St. Louis, 1940; m. Claire Schmuckel, Dec. 4, 1943; children—James, Susan, Kay. Intern, U. Chgo. Clinics, 1940-41, resident, 1941-42; mem. faculty U. Chgo. Sch. Medicine, 1946—, prof. medicine, 1959—; head sect. endocrinology, 1967-78; spl. research in endocrinologic aspects of reprodn., metabolic influence of progesterone. Served to capt. M.C., AUS, 1943-46. Decorated Bronze Star. Mem. Endocrine Soc. (council 1962-65), Central Soc. Clin. Research, Am. Soc. Clin. Investigation, A.M.A., Chgo. Soc. Internal Medicine (pres. 1968). Editor Perspectives in Biology and Medicine, 1973—; mem. editorial bd. Jour. Lab. and Clin. Medicine, 1957-62, Ann. Rev. Medicine, 1959-68. Home: 5732 Kenwood Ave Chicago IL 60637

LANDAU, SIEGFRIED, conductor; b. Berlin, Germany, Sept. 4, 1921; s. Ezekiel and Helen (Grynberg) L.; ed. Stern Conservatory, Klindworth-Scharwenka Conservatory, Berlin; L.G.S.M., Guildhall Sch. Music and Drama, London, Eng., 1939-40; condrs. degree Mannes Coll., N.Y., 1942; m. Irene Gabriel, May 2, 1954; children—Robert, Peter. Came to U.S., 1940, naturalized, 1946. Condr. Bklyn. Philharmonia, 1954-71, Music for Westchester Symphony Orch., 1961, Chattanooga Opera Assn., 1960-73; gen. music dir., chief condr. Westphalian Symphony Orch., West Germany, 1973-75. Recipient award Music Tchrs. Assn. outstanding contbn. music edn., 1963. Fellow Jewish Acad. Arts and Scis.; mem. Societa Mici Della Music Jesi (hon.), Nat. Jewish Music Council, ASCAP, Am. Musicol. Soc., Assn. Am. Condrs. and Composers. Works include opera, The Sons of Aaron, 1959, symphonic poem ballets, orchestral and choral scores. Home: 26 Ogden Rd Scarsdale NY 10583 Office: Box 35 Gedney Sta White Plains NY 10605

LANDAU, SYBIL HARRIET, lawyer, educator; b. N.Y.C., Nov. 26, 1937; d. Sidney and Janice (Katz) L.; B.A. in History with honors, Hunter Coll., 1958; LL.B. (Harlan Fiske Stone scholar), Columbia U., 1961; B.C.L., Oxford (Eng.) U., 1963. Admitted to N.Y. State bar, 1965, U.S. Supreme Ct. bar, U.K. Michaelmas bar; asst. lectr. in law U. Bristol (Eng.), 1963-65; asst. dist. atty. N.Y. County, 1965-72; asso. prof. law Hofstra U., 1972-74; vis. adj. asso. prof. law Bklyn. Law Sch., 1975; asso. prof. Benjamin N. Cardozo Sch. Law, 1975—, asst. dean, 1975-77; lectr. in field; mem. Brookdale Faculty, Brookdale Center of Aging, Hunter Coll., 1977-78. Bd. dirs. FDR-Woodrow Wilson Dem. Club, 1967-68; mem. Mayor's Task Force on Rape, 1974-77; mem. adv. bd. Gerontol. Inst., Yeshiva U., 1977-78. Named to Hunter Coll. Hall of Fame, 1974. Mem. Am. Law Inst., Am. Bar Assn., Women's Bar Assn., N.Y. State Bar Assn., Assn. Bar City N.Y., Hon. Soc. of Middle Temple, Hunter Coll. Alumni Assn. (dir. 1976-79), Met. Women's Law Tchrs. Assn. (v.p. 1976-78), N.Y. Polit. Action Council. Jewish. Club: N.Y.C. Women's. Home: 8 W 13th St New York NY 10011 Office: 55 Fifth Ave New York NY 10003

LANDAU, WALTER LOEBER, lawyer; b. New Orleans, Sept. 9, 1931; s. Walter Loeber and Mae (Wilzin) L.; B.A., Princeton U., 1953; LL.B., Harvard U., 1956; m. Barbara Jane Gordon, June 23, 1954; children—Donna Ellen, Blair Susan, Gordon Loeber. Admitted to N.Y. Ct. Appeals bar, 1956, U.S. Dist. Ct. bar for So. Dist. N.Y., 1962, U.S. Supreme Ct. bar, 1971; asso. firm Sullivan & Cromwell, N.Y.C., 1959-66, partner, 1966—; dir. U.S. Life Ins. Co., N.Y.C., Esselte Pendaflex Corp. Trustee Reece Sch., N.Y.C. Served to capt. USAF, 1956-59. Fellow Am. Bar Found.; mem. Am. Bar Assn., N.Y. State Bar Assn., Assn. Bar City N.Y., Fed. Bar Assn., Am. Law Inst., N.Y. Law Inst. (exec. com.). Republican. Office: 125 Broad St New York NY 10004

LANDAU, WILLIAM MILTON, neurologist; b. St. Louis, Oct. 10, 1924; s. Milton S. and Amelia (Rich) L.; student U. Chgo., 1941-43; M.D. cum laude, Washington U., St. Louis, 1947; m. Roberta Anne Hornbein, Apr. 3, 1947; children—David, John, Julia, George. Intern, U. Chgo. Clinics, 1947; resident St. Louis City Hosp., 1948; fellow Washington U., St. Louis, 1949-52, NIH, Bethesda, Md., 1952-54; instr. neurology Washington U., 1952-54, asst. prof., 1954-58, asso. prof., 1958-63, prof., 1963—, dept. head, 1970—, co-head dept. neurology and neur. surgery, 1975. Diplomate Am. Bd. Psychiatry and Neurology (dir. 1967, pres. 1975). Mem. ACLU (trustee East Mo. 1956—), Am. Neurol. Assn. (pres. 1977), Am. Acad. Neurology, Assn. U. Profs. Neurology (pres. 1978), Soc. Neurosci., Am. Physiol. Soc., Am. Electro-encephalography Soc. Editorial bd. Neurology, 1963, A.M.A. Archives Neurology, 1965, Annals Neurology, 1977. Research neurophysiology. Home: 4 Forest Ridge Clayton MO 63105 Office: 660 S Euclid Ave St Louis MO 63110

LANDAUER, JERRY GERD, journalist; b. Stuttgart, Germany, Jan. 16, 1932; s. Adolph and Meta (Marx) L.; came to U.S., 1938, naturalized, 1943; B.A., Columbia, 1953. Reporter, Washington Post, 1956-60, U.P.I., 1960-62, Wall St Jour., Washington, 1962—. Recipient Distinguished Service award Sigma Delta Chi, 1963; Raymond Clapper Meml. award, 1963; Drew Pearson prize, 1973; Worth Bingham prize for investigative reporting, 1973. Club: Nat. Press. Home: 4930 30th St NW NW Washington DC 20008 Office: 1025 Connecticut Ave NW Washington DC 20036

LANDAUER, ROLF WILLIAM, physicist; b. Stuttgart, Germany, Feb. 4, 1927; s. Karl and Anna (Dannhauser) L.; came to U.S., 1938, naturalized, 1944; S.B., Harvard U., 1945, A.M., 1947, Ph.D., 1950; m. Muriel Jussim, Feb. 26, 1950; children—Karen, Carl, Thomas. Solid state physicist Lewis Lab., NACA (now NASA), Cleve., 1950-52; with IBM Research and antecedent groups, 1952—, asst. dir. research T. J. Watson Research Center, Yorktown Heights, N.Y., 1966-69, IBM fellow, 1969—. Served with USNR, 1945-46. Fellow IEEE, Am. Phys. Soc.; mem. Nat. Acad. Engring. Contbr. articles on solid state theory, computing devices, statis. mechanics of computational process to profl. jours.; asso. editor Rev. Modern Physics, 1973-76; initiated IBM programs leading to injection laser, large scale integration. Office: IBM Research Center PO Box 218 Yorktown Heights NY 10598

LANDBACK, CHARLES RALPH, JR., mfg. co. exec.; b. Perth Amboy, N.J., July 5, 1918; s. Charles R. and Kirstine Marie (Nelson) L.; B.S., Rutgers U., 1940; m. Mildred McDonald, June 13, 1942; children—Charles, Samuel (dec.), Robert, Douglas. Salesman, DuPont Co., 1945-46; mgr. mfg. Taylor, Smith & Taylor, 1946-56; with Carborundum Co., Niagara Falls, N.Y., 1956—, group v.p., 1974-79, sr. v.p., world-wide product mgr., 1979—; dir. Toshiba Monofrax Co. Ltd. Served to capt. U.S. Army, 1941-45. Decorated Bronze Star. Mem. Am. Ceramic Soc. Republican. Episcopalian. Clubs: Niagara Falls Country, Youngstown Yacht. Office: Carborundum Center Niagara Falls NY 14302

LANDECKER, WERNER SIEGMUND, sociologist, educator; b. Berlin, Germany, Apr. 30, 1911; s. Adolf and Hertha (Kahn) L.; Jur. Utr. Dr., U. Berlin, 1936; Ph.D., U. Mich., 1947; m. Marjory Victoria Records, July 15, 1942; children—John Records, Thomas Franklin. Came to U.S., 1937, naturalized, 1944. Mem. faculty U. Mich., 1943—, prof. sociology, 1961—. Fulbright lectr. in Germany, 1968-69; Social Sci. Research Council, 1973-74. Mem. Internat., Am. sociol. assns., ACLU, AAUP, Internat. Sociol. Assn., Phi Sigma Delta. Author: (with others) Principles of Sociology, 1952; also articles. Home: 1113 Ferdon Rd Ann Arbor MI 48104

LANDEGGER, CARL CLEMENT, machinery and pulp mfg. co. exec.; b. Vienna, Austria, Sept. 20, 1930; s. Karl F. and Helena (Berger) L.; came to U.S., 1937, naturalized, 1947; B. Social Sci., Georgetown U., 1951; m. Cecilia Elizalde, June 30, 1951; children—Christine, Carl, Claudia, Cary, Celia. Chmn., Parsons and Whittermore, Inc., N.Y.C., 1953—; chmn., gen. mgr. Welser Papierfabrik GmbH, Wels, Austria, 1955-56; with Black Clawson Co., N.Y.C., 1956—, exec. v.p., 1959-65, pres., 1965—, chief exec. officer, 1967—; pres. St. Anne Nackawic Pulp & Paper Co., Prince Albert Pulp Co. Ltd.; dir. Downingtown Mfg. Co., N.Y.C. Chmn. Landegger Found.; bd. regents Georgetown U. Served to 1st lt. USAF, 1951-53. Club: Explorers (N.Y.C.). Office: Black Clawson Co 200 Park Ave New York NY 10017

LANDEN, ROBERT GERAN, historian, univ. dean; b. Boston, July 13, 1930; s. Harry James and Evelyn Gertrude (Geran) L.; A.B., Coll. of William and Mary, 1952; M.A., U. Mich., 1953; A.M., Princeton U., 1958, Ph.D. (Ford Found. fellow), 1961; m. Patricia Kizzia, July 19, 1958; children—Michael Geran, Robert Kizzia, Jill Arnett, Amy Patricia. Asst. prof. social sci. Ball State U., Muncie, Ind., 1959-60; asst. prof. near eastern studies U. Mich., Ann Arbor, 1960-61; asst. prof. history Dartmouth, Hanover, N.H., 1961-66, asst. dean of freshmen, 1963-64, asso. prof. history, 1966-67; prof., head dept. history Va. Poly. Inst. and State U., Blacksburg, 1967-69; prof. history U. S.C., Columbia, 1969-75, asso. vice provost, 1971-72, asso. provost, 1972-73, dean Coll. of Social and Behavioral Scis., 1972-75; prof. history U. Tex. at Arlington, 1975-77, dean Coll. Liberal Arts, 1975-77; prof. history U. Tenn., Knoxville, 1977—, dean Coll. Liberal Arts, 1977—. Served with AUS, 1953-55. Am. Council of Learned Socs. fellow, 1965-66, Comparative Studies Center Faculty fellow, 1965-66. Fellow Middle East Studies Assn. of N. Am.; mem. Am. Hist. Assn., Middle East Inst., Theta Delta Chi, Phi Kappa Phi. Roman Catholic. Author: Oman Since 1856, 1967; The Emergence of the Modern Middle East, 1970; (with Abid Al-Marayati) The Middle East, Its Governments and Politics, 1972. Contbr. articles to profl. jours. and book revs. to hist. publs. Office: Dean of Liberal Arts Univ of Tenn Knoxville TN 37916

LANDER, DAVID L., actor; b. Bklyn., June 22; s. Saul and Stella L.; ed. Carnegie Inst. Tech.; m. Kathy Fields. Mem., The Credibility Gap, satirical radio group; regular on ABC-TV series Laverne and Shirley, 1976—; other TV appearances include: Viva Valdez, Bob Newhart Show, Dinah, Merv Griffin Show, Mike Douglas Show, Rhoda, Barney Miller, Hollywood Squares, Kids Are People Too; recs. include: (with Michael McKean) Lenny and the Squiggstones. Office: care ABC Public Relations 1330 Ave of Americas New York NY 10019*

LANDER, EDWARD CLARK, found. exec.; b. Akron, Ohio, Apr. 3, 1937; s. Edward and Margaret (Warfield) L.; student U. Chgo., 1954-56; B.A., U. Akron, 1959; postgrad. Western Res. U. Sch. Law, 1959-61, Kent State U., 1961-63; M.A., N.Y. U., 1970. Exec. dir., program dir. Karamu House, Inc., Cleve., 1964-66; tng. coordinator Child Study Assn. Am., N.Y.C., 1966-69; project dir. N.Y. U. New Careers Tng. Lab., 1969-73; asso. dir. Dist. Council 37 Campus, Coll. New Rochelle, N.Y.C., 1973-75; exec. dir. Dance Theater Found., Inc., Alvin Ailey Am. Dance Theater, N.Y.C., 1975—. Mem. Cleve. Orch. Chorus, 1961-66. Recipient Headmaster's award Western Res. Acad., Clarence L. Hyde award U. Akron; U. Chgo. scholar, Western Res. U. Sch. Law scholar. Mem. Assn. Am. Dance Cos. (dir.), Nat. Council Negro Women (life). Author: (with others) A Curriculum of Training for Parent Participation, 1967. Contbr. to The Cleve Unitarian, 1965-66. Home: 372 Central Park W New York NY 10025 Office: 1515 Broadway New York NY 10036

LANDER, JACK ROBERT, historian; b. Hinckley, Eng., Feb. 15, 1921; s. Robert Arthur and Hilda Mary (Goodman) L.; B.A., Pembroke Coll., Cambridge (Eng.) U., 1942, M.A., 1945, M.Litt., 1950. Lectr., U. Ghana, Legon, 1950-63; asso. prof. history Dalhousie U., Halifax, N.S., Can., 1963-65; asso. prof. U. Western Ont. (Can.), Lindon, 1965-70, J.B. Smallman prof., 1970—. Leverhulme fellow, 1959-60. Fellow Royal Hist. Soc., Royal Soc. Can.; mem. Hist. Assn. Eng., Am. Hist. Assn., Medieval Acad. Am. Clubs: Reform (London); Faculty of U. Western Ont. Author: The Wars of the Roses, 1965; Conflict and Stability in Fifteenth Century England, 1969; Crown and Nobility, 1450-1509, 1976; England, 1450-1509, 1976; Power and Politics. Office: Dept History U Western Ont London ON N6A 5C2 Canada

LANDERS, ANN (MRS. ESTHER P. LEDERER), columnist; b. Sioux City, Iowa, July 4, 1918; d. Abraham B. and Rebecca (Rushall) Friedman; student Morningside Coll., 1936-39, L.H.D., 1964; Hum.D., Wilberforce (Ohio) Coll., 1972; L.H.D., U. Cin., 1974; L.H.D., Am. Coll. Greece, Deree-Pierce Coll., 1975, LL.D., 1979; m. Jules W. Lederer, July 2, 1939 (div. 1975); 1 dau., Margo (Mrs. Ken Howard). Syndicated columnist Pubs.-Syndicate-Field Enterprises, Chgo., 1955—; pres. Eppie Co., Inc., Chgo. Chmn. Eau Claire (Wis.) Gray-Lady Corps, A.R.C., 1947-53; chmn. Minn.-Wis. council Anti-Defamation League, 1945-49; asst. Wis. chmn. Nat. Found. Infantile Paralysis, 1951-53; hon. nat. chmn. 1963 Tb Christmas Seal Campaign; bd. sponsors Mayo Clinic, 1970; mem. sponsors com. Mayo Found., nat. adv. bd. Dialogue for the Blind, 1972; adv. com. on better health services AMA. County chmn. Democratic Party of

Eau Claire. Bd. dirs. Rehab. Inst. Chgo.; nat. bd. dirs. Am. Cancer Soc.; vis. com. bd. overseers Harvard Med. Sch.; trustee Menninger Found., Nat. Dermatology Found. Am. Coll. Greece, Deree-Pierce Coll., Athens, Meharry Med. Sch. Recipient award Nat. Family Service Assn., 1965; Adolf Meyer award Assn. for Mental Health, N.Y., 1965; Pres.'s Citation and nat. award Nat. Council on Alcoholism, 1966, 2d nat. award, 1975; Golden Stethoscope award Ill. Med. Soc., 1967; Humanitarianism award Internat. Lions Club, 1967; plaque of honor Am. Friends of Hebrew U., 1968; Gold Plate award Acad. Achievement, 1969; Nat. Service award Am. Cancer Soc., 1971; Robert T. Morse award Am. Psychiat. Assn., 1972; plaque recognizing establishment of chair in chem. immunology Weizmann Inst., 1974; Jane Addams Public Service award Hull House, 1977; Health Achievement award Nat. Kidney Found., 1978; Nat. award Epilepsy Found. Am., 1978; James Ewing Layman's award Soc. Surg. Oncologists, 1979; citation for distinguished service AMA, 1979; Thomas More medal Thomas More Assn., 1979; NEA award, 1979. Fellow Chgo. Gynecol. Soc. (citizen hon.); mem. League Women Voters (pres. 1948), Brandeis U. Women (pres. 1960). Author: Since You Asked Me, 1962; Teen-agers and Sex, 1964; Truth is Stranger..., 1968; Ann Landers Speaks Out, 1975; The Ann Landers Encyclopedia, 1978. Clubs: Chgo. Econs. (dir. 1975); Sigma Delta Chi. Office: Mrs Landers Chgo Sun-Times 401 N Wabash Ave Chicago IL 60611

LANDERS, MATTHEW PATRICK, pharm. co. exec.; b. Jamaica, N.Y., Oct. 12, 1916; s. Patrick and Sarah (Burke) L.; B.B.A. magna cum laude, Pace U., 1953; M.S. in Controllership Accounting, Columbia, 1955; postgrad. Bklyn. Law Sch., 1956-57; m. Barbara Teasley, Oct. 19, 1944; children—Gregory, Suzanne, Elizabeth. Payroll supr., N.Y.C., 1938-49; internal revenue agt., 1949-52; with Franke, Hannon & Withey, C.P.A.'s, N.Y.C., 1952-55, Scovell, Wellington & Co., C.P.A.'s, 1955-56; with Pfizer Inc., 1956—, treas., 1967—; dir. Pfizer Internat. subs., Hartford Trust Co. N.Y. Served to capt., inf., AUS, 1940-46; ETO. Decorated Bronze Star, Combat Inf. badge. Mem. Am. Inst. C.P.A.'s, N.Y. State Soc. C.P.A.'s, Fin. Execs. Inst. (sec. N.Y. chpt.), Tax Execs. Inst. (past pres. N.Y. chpt.), NAM (vice chmn. tax com.), Mfg. Chemists Assn., Beta Gamma Sigma. Club: Sleepy Hollow Country. Home: 30 Tavano Rd Ossining NY 10562 Office: 235 E 42d St New York City NY 10017

LANDES, DAVID SAUL, historian; b. N.Y.C., Apr. 29, 1924; s. Harry and Sylvia (Silberman) L.; A.B., Coll. City N.Y., 1942; A.M., Harvard, 1943, Ph.D., 1953; Docteur honoris causa, U. Lille; m. Sonia Tarnopol, Mar. 19, 1944; children—Jane, Richard Allen, Alison. Mem. Soc. Fellows, Harvard, 1950-53, prof. history, 1964-72, Leroy B. Williams prof. history and polit sci., 1972-75, Robert Walton Goelet prof. French History, 1975—, dir. Center for Middle Eastern Studies, 1966-68; asst. prof. econs. Columbia, 1952-55, asso. prof., 1955-58, fellow Center For Advanced Study Behavioral Scis., 1957-58; prof. history, econs. U. Cal. at Berkeley, 1958-64. Chmn., Council on Research Econ. History, 1963—. Served to 1st lt. Signal Corps, AUS, 1943-46. Fellow Am. Acad. Arts and Scis., Brit. Acad.; mem. Am. Hist. Assn., Econ. History Assn. (pres. 1976-77), Soc. French Hist. Studies, Royal Hist. Soc. (Gt. Britain), Econ. Hist. Soc. (Gt. Britain), Societe d'Histoire Moderne, Gesellschaft für Sozial-und Wirtschaftsgeschichte. Author: Bankers and Pashas, 1958; The Unbound Prometheus: Technological Change and Industrial Development in Western Europe, 1750 to the Present, 1969. Editor: Reader in the Rise of Capitalism, 1965; History as Social Science, 1971. Asso. editor Jour. Econ. History, 1954-60. Home: 24 Highland St Cambridge MA 02138

LANDES, ROBERT NATHAN, lawyer; b. N.Y.C., Dec. 24, 1930; s. Joseph William and Gertrude Ann (Sindeband) L.; A.B., Columbia, 1952, LL.B. (Harlan Fiske Stone scholar), 1954; m. Phyllis Markman, Apr. 16, 1964; children—Lucy Ann, Kathy Jill, Jeffrey Mark. Admitted to N.Y. State bar, 1954; asso. firm Shearman & Sterling, N.Y.C., 1957-61; asst. gen. counsel U.S. Industries, Inc., N.Y.C., 1961-70, v.p., gen. counsel U.S. Industries, Inc. Apparel Co., 1970-73; sr. v.p., gen. counsel, sec. McGraw-Hill, N.Y.C., 1974—. Served as lt. (j.g.) USNR, 1954-57. Mem. Am., N.Y. State, New York County bar assns., Assn. Bar City of N.Y. (mem. com. on corp. law 1978—), Mag. Pubs. Assn. (chmn. legal affairs com. 1977—), Columbia Coll. Alumni Assn. (v.p., dir. 1974-76), Democrat. Editor: Columbia Law Rev., 1953-54. Home: 1192 Park Ave New York NY 10028 Office: 1221 Ave of Americas New York NY 10020

LANDESBERG, STEVE, actor; b. N.Y.C., Nov. 23. Mem. The New York Stickball Team, comedy group; regular on TV series: Bobby Darin Amusement Company, 1972-73, Paul Sand in Friends and Lovers, 1974-75, Barney Miller, 1976—; guest appearances on TV shows: Ed Sullivan Show, Johnny Carson Show. Office: care Agy for Performing Arts Inc 900 Sunset Blvd Suite 315 Los Angeles CA 90069*

LANDGREBE, DAVID ALLEN, elec. engr.; b. Huntingburg, Ind., Apr. 12, 1934; s. Albert E. and Sarah A. L.; B.S. in Elec. Engring., Purdue U., 1956, M.S. in Elec. Engring., 1958, Ph.D., 1962; m. Margaret Ann Swank, June 7, 1959; children—James David, Carole Ann, Mary Jane. Mem. tech. staff Bell Telephone Labs., Murray Hill, N.J., 1956; electronics engr. Interstate Electronics Corp., Anaheim, Calif., 1958, 59, 62; mem. faculty Purdue U., West Lafayette, Ind., 1962—, dir. lab. for applications of remote sensing, 1969—, prof. elec. engring., 1970—; research scientist Douglas Aircraft Co., Newport Beach, Calif., 1964; dir. Univ. Space Research Assn., 1975-78. Recipient medal for exceptional sci. achievement NASA, 1973. Fellow IEEE; mem. Am. Soc. for Engring. Edn., AAAS, Am. Soc. Photogrammetry, Sigma Xi, Tau Beta Pi, Eta Kappa Nu. Club: Rotary. Author: (with others) Remote Sensing: The Quantitative Approach, 1978. Office: Purdue U Dept Elec Engring West Lafayette IN 47907

LANDIS, ELWOOD WINTON, editor; b. Wichita, Kans., June 14, 1928; s. Jacob Harrison and Christina (Fry) L.; B.A., Friends U., Wichita, 1950; M.S. in Journalism, Northwestern U., 1953; m. Nancy Gauss, Nov. 22, 1961; children—Frederic, Laura. Reporter, Wichita Eagle, 1953; copy editor Omaha World-Herald, 1955-57; publicity dir. Bethany (Kans.) Coll., 1957-61; publs. dir. tchr. edn. project Central Mich. U., 1961-64; mng. editor Teacher's Voice mag., E. Lansing, Mich., 1965—. Mem. Williamston (Mich.) City Planning Commn., 1972-75. Served with AUS, 1953-55. Recipient awards Edn. Press Assn. Am. Mem. Sigma Delta Chi, Phi Delta Kappa. Democrat. Home: 308 S Circle Dr Williamston MI 48895 Office: 1216 Kendale Blvd East Lansing MI 48823

LANDIS, FRED, educator; b. Munich, Germany, Mar. 21, 1923; s. Julius and Elsie (Schulhoff) L.; B.Eng., McGill U., 1945; S.M., Mass. Inst. Tech., 1949, Sc.D., 1950; m. Billie H. Schiff, Aug. 26, 1951; children—John David, Deborah Ellen, Mark Edward. Came to U.S., 1947, naturalized, 1954. Design engr. Canadian Vickers, Ltd., Montreal, Can., 1945-47; asst. prof. mech. engring. Stanford, 1950-52; research engr. Northrop Aircraft, Inc., Hawthorne, Calif., 1952-53; asst. prof., N.Y.U., 1953-56, asso. prof., 1956-61, prof., 1961-73, chmn. dept. mech. engring., 1963-73; dean, prof. mech. engring. Poly. Inst. N.Y., Bklyn., 1973-74; dean Coll. Engring. and Applied Sci., U. Wis.-Milw., 1974—; staff cons. Pratt & Whitney Aircraft Co., 1957—. Mem. Bd. Edn., Dobbs Ferry, N.Y., 1965-71, v.p., 1966-67, 70-71, pres. 1967-68; bd. dirs. Westchester County, Sch. Bds. Assn., 1969-70, v.p., 1970, pres., 1970-71. Fellow ASME (div. exec. com. 1965-73, policy bd. 1973—); asso. fellow Am. Inst. Aeros. and Astronautics; mem. Am. Soc. Engring. Edn., Sigma Xi, Tau Beta Pi, Pi Tau Sigma. Cons. editor Macmillan Co., 1960-68; cons. editorial bd. Funk & Wagnalls Ency. 1969—. Contbr. numerous research articles to profl. jours. Home: 2420 W Acacia Rd Milwaukee WI 53209

LANDIS, FREDERICK, U.S. judge; b. Logansport, Ind., Jan. 17, 1912; s. Frederick and Bessie (Baker) L.; student Wabash Coll., 1928-29; A.B., Ind. U., 1932, LL.B., 1934; m. E. Joyce Stevenson, July 4, 1945; children—Diana, Frederick, Susan, Gillian, Kenesaw Mountain. Admitted to Ind. bar, 1934; asso. Long and Yarlott, 1935-38; mem. Landis & Hanna, 1938-46, Landis & Landis, 1946-54, Landis & Michael, 1954-55; pros. atty. 29th Jud. Circuit, 1938-40; justice Supreme Ct. Ind., 1955-65; Judge U.S. Customs Ct., 1965—. Cass County rep. Ind. Ho. of Reps., 1950-52, state senator Cass and Fulton counties, 1952-55. Served from enlisted man to lt. USNR, 1942-46. Mem. Ind., Cass County (pres. 1948-51) bar assns., Am. Bar Assn., Am. Legion, V.F.W., Phi Delta Phi, Delta Tau Delta. Elk. Clubs: Columbia, Press (Indpls.). Office: US Customs Ct One Federal Plaza New York City NY 10007

LANDIS, JACOB, mgmt. research co. exec.; b. N.Y.C., Apr. 20, 1924; s. Joseph and Sarah (Wernick) L.; B.B.A., Coll. City N.Y., 1945; postgrad. N.Y.U., 1950; m. Marion Perl, June 8, 1952; children—Jeffry Steven, Cynthia Fay. Supr., Clarence Rainess & Co., N.Y.C., 1941-53; v.p. finance, treas., dir. Bobbie Brooks, Inc., Cleve., exec. v.p., 1953-68; pres. Mgmt. Research Asso., Inc., 1968—, Profit Mgmt., Inc., 1976—. Mem. Nat. Assn. Accountants, N.Y., Cleve. socs. C.P.A.'s, Cleve. Soc. Security Analysts, Cleve. Treasurer's Club. Jewish (pres., trustee temple). Home: 21950 E Byron Rd Shaker Heights OH 44122 Office: 3645 Warrensville Center Rd Cleveland OH 44122

LANDIS, LEWIS REX, indsl. engr., former govt. ofcl.; b. Polk, Ohio, Dec. 3, 1917; s. Cloyce Ivan and Lottie Pearl (McClure) L.; B.S. in Mech. Engring., B.S. in Indsl. Engring., Ohio State U., 1941; 1 son, Larry S. Various plant maintenance and engring. positions Gen. Electric Co., Ohio Boxboard Co., Army Ordnance Dept., 1941-57; indsl. engr., chief regional engr. Post Office Dept., 1957-59, dep. dir. research and engring., 1959-63, mgr. operations research, 1963-68, systems and indsl. engring. (now U.S. Postal Service), 1968-78; cons. indsl. engring., 1978—. Served to capt., indsl. ordnance U.S. Army, 1941-46. Registered profl. engr., Ohio. Club: Masons. Home: 1516 N Lake Dr Sun City Center FL 33570

LANDIS, RICHARD G., food processor; b. Davenport, Okla., Apr. 5, 1920; s. John W. and Venna (Perrin) L.; B.Social Sci., Laverne Coll.; postgrad. in social sci. Claremont Grad. Sch.; m. Leota Beth Throne, Nov. 6, 1943; children—Gary P., Dennis M., Kay E. With Del Monte Corp., San Francisco, 1942—, mgr. Eastern ops., San Francisco, 1965-66, v.p. Pacific Coast ops., 1966-68, v.p. U.S. prodn., 1968-72, pres., chief operating officer, 1972-77, chief exec. officer, 1977—, chmn., 1978—. Office: # 1 Market Plaza San Francisco CA 94119

LANDIS, ROBERT M., lawyer; b. Fleetwood, Pa., 1920; s. Jacob B. and Bertha (Moyer) L.; A.B., Franklin and Marshall Coll., 1941; J.D., U. Pa., 1947; m. Mary Elizabeth Hatton, Aug. 24, 1946; children—Christopher Hatton, Geoffrey Budd. Admitted to Pa. bar, 1947; asso. firm Dechert, Price & Rhoads, Phila., 1947-54, partner, 1954—; 1st dep. city solicitor, Phila., 1952-53; mem. Pa. Supreme Ct. Advisory Judicial Qualifications Commn., 1968; mem. U.S. Jud. Conf. Third Circuit. Chmn. Pa. Gov.'s Bd. Ethics, 1973-78; chmn. Bi-State Commn. Legislation Delaware River Port Authority Pa.-N.J., 1976-77. Co-chmn. Greater Phila. Partnership, 1977-79; bd. dirs. Greater Phila. Movement; pres. Children's Aid Soc. Pa., 1960-68; bd. dirs. Child Welfare League Am., 1964-66; pres. Fellowship Commn. Phila., 1972-74; past chmn. Pa. Council of Nat. Council Crime and Delinquency; mem. advisory council Villanova Inst. Correctional Reform, 1972-79; steering com. NAACP Legal Def. Fund; asso. trustee U. Pa.; chmn. bd. trustees Theodore F. Jenkins Law Library, 1970-71; elder, trustee First Presbyn. Ch. Lower Merion, Gladwyne, Pa. Fellow Am. Coll. Trial Lawyers, Am. Bar Found.; mem. Phila. Bar Assn. (numerous com. assignments, chmn. bd. govs. 1964, chancellor 1970—), Am. Bar Assn. (pres. Nat. Conf. Bar Presidents 1975-76, del. 1969-70, 77-78), Nat. Assn. R.R. Trial Counsel (pres. 1966-67), Am. Law Inst., Am. Judicature Soc. (dir. 1974-77). Clubs: Franklin Inn, Socialegal, Sunday Morning Breakfast, Racquet, Phila. Country. Home: 1401 Monk Rd Gladwyne PA 19035 Office: Dechert Price & Rhoads 3400 Centre Sq W 1500 Market St Philadelphia PA 19035

LANDMANN, WENDELL AUGUST, educator; b. Waterloo, Ill., Dec. 25, 1919; s. Fred William and Mary Anna (Tebbenhoff) L.; B.S., U. Ill., 1941; M.S., Purdue U., 1944, Ph.D., 1951; m. Rebecca Catharine Jones, Apr. 9, 1944; children—David Gard, Richard Frederick. Group leader Armour & Co., Chgo., 1951-55; asso. biochemistry Argonne Nat. Lab., Lemont, Ill., 1955-57; chief div. analytical and phys. chemistry Am. Meat Inst., Found., Chgo., 1957-64; prof. depts. biochemistry and biophysics, animal sci., also King Ranch prof. basic animal sci. Tex. A. and M. U., 1964-72, head dept. biochemistry and biophysics, 1970-78, prof. depts. biochemistry and biophysics, animal sci., 1978—; cons. U. Ill., Chgo., 1955-57. Pres. StageCenter, Inc., Bryan-College Station, Tex., 1967-68. Pres. bd. edn. Dist. 57, DuPage County, Ill., 1960-64. Bd. dirs. Brazos Valley Arts Council, 1971. Served with USNR, 1943-46. Mem. Inst. Food Technologists, AAAS, Am. Inst. Nutrition, Am. Meat Sci. Assn., Sigma Xi, Phi Kappa Phi, Phi Lambda Upsilon. Presbyn. Kiwanian (bd. dirs. College Station 1967-68). Author, patentee in field. Home: 1602 Dominik Dr College Station TX 77840

LANDOLT, ARLO UDELL, astronomer, educator; b. Highland, Ill., Sept. 29, 1935; s. Arlo Melvin and Vesta (Kraus) L.; B.A., Miami U., Oxford, Ohio, 1955; M.A., Ind. U., 1960, Ph.D., 1962; m. Eunice Jean Casper, June 8, 1966; children—Lynda, Barbara, Vicky, Debra Bess, Jennifer Louise. Mem. 1st wintering-over party Internat. Geophys. Year, Amundson-Scott South Pole Sta., Antarctica, 1957; asst. prof. physics and astronomy La. State U., 1962-65, asso. prof., 1965-68, prof., 1968—, dir. La. State U. Obs., 1970—, acting chmn. dept. physics and astronomy, summers 1972-73, pres. faculty senate, 1979-80; program dir. astronomy sect. NSF, 1975-76; guest investigator Kitt Peak Nat. Obs., Tucson, Cerro Tololo Inter-Am. Obs., La Serena, Chile, Dyer Obs., Vanderbilt U., Goethe Link Obs., Ind. U. NSF Research grantee, 1964, 66, 69, 71, 73, 75; NASA Research grantee, 1965; Research Corp. research grantee, 1964—; Air Force Office Sci. Research grantee, 1977, 78, 79. Fellow AAAS (sec. Sect. D 1970-78); mem. Am. Astron. Soc., Internat. Astron. Union, Royal Astron. Soc. (Eng.), Astron. Soc. Pacific, Am. Polar Soc., Am. Philatelic Soc., AAUP, Sigma Xi, Pi Mu Epsilon. Home: 1332 Knollwood Dr Baton Rouge LA 70808

LANDOLT, RUDOLPH FREDERICK, ins. co. exec.; b. Munich, Germany, June 13, 1922; came to U.S., 1927, naturalized, 1934; s. Casper Joseph and Marzellina L.; B.A., Pa. State U., 1948, postgrad. Law Sch., 1948-49; grad. exec. program Stanford U., 1977; m. Irmgard Mary Louise Fiene, Jan. 29, 1948; children—Richard Martin, Amy Landolt Eber, William Rudolph. With Kemper Ins. Group, 1949—, exec. v.p., Long Grove, Ill., 1978-79, sr. exec. v.p., chief ins. officer, 1979—; chmn. bd. Fed. Kemper Ins. Co., Iowa Kemper, Economy Fire & Casualty Ins. Co., Fed. Kemper Life, Fidelity Life Assn., Nat. Auto; dir. Kemsico, Ampico, Sequoia Ins. Co., Kemper County Mut. Bd. dirs. Chgo. Crime Commn.; mem. Chgo. Police Rev. Bd. Served with U.S. Army, 1942. Recipient various service awards. Mem. Ins. Info. Inst. (dir.). Republican. Roman Catholic. Club: Forest Grove (Ill.) Tennis. Home: 545 Red Barn Ln Barrington IL 60010 Office: Route 22 Long Grove IL 60049. *The only thing I am really interested in is if my acquaintances, friends, and especially my family think the world might have been just a little better place for my having been here.*

LANDON, EDWARD AUGUST, artist; b. Hartford, Conn., Mar. 13, 1911; s. Per August and Hannah Matilda (Anderson) L.; student Hartford Art Sch., 1928-29, Art Students League, 1930-31, U. Fine Arts, 1939; m. Rachel Meltzer, Feb. 20, 1948. Painter, 1931-39, printmaker, 1940—; numerous one-man shows including: Boston Printmakers, 1955, Paul Schuster Gallery, Cambridge, Mass., 1955, Meltzer Gallery, N.Y.C., 1956; U. Maine, 1970, Glass Gallery, N.Y.C., 1973, Gallery 2, Woodstock, Vt., 1974, So. Vt. Artists, Manchester, 1977; numerous group shows including Boston Printmakers, 1960, Springfield Art League, 1945, Oakland (Calif.) Art Assn., 1952, Phila. Print Club, 1960; represented in numerous permanent collections including Princeton Print Club, N.Y. Pub. Library, Pa. Acad., San Francisco Mus., Sao Paulo, Brazil, Seattle Art Mus., Tel Aviv (Israel) Mus., Turkee Mus., Finland, Victoria and Albert Mus., London. Recipient prize N.W. Printmakers, 1944, 46, Bklyn. Mus., 1947, San Francisco Art Assn., 1949, others including Nat. Serigraph Soc. purchase awards, 1952, 54, 57, 59. Solomon R. Gugenheim grantee, 1939-41; Fulbright research fellow, 1950-51. Mem. Nat. Serigraph Soc. (a founder 1942, editor Serigraph Quar. 1945-50, pres. 1952), Am. Color Print Soc., Boston Printmakers, Phila. Print Club, Print Council Am., So. Vt. Art Assn. Author: Picture Framing, 1960; contbr. articles to profl. publs., 1950-70; author film: Serigraphy, 1947; pioneer in devel. serigraphy, 1940; introduced serigraphy to Europe, 1950. Home: Lawrence Hall Rd Weston VT 05161

LANDON, MICHAEL (EUGENE MAURICE OROWITZ), actor; b. Forest Hills, N.Y., Oct. 21, 1937; s. Eli Maurice and Peggy (O'Neill) Orowitz; student U. So. Calif.; m. Lyn Noe; children—Mark, Josh, Cheryl, Michael, Leslie Ann, Shawna Leigh, Christopher Beau. Movie appearances include: I Was a Teenage Werewolf, 1957, God's Little Acre, 1958, The Legend of Tom Dooley, 1959, Maracaibo, 1958, The Errand Boy, 1961; TV film Little House on the Prairie, 1974; appeared on TV series Bonanza, 1959-73; star, dir., exec. producer, writer TV series Little House on the Prairie, 1974—; dir. It's Good to Be Alive for G.E. Theatre, 1974; writer, dir. TV film The Loneliest Runner, 1976; other TV appearances include: Dupont Theatre, Tales of Wells Fargo, Schlitz Playhouse of Stars, Studio One, Playhouse 90. Office: care NBC Press Dept 30 Rockefeller Plaza New York NY 10020*

LANDON, ROBERT GRAY, bus mfg. co. exec.; b. Portsmouth, Ohio, Dec. 22, 1928; s. Herman Robert and Hazel Ruth (Tener) L.; student Cornell U., 1947-49; B.A. in Econs., Wharton Sch., U. Pa., 1955; grad. advanced mgmt. program Harvard U., 1978; m. Sarah A. Newpher, July 2, 1954; children—Geoffrey, Suzanne. Loan officer Nat. City Bank, Cleve., 1955-60; SEC adminstr. Smith Kline Corp., 1960-64; controller, treas. Grumman Allied Industries, Inc., Garden City, N.Y., 1964-76, v.p., 1977—; v.p. investment mgmt. Grumman Corp., Bethpage, N.Y., 1978-79; pres. Grumman Flxible Corp., Delaware, Ohio, 1979—, also dir. Elder, 1st Presbyterian Ch., Northport, N.Y. Served with AC, USN, 1949-53. Clubs: Harvard of N.Y.; Northport (N.Y.) Yacht; Delaware Country. Home: 66 Glen Dr Worthington OH 43085 Office: 970 Pittsburgh Dr Delaware OH 43015

LANDON, ROBERT KIRKWOOD, ins. co. exec.; b. N.Y.C., Apr. 27, 1929; s. Kirk A. and Edith (Ungar) L.; student U. Va., 1946-48; B.S., Ga. Inst. Tech., 1950; m. Beulah Pair, Mar. 19, 1965; children—Chris Joseph, Kathleen Adele Staley, Kellyann Dorothy. With Am. Bankers Life Assurance Co. Miami, Fla., 1952—, pres., 1960-74, chmn., chief exec. officer, 1974—; dir. SE 1st Nat. Bank Miami; chmn. bd., pres. Am. Bankers Ins. Co., Miami; pres. Landon Corp., Dover, Del., 1971—; charter mem. advisory bd. Fla. Internat. U., 1972-74. Trustee Kirk A. and Dorothy P. Landon Found., 1969—. Served to lt. (j.g.) USNR, 1950-53. Mem. Met. Mus. and Art Centers, Council Internat. Visitors, World Bus. Council, Scabbard and Blade, Miami Ballet Co., Vizcayans, Phi Gamma Delta. Republican. Congregationalist. Clubs: Miami, Grove Isle, Palm Bay. Home: 2 Casuarina Concourse Coral Gables FL 33143 Office: 600 Brickell Ave Miami FL 33131

LANDON, SEALAND WHITNEY, lawyer; b. Burlington, Vt., Mar. 27, 1896; s. Sealand Whitney and Helen (Weeks) L.; student Bordentown Mil. Inst., 1908-13; B.S. cum laude, Princeton U., 1917; LL.B., Rutgers U., 1925, LL.M., 1926, J.D., 1974; L.H.D., Upsala U., 1977; m. Isabelle Morris Miller, June 25, 1924; children—Sealand Whitney III, Margot (Mrs. Paul S. Visher), Richard Warren, Lisa (Mrs. John B. Hewett). With Rockwood Sprinkler Co., Worcester, Mass., 1919-21, Western Electric Co., N.Y.C., 1923-26; admitted to N.Y. bar, 1926; prof. law Rutgers U. (N.J. Law Sch.), 1925-35; asso. firm Slayton & Jackson, N.Y.C., 1926-27; mem. firm Hulbert, Heermance & Landon, 1927-31, Swiger, Scandrett Chambers & Landon, 1932-34; atty. gen. legal dept. Am. Tel. & Tel. Co., 1934-37, gen. atty. long lines dept., 1937-51, asst. v.p., asst. sec., 1951-52, sec., asst. to pres., 1952-60, v.p., sec., 1960-61; dir. Nat. Newark & Essex Bank, Newark, 1962-69, emeritus, 1969—. Pub. gov. Am. Stock Exchange, 1962-68. Pres. Community Chest Oranges and Maplewood (N.J.), 1942-44, treas., 1947-50; past chmn. nat. quota com., vice chmn. nat. budget com. Community Chests and Councils (N.Y.) 1948-55; mem. planning bd. and zoning bd. adjustment, West Orange, 1931-54; chmn. bd. mgrs. Llewellyn Park, West Orange, 1937-45, trustee, 1957—; bd. mem. to survey Dept. Immigration and Naturalization, 1933; asso. counsel Moreland Commn. to investigate guaranteed mortgage and title cos. N.Y. State, 1934. Gov. Orange Meml. Hosp., 1946-49; hon. trustee Hosp. Center, Orange, pres., 1950-53, chmn. bd., 1962-65; hon. trustee N.J. Symphony Orch., trustee, 1950-75, chmn. bd., 1960-74; past trustee YMCA of the Oranges; trustee, treas. Victoria Found.; trustee, chmn. bd. Turrell Fund, pres., 1977; trustee Shelburne Mus.; chmn. Princeton U. Fund, 1956-62; dir. Bordentown Mil. Inst., 1930—, v.p., 1951-71, pres. 1934-51; trustee, v.p. Health Facilities Planning Council N.J., 1965-68; trustee Princeton, 1958-62, Edison Birthplace Assn., 1967—, Hosp. Service Plan N.J. (Blue Cross). Served as capt. CAC, U.S. Army, 1917-19. Recipient Citation outstanding citizen of the Oranges and Maplewood, N.J., 1953. Mem. Am. Arbitration Assn. (dir. 1929-37, 41-72, chmn. exec. com. 1950-56), Am. Bar Assn., Am. Soc. Corp. Secs. (past v.p., dir.; past pres. N.Y. regional group), Phi Beta Kappa. Republican. Presbyterian. Home: Llewellyn Park West Orange NJ 07052

LANDOR, JOHN HENRY, physician, educator; b. Canton, Ohio, Sept. 30, 1927; s. Henry and Alice Cecelia (Schaefer) L.; Ph.B., U. Chgo., 1948, M.D., 1953; m. Linda Marinelli, Dec. 26, 1953; children—Julia, Gina, Jenifer, Derric, John, Christopher. Intern U. Chgo., 1953-54, resident surgery, 1954-58, instr. surgery, 1958-59; instr. surgery U. Mo., 1959, asst. prof., 1959-62, asso. prof., 1962-68, prof. surgery, 1968-69; prof. surgery U. Fla., Gainesville, 1969-72; prof., chief div. gen. surgery Coll. Medicine and Dentistry of N.J., Rutgers Med. Sch., Piscataway, 1972—; chief dept. surgery Raritan Valley Hosp., Green Brook, 1972—. Served with AUS, 1946-47. Recipient Commonwealth Found. fellowship for research Royal Postgrad. Med. Sch., London, Eng., 1966-67. Mem. A.C.S., Am., Central surg. assns., Am. Gastroenterol. Assn., Soc. U. Surgeons, Societe Internationale de Chirurgie, Soc. Surgery Alimentary Tract, British Soc. Gastroenterology, Collegium Internationale Chirurgaie Digestivae. Home: 3 Greenholm Princeton NJ 08540

LANDOVITZ, LEON FRED, physicist, educator; b. Bklyn., May 24, 1932; s. Philip and Ethel (Leibman) L.; A.B., Columbia, 1953, Ph.D., 1958; m. Renee M. Altman, July 19, 1959; children—Keith S., Raphael J. NSF fellow Inst. Advanced Study, 1957-58; research asso. Brookhaven Nat. Lab., Upton, N.Y., 1958-60; asst. prof. physics Belfer Grad. Sch. Sci., Yeshiva U., N.Y.C., 1960-62, prof., 1967-74, also dir. computer center, chmn. info. scis. com., until 1974; dir. computer center Grad. Sch. and Univ. Center, City U. N.Y., 1974—, adj. prof. physics Hunter Coll., 1974—. Mem. Am., Italian phys. socs., Sigma Xi. Research and publs. in field of elementary particles, astrophysics, solid state physics. Home: 16 Locust Dr Great Neck NY 11021 Office: Grad School and Univ Center City U NY 33 W 42d St New York City NY 10036

LANDRES, MORRIS M., motion picture co. exec.; b. Lithuania; student Bklyn. Poly. Inst., N.Y.U.; civil engring. degree, Carnegie Inst. Tech., postgrad. edn. and art; m. Clara Pollock; 1 son, Peter David. Pres. Century Pictures Corp., Gen. Film Library Calif., Inc.; head Morris M. Landres Prodns., Morris M. Landres Enterprises, producers short subjects and features; v.p., asso. producer Adventure Pictures, Inc.; producer, co-owner, pres. Action Film Producers, Landres-Weiss Prodns.; also producer comml. films and exploitation features; studio cons., writer. Mem. Ind. Motion Picture Producers Assn., Acad. Motion Picture Arts and Scis. Home: 10501 Wilshire Blvd Los Angeles CA 90024. *Be ever vigilant to trends tending to dehumanize mankind. Actively participate with the younger generation in resisting such movements, either individual or mass attempts.*

LANDRIAULT, JACQUES, bishop; b. Alfred, Ont., Can., Sept. 23, 1921; s. Amedee and Marie-Louise (Brisebois) L.; B.A., U. Ottawa; Licence in Theology, St. Paul U. Sem., Ottawa. Ordained priest Roman Cath. Ch., 1947; curate in Noranda, Que.; chancellor Diocese Timmins, Ont., 1953; bishop of Cadi, aux. to bishop of Alexandria, Ont., 1962-64; bishop of Hearst, Ont., 1964-71, of Timmins, 1971—. Mem. Cath. Conf. Ont. Address: 65 Jubilee Ave E Timmins ON P4N 5W4 Canada

LANDRIEU, MOON, lawyer, sec. HUD; b. New Orleans, July 23, 1930; s. Joseph and Loretta (Bechtel) L.; B.B.A., Loyola U., New Orleans, 1952, LL.B., 1954; m. Verna Satterlee, Sept. 25, 1954; children—Mary, Mark, Melanie, Michelle, Mitchell, Madeleine, Martin, Melinda, Maurice. Admitted to La. bar, 1954; partner Landrieu, Calogero & Kronlage, New Orleans, 1958-69; mem. La. Ho. of Reps., 1960-65; councilman-at-large City of New Orleans, 1966-70, mayor, 1970-78; pres. Joseph C. Canzani Enterprises, 1978—; sec. HUD, Washington, 1979—. Mem. steering com. Nat. Urban Coalition, 1971—; coordinator S.W. region Nat. Conf. Democratic Mayors. Bd. regents Loyola U., New Orleans. Served with AUS, 1954-57. Recipient Humanitarian award B'nai B'rith, 1974; Weiss Ann. Brotherhood award NCCJ, 1978. Mem. Inter-Am. Municipal Orgn. (1st v.p. 1970—), La. Municipal Assn. (dist. v.p. 1970—), Nat. League Cities (mem. adv. bd. 1971-72, vice chmn. community devel. policy com.), U.S. Conf. Mayors (chmn. legis. action com. 1972, chmn. adv. bd. 1973-74, v.p. 1974-75, pres. 1975-76). Home: 4301 S Prieur St New Orleans LA 70125 Office: Office of Sec HUD 451 7th St SW Washington DC 20410

LANDRITH, HAROLD FOCHONE, univ. dean; b. Seneca, S.C., Dec. 23, 1919; s. Walter Louis and Ethel (Powell) L.; B.S., Clemson U., 1948; M.A., Vanderbilt U., 1949; Ed.D., U. Houston, 1960. Ednl. specialist, instr. tng. dept. Keesler AFB, Miss., 1951-55; head social sci. dept. South Tex. Coll., Houston, 1955-61; asso. prof. history and edn. Clemson U., 1961-65, dean Coll. Edn., 1965- -; cons. Internat. Tel. & Tel. Co., Fed. Labs., Modern Optics, Inc., Jr. Coll. Edn. Chmn. com. deans edn.; pres. dept. higher edn. S.C. State Supported Colls. Recipient Distinguished Service award S.C. Recreation and Park Soc., Distinguished Service award Jr. C. of C., 1954. Served with USAAF, 1939-45. Mem. S.C. Edn. Assn. (v.p.), Author: Introduction to The Community Junior College, 1971. Home: Fair Play Rd Seneca SC 29678

LANDRUM, THOMAS WALTER, elec. products mfg. co. exec.; b. Pickens, Miss., Jan. 4, 1919; s. Thomas Martin and Carrie Howard (Courts) L.; B.S. in Elec. Engring., Miss. State U., 1940; m. Blanche Martin, Mar. 31, 1956; 1 son, John Martin. Asst. elec. engr. Underwriters' Labs., Chgo., N.Y.C., 1940-41; with Westinghouse Elec. Corp., 1946-79, v.p. mktg., indsl. group, Pitts., 1964-68, v.p. lamp divs., Bloomfield, N.J., 1968-79. Served to lt. col. USAAF, 1941-45. Decorated Legion of Merit (U.S.), Croix de Guerre (France). Mem. IEEE (chmn. Shreveport, La., sect. 1955), Illuminating Engring. Research Inst., N.J. C. of C. (dir. 1968—). Club: Canoe Brook Country (Summit, N.J.). Home: 25 Cayuga Way Short Hills NJ 07078 Office: 1 Westinghouse Plaza Bloomfield NJ 07003

LANDRY, LIONEL, ednl. assn. exec.; b. Woonsocket, R.I., July 6, 1919; s. Lionel Daniel and Germaine (Desrochers) L.; A.B., Providence Coll., 1940; M.A., Harvard, 1941; student Brown U., 1941-42; m. Ruth Kin Maung, Sept. 24, 1955; children—Lisa, Peter, Christine. Lectr. Providence Coll., 1941-43; asst. dir. Centro Colombo-Americano, Bogota, Colombia, 1943-45; program officer Dept. State, Washington, 1945-50; lectr. Georgetown U. Sch. Fgn. Service, 1947-48; cultural attache Am. embassy, Rangoon, Burma, 1951-52; dir. USIS, also chmn. Burma Fulbright Found., 1953-55, country dir., Jakarta, Indonesia, 1955-58; regional dir. Fgn. Policy Assn., N.Y.C., 1958-62, asso. dir., 1962-64, dir., 1965-70; exec. v.p. The Asia Soc. Inc., N.Y.C., 1970—; moderator exec. seminars Aspen Inst. for Humanistic Studies, 1974—; pub. ASIA bimonthly, 1978—; lectr. various univs. U.S., also Burma. Mem. Council Fgn. Relations N.Y.C., Center Inter-Am. Relations, Assn. Asian Studies, Am. Com. for Borobudur (founding). Democrat. Roman Catholic. Club: Harvard. Author: The Land and People of Burma, 1968; The Land and People of Colombia, 1970. Contbr. articles on Asian affairs to Asia, Saturday Rev., Quadrant, others; contbr. essays to various books. Home: 10 Woodchuck Ln Wilton CT 06897 Office: 112 E 64th St New York NY 10021

LANDRY, TOM (THOMAS WADE), profl. football coach; b. Mission, Tex., Sept. 11, 1924; s. Ray and Ruth (Coffman) L.; B.S., U. Tex., 1949; degree indsl. engring. U. Houston, 1952; m. Alicia Wiggs, Jan. 28, 1949; children—Thomas, Kitty, Lisa. Player N.Y. Yankees All-Am. Football Conf., 1949; player N.Y. Giants, 1950-53, player-coach, 1954-55, defensive coach, 1956-59; head coach Dallas Cowboys, 1960—. First v.p. Nat. Fellowship Christian Athletes, chmn. bd. Dallas chpt.; bd. govs. Dallas Town North YMCA. Served with USAAF, World War II. Named to All-Pro team, 1954. Methodist (bd. govs.). Address: care Dallas Cowboys 6116 N Central Expressway Dallas TX 75206*

LANDS, WILLIAM EDWARD MITCHELL, educator; b. Chillicothe, Mo., July 22, 1930; s. Alonzo Mitchell and Bernice (Rubenstein) L.; B.S., U. Mich., 1951; Ph.D., U. Ill., 1954; m. Kay J. Rose; children—Susan Kay, Karen Jean (Mrs. James T. Keech), Edward Mitchell, Todd William. Mem. faculty Med. Sch., U. Mich., Ann Arbor, 1955—, asso. prof. biol. chemistry, 1963-67, prof., 1967—. Commr., Washtenaw County Bd. Commrs., 1969-72. NSF fellow, 1952-54, 54-55. Mem. Am. Soc. Biol. Chemists, Am. Chem. Soc., AAAS, Alpha Chi Sigma. Contbr. profl. jours.; editorial bd. Archives Biochem. Biophysics, Life Scis., Prostaglandins and Medicine, Prostaglandins and Therapeutics, Handbook of Lipid Research, Advances in Prostaglandin and Thromboxane Research. Home: 2753 Manchester Rd Ann Arbor MI 48104

LANDSHOFF, FRITZ HELMUT, publishing co. exec.; b. Berlin, July 29, 1901; s. Siegfried and Anna (Kirchheim) L.; Ph.D., U. Frankfurt (Germany), 1923; m. Sara Catharina Otte. Pres., Georg Kiepenheuer Verlag, Cologne, Germany, 1926-33, Querido Verlag, Amsterdam, Netherlands, 1933-40; v.p. L.B. Fischer Co., N.Y.C., 1940-46, Excerpta Medica, Amsterdam, 1946-50; exec. v.p. Harry N. Abrams, Inc., N.Y.C., 1951—. Office: 110 E 59th St New York NY 10022

LANDSTROM, KARL SIGURD, lawyer; b. Lebanon, Oreg., Feb. 12, 1909; s. Sigurd Hjalmar and Jessie (Ralston) L.; A.B., U. Oreg., 1930, A.M., 1932; postgrad. U. Calif. at Berkeley, 1930-31; J.D., George Washington U., 1959; m. Leora Lou Peetz, Dec. 31, 1937; children—Maris Lou (Mrs. Glenn E. Gutshall), Karen Bea (Mrs. Lester Harlow). Engaged in land econ. research Dept. Agr., 1937-48; agrl. econs. and land planning Bur. Land Mgmt., Dept. Interior, 1949-59, dir. bur., 1961-63, asst. to sec. interior, 1963-70; cons. pub. lands to com. interior and insular affairs Ho. of Reps., 1959-60; adminstrv. hearing officer State of Va., 1974—; spl. counsel. Geothermal Resources Internat., Inc., 1975—. Admitted to Va. bar, 1960, D.C. bar, 1970. Served to lt. col. AUS, 1942-46; ETO; col. ret. Mem. Fed. Bar Assn., Civil Affairs Assn. (nat. pres. 1961), Oreg. State Assn. of Washington, Ret. Officers Assn., Phi Beta Kappa. Presbyn. Home: 510 N Edison St Arlington VA 22203

LANDUYT, BERNARD FRANCIS, economist, educator; b. Monmouth, Ill., Mar. 22, 1907; B.Ed., Western Ill. Tchrs. Coll., 1929; A.M., State U. Iowa, 1936, Ph.D., 1938; A.M., Columbia, 1943; LL.D., U. Detroit, 1973; m. Meta Louise Bossong, June 2, 1928. Tchr. pub. schs., 1926-31; tchr., prin., pub. high schs., P.I., 1931-35; instr. State U. Iowa, 1937-38; mem. faculty, dept. econ. and bus. adminstrn. U. Detroit, 1938-71, chmn., 1947-63, prof. econs., 1949-71, chmn. M.B.A. program, 1948-74, asst. dean Coll. Commerce and Finance, 1958-63, dean, 1963-71, dean emeritus, 1971—, distinguished prof. adminstrn., 1974—; ret.; lectr. Nat. Mgmt. Assn., 1960—, CSC, 1958—, div. mgmt. edn. U. Mich., 1969—, Inst. for Career and Personal Devel. Central Mich. U., 1976—, Chrysler Inst., 1976—. Mem. Detroit St. Ry. Commn., 1963-72, pres., 1970-72; mem. Detroit Rapid Transit Commn.; mem. S.E. Mich. Transp. Authority, 1967-72. Served as mil. govt. officer, USNR, 1942-46; mem. fgn. trade sub-commn. Allied Control Commn. for Italy; econ. and agrl. officer U.S. Mil. Govt. Saipan; chief salvage sect. U.S. Mil. Govt. Okinawa; ret. comdr. USNR. Decorated Bronze Star. Mem. Am. Econs. Assn., Assn. Social Econs., Naval Res. Assn., Navy League U.S., U.S. Naval Acad. Found., U.S. Naval Inst., Res. Officers Assn., Alpha Phi Omega, Beta Alpha Psi, Alpha Sigma Lambda, Beta Gamma Sigma, Delta Phi Epsilon, Kappa Delta Pi, Order of Artus. Roman Catholic. Club: Economic (Detroit). Author, lectr. in econs. and mgmt. Co-author Administrative Strategy, 1961; Administrative Strategy and Decision Making, 1966. Home: 19780 Canterbury St Detroit MI 48221

LANDY, DAVID, anthropologist, educator; b. Savannah, Ga., June 4, 1917; s. Charles Edwin and Tillie (Rabinowitz) L.; B.A. in Psychology, U. N.C., 1949, M.A. in Sociology, 1950; Ph.D. in Anthropology, Harvard, 1956; m. Louise Fleming, Mar. 18, 1949; children—Laura, Lisa, Jonathan. Asst. dir. family life project Social Sci. Research Center, U. P.R., 1951-53, instr. social anthropology, 1952; lectr. Sch. Social Work Boston U., 1954-60; research anthropologist, prin. investigator, rehab. project Mass. Mental Health Center, Boston, 1956-60; research asso. anthropology Harvard Med. Sch., 1956-60; asso. prof. anthropology Grad. Sch. Pub. Health U. Pitts., 1960-63, prof., 1963-70, prof. anthropology, chmn. dept. in univ., 1963-70; prof. anthropology, 1970—, chmn. dept. U. Mass.-Boston, 1970-75; mem. adv. council 1st Internat. Council Social Psychiatry, London, Eng., 1964; dir. research project meaning work and mental illness Vocational Rehab. Adminstrn.-HEW, 1961-66; mem. exec. bd. Am. Indian Ethnohistoric Conf., 1964-65; coordinator, field dir. Tri-Instl. Program Anthrop. Field Tng., 1963-69; mem. Manuscripts Adv. Commn. Behavioral Sci., 1970-77. Fellow Am. Anthrop. Assn., A.A.A.S.; mem. Am. Ethnol. Soc., Am. Soc. for Ethnohistory, Soc. Applied Anthropology, Am. Mus. Natural History, Peabody Mus. (Harvard), Soc. for Med. Anthropology (exec. com. 1977-79). Author: Tropical Childhood, 2d edit., 1965; (with M. Greenblatt) Halfway House, 1964; co-author, editor Culture, Disease and Healing: Studies in Medical Anthropology, 1977; also articles, revs. Asso. editor Ethnology, 1961-70; co-editor spl. edit. jour. Social Issues, 1960. Home: 60 Endicott St Newton Highlands MA 02161

LANDY, MAURICE, microbiologist; b. Cleve., Mar. 8, 1913; s. Joseph and Rose (Eisenstein) L.; A.B., Ohio State U., 1934, M.A., 1934, Ph.D., 1940; m. Reba Altman, June 1, 1947. Chief biol. labs. SMA Corp., Cleve., 1936-42; chief dept. bacteriology Wyeth Inst., Phila., 1946-47; head typhoid research unit, chief dept. bacterial immunology Walter Reed Army Inst. Research, 1947-56; head immunology sect. Nat. Cancer Inst., 1956-62; chief lab. immunology Nat. Inst. Allergy and Infectious Diseases NIH, Bethesda, Md., 1962-67, chief allergy and immunology br., 1967-72; staff adviser Schweizerisches Forschunginstitut, Davos, Switzerland, 1973—. Sec. gen. 1st Internat. Congress of Immunology, Washington, 1971. Served to capt., San. Corps, AUS, 1942-46. Recipient Superior Service award HEW, 1966. Mem. Am. Acad. Microbiology, Am. Assn. Immunologists, Soc. Exptl. Biology and Medicine. Editor: (with Werner Braun) Bacterial Endotoxins, 1963, Immunological Tolerance, 1969; (with H. Sherwood Laurence) Mediators of Cellular Immunity, 1969; (with Richard T. Smith) Immune Surveillance, 1970; (with J.W. Uhr) Immunologic Intervention, 1971; (with H.O. McDevitt) Genetic Control of Immune Responsiveness, 1972; (with R.T. Smith) Immunobiology of the Tumor-Host Relationship, 1975; (with G. Cudkowicz) Natural Resistance Systems against Foreign Cells, Tumors, and Microbes, 1978; (with N.A. Mitchison) Manipulation of the Immune Response in Cancer, 1978. Asso. editor Jour. Immunology, Cellular Immunology; adv. editor Academic Press, N.Y.C. and London. Patentee in field. Home: Post Hotel 7270 Davos Switzerland Office: Schweizerisches Forschungsinstitut 7270 Davos Switzerland

LANE, ALVIN HUEY, JR., beverage co. exec.; b. Dallas, May 2, 1942; s. Alvin Huey and Marianne (Halsell) L.; B.A. (Western Electric scholar, J. Venn Leeds scholar), Rice U., Houston, 1964, B.S., 1965; m. Melanie Kadane, June 21, 1963; children—Alvin Huey, III, Michael, Lance, Marianne. Mgmt. positions with Procter & Gamble Mfg. Co., 1965-68; mgmt. cons. Ernst & Ernst, C.P.A.'s, Dallas, 1968-69; v.p. finance, sec. Balanced Investment Dynamics Co., Dallas, 1969-72; v.p. finance, sec. Dr Pepper Co., Dallas, 1972—, also dir. subs.'s; dir. MESBIC Fin. Corp., Dallas. Mem. U.S. Trademark Assn., Nat. Soft Drink Assn., Tex. Mfrs. Assn., Grocery Mfrs. Assn., Tau Beta Pi. Clubs: Lakewood Country, Lancer's. Home: 3415 Colgate St Dallas TX 75225 Office: PO Box 225086 Dallas TX 75265

LANE, ALVIN SEYMOUR, lawyer; b. Englewood, N.J., June 17, 1918; s. Martin Lane and Nettie (Gans) Daniels; Ph.B., U. Wis., 1940; LL.B., Harvard, 1947; m. Terese P. Lyons, Apr. 24, 1949; children—Mary-Jo, Judith Lyons. Admitted to N.Y. bar, 1947, since practiced in N.Y.C.; sr. partner firm Wien, Lane & Malkin. Chmn. Rapidata, Inc. Mem. adv. bd. to N.Y. atty. gen. on art legislation, 1966-71. Mem. bd. mgmt. Henry Ittleson Research Center Disturbed Children, Riverdale, N.Y., 1961-70; fellow Brandeis U., 1966—; sec., trustee Aldrich Mus. Contemporary Art, Inc., 1969-76; trustee Lexington Sch. Deaf, 1971; v.p., trustee Soho Center Visual Artists, Inc., 1974—. Served to lt. USNR, 1942-46. Mem. Assn. Bar City N.Y. (chmn. com. art 1963-65), Am. Bar Assn., N.Y. County Lawyers Assn. Club: Harvard (N.Y.C.). Contbr. articles to art publs. and legal jours. Home: 5251 Independence Ave Riverdale NY 10471 Office: 60 E 42d St New York City NY 10017

LANE, ARTHUR STEPHEN, lawyer; b. Arlington, Mass., Dec. 26, 1910; s. John J. and Catherine (Scannell) L.; grad. Exeter Acad., 1930; B.A., Princeton, 1934; LL.B., Harvard, 1937; m. Sally Kerney Kuser, May 24, 1947; children—Sally, Arthur Stephen, Mark, Cathy, Henry, Mary, Teresa. Law sec. N.J. vice chancellor, 1937-39; admitted to N.J. bar, 1939; asst. pros., Mercer County, 1946-56; partner Minton, Dinsmore & Lane, Trenton, 1946-56; judge Mercer County Ct., 1956-60, U.S. Dist. Ct., 1960-67; v.p., gen. counsel Johnson & Johnson, New Brunswick, N.J., 1967—, also dir.; partner firm Smith, Stratton, Wise & Heher, Princeton, N.J., 1976—; mem. N.J. State Commn. of Investigation, 1977—, N.J. Supreme Ct. Bd. Disciplinary Rev., 1978; spl. counsel CBS, 1977-78, I.U. Internat., 1978; dir. Trenton Times Newspapers. Pres. George Washington council Boy Scouts Am., mem. regional exec. com. Candidate N.J. Senate, 1953. Mem. Ad Hoc Com. for Creation Fed. Jud. Center; adv. com. Nat. Center State Cts. Bd. dirs. N.J. Children's Home Soc.; chmn. Nat. Council Crime and Delinquency; alumni trustee Princeton; trustee Princeton Country Day Sch. Served with USNR, 1941-46; capt. Res. Named mem. Sport's Illustrated Silver Anniversary Football Team. Mem. N.J., Mercer County, Am. bar assns., Alumni Assn. Exeter Acad. (exec. com.). Republican. Home: Pleasant Valley Rd Titusville NJ 08560 Office: 1 Palmer Sq Princeton NJ 08540

LANE, BERNARD BELL, furniture co. exec.; b. Lynchburg, Va., Nov. 23, 1928; s. Edward Hudson and Myrtle Clyde (Bell) L.; B.S., U.S. Naval Acad., 1950; m. Minnie Matthews Bassett, June 7, 1950; children—William R., Lucy H., Douglas B., Bernard Bell. With Lane Co., Altavista, Va., 1954—, v.p., then exec. v.p., 1960-76, pres., chmn. exec. com., 1976—, dir., 1956—. Bd. dirs. Va. Poly. Inst. and State U. Ednl. Found., 1968—; mem. Gov. Va. Adv. Bd. Indsl. Devel., 1970—, Gov. Va. Adv. Bd. Revenue Estimates, 1977—; chmn. com. urol. research, endowment and devel. Duke U. Med. Center, 1974—. Served as officer USAF, 1950-53. Methodist. Home: 302 Myrtle Ln Altavista VA 24517

LANE, BURTON (BURTON LEVY), composer; b. N.Y.C., Feb. 2, 1912; s. Lazarus and Frances Levy; student High Sch. of Commerce; studied piano with Simon Bucharoff 2 years; m. Marion Seaman, June 28, 1935 (div. 1961); 1 dau.; m. 2d, Lynn Daroff Kaye, Mar. 5, 1961. Former staff composer for Remick Music Pub.; wrote music for 2 songs in Three's a Crowd, 1930, 1 song in Third Little Word, 1931, entire score for 9th edit. Earl Carroll's Vanities, 1931, 2 songs in Singin' the Blues, 1931, 1 song in You're Not Pretty But You're Mine, 1932 for Americana; composed mus. scores for Hold on to Your Hats, 1940, Laffing Room Only, 1944, Finian's Rainbow, 1947, On a Clear Day You Can See Forever (Tony nomination, Grammy award); songs for motion pictures including Dancing Lady, 1933, including Everything I Have Is Yours, scores for Babes on Broadway, 1941, Royal Wedding, 1951, Give a Girl a Break, 1953, On a Clear Day You Can See Forever, 1966, Carmelina (with J. Lerner and J. Stein), 1979, animated film Heidi, 1979; composer music for Junior Miss, TV, 1958; songs include: Everything I Have Is Yours, How About You, Old Devil Moon, On a Clear Day You Can See Forever, How Could You Believe Me When I Said I Love You When You Know I've Been a Liar All My Life. Recipient 2 Acad. award nominations; award for Finian's Rainbow, Essex Symphony Soc., 1947. Mem. A.S.C.A.P. (10th term pres. 1957-67), Am. Guild Authors and Composers (Sigmund Romberg award), Songwriters Hall of Fame (dir.).

LANE, CHARLES AUGUSTINE, ins. co. exec.; b. N.Y.C., May 28, 1915; s. Jeremiah Joseph and Mary Frances (Tierney) L.; student N.Y. U., 1934-35; m. Margaretta Willett Connell, Apr. 24, 1939; 1 son, Charles A. Vice pres. Vigilant Ins. Co.; sr. v.p. Fed. Ins. Co.; pres. Pacific Indemnity Co., Los Angeles, also dir.; dir., pres. N.W. Pacific Indemnity Co.; dir. Tex. Pacific Indemnity Co., Chubb & Son Inc. Served with Armed Forces, World War II. Mem. Calif. Assn. Ins. Cos. (dir.), Pacific Ins. and Surety Conf. (pres.). Club: Los Angeles Country. Home: 1559 Club View Dr Los Angeles CA 90024 Office: 3200 Wilshire Blvd Los Angeles CA 90010

LANE, CHARLES WILLIAM, III, lawyer; b. Shreveport, La., Nov. 11, 1932; s. Charles William and Frances Duncan Conrad (Bailey) L.; B.B.A., Tulane U., 1954, LL.B., 1959; m. Shirley Lou Henderson, Aug. 18, 1957; children—Laura Frances, Susan Henderson, Charles William, IV. Admitted to La. bar, 1959, U.S. Supreme Ct. bar, 1964, other fed. bars; asso. firm Jones, Walker, Waechter, Poitevent, Carrere and Denegre, New Orleans, 1959-63, partner, 1964—, sr. partner, 1978—. Bd. dirs. Internat. House, New Orleans, 1977—. Served with USAF, 1955-58. Mem. Am. Bar Assn., La. Bar Assn., Am. Law Inst. Episcopalian. Clubs: Boston, Pickwick, Statford, New Orleans Country. Home: 103 Homestead Ave Metairie LA 70005 Office: 225 Baronne St New Orleans LA 70112

LANE, DAVID OLIVER, librarian; b. Flint, Mich., Oct. 17, 1931; s. Clinton Ellis and Mary Ailene (Sanders) L.; B.A., U. Mich., 1958, A.M. in L.S., 1959; doctoral fellow U. Chgo., 1968. Various library assignments, 1959-63; asst. dir. libraries Boston U., 1963-67; asst. univ. librarian U. Calif., San Diego, 1968-69; chief librarian, prof., dept. chmn. Hunter Coll., N.Y.C., 1969—. Dir. NSF funded study of library acquisitions, 1967-68; chmn. Council Chief Librarians, City U. N.Y., 1972-75; trustee N.Y. Met. Reference Library Agy., 1978—. Mem. A.L.A. (life), Assn. Coll. and Research Libraries, Beta Phi Mu. Club: Grolier. Author: Study of the Decision Making Procedures for the Acquisition of Science Library Materials, 1968. Home: 27D East

Hill Dr Somers NY 10589 Office: 695 Park Ave New York City NY 10021

LANE, EDWARD ELIOT, motion picture exec.; b. Boston, Aug. 12, 1911; s. Samuel and Rose (Kastenbaum) L.; A.B. cum laude, Harvard, 1933; postgrad. Coll. Bus. Adminstrn., Boston U., 1930-32, U. Calif. at Los Angeles, 1947-48; m. Louise Barbara Bertman, July 15, 1960 (div. June 1967); m. Beatrice Ruderman, June 15, 1975; 1 son by previous marriage, Eric J. Asst. to controller McCrory Stores Corp., N.Y.C., 1937-41; asst. controller John Irving Shoe Corp., Boston, 1941-42; spl. accountant Bulllocks's, Inc., Los Angeles, 1947-48; controller Gen. Cinema Corp., Boston, 1949—, treas., 1963—, fin. v.p., 1974-76, cons., 1976—, dir., 1968—; treas., dir. Smith Mgmt. Co., Boston, 1961—. Served to lt. comdr. USNR, 1942-46. Clubs: Newton (Mass.) Squash and Tennis, Emerald Hills Country, New Seabury Country. Home: 115 Tweedbrook Ln Hollywood FL 33021 Office: 27 Boylston St Chestnut Hill MA 02167

LANE, EDWARD WOOD, JR., banker; b. Jacksonville, Fla., Apr. 4, 1911; s. Edward Wood and Anna Virginia (Taliaferro) L.; A.B., Princeton, 1933; LL.B., Harvard U., 1936; m. Helen Spratt Murchison, Oct. 16, 1948; children—Edward Wood III, Helen Palmer, Anna Taliaferro, Charles Murchison. Admitted to Fla. bar, 1936; partner firm McCarthy, Lane & Adams, and predecessors, Jacksonville, 1941-60; pres. Atlantic Nat. Bank, Jacksonville, 1961-74, now dir.; chmn. Atlantic Bancorp.; dir. Fla. Pub. Co. Trustee Cummer Mus. Found. Served to lt. comdr. USNR, World War II. Mem. Jacksonville Area C. of C. (com. of 100), Phi Beta Kappa. Clubs: Florida Yacht, Timuquana Country, River, Univ. (Jacksonville); Ponte Vedra; Sawgrass. Home: 3790 Ortega Blvd Jacksonville FL 32210 Office: Atlantic Nat Bank General Mail Center Jacksonville FL 32203

LANE, GEORGE M., ambassador; b. Balt., Oct. 15, 1928; B.A., Cornell U., 1951; M.A., Fletcher Sch. Law and Diplomacy, 1957. Commd. fgn. ser. officer Dept. State, 1957; internat. relations officer, Beirut, Jidda, Aleppo, Rabat, Benghazi; personnel officer Dept. State, Washington, 1970-72, internat. relations officer, 1972-73; dep. dir., then acting dir. Office of N. African affairs, 1973-74, dep. chief of mission, Mbabane, 1974-76; dep. chief mission, Beirut, Lebanon, 1976-78; Am. ambassador to Yemen, Sana, Yemen Arab Republic, 1978—. Office: American Embassy Box 33 Sana Yeman Arab Republic

LANE, HAROLD EDWIN, educator, mgmt. cons.; b. Malden, Mass., Aug. 19, 1913; s. Edwin George and Annabel (Fraser) L.; B.S., Boston U., 1936, M.A., 1940; m. Constance Mason, June 1, 1940; children—Stephen Winslow, Harold Edwin, Nancy (Mrs. John H. Piper). Asst. sec. Greater Boston Community Fund, 1940-42; sr. economist Nat. War Labor Bd., Boston, also Portland, Oreg., 1943-46; dir. personnel Sordoni Industries, Wilkes-Barre, Pa., 1946-47; dir. personnel and labor relations Sheraton Corp. Am., Boston, 1947-54, v.p., 1954-68; mgmt. cons., 1968-69; v.p. Fred Harvey, Inc., Chgo., 1969-70; asso. prof. Bus. Coll. Mich. State U., East Lansing, 1970-78, prof., 1978—; summer sch. instr. Cornell U., 1949-67; spl. lectr. Harvard. Mem. Pres.'s Adv. Com. on Occupational Safety; mem. Council on Pres.'s Plans for Progress; nat. adv. com. Job Corps, Office Econ. Opportunity; chmn. Wage Deviation Bd. State Mich., 1974—; participant seminar Harvard Bus. Sch., 1963; cons. Ford Found. N.Y., 1963; seminar instr. Am. Mgmt. Assn., 1964. Mem. Soc. Advancement Mgmt., Am. Mgmt. Assn., Am. Sociol. Assn., Indsl. Relations Research Assn., Soc. Profls. in Dispute Resolution, Am. Hotel and Motel Assn., Council on Hotel, Restaurant and Instnl. Edn., AAUP, Friends East-West Center Honolulu, The Conf. Bd., U.S. C. of C. Conglist. Contbr. articles to profl. jours. Home: 4382 Okemos Rd Apt 216 G Okemos MI 48864 Office: 416 Eppley Center Coll Bus Mich State U East Lansing MI 48823

LANE, HOMER LOGAN, broadcasting co. exec.; b. Bklyn., June 21, 1923; s. Homer Logan and Mabel (Parker) L.; student Broadcast Mgmt. Devel. Seminar Harvard U., 1960; m. Doris Lanoue, Dec. 5, 1943; children—Barbara Lane Everett, Steven Homer, Mary Alice Cordalis, Thomas Harvey. Asst. supt. supt. network ops. CBS, N.Y.C., 1944-46; program dir. Sta.-KMHL, Marshall, Minn., 1946-51; v.p., gen. mgr. Kool Radio-TV Inc., Phoenix, 1951—, dir., 1967—, exec. v.p., 1972—; chmn. Met. Phoenix unit Radio Free Europe; mem. communications curriculum com. Maricopa County Jr. Coll. Dist., 1973—. Chmn. N.Mex. Gov.'s Com. on Employment of Handicapped, 1967—; mem. Mayor's Commn. Action Against Crime, 1967; planning com. Fund-raising banquet City of Hope, 1968; mem. Ariz. Gov.'s Commn. Energy Ariz. Industry Advisory Com.; exec. trustee TARPAC; Environment Growth, 1974—; chmn. broadcast services subcom. mem. Supreme Ct. Advisory Com. Lower Ct. Reorgn.; bd. dirs. Ariz. Acad.; mem. Phoenix Sister City Commn., 1972—. Recipient Abe Lincoln Merit award, 1972. Mem. Ariz. Broadcasters Assn. (pres. 1964), Broadcast Pioneers, Met. Phoenix Broadcasters Assn. (v.p. 1963-64), Nat. Broadcast Editorial Assn., Nat. Acad. TV Arts, Scis., Phoenix Press Club, Air Force Assn., Ariz. League United Latin Am. Citizens, Sales Mktg. Execs. Phoenix, Aircraft Owners Pilots Assn., Nat. Pilots Assn., Newcomen Soc., Sigma Delta Chi, Pi Sigma Epsilon. Clubs: Ariz. Country, Ariz. Press, Rotary. Home: 3839 E Whitton St Phoenix AZ 85018 Office: 511 W Adams St Phoenix AZ 85003

LANE, HOWARD RAYMOND, architect; b. Chgo., Oct. 13, 1922; s. Mose and Libbie (Sax) L.; student Carnegie Inst. Tech., 1943-44, Archtl. Assn. Sch., London, 1946; B.S. in Architecture, Ill. Inst. Tech., 1947; m. Shirley Robbins, June 14, 1947; children—Rod, Laura, Barbara. Asso., Skidmore, Owings & Merrill, Chgo., 1947, Allison & Rible, Architects, Los Angeles, 1948, A.C. Martin & Assos., 1949, Robert Alexander, 1949, Pereira & Luckman, 1950-53; pvt. practice architecture, Encino, Calif., 1953-79, Woodland Hills, Calif., 1979—; pres. Howard R. Lane Assos., 1953—. Founder, co-chmn. Valley Round Table Council, 1968-69. Served with U.S. Army, 1943-47. Fellow AIA (pres. Calif. council 1977, pres. So. Calif. chpt. 1974, vice-chmn. nat. energy com. 1979, chmn. designate 1980); mem. Nat. Council Archtl. Registration Bds., Encino C. of C. (past pres.). Office: 6150 Canoga Ave Suite 114 Woodland Hills CA 91367. *Nothing is more gratifying than creating, formulating and directing the opportunities and restrictions of aesthetics, engineering, economy, industry, and environment to bring to fruition a structure that fulfills a need for a community, business, government, or individual. Seeing a school, hospital, or office building successfully occupied and functioning, makes all the effort and occasional frustrations worth while.*

LANE, JAMES FRANKLIN, judge; b. Chattanooga, Mar. 4, 1931; s. Frank Scott and Thelma (Vickers) L.; B.A., Okla. Bapt. U., 1952; LL.B., U. Okla., 1954; m. Josephine Oleta Rennels, Jan. 26, 1954; children—James Nelson, Jeffrey Brian, Jerry Frank, Joe Creekmore. Admitted to Okla. bar, 1954; county atty. Beaver County, Okla., 1957-61; mem. firm Lane & Sharp, 1961-65; county judge Beaver County, 1964-69; asso. dist. judge 1st Jud. Dist. Okla., Beaver, 1969—. Mem. Beaver County Democratic Party Central Com., 1959-64. Bd. dirs. Beaver Med. Center, Inc.; bd. dirs., pres. Beaver County United Fund. Served with AUS, 1954-56. Mem. Okla., Panhandle, Beaver County (pres.) bar assns., Okla. Jud. Conf., Am. Judicature Soc., Beaver C. of C. Club: Beaver Golf (pres. 1964-65). Address: Box 609 Beaver OK 73932

LANE, JAMES GARLAND, JR., diversified co. exec.; b. Roxobel, N.C., Jan. 15, 1934; s. James Garland and Josie (Wembrow) L.; B.S., U. N.C., 1959; m. Janet Benthall Miller, Oct. 7, 1954; children—Bernice, Frances, Garland, Amy. Mem. audit staff S.D. Leidesdorf & Co., Greenville, S.C., 1959-65; v.p. finance Computer Servicenters, Inc., Greenville, 1965-68; exec. v.p., dir. Synalloy Corp., Spartanburg, S.C., 1968-73; pres. dir. Hewitt, Coleman & Assos., Greenville, 1973—. Served with USMCR, 1953-56. Home: 36 Sagamore Ln Greenville SC 29607 Office: Hewitt Coleman & Assos Greenville SC 29607

LANE, JAMES MCCONKEY, investment exec.; b. Pitts., July 9, 1929; s. Mortimer Bliss and Mary (Knapp) L.; B.A., Wheaton (Ill.) Coll., 1952; M.B.A., U. Chgo., 1953; postgrad. N.Y. U., 1956, U. Buffalo, 1960; m. Arlyne Ruth Nelson, Dec. 16, 1950; children—James, Theodore, Thomas, Karen, David. Credit corr. John Plain & Co., Chgo., 1951; trainee Chase Manhattan Bank, N.Y.C., 1953-55, account mgmt., mem. staff investment adv. div., 1955-59, investment officer, 1959-62, 2d v.p., 1962-64, v.p., mgr. corporate pension trust investments, 1964-66, v.p. div. exec. pension trust investment div., 1966-68, chmn. investment policy com., 1968-78, sr. v.p., investment group exec., 1968-70, exec. v.p. fiduciary investment dept., 1970-78; pres., dir. Chase Investors Mgmt. Corp., 1972-78; mng. dir. C.J. Lawrence Mgmt., N.Y.C., 1978—; dir. Cyrus J. Lawrence Inc.; dir. Capital Internat. S.A., 1972-77, Rockefeller Center, Inc., 1969-78. Bd. dirs. World Impact, Pocket Testament League Inc., Christian Camps Inc.; bd. dirs. Youth Devel., Inc., N.Y.C., 1970-75; trustee Wheaton Coll.; gov. Northeastern Bible Coll. Mem. Am. Finance Assn., N.Y. Soc. Security Analysts. Clubs: City Midday (N.Y.C.); Minisink (Chatham). Home: 105 Coleman Ave Chatham NJ 07928 Office: 115 Broadway New York NY 10006

LANE, JOHN DENNIS, lawyer; b. Norwalk, Conn., Nov. 23, 1921; s. John J. and Theresa A. (Donnelly) L.; B.S., Georgetown U., 1943, J.D., 1948; m. Elizabeth J. Galliher, Apr. 28, 1949; children—Elizabeth J., John Dennis, Margaret A., Robert E., Paul G. Admitted to D.C. bar, 1948, Conn. bar, 1950; atty. Office Chief Counsel, Bur. Internal Revenue, Washington, 1948-49; exec. sec. to U.S. Senator Brien McMahon, 1949-50; adminstrv. asst., 1950-52; pvt. practice, Washington and Norwalk, 1953—; partner firm Hedrick & Lane, 1954—. Mem. council Adminstrv. Conf. U.S., 1961; bd. regents Georgetown U., 1979—. Served to capt. USMCR, 1943-45. Recipient Citation of Merit. Fellow Am. Bar Found.; mem. Am. Bar Assn. (chmn. standing com. unauthorized practice of law 1971-73, chmn. standing com. nat. conf. groups 1973-75). Clubs: Met., Army and Navy (Washington); Columbia Country (Chevy Chase, Md.). Home: 5045 Van Ness St NW Washington DC 20016 Office: 1211 Connecticut Ave NW Washington DC 20036 also River St Plaza Norwalk CT 06852

LANE, JOHN MICHAEL, med. epidemiologist; b. Cambridge, Mass., Feb. 14, 1936; s. Alfred Gustavus Baker and Eileen Brenda (O'Connor) Lewis; B.A., Yale U., 1957; M.D., Harvard U., 1961; M.P.H., U. Calif., Berkeley, 1967; m. Carolina Hernandez, Sept. 19, 1969. Fellow, Mallory Inst., Harvard U., 1961; intern Bellevue Hosp., N.Y. U., 1962; med. officer USPHS, 1963—, resident Epidemic Intelligence Service, Center for Disease Control, Atlanta, 1963-65, epidemiologist smallpox eradication program, 1966-70, asst. dir. Bur. State Services, 1971-73, dir. Bur. Smallpox Eradication, 1974—; asso. prof. epidemiology U. Calif., Berkeley, 1970; asso. prof. preventive medicine Emory U. Med. Sch., 1971—; cons. WHO, Am. Acad. Pediatrics. Chmn. Atlanta Coalition on Transp. Crisis, 1972-74. Decorated Surg. Gen.'s Commendation medal. Mem. AMA, Am. Pub. Health Assn., Phi Beta Kappa. Author: Complications of Smallpox Vaccination, 1970; Routine Childhood Vaccination Against Smallpox Reconsidered, 1970; Smallpox and Smallpox Vaccination Policy, 1971. Home: 869 Clifton Rd NE Atlanta GA 30307 Office: 1600 Clifton Rd NE Atlanta GA 30333

LANE, KENNETH EDWIN, advt. agy. exec.; b. Orange, N.J., Sept. 30, 1928; s. Clarence Edwin and Erma Catherine (Kinser) L.; B.A., U. Chgo., 1947, M.A., 1950; m. Georgia Wilcoxon, Aug. 2, 1952 (div.); children—Kenneth, Laura, Linda, Katherine. Mgr. media Toni div. Gillette Co., 1953-63; media dir. MacParland-Aveyard Co., 1963-64; asso. media dir. Leo Burnett Co., Chgo., 1964-71, mgr. media dept., 1971-75, sr. v.p. media services, 1975—; bd. dirs. Traffic Audit Bur. Mem. Am. Assn. Advt. Agys., Media Dirs. Council. Home: 400 E Randolph St Chicago IL 60601 Office: Leo Burnett Agy Prudential Plaza Chicago IL 60601

LANE, KENNETH JAY, designer; b. Detroit, Apr. 22, 1932; s. Mack and Beatrice (Holinstat) L.; student U. Mich., 1951-52; B.F.A., R.I. Sch. Design, 1954. Mem. mdse. art staff Vogue, 1954-55; asst. designer Delman Shoes, N.Y.C., 1956-58; asso. designer Christian Dior Shoes, N.Y.C., 1958-63; owner Kenneth Jay Lane, Inc., N.Y.C., 1963—. Recipient Coty award, 1967, Harpers Bazaar Internat. award, 1967, Maramodo di Capri Tiberio D'oro award, 1967, Tobe Coburn Award-Spl. Swarowski award, 1967, Neiman Marcus award, 1968. Home: 23 Park Ave New York NY 10016 Office: 20 W 37th St New York NY 10018

LANE, LAURENCE WILLIAM, JR., publisher; b. Des Moines, Nov. 7, 1919; s. Laurence William and Ruth (Bell) L.; student Pomona Coll., 1938-40, LL.D. (hon.); B.J., Stanford U., 1942; m. Donna Jean Gimbel, Apr. 16, 1955; children—Sharon Louise, Robert Laurence, Brenda Ruth. With Lane Pub. Co., publisher Sunset Mag. and books, also producer Sunset Films, Menlo Park, Calif., 1930—, chmn. bd., 1974—; dir. Calif. Water Service Co., Crown Zellerbach Corp. Mem. adv. bd. Sec. Interior's Bd. Nat. Parks; mem. adv. council Grad. Sch. Bus., Stanford U.; former ambassador U.S. Dept. State; mem. Pacific Basin Econ. Council; trustee Colonial Williamsburg Found. Served to lt. USNR, World War II; PTO. Recipient Conservation Service award Sec. Interior. Fellow Coll. of Notre Dame; mem. Newcomen Soc. N.Am., Alaska Bus. Council, Pacific Area Travel Assn. (life; chmn. 1980—), Japan-Calif. Assn., Los Rancheros Vistadores, Advt. Club San Francisco, No. Calif. Alumni Assn., Alpha Delta Sigma. Republican. Presbyterian. Clubs: Bohemian, Pacific Union (San Francisco); Men's Garden (Los Angeles). Home: 880 Westridge Dr Portola Valley CA 94025 Office: Middlefield and Willow Rds Menlo Park CA 94025

LANE, LOUIS, musician, conductor; b. Eagle Pass, Tex., Dec. 25, 1923; s. William Bartlett and Virginia (Gardner) L.; B.Mus. summa cum laude, U. Tex., 1943; Mus.M., Eastman Sch. Music, 1947; Mus.D. (hon.), Akron U., 1973, Cleve. State U., 1974. Mem. Cleve. Orch., 1947-73, asso. condr., 1960-70, resident condr., 1970-73; condr. Akron (Ohio) Symphony Orch., 1959—; prin. guest condr. Dallas Symphony Orch., 1973-78; co-condr. Atlanta Symphony Orch., 1977—; guest condr. in Chgo., Seattle, St. Louis, Detroit, Houston, San Antonio, Vancouver, B.C., Can., Montevideo, Uruguay, Warsaw, Poland, Johannesburg, S.Africa, Helsinki, Finland; mus. dir. Lake Erie Opera Theatre, Cleve., 1964-72; co-dir. Blossom Festival Sch. of Cleve. Orch. and Kent State U., 1969-73; adj. prof. music Akron U., 1969—; vis. prof. music U. Cin., 1973-75; rec. artist for Columbia Records. Served with F.A., AUS, 1943-46. Recipient Mahler medal, 1971; Ditson award Columbia, 1972. Mem. Phi Mu Alpha, Pi Kappa Lambda. Home: 1325 Peachtree St NE Atlanta GA 30309 Office: Thomas Hall Hill and Center Sts Akron OH 44325

LANE, LYLE FRANKLIN, ambassador; b. Tacoma, Sept. 19, 1926; s. Lyle L. and Dorothy (Mahler) L.; B.A. magna cum laude, U. Wash., 1950; M.S.I.A., George Washington U., 1969; m. Jaclyn Fuller, Sept. 8, 1950; children—Thomas Grant, Timothy Fuller, Christopher Drew. Joined Fgn. Service, 1952; served in Guyaquil, Ecuador and Madrid, 1955-59, Washington, 1959-61; assigned to U. Calif., Berkeley, 1961-62; prin. officer, Cebu, Philippines, 1962-66; regional officer for Central Am. and Panama in Guatemala, 1966-68; assigned to Naval War Coll., 1968-69, Dept. State, Washington, 1969-73; dep. chief of mission, San Jose, Costa Rica, 1973-76, Lima, Peru, 1976-77; chief U.S. interests sect., Havana, Cuba, 1977-79; ambassador to Uruguay, 1979—. Served with U.S. Army, 1945-46; PTO. Mem. Fgn. Service Assn., Phi Beta Kappa. Home: Tacoma WA Office: Am Embassy Uruguay APO Miami FL 34035

LANE, MARK, lawyer, educator, author; b. N.Y.C., Feb. 24, 1927; s. Harry Arnold and Elizabeth (Brown) L.; LL.B., Bklyn. Law Sch., 1951; m. Anne-Lise Dabelsteen, Dec. 23, 1966; children—Anne-Marie, Christina. Admitted to N.Y. bar, 1951; practiced in N.Y.C., 1952-62; founder Mid-Harlem Community Parish Narcotics Clinic, 1953, East Harlem Reform Democratic Club, 1959; prof. law Catholic U., Washington, 1975—; mem. firm Ferguson & Lane, 1979—; dir. Citizens Commn. Inquiry, 1975—; founder Wounded Knee Legal Def.-Offense Com., 1973; founder The Covered Wagon, Mountain Home, Idaho, 1971; mem. N.Y. State Assembly, 1960-62. Served with AUS, 1945-47. Author: Rush to Judgment, 1966; A Citizens Dissent, 1968; Chicago Eye-Witness, 1969; Arcadia, 1970; Conversations with Americans, 1970; Executive Action, 1973; (with Dick Gregory) Code Name Zorro, 1977; The Strongest Poison, 1980; producer film (with Emile de Antonio) Rush to Judgment, 1967. Founder publs. Citizens Quar., 1975, Helping Hand, 1971. Home and office: 1177 Central Ave Memphis TN 38104. *I do not believe that our fate is pre-ordained. I do believe that women and men, working together, can determine their own destiny and that the people write their own history. What moves me most directly into action is the fact that I hate bullies. What concerns me the most in contemporary America is the influence of the police and spy organizations with the national news media. Together these are bullies to contemplate and oppose.*

LANE, MONTAGUE, physician, educator; b. N.Y.C., Aug. 28, 1929; s. George and Ida (Korn) L.; B.A., N.Y. U., 1947; M.B., Chgo. Med. Sch., 1952, M.D., 1953; M.S., Georgetown U., 1957; m. Carol Higley, June 30, 1957; children—Laura Diane, Adam Reuben. Clin. asso. Nat. Cancer Inst., NIH, 1954-56, sr. investigator Clin. Pharmacology and Exptl. Therapeutics Service, attending physician gen. med. br. Nat. Cancer Inst., 1957-60; asso. in medicine George Washington U., Med. Sch., 1957-60; asst. prof., asso. prof. depts. pharmacology and medicine Baylor U. Coll. Medicine, Houston, 1960-67; prof. depts. pharm. and medicine Baylor Coll. Medicine, 1967—, head div. clin. oncology dept. pharmacology, 1969—, head sect. med. oncology dept. medicine, 1961—. Mem. study sect. Nat. Cancer Inst., 1966-69, mem. cancer clin. investigations rev. com., 1972-75; chmn. new agts. com. S.W. Cancer Chemotherapy study group; cons. drug evaluations AMA, cons. Merck Manual; external adv. bd. Howard U. Cancer Center, 1977—. Diplomate Am. Bd. Internal Medicine (mem. subcom. on med. oncology 1974—). Named Disting. Alumnus, Chgo. Med. Sch., 1971. Fellow A.C.P.; mem. Am. Inst. Nutrition, Am. Soc. Clin. Oncology (program chmn. 1970), Am. Soc. Pharmacology and Exptl. Therapeutics (pres. 1971-72), Am. Soc. Hematology, Houston Soc. Internal Medicine (v.p. 1973-74), Am. Assn. Cancer Research, Harris County Med. Soc. Asso. editor Cancer Research, 1970—. Home: 1514 Bissonnet St Houston TX 77005 Office: 1200 Moursund Houston TX 77030

LANE, NANCY, editor; b. N.Y.C., Dec. 20, 1938; d. Morton and Lillian (Gelb) Lane; A.B. in Am. Civilization, Barnard Coll., 1960. Mem. staff N.Y. Times, 1959-61; asst. to mng. editor Polit. Sci. Quar., Columbia, N.Y.C., 1962-64, asst. editor, 1965-66, asso. editor, 1967-70, asst. to mng. editor Procs. Acad. Polit. Sci., 1962-64, asst. editor, 1965-66, asso. editor, 1967; asso. editor Am. Hist. Rev., Am. Hist. Assn., Washington, 1970-72, mng. editor, 1973-74; editor Oxford U. Press, N.Y.C., 1974—. Mem. Am. Hist. Assn., Orgn. Am. Historians. Home: 45 W 10th St New York NY 10011 Office: Oxford U Press 200 Madison Ave New York NY 10016

LANE, NEWTON ALEXANDER, lawyer; b. Boston, June 16, 1915; s. Samuel B. and Eva (Robbins) L.; A.B magna cum laude, Harvard, 1936, LL.B., 1939; Admitted to Mass. bar, 1939, since practiced in Boston; clk. to chief justice Mass. Supreme Ct., 1939-40; asst. atty. gen. Mass., 1941-42; individual practice, 1946—; asst. in math. Harvard. Dir. Zayre Corp. Served with AUS, 1942-46. Mem. Harvard Legal Aid Bur., Phi Beta Kappa. Home: 704 Dedham St Newton MA 02159 Office: 201 Devonshire St Boston MA 02110

LANE, PATRICK, poet; b. Nelson, B.C., Can., Mar. 26, 1939; s. A.S. and E.M. Lane; grad. high sch., Vernon, B.C.; children—Mark Hayden, Christopher Patrick, Kathryn Mary, Michael John, Richard Patrick. Tchr. creative writing course Notre Dame Coll., 1975; writer-in-residence U. Man., 1978-79, U. Ottawa, 1980; author: Letters From the Savage Mind, 1966, Separations, 1968, On The Street, 1969, Mountain Oysters, 1970, Hiway 401 Rhapsody, 1971, The Sun Has Begun to Eat The Mountain, 1972, Passing Into Storm, 1973, Beware The Months Of Fire, 1974, Unborn Things, 1975, Poems—New and Selected, 1978, (with Lorna Uher) No Longer Two People, 1979, There Are Still The Mountains, 1979, The Measure, 1980; contbr. to anthologies. Recipient Poetry award York U., 1971; Gov.-Gen.'s award, 1978; Can. Council jr. arts grantee, 1967, 70, sr. arts grantee, 1973, 76; Ont. Arts Council grantee, 1974, 78; Man. Arts Council sr. arts grantee, 1979. Mem. League Can. Poets. Office: care Dept English U Ottawa Ottawa ON Canada

LANE, RALPH, JR., educator; b. N.Y.C., May 8, 1923; s. Ralph and Mildred (Thompson) L.; A.B., Columbia, 1946, M.A., 1947; Ph.D., Fordham U., 1954; m. Joan Solari, June 28, 1958; children—Margaret A., Ralph III. Instr. sociology Fordham U., 1948-55; lectr. sociology Manhattan Coll., 1949-50; cultural affairs officer Am. embassy, Kabul, Afghanistan, 1955-58; mem. faculty U. San Francisco, 1958—, prof. sociology, 1967—, chmn. dept., 1961-70. Served with AUS, 1943-46. Mem. Am. Cath. Sociol. Soc. (pres. 1970-71), Am. Sociol. Assn., Assn. for Sociology of Religion. Home: 1230 23d Ave San Francisco CA 94122

LANE, REMBRANDT PEALE, corp. exec.; b. Washington, Oct. 11, 1927; s. Rembrandt Peale and Mabel Audrey (Herron) L.; B.A., Duke U., 1950; M.B.A., N.Y. U., 1953; m. Shirley Grace Meecham, Nov. 15, 1975; children—Russell F., Linda J. Asst. treas. Chase Manhattan Bank, N.Y.C., 1950-57; v.p. fin. and treas. N.E. Airlines, Boston, 1957-63; v.p. fin., dir. N.Am. Car Corp., Chgo., 1963-67; v.p. fin., dir. Rohr Industries, Inc., Chula Vista, Calif., 1967-71; exec. v.p., dir. Larwin Group, Beverly Hills, Calif., 1971-73; sr. v.p. adminstrn. and fin. Republic Corp., Los Angeles, 1973—, also dir.; dir. Butler

Aviation Co., 1964-68. Bd. dirs. San Diego Opera Co., 1967-71. Served with U.S. Army, 1945-47. Mem. Fin. Execs. Inst., Phi Beta Kappa. Republican. Club: Los Angeles Country. Office: 1900 Ave of the Stars Los Angeles CA 90067

LANE, RICHARD N., acoustical cons.; b. Eagle Pass, Tex., Feb. 6, 1919; s. William Bartlett and Virginia (Gardner) L.; B.A., U. Tex., Austin, 1940, M.A., 1941; m. Estelle Speed, Apr. 5, 1942; children—William B., Martha, Richard N., Laura. Acoustical engr. RCA, 1941; research asso. Underwater Sound Lab., Harvard, 1941-42; project engr. sonar sect. RCA, 1942-46; project physicist Def. Research Lab., U. Tex. at Austin, 1946-48, asst. dir., also charge acoustics div., 1950-57; mgr. airborne magnetic surveys sect. Edgar Tobin Aerial Surveys, San Antonio, 1948-49; cons. acoustics, 1950—; pres. Tracor, Inc., Austin, 1955-70, chmn. bd., 1955-72; chmn. bd. TCC, Inc. Austin, 1972—; dir. Data Disc, Inc., Am. First Corp.; pres. Lamac Environments, Inc., Austin, 1972-74; tech. dir. measurements and analysis L.R.A.P.P. of Office Naval Research, Arlington, Va., 1974-76; pres. Grug Fed., Inc., Houston, Arlington, Va., 1976—; vis. prof. architecture and planning U. Tex. at Austin, 1959-64. Mem. Am. Mgmt. Assn., Acoustical Soc. Am., IEEE, Explorers Club, Phi Beta Kappa, Sigma Xi, Beta Gamma Sigma. Contbr. articles to profl. jours. Home: 160 Litchfield Ln Houston TX 77024 Office: 2500 Tanglewilde Houston TX 77024

LANE, ROBERT EDWARDS, polit. scientist, educator; b. Phila., Aug. 19, 1917; s. Robert Porter and Bess (Edwards) L.; B.S., Harvard, 1939, Ph.D., 1950; m. Helen Sobol, Nov. 15, 1944; children—R. Lawrence, Thomas Edwards. Asst. sec. Internat. Student Service, 1940-41; tutor Harvard, 1946-48; mem. faculty Yale, 1948—, prof. polit. sci., 1962—, chmn. dept. polit. sci., 1967-70, 78-79, Ford Research prof. pub. affairs, 1963-64, fellow Inst. Human Relations, 1953-54; fellow Center Advanced Study Behavioral Scis., 1956-57, Woodrow Wilson Internat. Center for Scholars, 1970-71; sr. Fulbright-Hays scholar, 1972-73. mem. social sci. adv. com. NSF, 1968-71. Grantee Ford Found., 1954, Social Sci. Research Council, 1955-56, 65-66, Carnegie Found., 1961-62. Served with AUS, also USAAF, 1942-46. Fellow Am. Acad. Arts and Scis.; mem. Policy Studies Orgn. (pres. 1973), Internat. Soc. Polit. Psychology (pres. 1978-79), Am. Polit. Sci. Assn. (pres. 1970-71), Am. Sociol. Assn., Am. Psychol. Assn. Author: The Regulation of Businessmen, 1954; Political Life, 1959; The Liberties of Wit, 1961; Political Ideology, 1962; (with D. Sears) Public Opinion, 1964; Political Thinking and Consciousness, 1969; Political Man, 1972. Home: 3532 Yale Station New Haven CT 06520

LANE, SYLVIA, economist; b. N.Y.C.; A.B., U. Calif., Berkeley, 1934, M.A., 1936; postgrad. Columbia U., 1937; Ph.D., U. So. Calif., 1957; m. Benjamin Lane, Sept. 2, 1939; children—Leonard, Reese, Nancy. Lectr., asst. prof. U. So. Calif., Los Angeles, 1947-60; asso. prof. econs. San Diego State U., 1961-65; asso. prof. finance, asso. dir. Center Econ. Edn., Calif. State U., Fullerton, 1965-69, chmn. dept. finance, 1967-69; prof. agrl. econs. U. Calif., Davis, 1969—; vis. scholar Stanford U., 1975-76; econ. cons. Pres.'s Com. Consumer Interests, 1966—; cons. Calif. Adv. Commn. Tax Reform, 1963; project economist Los Angeles County Welfare Planning Council, 1956-59; del. White House Conf. on Food and Nutrition, 1969, Pres.'s Summit Conf. on Inflation, 1974; mem. adv. com. Center for Bldg. Tech., Nat. Bur. Standards, 1975—. Bd. dirs. Am. Council Consumer Interests, 1973, Consumers Union, 1975—. Ford Found. fellow U. Calif., Los Angeles, 1963, U. Chgo., 1965; fellow U. Chgo., 1968. Mem. Am. Econ. Assn., Am. Agrl. Econs. Assn. (dir. 1976—), Am. Council Consumer Info., Omicron Delta Epsilon (pres. 1973-75, trustee). Author: (with E. Bryant Phillips) Personal Finance, 1963, rev. edit., 1979; The Insurance Tax, 1965; California's Income Tax Conformity and Withholding, 1968; also articles. Home: 3028 N El Macero Dr El Macero CA 95618 Office: Dept Agrl Econs U Calif Davis CA 95616. *Select goals carefully . . .*

LANE, THOMAS HENRY, mktg. cons.; b. Hartford, Conn., Nov. 13, 1913; s. Thomas H. and Grace (O'Brien) L.; A.B., Dartmouth, 1935; m. Virginia Chalmers, Mar. 31, 1937; children—Christopher Thomas, Nia. Reporter, N.Y. Herald Tribune, 1935; pub. relations, radio sta. WOR, 1936; account exec., copywriter Young & Rubicam, N.Y.C., 1937-42; dir. advt., press and radio, war finance div. U.S. Treasury, 1942-45; dir. sales promotion and advt. Rexall Drug Co., Los Angeles, v.p., 1945-49; then v.p., dir. McCann-Erickson, Inc., N.Y.C.; sr. v.p. Lennen & Newell, Inc., N.Y.C., until 1966; sr. v.p. J. Walter Thompson Co., 1966-76; v.p. pub. affairs N.Y. C. of C. and Industry, 1977-78; pres. Tom Lane Assos. Inc., mktg. cons., Quechee, Vt., 1978—. Dir. adv. bd. Salvation Army N.Y.; trustee Loomis Sch., Quechee Lake Landowners Assn. Clubs: Dartmouth, Sales Executives, University, N.Y. Yacht (N.Y.C); Nat. Press (Washington); American Yacht; Apawamis (Rye, N.Y.). Home: Kingswood 3D Quechee VT 05059 Office: Tom Lane Assos Inc PO Box 3 Quechee VT 05059

LANE, WALTER BYRON, lawyer; b. Latah, Wash., Apr. 18, 1905; s. Walter McK. and Elizabeth (Peterman) L.; J.D., U. Wash., 1927; m. Genevieve Wing Casey, Apr. 8, 1967; children—Peter H., Patricia (Mrs. Harrison P. Sargent, Jr.), Linda (Mrs. Robert Brinkley). Admitted to Wash. bar, 1927; practice in Seattle, 1928—; mem. firm Lane, Powell Moss & Miller, 1936—. Dir., officer several cos. Mem. U. Wash. Alumni Assn. (pres. 1951-52), Psi Upsilon, Phi Delta Phi. Clubs: Seattle Golf (trustee 1956-59), Rainier (trustee 1960), University (Seattle). Home: 1574 NW 190th St Seattle WA 98177 Office: 3800 Rainier Bank Tower Seattle WA 98101

LANE, WARREN C., JR., lawyer; b. Providence, Aug. 9, 1923; s. Warren C. and Pauline (Newitt) L.; grad. Phillips Exeter Acad., 1942; A.B., Harvard, 1946, LL.B., 1949; m. Cynthia Rugg, Aug. 11, 1951; children—Corbin B., Kimberley R., Prescott N. Admitted to Mass. bar, 1949; asst. dist. atty. Middle Dist. Mass., 1953-55; mem. Worcester City Council, 1958-59; asso. firm Hartwell & Driscoll, Worcester, 1949-51; partner firm Bowditch & Lane, Worcester, 1951-77; individual practice, 1977—. Trustee Consumers Savs. Bank. Co-founder Internat. Center Worcester; past chmn. vol. services div. Golden Rule Fund campaign; past sec., dir. Worcester chpt. A.R.C. Trustee Becker Jr. Coll.; past trustee Shepherd Knapp Sch. Worcester Acad., Phillips Exeter Acad.; past bd. dirs. Legal Aid Soc. Worcester, Worcester Civic Music Assn., Worcester Meml. Homes for Blind; past mem. adv. bd. Worcester Salvation Army, Worcester Girls Club. Served to lt. (j.g.) USNR, World War II. Mem. Am., Mass., Boston, Worcester County (past pres.) bar assns., Phillips Exeter Acad. Alumni Assn. (past pres.). Republican. Unitarian. Mason, Rotarian (past pres. Worcester). Club: Worcester Harvard (past pres.) Office: 446 Main St Worcester MA 01608

LANE, WILLIAM GUERRANT, educator; b. Reidsville, N.C., June 15, 1919; s. Henry Pritchett and Eva (Smith) L.; A.B. magna cum laude, Furman U., 1939; M.A., Harvard, 1947, Ph.D., 1953; m. Kate Hodge, Sept. 5, 1953; 1 son, Richard Guerrant. Instr. English, Tufts U., 1947-50, Duke, 1952-56; asso. prof. S.W. Mo. State Coll., Springfield, 1956-60; asso. prof. U. Colo., 1960-63, prof., 1963-69, chmn. dept., 1964-67; prof. English, head dept. U. N.C., Greensboro, 1969—. Served to lt. comdr. USNR, 1941-45; PTO. Dexter Traveling scholar Harvard, 1952. Mem. Modern Lang. Assn. Am., South Atlantic Modern Lang. Assn., Keats-Shelley Assn. Am., Research Soc. for Victorian Periodicals, Am. Assn. Profs. Democrat. Author: Richard Harris Barham, 1968; Poetry: An Introduction, 1968. Gen. editor: English Language Notes, 1963-68. Home: 3700 Madison Ave Greensboro NC 27403

LANE, WILLIAM H., food co. exec.; b. Greenback, Tenn., Nov. 22, 1923; s. William Quincy and Vola (Stone) L.; student Ga. Inst. Tech., 1941-43; B.S., U. Tenn., 1946-47; m. Dorothy Dew, July 24, 1948; children—William H., Peggy Tipton, Timothy Dew. Sales engr. Ingersoll Rand Co., 1947-50; sales mgr. Woodman Co., Decatur, Ga., 1950-54; exec. v.p., gen. mgr. Red Dot Foods, Madison, Wis., 1954-60; pres. River Brand Rice Mills, Inc. (co. now Riviana Foods, Inc.), Houston, 1960—, also chief exec. officer, dir.; mem. bd. Tex. Commerce Bank. Trustee Rice U.; mem. devel. council U. Tenn. Mem. Sigma Chi. Episcopalian. Clubs: Augusta (Ga.) Nat. Golf (chmn.); Houston Country, River Oaks Country, Ramada (Houston). Office: PO Box 2636 Houston TX 77001

LANE, WILLIAM JAMES, diversified mfg. co. exec., lawyer; b. Detroit, May 29, 1921; s. William James and Evangeline Marie (Oates) L.; B.A. in Econs., U. Ill., 1942; J.D., U. Mich., 1948; m. Marie Frances Sheen, Sept. 5, 1942; children—William James, III, Sheryl Marie, Bryan Richard, Leigh Anne. With FBI, 1942; admitted to Mich. bar, 1948; atty. Kaiser-Frazer Corp., Willow Run, Mich., 1948-53; with Bohn Aluminium & Brass Corp., Detroit, 1953-62, corp. sec., 1954-62; v.p. legal, sec. Gulf & Western Metals Forming Co., Detroit, 1965-73; v.p., sec., legal counsel, dir. Gulf & Western Mfg. Co., Southfield, Mich., 1973—. Mem. Wayne County (Mich.) Republican Finance Com., 1960-65; mem. bus. contbns. com. Mich. Colls. Found., 1965—. Served to lt. USNR, 1942-45. Mem. Am., Mich., Detroit bar assns., Am. Soc. Corp. Secs. (past nat. v.p., pres. Detroit chpt.), Nat., Mich. mfrs. assns., Detroit C. of C., Alpha Tau Omega. Roman Catholic. Clubs: Detroit Athletic, Detroit Economic; Lochmoor (Grosse Pointe). Home: 1451 Oxford Rd Grosse Pointe Woods MI 48236 Office: 26261 Evergreen Southfield MI 48076

LANER, RICHARD WARREN, lawyer; b. Chgo., July 12, 1933; s. Jack E. and Esther G. (Cohon) L.; student U. Ill., 1951-54; B.S., Northwestern U., 1955, LL.B., 1956; m. Barbara Lee Shless, Aug. 15, 1954; children—Lynn, Kenneth. Admitted to Ill. bar, 1956; asso. firm Dorfman, DeKoven & Cohen (name changed to Dorfman, De Koven, Cohen & Laner 1973), Chgo., 1956-62, partner, 1962—. Mem. Chgo. Bar Assn. (chmn. com. labor law 1972-73), Chgo. Assn. Commerce, Industry, Order of Coif. Editor, Northwestern Law Rev., 1954-56. Contbr. articles to profl. jours. Home: 1590 Little John Ct Highland Park IL 60035 Office: 1 IBM Plaza Suite 3301 Chicago IL 60611

LANEY, JAMES JOSEPH, lawyer; b. Dallas, July 20, 1913; s. Edward Robertson and Olivia (Dickerson) L.; grad. Kemper Mil. Sch., 1932; LL.B., U. Tex., 1936; m. Jean Moroney, Dec. 10, 1943; children—Olivia, David. Admitted to Tex. bar, 1936; atty., asst. to v.p. Oil Well Supply Co., Dallas, 1937-42; partner firm Locke, Purnell, Boren, Laney & Neely, and predecessor, 1951-73, pres. Locke, Purnell, Boren, Laney & Neely, Profl. Corp., 1973—. Lectr. banking law Southwestern Grad. Sch. Banking, So. Meth. U.; dir. First Citizens Bank, Dallas, A.H. Belo Corp., Henry C. Beck Co. Served to lt. USNR, 1942-46. Mem. Am., Tex., Dallas bar assns., Am. Judicature Soc., Sigma Alpha Epsilon. Home: 4645 Fairfax St Dallas TX 75209 Office: Republic Bank Tower Dallas TX 75201

LANEY, JAMES THOMAS, univ. pres.; b. Wilson, Ark., Dec. 24, 1927; s. Thomas Mann and Mary (Hughey) L.; B.A., Yale, 1950, B.D., 1954, Ph.D. (D.C. Macintosh fellow 1965-66), 1966; D.D., Fla. So. Coll., 1977; L.H.D., Southwestern at Memphis, 1979; m. Berta Joan Radford, Dec. 20, 1949; children—Berta Joan, James T., Arthur Radford, Mary Ruth, Susan Elizabeth. Chaplain, Choate Sch., Wallingford, Conn., 1953-55; ordained to ministry Methodist ch., 1955; asst. lectr. Yale Div. Sch., 1954-55; pastor St. Paul Methodist Ch., Cin., 1955-58; sec. student Christian movement, prof. Yonsei U., Seoul, Korea, 1959-64; asst. prof. Christian ethics Vanderbilt U. Div. Sch., 1966-69; dean Candler Sch. Theology, Emory U., 1969-77, pres. univ., 1977—; vis. prof. Harvard Div. Sch., 1974; dir. Trust Co. of Ga. Pres. Nashville Community Relations Council, 1968-69; mem. Yale Council Com., 1972-77. Bd. dirs. Fund Theol. Edn., Christian Higher Edn. in Asia. Served with AUS, 1946-48. Selected for Leadership, Atlanta, 1970-71. Fellow Soc. for Religion in Higher Edn.; mem. Am. Soc. Christian Ethics, Atlanta C. of C. (dir.), Phi Beta Kappa, Omicron Delta Kappa. Author: (with J.M. Gustafson) On Being Responsible, 1968; also essays. Home: 1463 Clifton Rd Atlanta GA 30329 Office: Emory U Atlanta GA 30322

LANFORD, LUKE DEAN, electronics co. exec.; b. Greer, S.C., Aug. 4, 1922; s. John D. and Ethel W. (Ballenger) L.; B.S.E.E., Va. Polytechnic Inst., 1943; m. Donna Marie Cellar, Dec. 20, 1945; 1 dau., Cynthia Lea Lanford Brown. With Western Electric Co., Inc., 1946-78, asst. mgr. tng., N.Y.C., 1957-60, mgr. engring., Kansas City, 1960-63, asst. works mgr., Allentown, Pa., 1963-65; plant mgr., Reading, Pa., 1965-69, gen. mgr., Indpls., 1969-78; dir. Met. Indpls. Television Assn., Inc., Sta. WFYI-TV, 1970—, pres., 1975-79. Served with U.S. Army, 1943-46. Mem. IEEE, Telephone Pioneers Am., Eta Kappa Nu, Tau Beta Pi, Phi Kappa Phi. Republican. Presbyterian. Home: 7810 Camelback Dr Indianapolis IN 46250 Office: 2525 N Shadeland Indianapolis IN 46206

LANFORD, OSCAR ERASMUS, JR., ednl. adminstr.; b. Louisa County, Va., Dec. 19, 1914; s. Oscar E. and Ruth (Miller) L.; B.S., Va. Mil. Inst., 1934; A.M., Columbia, 1937, Ph.D., 1939; m. Caroline C. Sherman, Aug. 24, 1937; children—Oscar III, Caroline Aldrich (Mrs. William Eastman), Henry C. Sherman, William Armistead, Virginia Bowen (Mrs. Sedruddin Hemani). Research chemist Gold Dust Corp., 1934-36; instr. chemistry Columbia, 1937-40; prof. chemistry, chmn. dept. State U. N.Y. Coll., Albany, 1940-52, dean coll., 1952-61, first dir. Atmospheric Scis. Research Center, 1961; pres. Fredonia Coll., State U. N.Y., 1961-70; dir. panel on univ. purposes and goals, gen. mgr. constrn. fund, vice chancellor State U. N.Y. 1970—. Mem. Sigma Xi, Phi Lambda Upsilon. Club: University (Albany, N.Y.). Author textbooks, articles in sci. jours. Home: 2567 Brookview Rd Castleton-on-Hudson NY 12033 Office: State U Plaza PO Box 1946 Albany NY 12201

LANG, ARTHUR WILSON, JR., cons.; b. Austin, Tex., Sept. 12, 1929; s. Arthur Wilson and Parlee (Hocker) L.; student U. Tex., 1952-55, U. Denver, 1959-61; m. Charlene Rae Hammond, Sept. 15, 1960; children—Arthur Wilson II, Gregory Stephen. Night mgr. Stephen F. Austin Hotel, Austin, Tex., 1952; asst. mgr. Western Hills Hotel, Fort Worth, 1952-54, Trade Winds Motor Hotel, Corpus Christi, Tex., 1955-58; credit mgr. Denver Hilton, 1959-60; resident mgr. Jack Tar Hotel, Lansing, Mich., 1961-68; gen. mgr. Adolphus Hotel, Dallas, 1969-75; v.p., regional mgr. Metro Inns Mgmt. Co., Dallas, 1975-76; area rep. Holiday Inns, Inc., 1976-78; owner, operator Sheraton El Paso, 1978-79; pres., gen. mgr. El Paso G-H Inc.; guest computer lectr. IBM, Toronto, N.Y.C. and Dallas; lectr. Irving Ind. Sch. Dist., 1973-75, 76-77. Active Boy Scouts Am.; mem. President's Com. To Hire Handicapped, 1974. Recipient Distinguished Philanthopic Service award Nat. Jewish Hosp., 1972. Mem. Am. (Gold Key Pub. Relations award 1973), Dallas (v.p., bd. dirs.), Golden Triangle (pres.), Tex. (bd. dirs.) hotel and motel assns., Internat. Ind. Innkeepers (bd. dirs.), Skal Internat., Hotel Sales Mgmt. Assn. Methodist. Rotarian (bd. dirs. Orange club 1967), Mason (Shriner). Advisor Fast Foods mag., 1975; adv. bd. Hotel-Motel Mgmt. Mag., 1976. Address: Continental Inn 801 New Circle Rd NE Lexington KY 40505

LANG, CECIL YELVERTON, educator; b. Walstonburg, N.C., Sept. 18, 1920; s. Wilton Earl and Lillie (Yelverton) L.; A.B., Duke, 1941, A.M., 1942; M.A., Harvard, 1947, Ph.D., 1949; m. Violette Noelle Gúerin-Lésé Apr. 2, 1952; 1 son, Francois-Michel. Instr., then asst. prof. English, Yale, 1949-57; asso. prof. English, Claremont Grad. Sch., 1957-59; prof. English, Syracuse U., 1959-65, U. Chgo., 1965-67; prof. Center for Advanced Studies, U. Va., 1967-70, Commonwealth prof. English, 1970—. Served to 1st lt USAAF, 1942-46. Guggenheim fellow, 1951-52; Fulbright fellow, 1951-52; Morse fellow, 1956-57. Editor: The Swinburne Letters, 6 vols., 1959-62; New Writings of Swinburne, 1964; The Pre Raphaelites and Their Circle, 1968. Home: 1820 Edgewood Lane Charlottesville VA 22903

LANG, DANIEL, writer; b. N.Y.C., May 30, 1915; s. Nathan and Fanny (Cohen) L.; B.A., U. Wis., 1936; m. Margaret Altschul, July 19, 1942; children—Frances Altschul, Helen Goodhart, Cecily. Reporter, N.Y. Post, 1939-42; war corr. New Yorker mag., MTO, World War II, now staff writer. Mem. Greater N.Y. com. United Negro Coll. Fund. Recipient Soc. Mag. Writers award for excellence best article internat. relations; Sidney Hillman Found. award; Nat. Mag. award for reporting excellence; George Polk award for mag. reporting. Clubs: Century Assn., Skating (N.Y.C.). Author: Early Tales of the Atomic Age, 1948; The Man in the Thick Lead Suit, 1954; From Hiroshima to the Moon, 1959; (juvenile) A Summer's Duckling, 1963; An Inquiry into Enoughness, 1965; Casualties of War, 1969; Patriotism Without Flags, 1974; A Backward Look, 1979. Contbr. Story mag. New Republic, Sat. Rev., others. Home: Cove Island Mamaroneck NY 10543 Office: New Yorker Magazine 25 W 43d St New York City NY 10036

LANG, DANIEL S., artist; b. Tulsa, Mar. 17, 1935; s. Irving and Dorothy D. (Lauterer) L.; B.F.A., Tulsa U., 1953; M.F.A., Iowa U., 1959. Asst. prof. art SUNY, Fredonia, 1959-60, Art Inst. Chgo., 1962-64, Washington U., St. Louis, 1964-65; vis. artist Ohio State U., 1968-69, U. South Fla., 1971; one-man shows include: Boston Mus. Fine Arts, 1961, Galeria Ivan Spence, Ibiza, Spain, 1966, 71, Arthur Tooth & Sons, London, 1970, 74, Il Gabbiano Gallery, Rome, 1975, DM Gallery, London, 1975, Gimpel & Weitzenhofer, N.Y.C., 1976, Fischbach Gallery, N.Y.C., 1977, 79, Graphik Internat. GMBH, Stuttgart, W. Ger., 1979, Creiger Sesen, Boston, 1979; group shows include: Am. Fedn. of Arts travelling exhbn., 1968-69, U. Pa. Inst. Contemporary Art, 1970, Moore Coll. Art, 1971, Boston U., 1972, Joslyn Art Mus., Omaha and Sheldon Meml. Art Galleries, Lincoln, Nebr., 1973-74, Antarctica 2-man shows sponsored by NSF, organized by Smithsonian Instn., 1976-79, America 1976 travelling exhbn., 1976-78, including stops at Fogg Art Mus. Harvard U., Wadsworth Atheneum, Hartford, Conn. and Corcoran Gallery Art, Washington, Watson/de Nagy Gallery of Houston travelling exhbn., 1978-79; represented in permanent collections, including Mus. Modern Art, N.Y.C., Art Inst. Chgo., Library of Congress, Boston Public Library, Calif. Palace Legion of Honor, Nelson Rockefeller Collection, N.Y.C.; designer sets for Orfeo, Kent Opera Co., Eng. (later film by BBC), 1976. Served with U.S. Army, 1954-56. Home: 46 MacDougal St New York NY 10012 also 4 Lawrence Mansions Lordship Pl London SW 3 England also Montone Italy

LANG, ERICH KARL, physician, radiologist; b. Vienna, Austria, Dec. 7, 1929; s. Johann Hanns and Caecilia C. (Felkel) L.; came to U.S., 1950, naturalized, 1960; Arbitur, Realgymnasium, 1947; M.S., Columbia U., 1951; M.D., U. Vienna, 1953; m. Nicoli J. Miller, Apr. 21, 1956; children—Erich Christopher, Cortney Alexander Johann. Intern, U. Iowa Hosps., Iowa City, 1954-55, resident in internal medicine, 1955-56; resident in radiology Johns Hopkins U. Hosp., Balt., 1956-59, radiologist, 1956-61; instr. radiology Johns Hopkins U., 1956-61; radiologist, acting dir. radiology Methodist Hosp., Indpls., 1961-67; prof., chmn. dept. radiology La. State U. Med. Center, Shreveport, 1967-76, New Orleans, 1976—; prof., chmn. dept. radiology La. State U., Tulane U. schs. medicine, 1976—; dir. radiology Charity Hosp., New Orleans, 1976—. Served as maj. M.C., U.S. Army, 1961-65. Fellow A.C.P., Soc. Vascular Surgeons, Am. Coll. Radiology, Billroth Med. Soc.; mem. Radiol. Soc. N. Am., Am. Roentgen Ray Soc., Soc. Nuclear Medicine, Soc. Acad. Chmn. Radiology, Soc. U. Radiologists, La. New Orleans med. socs., Crescent City Radiol. Soc. Author numerous articles in field. Office: 1542 Tulane Ave New Orleans LA 70112

LANG, FRANCIS HAROVER, lawyer; b. Manchester, Ohio, June 4, 1907; s. James Walter and Mary (Harover) L.; A.B., Ohio Wesleyan U., 1929; J.D., Ohio State U., 1932; m. Rachel Boyce, Oct. 20, 1934; children—Mary Sue, Charles Boyce, James Richard. Admitted to Ohio bar, 1932; practice in East Liverpool, 1932-42, 45—; with War Dept., 1942-45. Chmn. bd. First Fed. Savs. & Loan Assn., East Liverpool; dir. First Na. Bank, Chester, W.Va., First Nat. Bank, East Liverpool; pres., dir., Walter Lang companies; dir. Sayre Electric companies. Bd. dirs. YMCA, Mary Patterson Meml.; past pres. Columbiana council Boy Scouts Am. regional com. E. Central region, mem. at large Nat. council, 1968-77; bd. dirs. Bd. Global Ministries of United Methodist Ch., 1968-76. Mem. E. Liverpool C. of C. (past pres.), Columbiana County Bar Assn. (past pres.), Ohio State Bar Assn. Methodist. Rotarian (past dist. gov.). Clubs: E. Liverpool Country, Masons (33d degree). Home: Highland Colony East Liverpool OH 43920 Office: Potters Savs and Loan Bldg East Liverpool OH 43920

LANG, FRANK CHRISTIAN, former marine corps officer; b. New Rochelle, N.Y., Sept. 13, 1918; s. Christian and Marie (Grab) L.; grad. Naval War Coll., 1968; m. Joyce Dillinder, June 16, 1946; children—Barbara Gayle, John Christian. Commd. 2d lt., U.S. Marine Corps, 1943, advanced through grades to maj. gen., 1973; comdg. officer Marine All Weather Fighter Squadron, 1956-58; operations staff officer Hdqrs U.S. European Command, Paris, 1960-63; comdg. officer Marine Helicopter Group, 1965-66; exec. officer Office of Dep. Chief of Staff Hdqrs. Marine Corps, 1968-69, dep. asst. dir. plans, programs and systems Def. Supply Agency, 1969-71; comdg. gen. 3d Marine Aircraft Wing and MCAS, El Toro, Calif., 1971-73; comdg. gen. 1st Marine Aircraft Wing, Japan, 1973-74; dir. for ops. Pacific Command, 1974-77; dep. comdr. Fleet Marine Force Pacific, 1977-78, ret., 1978. Mem. exec. council Boy Scouts Am., N.C., 1965-66, Calif., 1972-73. Decorated DSSM, Legion of Merit, D.F.C., Air Medal. Episcopalian. Home: 3111 Edith Ln San Diego CA 92106

LANG, GEORGE, restaurant cons. co. exec.; b. Székesfehérvár, Hungary, July 13, 1924; s. Simon and Ilona (Lang) Deutsch; student U. Szeged (Hungary), 1945, Mozarteum, Salzburg, Austria, 1945-46, U. Stranieri, Perugia, Italy, 1950-51; children—Andrea, Brian. Came to U.S., 1946, naturalized, 1950. Asst. banquet mgr. Waldorf-Astoria, 1953-58; v.p. sales and marketing Brass Rail Orgn., 1958-60; v.p. Restaurant Assos. Industries, 1960-71; pres. George Lang Corp., N.Y.C., 1971—. Pub. mem. Am. Revolution Bicentennial Commn.,

1969—, mem. exec. com., chmn. Festival U.S.A. coordinating art, internat. exchange and spl. events for Bicentennial celebrations. Author: The Cuisine of Hungary, 1971. Cons. editor: Time-Life Book div.'s Foods of the World series, 1966-70; contbg. editor Travel and Leisure mag. Contbr. to Ency. Brit., 1974; also columnist mags. Address: 33 W 67th St New York NY 10023. *Almost anyone can be creative given enough time, budget and space, but the ones who succeed today have the common denominator of being 'poets of the possible."*

LANG, GORDON, investment co. exec.; b. Sayre, Pa., Nov. 3, 1895; s. Herman and Martha (Levis) L.; B.S., Denison U., 1918; m. Harriet Kendig, Aug. 2, 1927 (dec. Mar. 1964); 1 son, Gordon; m. 2d, Constance W. Bates, Oct. 1965. Sales corr. B.F. Goodrich Rubber Co.; later bond salesman for Borton & Borton; then mgr. bond dept. Guarantee Title & Trust Co.; subsequently dir. sales devel. Gorham Co.; v.p., mgr. Black Starr & Frost-Gorham; pres. Spauding-Gorham; dir. Spaulding-Gorham, Black Starr & Frost-Gorham, Gorham, Inc., Gomanco, Inc.; pres., owner Spaulding and Co., Chgo., 1943-73, cons., 1973-75; owner Loring Andrews Co., jewelers, Cin., 1953-64, Rattermann & Co. (now Loring Andrews & Rattermann), 1958-64, Spaulding & Tatman, Evanston, Tatman, Chgo., 1958-60; pres., owner Gordco Inc., investments, 1972—. Dir., past pres. Chgo. Better Bus. Bur.; dir. Chgo. Area Project; past dir. Chgo. Crime Commn., Chgo. Retail Mchts. Assn.; past chmn. city planning adv. com., mem. exec. com. Chgo. Plan Commn.; mem. North Michigan Av. Assn. (1st pres.). Sec., dir. Chgo. Clubs Baseball for Boys. Past pres. Chgo. Latin Sch. Boys. Served as 2d lt. U.S. Army, World War I. Clubs: Chicago, Chicago Racquet (Chgo.); Old Elm, Commercial, Commonwealth; Onwentsia (Lake Forest); Bath and Tennis, Everglades (Palm Beach, Fla.). Developed place-setting method for sale flat silver. Home: 203 Bluff's Edge Dr Lake Forest IL 60045 also 313 Chilean Ave Palm Beach FL Office: Room 4600 First Nat Plaza Chicago IL 60670

LANG, H. JACK, advt. exec.; b. Cleve., June 24, 1904; s. Hascal Charles and Rosetta (Stettiner) L., B.A., Antioch Coll., 1928; m. Frances Wise, Aug. 10, 1935; children—Wendy, John. Founder, pres. Lang, Fisher, Stashower Inc., advt. agy., 1932-69, chmn. exec. com., 1969-72. Trustee Mt. Sinai Hosp. Cleve., 1947-72; mem. Found. Adv. Council; trustee Planned Parenthood Cleve. Served as lt. col. USAAF, 1942-46. Named to Hall of Fame, Cleve. Advt. Club. Mem. Manuscript Soc., Western Res. Hist. Soc. (library council), Friends of Library Council, Case-Western Res. U. Clubs: Rowfant Fellowe, Communications, Oakwood, Midday. Author: The Wit and Wisdom of Abraham Lincoln, 1941; Lincoln's Fireside Reading; Two Kinds of Christmases; Rowfant Manuscripts; newspaper syndicated feature and book, Letters of the Presidents. Editor The Wolf Mag. of Letters, 1934—, Lincoln's Log Cabin Library. Collector autograph letters. Home: 1737 Andrews Rd Cleveland Heights OH 44118 Office: 1010 Euclid Ave Cleveland OH 44115

LANG, HANS JOACHIM, engring. co. exec.; b. Crailsheim, Germany, Nov. 17, 1912; s. Karl Hermann and Marie (Muelberger) L.; came to U.S., 1920, naturalized, 1928; M.E., Stevens Inst. Tech., 1934; M.S., Mass. Inst. Tech., 1936; m. Emily Ruth Crowl, Feb. 26, 1944; children—Helen Marie (Mrs. Fay Logan, Jr.), Jacqueline Ruth (Mrs. Kirk Weaver), Anne Michelle (Mrs. Thomas Paolino), Robert Crowl. Process engr. Standard Oil Co. (N.J.), 1936-41; chief process engr. Day & Zimmermann, Inc., Phila., 1942-50; project mgr. C.F. Braun & Co., Alhambra, Cal., 1950-59, mgr. European sales, 1959-62; v.p. N. Am. operations Lummus Co., Bloomfield, N.J., 1962-68; pres. J.R. Pritchard & Co., Kansas City, Mo., 1968-69; group pres. Internat. Systems and Controls Engring. Group of Cos., 1969-74; exec. v.p. Procon Inc., Des Plaines, Ill., 1974-75, pres., 1975-77; pres. Lang Assos. Inc., Tenafly, N.J., 1978—; chmn. The Pritchard Corp., Kansas City, Mo., 1978—. Registered profl engr., N.Y., N.J., Pa., Calif., Tex. Mem. Am. Bar Assn., State Bar Calif., Am. Inst. Chem. Engrs., ASME, Am. Assn. Cost Engrs. Author articles in field. Home: 136 Westervelt Ave Tenafly NJ 07670 Office: 4625 Roanoke Pkwy Kansas City MO 64112

LANG, HOWARD JEROME, mfg. exec.; b. Galt, Ont., Can., June 15, 1912; s. Louis L. and Gertrude D. (Dietrich) L.; B. Chem. Engring., McGill U., 1935; m. Helen Mary Grant, Oct. 29, 1938; children—David, Christopher, Martha, Jennifer, Michael. With Canadian Industries, Ltd., also Defence Industries Ltd., 1935-45, Nat. Steel Car Corp., Ltd., Hamilton, Ont., 1945-60; pres., chief exec. officer, dir. Canron, Inc., 1960-67, chmn., pres., chief exec. officer, 1967-72, chmn., chief exec. officer, 1972-77, chmn., 1977—; v.p., dir. Canadian Imperial Bank Commerce; dir. Canadian Marconi Co., Texaco Can., Ltd., Canadian Pacific Ltd., Dominion Foundries and Steel, Ltd., Sun Life Assurance Co., Drummond McCall & Co. Ltd., Can. Fund, Inc., Can. Investment Fund Ltd. Mem. Conf. Bd. Hon. v.p. Que. Provincial council Boy Scouts Canada; bd. dirs. C.D. Howe Research Inst.; bd. govs. Appleby Coll., U. Waterloo. Mem. Assn. Profl. Engrs. Ont., Newcomen Soc. Eng., Delta Kappa Epsilon. Roman Catholic. Clubs: Hamilton; Knowlton Golf; Mt. Bruno Country; Mount Royal, St. James's (Montreal); Toronto, Toronto Golf, York. Home: 13 Rosedale Hts Dr Toronto ON M4T 1C2 Canada Office: 1 First Canadian Pl PO Box 134 Toronto ON M5X 1A4 Canada

LANG, JENNINGS BENTLY, producer; b. N.Y.C., May 28, 1915; s. Harry and Lillian (Saul) L.; B.S.S., M.S., St. John's U., 1934, J.D., 1937; m. Monica Lewis, Jan. 1, 1956; children—Michael Anthony, Robert Bruce, Jennings Rockwell. Admitted to N.Y. State bar, 1937; mem. firm Seligsberg & Lewis, N.Y.C., 1937; agt. Jaffe Agy., 1939-40, partner, v.p., 1942; pres., 1948-50; v.p., head prodn. M.C.A. Television, Universal Television, 1950-69; v.p., producer motion pictures Universal Pictures, 1969—. Bd. dirs. ACLU; bd. dirs. So. Calif. Public Television. Mem. Acad. Motion Picture Arts and Scis., Television Acad. Arts and Scis. Democrat. Clubs: Racquet, Friars. Home: 606 Mountain Dr Beverly Hills CA 90210 Office: 100 Universal City Plaza Universal City CA 91608

LANG, JOHN SANFORD, journalist, editor; b. Memphis, Sept. 10, 1941; s. John Hooper Caffee and Lillian Sanford (Owen) L.; B.S., Memphis State U., 1964; m. Lillian Pearl White, Sept. 17, 1960; children—James Christopher, Susan Sanford. Newsman A.P., Memphis and Nashville, 1963-64, spl. writer, New Orleans and Washington, 1966-72; asst. to pres. Tulane U., 1965; nat. corr., chief bur. N.Y. Post, Washington, 1972-77; asso. editor U.S. News and World Report, 1977-79; chief corr. White House, 1979—. Home: 3075 N Pollard St Arlington VA 22207 Office: 2300 N St NW Washington DC 20037

LANG, MABEL LOUISE, educator; b. Utica, N.Y., Nov. 12, 1917; d. Louis Bernard and Katherine (Werdge) Lang; B.A., Cornell U., 1939; M.A., Bryn Mawr Coll., 1940, Ph.D., 1943; Litt.D., Coll. Holy Cross, 1975, Colgate U., 1978. Mem. faculty Bryn Mawr Coll., 1943—, successively instr., asst. prof., 1943-50, asso. prof., 1950-59, prof. Greek, 1959—, chmn. dept., 1960—, acting dean coll. 2d semester 1958-59, 60-61; chmn. mng. com. Am. Sch. Classical Studies, Athens, 1975—, chmn. admissions and fellowship com., 1966-72; Blegen distinguished research prof. semester I, Vassar Coll., 1976-77. Guggenheim fellow, 1953-54; Fulbright fellow, Greece, 1959-60. Mem. Am. Philos. Soc., Am. Philol. Assn., Archaeol. Inst. Am., Soc. Promotion Hellenic Studies (Eng.), Classical Assn. (Eng.). Co-author: Athenian Agora Weights, Measures and Tokens; author: The Palace of Nestor, Vol. II; The Frescoes; Athenian Agora Graffiti and Dipinti, 1976. Contbr. articles profl. jours. Home: 905 New Gulph Rd Bryn Mawr PA 19010

LANG, NORTON DAVID, physicist; b. Chgo., July 5, 1940; s. Charles and Sadelle (Bilow) L.; A.B. summa cum laude, Harvard U., 1962, A.M., 1965, Ph.D., 1968; postgrad. (Knox fellow) London Sch. Economics, 1962-63; m. Enid Asher, June 8, 1969; 1 dau., Eugenie. Asst. research physicist, lectr. U. Calif., San Diego, 1967-69; mem. staff IBM Research Center, Yorktown Heights, N.Y., 1969—. Fellow N.Y. Acad. Scis., Am. Phys. Soc. (Davisson-Germer prize 1977); mem. Phi Beta Kappa. Contbr. articles on theoretical physics to profl. jours. Office: IBM Research Center Yorktown Heights NY 10598

LANG, OTTO EMIL, former Can. cabinet minister, grain co. exec.; b. Handel, Sask., Can., May 14, 1932; s. Otto T. and Maria (Wurm) L.; B.A., U. Sask., 1951, LL.B., 1953; B.C.L. (Rhodes scholar), Oxford (Eng.) U., 1955; m. Adrian Ann Merchant, Dec. 21, 1963; children—Maria, Timothy, Gregory, Andrew, Elisabeth, Amanda, Adrian. Called to Sask. bar, 1956, created Queen's counsel, 1972; mem. faculty Law Sch., U. Sask., 1956-68, asso. prof. law, 1958-61, prof., dean law, 1961-68; M.P. for Sask.-Humboldt, 1968-79; Canadian minister without portfolio, 1968-69, minister for energy and water, 1969—, minister of manpower and immigration, 1970-72, minister of justice, 1972-75, 78-79, minister transport, 1975-79, minister-in-charge Canadian Wheat Bd., 1970—; exec. v.p. Pioneer Grain Co. Ltd., Winnipeg, Man., Can., 1979—. Vice pres. Sask. Liberal Assn., 1956-62, fed. campaign chmn. Sask. 1963-64. Roman Catholic. Knight of Malta. Clubs: Manitoba; Curling; Winter (Winnipeg); Bridge (Ottawa); Golf (St. Charles, Sask.). Editor: Contemporary Problems in Public Law, 1967. Home: 12 Kingsway Winnipeg MB Canada Office: 25th Floor 1 Lombard Pl Winnipeg MB Canada

LANG, PEARL, dancer, choreographer; b. Chgo., May 1922; d. Jacob and Frieda (Feder) Lack; student Wright Jr. Coll., U. Chgo.; m. Joseph Wiseman, Nov. 22, 1963. Soloist, Martha Graham Dance Co., 1944-54; featured roles on Broadway include Carousel, 1945-47, Finian's Rainbow, 1947-48, role of Solvieg opposite John Garfield, ANTA Peer Gynt; formed own co., 1953; faculty Yale, 1954-68; tchr., lectr. Juilliard, 1953-69, Jacobs Pillow, Conn. Coll., Neighborhood Playhouse, 1963-68, Israel, Sweden, Netherlands; choreographer TV shows Omnibus, Frontiers of Faith, Look Up and Live, ABC Directions, CBC Folio; co-dir. T.S. Elliot's Murder in the Cathedral, Stratford, Conn.; co-dir., choreographer full length prodn. Dybbuk for CBC; dir. numerous Israel Bond programs; assumed roles Emily Dickinson, 1970, Clytemnestra, 1973, Jocasta in the Night Journey, 1974 for Martha Graham Dance Co. choreographer dance works Song of Deborah, 1952, Moonsung and Windsung, 1952, Legend, 1953, Rites, 1953, And Joy Is My Witness, 1954, Nightflight, 1954, Sky Chant, 1957, Persephone, 1958, Black Marigold, 1959, Shirah, 1960, Apasionada, 1961, Broken Dialoges, 1962, Shore Bourne, 1964, Dismembered Fable, 1965, Pray for Dark Birds, 1966, Tongues of Fire, 1967, Piece for Brass, 1969, Moonways and Dark Tides, 1970, Sharjuhm, 1971, At This Point in Place or Time, 1973, The Possessed, 1974, Prairie Steps, 1975, Bach Rondelays, 1977, I Never Saw Another Butterfly, 1977; A Seder Night, 1977; Kaddish, 1977; Icarus, 1978; Cantigas Ladino, 1978. Founder Pearl Lang Dance Found. Recipient 2 Guggenheim fellowships. Mem. Equity. Home: 382 Central Park W New York City NY 10025 Studio: care American Dance Center 1515 Broadway New York NY 10036

LANG, PHILIP DAVID, state legislator, ins. co. exec.; b. Portland, Oreg., Dec. 16, 1929; s. Henry W. and Vera (Kern) L.; student Lewis and Clark Coll., 1951-53, Northwestern Coll. Law, 1956; m. Marcia Jean Smith, May 29, 1952; 1 son, Philip David, III. Police officer Oreg. Dept. Police, Salem, 1953-55; claims adjuster Glenns Falls Ins. Co., Portland, 1955-57, Oreg. Automobile Ins. Co., Portland, 1959-61; adminstrv. asst. to mayor City of Portland, 1957-58; spl. agt., underwriter North Pacific Ins. Co., Portland, 1961-63, mgr., 1963-65, asst. v.p., 1965—; asst. v.p. Oreg. Automobile Ins. Co., 1965—; mem. Oreg. Ho. of Reps., 1960—, speaker of ho., 1975—. Div. leader Multnomah County (Oreg.) Democratic Com., 1956-60, mem. precinct com., 1956—. Served with USAF, 1947-50. Mem. Oreg. Ins. Underwriters Assn., Theta Chi. Methodist. Clubs: VFW, Masons, DeMolay (Legion Honor). Home: 7330 SE 42d Ave Portland OR 97206 Office: PO Box 74 Portland OR 97207. *Success is achieved through commitment to and perserverance in all that is undertaken balanced with tolerance and understanding of all persons.*

LANG, ROBERT TODD, lawyer; b. N.Y.C., July 2, 1924; s. Charles and Selma (Marks) L.; B.A., Yale, 1945, LL.B., 1947; m. Joann Rosenberger, Aug. 4, 1949; children—William Gerald, James David, Nancy, Carolyn. Admitted to N.Y. bar, 1947; asso. firm Weil, Gotshal & Manges, N.Y.C., 1948-56, partner, 1956—; vice chmn. bd. Coro, Inc., 1964-67, chmn. bd., 1967-69; dir. P.A. Bergner & Co., Richford Industries, Inc. Mem. N.Y. State Atty. Gen.'s Adv. Com. on Real Estate Syndication Act. Recipient Golden Torch award City of Hope, 1971. Mem. Am. (com. on fed. regulation of securities), N.Y. State bar assns., N.Y. County Lawyers Assn. (mem. com. on corp. law 1969—, chmn. 1971-76), Assn. Bar City N.Y. (com. on securities regulation 1973-76), Corby Ct. Yale Law Sch., N.Y. County Lawyers Assn. (spl. com. on legal opinions). Jewish. Contbr. articles to legal periodicals. Home: 28 Oxford Rd Scarsdale NY 10583 Office: 767 Fifth Ave New York City NY 10022

LANG, THOMPSON HUGHES, publishing co. exec.; b. Albuquerque, Dec. 12, 1946; s. Cornelius Thompson and Margaret Miller (Hughes) L.; student U. N.Mex., 1965-68, U. Americas, Mexico City, 1968-69. Advt. salesman Albuquerque Publ. Co., 1969-70, publisher, pres., treas., 1971—, also dir.; pres., treas., dir. Jour. Publ. Co., 1971—; pres., dir. Masthead, Internat., 1971—; pres. Magnum Systems, Inc., 1973—. Mem. H.O.W. Orgn. Home: 1615 Park St SW Albuquerque NM 87104 Office: 7th & Silver St SW Albuquerque NM 87102

LANG, WILLIAM CHARLES, corp. exec.; b. Bronx, N.Y., Jan. 29, 1944; s. Harold C. and Katherine L. (Pratt) L.; B.S. magna cum laude, Lehigh U., 1965; m. Marilyn Warshow, June 27, 1965; children—Kenneth William, Pamela Sue. Accounting supr. Peat, Marwick, Mitchell & Co., 1965-69; controller Pueblo Internat., Inc., N.Y.C., 1970-72, v.p. finance, 1972-77, now dir., mem. exec. com.; v.p. adminstrn. and fin. Kenyon & Eckhardt, Inc., 1978—, also dir. C.P.A. Mem. Financial Execs. Inst., Am. Inst. C.P.A.'s, Nat. Accounting Soc., N.Y. State Soc. C.P.A.'s, Beta Gamma Sigma, Sigma Phi. Home: 31 Gedney Way Chappaqua NY 10514 Office: 200 Park Ave New York NY 10022

LANG, WILLIAM HENRY, ret. steel co. exec.; b. Pitts., June 2, 1911; s. Charles Edward and Anna L. (Heachenroether) L.; A.B., Dartmouth, 1933; M.L., U. Pitts., 1938; grad. Advanced Mgmt. Program, Harvard, 1951; m. Llda Jones, June 23, 1938; children—Marjorie, Janet, Jean. With Gulf Oil Corp., 1933-34; with U.S. Steel Corp. and prior subsidiaries, N.Y.C., 1934-76, asst. treas., 1952-59, treas., adminstrv. v.p., 1959-70, exec. v.p. realty and fin., 1970-76; pres. U.S. Steel Credit Corp., 1954-76; vice chmn. 1st Nat. State Bank, Newark, 1968-70; dir. Extel Corp., Northbrook, Ill. Trustee St. Barnabas Med. Center, N.J. Mem. Am. Iron and Steel Inst. Clubs: Links (N.Y.C.); Baltusrol Country (Springfield, N.J.); Short Hills (N.J.); Pine Valley (N.J.). Home: 10 Delbarton Dr Short Hills NJ 07078

LANG, WILLIAM WARNER, physicist; b. Boston, Aug. 9, 1926; s. William Warner and Lilla Gertrude (Wheeler) L.; B.S., Iowa State U., 1946, Ph.D., 1958; M.S., M.I.T., 1949; m. Asta Ingard, Aug. 31, 1954; 1 son, Robert. Acoustical engr. Bolt Beranek and Newman, Inc., Cambridge, Mass., 1949-51; instr. in physics U.S. Naval Postgrad. Sch., Monterey, Calif., 1951-55; cons. engr. E.I. du Pont de Nemours & Co., Wilmington, Del., 1955-57; mem. research staff M.I.T., 1958; physicist IBM, Poughkeepsie, N.Y., 1958—, program mgr. acoustics tech., 1977—; pres. Noise Control Found., Poughkeepsie, 1975—; adj. prof. physics Vassar Coll., 1978—; chmn. working group Internat. Orgn. Standardization, 1969—, tech. com. 29 Internat. Electrotech. Commn., 1975—. Served with USN, 1944-47, 52. Decorated Meritorious Service medal. Fellow Audio Engring. Soc., IEEE (Group on Audio and Electroacoustics Achievement award 1970, dir. 1970-71), Acoustical Soc. Am.; mem. Nat. Acad. Engring., Inst. Noise Control Engring. (pres. 1978), AAAS. Episcopalian. Club: Rotary (pres. local club 1975-76). Editor: Procs. 1975 Nat. Conf. on Noise Control Engring.; Designing for Noise Control, 1978. Home: 29 Hornbeck Ridge Poughkeepsie NY 12603 Office: IBM Acoustics Lab C18/704 PO Box 390 Poughkeepsie NY 12602

LANGACKER, RONALD WAYNE, educator; b. Fond du Lac, Wis., Dec. 27, 1942; s. George Rollo and Florence (Hinesley) L.; A.B. in French, U. Ill., 1963, A.M. in Linguistics, 1964, Ph.D., 1966; m. Margaret G. Fullick, June 5, 1966. Asst. prof. U. Calif. at San Diego, La Jolla, 1966-70, asso. prof., 1970-75, prof. linguistics, 1975—. Guggenheim fellow, 1978. Mem. Linguistic Soc. Am., AAUP, ACLU. Author: Language and its Structure, 1968; Fundamentals of Linguistic Analysis, 1972; Non-Distinct Arguments in Uto-Aztecan, 1976; An Overview of Uto-Aztecan Grammar, 1977; asso. editor Lang., 1971-77; contbr. articles in field to profl. jours. Home: 3286 Galloway Dr San Diego CA 92122 Office: U Calif at San Diego Dept Linguistics C-008 La Jolla CA 92093

LANGBAUM, ROBERT WOODROW, educator, author; b. N.Y.C., Feb. 23, 1924; s. Murray and Nettie (Moskowitz) L.; A.B., Cornell U., 1947; M.A., Columbia, 1949, Ph.D., 1954; m. Francesca Levi Vidale, Nov. 5, 1950; 1 dau., Donata Emily. Instr. English, Cornell U., 1950-55, asst. prof., 1955-60; asso. prof. U. Va., Charlottesville, 1960-63, prof. English, 1963-67, James Branch Cabell prof. English and Am. lit., 1967—; vis. prof. Columbia U., 1960, 65-66, Harvard, summer 1965; mem. supervising com. English Inst., 1970-71, chmn., 1972. Served to 1st lt. M.I., AUS, 1942-46. Ford Found. fellow Center for Advanced Study, Stanford, Calif., 1961-62; Guggenheim fellow, 1969-70; sr. fellow Nat. Endowment for Humanities, 1972-73; Am. Council Learned Socs. grantee, 1961, 75-76. Mem. Modern Lang. Assn., Am. Assn. U. Profs. Author: The Poetry of Experience: The Dramatic Monologue in Modern Literary Tradition, 1957; The Gayety of Vision: A Study of Isak Dinesen's Art, 1964; The Modern Spirit: Essays on the Continuity of Nineteenth and Twentieth Century Literature, 1970; The Mysteries of Identity: A Theme in Modern Literature, 1977. Editor: The Tempest (Shakespeare), 1964; (anthology) The Victorian Age: Essays in History and in Social and Literary Criticism, 1967. Editorial bd. Victorian Poetry, 1963—, Style, 1967—, New Lit. History, 1969—, Bull. Research in Humanities, 1977, S. Atlantic Bull., 1978, Studies in English Lit., 1978, Nat. Forum, 1979. Home: 223 Montvue Dr Charlottesville VA 22901

LANGBEIN, WALTER B., hydrologist; b. Newark, Oct. 17, 1907; B.S., Cooper Union, 1931; Sc.D. (hon.), Fla. Coll., 1941; m. Rose Langbein, June 2, 1939; children—Laura, John. With Rosoff Constrn. Co., 1935; hydrologist U.S. Geol. Survey, 1935—, now in Washington; editor Water Resources Research; mem. adv. coms. and bds. Nat. Acad. Scis. Recipient Horton award, Horton medal, Bowie medal, Gano Dunn medal, Warren prize; Gold medal Dept. Interior. Mem. Nat. Acad. Scid., Am. Geophys. Union, ASCE, Geol. Soc. Am. Club: Cosmos (Washington). Contbr. articles to profl. publs. Home: 4452 N 38th St Arlington VA 22207 Office: US Geol Survey Reston VA 22092

LANGBO, ARNOLD GORDON, food co. exec.; b. Richmond, B.C., Can., Apr. 13, 1937; s. Osbjourn and Laura Marie (Hagen) L.; student U. B.C., 1955-56; m. Martha Miiller, May 30, 1959; children—Sharon Anne, Maureen Bernice, Susan Colleen, Roderick Arnold, Robert Wayne, Gary Thomas, Craig Peter, Keith Edward. With Kellogg Co., 1956—, account mgr. Kellogg Co. of Can. Ltd., Toronto, 1965-67, adminstrv. asst. to pres. Kellogg Co., Battle Creek, Mich., 1969-70, exec. v.p. Kellogg Co. of Can. Ltd., 1970-71, v.p. sales and mktg., 1971-74, sr. v.p. sales and mktg., 1974-76, pres. Kellogg Salada Can. Ltd., Toronto, 1976-79, pres. Kellogg U.S. Food Products div., Battle Creek, 1979—. Mem. Cereal Inst. (chmn. bd.). Roman Catholic. Office: 235 Porter St Battle Creek MI 49016

LANGDALE, NOAH NOEL, JR., coll. pres.; b. Valdosta, Ga., Mar. 29, 1920; s. Noah Noel and Jessie Katharine (Catledge) L.; A.B., U. Ala., 1941, LL.B., 1959; LL.B., Harvard U., 1948, M.B.A., 1950; m. Alice Elizabeth Cabaniss, Jan. 8, 1944; 1 son, Noah Michael. Asst. football coach U. Ala., 1942; admitted to Ga. bar, 1951, and practiced in Valdosta, 1951-57; instr., then asst. prof. econs. and social studies, chmn. dept. accounting, econs. secretarial sci., bus. adminstrn. Valdosta State Coll., 1954-57; pres. Ga. State U., Atlanta, 1957—; dir. Guardian Life Ins. Co. Am. Past mem. U.S. Adv. Commn. Ednl. Exchange. Served to lt. (s.g.) USNR, 1942-46. Recipient 1st Georgian of Year award Ga. Assn. Broadcasters, 1962; Silver Anniversary All-Am. award Sports Illustrated, 1966; Mrytle Wreath award Hadassah, 1970; Salesman of Yr. award Sales and Mktg. Execs. of Atlanta, 1975; Silver Knight of Mgmt. award Lockheed-Ga. chpt. Nat. Mgmt. Assn., 1978. Mem. Am., Ga. bar assns., Ga. Assn. Colls. (pres. 1962-63), SAR (past v.p. Ga.), Gridiron Soc., Phi Beta Kappa, Omicron Delta Kappa, Delta Chi, Phi Kappa Phi. Methodist. Clubs: Rotary, Capital City (Atlanta). Home: 3807 Tuxedo Rd NW Atlanta GA 30305 Office: Ga State Univ University Plaza Atlanta GA 30303

LANGDELL, ROBERT DANA, medical educator; b. Pomona, Cal., Mar. 14, 1924; s. Walter Irving and Florence Delsa (Reichenbach) L.; student Pomona Coll., 1941-43; M.D., George Washington U., 1948; m. Alice E. Pritt, June 3, 1948; children—Robert Dana, Sara Ellen. Intern Henry Ford Hosp., Detroit, 1948-49; mem. faculty Sch. Medicine, U. N.C., Chapel Hill, 1949—, asso. prof. pathology, 1959-61, prof., 1961—. Mem. hematology study sect. USPHS, 1968-71. Served to capt. M.C., AUS, 1955-56. USPHS sr. research fellow, 1957-61; Career Research fellow, 1962-66. Mem. Am. Assn. Blood Banks (pres. 1972-73), Am. Soc. Clin. Pathology, Am. Assn. Pathology, AMA, Coll. Am. Pathology (gov. 1977—), N.C. Med. Assn. Episcopalian. Editor-in-chief Transfusion, 1972—. Research in blood coagulation and hemostasis. Home: 707 William Circle Chapel Hill NC 27514

LANGDON, GEORGE DORLAND, JR., univ. pres.; b. Putnam Conn., May 20, 1933; s. George Dorland and Anne Claggett (Zell) L.; A.B. cum laude (Coolidge scholar), Harvard Coll., 1954; M.A., Amherst Coll., 1957; Ph.D. (Coe fellow), Yale U., 1961; m. Agnes Domandi; children—George Dorland, III, Campbell Brewster. Instr. in history and Am. studies Yale U., 1959-62, asst. provost, lectr. in history, 1969-70, asso. provost, lectr. in history, 1970-72, dep. provost, lectr. in history, 1972-78; asst. prof. history Calif. Inst. Tech., 1962-64; asst. prof. Vassar Coll., 1964-67, asso. prof., 1967-68, spl. asst. to pres., 1968; pres. Colgate U., 1978—, trustee, 1978—; trustee Salisbury Sch., Commn. on Ind. Colls. and Univs. of State of N.Y. Served to lt. U.S. Army, 1954-56. Fellow Pilgrim Soc. Author: Pilgrim Colony, A History of New Plymouth 1620-1691, 1966 (State and Local Assn. of History award of Merit). Office: Colgate U Hamilton NY 13346

LANGDON, HERSCHEL GARRETT, lawyer; b. Lowry City, Mo., Oct. 6, 1905; s. Isaac Garrett and Della (Park) L.; B.A., U. Iowa, 1930, J.D., 1931; m. Ethel Virginia Waterson, May 26, 1931; children—Richard G., Ann Virginia (Mrs. Charles Eugene Willoughby Ward). Admitted to Iowa bar, 1931, since practiced in Des Moines; mem. firm Herrick, Langdon & Langdon, and predecessors, 1935—. Dir. AID Ins. Co., Amco Ins. Co., Allied Life Ins. Co. Fellow Am. Coll. Trial Lawyers, Am. Bar Found.; mem. Am., Iowa, Polk County bar assns., Phi Beta Kappa, Delta Sigma Rho, Phi Delta Pi. Conglist. Mason. Home: 678 49th St Des Moines IA 50312 Office: 1300 Financial Center 7th and Walnut Des Moines IA 50309

LANGDON, JAMES LLOYD, banker, ret. food co. exec.; b. Smithfield, N.C., Oct. 6, 1918; s. James Uriah and Ruth (Dunn) L.; B.S., N.C. State U., 1940; postgrad. Asheville (N.C.) Law Sch., 1948, Northwestern U., 1953, Yale, 1955, Syracuse U., 1965; m. Madelyn Earl Pope, July 10, 1943; children—Madelyn Carol Langdon Kalkhurst, Sheila Jeanne Langdon Pierce. Agrl. devel. agt. Carolina Power & Light Co., 1946-49; gen. mgr. Farmer Supply Co., 1949-50; exec. v.p. N.C. Dairy Products Assn., Raleigh, 1950-59; dir. marketing dairy div. Pet, Inc., Johnson City, Tenn., 1959-69, v.p. mktg., 1969, v.p. ops., 1969, exec. v.p., gen. mgr., 1969-70, pres., 1970-75, group pres., 1975-79; pres., dir. Hamilton Bank; dir. Ancorp Bancshares, Inc. Bd. dirs., mem. exec. com., v.p. U.S. Indsl. Council; pres. Johnson City Med. Center Hosp. Served with USAAF, 1941-45; lt. col. Res., ret. So. Assn. Dairy Food Mfgrs. (dir., pres. 1973), Johnson City C. of C. (pres., dir.), Internat. Assn. Ice Cream Mfrs. (v.p., dir., pres. 1974-76), Phi Kappa Phi. Mem. Christian Ch. Clubs: Johnson City Country; Hurstleigh, Sphinx. Home: 3614 Bristol Hwy Knoll Vue Farm Johnson City TN 37601 Office: PO Box O CRS Johnson City TN 37601

LANGDON, JERVIS, JR., lawyer; b. Elmira, N.Y., Jan. 28, 1905; s. Jervis and Eleanor (Sayles) L.; A.B., Cornell U., 1927, LL.B., 1930; student Dijon (France) U., 1926; m. Irene Fortner, Aug. 26, 1949. Law clk., asst. gen. solicitor Lehigh Valley R.R. Co., 1930-33; commerce counsel N.Y.C. R.R. Co., 1934-36; asst. gen. atty. C.&O. Ry. Co., 1936-37, gen. atty., 1937-41, asst. v.p. traffic, 1941-42; spl. counsel Assn. Southeastern R.R.'s, Washington, 1947-53, chmn., 1953-56; gen. counsel B. & O. R.R., 1956-58, v.p., gen. counsel, 1958-61, pres., 1961-64; chmn. bd., pres. C.R.I. & P.R.R., 1965-70; trustee Penn Central Transp. Co., 1970-74, pres., 1974-76; of counsel Alston, Miller & Gaines, Washington, 1976—. Served from capt. to col., USAAF, 1942-46; asst. chief staff India-China div. Air Transp. Command, chief staff S.W. Pacific Wing. Decorated Legion of Merit with 2 oak leaf clusters, Distinguished Combat Unit award. Home: Quarry Farm Elmira NY 14902 Office: Suite 1000 1800 M St NW Washington DC

LANGDON, JOHN EMERSON, fin. exec.; b. Ottawa, Can., Apr. 13, 1902; s. Frederick William and Mary Ann (Allan) L.; m. Eustella Frances Burke, Mar. 28, 1931. With Financial Post, 1927-45; partner McLeod, Young, Weir & Co. Ltd., Toronto, Ont., Can., 1945-67; v.p., dir. Shell Realty Ltd. Hon. trustee, patron Royal Ont. Mus., Friends of Winterthur, Henry Francis du Pont-Winterthur Mus.; chmn. Toronto Symphony Found. Mem. Colonial Soc. Mass. of Boston Soc. (corr.), Silver Collectors Soc. (London), Ont. Heritage Found., Royal Soc. Arts (London), Am. Antiquarian Soc., John Howard Soc. (hon. life mem.). Clubs: Toronto Hunt, National (Toronto). Author: Canadian Silversmiths and Their Marks, 1960; Canadian Silversmiths 1700-1900, 1967; American Silversmiths in British North America 1776-1800, 1970; Canadian Clock and Watchmakers, 1976. Home: 43 Glenayr Rd Toronto ON M59 3B9 Canada Office: Toronto Dominion Centre PO Box 433 Toronto ON M5K 1M2 Canada

LANGDON, SUE ANE, actress; b. Paterson, N.J., Mar. 8; d. Albert and Grace Wallis (Huddle) Lookhoff; student N. Tex. State Coll., Denton; m. Jack Emrek, Apr. 4, 1959. TV appearances in series Arnie, 1970, Am. Scene Mag., 1962, Grandpa Goes to Washington, 1978, When the Whistle Blows, 1980, also numerous guest appearances; film appearances in Roustabout, 1967, Frankie and Johnny, 1966, A Fine Madness, 1968, The Rounders, 1967, Guide for the Married Man, 1969, The Great Imposter, 1960, The Cheyenne Social Club, 1971; star in Broadway prodn. The Apple Tree, 1967, in nat. co. of Most Happy Fella, 1958; numerous appearances dinner theatres; co-star with Sid Caesar at Sahara Hotel, Las Vegas, 1977. Trustee, Morris Animal Found., 1978—. Recipient Golden Globe award Hollywood Fgn. Press, 1971.

LANGDON, WILLIAM MONDENG, educator; b. LaGrange, Ill., Aug. 18,, 1914; s. Ernest Warren and Julia (Mondeng) L.; B.S., U. Ill., 1935, M.S., 1939, Ph.D., 1941; m. Redith Romine, Feb. 15, 1942; children—William Ernest, Suzanne; m. 2d, Nancy Drummond, Aug. 7, 1971. Asst. prof. chem engring. U. Ill. at Urbana, 1943-45; asso. prof. Renssalaer Poly. Inst., 1946-48; v.p., tech. dir. Graham Crowley and Assos., Chgo., 1948-55; sr. engr. I.T.T. Research Inst., Chgo., 1956-67; prof. chem. engring. Ill. Inst. Tech., 1968—; sr. materials engr. WPB, 1943-45; cons. in field, 1937-48, 68—. Mem. Am. Inst. Chem. Engrs., Am. Chem. Soc., A.A.A.S., Sigma Xi, Delta Upsilon, Sigma Tau, Omega Chi Epsilon, Phi Lambda Upsilon. Author, patentee in field. Home: 449 Lawndale Ave Woodstock IL 60098 Office: 10 W 33d St Chicago IL 60616

LANGE, BARBARA PEARSON (MRS. GORDON LANGE), coll. ofcl.; b. Swarthmore, Pa., July 5, 1910; d. Paul Martin and Edna (Wolfe) Pearson; student Swarthmore Coll., 1927-29, Yale Sch. Drama, 1929-31; m. Gordon C. Lange, June 15, 1932; children—Julia Alice (Mrs. James Parker Hall III), Jonathan Talbot, Josephine Pearson (Mrs. Richard de V. Seymour). Actress, Swarthmore Chatauqua, 1928-31, Pasadena Playhouse, 1934-35, summer stock, 1935; instr. Scripps Coll., Claremont, Cal., 1934-35; vocational adviser women, asst. alumni office Swarthmore Coll., 1940-43, dir. dramatics, 1946-62, lectr. English dept., 1954-62, dean of women, 1962-69, dir. career planning and placement, 1969-70, asso. dean of admissions, 1970—, dean of women emerita, 1975—; drama instr. Eastern Pa. Psychiat. Inst., 1956-57. Pres. Home and Sch., Swarthmore Sch. Dist., 1950; mem. internat. student seminar com. Am. Friends Service, 1953-59; com. mem. worship ministry Swarthmore Friends Meeting, 1957-59, 63—. Mem. bd. Hedgerow Theatre, 1957-60. Directed, appeared on University of the Air shows WFIL-TV, 1955, 56. Mem. Swarthmore Coll. Alumni Assn. (v.p. 1952), Kappa Alpha Theta. Mem. Soc. of Friends. Home: Wildman Arms Swarthmore PA 19081

LANGE, CHARLES HENRY, educator; b. Janesville, Wis., July 3, 1917; B.A., U. N.M., 1940, M.A., 1942, Ph.D., 1951; married; 3 children. Instr. anthropology U. Tex., 1947-51, asst. prof., 1951-55; asst. prof., curator So. Ill. U., Carbondale, 1955-58, asso. prof., 1958-63, prof., 1963-71, chmn. dept. anthropology, 1966-71; prof., chmn. dept. anthropology No. Ill. U., DeKalb, 1971-74, prof., 1974-79, part-time, 1979—. Served with AUS, 1942-45. NATO fellow, Tübingen, Germany, 1960-61. Fellow Am. Anthrop. Assn.; mem. Soc. Am. Archaeology, Archeol. Soc. N.M., Hist. Soc. N.M. Office: Dept Anthropology No Ill U DeKalb IL 60115

LANGE, CLIFFORD E., state librarian; b. Fond du Lac, Wis., Dec. 29, 1935; s. Elmer H. and Dorothy Brick (Smithers) L.; student St. Norbert Coll., 1954-57; B.S., Wis. State U., 1959; M.S.L.S. (Library Services Act scholar), U. Wis., 1960, Ph.D. (Higher Edn. Act fellow), 1972; m. Janet M. LeMieux, June 6, 1959; children—Paul, Laura, Ruth. Head extension dept. Oshkosh (Wis.) Public Library, 1960-62, head reference dept., 1962-63; asst. dir. Jervis Library, Rome, N.Y., 1962; dir. Eau Claire (Wis.) Public Library, 1963-66; asst. dir. Lake County Public Library, Griffith, Ind., 1966-68; asst. prof. Sch. Library Sci., U. Iowa, 1971-75; dir. Wauwatosa (Wis.) Public Library, 1973-75; asst. prof. U. So. Calif., 1975-78; state librarian N.Mex. State Library, Santa Fe, 1978—. Served with U.S. Army, 1958. Mem. ALA, N.Mex. Library Assn. Home: 1011 Calle Vianson Santa Fe NM 87501 Office: 300 Don Gaspar Santa Fe NM 87503

LANGE, FREDERICK MATTHEW, philanthropic adminstr.; b. Jersey City, N.J., Nov. 12, 1898; s. Mark and Lina (Fuchs) L.; B.A., Dickinson Coll., 1928; Ph.D. in Social Welfare, Internat. Free Protestant Episcopal U. (Eng.), 1946; D.C.L., Atlanta Law Sch., 1959; LL.D. (hon.), Hardin-Simmons U., 1956; L.H.D. (hon.), Taylor U., 1955; D.S.W. (hon.), Huston-Tillotson Coll.; D.P.A. (hon.), Fla. Meml. Coll.; M.A., Oxford (Eng.) U., 1974; m. Blanche Swanzy, Feb. 23, 1944. Pub. relations dir. Tex. div. Salvation Army, 1933-40, Dallas C. of C., 1940; exec. dir. Dallas Community Chest and War Chest, 1941-45; v.p., exec. dir. Southwestern Med. Found. and Med. Sch. Dallas, 1945-48; exec. v.p. Dallas County Community Chest, 1949-57; exec. v.p., Dallas Community Chest Trust Fund, 1957-68, pres., 1968—; internat. cons. Goodwill Industries, Christian Med. Soc.; fiscal cons. instns. and orgns. in S.W., 1948—. Lectr. All Souls Coll., also vis. fellow, mem. governing body St. Cross Coll., Oxford U., 1974; cons. nat. finance com. White House Conf. Children and Youth, 1960, mem. finance com. and nat. adv. council to conf. 1970; mem. nat. adv. arthritis and metabolic diseases council USPHS, 1960-62; specialist cultural exchange br. State Dept., 1961—; hon. consul gen. Dominican Republic, 1964—; vice chmn. Dallas Christian Com. for Israel. Trustee Hardin-Simmons U., Tex. Found. Decorated Duarte Sanchez y Mella medal (Dominican Republic); Royal Order Saint Sava (Yugoslavia); knight great band Liberian Humane Order African Redemption; Benemerenti medal (Vatican); knight Order of Hosp. of St. John Jerusalem; named first hon. life mem. in Southwest area of United Community Funds and Councils Am. 1953; recipient scroll of appreciation Central Community Chest Japan, 1959, citation Dallas region Nat. Conf. Christians and Jews, 1953, for humanitarian endeavors Republic Korea, 1967; Nat. award Nat. Com. Children and Youth, 1966; Order of Christopher Columbus medal (Dominican Republic), 1969; Plaque Bangkok Community Chest, 1973; community center named in his honor, Cheung Chou Island, Hong Kong, 1970, Fred M. Lange Hall Bishop Coll. and Fred M. Lange Hall Dallas Bapt. Coll. named in his honor. Mem. San Antonio Geneal. and Hist. Soc. Baptist. Clubs: Lakewood Country, Lancer (Dallas). Home: 3131 Maple Ave Apt C Dallas TX 75201 Office: Lange Center 4605 Live Oak St Dallas TX 75204

LANGE, HANS WILLIAM, mfg. co. exec.; b. Pitts., Mar. 13, 1930; s. Ewald and Elizabeth (Engle) L.; B.S., Carnegie Mellon U., 1952; M.B.A., Harvard U., 1956; m. Melissa McMurry, Dec. 19, 1953; children—Leslie, Allison, Hans William. Project mgr. Babcock & Wilcox Co., Lynchburg, Va., 1956-59; gen. mgr. Va. Indsl. Metals, Lynchburg, Va., 1959-65; plant mgr. Brenco, Inc., Petersburg, Va., 1965-67; v.p., gen. mgr. AMF, Inc., Richmond, Va., 1967-70; pres. Seamco, Inc., Stamford, Conn., 1970-72; with AMF, Inc., White Plains, N.Y., 1972—, exec. v.p. ops., 1977—. Bd. dirs. New Cannan Inn, Inc. Served with U.S. Army, 1952-54. Presbyterian. Office: AMF Inc 777 Westchester Ave White Plains NY 10604

LANGE, HOPE, actress; b. Redding Ridge, Conn., Nov. 28, 1931; d. John and Minnette (Buddecke) Lange; ed. Barmore Jr. Coll., Reed Coll. (Ore.); m. Don Murray. Appeared as dancer Jackie Gleason TV program, also Kraft TV plays; motion pictures include: Bus Stop, The True Story of Jesse James, Peyton Place, The Young Lions, In Love or War, A Pocketful of Miracles, Love is a Ball, Jigsaw, Death Wish, Hazard's People (TV), The Rivalry (TV), others; leading actress in TV series The Ghost and Mrs. Muir, New Dick Van Dyke Show. Recipient Emmy award, 1968.*

LANGE, JAMES BRAXTON, chem. co. exec.; b. Amory, Miss., Feb. 17, 1937; s. Oliver John and Sarah Nell (Gravlee) L.; B.S. in Psychology, Millsaps Coll., 1960; B.S. in Bus., Miss. Coll., 1970, M.B.A., 1973; m. Margaret Terry Terrell, Aug. 9, 1969. Sec., treas. 1st Mississippi Corp., Jackson, 1973—. Indsl. rep. Miss. CD, 1971-73; charter mem. Community Action Council, 1972-74; group leader United Givers Fund, 1970-73; mem. exec. com. YMCA. Served with USN, 1960-63. Mem. Am. Soc. Corporate Secs., Am. Soc. Personnel Adminstrn., Miss. Mfrs. Assn. (past chmn. indsl. relations com.), Jackson Personnel Assn., Indsl. Mgmt. Club Jackson, Jackson C. of C., Naval Res. Assn. (past v.p., treas.), Res. Officers Assn. (past v.p.), Navy League Jackson. Republican. Club: Lions. Home: 5056 Sunnyvale Dr Jackson MS 39211 Office: 700 North St Jackson MS 39205

LANGE, KURT, physician; b. Berlin, Germany, Oct. 31, 1906; came to U.S., 1939, naturalized, 1944; s. Georg and Pauline (Neumann) L.; M.D., U. Berlin, 1930; m. Helen Marcus, June 14, 1936; children—Peter, Monica. Intern, U. Berlin (Charite); resident in pathology 2d Med. U. Hosp., Berlin; instr. internal medicine U. Berlin, 1931-34; practice medicine specializing in internal medicine, Berlin, 1934-38, N.Y.C., 1939—; instr. medicine N.Y. Med. Coll., N.Y.C., 1939-44, asso. prof. medicine, 1945-62, prof. clin. pediatrics, 1962-71, prof. pediatrics, 1971—, prof. medicine, 1962—; attending physician Flower and Fifth Ave Hosps.; cons. physician Chenango Meml. Hosp., Norwich, N.Y., Horton Meml. Hosp., Middletown, N.Y.; resident asso. pathologist Lenox Hill Hosp., N.Y.C.; vis. physician Met. Hosp., Bird S. Coler Hosp.; dir. renal service N.Y. Med. Coll., 1952-78, Met. Med. Center, 1952-78. Chief renal service and lab. OSRD, U.S. Army, 1941-48. Recipient 2d award N.Y. State Med. Soc., 1946, hon. mention AMA, 1944-63, Bronze medal, 1946, certificate of merit, 1961, also Hectoen Gold medal AMA, 1966; First award N.Y. State Med. Soc., 1967; Franz Volhard medal German Nephrology Soc., 1976; Lester Hoenig award Kidney Found. N.Y., 1977. Fellow A.C.P., Am. Coll. Cardiology; mem. Harvey Soc., Soc. Exptl. Biology and Medicine, Soc. Exptl. Pathology, Alpha Omega Alpha. Am. editor: Clin. Nephrology. Club: Explorers. Home: 519 E 86th St New York NY 10028 Office: 11 E 68th St New York NY 10021

LANGE, LESTER HENRY, univ. dean, mathematician; b. Concordia, Mo., Jan. 2, 1924; s. Harry William Christopher and Ella Marie (Alewel) L.; student U. Calif., Berkeley, 1943-44; B.A. in Math., Valparaiso U., 1948; M.S. in Math., Stanford, 1950; Ph.D. in Math., U. Notre Dame, 1960; m. Anne Marie Pelikan, Aug. 17, 1947 (div. Oct. 1960); children—Christopher, Nicholas, Philip, Alexander; m. 2d, Beverly Jane Brown, Feb. 4, 1962; 1 son, Andrew. Instr., then asst. prof. math. Valparaiso U., 1950-56; instr. math. U. Notre Dame, 1956-57, 59-60; Danforth fellow, 1957-58, NSF faculty fellow, 1958-59; mem. faculty San Jose State U. (Calif.), 1960—, prof. math., head dept., 1961-70, dean Sch. Natural Scis. and Math., 1970—, Sch. Sci., 1972—. Served with inf., AUS, 1943-46; ETO. Mem. Math. Assn. Am. (bd. govs., L.R. Ford Sr. award 1972), Calif. Math. Council, London Math. Soc., Sigma Xi, Phi Kappa Phi. Author text on linear algebra. Contbr. to profl. jours. Home: 1644 Andalusia Way San Jose CA 95125

LANGE, PHIL C., educator; b. North Freedom, Wis., Feb. 26, 1914; s. Richard Samuel and Martha (Grosinske) L.; B.A., U. Wis., 1934, M.A., 1936, Ph.D., 1941; m. Irene Oyen, June 8, 1940; children—Dena Rae, Richard (dec.). Tchr., Reeseville (Wis.) Pub. Sch., 1935-37; chmn. English dept. Wayland Jr. Coll. and Acad., Beaver Dam, Wis., 1937-39; instr. English, student teaching supr. Beloit (Wis.) High Sch., 1939-40; asst. instr. U. Wis., Madison, 1940-41, summers 1938, 39; chmn. psychology dept., dean men. Ariz. State Coll., Flagstaff, 1941-42; chmn. edn. dept. State U. N.Y., Fredonia, 1942-50; prof. edn., coordinator student teaching Tchrs. Coll., Columbia U., 1950—; cons., expert for Dept. State, UNESCO, AID. Served with USNR, 1943-46. Recipient Filmstrip award Graphic Arts, 1966; Communication award Nat. Soc. Programmed Instrn., 1968; award Ednl. Press Assn. Am., 1969. Author, editor curriculum materials. Home: 727 Fox Hill Dr Sun City Center FL 33570 Office: Tchrs Coll Columbia Univ New York NY 10027

LANGE, ROLAND H., ins. co. exec.; b. Chgo., July 24, 1910; s. Robert and Elizabeth Lange; B.B.A. cum laude, Northwestern U., 1932; m. Florence E. Swartzloff, Apr. 10, 1937; children—Elizabeth Ann (Mrs. Hayden L. Leon, Jr.), Robert James. With Hartford Fire Ins. Co. (Conn.), 1930-70, pres., 1963-65, also dir.; vice chmn. bds. Hartford Ins. Group, 1965-68, cons., 1968-70. First pres., also chmn. Ins. Information Inst.; past chmn. bd. Factory Ins. Assn.; past trustee Ins. Inst. Am., Am. Fgn. Ins. Assn., Inst. Property and Liability Underwriters. Chmn. com. on financing higher edn. in State of Conn.; mem. nat. export expansion com. Dept. Commerce. Past chmn. bd. Greater Hartford chpt. ARC, spl. asst. to nat. chmn.; trustee, past chmn. bd. Ins. Coll. N.Y.; bd. dirs. Sch. Ins. at U. Conn., Hartford Salvation Army; bd. govs. Am. Nat. Red Cross; corporator Hartford Hosp., St. Francis Hosp., Mt. Sinai Hosp., Inst. Living; past pres. Conn. Opera Assn.; trustee, past chmn. Conn. Ednl. TV Corp.; trustee Hartt Coll., U. Hartford; past dir. Hartford C. of C. Recipient Greater Hartford C. of C. Leadership medal, 1968; Harriman award for distinguished service ARC, 1975. Clubs: Hartford, Hartford Golf. Home: 44 Stoner Dr West Hartford CT 06107

LANGE, TED, actor, dir.; b. Oakland, Calif., Jan. 5; s. Ted and Geraldine L.; attended San Francisco City Coll., Merritt Jr. Coll.; m. Sheryl; 1 son, Ted IV. Broadway debut in Hair; other stage appearances include: Dialogue Black and White, Tell Pharaoh, Big Time Buck White, Golden Boy, Ain't Supposed to Die A Natural Death; appearances with New Shakespearean Co.; dir. stage prodns.: The Odd Couple, Richard III, Hamlet; motion picture credits include: Trick Baby, 1972, Wattstax, 1973, Blade, 1973, Larry, 1974, Toe to Toe (dir.), Passing Through (screenplay); TV credits: That's My Mama, 1974-75, Mr. T. and Tina, 1976, The Last Detail, A.F.I. Salute to James Cagney; regular on ABC-TV series Love Boat, 1977—. Office: care Arnold Soloway Assos 118 S Beverly Blvd Beverly Hills CA 90212*

LANGE, VICTOR, educator; b. Leipzig, Germany, July 13, 1908; s. Walter and Theodora (Schellenberg) L.; student Thomasschule Leipzig, 1919-28, Oxford U., 1928, Sorbonne, 1929, U. Munich, 1929-30; M.A., U. Toronto (Gertrude Davis exchange fellow 1930-31), Ph.D., U. Leipzig, 1934; H.L.D., Monterey Inst., 1978; m. Frances Mary Olrich, Feb. 23, 1945; children—Dora Elizabeth, Thomas Victor. Came to U.S., 1932, naturalized, 1943. Dir. Akademische Auslandsstelle, U. Leipzig, 1931-32; lectr. German, Univ. Coll., Toronto, 1932-38; asst. prof. German, Cornell U., 1938-41, asso. prof., 1941-45, prof., 1945-57; prof. German lit. Princeton, 1957—, John N. Woodhull prof. modern. langs., 1968-77, emeritus, 1977—. Hon. prof. Free U., Berlin, 1962—; vis. prof. Smith Coll., U. Chgo., Berkeley, U. Cologne, U. Heidelberg, Munich, Columbia U., U. Mich., N.Y. U., Yale U., La Jolla, Davis; examiner in chief for German, Coll. Entrance Exam. Bd., 1942-50; cons. Dept. of State, 1950-53; external examiner U. Hong Kong, 1979—; vis. prof. U. Auckland (New Zealand), 1974. Bd. dirs. Nat. Carl-Schurz Found.; trustee Goethe House, N.Y.C. Guggenheim fellow, 1950-51, 67; McCosh fellow, 1966-67; Fulbright lectr., Australia, 1969; Phi Beta Kappa vis. scholar, 1968-69; Nat. Endowment Humanities sr. fellow, 1973-74; fellow Humanities Research Centre, Canberra, Australia, 1977. Decorated comdr.'s Cross (German Fed. Republic); recipient Gold medal Goethe Inst., 1966; prize for scholarship German Acad. Lang. and Lit., 1966. Mem. Internat. Assn. Germanists (pres. 1965-70), Am. Soc. 18th Century Studies (pres. 1975-76), Am. Council on German Studies, Modern Lang. Assn. Am. (exec. council, 1st v.p.), Am. Assn. Tchrs. German, Modern Humanities Research Assn. (chmn. Am. br.), German Acad. (Darmstadt), Am. Comparative Lit. Assn., Goethe Gesellschaft Weimar, Phi Beta Kappa. Clubs: Princeton, Grolier, P.E.N. (N.Y.C.). Author: Die Lyrik und ihr Publikum im England des 18. Jahrhunderts, 1936; Kulturkritik und Literaturbetrachtung in Amerika, 1938; Modern German Literature, 1945; Goethe's Fiction, 1953; Schlegel's Literary Criticism, 1955; Schillers Poetik, 1961; Contemporary German Poetry, 1964; The Reader in the Strategy of Fiction, 1973; Mann: Tradition and Experiment, 1976; The Classical Age of German Literature, 1980; (with W. R. Amacher) New Perspectives in German Literary Criticism, 1979, others. Editor: Deutsche Briefe, 1940; The Sorrows of Young Werther, 1949; Goethe's Faust, 1950; Great German Short Stories, 1952; Lessings Hamburg Dramaturgy, 1962; Goethe's Wilhelm Meister, 1962; German Classical Drama, 1962; Goethe: Twentieth Century Views, 1968; Humanistic Scholarship in America, 1968, Goethes Werke, 1972; also others; trans. Edith Wharton's Ethan Frome, 1948. Editorial bd. Comparative Lit., Germanistik, Rev. of Nat. Lit. Contbr. to lit. jours. Home: 343 Jefferson Rd Princeton NJ 08540

LANGELL, JEROME EDWIN, writer, feature editor; b. Cleve., Nov. 14, 1910; s. Alexander Hector and Agnes Helen (Jones) L.; B.S., Wharton Sch., U. Pa., 1933. Mdsg. and market research, Cleve. Press, 1933-38; market research, radio sta. WHK, Cleve., 1941; compliance investigator WPB, 1942-44; insp. Fisher Aircraft, 1944; asst. editor employee publs. Standard Oil Co. (O.), 1945; owner Allied Feature Syndicate (specializing in preparation and sale of editorial features to newspapers), Cleve., 1946—; collaborator and co-originator, nationally syndicated newspaper feature, Idea Chaser also founder

Ideacrafters of Am. Office: Allied Feature Syndicate Citizens Bldg Cleveland OH 44114

LANGELLA, FRANK, actor; b. Bayonne, N.J., Jan. 1. 1946; student Syracuse U., also studied with Seymour Falk; m. Ruth Weil, Nov. 1977. Apprenticed Pocono Playhouse, Mountain Home, Pa.; appeared Erie (Pa.) Playhouse, 1960; mem. original Lincoln Center repertory tng. co., 1963; off-Broadway debut in The Immoralist, 1963; other stage appearances include: Benito Cereno, 1964, The Old Glory (Obie award), 1964-65, Good Day (Obie award), 1965-66, The White Devil (Obie award), 1965-66, Long Day's Journey Into Night, The Skin of Our Teeth, The Cretan Woman, Yerma (all 1966), The Devils, Dracula, Iphigenia at Aulis (all 1967), A Cry of Players, 1968, Cyrano de Bergerac, 1971, A Midsummer Night's Dream, 1972, The Relapse, The Tooth of Crime, 1972, The Taming of the Shrew, 1973, The Seagull, 1974, Ring Round the Moon, 1975, The Prince of Hamburg; mem. Cleve. Playhouse co., 1967-68, L.I. Festival repertory, 1968; Broadway debut in Seascape (Drama Desk and Tony awards), 1974-75; appeared in Dracula, Boradway, 1977; stage directing debut in John and Abigail, 1969; performed in films Diary of a Mad Housewife (Nat. Soc. Film Critics award), 1970, The Twelve Chairs, 1970, The Deadly Trap, 1972, The Wrath of God, 1972, Dracula, 1979; TV appearances include On Stage, The Trials of O'Brien, Benito Cereno, 1965, Good Day, 1967, The Mark of Zorro, 1974, The Ambassador, 1974, The Seagull, 1975, The American Woman: Portraits of Courage, 1976, Eccentricities of a Nightingale, 1976. Bd. dirs. Berkshire Festival. Mem. Actors Equity, Screen Actors Guild.*

LANGEN, HERBERT JOHN, educator; b. Elkhorn, Wis., May 25, 1917; s. Ole J. and Frances (Koch) L.; B.Ed., U. Wis., Whitewater, 1939; M.A., U. Iowa, 1947, Ph.D., 1954; m. Dorothy L. Johnson, Nov. 22, 1941; children—William O., Nancy E. Bus. tchr. Morengo (Ill.) High Sch., 1939-40, East Dubuque (Ill.) High Sch., 1940-41; bookkeeper Skogman Constrn. Co., Cedar Rapids, Iowa, 1946; mem. faculty U. Ariz., Tucson, 1947—, prof., 1956—, head dept. bus. edn. and office adminstrn., 1949—, dir. career and vocat. tchr. edn., 1973—; cons. Ariz. Dept. Vocat. Edn., 1963—; del. Internat. Soc. Bus. Edn., Stockholm, Sweden, 1970, Amsterdam, Netherlands, 1971, pres., 1972-75. Served with USNR, 1941-46. Recipient Disting. Alumni Service award U. Wis., Whitewater, 1979. Mem. Nat. (exec. bd. 1969-71), Western, Ariz. bus. edn. assns., Internat. Soc. Bus. Edn. (pres. U.S. chpt. 1969-71), Delta Pi Epsilon, Pi Omega Pi (sponsor), Beta Gamma Sigma (sec.). Kiwanian (pres. Conquistador Club, Tucson 1969). Home: 4472 E 7th St Tucson AZ 85711

LANGENBERG, DONALD NEWTON, physicist, educator; b. Devils Lake, N.D., Mar. 17, 1932; s. Ernest George and Fern (Newton) L.; B.S., Iowa State U., 1953; M.S., U. Calif. at Los Angeles, 1955; Ph.D. (NSF fellow) U. Calif. at Berkeley, 1959; m. Patricia Ann Warrington, June 20, 1953; children—Karen Kaye, Julia Ann, John Newton, Amy Paris. Electronics engr. Hughes Research Labs., Culver City, Calif., 1953-55; acting instr. U. Calif. at Berkeley, 1958-59; mem. faculty U. Pa., Phila., 1960—, prof., 1967—, dir. Lab. for Research on Structure Matter, 1972-74, vice provost for grad. studies and research, 1974-79; maitre de conference associe Ecole Normale Superieure, Paris, France, 1966-67; vis. prof. Calif. Inst. Tech., Pasadena, 1971; guest researcher Zentralinstitut für Tieftemperatur forschung der Bayerischen Akademie der Wissenschaften and Technischen Universität München, 1974. Recipient John Price Wetherill medal Franklin Inst., 1975. NSF Postdoctoral fellow, 1959-60; Alfred P. Sloan Found. fellow, 1962-64; Guggenheim fellow, 1966-67. Fellow Am. Phys. Soc., Sigma Xi. Research and publs. on solid state and low temperature physics including electronic band structure in metals and semicondrs., quantum phase coherence and nonequilibrium effects in supercondrs. Home: 118 Penarth Rd Bala-Cynwyd PA 19004 Office: Dept Physics U Pa Philadelphia PA 19104

LANGENBERG, FREDERICK CHARLES, steel co. exec.; b. N.Y.C., July 1, 1927; s. Frederick C. and Margaret (McLaughlin) L.; B.S., Lehigh U., 1950, M.S., 1951; Ph.D., Pa. State U., 1955; postgrad. execs. program Carnegie-Mellon U., 1962; m. Jane Anderson Bartholomew, May 16, 1953; children—Frederick C., Susan Jane. With United States Steel Corp., 1951-53; vis. fellow Mass. Inst. Tech., 1955-56; with Crucible Steel Corp., Pitts., 1956-68, v.p. research and engrng., 1966-68; pres. Trent Tube div. Colt Industries, Milw., 1968-70; exec. v.p. Jessop Steel Co., Washington, Pa., 1970, pres., 1970-75, also dir.; pres., dir. Am. Iron and Steel Inst., Washington, 1975-78; pres., dir. Interlake, Inc., Oak Brook, Ill.; dir. Millcraft Industries, Inc. Active Pitts. Opera. Served with USNR, 1944-45. Alumni fellow Pa. State U., 1977. Fellow Am. Soc. Metals (trustee, David Ford McFarland award Penn State chpt. 1973, Pittsburgh Nite lectr. 1970, Andrew Carnegie lectr. 1976); mem. Am. Inst. M.E., Am. Chem. Soc., Am., Brit., Internat. iron and steel insts., Assn. Iron and Steel Engrs., Am. Ordnance Assn., U.S. C. of C. (mem. edn. and manpower devel. com. 1973), Phi Beta Kappa, Sigma Xi, Tau Beta Pi. Democrat. Clubs: Duquesne, University, St. Clair Country, Oakmont Country (Pitts.); Univ., Congressional, Burning Tree, Cosmos, Carlton (Washington); Butler Nat. Golf (Chgo.). Contbr. articles to tech. jours. Patentee in field. Home: 4416 Chalfont Pl Washington DC 20016 Office: Commerce Plaza 2015 Spring Rd Oak Brook IL 60521

LANGENDERFER, HAROLD QUENTIN, accountant; b. Swanton, Ohio, July 21, 1925; s. Omer Quintan and Minnie (Buckenmyer) L.; B.S. in Bus., Miami U., Oxford, Ohio, 1949; M.B.A., Northwestern U., 1950; D.B.A., Ind. U., 1954; m. Joan Mary Etzrodt, June 17, 1950; children—Thomas, Amy, Jeffry, Chris. Prof. intermediate accounting Ind. U., Bloomington, 1952-53; Peat, Marwick, Mitchell prof. profl. accounting U. N.C., Chapel Hill, 1953—; cons. mgmt. devel. to Ford Found., Cairo, 1961-63; tax cons. Served with U.S. Army, 1943-46. C.P.A., Ind., N.C. Mem. N.C. Assn. C.P.A.'s, Am. Inst. C.P.A.'s, Nat. Assn. Accountants, Am. Accounting Assn., Fin. Execs. Inst. Roman Catholic. Club: Chapel Hill Kiwanis (pres. 1966). Co-author: Income Tax Procedure, 1978; C.P.A. Examination—A Comprehensive Review, 3d edit., 1979; contbr. articles in field to accounting jours. Home: 1074 Canterbury Ln Chapel Hill NC 27514 Office: U NC 012-A Carroll Hall Chapel Hill NC 27514

LANGENFELD, NICHOLAS JOSEPH, clergyman, educator; b. Marytown, Wis., Aug. 11, 1901; s. John and Theresa (Brost) L.; B.A., St. Lawrence Coll., Wis., 1922; M.A., St. Francis Sem., Wis., 1926; Ph.D., Roman Acad., 1930; D.C.L., Collegio Angelico, Rome, 1931; Licencie es Sciences Sociales, U. Louvain (Belgium), 1933; diploma Acad. Internat. Law, The Hague, 1933. Ordained priest Roman Catholic Ch., 1926; asst. pastor St. Mary's Ch., Menasha, Wis., 1926-29; organized symphonic band St. Mary's High Sch., 1927; mem. faculty Fordham U. Sch. Social Service, 1934—, asso. prof., dir. research, 1934—, moderator Ann. Alumni Giving Fund, 1961—. Cath. chaplain on numerous ocean cruises. Recipient medal of merit Fordham U., 1955. Republican. Club: K.C. (hon. life mem.). Home: 355 W 22d St New York NY 10011

LANGENHEIM, RALPH LOUIS, JR., educator; b. Cin., May 26, 1922; s. Ralph Louis and Myrtle (Helmers) L.; B.S., U. Tulsa, 1943; M.S., U. Colo., 1947; Ph.D., U. Minn., 1951; m. Jean C. Harmon, Dec. 23, 1946; m. 2d, Virginia A.M. Knobloch, June 5, 1962; children—Victoria Elizabeth, Ralph Louis III; m. 3d, Shirley B. Ate, May 1, 1970. Teaching asst. U. Tulsa, 1941-43, U. Colo., 1947; fellow U. Minn., 1947-48, teaching asst., 1948-50; asst. prof. Coe Coll., 1950-52; asst. prof. paleontology U. Calif., Berkeley, 1952-59; asst. prof. geology U. Ill., Urbana, 1959-62, asso. prof., 1962-67, prof., 1967—; with Instituto Geologico Nacional de Colombia, summer 1953; Geol. Survey Can., summer 1958, Geol. Survey Iran, 1973. Served with USNR, 1943-46; lt. comdr. Res., ret. Mem. Paleontol. Soc. (sec. 1962-70), Geol. Soc. Am., Soc. Econ. Paleontologists and Mineralogists, Am. Assn. Petroleum Geologists, Societe Geologique Suisse, AAAS, Ill. Geol. Soc. (sec. 1978), Internat. Assn. Cnidaria Specialists (treas. 1977—), Ill. Acad. Sci., Rocky Mountain Biol. Lab., Geol. Soc. London, Wyo. Geol. Assn., Sigma Xi. Research and publs. in field. Home: 401 W Vermont Ave Urbana IL 61801

LANGENKAMP, R. DOBIE, govt. ofcl.; b. Tulsa, Aug. 14, 1936; s. Robert Darwin and Marybelle (Dobie) L.; B.A. magna cum laude, Stanford U., 1958; LL.B., Harvard U., 1961; m. Mary Alice Myers, Sept. 27, 1963; children—Heather Elizabeth, Matthew Dobie, Daniel Benjamin, Lucinda Turner. Admitted to D.C. bar, 1962, Okla. bar, 1964; mem. firm Collier, Shannon, Rill & Edwards, Washington, 1962-64; mem. firm Doerner, Stuart, Saunders, Daniel and Langenkamp, Tulsa, 1964-78, sr. partner, 1967-78; dep. asst. sec. for oil, natural gas and shale resources, resource applications Dept. Energy, Washington, 1978—; lectr. U. Tulsa, 1966-68. Chmn., Okla. State Police Task Force, 1976-77; mem. Gov.'s Adv. Com. on Criminal Justice; bd. dirs. Tulsa County Legal Aid Soc.; v.p., dir. Tulsa County Office of Econ. Opportunity. Served with U.S. Army, 1961-62, 1st lt. Res., 1962-68. Recipient Exceptional Service award Dept. Energy, 1979. Mem. Okla. Bar Assn. (exec. com.), Am. Bar Assn., D.C. Bar Assn., Harvard Law Sch. Assn. (pres. Okla.). Democrat. Episcopalian. Club: Tulsa Tennis. Home: 5280 Patridge Ln NW Washington DC 20016 Office: 12th and Pennsylvania Dept Energy Washington DC 20461

LANGER, GLENN ARTHUR, medical educator; b. Nyack, N.Y., May 5, 1928; s. A. Arthur and Marie Catherine (Doscher) L.; B.A., Colgate U., 1950; M.D., Columbia U., 1954; m. Marianne Phister, Oct. 12, 1977; 1 dau., Andrea Louise. Asst. prof. medicine Columbia, Coll. Phys. and Surg., 1963-66; asso. prof. medicine and physiology U. Calif. at Los Angeles Med. Sch., 1966-69, prof., 1969—, Castera prof. cardiology, 1978—, vice chmn. dept. physiology, 1967—; asso. dir. Los Angeles County Cardiovascular Research Lab., 1966—; vis. lectr., Sweden, 1970. Mem. exec. bd., basic sci. council Am. Heart Assn., 1973-74, vice chmn. basic sci. council, 1974-76, chmn., 1976-78, pres. Greater Los Angeles affiliate Am. Heart Assn., 1975-76; bd. dirs. Los Angeles County Heart Assn., 1968—; nat. bd. dirs. Am. Heart Assn., 1976—. Served to capt. M.C., AUS, 1955-57. Banbury fellow, 1950-54, 54-55, 57-59, 59-60, 60-62; Nat. Heart and Lung Inst. grantee, 1967—; Macy Found. fellow, 1979-80. Diplomate Am. Bd. Internal Medicine. Fellow Am. Coll. Cardiology; mem. Am. Physiol. Soc., Cardiac Muscle Soc., Harvey Soc., Soc. Gen. Physiologists, Assn. Am. Physicians, Phi Beta Kappa, Sigma Xi, Alpha Omega Alpha. Editor: (with A.J. Brady) The Mammalian Myocardium, 1974. Editorial bd. Am. Jour. Physiology, 1970-75, Jour. Molecular Cell Cardiology, 1970—, Circulation Research, 1971-76. Home: 101 Ocean Ave Santa Monica CA 90402 Office: School Medicine Univ California Los Angeles CA 90024

LANGER, JAMES JOHN, football player; b. Little Falls, Minn., May 16, 1948; B.S. in Econs., S.D. State U. With Miami Dolphins, 1970—; played in Pro-Bowl NFL All-Star game, 1973-78. Office: care Miami Dolphins 330 Biscayne Blvd Bldg Miami FL 33132

LANGER, LAWRENCE MARVIN, educator, physicist; b. N.Y.C., Dec. 22, 1913; s. Alexander H. and Anna (Brown) L.; B.S., N.Y. U., 1934, M.S., 1935, Ph.D., 1938; m. Beatrice Fisher, July 5, 1936. Teaching asst. research N.Y. U., 1934-38; mem. faculty Ind. U., Bloomington, 1938—, prof. physics, 1952—, chmn. dept., 1966-73; project engr., research asso. Radiation Lab., Mass. Inst. Tech., 1941-42; asso. physicist, group leader U. Cal. Div. War Research, 1943-45; alternate group leader Los Alamos Atomic Bomb Project, 1943-45; expert cons. AEC, 1948-61; adv. cons. nuclear data project Nat. Acad. Sci.-NRC, 1959. Fellow Am. Phys. Soc.; mem. A.A.A.S., Sigma Xi, Sigma Pi Sigma. Contbr. profl. jours. Home: 1342 Southdowns Bloomington IN 47401

LANGER, RALPH ERNEST, journalist; b. Benton Harbor, Mich., July 30, 1937; s. Ralph L. and Mary (Skuda) L.; student Central Mich. U., 1955-57; B.A. in Journalism, U. Mich., 1957-59; m. Katherine B. McGuire, June 25, 1960; children—Terri B., Tammi L. Telegraph editor, reporter Grand Haven (Mich.) Daily Tribune, 1959-60; mng. editor Port Angeles (Wash.) Evening News, 1962-66; copy desk Detroit Free Press, 1966-68; asst. mng. editor Dayton Jour. Herald, 1968, mng. editor, 1968-75; editor Everett (Wash.) Herald, 1975—. Served to 1st lt. AUS, 1960-62. Mem. Am. Soc. Newspaper Editors, A.P. Mng. Editors Assn., Scabbard and Blade, Alpha Phi Gamma, Sigma Phi Epsilon. Home: 2705 91st St SE Everett WA 98204 Office: Everett Herald Grand and California Sts Everett WA 98201

LANGER, ROBERT ADOLPH, photographer; b. Chgo., Oct. 8, 1942; s. Gerald and Constance Ann (Monforte) L.; student Wright Jr. Coll., 1962, Army Signal Corps Photog. Sch., 1963; m. Diana Marie Puig, Oct. 7, 1967; children—Robert Gerald, Jaime Maria, Gina Marie. Copy boy, lab. technician Chgo. Tribune, 1959-65; lab. technician, photographer Chgo. Sun-Times, 1965—. Served with Ill. N.G., 1964-70. Mem. Chgo. Press Photographers Assn. Office: 401 N Wabash Ave Chicago IL 60611

LANGERMAN, HAROLD A., advt. exec.; b. Phila., Dec. 20, 1923; s. Charles and Ida L.; B.A. in English, Gettysburg Coll., 1949; m. Ruth E., Apr. 15, 1953; 1 son, Stephen C. Copywriter, J. Walter Thompson Co., Tokyo, 1953-54; advt. mgr. Safeway Stores, Dallas, 1954-55; v.p., creative dir. Lewis & Gilman, Inc., Phila., 1956-69; exec. v.p., creative dir. Spiro & Assos., Phila., 1969-79, Smith-Langerman, Phila., 1979—; lectr. in field. Served with U.S. Army, 1943-46, 49-53. Decorated Bronze Star; recipient numerous advt. awards. Home: 303 Preston Rd Flourtown PA 19031 Office: 1616 Walnut St Philadelphia PA 19103

LANGEVIN, THOMAS HARVEY, univ. pres.; b. St. Paul, Mar. 20, 1922; s. Thomas E. and Myrtle (Damsgard) L.; B.S., Concordia Tchrs. Coll., Seward, Neb., 1947; M.A., U. Neb., 1949, Ph.D., 1951; m. Pearl E. Mattfeld, Aug. 29, 1942; children—Dennis, Timothy. Quarantine insp. USPHS, 1943-45; grad. asst., asst. instr. U. Neb., 1947-51; prof. Concordia Tchrs. Coll., 1951-63, dean coll., 1961-63, acting pres., 1961-63; dir. long-range planning project Luth. Ch.-Mo. Synod, 1964-65, also cons. Bd. Higher Edn.; acad. v.p. Pacific Luth. U., 1965-69; pres. Capital U., Columbus, Ohio, 1969—; cons., vis. fellow Battelle Seattle Research Center, 1976. Co-chmn. Tacoma Area Urban Coalition Edn. Task Force, 1967-69; mem., past chmn. Ohio Com. Pub. Programs in Humanities; exec. com. Fedn. Pub. Programs in Humanities; mem. Ohio Higher Edn. Facilities Commn.; former mem. Commn. on Future Lutheran Ednl. Conf. N. Am., pres., 1977-78; bd. dirs. Nat. Urban League. Mem. Columbus Urban League, Ohio Lutheran Forum, Met. Columbus Sch. Com.; bd. dirs. Tacoma Citizens Com. Pub. TV, 1967-69, Design for Progress Tacoma, 1969, Tacoma Area Urban Coalition, 1967-69; mem. adv. panel Air Force ROTC; adv. com. Center Sci. and Industry, Columbus; asso. in urban affairs Nat. Inst. Pub. Affairs; bd. control Concordia Coll., Portland, Oreg., 1965-69; bd. overseers Acad. Contemporary Problems, Columbus, 1972-75; trustee Columbus Symphony Orch., Columbus Sch. Girls; past trustee Columbus Met. Area Community Action; hon. trustee Internat. Council of Mid-Ohio; bd. govs. Goodwill Industries Central Ohio, Salesian Inner City Boys' Club; bd. dirs. Blue Cross Central Ohio, Franklin County Heart Br., Columbus Area Mental Health Center; bd. dirs. Battelle Meml. Inst. Found., chmn., 1977-78. Served with USCGR, 1943-45. Recipient Carnegie grant, postdoctoral fellow Center for Study Higher Edn., U. Mich., 1963-64. Mem. Assn. Ind. Colls. and Univs. Ohio (chmn. 1971-74), Am. Council Edn. (mem. Ohio panel nat. identification program for advancement women in higher edn. adminstrn.), Orgn. Am. Historians, Nebr., Ohio hist. socs., Am. Assn. Higher Edn., Newcomen Soc. N.Am., Navy League U.S. (dir. Columbus council), Columbus Area C. of C. (dir. 1971-74). Lutheran. Club: Columbus Rotary (dir.). Home: 569 Woodingham Pl Columbus OH 43213

LANGFITT, THOMAS WILLIAM, educator, neurosurgeon; b. Clarksburg, W.Va., Apr. 20, 1927; s. Frank and Veda (Davis) L.; A.B., Princeton, 1949; M.D., Johns Hopkins, 1953; m. Carolyn Louise Payne, Jan. 31, 1953; children—Thomas William, David Douglas, John Turner, Frank Davis. Intern Johns Hopkins Hosp., 1953-54, resident neurosurgery, 1957-61; chief neurology br. Med. Research Lab., Army Chem. Center, Edgewood, Md., 1956-57; chief neurosurgery Pa. Hosp., 1961-68, acting dir. dept. surgery, 1967-68; Charles Frazier prof., chmn. div. neurosurgery Sch. Medicine, U. Pa., 1968—, acting v.p. health affairs, 1973-74, v.p. for health affairs, 1974—; cons. neurosurgery Pa. Hosp., Children's Hosp. Phila., VA Hosp., Phila. Served with AUS, 1945-46, M.C., 1955-57. Diplomate Am. Bd. Neurosurgery. Mem. A.M.A., A.C.S., Am. Assn. Neurol. Surgeons, Am. Acad. Neurol. Surgery, Am. Neurol. Assn (council 1973—), Neurosurg. Soc. Am., Assn. Acad. Health Centers (dir. 1978), Research Soc. Neurol. Surgeons, Am. Surg. Assn., Am. Physiol. Soc., Phila. Neurol. Soc. (1st v.p. 1968). Editor Jour. Neurosurgery. Author papers on intracranial pressure, brain edema, cerebral blood flow. Home: 71 Merbrook Bend Merion PA 19006 Office: 3400 Spruce St Philidelphia PA 19104

LANGFORD, ANNA RIGGS, lawyer; b. Springfield, Ohio, Oct. 27, 1917; d. Arthur J. and Alice Riggs; J.D., John Marshall Law Sch., 1956; m. Lawrence W. Langford, Aug. 21, 1948 (div.); 1 son, Lawrence W. Admitted to Ill. bar; asso. Robinson, Farmer & Langford, Chgo., 1959-69; pvt. practice, Chgo., 1956—. Mem. Sparling Commn. investigating events of Democratic Conv., Chgo., 1968; del. Pres. Johnson's Conf. to Fulfill These Rights, Washington, 1968; mem. Gov. Olgilvie's Com. for Sr. Citizens and del. Pres. Nixon's Conf. on Aging, 1971; mem. Chgo. City Council from 16th Ward, 1971-75; del.-at-large Nat. Dem. Conv., Miami, Fla., 1972; del. World Congress of Peace Forces, Moscow, Russia, 1973; mem. Commn. of Inquiry into conditions in Chili after Mil. Coup, 1974; mem. Internat. Commn. of Inquiry into Crimes of Mil. Junta in Chili, Helsinki, Finland, 1974; chmn. Ill. Gov. Com. on Ethics, 1976. Founder, Pride Community Center, Inc. (Englewood), 1974; mem. N.A.A.C.P., Chgo. Urban League, Chgo. chpt. SCLC. Chmn. bd. dirs. Impact; bd. dirs. ACLU, 1970-71, Operation Breadbasket and successor orgn. Push. Recipient Iota Bus. Week award Alpha chpt. Iota Phi Lambda, 1969, James B. Anderson award for outstanding achievement in politics Montford Point Marine Assn., 1971, Achievement award 7th Ward Independent Polit. Orgn., 1971, Outstanding Service in Govt. award as alderman SCLC's Operation Breadbasket, 1971, certificate award Internat. Travellers Assn., 1971, Woman of Distinction award Etta Moten Civic and Ednl. Club, 1970, award of distinction Am. Friendship Club, 1971, Testimonial award Afro-Am. Patrolmens Assn., 1971, Community award WBEE Radio, 1971, Operation Bootstrap award, 1971; others. Hon. mem. Chgo. Police Capt.'s Assn., 1974. Mem. Nat., Cook County (dir., Civil Rights award 1970, Spl. Achievement award 1971) bar assns. Office: 1249 W 63d St Chicago IL 60636

LANGFORD, ERNEST, architect; b. Ballinger, Tex., May 30, 1891; s. Marcus Lafayette and Maude Clarence (Fewell) L.; B.S. in Architecture, Tex. A & M Coll., 1913; M.S., U. Ill., 1924; m. Lela Davidson, Dec. 24, 1913; 1 son, Keith. Architect, A.O. Watson Architect, Austin, Tex., 1913-15; instr. engring. drawing Tex. A & M Coll., 1915-19, prof., 1925-29, head Coll. Architecture, 1929-56, univ. archivist, 1957-71; instr. architecture U. Ill., 1920-25. Councilman City of College Station, Tex., 1938-42, mayor, 1942-66. Fellow AIA, Tex. Soc. Architects, Phi Kappa Phi, Tau Beta Phi. Club: Kiwanis.

LANGFORD, GEORGE CLEMENT, journalist; b. Johnson City, Tenn., May 24, 1939; s. Norris McCormick and Sarah Cartwright (Lacy) L.; B.A., Vanderbilt U., 1961; m. Anne Roberta Mirgain, June 13, 1964; children—Jennie Anne, Julie Beth. Reporter, UPI, St. Louis, 1961, Chgo., 1961-63, N.Y.C., 1963-65; reporter Chgo. Tribune, 1965-77, sports editor, 1977—. Mem. Asso. Press Sports Editors, Baseball Writers Assn. Am., Pro Football Writers Assn. Roman Catholic. Club: Chgo. Athletic Assn. Office: 435 N Michigan Ave Chicago IL 60611

LANGFORD, IRVIN JAMES, lawyer; b. Mobile, Apr. 28, 1927; s. Irvin Cobb and Wesley Blacksher (Coffin) L.; B.S., U. Ala., 1949, LL.B., 1951; m. Marylyn Judith Cleland Sept. 17, 1954; children—Debra Lynne, Kimberly Anne, Irvin James, David Wesley. Admitted to Ala. bar, 1951, since practiced in Mobile; partner firm Howell, Johnston, Langford, Finkbohner & Lawler, 1966—; spl. judge Probate Ct. Mobile County, 1970. Served with USNR, 1945-46. Mem. Am., Ala., Mobile bar assns., Ala. Trial Lawyers Assn., Farrah Order Jurisprudence, Sigma Chi, Phi Alpha Delta. Democrat. Presbyn. Mason (Shriner). Clubs: Athelstan, Internat. Trade (Mobile). Home: 4729 Wicker Way Mobile AL 36609 Office: PO Box 1643 Mobile AL 36601

LANGFORD, JAMES ROULEAU, univ. press adminstr.; b. South Bend, Ind., June 12, 1937; s. Walter McCarty and Alice M. (Joubert) L.; Ph.B., Aquinas Inst., 1960, M.A. in Philosophy, 1961, M.A. in Theology, 1964, S.T.L., 1965; m. Margaret Marie Hammerot, Aug. 30, 1968; children—Jeremy, Joshua. Instr. theology St. Thomas Coll., St. Paul, 1965-67; editor Doubleday & Co., N.Y.C., 1967-69; exec. editor U. Mich. Press, Ann Arbor, 1969-74; dir. U. Notre Dame Press (Ind.), 1974—. Mem. com. instnl. relations Assn. Am. U. Presses, 1974—. Democrat. Roman Catholic. Author: Galileo, Science and the Church, 1966, rev. 1971. Home: 109 Napoleon St South Bend IN 46617 Office: U Notre Dame Press Notre Dame IN 46556

LANGFORD, KENNETH ROYSTON, ret. railroad ofcl.; b. St. Louis, Oct. 13, 1916; s. William A. and Edna (Bethel) L.; certificate Mo. Inst. Accountancy and Law, 1954; m. Mary E. Dowdy, Aug. 30, 1941; children—Patricia Ann (Mrs. Frank Bearden), Kenneth Royston, Mary Elizabeth (Mrs. Frank C. Senn). With M.-K.-T. R.R., 1934-79, comptroller, 1969-79; comptroller, dir. Southwestern States Mgmt. Co.; comptroller Coordinated Transp. Co., Katy Transp. Co., Donland Devel. Co., San Antonio Belt and Terminal Ry. Co. Served with AUS, 1943-45. Lutheran. Home: 1012 S French St Denison TX 75020

LANGFORD, THOMAS ANDERSON, educator; b. Winston-Salem, N.C., Feb. 22, 1929; s. Thomas Anderson and Louie Mae (Hughes) L.; A.B., Davidson Coll., 1951, D.D., 1975; B.D., Duke, 1954, Ph.D., 1958; m. Ann Marie Daniel, Dec. 27, 1951; children—Thomas A., James Howard, Timothy Daniel, Stephen Hughes. Ordained to ministry Meth. Ch., 1952; from instr. to prof. religion Duke, 1956—, chmn. dept., 1965-71, dean Div. Sch., 1971—; vis. prof. U. N.C., 1962. World Meth. Council rep. in theol. discussions with Roman Catholic Ch. and Luth. World Fedn., 1975—; del. Gen. Conf. United Meth. Ch., 1976, Southeastern Jurisdictional Conf., 1972, 76; chmn. Duke self-study coordinating com. So. Assn. Colls. and Univs., 1975-76. Trustee Bennett Coll., Greensboro; exec. com. World Faith Council, 1976. N.C. Gurney Harris Kearns fellow, 1956-57; Dempster fellow, 1957; Am. Council Learned Socs. fellow, 1965-66; Soc. Religion in Higher Edn. fellow, 1969; named outstanding tchr., Duke, 1965; recipient E. Harris Harbison award, Danforth Found., 1965-66. Mem. Am. Theol. Soc., Phi Beta Kappa. Author: In Search of Foundations: English Theology 1900-1920, 1969; Introduction to Western Philosophy: Pre-Socratics to Mill, 1970. Editor: (with G.L. Abernathy) Philosophy of Religion, 1962, 2d edit., 1968, History of Philosophy, 1965; (with W.H. Poteat) Intellect and Hope, Essays in the Thought of Michael Polanyi, 1968; Christian Wholeness, 1979. Contbr. articles to profl. jours. Address: Divinity Sch Duke U Durham NC 27706

LANGFORD, THOMAS LEROY, constrn. co. exec.; b. Whittier, Calif., June 24, 1941; s. William Licurgus and Thecla (Rohr) L.; B.S., U. Calif. at Berkeley, 1963, M.B.A., 1964; grad. Advanced Mgmt. Program, Harvard U., 1976; m. Eugenia M. Falk, Jan., 1962; children—Carol, Thomas, Mary, Catherine. Audit mgr. Price Waterhouse & Co., Los Angeles, 1964-70; sr. v.p., chief fin. officer Parsons Corp., Pasadena, Calif., 1970—. C.P.A., Calif. Mem. Am. Inst. C.P.A.'s, Calif. Soc. C.P.A.'s. Home: 18515 Wells Dr Tarzana CA 91356 Office: 100 W Walnut St Pasadena CA 91124

LANGHAM, MICHAEL, theatrical dir.; b. Somerset, Eng., Aug. 22, 1919; s. Seymour and Muriel (Andrews Speed) L.; student Radley Coll., Abingdon, Eng., 1933-37, London U., 1937-39; D.Lit. (hon.), McMaster U., 1962, St. Scholastica Coll., 1973; LL.D., U. Toronto, 1966; m. Helen Burns, July 8, 1948 (div. 1972); 1 son, Christopher; m. Ellin Gorky, 1972. Engaged in theatrical profession, 1946—; dir. prodns. Arts Council Midland Theatre Co., 1946-48, Sir Barry Jackson's Birmingham Repertory Theatre, 1948-50, Glasgow Citizens' Theatre, 1953-54; now artistic dir. Guthrie Theater, Mpls., including direction Relapse, 1972, Oedipus the King, 1972, 73, The Government Inspector, 1973, The Merchant of Venice, 1973, King Lear, 1974, Love's Labor's Lost, 1974, The School for Scandal, 1974, Private Lives, Measure For Measure, 1975, The Matchmaker, 1976, Winter's Tale, 1977; dir. Julius Caesar at Stratford-upon-Avon, 1950, Stratford, Ont., 1955; dir. The Gay Invalid, London, 1950, Pygmalion, London, 1951, The Other Heart, London, 1951; dir. Old Vic Co. prodn. Othello at Berlin Festival, also London, 1951; Brit. Council lectr., Australia, 1952; dir. Richard III, Belgian Nat. Theatre, 1952, The Merry Wives of Windsor, The Hague, 1953; artistic dir. Stratford (Ont.) Shakespearean Festival, 1955—, including direction Hamlet, 1957, Henry IV, Part I, 1958, Much Ado About Nothing, 1958, Romeo and Juliet, 1960, Coriolanus, 1961, Love's Labour's Lost, 1961, Taming of the Shrew, 1962, Cyrano de Bergerac, 1962, Troilus and Cressida, 1963, Timon of Athens, 1963, King Lear, 1964, The Country Wife, 1964, also prodns. Love's Labour's Lost and Timon of Athens at Festival Theatre, Chichester, Eng., 1964; dir. Hamlet, Stratford-upon-Avon, 1956, Merchant of Venice, 1960, Much Ado About Nothing, 1961; dir. Henry V, Edinburgh Festival, 1956, Two Gentlemen of Verona, London, 1957, A Midsummer Night's Dream, London, 1960, Andorra, N.Y.C., 1963; compiler, dir. univ. tour Can. and U.S. on Shakespearean comedy, 1962; author, dir. The Affliction of Love for TV, 1963. Artistic cons. LaJolla (Cal.) Theater Project, 1965. Served with Brit. Army, 1939-45. Address: The Guthrie Theater Minneapolis MN 55403*

LANGHAUG, WOODROW PERSHING, ins. co. exec.; b. Evansville, Minn., Apr. 23, 1919; s. Ole and Mathilda E. L.; student St. Olaf Coll., 1937-39; m. Eunice Tande, Dec. 28, 1945; children—Mary Leeland, Kathleen. With Lutheran Brotherhood, Mpls., 1944—, dir., 1963—, sr. v.p. mktg., 1967-70, pres., 1970—; pres., dir. Luth. Brotherhood Fund, Inc., Luth. Brotherhood Income Fund, Inc., Luth. Brotherhood U.S. Govt. Securities Fund, Inc., Luth. Brotherhood Mcpl. Bond Fund, Inc., Luth. Brotherhood Money Market Fund, Inc.; dir. Luth. Brotherhood Research Corp., Luth. Orient Mission Soc. Chmn., Minn. Ins. Info. Center, 1975-77, mem. exec. com., 1977—; bd. dirs. Minn. Safety Council, 1976—; bd. regents Luther-Northwestern Sem., St. Paul, Golden Valley Luth. Coll., 1978—; bd. Met. Med. Center, Mpls., 1971-77; mem. advisory bd. U. Minn. Exec. Program; met. chmn. Nat. Alliance Bus., Mpls., 1978—, mem. met. adv. bd., 1979—. Mem. Nat. Assn. Life Underwriters, Internat. Assn. Health Underwriters, Nat. Assn. Fraternal Counsellors, Twin Cities Fraternal Underwriters Assn. Republican. Lutheran. Clubs: Minneapolis, Mpls. Athletic; Interlachen Country (Edina, Minn.). Home: 6113 Saxony Rd Minneapolis MN 55436 Office: 701 2d Ave S Minneapolis MN 55402

LANGHETEE, EDMOND JOSEPH, JR., oil and gas co. exec.; b. New Orleans, Sept. 29, 1928; s. Edmond Joseph and Hilda T. (Dureau) L.; B.S., La. State U., 1949; m. Rosalie A. D'Amico, Oct. 9, 1949; children—Edmond Joseph III, Jeanne, Leslie, Russell. With La. Land & Exploration Co., New Orleans, 1949—, v.p., 1962-65, sr. v.p., 1965-67, exec. v.p., 1967-74, vice chmn. bd., 1974—, dir. 1971—; chmn., dir. La. Land Offshore Exploration Co.; chmn. bd., dir. Kaluakoi Corp.; dir. Jacintoport Corp. Adv. bd. New Orleans area council Boy Scouts Am.; mem. La. State U. Found. Mem. Petroleum Club New Orleans (pres.), Petroleum Club Houston, New Orleans Geol. Soc., Houston, New Orleans (dir. 1976-78), Mobile (Ala.) chambers commerce, Am. Inst. Mining and Metall. Engrs., Ind. Petroleum Assn. Am., Am. Petroleum Inst. (dir.), Nat. Ocean Industries Assn. (dir.), Mid Continent Oil and Gas Assn. Democrat. Roman Catholic. Clubs: New Orleans Country; Metairie (La.) Country. Home: 765 Jewel St New Orleans LA 70124 Office: 225 Baronne St New Orleans LA 70112

LANGHOFF, SEVERIN PETER, JR., mgmt. cons.; b. Peoria, Ill., Apr. 21, 1910; s. Severin Peter and Amelia (Meyers) L.: B.S. in Engring., U. Ill., 1931, M.S. in Econs., 1932, Ph.D., 1935; m. Charlotte Hood, 1937; 1 son, Peter; m. 2d, Barbara K. Brumbaugh, Apr. 25, 1956; children—Christopher Severin, Andrew Petersen. With Nat. Resources Bd., 1934-35, Rural Electrification Adminstrn., 1935-40, Fed. Works Agy., 1940-42; chief statistician U.S. Army Service Forces, 1942-45; dir. research VA, 1945-46; cons. Commn. Orgn. Exec. Br. Govt., 1948, Office Sec. Def., 1948, Office Sec. Army, 1950-54; with Young & Rubicam, Inc., 1946-66, v.p., 1948-64, sr. v.p., 1964-66; pres. Am. Research Bur., 1966-71; dir. C-E-I-R, Inc., 1966-67; lectr. Grad. Sch. Bus., Columbia, 1963-64. Chmn. research com. Am. Assn. Advt. Agys., 1959-60; pres. Market Research Council, 1960-61; bd. dirs. Am. Marketing Assn., 1963-65; chmn. Advt. Research Found., 1966. Recipient Exceptional Civilian Service award War Dept., 1946. Mem. Tau Beta Pi. Editor, contbr. Models, Measurement and Marketing, 1965. Home: 7511 Hamilton Spring Rd Bethesda MD 20034

LANGHOLZ, ROBERT WAYNE, lawyer, investor; b. Sioux City, Iowa, Jan. 17, 1930; s. Harry H. and Alvina (Bockhop) L.; B.S. with distinction, U. Iowa, 1951, J.D., 1956; m. Edna Page, June 11, 1955; children—Robert W., Laurence Henry, Kristofer Page. Admitted to Okla. bar, 1957; research asst. to prof. Frank R. Kennedy, U. Iowa Coll. Law, 1955-56; trainee Gulf Oil Corp., 1956; mem. firm Carlson, Lupardus, Matthews, Holliman & Huffman, Tulsa, 1956-67; partner firm Holliman, Langholz, Runnels & Dorwart, Tulsa, 1967—; chmn. bd., chief exec. officer Skinner Bros. Co. Inc., Geophys. Research Corp., Indel-Davis Inc. Served with USAF, 1951-53. Mem. Am., Iowa, Okla. bar assns., Young Presidents Orgn. Methodist. Clubs: Tulsa, Summit, Masons Southern Hills Country (Tulsa); Eldorado Country (Palm Springs, Calif.). Home: 3848 S Atlanta Pl Tulsa OK 74105 Office: Holarud Bldg 10 E 3d St Suite 400 Tulsa OK 74103

LANGIE, LOUIS ANTOINE, JR., banker; b. Rochester, N.Y., May 11, 1928; s. Louis Antoine and Geraldine (Kreag) L.; A.B., Princeton, 1950; m. Sara Weaver, June 18, 1960; children—Roberta, Adele. Exec. v.p. Langie Fuel Service, Inc., Rochester, 1950-68; v.p., mgr. bus. services dept. Lincoln First Bank Rochester, 1968-70, sr. v.p., asst. mgr. banking div., 1970-71, exec. v.p., mgr. banking div., 1972-74, pres., 1974—. Pres., Cath. Youth Orgn., 1963-64; chmn. Rochester-Monroe County chpt. ARC, 1966-68; pres. Otetiana Council, Inc., 1969-71; v.p. Rochester Community Chest, 1968-71, pres., 1973-75; v.p. St. Mary's Hosp. Bd., 1971-73. Trustee, chmn. exec. com. Columbus Civic Centre; trustee, mem. exec. com. Colgate Rochester Div. Sch.; trustee Cath. Charities, Gleason Meml. Fund; treas. bd. trustees Allendale Columbia. Named Citizen of Day, Rochester Savs. Bank, 1954, N.Y. State Man of Year, Jr. C. of C., 1957; recipient LeRoy Snyder Meml. award C. of C., 1962; Silver Beaver award Boy Scouts Am., 1960, Distinguished Eagle award, 1975; St. George award, 1963; Civic award for Outstanding Contbn. to Commerce and Industry C. of C., 1971. Roman Catholic (ch. auditor 1971). Club: Rochester Ad (pres. 1963-64). Home: 1390 Clover St Rochester NY 14610 Office: 1 Lincoln First Sq Rochester NY 14643

LANGIUS, ADRIAN NELSON, architect, engr.; b. Zeeland, Mich., Nov. 8, 1903; s. Cornelius and Alberta (Dykhuizen) L.; student Hope Coll., 1922-25; B.Arch., U. Mich., 1928; LL.D., No. Mich. U., 1965; m. Dorothy Hewitt, Aug. 24, 1929; children—Mary Anne Delaney, Thomas Adrian. Architect, Mich. State Bldg. Div., 1929-39, dir., 1939-73, asst. dir. State Dept. Mgmt. and Budget, 1973-74, state architect emeritus, 1974; cons. architect and engr., 1975—. Sec., Mich. Capitol Devel. Commn.; mem. Gov.'s Com. on State Housing Code; chmn. Gov.'s Spl. Commn. on Art in state Bldgs.; bd. dirs. Lansing Downtown Devel. Council; chmn. Com. for Restoration of Biddle House, Mackinac Island; former dir. State Planning Commn.; sec. Postwar Victory Bldg. Program; mem. USPHS tech. adv. com. hosp. survey and constrn.; mem. adv. com. Mich. State Med. Soc. for Restoration of Beaumont House, Mackinac Island; chmn. com. on constrn. codes Gov.'s Fire Protection Conf.; mem. Gov.'s Constrn. Industry Conf. Recipient meritorius service award Mich. State Police, 1938; hon. alumnus Mich. State U., 1966; Sesquicentennial award U. Mich., 1967. Registered architect and engr., Mich. Fellow AIA (Gold medal Detroit chpt. 1964, dir. Mich. region and dir. 1962-65, pres. Western Mich. chpt. 1943-44, dir.), Mich. Soc. Architects (Gold medal 1955, past dir. 1942-43, 44-59, 62-65, 2d v.p. 1945, 51-55, pres. 1948-49), Mich. Soc. Profl. Engrs., Am. Automobile Assn., Mich. Engring. Soc. (dir. 1947-48), Mich. Assn. Professions (Distinguished Service award 1964, dir. 1960-61, pres. 1965-66), Nat. Cowmilkers Assn. Mem. Peoples Ch. of East Lansing. Clubs: U. Mich. (Lansing), Lansing City. Home and Office: 932 Westlawn East Lansing MI 48823

LANGLAND, JOSEPH THOMAS, author, educator; b. Spring Grove, Minn., Feb. 16, 1917; s. Charles M. and Clara Elizabeth (Hille) L.; B.A., U. Iowa, 1940, M.A., 1941; Ford fellow humanities, Harvard-Columbia, 1953-54; m. Judith Gail Wood, June 26, 1943; children—Joseph Thomas, Elizabeth Langland, Paul. Instr. in English, Dana Coll., Blair, Nebr., 1941-42; part-time instr. U. Iowa, 1946-48; asst. prof., then asso. prof. U. Wyo., 1948-59; mem. faculty U. Mass., Amherst, 1959—, prof. English, 1964—, dir. program for M.F.A. in writing, 1964-70, 78-79; vis. lectr. U. B.C., U. Wash., Seattle, San Francisco State Coll.; poetry reader, lectr., U.S. and Europe. Served to capt., inf., AUS, 1942-46; ETO. Amy Lowell Poetry fellow, 1955-56; Arts and Humanities fellow in poetry, 1966-67; recipient Melville Cane prize poetry Poetry Soc. Am., 1964. Democrat. Author: (poems) For Harold, 1945, The Green Town, 1956; The Wheel of Summer, 1963, 2d edit., 1966; An Interview and Fourteen Poems, 1973; The Sacrifice Poems, 1975. Co-editor: Poet's Choice, 1962; The Short Story, 1956. Co-translator: Poetry From the Russian Underground, 1973. Home: 16 Morgan Circle Amherst MA 01002

LANGLEBEN, MANUEL PHILLIP, educator; b. Poland, Apr. 9, 1924; s. David and Charna Molly (Shabason) L.; came to Can., 1929, naturalized, 1935; B.Sc., McGill U. (Can.), 1949, M.Sc., 1950, Ph.D., 1953; m. Rose Cohen, May 25, 1948; children—Adrian, David, Louise. Postdoctoral fellow Meterol. Office, Dunstable, Eng., 1953-54; research asso. McGill U., Montreal, Que., 1954—, asst. prof. physics, 1960-62, asso. prof., 1962-68, prof., 1968—, dir. McGill Centre for No. Studies and Research, 1977—. Mem. sub-com. snow and ice, asso. com. geotech. research Nat. Research Council Can., 1968-74; mem. working group on ice reconnaissance and glaciology Canadian Adv. Com. on Remote Sensing, 1971-75; mem. panel on ice, subcom. Arctic oceanography Canadian Com. on Oceanography, 1973—. Served with Royal Canadian Navy, 1941-45. Mem. Canadian Assn. Physicists, Royal Meteorol. Soc., Glaciological Soc., Am. Geophy. Union, Sigma Xi. Contbr. articles sci. jours. Home: 4753 Grosvenor Montreal PQ H3W 2L9 Canada

LANGLINAIS, JOSEPH WILLIS, univ. dean; b. San Antonio, Aug. 12, 1922; s. Joseph Willis and Marie Nellie (St. Julien) L.; B.S. in Edn., U. Dayton, 1943; S.T.D., U. Fribourg (Switzerland), 1954. Joined Soc. Mary, 1940, ordained priest Roman Cath. Ch., 1952; tchr. high schs. in Mo., Ill. and Man., Can., 1943-48; dir. admissions Chaminade Coll. Prep. Sch., St. Louis, 1957-59; dir. Archdiocesan High Sch. Sodality Union St. Louis, 1958-59; dir. Marianist Novitiate, Galesville, Wis., 1959-63; mem. faculty St. Mary's U., San Antonio, 1963—, dean Sch. Arts and Scis., 1964-75, acad. v.p., 1975—, dir. instnl. self-study, 1970-72. Mem. Cath. Theol. Soc. Am., Mariological Soc. Am., Am. Assn. U. Profs., Archaeol. Soc. Am., Torch Internat. Contbr. Cath. Ency. Am. Address: One Camino Santa Maria San Antonio TX 78284

LANGLITZ, DAVID CARL, trombonist; b. Rochester, N.Y., Feb. 8, 1953; s. Harold Nathan and Audrey Jane (De Santis) L.; Mus.B., Juilliard Sch. Music, 1975, Mus.M., 1976. Trombonist, Spoleto (Italy) Festival, summer 1972, Aspen (Colo.) Music Festival, summers 1973-74, Lincoln Center Chamber Music Soc., N.Y.C., 1978; prin. trombonist Met. Opera Orch., 1974—; instr. Montclair State Coll. Mem. Am. Fedn. Musicians. Rec. artist. Home and Office: 210 W 70th St Apt 614 New York NY 10023

LANGMAN, JAN, anatomist; b. Bodegraven, Netherlands, Oct. 21, 1923; s. Harm Jan and Adriana (van der Velde) L.; M.D., U. Amsterdam, 1948; Ph.D., univs. Amsterdam and Leiden, 1951; postdoctoral student U. Zurich, 1951; m. Margaretha Willemina Holtrust, Oct. 17, 1955; children—Ronald, Juliet. Came to U.S., 1964. Intern, 1952-55; asst., then asso. prof. U. Amsterdam, 1952-57; asso. prof. anatomy McGill U. Med. Sch., 1957-59, prof. anatomy and embryology, 1959-64; prof. anatomy, chmn. dept. U. Va. Med. Sch., Charlottesville, 1964—. Mem. So. Soc. Anatomists (pres. 1968), Am. Assn. Anatomists (v.p. 1972-74), Teratology Soc. (pres. 1969), Perinatal Research Soc. (pres. 1970). Author: Medical Embryology, 1963. Research in devel. anatomy, congenital malformations. Home: Somerset Farm Rural Route 6 Box 337 Charlottesville VA 22901

LANGMUIR, ALEXANDER DUNCAN, epidemiologist, ret. educator; b. Santa Monica, Calif., Sept. 12, 1910; s. Charles Herbert and Edith (Ruggles) L.; A.B., Harvard, 1931; M.D., Cornell U., 1935; M.P.H., Johns Hopkins, 1940, D.H.L. (hon.), 1978; D.Sc. (hon.), Emory U., 1970; m. Sarah A. Harper, June 1, 1940 (dec. 1969); children—Ann, Paul Harper, Susan, Lynn, Jane (dec.); m. 2d, Leona Baumgartner Elias, June 27, 1970. Intern, Boston City Hosp., 1935-37; with N.Y. Health Dept., 1937-41; dep. commr. Westchester County (N.Y.) Health Dept., 1941-42; epidemiologist Commn. on Acute Respiratory Diseases, Ft. Bragg, N.C., 1942-46; asso. prof. epidemiology Johns Hopkins Sch. Hygiene and Pub. Health, 1946-49; chief epidemiologist Center for Disease Control, USPHS, 1949-70; asso. clin. prof. Emory U., 1950-64, clin. prof., 1964-70; vis. prof. epidemiology Harvard Med. Sch., Boston, 1970-77; Thomas Francis Meml. lectr. U. Mich., 1971; cons. epidemiology Navy Dept., 1946-51, Research and Devel. Bd., 1947-53; cons. to asst. sec. def. for research and devel., 1953-59; mem. biol. and chem. def. planning bd. Dept. Def., 1959-61; mem. chem. corps adv. council Dept. Army, 1949-55; exec. com. div. med. scis. NRC, 1956-57; mem. adv. com. Atomic Bomb Casualty Commn., 1956-63; chief cons. tech. discussions 21st World Health Assembly, WHO, Geneva, Switzerland, 1968; mem. adv. com. Population Council, N.Y.C., 1968-71; cons. WHO, Easter Mediterranean region, 1973, smallpox edn. program, 1975, Western Pacific region, 1975; adv. com. immunization practices Center for Disease Control, HEW, 1971-75; mem. research adv. com. AID, 1969-73; cons. in survellance of communicable disease Govt. of Kuwait, 1976; chmn. Commn. on Eradication of Smallpox in Bangladesh and Burma, WHO, 1977; Heath Clark lectr. Sch. Hygiene and Trop. medicine, London U., 1977; Royal Soc. Medicine Found. vis. prof., London, 1978. Served as maj. M.C., AUS, 1944-46. Recipient Distinguished Service award Dept. Health, Edn. and Welfare, 1958; Bronfman prize pub. health achievement Am. Pub. Health Assn., 1965; Career Service award Nat. Civil Service League, 1968; Distinguished Alumnus award Med. Coll., Cornell U., 1969; James D. Bruce award A.C.P., 1973; mem. Soc. Fellows, Johns Hopkins, 1973; Harry Dowling Lecture award U. Ill. Sch. Medicine, 1974. Fellow Am. Pub. Health Assn. (John Snow award epidemiology sect. 1977), Am. Acad. Arts and Scis., Royal Soc. Medicine (hon.); mem. Am. Soc. for Clin. Investigation, Internat. Epidemiological Assn., Am. Soc. for Tropical Medicine and Hygiene, Am. Epidemiological Soc. (sec.-treas. 1946-51, pres. 1960), Am. Fedn. Clin. Research. Home: Abel's Hill Chilmark MA 02535

LANGMUIR, ROBERT VOSE, educator, elec. engr.; b. White Plains, N.Y., Dec. 20, 1912; s. Dean and Ethel (Ivimey) L.; A.B., Harvard, 1935; Ph.D. in Physics, Calif. Inst. Tech., 1943; m. Bertha Lee Lord, May 19, 1939 (div. 1970); children—Alan, Ann Langmuir Kellam. With Consol. Engring. Co., 1939-42; with research lab. Gen. Electric Co., 1942-48; mem. faculty Calif. Inst. Tech., 1948—, prof. elec. engring., 1957—, head dept., 1963-71; cons. in field, 1954—. Fellow Am. Phys. Soc.; mem. I.E.E.E. Author: Electromagnetic Fields and Waves, 1960. With others built 1st synchrotron in U.S., 1946. Office: Calif Tech 116-81 Pasadena CA 91125

LANGRIDGE, ROBERT, educator, scientist; b. Essex, Eng., Oct. 26, 1933; s. Charles and Winifred (Lister) L.; B.Sc. in Physics (1st class honours), U. London (Eng.), 1954, Ph.D. in Crystallography, 1957; m. Ruth Gottlieb, June 26, 1960; children—Elizabeth, Catherine, Suzanne. Came to U.S., 1957. Vis. research fellow biophysics Yale, 1957-59; research asso. biophysics Mass. Inst. Tech., 1959-61; research asso. pathology Children's Cancer Research Found., Boston, 1961-66; research asso. biophysics, lectr. biophysics, also tutor biochem. scis. Harvard, 1963-66; research asso. Project MAC, Lab. for Computer Sci., Mass. Inst. Tech., 1964-66; prof. biophysics and info. scis. U. Chgo., 1966-68; prof. chemistry and biochem. scis. Princeton, 1968-76; prof. pharm. chemistry, biochemistry and biophysics, med. info. scis. U. Calif., San Francisco, 1976—, dir. Computer Graphics Lab.; mem. organizing com. 1969 Internat. Biophysics Congress; mem. computer and biomath. research study sect. NIH, USPHS, 1968-72, chmn., 1975-77; mem. vis. com. biology dept. Brookhaven Nat. Lab., 1977—; cons. NIH, NSF, Nat. Acad. Sci., AEC, ERDA. Mem. Am. Soc. Biol. Chemists, Biophys. Soc. (editorial bd. 1970-73, council 1971-74), Assn. Computing Machinery, Sigma Xi. Mem. editorial bd. Handbook of Biochemistry and Molecular Biology, 1973—. Contbr. articles on molecular biology, x-ray diffraction and computing to profl. jours. Office: 926 Med Scis Bldg U Calif San Francisco CA 94143

LANGROCK, PETER FORBES, lawyer; b. N.Y.C., Feb. 2, 1938; s. Frank G. and Catherine F. (Preble) L.; B.A., U. Chgo., 1968, J.D., 1960; m. Joann Murphy, July 4, 1960; children—Frank H., Catherine L., Eric. Admitted to Vt. bar, 1960; partner firm Langrock, Sperry, Parker & Stahl, Middlebury, Vt., 1969—; state's atty. Addison County, Vt.. 1960-65; commr. Nat. Conf. Commrs. on Uniform State Laws, 1967—. Home: Salisbury VT 95769 Office: Langrock Sperry Parker & Stahl 15 S Pleasant St Middlebury VT 05753

LANGSAM, WALTER CONSUELO, ret. univ. pres.; b. Vienna, Austria, Jan. 2, 1906; s. Emery Bernhardt and Angela Virginia Bianca (Münz-Kleinert) L.; brought to U.S., 1906; B.S., Coll. City N.Y., 1925; M.A., Columbia, 1926, Ph.D., 1930; LL.D., Gettysburg Coll., 1950, Bucknell U., 1953, Loyola U., Chgo., 1965, Xavier U., Cin., 1966, U. Cin., 1975; Litt.D., Wagner Coll., 1955, St.Thomas Inst., 1974; Sc.D., Northeastern U., 1960; L.H.D., Hebrew Union Coll., 1961, Miami U., Oxford, O., 1965; Sc.D. Edn., Midland Coll., 1963; D.C.L., Youngstown (O.) U., 1965; m. Julia Elizabeth Stubblefield, Dec. 10, 1931; children—Walter Eaton, Geoffrey Hardinge. Tutor history Coll. City N.Y., 1926-27; instr. history Columbia, 1927-35, asst. prof., 1935-38, vis. prof. history, 1942; prof. history Union Coll., 1938-45; on leave to OSS, 1944-45; pres. Wagner Coll., 1945-52, Gettysburg Coll., 1952-55, U. Cin., 1955-71, ret., 1971; vis. prof. summers Duke, Ohio State U., N.Y.U., U. B.C., U. Colo.; radio news commentator Sta. WGY, Schenectady, 1941-43. Chmn. bd. Cin. br. Fed. Res. Bank Cleve., 1964-66; dir. Diamond Internat. Corp., So. Ohio Bank, Western-So. Life Ins. Co. Civilian aide to sec. army, 1962-66; chmn. hist. adv. com. Dept. of Army, 1967-72; chmn. exec. bd. commn. on colls. and univs. North Central Assn., 1968-70; pres. Ohio Coll. Assn., 1965-66; bd. cons. Nat. War Coll., 1972-76; U.S. del. Internat. Congress Peace and Christian Civilization, Florence, 1958. Mem. E. Central region adv. council Boy Scouts Am. Trustee Hamma Sch. Theology, 1967-70, Endicott Coll.; v.p. bd. theol. edn. Luth. Ch. Am., 1963-72; chmn. bd. Cin. Ballet Co., 1975-77. Recipient Townsend Harris medal, 1952; Outstanding Civilian Service medal with 2 laurel leaf clusters Dept. Army; Alumni medal City Coll. N.Y., 1972; comdr's. cross Order Merit (W. Germany), 1970; hon. consul of Finland, 1967-76. Mem. Cin. Hist. Soc. (v.p.)., Phi Beta Kappa, Phi Gamma Delta. Clubs: Commercial, Cincinnati Country, Queen City, Literary (Cin.); Poinciana (Palm Beach, Fla.). Author: The Napoleonic Wars and German Nationalism in Austria, 1930; The World since 1914, 6th edit., 1948; Major European and Asiatic Developments since 1935, 1939; In Quest of Empire: the Problem of Colonies, 1939; Documents and Readings in the History of Europe Since 1918, 1939; Since 1939: A Narrative of War, 1941; Francis the Good, the Education of an Emperor (1768-1792), 1949; The World Since 1919, 8th edit. (with O.E. Mitchell, Jr.), 1971; Franz der Gute. Die Jugend eines Kaisers, 1954; Historic Documents of World War II, 1958; World History since 1870, 1963; Where Freedom Exists, 1967; An Honor Conferred, A Title Awarded, A History of the Commercial Club of Cincinnati, 1880-1972, 1973; The World and Warren's Cartoons, 1977; Cincinnati in Color, with Photographs by Julianne Warren, 1978. Editor Lippincott Hist. Series, 1934-50. Contbr. The Shadow of War (L. Dodson, editor), 1934; War in the Twentieth Century (W. Waller, editor), 1940; War As a Social Institution (J.D. Clarkson, T. Cochran, editors), 1941; Nationalism and Internationalism: Essays Inscribed to Carlton J.H. Hayes (E.M. Earle, editor), 1950; Virtute Fideque; Festschrift für Otto Von Habsburg, 1965. Contbr. profl. jours. Address: Univ Cincinnati Cincinnati OH 45221. *Praying when one is not in trouble usually makes it unnecessary to pray for help in getting out of trouble. No fish ever was caught through keeping its mouth shut. Good administration involves the art of knowing when to make sensible exceptions to rules. Persons who have brilliant minds and are articulate, but who lack common sense, often seem to be more menace to, than furtherers of, civilization.*

LANGSDORF, ALEXANDER, JR., physicist; b. St. Louis, May 30, 1912; s. Alexander S. and Elsie (Hirsch) L.; B.A., Washington U., St. Louis, 1932; Ph.D., Mass. Inst. Tech., 1937; m. Martyl S. Schweig, Dec. 31, 1941; children—Suzanne M., Alexandra. NRC fellow U. Calif. at Berkeley, 1938; instr. Washington U., 1939-43; physicist Argonne (Ill.) Nat. Lab., 1943—, sr. physicist, 1947—. Mem. Dist. 211 High Sch. Bd., 1970-73. Recipient Alumni award Washington U., 1958. Fellow Am. Phys. Soc. Home: Route 1 Box 228 Schaumburg IL 60172 Office: 9700 S Cass Ave Argonne IL 60439

LANGSDORF, DAVID STANTON, former banker; b. Monrovia, Calif., Apr. 24, 1914; s. William Bell and Julia May (Tappan) L.; B.A., Occidental Coll., 1937; m. Mildred Weber, May 29, 1970; children by previous marriage—Richard Crane, Melinda Julia. With Bank of Am. Nat. Trust & Savs. Assn., San Francisco, 1937—, sr. v.p., controller, 1967-73, exec. v.p., controller, also controller BankAmerica Corp., 1973-75, exec. v.p., sr. adminstrv. officer, 1976-78; ret., 1979. Mem. Fin. Execs. Inst., Bankers Club San Francisco, Phi Beta Kappa, Sigma Alpha Epsilon. Republican. Episcopalian. Club: Contra Costa Country. Home: 1953 Bancroft Rd Walnut Creek CA 94598 Office: 555 California St San Francisco CA 94104

LANGSDORF, WILLIAM BELL, ednl. adminstr.; b. Denver, Oct. 24, 1909; s. William Bell and Julia (Tappan) L.; A.B., Occidental Coll., 1931, M.A., 1932; Ph.D., U. Calif., 1936, summer student, 1937; summer study U. Chgo., 1939, Stanford, 1940, Claremont Coll., 1946-47; m. Eileen Johnson, June 12, 1938; children—Sharon, William. Instr., asst. prof. Occidental Coll., 1934-39; vis. instr. U. Calif. at Los Angeles, summers 1938, 59; chmn. social sci. dept. Pasadena Jr. Coll., 1939-46, asst. prin., 1946-49, asso. prin., 1949-50; pres. Pasadena City Coll., 1950-59; pres. Calif. State Coll. at Fullerton, 1959-70, prof. history emeritus, 1973—; acad. vice chancellor Calif. State U. and Colls., 1970-73, vice chancellor emeritus, 1973—; asso. dir. sr. coll. and univ. accrediting commn. Western Assn. Schs. and Colls., 1973—; vis. summer prof. Harvard, 1948, U. Calif. at Los Angeles, 1959. Mem. Phi Beta Kappa, Phi Delta Kappa, Sigma Alpha Epsilon, Phi Alpha Theta. Republican. Presbyn. Author: Fighting for Freedom, 1947; others. Home: 301 Cameo Shores Rd Corona del Mar CA 92625 Office: Western College Assn Mills College Oakland CA 94613

LANGSLEY, DONALD GENE, psychiatrist; b. Topeka, Oct. 5, 1925; s. Morris J. and Ruth (Pressman) L.; B.A., State U. N.Y., Albany, 1949; M.D., U. Rochester, 1953; m. Pauline R. Langsley, Sept. 9, 1955; children—Karen Jean, Dorothy Ruth, Susan Louise. Intern, USPHS Hosp., San Francisco, 1953-54; resident psychiatry U. Calif., San Francisco, 1954-59, NIMH career tchr. in psychiatry, 1959-61; candidate San Francisco and Chgo. insts. for psychoanalysis, 1958-67; asst. prof., asso. prof. psychiatry U. Colo. Sch. Medicine, 1961-68; prof., chmn. dept. psychiatry U. Calif., Davis, 1968-77, U. Cin., 1977—; mem. psychiatry edn. com. NIMH, 1969-75. Served with AUS, 1943-46; med. officer USPHS, 1953-54. Recipient Spl. awards Colo. Assn. for Mental Health, 1968, Sacramento Area Mental Health Assn., 1973. Diplomate Am. Bd. Psychiatry and Neurology (dir. 1976—), Nat. Bd. Med. Examiners. Fellow Am. Psychiat. Assn. (Hofheimer award 1971, pres. 1980—, chmn. peer rev. com. 1975-77); mem. Central Calif. (pres. 1973-74), Colo. (pres. elect 1967-68) psychiat. socs. Author: The Treatment of Families in Crisis, 1968; Mental Health Education in the New Medical Schools, 1973; Peer Review Manual for Psychiatry, 1976. Contbr. articles to med. jours. Home: 700 Betula Ave Cincinnati OH 45229 Office: Dept Psychiatry U Cin Coll Medicine 231 Bethesda Ave Cincinnati OH 45267

LANGSTAFF, ELLIOT KENNEDY, corp. exec.; b. N.Y.C., Feb. 1, 1923; s. B. Meredith and Esther Knox (Boardman) L.; A.B., Harvard, 1947, M.B.A., 1949; m. Percy Lee, Dec. 20, 1952; children—David Hamilton, Lee Meredith, Maxim Kennedy. Asst. to dir. Fgn. Trade Adminstrn., Athens, Greece, 1949-52; asst. to spl. adviser, U.S. rep. to regional orgns. FOA, Paris, France, 1953-55; asst. sec. Am. Overseas Finance Corp., N.Y.C., 1955-59, asst. v.p., 1959-62, v.p., 1962-65; regional mgr. Africa, Asia, Middle East for Arbor Acres Farm, Inc., Glastonbury, Conn. subsidiary Internat. Basic Economy Corp., 1964-66; sec., dir. personnel Internat. Basic Economy Corp., N.Y.C., 1967-71, v.p. personnel, 1969-72; prin., dir. Ward Howell Assos., Inc., N.Y.C., 1972—; dir. Arbor Acres Pakistan, Ltd. Trustee Am. Farm Sch., Thessaloniki, Greece, Overseas Edn. Fund, LWV, Harvard Radcliffe Collegium Musicum. Served to 1st lt., inf. AUS, 1943-46. Decorated Army Commendation medal. Episcopalian. Club: Harvard of N.Y.C. Home: 307 Ingleside Rd Stamford CT 06903 Office: Ward Howell Assos Inc 99 Park Ave New York NY 10016

LANGSTAFF, GEORGE QUIGLEY, JR., footwear co. exec.; b. Paducah, Ky., July 28, 1925; s. George Quigley and Katherine Elizabeth (Irion) L.; B.A., U. of South, 1948; grad. Advanced Mgmt. Program, Harvard U., 1978; m. Maureen Black, Dec. 27, 1946; children—Patricia (Mrs. Charles Poole), Lynne (Mrs. Steve Frederick), Katherine (Mrs. Gregory Haag). Mfg. mgr. Genesco, Inc., Nashville, 1948-59, mktg. mgr., 1959-70, group pres., 1970-73, v.p., chief operating officer, 1974-78, exec. v.p., 1978—. Pres., Nashville Mental Health Assn., 1970, Episcopal Churchmen of Tenn., 1966; trustee, alumni v.p. U. of South. Mem. Republican State Exec. Com., 1952-53. Bd. dirs. United Fund, Jr. Achievement. Served with USNR, 1943-46. Clubs: Nashville Racquet; Bellemeade Country. Home: 6001 Andover Dr Nashville TN 37215 Office: Genesco Park Nashville TN 37202

LANGSTAFF, JOHN MEREDITH, musician; b. Bklyn., Dec. 24, 1920; s. Bridgewater Meredith and E Esther Knox (Boardman) L.; student Choate Sch., Curtis Inst. Music, Juilliard Sch. Music, Columbia; m. Diane Guggenheim; 1 dau., Carol; m. 2d, Nancy Graydon Woodbridge, Apr. 3, 1948; children—John Elliot, Peter Gerry, Deborah Graydon. Recitals, U.S., Can., Eng., Iceland, Europe; rec. for Odeon-Capital, Jupiter, RCA-Victor, Nixa, Renaissance, Conversa-Phone, Tradition, HMV, Desto, Weston Woods; soloist with Cantata Singers, N.Y. Philharmonic, Nat. Symphony, Montreal Symphony Orch., Little Orch. Soc., N.Y. Oratorio Soc., Collegium Musicum, Stratford Shakespeare Festival, Eng., Mpls. Symphony Orch.; radio, TV in U.S., Europe, Can., BBC (Eng.); dir. music dept. Potomac Sch., Washington, 1953-68, Shady Hill Sch., Cambridge, Mass., 1969-72; faculty Simmons Coll., Boston, 1970—, Wheelock Coll., Boston, 1974—, Mass. Coll. Art, 1977, Boston Coll., 1977, U. Conn., 1977—, Lesley Coll., 1977—; artistic dir. Young Audiences Mass., 1972—; artist-lectr. Assn. Am. Colls. Served as 1st lt., inf. AUS, World War II. Mem. Actors Equity, Country Dance and Song Soc. Am. (adv. bd.), Internat. Folk Music Council, English Folk Song Soc. (dir. Christmas Revels 1956, 57, 66, 70—, Spring Revels 1972—). Author: Frog Went a-Courtin', 1955 (Caldecott prize 1955); Over in the Meadow, 1957; On Christmas Day in the Morning, 1959; The Swapping Boy, 1960; Ol' Dan Tucker, 1963; Hi! Ho! The Rattlin' Bog, 1969; Jim Along, Josie, 1970; Gather My Gold Together, 1971; The Golden Vanity, 1971; Soldier, Soldier, Won't You Marry Me?, 1972; The Two Magicians, 1973; Shimmy, Shimmy Coke-a-pop!, 1973; St. George and the Dragon, 1973; A-Hunting We will Go, 1974; A Season for Singing, 1974; Sweetly Sings the Donkey, 1976; Hot Cross Buns, 1978. Home: 9 Burlington St Lexington MA 02173 Office: 74 Joy St Boston MA 02114

LANGSTON, HIRAM THOMAS, educator, surgeon; b. Rio de Janeiro, Brazil, Jan. 12, 1912 (derivative citizenship); s. Alva B. and Louise F. (Diguid) L.; student Collegio Batista, Rio de Janeiro, 1926-28, Georgetown (Ky.) Coll., 1929; A.B., U. Louisville, 1930, M.D., 1934; M.S. in Surgery, U. Mich., 1941; m. Helen M. Orth, June 22, 1941; children—Paula F., Thomas O., Carol E. Intern, Garfield Meml. Hosp., Washington, 1934-35, resident pathology, 1935-37; asst. resident surgery Univ. Hosp., Ann Arbor, Mich., 1937-38, resident surgery, 1938-39, resident thoracic surgery, 1939-40, instr. thoracic surgery Med. Sch., 1940-41; pvt. practice, also asso. surgery Northwestern U., 1941-42, asst. prof. surgery, 1946-48; pvt. practice thoracic surgery, Detroit, also asso. prof. surgery Wayne U., 1948-52; asso. prof. surgery U. Ill. Coll. Medicine, Chgo., 1952-62, prof. surgery, 1963-78; clin. prof. surgery Northwestern U. Sch. Medicine, Chgo., 1978—; chief surgeon Chgo. Tb Sanitarium, 1952-71; cons. thoracic surgery VA Hosp., Hines, Ill., 1952—; mem. staff St. Joseph's Hosp., chmn. dept. surgery, 1978—; mem. staff Grant Hosp. Served with M.C., AUS, 1942-46. Diplomate Am. Bd. Surgery, Am. Bd. Thoracic Surgery (a founder). Fellow A.C.S.; mem. A.M.A., Ill., Chgo. med. socs., Ill., Chgo. surg. socs., Chgo. Tb Soc., Am. Assn. Thoracic Surgery (pres. 1969-70), Am. Thoracic Soc., Am. Coll. Chest Physicians, Am., Pan-Pacific, Central, Western surg. assns., Theta Kappa Psi, Alpha Omega Alpha. Author numerous articles, chpts. in books. Mem. editorial bd. John Alexander Series, 1956-73, Jour. Thoracic and Cardiovascular Surgery, 1964-79. Home: 952 Pine Tree Ln Winnetka IL 60093 Office: 2913 N Commonwealth Ave Chicago IL 60657

LANGSTON, JAMES HORACE, educator; b. Garrison, Tex., Oct. 8, 1917; s. James Horace and Ruth (Green) L.; B.A., Stephen F. Austin State Coll., 1937; M.A., U. N.C., 1939, Ph.D., 1941. Research chemist Columbia Chem. div. Pitts. Plate Glass Co., Barberton, Ohio, 1941-46; mem. faculty Clemson (S.C.) Coll., 1946-58, prof. textile chemistry, 1951-58; prof. chemistry, head dept. Samford U., Birmingham, Ala., 1958—; Fulbright prof. chemistry Central U. and Nat. Poly. Sch., Quito, Ecuador, 1959-60, Nat. U. Honduras, Tegucigalpa, 1967-68; chem. cons. to pvt. cos., 1950-58. Fellow Am. Inst. Chemists; mem. Am. Chem. Soc., Sigma Xi. Contbr. articles to tech. jours. Discovered numerous new organic chem. compounds; research on polymerization, catalysis, pharmacol. effects, textile finishing. Home: 704 Canyon Creek Ln Birmingham AL 35216

LANGSTON, PAUL T., music educator, composer; b. Marianna, Fla., Sept. 15, 1928; s. Howard McGhee and Rosa (Jeffries) L.; pvt. study with Nadia Boulanger, 1962, 63; diploma Conservatoire Americaine, France; B.A., U. Fla., 1950; M.S. in Music, So. Bapt. Theol. Sem., 1953; S.M.D., Union Theol. Sem., 1963; m. Esther Howard, Aug. 12, 1950; children—Claire Beth, Erin, Howard. Organist-choirmaster St. John's Bapt. Ch., Charlotte, N.C., 1953-60; instr. music theory Davidson Coll., 1959-60; mem. faculty Stetson U., De Land, Fla., 1960—, dean Sch. Music, 1963—; asso. condr. Charlotte Oratorio Singers, 1954-60. Dir. Fla. Internat. Music Festival, Fla. Internat. Music Festival Inst. Bd. dirs. Fla. League Arts. Mem. Am. Guild Organists, Hymn Soc., Coll. Music Soc., Am. Assn. U. Profs., Music Tchrs. Nat. Assn., Pi Kappa Lambda, Delta Tau Delta. Composer organ, choral works. Home: 313 N Salisbury Ct De Land FL 32720

LANGSTON, ROY A., ins. co. cons.; b. Dallas, Feb. 13, 1912; s. Lamar Q. and Gertrude (McDaniel) L.; student Dallas Sch. Law, Mountain View Coll., Dallas; m. Edna Earle Scott, 1936; 1 dau., Peggy Ann (Mrs. Roland Orval Wright, Jr.). With Trinity Universal Ins. Co., 1929-33; with Traders & Gen. Ins. Co., 1933-73, sec.-treas., 1945-49, dir., 1949-73, v.p., sec., 1949-53, exec. v.p., 1953-56, pres., chief exec. officer, 1956-73; pres., chief exec. officer Traders Indemnity Co., Dallas, 1962-73. Past pres. Assn. Fire and Casualty Cos. Tex. Methodist (ofcl. bd.). Mason (32 deg., Shriner). Clubs: Insurance, High Noon (Dallas). Home: 2032 W Five Mile Pkwy Dallas TX 75224

LANGSTON, RUSSELL LEE, elec. engr.; b. Cape Girardeau, Mo., Nov. 15, 1931; s. Roland H. and Stella Jewell (Hicklin) L.; B.Elec. Engring., U. Mo. at Rolla, 1955; m. Betty Sue Johnston, Feb. 15, 1964; children—Russell Lee, Lyle Mark. With Gen. Motors Corp., 1954-57, Davis Electric Co., 1957-58; with U.S. Army Missile Command, Redstone Arsenal, Ala., 1958-77, electronic engr. program mgmt., 1972-77; cons. in field. Served with AUS, 1955-57. Recipient letter appreciation Office Sec. Def., 1970. Registered profl. engr., Ala. Mem. Nat., Ala. socs. profl. engrs. Methodist. Author tech. reports. Home: 822 Olivia Ave Huntsville AL 35802

LANGTON, BASIL CEDRIC, actor, stage dir.; b. Bristol, Eng., Jan. 9, 1912; s. Samuel Calvert and Ester (Shandel) L.; privately ed.; m. Louise Soelberg (div. 1959); 1 dau., Jessica Louise (Mrs. Chris Andrews); m. 2d, Nancy Wickwire (div. 1969). With Vancouver Little Theatre; scholar Theatre of Dance-Mime at Dartington Hall; played Hamlet at Shakespeare Meml. Theatre; with maj. Brit. Repertory Theatres, including Birmingham Repertory and Old Vic; has appeared in leading roles on Broadway in Soldiers, Camelot, The Affair and London's West End in Soldiers; founder Travelling Repertory Theatre during World War II; dir., actor Kings Theatre, Theatre Royal; on nat. tour of Hostile Witness; stock co. in Unknown Soldier and His Wife, Phila., 1967-68, Peg with Eartha Kitt, 1967-68; appeared on television shows The Secret Storm, 1967-68, Love of Life, Hallmark; moderator Lucien Clergue-CBS, 1967-68; stage dir. Medee, Volo di Notte, 1967-68, Ariadne Auf Naxos and The Would-Be Gentleman, Goyescas; exec. producer, v.p. Music Now Inc., 1970—; stage dir. world premiere Yerma opera by Villa-Lobos, Santa Fe, 1971, Arlesienne, N.Y.C., 1971; stage dir. N.Y. premiere Boulevard Solitude, 1972, Don Pasquale, Manhattan Sch. Music, N.Y.C., 1974, 13 Rue de l'Amour, Chgo., 1974; dir. Hay Fever, Chgo., 1975, Major Barbara, Juilliard, N.Y.C., 1976, 13 Rue de l'Amour, N.Y.C. and tour, 1978; stage dir., librettist The Free Lance (Sousa) at Iowa State Center and Acad. Music, Phila. for Opera Co. Phila., 1979; chmn. drama com. Fulbright-Hays-Inst. Internat. Edn.; faculty Sarah Lawrence Coll., Western Res. U., Cath. univs., Manhattan Sch. Music, N.Y.C., 1958—; lectr. Yale, Antioch Coll., Hunter Coll., Carnegie Inst. Tech., Am. Theatre Wing. Mem. Council Participating Dirs., Boston U.; co-founder, stage dir. Empire State Music Festival; narrator T.S. Eliot's The Wasteland with Cin. Symphony Orch. John Hay Whitney Found. grantee, 1949-50; Guggenheim fellow, 1957; MacDowell Colony grantee, 1960, 69; Nat. Endowment Arts grantee, 1974, 75. Mem. Nat. Opera Assn., Royal Photog. Soc., Actors Equity, Shaw Soc. Am. (dir.), A.F.T.R.A., A.G.M.A., English Speaking Union, A.S.C.A.P., Soc. Stage Dirs. and Choreographers. Home: 41 W 69th St New York NY 10023

LANGWORTHY, DAVID COLLIE, metal mfg. exec.; b. New Orleans, Dec. 3, 1917; s. William P. and Marjorie (Collie) L.; student Harvard, 1936-37, Yale Sch. Fine Arts, 1938-41; m. Norma Jane Shea, July 11, 1943; children—Collie S., Leslie Jane, Wilson B., Keith C. Exec. v.p. Magnetic Metals Co., Camden, N.J., 1947-1962, dir., 1947-75, pres., 1962-75; chmn. bd. Magnetco, Inc., Phila., 1975-77; past dir. The Bank of N.J. Past trustee Inst. Med. Research; chmn. com. Langworthy Found. Served to 2d lt. C.E., AUS, 1942-43. Clubs: Merion Cricket; Little Egg Harbor Yacht. Home: 18 W 11th St New York NY 10011

LANGWORTHY, ROBERT BURTON, lawyer; b. Kansas City, Mo., Dec. 24, 1918; s. Herman Moore and Minnie (Leach) L.; A.B., Princeton, 1940; J.D., Harvard, 1943; m. Elizabeth Ann Miles, Jan. 2, 1942; children—David Robert, Joan Elizabeth, Mark Burton. Admitted to Mo. bar, 1943, U.S. Supreme Ct., 1960; practiced in Kansas City, 1943—; asso., now sr. partner firm Linde, Thomson, Fairchild, Langworthy & Kohn, and predecessors, 1943—. Dir. Clarkson Power Flow, Inc., Miles Lumber Co. Commr., Housing Authority Kansas City, Mo., 1963-71, chmn., 1969-71; chmn. Bd. Election Commrs. Kansas City, 1973-77. Chmn. bd. West Central area YMCA, 1969—; mem. bd. Mid-Am. region YMCA, 1970—, vice chmn., 1970-73, chmn., 1973-78; pres. Met. Bd. Kansas City (Mo.) YMCA, 1965, bd. dirs., 1965—, mem. nat. bd., 1971-78, 79—; pres. Met. Area Citizens Edn., 1969-72; chmn. Citizens Assn. Kansas City, Mo., 1967; bd. dirs. Project Equality Kans.-Mo., 1967—, pres., 1970-72, treas., 1972-73, sec., 1973-76; 1st v.p. Human Resources Corp. Kansas City, Mo., 1969-71, 72-73, bd. dirs., 1965-73; hon. v.p. Am. Sunday Sch. Union (now Am. Missionary Fellowship), 1965—; vice chmn. trustee Kemper Mil. Sch., 1966-73; bd. dirs. YMCA of Rockies, 1974—; U.S. del. YMCA World Council, Buenos Aires, 1977. Bd. dirs. Mo. Republican Club, 1960—; del., mem. platform com. Rep. Nat. Conv., 1960; Rep. nominee for U.S. Congress, 1964. Served to lt. (j.g.) USNR, 1943-46; now capt. Res. ret. Mem. Am., Kansas City bar assns., Mo. State Bar, Lawyers Assn. Kansas City, Am. Judicature Soc., Harvard Law Sch. Assn. Mo. (v.p. 1973-74, pres. 1974-75). Presbyn. (elder). Clubs: University (Kansas City, Mo.); Leawood (Kans.) Country. Home: 616 W 69th St Kansas City MO 64113 Office: City Center Square 27th Floor PO Box 26010 Kansas City MO 64196

LANHAM, BENJAMIN TILLMAN, JR., coll. adminstr.; b. Edgefield, S.C., Apr. 5, 1917; s. Benjamin Tillman and Mary (Shaw) L.; B.S., Clemson U., 1937; M.S., U. Tenn., 1938; postgrad. Ia. State U., 1938-39; Ph.D., Mich. State U., 1960; m. Margaret Bernice Arnold, June 29, 1941; children—Benjamin Tillman III, Betty Anne. Mem. faculty Auburn (Ala.) U., 1939—, prof., head dept. agrl. econs., 1956-64, asso. dir. Agr. Expt. Sta., asst. dean agr., 1964-66, v.p. for research, 1966-72, v.p. for adminstrn., 1972—. Chmn. Ala. Water Resources Research Inst. Council; mem. council grad. edn. agrl. scis. So. Regional Edn. Bd.; mem. adv. com. Ala. Program Devel. Office. Served to maj., inf., AUS, 1942-46. Mem. A.A.A.S., Am. Farm Econ. Assn., Am. Econ. Assn., Am. Marketing Assn., Am. Acad. Polit. and Social Sci., Am. Sociol. Soc., Assn. So. Agrl. Workers, So. Econ. Assn., Internat. Conf. Agrl. Economists, Ala. Acad. Sci., Ala. Edn. Assn., Nat. Council U. Research Adminstrs., Land-Grant Coll. Assn., Sigma Xi, Gamma Sigma Delta, Omicron Delta Epsilon, Phi Delta Kappa, Omicron Delta Kappa. Baptist. Kiwanian. Past chmn. edit. bd. Jour. Ala. Acad. Sci. Contbr. profl. jours. Home: 536 S Gay St Auburn AL 36830

LANHAM, BETTY BAILEY, anthropologist; b. Statesville, N.C., Aug. 12, 1922; s. Clyde B. and Naomi (Bailey) L.; B.S., U. Va., 1944, M.A., 1947; Ph.D., Syracuse U., 1962. Mem. faculty River Falls State Tchrs. Coll., 1948-49, U. Md., 1949-50, Randolph Macon Women's Coll., 1954-55, Oswego State Tchrs. Coll., 1956-58, Hamilton Coll., 1961-62, Ind. U., 1962-65, Western Mich. U., 1965-67, Albany Med. Coll., 1967-70; prof. anthropology Indiana U. of Pa., 1970—. Wenner-Gren Found. for Anthrop. Research fellow, 1951-52; AAUW research fellow, 1959-60. Mem. Am. Anthrop. Assn., Soc. Applied Anthropology, Assn. Asian Studies. Democrat. Methodist. Contbr. articles profl. jours. Home: 121 Dolores Circle Indiana PA 15701 Office: Dept of Sociology and Anthropology Indiana University Indiana PA 15705

LANHAM, EDWIN MOULTRIE, writer; b. Weatherford, Tex., Oct. 11, 1904; s. Edwin Moultrie and Elizabeth (Stephens) L.; student Tome Sch., Port Deposit, Md., Polytech. Prep. Country Day Sch., Bklyn., Williams Coll., 1923-26; study art, Paris, 1926-30; m. Irene Stillman, June 3, 1940; 1 dau., Evelyn Linda (Mrs. Kazuto Ohira). Entered newspaper work, 1930; with N.Y. Eve. Post, 1930-33, N.Y.C. News Assn., 1934-39, N.Y. Herald Tribune, 1939-44; free lance writer, 1944—. Guggenheim fellow, 1940. Mem. Author's Guild, Phi Gamma Delta. Democrat. Author: Sailors Don't Care, 1929; The Wind Blew West, 1935; Banner at Daybreak, 1937; Another Ophelia, 1938; The Stricklands, 1939; Thunder in the Earth, 1941 (ann. award Tex. Inst. Letters 1942); The Iron Maiden, 1954; Slug It Slay, 1946; Politics is Murder, 1947; One Murder Too Many, 1952; Death of a Corinthian, 1953; Death in the Wind, 1956; Murder on My Street, 1958; Double Jeopardy, 1959; Six Black Camels, 1961; Passage to Danger, 1962; No Hiding Place, 1962; Monkey on a Chain, 1962; Speak Not Evil, 1964; The Paste-Pot Man, 1967; The Clock at 8:16, 1970. Contbr. short stories to nat. mags. Home: Grove Beach Clinton CT 06413 Died July 24, 1979.

LANHAM, ELIZABETH, educator; b. Santo, Tex., Mar. 10, 1912; s. James S. and Mina (Latimer) L.; B.B.A., Tex. Tech. U., 1934; M.B.A., U. Tex., Austin, 1939, Ph.D., 1950. Instr., N.Mex. State Coll., 1939-42; asst. prof. mgmt. U. Ariz., 1942-44; asst. dir. personnel State Farm Ins. Cos., Bloomington, Ill., 1944-47; prof. mgmt. U. Tex., Austin, 1947-78, chmn. dept. mgmt., 1971-76, prof. emeritus, 1978—, cons. div. extension, 1978—; cons. in field. Mem. Sigma Iota Epsilon, Beta Gamma Sigma, Chi Omega. Episcopalian. Author: Job

Evaluation, 1955, Spanish edit., 1962, Japanese edit., 1963; Administration of Wages and Salaries, 1963; author profl. monographs; contbr. articles, revs. to profl. jours. Home: 600 W 10th St Austin TX 78701

LANHAM, RICHARD ALAN, educator, lit. critic; b. Washington, Apr. 26, 1936; s. Roy Benjamin and Leolia Elizabeth (Reid) L.; A.B., Yale, 1956, M.A., 1960, Ph.D., 1963; m. Carol Dana, Sept. 7, 1957. Instr., Dartmouth Coll., 1962-64, asst. prof. English, 1964-65; asst. prof. UCLA, 1965-69, asso. prof., 1969-72, prof., 1972—, dir. writing programs, 1979—. Served with AUS, 1956-58. Nat. Endowment for Humanities Sr. fellow, 1973-74. Mem. Modern Lang. Assn. Am. Author: Sidney's Old Arcadia, 1965; A Handlist of Rhetorical Terms, 1968; Tristram Shandy: The Games of Pleasure, 1973; Style: An Anti-Textbook, 1974; The Motives of Eloquence: Literary Rhetoric in the Renaissance, 1976; Revising Prose, 1979. Home: 10792 Ashton Ave Los Angeles CA 90024

LANHAM, ROBERT LEE, holding co. exec.; b. Clarksburg, W.Va., Dec. 5, 1924; s. Dennis B. and Captolia H. (Carr) L.; B.S., W.Va. U., 1948; m. Janet Olds, Aug. 5, 1950; children—Robert L., Anne E. Acct., Arthur Andersen & Co., 1948-50; with Am. Natural Resources Co., Detroit, 1950—, controller, 1964-74, v.p. fin., 1974—, v.p., chief fin. officer, 1979—. Served with USN, 1943-46. Mem. Am. Gas Assn. (chmn. fin. com., chmn. fin. and adminstrv. sect.), Econ. Club Detroit. Republican. Methodist. Club: Detroit. Office: 1 Woodward Ave Detroit MI 48226

LANIER, JOHN HICKS, apparel co. exec.; b. Nashville, Apr. 12, 1940; s. Sartain and Claudia Gwynn (Whitson) L.; B.A., Vanderbilt U., 1962; M.B.A., Harvard U., 1964; m. Jane M. Darden, Oct. 15, 1966; children—Jay, Liza, Stephen. Pres., Oxford Industries, Inc., Atlanta; dir. Lanier Bus. Products, Crawford & Co., Trust Co. of Ga. Assos. Trustee, Westminster Schs., Henrietta Egleston Hosp. for Children. Served with USAFR, 1964-65. Mem. Am. Apparel Mfrs. Assn. (dir.). Republican. Office: 222 Piedmont Ave NE Atlanta GA 30308

LANIER, JOSEPH LAMAR, JR., mfg. co. exec.; b. Lanett, Ala., Feb. 9, 1932; s. Joseph Lamar and Lura Brown (Fowlkes) L.; B.S., Washington and Lee U., 1954; student Harvard Grad. Sch. Bus., 1954-55; m. Ann Morgan, Aug. 21, 1954; children—Joseph Lamar III, Ann M. Asst. mgr. Fairfax mill West Point-Pepperell, Inc., 1958-62, corp. v.p., 1962-68, pres. indsl. fabrics div., dir., 1968-70, corporate exec. v.p., 1970-74, pres., 1974—, chief exec. officer, 1975—; dir. Textile Hall Corp., Flower Industries, Inc., Trust Co. Ga., Liberty Nat. Ins.; dir. So. regional bd. Arkwright-Boston Ins. Co. Dir. Am. Textile Mfrs. Inst. Trustee LaGrange Coll.; bd. visitors Berry Coll. Mem. Ala. C. of C. (dir.). Home: Spring Rd Lanett AL 36863 Office: West Point Pepperell Inc PO Box 71 West Point GA 31833

LANIER, ROBERT JERRY, JR., profl. basketball player; b. Buffalo, Sept. 10, 1948; s. Robert Jerry and Nanette (Warford) L.; B.B.A., St. Bonaventure Coll., 1970; m. Shirley Neville, July 24, 1971; children—Jack, Kimberly, Tiffany. Center, Detroit Pistons, 1970—, team capt., 1975—. Active Boys Club Met. Detroit, Stroh Brewing Co. Mini Basketball Clinics. Mem. Nat. Basketball Assn. Players Assn. (sec.-treas.). Six-time mem. Nat. Basketball Assn. All-Star Team; named most valuable player 1974 All-Star Game. Office: 1200 Featherstone Pontiac MI 48057

LANIER, SARTAIN, apparel mfr., univ. trustee; b. Winchester, Tenn., Aug. 20, 1909; s. John Hicks and Nettie (Sartain) L.; B.A., Vanderbilt U., 1931; m. Elizabeth Moorman, July 19, 1977; children—Gwynn (Mrs. George C. Blount), Vance, Hicks. Partner Lanier Co., distbr. dictating machines, Nashville, 1934—; with Oxford Industries, Inc., apparel mfg., Atlanta, 1942—, pres., 1950-57, chmn. bd., 1957—; dir. Standard Brands, Inc., N.Y.C., Genuine Parts Co., Atlanta, Trust Co. Ga. Trustee Vanderbilt U., 1960—, Piedmont Hosp., Atlanta, 1969—. Mem. Vanderbilt U. Alumni Assn. (pres. 1958-59), Phi Beta Kappa. Clubs: Piedmont Driving, Capital City (Atlanta). Home: 100 Valley Rd NW Atlanta GA 30305 Office: 222 Piedmont Ave NE Atlanta GA 30312

LANIGAN, DENIS GEORGE, advt. agy. exec.; b. Eng., Jan. 25, 1926; ed. Cambridge (Eng.) U.; married; 2 children. With J. Walter Thompson Co., 1952—, mgr., Frankfurt, Germany, 1959-66, mng. dir., London, 1966-69, v.p., 1969-75, chmn., 1975—, also pres. European div., London. Office: 40 Berkeley Sq London W1 England

LANING, ROBERT COMEGYS, physician, govt. ofcl., former naval officer; b. Haiti, Sept. 20, 1922 (parents Am. citizens); s. Richard Henry and Marguerite C. (Boyer) L.; student U. Pa., 1941-43; M.D., Jefferson Med. Coll., 1948; m. Alice Teresa Lech, Sept. 9, 1961; 1 dau., Maria Alice. Intern, Jefferson Hosp., Phila., 1948-50; commd. lt. (j.g.) U.S. Navy, 1950, advanced through grades to rear adm., 1973; mem. astronaut recovery teams, 1960-66; chief of surgery Naval Hosp., San Diego, 1967-71; med. dir. Naval Hosp., Yokosuka, Japan, 1972-73; med. officer Pacific Fleet, 1973-75; asst. chief Bur. Medicine and Surgery for Operational Med. Support, Washington, 1975-77, ret., 1977; dep. dir. surg. service VA Central Office, Washington, 1977-79, dir. surg. service, 1979—. Diplomate Nat. Bd. Med. Examiners, Am. Bd. Surgery. Fellow A.C.S.; mem. Am. Assn. Mil. Surgeons. Roman Catholic. Home: 6532 Sunny Hill Ct McLean VA 22101 Office: 810 Vermont Ave NW Washington DC 20420

LANK, ROBERT BYRON, univ. dean; b. Kansas City, Mo., July 1, 1919; s. William John and Frances Blanche (Burton) L.; student Kan. State Tchrs. Coll., 1936-37; B.S., Kan. State U., 1940, D.V.M., 1942; M.S., Ia. State U., 1958; m. June Elaine Light, Nov. 28, 1946; children—Robert B., Judy Mae. Pvt. vet. practice, Ferriday, La., 1942, Bastrop, La., 1946-48; asso. prof., then prof., head dept. vet. sci. La. State U., 1948—, asso. dean Sch. Vet. Medicine, 1968—. Mem. vet. rev. com. NIH, 1969-72; mem. Nat. Com. for Accreditation Tng. Programs for Animal Technicians, 1972—; mem. Nat. Bd. Vet. Med. Examiners. Served to capt. Vet. Corps, AUS, 1942-46. Mem. Am. (chmn. council edn. 1969-71), La. (sec.-treas. 1950-55, exec. sec. 1961-64, pres. 1966, ho. dels. 1967—) vet. med. assns., Blue Key, Alpha Zeta, Gamma Sigma Delta, Alpha Gamma Rho. Methodist. Kiwanian. Research bovine vibriosis, bovine reproductive problems. Home: 246 Guava Dr Baton Rouge LA 70808

LANK, WILLIAM ALBERT, banker; b. Seaford, Del., Dec. 29, 1907; s. Albert J. and Elizabeth E. (Hayman) L.; pre-law student U. Del., 1925-27; m. Mary E. Hollis, Sept. 8, 1927; children—Merle Elizabeth, C. Richard Williams. Nat. bank examiner, controller of the currency, 1929-39; pres. Farmers Nat. Bank, Bloomsburg, Pa., 1939-64; sr. v.p., dir. United Penn Bank, Wilkes-Barre, Pa., 1964-72, now dir.; dir. United Penn Corp., Wilkes-Barre; pres. HLW Enterprises, Inc., Bloomsburg. Past mem. faculty Pa. Bankers Assn. Banking Sch., Bucknell U. Chmn. drives United Fund, 1960, 63; pres. Bloomsburg (Pa.) Hosp., 1950-62; past pres. Bloomsburg Civic Music Assn.; past treas. Salvation Army. Pres. bd. trustees Bloomsburg State Coll., 1964-71; former trustee Nat. Found. for Consumer Credit. Served to lt. USNR, 1943-46. Mem. Pa. (pres. 1962-63), Am. (exec. council) bankers assns., Union League Phila., Kappa Alpha. Republican. Presbyn. (treas. 1948-56). Mason (33 deg.), Elk, Moose. Club: Skytop (Pa.). Home: 1717 Old Berwick Rd Bloomsburg PA 17815 Office: 37 W Main St Bloomsburg PA 17815. *Early in life I learned perseverance—the willingness to follow through to a conclusion, whether it resulted in success or failure. I soon had to learn the difference between perseverance and stubbornness. Because stubbornness without adequate reasoning often led to expensive failure. I also learned that from daydreaming could come greatness and success. However, it was necessary to distinguish between wistful thinking and dreams that could lead to substance.*

LANKER, BRIAN TIMOTHY, photographer; b. Detroit, Aug. 31, 1947; s. Merrill Ross and Gertrude Pearl (Geisen) L.; student Phoenix Coll., 1967. Staff photographer Phoenix Gazette, 1966-69, Topeka Capital Jour., 1969-74; chief photographer Eugene (Oreg.) Register-Guard, 1974—. Named Nat. Newspaper Photographer of the Year, Nat. Press Photographers Assn., 1970, 76, Regional Photographer of the Year, 1968, 69, 70, 71, 72, 73; recipient Pulitzer prize for feature photography, 1973. Mem. Nat. Press Photographers Assn. Office: 1993 Kimberly Dr Eugene OR 97405. *For a time I lived wholly for the world of professional achievement; but one soon realizes that the most important aspect of life is closeness and sensitivity to people. The big moments in my life are not awards such as the Pulitzer but the sharing of thoughts, ideas, and love with people.*

LANKFORD, FRANCIS GREENFIELD, JR., educator; b. Morattico, Va., Feb. 14, 1906; s. Francis Greenfield and Alma (Coulbourne) L.; B.S., Randolph-Macon Coll., 1928, LL.D., 1959; M.A., U. Va., 1932, Ph.D., 1938; m. Florence Fleet, June 4, 1935; children—William Fleet, Francis Greenfield III. High sch. prin., 1928-31; from instr. to prof. edn. U. Va., Charlottesville, 1932-50; dir. research Richmond Pub. Schs., 1943-44; pres. Longwood Coll., Farmville, Va., 1955-65; prof. edn., dir. office instl. analysis U. Va., 1965-71, sesquicentennial scholar, 1971-72, Commonwealth prof., 1972, prof. edn. emeritus, 1972—; edn. adviser Ford Found.-U. Chgo. Pakistan Edn. Project, 1962-63. Dir. study high sch. edn. Va. C. of C., 1942-43; dir. div. ednl. research U. Va., 1951-55; mem. Charlottesville (Va.) Sch. Bd., 1952-55. Campaign chmn. Prince Edward Community Chest, 1958. Recipient Disting. Alumnus award U. Va. Sch. Edn., 1977. Gen. Edn. Bd. fellow U. Mich., 1939-40. Mem. Nat. Council Tchrs. Math. (v.p. 1955-57), Raven Soc., Phi Beta Kappa, Omicron Delta Kappa, Phi Delta Kappa (distinguished service award U. Va. chpt. 1944). Democrat. Episcopalian. Co-author: Mathematics for the Consumer, 1947, 2d edit., 1953; Basic Ideas of Mathematics, 1953; Algebra One and Algebra Two, 1955; Essential Mathematics, 1961, 2d edit., 1967, 3d edit., 1975; Contemporary Algebra I, 1962; Contemporary Algebra II, 1963; Algebra One, 1969, 72; Algebra Two, 1969, 72, 77; Numbers and Operations, 1970; Consumer Mathematics, 1971, 2d edit., 1974; also articles. Departmental editor: Math. Tchr., 1953-57. Home: Cavalier Dr Colthurst Farm Charlottesville VA 22901

LANKFORD, WILLIAM THOMAS, JR., steel co. exec.; b. Rockwood, Tenn., Nov. 1, 1919; s. William Thomas and Pearl (Chastain) L.; B.S. in Metall. Engring., Carnegie-Mellon U., 1941, Sc.D. in Metall. Engring., 1945; m. Gretchen Goldsmith, July 29, 1944; children—William T., Andrew James, John Robert, Kathleen. Devel. engr. Carnegie Steel Corp., 1945; chief research engr. specialty products U.S. Steel Corp., 1954-60, div. chief sheet products, 1960-63, asst. dir. steel products devel., 1963-67, mgr. steel processing, 1967-75, asso. dir., mgr. basic research Research Lab., Monroeville, Pa., 1975—. Recipient Charles B. Dudley medal, Richard L. Templin award ASTM, 1959. Registered profl. engr., Pa. Fellow ASME, Am. Soc. Metals, Metall. Soc. and Iron and Steel Soc. of Metall. Am. Inst. Mining, and Petroleum Engrs. (Howe Meml. lectr.); mem. Am. Iron and Steel Inst., AAAS. Republican. Club: University (Pitts.). Contbr. articles to profl. jours. Home: 200 Mayfair Dr Pittsburgh PA 15228 Office: Research Lab US Steel Corp 125 Jamison Ln Monroeville PA 15146

LANNAN, J. PATRICK, financial cons.; b. Sterling, Ill., June 30, 1905; s. Patrick Henry and Kathryn (Killen) L.; ed. pub. schs., Duluth, Minn.; LL.D., Duquesne U., 1955; m. Ora Mary Pelham, Aug. 20, 1924; children—Patricia Mary (Mrs. John H. Campbell), Michael Joseph, Lawrence Patrick, Colleen Margaret (Mrs. James L. Dillon), Sharon Ann (Mrs. Harve A. Ferrill), J. Patrick. With Ford Motor Co., Iron Mountain, Mich., 1924-26; indsl. cons., 1926-29; with Leight & Co., finance, Chgo., 1929-32; industrialist, partner Kneeland & Co., mems. Midwest Stock Exchange, Chgo., 1932-57; dir. Lannan & Co., ins. brokers, Chgo., Advance Ross Corp., Chgo.; mem. exec. com., dir. Internat. Tel. & Tel., Macmillan, Inc., N.Y.C.; chmn. bd., dir. JPL Enterprises, Inc.; dir. Gt. Falls Gas Co. (Mont.). Served as Dollar-a-Year man on WPB, World War II; spl. asst. to sub-com. Com. on Edn. and Labor of U.S. Congress which traveled throughout Europe, fall 1947. Chmn. bd. trustees Mag. Poetry; trustee Cancer Research Found. Roman Catholic. Clubs: Bondmen's (Chgo.); Rolling Rock (Pitts.). Contbr. articles to jours. Home: 1768 S Ocean Blvd Palm Beach FL 33480 Office: PO Box 6113 West Palm Beach FL 33405

LANNERS, FRED THOMAS, JR., chem. co. exec.; b. St. Paul, Nov. 14, 1917; s. Fred Thomas and Aurelia Marie (LeTourneau) L.; student River Falls State U., 1938-41; B. Chem. Engring., U. Minn., 1948; m. Leonette Mary Worm, Feb. 18, 1946; children—Michael, Aurelia, Shirley, Cynthia, F. Thomas, John, Alan, Carol, Robert, Kathleen. Chem. engr. Econ. Lab., St. Paul, 1948-51, asst. dir. research and devel., 1951-54, asst. to pres., 1954-57, adminstrv. v.p., 1957-60, pres. internat. ops., N.Y.C., 1960-70, St. Paul, 1970-72, corp. pres., 1972—, chmn. bd., chief exec. officer, 1978—; chmn. bd., pres., dir. Econ. Lab.; dir. First Nat. Bank St. Paul, Am. Hoist & Derrick. Bd. dirs. Profl. Econs. Bur.; trustee, bd. regents St. John's Coll. Served with AUS, 1942-45. Decorated Purple Heart, Bronze Star. Mem. St. Paul Area C. of C. (dir., 1st v.p.), NAM (dir.), Am. Mgmt. Assn., Nat. Security Indsl. Assn. Clubs: Minnesota, Athletic, Pool and Yacht. Contbr. articles profl. jours. Home: 2125 Lower St Dennis Rd St Paul MN 55116 Office: Osborn Bldg St Paul MN 55102

LANNI, JOSEPH TERRENCE, diversified industry exec.; b. Los Angeles, Mar. 14, 1943; s. Anthony Warren and Mary Lucille (Leahy) L.; B.S., U. So. Calif., 1965, M.B.A., 1967. Vice pres. Intervest, Inc., Los Angeles, 1967-69; treas. Republic Corp., Los Angeles, 1969-76; chief fin. officer C.W.I. Inc., 1977—; dir. OnLine Distributed Processing, Bd. dirs. Town Hall, Holy Family Services Counseling and Adoption; bd. regents Loyola Marymount U.; regional chmn. United Way. Mem. Los Angeles Jr. C. of C. (dir. Century City region), Am. Mgmt. Assn. (chmn. Ops. Enterprise, regional chmn. Speakers Bur.), Commerce Assos. (pres.-elect dir.), So. Calif. Civic Light Opera Assos. Clubs: Bachelors (past pres.); Crockfords (London); Beach; London. Author: Anthology of Poetry, 1965. Home: 1360 Warnall Ave Los Angeles CA 90024 Office: Suite 2600 1801 Century Park E Los Angeles CA 90067

LANNING, DAVID DAYTON, nuclear engr.; b. Baker, Oreg., Mar. 30, 1928; s. Oscar Dayton and Lillian Charlotte (Preatorius) L.; B.A. in Physics, U. Oreg., 1951; Ph.D. in Nuclear Engring., M.I.T., 1963; m. Gloria Rae Rogers, Aug. 27, 1950; children—Daniel Dayton, Stephen Allen, Davida Laurie. Physicist, Hanford Works, Gen. Electric Co., Richland, Wash., 1951-57; supt. M.I.T. Reactor, 1957-62, asst. prof. and project leader M.I.T. Reactor Lattice Studies, 1962-63, asso. prof., asst. dir. M.I.T. Reactor, 1963-65, prof. nuclear engring., co-dir. in charge M.I.T. Reactor Modification, 1969-75, prof., nuclear engring. dept. grad. admissions officer, 1975—. Recipient Patent award Gen. Electric Co., 1957; registered profl. engr., Mass. Mem. Am. Nuclear Soc. (contbr. to profl. meetings abstracts). Congregationalist. Home: Blueberry Circle Hampstead NH 03841 Office: 77 Massachusetts Ave Cambridge MA 02139

LANO, CHARLES JACK, mfg. co. exec.; b. Port Clinton, Ohio, Apr. 17, 1922; s. Charles Herbin and Antoinette (Schmitt) L.; B.S. in Bus. Adminstrn. summa cum laude, Ohio State U., 1949; m. Beatrice Irene Spees, June 16, 1946; children—Douglas Cloyd, Charles Lewis. With U.S. Gypsum Co., 1941-46, Ottawa Paper Stock Co., 1946-47; accountant Arthur Young & Co., C.P.A.'s, Tulsa, 1949-51; controller Lima div. Ex-Cell-O Corp., 1951-59, electronics div. AVCO Corp., 1959-61, Servomation Corp., 1961; asst. comptroller Scovill Mfg. Co., Waterbury, Conn., 1961-62, comptroller, 1962-67; controller CF&I Steel Corp., Denver, 1967-69, v.p., controller, 1969-70; controller Pacific Lighting Corp., 1970-76; exec. v.p. Arts-Way Mfg. Co., Armstrong, Iowa, 1976—. Served with USMCR, 1942-45. C.P.A., Okla. Mem. Am. Inst. C.P.A.'s, Calif. Soc. C.P.A.'s, Financial Execs. Inst., Nat. Assn. Accountants, Am. Mgmt. Assn. (lectr. financial control). Home: PO Box 198 Armstrong IA 50514 Office: Arts-Way Mfg Co Armstrong IA 50514

LANOUETTE, WILLIAM JOHN, journalist; b. New Haven, Sept. 14, 1940; s. Joseph Francis and Gertrude Veronica (Thied) L.; student USCG Acad., 1958-59; A.B., Fordham Coll., 1963; M.Sc., London Sch. Econs. and Polit. Sci., U. London, 1966, Ph.D., 1973; m. JoAnne Marie Sheldon, Apr. 12, 1969; children—Nicole Marie, Kathryn Ann. Researcher, reporter Newsweek, N.Y.C., 1961-64; news editor WVOX AM-FM Radio Sta., New Rochelle, N.Y., 1964; profl. staff mem., research and tech. programs subcom. Govt. Ops. Com., Ho. of Reps., Washington, 1967; legis. asst. to U.S. Rep. John S. Monagan, Washington, 1967-68; staff writer Nat. Observer, Washington, 1969-70, 72-77; staff corr. Nat. Jour., Washington, 1977—. Am. lectr. Hansard Soc. for Parliamentary Govt., London, 1965-66, 70-71; mem. Internat. Research Group on Drug Legis. and Programs, Geneva, 1972—. Served with USCG, 1958-59. Recipient Forum award, 1974. Mem. White House Corrs. Assn. Democrat. Clubs: Potomac Boat, Nat. Press (Washington). Contbr. articles to profl. publs. Home: 326 5th St SE Washington DC 20003 Office: 1730 M St NW Washington DC 20036

LANSBURY, ANGELA BRIGID, actress; b. London, Eng., Oct. 16, 1925; d. Edgar and Moyna (Macgill) Lansbury; student Webber-Douglas Sch. Drama (London), 1939-40, Feagin Sch. Drama, N.Y.C., 1940-42; m. Peter Shaw, Aug. 12, 1949; children—Anthony P., Deirdre A. Came to U.S., 1940, naturalized, 1951. Actress, Metro-Goldwyn-Mayer, 1943-50; free lance, 1950—; motion pictures include: Gaslight, 1944, Nat. Velvet, 1944, Dorian Gray, 1944, Harvey Girls, 1946, Till the Clouds Roll By, 1946, If Winter Comes, 1947, State of the Union, 1948, Samson and Delilah, 1949, Kind Lady, 1951, The Court Jester, 1956, The Long Hot Summer, 1957, Reluctant Debutante, 1958, Summer of the 17th Doll, 1959, A Breath of Scandal, 1959, Dark at the Top of the Stairs, 1960, Blue Hawaii, 1961, All Fall Down, 1962, Manchurian Candidate, 1963, In the Cool of the Day, 1963, World of Henry Orient, 1964, Out of Towners, 1964, Something for Everyone, 1969, Bedknobs and Broomsticks, 1970, Death on the Nile, 1978; appeared in plays Hotel Paradiso, 1957, A Taste of Honey, 1960, Anyone Can Whistle, 1964, Mame (on Broadway), 1966, Dear World, 1968, Gypsy, 1974, The King and I, 1978, Sweeney Todd, 1979, Hamlet (Nat. Theatre, London), 1976. Recipient Woman of Yr. award Harvard Hasty Pudding Theatricals, 1968; Antoinette Perry award, 1966, 69, 74, 79; Sarah Siddons award, 1974. Address: care Edgar Lansbury Suite 501 1650 Broadway New York NY 10019

LANSBURY, EDGAR GEORGE, producer; b. London, Jan. 12, 1930; s. Edgar Isaac and Charlotte Lillian (McIldowie) L.; came to U.S., 1941, naturalized, 1953; educated, U. Calif., Los Angeles; m. Rose Anthony Kean, Aug. 12, 1955; children—James, Michael, David, George, Brian, Kate. Designer stock and off-Broadway prodns., 1953-55; art dir. ABC-TV, 1955, CBS-TV, 1955-62, Channel 13, N.Y.C., 1962-63; motion picture art dir., 1963-64; formed Edgar Lansbury Prodns. Inc. for ind. prodn. in theatre and films, 1964—; producer Broadway plays: First One Asleep, Whistle, 1966, The Subject Was Roses, 1964, That Summer-That Fall, 1967, The Only Game in Town, 1968, Promenade, 1970, Look to the Lilies, 1970, Engagement Baby, 1971, Godspell, 1971, Elizabeth I, 1972, The Night That Made America Famous, 1974, The Magic Show, 1974, Gypsy, 1975, American Buffalo, 1977; producer films: The Subject was Roses, 1968, Godspell, 1973, The Wild Party, 1974, Squirm, 1976, Blue Sunshine, 1978; pres. Acting Co. Bd. dirs. Agni Yoga Soc., Nicholas Roerich Museum, N.Y.C.; bd. govs. League N.Y. Theatres and Producers. Served with U.S. Army, 1951-53. Recipient N.Y. Art Dirs. award for best comml. film, 1963, N.Y. Outercritics Circle award, N.Y. Critics Circle award, Antoinette Perry award for best produced play, 1965, nomination for Antoinette Perry award for best musical play, N.Y. Critics Circle award for best drama, 1977. Office: 1650 Broadway New York NY 10019

LANSDALE, BRUCE MCKAY, ednl. adminstr.; b. Worcester, Mass., Feb. 11, 1925; s. Herbert Parker and Marjorie Middleton (McKay) L.; B.S., U. Rochester, 1945; M.S. in Agrl. Edn., Cornell U., 1949; m. Elizabeth Joan Krihak, Jan. 22, 1949; children—David Parker, Jeffrey Dexter, Christine Kellog, Michael Lee. Chief interpreter Allied Mission for Greek Plebescite, Greece, 1946; vol. worker Am. Farm Sch., Thessaloniki, Greece, 1947, asst. dir., 1953-55, dir., pres., 1955—; Fulbright tchr., Greece, 1949-53; cons. World Council Chs.; bd. dirs. Fulbright program for Greece. Bd. dirs. Pinewood Sch., Thessaloniki Sch. Blind, Thessaloniki Tb Assn. Served with USNR, 1946-52. Decorated Order of George I (Greece); recipient (with wife) Disting. Alumni award U. Rochester, 1977. Mem. Modern Greek Lang. Assn., Greek Friends of Farmer Assn. Presbyterian. Clubs: Rotary, Yacht (Thessaloniki). Home: Am Farm Sch Box 140 Thessaloniki Greece Office: Am Farm Sch 380 Madison Ave 22d Ave New York NY 10017

LANSDALE, ROBERT TUCKER, social welfare cons.; b. Elmira, N.Y., Jan. 22, 1900; s. Herbert Parker and Lida Rachel (Eppley) L.; A.B., Oberlin Coll., 1921; diploma N.Y. Sch. Social Work, 1924; A.M., Columbia, 1925; postgrad. sociology U. Mich., 1925-27; LL.D., St. Lawrence U., 1953; m. Evelyn Gross, Dec. 31, 1925 (div. 1956); m. 2d, Carol Mary Standish, Jan. 28, 1956. Tchr. English and social sci. East High Sch., Rochester, N.Y., 1921-23; instr. sociology U. Mich., also exec. sec. Mich. Conf. Social Work, 1925-27; exec. sec. Council Social Agencies, Montclair, N.J., 1927-30; asst. to commr. U.S. Office Indian Affairs, 1930-34; adminstrv. asst. Fed. Emergency Relief Adminstrn., 1934-35; dir. state and local orgn. Gov. N.Y. Commn. Unemployment Relief, 1935-36; charge nat. study old-age assistance adminstrn., com. pub. adminstrn. Social Sci. Research Council, 1936-37; mem. faculty N.Y. Sch. Social Work, 1937-43; dir. Inst. Welfare Research, Community Service Soc., N.Y.C., 1941-43; commr. N.Y. State Dept. Social Welfare, 1943-53; cons. N.Y. State Commn. Fiscal Affairs State Govt., 1953-55; prof. Sch. Social

Welfare, Fla. State U., 1955-63; vis. prof. Sch. Social Work U. Md., Balt., 1964-66, prof. social work, 1966-70; cons. Md. Commn. on Aging, 1970-72, Gov. Md. Commn. Study Problems in Nursing Homes, 1972-73; research asso. Balt. Commn. on Aging and Retirement Edn., 1973-78; ret., 1978; cons. div. research Welfare Adminstrn., Dept. Health, Edn. and Welfare, Washington, 1964-66; cons. Inst. of Govtl. Research, Fla. State U., 1966-68; cons., lectr. numerous orgns., univs. Chmn. N.Y. State Youth Commn., 1949-53, N.Y. State Joint Hosp. Survey and Planning Commn., 1947-53; sec. Fla. Citizens Adv. Com. on Aged, 1959-61; v.p. Met. Sr. Citizens Center, Balt., 1969-70. Served with U.S. Army, 1918. Mem. Nat. Assn. Social Workers, Acad. Certified Social Workers, Am. Pub. Welfare Assn., Nat., Md. confs. social welfare. Author: The Florida Suitable Home Law, 1962; Inadequacies of Statewide Programs of Public Assistance in Urban Areas, 1967; Supplemental Security Income: The First Six Months, 1975; Supplemental Security Income: State Variations, 1977. Co-author: Administration of Old Age Assistance, 1938; County Welfare in Florida, 1968; Maryland's Older Citizens: an Assessment of Needs and Services, 1972; also articles, reports. Home: 3025 York St S Saint Petersburg FL 33707

LANSDEN, MERLE, ret. judge; b. nr. Beaver, Okla., July 8, 1907; s. William Arthur and Bridget Cecelia (Mulvey) L.; LL.B., U. Okla., 1939; m. Mildred I. Haught, July 5, 1957. Admitted to Okla. bar, 1939; practiced law, Beaver, 1939-55; with firm Lansden, Drum & Goetzinger, Beaver, 1955-67; dist. judge 1st Jud. Dist. Okla., 1967-77, ret., 1977. Pres., Okla. Jud. Conf., 1974. Mem. Okla. Ho. of Reps., 1940-46, 62-64, speaker, 1944; mem. Okla. Ct. Tax Rev., 1973. Served to maj. USMCR, 1943-46. Mem. Am., Okla. bar assns., Am. Judicature Soc., Order of Coif. Home: 2609 Fairfield Dr Norman OK 73069

LANSDOWNE, JAMES FENWICK, artist; b. Hong Kong, Aug. 8, 1937; s. Ernest and Edith (Ford) L.; grad. high sch. Exhibited one-man shows including Royal Ont. Mus., Toronto, Ont., 1956, Audubon House, N.Y.C., 1958, Tryon Galleries, London, Eng., 1961, 63, Kennedy Galleries, N.Y.C., 1962, Smithsonian Instn., Washington, 1969, 77, Oakland, Calif., 1976, Vancouver, B.C., 1976, Toronto, Ont., 1977; represented permanent collections Montreal Mus. Fine Arts, Art Gallery Victoria, Audubon House, Ulster Mus., Belfast, Ireland; represented pvt. collection Prince Philip. Decorated officer Order of Canada. Fellow Explorers Club; mem. Royal Canadian Acad. Arts, Fedn. Can. Artists, Can. Nature Fedn., Cornell Lab. Ornithology, Hakluyt Soc. Co-author: (with John A. Livingston) Birds of the Northern Forest, 1966; Birds of the Eastern Forest, 1968, Vol. II, 1970; author: Birds of the West Coast, Part I, 1976; illustrator: Rails of the World (S. Dillon Ripley), 1977. Studio: 941 Victoria Ave Victoria BC V8S 4N6 Canada Office: MF Feheley Arts Co Ltd 5 Drumsnab Rd Toronto ON Canada

LANSING, SHERRY LEE, motion picture prodn. exec.; b. Chgo., July 31, 1944; d. Norton and Margo Lansing; B.S. summa cum laude in Theatre, Northwestern U., 1966. Tchr. math. public high schs., Los Angeles, 1966-69; model TV commls. Max Factor Co., 1969-70, Alberto-Culver Co., 1969-70; appeared in movies: Loving, 1970, Rio Lobo, 1970; exec. story editor Wagner Internat., 1970-73; v.p. prodn. Heyday Prodns., Universal City, Calif., 1973-75; exec. story editor, then v.p. creative affairs MGM Studios, Culver City, Calif., 1975-77; sr. v.p. prodn. Columbia Pictures, Burbank, Calif., 1977-80; pres. prodn. 20th Century-Fox Prodns., Beverly Hills, Calif., 1980—. Office: 20th Century-Fox Prodns PO Box 900 Beverly Hills CA 90213

LANSNER, KERMIT IRVIN, editor, cons.; b. N.Y.C., May 9, 1922; s. David and Anna (Gordon) L.; B.A., Columbia, 1942; postgrad. Harvard, 1947, Columbia, 1948; Fulbright scholar, Sorbonne, Paris, France, 1950; m. Fay Gross, Sept. 10, 1948; children—Gabrielle, Erica. Asst. prof. philosophy Kenyon Coll., 1948-50; asso. editor Art News mag., 1953-54; mem. staff Newsweek mag., 1954-73, sr. editor, 1959-61, exec. editor, 1961-65, mng. editor, 1965-69, editor, 1969-72, contbg. editor, columnist, 1972-77, editor-in-chief Newsweek Books, 1972-73; cons. Louis Harris & Assos., 1973—. Served to lt. USNR, 1942-46. Mem. Council Fgn. Relations, Century Assn., Phi Beta Kappa. Contbr. Kenyon Rev., New Republic. Home: 317 W 80th St New York City NY 10024 Office: 317 W 80th St New York City NY 10024

LANTERMAN, JOSEPH BARNEY, indsl. exec.; b. Elkhart, Ill., Dec. 5, 1914; s. Fred J. and Bertha (Brown) L.; B.S., U. Ill., 1936; m. Marjorie Morton, June 7, 1947. With AMSTED Industries, Inc., 1936—, successively accountant, asst. to controller, asst. controller, controller, v.p., 1954-59, pres., chief exec. officer, 1959-69, chmn. bd., chief exec. officer, 1969-74, chmn., 1969—, dir., 1956—; dir. Midwest Stock Exchange, Trans Union Corp., I.C. Gulf R.R., Ill. Bell Telephone Co., Internat. Harvester Co., Harris Trust & Savs. Bank, Peoples Gas Co., Kemper Inc., A. E. Staley Mfg. Co. Past v.p. bd. govs., mem. exec. com. United Republican Fund Ill.; bd. dirs. Inst. Gas Tech., 1965-74; bd. dirs. Bus.-Industry Polit. Action Com., nat. chmn., 1967-69; bd. dirs. Met. Crusade of Mercy, 1961-69, pres., 1963-64; trustee Better Govt. Assn., 1964-74; vice chmn., trustee, exec. com., sec. Mus. Sci. and Industry, Chgo.; trustee, exec. com. Ill. Inst. Tech.; citizens bd. U. Chgo.; mem. bd. trustees Loyola U., Chgo., chmn., 1968-71, chmn. citizen's bd., 1973-75; mem. pres.'s com., dir. Lyric Opera Chgo., bd. dirs. Chgo. Boys Clubs, Protestant Found. Greater Chgo. C.P.A., Ill. Mem. Ill. Soc. C.P.A.'s, Ill. Mfrs. Assn. (dir. 1964-69), Ill. C. of C. (dir. 1957-63), The Conf. Bd., Northwestern U. Assos., Alpha Sigma Phi, Beta Alpha Psi. Clubs: Chicago, Economic (past pres., dir.), Mid-Am. (bd. govs., pres. 1968-70), Commercial (Chgo.); Glen View (Ill.); Garden of the Gods; Eldorado Country. Home: Rolling Acres Mundelein IL 60060 Office: Prudential Plaza Chicago IL 60601

LANTHIER, ANDRE, physician, biomed. research scientist; b. Montreal, Que., Can., Apr. 13, 1928; s. Eugene and Blanche (Paquette) L.; B.A., U. Montreal, 1947, M.D., 1953; m. Ghislaine Matte, Dec. 15, 1956; children—Francois, Gilbert, Stephane. Intern Notre Dame Hosp., Montreal, 1952-53, resident, 1953-55; research fellow Harvard U. Med. Sch. and asst. in medicine Peter Bent Brigham Hosp., Boston, 1955-57; faculty medicine, chmn. dept. medicine U. Montreal, 1968-72; physician-in-chief Notre-Dame Hosp., Montreal, 1967-72; asso. chmn. dept. medicine U. Montreal, 1972—; mem. Med. Research Council Can., 1966-72, chmn., 1971, Mem. Canadian Soc. Clin. Investigation (pres. 1967), Am. Fedn. Clin. Research, Am. Endocrine Soc., Royal Coll. Physicians, Surgeons Can. Contbr. numerous articles to biomed. research jours. Home: 1880 La Duchesse Saint Bruno PQ J3V 3L9 Canada Office: Notre-Dame Hosp Montreal PQ H2L 4K8 Canada

LANTHIER, RONALD ROSS, fin. exec.; b. Montreal, Que., Can., May 2, 1926; s. Emile Edgar and Edith (Martin) L.; Chartered Accountant, McGill U., 1952; m. Jacqueline Barbara Dyment, Nov. 7, 1944; children—April Carolyn, Bonnie Alice, Ronald Dyment, Andrea Elizabeth, John Elliott. Pub. accountant, 1944-51; chief accountant St. Lawrence Flour Co., 1951-52; controller Canadian Underwriters Assn., 1952-54; div. controller Canadian Aviation Electronics Co., 1954-56; treas. Webb & Knapp (Can.), 1956-62; dir. adminstrn. Greenshields, Inc., investment dealers, 1962-67; v.p. finance, treas. Canadian Marconi Co., 1967-72; v.p. finance, dir., mem. exec. com. Macdonald Tobacco, Inc., 1972-75; pres. Lanco Mgmt. Ltd., 1975—; v.p. finance MacDonald Stewart Textiles, 1976-77; v.p. fin. Electrolux Can., 1978—. Mem. Inst. Chartered Accountants Que., Financial Execs. Inst., Phi Kappa Pi. Anglican. Clubs: Royal Montreal Golf, Montreal Amateur Athletic Assn. Home: 6 Skyview Ln Aurora ON Canada Office: 2 Sheppard St Toronto ON Canada

LANTZ, MICHAEL, sculptor; b. New Rochelle, N.Y.; s. Frank and Mary (Jarvis) L.; student NAD, 1924-26, Beaux Arts Inst. Design, 1926-31. Asst. to Lee Lawrie, 1925-35; art instr. Adult Edn. Center, New Rochelle, 1935-38; instr. Nat. Acad. Sch. Fine Arts, 1964—, Old Lyme Acad. Fine Arts, 1977—; works include sculptural bronze History of Oil, Sinclair Oil Bldg., N.Y.C., sculptural panel Cement Industry, Lone Star Cement Corp., N.Y.C., 2 sculptural panels Architects Bldg., Albany, N.Y., sculptural panels in lobby Celanese Corp. Bldg., Charlotte, N.C., dining room DuPont Plaza Hotel, N.G. Meml. Bldg., Washington, Howard Trust Co., Burlington, Vt., dining room S.S. U.S. Ct. House, Lynchburg, Va.; U.S. Battle Monument St. Avold, France, City Hall Milw., 2 chapels Cathedral of Mary Our Queen, Balt., sculpture, Temple, Mobile, Ala., Court House, Mobile; exhbn. piece Christmas Font for Steuben Glass, 29 seals Pan Am. World Health Center, Washington; Thomas Bicentennial medal for U.S. Mint; New Rochelle Bicentennial Medal; 4-foot bronze Eagle, People's Bank for Savs., New Rochelle; Brookgreen Gardens Medallian for Soc. Medalists; Edenton (N.C.) Courthouse; exhibited at Nat. Acad., Archtl. League, Phila. Art Alliance, Pa. Acad.; 1st v.p. Nat. Acad.; academician NAD, mem. council, 1970-73. Recipient bronze, silver medals Beaux Arts Inst. Design; nat. competition, two equestrian groups FTC Bldg., Washington, 1938; 1st prize nat. competition Golden Anniversary medal City N.Y., 1948, Lindsay Morris Meml. award, 1950; silver medal Internat. Exhbn., Madrid, Spain; Hall of Fame medal N.Y. U.; Oliver Wendell Holmes Sr. medal; John Paul Jones medal; Saitus award for medallic art, 1969; Golden Plate award Am. Acad. Achievement, 1969; Elizabeth Watrous Gold medal, 1970, many others. Fellow Nat. Sculpture Soc. (exec. council, pres.), Fine Arts Fedn. N.Y. (v.p. 1970), Nat. Acad.; mem. Allied Artists Am. (silver medal), Acad. Artists Assn. Springfield (Mass.), Hudson Valley Artists Assn., Am. Artists Profl. League, Am. Numis. Soc. Club: N.Y. Athletic. Editor Nat. Sculpture Rev. Home: 979 Webster Ave New Rochelle NY 10804. *I have achieved success as a sculptor at the ripe young age of 24 through devotion, perserverance and talent. My main goal is to inspire young artists to achieve. I believe in good art.*

LANTZ, WALTER, animated cartoon producer; b. New Rochelle, N.Y., Apr. 27, 1900. Producer, Walter Lantz Cartunes; creator Woody Woodpecker, 1941, Chilly Willy, 1954; started dir. Gregory La Cava in 1916 with Katzenjamer Kids, Happy Hooligan and Krazy Kat; later producer, animator, actor, in Col. Heeza Liar for J.B. Bray; producer 1st technicolor cartoon screened (opening scenes King of Jazz); producer cartoons for army and navy, ednl. and comml. pictures for non-theatrical release and TV, The Woody Woodpecker Show for TV; pres. Walter Lantz Prodns., Inc. Recipient Acad. award, 1979. Address: care Walter Lantz Prodns Inc 6311 Romaine St Hollywood CA 90038

LANTZSCH, GUENTHER CHRISTIAN, banker; b. Krogis, Germany, Feb. 12, 1925; s. R. Edwin and Louise (Ettmeier) L.; B.A., Antioch Coll., 1951; M.B.A., U. Detroit, 1954; m. Margarette Joyce Kennedy, June 25, 1949; children—Barbara Ann, Geoffrey Christian. With Ford Motor Co., 1951-61, supr. budgets and profit analysis, 1957-61; planning mgr. Ford Motor Credit Co., 1961-62, mgr. marketing and planning, 1962-65; forward operations mgr. Ford Internat., 1965-69; v.p., comptroller Mellon Bank & Trust Co., Pitts., 1969-72; sr. v.p., comptroller Mellon Bank, N.A., Pitts., 1972—; v.p., treas. Mellon Nat. Corp., 1972—; sr. v.p., chief financial officer Mellon Bank, N.A., 1974-78, exec. v.p., chief fin. officer, 1978—; dir. Duquesne Light Co., Pitts. Bd. dirs., treas. Pitts. Symphony Soc., Heinz Hall for Performing Arts; bd. dirs. Am. Symphony Orch. League. Served to 1st lt., inf., AUS, 1943-47. Mem. Financial Execs. Inst., Am. Bankers Assn. Clubs: Sewickley Hunt; Duquesne (Pitts.); Allegheny Country; Rolling Rock; Flyfishers (London). Home: Spanish Tract Rd Sewickley PA 15143 Office: 525 William Penn Pl Pittsburgh PA 15230

LANYON, ELLEN (MRS. ROLAND GINZEL), artist; b. Chgo., Dec. 21, 1926; d. Howard Wesley and Ellen (Aspinwall) Lanyon; B.F.A., Art Inst. Chgo., 1948; M.F.A., State U. Ia., 1950; Fulbright fellow, Courtauld Inst., U. London, 1950-51; m. Roland Ginzel, Sept. 4, 1948; children—Andrew, Lisa. One woman shows Superior St. Gallery, Chgo., 1960, Stewart Richard Gallery, San Antonio, 1962, 65, Fairweather Hardin Gallery, Chgo., 1962, Zabriskie Gallery, N.Y.C., 1962, 64, 69, 72, B.C. Holland Gallery, Chgo., 1965, 68, Ft. Wayne Art Mus., 1967, Richard Gray Gallery, Chgo., 1970, 73, 76, 79, Madison Art Center, 1972, Nat. Collection at Smithsonian Instn., 1972, Odyssia Gallery, Rome, Italy, 1975, Krannert Performing Arts Center, 1976, Oshkosh Pub. Mus., 1976, U. Mo., 1976, Harcus Krakow, Boston, 1977—, Fendrick Gallery, Washington, 1978, Ky. State U., 1979, Ill. Wesleyan U., 1979, others; exhibited group shows, 1946—, including traveling exhbns. Am. Fedn. Arts, 1946-48, 50, 53, 57, 65, 66, 69, Art Inst. Chgo., 1946-47, 51-53, 55, 57-58, 60-62, 64, 66, 67, 68, 69, 71, 73, Corcoran Gallery Art, 1961, 76, Denver Art Mus., 1950, 52, Exhbn. Momentum, Chgo., 1948, 50, 52, 54, 56, Library of Congress, 1950, 52, Met. Mus. Art, 1952, Mus. Modern Art, 1953, 62, Phila. Mus. Art, 1946, 47, 50, 54, San Francisco Mus. Art, 1946, 50, U. Ill., 1953, 54, 57, Drawing Soc. Nat. Traveling Exhbn., 1965-66, The Painter and The Photograph traveling exhbn., 1964-65, Nostalgia traveling show, 1968-69, Violence, Mus. Contemporary Art, Chgo., 1969, Birds and Beasts, Graham Gallery, N.Y.C., 1969-71, Ill. painters Ill. Arts Council, 1968-71, Beyond Illustration HMH Publs. Europe, 1971, Chgo. Imagists, 1972, Chgo. Sch., 1972, Am. Women, 1972, Artists Books, 1973, Bicentennial American traveling exhibit, 1976, Chgo. Connection 1976-77, Downtown Whitney, N.Y.C., 1978—, Queens Mus., 1978, Dayton Art Inst., 1978, Odyssia Gallery, N.Y.C., 1979, Chgo. Cultural Center, 1979, others; represented permanent collections Art Chgo., Denver Art Mus., Library of Congress, Inst. Internat. Edn., London, Eng., Finch Coll., N.Y., Krannert Mus., U. Ill., U. Mass., N.J. State Mus., Ill. State Mus., Bklyn. Mus., Nat. Coll. Fine Arts, Boston Pub. Library, Des Moines Art Center, Albion Coll., Met. Mus., McNay Art Inst., Albion Coll., Kans. State U., U. Dallas, U. Houston, Cornell U., also numerous pvt. collections. Tchr. jr. sch. Art Inst. Chgo., 1952-54, past tchr. day sch.; tchr. Rockford Coll., summer 1953, Summer Sch. Painting, Saugatuck, Mich., 1961-62, 67-70, 71-72, 78, U. Ill., Chgo., 1970, U. Wis. Extension, 1971-72, Pa. State U., 1974, U. Calif., 1974, Sacramento State U., 1974, Stanford U., 1974, Boston U., 1975, Kans. State U., 1976, U. Mo., 1976, U. Houston, 1977; adj. vis. prof. So. Ill. U., No. Ill. U., SUNY, Purchase, 1978, Cooper Union, 1978-79, Parsons Sch. Design, 1979; disting. vis. prof. U. Calif., Davis, 1980—, others; founder, sec.-treas. Chgo. Graphic Workshop, 1952-55; participant Yaddo, 1973, 75, 76, Ossabow Island Project, 1976. Recipient Armstrong prize Art Inst. Chgo., 1946, 55, 77, Town and Country purchase prize, 1947, Blair prize, 1958, Palmer prize, 1962, 64, Chan prize, 1961, Vielehr prize, 1967; purchase prize Denver Art Mus., 1950, Library of Congress, 1950; Cassandra Found. award, 1970; Nat. Endowment for Arts grantee, 1974. Mem. Coll. Art Assn. (dir., exec. com.), Delta Phi Delta. Published Wonder Production Vol. I, 1971, Jataka Tales, 1975, Transformations, 1976. Illustrator: The Wandering Tattler, 1975. Address: 412 Clark St Chicago IL 60610 also 138 Prince St New York NY 10012

LANYON, WESLEY EDWIN, ornithologist; b. Norwalk, Conn., June 10, 1926; s. William J. and Frances A. (Merrill) L.; A.B. in Zoology, Cornell U., 1950; Ph.D., U. Wis., 1955; m. Vernia E. Hall, Jan. 29, 1951; children—Cynthia Hall, Scott Merrill. Interpretive specialist Nat. Park Service, summers 1947-51; instr. zoology U. Ariz., 1955-56; asst. prof. Miami U., Oxford, O., 1956-57; asst. curator birds Am. Mus. Natural History, N.Y.C., 1957-63, asso. curator, 1963-67, curator, 1967—, resident dir. Kalbfleisch Field Research Sta., 1958—. Adj. prof. biology City U. N.Y., 1968—; expdns. for mus. to C.Am. and Mexico, 1959, 60, 63, West Indies, 1960, 65, 66, S. Am., 1967-79. Fellow Ornithologists Union (Brewster award 1968, pres. 1976-78); mem. Cooper, Wilson ornithol. socs., Eastern Bird Banding Assn., Ecol. Soc. Am., Soc. Study Evolution, Soc. Systemic Zoology, Linnaean Soc. N.Y., Sigma Xi. Contbr. articles to profl. jours. Home: 100 LaSalle St New York NY 10027 Office: American Museum Natural History New York NY 10024

LANZ, JOHN ROBERT, ins. co. exec.; b. Oneida, N.Y., May 17, 1927; s. John Charles and Emma Regina (Phillips) L.; B.B.A., St. Bonaventure (N.Y.) U., 1950; M.S., U. Rochester (N.Y.), 1959; m. Ann T. Franz, Sept. 8, 1951; children—Catherine, Carolyn, Donna, John Charles. With Utica Mut. Ins. Co. (N.Y.), 1950—, asst. controller, then asst. treas., 1968-73, treas., controller, 1973—, also dir.; v.p. Uni Service Leasing Co.; pres. Mohawk Valley Workshop. Served with USNR, 1945-46, AUS, 1951-53; Korea. Decorated Purple Heart. C.P.C.U., 1962. Mem. Alliance Am. Insurers, Nat. Assn. Mut. Ins. Cos., C.P.C.U. Soc. Club: Utica Rotary. Home: 16 Barley Mow Run New Hartford NY 13413 Office: PO Box 530 Utica NY 13503

LANZET, MONROE, cosmetics co. exec.; b. N.Y.C., Aug. 12, 1930; s. Issac and Helen (Grummer) L.; B.S. in Chemistry, CCNY, 1954; postgrad. in organic chemistry N.Y. U., 1954-59; m. Judy Seidenfeld, Dec. 22, 1951; children—Steven Ira, Jeffery Adam, Lisa Ann; m. 2d, Barbara King Sheller, Dec. 26, 1978; stepchildren—Rhonda Eve Sheller, Lee Steven Sheller, Susan Mona Sheller. Mgr. internat. research Yardley of London Inc., Totawa, N.J., 1959-66; dir. cosmetic research Revlon Inc., N.Y.C., 1966-74; v.p. research and devel. and quality control Chanel Inc., N.Y.C., 1974-79; sr. v.p. research and devel. and quality assurance Max Factor & Co., Hollywood, Calif., 1979—. Fellow U.S. Soc. Cosmetic Chemists; mem. Cosmetic, Toiletries and Fragrance Assn. (chmn.; mem. exec. com. Sci. Affair Commn.). Contbr. articles to profl. publs.; patentee in field. Home: 4688 Alonzo Ave Encino CA 91316 Office: 1655 N McCadden Pl Hollywood CA 90028

LANZETTA, JOHN THOMAS, educator, psychologist; b. Long Beach, N.Y., Apr. 24, 1926; s. Michael and Anna del (Judice) L.; B.S., Lafayette Coll., 1948; Ph.D., U. Rochester, 1952; m. Jane L. Warner, Jan. 14, 1946; children—Joan L., Susan A., Thomas M., Patricia L., Donna Lynn, Michael J. Research asso. U. Rochester, 1951-53; supervisory research psychologist USAF, 1953-56; mem. faculty U. Del., 1956-65, prof. psychology, chmn. dept., also dir. Center Research Social Behavior, 1960-65, H. Rodney Sharp prof. psychology, 1962-65; prof. psychology Dartmouth, 1965—, Lincoln Filene prof., chmn. dept., 1975—; liaison scientist Office Naval Research, London, Eng., 1962-63; Ford Found. vis. prof. U. Louvain (Belgium), 1969-70, 73-74. Mem. adv. panel psychology and social scis. Dept. Def., 1960—; adv. com. civil def. Office Civil Def., 1961-67; cons. VA, 1961-67, also NSF, corps.; mem. navy surgeon gen.'s cons. panel neuropsychiatry. Research fellow Social Sci. Research Council, 1957. Mem. Am. (mem. publ. bd., mem. bd. editors), Eastern psychol. assns., AAAS, AAUP, N.Y. Acad. Scis., Social Sci. Research Council, Sigma Xi, Psi Chi. Author articles in field. Editor Jour. Personality and Social Psychology, 1967-76; cons. editor Jour. Exptl. Social Psychology, Jour. Applied Social Psychology, European Jour. Social Psychology. Home: 5 Meadow Ln Hanover NH 03755

LANZILLOTTI, ROBERT FRANKLIN, educator, economist; b. Washington, June 19, 1921; s. Vincent and Gilda S. (Incutti) L.; B.A., Am. U., 1946, M.A., 1947; student Dartmouth, 1943; Ph.D., U. Calif. at Berkeley, 1953; m. Patricia Joy Jackson, Oct. 27, 1945; children—Robert J., Donna J. Teaching fellow U. Calif. at Berkeley, 1947-49; mem. faculty Wash. State U., 1949-61, prof. econs., 1959-61; research asso. Brookings Instn., 1956-57, 1974-75; prof. econs., chmn. dept. Mich. State U., 1961-69; prof. econs., dean Coll. Bus. Adminstrn., U. Fla., Gainesville, 1970—; mem. U.S. Price Commn., 1971-72; dir. Jim Walter Corp.; chmn. Econ. Adv. Bd. to Gov. of Fla., 1973—; cons. Mich. Bankers Assn., attys. gen. Calif., Wis., Minn., Ill., Mich., Oreg., Washington, also Fed. Trade Commn., U.S. Dept. Justice, U.S. Govt. Accounting Office, U.S. Comptroller of the Currency, U.S. Census Bur. Served to lt. (j.g.) USNR, 1943-45; lt. comdr. Res. Decorated Bronze Star (2); NATO fellow, 1964. Mem. Am., So. (1st) v.p. 1972-73 econ. assn., Phi Beta Kappa (hon.), Beta Gamma Sigma, Omicron Delta Kappa. Author: Hard-Surface Floor Covering Industry, 1955; Pricing, Production & Marketing Policies of Small Manufacturers, 1964; Banking Structure in Michigan, 1945-63, 1966; co-author: Pricing in Big Business, 1959; Phase II in Review: The Price Commission Experience, 1975; Economic Effects of Government Mandated Costs, 1979. Contbr. profl. jours. Home: 2135 NW 28th St Gainesville FL 32605

LANZKOWSKY, PHILIP, physician; b. Cape Town, S. Africa, Mar. 17, 1932; came to U.S., 1965, naturalized, 1974; M.B., Ch.B., U. Cape Town, 1954, M.D., 1959; m. Rhona Chiat, Dec. 4, 1955; children—Shelley, David Roy, Leora, Jonathan, Mark. Intern, Groote Schuur Hosp., U. Cape Town, 1955-56; resident Red Cross Children's Hosp., U. Cape Town, 1957-60; fellow in pediatric hematology Duke U., 1961-62, U. Utah, Salt Lake City, 1962-63; dir. pediatric hematology N.Y. Hosp.-Cornell U. Med. Center, 1965-70; asst. prof., then. asso. prof. pediatrics Cornell U. Med. Sch., 1965-70; chmn. pediatrics L.I. Jewish-Hillside Med. Center, New Hyde Park, N.Y., 1970—; prof. pediatrics State U. N.Y. Med. Sch., Stony Brook, 1970—; cons. pediatrics Nassau County Med. Center, East Meadows, N.Y., 1970—, Cath. Med. Center, Queens, N.Y., Peninsula Hosp. Center, Far Rockaway, N.Y., Jamaica Hosp., Queens, St. John's Episcopal Hosp., Far Rockaway, Hillcrest Hosp., Queens, Health Ins. Plan of N.Y.; mem. med. adv. bd. L.I. chpt. Leukemia Soc. Am., Met. chpt. Hemophilia Soc. Am., St. Mary's Hosp. for Children, Bayside, N.Y., L.I. chpt. Nat. Found. Sudden Infant Death. Cecil John Adams Meml. traveling fellow, 1960; Hill-Pattison-Struthers burser, 1960; Nutrition Found. grantee, 1968; diplomate Child Health Eng. Fellow Royal Coll. Physicians Edinburgh, Am. Acad. Pediatrics; mem. Soc. Pediatric Research, Am. Pediatric Soc., Harvey Soc., Am. Hematology Soc., Am. Soc. Clin. Oncology, Am. Assn. Cancer Research, Am. Council Emigres in the Professions. Author: Pediatric Hematology-Oncology: A Treatise for the Clinician. Contbr. to med. jours. Home: 159 W Shore Rd Great Neck NY 11024 Office: LI Jewish-Hillside Med Center New Hyde Park NY 11040

LANZL, GEORGE FRANK, chemist, mfg. co. exec.; b. Chgo., Aug. 9, 1918; s. Hans and Elsa (Seitz) L.; B.S., Depauw U., 1940; Ph.D., Northwestern U., 1946; m. Eunice Brumm, Aug. 9, 1942; children—Steven G., Bruce F. With E. I. DuPont de Nemours & Co., Inc., Wilmington, Del., 1944—, lab. dir., 1956-58, dir. research and devel., 1958—. Mem. Am. Chem. Soc., Chem. Soc. U.K. Republican. Lutheran. Club: Columbia Yacht Racing Assn. Office: Textile Fibers Dept E I DuPont de Nemours & Co Inc Tenth and Market Sts Wilmington DE 19898

LANZONI, VINCENT, physician, med. sch. dean; b. Kingston, Mass., Feb. 23, 1928; s. Vincent and Caroline (Melloni) L.; B.S., Tufts U., 1949, Ph.D., 1953; M.D., Boston U., 1960; m. Phoebe Krey, June 12, 1960; children—Karen, Susan, Margaret. USPHS fellow Tufts U., 1953-54; intern in medicine Boston City Hosp., 1960-61, resident and fellow in medicine, 1961-65; asst. prof. pharmacology Boston U., 1964-67, asso. prof. medicine and pharmacology, 1967-73, prof., 1973-75, asso. dean Sch. Medicine, 1969-75; prof., dean Coll. Medicine Dentistry of N.J./N.J. Med. Sch., 1975—; bd. dirs., sec.-treas. Postgrad. Med. Inst., 1972-75; bd. dirs. Mass. Health Research Inst., Mass. Registration in Nursing, Roxbury Neighborhood Clinic. Served to 1st lt. USAF, 1954-56. Researcher cardiovascular pharmacology, hypertension. Home: 1 Farview Rd Millburn NJ 07041 Office: 100 Bergen St Newark NJ 07103

LAPALOMBARA, JOSEPH, educator; b. Chgo., May 18, 1925; s. Louis and Helen (Teutonico) LaP.; A.B., U. Ill., 1947, A.M., 1950; A.M. (Charlotte Elizabeth Proctor fellow, Class of 1883 fellow), Princeton, 1952, Ph.D., 1954; student U. Rome (Italy), 1952-53; M.A. (hon.), Yale, 1964; m. Lyda Mae Ecke, June 22, 1947 (div.); children—Richard, David, Susan; m. 2d, Constance Ada Bezer, June, 1971. Instr., then asst. prof. polit. sci. Oreg. State Coll., 1947-50; instr. politics Princeton, 1952; mem. faculty Mich. State U., 1953-64, prof. polit. sci., 1958-64, head dept., 1958-63; prof. polit. sci. Yale, 1964—, Arnold Wolfers prof., 1969—, chmn. dept. polit. sci., 1974-78, prof. Sch. of Orgn. and Mgmt., 1979—, chmn. Council Comparative and European Studies, 1966-71; vis. prof. U. Florence (Italy), 1957-58, U. Calif., at Berkeley, 1964, Columbia, 1966-67, U. Turin, 1974, U. Catania, 1974. Cons. FCDA, 1956, Carnegie Corp., 1959, Brookings Instn., 1962, Ford Found., 1965-76, Twentieth Century Fund, 1965-69, AID, 1967-68, Fgn. Service Inst., 1968-72, 74-76, Ednl. Testing Service, 1970-75; sr. research asso. Conf. Bd. N.Y., 1976—; exec. com. Inter U. Consortium Polit. Research, 1968-70; staff mem. Social Sci. Research Council, 1966-73; chmn. West European fgn. area fellowship program Social Sci. Research Council-Am. Council Learned Socs., 1972-74, mem., 1974-75; dir. Mich. Citizenship Clearing House, 1955. Decorated knight comdr. Order of Merit (Republic of Italy); Fulbright scholar, 1952-53, 57-58; Social Sci. Research Council fellow, 1952-53; Penfield scholar U. Pa., 1953; fellow Center Advanced Study Behavioral Scis., 1961-62; Rockefeller fellow, 1963-64; Ford Found. faculty fellow, 1969; Guggenheim fellow, 1971-72. Mem. Social Sci. Research Council (com. comparative politics 1958-72), Am. (exec. council 1963—, exec. com. 1967-68, v.p. 1979-80), So., Midwest polit. sci. assns., Am. Soc. Pub. Adminstrn., Am. Acad. Polit. and Social Sci., Soc. for Italian Hist. Studies, Internat. Polit. Sci. Assn., Società Italiana di Studi Elettorali, Associazione Italiana di Scienze Sociali, Consiglio Italiano di Scienze Sociali, Phi Beta Kappa, Phi Kappa Phi, Phi Eta Sigma. Club: Yale of N.Y., Elizabethan, Morys Assn., East India (London). Author: The Initiative and Referendum in Oregon, 1950; The Italian Labor Movement: Problems and Prospects, 1957; Guide to Michigan Politics, rev. edit., 1960; (with Alberto Spreafico), Elezioni e Comportamento Politico in Italia, 1963; Bureaucracy and Political Development, 1963; Interest Groups in Italian Politics, 1964; Italy: The Politics of Planning, 1966; (with Myron Weiner), Political Parties and Political Development, 1966; Clientela e Parentela, 1967; Burocracia y desarrolo politico, 1970; Crises and Sequences of Political Development (with others), 1972; Politics Within Nations, 1974; (with Stephen Blank) Multinational Corporations and National Elites: A Study in Tensions, 1975, Multinational Corporations in Comparative Perspective, 1976, Multinational Corporations and Developing Countries, 1979; bd. editors Midwest Jour. Polit. Sci., 1956-57; bd. editors Yale U. Press, 1965-72, 73-76; editorial bd. Comparative Politics, 1968—, Jour. Comparative and European Studies, 1969—; Am. Jour. Polit. Sci., 1976—. Series editor comparative politics Prentice-Hall Co., 1971—; mem. editorial adv. bd. Jour. Comparative Adminstrn., 1970-74, Adminstrn. and Soc., 1974—; adv. bd. ABC Polit. Sci. Contbr. articles to profl. jours. Address: 8 Reservoir St New Haven CT 06511

LAPENSKY, M. JOSEPH, airline exec.; b. Mpls., Nov. 27, 1918; s. Frank J. and Mary (Mulkern) L.; B.A., Coll. St. Thomas, St. Paul, 1940; m. Joan M. LaCroix, Nov. 14, 1942; children—John, Stephen, Rosemary, Julianne, Michael, Joseph. With Northwest Air Lines, Inc., 1945—, comptroller, 1960-66, v.p. econ. planning, 1966-73, v.p. fin., 1973-76, pres., chief operating officer, 1976—, chief exec. officer, 1979—, also dir.; dir. Northwest Bancorp., Mpls., Northwestern Nat. Bank-Southwest, Bloomington, Minn. Mem. bd. St. Marys Jr. Coll., Mpls.; chmn. bd. trustees Acad. Holy Angels; trustee St. Thomas Coll.; mem. Am. adv. bd. Sogang U., Seoul, Korea. Mem. Mpls. C. of C. (dir.). Clubs: Decathlon, Minneapolis (Mpls.); Minnesota (St. Paul). Home: 6621 Stevens Ave Minneapolis MN 55423 Office: Northwest Air Lines Inc Mpls-St Paul Internat Airport Saint Paul MN 55111

LAPHAM, LEWIS HENRY, editor; b. San Francisco, Jan. 8, 1935; s. Lewis Abbot and Jane (Foster) L.; grad. Hotchkiss Sch., 1952; B.A., Yale, 1956; postgrad. Cambridge U., 1956-57; m. Joan Brooke Reeves, Aug. 10, 1972; children—Lewis ANdrew, Elizabeth Delphine. Reporter, San Francisco Examiner, 1957-60, N.Y. Herald Tribune, 1960-62; author, editor USA-1, N.Y.C., 1962, Sat. Eve. Post, N.Y.C., 1963-67; writer Life mag., Harper's, N.Y.C., 1968-70; mng. editor Harper's, N.Y.C., 1971-75, editor, 1975—; v.p. Harper's Mag. Co., 1973—; dir. Harper-Atlantic Sales, N.Y.C. Mem. Council on Fgn. Relations. Club: Century Assn. (N.Y.C.). Home: 988 Fifth Ave New York NY 10021 Office: 2 Park Ave New York NY 10016

LAPHAM, LEWIS JAY, former govt. ofcl.; b. New Hampton, Iowa, Oct. 5, 1920; s. Percy Charles and Altha Theresa (Dygert) L.; A.B., State U. Iowa, 1942; M.S., Syracuse U., 1943; Ph.D., Harvard, 1954; m. Carol Helene Martens, June 5, 1943; children—Linda Kay (Mrs. Daniel F. Schick), David Lewis, Douglas Lowell. Asst. prof. pub. adminstrn. Fla. State U., 1948-50; cons. Dept. Def., 1950-51, 53-58; mem. staff subcom. mil. operations House Com. Govt. Operatins, 1951-53; attache U.S. mission NATO and European Regional Orgns., Paris, France, 1958-63; polit. officer Dept. State, 1963-66; spl. asst. to ambassador Am. embassy, Saigon, Viet Nam, 1967-68, Bangkok, Thailand, 1969-73; mem. Bd. Nat. Estimates, 1973; dir. office polit. research CIA, Washington, 1974-76, asst. to dep. dir., 1977-78. Served to lt. USNR, 1943-46. Mem. Am. Polit. Sci. Assn., Am. Soc. Pub. Adminstrn., Am. Acad. Polit. and Social Scis., Phi Beta Kappa, Phi Kappa Psi. Unitarian. Home: Route 1 Box 59B Naples Rd Harrison ME 04040

LAPHAM, ROBERT J., publishing co. exec.; b. Kansas City, Mo., Dec. 12, 1921; s. Jeffery Bowden and Margaret Estella (Moorhouse) L.; student U. So. Calif.; m. Edith Marie Huber, Oct. 29, 1949; children—Jeffery Christopher, Catherine Edith, Scott MacKenzie. West Coast mgr. Conde Nast Publs. Inc., Los Angeles, 1954-61, corp. advt. dir., N.Y.C., 1961-69, v.p., corp. advt. dir., 1969-74, gen. mgr., 1971-74, pres., 1974—. Served to lt. USCGR, 1942-46. Mem. Pubs. Info. Bur. (chmn. bd. 1973-75), Mag. Pubs. Assn. (dir. 1974—), Sigma Nu. Episcopalian. Clubs: N.Y. Yacht; Wee Burn Country. Home: 2 Midbrook Ln Darien CT 06820 Office: 350 Madison Ave New York City NY 10017

LAPICK, FRANK PAUL, former advt. agy. exec.; b. Cleve., Nov. 25, 1915; s. Salvatore and Catherine (Zaffarano) L.; B.S., U. Mich., 1938; m. Mary Martha Engeman, Jan. 13, 1940; children—Pamela M., Kim P. Advt. and display mgr. Gorton Coy, Elmira, N.Y., 1938-40; final test supt. Gen. Electric Co., Cleve., 1940-45; account exec. Fuller & Smith & Ross, Cleve., 1945-48, account supr., 1948-53, v.p., 1953-56; v.p., gen. mgr. Duffy, McClure & Wilder, Cleve., 1956-58; v.p. Carr Liggett Advt., Inc., 1958-60, exec. v.p., 1960-76, chmn. bd., chief exec. officer, 1976-78; ret., 1978. Recipient advt. excellence awards from various orgns. including Asso. Bus. Publs., Nat. Indsl. Advt. Assn., AIA, Cleve. Advt. Club, Chgo. Advt. Club. Mem. Indsl. Marketers, Cleve. Advt. Club, Sales and Mktg. Execs. Republican. Roman Catholic. Clubs: Cleve. Athletic; Duquesne (Pitts.). Home: 2602 La Gran Via Carlsbad CA 92008 Office: 815 Superior Ave Cleveland OH 44114

LAPIDES, JACK, medical educator; b. Rochester, N.Y., Nov. 27, 1914; s. Harry and Emma (Seldow) L.; B.A., U. Mich., 1936, M.A., 1938, M.D., 1941; m. Alice Jean Hatt, June 1948 (dec. Oct. 1971); m. 2d, Roberta de Vries Stadt, Sept. 1975. Rockefeller Research asso. fellow physiology U. Mich. Grad. Sch., 1936-38; intern U. Mich. Hosp., 1941-42, asst. resident surgery, 1946-47, resident sect. urology, dept. surgery, 1947-50; research fellow urology U. Chgo., 1947; USPHS postdoctorate fellow Nat. Cancer Inst., 1948-50; instr. urology U. Mich. Med. Sch., 1950-52, asst. prof. surgery, 1952-55, asso. prof., 1955-64, prof. surgery sect. urology, 1964—, head sect. urology, 1968—; chief sect. urology Wayne County Gen. Hosp., 1950—, VA Hosp., 1952—. Served with USAAF, 1942-46. Diplomate Am. Bd. Urology. Mem. Soc. Pediatric Urology, Washtenaw County Med. Soc., Fla. Urol. Soc., A.M.A., A.C.S., Am. Urol. Assn., A.A.A.S., Am. Assn. Genitourinary Surgeons, Pan-Am. Med. Assn., Phi Beta Kappa, Sigma Xi, Phi Eta Sigma, Phi Sigma, Phi Kappa Phi, Alpha Omega Alpha. Author: Fundamentals of Urology, 1976. Mem. editorial bd. Urology Digest. Contbg. author chpts. in numerous med. texts, also articles. Home: 2805 N Wagner Rd Ann Arbor MI 48103

LAPIDUS, JULES BENJAMIN, univ. dean; b. Chgo., May 1, 1931; s. Leo R. and Lillian D. (Davidson) L.; B.S., U. Ill., 1954; M.S., U. Wis., 1957, Ph.D., 1958; m. Anne Marie Liebman, June 8, 1970; children—Steven, Amy, Mark, Marilyn. Prof. medicinal and pharm. chemistry Ohio State U., 1958—, asso. dean Grad. Sch., 1972-74, vice provost for research, dean Grad. Sch., 1974—. Mem. pharmacology and toxicology tng. com. NIH, 1965-67, pharmacology program com., 1971-74. Mem. Am. Chem. Soc., A.A.A.S., Home: 197 W South St Worthington OH 43085 Office: 230 N Oval Mall Columbus OH 43210

LAPIDUS, MORRIS, architect, interior designer; b. Odessa, Russia, Nov. 25, 1902; s. Leon and Eva (Sherman) L.; came to U.S., 1903, naturalized, 1914; B. Arch., Columbia, 1927; m. Beatrice Perlman, Feb. 22, 1929; children—Richard L., Alan H. With Warren & Wetmore, N.Y.C., 1926-28, Arthur Weisner, N.Y.C., 1928-30; asso. architect Ross-Frankel, Inc., N.Y.C., 1930-42; prin. Morris Lapidus Assos., 1942—; pioneered use of modern in merchandising field; areas of work include housing, hosps., hotels, shopping centers, office bldgs., religious instns.; architect-designer Fontainebleau Hotel, 1954, Eden Roc Hotel, 1955, Americana Hotel, 1962, N.Y.C., Sheraton Motor Inn, 1962, N.Y.C., Fairfield Towers, Bklyn., 1966, Paradise Island Hotel, 1967, Nassau, Paradise Island Casino, 1968, Nassau, Out-Patient and Rehab. Center, continuing care wing Mt. Sinai Hosp., Miami Beach, Fla., 1967, congregation Beth Tfiloh, Pikesville, Md., 1967, Internat. Hdqrs. of Jr. Chamber Internat., Coral Gables, Fla., 1968, Cadman Plaza Urban Redevel., Bklyn., 1969, Penn-Wortman Housing Project, Bklyn., 1971, Bedford-Stuyvesant Swimming Pool and Park, Bklyn., 1970, El Conquistador Hotel, P.R., 1969, Trelawney Beach Hotel, Jamaica, W.I. 1973, Hassel Island Hotel and Condominium Complex, St. Thomas, V.I., 1970, Greater Miami Jewish Fedn. Hdqrs., 1970, Hertz Skycenter Hotel, Jacksonville Fla., 1971, Arentura, Miami, 1971, U. Miami (Fla.) Concert Hall, 1972, Griffin Sq. Office Bldg., Dallas, 1972, U. Miami Law Library, 1975, Citizens Fed. Bank Bldg., Miami, 1975, Miami Beach Theater of Performing Arts, 1976, Ogun State Hotel, Nigeria, 1977, others; asso. architect Keys Community Coll., Key West, Fla., 1977; lectr. store, hotel design; one-man exhibit 40 Yrs. Art and Architecture, Lowe Gallery, Miami U., 1967, Fedn. Arts and Archtl. League N.Y., 1970, Weiner Galleries, 1972. Mem. Miami Beach Devel. Commn., 1966-67. Winner nat. competition S.W. Urban Renewal Program in Wash., internat. competition for trade center on The Portal Site in Washington; recipient Justin P. Allman award Wallcovering Wholesaler's Assn., 1963; Outstanding Specifications award Gypsum Drywall Contractors Internat., 1968, certificate merit N.Y. Soc. Architects, 1971, others. Mem. AIA, Am. Inst. Interior Designers, Am. Artists Profl. League, Archtl. League, Nat. Inst. Archtl. Edn., Municipal Art Soc. N.Y., Miami Beach C. of C. (gov.). Kiwanian. Author: Architecture-A Profession and a Business, 1967; Prom Yesterdays Ghetto, 1972; Architecture of Joy, 1977. Home: 3 Island Ave Miami Beach FL 33139 Office: 1301 Dade Blvd Miami Beach FL 33139

LA PIERE, RICHARD TRACY, educator, author; b. Beloit, Wis., Sept. 15, 1899; s. Ernest and Ella (Brown) La P.; A.B. magna cum laude, Stanford, 1926, A.M., 1927, Ph.D. in Sociology, 1930; student London Sch. Econs. and Polit. Sci., 1927-28; m. Helen Halderman, Dec. 31, 1934. Asst. econs. Stanford, 1928-29, instr., 1929-33, asst. prof. sociology, 1932-38, asso. prof., 1938-49, prof., 1949-65, prof. emeritus, 1965—; prof. sociology U. Mich., 1938-39. Served with air service U.S. Army, 1917-19; AEF in France. Mem. Am., Pacific (pres. 1948) sociol. socs., Sociol. Research Assn., Social Sci. Conf. Pacific Coast, Phi Beta Kappa. Author: (textbook with P. R. Farnsworth) Social Psychology, 3d edit., 1947; (novel) Son of Han, 1937; Collective Behavior, 1938; When the Living Strive (report of 3 year survey of San Francisco's Chinatown pub. in novel form; winner Silver medal Commonwealth Club Cal.), 1941; Sociology, 1946; A Theory of Social Control, 1954; The Freudian Ethic, 1959; Social Change, 1965. Contbr. sci. jours. Home: 268 Searsville Rd Stanford University CA 94305

LAPIERRE, DOMINIQUE, author, historian; b. Chatelaillon, France, July 30, 1931; s. Jean and Luce (Andreotti) L.; student (Fulbright Exchange scholar), U. Polit. Sci., Paris, 1950-51; B.A., Lafayette Coll., Easton, Pa., 1952; m. Aliette Spitzer, Aug. 4, 1952. Editor Paris Match News mag., 1955-67; author, historian, Paris, 1967—. Co-author: (with Larry Collins) Is Paris Burning, 1964; Or I'll Dress You in Mourning, 1967; O Jerusalem, 1971; Freedom at Midnight, 1975; The Fifth Horseman, 1980. Home: 26 Ave Kleber Paris 75116 France Office: care Simon and Schuster Bldg 1230 Ave of the Americas New York NY 10020

LAPIN, RAYMOND HAROLD, mortgage banker; b. Inglewood, Calif., Feb. 13, 1919; s. Morris and Sarah (Goldberg) L.; B.S., U. Calif. at Berkeley, 1942; M.B.A. in Finance, U. Chgo., 1954; m. Mary Elizabeth Woodcock, Jan. 3, 1950 (div. 1972); 1 son, John Grattan. Asst. mgr. research dept. Fed. Res. Bank Chgo., 1949-54; founding pres., chief exec. officer Bankers Mortgage Co. Calif. (now Transam. Mortgage Co.), 1954-66; cons. Transam. Corp., 1966-67; pres. Fed. Nat. Mortgage Assn., Washington, 1967-68, dir., 1976—; pres., chmn. bd. pvt. owned corp. Fed. Nat. Mortgage Assn., 1968-70; mem. current reporting series com. Fed. Res. Bd., 1951-54; founding pres. Govt. Nat. Mortgage Assn., 1968; pres., chmn. bd. R.H. Lapin & Co., Inc., 1970—; dir. San Francisco Devel. Fund, 1965—; pres. San Francisco Municipal Ry. Improvement Corp., 1970-74; dir. Am. Savs. & Loan Assn. Fla., 1977—, L.B. Nelson Corp., 1977—, C.L. Assets (CNA), 1972—; hon. life mem. adv. com. FNMA. Commr., Art Commn. City and County San Francisco, 1964-65, Pub. Utilities Commn. City and County San Francisco, 1965-66; dir. Econ. Devel. Agy. Calif., 1966; mem. White House Task Force Mortgage Finance, 1967-68. Bd. dirs. Council for Civic Unity, 1962-65, Mt. Zion Hosp., San Francisco, 1964-67, 70-76, San Francisco Planning and Urban Renewal Assn., 1974-77, Nat. Housing Conf., 1975—; mem. San Francisco Mayor's Fiscal Adv. Com., 1977—. Served to capt. AUS, 1942-46; PTO. Recipient Outstanding Alumnus award U. Chgo., 1968; award for better communities and decent homes Nat. Housing Conf., 1977; numerous awards from nat. mortgage banking, savs. and loan, realtor and home builder assns. for initiating maj. changes in nat. secondary mortgage market. Mem. Lambda Alpha. Clubs: Federal City, Georgetown (Washington); Stock Exchange, St. Francis Yacht (San Francisco). Home: Hazel Mount Sausalito CA 94965 Office: 311 California St San Francisco CA 94104

LAPLANTE, JAMES GAMELIN, ins. co. exec.; b. Vincennes, Ind., Aug. 13, 1921; s. J.B.E. and Harriet (Jessup) LaP.; B.A., Washington and Lee U., 1943; M.B.A., Stanford, 1948; m. Margaret MacLaurin, Sept. 10, 1947; children—Lauren Margaret Younger, James Gamelin. Asst. treas. Indsl. Indemnity Co., San Francisco, 1964-67, treas., 1967-71, v.p., treas., 1971-72, sr. v.p., treas., 1972—; treas. Indsl. Underwriters Ins. Co., San Francisco, 1967—, 255 Cal. Corp., San Francisco, 1967—, Indsl. Indemnity Found., San Francisco, 1967—, Indsl. Underwriters, Inc., San Francisco, 1969—, Indsl. Ins. Co., San Francisco, 1970—, Indsl. Ins. Co. Hawaii, Ltd., 1971—, Indsl. Indemnity Alaska, 1972—, Indsl. Indemnity N.W., 1972—, Indsl. Indemnity Life Ins. Co., 1972—. Served to lt. USNR, 1943-46. Mem. Financial Execs. Inst. (pres. San Francisco chpt. 1977-78), Ins. Accountants Statis. Assn., Soc. Ins. Accountants, Phi Kappa Psi. Clubs: Foothills Tennis and Swim (Palo Alto, Cal.); Profits Unlimited (Atherton, Calif.); Bohemian (San Francisco); Menlo Country (Redwood City, Calif.). Home: 150 Hardwick Rd Woodside CA 94062 Office: 255 California San Francisco CA 94111

LAPOINTE, GUY GERARD, hockey player; b. Montreal, Que., Can., Mar. 18, 1948. Defenseman with Montreal Canadiens, Nat. Hockey League, 1968—. Office: care Montreal Canadiens 2313 Saint Catherine St West Montreal PQ H3H 1N2 Canada*

LAPOINTE, RENAUDE MARGUERITE, senator of Can.; b. Disraeli, Que., Can., Jan. 3, 1912; d. Alphonse F. and Marie L. (Poulin) Lapointe; Mus.B., Dominion Coll. Music, 1929; postgrad. Stanstead Coll., 1925-27, Laval U., Quebec City, 1933-38. Journalist, Le Soleil, Quebec City, 1939-59, La Presse, Montreal, Que., 1959-60, 61-70, Le Nouveau Jour., Montreal, 1960-61; info. officer Dept. Indian and No. Affairs, Ottawa, Ont., 1970-71; mem. Senate of Can., Ottawa, 1971—, speaker, 1974-79, corr. Time, Life, Variety mags., 1953-57; corr. CBC French Network, 1953-57. Rep. of Can. to UN Gen. Assembly, 1970-72; mem. nat. council Canadian Human Rights Found. Recipient Bowater award in journalism, 1962; named Journalist of Year, 1965. Mem. Commonwealth Parliamentary Assn., Inter-Parliamentary Union, NATO Parliamentary Assn., World Federalists (Canadian br.), Assn. des Parlementaires de Langue Française, Assn. France-Can., Cercle des Femmes Journalistes, Media Club Can. Liberal. Roman Catholic. Author: L'histoire bouleversante de Mgr. Charbonneau, 1961. Home: 180 MacLaren St Ottawa ON K2P 0L3 Canada Office: Senate of Can Ottawa ON K1A 0A4 Canada. *I owe my career in journalism and politics to many friends who had more faith in my possibilities than I had myself. I lost my youth but I did not lose my time.*

LAPONCE, JEAN ANTOINE, polit. scientist; b. Decize, France, Nov., 1925; s. Fernand and Fernande (Ramond) L.; came to Can., 1956, naturalized, 1972; diploma Institut d'études politiques, Paris, 1947; Ph.D., UCLA, 1955; m. Joyce Price, July, 1950; children—Jean-Antoine, Marc, Patrice; m. 2d, Iza Fiszhaut, Apr. 10, 1972; 1 dau., Danielle. Instr., U. Santa Clara, 1956; asst. prof. polit. sci. U. B.C., (Can.), Vancouver, 1956-61, asso. prof., 1961-66, prof., 1966—. Fellow Royal Soc. Can.; mem. Can. Polit. Sci. Assn. (pres. 1972-73), Am. Polit. Sci. Assn., French Polit. Sci. Assn., Internat. Polit. Sci. Assn. (pres. 1973-76). Author: The Protection of Minorities, 1961; The government of France under the Fifth Republic, 1962; People vs Politics, 1970. Office: Dept Polit Sci U BC Vancouver BC V6T 1W5 Canada

LAPORTE, CLOYD, JR., mfg. co. exec.; b. N.Y.C., June 8, 1925; s. Cloyd and Marguerite (Raeder) L.; A.B., Harvard, 1946, J.D., 1949; m. Caroline E. Berry, Jan. 22, 1949; children—Elizabeth, Marguerite, Cloyd III. Admitted to N.Y. State bar, 1949; asso. mem. firm Cravath, Swaine & Moore, N.Y.C., 1949-56; dir. adminstrn. Metals div. Olin Corp., N.Y.C., 1957-66; legal counsel Dover Corp., N.Y.C., 1966—, sec., 1971—. Served to 2d lt. A.C., AUS, World War II. Mem. Am., N.Y. State bar assns., Assn. Bar City N.Y. Clubs: Harvard, University (N.Y.C.); Gipsy Trail (Carmel, N.Y.). Home: 108 E 82d St New York City NY 10028 Office: 277 Park Ave New York City NY 10017

LAPORTE, LEO FREDERIC, educator; b. Englewood, N.J., July 30, 1933; s. Leo Frederic and Edea (Giacobbe) L.; student Fordham Coll., 1951-53; A.B., Columbia, 1956, Ph.D., 1960; m. Mary G. Dunlap, Apr. 6, 1956; children—Leo G., Eva R. From instr. to prof. dept. geol. scis. Brown U., Providence, 1959-71; prof. bd. earth scis. U. Calif. at Santa Cruz, 1971—, chmn., 1972-75, dean div. natural scis., 1975-76; vis. prof. Yale, 1964; geologist N.Y. State Geol. Survey, 1962-64; petroleum research cons. Mem. com. geol. scis. Nat. Acad. Sci.-NRC, 1970-72. Recipient President's award Am. Assn. Petroleum Geologists, 1969. Fellow A.A.A.S., Geol. Soc. Am.; mem. Am. Assn. Petroleum Geologists, Paleontological Soc., Soc. Econ. Mineralogists and Paleontologists (chmn. research com., paleontology councilor). Author: Ancient Environments, 1968, 79; Encounter with the Earth, 1975; prin. author: The Earth and Human Affairs, 1972; editor: Reefs in Time and Space, 1974; Evolution and the Fossil Record, 1978; contbr. articles profl. jours. Home: 110 Monterey St Santa Cruz CA 95060

LAPORTE, WILLIAM FREDERIC, chem. mfg. exec.; b. N.Y.C., Sept. 3, 1913; s. William Frederic and Florence M. (Kahn) L.; A.B., Princeton, 1936; M.B.A., Harvard, 1938; m. Ruth W. Hillard, June 15, 1946; children—Suzanne H., Lynn E., William Frederic III. With Am. Home Products Corp., N.Y.C., 1938—, asst. to pres. subsidiary Anacin Co., 1939-42, asst. to pres. corp., 1943-44, v.p., gen. mgr. Anacin Co., 1944, v.p., gen. mgr. subsidiary Whitehall Pharmacal Co.,

1944-48, pres. co., 1949-57, v.p., dir. corp., 1957-60, pres., dir., 1960-65, chmn. bd., pres., chief exec. officer, 1965-73, chmn. bd., chief exec. officer, 1973—; pres., dir. Buck Hill Falls Co.; dir. Mfrs. Hanover Trust Co., Am. Standard, Inc., B.F. Goodrich Co.; trustee Dime Savs. Bank of N.Y. Nat. chmn. Heart Fund campaigns, 1968, 69; trustee Columbia-Presbyn. Hosp. Mem. Proprietary Assn. (mem. exec. com.), Bus. Council, Bus. Roundtable. Clubs: Elm (Princeton); River, Pinnacle (N.Y.C.). Home: 435 E 52d St New York NY 10022 Office: 685 3d Ave New York NY 10017

LAPPEN, CHESTER I., lawyer; b. Des Moines, May 4, 1919; s. Robert C. and Anna (Sideman) L.; A.B. with highest honors in Econs., U. Calif., 1940; LL.B. magna cum laude (Faye diploma), Harvard, 1943; m. Jon Tyroler Irmas, June 29, 1941; children—Jonathan Bailey, Timothy, Andrea L., Sally Morris. Admitted to Calif. bar, 1943; practice in Los Angeles, 1946—; sr. partner firm Mitchell, Silberberg & Knupp, 1949—; advisory bd. Bank Am., 1962-65; chmn. bd., dir. Zenith Nat. Ins. Co., Zenith Nat. Ins. Corp., 1975-77; dir. Arden Group, Inc. (chmn. exec. com. 1978—), Data Products Corp., City Nat. Bank; trustee Citinat. Devel. Trust. Chmn. bd. trustees Immaculate Heart Coll. Served as spl. agt. CIA, AUS, 1943-46. Mem. Am., Los Angeles (dir. 1953), Los Angeles Jr. (pres. 1953), Beverly Hills, Calif. bar assns., Harvard Law Sch. Alumni Assn. So. Calif. (pres. 1973—); Artus (hon.). Republican. Editor-in-chief Harvard Law Rev., 1942-43. Office: 1800 Century Park E Los Angeles CA 90067

LAPSLEY, WILLIAM WINSTON, elec., gas and steam utility exec.; b. Selma, Ala., Jan. 14, 1910; s. Robert Kay and Ethel Baine (Pearce) L.; B.S., U.S. Mil. Acad., 1935; M.S. in Civil Engring., U. Calif., Berkeley, 1937; grad. Engr. Sch., 1938, Armed Forces Staff Coll., 1947, Army War Coll., 1951; m. June Louise English, June 15, 1935 (dec. 1952); children—Lynn (Mrs. George W. Jordan, Jr.), Robert A., Karen (Mrs. Jack Ellis); m. 2d, Frances Vivian Visart Lynn, June 14, 1953; stepchildren—Charles R., Jon V. Commn. 2d lt. U.S. Army, 1935, advanced through grades to maj. gen., 1962; various assignments U.S., ETO, Japan, 1935-56; comdg. gen. U.S. Army Eng. Maintenance Center, Columbus, Ohio, 1956-58; div. engr. U.S. Army Engr. Div., Ohio River, 1958-60; comdg. gen. 7th Logistical Command, USARPAC, Korea, 1960-61; div. engr. U.S. Army Engr. Div., N. Pacific, Portland, Oreg., 1962-65; comdg. gen. U.S. Army Mobility Command, Warren, Mich., 1965-67; retired, 1967; program mgr. fgn. operations Kaiser Jeep Corp., Taipei, Taiwan, 1967-68; with Consol. Edison Co. N.Y., Inc., 1969—, exec. v.p., 1971-73, pres., 1973-75, trustee, 1973—. Mem. Miss. River Commn., 1958-60; mem. Bd. Engrs. for Rivers and Harbors, 1958-60, 62—; U.S. del. U.S.-Can. treaty negogiating team joint use Columbia River water, 1961-62. Decorated Bronze Star with oak leaf cluster, Legion of Merit, D.S.M., numerous area and service ribbons. Mem. Assn. U.S. Army, Alumni Assn. U.S. Mil. Acad., Soc. Am. Mil. Engrs., Sigma Xi. Club: Sea Pines Country. Home: 41 Willow Oak Rd W Hilton Head SC 29928

LAPWING, LEO JOHN, metal cutting tool mfg. co. exec.; b. Detroit, July 1, 1917; s. Leon and Sarah Czajka; student Detroit Bus. Inst., 1939-40; m. Mary Kathryn Lepkojous; children—Carol, John, Janet. With Valeron Corp., Oak Park, Mich., 1942—, pres. and chmn. bd., 1944—, also dir. Roman Catholic. Club: K.C. Home: 4978 Malibu St Bloomfield Hills MI 48013 Office: 21100 Coolidge Hwy Oak Park MI 48237

LAQUEUR, WALTER, educator; b. Breslau, Germany, May 26, 1921; s. Fritz and Else (Berliner) L.; grad. Johannesgymnasium, Breslau, 1938; student Hebrew (Jerusalem) U., 1938-39; m. Barbara Koch, May 29, 1941; children—Sylvia, Shlomit. Agrl. worker, Palestine, 1940-44; newspaper corr., free-lance author, 1944-55; founder, editor Survey, London, Eng., 1955-67; vis. prof. Johns Hopkins, 1957, U. Chgo., 1958, Harvard, 1977; dir. Inst. Contemporary History, Wiener Library, London, 1964—; prof. history ideas and politics Brandeis U., Waltham, Mass., 1967-72; prof. history U. Tel Aviv, 1970—; chmn. research council Center Strategic and Internat. Studies Georgetown U., Washington, 1973—, counselor, 1976—, univ. prof. govt., 1977—. Recipient 1st Distinguished Writer's award Center Strategic and Internat. Studies, 1969. Mem. Royal Inst. Internat. Affairs. Author: Communism and Nationalism in the Middle East, 1956; The Soviet Union and the Middle East, 1959; Young Germany, 1962; Russia and Germany, 1966; The Fate of the Revolution, 1967; The Road to War, 1967; Road to Jerusalem, 1969; The Struggle for the Middle East, 1969; Europe Since Hitler, 1970; Out of the Ruins of Europe, 1971; Confrontation: The Middle East and World Politics, 1974; A History of Zionism, 1972; Weimar, 1975; Guerrilla, 1976; Terrorism, 1977; Guerilla Reader, 1977; Terrorism Reader, 1978; A Continent Astray, 1979. Co-editor, founder Jour. Contemporary History, 1966—; founder, editor Washington Papers, 1972—; founder, co-editor Washington Quar. of Strategic and Internat. Studies, 1977—. Home: Center Strategic and Internat Studies 1800 K St NW Washington DC 20006

LARAGH, JOHN HENRY, physician, scientist, educator; b. Yonkers, N.Y., Nov. 18, 1924; s. Harry Joseph and Grace Catherine (Coyne) L.; M.D., Cornell U., 1948; m. Adonia Kennedy, Apr. 28, 1949; children—John Henry, Peter Christian; m. 2d, Jean E. Sealey, Sept. 22, 1974. Intern medicine Presbyn. Hosp., N.Y.C., 1948-49, asst. resident, 1949-50; fellow cardiology, trainee Nat.. Heart Inst., 1950-51; research fellow N.Y. Heart Assn., 1951-52; asst. physician Presbyn. Hosp., 1950-54, asst. attending, 1954-61, asso. attending, 1961-69, attending physician, 1969—, pres. elect med. bd., 1972-74; dir. cardiology Delafield Hosp., N.Y.C., 1954-55; mem. faculty Columbia Coll. Phys. and Surg., 1950—, prof. clin. medicine, 1967—, spokesman exec. com. faculty council, 1971-73; Hilda Altschul Master prof. medicine, dir. Cardiovascular Center and Hypertension Center N.Y. Hosp.-Cornell Med. Center, 1975—, chief Cardiology div., 1976—; dir. Hypertension Center and Nephrology div. Columbia-Presbyn. Med. Center, 1971; cons. USPHS, 1964—. Mem. policy adv. bd. detection and follow-up program Nat. Heart and Lung Inst., 1971, bd. sci. counselors, 1972-78. Vice chmn. bd. trustees for profl., scientific affairs Presbyn. Hosp., 1974-75. Served with AUS, 1943-46. Recipient Stouffer prize med. research, 1969. Diplomate Am. Bd. Internal Medicine. Fellow A.C.P., Am. Coll. Cardiology; mem. Am. Heart Assn. (chmn. council high blood pressure research 1968-72), Am. Soc. Clin. Investigation, Assn. Am. Physicians., Am. Soc. Contemporary Medicine and Surgery (adv. bd.), Harvey Soc., Kappa Sigma, Nu Sigma Nu, Alpha Omega Alpha. Clubs: Winged Foot (Mamaroneck, N.Y.). Shinnecock Hills Golf (Southampton). Editor-in-chief Cardiovascular Reviews and Reports. Editor: Hypertension Manual, 1974. Editorial bd. Am. Jour. Medicine, Jour. Clin. Pharmacology, Circulation, Circulation Research, Jour. Clin. Endocrinology and Metabolism, Excerpta Medica (Internal Medicine), Kidney Internat., Am. Heart Jour. Research on hormones and electrolyte metabolism and renal physiology, on mechanisms of edema formation and on the causes and treatment of human high blood pressure. Home: 435 E 70th St New York NY 10021 Office: NY Hosp-Cornell Med Center 525 E 68th St New York NY 10021. *In scientific research, my greatest resource has been the ability to look at everyday clinical phenomena from a different point of view to develop new ideas and principles about human physiology. These perceptions have led to quantum leaps forward in creation of new knowledge and redirection of medical thinking.*

LARAMORE, DON NELSON, judge; b. Hamlet, Ind., Dec. 22, 1906; s. Louis Nelson and Pearl (Stephenson) L.; grad., Ind. Law Sch., 1927; m. Charlotte Schminke, Dec. 29, 1938; 1 dau., Prudence Ann. Ofcl. reporter Starke Circuit of Ind., 1924-31; judge Stark Circuit Ct., 1942-54; judge U.S. Ct. Claims, Washington, 1954—, sr. judge. Mem. Ind. Republican State Fin. Com., 1942-44, county chmn., 1936-42. Mem. Am. Bar Assn., D.C. Bar Assn., Fed. Bar Assn., Gamma Eta Gamma. Clubs: Nat. Lawyers, Congressional Country, Masons, Shriners, Elks. Home: 5017 Scarsdale Rd Washington DC 20016 Office: US State Ct of Claims 717 Madison Pl NW Washington DC 20005

LARDNER, HENRY PETERSEN, ins. co. exec.; b. Davenport, Iowa, Apr. 5, 1932; s. James Francis and Mary Catharine (Decker) L.; B.S.E. (Indsl. Engring.), U. Mich., 1954; m. Marion Cleaveland White, Dec. 28, 1954; children—Elisabeth, Emily, David, Peter, Sarah (dec.). Agt., H.H. Cleaveland Agy., Rock Island, Ill., 1956-60; with Bituminous Ins. Cos., Rock Island, 1960—, exec. v.p., 1968-72, pres., 1972—, also dir.; dir. 1st Nat. Bank of Rock Island. Bd. govs. State Colls. and Univs., 1971—; trustee Blackhawk Coll., 1964-72; mem. Ill. Bd. Higher Edn., 1976-77. Served with AUS, 1954-56. C.P.C.U. Home: 3227 29th Ave Rock Island IL 61201 Office: 320 18th St Rock Island IL 61201

LARDNER, RING WILMER, JR., author; b. Chgo., Aug. 19, 1915; s. Ring Wilmer and Ellis (Abbott) L.; grad. Phillips Acad., 1932; student Princeton, 1932-34; m. Silvia Schulman, Feb. 19, 1937 (div. 1945); children—Peter, Ann (Mrs. Waswo); m. 2d, Frances Chaney, Sept. 28, 1946; 1 son, James; stepchildren—Katharine (Mrs. Jones), Joseph. Reporter, N.Y. Daily Mirror, 1935; press agt. Selznick Internat. Pictures, Culver City, Calif., 1936-37; screenwriter various film companies, 1937—, including (with Michael Kanin) Woman of the Year, 1942, (with Leopold Atlas) Tomorrow the World, 1944, (with Albert Maltz) Cloak and Dagger, 1946, (with Philip Dunne) Forever Amber, 1947, (with Terry Southern), The Cincinnati Kid, 1965, (solo) MASH, 1970, The Greatest, 1977; also mag. and TV pieces. Recipient Acad. Motion Picture Arts and Scis. award for best original screenplay Woman of the Year, 1942, best screenplay adapted from another medium MASH, 1970. Author: (novel) The Ecstasy of Owen Muir, 1955, 72; The Lardners: My Family Remembered, 1976. Address: care Russell & Volkening Inc 551 Fifth Ave New York City NY 10017*

LARDNER, THOMAS JOSEPH, educator; b. N.Y.C., July 19, 1938; s. Thomas Joseph and Ann (Boyhan) L.; B.Aero. Engring., Poly. Inst. N.Y., 1958, M.S., 1959, Ph.D., 1961; m. Anne Jeanne Porter, Nov. 28, 1964; children—Joseph, Theresa, Deborah. Asst. prof. applied math. Mass. Inst. Tech., 1965-68, asso. prof. mech. engring., 1968-73; prof. theoretical and applied mechs., prof. bioengring. U. Ill., Urbana, 1973-78; prof. civil engring. U. Mass., Amherst, 1978—; Fulbright lectr., Nepal, 1965-66; cons. NIH, Ford Found., engring. firms. Served with AUS, 1961-63. Mem. Am. Soc. M.E., Am. Soc. Engring. Edn. (asso. editor Jour. Applied Mechs. 1972—), Soc. Indsl. and Applied Math., A.A.A.S. Club: Harvard Travellers. Editor: Mechanics of Solids, 2d edit., 1972. Contbr. numerous articles to profl. jours. Home: 175 Amity St Amherst MA 01002

LARDY, HENRY ARNOLD, educator; b. Roslyn, S.D., Aug. 19, 1917; s. Nick and Elizabeth (Gebetsreiter) L.; B.S., S.D. State U., 1939, D.Sc. (hon.), 1979; M.S., U. Wis., 1941, Ph.D., 1943; m. Annrita Dresselhuys, Jan. 21, 1943; children—Nick, Diana, Jeffrey, Michael. Mem. faculty U. Wis.-Madison, 1945—, asso. prof. biochemistry, 1947-50, prof., 1950—, Vilas prof. biol. scis., 1966—. Pres. Citizens vs. McCarthy, 1952. Recipient Paul-Lewis award enzyme chemistry Am. Chem. Soc., 1949, Neuberg medal Am. Soc. European Chemists, 1956. Mem. Nat. Acad. Sci., Am. Chem. Soc. (chmn. biol. div. 1958), Am. Soc. Biol. Chemists (pres. 1964), Am. Philos. Soc., Golden Retriever Club Am. (pres. 1962), Am. Acad. Arts and Scis., Endocrine Soc., Japanese Biochem. Soc. (hon.). Co-editor: The Enzymes. Home: Thorstrand Rd Madison WI 53705

LAREDO, RUTH, concert pianist; b. Detroit, Nov. 20, 1937; d. Ben and Miriam (Horowitz) Meckler; diploma Curtis Inst. Music, 1960; m. Jaime Laredo, June 1, 1960 (div. Nov. 1976); 1 dau., Jennifer. N.Y.C. debut with Leopold Stokowski and Am. Symphony, 1962; debut with Boulez and N.Y. Philharmonic, 1974; soloist with major Am. orchs., including those in N.Y.C., Cleve., Detroit, Phila., and Nat. and Am. symphonies; performed at Aspen, Marlboro, Spoleto, Israel and Caramoor festivals; recordings with Columbia Records include Ravel's La Valse, 1967, piano sonatas of Alexander Scriabin, 1970-71, complete solo piano works of Rachmaninoff; asst. prof. Yale U. Sch. Music, 1974. Address: c/o Hillyer Internat Inc 250 W 57th St New York City NY 10019

LARESE, EDWARD JOHN, airline pres.; b. Kimball, W.Va., Mar. 7, 1935; s. Innocente and Velia (Pais) L.; student U. Ky., 1953-54; A.B. in Accounting, Duke, 1957; m. Julianne Falotico, Aug. 15, 1964. Accountant, Price Waterhouse & Co., N.Y.C., 1957-65; mgr.-financial accounting Eastern Air Lines, Inc., N.Y.C., 1965-67, asst. to sr. v.p. finance and administrn., 1968-70, asst. controller finance planning and analysis, 1970-72, v.p., controller, 1972-76; v.p., controller IU Internat., Inc., Phila., 1976-79; chief exec. officer, pres. Altair Airlines, Inc., 1979—. Loaned exec. Dade County (Fla.) United Fund, 1965, corp. chmn., 1975-76. C.P.A., N.C. Mem. Air Transp. Assn. (vice chmn. corp. accounting com.), Am. Inst. C.P.A.'s, N.Y. Soc. C.P.A.'s, N.C. Assn. C.P.A.'s, Duke U. Alumni Assn., Sigma Nu. Episcopalian. Clubs: Bath (Miami Beach, Fla.); Radnor Hunt (Berwyn, Pa.). Home: 2490 White Horse Rd Berwyn PA 19312 Office: Altair Airlines Inc Scott Plaza II Philadelphia PA 19312

LARGE, JAMES MIFFLIN, JR., banker; b. Phila., Mar. 15, 1932; s. James Mifflin and Sarah Morris (Ellison) L.; B.S.E., Princeton U.; postgrad. Stonier Grad. Sch. Banking; m. Carol E. Large, Sept. 30, 1978; children—James Mifflin III, Richard C., Ginny, Dudly, Jon. Exec. v.p. Central Nat. Bank, Phila., until 1973; chmn. Everett Trust Co., 1973-75; exec. v.p., sr. loan officer Central Nat. Bank of Cleve., 1975—. Trustee, Cleve. Inst. Music; mem. adv. bd. Cleve. Natural History Mus.; chmn. adv. bd. John Carol U. Bus. Sch. Growth Assn. Served with USN, 1955-59. Mem. Res. City Bankers Assn., Robert Morris Assos. (trustee Cleve. chpt.). Episcopalian. Clubs: Union (Cleve.); Union League, Corinthian Yacht (Phila.); Princeton (N.Y.C.); Kurtland Country, Hunt. Author: Planning Secondary Defenses Against Loan losses; contbr. articles to trade jours. Home: River Rd Chagrin Falls OH 44022 Office: 800 Superior Ave Cleveland OH 44114

LARGE, JOHN WILLARD, research musician, educator; b. Appalachia, Va., Nov. 29, 1929; s. John Willard and Elma Elizabeth (Blankenship) L.; B.F.A., U. N.Mex., 1954, M.Mus., 1955; D.Mus., Ind. U., 1962; Licence de Concert, Ecole Normale de Musique, Paris, France, 1963; Ph.D. (NIH fellow), Stanford, 1971. Prof. music N.Y. State U. Coll., Potsdam, 1965-66, San Francisco State U., 1966-69, U. So. Calif., 1969-72, Santa Clara U., 1973-74, U. Calif. at San Diego, 1974-78, N. Tex. State U., Denton, 1978—; performing artist bass-baritone Eastman Boomer Concert Mgmt., N.Y.C., 1965-68. Served with USNR, 1955-59. Recipient Fulbright award, 1962-63. Mem. Nat. Assn. Tchrs. Singing, Acoustical Soc. Am. (dir. First Internat. Conf. on Research in Singing 1975), Internat. Assn. Exptl. Research in Singing (founder 1971, gen. sec. 1971—). Home: 1003 Eagle 120 Denton TX 76201 Office: Sch of Music North Texas State U Denton TX 76203

LARGEN, JOSEPH, book wholesaler; b. Union, N.J., June 13, 1940; s. Fred and Wilma L.; B.S. in Econs., U. Mo., 1963; m. Suzanne K. Otte, July 7, 1964; children—Lori, Lisa. Mgmt. trainee R.R. Donnelly Corp., Chgo., 1964-67; distbn. mgr., material control and distbn. Warwick Electronic Co., Niles, Ill., 1967-69; with Brodart, Inc., 1969—, v.p. prodn., Williamsport, Pa., 1973-75, exec. v.p., 1975-78, pres., 1978—. Served with USCG, 1963-64. Home: 3 Woodside Dr RD 3 Montoursville PA 17754 Office: 1609 Memorial Ave Williamsport PA 17705

LARIAR, LAWRENCE, cartoonist, editor, author; b. Bklyn., Dec. 25, 1908; s. Marcy and Ella (Poll) L.; student N.Y. Sch. Fine and Applied Arts, 1926-29, Academie Julien, Paris, Art Students League N.Y.C.; m. Susan Meyer, Oct. 19, 1935; children—Linda, Stephen. Comml. advt. artist, 1930-33; free lance illustrator and polit. cartoonist, 1933—; work has appeared in Sat. Eve. Post, Collier's, Am. Mag., Judge, New Yorker, Coll. Humor, Country Gentleman, N.Y. daily newspapers; cartoon editor Liberty Mag., 1941-48, Parade, 1957—; dir. Profl. Sch. Cartooning. N.Y. Sch. Fine and Applied Arts fellow, 1927. Mem. Am. Soc. Mag. Cartoonists (past pres., mem. war com.), Author's League Am. Author: Andrew the Ant; Cartooning For Everybody, 1941; Death Paints the Picture, 1943; Army Fun Book, 1943; He Died Laughing, 1943; The Man With the Lumpy Nose, 1944; Oh. Dr. Kinsey, 1953; Yankee Yiddish, 1953; Fish and Be Damned, 1953; Naked and Alone, 1953; Kiss and Kill, 1954; Golf and Be Damned, 1954; You've Got Me in Stitches, 1954; You've Got Me on the Hook, 1954; You've Got Me and How, 1955; Best Cartoons from Abroad, 1955; You've Got Me from 9 to 5, 1956; You've Got Me On the Rocks, 1956; The Real Lowdown, 1956; Hunt and Be Damned, 1956; Girl Running, 1956; Boat and Be Damned, 1957. Editor: Bed and Bored, 1945; The Girl With the Frightened Eyes, 1945; (with Col. Stoopnagle) Father Goosenagle, 1945; Run for Your Life, 1946; CBS TV Happy Headlines, 1947; Careers in Cartooning, 1949; Friday for Death, 1949; Easy Way to Cartooning, 1950; Stone Cold Blonde, 1951; American Salesman, 1951; Bantam Prince (N.Y. Herald-Tribune Syndicate); Murder for Madame, 1951; Knife at my Back, 1952; The Sunburned Corpse, 1952; The Day I Died, 1952; Don't Follow Me, 1953; How Green Was My Sex Life, 1955; You've Got Me in a Hole, 1955; The Salesman, 1955; Fix It and Be Damned, 1955. Editor: Best Cartoons of the Year, 1942—. Address: 248 Mt Joy Ave Freeport NY 11520

LARK, HOWARD (BILL) WILLIAM, ballet dancer; b. Sacramento, Dec. 10, 1944; s. Howard Alterson and Margaret Dolores (McMahan) L.; student Briggs Dance Sch., 1962, Crockett Dance Studio, 1963-64, Banff Sch. Fine Arts, summers 1962-63, Royal Winnipeg (Man., Can.) Sch., 1970. Mem. corps de ballet Joffrey Ballet, 1964; mem. corps de ballet Royal Winnipeg Ballet, 1971-75, soloist, 1975-78, prin. dancer, 1978-79, regisseur, 1977-79; prin. dancer 1st Chamber Dance Co., Seattle, 1979—; guest tchr., choreographer. Served with USAF, 1964-70. Office: 1st Chamber Dance Co PO Box 66252 Seattle WA 98166. *I cannot is a phrase you must forget. When one wants to, one always can.*

LARKIN, ARTHUR EDWARD, JR., food co. exec.; b. Mpls., Mar. 7, 1917; s. Arthur Edward and Lou (McCabe) L.; B.A. in Econs., Dartmouth, 1939; m. Margaret Davis, Sept. 17, 1941 (div. 1962); children—Wendy, Barbara, Margaret; m. 2d, Ellen Keenan, Jan. 23, 1963; children by previous marriage—Michael, Timothy, Peter, Annabel. With George A. Hormel & Co., 1946-58, v.p., dir., 1946-58; with Gen. Foods Corp., 1958-72, mktg. mgr. Maxwell House div., 1958-59, gen. mgr., 1959-62, v.p. corp., 1960, exec. v.p., 1962-66, pres., chief operating officer, 1966-72; pres., chief exec. officer Keebler Co., Elmhurst, Ill., 1972—, chmn., 1976—, chief exec. officer, 1976-78; chmn. fin. com. United Biscuits U.S., 1979—; dir. United Biscuits (Holdings) Ltd. Gt. Britain, Kemper Corp., H.P. Hood Co., Inc., Hercules Inc. Trustee Elmhurst Coll. Served to lt. comdr. USNR, 1940-45. Mem. Mgmt. Execs. Soc., Grocery Mfrs. Am. (dir.), Council on Fgn. Relations. Clubs: Economic, Presidents' (N.Y.C.). Home: Oak Brook IL 60521 Office: One Hollow Tree Ln Elmhurst IL 60126

LARKIN, BRIAN JAMES, ednl. corp. exec., educator; b. Austerlitz, N.Y., July 23, 1933; s. Charles Joseph and Marion Clair (Fosburgh) L.; B.A., U. N.Mex., 1961; M.A., Maxwell Grad. Sch., Syracuse U., 1967, Ph.D., 1973; m. Elizabeth Ann VanderPutten, 1977. Tchr. Fleischmanns (N.Y.) High Sch., 1961-64; asst. prof. social sci. and edn. and research asso. Social Sci., Syracuse (N.Y.) U., 1968-74; exec. dir. Nat. Council Social Studies, Washington, 1974-78; pres. Washington Ednl. Devel. Corp., 1978—. Served with AUS, 1954-57. NDEA fellow, 1964-65; NSF fellow, 1965-66, Experienced Tchr. fellow, 1966-67. Mem. Social Sci. Edn. Consortium, AAAS, World Future Soc., Am. Soc. Assn. Execs., Nat. Council Social Studies, Colo. Council Social Studies. Author: (with R.A. Price) Major Concepts for Social Studies (series), 1975; also numerous films and TV programs. Contbr. articles to profl. jours. Home: 1301 20th St Washington DC 20036 Office: 2025 Eye St NW Suite 314 Washington DC 20036

LARKIN, CHARLES EARLL, coast guard officer; b. Los Angeles, Oct. 21, 1927; s. Charles Earll and Effie (Van Wie) L.; B.S., U.S. Coast Guard Acad., 1949; M.S., George Washington U., 1968; grad. Air War Coll.; m. Katharine Phillips Buck, June 10, 1950; children—Charles, Michael, Lynn, James, Dale. Commd. seaman U.S. Coast Guard, 1945, advanced through grades to rear adm., 1976; deck watch officer/navigator Coast Guard, Boston, 1949-51; various assignments as aviator Coast Guard, 1951-65; comdg. officer Coast Guard Air Sta., Naples, Italy, 1965-67, Coast Guard Air Sta., San Francisco, 1970-73; chief aviation br. Coast Guard Hdqrs., Washington, 1973-75, chief of personnel, 1976-78; chief of staff 7th Coast Guard Dist., Miami, Fla., 1975-76; comdr. 13th Coast Guard Dist., Seattle, 1978—; mem. Seattle Seafair Sr. Council; bd. dirs. Sea Use Council; bd. dirs. USO-Puget Sound Area; regional emergency transp. coordinator, cargo security coordinator, Seattle-Tacoma. Mem. exec. bd. Chief Seattle council Boy Scouts Am. Decorated Silver Life Saving medal, Meritorious Service medal with 2 gold stars, Air medal, Coast Guard Commendation medal; subject of resolution of commendation County of San Mateo (Calif.), 1973. Mem. Nat. Def. Transp. Assn. (bd. hon. dirs.), Coast Guard Acad. Found. (hon. dir.). Clubs: Rainier, Seattle Yacht, 101, Transp. of Seattle. Home: 3201 Alki Ave SW Seattle WA 98116 Office: Comdr 13th Coast Guard Dist 915 2d Ave Seattle WA 98174

LARKIN, EMMET, historian; b. N.Y.C., May 19, 1927; s. Emmet and Annabell (Ryder) L.; B.A., N.Y. U., 1950; M.A., Columbia U., 1951, Ph.D., 1957; m. Dianne Willey, Aug. 13, 1966; children—Heather, Siobhan. Instr. history Bklyn. Coll., 1954-60; asst. prof. Mass. Inst. Tech., 1960-66; mem. faculty U. Chgo., 1966-71, prof. history, 1971—. Served with AUS, 1944-46. Fulbright scholar, 1955-56; fellow Howard Found., 1964-65, Newberry Library, 1976-77. Mem. Am. Com. Irish Studies (v.p. 1975-78). Author: James Larkin, Irish Labour Leader, 1876-1947, 1965; The Roman Catholic Church and the Creation of the Modern Irish State, 1878-1886, 1975; The Historical Dimensions of Irish Catholicism, 1976; The Roman

Catholic Church and the Plan of Campaign in Ireland, 1886-1888, 1978; The Roman Catholic Church in Ireland and The Fall of Parnell, 1888-1891, 1979. Home: 5021 S Woodlawn Ave Chicago IL 60615 Office: Dept History Univ Chicago 1126 E 59th St Chicago IL 60637

LARKIN, EUGENE DAVID, artist, educator; b. Mpls., June 27, 1921; s. John Peter and Martha Lavinia (Vandevere) L.; B.A., U. Minn., 1946, M.A., 1949; m. Audrey Jean Krueger, Jan. 29, 1947; children—Andrew, Alan. One man exhbns. include: Mpls. Inst. Arts, 1957, 60, 68, Syracuse U., 1962, Walker Art Center, Mpls., 1967, New Forms Gallery, Athens, Greece, 1967, U. Kans., 1972, Macalester Coll., 1974, U. Minn., St. Paul, 1973, 78; group exhbns. include: Phila. Printmakers Club, 1966, 20 American Artists, Geneva, Switzerland, 1964, Big Prints, N.Y. U., 1968, Midwestern Printmakers, Walker Art Center, 1973; represented in permanent collections: Mus. Modern Art, N.Y.C., Library Congress, Chgo. Art Inst., Mpls. Inst. Arts, U. Minn. Gallery, Des Moines Art Center, U. Tenn., Kans. State Tchrs. Coll., Minn. Mus. Art, Nat. Collection Fine Arts, Smithsonian Instn.; mem. faculty dept. art Kans. State Coll., Pittsburg, 1949-54; head printmaking dept., chmn. div. fine arts Mpls. Sch. Art, 1954-69; prof. design dept. U. Minn., St. Paul, 1969—. Mem. Coll. Art Assn. Am. Home: 64 Groveland Terr Minneapolis MN 55403 Office: Design Dept Univ of Minn 1985 Buford Ave St Paul MN 55108

LARKIN, FELIX EDWARD, corp. exec.; b. N.Y.C., Aug. 3, 1909; s. John A. and Maria C. (Henry) L.; A.B., Fordham U., 1931, LL.D. (hon.), 1978; M.B.A., N.Y. U., 1933; J.D., St. John's U., 1942; m. Evelyn Wallace, Dec. 28, 1937; children—Nancy Larkin Carr, John, James. Engaged security bus., 1933-37; lectr. Fordham U. Sch. Bus., 1937-42; law sec. Judge James Garrett Wallace, Ct. Gen. Sessions, N.Y.C., 1939-47; asst. gen. counsel Dept. Def., 1949, gen. counsel, 1949-51; v.p. charge indsl. relations W.R. Grace & Co., N.Y.C., 1951-58, exec. v.p. adminstrn., 1958-69, exec. v.p., sr. mem. office of pres., 1969-71, pres., 1971-74, chmn. corp., 1974—; dir. Marine Midland Banks, Inc., Winged Foot Holding Corp. Chmn. bd. trustees Fordham U., 1970-77, trustee, 1969-78, trustee emeritus, 1978—; bd. govs. New Rochelle (N.Y.) Hosp. Med. Center Assn. Recipient highest civilian award Dept. Def., 1951; named Man of Year, N.Y. U. Grad. Sch. Bus., 1963; named to Fordham U. Sports Hall of Fame, 1979. Mem. Friendly Sons St. Patrick, Am. Arbitration Assn. (dir. 1975—), Conf. Bd. Clubs: Winged Foot Golf (v.p., gov. 1967-72, 74—) (Mamaroneck); Larchmont (N.Y.) Yacht; N.Y. Univ., Pinnacle (gov.) (N.Y.C.); Delray Beach (Fla.); Pine Tree Golf (Boynton Beach, Fla.). Home: 1030 Old White Plains Rd Mamaroneck NY 10543 Office: 1114 Ave of Americas New York NY 10036

LARKIN, JOHN DAY, arbitrator; b. Huntland, Tenn., Sept. 15, 1897; s. John Day and Louanna (Erwin) L.; B.A., Berea (Ky.) Coll., 1923; M.A., U. Chgo., 1925; Ph.D., Harvard, 1935; m. Ruth Ormsby, Aug. 22, 1922 (dec.); children—Margaret (Mrs. Stuart A. Pettingill), John Day III; m. 2d, Kathleen Ormsby, Sept. 8, 1928. Bank clk., 1919; field agt. Ralston Purina Co., St. Louis, 1923-24; instr. history Hamline U., St. Paul, 1925-27; instr. Rutgers U., summer 1927; instr. polit. sci. U. N.D., 1927-28; asst. govt. Harvard, 1928-30; successively tutor, instr., asst. prof. govt. Coll. City N.Y., 1930-37; asso. prof. polit. sci. Armour Inst. Tech., 1937-40; head dept. polit. and social sci. Ill. Inst. Tech., 1940-46, dean div. liberal studies, 1945-62; spl. mediation rep. NWLB, 1942-43; pub. mem. 6th Regional War Labor Bd., 1943-45; vice-chmn. Chgo. Regional WLB, 1944-45; mem. labor panel Am. Arbitration Assn., 1947—; arbitrator Fed. Mediation and Conciliation Service, 1947—, Franklin Assn. and Typographical Union, 1961—; referee Nat. Ry. Adjustment Bd., 1954—; mem. Pres.'s Ry. Emergency Bd. No. 114, 1955; permanent arbitrator Deere & Co. and UAW, 1958-61, Wilson & Co. and UPWA, 1962-67. Mem. Nat. Acad. Arbitrators (pres. 1956), Am. Polit. Sci. Assn., Indsl. Relations Research Assn., Am. Soc. Pub. Adminstrn., Armour Faculty Club Ill. Inst. Tech. (hon. life). Club: University. Author: The President's Control of the Tariff, 1936; Trade Agreements, 1940. Home: 860 Lake Shore Dr Chicago IL 60611 Office: 33 N LaSalle St Chicago IL 60602

LARKIN, JUNE NOBLE, found. exec.; b. N.Y.C., June 17, 1922; d. Edward John and Ethel Louise (Tinkham) Noble; B.A., Sarah Lawrence Coll., 1944; m. David Shiverick Smith, Dec. 8, 1945 (div. 1968); children—E.J. Noble, David S., Jeremy T., Bradford D.; m. 2d, Frank Yoakum Larkin, Mar. 4, 1968. Trustee, Sarah Lawrence Coll., 1964-73, chmn. bd., 1971-73, now hon. trustee; trustee Mus. Modern Art, 1969—, v.p., 1978—; trustee The Juilliard Sch., 1974—, Museums Collaborative, 1973-76, The Eaglebrook Sch., 1974—, Greenwich Hosp., 1967—, Cultural Council Found., 1976-79; bd. dirs. Repertory Theatre of Lincoln Center, 1969-72; chmn. bd. trustees Edward John Noble Found., N.Y.C., 1972—. Mem. N.Y.C. Cultural Council, 1971-74; mem. Nat. Parks Centennial Commn., 1972-73; mem. Mayor's Com. Cultural Policy, N.Y.C., 1974; trustee N.Y. Philharm., 1979—, Cultural Assistance Center, 1978—; hon. chmn. bd. trustees North Country Hosps., Gouverneur, N.Y., 1959-78. Mem. Nat. Soc. Colonial Dames State of N.Y. Clubs: Colony (N.Y.C.); Sulgrave (Washington). Home: 600 Lake Ave Greenwich CT 06830 Office: 32 E 57th St New York NY 10022

LARKIN, KENNETH VINCENT, bank exec.; b. Bklyn., July 10, 1921; s. William H. and Cecile (Breslen) L.; B.A. in Chemistry and Physics, Hofstra Coll., 1943; postgrad. Midwestern Grad. Sch. Banking; grad. Advanced Mgmt. Program, Harvard U.; m. Sylvia Repetto, June 30, 1945; children—Kenneth, Christine, William, Maureen, Mary, Anne-Marie. With Bank of Am., 1945—, head Timeplan Bank Card/Visa/Master Charge operation, San Francisco, 1971-78; dir. VISA U.S.A., VISA Internat.; mem. Nat. Bus. Council for Consumer Affairs, 1972; chmn. bd. BA Ins. Co., BA Ins. Agy. Co.; lectr. on banking at univs.; 1st v.p., bd. dirs. Better Bus. Bur. Mem. lay bd. St. Mary's Hosp., San Francisco. Served with USN, 1943-45; PTO. Decorated knight Order Malta. Clubs: Bankers, Olympic, Meadow, Silverado Country; Rotary (San Francisco). Office: PO Box 37000 San Francisco CA 94137

LARKIN, PETER ANTHONY, educator; b. Auckland, New Zealand, Dec. 11, 1924; s. Frank Wilfred and Caroline Jane (Knapp) L.; B.A., M.A., U. Sask., 1946; D.Phil. (Rhodes scholar), Oxford U., 1948; m. Lois Boughton Rayner, Aug. 21, 1948; children—Barbara, Kathleen, Patricia, Margaret, Gillian. Bubonic plague survey Govt. of Sask., 1942-43; fisheries investigator Fisheries Research Bd. of Can., 1944-46; chief fisheries biologist B.C. Game Commn., 1948-55; asst. prof. U. B.C., 1948-55, prof. dept. zoology, 1959-63, 66-69, prof. Inst. Animal Resource Ecology, 1969—, also dir. fisheries, 1955-63, 66-69, head dept. zoology, 1972-75, dean grad. studies, 1975—. Hon. life gov. Vancouver Pub. Aquarium; mem. Canadian nat. com. Spl. Com. on Problems Environment, 1971—; mem. Killam selection com. Can. Council, 1974—; mem. Sci. Council Can., 1971—, govtl. research coms. Recipient Centennial medal Govt. of Can., 1967, Master Tchr. award U. B.C., 1970, Silver Jubilee medal, 1977. Nuffield Found. fellow, 1961-62. Fellow Royal Soc. Can.; mem. Internat. Limnological Assn., Am. Fisheries Soc., B.C. Natural Resources Conf. (pres. 1954), B.C. Wildlife Fedn., Brit. Ecology Soc., Canadian Soc. Wildlife and Fisheries Biologists (v.p. 1961), Canadian Soc. Zoologists (pres. 1972). Contbr. articles to profl. jours. Home: 4166 Crown Crescent Vancouver BC V6R 2A9 Canada

LARKIN, RICHARD XAVIER, army officer; b. Omaha, Sept. 29, 1929; s. Michael Francis and Angela Frances (Cain) L.; B.S., U.S. Mil. Acad., 1952; M.A., Columbia U., 1964; grad. Command and Gen. Staff Coll., 1965, Armed Forces Staff Coll., 1967, Army War Coll., 1971; M.A., George Washington U., 1974; m. Donna Claire Griffith, June 28, 1952; children—M. Colleen, Richard J., Maureen A., Michael P., Mark C. Commd. 2d lt. U.S. Army, 1952, advanced through grades to maj. gen.; co. comdr. 8th Div., Colo., W. Ger., 1954-59; asst. prof. fgn. lang. U.S. Mil. Acad., West Point, N.Y., 1961-64; mem. Army Gen. Staff, 1967-68; bn. comdr. 4th Div., Vietnam, 1968-69, mem. Joint Chiefs of Staff, Washington, 1971-72, brigade comdr. 4th Div., Colo., 1972-74, asst. div. comdr., 1975-77, def. attache, Moscow, 1977-79, chief of staff Def. Intelligence Agy., Washington, 1979—. Decorated Silver Star, Legion of Merit with oak leaf cluster, D.F.C., Bronze Star with oak leaf cluster, Air medals, Combat Infantryman's Badge. Roman Catholic. Club: K.C. Office: Chief of Staff Def Intelligence Agy Washington DC 20301

LARKIN, ROGER ALLEN, grain co. exec.; b. Oklahoma City, Oct. 30, 1926; s. William P. and Agnes A. (Mathies) L.; B.S., Okla. State U., 1948; M.S., U. Nebr., 1950; m. Shirley F. Isley, Sept. 25, 1950; children—Ann, Beth, Bob. Research scientist Dept. Agr., Peoria, Ill., 1950-53; grain buyer Pabst Brewing Co., Peoria, 1953-57; grain merchandiser Ill. Grain Corp., Peoria, 1957-60, Chgo., 1960-65, Producers Export Co., N.Y.C., 1965; asst. head grain div. Farmers Union Grain Terminals Assn., St. Paul, 1965-69; pres. Tidewater Grain Co., Phila., 1969—, also dir.; dir. Comml. Exchange of Phila., Gen. Grain Co., Early and Daniel Co., bd. dirs. Nat. Grain Trade Council. Contbr. articles to profl. jours.; patentee in field. Office: 346 Pub Ledger Bldg Philadelphia PA 19106

LARKINS, JOHN DAVIS, JR., judge; b. Morristown, Tenn., June 8, 1909; s. John D. and Emma (Cooper) L.; B.A., Wake Forest Coll., 1929, law student, 1930; LL.D., Belin U., 1957, Wake Forest U., 1977; m. Pauline Murrill, Mar. 15, 1930; children—Emma Sue (Mrs. D.H. Loftin), Polly (Mrs. J.H. Bearden). Admitted to N.C. bar, 1930, since practiced in Trenton; U.S. dist. judge Eastern Dist. N.C., 1961—, chief judge, 1975—, sr. judge, 1979—. Sec. Larkins Stores, Inc.; dir. Life Ins. Co. of N.C. Del.-at-large Democratic Nat. Conv., 1940, 44, 48, 56, 60; sec. N.C. Dem. Exec. Com., 1952-54, chmn., 1954-58; mem. Dem. Nat. Com., 1958-60; mem. N.C. Senate 7th dist., 1936-44, 48-54, pres. pro tem, 1941-42. Chmn. gov.'s adv. budget commn., 1951-53, liaison officer, legislative counsel, 1955. Mem. nat. bd. dirs., vice chmn. Am. Cancer Soc.; trustee U. N.C., Bapt. Hosp., Wake Forest U. Served as pvt. AUS, 1945. Recipient Distinguished Service award Am. Cancer Soc., Wake Forest U. Sch. Law, 1968. Mem. Am. Legion, 40 and 8, Woodmen of World, Am., Fed., N.C. bar assns., N.C. Bar, Inc., Phi Alpha Delta. Baptist (chmn. bd. deacons 1930-78, hon. deacon for life). Clubs: Masons, Shriners, Elks, Moose. Home: Trenton NC 28585 Office: US Dist Ct US Courthouse PO Box 126 Trenton NC 28585

LARMON, WILLIAM ALEXANDER, physician; b. Sunnyvale, Calif., Oct. 23, 1916; s. William A. and Eleanor (Bradford) L.; student San Jose State Coll., 1933-36, Stanford, 1936-37; B.S., Northwestern U., 1941, M.B., M.D., 1942; m. Irene Traska, Oct. 13, 1945 (dec. Oct. 1976); m. Jane Alderson, Mar. 14, 1977. Intern, Harper Hosp., Detroit, 1941-42, asst. resident pathology, 1942; Kemper fellow bone and joint dept. Northwestern U. Hosp., 1942-45, fellow bone and joint dept., 1945-46; faculty Northwestern U. Med. Sch., 1947—, prof. bone and joint surgery, 1974, acting chmn. dept. orthopedic surgery, 1971; pvt. practice, Chgo., 1947—; chief staff Northwestern Meml. Hosp., 1974, bd. dirs., 1974—; attending staff VA Hosp., Hines, Ill. Orthopaedic rep. Adv. Bd. Med. Specialists, 1962—; chmn. nat. adv. com. orthopaedic surgery VA, 1969—. Bd. dirs. Nat. Interne and Residency Program. Diplomate Am. Bd. Orthopaedic Surgery (sec.-treas. 1962-68). Fellow A.C.S. (gov. 1968—); mem. A.M.A., Ill., Chgo. med. socs., Am. Acad. Orthopaedic Surgery, Clin-Orthopaedic Soc., Am. Rheumatism Soc., Chgo. Rheumatism Assn., Chgo. Orthopaedic Soc. (pres. 1961-62), Chgo. Surg. Soc., Am. Assn. Ry. Surgeons, Hines Surg. Assn., Assn. Bone and Joint Surgeons, Am. Orthopaedic Assn., Alpha Kappa Kappa. Contbr. articles to profl. jours., chpts. to books. Editor instructional course vol. 15, Am. Acad. Orthopaedic Surgeons, 1958. Home: 1412 Sandburg Terr Chicago IL 60610 Office: 233 E Erie St Chicago IL 60611

LARNED, WILLIAM EDMUND, JR., internat. devel. and venture capital co. exec.; b. Albany, N.Y., July 3, 1919; s. William Edmund and Augusta Danforth (Geer) L.; B.S., U.S. Mil. Acad., 1943; m. Margaret Auguste Klipstein, Jan. 22, 1943; children—Gay, William August, Cynthia Troy. Commd. 2d lt. U.S. Army, 1943, advanced through grades to maj., 1953; small unit comdr. 3d and 4th Mech. Cav. groups ETO, 1943-46; with CIC, Europe, U.S., 1946-52; gen. staff officer Dept. Army, Washington, 1953-55, ret., 1955; mgr. market planning Servomechanisms, Inc., N.Y.C., Los Angeles, 1956-59; chief requirements br. Ramo-Wooldridge div. TRW, Canoga Park, Calif., 1959-60; pres., dir. DMS, Inc. div. McGraw-Hill Publs., Greenwich, Conn., Beverly Hills, Calif., 1960-70; pres., dir. Internat. Bus. Services Corp., Greenwich, Conn., 1970-72; v.p., dir. GMS Assos. Internat., Arlington, Va., 1971-73; v.p., dir. Halaby Internat. Corp., N.Y.C., 1973—; dir. Safeflight Internat. Corp., Pearl River, N.Y., 1978—. Author: The Aerospace Marketing Handbook, 1960; Aerospace Market Intelligence Report, 1961. Home: 37 Burying Hill Rd Greenwich CT 06830 Office: One Blue Hill Plaza Pearl River NY 10965

LARNER, JEREMY, writer; b. Olean, N.Y., Mar. 20, 1937; s. Martin L. and Clara (Bronstein) L.; A.B., Brandeis U., 1958. Editor, Dissent Mag., N.Y.C., 1965—; with Inst. Politics, Harvard, 1970-71. Recipient Aga Kahn prize for best Paris Rev. story, 1964; award Nat. Council Arts, 1966-67. Author: Drive, He Said (Delta prize), 1964; (with Ralph Tefferteller) The Addict in the Street, 1965; The Answer, 1968; (with Irving Howe) Poverty: Views From The Left, 1968; Nobody Knows: Reflections on the McCarthy Campaign of 1968, 1970; The Candidate (Acad. award best screenplay), 1973. Address: care Ziegler-Ross 9255 Sunset Blvd Los Angeles CA 90069*

LARNER, JOSEPH, pharmacologist; b. Brest-Litovsk, Poland, Jan. 9, 1921; naturalized Am. citizen; B.A., U. Mich., 1942; M.D., Columbia U., 1945; M.S. (NIH fellow), U. Ill., 1949; Ph.D. in Biochemistry (Life Ins. Med. Research Fund fellow), Washington U., St. Louis, 1951; married; 3 children. Instr. biochemistry Washington U., 1951-53; asst. prof. Noyes Lab. Chemistry, U. Ill., 1953-57; asso. prof. pharmacology Sch. Medicine Western Res. U., 1957-63, prof., 1963-65; Hill prof. metabolic enzymology Coll. Med. Sci. U. Minn., Mpls., 1965-70; prof., chmn. dept. pharmacology U. Va., 1970—. Mem. metabolic study sect. NIH, 1962-66; mem. enzyme subcom. NRC-Nat. Acad. Sci.; bd. dirs. U. Va. Diabetes Research and Tng. Center. Served to capt. M.C., U.S. Army, 1946-48. Recipient Research Career award NIH, 1963-64; Travel award Internat. Congress Biochemists, 1955. Fellow Royal Coll. Medicine; mem. Am. Chem. Soc., Am. Soc. Biol. Chemistry, Am. Pharm. Soc., Am. Diabetes Assn. (established investigator). Office: U Va Sch Medicine Charlottesville VA 22901

LARO, ARTHUR EMMETT, editor; b. Brownsville, Tex., Feb. 19, 1912; s. Arthur Elmo and Anna Maude (Hale) L.; ed. San Antonio pub. schs.; m. Dorothy Vernon Jones, June 5, 1937 (dec.); 1 dau., Mary Ann; m. 2d, Kay Dalton, Aug. 25, 1973. Reporter, San Antonio Light, 1929-36, Houston Press, 1936-37; real estate editor, spl. edit. editor Houston Post, 1937-45, city editor, 1945-46, mng. editor, 1946, past exec. editor, v.p.; dir. Houston Post Co., 1949-60; exec. editor Los Angeles Mirror, 1960, editor, pub., 1960-62; editor Newhouse Nat. News Service, 1962-64; exec. v.p., editor Chgo. Tribune-N.Y. News Syndicate, Inc., 1964-66, pres., editor, 1966-74; cons., 1974—; partner Laro/Donahue Ltd., Houston, 1974-76; gen. mgr. Booke and Co., Inc., 1977—. Dir. Energy Research and Edn. Found., 1970—. Mem. Sigma Delta Chi. Methodist. Clubs: National Press; Houston. Home: 661 Bering Dr Apt 309 Houston TX 77057 Office: 3630 Wake Forest Houston TX 77098

LAROCCA, JOSEPH PAUL, educator; b. La Junta, Colo., July 5, 1920; s. Vito Michael and Mary (Parlapiano) L.; B.S., U. Colo., 1942; M.S. (Nat. Formulary fellow), U. N.C., 1944; Ph.D., U. Md., 1948; m. Blair Camak, Apr. 19, 1947; children—Carl Anthony, Mary Blair, Charlotte Ann, Elizabeth. Research chemist U.S. Naval Research Lab., Washington, 1947-49; asso. prof. medicinal chemistry U. Ga., 1949-50, prof., 1950—, head dept., 1968—; lectr. Oak Ridge Asso. Univs. Mobile Radioisotope Program, 1965, 66; cons. physician manpower USPHS, 1967. Bd. dirs. Am. Assn. Colls. Pharmacy, 1974-76. Chmn. bd. Clark County unit Am. Cancer Soc., 1965-66, pres., 1964-65; chmn. bd. Clark County Community Chest, 1963-64, pres., 1962-63; pres. Athens Assn. Retarded Children, 1960-61. Served with AUS, 1944-46. Gustauus A. Pfeiffer Meml. Research fellow, 1964-65; Orins Research participant, 1964, 65, 66. Fellow A.A.A.S.; mem. Am. Pharm. Soc., Am. Chem. Soc., Ga. Pharm. Assn., Ga. Acad. Sci., Sigma Xi, Phi Kappa Phi, Rho Chi, Phi Delta Chi. Rotarian. Author research papers, reports. Home: 115 Fortson Circle Athens GA 30601

LAROCHE, ROBERT EUGENE, fin. co. exec.; b. Washington, Ind., Dec. 26, 1926; s. Henry Arther and Donna Alma (Armes) LaR.; student Washington U., 1944-47; m. Kathleen Grace Wood, Nov. 17, 1973; children from previous marriage—Michele Marie LaRoche Mutzke, Debrah Verlene LaRoche Vaughan. Vice pres. Borg-Warner Acceptance Corp., Chgo., 1959-67, pres., 1967-72, chmn. bd. dirs., 1972—; dir. Marina Bank, Chgo., Borg-Warner Acceptance Can., Ltd., Borg-Warner Acceptance Corp., Australia, Borg-Warner Acceptance Ltd., London, Borg-Warner Financieringsmaatschappij B.V., Amsterdam, Borg-Warner Finanzierungs GmbH, W. Germany, S.A. Borg Warner Acceptance Corp. N.V., Brussels. Served with inf., U.S. Army, 1944-45. Address: Borg Warner Acceptance Corp 1 IBM Plaza Chicago IL 60611

LAROCHELLE, DONALD RAYMOND, engr., engring. co. exec.; b. Lewiston, Maine, Nov. 26, 1930; s. Philip Joseph and Dora Alexena (Poisson) LaR.; B.S., U. Maine, 1953; m. Anne Marie Albert, Oct. 31, 1953; children—Paul, Gary, Theresa, Jane, Stephan, Patti. Asst. city engr., Lewiston, 1953-55; pres. Aliberti, LaRochelle & Hodson Engring. Corp., Lewiston, 1955—; chmn. bd. AL&H Constrn. Mgmt. Inc., 1976—; pres. Comtect, Inc., Lewiston, 1969—; trustee Androscoggin County Savs. Bank, 1976—. Commr. Maine Manufactured Housing Commn., 1977. Corporator, Central Maine Gen. Hosp., Lewiston, 1969—; bd. dirs. St. Mary's Gen. Hosp. Registered profl. engr., Maine, N.H., Vt., Mass., R.I., Conn. Fellow Am. Cons. Engrs. Council; mem. ASCE, Nat. Soc. Profl. Engrs., Cons. Engrs. of Maine (pres. 1971-72), Auburn-Lewiston C. of C. (pres. 1976-77), Phi Kappa Sigma. Republican. Roman Catholic. Home and office: 21 Bristol Rd Lewiston ME 04240

LA ROCQUE, EUGENE PHILIPPE, bishop; b. Windsor, Ont., Can., Mar. 27, 1927; s. Eugene Joseph and Angeline Marie (Monforton) LaR.; B.A., U. Western Ont., 1948; M.A., Laval U., 1956. Ordained priest Roman Catholic Ch., 1952, consecrated bishop, 1974; asst. parish priest Ste. Therese Ch., Windsor, 1952-54; registrar, then dean men, lectr. Christ The King Coll., U. Western Ont., 1956-64, asst. spiritual dir. St. Peter's Sem., 1964-65, prin., dean King's Coll., 1965-68; pastor St. Joseph's Ch., Rivière-aux-Canards, Ont., 1968-70, Ste. Anne's Ch., Tecumseh, 1970-74; bishop of Alexandria, Ont., 1974—; dean Essex County, 1970-73; trustee Essex County Roman Cath. Separate Sch. Bd., 1972-74; 1st chmn. liaison com. between Can. Jewish Congress, Can. Council Chs. and Can. Cath. Conf. Bishops, 1977—; mem. Can. Cath. Conf. Bishops, pres. Senate Priests Can., 1973-74. Club: K.C. (3 deg.; chaplain Ont. 1977—). Address: 200 Montreal Rd Box 1388 Cornwall ON K6H 5V4 Canada

LA ROCQUE, GENE ROBERT, ret. naval officer, former govt. ofcl.; b. Kankakee, Ill., June 29, 1918; s. Edward and Lucile (Eddy) LaR.; student U. Ill., 1936-40; B.A., George Washington U., 1958; hon. doctorate, Hanyang U., Seoul, Korea, 1975; m. Sarah Madeline Fox, Apr. 17, 1945 (dec.); children—John C., James C., Annette D. Commd. ensign USN, 1941, advanced through grades to rear adm., 1965; comdr. Task Group in 6th Fleet Mediterranean Sea, 1965-66; mem. faculty Naval War Coll., 1951-53; dir. Inter-Am. Def. Coll. Washington, 1969-72; ret., 1972; dir. Center Def. Info., Washington, 1972—. Decorated Bronze Star medal with combat V, Legion of Merit; Abdon Calderón 1st Class (Ecuador); Order Naval Merit (Brazil); Mil. Order Gt. Star (Chile). Mem. Naval Inst. Clubs: New York Yacht; Army-Navy (Washington). Home: 5015 Macomb St NW Washington DC 20016 Office: 122 Maryland Ave NE Washington DC 20002

LARONGE, MARVIN JOSEPH, lawyer; b. Cleve., Mar. 20, 1905; s. Joseph and Retta (Rosenthal) L.; B.S., Wharton Sch., U. Pa., 1925; LL.B., Western Res. U., 1928; m. Bernice Goldrich, Sept. 6, 1928; children—Donald M., Mary Jo. Admitted to Ohio bar, 1928, since practiced in Cleve.; mem. Cleve. City Law Dept., 1935-41; now mem. firm Ulmer, Berne, Laronge, Glickman & Curtis. Dir. Columbia Iron & Metal Co., Atlas-Lederer Co., Atlas Metals Co. Past trustee United Negro Coll. Fund; v.p. Mt. Sinai Hosp., Cleve.; pres. Cleve. Soc. for Blind. Fellow Am., Ohio bar founds.; mem. Am., Ohio, Cleve. bar assns., Case Western Res. U. Law Alumni Assn. (pres. 1965-67). Clubs: Cleveland District Golf Assn. (past pres.); Oakwood Country (past pres.). Home: 13800 Shaker Blvd Cleveland OH 44120 Office: 900 Bond Court Bldg Cleveland OH 44114

LAROQUE, PAUL DE SALABERRY, lawyer, former aluminum co. exec.; b. Montreal, Que., Can., Apr. 26, 1908; s. Roquebrune-Paul and Adine (Lesage) L.; B.A., Coll. Sainte-Marie, Montreal, 1926; LL.L., U. Montreal, 1929; L.S.C., Ecole des Hautes Etudes Commerciales de Montreal, 1931; student Harvard Grad. Sch. Bus. Adminstrn., 1930-31; m. Line Leman, Jan. 20, 1934; children—Francois, Jeanne. Called to Que. bar, 1929; with Banque Canadienne Nationale, 1931-41, head investment dept., 1935-41; with Alcan Aluminium Ltd. Group Cos., 1941-72; sec. Alcan Aluminium Ltd., 1962-72, v.p., legal officer, 1963-72, dir., 1947-72; counsel firm Geoffrion & Prud'homme, and predecessor, Montreal, 1972—; past dir. several Alcan subsidiaries, Aluminum Co. Can. Ltd. Mem. Royal Commn. Enquiry Edn. Que. Fellow Chartered Inst. Secs. and Adminstrs. Can.; mem. Am. Soc. Corp. Secs., Home: Ten Eyck Rd Dunham PQ J0E 1M0 Canada Office: 500 Place d'Armes Montreal PQ H2Y 2W4 Canada

LAROS, GERALD SNYDER, II, orthopedic surgeon; b. Los Angeles, July 19, 1930; s. Gerald Snyder and Josephine (Kutish) L.; student Stanford U., 1948-51; B.S., Northwestern U., 1952, M.D., 1955; M.S., U. Iowa, 1970; m. Marilyn Muir Wald, Aug. 9, 1958; children—Ann, David, Sarah. Intern, Phila. Gen. Hosp., 1955-56; resident orthopedic surgery Hines (Ill.) VA Hosp., 1956-59, Shriners Hosp. for Crippled Children, Honolulu, 1960; attending orthopedist Moline Pub. and Moline Luth. hosps. (Ill.), 1961-67; research fellow orthopedics U. Iowa, 1968-70, asst. prof., 1970-71; asso. prof. orthopedics U. Ark., 1971-73; prof., chmn. orthopedics U. Chgo., 1973—. Mem. Am. Acad. Orthopedic Surgeons, Am. Orthopedic Assn., Orthopedic Research Soc., A.C.S. Home: 1225 E 56th St Chicago IL 60637 Office: 950 E 59th St Chicago IL 60637

LAROSE, ROGER, univ. adminstr., pharm. co. exec.; b. Montreal, Que., Can., July 28, 1910; s. Alfred and Anna (Contant) L.; B.A., U. Montreal, 1929; B.Sc. in Pharmacy, 1932; Licentiate in Social, Polit., and Econ. Scis., 1934; m. Rita Dagenais, Aug. 10, 1936 (dec. Oct. 1960); 1 dau., Louise Larose Cuddihy; m. 2d, Julienne Begin, Aug. 4, 1961. Asst. prof. pharmacy U. Montreal, 1934, dean Faculty Pharmacy, 1960-65, vice rector, 1969—; with Ciba Co. Ltd., Montreal, 1936-71, v.p., 1958-68, pres., 1968-71, dir., 1958-71; pres. Ciba-Geigy Can. Ltd., 1971-73, dep. chmn. bd., 1973-78, chmn. bd., 1978—; vice chmn. bd., mem. exec. com. Bank Canadian Nat.; chmn. bd. Yvon-Fournier Co. Ltd., 1978—; mem. Sci. Council Can., 1966-71; pres. com. Sci. Council on Health Scis., 1969-73. Bd. dirs. Institut de diagnostic et de recherches clinique de Montreal, 1968—, Hotel-Dieu de Montreal; pres. Hopital St.-Luc de Montreal, 1978—; bd. govs. Canadian Bankers Inst., 1973—; pres. Montreal Symphony Orch., 1978—. Decorated officer Order Can. Mem. Acad. Pharmacy (France), Pharm. Soc. Gt. Britain (hon.). Clubs: St.-Denis (Montreal); Forest and Stream (Dorval). Home: 65 Springgrove Crescent Outremont Montreal PQ H2V 3J1 Canada Office: Office of the Vice Rector 2900 Boulevard Edouard Montpetit Montreal PQ H3C 3J7 Canada

LA ROSSA, JAMES M(ICHAEL), lawyer; b. Bklyn., Dec. 4, 1931; s. James Vincent and Marie Antoinette (Tronolone) La R.; B.S., Fordham U., 1953, J.D., 1958; m. Gayle Marino, Sept. 20, 1958; children—James M., Thomas, Nancy, Susan. Admitted to N.Y. State bar, 1958, U.S. Dist. Ct. bar, 1961, U.S. Supreme Ct. bar, 1969; individual practice law, N.Y.C., 1958-62, 67-74, 76—; asst. U.S. atty. Eastern Dist. N.Y., Bklyn., 1962-65; partner firm Lefkowitz & Brownstien, N.Y.C., 1965-67, La Rossa, Shargel & Fishetti, N.Y.C., 1974-76; participant Debate on Legal Ethics, Criminal Cts. Bar Assn. Queens County (N.Y.), 1978, Criminal Trial Advocacy Workshop, Harvard U. Law Sch., 1978. Served to 1st lt. USMC, 1953-55. Recipient Guardian of Freedom award B'nai B'rith, 1978. Mem. N.Y. State Bar Assn., Fed. Bar Counsel, Assn. Bar City N.Y., Am. Bar Assn. Author: White Collar Crimes: Defense Strategies, 1977; Federal Rules of Evidence in Criminal Matters, 1977; White Collar Crimes, 1978. Office: 522 5th Ave New York NY 10036

LAROUNIS, GEORGE PHILIP, mfg. co. exec.; b. Bklyn., Mar. 19, 1928; s. Philip John and Helen (Cormentelou) L.; B.E.E., U. Mich., 1950; postgrad. in Law U. Mich.; J.D., N.Y. U., 1954; m. Mary G. Efthymiatou, Jan. 13, 1958; 1 dau., Daphne H. Electronics engr. in research and devel. Columbia U. Electronics Research Lab., 1952-54; asso. firm Pennie, Edmonds, Morton, Barrows & Taylor, N.Y.C., 1954-58; fgn. patent atty. Western Electric Co., N.Y.C., 1958-60; asst. dir. Bendix Internat., Paris, 1960, dir. licensing and indsl. property rights, to 1974; v.p. staff ops. Bendix Europe, 1974-77; v.p. Europe, Bendix Internat., Paris, also dir. European affiliates; v.p. Bendix Internat. Fin. Corp., Bendix Internat. Cons. Corp.; dir. Société Anonyme D.B.A., France, Digue, France, Renix, France, Bendiberica, Spain, Benditalia, Italy, B.W. Ltd., U.K., Bendix Ltd. U.K. Served with U.S. Army, 1946-47. Recipient Spl. Distinguished Achievement award Bendix Internat. Mem. N.Y., Fed. Patent bar assns., Licensing Execs. Soc., Internat. C. of C., Tau Beta Pi, Eta Kappa Nu. Clubs: Racing de France, Polo de Paris. Home: 9 Blvd du Chateau Neuilly-sur-Seine 92200 France Office: 44 Rue Francois Ier Paris 75008 France

LARRABEE, CARROLL BURTON, former publisher; b. Coudersport, Pa., June 21, 1896; s. Leon E Eugene and Louise (Berfield) L.; student Peddie Sch., 1913-14, Brown U., 1914-17, 19-20, Univ. Coll., London, Eng., 1919; m. Kathryn White, May 25, 1921; children—Donna Louise Rigali, Elizabeth Ann Nelson. Reporter, Bradford Daily Era, 1920; editorial writer Printers' Ink Pub. Co., Inc., 1920-23, asso. editor, 1923-33, mng. editor, 1932-42, dir., 1941-55, pres., 1942-44, pres., pub., 1944-54, chmn. bd., 1954-55; dir. publs. Applied Jours., Am. Chem. Soc., 1955-62, ret. Dir. Mag. Pubs. Assn., 1942-55. Pres. Peddie Alumni Assn., 1927-28; dir. Nat. Com. for Edn. Alcoholism, 1948-50; bd. dirs. Delta Upsilon, 1927-47, editor quar. 1926-47. Served as pvt. Battery A, 103d F.A., U.S. Army, 1918-20; with AEF. Decorated Purple Heart; recipient medal for spl. service to journalism U. Mo., 1953; Golden Fifty award Alpha Delta Sigma, 1963. Mem. Advt. Club N.Y.C. Author: (with R.B. Franken) Packages that Sell, 1928; How to Package for Profit, 1935; (with H.W. Marks) Tested Selling of Ideas, 1936, Check List of Advertising, Selling and Merchandising Essentials, 1937; Tested Display Ideas, 1938; (with E.B. Weiss) How to Sell Through Wholesalers, 1937. Editor: (with E.B. Weiss, F.C. Kendall) Handbook of Advertising, 1938. Home: 7708 Killebrew Dr Annandale VA 22003

LARRABEE, DONALD RICHARD, publishing co. exec.; b. Portland, Maine, Aug. 8, 1923; s. Henry Carpenter and Marion (Clapp) L.; student Syracuse U., 1941-43; m. Mary Elizabeth Rolfs, Oct. 9, 1948; children—Donna Louise, Robert Rolfs. Reporter, Portland Press Herald, 1941-43, Syracuse Post Standard, 1943; reporter Griffin-Larrabee News Bur., Washington, 1946-54, mng. editor, 1954-67, bur. chief, 1967-69, owner, 1969-78; dir. Washington office State of Maine, 1978—; dir. Nat. Press Bldg. Corp., 1973—. Bd. dirs. Nat. Press Found., 1978—. Served with USAAF, 1943-45. Mem. Me. Soc. Washington (pres. 1950-53), Corrs. for Congl. Press Galleries (standing com. 1959-60), White House Corrs. Assn. Conglist. (moderator 1962). Clubs: Gridiron, National Press (sec. 1953-54, treas. 1966-67, chmn. bd. 1969, pres. 1973) (Washington). Home: 4704 Jamestown Rd Washington DC 20016 Office: Room 5 National Press Bldg Washington DC 20045

LARRABEE, ERIC, writer, educator; b. Melrose, Mass., Mar. 6, 1922; s. Harold Atkins and Doris (Kennard) L.; A.B. cum laude, Harvard, 1943; LL.D., Keuka Coll., 1961; m. Eleanor Barrows Doermann, Apr. 4, 1944. Asso. editor Harper's mag., 1946-58; exec. editor Am. Heritage, 1958-61, mng. editor, 1961-62; mng. editor, Horizon, 1962-63; editorial cons. Doubleday & Co., N.Y.C., 1963-69; provost arts and letters State U. N.Y. Buffalo, 1967-70, prof., 1967-72; exec. dir. N.Y. State Council on Arts, N.Y.C., 1970-75; pres. Nat. Research Center Arts, N.Y.C., 1976-78. Mem. N.Y. Council for Humanities, 1976—. Served to 1st lt. AUS, World War II. Decorated Bronze Star medal; recipient Gold medal of honor Nat. Arts Club, 1971. Mem. Am. Council Learned Socs. (mem.-at-large 1955-59), Phi Beta Kappa (hon.). Author: The Self-Conscious Society, 1960; The Benevolent and Necessary Institution, 1971. Editor: American Panorama, 1957; (with Rolf Meyersohn) Mass Leisure, 1958; Museums and Education, 1968. Co-editor (with Robert E. Spiller) American Perspectives, 1961. Contbr. articles nat. mags. Home: 448 W 20th St New York NY 10011 also 118 Summit Ave Buffalo NY 14214

LARRABEE, MARTIN GLOVER, educator; b. Boston, Jan. 25, 1910; s. Ralph Clinton and Ada Perkins (Miller) L.; B.A., Harvard, 1932; Ph.D., U. Pa., 1937; M.D. (hon.), U. Lausanne (Switzerland), 1974; m. Sylvia Kimball, Sept. 10, 1932 (div. 1944); 1 son, Benjamin Larrabee Scherer; m. 2d, Barbara Belcher, Mar. 25, 1944; 1 son, David Belcher Larrabee. Research asst., fellow U. Pa., Phila., 1934-40, asso. to asso. prof., 1941-49; asst. prof. physiology Cornell U. Med. Coll., N.Y.C., 1940-41; asso. prof. Johns Hopkins, Balt., 1949-63, prof. biophysics, 1963—. Mem. Am. Physiol. Soc., Biophys. Soc., Am. Soc. Neurochemistry, Internat. Neurochem. Soc., Nat. Acad. Scis., Soc. for Neurosci. (treas. 1970-75), Physiol. Soc. (asso., Eng.), Phi Beta Kappa. Clubs: Appalachian Mountain, Sierra, Mountain of Md. Contbr. articles to scientific jours. Research on circulatory, respiratory and nervous systems of animals, especially on synaptic and metabolic mechanisms in sympathetic ganglia, 1934—; wartime research on oxygen lack, decompression sickness, nerve injury, infrared viewing devices, 1941-45. Home: 4227 Long Green Rd Glen Arm MD 21057 Office: Biophysics Dept Johns Hopkins Univ Baltimore MD 21218

LARROW, ROBERT WILLIAM, justice Supreme Ct. Vt.; b. Vergennes, Vt., Apr. 27, 1916; s. William Edward and Melissa (Young) L.; A.B., Holy Cross Coll., 1936; LL.B., Harvard U., 1939; m. Marion E. Leonard, May 21, 1940; children—Anne Larrow Newman, Mary Larrow Bernardina, Barbara Larrow Walsh, Joan Larrow Finnegan, Judith Larrow Leroux, William, Robert William, John. Admitted to Vt. bar, 1939; mem. firm McNamara and Larrow, Burlington, Vt., 1940-66; corp. counsel City of Burlington, 1944-63; chmn. Vt. Liquor Control Bd., 1963-66; judge Superior Ct. Vt., Burlington, 1966-74; asso. justice Vt. Supreme Ct., Mdntpelier, 1974—; mem. Vt. Ho. of Reps., 1949-51. Del. Democratic Nat. Conv., 1952, 60. Mem. Vt., Chittenden County (Vt.) bar assns., Am. Judicature Soc. Roman Catholic. Club: Ethan Allen (Burlington). Home: 85 Crescent Rd Burlington VT 05401 Office: Vt Supreme Ct Montpelier VT 05602

LARROWE, CHARLES PATRICK, economist; b. Portland, Oreg., May 1, 1916; s. Albertus and Helen (Maginnis) L.; B.A., U. Wash., Seattle, 1946, M.A., 1948, Ph.D., Yale U., 1952; 1 son, Peter. Asst. instr. econs. U. Wash., 1946-49, Yale U., 1949-52; asso. prof. U. Utah, 1952-56; mem. faculty Mich. State U., East Lansing, 1956—, prof. econs., 1961—, faculty grievance ofcl., 1976—; cons. to govt. Served with Am. Field Service, 1942-43, AUS, 1943-45. Decorated Silver Star, Purple Heart with oak leaf cluster, Combat Infantryman's badge; grantee Rabinowitz Found., 1962. Democrat. Mem. ACLU, NAACP. Author: Shape-Up and Hiring Hall, 1955; Harry Bridges, 2d edit., 1977. Home: 537 Gunson St East Lansing MI 48823 Office: Dept Econs Mich State Univ East Lansing MI 48824

LARRY, R. HEATH, corp. exec.; b. Huntingdon, Pa., Feb. 24, 1914; s. Ralph E. and Mabel (Heath) L.; A.B., Grove City Coll., 1934, LL.D., 1964; J.D., U. Pitts., 1937; m. Eleanor Ketler, Sept. 10, 1938; children—David Heath, Dennis Ketler, Thomas Richard. Admitted to Pa. bar, 1937; pvt. practice, 1937-38; atty. Nat. Tube Co., 1938-44, sec., dir., 1944-48; gen. atty. U.S. Steel Corp., Pitts., 1948-52, asst. gen. solicitor, 1952-58, adminstrv. v.p. labor relations, 1958-66, adminstrv. v.p., asst. to chmn., 1966, exec. v.p., asst. to chmn., 1966-69, vice chmn. bd., 1969-77; pres. N.A.M., 1977—; dir. Cyclops Corp., Pitts. Nat. Bank, Textron, Inc. Bd. dirs. Bus. Com. for the Arts, Fgn. Policy Assn., Internat. Execs. Service Corps; bd. visitors U. Pitts. Sch. Law; trustee Grove City Coll.; chmn. Nat. YMCA Retirement Fund Bd.; trustee Com. for Econ. Devel., Conf. Bd. Mem. Pa. Soc., Newcomen Soc. N.Am., Internat. C. of C. (trustee U.S. Council), Council Fgn. Relations, Am. Iron and Steel Inst., Pilgrims U.S., Nat. Mfrs. Assn. (dir., regional v.p.). Presbyn. Clubs: Duquesne (Pitts.); Metropolitan (Washington); Union, Economic, (N.Y.C.); Gulf Stream Golf, Delray Beach Yacht. Home: Apt 903 Seagate Towers South 220 MacFarlane Dr Delray Beach FL 33444 Office: 8th Floor 1776 F St Washington DC

LARSEN, ALLAN FRANKLIN, farmer, implement dealer, former state legislator; b. Firth, Idaho, Apr. 4, 1919; s. James Berkeley and Florence (Tingey) L.; student Utah State Agrl. Coll., 1938-39; m. Barbara Grace Elswood, June 24, 1942; children—Stephen, Gary, Stafford, Jeanie, Mark, Richard, Karen. Farmer, nr. Blackfoot, Idaho, pres., stockholder Rocky Mountain Machinery Co., Blackfoot, Idaho; mem. Idaho Ho. of Reps., 1967-78, speaker of ho., 1975-76, 77-78. Republican precinct committeeman, Moreland, Idaho, 1964-65; Rep. candidate for Gov. of Idaho, 1978; pres. Nat. Potato Council, 1968; stake pres. Ch. of Jesus Christ of Latter-day Saints, 1966-78, now regional rep. Mem. Western Farmers Assn. (exec. bd. 1969-75, vice chmn. bd. 1973-74), Potato Growers Idaho (pres. 1966; Hall of Fame award). Home: Route 7 Box 262 Blackfoot ID 83221

LARSEN, ARNOLD, energy co. exec.; b. Lakeview, Mich., July 12, 1917; s. Niels Otto and Julia (Peterson) L.; B.Econs., U. Mich., 1947; m. Maxine Patricia Delaurante, June 23, 1951; children—Jon Lawrence, Gregg Thomas, Mark Andrew, Rande William, Julie Catherine. Office clk. Atlantic Commn. Co., 1936-38; jr. accountant White, Bower & Prevo, C.P.A.'s, 1947-48; intermediate accountant Congdon, O'Hara & Becker (merged with Peat, Marwick, Mitchell & Co. 1952), 1948-52, successively supr., mgr., mgr. area office, 1952-53; v.p. finance, treas., asst. sec., dir. Husky Oil & Refining, Ltd., 1953-61, also its successor co. Canadian Husky Oil, Ltd., 1962-64; sr. v.p. Husky Oil Co., Husky Oil Ltd., 1964-67, exec. v.p., 1967-73, sr. v.p., asst. sec., 1973-75; past v.p. Husky Petroleum Corp.; past sr. v.p. Husky Oil Operations Ltd.; past v.p., dir. No. Natural Gas Co. Ltd., Husky Oil (Alta.), Lloydminster Pipeline Ltd., Husky Pipeline, Ltd., other subsidiaries; past dir. Husky Leasebacks, Ltd., Gate City Steel Corp., Peace Pipe Line Co., Ltd.; past v.p. Husky Oil Exploration, Inc.; past mng. dir. Husky Finance Co. N.V.; past v.p. Alta. Energy Co. Ltd., now sr. corp. advisor; chmn., dir. AEC Power Ltd.; dir. Interprovincial Steel & Pipe Co. Ltd., Steel Alta. Ltd. Served to capt. AUS, 1941-46. C.P.A., Wyo. Mem. Ind. Petroleum Assn. Can. (dir. 1963-67, 72-75), Can. Petroleum Assn. (dir. 1972-75), Wyo. Inst. C.P.A.'s. Methodist. Home: 68 Massey Pl Calgary AB T2V 2G8 Canada Office: 1000 540 5th Ave SW Calgary AB T2P 0M2 Canada

LARSEN, ARTHUR HOFF, educator; b. Boston, Mar. 9, 1907; s. Peter Marinus and Eleonora (Pedersen) L.; B.Ed., U. Wis. Ph.M., U. Wis., 1931, Ph.D., 1939; postgrad. U. Chgo., 1934; m. Faith Elaine Herrick, Aug. 5, 1933; 1 son, Richard Herrick. Prin. state graded sch., Siren, Wis., 1929-30; tchr. math. York Community High Sch., Elmhurst, Ill., 1931-35; mem. faculty Ill. State U., Normal, 1935—, prof. edn., 1935-65, head dept. edn. and psychology, 1945-49, v.p. univ., dean faculty, 1949-65, Distinguished prof. higher edn., 1965-72, prof. emeritus, 1972—. Former pres. bd. Bank of Ill., Normal; mem. adv. council Asso. Orgns. Tchr. Edn., 1961-64, adv. council Degree Granting Instns. in Ill., 1962-76. Mem. Ill. Council on Aging, 1974—. Mem. Nat., Ill. edn. assns., Am. Ednl. Research Assn. Methodist. Home: 608 Normal Ave Normal IL 61761

LARSEN, D. FRANKLIN, banker; b. Toronto, Ont., Can., Aug. 9, 1934; came to U.S. 1953, naturalized, 1958; s. Otto and Doris P. (Clark) L.; grad. degree in comml. banking Stonier Grad. Sch. Banking, Rutgers U., 1970; m. Elizabeth Marie Osborne, Jan. 9, 1959; children—David, James. With Rockland Nat. Bank, New City, N.Y., 1956-66, br. mgr., 1963-64, credit mgr., 1964-66; br. mgr. Garden State Nat. Bank, Paramus, N.J., 1966-71, lending officer, 1971-79, exec. v.p., sr. lending officer, 1976—; instr. Am. Inst. Banking. Mem. Robert Morris Assos. v.p. No. N.J. chpt. 1979-80). Methodist. Home: Monsey NY 10952 Office: 10 Forest Ave Paramus NJ 07652

LARSEN, DON HYRUM, educator; b. Vineyard, Utah, Sept. 22, 1917; s. Hyrum and Ann (Ellis) L.; B.S., Brigham Young U., 1940; M.S., U. Neb., 1942; Ph.D., U. Utah, 1950; m. Ila Mower, Aug. 14, 1941; children—Marilyn (Mrs. LeGrand L. Baker), Lloyd Don, Wayne Hyrum. Chemist, Hercules Powder Co., 1943; microbiologist Comml. Solvents Corp., 1943-46; instr. U. Utah, 1947-50; asst. prof. U. Nebr., 1950-52; mem. faculty Brigham Young U., Provo, Utah, 1952—, prof. microbiology, 1961—, chmn. dept., 1955-60, 64-72; microbiologist U. Calif. Naval Biol. Lab., 1960-61. Mem. Am. Soc. Microbiology (pres. Intermountain br. 1965, Nat. councilor 1958-59), A.A.A.S., Soc. Indsl. Microbiology, Utah Acad. Arts and Scis., Sigma Xi (pres. Beigham Young U. chpt. 1966), Phi Kappa Phi, Phi Lambda Upsilon. Author, patentee in field. Home: 140 E 2000 South St Orem UT 84057 Office: 893 Widtsoe Bldg Brigham Young Univ Provo UT 84601

LARSEN, EDWIN MERRITT, educator, chemist; b. Milw., July 12, 1915; s. Howard Reynolds and Ella (Tees) L.; B.S., U. Wis., 1937; Ph.D., Ohio State U., 1942; m. Kathryn Marie Behm, Aug. 17, 1946; children—Robert, Lynn, Richard. Chemist, Rohm & Haas, Phila., 1937-38; teaching asst. Ohio State U., 1938-42; group leader Manhattan Dist. polonium project Monsanto Chem. Co., 1943-46; mem. faculty dept. chemistry U. Wis.-Madison, 1942-43, 46—, prof., 1958—, asso. chmn. dept., 1977—; vis. prof. U. Fla., 1958; Fulbright lectr. Technische Hochschule, Vienna, Anorganische Institut, 1966-67. Mem. A.A.A.S., Am. Chem. Soc. (chmn. Wis. sect.), Wis. Acad. Scis., Arts and Letters, Sigma Xi (chmn. Wis. chpt.), Phi Lambda Upsilon. Author: Transitional Elements, 1965. Contbr. articles profl. jours. Research on transitional elements, titanium, zirconium, thorium, hafnium. Home: 109 Standish Ct Madison WI 53705

LARSEN, ELMER CONRAD, former paint mfg. co. exec.; b. Owen, Wis., Oct. 23, 1912; s. Emil and Kristine (Braathen) L.; B.A., St. Olaf Coll., 1934; M.S., Mont. Sch. Mines, 1936; D.Tech. Sci. (Exchange fellow), Tech. Hochsch. Stuttgart, Germany, 1938; Ph.D. (Univ. fellow), U. Wis., 1939; m. Nancy Wescott Skinner, May 1960; children—Charles, Sandra, Robert, Henry, Elizabeth. Instr. chemistry Mont. Sch. Mines, 1934-36; research chemist, mem. tech. staff Bell Telephone Labs., Inc., N.Y.C., 1939-45; asst. dir. research J.T. Baker Chem. Co., Phillipsburg, N.J., 1945-49, v.p., tech. dir., dir., 1954-59; chief engr. Tungsten & Chem. div. Sylvania Electric Products, Inc., Towanda, Pa., 1949-54; dir. comml. devel., paint and brush div. PPG Industries, 1959-62, dir. planning, devel., coatings and resins div., 1963-66, v.p., gen. mgr. coatings and resins div., 1966-78; former pres., mng. dir., dir. Italver-Pitts. Paints (Italy); former dir. subsidiaries including Peintures Corona (France), Pinco-Pitts. (Venezuela), Pinturas Pitts. de Mexico (Mexico). Club: P.A.A. Home: 46 Ordale Blvd Pittsburgh PA 15228

LARSEN, ERIK, educator; b. Vienna, Austria, Oct. 10, 1911; s. Richard and Adrienne (Schapringer de Csepreg) L.; came to U.S., 1947, naturalized, 1953; Candidate, Institut Superieur d'Histoire de l'Art et d'Archeologie, Brussels, 1931; Licentiate, Louvain (Belgium) U., 1941; Docteur en Archeologie et Histoire de l'Art, 1959; m. Lucy Roman, Oct. 4, 1932; children—Sigurd-Yves, Annik-Eve. Dir., editor-in-chief on semi-ofcl. cultural mission for Belgian Govt., Pictura, art mag., Brussels, Rio de Janeiro, Brazil, 1946-47; research prof. art Manhattanville Coll. of Sacred Heart, 1947-55; instr. CCNY, 1948-55; lectr, then vis. prof. Georgetown U., 1955-58, asso. prof. fine arts, 1958-63, prof., 1963-67, head dept. fine arts, 1960-67; prof. history of art U. Kans., '67—, dir. Center for Flemish Art and Culture, 1970—; cons. old masters' paintings; mem. Kans. Cultural Arts Commn., 1971-73, Kans. Cultural Arts Adv. Council, 1973-79. Served with Belgian Underground, 1942-45. Decorated knight's cross Order Leopold, knight's cross Order of Crown (Belgium); recipient prix Thorlet, laureate Inst. France, Academie des sciences morales et politiques, 1962; named hon. Ky. col., 1977. Fellow Soc. Antiquaries of Scotland; mem. AAUP, Appraisers Assn. Am., Association des Diplomes en Histoire de l'Art et Archeologie de l'Universite Catholique de Louvain, Academie d'Aix-en Provence (France) (corr.), Academie de Macon (France) (asso.), Academie d'Alsace (France) (corr.), Comite Cultural Argentino (hon.), Schweizerisches Institut fuer Kunstwissenschaft (Zurich, Switzerland), Academia di Belle Arti Pietro Vanucci (Perugia, Italy),(hon.), Royal Soc. Arts (London) (Benjamin Franklin fellow, hon. corr. mem. for Kans.); correspondent-academician Real Academia de Bellas Artes de San Telmo (Malaga, Spain), Real Academia de Bellas Artes de San Jorge (Barcelona, Spain), Accademia Tiberina (Rome). Author books, the most recent being: La Vie, Les Ouvrages et Les Eleves de Van Dyck, 1975; Calvinistic Economy and 17th Century Dutch Art, 1979; contbr. numerous articles, revs. to profl. publs., newspapers. Home: 3103 Trail Rd Lawrence KS 66044 Office: U Kans Kress Found Dept Art History Lawrence KS 66045

LARSEN, HAROLD CECIL, educator; b. Granite, Utah, June 15, 1918; s. John L. and Sarah (Markham) L.; B.Sc., U. Utah, 1941; M.Sc., Cal. Inst. Tech., 1946, Aero. Engr., 1955; m. Ada Caroline Kelly, June 28, 1956; children—John H., Kristin L., Robert G. With Lockheed Aircraft Co., 1941; mem. faculty USAF Inst. Tech., 1949—, prof. aeros., 1957—, head dept., 1957—, dir. Aero. Design Center, 1970—, Hanneman Assos., 1958—. Cons. in field, 1952—. Served with AUS, 1942-45, USAAF, 1945-49. Mem. Am. Inst. Aeros. and Astronautics, Am. Assn. U. Profs., Am. Soc. Engring. Edn., Sigma Xi, Tau Beta Pi. Research design, calibration and test high altitude air sampler, coin aircraft study and design, turbulent mixing of radial flow jets, vortex theory cyclogiro, design inter city cyclogiro transport, application of vortex theory to wind and water flow energy conversion, design cruise missile and airborne launching system for carrier aircraft. Home: 2829 Rugby Rd Dayton OH 45406 Office: Air Force Inst Tech Wright Patterson AFB OH 45433

LARSEN, JACK LENOR, fabric designer; b. Seattle, 1927; student Sch. of Architecture, U. Wash.; M.F.A., Cranbrook Acad. Art, Mich. Founder, dir. Jack Lenor Larsen Inc., 1953; cons. to U.S. State Dept. for grass weaving projects in Taiwan and Vietnam, 1957, 59; designer fabrics for Pan Am. Airlines, 1958; co-founder Larsen Design Studio, 1958; co-dir. fabric design dept. Phila. Coll. Art, 1961-63; designer, dir. traveling exhbn. Fabrics Internat., West Africa, Morocco, Transvaal, 1962; founder Jack Larsen Internat., Zurich, Switzerland, 1963; co-dir. wall hangings exhbn. Mus. Modern Art, N.Y.C., 1968; designer fabrics for 747 Jets, Pan Am. and Braniff Airlines, 1969; designer Visiona IV exhbn., Frankfurt, W. Ger., 1974; artist-in-residence Royal Coll. Art, London, 1975; dir. wall hangings exhbn. Mus. Modern Art, N.Y.C., 1977, now adv; chmn. Haystack Mountain Sch. Crafts; bd. dirs. Pilchuck Glass Center, Seattle;

overseer Parsons Sch. Design; one-man show of fabric design, Portland, Oreg., 1949; group shows include: Mus. of Modern Art, N.Y.C., 1951, 55, Mus. of Fine Arts, Boston, Stedelijk Mus., Amsterdam, Holland, Renwick Mus., Washington, Kunstindustriestmuseum, Copenhagen, Denmark, 1976, Fashion Inst. Tech., N.Y.C., 1978; represented in permanent collections: Mus. Modern Art, N.Y.C., Phoenix Civic Plaza, Sears Bank & Trust Co., Chgo., Royal Coll. Art, London, Khartoum Hilton, Sudanese Republic, others. Recipient numerous awards including: Gold Medal award 13th Milan Triennale, 1964, Gold Medal award AIA, 1968, Pace Setter award House Beautiful, 1973. Fellow Royal Soc. Art, Am. Craft Council, Am. Inst. Interior Designers (hon., Elsie De Wolfe award 1971); mem. Mcpl. Art Soc. Author: (with Azalea Thorpe) Elements of Weaving, 1967; (with Mildred Constantine) Beyond Craft: The Art Fabric, 1972; (with Jeanne Weeks) Fabrics for Interiors, 1975. Address: 41 E 11th St New York NY 10012

LARSEN, JOHN WALTER, banker; b. N.Y.C., Sept. 7, 1914; s. Carl and Ella (Olsen) L.; B.S., N.Y. U., 1939; postgrad. Rutgers U., 1946-48, Columbia U., 1957; m. Eleanor Waterhouse, June 10, 1939; children—John Walter, Nancy Larsen Farrell, Gregory, Melissa. Clk., auditor, asst. sec., treas., asst. v.p. North River Savs. Bank, 1933-49; v.p. Bowery Savs. Bank, N.Y.C., 1949-53, v.p., treas., 1953-59, exec. v.p., treas., 1959-61, pres., 1962-76, vice chmn. bd., 1976-79, trustee, 1962—; dir. United Jersey Banks, Diebold Computer Leasing, Inc. Pres. Citizens Budget Commn., N.Y.C., 1974—; bd. dirs. Fifth Ave. Assn., Realty Found. N.Y.; trustee Nat. Jewish Hosp. at Denver, Mus. City N.Y., Inner-City Scholarship Fund; mem. Region II exec. com. Boy Scouts Am. Recipient Silver Beaver, Silver Antelope, Good Scout awards Boy Scouts Am., Dean John T. Madden award N.Y. U., 1964, Meritorious Service award N.Y. U. Alumni, 1965, Nat. Jewish Hosp. at Denver award, 1973, Interfaith Achievement award, 1974, N.Y. U. Urban Leadership award, 1977; C.P.A., N.Y. State. Mem. Savs. Banks Assn. N.Y. State, Phi Alpha Kappa. Presbyterian. Clubs: Union League; Arcola Country; N.Y. U. Home: 362 Crest Rd Ridgewood NJ 07450 Office: 110 E 42d St New York NY 10017

LARSEN, JONATHAN ZERBE, journalist; b. N.Y.C., Jan. 6, 1940; s. Roy Edward and Margaret (Zerbe) L.; B.A., Harvard, 1961; M.A.T., 1963; m. Katharine Wilder, May 28, 1966. Contbg. editor Time mag., N.Y.C., 1965-66, corr., Chgo., 1966-68, Los Angeles, 1968-70, bur. chief, Saigon, Vietnam, 1970-71, asso. editor, 1972-73; editor New Times mag., N.Y.C., 1974-79; Nieman fellow Harvard U., 1979-80. Trustee Lehrman Inst., N.Y.C. Club: Harvard. Home: 439 E 51st St New York NY 10022

LARSEN, JOSEPH REUBEN, educator; b. Ogden, Utah, May 27, 1927; s. Joseph Reuben and Anna Charlotte (Anderson) L.; B.S., U. Utah, 1950, M.S., 1952; Sc.D., Johns Hopkins, 1958; m. Shauna Stewart, Dec. 15, 1948; children—Pamela Larsen McClure, Deborah Larsen Swensen, Jennifer. Asst. prof. entomology U. Wyo., 1962-63; asst. prof. entomology U. Ill., Urbana, 1963-65, asso. prof., 1965-67, prof., 1967-69, head dept. entomology, 1969-75, dir. Sch. Life Scis., 1975—. Invited participant symposiums XVI Internat. Congress Zoology, 1963, Functional Orgn. of Compound Eye in Sweden, 1965, Entomol. Soc. Am., 1973. Served with M.C., AUS, 1944-47. Mem. Entomol. Soc. Am., Am. Physiol. Soc., Am. Soc. Zoologists, Electron Microscope Soc. Am., Sigma Xi. Mem. Ch. of Jesus Christ of Latter-day Saints (stake pres.). Author: A Laboratory Manual in Biology, 1979; (with others) Bionomics and Embryology of Aedes vexans, 1973. Home: 3913 Clubhouse Dr Champaign IL 61820 Office: U Ill 387 Morrill Hall Urbana IL 61801. *Aristotle stated many years ago that "the search for truth is in one way hard and in another easy. For it is evident that no one can master it fully nor miss it wholly. But each adds a little to our knowledge of nature and from all the facts assembled there arises a certain grandeur." This statement has been a guiding philosophy in my pursuit of knowledge and understanding.*

LARSEN, LOUIS ROYTER, electronics co. exec.; b. Phila., July 4, 1916; s. Lauritz and Anna (Royter) L.; B.S. in Econs., U. Pa., 1949, M.B.A., 1956; m. Eugenia Riddell Jacobs, Oct. 20, 1944; children—Louis Royter, Eric Risor, Peter Christian, Geoffrey Stang. Instr., U. Pa., 1949-51; with Sprague Electric Co., North Adams, Mass., 1951—, controller, 1967—. Served with USAAF, 1942-45. Mem. Nat. Assn. Accountants. Home: Valley Rd Wellfleet MA 02667 Office: 87 Marshall St North Adams MA 01247

LARSEN, LYLE VERNON, ret. engring. research co. exec.; b. Corvallis, Oreg., Aug. 8, 1921; s. Walter Winfred and Nellie Lyle (Gellatly) L.; B.C.E., Oreg. State U., 1943; m. Viola Grace Hoefer, July 7, 1943; children—Linda Louise, Diane Wynne, Lee Alan. With Chgo. Bridge & Iron Co., 1943—, design engr., Eureka, Calif., 1943-46, Chgo., 1946-57, sales engr., N.Y.C., 1957-61, project mgr., Oak Brook, Ill., 1961-63, engring. mgr., 1963-65, Rijswijk, Netherlands, 1965-67, mgr. patents and licenses, Oak Brook, 1967-72, mgr. research, Plainfield, Ill., 1972-74, dir. research, 1974-77. Mem. ASCE. Republican. Presbyterian. Patentee in field. Home: 2545 Pine St North Bend OR 97459

LARSEN, OTTO NYHOLM, educator; b. Tyler, Minn., Jan. 23, 1922; s. Lars Christian and Sigrid Marie (Knudsen) L.; student Grand View Coll., 1940-42, U. Oreg., 1942-43; B.A., U. Wash., 1947, Ph.D., 1955; m. Greta Lillian Petersen, Sept. 5, 1947; children—Paul N., Lork K., Chris N., John A.N. Instr., U. Wash., Seattle, 1951-54, asst. prof., 1954-57, asso. prof. sociology, 1958-62, prof., 1962—, dir. sociol. research, 1961-67, chmn. dept. sociology, 1971-72; Fulbright prof. U. Copenhagen (Denmark), 1959-60; vis. prof. San Diego State U., 1955, U. Colo., 1967, U. Hawaii, 1969. Commr. U.S. Commn. on Obscenity and Pornography, 1968-70. Bd. dirs. Social Sci. Research Council, 1976—, chmn. bd., 1978-79; bd. govs. Nat. Enquiry into Scholarly Communication, 1977-79. Served with USAAF, 1943-46. Mem. Pacific (pres. 1968-69), Am. (exec. officer 1972-75) sociol. assns., Alpha Kappa Delta (pres. united chpts. 1970-72). Editor: Violence and the Mass Media, 1968. Author: (with M. deFleur) The Flow of Information, 1958; (with G. Lundberg, C. Schrag and W. Catton) Sociology, 4th edit., 1968; (with W. Catton) Conceptual Sociology, 1971; co-editor: (with J. Demerath and K. Schuessler) Sociology and Social Policy, 1975; (with L. Coser) The Uses of Controversy in Sociology, 1976. Contbr. articles to profl. publs. Home: 5407 Ravenna Ave NE Seattle WA 98105 Office: Dept Sociology Univ Wash Seattle WA 98195

LARSEN, R. BRUCE, newspaper editor; b. Grandview, Man., Can., June 19, 1927; s. Lewis Joseph and Stella Marie (White) L.; student U. Man.; m. Jennifer Hurst, Mar. 1, 1969; children by previous marriage—Tim, Eric, Karen. Reporter, Winnipeg Tribune, 1946-50, Vancouver News-Herald, 1950-51; reporter, then city editor Vancouver Province, 1951-59; city editor, then asst. mng. editor Vancouver Sun, 1959-74, mng. editor, 1974—; bd. dirs. Can. Mng. Editors Conf. Mem. B.C. Racing Commn., 1970-75. Recipient Can. Nat. Newspaper award, 1956; named B.C. Harness Horse Breeder of Year, 1970. Mem. AP Mng. Editors. Mem. United Ch. Can. Club: Richmond Winter. Office: 2250 Granville St Vancouver BC Canada

LARSEN, ROLF, justice Supreme Ct. Pa.; b. Pitts., Aug. 26, 1934; s. Thorbjorn Ruud and Mildred (Young) L.; ed. Pa. State U., U. Pitts., Duquesne U. Sch. Philosophy, U. Santa Clara; LL.B., Dickinson Sch. Law, 1960. Admitted to Pa. bar, 1960; judge Pa. Ct. Common Please, 5th Jud. Dist., Civil Div., 1974-77; justice Pa. Supreme Ct., 1978—. Served with U.S. Army, 1954-56. Office: 707 City-County Bldg Pittsburgh PA 15219*

LARSEN, ROY EDWARD, ret. publisher; b. Boston, Apr. 20, 1899; s. Robert and Stella (Belyea) L.; grad. Boston Latin Sch., 1917; A.B., Harvard, 1921, LL.D., 1953, Marietta (O.) Coll., 1946, Bucknell (Pa.) U., 1950, N.Y. U., 1952, Dartmouth, 1954; L.H.D., Bard Coll., 1951, Kalamazoo Coll., 1951; m. Margaret Zerbe, June 20, 1927; children—Anne (Mrs. Drew Simonson), Robert, Christopher, Jonathan. With Time Mag., from 1922, circulation mgr., 1922-27; pres. Time Inc., 1939-60, vice chmn. bd., 1961-79, ret., 1979. Chmn. bd. Time, Inc. Organizer, chmn. Nat. Citizens Commn. for Pub. Schs., 1959-66; mem. Pres.'s Com. for White House Conf. on Edn. and Conf. on Edn. Beyond High Sch. Bd. dirs. United Hosp. Fund N.Y.; chmn. bd. Fund for Advancement Edn., 1955-67; trustee Ford Found., 1957-69, N.Y. Pub. Library, N.Y.C.; bd. overseers Harvard, 1940-46, 53-59; vice chmn., chmn. arts com. U.S. Adv. Commn. on Internat. Ednl. and Cultural Affairs, 1963-69; gov. Nature Conservancy. Chmn. bd. Nantucket Conservation Found. Clubs: Harvard, Century, River, University, Links (N.Y.C.); Lyford Cay. Home: 4900 Congress St Fairfield CT 06430 Office: Time and Life Bldg Rockefeller Center New York City NY 10020

LARSEN, SUSAN CAROL, art historian; b. Chgo., Oct. 3, 1946; d. Ingvald and Esther Martha (Lang) L.; B.A. in Art History, Northwestern U., 1968, M.A. (grad. fellow), 1972, Ph.D., 1975. Asst. prof. Sch. Fine Arts, U. So. Calif., 1975—; Los Angeles corr. Art News mag.; art cons. Environ. Communications, Inc.; curator exhbns. contemporary art, cons. in field. Mem. Internat. Assn. Critics Art, Coll. Art Assn., Los Angeles Inst. Contemporary Art, Am. Studies Assn. Contbr. articles to profl. jours. Office: Sch Fine Arts Watt Hall Univ So Calif Los Angeles CA 90007

LARSEN, WESLEY BERNARD, osteopathic surgeon; b. Aurora, Ill., Sept. 5, 1908; s. Thomas Ludwig and Amalie (Anjou) L.; student Northwestern U., 1927-30, Chgo. Coll. Osteopathy, 1945; m. Lila Caroline Anderson, June 2, 1936; 1 dau., Linda Sue. Intern, Chgo. Osteo. Hosp., 1945-46, mem. staff, 1946-78, hon. staff, 1978—; pvt. practice, Chgo., 1946—, Hinsdale, Ill., 1957—; asst. prof. dept. practice Chgo. Coll. Osteopathy, 1947-55, trustee coll., 1954-57. Pres. Am. Osteo. Found., 1960-65; vice chmn. corp. Nat. Osteo. Found., 1962-65, bd. dirs., 1963-65, 74—, mem. corp., 1976—; v.p. A.T. Still Osteo. Found. and Research Inst., 1962-65; mem. Pres. Johnson's White House Conf. on Health, 1966; pres. Ill. Inter-Profl. Council 1973-74, 3d v.p., 1975-76, 2d v.p., 1976-77. Recipient Specialty certificate Am. Coll. Gen. Practice; named hon. chieftain Acoma Indian Tribe Okla., 1966; hon. citizen of Tex. Gov. John Connally, 1966, Corpus Christi Mayor McIver Furman, 1966; ambassador goodwill Mayor Kenneth A. Schmied of Louisville, 1966. Diplomate Am. Osteo. Bd. Gen. Practice. Fellow Am. Coll. Gen. Practice in Osteopathic Medicine and Surgery (pres. Ill. chpt. 1974—, mem. congress dels. 1975); mem. Internat. Acad. Preventive Medicine (hon. citation, trustee), Am. (exec. com. 1959—, cons. conf. com. 1964-65, chmn. div. pub. and profl. service, mem. exec. com. 1957-58, chmn. com. pension trust 1957-58, chmn. com. ethics 1958-62, chmn. dept. pub. affairs 1962-64, chmn. publs. com. 1960- 62, chmn. com. coordination 1963-64, chmn. dept. bus. affairs 1964-65, 1st v.p. 1959-62, trustee 1962-65, pres. 1965-66, cons.-adviser to aux.), Ill. (pres. 1955-57, trustee, past dist. pres.) osteo. assns., Ill. Assn. Osteo. Physicians and Surgeons (hon. life), Am. Acad. Osteopathy (bd. govs., chmn. coll. assistance com. 1968-71), Nat., Ill. assns. parliamentarians. Club: Atlas. Mason (32 deg., Shriner). Columnist Osteo. Annals. Home: 935 S Bodin St Hinsdale IL 60521 Office: 34 S Vine St Suite 2 Hinsdale IL 60521

LARSH, HOWARD WILLIAM, educator; b. East St. Louis, Ill., May 20, 1914; s. John Edgar and Margaret (Kays) L.; B.A., McKendree Coll., 1936; student mycology Washington U., St. Louis, 1936-37; M.S., U. Ill. at Urbana, 1938, Ph.D., 1941; postgrad med. mycology Duke, also U. N.C., summer, 1946; m. Georgia Lee Thomson, Sept. 4, 1938; 1 son, Jonathan Thomson. Mem. faculty U. Okla., 1941—, prof. med. mycology, 1948—, research prof., 1962—, chmn. dept. botany and microbiology, 1966-76; cons. in field, 1950—; dir. labs. Mo. State Chest Hosp., 1977—; mem. Lunar Quarantine Operations Team; research reviewer immunology and infectious diseases com. VA Hosp., Oklahoma City, 1972. Diplomate Am. Bd. Med. Microbiology, Am. Bds. Bioanalysis; recipient Rhoda Benham award Am. Soc. for Microbiology, 1977. Fellow AAAS, Am. Pub. Health Assn., Okla. Acad. Sci., Am. Acad. Microbiology; mem. Bot. Soc. Am., Soc. Am. Bacteriologists, Am. Soc. Tropical Medicine and Hygiene, Soc. Exptl. Biology and Medicine, Internat. Soc. Human and Animal Mycology (editor in chief Jour.); Reticuloendothelial Soc., Med. Mycology Soc. Ams. (pres. 1973-74), Sigma Xi, Phi Sigma, Lambda Tau. Author articles in field. Home: 611 Broad Ln Norman OK 73069 Office: Botany Microbiology Univ Okla 770 Van Vleet Oval Norman OK 73019

LARSH, JOHN EDGAR, JR., educator; b. East St. Louis, Ill., Oct. 3, 1917; s. John Edgar and Margaret (Kays) L.; student McKendree Coll., 1935-37; A.B., U. Ill., 1939, M.S., 1940; student U. Mich. Biol. Sta., summer 1939-40; Sc.D., Johns Hopkins Sch. Hygiene and Pub. Health, 1943; m. Ruth Ella Neal, Aug. 12, 1939; children—Robert Neal, John Charles, Margaret Jane. Instr. parasitology U. N.C. Sch. Pub. Health and Sch. Medicine, Chapel Hill, 1943-44, asst. prof., 1944-45, asso. prof., 1945-47, prof., 1947—, head dept., 1945—, asst. dean Sch. Pub. Health, 1964-70, asso. dean, 1971-76; asso. parasitology Duke U. Sch. Medicine, 1944-55, asso. prof., 1956-58, prof., 1959—; mem. Am. Bd. Med. Microbiology, 1973—; cons. parasitology Dominican Republic, summers 1949-52, Peru, 1956, Bur. State Services, HEW, 1964-66, Bur. Health, Manpower, 1966-68; mem. tropical medicine and parasitology study sect. NIH, 1969-73, chmn., 1971-73; pres. Internat. Commn. Trichinellosis, 1972-76; exec. dir. 3d Internat. Conf. Trichinellosis, Miami Beach, Fla., 1972—. Diplomate Am. Bd. Microbiology. Fellow A.A.A.S., Am. Pub. Health Assn.; mem. Am. Soc. Tropical Medicine and Hygiene (pres. 1965-66), Royal Soc. Tropical Medicine and Hygiene, Belgian Soc. Tropical Medicine (fgn. corr.), Am. Soc. Parasitologists, Am. Inst. Biol. Scis., Am. Acad. Microbiology, Sigma Xi. Conglist. Author: Outline of Medical Parasitology, 1964. Editorial bd. Jour. Parasitology, 1966—. Home: Route 5 Chapel Hill NC 27514 Office: Sch Pub Health (201H) Chapel Hill NC 27514

LARSON, ALLAN LOUIS, polit. scientist, educator; b. Chetek, Wis., Mar. 31, 1932; s. Leonard Andrew and Mabel (Marek) L.; B.A. magna cum laude, U. Wis., Eau Claire, 1954; Ph.D., Northwestern U., 1964. Instr., Evanston Twp. (Ill.) High Sch., 1958-61; asst. prof. polit. sci. U. Wis., 1963-64; asst. prof. Loyola U., Chgo., 1964-68, asso. prof., 1968-74, prof., 1974—; Norman Wait Harris fellow in polit. sci. Northwestern U., 1954-56. Mem. Am. Polit. Sci. Assn., AAAS, Am. Acad. Polit. and Social Sci., Acad. Polit. Sci., Midwest Polit. Sci. Assn., AAUP, Kappa Delta Pi, Pi Sigma Alpha, Phi Sigma Epsilon. Roman Catholic. Author: Comparative Political Analysis, 1980; (with others) Progress and the Crisis of Man, 1976; contbr. articles to profl. jours. Home: 2015 Orrington Ave Evanston IL 60201 Office: Damen Hall Room 915 6525 N Sheridan Rd Chicago IL 60626. *My personal and professional life has been based on the principle that man does not live by bread alone. Values and ideals are not illusions or delusions. The very survival of mankind may depend on our constructing a culture rooted in altruism and the most sublime ideals of conduct. The solution to current problems will not be found in a retreat from the Judeo-Christian tradition. Material power not enlightened by wisdom and love is a curse. Higher goals and values give our society purpose and direction.*

LARSON, CARL MARTIN, educator; b. Council Bluffs, Iowa, Feb. 11, 1916; s. Carl Emil and Anna Fredrickson L.; B.S., U. Ill., Urbana, 1939; M.B.A., Northwestern U., 1950; m. Mary Jane Jacobson, Mar. 7, 1942; 1 dau., Deborah Rae Larson Poat. Asst. instr. U. Ill., 1946-49, instr., 1949-62, asst. prof., 1962-66, asso. prof. Chgo. campus, 1966-70, prof. mktg., 1970—; cons. in field; dir. Paddock Publs. Inc., Arlington Heights, Ill.; mem. Nat. Council for Small Bus. Mgmt. Devel., nat. steering com. Small Bus. Inst., 1975-77. Served with U.S. Army, 1941-46. Decorated Bronze Star. Mem. Am., So. mktg. assns., Nat. Assn. Mgmt. Educators (v.p. research 1976), Alpha Kappa Psi, Beta Gamma Sigma. Lutheran. Author: (with James Engel and Wayne Tolarzyk) Cases in Promotional Strategy, 1971; (with Robert Weigand and John Wright) Basic Retailing, 1976; Student Guide to Basic Retailing, 1976; contbr. articles to profl. jours. Home: 8 N Donald St Arlington Heights IL 60004 Office: U Ill Chgo Circle Campus Box 4348 Chicago IL 60680. *The joy of success can best be achieved by placing one's trust in God and secondly one's own talents. Dedication to the completion of any task is a must, and perseverance is a trait to cultivate. It helps to have a sense of humor, humility, faith, and a friendly attitude. Perhaps the most important ingredient for achieving success is love of a wife and friends.*

LARSON, CARL THEODORE, architect, educator; b. Kansas City, Mo., Jan. 6, 1903; s. Peter and Bengta (Swenson) L.; A.B. magna cum laude, Harvard, 1925, M.Arch., 1929, Nelson Robinson Traveling fellowship, 1929-30; m. Marjorie W. MacNaught, Apr. 24, 1930 (dec. Dec. 1963); children—Ronal W., Dana W.; m. 2d, Myra Ann Gulick, July 2, 1970. Asso. editor Archtl. Record, 1930-36; research cons. F.W. Dodge Corp., N.Y.C., 1937; architect, project planner U.S. Housing Authority, 1938; tech. editor Archtl. Forum, 1939-42, 48; field rep. adminstrator's office Nat. Housing Agy., 1942-43; tech. cons. mil. affairs sub-com. U.S. Senate, 1944-45; asst. tech. dir. Nat. Housing Agy, 1946; tech. dir. Gen. Homes, Inc., Columbus, Ohio, 1947; prof. architecture U. Mich., 1948-73, prof. emeritus, 1973—, coordinator archtl. research lab., 1948-73; pvt. practice research and planning cons., 1973—; dir. research project facilities early childhood devel. Ednl. Facilities Labs., Inc., 1969-72; sr. cons. social econs. UN Tech. Assistance Adminstrn. regional housing centre, Indonesia, 1956; archtl. cons. ICA, Ethiopia and Tunisia, 1960; cons. archtl. research USPHS, 1965. Mem. bldg. research adv. bd. Nat. Acad. Scis.-NRC, 1966-68, Fed. Constrn. Council, 1967-68. Fellow A.I.A.; mem. Am. Soc. Info. Sci., World Future Soc., Soc. for Internat. Devel., Bldg. Research Inst., Phi Beta Kappa. Author: (with K. Lonberg-Holm) Planning for Productivity, 1940, Plan Europe 2000: Role of Mass Media of Information and Communication, 1972; Development Index, 1953; (with S.C.A. Paraskevopoulos and K. Lonberg-Holm) Environmental Analysis, vol. 3 in School Environment Research series, also dir. series project; also articles. Home: 3575 E Huron River Dr Ann Arbor MI 48104

LARSON, CHARLES FRED, assn. exec.; b. Gary, Ind., Nov. 27, 1936; s. Charles F. and Margaret J. (Taylor) L.; B.S.M.E., Purdue U., 1958; M.B.A. summa cum laude, Fairleigh Dickinson U., 1973; m. Joan Ruth Grupe, Aug. 22, 1959; children—Gregory Paul, Laura Ann. Project engr. Combustion Engring., Inc., East Chicago, Ind., 1958-60; sec. Welding Research Council, N.Y.C., 1960-70, asst. dir., 1970-75, editor bulls. and Welding Research Abroad, 1960-76; exec. dir. Indsl. Research Inst., Inc., N.Y.C., 1975—, sec. I.R.I. Research Corp. Mem. Wyckoff (N.J.) Bd. Edn., 1973-78, pres., 1976-77; reader In Touch Networks, Inc., N.Y.C., 1979—. Served with U.S. Army, 1959. Registered profl. engr., N.J. Mem. AAAS, Am. Soc. Assn. Execs., ASME, Assn. Research Dirs., Council Engring. and Sci. Soc. Execs., Soc. Research Adminstrs. Republican. Methodist. Clubs: High Mountain Golf, 60 East, Masons. Asso. editor Jour. Pressure Vessel Tech., 1973-75. Office: 100 Park Ave Suite 2209 New York NY 10017

LARSON, CHARLES PHILIP, pathologist; b. Eleva, Wis., Aug. 15, 1910; s. Clarence P. and Louise (Steig) L.; B.A., Gonzaga U., 1931; M.D., C.M., McGill U., 1936; postgrad. neuropathology U. Mich., 1939; m. Margaret I. Kobervig, Dec. 10, 1944; children—C. Phillip, Lillian L., Charles P., Christine, Elizabeth, Paul, Lawrence. Intern, Pierce County Hosp., Tacoma, 1936-37; instr. U. Oreg. Med. Sch., 1939-41; pathologist, dir. labs. Tacoma Gen. Hosp., Tacoma Med. Labs., others, 1946—; sr. partner Drs. Larson, Wicks, Elder & Apa; asso. clin. prof. pathology U. Wash.; criminologist, med.-legal crime investigator, lectr. crime detection; sr. partner Lakewood Clin. Lab.; dir. Tacoma Police Lab. Vis. prof. forensic pathology U. Tex., 1960; dir. Nat. Careers Com. for Med. Tech.; trustee Pierce County Blood Bank. Served as lt. col. AUS, 1942-45. Diplomate Am. Bd. Pathology, Am. Bd. Legal Medicine. Fellow Am. Soc. Clin. Pathologists (dir. 1966, chmn. forensic pathology council), Am. Psychiat. Assn., Internat. Assn. Identification, Am. Acad. Forensic Scis.; mem. Nat. Assn. Med. Examiners (pres. 1972), Internat. Soc. Clin. Pathology (v.p.), AMA, Coll. Am. Pathologists (pres.), Am. Cancer Soc. (pres. Wash. div.), Nat. Mental Assn., N. Pacific Soc. Neurology and Psychiatry, Pacific N.W. Soc. Pathologists, Wash. Soc. Pathologists, Pierce County Med. Soc. (pres. 1967), Wash. Med. Assn. (v.p. 1967), McGill Grads. Soc. (past pres.), Nat. (pres. 1962), World (pres. 1963) boxing assns. Elk, Rotarian. Author: Manual of Neuropathology, 1940. Contbr. articles to profl. jours. Home: 2018 N 30th St Tacoma WA 98403 Office: 1211 S 12th St Tacoma WA 98405

LARSON, CLARENCE EDWARD, former govt. ofcl., energy cons.; b. Cloquet, Minn., Sept. 20, 1909; s. Louis and Caroline (Ullman) L.; B.S., U. Minn., 1932; Ph.D., U. Calif., 1936; 1 son, Robert Edward; m. 2d, Jane R. Warren, Apr. 20, 1957; children—Ernest Lawrence, Lance Stafford. Nat. Tb Assn. fellow, research asso. Mt. Zion Resarch Lab., 1936-37; prof. chemistry Coll. of Pacific, 1937-40, chmn. chemistry dept., 1940-42; civilian staff OSRD, 1942; chief analytical sect. radiation lab. U. Calif., 1942-43; asst. supt. Tenn. Eastman Corp., Oak Ridge, 1943-46; dir. research and devel. electromagnetic plant Carbide & Carbon Chem. Corp., 1946-48, plant supt., 1948-50; became dir. Oak Ridge Nat. Lab., 1950, now mem. adv. com. for chemistry; v.p. research Nat. Carbon Co. div. Union Carbide and Carbon Corp., 1955-59; asso. mgr. research Union Carbide Corp., 1959-61; v.p. Union Carbide Nuclear Co., also gen. mgr. Oak Ridge ops., 1961-65, pres. Union Carbide nuclear div., 1965-69; commr. AEC, 1969-74; energy cons., 1974—; dir. Oak Ridge Inst. Nuclear Studies, 1961-69; chmn. Nat. Battery Adv. Com., 1976—; ofcl. del. U.S. del. Internat. Conf. Peaceful Uses Atomic Energy, Geneva, Switzerland, 1955; mem. U.S.-USSR Joint Commn. on Sci. and Tech. Cooperation. Fellow Am. Nuclear Soc.; mem. Am. Chem. Soc., AAAS, Soc. Exptl. Biology and Medicine, Nat. Acad. Engring., Sci. Research Soc. Am., Inc. (charter), Sigma Xi, Phi Lambda Epsilon, Tau Beta Pi. Clubs: Rotary (pres. Oak Ridge 1953); Cosmos (Washington). Contbr. to sci. periodicals. Home: 6514 Bradley Blvd Bethesda MD 20034 Office: 1911 N Ft Myer Dr Suite 402 Arlington VA

LARSON, CURTIS LUVERNE, educator, cons.; b. Cottonwood, Minn., Oct. 10, 1920; B. Agrl. Engring., U. Minn., 1943, M.S. in Civil Engring., 1949; Ph.D. in Civil Engring., Stanford, 1965; m. Miriam R. Johnson, July 3, 1944; children—Mark C., Reed W., Jean M. Engring. trainee Allis-Chalmers Mfg. Co., Milw., 1944; research fellow civil engring. U. Minn., 1946-48, from instr. to prof. agrl. engring., 1948—; on leave teaching, research Colombian Inst. Agr. (S.Am.), 1972-73. Served with USNR, 1944-46. Mem. Am. Soc. Agrl. Engrs., Soil Conservation Soc. Am., Am. Geophys. Union, Am. Water Resources Assn., Sigma Xi, Gamma Sigma Delta. Contbr. articles to profl. jours. Home: 1885 Tatum St St Paul MN 55113 Office: U Minn Dept Agrl Engring St Paul MN 55108

LARSON, DOYLE EUGENE, air force officer; b. Madelia, Minn., Oct. 2, 1930; s. Edgar Louis and Gyneth Mae (Weldy) L.; B.A., Hardin-Simmons U., 1962; M.S. in Polit. Sci., Auburn U., 1971; postgrad. Armed Forces Staff Coll., 1965, Air War Coll., 1971; m. Lois James, May 29, 1953; children—James, Nancy, Mary, Mark. Enlisted U.S. Air Force, 1951, commd. 2d lt., 1953, advanced through grades to maj. gen., 1977; sr. military rep. Nat. Security Agy., Pentagon, 1971-72; asst. for joint matters, asst. chief of staff intelligence Air Staff, 1972-73, dir. policy and resource mgmt., 1973-74; dir. intelligence Hdqrs. Pacific Command, Camp H.M. Smith, Hawaii, 1974-77; dep. chief of staff for intelligence Hdqrs. SAC, 1977-79; comdr. Electronic Security Command, San Antonio, Tex., 1979—. Mem. San Antonio Community Council. Decorated D.S.M., Legion of Merit with 2 oak leaf clusters, Air medal with 3 oak leaf clusters. Mem. Air Force Assn. Presbyterian. Home: 9 2d St Madelia MN 56062 Office: HQ ESC/CC Kelly AFB San Antonio TX 78243

LARSON, EARL RICHARD, judge; b. Mpls., Dec. 18, 1911; s. Axel R. and Hannah (Johnson) L.; B.A., U. Minn., 1933, LL.B., 1935; m. Cecill Frances Carlgren, Dec. 30, 1939; children—Jane, Earl R. Admitted to Minn. bar, 1935; U.S. dist. judge Minn., Mpls., 1961—. Served to lt. (s.g.) USNR, 1943-46. Home: 2036 Kenwood Pkwy Minneapolis MN 55405 Office: US Court House Minneapolis MN 55401

LARSON, ERIC GUSTAV, publishing co. exec.; b. Detroit, Dec. 30, 1924; s. Carl Johann and Serafia Wicturia (Peterson) L.; B.S., U. Pa., 1950; m. Ann Warnock, Aug. 27, 1955; children—Karen, Andrew. With mktg. dept. Armstrong Cork Co., Lancaster, Pa., 1950-53; with TV Guide mag., Radnor, Pa., 1954—, advt. dir., 1963—. Served with AUS, 1944-46. Bd. dirs. Publishers Info. Bur. Club: Detroit Athletic. Home: 317 Echo Valley Ln Newtown Square PA 19073 Office: TV Guide Radnor PA 19088

LARSON, FRANK CLARK, educator; b. Columbus, Neb., Jan. 17, 1920; s. Albin Victor and Wilhelmina (Herold) L.; B.A., Neb. State Coll., 1941; M.D., U. Neb., 1944; m. June Adele Herling, June 12, 1948 (div. Dec. 1969); children—Karen Lee Larson Dewitt, Alan Clark, Donn Christopher; m. 2d, Myrna Irene Traver, Dec. 18, 1970. Intern, Detroit Receiving Hosp., 1944-45; resident U. Neb. Hosp., 1947, Univ. Hosps., Madison, Wis., 1947-50; practice medicine specializing in internal medicine, Madison, 1951—; asst. chief medicine and Tb service VA Hosp., Madison, 1951-56; mem. faculty U. Wis. Med. Sch.-Madison, 1951—, prof. medicine, 1963—; dir. clin. labs. U. Wis. Hosps., dir. Sch. Med. Tech., 1958—. Served with AUS, 1945-47. Diplomate Am. Bd. Internal Medicine. Fellow A.C.P.; mem. Central Soc. Clin. Research, Endocrine Soc., A.M.A., Acad. Clin. Lab. Physicians and Scientists, Am. Soc. Clin. Pathologists, Wis. Soc. Pathologists, Sigma Xi, Alpha Omega Alpha. Research metabolism thyroid hormone. Home: 2621 Marshall Pkwy Madison WI 53713

LARSON, GODFREY EDWARD, former govt. ofcl.; b. St. Paul, July 14, 1920; s. Peter Edward and Wilhelmina (Issel) L.; student Miss. State Coll., 1943, U. Pa., 1949-52; m. Elizabeth B. Glauner, Jan. 9, 1942; children—Susan (Mrs. Sydney R. Robertson), Nancy (Mrs. David E. Warner), Terrence, Cheryl, Kristin (Mrs. Gabriel D. Chikes). Student, clk., 1938-42; chief clk. M.-K.-T. Ry., 1946-47; personal campaign asst., 1947-48; asst. to pres. U. Pa., 1948-53; asst. to dir. FOA, 1953-55; asst. to spl. asst. to Pres. (disarmament), 1955-58, spl. asst. sec. Dept. Interior, 1958-61; chief contracts, adminstrn. and budget Office of Coal Research, Dept. Interior, Washington, 1961-74, acting asst. dir. contracting, 1974-75; dep. dir. procurement ops. ERDA, Washington, 1975-77; asso. dir. Office of Procurement Ops., U.S. Dept. Energy, 1977-79; ret., 1979; energy distbn. and procurement cons., 1979—; adv. to U.S. del. to UN subcom. on disarmament, 1956-57. Served from pvt. to 1st lt. AUS, 1942-46. Mem. Am. Legion, Soc. for Pub. Adminstrn., Nat. Contract Mgmt. Assn. Presbyn. Home and office: 14412 Brookmead Dr Germantown MD 20767

LARSON, HAROLD VERNON, communications co. exec.; b. Strong, N.D., May 7, 1918; s. Arthur O. and Anna (Stenberg) L.; B.S., U. Ore., 1946; student econs. U. Uppsala (Sweden), 1946-47, internat. affairs George Washington U., 1963-65; m. Signe Marie Eklund, July 20, 1946; children—Harold Vernon, Jennifer Signe, Jon Eric, Christina Marie. Flying cadet, 1940; commd. 2d lt. USAAF, 1941, advanced through grades to brig. gen. USAF, 1966; bomber pilot, squadron operations officer, Guadalcanal, World War II; assigned 1st Air Force, Mitchel Field, N.Y., 1944-45, operations div. Hdqrs. USAF, 1947, Mil. Assistance Adv. Group, Oslo, Norway, 1950-52, Hdqrs. USAF, 1952-55, Air Force ROTC, 1955-58, Army War Coll., 1958-59, Hdqrs. Pacific Command, 1959-62, Joint Chiefs Staff, 1962-65; dir. mil. assistance and sales Hdqrs. USAF, 1966-70, ret. 1970; mgr. internat. mil. marketing, aircraft div. Hughes Tool Co., Washington, 1970-71; dir. mil. assistance and sales Internat. Security Affairs office sec. def., Washington, 1971-72; dep. dir. Def. Security Assistance Agy., Washington, 1972-73; mgr. internat. mil. mktg. Rockwell Internat., 1973—. Active local Boy Scouts Am. Decorated Legion of Merit, Air medal with oak leaf cluster. Mem. Air Force Assn., Air Force Hist. Found., Delta Tau Delta. Lutheran. Home: 3711 N Oakland St Arlington VA 22207

LARSON, HENRIETTA MELIA, educator, author; b. Ostrander, Minn., Sept. 24, 1894; d. Hans Olaf and Karen Maria (Norgaarden) Larson; B.A., St. Olaf Coll., 1918, Litt.D., 1943; postgrad. U. Minn., 1922-24; Ph.D., Columbia, 1926; M.A. (hon.), Harvard, 1960. Instr., So. Ill. U., 1926-28; with Harvard Grad. Sch. Bus. Adminstrn., 1928—, successively, research asso., asst. prof., 1938-42, asso. prof., 1942-59, prof., 1960-61, prof. emerita, 1961—. Trustee Bus. History Found., 1947—; cons. Ford Found., Indian Inst. Mgmt., Ahmedabad, 1966. Mem. Am., Norwegian-Am., Econ. (v.p.) hist. assns., Econ. History Soc., Am. Assn. U. Women, Phi Beta Kappa. Lutheran. Author: Farmer and the Wheat Market, 1926; Jay Cooke, Private Banker, 1936; (with N.S.B. Gras) Casebook in American Business History, 1939; Guide to Business History, 1948; (with K.W. Porter) History of Humble Oil and Refining Company, 1959; (with E.H. Knowlton and C.S. Popple) History of Standard Oil Company (New Jersey), vol. 3, 1971. Editor, Harvard Studies in Bus. History, 1950-64. Home: 1110 W 1st St Northfield MN 55057

LARSON, JERRY L., state supreme ct. justice; b. Harlan, Iowa, May 17, 1936; s. Gerald L. and Mary Eleanor (Patterson) L.; B.A., State U. Iowa, 1958, J.D., 1960; m. Linda R. Logan; children—Rebecca, Jeffrey, Susan, David. Admitted to Iowa bar; partner firm Larson & Larson, 1961-75; dist. judge 4th Jud. Dist. Ct. of Iowa, 1975-78; justice Iowa Supreme Ct., 1978—; county atty. Shelby County (Iowa), 1965-69. Mem. Iowa State Bar Assn., Iowa Judges Assn., Am. Judicature Soc. Office: State House Des Moines IA 50319

LARSON, JESS, lawyer; b. Mill Creek, Indian Terr., June 22, 1904; s. Leonard and Bessie (Downard) L.; student U. Okla., 1922-26, 33, Emerson Coll. Oratory, Boston, 1926-27; LL.D., Duquesne U., 1950; m. Germaine Moreau, Dec. 25, 1929 (dec. May 1964); m. 2d, Mrs. Zdenka Sokitch, Apr. 18, 1967. Rancher, engaged in dairy bus., Okla., 1927-28; mayor, Chickasha, Okla., 1929-33; admitted to Okla. bar, 1935, D.C. bar, 1955, also U.S. Supreme Ct.; practice in Oklahoma City, 1934-35, 39-40, Washington, 1954—; exec. dir. Okla. Sch. Land Commn., 1935-39; asst. gen. counsel War Assets Adminstrn., 1946, gen. counsel, 1946-47, asso. adminstr., 1947, adminstr., 1947-49; adminstr. Fed. Works Agy., 1949, Gen. Services Adminstrn., 1949-53, adminstr. Def. Materials Procurement Agy., 1951-53; partner firm Alvord & Alvord, Washington, 1965—. Chmn. bd. Nat. Patent Devel. Corp., N.Y.C., 1959—. Entered Okla. N.G. as pvt., 1923, commd. 2d lt., 1923, advanced through grades to col., 1944; served in Mediterranean, Italian theatres, 1942-43; dir. tactics F.A. Sch., Ft. Sill, Okla., 1944-45; assigned War Dept. Gen. Staff, 1945; transferred to USAF Res., 1952, now maj. gen., ret. Decorated Legion of Merit, Purple Heart. Mem. Am., Okla. bar assns., Bar Assn, D.C., Air Force Assn. (pres. 1964-67), Delta Tau Delta. Mason (32 deg.). Clubs: Metropolitan (Washington and N.Y.C.); Army and Navy (Washington). Home: 2925 43d St NW Washington DC 20016 Office: World Center Bldg Washington DC 20006. *For whatever success I might have achieved in my life, I would attribute it basically to the following facts: (1) I have been blessed with a great family which has endowed me with love, respect, and confidence. (2) I have had the good fortune to have been a part of a family which was in itself an economic unit, living on the edge of the frontier, close to the earth, and from which experience I developed a basic and, I believe, a sound sense of spiritual, human, and economic values.*

LARSON, JOHN DAVID, life ins. co. exec.; b. Madison, Wis., July 6, 1941; s. Lawrence John and Anna Mathilde (Furseth) L.; B.B.A., U. Wis., 1964, J.D., 1965, M.B.A., 1966; m. Evelyn Vie Smith, Jan. 22, 1966; children—Eric John, Karen Annette. Admitted to Wis. bar, 1965, U.S. Ct. Mil. Appeals bar, 1966; with Nat. Guardian Life Ins. Co., Madison, 1969—, exec. v.p., treas., 1973, pres., 1974—, dir., 1974—; dir. 1st Wis. Nat. Bank, Madison. Chmn. Madison chpt. ARC, 1974-75; pres. United Way Dane County, 1975. Served with U.S. Army, 1966-69. Recipient Know Your Madisonian award Wis. State Jour., 1973; C.P.A., Wis. Mem. Am. Bar Assn., State Bar Wis., So. Chpt. Wis. Inst. C.P.A.'s, Am. Soc. C.L.U.'s, Madison C. of C. (dir. 1976—). Lutheran. Clubs: Maple Bluff (dir. 1974—), Rotary. Home: 401 New Castle Way Madison WI 53704 Office: PO Box 1191 Madison WI 53701

LARSON, JOHN WILLIAM, lawyer; b. Detroit, June 24, 1935; s. William and Sara Eleanor (Yeatman) L.; B.A. with distinction, honors in Economics, Stanford, 1957, LL.B., 1962; m. Pamela Jane Wren, Sept. 16, 1959; 1 dau., Jennifer Wren. Admitted to Calif. bar, 1962; asso. firm Brobeck, Phleger & Harrison, San Francisco, 1962-68, partner, 1968-71, 73—; asst. sec. Dept. Interior, Washington, 1971-73; exec. dir. Natural Resources Com., Washington, 1973; counsellor to chmn. Cost of Living Council, Washington, 1973. Dir. Measurex Corp. Mem. faculty Practising Law Inst. Mem. U.S.-USSR Joint Com. on Environment; mem. bd. visitors Stanford Law Sch., 1974-77; trustee Katharine Branson Sch./Mt. Tamalpais Sch. Served with AUS, 1957-59. Mem. Am., Calif. bar assns., Order of Coif. Clubs: Pacific Union, Burlingame (San Francisco); University, Chevy Chase (Washington). Home: PO Box 349 Ross CA 94957 Office: One Market Plaza San Francisco CA 94105

LARSON, KERMIT DEAN, educator; b. Algona, Iowa, Apr. 7, 1939; s. Loren L. and Hansena Laurena (Andersen) L.; A.A., Ft. Dodge Jr. Coll., 1960; B.B.A., U. Iowa, 1962, M.B.A., 1963; D.B.A., U. Colo., 1966; m. Nancy Lynne Weber, June 17, 1961; children—Julie Renee, Timothy Dean, Cynthia Lynne. Mem. faculty U. Tex., Austin, 1966—, Arthur Andersen & Co. Alumni prof., 1975—, chmn. dept. accounting, 1971-75. Vis. asso. prof. Tulane U., New Orleans, 1970-71; cons. sales tax audit litigation, pvt. anti-trust litigation, expropriation ins. arbitration. C.P.A., Tex. Mem. Am. Acctg. Assn. (v.p. 1978-79), Am. Finance Assn., Am. Inst. C.P.A.'s, Am. Inst. Decision Scis., Tex. Soc. C.P.A.'s, Beta Gamma Sigma, Beta Alpha Psi. Baptist. Author: (with C.H. Griffin and T.H. Williams) Advanced Accounting, 3d edit., 1977; (with W.W. Pyle and J.A. White) Fundamental Accounting Principles, 8th edit., 1978. Contbr. articles to profl. jours. Home: 1310 Falcon Ledge Austin TX 78746 Office: Dept Accounting U Tex Austin TX 78712

LARSON, MARTIN ALFRED, author, lectr.; b. Whitehall, Mich., Mar. 2, 1897; s. Alfred and Augusta (Lindblad) L.; student Parsons Bus. Coll., 1916; A.B., Kalamazoo Coll., 1920; M.A. (fellow), U. Mich., 1921, Ph.D., 1923; m. Lillian Davis, Aug. 9, 1922 (div. June 1932); children—John Alfred, David William; m. 2d, Emma Bruder, June 19, 1951. Mem. faculty Mich. Eastern U., 1923-25, U. Ida., 1925-27; owner, mgr. Larson Paint Co., Detroit, 1935-50; pres. Martin A. Larson Co., 1946-60; lectr., writer various mags. and periodicals, 1925—. Operator, Detroit Open Forum, 1935-48; pres. Detroit Taxpayers Assn., 1942-49; lectr., spl. researcher Liberty Lobby, United, 1964-75; research cons., spl. researcher Americans United, 1967—. Recipient Religious Liberty citation Americans United, 1970. Mem. Phoenix Philos. Soc., Am. Humanist Assn., Soc. Religious Humanism, Pi Kappa Delta. Unitarian. Author: Milton and Servetus, 1926; The Modernity of Milton, 1927; The Plaster Saint, 1953; The Religion of the Occident, 1959; Wanton Sinner, 1962; Church Wealth and Business Income, 1965; Tax-Exempt Property in Key American Cities, 1965; The Essene Heritage, 1967; The Great Tax Fraud, 1968; (with C. Stanley Lowell) The Churches: Their Riches, Revenues, and Immunities, 1969; Praise the Lord for Tax Exemption, 1969; When Parochial Schools Close, 1972; Tax-Revolt: U.S.A., 1973; Tax-Rebellion: U.S.A., 1974; The Federal Reserve and Our Manipulated Dollar, 1975; The Religious Empire, 1975; How to Defend Yourself Against the IRS, 1976; The Story of Christian Origins, 1977; The Essence of Jefferson, 1978; How To Save Money on Your Taxes This Year, 1978; How to Establish a Trust and Reduce Taxation, 1978; The Continuing Tax Rebellion, 1979; The Essene-Christian Faith, 1979; The Middle Class and the IRS, 1980. Home: 4108 E Stanford Dr Phoenix AZ 85018. *Even as a boy, I dreamed of the day when I might devote my life to research and the writing of books which might have social value, even if they did not provide any substantial economic benefit to myself. In 1950, at the age of 53, I was at last in a position to do this, and have since constantly pursued my ideal. I have now published 22 books of which more than 300,000 copies are in print; I have written extensively for various publications; and in all this I feel that my life has achieved a certain degree of significant fulfillment. The good life must consist of something more than the mere earning of money or satisfying of material needs.*

LARSON, MAURICE ALLEN, chem. engr., educator; b. Missouri Valley, Iowa, July 19, 1927; s. Albert Juluis and Grace Elizabeth (Chambers) L.; B.S., Iowa State U., 1951, Ph.D., 1958; m. Ruth Elizabeth Gugeler, Dec. 5, 1953; children—Richard Alan (dec.), Janet Ann, John Albert. Chem. engr. Dow Corning Corp., Midland, Mich., 1951-54; teaching asst. Iowa State U., 1954-55, instr. dept. chem. engring., 1955-58, asst. prof., 1958-61, asso. prof., 1961-64, prof., 1964—, Anson Marston Disting. prof., 1977—, chmn. dept. chem. engring., 1978—; cons. fertilizer tech. and crystallization, 1960—; cons. AID, Kharagpur, India, 1968; Shell vis. prof. Univ. Coll., London, 1971-72; sci. exchange visitor, Czechoslovakia and Poland, 1974. Served with U.S. Army, 1946-47. Recipient H.A. Webber Teaching award Iowa State U., 1967, Western Electric Fund award Am. Soc. Engring. Edn. 1970, Faculty citation Iowa State U. Alumni, 1972; NSF fellow, 1965-66. Mem. Am. Inst. Chem. Engrs. (pres. Iowa 1970-71), Am. Chem. Soc. (chmn. div. fertilizer and soil chemistry 1975), Am. Soc. Engring. Edn., Sigma Xi, Tau Beta Pi, Phi Lambda Upsilon. Democrat. Methodist. Club: Lions (pres. Ames 1979-80). Author: (with A.D. Randolph) Theory of Particulate Processes, 1971; contbr. articles to profl. jours. Home: 2710 Thompson Dr Ames IA 50010

LARSON, MILTON B., educator; b. Portland, Ore., July 3, 1927; s. Oscar Gilbert and Martha (Opedal) L.; B.S. in Mech. Engring., Ore. State U., 1950, M.S. in Physics, 1955; M. Engring., Yale, 1951; Ph.D., Stanford, 1961; m. Wilma Eloise Lawrence, Sept. 9, 1950; children—Steven Leroy, Gregory Lawrence, Arnold William, Linda Louise. Design engr. J. Donald Kroeker, Portland, Ore., 1950; research engr. Boeing Airplane Co., Seattle, 1951-52; from instr. to asso. prof. Ore. State U., Corvallis, 1952-64, prof. mech. engring., 1969—; dean Sch. Engring. U. N.D., 1964-68. Ford Found. resident plastics dept. DuPont, Parkersburg, W.Va., 1968-69; summer indsl. positions, 1953-63; cons. to govt. Served in AUS, 1945-46. Recipient Lloyd Carter award outstanding and inspirational teaching Ore. State U., 1956; NSF sci. faculty fellow, 1957-59. Mem. Am. Soc. Engring. Edn., Am. Soc. M.E.'s, Tau Beta Pi, Pi Tau Sigma, Sigma Tau. Republican. Lutheran. Address: 206 N W 30 Corvallis OR 97330

LARSON, NETTABELL GIRARD, lawyer; b. Riverton, Wyo.; d. George and Arranetta (Bell) Girard; student Idaho State U., 1957-58; B.S., U. Wyo., 1959, LL.B., 1961; m. Dean M. Larson, Dec. 30, 1970. Admitted to Wyo. bar, 1961, U.S. Supreme Ct. bar, 1969, D.C. bar, 1969; practiced in Riverton, 1963-69; atty.-adviser on gen. counsel's staff Dept. Housing and Urban Devel., assigned Office Interstate Land Sales Registration, Washington, 1969-70, sect. chief interstate land sales Office Gen. Counsel, 1970-73; partner firm Larson & Larson, Riverton, 1973—. Guest lectr. at high schs.; condr. seminar on law for layman Riverton br. A.A.U.W., 1965; condr. course on women and law; lectr. equal rights, job discrimination, land use planning. Chmn. fund drive Wind River chpt. A.R.C., 1965; chmn. Citizens Com. for Better Hosp. Improvement. 1965; chmn. sub-com. on polit., legal rights and responsibilities Gov.'s Commn. on Status Women, 1965-69, adv. mem. 1973—, rep. Nat. Conf. Govs. Commn., Washington, 1966; local chmn. Law Day, 1966, 67; mem. state bd. Wyo. Girl Scouts U.S.A., sec., 1974-76, mem. nat. bd., 1978—; state vol. adviser Nat. Found., March of Dimes, 1967-69; legal counsel Wyo. Women's Conf., 1977. Recipient Spl. Achievement award HUD, 1972; Distinguished Leadership award Girl Scouts U.S.A., 1973. Mem. Wyo., Fremont County, D.C. bar assns., Women's Bar Assn. for D.C., Internat. Fedn. Women Lawyers, Am. Judicature Soc., Am. Trial Lawyers Assn., Nat. Assn. Women Lawyers (del. Wyo., nat. sec. 1969-70, v.p. 1970-71, pres. 1972-73), AAUW (br. pres.), Wyo. Fedn. Womens Clubs (state editor, pres. elect 1968-69, treas. 1974-76), Kappa Delta, Delta Kappa Gamma (hon. mem. state chpt.). Clubs: Riverton Chautauqua (pres. 1965-67). Editor: Wyoming Clubwoman, 1966-68; bd. editors Wyo. Law Jour., 1959-61. Writer Obiter Dictum column Women Lawyers Jour.; also articles in legal jours. Home: 224 W Sunset St PO Box 687 Riverton WY 82501 Office: 513 E Main St Riverton WY 82501. *I believe first and foremost in the freedom of the individual—the right of the individual to be different, to be unique, and to pursue his or her particular heart's desire so long as that pursuit does not endanger the life or freedom of another. Perhaps because as a woman lawyer in predominately a man's profession, I have experienced the bitterness and dissolutionment of discrimination, I have actively worked through the equal rights movement toward the realization of individual freedom for all people. I support equality, not in the sense of "sameness," but in the realization of greater opportunities for individual development and differentiation.*

LARSON, OLIVER C., assn. exec.; b. Portland, Oreg., Nov. 6, 1919; s. Andrew G. and Hannah L. L.; student Reed Coll., 1940-41; B.A. in Journalism, U. Oreg., 1948; m. Vivian Maxine Westerlund, Jan. 8, 1949; children—Signe Ann, Bruce Warner, Sara Beth. Mgr., Lebanon (Oreg.) C. of C., 1949-51, Springfield (Oreg.) C. of C., 1951-54; indsl. mgr. Tacoma (Wash.) C. of C., 1962-65; indsl. mgr. Portland (Oreg.) C. of C., 1962-65, exec. v.p., 1965—, pub. Portland mag. Served with inf. U.S. Army, 1941-45. Democrat. Methodist. Home: 7725 SE 19th Ave Portland OR 97202 Office: 824 SW 5th Ave Portland OR 97204

LARSON, PAUL FRANK, neurologist, univ. adminstr.; b. Washington, Aug. 23, 1934; s. John David and Catherine (Jones) L.; student Wheaton Coll., 1952-55; M.D., George Washington U., 1959; m. Lillian Ruth Bateman, Sept. 18, 1961; children—Donald, Catherine, Andrea, Craig. Instr. in neurology La. State U. Sch. Medicine, New Orleans, 1967-68, asso. prof. neurology and physiology, 1972-77, prof., 1977—, asso. dean student affairs and records, 1975-77, acting dean Sch. Medicine, 1977-78, dean, 1978—. Served as capt. M.C., U.S. Army, 1962-64. Recipient Neurology award AMA; Muscular Dystrophy Assn. Am., George Meany fellow, 1968-72. Home: 55 Grand Canyon New Orleans LA 70114 Office: 1542 Tulane Ave New Orleans LA 70112

LARSON, ROBERT EDWARD, engring. research and cons. co. exec.; b. Stockton, Calif., Sept. 19, 1938; s. Clarence Edward and Gertrude Ellen (Ruben) L.; S.B., Mass. Inst. Tech., 1960; M.S., Stanford U., 1961, Ph.D., 1964; m. Susan Louise Rollefson, June 20, 1964; children—Carrie Ellen, Lucinda Louise, Robert Erik. Engr., IBM Corp., Poughkeepsie, N.Y., 1956-59; mem. tech. staff Hughes Aircraft Co., Culver City, Calif., 1960-62; research engr. Stanford Research Inst., Menlo Park, Calif., 1964-68; sr. research engr. Wolf Mgmt. Services, Palo Alto, Calif., 1968-69; v.p. Systems Control, Inc., Palo Alto, 1969-72, exec. v.p., 1972—. Precinct worker Republican Party, 1964, 66, 68, 72. Recipient Donald P. Eckman award Am. Automatic Control Council, 1968, Outstanding Elec. Engr. citation Eta Kappa Nu, 1969; Registered profl. engr., Calif. Fellow IEEE (asso. editor Trans. on Automatic Control 1967-72, v.p. Control Systems Soc. 1973-74, pres. soc. 1975-76, dir. inst. 1978-79, mem. long-range planning com. 1977-79, mem. audit com. 1978-79, chmn. com. 1979—, U.S. activities bd. ops. com. 1979—, nominations and appointments com. 1979—); mem. AAAS, Sigma Xi, Delta Tau Delta, Tau Beta Pi, Eta Kappa Nu. Author: State Increment Dynamic Programming, 1968; Principles and Problems of Dynamic Programming, 1973; Principles of Dynamic Programming, Par I, 1978; contbr. numerous articles on control theory and its applications to profl. jours. Home: 26515 Anacapa Dr Los Altos Hills CA 94022 Office: 1801 Page Mill Rd Palo Alto CA 94304

LARSON, ROY, journalist; b. Moline, Ill., July 27, 1929; s. Roy W. and Jane (Beali) L.; A.B., Augustana Coll., Rock Island, Ill., 1951; M.Div., Garratt Theol. Sem., 1955; m. Dorothy Jennisch, June 7,

1950; children—Mark, Bruce, Jodie, Bradley. Ordained to ministry Methodist Ch., 1956; minister Covenant United Meth. Ch., Evanston, Ill., 1963-68, First United Meth. Ch., Elmhurst, Ill., 1968-69; religion editor Chgo. Sun-Times, 1969—. Home: 9410 Lincolnwood Evanston IL 60203 Office: 401 N Wabash Chicago IL 60611

LARSON, RUBY ILA, cytogeneticist; b. Hatfield, Sask., Can., May 30, 1914; d. Albert and Esther Naomi (Lofgren) L.; B.A., U. Sask., 1943, M.A., 1945; Ph.D., U. Mo., 1952; D.Sc. (hon.), U. Lethbridge, 1977. Cytogeneticist cereal div. Dominion Exptl. Sta., Swift Current, Alta., Can., 1945-48, Agr. Can.-Sci. Service Labs., Lethbridge, Alta., 1948-59, Research Sta., Lethbridge, 1959—. Named Woman of Year Lethbridge YWCA, 1975. Fellow Agrl. Inst. Can.; mem. Genetics Soc. Can. (life mem.), Alta. Inst. Agrology, Entomol. Soc. Alta., Agronomy Soc. Can. Contbr. articles on the cytogenetics of insect, disease resistance and nitrogen fixation in wheat to profl. jours. Office: Research Station Lethbridge AB T1J 4B1 Canada

LARSON, TAFT ALFRED, state legislator, ret. educator; b. Wakefield, Nebr., Jan. 18, 1910; s. Fred and Jennie (Larson) L.; A.B., U. Colo., 1932, A.M., 1933; postgrad. U. Chgo., 1934-35, U. London (Eng.), 1937-38; Ph.D., U. Ill., 1937; m. Aylein Eckles Hunt, June 11, 1941 (div. Nov. 1947); 1 adopted dau., Nancy Jo; m. 2d, Mary Adrienne Hawkins, Aug. 20, 1949; 1 dau., Mary Lou. Mem. faculty U. Wyo., Laramie, 1936-75, prof., head history dept., 1948-68, William R. Coe Distinguished prof. Am. studies, 1968-75, emeritus, 1975—, dir. Sch. Am. Studies, 1959-68. Vis. prof. history Columbia, 1950-51; mem. U.S. nat. commn. for UNESCO, 1963-66. Mem. Wyo. Ho. Reps., 1977—. Recipient G.D. Humphrey Distinguished faculty award U. Wyo., 1966. Served to lt. USNR, 1943-46. Mem. Western (pres. 1970-71), Am. (mem. council Pacific Coast br. 1951, 57-59, 66-69) hist. assns., Orgn. Am. Historians (exec. com. 1961-64), Wyo. Hist. Soc. (pres. 1957- 58), Phi Beta Kappa, Delta Sigma Phi. Democrat. Rotarian. Author: Wyoming's War Years, 1941-45, 1954; History of Wyoming, 1965, rev. edit., 1978; Wyoming: A Bicentennial History, 1977. Editor: Bill Nye's Western Humor, 1968. Bd. editors Pacific Hist. Rev., 1953-55, 69-72. Contbr. articles Medieval English and Western Am. history to profl. jours. Home: 810 Clark St Laramie WY 82070

LARSON, THOMAS BRYAN, educator, former govt. ofcl.; b. Kansas City, Mo., Nov. 16, 1914; s. Gustave Leonard and Mary (Thomas) L.; A.B., U. Neb., 1937; M.A., U. Chgo., 1938; Ph.D., Columbia, 1971; m. Helen Ruth Sapir, June 21, 1942; children—John Daniel, Karen (Mrs. Orkin). Instr. polit. sci. Northeastern U., Boston, 1939-41, Amherst Coll., 1941-42, Williams Coll., 1942-43; with Dept. of State, 1947-66, dep. chief Div. Research for USSR, 1955-57, chief, 1957-58; first sec. Am. embassy, Paris, France, 1959-62; chmn. dept. polit. affairs Nat. War Coll., 1963-64; spl. studies group Bur. Intelligence Research, Dept. State, 1964-66; lectr., sr. fellow Columbia Russian Inst., 1966-68; lectr. Johns Hopkins, 1958-59, George Washington U., 1964-66; vis. prof. U. Kan., 1972; SAIS, Johns Hopkins, 1973-74. Served as 1st lt. AUS, 1943-46. Mem. Am. Polit. Sci. Assn., Phi Beta Kappa. Author: Disarmament and Soviet Policy, 1964-68, 1969. Co-editor Soviet Politics since Khrushchev, 1968; Soviet-American Rivalry, 1978. Home: 8613 Seven Locks Rd Bethesda MD 20034

LARSON, THURSTON ERIC, state ofcl., educator; b. Chgo., Mar. 3, 1910; s. Gustav W. and Selma (Bergstrom) L.; B.S. in Chem. Engring., U. Ill., 1932, Ph.D. in San. Chemistry, 1937; m. Veda E. Taylor, Nov. 24, 1938; children—Byron G., Bruce T. With Ill. Water Survey, 1932-77, head chemistry sect., 1950-77, asst. chief, 1956-77, ret., 1977, prin. scientist emeritus; prof. san. engring. U. Ill., Urbana, 1961—; mem. Am. Water Works Assn., 1937—, bd. dirs., 1961-67, v.p., 1968-69, pres., 1970-71, trustee research found., 1967-69, recipient Outstanding Service medal Am. Water Works Assn., 1966, research award, 1972, hon. mem., 1974; diplomate Am. Acad. Environ. Engring. Mem. Am. Chem. Soc. (councillor 1948-55, 57-76, pollution control award), AAAS, Nat. Assn. Corrosion Engrs., Water Pollution Control Fedn., Internat. Assn. Water Pollution Research, Nat. Acad. Engring., Internat. Water Supply Assn. Co-inventor steam purity analyzer. Home: 706 LaSell Dr Champaign IL 61820 Office: 605 E Springfield St Champaign IL 61820

LARSON, WARD JEROME, bank exec., lawyer; b. Mpls., Mar. 3, 1924; s. Philip Jerome and Inez (Sandstrom) L.; B.A., N. Central Coll., Naperville, Ill., 1948; LL.B., Harvard, 1951; m. Phyllis Jean Lindahl, June 18, 1949; children—Eric, Peter, David, Barbara. Admitted to Ill. bar, 1951; atty. First Nat. Bank Chgo., 1951-56; asst. trust officer, v.p. DuPage Trust Co., Glen Ellyn, Ill., 1956-62; with Fed. Res. Bank Chgo., 1962—, v.p., gen. counsel, sec., 1968, sr. v.p., gen. counsel, sec., 1970—. Chmn. ins. com. Fed. Res. Banks, 1968—; mem. adminstrv. bd. Fed. Res. Employee Benefits System, 1970-74, vice chmn., 1973-74. Mem. bd. edn. sch. dist. 41, Glen Ellyn, Ill., 1961-67, pres., 1964-67; chmn. estate planning com. N. Central Coll., 1962-68. Bd. dirs., v.p. B.R. Ryall YMCA, Glen Ellyn, 1968-70; bd. dirs. United Meth. Found.-N. Ill. Conf., 1973-76; mem. exec. com. Chgo. chpt. March of Dimes. Served to 1st lt., inf. AUS, 1943-46. Mem. Am., Chgo. bar assns., Alumni Assn. North Central Coll. (dir. 1976—, sec. 1977). Methodist (chmn. trustees 1968-69, chmn. council ministries 1969-71, chmn. membership commn. 1973-75, chmn. social concerns com. 1977, lay leader 1979). Home: 196 Bryant Ave Glen Ellyn IL 60137 Office: 230 S LaSalle St Chicago IL 60690

LARSON, WILFRED JOSEPH, chem. co. exec.; b. N.Y.C., July 12, 1927; s. Fred Wilfred and Mabel Louise (Messier) L.; B.S. in Econs., U. Pa., 1951; postgrad. U. Chgo., 1958-59, Seton Hall U., 1960-61, U. Cin., 1964-65; m. Joan Jesslyn Tilford, Sept. 4, 1949; children—Linda Sue, Robert Wilfred. With Ward Foods, N.Y.C., 1953-63, controller, chief financial officer, 1961-63, Drackett Co., Cin., 1963—, financial v.p., 1966-67, adminstrv. v.p., 1967-68, exec. v.p., 1969-79; pres. Bristol-Myers Products Can., 1977-79; pres. Westwood Pharms., Inc., 1979—; dir. Cin. Savs. Assn. Pres., trustee Cin. Adolescent Clinic, Inc., 1968—; trustee, treas., mem. adminstrv. investment and exec. coms., chmn. audit budget coms. Childrens Hosp. Med. Center. Served with USNR, 1945-47, AUS, 1951-53. Mem. Financial Exec. Inst. (treas. sec. 1965-68). Republican. Episcopalian (vestryman, treas. 1966-69). Clubs: Wyoming (O.) Golf (treas., v.p.); Racquet, Bankers, Queen City, Commonwealth (Cin.). Home: 188 Mt Pleasant Ave Cincinnati OH 45215 Office: 5020 Spring Grove Ave Cincinnati OH 45232

LARSON, WILLIAM G., photographer; b. N. Tonawanda, N.Y., Oct. 14, 1942; s. John E. and Virginia (Moyer) L.; B.S., SUNY, Buffalo, 1964; M.S., Ill. Inst. Tech., 1968; m. Catherine Jansen, Aug. 25, 1973; 1 dau., Erika Danese. Mem. faculty Tyler Sch. Art, Temple U., Phila., 1968—, prof. photography, 1979—, chmn. dept., 1972—; condr. workshops, speaker in field; rep. permanent collections Mus. Art and History, Freibourg, Switzerland, Mus. Modern Art, N.Y.C., Phila. Mus. Art, Mus. of Art, R.I. Sch. Design, Providence, U. Exeter (Eng.), New Orleans Mus. Arts, U. Hartford (Conn.) Mus., Kalamazoo Inst. Art, U. Tenn., Knoxville, U. Louisville Photog. Archives, Sun Valley (Idaho) Center Arts and Humanities. Grantee Nat. Endowment Arts, 1971, 79, Polaroid Corp., 1979. Mem. Soc. Photog. Edn. Works rep. numerous photog. publs., also in mags.; co-editor Quiver, 1978—. Office: Tyler Sch Art Temple Univ Philadelphia PA 19126

LARUE, CARL FORMAN, lawyer; b. Ann Arbor, Mich., Aug. 4, 1929; s. Carl D. and Evelina F. LaR.; A.B., Harvard U., 1952; LL.B., U. Mich., 1957; m. Ann Williams Lindbloom, June 28, 1971; children—Steve, Ned; stepchildren—Eric, Sarah Relyea. Admitted to Ohio bar, 1957, Ill. bar, 1964, Calif. bar, 1969; asso. firm Fuller, Henry, Hodge & Snyder, Toledo, 1957-59; asst. U.S. atty. for Northwestern Ohio, Dept. Justice, 1959-61; staff atty. Libbey-Owens-Ford Co., Toledo, 1961-64, v.p., gen. counsel, sec., 1978—; sr. atty. Armour and Co., Chgo., 1964-68; asst. gen. counsel Rockwell Internat., Los Angeles, 1968-78. Served with U.S. Army, 1952-54. Mem. Am. Bar Assn., Ohio Bar Assn., Toledo Bar Assn. Clubs: Toledo, Press. Home: 3553 Brookside Rd Toledo OH 43606 Office: 811 Madison Ave Toledo OH 43695

LARUE, (ADRIAN) JAN (PIETERS), musicologist, educator; b. Kisaran, Sumatra, Indonesia, July 31, 1918 (parents Am. citizens); s. Carl Downey and Evelina Brown (Forman) LaR.; S.B., Harvard, 1940, Ph.D., 1952; M.F.A., Princeton, 1942; m. Helen Claire Robison, Aug. 21, 1940; children—Charlotte (Mrs. Jonathan Isaacs), Christine (Mrs. Dan Honig). Instr. music Wellesley Coll., 1942-43, 46-48, asst. prof., 1948-50, asso. prof., 1950-57, chmn. dept. music, 1950-57; prof. N.Y. U., 1957—, exec. dean arts and sci., 1962-63, chmn. dept. music, 1970-73, dir. grad. studies in music, 1973—. Vis. prof. U. Calif. at Los Angeles, 1947, U. Mich., 1962. Mem. council Smithsonian Instn., 1967-73; mem. Zentralinstitut für Mozartforschung, Salzburg (Austria) Mozarteum, 1969—; first musicologist-in-residence Mozart Festival Kennedy Center, 1975. Served to 1st lt. Transp. Corps, AUS, 1943-46; Okinawa. Ford fellow, 1954; Fulbright fellow, 1954-56; Am. Council Learned Socs. fellow, 1964; Guggenheim fellow, 1965; NEH grantee for summer seminar in style analysis, 1978. Mem. Music Library Assn., Soc. Ethnomusicology, Am. Musicological Soc. (pres. 1966-68), Am. Soc. Eighteenth-Century Studies (exec. bd.), Phi Beta Kappa. Author: Guidelines for Style Analysis, 1970; contbg. author: Die Musik in Geschichte und Gegenwart, 1968; Grove's Dictionary of Music and Musicians, 1978. Editor: Congress Report of the Internat. Musicological Soc., 2 vols., 1961; Festschrift Otto Erich Deutsch, 1963; Aspects of Medieval and Renaissance Music, 1966. Contbr. numerous articles on 18th century symphony and concerto, musical analysis, watermarks, music manuscripts and computer applications to music to profl. jours. Home: 15 Edgehill Dr Darien CT 06820 Office: Dept of Music 268 Waverly Bldg NYU New York City NY 10003

LARUS, CHARLES TAFT, investment banker; b. Hartford, Conn., June 28, 1919; s. John Ruse and Elizabeth (Taft) L.; B.S., Yale U., 1941; m. Ethel Thompson, June 30, 1956; children—Margery (Mrs. Gunnar S. Overstrom), Elizabeth (Mrs. Gilbert Keegan). Underwriting clk. Conn. Mut. Life Ins. Co., Hartford, 1941-42; trainee-draftsman Niles-Bement-Pond, West Hartford, Conn., 1942-45; analyst Advest Co., Hartford, 1945-50, syndicate mgr., 1950-54, partner, 1954-66, exec. partner, 1966-76, pres., 1977-79, chmn., 1979—; dir. Conn. Water Service Co., Unionville Water Co. (Conn.); hon. trustee State Bank for Savs., Hartford. Chmn. Avon Bd. Finance, 1965-67; treas. Town of Avon, 1968—. Incorporator Inst. Living, Hartford, Hartford Hosp. Mem. Securities Industry Assn. (mem. governing council 1974-76). Club: Hartford. Home: 385 Waterville Rd Avon CT 06001 Office: 6 Central Row Hartford CT 06103

LARUSSA, JOSEPH ANTHONY, optical co. exec.; b. N.Y.C., May 10, 1925; s. Ignacio and Jennie (Bellone) LaR.; B.S. in Mech. Engring., Coll. City N.Y., 1949; M.S., Columbia, 1955, postgrad. math., mechanics, 1955-59; postgrad. math., physics N.Y. U., 1959-62; m. Stella M.A. Braconnier, July 2, 1946; children—Joseph, Raymond Paul, Debra Marie. Vice pres. charge advanced engring. Farrand Optical Co., Inc., Valhalla, N.Y., 1952—. Served with inf. AUS, World War II: ETO. Registered profl. engr., N.Y. Mem. Am. Inst. Aeros. and Astronautics (DeFlorez award 1968), Tau Beta Pi, Pi Tau Sigma. Patentee in field. Home: 451 Rutledge Dr Yorktown Heights NY 10598 Office: 117 Wall St Valhalla NY 10595

LASAGNA, LOUIS CESARE, physician, educator; b. N.Y.C., Feb. 22, 1923; s. Joseph and Carmen (Boccignone) L.; B.S., Rutgers U., 1943; M.D., Columbia, 1947; m. Helen Chester Gersten, July 20, 1946; children—Nina, David, Maria, Kristin, Lisa, Peter, Christopher. Intern, Mt. Sinai Hosp., N.Y.C., 1947-48; resident Maimonides Hosp., Bklyn., 1948-50; instr. pharmacology and exptl. therapeutics Johns Hopkins Med. Sch., 1950-52, asst. prof. medicine, 1954-57, asso. prof. medicine, 1957-70, asst. prof. pharmacology and exptl. therapeutics, 1954-59, asso. prof. pharmacology and exptl. therapeutics, 1959-70; prof. pharmacology and toxicology, prof. medicine U. Rochester Sch. Medicine, 1970—; research asso. Harvard, 1953-54, 67-68. Served with USNR, 1943-46; with USPHS, 1952-54. Mem. Am. Soc. Pharmacology and Exptl. Therapeutics, Am. Soc. Clin. Investigation, Assn. Am. Physicians, Inst. Medicine, Phi Beta Kappa, Sigma Xi, Alpha Omega Alpha. Author: The Doctors' Dilemmas, 1962; Life, Death, and the Doctor, 1968; The VD Epidemic, 1975. Research on placebos, clin. pharmacology. Home: 465 Clover Hills Dr Rochester NY 14618

LASALLE, JOSEPH PIERRE, mathematician; b. State College, Pa., May 28, 1916; s. Leo Joseph and Aline (Mistric) LaS.; B.S., La. State U., 1937; Ph.D. (Henry Laws fellow), Calif. Inst. Tech., 1941; m. Eleanor Seip, June 12, 1942; children—Nannette Maria, Marc Joseph. Instr., U. Tex., 1941-42, Radar Sch., Mass. Inst. Tech., 1942-43; research asso. Princeton, 1943-44, Cornell U., Ithaca, N.Y., 1944-46; mem. faculty U. Notre Dame, 1946-47, 48-58, prof. math., 1951-58; asso. dir. Math. Center, Research Inst. for Advanced Studies, Balt., 1958-64; prof., dir. Lefschetz Center for Dynamical Systems, Brown U., Providence, 1964—, also chmn. div. applied math., 1968-73. Guggenheim fellow, 1975. Fellow A.A.A.S., Am. Acad. Mechanics; mem. Soc. for Indsl. and Applied Math. (past pres.), Am. Math. Soc., Math. Assn. Am. (Chauvenet prize 1965). Author: (with N. Haaser, J. Sullivan) Introduction to Analysis, Vol. 1, 1959; (with S. Lefschetz) Stability by Liapunov's Second Method with Applications, 1961, Recent Soviet Contributions to Mathematics, 1962; (with S. Lefschetz and L. Cesari) International Symposium on Nonlinear Differential Equations and Nonlinear Mechanics, 1963; (with N. Haaser, J. Sullivan) Intermediate Analysis, Vol. 2, 1964; (with Jack K. Hale) Differential Equations and Dynamical Systems, 1967; (with Henry Hermes) Functional Analysis and Time Optimal Control, 1969; (with L. Cesari and J.K. Hale) Dynamical Systems, Vols. I and II, 1976; The Stability of Dynamical Systems, 1976; also articles. Editor-in-chief Jour. Differential Equations; editor Jour. Math. Analysis and Applications, SIAM Jour. Control, Nonlinear Analysis: Theory, Methods and Applications. Pioneered devel. modern theory of optimal control; contbr. to theory of differential equations, dynamical systems and theory of stability. Home: Point Meadows Little Compton RI 02837 Office: Div Applied Math Brown U Providence RI 02912

LASANSKY, MAURICIO, artist, educator; b. Buenos Aires, Argentina, Oct. 12, 1914; s. Abraham and Ana (Kahan) L.; student Superior Sch. Fine Arts, 1933-35; D.Arts (hon.), Iowa Wesleyan Coll., 1959; D.F.A., Pacific Luth. U., 1969; D.Hum. (hon.), Hamline U., 1977; m. Emilia Barragan, Dec. 16, 1937; children—Guillermo Abraham, Rocio Altana, Leonardo, Marja Jimena, Luis Philip, Thomas. Came to U.S., 1943, naturalized, 1952. Dir., Free Fine Arts Sch., Cordoba, Argentina, 1936-39, Taller Manualidades, Cordoba, 1939-43; Guggenheim fellow for research in black and white, N.Y.C., 1943-45; vis. lectr., apptd. to create graphic arts dept. State U. Iowa, 1946, asst. prof., 1947-48, prof., 1948—, research prof., 1965, 72, 78, Virgil M. Hancher prof. art, 1967—; Lucas lectr. Carleton Coll., Northfield, Minn., 1965; condr. seminar in printmaking Webster Coll., St. Louis, 1975; lectr., condr. seminar, workshop Grand Valley Coll., Allendale, Mich., 1975; represented in museums, Argentina, Spain and U.S. including Nat. Gallery, Library of Congress, Mus. Modern Art N.Y.C., Art Inst., Chgo., Bklyn. Mus., Whitney Mus. Am. Art, N.Y.C., Phila. Mus., Seattle Mus., Okla. Mus., Tulsa, N.Y. Pub. Library, Rosenwald Collection, Phila., City Art Mus., St. Louis, Washington U. Collection, Nat. Gallery of Victoria, Melbourne, Uff 121 Gallery, Florence, Italy, Am. Embassy, Mexico City, and others; USIA tour of works to Latin Am., 1959-61; one-man shows Washington, San Francisco Mus. Art, 1945, Art Inst., 1947, Museo de Arte Contemporaneo, Madrid, Spain, Museo de Arte Moderno, Barcelona, Spain, 1953-54, Retrospective Exhbn. U. Iowa, 1957, 76, Ford Found. Retrospective Exhbn., 1959, Los Angeles County Mus., Seattle Mus., Bklyn. Mus., 1961, Palace of Fine Arts, Mexico City, 1969, U. Iowa, 1970, Dickinson Coll., Carlisle, Pa., 1972, Creighton U., 1977, U. S.C., 1977, Fla. Internat. U., 1977, Ft. Lauderdale Mus. Arts, 1978, Charles H. McNider Mus., Mason City, Iowa, 1978, numerous others, U.S., Europe, Japan, S.Am., Australia; Phila. Mus. Art, 1967, Whitney Mus. Am. Art, N.Y.C., 1967, Palace Fine Arts, Mexico City, 1969, Mus. Art, U. Iowa, 1970, exhibited in group shows Am. Art Today at N.Y. World's Fair, 1964-65, Albertine Mus., Vienna, Austria, 1st Nat. Biennial, Honolulu, 1st Biennial, Honolulu, Internat. Graphic Art, 1945-70, Albertine Mus. Venice, 1971, 3d Internat. Biennial, San Juan, P.R., 1974, 3d Am. Biennial, Cali, Columbia, 1976, OAS, 1976, So. Conn. State Coll., 1976, Jewish Mus., N.Y.C., 1976, Miami U. Art Center, Oxford, Ohio, 1976, Internat. Invitation Exhbn., P.R., 1979, numerous others. Mem. com. selection graphic arts John Simon Guggenheim Meml. Found., 1965-72. Recipient numerous awards including 1st prize 17th Internat. Exhbn. Prints, Seattle, 1944; 1st prize Print Group, Phila., 1945; prize Library of Congress Exhbn., 1945; prizes Phila. Print Club, Denver Art Mus. 52d Ann. Exhbn., Des Moines Salon, 1946; 1st purchase prize for print Denver 53d Ann. exhbn. 1947, Library of Congress, 1950, 62, 63, purchase prize, nat. exhbn. Soc. Washington Printmakers, Charles M. Lea prize Phila. Print Club, 1957, 62; Eyre Medal award and purchase Pa. Acad. Fine Arts 152d exhbn., 1957; Instituto Nacional De Bellas Artes Posada Prizes, 1st Mexican Biennial, 1958; Calif. Soc. Etchers Open award, 1959; Ford Found. Purchase award, 1962; Accademico Onorario of Classe de Incisione, Accademia Delle Arti del Disegno, Florence, Italy, 1965; 1st prize, 1st Biennial del Grabado, Latino Americano en San Juan de P.R., 2d Internat. Biennial of Graphic Art, Florence, Italy, Honolulu, 1971; 1st prize Color Prints of Americas, N.J. State Mus., spl. mention Pan Am. show prints and drawings Cali, Colombia, 1971; Dickinson Coll. Art award, 1974. Guggenheim fellow, Spain and S.Am., 1953-54, 65. Mem. Coll. Art Assn. (dir.). Club: Iowa Print Group (Iowa City). Works included in numerous art books, including Lasansky: Printmaker, 1976. Address: Quail Creek Condominium Apt 3D North Liberty IA 52317

LASATER, DONALD E., banker; b. St. Louis, Dec. 8, 1925; s. Jacques and Kathryne (Haessel) L.; student S.E. Mo. State Coll., 1942-43, U. Iowa, 1943; LL.B., U. So. Calif., 1948; student Nat. Trust Sch., 1960; m. Mary E. McGinnis, Apr. 4, 1951; children—Kevin Michael, Timothy Patrick, Thomas Brady, Laura Clark, John Robert. Admitted to Mo. bar; practice law, St. Louis, 1949-54; asst. pros. atty. St. Louis County, 1955-56, counselor, 1957-58; with Merc. Trust Co., St. Louis, 1959—, v.p. trust dept., 1965-67, dir., pres., 1967-70, chmn. bd., 1970—; dir. Gen. Am. Life Ins. Co., St. Louis, Interco Inc. Mem. exec. com. St. Louis Area council Boy Scouts Am. Bd. dirs. Barnes Hosp., St. Louis, Jr. Achievement Miss. Valley, Met. YMCA; trustee Washington U., St. Louis. Served with USNR, 1943-45. Mem. Mo. Bar Assn., Bar Assn. St. Louis, Am. Bankers Assn. (legis. council), Republican. Roman Catholic. Clubs: Noonday, St. Louis; Bogey; Old Warson Country. Home: 751 Cella Rd Ladue MO 63124 Office: 721 Locust St Saint Louis MO 63166

LASATER, HUBERT L., economist; b. Paul's Valley, Okla., Aug. 10, 1912; s. Luke L. and Jennie Lee (Munday) L.; B.S., Okla. State U., 1933, M.S., 1948; postgrad. Cornell U., Ithaca, N.Y., 1948-50; m. Ruby Jean Kinser, Aug. 10, 1935; children—Betty Jean (Mrs. Byron D. Spargo), Lois Elaine (Mrs. Wilfred E. McMurphy). Supt. Liberty Sch., Paul's Valley, Okla., 1933-35; exec. asst. Okla. A.A.A., 1934-35; county agrl. agt., Okla., 1935-44, asso. state 4-H Club leader, 1944-46; extension poultryman Okla., 1946-48, extension poultry marketing specialist, 1950-52; asso. prof. poultry husbandry Cornell U., Ithaca, N.Y., 1948-49; agriculturist, livestock sci. cons. U.S. Operations Mission, Republic of Lebanon, 1952-53, dir. agr. extension, 1953-56, dep. chief agriculturist, 1956-57, chief agriculturist, 1957-58; dep. food and agr. officer U.S. Operations Mission, Ethiopia, 1958-59, acting food and agrl. office, 1959-60; agriculturist ICA-Washington-Africa-Europe br. of O/Food, 1960-61; chief agrl. tng. AID, Washington, 1962-68; food and agr. officer, Accra, Ghana, 1968-71; agrl. cons. AID, 1971-74, now ret. Licenced judge Am. Poultry Assn., 1946. Served with USNR, 1944-46. Decorated Order Cedars of Lebanon. Mem. Scientists and Engrs. Fed. Service, Nat. Biol. Scientists, Nat. Poultry Sci. Assn., Epsilon Sigma Phi, Alpha Zeta. Mason (32 deg.). Address: 4901 Country Club Dr Stillwater OK 74074

LASCARA, VINCENT ALFRED, naval officer; b. Norfolk, Va., Dec. 24, 1919; s. Joseph and Mary (Caleo) L.; student Belmont Abbey Jr. Coll., 1938-40; B.A., Coll. William and Mary, 1942; M.B.A., Stanford U., 1951; postgrad. Naval War Coll., 1967; m. Elizabeth Irma Lyons, Feb. 22, 1951; children—Elisa Mary, Vincent Joseph, William Anthony, Virginia Anna. Commd. ensign USN, 1942, advanced through grades to vice adm., 1976; supply officer U.S.S. Enterprise, 1960-64; dir. inventory control Naval Supply Center, Norfolk, 1964-66; exec. officer Ships Parts Control Center, Mechanicsburg, Pa., 1967-68; comdg. officer Fleet Materials Support Office, Mechanicsburg, 1968-69; asst. comptroller Office Navy Comptroller, Washington, 1969-73, also comdr. Navy Accounting and Fin. Center, 1969-73; comdg. officer Navy Supply Center, Norfolk, 1973. Chmn. bd. dirs. Navy Fed. Credit Union, Washington. Mem. Am. Soc. Mil. Comptrollers (v.p.). Home: 912 Cardinal Rd Virginia Beach VA 23451

LASCH, ROBERT, former journalist; b. Lincoln, Neb., Mar. 26, 1907; s. Theodore Walter and Myrtle (Nelson) L.; A.B., U. Neb., 1928; A.B., (Rhodes scholar 1928-30), Oxford, 1930; Nieman fellow, Harvard, 1941-42; m. Zora Schaupp, Aug. 22, 1931; children—Christopher, Catherine. Reporter, state editor, editorial writer Omaha World-Herald, 1931-41; editorial writer, then chief editorial writer Chgo. Sun and Sun-Times, 1942-50; editorial writer St. Louis Post-Dispatch, 1950-57, editor editorial page, 1957-71, ret. Recipient St. Louis Civil Liberties award, 1966; Pulitzer prize for distinguished editorial writing, 1966. Contbr. to Newsmen's Holiday,

1942. Author: For a Free Press (Atlantic Monthly prize), 1944; Breaking The Building Blockade, 1946. Home: PO Box 728 342 E El Pinon Green Valley AZ 85614

LASCHUK, ROY BOGDAN, lawyer; b. Saskatoon, Sask., Can., Aug. 13, 1932; s. Nicholas and Agatha (Schyhol) L.; B.A., U. Sask., 1953; LL.B., 1955; m. Tairroyn Riley, Aug. 21, 1964; children—Tonia Jane, Stephen Clare, Graham Christopher. Called to Sask. bar, created queen's counsel, 1978; asso. firm Balfour, Moss, Laschuk, Kyle, Vancise & Cameron and predecessors, Regina, Sask., 1956-61, partner, 1961—; dir. Key Pipe Line Co. Ltd., Arctic Constructors Ltd. Spl. lectr. bar admissions U. Sask. Coll. Law, 1967—. Exec. mem. Progressive Conservative Assn., 1956-62, 70—. Bd. dirs. Regina Housing Authority, 1973—. Mem. Law Soc. Sask., Canadian (mem. council), Regina (dir. 1975—, v.p. 1977-78, pres. 1978) bar assns., Canadian Petroleum Assn. (chmn. legal com. Sask. 1972-78), Canadian Assn. Occupational Therapists (hon. exec. mem. 1970-75). Baptist. Rotarian. Clubs: Assiniboia, Lake Shore Estates (Regina). Home: 85 Compton Rd Regina SK S4S 2Y4 Canada Office: 1850 Cornwall St Regina SK S4P 2K3 Canada

LASDON, LLOYD I., bus. exec.; b. N.Y.C., Nov. 9, 1927; s. Philip S. and Shirley (Davidson) L.; B.S. in Chemistry, Purdue U., 1949; m. Sandra Rubin, Mar. 1, 1952; children—Laurie M., Douglas H. Prin., officer Reduction & Refining Co., Kenilworth, N.J., 1949-62; founder, chmn. bd. Barrier Chems, Inc., Vernon, N.J., 1962-69; v.p. CBWL-Hayden Stone Co., N.Y.C., 1969-70; exec. v.p. Aurora Products Corp., West Hempstead, N.Y., 1970-73; pres. Metron Industries and subs. including Met. Mirror Corp., Mt. Vernon, N.Y., 1974—. Trustee Sarah Lawrence Coll., 1976—. Club: Beach Point (Mamaroneck, N.Y.). Patentee in field. Sculptor, represented in permanent collections. Home: Beverly Rd Purchase NY 10577 Office: 31 Warren Pl Mount Vernon NY 10552

LASDON, WILLIAM STANLEY, pharm. co. exec.; b. Bklyn., Mar. 14, 1896; LL.D., Nat. U. Ireland, 1954; L.H.D., Yeshiva U., 1969; m. Mildred D. Silverman, May 30, 1922; children—Nanette L. (Mrs. Laitman), Robert Steven. With research dept. Stanley Securities, N.Y.C., 1914-26; sec.-treas. Pyridium Corp., 1926-36, pres., chmn. bd., 1936-50; pres. Anahist Co., Inc., 1949-55; pres., chmn. bd. Nepera Chem. Co., 1950-56; dir. Nepera Internat. Corp., 1946; dir. Warner-Lambert Pharm. Co., Inc., Morris Plains, N.J., 1956—, chmn. exec. com., 1960-72, vice chmn. bd., 1973—, cons., 1973—; dir. Capital Cities Communications Inc., 1957—. Pres. Lasdon Found., 1946—; bd. overseers Albert Einstein Coll. Medicine, 1954—; bd. dirs. Cerebral Palsy Assn.; mem. adv. com. John F. Kennedy Center for Performing Arts, 1970—; patron Lincoln Center Performing Arts, Mus. Modern Art. Clubs: Harmonie, Sky, Board Room; Rockrimmon (Conn.) Country; Palm Beach (Fla.) Country. Home: Amawalk Rd Katonah NY 10536 Office: Hotel Pierre New York City NY 10021

LASER, MARVIN, educator; b. Chgo., Nov. 2, 1914; s. Harry and Ida (Preskill) L.; Ph.B., U. Chgo., 1935, M.A., 1937; Ph.D., Northwestern U., 1948; m. Dorothy Kort, Feb. 8, 1948; children—Harvey R., Steven A. Instr. English, Wilson Jr. Coll., Chgo., 1938-42, 46-53; lectr. English, Northwestern U., Chgo., 1947-49; prof. English, Chgo. Tchrs. Coll., 1953-56, Calif. State U., Los Angeles, 1956-65, chmn. div. lang. arts, 1956-63; prof. English, dean Sch. Humanities and Fine Arts, Calif. State U., Dominguez Hills, 1965—. Served to capt. USAAF, 1942-46. Mem. Modern Lang. Assn., Coll. English Assn. (past dir.), Internat., Calif. councils fine arts deans, Phi Beta Kappa. Co-author: Language in Your Life, 4 vols., 1965-70. Co-editor Television for the California State Colleges, 1962, Ideas and Issues, 1963, Studies in J.D. Salinger, 1963, Student, School, and Society, 1964, Channel One, 1970; co-editor, joint author Harper & Row Scope series, 1965-67. Home: 3017 Palos Verdes Dr W Palos Verdes Estates CA 90274 Office: 1000 E Victoria St Carson CA 90747

LASH, JOSEPH P., author; b. N.Y.C., Dec. 2, 1909; s. Samuel and Mary (Avchin) L.; A.B., Coll. City N.Y., 1931; A.M., Columbia, 1932; m. Trude Wenzel, Nov. 8, 1944; 1 son, Jonathan. Editor, Student Outlook, 1933-35; nat. sec. Am. Student Union, 1936-39; gen. sec. Internat. Student Service, 1940-42; N.Y. sec. Ams. for Democratic Action, 1946-48; asst. to Elliott Roosevelt, 1948-50; UN corr. N.Y. Post, 1950-61, asst. editor editorial page, 1961-66. Served to 2d lt. USAAF, 1942-45. Decorated Air Medal. Recipient Pulitzer prize for biography, 1972, Nat. Book award, 1972, Francis Parkman prize, 1972, first Samuel E. Morison award, 1976. Author: Dag Hammarskjold: Custodian of the Brushfire Peace, 1962; A Friend's Memoir, 1964; Eleanor and Franklin, 1971; Eleanor: The Years Alone, 1972; From the Diaries of Felix Frankfurter, 1975. Asst. editor F.D.R., His Personal Letters, Vols. III-IV, 1950; Roosevelt and Churchill: 1939-41, 1976. Home: Skyline Dr Oakland NJ 07436

LASH, KENNETH, educator; b. New Britain, Conn., July 27, 1918; s. Jack Edward and Lillian (Miller) L.; B.A., Yale, 1939; M.A., U. N.Mex., 1948; postgrad. (Fulbright scholar), U. de Lille (France), 1950-51. Instr. dept. English, U. N.Mex., Albuquerque, 1948-54; editor N.Mex. Quar. Rev., Albuquerque, 1951-55; lectr. dept. humanities San Francisco Art Inst., 1959-70, chmn. dept., 1964-70; head art dept. U. No. Iowa, Cedar Falls, 1970-76, dir. Humanities program, 1976—; ednl. cons. Mem. role of the arts task force Pres.'s Commn. on Mental Health, 1977-78. Served with USNR, 1943-46. Rockefeller Found. traveling grantee, 1954-55. Mem. Phi Beta Kappa. Writer poetry, drama, fiction, edn., 1946—. Contbg. editor, columnist N.Am. Rev., 1972—. Home: 2725 Rainbow Dr Cedar Falls IA 50613. *The major life-giving principles of the human are kindness and humor. The latter requires activity of mind, the former activity of spirit. To the extent that these activities are institutionalized, become spectator sports, an individual, a society, a civilization, is in trouble—that trouble called dying. Enmity, like charity, begins at home. Three of our most grotesque enemies are TV, sentimentality, and test-scores.*

LASHINSKY, HERBERT, educator; b. N.Y.C., Dec. 14, 1921; s. Isodore Meyer and Leah (Abrams) L.; B.Sc., Coll. City N.Y., 1950; Ph.D., Columbia U., 1961; div.; 1 dau., Karen. Engr., Western Electric Co., 1940-43; research asso. Princeton, 1961-64; prof. Inst. Phys. Sci. and Tech., Math., U. Md., College Park, 1964—. Served with AUS, 1943-46. Mem. Am. Phys. Soc., IEEE. Editor: Soviet Physics-Tech. Physics. Translator Reviews of Plasma Physics. Patentee in field. Home: 5400 Pooks Hill Rd Bethesda MD 20014 Office: Inst Phys Sci U Md College Park MD 20740

LASHLY, JOHN HENDERSON, lawyer; b. St. Louis, Aug. 20, 1916; s. Jacob Mark and Bessie (Henderson) L.; A.B., Swarthmore Coll., 1938; J.D., Washington U., 1941; m. Jean McCrory, 1942; children—Mark, James, Patrick, Bonnie Jean; m. 2d, Louise Champion, 1973. Admitted to Mo. bar, 1941; practice law, St. Louis, 1941—, partner firm Lashly, Caruthers, Thies, Rava & Hamel, 1950—, chmn. bd., 1973—. Pres. St. Louis Mcpl. Opera Bd., 1973-74, dir., 1955—; pres. St. Lukes Hosp., 1964-66; pres. St. Louis Mercantile Library, 1962-64. Served with USAAF, World War II. Mem. Am. Bar Assn. (ho. of dels. 1966-70, bd. govs. 1970-73), Mo. Bar (bd. govs., pres. 1966-67), Bar Assn. St. Louis (pres. 1960-62), St. Louis C. of C. (dir. 1957-61), Phi Delta Theta (Phi of Yr. 1978), Phi Delta Phi. Clubs: Media, Noonday, Racquet, Stadium, Yacht. Office: 714 Locust St Saint Louis MO 63101

LASHLY, PAUL WEBSTER, lawyer, urban redeveloper, financier; b. Joplin, Mo., Nov. 15, 1917; s. Walter W. and Grace (Hastings) L.; student St. Louis U., 1935-38; LL.B., Washington U., St. Louis, 1941; postgrad. Cambridge (Eng.) U., 1942-43, Algiers U., 1943-44. Admitted to Mo. bar, 1941, U.S. Supreme Ct. bar, 1951; practiced in St. Louis, 1941—; now sr. partner Lashly Neun & Johnson; provisional judge, 1948-52. Lectr. corps. and corp. finance St. Louis Law Sch., 1946-50, Law Sci. Found.; ltd. partner Mansion House Center Redevel. Corp.; pres. Viburnum Community Devel. Corp., Emeritus Corp., Kingswater Devel. Corp.; dir. Washington Ct. Devel. Co., Regional Indsl. Redevel. Corp., Resources, Inc.; past chmn. urban redevel. com. City Planning Commn. St. Louis, 1951-56; mem. Municipal Bus. Devel. Commn. and Planned Indsl. Expansion Authority, 1969-75. Past pres. bd. Epilepsy League St. Louis, Neuromed. Found. Served to lt. comdr. USNR, 1942-46. Mem. Am. (past nat. chmn. Am. bar young lawyers conf., mem. ho. of dels.), Inter-Am., Internat., Mo., St. Louis, Lawyers bar assns., Phi Delta Phi. Mason (32 deg., Shriner). Clubs: Racquet, Media, Mo. Athletic, Lawyers (St. Louis); Bridlespur Hunt; Squash. Contbr. numerous articles to profl. jours. Home: 9 Kingsbury Pl Saint Louis MO 63112 Office: 457 N Kingshighway Saint Louis MO 63102. *A person's life is much like the rays of the sun or moon; either illuminating and making easier the efforts of others or obscuring to the point of total eclipse those lives.*

LASHOF, JOYCE R. COHEN, physician, govt. ofcl.; b. Phila., Mar. 27, 1926; d. Harry and Rose (Brodsky) Cohen; A.B., Duke U., 1946; M.D., Womans Med. Coll. Pa., 1950; m. Richard Kenneth Lashof, June 11, 1950; children—Judith, Carol, Danny. Intern, Bronx Hosp., N.Y.C., 1950-51; resident, 1951-52; resident Montefiore Hosp., N.Y.C., 1952-53; fellow Yale U., 1953-54; USPHS fellow U. Oxford, Eng., 1964-65; practice medicine specializing in preventive medicine, Chgo., 1954-73; dep. asst. sec. for health programs HEW, Washington, 1977-78; asst. dir. Office Tech. Assessment, U.S. Congress, Washington, 1978—; dir. sect. community medicine Presbyn.-St. Luke's Hosp., Chgo., 1967-71, chmn. dept. preventive medicine, 1971-73; project dir. Mile Sq. Health Center, Chgo. 1967-71; instr. medicine U. Chgo., 1956-58; asst. prof., 1958-60; clin. asst. prof. preventive medicine U. Ill., 1960-61, asst. prof., 1961-64, asso. prof., 1964-68, prof. preventive medicine and community health, 1968-71; prof. preventive medicine Rush Med. Coll., Chgo., 1971-73; dir. pub. health, State of Ill., Springfield, 1973-77; research dir. Chgo. Bd. Health, 1965. Diplomate Am. Bd. Internal Medicine. Fellow Am. Pub. Health Assn., A.C.P.; mem. Am. Assn. Tchrs. Preventive Medicine. Contbr. articles in field to profl. jours. Office: OTA US Congress Washington DC 20510

LASKE, ARTHUR CHARLES, found. exec.; b. Bridgeport, Conn., Oct. 3, 1899; s. August A. and Mary (Miller) L.; grad. pub. schs. Bridgeport; m. Evelyn R. Strasburger, Oct. 12, 1921; children—Marilyn F. Laske Chisnall, Arthur Charles. Pres. dir. Sormir Petroleum Corp., 1937—; pres., dir. Wm. T. Morris Found., Inc., N.Y.C., 1939—, Circle Petroleum Corp., 1960—. Club: Algonquin. Home: 5081 Main St Trumbull CT 06611 Office: William T Morris Found Inc PO Box 5786 230 Park Ave New York NY 10017

LASKER, EDWARD, lawyer; b. Chgo., May 15, 1912; s. Albert D. and Flora (Warner) L.; grad. Phillips Exeter Acad., 1929; B.A., Yale, 1933; LL.B., U. Cal. at Los Angeles, 1955; m. Cynthia S. Palmer, Nov. 1963; children by previous marriage—Albert, Lawrence, Steven. Engaged as account exec., v.p. charge radio, 1st v.p., gen. mgr. Lord & Thomas, 1933-41; spl. asst. to sec. navy, 1941-42; motion picture producer, 1946- 52; admitted to Calif. bar, 1955; counsel firm McKenna & Fitting, Los Angeles. Dir. Great Western Financial Corp., Gt. Western Savs. & Loan Assn., Philip Morris, Inc., Mission Viejo Co. Del. Democratic Nat. Conv., 1956, 60. Asst. chief disciplinary referee Calif. State Bar, 1976-77, mem. disciplinary bd., 1978—. Trustee Pomona Coll. Served from lt. (j.g.) to lt. comdr., USNR, 1942-45. Home: 901 Airole Way Los Angeles CA 90024 Office: 3435 Wilshire Blvd 28th Floor Los Angeles CA 90010

LASKER, GABRIEL WARD, anthropologist, educator; b. Huntington, Yorkshire, Eng., Apr. 29, 1912; s. Bruno and Margaret Naomi (Ward) L.; student U. Wis., 1928-30; A.B., U. Mich., 1934; A.M., Harvard, 1940, Ph.D., 1945; m. Bernice Kaplan, July 31, 1949; children—Robert Alexander, Edward Meyer, Ann Titania. Instr. English, Chiao T'ung U., Peking, China, 1936-37; teaching fellow in anatomy Harvard Med. Sch., 1941-42; mem. faculty dept. anatomy Wayne U. Sch. Medicine, Detroit, 1946—, asst. prof., 1947-55, asso. prof., 1955-64, prof., 1964—, conducted Wayne U.-Viking Fund field trip to Mexico to study effects of migration on phys. characteristics of Mexicans, 1948. Fellow Am. Anthropol. Assn., A.A.A.S. (v.p. 1968); mem. Am. Assn. Phys. Anthropologists (sec.-treas. 1947-51, v.p. 1960-62, pres. 1963-65), Am. Assn. Anatomists, Am. Soc. Human Genetics, Council Biology Editors (chmn. 1963-65), Sigma Xi, Author: Physical Anthropology; The Evolution of Man. Editor Yearbook of Phys. Anthropology, 1945-51, Human Biology, 1953—. Contbr. articles to profl. jours. Office: 540 E Canfield Ave Detroit MI 48201

LASKER, JOSEPH L., artist; b. N.Y.C., June 26, 1919; s. Isidore and Rachel (Strollowitz) L.; student Cooper Union Art Sch., evenings 1936-39, Escuela Universitaria de Bellas Artes, Mexico, 1948; m. Mildred Jaspen, Nov. 28, 1948; children—David Raymond, Laura, Evan. Tchr. Coll. City N.Y., 1947; vis. asso. prof. art U. Ill., 1953-54; exhibited one-man show Kraushaar Galleries, N.Y.C., 1951, 53, 58, 63, 70, 74, 76, 78; works represented in permanent collections Whitney Mus., Cal. Palace Legion of Honor, Phila., Springfield Mus. (Mass.), Joseph Hirschorn Collection, Balt. Mus., Munson-Williams Proctor Inst., Phila. Mus. Art; murals in Calumet (Mich.) P.O., Millbury (Mass.), Henry Street Settlement Play House, N.Y.C. Abbey Meml. scholar, 1946, 47; Pris de Rome fellow, 1950, 51; Guggenheim fellow, 1954; Benjamin Altman prize (figure) Nat. Acad. Design, 1958; grantee Nat. Inst. Arts and Letters, 1968. Illustrator children's books. Office: care Kraushaar Galleries 1055 Madison Ave New York NY 10021

LASKER, MARY (MRS. ALBERT D. LASKER), civic worker; b. Watertown, Wis.; d. Frank Elwin and Sara (Johnson) Woodard; A.B. cum laude, Radcliffe Coll.; LL.D., U. Wis.; postgrad. Oxford U.; L.H.D. (hon.), U. So. Calif., U. Calif., Berkeley, Bard Coll., Woman's Med. Coll. Pa., N.Y. U., N.Y. Med. Coll., Jefferson Med. Coll., Phila.; LL.D., Columbia U.; m. Paul Reinhardt (div.); m. 2d, Albert D. Lasker. Art dealer; connected with Reinhardt Galleries, N.Y.C., arranging benefit loan exhbns. outstanding old and modern French masters and selling pictures to collectors and museums; with husband established med. research found. Albert and Mary Lasker Found. which gives awards for contbns. med. research, pub. health adminstrn., 1942. Trustee Research to Prevent Blindness; hon. chmn. bd. dirs. Am. Cancer Soc.; pres. bd. United Cerebral Palsy Research and Ednl. Found.; mem. nat. adv. bd. Nat. Cancer Inst.; chmn. Nat. Health Edn. Com.; adv. council Ad Council; bd. dirs. Norton Simon Mus. Decorated chevalier, officer French Legion of Honor; recipient Presdl. Medal of Freedom, 1969. Home: 870 UN Plaza New York NY 10017 Office: 865 UN Plaza New York NY 10017

LASKI, FRANK JOSEPH, lawyer, banker; b. Bklyn., May 1, 1929; s. Frank A. and Catherine V. (Corcoran) L.; B.S. in Econs., Coll. Holy Cross, 1951; LL.B., J.D., Buffalo Law Sch., 1954; m. Catherine E. Augustine, Aug. 8, 1953; children—John, Ruth, William, Richard, Mary, James, Ann. Admitted to N.Y. bar, 1954; partner firm Phillips, Lytle, Hitchcock, Blaine & Huber, Buffalo, 1957-73; gen. counsel, sec. Marine Midland Banks, Inc., Buffalo, 1973—, Marine Midland Bank, Buffalo, 1976—. Served to lt. (j.g.), USNR, 1955-57. Mem. Am., N.Y. State, Erie County bar assns., Am. Soc. Corporate Secs., Assn. Bank Holding Cos. Roman Catholic. Clubs: Buffalo, Park Country (Buffalo); Bd. Room (N.Y.C.). Office: 2400 Marine Midland Center Buffalo NY 14203

LASKIN, BORA, chief justice Can.; b. Ft. William, Ont., Can., Oct. 5, 1912; s. Max and Bluma (Singel) L.; B.A., U. Toronto, 1933, M.A., 1935, LL.B., 1936; postgrad. Osgoode Hall Law Sch., 1933-36; LL.M., Harvard U., 1937; hon. LL.D., D.Phil., D.H.L., D.C.L. numerous univs.; m. Peggy Tenenbaum, 1938; children—John, Barbara. Read law with W.C. Davidson, 1933-36; called to bar Ont., 1937, created Queen's counsel, 1956; lectr. in law and asst. prof. U. Toronto, 1940-45, prof., 1949-65; lectr. in law Osgoode Hall Law Sch., 1945-49; labor arbitrator and conciliator, 1942-65; asso. editor Dominion Law Reports and Canadian Criminal Cases, 1943-65; justice Ont. Ct. Appeal, 1965-70; Puisne judge Supreme Ct. Can., 1970-73, chief justice, 1973—; chancellor Lakehead U., 1971—. Chmn., mem. bd. govs. Ont. Inst. Studies in Edn., 1965-69; bd. govs. York U., 1967-70, Carleton U., 1970-73. Mem. Assn. Canadian Law Tchrs. (pres. 1953-54), Canadian Assn. Univ. Tchrs. (pres. 1964-65), Nat. Acad. Arbitrators; fellow Royal Soc. Can., Brit. Acad. (corr.). Recipient Milner award Canadian Assn. Univ. Tchrs., 1971. Author: Canadian Constitutional Law, 3d edit., 1966; Cases and Notes on Land Law, new edit., 1964; The British Tradition in Canadian Law, 1969; The Institutional Character of the Judge, 1972; also articles. Office: Supreme Ct Can Supreme Ct Bldg Wellington St Ottawa ON K1A 0J1 Canada

LASKIN, DANIEL M., oral and maxillofacial surgeon, educator; b. Ellenville, N.Y., Sept. 3, 1924; s. Nathan and Flora (Kaplan) L.; student N.Y. U., 1941-42; B.S., Ind. U., 1947; M.S., U. Ill., 1951; m. Eve Pauline Mohel, Aug. 25, 1945; children—Jeffrey, Gary, Marla. Mem. faculty U. Ill., Chgo., 1949—, prof. dept. oral and maxillofacial surgery, 1960—, head dept., 1973—, clin. prof. surgery, 1961—, dir. temporomandibular joint and facial pain research center, 1963—; head dept. dentistry U. Ill. Hosp., Chgo.; attending oral surgeon Edgewater, Swedish Covenant, Ill. Masonic, Skokie Valley Community hosps. (all Chgo.); dep. chmn. dept. oral surgery Cook County Hosp., Chgo.; cons. oral surgery to Surgeon Gen. Navy, 1977. Recipient Distinguished Alumni Service award Ind. U., 1975; William J. Gies editorial award hon. mention, 1975, 76, 77; Simon P. Hullihen Meml. award, 1976, Arnold K. Maislen Meml. award, 1977. Diplomate Am. Bd. Oral and Maxillofacial Surgery. Fellow Am., Internat. colls. dentists, AAAS; fellow in gen. anesthesia Am. Dental Soc. Anesthesiology; mem. Ill. Splty. Bd. Oral Surgery, Am. Dental Assn., Am. Assn. Oral and Maxillofacial Surgeons (editor Forum 1965—, distinguished service award 1972, pres. 1976-77 research recognition award 1978, William J. Gies award 1979), Internat. Assn. Dental Research, Internat. Assn. Oral Surgeons, Am. Dental Soc. Anesthesiology (pres. 1976-78), Am. Soc. Exptl. Pathology, Am. Assn. Dental Editors, Sigma Xi, Omicron Kappa Upsilon. Editor: Jour. Oral Surgery, 1972—; editorial bd. Internat. Jour. Oral Surgery, 1978—. Research and publs. on connective tissue physiology and pathology, particularly cartilage and bone metabolism, craniofacial growth and pathology of temporomandibular joint. Office: U Ill Med Center Dept Oral and Maxillofacial Surgery PO Box 6998 Chicago IL 60680

LASKIN, SYLVESTER, utility exec.; b. Duluth, Minn., June 18, 1914; s. David and Esther (Kernes) L.; B.E.E., U. Minn., 1935; m. Betty Cornfeldt, Jan. 12, 1941; children—Eileen (Mrs. James Mitson), Harold, Michael. With Minn. Power & Light Co., Duluth, 1935—, v.p. comml., 1963-68, pres., chief exec. officer, 1969-79; ret., 1979; chmn. bd. Superior Water Light & Power Co.; dir. Northwest Bancorp., First & Am. Nat. Bank. Chmn. Minn. Safety Council, 1976-77; pres. Northeast Minn. Devel. Assn., 1976-77; chmn. St. Louis County Heritage and Arts Center, 1976-77; adv. com. Edison Electric Inst.; trustee U. Minn. Found., 1974-78. Registered profl. engr., Minn. Mem. IEEE, N.A.M. (dir. 1970). Jewish (pres. temple 1967-68). Mason (Shriner). Home: 3609 E Superior St Duluth MN 55804

LASKOWSKI, LEONARD FRANCIS, JR., microbiologist; b. Milw., Nov. 16, 1919; s. Leonard Francis and Frances (Cyborowski) L.; B.S., Marquette U., 1941, M.S., 1948; Ph.D., St. Louis U., 1951; m. Frances Bielinski, June 1, 1946; children—Leonard Francis III, James, Thomas. Instr. bacteriology Marquette U., 1946-48; mem. faculty St. Louis U., 1951—, prof. pathology, 1969—, asso. prof. internal medicine, 1977—; dir. clin. microbiology sect. St. Louis U. Hosps. Labs., 1965—; cons. clin microbiology Firmin Desloge Hosp., St. Louis U. Group Hosps., St. Marys Group Hosps.; cons. bacteriology VA Hosp., asst. dept. chief Pub. Health Lab., St. Louis Civil Def., 1958—; cons. St. Elizabeths Hosp., St. Louis County Hosp., St. Francis Hosp.; Health and tech. tng. coordinator for Latin Am. projects Peace Corps, 1962-66. Served with M.C., AUS, 1942-46. Diplomate Am. Bd. Microbiology. Fellow Am. Acad. Microbiology; mem. Soc. Am. Bacteriologists, N.Y. Acad. Scis., Am., Mo. pub. health assns., AAUP, Med. Mycol. Soc. Am., Alpha Omega Alpha. Contbr. articles to profl. jours. Home: Rte 1 Box 117 Villa Ridge MO 63089 Office: 1402 Grand Blvd S St Louis MO 63104

LASKOWSKI, MATTHEW LUDWIG, mfg. co. exec.; b. N.Y.C., Nov. 2, 1919; s. Adam John and Ludwika (Syp) L.; B.A. in Social Sci., Bklyn. Coll., 1939; J.D., Columbia, 1942; M.B.A., N.Y. U., 1961; m. Henryka Poltorak, June 25, 1949; children—Matthew Ludwig, Mark. Admitted to N.Y. bar, 1942; atty. Gammans & Goldin, 1946-52; atty. Western Electric Co., 1952-63, asst. sec., 1963-73, asst. treas., 1973—, asst. treas. Western Electric Internat. Inc., 1978—; sec. Nassau Smelting & Refining Co. subsidiary Western Electric Co., S.I., N.Y., 1963-73, asst. treas., 1977—; sec. Mfrs. Junction Ry. Co., Cicero, Ill., 1965-73; asst. sec. Teletype Corp., Skokie, Ill., 1963-73, asst. treas., 1973—; treas. Western Electric Fund, 1973-79; asst. treas. Western Electric Polit. Action Com., 1978; mem. Short Term Investment Group, N.Y.C., 1973—; alt. mem. Treas.' Group, N.Y.C., 1973—. Adj. asst. prof. econs. N.Y. U., 1961-62, Fairleigh-Dickinson U., 1962-63, Pace U., 1963-73. Mem. Kosciuszko Found., Polish Cultural Found. N.J. Served with USAAF, 1942-46. Recipient Alumni award N.Y. U. Grad. Sch. Bus. Adminstrn., 1961. Mem. Adminstrv. Mgmt. Soc. (v.p. research and study 1971-73), Am. Mgmt. Assn. (planning council 1970—), Assn. Record Execs. and Adminstrs. (charter), Corp. Cash Mgrs. Assn., Bergen County Players (life). Club: Polish Univ. (N.J.). Home: 27 Isabella Pl Glen Rock NJ 07452 Office: 222 Broadway New York NY 10038

LASKOWSKI, MICHAEL, JR., chemist; b. Warsaw, Poland, Mar. 13, 1930; s. Michael and Maria (Dabrowska) L.; came to U.S., 1947, naturalized, 1955; B.S. magna cum laude, Lawrence Coll., 1950; Ph.D. (NIH fellow), Cornell U., 1954, postgrad., 1954-55; postgrad. Yale U., 1955-56; m. Joan Claire Heyer, Nov. 29, 1957; children—Michael Christopher, Marta Joan. Research asst. Marquette U., 1949-50; instr. Cornell U., 1956-57; asst. prof. chemistry Purdue U., 1957-61, asso. prof., 1961-65, prof., 1965—; chmn. Gordon Research Conf. Physics and Phys. Chemistry Biopolymers, 1966; mem. study sect. NIH, 1967-71. Recipient McCoy award Purdue U., 1975; co-recipient award in biol. scis. Alfred Jurzykowski Found., 1977. Mem. Am. Chem. Soc. (chmn. sect. 1968-69), Am. Soc. Biol. Chemists, AAAS, AAUP, Polish Acad. Arts, Sci. Am., ACLU, Sigma Xi. Editorial bd. Archives Biochemistry, Biophysics, 1972—, Biochemistry, 1973-78; contbr. articles to profl. jours. Home: 1717 Maywood Dr West Lafayette IN 47906 Office: Dept Chemistry Purdue U West Lafayette IN 47907

LASKY, BURTON S., publishing cons.; b. N.Y.C., Dec. 18, 1924; s. Joseph and Celia (Levowitz) L.; B.A., Coll. City N.Y., 1943; m. Lorraine Lanouette, Apr. 7, 1950; children—Michael, Andrew, Alan. Book prodn. mgr. Acad. Press, Inc., N.Y.C., 1952-55; founder, 1955, since pres. Burton Lasky Assos., Inc., editorial agy., N.Y.C.; founder, pres. Agathon Press, Inc., pubs., N.Y.C., 1969-76; co-founder, pres. APS Publns., Inc., jour. and book pubs., N.Y.C., 1971-76; lectr. graphic arts and pub. div. Sch. Continuing Edn., N.Y. U., 1958-73. Vice pres. bd. dirs. Riverdale Mental Health Assn., Bronx, N.Y., 1968—, Exptl. Systems, Inc., Creative Teaching Workshop, 1974—. Served with AUS, 1943-46. Contbr. articles to profl. jours. Home: 2741 Arlington Ave Bronx NY 10463 Office: 111 8th Ave New York City NY 10011

LASKY, DAVID, lawyer; b. N.Y.C., Nov. 12, 1932; s. Benjamin and Rebecca (Malumed) L.; B.A., Bklyn. Coll., 1954; LL.B., Columbia, 1957; m. Phyllis Beryl Sumper, Apr. 14, 1957; children—Jennifer Lee, Robert Barry. Admitted to N.Y. bar, 1957; atty. N.Y.C. R.R. Co., 1957-62; with Curtiss-Wright Corp., N.Y.C., 1962—, corp. counsel, 1966-67, gen. counsel, 1967-72, v.p., 1972—. Chmn. zoning bd. appeals, Ramapo, N.Y., 1968-72. Served with AUS, 1957-58. Mem. Am., N.Y. bar assns., Assn. Bar City N.Y., Phi Beta Kappa. Home: 354 Manchester Rd Ridgewood NJ 07450 Office: One Passaic St Wood-Ridge NJ 07075

LASKY, MELVIN JONAH, editor, publisher; b. N.Y.C., Jan. 15, 1920; s. Samuel and Esther (Kantrowitz) L.; B.S.S., Coll. City N.Y., 1939; M.A., U. Mich.; postgrad. Columbia, 1941-43; m. Brigitte Newiger, 1947 (div. 1974); children—Vivienne, Oliver. Lit. editor The New Leader, N.Y.C., 1942-43; fgn. corr., 1946-48; editor, publisher Der Monat, Berlin, Germany, 1948-58, 78—; co-editor Encounter mag., London, Eng., 1958—; editorial dir. Library Press, N.Y.C., 1970—; publisher Alcove Press, London, 1972—. Served to capt. U.S. Army, 1943-46; ETO. Recipient U. Mich. Sesquicentennial award, 1967; Resident Scholar award CCNY, 1978. Club: Garrick (London). Author: Reisenotizen und Tagebücher, 1958; Africa for Beginners, 1962; Utopia and Revolution, 1976; contbg. author: America and Europe, 1951, New Paths in American History, 1965, Sprache und Politik, 1969, Festschrift for Raymond Aron, 1971. Editor The Hungarian Revolution, 1957. Home: 37 Godfrey St Chelsea London SW3 England Office: 59 St Martin's Ln London WC2N 4JS England

LASKY, MOSES, lawyer; b. Denver, Nov. 2, 1907; s. Juda Eisen and Ida (Grossman) L.; A.B. magna cum laude, U. Colo., 1926, J.D., 1928; LL.M., Harvard, 1929; m. Ruth Helen Abraham, July 6, 1933; children—Morelle, Marshall. Asst. dept. econs. U. Colo., 1925-26; salesman, local sales mgr. R.C. Barnum Co., Cleve., 1927-28; admitted to Calif. bar, 1930, U.S. Supreme Ct., 1947; asso. Brobeck, Phleger & Harrison, San Francisco, 1929-41, partner, 1941-79; partner firm Lasky, Haas, Cohler & Manter, San Francisco, 1979—; instr. Golden Gate Law Sch., 1934-35. Pres. bd. dirs. San Francisco Mus. Art, 1963-64, now trustee; pres. Regional Arts Council San Francisco, 1963-64; v.p. bd. dirs. San Francisco Art Inst., 1964; trustee War Meml. San Francisco, 1969-75; co-chmn. San Francisco Crime Com., 1968-71; bd. dirs. The Exploratorium, San Francisco, 1979—; bd. overseers Los Angeles br. Hebrew Union Coll. Recipient Disting. Alumnus award U. Colo. Law Sch., 1977. Fellow Am. Coll. Trial Lawyers; mem. Am. Bar Assn., Phi Beta Kappa, Delta Sigma Rho. Contbr. articles in legal field and on Jewish life to jours. and mags. Home: 10 Mountain Spring Ave San Francisco CA 94114 Office: Stewart St Tower Suite 1605 No 1 Market Plaza San Francisco CA 94105

LASKY, ROYLE LAUNCEY (ROYLE LAUNCEY), hobby kit mfg. co. exec.; b. Milw., June 14, 1930; d. Leroy and Anne (Edelman) Michel; children—Kim Glaser Selbert, Leslie Glaser Kanner. With Revell, Inc., Venice, Calif., 1958—, pres., chief exec. officer, 1970-72, chairwoman bd., 1972-79, vice chairwoman bd., 1979—; video-tape participant UCLA mgmt. course, 1974. Mem. Toy Mfrs. Assn. (dir. 1975), Hobby Industry Assn. Am. (dir. 1974-75, sec. 1975, exec. com. 1975), Young Pres.'s Orgn. (exec. com. 1976-77). Office: 4223 Glencoe Ave Venice CA 90291

LASKY, VICTOR, news columnist, author; b. Liberty, N.Y., Jan. 7, 1918; s. Max and Bella (Polen) L.; B.A., Bklyn. Coll., 1940; m. Patricia Pratt, Sept. 6, 1952. Reporter, Chgo. Sun, 1941-47; corr. Stars and Stripes, ETO, 1943-45; rewriteman-reporter N.Y. World-Telegram, 1947-50; screenwriter Metro-Goldwyn-Mayer, Culver City, Calif., 1951-52; writer RKO Gen.-Teleradio, 1955; pub. relations exec. Radio Liberty, N.Y.C., 1956-60; news columnist N.Am. Newspaper Alliance, 1962—. Clubs: Overseas Press (N.Y.C.); Nat. Press (Washington). Author: (with R. de Toledano) Seeds of Treason, 1950; J.F.K., The Man and The Myth, 1963; The Ugly Russian, 1965; Robert F. Kennedy, The Myth and the Man, 1968; (with George Murphy) Say, Didn't You Used to be George Murphy, 1970; Arthur J. Goldberg, The Old and the New, 1970; It Didn't Start with Watergate, 1977; Jimmy Carter: The Man and The Myth, 1979; also chpts. in books. Editor: American Legion Reader, 1953. Home: 700 New Hampshire Ave NW Washington DC 20037

LASLEY, JAMES BERNARD, textile co. exec.; b. nr. Reidsville, N.C., Oct. 10, 1918; s. Joseph B. and Sallie L. (Strader) L.; B.S. in Mech. Engring., N.C. State U., 1939; grad. exec. program U. N.C., 1961; m. Myrtle Edna Bailey, Sept. 20, 1941; children—Jansen B., John H., Justina. Supt. bldgs. and grounds Meredith Coll., Raleigh, N.C., 1939-41; asst. plant engr. N.C. Shipbldg. Co., Wilmington, N.C., 1941-46, profl. mech. engr., 1946-47; with Springs Mills, Inc., 1947—, plant engr., 1948-60, asst. to v.p. finishing, 1960-62, dir. finishing, 1962-64, v.p. finishing, 1964-66, v.p. corp. devel., 1966-67, exec. v.p. ops., 1968-69, exec. v.p. engring., research and corp. devel., 1969—, also dir., mem. corp. mgmt., corp. long-range planning, exec., fin. coms. Trustee Textile Research Inst. Registered profl. engr., N.C. Mem. Am. Soc. M.E. (past sect. chmn.), N.C. State U. Alumni Assn. (bd. 1972—), Phi Kappa Phi, Theta Tau, Pi Tau Sigma. Methodist. Patentee open-width wet processing apparatus, mercerizing frame washing system, pillow tubing opening and detwister. Home: Route 4 Box 334 Lancaster SC 29720 Office: Springs Mills Inc Fort Mill SC 29715

LASNICK, JULIUS, business exec.; b. Paterson, N.J., Aug. 15, 1929; s. Herman and Badana L.; B.S. in Textiles, N.C. State U., 1951; m. Ann Kaplan, July 20, 1958; children—David, Laurie. With Milliken & Co., N.Y.C., 1951-78, gen. mgr., until 1978; exec. v.p. mktg. M. Lowenstein Corp., N.Y.C., 1978—. Served with U.S. Army, 1953-55. Office: M Lowenstein Corp 1430 Broadway New York NY 10018

LASOR, WILLIAM SANFORD, clergyman, educator; b. Phila., Oct. 25, 1911; s. William Allan and Sara (Lewis) LaS.; A.B., U. Pa., 1931; Th.B., Princeton Sem., 1934, Th.M., 1943; M.A., Princeton, 1934; Ph.D. (Dropsie fellow in Assyriology), Dropsie U., 1949; Th.D., U. So. Cal., 1956; m. Elizabeth Granger Vaughan, June 16, 1934; children—William Sanford, Elizabeth Ann La Sor Kirkpatrick, Frederick Eugene, Susanne Marie La Sor Whyte. Ordained to ministry Presbyn. Ch., 1934; pastor First Presbyn. Ch., Ocean City, N.J., 1934-38, Green Ridge Presbyn. Ch., Scranton, Pa., 1938-43; prof., chmn. dept. religion Lafayette Coll., 1946-49; prof. O.T., Fuller Theol. Sem., Pasadena, Calif., 1949-77, sr. prof. O.T., 1977—. Vis. prof. Israel-Am. Inst., 1962, mem. Pre-Holy Year Ecumenical Pilgrimage, 1974. Comdg. officer Naval Res. Chaplain Co., Los Angeles, 1968-70. Pres. bd. dirs. Tokyo Evangelistic Center. Served as chaplain USNR, 1943-46. Fellow Am. Assn. Theol. Schs., 1961-62. Mem. Am. Assn. Profs. Hebrew, Soc. Bibl. Lit. and Exegesis, Internat. Orgn. O.T. Scholars, Soc. O.T. Scholars (Brit.), Mil. Chaplains Assn. (pres. So. Cal. chpt. 1967-69), Alpha Sigma Phi. Republican. Author: Hebrew Handbook, 1951; Dead Sea Scrolls, 1956; Great Personalities of the Old Testament, 1959; Great Personalities of the New Testament, 1961; Handbook of New Testament Greek, 1964, 2d edit., 1973; Daily Life in Bible Times, 1966; Men Who Knew God, 1970; Men Who Knew Christ, 1971; Church Alive!, 1972; Dead Sea Scrolls and the Old Testament, 1972; Israel, 1976; Handbook of Biblical Hebrew, 1978-79; author, photographer documentary film on Ghana Miracle in Black, 1964. Editor Bibliographie Revue de Qumrân, 1960-65; contbr. articles to profl. jours. honored by Festschrift, Biblical and Near Eastern Studies; Essays in Honor of William Sanford La Sor (editor Gary A. Tuttle), 1978. Holds comml. pilots license. Home: 1790 E Loma Alta Dr Altadena CA 91001 Office: 135 N Oakland Ave Pasadena CA 91101. *I have always been aware of God's leading my life. This does not imply that I have always been right or successful. At every moment I am faced with choices. But once I have made a choice, I act on the conviction that this is God's will. Tensions, worry about whether I have done the right thing, and pressures disappear. Whether I succeed or fail, I know that God is leading me to His ultimate goal and teaching me through the experience.*

LASORDA, TOM CHARLES, profl. baseball team mgr.; b. Norristown, Pa., Sept. 22, 1927; s. Sam and Carmella (Covatto) L.; student pub. schs., Norristown; m. Joan Miller, Apr. 14, 1950; children—Laura, Tom Charles. Profl. player with Bklyn. Dodgers, 1954-55, Kansas City A's, 1956; with Los Angeles Dodgers, 1956—, mgr., 1977—. Served with U.S. Army, 1945-47. Los Angeles Dodgers winner Nat. League pennant, 1977, 78 played in World Series, 1977, 78; 2d Nat. League mgr. to win pennant first two yrs. as mgr. Mem. Profl. Baseball Players Am. Roman Catholic. Club: Variety of Calif. (v.p.). Home: 1473 W Maxzim St Fullerton CA 92633 Office: 1000 Elysian Park Ave Los Angeles CA 90012

LASOTA, JOHN ALBERT, JR., lawyer; b. Paterson, N.J., Oct. 19, 1941; LL.B., U. Ariz., 1966. Admitted to Ariz. bar, 1966; police legal advisor Phoenix Police Dept., 1967-72; asst. prof., asst. dean Ariz. State U., 1972-75; chief asst. atty. gen. State of Ariz., Phoenix, 1975-78, acting atty. gen., 1978, atty. gen., 1978. Chmn. police sect. Phoenix Citizens Bond Adv. Council, 1975; mem., chmn. City of Phoenix Criminal Justice Adv. Com., 1972-75. Mem. Nat. Assn. Attys. Gen. Office: 100 W Washington St Phoenix AZ 85003

LASS, ERNEST WILLIAM, newspaper and radio sta. exec.; b. Roselle, N.J., Jan. 7, 1907; s. Ernest Charles and Elizabeth (Otter) L.; Litt.B., Rutgers U., 1928; L.H.D. (hon.), Monmouth Coll., 1971; m. Frances F. Felger, Apr. 14, 1933; children—E. Donald, Barbara Ann Lass Carr. With Asbury Park Press, Inc. (N.J.), 1928—, sec.-treas. 1945-74, pub., 1974, chmn. bd., 1974—; dir. emeritus Midlantic Nat. Bank-Mchts.; dir. F. & F. Felger, Inc. Mem. N.J. Water Resources Com., 1952, N.J. Commn. to Study Adminstrv. and Profl. Salaries, 1958; chmn. Monmouth County (N.J.) Welfare Bd., 1962-68. Recipient Brotherhood award NCCJ, 1972; Disting. Citizen award Boy Scouts Am., 1977; Achievement award State of Israel, 1968. Mem. N.J. Press Assn. (pres. 1957-58, Four Freedoms award 1942), Am. Newspaper Pubs. Assn., Internat. Press Inst., Asbury Park C. of C. (pres. 1955-56). Club: Deal Golf and Country. Home: 511 Woodmere Rd Interlaken NJ 07712 Office: Press Plaza Asbury Park NJ 07712

LASSAW, IBRAM, sculptor; b. Alexandria, Egypt, May 4, 1913 (derivative citizen); s. Philip and Bertha (Zaleski) L.; student Clay Club, 1927-32, Beaux Arts Inst. Design, N.Y.C., 1930-31, Coll. City N.Y., 1931-32; student art Amedée Ozenfant; m. Ernestine Blumberg, Dec. 15, 1944; 1 dau., Denise. One-man shows: Kootz Gallery, N.Y.C., 1951, 52, 54, 58, 60, 63, 64, Mass. Inst. Tech., 1958, Duke, 1963, Benson Gallery, 1966, Gertrude Kasle Gallery, Detroit, 1968, Zabriskie Gallery, N.Y.C., 1977; others; exhibited at museums, univs., art insts. in U.S., Japan, France, Italy, Holland, Denmark, Switzerland, Eng., S. Am., USSR, also Internat. Exhbn. Sculpture, Musée Rodin, Paris, 1956, retrospective Heckscher Mus., Huntington, N.Y., 1973, Smithsonian Instn., 1975, Whitney Mus. Am. Art, 1976, 78, U. N.Mex., Albuquerque, 1977, Guild Hall, East Hampton, N.Y., 1978; represented in permanent collections; Mus. Modern Art, N.Y.C., Whitney Mus. Am. Art, N.Y.C., Museu de Arte Moderna, Rio de Janeiro, Brazil, Gallery Contemporary Art, Carnegie-Mellon U., Pitts., Balt. Mus. Art, Washington U., St. Louis, Albright Knox Art Gallery, Buffalo, Nat. Collection Fine Arts, Smithsonian Instn., Wadsworth Atheneum, Hartford, Conn., Fogg Mus. of Harvard U., Newark Mus., Worcester (Mass.) Art Mus., U. Calif. Mus., Berkeley, U. N.C., Greensboro, Birla Mus., Calcutta, India, Israel Mus., Jerusalem, Wichita (Kans.) Art Mus., Bklyn. Mus.; works in pvt. collections including Nelson Rockefeller, William A. M. Burden; one of five U.S. reps. to Venice Biennale, 1954; prin. commns. include large sculpture Pillar of Fire, Temple Beth-El, Springfield, Mass., 1953, sculptures Temple Beth-El, Providence, 1954, editorial room Seventeen mag., 1954, Sculpture Pantheon, Celanese Bldg., N.Y.C., also residential archtl. sculpture; Benjamin N. Duke prof. Duke U., 1962-63; tchr. U. Calif. at Berkeley, 1965-66, Am. U., 1950, Colo. Coll., Colorado Springs, 1965; adj. faculty Southampton (L.I.) Coll., 1966—; vis. prof. Brandeis U., 1975, Mt. Holyoke Coll., 1978. Served as pvt. AUS, World War II. Mem. Am. Abstract Artists (pres. 1946-48). Pioneer welding techniques in sculpting. Work reproduced in numerous books. Home and Studio: PO Box 487 East Hampton NY 11937

LASSER, DAVID, former labor exec.; b. Balt., Mar. 20, 1902; s. Leonard and Lena (Jaffee) L.; student engring. Mass. Inst. Tech., 1920-24; m. Florence Glassberg, Aug. 26, 1927; 1 son, Daniel Joseph; m. 2d, Helen Gerber, Sept. 25, 1937; 1 stepdau., Elaine Karen; m. 3d, Amelia Tolbert, Dec. 23, 1963. Engr. Rossendale Reddaway Co., Newark, 1924; prodn. mgr. Halperin Mills, Bklyn., 1925-26; ins. agt. Met. Life Co., 1927; tech. writer N.Y. Edison Co., 1927-29; mng. editor Gernsback Publs., N.Y.C., 1929-33; chmn. Workers Unemployed Union, N.Y.C., 1933-35; pres. Workers Alliance Am. until resignation 1940; pres. Am. Security Union, 1940-41; labor cons. Work Projects Adminstrn., 1941, WPB, 1942, asst. dir. plant productivity div., 1943-45, office labor requirements Civilian Prodn. Adminstrn.; dir. office labor adv. coms., 1944-47; spl. labor adviser, sec. commerce, 1947-48; asst. to pres. for econs. and collective bargaining Internat. Union Elec., Radio and Machine Workers AFL-CIO, 1950-69, ret. 1969. Served with U.S. Army, 1918; to sgt. 49th Inf., A.E.F., 1918-1919. Mem. Indsl. Relations Research Assn., DAV World War, Soc. Advancement Mgmt., Am. Inst. Indsl. Engrs. Sigma Alpha Mu. Author: Conquest of Space 1931; Private Monopoly-The Enemy at Home, 1945; also numerous articles. Home: 12539 Plaza Centrada San Diego CA 92128

LASSER, ELLIOTT CHARLES, physician, educator; b. Buffalo, Nov. 30, 1922; s. Isydor and Rosa (Goldstein) L.; B.S., Harvard, 1943; M.D., U. Buffalo, 1946; M.S., U. Minn., 1952; m. Phyllis Adler, Sept. 24, 1944; children—Andrew, Kenneth, Theodore, Robin. Intern. Buffalo Gen. Hosp., 1946-47; resident and instr. radiology U. Minn. Med. Sch., 1949-53; dir. diagnostic radiology Roswell Park Meml. Inst., Buffalo, 1953-56; asst. prof. radiology U. Buffalo Sch. Medicine, 1956; prof., chmn. dept. radiology U. Pitts. Sch. Medicine, 1956-68; prof. radiology Med. Sch., U. Calif. at San Diego, 1968—, chmn. dept., 1968-77. Mem. Am. Coll. Radiology, A.M.A., Assn. Univ. Radiologists, Radiol. Soc. N.A., Calif., San Diego radiol. socs. Home: 8081 Calle del Cielo La Jolla CA 92037

LASSER, LOUISE, actress; b. N.Y.C.; ed. Brandeis U., New Sch. for Social Research; student Sanford Maisner; m. Woody Allen, 1966 (div.). Appeared in: (plays) I Can Get It For You Wholesale, 1962, The Third Ear, 1964, Henry, Sweet Henry, 1967, Lime Green/Khaki Blue, 1969, The Chinese, 1970; (films) What's New, Pussycat?, 1965, What's Up, Tiger Lily?, 1966, Take the Money and Run, 1969, Bananas, 1971, Everything You Always Wanted to Know About Sex But Were Afraid to Ask, 1972, Such Good Friends, 1971, Slither, 1973; (TV drama) The Lie, 1976; (TV movies) Isn't It Shocking?, 1973, Just Me and You, 1978; (TV series) Masquerade, Mary Hartman, Mary Hartman. Address: care Tandem Productions 1901 Ave of Stars Los Angeles CA 90067*

LASSERS, WILLARD J., judge; b. Kankakee, Ill., Aug. 24, 1919; s. Henry and Sylvia (Oppenheim) L.; A.B., U. Chgo., 1940, J.D., 1942; m. Elisabeth Stern, June 30, 1946; 1 dau., Deborah Lassers Hauser. Admitted to D.C. bar, 1941, Ill. bar, 1942, U.S. Supreme Ct. bar, 1965; practiced in Chgo., 1946—; practice with Alex Elson, Chgo., 1946-48, Elson and Cotton, 1948-49; atty. RFC, Chgo., 1950-51; atty. Office Price Stablzn., Chgo., 1951-53; individual practice law, Chgo., 1953-60; partner Elson, Lassers and Wolff, Chgo., 1960-78; judge Circuit Ct. Cook County, Chgo., 1978—; lectr. taxation U. Chgo., 1954-55. Mem. Gov.'s Com. to Study Consumer Credit Laws, 1962-63; chmn. Com. Ill. Govt., 1962-63. Bd. dirs. Ill. div. ACLU, to 1978. Served with AUS, 1943-46. Mem. Ill., Chgo. bar assns., Am. Arbitration Assn. (mem. panel labor arbitrators 1965-78). Author: (with Alex Elson and Aaron S. Wolff) Civil Practice Forms Annotated, Illinois and Federal, 1952, 65; Scapegoat Justice: Lloyd Miller and the Failure of the Legal System, 1973; reviser: Fletcher Corporation Forms, 5 vols., 1957-60. Home: 1509 E 56th St Chicago IL 60637 Office: Richard J Daley Center Chicago IL 60602

LASSETTRE, EDWIN NICHOLS, educator, phys. chemist; b. Monroe County, Ga., Oct. 26, 1911; s. Carlos E. and Jennie J. (Nichols) L.; B.Sc., Mont. State Coll., 1933; Ph.D., Calif. Inst. Tech., 1938; D.Tech. (hon.), Royal Inst. Tech., Stockholm, 1977; m. Ilse R. Sturies, Dec. 22, 1951. Mem. faculty Ohio State U., 1937-62, prof. chemistry, 1950-62; group leader, research scientist Manhattan Project, SAM Labs., Columbia, 1944, Carbide and Carbon Chems. Corp., 1945; staff fellow, mem. adv. com. Mellon Inst., Pitts., 1962-67; staff fellow, prof. chem. physics Carnegie-Mellon U., 1967-74, univ. prof. chem. physics, 1974-77, emeritus, 1977—, dir. Center for Spl. Studies, 1971-73. Cons. gaseous diffusion plant Oak Ridge Nat. Lab., 1954-67, rev. com. radiol. physics div. Argonne Nat. Lab., 1968-70, del. Argonne Univs. Assn., 1971-74. Fellow Am. Phys. Soc.; mem. Am. Chem. Soc., Optical Soc. Am. Editorial bd. Jour. Chem. Physics, 1967-69, Jour. Electron Spectroscopy and Related Phenomena, 1971-75. Contbr. articles in field. Home: 224 E Waldheim Rd Pittsburgh PA 15215 Office: 4400 5th Ave Pittsburgh PA 15213

LASSITER, CHARLES ALBERT, educator; b. Murray, Ky., Feb. 20, 1927; s. E.A. and Helen (Wells) L.; student Murray State Coll., 1946-48; B.S., U. Ky., 1949, M.S., 1950; Ph.D., Mich. State U., 1952; m. Robbie Richerson, Sept. 9, 1946; children—John Wells, Barbara Marie. Faculty dairy sci. U. Ky., 1952-56, Mich. State U., 1956-76, prof. dairy sci., chmn. dept., 1959-76; head dept. animal sci. N.C. State U., 1976—. Mem. fgn. mission bd. So. Bapt. Conf., 1965-71; mem. exec. com. Bapt. State Conv., 1972—. Trustee, Golden Gate Bapt. Theol. Sem., 1971-76. Served with USNR, 1945-46. Recipient award for nutrition research Am. Feed Mfrs. Assn., 1958. Mem. Am. Dairy Sci. Assn. (dir. 1968-71), Am. Soc. Animal Sci., Sigma Xi, Phi Kappa Phi, Zeta Phi, Alpha Zeta. Home: 138 Castlewood Dr Cary NC 27511

LASSITER, RONALD CORBETT, business exec.; b. Houston, Aug. 2, 1932; s. Mance and Pauline Marie (Lloyd) L.; B.A., Rice U., 1955; M.B.A., Harvard, 1964; m. Ella Lee Moechel, Dec. 26, 1951; children—Rona Lee, James Mance, Jennifer Lynn, Lynda Fay. Controller, Agrico div. Continental Oil Co., N.Y.C., 1966-69; v.p. Marathon Mfg. Co., Houston, 1969-70; sr. v.p. Zapata Corp., Houston, 1970-71, exec. v.p., 1971-77, sr. exec. v.p., 1977-78, pres., chief operating officer, 1978—, also dir.; chmn. bd. Paramount Pacific, Inc., Penn West Fuels, Inc., Zapata Coastal Transport, Inc., Zapata Colo. Mining Corp., Zapata Elkhorn, Inc., Zapata Fuels, Inc., Zapata Ocean Carriers, Inc., Zapata Products, Inc., Zapata Protein, Inc., Zapata Sea Services, Inc., Zapata Tankships, Inc., Zapata Western LNG, Inc.; dir. Granby Mining Co., Granisle Copper, Ltd., Houston, Pesquera Zapata S.A. Mem. Soc. Mining Engrs., Am. Inst. Mining, Metall. and Petroleum Engrs., Petroleum Club Houston. Club: Athletic (Houston). Home: 10811 Bridlewood Dr Houston TX 77024 Office: Zapata Tower Houston TX 77002

LASSLO, ANDREW, medicinal chemist, educator; b. Mukacevo, Czechoslovakia, Aug. 24, 1922; s. Vojtech Laszlo and Terezie (Herskovicova) L.; M.S., U. Ill., 1948, Ph.D., 1952, M.L.S., 1961; m. Wilma Ellen Reynolds, July 9, 1955; 1 dau., Millicent Andrea. Came to U.S., 1946, naturalized, 1951. Research chemist organic chems. div. Monsanto Chem. Co., St. Louis, 1952-54; asst. prof. pharmacology, div. basic health scis. Emory U., 1954-60; prof., chmn. dept. medicinal chemistry Coll. Pharmacy, U. Tenn. Center for Health Scis., 1960—; cons. Geschickter Fund for Med. Research Inc., 1961-62; dir. postgrad. tng. program sci. librarians USPHS, 1966-72; dir. postgrad. tng. program organic medicinal chemistry for chemists FDA, 1971; exec. com. adv. council S.E. Regional Med. Library Program, 1969-71; mem. president's faculty adv. council U. Tenn. System, 1970-72; chmn. energy authority U. Tenn. Center for Health Scis., 1975-77, chmn. council departmental chmn., 1977; chmn. Internat. Symposium on Contemporary Trends in Tng. Phamacologists, Helsinki, 1975. Served to capt. M.S.C., U.S. Army Res., 1953-62.

Recipient Sigma Xi Research prize, 1949, Honor Scroll Tenn. Inst. Chemists, 1976; Americanism medal D.A.R., 1976; U. Ill. fellow, 1950-51; Geschickter Fund Med. Research grantee, 1959-65; USPHS Research and Tng. grantee, 1958-64, 66-72; NSF research grantee, 1964-66. Fellow A.A.A.S., Am. Inst. Chemists (nat. councillor for Tenn. 1969-70); mem. A.L.A. (life), Am. Chem. Soc. (sr.), Am. Pharmaceut. Assn., Am. Soc. Pharmacology and Exptl. Therapeutics (chmn. subcom. pre-and postdoctoral tng. 1974-78, exec. com. ednl. and profl. affairs 1974-78), Drug Info. Assn. (bd. dirs. 1968-69, chmn. com. edn. 1966-68), Med. Library Assn. (chmn. com. regional med. library programs 1971-72), Sigma Xi (pres. elect U. Tenn. Center for Health Sci. chpt. 1975-76, pres. 1976-77), Beta Phi Mu, Rho Chi. Methodist (past trustee, ofcl. and adminstrv. bd., chmn. com. edn. and social concerns). Club: Health Scis. Center Faculty Club (charter bd. dirs. 1966-68, exec. com. 1967-68). Producer, moderator TV and radio series Health Care Perspectives, 1976-78. Editor: Surface Chemistry and Dental Intequments, 1973. Contbr. numerous articles in sci. and profl. jours. Mem. editorial bd. Jour. Medicinal and Pharm. Chemistry, 1961, U. Tenn. Press, 1974-77. Inventor, patentee. Composer: Synthesis in C Minor (piano), 1968. Home: 5479 Timmons Ave Memphis TN 38117 Office: 26 S Dunlap St Memphis TN 38163. *Of all the pleasures a human being can savor, none exceeds the satisfaction of a genuine sense of accomplishment. It undergirds all elements of creative living and surmounts vicissitudes exceeding conventional human endurance.*

LASSNER, FRANZ GEORGE, found. exec.; b. Leipzig, Germany, May 6, 1926; s. Oscar and Marga (Treskow) L.; A.B. in History, Rutgers U., 1947; M.A. in History, Georgetown U., 1951, Ph.D. in Govt., 1960; m. Marguerite Sansone, Aug. 18, 1961; children—Alexander Nicholas, John Paul. With various research projects Georgetown U., Washington, 1951-62; research supt. Russian Studies Project, Washington, 1956-57; research asso., curator spl. collections Hoover Inst., Stanford, Calif., 1962-63, dir. archives, 1969-74, spl. rep., 1974—; dir. devel. Phila. Coll. Textiles and Sci., 1974-76; sr. v.p. programs Freedoms Found., Valley Forge, 1977—; dir. Herbert Hoover Presdl. Library, West Branch, Iowa, 1963-67; dir. research and publs. Hoover Found., Des Moines, 1968; dir. polit. studies program Balzekas Mus. of Lithuanian Culture. Mem. Phila. Soc., Lambda Chi Alpha, Delta Phi Alpha. Roman Catholic. Clubs: University (Washington). Home: 9503 Meadowbrook Ave Philadelphia PA 19118 Office: Freedoms Found Valley Forge PA 19481

LASSWELL, MARCIA LEE, psychologist; b. Oklahoma City, July 13, 1927; d. Lee and Stella (Blackard) Eck; B.A., U. Calif., Berkeley, 1949; M.A., U. So. Calif., 1952; postgrad. U. Calif., Riverside, U. So. Calif., U. N.C.; m. Thomas Lasswell, May 29, 1950; children—Marcia Jane, Thomas Ely, Julia Lee. Individual practice psychotherapy, marriage and family counseling, Pomona, Calif.; asst. prof. Pepperdine Coll., Los Angeles, 1959-60; asst. prof. psychology behavioral sci. dept. Calif. State U., Pomona, 1960-64, asso. prof., 1965-69, prof., 1970—, chmn. dept., 1964-69; asso. clin. dir. Human Relations Center, U. So. Calif., 1975—; vis. asso. prof. Scripps Coll., 1968-69, U. So. Calif., 1969-70, Occidental Coll., 1971-72; lectr. various Calif. univs.; columnist McCall's mag.; mem. staff spl. project alcoholics and narcotics offenders Calif. Prison System, 1970-73; mem. Calif. Accreditation Com. Secondary Schs. and Colls., 1965—. Bd. dirs. Calif. Mental Health Authority, Planned Parenthood San Gabriel Valley, Open Door Free Clinic. Recipient Outstanding Tchrs. award Calif. State U., 1971. Fellow Am. Assn. Marital and Family Therapy (dir. 1970-72); mem. Am. Sociol. Assn., Pacific Sociology Assn., Nat. Council Family Relations (exec. com. 1978-80), AAAS, Conf. Conciliation Cts., So. Calif. Assn. Marital and Family Therapy (pres. 1972-73), Alpha Kappa Delta, Phi Delta Gamma, Pi Gamma Mu. Author: College Teaching of General Psychology, 1967; Love, Marriage and Family, 1973; No-Fault Marriage, 1976; Styles of Loving, 1980. Home: 875 Hillcrest Dr Pomona CA 91768

LASSWELL, MARY CLYDE GRAYSON LUBBOCK (MRS. DUDLEY WINN SMITH), author; b. Glasgow, Scotland, Feb. 8, 1905 (parents Am. citizens); d. William Robinson and Mary Clyde (Caskey) Lubbock; B.S., U. Tex., 1930; m. Clyde Lasswell, Jan. 3, 1938; m. 2d, Dudley Winn Smith, Feb. 3, 1964. Mem. Tex. Civil War Centennial Commn. Mem. Authors League Am., Dramatists Guild, Tex. Inst. Letters, Daus. Republic Tex., ASCAP, Theta Sigma Phi. Episcopalian. Columnist Houston Chronicle, 1959-64. Author: Suds in Your Eye, 1942 (Broadway play dramatized by Jack Kirkland, 1943); High Time, 1944; Mrs. Rasmussen's Book of One Arm Cookery, 1946; Bread for the Living, 1948; One on the House, 1949; Walt for the Wagon, 1951; Tooner Schooner, 1953; (with Bob Pool) I'll Take Texas, 1958; Let's Go For Broke, 1962; Tio Pepe (wrote words, music, libretto for musical comedy 1968), 1963; Biography John Henry Kirby, 1966; Mrs. Rasmussen's Book of One Arm Cookery With Second Helpings, 1970; also wrote lyrics, music, and book for mus. Lonely Star set in Republic of Texas, 1951. Editor, compiler Rags and Hope. Address: PO Box 316 Los Alamos CA 93440

LASSWELL, THOMAS ELY, author, educator; b. St. Louis, Oct. 29, 1919; s. Gustavus and Miriam (Ely) L.; student Westminster Coll., 1936-38; A.B., Ark. Coll., 1940; M.S. in Edn., U. So. Calif., 1947, Ph.D. in Sociology, 1953; m. Marcia Lee Eck, May 29, 1950; children—Marcia Jane, Thomas Ely, Julia Lee. Prin., Highland Instn., Guerrant, Ky., 1941-42; asst. prof. Pepperdine Coll., Los Angeles, 1950-54; asso. prof. sociology Grinnell Coll., 1954-59; mem. faculty U. So. Calif., Los Angeles 1959—, prof., 1963—, chmn. dept. sociology and anthropology, 1965-66, dir. resident honors, 1961-70; vis. prof. Stephen F. Austin State Coll., Nacogdoches, Tex., 1950, 56, 58, Whittier Coll., 1957, Northwestern U., 1960, Pomona Coll., 1967-68, U. Calif., San Diego, 1967-68, U. Hawaii, 1975; cons. Deasy & Bolling Architects, 1965—, Warren V. Bush Prodns., Inc., 1977—. Vice pres. bd. Iowa Council Family Relations, 1958-59; mem. Nat. Council on Family Relations, 1957—; pres. Faculty Center Assn., 1966-67. Bd. dirs. Hacker Found., Beverly Hills, Calif., 1970—. Served to lt. USNR, 1942-46. Fellow Am. Sociol. Assn.; mem. Internat., Pacific sociol. assns., Internat. Council on Social Welfare, Soc. for Study Symbolic Interaction, Am. Assn. Marriage and Family Counselors (dir.) So. Calif. Assn. Marriage and Family Therapy (pres. 1978-79), Alpha Kappa Delta, Phi Kappa Phi. Club: Yorke House. Author: Class and Stratum, 1965; (with Burma and Aronson) Life in Society, 1965, 2d edit., 1970; (with Marcia E. Lasswell) Love, Marriage and Family, 1973; (with Jerry G. Bode) Sociology in Context, 1974. Mng. editor Sociology and Social Research, 1960-65, asso. editor, 1965-70; series editor Schenkman series in stratification; series editor Gen. Learning Press Instructional System: Sociology. Home: 875 Hillcrest Dr Pomona CA 91768 Office: Dept Sociology Univ Southern California Los Angeles CA 90007

LASTER, HOWARD JOSEPH, univ. dean; b. Jersey City, Mar. 13, 1930; s. Harry and Yetta (Adelman) L.; A.B., Harvard U., 1951; Ph.D., Cornell U., Ithaca, N.Y., 1957; m. Miriam Sargeant, Apr. 26, 1952; children—Elizabeth, Jonathan, Jane, Sarah. Mem. faculty U. Md., College Park, 1956-77, prof., 1965-77, chmn. dept. physics and astronomy, 1965-75; dean Coll. Liberal Arts, U. Iowa, Iowa City, 1977—. Mem. Md. Gov.'s Sci. Resources Adv. Bd., 1965-70; mem. Md. Gov.'s Sci. Adv. Council, 1970-77, chmn., 1973-75. Vis. fellow Clare Hall, Cambridge (Eng.) U., 1970-71; vis. program asso. NSF, 1975-76; dir. Atlantic Research Corp., 1972—. Fellow Am. Phys. Soc., Royal Astron. Soc., Washington Acad. Scis.; mem. AAAS, Am. Astron. Soc., Am. Assn. Physic Tchrs., ACLU, AAUP, Washington Philos. Soc., Chesapeake Physics Assn., Md. Acad. Sci., Phi Beta Kappa, Sigma Xi. Democrat. Research in cosmic ray theory, astrophysics and science policy. Office: Coll Liberal Arts U Iowa Iowa City IA 52242

LASTER, LEONARD, physician; b. N.Y.C., Aug. 24, 1928; s. Isaac and Mary (Ehrenreich) L.; A.B., Harvard U., 1949, M.D., 1950; m. Ruth Ann Leventhal, Dec. 16, 1956; children—Judith Eve, Susan Beth, Stephen Jay. From intern to resident in medicine Mass. Gen. Hosp., Boston, 1950-53; fellow gasteronterology Mass. Meml. Hosp., 1958-59; vis. investigator Pub. Health Research Inst., N.Y.C., 1953-54; commd. lt. USPHS, 1954, advanced through grades to asst. surgeon gen. (rear adm.), 1971; mem. staff Nat. Inst. Arthritis, Metabolic and Digestive Diseases, NIH, Bethesda, Md., 1954-73, chief digestive and hereditary diseases br., 1969-73; spl. asst., then asst. dir. human resources President's Office Sci. and Tech., 1969-73; exec. dir. Assembly Life Scis., also div. med. scis. Nat. Acad. Scis.-NRC, 1973-74; resigned USPHS, 1973; v.p. acad. affairs and clin. affairs Med. Center, also dean Coll. Medicine, prof. medicine Downstate Med. Center, State U. N.Y., Bklyn., 1974-78; pres. U. Oreg. Health Scis. Center, Portland, 1978—, prof. medicine Sch. Medicine, 1978—; dir. Blue Cross. Bd. dirs. Found. Advanced Edn. Scis., Bethesda, 1965-69, Bedford Stuyvesant Family Health Center, Bklyn., 1976-78, Med. Research Found. Oreg., Oreg. Symphony, 1979—; pres. Burning Tree Elementary Sch. PTA, Bethesda, 1972-73. Diplomate Nat. Bd. Med. Examiners, Am. Bd. Internal Medicine (gastroenterology). Fellow ACP; mem. Am. Assn. Study Liver Diseases, Am. Fedn. Clin. Research, Am. Gastroenterol. Assn., Am. Soc. Biol. Chemists, Am. Soc. Clin. Investigation, Assn. Am. Med. Colls. (council deans 1974-78), Eastern Gut Club, Marine Biol. Lab. Corp., Portland C. of C. (dir.), Phi Beta Kappa, Alpha Omega Alpha. Clubs: Cosmos (Washington); Harvard (N.Y.C.); University, Downtown Rotary (Portland). Author articles gastrointestinal disease, inborn errors metabolism, devel. biology. Editorial bds. med. jours. Home: 1265 SW Davenport St Portland OR 97201 Office: 3181 SW Sam Jackson Park Rd Portland OR 97201. *Education is nurturing excellence in others and the facilitating its spread as an infectious disease.*

LASTER, RICHARD, food co. exec.; b. Vienna, Austria, Nov. 19, 1923; s. Alan and Caroline L.; naturalized U.S. citizen, 1944; student U. Wash., 1941-42; B.Ch.E. cum laude, Poly. Inst. Bklyn., 1943; postgrad. Stevens Inst. Tech., 1945-47; m. Liselotte Schneider, Oct. 17, 1948; children—Susan (Mrs. Franklin Rubenstein), Thomas. With Gen. Foods Corp., 1944—, with corp. research and devel., Hoboken, N.J., 1944-58, ops. mgr. Franklin Baker div., Hoboken, and Atlantic Gelatin div., Woburn, Mass., 1958-64, mgr. research devel. Jell-O div., White Plains, N.Y., 1964-67, corp. mgr. quality assurance, White Plains, 1967-68, ops. mgr. Maxwell House div., White Plains, 1968-69, exec. v.p. Maxwell House div., 1969-71, pres. Maxwell House div., 1971-73, corp. group v.p., White Plains, 1973-74, exec. v.p. Gen. Foods Corp., 1974—, also dir., pres. research, devel. and food-away-from-home, 1975—; dir. Firestone Tire & Rubber Co. Mem. sch. bd., Chappaqua, N.Y., 1971-73, pres., 1973-74; chmn., mem. bd., 1st v.p. United Way of Westchester, 1978; chmn. adv. com. Poly. Inst. of Westchester, 1977; bd. dirs. Nat. Center for Resource Recovery; trustee Nutrition Found. Inc., Poly. Inst. N.Y.; mem. coll. council SUNY, Purchase. Recipient Distinguished Alumnus award, elected fellow Polytech. Inst. N.Y. Mem. Am. Inst. Chem. Engrs. (Food and Bioengring. award 1972), Am. Chem. Soc., Am. Inst. Chemists, AAAS, Tau Beta Pi, Phi Lambda Upsilon. Clubs: Birchwood Tennis; Woodstock (Vt.) Country. Contbr. articles on food sci. to profl. publs. Patentee in field. Home: 23 Round Hill Rd Chappaqua NY 10514 Office: 250 North St White Plains NY 10625

LASTFOGEL, ABE, talent rep.; b. N.Y.C., May 17, 1898; m. Frances Arms, Apr. 6, 1927. Asso. with William Morris Agy., 1912—, pres., 1952—, chmn. bd., 1969-76, co-chmn. bd., 1976—. Bd. govs. USO; pres. St. Jude Hosp.; bd. dirs. Nat. Jewish Welfare Bd., Big Bros. Greater Los Angeles; asso. Calif. Inst. Tech.; hon. life mem. Am. Theatre Wing. Recipient medal of Freedom and Presdl. certificate of merit from Pres. Truman, 1945. Office: William Morris Agy 151 El Camino Dr Beverly Hills CA 90212*

LASWELL, TROY JAMES, educator; b. Ottawa, Ky., Nov. 12, 1920; s. John Henry and Mattie Mae (Purcell) L.; A.B. in Geology and Geography, Berea Coll., 1942; postgrad. U. Heidelberg (Germany), 1945, Ky. Eastern State U., summer 1946; A.M. in Geology and Geography, Oberlin Coll., 1948; Ph.D. in Geology, U. Mo., 1953; m. Dorothy I. Howard, Mar. 25, 1943; 1 son, David Morris. Instr. geology U. Mo., 1948-53; asst., then asso. prof. geology Washington and Lee U., 1953-57; asso. prof., then prof. geology La. Poly. Inst., 1957-62; prof., head dept. geology and geography Miss. State U., 1962—. Geologist Mo. Geol. Survey, summer 1952, 52-53; cons. geologist Va. Minerals, Inc., 1955-56, So. River Mining Co., 1957, Humble Oil & Refining Co., summers 1955-58; chmn. geology sect. Va. Acad. Scis., 1956-57; dir. NSF Inst. Outstanding High Sch. Students, La. Poly. Inst., summer 1960. Bd. dirs. Miss. Geol. Survey, 1970-78, vice chmn., 1972-73, 74-75, 76-77. Served to capt., C.E., AUS, 1942-46: ETO. Fellow Geol. Soc. Am. (sec. S.E. sect. 1970-75); mem. Am. Assn. Petroleum Geologists, Nat. Assn. Geology Tchrs., Miss. Geol. Soc., Miss. Acad. Scis., Sigma Xi, Phi Kappa Phi, Sigma Gamma Epsilon. Kiwanian. Contbr. articles to profl. jours. Office: PO Box 824 Mississippi State MS 39762

LASZLO, ERNEST, dir. motion picture photography, photographer; b. Szabadka, Yugoslavia, Apr. 23, 1905; s. Max and Gizella (Steiner) L.; grad. Gymnasium, Budapest, Hungary, 1922; m. Rose Ellen Nelson, July 3, 1925; 1 dau., Joan Ellen. Came to U.S., 1923, naturalized, 1928. Camerman, Paramount Studios until 1943, dir. motion picture photography, 1943-49; free-lance, 1949—. Vice pres. Am. Soc. Cinematographers Holding Corp., Hollywood, 1961—. Recipient Acad. award for best photography, 1965. Mem. Acad. Motion Pictures Arts and Scis. (bd. govs.), Am. Soc. Cinematographers (pres. 1972-74). Mason (Shriner, 32 deg.). Photog. dir.: Inherit the Wind, 1960; Judgement at Nuremberg, 1961; Mad, Mad, Mad World, 1963; Ship of Fools, 1965; Fantastic Voyage, 1966; Star, 1968; Airport, 1970; Logans Run, 1977. Home: 4445 Gainsborough Ave Los Angeles CA 90027

LATANE, JAMES WILSON, regional farm coop. exec.; b. Washington, Nov. 12, 1917; s. James and Martchen Lindenkohl (Flemer) L.; B.S., Va. Poly. Inst. and State U., 1938; m. Margaret DeRoulhac Hill, July 18, 1947; children—James Wilson, William Catesby, III, Martha Ellen. Field surveyor Rural Electrification Coops., Palmyra, Va., 1938-39; supr. field office Fed. Land Bank, Tappahannock, Va., 1940-41; farmer, Oak Grove, Va., 1947—; pres. No. Neck Grain Coop., Inc., Nomini Grove, Va., 1958-60; bd. dirs. So. States Coop. Inc., Richmond, Va., 1968-78, pres., 1977-78. Mem. Westmoreland County Selective Service Bd., 1955-75; mem. Westmoreland County, Va. Planning Commn., 1970-77; lay reader St. Peter's Episcopal Ch., Oak Grove. Served with C.E. U.S. Army, 1942-46. Decorated Bronze Star with oak leaf cluster. Mem. Va. Agribus. Council, Va. Beef Cattle Assn. (pres. 1967-70), Fredericks-Feeder Cattle Assn. Home: Oak Grove VA 22443 Office: PO Box 1656 Richmond VA 23213

LATCHUM, JAMES LEVIN, judge; b. Milford, Del., Dec. 23, 1918; s. James H. and Ida Mae (Robbins) L.; grad. Peddie Sch., 1936; A.B. cum laude, Princeton, 1940; J.D., U. Va., 1946; m. Elizabeth Murray McArthur, June 16, 1943; children—Su-Allan, Elizabeth M. Admitted to Del. bar, 1947; asso. Berl, Potter & Anderson, Wilmington, 1946-53, partner, 1953-68; chief judge U.S. Dist. Ct. Del., Wilmington, 1968—. New Castle County atty. Del. Hwy. Dept., 1948-50; asst. U.S. atty., 1950-53; atty. Del. Interstate Hwy. Div., 1955-62, Delaware River and Bay Authority, 1962-68. Chmn. New Castle County Democratic Com., 1953-56, Wilmington City Com., 1959-63. Served to maj. Insp. Gen. Corps, AUS, 1942-46: PTO. Mem. Am., Del., Va., N.Y.C. bar assns., Order of Coif, Sigma Nu Phi. Presbyn. Club: Wilmington Country. Home: 2209 Baynard Blvd Wilmington DE 19899 Office: U S Dist Ct Wilmington DE 19899

LATEINER, JACOB, pianist; b. Havana, Cuba, May 31, 1928; s. Max and Rebecca (Weintraub) L.; student at age of four; 1st concert at age eight, Havana; pupil of Isabelle Vengerova, Curtis Inst. Music, 1940-47. Solo debut Phila. Orch., 1945; recital debut Carnegie Hall, 1948; 1st U.S. tour, 1947-48, now annually; Australian tours, 1948, 56; 1st European tour, 1957, now annually; solo appearances N.Y. Philharmonic, Berlin Philharmonic, BBC-London Symphony orchs., Concertgebouw Orkest, Chgo., Boston, Cleve., Mpls. and Los Angeles orchs.; chamber music concerts with Jascha Heifetz and Gregor Piatigorsky, 1962-68; rec. artist for Westminster, RCA records; mem. piano faculty Mannes Coll. Music, 1963-70, Juilliard Sch., 1966—. Ford Found. fellow performing artists, 1959. Address: care Tornay Mgmt 1995 Broadway New York City NY 10023

LATHAM, ALLEN, JR., mfg. co. exec.; b. Norwich, Conn., May 23, 1908; s. Allen and Caroline (Walker) L.; B.S. in Mech. Engring., Mass. Inst. Tech., 1930, Sloan fellow, 1936; m. Ruth Nichols, Nov. 11, 1933; children—W. Nichols, Harriet (Mrs. William S. Robinson), David W., Thomas W. Devel. engr. E.I. duPont, Belle, W.Va., 1930-35; engr., treas. Polaroid Corp., Cambridge, Mass., 1936-41; engr., v.p. Arthur D. Little, Cambridge, 1941-66; pres. Cryogenic Tech., Waltham, Mass., 1966-71; chmn. bd. Haemonetics, Braintree, Mass., 1971—, also dir.; trustee Elliot Savs. Bank, Boston. Named Engr. of Yr., Socs. New Eng. Engring., 1970. Mem. ASME, Am. Inst. Chem. Engrs., Instrument Soc. Am., AAAS, Nat. Acad. Engring. Club: Country (Brookline, Mass.). Patentee in blood processing equipment and processes. Home: 66 Malcolm Rd Jamaica Plain MA 01230 Office: 400 Wood Rd Braintree MA 02184

LATHAM, GARY VINCENT, geophysicist; b. Conneautville, Pa., Sept. 2, 1935; s. Vincent Ernest and Corolyn Jane (Myers) L.; B.S., Pa. State U., 1958; Ph.D., Columbia U., 1965; m. Karen Nicola Christiansen, July 26, 1971; 1 dau., Kary Anne. Sr. research asso. Columbia U., 1958-72; prof. marine scis. Marine Sci. Inst., U. Tex., 1972—, asso. dir. geophysics lab., 1975—; vis. asso. geophysics Calif. Inst. Tech., 1975; mem. lunar and planetary sci. council Univs. Space Research Assn.; expert to sci. and applications directorate NASA; tech. cons. Ency. Brit.; trustee Palisades Geophys. Inst., Blauvelt, N.Y. Recipient Exceptional Sci. Achievement medal NASA, 1972. Mem. Am. Geophys. Union, Seismol. Soc. Am., Soc. Exploration Geophysicists, N.Y. Acad. Scis., Am. Soc. Oceanography. Editorial bd. Space Sci. Instrumentation, 1975. Home: 2905 Frostwood Circle Dickinson TX 77539 Office: 700 The Strand Galveston TX 77550

LATHAM, JEAN LEE, writer; b. Buckhannon, W.Va., Apr. 19, 1902; d. George Robert II and Winifred Ethelda (Brown) Latham; A.B., W.Va. Wesleyan Coll., 1925, Litt.D., 1956; B.D.E., Ithaca Coll., 1928; M.A., Cornell U., 1930; student W.Va. Inst. Tech., 1942. Head English dept. Upshur County High Sch., 1926-27; substitute tchr. speech W.Va. Wesleyan Coll., 1927; tchr. dramatic and acad. depts. Ithaca Coll., 1928-29; editor in chief Dramatic Pub. Co., Chgo., 1930-36; free lance writer, 1936-41, 45—. Trainer insps. Signal Corps, U.S. War Dept., 1943-45; substitute librarian Warm Springs Found., summer 1951. Publicity dir. South Pinellas chpt. A.R.C., St. Petersburg, Fla., 1949. Bd. dirs. Friends of U. Miami (Fla.) Library. Mem. Nat. League Am. Pen Women, Women's Aux. U.S. Power Squadron, Phi Kappa Phi, Zeta Phi Eta. Democrat. Club: Zonta. Methodist. Playwright: The Blue Teapot, 1932; Old Doc, 1941; Gray Bread, 1941; Senor Freedom, 1941; The Nightmare, 1953. Author: Do's and Don'ts of Drama, 1935; The Story of Eli Whitney, 1953; Medals for Morse, 1954; Carry On, Mr. Bowditch (Jr. Literary Guild selection, Newbery Medal, hon. mention Internat. Bd. Books for Young People), 1955; Trail Blazer of the Seas, 1956; This Dear Bought Land (Jr. Lit. Guild selection May 1957), 1957; On Stage, Mr. Jefferson 1958; Young Man in a Hurry; The Story of Cyrus W. Field, 1958; Nutcracker, Puss in Boots, Jack the Giant Killer, Hop O' My Thumb, When Homer Honked, The Dog that Lost His Family, The Cuckoo Who Couldn't Count, The Man Who Never Snoozed; Drake: The Man They Called a Pirate, 1960; Man of the Monitor: The Story of John Ericsson, 1962; The Story of Eli Whitney, 1963; The Chagres: Power of the Panama Canal, 1964; Sam Houston: Hero of Texas, 1965; Retreat to Glory, The Story of Sam Houston, 1965; George W. Goethals: Panama Canal Engineer, 1965; The Frightened Hero, 1965; David Glasgow Farragut: Our First Admiral, 1967; The Columbia: Powerhouse of North America, 1967; Anchor's Aweigh: The Story of David Glasgow Farragut, 1968; Far Voyager: The Story of James Cook, 1970; Rachel Carson: Who Loved the Sea, 1973; Elizabeth Blackwell: Pioneer Woman Doctor, 1975. Recorded Carry On Mr. Bowditch for Talking Books, 1956. Home: 12 Phoenetia Ave Coral Gables FL 33134. *I grew up in a home where BELIEF was the net under the tightrope walker. It was not tangled around his ankles. A home where I dared to believe was the secret of success.*

LATHAM, WILLARD, army officer; b. El Dorado, Ark., Dec. 12, 1927; s. David A. and Jewel E. (Houser) L.; A.A., N. Tex. Agr. Coll., 1949; B.A., Tex. Christian U., 1960; grad. Airborne Sch. and Inf. Officer's Basic Course, Ft. Benning, Ga., 1949, Inf. Officers' Advanced Course, Ranger Tng., Ft. Benning, 1957, Command and Gen. Staff Coll., Ft. Leavenworth, Kans., 1961, Armed Forces Staff Coll., 1962, Army War Coll., 1968; m. Myra Nell Turner, June 25, 1949; children—Cynthia A., Mark B., Susan L., Scott M., Rebecca L., Thomas M., Sara E. Commd. 2d lt. U.S. Army, 1949, advanced through grades to maj. gen., 1975; served with 8th Cavalry Regt., Japan, Korea, 1949-51, 82d Airborne Div., U.S., 1951-53, 7th Army, Germany, 1953-56; instr. ROTC, U. Tex., 1960; served with Iceland Def. Force, 1961-62; personnel mgmt. officer inf. career mgmt. div. office personnel ops. and office chief of staff Pentagon, 1963-66; comdr. 2d Bn., 6th Inf., Berlin, 1966-67, 1st Bn., 16th Inf., 1st Inf. Div., Vietnam, 1967-68, 5th Bn., 60th Inf., 9th Inf. Div., 1968; asst. chief of staff G3, 1st Inf. Div., Vietnam, 1968-69; mem. faculty Command and Gen. Staff Coll., 1969-70; comdr. 197th Inf. Brig., Ft. Benning, 1970-71, chief staff, dep. comdr. Inf. Center, 1972-73; asst. div. comdr. 3d Inf. Div., Germany, 1973-74; comdr. 172d Inf. Brigade, Alaska, 1975; comdg. gen. U.S. Inf. Center, Ft. Benning, 1975-77; chief Joint U.S. Mil. Mission for Aid to Turkey, Ankara, 1977—. Decorated Silver Star with oak leaf cluster, Legion of Merit with 2 oak leaf clusters, D.F.C. with 2 oak leaf clusters, Bronze Star with 2 oak leaf clusters and V device, Meritorious Service medal,

Army Commendation medal with oak leaf cluster, Air medal with 13 oak leaf clusters, Purple Heart with oak leaf cluster, Civil Action Honor medal 1st class (U.S.); Cross of Gallantry with palm (3), Armed Forces Honor medal (Vietnam). Mem. Assn. U.S. Army. Author: The Modern Volunteer Army Program: The Benning Experiment, 1970-72, 1974. Home and Office: Hdqrs Joint US Mil Mission for Aid to Turkey APO NY 09254

LATHAM, WILLIAM PETERS, composer, educator; b. Shreveport, La., Jan. 4, 1917; s. Lawrence L. and Eugenia (Peters) L.; student Asbury Coll., Wilmore, Ky., 1933-35, Cin. Conservatory Music, 1936-38; B.Sc. in Music Edn., U. Cin., 1938; B.Mus., Coll. Music Cin., 1940, M.Mus., 1941; Ph.D., Eastman Sch. Music, 1951; pupil composition with Eugene Goossens, Howard Hanson, Herbert Elwell; m. Joan Seyler, Apr. 18, 1946; children—Leslie Virginia, William Peters, Carol Jean. Mem. faculty N. Tex. State Tchrs. Coll., 1938-39, Eastern Ill. State Tchrs. Coll., 1946, State Coll. Ia., 1946-65, prof. music, 1959-65; prof. composition N. Tex. State U. Sch. Music, Denton, 1965—, dir. grad. studies, 1969, disting. prof., 1978—. Served to 2d lt. AUS, 1942-46. Scholar in composition Cin. Coll. Music, 1939-41; recipient 1st prize, grad. div. Phi Mu Alpha, 1952. Mem. ASCAP (ann. awards com. 1962—), Music Educators Nat. Conf., Phi Mu Alpha, Pi Kappa Lambda. Composer numerous works, 1938—, most recent being: (orch.) Jubilee 13/50, 1978; (chamber music) Bravoure for piano, 1976, Eidolons for euphonium and piano, 1977, Ex Tempore for alto saxophone, solo, 1978; (chorus) St. David's Mass, 1977, Epigrammata, 1978; (band) Revolution, 1975, Fusion, 1975, March 6, 1978. Home: 1815 Southridge Dr Denton TX 76201

LATHEM, EDWARD CONNERY, educator, librarian, editor; b. Littleton, N.H., Dec. 15, 1926; s. Belton Gilreath and Myrtie Etta (Connery) L.; A.B., Dartmouth Coll., 1951; M.S., Columbia U., 1952; D.Phil., Oxford U., 1961; m. E. Elizabeth French, Nov. 27, 1957. With Library, Dartmouth Coll., 1952-78, librarian, 1968-78, dean of libraries, 1973-78; officer, dir. Stinehour Press Inc., 1958-77, Plymouth Cheese Corp., 1959—, N. Country Pub. Co., 1970-78, Vt. Provisioners Inc., 1972—, Meriden-Stinehour Inc., 1977—; co-publisher Coös County Democrat, 1970-78, fence viewer, Hanover, 1962—; advisory editor Dodd, Mead & Co., 1974—. Corp. mem. Hanover Improvement Soc., 1971—; trustee N.H. Hist. Soc., 1956-76, Howe Library, Hanover, 1967—; pres. Assn. Research Libraries, 1976-77. Woodward fellow, Dartmouth Coll., 1978—. Mem. Am. Antiquarian Soc., Bibliog. Soc. Am., Phi Beta Kappa. Clubs: Century, Dartmouth, Grolier (N.Y.C.); Odd Volumes, St. Botolph (Boston). Organizer microfilm edit. Papers of Daniel Webster, 1971; initiator Univ. Press of New Eng.; editor and compiler numerous books including: (with Hyde Cox) Selected Prose of Robert Frost, 1966; Interviews with Robert Frost, 1966; (with Lawrance Thompson) Robert Frost and the Lawrence, Mass. High Sch. Bulletin, 1966; Your Son, Calvin Coolidge, 1968; The Poetry of Robert Frost, 1969; A Concordance to the Poetry of Robert Frost, 1971; (with Lawrance Thompson) Robert Frost: Poetry and Prose, 1972; Calvin Coolidge Says, 1972; Chronological Tables of American Newspapers 1690-1820, 1972; Calvin Coolidge: Cartoons of His Presidential Years, 1973; Robert Frost 100, 1974; 76 United Statesiana, 1976; North of Boston Poems (R. Frost), 1977; Thirteen Colonial Americana, 1977; The Dartmouth Experience (John Sloan Dickey), 1977; American Libraries as Centers of Scholarship, 1978. Home: Hanover NH 03755 Office: 213 Baker Library Dartmouth Coll Hanover NH 03755

LATHROP, GRAYSON FARQUHAR, advt. agy. exec.; b. Springfield, Ohio, Mar. 5, 1917; s. Grayson Farquhar and Maureen (Curtis) L.; ed. Harvard U., 1938; m. Muriel Jacobs, Dec. 17, 1955; children—Grayson Farquhar, Kevin Halsey, Gavin Curtis. Salesman, H. J. Heinz Co., 1939-40; v.p., account supr. Kenyon & Eckhardt, Inc., 1940-58; with Al Paul Lefton Co. Inc., N.Y.C., 1958—, exec. v.p., 1967-72, chmn. bd. 1972—, also dir. Served to 1st lt. USAAF, 1942-45. Decorated Bronze Star. Mem. Am. Assn. Advt. Agys., Asia Soc. Home: 26 W 11th St New York NY 10011 Office: 71 Vanderbilt Ave New York NY 10017

LATHROP, IRVIN TUNIS, educator; b. Platteville, Wis., Sept. 23, 1927; s. Irvin J. and Marian (Johnson) L.; B.S., Stout State Coll., 1950; M.S., Iowa State U., 1954, Ph.D., 1958; m. Eleanor M. Kolar, Aug. 18, 1951; 1 son, James I. Tchr., Ottumwa (Iowa) High Sch., 1950-55; mem. faculty Iowa State U., 1957-58, Western Mich. U., 1958-59; mem. faculty Calif. State Coll., 1959—, prof. indsl. arts, 1966—, chmn. dept. indsl. edn., 1969—. Cons. Naval Ordnance Lab., Corona, Calif., 1961-63. Mem. adv. com. El Camino and Orange Coast Coll. Served with USAAF, 1946-47. Mem. Nat. Soc. for Study Edn., Am. Council on Indsl. Arts Tchr. Edn., Am. Vocational Assn., Nat. Assn. Indsl. and Tech. Tchrs., Am. Indsl. Arts Assn., Am. Ednl. Research Assn., Epsilon Pi Tau, Psi Chi, Phi Delta Kappa, Phi Kappa Phi. Author: (with Marshall La Cour) Photo Technology, 1966, rev. edit., 1977, Photography, 1979, The Basic Book of Photography, 1979; Laboratory Manual for Photo Technology, 1973; (with John Lindbeck) General Industry, 1969, rev. edit., 1977; (with Robert Kunst) Photo-Offset, 1979. Editorial cons. Am. Tech. Soc. Contbr. articles to profl. jours. Home: 819 E Clemensen St Santa Ana CA 92701 Office: 6101 E 7th St Long Beach CA 90801

LATHROP, KAYE DON, nuclear scientist; b. Bryan, Ohio, Oct. 8, 1932; s. Arthur Quay and Helen Venita (Hoos) L.; B.S., U.S. Mil. Acad., 1955; M.S., Calif. Inst. Tech., 1959, Ph.D., 1962, m. Judith Marie Green, June 11, 1957; children—Braxton Landess, Scottfield Michael. Staff mem. Los Alamos Sci. Lab., 1962-67; group leader methods devel. Gen. Atomic Co., San Diego, 1967-68; with Los Alamos Sci. Lab., 1968—, asso. div. leader reactor safeguards and reactor safety and tech. div., 1975-77, alt. div. leader energy div., 1977-78, div. leader computer sci. and services div., 1978-79, asso. dir. for engrng. scis., 1979—; vis. prof. U. N.Mex., 1964-65, adj. prof., 1966-67; guest lectr. Internat. Atomic Energy Agy., 1969; mem. adv. com. reactor physics ERDA, 1973—; cons. in field. Served to 1st lt. C.E., U.S. Army, 1955-58. Spl. fellow AEC, 1958-61; R.C. Baker Found. fellow, 1961-62; recipient E.O. Lawrence Meml. award ERDA, 1976. Fellow Am. Nuclear Soc. (chmn. math. and computation div. 1970-71, nat. dir. 1973-76, 79—, treas. 1977-79); mem. Am. Phys. Soc., AAAS, Sigma Xi. Republican. Episcopalian. Author reports, papers, chpts. to books. Home: 199 San Ildefonso Rd Los Alamos NM 87544 Office: MS 145 PO Box 1663 Los Alamos NM 87545

LATIES, ALAN MALEV, physician, educator; b. Beverly, Mass., Feb. 8, 1931; s. Simon Gregory and Rima (Kapnik) L.; B.A., Harvard Coll., 1954; M.D., Baylor U., 1959; m. Marguerite Leiken, Apr. 2, 1955; children—Nicholas, Jane. Intern Mt. Sinai Hosp., N.Y.C., 1959-60; resident ophthalmology Hosp. of U. Pa., 1960-63; USPHS spl. fellow Inst. Neurol. Sci., U. Pa., 1963-64, instr. ophthalmology, 1961-63, asst. prof., 1966-68, mem. Inst. Neurol. Scis., 1967—, asso. prof. ophthalmology, 1968-70, Irene Heinz Given and John LaPorte Given prof. ophthalmology, 1970—. Mem. vision research and tng. com. Nat. Eye Inst., 1971—; chmn. sci. adv. bd. Nat. Retinitis Pigmentosa Found., recipient Humanitarian award, 1978; mem. Nat. Adv. Eye Council, 1979—. Recipient Friedenwald award for research in ophthalmology, 1972. Editorial bd. Investigative Ophthalmology, 1972—, editor-in-chief, 1977—. Home: 2403 Spruce St Philadelphia PA 19103 Office: Scheie Eye Inst 51 N 39th St Philadelphia PA 19104

LATIES, VICTOR GREGORY, psychologist; b. Racine, Wis., Feb. 2, 1926; s. Simon Gregory and Rima (Kapnik) L.; A.B., Tufts U., 1949; Ph.D., U. Rochester, N.Y., 1954; m. Martha Ann Fisher, July 29, 1956; children—Nancy, Andrew, Claire. Ford Found. teaching intern Brown U., 1954-55; instr., asst. prof. dept. pharmacology Johns Hopkins U. Sch. Medicine, 1955-65; asso. prof. U. Rochester Sch. Medicine and Dentistry, 1965-71, prof. dept. radiation biology and biophysics, psychology, pharmacology and toxicology, 1971—; mem. NIMH preclinical psychopharmacology research rev. com., 1967-71; mem. Nat. Acad. Sci.-NRC bd. on toxicology and environ. health hazards, 1977—. Served with USN, 1944-46. Fellow Am. Psychol. Assn. (pres. div. psychopharmacology 1968-69, div. exptl. analysis of behavior 1979—), Behavioral Pharmacology Soc. (pres. 1966-68), Am. Soc. Pharmacology and Exptl. Therapeutics, Psychonomic Soc., Soc. for Neuroscience, Eastern Psychol. Assn., Soc. for Exptl. Analysis of Behavior (sec.-treas. 1966—). Editor: Jour. of Exptl. Analysis of Behavior, 1972-76; (with B. Weiss) Behavioral Toxicology, 1975; Behavioral Pharmacology, 1976; mem. editorial bd. Jour. of Pharmacology and Exptl. Therapeutics, 1965-71, Psychopharmacologia, 1968-78. Contbr. sci. articles to profl. jours. Home: 55 Dale Rd E Rochester NY 14625 Office: Dept Radiation Biology and Biophysics U Rochester Med Center Rochester NY 14642

LATIMER, ALLIE B., lawyer, govt. ofcl.; b. Coraopolis, Pa.; d. Lawnye S. and Bennie Latimer; B.S., Hampton Inst., 1947; J.D., Howard U., 1953; LL.M., Catholic U., 1958; postgrad. Am. U., 1960-61; m. Albert Starks Weeden, Apr. 2, 1966. Admitted to N.C. bar, 1955, D.C. bar, 1960; vol. in projects Am. Friends Service Com., N.J. and Europe, 1948-49; correctional officer Fed. Reformatory for Women, Alderson, W.Va., 1949-51; personnel clk. NIH, Bethesda, 1953-55; realty officer Mitchell AFB, N.Y., 1955-56; with Office Gen. Counsel, GSA, Washington, 1957—, chief counsel, after 1966, asst. gen. counsel, 1971-76, gen. counsel, 1977—; asst. gen. counsel NASA, 1976-77; past chmn. central office com. Fed. Women's Program, GSA; mem. membership and budget com. Health and Welfare Council, 1967-72. Bd. dirs., pres. D.C. Mental Health Assn., Friendship House, Washington; elder Presbyn. Ch., pres. Interacial Council, 1964-75; chmn. Presbyn. Econ. Devel. Corp. Recipient GSA Sustained Superior Service award, 1959, Meritorious Service award, 1964, Commendable Service award, 1964, Pub. Service award, 1971, Outstanding Performance award, 1971. Mem. Am. Nat. (sec. 1966-74), Fed., Washington, N.C. bar assns., Nat. Bar Found. (dir. 1970-71, pres. 1974-75), Hampton (pres. Washington chpt. 1970-71), Howard Law (v.p. 1962-63) alumni assns., Links (pres. Washington chpt. 1971-74, nat. v.p. 1976-79), Federally Employed Women (1st pres.). Home: 1721 S St NW Washington DC 20009 Office: Office of Gen Counsel Gen Services Adminstrn 18th and F Sts NW Washington DC 20405

LATIMER, JOHN FRANCIS, educator; b. Clinton, Miss., May 16, 1903; s. Murray and Myrtle (Webb) L.; A.B., Miss Coll., 1922, Litt.D., 1964; M.A., U. Chgo., 1926; Ph.D., Yale, 1929; m. Helen Blundon, July 27, 1946. Tchr., prin. Clinton High Sch., 1922-24; instr. classics Vanderbilt U., 1926-27; master in Greek, Taft Sch., 1929-31; asst. prof. classics Knox Coll., 1931-33; chmn. dept. classics Drury Coll., 1933-36; chmn. dept. classics George Washington U., 1936-71, asst. dean Coll. Gen. Studies, 1951-56, asst. dean faculties, 1956-59, asso. dean, 1959-64, dir. fgn. student affairs, 1964-66, prof. classics emeritus, 1973—. Mem. Com. Internat. Exchange of Persons, 1959-71. Trustee St. John's Child Devel. Center, Washington, pres. bd. trustees, 1973-77; pres. Friends of Libraries, George Washington U., 1977-78; pres. Soc. of Emeriti, George Washington U., 1978—. Served to comdr. USNR, 1942-47; capt. Res. (ret.). Mem. Am. Philol. Assn., Archeol Inst. Am., Classical Assn. Atlantic States (pres. 1955-57), Am. Sch. Classical Studies, Am. Classical League (pres. 1960-66, exec. sec. 1966-73), Omicron Delta Kappa. Club: Cosmos (Washington). Author: What's Happened to Our High Schools?, 1958; The Oxford Conference and Related Activities, 1968. Editor: (with introduction) A Life of George Washington in Latin Prose (Francis Glass), 1976; (with foreword) A Grammatical and Historical Supplement to the Glass Washington, 1976, A Composite Translation of the Glass Washington, 1976. Contbr. articles to profl. jours. Home: 3601 Connecticut Ave NW Washington DC 20008. *Real success is found in the satisfaction one gets in doing one's daily work with undiminished enthusiasm because of a strong conviction that it is worth doing to the best of one's ability. This philosophy can be a permanent possession that increases in value each year and gives added meaning to all of the various activities and relationships of one's life.*

LATIMER, JONATHAN WYATT, author; b. Chgo., Oct. 23, 1906; s. Jonathan Guy and Evelyn (Wyatt) L.; ed. Mesa (Ariz.) Ranch Sch., 1922-25; A.B., Knox Coll., 1929; m. Ellen Baxter Peabody, Dec. 11, 1937; children—Ellen Jane, Jonathan, Nicholas; m. 2d, Jo Ann Hanzlik, Dec. 18, 1954. Began as newspaperman, 1929; reporter Chgo. Herald-Examiner, later Chgo. Tribune, 1930—35; writer Paramount, Metro-Goldwyn-Mayer, 1940-41, RKO, Paramount, 1946-47. Served with USNR, 1942-45. Mem. Screen Writers Guild, Acad. Motion Picture Arts and Scis., Phi Beta Kappa, Phi Delta Theta. Club: Beach and Tennis (La Jolla, Calif.). Author: Murder in the Madhouse, 1935; Headed for a Hearse, 1935; The Lady in the Morgue, 1936, The Dead Don't Care, 1937; Red Gardenias, 1939; Dark Memory, 1940; Topper Returns, 1941; Night in New Orleans, 1942; The Glass Key, 1942; The Fifth Grave, Nocturne, 1946; They Won't Believe Me, 1947; The Big Clock, 1947; Sealed Verdict; Beyond Glory, 1948; Night Has A Thousand Eyes; Alias Nick Beal, 1949; Copper Canyon, 1950; The Redhead and the Cowboy; Submarine Command, 1951; Botany Bay, 1952; Plunder of the Sun, 1955; Sinners and Shrouds; The Strange Case of the Cosmic Rays; Back from Eternity, 1956; The Lady and the Prowler, 1957; The Unchained Goddess, 1957; The Whole Truth, 1958; Tiger by Night, 1959; Black Is the Fashion for Dying, 1959; The Mink- Lined Coffin, 1960; CBS Perry Mason Series, 1960-65. Home: 1532 Copade Oro Dr La Jolla CA 92037

LATIMER, MURRAY WEBB, economist, social ins. specialist; b. Clinton, Miss., Jan. 6, 1901; s. Murray and Myrtle (Webb) L.; A.B., Miss. Coll., Clinton, 1919; M.B.A., Harvard, 1924; grad. work Columbia, 1926-28; m. Edith Sonn, May 18, 1928; children—Hugh, Lenore Judith, Margaret Webb. Mem. bus. research staff Harvard, 1923, supr., 1924-25, instr. finance, 1925; economist, old age ins. expert Indsl. Relations Counselors, Inc., N.Y.C., 1926-33; mem. adv. com. Dept. Labor, 1933-35; staff com. on govt. statistics and information services, 1933; spl. agt. U.S. Bur. Labor Statistics, also cons. Fed. Coordinator Transp., in charge econ. and actuarial studies of old age, retirement and unemployment ins., 1933-34; chmn. 1st U.S.R.R. Retirement Bd., 1934-35; chmn. 2d U.S.R.R. Retirement Bd., 1935-46; research dir. President's Guaranteed Wage Study, 1945-47; cons. economist, 1947—. Dir. Federal Bur. Old Age Benefits, U.S. Social Security Bd., 1936; lectr. economics Wharton Sch., U. Pa., 1936-37; chief exec. officer Office Fgn. Relief, State Dept. and FEA, 1943; mem. Am. del. UNRRA council meeting, Atlantic City, 1943; participated in formulation R.R. Retirement Act of 1937, Carriers Taxing Act of 1937, also R.R. Unemployment Ins. Act; mem. tech. bd. to President's Com. Econ. Security, also chmn. sub-com. old age security, 1934-35; reviewer actuarial assumptions underlying cost estimates Social Security, 1970-71; mem. panel on contingent employer liability ins. of adv. com. Pension Benefit Guaranty Corp., 1977—. Served in S.A.T.C., 1918. Fellow Gerontol. Soc., Casualty Actuarial Soc., Conf. Actuaries in Pub. Practice, Canadian Inst. Actuaries; mem. Am. Acad. Actuaries, Am. Econ. Assn., Am. Statis. Assn., Am. Mgmt. Assn., Am. Pension Conf., Indsl. Relations Research Assn. Democrat. Author: (with K.S. Boardman) Distribution of Textiles, 1926; Trade Union Pension Systems in U.S. and Canada, 1932; Industrial Pension Systems in U.S. and Canada, 1933; (with K. Tufel), Trends in Industrial Pensions, 1940; (with others) Guaranteed Wages, 1947; A Guaranteed Wage Plan for Workers in the Steel Industry, 1952; A Guaranteed Wage Plan for the Employees of the Aluminum Co. of Am.; The Relationship of Employee Hiring Ages to the Cost of Pension Plans, 1965. Contbr. articles to econ. and statis. reviews. Home: 2951 Albemarle St NW Washington DC 20008 Office: 1625 K St NW Washington DC 20006

LATIMER, PAUL HENRY, biophysicist; b. New Orleans, Nov. 25, 1925; s. Claiborne Green and Frieda (Hildebrandt) L.; student U. Ky., 1943-44, 46-47; B.S., Northwestern U., 1949; M.S., U. Ill., 1950, Ph.D., 1956; m. Margaret Kinard, Aug. 16, 1952; children—Margaret Gwyn, Marianne Mason, Susan Pauline. Instr. physics Coll. William and Mary, Williamsburg, Va., 1950-51; postdoctoral fellow Carnegie Instn., Stanford, Calif., 1956-57; asst. prof. dept. physics, investigator Howard Hughes Med. Inst., Vanderbilt U., Nashville, 1957-62; asso. prof. dept. physics Auburn (Ala.) U., 1962-71, prof., 1971—; lectr. Escuela de Espectroscopia, U. Nacional Autonoma de Mex., Mexico City, 1979; cons. Dept. Justice, 1959; ASEE-NASA fellow Marchall Space Flight Center, Ala., summer 1971; cons. So. Research Inst., Birmingham, Ala., 1976; contractor U.S. Army, 1977. Wellcome Trust grantee U. Cambridge (Eng.), summer 1974. Served with AUS, 1944-46; ETO. Decorated Bronze Star. Mem. Optical Soc. Am., Biophys. Soc., Am. Phys. Soc., AAUP, Sigma Xi, Kappa Alpha. Presbyterian. Club: Kiwanis. Contbr. articles to profl. jours. Home: 530 Forestdale Dr Auburn AL 36830

LATIMER, PEYTON RANDOLPH, textile co. exec.; b. Washington, May 25, 1938; s. Samuel Edwin and Mary Kensett (Reese) L.; B.S., U.S. Naval Acad., 1960; m. Diane Frances Dooley, Aug. 25, 1962; children—Bronwen Elizabeth, Jonathan Carroll. Commd. ensign U.S. Navy, 1960, served to lt. comdr., resigned, 1968; asst. v.p. Chem. Bank, N.Y.C., 1969-72; mgr. acquisitions The Singer Co., 1973-75; treas. Singer Sewing Machine Co., N.Y.C., 1975-76; treas. Burlington Industries, Inc., N.Y.C., 1976—. Republican. Episcopalian. Clubs: N.Y. Athletic, Army-Navy Country. Home: 30 Waterside Plaza Apt 35A New York City NY 10010 Office: 1345 Ave of Americas New York City NY 10019

LATNO, ARTHUR CLEMENT, JR., telephone co. exec.; b. Ross, Calif., May 14, 1929; s. Arthur Clement and Marie (Carlin) L.; B.S., Santa Clara U., 1951; m. Dorothy Sheldon Guess, June 27, 1953; children—Jeannine Marie, Michele Claire, Arthur Clement III, Mary Suzanne, Patrice Anne. With Pacific Tel. & Tel. Co., San Francisco, 1952—, v.p., 1972-78, exec. v.p., 1978—; dir., mem. exec. com. Intermountain Gas Co., Boise; dir. Bell Tel. Co., Nev., Pacific Coast Elec. Assos., Inc. Bd. dirs. Fromm Inst. Lifelong Learning, Nazareth House, San Rafael, Calif., 1972—; regent St. Mary's Coll. Calif., 1971—; chmn. bd. dirs. and chmn. exec. com. Bilingual Children's TV, Inc., 1972—; trustee Marin Gen. Hosp. Mem. Knights of Malta (vice chancellor), Alpha Sigma Nu. Club: Meadow. Home: 67 Convent Ct San Rafael CA 94901 Office: Pacific Tel & Tel Co 140 New Montgomery St San Francisco CA 94105

LATOUR, WALLACE CHARLES, home products co. exec.; b. N.Y.C., June 25, 1924; s. Casper Charles and Emily Marion (Tether) L.; grad. Philips Acad., Andover, Mass., 1942; B.A., Princeton, 1948; m. Margaret Ann Moore, Sept. 20, 1952; children—William Charles, Richard Tether, Emily Louise. With Merrill Lynch, Pierce, Fenner & Smith, N.Y.C., 1948-62; gen. partner F.I. duPont, Glore Forgan & Co., N.Y.C., 1962-70, sr. mng. partner, 1969-70; sr. v.p., dir. Bache & Co., Inc., N.Y.C., 1971-73; asst. to pres. Am. Home Products Corp., 1974-77; sr. v.p. Sogen Swiss Internat. Corp., 1977—; Served with AUS, 1943-46. Mem. Phi Beta Kappa. Clubs: Bond (N.Y.C.); Bronxville (N.Y.) Field; Elm (Princeton); Stratton Mountain Country (Vt.). Home: 31 Edgewood Ln Bronxville NY 10708 Office: Suite 3104 405 Lexington Ave New York NY 10017

LA TOURETTE, JOHN ERNEST, univ. ofcl.; b. Perth Amboy, N.J., Nov. 5, 1932; s. John Crater and Charlotte Ruth (Jones) LaT.; B.A., Rutgers U., 1954, M.A., 1955, Ph.D., 1962; m. Lillie M. Drum, Aug. 10, 1957; children—Marc Andrew, Yanique Renee. Instr., Rutgers U., 1960-61; asst. prof. econs. SUNY, Binghamton, 1961-65, asso. prof., 1965-69, chmn. dept. econs., 1967-76, acting provost for grad. studies and research, 1975-76; dean Grad. Coll., vice provost for research Bowling Green State U., 1976-79; provost, v.p. No. Ill. U., 1979—; vis. prof. Karlsruhe (W. Ger.) U., 1974; research prof. Brookings Inst., 1966-67; vis. scholar Ariz. State U., 1969, 70; lectr. Econs. Inst., U. Colo., 1966; dir. NSF Departmental Sci. Devel. Grant, 1970-75. Served to capt. USAF, 1955-58. Ford Found. grantee, 1963; SUNY Found. grantee, 1963, 65, 70. Mem. Am. Econ. Assn., Can. Econ. Assn. Contbr. articles to profl. jours. Home: 630 Joanne Ln DeKalb IL 60115 Office: Lowden Hall 307 No Ill U DeKalb IL 60115

LATOURRETTE, JAMES THOMAS, educator; b. Miami, Ariz., Dec. 26, 1931; s. Emery Everest and Carrie D. (Hoffman) LaT.; B.S., Calif. Inst. Tech., 1953; M.A. (Gen. Communication Co. fellow), Harvard, 1954, Ph.D. (NSF fellow), 1958; m. Muriel Ashe, Aug. 28, 1955; children—Mary Beth, John Emery, James Thomas, Joanne. Research asso., lectr. physics Harvard, 1957-59; physicist Gen. Electric Research Lab., Schenectady, 1960-62; sr. supervisory scientist TRG, Inc., Melville, N.Y., 1962-66; sect. head TRG div. Control Data Corp., Melville, 1966-67; prof. electrophysics Poly. Inst. N.Y. (formerly Poly. Inst. Bklyn.), Farmingdale, N.Y., 1967—; cons. Smithsonian Instn. NSF postdoctoral fellow Physikalisches Institut der Universitat Bonn, Germany, 1959-60. Mem. Am. Phys. Soc., I.E.E.E., AAAS, AAUP, Sigma Xi, Tau Beta Pi. Contbr. articles to profl. jours. Home: 2 Candlewood Ct Huntington NY 11743 Office: Poly Inst NY Route 110 Farmingdale NY 11735

LA TOZA, CHARLES ANTON, chem. co. exec.; b. Chgo., Feb. 2, 1928; s. Charles Joseph and Mildred Roberta (Anton) La T.; Ph.B., Northwestern U., 1949; J.D., De Paul U., 1956; m. June Anderson, Aug. 20, 1949; children—Kenneth, Dennis, Gregory, Patricia, Judy, Sandra. Chemist, Nalco Chem. Co., Oak Brook, Ill., 1949-55, mem. staff legal dept., 1955-68, asst. sec., 1968-74, sec., asst. treas., 1974—; pres. Nalco Found.; condr. seminars. on corp. sec.'s functions Am. Mgmt. Assn. Exec. officer Lutheran Ch. of the Good Shepherd; mem. pres.'s adv. council, mem. council on univ. priorities and planning Valparaiso U., 1979-80; mem. adv. council Associated Colls. Ill. Mem. Am. Soc. Corp. Secs., Am. Mgmt. Assn., Am. Chem. Soc., Am. Bar Assn., Ill. Bar Assn., Chgo. Bar Assn. Patentee (Italy). Office: 2901 Butterfield Rd Oak Brook IL 60521

LATSHAW, JOHN, stock broker; b. Kansas City, Dec. 10, 1921; s. Ross W. and Edna (Parker) L.; student Kansas City Jr. Coll., 1938-40; B.S., Mo. U., 1942; m. Barbara Haynes, Nov. 13, 1954 (div. Dec. 1975); children—Constance, Elizabeth. Mgr. trading dept. Harris, Upham & Co., 1943-49; partner Uhlmann & Latshaw, 1949-53, E.F. Hutton & Co., 1954-62, v.p. E.F. Hutton & Co., Inc., Kansas City, 1962-73, exec. v.p., 1972—, dir., 1968—, mem. exec. com., 1970—; chmn. bd. Bus. Communications, Inc.; dir. E. F. Hutton London Ltd., Guy's Foods, Inc., Kansas City Life Ins. Co., Western Ins. Securities; chmn. bd., mem. exec. com. Cable TV of Kansas City, Inc., Cablevision of Kansas City, Inc. Mem. Kansas City Bd. Trade; gov. Midwest Stock Exchange, 1966-68. Past Chmn. Key Men's Council; past pres. Friends of Zoo, 1970; mem. exec. com. Religious Heritage Am., Starlight Theatre, Performing Arts Kansas City; v.p., mem. exec. bd. Am. Cancer Soc., 1970, 71, mem. Jackson County and Crusade Adv. Com.; mem. Gov.'s Com. on Higher Edn.; bd. dirs. Kansas City Theatre Guild Council; trustee City Employees Pension Plan, St. Andrew's Episcopal Ch. Meml. and Res. Trust Fund; bd. govs. Am. Royal; exec. bd. Kansas City Area council Boy Scouts Am., 1970-72, adv. bd., 1973, chmn. patriotism program, 1970; hon. bd. dirs. Rockhurst Coll.; past pres. Kansas City Soccer Club, Inc.; mem. exec. com. N.Am. Soccer League, 1968, 69; bd. govs. Invest-In-Am. Nat. Council, mem. Central Region exec. com., regional chmn. Invest-in-Am. Week Liaison, 1958—; mem. fin. com. Mayor's Profl. Theater; mem. Univ. Assos. of U. Mo. of Kansas City; chmn. hon. trustees YWCA, 1968-69; trustee Midwest Research Inst.; mem. chancellor's adv. council Met. Community Colls., 1976-77; mem. pres.'s council bd. hon. trustees Kansas City Art Inst.; bd. govs. Agr. Hall of Fame, 1976-77; bd. dirs., mem. fin. com. Mayor's Christmas Tree Assn.; mem. Civic Council Greater Kansas City. Recipient citation of merit U. Mo., 1957; Golden Eagle award Nat. Invest in Am. Council, 1970; named hon. consul Thailand; decorated knight hospitaller of Malta, Sovereign Order of St. John of Jerusalem. Mem. Kansas City C. of C. (dir., past pres.), Bus. and Profl. Assn. Western Mo. (mem. adv. bd.), Kansas City Security Traders Assn. (past pres.), Nat. Security Traders Assn. (past v.p.), Order Jim Daisy, Sigma Nu. Episcopalian (trustee). Clubs: Carriage, Kansas City, Mission Hills Country, University. Home: 3 Dunford Circle Kansas City MO 64112 Office: 920 Baltimore Kansas City MO 64105

LATTA, DELBERT L., congressman; b. Weston, Ohio, Mar. 5, 1920; A.B., LL.B., Ohio No. U.; m. Rose Mary Kiene; children—Rose Ellen, Robert Edward. Admitted to Ohio bar, 1944; state senator, Ohio, 3 terms; mem. 86th-96th Congresses, 5th Ohio Dist. Republican. Home: Bowling Green OH 43402 Office: House Office Bldg Washington DC 20515

LATTA, GORDON ERIC, educator; b. Vancouver, B.C., Can., Mar. 8, 1923; s. Eric Robert and Ethel (Titley) L.; B.A., U. B.C., 1948; Ph.D., Calif. Inst. Tech., 1951; m. Irene Thomson Blais, Apr. 2, 1945; children—Robin Leslie, Gail Arlene, Brian David. Came to U.S., 1953, naturalized, 1959. Fine instr. Princeton, 1951-52; asst. prof. U. B.C., 1952-53; prof. Stanford, 1953-67; William Stanfield Calcott prof. applied math. U. Va., Charlottesville, 1967—. Served with RCAF, 1943-45. Mem. Math. Assn. Am., Soc. Indsl. and Applied Math. Contbr. articles to profl. jours. Home: 511 N 1st St Apt 401 Charlottesville VA 22901

LATTA, WILLIAM CHARLTON, clergyman; b. College Corner, Ohio, Mar. 30, 1902; s. Linton Thomas and Minnie Isadora (Rex) L.; B.A., Miami (Ohio) U., 1924; Th.B., Xenia Theol. Sem., St. Louis, 1927, Th.M., 1928; D.D., Westminster Coll., 1951; m. Marjorie Faye Clippard, May 4, 1928; children—William Charlton, John Linton, Bruce. Ordained to ministry United Presbyn. Ch., 1928; pastor, Wellsville, Ohio, 1928-31, Oil City, Pa., 1932-45, 1st United Presbyn. Ch., Oakmont, Pa., 1945-72, emeritus, 1972—. Bd. dirs. Am. missions United Presbyn. Ch. N.Am., 1954-58, pres., 1956-58, chmn. gen. council Evangelism, 1951-58, co-chmn. commn. Evangelism, 1958-60, v.p. bd. nat. missions, 1958-62, pres., 1962-65, mem. gen. council, 1958-60, 62-64, chmn. exec. com. bd. nat. missions, 1962-65; vice moderator Pitts. Synod, 1956-57; mem. N. Am. council World's Presbyn. Alliance, 1966-68, del. meeting, Sao Paulo, Brazil, 1959; mem. gen. assembly Nat. Council Chs., 1963-66, mem. div. home missions, 1963-66, mem. joint com. Evangelism, 1951-65; mem. gen. council Pitts. Presbytery, 1962-74, chmn., 1962-63, chmn. nominating com., 1966-68, mem. evaluating com., 1969-74, trustee, 1976—, mem. fin. com., 1976—, trustee, mem. fin. com., 1976—; mem. Oakmont Ministerial Assn., 1945-73, pres., 1970-73; chmn. com. to unite work bd. nat. missions Presbyn. Ch. U.S.A. and bd. Am. missions United Presbyn. Ch. N. Am., 1957-58; chmn. structure com. Bd. Nat. Missions, 1961-62; dir., tchr. at youth confs. Bd. dirs. Pitts.-Xenia Theol. Sem., 1941-45, v.p., 1944-45; bd. dirs. Carnegie Library Oakmont (Pa.), 1965-72; trustee Knoxville (Tenn.) Coll., 1954-75, v.p., 1970-72, chmn. com. personnel policies and salary adminstrn., mem. finance and bldg. and grounds coms., 1970-75. Contbr. articles to religious publs. Home: 6675 Saltsburg Rd Pittsburgh PA 15235

LATTES, RAFFAELE, physician, educator; b. Torino, Italy, May 22, 1910; s. Attilio Marco and Dolce (Noemi) L.; M.D., U. Torino, 1933; D.M.S., Columbia, 1946; m. Eva H. Hahn, 1936; children—Conrad George, Robert George. Came to U.S., 1940, naturalized, 1947. Tng. surgery, surg. pathology U. Torino Med. Sch., 1934-38; instr. pathology Woman's Med. Coll. Pa., Phila., 1941-43; asst. prof. pathology N.Y. Postgrad. Hosp. and Med. Sch., 1946-48; instr. surg. pathology Coll. Phys. and Surg., Columbia, 1943-46, asst. prof., 1948-49, asso. prof. surgery, surg. pathology, 1949-51, prof. surgery, surg. pathology, 1958-78, prof. emeritus, 1978—, spl. lectr. in surgery, 1978, dir. lab. surg. pathology, 1951—. Diplomate Am. Bd. Pathology. Fellow A.M.A., Coll. Am. Pathologists, N.Y. Acad. Medicine, Internat. Acad. Pathology; mem. N.Y. Path. Soc., Am. Assn. Pathologists and Bacteriologists, A.A.A.S., Am. Assn. Cancer Research, Am. Soc. Clin. Pathologists, Allen O. Whipple Soc. Home: 597 Rutland Ave Teaneck NJ 07666 Office: 630 W 168th St New York City NY 10032

LATTIMER, JOHN KINGSLEY, physician, educator; b. Mt. Clemens, Mich., Oct. 14, 1914; s. Eugene and Gladys Soulier (Lenfestey) L.; A.B., Columbia, 1935, M.D., 1938, Sc.D., 1943; student Balliol Coll., Oxford (Eng.) U., 1944, Med. Field Service Sch., Paris, France, 1945; m. Jamie Elizabeth Hill, Jan. 1948; children—Evan, Jon, Gary. Surg. intern Meth.-Episcopal Hosp., N.Y.C., 1938-40; urol. resident Squier Urol. Clinic, Presbyn. Hosp., N.Y.C., 1940-43, dir. Squier Urol. Clinic, 1955—, dir. urol. service Presbyn. Hosp., 1955—, also dir. urology Sch. Nursing; staff asst., instr. urology Columbia Coll. Physicians and Surgeons, 1940-53, asst. prof. clin. urology, 1953-55, prof. urology, chmn. dept. urology, 1955—; vis. prof. Mayo Clinic Med. Sch., Rochester, Minn., 1977; guest lectr. Akron City Hosp., 1977, Reno Surg. Soc., 1977; chief urology Babies Hosp., Vanderbilt Clinic, Frances Delafield Hosp., N.Y.C., 1955; cons. urology VA, N.Y.C., 1947—, USPHS Hosp., S.I., N.Y.C., Meth. Hosp., Bklyn., Englewood (N.J.), Yonkers (N.Y.) gen. hosps., Harlem, Roosevelt, St. Lukes hosps. (all N.Y.C.); mem. com. surgery in Tb, genito-urinary Tb, VA; med. cons. Time mag.; cons. to com. on therapy Nat. Tb Assn.; mem. expert adv. panel biology human reprodn. WHO; mem. N.Y. Supreme Ct. Med. Arbitration Panel, 1975; Am. Urol. Assn. rep. to NRC-Nat. Acad. Scis.; mem. tng. grants com. NIH, 1968—. Trustee Presbyn. Hosp., 1974—; mem. vis. com. sect. arms and armour Met. Mus. Art, 1978. Served from 1st lt. to maj. M.C., AUS, 1943-46; chief urol. sect. gen. hosps. Recipient Joseph Mather Smith prize for research kidney disease Columbia, 1943; 1st prize for clin. research Am. Urol. Assn., 1950, 60; prize research kidney Tb A.M.A., 1953; honor award for meritorious work in field of Tb, Am. Acad. Tb Physicians, also prizes for sci. exhibits; gold medal alumni assn. Coll. Physicians and Surgeons, 1971; Hugh Young medal for outstanding work in infectious diseases, 1973; Belfield medal Chgo. Urol. Soc.; Burpeau medal N.J. Acad. Medicine; Edward Henderson Gold medal Am. Geriatrics Soc., 1978; Gt. medal City of Paris, 1979; Richard Chute lectr., 1973; Stoneburner lectr. Med. Coll. Va., 1973. Diplomate Am. Bd. Urology. Fellow A.C.S. (chmn. adv. com. urology 1962-64, gov. 1966—, com. on undergrad. tng. 1967—, chmn. nominating com. 1976-77, com. to study size and composition of bd. govs.), AMA, Am. Acad. Pediatrics (chmn. com. on pediatric urology, pres. sect. urology 1973—); mem. N.Y. Acad. Medicine (chmn. genito-urinary surg. sect. 1956-57), Am. Assn. Genito-Urinary Surgeons, Am. Urol. Assn. (pres. 1975-76; chmn. com. on pediatric urology, pres. N.Y. sect. 1966, exec. com. 1967—, com. on surgery, mem. rev. and long range planning com., editorial bd. Jour. Urology 1965—, chmn. com. to gather info. about urology; chmn. coordinating council for urology, chmn. nominating com. 1976-77), Alumni Assn. Presbyn. Hosp. (pres. N.Y.C. 1967-68), Am. Thoracic Soc., AAUP, N.Y. State Pediatrics Soc., Soc. U. Urologists (pres. 1969—), Nat. Inst. Social Scis., St. Nicholas Soc., Assn. Mil. Surgeons, Harvey Soc., Nat. Tb Assn., N.Y., New York County med. socs., Soc. Pediatric Urology (pres. 1961-62), Brit. Assn. Urol. Surgeons (corr. mem.), N.Y. Soc. Surgeons, N.Y. Soc. Professions, Internat. Société d'Urology (pres. 1973—), S.A.R., Assn. Pediatric Urology (pres. 1961), A.A.A.S., Am. Assn. Clin. Urologists, Assn. Am. Med. Colls., Clin. Soc. Genito-Urinary Surgeons, N.Y. Acad. Sci., Assn. Mil. Historians, Soc. War 1812, Mil. Order Fgn. Wars U.S., Order of Founders and Patriots, Arms and Armour Soc. N.Y., Arms and Armour Soc. Eng., Arms and Armour Soc. Gueurnsey, Soc. Colonial Wars, Manuscript Soc., Revolutionary War Round Table of N.Y. Club: Metropolitan. Contbr. numerous articles on urology and history to various publs., also chpts. in books; researcher, writer, speaker on assassinations of Pres. Lincoln and Kennedy. Office: Columbia U Med Sch New York NY 10032

LATTIMORE, OWEN, author, historian; b. Washington, July 29, 1900; s. David and Margaret (Barnes) L.; ed. Coll. Classique Cantonal, Lausanne, Switzerland, 1913-14, St. Bees Sch., Cumberland, Eng., 1915-19, Grad. Sch., Harvard, 1929; D.Litt., Glasgow U. (Scotland), 1964; Ph.D. (hon.), U. Copenhagen (Denmark), 1972; LL.D., Brown U., 1975; m. Eleanor Holgate, Mar. 4, 1926 (dec. Mar. 1970); 1 son, David. Engaged in business, Shanghai, China, 1920; newspaper work, Tientsin, 1921; with Arnhold & Co., Ltd., Tientsin and Peking, 1922-26; engaged in travel and writing, 1926—; research in Manchuria under Social Sci. Research Council, 1929-30, in Peiping under Harvard-Yenching Inst., 1930-31, under J.S. Guggenheim Meml. Found., 1931-33; field work in Mongolia and research in Peiping under Inst. of Pacific Relations, 1934-37; editor Pacific Affairs, 1934-41; lectr. Johns Hopkins, 1938-63, dir. Walter Hines Page Sch. Internat. Relations, 1939-53; prof. Chinese studies U. Leeds (Eng.), 1963-70; Chichele lectr. Oxford (Eng.) U., 1965; polit. adviser to Chiang Kai-shek, 1941-42; dep. dir. Pacific ops. OWI, 1942-44; mem. Reparations Mission to Japan, 1945-46; chief UN Tech. Aid Exploratory Mission to Afghanistan, 1950. Mem. X, XI XIV Congresses Hist. Scis. Recipient Cuthbert Peek award Royal Geog. Soc., 1929; Patron's medal, 1942; Gold medal Phila. Geog. Soc., 1933, U. Ind. medal, 1974. Mem. Assn. Asian Studies, Royal Asiatic Soc., Royal Geog. Soc. (mem. council 1965-66), Royal Central Asian Soc., Am. Geog. Soc. (hon.), Am. Philos. Soc., Am. Hist. Assn., Acad. Scis. Mongolian People's Republic (fgn. mem.), Czsoma Körösi Soc. (hon.), Phi Beta Kappa (hon.). Author: The Desert Road to Turkestan, 1928; High Tartary, 1930; Manchuria, Cradle of Conflict, 1932; The Mongols of Manchuria, 1934; Inner Asian Frontiers of China, 1940; Mongol Journeys, 1941; (with Eleanor Lattimore) China, A Short History, 1947; Solution in Asia, 1945; The Situation in Asia, 1949; Ordeal by Slander, 1950; Pivot of Asia, 1950; Nationalism and Revolution in Mongolia, 1955; Nomads and Commissars, 1962; Studies in Frontier History, 1963; (with Eleanor Lattimore) Silks, Spices and Empire, 1968; History and Revolution in China, 1974. Contbr. articles to learned jours., encys., and mags. Office: care Greenwood Press 51 Riverside Ave Westport CT 06880*

LATTIN, CLARK PARKER, JR., engring. and constrn. co. exec.; b. Yonkers, N.Y., Feb. 11, 1916; s. Clark Parker and Kathryn (Hanson) L.; B.Mech. Engring., U. Del., 1938; m. Ruth Cantwell, Oct. 21, 1939; children—Anne Drake, Nancy Booker, Kathryn Martin, Clark Parker, III. With Foster Wheeler Corp., 1938-60, v.p., dir., 1958-60; v.p. Chem. Constrn. Corp., 1960-65; with Pullman Kellogg, div. Pullman Inc., 1965—, sr. v.p., 1968-70, pres., 1971—, v.p. parent corp., 1973—; chmn., dir. Kellogg Internat. Corp., Kellogg Continental, B.V., Heat Research Corp., Gordian Assos., Inc., HLK Services, Ltd. Registered profl. engr., N.J. Mem. Am. Inst. Chem. Engrs., Am. Petroleum Inst., Houston C. of C. (dir.). Republican. Episcopalian. Clubs: River Oaks Country, Petroleum (Houston); University (N.Y.C.). Office: 3 Greenway Plaza E Houston TX 77046

LATTING, PATIENCE SEWELL (MRS. TRIMBLE B. LATTING), mayor; b. Texhoma, Okla., Aug. 27, 1918; d. Frank Asa and Leila (Yates) Sewell; A.B. magna cum laude, U. Okla., 1938; M.A., Columbia U., 1939; m. Trimble B. Latting, Aug. 23, 1941; children—Francelia Latting Wilson, Nancy Sewell Latting Spelman, James Trimble, Cynthia Longley. Asst. to research librarian Chase Nat. Bank, N.Y.C., 1938-39. Mem. Oklahoma City Council, 1967-71; mayor, Oklahoma City, 1971—. Legislation chmn. Okla. Congress Parents and Tchrs., 1960-67; mem. exec. com. Oklahoma City Council PTA's, 1960-62; pres. Edgemore PTA, Oklahoma City, 1963-64; mem. Okla. Gov's Reapportionment Com., 1960, Gov.'s Adv. Com. on Edn., 1964, Oklahoma City Citizens Emergency Fin. Com., 1965; trustee U.S. Conf. Mayors; apptd. officer of ct. to aid in reapportionment Okla. Legislature, 1964; Named Outstanding Sr. Woman, Theta Sigma Phi, U. Okla., 1938; recipient Amy B. Onken award to outstanding undergrad. mem. Pi Beta Phi, 1938, Phi Beta Kappa award to Outstanding Oklahoman, 1976; named Woman of Yr. in Civic Work, Oklahoma City chpt. Theta Sigma Phi, 1961, Outstanding Woman award, 1968; named Outstanding Woman of Okla., Soroptimists, 1969; named hon. col. Okla., 1960. Mem. LWV (mem. Oklahoma City bd. 1958-59), Oklahoma City Tennis Assn. (mem. bd. 1965—), Mortar Bd., Huguenot Soc. Founders of Manakin in the Colony Va., Phi Beta Kappa (v.p. Oklahoma City alumni, 1965—), Alpha Lambda Delta, Sigma Alpha Iota, Chi Delta Phi, Pi Mu Epsilon, Pi Beta Phi (pres. Oklahoma City alumni 1947-48), Delta Kappa Gamma (hon.). Clubs: 20th Century (sec. 1961-62), Oklahoma City Golf and Country, Altrusa (hon.). Instrumental in securing passage of state law permitting local sch. bds. to prohibit high sch. fraternities and sororities, 1953; author of amicus curiae brief filed on behalf of Okla. Congress Parents and Tchrs. dealing with reapportionment of state legislature, 1962. Office: City Hall 200 N Walker St Oklahoma City OK 73102*

LATTMAN, LAURENCE HAROLD, educator; b. N.Y.C., Nov. 30, 1923; s. Jacob and Yetta (Schwartz) L.; B.S. in Chem. Engring., Coll. City N.Y., 1948; M.S. in Geology, U. Cin., 1951, Ph.D. (Fenneman fellow), 1953; m. Hanna Renate Cohn, Apr. 12, 1946; children—Martin Jacob, Barbara Diane. Instr., U. Mich., 1952-53; asst. head photogeology sect. Gulf Oil Corp., Pitts., 1953-57; asst. prof. to prof. geomorphology Pa. State U., 1957-70; prof., head dept. geology U. Cin., 1970-75; dean Coll. of Mines, U. Utah, 1975-78, dean Coll. Engring., 1978—. Cons. U.S. Army Engrs., Vicksburg, Miss., 1965-69, also maj. oil cos. Served with AUS, 1943-46. Recipient Distinguished Teaching award Pa. State U., 1968. Fellow Geol. Soc. Am.; mem. Am. Assn. Petroleum Geologists, Am. Soc. Photogrammetry (Ford Bartlett award 1968), Soc. Econ. Paleontologists and Mineralogists, Sigma Xi. Author: (with R.G. Ray) Aerial Photographs in Field Geology, 1965. Contbr. articles to profl. jours. Home: 2119 Lakeline Dr Salt Lake City UT 84109

LATTO, LAWRENCE JAY, lawyer; b. Bklyn., Sept. 23, 1920; B.S., Coll. City N.Y., 1941; LL.B., Columbia U., 1948. Admitted to N.Y. bar, 1948, D.C. bar, 1949, Va. bar, 1954; asso. firm Shea & Gardner, Washington, 1948-54, mem. firm, 1954—. Mem. Am., D.C. (chmn. bd. profl. responsibilities), Va. bar assns., Am. Law Inst., Center Law and Social Policy (vice-chmn., trustee). Editor-in-chief Columbia Law Rev., 1948. Home: 928 S 26th St Arlington VA 22202 Office: Shea & Gardner Walker Bldg Washington DC 20005

LATZ, G. IRVING, II, econ. urban affairs cons.; b. Ft. Wayne, Ind., Feb. 12, 1920; s. G. Irving and Carrie (Stiefel) L.; B.S. in Econs., U. Pa., 1941; M.B.A., U. Chgo., 1971; m. Janet Horwitz Simon, Oct. 16, 1949; children—Sara Rose, G. Irving III. Trainee, F.R. Lazarus Co., Columbus, O., 1941; with Wolf & Dessauer Co., Ft. Wayne, 1946-66, treas., 1947-66, pres., 1957-66; Model Cities adminstr., Columbus, 1967-68; cons. urban affairs Michael Reese Hosp. and Med. Center, Chgo., 1973-74; Latz Assos., Ft. Wayne, 1974—; dir. Ft. Wayne Future, Inc., Ft. Wayne Nat. Bank. Pres. Ind. Retail Council, 1965-66. Gen. chmn. Ft. Wayne United Fund; gen. chmn. Ft. Wayne Fine Arts Found., 1958-67, pres., 1967-69. Bd. dirs. Ft. Wayne Jewish Fedn., United Community Services. Served with AUS, 1941-46. Mem. Fort Wayne C. of C. (v.p.). Jewish. Club: Ft. Wayne Country. Home: 1919 Hadley Rd Fort Wayne IN 46804

LATZ, MURRAY JESSE, retail trade exec.; b. N.Y.C., June 1, 1921; s. Irving and Hattie (Steinthal) L.; B.A., Dartmouth, 1942, M.C.S., 1942; m. Marjorie Jane Kleinberg, Dec. 16, 1951; children—Michael, Ronald. Staff accountant S.D. Leidesdorf, N.Y.C., 1946-52; supr. Touche Ross & Co., N.Y.C., 1952-58; with Allied Stores Corp., N.Y.C., 1958—, asst. treas., 1960-61, treas., 1971—, v.p., 1978—; v.p., treas. Allied Stores Credit Corp., 1972—. Treas Morton H. Steinthal Meml., Inc. Served with Finance Corps, AUS, 1943-46. C.P.A. Mem. Am. Inst. C.P.A.'s. Home: 1668 Sherbourne Rd Valley Stream NY 11580 Office: Allied Stores Corp 1114 Ave of Americas New York City NY 10036

LATZER, THOMAS FRANKLIN, former food co. exec., lawyer; b. Wellsboro, Pa., Mar. 12, 1912; s. John Albert and Louise (Briggs) L.; B.S. in Gen. Bus., U. Ill., 1935; J.D., Harvard, 1938; LL.D., John Brown U., 1965; m. Elisabeth Addington Good, Jan. 1, 1938; children—Robert W., Elizabeth L. Pooley, Margaret L. Grindley, Louis A. Law clk. Owlett and Webb, Wellsboro, Pa., 1938-39; legal dept. Pet Milk Co. (now Pet, Inc.), St. Louis, 1939-54, asst. sec., 1949-54, sec., 1954-69, v.p., 1969-77, also dir., 1952—. Trustee Louis Latzer Meml. Pub. Library, Highland, Ill., YMCA of U. Ill., Coro Found.; chmn. Midwestern Center; bd. dirs. Consol. Neighborhood Services, Inc., Goodwill Industries Mo.; pres. Downtown Day Care. Mem. Am., St. Louis bar assns., Beta Gamma Sigma. Episcopalian. Home: 55 Loren Woods St Louis MO 63124 Office: 400 S 4th St St Louis MO 63166

LAUB, WILLIAM MURRAY, utility exec.; b. Ft. Mills, Corregidor, Philippines, July 20, 1924 (parents Am. citizens); s. Harold Goodspeed and Marjorie M. (Murray) L.; B.S. in Bus. Adminstrn., U. Calif. at Berkeley, 1947, LL.B., 1950; m. Mary McDonald, July 26, 1947; children—William, Andrew, Mary, David, John. Admitted to Calif. bar, 1951; practiced in Los Angeles, 1951-55; with Southwest Gas Corp., Las Vegas, Nev., 1948—, v.p., gen. counsel, 1958-60, exec. v.p., 1960-64, pres., 1964—; also dir.; dir. 1st Nat. Bank Nev., Las Vegas. Pres., Boulder Dam Area council Boy Scouts Am., 1967-69, So. Nev. Indsl. Found., 1967-68, So. Nev. Meth. Found., 1968—; chmn. Nev. Equal Rights Commn., 1966-68. Chmn., Clark County Republican Central Com., 1964-66; nat. committeeman Nev. Rep. Com., 1968—; trustee Sch. Theology at Claremont (Calif.), 1977—. Served to lt. (j.g.), USNR, 1941-55. Methodist (trustee). Clubs: Jonathan (Los Angeles); Pauma Valley (Calif.) Country. Home: 1000 Rancho Circle Las Vegas NV 89107 Office: PO Box 15015 Las Vegas NV 89114

LAUBACH, GERALD DAVID, chem. co. exec.; b. Bethlehem, Pa., Jan. 21, 1926; s. Steward Lovine and Bertha (Rader) L.; student Mt. St. Mary's Coll., 1944-45; A.B. in Chemistry, U. Pa., 1947; Ph.D., Mass. Inst. Tech., 1950; D.Sc. (hon.), Hofstra U., 1979; m. Winifred Isabel Taylor, Oct. 3, 1953 (dec. Oct. 1979); children—Stephen, Andrea, Hilary. With Chas. Pfizer & Co., Inc., Groton, Conn., 1950—, mgr. medicinal products research, 1958-61, dir. dept. medicinial chemistry, 1961-63, group dir. medicinal research, 1963-64, v.p. medicinal products research and devel., 1964-68, dir., 1968—; mem. exec. com. Pfizer Pharms., 1969—, pres., 1969-71; exec. v.p. Pfizer Inc., 1971-72, pres., 1972—; dir. Loctite Corp., PMA, Conn. Gen. Ins. Corp., Hartford. Chmn. bd. trustees Conn. Coll.; mem. council Rockefeller U. Served with USNR, 1944-46. Mem. Am. Chem. Soc., AAAS, Soc. Chem. Industry, Am. Mgmt. Assn., N.Y. Acad. Scis., Chemists Club N.Y. (dir. 1968—, exec. com. 1969—). Contbr. articles to tech jours. Patentee in field. Home: Blood St Lyme CT 06371 Office: 235 E 42d St New York NY 10017

LAUBE, ROGER GUSTAV, banker; b. Chgo., Aug. 11, 1921; s. William C. and Elsie (Drews) L.; student Roosevelt U., 1938-42, John Marshall Law Sch., 1942, 48-50, Nat. Trust Sch., Northwestern U., 1960, Trust Div., Pacific Coast Grad. Sch. Banking, 1962-64; m. Irene Mary Chadbourne, Mar. 30, 1946; children—David Roger, Philip Russell, Steven Richard. With Chgo. Title & Trust Co., Chgo., 1938-42, 48-50, Nat. Bank Alaska, Anchorage, 1950-72, mgr. mortgage dept., 1950-57, v.p., trust officer, mgr. trust dept., 1957-72; v.p., trust officer, chmn. marketing div. Bishop Trust Co., Ltd., Honolulu, 1972—. Pres., Anchorage Estate Planning Council, 1960-62, mem., 1963-72. Pres. Anchorage Community Chorus, 1959-60, mem., 1947-72; pres. Anchorage camp Gideons Internat., 1950-72, Honolulu, 1972—; mem. adv. bd. Faith Hosp., Glennallen, Alaska, 1960—, Central Alaska Mission of Far Eastern Gospel Crusade, 1960—; sec.-treas. Alaska Bapt. Found., 1955-72; bd. dirs. Alaska Festival Music, 1960-72, Anchorage Symphony, 1965-72; bd. advisers Salvation Army, Alaska, 1961-72, bd. advisers, Honolulu, 1972—, chmn. bd. advisers, 1976-77. Served to 1st lt. with J.A.G., AUS, 1942-48. Recipient Others award Salvation Army, 1972. Mem. Am. Inst. Banking (instr. trust div. 1961—), Am. Bankers Assn. (mem. legislative council trust div. 1961-72), Hawaii Estate Planning Council (v.p. 1979, pres. 1980), Nat. Assn. Life Underwriters (asso.), Anchorage C. of C. (mem. awards com. 1969-71), Honolulu C. of C.,

Internat. Assn. Financial Planners. Baptist (exec. com. conv. 1959-61, dir. music Alaska 1950-72, Hawaii 1972—, chmn. trustees 1970-72). Home: 1879 Halekoa Dr Honolulu HI 96821 Office: Bishop Trust Co Ltd 140 S King St Box 2390 Honolulu HI 96804

LAUBER, THORNTON STUART, cons. engr., educator; b. Cornwall, Ont., Can., Jan. 5, 1924; s. Thornton Woodburn and Gertrude (Hirst) L.; brought to U.S., 1924, naturalized, 1932; B.S., Cornell U., Ithaca, N.Y., 1944; M.S., Ill. Inst. Tech., 1951; Ph.D., U. Pa., 1964; m. Lois Marie Pearson, Feb. 11, 1956; children—Judith Marie, Pamela Jean, Thornton Bruce, Mary Alane. Engr., Commonwealth Assos., Inc., Jackson, Mich., 1946-50; heat transfer engr. Gen. Electric Co., Pittsfield, Mass., 1951-58, sr. analytical engr., Phila., 1958-69, cons., 1969—; prof. electric power engring. Rensselaer Poly. Inst., Troy, N.Y., 1969—, S.B. Crary prof. engring., 1970—. Served to 2d lt., inf., Signal Corps, AUS, 1944-46. Mem. IEEE, ASME, Sigma Xi, Eta Kappa Nu, Tau Beta Pi. Home: 1005 Seminole Rd Scotia NY 12302 Office: Jonsson Engring Center 5004 Rensselaer Poly Inst Troy NY 12181

LAUCHNER, JULIAN HAWTHORNE, coll. dean; b. Centralia, Ill., Oct. 8, 1924; s. Aaron H. and Ruth B. (Ford) L.; B.S., U. Ill., 1949, B.S. in Chem. Engring., 1950, M.S. in Ceramic Engring., 1954, Ph.D. in Materials Engring., 1956; m. Virginia L. Slater, Sept. 9, 1950; children—Linda Sue, Julia Anne, Mark Alan, Lenora Jayne, Carol Jo, Ruth Ellen. Devel. engr. Ferro Corp., 1950-54; faculty U. Ill., 1956-60, research asso. prof., 1958-60; prof. ceramic engring., head dept. Miss. State U., 1960-62, dir. materials research center, 1962; dean So. Ill. U. Sch. Tech., Carbondale, 1962-72 (on leave); sci. and tech. adviser Latin Am. program Ford Found., Rio de Janeiro, 1967-72; dean Cleve. State U. Fenn Coll. Engring., 1972—. Cons. Am. Metal Climax, Inc., Ford Found., Dept. State-AID, Gen. Electric Co., Herschede Enterprises. Mem. Ill. Bd. of Registration for Sanitarians, Dept. Registration and Edn. Served with USAAF, 1943-45. Registered profl. engr. Mem. Am. Soc. Engring. Edn., Am. Chem. Soc., Nat., Ill. socs. profl. engrs., Am. Inst. Aeros. and Astronautics, Internat. Soc. for Engring. Sci., Ill. Assn. Professions (dir.), Sigma Xi. Address: Box 176 Philo IL 61864

LAUCK, ANTHONY JOSEPH, clergyman, artist; b. Indpls., Dec. 30, 1908; s. Anthony Peter and Marie Elizabeth (Habig) L.; diploma fine arts John Herron Art Sch., 1936; A.B., U. Notre Dame, 1942; certificate carving, painting Corcoran Sch. Art, 1948. Entered Congregation of Holy Cross, 1937; ordained priest Roman Catholic Ch., 1946; priest aux. St. Martin's Ch., Washington, 1946-48, Holy Cross Ch., N.Y.C., 1948-49, U. Notre Dame (Ind.) Univ. Ch., 1950—, faculty dept. art univ., 1950—, asso. prof. sculpture, 1958-70, prof. sculpture, 1970-72, emeritus, 1973—, head dept. art, 1960-67, dir. Univ. Art Gallery, 1962-74, dir. emeritus, 1974—. Exhibited exhbns. John Herron Art Inst., Ind. State Fair, Indpls., Corcoran Gallery Art, Nat. Mus. Art, Washington, N.A.D., Audubon Artists, N.Y.C., Pa. Acad. Fine Arts, Phila., Conn. Acad. Fine Art, Hartford, Provincetown (Mass.) Art Assn., Newport (R.I.) Art Assn.; represented permanent collections 3d Sculpture Internat., Phila. Mus. Art, 1949, Corcoran Gallery Art, Pa. Acad. Fine Arts, Norfolk Mus. Art, South Bend Art Assn., Indpls. Mus. Art, Notre Dame U., Ind. State Museum, Grand Rapids Art Mus., Evansville Mus. Arts and Sci., Ball State U. Art Mus., Gary Art Center, Hartwick Coll., also pvt. collections. Chmn. art jury Nat. Sacred Heart Drawing Competition, Xavier U., 1956. Recipient Fairmount Park purchase prize Third Sculpture Internat., 1949; George D. Widener Gold medal for sculpture Am. art exhbn. Pa. Acad. Art, 1953; John Herron Art Inst. citation, 1957; 1st prize for sculpture Hammond (Ind.) Art Salon, 1967, Newport (R.I.) Art Assn.; inducted medalist Ind. Acad., 1973. Mem. Audubon Artists, Arts Club Chgo., Indiana Artists Club. Contbr. articles on sacred art to jours. and mags. Home: Moreau Seminary Notre Dame IN 46556. *For subject matter, I look about and try to use whatever in God's creation seems to have visual impact for me, something which arouses a personal experience of value. The medium is the language which I speak, and these are the languages, the tongues, I love.*

LAUCK, DANIEL WAYNE, journalist; b. Topeka, Dec. 1, 1948; s. Homer Robert and Opal LaVerne (Murphy) L.; student Washburn U., 1966-67; B.A., Kans. State U., 1970; m. Barbara Jo Stadler, Dec. 26, 1967; children—Jamie Layne, Macie Jayne. Sports editor Manhattan (Kans.) Mercury, 1969; sports writer Topeka Capital-Jour., 1970-74; columnist Wichita (Kans.) Eagle-Beacon, 1974-75; sports writer Newsday, 1976—; tchr. reporting Washburn U., 1973-74. Recipient News-feature award Best Sports Stories of 1973; Sports-Feature award N.Y. State Asso. Press, 1978, 79; named Kans. Sportswriter of Year, 1974. Mem. Nat. Assn. Sports Writers and Broadcasters, Sigma Delta Chi. Contbr. to various sports publs. Home: 10 W Lyons St Melville NY 11747 Office: 1 Newsday Plaza Melville NY 11747

LAUDEMAN, RANDOLPH DOUGLASS, lawyer; b. Balt., Apr. 8, 1909; s. Randolph and Mary M. (Treut) L.; LL.B., U. Balt., 1929; m. Dorothy Irving Remington, Sept. 24, 1935; children—Arthur N., Dorothy L. (Mrs. Frank L. Mitchell). With B. & O. R.R., Balt., 1926-31; admitted to Md. bar, 1931, Ill. bar, 1951, also Fed. Ct., U.S. Tax Ct., U.S. Ct. of Claims; practice in Balt., 1931-35, Bloomington, Ill., 1951—; pvt. practice, 1931-35, 51—; investigator alcohol tax unit Treasury Dept., Balt., 1934-35, Raleigh, N.C., 1935, Balt., 1936, Salisbury, Md., 1937-38, examiner, revenue agt. estate and income tax unit, Bloomington, 1939-51. Auditor, Bloomington-Normal Community Chest, 1940; first aid instr. McLean County chpt. ARC, 1942-65, first aid chmn., 1945, disaster chmn., 1947-49, chpt. chmn., 1949; chmn. McLean County unit Am. Cancer Soc., 1964-70; pres. McLean County Hist. Soc., 1967-69; chmn. Bloomington-Asahigawa Sister City Com., 1969-74; bd. dirs. Credit Bur. of Bloomington. Republican precinct committeeman, 1960-65. Mem. Am., Ill., McLean County bar assns. Presbyn. (elder, trustee). Mason (Shriner). Home: 805 S Mercer Ave Bloomington IL 61701 Office: 221 E Washington St Boomington IL 61701

LAUDER, ESTEE, cosmetics co. exec.; b. Vienna, Austria; m. Joseph Lauder; children—Leonard, Ronald. Partner Estee Lauder Inc., 1946—. Named One of 100 Women of Achievement Harpers Bazaar, 1967, Top Ten Outstanding Women in Business, 1970; recipient Spirit of Achivement award Albert Einstein Coll. Medicine, 1968, Internat. Achievement award Frost Bros., 1971. Office: 767 Fifth Ave New York NY 10022*

LAUDERDALE, FRANK, JR., univ. dean; b. Wellington, Mo., Jan. 11, 1916; s. Frank Lee and Ethel (Larkin) L.; B.S., Central Mo. State Coll., 1936; postgrad. U. Ia., 1938; M.Ed., U. Mo., 1941; Ph.D., U. Tex., Austin, 1966; m. Frances Prideaux, Sept. 12, 1946; children—Lee, Lou Azile, Susan, Paul Michael. Tchr. various Mo. high schs., 1936-41; instr. U. Mo., 1946; accountant Haskins & Sells, Dallas, 1947-50; instr. U. Tex., Austin, 1950-52; dept. head Stephen F. Austin State U., Nacogdoches, Tex., 1952-68, dean Sch. Bus., 1968—; pvt. practice pub. accounting. Served to capt. USAAF, 1942-46. Mem. Tex. Soc. C.P.A.'s, Am. Accounting Assn., Beta Gamma Sigma, Beta Alpha Psi, Alpha Kappa Psi. Home: 4101 Raguet St Nacogdoches TX 75961

LAUER, DOLOR JOHN, indsl. physician; b. St. Paul, July 8, 1912; s. John H. and Gertrude (Berning) L.; B.S., M.B., U. Minn., 1937, M.D., 1938; doctorate in Indsl. Medicine, U. Pitts., 1950; m. Helene Sheran, Oct. 26, 1940; children—Wallace, Richard, Stephen, John, Camille, Phillip, Elizabeth. Gen. practice medicine and surgery, St. Paul, 1938-40; fellow indsl. medicine U. Pitts., 1946-47; asst. prof. occupational medicine Kettering Lab., U. Cin., 1948-51; med. dir. Jones & Laughlin Steel Corp., also clin. asso. prof. occupational med. U. Pitts., 1951-60; clin. asso. prof. occupational medicine N.Y. U. Post Grad. Medicine, 1961—; med. dir. ITT, N.Y.C., 1960-78, cons., 1978—. Mem. Pa. Adv. Bd. Health, 1956-60, Allegheny County Bd. Health, chmn. 1957-60; pres. Allegheny County unit Am. Cancer Soc., 1955-56; del. Internat. Conf. Health and Health Edn. to Pub. Trustee Nat. Health Council. Served from lt. (j.g.) to comdr. USNR, 1940-45. Diplomate pub. health and occupational medicine Am. Bd. Preventive Medicine. Mem. AMA, Am. Occupational Med. Assn. (pres. 1959-60, Knudsen award 1977), N.Y. Acad. Medicine, Med. Soc. N.Y., N.Y. County Med. Soc., Am. Acad. Occupational Medicine (Kehoe award 1977), Internat. Assn. for Occupational Health, Am. Indsl. Hygiene Assn., Am. Coll. Preventive Medicine (pres. 1963-64), Ramazzini Soc., Sigma Xi. Club: University (N.Y.C.). Home: 3 Washington Sq Larchmont NY 10538 Office: 320 Park Ave New York NY 10022

LAUER, JAMES LOTHAR, physicist; b. Vienna, Austria, Aug. 2, 1920; came to U.S., 1938, naturalized, 1943; s. Max and Friedericke (Rappaport) L.; A.B., Temple U., 1942, M.A., 1944; Ph.D., U. Pa., 1948; postgrad. U. Calif., San Diego, 1964-65; m. Stefanie Dorothea Blank, Sept. 5, 1955; children—Michael, Ruth. Scientist, Sun Oil Co., Marcus Hook Pa., 1944-52, spectroscopist, 1952-64; asst. prof. U. Pa., 1952-55; lectr. U. Del., 1952-58; research fellow mech. engring. U. Calif., San Diego, 1964-65; research prof. mech. engring. Rensselaer Poly. Inst., Troy, N.Y., 1978—; cons. Sun Oil Co. Pa., 1978—, Aluminum Co. Can. Ltd., 1976—. Active Penn Wynne Civic Assn., 1959-77. Sun Oil Co. fellow, 1964-65; Air Force Office Sci. Research grantee, 1974-78; NASA Lewis Research Center grantee, 1974-78. Mem. Am. Chem. Soc., Am. Phys. Soc., Soc. Applied Spectroscopy, Spectroscopy Soc. Can., Sigma Xi. Jewish. Author: Infrared Fourier Spectroscopy—Chemical Applications, 1978; author numerous tech. papers, patentee in field. Home: 7 Northeast Ln Ballston Lake NY 12019 Office: Dept Mech Engring Rensselaer Poly Inst Troy NY 12181. *My advice to those contemplating a career in experimental research is to give much thought to these points: (1) interest, enthusiasm, willingness to work are only basics, (2) a loving and understanding wife is essential, and (3) the knowledge that you can create your own success at any time is the driving force.*

LAUERMAN, HAROLD WILLIAM, ret. found. cons.; b. Washington, Pa., July 11, 1914; s. Nicholas John and Nellie Gertrude (Schmidt) L.; m. Hazel M. Ruth, Apr. 15, 1943. With Donora (Pa.) Herald-Am., 1935-42; asst. to mgr. indsl. relations Nat. Tube Co., McKeesport, Pa., 1942-43; editor house organ H.J. Heinz Co., Pitts., 1946-48; head employee publs. and community relations, 1948-56; account supr., pub. relations W.S. Walker Advt. Agy., Pitts., 1956-58; mgr. pub. relations dept. Erwin, Wasey, Ruthrauff & Ryan, Pitts., 1958-61, dir. pub. relations, 1961-63; adminstrv. officer Sarah Scaife Found., Inc., Pitts., 1963-70, chief adminstrv. officer, 1970-74, cons. to found., 1974-76. Bd. dirs., past pres. Donora Community and Library Center; bd. dirs. Meadowcroft Village, Avella, Pa.; mem. adv. com. Monongahela Valley Hosp. Served with USAAF, 1943-46. Mem. Pitts. Press Club, Am. Legion. Elk. Home: 39 2d St Extension Donora PA 15033

LAUFE, LEONARD EDWARD, physician; b. Pitts., July 22, 1924; s. Myer L. and Ethel (Terner) L.; B.S., U. Pitts., 1944; student U. Rochester, 1944-45; M.D., U. Louisville, 1949; m. Symoine K. Kamin, July 28, 1946; children—Lucy, Jennifer. Intern, Mercy Hosp., Pitts., 1949-50; resident obstet.-gynecol. pathology Magee Hosp., Pitts., 1950-51, resident in obstetrics and gynecology, 1953-56; clin. asso. prof. U. Pitts.; mem. staff Magee-Womens Hosp., Western Pa. Hosp., chief obstetrics and gynecology, 1965-75; med. dir. Internat. Fertility Research Program, Research Triangle Park, N.C., 1975—; clin. prof. obstetrics and gynecology Duke U. Med. Center; dir. Internat. Pregnancy Adv. Service. Served to capt. M.C., AUS, 1951-53. Pitts. Found. fellow, Radiumhemmet-Stockholm and Newcastle, 1956. Diplomate Am. Bd. Obstetrics and Gynecology. Fellow Pitts. Obstet.-Gynecol. Soc., Am. Coll. Obstetrics and Gynecology (founder resident's div. 1954, pres. dist. III 1955-56); mem. Orange County Med. Soc., Alpha Omega Alpha. Author: Obstetric Forceps, 1968. Designer 3 obstet. forceps. Home: 1721 Allard Rd Chapel Hill NC 27514 Office: Internat Fertility Research Program Research Triangle Park NC 27709

LAUFER, HANS, biologist, educator; b. Germany, Oct. 18, 1929; s. Sol and Margarete (Freundlich) L.; B.S., Coll. City N.Y., 1952; M.A., Bklyn. Coll., 1953; Ph.D. (James fellow), Cornell U., Ithaca, N.Y., 1957; m. Evelyn Green, Oct. 31, 1953; children—Jessica, Marc, Leonard. Research and teaching asst. Cornell U., 1953-57; NRC fellow Carnegie Instn. of Washington, 1957-59; asst. prof. biology Johns Hopkins, 1959-65; asso. prof. U. Conn., Storrs, 1965-72, prof., 1972—; vis. prof. Karolinska Inst., Stockholm, 1972, Charles U., Prague, 1974; participant Nat. Acad. Scis.-Czechoslovak Acad. exchange program, 1974, 77. Conklin Meml. fellow Marine Biology Lab., Woods Hole, Mass., 1956, Lalor fellow, 1962, 63, mem. staff, embryology course, 1968-72, mem. corp., 1962—, corp. trustee, 1978—; vis. scholar Case Western Res. U., 1962; mem. NSF-NATO Fellowship Rev. Panel, 1974-76; NATO Sr. fellow, 1972; NIH Spl. fellow, 1973; Rosenstiel scholar Brandeis U., 1973. Fellow AAAS (chmn. sect. biology 1975); mem. Internat. Soc. Devel. Biology, Assn. Research Councils (nat. bd. on grad. edn. of conf. bd., 1971-75), Am. Soc. Zoology, Soc. Devel. Biology, Am. Soc. Cell Biology, European Soc. Comparative Endocrinology, Am. Assn. Advancement Aging Research, Internat. Soc. Differentiation, Tissue Culture Assn. Contbg. author numerous books. Asso. editor Jour. Exptl. Zoology, 1969-73. Contbr. numerous articles to profl. jours. Home: 49 Constance Dr Manchester CT 06040 Office: U-42 Biol Scis U of Conn Storrs CT 06268

LAUFER, JOHN, aero. engr.; b. Szekesfehrvar, Hungary, Sept. 22, 1921; s. Eugen Jeno and Ella (Possel) L.; came to U.S., 1939, naturalized, 1949; B.S., La. State U., 1942; M.S., Calif. Inst. Tech., 1943, Engr., 1944, Ph.D., 1948; m. Suzan Irma Ullman, Mar. 29, 1947; children—Karen Elizabeth, Eric Gene. Physicist, Nat. Bur. Standards, Washington, 1949-52; sr. research engr. Jet. Propulsion Lab., Pasadena, Calif., 1952-58, research specialist, 1958-60, chief sect. gas dynamics, 1960-64; prof. aerospace engring., chmn. dept. aerospace engring. U. So. Calif., 1964—; cons. to industry. Recipient Disting. Faculty award U. So. Calif. Sch. Engring., 1967; John Simon Guggenheim fellow, 1958; Fulbright-Hayes fellow, 1958; NATO sr. fellow in sci., 1977. Fellow Am. Phys. Soc., AIAA; mem. Nat. Acad. Engring., Sigma Xi, Tau Beta Pi. Contbr. numerous articles to profl. jours. Home: 1912 Homewood Dr Altedena CA 91001 Office: Dept Aerospace Engring U So Calif Los Angeles CA 90007

LAUFF, GEORGE HOWARD, biologist; b. Milan, Mich., Mar. 23, 1927; s. George John and Mary Anna (Klein) L.; B.S., Mich. State U., 1949, M.S., 1951; postgrad. U. Mont., 1951, U. Wash., 1952; Ph.D., Cornell U., 1953. Fisheries research technician Mich. Dept. Conservation, 1950; teaching asst. Cornell U., 1952-53; instr. U. Mich., 1953-57, asst. prof., 1957-61, asso. prof., 1961-62; research asso. Gt. Lakes Research Inst., U. Mich., 1954-59; dir. U. Ga. Marine Inst., 1960-62; asso. prof. U. Ga., 1960-62; research coordinator Sapelo Island Research Found., 1962-64; dir. Kellogg Biol. Sta., dept. fisheries and wildlife and zoology Mich. State U., East Lansing, 1964—; mem. cons. and rev. panels for Smithsonian Inst., Nat. Water Commn., NSF, Nat. Acad. Sci., Am. Inst. Biol. Sci., U.S. AEC, Inst. Ecology, others. Served with inf. U.S. Army, 1944-46. Office of Naval Research grantee; U.S. Dept. Interior grantee, NSF grantee, others. Fellow AAAS; mem. Am. Inst. Biol. Sci., Am. Soc. Limnology and Oceanography (pres. 1972-73), Ecol. Soc. Am., Freshwater Biology Assn., INTECOL, Societas Internationalis Limnologiae, Orgn. Biol. Field Stas., Sigma Xi, Phi Kappa Phi. Editor: Estuaries, 1967; Experimental Ecological Reserves, 1977. Home: 3818 Heights Dr Hickory Corners MI 49060 Office: 3700 E Gull Lake Dr Hickory Corners MI 49060

LAUFFER, MAX AUGUSTUS, JR., biophysicist, educator; b. Middletown, Pa., Sept. 2, 1914; s. Max Augustus and Elsie (Keiper) L.; B.S., Pa. State Coll., 1933, M.S., 1934; Ph.D., U. Minn., 1937; m. Dorothy Easton, Dec. 20, 1936 (dec. 1963); 1 son, Edward William; m. 2d, Erika Erskine, Mar. 21, 1964; children—Susan, Max, John. Asst., instr. biochemistry U. Minn., 1935-37; fellow, asst., asso. Rockefeller Inst. Med. Research, Princeton, 1937-44; asso. prof. U. Pitts., 1944-47, prof. biophysics, 1947—, head dept., 1949-56, dean div. natural scis., 1956-63, Andrew Mellon prof. biophysics, 1963—, chmn. dept., 1963-67, 71-75. Vis. prof. U. Bern (Switzerland), 1952, Max Planck Inst. Virus Research, Tubingen, Germany, 1965-66, Philippines, 1967; sci. adv. bd. Delta Regional Primate Research Center, Tulane U., 1964-67; nat. advisory gen. med. scis. council NIH, 1963-67; mem. teaching staff Marine Biol. Lab., Woods Hole, Mass., 1953-56; sci. adv. com. Boyce Thompson Inst. Plant Research, 1953—; cons. Research and Devel. Bd., 1947-53, surgeon gen., 1961-63. Mem. bd. Christian edn. U.P. Ch. U.S.A., 1963-72, mem. council of ch. and soc., 1963-71, chmn., 1968-71. Trustee Pitts. Theol. Sem., 1964-79, pres., 1971-74; bd. dirs. Health Research and Services Found., Pitts., 1961-67, 75—; trustee Coll. of Wooster, 1967—. Recipient Eli Lilly Research award in biochemistry Am. Chem. Soc., 1945; Outstanding Achievement award U. Minn., 1964. Fellow N.Y. Acad. Sci.; mem. Am. Chem. Soc. (chmn. div. biol. chemistry 1949-50, Pitts. award 1958), Fedn. Am. Scientists (chmn. Pitts. br. 1958-59), Biophys. Soc. (exec. bd. 1958-62, pres. 1961), Am. Soc. Biol. Chemists, Soc. Exptl. Biology and Medicine, Phi Beta Kappa, Sigma Xi, Alpha Zeta, Alpha Chi Sigma, Gamma Alpha, Phi Kappa Phi, Phi Eta Sigma, Gamma Sigma Delta, Phi Lambda Upsilon, Sigma Pi Sigma, Phi Sigma. Presbyn. Clubs: Faculty (U. Pitts.); University (Pitts.). Author: Entropy-Driven Processes in Biology, 1975. Bd. editors Archives Biochemistry and Biophysics, 1944-54, Biophys. Jour., 1960-64, editor, 1969-73; co-editor Advances in Virus Research, 1953—. Contbr. articles to profl. jours. Home: 1273 Folkstone Dr Pittsburgh PA 15243 also 190 Lauffer Rd Middletown PA 17057

LAUFMAN, HAROLD, surgeon; b. Milw., Jan. 6, 1912; s. Jacob and Sophia (Peters) L.; B.S., U. Chgo., 1932, M.D., 1937; M.S. in Surgery, Northwestern U., 1946, Ph.D., 1948; children—Dionne Laufman Weigert, Laurien. Intern, Michael Reese Hosp., Chgo., 1936-39; resident in gen. surgery St. Marks Hosp., London, Eng., Northwestern U. Med. Sch., Cook County Hosp., Hines VA Hosp., 1939-46; faculty Northwestern U., Chgo., 1941-65, from clin. asst. to prof., attending surgeon Passavant Meml. Hosp., Chgo., 1953-65; prof. surgery, history of medicine Albert Einstein Coll. Medicine, N.Y.C., 1965-79, emeritus, 1979—; dir. Inst. Surg. Studies, Montefiore Hosp. and Med. Center, Bronx, N.Y., 1965—; practice medicine specializing in gen. surgery, Chgo., 1941-65, N.Y.C., 1965—; professorial lectr. surgery Mt. Sinai Sch. Medicine, 1979—; adj. attending surgeon Mt. Sinai Hosp., 1979—; James IV vis. prof., Israel, 1962; cons., lectr. in field; chmn. FDA Classification Panel Gen. and Plastic Surgery Devices, 1975-78; pres. Harold Laufman Assos., Inc., cons., 1977—. Chmn. bd. N.Y. Chamber Soloists, 1974—. Served to maj. AUS, 1942-46. Diplomate Am. Bd. Surgery. Fellow A.C.S.; mem. Assn. Advancement Med. Instrumentation (pres. 1974-75, chmn. bd. 1976-77), Am. Assn. Hosp. Cons., Am. Med. Writers Assn. (pres. 1968-69), Am. Surg. Assn., Societe Internationale de Chirurgie, Western Surg. Assn., Central Surg. Assn., N.Y. Surg. Soc., Soc. Vascular Surgery, Internat. Cardiovascular Soc., Soc. Surgery Alimentary Tract, Chamber Music Conf. and Composers Forum of East (pres. 1975—), Sigma Xi, Alpha Omega Alpha, Phi Sigma Delta. Jewish. Clubs: Standard (Chgo.); Tammy Brook Country (Cresskill, N.J.). Author: (with S.W. Banks) Surgical Exposures of the Extremities, 1953; (with R.B. Erichson) Hematologic Proglems in Surgery, 1970; chmn. editorial bd. Diagnostica, 1974—; mem. editorial bd. Surgery, Gynecology and Obstetrics, 1974—, Med. Instrumentation, 1972—, Med. Research Engring., 1972—; contbg. author; contbr. articles to sci. pubs. Home: 31 E 72d St New York NY 10021 Office: 111 E 210th St New York NY 10467

LAUFMAN, SIDNEY, artist; b. Cleve., Oct. 29, 1891; s. George and Bertha (Toffler) L.; student Cleve. Sch. Art, 1911-12, Chgo. Art Inst., 1913-18, Art Students' League N.Y., 1919-20; m. Beatrice Ratner, Aug. 27, 1916. Lived and worked in France, 1920-33; instr. painting Art Students League, N.Y.C., 1938-50; vis. lectr. fine arts Brandeis U., 1959-60; represented in permanent collections large museums throughout U.S. represented by Forum Gallery, N.Y.C. Recipient numerous prizes and awards A.N.A., 1939, N.A., 1944. Mem. NAD (council 1947-50), Artists Equity Assn. (nat. sec., pres. N.Y. chpt. 1950-52), Woodstock Artists Assn., Woodstock Art Conf. (chmn. 1950). Home: 1038 S Osprey Ave Sarasota FL 33577

LAUGHERY, JACK ARNOLD, restaurant chain exec.; b. Guthrie Center, Iowa, Feb. 25, 1935; s. Gerald Reve and Mildred Eva (Ansberry) L.; B.C.S., U. Iowa, 1957; grad. exec. program U. N.C., Chapel Hill, 1976; m. Helen Herboth, Sept. 14, 1968; children—Brenda, Kelly, Christine, Sarah. Salesman, Conn. Gen. Ins. Co., 1957-62; with Sandy's Systems, 1962-72, pres., 1969-72, chief operating officer, 1970-72, chief exec. officer, 1971-72; exec. v.p. Hardee's Food Systems, Inc., Rocky Mount, N.C., 1972-73, pres., 1973—, chief operating officer, 1973-75, chief exec. officer, 1975—, also dir.; dir. First Union Nat. Bank, Charlotte, N.C., First Union Nat. Bank, Charlotte. Bd. dirs. Wesleyan Coll., Rocky Mount. Served with AUS, 1957-60. Mem. Nat. (dir. 1977—), N.C. (dir. 1975—) restaurant assns., Rocky Mount C. of C. (dir. 1976—), Am. Mgmt. Assn. Republican. Episcopalian. Home: 150 Hunter Hill Rd Rocky Mount NC 27801 Office: Hardee's Food Systems Inc PO Box 1619 Rocky Mount NC 27801

LAUGHLIN, CHARLES VAILL, educator, lawyer; b. Pittsfield, Ill., May 26, 1907; s. Ely Vaill and Anne (Hawker) L.; student Lenox Coll., 1924-26; LL.B., George Washington U., 1929, A.B., 1930; LL.M., Harvard, 1940; J.S.D., U. Chgo., 1942; m. Hope Lorraine Edson, June 5, 1948; 1 son, Richard Vaill. Admitted to D.C. bar, 1929, Ill. bar, 1930, Va. bar, 1948; with Davies, Jones, Beebe and Busick, Washington, 1929-30, Shanner and Shanner, Chgo., 1931, 32-38, Vedder, Price, Kaufman and Kammholz, Chgo., summer 1952; tchr. polit. sci. Lenox Coll., Hopkinton, Iowa, 1931-32, 38-39; mem. faculty

Washington and Lee U., Lexington, Va., 1940-42, 46—, prof. law, 1950—; vis. prof. George Washington U., 1960, U. Va., 1961; tchr. classes mil. law U.S. Army Res. program, 1953-60; U.S. commnr., 1962-71, labor arbitrator, 1970—, magistrate, 1971-75; Fulbright lectr. Am. law U. Helsinki (Finland), 1963-64. Chmn. Va. Republican Com. on Issues, 1957. Republican candidate for Iowa Legislature, 1932; mem. Rockbridge County (Va.) Rep. Com., 1952-59, 64—, Lexington (Va.) Electoral Bd., 1966-72, chmn., 1971-72; del., key note speaker dist. Rep. conv., 1952. Served to capt. Judge Adv. Gen. Corps, AUS, 1942-46. Recipient John B. Learner medal George Washington U., 1929. Mem. Am. Law Inst., Order of Coif, Am. Judicature Soc., Am. Assn. Arbitrators, Judge Advs. Assn., Delta Theta Phi, Acacia. Republican. Presbyterian. Contbr. articles to legal jours. Home: 209 Barclay Ln Lexington VA 24450. *I regret practically nothing that I have done. My greatest regrets are things that I have had the opportunity to do, but have left undone.*

LAUGHLIN, JAMES, publishing co. exec., writer, lectr.; b. Pitts., Oct. 30, 1914; s. Henry Hughart and Marjory (Rea) L.; A.B., Harvard U., 1939; Litt.D. (hon.), Hamilton Coll., 1969; Litt.D. (hon.), Colgate U., 1978; m. Margaret Keyser, Mar. 13, 1942 (div. 1952); children—Paul, Leila; m. 2d, Ann Clark Resor, May 19, 1956; children—Robert, Henry. Founder New Directions (now New Directions Pub. Corp.), N.Y.C., 1936, pres., 1964—; pres. Intercultural Publs., Inc; pub. Perspectives, USA and Perspectives supplements The Atlantic Monthly Jour.; cons. Indian So. Langs. Book Trust, Madras, 1955; vis. Regents prof. U. Calif. at San Diego, 1974. Chmn. creative writing panel Inst. Internat. Edn. Conf. on Arts Exchange, 1956—. Bd. dirs. Goethe Bi-Centennial Found., 1949, Aspen (Colo.) Inst. Humanities, 1950; mem. Nat. Citizens Commn. for Internat. Cooperation; mem. U.S. Nat. Commn. for UNESCO, 1960-63, Nat. Commn. for Internat. Coop. year, 1966; past trustee Allen-Chase Found.; mem. vis. com. dept. German, Princeton U.; mem. vis. com. dept. Romance langs. Harvard U.; co-trustee Merton Legacy Trust, 1969—; trustee Rosenbach Found., Phila. Decorated chevalier Legion of Honor; hon. fellow Coll. Five, U. Calif. at Santa Cruz, 1972—; recipient Distinguished Service award Am. Acad. Arts and Letters, 1977; award for pub. PEN, 1979; Carey-Thomas citation Pubs. Weekly, 1978. Mem. Am. Acad. Arts and Scis., Salt Lake City Winter Sports Assn. (dir. 1939—, v.p. 1958), Alta Lodge Co. (v.p. 1948-58, pres. 1958-59), P.E.N., Asia Soc. (chmn. publs. com. 1959-67). Clubs: Century Assn., Harvard (N.Y.C.). Author: Some Natural Things, 1945; A Small Book of Poems, 1948; The Wild Anemone and Other Poems, 1957; Selected Poems, 1960; The Pig, 1970; In Another Country, 1978; contbr. to mags. and books. Collector lit. mags. (little mag. type). Home: Meadow House Norfolk CT 06058 Office: 80 8th Ave New York NY 10014

LAUGHLIN, JOHN SETH, physicist, educator; b. Canton, Mo., Jan. 26, 1918; s. Sceva Bright and Catherine (Goodall) L.; A.B., Willamette U., 1940, D.Sc., 1968; M.S., Haverford Coll., 1942; Ph.D., U. Ill., 1947; m. Barbara Kester, June 14, 1943; children—Catherine Ann, Frances Elizabeth, Janet Judd; m. 2d, Eunice Byersdorf, June 23, 1979. Research physicist OSRD, 1944-45; asst. prof. dept. physics U. Ill., 1946-48, asso. prof. radiology, 1951-52; attending physicist Meml. Hosp., chmn. dept. med. physics, 1952—, chief div. biophysics Sloan-Kettering Inst., N.Y.C., 1952—, v.p. Sloan-Kettering Inst., 1966-72, prof. biophysics Sloan Kettering div. Cornell U. Grad. Sch., 1955—; dir. N.E. Center for Radiol. Physics, 1974—; John Wiley Jones lectr. Rochester Inst. Tech., 1977. Recipient Distinguished Service Alumni award U. Ill. Coll. Engring., 1972; Alumni citation Willamette U., 1964. Diplomate Am. Bd. Radiology. Fellow Am. Phys. Soc., Am. Coll. Radiology, N.Y. Acad. Scis., Sigma Xi; mem. Health Physics Soc. (pres. 1960-61), Assn. Tchrs. Physics, AAAS, Radiol. Soc. N.Am., Soc. Nuclear Medicine (dir.), Am. Radium Soc., Internat. Orgn. Med. Physics (v.p. 1965-69, pres. 1969-72), Radiation Research Soc. (pres. 1970-71), Am. Assn. Physicists in Medicine (pres. 1964-65, chmn. sci. com. 1968—, Coolidge award 1974). Author: Physical Aspects of Betatron Therapy, 1954. Home: 345 E 68th St New York NY 10021 Office: 1275 York Ave New York NY 10021

LAUGHLIN, LARRY, lawyer; b. Chgo., Aug. 12, 1918; s. Harmon L. and Mabel (Rorke) L.; student Columbia U., 1935-37; B.A., UCLA, 1941; J.D., U. Ariz., 1954; m. Sylvia Stauffer, Feb. 1, 1946; children—Sheila, Nora, Evan. Reporter, San Francisco Chronicle, 1946-49, Phoenix Republic, 1949-51; admitted to Ariz. bar, 1954, since practiced in Phoenix; mem. firm Carson Messinger Elliott Laughlin & Ragan, 1954—. Mem. exec. com. Roosevelt council Boy Scouts Am., 1955—, pres., 1973-75; trustee Phoenix Country Day Sch., 1963-68, pres., 1967-68; trustee Heard Mus., Phoenix, 1963—, pres., 1969-70; bd. dirs. Phoenix Dist. Tennis Assn., 1967-72, v.p., 1968; bd. dirs. Southwestern Tennis Assn., 1967-72, v.p., 1968-70; bd. dirs. Phoenix Arts Council, 1972-75, Ariz. Ballet Theatre, 1976—. Served with USAAF, 1941-46. Decorated Air medal with 3 oak leaf clusters; recipient Silver Beaver award Boy Scouts Am. Mem. Am. Bar Assn., State Bar Ariz., Phi Delta Phi. Episcopalian. Clubs: Univ., Ariz. (dir. 1970-72), Rotary. Home: 75 E Orangewood Ave Phoenix AZ 85020 Office: 3550 N Central Ave Phoenix AZ 85012

LAUINGER, PHILIP CHARLES, publisher; b. Oil City, Pa., Aug. 8, 1900; s. Frank T. and Helen (Boyle) L.; A.B., Georgetown U., 1922, LL.D., 1958; Sc.D., St. Bonaventure U., 1957; m. Frances Flaherty, Jan. 19, 1933; children—Philip, Helen, Mary, Frank, Frances, Anthony, Joseph (dec.). Staff rep. Oil and Gas Jour., Tulsa, 1922-31, pres. 1931-69, chmn. bd., 1969—; dir. Derrick Pub. Co., Oil City, Petroleum Pub. Co., Tulsa. Decorated knight of Malta, knight of Holy Sepulchre Grand Cross. Mem. Tex. Mid-Continent Oil and Gas Assn., Natural Gas Assn., Am. Petroleum Inst. Clubs: Tulsa, Southern Hills Country. Author in field. Home: 1357 E 27th Pl Tulsa OK 74114 Office: 1421 S Sheridan St Tulsa OK 74112

LAUMANN, EDWARD OTTO, sociologist; b. Youngstown, Ohio, Aug. 31, 1938; A.B. summa cum laude, Oberlin Coll., 1960; A.M., Harvard U., 1962, Ph.D., 1964. Asst. prof. sociology U. Mich., 1964-69, asso. prof., 1969-72; prof. sociology U. Chgo., 1973—, dir. Center for Social Orgn. Studies, 1973—. Mem. sociology panel NSF, Washington, 1972-74. Mem. Internat., Am. sociol. assns., AAAS, Public Choice Soc. Editor: Am. Jour. Sociology, 1978—. Office: 1126 E 59th St Chicago IL 60637

LAUN, HAROLD GEORGE, investment banker; b. Elkhart Lake, Wis., Apr. 14, 1905; s. Louis and Adele (Gutheil) L.; student U. Calif. at Berkeley; A.B., U. Wis., 1927; m. Mary Rapp, Nov. 8, 1930; children—Mary Georgina, Katherine Louise; m. 2d, Margaret Widmark, Feb. 14, 1951. Gen. clk. First Nat. Bank of Chgo., 1927-28; salesman Bonbright & Co., Chgo., 1928-32, Chase, Harris Forbes Co., 1932-33, F.S. Moseley & Co., Chgo., 1933-46, partner, 1946-71; account exec. Moseley, Hallgarten and Estabrook, Inc., 1971—; founder, organizer Technology Fund, 1948; chmn. TV Shares Mgmt. Corp., 1948-54; past dir. Diversey Corp. Past bd. dirs. U. Wis. Found.; trustee Lakeland Coll., Sheboygan, Wis., 1976—. Mem. Sigma Phi. Clubs: University, Skokie Country, Mid-Am., Cliff Dwellers. Home: 2244 Lincoln Park W Chicago IL 60614 Office: 135 S LaSalle St Chicago IL 60603

LAUN, LOUIS FREDERICK, trade assn. exec.; b. Battle Creek, Mich., May 19, 1920; s. Louis Frederick and Roena (Graves) L.; B.A., Yale U., 1942; m. Margaret West, Jan. 25, 1947; children—Nancy Laun Perez, Kathryn Laun Spaulding, Margaret. Asst. advt. mgr. Bates Fabrics, Inc., N.Y.C., 1946-48; asst. to pres., indsl. and public relations Bates Mfg. Co., Lewiston, Maine, 1948-55; advt. dir., out-of-town sales mgr. Burlington Industries, N.Y.C., 1955-57; gen. merchandising mgr. Celanese Fibers Co., N.Y.C., 1957-60, v.p., dir. mktg., 1960-63, exec. v.p. mktg., 1963-64; pres. Celanese Fibers Mktg. Co. div. Celanese Corp., 1964-71, also v.p. corp., 1964-71; asso. adminstr. ops. SBA, Washington, 1973, dep. adminstr., 1973-77; pres. Am. Paper Inst., N.Y.C., 1977—; U.S. pulp and paper rep. food and agrl. orgns. UN; past dir. Anchor Group of Mut. Bd. dirs. N.Y. Bd. Trade, Better Bus. Bur. N.Y., Alliance to Save Energy; indsl. asst. to chmn. Opportunities Industrialization Centers Am.; chmn. Republican Industry Workshop program; field dir. Com. for Re-election of Pres., 1972; trustee Taft Sch. Served with USMCR, 1942-46. Decorated Bronze Star; recipient Human Rights award Anti-Defamation League, 1968; Achievement award Textile Vets. Assn., 1970; named Young Man of Yr., Lewiston-Auburn C. of C., 1953, Man of Yr., Textile Salesman Assn., 1970, Fabric Salesmen's Guild, 1971; Gold medal for disting. service SBA. Mem. Color Assn. U.S. (sec.), Man-Made Fiber Producers Assn. (chmn. 1967-69). Clubs: Union League, Yale (N.Y.C.); Sleepy Hollow Country (Scarborough, N.Y.); Met., Capitol Hill (Washington); Mid-Ocean (Bermuda). Home: 26 Spring Ln Chappaqua NY 10514 Office: 260 Madison Ave New York NY 10016

LAUNIUS, MELVIN RAY, mfg. co. exec.; b. McLeansboro, Ill., Mar. 4, 1935; s. Jeff H. and Delcie J. (Jenkins) L.; B.A., So. Ill. U., 1956; m. Ardeth Jean Meyer, Mar. 8, 1958; children—Laurie Kay, Melvin Ray, Jeff L., John. Agy. builder All Am. Life and Casualty Co., Greenville, S.C., 1956—; pres. Launius Enterprises Inc.; owner Holiday Apts., Morristown, Tenn., Launius Ford Inc., Whitmire, S.C., Sonny Acres Farms Inc., Louisville, also dental lab., farms in S.C. and Mo.; co-owner Ky. Bourbons Profl. Slow Pitch Softball Franchise. Sec., Ill. Young Democrats, 1954-55. Served to capt. USAF, 1957-67. Named jr. agy. builder of year All Am. Life and Casualty Co., 1964. Mem. Ch. Jesus Christ of Latter-day Saints (elder 1969—). Mason, Eagle. Home: 26 Stevenson Rd Taylors SC 29687 Office: 134 Donaldson Rd Greenville SC 29606

LAUNSTEIN, HOWARD CLEVELAND, educator; b. Flushing, Mich., Oct. 15, 1922; s. John Henry and Jennie Grace (Cleveland) L.; student Central Mich. U., 1941-43; B.A., Mich. State U., 1947, M.A., 1948; Ph.D., Ohio State U., 1956; m. Elizabeth June Snyder, May 22, 1943; children—Robert John, Howard Elmer. Grad. asst. Mich. State U., 1947-48, instr. accounting, 1948-56; asst. prof. State U. Iowa, Iowa City, 1956-58; asso. prof. Marquette U., Milw., 1958-64, prof. finance, 1964—, chmn. dept., 1959-67; ins. agt. Guarantee Mut. Life Ins. Co., Lansing, Mich., 1948-51; instr. C.P.C.U. program, 1954-55, C.L.U. programs, 1959—; ins. cons. Marquette U., 1958—; mem. edn1. adv. com. Wis. Real Estate Examining Bd., 1976-78; dir., auditor Red Cedar Coop. Assn., East Lansing, 1949-52. Asst. cub master, treas. Greendale (Wis.) cub pack Boy Scouts Am., 1960-66, committeeman Boy Scouts, 1963-66; mem. citizens com. bonding issues Greendale Sch., 1959-61. Bd. govs., dir. Nat. Inst. Consumer Credit Mgmt., 1965—. Served with USAAF, 1942-45. Decorated Air medal. Mem. Internat. Ins. Seminars (bd. govs. 1965—, moderator 1965-71), Am. Finance Assn., Midwest Econ. Assn., Am. Accounting Assn., Am. Financial Mgmt. Assn., Am. Risk and Ins. Assn., Beta Alpha Psi, Delta Sigma Pi, Sigma Epsilon, Beta Gamma. Methodist. Contbr. chpts. to books, articles to profl. jours. Chmn. awards com. Nat. Assn. Ind. Insurers Jour. Ins., 1962-63, 68-69, 72—. Home: 5854 Glen Flora Greendale WI 53129 Office: Marquette U Milwaukee WI 53233

LAUPUS, WILLIAM EDWARD, physician, educator; b. Seymour, Ind., May 25, 1921; s. John George and Laura Kathryne (Hancock) L.; B.S., Yale, 1943, M.D., 1945; m. Evelyn Estelle Fike, Mar. 6, 1948; children—Patricia, John Richard, Laura, William Edward. Intern N.Y. Hosp.-Cornell Med. Center, 1945-46; resident, 1948-51; instr. pediatrics Cornell U. Sch. Medicine, 1950-52; asst. prof., then asso. prof., prof. pediatrics Med. Coll. Ga., 1959-63; prof. pediatrics, chmn. dept. Med. Coll. Va., Va. Commonwealth U., Richmond, 1963-75; pediatrician-in-chief Med. Coll. Va. Hosps.; dean, prof. pediatrics Sch. Medicine, East Carolina U., 1975—. pres. Richmond Area Community Council, 1973-75. Served with AUS, 1946-48. Diplomate Am. Bd. Pediatrics (ofcl. examiner 1966—, mem. exec. bd. 1972-77, pres. 1976-77). Mem. Am. (past pres. Va. chpt.), Va. acads. pediatrics, Am., Va. (pres.), Richmond pediatric socs., A.M.A., Med. Soc. Va., Richmond Acad. Medicine, Alpha Omega Alpha. Club: Bull and Bear (Richmond). Contbr. to Nelson's Textbook of Pediatrics, 1964, 69, 75, Kendig's Respiratory Diseases in Children, 1969, 72, 77, Gellis and Kagen's Current Therapy, 1969-77. Home: 218 Country Club Dr Greenville NC 27834 Office: East Carolina U Greenville NC 27834

LAURENCE, DAN H., lit. and dramatic specialist; b. N.Y.C., Mar. 28, 1920; B.A., Hofstra U., 1946; M.A., N.Y. U., 1950. Performed in profl. theatre, 1932-41; writer, performer Armed Forces Radio, 1942-45; writer for radio, TV, U.S. and Australia, 1946-48; grad. asst. N.Y. U., 1950-52, asso. prof. English, 1962-67, prof., 1967-70; instr. Hofstra U., 1953-58; editor Readex Microprint Corp., 1959-60; lit. and dramatic adv. Estate of George Bernard Shaw, London, 1973—; vis. prof. Ind. U., 1969, U. Tex., 1974-75; vis. fellow Inst. Arts and Humanistic Studies, Pa. State U., 1976; spl. cons. Humanities Research Center, U. Tex., Austin, 1975-77. Served with USAAF, 1942-45; PTO. John Simon Guggenheim Meml. fellow, 1960, 61, 72. Mem. MLA, Royal Acad. Dramatic Art (asso.), Phi Beta Kappa, Phi Gamma Delta. Author: (with Leon Edel) Henry James: a bibliography, 3d edit., 1980; Robert Nathan: A Bibliography, 1960; playwright: The Black Girl in Search of God, 1977; editor: Uncollected Writings of Bernard Shaw: How to Become A Musical Critic, 1961; Platform and Pulpit, 1961; (with David H. Greene) The Matter with Ireland, 1962; Selected Non-Dramatic Writings of Shaw, 1965; Collected Letters of Bernard Shaw, 1965—; Bernard Shaw's Collected Plays with Their Prefaces, 7 vols., 1970-74; (with Daniel J. Leary) Flyleaves, 1977; Shaw's Music, 1980. Home and Office: 2500 Jackson Keller Rd 1103 San Antonio TX 78230

LAURENCE, JOHN, fgn. corr.; b. Bridgeport, Conn.; ed. Rensselaer Poly. Inst., U. Pa.; m. Joy Baker. Former news editor radio sta. WIIC, Bridgeport, Conn., then radio sta. WWDC, Washington; writer-reporter radio sta. WNEW, N.Y.C., 1961-64; with CBS News, 1964-78, fgn. news corr., Vietnam, 1965-66, 67-71, fgn. news corr., London, 1971-78; corr. ABC News, London, 1978—. Recipient Emmy award for achievement within regular newscasts, 1967-68, 70-71; Sigma Delta Chi award, 1967; Alfred I. duPont-Colombia U. award, 1969-70; Overseas Press Club award, 1971, 73, 75. Address: care ABC News World Hdqrs 7 W 66th St New York NY 10023*

LAURENT, DON, hosp. cons.; b. Cadillac, Mich., June 27, 1912; s. Simon Harry and Bertha Lenora (Anderson) L.; B.S. in Med. Biology, Mich. State Coll., 1937, postgrad., 1939; postgrad. hosp. adminstrn., U. Chgo., 1952; m. Marjorie Vivian Nixon, Feb. 2, 1935; children—Don Harry II, Judith Rae (Mrs. James Taggart, Jr.), Nina Kay Laurent Kurtz. Asst. dir. bur. labs. Mich. Health Dept., 1937-47; dir. Meml. Hosp., Sarasota, Fla., 1948-56, exec. dir., 1956-76; founder Laurent Hosp. and Sci. Cons. Services, and Assos., 1976—; preceptor U. Fla.; mem. adv. com. Fla. Bd. Health; sec. Fla. Blue Cross. Mem. bd. Indsl. Devel. Council; pres. Sarasota Area-Wide Planning Council, West Coast (Fla.) Areawide Health Planning Council, 1974—; mem. adv. bd. Sarasota United Appeal, 1968—, Sarasota Vocational Edn. Bd., 1958—. Trustee Sarasota Non Profit Assn.; bd. dirs. Sarasota chpt. A.R.C., Mil. Assistance to Safety and Traffic, 1974—. Recipient award of merit Fla. Hosp. Research and Edn. Found., 1974. Fellow Am. Coll. Hosp. Adminstrs., Royal Soc. Health; mem. Am. (council adminstrn. 1965-68, ho. dels. 1963-68), Fla. (pres. 1964) hosp. assns., Am. Pub. Health Assn., U.S. Coast Guard Aux. Republican. Methodist (chmn. bd. stewards 1966). Mason (32 deg., Shriner), Rotarian (past pres. Sarasota Bay). Clubs: Lambs (N.Y.C.); University (Sarasota); Bradenton (Fla.) Yacht. Home and office: 3327 Sheffield Circle Sarasota FL 33580

LAURENT, LAWRENCE BELL, journalist, educator; b. Monroe, La., Mar. 9, 1925; s. Lewis Emeal and Ethel (Dawkins) L.; student U. Va., 1946-49; pvt. study with Dr. W.Y. Elliott, 1954-56, Dr. Franklin Dunham, 1957-58; m. Margaret F. Goodwillie, Nov. 1, 1949; children—Richard Sandford, Arthur Halliday, Margaret Funsten, Elizabeth MacLean. With Bluefield (W.Va.) Daily Telegraph, 1949-50, Charlottesville (Va.) Daily Progress, 1950-51; with Washington Post, 1951—, radio-TV editor, 1953—; adj. prof. communications Am. U., Washington, 1963—; chmn. editorial bd. TV Quar., 1963-73; guest prof. Syracuse U., 1965; vis. prof. U. Detroit, 1967; formerly judge Alfred I. duPont awards, Saturday Rev. Lit. TV awards, Sigma Delta Chi pub. service TV awards, Humanitas awards. Bd. dirs. Family Inst. Served with USNR, 1943-45. Recipient Front Page award Am. Newspaper Guild, 1964; Disting. Tchr. award Am. U., 1978. Mem. Nat. Acad. TV Arts and Scis., Nat. Press Club, White House Corrs. Assn., AAUP, Sigma Delta Chi, Pi Delta Epsilon. Episcopalian. Editor, author: (with Newton N. Minow) Equal Time, 1964. Contbr. to books, mags. Home: 215 Jefferson St Alexandria VA 22314 Office: 1150 15th St NW Washington DC 20071

LAURENT, RONALD P., govt. ofcl.; b. Evanston, Ill., May 11, 1937; B.A., Fisk U., 1960. Housing insp. Evanston (Ill.) Dept. Health, 1962-64; loan officer Salk, Wood and Salk, Inc., 1964-69; asst. v.p. Percy Wilson Mortgage & Fin. Corp., 1969-70; v.p., then sr. v.p. McElvain-Reynolds Co., 1970-79; pres. Govt. Nat. Mortgage Assn., Washington, 1979—. Address: Nat Mortgage Assn 451 7th St SW Washington DC 20410*

LAURENTS, ARTHUR, playwright; b. N.Y.C., July 14, 1918; s. Irving and Ada (Robbins) L.; A.B., Cornell U., Ithaca, N.Y., 1937. Radio script writer, 1939-40. Served with AUS, 1941-45. Received Variety Radio award for writing Assignment Home series, 1945; Am. Acad. Arts and Letters awards for play Home of the Brave, 1946, co-winner Sidney Howard award, 1946. Mem. Dramatists Guild Council, P.E.N., Authors League, Screenwriters Guild, Acad. Motion Picture Arts and Scis. Author: The Way We Were (novel), 1972; (screen plays) The Snake Pit, 1948, Rope, 1948, Caught, 1948, Anna Lucasta, 1949, Anastasia, 1956, Bonjour Tristesse, 1958, (novel) The Way We Were, 1973; The Turning Point (novel) (Writers Guild Am. award), 1977; (plays) Home of the Brave, 1946, The Bird Cage, 1950, The Time of the Cuckoo, 1952, A Clearing in the Woods, 1956, Invitation to a March, 1960, The Enclave, 1973, Scream, Houston, 1978; (mus. plays) West Side Story, 1957, Gypsy, 1959, Do I Hear a Waltz?, 1964, Hallelulah, Baby (Tony award) 1967; screenwriter, co-producer film The Turning Point, 1977; co-author, dir. My Mother was a Fortune Teller (Drama Desk award), 1978, The Madwoman of Central Park West; radio plays in anthologies Radio Drama in Action, 1945, Best One Act Plays of 1944-45, 1945-46; dir. Broadway prodns. Invitation to a March, 1960, I Can Get It For You Wholesale, 1962; writer, dir. Anyone Can Whistle, 1964, The Enclave, 1973; dir. London prodn. Gypsy, 1973, N.Y. revival (Drama Desk award), 1974. Home: Quogue NY 11959

LAURENZO, VINCENT DENNIS, farm equipment mfg. co. exec.; b. Des Moines, May 31, 1939; s. Vincent C. and B.J. (Garver) L.; B.B.A., U. Notre Dame, 1961; M.A., U. Mich., 1964; m. Sherrill S. Mullen, Sept. 10, 1960; children—Lisa, David, Susan, Nancy, James. With Ford Motor Co., Dearborn, Mich., 1961-66; plant controller Massey Ferguson Inc., 1967-70; with parent co. Massey Ferguson Ltd., Toronto, Ont., Can., 1971—, dir. fin. Americas, 1977-78, v.p., comptroller, 1978—. Roman Catholic. Office: 200 University Ave Toronto ON Canada

LAURETA, ALFRED, U.S. judge; b. Ewa, Oahu, Hawaii, May 21, 1924; s. Laureano and Victoriana (Pascua) L.; B.Ed., U. Hawaii, 1947, teaching cert., 1948; LL.B., Fordham U., 1953; m. E. Evelyn Reantillo, Feb. 21, 1953; children—Michael, Gregory, Pamela Ann, Lisa Lani. Admitted to Hawaii bar; partner firm Kobayashi, Kono, Laureta & Ariyoshi, Honolulu, 1954-59; adminstr. to U.S. Congressman Inouye, 1959-63; dir. Hawaii Dept. Labor and Indsl. Relations, 1963-67; judge 1st Circuit Ct., Honolulu, 1967-69, 5th Circuit Ct., Kauai, 1969-78, U.S. Dist. Ct. No. Mariana Islands, Saipan, 1978—. Mem. Nat. Council Juvenile Ct. Judges, Am. Judicature Soc., Hawaii Bar Assn., Kauai Bar Assn. Democrat. Roman Catholic. Office: PO Box 687 Saipan CM TT 96950

LAURIE, JAMES ANDREW, journalist, broadcaster; b. Eustis, Fla., June 16, 1947; s. Andrew Louis and Geneva Lavina (Pryor) L.; B.A. in History, Am. U., Washington, 1969; postgrad. George Washington U., 1974. Freelance writer and reporter for Metromedia Radio-TV, Washington, 1969, Phnom Penh, Cambodia and Saigon, Vietnam, 1970-71; reporter NBC News, Saigon, 1971-74, 75, corr., Tokyo, 1975-78; corr., bur. chief ABC News, Hong Kong, 1978—. Recipient George Foster Peabody Broadcasting award for reporting fall of Saigon, 1976. Address: ABC News 1253 New Mercury House Wanchai Hong Kong BCC

LAURIE, PIPER (ROSETTA JACOBS), actress; b. Detroit, Jan. 22, 1932; student Los Angeles pub. sch.; m. Joseph Morgenstern, 1962; 1 child. Acted in sch. plays; motion picture debut in Louisa; other motion pictures include The Milkman, Francis Goes to the Races, Prince Who Was A Thief, Son of Ali Baba, Has Anybody Seen My Gal, No Room for the Groom, Mississippi Gambler, Kelly and Me, Golden Blade, Dangerous Mission, Johnny Dark, Dawn at Socorro, Smoke Signal, Ain't Misbehavin', Until They Sail, The Hustler, Carrie, 1976, Tim, 1978; TV appearances include Days of Wine and Roses, Playhouse 90, The Deaf Heart, The Ninth Day, G.E. Theatre, Play of the Week, Hallmark Hall of Fame, Nova: Margaret Sanger, The Woman Rebel, In the Matter of Karen Ann Quinlan, Rainbow, Skag; appeared Broadway play Glass Menagerie, 1965, off-Broadway plays Rosemary and The Alligators, 1961; Acad. award nominee for The Hustler, 1962, Carrie, 1976. Mem. Acad. Motion Picture Arts and Scis. Address: care Susan Smith & Assos 9869 Santa Monica Blvd Beverly Hills CA 90212

LAURILA, SIMO HEIKKI, geodesist, educator; b. Kangasala, Finland, Jan. 15, 1920; s. Juho H. and Fanny (Heikkila) L.; B.Sc., Finland's Inst. Tech., 1946, M.Sc., 1948, Ph.D., 1953; m. Mary Isabel Kouki, Feb. 10, 1946; children—Helena Laurila Moore, Marketta, Kristina Laurila Horton, Taina Laurila Krieg, Paula. Came to U.S., 1953, naturalized, 1961. Research asso. photogrammetric bur. Govt.

of Finland, Helsinki, 1948-53; geodesist Finnish Geodetic Inst., Helsinki, 1953; research asso. Ohio State U., Columbus, 1953-59, asso. research supr., 1960-66, faculty, 1956-66, prof. geodesy, 1962-66; research specialist N.Am. Aviation Corp., Columbus, 1966; head geodesy program U. Hawaii, Honolulu, 1966—, prof. geodesy, 1966—, chmn. dept. geoscis., 1969-73; lectr. Finland's Inst. Tech., 1950-52, Finland's Mil. Acad., 1950-52; UN specialist, Ceylon, 1972, 74. Recipient award Tech. Found. Advanced Sci., Finland, 1960, Kaarina and W.A. Heiskanen award Ohio State U., 1965. Fulbright sr. lectr., Finland, 1973. Mem. Am. Geophys. Union. Author: Electronic Surveying and Mapping, 1960; Electronic Surveying and Navigation, 1976. Contbr. articles to profl. jours. Home: 46-075 Aliipapa Pl Apt 1424 Kaneohe HI 96744 Office: Inst Geophysics U Hawaii Honolulu HI 96822

LAURIN, J(OSEPH) W(ILFRED) PAUL, assn. exec.; b. Ottawa, Ont., Apr. 24, 1938; s. Wilfred and Rose-Anna L.; m. Florence A. Coey, Feb. 5, 1958; children—Suzanne I., Yvonne M. Commd. officer RCAF, 1955, ret., 1965; mem. public relations and advt. staff Bank of Montreal, 1965-71; regional dir. public relations Can. Bankers Assn., 1971-76; dir. communications Montreal Urban Community, 1976-78; exec. sec. Can. Assn. Chiefs of Police, Ottawa, 1978—. Mem. Can. Public Relations Soc., Royal Can. Mil. Inst., Inst. Assn. Execs. Office: 1002 116 Albert St Ottawa ON K1P 5G3 Canada

LAURITZEN, JOHN RONNOW, banker; b. Mpls., Mar. 28, 1917; s. Max R. and Margaret (Flannery) L.; student Princeton, 1937-38, U. Minn., 1939, U. Wis. Sch. Banking, 1947-49; m. Elizabeth Ann Davis, Nov. 4, 1939; children—Bruce Ronnow, Ann Davis (Mrs. Ray Pape). With First Nat. Bank, Omaha, 1943—, v.p., 1949-61, pres., 1967-70, chmn. exec. com., pres., 1962-71, chmn. bd., chmn. exec. com., 1971—, also dir.; pres., dir. Emerson State Bank (Iowa), First State Bank, Loomis, Nebr., Washington County Bank, Blair, Farmers & Mchts. State Bank, Bloomfield, Burt County State Bank, Tekamah, Nebr., Lauritzen Co., Omaha, Emerson Ins. Agy., Inc., Blair Ins. Agy., Inc., Burt County Ins. Agy., Inc., Farmers & Mchts. Co. of Bloomfield, Farmers & Ranchers Service Co., Financial Service Co. Clubs: Omaha, Omaha Country, University Cottage, Alexandria Golf, Marco Island Golf. Home: 6621 Underwood St Omaha NE 68132 Office: First Nat Bank of Omaha Omaha NE 68102

LAURITZEN, PETER OWEN, elec. engr.; b. Valparaiso, Ind., Feb. 14, 1935; s. Carl W. and Edna B. (Seebach) L.; B.S., Calif. Inst. Tech., 1956; M.S., Stanford U., 1958, Ph.D., 1961; m. Helen M. Janzen, Apr. 6, 1963; children—Beth K., Margo S. Asso. evaluation engr. Honeywell Aero. Div., Mpls., 1956-57; mem. tech. staff Fairchild Semoconductor Div., Palo Alto, Calif., 1961-65; asst. prof. elec. engring. U. Wash., Seattle, 1965-68, asso. prof., 1968-73, prof., 1973—, adj. prof. social mgmt. of tech., 1977—; engring. mgr. Autoch Corp., Seattle, 1979-80; cons. x-ray div. Chgo. Bridge & Iron Works, 1967-71. Pres., Coalition for Safe Energy, Wash. Citizens Group, 1975-76. Danforth asso., 1966-78; NASA-Am. Soc. Engring. Edn. summer faculty fellow, 1974. Mem. IEEE, Am. Soc. Engring. Edn., AAAS. Home: 7328 58th Ave Seattle WA 98115 Office: Elec Engring Dept U Wash Seattle WA 98195

LAURRELL, ROBERT WILLIAM, chem. engr.; b. Wheeling, W.Va., Feb. 21, 1920; s. William Henry and Louise Rose (Wasemann) L.; B.Chem.Engring., Ohio State U., 1950, M.S. in Chem. Engring., 1950; m. Lizbeth Jean Day, Nov. 13, 1976; children—Sherron Laurrell Cook, Nanci E., Patricia L., R. David. With E.I. DuPont DeNemours & Co., Inc., 1950—, product mgr. consumer paints Marshall Research and Devel. Lab., Phila., 1968-70. tech. mgr. finishes div., 1970-72, dir. lab., 1972—. Served to capt. U.S. Army, 1941-46. Republican. Lutheran. Home: 50 Chapel Hill Rd Media PA 19063 Office: 3500 Grays Ferry Ave Philadelphia PA 19146

LAUSHEY, LOUIS MCNEAL, educator; b. Columbia, Pa., May 13, 1917; s. Walter Ralph and Laura Ford (McNeal) L.; B.S., Pa. State Coll., 1942; M.S., Carnegie Inst. Tech., 1947, Sc.D., 1951; m. Sophia Ann King, Sept. 3, 1949. With Am. Bridge Co., 1942; instr. to asso. prof. Carnegie Inst. Tech., 1942-54, chmn. engring. and sci. faculty, 1952-53; prof., head dept. civil engring. Norwich (Vt.) U., 1954-58; William Thoms prof., head dept. civil engring. U. Cin., 1958-78, prof. civil engring., 1978—, chmn. univ. faculty, 1967-70; engring. cons. Served as lt. (j.g.) C.E.C., USNR, 1944-46. Recipient Profl. Achievement award, Cin., 1976. Registered profl. engr. Fellow ASCE (pres. Vt. 1956, v.p. Maine 1957, pres. Cin. 1965, chmn. dist. 9 council 1972, pres. Ohio council 1973); mem. Internat. Assn. Hydraulic Research, Internat. Assn. Shell Structures, Am. Soc. Engring. Edn. (chmn. Ohio), Am. Geophys. Union, Soc. Am. Mil. Engrs., Navy League, Engring. Soc. Cin., Sigmi Xi, Tau Beta Pi, Sigma Tau, Chi Epsilon. Episcopalian. Contbr. articles to profl. jours. Home: 9066 Eldora Dr Cincinnati OH 45236

LAUSON, HENRY DUMKE, physician, emeritus educator; b. New Holstein, Wis., Aug. 20, 1912; s. Henry Detlef and Lydia (Dumke) L.; B.S., U. Wis., 1936, Ph.D. in Physiology, 1939, M.D., 1940; m. Eleanor Catchis, Sept. 4, 1936 (dec. Sept. 1975); m. 2d, Ruth Eckart Laun, Aug. 27, 1977. Intern U. Kans. Hosp., 1940-41; resident medicine Henry Ford Hosp., Detroit, 1941-42; OSRD fellow physiology and medicine N.Y. U. Coll. Medicine, 1942-43, instr. physiology, 1943-46; asso. Rockefeller Inst. Med. Research, 1946-50; asso. prof. physiology Cornell U. Med. Coll., 1950-55; prof. physiology, chmn. dept. Albert Einstein Coll. Medicine, Yeshiva U., 1955-78, prof. emeritus, 1978—. Cons., NIH, USPHS, 1962-65. Mem. Am. Physiol. Soc., Am. Soc. Clin. Investigation, Soc. Exptl. Biology and Medicine, Harvey Soc. (sec. 1952-55), Phi Beta Kappa, Sigma Xi, Alpha Omega Alpha. Contbr. research papers endocrinology, circulation, kidney physiology to profl. jours. Home: Leather Hill Rd Wingdale NY 12594

LAUTENBERG, FRANK R., computer service co. exec.; b. Paterson, N.J., Jan., 1924; s. Samuel and Mollie L.; B.S., Columbia U., 1949; D.H.L., Hebrew Union Coll., Cin. and N.Y.C., 1977; Ph.D. (hon.), Hebrew U., Jerusalem, 1978; married; children—Ellen, Nan, Lisa, Joshua. Founder, Automatic Data Processing, Inc., Clifton, N.J., 1953—, exec. v.p. adminstrn., 1961-69, pres., 1969—, chief exec. officer, 1975—, also chmn. bd.; mem. policyholder's adv. com. New Eng. Life Ins. Co., Boston; adv. bd. Present Tense mag., N.Y.C.; commr. Port Authority N.Y. and N.J. Asso., Sch. Bus., Columbia U.; nat. pres. Am. Friends Hebrew U., 1973-74; former gen. chmn., now pres. Nat. United Jewish Appeal, 1975-77; bd. govs. Am. Jewish Com.; mem. internat. bd. govs. Hebrew U., Jerusalem; mem. bd. overseers N.J. Symphony Orch.; bd. govs. Am. Jewish Com.; mem. Pres.'s Commn. on the Holocaust; founder Lautenberg Center for Gen. and Tumor Immunology, Med. Sch., Hebrew U., Jerusalem, 1971; v.p. Jewish Community Fedn. Met. N.J., East Orange; mem. fin. council Nat. Democratic Com. Served with Armed Forces, 1943-46; ETO. Recipient Torch of Learning award Am. Friends Hebrew U., 1971, Scopus award, 1975. Mem. Nat. Assn. Data Processing Service Orgns. (pres. 1968-69, dir. 1974—), Patrons Soc. Met. Opera. Office: 405 Route 3 Clifton NJ 07015

LAUTERBACH, HENRY SEBASTIAN, elec. equipment mfg. co. exec.; b. Bronxville, N.Y., Apr. 19, 1915; s. Henry and Kathryn (Hyde) L.; B.A., Rollins Coll., 1937; m. Shirley Mae Kroll, Mar. 27, 1964; children—Henry William, Kathryn Hyde, Craig Alan, Paul Henry, Lynn Marie. Gen. mgr. Sta-Rite Products, Delavan, Wis., 1939, treas. Sta-Rite Products, Inc., 1939-43, v.p., gen. mgr., 1943-44, pres., 1944-52, pres., chmn. bd., 1952-66, chmn. bd., chief exec. officer Sta-Rite Industries, 1966-70, pres., chief exec. officer, 1970-73, chmn. bd., chief exec. officer, 1973-75, 77—; pres., chief exec. officer Superior Stainless, Inc.; dir. Koehring Co., Milw., Citizens Bank Delavan. Mem. Polish-U.S. Econ. Council. Metro chmn. Southeastern Wis. Nat. Alliance Business, Racine, Wis.; past bd. dirs. Boy Scouts Am., Whitewater State Found., U. Wis. at Whitewater, Wis. Assn. for Mental Health; bd. dirs., pres. Gateway Tech. Found., Kenosha, Wis., 1977—; mem. president's exec. senate Marquette U., 1976—; trustee Walworth County (Wis.) Nursing Home and Farm, 1977—. Recipient Marquis award AIM; ann. award for supplier and Man of Yr. award Sears Plumbing & Heating Div., 1965. Mem. Wis. Mfrs. Assn. (dir.), Navy League (life), Am. Ordnance Assn. Clubs: Big Foot Country (Fontana, Wis.); Wisconsin, Milwaukee (Milw.); Home: Route 2 Box 157 Delavan WI 53115 Office: 211 Sugar Creek Rd Delavan WI 53115. *Success must be achieved with the support of your fellow man, not at his expense.*

LAUTERBACH, ROBERT ALAN, ret. accountant; b. Sac City, Iowa, Aug. 26, 1921; s. Paul A. and Ada (Johnson) L.; B.S.C., Iowa U., 1946; LL.B., Denver U., 1948; m. Sarah M. Messenger, Apr. 27, 1943; children—Marian, Michael, John. Admitted to Colo. bar, 1949; practice in Denver, 1949-50; with Ernst & Ernst, C.P.A.'s, Denver, 1950-77, partner, 1961-77, partner-in charge Denver office, 1964-76. Served with USAAF, 1943-45: ETO. C.P.A. Mem. Colo. Soc. C.P.A.'s (past dir.), Sigma Alpha Epsilon. Clubs: University, Cherry Hills Country (past dir., treas.) (Denver); Garden of the Gods (Colorado Springs); Tucson Nat. Golf. Home: 3860 S Glencoe St Denver CO 80237

LAUTERBACH, ROBERT EMIL, steel co. exec.; b. Erie, Pa., May 31, 1918; s. Emil and Inez (Ricci) L.; B.B.A., Westminster Coll., 1939; postgrad. U. Pitts., 1939-41; LL.D., Wheeling Coll., 1975; m. Jane Stonerod, Nov. 5, 1919; children—Jeffrey R., Marsha J., Mark S. With Wheeling-Pitts. Steel Corp. and subsidiaries, 1939—, treas. Johnson Steel & Wire Co., 1947-50, asst. sec. parent firm, 1950-52, sec., 1952-58, v.p., 1958-68, exec. v.p. Wheeling Pitts. Steel Corp., 1968-70, pres., 1970—, chmn., 1973-78, now dir.; dir. Pitts. Nat. Bank, H.H. Robertson Co., Universal-Rundle Corp. Bd. dirs. Jr. Achievement Pitts., 1950-60, United Way of All County, Boy Scouts Am.; treas. local br. Am. Cancer Soc., 1953-62; pres. Mt. Lebanon Library Bd., 1962-73; pres. bd. trustees Westminster Coll., 1970—. Served with AUS, 1943-46. Recipient George Washington Honor medal Freedoms Found. at Valley Forge. Mem. Am. Petroleum Inst., Am., Internat. iron and steel insts. Clubs: Duquesne, Laurel Valley Golf, Rolling Rock, Fox Chapel Golf (Pitts.). Home: 115 Forest Dr Pittsburgh PA 15238 Office: 4 Gateway Center Pittsburgh PA 15230

LAUTERMILCH, PAUL ANTHONY, naval officer; b. Cleve., Nov. 11, 1927; s. Paul Albert and Clara Agnes (Grzesk) L.; B.S., U.S. Naval Acad., 1951; B.S. in Communications Engring., U.S. Navy Postgrad. Sch., 1959; M.A. in Internat. Affairs, George Washington U., 1961; student Naval War Coll., 1962; m. Dorthy Ann Mescher, Aug. 27, 1953; children—Dorothy Ann Lautermilch Friday, Paul Andrew, Kathleen Marie, John David, Susan Claire, Ann Elizabeth. Enlisted man U.S. Navy, 1946-47, commd. ensign, 1951, advanced through grades to rear adm., 1977; served in U.S.S. Taussig, destroyer, Korean War, 1951-54; aide to comdr. Destroyer Flotilla Four, 1954-55; comdg. officer U.S.S. Hawk, coastal minesweeper, 1955-57; served in U.S.S. Rochester, heavy cruiser, 1959-61; mem. staff Chief Naval Ops., Washington, 1962-64, 66-68, 71-74; exec. officer Guided Missile Frigate U.S.S. Macdonough, 1964-66; comdg. officer Guided Missile Destroyer U.S.S. Goldsborough, 1968-70; asst. chief of staff (ops.) Navy Staff, Vietnam, 1970-71; comdr. Destroyer Squadron 31, 1974-75; chief of staff 7th Fleet in Western Pacific, 1975-77; dep. chief of staff (mgmt.), fleet insp. gen., to comdr. in chief U.S. Pacific Fleet, Pearl Harbor, Hawaii, 1977-79; comdr. Cruiser-Destroyer Group Five, 1979—. Decorated Legion of Merit with 2 gold stars, Bronze Star, Navy Commendation medal. Mem. U.S. Naval Acad. Alumni Assn., U.S. Naval Inst. Roman Catholic. Office: Comdr Crudesgru 5 FPO San Francisco CA 96601

LAUTH, DAVID FRANCIS, coast guard officer; b. Buffalo, Jan. 21, 1928; s. Cletus George and Katherine Veronica (Sharpe) L.; B.S., U.S. Coast Guard Acad., 1949; M.P.A., U. Pitts., 1964; m. Catherine Irene McDermott, Feb. 11, 1956; children—Mary Kay, Susan Ann. Commd. ensign U.S. Coast Guard, 1949, advanced through grades to rear adm., 1975; comdg. officer USCG Loran Sta., Talampulan, Philippines, 1953-54; capt. Port Office, San Francisco, 1954-57; Comdg. officer USCG Cutter Magnolia, 1957-59, Coast Guard Base, Galveston, Tex., 1959-60, USCG Cutter Iris, 1961-63; assigned to Office Personnel, 1964-67; assigned to asst. sec. Transp., 1967-69; comdg. officer USCG Cutter Minnetonka, 1969-71; assigned to Office Boating Safety, 1971-73, chief, 1975-78; dep. chief Office Personnel, 1973-74; comdr. 14th Coast Guard Dist., Honolulu, 1978—. Mem. Nat. Sea Explorer Council, 1976; chmn. Explorer div. Aloha council Boy Scouts Am., 1979; vice chmn. Combined Fed. Campaign, Honolulu, 1979. Decorated Meritorious Service medal, USCG Commendation medal with 2 gold stars, USCG Achievement medal; recipient Nat. Water Safety Congress award, 1978, Disting. Service award Boating Writers Internat., 1978, Am. Boat and Yacht Council commendation, 1979. Mem. USCG Acad. Alumni Assn. (Eagle Club), U.S. Naval Inst., Nat. Def. Transp. Assn. (dir.). Clubs: Rotary Internat.; Propeller (Honolulu). Home: 3399 Diamond Head Rd Honolulu HI 96815 Office: PJKK Fed Office Bldg Honolulu HI 96850

LAUTHER, SAMUEL EDGAR, banker; b. Ft. Madison, Iowa, Oct. 3, 1913; s. Irwin S. and Grace (Liddle) L.; student Missouri Valley Coll., 1931-34, Duke, 1941-42; m. DeLora Whisnant, June 21, 1941; 1 son, Richard C. Asst. cashier State Bank Nauvoo (Ill.), 1934-40, 1st Nat. Bank, Gibson City, Ill., 1940-41; asst. nat. bank examiner 7th Fed. Res. Dist., Office Comptroller of Currency, 1941-42; v.p. Irwin Union Bank & Trust Co., Columbus, Ind., 1946-47, exec. v.p., 1947-51, pres., 1951-64; sr. v.p. Crocker Citizens Nat. Bank, Los Angeles, 1964-65, exec. v.p., 1965-68; chmn. bd., chief exec. officer Am. Fletcher Nat. Bank & Trust Co., Indpls., 1968-74, chmn. exec. com., to 1975, now dir.; past pres. Columbus Growth, Inc.; chmn. bd. Am. Fletcher Corp., 1970-74, chmn. exec. com., to 1975, now dir.; dir. Indpls. Water Co.; lectr. Am. Bankers Assn., Rutgers U. Chmn. United Fund Campaign, Indpls., 1971; pres. Indpls. Progress Com., 1970. Past trustee Hanover Coll., U. Redlands, Butler U., Columbus Redevel. Commn. Served to maj. AUS, 1942-46. Mem. Am. Bankers Assn. (pres. savs. div. 1962-63, mem. exec. council), Ind. C. of C. (dir. 1969—). Presbyterian (deacon 1960-61, elder 1962—, trustee 1963—). Clubs: Annandale Golf (Pasadena, Calif.); 100 California, Downtown (Los Angeles); University, Valley Hunt. Contbg. author: The Bankers Handbook, 1966. Home: 452 S Orange Grove Blvd Pasadena CA 91105 Office: 301 E Colorado Blvd Suite 527 Pasadena CA 91101

LAUX, PETER JOHN, librarian; b. New Lond, Wis., Jan. 7, 1922; s. Peter John and Cecilia (Bolinski) L.; B.S. cum laude, St. Norbert Coll., 1948; M.A., Marquette U., 1950; M.S. in Library Sci., U. Wis., 1952; m. Bernice Elizabeth Dorn, Jan. 25, 1943; children—Peter, Barbara, Gregory, Charles, Nicholas, Ronald, Linda, Laura. Asst. dept. philosophy, religion and edn. Milw. Pub. Library, 1954-54; asso. librarian Georgetown U., Washington, 1954-60; dir. library Canisius Coll., Buffalo, 1960—. Spl. cons. periodicals USIA, 1959-60. Chmn. lay adv. council Milw. Archdiocesan Cana Conf., 1954; mem. com. alcoholism Milw. County Mental Health Soc., 1953-54. Pres. bd. trustees Western N.Y. Library Resources Council, 1974. Author: A Man's Home Is His Hassle, 1969; also book revs., bibliographies. Contbg. editor Cath. Library World, 1964-66. Home: 251 Parkside Ave Buffalo NY 14214

LAVATELLI, LEO SILVIO, physicist, educator; b. Mackinaw Island, Mich., Aug. 15, 1917; s. Silvio E. and Zella (Cunningham) L.; B.S., Calif. Inst. Tech., 1939; M.A., Princeton, 1943; M.A., Harvard, 1947, Ph.D., 1951; m. Anna Henderson, June 14, 1941; children—Nancy Jack, Mark Leo; m. 2d, Celia Burns Stendler, Jan. 23, 1967; m. 3d, Barbara Gow Deemer, Nov. 22, 1976. Instr., Deep Springs Jr. Coll., 1939-41; instr., research asst. Princeton, 1941-43; staff Los Alamos Sci. Lab., 1943-46; research asst. Harvard, 1946-50; prof. physics U. Ill., 1950—. Cons. Phys. Sci. Study Com., 1957-59, Mass. Inst. Tech. Sci. Teaching Center, 1966, Harvard Project Physics, 1966; phys. sci. cons. Macmillan Sci. Series, 12 vols., 1970. Recipient undergrad. instructional award, U. Ill., 1965. Guggenheim Meml. Found. fellow Istituto di Fisica, U. Bologna (Italy), 1957-58. Fellow Am. Phys. Soc. Contbr. articles to profl. jours. Home: 2403 W Springfield Ave Champaign IL 61820 Office: Univ Illinois Urbana IL 61801

LAVECK, GERALD DELOSS, physician; b. Seattle, Apr. 19, 1927; s. DeLoss Francis and Helen Marie (Keller) LaV.; B.S., U. Wash., 1948, M.D., 1951; m. Beverly Beers Vander Veer, July 22, 1976; children—Gerald DeLoss, Roxanne M., Julie B., Amy B., Jill M. Clin. dir. Rainier Sch. Buckley, Wash., 1958-62; head crippled children's service Wash. Health Dept., 1962-63; dir. Nat. Inst. Child Health and Human Devel., Bethesda, 1966-73; clin. prof. pediatrics Georgetown U., Washington, 1966-73; mem. faculty U. Wash., Seattle, 1973—; dir. research Bur. Community Health Services, USPHS, Rockville, Md., 1976-77; med. cons. Region X, USPHS, Seattle, 1977—. Served with USPHS, 1953-55, 72—. Recipient Superior Service award HEW, 1966. Fellow Am. Acad. Pediatrics, Am. Pub. Health Assn., Assn. Mental Deficiency. Home: 6633 NE Windermere Rd Seattle WA 98115 Office: USPHS Region X 1321 2d Ave MS/833 Seattle WA 98101

LAVELLE, ARTHUR, educator; b. Fargo, N.D., Nov. 29, 1921; s. Frank and Lillie (Hanson) LaV.; B.S., U. Wash., 1946; M.A., Johns Hopkins, 1948; Ph.D., U. Pa., 1951; m. Faith Evelyn Wilson, Sept. 6, 1947; 1 dau., Audrey Anne. USPHS postdoctoral fellow U. Pa., Phila., 1951-52; mem. faculty dept. anatomy U. Ill. Coll. Medicine, Chgo., 1952—, asso. prof., 1958-65, prof., 1965—; vis. prof. U. Calif. at Los Angeles, 1968-69; cons. Galesburg (Ill.) State Research Hosp., 1965-68; mem. biol. stain commn. Am. Assn. Anatomists, 1953—. USPHS research grantee, 1953-70; Cerebral Palsy Found. grantee, 1964-68; Guggenheim fellow, 1968-69. Mem. Am. Assn. Anatomists, Am. Soc. Cell Biology, Am. Soc. Zoologists, Soc. Developmental Biology, A.A.A.S., Am. Inst. Biol. Scis., Soc. for Neurosci., Sigma Xi. Contbr. articles to profl. jours. Home: 462 Highland Ave Elmhurst IL 60126 Office: 1853 W Polk St Chicago IL 60612

LAVELY, JOHN HILLMAN, educator; b. Des Moines, Sept. 25, 1916; s. Horace Thomas and Gertrude (Hillman) L.; A.B., Allegheny Coll., 1938; S.T.B. cum laude, Boston U., 1941, Ph.D., 1950; m. Josephine G. Magee, Sept. 3, 1941; children—Anthony Magee, John Hillman, Lisa, Kim. Ordained to ministry Meth. Ch., 1941; minister, Framingham, Mass., 1941-45, Ligonier, Pa., 1945-47; asso. prof. philosophy Albion Coll., 1947-51; mem. faculty Boston U., 1951—, prof. philosophy, 1957—, dir. grad. studies dept. philosophy, 1967-69, chmn. dept., 1962-67, 73-76, dir. undergrad. studies dept. philosophy, 1970-72, 76—. Mem. So. New Eng. Conf. United Meth. Ch. Mem. Am. Philos. Assn., Am. Acad. Religion, Metaphys. Soc. Am., Soc. Sci. Study Religion, A.A.U.P. Editor: Philos. Forum, 1955-67. Contbr. articles to profl. jours. Home: 304 Central St Auburndale MA 02166 Office: 745 Commonwealth Ave Boston MA 02215

LAVENDER, DAVID CHARLES, mag. editor; b. Pitts., Nov. 27, 1944; s. Charles Malcolm Clarke and Esther Devereaux (Stevenson) L.; A.S. in Journalism, Point Park Coll., Pitts., 1964; m. Ellen Ruth Exler, May 10, 1969. Advt. asst. Buhl Optical Co., Pitts., 1968-69; editor Sewickley (Pa.) Herald, 1969-70; copywriter Gateway Mktg. Services, Pitts., 1970-73; editor Pollution Equipment News, Pitts., 1973—, editor, asst. pub. Indsl. Hygiene News, 1978—. Served with AUS, 1965-68. Decorated Joint Service Commendation medal. Address: 433 Sangree Rd Pittsburgh PA 15237

LAVENDER, ROBERT EUGENE, chief justice Okla. Supreme Ct.; b. Muskogee, Okla., July 19, 1926; s. Harold James and Vergene Irene (Martin) L.; LL.B., U. Tulsa, 1953; grad. Appellate Judges Seminar, 1967, Nat. Coll. State Trial Judges, 1970; m. Maxine Knight, Dec. 22, 1945; children—Linda (Mrs. Dean Courter), Robert K., Debra Lucille, William J. Admitted to Okla. bar, 1953; with Mass. Bonding & Ins. Co., Tulsa, 1951-53, U.S. Fidelity & Guaranty Co., Tulsa, 1953-54; asst. city atty., Tulsa, 1954-55; practice, Tulsa, 1955-60, Claremore, Okla., 1960-65; justice Okla. Supreme Ct., 1965—, now chief justice; guest lectr. Okla. U., Oklahoma City U., Tulsa U. law schs. Republican committeeman Rogers County, 1961-62. Served with USNR, 1944-46. Mem. Am., Okla., Rogers County bar assns., Am. Judicature Soc., Okla. Jud. Conf., Phi Alpha Delta (hon.). Methodist (adminstrv. bd.). Mason (32 deg.). Home: 2910 Kerry Ln Oklahoma City OK 73120 Office: Room 240 State Capitol Bldg Oklahoma City OK 73105

LAVENSON, JAMES H., corp. exec.; b. Phila., 1919; grad. Williams Coll., 1941. Pres., chief exec. officer SYR Corp.; pres. Lavenson Mgmt. Enterprises, Inc., N.Y.C., 1976—; pres. Plaza Hotel, N.Y.C.; Plaza Hotel, N.Y.C., 1972-75, Sunwear, Inc.; chmn. Doxsee Food Co.; pres. Lavenson Bur. Advt., Inc., 1950-64; dir. Sonesta Hotels, TLC Corp. Bd. dirs. Am. Field Service, Chief Execs. Forum. Author: Selling Made Simple; Jaundiced Eye; Think Strawberries; Sensuous Animal. Home: 1831 E Mountain Dr Montecito CA 93108 Office: San Ysidro Ranch Montecito CA 93108

LAVENTHOL, DAVID ABRAM, journalist; b. Phila., July 15, 1933; s. Jesse and Clare (Horwald) L.; A.B., Yale U., 1957; M.A., U. Minn., 1960; Litt.D., Dowling Coll., 1979; m. Esther Coons, Mar. 8, 1958; children—Peter, Sarah. Reporter, news editor St. Petersburg (Fla.) Times, 1957-62; asst. editor, city editor N.Y. Herald-Tribune, 1963-66; asst. mng. editor Washington Post, 1966-69; asso. editor Newsday, L.I., N.Y., 1969, exec. editor, 1970, v.p., 1971-74, editor, 1971—, exec. v.p., 1974-78, pub., chief exec. officer, 1978—. Trustee L.I. U., 1979—; bd. dirs. Advt. Council, 1979—. Served with Signal Corps, AUS, 1953-55. Mem. Am. Soc. Newspaper Editors, China Council. Club: Century. Home: 22 Bayview Ave Port Washington NY 11050

LAVENTURE, WILLIAM BURROWS, lawyer; b. Davenport, Iowa, Jan. 29, 1905; s. William Mason and Bessie (Burrows) LaV.; grad. Asheville (N.C.) Sch., 1922; Ph.B., Yale, 1926, LL.B., 1928; m.

Barbara Walton, Nov. 5, 1938. Admitted to N.Y. bar, 1928, since practiced in N.Y.C.; partner firm Reynolds, Richards, LaVenture, Hadley & Davis, and predecessors, 1944—. Mem. Am. Bar Assn., Assn. Bar City N.Y. Clubs: Down Town Association, University (N.Y.C.). Home: Matthiessen Park Irvington NY 10533 Office: 67 Wall St New York City NY 10005

LAVER, RODNEY GEORGE, tennis player; b. Rockhampton, Queensland, Australia, Aug. 9, 1938; ed. pub. schs.; m. Mary Benson, 1966; 1 son. Played on Australian Davis Cup team, 1958-63, 73; Australian champion, 1960, 62, 69, Wimbledon champion, 1961, 62, 68, 69, U.S.A. champion, 1962, 69, French champion, 1962, 69, 1st player to win Grand Slam twice, 1962, 69; French champion, 1962, 69, 1st player to win Grand Slam, 1962, 69; joined World Championship Tennis, 1970, played for San Diego Friars, 1976, 77, 78. Decorated Order Birt. Empire. Author: How to Play Winning Tennis, 1964; Education of a Tennis Player, 1971.

LAVERCOMBE, ROBERT RIESER, lawyer; b. Cin., Aug. 6, 1920; B.B.A., U. Cin, 1948, LL.B., 1949. Admitted to Ohio and U.S. Dist. Ct. bars; partner firm Beckman, Lavercombe, Fox & Weil, gen. practice law, Cin. Office: Beckman Lavercombe Fox & Weil 1714 First Nat Bank Bldg Cincinnati OH 45202

LAVERGE, JAN, tobacco co. exec.; b. Amsterdam, Netherlands, Nov. 17, 1909; s. Hendrik Johannes and Margaretha (Van Gelder) L.; M.E., Higher Tech. Sch., Amsterdam, 1930; m. Henriette Amelia Boelen, May 21, 1935; children—Bart Jan, Eva S., Charlotte M. Came to U.S., 1934, naturalized, 1942. With Am. Tobacco Co., Amsterdam, 1930-34; with Universal Leaf Tobacco Co., Inc., Richmond, Va., 1934—, asst. v.p., 1946-51, v.p., 1951-66, sr. v.p., 1966-78, dir., 1953—, chmn. exec. com., 1974-78, cons., 1978—. Served to maj. AUS, 1943-46. Decorated Legion of Merit, Croix de Guerre (France); Netherlands Order Orange Nassau. Home: 6120 St Andrews Ln Richmond VA 23226 Office: Universal Bldg Broad and Hamilton Richmond VA 23230

LAVERTY, ROBERT E., hosp. adminstr.; b. Toledo, May 8, 1945; s. Donald J. and Kathryn A. L.; B.B.A. in Adminstrn., U. Mich., 1969, M.H.A., 1972; m. Suzanne, June 12, 1968; children—Sarah, Michael. Adminstrv. asst. St. Joseph Mercy Hosp., Ann Arbor, Mich., 1967-72, asst. to exec. dir., 1972-76, exec. dir., 1976—; chmn. fin. com. Eastern Mich. Regional Bd., Sisters of Mercy Health Corp.; trustee, mem. exec. com. Greater Detroit Area Hosp. Council; corp. mem. Blue Cross Blue Shield of Mich.; dir. Nat. Bank & Trust Co. Bd. dirs. Washetenaw (county, Mich.) United Way. Mem. Am. Hosp. Assn., Mich. Hosp. Assn., Am. Coll. Hosp. Adminstrn., Am. Mgmt. Assn., Ypsilanti (Mich.) Area C. of C. (trustee, chmn. bd. trustees, mem. services council). Home: 2116 Devonshire St Ann Arbor MI 48104 Office: PO Box 995 Ann Arbor MI 48106*

LAVERY, CHARLES JOSEPH, coll. chancellor; b. Toronto, Ont., Can., May 1, 1915; s. Charles James and Eleanor (Bradley) L.; B.A., U. Toronto, 1937, M.A., 1940; Ph.D., U. Chgo., 1950; D.D. (hon.), Hofstra U., 1968; LL.D., Hobart and William Smith Coll., 1975, Nazareth Coll., 1978, U. Rochester, 1979. Joined Congregation of St. Basil, 1937; ordained priest Roman Cath. Ch., 1942; instr. Aquinas Inst., Rochester, N.Y., 1940-41; dir. devel. U. St. Thomas, Houston, 1948; registrar, v.p. St. Michaels Coll., U. Toronto, 1949-58; pres. St. John Fisher Coll., Rochester, 1958-80, chancellor, 1980—; mem. exec. com. Rochester Area Colls., 1965—; mem. Gov.'s Task Force on Higher Edn., 1975—; chmn. pub. affairs com. Commn. Ind. Colls. and Univs. Chmn. Rochester Clean City Com.; mem. Inter-Faith Com. for Israel; mem. adv. bd. Jr. League; bd. dirs. Ednl. TV Assn., Rochester/Monroe County Athletes Hall of Fame, United Community CHest. Recipient County Civic medal, 1972; Monroe County Citizens Civic award, 1972; named Kiwanis Citizen of Yr., 1971. Mem. Rochester C. of C. (dir.). Clubs: Fortnightly, Oak Hill Country, University, Genesee Valley (Rochester). Home: 3690 East Ave Rochester NY 14618

LAVERY, EMMET GODFREY, writer; b. Poughkeepsie, N.Y., Nov. 8, 1902; s. James A. and Katharine T. (Gilmartin) L.; LL.B., Fordham, 1924; L.H.D., Mount St. Paul Coll., 1968; m. Genevieve E. Drislane, Nov. 3, 1925; children—Emmet, Elizabeth. Admitted to N.Y. bar, 1925; city editor Poughkeepsie Sunday Courier, 1925-35; vis. lectr. drama Fordham U., 1939; research grant drama from Rockefeller Found. at Vassar, 1940, head research staff for Hallie Flanagan's history of Fed. Theatre, Arena; resident playwright Smith Coll. on grant from Rockefeller Found., 1942; writer for stage and screen, 1935—; stage plays include: The First Legion (trans. fourteen langs.), 1934; Monsignor's Hour, 1935; Second Spring (life of Cardinal Newman), 1938; The Magnificent Yankee, 1946, on tour, 1947; (opera) Tarquin, 1950; Fenelon (Basle), 1956; Hail to the Chief, 1958; American Portrait, 1958; Dawn's Early Light, 1959; Ladies of Soissons, 1964; screen plays: Hitler's Children (dramatization of Gregor Ziemer's Education for Death), 1942; Behind the Rising Sun (dramatization of book by James R. Young), 1943; Guilty of Treason, 1950; The First Legion, 1951; The Magnificent Yankee, 1951; Bright Road, 1953 (adaptation See How They Run); The Court Martial of Billy Mitchell (collaboration), 1955; Williamsburg, 1957; published plays: Brother Petroc's Return (from English novel by S.M.C.), 1940; Kamiano (Damien) (with Grace Murphy) in trilogy Theatre for Tomorrow, 1940; Murder in a Nunnery (based on novel by Eric Shepherd), 1944; Brief Music, 1940; The Gentleman from Athens, 1948; Song at the Scaffold (adaptation from novel by Gertrud von le Fort), 1949; Yankee Doodles (ballet), 1964; writer, producer El Dorado (folk ballet), 1968; writer Continental Congress: 1976, KNBC-TV, 1971, Prairie Lawyer TV program, 1975, The Magnificant Yankee (Bicentennial revival), Kennedy Center, Washington, 1976; War Dept. made arrangements, 1947, 48, for special prodn. The First Legion and the Magnificent Yankee in Austria as part of re-edn. program; co-licensor Dialogues des Carmelites (Poulene), 1954—; propr. film The First Legion. A founder Nat. Cath. Theatre Conf., 1937; dir. Nat. Service Bur. Fed. Theater, 1937-39; chmn. Hollywood Writers Moblzn., 1944-45. Pres. bd. aldermen, Poughkeepsie, 1929-33; mem. Joint Commn. on Fair Jud. Election Practices, Calif., 1976. Mem. Screen Writers Guild (pres. 1945-47), Motion Picture Acad. Arts and Scis. (v.p. 1946), Authors League, Dramatists Guild (N.Y.), Am. Bar Assn. (Gavel award for Magnificent Yankee 1965). Democrat. Roman Catholic. Clubs: The Players (N.Y.C.); Poughkeepsie Tennis; Newman (Los Angeles). Address: 17925 Tarzana St Encino CA 91316. *My friends suggest that I am always writing the same story. To a certain extent, true. Whether the play is about Justice Holmes or Cardinal Newman or Fenelon, the point of being is faith.*

LAVERY, OWEN SEAN, ballet dancer; b. Harrisburg, Pa., Aug. 16, 1956; s. Eugene Delbert and Rose Ann (Flood) L.; Debut with San Francisco Ballet, 1972; with Frankfurt Ballet, 1975-77, prin. dancer, 1977; prin. dancer N.Y.C. Ballet, 1977—, U.S. Terpsichore, 1977. Roman Catholic. Office: care New York City Ballet Lincoln Center Plaza New York NY 10023

LAVERY, WILLIAM EDWARD, univ. pres.; b. Geneseo, N.Y., Nov. 20, 1930; s. John Raymond and Mary Irene (O'Brien) L.; B.S., Mich. State U., 1953; M.A., George Washington U., 1959; Ph.D., U. Wis., 1962; m. Peggy J. Johnson, Apr. 7, 1956; children—Debra, Kevin, Lori, Mary. Tchr. Clarence (N.Y.) Central High Sch., 1953-54; asst. to adminstr. Fed. Extension Service Dept. Agr., Washington, 1956-66; dir. adminstrn.-extension div. Va. Polytech. Inst. and State U., Blacksburg, 1966-68, v.p. finance, 1968-73, exec. v.p., 1973-75, pres., 1975—. AID cons. to El Salvador, 1969. Dir. Dominion Bankshores Corp. Mem. United Fund-Community Fedn., 1968-72. Bd. dirs. Montgomery County Hosp. Served with AUS, 1954-56. Kellogg Found. fellow, 1960-62. Mem. Omicron Delta Kappa, Epsilon Sigma Phi, Phi Kappa Phi, Phi Delta Kappa. Club: Rotary (Blacksburg). Home: 604 Rainbow Ridge Blacksburg VA 24060

LAVEY, KENNETH HENRY, advt. agy. exec., designer; b. Palermo, Calif., Aug. 25, 1923; s. Rudolph Charles and Margaret S. (Williams) L.; B.A., Calif. Coll. Arts and Crafts, 1948; grad. Pratt Inst., 1949; m. Joann Lucile Miller, July 11, 1948; children—Brian Benton, Neil Bruce. With L. W. Frolich, pharm. advt. co., N.Y.C., 1949-72, creative dir., 1962-66, sr. v.p., dir. creative planning, 1966-72; co-founder Lavey/Wolff/Swift, Inc., health care communications agy., N.Y.C., 1972, exec. v.p., dir. creative services, 1972—; lectr. Pratt Inst., 1976-77, participant Ten Alumni exhibit, 1962, Fifty Alumni exhibit, 1966; panel mem. Pharm. Advt. Club Seminar. Served with USAAF, 1943-46. Recipient Student medal for advt. design Pratt Inst., 1949. Mem. Art Dirs. Club N.Y., Am. Ethical Union, Riverdale-Yonkers Ethical Soc. (v.p. 1969-71, 76-77). Designer (with Harvard Med. Sch. dept. physiology) anatomical graphics. Office: 488 Madison Ave New York City NY 10022

LAVIDGE, ROBERT JAMES, marketing research exec.; b. Chgo., Dec. 27, 1921; s. Arthur Wills and Mary Beatrice (James) L.; A.B., DePauw U., 1943; M.B.A., U. Chgo., 1947; m. Margaret Mary Zwigard, June 8, 1946; children—Margaret, Kathleen, William, Lynn Elizabeth. Asst. to dir. marketing research Pepsodent div. Lever Bros., 1947-48, new products marketing research mgr., 1948-49; asst. dir. marketing Am. Meat Inst., Chgo., 1950-51; partner Elrick, Lavidge and Co., Chgo., 1951-56; pres. Elrick and Lavidge, Inc., Chgo., 1956—; dir. Mid-Am. Industries; lectr. mktg. research, sales adminstrn. Northwestern U., 1950—. Mem. Nat. Marketing Adv. Com., 1967-71, also exec. com. Trustee, Village Western Springs (Ill.), 1957-61, pres., 1973-77; chmn. Cook County Council Govts., 1974-76. Mem. alumni bd. U. Chgo., DePauw U., pres. alumni assn., 1967-68. Served with USNR, 1943-46. Mem. Am. Marketing Assn. (v.p. 1963-64, pres. 1966-67), Internat. Relations Soc. (chmn. 1961-65), Am. Assn. Pub. Opinion Research, Econ. Club Chgo., Phi Beta Kappa, Beta Gamma Sigma, Sigma Delta Chi, Pi Sigma Alpha, Delta Upsilon. Presbyn. Clubs: La Grange (Ill.) Country; Klinger Lake (Mich.); Metropolitan (Chgo.). Home: 4901 Grand Ave Western Springs IL 60558 Office: 10 S Riverside Plaza Chicago IL 60606

LAVIN, BERNICE E., business exec.; b. 1925; student Northwestern U.; m. Leonard H. Lavin, Oct. 30, 1947; children—Scott Jay, Carol Marie, Karen Sue. Sec., v.p., treas. Alberto-Culver Co., 1961—, also dir.; sec.-treas., dir. Alberto-Culver Export, Inc., John A. Frye Shoe Co., Inc., Leonard H. Lavin & Co., Masury-Columbia Co., Milani Foods, Inc., Draper Daniels, Inc. Home: Glencoe IL 60022 Office: 2525 Armitage Ave Melrose Park IL 60160

LAVIN, DAVID J., writer, fast food co. exec.; b. Canton, Ohio, Aug. 2, 1923; s. William Lewis and Celia (Yassenoff) L.; student U. Wis., 1941-43; B.S., Ohio State U., 1945; grad. Advanced Mgmt. Program, Harvard, 1959; m. Elinor Rose Golden, June 24, 1951; children—Nancy, Susan, William II. With Sugardale Foods, Inc., Canton, 1959-76, v.p. mdsg., dir., 1961—, chmn. bd., chief exec. officer, 1969-76; chmn. bd., chief exec. officer Morgan's Restaurants, Inc., 1976-77, Royal Castle, Inc.; gen. partner Laar Ltd.; realtor asso. Walker & Lee; pres. Imperial Realty, Niles Realty Co. Originator, co-author with wife nat. syndicated column Teenage Corner, 1960—; co-founder Camp Conestoga for Boys. Chmn. Canton chpt. ARC, Stark County chpt. Am. Heart Soc.; mem. finance and bldg. commn. Canton Philomatheon Soc. for Blind; mem. exec. com., men's chmn. Canton Sesquicentennial; pub. rep. to bd. trustees Blue Cross Hosp. Plan, Inc.; mem. Aultman Hosp. Assn.; asso. chmn. Nat. Bible Week, 1972; past pres. Rolling Acres Home Owners Assn.; mem. Palm Desert Real Estate Bd. Mem. exec. finance com. Stark County Republican party. Hon. life mem. bd. dirs. Canton Symphony, Blossom Music Center; bd. dirs. Nat. Council U.S.O.; bd. dirs., 1st v.p. Canton Players Guild; bd. dirs., sec. Walsh Coll. Recipient certificate merit Canton Philomatheon Soc. for Blind; Silver medal Advt. Fedn. Am. and Printer's Ink mag., 1963. Mem. Canton C. of C., Stark County Hist. Soc., Arts Unlimited, Mus. Arts Assn., Western Res. Acad. Alumni Assn. (v.p.), Palm Springs Friends of Los Angeles Philharmonic, Desert Mus. Palm Springs, Palm Springs Opera Guild. Clubs: Canton, Harvard, Canton Advertising (past pres., dir.); Rotary (Rancho Mirage, Calif.); Arrowhead Country (past treas., dir.), Lakeview Country; Racquet, Tamarisk Country (Palm Springs, Calif.). Home: 70-540 Gardenia Ct Rancho Mirage CA 92270 Office: 73-261 Hwy 111 Palm Desert CA 92260

LAVIN, IRVING, art historian; b. St. Louis, Dec. 14, 1927; B.A., Washington U., 1949; postgrad. Cambridge U., 1948-49; M.A., N.Y. U., 1952; M.A., Harvard U., 1953, Ph.D., 1955; m. Marilyn Aronberg Lavin, 1952; children—Amelia, Sylvia. Lectr. art history Vassar Coll., 1959-62; asso. prof., then prof. art history N.Y. U., 1963-73; prof. Faculty of Sch. of Hist. Studies, Inst. Advanced Study, Princeton, N.J., 1973—; mem. vis. com. dept. art and archaeology Princeton U., 1973—; vis. com. dept. fine arts Harvard U., 1977; mem. Nat. Com. for the History of Art, 1975—; mem. steering com. Corpus Ancient Mosaics Tunisia, 1969—. Served with U.S. Army, 1955-57. Fulbright fellow, 1961-62, 62-63; Am. Council Learned Socs. fellow, 1965-66; Guggenheim Found. fellow, 1968-69. Fellow Am. Acad. Arts and Scis.; mem. Coll. Art Assn. (dir. 1976—), Soc. Archtl. Historians, Renaissance Soc. Am., Assn. Internat. pour l'étude des mosaïques antiques. Author works in field. Home: 56 Maxwell Ln Princeton NJ 08540 Office: Sch Hist Studies Inst Advanced Study Princeton NJ 08540

LAVIN, JOHN HALLEY, editor; b. Queens County, N.Y., Oct. 27, 1932; s. John Joseph and Dorothy Monica (Halley) L.; B.A., Queens Coll., 1958; participant health adminstrv. devel. program, Cornell U., 1969; m. Bernadette Manning, Mar. 2, 1957; children—John Stephen, Michael James, Eileen Mary, Monica Ann. Editor L.I. Graphic, weekly, 1958; copy editor New Haven Register, 1958-59; newsman, state news editor A.P., Newark, 1959-65, gen. news supr., N.Y.C., 1965-66; editor-writer Med. Econs. Co., mag. pubs., Oradell, N.J., 1966—; Atlantic bur. chief Soccer Am. Mag., 1977-78; sr. editor, news div. chief, mem. editorial bd. Med. Econs., 1968-73; editor RN, 1973-75, Nursing Opportunities, 1973-75, RN Recruiter, 1974-75. Publicity chmn. Glen Rock (N.J.) Cub Scouts and Boy Scouts Am. 1968-73; founder, mem. Glen Rock Jr. Soccer Club, 1970-74, publicity chmn., 1970-72, trustee, 1973-74, grounds mgr., 1972-74. Served with USN, 1951-55; Korea. Recipient Jesse H. Neal award Am. Bus. Press, 1976, certificate, 1976. Mem. Soc. Profl. Journalists, Am. Soc. Journalists and Authors. Roman Catholic. Contbr. articles to profl. and gen. interest publs. Home: 83 Rodney St Glen Rock NJ 07452 Office: 680 Kinderamack Rd Oradell NJ 07649. *An editor's primary responsibility is to his reader. If he has performed his corporate duties well, endeared himself to his publisher, pleased his writers and advertisers, fed his ego among his fellow editors, but has allowed the editorial excellence of his publication to be compromised, he has not met his primary responsibility. If he loses touch with the copy or the reader, he is no longer an editor; he is a manager. And he might as well be in some other business.*

LAVIN, LEONARD H., toiletries co. exec.; b. Chgo., Oct. 29, 1919; s. Samuel and Ella (Rissman) L.; B.A., U. Wash., 1940; D.H.L., DePaul U., 1971; m. Bernice Elizabeth Weiser, Oct. 30, 1947; children—Scott Jay, Carol Marie (Mrs. Howard Bernick), Karen Sue. With Lucien LeLong, 1940-41, 45-46; sales mgr. Halgar Co., 1946-49; mgr. selling and advt. Jules Montenier, Inc., 1950-53; organizer Leonard H. Lavin & Co., Chgo., 1953-55; pres. Alberto-Culver Co., Melrose Park, Ill., 1955—. Bd. overseers Johnston Coll. at U. Redlands, until 1973; bd. dirs. Rehab. Inst. Chgo. Served with USNR, 1941-45. Mem. Young Pres. Orgn., Sales Marketing Execs. Internat. (pres. panel). Home: Glencoe IL 60022 Office: 2525 Armitage Ave Melrose Park IL 60160

LAVIN, LINDA, actress; b. Portland, Maine, Oct. 15, 1937; d. David J. and Lucille (Potter) Lavin; B.A., Coll. William and Mary, Williamsburg, Va., 1959. Off-Broadway debut in Oh, Kay!, 1960, Broadway debut in A Family Affairs, 1962; appearances in revues Wet Paint, 1965, The Game Is Up, 1965, The Mad Show, 1966; with nat. touring company On a Clear Day You Can See Forever, 1966-67; mem. acting company Eugene O'Neil Playwrights Unit, 1968; other stage appearances include It's a Bird... It's a Plane... It's Superman, 1966, Something Different, 1967, Little Murders, 1969, Cop-Out, 1969, The Last of the Red Hot Lovers (Tony nominee), 1969, Story Theatre, 1970, The Enemy is Dead, 1973, Love Two, 1974, The Comedy of Errors, 1975, Dynamite Tonite!, 1975; star TV series Alice, 1976—, recipient Golden Globe award, 1979; other TV appearances on CBS Playhouse, Barney Miller, Rhoda, Harry O, Phyllis, also in The Beggar's Opera, Damn Yankees; nightclub appearances, also pvt. drama tchr. and rec. artist. Recipient Sat. Rev., Outer Critics Circle awards for Little Murders; Theater World award for Wet Paint. Address: care CBS CBS Television City Los Angeles CA 90036

LAVINE, HAROLD, editor, writer; b. N.Y.C., Feb. 19, 1915; s. Elias and Pauline (Bershadsky) L.; student Townsend Harris Hall, 1927-30; m. Violet Edwards, Dec. 24, 1936; 1 dau., Cammie Caroline Edwards. Reporter N.Y. Am., 1932-33, N.Y. Evening Jour., 1933-34, N.Y. Evening Post, 1934-36; asst. mng. editor PM, 1941-44; with U.S. Army News Service, 1944-46; sr. editor Newsweek mag., 1946-63, Forbes mag., 1963-74; editorial writer, columnist Ariz. Republic, 1974—. Recipient Page One award, 1961. Club: The Lotos (N.Y.C.). Author: Fifth Column in America, 1940; (with James A. Wechsler) War Propaganda and the United States, 1940; Central America, 1964; Smoke-Filled Rooms, 1970. Home: 6505 N 12th Way Phoenix AZ 85014 Office: PO Box 1950 Phoenix AZ 85001

LAVIS, RICK COMSTOCK, govt. ofcl.; b. Mt. Kisco, N.Y., Feb. 1, 1940; s. Fred and Kathleen Comstock L.; student Claremont Men's Coll., 1959-60; B.S. in Polit. Sci., Ariz. State U., 1964, postgrad., 1964-68; m. Martha Luella Ives, July 16, 1966; children—Daniel, Benjamin. Teaching asst. Am. govt. U. Ariz., 1966-68; dir. devel. Orme Sch., Mayer, Ariz., 1968-71; legis. and adminstrv. asst. Sen. Paul J. Fannin, Washington, 1971-76; legis. rep. El Paso Natural Gas Co., Washington, 1976-77; dep. asst. sec. for Indian Affairs, Dept. Interior, Washington, 1977—. Trustee, Orme Sch. Republican. Presbyterian. Office: Dept Interior Washington DC 20245. *If anything can characterize my life it is my interest and active participation in public affairs. The opportunity to resolve public issues by helping to create and fashion solutions to often difficult problems has proved to be not only challenging but personally rewarding. Public service is an essential requirement of all citizens in a democracy and to have participated in public life will, I hope, prove to be a positive legacy for my family.*

LAVOIE, LÉO, banker; b. Notre-Dame-du-Lac, Que., Can., Mar. 18, 1913; s. Phydime and Caroline (Viel) L.; ed. St.-Francois-Xavier Coll., Riviere-du-Loup, Que.; grad. Advanced Mgmt. Program, Harvard, 1954; D.Sc. Comm. honoris causa, U. Montreal, 1970; m. Claire Maranda, June 10, 1940; 1 dau., Lise (Mrs. Leon Courville). With Provincial Bank of Can., 1930—, v.p., gen. mgr., 1966-67, pres., 1967-76, chief exec. officer, 1967-77, chmn. bd., 1974—; chmn. bd. Canadair Ltd., Ciné Monde Inc.; dir. Alliance Mut. Life Ins. Co., Compagnie France Film, Télé-métropole Inc., Canadian Reins. Co., Canadian Reassurance Co., others. Active various social and cultural orgns., clubs and assns. Office: 221 St James St Montreal PQ H2Y 1M7 Canada

LAW, BERNARD FRANCIS, bishop; b. Torreon, Mex., Nov. 4, 1931 (parents Am. citizens); s. Bernard A. and Helen A. (Stubblefield) L.; B.A., Harvard U., 1953; postgrad. St. Joseph Sem., St. Benedict, La., 1953, Pontifical Coll. Josephinum, Worthington, Ohio, 1955. Ordained priest Roman Catholic Ch., 1961, consecrated bishop, 1973; asst. pastor St. Paul's Ch., Vicksburg, Miss., 1961-63; editor Natchez-Jackson Diocesan newspaper, 1963-68, dir. Natchez-Jackson Diocesan Family Life Bur., asst. dir. vocations, moderator Diocesan Council of Cath. Men and Council of Cath. Women, spiritual dir. minor Sem.; exec. dir. U.S. Bishops Com. for Ecumenical and Interreligious Affairs, 1968-71, chmn., 1975—; vicar gen. Diocese of Natchez-Jackson, 1971-73; bishop Diocese of Springfield-Cape Girardeau, Mo., 1973—. mem. adminstrv. com. Nat. Conf. Cath. Bishops, 1975—; mem. communication com. U.S. Cath. Conf., 1974; mem. adminstrv. bd. U.S. Cath. Conf., 1975—; mem. Vatican Secretariat for Promoting Christian Unity, 1976—; consultor Vatican Commn. Religious Relations with the Jews, 1976—. Trustee, Pontifical Coll. Josephinum, 1974—, Nat. Shrine of Immaculate Conception, 1975—; bd. regents Conception (Mo.) Sem. Coll., 1975—. Home: 1320 E Walnut St Springfield MO 65802 Office: 200 McDaniel Bldg Springfield MO 65806

LAW, CURSEY SHELBY, bus. exec.; b. Trenton, Tenn., Feb. 23, 1933; s. Lawson S. and Doris J. (Haller) L.; B.S. in Mech. Engring., Mich. State U., 1959; m. Marilyn Mehney, June 18, 1960; children—Jeffrey, Catherine, James. Supr. prodn. Excello Corp., Lima, Ohio, 1959-64; group v.p. fluid power Cessna Aircraft Co., Wichita, Kans., 1973-77; now pres. Hutch-Line Inc., Hutchinson, Kans. Bd. dirs. Hutchinson (Kans.) Hosp. Corp., 1972-74, Indsl. Dist. Hutchinson, 1969—. Served with USN, 1951-55. Mem. Wichita C. of C. Conglist. Mason. Home: Route 3 Box 46 Willowbrook Hutchinson KS 67501 Office: Hutch-Line Inc 413 E 3d St Hutchinson KS 67501

LAW, DAVID HILLIS, IV, educator, physician; b. Milw., July 24, 1927; s. David Hillis and Hazel-Janice (May) L.; A.B., Cornell U., Ithaca, N.Y., 1950, M.D., 1954; m. Patricia Bicking Thornton, Sept. 13, 1949; children—Linda (Mrs. Clark), Wendy Anne, David Hillis V, Kimberly Bicking, Cassandra McGibeny. Intern, resident N.Y. Hosp.-Cornell Med. Center, 1954-57, research fellow medicine, 1957-58, dir. personnel health service, 1958-60; med. dir. outpatient dept., chief div. gastroenterology Vanderbilt U. Hosp., Nashville, 1960-69; attending physician gastroenterology Thayer Vets. Hosp., 1960-69; spl. cons. NIH, 1962-63; asst. prof. medicine Vanderbilt U. Sch. Medicine, 1960-66, asso. prof., 1966-69; chief med. service VA

Hosp., Albuquerque, 1969—; prof. medicine, vice chmn. dept. medicine U. N.Mex. Sch. Medicine, Albuquerque, 1969—; mem. numerous adv. coms. VA; mem. U.S. Pharmacopeia Com. on Revision, 1975—; participant nutrition surveys, Jordan, 1962, Ky. 1969; lectr. A.M.A., 1971—. Served with AUS, 1945-46. Fellow A.C.P., Am. Pub. Health Assn., Am. Gastroent. Assn., Am. Coll. Nutrition; mem. Am. Fedn. Clin. Research, So., Western socs. clin. research, Western Assn. Physicians, Am. Inst. Nutrition, Am. Soc. Clin. Nutrition, A.M.A., Pan Am. Med. Assn., Alpha Omega Alpha. Editorial bd. Am. Jour. Digestive Diseases, 1968-75. Co-editor: Parenteral Nutrition, 1970. Contbr. articles to profl. jours., also chpts. to books. Home: 8220 Pickard Ct Albuquerque NM 87110 Office: VA Hosp Albuquerque NM 87108

LAW, EDWARD, paper co. exec.; b. Niles, Ohio, Aug. 31, 1923; s. Edward and Edith (Shoup) L.; student Baldwin-Wallace Coll., 1941-42; B.S. in Mech. Engring., U. Mich., 1948; grad. Advanced Mgmt. Program, Harvard, 1963; m. Patricia Reid, June 25, 1948; children—Jeffrey, Reid, Carol Lynn, Stephen Edward. With W.Va. Pulp & Paper Co., Covington, Va., 1948-52, Waldorf Paper Products Co., St. Paul, 1952-67; sr. v.p. Clevepak Corp., N.Y.C., 1967—; v.p. Waste Mgmt. Inc., Oak Brook, Ill., 1973-75; owner, mgr. Flom Corp., Des Plaines, Ill., 1975—, Flour City Press-Pak, Mpls., 1975—. Mem. exec. bd. Indian head council Boy Scouts Am. Served with USAAF, 1942-46. Mem. T.A.P.P.I., Paper Industry Mgmt. Assn., St. Paul C. of C., Lambda Chi Alpha. Home: 3225 Woodbridge St St Paul MN 55112 Office: 375 Park Ave New York City NY 10022

LAW, JOHN MANNING, lawyer; b. Chgo., Dec. 5, 1927; s. Fred Edward and Elisabeth Manning (Emmons) L.; student U. Chgo., 1944-45, St. Ambrose Coll., 1945; B.A., Colo. Coll., 1948; LL.B., U. Colo., 1951; m. Carol Lufkin Ritter, May 14, 1955; children—John Emmons, Lucy Lufkin, Frederick Ritter, Beth Kimball. Admitted to Colo. bar, 1951, Ill. bar, 1952; atty. trust dept. Harris Trust & Savs. Bank, Chgo., 1951-52; asso. firm Dickerson, Morrissey & Dwyer, Denver, 1952-57; partner firm Law, Clark & Scheid, Denver, 1958—; mem. Colo. State Bd. Law Examiners, 1971—. Commr. Moffat Tunnel Commn., 1966-78. Served to capt. JAGC, USNR. Fellow Internat. Soc. Barristers, Colo. Bar Found. (charter); mem. Am. (standing com. on legal assistance to servicemen 1971-78, chmn. 1972-73), Colo. (bd. govs. 1968-71), Arapahoe County (Colo.), Denver (trustee 1971-74) bar assns., Phi Gamma Delta, Phi Delta Phi, Denver Law Club. Republican. Presbyterian. Clubs: Univ., Perry Park Country (past pres.). Home: 2000 S Madison St Denver CO 80210 Office: First of Denver Plaza Bldg Suite 3100 Denver CO 80202

LAW, JOHN PHILIP, actor; b. Hollywood, Calif., Sept. 7, 1937; attended Calif. State Poly. Inst., U. Hawaii; studied dramatics at Repertory Theatre of Lincoln Center, N.Y.C. Made acting debut as lead in play The Changeling at Lincoln Center Repertory Co.; films appeared in include: The Love Machine, Von Richthofen and Brown, The Last Movie, The Russians Are Coming The Russians Are Coming, Hurry Sundown, Barbarella, Skidoo, The Sergeant, The Cassandra Crossing, Dancer: Diabolik, The Hawaiians, The Golden Voyage of Sinbad. Office: care William Morris Agy 151 El Camino Dr Beverly Hills CA 90212*

LAW, LLOYD WILLIAM, geneticist; b. Ford City, Pa., Oct. 28, 1910; s. Craig Smith and Cora Jane (Whiteley) L.; B.S., U. Ill., 1931; A.M., Harvard, 1935, Ph.D. (Austin fellow), 1937; Harvard Sheldon fellow Stanford U., 1937-38; m. Bernette Bohen, May 4, 1942; children—Lloyd William, David Bradford. Tchr. high sch., Charleston, Ill., 1931-34; Finney-Howell Med. research fellow Jackson Meml. Lab., Bar Harbor, Maine, 1938-41, Commonwealth Fund fellow, 1941-42, research assoc., 1946, sci. dir., 1947, now trustee; geneticist Nat. Cancer Inst., Bethesda, Md., 1947-52, head leukemia studies sect., 1952—, chief lab. cell biology, 1970—, mem. sci. directorate, 1970—. Panel mem. com. on growth NRC, 1952-56; mem. pharmacology and exptl. therapeutics study sect. NIH, 1955—; mem. screening panel cancer chemotherapy Nat. Service Center, 1955—; mem. adv. bd. Nat. Blood Research Found., 1954—, adv. bd. cancer research Am. Cancer Soc., 1965—, mem. panel on etiology of cancer, 1960—; sci. bd. Childrens Cancer Fund Am., 1956—; bd. sci. advisers Roswell Park (N.Y.) Cancer Inst., 1957—; expert adv. com. cancer WHO, 1960—; mem. U.S.A. nat. com. Internat. Union Against Cancer, 1969—; mem. bd. sci. advs. Chemotherapy Found. N.Y., 1974—. Served as capt. 2d Air Force, USAAF, 1942-46. Recipient Anne Frankel Rosenthal award A.A.A.S., 1955; USPHS Meritorious Service award, 1965; G.H.A. Clowes Meml. award in cancer research, 1965; Allesandro Pascoli prize, 1969; Distinguished Service medal USPHS, 1969; G.B. Mider lecture award NIH, 1970. Mem. Soc. Exptl. Biology and Medicine, N.Y. Acad. Sci., Am. Soc. Exptl. Pathology, Am. Assn. Cancer Research (dir. 1956-59, 65—, pres. 1967-68), Italian Cancer Soc., Royal Soc. Medicine. Author: Advances in Cancer Research (vol. II), 1954; Leukemia Research, 1955; Origins of Resistance to Toxic Agents, 1955, other books in field. Contbr. articles to profl. jours., books and pamphlets. Home: 9810 Fernwood Rd Bethesda MD 20034 Office: Nat Cancer Institute Public Health Service Rockville Pike Bethesda MD 20205

LAWARE, JOHN PATRICK, banker; b. Columbus, Wis., Feb. 20, 1928; s. John Henry and Ruth (Powles) L.; B.A., Harvard, 1950, grad. Advanced Mgmt. Program, 1975; M.A., U. Pa., 1951; m. Margery Ann Ninabuck, Dec. 22, 1952; children—John Kevin, Margaret Ann. Trainee, Chem. Bank & Trust Co., N.Y.C., 1953-54, with credit dept., 1954-56, asst. sec., 1957-60, asst. v.p., 1960-62, v.p., 1962-65, v.p. in charge mktg. div., 1965-68, sr. v.p., 1968-72; sr. v.p. in charge holding co. ops. Chem. N.Y. Corp., from 1972; pres., dir. Shawmut Corp., 1978—, Shawmut Bank of Boston N.A., 1978—, Shawmut Assn., Inc., 1978—, Devonshire Fin. Service Corp., 1978—; dir. Shawmut Corp. subs.; alt. dir. Atlantic Internat. Bank Ltd., London; alt. mem. Internat. Monetary Conf. Bd. dirs. Mass. Taxpayers Found. Served from pvt. to 2d lt. USAF, 1951-53. Mem. Harvard Advanced Mgmt. Assn., Assn. Res. City Bankers, Mass. Bankers Assn. (vice chmn.), Greater Boston C. of C. (dir.), Mus. of Sci. Clubs: Harvard (N.Y.C.); Scarsdale Golf; Fox Meadow Tennis; Harvard, Algonquin, Comml., Union (Boston). Home: 100 Codman Rd Brookline MA 02146

LAWATSCH, FRANK EMIL, JR., banker; b. Avenel, N.J., May 11, 1944; s. Frank Emil and Jessie Margaret Lawatsch; B.A., Colgate U., 1966; J.D., Cornell U., 1969; m. Deanna Conover, May 25, 1969; children—Amanda, Abigail, Frank. Admitted to N.Y. bar, 1969; atty. firm Shearman & Sterling, N.Y.C., 1969-78; v.p., gen. counsel Midlantic Banks Inc., W. Orange, N.J., 1978—. Mem. Am. Bar Assn., N.J. Bar Assn., Bar Assn. City N.Y. Episcopalian. Home: 185 Park St Montclair NJ 07042 Office: 95 Old Short Hills Rd West Orange NJ 07052

LAWDER, STANDISH DYER, artist, film maker; b. N.Y.C., Feb. 4, 1936; s. Douglass Ward and Janice (Chapman) L.; B.A., Williams Coll., 1958; M.A., Yale U., 1962, Ph.D., 1967; children—Katherine Ward, Cynthia R. Mem. faculty Yale U., 1967-75, Harvard U., 1971-72; curator collection classic films Yale U., 1969-75; prof. art and film, chmn. dept. visual arts, U. Calif., San Diego, 1975—; films include: Necrology, 1969, Corridor, 1970, Runaway, 1970, Colorfilm, 1972, Raindance, 1973, Catfilm for Katy and Cynnie, 1973; films in permanent collection: Mus. Modern Art, N.Y.C.; designer steroscopic motion picture system, 1973—. Served with U.S. Army, 1958-60. Guggenheim fellow, 1972. Home: 1552 Camino del Mar Apt 640-B Del Mar CA 92014 Office: Dept Visual Arts Univ Calif San Diego La Jolla CA 92037

LAWFORD, PETER, actor; b. London, Eng., Sept. 7, 1923; s. Sir Sidney and Lady Lawford; ed. pvt. tutors. m. Patricia Kennedy (div. 1966); children—Christopher, Sydney, Victoria, Robin; m. 2d, Mary Ann Rowan, Nov. 2, 1971 (div. 1973). Motion pictures: White Cliffs Dover, Paris After Dark, Canterville Ghost, Two Sisters From Boston, Good News, Easter Parade, Julia Misbehaves, Rogue's March, Ocean's Eleven, Exodus, numerous others; TV series Dear Phoebe, 1956-57; role of Nick Charles, Thin Man series, NBC-TV, 1957-59; recent films include: The Longest Day, 1962; Advise and Consent, 1962; Sargeants Three, 1961; Dead Ringer, 1963; Harlow; The Oscar; Skidoo; Hook, Line and Sinker; Buona Serra Mrs. Campbell; April Fools; One More Time; They Only Kill Their Masters; That's Entertainment, 1974; Rosebud, 1975; Won Ton Ton, 1976; TV prodn. Ellery Queen, 1971; pres. Chrislaw Prodns., Inc. Address: care Lew Sherrell Agy 7060 Hollywood Blvd Los Angeles CA 90028*

LAWHON, JOHN E., III, lawyer, former county ofcl.; b. Denton, Tex., Dec. 14, 1934; s. John E. and Gladys (Barns) L.; student North Tex. State Univ., 1951-53; B.B.A., U. Houston, 1958, J.D., 1958; m. Tommie Collins, Aug. 27, 1967; 1 son, David Collins. Admitted to Tex. bar, 1958; asst. dist. and county atty. Denton County, Tex., 1958-61, dist. and county atty., 1961-77; dir. Southridge, Inc., Denton, 1962-72, Lawyers Title Agy. Denton, 1965-74; Legal adviser Denton City-County Day Nursery; tchr. bus. law, North Tex. State U., Denton, 1969-71; mem. adv. bd. Tex. Criminal Justice Council, 1973-79; univ. atty. Tex. Women's U., 1977—. Bd. dirs. Denton County Welfare Council, 1970-78, Denton Community Council, 1978-79. Mem. Tex., Denton (pres. 1968-69, dir. 1978—) bar assns., Tex. Dist. and County Attys. Assn. (dir. 1964-66), Denton Jaycees (sec. 1961), Denton C. of C., Tex. Bar Assn. Baptist (deacon 1968—). K.P., Kiwanian (dir.). Home: 2810 Carmel Denton TX 76201 Office: Adminstrn Tower Bldg Tex Women's Univ PO Box 23025 Denton TX 76204

LAWHORN, DONALD SAMUEL, ins. co. exec.; b. Indpls., Sept. 7, 1925; s. Roy D. and Angie (Blunt) L.; B.S., Ind. U., 1949; m. Juanita E. Freeland, June 15, 1947; children—Cynthia D., Deborah A., Bruce L. Investment analyst Am. United Life, Indpls., 1949-61; v.p., treas. Vol. State Life, Chattanooga, 1962-68; v.p., chief investment officer Indpls. Life Ins. Co., Indpls., 1968—. Served with USAAF, 1943-45. Mem. Indpls. Analysts Soc. (pres. 1960-61). Home: 1214 Hillcrest Dr Carmel IN 46032 Office: 2960 N Meridian St Indianapolis IN 46208

LAWI, DAVID STEVEN, electronics co. exec.; b. Baghdad, Iraq, Aug. 3, 1935; s. Steven David and Marcelle (Masry) L.; came to U.S., 1946, naturalized, 1952; A.A. in Sci., N.Y. State Coll., 1955; m. Anne Shamash, June 9, 1968; children—Nicole, Neil. Registered rep. Bear, Stearns & Co., N.Y.C., 1956-62; dir. Adobe Brick & Supply, West Palm Beach, Fla., 1962-64; v.p. Molly Corp., Reading, Pa., 1962-64; gen. mgr. United Shoe Machinery Corp., Reading, 1964-65; a founder, sec., treas., dir. Unimax Group Inc. (formerly Riker-Maxson Corp.), N.Y.C., 1966—, also dir. all subsidiaries. Served with AUS, 1968. Home: Ramapo Trail Harrison NY 10528 Office: 425 Park Ave New York NY 10022

LAWLER, BEVERLEY RHEA, advt. and pub. relations exec.; b. Norfolk, Va., Nov. 5, 1926; s. Frank Porter and Virginia Broughton (Rhea) L.; A.A. with honors, Coll. William and Mary, 1948; B.A., U. N.C., 1950; postgrad. Army Command and Gen. Staff Coll., 1959-60; m. Ann Fitzpatrick, June 14, 1952; children—Ann Lynn, Susan Rhea, Andrew Francis. Pub. info. specialist U.S. Army Field Forces, 1950-54; founder, pres. Pub. Relations Inst., Norfolk, 1954—, Lawler Ballard Advt., Norfolk, 1954—. Mem. adv. bd. Old Dominion U., Norfolk, 1964—; mem. found. bd. Norfolk State Coll., 1972—; mem. S.E. regional cabinet Boy Scouts Am., 1972-79, chmn. communications com., 1972-78, mem. nat. pub. relations com., 1977—; chmn. civic affairs com. Norfolk C. of C., 1965-66; chmn. publicity com. United Community Fund, Norfolk, 1966-68; bd. dirs. Cruise Internat., 1972—, Norfolk YMCA, 1973—, Tidewater chpt. ARC, 1965-67, Va. Travel Council, 1963-64, Internat. Azalea Festival, 1967-68. Served to sgt. U.S. Army, 1943-45. Decorated Combat Inf. badge; Bronze Star; recipient Silver Antelope award Boy Scouts Am., 1976; named Ad Man of Year Eastern Va. Advt. Club, 1965; Norfolk YMCA Man of Year, 1978. Mem. Nat. Fedn. Advt. Agys. (past pres.), Accredited Advt. Agys. of Tidewater (past pres.), Pub. Relations Soc. Am. (past pres. Va. chpt.; recipient Silver Anvil 1962, 69), Am. Assn. Advt. Agys. Roman Catholic. Clubs: Norfolk Yacht and Country, Harbor (Norfolk); Commonwealth (Richmond, Va.). Home: 6103 Studeley Ave Norfolk VA 23508 Office: 248 W Bute St Norfolk VA 23501

LAWLER, BRUCE GIBBS, railroad exec.; b. Clifton Forge, Va., Jan. 1, 1927; s. Michael Francis and Lucy (Gibbs) L.; B.S., U. Notre Dame, 1951; m. Mary Eleanor Neely, July 16, 1955; children—Susan Gibbs, Sarah Summers. With Chesapeake & Ohio Ry. Co. (merged with Balt. & Ohio R.R. 1963), Balt., and other locations, 1951—, dep. comptroller, 1970-72, comptroller, 1972—, also asst. v.p., 1974—; dir. Fruit Growers Express Co. Served with USAAF, 1945-46. Home: 6649 Walnutwood Circle Baltimore MD 21212 Office: 2 N Charles St Baltimore MD 21201

LAWLER, CHARLES ALTON, civil engr.; b. Luling, Tex., Apr. 24, 1921; s. Charlie Albert and Annie Laura (New) L.; B.C.E., U. Tex., 1942; m. Mary Sue Thrift, Sept. 22, 1973; children—Kathlin Bounds, Susan Dalby. Design engr. Exxon Co. USA, Baytown, Tex., 1942-44, Brown & Root, Inc., Houston, 1946-47; sr. engr., then partner H.E. Bovay, Jr. Cons. Engrs., Houston, 1947-62; exec. v.p. Bovay Engrs., Inc., Houston, 1962-74, pres., chmn. exec. com., dir., 1974—; dir. Limbaugh Engrs., Inc., Albuquerque. Served to lt. (j.g.) USNR, 1944-46. Registered profl. engr., Tex. Mem. Nat., Tex. socs. profl. engrs., ASCE, Soc. Am. Mil. Engrs., Houston Engring. and Sci. Soc., Am. Water Works Assn., Marine Tech. Soc., Houston C. of C. Methodist. Club: Champions Golf. Author papers in field. Co-inventor lumber sorter, 1952, granular product storage bin to prevent graded particle segregation, 1967. Home: 625 Wellesley Dr Houston TX 77024 Office: 5619 Fannin St Houston TX 77004

LAWLER, EDMUND G., hosp. adminstr.; B.S., Loyola U., Chgo.; M.S., Northwestern U.; m. Jean Oliver; children—Edmund, Timothy, Marianne, Eileen, Daniel, Elizabeth. Dir., Oak Forest (Ill.) Hosp. of Cook County; guest lectr. Govs. State U. Chmn. South Cook County Health Care Planning Com.; chmn. long term care adv. com. CHP, Inc., Chgo.; mem. St. Damian Sch. Bd., Oak Forest; bd. dirs. Suburban Cook-DuPage County Health Systems Agy. Recipient Ill. Superior Pub. Service award, 1969, Ill. Juvenile Officers Assn. spl. award, 1971, Mem. Am. (chmn. governing council rehab. and chronic disease), Ill. hosps. assns., Am. Coll. Hosp. Adminstrs., Am. Pub. Health Assn., Chgo. Assn. Commerce and Industry, Chgo. Hosp. Council, Chgo. Council Fgn. Relations, Assn. Rehab. Facilities (dir.). Clubs: Midlothian (Ill.) Country; Rotary Internat.; Grand Beach (Mich.). Contbr. articles to profl. jours. Address: Oak Forest Hosp 159th St and Cicero Ave Oak Forest IL 60452

LAWLER, EUGENE PATRICK, advt. agy. exec.; b. Milw., Dec. 22, 1922; s. John Robert and Cecile Bridget (Murphy) L.; B.S., U.S. Naval Acad., 1947; m. Joyce L. Moorbeck, Nov. 30, 1946; children—Kathleen, Patrick, Michael, John, Mark, Joseph, Charles, David. Engring. trainee Allis-Chalmers, 1946-47, staff advt. exec., 1947-48; internat. sales promotion mgr. Nordberg (now Rexnord), 1948-50; account group supr. Gittins Agy., Milw., 1950-61; pres. Lawler, Kenney & Reichert, Milw., 1961-63; exec. v.p. Hoffman-York, Milw., 1963-66, pres., chief exec. officer, 1966—; dir. Godfrey Co. Bd. overseers Milw. Archdiocesan Sem. Served with U.S. Navy, 1940-46. Recipient Silver medal award for disting. service Am. Advt. Fedn., 1974; Disting. Service award as chmn. bd. Nat. Advt. Agy. Network, 1971. Mem. Am. Assn. Advt. Agys., Met. Milw. Assn. Commerce (dir.), President's Assn., Am. Mgmt. Assn., Public Relations Soc. Am., Milw. Advt. Club. Republican. Roman Catholic. Clubs: Blue Mound Golf and Country, Milw. Univ. Home: 1640 Lindhurst Ct Elm Grove WI 53122 Office: 2300 N Mayfair Rd Milwaukee WI 53226

LAWLER, GORDON JOSEPH, publishing co. exec.; b. Mpls., Oct. 11, 1911; s. Joseph Earle and Mabel (McGregor) L.; B.A. in Journalism, U. Minn., 1935; m. Edith Anne Nixon, July 11, 1950; 1 son, Michael John. Asst. advt. mgr. Minn. & Ont. Paper Co., Mpls., 1946-50; editor Vance Pub. Co., Chgo., 1951-60; sales promotion mgr. Celotex Corp., Chgo., 1960-64; sr. v.p. Daniel J. Edelman, Inc., Chgo., 1964-72; dir. communications Cahners Pub. Co., Chgo., 1972—. Pub. relations adviser Chgo. Mag., 1969—; industry adviser Chgo. State Coll., 1970—. Mem. hosp. adv. bd. Booth Meml. Hosp., Chgo., 1971—. Served with USAAF, 1942-46. Mem. Pub. Relations Soc. Am. Home: 1175 Beech Ln Highland Park IL 60035 Office: 5 S Wabash Chicago IL 60603

LAWLER, JOSEPH CHRISTOPHER, engring. exec.; b. Lynn, Mass., May 3, 1920; s. Joseph Christopher and Clara Mae (Emerson) L.; B.S. cum laude (Desmond Fitzgerlad scholar 1943), Northeastern U., 1943, D.Eng. (hon.), 1972; M.S., Harvard, 1947; children—Susan Vivian, Joseph Christopher III, William Douglas. Project engr. Camp Dresser & McKee Inc., Boston, 1947-52, partner, 1952—, pres., 1970-78, chmn. bd., 1970—, chief exec. officer, 1978—. Mem. North Reading Pub. Sch. Bldg. Com., 1956-60, North Reading Sch. Com., 1960-61. Trustee Northeastern U., 1977—, mem. corp., 1965—. Served to lt. (j.g.) C.E.C., USN, 1944-46. Recipient New Eng. Engr. of Year award, 1972; named Alumni Man of Yr., Northeastern U., 1972, Outstanding Civil Engring. Alumnus, 1979. Registered profl. engr., N.H., Vt., R.I., Conn., Maine, Mass., N.Y., Calif., Va. Diplomate Am. Acad. Environ. Engrs., recipient Gordon Maskew Fair award, 1979. Fellow ASCE, Water Pollution Control Fedn. (dir. at large 1972-75, exec. com., 1972-73), Am. Cons. Engrs. Council; mem. Nat. Acad. Engring., Northeastern U. Alumni Assn. (dir. 1958-60, v.p. 1960-62), Engring. Socs. New Eng. (pres. 1962-63), Nat. Council Profl. Services Firms (dir., 1972—, pres. 1976), New Eng. Water Pollution Control Assn. (pres. 1970), Am. Water Works Assn., Nat. Soc. Profl. Engrs. (Profl. Engrs. in Pvt. Practice award 1977), Tau Beta Pi, Chi Epsilon (hon.). Contbr. to Handbook of Applied Hydraulics (Davis), 1969, articles to profl. jours. Home: 16 Winter St North Reading MA 01864 Office: One Center Plaza Boston MA 02108

LAWLER, OSCAR THOM, banker; b. Los Angeles, Nov. 23, 1914; s. Oscar and Hilda (Brode) L.; B.A., Yale, 1936; m. Joan Day Pattinson, July 27, 1937; children—Daniel Day (dec.), Charles Frederick, Joan Day (Mrs. Joseph Ray Sutton). Pres., Farmers & Mchts. Nat. Bank of Los Angeles, 1953-56; chmn. exec. com., dir. Security Pacific Nat. Bank, Los Angeles, 1956-77; cons. Security Pacific Nat. Bank; dir. Security Pacific Internat. Bank, Cyprus Mines Corp., Union Pacific Corp. Chmn. bd. Barlow Hosp.; vice chmn. Los Angeles Civic Light Opera Assn.; sec.-treas. Oak Tree Found.; trustee Union Pacific Found., Hollenbeck Home, Rancho Santa Ana Bot. Garden, Dan Murphy Found., Good Hope Med. Found.; mem. Bus. Com. for the Arts, Inc. Mem. Los Angeles C. of C. (dir. 1954-56, 62-65, pres. 1964), Soc. Friendly Sons St. Patrick of Los Angeles (pres. 1962-63), Founders of Music Center, Calif. Tech. Assos. (dir.), Los Angeles Stock Exchange Club (dir., past pres.), Los Angeles World Affairs Council, Friends of Claremont Colls., Friends of Huntington Library, Honnold Library Soc., Calif. Hist. Soc. (dir.), Newcomen Soc. N.Am., Assos. Calif. Inst. Tech. Mason. Clubs: California; India House, Yale (N.Y.C.); Los Angeles, Lincoln (pres. 1967-68), Sunset, Yale of So. Calif. Home: 5224 W 2d St Los Angeles CA 90004 Office: PO Box 2097 Terminal Annex Los Angeles CA 90051

LAWLER, THOMAS NEWMAN, lawyer; b. N.Y.C., Apr. 18, 1908; s. Thomas B. and Margaret A. (Brennan) L.; A.B., Princeton, 1929; LL.B., Harvard, 1932; m. Martha E. Reynolds, Nov. 15, 1934; children—Ann (Mrs. Thomas E. Dewey, Jr.), Martha Elisabeth (Mrs. David T. Schiff). Admitted to N.Y. bar, 1932, since practiced N.Y.C.; asso. Breed, Abbott & Morgan, 1932-34, O'Brien, Driscoll & Raftery, 1934-44; partner firm O'Brien, Driscoll, Raftery & Lawler, 1944-51, Lawler & Rockwood, N.Y.C., 1951-66, Lawler, Sterling & Kent, 1966-74, Hall, Dickler, Lawler, Kent & Howley, 1974—. Dir. Philip Morris, Inc., Bank of Commerce, Wheelock Signals, Inc., Irving Berlin Music Corp. Trustee Irving Berlin Charitable Fund, Fred C. Gloeckner Found. Mem. Am. (chmn. copyright com. 1946-48), N.Y. bar assns. Club: Sleepy Hollow Country (Scarborough, N.Y.). Home: 54 Hemlock Dr North Tarrytown NY 10591 Office: 460 Park Ave New York NY 10022

LAWLESS, WILLIAM B(URNS), lawyer; b. North Tonawanda, N.Y., June 3, 1922; s. William B. and Margaret H. (Welton) L.; J.D., U. Notre Dame, 1944; A.B., U. Buffalo, 1949; LL.M., Harvard U., 1950; m. Jeanne Offermann, Mar. 9, 1944; children—Sharon M., Barbara Lawless Bourhis, William B., III, Cathy Lawless Joyce, Gregory F., Richard A., Robert C., Jeannie W., Therese M., John Rutledge, Maria, Thomas More. Admitted to N.Y. bar, 1946, D.C. bar, 1972, U.S. Tax Ct., 1950, U.S. Supreme Ct. bar, 1955, Mass. bar, 1976; asso. firm Kenefick, Cooke, Mitchell, Bass & Letchworth, Buffalo, N.Y., 1946-50; partner firm Williams, Crane & Lawless, Buffalo, 1950-54; sr. partner firm Lawless, Offermann, Fallon & Mahoney, Buffalo, 1954-56; justice N.Y. Supreme Ct., 8th Jud. Dist., Buffalo, 1960-68; dean Faculty of Law Notre Dame U., 1968-71; partner firm Mudge, Rose, Guthrie & Alexander, N.Y.C., 1971-75, Hawkins, Delafield & Wood, N.Y.C., 1975-79, Lawless & Crowley, 1979—; bd. dirs. Nat. Jud. Coll.; mem. N.Y. State Joint Legis. Com. on Ct. Reorgn.; Robert H. Jackson lectr. Nat. Coll. State Trial Judges, 1962. Pres. Buffalo Common Council, 1956-60; trustee Pace U. Served with USN, 1943-46; PTO. Fellow Am. Bar Found., Am. Coll. Trial Lawyers; mem. Am. Bar Assn., N.Y. State Bar Assn., Assn. Bar City N.Y., Am. Law Inst., Fed. Bar Council, Inst. Jud. Adminstrn., Law Students Civil Rights Research Counsel, U.S. Supreme Ct. Hist. Soc., Union Internationale des avocats, Internat. League Human Rights, Citizens Union N.Y., Alumni Assn. U. Buffalo, Alumni Assn. Harvard U., Alumni Assn. U. Notre Dame. Clubs: Downtown Assn., Harvard of N.Y.C. Author: (with others) New York Pattern Jury Instructions, vol. 1, 1965, vol. 2, 1968; adv. bd. Am. Bar Assn. Jour., 1976—;

contbr. articles to law jours. Office: 720 Fifth Ave New York NY 10019

LAWLESS, WILLIAM JOSSELYN, JR., bus. exec., state legislator; b. Newton, Mass., Apr. 13, 1919; s. William Josselyn and Anna (Lemon) L.; A.A., George Washington U., 1949, B.A. with distinction in Math. Statistics, 1952; m. Ruth Atwood Gammons, Jan. 1, 1941; children—William Josselyn III, Philip Gammons. Sr. analytical officer, then chief Office Machine Prodn., U.S. Dept. Def., 1946-53; with IBM Corp., 1952-62, 65-74, corp. staff dir. systems engring., 1960-62, dir. corporate planning, 1965-68, gen. mgr. South Am. hdqrs., 1968-69, gen. mgr. Latin Am. hdqrs., Buenos Aires, Argentina, 1969-74; mgmt. cons., 1974-78; pres. Cognitronics Corp., 1978—; mem. Conn. Ho. of Reps., 1974-78, asst. majority leader, 1975-78. Dir., AID mission to Ghana, 1962-64, to Nigeria, 1964-65; mem. sci. orgn. devel. bd. NRC of Nat. Acad. Scis., 1966-68. Chmn. bd. Rowayton (Conn.) Civic Assn., 1960-61; mem. Norwalk Citizens Action Com., 1959-61; commr. police, Norwalk, Conn. Bd. dirs. Overseas Devel. Council. Served to capt. AUS, 1942-46. Decorated Legion of Merit. Mem. IEEE (sr.), AAAS, Assn. Computing Machinery, Inst. Mgmt. Sci., Phi Beta Kappa. Democrat. Contbr. articles to profl. jours. papers. Home: 6 New St East Norwalk CT 06855

LAWLEY, ALAN, educator; b. Birmingham, Eng., Aug. 29, 1933; s. Archibald and Millicent A. (Olorenshaw) L.; B.Sc., U. Birmingham, 1955, Ph.D., 1958; m. Nancy A. Kressler, Mar. 26, 1960; children—Carolyn Ann, Elizabeth Ann, Jennifer Ann. Research asso. U. Pa., 1958-61; lab. mgr. research labs. Franklin Inst. Labs., 1961-66; prof. materials engring. Drexel U., Phila., 1966—, chmn. dept., 1966-79. Cons. to govt., industry. Fellow Am. Soc. Metals; mem. Am. Inst. Metall. Engrs., Am. Soc. Engring. Edn., Metals Soc., Electron Microscopy Soc. Am., Am. Powder Metallurgy Inst., Sigma Xi, Phi Kappa Phi, Tau Beta Pi, Alpha Sigma Mu. Contbr. chpts. to books, articles to profl. jours. Home: 336 Hathaway Ln Wynnewood PA 19096 Office: Dept Materials Engring Drexel Univ Philadelphia PA 19104

LAWLIS, MERRITT EUGENE, educator; b. Columbus, Ind., Nov. 22, 1918; s. Daniel Webber and Mabel (Locke) L.; A.B., Wabash Coll., 1940; Ph.D. (Dexter fellow), Harvard U., 1951; postgrad. (Mellon fellow) U. Pitts., 1965-66; m. Naomi Abel, Aug. 3, 1946; children—Marcia, Barbara, Abigail. Mem. staff newspaper, Phoenix, 1940; instr. Ind. U., 1951-54, asst. prof. English and comparative lit., 1955-59, asso. prof., 1960-64, prof., 1965—; fellow Folger Library, Washington, 1966. Served to lt. col. A.C., U.S. Army, 1940-46. Decorated Purple Heart, Bronze Star. Unitarian. Club: Renaissance. Author: Apology for the Middle Class, 1961; contbr. articles to profl. jours.; editor: The Novels of Thomas Deloney, 1961; Elizabethan Prose fiction, 1967; The Shoemakers' Holiday (Dekker), 1979. Home: 1900 E Hunter Ave Bloomington IN 47401 Office: Dept English/Comparative Lit Ind U Bloomington IN 47401

LAWLOR, WILLIAM JAMES, former investment banker; b. Chgo., May 21, 1907; s. William J. and Mary (Garvy) L.; A.B., Georgetown U., 1928; m. Mary Fortune, June 1, 1933; 1 son, William J. III. Trader, Hickey, Doyle and Co., 1928-37; v.p. Hickey and Co., 1937-47; mgr. investment dept. Hornblower and Weeks, Chgo., 1947-50, partner, 1950-72; sr. v.p., dir., mem. exec. com. Loeb, Rhoades, Hornblower & Co. Former vice chmn., mem. exec. com. Midwest Stock Exchange. Bd. dirs. Cath. Charities Chgo.; mem. citizens bd. Loyola U., Chgo.; presdl. counselor Georgetown U. Served from apprentice seaman to lt. USNR, 1943-46. Mem. Investment Bankers Assn. (chmn. Central States group 1956-57, gov. 1958-61). Clubs: Mid-Day, University, Bond, Georgetown, Exmoor, Indian Hill, Chicago Curling; Hobe Sound Yacht, Island (Hobe Sound, Fla.). Home: 1630 Sheridan Rd Apt 8-N Wilmette IL 60091 Office: 72 W Adams St Chicago IL 60603

LAWRASON, F. DOUGLAS, physician, educator; b. St. Paul, July 30, 1919; s. Joseph F. and Clara (Mueller) L.; student U. Chgo., 1937-40; B.A., U. Minn., 1941, M.A., 1944, M.D., 1944; m. Elaine J. Wilson, Mar. 18, 1944; children—Peter D., Jock D., Susan E. Intern, resident, fellow Yale Sch. Medicine and New Haven Hosp., 1944-49; instr., asst. prof. medicine Yale, 1949-53; profl. asso. NRC, 1950-53; asst. prof. medicine, asst. dean Sch. Medicine, U. N.C., 1953-55; prof. medicine, provost U. Ark., dean U. Ark. Sch. Medicine, 1955-61; exec. dir. med. research Merck Sharp & Dohme Research Labs., West Point, Pa., 1961-66, v.p. med. research, 1966-69; prof. medicine, dean acad. affairs U. Tex. Southwestern Med. Sch., Dallas, 1969-72, dean, 1972-73; sr. v.p. sci. affairs Schering-Plough, 1973—, pres. Schering-Plough research div., 1975—, also corporate dir. Served with M.C., USNR, 1946-47. Mem. N.Y. Acad. Sci., A.A.A.S., Fedn. for Clin. Research, Am. Heart Assn., Acad. Hematology, Am. Coll. Cardiology, Sigma Xi. Home: 53 Spring Valley Rd Convent NJ 07961

LAWRENCE, ALLAN, Canadian govt. ofcl.; b. Toronto, Ont., Can.; student U. Toronto, Osgoode Hall Law Sch.; married; 2 children. Called to Ont. bar, 1954; mem. Ont. Legislature, 1958-72, minister of mines for Ont., 1968, later minister Ont. Dept. No. Affairs; atty. gen. for Ont., 1971; provincial sec. Dept. Justice, 1972; mem. Can. Ho. of Commons for Durham-Northumberland, 1972—, chmn. public accounts com.; solicitor gen., minister of consumer and corp. affairs Govt. of Can., 1979—. Mem. Progressive Conservative Party. Office: Ministry of Solicitor General 340 Laurier Ave W Ottawa ON K1A 0P8 Canada

LAWRENCE, CHARLES BARNES, JR., cons., ret. govt. ofcl.; b. St. Louis, Dec. 25, 1908; s. Charles Barnes and Mabel Maud (Case) L.; student St. John's Mil. Acad., 1928; A.B., Columbia U., 1934, A.M., 1939, postgrad., 1940-41, Am. U., 1962-69; m. Catherine Marie Saponar, July 23, 1935; 1 son, Larry James. Coordinator statis. projects Central Statis. Bd. and WPA, 1935-41; dir. statis. standards OPA, 1942-43; asst. dir. Pres.' Com. for Congested War Prodn. Areas, 1943-44; regional dir. PHA, 1945-48; pres. Reliance Homes of Washington, Inc., 1948-51; dir. AEC Community Surveys, 1952; UN statis. cons., Columbia, Cuba, Ecuador, Haiti, 1952-53, Indonesia, 1975; dep. asst. to sec. HEW, 1954-60; statis. cons. spl. studies Rockefeller Bros. Fund, 1958; chief statis. adv. group to Republic Korea, 1959-60; asst. dir. ops. Bur. Census, 1960-65, asst. dir. internat. statis. programs, 1966-70, chief statis. adv. group to Govt. Brazil, 1971-73; statis. cons. Fed Energy Adminstrn., 1974-75; mgmt. and statis. cons., 1976—, hon. prof. statistics Myeongji U., Seoul, Korea; Collector, mus. instruments of indigenous people of world; composer situational music. Awarded Korean Order Civil Merit Mogryeon medal. Fellow Am. Statis. Assn.; mem. Brazilian, Korean statis. assns., Internat. Assn. Survey Statisticians, D.C. Sociol. Soc., Internat. Assn. Agrl. Economists (rapporteur), Soc. Internat. Devel. (sec.-treas. Washington chpt. 1962-63, pres. 1963-65, del. to People's Republic of China 1978), El Club de Las Americas (pres. 1957-59), Fed. Bus. Assn. (pres. Cleve. 1946-47), Washington Statis. Soc. (v.p. 1957-58), Inter-Am. Statis. Inst. (constituent), Aircraft Owners and Pilots Assn., Pi Sigma Alpha. Club: Kiwanis (v.p. 1979—). Editor: Health, Education and Welfare Indicators, 1957-59; The Status of Statistics in Central America at the Inception of the Alliance for Progress, 1962; Statistics for Planning in the U.S.S.R., 1969; A.D.P. as a Tool of Modern Management, 1971; A Series of Reports on The Status of Statistics in Developing Countries, 1969-73; Combination Way, 1977. Home: 15137 Vantage Hill Rd Silver Spring MD 20906

LAWRENCE, CHARLES EDMUND, architect; b. Victoria, Tex., Jan. 24, 1927; s. Robert Lee and Josephine Amelia (Jecker) L.; student Tex. A and M U., 1944-45; B.Arch., U. Tex., 1951; m. Nancy Jo Mell, June 23, 1951; children—Lise Ann, Charles Mell, Mia Michele, Joshua Jon. Designer, Caudill Rowlett Scott, Inc., Bryan, Tex., 1951-58, dir. design, 1958-72, partner, 1958—, dir., Houston, 1967—; vis. prof. Rice U. Sch. Architecture, 1960; mem. adv. bd. Ednl. Facilities Lab., Sch. Constrn. System Devel. Project Calif., 1961-63; mem. adv. council U. Tex. Sch. Architecture, 1975—. Served with USN, 1945-46. Fellow AIA; mem. Tex. Soc. Architects. Roman Catholic. Prin. works include Brownsville Acad., Jesse Jones Hall for Performing Arts, H.L.&P. Energy Control Center, Edwin Thomas Hall for Performing Arts, U. of Petroleum and Minerals. Home: 11715 Timberknoll St Houston TX 77024 Office: 1111 W Loop S Houston TX 77027

LAWRENCE, CHARLES HARRIS, physician; b. Chgo., Mar. 27, 1913; s. Louis James and Hattie (Abrams) L.; B.S., U. Chgo., 1934; M.D., Rush Med. Sch., Chgo., 1937; m. Elise Lieberman, Nov. 20, 1947; children—Nancy, Ann. Intern, then resident pathology Cook County Hosp., Chgo., 1937-39, asso. attending physician, 1947-50, attending physician, 1953-59; pvt. practice medicine specializing in internal medicine, Chgo., 1946—; mem. staff Ill. Research and Edn. Hosp., 1960-64, Michael Reese Hosp., and Med. Center, 1947—, pres. med. staff, 1964-65, coordinator clin. services, 1967-69, med. dir., 1969-73, v.p. profl. affairs, 1973—; clin. asst. prof. medicine U. Ill. Sch. Medicine, 1953-64. Served to maj. M.C., AUS, 1940-46: PTO. Decorated Purple Heart, Combat Med. Badge. Diplomate Am. Bd. Internal Medicine. Mem. A.C.P., Am., Ill., Chgo., Cook County med. assns., Inst. Medicine, Chgo. Soc. Internal Medicine, Ill. Soc. Med. Research, Am. Heart Assn., Sigma Xi, Pi Lambda Phi. Jewish religion. Club: Ravisloe Country (Homewood, Ill.). Contbr. articles and med. bulls. to profl. lit. Home: 5555 S Everett Ave Chicago IL 60637 Office: 2929 S Ellis Ave Chicago IL 60616

LAWRENCE, CHARLES SEELY, III, ins. co. exec.; b. Passaic, N.J., Feb. 9, 1932; s. Charles Seely and Gladys (Smith) L.; B.S., Rutgers U., 1954; postgrad. Dartmouth Coll., summers 1967, 68, 69; m. Lilles Ann Tillinghast, June 28, 1958; children—David, Stephen, Todd. With Chase Manhattan Bank, N.Y.C., 1954-62; with Central Nat. Bank, Cleve., 1962-78, sr. v.p., 1970, exec. v.p., 1971-74, pres., 1975-78, also dir.; pres., dir. Central Cleve. Internat. Bank, N.Y.C., 1970-78; v.p., dir. Centran Corp., 1972-78; pres., chief exec. officer, dir. Guardian Title Ins. Co., Cleve., 1979—; dir. Cole Consumer Products Co. Mem. citizens com., Shaker Heights; trustee Cleve. State U. Devel. Found. Served with U.S. Army, 1955-57. Mem. Ohio Land Title Assn., Newcomen Soc. N.Am. Episcopalian. Clubs: Cleve. Skating (trustee 1977), Racquet, Mayfield Country (Cleve.). Home: 2866 Sedgewick Rd Shaker Heights OH 44120 Office: 3861 Green Rd Beachwood OH 44122

LAWRENCE, DAVID, JR., newspaper editor; b. N.Y.C., Mar. 5, 1942; s. David and Nancy Wemple (Bissell) L.; B.S., U. Fla., 1963; m. Roberta Phyllis Fleischman, Dec. 21, 1963; children—David III, Jennifer Beth, Amanda Katherine. News editor St. Petersburg (Fla.) Times, 1963-67; news editor/style Washington Post, 1967-69; mng. editor Palm Beach (Fla.) Post, 1969-71, Phila. Daily News, 1971-75; exec. editor Charlotte (N.C.) Observer, 1975-76, editor, 1976-78; exec. editor Detroit Free Press, 1978—. Home: 1022 Yorkshire Rd Grosse Pointe MI 48230 Office: 321 W Lafayette Blvd Detroit MI 48231

LAWRENCE, DICK, newspaperman; b. Bonners Ferry, Idaho, Jan. 6, 1916; s. Don and Mabel (Hider) L.; A.B., U. Wash., 1937; m. Jean Wingate, May 22, 1939; children—Rick, Sherril Lee. News editor Puyallup Valley (Wash.) Tribune, 1937-39; editor, co-publisher Olympia News, 1939-41; telegraph editor Daily Olympian, 1941-51, news editor, 1951-60, editor, 1960-64, editor mgr., 1964-67, pub., 1967-69, communications cons., 1969—. Served to lt. (s.g.) USNR, 1942-45. Mem. Alpha Delta Phi, also Sigma Delta Chi. Home: 2119 E Bay Dr Olympia WA 98506

LAWRENCE, GEORGE H., assn. exec.; b. Bartlesville, Okla., Nov. 1, 1925; s. Chester Allen and Pearl (Nation) L.; B.S. in Indsl. Engring., Okla. State U., 1949; LL.B., S. Tex. Coll. Law, 1957; m. Shirley Jo Thompson, Sept. 4, 1948; children—Michael, Linda, George H., Amy Jo. Petroleum engr. Humble Oil & Refining Co., Houston, 1949-59; atty., then asst. mgr. natural gas div. Humble Oil Co., 1959-63; individual legal practice, also petroleum engring. cons., Houston, 1963-64; natural gas coordinator Am. Petroleum Inst., Washington, 1964-68; mgr. Washington office, then dir., v.p., exec. v.p. Am. Gas Assn., 1968-76, pres., Arlington, Va., 1976—; vice chmn., bd. dirs. Nat. Energy Found.; bd. dirs., treas. Center Urban Studies, Washington; bd. dirs. Council Energy Studies, Tulsa. Trustee, Ford Theatre Found., Washington. Served with USMCR, 1943-46. Recipient award Center Urban Environ. Studies, 1979. Men. Am. Bar Assn., Soc. Petroleum Engrs., Am. Soc. Assn. Execs., Tex. Bar Assn., Sigma Chi. Democrat. Methodist. Clubs: Nat. Democratic, Capitol Hill, Kiwanis, Univ. (Washington); Congressional Country (Bethesda, Md.). Author monographs, reports in field. Home: 8707 Eaglebrook Ct Alexandria VA 22308 Office: 1515 Wilson Blvd Arlington VA 22209

LAWRENCE, HALLETT THOMPSON, advt. agy. exec.; b. Pueblo, Colo., Oct. 7, 1921; s. Chauncey Wynkoop and Laura (Gallup) L.; B.S. in Elec. Engring., U.S. Naval Acad., 1944; m. Dorothy McElroy, Dec. 30, 1945 (div. 1966); children—Lindalee Climo, Laura Louise. Commd. ensign U.S. Navy, 1944, advanced to lt. (j.g.), 1947, resigned, 1947; advt. writer Foxboro Co., 1948-52; gen. mgr. Spir-it, Inc., Malden, Mass., 1952-54; with Griswold-Eshleman, 1954-55, Boland Assos., 1956-57; founder Hal Lawrence Inc., advt., 1957, now pres., chmn.; founder, dir. AviAm. Corp., Palo Alto, 1971—; founder Aero-Crafters, Tokyo, also Palo Alto; partner Daly Travel Services, Inc., San Francisco; founding dir. Heil Sci. Labs., Inc., 1962, Founding dir., chmn. bd. Golden Triangle Assos., Inc., Minden, Nev. Mem. Bay Area Soaring Assos. (founder, dir.), Internat. Assn. Shipboard Edn. (dir.), Pan Pacific Music and Art Soc. (treas., dir.). Organizer, pilot 1st flight around perimeter continental U.S. in motorglider, 1978. Home: 147 Degas Rd Portola Valley CA 94025 Office: 2440 Embarcadero Way Palo Alto CA 94303

LAWRENCE, HARDING LUTHER, airline exec.; b. Perkins, Okla., July 15, 1920; s. Moncey Luther and Helen Beatrice (Langley) L.; student Kilgore Coll., 1938-39; B.B.A., U. Tex., 1942; LL.B., S. Tex. Coll. Law, 1949, J.D., 1972; LL.D., U. Portland, 1968; m. Jimmie G. Bland, Jan. 2, 1942; children—James B., Deborah M., State R.; m. 2d, Mary G. Wells, Nov. 25, 1967; children (adopted)—Pamela, Katy. Gen. sales mgr., then v.p. sales, dir. Pioneer Air Lines, 1947-55; v.p. sales Continental Air Lines, Inc., 1955-57, v.p.-exec. adminstrn., 1957-58, exec. v.p., dir., 1958-65; pres. dir. Braniff Airways, Inc., Dallas, 1965-68; chmn. bd., pres. Braniff Internat., 1968-70, chmn. bd., chief exec. officer, dir., 1970—; dir. First Internat. Bancshares. Decorated Order of Balboa; Order of Sun; comdr. Order of O'Higgins; recipient Americas award, 1978. Mem. Air Transport Assn. Am. (dir.), Dallas Council on World Affairs (dir.). Mailing address: PO Box 61747 Dallas-Fort Worth Airport TX 75261 Office: Braniff Internat Corp Braniff Pl Dallas-Fort Worth Airport TX 75261

LAWRENCE, HAROLD, orch. exec.; b. N.Y.C., Oct. 22, 1923; s. Nat and Lila (Karsenty) L.; ed. City Coll., N.Y.; m. Mary Morris, Apr. 6, 1963. Dir. recorded music radio sta. WQXR, N.Y.C., 1950-56; dir. classical div. Mercury/Philips Records, 1956-68; gen. mgr. London Symphony Orch., 1968-73; mgr. N.Y. Philharmonic, 1973-75; pres., gen. mgr. Buffalo Philharmonic Orch., 1975-77; now pres., gen. mgr. Oakland (Calif.) Symphony Orch.; lectr. music Bklyn. Coll., also N.Y.C. Bd. Edn., 1951-53; lectr. arts adminstrn. Coll. B, U. Buffalo, 1975-76; cons. Wolf Trap Found., Vienna, Va., 1973-74. Mem. ASCAP. Writer, lectr., composer, producer rec. and radio programs. Home: 4250 Wilshire Blvd Oakland CA 94602

LAWRENCE, HENRY SHERWOOD, physician, educator; b. N.Y.C., Sept. 22, 1916; s. Victor John and Agnes (Whalen) L.; A.B., N.Y. U., 1938, M.D., 1943; m. Dorothea Wetherbee, Nov. 13, 1943; children—Dorothea, Victor, Geoffrey. Mem. faculty N.Y. U. Sch. Medicine, N.Y.C., 1947—, John Wyckoff fellow in medicine, 1948-49, dir. student health, 1950-57, head infectious disease and immunology div., 1959—, prof. medicine, 1961—, co-dir. med. services, 1964—, dir. cancer center, 1974-79. Vis. physician Univ. Hosp., Bellevue Hosp., 1964—; cons. medicine Manhattan VA Hosp., 1964—, infectious disease program com. VA Research Service, 1960-63; cons. allergy and immunology study sect. USPHS, 1960-63, chmn., 1963-65; asso. mem. commn. on streptococcal and staphylococcal diseases Armed Forces Epidemiological Bd., Dept. Def., 1956-73; mem. coms. Nat. Acad. Scis.-NRC, 1957-62, chmn. com. transplantation, 1968-70; mem. NRC, 1970-72; mem. allergy and infectious disease panel Health Research Council, N.Y.C., 1962-75, co-chmn., 1968-75; mem. sci. adv. council Am. Cancer Soc., 1973-77. Served to lt. M.C., USNR, World War II. Commonwealth Found. fellow Univ. Coll., London, Eng., 1959; recipient Research Career Devel. award USPHS, 1960-65; prize Alpha Omega Alpha, 1943; Meritorious Sci. Achievement award N.Y. U. Alumni Assn., 1970; von Pirquet Gold medal Ann. Forum on Allergy, 1972; award A.C.P., 1973; Sci. Achievement award Am. Coll. Allergists, 1974; Sci. medal N.Y. Acad. Medicine, 1974; Bristol Sci. award Infectious Diseases Soc. Am., 1974; Charles V. Chapin medal, 1975; Lila Gruber honor award Am. Acad. Dermatology, 1975; Alumni Achievement award N.Y. U. Washington Sq. Coll., 1979; diplomate Am. Bd. Internal Medicine. Fellow A.C.P. (Bronze medal 1973), Am. Acad. Allergy (hon.), Royal Coll. Physicians and Surgeons Glasgow (hon.); mem. Nat. Acad. Scis., Assn. Am. Physicians, Am. Soc. for Clin. Investigation, Am. Assn. Immunologists, Soc. for Exptl. Biology and Medicine (editorial bd. procs.), Interurban Clin. Club, Harvey Soc. (sec. 1957-60, lectr. 1973—, councillor 1974-77), Peripatetic Clin. Soc., Infectious Diseases Soc. (charter, councillor 1970-72), Royal Soc. Medicine (affiliate) (Eng.), Internat. Transplantation Soc. (chmn. constn. com., councillor), Societe Francaise D'Allergie (corr.), Alpha Omega Alpha. Editor: Medical Clinics of North America, 1957; Cellular and Humoral Aspects of Hypersensitive States, 1959; (with M. Landy) Mediators of Cellular Immunity, 1969. Editorial bd. Transplantation, Ann. of Internal Medicine; founder, editor-in-chief Cellular Immunology. Research, publs. on characterization transfer factor in cellular immunity, mechanisms tissue damage and homograft rejection in man. Home: 343 E 30th St New York NY 10016

LAWRENCE, JACOB, educator, painter; b. Atlantic City, Sept. 7, 1917; s. Jacob and Roselee (Armstead) L.; student Harlem Art Workshop, N.Y.C., 1932-39; scholar Am. Artists Sch., N.Y.C., 1938-39; A.F.D., Denison U., 1970; Dr. Fine Arts (hon.), Pratt Inst., 1970, Colby Coll., 1976; m. Gwendolyn Knight, July 24, 1941. Exhibited John Brown Series under auspices Am. Fedn. Art, 1947, 30 paintings on history U.S., Alan Gallery, 1957; one-man shows including Migration Series, Mus. Modern Art, 1944, Downtown Gallery, N.Y.C., 1941, 43, 45, 47, 50, 53, M'Bari Artists and Writers Club, Nigeria, 1962, Terry Dintenfass Gallery, N.Y.C., 1963; works included Johnson Wax Co. World tour group exhbn., 1963, U.S. State Dept. group exhbn. in Pakistan, 1963; retrospective exhbn. Whitney Mus. Am. Art, 1974; commd. for graphic impressions 1977 Inauguration, Washington; represented in Met. Mus. Art, Mus. Modern Art, Whitney Mus., Phillips Meml. Gallery, Wash., Portland (Oreg.) Mus., Worcester (Mass.) Mus., Balt. Mus. Art, Wichita Art Mus., Albright Art Gallery, Buffalo, AAAL, N.Y.C., Mus. Modern Art, S ao Paulo, Brazil, R.I. Sch. Design, Va. Mus. Fine Arts, Bklyn. Mus., IBM Corp., Container Corp. Am., various univs.; artist Yaddo Found., Saratoga, 1954-55; instr. Pratt Inst. Art Sch., N.Y.C., 1958-65, Art Students League, N.Y.C., 1967-69, New Sch. Social Research, N.Y.C., 1966-71; artist in residence Brandeis U., 1965—; coordinator of the arts Pratt Inst., 1970—, prof. art, 1970; prof. art U. Wash., Seattle, 1970—, Disting. Faculty lectr., 1978. Bd. govs. Skowhegan Sch. Painting and Sculpture; mem. Fulbright Art Com., 1966-67; mem. Wash. State Arts Commn., 1976—; elector Hall of Fame for Gt. Americans, 1976—; mem. Nat. Endowment for Arts, 1978—. Rosenwald fellow, 1940, 41, 42; recipient purchase prize Artists for Victory, 1942, Atlanta U., 1948; Guggenheim fellow, 1945; Opportunity mag. award, 1948; Norman Wait Harris medal Art Inst. Chgo., 1948; Acad. Arts and Letters grantee, 1953; Chapelbrook Found. grantee, 1955; 1st prize in mural competition for UN Bldg., Nat. Council U.S. Art, Inc., 1955; recipient Retrospective Exhbn. with Definitive Catalogue, Ford Found., 1960, Whitney Mus. Modern Art, 1974; works selected as part of exchange exhibit with Soviet Union, 1959; Spingarn medal N.A.A.C.P., 1970; ann. citation Nat. Assn. Schs. Art, 1973. Mem. Artist Equity Assn. (past sec., pres. N.Y. chpt. 1957), Nat. Inst. Arts and Letters. Author: Harriet and the Promised Land, 1968; illustrator Aesop's Fables, 1970. Address: 4316 37th Ave NE Seattle WA 98105. *As an artist, I hope to contribute something of value to life in general and to my fellow-man in particular. I hope that when my life ends... I would have added a little beauty, perception and quality for those who follow. During my life-time also...I hope to learn and add further motivation, insight and dimension as to my own thinking.*

LAWRENCE, JAMES, architect; b. Milton, Mass., May 30, 1907; s. James and Marion Lee (Peabody) L.; B.A., Harvard U., 1929; postgrad. Cambridge (Eng.) U., 1929-30; spl. student M.I.T., 1932-35; m. Martina Louise Brandegee, Sept. 9, 1933 (div. 1959); children—James, Martina, Edward Peabody, Robert Prescott; m. 2d Frances Weeks, Jan. 9, 1973. Mem. staff Leland & Larsen, Boston, 1939-42, 45-55; partner Child Lawrence & Shannon, Boston, 1955-60, Lawrence Shannon & Underwood, Boston, 1960-63; prin. James Lawrence, Architect, Brookline, Mass., 1963—; mem. Mass. Art Commn. Trustee Wellesley Coll., 1948-66, Gardner Museum, Boston, 1942-45. Served to maj. USAAF, 1942-45. Decorated Bronze Star. Fellow AIA (nat. dir.), Am. Acad. Arts and Scis., Royal Soc. Arts (Benjamin Franklin fellow); mem. Mass. State Assn. Architects (pres. 1953-55), Boston Soc. Architects (pres. 1962-64), English Speaking Union (pres. Boston chpt. 1947-52). Democrat. Episcopalian. Clubs: Tavern, Harvard, Union Boat; The Country (Brookline). Home and Office: 282 Newton St Brookline MA 02146

LAWRENCE, JAMES HAROLD, JR., mech. engr., educator; b. Beatrice, Nebr., Feb. 9, 1932; s. James Harold and Doris Edris (Wheeler) L.; B.S. in Mech. Engring., Tex. Tech. U., 1956, M.S. in

Mech. Engring., 1960; Ph.D. (Ford Found. fellow), Tex. A. and M. U., 1965; m. Jane Lenore Matthews, Jan. 16, 1955; children—Jenny Ann, Julie Kay. Design engr. Gen. Electric Co., Richland, Wash., 1957; prof. mech. engring. Tex. Tech. U., Lubbock, 1956—, now chmn. dept. mech. engring. Cons. to various law firms. Mem. Emergency Med. Service Study Group, Lubbock, 1973. Mem. Am. Soc. Engring. Edn. (chmn. ann. conf. 1973), ASME, Am. Soc. Heating, Refrigerating and Air-Conditioning Engrs., Lubbock C. of C., Pi Tau Sigma, Phi Kappa Phi. Methodist (chmn. bd. trustees 1970—). Home: 6027 Norfolk St Lubbock TX 79413

LAWRENCE, JEROME, writer; b. Cleve., July 14, 1915; s. Samuel and Sarah (Rogen) Schwartz; B.A., Ohio State U., 1937, L.H.D. (hon.), 1963; D.Litt., Fairleigh Dickinson U., 1968; Dr. Fine Arts (hon.), Villanova U., 1969. Reporter, telegraph editor Wilmington (O.) News Jour., 1937; editor Lexington (O.) Daily News, 1937; continuity editor radio sta. KMPC, 1937-39; staff writer CBS, 1939-41; scenario writer Paramount Studios, 1941; free lance writer-dir. as Lawrence and Lee, 1942—; master playwright N.Y. U. Inst. Performing Arts, 1967-69; vis. prof. Ohio State U., 1969—; author-dir. for radio and television: The Railroad Hour, Columbia Workshop, Favorite Story, They Live Forever, Date with Judy, Hallmark Playhouse, Frank Sinatra Show; Army-Navy programs: D-Day, VE- Day, VJ-Day; appeared in The Life and Times of Paul Muni, 1974; a founder, overseas corr. Armed Forces Radio Service; founder, trustee Am. Playwrights Theatre, pres., 1968—; co-founder, judge Margo Jones award; bd. mem. Bd. Standards of Living Theatre; bd. dirs. Nat. Repertory Theatre, Am. Conservatory Theatre; mem. adv. bd. Eugene O'Neill Found., USDAN Center for Creative and Performing Arts. Mem. State Dept. Cultural Exchange Drama Panel, 1961-69. Recipient N.Y. Press Club award 1942; Coll. City N.Y. award, 1948; Radio-TV Life award, 1948, 52, Peabody award, 1949, 52; Radio-TV Mirror award, 1952, 53; Variety Showmanship award, 1954; Donaldson award, 1955; Variety Critics poll, 1955; Outer-Circle Critics award, 1955, Ohioana award, 1955; spl. citation War Dept.; Brit. Drama Critics award, 1960; Ohio Press Club award, 1959; State Dept. medal, 1968; Regasus award, 1970; named playwright of year Baldwin-Wallace Coll., 1960; Centennial Award medal Ohio State U., 1970. Mem. Acad. Motion Picture Arts and Scis., Acad. TV Arts and Scis., ANTA (dir., v.p.), Ohio State U. Assn. (dir.), Radio Writers' Guild (a founder, pres.), Writers Guild Am. (dir., founding mem.), Dramatists Guild (council), A.S.C.A.P., Phi Beta Kappa, Sigma Delta Chi, Zeta Beta Tau. Club: Players (N.Y.C.). Co-author, dir.; (album) One God. Author: Live Spelled Backwards, 1969, Off Mike; co-author (all with Robert E. Lee): (musicals) Look, Ma, I'm Dancin', 1948 Shangri-La, 1956, Mame, 1966, Dear World, 1969; (plays): Inherit the Wind (named best fgn. play of year London Critics Poll 1960; 7 Antoinette Perry awards), 1955, Auntie Mame, 1956,, the Gang's All Here, 1959, Only in America, 1959, A Call on Kuprin, 1961, Diamond Orchid (revised as Sparks Fly Upward, 1966), 1965, The Incomparable Max, 1969, The Crocodile Smile, 1970, The Night Thoreau Spent in Jail, 1970; (screenplay) The Night Thoreau Spent in Jail, 1971; Jabberwock, 1974; Decca Dramatic Albums, Musi-Plays.*

LAWRENCE, JOHN FREDERICK, newspaper editor; b. Cleve., Feb. 6, 1934; s. Charles Wesley and Helen Mary (Defenbacher) L.; B.A., Oberlin Coll., 1956; m. Elinor Georgette Holzinger, Sept. 4, 1955; children—Deborah, Wesley, David, William. Corr. from Oberlin (Ohio) for Cleve. Plain Dealer, 1954-56; reporter Wall St. Jour., N.Y.C., 1956, Cleve., 1957-58, Chgo., 1959-61, bur. chief, Phila., 1962-63, Pitts., 1963-65, asst. mng. editor Pacific Coast edit., San Francisco, 1965-68; financial editor Los Angeles Times, 1968-72, Washington bur. chief, 1972-75, asst. mng. editor-econ. affairs, 1975—; corr. Economist of London, 1960-72. Coach Lafayette (Calif.) Youth Basketball, 1967-68; den leader San Gabriel Valley council Boy Scouts Am., 1969-70; chmn. sch. site council Paradise Canyon Sch., 1978. Recipient Best Sports Story award San Francisco Press Club, 1968; Loeb Achievement award, 1971; John Hancock award, 1971. Author: (with Paul E. Steiger) The '70s Crash and How To Survive It, 1970. Home: 5302 Ivafern Ln La Cañada CA 91011 Office: Times Mirror Sq Los Angeles CA 90053

LAWRENCE, JOHN MILLER, biologist; b. Cape Girardeau, Mo., Oct. 11, 1937; s. John Thanet and Georgia Lee (Miller) L.; B.S., S.E. Mo. State Coll., 1958; M.A., U. Mo., 1960; Ph.D., Stanford U., 1965. Asst. prof. U. South Fla., 1965-71, asso. prof., 1971-75, prof. biology, 1975—. Mem. Am. Soc. Zoologists, Marine Biol. Assn. U.K. (life), Scottish Marine Biol. Assn., Fla. Acad. Sci., Ecol. Soc. Am., Am. Soc. Limnology and Oceanography. Research in physiol. ecology of marine invertebrates. Office: Dept Biology U South Fla Tampa FL 33620

LAWRENCE, JUSTUS BALDWIN, pub. relations exec.; b. Cleve., Dec. 16, 1903; s. L. N. and Dorothy (Lyman) L.; Ph.B., Yale, 1927; m. Mary Peace (dec.); m. 2d, Carlene Roberts Teetor. Newspaperman and mag. writer, 1928-33; advt. and publicity dir., asst. to Samuel Goldwyn, motion pictures, 1933- 39; pub. relations dir. Assn. Motion Picture Producers, Hollywood, Calif., 1939-41; exec. v.p. J. Arthur Rank Orgn., Inc., N.Y.C., 1945-51; now pres. J.B. Lawrence, Inc., pub. relations and research, N.Y.C. Dep. chief pub. information, SHAPE, Paris, 1951-52. U.S. del. 10th UNESCO Conf., 1958; presdl. mem. U.S.O. Corp., 1960-62. Served as pub. relations aide to Lord Mountbatten, Commandos, attached to Brit. Army, 1942-43; col., gen. staff U.S. Army, chief pub. relations officer ETO, 1943-45. Decorated Legion of Merit, Bronze Star (U.S.); Legion of Honor (France); Order Brit. Empire. Clubs: Yale, Sky (N.Y.C.); Army and Navy, Nat. Press, 1925 F St. (Washington); The Travellers (Paris); Bucks (London); University (Mexico City); Pilgrims U.S. Contbr. articles to popular mags. Home: 580 Park Ave New York NY 10021 Office: 280 Madison Ave New York NY 10016

LAWRENCE, KENNETH MORRISON, exploration cons.; b. Gilmer, Tex., June 24, 1908; s. Eunice Lee and Valona (Morrison) L.; B.A. in Physics, U. Tex., 1937; m. Marian Tarlton, July 1, 1938; children—Kenneth Lee, Linda. With Amerada Petroleum Corp., Tulsa, 1929-69, chief geophysicist, 1951-62, v.p., 1962-68, sr. v.p., 1968-69; pres. subsidiary Geophys. Research Corp., 1961-71; sr. v.p. Amerada div. Amerada Hess Corp., 1969, exec. v.p., 1970; exploration cons., 1971—; ind. producer oil and gas. Mem. Soc. Exploration Geophysicists, European Assn. Exploration Geophysicists, Tulsa Geol. Soc. Geophys. Soc. Tulsa. Address: 3910 S Gary Pl Tulsa OK 74105

LAWRENCE, LES (EDWIN), artist, educator; b. Corpus Christi, Tex., Dec. 17, 1940; s. Raymond Leslie and Florence Edith (LaCompt) L.; B.A., Southwestern State Coll., Weatherford, Okla., 1961; M.F.A., Ariz. State U., 1970; m. Jaye Ackman, June 18, 1969; 1 dau., Laurie L. Mem. faculty Hardin-Simmons U., Abilene, Tex., 1966-68; mem. faculty Grossmont Coll., El Cajon, Calif., 1970—; exhibited in one man shows including: Gallery A., Taos, N.Mex., 1967, San Angelo (Tex.) State Coll., 1968, Ariz. State Coll., 1970, Palomar Coll., San Marcos, Calif., 1973, Elaine Horwitch Gallery, Scottsdale, Ariz., 1974, Ariz. State U., Tempe, 1974, Mira Costa Coll., Oceanside, Calif., 1976, Triad Gallery, San Diego, 1976; exhibited in group shows including: Gallery A, Toas, N.Mex., 1968, W. Tex. Mus., Lubbock, 1969, Heard Mjs., Phoenix, 1969, Yuma (Ariz.) Fine Art Center, 1971, Grossmont Coll. Gallery, El Cajon, 1972, Oakland (Calif.) Mus., 1974, Mus. Contemporary Crafts, N.Y.C., 1974, Robinson Gallery, Houston, 1975, Fairtree Gallery, N.Y.C., 1975, Elaine Horwitch Gallery, Scottsdale, Ariz., 1975, E.B. Crocker Gallery, Sacramento, 1975, Galeria Del Sol, Santa Barbara, 1976; represented in permanent collections including: Whitty Mus., San Antonio, Lubbock (Tex.) Municipal Art Center, Hardin-Simmons U., Ariz. State U., Tempe, Yuma (Ariz.) Fine Arts Assn., Pacific Luth. U., Tacoma, Wash., E.B. Crocker Art Gallery, Sacramento, Calif., Phoenix Art Mus., Western Wash. State U. Mem. World Crafts Council, Am. Crafts Council, Allied Craftsmen San Diego. Baptist. Home: 2097 Valley View Blvd El Cajon CA 92020 Office: Grossmont Coll Art Dept 8800 Grossmont Dr El Cajon CA 92020

LAWRENCE, LOREN E., ambassador; b. Hamilton, Kans., Jan. 26, 1926; ed. Washington U., St. Louis; grad. sr. seminar in fgn. policy Fgn. Service Inst., 1974. Commd. fgn. service officer Dept. State, 1954; spl. officer Refugee Relief Program, Rotterdam, Netherlands, from 1954; consular officer U.S. consulate, Hong Kong, Macao, Tel Aviv, until 1966; personnel mgmt. specialist Dept. State, Washington, from 1966, career mgmt. officer, until 1970, dep. dir. personnel for mgmt., 1974-75, dep. adminstr. Bur. Consular Affairs, 1975-76; counselor for consular affairs U.S. consulate, Manila, Philippines, 1970-73; London, 1976-77; dep. asst. sec. of state for passport services Dept. State, Washington, 1977-79; AEC to Jamaica, 1979—. Served with U.S. Army, 1944-45, 47-53. Office: US Embassy Jamaica Mut Life Center 2 Oxford Rd Suite D Floor Kingston Jamaica*

LAWRENCE, MARK HOWARD, trombonist; b. Ames, Iowa, Oct. 6, 1948; s. Howard Wallace and Lois Wanda (Miller) L.; student U. Mich., 1967-68; B.M., Curtis Inst. Music, 1972; m. Janet Louise Ketchum, June 15, 1974. Prin. trombonist Nat. Symphony of Colombia, 1972, Denver Symphony, 1973-74, San Francisco Symphony, 1974—; mem. faculty Dominican Coll., San Rafael, Calif., 1975, San Francisco Conservatory Music, also San Francisco State U. tchr. trombone; condr. clinics; recitalist. Mem. Am. Fedn. Musicians, Internat. Trombone Assn. Office: 107 War Memorial Vets Bldg San Francisco CA 94102

LAWRENCE, MARY GEORGENE WELLS (MRS. HARDING LAWRENCE), advt. agy. exec.; b. Youngstown, Ohio, May 25, 1928; d. Waldemar and Violet (Berg); ed. Carnegie Inst. Tech., 1949; LL.D., Babson Coll., 1970; m. Harding Lawrence, Nov. 25, 1967; children—James, State, Deborah, Kathryn, Pamela. Copywriter, McKelvey's Dept. Store, Youngstown, 1951-52; fashion advt. mgr. Macy's, N.Y.C., 1952-53; copy group head McCann-Erickson, N.Y.C., 1953-56; with Doyle, Dane, Bernbach, N.Y.C., 1957-64, v.p., asso. copy chief, 1963-64; sr. partner, creative dir. Jack Tinker & Partners, N.Y.C., 1964-66; chmn. bd., chief exec. officer Wells, Rich, Greene, Inc., N.Y.C., 1966—. Named to Copywriters Hall of Fame, Copy Club, 1969; named Mktg. Stateswoman of Year, Sales Execs. Club N.Y., 1970, Advt. Woman of Year, Am. Advt. Fedn., 1971. Mem. Dallas Advt. Club. Office: Wells Rich Greene Inc 767 Fifth Ave New York NY 10022*

LAWRENCE, MERLE, med. educator; b. Remsen, N.Y., Dec. 26, 1915; s. George William and Alice Rutherford (Bowne) L.; A.B., Princeton, 1938, M.A., 1940; Ph.D., 1941; m. Roberta Ashby Taylor Harper, Aug. 8, 1942; children—Linda Alice Lawrence Nolt, Roberta Harper Lawrence Henderson, James Bowne. NRC fellow Johns Hopkins Hosp., 1941; asst. prof. psychology Princeton, 1946-50, asso. prof., 1950-52; asso. research Lempert Inst. Otology, N.Y.C., 1946-52; asso. prof. dept. otolaryngology U. Mich. Med. Sch., 1952-57, prof. otolaryngology, 1957—, research asso. Inst. Indsl. Health, 1952—; prof. psychology U. Mich. Coll. Lit. Sci. and Arts, 1957—, dir. Kresge Hearing Research Inst., 1961—; mem. Nat. Adv. Neurol. and Communicative Disorders and Stroke Council, 1976—; chmn. bd. Pan-Cayman House, Grand Cayman, B.W.I., 1972—; mem. communicative disorders research tng. com. Nat. Inst. Neurol. Diseases and Blindness, 1961-65; mem. communicative scis. study sect. div. research grants NIH, 1965-69, chmn., 1967-69, mem. communicative disorders rev. com., 1972-76. Served as naval aviator USNR, 1941-46, 50-51; PTO; Korean conflict. Decorated Purple Heart, Air medal with nine gold stars; recipient Sec. Navy Commendation, award merit Am. Acad. Ophthalmology and Otolaryngology, 1965, Assn. Research in Otolaryngology, 1979, Am. Otol. Soc., 1967, Distinguished Service award Princeton Class of 1938. NRC fellow, 1941. Fellow Otosclerosis Study Group, Am. Laryngol., Rhinolog. and Otolaryngol. Soc.; mem. AAAS, Acoustical Soc. Am., Mich. Acoustical Soc. (pres. 1956), Am. Acad. Ophthalmology and Otolaryngology, Am. Otological Soc., Collegium Oto-Rhino-Laryngologicum Amicitiae Sacrum, Soc. U. Laryngologists, Assn. Research Otolaryngology, Am. Auditory Soc. (council 1978-82), Am. Tinnitus Assn., Quarter Century Wireless Assn. Rotarian. Clubs: Centurion; Mich. Masters Swim, Ann Arbor Racquet. Home: 2029 Vinewood Blvd Ann Arbor MI 48104

LAWRENCE, MERLOYD LUDINGTON, editor; b. Pasadena, Calif., Aug. 1, 1932; d. Nicholas Saltus and Mary Lloyd (Macy) Ludington; A.B., Radcliffe Coll., 1954, M.A., 1957; m. Seymour Lawrence, June 21, 1952; children—Macy, Nicholas. With Houghton Mifflin Co., 1955-57; free lance translator, 1957-65; editor, treas., v.p. Seymour Lawrence Inc., Boston, 1965—. Treas., v.p. Milford House Properties, Ltd., N.S., Can., 1975—; trustee Milton (Mass.) Acad., 1974—; mem. com. on clin. investigations Beth Israel Hosp. Mem. Am. Translators Assn., Mass. Audubon Soc. (dir. 1979—), Phi Beta Kappa. Translator works of Flaubert and Balzac, modern French fiction, German and Swedish children's books. Contbr. articles to nat. mags. Home: 102 Chestnut St Boston MA 02108 Office: 61 Beacon St Boston MA 02108

LAWRENCE, NATHANIEL MORRIS, educator; b. Okmulgee, Okla., June 28, 1917; s. Nathaniel Morris and Anna (Trask) L.; A.B., Stanford, 1938; S.T.B., Harvard, 1942, M.A. in Philosophy, 1946, Ph.D., 1949; m. Mary Elizabeth Wood, Oct. 9, 1939; children—Mary Ellen, Nathaniel Spencer, Roger Trask Wood. Instr. philosophy Wellesley Coll., 1945-47, U. Ill., 1947-50; asst. prof. La. State U., 1950-52; lectr. Harvard, 1952-53; asst. prof. U. Calif. at Los Angeles, 1953-55; vis. lectr. Yale, 1955-56, asso. prof., 1956-60; prof. philosophy Williams Coll., 1960—, Mass. prof. philosophy, 1976—. Mem. Metaphys. Soc. Am., Internat. Soc. for Study Time, Soc. for Phenomenology and Existential Philosophy. Author: Whitehead's Philosophical Development, 1956; (with R. Brumbaugh) Six Philosophers on Education, 1963; (with R. Brumbaugh) Philosophical Themes in Modern Education, 1973; Alfred North Whitehead, 1974. Editor: (with Daniel O'Connor) Readings in Existential Phenomenology, 1967; (with J.T. Fraser) The Study of Time II, 1975; (with J.T. Fraser and D. Park) The Study of Time III, 1978. Contbr. articles to J.T. profl. jours. Home: 80 South St Williamston MA 01267

LAWRENCE, PAUL ROGER, educator; b. Rochelle, Ill., Apr. 26, 1922; s. Howard Cyrus and Clara (Luther) L.; student Grand Rapids Jr. Coll., 1939-41; A.B., Albion Coll., 1943; M.B.A., Harvard, 1947, D.C.S., 1950; m. Martha G. Stiles, Dec. 14, 1948; children—Anne Talcott, William Stiles. Faculty, Harvard Bus. Sch., Boston, 1947—, asst. prof., 1951-56, asso. prof., 1956-61, prof. organizational behavior, 1961-68, Donham prof. organizational behavior, 1968; dir. Millipore Corp. Served to lt. USNR, 1943-46. Mem. Am. Sociol. Assn., Acad. Mgmt. Author: The Changing of Organizational Behavior Patterns; (with others) Management Behavior and Foreman Attitude, Administering Changes, Organizational Behavior and Administration, Top Management Behavior in a Large Organization, Industrial Jobs and the Worker, Organization and Environment, Studies in Organization Design; Mayors in Action; Developing Organizations: Diagnosis and Action; Matrix. Home: 17 Willard St Cambridge MA 02138 Office: Humphrey House Soldiers Field Boston MA 02164

LAWRENCE, PHILIP SIGNOR, health statistics cons.; b. Oak Park, Ill., Nov. 6, 1914; s. Philip S. and Mary (Phillips) L.; B.A., Denison U., 1937; D.Sc., Johns Hopkins, 1940; m. Elizabeth Scott, Sept. 6, 1941; children—Philip, Robert, William, Patricia. Research asst. Johns Hopkins Sch. Pub. Health, Balt., 1940-41, Harvard, 1941; chief family studies USPHS, Washington, 1946-56, chief div. health interview statistics, 1957-66, cons. in genetics, 1940-41; asso. dir. Nat. Center for Health Statistics, Washington, 1966-73, dep. dir., 1973-76; cons. on health statistics, 1976—; cons. to internat. orgns. Bd. dirs. Washington Area council Boy Scouts Am., 1955-56. Served to lt. comdr. USNR, 1941-45; capt. Res. ret. Recipient Superior Service award USPHS, 1973. Fellow Am. Statis. Assn.; mem. Wash. Statis. Soc., Internat. Assn. Survey Statisticians, Interam. Statis. Inst., Internat. Union Sci. Study Population, Phi Beta Kappa, Omicron Delta Kappa, Delta Omega. Contbr. articles to profl. jours. Home: 9848 Singleton Dr Bethesda MD 20034

LAWRENCE, RICHARD DAY, army officer; b. Eastland, Tex., July 31, 1930; s. Milton Elmer and Mary (Day) L.; student Va. Military Inst., 1947-49; B.S., U.S. Military Acad., 1953; M.S., U. So. Calif., 1961; Ph.D., Ohio State U., 1968; postgrad. U.S. Army War Coll., 1970-71; m. Patsy Ann Wiese, June 6, 1953; children—Anne Hunter, Kevin Scott. Commd. 2d lt., U.S. Army, 1953, advanced through grades to maj. gen., 1978; chief of armor and infantry weapons systems analysis, Office of Asst. vice chief of staff U.S. Army, Washington, 1971-72; fed. exec. fellow Brookings Instn., Washington, 1972-73; armor brigade comdr. 1st cavalry div., Fort Hood, Tex., 1973-75; project mgr. Saudi Arabian N.G. modernization, 1975-77; chief tank forces mgmt. Office of Chief of Staff, Washington, 1977-78; mil. negotiator U.S. Del. Egyptian-Israeli Peace Talks, Washington, 1978; chief spl. military mission to Saudi Arabia and North Yemen, 1979; chief Army Force Modernization Coordination, Office of Chief of Staff, U.S. Army, Washington, 1979—. Decorated Silver Star, Legion of Merit, and others. Mem. Assn. U.S. Army, U.S. Army Armor Assn., Sigma Xi. Methodist. Office: Hdqrs Dept Army Washington DC 20310

LAWRENCE, RICHARD ELMER, educator; b. St. Paul, Aug. 10, 1920; s. Arthur E. and Gladys (Steele) L.; B.S., U. Minn., 1942; M.A., Columbia, 1948, Ed.D., 1953; m. Joy Lynn Rotton, Aug. 15, 1975; children by previous marriage—Arthur Michael, Patti Jean (Mrs. Stephen Teague), Cheryl Marion. Tchr. jr. and sr. high sch. N.Y., 1946-53; asst. prof. edn. No. Ill. State Tchrs. Coll., 1953-55; asso. sec. Am. Assn. Colls. for Tchr. Edn., Washington, 1955-57, asso. exec. sec., 1961-68; asso. prof. edn., asso. dean summer sessions Syracuse U., 1957-61; dean Coll. of Edn. of U. N.Mex., 1969-73, prof. ednl. adminstrn., 1973—. Dir. NDEA Nat. Inst. Advanced Study in Teaching Disadvantaged Youth, 1966-68; mem. Commn. on Edn. for the Teaching Profession, 1969-71; mem. exec. com. Assn. Colls. and Schs. of Edn. in State Univ. and Land Grant Colls., 1969-73. Cons. Albuquerque Goals Program, 1969. Served with USNR, 1942-45. Mem. AAAS, Am. Ednl. Research Assn., Assn. Tchr. Educators, Assn. Supervision and Curriculum Development, Nat. Soc. Study of Edn., NEA, Phi Delta Kappa. Unitarian. Home: 17 Berm NW Albuquerque NM 87120

LAWRENCE, RICHARD WESLEY, JR., business exec.; b. N.Y.C., Jan. 16, 1909; s. Richard Wesley and Ruth (Earle) L.; B.S., Princeton, 1931; LL.B., Columbia, 1934; m. Marjorie Fitch, June 23, 1933 (dec. Feb. 1945); children—Ruth Earle (Mrs. Bates Wilson), Alida (Mrs. Lloyd W. Currey); m. 2d, Elizabeth Hand Wadhams, Apr. 13, 1946; 1 dau., Elizabeth Lawrence Lojeski. Admitted to N.Y. bar, 1935, practiced in N.Y.C., 1935-42; former chmn. bd. Printers Ink Pub. Co., Bankers Comml. Corp.; pres. Conservation Mgmt., Inc., Elizabethtown; dir. Elizabethtown Builders, Elizabethtown Publs., Umont Mining, Inc., Eviron. Resource Cons., Inc. Chmn. Adirondack Park Agy., 1971-75; chmn. Commr. Edn.'s com. on Reference and Research Library Resources; mem. Gov.'s Commn. on Future of Adirondacks; past chmn. council State U. Coll., Plattsburgh. Past chmn. bd. trustees North Country Community Coll.; trustee Adirondack Conservancy, Assn. for Protection Adirondacks, Adirondack Council; pres. Crary Edn. Found., Elizabethtown Library, Crown Point Found. Served as capt. USAAF, 1942-44; lt. col. ret. Recipient North Country citation St. Lawrence U., 1969. Hon. mem. N.Y. Library Assn. (Velma Moore award), N.Y. State Hist. Assn. (trustee), Essex County Hist. Soc. (v.p., dir.); mem. Def. Orientation Conf. Assn. (v.p., dir.). Clubs: Union League, Princeton, Explorers (N.Y.C.); Ausable. Home: Elizabethtown NY 12932 Office: Church St Elizabethtown NY 12932

LAWRENCE, ROBERT, conductor, music critic; b. N.Y.C, Mar. 18, 1912; s. Robert Julian and Isabelle (Lawrence) L.; B.A., Coll. City N.Y., 1931; M.A., Columbia, 1934; fellow in conducting Juilliard Grad. Sch., 1933-36. Joined N.Y. Herald Tribune's music staff, 1939; condr. N.Y.C. WPA Symphony Orch., 1940; made recs. Wagner's Ring of the Nibelung (speech and piano) for RCA Victor, 1940; ofcl. lectr. Phil. Orch.'s N.Y. season, 1940-41; guest condr. Ill., R.I., N.Y.C. symphonies, Wallenstein Sinfonietta, Radio City Music Hall Broadcasting Symphony, 1941-42; condr. Thais with Met. Opera Co. singers in Montreal, 1942, Trojans with Am. Opera Soc., 1960; guest condr. Ballet Theater, 1942, Buenos Aires Philharmonic, Nat. Symphony Peru, Brazilian Symphony Orch., Nat. Orch. Guatemala, 1960; apptd. dance critic N.Y. Herald Tribune, 1942; the quiz expert in nat. broadcast every week of Met. Opera Saturday matinee, 1941-42, permanent quizmaster, 1952-57; noted as authority on music of Hector Berlioz; guest condr., opera and symphony, Italy, May-June, 1944; dir. Tosca, Royal Opera, Rome, 1 1944-45; symphony concerts, 1945; Rome Radio Orch. 1944; guest condr. St. Cecilia Acad. Orch., Rome, 1945; dir. Maggio mus. Orch., Florence, 1945; debut as condr. N.Y. Philharmonic-Symphony, 1948; condr., music dir. Phoenix Symphony Orch., 1949-52; guest condr. NBC Symphony, 1953, Orquesta Sinfonica Nacional, Mexico, 1953, Royal Philharmonic (London), 1955, Presdl. Philharmonic (Ankara), 1955, Symphony of the Air (N.Y.), 1955; conducted Damnation of Faust, at Carnegie Hall, with Schola Cantorum, N.Y. Philharmonic, 1954. Condr., music dir. Presdl. Symphony Orch. Turkey (Ankara), 1957-59; artistic dir., condr. Friends of French Opera, 1962—; featured music commentator Station WQXR, 1963-68. Dir. dept. opera Peabody Inst., Balt., 1968-73; lectr. opera N.Y. State U., Purchase, 1971-72; adj. prof. opera Temple U., Phila., 1976—. Author adaptations Carmen, Aida, Lohengrin, Haensel and Gretel, 1937; The Ring of the Nibelung, 4 vols., 1938; Pinafore, The Mikado, The Gondoliers, 1939; Petrouchka, The Three Cornered Hat, 1940; Boris Godounoff, Bartered Bride, Magic Flute, 1942; (in collaboration), Metropolitan Opera Guide, 1939; Victor Book of Ballets and Ballet

Music, 1950; The World of Opera, 1955. Author: A Rage for Opera, 1971. Address: 140 E 28th St New York NY 10016

LAWRENCE, ROBERT THEODORE, real estate exec.; b. Babylon, N.Y., Aug. 29, 1913; s. Joseph William and Mary (Byrns) L.; B.A., Columbia, 1934; m. Shirley Winberg, Oct. 11, 1947; children—Karin, Kristin, Karla, Kimberly. Vice pres., dir. Charles F. Noyes, N.Y.C., 1935-60; sr. v.p. Wm. A. White & Sons, N.Y.C., 1960—; dir. Knickerbocker Fed. Savs. & Loan Assn. Trustee Clinton Hall Assn., Merc. Library, N.Y. Optometric Soc. Served with USNR, 1941-45. Mem. Friendly Sons St. Patrick. Rotarian. Clubs: Babylon Yacht (West Islip); Southward Ho Country (Brightwaters, N.Y.). Home: 39 Davison Ln East Ilsip NY 11795 Office: 51 E 42d St New York NY 10017

LAWRENCE, RUDDICK CARPENTER, bus. exec.; b. Marquette, Mich., Jan. 5, 1912; s. Willard Carpenter and Verna (Ruddick) L.; B.A. in Journalism cum laude, U. Wash., 1934; m. Barbara Dole, June 5, 1937 (div. 1971); children—Dana Ann (Mrs. Scott Wetstone), Sara Hilary (Mrs. Dean Lee Engelhardt), Megan Elizabeth (Mrs. Roger Cumming), Jean Hathaway (Mrs. Peter Petri), Ruddick C., Daniel Dole; m. 2d, Cherry McDonnell Swasey, Oct. 27, 1973; stepchildren—Leslie Denison Black, Caroline McDonnell Black. Dir. publicity Detroit Inst. Arts, 1934-36; asso. dir. World Adventure Series, Detroit, 1934-36; Western mgr. Am. Boy mag., Chgo., 1936-39; So. mgr. Fortune mag., Time, Inc., Phila., 1939-44, N.Y. mgr., asso. advt. mgr. Fortune mag., N.Y.C., 1946-50; dir. sales devel. TV network, dir. promotion, planning, devel. radio and TV networks NBC, N.Y.C., 1950-53; v.p. N.Y. Stock Exchange, 1953-68; v.p. Continental Oil Co., 1968-77; pres. Lawrence Assos., 1977—; chmn. bd. trustees Sarah Lawrence Coll., 1964-69; bd. mgrs. N.Y. Bot. Garden; chmn., bd. dirs. N.Y. Bd. Trade; bd. dirs. Internat. Film Found., World Adventure Series; gov. Invest-in-Am. Nat. Council, Inc.; dir. U.S.-Arab C. of C., pres. 1976-79. Served from lt. (j.g.) to lt. USNR, 1944-46, staff requirements rev. bd. Office Sec. Navy, Chief Naval Operations. Decorated Star of Jordan, Cedars of Lebanon. Mem. Pub. Relations Soc. N.Y., Pilgrims Soc., Phi Kappa Psi (trustee Endowment Fund Corp.), Sigma Delta Chi. Episcopalian. Clubs: Explorers, Circumnavigators, Bronxville Field, Hemisphere, University, Economic (N.Y.C.); Shelter Island Racquet. Home: 3 Wellington Circle Bronxville NY 10708 (summer) Menantic Rd Shelter Island NY 11964 Office: 30 Rockefeller Plaza Suite 4515 New York NY 10020

LAWRENCE, SEYMOUR, editor, publisher; b. N.Y.C., Feb. 11, 1926; s. Jack and Sophie (Luby) L.; A.B., Harvard, 1948; m. Merloyd Ludington, June 21, 1952; children—Macy, Nicholas. Editor, pub. of Wake, 1945-54; coll. traveler D. Van Nostrand Co., 1948-50; coll. traveler, field editor Ronald Press, 1950-51; spl. asst. to editor Atlantic Monthly, 1952-54, asso. editor Atlantic Monthly Press, 1954, dir., 1955-64; v.p. Alfred A. Knopf, Inc., 1964; founder Seymour Lawrence, Inc., 1965, pres., editor in chief, 1965—. Clubs: Signet Society (Cambridge, Mass.); Union Boat (Boston); Harvard, Century Assn. (N.Y.C.). Home: 102 Chestnut St Boston MA 02108 Office: 61 Beacon St Boston MA 02108

LAWRENCE, STEVE, entertainer; b. Bklyn., July 8; m. Eydie Gorme, Dec. 29, 1957; children—David, Michael. Mem. cast Tonight Show; host Steve Lawrence Show, CBS-TV, 1965; has starred with Eydie Gorme in TV spls. honoring Gershwin, Porter and Berlin (7 Emmy awards); numerous TV guest appearances; performs in leading night clubs; made stage debut in What Makes Sammy Run, 1964; co-starred with wife in Golden Rainbow, N.Y.C., 1967. Hon. chmn. entertainment com. Cerebral Palsy; bd. govs. Brookdale Hosp., N.Y.C. Served with AUS, 1958-60. Recipient N.Y. Drama Critics award for best male performance in mus. comedy, 1964; Emmy award for outstanding TV spl., 1975-76; (with Eydie Gorme) TV Critics Circle award for achievement in music, 1976-77. Club: Friars (gov.) (N.Y.C.). Address: care Arnold Lipsman Steinberg Lipsman & Assos 8961 Sunset Blvd Los Angeles CA 90069

LAWRENCE, THOMAS HOEL, mgmt. cons.; b. New Orleans, July 21, 1913; s. Thomas Hoel and Billie (Marks) L.; grad. Phillips Acad., Andover, Mass., 1931; A.B., Yale, 1935; postgrad. U. Cin., 1938-39; m. Bettie Byrd Rogers, Oct. 17, 1936; children—Thomas Hoel III, Kathryn Byrd (Mrs. William P. Harsh, Jr.). Mgmt. trainee to dir. tng. mfg. dept. Procter & Gamble Co., 1935-48; dir. tng. Hallmark, Inc., 1948-49; asst. to pres. Gt. Lakes Pipeline Co., 1949-50; mgmt. cons., 1950-53; pres. Lawrence-Leiter & Co., Kansas City, Mo., 1953-76, chmn. bd., 1976-78, chmn. emeritus, 1978—; speaker on mgmt., 1950—. Bd. dirs. Nat. Safety Council, 1949-51, Jackson County chpt. ARC, 1960-64. Mem. Am. Mgmt. Assn., Assn. Cons. Mgmt. Engrs. (past pres.), Soc. Advancement Mgmt. (past dir.), Inst. Mgmt. Consultants (founding mem., pres. 1978-79). Clubs: University, Kansas City Country, Mercury (Kansas City, Mo.). Home: 221 W 48th St Kansas City MO 64112 Office: 427 W 12th St Kansas City MO 64105

LAWRENCE, VERA BRODSKY, music historian; b. Norfolk, Va., July 1, 1909; d. Simon and Rose Brodsky; student music (fellow) Juilliard Found., 1928-32; Mus.D. (hon.) N.E. Conservatory, 1976; m. Theodore Lawrence, Feb. 22, 1944 (dec.). Concert pianist, 1930-65; mem. faculty Curtis Inst. Music, Juilliard Sch., 1930's and 40's; mem. music staff CBS, 1939-46; adminstr. publs. Contemporary Music Project, Washington, 1967-70; free-lance writer, editor, historian Am. music, 1970—; artistic cons. Houston Opera production and Deutsche Grammophon rec. of Scott Joplin's Treemonisha, 1975; music adv. and planning panelist, cons. Nat. Endowment for Arts, 1977-79; mem. advisory bd. Gunther Schuller Fund for Studies in Am. Music; editor and compiler: The Piano Works of Louis Moreau Gottschalk, 1969; The Wa-Wan Press, 1970; The Collected Works of Scott Joplin, 1971; author: Music for Patriots, Politicians, and Presidents, 1975; editor: CMP Library and Catalog, 1968. Rockefeller Found. grantee, 1970, 71; Guggenheim fellow, 1976; Nat. Endowment for Humanities grantee, 1978—. Mem. Music Library Assn., N.Y. Hist. Soc. (life), Authors Guild.

LAWRENCE, VICKI ANN, singer, dancer, comedienne; b. Los Angeles, Mar. 26, 1949; d. Howard Axelrad and Ann Alene (Loyd) Lawrence; student U. Calif. at Los Angeles, 1967-70; m. Alvin Adolph Schultz, Jr., Nov. 16, 1974; 1 dau., Courtney Allison. Singer, dancer, comedienne The Carol Burnett Show, CBS, 1967-78, ABC, 1979; appeared in TV movie Having Babies, 1976; recs. include The Night the Lights Went Out in Georgia (Gold record). Recipient Emmy award, 1975-76. Office: 7800 Beverly Blvd Los Angeles CA 90036*

LAWRENCE, VICTOR DANIEL, lawyer; b. Seattle, Apr. 29, 1913; s. Aubrey Daniel and Esther Pauline (Jensen) L.; student So. br. U. Idaho, 1930-32; B.A., U. Wash., 1934, LL.B. cum laude, 1937; m. Mabel Andersen, July 5, 1941; 1 son, Robert Daniel. Admitted to Wash. bar, 1937, since practiced in Seattle; asso. Weter, Roberts & Shefelman, 1937-41, 46-50; partner Hall, Cole & Lawrence, 1950-62, Roberts, Shefelman, Lawrence, Gay & Moch, 1962—. Trustee, Seattle Gen. Hosp., 1969—, pres. trustees, 1972-74; trustee Swedish Hosp. Med. Center, 1978—, sec. trustees, 1978—. Served to capt., judge adv. gen. dept., AUS, 1941-46. Mem. Seattle (trustee 1955-58), Seattle-King County (pres. 1958-59) bar assns., Order of Coif, Delta Theta Phi. Conglist. Club: College (pres. 1966-67) (Seattle). Editorial staff Washington Law Rev., 1935-37. Home: 8203 42d Ave NE Seattle WA 98115 Office: 1818 IBM Bldg Seattle WA 98101

LAWRENCE, WALTER, JR., surgeon; b. Chgo., May 31, 1925; s. Walter and Violette May (Matthews) L.; student Dartmouth, 1943-44; Ph.B., U. Chgo., 1944, S.B., 1945, M.D. with honors, 1948; m. Susan Grayson Shryock, June 20, 1947; children—Walter Thomas, Elizabeth, William Amos, Edward Gene. Intern, Johns Hopkins, 1948-49, asst. resident, 1949-51; resident Meml. Sloan-Kettering Cancer Center, 1951-52, 54-56, research fellow, 1956, asst. mem., asst. attending surgeon, 1957-60, asso. mem., asso. attending surgeon, 1960-66; practice medicine specializing in surgery, N.Y.C., 1956-66, Richmond, Va., 1966—; instr. surgery Cornell U., 1957-58, asst. prof. clin. surgery, 1958-63, clin. asso. prof., 1963-66; vis. investigator Queen Victoria Hosp., East Grinstead, Eng., 1964-65; prof. surgery Med. Coll. Va., Richmond, 1966—, chmn. div. surg. oncology, 1966-76, exec. vice chmn. dept. surgery, 1966-73, acting chmn., 1973-74, Am. Cancer Soc. prof. clin. oncology, 1972-77, dir. Cancer Center, 1974—; chmn. surgery test com. Nat. Bd. Med. Examiners, 1973-77; examiner Am. Bd. Surgery, 1974-78, sr. mem., 1978—; med. dir.-at-large Am. Cancer Soc., 1967—, med. v.p. Va. div., 1975-77, pres., 1977-79, mem. council for research and clin. investigation, 1974-78; bd. sci. counsellors Nat. Cancer Inst., 1978—. Served with USNR, 1942-46, U.S. Army, 1952-54. Recipient Cancer Research award Alfred P. Sloan Found., 1964; J. Shelton Horsley award Am. Cancer Soc., 1973; Distinguished Service award U. Chgo., 1976. Diplomate Am. Bd. Surgery. Fellow A.C.S. (commn. on cancer 1973—, chmn. 1979—), N.Y. Acad. Scis., Royal Soc. Medicine; mem. AAAS, Am. Assn. Cancer Edn., Am. Assn. Cancer Research, Am. Gastroenterol. Assn. (council on cancer 1972-76), Am. Surg. Assn., AMA, Halsted Soc. (past pres.), James Ewing Soc., Soc. Head and Neck Surgeons, Soc. Surgery Alimentary Tract (founder), Soc. Surg. Oncology (exec. com. 1976-77, v.p. 1977-78, pres. 1979-80), Soc. Univ. Surgeons, Surg. Biol. Club, Transplantation Soc., Collegium Internat. Chirurgiae Digestive, Southeastern Surg. Congress, Pan Am. Med. Assn., Société Internationale de Chirurgie, Va. Surg. Soc. (v.p. 1973-74), Argentine Surg. Assn. (hon.), Sigma Xi, Alpha Omega Alpha. Author: (with J.J. Terz) Cancer Management, 1977; mem. editorial bd. Jour. Surg. Oncology, 1978—; asst. editor Cancer, 1962-65. Contbr. articles to med. jours. Home: 6501 Three Chopt Rd Richmond VA 23226 Office: Box 11 Med Coll Va Sta Richmond VA 23298

LAWRENCE, WALTER DAVID, former fgn. service officer, cons. engr.; b. Denver, Nov. 14, 1917; s. Walter David and Eline Olivia (Kronstedt) L.; B.S. in Elec. Engring., U. Colo., 1940; m. Mary Margaret Roosa, July 4, 1941; children—Sherryl Ann (Mrs. Michael D. Lodge), Kirkland Wayne, Glen Alan. Elec. draftsman Giffels & Vallet, architects-engrs., Detroit, 1940; test engr. Gen. Electric Co., 1940-41, contract service engr., 1941-43, factory engr., 1943-45; resource and devel. engr. Bur. Reclamation, 1945-54; elec. engring. adviser Govt. India, 1954-57; rural electrification adviser to Govt. Lebanon, 1957-58; elec. power adviser to Govt. Ceylon, 1958-62; capital loans engrs. USAID/India, 1962-66; assigned Washington, 1966-68; capital project engr., Ankara, Turkey, 1968-73, Jakarta, Indonesia, 1973-77; cons. engr., 1977—. Registered profl. engr., Wyo. Mem. Internat. Inst. String Bass. Toastmaster. Address: 6423 Princeton Dr Alexandria VA 22307

LAWRENCE, WILLARD EARL, educator; b. Chassell, Mich., Apr. 8, 1917; s. William and Ruth Marie (Messner) L.; student Ripon Coll., 1947-49; B.S., Marquette U., 1951, M.S., 1953; postgrad. U. Wyo., summer 1959, Iowa State U., summer 1961; M.S., U. Wis., 1962, Ph.D., 1964; m. Lorayne Adalayde Williams, June 12, 1943; children—Victoria (Mrs. Joseph C. Barton), Barbara (Mrs. Timothy F. Columbia), Joan (Mrs. James A. Wilger), Willard, Mark. Prof. math. and statistics Marquette U., Milw., 1953, chmn. dept., 1973-79; statis. cons. Served with USAAF, 1941-45. Decorated Bronze Star medal. NSF faculty fellow, 1961-62. Mem. Math. Assn. Am., Am. Statis. Assn., Inst. Math. Statistics. Roman Catholic. Author: Introduction to the Theory of Probability, 1967; Probability: An Introductory Course, 1970. Home: 6823 Kinsman St Wauwatosa WI 53213 Office: William Wehr Physics Bldg Marquette U Milwaukee WI 53233

LAWRENCE, WILLIAM JOSEPH, JR., bus. exec.; b. Kalamazoo, Feb. 1, 1918; s. William J. and Borgia M. (Wheeler) L.; postgrad. Cranbrook Sch., Bloomfield Hills, Mich., 1937; A.B., Kalamazoo Coll., 1941; m. Doris Luella Fitzgerald, Aug. 19, 1955; children—Aaron Frances, Cleve Moren, Julie Anne, William III. Engaged in personal investments; chmn. bd., dir. Superior Pine Products Co.; dir., asst. treas. Ill. Envelope Co.; mem. exec. com., dir. Am. Nat. Holding Co., Am. Nat. Bank & Trust Co. of Mich.; chmn. bd., dir. Channel 41, Inc.; dir. Ban-Pro Corp., Am. Nat. Discount Co., Am. Nat. Bank Credit Corp., Am. Nat. Mortgage Co., ANB Leasing. Pres., trustee Kalamazoo Found.; chmn. bd., trustee Borgess Hosp.; mem. fin com. Kalamazoo Inst. Arts; trustee, mem. exec. com. Kalamazoo Coll. Served with AUS, 1942-46. Mem. Kalamazoo C. of C. Roman Catholic. Kiwanian. Clubs: Gull Lake Yacht, Gull Lake Country, Park. Home: Drawer 37 Richland MI 49083 Office: 1000 Am Nat Bank Bldg Kalamazoo MI 49007

LAWRENCE, WILLIAM PORTER, naval officer; b. Nashville, Jan. 13, 1930; s. Robert Landy and Tennie (Brewer) L.; B.S. in Elec. Engring., U.S. Naval Acad., 1951; M.S. in Internat. Affairs. George Washington U., 1974; m. Diane Wilcox, 1974; children—William Porter, Laurie, Wendy. Commd. ensign U.S. Navy, 1951, advanced through grades to rear adm., 1975, designated naval aviator, 1952; test pilot, service in Korea and Vietnam; prisoner-of-war, 1967-73; comdr. Light Attack Wing, Pacific Fleet, 1974-75; dir. aviation programs div. Navy Dept., Washington, 1975-78; supt. U.S. Naval Acad., 1978—. Decorated D.S.M., Silver Star, D.F.C., Air medal, Bronze Star, Purple Heart; recipient Gold medal Nat. Football Hall of Fame, 1979. Mem. Naval Inst. (v.p.), Am. Legion, VFW. Methodist. Club: Kiwanis. Author: Oh Tennessee My Tennessee, 1974. Home: 1 Buchanan Rd US Naval Acad Annapolis MD 21402

LAWRIE, ROY THOMAS, automotive co. exec.; b. Windsor, Ont., Can., Nov. 21, 1925; s. Thomas and Maude Ellen (Dollar) L.; student U. Mich., 1954-58; m. Olga Collette, Oct. 1, 1949; children—Jay, Brett, Todd, Jodi, Kip. Mgr. budget dept. Windsor mfg. operations Ford of Can., 1956-59, budgeting control mgr., 1959-60, divisional controller, 1960-65, spl. asst. to v.p. finance, 1967-68; controller Ford of Australia, 1965-67; operational controller Am. Motors Corp., Detroit, 1968-72, corp. controller, 1972—, v.p., 1975—. Served with RCAF, 1943-45. Office: Am Center 27777 Franklin Rd Southfield MI 48076

LAWROSKI, HARRY, nuclear co. exec.; b. Dalton, Pa., Oct. 10, 1928; s. Alexander and Nancy (Lutchka) L.; B.S. in Chem. Engring., Pa. State U., 1950, M.S., 1956, Ph.D., 1959; m. Mary Ann DeWoody, Oct. 6, 1962. Research and devel. work in petroleum refining Pa. State U., 1950-58; instr., thesis advisor Argonne (Ill.) Nat. Lab., 1958-63; supt., asso. project dir. exptl. breeder reactor II power plant, Idaho Nat. Engring. Lab., 1968-73; gen. mgr. quality assurance and environmental services Nuclear Services Corp., Campbell, Calif., 1973-76; asst. gen. mgr. nuclear fuel processing and waste mgmt. tech. Idaho chem. programs Allied Chem. Corp., Idaho Falls, 1976-79, cons., 1979—; lectr. Idaho Acad. Scis.; cons. in field. Fellow Am. Nuclear Soc. (treas. 1973-77, dir. 1969-77, pres.-elect 1979—), Am. Inst. Chem. Engrs. (chmn. nuclear engring. div. 1974), Skull and Bones, Sigma Xi, Tau Beta Pi, Sigma Tau, Phi Lambda Upsilon. Clubs: Rotary, Elks. Author, patentee in field. Home: 2375 Belmont St Idaho Falls ID 83401 Office: 550 2d St Idaho Falls ID 83401

LAWROSKI, STEPHEN, chem. engr.; b. Scranton, Pa., Jan. 17, 1914; s. Alex and Nancy (Lutzka) L.; B.S., Pa. State U., 1934, M.S., 1939, Ph.D., 1943; m. Helen Wilson, Sept. 14, 1947; children—Nancy Ann, Stephen Wilson. Research asst. Petroleum Refining Lab., 1934-43; research engr. Standard Oil Devel. Co., Elizabeth, N.J., 1943-44; group leader Manhattan project Metall. Lab., Chgo., 1944-46; dir. chem. engring. div. Argonne (Ill.) Nat. Lab., 1947-63, coordinator engring., research, devel., 1959-63, asso. lab. dir. Nuclear Reactor Research and Devel., 1963-70, sr. chem. engr., 1970—. Cons. to U.S. Army Chem. Corps on engring. and prodn., 1961-66; mem. gen. adv. com. for AEC, 1964-70, mem. adv. com. on reactor safeguards, 1974—. Fellow Am. Nuclear Soc., Am. Inst. Chem. Engrs.; mem. Am. Chem. Soc. (chmn. nuclear tech. subdiv. div. indsl. and engring. chemistry 1957), Research Soc. Am., Nat. Acad. Engring. Editor: The Reactor Handbook, 1955; Reactor Fuel Processing, quar. AEC. Home: 144 S Sleight St Naperville IL 60540 Office: Argonne Nat Lab Argonne IL 60439

LAWRY, SYLVIA (MRS. STANLEY ENGLANDER), assn. exec.; b. N.Y.C.; d. Jack and Sonia (Tager) Friedman; A.B., Hunter Coll., 1936; m. Michael Lawry, Mar. 1944 (div. 1946); m. 2d, Stanley Englander, Apr. 1957 (dec. 1968); children—Franklin Myles, Steven Jon. Practiced law, also hearing reporter for State Arbitrator, 1937-40, U.S. Atty.'s office, N.Y., 1943-44; asst. dir. radio prodn. Civilian Def. Reporting, sponsored by N.Y.C., 1942-43; with sister, Alice Friedman, founded Nat. Multiple Sclerosis Soc., N.Y.C., 1946, became exec. sec. and dir., now exec. dir.; sec. Internat. Fedn. Multiple Sclerosis Socs. Mem. President's Com. on Employment of Handicapped; mem. Nat. Com. Research Neurol. and Communicative Disorders; bd. dirs. Nat. Health Council. Mem. Acad. Polit. Sci., Am. Judicature Soc., Internat. Soc. Rehab. of Disabled., Am. Public Health Assn., Internat. Platform Assn. Office: Nat Multiple Sclerosis Society 205 E 42d St New York NY 10017

LAWS, HUBERT, flutist; b. Houston, Nov. 10, 1939; s. Hubert and Miola (Donahue) L.; student Tex. So. U., 1956-58, Los Angeles State Coll., 1958-60; B. Music, Juilliard Sch. Music, 1964. Recording artist, 1965—; flutist Met. Opera Orch., N.Y.C., 1968-72, N.Y. Philharmonic, N.Y.C., 1970—. Winner Downbeat poll, 1971-77, Playboy mag. poll, 1974, Ebony black music poll, 1974, Swing Jour. jazz flute poll, Japan, 1974-76. Office: care Liz Dapin 21 W 86th St Suite 1609 New York NY 10024*

LAWS, ROBERT HARRY, economist, engring. and cons. co. exec.; b. Mountain City, Tenn., Apr. 17, 1917; s. William R. and Charlotte (Seehorn) L.; A.B., Carson-Newman Coll., 1940, LL.D. (hon.), 1974; M.A., U. Tenn., 1942; postgrad. U. Tex., 1948-50. Economist, TVA, 1941-42; asst. prof. econs. U. Tenn., 1947-50, asso. prof., 1950-53; teaching fellow in econs. U. Tex., 1948-50; dir. econ. research Soc. Advancement Mgmt., 1953-56; with Commonwealth Services, Inc., N.Y.C., 1956-74, v.p., 1960-64, exec. v.p., 1965-67, pres., chief exec. officer, 1967-74, dir., 1960—; sr. v.p., dir. Gilbert/Commonwealth, Reading, Pa., 1973—, also dir.; pres. Gilbert Commonwealth Internat. Inc., Reading, 1973—; sr. v.p., chief adminstrv. officer, dir. Gilbert Assos., Inc., Reading, Pa., 1979—; dir. APC Graphics, Inc., Gai-tronica, Inc.; dir., mem. exec. com. Peoples Gas System (Fla.), 1962-76. Served with USN, 1942-47. Recipient Disting. Alumni award Carson-Newman Coll., 1972. Mem. Am. Econ. Assn., Am. Acad. Mgmt., Indsl. Relations Research Assn., Am. Arbitration Assn., Am. Acad. Polit. and Social Sci., Newcomen Soc. N. Am., Delta Sigma Pi, Pi Gamma Mu, Delta Nu Alpha. Clubs: Bd. Room, N.Y., Pinnacle, Lawyers (N.Y.C.); City (Knoxville). Author: Labor Relations in the Motor Freight Industry, 1953; contbg. editor Advanced Mgmt., 1953-56. Home: PO Box 268 Point Pleasant PA 18950 Office: PO Box 1498 Reading PA 19603

LAWS, ROBERT JULIAN, equipment mfg. co. exec.; b. Hot Springs, Ark., Oct. 23, 1922; s. Wiley Luther and Elizabeth (Fisher) L.; B.S. in Mech. Engring., U.S. Naval Acad., 1946; postgrad. U. Cal. at Los Angeles, 1948-50; m. Alice Elizabeth Dick, June 9, 1946; children—Robert David, John Luther. Asst chief engr., sales dir. Baker div. Otis Elevator, 1955-59; mgr. European operations Cascade Corp., Portland, Ore., 1959-65, exec. v.p., chief operating officer, dir., 1965-72, pres. Cascade Corp. Internat., 1972—, dir., 1972—; pres., dir. Cascade (Japan) Ltd., 1974—. Served to maj. USMC, 1946-55. Home: 315 Harbor Dr Indian Rocks Beach FL 33535

LAWSON, CHRIS ANDERSON, advt. agy. fin. exec.; b. Detroit, June 29, 1951; s. Jack Anderson and Janice A. (Schmitz) L.; B.S. in Acctg., Mich. State U., 1973; m. Debra A. Seed, June 23, 1973; 1 son, Chad Anderson. Audit sr. Arthur Andersen & Co., Detroit, 1973-78; internal auditor Ross Roy, Inc., Detroit, 1978-79, treas., 1979—. C.P.A., Mich. Mem. Am. Inst. C.P.A.'s, Mich. Assn. C.P.A.'s. Republican. Lutheran. Office: 2751 E Jefferson Ave Detroit MI 48207

LAWSON, DONALD ELMER, publishing co. exec.; b. Chgo., May 20, 1917; s. Elmer Daniel and Christina (Grass) L.; B.A., Cornell Coll., Mt. Vernon, Iowa, 1939, Litt.D. (hon.), 1970; postgrad. U. Iowa Writers Workshop, 1939-40; m. Beatrice M. Yates, Mar. 30, 1945. Editor, The Advertiser, Nora Springs, Iowa, 1940-41; with Compton's Ency., Chgo., 1946-73, mng. editor, 1960-65, editor-in-chief, 1965-73; v.p., editor-in-chief Compton's Ency.-Ency. Brit. 1972-73; exec. editor Am. Educator Ency., 1973-74, editor-in-chief, 1974—. Bd. dirs. Marcy-Newberry Assn. Settlement Houses. Served with USAAF, 1941-45; ETO. Mem. Authors Guild, Chgo. Book Clinic. Internat. Platform Assn., Chgo. Lit. Club, Soc. Midland Authors, Phi Beta Kappa. Methodist. Clubs: Cliff Dwellers, Press (Chgo.). Author: A Brand for the Burning, 1961; Young People in the White House, 1961, rev. edit., 1970; The United States in World War I, 1963; The United States in World War II, 1963; The United States in the Korean War, 1964; Famous American Political Families, 1965; The War of 1812, 1966; Frances Perkins First Lady of the Cabinet, 1967; Great Air Battles: World Wars I and II, 1968; The Lion and the Rock: The Story of the Rock of Gibraltar, 1969; Youth and War: From World War I to Vietnam, 1969; Ten Fighters for Peace, 1971; The Colonial Wars, 1972; The American Revolution, 1974; The United States in the Indian Wars, 1975; The United States in the Mexican War, 1976; The United States in the Spanish-American War, 1976; The United States in the Civil War, 1977; Education Careers, 1977; Democracy, 1978; THe Secret World War II, 1978; Morocco, Algeria, Tunisia, and Libya, 1978; The Changing Face of the Constitution, 1979; FOR's New Deal, 1979. Home: 1122 W Lunt Ave Chicago IL 60626. *"Tomorrow always comes" is a truism I like to think I have learned to live by after several decades of meeting deadlines—both in the publishing business and in my personal life. It means, purely and simply, facing up to responsibilities, initiating action rather than being pushed into it, treating friends, colleagues, and employees honestly* *and decently, and endeavoring to maintain one's integrity in an all-too permissive society.*

LAWSON, ERNEST THOMAS, educator; b. Cape Town, South Africa, Nov. 27, 1931; s. Robert Edward and Emily (Swart) L.; B.D., M.A., Ph.D., U. Chgo., 1963; m. Ruth Ann Jones, July 30, 1966; children—Sonya Ruth, Jennifer. Instr., Western Mich. U., Kalamazoo, 1961-63, asst. prof., 1963-65, asso. prof., 1965-67, prof., 1967—, head dept. religion, 1965-72, 76—. Recipient Internat. and Area Studies award, 1962; Soc. for Religion in Higher Edn. post doctoral fellow. Mem. Am. Acad. Religion, ACLU, Philosophy of Sci. Assn. Home: 2642 Fairgrove Ave Kalamazoo MI 49009

LAWSON, JAMES DEAN, corp. exec.; b. Ramey, Pa., Apr. 26, 1918; s. Alexander Dean and Elizabeth Jane (Alsop) L.; B.S., Calif. State Tchrs. Coll., 1941; M.Ed. in Edn. and Sociology, U. Pitts., 1948, Ed.D. in Adminstrn., 1961; m. Pearle Lorenda Tyler, Apr. 9, 1944; children—James Tyler, Jennifer Lynn Lawson Kaufmann, Timothy Arthur, Rodger Bruce. Miner, Westmoreland Coal Co., Yukon, Pa., 1936; tchr. Hempfield Twp. Schs., Greensburg, Pa., 1937-41, Butler (Pa.) Area Joint Schs., 1949-55, dir. curriculum and supervision, 1955-60; asst. supt. in charge of instruction Bethpage (N.Y.) Pub. Schs., 1960-65; pres. Butler County (Pa.) Community Coll., 1965-70; v.p. planning Halstead Industries, Inc., Zelienople, Pa., 1971-72, pres., 1972—, also dir.; asst. dir. Butler County Community Resources Workshop for Tchrs., 1955-56; guest instr. pub. speaking and psychology of indsl. relations Armco Steel Corp., 1952-56; cons. to Hill & Knowlton, Inc., N.Y.C., Iron and Steel Inst., charter banks in state of N.Y., 1960-65. Served to maj. Signal Corps, U.S. Army, 1941-46. Recipient Community Service citation Butler (Pa.) Bd. Edn., 1954. Mem. NEA, Copper Devel. Assn., St. Andrews Soc., Phi Delta Kappa. Republican. Presbyterian. Contbr. articles to edn. jours. Home: RFD 1 Valencia PA 16059 Office: Halstead Industries Inc W New Castle St Zelienople PA 16063

LAWSON, JAMES RAYMOND, carillonneur; b. Cody, Wyo., May 25, 1919; s. Leslie and Celeste (Sellers) L.; B.A., U. Chgo., 1941; postgrad. Stanford, 1942; laureate Ecole de Carillon Malines, Belgium, 1949. Carillonneur, Hoover War Library, Stanford, 1941-48; guest carillonneur Scottish Rite Cathedral, Indpls., 1946-47; carillonneur Rockefeller Chapel, U. Chgo., 1953-60, Riverside Ch., N.Y.C., 1960—; lectr. dept. music Lehman Coll., U. City N.Y., 1969—. Mem. Guild Carillonneurs N.A., Coll. of Campanology (Eng.), Sussex County Assn. Change Ringers (Eng.). Editor Overtones (quart. jour. Am. Guild English Handbell Ringers), 1960-64. Address: 490 Riverside Dr New York City NY 10027

LAWSON, JOHN SHULTS, investment co. exec.; b. N.Y.C., Aug. 1, 1924; B.A. in English, Harvard U., 1948; D.Bus Adminstrn. (hon.), St. John's U., Staten Island, 1975; m. Charlotte Chevalier, May 16, 1947; children—Catherine C., Elizabeth E. Asst. treas. J.P. Morgan & Co., Inc.; v.p. Discount Corp. N.Y.; v.p. Clark, Dodge, Inc., 1964-67; with Marine Midland Bank, N.Y.C., 1967-75, pres., 1972-75, chmn., 1973-75; dir. Marine Midland, Inc., 1972-75, pres., 1972-75; pres. Nat. Investors Corp., N.Y.C., 1975—; vice chmn., dir. Union Data Service Center, Inc.; partner J.&W. Seligman & Co.; dir., mem. exec. com. Tri-Continental Corp.; mem. investment com., Union Capital Fund, Inc.; dir. Broad St. Investing Corp., Union Cash Mgmt. Fund, Inc., Union Income Fund, Inc., Union Service Corp., Victory Carriers, Inc. Nat. treas., bd. dirs. Am. Cancer Soc.; mem. internat. adv. council Bryn Mawr Coll. Served with AUS, 1943-46. Decorated Bronze Star; recipient Hornbook award Boston Globe, 1967. Clubs: Board Room, Bond, Economic, Links (N.Y.C.). Author: The Spring Rider, 1968; You Better Come Home With Me, 1966. Home: 1 Merestone Terr Bronxville NY 10708 Office: 1 Bankers Trust Plaza New York City NY 10006

LAWSON, JUAN OTTO, physicist; b. Bluefield, W.Va., Apr. 18, 1939; s. Harold Lomain and Eliza Serena (Fullen) L.; B.S., Va. State Coll., 1960; M.S., Howard U., 1962, Ph.D., 1966; m. Marjorie Payton, Dec. 21, 1963; children—Michael Steven, Edith Serena. Asst. prof. physics U. Tex., El Paso, 1967-70, asso. prof., 1970-74, prof., 1974—, asst. grad. dean, 1970-71, dean Coll. Sci., 1975—. Served to capt. arty. U.S. Army, 1965-67. Decorated Army Commendation medal. Mem. Am. Assn. Physics Tchrs., Am. Phys. Soc., Sigma Xi. Mem. Ch. of God in Christ. Office: U Tex El Paso TX 79968

LAWSON, RAY SHEPHERD, hotel exec.; b. Binghamton, N.Y., July 13, 1943; s. Stuart Wellington and Betty (Shepherd) L.; A.A.S., Broome Coll., 1965; m. Judith Kuczynski, Sept. 6, 1965. Regional sales mgr. Sheraton Corp., Chgo., 1970-71; gen. mgr. Travelodge-Wharf, San Francisco, 1971-73; gen. mgr. Travelodge-Harbor Island, San Diego, 1973-75; gen. mgr. Holiday Inn Embarcadero, San Diego, 1975—. Served with U.S. Army Res., 1965-71. Mem. Am. Hotel and Motel Assn., Calif. Hotel and Motel Assn., Hotel Sales Mgrs. Assn. Republican. Office: 1355 Harbor Dr San Diego CA 92101

LAWSON, RICHARD HENRY, educator; b. San Francisco, Jan. 11, 1919; s. Henry Porter and Alice (Hanchett) L.; student Multnomah Coll., 1937-39; B.A., U. Oreg., 1941, M.A., 1948; Ph.D., UCLA, 1956; m. Eldene Laura Balcom, Aug. 26, 1950. Instr., Wash. State U., 1953-57; asst. prof. San Diego State U., 1957-62, asso. prof. German, 1962-66, prof. German, 1966-76, chmn. dept. German and Russian, 1965-68, chmn. div. humanities, 1968-69, asst. dean grad. studies, 1970-72, 73-74, acting asso. dean grad. studies, 1972-73; prof. U. N.C., Chapel Hill, 1976—, chmn. dept. Germanic langs., 1976-79; cons. Webster's New Internat. Dictionary, 1956-58. Served from pvt. to 1st lt. USAAF, 1941-46; maj. Res. Decorated Air medal. Mem. MLA, Am. Assn. Tchrs. German, Am. Com. for Study of Austrian Lit., Am. Comparative Lit. Assn., Internat. Arthur Schnitzler Research Assn., Internationale Vereinigung fuer germanische Sprach und Literaturwissenschaft. Author: Edith Wharton and German Literature, 1974; Edith Wharton, 1977; contbr. articles to profl. jours.; bibliog. editor 20th Century Lit., 1967—. Research in Germanic linguistics, modern German lit. and comparative lit. Home: 904 The Oaks Apts Chapel Hill NC 27514

LAWSON, RICHARD LAVERNE, air force officer; b. Fairfield, Iowa, Dec. 19, 1929; s. Vernon C. and Wilma A. (Rabel) L.; B.S., Parsons Coll.; M.P.A., George Washington U., 1964; grad. Nat. War Coll., 1969; m. Joan Graber, Aug. 28, 1949; children—Leslie D., Wendy L., Richard H., Randolph S. Joined USAF, advanced through grades to lt. gen.; now dir. plans and policy Orgn. of Joint Chiefs of Staff, Washington. Decorated D.S.M., Legion of Merit with oak leaf cluster, Bronze Star medal, Air medal with oak leaf cluster, citation and unit decorations. Home: Quarters 71 Bolling AFB Washington DC 20336 Office: Dir J-5 OJCS Pentagon Washington DC 20301

LAWSON, ROBERT BARRETT, physician, educator; b. Oakland, Calif., Aug. 24, 1911; s. W. Elsworth and Florence (Shera) L.; B.A., Harvard, 1932, M.D, 1936; NRC fellow U. Calif., Yale, 1945; m. Elsie C. Earle, 1939; children—Edward, Richard. Rotating intern Rochester (N.Y.) Gen. Hosp., 1936-37; house officer pediatric service Johns Hopkins Hosp., 1937-38; asst. resident pediatrics Strong Meml. Hosp., 1938-39, resident pediatrics outpatient dept., 1939-40; prof. pediatrics U. N.C. Sch. Pub. Health, 1940-42; asso. pediatrics Duke U. Med. Sch., 1940-42; asst. prof. pediatrics Bowman Gray Sch. Medicine, Wake Forest Coll., 1942-45, asso. prof. pediatrics, 1945-50, prof. pediatrics, dir. dept., 1950-54; prof. pediatrics, chmn. dept. Sch. Medicine, U. Miami (Fla.), 1954-62, clin. prof., 1971—; prof. pediatrics Northwestern U., 1962-71, chmn. dept., 1962-70, v.p. for health scis., 1970-71; chief staff Children's Meml. Hosp., Chgo., 1962-70, Variety Children's Hosp., Miami, 1971—. Pediatric cons. N.C. State Bd. Health, 1940-42. Diplomate Am. Bd. Pediatrics (pres. 1968-70). Mem. Am. Acad. Pediatrics, Am., Fla. pediatric socs., A.M.A., Soc. Pediatric Research. Former editor Am. Jour. Diseases of Children. Home: 5450 Banyan Dr Miami FL 33156 Office: 6125 SW 31st St Miami FL 33155

LAWSON, ROBERT WILLIAM, JR., lawyer; b. South Boston, Va., Sept. 20, 1908; s. Robert William and Mary Easley (Craddock) L.; B.A., Hampden-Sydney Coll., 1930; LL.B., U. Va., 1935; m. Virginia Peyton Broun, Nov. 19, 1938; children—Robert William III, Fontaine Broun, Lewis Peyton. Master, Episcopal High Sch., Alexandria, Va., 1930-32; admitted to Va. bar, 1934, W.Va. bar, 1935, since practiced in Charleston; mem. Steptoe & Johnson, 1935—. Dir. Fed. Res. Bank of Richmond, 1967-75, dep. chmn., 1968-72, chmn., 1972-75; dir. Eagle Land Co., Slab Fork Coal Co. Chancellor P.E. Ch. Diocese W.Va., 1956-79. Past bd. dirs. Community Music Assn.; past trustee Hampden-Sydney Coll., Episcopal High Sch. Served with USMCR, World War II; to lt. comdr. USNR, World War II. Mem. Am. (ho. of dels., state del. 1975—), W.Va., Kanawha County bar assns., Am. Law Inst., Charleston C. of C. (past dir.), Raven Soc., Kappa Sigma, Omicron Delta Kappa. Democrat. Episcopalian. Home: 10 Grosscup Rd Charleston WV 25314 Office: PO Box 1588 Charleston WV 25326

LAWSON, RUSTON WILLIAM, banker; b. Glenboro, Man., Can., Oct. 19, 1917; s. Clarke B. and Florence (Ruston) L.; B.A., U. Man., 1938, B.A., U. Oxford, 1940, M.A., 1945; LL.D., U. Winnipeg, 1975; m. Katharine Macdonnell, Aug. 1, 1964; 1 dau., Anne. With Fgn. Exchange Control Bd., Ottawa, Ont., Can., 1940-42, 47-50; economist Royal Commn. on Coal, 1945-47; with Bank of Can., 1950—, now sr. dep. gov., Ottawa. Served with Can. Army, 1942-45. Home: 158 Carleton St Rockcliffe Ottawa ON K1M 0G7 Canada Office: 234 Wellington St Ottawa ON K1A 0G9 Canada

LAWSON, THOMAS ELSWORTH, advt. agy. exec.; b. Taunton, Mass., May 30, 1937; s. Wilbur Lougheed and Margaret Mary (Walsh) L.; B.A., Harvard, 1959; 1 son, Patric. Media trainee, media supr., account exec., v.p. account supr., sr. v.p. mgmt. supr. Ogilvy & Mather Inc., advt. agy., N.Y.C., 1961-70; co-founder, pres. Rosenfeld, Sirowitz & Lawson Inc., N.Y.C., 1971—. Served to 1st. lt. Inf., Paratroops, AUS. Mem. Am. Assn. Advt. Agys. (bd. dirs.), chmn. Eastern region), Young Pres.'s Orgn. Club: Harvard (N.Y.C.). Home: 157 E 61st St New York NY 10021 Office: 1370 Ave of Americas New York NY 10019

LAWSON, THOMAS SAWYER, banker; b. Washington, May 25, 1921; s. June Keith and Susette (Sawyer) L.; student Benjamin Franklin U., 1941, George Washington U., 1946; postgrad. Rutgers U. Sch. Banking, 1954-56; m. Ruth Oliver, Mar. 23, 1946; 1 dau., Susan Lorraine. Clk., Union Trust Co. D.C., 1940-42, asst. trust officer, 1946-60; trust officer Suburban Trust Co., Hyattsville, Md., 1960—, v.p., 1967-73, sr. v.p., 1973-76, exec. v.p., 1976—; officer, dir. numerous small corps. Instr. financial counseling Montgomery Coll., 1977—. Served with USNR, 1942-46; PTO. Mem. Washington Estate Planning Council (past pres.), Md. Bankers Assn. (trust com. 1969-79). Methodist (trustee). Rotarian (pres. club 1975-76, dist. gov. 1979-80). Home: 12519 Meadowood Dr Silver Spring MD 20904 Office: 6495 New Hampshire Ave Hyattsville MD 20783

LAWSON, TOM F., printing co. exec.; b. London, Ont., Can., Nov. 12, 1915; s. R. Ray and Helen (Newton) L.; B.A. (Scholar), U. Western Ont., 1935; D.C.L. (hon.), Kings U., 1977; m. Margaret Otton, Sept. 10, 1938; children—Constance, Joan, Tom, Marilyn, Tim, Peter. Joined Lawson & Jones Co., London, Ont., Can., 1933, gen. mgr., 1948-53, pres., 1953—, chmn., 1976—; v.p. Can. Trust Co., 1958—. Served to lt. col. Can. Army, 1940-45. Recipient Distinguished Service medal Salvation Army, 1975. Mem. Can. (past v.p.), Ont. (past pres.), London (past pres.) chambers commerce. Liberal. Anglican. Club: Rotary (past pres.). Home: 1384 Hutton St London ON N6G 2C1 Canada Office: Lawson & Jones 395 Wellington Rd S London ON N6A 4Z9 Canada

LAWSON, WALTER REYNOLDS, mfg. co. exec.; b. Amherst, N.S., Can., Feb. 11, 1918; s. Gerald and Rose (Smith) L.; B.S. in Chem. Engring., Dalhousie U., Halifax, N.S., 1940; m. Harriet Senior, June 22, 1946; children—Cecily, Geoff, Tim, Heather. Plant engr. Domtar Ltd., Toronto, Ont., 1945-47, works mgr., 1950-51, project engr., Montreal, Que., 1952-54, gen. sales mgr., 1954-57, v.p., 1957-62, v.p. purchasing and traffic, 1966-70; v.p., gen. mgr. Domtar Packaging Co., 1970-76, pres., 1976-79; exec. v.p. Domtar Inc., 1979—; plant mgr. Sifto Salt Co., Sarnia, Ont., 1947-50; plant mgr. Manistee (Mich.) Salt Works, 1951-52. Mem. bus. and industry adv. com. OECD. Bd. govs. Montreal Gen. Hosp., 1965-75. Served to maj. Can. Army, 1940-45. Mem. Can. Mfrs. Assn. (nat. pres. 1974-75, chmn. Que. div. 1964-65), Inst. Applied Econ. Research (bd. govs. 1975—). Clubs: Royal Montreal Golf (dir. 1964-67), Granite, St. James (dir. 1976-77). Home: 224 Senneville Rd Senneville PQ H9X 3L2 Canada Office: 395 de Maisonneuve Blvd W Montreal PQ Canada

LAWSON, WARREN ROBERT, state ofcl., physician; b. Mpls., Jan. 18, 1920; s. Wilbert F. and Lillian B. (Koepsel) L.; B. Chem. Engring., U. Minn., 1941, M.P.H., 1942, B.S., 1955, M.D., 1956. With Minn. Dept. Health, Mpls., 1942-52, 57—, supr. health services for state employees, 1960 and after, dep. exec. officer dept., 1967-70, exec. officer, 1971-73, state commr. health, 1973—, also sec.; intern Mpls. Gen. Hosp., 1956-57; vis. lectr. U. Minn. Med. Sch., Sch. Pub. Health, 1960—; mem. Minn. Environ. Quality Bd., 1974—, Minn. Water Resources Bd., 1977—, statewide health coordinating council Minn. Planning Agy., 1977—; mem. advisory com. Indian Health Bd. of Mpls., 1972—; mem. med. adv. bd. Kidney Found. Upper Midwest; bd. dirs. Mpls. War Meml. Blood Bank, 1970-79. Registered profl. engr., Minn. Fellow Am. Pub. Health Assn.; mem. Intersoc Engring. Bd. (diplomate), Am., Minn. med. assns., Am., Minn. pub. health assns., Hennepin County (Minn.) Med. Soc., Minn. Acad. Medicine, Minn. Acad. Occupational Medicine Surgery, Indsl. Med. Assn., Health Physics Soc., Conf. State San. Engrs., Am. Acad. Govtl. Indsl. Hygienists, Am. Assn. Pub. Health Physicians, Minn. Human Genetics League (dir. 1962—), Alpha Chi Sigma, Phi Chi. Clubs: Masons, Shriners. Home: 5133 Mirror Lakes Dr Minneapolis MN 55436 Office: 717 Delaware St SE Minneapolis MN 55440

LAWSON, WILLIAM DAVID, III, cotton mcht.; b. Jackson, Miss., Oct. 30, 1924; s. William David, Jr. and Elizabeth Vaiden (Barksdale) L.; B.S., Davidson (N.C.) Coll., 1948; M.B.A., Wharton Sch., U. Pa., 1949; m. Elizabeth Coppridge Smith, June 9, 1948; children—Margaret Monroe Headrick, William David, IV, Susan Barksdale, Thomas Nelson. Pres. W.D. Lawson & Co., Gastonia, N.C., 1971—; bd. mgrs. N.Y. Cotton Exchange; chmn. bd. First Union Nat. Bank, Gastonia; v.p. Avon Bonded Warehouse, Automatic Machine Handling, Inc.; past pres. Nat. Cotton Council, Am. Cotton Shippers Assn., Atlantic Cotton Assn., Cotton Council Internat.; v.p. Avon and Peoples Warehouse, Gastonia. Bd. visitors Davidson Coll.; pres. Covenant Village. Served to 1st lt., inf., AUS, 1943-46. Named Cotton Man of Year, Cotton Digest, 1969, 76. Mem. Newcomen Soc., Gaston County C. of C. (past pres.), Am. Legion, Kappa Sigma. Republican. Presbyterian (elder). Clubs: Gaston Country, Gastonia Rotary (past pres.). Home: 2444 Armstrong Circle Gastonia NC 28052 Office: 104 S Avon St Gastonia NC 28052

LAWSON, WILLIAM HOGAN, III, housing and recreational vehicle mfg. co. exec.; b. Lexington, Ky., Feb. 3, 1937; s. Otto Kirsky and Glady (McWhorter) L.; B.S. in Mech. Engring., Purdue U., 1959; M.B.A., Harvard U., 1961; m. Martha G. Grubb, Aug. 24, 1963; children—Elizabeth, Cynthia. Gen. mgr. service div. Toledo Scale Corp., 1964-66; exec. v.p., chief ops. officer Skyline Corp., Elkhart, Ind., 1963—; dir. JSJ Corp.; instr. U. Toledo, 1966-67. Served with U.S. Army, 1961-63. Mem. Harvard U. Bus. Sch. Assn. Republican. Presbyterian. Home: 5 Holly Ln Elkhart IN 46514 Office: 2520 By-Pass Rd Elkhart IN 46514

LAWSON, WILLIAM VAUGHN, II, constrn. co. exec.; b. Chgo., Mar. 6, 1924; s. William Vaughan and Violet Justine (Behrendt) L.; student Columbia, N.Y. U., U. Calif., m. Mary Lou Crandall, Nov. 17, 1947; children—William Vaughan, Marguerite, Victoria Lou, Jacquelyn. With Shell Oil Co., 1947-48, George A. Fuller Co., N.Y.C. 1948, Los Angeles, 1951—, pres., 1964—, also dir.; pres. George A. Fuller Internat., 1964—; chmn. bd. George A. Fuller Co., P.R., 1964—. Served to capt., pilot, USAAF, World War II: PTO. Decorated Air medal. Clubs: Bel Air Country (Los Angeles); Fifth Avenue, River, Economic (N.Y.C.); Links. Home: 469 St Pierre Rd Los Angeles CA 90024 Office: 1070 Casiano Rd Los Angeles CA 90049

LAWSON-JOHNSTON, PETER ORMAN, mining co. exec.; b. N.Y.C., Feb. 8, 1927; s. John R. and Barbara (Guggenheim) L.; student Lawrenceville Prep. Sch., 1940-45; B.A., U. Va., 1951; m. Dorothy Stevenson Hammond, Sept. 30, 1950; children—Wendy, Tania, Peter, Mary. Reporter, yachting editor Balt. Sun Papers, 1951-53; exec. dir. Md. Classified Employees Assn., Balt., 1953-54; pub. information dir. Md. Civil Def. Agy., Pikesville, 1954-56; v.p. Feldspar Corp., N.Y.C., 1956-59; sr. partner Guggenheim Bros.; chmn. bd., dir. Pacific Tin Consol. Corp., Anglo Co., Ltd., Feldspar Corp., Brazilian Mining and Dredging Co., Inc.; v.p., dir. Elgerbar Corp.; dir. McGraw-Hill, Inc., Barber Oil Co., Nabors Drilling Co., Printex Corp., Kennecott-Copper Corp., R.L. Manning Co.; ltd. partner Alex Brown & Co. Trustee, pres. S.R. Guggenheim Found.; chmn. bd. dirs. H.F. Guggenheim Found.; trustee The Lawrenceville Sch. Served with AUS, 1945-47. Mem. Am. Ceramic Soc., Pilgrims of U.S., Carolina Plantation Soc. Republican. Episcopalian. Clubs: Edgartown Yacht, Edgartown Reading Room; American (London); Green Spring Valley Hunt (Garrison, Md.); River, Century Assn., City Midday (N.Y.C.); Nassau Gun, Beden's Brook, Pretty Brook Tennis (Princeton, N.J.); Maryland; Seminole Golf (North Palm Beach, Fla.); Island (Hobe Sound, Fla.). Home: Princeton NJ Office: Guggenheim Bros Suite 3555 120 Broadway New York NY 10005

LAWTON, ALFRED HENRY, physician; b. Carson, Iowa, July 26, 1916; s. George A. and Cora Anna L.; A.B., Simpson Coll., 1937, D.Sc. (hon.). 1958; M.S., Northwestern U., 1939, B.M., 1940, M.D., 1941, Ph.D., 1943; m. Mary Ellen Swick, Aug. 20, 1940 (dec. 1974); children—George W., Dianna M., Lola J.; m. 2d, Ruth S. Allen, Aug. 11, 1974. Rotating interne Passavant Hosp., Chgo., 1940-41; surg. residency Henry Ford Hosp., Detroit, 1941-42; surgeon (lt. comdr.) USPHS, Apr. 1942-46; asst. prof. physiology, pharmacology and medicine U. Ark. Med. Sch., 1946-47; dean Sch. Medicine, prof. physiology and pharmacology U. N.D., 1947-48; chief research VA div. research and edn.; asst. clin. prof. medicine George Washington U.; dir. med. research, DCS-D, Hdqurs. USAF, 1951-55; cardiologist and dir. research lab. VA Center, Bay Pines, Fla., 1955-60, asst. chief profl. services for research and edn., 1960-62; dir. research accidents and aging study group USPHS div. accident prevention, St. Petersburg, 1962-64; dir. human devel. study center Nat. Inst. Child Health and Human Devel., HEW, 1964-66; asso. dean acad. affairs U. South Fla., Tampa, 1966-70, acting dean Coll. Medicine, 1968-69, acting v.p. and dean acad. affairs, 1970-71; physician outpatient dept. VA Hosp., Tampa, 1971-72; exec. dir. tech adv. com. aging HEW, 1972-73; asst. chief ambulatory care service VA Hosp., Tampa, 1973-74; dir. geriatric research, edn. and clin. center VA Center, Bay Pines, 1974-77, also asso. chief staff for research and devel.; dir. gerontol. edn. Advent Christian Village, Dowling Park, Fla., 1979—. Named Scientist of Year, Fla. Acad. Scis., 1967. Fellow AAAS, Am. Gerlatrics Soc., Gerontol. Soc., Inc.; mem. Am. Chem. Soc., A.M.A., Am. Heart Assn., Fla. Council on Aging, Am. Soc. Pharmacology and Exptl. Therapeutics, Am. Physiol. Soc., Sigma Xi, Phi Beta Pi, Lambda Chi Alpha, Pi Kappa Delta, Sigma Tau Delta. Methodist. Contbr. articles to profl. jours. Home and office: Advent Christian Village Dowling Park FL 32060

LAWTON, EUGENE ALFRED, banker; b. Yonkers, N.Y., Mar. 30, 1936; s. Charles Phineas and Jean (Pagnotta) L.; student Westchester Community Coll., 1954-56, Am. Inst. Banking, 1958-63, Sch. Bank Adminstrn. U. Wis., 1971; m. Elizabeth Anne Nicoletti, Oct. 20, 1956; children—Glenn Michael, Gary Paul, Melissa Anne. With Nat. Bank Westchester, White Plains, N.Y., 1956-61; sr. auditor County Trust Co., White Plains, 1961-68; v.p., auditor City trust, Bridgeport, Conn., 1968-77; v.p. Bay Banks Inc., Boston, 1978—. Active Boy Scouts Am. Mem. Bank Adminstrn. Inst. (guest lectr.), Am. Mgmt. Assn., Am. Inst. Banking, EDP Auditors Assn., Inst. Internal Auditors. Republican. Roman Catholic. Club: Masons. Home: 55 Paul Revere Rd Lexington MA 02173 Office: 175 Federal St Boston MA 02110

LAWTON, GEORGE ALBERT, air conditioning co. exec.; b. Dorchester, Mass., Apr. 10, 1914; s. George F. and Mary Ann (Newman) L.; A.B., U. Notre Dame, 1935; m. Mary Patricia Walsh, Jan. 1, 1937; children—Paula M. (Mrs. Bevington), Maria Elena (Mrs. Torruella), George Albert. Agt., then gen. agt., dir. agys. Aetna Life Ins. Co., 1939-55; v.p., then pres., dir. Security-Conn. Ins. Cos., 1955-57; pres., dir. Bankers Security Life Ins. Soc., 1957; v.p., sec. Home Ins. Co., 1958; chmn., dir. Ga. Internat. Life Ins. Co., Great Internat. Life Ins. Co. N.Y., Abbey Life Assurance Co., Ltd., London, Abbey Internat. Corp., Atlanta, Abby Leven Nederland, Amsterdam, 1959-69; sr. v.p. U.S. Life Corp., N.Y.C., 1970-71; mgmt. cons., 1971-73; project cons. Gen. Telephone and Electronics, 1973-75; v.p. Servidyne Inc., 1975—. Trustee, bd. govs. NCCJ; bd. regents Gonzaga U., Spokane, Wash. Mem. Am. Coll. Life Underwriters. Clubs: Piedmont Driving (Atlanta); Watch Hill (R.I.) Yacht. Home: 30 Cherokee Rd NW Atlanta GA 30305

LAWTON, RICHARD GRAHAM, chemist, educator; b. Berkeley, Calif., Aug. 29, 1934; s. John H. and Dorothy (Hoffman) L.; B.S., U. Calif., Berkeley, 1956; Ph.D., U. Wis., 1962; m. Anne Bender, June 14, 1958; children—Stephen, John, Eric, David, Deborah. Research chemist Merck, Sharp, and Dohme Research Labs., 1956-57; prof. chemistry U. Mich., Ann Arbor, 1962—; cons. in field. Served with U.S. Army, 1957-59. Mem. AAAS, Am. Chem. Soc. Presbyterian. Home: 2888 Daleview Dr Ann Arbor MI 48103 Office: Dept Chemistry Univ Mich Ann Arbor MI 48109

LAWTON, ROBERT OSWALD, educator; b. Greenwood, S.C., Dec. 28, 1924; s. Robert O. and Anne (Simpson) L.; student Wofford Coll., 1941-43, Litt. D., 1969; A.B., Duke, 1946, M.A., 1947, Ph.D., 1953; m. Elise Bates Nicholson, Aug. 15, 1945; children—Robert O., Elise Bates. Mem. faculty Fla. State U., Tallahassee, 1949—, prof. English, 1964—, dean Coll. Arts and Scis., 1966-72, v.p. acad. affairs, 1977—. Profl. cons. So. Assn. Colls. and Secondary Schs., 1960—. Served with AUS, 1943-45. Decorated D.S.C. Mem. S. Atlantic Modern Lang. Assn., Shakespeare Assn., So. Conf. Acad. Deans, Am. Assn. Acad. Deans, Council Arts and Scis., Omicron Delta Kappa. Home: 1403 N Randolph St Tallahassee FL 32306

LAWWILL, THEODORE, ophthalmologist; b. Chattanooga, Oct. 16, 1937; s. Stewart and Sue (Frierson) L.; B.A., Vanderbilt U., 1958, M.D., 1961; m. Charlene Lascody, May 25, 1963; children—Joseph Charles, Andrea. Intern, U. Iowa Hosps., 1961-62; resident ophthalmology (NIH trainee) U. Ill., 1963-64, NIH trainee in ophthalmology, 1965-66; research asso. dept. ophthalmology U. Iowa, 1964-65; research ophthalmologist Walter Reed Army Inst. Research, faculty mem. ophthalmology service Walter Reed Army Hosp., 1966-68; asst. prof. ophthalmology, asso. in physiology and biophysics U. Louisville, 1968-70, asso. prof. ophthalmology, asso. in physiology and biophysics, 1970-73, asso. prof. ophthalmology, asso. in physiology and biophysics, asso. in pediatrics, 1974-77, prof. ophthalmology, asso. in physiology and biophysics, asso. in pediatrics, 1978—; dir. ophthalmology children's div. Norton-Children's Hosps., Inc., 1971—; mem. com. on vision Nat. Acad. Sci., NRC. Served to capt., M.C., U.S. Army, 1966-68. Diplomate Am. Bd. Ophthalmology. Fellow A.C.S., Am. Acad. Ophthalmology; mem. Am. Acad. Ophthalmology and Otolaryngology, Assn. Research in Vision and Ophthalmology, AAAS, Internat. Soc. Clin. Electrophysiology of Vision, Internat. Strabismological Assn., Optical Soc. Am., AMA, Ky. Med. Assn. Presbyterian. Club: Louisville Boat. Editor: Perspectives in Ophthalmology; contbr. articles to profl. jours. Home: 2500 Woodside Rd Louisville KY 40207 Office: 301 Muhammad Ali Blvd Louisville KY 40202

LAWYER, VERNE, lawyer; b. Indianola, Iowa, May 9, 1923; s. Merrill Guy and Zella (Mills) L.; LL.B., Drake U., 1949; m. Sally Hay, Oct. 5, 1946; 1 dau., Suzanne; m. 2d, Vivian Jury, Oct. 25, 1959; children—Michael Jury, Steven Verne. Admitted to Iowa bar, 1949, U.S. Supreme Ct. bar, 1957; practice law, Des Moines, 1949—; mem. firm Lawyer, Lawyer, Dunn & Jackson. Mem. Iowa Aeros. Commn., 1973-75; trustee ATL Roscoe Pound Found., 1965-71, fellow, 1973—. Recipient Outstanding Law Alumni award Phi Alpha Delta, 1964. Fellow Internat. Acad. Trial Lawyers, Am. Bar Found., Internat. Soc. Barristers; mem. Am. (state chmn. membership com. ins., negligence and compensation law 1970—, com. trial techniques 1969-70), Iowa (spl. commn. fed. practice 1971-78, spl. automobile reparations com. 1972—), Polk County bar assns., Assn. Trial Lawyers Am. (v.p. Iowa chpt. 1956-57, nat. sec. 1963-64, 67-68, gov. 1962-63, mem. com. internat. aviation 1973—, trial advs. scholarship soc. com. 1973—), Iowa Acad. Trial Lawyers (sec.-treas. 1962—, editor Newsbull. 1962—, editor Weekly Verdict Summary 1970—, editor Acad. Alert), Assn. Trial Lawyers Iowa, Law Sci. Acad. Am., Lawyer-Pilots Bar Assn., Am. Judicature Soc., World Assn. Lawyers (founding), World Peace Through Law Center, Trial Lawyers Assn. Des Moines, Phi Alpha Delta, Sigma Alpha Epsilon. Author: Trial by Notebook, 1964; co-author: Art of Persuasion in Litigation, 1966; How to Defend a Criminal Case from Arrest to Verdict, 1967; contbr. articles to law jours. Home: 5831 N Waterbury Rd Des Moines IA 50312 Office: Fleming Bldg Des Moines IA 50309

LAX, BENJAMIN, physicist, educator; b. Miskolz, Hungary, Dec. 29, 1915; brought to U.S., 1926, naturalized, 1940; B.Mech. Engring., Cooper Union, 1941; Ph.D. in Physics, Mass. Inst. Tech., 1949; D.Sc. (hon.), Yeshiva U., 1975; m. Blossom Cohen, 1942; children—Daniel R., Robert M. Mech. engr. U.S. Engring. Office, 1941-42; cons. Sylvania Elec. Products, Inc., 1946; with USAF Cambridge (Mass.) Research Center, 1946-51; mem. staff solid state group Lincoln Lab., Mass. Inst. Tech., 1951-52, head ferrites group, 1955-57, asso. head communications div., 1957-58, head solid state group, 1958-64, dir. Francis Bitter Nat. Magnet Lab., 1960—, asso. dir. Lincoln. Lab., 1964-65; prof. physics Mass. Inst. Tech., 1965—. Mem. solid state sci. panel Nat. Acad. Scis.; chmn. 10th Internat. Semicondr. Conf., Cambridge, 1970; mem. exec. com. Transp. Research Bd., 1974—; past chmn. Joint Council Quantum Electronics. Recipient Oliver E. Buckley prize, 1960; citation profl. achievement Cooper Union, 1964; citation outstanding achievement USAF, 1965; Gano Dunn medal Cooper Union Alumni Assn.; Outstanding Achievement award OAR, 1970. Fellow Am. Physics Soc. (asso. editor Physics Rev. 1960-63), Optical Soc. Am., Am. Acad. Arts and Scis.; mem. Nat. Acad. Scis., Sigma Xi, Tau Beta Pi. Author: (with K.J. Button) Microwave Ferrites and Ferrimagnetics. Editor: (with others) High Magnetics Fields, Physics of Quantum Electronics; asso. editor Jour. Applied Physics, 1957-59, Microwave Jour. U.S., 1960-63. Research radar, microwave discharges, plasma physics, ferrites, semiconductors, magneto-optical studies solids and high magnetic fields, cyclotron resonance, quantum electronics and quantum magneto-optics. Address: Francis Bitter Nat Magnet Lab Mass Inst Tech Cambridge MA 02139

LAX, PETER DAVID, mathematician; b. Budapest, Hungary, May 1, 1926; s. Henry and Klara (Kornfeld) L.; came to U.S., 1941, naturalized, 1944; B.A., N.Y. U., 1947, Ph.D., 1949; D.Sc. (hon.), Kent State U., 1976; D. honoris causa U. Paris, 1979; m. Anneli Cahn, 1948; children—John, James D. Asst. prof. N.Y. U., 1949—, dir. Courant Inst. Math. Scis., 1972—. Mem. Pres.'s Com. on Nat. Medal of Sci., 1976—. Served with AUS, 1944-46. Recipient Semmelweis medal Semmelweis Med. Soc., 1975. Mem. Am. Math. Soc. (pres. 1979-80, Norbert Wiener prize), Nat. Acad. Scis., Am. Acad. Scis., Math. Assn. Am. (bd. govs.; Chauvenet prize), Soc. Indsl. and Applied Math. Author: (with Ralph Phillips) Scattering Theory, 1967, Scattering Theory for Automorphic Functions, 1976; (with A. Lax and S.Z. Burstein) Calculus with applications and computing), 1976; Hyperbolic Systems of Conservation Laws and the Mathematical Theory of Waves, 1973. Home: 300 Central Park W New York NY 10024 Office: 251 Mercer St New York NY 10012

LAX, PHILIP, interior design co. exec.; b. Newark, Apr. 22, 1920; s. Nathan and Beckie (Hirschhorn) L.; B.S., N.Y. U., 1940, postgrad., 1941-42; m. Mildred Baras, Feb. 15, 1948; children—Corinne Lax Gehr, Barbara Lax Rogal. With Lax & Co., Newark, 1942-77, v.p., 1950-77; pres. Chathill Mgmt., Inc., 1977—. Pres., B'nai B'rith Center, Rochester, Minn., 1965-70, now hon. pres.; pres. Rutgers U. Hillel Found., 1969—; chmn. United Jewish Appeal, Maplewood, N.J., 1966, 76; mem. Gov.'s Conf. on Edn., N.J., 1966, Mayor's Budget Com., Maplewood, 1958-59; co-chmn. N.J. Opera Ball, 1977; trustee B'nai B'rith Found., Washington, 1967—, chapel named for him 1975, Philip Lax Gallery of B'nai B'rith History and Archives named for him; co-chmn. B'nai B'rith Internat. Council, 1979; trustee Rutgers U. Hillel; trustee Henry Monsky Found., Washington, 1968—, Leo N. Levi Hosp., Hot Springs, Ark., 1968-71; Nat. Arthrities Hosp., 1976—; mem. Econ. Devel. Commn., Twp. of Maplewood, 1979—; mem. steering com. to Restore Ellis Island, 1977—; nat. pres. Ellis Island Restoration Commn., 1978—; Recipient Found. award B'nai B'rith, 1968, Humanitarian award, 1969, Pres.'s Gold medal, 1975; Pro Mundi Beneficio medal Brazilian Acad. Humanities, 1976. Mem. Am., Nat. (trustee 1970-73) socs. interior designers, Am. Arbitration Assn., Phi Alpha Kappa. Clubs: Masons (32 deg.); Shriners; B'nai B'rith (v.p. Supreme Lodge 1968-71, internat. bd. govs. 1971—) New York University (founder N.Y.C. 1956). Home: 35 Claremont Dr Maplewood NJ 07040 Office: Chathill Mgmt 830 Morris Turnpike Short Hills NJ 07078

LAXALT, PAUL, U.S. Senator; b. Reno, Aug. 2, 1922; s. Dominique and Theresa (Alpetche) L.; student Santa Clara U., 1940-43; B.S., LL.B., Denver U., 1949; m. Jackalyn Ross, June 23, 1946 (div.); children—Gail, Sheila, John, Michelle, Kevin, Kathleen; m. 2d, Carol Wilson, Jan. 27, 1976. Admitted to Nev. bar, 1949; practice in Carson City; partner firm Laxalt, Ross & Laxalt, 1954-62; dist. atty. Ormsby County, 1951-54; city atty. Carson City, 1954-55, lt. gov. Nev., 1963-66, gov. Nev., 1966-70, sr. partner Laxalt, Berry & Allison, Carson City, 1970-74; U.S. senator, 1975—; pres., gen. mgr. Ormsby House Hotel and Casino, Carson City, 1972—. Mem. Am. Bar Assn., Am. Legion, V.F.W. Eagle. Office: US Senate Washington DC 20510*

LAXSON, RUSSELL WILLIAM, govt. ofcl., former mfg. co. exec.; b. Mpls., June 11, 1913; s. Albert C. and Minnie A. (Brandt) L.; B.B.A. with distinction, U. Minn., 1934; m. Margot M. Jasnowski, Jan. 22, 1937; children—David C., John R. Accountant, Arthur Andersen & Co., Chgo., 1934-38; asst. auditor Middle West Service Co., Chgo., 1938-41; with Island Creek Coal Co., Huntington, W.Va., 1941-47, controller, 1949-52, v.p., controller, 1952-55, adminstrv. v.p., 1955-56; treas. Honeywell Inc., Mpls., 1956-68, v.p., 1968-78; mem. Nat. Commn. Social Security, 1978—. Recipient Elijah Watt Sells Gold medal Am. Inst. Accountants, 1939. C.P.A., Ill. Mem. Minn. Assn. Commerce and Industry (past pres.), N.A.M. (past dir.), Pub. Affairs Council (chmn. dir.), Phi Beta Kappa, Beta Gamma Sigma. Home: 1701 Archer Ct Plymouth MN 55447

LAY, DONALD POMEROY, U.S. judge; b. Princeton, Ill., Aug. 24, 1926; s. Hardy W. and Ruth (Cushing) L.; student U.S. Naval Acad., 1945-46; B.A., U. Iowa, 1948, J.D., 1951; m. Miariam Elaine Gustafson, Aug. 6, 1949; children—Stephen Pomeroy (dec.), Catherine Sue, Cynthia Lynn, Elizabeth Ann, Deborah Jean, Susan Elaine. Admitted to Nebr. bar, 1951, Iowa bar, 1951, Wis. bar, 1953; with firm Kennedy, Holland, DeLacy & Svoboda, Omaha, 1951-53, Quarles, Spence & Quarles, Milw., 1953-54, Eisenstatt, Lay, Higgins & Miller, 1954-66; U.S. circuit judge 8th Circuit U.S. Ct. Appeals, 1966—; faculty mem. on evidence Nat. Coll. Trial Judges, 1964-65; part-time instr. bus. law Omaha U., 1956-57. Pres., Douglas County (Nebr.) Dystrophy Assn., 1964. Bd. dirs. Hattie B. Monroe Home, Omaha, 1961-67. Served with USNR, 1944-46. Fellow Internat. Acad. Trial Lawyers; mem. Am., Nebr., Iowa, Wis. bar assns., Am. Judicature Soc. (dir. 1976—, exec. bd. 1979—), Law Sci. Acad. (v.p. 1960), Am. Trial Lawyers Assn. (bd. govs. 1963-65), U. Iowa Alumni Assn. (pres. Omaha-Council Bluffs chpt. 1958), Order of Coif, Delta Sigma Rho, Phi Delta Phi. Methodist (ofcl. bd. 1965-68). Mem. editorial bd. Iowa Law Rev., 1950-51. Contbr. articles to legal jours. Home: 6425 S 118 Plaza Omaha NE 68137 Office: PO Box 1538 Omaha NE 68101

LAY, HENRY ANTHONY, lawyer, retail store exec.; b. Long Beach, Calif., Apr. 11, 1941; s. Aubrey and Antonia (Siemer) L.; LL.B. cum laude, St. Louis U., 1964; children—Matthew, Andrew, Susan. Mem. firm Greensfelder, Hemker, Wiese, Gale and Chappelow, St. Louis, 1964-70, partner, 1970; with May Dept. Stores Co., St. Louis, 1970—, corp. v.p., 1972-75, v.p. real estate, 1975-77, exec. v.p. real estate and improvements, 1977—, dir., mem. exec. com., 1978—. Mem. Am. Bar Assn., Mo. Bar Assn. Club: Mo. Athletic. Office: 611 Olive St Suite 1350 Saint Louis MO 63101

LAY, HERMAN WARDEN, soft drink co. exec.; b. Charlotte, N.C., June 3, 1909; s. Jesse N. and Bertha Erma (Parr) L.; student Furman U., 1926-28; LL.D., Drury Coll., Springfield, Mo., 1966; Furman U., 1967; m. Amelia Harper, Dec. 28, 1935; children—Linda (Mrs. Henry Chambless, Jr.) (dec.), Susan LayWhite, H. Ward, Dorothy (Mrs. James Rutledge). Founder, pres., chmn. H. W. Lay & Co., Inc., 1939-61; pres. Frito-Lay, Inc., 1961-62, chmn. exec. com., chief exec. officer, 1962-65, chmn. bd., 1964-65; chmn. bd., chmn. finance com. Pepsi Co. Inc., 1965-71, chmn. exec. com., 1971—, also dir.; dir. Southwestern Life Corp., Braniff Internat. Corp., First Internat. Bancshares, Inc.; adv. dir. Third Nat. Bank of Nashville. Pres. Potato Chip Inst. Internat., 1949; chmn. Baylor U. Med. Center Found.; bd. dirs. Dallas chpt. Am. Cancer Soc., Dallas Civic Opera; former dir. Am. Mgmt. Assn.; mem. adv. council to trustees Furman U. Named Alumnus of Year, Furman U., 1965; recipient Golden Plate award Am. Acad. Achievement, 1975. Mem. Chief Execs. Forum. Clubs: Piedmont Driving (Atlanta); Preston Trl. Golf, Petroleum, Brook Hollow Golf (Dallas). Office: Pepsico Inc PO Box 35034 Dallas TX 75235

LAY, KENNETH LEE, energy cos. exec.; b. Tyrone, Mo., Apr. 15, 1942; s. Omer and Ruth E. (Reese) L.; B.A., U. Mo., 1964, M.A., 1965; Ph.D., U. Houston, 1970; m. Judith Diane Ayers, June 10, 1966; children—Mark Kenneth, Elizabeth Ayers. Corp. economist Exxon Corp., Houston, 1965-68; asso. prof. and lectr. in econs. George Washington U., 1969-73; tech. asst. to commr. FPC, 1971-72; dep. undersec. for energy Dept. Interior, 1972-74; v.p. Fla. Gas Co., (now Continental Resources Co.), Winter Park, Fla., 1974-79, pres., 1979—; pres. Fla. Gas Transmission Co., Winter Park, 1976-79; chmn. bd. dirs. Slurry Transport Assn., 1969-70; dir. Gas Research Inst. Bd. dirs. John Young Museum, Orlando, Fla., 1974-76, Winter Park Library, 1977-78. Served with USN, 1968-71. Decorated Navy Commendation award; N.A.M. fellow; State Farm fellow; Guggenheim fellow. Mem. Am. Econ. Assn., Am. Gas Assn., So. Gas Assn. (dir.), Interstate Natural Gas Assn., Young Presidents Assn. Republican. Methodist. Clubs: Winter Park Racquet, Citrus. Office: PO Box 44 Winter Park FL 32790

LAY, NORVIE LEE, lawyer, univ. dean, educator; b. Cardwell, Ky., Apr. 17, 1940; s. Arlie H. and Opha (Burns) L.; B.S., U. Ky., 1960; J.D., U. Louisville, 1963; LL.M. (Cook fellow), U. Mich., 1964, S.J.D., 1967; m. Judith Anne Finnell, June 12, 1960; 1 dau., Lea Anne. Admitted to Ky. bar, 1963; asst. prof. law U. Louisville, 1964-67, asso. prof., 1967-70, prof., 1970—, asst. dean Sch. Law, 1971-73, asso. dean, 1973—; grad. faculty Nat. Trust Sch., Northwestern U., 1975—; police ct. judge, Barbourmeade, Ky., 1972-78. Trustee, St. Joseph's Infirmary, 1974-78, S.W. Jefferson Community Hosp., 1979—. Recipient Scholarship Key, Delta Theta Phi, 1963, Outstanding Graduating Sr. award Omicron Delta Kappa, 1963. Mem. Am., Ky., Louisville bar assns., Am. Judicature Soc. Republican. Baptist. Author: Tax and Estate Planning for Community Property and the Migrant Client, 1970; contbr. articles to profl. jours. Home: 3501 Sorrento Ave Louisville KY 40222

LAY, S. HOUSTON, lawyer, diplomat, educator; b. Virden, Ill., Jan. 31, 1912; s. Samuel Houston and Pearl (Jones) L.; A.A., Blackburn Coll., 1931; A.B., U. Ill., 1936, J.D., 1937; LL.M., Columbia U., 1938; m. Eleanore Erikson, Sept. 9, 1939; 1 son, Samuel Houston, III. Admitted to Ill. bar, 1937, U.S. Supreme Ct. bar, 1950, D.C. bar, 1952; sr. atty. Office of Gen. Counsel, REA, Dept. Agr., 1938-42; dep. asst. legal adviser adminstrn. and fgn. sers. Dept. State, 1946-50; chief adminstrv. law sect. Office of Gen. Counsel, Office of U.S. High Commr., Germany, Frankfort and Bonn, 1950-51, dir. law com. and legis. affairs div., 1951-53, asst. gen. counsel, 1953-54; dep. dir. then acting dir. Office of Spl. Consular Services, U.S. Dept. State, 1954-55; counsel mut. security affairs, NATO officer Am. embassy, Athens, Greece, then sr. insp. Fgn. Service Inspection Corps, U.S. Dept. State, 1955-58; head team to survey ops. Visa Office, U.S. Dept. State, 1961-62; dir. internat. affairs and legal profession programs Am. Bar Found., 1962-67; partner firm Rose, Stansbury, Albright, Mason and Lay, San Diego, 1965-67; prof. law Calif. Western Sch. Law, 1966—; dir. Inst. Study of Internat. Law, 1974—. Mem. Inter-Am., Am. (cons. standing com. law and nat. security), Fed., Ill., Chgo. bar assns., Am. Soc. Internat. Law, Fgn. Law Assn., Am. Inst. Aeros. and Astronautics, Am. Assn. Law Schs. (chmn. admiralty sect.), World Peace Through Law Center, Chgo., San Diego councils fgn. relations, Am. Fgn. Service Assn., Am. Acad. Polit. and Social Sci. Author: (with Howard Taubenfeld) The Law of Man's Activity in Space, 1970; New Dimensions on Law of the Sea, Vols. 1-4, 1973, Vols. 5 and 6, 1977, Vols. 7 and 8, 1979. Contbr. articles to profl. publs. Home: 5930 Folsom Dr La Jolla CA 92037 Office: Calif Western Sch Law 350 Cedar St San Diego CA 92101

LAYBOURNE, EVERETT BROADSTONE, lawyer; b. Springfield, Ohio, Oct. 26, 1911; s. Lawrence Everett and Jean (Broadstone) L.; B.A., Ohio State U., 1932; J.D., Harvard, 1935; m. Dorrise Barclay, Sept. 19, 1936 (dec. Nov. 1973); m. 2d, Ottilie Kruger, July 31, 1974. Admitted to Calif. bar, 1936; mem. firms Macdonald, Schultheis & Pettit, 1936-40, Schultheis & Laybourne, 1940-54, Schultheis, Laybourne & Dowds, 1954-68, Laybourne, Keeley & MacMahon, 1968-69; sr. partner Macdonald, Halsted & Laybourne, Los Angeles, 1969—; dir. Viking Industries, Pacific Energy Corp., McBain Instruments, Coldwater Investment Co., Brouse-Whited Packaging Co.; trustee Brite-Lite Corp. Calif. chmn. UN Day, 1960; regional vice chmn. U.S. Com. for UN, 1961-64; mem. adv. council Stamp Out Smog, 1963-75; mem. spl. rev. com. Los Angeles Air Pollution Control Dist., 1964-65. Bd. dirs. Fedn. Hillside, Canyon Assos., Los Angeles, 1952-59, chmn. bd., 1957-59; bd. dirs. WAIF, Inc., 1977—, chmn. bd., 1978—; bd. dirs. UN Assn. U.S.A., 1964-65, Ralph M. Parsons Found., 1977—, v.p., 1978—; trustee, sec. Beta Theta Pi Scholastic Found. So. Calif., 1947-58. Served as lt. USNR, 1944-46. Recipient Commendation Los Angeles City Council, 1957, Alumni Centennial award Ohio State U., 1970. Mem. Big Ten Univs. Club So. Calif. (pres. 1941-42), Los Angeles Bar Assn. (exec. com. internat. law sect. 1968-74), World Affairs Council, Selden Soc., Roscomare Valley Assn. (pres. 1952-54), Phi Beta Kappa, Republican. Episcopalian (sr. warden 1966-67). Clubs: Calif., Bel-Air Country, Town Hall. Office: 1200 Wilshire Blvd Los Angeles CA 90017

LAYDE, DURWARD CHARLES, educator; b. La Crosse, Wis., Dec. 29, 1912; s. Joseph B. and Anna (Garvey) L.; B.A., St. Norbert Coll., 1933; Ph.D., U. Wis., 1940; m. Mary Agnes Lee, Nov. 20, 1943; children—Margaret, Michael, Thomas, Peter, Joseph. Mem. faculty U. Wis. System, 1939—, faculty U. Wis., Milw., 1956—, prof. chemistry, 1963—, asso. chmn., 1970-74, chmn., 1974-76. Mem. Am. Chem. Soc., A.A.A.S., Sigma Xi, Phi Lambda Upsilon. Roman Catholic. Author: Experiments in Qualitative Analysis, 1962; (with Daryle H. Busch) Introduction to Qualitative Analysis, 1961. Home: 4968 N Idlewild Ave Whitefish Bay WI 53217 Office: U Wis Milwaukee WI 53201

LAYDEN, ANDREW JAMES, parking co. exec.; b. Forney, Tex., July 1, 1930; s. Martin Patrick and Gertrude Marie (Campbell) L.; student U. St. Thomas, 1947-48; B.S., Spring Hill Coll., 1951; m. Alberta Ann Coleman, June 12, 1954; children—Mary Ann, Andrew James. With Allright Auto Parks, Inc., Houston, 1948, Mobile, Ala., 1948-51, Dallas, 1951-66, Houston, 1966—, exec. v.p., 1965-66, pres., 1966—, also chief exec. officer. Served with USMC, 1951-53. Named adm. Tex. Navy. Mem. Nat. Parking Assn. (pres.), Young Pres.'s Club, Sierra Club. Roman Catholic. Clubs: River Oaks Country, Dallas Country. Home: 2156 Troon Rd Houston TX 77019 Office: 1625 Esperson Bldg Houston TX 77002

LAYMAN, EMMA MCCLOY (MRS. JAMES W. LAYMAN), psychologist, educator; b. Danville, Va., Feb. 25, 1910; d. Charles Harold and Anna (Fisher) McCloy; A.B., Oberlin Coll., 1930; M.A., N.Y.U., 1931; Ph.D., U. Iowa, 1937; m. James Walter Layman, Dec. 12, 1936 (dec. May 4, 1978). Psychol. examiner Iowa Psychopathic Hosp., Iowa City, 1934-35, 37; clin. psychologist Mich. Children's Inst., Ann Arbor, 1935-36; supr. psychol. services Iowa Bd. Social Welfare, Des Moines, 1937-41; asso. prof. psychology Woman's Coll., U. N.C., 1947-52; supervisory clin. psychologist Brooke Army Hosp., Ft. Sam Houston, 1952-54; chief psychologist Children's Hosp., Washington, 1954-60; head dept. psychology Iowa Wesleyan Coll., Mt. Pleasant, 1960-75, asso. prof., 1960-61, prof., 1961-75, emeritus, 1975, chmn. social sci. div., 1969-75, dir. East Asian Inst., 1963-75, dir. internat. studies, 1970-75; pvt. practice clin. psychology, 1941—; lectr. U. Chattanooga, 1946-47; vis. prof. edn. Duke, summers 1948-50; adj. prof. Am. U., 1954-60; lectr. Howard U., 1956-60; cons. Walter Reed Army Hosp., 1956-60. Served from lt. (j.g.) to lt., USNR, 1943-46. Diplomate Am. Bd. Examiners Profl. Psychology. Fellow Am. Psychol. Assn., Internat. Council Psychologists (editor newsletter 1956-58, past pres., dir.); mem. Interam. Psychol. Soc., Am. Psychopath. Assn., Assn. Asian Studies, Phi Beta Kappa, Sigma Xi. Episcopalian. Author: Mental Health Through Physical Education and Recreation, 1955; Airesboro Castle, 1974; Buddhism in America, 1976; also articles. Home: 403 S Walnut St Mount Pleasant IA 52641

LAYMAN, WILLIAM ARTHUR, psychiatrist; b. West New York, N.J., Feb. 8, 1929; s. Frank Kyle and Lucy Geraldine (Rooney) L.; student N.Y. U., 1946, 48; B.S. cum laude, St. Peter's Coll., 1951; M.D., Georgetown U., 1955; 1 son, William Kraft. Intern, Hackensack (N.J.) Hosp., 1955-56; resident in psychiatry Lyons (N.J.) VA Hosp., 1956-57, Fairfield Hills Hosp., Newton, Conn., 1957-58; fellow in psychiatry Yale U., 1958-59; instr. psychiatry Seton Hall Coll. Medicine, 1959-61, asst. prof., 1961-65; asso. prof. psychiatry N.J. Med. Sch., Newark, 1965-74, clin. prof., 1974-77, prof., 1977—; pvt. practice medicine specializing in psychiatry, Newark, 1959—; dep. chmn. ednl. services, dept. psychiatry and mental health sci. N.J. Med. Sch., 1976—; cons. Greystone Park State Hosp.; mem. staff Martland Hosp. Served with U.S. Army, 1946-48. Diplomate Am. Bd. Psychiatry and Neurology. Fellow Am. Psychiat. Assn.; mem. N.J., Bergen County med. socs., AAUP. Contbr. articles to profl. jours. Home: 208 Anderson St Hackensack NJ 07601 Office: 100 Bergen St Newark NJ 07103

LAYMON, CHARLES MARTIN, clergyman, educator, editor, author; b. Dayton, Ohio, Aug. 11, 1904; s. Charles Burch and Sarah Pearl (Hinkle) L.; A.B., Ohio Wesleyan U., 1927, D.D., 1959; postgrad. U. Edinburgh, 1930-31, Harvard, 1940; S.T.B., Boston U., 1931, Th.D., 1941; m. Lillian Christina Stenberg, June 18, 1932 (dec. Oct. 1964); children—Douglas, John, Sarah; m. 2d, Virginia Love Point, May 7, 1967. Entered ministry M.E. Ch., 1924, ordained deacon, 1929, elder, 1931; pastor Red Lion (Ohio) Meth. Ch., 1924-26; asso. pastor Leyden Congl. Ch., Brookline, Mass., 1927-29; instr. English Bible, Ohio Wesleyan U., 1931-35; pastor St. Paul Meth. Ch., Delaware, Ohio, 1933-35; prof. Bible and philosophy Union Coll., Barbourville, Ky., 1935-43; dean, prof. lit. and Bible history Scarritt Coll., Nashville, 1943-50; pastor Indianola Meth. Ch.,

Columbus, Ohio, home of Wesley Found. Ohio State U., 1951-53; editor adult publs., bd. edn. Meth. Ch., Nashville, 1953-60; chmn. dept. religion, prof. religion Fla. So. Coll., Lakeland, 1960-63, prof. emeritus, 1973—. Chmn. bd. ministerial tng. and qualifications Ohio Conf. of Meth. Ch., 1951-53, also mem. exec. com. conf. bd. edn., chmn. regional personnel com. bd. missions, mem. gen. bd. edn., 1951-53. Recipient Distinguished Alumnus award Boston U. Sch. Theology, 1964. Mem. N.E.A., Nat. Assn. Bibl. Instrs., Franklin County Hist. Soc., Martha Kinney Cooper Ohioana Library Assn., Tau Kappa Epsilon, Theta Alpha Phi. Clubs: Civitan, Torch (Nashville). Author: Readings in the Gospel of St. John, 1946; Great Prayers of the Bible, 1947; Our Faith in Christ, 1949; Primer of Prayer, 1949; A New Life in Christ, 1950; The Life and Teachings of Jesus, 1955, rev., 1962; Great Moments in the Life of Christ, 1950; I Follow, 1956; Christ in the New Testament, 1958; Luke's Portrait of Christ, 1959; The Message of the Bible, 1960; The Book of Revelation, 1960; The Teachings of Jesus for Evangelism, 1961; The Challenge of the Protestant Faith to Communism, 1962; The Use of the Bible in Teaching Youth, 1962; Thy Crown Him Lord of All, 1976. Kingdom Come, 1964; New Testament Guide, 1964; Old Testament Guide, 1964; Editor, author: The Internat. Lesson Ann., 1956—; The Lord's Prayer in Its Biblical Setting, 1968; editor: The Interpreters One Volume Commentary on The Bible, 1971; Agape Love, 1972; They Dared to Speak for God, 1974; Crown Him Lord of All, 1976; editor Chinese edit. Interpreter's One Volume Commentary, 1979; contbr. articles to religious publs. Home: Route 1 Valley High Gatlinburg TN 37738

LAYNE, DONALD SAINTEVAL, biochemist, educator; b. Lime Ridge, Que., Can., Apr. 5, 1931; s. John Graham and Kathleen (Atkinson) L.; B.S., McGill U., 1953, Ph.D., 1957; m. Edith Common, Apr. 25, 1959; children—Donald Graham, Kathleen Renate, Geoffrey Haddon. With Worcester Found. for Exptl. Biology, Shrewsbury, Mass., 1959-66, dir. steroid tng. program, 1964-66; asso. prof. biology Clark U., Worcester, Mass., 1964-66; prof. biochemistry U. Ottawa (Ont., Can.), 1966-79; v.p. research Connaught Labs., Toronto, Ont., 1979—. Mem. Can. Biochem. Soc., A.A.A.S., Am. Physiol. Soc., Am. Soc. Biol. Chemists. Research, publs. in isolation Metabolites natural estrogens, metabolism norsteroids. Home: 15 Allenwood Crescent Willowdale ON M2J 2R1 Canada

LAYNE, JAMES NATHANIEL, biologist; b. Chgo., May 16, 1926; s. Leslie Joy and Harriet (Hausman) L.; B.A., Cornell U., Ithaca, N.Y., 1950, Ph.D., 1954; m. Lois Virginia Linderoth, Aug. 26, 1950; children—Linda Carrie, Kimberly, Jamie Linderoth, Susan Nell, Rachel Pratt. Grad. teaching asst. Cornell U., Ithaca, N.Y., 1950-54, asso. prof. zoology, 1963-67; asst. prof. zoology So. Ill. U., Carbondale, 1954-55; asst. prof., then asso. prof. biology U. Fla., 1955-63; asst. curator, then asso. curator mammals Fla. State Mus., Gainesville, 1955-63, research asso., 1963-65; dir. research, then resident dir. Archbold Biol. Sta., Archbold curator mammals Am. Mus. Natural History, 1967—, exec. dir. Archbold Expdns., also mem. adv. bd. and bd. dirs. Archbold expdns. Adj. prof. zoology U. South Fla.; research asso. Fla. State Collection of Arthropods; vis. scientist primate ecology sect. Nat Inst. Neurol. Diseases and Blindness, summers 1961, 62. Trustee Fla. Defenders of Environment; bd. dirs. Fla. Audubon Soc. Served with USAAF, 1944-46. Fellow A.A.A.S.; mem. Am. Soc. Zoologists, Am. Inst. Biol. Scientists, Am. Soc. Mammalogists (pres. 1970-72), Ecol. Soc. Am., Soc. for Study Evolution, Am. Soc. Naturalists, Wildlife Soc., Wildlife Disease Assn., Fla. Acad. Scis., Soc. Systematic Zoologists, Phi Beta Kappa, Sigma Xi, Phi Kappa Phi, Phi Sigma. Contbr. articles and chpt. to profl. jours. and books. Home: Box 1022 Lake Placid FL 33852 Office: Archbold Biol Sta Route 2 Box 180 Lake Placid FL 33852

LAYNE, JOHN ANTHONY, physician; b. Lanesboro, Minn., July 4, 1910; s. John Anthony and Clara (Hayes) L.; M.B., U. Minn., 1934, M.D., 1935, Ph.D., 1941; m. Margaret Hyland, Aug. 11, 1937; children—John, Robert, George, Michael. Intern, Cin. Gen. Hosp., 1934-35; teaching fellow internal medicine U. Minn., 1935-38, instr. medicine, 1938-41; practice medicine specializing in internal medicine, Great Falls (Mont.) Clinic, 1941—, partner, 1948—; dir. Great Falls Savs. and Loan Assn.; chmn. bd. commrs. Joint Commn. on Accreditation of Hosps., 1973-74; mem. nat. adv. council on med., dental, optometric and podiatric edn. HEW, 1969-70; pres. bd. trustees Mont. Physicians Service, 1970-73; pres. Mont. Bd. Med. Examiners, 1973. Served with M.C., U.S. Army, 1943-46. Decorated Legion of Merit. Diplomate Am. Bd. Internal Medicine. Mem. A.C.P. (chmn. bd. govs. 1964-66, regent 1968-73, v.p. 1973-74), AMA (commn. on cost of med. care 1959-64), Alpha Omega Alpha, Sigma Xi. Democrat. Catholic. Clubs: Internat. (Chgo.); Mont. (Helena). Contbr. articles to profl. jours. Home: 817 5 Ave N Great Falls MT 59401 Office: Great Falls Clinic PO Box 5012 Great Falls MT 59403

LAYTON, BILLY JIM, composer; b. Corsicana, Tex., Nov. 14, 1924; s. Roy William and Jimmie Vera (Franks) L.; Mus.B., New Eng. Conservatory Music, 1948; Mus.M., Yale, 1950; postgrad. (Alfred M. Hertz Travelling fellow), U. Cal. at Berkeley 1954; Ph.D., Harvard, 1960; m. Evro Zeniou, Feb. 2, 1949; children—Alexis Roy, Daphne Niobe. Faculty, New Eng. Conservatory Music, 1959-60, Harvard, 1960-66; prof. State U. N.Y. at Stony Brook 1966—, chmn. dept. music, 1966-72. Rome Prize fellow, 1954-57; grantee Nat. Inst. Arts and Letters, 1958; Guggenheim fellow, 1963; grantee Thorne Music Fund, 1968-70. Recipient Creative Arts award Brandeis U., 1961. Mem. Am. Music Center (dir. 1972-74), Am. Soc. Univ. Composers (founding), A.S.C.A.P., Am. Musicological Soc., Coll. Music Soc. (mem. council 1970-72), Internat. Soc. Contemporary Music (dir. U.S.A. sect. 1968-70), Soc. for Music Theory (founding) Composer: Five Studies for Violin and Piano, 1952; An American Portrait (symphonic overture), 1953; Three Dylan Thomas Poems (mixed chorus, brass sextet), 1954-56; String Quartet in Two Movements, 1956; Three Studies for Piano, 1957; Divertmento, 1958-60; Dance Fantasy for Orchestra, 1964. Home: 4 John's Rd Setauket NY 11733 Office: Dept Music State U N Y Stony Brook NY 11794

LAYTON, CALEB RODNEY, III, judge; b. Georgetown, Del., July 4, 1907; s. Daniel John and Laura (Schimpf) L.; grad., Phillips Andover Acad., 1926; A.B., Princeton, 1930; student Pa. Law Sch.; m. Marion Marie Brooke, Nov. 28, 1934; children—Marion (Mrs. Richard L. Laird), Caleb Rodney, D. Brooke. Asso. judge Superior Ct. Del., 1947-57; U.S. judge for Dist. of Del., 1957—. Mem. Del. Hist. Soc., Del. State Bar Assn. Clubs: Wilmington; Bidermann Golf; Greenville Country. Address: 844 King St Box 19 Wilmington DE 19801*

LAYTON, EMMET JOHN, landscape architect, city planner; b. St. Louis, Mar. 27, 1905; s. Felix Emmet and Dora Ieabelle (Milster) L.; B.Arch., Washington U., St. Louis, 1931, M.Arch., 1933; spl. student Mo. Bot. Garden, U. Mass., Amherst; m. Ruth Cornelius, June 6, 1936; children—Christopher C., Anthony E.; m. 2d, Mary C. Mackey, June 15, 1973; stepchildren—Eugene III, Ellen, John. Pvt. practice landscape architecture and city planning, St. Louis, 1945-70; lectr. city planning and landscape architecture Sch. Architecture, Washington U., 1948-59; campus landscape architect dept. facilities planning, lectr. environ. control and landscape architecture Coll. Environ. Sci., U. Wis., Green Bay, 1969-78, environ. investigator to establish Cofrin Arboretum, 1970, designer site devel. and devel. Arboretum, 1977; prin. works include master plan Mo. Bot. Garden, Nat. Shrine for Our Lady of Snows, Belleville, Ill., restoration Jefferson Barracks Hist. Park and Archives, St. Louis County, master plan Nat. Shrine for Our Lady of Miraculous Medal at St. Mary of Berrens Sem., Perryville, Mo., Winston Churchill Meml. at Westminster Coll., Fulton, Mo., design for site devel. and constrn. Cofrin Arboretum, U. Wis. at Green Bay, 1977. Mem. plan commn. City of Clayton, Mo., 1955-59; bd. govs. Tower Grove Park, St. Louis, 1955-69; trustee Wydown; Forest Subdiv., 1964-69. Recipient bd. advisers Environic Found. Internat.; mem. Lake Michigan Regional planning Council. Churchill Fellow Westminster Coll., 1969. Registered architect, Mo.; registered landscape architect, Calif., N.Y. State. Fellow Am. Soc. Landscape Architects; asso. Am. Inst. Planners (a founder, past officer St. Louis chpt.); mem. AIA, Mo. Soc. Registered Architects, Nat. Trust Historic Preservation, Landsmarks Assn. St. Louis, Mo. Parks and Recreation Assn., Ozark Rivers Assn. Address: 644 Island Way Clearwater FL 33515

LAYTON, JACK MALCOLM, pathologist; b. Ossian, Iowa, Sept. 27, 1917; s. Willis Harry and Grace Mina (Thompson) L.; A.B. magna cum laude, Luther Coll., 1939, D.Sc. (hon.), 1974; M.D., State U. Iowa, 1943; m. Lois Leone Wilson, Mar. 26, 1943 (dec. 1970); children—Jack Malcolm, Mary Mina Layton Cilek; m. 2d, Elizabeth Yerxa Sharp, June 2, 1971. Rotating intern Univ. Hosps., Iowa City, Iowa, 1943, resident, 1946-50; mem. faculty U. Iowa, 1946-67, asst. prof., 1950-54, asso. prof., 1954-61, prof., 1961-67; mem. faculty U. Ariz. Coll. Medicine, 1967—, prof., head dept. pathology, 1967—, acting dean Coll. Medicine, 1971-73; acting dir. Ariz. Med. Center, 1971-73; med. dir. U. Ariz. Med. Tech. Program, 1976—; dir. clin. pathology Ariz. Health Scis. Center, 1967—; regent Nat. Library Medicine, 1969-73, chmn., 1973; mem. spl. med. adv. group to adminstr. VA, 1975-79; mem. nat. pathology adv. council VA, 1971—. Served with USNR, 1944-46. Recipient Outstanding Tchrs. award U. Iowa, 1954, 67; Disting. Service award Iowa chpt. Arthritis and Rheumatism Found., 1963, Iowa Assn. Pathologists, 1969; Merit award Iowa Med. Soc., 1968; Outstanding Tchr. award U. Ariz., 1969, Outstanding Prof. award, 1971; Disting. Faculty award U. Ariz. Coll. Medicine Alumni Assn., 1976; Appreciated Citizens award Ariz. Soc. Med. Technologists, 1979, others; diplomate Am. Bd. Pathology (trustee 1974—). Fellow AAAS; mem. AMA (mem. ho. of dels. 1978—), Am. Soc. Clin. Pathologists (pres. 1973), Internat. Acad. Pathology (pres. U.S.-Can. div. 1976-77, v.p. N. Am. 1978—), Assn. of Pathology Chairmen (pres. 1973-74), Coll. Am. Pathologists, Am. Assn. Pathologists, Intersoc. Pathology Council (pres. 1979—), Electron Microscopy Soc. Am., AAUP, Soc. Exptl. Biology and Medicine, Ariz. Med. Assn. (So. dist. dir. 1977—), Sigma Xi (pres. U. Iowa 1965, pres. U. Ariz. 1977), Alpha Omega Alpha. Congregationalist. Home: 5642 N Mina Vista Tucson AZ 85718 Office: U Ariz Health Scis Center 1501 N Campbell Ave Tucson AZ 85724

LAYTON, JOE, dir., choreographer; b. N.Y.C., May 3, 1931; s. Irving J. and Sadie (Fischer) Lichtman; grad. high sch.; m. Evelyn Russell, Oct. 6, 1959; 1 son, Jeb James. Choreographer Broadway prodns. Sound of Music, 1959, Green Willow, 1960, Tenderloin, 1960, Sail Away, 1960; choreographer Off-Broadway prodns. On The Town, 1959, Once Upon A Mattress, 1959; dir., choreographer Broadway prodns. No Strings, 1962, The Girl Who Came To Supper, 1963, Drat the Cat, 1966, Sherry, 1967, South Pacific, 1967, George M., 1968, Dear World, 1969, (non-musical) Peterpat, 1964, Scarlett, Tokyo, 1970, Two by Two, touring prodn. Gone with the Wind, 1973; prodns. in Eng. include Sound of Music, Sail Away, No Strings, On The Town, Carol Channing and Her Ten Stout-Hearted Men, 1970; choreographer TV prodns. Mary Martin's Easter Special, 1959; dir., choreographer TV prodns. Gershwin Years, 1960, Once Upon A Mattress, 1961, My Name is Barbra, 1965, Color Me Barbra, 1966, Jack Jones Special, 1966, Belle of 14th Street-Barbra Streisand, 1967, Flip Side, 1967, Androcles and the Lion, 1968, Debbie Reynolds Special, 1968, Infancy, 1968, Littlest Angel, 1969, Theater of the Deaf, NBC Special, 1967, Lorelei, U.S. tour, 1973, Raquel Welch, Las Vegas, 1973, Raquel Welch, TV, 1974, Barbra Streisand, and Other Musical Instruments, 1974, World Tour-Carpenters, 1976, A Special Olivia Newton-John, 1976; choreographer motion picture Thoroughly Modern Millie, 1967, Harry & Walter Go to New York; stage show An Evening with Diana Ross; choreographer Overture, Grand Tour, O.W. for Royal Ballet, London, 1970, Double Exposure for City Center Joffrey Ballet, N.Y.C., 1972; dir., choreographer mus. stage prodn. Gone With the Wind, London, 1972, U.S. tour, 1973-74; pres. Jove Enterprises; dir. Lost Colony prodn. Roanoke Island Hist. Assn., 1965—, Nat. Theater of Deaf, Waterford Conn.; staged Las Vegas night club acts of Connie Stevens, Diahann Carroll, Dyan Cannon; dir., choreographer Bette Midler's Clams on the Half-Shell Revue. Served with AUS, 1952-54. Recipient Antoinette Perry awards for No Strings, 1962, Greenwillow, George M, 1969, Emmy award for My Name is Barbra, 1965.*

LAYTON, LEROY, accountant, assn. exec.; b. North Plainfield, N.J., July 16, 1914; s. LeRoy and Harriet (Randall) L.; B.S. in Commerce and Engring., Drexel U., 1937; m. Marian Louise Hall, Aug. 20, 1938; children—Nancy L. (Mrs. Ralph Schultheis Jr.), Marian L. (Mrs. Richard Lloyd), Carol L. (Mrs. David Caffery), LeRoy H. With Main Lafrentz & Co. (formerly Main & Co.), Phila. and N.Y.C., 1937-75, mng. partner, chmn. mgmt. com., 1963-72, sr. partner, 1972-75; partner McLintock Main Lafrentz-Internat., N.Y.C. and London, 1964-77, mem. adminstrv. and policy com., 1964-74, chmn. bd. mgmt., 1974-77; dir. C.I.T. Fin. Group; treas. Barclay White & Co., Phila., 1949-63. Adv. asso., div. profl. accounting Rutgers U., 1963—; mem. Commn. on Auditor's Responsibilities, 1974-78. Active Boy Scouts Am., 1954-77; dist. gov., pres. Del. County chpt., Nat. Exchange Club, 1951-53. Vice chmn. bd. trustees, chmn. exec. com. Drexel U., Phila., also chmn. vis. com. Coll. Bus. and Adminstrn., 1971—; trustee Financial Accounting Found., 1972-73; mem. adv. council Manhattan Coll. Sch. Bus., 1978—. Recipient A.J. Drexel Paul award Drexel U., 1961, 65th Anniversary citation, 1956. C.P.A., Pa., N.Y., N.J. Mem. Am. Inst. C.P.A.'s (council 1969—, nat. v.p. 1970-71, nat. pres. 1972-73, mem. acctg. principles bd. 1963-70; Gold medal award 1975), Pa., N.Y., N.J. socs. C.P.A.'s, Am. Accounting Assn., Accountants for Pub. Interest (dir. 1975—), Nat. Alumni Assn. Drexel U. (gov., past pres.), Nat. Eagle Scout Assn., Beta Alpha Psi (hon.), Beta Gamma Sigma (hon.). Republican. Methodist (treas. bd. trustees, chmn. finance com.). Club: Union League (gov. 1976-78, v.p. 1978—) (N.Y.C.). Home: 667 Navaho Trail Dr Franklin Lakes NJ 07417 Office: 280 Park Ave New York NY 10017

LAYTON, ROBERT LYNN, educator; b. Salt Lake City, May 31, 1925; s. Lynn C. and Leone (Gedge) L.; B.S., U. Utah, 1951, M.S., 1952; Ph.D., Syracuse U., 1962; m. Betty M. James, Sept. 5, 1951; children—Christine, James, Joan, Raymond, Carol, Roger, Bill. With Brigham Young U., 1954—, prof., chmn. dept. geography, 1960-65, 67—; vis. prof. U. Man., summer 1964, Portland State Coll., summer 1968; cons. cartography, land use inventory, edn. Adviser planning AID, Guatemala, 1965-66. Served to staff sgt. USAAF, 1943-46. Mem. Assn. Am. Geographers, Nat. Council Geog. Edn., Conf. Latinamericanist Geographers, Am. Soc. Planning Ofcls., Phi Beta Kappa, Sigma Xi, Phi Kappa Phi. Contbr. articles to profl. jours. Home: 490 E 1980 N Provo UT 84601

LAYTON, WILBUR LESLIE, psychologist, educator; b. Atlantic, Iowa, Mar. 26, 1922; s. Charles Emory and Helen Marie (Dorsey) L.; B.S., Iowa State U., 1943; M.A., Ohio State U., 1947, Ph.D., 1950; m. Gloria M. Madsen, Aug. 26, 1944; children—Gregory Jon, Patricia Lynn, Charles Frederick. From asst. prof. to prof. psychology also asst. dir. student counseling bur. U. Minn., 1948-59; psychol. cons. to bus. and industry, 1950—; prof. psychology Iowa State U., 1960—, chmn. dept., 1960-67, v.p. student affairs, 1967-76; vis. summer prof. Central Wash. Coll., Ellensburg, 1960, N.C. State Coll., 1962, Ohio State U., 1966; field selection officer Peace Corps, 1963-69. Mem. Iowa Policy Bd. Statewide Planning for Vocational Rehab. Services; mem. Gov. Minn. Adv. Com. Vocational Rehab., 1955-59, Gov. of Iowa's Com. Mental Health, 1961-62; mem. exec. council Minn. Psychol. Assn., 1957-59. Bd. dirs. Minn. Council for Gifted, 1956-59. Served with AUS, 1943-46. Diplomate Am. Bd. Examiners Profl. Psychology. Fellow Am. Psychol. Assn., A.A.A.S.; mem. ACLU, Am. Coll. Personnel Assn., Iowa (pres. 1962-63), Midwestern psychol. assns., Nat., Iowa rehab. assns., Nat. Council on Measurement in Edn. (pres. 1966-67), Psychometric Soc., Psychonomic Soc., Phi Kappa Phi, Sigma Xi, Psi Chi (pres. Iowa State U. chpt. 1942-43), Alpha Psi Delta. Rotarian. Author: Counseling Use of the Strong Vocational Interest Blank, 1958; (with others) Testing in Guidance and Counseling, 1963. Editor: The Strong Vocational Interest Blank: Research and Uses, 1960. Pub. Ohio State Psychol. Test, Minn. Scholastic Aptitude Test. Home: 3604 Ross Rd Ames IA 50010

LAZAR, IRVING PAUL, artists rep., lawyer; b. Stamford, Conn., Mar. 28, 1907; s. Samuel Mortimer and Stari (DeLongpre) L.; student Fordham U., 1926; LL.B., St. Lawrence U., 1931; m. Mary Van Nuys, Jan. 1963. Admitted to N.Y. bar, 1931; practiced in N.Y.C. until 1935; with Music Corp. Am., 1936-42; artists rep. service for writers/dirs. for legitimate theatre and motion pictures, N.Y.C., Beverly Hills, London and Paris, 1933—. Served to capt. USAAF, 1942-45. Office: 211 S Beverly Dr Beverly Hills CA 90212 also One E 66th St New York City NY 10021

LAZAREVICH, EMIL ROBERT, sculptor; b. San Francisco, Apr. 11, 1910; s. Zsivko and Hermine (Lyall) L.; student U. Calif., Berkeley, 1927-29, U. San Francisco, 1935-37; m. Jean E. Kane, Feb. 26, 1938 (dec. July 1962); 1 dau., Ann Jean (Mrs. Harold A. Papazian); m. 2d Virginia Owens Sciaroni, June 28, 1974 (div. Sept. 1979). One-man shows: Santa Barbara (Calif.) Mus. Art, 1945, 49, 69, M.H. de Young Meml. Mus., San Francisco, 1946, Jepson Art Inst., Los Angeles, 1949, Ankrum Gallery, Los Angeles, 1961, 63, 66, Ventura (Calif.) Coll., 1970, Santa Barbara City Coll., 1978; exhibited in numerous group shows, including: Palace Legion of Honor, San Francisco, 1960, Long Beach (Calif.) Mus. Art, 1962, La Jolla (Calif.) Art Center, 1962, Cedars-Sinai Fellowship Council, Los Angeles, 1963, Fullerton (Calif.) Jr. Coll., 1964, Fullerton Art League, 1966, Esther Bear Gallery, Santa Barbara, 1966, 67, 68, 69, 70, 71, 74; represented in permanent collections: Crocker Art Gallery, Sacramento, Denver Mus. Art, Hirshhorn Mus. and Sculpture Garden at Smithsonian Instn., Washington, San Francisco Art Inst., also numerous pvt. collections. Recipient award Santa Barbara Mus. Art, 1944, Am. Sculpture, Met. Mus. Art, 1951, Sacramento State Fair, 1954, 58; purchase awards San Francisco Art Commn., 1955, San Francisco Art Inst., 1958. Home: 1125 N Nopal St Santa Barbara CA 93103. *I have dedicated my life to creating sculpture that is music to the eye and nourishment for the soul. I have always before me the image of MAN, not as a delectation, but as something awesome.*

LAZARUS, A(RNOLD) L(ESLIE), educator, author; b. Revere, Mass., Feb. 20, 1914; s. Benjamin and Bessie (Winston) L.; student Coll. William and Mary, 1931-32; B.A., U. Mich., 1935; M.A., U. Calif. at Los Angeles, 1941, Ed.D., 1957; m. Keo Smith Felker, July 24, 1938; children—Karie (Mrs. John Friedman), Dianne (Mrs. James Runnels), David, Peter. Tchr., Calif. pub. schs., 1945-53; instr. Santa Monica (Calif.) City Coll., 1953-58; lectr. Los Angeles State Coll., 1958-59; asso. prof. U. Tex., 1959-62; prof. English, dir. tchr. edn. in English, Purdue U., Lafayette, Ind., 1962—, dir. English Curriculum Center, 1963—; gen. editor Purdue Research Found. Project English Study Units, 1969—. Mem. English commn. Coll. Entrance Examination Bd., Bd. judges Book-Of-The-Month Club Writing Fellowships, 1967-70. Served with AUS, 1942-44. Recipient Best Tchr. award Purdue Sch. Humanities, 1974; Kemper McComb award, 1976. Ford Found. fellow, 1954. Mem. Nat. Council Tchrs. of English (exec. com. Conf. English Edn. 1966-72), Poetry Soc. Am., N.E.A., Modern Lang. Assn., Coll. English Assn., Phi Beta Kappa. Author: Your English Helper, 1953; Adventures in Modern Literature, 1956, 62, 70; Harbrace English Language Series, 1963; Selected Objectives in the Language Arts, 1967; Entertainments and Valedictions, 1970; (with others) A Catalogue of Performance Objectives in English, 1971; (with others) The Grosset and Dunlap Glossary to Literature and Language, 1971, 72, 73; (with others) A Suit of Four, 1973; The Indiana Experience, 1977; poems, stories in lit. jours. Editor: Quartet mag., 1962-68, poetry editor, 1968-73. Contbg. author to New Book of Knowledge, 1967, Foundations of Education, 1967, College English: The First Year, 1968, 73, 78; also articles profl. jours. Home: 945 Ward Dr #69 Santa Barbara CA 93111. *As you unravel the threads/ swaying in your exegesis of I-thou/ Do your students divine/ the incredible whole cloth of your own denouement?*

LAZARUS, CHARLES YONDORF, merchant; b. Columbus, Ohio, Apr. 27, 1914; s. Simon and Edna (Yondorf) L.; B.A., Yale U., 1936; LL.D. (hon.), Capital U., Columbus, 1962; H.H.D., Ohio Dominican Coll., Columbus, 1968; m. Frances Nathan, May 12, 1946; children—Marjorie Lazarus Schwartz, Wendy and Stuart (twins). With F.&R. Lazarus Co., Columbus, 1936—, exec. v.p., 1950-59, pres., 1959-69, chmn. bd., chief exec. officer, 1969—; v.p., dir. Federated Dept. Stores, Inc.; dir. Asso. Mdsg. Corp., Fed. Res. Bank Cleve., Midland Mut. Life Ins. Co. Served to lt. col. USAAF, 1941-45. Decorated Legion of Merit, Bronze Star; recipient Distinguished Service award Coll. Adminstrv. Sci., Ohio State U., 1970; Centennial Achievement award Ohio State U., 1970; Columbus award Columbus C. of C., 1972; Nat. Honoree award Beta Gamma Sigma, 1972. Clubs: University, Athletic, Winding Hollow Country, LaQuinta Country, Muirfield Village Golf, Rocky Fork Country. Home: 236 N Columbia Ave Columbus OH 43209 Office: F&R Lazarus Co Town and High Sts Columbus OH 43216

LAZARUS, DAVID, physicist, educator; b. Buffalo, Sept. 8, 1921; s. Barney B. and Lillian (Markel) L.; B.S., U. Chgo., 1942, M.S., 1947, Ph.D., 1949; m. Betty Jane Ross, Aug. 15, 1943; children—Barbara, William, Mary Ann, Richard. Instr. electronics U. Chgo., 1942-43, electronics engr., 1946-49, instr. physics, 1949; research asso. radio research lab. Harvard, 1943-45, vis. prof., 1978-79; faculty physics U. Ill., Champaign, 1949—, prof., 1959—; asso. prof. U. Paris, 1968-69; vis. prof. M.I.T., 1978-79. Vis. scientist Am. Inst. Physics, N.Y.C., 1962-69; cons. phys. sci. study com. Halicrafters Co., Chgo., 1957-69, Gen. Electric Co., Cin., 1960-68, Gen. Atomic, La Jolla, Calif., 1962-63, Lawrence Radiation Lab., 1967-68, Sandia Lab., 1970-72, Addison-Wesley Pub. Co., Reading, Mass., 1964—. Guggenheim fellow, 1968-69. Fellow Am. Phys. Soc. (mem. council 1974-78, mem. exec. com. div. condensed matter physics 1968-70, 74-78, chmn. New Materials prize com. 1976, chmn. Buckley prize com. 1979). Author: (with H. de Waard) Modern Electronics, 1966; (with R.I. Hulsizer)

The World of Physics, 1972; also articles. Home: 502 W Vermont Ave Urbana IL 61801

LAZARUS, GUSTAV, ret. mfg., distbg. co. exec., lawyer; b. Pitts., June 8, 1911; s. Ruben Harry and Dora (Brooks) L.; LL.B., St. John's U., 1932; m. Sally Carr, Oct. 17, 1937; children—John, Eric, Robert. Admitted to N.Y. State bar, 1933; practice law, N.Y.C., 1933-43, 46-77; presiding insp. Immigration and Naturalization Service, Dept. Justice, 1943-46; gen. counsel Garcia Corp., Teaneck, N.J., 1953-77, dir., 1957-77, exec. v.p. law, 1975-77, ret., 1977. Mem. Am. (chmn. immigration and nationality com., adminstrv. law sect. 1959-60), Fed. bar assns., Assn. Immigration and Naturalization Lawyers (nat. pres. 1951), N.Y. County Lawyers Assn., Am. Arbitration Assn. Mason. Home: 190 Beverly Rd White Plains NY 10605

LAZARUS, HERMAN, lawyer; b. Phila., Apr. 21, 1910; s. Samuel and Fannie (Levin) L.; B.S. in Edn., Temple U., 1933, LL.B., 1937; LL.M., U. Pa., 1941; m. Sarah Edith Goldstein, Oct. 14, 1933; 1 dau., Ruth Helen Holmes. Admitted to Pa. bar, 1938, D.C. bar, 1951; atty. N.L.R.B., 1942-46, asst. to gen. counsel, 1946-47; head labor-mgmt. sect. Pub. Affairs Inst., 1947-49; counsel U.S. Senate Com. on Labor and Pub. Welfare, 1949-51; pub. mem. rev. and appeals com. W.S.B., 1951-52, also pub. mem. and vice chmn., 1952-53; practice law in Phila., 1953—; sr. partner firm Cohen, Shapiro, Polisher, Shiekman & Cohen, 1972—. Hon. Pres. Jewish Employment and Vocational Soc. Mem. Am., Pa., Phila. bar assns. Home: William Penn House 1919 Chestnut St Philadelphia PA 19103 Office: 22d Floor 12 S 12th St Philadelphia PA 19107

LAZARUS, KENNETH ANTHONY, lawyer; b. Passaic, N.J., Mar. 10, 1942; s. John Joseph and Margaret (Di Cenzo) L.; B.A., U. Dayton, 1964; J.D., U. Notre Dame, 1967; LL.M. in Taxation, George Washington U., 1971; m. Marylyn Jane Flemming, Aug. 13, 1966; children—Maggi Ann, John, Joseph. Admitted to N.J. bar, 1967, U.S. Tax Ct. and Ct. Claims, 1970, U.S. Supreme Ct., 1971, D.C. bar, 1976; trial atty. U.S. Dept. Justice, 1967-71; asso. counsel and chief counsel to Minority Com. on Judiciary, U.S. Senate, 1971-74; asso. counsel to Pres. U.S., 1974-77; partner firm Bierbower & Rockefeller, Washington, 1977—; mem. adv. bd. U. Dayton Sch. Law, 1975—; adj. prof. Georgetown U. Law Sch. U.S. reporter to UN, 1975-77; mem. adv. council Republican Nat. Com., 1977—. Mem. D.C. Bar Assn., Bar Assn. D.C., Am. Bar Assn., Fed. Bar Assn., N.J. Bar Assn., Am. Judicature Soc., Am. Law Inst., Gray's Inn. Clubs: Westwood Country, Metropolitan. Contbr. numerous articles to profl. pubs. Home: 2600 Hickory Hollow Oakton VA 22124 Office: 1625 K St NW Washington DC 20006

LAZARUS, MAURICE, retail exec.; b. Columbus, Ohio, June 27, 1915; s. Fred, Jr., and Meta (Marx) L.; student Ohio State U.; B.A., Harvard, 1937; LL.D., Am. Internat. Coll., 1969; m. Nancy Stix, June 7, 1942; children—Carol, Jill. Div. mdse. mgr. John Shillito Co., Columbus, 1937-41; head service and control Foley's, Houston, 1945-48, exec. v.p., 1948-58; pres., treas. Filene's, Boston, 1958-64, chmn. bd., 1964-65; vice chmn. Federated Dept. Stores, Inc., Boston, 1965-70, chmn. finance com., 1971—, also dir.; dir. Arthur D. Little Inc., Itek Corp., New Eng. Tel. & Tel. Co., Mass. Mut. Life Ins. Co., Cambridge Center Adult Edn., 1974-78. Mem. adv. com. on nat. health ins. issues HEW, 1977-78; mem. adv. Council Pres.'s Commn. on Status of Women, 1963-68; chmn. exec. com. Public Agenda Found.; mem. div. health scis. and tech. Harvard U.-M.I.T.; mem. adv. bd. Schlesinger Library Women's Archives, Radcliffe Coll., 1972-76; mem. bd. overseers Harvard Coll.; mem. ethics adv. bd. HEW; vis. com., chmn. central services Med. Sch., dental medicine, Sch. Pub. Health, dept. Romance langs. and lits. Harvard U., 1974-77, mem. governance com., 1968-71; chmn. adv. com. Joint Center Urban Studies. Trustee Mass. Gen. Hosp., Old Sturbridge Village, 1965-78, Marine Biol. Lab., Tufts U. Civic Edn. Found. of Lincoln Filene Center for Citizenship and Pub. Affairs, New Eng. Med. Center Hosp., 1960-78, Beaver Country Day Sch., 1960-64, Beth Israel Hosp., 1958-65, Bennington Coll., 1965-72, Combined Jewish Philanthropy Greater Boston, 1962-65; bd. dirs. Boston chpt. A.R.C., 1962-64, Harvard Community Health Plan. Asso. Harvard Alumni, 1966-73, pres., 1972-73; mem. Mass. Higher Edn. Facilities Commn., 1970-74; mem. corp. Northeastern U., Peter Bent Brigham Hosp.; bd. overseers Boston Symphony Orch., 1971-74; vis. com. Univ. Cancer Found., Houston; mem. Mass. Inst. Tech. Council Arts, 1972-77, Harvard Med. Center, 1977-79. Clubs: Belmont (Mass.) Country; Bay, Harvard (Boston, N.Y.C.); University (N.Y.); St. Botolph (Boston); Commercial-Merchants (Boston). Home: 144 Brattle St Cambridge MA 02138 Office: 50 Cornhill St Boston MA 02108

LAZARUS, MELL, cartoonist; m. Eileen Hortense Israel, June 19, 1949; children—Marjorie, Susan, Catherine. Cartoonist-writer Miss Peach, 1957—, Momma, 1970—. Served with USNR, 1945, USAFR, 1951-54. Mem. Nat. Cartoonists Soc. (chmn. membership com. 1965, Humor Strip Cartoonist of Year, 1973), Writers Guild Am. West, Sigma Delta Chi. Author: (anthologies) Miss Peach; Miss Peach Are These Your Children?, Future Doctors of America; Miss Peach, Again; Momma; The Momma Treasury; Miss Peach of the Kelly School; Momma, We're Grownups Now!; (novel) The Boss is Crazy, Too, 1964; (plays) Everybody Into the Lake, Elliman's Fly, Lifetime Eggcreams, 1969-70; (juvenile) Francine, Your Face Would Stop a Clock, 1975; co-author Miss Peach TV spl. programs Turkey Day Pageant and Annual Heart Throb Ball. Office: Field Newspaper Syndicate 401 N Wabash Ave Chicago IL 60611

LAZARUS, RALPH, merchant; b. Columbus, Ohio, Jan. 30, 1914; s. Fred and Meta (Marx) L.; B. A., Dartmouth Coll., 1935, LL.D., 1965; LL.D., U. Miami, 1961; D.C.S., Suffolk U., 1962; LL.D., Xavier U., 1965; m. Gladys Kleeman, June 24, 1939; children—Mary (dec.), Richard (dec.), John, James. Vice pres., gen. mdse. mgr. F. & R. Lazarus & Co., 1935-51; with OPA, WPB, 1941-43; exec. v.p. Federated Dept. Stores, Inc., Cin., 1951-57, pres., 1957-67, chmn. bd., 1967—, chief exec. officer, 1966—; dir. Chase Manhattan Corp., Chase Manhattan Bank, Scott Paper Co., Gen. Electric Co.; mem. President's Adv. Com. on Trade Negotiations. Dir., Nat. Com. on U.S.-China Relations; mem. Cin. Council on World Affairs; mem. Council Better Bus. Burs., Nat. Center for State Cts., Cin. Bus. Com., Nat. Urban League, Bus. Com. for Arts, Inc., Eisenhower Exchange Fellowships; Rockefeller U. Council; trustee Com. Econ. Devel., Dartmouth Coll. Served to lt. USAAF, World War II. Recipient Gold Medal award Nat. Retail Mchts. Assn., 1974; Brotherhood award NCCJ, 1975. Mem. Council on Fgn. Relations, Bus. Council. Clubs: Athletic, University, Winding Hollow Country (Columbus); Harmonie, Sky (N.Y.C.); Blind Brook Country (White Plains, N.Y.); Losantiville Country, Camargo Country, Commonwealth, Comml., Dartmouth, Queen City (Cin.); La Quinta (Calif.) Country. Home: 1009 Catawba Valley Dr Cincinnati OH 45226 Office: 7 W 7th St Cincinnati OH 45202

LAZARUS, RICHARD STANLEY, scientist, educator; b. N.Y.C., Mar. 3, 1922; s. Abe and Matilda (Marks) L.; A.B., City Coll. N.Y., 1942; M.S., U. Pitts., 1947, Ph.D., 1948; m. Bernice H. Newman, Sept. 2, 1945; children—David Alan, Nancy Eve. Asst. prof. Johns Hopkins, 1948-53; psychol. cons. VA, 1952—; asso. prof. psychology, dir. clin. tng. program Clark U., Worcester, Mass., 1953-57; asso. prof. psychology U. Calif. at Berkeley, 1957-59, prof. psychology, 1959—; prin. investigator Air Force contracts dealing with psychol. stress, 1951-53, USPHS grant on personality psychol. stress, 1953-70; NIA and NCI grantee on stress, coping and health, 1977—; USPHS spl. fellow Waseda U., Japan, 1963-64. Served to 1st lt. AUS, 1943-46. Guggenheim fellow, 1969-70; Army Research Inst. research grantee, 1973-75. Diplomate in clin. psychology Am. Bd. Examiners in Profl. Psychology. Fellow AAAS, Am. Psychol. Assn.; mem. Western Psychol. Assn. Author several books, numerous publs. in profl. jours. Home: 3255 Woodview Dr Lafayette CA 94549 Office: Dept Psychology U Calif Berkeley CA 94720

LAZENBY, FRED WIEHL, ins. co. exec.; b. Chattanooga, Jan. 13, 1932; s. John Wesley and Adela (Valenzuela) L.; B.A. cum laude, Vanderbilt U., 1954; m. Kathryn Woodard, Sept. 20, 1958; children—Kathryn Wesley, Grace Woodard. With Nat. Life & Accident Ins. Co., Nashville, 1956—, field supr., 1961-62, dist. mgr., 1962-64, mgr. mktg. research, 1964-65, asst. v.p., regional mgr., 1965-71, 2d v.p., exec. asst., 1971-72, 2d v.p., dir. agys., 1972-74, sr. v.p., 1974-77, exec. v.p., 1977—, also dir.; dir. Nat. Property Owners Ins. Co. Served to 1st lt. U.S. Army, 1954-56. C.L.U. Republican. Methodist. Clubs: Belle Meade Country, Nashville City. Office: Nat Life Center Nashville TN 37250

LAZEROWITZ, ALICE AMBROSE (MRS. MORRIS LAZEROWITZ), educator, author; b. Lexington, Ill., Nov. 25, 1906; d. Albert Lee and Bonnie (Douglass) Ambrose; A.B., James Millikin U. (now Millikin U.), 1928, LL.D., 1958; M.A., U. Wis., 1929, Ph.D., 1932, Cambridge (Eng.) U., 1938; m. Morris Lazerowitz, June 15, 1938. Instr. philosophy U. Mich., 1935-37; asst. prof. Smith Coll., 1937-43, asso. prof., 1943-51, prof. philosophy, 1951-64, chmn. dept., 1958-70, Sophia and Austin Smith prof. philosophy, 1964-72, prof. emeritus, 1972—; vis. Disting. prof. U. Del., 1975; prof. in emeritus program Hampshire Coll., 1977, 79. Mem. Am. Philos. Assn. (pres. Eastern div. 1975). Author: (with Morris Lazerowitz) Fundamentals of Symbolic Logic, 1948, rev. edit., 1962; Logic: The Theory of Formal Inference, 1961, rev. edit., 1972; Essays in Analysis, 1966; (with Lazerowitz) Philosophical Theories, 1975. Author and editor: (with Morris Lazerowitz) G.E. Moore—Essays in Retrospect, 1970, Ludwig Wittgenstein, Philosophy and Language, 1972. Editor Jour. Symbolic Logic, 1953-68. Home: Newhall Rd Conway MA 01341

LAZRUS, BENJAMIN, watch mfr.; b. N.Y.C., Apr. 29, 1894; s. Israel and Ella (Cohn) L.; student Columbia Coll., 1912-13, 15; m. Bess Feldman, Feb. 24, 1924; children—Natalie Louise, Jonathan Ezra. A founder Benrus Watch Co., 1923, chmn. bd. Benrus Watch Co., Inc. Mem. Watch Mfs. Adv. Com., WPB. Trustee Congregation Emanu-El, New York, Jewish Community Center White Plains, Nat. Jewish Hosp., Denver. Mem. exec. com. Am. Jewish Com., Jewish Bd. Guardians. Chmn., Jewish Big Brother Movement of N.Y.; v.p. Council Jewish Fedns. and Welfare Funds, Inc.; chmn. nat. adv. council Syngogue Council Am.; bd. dirs. Nat. Jewish Welfare Bd., Nat. Refugee Service; trustee, v.p. Fedn. Jewish Philanthropies N.Y.; treas. Am. Jewish Tercentenary Com.; dir. U.S.O. Greater N.Y. Jewish religion (v.p., trustee congregation). Clubs: Harmonie, Quaker Ridge Golf, Metropolis Country, Jewelers 24 Karat (N.Y.C.). Home: 150 E 69th St New York City NY 10021 Office: 1776 Broadway New York City NY 10019

LAZRUS, OSCAR M., lawyer; b. Jassy, Rumania, July 12, 1887; s. Israel and Ella (Cohn) L.; came to U.S. 1889, naturalized citizen; LL.B., St. Lawrence U., 1909; m. Paula Kronheim, Feb. 11, 1913 (dec. 1952); children—Julian, Jay K.; m. 2d, Anna Leitner, 1953 (dec. 1961); m. 3d, Rose Lazrus, 1962. Apprentice law office Samuel Untermeyer, 1905-06; pvt. practice, N.Y.C., 1909-24; a founder, past pres., past chmn. bd. Benrus Watch Co. Nat. sec. NCCJ; mem. exec. com. Am. Jewish Com.; mem. pres.'s council Brandeis U. Bd. dirs. Am. Joint Distbn. Com.; life trustee Fedn. Jewish Philanthropies N.Y.; bd. govs. Union Am. Hebrew Congregations. Recipient certificate of appreciation Mayor John V. Lindsay of N.Y.C., 1967; cited by NCCJ, gifted $100,000 to Conf. for Oscar M. Lazrus Center for Interreligious Affairs, 1972. Mem. Am. Bar Assn. Jewish. Clubs: Harmonie, Bankers, 24 Karat. Home: 936 Fifth Ave New York City NY 10021 Office: 43 W 57th St New York City NY 10019

LAZZARO, ANTHONY DEREK, univ. ofcl.; b. Utica, N.Y., Jan. 31, 1921; s. Angelo Michael and Philomena (Vanilla) L.; B.S. in Indsl. Engring., U. So. Calif., 1948; LL.D., Pepperdine U., 1974; m. Shirley Margaret Jones, Dec. 20, 1941; 1 dau., Nancy Lee (Mrs. Sergio G. Ferri). Asst. bus. mgr. U. So. Calif., Los Angeles, 1948-60, asst. bus. mgr., dir. campus devel., 1960-65, asso. bus. mgr., dir. campus devel., 1965-71, asso. v.p. bus. affairs, 1971-72, v.p. bus. affairs, 1972—. Mem. nat. adv. council United Student Aid Funds, N.Y.C., 1973—, chmn., 1976-77; dir. Republic Fed. Savs. & Loan Assn., and subs. corps., Los Angeles; spl. studies cons., phys. facilities br. Div. Higher Edn., Office Edn., HEW, 1956-59. Mem. citizens com. Palos Verdes Bd. Edn., 1955-57; mem. Hoover urban renewal adv. com. Community Redevel. Agy., City of Los Angeles, 1960—. Served to lt. USNR, 1941-46. Registered profl. engr., Calif. Mem. Nat. (pres. 1979, dir. 1972—, chmn. goals and programs com. 1978), Western (pres. 1972), assns. coll. and univ. bus. officers, Soc. for Coll. and Univ. Planning, Phi Kappa Phi, Tau Beta Pi. Clubs: University, Jonathan (Los Angeles). Editorial cons. College and University Business, 1955-58. Home: 4012 Via Largavista Palos Verdes Estates CA 90274 Office: University Park OWH 100 Los Angeles CA 90007

LEA, LOLA STENDIG, lawyer; b. N.Y.C., Sept. 20, 1934; d. Hershel and Sophie (Golub) Stendig; B.A. cum laude, N.Y. U., 1954; LL.B., Yale U., 1957; m. Robert M. Lea, Sept. 12, 1953 (div. Apr. 1976); 1 dau., Jennie. Admitted to N.Y. State bar, 1958; law clk. to U.S. dist. judge So. Dist. N.Y., 1957-59; asst. U.S. atty. So. Dist. N.Y., 1959-61, asso. C.C. Davis, N.Y.C., 1961-67; mem. firm Davis & Cox, N.Y.C., 1967-71, Lea, Goldberg & Spellun, P.C., N.Y.C., 1971-77, Trubin, Sillcocks, Edelman & Knapp, N.Y.C., 1977—; spl. counsel to N.Y. 1st dept. joint interprofl. com. Jrs. and Lawyers, 1972—; lectr. Practicing Law Inst., N.Y.C., 1969-70, 74, 79; spl. mediator Med. Malpractice Mediation part Supreme Ct. N.Y., 1971—. Fellow Am. Bar Found.; mem. Am. Bar Assn., N.Y. Bar Assn. (del. 1972-77, mem. exec. com. 1976-77), Assn. Bar City N.Y. (chmn. grievance com. 1978—, chmn. medicine and law com. 1969-71, mem. other coms.), N.Y. County Lawyers Assn. (dir. 1978—). Home: 24 Garden Pl Brooklyn NY 11201 Office: Trubin Sillcocks Edelman & Knapp 375 Park Ave New York NY 10022

LEA, LORENZO BATES, lawyer; b. St. Louis, Apr. 12, 1925; s. Lorenzo Bates and Ursula Agnes (Gibson) L.; B.S., M.I.T., 1946; J.D., U. Mich., 1949; grad. Advanced Mgmt. Program, Harvard U., 1964; m. Marcia Gwendolyn Wood, Mar. 21, 1953; children—Victoria, Jennifer, Christopher. Admitted to Ill. bar, 1950; with Standard Oil Co. (Ind.), Chgo., 1949—, asst. gen. counsel, 1963-71, asso. gen. counsel, 1971-72, gen. counsel, 1972-78, v.p., gen. counsel, 1978—. Trustee Village of Glenview (Ill.) Zoning Bd., 1961-63; bd. dirs. Chgo. Crime Commn., 1978—, United Charities of Chgo., 1973—, Midwest Council for Internat. Econ. Policy, 1973—. Served with USNR, 1943-46. Mem. Am. Bar Assn., Ill. Bar Assn., Chgo. Bar Assn., Am. Petroleum Inst., Assn. Gen. Counsel, Order of Coif, Sigma Xi. Republican. Mem. United Ch. of Christ. Clubs: Econs., Legal, Mid-Am. (Chgo.); Glen View. Office: 200 E Randolph Dr Chicago IL 60601

LEA, SCOTT CARTER, packaging exec.; b. New Orleans, Nov. 14, 1931; s. Leonard G. and Helen (Stoughton) L.; B.A., Amherst Coll., 1954; M.B.A., U. Pa., 1959; m. Marilyn Ruth Blair, Oct. 25, 1957; children—Scott, Nancy B., Mark S. Sales and mktg. positions Riegel Paper, 1959-66, sales mgr. folding carton dept. southeastern div., 1966-67, gen. sales mgr., 1967-69, v.p. folding carton dept., 1969-71; v.p. bd. conversion div. Rexham Corp., Charlotte, N.C., 1971-73, v.p. packaging group, 1973-74, pres., 1974—. Mem. adv. bd. Bernard M. Baruch Coll., N.Y.C.; trustee Johnson C. Smith U., Charlotte, N.C. Served with U.S. Army, 1954-57. Mem. Paperboard Packaging Council (sr. adv. council), Charlotte C. of C. (dir. 1977-78). Club: Carmel Country (Charlotte). Home: 3704 Stone Ct Charlotte NC 28211 Office: Greenwood Cliff Charlotte NC 28204

LEA, TOM, painter, writer; b. El Paso, Tex., July 11, 1907; s. Tom and Zola (Utt) L.; student Art Inst. Chgo., 1924-26; Litt.D., Baylor U., 1967; L.H.D., So. Meth. U., 1970; m. Sarah Catherine Dighton, July 14, 1938; 1 son, James Dighton. Mural painter, comml. artist, art tchr., Chgo, 1926-33; student in Italy; 1930, N.M. 1933-35; staff Lab. Anthropology, Santa Fe, 1933-35; muralist, easel painter, book illustrator, El Paso, 1936—, writer, 1947—; war corr. Life mag., 1941-46; executed murals pub. bldgs. El Paso, Washington, Dallas, Odessa, Tex., Pleasant Hill, Mo.; easel works represented in Dallas Mus. Fine Arts, Life mag. World War II art, collection in Pentagon, El Paso Mus. Art, Humanities Research Center, U. Tex., Austin, pvt. collections. Author, illustrator: Peleliu Landing, 1945; The Brave Bulls, 1949; The Wonderful Country, 1952; The King Ranch, 2 vols., 1957; The Primal Yoke, 1960; The Hands of Cantú, 1964; A Picture Gallery 1968; In the Crucible of the Sun, 1974. Address: 2401 Savannah St El Paso TX 79930

LEA, WILLIAM SENTELLE, clergyman; b. Easton, Wash., Nov. 24, 1911; s. Joseph Marshall and Kitty May (Sentelle) L.; B.S., Davidson Coll., 1932; B.D., U. of South, 1935, D.D., 1952, M.Div., 1965; postgrad. Oxford (Eng.) U., 1968, St. Andrews U., 1970; m. Jean Emert, July 10, 1940; children—Anne (Mrs. John Tuohy), Jean (Mrs. Dennis Scully). Ordained to ministry Episcopal Ch., 1935; rector St. Paul's Ch., Kingsport, Tenn., 1937-40, Ch. of Advent, Spartanburg, S.C., 1940-44, Christ Ch., Raleigh, N.C., 1944-46, St. Andrew's Ch., Maryville, Tenn., 1946-47, St. Johns Ch., Knoxville, Tenn., 1947-56; editor Episcopal Churchnews, 1956-57; dean St. John's Cathedral, Denver, 1957-62; rector Christ Ch., Winnetka, Ill., 1962-78; now free lance writer; also with exec. council Episcopal Ch. Instr., Maryville (Tenn.) Coll., 1945-46, Seabury-Western Theol. Sem., Evanston, Ill., 1964-66; pres. Denver Council Chs., 1960-61. Chmn., Mayor's Commn. on Human Relations, Denver, 1960-62. Bd. dirs. Episcopalian mag., 1957—; mem. selection com. Rockefeller Fund for Theol. Edn., 1968—. Mem. Phi Gamma Delta. Clubs: Indian Hill (Winnetka); Glenview (Golf, Ill.); University (Chgo.); Mission Valley (Nakomis, Fla.). Author: Is God Dead?, 1968; This We Can Believe, 1972; Life and Work of Theodore Wedel, 1972; Faith and Science—Mutual Responsibility for a Human Future, 1979; asso. editor: Anglican Theol. Rev., 1972—, Living Church, 1957-74. Home: 5646 Cape Leyte Dr Sarasota FL 33581 also Gen Delivery Ephraim WI 54211

LEABO, DICK ALBERT, educator; b. Walcott, Iowa, Oct. 30, 1921; s. Albert Thomas and Clara (Beinke) L.; B.S., U. Iowa, 1949, M.A., 1950, Ph.D., 1953; m. Artus M. Vande Voort, June 11, 1955; 1 son, Thomas William (dec.). Research asst., then research asso. U. Iowa, 1948-53, asst. prof., asst. dir. Bur. Bus. and Econ. Research, 1953-56; asst. prof., asst. dir. Bur. Bus. and Econ. Research, Mich. State U., 1956-57; faculty U. Mich., 1957-78, prof. statistics, 1963—, Fred M. Taylor Endowed Disting. prof., 1978—, asso. dean Grad. Sch. Bus. Adminstrn., 1962-65, dir. doctoral studies program, 1965. Cons. Brookings Instn., 1957-59; Exchange prof. Nederlandsche Econ. Hoogesch., 1965. Served to 1st lt. USAAF, 1943-45; CBI. Decorated D.F.C., Air medal. Mem. Am. Statis. Assn. (exec. com. faculty reps. 1965-68, U. Mich. faculty rep. 1965-68), Am. Econs. Assn., Am. Finance Assn., Nat. Assn. Bus. Economists, Omicron Delta Epsilon, Phi Kappa Phi (nat. v.p. 1977—, exec. com. pres. U. Mich.). Presbyn. (deacon, elder). Author: Basic Statistics, 5th edit., 1976; (with F.A. Bond, A.W. Swinyard) Preparation for Business Leadership, 1964; (with L.F. Hampel) Workbook in Business and Economic Statistics, 5th edit., 1962. Contbr. articles to profl. jours. Office: Grad Sch Bus Adminstrn U Mich Ann Arbor MI 48109

LEACH, DANIEL EDWARD, govt. ofcl.; b. Detroit, Apr. 2, 1937; s. Vincent George and Helen (Goldike) L.; A.B., Colgate U., 1958; LL.B., Detroit Coll. Law, 1961; M.Law, Georgetown U., 1963; m. Jean Carter, 1960; children—Robin, Jennifer, Carter. Trial atty. civil div. Dept. Justice, 1962-65; mem. firm Sullivan, Eaimes, Moody and Petrillo, Detroit, 1965-66; gen. counsel Democratic Policy Com., U.S. Senate, Washington, 1966-76; vice chmn. U.S. Equal Employment Opportunity Commn., Washington, 1977—; mem. Pres.' Regulatory Council, Task Force on Youth Unemployment, Adminstrv. Conf. of U.S.; vis. prof. law U. Denver, 1972, Cath. U. Am., 1973. Mem. D.C. Bar Assn. Author works in field. Home: 3419 Woodside Rd Alexandria VA 22310 Office: 2401 E St NW Washington DC 20506

LEACH, DAVID GOHEEN, plant geneticist; b. New Bethlehem, Pa., Jan. 18, 1913; s. Andrew Steelman and Nellie (Goheen) L.; A.B., Coll. of Wooster (Ohio), 1934, D.Sc., 1966; children by former marriage—Robin, David Goheen, Brian. Partner, Western Bldg. Devel. Co., Denver, Boyd & Shriver, Indiana, Pa., Mt. Lebanon Shopping Center, Pitts.; genetics research ornamental plants; vis. lectr. plant genetics colls., univs., state expt. stas.; cons. plant and animal genetics USSR, 1962, U.S. Dept. Agr., DuPont affiliated founds.; lectr. bot. gardens and arboretums; lectr. U. Szechuan, People's Republic of China; exhbn. photographs of wilderness explorations Photography in Fine Arts tour, sponsored Sat. Rev., 1960; dir. Western Pa. Laurel Festival; mem. Gov.'s Adv. Commn. Cook's Forest, 1956-59; research expt. sta., Brookville, Pa., 1954-70, North Madison, Ohio, 1970—; co-chmn. Internat. Conf. on Chemotaxonomy, N.Y. Bot. Garden, 1978; plant explorer central highlands of New Guinea, 1979, Western China, 1979. Dir. Local YMCA, A.R.C., Am. Cancer Soc., Gateway Players. Recipient certificate of Merit, Pa. Hort. Soc., Dr. Walter Dick Meml. award, 1951; Recognition award C. of C., 1959; Ann. award Pa. Festival, 1962; Great Lakes Region award for research and publs., 1962; gold medal Am. Rhododendron Soc., 1965, Garden Club Am., 1969; Loder Cup, Royal Hort. Soc. (Eng.), 1970; Jackson Dawson medal Mass. Hort. Soc., 1973; Research award Pa. Nurserymen's Assn., 1979. Fellow Royal Hort. Soc.; mem. Internat. Soc. Hort. Sci., Am. Assn. Bot. Gardens and Arboretums, Am. Hort. Soc. (pres. 1970-74), Am. Rhododendron Soc. (dir.), Internat. Plant Propagator's Soc. (dir.), Nat., Western Pa. conservancies, Am. Audubon Soc., Nat. Wildlife Fedn. Republican. Presbyn. Clubs: Hope Island (Maine) (pres.); Batteaux Bay (Charlottesville, Tobago, W.I.). Author: Rhododendrons of the World, 1961. Contbr. to Ency. Brit., also numerous articles to books, popular and profl. hort. publs.

LEACH, DAVID MILES, educator; b. South Bend, Wash., Mar. 31, 1923; s. Kenneth Mallory and Burdella DeEtte (Deach) L.; A.B., Whitman Coll., 1949; Ph.D., U. Rochester, 1959; m. Mattie Arvilla Caldwell, Sept. 8, 1943; children—David Michael, Patrick Eugene (dec.). Faculty, Alfred (N.Y.) U., 1952-69, prof. history and polit. sci., 1963-69, chmn. dept., 1964-68, dean Coll. Liberal Arts, 1967-68; prof. history, chmn. dept., chmn. div. social scis. Wilkes Coll., Wilkes-Barre, Pa., 1969—. Served with USAAF, 1943-45. Recipient Dexter Perkins prize history U. Rochester, 1956; Achievement award Sigma Chi, 1947. History fellow U. Rochester, 1949-52. Mem. Am. Hist. Assn., Orgn. Am. Historians, AAUP, Phi Beta Kappa. Home: 53 Crisman St Forty Fort PA 18704

LEACH, EDWARD CURTIS, former hotel exec.; b. Cleve., Mar. 21, 1913; s. Frank L. and Marguerite (Sullivan) L.; student U.S. Mil. Acad., 1932-33; m. Elsie Pauline Norwood, May 18, 1942; children—Marguerite Ann, Betsy Kay, Edward Curtis. With hotels in Mineral Wells, Tex., 1933-35, Wichita Falls, Tex., 1935, Waco, Tex., 1937-38, Ft. Worth, 1938-40; exec. asst. mgr. Texas Hotel, Ft. Worth, 1938-40; mgr. Jack Tar Hotel, Galveston, 1940-52; pres. successor orgn. Jack Tar Mgmt. Co., owners or operators 13 hotels, Galveston, 1952-69; dir., mem. exec. com., trust investment com., chmn. dir.'s examining com. U.S. Nat. Bank, Galveston; now hotel cons. Mem. Texas City Disaster Com., 1947-48; pres. Galveston County Municipal Utility Dist. No. 1; adv. council naval affairs 6th Naval Dist., 1961-62; permanent chmn. for Galveston, Tex. Com. Employment Physically Handicapped, 1956—; founder, past v.p., dir. Galveston Conv. and Tourist Bur., 1958-62, mem. exec. com.; chmn. bd. trustees Beach Park; pres. Galveston Beach Assn., 1949, Galveston Citizens Com., 1962; v.p. regional dir. Tex. Tourist Council, 1961-62; chmn. Park Bd. Trustees, Galveston, 1969-71. Recipient Horatio Alger award, 1960, spl. award Rotary Internat., 1960; Ed Leach Day proclaimed by Mayor of Galveston, 1960; recipient spl. resolution City San Francisco, 1960. Mem. Am. (fellowship award 1958, nat. dir., treas. 1965, pres. 1968—, certified hotel adminstr. 1977), Tex. (exec. com., 1st v.p. 1965—, chmn. bd. 1968—) hotel and motel assns., C. of C. (mem. exec. com.; Distinguished Community Service award 1960), Master Hosts (spl. award 1960; original mem., past pres.). Address: Route 1 Box 149E Galveston TX 77551

LEACH, JAMES ALBERT SMITH, Congressman; b. Davenport, Iowa, Oct. 15, 1942; s. James Albert and Lois (Hill) L.; B.A., Princeton, 1964; M.A., Johns Hopkins, 1966; student London Sch. Econs., 1966-68; m. Elisabeth Foxley, Dec. 6, 1975. Mem. staff Congressman Donald Rumsfeld, 1965-66; U.S. Fgn. Service officer, 1968-69; spl. asst. to dir. OEO, 1969-70; mem. U.S. del. Geneva Disarmament Conf., 1971-72, UN Gen. Assembly, 1972, UN Natural Resources Conf., 1975; pres. Flamegas Companies Inc., Bettendorf, Iowa, 1973-76; chmn. bd. Adel Wholesalers, Inc., Bettendorf, 1973-76; mem. 95th and 96th Congresses from 1st Dist. of Iowa; mem. U.S. Adv. Commn. Internat. Ednl. and Cultural Affairs, 1975-76. chmn. Iowa Republican Directions '76 Com. Episcopalian. Home: 2625 Wood Ln Davenport IA 52803 Office: US House of Reps Washington DC 20515

LEACH, JAMES LINDSAY, educator; b. Lawrenceville, Ill., Apr. 9, 1918; s. James Gard and Nellie Irene (Biesecker) L.; B.S., U. N.Mex., 1942; M.S., U. Ill., 1949; Ph.D., Ill. State U., 1974; m. Mary Jane Zipprodt, Oct. 13, 1945; children—James Lindsay, Charles, Robert, Janet Sue. Mem. faculty U. Ill., Urbana, 1946—, asso. prof. mech. engring., 1949-53, prof., 1953—; mech. engr. foundry div. Gen. Motors, Danville, Ill., 1949-51; engr. Tex. Co. Lawrenceville, 1946-47; cons. in field; vis. prof. Indian Inst. Tech., Kharagpur, 1960-61, Summer Sch. for Engring. Tchrs. India, New Delhi, summer, 1964—, Bengal Engring. Coll., Calcutta, 1964, U. Wis., New Delhi, summer 1965, Thermal Fabircation Inst., Coimbatore, India, summers, 1966-67, Survey Tech. Edn., Kenya Vista, 1971, Evaluation and Tng. Tech. Edn. Tchrs., 1972; cons. Acad. Ednl. Devel. and Ministry Transport, Iran, 1976. Served to lt. col. USAAF, 1943-45. Recipient citation Am. Soc. Die Casting Engrs., 1975. Mem. ASME, Am. Soc. Mil. Engrs., Am. Soc. Petroleum Engrs., Nat. Soc. Engring. Edn., Nat. Soc. Profl. Engrs., Sci. Research Soc. Am., Fedn. Am. Scientists, Am. Foundrymen's Soc. (dir. Central Ill. chpt. 1960—, citation 1968). Author: (with others) Manufacturing Processes and Materials for Engineers, 2d. edit., 1969; contbr. articles to profl. jours. Home: 910 N Broadway Urbana IL 61801 Office: Foundry Lab U Ill Urbana IL 61801

LEACH, JOHN FRANK, printing and forest products co. exec.; b. New Ross, Wexford, Ireland, Mar. 11, 1921; s. John Reginold and Evelyn Muriel (Ard) L.; came to U.S., 1921, naturalized, 1926; B.S. in Indsl. Mgmt., Wayne U., 1950; m. Lee Marie Serre, Dec. 1, 1945; children—John Michael, Suzanne Lee (Mrs. David Born). Apprentice tool, die maker Ford Motor Co., Dearborn, Mich., 1934-38, various mfg. positions, 1938-50, prodn. mgr. Cleve. engine plant, 1950-54; dir. mfg. Studebaker-Packard Corp., Detroit, 1954-56; v.p. mfg. Bunker-Ramo Corp. (formerly Amphenol Electronics Corp.), Chgo., 1956-59, div. pres., 1959-63, group exec., Electronics Corp.), Chgo., 1956-59, div. pres., 1959-63, group exec., 1963-68, exec. v.p., chief operating officer, 1968-72; pres., chief exec. officer Arcata Corp., Menlo Park, Calif., 1972—, also dir.; dir. Ampex Corp., Tymshare, Inc., SRI Internat. Council, Real Estate Data, Inc., Consol. Freightways Corp.; dir., chmn. exec. com. Henry Pratt Co. Bd. dirs. Bus. Sch., U. Calif. Berkeley, Bay Area Council, Resource Center for Women. Served to 2d lt. USAAF, 1943-45. Recipient Medal of Honor Electronic Industries Assn., 1972. Mem. Stock Exchange Club, Assn. Bus. Edn. (dir.). Clubs: Desert Forest Golf, Menlo Country, Sunset Ridge Country. Home: 121 Sheridan Way Woodside CA 94062 Office: 2750 Sand Hill Rd Menlo Park CA 94025

LEACH, JOSEPH LEE, educator, author; b. Weatherford, Tex., May 2, 1921; s. Austin Felix and Eula Lee (Gose) L.; B.A., So. Methodist U., 1942; Ph.D., Yale U., 1948; m. Dorothy Ann Stuart, June 5, 1958; children—Joseph Lee, Jonathan Stuart, Anne Stuart, Christopher Bryan, Timothy Peter, Hilary, Melinda. Prof. English, U. Tex., El Paso, 1947—; prof. U. Ark., Fayetteville, 1957, European div. U. Md., 1957-58. Pres., Festival Theatre, El Paso, 1969, El Paso County Hist. Soc., 1961. Served with inf. AUS, 1946-47. U. Tex. Research grantee, 1969-70. Mem. MLA, Nat. Council Tchrs. English, Sierra Club (pres. El Paso group 1970-71), Pi Kappa Alpha. Republican. Episcopalian. Club: Yale. Author: The Typical Texan, 1952; Bright Particular Star, 1970; co-editor: World Literature Written in English, 1969; contbr. articles on history and English to scholarly publs. Home: 735 DeLeon St El Paso TX 79912

LEACH, MAURICE DERBY, JR., librarian; b. Lexington, Ky., June 23, 1923; s. Maurice Derby and Sallie Eleanor (Woods) L.; A.B., U. Ky., 1945; B.L.S., U. Chgo., 1946; m. Virginia Stuart Baskett, Mar. 16, 1953; 1 dau., Sarah Stuart. Bibliographer, Dept. State, 1947-50; fgn. service officer Dept. State (USIS), vice consul, attache, Cairo and Alexandria, U.A.R., Beirut, 1950-59; chmn. dept. library sci. U. Ky., 1959-66; regional program officer Ford Found., Beirut, 1967-68; librarian, prof. Washington and Lee U., Lexington, Va., 1968—; library adviser Nat. Library, Egypt, Lebanon and acad. libraries in Middle East. Served with AUS, 1948-49. Mem. English Speaking Union, Va. (pres. 1976), Southeastern library assns., Assn. Preservation of Va. Activitied (dir. Lexington br.). Episcopalian. Club: Rotary. Contbr. articles to profl. jours. Home: 1 Courtland Center Lexington VA 24450

LEACH, RALPH F., banker; b. Elgin, Ill., June 24, 1917; s. Harry A. and Edith (Sanders) L.; A.B., U. Chgo., 1938; m. Harriet C. Scheuerman, Nov. 18, 1944; children—C. David, H. Randall, Barbara E. Investment analyst Harris Trust & Savs. Bank, Chgo., 1940-48, Valley Nat. Bank, Phoenix, 1948-50; chief govt. finance sect. Fed. Res. Bd., Washington, 1950-53; treas. Guaranty Trust Co., N.Y.C., 1953-59, v.p., 1958-59; v.p., treas. Morgan Guaranty Trust Co., N.Y.C., 1959-62, sr. v.p., treas., 1962-64, exec. v.p., treas., 1964-68, vice chmn. bd. dirs., 1968-71, chmn. exec. com., 1971-77; dir. So. R.R. Co., Urban Nat. Corp., Continental Corp., Merrill Lynch & Co., Energy Conversion Devices, Inc.; trustee Bowery Savs. Bank. Trustee Com. for Econ. Devel., Presbyn. Hosp., Juilliard Sch. Served to capt. USMCR, 1940-45. Mem. Phi Kappa Psi. Clubs: Bronxville Field; Siwanoy Country. Home: 60 Hampshire Rd Bronxville NY 10708 Office: 23 Wall St New York City NY 10015

LEACH, REGINALD (REGGIE) JOSEPH, hockey player; b. Riverton, Man., Can., Apr. 23, 1950. Right wing with Boston Bruins, 1970-72, Calif. Golden Seals, 1972-74, Phila. Flyers, 1974—. Recipient Conn Smythe Trophy, 1976. Office: care Phila Flyers Pattison Pl Philadelphia PA 19148*

LEACH, ROBERT DAVID, railroad exec.; b. Chgo., Sept. 4, 1925; s. Alphus L. and Helen (Junk) L.; B.S. in Acctg., U. Ill., 1949; m. Elizabeth Wittich, June 11, 1953; children—David Edward, Diane Elizabeth. Mgr. utilities dept. Arthur Andersen & Co., 1949-57; with Chgo. and North Western Transp. Co., C&NW Railway Co., 1957—, v.p. systems and corp. indsl. engring., 1973-79, sr. v.p. systems and materials, 1979—, dir. Mem. Assn. Am. Railraods, Ill. C.P.A. Soc., Am. Inst. C.P.A.'s. Club: Tower. Home: 629 Argyle Flossmoor IL 60422 Office: 400 W Madison Chicago IL 60606

LEACH, ROBERT ELLIS, physician, educator; b. Sanford, Maine, Nov. 25, 1931; s. Ellis and Estella (Tucker) L.; A.B., Princeton, 1953; M.D., Columbia, 1957; m. Laurine Seber, Aug. 20, 1955; children—Cathy, Brian, Michael, Craig, Karen, Diane. Resident orthopedic surgery U. Minn., 1957-62; orthopedic surgeon Lahey Clinic, Boston, 1964-68, chmn. dept., 1968-70; prof., chmn. dept. Boston U. Med. Sch., 1970—; lectr., Tufts U. Med. Sch., Medford, Mass., 1971—. Served to lt. comdr. USNR, 1962-64. Am., Brit., Canadian Orthopedic Travelling fellow, 1971. Mem. Am. Acad. Orthopedic Surgeons, Continental Orthopedic Soc. (sec. 1966—), Orthopedic Research Soc., Am. Orthopedic Soc. Sports Medicine. Club: Longwood Cricket (Brookline). Contbr. articles to profl. jours. Home: 40 Rockport Rd Weston MA 02193 Office: 75 E Newton St Boston MA 02118

LEACH, WILFORD, playwright, dir.; b. Petersburg, Va., Aug. 26, 1932; s. Carson W. and Louise (Shupin) L.; A.B., Coll. William and Mary, 1950; M.A., U. Ill., 1955, Ph.D., 1957. Prof. theatre and film Sarah Lawrence Coll., 1958—; mem. directing faculty Yale Sch. Drama, 1978—; dir. film The Wedding Party, 1967; co-dir. ETC Company of LaMama, N.Y.C., 1969—; artistic dir. LaMama Theatre, N.Y.C., 1970—; dir., designer Joseph Papp's N.Y. Shakespeare Festival, 1978; asso. to Joseph Papp, also prin. dir. Shakespeare Festival, 1979—; dir., designer The Mandrake, All's Well, Taming of the Shrew, Coriolanus, Othello, others; mem. faculty Yale U. Sch. Drama, 1978-79. Guggenheim fellow, 1972-73; recipient Obie award direction, 1972. Nat. Endowment for Arts grantee, 1975. Author: (plays) Trapdoors, 1958, Gertrude, 1959, In 3 Zones, 1965, Carmilia, 1970, Demon, 1971, Corfax (Don't Ask), 1974, Undine, 1975, Road House, 1976. Address: 47 Great Jones St New York NY 10012 Office: care Shakespeare Festival 425 Lafayette St New York NY 10003

LEACHMAN, CLORIS, actress; b. Des Moines; ed. Northwestern U.; m. George England, 1953; 5 children. Motion picture appearances include Kiss Me Deadly, Butch Cassidy and the Sundance Kid, The Last Picture Show, W.U.S.A., Dillinger, Daisy Miller, Young Frankenstein, 1974, Crazy Mama, High Anxiety, 1977, The North Avenue Irregulars, 1979, Scavenger Hunt, 1979; TV appearances include Lassie, 1957, Route 66, Laramie, Trials of O'Brien, Mary Tyler Moore Show, Phyllis, 1975-77; appeared in TV movie Brand New Life, The Migrants, Death Scream, 1975, A Girl Named Sooner, 1975, Ladies of the Corridor (play), 1975, The New Original Wonder Woman, 1975, The Love Boat, 1976. Recipient Oscar award as best supporting actress in The Last Picture Show, Nat. Acad. Motion Picture Arts and Scis., 1971; 4 Emmy awards for Mary Tyler Moore Show and others. Address: Creative Artists Agy Inc 1888 Century Park E Suite 1400 Los Angeles CA 90067*

LEACHMAN, ROBERT BRIGGS, physicist, govt. ofcl.; b. Lakewood, Ohio, June 11, 1921; s. Milton George and Wilma (Rothenbecker) L.; B.S., Case Inst. Tech., 1942; Ph.D., Iowa State U., 1950; m. Lenore Jean Collins, June 16, 1946; children—Elaine Alice, Mark Collins, Gregg Milton. Staff mem. radiation lab. Mass. Inst. Tech., Cambridge, 1943-45; instr. Ia. State U., Ames, 1947-48; staff mem., group leader Los Alamos Sci. Lab., 1950-67, head cyclotron research, 1957-67; prof. physics Kan. State U., 1967-72, head dept., 1967-71, dir. Nuclear Sci. Labs., 1967-72; asst. to dep. dir. Def. Nuclear Agy., Washington, 1972-74; asst. to dep. dir. regulations AEC, Washington, 1974-75, Nuclear Regulatory Commn., Washington, 1975-78; with Office of Tech. Assessment, U.S. Congress, Washington, 1978-79, with Sci. and Tech. Com., 1979—; prof. U. N.Mex., Los Alamos, part-time 1964-65; lectr. Montgomery Coll., Takoma Park, Md., 1978. Guggenheim fellow Nobel Inst., Stockholm, Sweden, 1955-56; Fulbright fellow Inst. Theoretical Physics, Copenhagen, Denmark, 1962-63. Fellow Am. Phys. Soc. Research. Co-author book on safeguarding nuclear material. Contbr. numerous publs. in physics of nuclear fission, atomic stopping properties, nuclear reactions. Home: 929 6th St SW Washington DC 20024

LEACOCK, ELEANOR BURKE, anthropologist, educator; b. Weehawken, N.J., July 2, 1922; d. Kenneth Duva and Lily Mary (Batterham) Burke; A.B. cum laude, Barnard Coll., 1944; M.A., Columbia, 1946, Ph.D., 195l; m. Richard Leacock, Dec. 27, 1941 (div. May 1962); children—Elspeth, Robert, David, Claudia; m. 2d, James Haughton, 1966. Staff, Yorkville Mental Health Project, research asst. Cornell U. Med. Coll., N.Y.C., 1952-55; lectr. Queens Coll., N.Y.C., 1955-56, Coll. City N.Y., 1956-60; research asso. Bank St. Coll. Edn., N.Y.C., 1958-65; asso. prof. Poly. Inst., Bklyn., 1964-67, prof., 1967-72; prof. anthropology City Coll., City U. N.Y., 1972—, chmn. dept., 1972-75, 78—; pres. Council on Anthropology and Edn., 1979-80; Danforth asso., 1975-81. Fellow Soc. Applied Anthropology (exec. com. 1972-75). Am. Anthrop. Assn. (exec. bd. 1971-73); mem. Am. Indian Ethnohistoric Conf. (sec.-treas. 1961-65), A.A.A.S. (program chmn. 1960, sec. anthropology sect. 1962-65), Am. Ethnol. Soc., Phi Beta Kappa. Author: Teaching and Learning in City Schools, 1969. Editor: The Culture of Poverty, A Critique, 1971; editor, author intro. Origin of the Family, Private Property and the State (Frederick Engels). Co-editor: North American Indians in Historical Perspective, 1971; gen. editor Abstracts in Anthropology, 1973-76. Contbr. articles to profl. publs. Home: 135 Duane St New York City NY 10013

LEADER, ROBERT WARDELL, pathologist; b. Tacoma, Jan. 16, 1919; s. Robert Joseph and Edith May (Wardell) L.; B.S., Wash. State U., 1952, D.V.M., 1952, M.S., 1955; Sc.D. (hon.), Med. Coll. Ohio, 1976; m. Isabel Parma, Sept. 20, 1969; children—Cheri, Mary, Robert, Lorraine, Carol. From instr. to prof. pathology Wash. State U., 1952-65; asso. prof., head comparative pathology lab. Rockefeller U., 1965-71; prof., head dept. pathobiology U. Conn., 1971-75; prof. pathology, chmn. dept. Mich. State U., East Lansing, 1975—; mem. path. tng. grant com. NIH, 1967-71, virology study sect., 1971-75; med. adv. com. Leukemia Soc., 1965-71; Robert Miller lectr. Dartmouth Coll., 1968. Served with USNR, 1937-46. Borden scholar, 1951; postdoctoral fellow NIH, 1954-55, tng. grantee, 1959-65. Mem. Am. Assn. Pathologists, Am. Coll. Vet. Pathologists, AAAS, AVMA, Internat. Acad. Pathology, Harvey Soc., Reticuloendothelial Soc., Mich. Soc. Pathologists. Author: Dictionary of Comparative Pathology, 1971; also articles. Editorial bd. Jour. Reticuloendothelial Soc. Address: Dept Pathology Mich State Univ East Lansing MI 48824

LEADER, SOLOMON, educator; b. Spring Lake, N.J., Nov. 14, 1925; s. William and Mary (Weinstein) L.; B.S., Rutgers U., 1949; M.A., Princeton, 1951, Ph.D., 1952; m. Elvera Grutter, Dec. 17, 1960; children—Jeremy, Shana, Rachel. Faculty math. Rutgers U., New Brunswick, N.J., 1952—, asso. prof., 1957-61, prof., 1961—. Served with AUS, 1944-46. Decorated Combat Inf. Badge. Research in gen. topology, functional analysis. Home: 9 Monroe Ct RD 4 Princeton NJ 08540 Office: Rutgers U New Brunswick NJ 08903

LEAF, ALEXANDER, physician, educator; b. Yokohama, Japan, Apr. 10, 1920; s. Aaron L. and Dora (Hural) L.; came to U.S., 1922, naturalized, 1936; B.S., U. Wash., 1940; M.D., U. Mich., 1943; M.A., Harvard, 1961; m. Barbara Louise Kincaid, Oct. 1943; children—Caroline Joan, Rebecca Louise, Tamara Jean. Intern, Mass. Gen. Hosp., Boston, 1943-44, mem. staff, 1949—, physician-in-chief, 1966—; resident Mayo Found., Rochester, Minn., 1944-45; research fellow U. Mich., 1947-49; practice internal medicine, Boston, 1949—; faculty Med. Sch., Harvard, 1949—, Jackson prof. clin. medicine, 1966—. Served to capt. M.C., AUS, 1945-46. Recipient Outstanding Achievement award U. Minn., 1964; vis. fellow Balliol Coll.; Oxford, 1971-72; Guggenheim fellow, 1971-72. Fellow Am. Acad. Arts and Scis.; mem. Am. Soc. Clin. Investigation (past pres.), Biochem. Soc., Am. Physiol. Soc., Biophys. Soc., Assn. Am. Physicians, Nat. Acad. Sci. Home: 1 Curtis Circle Winchester MA 01890 Office: Mass Gen Hosp Boston MA 02114

LEAF, BORIS, physicist, educator; b. Yokohama, Japan, Mar. 4, 1919; s. Aron L. and Dora (Guralsky) L.; came to U.S., 1922, naturalized, 1936; B.S. summa cum laude, U. Wash., 1939; Ph.D., U. Ill., 1942; m. Genevieve Lukman, Aug. 28, 1947; children—Evelyn Marie, David Alexander, Michael Leon. Research asst. NDRC, U. Ill., 1942-43; faculty U. Ill., 1943-44; asso. chemist metall. lab. U. Chgo., 1944-45; Frank B. Jewett fellow Yale, 1945-46; faculty Kans. State U., 1946-65; prof., chmn. dept. physics State U. N.Y., Cortland, 1965—; prof. State U. N.Y. at Binghamton, 1968-71. Faculty scis. Free U. Brussels (Belgium), 1958-60; research physicist U.S. Naval Radiol. Def. Lab., San Francisco, summers 1963, 64, 66; vis. prof. Cornell U., 1973-74; faculty exchange scholar State U. N.Y., 1974—. Fellow Am. Phys. Soc. (exec. com. N.Y. State sect. 1971-73), A.A.A.S.; mem. A.A.U.P. (nat. council 1963-66, nat. com. C 1965-71), N.Y. Acad. Sci., Am. Assn. Physics Tchrs., Sigma Xi, Phi Beta Kappa, Pi Mu Epsilon, Sigma Pi Sigma, Phi Lambda Upsilon. Asso. editor Am. Jour. Physics, 1976-79. Research on statis. mechanics and thermodynamics. Home: 28 Melvin Ave Cortland NY 13045

LEAF, HOWARD WESTLEY, air force officer; b. Menominee, Mich., Sept. 22, 1923; s. Joseph Conrad and Hilda Eugene (Lavoy) L.; B.S., Colo. Sch. Mines, 1950; M.S., St. Louis U., 1955; grad. Command and Staff Coll., 1961, Indsl. Coll. Armed Forces, 1969; m. Madonna Anne Ronan, May 21, 1955; children—Mary Beth, Barbara, Timothy, Anne Marie, Thomas, James. Commd. 2d lt. U.S. Air Force, 1951, advanced through grades to maj. gen., 1976; aviation cadet, 1950-51; jet pilot, Korea, 1952-53; test pilot, 1955-60; geophysicist, 1961-64; ops. officer 49th Tactical Fighter Wing, Europe, 1965; squadron comdr., S.E. Asia, 1966; staff officer Hdqrs. USAF, 1966-68, 69-71; wing comdr., 1971-74; dep. chief of staff/requirements Tactical Air Command, 1974-76; comdr. AF Test and Evaluation Center, Kirtland AFB, New Mex., 1976—. Decorated D.S.M., Silver Cross, Legion of Merit, D.F.C.; recipient Eugene M. Zuckert Mgmt. Award, 1978. Presbyterian. Home: 2237 Stockton Loop Kirtland Air Force Base NM 87118 Office: Commander Air Force Test and Evaluation Center Kirtland Air Force Base NM 87118

LEAF, PAUL, producer, director; b. N.Y.C., May 2, 1929; s. Manuel and Anna (Dardick) L.; B.A. in Drama with honors, CCNY, 1952; m. Nydia Ellis, Oct. 22, 1955; children—Jonathan, Alexandra, Ellen. Dir., producer various Broadway prodns., the most recent being The Subject Was Roses, 1964; films include: Judge Horton and the Scottsboro Boys (Peabody award), 1976, Desperate Characters, 1972, Sister Aimee, 1977, Every Man a King, 1977; TV prodns. include: Sgt. Matlovich vs. the U.S. Air Force, 1978; pres. Sea Gate Co.; guest lectr. at colls.; juror U. Ohio TV Awards. Served with U.S. Army, 1952-54. Decorated Meritorious Service medal; recipient 20 internat. festival and profl. awards, including Venice, 1967, London, 1967, 68, 69, N.Y., 1967, 68, 69, Berlin, 1972. Mem. Dirs. Guild Am., Writers Guild Am. Home: 924 23d St Santa Monica CA 90403 Office: 20th Century Fox Beverly Hills CA

LEAGUE, ARCHIE WILLIAM, ret. govt. ofcl.; b. Poplar Bluff, Mo., Aug. 19, 1907; s. Achen and Itasca (Magner) L.; student Washington U., St. Louis, 1926; grad. U.S. Command and Gen. Staff Sch., 1940, USAF Sch. Applied Tactics, 1945; m. Ida Margaret Wood, Feb. 16, 1946; 1 dau., Patricia Annette. Profl. pilot, 1926-29; asst. airport mgr., St. Louis, 1929-37; with FAA, and predecessors, 1937—, regional dir., 1960-65, dir. air traffic control service, 1965-68, asst. adminstr., 1968-73, aviation cons., 1973—. Cons., lectr. in field. Bd. dirs. Tarrant County (Tex.) United Fund, 1960-64. Served to col. USAAF, World War II; PTO. Decorated D.F.C., Bronze Star, Air medal; named hon. adm. Tex. Navy, 1965; brig. gen. to gov. La., 1965; col. to gov. N.M., 1965; named Ark. Traveler, 1965; received Meritorious Service award FAA, 1965, Distinguished Career Service award, 1973; enshrined in Air and Space Mus., Smithsonian Instn., 1973. Mem. Quiet Birdmen, Airway Pioneers, Order of Daedalians, Ox-5 Aviation Pioneers. Club: Elgin (Ill.) Adventures (charter). Collaborator: Meteorology for Pilots, 1930; Learning to Fly, 1935. Contbr. articles to profl. jours. Home: 3715 King Arthur Rd Annandale VA 22003

LEAHY, CHARLES FARRINGTON, lawyer; b. Claremont, N.H., Feb. 27, 1935; s. Albert Dennis and Helen Barr (Farrington) L.; B.A., Yale Coll., 1957; J.D., Harvard U., 1963; m. Mary Susan Stein, Oct. 22, 1977; children—Mary Siobhan, Charles Farrington, Matthew Edward, Susan Barr, Jonathan Norton. Admitted to N.H. bar, 1963, also fed. cts.; asso. firm Orr & Reno, P.A., Concord, N.H., 1963-67, partner, 1967—; dir. Bank N.H., N.A., United Life & Accident Ins.

Co.; legis. counsel to Walter Peterson, Jr., Gov. N.H., 1971, 72. Mem. Bd. Edn., Concord Union Sch. Dist., 1977—. Served with U.S. Army, 1957-60. Mem. Am. Bar Assn., N.H. Bar Assn., Am. Law Inst. Republican. Episcopalian. Home: 10 Bishopsgate Concord NH 03301 Office: 95 N Main St Concord NH 03301

LEAHY, JOHN JACOB, fin. cons.; b. Long Island City, N.Y., Jan. 18, 1921; s. Frank Joseph and Louise (Huther) L.; B.S., N.Y. U., 1949; m. Martha Goedl, July 6, 1946; children—Michael John, Robert John. Financial analyst, mem. financial staff Gen. Motors Corp., N.Y.C., 1949-52; ofcl. asst. First Nat. City Bank, N.Y.C., 1952-56; investment mgr. Prudential Ins. Co. Am., Newark, 1956-61; asst. treas. Ryder System, Inc., Miami, Fla., 1961-65; asst. treas. AMF, Inc., N.Y.C., 1965-68; asst. treas. Norton Simon, Inc., Fullerton, Calif., 1968-69, treas., 1969-70; v.p. United Calif. Bank, Los Angeles, 1970-76, mgr. cash mgmt. dept., 1973-76; fin. cons., 1976—; mem. cash mgmt. adv. group GSA, 1975-76. Served with AUS, 1942-45. Mem. Am. Mgmt. Assn. (mem. finance div. planning council 1971-76), Cash Mgmt. Group So. Calif. (program chmn. 1974-75). Roman Catholic. Club: Los Angeles Treasurers (pres. 1976, dir. 1976-79). Pub., Leahy Fin. Newsletter. Home: 212 Alvarado Circle Fullerton CA 92635

LEAHY, PATRICK JOSEPH, senator; b. Montpelier, Vt., Mar. 31, 1940; s. Howard and Alba (Zambon) L.; B.A., St. Michael's Coll., Vt., 1961; J.D., Georgetown U., 1964; m. Marcelle Pomerleau, Aug. 25, 1962; children—Kevin, Alicia, Mark. Admitted to Vt. bar, 1964; U.S. Supreme Ct. bar; former asso. with Black, Wilson & Hoff; city atty. Burlington, Vt., 1964-66; state's atty., Chittenden County, Burlington, 1966-75; U.S. senator from Vt., 1975—; vis. lectr. U. Vt.; cons. Nat. Center Prosecution Mgmt. Mem. adv. commn. Vt. Supreme Ct. Mem. Vt. Bar Assn. (past chmn. criminal law sect.), Vt. State's (past pres.), Nat. Dist. (v.p.) attys. assns. Office: 232 Russell Senate Office Bldg Washington DC 20510

LEAHY, THOMAS FRANCIS, broadcasting exec.; b. N.Y.C., June 30, 1937; s. Thomas Donald and Mary Ann (McCarthy) L.; B.E.E., Manhattan Coll., 1959; m. Patricia B. Flanagan, May 5, 1962; children—Patricia Ann, Allison, Thomas Francis, Kirsten Elizabeth. Sales service ABC-TV, N.Y.C., 1960-61; account exec. WGN, N.Y.C., 1961-62; account exec. WCBS-TV, N.Y.C., 1962-64, account exec. CBS Television Network Sales, Chgo., 1964-66, N.Y.C., 1966-69, dir. daytime sales, 1969-71; v.p. sales CBS Television Stas., N.Y.C., 1971-73, v.p., gen. mgr., 1973-77, pres., 1977—. Mem. pres.'s council Manhattan Coll., Fordham U., Coll. of New Rochelle; formerly bd. dirs. Red Cross of Greater N.Y.; trustee Fordham Prep. Sch.; bd. dirs. Big Brothers of New York. Served with U.S. Army 1959-65. Mem. Internat. Soc. Radio and TV (dir.), Nat. Acad. TV Arts and Scis., TV Advt. Bur. Clubs: Friars; Siwanoy Country. Home: 25 Studio Ln Bronxville NY 10708 Office: 51 W 52d St New York City NY 10019

LEAHY, THOMAS RICHARD, clergyman, editor; b. Milw., May 5, 1921; s. Thomas Edward and Ruby (Hughes) L.; A.B., Northwestern U., 1943; postgrad. advt. and communications, Columbia, 1946-47, philosophy, St. Francis Sem.; Licentiate in Sacred Theology, U. Fribourg (Switzerland), 1955; postgrad. journalism, Marquette U., 1962-63. Copywriter, jr. account exec. Keller-Crescent, Evansville, Ind., 1947-49; ordained priest Roman Catholic Ch., 1955; parish work, Milw., 1955-62; feature editor Catholic Herald Citizen, 1962, exec. editor, 1967—. Mem. liturgical commn. Milw. Archdiocese, 1965—. Served with AUS 1943-46. Recipient First prize Best Human Interest Feature Story, Catholic Press Assn., 1962, Third prize for Best Editorial, 1970, First prize layout design, 1978. Mem. Sigma Delta Chi, Alpha Tau Omega. Club: Milw. Press. Address: 2170 N Prospect Ave Milwaukee WI 53202

LEAHY, WILLIAM F., lawyer, ins. co. exec.; b. N.Y.C., July 28, 1913; s. William F. and Anna (Murphy) L.; pre-law certificate Coll. City N.Y., 1936; LL.B. cum laude, Bklyn. Law Sch., 1939, LL.M., 1940; m. Catherine Patricia Carlin, Oct. 19, 1940; children—William C., Michael J. Admitted to N.Y. bar, 1940; with Met. Life Ins. Co., N.Y.C., 1932-78, asso. gen. counsel, 1962-65, v.p. real estate financing, 1965 and after, sr. v.p., 1976-78; sr. real estate cons. Goldman Sachs Realty Co.; dir. City Title Ins. Co., Dollar Fed. Savs. & Loan Assn., Malverne, N.Y., Pulte Home Corp. Served to lt. col. USAAF, 1941-46. Mem. Am. Bar Assn., N.Y. State Title Assn. Home: 34 Roosevelt Ave Lynbrook NY 11563 Office: 444 Madison Ave New York NY 10022

LEAK, DAVID KEITH, mfg. co. exec.; b. Flint, Mich., Mar. 18, 1932; s. Keith Laverne and Helen May (Rasmussen) L.; student U. Mich., 1949-50, Flint Jr. Coll., 1950-51; B.A. in Engring. and Accounting, Albion Coll., 1954; mgmt. devel. certificate Wayne State U., 1966; m. Sally Chappell Stormer, June 21, 1953; children—Brian David, Scott Howard, Jeffrey Keith. Jr. auditor Arthur Young & Co., Chgo., 1954-55; office mgr. Olin Mathieson Co., Chgo., 1955-56; with Fed.-Mogul Corp., 1956—, controller Bower div., Detroit, 1969-71, mgr. planning Bearing Group, Southfield, Mich., 1971-73, adminstrv. mgr. Powdered Metals div., 1973-74, corp. controller, 1974-78, v.p., controller, 1979—. Mem. com. spl. edn. Oakland County (Mich.) Intermediate Schs., 1974. Trustee Village of Clarkston, Mich., 1967-68; trustee Clarkston Pub. Schs., 1970-78, pres., 1972-78. Mem. Oakland County Sch. Bd. Assn., Financial Exec. Inst. Episcopalian (trustee diocese 1975-78, exec. council diocese 1971-74). Home: 6195 Middle Lake Rd Clarkston MI 48016 Office: PO Box 1966 Detroit MI 48235

LEAK, ROBERT E., state ofcl.; b. Charlotte, N.C., Sept. 15, 1934; s. James Pickett and Cornelia (Edwards) L.; B.S., Duke, 1956; M.S., U. Tenn., 1957; m. Martha Councill, Aug. 25, 1956; children—Robert E., James Councill. With Pan Am. Petroleum Co., Lafayette, La., 1957-59, Allied Securities Corp., Raleigh, N.C., 1961-62, Cameron Brown Mortgage Co., Raleigh, Charlotte, 1962-64; with N.C. Dept. Natural and Econ. Resources, Raleigh, 1959-61, 64-76, dir. div. econ. devel., until 1976; dir. S.C. State Devel. Bd., Columbia, 1976—; mem. U.S. Dept. Commerce Small Bus. Adv. Council; mem. indsl. devel. com. Coastal Plains Regional Commn.; leader industry organized govt. approved trade and indsl. devel. missions to Can., Europe, S.Am., Australia, Far East. Past mem. bd. dirs. Raleigh YMCA. Mem. Am. Indsl. Devel. Council (past pres.), So. Assn. Planning and Devel. Agys. (pres.), Nat. Assn. state Devel. Agys. (v.p.). Episcopalian (pres. mem. of ch., lay reader). Home: 6030 Lakeshore Dr Columbia SC 29206 Office: SC State Devel Bd Bankers Trust Bldg Columbia SC 29206

LEAKE, DONALD LEWIS, oral and maxillofacial surgeon; b. Cleveland, Okla., Nov. 6, 1931; s. Walter Wilson and Martha Lee (Crow) L.; A.B., U. So. Calif., 1953, M.A., 1957; D.M.D., Harvard U., 1962; M.D., Stanford U., 1969; m. Rosemary Dobson, Aug. 20, 1964; children—John Andrew Dobson, Elizabeth, Catherine. Intern, Mass. Gen. Hosp., Boston, 1962-63, resident, 1963-64; postdoctoral fellow Harvard U., 1964-66; practice medicine specializing in oral and maxillofacial surgery; asso. prof. oral and maxillofacial surgery Harbor-UCLA Med. Center, Torrance, 1970-74, dental dir., chief oral surgery, 1970—, prof., 1974—; cons. to hosps.; dental dir. coastal health services region, Los Angeles County, 1974—. Recipient 1st prize with greatest distinction for oboe and chamber music Brussels Royal Conservatory Music, Belgium, 1956. Fellow A.C.S.; mem. So. Calif. Acad. Oral Pathology, Internat. Assn. Dental Research, Am., So. Calif. socs. oral surgeons, Med. Research Assn. Calif., Internat. Assn. Oral Surgeons, Am. Acad. Oral Medicine, Am. Assn. Hosp. Dentists, AAAS, Soc. for Biomaterials, ASTM, European Assn. Maxillofacial Surgeons, Brit. Assn. Oral Surgeons, Internationale Gesellschaft fur Kiefer-Gesichts-Chirurgie, Phi Beta Kappa, Phi Kappa Phi. Club: Harvard of Boston. Contbr. articles to med. jours. Home: 2 Crest Rd W Rolling Hills CA 90274 Office: Harbor-UCLA Med Center 1000 W Carson St Torrance CA 90509

LEAKE, GEORGE JUNIUS, bishoo; b. Wilson, N.C., Nov. 21, 1929; s. David and Elsie Mae (Barnes) L.; B.A., Livingstone Coll., Salisbury, N.C., 1957; D.D. (hon.), 1972; M.Div., Hood Sem., Salisbury, 1960; LL.D. (hon.), Clinton Coll., Rock Hill, S.C., 1969; m. Vilma Louise Dew, Sept. 7, 1953; children—George Jacob, Yolanda Georgetta. Ordained to ministry A.M.E. Zion Ch., 1950; pastor Little Rock A.M.E. Zion Ch., Charlotte, N.C., 1963-72; cons. City of Charlotte Redevel. Commn., 1966-67; dir. Opportunity Industrialization Center, Charlotte, 1967-71; pres. Pride Inc., cons., Charlotte, 1970-72; bishop A.M.E. Zion Ch., Charlotte, 1972—; exec. dir. Innovative Drug Abuse Program, Charlotte, 1974—; pres. Leake & Green Realty & Ins. Co., 1970—; dir. Dynamics Assos. Recipient Meritorious Service award Livingstone Coll., 1972; also various certificate appreciation. Mem. Alcohol Profls. N.C., Nat. Assn. Real Estate Brokers, N.C. Real Estate Brokers Assn., Nat. Council Chs., Livingstone Coll. Alumni Assn., Omega Psi Phi (named Omega Citizen of Year, 1969). Clubs: Masons, Elks. Author: Out Reach Concept for Helping Alcoholics, 1977. Office: 2220 W 10th St Charlotte NC 28208*

LEAMAN, J. RICHARD, JR., paper co. exec.; b. Lancaster, Pa., Sept. 22, 1934; s. J. Richard and Margaret B. Leaman; B.A., Dartmouth Coll., 1956, M.B.A., Amos Tuck Sch., 1957; m. Helen Brown, June 15, 1957; children—Lynda B., J. Richard, III. With Scott Paper, Phila., 1967—, v.p. comml. products, 1975-78, sr. v.p. mktg. and sales, 1978—; adv. bd. Assn. Nat. Advertisers. Mem. admission com. Dartmouth Coll. Served to capt. USAF, 1957-61. Mem. Pa. C. of C. Republican. Episcopalian. Clubs: Dartmouth (Phila.); Rose Tree Media Optimists. Home: 103 Wilton Woods Ln Media PA 19063 Office: Scott Plaza Philadelphia PA 19113

LEAN, MARTIN EDWIN, educator; b. Chgo., Nov. 22, 1918; s. Edwin Samuel and Mary (Levinson) L.; A.B., Roosevelt U., 1940; M.A., U. Nebr., 1942; Ph.D., Columbia, 1948; m. Marjorie Ann Bason, June 8, 1946 (dec. Mar. 1958); children—Deborah Bason, Patricia Albright; m. 2d, Judith A. Lutzky, Aug. 2, 1964 (div. Aug. 1972). Instr., U. N.C., Chapel Hill, 1945-46, asst. prof., 1946-49; asst. prof. Bklyn. Coll. of City U. N.Y., 1949-56, asso. prof., 1956-64, prof., chmn. dept. philosophy, 1964-73; prof., dir. Sch. Philosophy, U. So. Calif., Los Angeles 1973—; chmn. conf. on methods in philosophy and the scis. New Sch. for Social Research, 1964-65, adj. prof., 1965-73; vis. prof. Swarthmore Coll., 1964, U. Western Ont., also U. Calgary, 1966, U. So. Calif., 1969, 71, 72-73; cons. philosophy Macmillan, St. Martin's Press, Random House, others. Recipient Woodbridge Prize for Essay in Philosophy, Columbia U., 1950; sr. Fulbright Research Scholar, Oxford U., 1956-57. Mem. Am. Philos. Assn., Mind Assn. (Eng.), Aristotelian Soc. (Eng.). Author: Sense Perception and Matter, 1953. Editorial bd. Ency. Philosophy, 1967. Bd. cons. editors Philosophia. Home: 1513 Queens Rd Los Angeles CA 90069

LEAR, EVELYN, soprano; b. Bklyn.; vocal student in N.Y.C.; student N.Y. U., Hunter Coll.; children—Jan, Bonni; m. 2d, Thomas Stewart. Song recitals Phillips Gallery, Washington; mem. Juilliard Sch. Music Workshop; recital Town Hall, N.Y.C., 1955; lead in Marc Blitzstein's Reuben, Reuben; performed Strauss's Four Last Songs with London Symphony Orch., 1959; mem. Deutsche Opera, 1959; appeared in Lulu at Vienna Festival, 1962, The Marriage of Figaro at Salzburg Festival, 1962; appeared throughout world, 1962-66; debut Vienna State Opera, 1964, Frankfurt Opera, 1965, Covent Garden, 1965, Kansas City (Mo.) Performing Arts Found., 1965, Chgo. Lyric Opera, 1966, La Scala Opera, 1971, also in Brussels, San Francisco, Los Angeles, Buenos Aires; debut at Met. Opera, 1967, mem. co., 1967—; roles include Tosca, Manon, Marshallin; TV appearance in La Boheme, 1965; numerous solo appearances, 1960—; appeared in film Buffalo Bill, 1976; rec. artist Angel Records, Deutsche Grammophon. Recipient Concert Artists Guild award, 1955; Liederabend, Salzburg Festival, 1964; Grammy award for best operatic recording (Marie in Wozzeck), 1965. Fulbright scholar, 1957. Address: care Columbia Artists Mgmt Inc 165 W 57th St New York City NY 10019

LEAR, JOHN, writer, editor; b. nr. Allen, Pa., Aug. 10, 1909; s. Charles D. and Esther M. (Sourbeer) L.; D.Sc. (hon.), Dickinson Coll., 1968; m. Dorothy Leeds, Sept. 26, 1931 (dec. May 1965); m. 2d, Marie Nesta, Aug. 28, 1966. Editor, Daily Local News, Mechanicsburg, Pa., 1927-28; reporter Patriot, Harrisburg, 1928-34; writer-editor A.P., Phila., Chgo., N.Y.C., Washington, Buenos Aires, roving assignments Eastern U.S., Can., S.Am., 1934-42; coordinator info. staff gov. P.R., 1942-43; radio news writer Press Assn., N.Y.C., 1943; free lance mag. corr., 1944-48; mng. editor Steelways mag., 1948-49; chief articles editor Collier's mag., 1949-50, asso. editor, 1950-53; cons. publs. IBM Corp., 1953-54; dir. spl. atomics and automation studies Research Inst. Am., 1954-55; sci. editor Sat. Rev., 1956-71, sr. editor, 1971-72; v.p. Bauer Engring., Inc., 1972; v.p., chief editor Bauer, Sheaffer & Lear, Inc., Chgo., 1972-75; chief editor Keifer & Assos., Inc., 1975-76; Am. corr. New Scientist, London, 1956-62; editorial cons. Russell Sage Found., 1967-68, Inst. for Social Research, U. Mich., 1972-73; columnist King Features Syndicate, 1973; sci. cons. Crown Publishers, Inc., 1974; editorial cons. Rockefeller Found., 1978—; cons. Office of Tech. Assessment, U.S. Congress, 1975; publs. cons. Acad. Forum, Nat. Acad. Scis., 1976. Recipient Westinghouse award AAAS, 1951; Albert Lasker Med. Journalism award, 1952; citation for sci. writing Deadline Club, 1971. Mem. Authors Guild, Sigma Delta Chi (Disting. Pub. Service award 1950, 61). Author: Forgotten Front, 1942; Kepler's Dream, 1965; Recombinant DNA—The Untold Story, 1978. Contbg. editor World Press Rev., 1976—. Home: 130 S Madison St Harrisburg PA 17109 Office: Exec House Suite 1214 101 S 2d St Harrisburg PA 17101

LEAR, NORMAN MILTON, writer, producer, dir. TV and films; b. New Haven, July 27, 1922; s. Herman and Jeanette (Seicol) L.; student Emerson Coll., 1940-44, H.H.D., 1968; m. Frances A. Loeb, Dec. 7, 1956; children—Ellen (Mrs. Jeffrey Reiss), Kate B., Maggie B. Engaged in pub. relations, 1945-49; comedy writer for TV, 1950-54; writer, dir. for TV and films, 1954-59; writer, dir., producer for TV and films, 1959—; writer, producer films Come Blow Your Horn, 1963, Divorce American Style, 1967, The Night They Raided Minsky's, 1968; writer, producer, dir. film Cold Turkey, 1971; creator, producer TV shows TV Guide Awards Show, 1962, Henry Fonda and the Family, 1963, Andy Williams Spls., also Andy Williams Series, 1965, Robert Young and the Family, 1970; developer TV shows All in the Family, 1971—; creator, developer Maude, 1972—; co-developer TV show Sanford and Son, 1972—; developer Good Times, 1974—, The Jeffersons, 1975—, Hot L Baltimore, 1975—, Mary Hartman, 1976—, The Dumplings, 1976—, One Day At a Time, 1976, All's Fair, 1976—, A Year at the Top, 1977; Co-creator All That Glitters, 1977; creator Fernwood 2 Night, 1977; developer The Baxters, 1979. Pres. Am. Civil Liberties Found. So. Calif., 1973—. Bd. dirs. Calif. Citizens Action Group. Served with USAAF, 1941-45. Decorated Air medal with 4 oak leaf clusters; named One of Top Ten Motion Picture Producers, Motion Picture Exhibitors, 1963, 67, 68; Showman of Year, Publicists Guild, 1971, Assn. Bus. Mgrs., 1972; Broadcaster of Year, Internat. Radio and TV Soc., 1973; Man of Year, Hollywood chpt. Nat. Acad. Television Arts and Scis., 1973; recipient Emmy awards for All in the Family, 1970-73, Peabody award for all in the Family, 1978. Mem. Writers Guild Am., Dirs. Guild Am., AFTRA. Office: 1901 Ave of The Stars Los Angeles CA 90067

LEAR, ROBERT WILLIAM, holding co. exec; b. Canon City, Colo., May 10, 1917; s. Louis and Bertha (May) L.; B.A., U. Colo., 1938; M.B.A. with distinction, Harvard, 1940; m. Dorothy Schureman, Sept. 16, 1941; children—William S., Andrew R. Market research analyst U.S. Steel Corp., 1940-43; sales promotion mgr. Duff-Norton Co., 1946-47; corp. dir. marketing services Am. Standard Co., 1947-61; v.p. marketing Carborundum Co., 1961-64, group v.p., 1964-67; pres., dir. Indian Head Inc., 1967-72; pres., chief exec. officer, chmn., dir. F. & M. Schaefer Corp., N.Y.C., 1972-77, now dir.; exec.-in-residence Columbia Grad. Bus. Sch., 1977—; dir. Church & Dwight Co., Inc., Interpace Corp., Combustion Equipment Assos., St. Regis Paper Co., Turner Constrn. Co., Welsh, Carson, Anderson Assos. Venture Funds, others; adv. dir. Chem. Bank. Bd. dirs. Waveny Care Center. Served as lt. USNR, 1943-46. Clubs: Harvard (N.Y.C.); New Canaan Country; Blind Brook. Home: 429 Silvermine Rd New Canaan CT 06840 Office: 404 Uris Hall Columbia U New York NY 10027

LEAR, WILLIAM EDWARD, univ. dean; b. Lexington, Ky., Aug. 29, 1918; s. William Harry and Hattie (Blakeman) L.; student Lincoln Meml. U., 1935-36, U. Cin., 1937-39; B.S. in Elec. Engring., U. Ala., 1942; M.S. in Elec. Engring., Stanford, 1949; Ph.D., U. Fla., 1953; D.Eng., Pusan (Korea) Nat. U., 1975; m. Mary Etta Tyson, June 7, 1947; children—John Tyson, Gene Herbert, William Edward, Elizabeth Tyson. Engr., RCA, 1942-44; instr. elec. engring. U. Ala., 1946-48; asst. prof. elec. engring. U. Fla., 1949-53; asso. prof. elec. engring. U. Tenn., 1953-54; faculty U. Fla., 1954-66, asso. prof. elec. engring., 1954-57, prof., 1957-66; asso. dean engring. U. Ala., 1966-67, dean Engring. Coll., 1967—; dir. First Ala. Bank Tuscaloosa; research participant Oak Ridge Nat. Lab., 1949-50; cons. to govt., industry, 1953—; research asso. Stanford, summers 1957, 61; program dir. engring. systems, head engring. sect. NSF, 1963-64; chmn. Engring. Coll. Council; chmn. Ala. Bd. Registration for Profl. Engrs.; mem. Panel on Alternate Approaches to Grad. Edn.; mem. planning commn. for expanding minority opportunities in engring. Sloan Found. mem. engring. edn. and accreditation com. Engrs. Council for Profl. Devel.; chmn. consortium adv. com. U. Petroleum and Minerals, Dhahran, Saudi Arabia; project dir. Southeastern Consortium for Minorities in Engring.; cons. House Com. on Sci. and Tech., 95th Congress. Served to lt. (j.g.) USNR, 1944-46. Grantee Office Naval Research 1952-53, tube div. Sperry Electronic Co., 1957-63, NSF, 1960-61, Air Force Office Sci. Research, 1964-66. Mem. IEEE (sr.), Nat. Commn. Engring. Examiners, Am. Soc. for Engring. Edn. (v.p., dir.), Ala. Soc. Profl. Engrs. (dir.), Sigma Xi, Tau Beta Pi, Alpha Tau Omega. Home: 54 Arcadia Dr Tuscaloosa AL 35401 Office: Coll Engring U Ala University AL 35486

LEARD, JOHN EARNSHAW, newspaperman; b. Boston, Aug. 15, 1916; s. John S.H. and Isabelle (Earnshaw) L.; A.B., Bates Coll, 1938; M.S. in Journalism, Columbia, 1939; m. Hazel Elsie Turner, Sept. 28, 1940; children—Linda Earnshaw (Mrs. Raymond B. Parkin, Jr.), Judith Alden (Mrs. Richard J. Nicholas). Mem. staff Lewiston (Me.) Sun-Jour., 1937; Pulitzer traveling scholar, S.Am., 1939-40; editorial asst. Richmond (Va.) News Leader, 1939, reporter, copy editor, asst. city editor, 1941-43, asst. city editor, 1947-51, city editor, 1951-63; asst. editor Atlantic Monthly mag., Boston, 1940-41; telegraph editor New Haven Register, 1946-47; mng. editor Richmond Times-Dispatch, 1963-69; v.p. Richmond Newspapers, Inc., exec. editor Richmond Times-Dispatch, Richmond News Leader, 1969—. Trustee Bates Coll, 1958-63. Served with AUS, 1943-46. Mem. Am. Soc. Newspaper Editors, Va. Press Assn. (past pres.), A.P. Mng. Editors Assn. (past pres. 1976-77), Sigma Delta Chi. Episcopalian. Clubs: Hermitage Country, Westwood (pres. Richmond 1958-60). Home: 6207 Monument Av Richmond VA 23226 Office: 333 E Grace St Richmond VA 23219. *Listen, get both sides, and communicate.*

LEAREY, FRED DON, telephone co. exec.; b. Findlay, Ohio, Mar. 7, 1906; s. Fred B. and Iris A. (Galleher) L.; A.B., Ohio Wesleyan U., 1928; m. Marian E. Van Valkenburgh, Jan. 13, 1935; children—Fred K., Richard N. Student engr., lineman, installer, traffic student Ohio Bell Telephone Co., 1928-36, comml. mgr., comml. tng. supr., dist. sales mgr., 1936-43, dir. mktg., 1960-61; with AT&T, N.Y.C., 1943-46, div. comml. mgr., gen. comml. mgr., Columbus, Ohio, 1946-60; pres. Gen. Telephone Co. Fla., Tampa, 1961-71, chmn. bd., 1971, also dir.; dir. Founders Life Assurance Co., Century First Nat. Bank, St. Petersburg, Tampa Ship Repair & Dry Dock Co. Chmn. Civil Service Bd. of Tampa, 1974. Bd. dirs. United Fund, pres. 1965-66; bd. dirs. Boy Scouts Am.; bd. dirs. Fla. Council 100, also past chmn.; bd. dirs. New Coll., Sarasota; past interim pres., chmn. bd. U. Tampa. Mem. Tampa C. of C. (past pres.), Com. 100 (chmn. exec. com.), Fla. Telephone Assn. (past pres.), Ye Mystic Krewe of Gasparilla. Conglist. Rotarian. Clubs: Tampa Yacht and Country, Palma Ceia Golf and Country, University (Tampa). Home: 2407 Ardson Pl Tampa FL 33609 Office: PO Box 110 Tampa FL 33601

LEARN, ELMER WARNER, univ. ofcl.; b. Sayre, Pa., Jan. 19, 1929; s. John Walter and Naomi Ruth (Warner) L.; B.S., Pa. State U., 1950, M.S., 1951, Ph.D., 1957; student U. Minn., 1954-55; m. Theresa Arlene Green, Sept. 22, 1956; children—Diane Marie, Linda Jean. Grad. research asst., instr. Pa. State U., 1950-51, 53-54, 55-56; successively asst. prof., asso. prof., prof. U. Minn., 1956-69, head dept. agrl. econs., 1963-64, asst. to pres. then exec. asst. to pres., also dir. planning, 1964-69; exec. vice chancellor U. Calif. at Davis, 1969—; cons. 4th Dist. Fed. Res. Bank, 1960, Dept. Agr., 1962-65. Served with AUS, 1951-53. Recipient Grad. Student award Am. Farm Econs. Assn., 1956. Mem. Am. Agrl. Econs. Assn., Am. Econ. Assn., AAUP, Nat. Planning Assn. (mem. agrl. com.), Gamma Sigma Delta. Contbr. articles on agrl. policy, prices, fgn. trade policy to profl. jours. Home: 1702 Sycamore Ln Davis CA 95616

LEARNED, MICHAEL, actress; b. Washington, Apr. 9; ed. Austria, Eng.; m. Peter Donat (div.); children—Caleb, Christopher, Lucas; m. 2d, William Parker, Dec. 18, 1979. Apprentice, Conn. Shakespeare Festival; with resident and touring cos. Can. Stratford Shakespeare Festival, Am. Conservatory Theatre, also San Diego Shakespeare Festival; stage appearances include The Three Sisters, A God Slept Here, Antony and Cleopatra, Under Milkwood, Tartuffe, Deedle Dumpling, My Son, God, The Merchant of Venice, Private Lives, Importance of Being Earnest, Miss Margarida's Way, Dear Liar; TV appearances include Gunsmoke, Police Story, (movies) Hurricane, 1974, It Couldn't Happen to a Nicer Guy, 1974, Widow, 1976, Little Mo, 1978; appeared in film Apocalypse Now, 1977; appeared on TV series The Waltons, 1972—; also numerous roles in Canadian Broadcasting Corp. prodns. Recipient Photoplay award, 1974; Emmy award Nat. Acad. TV Arts and Scis., 1973, 74, 76. Office: care

Henderson/Hogan Agy Inc 247 S Beverly Dr Beverly Hills CA 90212*

LEARY, JAMES FRANCIS, financial co. exec.; b. Phila., Mar. 9, 1930; s. Cornelius J. and Marie C. (Canisius) L.; B.A., Georgetown U., 1951; M.B.A., N.Y. U., 1958; m. Joanne L. Quiros, May 1, 1976; children—Pamela, Neil, Beth. With CIT Financial Corp., N.Y.C., 1960-71, various exec. positions, 1962-71; sr. v.p. Nat. Div. Nat. Bank N. Am., N.Y.C., 1971-73; treas. Assos. Corp. N.Am., N.Y.C., 1973-74, South Bend, Ind., 1974—, sr. v.p. fin., 1974-76, exec. v.p., chief fin. officer, Dallas, 1976—; dir. Tex. Am. Bank, Dallas; mem. adv. com. Regional Fin. Enterprises, Stamford, Conn. Served with USMCR, 1952-54. Home: 7225 S Janmar Circle Dallas TX 75230 Office: Assos Corp N Am PO Box 22822 Dallas TX 75222

LEARY, JOHN CHARLES, fgn. service officer; b. Hartford, Conn., Feb. 3, 1924; s. Paul Edward and Hannah Moylan (Lynch) L.; B.A. in Internat. Relations, Yale, 1947, M.A. in Econs., 1959; student Wharton Grad. Sch., U. Pa., 1948-49; m. Nancy Fay Smith, July 8, 1950; children—Suzanne Elizabeth Leary Connolly, Robert Edward, Barbara Jean Leary Jones, Patricia Fay (dec.), John Charles, Margaret Hannah. Joined U.S. Fgn. Service, 1949; vice consul, Cherbourg, France, 1950-52; econ. officer, Duesseldorf, Germany, 1953-56; consul, Istanbul, Turkey, 1956-58; internat. economist State Dept., 1959-63; 1st sec., chief fgn. econ. br. embassy, Tokyo, Japan, 1964-68, chief gen. comml. policy div. State Dept., Washington, 1968-72, dep. dir. Office Internat. Trade, 1970-72, mem. 15th sr. seminar on fgn. policy, 1972-73, counselor for econ. and comml. affairs Am. Embassy, Ottawa, Ont., 1973-77; minister-counselor, U.S. rep. UN Indsl. Devel. Orgn., Vienna, Austria, 1977—. Chmn. U.S. delegation balance-of-payments com. GATT, 1961, 62, 63. Mem. Yale Alumni Bd., 1966-68. Mem. adv. council St. Mary's Internat. Sch., Tokyo, Japan, 1967-68; v.p. Brookville-Seminary Valley Civic Assn., Alexandria, Va., 1969-71; pres. exec. bd. Am. Internat. Sch., Vienna, Austria, 1978—. Served to 1st lt., pilot, USAAF, 1943-45; ETO. Decorated Air medal with 4 oak leaf clusters; recipient Commendable Service award State Dept., 1963. Mem. Am. Fgn. Service Assn., Am. Econ. Assn. Home: Sternwartestrasse 59 A-1180 Vienna Austria Office: Am Embassy Boltzmanngasse 16 A-1091 Vienna Austria also Vienna Dept State Washington DC 20521

LEARY, LEWIS, writer, lectr.; b. Blauvelt, N.Y., Apr. 18, 1906; s. Lewis Gaston and Beatrice Emily (Knight) L.; B.S., U. Vt., 1928, LL.D., 1963; A.M., Columbia, 1932, Ph.D., 1941; m. Mary Warren Hudson, Mar. 7, 1932; children—Carolyn (Mrs. William Bartholet), Martha Hudson (Mrs. Theodore Allen). Instr. English, Am. U., Beirut, 1928-31; faculty U. Miami, 1935-40, asso. prof. English, 1938-40; faculty Duke, 1941-52, prof. Am. lit., 1950-52; prof. English, Columbia, 1952-68, chmn. dept., 1962-68; William Rand Kenan, Jr. prof. English, U. N.C., 1968-76; asso. Nat. Humanities Center, 1978-79. Spl. asst. OSS, Washington, Cairo, 1942-45; Fulbright lectr. U. Amsterdam, 1957-58; vis. prof. U. Pa., 1958-59, Swarthmore Coll., 1959-60, Duke U., 1978. Recipient Jay B. Hubbell medallion for distinction in Am. lit., 1976. Mem. Modern Lang. Assn., Bibliog. Soc. Am., Am. Antiquarian Soc. Clubs: Grolier, Century (N.Y.C.). Author: Idiomatic Mistakes in English, 1932; That Rascal Freneau: A Study in Literary Failure, 1941, 60, 71; The Literary Career of Nathaniel Tucker, 1951; Mark Twain, 1960; Mark Twain's Letters to Mary, 1961; John Greenleaf Whittier, 1962; Washington Irving, 1963; Norman Douglas, 1967; Southern Excursions, 1971; William Faulkner of Yoknapatawpha County, 1973; Soundings: Some Early American Writers, 1975; American Literature: A Study and Research Guide, 1976. Editor: The Last Poems of Philip Freneau, 1945, 71; Articles on Am. Literature, 1947, rev. and extended, 1954, 70, 79; Method and Motive in the Cantos of Ezra Pound, 1954; The Unity of Knowledge, 1955; Contemporary Literary Scholarship: A Critical Review, 1958; American Literary Essays, 1960; Mark Twain's Wound, 1962; The Teacher and American Literature, 1965; Mark Twain's Correspondence with Henry Huttleston Rogers, 1969; Criticism: Some Major American Writers, 1971. Contbr. articles to profl. periodicals. Home: Greenlaw Hall U NC Chapel Hill NC 27514

LEARY, ROBERT MICHAEL, investment counsellor; b. Omaha, Oct. 9, 1913; s. Henry Shellington and Nell (Swift) L.; B.S.C., Creighton U., 1934; M.B.A., Northwestern U., 1936; m. Alyce Rita Popp, Sept. 21, 1939; children—Sharon (Mrs. George Reichert), Sheila Leary Daly, Michele (Mrs. Dale Alexander), Kathleen (Mrs. Jeffrey Lee), Suzanne. Pres., 7-Up Bottling Co., Hastings, Nebr., 1946-52; zone mgr. Investors Diversified Services, Inc., Hays, Kans., 1953-55; div. mgr. King Merritt & Co., Hays, 1956-60; v.p. Westamerica Securities Inc., Denver, 1960-68; pres., dir. Meridian Capital Corp., San Francisco, 1969-70; pres. Excalibur, Ltd., Denver, 1970-72; v.p., dir. Mountain Haus Devel. Co., Vail, Colo., 1970-75; chmn. Refinery Corp., Denver, 1970-72; v.p. Petro-Silver, Inc., Denver, 1971-79; v.p., dir. Carr Mason & Leary Inc., Beverly Hills, Calif., 1972-78; pres. R.M. Leary & Co., Inc., Denver, 1978—; trustee First Gen. Resources Co., 1970-73. Trustee Soc. Fin. Counseling Ethics, Denver, 1969-71, Internat. Assn. Fin. Planners, Denver, 1969-73. Served to lt. (j.g.) USNR, 1944-45. Mem. Am. Legion, VFW, 40 and 8, Delta Sigma Pi. Democrat. Roman Catholic. Clubs: Elks, K.C., Mount Vernon Country; 26; Optimist (past pres. St. Joseph, Mo.); La Costa Country (Calif.). Home: 3131 E Alameda Ave Denver CO 80209 Office: 2800 First Nat Bank Bldg Denver CO 80293

LEARY, THOMAS SAMUEL, univ. pres.; b. Rochester, N.Y., May 8, 1915; s. Samuel W. and Alta (Kemp) L.; B.Ch.E., Rensselaer Poly. Inst., 1938, M.S., 1939; Ph.D., Iowa State U., 1942; m. Geraldine Ruth Kempnich, Nov. 14, 1942; children—Patricia Leary Davenport, Kathleen Leary Briggs. Tech. aide, supt. Holston Ordnance Works, Kingsport, Tenn., 1942-44; responsible engr. Stromberg Carlson Co., Rochester, 1944-46; chief devel. chemist Am. Cyanamid Co., Bound Brook, N.J., 1946-55; mgr. research lab. Cities Service Oil Co., Lake Charles, La., 1955-61; prof., head dept. engring. McNeese State Coll., Lake Charles, 1961-69, pres., 1969—. Cons. engr. Ernest Levingston & Assos. Bd. dirs. McNeese State U. Found., W.T. and E.L. Burton Found., St. Patrick's Hosp. Registered profl. engr., La., Tex. Fellow Am. Inst. Chem. Engrs.; mem. Am. Assn. Sch. Adminstrs., Greater Lake Charles C. of C. (dir.), Sigma Xi. Contbr. articles to profl. jours. Patentee in field. Office: Office of Pres McNeese State U Lake Charles LA 70609

LEARY, TIMOTHY, psychologist, author; b. Springfield, Mass., Oct. 22, 1920; s. Timothy and Abigail (Ferris) L.; student Holy Cross Coll., 1938-39, U.S. Mil. Acad., 1940-41; A.B., U. Ala., 1943; M.S., Wash. State U., 1946; Ph.D. in Psychology, U. Calif. at Berkeley, 1950; m. Rosemary Woodruff, Aug. 17, 1965; children—Susan, John Busch. Asst. prof. U. Calif. at Berkeley, 1950-55; dir. psychol. research Kaiser Found., Oakland, Calif., 1955-58; lectr. Harvard, 1959-63; first guide League Spiritual Discovery, 1964—; psychol. cons. to mgmt., 1953-63; cons. Mass. Dept. Corrections, 1961-63, Afghanistan Export Assn., 1966-69, Appellant in U.S. Supreme Ct. decision which invalidated Fed. marijuana law test case, 1969; producer Psychedelic Celebrations, 1965-66; writer, actor film Turn On, Tune In, Drop Out. Candidate for gov. Calif., 1969-70. Served with U.S. Army, 1942-45. Mem. Am. Psychol. Assn. Author: Social Dimensions of Personality, 1950; Interpersonal Diagnosis of Personality, 1950; Multi-level Assessment of Personality, 1951; Psychedelic Experience, 1964: (with G. Weil) Psychedelic Reader, 1965: Psychedelic Prayers, 1964; High Priest, 1968; Politics of Ecstasy, 1968; The Psychology of Pleasure, 1969; Jail Notes, 1970; Confessions of a Hope Fiend, 1973; Neurologic, 1973; Terra II, 1973; The Intelligence Agents, 1978; Exo-Psychology, 1979. Recordings: (with J. Lennon) Give Peace a Chance, 1969; Seven Up, 1973. Address: care Peace Press Inc 3828 Willat Ave Culver City CA 90230*

LEARY, WILLIAM EDWARD, ins. co. exec.; b. Boston, Oct. 14, 1923; s. William Edward and Mary Elizabeth (Lee) L.; A.B., Harvard Coll., 1948; m. Ellen Elizabeth Pickett, Sept. 9, 1950; children—William E., Ellen M., James T. With John Hancock Mut. Life Ins. Co., Boston, 1950—, asst. treas., 1964-66, 2d v.p., 1966-68, v.p., 1968-70, sr. v.p., 1970—, now head mortgage and real estate dept.; mem. Greater Boston Real Estate Bd.; dir. Commonwealth Bank & Trust Co., Commonwealth Nat. Corp.; trustee N. Am. Mortgage Investors; bd. dirs. Boston Mcpl. Research Bur.; mem. adv. com. Fed. Nat. Mortgage Assn., 1975-76, 78-79; mem. Mass. Gov.'s Commn. to Simplify Regulations, 1979. Served with U.S. Army, 1943-46. Mem. Mortgage Bankers Assn., Am., Internat. Council Shopping Centers. Roman Catholic. Office: John Hancock Mut Life Ins Co John Hancock Pl Boston MA 02117

LEARY, WILLIAM JAMES, supt. schs.; b. Boston, Oct. 1, 1931; s. John Gilbert and Josephine Marie (Kelley) L.; S.B., Boston Coll., 1953; M.Ed., Boston State Coll., 1954; postgrad. (Fulbright fellow), Sophia U., Tokyo, Japan, 1967; certificate advanced study Harvard U., 1972, Ed.D., 1973; Ed.D., Boston U., 1971; m. Joann Linda Parodi, June 25, 1960; children—Lorraine, Lisa, Linda. Tchr. pub. schs., Boston, 1957-67; chmn. dept. social studies Dorchester High Sch., Boston, 1967-68; dir. curriculum Boston Dist. Pub. Schs., 1969-71, supt. schs., 1972-75; exec. dir. Met. Planning Project, Newton, Mass., 1975-77; supt. schs., Rockville Centre, N.Y., 1977—; asso. prof. dept. continuing studies Boston State Coll., 1970-72; asso. in edn. Harvard Grad. Sch. Edn., 1972-75; adj. prof. edn. Boston U., 1973-75; prof. edn. Suffolk U., 1975-77; adj. prof. edn. C.W. Post Center, L.I. U., 1979—; mem. meml. scholarship fund com. Harvard U., 1977—; TV commentator Channel 5, Boston, 1975-76. Edn. coordinator United Way, 1974. Trustee Museum Fine Arts, Boston, 1972—; bd. dirs. Boston Youth Symphony, 1972—, Edn. Devel. Center, 1972—; mem. nat. alumni bd. Boston U., 1975-78; mem. vis. com. Suffolk U., 1978—. Served with M.C., AUS, 1955-56. Recipient Ida M. Johnston Outstanding Alumni award Boston U. Sch. Edn., 1976; Man of Yr. award Pope's Hill. Assn., 1976. Mem. Am. Assn. Sch. Adminstrs. (del. assembly 1980), Am. Hist. Assn., Assn. for Asian Studies, Nat. Council for Social Studies, Internat. Reading Assn., Assn. for Supervision and Curriculum Devel., Phi Delta Kappa. Roman Catholic. K.C. Edn. columnist Boston Herald Am., 1976—. Home: 3 Bennett St Rockville Centre NY 11570 Office: Shepherd St Rockville Centre NY 11570. *A person's ability for creative and imaginative thinking is limited only by his/her fear to dream.*

LEASURE, JOHN KEITH, educator; b. Sidell, Ill., Nov. 2, 1920; s. Onam Henry and Dorothy (Bever) L.; B.S., U. Ill., 1942, Ph.D., 1953; M.S., Mich. State U., 1946; m. Betty Jean Wille, May 20, 1945; children—Karol Lynn (Mrs. Dan M. Johnson), Bruce Robert. Asst. prof. U. Tenn., 1947-53, asso. prof., 1953-55; research group leader Dow Chem. Co., Midland, Mich., 1955-64, mgr. govt. affairs, bioproducts dept., 1964-66; prof., chmn. dept. plant industries So. Ill. U., Carbondale, 1966-72, asst. provost, 1972-73, v.p. for acad. affairs, provost, 1973-76, prof. dept. plant and soil sci., 1976—. Mem. dist. com. Boy Scouts Am., 1952-66. Served to capt. USNR, 1942-45; Res., ret., 1973. Mem. Am. Soc. Agronomy (nat. com. 1967-71), Am. Soc. Plant Physiologists, Am. Chem. Soc., Weed Sci. Soc. Am. (nat. com. 1968-79), Sigma Xi, Phi Kappa Phi, Alpha Zeta, Gamma Sigma Delta. Methodist. Patentee in field. Home: Rural Route 4 Carbondale IL 62901. *I have found that there are two things that I can never quite accomplish: the first is to learn all I need to know; and the second is to use all I have learned. I try to balance learning and doing.*

LEATH, JAMES MARVIN, congressman; b. Rusk County, Tex., May 6, 1931; s. Ned Morris and Linnie Faye (Jacobs) L.; B.B.A., U. Tex., 1954; m. Alta Ruth Neill, May 24, 1954; children—James Gregory (dec.), Thomas Milton. Officer, dir. numerous banks, Marlin, Bermond, Kosse, Tex., 1962-77; chmn. bd., pres. Central Nat. Bank, Waco, Tex., 1977; dir. Marlin Mills, Inc. (Tex.), 1966-77, Clifton Corp., Waco, 1977-78; mem. 96th Congress from 41st Tex. Dist. Served to 1st lt., U.S. Army, 1954-56. Democrat. Presbyterian. Office: 1331 Longworth House Office Bldg Washington DC 20515

LEATHAM, JOHN TONKIN, ins. co. exec.; b. Chgo., July 4, 1936; s. Chester and Betty (Collins) L.; B.A., Lawrence U., Appleton, Wis., 1958; m. Sheila K. Andersen, Sept. 13, 1958; children—Lisa M., John A., Bronwen Gay, Douglas Q. Asst. cashier, lending officer Continental Ill. Nat. Bank & Trust Co., Chgo., 1962-68; with Reliance Group, Inc., N.Y.C., 1968—, sr. v.p., chief financial officer, 1971-72, exec. v.p., chief operating and chief financial officer, 1972—, dir., mem. exec. com., 1974—; dir., mem. exec. com. Ops. Research, Inc., Reliance Ins. Co., 1976—. Nat. dir. Reading is FUN-damental, Inc., 1975—. Served to 1st lt. USAF, 1958-62. Decorated Air Force Commendation medal. Mem. Lawrence U. Alumni Assn. (v.p. 1963-70, dir. 1965-71). Club: Union League (Chicago); Country (Darien, Conn.). Home: 6 Hummingbird Ln Darien CT 06820 Office: 919 3d Ave New York City NY 10022

LEATHER, RICHARD BRENK, mining exec.; b. N.Y.C., Feb. 22, 1932; s. Basil Henry and Elizabeth Marie (Brenk) L.; B.A., Yale, 1953; certificate, U. Paris, 1952; LL.B., Harvard, 1958; m. Penelope Jessie Pope, May 28, 1960; children—Edward, Ann, Charles. Admitted to N.Y. bar, 1959; atty. firm Chadbourne Parke Whiteside & Wolff, 1958-70, partner, 1966-70; atty. Newmont Mining Corp., N.Y.C., 1970—, gen. counsel and sec., 1971-74, v.p., gen. counsel, 1975-78, sr. v.p., 1978-79, exec. v.p., 1979—, also dir.; dir. Magma Copper Co., Foote Mineral Co. Trustee L.W. Frohlich Found. Served with AUS, 1954-56. Mem. Am., N.Y. State bar assns., Am. Inst. Mining, Metall. and Petroleum Engrs., Copper Devel. Assn. (sec.), Smelter Environ. Research Assn. (trustee), Am. Bur. Metal Stats. (trustee). Clubs: Racquet and Tennis (N.Y.C.); Manhasset Bay Yacht (Port Washington, N.Y.). Home: 50 Valley Rd Plandome NY 11030 Office: 300 Park Ave New York NY 10022

LEAVELL, BYRD STUART, physician; b. Washington, Dec. 29, 1910; s. Byrd and Lucie (Browning) L.; B.S., Va. Mil. Inst., 1931; M.D., U. Va., 1935; m. Nancy Butzner, Oct. 7, 1939; children—Anne Leavell Reynolds, Lucie Leavell Vogel, Byrd Stuart, Jr. Intern, N.Y. Hosp., N.Y.C., 1935-36, asst. resident, 1936-38; practice medicine specializing in internal medicine, Charlottesville, Va., 1946—; fellow U. Va., 1938-39, asst. dir. student health, 1939-40, instr. medicine Sch. Medicine, 1940-42, asst. prof., 1946-54, prof., 1954—, chmn. dept. internal medicine, 1966-68, asst. dean Sch. Medicine, 1958-61, head div. hematology, 1945-70. Served to maj., M.C., AUS, 1942-46. Decorated Bronze Star. Mem. AMA, A.C.P., Internat., Am. socs. hematology, AAAS, So. Soc. Clin. Investigation, Am. Clin. and Climatol. Assn., Kappa Alpha, Alpha Omega Alpha, Omicron Delta Kappa. Episcopalian. Clubs: Colonnade (pres. 1960), Farmington Country (Charlottesville). Author: The 8th Evac., 1970; (with O.A. Thorup) Fundamentals of Clinical Hematology, 4th edit., 1976. Home: Box 229 Route 2 Charlottesville VA 22901

LEAVELL, JEROME FONTAINE, lawyer, educator; b. Blue Mountain, Miss., Feb. 14, 1928; s. William Nelson and Lillian Grace (Farley) L.; B.A., U. Miss., 1951, LL.B., 1951, J.D., 1969; Ford Found. fellow, Balliol Coll., Oxford U., 1969; LL.M. (Sterling fellow), Yale 1964, J.S.D., 1972; m. Martha Naomi Roll, Aug. 15, 1964; children—Glenn Farley, Naomi Fontaine. Admitted to Miss. bar, 1951, Fed. bar, 1952, N.Y. bar, 1957, Ga. bar, 1965, Ark. bar, 1972, Va. bar, 1975, also U.S. Supreme Ct. bar; atty. FTC, Washington, 1951-52; law clk. Edwin R. Holmes, U.S. Ct. of Appeals, 5th Circuit, 1952; asso. Brewer & Brewer, Clarksdale, Miss., 1953-54, Cadwalader, Wickersham & Taft, N.Y.C., 1955-57; atty. Chase Manhattan Bank, N.Y.C., 1958-62; practiced in N.Y.C., 1962-63; trial atty. N.Y. State Tax Commn., 1962-63; atty. Merrill, Lynch, Pierce, Fenner & Smith, N.Y.C., 1963-64; pvt. practice, Atlanta, 1965; spl. lectr. on constl. law Woodrow Wilson Sch. Law, Atlanta, 1965; asst. prof. U. Ark., 1966-67, asso. prof., 1967-72, placement dir., faculty adviser law rev., 1972; vis. prof. La. State U., 1972; asso. prof. Coll. William and Mary, Williamsburg, Va., 1972-75; prof. Sch. Law, Miss. Coll., Clinton, 1975-77; mem. firm Dodson, McLaurin & Leavell, Oxford, Miss., 1977—; spl. dep. pros. atty., Ark., 1972; Disting. vis. prof. U. Ark., Little Rock, 1972; cons. Ark. Dept. Securities, 1968; case editor Brief mag. Ark. Lawyers Assn., 1967-69; spl. cons. Nat. Commn. for Protection of Human Subjects of Biomed. and Behavioral Research, 1977. Served with AUS, 1946-48. Recipient Cannon prize Chase Manhattan Bank, 1959, Outstanding Prof. award Delta Theta Phi, 1971, Outstanding Tchr. award Phi Alpha Delta-Student Bar Assn., 1968, certificate merit Law Sch. William and Mary, Delta (hon.), Mem. Am., Fed., Va., Hinds County, Lafayette County bar assns., Assn. Am. Law Schs., Am. Judicature Soc., Inner Temple (hon.), Oxford Soc., Oxford Law Soc., Soc. for Legal History, Am. Soc. Internat. Law, English Speaking Union, Mary Ball Soc., Sigma Alpha Epsilon, Phi Alpha Delta, Delta Theta Phi. Clubs: Yale, Oxford at William and Mary, Rotary. Episcopalian. Author: A Treatise on the Law and Ethics of Organ Transplants, 1972; Survey of American Law of Advertising, 1972. Contbr. articles to profl. jours. Home: 65 Country Club Terr Oxford MS 38655

LEAVENGOOD, VICTOR PRICE, telephone co. exec.; b. Ocala, Fla., June 2, 1924; s. Hansel Devane and Mildred (Price) L.; B.S. in Bus. Adminstrn., U. Fla., 1947; M.B.A., Harvard, 1949; m. Elizabeth Lee Bird, Sept. 12, 1950; children—Sally, Ann, Hansel. Bus. mgr. Ocala (Fla.) Star Banner, daily newspaper, 1952-59; circulation dir. Tampa (Fla.) Tribune, 1959-60, dir. community affairs, 1960-64; asst. v.p. Gen. Telephone Co. Fla., Tampa, 1964-70, sec., treas., 1970—; dir. Barnett Bank Tampa. Pres. Hills County Community Coordination Council, 1964-65, Tampa Econ. Opportunity Council, 1965-66, Fla. Clergy Econ. Edn. Found., 1964-68; pres. United Fund Greater Tampa Inc., 1964-68, treas., 1970-75; mem. Fla. Council Mental Health Tng. and Research, 1967-74; pres. Fla. chpt. United Way, 1969—; mem. Pres.'s Round Table, Eckerd Coll., St. Petersburg, Fla., 1969—; mem. Hillsborough County Hosp. Council; mem. president's council U. South Fla., 1974—, treas. U. South Fla. Found., 1975—; bd. dirs. Suncoast council Girl Scouts U.S.A. Served to comdr. USNR, 1942-47. Mem. Greater Tampa (bd. dirs.), Fla. (edn. com. 1968-71), U.S. (edn. com.) chambers commerce, Phi Eta Sigma, Phi Delta Theta. Democrat. Methodist (ofcl. bd.). Kiwanian; mem. Ye Mystic Krewe of Gasparilla. Clubs: University, Tower, Tampa Yacht and Country (Tampa). Home: 4516 Sylvan Ramble Tampa FL 33609 Office: 610 Morgan St Tampa FL 33601

LEAVERTON, PAUL EMMETT, JR., educator; b. Irvington, Iowa, July 30, 1934; s. Paul Emmett and Muriel Kay (Body) L.; B.S., Iowa State U., 1956, M.A., 1961, Ph.D., 1963; children—Scott Allen, Thomas Stuart. Statistician, Epidemic Intelligence Service, Atlanta, 1957-59; asst. prof. U. Colo. Med. Coll., 1963-64; mem. faculty U. Iowa Coll. Medicine, 1964-74, prof. biostatistics dept. community health, 1967-74; asso. dir. for research Nat. Center for Health Statistics, Hyattsville, Md., 1974—; cons. WHO. Served with USPHS, 1957-59. Named Outstanding Young Alumnus, Iowa State U., 1969. Fellow A.A.A.S.; mem. Am. Statis. Assn., Biometric Soc., Am. Pub. Health Assn. Author: A Review of Biostatistics, 1978; co-author: Statistical Inference in the Biomedical Sciences, 1970. Home: 10661 Montrose Ave 202 Bethesda MD 20014. *Continual reevaluation of life goals to avoid long-term commitments to obsolete plans.*

LEAVEY, H. HAROLD, lawyer, assn. exec.; b. Sacramento, July 19, 1906; s. Charles L. and Eva E. (Elliott) L.; A.B., U. Calif. at Berkeley, 1928, J.D., 1932; m. Harriet T. Ferguson, June 23, 1934; children—Anna Rita (Mrs. William R. Neuman), Patricia Z. (Mrs. Robert E. Krisch), Terrance C. Admitted to Calif. bar, 1932; practiced law, Sacramento, 1932-33; tax atty. Calif. Bd. Equalization, 1933-35; with Calif.-Western States Life Ins. Co., 1935-71, gen. counsel, 1945-68, sec., 1957-68, exec. v.p., 1967-68, pres., 1968-70, chmn., 1970-71; v.p. Westerlic Corp., Ltd., 1939-68, gen. counsel, 1950-68, dir., 1954-71; v.p. Am. Health Systems Inc., 1971-75, dir., 1973-75; legal counsel Am. Assn. Founds. for Med. Care, San Francisco, 1972-76, United Founds. for Med. Care, 1973—. Dir., sec. Western 65 Health Ins. Assn., 1965-67; sec. legal sect. Am. Life Conv., 1958, chmn., 1959; exec. com. Assn. Calif. Life Ins. Co., 1963-65; dir. Unemployment Ins. Assn., 1958-71, pres., 1960-61. Mem. Sacramento Redevel. Agy., 1950-73, chmn., 1950-54; adv. com. urban renewal League Calif. Cities, 1960-67, chmn., 1960-63; nat. adv. council Urban Am., 1965-70. Bd. dirs. Sacramento area USO, 1945-64, chmn., 1950-53; bd. dirs. Cath. Welfare Bur. Sacramento, 1950-68, pres., 1950-57; bd. dirs. Sacramento Area United Crusade, 1954-65, drive chmn., 1957-58, pres., 1964; bd. dirs. Sacramento Vol. Bur., 1963-68, exec. com., 1966-68. Recipient Community Welfare Council award, 1958; Distinguished Service awards USO, 1966, Sacramento City Council, 1973; United Crusade Distinguished Service award, 1966. Mem. Am., Sacramento County (pres. 1965) bar assns., Calif. State Bar, Sierra Club. Republican. Roman Catholic. Club: Olympic (San Francisco). Home: 56 Northlite Circle Sacramento CA 95831 Office: 1006 4th St Suite 1300 Sacramento CA 95814

LEAVITT, CHRISTOPHER PRATT, educator; b. Boston, Nov. 20, 1927; s. Richard C. and Helen (Pratt) L.; B.S., Mass. Inst. Tech., 1948; Ph.D., 1952; m. Joyce Ann Carlson, Jan. 3, 1959; children—Stephen C., Richard C., Karin E., Suzanne M., Jonathan P. Research asso. Brookhaven Nat. Lab., Upton, L.I., 1952-54; asso. physicist, 1954-56; mem. faculty U. N.Mex., Albuquerque, 1956—, asso. prof. physics, 1961-65, prof., 1965—; cons. Air Force Spl. Weapons Center, Kirtland AFB, N.Mex., 1959. Pres. Albuquerque United World Federalists, 1963—. Mem. Am. Phys. Soc., Sigma Xi. Research on solar neutrons, satellite expt., 1969-74, nucleon-nucleon interactions, 1973—. Home: 944 Green Valley Rd NW Albuquerque NM 87107

LEAVITT, DANA GIBSON, corp. exec.; b. Framingham, Mass., Dec. 4, 1925; s. Luther C. and Margaret (Gibson) L.; B.A., Brown U., 1948; postgrad. Harvard Bus. Sch., 1954-55; m. Frances Smith, Apr. 12, 1952; children—Margaret Gibson, Jonathan. Home office rep. Aetna Life Ins. Co., Boston, also Long Beach, Calif., 1949-54; v.p., sec.-treas., exec. v.p. N. Am. Title Ins. Co., Oakland, Calif., 1955-64; pres. Transam. Title Ins. Co., Oakland, 1964-72; v.p. Transam. Corp.,

1969-71, group v.p., 1971-77, exec. v.p., 1977—; chmn. bd. Transam. Financial Corp., Transam. Ins. Co., Occidental Life Ins. Co. of Calif.; dir. United Artists Corp., Trans Internat. Airlines, Transam.-DeLaval Inc., Lyon Moving & Storage Co., Transam Corp. Regional chmn. Brown U. Fund, 1969-72. Bd. dirs. Children's Hosp. Med. Center and Found., 1969-72; trustee Lewis and Clark Coll., Portland, Oreg., 1972-75; trustee Brown U., Providence, 1973-78, trustee emeritus, 1978—. Served with USMCR, World War II. Mem. Delta Kappa Epsilon. Republican. Clubs: Brown U. of No. Calif., Harvard Bus. Sch. of No. Calif., Orinda Country; Bohemian (San Francisco). Office: 600 Montgomery St San Francisco CA 94111

LEAVITT, HAROLD JACK, psychologist; b. Lynn, Mass., Jan. 14, 1922; s. Joseph and May (Lopata) L.; B.A., Harvard Coll., 1943; M.S., Brown U., 1944; Ph.D., Mass. Inst. Tech., 1949; m. Gloria Rosenthal, Jan. 31, 1943; children—John, Emily, David. Asst. prof. psychology Rensselaer Poly. Inst., 1949-50; asso. prof. Sch. Bus., U. Chgo., 1954-58; prof. indsl. adminstrn. and psychology GSIA, Carnegie Inst. Tech., 1958-66; Walter Kenneth Kilpatrick prof. orgn. behavior and psychology Grad. Sch. Bus., Stanford U., 1966—; vis. prof. London Grad. Sch. Bus. Studies, 1972; v.p. Nejelski & Co., 1951-53; cons. European Prod. Agy., Paris, 1956; faculty prin. Mgmt. Analysis Center, Inc., 1971—. Served to lt. (j.g.) USNR, 1944-46. Fellow Am. Psychol. Assn.; mem. Inst. Mgmt. Scis. (v.p. 1959-60), Nat. Tng. Labs. (nat. bd. 1962-64, adviser 1970—). Author: Managerial Psychology, 4th edit., 1978; (with W. Dill and H. Eyring) The Organizational World, 1973. Co-editor: Organizations of the Future, 1974; mem. editorial bd. Omega, 1974—. Home: 743 Cooksey Ln Stanford CA 94305 Office: Grad Sch Bus Stanford U Stanford CA 94305

LEAVITT, JEROME EDWARD, educator; b. Verona, N.J., Aug. 1, 1916; s. Thomas Edward and Clara Marie (Sonn) L.; B.S., Newark State Coll., 1938; M.A., N.Y. U., 1942; Ed.D., Northwestern U., 1952; m. Florence Elizabeth Wilkins, Aug. 23, 1963. Tchr. pub. schs., Roslyn Heights, N.Y., 1938-42; instr. Sperry Gyroscope, Bklyn., 1942-45; prin., supr. pub. schs., Los Alamos, N.Mex., 1945-49; prof. edn., exec. asst. to dean Portland (Oreg.) State U., 1952-66; prof. edn. U. Ariz., Tucson, 1966-69; prof. elem. edn., coordinator Child Abuse Project, Calif. State U., Fresno, 1969—; ednl. cons. Mem. Assn. Childhood Edn. Internat. (life), Assn. Supervision and Curriculum Devel., Nat. Soc. Study Edn., N.E.A. (life), Soc. Profs. Edn., Calif. Tchrs. Assn., Profs. Curriculum, Phi Delta Kappa, Kappa Delta Pi, Epsilon Pi Tau. Author: By Land, By Sea, By Air, 1969; The Beginning Kindergarten Teacher, 1971; America and Its Indians, 1971; The Battered Child, 1974; and others; contbr. articles to profl. jours. Home: 1338 E Almendra Dr Fresno CA 93710 Office: Dept Elem Edn Calif State Univ Fresno CA 93740

LEAVITT, JOAN KAZANJIAN, state health ofcl., physician; b. Boston, Jan. 14, 1926; d. Varaztad Hovannes and Marion V. (Hanford) Kazanjian; A.B., Radcliffe Coll., 1947; M.A., Smith Coll., 1949; M.D., Boston U., 1953; m. Don K. Leavitt; children—Mark S., Lynda Donn. Intern in pediatrics Boston City Hosp., 1953-54, resident in pediatrics, 1954-55; resident in pediatrics Mass. Gen. Hosp., Boston, 1955-56, 57-58; pediatrician Comanche County (Okla.) Guidance Center, 1959; practice medicine specializing in pediatrics, Altus, Okla., 1959-64; med. dir. Jackson County (Okla.) Health Dept., 1960-67, Kay County (Okla.) Health Dept., 1967-76; chief maternal and child health service Okla. Health Dept., Oklahoma City, 1976, dep. commr. for personal health services, 1976-77, commr. of health, 1977—. Mem. AMA, Okla. State Med. Assn., Okla. Public Health Assn., Oklahoma County Med. Soc., Assn. State and Territorial Health Ofcls., Sigma Xi. Home: 6235 NW Grand St Oklahoma City OK 73118 Office: 1000 NE Tenth St PO Box 53551 Oklahoma City OK 73152

LEAVITT, JOSEPH, producer, musician; b. Chelsea, Mass., Feb. 13, 1916; s. Abraham and Mildred (Leavitt) L.; grad. New Eng. Conservatory Music, 1940; B.A., Am. U., 1954; student Boston U., 1941, Manhattan Sch. Music, 1946; m. Sally Elissa, Aug. 30, 1942; children—Howard R., Joan E. Successively musician, pianist, prin. musician, dir. ops. and asst. mgr. Nat. Symphony Orch., Washington, 1949-69; gen. mgr. N.J. Symphony Orch., 1969-71; exec. dir., exec. producer all Wolf Trap prodns., Wolf Trap Found. Performing Arts, Vienna, Va., 1970-73; gen. mgr. Balt. Symphony Orch., 1973—; engagements with Boston Pops, Balt. Symphony Orch.; rec. artist RCA Victor, Westminster, Columbia records; mem. faculty tympani percussion Peabody Conservatory, 1948-49; faculty arts mgmt. U. Md. summer sch., 1974-76; adj. prof. arts mgmt. Goucher Coll., 1977—. Mem. adv. com. Fairfax County Council Arts, 1971-73, Balt. Mayor's Com. on Art and Culture; bd. dirs., v.p. Md. Council for Dance, 1976-78; mem. exec. com. Regional Cultural Commn.; field reader Program for Gifted and Talented, HEW. Served with USAAF, World War II. Mem. Internat. Assn. Performing Arts Adminstrs. (dir.). Club: Rotary. Author: The Rhythms of Contemporary Music, 1963; Reading by Recognition, 1960. Home: 1110 Hampton Garth Towson MD 21204 Office: 5204 Roland Ave Baltimore MD 21210.
A friend once advised "Don't try to get out of things—get into things." I have found this most valuable.

LEAVITT, LLOYD RICHARDSON, JR., air force officer; b. Alpena, Mich., Nov. 18, 1928; s. Lloyd Richardson and Grace Katherine (Hagen) L.; B.S., U.S. Mil. Acad., 1950; M.A., George Washington U., 1965; postgrad. Nat. War Coll., 1966-67; m. Anne Sullivan, July 21, 1950; children—Anne (Mrs. Richard D. Whitmyre), Lloyd Richardson III, Mary C. Commd. 2d lt. USAF, 1950, advanced through grades to lt. gen., 1978; various assignments in fighters, bombers, reconnaissance aircraft; dir. operational readiness USAF, Europe, 1968-70; comdr. 432d Tactical Ftr-Recce Wing, Udorn, Thailand, 1970-71; dir. strike forces Hdqrs. USAF, 1971-72; dep. dir. operations Joint Chiefs Staff, Washington, 1972-74; comdr. Chanute Tech. Tng. Center, Rantoul, Ill., 1974-77; dep. chief staff, ops. and intelligence Hdqrs. USAFE, Ramstein, W. Ger., 1977-78; vice comdr.-in-chief SAC, Offutt AFB, Nebr., 1978—. Bd. advisers U. Nebr., Omaha. Decorated D.S.M. with 1 oak leaf cluster, Legion of Merit with 2 oak leaf clusters, D.F.C. with 2 oak leaf clusters, Bronze Star, Meritorious Service medal, Air medal with 2 silver, 3 bronze oak leaf clusters. Mem. Air Force Assn. Episcopalian (vestryman). Home: Quarters 9 Offutt AFB NE 68113 Office: Vice Comdr-in-chief SAC Offutt AFB NE

LEAVITT, MILO DAVID, JR., physician, govt. ofcl.; b. Beloit, Wis., June 24, 1915; s. Milo David and Helen (Hubner) L.; B.A., U. Wis., 1938; M.D., U. Pa., 1940; M.Sc., U. Minn., 1948; M.P.H., Harvard, 1959. Rotating intern Phila. Gen. Hosp., 1940-42; fellow internal medicine Mayo Clinic, Rochester, Minn., 1945-49; clin. asst. prof. medicine Woman's Med. Coll. Pa., Phila., 1949-58; with NIH, Bethesda, 1959—, asst. chief perinatal research br., 1960-62, head spl. internat. programs sect. Office Internat. Research, 1962-66, dep. asst. sec. for sci. and population HEW, 1966, dep. dir., acting dir. office program planning, 1967-68, dir. Fogarty Internat. Center, 1968-78; spl. asst. to dir. Nat. Inst. Aging, NIH, 1978—; cons. VA, Phila., 1954-58; mem. U.S. del. 25th-27th, 29th World Health Assemblies. Bd. dirs. Gorgas Meml. Inst. Tropical and Preventive Medicine. Served to capt. M.C., AUS, 1942-45. Mem. A.M.A., Indsl. Med. Assn., Am. Geriatrics Soc., Gerontol. Soc., Phila. County Med. Soc., Am. Diabetes Assn., Assn. Am. Med. Colls., N.Y. Acad. Scis., A.A.A.S., Alumni Assn. Mayo Found., Am. Heart Assn., Am. Pub. Health Assn., Am. Soc. Pub. Health Adminstrs., Phila. Coll. Physicians, Sigma Xi, Kappa Sigma, Alpha Mu Pi Omega. Episcopalian. Contbr. articles to profl. jours. Home: 8017 Eastern Ave Silver Spring MD 20910 Office: NIH Nat Inst on Aging Bethesda MD 20205

LEAVITT, THOMAS WHITTLESEY, mus. dir., educator; b. Boston, Jan. 8, 1930; s. Richard C. and Helen M. (Pratt) L.; A.B., Middlebury (Vt.) Coll., 1951; M.A., Boston U., 1952; Ph.D., Harvard, 1958; m. Jane O. Ayer, June 23, 1951 (div. 1969); children—Katherine, Nancy, Hugh; m. 2d, Lloyd B. Carter, Sept. 14, 1978. Asst. to dir. Fogg Mus., Harvard, 1954-56; exec. dir. fine arts com. People to People Program, 1957; dir. Pasadena (Calif.) Art Mus., 1957-63, Santa Barbara (Calif.) Mus. Art, 1963-68; dir. Andrew Dickson White Mus. Art, Cornell U., Ithaca, N.Y., 1968-73, Herbert F. Johnson Mus. Art, 1973—, univ. prof. history art, 1968—. Dir. mus. program Nat. Endowment for Arts, 1971-72, mem. museum panel, 1972-75; vice chmn. Council on Museums and Edn. in Visual Arts, 1972-76; trustee Gallery Assn. N.Y. State, 1972-78; mem. mus. panel N.Y. State Council Arts, 1975-78. Trustee Am. Fedn. Arts, 1972—; bd. govs. N.E. Museums Conf., 1973-76. Mem. Am. Assn. Art Mus. Dirs. (treas. 1973-76, pres. 1977-78, trustee 1978—), Am. Assn. Museums (council 1976-79), Coll. Art Assn. Author exhbn. catalogs, articles. Home: 1151 Taughannock Blvd Ithaca NY 14850 Office: Herbert F Johnson Mus of Art Cornell U Ithaca NY 14853

LEAVY, HERBERT THEODORE, publisher; b. Detroit, July 10, 1927; s. Morris and Thelma (Davidson) L.; B.S. in Journalism, Ohio U., 1951; m. Patricia J. Moran, June 20, 1953; children—Karen, Kathryn, Jill, Jacqueline. Supervisory editor Fawcett Books, N.Y.C., 1951-60; v.p., editorial dir. Davis Publs., N.Y.C., 1960-69; founder, pres. Internat. Evaluations, Hauppage, N.Y., 1969-70; publisher, dir. Countrywide Publs. Inc., N.Y.C., 1970-75; pres. Communications Devel. Co., N.Y.C., 1975-77; publs. supr. J.C. Penney Co., N.Y.C., 1977—. Served to sgt. USAAF, 1945-47. Mem. Sales Exec. Club, Am. Soc. Mag. Editors, Nat. Sporting Goods Assn., Am. Mgmt. Assn., Mag. Advts. Sales Club, Electronics Press Club, U.S. Tennis Ct. and Track Builders Assn., Am. Motorcycle Assn., Am. Horse Council, Author's Guild, Motorcycle Industry Council, Nat. Indoor Tennis Assn., Bus./Profl. Advt. Assn., Sigma Delta Chi. Author: The Pleasure, 1958; Executive Handbook, 1969; Carpentry, 1970—; Shoe and Leather Repair at Home; The Complete Book of Beards and Moustaches; Air Conditioning-Repair and Maintenance; Designing and Building Beds, Lofts and Sleeping Areas; Wallcovering; Floor Stripping and Refinishing, Packing and Moving; Recreational Vehicles; Appliance Repair; Plumbing Handbook; Successful Small Farms; numerous others. Home: 7 Radburn Dr Commack NY 11725 Office: JC Penney Co 1301 Ave of Americas New York NY 10019

LEBAN, MICHAEL EUGENE, home builder; b. Chgo., May 23, 1932; s. Michael and Leona Mae (Newell) L.; student U. Detroit, 1950-51; B.S.C., Loyola U., Chgo., 1956; m. Nancy Clare Knowles, June 4, 1955; children—Beth, Gail, Brian, Lisa, Regina, Matthew. Gen. supr. Gary (Ind.) steel works U.S. Steel Co., 1956-65; mgr.-in-charge dept. mgmt. cons. Peat, Marwick, Mitchell, Milw., 1965-72; co-dir. fin. systems Monsanto Co., St. Louis, 1972-73; controller-treas. Fisher Controls Co. Inc., Marshalltown, Iowa, 1973-78; corp. controller Fox & Jacobs Inc., Dallas, 1978—. Bd. dirs. Marshalltown Hosp., 1973-78, Marshalltown Community Hosp., Marshalltown YMCA, 1974-78. Served with U.S. Army, 1952-54; Korea. Roman Catholic. Clubs: Rotary, K.C. Home: 13859 Peyton Dr Dallas TX 75240 Office: PO Box 934 2900 Surveyor Blvd Carrollton TX 75006

LEBARON, EDWARD WAYNE, JR., profl. football team mgr.; b. San Rafael, Calif., Jan. 7, 1930; s. Edward Wayne and Mabel Butler (Sims) LeB.; B.A., Coll. Pacific, 1950; LL.B., George Washington U., 1959; m. Doralee M. Le Baron, June 4, 1954; children—Edward Wayne, William Bruce, Richard Wilson. Football quarterback Washington Redskins, 1952-59; admitted to Calif. bar, 1960, Tex. bar, 1960, Nev. bar, 1967; with Dallas Cowboys, 1960-63; exec. v.p. Nevada Cement Co., 1964-65; mem. firm Wynne & Wynne, Dallas, 1960-63; mem. firm Bible, McDonald & Carano, Reno, 1966-68; mem. firm Laxalt & Berry, Carson City, Nev., 1969-70; partner firm Jones, Jones, Bell, LeBaron and Brown, Las Vegas, Nev., 1970-76; gen. mgr. Atlanta Falcons Football team, 1977—; dir. Tom Brown, Inc., Ormand Industries; partner LeBaron Ranches. Served with USMC, 1950-52. Decorated Purple Heart, Bronze Star. Named Sportsman of Year in Ga., 1978-79. Mem. Am. Bar Assn. Republican. Clubs: Commerce, Capital City. Office: I-85 at Suwanee Rd Suwanee GA 30174

LEBARON, FRANCIS NEWTON, educator; b. Framingham, Mass., July 26, 1922; s. Paul Burrows and Dorothy (Lamson) LeB.; S.B., Mass. Inst. Tech., 1944; M.A., Boston U., 1948; Ph.D., Harvard, 1951; m. Margaret Lenore Shaw, July 8, 1953; 1 son, Geoffrey Shaw. Asso. biochemist McLean Hosp., Belmont, Mass., 1957-64; asso. biol. chemist Harvard Med. Sch., 1959-64; asso. prof. biochemistry U. N.Mex. Med. Sch., 1964-69, prof., 1969—, chmn. dept., 1971-78, chmn. ad hoc nutrition planning commn., 1969; vis. scholar Mass. Inst. Tech., 1974-75. Served with USNR, 1943-46. Mem. Am. Chem. Soc., Biochem. Soc. (London), Am. Soc. Biol. Chemists, Assn. Am. Med. Colls., A.A.A.S., Internat., Am. (pres. 1969-71) socs. neurochemistry, Sigma Xi, Theta Delta Chi, Editorial bd. Jour. Neurochemistry, 1965—. Contbr. articles to profl. jours. Home: 1713 Morningside Dr NE Albuquerque NM 87110

LEBEAU, EDWARD CHARLES, lawyer; b. Marshall, Minn., Oct. 13, 1929; s. Edward and Dorilda (Brouillette) LeB.; A.B., U. Neb., 1951; J.D., Harvard, 1957; m. Carolyn Maria Sanroma, June 15, 1957; children—Melinda, Christopher, David, Paula, Carol, James. Admitted to Ariz. bar, 1957, since practiced in Phoenix; asso. Evans, Kitchel & Jenckes, 1957-61, partner, 1962—. Instr. Am. Inst. Banking, Maricopa chpt., 1958-62. Served to lt. (j.g.) USNR, 1951-54. Mem. Am., Ariz., Maricopa County bar assns., Harvard Law Sch. Assn. Ariz. (dir., past pres.), Phi Beta Kappa. Republican. Roman Catholic. Home: 5800 Kiva Ln Scottsdale AZ 85253 Office: 363 N 1st Ave Phoenix AZ 85003

LEBECK, WARREN WELLS, assn. exec.; b. Chgo., Mar. 13, 1921; s. Emil and Hazel (Wells) L.; B.A., North Central Coll., Naperville, Ill., 1942; m. Dorothy Lester, Feb. 1, 1943; children—Sara Beth, Kenneth, Clayton A., Frederick E. With Montgomery Ward & Co., Chgo., 1941-42, 46-54; with Chgo. Bd. Trade, 1954—, sec., then exec. v.p., 1957-73, pres., 1973-77, sr. exec. v.p., 1977—; past dir. Bank of Hinsdale (Ill.); past chmn. bd., pres. South Loop Improvement Project; mem. U.S. Agrl. Policy Adv. Com., 1976—. Former mem. bd. edn. Downers Grove (Ill.) Twp. High Sch. Served with USNR, 1942-45. Clubs: Union League (past dir.), Economic, Commodity, Metropolitan, Mid Day (Chgo.); Salt Creek. Home: 432 Minneola St Hinsdale IL 60521 Office: 141 W Jackson Blvd Chicago IL 60604

LEBED, HARTZEL ZANGWILL, ins. co. exec.; b. Columbia, Pa., Mar. 1, 1928; B.S. in Commerce, U. N.C., 1950; m. Ann Kronick, June 12, 1956; children—Holly, Jay, Alex. With Conn. Gen. Life Ins. Co., Hartford, 1950—, v.p. group sales, 1971-73, sr. v.p. group pension ops., 1973-76, exec. v.p. group pension ops. and reinsurance ops., 1976-78, exec. v.p., chief investment officer, 1978—; dir. CG Fund, CG Investment Mgmt. Co., Congen Realty Adv. Co., Congen Properties. Bd. dirs. Hartford Jewish Fedn.; trustee Mt. Sinai Hosp., Hartford, Kingswood-Oxford Sch., West Hartford, Conn. Served with USN, 1945-47. Mem. Phi Beta Kappa. Office: Conn Gen Life Ins Co Hartford CT 06152

LEBEDOW, AARON LOUIS, cons. co. exec.; b. Chgo., Aug. 19, 1935; s. Isidor and Fannie (Perchikoff) L.; B.S. in Indsl. Engring., Ill. Inst. Tech., 1957; M.B.A., U. Mich., 1958; m. Rosalie Schar, Nov. 12, 1961; children—Ellen, Francine, Sheri. Asst. marketing mgr. Imperial-Eastman, Chgo., 1960-61; mgr. Corplan Assos., Chgo., 1961-66; chmn. bd. Technomic Consultants, Chgo., 1966—. Served to 1st lt. USAF, 1958-60. Cert. mgmt. cons. Mem. Am. Mgmt. Assn., Am. Mktg. Assn., Inst. for Mgmt. Consultants, Tau Epsilon Phi. Mem. B'nai B'rith. Home: 715 LaCrosse St Wilmette IL 60091 Office: 1 N Wacker Dr Chicago IL 60606

LEBEL, ROBERT, bishop; b. Trois Pistoles, Que., Can., Nov. 8, 1924; s. Wilfrid and Alexina (Belanger) L.; L.Theol., St. Paul U., Ottawa, 1950; D.Theol., Athenee Angelicum, Rome, 1951. Ordained priest Roman Catholic Ch., 1950, consecrated bishop, 1974; tchr. theology Major Sem., Rimouski, Que., 1951-65, rector, 1963-65, rector Minor Sem., 1965-68; tchr. domatic theology U. Rimouski, 1970-74; aux. bishop, St. Jean, Que., 1974-76; bishop, Valleyfield, Que., 1976—; bd. dirs. Fedn. des Colls. Classiques, 1965-68, Soc. Nat. de l'est du Que., 1970-74. Mem. Assemblee des Eveques Que. (pres. com. theology), Conf. Can. Cath. Bishops (dir.), Soc. Canadienne de Theologie. Club: K.C. Contbr. ch. publs. Address: 31 Fabrique Valleyfield PQ J6T 4G9 Canada

LEBENSOHN, ZIGMOND MEYER, psychiatrist, educator; b. Kenosha, Wis., Sept. 8, 1910; s. Morris P. and Bertha (Schiffman) L.; student U. Wis., 1926-29; B.S., Northwestern U., 1930, M.B., 1933, M.D., 1934; m. Mary Bates, Feb. 15, 1940 (dec. May 1975); children—Valerie, Jeremy, Marya Lebensohn Huseby, Lucia; m. 2d, Nancy Leach Shields, Mar. 18, 1979. Intern Cook County Hosp., Chgo., 1934-35; psychiat. med. officer St. Elizabeths Hosp., Washington, 1935-39; chief psychiatry Sibley Meml. Hosp., 1956-75, chief emeritus, 1976—; mem. faculty George Washington U. Med. Sch., 1936-41; prof. clin. psychiatry Georgetown U. Sch. Medicine, 1941—; cons. to govt., 1946—. Mem. med. adv. panel FAA, 1961-66; mem. D.C. Commnr. Youth Council, 1954-55. Served as med. officer USNR, 1941-45. Kober lectr. Georgetown U., 1962. Diplomate Am. Bd. Psychiatry and Neurology. Life fellow Am. Psychiat. Assn. (chmn. com. pub. information 1964-67, 70-73, trustee 1967-70); fellow A.M.A.; mem. Assn. Research Nervous and Mental Diseases, Am. Psychopathol. Assn., Group Advancement Psychiatry (chmn. com. psychiatry and law 1966-70), D.C. Med. Soc. (1st v.p. 1953-54; certificate meritorious service 1963), Washington Psychiat. Soc. (pres. 1952), Phi Beta Kappa, Alpha Omega Alpha. Contbr. articles to profl. jours., chpts. to books. Home: 4840 Hutchins Pl NW Washington DC 20007 Office: 2015 R St NW Washington DC 20009

LEBER, LESTER, advt. agy. exec.; b. Newark, June 11, 1913; B.A., Columbia, 1934; m. Magdalena Maurer, July 15, 1968; children by previous marriage—Frederick, Laura (Mrs. Ernest Wood), Daniel. With Grey Advt. Agy., N.Y.C., 1935-52; founder, chmn. bd. Leber Katz Partners Inc., N.Y.C., 1953—; columnist advt. publs. Served with USNR, 1943-45. Mem. Am. Assn. Advt. Agys. (sec. N.Y. region 1955-56). Home: 9 Court Dr Shillingford Oxfordshire England Office: 767 Fifth Ave New York City NY 10022

LEBER, WALTER PHILIP, engring. co. exec., ret. army officer; b. St. Louis, Sept. 12, 1918; s. Walter and Bonnie Vera (Blackman) L.; B.S., Mo. Sch. Mines, 1940; M.B.A., George Washington U., 1961; grad. Command and Gen. Staff Coll., 1956, Indsl. Coll. Armed Forces, 1958; m. Bernice Jean Palus, Sept. 9, 1950; children—Randolph Frank, Bonnie Gay, Philip Kevin. Petroleum engr. Stanolind Oil & Gas Co., 1940-41; commd. 2d lt. C.E., U.S. Army, 1941, advanced through grades to lt. gen., 1971; comdr. engring. troops 2d Inf. Div., 1941-42; faculty Engrs. Sch., Ft. Belvoir, Va., 1942; assigned Office Chief Engr. and Advanced Sect. Communications Zone, ETO, 1942-46, Manhattan Engring. Dist., Oak Ridge, 1946-47; chief tech. div. mil. liaison com. AEC, 1947-49; asst. dist. engr., exec. officer Seattle and Walla Walla dist., C.E., 1949-50; comdr. 46th Engr. Bn., Ft. Sill, Okla., 1950-51; assigned gen. staff logistics Dept. Army, 1951-55; dep. engr. 8th U.S. Army, Korea, comdr. 2d Engr. Group, Korea, 1956-57; exec. officer to chief engrs. U.S. Army, 1958-61; lt. gov. C.Z., v.p., dir. Panama Canal Co., 1961-63; div. engr. Army Engr. Div., Ohio River, 1963-66; dir. civil works Office Chief Engrs., U.S. Army, Washington, 1966-67; gov. C.Z., pres. Panama Canal Co., 1967-71; system mgr. Safeguard Anti-ballistic Missile System, 1971-74, ret., 1974; area mgr. Middle East, Harza Engring Co., Chgo., 1974-76, dir. Eastern Hemisphere mgmt., 1977—, v.p., 1978—. Chmn. gov. C.Z. Council Vol. Giving, 1961—; mgmt. com. Balboa YMCA; exec. bd. C.Z. council Boy Scouts Am. Trustee, exec. com. C.Z. United Fund. Decorated D.S.M. with oak leaf cluster, Legion Merit with 2 oak leaf clusters, Bronze Star medal; Order Brit. Empire; L'Orde de Leopold II (Belgium). Registered profl. engr., D.C., Fla. Mem. Soc. Am. Mil. Engrs., Tau Beta Pi, Phi Kappa Phi. Episcopalian. Home: 3231 SE Fairway West Stuart FL 33494 Office: care Harza Engring Co 150 S Wacker Dr Chicago IL 60606

LEBERTHON, EDWARD LYNCH, lawyer; b. Los Angeles, Jan. 4, 1928; s. James and Ruth Adele (Giltner) LeB.; J.D., Loyola U., Los Angeles, 1953; m. Veronica Franks, June 17, 1961; children—Adam, Michael. Admitted to Calif. bar, 1954, since practiced in Los Angeles; counsel for Northwestern Nat. Ins. Group, 1965—, Continental Ins. Cos., 1962—, Mobil Oil Corp., 1970—, Allstate Ins. Co., 1971—, others. Mem. Am., Calif., Los Angeles County bar assns., Assn. So. Calif. Def. Counsel, Am. Bd. Trial Advocates. Republican. Home: 10412 Keokuk Ave Chatsworth CA 91311 Office: 7060 Hollywood Blvd Los Angeles CA 90028

LEBLANC, HUGUES, educator; b. Ste-Marie de Beauce, Que., Can., Mar. 19, 1924; s. Edmond and Alice (Caron) L.; came to U.S., 1946, naturalized 1952; M.A., Montreal (Can.) U., 1946; Ph.D., Harvard, 1948; m. Virginia Southall Graham, June 10, 1950; children—Gabrielle, Suzanne, Stephen. Prof. philosophy Bryn Mawr (Pa.) Coll., 1948-67, Temple U., Phila., 1967—. Fulbright fellow, 1953-54; Guggenheim fellow, 1965-66. Author: An Introduction to Deductive Logic, 1955; Statistical and Inductive Probabilities, 1962; Techniques of Deductive Inference, 1966; Deductive Logic, 1972; Truth, Syntax and Modality, 1973; Truth-Value Semantics, 1976; also numerous papers on logic and probability. Home: 447 Barclay Rd Rosemont PA 19010 Office: Temple U Philadelphia PA 19122

LE BLANC, MORELAND PAUL, JR., public accountant; b. Baton Rouge, Aug. 9, 1921; s. Moreland Paul and Carmen Marie (Haydel) LeB.; student Loyola U., New Orleans, 1937-40; B.S., La. State U., 1948, M.B.A., 1949; m. Lillian Frances Lanford, Sept. 16, 1946; children—Sharon Frances, Julie Ann, Paul Lanford, Mary Martha. With Arthur Andersen & Co., 1949—, partner, 1956—, vice chmn., 1972-75, co-chmn., 1975—. Nat. bd. dirs. Jr. Achievement; mem. adv.

council Columbia U. Sch. Bus., Tulane U. Sch. Bus.; bd. dirs. Greater N.Y. Fund, Citizens Union of City N.Y. Served to lt., jr. grade, USN, 1943-46. C.P.A., N.Y. Mem. Am. Inst. C.P.A.'s, N.Y. State Soc. C.P.A.'s. Clubs: Univ., Union League, Recess, Racquet and Tennis, Golf at Aspetuck, Wee Burn Country, Landmark, Chgo. Home: 6 Cloudy Ln Darien CT 06820 Office: 1345 Ave of Americas New York City NY 10019

LEBLOND, CHARLES PHILIPPE, educator, researcher; b. Lille, France, Feb. 5, 1910; s. Oscar and Jeanne (Desmarchelier) L.; L.Sc., U. Lille, 1932; M.D., U. Paris (France), 1934, D. Sc., 1945; Ph.D., U. Montreal, 1942; D.Sc., Acadia U., 1972; m. Gertrude Sternschuss, Oct. 22, 1936; children—Philippe L., Paul N., Pierre F., Marie Pascale. Asst. histology U. Lille and U. Paris (France), 1934-35; Rockefeller fellow anatomy Yale, 1935-37; charge biology div. Lab. Synthese Atom, Paris, 1937-40; research fellow U. Rochester (N.Y.), 1940-41; mem. faculty McGill U., Montreal, Que., Can., 1941—, prof. anatomy, 1948—, chmn. dept., 1957—. Fogarty scholar NIH, 1975. Fellow Royal Soc. London, Royal Soc. Can., Am. Assn. Anatomy, Canadian Assn. Anatomists. Author: L'Acide Ascorbique dans les Tissues et sa Detection, 1936; Radioautography as a Tool in the Study of Protein Synthesis, 1965. Home: 68 Chesterfield St Montreal PQ Canada

LEBLOND, RICHARD EMMETT, JR., arts adminstr.; b. Cin., Nov. 19, 1924; s. Richard Emmett and Mildred (Ziegler) LeB.; A.B., U. Cin., 1950, A.M., 1950; Ph.D. in Sociology, U. Mich., 1968; children by previous marriage—Helen LeBlond Banister, Richard Emmett, III, Anne W., Laurence Z. Instr., U. Mich., 1955-57; instr. Temple U., 1957-61, asst. prof. sociology, 1961-66; asso. prof. Rider Coll., 1966-73, chmn. dept. sociology, 1970-73; pres., gen. mgr. Pa. Ballet, Phila., 1973-75, San Francisco Ballet, 1975—; bd. dirs. San Francisco Conv. and Vis. Bur. Served with USN, 1943-46. Mem. Am. Arts Alliance (dir.), Assn. Am. Dance Cos. (dir. 1966—, chmn. bd. 1970-75), Calif. Assn. Dance Cos. (dir.), San Francisco Bay Area Dance Coalition (dir.), San Francisco Arts Advs. (dir.), Calif. Confedn. Arts (pres.). Club: Commonwealth of Calif. Office: San Francisco Ballet 378 18th Ave San Francisco CA 94121

LEBLOND, RICHARD KNIGHT, II, banker; b. Cin., Nov. 16, 1920; s. Harold R. and Elizabeth (Conroy) LeB.; grad. Hill Sch., 1940; B.A., Princeton, 1944; postgrad. Columbia Grad. Sch. Bus. Adminstrn., 1960, Harvard Bus. Sch., 1967; m. Sally C. Chapman, Dec. 11, 1948; children—Mary, Richard Knight III, Edward, Elizabeth, David, Virginia, William, Thomas, Sara, Joseph. With Chem. N.Y. Bank, and predecessor, 1946—, sr. v.p., 1966-68, exec. v.p., 1968-73, vice chmn., 1973—; dir. LeBlond, Inc., Cin., Barnes Group Inc., Bristol, Conn., Home Life Ins. Co., N.Y.C. Mem. Cardinal's Com. for Edn. N.Y.C. Served to 1st lt. AUS, 1943-46. Mem. Assn. Res. City Bankers, N.Y.C. Council on Fgn. Relations (dir.). Clubs: Country of New Canaan (Conn.); Pine Valley (N.J.) Golf; Links, University (N.Y.C.); Blind Brook (Port Chester, N.Y.); Augusta (Ga.) Nat. Golf. Home: 194 Sunset Hill Rd New Canaan CT 06840 Office: 20 Pine St New York City NY 10015

LEBOR, JOHN F(RANCIS), corporate exec.; b. Portland, Oreg., Mar. 22, 1906; s. John G. and Jettie P. (Cook) L.; B.B.A., U. Oreg., 1928; M.B.A., Harvard, 1930; m. Violette Steinmetz, Oct. 7, 1931; children—Andrew Scott, John Cook. Investment analyst Scudder, Stevens & Clark, N.Y.C., 1930-33; financial staff Radio-Keith-Orpheum Corp., 1933-40; sec.-treas. York (Pa.) Corp., 1940-46; treas. Federated Dept. Stores, Inc., Cin., 1946-51, v.p., treas., dir., 1951-57, v.p., dir., 1958-60, exec. v.p., dir., 1960-65; dir. Bobbie Brooks, Inc., Cleve., Carlisle Retailers, Ashtabula, Ohio, Diamond Crystal Salt Co., St. Clair, Mich., Gateway Option Income Fund, Cin., U.S. Shoe Corp., Cin. Mem. Phi Beta Kappa, Beta Gamma Sigma, Beta Alpha Psi, Alpha Kappa Psi, Episcopalian. Clubs: Queen City, Bankers (Cin.); Chgo. Home: 222 Oliver Rd Cincinnati OH 45215 Office: 511 Walnut St Cincinnati OH 45202. *An important guiding principle for evaluating myself and others has been dependability and a record of "mission accomplished," as opposed to offering alibis.*

LEBOUTILLIER, MARTIN, broker; b. Phoenix, Dec. 7, 1921; s. Martin and Cornelia Throop (Geer) LeB.; grad. Hotchkiss Sch., Lakeville, Conn., 1940; A.B., Yale, 1943; m. Clelia Delafield, Sept. 11, 1948 (div.); children—Clelia, Cynthia (dec.); m. 2d, Polly Kinnear, Sept. 28, 1957; children—Martin, John. With Firestone Tire & Rubber Co., 1946, Fred Eldean Orgn., Inc., 1947; gen. partner Delafield & Delafield, 1950-54; with new bus. dept. Dean Witter & Co., investment bankers, 1955-61; gen. partner Dean Witter & Co., 1961-68; gen. partner Paine, Webber, Jackson & Curtis, 1968-70; exec. v.p., chief operating officer Paine, Webber, Jackson & Curtis, Inc., 1970-71, pres., exec. com., dir., 1971-74, chmn. exec. com., dir., 1974—; dir. Paine Webber Inc., Paine Webber Mitchell Hutchins Inc., Paine Webber Far East Ltd., Paine Webber Internat. Inc., Paine Webber Real Estate Servicing, Inc., Paine, Webber, Jackson & Curtis Securities Ltd., Paine, Webber, Jackson & Curtis Internat., S.A., Abacus Fund Security Corp., Bd. dirs. Sheltering Arms Childrens Service, N.Y., Francis Ward Paine Found., Inc. Mem. St. Nicholas Soc., Pilgrims of U.S., Soc. Colonial Wars, Delta Kappa Epsilon. Clubs: Bankers of Am. (N.Y.C.); N.Y. Yacht; Clove Valley Rod and Gun (LaGrangeville, N.Y.); Bohemian (San Francisco). Home: 1165 Fifth Ave New York City NY 10029 Office: 140 Broadway New York City NY 10005

LEBOUTILLIER, PHILIP, JR., banker; b. N.Y.C., Feb. 24, 1916; s. Philip and Gertrude H. (Tifft) LeB.; grad. Choate Sch., 1934; B.A., Princeton, 1938; m. Felia Ford, July 13, 1940; children—Philip G., George F., Ford. With Bethlehem Shipbldg. Corp., Quincy, Mass., 1938-39, Electric Auto-Lite Co., Toledo, 1939-42; asst. to pres. Toledo Scale Co., 1945-47; pres. Ottawa River Paper Co., Toledo, 1947-58; v.p. Mead Containers, Inc., 1958-59; pres. Hixon-Peterson Lumber Co., 1959-61; dep. asst. sec. def., supply and logistics, Washington, 1959-61; partner Collin, Norton & Co., 1961-64; v.p. Clark, Dodge & Co., 1964-74; pres. Tropic Isle Pubs., Inc., Miami, Fla., 1972—; chmn. bd. First Nat. Bank, Toledo, 1975—; dir. Aro Corp., Bryan, Ohio, Kysor Indsl. Corp., Cadillac, Mich., Canrad-Hanovia, Newark, Libbey-Owens-Ford Co., Toledo. Served from ensign to comdr. USNR, 1942-45. Decorated Silver Star medal. Home: 20547 Tontogany Creek Rd Bowling Green OH 43402 Office: 606 Madison Ave Toledo OH 43604

LEBOVITZ, HAROLD PAUL, newspaperman; b. Cleve., Sept. 11, 1916; s. Isaiah and Celia (Levy) L.; B.A., Western Res. U., 1938; M.A., 1942; m. Margie Glassman, Feb. 20, 1938; children—Neil Ross, Lynn Gail. Sci. tchr., coach Euclid (Ohio) High Sch., 1938-46; reporter, baseball writer, columnist Cleve. News, 1946-60; columnist Cleve. Plain Dealer, 1960—, sports editor, 1964—; columnist The Sporting News, 1976—, Gannett Syndicate, 1979—; dir. Cleve. Jewish News, 1971—; baseball umpire, 1937-50; football ofcl., 1940-71; basketball ofcl., 1940-60; Cleve. corr. Sporting News, 1950-64. Mem. recreation com., University Heights, O., 1965—. Bd. dirs. Jewish Community Center, Cleve., 1962-63, Alumni Assn. Adelbert Coll. of Case-Western Reserve U., 1969—. Named Citizen of Year, Univ. Heights, 1964, Sportsman of Year, Brith Emeth Men's Club, 1964, Top Sportswriter, Cortron Twelve of Atlantic Fleet, 1961, Sporting News Top Feature Writer, 1963-64; recipient ten best writing awards Cleve. Newspaper Guild, 1948-60. Mem. Baseball Writers Assn. Am. (pres. 1965-66, bd. dirs. 1966-67), Ohio Sports Editors Assn. (pres. 1965-66), Cleve. Football Ofcls. Assn., Ohio Football Ofcls. Assn., Cleve. Umpires Assn., Sigma Delta Chi. Author: Pitchin' Man, 1948; (with Phil R. Gilman) Springboards to Science, 1967; also numberous articles; rep. sports anthologies. Inventor outdoor playground game Four Sq. Tennis. Home: 2380 Edgerton Rd University Heights OH 44118 Office: 1801 Superior Ave Cleveland OH 44114

LEBOW, IRWIN LEON, electronics engr.; b. Boston, Apr. 27, 1926; s. Samuel and Ruth (Tobey) L.; S.B., M.I.T., 1948, Ph.D., 1951; m. Grace H. Hackel, July 8, 1951; children—Judith, William, David. Staff mem. M.I.T. Lincoln Lab., 1951-60, asso. leader satellite communications surface techniques group, 1960-65, leader, 1965-70, asso. head communications div., 1970-72, asso. head data systems div., 1972-75, mem. steering com., 1970-75; chief scientist, asso. dir. tech. Def. Communications Agy., Dept. Def., Washington, 1975—. Served with USNR, 1944-46. Fellow Am. Phys. Soc., IEEE; mem. AAAS, Armed Forces Communications and Electronics Assn., Sigma Xi. Author: (with others) Theory and Design of Digital Machines, 1962. Home: 12297 Greenleaf Ave Potomac MD 20854 Office: Code 101A Def Communications Agy Washington DC 20305

LEBOW, SYLVAN, orgn. exec.; b. Balt., July 23, 1912; s. Joseph and Marie (Propp) L.; A.B., Johns Hopkins, 1932; B.J., U. Mo., 1933; m. Ruth Lebowitz, Jan. 30, 1934; children—Mark D., Joy Ann. Newspaper reporter Balt. Post, Harrisburg (Pa.) Patriot-News, Phila. Record, 1934-40; pub. Harrisburg Guide, 1946-48; pub. relations dir. Pa. Motor Truck Assn., 1940-42; pres. Pa. Pub. Relations Service, 1942-49; exec. dir. Nat. Fedn. Temple Brotherhoods and Jewish Chautauqua Soc., N.Y.C., 1949-78, exec. cons., 1978—; editor Brotherhood mag., 1966-78; devel. cons. Synagogue Council Am., 1978—; nat. cons. Zionist Orgn. Am.; bd. dirs., past vice chmn. Religion in Am. Life; bd. dirs. World Union Progressive Judaism. Pub. relations dir. Commonwealth Pa., Democratic Com., Harrisburg, 1941-42. Recipient George Washington honor medal Freedoms Found., 1958. Fellow Jewish Chautauqua Soc. mem. Pub. Relations Soc. Am. (charter), Pi Lambda Phi. Author: The Temple Brotherhood, 1963. Producer motion pictures about Judaism for TV, 1954—. Home: 360 E 72d St New York NY 10021 Office: 838 Fifth Ave New York NY 10021

LEBOWITZ, ALBERT, lawyer, author; b. St. Louis, June 18, 1922; s. Jacob and Lena (Zemmel) L.; A.B., Washington U., St. Louis, 1945; LL.B., Harvard, 1948; m. Naomi Gordon, Nov. 26, 1953; children—Joel Aaron, Judith Leah. Admitted to Mo. bar, 1948; asso. Frank E. Morris, St. Louis, 1948-55; partner firm Morris, Schneider & Lebowitz, St. Louis, 1955-58, Crowe, Schneider, Shanahan & Lebowitz, St. Louis, 1958-66; counsel firm Murphy & Roche, St. Louis, 1966-67, Murphy & Schlapprizzi, St. Louis, 1967—; editor lit. quar. Perspective, 1961—. Served as combat navigator USAAF, 1943-45; ETO. Decorated Air medal with 3 oak leaf clusters. Mem. Am., Mo., St. Louis bar assns., Phi Beta Kappa. Author: (novel) Laban's Will, 1966; The Man Who Wouldn't Say No (novel), 1969; also short stories. Home: 743 Yale Ave St Louis MO 63130 Office: 1015 Locust St St Louis MO 63101

LEBOWITZ, JOEL LOUIS, physicist, educator; b. Taceva, May 10, 1930; B.S., Bklyn. Coll., 1952; M.S., Syracuse U., 1955, Ph.D., 1956; hon. doctorate Ecole Polytechnique Federale, Lausanne, Switzerland, 1977; m. Estelle Mandelbaum, June 21, 1953. Came to U.S., 1946, naturalized, 1951. NSF postdoctoral fellow Yale, 1956-57; mem. faculty Stevens Inst. Tech., 1957-59; mem. faculty Yeshiva U., N.Y.C., 1959-77, prof. physics, 1965-77, acting chmn. dept. physics Belfer Grad. Sch. Sci., 1964-67, chmn. dept., 1967-76; prof. math. and physics, dir. Center for Mathematical Scis., Rutgers U., New Brunswick, N.J., 1977—. Guggenheim fellow, 1976-77. Fellow Am. Phys. Soc.; mem. AAAS, N.Y. Acad. Scis. (pres. 1979), AAUP, Am. Math. Soc., Phi Beta Kappa, Sigma Xi. Editor: Jour. Statis. Physics, 1975—, Studies in Statis. Mechanics, 1973—, Com. Math. Physics, 1973—; contbr. articles to profl. jours. Office: Dept Math Hill Center Busch Campus Rutgers U New Brunswick NJ 08903

LEBRA, WILLIAM PHILIP, educator; b. St. Paul, Sept. 2, 1922; s. William Charles and Stella Bertha (Welker) L.; B.A., U. Minn., 1948, M.A., 1949; Ph.D., Harvard, 1958; m. Takie Sugiyama, Apr. 25, 1963. Field asso. in anthropology NRC, 1953-54; teaching fellow in anthropology Harvard, 1954-55; instr. anthropology Pitts. U., 1957-58, asst. prof., 1958-61; vis. scholar East-West Center, Honolulu, 1961-62; asso. prof. anthropology and Asian studies U. Hawaii, 1962-64, prof., 1964—, dir. Social Sci. Research Inst., 1962-70, dir. culture and mental health program, 1967-77. Served with AUS, 1943-46. Prin. investigator NIMH grant, 1959-62, 67-77. Fellow Am. Anthrop. Assn., Royal Anthrop. Inst. Gt. Britain; mem. Japanese Soc. Ethnology, Asiatic Soc. Japan, Assn. Asian Studies, Soc. Applied Anthropology, Am. Ethnol. Soc. Author: Okinawan Religion, 1966; (with F.R. Pitts and W.P. Suttles) Post-war Okinawa, 1955; Okinawa no shukyo to shakai kozo, 1974. Editor: Transcultural Research in Mental Health, 1972; Youth, Socialization and Mental Health, 1974; (with T.S. Lebra) Japanese Culture and Behavior, 1974; Culture-Bound Syndromes, Ethnopsychiatry, and Alternate Therapies, 1976. Home: 3625 Woodlawn Terrace Pl Honolulu HI 96822

LEBUHN, ROBERT, airline co. exec.; b. Davenport, Iowa, May 2, 1932; s. Dick and Mable (Blom) LeB.; B.S., Northwestern U., 1954; M.B.A., U. Pa., 1957; m. Jo-Ann Fitzsimmons, June 19, 1954; children—Anne, Ellen, Robert, Richard. Security analyst Cyrus J. Lawrence & Sons, N.Y.C., 1957-62; v.p. Eppler & Co., Inc., Morristown, N.J., 1962-72; chmn. fin. and plan com., dir. USAIR; dir. Chem Systems, Inc., RSC Industries, Heritage Bancorp. Served to lt. (j.g.) USNR, 1954-56. Home: Fawn Hill Dr New Vernon NJ 07976 Office: One Madison Ave Morristown NJ 07960

LECAM, LUCIEN MARIE, educator; b. Croze Creuse, France, Nov. 18, 1924; s. Francois Marie and Marie Renee (Jouanno) LeC.; Licence es Scis., U. Paris, 1947; grad. student Sorbonne, Paris, 1947-48; Ph.D., U. Calif. at Berkeley, 1952; m. Louise E. Romig, Apr. 19, 1952; children—Denis A., Steven D., Linda M. Came to U.S., 1950. Mem. faculty U. Calif. at Berkeley, 1952—, prof. statistics, 1953—, Miller prof., 1971-72, prof. math., 1973—, chmn. dept., 1961-65. Dir. Centre de Recherches Mathématiques, U. Montreal, 1972-74. Fellow AAAS, Am. Acad. Arts and Scis.; mem. Inst. Math. Statistics (pres. 1972-73), Internat. Statis. Inst., Am. Math. Soc., Internat. Assn. for Statistics in Phys. Scis. (council 1973), Societé Mathematique France, Societé Mathematique Can. Home: 101 Kensington Rd Kensington CA 94707 Office: Univ California Berkeley CA 94720

LECHAY, JAMES, painter; b. N.Y.C., July 5, 1907; s. Charles and Augusta (Wolfson) L.; A.B., U. Ill., 1928; D.F.A. (hon.), Coe Coll., 1961; m. Rose David, Mar. 26, 1934; children—Jo, Daniel. Asst. prof. art U. Iowa, 1945-49, asso. prof., 1949-56, prof., 1956-75, prof. emeritus, 1975—; tchr. Stanford, 1949, N.Y. U., 1953, Skowhegan (Maine) Sch. Painting and Sculpture, 1961; artist in residence Tamarind Inst., 1973; vis. artist New Asia Coll., Chinese U. of Hong Kong, 1976; 18 one-man shows, N.Y.C., others in Trieste, Italy, Chgo., Cedar Rapids, Iowa City, Des Moines Art Center, Toledo, Louisville, Springfield, Ill., Ft. Dodge, Cedar Falls and Davenport, Iowa Wesleyan U., Sioux City, Iowa, Wellfleet, Mass.; exhibited group shows Met. Mus. Art, N.Y.C., Pa. Acad. Fine Arts, Va. Mus. Fine Arts, Bklyn. Mus., Chgo. Art Inst., Phillips Meml. Gallery, Whitney Mus. Am. Art, Corcoran Gallery Art, Carnegie Instn., others; represented permanent collections Nat. Collection Fine Arts Smithsonian Instn., Pa. Acad. Fine Arts, U. Ariz., U. Iowa, Bklyn. Mus., New Britain Inst., U. Nebr., Memphis Mus., Ill. Wesleyan U., Chgo Art Inst., Wichita Art Center, Philbrook Mus., Tulsa, Des Moines Art Center, Coe Coll., Joslyn Art Mus., U. No. Iowa, Rochester Meml. Gallery, others; also pvt. collections. Recipient Norman Wait Harris bronze medal, 52 ann. exhbn. Am. Painting, 1941; Lambert purchase prize Pa. Acad., 1942; hon. mention for water color Art Inst. Chgo., 1943, prize for oil 2d Ann. Portrait of Am. Exhbn., 1945; hon. mention Denver Mus., 1946; 1st prize for oil Iowa State Fair Exhbn., 1946, 51, 53, 55; 1st prize First Biennial Walker Art Center, Mpls., 1947, Minn. Centennial, 1949; Edmundson trustee prize Des Moines Art Center, 1950, 1st prize 1952, 53; 1st prize Davenport Municipal Art Gallery, 1950; Rosenfield Collection purchase prize, Des Moines Art Center, 1959; Childe Hassam purchase prize, 1974; Benjamin Altman prize NAD, 1977, Henry Ward Ranger Fund purchase prize, 1979. Home: Wellfleet MA 02667 Office: Kraushaar Galleries 1055 Madison Ave New York NY 10028

LECHNER, VINCENT FRANCIS, ret. hosp. equipment mfr.; b. Erie, Pa., Nov. 2, 1911; s. Bernard Joseph and Katherine (Klang) L.; B.S. In Bus. Adminstrn., U. Pitts., 1933; m. Dorothy Casey, Sept. 7, 1939; children—Thomas Mark, Robert Michael, Bernard Joseph, Anne Katherine. With Am. Sterilizer Co., Erie, 1937-75, exec. v.p., 1961-62, pres., 1962-71, chmn. bd., chief exec. officer, 1971-74, cons., dir., 1971—. Bd. dirs. Erie Conf. on Community Devel.; incorporator, trustee emeritus St. Vincent Hosp., Erie; corporator Hamot Hosp., Erie; bd. dirs. Pa. Med. Care Found.; trustee emeritus Gannon Coll., Erie. Clubs: Erie, Aviation Country, Erie Maennerchor, Erie Yacht. Home: 407 Kahkwa Ave Erie PA 16505

LECHOWICH, RICHARD VICTOR, food microbiologist; b. Chgo., June 23, 1933; s. Victor Vincent and Stella Barbara Patrick L.; A.B., U. Chgo., 1952, M.S., 1955; Ph.D., U. Ill., 1958; m. Joan Marie MacDonald, June 15, 1957; children—Ronald C., Richard A., Steven P., Karen J., Ellen J. Microbiologist, asst. to dir. container devel. Continental Can Co., Chgo., 1958-63; asst. prof. food sci. Mich. State U., East Lansing, 1963-66, asso. prof., 1966-70, prof., 1970-71; prof., head dept. food sci. and tech. Va. Poly. Inst. and State U., Blacksburg, 1971—; cons. food industry. Mem. Nat. Inst. Food Technologists (chmn. expert panel on food safety and nutrition 1973-77), Am. Soc. Microbiology, Soc. Applied Bacteriology, AAAS, Internt. Assn. Mil., Food and Environ. Sanitarians, Carlina-Va. Inst. Food Technologists, Sigma Xi, Phi Tau Sigma, Gamma Sigma Delta. Contbg. author books; contbr. articles to sci. jours.; edit. bd. Jour. Food Protection, 1971—. Club: Rotary. Home: 903 Mason Dr NE Blacksburg VA 24060

LECHT, LEONARD A., economist; b. Providence, Oct. 16, 1920; s. Harry and Sarah (Finkle) L.; B.A., U. Minn., 1942; Ph.D., Columbia, 1953; m. Jane A. Gillespie, Sept. 15, 1951; 1 son, David Jonathan. Lectr. econs. Columbia, 1947-49; asst. prof. econs. U. Tex., 1949-53, Carleton Coll., 1953-54; asso. prof. L.I. U., 1954-56, chmn. dept. econs. and sociology, 1954-63, prof., 1956-63; faculty fellow Ford Found., 1951-52; dir. nat. goals project Nat. Planning Assn., Washington, 1963-66, dir. center for priority analysis, 1967-74; dir. spl. projects The Conf. Bd., N.Y.C., 1974—. Adj. prof. econs. Temple U., 1967-68; lectr. New Sch. for Social Research, 1977—; econ. cons. Served with AUS, 1943-45. Mem. Am. Econ. Assn., Indsl. Relations Research Assn., Nat. Econs. Club, Nat. Assn. Bus. Economists, Am. Statis. Assn., Phi Beta Kappa. Author: Experience Under Railway Labor Legislation, 1955; The Dollar Cost of Our National Goals, 1965; (with others) Requirements for Scientific and Engineering Manpower in the 1970's, 1964; Goals, Priorities and Dollars-The Next Decade, 1966; Manpower Needs for National Goals in the 1970's, 1969; National Priorities, Manpower Needs and the Impact of Diminished Defense Purchases for Vietnam, 1968; Changes in National Priorities During the 1960's, Their Implications for 1980, 1972; Dollars for National Goals—Looking Ahead to 1980, 1974; Evaluating Vocational Education: Policies and Plans for the 1970's, 1974; Changes in Occupational Characteristics—Planning Ahead to the 1980's, 1976; Occupational Choices and Training Needs, 1977. Contbr. articles to profl. jours. Home: 625 Main St Roosevelt Island New York NY 10044 Office: 845 3d Ave New York NY 10022

LECKER, ABRAHAM, banker; b. Rumania, Mar. 29, 1916; s. Schaje and Lisa (Schimmel) L.; B.Sc. in Econs., Certified Assn. Brit. Inst. Bankers, London; LL.B., Sch. of Law, Tel Aviv, Israel; student Harvard Bus. Sch.; m. Minnie Kamenetzky, Aug. 29, 1954; 1 dau., Lisa Joy. Came to U.S., 1957. With banks in Palestine, 1934-36, Barclays Bank DCO, Palestine, 1936-49; dep. treas., comptroller City of Haifa (Israel), 1949-57; with Exchange Nat. Bank, Chgo., 1957—, sr. v.p., cashier, 1966—, exec. v.p., 1973—. Served with Brit. Army, World War II, Israeli Army, 1948-49. Mem. Chgo. Council Fgn. Relations, Chgo. Assn. Commerce and Industry, Am. Jewish Com., Brit. Inst. Bankers, Am. Inst. Bankers, Ill. Mrs. Assn., Bankers' Assn. for Fgn. Trade, Ill. C. of C. Mem. B'nai B'rith. Clubs: International Trade, Bankers (Chgo.). Home: 3750 Lake Shore Dr Chicago IL 60613 Office: 130 S LaSalle St Chicago IL 60690

LECLAIR, CHARLES GEORGE, painter, educator; dean; b. Columbia, Mo., May 23, 1914; s. Carl Amie and Marie (Fess) LeC.; B.S., M.S., U. Wis., 1935; student Academie Ranson, Paris, 1937; grad. study, Columbia, 1940-41; m. Margaret Foster, May 30, 1945. Instr. art U. Ala., 1935-36, asst. prof., head dept., 1937-42; asst. prof. art, head dept. Albion Coll., 1942-43; tchr. painting and design Albright Art Sch., Buffalo, 1943-46; asso. prof., head dept. Chatham Coll., 1946-52, prof., 1952-60; dean Tyler Sch. of Art, Temple U., Phila., 1960-74, prof. painting, 1974—, chmn. painting and sculpture dept., 1979—; established Tyler Sch. Art, Rome, Italy, 1966; works exhibited Pa. Acad., Met. Mus. Art, Carnegie Inst., Whitney Mus., Corcoran Mus., Chgo. Art Inst., Richmond Mus., Butler Mus. Art, Am. Watercolor Soc., Bklyn. Mus.; one-man shows Carnegie Inst., 1954, Salpeter Gallery, N.Y. C., 1956, 59, 65, Rochester Inst. Tech., 1958, Phila. Art Alliance, 1962, 73, Franklin and Marshall Coll., 1969; Galleria 88, Rome, Italy, 1970, 40-yr. Retrospective, Temple U., 1978, Visual Images, Wellfleet, 1978, Gross-McCleaf Gallery, Phila., 1979. Fellow Fund for Advancement Edn. (Ford Found.), 1952-53; named Pitts. Artist of Year, 1957. Contbr. chpt. Accent on Teaching (edited Sidney J. French), 1954. Home: 2052 Lombard Ave Philadelphia PA 19146

LECLERC, IVOR, philosopher, educator; b. Dordrecht, South Africa, Feb. 9, 1915; B.A., U. South Africa, 1941; M.A., U. Cape Town, 1946; Ph.D., King's Coll., U. London (Eng.), 1949; m. Joan Pirie, Sept. 6, 1975. Lectr. U. Glasgow (Scotland), 1950-61, sr. lectr., 1962-63; vis. prof. Bonn (Germany) U., 1961, 73; prof. philosophy Emory U., 1963—. Served to capt. S. African Forces, 1942-45. Mem. Royal Inst. Philosophy, Kant-Gesellschaft, Leibniz-Gesellschaft, Am. Philos. Assn., Metaphys. Soc. Am., Internat. Soc. for Metaphysics, AAUP. Author: Whitehead's Metaphysics, 1958; The Nature of

Physical Existence, 1972. Editor: The Relevance of Whitehead, 1961; The Philosophy of Leibniz and the Modern World, 1972. Home: 888 Oakdale Rd NE Atlanta GA 30307 Office: Dept Philosophy Emory U Atlanta GA 30322

LE COMTE, EDWARD SEMPLE, educator, author; b. N.Y.C., May 28, 1916; s. John Radway and Mary (Semple) Le C.; A.B., Columbia, 1939, A.M., 1940, Ph.D., 1943; m. Marie Munzer, Jan. 19, 1945; 1 son, Douglas Munzer. Instr. English, Columbia, 1943-45; asst. prof. English, U. Calif. at Berkeley, 1945-48; asst. prof. English, Columbia, 1948-56, asso. prof., 1956-64; prof. English, State U. N.Y. at Albany, 1964—. Mem. Milton Soc., Renaissance Soc., Authors Guild, Phi Beta Kappa. Author: Endymion in England: The Literary History of a Greek Myth, 1944; Yet Once More: Verbal and Psychological Pattern in Milton, 1953; A Dictionary of Last Words, 1955; The Long Road Back, 1957; (novel) He and She, 1960; A Milton Dictionary, 1961; Grace to a Witty Sinner: A Life of Donne, 1965; The Notorious Lady Essex, 1969; The Man Who Was Afraid, 1969; Milton's Unchanging Mind, 1973; Poets' Riddles: Essays in Seventeenth-Century Explication, 1975; Sly Milton: The Meaning Lurking in the Contexts of His Quotations, 1976; Milton and Sex, 1978; The Professor and the Coed, 1979; A Dictionary of Puns and Cruxes in Milton's English Poetry, 1980; also various articles in scholarly jours. on 17th Century lit.; editor: Paradise Lost and Other Poems, 1961; Justa Edovardo King, 1978. Home: Box 113 North Egremont MA 01252 Office: State U of NY Albany NY 12222

LE DAIN, GERALD ERIC, fed. judge Can.; b. Montreal, Que., Can., Nov. 27, 1924; s. Eric George and Antoinette Louise (Whithard) Le D.; B.C.L., McGill U., Montreal, 1949; Docteur del'Universite, U. Lyon (France), 1950; LL.D. (hon.), York U., Can., 1976, Concordia U., N.S., 1976; D.C.L. (hon.), Acadia U., N.S., 1978; m. Cynthia Roy, Sept. 13, 1947; children—Jacqueline, Catherine, Barbara, Caroline, Eric, Jennifer. Called to Que. bar, 1949, Ont. bar, 1968; created Queen's counsel, 1961; asso. prof. law McGill U., 1953-59, prof., 1966-67; dean, prof. Osgoode Hall Law Sch., York U., 1967-72, prof., 1972-75; practiced law with Walker, Martineau & Co., Montreal, 1950-53; with legal dept. CDN Internat Pap Co., Montreal, 1959-61; partner Riel, LeDain & Co., Montreal, 1961-66; judge Fed. Ct. of Appeal of Can., Ottawa, Ont., 1975—; chmn. Commn. of Inquiry Into Non-Med. Use of Drugs (Le Dain Commn.), 1969-73. Served with arty. Can. Army, 1943-46; France, Germany. Recipient Elizabeth Torrance Gold medal McGill U., 1949; MacDonald Travelling scholar, 1949-50. Club: Rideau (Ottawa). Contbr. articles to legal jours. Office: Fed Ct of Can Wellington St Ottawa ON K1A 0H9 Canada

LEDBETTER, CALVIN (CAL) REVILLE, JR., former legislator, educator; b. Little Rock; s. Calvin Reville and Virginia Mae (Campbell) L.; B.A., Princeton, 1951; LL.B., U. Ark., 1954; Ph.D., Northwestern U., 1960; m. Mary Brown Williams, July 26, 1953; children—Grainger, Jeffrey, Snow. Admitted to Ark. bar; pvt. practice law, Little Rock, 1954; grad. asst. Northwestern U., Evanston, Ill., 1959-60; mem. faculty dept. polit. sci. U. Ark., Little Rock, 1960—, now prof., head dept., dean Coll. Liberal Arts, cons. law enforcement program, advisor pre-law program; mem. Ark. Ho. of Reps., 1967-76, chmn. spl. legis. com., com. on legis. orgn.; vice chmn. legis. com. state agys. and govt. affairs; cons. pub. schs.; mem. Nat. Adv. Com. on Criminal Justice Goals and Standards; mem. adv. com. Nat. Inst. Law Enforcement and Criminal Justice. Mem. Ark. Adv. Council on Pub., Elementary and Secondary Edn.; Gov.'s rep. So. Regional Growth Policies Bd.; mem. Ark. Legis. Council; del. Ark. Constl. Conv., 1979, v.p., 1979-80; chmn. law enforcement and criminal justice task force Nat. Legis. Conf. Former chmn. coll. and univ. sect. United Fund. Del. Democratic Nat. Conv., 1968; mem. exec. com. Ark. Young Dem. Orgn. Bd. dirs. Health and Welfare Council Pulaski County; trustee Philander Smith Coll.; trustee, chmn. council community advisers St. Vincent's Infirmary. Served with Judge Adv. Gen. Corps, AUS, 1955-57; Germany. Named Educator of Year, Greater Little Rock Fedn. Women's Clubs, 1968. Mem. Nat. Conf. State Legislators (exec. com.), Am., Ark., Pulaski County bar assns., Am., So., Ark. (v.p.) polit. sci. assns., Ark. Acad. Sci., Am. Acad. Polt. and Social Sci., Ark. Hist. Assn., Ark. Edn. Assn. Democrat. Presbyn. (former elder, moderator and deacon). Rotarian (v.p. West Little Rock). Co-author: Politics in Arkansas: The Constitutional Experience, 1972; The Arkansas Plan: A Case Study in Public Policy; contbr. articles, book reviews to profl. jours. Home: 3230 Ozark St Little Rock AR 72205 Office: Coll Liberal Arts U Ark Little Rock AR 72204

LEDBETTER, J. LEE, steel co. exec.; b. Hull, Ill., Dec. 2, 1931; s. Fred L. and Alta J. (Spidle) L.; B.S., Western Ill. U., 1956; postgrad. U. Ill., 1956-58; m. Patricie L. Mayes, June 1, 1952; children—Christine, Jeffery, Rachelle, Stephen. Tchr. econs. and bookkeeping Annawan (Ill.) High Sch., 1956-58; acct. Arthur Andersen & Co., Chgo., 1958-60; with Monsanto Co., St. Louis, 1960-72, asst. corp. controller, to 1972; v.p. fin. Lukens Steel Co., Coatesville, Pa., 1972—. Bd. dirs. Southeastern chpt. Brandywine br. ARC, 1979. Served with USN, 1949-53. C.P.A., Ill. Mem. Fin. Execs. Inst. (treas. Phila. chpt.), Am. Iron and Steel Inst., NAM, Am. Mgmt. Assn., Pa. Economy League. Home: 83 Winding Way Downingtown PA 19335 Office: Lukens Steel Co S First Ave Coatesville PA 19320

LEDBETTER, WILLIAM JOE, mfg. co. exec., lawyer; b. Memphis, Jan. 24, 1927; s. Andrew F. and Jessie (Williams) L.; student Memphis State Coll., 1944-45, 46-47, U. Neb., 1945-46; LL.B., Washington and Lee U., 1950; m. Shirley Ann Good, May 5, 1956; children—Gleghn Andrew, Sally Ann. Admitted to Tenn. bar, 1949, N.Y. bar, 1951, Minn. bar, 1964; asso. firm Townsend & Lewis, N.Y.C., 1950-51, Cravath, Swaine & Moore, N.Y.C., 1951-57; atty., then asso. corp. counsel Gen. Electric Co., 1957-64; corp. counsel Honeywell Inc., Mpls., 1964-65, sec., gen. counsel, 1965-69; v.p., sec., gen. counsel Magnavox Co., N.Y.C., 1969-71; sr. v.p. adminstrn. and finance Addressograph Multigraph Corp., Cleve., 1971-72, exec. v.p. internat. operations, dir., 1972-74; v.p. finance Textron Inc., Providence, 1974-78, sr. v.p. fin., 1978-79, exec. v.p. fin. and adminstrn., 1979—. Mem. Am. Bar Assn., Phi Beta Kappa, Order of Coif. Clubs: Hope, Turk's Head, Agawam Hunt. Home: 141 Morris Ave Providence RI 02906 Office: 40 Westminister St Providence RI 02903

LEDDER, EDWARD JOHN, pharm. co. exec.; b. Chgo., Aug. 3, 1917; s. Edward John and Amanda C. (Heininger) L.; B.A., U. Chgo., 1939, M.B.A., 1954; m. Esther Jane Putman, July 20, 1940; children—Diane Alison, Mark Stephen. With Abbott Labs., North Chicago, Ill., 1939—, v.p. pharm. marketing, 1963-66, exec. v.p. mktg. ops., 1966-67, pres., 1967-76, chief exec. officer, 1974—, chmn. bd., 1976—. Served to lt. (j.g.) USNR, World War II. Mem. Sigma Chi. Presbyn. Office: Abbott Labs North Chicago IL 60064*

LEDECKY-JANECEK, EMANUEL V.A., curator; b. Pilsen, Bohemia, Czechoslovakia, Sept. 27, 1933; s. Emanuel Ledecky and Eugenie Egertova; came to U.S., 1946, naturalized, 1966; B.A., Queen's Coll., 1956; divorced; 1 dau., Nina Marie. Asst. dept. fishes Am. Museum Natural History, N.Y.C., 1961-62; curator exhibits New Eng. Aquarium, Boston, 1962-63; asst. gen. curator Cin. Zool. Soc., 1963-66; curator exhibits John G. Shedd Aquarium, Chgo., 1966—. Pres. Czechoslovak Cultural Assn., 1972-74, 76-79. Served with AUS, 1957-59. Mem. Am. Assn. Zool. Parks and Aquariums (profl. mem.), Am. Soc. Ichthyologists and Herpetologists, Nature Conservancy (life), Internat. Platform Assn., Czechoslovak Soc. Arts and Scis. in Am. Club: Adventurers (profl. mem.). Office: 1200 S Lake Shore Dr Chicago IL 60605

LEDEEN, ROBERT WAGNER, neurochemist, educator; b. Denver, Aug. 19, 1928; s. Hyman and Olga (Wagner) L.; B.S., U. Calif., Berkeley, 1949; Ph.D., Oreg. State U., 1953. Postdoctoral fellow in chemistry U. Chgo., 1953-54; research asso. in chemistry Mt. Sinai Hosp., N.Y.C., 1956-59; research fellow Albert Einstein Coll. Medicine, Bronx, N.Y., 1959, asst. prof., 1962-69, asso. prof., 1969-75, prof., 1975—. Mem. neurol. scis. study sect. NIH. Served with U.S. Army, 1954-56. NIH grantee, 1963-79; Nat. Multiple Sclerosis Soc. grantee, 1967-74. Mem. Internat. Soc. Neurochemistry, Am. Soc. Neurochemistry, Am. Chem. Soc., Am. Soc. Biol. Chemists, N.Y. Acad. Sci., Am. Oil Chemists Soc. Jewish. Contbr. articles to profl. jours.; mem. editorial bd. Jour. Lipid Research, Jour. Neurochemistry. Home: 111 Wadsworth Ave New York NY 10033 Office: 1300 Morris Park Ave Bronx NY 10461

LEDERBERG, JOSHUA, univ. pres., geneticist; b. Montclair, N.J., May 23, 1925; s. Zwi Hirsch and Esther (Goldenbaum) L.; B.A., Columbia, 1944; Ph.D., Yale, 1947, Sc.D. (hon.), 1960; Sc.D. m. Marguerite S. Kirsch, Apr. 5, 1968; children—David Kirsch, Anne. With U. Wis., 1947-58; prof. genetics Stanford Sch. Medicine, 1959-78; also bd. dirs. Center Advanced Studies Behavioral Sci., Stanford; pres. Rockefeller U., N.Y.C., 1978—; mem. bd. sci. advisers Cetus Corp., Berkeley, Calif.; dir. Inst. Sci. Info. Inc., Phila., Ann. Revs., Inc., Palo Alto, Calif. Bd. dirs. Natural Resources Def. Council, N.Y.C. Recipient Nobel prize in physiology and medicine for research genetics of bacteria, 1958. Office: Office of Pres Rockefeller U 66th and York Ave New York NY 10021

LEDERER, ALBRECHT MISA, mgmt. cons.; s. Richard M. and Helen (Leod) L.; ed. privately in chem. engring.; m. Eileen Farrell, 1931. Engr., mgmt. cons. Morris & Van Wormer, N.Y.C., 1924-58, gen. partner, 1934-58, offices Rio de Janeiro, Caracas, Lima, Santiago, Washington; pres. Am. Lederer & Co., Inc., N.Y.C., 1958—. Sr. adviser to adminstr. UN Devel. Programme, N.Y.; cons. to ECA; mem. commerce mission to Europe, 1949; cons. Mut. Security Agy., adv. group on European productivity; v.p. Nat. Mgmt. Council U.S., 1945-51, pres., 1951-60; v.p., trustee, exec. com. China Inst. in Am., 1949-55; rep. Com. Econ. Devel., adv. com. to State, Commerce depts. comml. activities of fgn. service; adviser on mgmt. to Ministry of Finance Brazil; bd. councilors Rock Island (Ill.) Arsenal, 1955-63; cons. to bd. adviser, dir., former mem. exec. com. Internat. Exec. Service Corps; chmn. bd., mem. exec. com. Technoserve, Inc.; mem. Seminar Orgn. and Mgmt. Colo. U. Past pres., chmn. bd. Council Internat. Progress Mgmt., Inc., also dir.; pres. World Council Mgmt., 1960-63. Bd. dirs. Inst. Mgmt. Consultants. Decorated knight comdr. Order Lion (Finland); recipient Gold medal award Internat. U., Rome, Italy, 1957; Mgmt. Man of Year award Nat. Mgmt. Assn., 1963; Wallace Clark award, 1964; Mgmt. Cons. award for Excellence, 1977. Fellow Internat. Acad. Mgmt. (past vice chancellor); mem. Nat. Sutures Corp. (past pres.), ASME, Bombay Mgmt. Assn. (hon.), Assn. Mgmt. and Indsl. Engrs. P.I. (hon.), Malaysian Inst. Mgmt. (hon.), ASME. Club: Downtown Athletic (N.Y.C.). Author: Philosophy of Management; The Present Position of the International Management Movement: The Role of the Professional Manager of Industrial Enterprises in the Building of Nations; World Business Education: An Investment Opportunity. Home: 41 Fifth Ave New York NY 10003 Office: 515 Madison Ave New York NY 10022

LEDERER, EDITH MADELON, journalist; b. N.Y.C., Mar. 27, 1943; d. Samuel B. Weiner and Frieda (Rich) Weiner Lederer; adopted dau. Irving A. Lederer; B.S. with distinction, Cornell U., 1963; M.A., Stanford, 1964. With Sci. Service, Washington, 1964-65; freelance writer, 1965-66; mem. staff A.P., 1966—, chief bur., Lima, Peru, 1975, chief Caribbean services, San Juan, P.R., 1975-78, corr., Hong Kong, 1978—. Recipient resolution Calif. Assembly, 1974. Mem. Mortar Bd., Phi Kappa Phi, Omicron Nu, Sigma Delta Chi. Address: care Asso Press 50 Rockefeller Plaza New York NY 10020. *Women should take more risks to live their dreams, which otherwise turn to nightmares of frustration as empty years pass. It is better to fail and touch the essence of life than to stand forever on the threshold as a gutless spectator.*

LEDERER, MARION IRVINE, cultural adminstr.; b. Brampton, Ont., Can., Feb. 10, 1920; d. Oliver Bateman and Eva Jane (MacMurdo) L.; student U. Toronto, 1938, U. Calif. at Los Angeles, 1942-45; m. Francis Lederer, July 10, 1941. Owner Canoga Mission Gallery, Canoga Park, Calif., 1967—, cultural heritage monument, 1974—. Vice pres. Screen Smart Set women's aux. Motion Picture and TV Fund, 1973—; founder sister city program Canoga Park-Taxco (Mexico), 1963. Mem. mayor's cultural task force San Fernando Valley, 1973—. Bd. dirs. Muses (Mus. Sci. and Industry Los Angeles). Recipient numerous pub. service awards from mayor, city council, C. of C. Mem. Canoga Park C. of C. (cultural chmn. 1973-75, dir. 1973-75). Presbyn. Home: 7209 Woodlake St Canoga Park CA 91305 Office: 23130 Sherman Way Canoga Park CA 91307

LEDERER, RAYMOND FRANCIS, Congressman; b. Phila., May 19, 1937; s. Miles W. and Susan (Scullin) L.; student Phila. Community Coll., St. Joseph's Coll. Phila., Pa. State U.; m. Eileen Coyle, Apr. 15, 1961; children—Miles, Mary Beth, Joseph, Patricia, Diane, Claire. Probation officer, dir. Phila. Probation Dept.; mem. Pa. Ho. of Reps., 1974-77; mem. 95th-96th Congresses from 3d Dist. Pa., mem. Ways and Means Com. Active city and ch. youth athletic programs; past pres. St. Michaels Home and Sch. Assn.; bd. dirs. Roman Cath. High Sch., Phila.; football commr. Cath. Youth Orgn., Phila.; chmn. Young Democrats for Kennedy and Johnson, Phila., 1960; mem. Phila. Dem. Com. Recipient Gold Star Mothers' award, 1976; elected to Phila. Police Athletic League Hall of Fame, 1977. Office: 119 Cannon House Office Bldg Washington DC 20515*

LEDERER, WILLIAM JULIUS, author; b. N.Y.C., Mar. 31, 1912; s. William J. and Paula (Franken) L.; B.S., U.S. Naval Acad., 1936; asso. Nieman fellow, Harvard, 1950-51; m. Ethel Hackett, Apr. 21, 1940 (div. Jan. 1965); children—Brian, Jonathan, Bruce; m. 2d, Corinne Edwards Lewis, July 1965 (div. May 1976). Enlisted USN, 1930, commd. ensign, 1936, advanced through grades to capt., 1952, ret., 1958; Far East corr. Reader's Digest, 1958-63; lectr. colls. and univs., 1949—; author in residence Harvard, 1966-67. Author: All the Ship's at Sea, 1950; The Last Cruise, 1950; Spare Time Article Writing for Money, 1953; Ensign O'Toole and Me, 1957; A Nation of Sheep, 1961; Timothy's Song, 1965; Pink Jade, 1966; (with Eugene Burdick) The Ugly American, 1958, Sarkhan, 1965; Our Own Worst Enemy, 1967; (with Don D. Jackson) The Mirages of Marriage, 1968; (with Joe Pete Wilson) Complete Cross-Country Skiing and Ski Touring, 1970; (with others) Marriage for and Against. Mem. Signet Soc., Authors Guild, Sigma Delta Chi. Clubs: Lotos, Trap Door Spiders, National Press, Harvard Faculty. Address: East Hill Farm Peacham VT 05862. *If one works at being joyful and physically functional, almost everything else seems to come along on its own. Put energy into the "here and now" and do not distract from it by worrying about either the past or the future.*

LEDERLE, JOHN WILLIAM, educator; b. Royal Oak, Mich., May 26, 1912; s. Emil John and Minnie Louise (Shore) L.; A.B., U. Mich., 1933, A.M., 1934, LL.B., 1936, Ph.D., 1942; Litt.D., Amherst Coll., 1963, Holy Cross, 1963, Boston U., 1965; LL.D., Hokkaido U., Japan, 1963, U. Mass., 1970; Dr.Pub. Adminstrn., Northeastern U., 1964; D.Sc. in Edn., Lowell State Coll., 1970; m. Angie Pamela King, Apr. 16, 1938; children—Pamela Jean, Thomas Paine. Admitted to Mich. bar, 1936, U.S. Supreme Ct. bar, 1947; with firm Lucking, Van Auken & Sprague, Detroit, 1936-40; staff atty. Mich. Municipal League, 1945-48, gen. counsel, 1948-51; instr. polit. sci. Brown U., 1941-44, asst. prof., 1944, asst. to dean coll., 1942-44, asst. dean coll., 1944; asst. prof. polit. sci. U. Mich., 1944-48, asso. prof., 1948-50, prof., 1950-60, on leave, 1953-54, sec. Inst. Pub. Adminstrn., 1947-48, dir. curriculum, 1948-50, dir., 1950-60; pres. U. Mass., 1960-70, Joseph B. Ely prof. govt., 1970—. Dir. Northampton Coop. Bank. Controller, State of Mich., 1953-54; sec. State Adminstrv. Bd., 1953-54; mem. Mich. State Bldg. Commn., 1953-54; chmn. Mich. Commn. on Interstate Cooperation, 1953-54; mem. exec. com. Flint Coll., U. Mich., 1958-59, Dearborn Center, U. Mich., 1959-60. cons. to U.S. Senate spl. campaign expenditures coms. of 1944 and 1946, to U.S. Ho. of Reps. spl. campaign expenditures com. of 1950; cons. sub-com. on privileges and elections, U.S. Sen. Com. on Rules and Adminstrn., 1952; cons. Mut. Security Agy., 1952; dir., adviser Inst. Pub. Adminstrn., U. Philippines, 1952-53; collaborator U.S. Forest Service; cons. Com. on Govt. and Higher Edn., 1958-59; mem. Mass. Bd. Ednl. Assistance, 1960-65; mem. New Eng. Bd. Higher Edn., 1961-73; mem. Mass. adv. bd. Higher Edn. Policy, 1962-65, Mass. Bd. Regional Community Colls., 1960-70. Mem. state com. YMCA Mich., 1957-60; chmn. Mass. Gov.'s Spl. Com. on Local Govt. Mgmt. Capacity, 1976-78. Trustee Hampshire Coll., 1965-70, Clarke Sch. for Deaf, 1975—. Mem. Am. Soc. Pub. Adminstrn. (chmn. conf. of dirs. bur. govt. research 1958-61), Assn. State U. and Land Grant Colls. (exec. com. 1967-70), Am. Polit. Sci. Assn., Mich. Municipal Attys. Assn. (sec.-treas. 1947-48), Mich. Union, Mich. Municipal League (hon. life). Bd. editors Pub. Adminstrn. Rev., 1954-56. Contbr. articles to profl. jours. Home: Laurel Ledge Rural Route 2 Amherst MA 01002

LEDERMAN, LEON MAX, physicist, educator; b. N.Y.C., July 15, 1922; s. Morris and Minna (Rosenberg) L.; B.S., Coll. City N.Y., 1943; A.M., Columbia, 1948, Ph.D., 1951; m. Florence Gordon, Sept. 19, 1945; children—Rena S., Jesse A., Heidi R. Asso. in physics Columbia, N.Y.C., 1951, asst. prof., 1952-54, asso. prof., 1954-58, prof., 1958—, Eugene Higgins prof. physics, 1973—; dir. Fermi Nat. Accelerator Lab., Batavia, Ill., 1979—. Dir. Nevis Labs., Irvington, N.Y., 1960-67, 69—; guest scientist Brookhaven Nat. Labs., 1955—; cons., nat. accelerator lab. European Orgn. for Nuclear Research (CERN), 1970—; mem. high energy physics adv. panel AEC, 1966-70; mem. adv. com. to div. math. and phys. scis. NSF, 1970-72. Served to 2d lt. Signal Corps, AUS, 1943-46. Recipient Nat. Medal of Sci., 1965. NSF fellow, 1967; Guggenheim fellow, 1958-59; Ford Found. fellow European Center For Nuclear Research, Geneva, 1958-59; recipient Townsend Harris medal City U. N.Y., 1973; Elliot Cresson medal Franklyn Inst., 1976. Fellow A.A.A.S., Am. Phys. Soc.; mem. Italian Phys. Soc., Nat. Acad. Sci. Contbr. articles to profl. jours. Home: 34 Overlook Rd Dobbs Ferry NY 10522

LEDERMAN, LEONARD LAWRENCE, govt. research exec.; b. N.Y.C., Nov. 23, 1931; s. Hyman G. and Yetta (Dreyfus) L.; B.A. in Econs., Coll. City N.Y., 1953; M.A. in Econs., N.Y. U., 1957; postgrad. Columbia, 1955-56, Princeton, 1957-58; m. Florence Krinsky, May 19, 1956; children—Hugh Daniel, Steven Mark, Michael Jay. Statistician, Barnard Research Inc., N.Y.C., 1953-54; research analyst Maidenform Inc., Bayonne, N.J., 1954-58; asst. mgr. mfg. dept., exec. sec. coms. on sci. and tech., also comml. use atomic energy U.S. C. of C., Washington, 1958-62; fellow, sr. research advisor Battelle Meml. Inst., Washington, 1963-70; dep. head Office Econ. and Manpower Studies, dir. Office Exploratory Research and Problem Assessment, Research Applied to Nat. Needs Directorate, NSF, Washington, 1970-72, detailed to Exec. Office of Pres. as program mgr. Productivity and New Tech. Opportunities Program, 1971-72, dir. Office Nat. Research and Devel. Assessment, 1972-76, acting dep. asst. dir. planning and programs Directorate for Sci., Technol. and Internat. Affairs, 1976-77, dep. asst. dir. and dir. strategic planning and assessment, 1977—; cons. Pres.'s Task Force on Hwy. Safety. Recipient certificates of accomplishment for staff work NSF, 1972, 74, Spl. Achievement award NSF, 1972, Outstanding Performance rating for Nat. Research and Devel. Assessment Program NSF, 1974, Superior Accomplishment award NSF, 1979. Mem. Am. Econ. Assn., Am. Mgmt. Assn., Am. Standards Assn., Am. Aero. Soc., A.A.A.S., World Future Soc. Author: An Analysis of the Allocation of Federal Budget Resources as an Indicator of National Goals and Priorities, 2 vols., 1969; Federal Funding and National Priorities, An Analysis of Programs, Expenditures, and Research and Development, 1971; contbg. author; A Review of the Relationship Between Research and Development and Economic Growth/Productivity, 1971. Home: 5602 Ridgefield Rd Bethesda MD 20016 Office: 1800 G St NW Room 1225 Washington DC 20550

LEDERMAN, WILLIAM RALPH, lawyer, educator; b. Regina, Sask., Can., Jan. 6, 1916; s. Ralph and Margaret (McDonald) L.; B.A., U. Sask., 1937, LL.B., 1950, LL.D. (hon.), 1967; B.C.L. (Rhodes scholar, Vinerian scholar), Oxford U., 1948; LL.D. (hon.), U. Victoria, 1975, Dalhousie U., 1978, York U., 1979; m. Edna E. Thompson, July 17, 1948; children—Lewis, Peter, William Ralph. Called to Sask. bar, 1946, N.S. bar, 1954, Ont. bar, 1959; created queen's counsel, Ont., 1964; prof. law U. Sask., 1948-49; Sir James Dunn prof. law Dalhousie U., 1949-58; dean of law Queen's U., Kingston, Ont., 1958-68, prof. law, 1968—. Served with Royal Can. Arty., 1941-45. Fellow Royal Soc. Can. Presbyterian. Contb. articles on constitutional law and pvt. internat. law to legal jours. Home: 815 Johnson St Kingston ON K7L 2B7 Canada Office: Faculty of Law Queen's U Kingston ON K7L 3N6 Canada

LEDFORD, FRANK FINLEY, JR., surgeon, army officer; b. Jacksonville, Fla., Apr. 22, 1934; s. Frank F. and Hazel H. (Barrette) L.; B.S., U. Dayton, 1955; M.D., U. Cin., 1959; postgrad. Indsl. Coll. Armed Forces, 1976—; m. Marilyn Sue Kain, Aug. 23, 1957; 1 dau., Cheryl Lynn. Intern, Brooke Army Hosp., San Antonio, 1959-60; resident Letterman Army Hosp., San Francisco, 1960-65; commd. 2d lt. U.S. Army, 1958, advanced through grades to col., 1973; surgeon, 1958-69; chief orthopedic surgery Army Hosp., Landstuhl, W.Ger., 1969-71; dep. commr. Army Hosp., Heidelberg, W.Ger., 1971-72; asst. chief surg. cons. Office of Surgeon Gen., Washington, 1972-73, chief grad. med. edn., 1973-76; comdr. U.S. Army Hosp., Fort Riley, Kans., 1977—. Diplomate Am. Bd. Orthopedic Surgery. Fellow A.C.S., Am. Acad. Orthopedic Surgeons; mem. AMA, Assn. Mil. Surgeons, Soc. Mil. Orthopedic Surgeons. Methodist. Club: Tantallon Country. Contbr. articles to med. jours. Address: 26 Sheridan Ave Fort Riley KS 66442

LEDFORD, HUBERT FRANCIS, life ins. co. exec.; b. Wake County, N.C., Aug. 30, 1906; s. Arthur Raymond and Arrada Frances (Coley) L.; student Kings Bus. Coll., 1924-26, Internat. Corr. Schs., 1926-29, Life Office Mgmt. Assn., 1946-51; m. Lola Marshburn, Nov. 6, 1926. Sec.-treas. Atlantic Joint Stock Land Bank, Raleigh, N.C., 1931-41, Greensboro Joint Stock Land Bank (N.C.), 1936-39; with

State Capital Life Ins. Co., Raleigh, 1936-70, pres., 1954-70; with State Life Ins. Co., Columbia, S.C., 1949-71, pres., 1954-71; co. merged with Durham Life Ins. Co. (N.C.), 1970; co-chmn. bd. dirs. Durham Life Ins. Co., 1971—; dir. Am. Hog Co., FALCO Corp., State Capital Ins. Co., State Capital Ins. Co., WPTF Broadcasting Co. Bd. dirs. ARC, YMCA, Salvation Army. Served with AUS, 1943-45. Mem. Am. Life Conv., Inst. Life Ins., Life Ins. Agy. Mgmt. Assn., Life Insurers Conf., Newcomen Soc. Democrat. Baptist. Clubs: Rotary, Carolina Country, Raleigh Execs. Home: 3030 Randolph Dr Raleigh NC 27609 Office: 2610 Wycliff Dr Raleigh NC 27607

LEDFORD, JACK C., aircraft co. exec.; b. Blairsville, Ga., Sept. 1, 1920; s. Jack Raymond and Clara Mae (Duckworth) L.; B.S., Ohio State U.; M.B.A., George Washington U.; m. Pauline F. Knight, Dec. 9, 1973; children—Barbara Jan (Mrs. Russell J. Thomas), Jack Michael, Joseph Dan. Commd. 2d lt. Air Corps U.S. Army, 1941, advanced through grades to brig. gen. USAF, 1965; dep. chief staff Def. Atomic Support Agy., Washington, 1958-61; dir. spl. projects USAF, 1961-63; asst. dir. CIA, 1963-66; dir. inspection USAF, 1966-68; comdr. 12th Strategic Air Div., Tucson, 1968-70; ret. 1970; v.p. area devel. So. Ariz. Bank & Trust Co., Tucson., 1970-71; v.p. Hughes Aircraft Internat. Service Corp., 1971—. Pres. Old Pueblo Boys Club. Bd. dirs. Tucson United Community Campaign, Catalina council Boy Scouts Am., Pima County Air Mus. Decorated D.S.C., D.S.M. (2), Legion of Merit, Air Medal, Purple Heart; Order of Flying Cloud and Banner (China). Mem. Air Force Assn., Delta Upsilon. Rotarian. Office: Hughes Aircraft Co Bldg 373 7120 PO Box 92919 Los Angeles CA 90009

LEDOGAR, RAYMOND ANTHONY, corp. exec., lawyer; b. N.Y.C., May 16, 1926; s. Joseph A. and Mary (Wium) L.; A.B., Harvard, 1948, LL.B., 1951, J.D., 1969; LL.M., N.Y.U., 1962; m. Judith I. Wolfinger, June 27, 1959; children—Leslie W., Felicia W. Admitted to N.Y. bar, 1951, N.M. bar, 1962, Ill. bar, 1974, N.C. bar, 1975; atty. Bell Telephone Labs., Inc., N.Y.C., 1953-61; atty. Sandia Corp., Albuquerque, 1961-65; atty. Western Electric Co. Inc., N.Y.C., 1965-73, labor atty., asst. sec., 1973—; gen. atty., asst. sec. Nassau Smelting & Refining Co. Inc., Tottenville, S.I., N.Y., 1971-73. Bd. dirs. United Fund of Manhasset Inc. Served with USAAF, 1944-46. Mem. Am., N.M., Ill., Chgo., N.C. bar assns. Am. Acad. Polit. and Social Sci. Clubs: Harvard (N.Y.C.); Plandome (N.Y.) Country. Home: 5 Roswell Ct Irving Park Greensboro NC 27408 Office: Western Electric Co PO Box 25000 Greensboro NC 27420

LEDOUX, HAROLD ANTHONY, cartoonist; b. Port Arthur, Tex., Nov. 7, 1926; s. Antoine Ovide and Pauline Zulma (Bernard) LeD.; student Chgo. Acad. Fine Arts, 1948-49; children—Lorraine Marthe, Noelle Pauline. Cartoonist, Famous Funnies, N.Y.C., 1950-53; asst. cartoonist to Judge Parker syndicated comic strip, 1953-65, cartoonist, illustrator, Judge Parker, 1965—. Advisor, Council for Devel. of French in La. Served with U.S. Mcht. Marine, 1944-47. Mem. Nat. Cartoonists Soc., Comics Council. Roman Catholic. Club: Alliance Francaise. Address: 1100 Harness Ln Richardson TX 75081

LE DUC, DON RAYMOND, lawyer, educator; b. South Milwaukee, Wis., Apr. 7, 1933; s. Raymond Joseph and Roberta (Jones) Le D.; B.A., U. Wis., 1959, Ph.D., 1970; J.D., Marquette U., 1962; m. Alice Marie Pranica, Oct. 24, 1959; children—Paul, Marie. Admitted to Wis. bar, 1962; asso. firm Arnold, Murray & O'Neill, Milw., 1962-63; Ford fellow in comparative law U. Wis., Madison, 1963-63, prof., 1973—, chmn. W. European studies program, 1979—; individual practice law, Green Bay, Wis., 1964-67; chief counsel Wis. Dept. Ins., Madison, 1967-69; asst. prof. communications law U. Md., 1970-71; asso. prof. Ohio State U., 1971-73; dir. Comparative Telecommunications Research Center, Madison, 1974—; chief counsel Wis. Gov.'s Task Force on Telecommunications, 1971-72; cable TV advisory com. mem. FCC, 1972—. Served as spl. agt. CIC, U.S. Army, 1954-57. Recipient award Ohio State U., 1971, Wis. Alumni Research Found., 1974, 75, 77; grantee Am. Philos. Soc., 1975, 77; research fellow NATO, 1979, Council European Studies, 1979. Mem. FCC, Wis. bar assns., Broadcast Edn. Assn., Internat. Inst. Communication. Republican. Roman Catholic. Author: Cable Television and the FCC, 1973; Issues in Broadcast Regulation, 1974; asso. editor: Jour. Broadcasting, 1974—, Jour. Communication, 1978—; contbr. articles to profl. publs.; editor Client mag., 1972—. Home: 305 Cheyenne Tr Madison WI 53705 Office: Vilas Communication Hall U Wis Madison WI 53706

LEDUC, ELIZABETH HORTENSE, biologist; b. Rockland, Maine, Nov. 19, 1921; d. Arthur Eli and Rosina Zeneda (Gladu) Leduc; B.S., U. Vt., 1943; M.A., Wellesley Coll., 1945; Ph.D., Brown U., 1948. Fellow NIH, Washington, 1948-49; instr. anatomy Harvard Med. Sch., 1949-51, asso. in anatomy, 1951-53; asst. prof. biology Brown U., 1953-57, asso. prof., 1957-64, prof., 1964—, dir. biology, 1967-68, dean of biol. scis., 1973-77, Frank L. Day prof. biology, 1973—; annual guest investigator Inst. de Recherces sur le Cancer, Villejuif, France, summers, 1959—; mem. study sect. for cell biology NIH, 1969-72; mem. Pres.'s Com. on Sci. and Tech., 1976-77; mem. nat. adv. Gen. Med. Scis. Council, 1972-76; mem. study sect. for cell and devel. biology Am. Cancer Soc., 1979—. Mem. Biol. Stain Comm., Histochemistry Soc., Am. Assn. Cancer Research, Am. Soc. Exptl. Pathology, Soc. Devel. Biology, AAAS, Am. Asso. Anatomists, Am. Soc. Cell Biology, Soc. Francaise de Microscopic Electronique. Cons. editor Anatomical Record, 1968-74, Jour. de Biologie Cellulaire, 1976—, Micron, 1975-78; mem. editorial adv. bd. Cancer Research, 1968-76. Contbr. articles to profl. jours. Home: 51 Holly St Providence RI 02906 Office: Brown U Box G Providence RI 02912

LEDUC, GILLES GERMAIN, cardiologist; b. Montreal, Que., Can., Oct. 14, 1923; s. Octave Joseph and Elisabeth Marie (Lussier) L.; B.A., U. Ottawa (Ont., Can.), 1944; M.D., U. Montreal, 1950; m. Francine Mercier, Sept. 12, 1959; children—Bertrand, Martin. Intern, Hotel-Dieu de Montreal, 1950, resident, 1951-52, attending physician, 1955; resident in cardiology St. Luke's Hosp., N.Y.C., 1952-54, Hopital Boucicaut, Paris, 1954-55; practice medicine specializing in internal medicine and cardiology, Montreal, 1955—; cons. physician St. Justine Hosp., 1956—; prof. medicine U. Montreal, 1956—; sr. mem. Inst. Research, Montreal. Fellow Am. Heart Assn., Am. Coll. Cardiology; mem. Montreal Cardiac Soc. (past pres.), Acad. Regliion and Mental Health (mem. adv. council). Roman Catholic. Contbr. sci. papers to profl. jours. Home: 82 Lockhart St Mont Royal PQ Canada Office: 110 Pine Ave Montreal PQ Canada

LEDWIDGE, PATRICK JOSEPH, lawyer; b. Detroit, Mar. 17, 1928; s. Patrick Liam and Mary Josephine (Hooley) L.; A.B., Coll. Holy Cross, 1949; J.D., U. Mich., 1952; m. Rosemary Lahey Mervenne, Aug. 3, 1974; stepchildren—Anne Marie, Mary Clare, John, David, Sara Mervenne. Admitted to Mich. bar, 1952; asso. firm Dickinson, Wright, McKean, Cudlip & Moon, Detroit, 1956-63, partner, 1964—; mem. exec. com. Inst. Continuing Legal Edn., Ann Arbor, Mich. Served to lt. j.g. U.S. Navy, 1952-55. Mem. Am. Bar Assn., Mich. Bar Assn., Detroit Bar Assn., Am. Law Inst. Roman Catholic. Clubs: Detroit, Detroit Athletic, Detroit Golf. Home: 777 N Williamsburg St Birmingham MI 48010 Office: 800 1st National Bldg Detroit MI 48226

LEDYARD, ROBINS HEARD, ins. co. exec.; b. Nashville, Oct. 14, 1939; s. Quitman Robins and Alma Elizabeth (Stevenson) L.; B.A., Vanderbilt U., 1965, J.D., 1966; m. Julia Bordeaux Gambill, Dec. 19, 1962; children—Stevenson Gambill, Quitman Robins, Margaret Dabney. Admitted to Tenn. bar, 1966; atty. Nat. Life & Accident Ins. Co., Nashville, 1966-68, asst. counsel, 1968-69, asso. counsel, 1969-70, counsel, 1970-72, asso. gen. counsel, 1972-75, gen. counsel, 1975—; tchr. C.L.U.'s, 1967-75. Active United Way, Nashville, 1967—, Heart Fund, 1970-73; vice chmn. United Diocesan Givers, 1975. Served with USMC, 1958-61. Recipient Bennett Douglas Bell Meml. prize, 1966; Marr scholar, 1965-66. Mem. Am. Council Life Ins. (chmn. tax com. 1978—), Assn. Life Ins. Counsel (chmn. tax com. 1979—), Nashville Bar Assn., Internat. Assn. Ins. Counsel, Order of Coif, Phi Delta Phi, Alpha Tau Omega. Democrat. Roman Catholic. Clubs: Belle Meade Country, Capitol of Nashville, K.C. Asst. editor Vanderbilt Law Rev., 1965-66; contbr. articles in field to profl. jours. Home: 1215 Chickering Rd Nashville TN 37205 Office: 2540 National Life Center Nashville TN 37250

LEE, ADDISON EARL, educator; b. Maydell, Tex., June 18, 1914; s. Earl and Alma (Fletcher) L.; B.S., Stephen F. Austin Tchrs. Coll., 1934; M.S., Tex. A. and M. Coll., 1937; Ph.D., U. Tex., 1949; m. Neta Edith Warren, Aug. 29, 1937; children—Donald Addison, Neta Susan. Tchr. biology Austin High Sch., 1937-46; instr. U. Tex., Austin, 1946-49, asst. prof., 1949-53, asso. prof. botany, 1953-59, prof. sci. edn., 1959-65, prof. sci. edn. and biology, dir. Sci. Edn. Center, 1965—. Vis. prof. dept. biology U. Va., 1957; dir. NSF Summer Inst., 1958-73, NSF Acad. Yr. Inst., 1967-73, U. Tex. Fellow Tex. Acad. Sci. (pres. 1963), mem. N.E.A., Nat. Sci. Tchrs. Assn. (pres. 1966-67, Robert H. Carleton award 1975), Nat. Assn. Biology Tchrs. (v.p. 1965-66, pres. 1973, hon. mem. 1977—), Nat. Assn. Research Sci. Teaching, Assn. Tchrs. Sci. Author numerous books, articles in profl. jours. Home: 4506 Balcones Dr Austin TX 78731

LEE, ADRIAN ISELIN, JR., journalist; b. Miami, Fla., Nov. 6, 1920; s. Adrian Iselin and Adriana Lanier (Owen) L.; B.A., Spring Hill Coll., Mobile, Ala., 1943; m. Marie Laine Santa Maria, Oct. 14, 1950; children—Adrian Iselin III, Catherine Taney, Thomas Sim, William Owen, Anne Marie, Louisa Carrell. With The Bulletin, Phila., 1948—, gen. assignment reporter, 1960—, editorial writer, 1967-72, columnist op-ed page, 1972—; tchr. editorial writing, dept. journalism Temple U. Active, Chestnut Hill Community Assn. Served to lt. (j.g.) USNR, 1943-46; PTO. Decorated Navy Unit Commendation medal. Mem. Nat. Press Club, Pen and Pencil Club, Phila. Press Assn. (prize for coverage John F. Kennedy assassination 1963), Sigma Delta Chi (prize for column writing 1978). Republican. Roman Catholic. Home: 119 W Springfield Ave Philadelphia PA 19118 Office: Phila Bull 30th and Market Sts Philadelphia PA 19101

LEE, ALFRED MCCLUNG, social scientist, educator; b. Oakmont, Pa., Aug. 23, 1906; s. Alfred McClung and Edna (Hamor) L.; A.B., U. Pitts., 1927, A.M., 1931; Ph.D., Yale, 1933; m. Elizabeth Riley Briant, Sept. 15, 1927; children—Alfred McClung 3d, Briant Hamor. Newspaper, civic experience, Pitts., 1927-31, New Haven, 1931-34; Kennedy T. Friend fellow in sociology Yale, 1931-33, Sterling post-doctoral fellow, 1933-34, asst. prof. Inst. Human Relations, 1937-38; asst. prof. U. Kans., 1934-35, asso. prof., 1935-38; pub. affairs specialist Twentieth Century Fund, 1938-40; lectr. sociology N.Y. U., 1938-39, asst. prof., 1939-42, vis. grad. prof., 1951-55; prof. sociology, anthropology Wayne U., 1942-49, research sociologist, 1948-49; prof. sociology, anthropology Bklyn. Coll. and Grad. Center City U. N.Y., 1949-71, prof. emeritus, 1971—. Vis. prof. U. Mich., 1947-48; UNESCO prof. sociology, Milan, Italy, 1957-58; exec. dir., treas. Inst. for Propaganda Analysis, 1940-50; cons. FCC, 1941, U.S. Dept. Justice, 1943-44, U.S. Office Edn., 1947-49; research cons. Met. Applied Research Center, N.Y.C., 1967-76; vis. scholar Drew U., Madison, N.J., 1975—; cons. to civic, edn. orgns. Pres., Friends of Danilo Dolci, 1971-73. Recipient Fulbright award U. Rome, 1960-61; Honor award Corriere della Sera Newspapers, 1967 (Italy). Marshall Field research grantee, 1947-48; Am. specialist grantee U.S. State Dept., 1967; Am. Humanist Assn. humanist fellow, 1977. Fellow AAAS, Am. Anthrop. Assn., Am. Sociol. Assn. (pres. 1975-76), Assn. Italiana di Scienze Sociali; mem. Internat. Sociol. Assn. (U.S. del. 1966-70), Inst. Internat. de Sociologie (Rome), Eastern Sociol. Soc. (pres. 1954-55, Ann. Merit award 1974), Soc. Study Social Problems (founder 1950-51, pres. 1953-54), Soc. for Psychol. Study Social Issues, Assn. Humanist Sociology (acting pres. 1975-76, pres. 1976-77), Nat. Soc. Profs., Profl. Staff Congress, Am. Fedn. Tchrs., NEA, Irish Texts Soc. (Dublin), ACLU, NAACP (chmn. com. social sci. cons. legal def. and ednl. fund 1954-57), Am. Com. Irish Studies, Irish Sociol Assn. (hon.), Deutsche Gesellschaft für Soziologie (corr.), Sigma Xi, Omicron Delta Kappa, Sigma Delta Chi (Nat. Research award 1937), Alpha Kappa Delta, Sigma Chi. Clubs: Art Center (Summit, N.J.); Yale (N.Y.C.). Author several books, latest being: How to Understand Propaganda, 1952; Fraternities Without Brotherhood, 1955; La Sociologia delle Comunicazioni, 1960; Che Cos'E' la Propaganda, 1961; Multivalent Man, 1966; The Daily Newspaper in America, 1973; Toward Humanist Sociology, 1973; Sociology for Whom?, 1978; co-author: Marriage and the Family, rev. edit., 1967; Race Riot, 1968; The Participant Observer, 1970; The Fine Art of Propaganda, 1972. Editor, co-author textbooks in sociology. Mem. bd. Pub. Affairs Pamphlets, 1950—, vice chmn., 1970—; bd. mem. Sociol. Abstracts, 1965—; asso. editor The Humanist, 1979—. Contbr. to mags., jours. Home: 100 Hemlock Rd Short Hills NJ 07078. *Both in my writing and in my teaching, I have tried to identify and to help others grasp opportunities to magnify the potential of individuals in society. I have opposed the development of elitist theories and of other controls that would diminish human stature and dignity. I have contended that people need not be deformed into mere tools of impersonal bureaucracies or of rash power-seekers, and I believe that they will not be.*

LEE, ALLAN WREN, clergyman; b. Yakima, Wash., June 3, 1924; s. Percy Anson and Agnes May (Wren) L.; B.A., Phillips U., Enid, Okla., 1949; M.A., Peabody Coll. Tchrs., 1953; B.D., Tex. Christian U., 1955, D.D. (hon.), 1968; m. Mildred Elaine Ferguson, June 16, 1946; 1 dau., Cynthia Ann. Ordained minister Christian Ch. (Disciples of Christ), 1949; pastor chs. in Tex. and Wash., 1955-71; gen. sec. World Conv. Chs. of Christ, Dallas, 1971—; mem. gen. bd. Christian Ch., 1971-73; pres. Seattle Christian Ch. Missionary Union, 1964-66, Wash.-No. Idaho Conv. Christian Chs., 1966. Recipient Distinguished Service citation Children's Home Soc. Wash., 1967, Distinguished Service award Bremerton Jaycees, 1959. Founder, life mem. Disciples of Christ Hist. Soc. Club: Seattle Civitan (pres. 1962-64, lt. gov. Orewa dist. 1965). Author: Bridges of Benevolence, 1962; Wit and Wisdom, 1963; The Burro and the Bibles, 1968; Under the Shadow of the Nine Dragons, 1969; Reflections Along the Reef, 1970; Disciple Down Under, 1971; Meet My Mexican Amigos, 1972; One Great Fellowship, 1974; also articles. Office: 8609 NW Plaza Dr Suite 405 Dallas TX 75225. *I make every effort to live a life patterned after the life and teachings of the Man of Nazareth, Jesus Christ—that is, to be compassionate, understanding, peaceful and loving.*

LEE, ARMISTEAD MASON, research dir.; b. Anking, China, Apr. 2, 1916 (parents Am. citizens); s. Edmund Jennings and Lucy Mitchell (Chaplin) L.; B.A., Yale, 1938, M.A., 1941; Rhodes scholar, Oxford U., 1938-39; M.P.A., Harvard, 1957; m. Eleanore Ruggles Cobb, June 20, 1942; children—Eleanore Ruggles (Mrs. Robert P. Browning), Rebecca Rust, Jeffrey Armistead. Vice consul, Toronto, Ont., Can., 1943, Dakar, French West Africa, 1944, Melbourne, Australia, 1946; 2d sec., polit. officer Am. embassy, Wellington, New Zealand, 1948-51; asst. labor adviser, bur. European affairs Dept. State, 1951, Commonwealth affairs officer charge Australia, N.Z., South African affairs, 1952-54; consul, Kingston, Jamaica, 1954-56; econ. officer Am. embassy, Reykjavik, 1957-58; head econ. unit Am. embassy, Brussels, 1959, 1st sec., 1960; dep. U.S. commr. Tripartite Commn. for Restitution Monetary Gold, Brussels, 1960-63; alternate country dir. (econ.) Central African and Malagasy Affairs, Dept. State, 1963-67; dir. econ. research Pharm. Mfrs. Assn., Washington, 1967-72, asst. v.p. research and planning, 1972—. Ad hoc adviser U.S. delegation 7th Gen. Assembly UN, 1952; adviser U.S. delegation West Indian Conf., San Juan, 1955. Mem. Assn. Am. Rhodes Scholars, Soc. Lees Va. (pres.), Phi Beta Kappa. Club: National Economists (sec. 1976, v.p. 1978) (Washington). Home: 2367 N Kenmore St Arlington VA 22207 Office: 1155 15th St Washington DC 20005

LEE, AUDREY, author; b. Phila.; student in Liberal Arts Temple U.; student writers workshop Columbia U., 1966. Author novels: The Clarion People, 1968; The Workers, 1969; contbg. author: (short story in anthology) What We Must See, 1971, (poetry in anthology) Keeping the Faith, 1974; (short story in textbook) Reading Tactics E, 1977; Question and Form in Literature, 1979; contbr. short stories to popular and lit. mags., including Essence Mag., Negro Digest, Black World Mag., Playgirl mag.; contbr. poetry, revs., articles to lit., jours., popular mags., newspapers. Home: Philadelphia PA . *Even the most reasonable principles are costly; and their maintenance often requires stamina, courage and patience. One must constantly work at the maintenance of one's interior to provide a comfortable place for the conscience and the psyche. Were I required to choose between decency and talent, I should choose decency. The essence of success is survival, with dignity.*

LEE, BERT GENTRY, aerospace exec.; b. N.Y.C., Mar. 29, 1942; s. Harrell Estes and Peggy (Harding) L.; B.A. summa cum laude, U. Tex., Austin, 1963; M.S., Mass. Inst. Tech., 1964; postgrad. U. Glasgow (Scotland), 1964-65; m. Catharine Sue Cooper, Oct. 5, 1975; 1 son, Cooper Gentry. Staff engr. Martin Marietta Aerospace Co., Denver, 1965-72, mgr. Viking mission ops. and design, Denver, 1972-74, dir. Viking sci. analysis and mission planning, Pasadena, Calif., 1974-76; sect. mgr. mission design Jet Propulsion Lab., Pasadena, 1976-78, mgr. mission ops. and engring. Project Galileo, 1978—; project mgr. Cosmos for PBS, 1978—; v.p., gen. mgr. Carl Sagan Prodns., Inc., sci. for media, 1976-79; lectr. sci., space and the future, 1975—. Woodrow Wilson fellow, 1963; Marshall fellow, 1964; recipient Exceptional Sci. Achievement medal NASA, 1977. Mem. Phi Beta Kappa. Contbr. profl. jours. Home: 5441 Rock Castle Rd La Canada CA 91011 Office: 4800 Oak Grove Dr Pasadena CA 91103

LEE, BLAIR, III, acting gov. Md.; b. Silver Spring, Md., May 19, 1916; s. E. Brooke and Elizabeth (Wilson) L.; A.B., Princeton, 1938; m. Mathilde Boal, July 6, 1944; children—Blair IV, Joseph W., Christopher G., Frederick B., Philip L., John F., Jeanne M. Editor Md. News, Silver Spring, 1945-49; pres. Silver Spring Bd. Trade, 1948-49, Md. Press Assn., 1949; vice chmn., park commnr. Md. Nat. Capital Park and Planning Commn., 1949-51, mem., 1965-66; pvt. planning and zoning cons., 1954-59, property mgmt., 1959—; mem. Md. Ho. of Dels., 1955-62, Md. Senate, 1967-69; sec. state Md., 1969-71, lt. gov., 1971-77, acting gov., 1977—. Del. Democratic Nat. Conv., 1948, 60, 64, 72, 76, alternate, 1968; Montgomery County campaign mgr. John F. Kennedy, 1960; regional coordinator Middle Atlantic States, Johnson-Humphrey, 1964. Served to lt. comdr. USNR, 1941-45. Home: 400 Warrenton Dr Silver Spring MD 20904 Office: State House Annapolis MD 21404

LEE, BRENDA, entertainer; b. Atlanta, Dec. 11, 1944; d. Reuben Lindsey and Grayce (Yarbrough) Tarpley; grad. Hollywood Profl. Sch., 1963; m. Ronald Shacklett, Apr. 24, 1963; children—Julie Leann, Jolie Lenee. Night club appearances at The Flamingo, Las Vegas, 1962, The Deauville, Miami, Fla., 1962, The Sahara, Las Vegas, 1961; TV appearances on shows of Ed Sullivan, Perry Como, Bob Hope, Red Skelton, Danny Thomas, Steve Allen, Tennessee Ernie Ford, also Tonight, Hullabaloo, Kraft Music Hall, Johnny Cash Show; motion picture feature role in Two Little Bears, 1962; command performance for Queen Elizabeth, 1964. Named Worlds' Number One Female Vocalist, New Mus. Express Polls, Eng., 1962-65; recipient Edison award in Belgium, 1962, Outstanding Vocalist Naras award, 1962, Cashbox and Billboard Best Female Vocalist award, 1962, 63. Office: care Buckskin Co 7 Music Circle N Nashville TN 37203*

LEE, BRUCE, editor; b. N.Y.C., Dec. 3, 1930; s. Edward Brooke and Thelma Llewellyn (Lawson) L.; B.A., Rollins Coll., 1954; M.F.A., Fordham U., 1959; m. Nancy Faye Hatch, Sept. 28, 1958; children—Evalyn, Bruce H. Reporter, Adirondack Daily Enterprise, Saranac Lake, N.Y., 1952-53, N.Y. Daily News, N.Y.C., 1954; asso. editor Newsweek, N.Y.C., 1954-61; Washington corr. Reader's Digest mag., 1961-65, asso. editor, N.Y.C., 1965-66, sr. editor, 1966-72; editor Reader's Digest Press, N.Y.C., 1972-78; sr. editor Gen. Book div. McGraw-Hill, N.Y.C., 1978—. Clubs: N.Y. Yacht, Seawanhaka Corinthian Yacht. Author: Boy's Life of John F. Kennedy, 1962. Home: 1192 Park Ave New York NY 10028 Office: 1221 Ave of Americas New York NY 10020

LEE, BURNS WELLS, pub. relations co. exec.; b. St. Louis, July 21, 1913; s. Channing B. and Rae (Wells) L.; A.B., Occidental Coll., 1935; m. Pauline Slocum, Apr. 10, 1939 (div.); m. 2d, Kathleen Booth Strutt, July 1, 1960. Publicity dir., mem. staff Benton & Bowles, Inc., N.Y.C., Hollywood, 1935-42; sr. specialist war savs. staff Treasury Dept., Washington, 1942-43; pub. relations mgr. Rexall Drug Co., Los Angeles, 1946-49; pres. Burns W. Lee Assos., Los Angeles, 1949-61; pres. Bergen & Lee, Inc., Los Angeles, 1961—. Served as pub. relations officer USMCR, 1943-46. Mem. Pub. Relations Soc. Am. (chmn. com. standards of profl. practice 1951, regional v.p. 1952-53, chmn. PR reference round table 1954-55, chmn. eligibility com. 1962, chmn. grievance bd. 1965-66, chmn. spl. task force on pub. relations, 1975-77, 1st ann. professionalism award Los Angeles chpt. 1964), Regional Plan Assn. So. Cal. (dir., chmn. pub. relations com. 1967-70), Central City Assn. (dir. 1971—), Los Angeles C. of C. (pub. relations chmn., bus. outlook conf. 1974 mem. exec. com. 1979—, internat. commerce com. 1979—). Rotarian. Home: 870 Rome Dr Los Angeles CA 90065 Office: 1533 Wilshire Blvd Los Angeles CA 90017

LEE, CALVIN BOW TONG, ins. co. exec.; b. N.Y.C., Feb. 18, 1934; s. George G. and Lin (Hong) L.; A.B., Columbia, 1955, LL.B., 1958; LL.M., N.Y.U., 1965, J.S.D., 1968; m. Beverly Song, June 8, 1957 (div.); children—Christopher, Craig; m. 2d, Audrey A. Evans, Sept. 11, 1971. Gen. mgr. Lee's Restaurant, N.Y.C., 1951-58; admitted to N.Y. bar, 1959; U.S. Supreme Ct. bar; atty. Emmet, Marvin & Martin N.Y.C., 1958-61; asst. dean, dir. Citizenship Program, lectr. polit. sci. Columbia, 1961-65; Am. Council Edn. fellow in acad. adminstrn. Bryn Mawr Coll., 1965-66; staff asso. Am. Council on Edn., 1966-67; asst. dir. div. of coll. support Bur. Higher Edn., U.S. Office Edn., 1967-68; dean Coll. Liberal Arts, Boston U., 1968-70, acting pres.,

1970, exec. v.p., 1971; chancellor U. Md., Baltimore County, 1971-76; v.p. Prudential Ins. Co. Am., Newark, 1976—. Mem. Authors Guild, Phi Alpha Delta. Author: Chinese Cooking for American Kitchens, 1958; Chinatown, U.S.A., 1965; One Man, One Vote, 1967; The Campus Scene: 1900-1970, 1970; co-author: The Invisible Colleges, 1972; The Gourmet Chinese Regional Cookbook, 1976. Editor, contbr. Improving College Teaching, 1967; co-editor, contbr. Whose Goals for American Higher Education, 1968. Home: 369 Fairmount Ave Chatham Township NJ 07928 Office: Corp Office Prudential Plaza Newark NJ 07101

LEE, CARL E., broadcasting co. exec.; b. Reading, Mich., Nov. 7, 1918; s. Bert H. and Mary L. (Nash) L.; grad. Mich. Acad. Radio Sci., 1939; m. Winifred E. Fulton, Oct. 12, 1940; 1 dau., Cheryl Ann Lee. Engr. radio sta. WKZO, 1939-42, chief engr., 1942-51; adminstrv. asst., dir. engring. Fetzer Broadcasting Co., Kalamazoo, 1951-53, mng. dir., 1953-54, v.p., 1954-58, exec. v.p., gen. mgr., 1958-73, pres., gen. mgr., 1973—, also dir.; pres., gen. mgr. Fetzer TV Corp., 1973—, also dir.; vice chmn. bd. Cornhusker TV Corp., 1973—, Medallion Broadcasters Inc., 1973—; v.p., dir. Fetzer Communications Inc., Wolverine Calbevision Inc., Detroit Baseball Club; dir., mem. exec. com. First Nat. Bank & Trust Co., Kalamazoo, First Nat. Financial Corp., Kalamazoo Broadcast Music Inc. Mem. nat. industry adv. com. Emergency Broadcast System, 1966, mem. Kalamazoo local industry adv. com., 1966; mem. airport adv. com., Kalamazoo, 1970—; mem. blue ribbon study com. Dist. Ct., Kalamazoo, 1974; chmn. Southwestern Mich. Operational Area Emergency Communications Com., 1974—. Bd. dirs. Broadcasters' Found. Inc., Broadcast Pioneers Ednl. Fund; trustee, sec. John E. Fetzer Found. Inc. Recipient Liberty Bell award. Mem. Kalamazoo County C. of C. (v.p. 1973-74, chmn. Kalamazoo Community Devel. 1973-74, dir. Community Service award), Broadcast Pioneers (dir.), I.E.E.E., Soc. TV Pioneers. Presbyn. Mason (32 deg., Shriner), Lion. Clubs: Kalamazoo Park, Kalamazoo Country. Home: 1902 Chevy Chase Blvd Kalamazoo MI 49008 Office: 590 W Maple St Kalamazoo MI 49008

LEE, CHARLES, educator; b. Phila., Jan. 2, 1913; s. Benjamin and Lillian (Potash) Levy; A.B., U. Pa., 1933, M.A., 1936, Ph.D., 1955; div.; children—Myles E., Gail M. Lit. editor Boston Herald-Traveler, 1936-40, Phila. Record, 1940-47; faculty U. Pa., 1949-65, prof. communications, 1959-65, prof. English, 1959—, vice dean Annenberg Sch. Communications, 1959-65, roving critic WCAU radio, 1964-65, WCAU-TV, 1965-73; entertainments editor WCAU radio, 1974-79. Creative cons. Four-Star Internat., Hollywood. Exhibited one-man art show Janet Fleisher Gallery, Phila., 1972. Recipient 1st award for meritorious achievement in journalism U. Pa., 1944. Mem. Soc. Am. Historians, A.A.U.P., Phi Beta Kappa. Author: Exile: A Book of Verse, 1936; How to Enjoy Reading, 1939; An Almanac of Reading, 1940; Weekend at the Waldorf, 1945; North East, South, West, 1945; The Twin Bedside Anthology, 1946; Snow, Ice and Penguins, 1950; I'll Be Waiting, 1958; The Hidden Public, 1958. Editor (author preface): The State of the Nation, 1963; Sevens Come Eleven, 1972. Home: Presdl Apts Philadelphia PA 19131

LEE, CHARLES HENRY, lawyer, internat. exec.; b. Santiago, Chile, June 28, 1909; s. Charles Henry and Ellen Scott (Wilson) L.; student Columbia, 1927-28; Ph.B. cum laude, Georgetown U., 1931; postgrad. George Washington, Columbia, 1932-33; LL.B., Fordham U., 1937; m. Lulu Vargas-Vila, Aug. 20, 1938; children—Patricia Ellen (Mrs. Lars Schonander), Charles Henry III (dec.), Elizabeth (Mrs. John D. Sevier). Asst. to arbitrator Guatemala-Honduras Boundary Arbitration Tribunal, Washington, 1931-33; admitted to N.Y. bar, 1938, D.C. bar, 1946; pvt. practice, N.Y.C., 1937-41; atty. Coordinator Inter-Am. Affairs, Washington, 1941; atty. Tex. Co., N.Y.C., 1941-46; spl. asst. to asst. sec. state Inter-Am. affairs Dept. State, Washington, 1946-47; mng. dir. E.R. Squibb & Sons Argentina, Buenos Aires, 1947-49; asst. v.p., asst. to pres. E.R. Squibb & Sons, N.Y.; dir. Brazilian subsidiary, 1949-56; mng. dir. internat. practice McKinsey & Co., mgmt. cons., N.Y.C., 1956-58; mng. partner Lee, Altieri, Sisto & Assos., mgmt. cons., Mexico City, 1958-61; partner Rado & Lee, attys., N.Y.C., 1958-61; dir. U.S. Econ. Mission to Chile, Santiago, 1961-64; v.p., chmn. bd. Hooker Mexicana S.A. de C.V., v.p. Hooker Internat. Corp., 1972—; partner Sintemex. Mem. Council on Fgn. Relations N.Y., 1951—; hon. mem. faculty Cath. U. Chile. With Inter-Am. Def. Bd., Washington, 1942; mil. attache Div. G-2 War Dept., Washington, 1942-43; asst. mil. attache Am. embassy, Argentina, 1943-45. Bd. dirs., v.p. Mexican-N.Am. Cultural Inst. Decorated comdr. Order al Merito (Chile). Mem. Am. C. of C. Mexico (dir., past pres., chmn. bus. adv. council), Am. Chamber of Mex., Assn. Am. Chambers Commerce Latin Am. (v.p.), Mexican Acad. History and Geography, Am. Bar Assn. (past sec., chmn. Latin Am. law com.), Assn. Bar City N.Y., Pan Am. Soc. U.S. Roman Catholic. Clubs: University (Washington, N.Y.C. and Mexico City); Campestre Churubusco (Mexico City). Internat. relations editor: Handbook of Latin Am. Studies, 1941. Home: Platon 445 Mexico 5 DF Mexico Office: Mariano Escobedo 510 Mexico 5 DF Mexico

LEE, CHARLES ROBERT, holding co. exec.; b. Pitts., Feb. 15, 1940; s. John Anthony and Margaret V. (English) L.; B.Metall. Engring., Cornell U., 1962; M.B.A. with distinction, Harvard U., 1964; m. Ilda Gerhardt, Dec. 31, 1958; children—Douglas, Dana, Debra, Dawn, Daryyn. Mgr. bus. research U.S. Steel Corp., Pitts., 1964-70; asst. treas. corp. investments Penn Central Transp. Co., Phila., 1970-71; v.p. fin. Pa. Co., Arlington, Va., 1971—; sr. v.p. fin. The Penn Central Corp., N.Y.C., 1979—; dir. Great S.W. Corp., Buckeye Pipe Line Co., Arvida Corp., Edgington Oil Co., Clearfield Bituminous Coal Corp., Penn Towers Inc. Home: 9609 Persimmon Tree Rd Potomac MD 20854 Office: The Penn Central Corp 245 Park Ave New York NY 10003

LEE, CHESTER MAURICE, govt. ofcl.; b. New Derry, Pa., Apr. 6, 1919; s. Joseph and Mary L.; B.S., U.S. Naval Acad., 1941; postgrad. George Washington U., 1962-63; m. Rose McGinnis, Apr. 18, 1942; children—Suzanne D., David J., Virginia A., Nancy M. Commd. ensign U.S. Navy, 1941, advanced through grades to capt., 1961; comdg. officer U.S.S. Rodman, Charleston, S.C., 1952-53; instr. Gen. Line Sch., Long Beach, Calif., 1953-56; with Spl. Projects Office, Bur. Naval Weapons, Washington, 1956-58, 60-62; comdg. officer U.S.S. Gyatt, Washington, 1958-60; comdr. Destroyer Div. 132, Long Beach, 1963-64; with Office Sec. Def., Washington, 1964-65; ret., 1965; with NASA, Washington, 1965—, dir. Apollo Mission, 1969-72, program dir. Apollo/Soyuz Test Project, 1973-75, dir. space transp. systems ops., 1975—. Decorated Navy Commendation medal; recipient two Exceptional Service medals, 1969, Distinguished Service medals, 1973, 75, NASA. Mem. Am. Inst. Aeros. and Astronautics, Am. Astronautic Soc. Office: 600 Independence Ave SW Washington DC 20546*

LEE CHING WEN, educator; b. Yunnan, China, Nov. 19, 1921; s. S.C. and S. (Lee) L.; B.S., Nat. Inst. Tech., China, 1944; M.S., Ill. Inst. Tech., 1956, Ph.D., 1958; m. Chi-en Chiang, Oct. 20, 1951; 1 son, Harry F. Came to U.S., 1954, naturalized, 1964; staff mem. IBM Corp. Lab., Edicott, N.Y., 1959-60; asst. prof. Case Inst. Tech., 1960-62; asso. prof. U. Tenn., 1962-66, prof. engring. sci., 1966—; cons. Oak Ridge Nat. Lab., 1967-72. Mem. ASME, Am. Soc. Engring. Edn., Am. Acad. Mechanics, Sigma Xi. Contbr. articles to profl. jours. Home: 8300 Bennington Dr Knoxville TN 37919

LEE, CHONG-SIK, polit. scientist; b. Anju, Korea, July 30, 1931; s. Bong-Joo and Bong-kye (Moon) L.; came to U.S., 1954, naturalized, 1969; B.A., U. Calif., Los Angeles, 1956, M.A., 1957, Ph.D., Berkeley, 1961; m. Myung-Sook Woo, Mar. 19, 1962; children—Sharon, Gina, Roger. Instr. polit. sci. U. Colo., Boulder, 1960-61, Dartmouth Coll., Hanover, N.H., 1961-63; asst. prof. U. Pa., Phila., 1963-65, asso. prof., 1965-73, prof., 1973—; chmn. joint com. on Korean Studies, Social Sci. Research Council and Am. Council Learned Socs., 1970-77. Mem. Task Force on Equal Ednl. Opportunity and Quality Edn., Pa. Higher Edn. Planning Commn., 1977. Social Sci. Research Council grantee, 1963, 66-67, 72, 73-74; Rockefeller Found. grantee, 1965-66; Ford Found. faculty fellow, 1969-70. Mem. Am. Polit. Sci. Assn. (Woodrow Wilson Found. award for best book in polit. sci. 1974), Assn. Asian Studies. Author: The Politics of Korean Nationalism, 1963; Counterinsurgency in Manchuria: The Japanese Experience, 1931-40, 1967; (with Robert A. Scalapino) Communism in Korea, 1973; The Life of Kim Kyu-sik, 1974; Materials on Korean Communism, 1945-47, 1977; The Korean Workers' Party: A Short History, 1978; mem. editorial bd. Asian Survey, 1973—. Home: 8 Cypress Ln Berwyn PA 19312 Office: Dept Polit Sci Univ Pa Philadelphia PA 19104. *Life is full of disappointments and even calamities that turn out to be disguised blessings. Work hard, be true to yourself, and hope that the opportunity will knock one more time.*

LEE, CHRISTOPHER FRANK CARANDINI, actor, author; b. London, May 27, 1922; U.S. resident, 1976; s. Geoffrey Trollope and Estelle Marie (Carandini) L.; student Brit. schs.; m. Birgit Kroencke, Mar. 17, 1971; 1 dau., Christina Erika. With theatrical and film industry, 1947—; films include: Corridor of Mirrors, 1947, The Curse of Frankenstein, 1956, Dracula, 1958, The Three Musketeers, 1974, The Man with the Golden Gun, 1974, Airport 77, 1977, Caravans, 1978, Return from Witch Mountain, 1978, Circle of Iron, 1979, The Passage, 1979, The Wicker Man, 1979, Jaguar Lives, 1979; author: (autobiography) Tall Dark and Fearsome, 1977, The Great Villains, 1979, Archives of Evil. Served with RAF, 1941-46. Decorated Polonia Restituta, Czechoslovak Medal for Valor, officer Arts, Lettres et Scis. France. Mem. Acad. Motion Picture Arts and Scis., Am. Film Inst., Screen Actors Guild, Brit. Actors Equity, Variety, Clubs Internat. Conservative. Mem. Ch. of Eng. Clubs: Hon. Company Edinburgh Golfers; Marylebone Cricket, Bucks's (London); Travellers (Paris); Bel-Air Country (Los Angeles). Office: care Littman/Addis Co 409 N Camden St Beverly Hills CA 90210

LEE, DAVID MORRIS, physicist, educator; b. Rye, N.Y., Jan. 20, 1931; s. Marvin and Annette (Franks) L.; A.B., Harvard, 1952; M.S., U. Conn., 1955; Ph.D. in Physics, Yale, 1959; m. Dana Thorangkul, Sept. 7, 1960; children—Eric B., James M. Mem. faculty Cornell U., 1959—, prof. physics, 1968—; vis. asso. scientist Brookhaven Nat. Lab., Upton, N.Y., 1966-67; vis. prof. U. Fla., 1974-75. Served with AUS, 1952-54. Co-recipient Sir Francis Simon Meml. prize Brit. Inst. Physics, 1976. DuPont grad. fellow, 1957-58; Guggenheim fellow, 1966-67, 74-75; Japan Soc. for Promotion of Sci. fellow, 1977. Mem. Am. Phys. Soc., AAAS. Co-discoverer superfluid phases of liquid 3He. Home: 38 Woodcrest Ave Ithaca NY 14850

LEE, DON L. (HAKI R. MADHUBUTI), writer, educator; b. Little Rock, Feb. 23, 1942; s. Jimmy and Maxine (Graves) L. Writer-in-residence Howard U., 1970-75; dir. Inst. Positive Edn.; editor, pub. Third World Press; editor Black Books Bull. Author: Black Pride, 1968; Directionscore-Selected and New Poems, 1971; Don't Cry, Scream, 1969; Think Black, 3d edit., 1967; We Walk the Way of the World, 1970; Dynamite Voices—Black Poets of the 1960's; From Plan to Planet; Life Studies: The Need for African Minds and Institutions; Book of Life, 1974; Enemies: The Clash of Races, 1978. Served with AUS, 1960-63. Address: 7524 S Cottage Grove Ave Chicago IL 60619

LEE, E. BRUCE, educator; b. Brainerd, Minn., Feb. 1, 1932; s. Ernest R. and Hazel A. (Bruce) L.; B.S., U. N.D., 1954, M.S., 1955; Ph.D., U. Minn., 1960; m. Judith D. Paine, Sept. 4, 1954; children—Brian, Kevin, Timothy, Joel, Cara Lyn, Elizabeth. Instr., U. N.D., 1954-55; research scientist Honeywell, Inc., Mpls., 1955-62; vis. scientist Research Inst. for Advanced Studies, Balt., 1962-63; prof. computer sci., control sci. and elec. engring. U. Minn., Mpls., 1963—, head dept. computer information and control sci., 1969-71, head dept. elec. engring., 1976—; cons. problems of systems Honeywell, Inc., Univac. Recipient Gold Medal award Pi Tau Sigma, 1961. Sigma Tau fellow, 1954-55. Mem. IEEE, Soc. for Indsl. and Applied Math., Sigma Xi, Sigma Tau. Author: Foundations of Optimal Control Theory, 1967. Home: 1705 Innsbruck Pkwy Minneapolis MN 55421

LEE, E(UGENE) STANLEY, engr., mathematician, educator; b. Hopeh, China, Sept. 7, 1930; s. Ing Yah and Lindy (Hsieng) L.; came to U.S., 1955, naturalized, 1961; M.S., N.C. State U., 1957; Ph.D., Princeton U., 1962; m. Mayanne Lee, Dec. 21, 1957; children—Linda J., Margaret H. Research engr. Phillips Petroleum Co., Bartlesville, Okla., 1960-66; asst. prof. Kans. State U., Manhattan, 1966-67, asso. prof., 1967-69, prof. indsl. engring., 1969—; prof. U. So. Calif., 1972-76; cons. govt. and industry. Dept. Def. grantee, 1967-72; Office Water Resources grantee, 1968-75; EPA grantee, 1969-71; NSF grantee, 1971—; Dept. Agr. grantee, 1978—. Mem. Am. Inst. Chem. Engrs., Soc. Indsl. and Applied Math., Ops. Research Soc. Am., Sigma Xi, Tau Beta Pi, Phi Kappa Phi. Author: Quasilinearization and Invariant Imbedding, 1968; Coal Conversion Technology, 1979; editor Energy Sci. and Tech., 1975—; asso. editor Jour. Math. Analysis and Applications, 1974—, Computers and Mathematics with Applications, 1974—. Office: Dept Indsl Engring Kans State U Manhattan KS 66506

LEE, EDWARD MATTHEW, JR., pub. co. exec.; b. Springfield, Mass., Sept. 28, 1935; s. Edward M. and Helen L. (Patrell) L.; B.B.A., U. Mass., 1957; M.B.A., Harvard U., 1964; m. Jill Dana, Aug. 22, 1964; children—Dana Elizabeth, Deborah Ellen, R. Michael, Edward Matthew III. Field rep. Aetna Life & Casualty, Hartford, Conn., Providence, Buffalo, Boston, 1957-62; with Basic Systems, Inc., 1964-67, regional mgr., Chgo., 1965, nat. sales mgr., N.Y.C., 1965, dir. sales and mktg., 1966, asst. to v.p. ops. Xerox Edn. Group, 1967; asst. to pres., dir. corporate communications Indian Head, Inc., N.Y.C., 1968-70, v.p. mktg., info. handling services div., Denver, 1970; pres. Info. Handling Services, Englewood, Colo., 1971—; dir. Research Media Inc., Cambridge, Mass., 1968-77, Nat. Micrographics Assoc., Silver Spring, Md., 1971—, dir., 1974-77, treas., 1976-79; dir. Visa Oil Corp., 1978—, Women's Bank of Denver, 1979—, Energy Mgmt. Corp., 1979—; participant U.S./China trade agreement negotiations, Peking, 1979. Chmn. bus. adv. bd. Colo. Women's Coll., Denver, 1977—; exec. in residence U. Denver, 1978, mem. Career Adv. Com.; bd. dirs. Kent-Denver Country Day Sch., 1978—, Leadership Denver, 1974—, Colo. Dist. Export Council, 1978—. Served with U.S. Army, 1957-58. Recipient Employer of the Year award, Pres.'s Com. on Employment of Handicapped and Nat. Assn. for Mental Health, 1973; Mobil Oil Corp. Internat. scholar, 1963. Mem. Info. Industry Assn. (dir. 1976—), Young Pres. Orgn. Clubs: Antique Automobile of Am., Vet. Motor Car of Am., Metro Denver Exec. (dir. 1977—), Classic Car Am., Rolls Royce Owners, Denver Athletic, Harvard of N.Y.C., Arapahoe Tennis, Arlberg, Cherry Hills Country. Home: 2655 Cherryridge Rd Cherry Hills CO 80110 Office: 15 Inverness Way E Englewood CO 80150

LEE, EUGENE CANFIELD, educator, univ. ofcl.; b. Berkeley, Calif., Sept. 19, 1924; s. Edwin Augustus and Edna (Canfield) L.; B.A., U. Calif. at Los Angeles, 1946; M.A., U. Calif., Berkeley, 1950, Ph.D., 1957; m. Jane Gale Myers, Apr. 18, 1953; children—Douglas Edwin, Nancy Gale. Asst. to city mgr. San Leandro, Calif., 1948-50; faculty U. Calif. at Berkeley, 1955—, asso. prof., 1962-69, prof., 1969—, asst. to chancellor, 1955-57, asst. to pres., 1958-59, 73-76, asst. dir. Inst. Govt. Studies, 1959-63, asso. dir., 1964-65, dir. inst., 1967—; research polit. scientist (Rockefeller grantee to polit. sci. dept.) Inst. Pub. Adminstrn., U. Coll. Dar es Salaam, Tanganyika, 1963-64, v.p.-exec. asst. U. Calif., 1965-67; adviser to pres. U. P.R., 1976-77; cons. UN U., Tokyo, 1976; staff cons. Calif. Congressional del., 1979. Chmn. Commn. Calif. Govt. Orgn. and Economy, 1961-63; mem. Calif. Fair Campaign Practices Com., 1962-66; tech. adv. com. Carnegie Commn. Higher Edn., 1970-76. Trustee Pub. Adminstrn. Service, 1968-76; chmn. bd. dirs. Calif. Center for Research and Edn. in Govt., 1972—. Exec. asst. Democratic gov. candidate Calif., 1954. Mem. Am. Polit. Sci. Assn., Am. Soc. Pub. Adminstrn., No. Calif. Polit. Sci. Assn. (pres. 1965-66). Conglist. Author: The Politics of Nonpartisanship: A Study of California City Elections, 1960; California Votes, 1928-60, 1963; co-author: The California Governmental Process, 1966; The Challenge of California, 1970, 2d edit., 1976; The Multicampus University: A Study of Academic Governance, 1971; California Votes, 1960-72, 1974; Managing Multicampus Systems, 1975. Contbr. articles to profl. jours. Home: 3805 Palo Alto Dr Lafayette CA 94549 Office: U Calif Berkeley CA 94720

LEE, FRANK HERBERT, educator; b. Mansfield, Ohio, Dec. 13, 1900; s. Howard Edgar and Helena (Frank) L.; A.B., Miami U., Oxford, Ohio, 1923; A.M., Columbia, 1932; D.Sc. (hon.), Marlboro Coll., 1956, LL.D., Hendrix Coll., 1962; m. Carolynn Lampson, Sept. 15, 1923; children—Mary Emilie, Frank Lampson; m. 2d, Lorraine A. Leland, Apr. 6, 1958. Asst. dept. drawing Miami U., 1922-23; teaching fellow Ohio State U., 1923-24; instr. drafting Columbia, 1924-34, asso., 1934-42, asst. prof., 1942-46, asso. prof., 1946-52, prof., 1952-69, prof. emeritus, 1969—, dir. spl. projects Henry Krumb Sch. Mines, Sch. Engring. and Applied Sci., 1969—, chmn. dept. graphics, 1952-69, asst. to dean Columbia Coll., 1942—, adminstrv. asst. to dean engring. 1952—, co-founder faculty childrens tuition remission plan, co-founder, chmn. bd. Tuition Exchange; chief draftsman Peele Co., Bklyn., 1929; cons. Richmond Fireproof Door Co., N.Y.C.,; mem. scholarship com., tng. cons. Grumman Aircraft, 1942—. Recipient Great Tchr. award Soc. Older Grads., 1961. Mem. ASME, Am. Soc. Engring. Edn., Sigma Chi. Ind. Democrat. Episcopalian. Clubs: Men's Faculty, Columbia University (N.Y.C.). Home: 2 Bayberry Ridge Roslyn NY 11576 Office: 814 S W Mudd Columbia U New York City NY

LEE, FREDERICK BILLINGS, lawyer; b. Woodstock, Vt., Aug. 2, 1906; s. Frederic Schiller and Laura (Billings) L.; student Stanford, 1924-25; A.B. cum laude, Harvard, 1928, LL.B., 1931; m. Jane Pillow Rightor, May 7, 1938; children—Jane Lee Wolfe, Frederick Billings, Laura Lee Kent. Admitted to N.Y. bar, 1932, D.C. bar, 1949, U.S. Supreme Ct. bar, 1954; gen. practice law Simpson Thacher & Bartlett, N.Y.C., 1931-41; asso. with CAA as program planning officer, exec. asst. to adminstr., dep. adminstr., acting adminstr., then dep. adminstr., 1952-53, adminstr., 1953-55; gen. practice law, 1955-56, 72—; v.p., asso. counsel Olin Corp., Washington, 1956-72. Served to comdr. UNSR, 1941-45. Mem. Inst. Aero. Scis., United Planing Orgn. (pres., chmn. bd. 1962-71), Assn. Bar City N.Y. Clubs: Century, Harvard (N.Y.C.); Metropolitan, International (Washington); Chevy Chase (Md.). Author: Instrument Flight, 1943; Instrument Flight—Theory and Practice, 1943; Notes on Contact Cross-Country Flying, 1942; Charging for Federal Airways Services, 1946. Home: 1327 Potomac School Rd McLean VA 22101 Office: 1825 K St NW Washington DC 20006

LEE, FREDERICK YUK LEONG, physician, educator; b. Honolulu, Sept. 18, 1937; s. Harold K.L. and Frances Y. (Sugai) L.; student U. Hawaii, 1955-58; M.D., Tulane U., 1962; m. Linda Scott Partridge, June 21, 1974; 1 dau., Suelin K.O.; children by previous marriage—Mark K.C., Michelle Y.C., Monica Y.Y. Rotating intern Charity Hosp., New Orleans, 1962-63, resident obstetrics and gynecology, 1966-69, instr., chief resident, 1968-69; mem. faculty Tulane U. Sch. Medicine, 1969-78; John Rock prof. reproductive physiology dept. obstetrics and gynecology, 1974-78, clin. prof., 1978—, dir. sec. reproductive physiology, 1975-78, program dir. studies infertility and fertility, 1973-78, dir. ultra-sound unit, 1974-78. Served to capt. M.C., USAF, 1962-66. Recipient Sidney K. Simon Meml. prize Tulane U. Med. Sch., 1962; fellow USPHS, 1969-70. Fellow A.C.S., Am. Coll. Obstetricians and Gynecologists; mem. La., New Orleans, Conrad G. Collins and Jefferson obstetrics and gynecol. socs., New Orleans Grad. Med. Assembly, Am. Fertility Soc., Am. Inst. Ultrasound in Medicine, Central Assn. Obstetricians and Gynecologists, La., Orleans Parish med socs., Sigma Xi. Contbr. articles to med. jours. Home: 1401 Colony Rd Metairie LA 70003 Office: 4720 I-10 Service Rd Metairie LA 70002

LEE, GARY A., congressman; b. Buffalo, 1933; B.A., M.A., Colgate U., 1960; postgrad. Cornell U., 1963; m. Kathleen Ann O'Brian, 1958; children—Karen, Brian, Jeffrey, Diane. Tchr., Corning (N.Y.) City Sch. Dist., 1960-63; dir. scholarships and fin. aid Cornell U., 1963-75; mem. N.Y. Assembly from 128th Dist., 1974-78; mem. 96th Congress from N.Y. 33d dist.; mem. adv. com. univ. fin. N.Y. State Regents, 1970-72. Alderman Corning Common Council, 1961-63; councilman Town of Dryden (N.Y.), 1965-67, supr., 1968-69; mem. Tompkins County (N.Y.) Bd. Suprs., 1968-69, 70-74, chmn., 1974; chmn. Tompkins County Republican Party, 1969-74; mem. N.Y. State Rep. Com., 1972. Served with AUS, 1952-56; Korea. Mem. Am. Legion, Tompkins County C. of C., Finger Lakes Assn., Varna Community Assn. Home: 940 Dryden Rd Ithaca NY 14850 Office: Ho of Reps care Postmaster of House Room 513 Cannon House Office Bldg Washington DC 20515

LEE, GARY EDWIN, lawyer; b. Pampa, Tex., Dec. 15, 1944; s. Walter E. and Nancy (Caudell) L.; B.S., W. Tex. State U., 1967; J.D., U. Houston, 1970; m. Ruth Ocine Chism, Feb. 23, 1962; children—Beverli Jean, Greg Anthony. Admitted to Tex. bar, 1970; mem. firm Funderburk & Funder-Burk, Houston, 1970-71; partner Lee & Pettitt, Houston, 1971, Werner & Rusk, and predecessor firm, Houston, now partner firm Bates, Lee and McCool. Mem. Am., Tex., Houston, Houston Jr. bar assns., U. Houston Coll. Law Alumni Assn. (dir.), Phi Alpha Delta. Home: 9322 Willow Meadow Houston TX 77071 Office: 9809 Rowlett Suite 200 Houston TX 77002

LEE, GEORGE C., civil engr., univ. adminstr.; b. Peking, China, July 17, 1933; s. Shun C. and J. T. (Chang) L.; B.S., Taiwan U., 1955; M.S. in Civil Engring., Lehigh U., 1958, Ph.D., 1960; m. Grace S. Su, July 29, 1961; children—David S., Kelvin H. Research asso. Lehigh U., 1960-61; mem. faculty dept. civil engring., SUNY, Buffalo, 1961—, prof., 1967—, chmn. dept., 1974-77, dean faculty of engring. and applied scis., 1978—; head engring. mechanics sect. NSF, Washington, 1977-78; sci. cons. Nat. Heart Lung and Blood Inst. Recipient Adams Meml. award Am. Welding Soc., 1974; Superior Accomplishment award NSF, 1977. Mem. ASCE, Am. Welding Soc., Welding Research Council, Structural Stability Research, Council,

Am. Soc. Engring. Edn., AAAS, Sigma Xi, Chi Epsilon, Tau Beta Pi. Author: Structural Analysis and Design, 1979. Contbr. articles to profl. jours. Home: 288 Countryside Ln Williamsville NY 14221 Office: 203 Fronczak Hall SUNY Buffalo Amherst NY 14260

LEE, GEORGE HAMOR, scientist, educator; b. Oakmont, Pa., June 3, 1908; s. Alfred McClung and Edna (Hamor) L.; B.S., U. Pitts., 1936; M.S. in Engring. (Westinghouse Research asso.), Cornell U., 1937, Ph.D. (McMullen research scholar), 1940; m. Dora Maye Raymo, Oct. 12, 1929 (div. 1963); 1 son, George Hamor II; m. 2d, Lola Frances Madagan, Sept. 19, 1963. With Aluminum Research Labs., New Kensington, Pa. and Massena, N.Y., 1927-33; instr. mechanics Cornell U., 1937-40, asst. prof., 1941-45, asso. prof., 1945, coordinator, supr. math. and mechanics for engring., sci. and mgmt. war tng. program, 1941-45; instr. mechanics Carnegie Inst. Tech., 1940-41; asso. prof. mech. engring. U.S. Naval Postgrad. Sch., 1945-50, prof., 1950-51; prof. mechanics Rensselaer Poly. Inst., 1951-61, asso. head dept., 1952-53, head dept., 1953-55, dir. div. research, 1954-60; chief scientist, dir. research and devel. Office Chief Ordnance, U.S. Army, 1960-62; chief ground warfare tech. Mpls.-Honeywell Regulator Co., Washington, 1962-63; prof. aerospace engring. U. Cin., 1963-74, emeritus, 1974—, adminstr. univ. research, asso. dean Grad. Sch., 1963-67, asst. v.p. for research (scis. and engring.), 1967-74, cons. to exec. v.p. for acad. affairs, 1971—. Cons. Babcock & Wilcox Co., 1942, Naval Ordnance Lab., 1949-51; chmn. sci. adv. com. KDI, Inc., Cin., 1963-64; mem. adv. com. Eglin AFB, U. Pa.; dir. Center Study Aging, Inc.; Albany, N.Y. Mem. exec. com. Nat. Conf. Adminstrn. Research, 1958-59; mem. Nat. Miniturization Awards Com., 1957—. Fellow A.A.A.S.; mem. ASME (sponsor exptl. stress analysis applied mech. div. 1952-54, research com. mech. pressure responsive elements 1953—), A.A.U.P., Am. Soc. Engring. Edn., Am. Ordnance Assn., Assn. U.S. Army, Sigma Xi, Sigma Chi, Atmos. Clubs: University (pres. 1950-51); Annapolis (Md.); Engineers (N.Y.C.); Troy (N.Y.) Country; Albany Camera. Author: An Introduction to Experimental Stress Analysis, 1950. Contbr. articles to profl. jours., Am. Civil Engring. Practice. Home: 2856 Almester Dr Cincinnati OH 45211

LEE, GILBERT LAMONT, JR., univ. adminstr.; b. Pontiac, Mich., Aug. 10, 1919; s. Gilbert Lamont and Delia (Flint) L.; B.A., Mich. State U., 1941; M.B.A., U. Mich., 1947; m. Lorraine Merton, Feb. 4, 1944; children—Linda (Mrs. Jeffrey Swope), Barbara (Mrs. John Nama), Nancy. Auditor, Iceman, Johnson & Hoffman, Ann Arbor, Mich., 1947-51; successively accountant, controller, v.p. bus. affairs U. Mich., 1951-67; v.p. bus. and finance U. Chgo., 1967-72; pres. Assn. Univs. for Research in Astronomy, 1972-78; asst. chancellor U. Wis. at Milw., 1978—; mem. faculty workshop for coll. bus. mgmt. U. Nebr., 1958—; cons. examiner N. Central Assn. Bd. dirs. Ann Arbor United Fund, 1965-67, Episcopal Student Found., 1955-67, Mich. Children's Aid Soc., 1959-65, Univ. Corp. Atmospheric Research, 1959; trustee Tucson Med. Center, 1973-78; mem. vis. com. Harvard, 1969-74. Served to lt. col. USAAF, 1941-46. C.P.A., Mich. Mem. Nat. Assn. Coll. and Univ. Bus. Officers (chmn. com. accounting principles), Am. Inst. C.P.A.'s, Mich. Assn. C.P.A.'s, Tucson C. of C., Phi Kappa Phi, Beta Gamma Sigma, Beta Alpha Psi. Episcopalian. Clubs: Old Pueblo, Tucson Nat. Golf. Home: 9620 N Linde Ct Mequon WI 53092 Office: Chapman Hall U Wis Milwaukee WI 53201

LEE, GLENN RICHARD, univ. adminstr.; b. Ogden, Utah, May 18, 1932; s. Glenn Edwin and Thelma (Jensen) L.; B.S., U. Utah, 1953, M.D., 1956; m. Pamela Marjorie Ridd, July 18, 1969; children—Jennifer, Cynthia. Intern, Boston City Hosp.-Harvard U., 1956-57, resident 1957-58; clin. asso. Nat. Cancer Inst., NIH, 1958-60; postdoctoral fellow U. Utah, 1960-63; instr., U. Utah Coll. Medicine, 1963-64, asst. prof. internal medicine, 1964-68, asso. prof., 1968-73, prof., 1973—, asso. dean for acad. affairs, 1973-76, dean Coll. Medicine, 1978—. Served with USPHS, 1958-60. Markle Found. scholar, 1965-70; Nat. Inst. Arthritis, Metabolic and Digestive Disease grantee, 1977—. Mem. A.C.P., Am. Soc. Hematology, Am. Soc. Clin. Investigation, Western Assn. Physicians, Am. Inst. Nutrition. Mormon. Author: (with others) Clinical Hematology, 7th edit., 1974. Contbr. numerous articles to profl. jours.; editorial bd. Am. Jour. Hematology, 1976-79. Home: 3781 Ruth St Salt Lake City UT 84117 Office: 60 N Medical Dr Salt Lake City UT 84132

LEE, GUS CHARLES, govt. ofcl.; b. Galveston, Tex., July 28, 1914; s. Jack L. and Stella (Deussen) L.; B.A., U. Tex., 1938, M.A., 1940, LL.B., 1941; m. Elizabeth Sharp, Mar. 16, 1940; children—Charles Richard, Anna Elizabeth, James Holland. Personnel dir. City of Austin, Tex., 1940; asst. dir. Tex. Merit System Council, 1941-42; personnel methods cons. Social Security Bd., 1943; personnel tng. dir. U.S. Employmnt Service for Tex., 1944-46; dir. orgn. and methods div., zone office War Assets Adminstrn., 1946-47; orgn. analyst Office Sec. Def., 1948, dir. orgn. and methods div., 1949-51, chief manpower utilization surveys div., 1951-53, dir. manpower utilization, 1953-59, dir. manpower requirements and utilization, 1959-61, dir. manpower requirements, utilization and civilian personnel, 1961-67, dir. manpower mgmt. and utilization, 1967-70, dir. procurement policy, staff dir. Project Vol. for ending the draft, 1970—, spl. asst. for All Vol. Force, 1974-75; sr. staff scientist Human Resources Research Orgn., 1975—. Bd. dirs. YMCA Boy's Camp. Mem. Armed Forces Mgmt. Assn. (dir.), Am. Assn. Pub. Adminstrn., Soc. for Advancement Mgmt. Club: Tejas (Austin). Author: Ending the Draft: The Story of the All Volunteer Force, 1977. Home: 5309 Falmouth Rd Westmoreland Hills MD Office: The Pentagon Washington DC 20301

LEE, HARLEY CLYDE, cons., mining engr., indsl. exec., b. Belleville, Ohio, Nov. 7, 1901; s. Charles H. and Clara (Hissong) L.; B.M.E., Ohio State U., 1927; m. Elizabeth Keedick, June 4, 1932. Dir. research Basic, Inc., Cleve., 1931-41, v.p., tech. dir., 1945-61, dir., 1953—, vice chmn., 1961-64, v.p. tech., 1962-74; supt. tech. dept. Basic Magnesium Inc., 1941-45; dir. Elgin Electronics, Inc. Recipient Lamme medal eminence in engring. Ohio State U., 1958. Fellow Am. Ceramic Soc., Am. Mineral Soc.; mem. Am. Chem. Soc., Am. Inst. Mining and Metall. Engrs., Am. Soc. Metals, ASTM, Geol. Soc. Am., Electrochem. Soc., Sigma Xi, Tau Beta Pi. Clubs: Union, Mayfield Country, Skating (Cleve.). Contbr. papers to tech. lit. Patentee in field. Home: 2675 Ashley Rd Cleveland OH 44122 Office: Hanna Bldg Cleveland OH 44115

LEE, HELEN, clothing designer; b. Knoxville, Tenn., Aug. 15, 1908; d. William Baxter and Elizabeth Douglas (Matthews) Lee; student U. Tenn., 1927-28, Traphagen Sch. Design, N.Y.C., 1929-30; m. Robert Graham Lewis, Apr. 7, 1933; 1 dau., Lee Lewis Ball; m. 2d, Theodore Grant Caldwell, Jan. 16, 1940; 1 dau., Jenni Caldwell Higginbotham. Designer, Joseph Love, N.Y.C., 1930-34, L. Wohl, N.Y.C., 1934-50, Rosenau Bros., N.Y.C., 1950-51, Sam Landorf & Co., N.Y.C., 1951-59; head designer, v.p. Alyssa, N.Y.C., 1959-71; founder, pres. Designs by Helen Lee, N.Y.C., 1971—; design critic Parsons Sch. Design, 1960-67. Recipient Coty award, 1953. Mem. Council Am. Fashion Designers (dir.), Fashion Group. Office: 1441 Broadway New York City NY 10018

LEE, JACK (JIM SANDERS BEASLEY), broadcast exec.; b. Buffalo Valley, Tenn., Apr. 14, 1936; s. Jesse McDonald and Nelle Viola (Sanders) Beasley; student Wayne State U., 1955-57; B.A Albion Coll., 1959; m. Barbara Sue Looper, Sept. 1, 1961; children—Laura Ann, Elizabeth Jane, Sarah Kathleen. Announcer, WHUB, Cookeville, Tenn., 1956; news dir., program dir. WALM, Albion, Mich., 1957-59; radio-TV personality WKZO-Radio-TV, Kalamazoo, 1960-62; prodn. dir. WKMH-WKNR, Detroit, 1962-63; gen. mgr. WAUK-AM-FM, Waukesha, Wis., 1963-65; asst. program mgr. WOKY, Milw., 1965-70; program mgr. WTMJ-WKTI, Milw., 1970-76; gen. mgr. WEMP-WNUW, Milw., 1976—; pres. Jack Lee Enterprises, Ltd.; instr. dept. mass communication U. Wis.-Milw.; adviser Nat. Bahal Info. Office; maj., CAP, 1964—; bd. dirs. Milw. Summerfest, Variety Club of Wis. Served with U.S. Army, 1959, 61-62. Decorated Army Commendation medal; Billboard radio program dir. finalist, 1975. Mem. Sales and Mktg. Execs. of Milw., Am. Fedn. Television and Radio Artists, Omicron Delta Kappa, Alpha Epsilon Rho. Home: W 183 N 8521 Lawrence Ct Menomonee Falls WI 53051 Office: 11800 W Grange Ave Hales Corners WI 53130. *It is a constant struggle to balance my greatest gift-the ability to express myself-with my biggest failing-the inability to keep my mouth shut.*

LEE, JAMES BRACKEN, lawyer; b. Price, Utah, Apr. 28, 1930; s. J. Bracken and Margaret D. Lee; B.S., U.S. Mil. Acad., 1952; J.D., George Washington U., 1961; m. Evelyn Brown, Nov. 22, 1978; children—Jamie, Johanna, Jonathan. Admitted to Utah bar; law clk. Utah Supreme Ct., 1960-61; atty. Office of Sec. of State, Utah, 1961-62; mem. firm Parsons, Beale & Latimer, Salt Lake City, 1962—, v.p., 1973-78, pres., 1978—. Chmn. bd. Salt Lake County Bar Legal Services, 1972-75; chmn. bd. Utah Legal Services, 1978—. Served with U.S. Army, 1952-55; served to brig. gen. Army N.G. Mem. Am. Bar Assn., Utah State Bar Assn. (pres. 1977-78), Salt Lake County Bar Assn. (pres. 1968-69). Home: 680 Northcrest Salt Lake City UT 84103 Office: 79 S State Salt Lake City UT 84111

LEE, JAMES EDWARD, petroleum co. exec.; b. Kiln, Miss., Dec. 13, 1921; s. Fitzhugh and Bonnie Mae (Lenoir) L.; B.S., La. Tech. U., 1942; m. Kathleen Ruth Edwards, Apr. 18, 1943; children—Kay Lee Strickland, Janet Lee Havens, Douglas B., James Stephen. Chem. engr. Gulf Oil Corp., Port Arthur, Tex., 1942-47, asst. foreman, Phila., 1947-52, supt., 1953-59, area rep., coordinator, Manila, 1959-63, Tokyo, 1963-66, mng. dir. Kuwait Oil Co., 1966-69, pres. Gulf Oil Co.-Eastern Hemisphere, London, 1969-72, corp. exec. v.p., 1972-73, pres., 1973—, also dir.; dir. Joy Mfg. Co. Bd. dirs. Carnegie-Mellon U., Hwy. Users Fedn., La. Tech. Engring. Found., Pitts. Nat. Bank, Pitts. Theol. Sem., Shady Side Acad., West Penn Hosp. Mem. Am. Petroleum Inst. (dir.), C. of C. Greater Pitts., Internat. Petroleum Expn. and Congress, YMCA. Clubs: Pitts. Field, Rolling Rock, Duquesne. Office: Gulf Bldg Pittsburgh PA 15219

LEE, JAMES GILLIS, pulp and paper mill exec.; b. Panama City, Fla., July 11, 1927; student U. Fla., 1943-45; B. Marine Engring., U.S. Merchant Marine Acad., 1949; m. Barbara L.; children—James Gillis, Douglas, Stephen, Laura. Chief engr. Lykes Bros. Steamship Co., New Orleans, 1949-51; test engr. Combustion Engring. Co., N.Y.C., 1952-55; power plant supt., maintenance supt. Eastex Pulp & Paper Co., Silsbee, Tex., 1955-60; pulp mill supt. Tenn. River Pulp & Paper Cl., Counce, 1960-67; supt. chem. and power depts. Pineville Kraft Corp. (La.), 1967-68; mill mgr. Continental Can Co., Hodge, La., 1968-70, gen. mgr. mfg. Greenwich, Conn., 1970-74; exec. v.p., gen. mgr. Ga. Kraft Co., Rome, 1974—; dir. First Nat. Bank, Rome, Ga.; trustee N.C. State Pulp and Paper Found., Raleigh, 1974-78; me. bus. and industry liaison council Ga. Bus. and Industry Assn.-Ga. Inst. Tech. Mem. TAPPI. Presbyterian. Patentee paper mfg. Home: 7 Saddle Tr Rome GA 30161 Office: 1700 Redmond Circle Rome GA 30161

LEE, JAMES MADISON, army officer; b. Scotts Hills, N.C., Oct. 15, 1926; s. Fitzhugh and Bessie (Peace) L.; B.S., U.S. Mil. Acad., 1950; postgrad. Air Command and Staff Coll., 1959, Armed Forces Staff Coll., 1963, Army War Coll., 1966; m. Martha Jeanne Purcell, Feb. 13, 1954; children—William, Robert, Jennifer. Commd. 2d. lt. U.S. Army, 1950, advanced through grades to lt. gen., 1978; adviser U.S. Mil. Assistance Command, Vietnam, 1964-65; BCT bn. comdr. Ft. Leonard Wood, Mo., 1965-66; br. chief war plans div., asst. dir. plans directorate ODCSOPS, 1967-69; comdg. officer 196th Inf. Brigade, Americal Div., Vietnam, 1969-70; dep. chief legis. liaison Army Dept., Office Sec. Army, Washington, 1971-73; asst. div. comdr. Hdqrs. 1st Cav. Div., Ft. Hood, Tex., 1973-74; chief legis. liaison Office Sec. Army, Washington, 1974-78; chief of staff Allied Forces So. Europe, Naples, Italy, 1978—. Decorated Silver Star, Legion of Merit with two oak leaf clusters, D.F.C., Bronze Star with oak leaf cluster, Purple Heart, Air medal with eleven oak leaf clusters, Vietnamese Cross of Gallantry with palm and gold star. Office: Chief Staff Allied Forces So Europe Box 130 FPO New York NY 09524

LEE, JAMES MICHAEL, educator; b. Bklyn., Sept. 29, 1931; s. James and Emma (Brenner) L.; A.B., St. John's U., 1955; A.M., Columbia, 1956, Ed.D., 1958; m. Marlene Mayr, Oct. 16, 1976. Tchr. gen. sci. N.Y.C. secondary sch., 1955-56, chmn. sci. dept. and coordinator audio-visual aids, 1956-59, substitute tchr. adult edn., 1955-60; lectr. Hunter Coll. Grad. Sch., N.Y.C., 1959-60, Sch. Edn. Seton Hall U., South Orange, N.J., 1959; asst. prof. grad. dept. edn. St. Joseph Coll., West Hartford, Conn., 1959-62, U. Notre Dame, South Bend, Ind., 1962-65, asso. prof., 1965-68, prof., 1968-77, chmn. dept. grad. studies in edn., 1966-71, dir. religious edn. program, 1967-77; prof. U. Ala. in Birmingham, 1977—, chmn. dept. secondary instrn. and ednl. founds., 1977-79; founder, pub. Religious Edn. Press; cons. in field. Fulbright sr. research scholar U. Munich, 1974-75; Religious Edn. Assn. Lilly research tng. fellow, 1974-75. Mem. Assn. Profs. and Researchers in Religious Edn. (exec. com. 1972-73, 78—), Am. Ednl. Research Assn., Nat. Soc. Study Edn., Religious Edn. Assn. (research com. 1970—, dir. 1979—), Soc. for Sci. Study Religion. Author: Principles and Methods of Secondary Education, 1963; Guidance and Counseling in Schools; Foundations and Processes, 1966; Purpose of Catholic Schooling, 1968; Shape of Religious Instruction, 1971; The Flow of Religious Instruction, 1973; Forward Together, 1973. Editor, contbr.: Seminary Education in a Time of Change, 1965, Readings in Guidance and Counseling, 1966, Catholic Education in the Western World, 1967, Toward A Future For Religious Education, 1970, The Religious Education We Need, 1977. Home: 1531 Wellington Rd Homewood AL 35209

LEE, JOANNA, TV writer, dir., producer; b. Newark, N.J., Apr. 7, 1938; d. Harry I. Jacobs; student in theatre arts U. Calif. at Los Angeles, 1952-53; children by previous marriages—Craig Lee, Christopher Ciampa. TV writer, 1960-75; writer The Waltons, CBS-TV, 1973-74; writer-dir.-producer A Pocket Filled With Dreams, 1975 entry to Cannes Film Festival; writer-asso. producer movie Babe, CBS-TV, 1975; writer-producer programs I Want To Keep My Baby, CBS-TV, The Women, ABC-TV, Ziegfeld, CBS-TV; pres. Christiana Prodns.; broadcast preceptor San Francisco State U., 1975—. Recipient Emmy award for Waltons Thanksgiving Spl., Nat. Acad. TV Arts and Scis., 1974; 2 nominations for best TV dramatic episode Writers Guild Am., 1974; Hon. mention Population Inst., 1974. Mem. Women in Film (v.p.). Office: Paramount Studios Marathon St Hollywood CA 90028*

LEE, JOE R., restaurant chain exec.; b. Blackshear, Ga., Dec. 18, 1940; s. John Pope and Audice L. Lee; student Valdosta (Ga.) State Coll., 1966-67; m. Carolyn Dale, Sept. 5, 1961; children—Michael Frederick, Keena Rene. Restaurant mgr. Darden Enterprises, Waycross, Ga., 1967-68; with Red Lobster Inns, Orlando, Fla., 1968-76, 1975-76; v.p. Gen. Mills, Inc., Orlando, 1975—, Gen. Mills Restaurant Group, Inc., Orlando, 1979—; dir. Sun First Nat. Bank, Orlando. Bd. dirs. John Young Museum and Planetarium, Orlando. Mem. Nat. Restaurant Assn. (dir.), Orlando Area C. of C. (dir.). Baptist. Club: Citrus (Orlando). Home: PO Box 38 Gotha FL 32734 Office: PO Box 1431 Orlando FL 32802

LEE, JOHN FRANKLIN, lawyer, assn. exec.; b. Idaho Falls, Idaho, Dec. 7, 1927; s. Wilford D. and Lorine (Hutchinson) L.; B.A., Brigham Young U., 1950; J.D., George Washington U., 1956; diploma Stonier Grad. Sch. Banking, Rutgers U., 1966; m. Patricia Anne Mason, Sept. 15, 1950; children—Randall Mason, Laurelei, John F. Admitted to D.C. bars, 1956; atty. SEC, 1956-59; practice in Salt Lake City, 1959-64; asst. to chmn. Fed. Deposit Ins. Corp., Washington, 1964-66, gen. counsel, 1966-68; exec. v.p. N.Y. Clearing House Assn., N.Y.C., 1968—. Adv. council Brigham Young U. Bd. dirs. Nat. Automated Clearing House Assn., N.Y.C. Community Preservation Corp., Consumer Credit Counseling Service Greater N.Y. Served to lt. comdr. USNR, 1945-46, 51-54. Mem. Order of Coif, Phi Delta Phi. Mem. Ch. of Jesus Christ of Latter-day Saints. Clubs: Recess, Canoe Brook Country. Home: 30 Slope Dr Short Hills NJ 07078 Office: 100 Broad St New York City NY 10004

LEE, JOSEPH BRACKEN, ret. city ofcl.; b. Price, Utah, Jan. 7, 1899; s. Arthur J. and Ida. M. (Leiter) L.; ed. pub. schs.; m. Margaret Draper, Feb. 23, 1928; children—Helen, James B., Margaret Jon, Richard L. Postal clk. U.S. P.O. 1919; ins. agt. Equitable Ins. Co. agy., Price, 1919-30, mgr., owner, 1930—; dir. Equitable Finance Co., Time Finance Co. Salt Lake; mayor Price, 1936-47; gov. Utah, 1949-57; mayor Salt Lake City, 1960-75. Nat. chmn. For America, 1957—; dir. nat. com. to repeal 16th amendment; hon. chmn. Utah Tax Limitation Com., 1978; mem. Utah Bd. Bond drive, World War I; chmn. Carbon Co. Red Cross, 1944-47. Served with inf. U.S. Army, 1917-19; commd. officer Res. Corps, 1919-29. Recipient Freedom Found. award, 1952; Tom McCoy award as outstanding municipal officer Utah, 1967. Mem. Utah Mnicipal League (pres. 1939-40), Carbon Water Conservancy Dist. (sec. 1942—). Republican. Elk (charter), Mason (33 deg., Shriner, knight comdr. Ct. Honor). Home: 2031 Laird Dr Salt Lake City UT 84108

LEE, LAURENCE RAYMOND, pharm. co. exec.; b. Chgo., Feb. 3, 1928; s. Victor L. and Evelyn W. (Plumhoff) L.; Ph.B., U. Chgo., 1946, J.D., 1951; m. Barbara E. Rogers, Jan. 28, 1956; children—Justin, David. Admitted to Ill. bar; atty. Abbott Labs., North Chicago, Ill., 1955-63, sec., gen. counsel, 1963—, v.p., 1972—. Served with U.S. Army, 1946-48. Mem. Am., Chgo. bar assns., Am. Soc. Corporate Secs., Order of Coif. Office: Abbott Labs Abbott Park North Chicago IL 60064

LEE, LAWRENCE JOHN, lawyer; b. St. Louis, Nov. 15, 1934; s. George and Jennie L.; B.A., U. Ill., Urbana, 1955; LL.B. in Internat. Law, Cornell U., 1958; LL.M. in Taxation, Georgetown U., 1961; postgrad. U. Pa. Law Sch.; m. Carol Portante, Nov. 28, 1975; children—Shannon, Erin. Admitted to N.Y. bar, 1958, D.C. bar, 1959, Colo. bar, 1964, Calif. bar, 1967, Pa. bar, 1970, Ariz. bar, 1974; law clk. to judge Tax Ct. U.S., Washington, 1960-62; with firm Robbins, Green, O'Grady & Abbuhl, Phoenix; spl. counsel on taxes City of Phoenix, 1975—; chmn. com. continuing legal edn. State Bar Ariz; speaker at nat., local tax insts. and programs. Mem. Colo. Civil Rights Commn., 1965-67. Served to lt. comdr. Judge Adv. Gen Corps, USNR. Mem. Am. Bar Assn. (spl. adv. com. on continuing legal edn. sect. taxation), Fed. Bar Assn. (chmn. Los Angeles chpt. tax com., vice chmn. estate and gift tax com., pres. Phoenix chpt. 1976), 9th Circuit Fed. Bar Assn. (v.p.), Am. Law Inst., Ariz. State Bar Assn. (v.p. tax com., Outstanding Achievement award 1977). Contbr. numerous articles to profl. jours.; columnist Rev. Taxation of Individuals; bd. editors Practical Lawyer. Office: Robbins Green O'Grady & Abbuhl 1900 Valley Bank Center Phoenix AZ 85073

LEE, LEROY WILLIAM, urol. surgeon; b. Omaha, July 29, 1914; s. Herman Charles and Charlotte May (Du Bois) L.; student U. Chgo., 1932-34; B.Sc., U. Nebr., 1936, M.Sc., 1938, M.D., 1939; m. Dorothy Reed, Dec. 21, 1937; children—Marcia E. (Mrs. Clifford H. Hollestelle), Marie A. (Mrs. William Robert Johnson), Harry R., Roger E. Intern, Phila. Gen. Hosp., 1939-41, resident surgeon, 1943-44; resident urology Hosp. U. Pa., 1941-43; pvt. practice urol. surgery Drs. Lee, Malashock & Frank, Omaha, 1945—; prof., chmn. dept. urology U. Nebr. Coll. Medicine, 1952-70, prof., vice chmn. dept., 1970—; sr. urologist, pres. med. staff Clarkson Meml. Hosp., Omaha; sr. urologist Univ. Hosp., Omaha. Cons. SAC, Offutt AFB, 1950-65, VA Hosp., Omaha, 1956—. Diplomate Am. Bd. Urology. Mem. Nat. Huguenot Soc., Alumni Assn. U. Nebr. Coll. Medicine (pres.), AMA, Am. Urol. Assn., Omaha-Midwest Cln. Soc., Nebr. Med. Assn. (councilor 1963-69), Soc. U. Urologists, S.A.R., Sigma Xi, Alpha Omega Alpha, Phi Chi. Presbyn. (elder). Mason. Contbr. articles to profl. jours. Home: 2517 N 55th St Omaha NE 68104 Office: Doctor's Bldg Omaha NE 68131

LEE, LINWOOD LAWRENCE, JR., educator; b. Trenton, N.J., Aug. 5, 1928; s. Linwood Lawrence and Lucy (Litterst) L.; A.B., Princeton, 1950; M.S., Yale, 1951, Ph.D., 1955; m. Dorothy Tutt, May 18, 1957; 1 son, Linwood L. III. Physicist Argonne Nat. Lab., 1954-65; prof. dept. physics, dir. nuclear structure lab. State U. N.Y. at Stony Brook, 1965—. Fellow Am. Phys. Soc.; mem. Sigma Xi. Home: 8 John's Rd Setauket NY 11733 Office: Dept Physics State Univ NY Stony Brook NY 11790

LEE, M. O., textile co. exec.; b. Indianola, Nebr., Nov. 11, 1911; s. Rual O. and Mayme (Mann) L.; m. Rosalie Hakel, Nov. 27, 1935 (dec.); children—William Frank, Regina Ann, Mary Sylvia, John Manford. With VF Corp. (formerly Vanity Fair Mills, Inc.), Reading, Pa., 1942—, v.p., 1948-59, pres., 1959—, dir., chmn. bd., 1965-69, chmn., 1969—, chief exec. officer, 1969-75; dir. Nat. Central Bank, First Nat. Bank Mobile. Mem. adv. com. Profl. Golf Assn. Clubs: Athelstan, Lakewood Golf (Mobile); Country of N.C. (Pinehurst) Berkshire Country (Reading); Dunes (Cal.) Country; Hemisphere, Metropolitan (N.Y.C.); Kansas City (Mo.). Home: 1333 Van Steffy Ave Wyomissing PA 19610 Office: Box 1022 Reading PA 19603

LEE, MELVIN, educator; b. N.Y.C., Jan. 5, 1926; s. Herman and Rebecca (Panish) L.; B.A., U. Calif. at Los Angeles, 1947, M.Sc., at Berkeley, 1950, Ph.D., 1958; m. Beverly M. Low, Feb. 4, 1949; children—David M., Janice Naomi, Jeffrey Wayne, Ronald Alan. Mem. faculty U. Calif. at San Francisco, 1950-67, asst. prof. nutrition, 1959-67; prof. nutrition, dir. Sch. Home Econs., U. B.C., 1967-74, acting dir., 1975-76, 79-80, prof. nutrition, 1976—; vis. research asso. Nihon U. Sch. Dentistry, Jikei U. Sch. Medicine, Tokyo, Japan, 1976-77. Mem. Am. Inst. Nutrition, Nutrition Soc. Can., Soc. Latinoamericana de Nutricion. Home: 2194 W 33d Ave Vancouver BC V6M 1B9 Canada

LEE, MICHAEL EDWARD, journalist; b. Dallas, Apr. 30, 1942; s. Robert Edward and Jane (Riley) L.; student Lon Morris Jr. Coll., 1960-62, U. Tex., Austin, 1962-65; m. Christine Wilcox, Apr. 15, 1977; children by previous marriage, Aaron, Kate. Reporter, Sta.-KHFI-Radio-TV, Austin, Tex., 1965-66, Sta.-WFAA-Radio-TV, Austin, 1966-68, Sta.-KPIX-TV, San Francisco, 1968-75; news corrs. CBS News, N.Y.C., 1975, Beirut, 1975, London, 1977—; radio and TV coverage Lebanese Civil War, 1975-77 (Sigma Delta Chi Disting. Service award 1976, Overseas Press Club Am. Best Radio Spot News from Abroad 1976, Overseas Press Club award for Best TV Spot, 1976); coverage of Sadat Peace Initiative, 1977-79 (Overseas Press Club award for Best Radio Spot News 1977), Iranian Revolution, 1979. Office: 524 W 57th St New York NY 10019

LEE, NELLE HARPER, author; b. Monroeville, Ala., Apr. 28, 1926; d. Amasa Coleman and Frances (Finch) Lee; student Huntingdon Coll., 1944-45, U. Ala., 1945-49. Author: To Kill a Mockingbird, 1960 (Pulitzer prize for fiction 1961); contbr. to Vogue. Mem. Nat. Council on Arts, 1966-72. Recipient Ala. Library Assn. award, 1961, NCCJ Brotherhood award, 1961. Office: care McIntosh & Otis Inc 18 E 41st St New York NY 10017*

LEE, NORMAN RAY, utility exec.; b. Grayson, La., Oct. 24, 1924; s. John Wesley and Lillie Ellen (Bozone) L.; student La. State U., 1941-43; B.S. in Elec. Engring., Calif. Inst. Tech., 1947; postgrad. Advanced Mgmt. Program, Harvard, 1967; m. Nell Edna Ray, Jan. 15, 1950; children—Norman Ray, Rebecca Nell. Engr., Standard Oil Cal., El Segundo, 1946, Allis-Chalmers, West Allis, Wis., 1947-48; with Gulf States Utilities Co., 1949—, v.p. Baton Rouge div., 1967-68, v.p. La. operations, 1968-69, v.p. div. operations, 1969-70, sr. v.p., 1970-72, exec. v.p., Beaumont, Tex., 1972-73, pres., 1973—, also dir.; dir. Am. Nat. Bank, Beaumont. Served with USNR, 1943-46, 51-52. Registered profl. engr., Tex. Mem. Fellowship Christian Athletes, Beaumont C. of C. (dir., pres.). Methodist. Clubs: Rotary, Beaumont Country. Home: 1220 Wilchester Circle Beaumont TX 77706 Office: PO Box 2951 Beaumont TX 77704

LEE, PEGGY (NORMA DELORES EGSTROM), singer, actress; b. Jamestown, N.D., May 26, 1920; d. Marvin Engstrom; ed. high sch.; m. Dave Barbour, 1943 (div. 1951); 1 dau., Nicki; m. 2d, Brad Dexter, Jan. 4, 1955 (div. 1955); m. 3d, Dewey Martin, Apr. 25, 1956 (div. 1959); m. 4th, Jack del Rio, Mar. 1964 (div. Dec. 1964). Singer Sta. WDAY, Fargo, N.D.; various singing engagements, Mpls.; vocalist Will Osborne's band, Doll House, Palm Springs, Ambassador Hotel West, Chgo., Americana Hotel, Basin St. East, Benny Goodman's Band, 1941-43; concert with Benny Goodman at Melodyland Theatre, Anaheim, Calif., Circle-Star Theatre, San Carlos, Calif.; screen appearance in Mr. Music, 1950, The Jazz Singer, 1953, Pete Kelly's Blues, 1955; performer Revlon Revues CBS-TV, 1960, also mus. variety TV shows, dramatic role Gen. Electric Theater, 1960; composer mus. themes for motion pictures including Johnny Guitar, About Mrs. Leslie, musical score for cartoon feature Tom Thumb; lyricist, supplied several voices for Lady and the Tramp; numerous recs. Capitol Records, 1944, including Golden Earings, You Was Right Baby, It's A Good Day, Manana, and I Don't Know Enough About You, Is That All There Is, (album) I'm A Woman; A and M Records include Mirrors; conducted research, wrote program, performed The Jazz Tree, Philharmonic Hall Lincoln Center for Performing Arts, N.Y.C., 1963. Named Best Female Vocalist, Metronome, Downbeat mags., 1946; Most Popular Vocalist citation Billboard, 1950. Author: (verse) Softly, With Feeling, 1953. Address: care Norby Walters 1290 Ave of Americas Suite 264 New York NY 10019*

LEE, R(AYMOND) WILLIAM, JR., apparel co. exec.; b. Richmond, Va., Apr. 24, 1930; s. Raymond William and Sally (Beal) L.; A.B., Duke U., 1951; m. Marianne Hollingsworth, June 21, 1952; children—Lelia, Carol, Raymond William, III, Sally. With Oxford Industries, Inc., Atlanta, 1955—, v.p. menswear, 1970-77, v.p. fin. and adminstrn., 1977—, also dir. Mem. fin. com. Ga. Republican Com., 1974-75; bd. dirs. Ga. Coop. Services for Blind, 1974—, pres., 1979-80. Served with USMCR, 1951-53. Mem. Am. Apparel Mfrs. Assn. (dir. 1964-70), Men's Fashion Assn. (dir. 1974—), Father's Day Council (dir. 1975—). Republican. Episcopalian. Clubs: Cherokee Town and Country (treas. 1977-78, dir. 1979—), Kiwanis. Home: 6265 Riverside Dr NW Atlanta GA 30328 Office: 222 Piedmont Ave NE Atlanta GA 30308

LEE, RENSSELAER WRIGHT, art historian; b. Phila., June 15, 1898; s. Francis Herbert and Helen (Stavers) L.; A.B., Princeton, 1920, Ph.D., 1926; L.H.D., Northwestern U., 1971; m. Stella Wentworth Garrett, May 27, 1925; children—Julia Rensselaer, Mary Josephine Garrett (Mrs. Cyril Muroncew), Rensselaer Wright. Instr. English, Princeton, 1922-23, 25-28; asso. prof. history art, chmn. dept. Northwestern U., 1931-34, prof., 1934-40, Harris lectr., 1966; prof. art Smith Coll., 1941-48, Columbia, 1948-54, N.Y. U. Inst. Fine Arts, 1954-55; vis. prof. Princeton, 1948, 68-69, chmn. dept. art and archeology, 1955-64, Marquand prof. art and archaeology, 1961-66, prof. emeritus, 1966—, chmn. adv. council dept. classics, 1942-55. Mem. vis. com. dept. fine arts Fogg Mus., Harvard, 1957-63; mem. Inst. Advanced Study, 1939, 42-44, 46-47; adv. council Inst. Fine Arts, N.Y. U. Vice pres. Internat. Fedn. Renaissance Socs. and Insts., 1961-70; v.p. Internat. Council Philosophy and Humane Scis., 1965-71; chmn. presdl. adv. com. on Yale Center for Brit. Art and Brit. Studies, 1972—. Fellow Am. Council Learned Socs., 1930-31, chmn. com. research and publ. fine arts, 1942-44, exec. sec. com. protection cultural treasures in war areas, 1944-45, dir., 1953-61; trustee Am. Acad. in Rome, 1958—, pres., 1968-71. Fellow Am. Acad. Arts and Scis.; mem. Am. Philos. Soc., Archeol. Inst. Am., Coll. Art Assn. Am. (sec. 1939-42, 49-50, pres. 1945-46, hon. dir. 1974—), Mediaeval Acad. Am. (councilor 1961-64), Union Académique Internationale (pres. 1962-65), Renaissance Soc. Am. (exec. bd. 1960-70, pres. 1977—). Episcopalian. Clubs: Grolier, Princeton, Century (N.Y.C.); Cosmos (Washington); Athenaeum (London). Author: Ut pictura poesis, The Humanistic Theory of Painting, 2d edit., 1967, Italian transl., 1974; Names on Trees: Ariosto into Art, 1977. Editor-in-chief Art Bull., 1942-44, editorial bd., 1945—. Contbr. articles and revs. to profl. jours. Home: 120 Mercer St Princeton NJ 08540

LEE, RICHARD VAILLE, physician; b. Islip, N.Y., May 26, 1937; s. Louis Emerson and Erma Natalie (Little) L.; B.S., Yale U., 1960, M.D. cum laude, 1964; m. Susan Bradley, June 25, 1961; children—Matthew, Benjamin. Intern, Grace-New Haven Hosp., 1964-65, asst. resident in internal medicine, 1965-66, 69-70; fellow in inflammatory disease Yale U., New Haven, 1970-71; practice medicine specializing in internal medicine, New Haven, 1969-76, Buffalo, 1976—; practice medicine specializing in family practice, Poplar, Mont., 1966-68, Chester, Mont., 1968-69; asst. prof. medicine Yale U., 1971-74, asso. prof. clin. medicine, 1974-76; prof. medicine State U. N.Y., Buffalo, 1976—, chief div. gen. internal medicine, 1979—; dir. primary care center Yale-New Haven Hosp., 1975-76, dir. med. clinics, 1971-75; chief med. service, Buffalo VA Hosp., 1976-79; head dept. medicine Children's Hosp. of Buffalo, 1979—; cons. internal medicine N.Y. Zool. Soc., 1973—. Served with USPHS, 1966-68. Diplomate Am. Bd. Internal Medicine, Am. Bd. Family Practice. Fellow Am. Acad. Family Practice, A.C.P.; mem. N.Y. Acad. Sci., Am. Fedn. Clin. Research, AMA, Soc. Research and Edn. in Primary Care Medicine, Flying Physicians Assn., Infectious Diseases Soc. Am., Alpha Omega Alpha. Contbr. articles on gen. medicine and infectious diseases to med. jours., also articles on health problems of isolated S. Am. Indian tribes; contbr. chpts. to books on obstetrics; cons. editor Am. Jour. Medicine. Home: 7664 E Quaker Rd Orchard Park NY 14127 Office: 219 Bryant St Buffalo NY 14222

LEE, RICHARD WAYNE, electronics co. exec.; b. Hastings, Nebr., Aug. 20, 1916; s. John C. and Jessie (Reynolds) L.; A.B., Hastings Coll., 1937; A.M., U. Nebr., 1939; postgrad. U. Ill., 1939-42; m. Norma G. Cope, July 27, 1940; children—Karen, Richard, Nancy, Terry. Research asso. radiation lab. Mass. Inst. Tech., 1942-45; project engr. GPL div. Gen. Precision, Inc., Pleasantville, N.Y., 1945-49, dept. head, 1949-52, div. head, 1952-58, v.p. engring., 1956-59, v.p. engring. and research, 1959, pres., 1959-63, pres. Librascope group, 1963-68; v.p., dir. Singer Gen. Precision, Inc., 1968-69; pres. Avionics div. ITT, Nutley, N.J., 1969-71, gen. mgr. Electro-components group, 1971-74, group gen. mgr. Energy Products group, 1974—. Sr. mem. I.E.E.E. Home: 18 Canaan Pl Allendale NJ 07401 Office: 320 Park Ave New York NY 10022

LEE, ROBERT, educator, author; b. San Francisco, Apr. 28, 1929; s. Frank and Shee (Fong) L.; A.B., U. Calif. at Berkeley, 1951; M.A., Pacific Sch. Religion, 1953; B.D. magna cum laude, Union Theol. Sem., 1954; Ph.D., Columbia, 1958; m. May Gong, Feb. 4, 1951; children—Mellanie Lynn, Marcus Arthur, Matthew John, Wendy Gale, Michelle Micho. ordained to ministry United Ch. Christ, 1954, transferred to U.P. Ch., 1961; Western regional exec. sec. Chinese Student Christian Assn., 1949-50; asso. sec. Stiles Hall, Univ. YMCA, Berkeley, Calif., 1950-52; dir. research Protestant Council N.Y., 1954; from instr. to asst. prof. ch. and community Union Theol. Sem., 1955-61; lectr. philosophy Mills Coll. Edn., 1956-57; Margaret Dollar prof. social ethics, dir. Inst. Ethics and Soc., San Francisco Theol. Sem., 1961—; prof., area chmn. Grad. Theol. Union, 1962—. Vis. prof. Union Theol. Sem., summer 1964, Internat. Christian U., Tokyo, Japan, 1964-65, Assn. S.E. Asian Sems., Hong Kong, 1966; vis. scholar Stanford Grad. Sch. Bus., 1971-72; co-optd staff World Council Chs. Conf. Ch. and Soc., Geneva, Switzerland, 1966; lectr., TV appearances, 1956—; cons. ISI Corp., 1971-72, World Coll. West, 1977—; theologian-in-residence Windward Coalition, Kilau, Hawaii, 1980; moderator Inst. Religion and Social Studies, Jewish Theol. Sem., 1960; asso. Columbia Seminar, 1961; sr. fellow East-West Center, Honolulu, 1972-73; bd. advisors Walden U. Adv. com. problems met. soc. U.P. Ch., 1961—, Center Study Democratic Instns., Coll. Marin, 1965—. Bd. sponsors Christianity and Crisis; bd. dirs. Am. Soc. Christian Ethics, Family Service Agy. of Marin, Festival Theatre Found., Planned Parenthood Assn. Marin County, Pacific S.W. Student YMCA, ISI Trust Fund, ISI Growth Fund, ISI Income Fund, Found. for Theol. Edn. S.E. Asia. Mem. Religious Research Assn. (book rev. editor jour. 1959-65), Am. Sociol. Assn., Soc. Religion Higher Edn., Soc. for Sci. Study Religion, Pacific Coast Theol. Group, Center for Ethics and Social Policy. Author: Social Sources of Church Unity (selected for Kennedy White House Library); 1960; Religion and Leisure in America, 1964; Dictionary of Centers for the Study of Society, 1965; Stranger in the Land, 1967; (with Russ Galloway) The Schizophrenic Church, 1969; The Promise of John C. Bennett, 1969; (with Marjorie Casebier) The Spouse Gap, 1971; Marriage Enrichment Sharing Sessions, 1979; Faith and the Prospects of Economic Collapse, 1980; editor: Cities and Churches, 1962; (with Martin E. Marty) Religion and Social Conflict, 1964; The Church and The Exploding Metropolis, 1965. Editor: Action/Reaction; Pacific Theol. Rev. Contbr. to profl. jours., books. Home: 18 Kensington Ct San Anselmo CA 94960

LEE, ROBERT BARTLETT, state justice; b. South Bend, Ind., Nov. 16, 1912; s. Clarence Eugene and Mary Lillian (Jennings) L.; A.B. (Rector scholar), DePauw U., 1935; LL.B. magna cum laude, U. Notre Dame, 1940; grad. Appellate Judges Seminar N.Y. U. Law Sch., 1971; m. Ruth Elisabeth Wade, Sept. 27, 1941; children—Nancy W. (Mrs. Bernard Shavill), Edward B., William P., Judith Ann. Admitted to Ind. bar, 1940, Colo. bar, 1941; practice law, Englewood, Colo., 1941-61; partner firm Lee, Shivers & Banta, 1958-61; dep. dist. atty., Arapahoe County, Colo., 1943-49; dist. judge 18th Jud. Dist. Colo., 1960-69; justice Supreme Ct. Colo., 1969—, mem. com. civil jury instrns., 1965-69; vis. lectr. U. Colo. Law Sch., 1968-77. Mem. adv. com. to com. on amendment no. 1 Colo. Legislative Council, 1963, adv. com. to com. on appellate cts., 1968; chmn. Colo. Commn. Jud. Qualifications, 1967-69; mem. commn. Calif. rural legal assistance Office Econ. Opportunity, 1971. Pres. Englewood Old Timers Assn., 1948; mem. civic adv. council Porter Meml. Hosp., Denver. Mem. Am., Colo., 18th Jud. Dist. (pres. 1959) bar assns., Am. Judicature Soc., Nat. Coll. State Trial Judges, Englewood C. of C. (past dir.). Mason, Elk, Lion (past pres. Englewood). Home: 3144 S Wheeling Way Aurora CO 80014 Office: Colo State Judicial Bldg 2 14th Ave Denver CO 80203

LEE, ROBERT E., govt. ofcl.; b. Chgo., Mar. 31, 1912; s. Patrick and Delia (Ryan) L.; grad. DePaul U., 1935; hon. doctorates U. Notre Dame, St. John's U., N.Y.C.; m. Wilma Rector (dec. Sept. 1972); children—Patricia, Robert E., Michael B.; m. 2d, Rose Bente. Agt., fiscal asst. to J. Edgar Hoover, FBI, 1939-47; dir. surveys and investigations house appropriations com. U.S. Congress, 1947-53; commr. FCC, 1953—, also vice chmn. Vice chmn. space conf., Geneva, Switzerland, 1971, Plenipotentiary Conf., Torremolinos, Spain, 1973; organizer, chmn. Com. for Full Devel. All-Channel Broadcasting, Com. for Full Devel. Instrnl. TV Fixed Service; mem. Radio Tech. Commn. for Aeros.; chmn. U.S. del. to World Adminstrv. Tel. & Tel. Conf., 1973, to World Adminstrv. Radio Conf. for Maritime, 1974, to Conf. for Broadcast Satellites, 1977; mem. telecommunications advisory com. Telecommunications Program, U. Notre Dame, South Bend, Ind.; mem. communications arts advisory council St. John's U.; founder Cath. Apostolate for the Mass Media. Recipient Marconi gold medal, Quarter Century wireless award. Mem. I.E.E.E. Clubs: Capitol Hill, Bolling Air Force Officer's, Congressional County. Home: 2411 N Quebec St Arlington VA 20227

LEE, ROBERT EDWIN, playwright; b. Elyria, Ohio, Oct. 15, 1918; s. Claire Melvin and Elvira (Taft) L.; student Ohio Wesleyan U., 1935-37, Litt.D., 1962; H.H.D., Ohio State U., 1979; m. Janet Waldo, Mar. 29, 1948; children—Jonathan, Lucy. Vice pres. Lawrence & Lee, Inc., 1946—; prof. playwriting Pasadena (Calif.) Playhouse Coll. Theatre Arts, 1964; adj. prof. dept. theatre arts U. Calif. at Los Angeles, 1966—; author (with J. Lawrence) radio program Railroad Hour, 1948-54; author, producer radio and TV program Favorite Story, 1946-54; pres. Am. Playwrights Theatre, 1973; participant Cultural Exchange Mission to USSR, 1971. Recipient Peabody award for best radio program, UN series, 1948; Donaldson award best first play, 1955; Outer Critics Circle award, 1955; Variety Critics Poll award, 1955; citation for disting. service to theatre Am. Theatre Assn., 1979. Author: (book) Television the Revolution, 1945; (Broadway plays) (with Jerome Lawrence) Inherit the Wind, 1955, Auntie Mame, 1956, The Gang's All Here, 1959, Only In America, 1959, A Call on Kuprin, 1961, Diamond Orchid, 1965, The Night Thoreau Spent in Jail, 1970, The Incomparable Max, 1971, Jabberwock, 1972, 10 Days That Shook the World, 1973; Sounding Brass, 1975; First Monday in October, 1977; (Broadway musicals) Look Ma I'm Dancin', 1948, Shangri-La, 1956; (with J. Herman, J. Lawrence) Mame, 1966, Dear World, 1968. Trustee Margo Jones Award. Congregationalist. Home: 15725 Royal Oak Rd Encino CA 91316 Office: MacGowan Hall U Calif at Los Angeles Los Angeles CA 90024. *I believe in change. I believe it is the purpose of the artist—particularly the playwright—to anticipate tomorrow—to project his imagined view of it—so we can prepare for the future with a maximum of sanity and a minimum of despair. To make change enriching, not debasing, is the aim of my work and my life.*

LEE, RONALD BARRY, business exec.; b. N.Y.C., May 26, 1932; s. Kermit James and Lillian Byrant (Jackson) L.; B.S. in Engring., U.S. Mil. Acad., 1954; M.B.A., Syracuse U., 1964; LL.D., Western New Eng. Coll., 1969; M.A., Am. U., 1977, postgrad., 1977—; m. Joyce A. Thomas, 1960 (div. Oct. 1975); 2 sons. Commd. 2d lt. U.S. Army, 1954, advanced through grades to maj., 1965; communications officer 3d Armored Corps, 1954-56; radio and wire communications constrn. engring., Okinawa, 1956-59; part-time radio announcer sta. KSBK, Okinawa, 1957-59; instr. orgn. and staff procedures U.S. Army Signal Sch., 1960-61, instr. plans and operations, 1961, chief operations, officer dept., 1961-62; asst. G-3 (operations) adviser Vietnamese 9th Div., 1962-63; chief electronic system sect., evaluation br. systems analysis Army Material Command, 1964-65; White House fellow, 1965-66; resigned commn., 1966; mem. staff Lawrence F. O'Brien, The White House, 1965; asst. to postmaster gen., 1965-66, dir. office planning and systems analysis, 1966-68; asst. provost, dir. Center for Urban Affairs, prof. Mich. State U., 1968-69; asst. postmaster gen. for planning and marketing, 1969-72; with Xerox Corp., Stamford, Conn., 1972-73, White Plains, N.Y., 1973-75, regional mgr. Des Plaines, Ill., 1975-78, mgr. govt., edn. and med. mktg., Rochester, N.Y., 1978-79, mgr. bus. and community affairs, Washington, 1979—; pres. LPX, Inc., N.Y.C., 1976—; lectr. in field. Mem. Weston (Conn.) Police Commn., 1973-75. Trustee Western New Eng. Coll., 1969-75; bd. advisers, trustee Woodrow Wilson Sch. (Princeton), 1969-75; bd. dirs. Zion Investment Assn., 1970-76. Decorated Army Commendation medal with oak leaf cluster; named Neighbor of Month, Springfield, Mass., June 1950; recipient Arthur S. Flemming award, 1968. Mem. N.A.A.C.P., Nat. Urban League, Assn. West Point Grads, Assn. Syracuse Army Comptrollers, Am. Soc. Pub. Adminstrn., White House Fellows Assn. (1st pres. 1966), Am. Acad. Polit. and Social Sci., Nat. Acad. Pub. Adminstrn. (trustee), Beta Gamma Sigma, Alpha Phi Alpha. Contbr. articles to profl. jours. Home: 3912 Harrison St NW Washington DC 20015 Office: Xerox Corp Xerox 1616 N Ft Myer Dr Arlington VA 22209. *All problems are solvable by intelligent people of goodwill.*

LEE, SHERMAN EMERY, art mus. ofcl.; b. Seattle, Apr. 19, 1918; s. Emery H. and Adelia (Baker) L.; B.A., M.A., Am. U.; Ph.D., Western Res. U.; m. Ruth A. Ward, Sept. 3, 1938; children—Katharine C. Lee Keefe, Margaret A. (Mrs. Arne Gray), Elizabeth K. (Mrs. William Chiego), Thomas W. Curator, Far Eastern art Detroit Inst. Art, 1941-46; with dept. arts and monuments, div. civil information and edn. sect. Gen. Hdqrs. Supreme Comdr. Allied Powers, Tokyo, 1946-48; asst. dir., then asso. dir. Seattle Mus. Art, 1948-52; curator Oriental art Cleve. Mus. Art, 1952—, asst. dir., 1956, asso. dir., 1957, dir., 1958—; prof. art Western Res. U., 1962—. Cons. com. Artibus Asiae. Chmn. Am. Arts Alliance; trustee Amon Carter Mus. Western Art. Served from ensign to lt. (j.g.) USNR, 1944-46. Decorated Legion of Honor; Order North Star; Order of Sacred Treasure 3d class. Mem. Am. Acad. Arts and Scis., Am. Assn. Museums, Assn. Art Mus. Dirs. (past pres.), Coll. Art Assn., Asia Soc. (trustee). Clubs: Union (Cleve.); Century Assn. (N.Y.). Author: Chinese Landscape Painting, rev. edit., 1962; (with Wen Fong) Streams and Mountains Without End, 1955; Japanese Decorative Style, 1961; History of Far Eastern Art, 2d edit., 1973; (with W.K. Ho) Chinese Art Under the Mongols, 1968. Editor: On Understanding Art Museums, 1977. Home: 2536 Norfolk Rd Cleveland OH 44106 Office: Cleve Museum Art Cleveland OH 44106

LEE, SHIH-YING, educator; b. Peking, China, Apr. 30, 1918; s. Tse-Kung and Pei-Jou (Tao) L.; B.S., Tsing-Hua U., Peking, 1940; Sc.D., Mass. Inst. Tech., 1945; m. Lena Ying, Aug. 18, 1973; children from previous marriage—Carol Sana, David, Linda Grace. Came to U.S., 1942, naturalized, 1952. Bridge design engr. Chinese Govt., 1940-41, hydraulic power research engr., 1941-42; design engr. Cram & Ferguson Co., Boston, 1945-47; research engr. Mass. Inst. Tech., 1947-52, faculty, 1952—, prof. mech. engring., 1966—; pres. Setra Systems Inc., Natick, Mass. Inventor field instrumentation, fluid power control. Home: Huckleberry Hill Lincoln MA 01773 Office: Setra Systems Inc 1 Strathmore Rd Natick MA 01760

LEE, SIDNEY PHILLIP, chem. engr., state senator; b. Pa., Apr. 20, 1920; s. Samuel L. and Mollie (Heller) L.; B.Sc., U. Pa., 1939; McMullin fellow Cornell U., 1939-40, then M.Ch.E. Chem. engr. Atlantic Richfield Co., 1938-42, sr. chem. engr., 1942-45; pres. Dallas Labs., 1945—, Asso. Labs., Dallas, 1945—, West Indies Investment Co., 1957—; chmn. exec. com. West Indies Bank & Trust Co.; dir. Am. Ship Bldg. Co.; prin. West Indies Investment Co., St. Croix, 1956—; mem. V.I. Senate, 1976—, now v.p.; chmn. com. govt. ops. V.I. Govt. Democratic nat. committeeman for V.I., 1969—; mem. V.I. Bd. Edn., 1969—. Fellow Am. Inst. Chemists; sr. mem. Am. Inst. Chem. Engring., Am. Inst. Mining and Petroleum Engring.; mem. Tau Beta Pi, Sigma Tau. Clubs: Rotary (pres. 1971-73), Lions (pres. 1960). Home: PO Box 130 Christiansted St Croix US VI 00820 also 1323 Wall St Dallas TX 75215 Office: PO Box 15705 Dallas TX 75215. *In retrospect, elation from supposed triumphs or defeats is blurred in memory; and of greater importance is the quality of one's life or how one played the game.*

LEE, SIDNEY S., physician, educator; b. New Haven, Dec. 5, 1921; s. Nathaniel and Anna (Dickstein) L.; B.S., Yale, 1942, M.D., 1950, M.P.H., 1952, Dr.P.H., 1953; m. Vera Cohen, June 23, 1946 (div.); 1 dau., Amanda; m. 2d, Frances Zellick, Dec. 11, 1959; children—Civia, Jonathan, Michael. Sr. asst. surgeon USPHS, 1950-54, dir. Bur. Venereal Disease Control, W.Va. Health Dept., 1952-53, chief dept. Ohio Dept. Health, 1953-54; asst. dir. Beth Israel Hosp., Boston, 1954-57, head dept. preventive medicine, 1955-66, dir. clin. services, 1958-60, gen. dir., 1960-66; instr. pub. health practice Harvard, 1955-58, asso. pub. health practice, 1958-60, lectr., 1960-63, lectr. preventive medicine, 1963-67, asso. dean faculty medicine for hosp. programs, 1966-72, clin. prof. hosp. and med. care adminstrn., 1967-72, cons. to dean, 1972-73; prof. social medicine McGill U., Montreal, Que., Can., 1972—, asso. dean faculty medicine, 1972—, dir. Health Care Centre, 1972—; cons. Royal Victoria Hosp., Montreal, Montreal Gen. Hosp., Montreal Children's Hosp., Jewish Gen. Hosp., Montreal, Montreal Chest Hosp., 1973—; mem. Nat. Health Grants Com. Can., 1973-75. Trustee, Dimock Community Health Center, 1968-72; bd. mgrs. Vis. Nurse Assn. Boston, 1966-72. Trustee, Royal Victoria Hosp., Jewish Gen. Hosp. Served with AUS, 1943-45; ETO; surgeon USPHS (R), 1960—. Decorated chevalier Ordre de Sante Publique (France), 1954. Diplomate Nat. Bd. Med. Examiners, Am. Bd. Preventive Medicine. Fellow Am. Pub. Health Assn. (governing council 1970-71, 73-74), A.A.A.S.; mem. Am. Assn. Med. Coll., Internat. Hosp. Fedn., Assn. Tchrs. Preventive Medicine, Am. Coll. Preventive Medicine (regent 1976-78), Royal Soc. Health, Soc. Med. Adminstrs. (pres. 1974-76), Conseil de Recherche Santé du

Quebec. Home: 4905 Cote St Luc Rd Apt 311 Montreal PQ H3W 2H7 Canada Office: 3655 Drummond St Montreal PQ H3G 1Y6 Canada

LEE, STAN, publisher, writer; b. N.Y.C., Dec. 28, 1922; s. Jack and Celia (Solomon) Lieber; student pub. schs., N.Y.C.; m. Joan Clayton Boocock, Dec. 5, 1947; 1 dau., Joan C. With Marvel Comics, N.Y.C., 1939—, pub., creative dir., 1970—; adj. prof. popular culture Bowling Green (Ky.) State U.; author: Origins of Marvel Comics, 1974; Son of Origins, 1975; Bring On The Bad Guys, 1976; The Superhero Women, 1977; The Silver Surfer; How to Draw Comics the Marvel Way, 1978; Marvel's Greatest Superhero Battles, 1978; Incredible Hulk, 1978; Fantastic Four, 1979; Doctor Strange, 1979; Complete Adventures of Spiderman, 1979; Captain America, 1979; The Best of the Worst, 1979; others; coll. lectr., TV script editor. Served with AUS, 1942-45. Recipient ann. award Popular Culture Assn., 1974. Mem., founder Acad. Comic Book Arts (award 1973), Nat. Acad. TV Arts and Scis., Nat. Cartoonists Soc., AFTRA. Club: Friars (N.Y.C.). Office: 575 Madison Ave New York NY 10022

LEE, STANLEY LEROY, physician; b. Newburgh, N.Y., Aug. 27, 1919; s. Philip H. and Bessie (Stember) L.; B.A., Columbia U., 1939; M.D., Harvard U., 1943; m. Ann Rosenthal, Dec. 23, 1947; children—Nancy E., Edward J., Kenneth R. Intern, resident, fellow in medicine and pathology Mt. Sinai Hosp., N.Y.C., 1943-44, 46-49, research asst., asst. attending physician, 1949-59; practice medicine, specializing in internal medicine, N.Y.C.; dir. hematology Maimonides Med. Center, Bklyn., 1959-71; dir. medicine Jewish Hosp. and Med. Center, 1971-77; asso. prof. SUNY Downstate, Bklyn., 1959-69, prof., 1969—, dean faculty, 1978—, acting pres., 1979—. Served with AUS, 1944-46. Decorated Combat Med. badge. Diplomate Am. Bd. Internal Medicine. Fellow A.C.P.; mem. Am. Soc. Hematology, Am. Soc. Human Genetics, Am. Soc. Clin. Oncology, Am. Rheumatism Assn., Soc. Exptl. Biology and Medicine, Harvey Soc., N.Y. Acad. Medicine, AAAS, Am. Fedn. Clin. Research. Jewish. Club: Harvard (N.Y.C.). Office: 450 Clarkson Ave Brooklyn NY 11203

LEE, SUL HI, univ. library adminstr.; b. Taegu, Korea, July 13, 1936; s. Sang Moo and Won Nim L.; B.A., Bowling Green State U., 1961; M.A., U. Toledo, 1964; M.A., U. Mich., 1966; m. Seol Bong Ryu, Sept. 6, 1962; 1 dau., Melissa Jemee. Reference librarian Toledo Public Library, 1961-67; supr. info. analysts Owens-Ill., Inc., 1967-68; dir. Center for Library and Info. Systems, U. Toledo, 1968-70; asso. dir. library Eastern Mich. U., 1970-73; asso. dir. libraries U. Rochester, 1973-75; dean library services Ind. State U., 1975-78; dir. univ. libraries U. Okla., Norman, 1978—; vis. asso. prof. library sci. U. Mich., 1969-73; cons. in field; bd. dirs. Ind. Coop. Library Services Authority, 1978, FOLIO, 1979—. Author: Library Orientation, 1972; A Challenge for Academic Libraries, 1973; Planning-Programing-Budgeting System, 1973; Library Budgeting, 1977; Dynamics of Library Organization, 1978. Office: 401 W Brooks St Norman OK 73069

LEE, THOMAS EDISON, judge; b. Winter Park, Fla., Jan. 29, 1915; s. Andrew Jackson and Leila (Moss) L.; B.B.A., U. Miami, 1946; J.D., Stetson U., 1949; m. Margaret Tough, Dec. 8, 1951; 1 son, Thomas Gregory. Admitted to Fla. bar, 1949; practice law, Miami, Fla., 1949-64; asst. atty. gen. State of Fla., 1957-58, 61-64; judge Met. Ct. Dade County, Fla., 1964-71; judge State Circuit Ct. 11th Jud. Circuit, Dade County, Fla., 1971—. Adviser, dir. Peoples First Nat. Bank of Hialeah, 1967-74, Peoples Liberty Nat. Bank of North Miami, 1967-74; mem. adv. bd. Am. Automobile Assn. Hearing examiner Fla. Real Estate Commn., 1961-64. Chmn. adv. bd. Fla. Fedn. Blind, 1967-69; mem. SSS bd.; 20 years. Served with AUS, World War II. Recipient Greater Miami Jaycees Cooper-Taylor award, 1970; D.A.V. Americanism award, 1968; Good Govt. award North Miami Jaycees, 1972. Mem. Fla., Am. (subcom. nat. conf. spl. ct. judges 1966—), Dade County, Hialeah-Miami Springs (hon.) bar assns., Acad. Trial Lawyers, North Am. Judges Assn., Am. Judicature Soc., Internat. Acad. Law and Sci., Miami Shores C. of C. (dir. 1961-78), Am. Legion, Fraternal Order Police Assn., Lawyers Club of Dade County, Beta Gamma Sigma, Pi Kappa Alpha. Democrat. Mason (Shriner). Clubs: Marching Chowder Soc. Miami Shores, Sertoma (chmn. bd. 1956-57), Miami Shores Mens, Flamingo Dinner (dir. 1959-60, pres. 1969), Com. of 100. Home: 11490 W Biscayne Canal Rd Miami FL 33161 Office: Dade County Court House Miami FL 33130. *During a law school lecture in my Equity Jurisprudence class several years ago, Dr. Leonard Curtis stated that "every lawyer should submit himself to a Supreme Diety." He went on to explain the unbridled power that a lawyer has over the money, property, and lives of his clients. This innocuous classroom statement coupled with the oath of office of a lawyer had a lasting effect on my legal and now judicial career.*

LEE, THOMAS LEROY, supt. schs.; b. Hickory Flat, Miss., June 2, 1912; s. Arthur and Leeanna (Barker) L.; A.B., Ark. State Tchrs. Coll., 1936; M.A., U. Ark., 1943; Ed.D., U. Houston, 1952; m. Irene Wood, June 1, 1941; children—Robert L., Lawrence W. Tchr. jr. high sch., Little Rock, 1934-35; tchr. Ark. State Tchrs. Coll., Conway, 1935-36; tchr. high sch., Texarkana, Tex., 1936-38, North Little Rock, Ark., 1938-41; tchr., prin., Marianna, Ark., 1941-42, Hughes, Ark., 1942-44; prin. Fort Smith, Ark., 1946-56, curriculum supr., 1956-57; asst. supt. secondary edn. Tucson Pub. Schs., 1957-65, dept. supt., 1965-68, supt., 1968—. Mem. Pima County Council on Alcoholism, 1967-71. Bd. dirs. Jr. Achievement, Boy Scouts Am., Goodwill Industries, Tucson Boys Choir. Mem. N.E.A., Ariz., Tucson edn. assns., Am., Ariz. assns. sch. adminstrs., Tucson C. of C. (Tucson Beautiful com.). Methodist. Rotarian. Home: 4462 E Holmes St Tucson AZ 85711 Office: 1010 E 10th St Tucson AZ 85719

LEE, TSUNG-DAO, educator; b. Shanghai, China, Nov. 25, 1926; s. Tsing-Kong Lee and Ming-Chang Chang; student Nat. Chekiang U., Kweichow, China, 1943-44, Nat. S.W. Asso. U., Kunming, China, 1945-46; Ph.D., U. Chgo., 1950; m. Jeannette Chin, June 3, 1950; children—James, Stephen. Research asso. astronomy U. Chgo., 1950; research asso., lectr. physics U. Calif., 1950-51; mem. Inst. Advanced Study, Princeton, 1951-53, prof. physics, 1960-63; asst. prof. physics Columbia, 1953-55, asso. prof., 1955-56, prof., 1956-60, 63—, Enrico Fermi prof. physics, 1964, adj. prof., 1960-62; Loeb lectr. Harvard, 1957, 64. Recipient Albert Einstein award in sci. Yeshiva U., 1957; (with Chen Ning Yang) Nobel Prize in physics, 1957. Mem. Nat. Acad. Sci. Address: Dept Physics Columbia U New York City NY 10027

LEE, W. WARREN, food co. exec.; b. Bronxville, N.Y., Aug. 31, 1924; s. William C. and Ruth (Cramond) L.; A.B., Bucknell U., 1948, M.A., 1949; m. Jean Anne Perkins, Sept. 10, 1949; children—Kathryn, Richard, Barbara, Douglas. Auditor Arthur Andersen & Co., N.Y.C., 1949-54; controller Holly Corp., N.Y.C., 1954-56; asst. controller Warner-Lambert, Morris Plains, N.J., 1955-69; controller PepsiCo., Inc., Purchase, N.Y., 1969-75; v.p. finance Welch Foods, Inc., Westfield, N.Y., 1975-76; v.p. finance Hunt-Wesson Foods, Inc., Fullerton, Calif., 1976—. Pres., Morris Plains Bd. Edn., 1959-65. Served with USAF, 1942-45. Decorated Air medal. Mem. Financial Execs. Inst., Nat. Assn. Accountants, Phi Beta Kappa. Presbyterian. Club: Yorba Linda (Calif.) Country. Home: 1540 Miramar Dr Fullerton CA 92631 Office: 1645 W Valencia Dr Fullerton CA 92634

LEE, WALLACE WILLIAMS, JR., hotel exec.; b. Nacogdoches, Tex., June 28, 1915; s. Wallace Williams and Caryl (Ames) L.; B.S. in Hotel Adminstrn., Cornell U., 1936; postgrad. in Advanced Bus. Mgmt., Columbia, 1954; m. Doris Card, Sept. 19, 1942; children—Doris, Frederic Williams. Asst. mgr. Broadmoor Hotel, Colorado Springs, Colo., 1938-42; resident mgr. Hotel Thayer, West Point, N.Y., 1945-47; mgr. Hotel Anderson (Ind.), 1947-48; resident mgr. Hotel Roosevelt, N.Y.C., 1951-53, gen. mgr., 1954; asst. mgr. Waldorf-Astoria, N.Y.C., 1948-51, mgr., 1954-59, v.p., resident mgr., 1959-61; gen. mgr. The Barclay and Park Lane Hotels, N.Y.C., 1961-63; group v.p. accommodations Howard Johnson Co., 1963—. Vice chmn. adv. com. to Statler Found., 1966-72; mem. exec. bd. Greater N.Y. councils Boy Scouts Am., 1960-71, mem. exec. bd. Boston council, 1971-79, chmn. camping Northeast region, 1972-73; v.p. bd. dirs. YMCA of Greater N.Y., 1965-71; bd. dirs. Travelers Aid Soc., N.Y.C., 1959-66; trustee Am. Hotel Found., 1973-78; pres. Hospitality, Lodging and Travel Research Found., 1975—. Served to capt. AUS, 1942-45. Recipient Silver Beaver award Boy Scouts Am., 1964; certified hotel adminstr. Mem. Am., Hotel/Motel Assn. (mem. industry adv. council 1973—), Discover Am. Travel Orgn., Cornell Soc. Hotelmen (pres. 1953-54), Hotel Sales Mgrs. Assn., Nat. Restaurant Assn. Conglist. Club: Timber Trails. Home: Box 300 Sherman CT 06784 Office: Howard Johnson Co 220 Forbes Rd Braintree MA 02184

LEE, WILLIAM FRANKLIN, III, univ. dean; b. Galveston, Tex., Feb. 20, 1929; s. William Franklin Jr. and Anna Lena (Keis) L.; B.Mus., N. Tex. State U., 1949, M.S., 1950; M.Mus., U. Tex., 1956, Ph.D., 1956; children—William Franklin IV, Robert Terry, Patricia Lynn, Peggy Ann. Prof. music St. Mary's U., San Antonio, 1952-55; asst. to dean fine arts U. Tex., 1955-56; chmn. dept. music Sam Houston State Coll., 1956-64; dean Sch. Music, U. Miami (Fla.), 1964—. Performances with Houston, Dallas symphony orchs., also Gene Krupa and Artie Shaw; guest clinician, condr., composer, 1952—. Mem. ASCAP (recipient 11 awards 1968-78), Nat. Assn. Am. Composers and Condrs., A.A.U.P., Music Educators Nat. Conf., Am. Fedn. Musicians, Music Tchrs. Nat. Assn., Pi Kappa Lambda, Kappa Kappa Psi, Phi Mu Alpha. Composer, author, arranger more than 100 published works. Author: Music Theory Dictionary, 1962; also articles, music publs. Editor, co-founder Southwestern Brass Jour., 1958. Home: 4913 SW 71st Pl Miami FL 33155

LEE, WILLIAM JAMES, clergyman, sem. adminstr.; b. Wooster, Ohio, Apr. 14, 1922; s. Norbert Henry and Matilda Rose (Sohl) L.; grad. St. Charles Coll., Balt., 1941; B.A., St. Mary's Sem., Balt., 1943; M.A., Catholic U. Am., 1947, Ph.D., 1961. Ordained priest Roman Catholic Ch., 1946; tchr. St. Joseph's High Sch., Mountain View, Calif., 1946-48; mem. Priests of St. Sulpice, 1949—; instr., registrar St. Edward's Sem., Kenmore, Wash., 1949-55; prof. social scis. St. Mary's Sem. Coll., Balt., 1958-68, acad. dean, 1961-66, rector, 1966-72, pres., 1972—. Mem. Urban Commn., Archdiocese of Balt., 1964-68, chmn. Justice and Peace Commn., 1973—; cons. U.S. province Priests of St. Sulpice, 1972—, gen. treas., 1978—. Bd. govs. Citizens Planning and Housing Assn. Balt., 1963-73, v.p., 1965-67; bd. dirs. Balt. Neighborhoods, 1970-73. Mem. Am. Econs. Assn., Am. Assn. Higher Edn., Nat. Catholic Ednl. Assn. (chmn. sem. dept. 1974-75). Democrat. Author: Economic and Ethical Aspects of Right to Work Laws, 1961; (with Howes and Wood) Baltimore Urban Parish Study, 1967. Address: St Mary's Seminary 5400 Roland Ave Baltimore MD 21210

LEE, WILLIAM JOHN, petroleum engr.; b. Lubbock, Tex., Jan. 16, 1936; s. William Preston and Bonnie Lee (Cook) L.; B.Chem. Engring., Ga. Inst. Tech., 1959, M.S. (NSF fellow), 1961, Ph.D., 1963; m. Phyllis Ann Bass, June 10, 1961; children—Anne Preston, Mary Denise. Sr. research specialist Exxon Prodn. Research Co., Houston, 1962-68; asso. prof. petroleum engring. Miss. State U., Starkville, 1968-71; tech. advisor Exxon Co., Houston, 1971-77; prof. petroleum engring. Tex. A. and M. U., College Station, 1977—; continuing edn. lectr. Am. Assn. Petroleum Geologists, 1977-79, Soc. Petroleum Engrs., 1970-79, Exxon Co. U.S.A., 1978-79. Registered profl. engr., Miss. Mem. Soc. Petroleum Engrs. of Am. Inst. Mining, Metal. and Petroleum Engrs. (mem. career guidance com. 1971—, chmn. formation evaluation com. 1973; chmn. Gulf Coast sect. student affairs 1972-73, sec. treas. 1973-74, dir. 1974-76, mem. long-range planning implementation com. 1977, editorial rev. com. 1977-78, continuing edn. com. 1977-79, chmn., 1979-80, disting. lectr. 1978-79, nat. officer nominating com. 1979. Home: Box 483 College Station TX 77840 Office: Dept Petroleum Engring Tex A and M U College Station TX 77843. *Setting the most ambitious goals consistent with my abilities and proceeding to try to achieve them in a systematic way has produced more results for me than any other personal trait or strategy.*

LEE, WILLIAM MARSHALL, lawyer; b. N.Y.C., Feb. 23, 1922; s. Marshall McLean and Marguerite (Letts) L.; student U. Wis., 1939-40; B.S., Aero. U. Chgo., 1942; postgrad. U. Calif., Los Angeles, 1946-48; J.D., Loyola U., Chgo., 1952; m. Lois Kathryn Plain, Oct. 10, 1942; children—Marsha (Mrs. Thomas J. Johnson), William Marshall, Victoria C. (Mrs. Larry Nelson). Thermodynamicist Northrop Aircraft Co., Hawthorne, Calif., 1947-49; patent agt. Hill, Sherman, Meroni, Gross & Simpson, Chgo., 1949-51, Borg-Warner Corp., Chgo., 1951-53; admitted to Ill. bar, 1953, partner Hume, Clement, Hume & Lee, Chgo., 1953-72; pvt. practice, law firm William Marshall Lee, Chgo., 1973-74; sr. partner Lee & Smith, Chgo., 1974—; v.p., dir. Power Packaging, Inc.; dir. Strenger Assos., Inc., Perfection Equipment, Inc. Pres., Glenview (Ill.) Citizens Sch. Com., 1953-57; v.p. Glenbrook High Sch. Bd., 1957-63. Served as lt. USNR, 1942-46; CBI. Recipient Pub. Service award Glenbrook High Sch. Bd., 1963. Mem. Am. (sec. sect. patent, trademark and copyright law 1977—), Ill., Chgo., 7th Fed. Circuit bar assns., Internat., Am., Chgo. patent law assns., Licensing Execs. Soc. (treas. 1977—), Phi Delta Theta, Phi Alpha Delta. Republican. Episcopalian. Clubs: Law, University (Chgo.); Tower, Snow Chase Chgo. (pres. 1963-64). Speaker and contbr. articles on legal topics. Home: 84 Otis Rd Barrington IL 60010 Office: 10 S Riverside Plaza Chicago IL 60606

LEE, WILLIAM STATES, utility co. exec.; b. Charlotte, N.C., June 23, 1929; s. William States and Sarah (Everett) L.; B.S. in Engring. magna cum laude, Princeton, 1951; m. Janet Fleming Rumberger, Nov. 24, 1951; children—Lisa, States, Helen. With Duke Power Co., Charlotte, 1955—, engring. mgr., 1962-65, v.p. engring., 1965-71, sr. v.p., 1971-75, exec. v.p., 1976-77, pres., chief operating officer, 1978—, also dir., mem. exec. and fin. coms.; mem. U.S. Com. on Large Dams, 1963—; dir. J.A. Jones Constrn. Co., Liberty Corp. mem. N.C. Energy Policy Council. Bd. dirs. United Community Services, Atomic Indsl. Forum, S.C. Energy Research Inst.; trustee Queens Coll., U. N.C. Charlotte Found., N.C. State Engring. Found. Served with C.E., USNR, 1951-54. Named Outstanding Engr., N.C. Soc. Engrs., 1969. Registered profl. engr., N.C., S.C. Fellow ASME (George Westinghouse gold medal 1972), ASCE; mem. Nat. Acad. Engring., Nat. Soc. Profl. Engrs., Edison Electric Inst. (nuclear power policy com.), Charlotte C. of C. (chmn. 1979), Am. Nuclear Soc., Phi Beta Kappa, Tau Beta Pi. Presbyn. (ruling elder). Home: 1632 Beverly Dr Charlotte NC 28207 Office: Box 2178 Charlotte NC 28242

LEE, YUAN T(SEH), chemist; b. Taiwan, Nov. 29, 1936; s. Tsefan and Pei (Tsai) L.; came to U.S., 1962, naturalized, 1974; B.S., Taiwan U., 1959; M.S., Tsinghua (China) U., 1961; Ph.D., U. Calif., Berkeley, 1965; m. Bernice W., June 28, 1963; children—Ted, Sidney, Charlotte. Successively asst. prof., asso. prof., prof. chemistry U. Chgo., 1968-74; prof. U. Calif., Berkeley, 1974—. Fellow Am. Phys. Soc.; mem. Nat. Acad. Scis., Am. Acad. Arts and Scis., Am. Chem. Soc. Contbr. numerous articles on chem. physics to profl. jours. Office: Dept Chemistry U Calif Berkeley CA 94720

LEE, YUNG-KEUN, physicist, educator; b. Seoul, Korea, Sept. 26, 1929; s. Kwang-Soo and Young-Sook (Hur) L.; came to U.S., 1953, naturalized, 1968; B.A., Johns Hopkins, 1956; M.S., U. Chgo., 1957; Ph.D., Columbia, 1961; m. Ock-Kyung Pai, Oct. 25, 1958; children—Ann, Arnold, Sara, Sylvia, Clara. Research scientist Columbia U., N.Y.C., 1961-64; prof. physics Johns Hopkins U., Balt., 1964—; vis. mem. staff Los Alamos Sci. Lab., 1971; vis. researcher Institut Scis. Nucléaires, Grenoble, France, 1975. Mem. Am. Phys. Soc. Democrat. Methodist. Club: Johns Hopkins. Contbr. articles to profl. jours. Home: 1318 Denby Rd Towson MD 21204 Office: Johns Hopkins U 34th and Charles Sts Baltimore MD 21218

LEECH, CHARLES RUSSELL, JR., lawyer; b. Coshocton, Ohio, July 29, 1930; s. Charles Russell and Edna (Henry) L.; A.B. cum laude, Kenyon Coll., 1952; J.D., Ohio State U., 1955; M.A., U. Toledo, 1969; m. Patricia Ann Tubaugh, June 20, 1953; children—Charles Russell III, Timothy David (dec.), Wendy Ann. Admitted to Ohio bar, 1955; asso. firm Fuller, Henry, Hodge & Snyder and predecessors, Toledo, 1957-64, partner, 1964—. Mem. exec. com. alumni council Kenyon Coll., 1967-72, trustee coll., 1974—. Served with USNR, 1955-57. Mem. Am., Ohio, Toledo bar assns., Kenyon Coll. Alumni Assn. Maumee Valley (past pres.), Beta Theta Pi, Phi Delta Phi. Republican. Mng. editor Ohio State Law Jour., 1955. Home: 10953 Springbrook Ct Whitehouse OH 43571 Office: 300 Madison Ave Toledo OH 43604

LEECH, GEOFFREY BOSDIN, geologist; b. Montreal, Que., Can., Aug. 28, 1918; s. Daniel Herbert and Olive Roberta (Shepherd) L.; B.A.Sc. in Geol. Engring., U. B.C. (Can.), Vancouver, 1942; M.Sc., Queen's U., Kingston, Ont., 1943; Ph.D. (Proctor fellow), Princeton U., 1949; m. Mary Jean Winters, Oct. 1, 1946; 1 dau., Joan Elizabeth. Geologist, Internat. Nickel Co., Can. and Venezuela, 1943-46, B.C. Dept. Mines, Victoria, 1947-48; geologist Geol. Survey Can., Ottawa, Ont., 1949-72, head econ. geology subdiv., 1972-79, dir. econ. geology div., 1979—; mem. Commn. for Metallogenic Map N. Am., Commn. for Tectonics of Ore Deposits. Fellow Royal Soc. Can.; mem. Geol. Soc. Am., Geol. Assn. Can., Can. Inst. Mining and Metallurgy, Soc. Econ. Geologists, Internat. Assn. on Genesis of Ore Deposits (asst. sec. gen.). Unitarian. Contbr. numerous articles to profl. jours. Home: 1113 Greenlawn Crescent Ottawa ON K2C 1Z4 Canada Office: Geol Survey Can 601 Booth St Ottawa ON K1A 0E8 Canada

LEECH, NOYES ELWOOD, lawyer, educator; b. Ambler, Pa., Aug. 1, 1921; s. Charles S. and Margaret Owens (Reid) L.; A.B., U. Pa., 1943, J.D., 1948; m. Louise Ann Gallagher, Apr. 19, 1954; children—Katharine, Gwyneth. Admitted to Pa. bar, 1949; asso. firm Dechert, Price & Rhoads, and predecessors, Phila., 1948-49, 51-53; instr. law U. Pa., Phila., 1949-56, prof., 1957-78, Ferdinand Wakeman Hubbell prof. law, 1978—. Mem. Am. Law Inst., AAUP, Am. Soc. Internat. Law, Order of Coif, Phi Beta Kappa. Co-author: The International Legal System, 1973; Cases and Materials on Corporations, 1977; gen. editor Jour. Comparative Corp. Law and Securities Regulation. Home: 162 W Queen Ln Philadelphia PA 19144 Office: U Pa Law Sch 3400 Chestnut St Philadelphia PA 19104

LEECH, ROBERT MILTON, educator; b. Cameron, Tex., June 23, 1921; s. Robert Earl and Annette Elizabeth (Laird) L.; B.F.A., U. Tex., 1948, M.F.A., 1949, Ph.D., 1962; m. Carolyn Hotchkiss, Sept. 19, 1942; children—Janis Teague, Susan Williams. Mem. faculty U. Tex. at El Paso, 1949—, prof. drama and speech, 1962—, head dept., 1960-63, dean adminstrn., 1964-65, v.p., 1965-71, acting pres., 1968-69, v.p. acad. affairs, 1969-71; dir. 50 theatrical prodns. for coll., devel. summer play festival and children's theatre program. Exec. dir. Mission '73 (citizens commn. to study coll.), 1962—; pres. El Paso Mental Health Assn., Nat. (v.p. region IV), Tex. (pres.) assns. mental health, El Paso Arts Council. Bd. dirs., exec. com., v.p. Nat. Assn. Mental Health. Served to capt. USAAF, 1942-45, USAF, 1951-53. Home: 804 Don Quixote Ct El Paso TX 79922

LEECH, WILLIAM MCMILLAN, JR., atty. gen. Tenn.; b. Charlotte, Tenn., Nov. 5, 1935; B.S., Tenn. Tech. U., 1958; J.D., U. Tenn. 1966; married; 3 children. Admitted to Tenn. bar; practiced law, 1967-78; judge (Tenn.) Mcpl. Ct.; asst. dist. atty. gen. Tenn.; atty. gen. State of Tenn., 1978—. Bd. dirs. Tenn. Performing Arts Found.; chmn. U. Tenn. Coll. Law Alumnae Adv. Com. Fellow Am. Bar Found.; mem. Am. Bar Assn., Tenn. Bar Assn., Maury County Bar Assn., Tenn. Def. Lawyers Assn., Nat. Assn. Criminal Def. Lawyers, Maury County C. of C., Nat. Assn. Attys. Gen. Democrat. Office: Office Atty Gen 450 James Robertson Pkwy Nashville TN 37219*

LEED, RICHARD LEAMAN, educator; b. Lititz, Pa., Jan. 31, 1929; s. Jacob McHugh and Ada (Leaman) L.; B.A., Oberlin Coll., 1954; Ph.D., Cornell U., 1958; m. Gretel Edwards Reinhold, June 9, 1956; children—Andrew, Noah, Jessica. Asst. prof. linguistics Cornell U., 1958-69, prof., 1969—. Author: (with G.H. Fairbanks) Basic Conversational Russian, 1964; contbr. articles to profl. jours. Home: 58 Garrett Rd Ithaca NY 14850

LEEDS, ANTHONY, anthropologist, educator; b. N.Y.C., Jan. 26, 1925; s. Arthur S. and Polly (Cahn) L.; B.A. with honors in Anthropology, Columbia, 1949; Ph.D. in Anthropology, 1957; postgrad., 1957-60; m. Elizabeth Rachel Plotkin, Jan. 28, 1967; children—Madeleine, John Christopher, Anne Lowrey, Jeremy, Jared. Teaching asst. anthropology dept. Columbia, N.Y.C., 1952-53, adminstrv. asst., 1953-54, part time instr., 1953-54, 59-60; sci. instr. Baldwin Sch., N.Y.C., 1954-56; instr. dept. sociology and anthropology, Hofstra U., Hempstead, N.Y., 1956-59; instr. dept. sociology and anthropology, City U. N.Y., 1956-59, asst. prof., 1959-61; chief program urban devel., dept. social affairs Pan Am. Union, Washington, 1961-63; asso. prof. U. Tex., Austin, 1963-67, prof., 1967-72, research asso. Inst. Latin Am. Studies, 1963-72; prof. Boston U., 1972—; research asso. Center for Study History and Philosophy of Sci., 1973—, African Studies Center, 1977—; lectr. Am. U., Washington, 1962-63, U.S. Fgn. Service Dept., 1961-62; vis. prof. Fed. U. Rio de Janeiro, Brazil, Museu Nacional, 1969; Fulbright lectr. Oxford and London Univs., Eng., 1972-73; tech. cons., evaluator, AID, Guanabara, Brazil, 1966; cons. Columbia U. Inst. Urban Environment, 1968, Southwest Ednl. Devel. Lab., Austin, 1970-72; exhibited photographs Hobart Coll., 1976, Coll. Atlantic, 1977. Mem. Nat. Acad. Scis.-Nat. Research Council-Conselho Nacional de Pesquisas Joint Brazilian-Am. Commn. on Indsl. Research Devel., 1966-68. Brazilian Govt. exchange scholar, 1951-52; Social Sci. Research Council Grantee, 1958; Columbia U. Council for Social Sci. Research grantee, 1959; Am. Philos. Soc. grantee, 1960;

Wenner-Gren Found. grantee, 1962, 64, 65; Instituto Nacional de Estudos Pedagógicos grantee, 1962; U. Tex. Univ. Research Inst. grantee, 1964, 67-68, 68-69; Ford Found. grantee, 1965-66; Fulbright Found. grantee, 1969-70; U. Tex. Inst. Latin Am. Studies grantee, 1967, 68, 71; Fulbright fellow, 1972-73; Gulbenkian Found. grantee, 1977-79; Wenner-Gren Found. grantee, 1978-79; numerous other grants. Fellow Royal Anthrop. Soc., A.A.A.S. (sect. sec. 1965-73); mem. Am. Anthrop. Assn. (grantee 1960, vis. lectr. 1963), Soc. for Am. Archaeology, Soc. for Gen. Systems Research, Soc. for History of Tech., Am. Ethnol. Soc., Phi Beta Kappa, Sigma Xi. Editor: (with A.P. Vayda) Man, Culture and Animals: The Role of Animals in Human Ecological Adjustment, 1965; Social Structure, Stratification, and Mobility, 1967; A Sociologia de Brasil Urbane, 1978. Contbr. chpts. to books, articles to profl. publs. and encys. Home: 62 River Pl Dedham MA 02026 Office: Department of Anthropology Boston University Boston MA

LEEDS, LAURENCE CARROLL, JR., apparel mfg. co. exec.; b. N.Y.C., June 17, 1929; s. Laurence Carroll and Kathryn (Emsheimer) L.; grad. Lawrenceville Sch., 1946; B.A., Yale, 1950; M.B.A., U. Pa., 1952; m. Dalia Benary, Oct. 16, 1955; children—Laurence Carroll III, Ashley, Tracy. With Manhattan Industries (formerly Manhattan Shirt Co.), N.Y.C., 1955—, mdse. mgr., 1958-59, v.p., dir., 1959-65, exec. v.p., 1965-66, pres., chief operating officer, 1966-74, chmn. bd., chief exec. officer, 1974—; mem. region IV adv. bd. Mfrs. Hanover Trust Co. Former mem. N.Y.C. Youth Bd. Mem. N.Y. County Republican Finance Com.; Rep. dist. leader, 66th Assembly Dist., N.Y.C. Bd. dirs. Yale U. Devel. Bd., Fashion Inst. Tech.; trustee Carnegie Hall. Served to lt. USNR, 1952-55. Mem. Am. Apparel Mfrs. Assn. (bd. dirs.). Home: 1016 Fifth Ave New York NY 10028 Office: 1271 Ave of Americas New York NY 10020

LEEDS, ROBERT LEWIS, JR., mfg. co. exec.; b. N.Y.C., Feb. 9, 1930; s. Robert Lewis and Elisabeth (Bandler) L.; B.A., Amherst Coll., 1951; M.B.A., U. Pa., 1953; m. Irene Osterweil, July 9, 1958; children—Leslie Anne, Robert Lewis III. With Manhattan Industries, Inc., N.Y.C., 1955-74, v.p. marketing, 1958-65, exec. v.p., 1965-66, chmn. bd., chief exec. officer, 1966-74, also dir.; v.p. corporate devel. Benrus Corp., 1975-77; adv. bd. Mfrs. Hanover Trust Co., 1973-74; prof. mktg. Bklyn. Coll., 1979—, Pace U., 1979—. Bd. dirs. Hillside Hosp., Glen Oaks, N.Y. Served with USAF, 1953-55. Mem. Men's Fashion Assn. (chmn. bd. 1972-74, dir.). Home: 860 Fifth Ave New York NY 10021

LEEDS, WILLIAM LATHAM, lawyer; b. Dallas, July 24, 1910; s. William Latham and Kathleen (Francis) L.; B.B.A., So. Methodist U., 1932; LL.B. with highest honors, U. Tex., 1936; m. Geneva Freeman, Mar. 27, 1959; children—Patricia Ann, Cheryl Francis. Admitted to Tex. bar, 1936, since practiced in Dallas; partner firm Johnson, Bromberg, Leeds & Riggs, and predecessors, 1945—. Sec., Temco Aircraft Corp., 1952-60, United Nuclear Corp., 1955-57; dir., mem. exec. com. UNC Resources, Inc. (formerly United Nuclear Corp.), 1959—; dir. Channel 6, Inc., Bell Pub. Co., County Developers, Inc., Killeen Pub. Co., Temtex Industries, Inc. Served with USNR, 1942-44. Mem. Am., Tex., Dallas bar assns., Order of Coif, Phi Delta Phi, Alpha Kappa Psi, Kappa Sigma. Methodist (steward). Clubs: Dallas Country, Terpsichorean, Idlewild (Dallas). Student editor Tex. Law Rev. Home: 5555 Nakoma Dr Dallas TX 75209 Office: 4400 Republic Bank Tower Dallas TX 75201

LEEDY, DANIEL LONEY, ecologist; b. Butler, Ohio, Feb. 17, 1912; s. Charles Monroe and Bernice Camille (Loney) L.; A.B. with honors, Miami U., Oxford, O., 1934, B.Sc., 1935; M.Sc., Ohio State U., 1938, Ph.D., 1940; m. Barbara E. Sturges, Nov. 25, 1945; children—Robert Raymond, Kathleen Eleanor. Asst. geology and zoology depts. Miami U., 1933-35; instr. wildlife mgmt. Ohio State U., 1940-42; leader Ohio Coop. Wildlife Research Unit, 1945-48; biologist charge coop. wildlife research units U.S. Fish and Wildlife Service, Washington, 1949-57; mem. biol. sci. com. Dept. Agr. Grad. Sch., 1950-75; pres. Wildlife Soc., 1952, exec. sec., 1953-57; chief br. wildlife research U.S. Fish and Wildlife Service, 1957-63; chief div. research Bur. Outdoor Recreation, Dept. Interior, 1963-65, water resources research scientist Office Water Resources Research, 1965-74; ret., 1974; research dir. Urban Wildlife Research Center, Ellicott City, Md., 1975—. Served to capt. USAAF, 1942-45. Decorated Bronze medal. Recipient certificate of merit Nash Conservation Awards program, 1953; Am. Motors Conservation award, 1958; U.S. Dept. Interior Distinguished Service award, 1972; Distinguished Alumni award Ohio State U., 1975. Fellow A.A.A.S.; mem. Wildlife Soc. (hon.), Am. Ornithologist's Union, Am. Soc. Mammalogists, Wilson Ornithol. Soc., Am. Fisheries Soc., Internat. Assn. Fish and Wildlife Agys., Soil Conservation Soc., Ecol. Soc. Am., Wildlife Disease Assn., Sigma Xi. Clubs: Field Biologists, Cosmos (Washington). Contbr. articles to profl. publs. Home: 10707 Lockridge Dr Silver Spring MD 20901 Office: 4500 Sheppard Ln Ellicott City MD 21043

LEEDY, PAUL FRANCIS, former educator; b. Battle Creek, Mich., May 10, 1903; s. Francis I. and Loretta (Dunne) L.; A.B., U. Mich., 1930, A.M., 1931, Ph.D., 1940, A.B. in L.S., 1946; LL.D., Bowling Green State U., 1971; m. Thelma Farlin, Sept. 6, 1925. Asst. English, U. Mich., 1930-31, teaching fellow, 1932-38, 39-40; faculty Bowling Green (Ohio) State U. 1938-69, prof. English, 1946-69, librarian, 1943-56, dir. library, 1956-61, prof., chmn. dept. library sci., 1946-61, provost, 1961-68, trustee prof. English, 1968-69, provost emeritus, prof. emeritus, 1969—. Mem. Modern Lang. Assn. Am., A.L.A., A.A.U.P., Ohio Library Assn. (chmn. coll. and univ. sect. 1960-61), Ohio Coll. Assn. (chmn. library sect. 1953-54), Phi Kappa Phi, Alpha Tau Omega, Omicron Delta Kappa. Club: Torch (pres. 1965-66) (Toledo). Home: 865 Parker St Bowling Green OH 43402. *Talent, luck, and timing are important factors.*

LEEDY, ROBERT ALLAN, lawyer; b. Portland, Oreg., Aug. 5, 1909; s. Harry E. and Loretta (Viles) L.; J.D., U. Oreg., 1933; m. Annapauline Rea, Sept. 14, 1935; children—Douglas Harry, Robert Allan, Jr. Admitted to Oreg. bar, 1933, practice in Portland, 1934—; mem. firm Bullivant, Wright, Leedy, Johnson, Pendergrass & Hoffman; U.S. commr., 1943-56. Mem. Oreg. Bar Examiners, 1947-48, chmn., 1949. Chancellor, Episcopal Diocese Oreg., 1970—. Mem. Am., Oreg. (pres. 1953), Multnomah County bar assns., Western Bar Conf. (pres. 1952), Alpha Tau Omega, Phi Delta Phi. Home: 10360 SE Waverley Ct Milwaukie OR 97222 Office: Willamette Center Portland OR 97204

LEEDY, WILLIAM HUDSON, lawyer; b. Kansas City, May 18, 1928; A.B., Washington and Lee U., 1949; LL.B., U. Mo., 1952; LL.M. in Taxation, N.Y. U., 1957. Admitted to Mo. bar, 1952; asso., then mem. firm Lathrop, Koontz, Righter, Claggett, Park & Norquist and predecessors, Kansas City, 1954-62, 69—; gen. counsel Fed. Res. Bank of Kansas City, 1962-64; mem. firm Gage & Tucker, Kansas City, 1964-69; mem. Appellate Jud. Commn. Mo., 1974—; dir., gen. counsel Columbia Union Nat. Bank, 1968—. Mem. Bd. Police Commrs. Kansas City, 1961-62. Mem. Am., Kansas City bar assns., Am. Law Inst., Am. Judicature Soc., Mo. bar (gov. 1967-73), Lawyers Assn. Kansas City. Home: 814 Westover Rd Kansas City MO 64113 Office: 1500 Ten Main Center Kansas City MO 64105

LEEFE, JAMES MORRISON, architect; b. N.Y.C., Aug. 28, 1921; s. Charles Clement and Suzanne (Bernhardt) L.; cert. U.S. Mcht. Marine Acad., 1943; B.Arch., Columbia U., 1950; m. Miriam Danziger, Oct. 31, 1949; 1 dau., Molly Elizabeth. Practice architecture, San Francisco, 1955-60; chief architect power and indsl. div. Bechtel Inc., San Francisco, 1960-64, prin. urban designer, 1974—; v.p., asst. sec. Bechtel Assos. P.C., N.Y., 1978—; v.p. Bechtel Assos. P.C., D.C. and Va., 1978—; partner Leefe & Ehrankrantz Architects, San Francisco, 1964-68; v.p. Bldg. Systems Devel. Inc., San Francisco and Washington, 1965-70, also dir.; dir. architecture Giffels Assos. Inc., Detroit, 1971-74; lectr. in architecture Columbia U., 1951-52, U. Calif., Berkeley, 1954-60; mem. faculty U. for Pres's., Young Pres's. Orgn., 1967; adj. prof. U. Detroit, 1971-72; mem. adv. bd. Nat. Clearing House for Criminal Justice Planning and Architecture, 1974-76. Chmn. bd. Museum West of Am. Crafts Council, San Francisco, 1966-68; vice chmn. Franklin (Mich.) Hist. Dist. Commn., 1973-74. Served with U.S. Mcht. Marine, 1942-46. Recipient Hirsh Meml. prize Columbia U., 1950, 1st prize (with Miriam Leefe) Dow Chem. Co. Competition for Interior Design, 1960. Fellow AIA (del. Internat. Union Architects work group in housing). Works include: Mus. West of Am. Craftsmen's Council, San Francisco, 1964 (Archtl. Record award for interior design 1971); Wells Hydrocombine Dam and Power Generating Facility, Columbia River, Wash., 1965; Boundary Dam, Pend Orielle River, Wash., 1965, (Am. Public Power Assn. honor award 1975); Detroit Automobile Inter-Ins. Exchange Corp. Hdqrs., Dearborn, Mich., 1972 (Detroit chpt. AIA honor award 1975), PPG Industries Research Center, Allison Park, Pa., 1973 (Detroit chpt. AIA honor award 1975, Am. Inst. Steel Constrn. Archtl. award of excellence 1975, Mich. Soc. Architects honor award 1976); Gen. Electric Research Center, Twinsburg, Ohio, 1973 (Detroit chpt. AIA honor award 1977); Appliance Buyers Credit Corp. Hdqrs. Office, Benton Harbor, Mich., 1974 (Engring. Soc. Detroit Design award 1976); contbr. articles to profl. jours. Home: 131 Spencer Ave Sausalito CA 94965 Office: Bechtel Inc 45 Fremont St San Francisco CA 94105. *I think of architecture as a celebration of life, of the buildings we make for ourselves as stepping stones on the path of history. This forces me to be an optimist, always searching to find a manifestation of the joy of being in my work.*

LEEHEY, PATRICK, educator; b. Waterloo, Iowa, Oct. 27, 1921; s. Florance Patrick and Monica (White) L.; B.S., U.S. Naval Acad., 1942; postgrad. U.S. Naval Postgrad. Sch., 1946-47; Ph.D., Brown U., 1950; m. Dorothy Feltus, Feb. 3, 1944; children—Patrick M., David J., Christopher M., Jonathan R., Susan E., Jennifer A. Commd. ensign USN, 1942, advanced through grades to capt., 1962; hydrofoil project officer, 1951-53; design supt. Puget Sound Naval Shipyard, 1956-58; head ship silencing br. USN Bur. Ships, 1958-63; head acoustics lab. David Taylor Model Basin, 1963-64; ret., 1964; asso. prof. naval architecture Mass. Inst. Tech., 1964-66, prof., 1966—. Cons. Rand Corp., Litton Industries, Office Naval Research. Mem. Am. Math. Soc., Acoustical Soc. Am., Am. Soc. Naval Engrs., Sigma Xi. Patentee in field. Home: 48 Bellevue Rd Swampscott MA 01907 Office: 77 Massachusetts Ave Cambridge MA 02139

LEEK, SYBIL, astrologer, author; b. Eng. Author numerous books including Diary of a Witch, 1968; Complete Art of Witchcraft, 1971; Reincarnation, The Second Chance, 1974; Driving Out the Devils, 1975; Herbs, Medicinal and Mystical, 1975; (with Stephen B. Leek) Ring of Magic Islands, 1976; (with Bert Sugar) The Assassination Chain, 1976; Moonsigns, 1977; asso. editor MacFadden Womens Group; columnist Globe Communications. Address: PO Box 158 Melbourne Beach FL 32951

LEEN, WALTER VICTOR, lawyer; b. Chgo., Jan. 13, 1911; s. Harry and Sadie (Izaks) L.; student U. Mich., 1928-31; Ph.B., U. Chgo., 1933, J.D., 1934; m. Molly S. Sheras, June 26, 1948; 1 dau., Barbara Ellen. Admitted to Ill. bar, 1934; asso. firm Sidney J. and Arthur Wolf, Chgo., 1934-39; spl. atty. Ill. Dept. Revenue, 1939-41; legal counsel Golan Wine, Inc., Los Angeles, 1942; individual practice, Chgo., 1946-47; staff asst. Law Sch., U. Chgo., 1947-48, legal counsel Spl. Constrn. Staff, 1948-50, mem. legal dept., 1950-53, asso. legal counsel, 1953-62, sec. bd. trustees, gen. counsel, 1962-77, spl. asst. to pres., 1977-78; individual practice, Chgo., 1979—. Bd. dirs., officer Country Home Convalescent Children, 1962-78; trustee Chgo. Sinai Congregation, 1976—, treas., 1979—. Served with USAAF, 1942-46. Mem. Am. Bar Assn., Fed. Bar Assn., Nat. Assn. Coll. and Univ. Attys. (a founder), Ill. Bar Assn., Chgo. Bar Assn., Order Wig and Robe, Zeta Beta Tau, Phi Sigma Delta. Club: Quadrangle (Chgo.). Bd. editors U. Chgo. Law Rev., 1933-34. Address: 1243 E 50th St Chicago IL 60615

LEENEY, ROBERT JOSEPH, newspaper editor; b. New Haven, May 10, 1916; s. Patrick Joseph and Mary Alice (Ross) L.; student pub., pvt. schs.; m. Anne King Coyne, June 28, 1941; children—Robert Joseph, David Coyne, Anne Patricia. Reporter, book page editor, drama critic New Haven Register, 1940-47, editorial writer, 1947-55; editor editorial page New Haven Jour.-Courier, New Haven Register, 1956-61, exec. editor, 1961-72, editor, 1972—, v.p., dir., 1970—; v.p., sec. Register Pub. Co.; dir. Conn. Savs. Bank. Examiner adminstrv. reports, editor Ofcl. Digest State Reports, Conn., 1951-52. Conn. pub. info. chmn. Am. Cancer Soc.; v.p. Arts Council of Greater New Haven; mem. Conn. Edn. Council, Edn. Commn. of States Served with USAAF, World War II. Named to New Eng. Journalism Hall of Fame, 1977. Mem. Nat. Conf. Editorial Writers, Am., New Eng. (pres. 1961) socs. newspaper editors, New Eng. A.P. News Execs. Assn. (pres. 1977), Conn. Editorial Assn., Conn. Circuit Assn. Press (pres.), New Haven C. of C. (v.p., dir., distinguished service award), Outer Circle, Sigma Delta Chi (pres. Conn. chpt. 1963-69). Clubs: Kiwanis, Woodbridge, Mory's, Quinnipiak. Home: Carrington Hill Rd R 69 Bethany CT 06525 Office: 367 Orange St New Haven CT 06511

LEENHOUTS, WILLIS CORNELIUS, architect; b. Milw., May 2, 1902; s. Cornelius and Adrianja (Ouweneel) L.; extension student U. Wis., 1920-24; student Columbia U., 1924-25; m. Lillian May Scott, July 21, 1943; 1 dau., Robin Scott. Draftsman archtl. firms, Milw., 1920-28; pvt. archtl. practice, Milw., 1928-45; partner firm Willis & Lillian Leenhouts, Milw., 1945—. Served with AUS, World War II. Fellow AIA; mem. Wis. Soc. Architects. Unitarian-Universalist. Club: Walrus. Home: 1204 E Concordia Ave Milwaukee WI 53212 Office: 3332 N Dousman St Milwaukee WI 53212

LEEPER, CHARLES KENDAL, indsl. products co. exec.; b. DeQueen, Ark., June 20, 1923; s. John Cleveland and Cadenza Vae (Winters) L.; B.M.E., U. Tex., 1944; M.S., Mass. Inst. Tech., 1948, Sc.D., 1954; m. Mavourneen Anne Byrns, July 26, 1974; children by previous marriage—David Scott, Gregory Kevin, Rebecca Jeanean. Jr. engr. Am. Mfg. Co. of Tex., Ft. Worth, 1944-45, Johns Hopkins U. Applied Physics Lab., Silver Spring, Md., 1945-46; research asst., instr. Mass. Inst. Tech., 1946-54; sr. engr., design mgr., devel. mgr. Nuclear Devel. Assos., White Plains, N.Y., 1954-59; div. dir. Atlantic Research Co., Alexandria, Va., 1960-63, also cons.; mem. tech. staff, mgr. engring. Aerojet Liquid Rocket Co., Sacramento, 1963-69; v.p., tech. dir. Aerojet Nuclear Systems Co., Sacramento, 1969-71; asst. gen. mgr. research and engring., pres., gen. mgr. Aerojet Nuclear Co., Idaho Nat. Engring. Lab., Idaho Falls, 1971-77; v.p. engring. C-E Air Preheater Combustion Engring. Co., Wellsville, N.Y., 1977-79; v.p. corp. tech. Combustion Engring. Corp., Stamford, Conn., 1979—; chmn. bd. Prewitt Aircraft Co.; cons. United Aircraft Corp. Mem. advisory com. Sacramento State Coll. Served with USNR, 1943-44. Fellow N.Y. Acad. Scis., Am. Inst. Aeros. and Astronautics; mem. ASME, Am. Nuclear Soc., Fairfield County Astronomy Soc., Combustion Inst., Royal Astron. Soc. (Can.), Photog. Soc. Am., Sigma Xi. Contbr. tech. articles to profl. jours. Patentee valves, control systems and solid rocket designs. Home: PO Box 458 New Canaan CT 06840 Office: 900 Long Ridge Rd Stamford CT 06902

LEEPER, MICHAEL EDWARD, ret. army officer, corp. exec.; b. Republic, Pa., Jan. 28, 1917; s. Samuel and Elizabeth (Augustine) L.; B.S., U. Pitts., 1940; M.B.A., Stanford U., 1949; grad. Indsl. Coll. Armed Forces, 1961; m. Betty Jane Marshall, June 5, 1943 (dec.); children—Michael E., Richard A., James R.; m. 2d, Mary Hoke Austin, July 20, 1974. Credit mgr. finance div. Ford Motor Co., Uniontown, Pa., 1940-41; commd. 2d lt. U.S. Army, 1942, advanced through grades to brig. gen., 1969; ret., 1971; staff positions as comptroller, procurement and mil. logistics, 1942-71; G-4, 8th U.S. Army, Korea, 1970-71; chmn. bd. Aloha Corp., Honolulu, 1973—; pres. DRC of Hawaii, Inc., Honolulu, 1974—. Decorated D.S.M., Legion of Merit, Army Commendation medal (U.S.); Order of Merit (Korea). Mem. Beta Gamma Sigma, Lambda Chi Alpha. Lion. Rotarian. Home: 4116 Black Point Rd Honolulu HI 96816

LEER, JOHN W., business exec.; b. 1925; student U. So. Calif.; m. Jo Ann Smoyer; children—Jeri, Kerri, Wendy. Dir. marketing and sales devel. Am. Tobacco Co., 1954-64; v.p., dir. marketing Houston Sports Assn., 1964-66; with Braniff Airways, Inc., v.p. sales 1966, sr. v.p. corp. and marketing planning, 1967, pres. hotel div., 1970-75; asso. R.E. Smith Interests, Houston, 1975—. Office: 2000 West Loop S Suite 1900 Houston TX 77027

LEES, BENJAMIN, composer; b. Harbin, China, Jan. 8, 1924; came to U.S., 1925; studied piano with K.I. Rodetsky, 1931, Marguerite Bitter, 1945-48, compostion with Halsey Stevens at U. So. Calif., 1945-48, with George Antheil, 1949-54. Prof. composition Peabody Conservatory, Queen's Coll., Manhattan Sch. Music. Recipient Fromm Found. award, 1953; William and Norma Copley Found. award, 1955; UNESCO award, 1958; Sir Arnold Bax medal, 1958; Guggenheim fellow, 1954, 66; Fulbright fellow, 1956. Composer: (orch.) Profile, 1952, Declamations for piano and strings, 1953, Symphony Number 1, 1953, Number 2, 1958, Piano Concerto Number 1, 1955, Divertimento Burlesca, 1957, Songs of the Night for Soprano and Orch., 1952, Violin Concerto, 1958, Prologue, Capriccio and Epilogue, 1958, Concerto for Orch., 1959, Concertante Breve, 1959, Interlude for Strings, 1957; Visions of Poets for Soprano and Tenor Solo, Chorus and Orch., 1961; (operas) The Oracle, 1956, The Gilded Cage; (chamber music) String Quartet Number 1, 1952, Evocation for Solo Flute, 1953, Violin Sonata Number 1, 1953, Movement da Camera for Flute, Clarinet, Cello and Piano, 1954, String Quartet Number 2, 1955, Three Variables for Winds and Piano, 1956; (piano) Sonata for Two Pianos, 1951, Toccata, 1953, Fantasia, 1954, Kaleidoscopes, 1959, Sonata Breve, 1956, Six Ornamental Etudes, 1957, Epigrams, 1961; (songs) Cyprian Songs for baritone, 1961; Concerto for Oboe and Orch., 1964; Piano Sonata 4, 1965; Piano Concerto 2, 1966; Symphony No. 3, 1968; (opera) Medea in Corinth, 1970; Study for Solo Cello, 1972; Sonata No. 2 for Violin and Piano, 1973; Etudes for Piano and Orch., 1974; Labyrinths for Symphonic Band, 1975; Variations for Piano and Orch., 1975; Passa caglia for Orch., 1976; Concerto for Woodwind Quintet and Orch., 1976; Staves (soprano and piano), 1977; Scarlatti Portfolio (transcriptions for orch.), 1978; String Quartet No. 3, 1978-79; Dialogue for Cello and Piano, 1977. Address: 28 Cambridge Rd Great Neck NY 11023

LEES, FRANCIS ANTHONY, educator; b. Bklyn., Jan. 19, 1931; s. Roy A. and Mary (Ozustowicz) L.; B.A., Bklyn. Coll., 1952; M.A., St. Louis U., 1953; Ph.D., N.Y. U., 1961; m. Kathryn V. Murphy, June 6, 1959; children—Veronica Ann, Francis, Daniel, Jeannette Marie. Lectr. econs. St. Louis U., 1952-53; instr. Fordham U., 1956-60; asst. prof. St. John's U., Jamaica, N.Y., 1960-61, asso. prof., 1962-65, prof., 1965—; financial analyst, econ. cons. Dominick & Dominick, N.Y.C., 1961-62. Served with AUS, 1953-56. Am. Bankers Assn. Summer Research fellow, 1969. Author: Foreign Investment, Capital Controls and the US Balance of Payments, 1968; International Banking and Finance, 1974; International Financial Markets, 1975; Foreign Banking and Investment in the United States, 1976; Economic and Political Development of the Sudan, 1977. Editor: Rev. of Bus., 1967-75. Contbr. articles to profl. jours. Home: 192 Coolidge Dr East Meadow NY 11554 Office: Bus Research Inst St John's U Jamaica NY 11439

LEES, LESTER, educator; b. N.Y.C., Nov. 8, 1920; s. Harry and Dorothy (Innenberg) L.; B.S., Mass. Inst. Tech., 1940, M.S., 1941; m. Constance Louise Morton, Aug. 30, 1941; 1 son, David Grayson. Research fellow, instr. math. Calif. Inst. Tech., 1942-44, asso. prof. aeros., 1953-55, prof., 1955-74, dir. environ. quality lab., 1970-74, prof. environ. engring. and aeronautics, mem. sr. staff environ. quality lab., 1974—; aero. engr. Nat. Adv. Com for Aeros., Langley Field, Va., 1944-46; asst. prof. aero. engring. Princeton U., 1946-48, asso. prof., 1948-53; cons. TRW, 1953—, Aerospace Corp., 1960-65. Fellow Am. Acad. Arts and Scis., Am. Inst. Aeros. and Astronautics; mem. Nat. Acad. Engring. Democrat. Jewish. Contbr. articles to profl. jours. Home: 1911 N Pepper Dr Altadena CA 91001 Office: Calif Inst Tech 1201 E California Blvd Pasadena CA 91125

LEES, SIDNEY, educator; b. Phila., Apr. 17, 1917; s. Charles K. and Bess Rose (Segal) L.; A.B., Coll. City N.Y., 1938; S.M., Mass. Inst. Tech., 1948, Sc.D., 1950; m. Marjorie Berman, Sept. 17, 1947; children—David E.B., P. Andrew, Eliot Jay. Observer, U.S. Weather Bur., 1938-40; meteorol. instrument engr. U.S. Signal Corps, 1940-43; research asso. Mass. Inst. Tech., 1947-50, asst. prof. aero. dept., 1950-57; cons engr., 1957-62; prof. engring. Thayer Sch., Dartmouth, 1962-66; head bioengring. dept., sr. mem. staff Forsyth Inst. Research and Advanced Study, Boston, 1966—; vis. scientist U. Amsterdam, 1975; chmn. 1965 Joint Automatic Control Conf., Research Conf. on Instrumentation Sci., 1971; chmn. Conf. on Ultrasonics in Bioengring. and Biophysics, 1978. Served with AUS, 1943-46. Mem. Am. Phys. Soc., ASME, IEEE, Sigma Xi (pres. Dartmouth chpt. 1964-65). Co-author: Instrument Engineering, 3 vols., 1952-55. Editor: Air, Space and Instruments, Draper Anniversary vol., 1963. Contbr. articles to profl. jours. Home: 50 Eliot Memorial Rd Newton MA 02158 Office: Forsyth Dental Center 140 The Fenway Boston MA 02115

LEE-SMITH, HUGHIE, artist; b. Eustis, Fla., Sept. 20, 1915; s. Luther and Alice (Williams) S.; student Art Sch. of Detroit Soc. Arts and Crafts, 1934-35; grad. Cleve. Inst. Art, 1938; B.S., Wayne State U., 1953; m. Mabel Louise Everett, 1940 (div. 1953); 1 dau., Christina. Exhibited in group shows Cleve. Mus. Art, Detroit Inst. Arts, Butler Inst. Am. Art, Youngstown, Ohio, Bklyn. Mus., Wadsworth Atheneum, Boston Mus., San Francisco Mus., Mus. Modern Art, Whitney Mus.; represented in permanent collections Detroit Inst. Arts, Parrish Mus., Southampton, L.I. U., U. Mich., Wayne State U., Atlanta U., Howard U., Art Sch. of Detroit Soc. Arts and Crafts, U.S.

Navy Art Center; one man shows Detroit Artists Market, Howard U. Gallery, Washington, Grand Central Art Galleries, N.Y.C., Janet Nessler Gallery, N.Y.C., U. Chgo., others; work acquired by Lagos (Nigeria) Mus.; instr. painting Studio-on-the-Canal, Princeton, N.J., 1959-64; art tchr. Princeton Country Day Sch., 1964-65, instr. painting Art Students League, N.Y.C. Served with USNR, 1944-45. Recipient Thomas B. Clark prize N.A.D., 1959; prize Allied Artists Am. 1958; Emily Lowe award, 1957; Founders prize Detroit Inst. Arts, 1953; certificate of commendation USN, 1974, others; named Mich. Painter of Year, Detroit News, 1953. Mem. Artists Equity Assn., Allied Artists Am., Princeton Art Assn., Mich. Acad. Sci., Arts and Letters, NAD, Audubon Artists, Artists Fellowship. Club: Players (N.Y.C.). Home: 330 W 58th St Apt 4G New York NY 10019

LEESON, CHARLES ROLAND, physician, educator; b. Halifax, Eng., Jan. 26, 1926; s. Charles Ernest and Gladys (Stott) L.; B.A., Cambridge (Eng.) U., 1947, B. Medicine and Surgery, 1950, M.A., 1951, M.D., 1959, Ph.D., 1971; m. Marjorie Martindale, Apr. 22, 1954; children—Roland Mark, Nicola Jane, Christine Ann, David Neil, Paula Suzanne. Came to U.S., 1963. Intern, King's Coll. Hosp., London, 1950-51; lectr. U. South Wales, 1955-58; asso. prof. anatomy Dalhousie U., N.S., 1958-61, Queen's U., Kingston, Ont., 1962-63; prof. anatomy U. Iowa, 1963-66; prof. U. Mo., Columbia, 1966-78, chmn. dept. anatomy, 1966-77; prof. anatomy U. Ill., Urbana, 1978—. Served with med. br. RAF, 1951-55. Mem. Anat. Soc. Gt. Britain, Canadian, Am. assns. anatomists, Electron Microscopy Soc. Am. Author: (with T.S. Leeson) Histology, 3d edit., 1976; Human Structure, 1972; Practical Histology, 1973; A Brief Atlas of Histology, 1979. Home: 2503 Melrose Dr Champaign IL 61820

LEESON, THOMAS SYDNEY, educator, physician; b. Halifax, U.K., Jan. 26, 1926; s. Charles Ernest and Gladys (Stott) L.; B.A., U. Cambridge (Eng.), 1945, M.A., M.B., B.Chirg., 1950, M.D., 1959, Ph.D., 1971; m. Catherine Mary Whitcomb, Sept. 6, 1951; children—Roland Paul, Susan Gillian, Helen Clare. Intern King's Coll. Hosp., London, 1950-51; lectr. anatomy U. Cardiff, 1955-57; asst. prof. U. Toronto, 1957-60, asso. prof., 1960-63; prof., chmn. dept. anatomy U. Alta. Med. Sch., Edmonton, Can., 1963—. Mem. Med. Research Council Can., 1968-72. Served with RAF, 1951-55. Recipient Starr medal U. Toronto, 1959. Fellow Brit. Assn. Clin. Anatomists; mem. Brit. Anat. Soc., Am. Assn. Anatomists, Renal Assn., Electron Microscope Soc. Am. Author: (with A.W. Ham) Histology, 1961; (with C.R. Leeson) Histology, 3d edit., 1976; Human Structure, 1972; Practical Histology, 1973; A Brief Atlas of Histology, 1979. Home: 11739 83d Ave Edmonton AB Canada Office: Dept Anatomy U Alta Edmonton AB Canada

LEESTAMPER, ROBERT EUGENE, univ. pres.; b. St. Paul, July 2, 1929; s. Sidney L. and Virginia May (Peterson) L.; B.A., U. Minn., 1952; M.A., Columbia, 1955; Ed.D., Harvard, 1964; m. Barbara Jean Dunigan; children—Michael, David. Research psychologist Personnel and Tng. Research Center, San Antonio, 1955-57, Cambridge Research Center, Bedford, Mass., 1957-59; prof. psychology Northland Coll., 1960-62; asst. dir. housing N.Mex. State U., 1962-63, dir. housing and placement, 1963-64, registrar, 1964-68, asso. prof. dir. instnl. studies, 1965-68; asst. exec. dir. Minn. Higher Edn. Coordinating Commn., 1968-70; pres. Worcester State Coll., 1970-75; pres. S.E. Mo. State U., 1975—. Served to capt. USAF, 1952-55. Mem. A.A.U.P., Bon-Aire Ednl. Found. (chmn. scholarship com. 1970-74, chmn. bd. 1974—), Blue Key, Kappa Delta Pi, Alpha Kappa Lambda. Contbr. articles to profl. jours. Home: 614 W Main Fredericktown MO 63645

LEESTMA, ROBERT, govt. ofcl., educator; b. Detroit, Oct. 15, 1927; s. Richard and Jeanne (Nivarre) L.; A.B., U. Mich., 1949, A.M., 1951, Ph.D., 1956; m. Margaret Elizabeth Bell, Aug. 13, 1955. Research, teaching asst. community adult edn. program U. Mich., 1949-50, asst. dir. Audio-Visual Edn. Center, lectr. Sch. Edn., 1951-55; tchr. English and social studies Ann Arbor (Mich.) pub. schs., 1950-51; ICA edn. and mass communications adv. govt. Vietnam, 1955-58, edn. adviser govt. Thailand, 1958-61; asso. prof., dir. Peace Corps tng. program U. Mich., 1961-64; dep. chief edn. div. Bur. Africa, AID, 1964-65, dir. Office Multilateral Policy and Programs and dir. Multilateral Policy Planning Staff, Bur. Ednl. and Cultural Affairs, State Dept., 1965-67; asst. to asst. sec. edn. (internat. edn.) HEW, 1967-68; dir. Inst. Internat. Studies, asso. commr. internat. edn. U.S. Office Edn., 1968-74, asso. commr. instl. devel. and internat. edn., 1974—. Mem. chmn. and/or adviser U.S. delegations internat. confs.; now U.S. rep., chmn. edn. com. OECD; mem. Indo-U.S. Subcommn. on Edn. and Culture, U.S.-Egyptian Joint Working Group on Edn. and Culture, U.S.-Japan Culcon Edn. Com., U.S. Nat. Commn. for UNESCO; alt. mem. U.S.-Japan Friendship Commn., also Am. panel, Joint Culcon Com.; HEW rep. to OAS Inter-Am. Com. on Edn. Served with AUS, 1946-47. Payne scholar U. Mich., 1951-52; Hinsdale scholar, 1953-54. Mem. Am. Ednl. Research Assn., Comparative and Internat. Edn. Soc., Assn. Asian Studies, Soc. Internat. Devel. Contbr. chpts. to books, articles to profl. jours. Home: 2712 George Mason Pl Alexandria VA 22305 Office: US Office Edn 7th and D Sts SW Washington DC 20202

LEET, GLEN, found. exec., author; b. Brockton, Mass., Apr. 21, 1908; s. Alexander Fisher and Alice (Horn) L.; B.A., Norwich U., 1930, Ph.D., (hon.), 1973; M.S., Syracuse U., 1931; postgrad. U. Chgo., 1935, Am. U., 1937, Boston Coll., 1943; grad. tng. program UNRRA, U. Md., 1944; m. Marsha Hatch, June 11, 1940 (dec. Feb. 19, 1971); children—Carla Ruth, Glen, Frederika Athena; m. 2d, Mildred Robbins, Aug. 9, 1974; stepchildren—Jane Marla Robbins, Aileen Robbins Friedman. Apprentice to city mgr., Norfolk, Va., 1931; spl. agt. Va. Dept. Social Welfare, 1931; asst. dir. Am. Municipal Assn., 1932-34; asst. sec. U.S. Conf. Mayors, 1933-34; field rep. Am. Pub. Welfare Assn., Chgo., 1934-37; editor Washington News Letter Social Legislation, also dir. spl. program social security Grad. Sch. Am. U., Washington, 1937-39; R.I. state adminstr. pub. assistance, 1939-44; dir. welfare Greece UNRRA, Athens, 1944-46; as UN adviser on social policy to govt. Greece, organized 1st nat. community devel. program with UN tech. assistance, 1947-50; chief community devel. unit UN secretariat, N.Y.C., 1950-52; cons. community devel. to govts. in Asia, Africa, Europe, Middle East, Latin Am., also mem. UN Mission to survey community devel. in Africa, 1953-57; program dir. Save the Children Fedn., N.Y.C., 1957-61, exec. dir., 1961-71, pres., 1971—, bd. dirs., 1975—; pres. Community Devel. Found., 1971-75, exec. dir., 1960-71, bd. dirs., 1975—; co-dir. Hotline Internat., computer info. sharing system; co-dir. Leet & Leet, cons. Mem. Mission to Study Child Welfare in China, 1973, Study Tour to Study Child Welfare in USSR, 1973; mem. Am. Com. Community Devel. in Tanzania; observer UN Conf. Protection Human Environment, Stockholm, 1972, Seminar on Human Rights in Relation to Sci. and Tech., Vienna, 1972, World Population Conf., Bucharest, 1974, World Food Conf., Rome, 1974 UN Conf. on Human Settlements, Vancouver, 1976, UN Conf. on Water, Mar del Plata, Argentina, 1977; convener Non-Govtl. Orgn. Conf. Protection Human Environment, UN, N.Y.C., 1972; mem. convening com. 1st World Assembly Non-Govtl. Orgns. concerned with Global Environment, UN, Geneva, Switzerland, 1973; mem. advisory com. Habitat, U.S. Dept. State, 1976. Founder, Ind. Voters League U. Chgo., 1934. Bd. dirs. CARE, Am. Council Vol. Agys. Fgn. Service, Overseas Edn. Fund League Women Voters. Decorated Gold Cross of George (Greece). Mem. Internat. Soc. Community Devel. (pres.), Am. Pub. Welfare Assn., Am. Soc. Pub. Adminstrn. (past pres. Athens), Internat. Conf. Social Work, Nat. Conf. Social Welfare, Nat. Assn. Social Workers, Center Inter-Am. Relations. Club: Fairfield County Hunt. Author: Handbook on Social Legislation, 1957; The Role of Specific Ministries and Services in Comprehensive National Community Development Programs, 1962; The Analysis and Evaluation of New Community Development Project Proposals, 1962; Commodity Aided Community Development in Mexico, 1963; Computer Aided Community Development Reporting in Mexico, 1964; Ten Concepts Concerning Computer Aided Community Action Reporting, 1964; The International Community Development Statistical Bulletin; Full Employment for Refugees; Basic Elements of Comprehensive National Community Development Programs; Child Welfare in the Space Age; People Needing Water, 1977; Aided Self Employment as a Means of Enabling the Poorest of the Poor to Contribute to Development, 1978; (with Mildred Robbins Leet) The Augmentation of International Conferences Through Computer Communications, 1978; editor: (with Robert M. Paige) Property Tax Limitation Laws, 1936; testimony on self help policies before U.S. Ho. of Reps. Appropriations Com., 1978. Home: 54 Riverside Dr New York NY 10024 also 2 Briar Oak Dr Weston CT 06883

LEET, RICHARD HALE, oil co. exec.; b. Maryville, Mo., Oct. 11, 1926; s. Theron Hale and Helen Eloise (Rutledge) L.; B.S. in Chemistry, N.W. Mo. State Coll., 1948; Ph.D. in Phys. Chemistry, Ohio State U., 1952; m. Phyllis Jean Combs, June 14, 1949; children—Richard Hale II, Alan Combs, Dana Ellen. Research chemist Standard Oil Co. (Ind.), Whiting, 1953-64; dir. long-range and capital planning, mktg. dept. Am. Oil Co., Chgo., 1964-68, mgr. ops. planning, mfg. dept., 1968-70, regional v.p., Atlanta, 1970-71, v.p. supply, Chgo., 1971-74; v.p. planning and adminstrn. Amoco Chems. Corp., Chgo., 1974-75, v.p. mktg., 1975-77, exec. v.p., 1977-78, pres., 1978—. Vice chmn. bd. mgrs. Met. YMCA, Chgo.; area v.p. Boy Scouts Am.; trustee Crusade of Mercy; bd. visitors Emory U., 1970-71. Served with USNR, 1944-46. Mem. Am. Chem. Soc., Am. Petroleum Inst., Chem. Mfrs. Assn. (dir.), Phi Sigma Epsilon, Gamma Alpha. Methodist. Home: 2504 Brookwood Dr Flossmoor IL 60422 Office: 200 E Randolph St Chicago IL 60601

LEETE, EDWARD, educator; b. Leeds, Eng., Apr. 18, 1930; s. Edward Cecil and Elsie (Griffith) L.; B.Sc., U. Leeds, 1948, Ph.D., 1950, D.Sc., 1965; m. Sheila Anne Slattery, Dec. 4, 1976; children—Jennifer Anne, Carolyn Marie; children by previous marriage—Peter Andrew, Allison Jane. Came to U.S., 1954, naturalized, 1961. Postdoctoral fellow NRC Can., 1950-54; asst. prof. U. Calif. at Los Angeles, 1954-58; faculty U. Minn., Mpls., 1958—, prof. chemistry, 1963—. Cons. NIH, 1962-65, Philip Morris Tobacco Co., 1974-77. Guggenheim fellow U. Oxford (Eng.), 1965; recipient Disting. Tchr. award U. Minn., 1976. Fellow Chem. Soc. London; mem. Am. Chem. Soc. Mem. editorial bd. Phytochemistry. Research on origin natural products and alkaloids. Home: 399 Otis Ave Saint Paul MN 55104

LEETE, WILLIAM WHITE, artist; b. Portsmouth, Ohio, June 12, 1929; s. Bernard Emerson and Lois Trowbridge (Denison) L.; B.A., Yale U., 1951, B.F.A., 1955, M.F.A., 1957; m. Doris Louise Knight, Sept. 19, 1952; children—Amy Knight, Robin Ellen. Mem. faculty dept. art, U. R.I. Kingston, 1957—, now prof., acting chmn. dept., 1968, 69-70, 76; represented in permanent collections: De Cordova Mus., Lincoln, Mass., Cleve. Mus., Worcester Mus., R.I. Hosp. Trust Bank, also various pvt. collections. Served with USMC, 1951-53. Mem. Coll. Art Assn., AAUP. Home: 50 Silver Lake Ave Wakefield RI 02879 Office: Dept Art Univ of RI Kingston RI 02881

LEFEBVRE, ARTHUR HENRY, mech. engr.; b. Long Eaton, Eng., Mar. 14, 1923; s. Henri and May (Brown) L.; came to U.S., 1976; B.Sc., Nottingham U., 1946; Ph.D., Imperial Coll., London, 1952, D.Sc., 1975; m. Elizabeth Marcella Betts, Dec. 20, 1952; children—David Ivan, Paul Henry, Anne Marie. Combustion engr. Rolls Royce, Derby, Eng., 1952-61; prof. aircraft propulsion Cranfield Inst. Tech., Eng., 1961-71, prof., head Sch. Mech. Engring., 1971-76; prof., head Sch. Mech. Engring, Purdue U., West Lafayette, Ind., 1976—; cons. on combustion to various cos. in Britain, Sweden and U.S.A.; mem. propulsion and energetics panel Adv. Group for Aero. Research and Devel., 1972-76. Fellow Royal Aero. Soc., Instn. Mech. Engrs., Royal Soc. Arts. Contbr. tech. articles to profl. jours. Patentee combustion equipment. Home: 1741 Redwood Ln Lafayette IN 47905 Office: Sch Mech Engring Purdue U West Lafayette IN 47907

LEFEBVRE D'ARGENCÉ, RENÉ-YVON MARIE MARC, museum dir.; b. Plouescat, France, Aug. 21, 1928; s. Marc and Andrée (Thierry) L. d'A.; came to U.S., 1962; Licencié-ès-Lettres, Sorbonne, Paris, 1952; Brevete de l'Ecole Nationale des Langues Orientales Vivantes, Paris, Chinese, 1950, Japanese, 1951, Finnish, 1952; Ph.D. (hon.), Chinese Acad., Taiwan, 1969; m. Ritva Pelanne, Nov. 2, 1955; children—Chantal, Yann, Luc. Curator, Musée Cernuschi, Paris, 1953, Blanchard de la Brosse Mus., Saigon, 1954-58, Louis Finot Mus., Hanoi, N. Vietnam, 1954-58; prof. art history U. Calif., Berkeley, 1962-65; curator Asiatic collections M.H. de Young Meml. Mus., San Francisco, 1964; dir. Avery Brundage Found., San Francisco, 1965-68; dir., chief curator Asian Art Mus. San Francisco, 1969—. Pres. French-Am. Bilingual Sch., San Francisco, 1975—; founder, bd. dirs. Ecole Française San Francisco, 1967—; bd. dirs. Alliance Française, San Francisco, 1974—, Asian Art Found. San Francisco, 1978—. Named chevalier de l'Etoile du Nord (Sweden), 1968, chevalier de l'Ordre National du Mérite (France), 1970; recipient Médaille de la Reconnaissance Française, Govt. France, 1957, Order of Merit, Avery Brundage Found., 1968; Quai d'Orsay grantee, Taiwan and Japan, 1959-61. Mem. Sociedad Asiatica de la Argentina, Soc. Asian Art (adv. com. 1972—). Author: Chinese Jades in the Avery Brundage Collection, 1972; Chang Dai-chien, 1972; The Hans Popper Collection, 1973; Avery Brundage Collection: Chinese, Korean, and Japanese Sculpture, 1974; A Decade of Collecting, 1976; Bronze Vessels of Ancient China in the Avery Brundage Collection, 1977; gen. editor: Asian Art Museum and University Collections in the San Francisco Bay Area, 1977, 5,000 Years of Korean Art, 1979. Home: 16 Midhill Dr Mill Valley CA 94941 Office: Asian Art Museum San Francisco Golden Gate Park San Francisco CA 94118

LEFER, ALLAN MARK, physiologist; b. N.Y.C., Feb. 1, 1936; s. I. Judah and Lillian G. (Gastwirth) L.; B.A., Adelphi Coll., 1957; B.A., Western Res. U., 1959; Ph.D. (NSF fellow), U. Ill., Urbana, 1962; m. Mary E. Indoe, Aug. 23, 1959; children—Debra Lynn, David Joseph, Barry Lee and Leslie Ann (twins). Instr. physiology, USPHS-NIH fellow Western Res. U., 1962-64; asst. prof. physiology U. Va., 1964-69, asso. prof., 1969-71, prof., 1972-74; vis. prof. Hadassah Med. Sch., Jerusalem, Israel, 1971-72; prof., chmn. dept. physiology Jefferson Med. Coll., Thomas Jefferson U., Phila., 1974—; cons. Merck & Co., Upjohn Co., Organon Co., NIH. Active, Acad. Com. on Soviet Jewry, 1970—; chmn. United Jewish Appeal, 1973-74; coach basketball and baseball Huntingdon Valley Athletic Assn., 1975-78. Recipient Pres. and Visitor's prize in research U. Va., 1970. Fellow Am. Coll. Cardiology; mem. Am. Physiol. Soc., Am. Soc. Pharmacology and Exptl. Therapeutics, Internat. Heart Research Soc., Am. Heart Assn. (established investigator 1968-73), Shock Soc., AAAS, Soc. Exptl. Biology and Medicine, Israel Soc. Physiology and Pharmacology, Phila. Physiol. Soc. (pres. 1978-79), Sigma Xi. Democrat. Club: B'nai B'rith (v.p. 1967-68, pres. 1970-71 Charlottesville, chmn. Va. Hillel 1970-71). Author: Pathophysiology and Therapeutics of Myocardial Ischemia, 1977; Prostaglandins in Cardiovascular and Renal Function, 1979. Editor: Circulatory Shock, 1973—. Contbr. to World Book Ency. Sci. Yearbook, 1979. Contbr. sci. articles to profl. jours. Home: 3590 Walsh Ln Huntingdon Valley PA 19006 Office: 1020 Locust St Philadelphia PA 19107

LEFEVRE, ELBERT WALTER, JR., educator; b. Eden, Tex., July 29, 1932; s. Elbert Walter and Hazie (Davis) LeF.; B.S. in Civil Engring., Tex. A. and M. U., 1957, M.S. in Civil Engring., 1961; Ph.D., Okla. State U., 1966; m. Joyce Ann Terry, Nov. 28, 1957; children—Terry Ann, Charmaine Rene, George Walter, John Philip. Faculty, Tex. A. and M. U., Bryan, 1958, Tex. Technol. Coll., Lubbock, 1959-63, Okla. State U., Stillwater, 1963-66; faculty U. Ark., Fayetteville, 1966—, head dept. civil engring., 1971—; sr. v.p. Engring. Services, Inc., Springdale, Ark., 1973—. Served to 1st lt. AUS, 1953-56. Registered profl. engr., Ark., Tex. Mem. Am. Soc. C.E. (pres. Mid-South sect. 1972, chmn. dist. 1977-80, mem. transp. research bd. 1966—), Am. Soc. Engring. Edn. (pres. Midwest sect. 1976-77), Ark. Soc. Profl. Engrs. (pres. 1979-80), Sigma Xi, Chi Epsilon. Mason, Rotarian (pres. 1973). Home: 300 Paradise Ln Springdale AR 72764 Office: Dept Civil Engineering University Arkansas Fayetteville AR 72701

LEFEVRE, GEORGE, JR., educator; b. Columbia, Mo., Sept. 13, 1917; s. George and Julia (Faris) L.; A.B., U. Mo., 1937, M.A., 1939, Ph.D., 1949; m. Elsbeth Victoria Wahlin, June 11, 1943 (dec.); children—George W., Julia L. (Mrs. Robert Phelps), Kathryn E.; m. 2d, Dora Elizabeth Tincher, Dec. 16, 1972. Biologist, Oak Ridge Nat. Lab., 1946-47; asst. prof. U. Utah, Salt Lake City, 1949-54, asso. prof., 1954-56; program dir. genetic biology NSF, Washington, 1956-59; dir. biol. labs. Harvard, 1959-65; prof. San Fernando Valley State Coll. (now Calif. State U.), Northridge, 1965—, chmn. dept. biology, 1965-79. Served with C.E., AUS, 1942-46. Mem. Genetics Soc. Am. (treas. 1972-75), Phi Beta Kappa, Sigma Xi, Beta Theta Pi. Editor: Genetics, 1976—. Home: 10132 Eton Ave Chatsworth CA 91311 Office: Biology Dept Calif State U Northridge CA 91330

LEFEVRE, PERRY DEYO, clergyman, educator; b. Kingston, N.Y., July 12, 1921; s. Johannes and Faye (McFerran) LeF.; A.B., Harvard, 1943; B.D., Chgo. Theol. Sem., 1946; Ph.D., U. Chgo., 1951; m. Carol Baumann, Sept. 14, 1946; children—Susan Faye, Judith Ann, Peter Gerret. Ordained to ministry Conglist. Ch., 1946; instr. religion Franklin and Marshall Coll., 1948-49; asst., then asso. prof. religion Knox Coll., 1949-53, Fed. Theol. Sem., U. Chgo., 1953-61; prof. constructive theology, dean faculty Chgo. Theol. Sem., 1961—. Sr. fellow Danforth Found. Mem. Nat. Council Religion in Higher Edn., Phi Beta Kappa. Author: The Prayers of Kierkegaard, 1956; The Christian Teacher, 1958; Introduction to Religious Existentialism, 1963; Understandings of Man, 1966; Philosophical Resources for Christian Thought, 1968; Conflict in a Voluntary Association, 1975. Address: 5757 University Ave Chicago IL 60637

LEFEVRE, THOMAS VERNON, utility co. exec., lawyer; b. Dallas, Dec. 5, 1918; s. Eugene H. and Callie E. (Powell) F.; B.A., U. Fla., 1939; LL.B., U. Fla., 1942; LL.M., Harvard U., 1946; m. Lillian Herndon Bourne, Oct. 12, 1946; children—Eugene B., Nicholas R., Sharon A., Margot P. Admitted to Fla. bar, 1945, N.Y. bar, 1947, D.C. bar, 1951, Pa. bar, 1955, U.S. Supreme Ct. bar, 1953; atty. Sullivan & Cromwell, N.Y.C., 1946-48; spl. atty. IRS, 1949-51; partner firm Pepper, Lefevre, Orr & Faircloth, Washington, 1951-52; atty. Paul, Weiss, Rifkind, Wharton & Garrison, Washington, 1952-54, Chapman, Walsh & O'Connell, Washington, 1954-55; atty. Morgan, Lewis & Bockius, Phila., 1955, partner, 1956-79; pres., chief exec. officer, dir. UGI Corp., Valley Forge, Pa., 1979—; dir. AVC Corp.; mem. Commr.'s Adv. Group IRS, 1976-77; mem. adv. bd. N.Y. U. Tax Inst., 1962-67; mem. adv. bd. U. Pa. Tax Conf., 1970-79. Bd. dirs. Greater Phila. Found., 1965-79; v.p., mem. exec. com., dir. Delaware Valley Housing Assn., 1959-66; chmn. bd. trustees Agnes Irwin Sch., 1968-74; mem. health affairs com., asso. trustee U. Pa., 1976-78; mem. long range planning com. U. Pa. Med. Sch., 1975-79; trustee Inst. Cancer Research, 1979—. Served with USMC, 1942-46. Fellow Am. Bar Assn. (vice chmn. govt. relations sect. of taxation 1976-79), Greater Phila. C. of C. (exec. com., dir., gen. counsel), Pa. Bar Assn., Phila. Bar Assn., Fla. Bar Assn. Episcopalian. Clubs: Sunday Breakfast, Union League (Phila.); Merion Cricket (Ardmore, Pa.). Office: PO Box 858 Valley Forge PA 19482

LEFEVRE (STERNE), RICHARD GREGG, educator; b. Phila., May 9, 1921; s. Leon Thomas and Elizabeth Gertrude (Limburg) LeF.; B.A. with honors, Swarthmore Coll., 1942; M.A., Duke U., 1947; Ph.D., U. Pa., 1962; m. Mary Louise Stowe, May 30, 1948; children—Christopher Stowe, Mary Elizabeth, John Stephen. Research asst. Pa. Commn. on Penal Affairs, Phila., 1946; instr. sociology Tufts Coll., Medford, Mass., 1948-49, Northeastern U., Boston, 1950-51; dir. budgeting Providence Community Fund, 1955-60; dir. research Social Service Council, Trenton, N.J., 1960-62, Welfare Planning Council, Miami, Fla., 1962-68; dir. social research Citizen's Planning Council, Rochester, N.Y., 1968-73; asso. prof. urban studies, sociology U. Akron (Ohio), 1973-78, asso. prof. urban studies, 1978—. Adj. asso. prof. sociology U. Miami, 1962-68; lectr. sociology St. John Fisher Coll., Rochester, N.Y., 1970-73; mem. Consortium on Aging, Akron U.-Kent State U., Akron, 1973—; cons. Age Discrimination Study, U.S. Commn. Civil Rights, 1977. NIMH grantee, 1965. Mem. Soc. of Friends (Indian Affairs com. N.Y. Yearly Meeting 1971—), Assn. Humanist Sociology (dir. 1976-79), Gamma Mu. Author: Delinquent Conduct and Broken Homes, 1964; (with James E. Phillips, Alvin Rabushka) The Urban Elderly Poor: Racial and Bureaucratic Conflict, 1974; (with Frank J. Costa) Public Rule or Ruling Classes-Value Debates in Administration and Planning, 1978. Author govt. reports. Contbr. articles, revs. to profl. and religious jours. Home: 4062 Greenwich Rd Norton OH 44203 Office: Dept of Urban Studies U Akron Akron OH 44325

LEFF, ARTHUR, govt. ofcl.; b. N.Y.C., Mar. 19, 1908; s. Isadore Isaac and Bessie (Mansion) L.; A.B., Cornell U., 1929, LL.B., 1930; m. Miriam Kapit, Feb. 23, 1934; 1 dau., Joanna (Mrs. Mark Pinsky). Admitted to N.Y. bar, 1931; practice in N.Y.C., 1931-42; adminstrv. law judge NLRB, SEC, Fed. Res. Bd., 1943-63; chief counsel to chmn. NLRB, 1963-70, asso. chief adminstrv. law judge, 1970—. Mem. Adminstrv. Conf. U.S., 1972-74. Mem. Am., Fed. bar assns., Conf. Adminstrv. Law Judges, Fed. Execs. League. Home: 2207 Richland Pl Silver Spring MD 20910 Office: 1717 Pennsylvania Ave Washington DC 20570

LEFF, CARL, mfg. co. exec.; b. N.Y.C., Oct. 23, 1897; s. Max and Sarah (Weinstein) L.; D.D.S., Columbia U., 1919; m. Eleanor Wiesen, Jan. 14, 1930; children—Marjorie (Mrs. Morgan Miller), Maxine (Mrs. George Myers). With Nat. Spinning Co., N.Y.C., 1919—, chmn., 1978—; dir. Beneficial Life Ins. Co. Trustee L.I. Coll. Medicine, 1945-49, Jewish Hosp., Bklyn., 1926—, Fedn. Jewish Philanthropies, United Jewish Appeal, N.Y.C., 1939—. Fellow Brandeis U., 1966—. Clubs: Masons, Metropolis Country (White Plains, N.Y.); Palm Beach (Fla.) Country; Harmonie (N.Y.C.). Home:

100 Sunrise Ave Palm Beach FL 33480 Office: 183 Madison Ave New York City NY 10016

LEFF, JULIUS JACK, publishing co. exec.; b. N.Y.C., Feb. 24, 1910; s. Harry and Sarah (Goodman) L.; student Columbia U., 1929-30, N.Y. U., 1932; m. Helen Elinne Milstein, Nov. 16, 1935; children—Howard, Stephen, Nancy. Reader, rewrite man newspaper The PM, N.Y.C., 1940-50; rewrite man N.Y. Star, 1950-51, N.Y. Times, 1951-53; v.p. Cambridge Book Co. div. N.Y. Times, N.Y.C., 1951—, editor-in-chief, editorial dir., 1951-75, advtg. dir., 1972-74, area sales rep., 1977—; v.p. Expn. Press, Inc., N.Y.C., 1975-76; pres. Edu-Services, Inc. Mem. Nat. Sch. Pub. Relations Assn., Nat. Sci. Tchrs. Assn., Nat. Assn. Book Editors, Nat. Council Social Studies, Fla. Vocat. Assn. Author: Unit Review Social Studies, 1942; Unit Review Math, 1943; Unit Review General Science, 1944; Safe Driving, 1953; Better and Faster Reading for Managers, 1968. Home: 7204 NW 92d Terr Fort Lauderdale FL 33321 Office: 488 Madison Ave New York City NY 10022

LEFF, STEPHEN M., advt. agy. exec.; b. N.Y.C., Oct. 30, 1939; s. Maurice and Hattie L.; B.S., Syracuse U., 1961; m. Bonnie Greenwald, Nov. 19, 1961; children—Lisa Jill, Samantha Lynn. With Screen Gems/Audience Studies Inc., N.Y.C., 1961-63, McManus John & Adams, N.Y.C., 1963-69; sr. radio-TV exec. McCann-Erickson, N.Y.C., 1969-70, sr. v.p., dir. radio/TV programming, 1971-78, exec. v.p., dir. media services, 1978—; v.p. spl. projects Winters Rosen, Inc., N.Y.C., 1970-71. Served with USAR, 1961. Mem. Am. Assn. Advt. Agys. Office: 485 Lexington Ave New York NY 10017

LEFFALL, LASALLE DOHENY, JR., physician, educator; b. Tallahassee, May 22, 1930; s. LaSalle Doheny and Martha Lula (Jordan) L.; B.S., Fla. A. and M. U., 1948; M.D., Howard U., 1952; m. Ruth Juanita McWilliams, Aug. 18, 1956; 1 son, LaSalle Doheny III. Intern, Homer G. Phillips Hosp., St. Louis, 1952-53; resident Freedmen's, D.C. Gen. hosps., Washington, 1953-57, Meml. Sloan Kettering Cancer Center, N.Y.C., 1957-59; practice medicine specializing in surgery, cancer disease, Washington, 1962—; asst. prof. surgery Howard U. Coll. Medicine, 1962-66, asso. prof., 1966-69, prof., chmn. dept. surgery, 1970—, mem. staff U. Hosp. Served with M.C., AUS, 1960-61. Diplomate Am. Bd. Surgery. Mem. Am. Cancer Soc. (pres. 1978-79, nat. dir.), Soc. Surg. Oncology (pres. 1978-79), Am. Gastroent. Assn., Inst. Med., Am. Surg. Assn., Soc. U. Surgeons, Soc. Head and Neck Surgeons, A.C.S., Southeastern Surg. Congress, N.A.A.C.P., Urban League, Alpha Phi Alpha. Club: Cosmos. Home: 2900 Ellicott St NW Washington DC 20008 Office: Howard Univ Hosp Washington DC 20060. *One of the highest standards of surgical discipline is "Equanimity under duress". This applies equally to one's personal life and professional life. One should set aside time at the end of the day as "Moments of Reflection"—to decide what did he do that he shouldn't have done, what didn't he do that he should have done. The prime goal is to help someone in some way each day.*

LEFFEK, KENNETH THOMAS, chemist, educator; b. Nottingham, Eng., Oct. 15, 1934; s. Thomas and Ivy Louise (Pye) L.; came to Can., 1959, naturalized, 1966; B.S., Univ. Coll., London, Eng., 1956, Ph.D., 1959; m. Janet Marilyn Wallace, Sept. 26, 1958; children—Katharine, Geoffrey. Asst. prof. chemistry Dalhousie U., Halifax, N.S., 1961-67, asso. prof., 1967-72, prof., dean grad. studies, 1972—. Chmn. Atlantic Provinces Interuniv. Com. on Scis., 1975-77. Leverhulme fellow U. Kent (Eng.), 1967-68. Fellow Chem. Inst. Can., Royal Soc. Arts (London); mem. Chem. Soc. London, Chem. Inst. Can. (chmn. Atlantic sect. 1973-74). Club: Waegwoltic (Halifax). Contbr. articles on phys.-organic chemistry to profl. jours. Office: Faculty Grad Studies Dalhousie U Coburg Rd Halifax NS B3H 4H6 Canada

LEFFEL, CHARLES POAGUE, elec. appliances co. exec.; b. Evanston, Ill., May 30, 1928; s. Philip Clark and Catherine Smith (Poague) L.; A.B., Amherst Coll., 1950; m. Grace Ann Hartnett, June 2, 1962; 1 dau., Kay. Salesman, Goodbody & Co., Chgo., 1950-51, Internat. Paper Co., Cleve., 1951-54; exec. v.p. No. Electric Co., 1957-67, pres., 1967-72; v.p., pres. non-Sunbeam domestic consumer products group Sunbeam Corp., Oak Brook, Ill., 1974-76, exec. v.p. parent co., 1976-77, pres. domestics consumer products group, 1976-77, pres. corp., 1977—, also dir. Bd. mgrs. Chgo. Boys Club Camps, Robert E. Wood Boys Club. Served with AUS. Clubs: Metropolitan, Racquet (Chgo.); Glen View (Golf, Ill.); Deke (N.Y.C.). Home: 30 E Scott St Chicago IL 60610 Office: 2001 S York Rd Oak Brook IL 60521

LEFFERTS, GEORGE, writer, producer, dir.; b. Paterson, N.J.; s. Morris and Elinor (Jacobs) L.; B.A. in Engring. (Nat. Merit scholar, William Rose scholar), Drew U., 1940; B.A. in English, U. Mich., 1942; m. Elizabeth Ruth Schaul, Dec. 29, 1942; children—Lauren Ruth, Barbara Ellen. Exec. producer, writer, dir. NBC, 1947-57; prodns. include Biographies in Sound (Peabody award 1956), NBC Theatre (Ohio State award 1955), Kraft Theatre, Armstrong Circle Theatre, Studio One, Lights Out, Frank Sinatra Show, spl. program Pain, 1971, Bravo Picasso!, 1972, What Price Health program NBC Investigative Reports, 1972, CBS Ben Franklin Series (Peabody award 1975, Emmy award 1975); exec. producer, writer, dir. NBC Spls. for Women series (Emmy award 1962, Golden Globe award 1961), 1961; exec. producer series Breaking Point (Producers Guild Plaudit award 1963), 1962-64, CBS Smithsonian Spls., 1974-75, ABC Wide World of Entertainment, 1973-74; exec. producer Bing Crosby Prodns., 1962-64, Wolper Prodns., 1974-75, Time/Life Films, 1978-79; original Films include The Living End, 1959, The Stake, 1960, The Teenager, 1965, The Harness, 1972, Miss Beautiful, 1977, Bud & Lou, 1978; Mean Dog Blues, 1979; producer Hallmark Hall of Fame, 1969-70; producer Teacher, Teacher (Emmy award 1970), 1968; pres. George Lefferts Assos., 1968—; exec. producer ABC, 1966-67; exhibited sculpture Sculpture Gallery, N.Y.C., 1960; producer Report from America series U.S. Dept. State, Tactic series Am. Cancer Soc., others. Served with AUS, 1942-45. Recipient Nat. Media award, 1961, Fame award, 1962, Fgn. Press award, 1963, Golden Globe award, 1967, Plaudit award Producers Guild, 1968, 69, Cine Golden Eagle award, 1974, Peabody award, 1970, 75, 1st prize San Francisco Film Festival, 1970. Mem. Nat. Acad. TV Arts and Scis., Am. Acad. Motion Picture Arts and Scis., Christopher Morley Knothole Assn. Club: South Bay Cruising (Babylon, (N.Y.). Author: (plays) Nantucket Legend, 1960; The Boat, 1968; Hey Everybody, 1969; also mag. articles, works on piano method, syndicated guest columns, others. Address: Glen Goin Alpine NJ 07620 also Robbins Rest Fire Island NY 11776. *I have never tried to accomplish anything, only to experience the poetry of living—and to share that poetry by loving, writing, and creating.*

LEFFERTS, GILLET, JR., architect; b. N.Y.C., May 6, 1923; s. Gillet and Helen Willets (Lambert) L.; grad. Deerfield Acad., 1941; A.B., Williams Coll., 1947; M.F.A., Princeton, 1950; m. Lucia Beverly Hollerith, Apr. 21, 1951; children—Helena Gillet (dec.), Robert Beverly, John Willets, Sarah Fox, David Hollerith. Apprentice, Moore & Hutchins, N.Y.C., 1947-48, 50-55, asso. mem., 1955-66, partner, 1967-72; partner Hutchins, Evans & Lefferts, N.Y.C., 1972—; instr. Mechanics Inst., N.Y.C., 1955-58. Mem. Zoning Bd. Appeals, Darien, Conn., 1961-69; mem. Planning and Zoning Commn., 1969-77, chmn., 1973-77. Served as pilot USAAF, 1943-46. Decorated Air medal with oak leaf cluster. Fellow AIA; mem. Fairfield County Alumni Assn. Williams Coll. (v.p. 1965-67), Nat. Inst. Archtl. Edn. (chmn. bd. trustees 1963-65, treas. 1970-73), Delta Psi. Episcopalian. Clubs: Century Assn., St. Anthony, Williams (N.Y.C.); Norwalk (Conn.) Yacht. Architect master plan and ednl. facilities SUNY, Binghamton, 1956-79; master plan Coll. Agr. Malaya, 1970; St. Johnland Home, L.I., N.Y., 1976. Office: 155 E 44th St New York NY 10017

LEFKOWITZ, IRVING, educator; b. N.Y.C., July 8, 1921; s. Adolph and Celia (Berko) L.; B.S. in Chem. Engring., Cooper Union, 1943; M.S. in Instrumentation Engring., Case Inst. Tech., 1955, Ph.D., 1958; m. Madelyn I. Moinester, July 3, 1955; children—Deborah, Daniel. With J.E. Seagram & Sons, 1943-53, dir. instrumentation research, 1951-53; faculty Case Inst. Tech., 1953—, prof. engring., 1965—, dir. research group in control complex systems, 1960—, acting head systems engring. dept. Case Western Res. U., 1972-76. Mem. sci. staff Internat. Inst. for Applied Systems Analysis, Austria, 1974-75. Cons. in field, 1959—. NATO postdoctoral fellow, 1962-63. Mem. AAAS, IEEE (adv. com. systems sci. and cybernetics group 1969-72), Am. Automatic Control Council (chmn. systems engring. com. 1968-69), IFAC (vice-chmn. systems engring. com. 1975-78, chmn. com. 1978—), Instrument Soc. Am., Sigma Xi. Contbr. papers to profl. lit. Editorial adv. bd. Jour. Dynamic Systems, Measurement and Control, 1972-77. Home: 3532 Meadowbrook Blvd Cleveland Heights OH 44118 Office: University Circle Cleveland OH 44106

LEFKOWITZ, LOUIS J., lawyer; b. N.Y.C., July 3, 1904; s. Samuel and Mollie (Isaacs) L.; LL.B. cum laude, Fordham U., 1925; m. Helen Schwimmer, June 14, 1931; children—Joan (Mrs. Harold Feinbloom), Stephen Allan. Admitted to N.Y. bar, 1926; pvt. practice law, N.Y.C.; justice Municipal Ct., N.Y.C., 1935, City Ct., 1954; atty. gen. N.Y., Albany, 1957-79; mem. firm Phillips, Nizer, Benjamin, Krim & Ballon, N.Y.C., 1979—. Mem. N.Y. Assembly, 1928-30; del. Republican Nat. Conv., 1944, 48, alt. del., 1956. Active numerous civic activities. Bd. dirs. Florence Crittenton League. Mem. Assn. Bar City N.Y., N.Y. County Lawyers Assn., Fed., Am. bar assns., Nat. Assn. Attys. Gen. (pres.), Assn. Lawyers Criminal Cts. Manhattan, Grand St. Boys Assn., Am. Jewish Congress. Jewish. K.P.; mem. B'nai B'rith. Home: 575 Park Ave New York NY 10021 Office: 40 W 57th St New York NY 10019

LEFKOWITZ, NAT, talent agy. exec.; b. Bklyn., July 24, 1905; s. Henry and Rose (Berkowitz) L.; diploma Coll. City N.Y., 1922-26; LL.M., Bklyn. Law Sch., 1938; m. Sally Feigelman, Feb. 27, 1932; children—Dorothy Beth (Mrs. Burton L. Litwin), Rona Carol Lefkowitz Pinkus, Helene Andrea (Mrs. Robert D. Nachtigall). Accountant, Gottheimer, Getz & Co., 1924-26; comptroller, treas., exec. v.p., treas. William Morris Agy., Inc., N.Y.C., 1927-69, pres., 1969-76, co-chmn., 1976—, also dir.; admitted to N.Y. bar, 1938; v.p. Jewish Theatrical Guild. Active amusement and entertainment divs. United Jewish Appeal and Fedn. Jewish Philanthropies, 1945—, chmn. television industry's campaign for fedn., 1968, recipient award in honor entertainment div., 1975. Trustee Will Rogers Hosp., O'Donnell Meml. Research Labs. Recipient Human Rights award Anti-Defamation League, 1969; Man of Year award Variety Club Found. N.Y., 1978; C.P.A., N.Y. Mem. Motion Picture Pioneers, Nat. Acad. TV Arts and Scis., Variety Clubs Internat. Jewish. Mem. B'nai B'rith. Clubs: City Athletic; Friars; Dellwood Country. Home: 91 Central Park W New York NY 10023 Office: 1350 Ave of Americas New York NY 10019

LEFLAR, ROBERT ALLEN, legal educator; b. Siloam Springs, Ark., Mar. 22, 1901; s. Lewis D. and Viva (Pilkington) L.; B.A., U. Ark., 1922; LL.B. cum laude, Harvard, 1927, S.J.D., 1932; m. Doris Drake, June 20, 1928; 1 foster dau., Helen; m. 2d, Helen Finger, Oct. 18, 1946; children—Robert B., Charles J.F. Tchr. high sch., Stuttgart, Ark., 1922; prof. journalism John E. Brown Coll., Siloam Springs, 1923-24; admitted to Ark. bar, 1928, U.S. Supreme Ct. bar, 1943; asso. justice Ark. Supreme Ct., 1949-51; tchr. law U. Ark., 1927—, dean Law Sch., 1943-54, now distinguished prof. law; prof. law N.Y. U., 1954—, dir. Appellate Judges Seminars, 1956-77, cons. dir., 1977—. Regional atty., then asst. solicitor War Relocation Authority, 1942-44; pub. mem. Regional War Labor Bd., 1944-45. Sec., Ark. Criminal Law Reform Commn., 1934-37; chmn. Ark. Statute Revision Commn., 1945-54; Ark. commr., life mem. Nat. Conf. Commrs. Uniform State Laws; chmn. Ark. Constl. Revision Com., 1967; pres. Ark. Constl. Conv., 1969-70, 79-80; past pres. S.W. Athletic Conf. Mem. Am., Ark. bar assns., Am. Judicature Soc., Phi Beta Kappa. Methodist. Author: American Conflicts Law, 3d edit., 1977; The First 100 Years (U. Ark. history), 1972; Appellate Judicial Opinions, 1974; Internal Operating Procedures of Appellate Courts, 1976. Home: 1717 W Center St Fayetteville AR 72701. *My purpose has been to help those who work in the law to understand not only what the law has been and is, but also what it can become as it increasingly serves its true function in society—good and peaceful order among mankind.*

LEFLORE, BYRON LOUIS, banker; b. San Antonio, Feb. 6, 1936; s. Louis and Margaret (Byron) LeF.; B.B.A., U. Tex. at Austin, 1958, postgrad., 1958-59; grad. Grad. Sch. Credit and Fin. Mgmt. Harvard, 1973; m. Kathryn Barragan, June 22, 1962; children—Byron Louis Jr., Elizabeth Barragan, James Milo, Campbell Joseph. With Mission City Bank, San Antonio, 1959-69, v.p., 1960-69, exec. v.p., 1969; v.p. Nat. Bank Commerce, San Antonio, 1969-71, sr. v.p., 1971-73; exec. v.p. Baxar County Nat. Bank, San Antonio, 1973-74, pres., chief exec. officer, 1974—. Former chmn., pres. Travelers Aid Soc., Central Index San Antonio, Madonna Neighborhood Centers; past pres. Creative Arts San Antonio, Inc.; former treas., past mem. exec. com., past chmn. San Antonio chpt. Am. Heart Assn.; former chmn. devel. drive council Boy Scouts Am. Former bd. dirs. S.W. Heart and Lung Center, San Antonio Fedn. Neighborhood Centers; bd. dirs. Catholic Family and Childrens Service, Community Welfare Council, Econ. Opportunity Devel. Corp., Tex. Assn. Bus., United Way, Met. YMCA Downtown, Inc.; bd. dirs., Cath. co-chmn. NCCJ; past chmn. Archdiocesan exec. com.; mem. Centro Downtown Transp. Center Com., City and County Coop. Com., Santa Rosa Children's Hosp., Sunsline Cottage investment com., numerous other civic activities; trustee Incarnate Word Coll.; past mem. exec. com. Am. Heart Assn.; mem. adv. council U. Tex. at San Antonio Coll. Bus. Mem. San Antonio C. of C. (dir., former vice chmn. devel. fund council, steering com. econ. devel. council), Beta Theta Pi. Home: 214 Morton St San Antonio TX 78209 Office: PO Box 300 San Antonio TX 78291

LEFRAK, JOSEPH SAUL, lawyer, accountant; b. N.Y.C., Sept. 23, 1930; s. Paul B. and Elizabeth (Iken) L.; student N.Y. U., 1948-52; B.S., Bklyn. Law Sch., 1955, J.D., 1955; m. Susan Siskind, Sept. 14, 1952; children—Babette C., Mark P. Admitted to N.Y. State bar, 1955, Fla. bar, 1978, U.S. Supreme Ct. bar, 1960; practiced in N.Y.C.; partner firm Winter & Lefrak, C.P.A.'s, N.Y.C., 1959-66, Blackman, Lefrak & Blackman, C.P.A.'s, 1966-72, Lefrak, Fischer, Myerson & Mandell, and predecessors, 1966—. Bd. dirs. Asso. Camps YM-YWHA; trustee Reece Sch. Mem. Am., N.Y. State bar assns., Am. Inst. C.P.A.'s, N.Y. Soc. C.P.A.'s, Am., N.Y. assns. atty. C.P.A.'s. Jewish (trustee, v.p. congregation). Clubs: City Athletic, Merchants (N.Y.C.). Home: 983 Park Ave New York City NY 10024 Office: 575 Madison Ave New York City NY 10022 also 249 Royal Palm Way Palm Beach FL

LEFRAK, JOSEPH SAUL, lawyer, accountant; b. N.Y.C., Sept. 23, 1930; s. Paul B. and Elizabeth (Iken) L.; student N.Y. U., 1948-52; B.S., Bklyn. Law Sch., 1955, J.D., 1955; m. Susan Siskind, Sept. 14, 1952; children—Babette C., Mark P. Admitted to N.Y. State bar, 1955, Fla. bar, 1978, U.S. Supreme Ct. bar, 1960; practiced in N.Y.C.; and Palm Beach, partner firm Winter & Lefrak, C.P.A.'s, N.Y.C., 1959-66, Blackman, Lefrak & Blackman, C.P.A.'s, 1966-72, Lefrak, Fischer, Attys. at Law, Myerson & Mandell, and predecessors, 1966—. Bd. dirs. Asso. Camps YM-YWHA; trustee Reece Sch. Mem. Am., N.Y. State, Fla. bar assns., Am. Inst. C.P.A.'s, N.Y. Soc. C.P.A.'s, Young Men's Philanthropic League, Am., N.Y. assns. atty. C.P.A.'s. Jewish (trustee, v.p. congregation). Clubs: City Athletic, Merchants (N.Y.C.). Home: 983 Park Ave New York NY 10028 Office: 575 Madison Ave New York NY 10022

LEFRAK, SAMUEL J., housing and bldg. corp. exec., real estate devel., fin., oil and gas exploration, instant communication, music pub., motion picture exec., pub. ofcl.; b. N.Y.C., Feb. 12, 1918; s. Harry and Sarah (Schwartz) L.; grad. U. Md., 1940; postgrad. Columbia, Harvard; Sc.D., London Coll. Applied Sci., 1970; LL.D. N.Y. Law Sch., 1975, Colgate U., 1979; consulate laureate Univ. Studies, Rome, 1972; m. Ethel Stone, May 14, 1941; children—Denise, Richard, Francine, Jacqueline. Pres., Lefrak Orgn., 1948—, chmn. bd., 1975—; creator, sponsor, builder Lefrak City; mem. adv. bd. Sta. WHLI, 1955; commr. Landmarks Preservation Commn. N.Y.C., 1966; commr. pub. works Borough Manhattan, 1956-58; commr. Interstate Sanitation Commn., 1958; Saratoga Springs Commn., 1962—. Mem. adv. bd. Chem Bank.; guest lectr. Harvard Grad. Sch. Bus. Adminstrn., 1971, Yale, 1975, N.Y. U., 1977; guest speaker Financial Women's Assn. N.Y., 1975; featured speaker Instl. Investment Real Estate Conf., 1975; U.S. del. Internat. Conf. Housing and Urban Devel., Switzerland, 1967; dir. N.Y. World's Fair Corp., 1964-65, N.Y. Indsl. Devel. Corp., 1975—; chmn. bd. L.I. Post; pres. N.Y.C. Comml. Devel. Corp., 1967-71, chmn., 1971—; founding mem. World Business Council, Inc., 1970; mem. Gov. N.Y. finance and adv. com. N.Y. State Traffic Safety Council, 1966; mem. Pres.'s Com. Employment Handicapped; spl. cons. urban affairs State Dept., 1969; mem. adv. council Real Estate Inst., N.Y. U., 1970—; commr. Saratoga-Capital dist. N.Y. State Park and Recreation Commn., 1973; mem. N.Y.C. Pub. Devel. Corp.; mem. Nat. Energy Council, U.S. Dept. Commerce; mem. Mayor's Com. on Housing Devel., N.Y.C., 1974—; mem. exec. com. Citizen's Com. for N.Y.C., Inc., 1975—; mem. N.Y. State Gov.'s Task Force on Housing, 1974. vice chmn.-at-large A.R.C. in N.Y.; mem. U.S. com. UN Orgn., 1957; chmn. nat. bd. Histadrut, 1967—; chmn. bldg. com. Saratoga Performing Arts; mem. Fifth Ave. Assn.; dir., chmn. real estate div. Greater N.Y. Fund; hon. com. A.A.U.; Queens chmn. United Greek Orthodox Charities, 1973; chmn. Celebrity Sports Night-Human Resources Center, 1973-74. Trustee, dir. Beth-El Hosp.; bd. dirs. U.S.O., Citizens Housing and Planning Council N.Y., 1957—, Interfaith Movement, Diabetics Found., Queens Cultural Assn., Consumer Credit Counseling Service Greater N.Y., Astoria Motion Picture and TV Center Found.; trustee N.Y. Law Sch., Queens Art and Cultural Center, N.Y. Citizens Budget Com., Jewish Hosp. at Denver, Brookdale Hosp. Med. Center; trustee, mem. adv. bd. Pace U.; mem. exec. bd. Greater N.Y. councils Boy Scouts Am.; founder Albert Einstein Sch. Medicine; bd. govs. Invest-in-Am. Nat. Council. Decorated Order St. John of Jerusalem (Pope John); recipient Mayor N.Y.C. award outstanding citizenship, 1960; Nat. Boys Club award, 1960; Citizen of Year award B'nai B'rith, 1963, Distinguished Achievement award, 1967; Man of Year award V.F.W., 1963; Brotherhood award NCCJ, 1964; Chief Rabbi Herzog gold medal, Torah Fellowship citation Religious Zionist Am., 1966; John F. Kennedy Peace award, 1966; Man of Year award Bklyn. Community Hosp., 1967; Builder of Excellence award Brandeis Sch., 1968; Master Builder award N.Y. Cardiac Center, 1968; Distinguished Citizen award M Club Found. U. Md., 1970; Distinguished Alumnus award U. Md. Alumni Assn., 1970; Am. Eagle award nat. council Invest-in Am., 1972; Exec. Sportsman award Human Resources Center, 1973; Archtl. award Fifth Av. Assn., 1974; Excellence in Design award Queens C. of C., 1974; named hon. citizen Md., 1970. Mem. Sales Execs. Club N.Y. (dir.), United Hunts Racing Assn., Philharmonic Symphony Soc. N.Y., Explorers Club (dir.), Phi Kappa Phi, Tau Epsilon Phi (established Samuel J. LeFrak scholarship award 1975). Clubs: Masons, Shriners; Lotos (dir. 1975—, Merit award 1973), Grand Street Boys, Friars (dir. Found.), Advertising, Economic, Downtown Athletic (N.Y.C.); Town; Turf and Field; Cat Cay (Nassau, Bahamas); Xanadu Yacht (Freeport, Grand Bahamas); Palm Bay (Miami Beach, Fla.); Seawane; Ocean Reef (Key Largo); Sag Harbor Yacht (L.I.). Office: 97-77 Queens Blvd Forest Hills NY 11374

LEFTON, AL PAUL, JR., advt. exec.; b. Wilmington, Del., July 11, 1928; s. Al Paul and Clara Belle (Ginns) L.; B.A., Yale, 1950; m. Amarilice Miller, Dec. 28, 1951; children—Alice, Marie, Al Paul III. With Al Paul Lefton Co., Inc., Phila., 1950—, v.p., sec., 1961-64, pres., chief exec. officer, 1964—. Bd. dirs. Eaglesville Sanitarium, 1965-79, Robin Hood Dell, Med. Coll. Pa., Phila. Coll. Art; trustee No. Home for Children. Served with AUS, 1951-53. Clubs: Yale (N.Y.C., Phila.); Union League (Phila.). Office: Rohm & Haas Bldg Independence Mall W Philadelphia PA 19106 also 71 Vanderbilt Ave New York NY 10017

LEFTWICH, JAMES ADOLF, writer, publisher, pub. relations exec.; b. Newport News, Va., July 23, 1902; s. David and Eugenia Leftwich; student Augusta Mil. Acad., 1920; archtl. course U. Va., 1921-25; hon. alumnus U. Calif. at San Diego, 1964; m. Ilka Renwick, Sept. 2, 1947; 1 dau., Jean Renwick (Mrs. Tom Bushnell); m. 2d, Merry Ann Ottosen, Mar. 12, 1963. Feature writer Miami (Fla.) Tab, 1926; editorial dept. Sun, N.Y.C., 1926-29; with book rev. sect. N.Y. Am., 1930-31; feature editor Nat. Radio Press Syndicate, 1932-35, Newport News Times Herald, 1934-36; feature writer, editor various publs., 1936—; dir. art, pub. relations Art Assos., N.Y.C., 1939-42; pub. relations dir. Congl. Com. for Investigation FCC, 1943; pub. relations asso. Com. Internat. Econ. Policy, Reciprocal Trade Agreements Act, 1944, Com. Internat. Econ. Policy for Loan Agreement to Gt. Britain, 1946; pub. relations counsel N.Y. Bd. Trade, 1943-50, vice chmn. aviation sect., 1947; mem. Leftwich & Barkley, pub. relations cons., N.Y.C., 1951-56; pub. relations Ryan Aero. Co., 1957; pub. relations dir. Sorrento Valley Indsl. Park, Indsl, Developers, Ltd., San Diego; advt. dir., pub. relations counsel La Jolla Fed. Savs. & Loan Assn., La Jolla Town Council, La Jolla Decent Lit. Com.; pub. relations dir. La Jolla br. Am. Cancer Soc., 1959-60; established La Jolla Press, 1968. Initiated nat. program to raise Civil War ironclad Monitor sunk off Cape Hatteras, 1947, 68. Served as athletic officer 111th F.A., Va. N.G., 1926. Named col. Ky. Gov.'s staff, 1952. Mem. John Erisson Soc., U.S. Olympians (v.p. 1954-55, exec. com.), San Diego Arms Collectors, Soc. Profl. Journalists, Thomas Jefferson Soc. of Alumni of U. Va., U. Va. Club So. Calif. (founder, pres.), Sigma Delta Chi. Episcopalian. Clubs: Nat. Press (Washington); Advertising (N.Y.C.); Country; Racquet (pub. relations and advt. dir.), La Jolla Gun, Sportsmens, Beach and Tennis (La Jolla); Sportsmens (New Hope, Pa.); New Jersey Gun Collectors; Navesink River (N.J.) Rod and Gun; Maine Biggest Bucks; Mt. Desert Isle (Maine) Game Assn.; San Diego Duck and Skeet (pub. relations dir.); Press and Union League (San Francisco). Author: Frank Forester, 1931; O'Malley and other Stories, 1951; Meet Sir

George Carteret, 1953; La Jolla's House of Many Legends, 1960; The Record and Legend of the Ancient Aztec Calendar, 1967; also articles in gun publs. Editor: Pathology Laboratory Careers for Tissue Technicians; A Pathology Laboratory Can Be Attractive As Well As Efficient. Editor mag. Am. Soc. Swedish Engrs., 1945-48. Contbr., research dir. Merrimack and Monitor, also Duel of the Ironclads, 1969. Mem. U.S. Olympic Boxing Team, 1924, U.S. Nat. Middleweight Champion. Home: PO Box 3333 2056 Torrey Pines Rd La Jolla CA 92038

LEFTWICH, RICHARD HENRY, educator; b. Burden, Kans., Feb. 1, 1920; s. Rush F. and Nellie (Bailiff) L.; B.A., Southwestern Coll., 1941; M.A., U. Chgo., 1948, Ph.D., 1950; m. Maxine Ellen Dieterich, Mar. 11, 1945; children—Judith E., Gregory V., Bradley R. Asst. prof., asso. prof. Okla. State U., Stillwater, 1948-55, prof. econs., 1955-75, head dept. econs., 1966-75, Regents prof. econs., 1975—, Ford Found. faculty research fellow, 1959-60; vis. prof. U. Chgo., 1962-63. Dir. Ford Found. Faculty Research Seminar, 1960. Served with USAAF, 1942-45. Decorated Bronze Star medal. Mem. Am., Midwestern (pres. 1977), So. (pres. 1965) econ. assns., Southwestern, Western (pres. 1973) social sci. assns. Author: The Price System and Resource Allocation, 1955, 7th edit., 1979; An Introduction to Economic Thinking, 1969; (with Ansel M. Sharp) The Economics of Social Issues, 4th edit., 1980; A Basic Framework for Economics, 1980. Home: 818 W Knapp Ave Stillwater OK 74074

LEFTWICH, SAMUEL GILMER, retail co. exec.; b. Homer, Nebr., Dec. 10, 1926; s. Samuel Abel and Norma Emma (Ritchison) L.; B.S. in Bus. Adminstrn., U. Nebr., Omaha, 1949; m. Doris Mae Krupa, Oct. 1, 1950; children—James, Scott, Sharon, Thomas, Robert, William. With K Mart Corp. (formerly S.S. Kresge Co.), 1949—, dir. food ops. K mart Internat. Hdqrs., Troy, Mich., 1974-75, v.p. personnel and employee relations, Troy, 1976-79, sr. v.p. personnel and mgmt. devel., Troy, Mich., 1979—. Served with AC, USN, 1944-46; PTO. Office: 3100 W Big Beaver Troy MI 48084

LE GALLIENNE, EVA, actress; b. London, Jan. 11, 1899; d. Richard and Julie (Norregaard) Le G.; ed. Collège Sévigne, Paris; M.A. (hon.), Tufts Coll., 1927; D.H.L., Smith Coll., 1930, Ohio Wesleyan U., 1959, Goucher Coll., 1960, U. N.C., 1964, Barr's Coll., 1965, Fairfield U., 1966; Litt.D., Russell Sage Coll., 1930, Brown U., 1933, Mount Holyoke Coll., 1937. Debut in The Laughter of Fools, Prince of Wales Theatre, London, 1915; New York debut in The Melody of Youth, 1916; appeared in New York and on tour in Mr. Lazarus, 1916-17; with Ethel Barrymore in The Off Chance, 1917-18; Not So Long Ago, 1920-21; Liliom, 1921-22; The Swan, 1923; Hannele in The Assumption of Hanele, by Hauptmann, 1923; Jeanne d'Arc, by Mercedes de Acosta, 1925; The Call of Life, by Schnitzler, 1925; The Master Builder, by Ibsen, 1925-26; founder, dir. Civic Repertory Theatre, N.Y.C., opening October 25, 1926; presented over 30 plays in 7 years including Three Sisters, Cradle Song, Inheritors, Peter Pan, Romeo and Juliet, Camille, Allison's House (Pulitzer prize), Alice in Wonderland; starred in Therese, 1945; co-founder with Margaret Webster of Am. Repertory Theatre, which produced (1946, 47), Shakespeare's Henry the Eighth, Barrie's What Every Woman Knows, Ibsen's John Gabriel Borkman, Shaw's Androcles and the Lion, Howard's Yellow Jack, Lewis Carroll's Alice in Wonderland, Ibsen's Hedda Gabler and Ghosts, 1948; toured in The Corn Is Green, 1949-50; on Broadway in The Southwest Corner, 1955; as Queen Elizabeth in Schiller's Mary Stuart, N.Y.C., 1957, on tour, 1959-60; in Maxwell Anderson's Elizabeth the Queen, 1961-62; toured in Sea Gull, Nat. Repertory Theatre, 1963-64, in Madwoman of Chalilot and The Trojan Women; appeared with APA Repertory Theatre, N.Y.C. as Marguerite in Exit The King; also directed Chekov's The Cherry Orchard, 1967-68, Doll's House, Seattle Repertory, 1975; appeared as Countess in All's Well That Ends Well, Shakespeare Festival Theatre, Stratford, Conn., 1970, in The Dream Watcher, White Barn Theatre, 1975; The Royal Family, Helen Hayes Theatre, N.Y.C., 1976, nat. tour, 1976-77; appeared in movie The Resurrection, 1979. Recipient Brandeis U. award for drama, 1966; winner of Pictoral Rev. Achievement award, 1926; gold medal Soc. Arts and Town Hall Club award, 1934; Am. Acad. Arts and Letters medal for good diction on the stage 1945; Outstanding Woman of Year award Women's Nat. Press Club, 1947; spl. award ANTA, 1964, award, 1977; Spl. Tony award Am. Theatre Wing, 1964; Handel medallion City N.Y., 1976; Emmy award, 1978; decorated cross Royal Order St. Olaf, 1961. Mem. Actors' Equity Assn., Dramatists Guild. Author: At 33 (autobiography), 1934; Flossie and Bossie, 1949 (London edit. 1950); With a Quiet Heart, 1953; The Mystic in the Theatre, a study of Eleonora Duse, 1966. Translator many works of Henrik Ibsen, Hans Christian Anderson. Home: Hillside Rd Weston CT 06880

LEGARE, HENRI FRANCIS, clergyman; b. Willow-Bunch, Sask., Can., Feb. 20, 1918; s. Phillippe and Amanda (Douville) L.; B.A., U. Ottawa, 1940; theol. student, Lebret, Sask., 1940-44; M.A., Laval U., 1946; Dr. Social Sci., Cath. U. Lille (France), 1950; LL.D. (hon.), Carleton U., Ottawa, 1959, Windsor (Ont.) U., 1960, Queens U., Kingston, Ont., 1961, U. Sask., 1963, Waterloo (Ont.) Luth. U., 1965. Ordained priest Roman Cath. Ch., 1943; prof. sociology Laval U., 1947, U. Ottawa, 1951; exec. dir. Cath. Hosp. Assn. Can., 1952-57; dean faculty social scis. U. Ottawa, 1954-58, pres., 1958-64; provincial Oblate Fathers, Winnipeg, Man., 1966-67; bishop of Labrador, 1967-72; archbishop Grouard-McLennan, Alta., 1972—. Chmn., Canadian Univs. Found., 1960- 62. Decorated grand cross merit Order Malta, 1964; order merit French Lang. Assn. Ont., 1965. Mem. Assn. Canadian Univs. (pres. 1960-62), Internat. Assn. Polit. Sci. Contbr. articles to profl. jours. Address: Archbishop's House CP 388 McLennan AB T0H 2L0 Canada

LEGAULT, ALBERT, polit. scientist; b. Montreal, Que., Can., June 7, 1938; s. Fortunat and Felecilda (Geoffrion) L.; B.A., U. Montreal, 1959; M.A., U. Chgo., 1961; Ph.D., U. Geneva, 1964; degree in law (hon.), U. Paris, 1976; 1 dau., Cornelia. Chmn. strategic studies Queen's U., Kingston, Ont., Can., 1968-69; prof. polit. sci. Laval U., Quebec, Que., 1969—, dir. gen. Centre Quebecois de Relations Internationales, 1973—; asso. dir. Can. Inst. Internat. Affairs, Toronto, Ont., 1975—. Fellow Royal Soc. Can.; mem. Can. Inst. Internat. Affairs, Internat. Inst. Strategic Studies, Atlantic Inst. Can., Can. Polit. Sci. Assn. Roman Catholic. Author: with George Lindsey) The Dynamics of the Nuclear Balance, 1974, 2d, rev. edit., 1976. Office: Laval U Faculte des Sciences Sociales Quebec PQ G1K 7P4 Canada

LEGER, JULES, former gov. gen. of Can.; b. St. Anicet, Que., Can., Apr. 4, 1913; s. Ernest and Alda (Beauvais) L.; B.A., Coll. of Valleyfield, 1933; postgrad. U. Montreal, 1933-36; LL.D., U. Sorbonne, 1938; m. Gaby Carmel, 1938; 1 dau., Helene. Asso. editor Ottawa daily Le Droit, 1938-39; prof. history of diplomacy U. Ottawa, 1939-42; 3d sec. Dept. External Affairs, 1940-43; mem. Canadian mission in Chile, 1943-47; 1st sec. to London, 1947; adviser Canadian del. Gen. Assembly UN, Paris, 1948-49; exec. asst. to prime minister, 1949; participant Commonwealth Prime Ministers Meeting, London, 1950; chief European Div., 1950; asst. under-sec. state for external affairs, 1951-53; ambassador to Mexico, 1953-54; under-sec. state for external affairs, 1954-58; ambassador, permanent rep. N.Atlantic Council, Canadian rep. OEEC, Paris, 1958-62; participant ministerial meetings NATO, 1958-62, Atlantic Congress, London, 1959; ambassador to Italy, 1962-64, to France, 1964-68; under-sec. state in fields of arts and cultural support, bilingualism, edn. and citizenship, 1968-73; ambassador to Belgium and Luxembourg, 1973-74; gov. gen., comdr.-in-chief of Can., 1974-79; apptd. to Privy Council, 1979. Decorated companion Order of Can., comdr. Order Mil. Merit. Office: 3-B-132 Pearson Bldg Ottawa ON Canada

LEGER, PAUL-EMILE, cardinal; b. Valleyfield, Que., Can., Apr. 26, 1904; s. Ernest and Alda (Beauvais) L.; student Sem. St. Therese; L.Th., Grand Sem. Montreal; J.C.L., Inst. Catholique, Paris, France; S.T.D., Laval U., 1951, U. Ottawa, 1961; Litt.D., Assumption Coll., 1954; LL.D., McGill U., 1960, St. Francis Xavier U., 1961, U. Toronto, 1965, U. Alta., 1967; D.C.L. (hon.), Bishop's U., Lennoxville, Que., 1965; L.H.D., Waterloo Lutheran U., 1969; Dr. honoris causa, U. Montreal, 1974, U. Sherbrooke, 1974, U. Kingston, 1979; Ordained priest Roman Catholic Ch., 1929, consecrated bishop, Rome, 1950, elevated to Sacred Coll. Cardinals, 1953; with Inst. Catholique, Paris, 1930-31; prof. Issy-les-Moulineaux, 1931-32, asst. master novices, 1932-33; founder, superior Sem. of Fukuoka, Japan, 1933-39; vicar gen., pastor cathedral Diocese of Valleyfield, 1940-47; rector Canadian Coll., Rome, Italy, 1947-50; archbishop of Montreal, Can., 1950-67, resigned for mission fields of Africa, 1967; chancellor U. Montreal, 1950; nominated as parish priest St. Madelein Sophie Barat's Parish, 1974, resigned, 1975. Papal legate closing Marian Year, Lourdes, France, 1954, St. Joseph's Oratory, Montreal, 1955, Ste. Anne de Beaupré, Quebec, Can., 1958. Mem. Central Commn. preparatory to Vatican II, 1961; mem. Council Commn. on Sacred Theology, 1962; mem. Sacred Consistorial Congregation Rome, 1963; mem. commn. canon law Council Vatican II, 1963; mem. del. Can. bishops Synod of Bishops, Rome, 1967; mem. Council Propagation of Faith, Rome, 1972; mem. Pontifical Commn. Pastoral of Tourism, Rome, 1972; co-pres. Can. Found. for Refugees, 1979—. Decorated knight grand cross Equestrian of Holy Sepulchre of Jerusalem, 1950; bailiff grand cross of honour and devotion Sovereign Order of Malta, 1954; knight grand cross Legion Honour (France), 1958; grand cross de Benemerencia (Portugal), 1965; comdr. Order of Valor and Merit (Cameroun Republic), 1969; recipient award for service to humanity Royal Bank Can., 1969; Humanitarian award Variety Clubs Internat., 1976; Pearson medal for peace Can. Assn. UN, 1979. Address: 2065 Sherbooke St W St W Montreal PQ H3H 1G6 Canada

LEGERE, LAURENCE JOSEPH, govt. ofcl.; b. Fitchburg, Mass., Jan. 2, 1919; s. Laurence Joseph and Aurore Hermine (Bean) L.; B.S., U.S. Mil. Acad., 1940; M.P.A., Harvard, 1948, A.M. (Littauer fellow), 1949, Ph.D., 1951; m. Mary Yesley Keville, Oct. 25, 1973. Commd. 2d lt. U.S. Army, 1940, advanced through grades to col., 1959; asst. prof. internat. relations U.S. Mil. Acad., 1945-47; student Nat. War Coll., 1960-61; asst. to mil. rep. of Pres. U.S., Washington, 1961-62; sr. staff mem. NSC, Washington, 1962-63; ret., 1966; sr. staff mem. Center for Internat. Studies, Mass. Inst. Tech., Cambridge, 1966-67; dir. office nat. security studies Bendix Corp., Ann Arbor, 1967-68; dir. internat. and social studies div. Inst. Def. Analyses, Arlington, Va., 1968-74; def. advisor U.S. Mission to NATO, Brussels, 1974—; mem. policy panel on Europe, UN Assn., 1967-69, policy panel on satellite communications, 1971-73. Decorated Silver Star, Legion of Merit, Bronze Star, Purple Heart, Distinguished Civilian Service medal; recipient Presidential Service Badge, 1956-57, 61-63, medal Outstanding Pub. Service, 1976, medal Disting. Pub. Service, 1978. Mem. Am. Polit. Sci. Assn., Internat. Studies Assn., Am. Mil. Inst. Democrat. Roman Catholic. Clubs: Army-Navy, Harvard (Washington). Contbg. author, editor: The President and the Management of National Security, 1969. Contbr. numerous articles on foreign and def. policies to profl. jours. Home: 154 Route Gouvernementale 1950 Kraainem Belgium Office: US Mission to NATO APO New York City NY 09667

LEGERTON, CLARENCE WILLIAM, JR., physician, educator; b. Charleston, S.C., July 8, 1922; s. Clarence William and Winnie Davis (McMaster) L.; student Davidson Coll., 1939-43; M.D., Med. Coll. S.C., 1946; m. Mitzi Foster Herrin, May 31, 1958; children—Clarence William, Mary Pringle, Gregg McMaster. Intern, Univ. Hosp., Balt., 1946-47, med. resident, 1947-48; instr. medicine Duke U. Sch. Medicine, 1950-53; practice medicine specializing in gastroenterology, Conway, S.C., 1953-56, Charleston, 1956-66; prof. medicine, dir. div. gastroenterology Med. U. S.C., Charleston, 1966—, asst. to pres., 1975—; med. dir. Nat. Miss U.S.A. Pageant, 1977-79; dir. Citizens and So. Nat. Bank, Charleston, chmn. Charleston bd., 1974—. Vice chmn. Charleston Commn. Public Works, 1959—; chmn. water supply City of Charleston; pres. Charleston Symphony Orch. Assn., 1967-68; chmn. bd. dirs. Legerton & Co., Inc. Mem. City Council Charleston, 1959-76, mayor pro-tem, 1960; pres. Charleston County Democratic Conv., 1960; trustee Montreat-Anderson Coll., vice chmn., 1962-74, chmn., 1974—; trustee Queens Coll., Nat. Found. Ileitis and Colitis; bd. visitors Davidson (N.C.) Coll., 1979—; chmn. bd. Charleston Mcpl. Auditorium; chmn. adv. bd. Comprehensive Health Planning Council Charleston, Berkeley and Dorchester Counties. Served to capt. AUS, 1948-50. Fellow A.C.P. (gov. S.C. 1978—), Am. Coll. Gastroenterology; mem. S.C. Soc., New Eng. Soc., Alpha Omega Alpha, Sigma Phi Epsilon, Alpha Kappa Kappa. Presbyterian (ruling elder 1956— pres. corp. 1965—, moderator 1963). Clubs: Carolina Yacht (Charleston); Biltmore Forest Country (Asheville, N.C.). Home: 32 Council St Charleston SC 29401 Office: Medical University Hospital Charleston SC 29402. *I believe life confers upon each individual a responsibility to his Creator, his community, his family, and his own person. This responsibility is discharged by the demonstration of religious faith through both precept and example, by involvement in various forms of community service for the betterment of society, by faithfulness to the family unit, and by a concern for the avoidance of those things which impair personal health, whether mental or physical.*

LEGG, ROBERT HENRY, real estate, financial cons.; b. Geneva, N.Y., Aug. 22, 1917; s. Charles Quested and Alice Burton (Fothergill) L.; student Hobart Coll., Geneva, 1935-36; A.B. magna cum laude, Kenyon Coll., Gambier, Ohio, 1939; M.S., Mass. Inst. Tech., 1942; LL.B., Columbia, 1946; m. Jane Elizabeth Morris, Feb. 7, 1942; children—Robert Austin, Judy Ann Legg Shontze. Admitted to N.Y. bar, 1946; atty. Cravath, Swaine & Moore, N.Y.C., 1946-49; partner Hammond, Kennedy & Legg Co., 1949-62; v.p. Uris Bldg. Corp., N.Y.C., 1962-71, dir., 1965-73, exec. v.p., 1971, chmn. bd., chief exec. officer, 1971-73; trustee Westchester County Savs. Bank, 1959-74. Mem. bus. adv. com., Briarcliff Manor, N.Y., 1958-62, mem. planning bd., 1962-66. Sec.-treas. Briarcliff Found., 1964-74; bd. dirs. Phelps Meml. Hosp., 1960-66; trustee Kenyon Coll., 1965-78. Served from 2d lt. to capt. USAAF, 1942-46. Recipient Gregg Cup award Kenyon Alumni Council, 1966. Mem. Phi Beta Kappa, Alpha Delta Phi, Phi Delta Phi. Clubs: Sleepy Hollow Country (Scarborough, N.Y.); Four Hills Country (Albuquerque). Home: 1308 Wagontrain Dr SE Albuquerque NM 87123

LEGG, WILLIAM JEFFERSON, lawyer; b. Enid, Okla., Aug. 20, 1925; s. Garl Paul and Mabel (Gensman) L.; grad. Enid Bus. Coll., 1943; student Pittsburg (Kans.) State U., 1944; B.B.A., U. Tex., 1946; J.D., U. Tulsa, 1954; m. Eva Imogene Hill, Dec. 16, 1950; children—Melissa Lou, Eva Diane, Janet Sue. With Marathon Oil Co., Tulsa, 1949-61, atty., 1954-61; admitted to Okla. bar, 1954; practice in Oklahoma City, 1962—; mem. firm Andrews, Davis, Legg, Bixler, Milsten & Murrah, Inc., and predecessor, 1962—; adj. prof. law Oklahoma City U., 1975—; lectr. energy seminars. Ordained Reorganized Ch. of Jesus Christ of Latter-Day Saints, 1964, dist. pres., 1975—. Mem. com. Okla. Energy Adv. Council, 1973—. Chmn. bd. trustees Am. Inst. Discussion, 1969-72, now trustee, counsel; trustee Jenkins Found. Research, sec., 1975—; trustee Restoration Trails Found., 1975—. Served with USNR, 1943-46. Mem. U.S. Supreme Ct. Am., Okla. (past com. chmn.), Oklahoma County (past com. chmn.) bar assns. Contbr. articles to profl. jours. Home: 3017 Brush Creek Rd Oklahoma City OK 73120 Office: 1600 Midland Center Oklahoma City OK 73102

LEGGETT, GLENN, former educator; b. Ashtabula, Ohio, Mar. 29, 1918; s. Glenn H. and Celinda (Sheldon) L; A.B., Middlebury (Vt.) Coll., 1940, LL.D., 1971; M.A., Ohio State U., 1941, Ph.D., 1949; L.H.D., Rockford Coll., 1967, Ripon Coll., 1968, Coll. Idaho, 1974, Grinnell Coll., 1975; LL.D., Morningside Coll., 1975; Litt.D., Lawrence U., 1968; m. Doris Ruth James, June 14, 1941 (dec.); children—Leslie Ann (Mrs. David K. Leonard), Susan Cady (Mrs. Michael Baxter Jones), Celinda Sheldon (Mrs. Raymond Riecke), Joanna Ruth (Mrs. Alan Sinnwell); m. 2d, Russelle Seeberger Jones, Mar. 11, 1973; children—Brian Edward Jones, Sarah Lorene Jones. Instr. in English, Mass. Inst. Tech., 1942-44; instr., then asst. prof. English, Ohio State U., 1946-52; asso. prof. English, U. Wash., 1952-58, asst. to pres., 1958-61, vice provost, 1961-63, provost, 1963-65; prof. English, pres. Grinnell Coll., 1965-75, pres. emeritus, 1979—; v.p. corporate communications Deere & Co., 1975-79. Mem. commn. English, Coll. Entrance Exam. Bd., 1957-65, trustee, 1965-76, vice chmn., 1970-72, chmn., 1972-74; chmn. Ill.-Iowa Assn. Children with Learning Disabilities, 1976-79; bd. dirs. Quad-Cities Grad. Study Center, 1975—, chmn., 1977-79; chmn. Conf. Coll. Composition, 1959; chmn. Iowa Coll. Found., 1974-75; trustee Marycrest Coll., 1975—; curator Stephens Coll., 1976—. Served with USNR, 1944-46. Mem. Modern Lang. Assn., Nat. Council Tchrs. English (chmn. coll. sect. 1963-65, chmn. survey undergrad. curriculum in English 1964-67, task force career edn. 1978-79), Iowa Assn. Pvt. Colls. (pres. 1969-71), Assn. Colls. Midwest (chmn. 1971-73), Chi Psi. Conglist. Author: (with Mead, Charvat) Handbook for Writers, 7th edit., 1978; A Conservative View, The New Professors, 1960. Editor: Twelve Poets, 1959; (with Daniel, Beardsley) Theme and Form; An Introduction to Literature, 4th edit., 1975; (with Daniel) The Written Word, 1960; (with Steiner) Twelve Poets, Alternate Edition, 1967; Years of Turmoil: Years of Change, 1978; Teacher to Teacher: Selected Papers on Teaching, Writing, and Higher Education, 1979. Home: 6 College Park Rd Grinnell IA 50112

LEGGETT, ROBERT LOUIS, congressman; b. Richmond, Calif., July 26, 1926; s. Elmer and Victoria (Toffoli) L.; B.A., U. Calif. at Berkeley, 1947; LL.B., U. Calif., Boalt Hall, 1950; m. Barbara Burnett, Aug. 16, 1947; children—Diana Elise, Jeanne Barbara, Robert Neal. Admitted to Calif. bar, 1951, since practiced in Vallejo; sr. partner Leggett & Gianola, 1956—; mem. Calif. Legislature, 1960-62; mem. 88th-96th U.S. Congresses from 4th Calif. Dist.; mem. Armed Forces Com., ranking majority mem. investigations subcom., research and devel. subcom.; mem. Mcht. Marine and Fisheries Com., chmn. subcom. on fisheries and wildlife conservation and environ.; mem. House Budget Com.; chmn. Task Force on Nat. Security. Served with USNR, 1944-46. Mem. Vallejo C. of C., Am., Solano County bar assns., Navy League, Sons of Italy, Am. Legion. Democrat. Elk, Kiwanian, Order Redmen. Home: 3606 Pinetree Terrace Falls Church VA 22041 Office: House Office Bldg Washington DC 20515

LEGO, PAUL EDWARD, lamp mfg. co. exec.; b. Centre County, Pa., May 16, 1930; s. Paul Irvin and Sarah Elizabeth (Montgomery) L.; B.S. in Elec. Engring., U. Pitts., 1956, M.S., 1958; m. Ann Sepety, July 7, 1956; children—Paul Gregory, Debra Ann, Douglas Edward, Michael John. With Westinghouse Electric Corp., 1956—, bus. unit mgr. electronic components divs., Pitts., 1974-77, v.p., gen. mgr. lamp divs., Bloomfield, N.J., 1977—; dir. Compagnie Des Dispostifs Semiconducteurs, LeMans, France; curriculum adv. bd. Syracuse (N.Y.) U., 1975-77; adv. bd. N.J. Inst. Tech., 1978—. Bd. dirs. Capabilities, Inc., Elmira, N.Y., 1974-77. Served with AUS, 1948-52. Recipient Westinghouse Order of Merit, 1975. Mem. IEEE, Electronics Industries Assn., N.J. C. of C., Sigma Xi. Democrat. Roman Catholic. Club: Canoe Brook Country (Summit, N.J.). Author papers in field. Office: 1 Westinghouse Plaza Bloomfield NJ 07003. *When a person moves into management, his emphasis must shift from what he can personally achieve to what he can achieve through others. He now becomes responsible for choosing capable people to work for him, providing them the right environment to work in, seeing that they have the proper leadership to get the job done. A little friendship applied at the right time will cement this team formula.*

LEGORRETA, LUIS G., utility co. exec.; b. Zamora, Mex., Jan. 30, 1898; s. Juan de Dios Legorreta and Guadalupe Garcia de Legorreta; student Instituto Cientifico de Mexico City, 1911; m. Gudalupe Vilchis, Dec. 2, 1926; children—Xavier, Isabel, Ricardo, Fernando. With Banco Nacional de Mexico S.A., Mexico City, 1913—, pres., 1933-52, vice chmn., dir. dels., 1952-58, chmn. bd., dir. dels., 1958-70, hon. chmn., 1970—; chmn. bd. Industria Electric de Mexico, Mexico City, 1945-76; dir. until 1976, Banco de Mexico, Cia Fundidora de Fierro y Acero de Monterrey, Celanese Mexicana. Chmn. bd. trustees Fundacian Mier y Pesado, pvt. charity orgn., 1940—. Clubs: Bankers, Univ. of Mex., Campestre de la Ciudad de Mexico, Jockey Mexicano (Mexico City). Home: Montanas Calizas 490 Mexico City DF 10 Mexico Office: Isabel La Catolica 44 Mexico City DF Mexico

LEGRAND, CLAY, state justice; b. St. Louis, Feb. 26, 1911; s. Nicholas and Mary Margaret (Leifield) LeG.; student St. Ambrose Coll., Davenport, Iowa, 1928-31; LL.B., Catholic U. Am., 1934; m. Suzanne Wilcox, Dec. 30, 1935; children—Mary Suzanne (Mrs. Thomas J. Murray), Julie A., Nicholas W. Admitted to Iowa bar, 1934, practice law, Davenport, 1934-57; judge Dist. Ct., 1957-67; justice Supreme Ct. Iowa, Davenport, 1967—; lectr. St. Ambrose Coll., 1957-67. Mem. law alumni council Catholic U. Am. Law Sch. Recipient award for outstanding achievement in field of law and the cts. Cath. U. Am., 1969; award of merit for profl. achievement St. Ambrose Coll., 1976. Mem. Am., Iowa, Scott County bar assns., Am. Judicature Soc., Inst. Jud. Adminstrn. Home: Rural Route 1 LeClaire IA 52753 Office: 416 W 4th St Davenport IA 52801

LE GUIN, URSULA KROEBER, author; b. Berkeley, Calif., Oct. 21, 1929; d. Alfred Louis and Theodora (Kracaw) Kroeber; B.A., Radcliffe Coll., 1951; M.A., Columbia, 1952; m. Charles A. Le Guin, Dec. 22, 1953; children—Elisabeth, Caroline, Theodore. Recipient Boston Globe-Hornbook award for excellence in juvenile fiction, 1968; Nebula award, 1969, 75; Hugo award for best novel, 1969, 75, best novella, 1973, best short story, 1974; Newbery honor medal, 1971; Nat. Book award, 1973. Fulbright fellow, France, 1953-54. Mem. Sci. Fiction Research Assn., Authors Guild, PEN, Phi Beta Kappa. Author: Rocannon's World, 1966; Planet of Exile, 1967; City of Illusion, 1967; A Wizard of Earthsea, 1968; The Left Hand of Darkness, 1969; The Tombs of Atuan, 1971; The Lathe of Heaven, 1971; The Farthest Shore, 1972; The Dispossessed, 1974; The Wind's Twelve Quarters, 1975; A Very Long Way from Anywhere Else, 1976; Orsinian Tales, 1976; The Language of the Night, 1978; Leese

Webster, 1979; Malafrena, 1979. Address: 3321 NW Thurman St Portland OR 97210

LEH, JOHN HENRY, banker; b. Allentown, Pa., May 24, 1899; s. John and Irene (Keck) L.; A.B., Princeton U., 1921; m. Dorothea Backenstoe, Sept. 8, 1921 (dec. 1955); 1 dau., Jean Robinson Graham; m. 2d, Eleanore Bear Pope, Feb. 16, 1957; stepchildren—Robert Bear, William Henry, Richard Warren, James Webster. Dir. Second Nat. Bank, Allentown, 1928-54, v.p., 1941-54; with First Nat. Bank, Allentown, 1954—, v.p., mem. exec. com., 1954-75, chmn. bd., 1968-75, chmn. emeritus, 1975—; partner H. Leh & Co., 1921-78, Leh Bros., 1932—; dir., sec. Internat. Film Found., 1946-71. Treas., Allentown Redevel. Authority, 1956-73; mem. Lehigh-Northampton Airport Authority, 1946-72, chmn., 1955-70, chmn. emeritus, 1970—; pres. Great Valley council Girl Scouts U.S.A., 1961-64, mem. nat. equipment com., 1960-70; mem. bd., exec. com. Pa. div. Am. Cancer Soc., 1962-63, Pa. crusade chmn., 1962. Trustee, Cedar Crest Coll., 1963-71, mem. exec. com., treas., 1965-71. Served with U.S. Army, 1917-18. Recipient Distinguished Aviation Citizens award, 1964; Founders award Lehigh U., 1963; Distinguished Service award Allentown C. of C., 1967; We Point With Pride award FAA, 1972; Service award Princeton Alumni Council, 1973. Lutheran (past deacon, elder). Kiwanian. Home: 1761 Lehigh Pkwy North Allentown PA 18103 Office: 626 Hamilton Mall Allentown PA 18101. *Any success which I may have had in my life has been in a large part due to the fact that I like people. I am an extrovert. Two phrases, "Please" and "Thank You" (in all languages) have paid dividends to me in the most unexpected places. I have had a very full life. It's been fun. But, I add that I have also worked hard!*

LEHING, CHARLES CONRAD, banker; b. N.Y.C., Feb. 5, 1922; s. Theodore Henry and Josephine (Seebach) L.; B.S. in Bus., Fordham U., 1950, LL.B., 1954; m. Carol Yvonne Fuhro, Oct. 2, 1954; children—Peter Conrad, Andrew Charles, Susan Carol. With Corn Exchange Bank & Trust Co., N.Y.C., 1940-54, mgr. credit dept., 1950-51, asst. sec., 1951-53, asst. v.p., 1953-54; Admitted to N.Y. bar, 1955. asst. v.p. Chem. Bank N.Y. Trust Co. (now Chem. Bank), N.Y.C., 1954-61, v.p., 1961-69, sr. v.p., 1969—; dir. Bancap Corp., N.Y. Bus. Devel. Corp. Served with AUS, 1941-45. Mem. N.Y. State Bar Assn., Beta Gamma Sigma, Delta Theta Phi. Home: 367 Harvey Ct Wyckoff NJ 07481 Office: 20 Pine St New York City NY 10015

LEHISTE, ILSE, educator; b. Tallinn, Estonia, Jan. 31, 1922; d. Aleksander and Julie M. (Sikka) L.; Dr.Phil., U. Hamburg (Germany), 1948; Ph.D., U. Mich., 1959; D.Univ. (hon.), U. Essex (Eng.), 1977. Came to U.S., 1949, naturalized, 1956. Lectr., U. Hamburg, 1948-49; asso. prof. modern langs. Kans. Wesleyan U., 1950-51, Detroit Inst. Tech., 1951-56; research asso. U. Mich., 1957-63; faculty Ohio State U., Columbus, 1963—, prof. linguistics, 1965—, chmn. dept., 1965-71, dir. Linguistic Inst., 1970; vis. prof. U. Cologne (Germany), 1965, U. Calif. at Los Angeles, 1966, U. Vienna, 1974. Guggenheim fellow, 1969, 75; grantee Am. Council Learned Socs., 1971. Fellow Center for Advanced Study in Behavioral Scis., 1975-76. Fellow Acoustical Soc. Am.; mem. Linguistic Soc. Am. (exec. com. 1971-73, pres.-elect 1979), MLA, Internat. Soc. Phonetic Scis., AAAS, Societas Linguistica Europaea. Author 7 books, latest being: (with R.J. Jeffers) Principles and Methods for Historical Linguistics, 1979; contbr. articles to profl. jours., book revs. Home: 985 Kennington Ave Columbus OH 43220

LEHMAN, ARNOLD LESTER, museum ofcl.; b. N.Y.C., July 18, 1944; s. Sidney and Henrietta F. L.; B.A., Johns Hopkins, 1965, M.A., 1966; M.A., Yale U., 1968, Ph.D., 1973; m. Pamela Gimbel, June 21, 1969; children—Nicholas Richard, Zachary Gimbel. Chester Dale fellow Met. Mus. Art, N.Y.C., 1969-70; lectr. art history Cooper Union and Hunter Coll., 1969-72; dir. Urban Improvements Program, N.Y.C., 1970-72, Parks Council of N.Y.C., 1972-74, Met. Mus. and Art Centers, Miami, Fla., 1974-79, Balt. Mus. Art, 1979—. Active N.Y. Fine Arts Fedn., Dade Heritage Trust. Mem. Soc. Archtl. Historians, Coll. Art Assn. Club: Harmonie (N.Y.C.). Author: The Architecture of Worlds Fairs 1900-1939, 1972; The New York Skyscraper: A History of its Development 1870-1939, 1974; also various mus. catalogs. Office: Balt Mus Art Art Museum Dr Baltimore MD 21218

LEHMAN, ERNEST, author, film writer, dir., producer; m. Jacqueline Lehman; children—Roger, Alan. Copy editor Wall Street financial mag.; Broadway press agt.; radio comedy writer; free-lance journalist and short story writer, in nat. mags.; debut as prod.-writer film Who's Afraid of Virginia Woolf?; writer screen plays Executive Suite, West Side Story, The King and I, North by Northwest, The Prize, Sabrina, Somebody Up There Likes Me, From the Terrace, Sweet Smell of Success, The Sound of Music; writer, producer film version Hello, Dolly; writer, producer, debut as dir. Portnoy's Complaint; writer screenplay Family Plot, Black Sunday; author (novel) The French Atlantic Affair, 1977; monthly columnist Am. Film mag. Address: care Chenault Prodns Inc 315 S Beverly Dr Beverly Hills CA 90212

LEHMAN, FREDERIC K(RIS), anthropologist, linguist; b. U.S., Feb. 5, 1924; s. David H. and Olga (Lurie) L.; student Sch. Asiatic Studies, 1945-50; B.A., N.Y. U., 1949; Ph.D., Columbia U., 1959; postgrad. U. Pa., 1953-54; m. Sheila Geyer, Sept. 10, 1955; children—Mark A., Charles F.A. Research asso. U. Ill., Urbana, 1952-53, 59-60, asst. prof. anthropology and linguistics, 1963-65, asso. prof., 1965-68, prof., 1968—, lectr. in Thai and Burmese, 1965—; lectr. U. Rangoon (Burma), 1961-62. Social Sci. Research Council grantee, 1957-58; NSF grantee, 1960-62; U.S. Army M.C. grantee, 1967-68; NSF grantee, 1965. Mem. Am. Anthrop. Soc., Assn. Asian Studies (chmn. Burma studies group), Linguistic Soc. Am., Siam Soc. Buddhist. Author: The Structure of Chin Society, 2d edit., 1979; Kayah Society, 1967; Who are the Karen, 1979; editor occasional papers of Wolfenden Soc. on Tibeto-Burman linguistics, 1970—. Home: 1316 Grandview Dr E Champaign IL 61820 Office: Dept Anthropology U Ill Urbana IL 61801

LEHMAN, HARVEY EUGENE, biologist; b. Yuhsien, China, Apr. 19, 1919; s. Algie Elsworth and Mabel (Burke) L.; B.A., Maryville Coll., 1941; M.A., U. N.C., 1944; Ph.D., Stanford, 1948; m. Lilliam Margot Youngs, July 26, 1958. Mem. faculty U. N.C., Chapel Hill, 1948—, prof. zoology, 1959—, chmn. dept., 1962-67, 76—, chmn. div. natural scis., 1965-66; dir. NSF grad. tng. program exptl. embryology Bermuda Biol. Sta., St. George's, 1960-74. NSF postdoctoral fellow U. Berne (Switzerland), 1952-53; recipient Tanner award in teaching U. N.C., 1961. Mem. Soc. Devel. Biology, Am. Soc. Zoologists (soc. div. devel. biology 1969-71), Western Soc. Naturalists, AAAS, Internat. Inst. Embryology and Devel., Am. Micros. Soc., Am. Soc. Cell Biology, Am. Inst. Biol. Scis. Author: Chordate Development, 1977; A Narrative of Animal and Human Evolution, 1978; Laboratory Guide for General Zoology, rev. edit., 1979; Laboratory Handbook of Vertebrate Embryology, rev. edit., 1965; also articles. Home: 47 Arboretum Dr Chapel Hill NC 27514

LEHMAN, IRVING GEORGE, artist; b. Russia, Jan. 1, 1900; s. Aaron and Pearl (Feller) L.; student Nat. Acad.; m. Martha Weingard, June 26, 1934. Painter, sculptor; exhibited ACA Gallery, 1934, Uptown Gallery, 1938, 39, 40 Seattle Mus., Chgo., Art Inst., Albany Inst. History and Art, Bklyn. Museum's Internat. water-color shows and sculpture shows, Harry Salpeter Gallery, 1947, 48, wood sculpture Whitney Mus., 1949, New Sch. Social Research, 1948-49, Riverside Mus., N.Y.C., 1948, 49, Bklyn. Mus. Water Color Show, 1949, oils Am. Abstract Artists, 1950, woodcut and sculpture Nebr. Art Assn., 1950, Bibliotheque Nationale, Paris, 1951; one-man shows: Phila. Art Alliance, 1950, Harry Salpeter Gallery, 1950, 54, 55, Oxford U., 1950, Mus. of Columbia (S.C.), 1958, The Gallery Ten, Mt. Vernon, N.Y., 1959, Gladstone Galleries, Woodstock, N.Y., 1961-64, 66, Berkshire Playhouse Gallery, Stockbridge, Mass., 1963, Knapnick Galleries, N.Y.C., 1962, Gallery One, Hillsdale, N.Y., 1966, 67, Atelier 5, Canaan, N.Y., 1969, 70, Gallery at Shelter Rock Library, Albertson, N.Y., 1973, Simon's Rock, Great Barrington, Mass., 1973, Red Rock Gallery, East Chatham, N.Y., Cordy Gallery, N.Y.C., 1977; exhibited Nocturne, Worship, Evening Traffic, Mardi Gras, Fog, Evening, at Harry Salpeter Gallery, 1947, Paris, Denmark, Belgium, Italy, Munich, 1951; Italy, Japan, 1955; exhibited at Berkshire Mus., Pittsfield, Mass., 1977, Union Carbide Gallery, N.Y.C., 1977, Parsons Sch. Design, N.Y.C., 1977, Patterson (N.J.) Coll., 1977; works included U.S. internat. traveling show in Europe, 1951—; metal sculpture Passing Forms in Kaback collection, 1968. Recipient Water Color Soc. Ala. award, 1948, Kate W. Arms Meml. prize for print in miniature sec. 33d ann. exhbn. Soc. Am. Etchers, Gravers, Lithographers and Woodcutters Am., 1947; hon. mention Washington Watercolor, 1949; Terry Art Inst. award for oils, 1952; Victor Wyler Found. award for oils, 1958, Mary and Gustave Kellner award sculpture Bklyn. Soc. Artists, 1959; Bklyn. Soc. Artists 44th Ann. award for oils, 1961. Mem. Am. Abstract Artists, Audubon Artists, Am. Soc. Contemporary Artists. Home: RD Box 122 Red Rock East Chatham NY 12060 also 70 La Salle St New York City NY 10027. *I see the nature and configurations of life in visual and tactile terms. In painting, color-form-line-space express deeply the emotions and thoughts that move me. In sculpture, wood, stone and metal, both in their natural form and the forms man has evolved while using these materials, stimulate and energize my imagination. In them, alone and in combination, I believe I can see the hopes, the longings, the plans of man's development. With all these I hope to create the symbols that express what I feel and think. And I am especially concerned that I an not beguiled by the compelling competence of the machines of our age into polishing these symbols into slick and deceptive images.*

LEHMAN, ISRAEL ROBERT, biochemist; b. Lithuania, Oct. 5, 1924; s. Herman Bernard and Anne (Kahn) L.; came to U.S., 1927, naturalized, 1936; A.B., Johns Hopkins U., 1948, Ph.D., 1954; m. Sandra Lee Teper, July 5, 1959; children—Ellen, Deborah, Samuel. Instr. microbiology Washington U. Med. Sch., St. Louis, 1957-59; mem. faculty Stanford U. Med. Sch., 1959—, prof. biochemistry, 1966—, chmn. dept., 1974-79. Service with U.S. Army, 1943-46. Mem. Am. Soc. Biol. Chemists, Am. Acad. Arts and Scis., Nat. Acad. Scis. Home: 895 Cedro Way Stanford CA 94305 Office: Dept Biochemistry Stanford Univ Stanford CA 94305

LEHMAN, JOHN HOWARD, lawyer; b. nr. Abilene, Kans., Nov. 19, 1905; s. Henry L. and Anna (Burkholder) L.; A.B., McPherson Coll., 1931; LL.B., U. Kans., 1935; m. Vivian Canary, Dec. 21, 1935; children—Stanley, Carolyn, Patricia, Virginia. Admitted to Kans. bar, 1935, since practiced in Abilene; county atty. Dickinson County, Kans., 1937-41; sr. partner firm Lehman, Guilfoyle & Hinkle, and predecessor, 1948—. Dir. Citizens Bank, Abilene. Mem. Abilene Bd. Edn., 1941-56, pres., 1955-56; spl. counsel Eisenhower Library Commn. Kans., 1961-68; incorporator Dwight D. Eisenhower Library Assos., Inc., 1963. Mem. Kans. Ho. of Reps., 1941-43, Kans. Senate, 1945-49. Trustee, Brown Meml. Found., Kans. Scottish Rite Found.; incorporator, trustee Eisenhower Found. Mem. Am. Bar Assn., Bar Assn. State Kans., Am. Judicature Soc., Order of Coif, Phi Alpha Delta. Mem. Ch. of Brethren. Mason (33 deg., Shriner). Home: 203 NW 10th St Abilene KS 67410 Office: 306 NW 2d St Abilene KS 67410

LEHMAN, JOHN HOWARD, lawyer; b. nr. Abilene, Kans., Nov. 19, 1905; s. Henry L. and Anna (Burkholder) L.; A.B., McPherson Coll., 1931; LL.B., U. Kans., 1935; m. Vivian Canary, Dec. 21, 1935; children—Stanley, Carolyn, Patricia, Virginia. Admitted to Kans. bar, 1935, since practiced in Abilene; county atty. Dickinson County, Kans., 1937-41; sr. partner firm Lehman & Guilfoyle, and predecessor, 1948—. Dir. Citizens Bank, Abilene. Mem. Abilene Bd. Edn., 1941-56, pres., 1955-56; spl. counsel Eisenhower Library Commn. Kans., 1961-68; incorporator Dwight D. Eisenhower Library Assos., Inc., 1963. Mem. Kans. Ho. of Reps., 1941-43, Kans. Senate, 1945-49. Trustee Brown Meml. Found., Kans. Scottish Rite Found.; incorporator, trustee Eisenhower Found. Mem. Am. Bar Assn., Bar Assn. State Kans., Am. Judicature Soc., Order of Coif, Phi Alpha Delta. Mem. Ch. of Brethren. Mason (33 deg., Shriner). Home: 203 NW 10th St Abilene KS 67410 Office: 306 NW 2d St Abilene KS 67410

LEHMAN, KIEFFER ROSS, livestock co. exec.; b. Fortuna, Mo., Nov. 29, 1930; s. Kieffer Roland and Lee Anna (Ross) L.; B.S. in Agr., U. Mo., 1956; m. Betty Louise Gammell, Feb. 5, 1955; children—Debra, Angela, James, Dee Ann, Wendy. Dir., St. Joseph Market Found., 1957-60; v.p. St. Joseph Stock Yards Co., 1961; pres., gen. mgr. Union Stockyards Co., Fargo, N.D., 1961-67, Sioux Falls Stockyards Co. (Iowa), 1967-72; asst. gen. mgr. Central Livestock Assn., South St. Paul, Minn., 1973-74, pres., gen. mgr., 1974—; dir. Northwestern Nat. Bank, South St. Paul. Bd. dirs. Minn. State Council on Econ. Edn. Served with U.S. Army, 1952-54. Mem. St. Paul C. of C. (chmn. agr. com. 1977), Minn. Taxpayers Assn., St. Paul Winter Carnival Assn., Wis. Livestock and Meat Council, Am. Inst. Coop., S.E. Met. C. of C., Nat. Livestock Feeders Assn., Minn. Assn. Commerce and Industry, Minn., Wis. assns. coops., Nat. Council Farmers Coops., Greater N.D. Assn. Clubs: St. Paul Athletic, Pool and Yacht, Mendakota Country; Sioux Falls Elks; St. Joseph Masons. Home: 2131 Theresa St Saint Paul MN 55120 Office: Central Livestock Assn Exchange Bldg South Saint Paul MN 55075

LEHMAN, RALPH MALCOLM, mfg. co. exec.; b. Cannelton, Ind., Oct. 7, 1922; s. Edgar A. and Elenora M. (Baertich) L.; B.S. in Mech. Engring., Purdue U., 1947; m. Julia S. Jones, Feb. 16, 1946; children—Constance S., Gary. With Ross Gear & Tool Co., Lafayette, Ind. (now div. TRW, Inc.), 1947-76, v.p., gen. mgr., 1966-76, v.p., gen. mgr. steering components group Automotive Worldwide div., 1976—; dir. Lafayette Nat. Bank, 1968-78, Schwab Safe Co., Inc. Pres., Lafayette Jr. Achievement, 1967; chmn. Tippecanoe County chpt. ARC, 1959-61; bd. dirs. Lafayette United Fund, 1966-68; bd. dirs. Lafayette Home Hosp., 1967—, pres. hosp., 1972; bd. dirs. Wabash Valley Sanitarium, to 1976; exec. bd. Harrison Trails council Boy Scouts Am.; bd. govs. Am. Nat. Red Cross; trustee Purdue Found.; bd. dirs. Purdue Research Found., YMCA of Cleve.; corp. gift team mem. United Way, 1977, 78, 79. Served to 1st lt. USAAF, 1943-46. Recipient Disting. Alumni award Purdue U., 1978, Disting. Engr. Alumnus award, 1978. Mem. Soc. Automotive Engrs., Am. Mgmt. Assn., Farm Indsl. Equipment Inst., Theta Chi. Presbyn. (elder). Club: Masons. Home: 31649 S Woodland Rd Pepper Pike OH 44124 Office: 23555 Euclid Ave Euclid OH 44117

LEHMAN, RICHARD LEROY, lawyer; b. Johnstown, Pa., Feb. 4, 1930; s. John S. and Deliah E. (Chase) L.; A.B. in Social Work, U. Ky., 1957; LL.B., U. Detroit, 1960. Admitted to Mich. bar, 1961, since practiced in Detroit; mem. firm Garan, Lucow, Miller, Lehman, Seward & Cooper, 1961—; dir. Bros. Specifications, Inc., Detroit; v.p., gen. counsel, dir. Matvest Corp.; pres. Home Bldg. Plan Service, Inc., Portland, Oreg.; vis. lectr. U. Detroit Law Sch., 1970-74, also Inst. Continuing Legal Edn.; del. 6th Circuit Jud. Conf., 1977-79. Mem. exec. com. pres.'s cabinet U. Detroit, 1975-79; bd. dirs. Old Newsboys Goodfellow Fund Detroit, 1975-78. Served to 1st lt. AUS, 1947-53. Recipient Algernon Sydney Sullivan Medallion, U. Ky., 1957. Mem. Am., Fed., Genesee County (bench and bar com. 1975-78), Detroit bar assns., State Bar Mich. (mem. negligence council 1972-74), Am. Judicature Soc., Am. Arbitration Assn., Assn. Def. Trial Counsel, Def. Research Inst., U. Ky. Alumni Assn., U. Detroit Law Sch. Alumni Assn. (dir. 1970-77, pres. 1974-75), U. Detroit Alumni Assn., Order Sons of Italy. Home: 4052 Waterwheel Ln Bloomfield Hills MI 48013 Office: 1475 E Outer Dr Detroit MI 48234

LEHMAN, ROBERT NATHAN, medical educator; b. Lancaster, Pa., Oct. 22, 1911; s. Harry Nathan and Mable May (Shenk) L.; B.S., Franklin and Marshall Coll., 1933; M.D., Temple U., 1937; m. Clara May Hileman, Apr. 24, 1938; 1 dau., Mary Dorcas. Intern, Temple U. Hosp., 1937-39, resident, 1947-48; resident Walter Reed Hosp., Washington, 1948-50, Armed Forces Inst. Pathology, Washington, 1950-51; chief ophthalmology VA Hosp., Pitts., 1954—; prof. ophthalmology U. Pitts. Med. Sch., 1954—, lectr. pathology, 1966—. Served with AUS, 1939-54. Decorated Bronze Star; Croix de Guerre (2) (France). Mem. Am. Acad. Ophthalmology and Otolaryngology, A.C.S., Pitts. Ophthal. Soc., Eastern Ophthal. Pathology Soc., Soc. Mil. Surgeons. Club: University (Pitts.). Contbr. articles to profl. jours. Home: 801 Washington Ave Tyrone PA 16686

LEHMAN, WILLIAM, congressman; b. Selma, Ala., Oct. 5, 1913; s. Maurice M. and Corinne L. (Leva) L.; m. Joan Feibelman, 1939; children—William, Kathy (Mrs. Donald Weiner) (dec.), Tom. Owner car sales and finance bus., Miami, 1936-41, 46-66, William Lehman Buick, North Miami Beach, 1966—; mem. 93d-96th congresses from 13th Dist. Fla. Mem. Dade County Sch. Bd., Miami, 1966-72, chmn., 1971-72. Recipient Humanitarian of Yr. award Am. Jewish Com., 1972. Democrat. Office: 2440 Rayburn House Office Bldg Washington DC 20515*

LEHMANN, CHARLES FREDERICK, educator; b. Bluffton, Ohio, Dec. 25, 1922; s. Gustav Adolph and Huldah (Moser) L.; A.B. in History, A.M. in History, U. Mich., 1948, Ph.D. in Edn., 1957; m. Judith Taylor, June 15, 1946; children—Christopher Frederick, Timothy James, Jane Elizabeth, Sarah Taylor. Supervising tchr. Univ. High Sch., Ann Arbor, Mich., 1948; asst. prof. No. Mich. Coll., Marquette, 1948-50; cons. Mich. Dept. Pub. Instrn., 1950-53; research asso. U. Mich., Ann Arbor, 1953-55, prof. edn., 1962—, asso. dean Sch. Edn., 1962-71. Cons. to sch. dists., architects, law firms; pres. Edn. Audit, Inc., Ann Arbor. Served with AUS, 1943-46. Mem. AAUP, Profs., Am. Assn. for Higher Edn., Am. Sociology Assn., Nat. Soc. for Study Edn., Phi Kappa Phi, Phi Delta Kappa. Author articles, bulls. Home: 2824 Glacier Way Ann Arbor MI 48105

LEHMANN, ERICH LEO, educator; b. Strasbourg, France, Nov. 20, 1917; s. Julius and Alma Rosa (Schuster) L.; M.A., U. Calif. at Berkeley, 1943, Ph.D., 1946; m. Juliet Popper Shaffer; children—Stephen, Barbara, Fia. Came to U.S., 1940, naturalized, 1945. Asst. dept. math. U. Calif. at Berkeley, 1942-43, asso., 1943-46, instr., 1946-47, asst. prof., 1947-51, asso. prof., 1951-54, prof., 1954-55, prof. dept. statistics, 1955—, chmn. dept. statistics, 1973-76; vis. asso. prof. Columbia, 1950-51, Stanford, 1951-52; vis. lectr. Princeton, 1951. Guggenheim fellow, 1955, 66, 79; Miller research prof., 1962-63, 72-73. Fellow Inst. Math. Statistics, Am. Statis. Assn.; mem. Internat. Statis. Inst., Nat. Acad. Scis., Nat. Acad. Sci., Am. Acad. Arts and Scis. Author: Testing Statistical Hypotheses, 1959; Basic Concepts of Probability and Statistics, 1964, 2d edit. (with J.L. Hodger, Jr.), 1970; Nonparametrics: Statistical Procedures Based on Ranks, 1975. Office: Dept Statistics U Calif Berkeley CA 94720

LEHMANN, GILBERT MARK, mech. engr., educator; b. Libertyville, Ill., Aug. 4, 1933; s. William Henry and Muriel Loise (Fischer) L.; B.S.M.E., Valparaiso U., 1955; M.S.M.E., Ill. Inst. Tech., 1957; Ph.D., Purdue U., 1966; m. Marilyn Ann Hoffman, July 5, 1958; children—Susan, Christopher. Mem. faculty dept. mech. engring. Valparaiso (Ind.) U., 1956—, prof., 1973—, dean Coll. Engring., 1971—. Served with USCG, 1958. Mem. ASME, Am. Soc. Engring. Edn. Lutheran. Office: Valparaiso Univ Valparaiso IN 46383

LEHMANN, HEINZ EDGAR, psychiatrist; b. Berlin, July 7, 1911; s. Richard R. and Emmy (Gronke) L.; came to Can., 1937, naturalized, 1948; ed. U. Freiburg (Germany), 1929, 30-31, U. Marburg, 1929-30, U. Vienna (Austria), 1931; M.D., U. Berlin, 1935; m. Annette Joyal, July 28, 1940; 1 son, Francois. Intern, Martin Luther Hosp., Berlin, 1935, Children's Meml. Hosp., Montreal, Que., Can., 1937; resident Verdun Protestant Hosp., Montreal, 1938, psychiatrist, 1935-47; clin. dir. Douglas Hosp., Verdun, 1947-66, dir. research, 1966-76; prof. psychiatry McGill U., Montreal, 1965—, chmn. dept. psychiatry, 1971-74, dir. div. psychopharmacology, 1976-77; adminstr. N.Y. State Office Mental Hygiene, dir. research ops., 1979—. Decorated officer Order Can.; recipient Albert Lasker award Am. Public Health Assn., 1957; Psychiat. award Taylor Manor Hosp., 1978. Fellow Royal Soc. Can., Royal Coll. Can.; mem. Am. Coll. Neuropsychopharmacology (pres. 1968), Collegium Internationale Neuro-Psychopharmacologium (pres. 1970), Can. Psychiat. Assn. (McNeil award 1969, 70, 74), Am. Psychiat. Assn., Royal Coll. Psychiatrists (U.K.) (found. fellow). Author: (with T. A. Ban) Experimental Approaches to Psychiatric Diagnosis, 1971, Pharmacotherapy of Tension and Anxiety, 1970; contbr. numerous articles on psychiatry and psychopharmacology to profl. publs. Home: 1212 Pine Ave W Montreal PQ H3G 1A9 Canada Office: 1033 Pine Ave W Montreal PQ H3A 1A1 Canada

LEHMANN, PAUL LOUIS, educator, clergyman; b. Balt., Sept. 10, 1906; s. Timothy and Martha Emilie (Menzel) L.; B.A. with honors, Ohio State U., 1927, B.Sc. in Edn., 1927; B.D., Union Theol. Sem., 1930, Th.D., 1936; Fogg traveling fellow U. Zurich, 1932-33, U. Bonn, 1933; D.D., Lawrence Coll., 1949; Fulbright research fellow U. Strasbourg (France), 1955; M.A. (hon.), Harvard, 1956; Litt.D., Elmhurst (Ill.) Coll. 1967; D.Theol. (hon.), U. Tübingen (Germany), 1971; LL.D., Colo. Coll., Colorado Springs, 1973; m. Marion Nelle Lucks, Aug. 29, 1929; 1 son, Peter Michael (dec.). Ordained to ministry Evang. and Ref. Ch., 1937; mem. Presbytery of Boston, U.P. Ch. in U.S.A., 1946—; asst. prof. religion and philosophy Elmhurst (Ill.) Coll., 1933-35, asso. prof., 1935-38, prof., chmn. dept., 1938-40; asso. prof. Bibl. and systematic theology Eden Theol. Sem., Webster Groves, Mo., 1940-41; asst. prof. Bibl. lit., history and interpretation Wellesley Coll., 1941-42, asso. prof., 1942-46; asso. religious editor Westminster Press, Phila., 1946-47; asso. prof. applied Christianity, Princeton Theol. Sem., 1947-49, Stephen Colwell prof., 1949-56; Parkman prof. theology Harvard Div. Sch., 1956-57, Florence Corliss Lamont prof. div., 1957-63, William Belden Noble lectr., 1968; Auburn prof. systematic theology Union Theol. Sem., N.Y.C., 1963-68, Charles A. Briggs prof. systematic theology, 1968-74, emeritus, 1974—; prof. theology and ethics Union Theol. Sem., Richmond, Va., 1974-76; Earl lectr. Pacific Sch. Religion, 1971; James A. Gray lectr. Duke Div. Sch., 1971; Roian Fleck resident in religion Bryn Mawr (Pa.) Coll., fall semester 1976-77; vis. prof. theology and ethics San Francisco Theol. Sem., San Anselmo, Calif. and Grad. Theol. Union U. Calif., Berkeley, 1976, spring 1977; Larkin-Stuart lectr. Victoria Coll. U. Toronto (Ont., Can.), 1975; Enoch Pond lectr. Bangor (Maine) Theol. Sem., 1976; vis. prof. theology and ethics Moravian Theol. Sem., Bethlehem, Pa., fall semester 1977-78; Benjamin B. and Annie Kinkead Warfield lectr. Princeton Theol. Sem., March 1979; Niebuhr Convocation lectr. Eden Theol. Sem., Webster Groves, Mo., Apr. 1979. Mem. Am. Soc. Christian Ethics, Duodecim, Am. (pres. 1969-70) theol. socs., Phi Beta Kappa. Author: Forgiveness, 1940; Re-educating Germany (translated from German, Werner Richter), 1945; Ethics in a Christian Context, 1963; The Transfiguration of Politics, 1975. Contbr. articles to religious publs. Home: 176 E 77th St New York NY 10021

LEHMANN, PHYLLIS WILLIAMS, educator, archaeologist; b. Bklyn., Nov. 30, 1912; d. James Barnes and Florence Lourene (Richmond) Williams; B.A., Wellesley Coll., 1934, L.H.D., 1976; Ph.D., N.Y. U., 1943; Litt.D., Mt. Holyoke Coll., 1971; D.F.A., Coll. Holy Cross, 1973; m. Karl Lehmann, Sept. 14, 1944 (dec. Dec. 1960). Asst. charge classical collection Bklyn. Museum, 1934-36; part-time instr. history art Bennett Jr. Coll., 1936-39; mem. faculty Smith Coll., 1946—, prof. art, 1955-67, Jessie Wells Post prof. art, 1967-72, William R. Kenan, Jr. prof. art, 1972-78, prof. emeritus, 1978—, dean, 1965-70; asst. field dir. excavations conducted by Archaeol. Research Fund of N.Y. U. at Samothrace, 1948-60, acting dir., 1960-62, adv. dir., 1962—; research prof. Inst. Fine Arts, N.Y. U., 1962-65, adj. prof., 1965—; Flexner lectr. Bryn Mawr Coll., 1977. Named hon. citizen of Samothrace, 1968; Fulbright research grantee, Italy, 1952-53; Guggenheim fellow, 1952-53; Bollingen fellow, 1960; recipient Wellesley Coll. Alumni Assn. Achievement award, 1976. Fellow Am. Acad. Arts and Scis.; mem. Archaeol. Inst. Am. (trustee 1970-72), Coll. Art Assn. Am., Am. Numis. Soc., Soc. Archtl. Historians (Alice D. Hitchcock award 1969), AAUW, Renaissance Soc. Am., Am. Sch. Classical Studies in Athens (exec. com. 1971-75, publ. com. 1975—, chmn. 1977-80), Williamsburg Hist. Soc., Phi Beta Kappa. Club: Cosmopolitan. Author: Statues on Coins of Southern Italy and Sicily in the Classical Period, 1946; Roman Wall Paintings from Boscoreale in the Metropolitan Museum of Art, 1953; The Pedimental Sculptures of the Hieron in Samothrace, 1962; Samothrace, vol. 3, 1969; (with Karl Lehmann) Samothracian Reflections, Aspects of the Revival of the Antique, 1973; Skopas in Samothrace, 1973; Cyriacus of Ancona's Egyptian Visit and Its Reflections in Gentile Bellini and Hieronymus Bosch, 1978; also articles to profl. jours. Editor: Samothrace, 1961—; asst. editor: Art Bull., 1945-47, book rev. editor, 1949-52. Home: Main St Haydenville MA 01039 Office: Hillyer Hall Smith Coll Northampton MA 01063

LEHMANN, WINFRED PHILIPP, educator; b. Surprise, Nebr., June 23, 1916; s. Phillip Ludwig and Elenore Friederike (Grosnick) L.; B.A., Northwestern Coll., Watertown, Wis., 1936; M.A., U. Wis., 1938, Ph.D., 1941; m. Ruth Preston Miller, Oct. 12, 1940; children—Terry Jon, Sandra Jean. From instr. to asst. prof. Wash. U., 1946-49; from asso. prof. to prof. U. Tex., 1949-63, Ashbel Smith prof. linguistics, 1963—, chmn. dept. Germanic langs., 1953-65, chmn. dept. linguistics, 1965-72. Dir. Georgetown English lang. program, Ankara, Turkey, 1955-56; chmn. linguistics delegation People's Republic of China, 1974. Chmn. bd. dirs. Center for Applied Linguistics, 1973-78. Served from pvt. to 1st lt. Signal Corps, AUS, 1942-46. Recipient Jakob Grimm prize, 1975. Fulbright research fellow, Norway, 1950-51; Guggenheim fellow, 1972-73. Mem. Linguistic Soc. Am. (pres. 1973), Modern Lang. Assn. (exec. council), Am. Council Learned Socs. (dir.), Danish Acad. Scis., others. Lutheran. Author: (with L. Faust) A Grammar of Formal Written Japanese, 1951; Proto-Indo-European Phonology, 1952; The Alliteration of Old Saxon Poetry, 1953; The Development of Germanic Verse Form, 1956; Historical Linguistics; an Introduction, 1962, 2d edit., 1973; Descriptive Linguistics: an Introduction, 1972, 2d edit., 1976; Proto-Indo-European Syntax, 1974. Editor: Language and Linguistics in the People's Republic of China, 1974; (with R.P.M. Lehmann) An Introduction to Old Irish, 1975; Syntactic Typology; contbr. articles to profl. jours. Home: 3800 Eck Ln Austin TX 78734

LEHMANN, WOLFGANG JOHN, fgn. service officer; b. Berlin, Sept. 18, 1921; came to U.S., 1934, naturalized, 1941; s. Karl and Elwine (Hartleben) L.; student Haverford Coll., 1940-42, U.S. Army War Coll., 1964-65; m. Odette Chatenet, Oct. 30, 1947; children—Mark Ernest, Michael David. Commd. fgn. service officer Dept. State, 1951; attache Am. Embassy, Rome, 1954-55; supr. refugee relief program U.S. Mission, Geneva, 1955-56; 2d sec. Am. Embassy, Vienna, 1956-57; public affairs adviser European Bur., Dept. State, Washington, 1957-62; 1st sec. Am. Mission to European communities, Brussel, 1962-64; spl. asst. for European affairs, Dept. Def., Washington, 1965-68; dir. atomic energy and space Dept. State, Washington, 1968-70; polit. adviser U.S. European Command, Germany, 1970-73; consul gen., Can Tho, Vietnam, 1973-74; U.S. minister Am. Embassy, Saigon, Vietnam, 1974-75; consul gen., Frankfurt, Germany, 1975—. 1st v.p. USO Council of Germany, 1976—. Served with U.S. Army, 1942-47. Decorated Bronze star. Mem. Acad. Polit. Sci. Office: 21 Siesmayer Strasse Frankfurt Federal Republic Germany 6000

LEHN, WALTER, linguist; b. Herschel, Sask., Can., Mar. 22, 1926; s. Isaak and Anna (Bartel) L.; B.A., Tabor Coll., Hillsboro, Kans., 1951; Ph.D., Cornell U., 1957; m. Violet Stewart, Sept 1, 1951; children—Steven (dec.), Frederick. Linguist, Arabian Am. Oil Co., Saudi Arabia and Lebanon, 1952-54; asst. prof. linguistics, dir. English Lang. Inst., Am. U. Cairo, 1957-60; asso. prof. linguistics, asso. dir. Middle East Center, U. Tex., Austin, 1960-62, asso. prof., dir., 1962-66; prof., chmn. dept. linguistics U. Minn., Mpls., 1966-74. Cons. on teaching English, Egyptian Ministry Edn., 1961-66. Mem. Am. Oriental Soc., Canadian Linguistic Assn., Linguistic Soc. Am., Middle East Inst. Contbr. articles to profl. jours. Home: Rural Route 2 Palmerston ON N0G 2P0 Canada

LEHNE, HENRY, former electronics co. exec.; b. Pitts., July 16, 1914; s. Henry and Fannie Louise (Kreis) L.; B.S., Carnegie Inst. Tech., 1937; grad. Harvard Advanced Mgmt. Program, 1950; m. Charlotte Fay Hiehle, July 15, 1939 (div. 1972); children—H. Theodore, C. Richard; m. 2d, Ruth T. Gormley, 1972. With Republic Aviation Corp., 1939-52, v.p., 1950-52; dir. electronic def. labs. Sylvania Electric Products, Inc., 1953-54, gen. mgr. Sylvania Electronic Systems div., 1954-58, sr. v.p., 1959-69; asst. postmaster gen. Bur. Facilities, U.S. Post Office Dept., 1969-71; v.p. Schlumberger Ltd., N.Y.C., 1971-73; v.p. GTE Info. Systems, 1973-74, pres., 1977-79; sr. v.p. mfg. services GTE Sylvania Inc., 1974-76. Trustee Carnegie-Mellon U. Mem. Carnegie-Mellon Alumni Assn. Club: Kenwood Golf and Country (Bethesda, Md.); University (N.Y.C.); Capitol Hill (Washington); Kingsmill Golf (Williamsburg, Va.). Home: 32 Ensigne Spence St Williamsburg VA 23185

LEHNERT, HERBERT HERMANN, educator; b. Luebeck, Germany, Jan. 19, 1925; s. Bernhard Alfred and Elisabeth (Doemel) L.; Ph.D., U. Kiel (Germany), 1952; m. Ingeborg Poth, Aug. 13, 1952; children—Bernard (dec.), Brigitte, Bettina. Came to U.S., 1958, naturalized, 1971. Lectr., U. Western Ont. (Can.), 1957; faculty Rice U., 1958-68, prof. German, 1966-68; prof. German, U. Kans., 1968-69; prof. German, U. Calif. at Irvine, 1969—, chmn. dept., 1974-76; vis. prof. Harvard, fall 1970. Served with German Army, 1943-46; prisoner of war. Nat. Endowment for Humanities fellow, 1973, 78; Guggenheim fellow, 1978-79. Mem. Internat. Assn. Germanic Studies, Modern Lang. Assn., Am. Assn. Tchrs. German. Author: Thomas Mann; Fiktion, Mythos, Religion, 1965; Struktur und Sprachmagie, 1966; Thomas Mann Forschung, 1969; Geschichte der deutschen Literatur: Vom Jugendstil zum Expressionismus, 1978; contbr. articles to profl. jours. Home: 10 Aspen Tree Ln Irvine CA 92715

LEHNINGER, ALBERT LESTER, educator, biochemist; b. Bridgeport, Conn., Feb. 17, 1917; s. Albert O. and Wally Selma (Heymer) L.; B.A., Wesleyan U., 1939, D.Sc. (hon.), 1954; M.S., U. Wis., 1940, Ph.D., 1942; D. Sc. (hon.), U. Notre Dame, 1968, Acadia U., 1972, Meml. U., Nfld., 1973, U. Paris, 1977, U. Louvain, 1978; M.D. (hon.), U. Padua (Italy), 1966; m. Janet Wilson, Mar. 12, 1942. Instr. physiol. chemistry U. Wis., 1942-45; asst. prof. biochemistry U. Chgo., 1945-49, asso. prof., 1949-52; DeLamar prof. physiol. chem., dir. dept. Sch. Med., Johns Hopkins, 1952-78, Univ. prof. med. sci., 1978—; vis. prof. U. Frankfurt (Germany), 1951. Mem. Pres.'s Panel on Biomed. Research, 1975-76. Recipient Paul Lewis award enzyme chemistry Am. Chem. Soc., 1948; Remsen award, 1969; Guggenheim fellow, 1951-52, 64. Mem. Am. Chem. Soc., AAAS, Nat. Acad. Scis. (councilor 1976—), Am. Soc. Biol. Chemists (pres. 1972-73), Am. Philos. Soc. (v.p. 1975—), Am. Acad. Arts and Scis., Inst. Medicine (councilor 1976—), Biochem. Soc. (London), Phi Beta Kappa, Sigma Xi, Phi Nu Theta. Clubs: 14 West Hamilton St., Johns Hopkins (Balt.); Green Spring Valley Hunt; Gibson Island Yacht Squadron. Author: The Mitochondrion, 1964; Bioenergetics, 2d edit., 1971; Biochemistry, 1970, 2d edit., 1975; Short Course in Biochemistry, 1973; also articles in field. Mem. editorial bds. jours. Home: 15020 Tanyard Rd Sparks MD 21152 Office: Sch Medicine John Hopkins U Baltimore MD 21205

LEHR, DAVID, physician, scientist, educator; b. Sadagura, Austria, Mar. 22, 1910; s. Salomon and Esther (Buck) L.; M.D., U. Vienna, 1935; m. Lisa Fellner; children—Karin Elizabeth, Jonathan Mathias. Came to U.S., 1939, naturalized, 1945. Intern, Krankenhaus Wieden, Vienna, 1935-36; instr. pharmacology Royal U. Lund (Sweden), 1938-39; pharmacologist, research asso. dept. pathology Newark Beth Israel Hosp., 1939-42; instr. pharmacology and medicine N.Y. Med. Coll., Flower and Fifth Av. Hosp., 1941-44; asst. prof. pharmacology and medicine N.Y. Med. Coll., 1944-49, asso. prof., 1949-54, prof., dir. dept. pharmacology, 1954-56, prof., chmn. dept. physiology and pharmacology, 1956-64, asso. prof. medicine, 1949—, prof., chmn. dept. pharmacology, 1964-79; asst. vis. physician Met. Hosp., Welfare Island, N.Y., 1942-54; asso. attending physician Flower and Fifth Ave. Hosps., 1949-78, poison control officer, 1955-78; vis. physician Met. and Bird S. Coler hosps., 1954—; Claude Bernard prof. Inst. Exptl. Medicine and Surgery, U. Montreal, 1961. Recipient certificate merit for exhibit Med. Soc. N.J., 1941; certificate proficiency Chem. Warfare Sch., 1942; certificate merit original investigation A.M.A., 1948; 1st award clin. research Med. Soc. N.Y., 1949; certificate merit excellence sci. exhibit Assn. Am. Mil. Surgeons, 1949; medal alumni distinguished service N.Y. Med. Coll., 1965, 76; Edward Henderson gold medal award Am. Geriatric Soc., 1972; Med. Students award for excellence of teaching, 1976, 77, 78, 79. Fellow A.C.P., AAAS, N.Y. Acad. Medicine, N.Y. Acad. Scis., Am. Coll. Cardiology, Am. Heart Assn., Am. Coll. Clin. Pharmacology and Chemotherapy, Am. Coll. Nutrition (hon.); mem. AMA, Am. Soc. Pharmacology and Exptl. Therapeutics, Soc. Exptl. Biology and Medicine, Sci. Research Soc. Am., Harvey Soc., Internat. Soc. Internal Medicine, Am. Soc. Arteriosclerosis, AAUP, Pirquet Soc. Clin. Medicine (distinguished mem. award 1973), Virchow-Pirquet Med. Soc. (v.p. 1977-78, pres. 1979), Internat. Study Group Research Cardiac Metabolism (founding com.), Rudolf Vichow Med. Soc. (pres. 1970-72), Pirquet Soc. (pres. 1958-60), Contin Soc. (hon.), Med. Soc. N.Y., Med. Soc. County N.Y., Alumni Assn. N.Y. Med. Coll., Assn. Am. Med. Colls., Assn. Med. Sch. Pharmacology, Am. Soc. Exptl. Pathology, N.Y. Soc. Med. Research (v.p. 1961-63), German Soc. Magnesium Research (editorial bd. magnesium bull. 1979—), N.Y. Heart Assn., Royal Soc. Promotion Health, Council Arteriosclerosis, Sigma Xi, Alpha Omega Alpha. Editorial bd. Jour. Clin. Pharmacology, 1969—, Jour. Cardiovascular Pharmacology, 1977—, Magnesium Bull., 1979—; contbr. numerous articles to profl. jours. Home: 79 Lloyd Rd Montclair NJ 07042 Office: Munger Pavilion Bldg NY Med College Valhalla NY 10595

LEHR, FRANK HENRY, engring. co. exec.; b. Easton, Pa., Apr. 2, 1925; s. Francis H. and Sadie (Fulse) L.; B.S. in Engring., Pa. State U., 1950; M.S., Newark Coll. Engring., 1956; m. Veronica Shevock, June 24, 1950; children—Diane C., Frank F., Janice S. Field engr. C.R.R. of N.J., Jersey City, 1950-51; structural designer Arthur G. McKee & Co., Union, N.J., 1951, 53-54; constrn. engr. Jersey Testing Lab., Inc., Newark, 1954-57; pres. Frank H. Lehr Assos., cons. civil engrs., East Orange, N.J., 1957—; treas. Investment Casting Corp., 1972-76, Chmn., Joint Meeting Sewer Commn. Union and Essex Counties (N.J.), 1969-76; mem. Summit (N.J.) Bd. Appeals, 1958-75, City Council, Summit, 1962-76, pres., 1970-76; mem. Summit Bd. Sch. Estimates, 1964-69; mayor City of Summit, 1976-80. Served to capt. USMCR, 1943-47, 51-53. Registered profl. engr., N.J., N.Y., Pa., Mass., Conn., Ohio. Fellow Am. Cons. Engrs. Council, ASCE; mem. Union County Soc. Profl. Engrs. (past pres.), Marine Corps Res. Officers Assn., ASTM, Bldg. Ofcls. N.J. Club: Kiwanis (dir. East Orange chpt.). Home: 16 Myrtle Ave Summit NJ 07901 Office: 15 Freeman Ave East Orange NJ 07018

LEHR, LEWIS WYLIE, diversified mfg. corp. exec.; b. Elgin, Nebr., Feb. 21, 1921; s. Lewis H. and Nancy (Wylie) L.; B.S. in Chem. Engring., U. Nebr., 1947, Sc.D. (hon.), 1977; m. Doris Stauder, Oct. 13, 1944; children—Mary A. Lehr Makin, William L., Donald D., John M. With 3M Co., St. Paul, 1947—, v.p. med. products div., 1960-72, health care products group, 1972-74, tape and allied products group, 1974-75, pres. U.S. ops., 1975-79, vice chmn., chief exec. officer, 1979—; dir. 1st Bank Systems, Inc., Mpls., Gen. Mills, Inc., Mpls. Trustee Hamline U., St. Paul, 1978—; bd. overseers Harvard Coll. Vis. Com. Med. and Dental Schs., 1977-79; bd. dirs. United Way of St. Paul Area, 1977—, Guthrie Theater Found., 1977—. Served with AUS, 1943-46; ETO. Recipient Alumni Achievement award U. Nebr. Alumni Assn., 1976. Mem. Am. Chem. Soc., Health Industry Mfrs. Assn., Bus. Roundtable. Clubs: North Oaks Golf, St. Paul Athletic, White Bear Yacht, Minnesota. Office: Minn Mining & Mfg Co 3M Center Saint Paul MN 55101

LEHRER, JAMES CHARLES, television journalist; b. Wichita, Kans., May 19, 1934; s. Harry Frederick and Lois Catherine (Chapman) L.; A.A., Victoria Coll., 1954; B.J., U. Mo., 1956; m. Kate Staples, June 4, 1960; children—Jamie, Lucy, Amanda. Reporter, Dallas Morning News, 1959-61; reporter, columnist, city editor Dallas Times Herald, 1961-70; exec. producer, corr. Sta. KERA-TV, Dallas, 1970-72; public affairs coordinator Public Broadcasting Service, Washington, 1972-73; corr. NPACT-WETA-TV, Washington, 1973—, now asso. editor-co-anchor, MacNeil/Lehrer Report; instr. creative writing Dallas Coll., So. Meth. U., 1967-68. Served with USMC, 1956-59. Recipient Columbia-Dupont award; George Polk award; Peabody award; Emmy award. Mem. Tex. Inst. Letters, Council Fgn. Relations. Author: (fiction) Viva Max, 1966; We Were Dreamers, 1975. Home: 3356 Macomb Washington DC 20016 Office: WETA-TV PO Box 2626 Washington DC 20013

LEHRER, KEITH EDWARD, educator; b. Mpls., Jan. 10, 1936; s. Abraham I. and Estelle (Mayrick) L.; B.A. magna cum laude, U. Minn., 1957; A.M., Brown U., 1959, Ph.D., 1960; m. Adrienne Joyce Kroman, July 21, 1957; children—Mark Alan, David Russell. Instr. Wayne State U., Detroit, 1960-63, asst. prof., 1962-63; asst. prof. U. Rochester (N.Y.), 1963-65, asso. prof., 1965-68, prof. philosophy, 1968-74; prof. U. Ariz., Tucson, 1974—, head dept., 1976-78; vis. prof. U. Alta. (Can.), Calgary, summer 1966, Vanderbilt U., Nashville, 1970, U. Ill., Chgo., 1979; dir. Summer Inst. in Theory of Knowledge, Amherst (Mass.) Coll., 1972. Democratic party committeeman, 1970-72. NSF sr. postdoctoral fellow, 1966; NSF grantee research inductive logic, 1970-72; Am. Coll. Learned Socs. sr. fellow Center for Advanced Study, Palo Alto, Calif., 1973-74, dir. Mellon Found. Summer Seminar Freedom and Causation, 1977; dir. Summer Seminar Rationality and Skepticism, Nat. Endowment Humanities, 1975, fellow, 1980. Mem. Am. Philos. Assn. (exec. com. 1969-71), Philosophy Sci. Assn. (governing bd. 1977-78), Phi Beta Kappa. Author: Freedom and Determinism, 1966; (with J.W. Cornman) Philosophical Problems and Arguments, 1968, 2d edit., 1974; (with Adrienne Lehrer) Theory of Meaning, 1970; (with H. Feigland W. Sellars) New Readings in Philosophical Analysis, 1972; Knowledge, 1974; (with Ronald Beanblossom) Reid's Inquiries and Essays, 1975; Analysis and Metaphysics, 1975. Adv. bd. Philos. Forum, 1969—, Am. Philos. Quar., 1974—; editor-in-chief Philos. Studies, 1974—. Home: 65 Sierra Vista Dr Tucson AZ 85719

LEHRER, LEONARD, artist, educator; b. Phila., Mar. 23, 1935; s. Abraham and Bessie L.; B.F.A., Phila. Coll. Art, 1956; M.F.A., U. Pa., 1960; m. Marilyn Bigard, May 29, 1977; 1 dau., Anna-Katrina Picard; stepchildren—Tracy, Jamye, Janna, John Peel. Mem. faculty Phila. Coll. Art, 1956-70, co-dir. found. program, 1965-70; prof. art U. N.Mex., 1970-74, chmn. dept., 1970-73; prof. U. Tex., San Antonio, 1974-77, dir. div. art and design, 1974-75; prof., chmn. dept. art Ariz. State U., Tempe, 1977—; one-man shows: Utah Mus. Fine Arts, Salt Lake City, 1973, Marian Locks Gallery, Phila., 1974, 77, McNay Art Inst., San Antonio, 1975, Galerie Kühl, Hannover, W. Ger., 1976, 79, numerous others; represented in permanent collections: Phila. Mus. Art, Nat. Gallery Art, Washington, Library of Congress, Mus. Modern Art, N.Y.C., Cleve. Mus. Art, Sprengel Mus. Modern Art, W. Ger., numerous others. Jewish. Office: Dept Art Ariz State Univ Tempe AZ 85281

LEHRER, ROBERT NATHANIEL, indsl. engr., educator; b. Sandusky, Ohio, Jan. 17, 1922; s. Henry William and Margaret (Boyd) L.; B.S. in Mech. Engring. with distinction, Purdue U., 1945, M.S., 1947, Ph.D., 1949; student engring. Midshipman Sch., 1945; m. Patricia Lee Martin, July 7, 1945; children—Joan Elizabeth. Research asst., instr. Purdue U., 1946-49; asst. prof. indsl. engring. Oreg. State Coll., 1949-50; asso. prof. indsl. engring., research asso. Ga. Inst. Tech., 1950-54, prof. indsl. engring., research asso., 1954-58; prof. indsl. engring., chmn. dept. Technol. Inst., Northwestern U., 1958-63; prof., asso. dir. Sch. Indsl. Engring., Ga. Inst. Tech., Atlanta, 1963-66, dir. Sch. Indsl. and Systems Engring., 1966-78, prof., 1978—; asso., vis. sr. adv. Am. Productivity Center, 1978-79; cons. indsl. engring. operations research, 1950—; cons. editor Reinhold Pub. Corp., textbook series, 1960-67. Adv. bd. mil. personnel supplies NRC, 1965-68; mem. nat. research council Am. Acad. Scis., 1965-68; expert indsl. engring. UNESCO, Mexico, 1962-63; mem. Nat. Acad. Scis. Panel to Indonesia, 1971. Served with USNR, 1943-46. Designated Distinguished Alumnus, Purdue U., 1964. Registered profl. engr. Fellow Am. Inst. Indsl. Engrs. (Outstanding Indsl. engr. in Southeast 1957, v.p. publs. 1960-62), A.A.A.S.; mem. Inst. Mgmt. Scis., Operations Research Soc. Am., Am. Soc. Engring. Edn., Sigma Xi, Tau Beta Pi, Phi Kappa Phi, Alpha Pi Mu, Pi Tau Sigma, Phi Delta Theta. Episcopalian. Author: Work Simplification: Creative Thinking About Work Problems, 1957; The Management of Improvement; Concepts, Organization and Strategy, 1965; others. Editor-in-chief Jour. Indsl. Engring., 1953-61, exec. editor, 1961-62. Contbr. articles to tech. jours. Home: 1506 Hanover West Dr NW Atlanta GA 30327

LEHRER, STANLEY, publisher; b. Bklyn., Mar. 18, 1929; s. Martin and Rose L.; B.S. in Journalism, N.Y. U., 1950; postgrad. in edn. San Antonio Coll., 1952; m. Laurel Francine Zang, June 8, 1952; children—Merrill Clark, Randee Hope. Editor and pub. Crossroads mag., Valley Stream, N.Y., 1949-50; youth service editor Open Road mag., N.Y.C., 1950-51; mng. editor School & Society, N.Y.C., 1953-68, v.p., 1956-68, pub. School & Society Books, N.Y.C., 1963—, pub. School & Society mag., 1968-72, Intellect mag., N.Y.C., 1972-78, editorial dir., 1974-78; pub., editorial dir. USA Today Mag., 1978—; cons. Child Care Publs., N.Y.C., 1955; producer Report on Edn., Sta. WBAI-FM, N.Y.C., 1960-61. Vice pres. Garden City Park (N.Y.) Civic Assn., 1961-63; treas. Citizens' Com. Edn. Garden City Park, 1962; mem. nat. jr. book awards com. Boys' Clubs Am., 1954. Served with Signal Corps, U.S. Army, 1951-53. Recipient Non-fiction awards Midwestern Writers Conf., Chgo., 1948. Mem. New Hyde Park (N.Y.) C. of C. (dir. 1961-62), Titanic Hist. Soc., S.S. Hist. Soc. Am., Soc. Advancement of Edn. (treas. 1953—, trustee 1963, pres. 1968—), Psi Chi Omega. Author: John Dewey: Master Educator, 1959; Countdown on Segregated Education, 1960; Religion, Government, and Education, 1961; A Century of Higher Education: Classical Citadel to Collegiate Colossus, 1962; Automation, Education and Human Values, 1966; Conflict and Change on the Campus: The Response to Student Hyperactivism, 1970; Leaders, Teachers, and Learners in Academe: Partners in the Educational Process, 1970; Education and the Many Faces of the Disadvantaged: Cultural and Historical Perspectives, 1972; contbr. articles to profl. jours. Home: 82 Shelbourne Ln New Hyde Park NY 11040 Office: USA Today 1860 Broadway New York NY 10023

LEHRER, THOMAS ANDREW, songwriter, entertainer, lectr.; b. N.Y.C., Apr. 9, 1928; s. James and Anna (Waller) L.; B.A., Harvard, 1946, M.A., 1947, postgrad., 1947-53, 60-65; postgrad. Columbia U., 1948-49. Entertainer in night clubs, concerts, 1953-54, 57-60, 65; mathematician Baird-Atomic, Inc., Cambridge, Mass., 1953-54; lectr. bus. adminstrn. Grad. Sch. Bus. Adminstrn., Harvard, 1962, lectr. edn. Grad. Sch. Edn., 1963-66; lectr. polit. sci. Mass. Inst. Tech., 1962-71; lectr. psychology Wellesley Coll., 1966; lectr. U. Calif. at Santa Cruz, 1972—. Served with U.S. Army, 1955-57. Mem. Am. Math Soc., Math. Assn. Am., Am. Statis. Assn., ASCAP, Composers and Lyricists Guild Am., Am. Fedn. Musicians. Author: Tom Lehrer Song Book, 1954; Tom Lehrer's Second Song Book, 1968. Records: Song by Tom Lehrer, 1953; More of Tom Lehrer, 1959; An Evening Wasted With Tom Lehrer, 1959; Tom Lehrer Revisited, 1960; That Was The Year That Was, 1965. Home: 11 Sparks St Cambridge MA 02138

LEHRMAN, EDGAR HAROLD, educator; b. N.Y.C., Apr. 13, 1926; s. Jacob and Frances (Wittenberg) L.; A.B., Cornell U., 1948; M.A., Columbia, 1951, Ph.D., 1954, certificate Russian Inst., 1956; m. Ruffa (Ruth) Makarova, Mar. 28, 1963; children—Tanya Elise, Ellen

Rose, Julie Sarah. Instr. Russian, Duke, 1951-52, Dartmouth, 1954-55; adminstrv. asst. to dir. Russian Inst., Columbia, 1955-56; asst. prof. Pa. State U., 1956-59; asso. prof. Emory U., 1959-67, also chmn. dept. Russian; prof. Washington U., St. Louis, 1967—, also chmn. dept. Russian. Served with AUS, 1944-46. Decorated Purple Heart. Mem. Am. Assn. Advancement Slavic Studies, Am. Assn. Tchrs. Slavic and E. European Langs. (v.p.), AAUP. Author: Handbook to Russian Text of Crime and Punishment, 1977. Editor, translator: Turgenev's Letters: A Selection (Ivan Turgenev), 1961. Contbr. articles to profl. jours. Office: Dept of Russian 302 Ridgley Bldg Box 1052 Washington U Saint Louis MO 63130

LEHRMAN, IRVING, clergyman; b. Poland, June 15, 1911; s. Abraham and Minnie (Dinowitz) L.; came to U.S., 1920; grad. Jewish Inst. Religion; M.H.L., Jewish Theol. Sem. Am., 1942, D.H.L., 1958, D.D. (hon.), 1968; m. Bella Goldfarb, May 21, 1935; children—Dr. David, Rosalind. Rabbi, 1942; rabbi Temple Emanu-El, Miami Beach, Fla., 1943—. Former vis. prof. homiletics Jewish Theol. Sem. Am. Mem. rabbinic cabinet and bd. rabbinic visitors Jewish Theol. Sem. Am.; dir. Internat. Synagogue Kennedy Airport; pres. Synagogue Council Am., 1971-73, hon. pres., 1973—. Mem. Pres.'s Commn. Obscenity and Pornography, Pres.'s Commn. Aging; fellow Hebrew U.; dir. Greater Miami Jewish Fedn.; mem. nat. council Boy Scouts Am.; chmn. religious task force White House Conf. Food, Nutrition and Health, 1969; dir. Dade County ARC, United Fund Dade County; pres. Travelers Aid, 1958; trustee Ency. Judaica Research Found.; pres. council Brandeis U.; nat. bd. dirs. NCCJ; nat. commr. Hillil Found.; nat. bd. dirs. Jewish Nat. Fund; chmn. bd. govs. Israel Bonds Greater Miami. Recipient Silver Medallion award Nat. Conf. Christians and Jews, 1972, Prime Minister's Medallion of State of Israel, 1969. Mem. Zionist Orgn. Am. (v.p.), Rabbinical Assn. S.W. Region (hon. pres.), Rabbinical Assn. Greater Miami (past pres.), Rabbinical Assembly Am. (past sec.), Am. Technion Soc. (nat. dir., Albert Einstein brotherhood award 1973). Kiwanian. Home: 2925 Flamingo Dr Miami Beach FL 33140 Office: 1701 Washington Ave Miami Beach FL 33139

LEHRMAN, LEWIS EDWARD, business exec.; b. Harrisburg, Pa., Aug. 15, 1938; s. Benjamin S. and Rose (Herman) L.; grad. Hill Sch., 1956; B.A. Yale, 1960; M.A. (Woodrow Wilson fellow), Harvard, 1962; m. Louise Lombard Stillman, May 27, 1966; children—R. Leland, John S., Thomas D., Eliza D., Peter R. Carnegie teaching fellow Yale, 1961; pres., treas. Rite Aid Corp., Shiremanstown, Pa., 1969-77, chmn. exec. com., 1977—. Chmn. bd. trustees, pres. Lehrman Inst., N.Y.C.; trustee Collegiate Sch., N.Y.C., Lenox Hill Hosp., N.Y.C., Citizens Com. for N.Y.C., Boys Club of N.Y., Daytop Village, N.Y.C., Eisenhower Coll., Am. Enterprise Inst., Washington, Inner-City Scholarship Fund Inc., Archdiocese of N.Y., N.Y.C.; bd. dirs. U.S. Com. for Refugees, N.Y.C., Episcopal Sch., N.Y.C.; chmn. N.Y. State Republican Platform com., 1978, N.Y. Rep. Econ. Adv. Council, 1979. Served with AUS, 1963. Home: 778 Park Ave New York NY 10021 Office: 641 Lexington Ave New York NY 10022

LEHRMAN, NAT, magazine editor; b. Bklyn., Aug. 5, 1929; s. Louis and Lena (Goldfarb) L.; B.A., Bklyn. Coll., 1953; M.A., N.Y. U., 1960; m. Kazuko Miyajima, Nov. 13, 1956; children—Jerome M., Cynthia H. Travel editor internat. travel dept. Am. Automobile Assn., 1955-57; editor Relax mag., 1958; mng. editor Dude, also Gent mags., 1959-61; editor, then asso. to asst. mng. editor Playboy mag., Chgo., 1961-71; editor new publns., Playboy Enterprises, 1972; editor, then asso. pub. Oui mag., 1973-75; sr. v.p., asso. pub. Playboy mag., 1976—; tchr. fiction Columbia Coll., Chgo., 1967; author: Masters and Johnson Explained, 1970. Served with U.S. Army, 1953-55. Office: 919 N Michigan Ave Chicago IL 60611

LEIBENSTEIN, HARVEY, educator; b. Russia, Aug. 7, 1922; s. Joseph and Gusta (Bendick) L.; came to Can., 1925; came to U.S., 1942, naturalized, 1949; B.S., Northwestern U., 1945, M.A., 1946; Ph.D. (Social Sci. Research Council fellow), Princeton, 1951; m. Margaret Libnic, 1954. Instr. econs. Ill. Inst. Tech., 1946-47; instr. Princeton, 1947-48; asst. prof. U. Calif. at Berkeley, 1951-60, prof., 1960-67; vis. prof. Harvard, 1966-67, Andelot prof. econs. and population, 1967—; mem. Inst. Advanced Study, Princeton, N.J., 1978-79. Social Sci. Research Council faculty research fellow U. Calif. at Berkeley, 1957-60; Guggenheim fellow, 1963. Mem. Am. Econ. Assn., Population Assn. Am., Internat. Union Sci. Study of Population. Author: A Theory of Economic Demographic Development, 1954; Economic Backwardness and Economic Growth, 1957; Economic Theory and Organizational Analysis, 1960; Beyond Economic Man—New Foundations of Micro Economics, 1975; General X-Efficiency Theory and Economic Development, 1978. Home: 47 Larchwood Dr Cambridge MA 02138 Office: 204 Littauer Center Harvard U Cambridge MA 02138

LEIBER, GERSON AUGUST, artist; b. Bklyn., Nov. 12, 1921; s. William and Rebecca (Margulis) L.; student art, Hungary, 1946, Art Students League N.Y., 1947-52, Bklyn. Mus. Art Sch., 1952-53; m. Judith Maria Peto, Feb. 5, 1946. One-man shows Oakland (Calif.) Mus., 1960, N.Y.C., 1961, 62, 63, 64, 68, 69, 72, 76; exhibited in numerous nat. and internat. group shows; prints and paintings represented in pvt. and permanent collections; instr. Newark Sch. Fine and Indsl. Arts; v.p. Judith Leiber, Inc., N.Y.C., 1963—. Served with AUS, 1942-47. Recipient numerous prizes including Bklyn. Mus. Purchase awards, 1953-66, 2d prize of $1,000, Asso. Am. Artists Nat. Print Exhbn., 1959, Soc. Washington Printmakers prize, 1962, purchase award Hunterdon County Art Center 6th nat. print exhbn., 1962, Audubon medals of Honor for Graphics, 1963, 65; Sonia Watter award Am. Color Print Soc., 1968; $1000 Purchase award Assn. Am. Artists, 1968; John Taylor Arms Meml. prize NAD, 1971. Tiffany fellow, 1957, 60. Mem. Boston Printmakers Soc., NAD (asso.), Soc. Am. Graphic Artists (pres.), Art Students League N.Y. Home: 20 E 35th St New York City NY 10016 Office: 14 E 32d St New York City NY 10016

LEIBER, JUDITH MARIA, designer, mfr.; b. Budapest, Hungary, Jan. 11, 1921; d. Emil and Helen (Spitzer) Peto; came to U.S., 1947, naturalized, 1949; student pvt. schs., Hungary and Eng.; m. Gerson Leiber, Feb. 6, 1946. Master handbag maker, Hungary, 1942; pattern maker, designer Nettie Rosenstein, N.Y.C., 1947-60, Koret, N.Y.C., 1960-61; owner, mgr. Judith Leiber, Inc., N.Y.C., 1963—. Recipient Swarovski award and Am. Handbag Designer award Leather Industries Am., 1970; Coty award Am. Fashion Critics, 1973. Mem. Nat. Handbag Authority (dir. 1972—), Fashion Group. First woman master handbag maker, Hungary; first woman patternmaker Am. handbag industry. Home: 20 E 35th St New York City NY 10016 Office: 14 E 32d St New York City NY 10016

LEIBHAM, JOHN ALBERT, canning co. exec.; b. Sheboygan, Wis., Jan. 5, 1930; s. Jacob Albert and Madeline Josephine (Burkard) L.; grad. Sheboygan Bus. Coll., 1954; m. Genevieve Hipke, June 19, 1954; children—Terrence, Mark, Carrie, Jeffrey. Accountant, Firestone Co. Store, Sheboygan, 1954-55; accountant A.T. Hipke & Sons, Inc., New Holstein, Wis., 1955-60, dir., 1959—, v.p. sales, 1960—; v.p. sales, dir. Hipke Packaging Corp., New Holstein, 1965—. Served with AUS, 1948-52. Decorated Purple Heart, Bronze Star. Mem. Nat. Canners Assn., Wis. Canners and Freezers Assn., Young Guard. Roman Catholic. Club: Calumet (New Holstein). Home: 2105 Mary Ave New Holstein WI 53061 Office: AT Hipke & Sons Inc Park and Broadway New Holstein WI 53061

LEIBMAN, MORRIS IRWIN, lawyer; b. Chgo., Feb. 8, 1911; s. Isadore M. and Clara (Leibman) L.; Ph.B., U. Chgo., 1931, J.D., 1933; m. Molly Meyers, July 5, 1936; 1 dau., Linda. Admitted to Ill. bar, 1933, since practiced in Chgo.; partner firm Sidley & Austin; lectr. law schs. U. Chgo., U. Ill., DePaul U., Northwestern U. Chmn. Nat. Adv. Council Econ. Opportunity; mem. Sec. Def. Adv. Com. Non-Mil. Instn., President's Panel Cons. Internal Affairs and Nat. Security; bd. dirs. Nat. Strategy Information Center; mem. adv. bd. Edn. for Freedon, Atlanta; exec. bd. Center Strategic Studies, Georgetown U. Trustee Loyola U. Fellow Am. Bar Assn. (chmn. law and nat. security); mem. Def. Orientation Conf. Assn., Ill., Chgo., N.Y. bar assns., Assn. Bar City N.Y., Chgo. Law Inst., Am. Judicature Soc. Clubs: Law, MidDay, Standard, Carlton (Chgo.); Sky (N.Y.C.); Army and Navy (Washington). Home: 1550 Lake Shore Dr Chicago IL 60610 Office: 1 First Nat Plaza Chicago IL 60603

LEIBMAN, RON, actor; b. N.Y.C., Oct. 11, 1937; s. Murray and Grace (Marks) L.; student Ohio Wesleyan U., Actors Studio, N.Y.C.; m. Linda Lavin, Sept. 7, 1969. Acting debut Barnard Summer Theatre in A View from the Bridge, 1959; off-Broadway debut: Legend of Lovers, 1959; Broadway debut: Dear Me, the Sky is Falling, 1963; Broadway appearances include: Bicycle Ride to Nevada, The Deputy, We Bombed In New Haven (Theatre World award); off-Broadway appearances include: John Brown's Body, Scapino, Dead End, Poker Session, The Premise, Transfers, Room Service; film appearances include: Where's Poppa, 1970, Hot Rock, 1972, Slaughterhouse Five, 1972, Your Three Minutes Are Up, 1973, The Super Cops, 1974, Law and Disorder, 1974, Won Ton Ton, 1976, Norma Rae, 1979; television films include: A Question of Guilt, The Art of Crime, Martinelli: Outside Man; starred in television series Kaz (recipient Emmy award), 1978-79; mem. Yale Repertory Co., 1967-68. Recipient Drama Desk award for role in We Bombed in New Haven, Transfers; Obie award for role in Transfers. Office: care Agy for the Performance Arts 9000 Sunset Blvd Suite 315 Los Angeles CA 90069*

LEIBOLD, ARTHUR WILLIAM, JR., lawyer; b. Ottawa, Ill., June 13, 1931; s. Arthur William and Helen (Cull) L.; A.B., Haverford Coll., 1953; J.D., U. Pa., 1956; m. Nora Collins, Nov. 30, 1957; children—Arthur William II, Alison Aubry, Peter Collins. Admitted to Pa. bar, 1957; with firm Dechert, Price & Rhoads, Phila., 1956-69, partner, 1965-69, Washington, 1972—; gen. counsel Fed. Home Loan Bank Bd. and Fed. Savs. & Loan Ins. Corp., Washington, 1969-72, Fed. Home Loan Mortgage Corp., 1970-72; lectr. English, St. Joseph's Coll., Phila., 1957-59. Mem. Pres. Kennedy's Lawyers Com. Civil Rights, 1963, Adminstrv. Conf. U.S., 1969-72; bd. dirs. Marymount Coll. Va., 1974-75. Mem. Phila. Com. 70, 1965-74, Fellowship Commn. Mem. Am. (ho. dels. 1967-69, 79—, treas. 1979—, fin. com., bd. govs. 1977—), Fed. (nat. council 1971—), D.C., Phila. bar assns., Am. Bar Found. (treas. 1979—), Am. Bar Ret. Assn. (dir. 1978—), Order of Coif, Phi Beta Kappa. Roman Catholic. Republican. Clubs: Phila. Country (Gladwyne, Pa.); Skating, Orpheus (Phila.). Contbr. articles to profl. publs. Home: 3604 Prospect St NW Washington DC 20007 Office: 888 17th St NW Washington DC 20006

LEIBOWITZ, HARRY, real estate co. exec.; b. N.Y.C., June 6, 1930; s. Isidore and Gussie (Gruenstein) L.; B.B.A., Bernard Baruch Sch. Bus., 1952; m. Helene Wachtel, Apr. 7, 1957; children—Lori F., Stuart I. With S.D. Leidesdorf & Co., C.P.A.'s, N.Y.C., 1952-60, v.p., treas., controller, dir. Uris Bldgs. Corp., N.Y.C., 1960-76; sr. v.p. Cross & Brown Co., N.Y.C., 1976-78; exec. v.p. Peter Pattison Assos., Inc., N.Y.C., 1978—. C.P.A., N.Y. Mem. Fin. Execs. Inst. (pres. N.Y.C. chpt. 1974-75), Am. Inst. C.P.A.'s, N.Y. State Soc. C.P.A.'s. Home: 555 Kappock St Riverdale NY 10463 Office: 380 Madison Ave New York NY 10017

LEIBOWITZ, HERSCHEL WELDON, educator, psychologist; b. York, Pa., Feb. 21, 1925; s. Lewis and Nettie (Wolfson) L.; student U. Paris, 1945-46; B.A., U. Pa., 1948; M.A., Columbia, 1950, Ph.D., 1951; m. Eileen Diane Wirtshafter, June 12, 1949; children—Maryee Ellen, Michael W. From instr. to prof. psychology U. Wis., 1951-61; mgr. behavioral scis. IBM Corp., Bethesda, Md. and Yorktown Heights, N.Y., 1960-62; prof. psychology Pa. State U., 1962—, Evan Pugh prof. psychology, 1977—; vis. prof. U. Mich., summer 1962, Mass. Inst. Tech., 1963, Fla. State U., 1972; guest Max Planck Inst. fur Verhaltensphysiologie and U. Munich, 1957, Inst. for Perception, Soesterberg, Holland, 1967; vis. prof. neurology U. Freiburg, 1976-79; vis. prof. ophthalmology U. Fla., 1977. Mem. psychobiology adv. panel NSF, 1962-65, sensory physiology and perception adv. panel, 1979—; cons. VA, 1959—, Inst. Def. Analysis, 1964—, Dept. Interior, 1965-67, Dept. Def., 1966—, U. Mich. Infrared Physics Lab., 1967-68, Inst. Environ. Medicine, 1970-75; vis. scientist U.S. Japan Coop. Sci. Program, 1965; mem. NRC-Nat Acad. Sci. vision com., 1963—, mem. exec. council, 1973-76; mem. exptl. psychology study sect. NIH, 1970-74; mem. adv. bd. Applied Research Lab., 1973-76; mem. Assembly Behavioral and Social Scis., NRC, 1973—. Served with inf. AUS, 1943-46; ETO. Guggenheim fellow, 1957; recipient Heineman stipend, 1967; Von Humboldt sr. scientist, 1976-77. Fellow Am. Psychol. Assn. (bd. sci. affairs, sci. awards com.), AAAS, Am. Acad. Optometry, Optical Soc. Am., Soc. Exptl. Psychologists, Psychonomic Soc. Club: Cosmos. Author: Visual Perception, 1965. co-editor: Psychological Research, 1965—, Perception and Psychophysics, 1969—, Handbook of Sensory Physiology; cons. editor Behavioral Research Methods & Instrumentation, 1970—, Jour. Exptl. Psychology, 1960-74, Science, 1964—, Internat. Jour. Vision Research, 1959-65, 73—, Psychology Bull., 1964-68; adv. editor Contemporary Psychology, 1973—. Home: 160 Sandy Ridge Rd State College PA 16801 Office: 614 Moore Bldg Pa State U University Park PA 16802

LEIBOWITZ, IRVING, newspaper editor; b. N.Y.C., Aug. 5, 1922; s. Max and Freida (Scheiner) L.; student Bordentown (N.J.) Mil. Inst., 1937; m. Freida Greenwald, Dec. 10, 1950; 1 dau., Marilyn; stepchildren—Dennis Howard, Alan Leslie. Reporter, Suffolk (Va.) New Herald, 1945-46; sports editor Portsmouth (Va.) Star, 1946-47; state editor Mansfield (Ohio) News-Jour., 1947-48; with Indpls. Times, 1948-66, columnist, 1951-61, asst. mng. editor, 1954-60, mng. editor, 1960-66; editor Lorain (Ohio) Jour., 1966-79; founder, dir. Ind. Press Inst., Ind. U., 1958-79. Guest lectr. Ind. U., 1960; editor-in-residence Iowa State U., 1976. Served to sgt. AUS, World War II; maj. USMC Res., ret. Decorated Bronze Star. Recipient Distinguished Service award Jr. C. of C. Indpls., 1957; designated Old Master, Purdue U., 1965. Mem. Am. Soc. Newspaper Editors, Sigma Delta Chi (past pres. Indpls.). Club: Indpls. Press (past pres.). Author: My Indiana, 1963. Died Apr. 28, 1979. Home: 5537 Beaver Crest Dr Lorain OH 44053

LEIBSON, IRVING, indsl. co. exec.; b. Wilkes Barre, Pa., Sept. 28, 1926; s. Henry and Sonia (Rose) L.; B.Chem. Engring. cum laude, U. Fla., 1945, M.S., 1947; M.S., Carnegie Inst. Tech., 1949; D.Sc., 1952; m. Lola Pavalow, Feb. 16, 1950; children—Russell, Sandra Eve. Chem. engr. to supr. Humble Oil and Refining Co., Baytown, Tex., 1952-61, mgr. process engring., 1961-63, tech. mgr., 1963-65, dir. research and devel., 1965-67, gen. mgr. ABS div., 1967-68; v.p. Dart Industries Chem. Group, Paramus, N.J., 1969-74; asst. to sr. v.p., investment dept. Bechtel Corp., San Francisco, 1974-75, mgr. process and environment, v.p. C & I/Girdler Inc. (a Bechtel Co.), 1976-78, v.p., mgr. research and engring. Bechtel Nat. Inc., 1978-79, Bechtel Inc., 1979—; part time prof. Rice U., 1957, U. Md., 1954. Vice chmn. Intersoc. Task Force Energy, 1973. Dist. commr. E. Harris County dist. Boy Scouts Am., 1958-61. Served with AUS, 1953-54. Registered profl. engr., Calif., N.J., Tex. Fellow Am. Inst. Chem. Engrs. (dir. 1967-69, v.p. 1973, pres. 1974; Publ. award S. Tex. chpt. 1957, Founders award 1976); mem. Comml. Devel. Assn., Am. Chem. Soc., Engrs. Joint Council (dir. 1969—), Engrs. Manpower Commn. Kiwanian. Clubs: Round Hill Golf and Country, Stock Exchange (San Francisco). Patents, publs. in field. Home: 2525 Round Hill Dr Alamo CA 94507 Office: PO Box 3965 San Francisco CA 94119

LEICHLITER, VAN HANDLIN, ret. mfg. exec.; b. Mt. Braddock, Pa., Sept. 9, 1906; s. Braden Boyd and Nana (Handlin) L.; B.S., Pa. State Coll., 1930; m. Helen Rodgers, Nov. 26, 1936; 1 son, Van Handlin. Mill metallurgist Am. Steel & Wire Co., Worcester, Mass., 1930-34, metallurgist, Cleve., 1934-35, dist. metallurgist, 1935, asst. supt. Newburgh works, Cleve., 1936-39, supt. wire mills Cuyahoga works, 1939-41, supt. wire mills So. works, Worcester, 1941-44, div. supt., 1944, gen. supt., 1945-50, asst. v.p. ops., Cleve., 1950-53, v.p. ops., 1953-56, pres. Am. Steel and Wire div., Cleve., 1956-64; v.p. wire ops. U.S. Steel Corp., Pitts., 1964-70. Hon. v.p. Boy Scouts Am., Cleve.; bd. dirs. Cleve. Mus Arts Assn.; v.p., trustee Coronary Club, Inc.; hon. trustee John Carroll U.; trustee Lake Erie (Ohio) Coll., Coll. Wooster, Ednl. Research Council Am., Fenn Ednl. Found. Recipient David Ford McFarland award Pa. State U., 1956, Distinguished Alumnus award, 1959; Distinguished Service award Cleve. C. of C., 1964. Mem. Am. Iron and Steel Inst., Am. Soc. Metals, Penn State Alumni Assn., Alpha Phi Sigma, Delta Chi. Clubs: Masons (33 deg.); Union, Fifty (Cleve.); Pepper Pike. Home: 21200 Almar Dr Shaker Heights OH 44122

LEIDEL, FREDERICK OTTO, engr., educator; b. Milw., Dec. 3, 1916; s. Otto Frederick and Alma (Losse) L.; B.S. in Mech. Engring., U. Wis., 1940; m. Margarette Frona Underwood Lerum, June 5, 1963; children—Linda K., James M.; stepchildren—Dennis, Russell, James. Design engr. Hamilton Standards Propeller div. United Aircraft Corp., East Hartford, Conn., 1940-45; instr. U. Ill., Champaign, 1946; mem. faculty Coll. Engring., U. Wis.-Madison, 1946—, prof., 1962—, asso. dean Coll. Engring., 1966—; dir. Univ. Book Store, 1967-75, chmn., 1973-75. Bd. dirs. Univ. YMCA, 1962-69. Registered profl. engr., Wis. Clubs: Masons, Shriners, Order Eastern Star. Office: Coll Engring Univ Wis Madison WI 53706. *The rewards for effort are almost always greater than the effort. Therefore effort seems to be a good way of getting something for nothing. The result is an upward spiral, for the pleasure of the reward leads to greater effort.*

LEIDER, GERALD J., TV/motion picture producer; b. Camden, N.J., May 28, 1931; s. Myer and Minnie Leider; B.A., Syracuse U., 1953; m. Susan Trustman, Dec. 21, 1968; children—Matthew Trustman, Kenneth Harold. Theater producer in N.Y.C., London, 1956-59, producer Gielgud's Ages of Man, 1958-59; dir. spl. programs CBS-TV, 1960-61, dir. program sales, 1961-62; v.p. TV ops. Ashley Famous Agy., Inc., N.Y.C., 1962-69; pres. Warner Bros. TV, Burbank, Calif., 1969-74; exec. v.p. fgn. prodn. Warner Bros. Pictures in Rome (Italy), 1975-76; ind. producer motion pictures and TV GJL Prodns., Inc., Los Angeles, 1977—; feature motion pictures include The Jazz Singer with Neil Diamond, 1980; TV films include: And I Alone Survived, 1978, Willa, 1979, The Hostage Tower, 1980. Recipient Arents Alumni medal Syracuse U., 1977. Fulbright fellow U. Bristol (Eng.), 1954. Mem. Acad. TV Arts and Scis., Am. Film Inst., Hollywood Radio and TV Soc. (pres. 1975-76), Second Decade Council. Office: Samuel Goldwyn Studio 1041 N Formosa Ave Los Angeles CA 90046

LEIDESDORF, ARTHUR DAVID, accountant; b. N.Y.C., July 31, 1918; s. Samuel D. and Elsa (Grunwald) L.; grad. Blair Acad., 1937; B.S. in Accounting, N.Y. U., 1941; m. Joan Rose Wheeler, June 1, 1939 (div.); children—Samuel David II, William Alfred; m. 2d, Tova Dryman, Apr. 10, 1966; children—Edmond Hugo, Nicole Elsa. Vice pres., past dir. Murray Hill Operating Co., Inc., N.Y.C., 1946, pres., 1968—; past pres., dir. Pershing Square Bldg. Corp., N.Y.C.; past chmn. bd., dir. 100 Park Ave., N.Y.C.; past mng. partner S.D. Leidesdorf & Co., N.Y.C.; past sec.-treas. Harbor Universal, Inc.; past v.p., dir. Sherman-Taylor Corp., N.Y.C., Beaux Arts Properties, Inc.; past chmn. bd. Mid-Central Properties Ltd. Mem. nat. panel arbitrators Am. Arbitration Assn., 1955—. Vice chmn., past chmn. finance com., exec. com. trustee Citizens Budget Commn.; past asst. sec., asst. treas. Inst. for Advanced Study; past pres., past treas., also dir., exec. com. 92d St. br. YMHA-YWHA; past mem. instnl. trustees council Fedn. Jewish Philanthropies N.Y.; pres. Leidesdorf Found. Served to 1st lt. AUS, 1942-46. Recipient Silver Beaver award Boy Scouts Am. C.P.A., N.Y. Mem. Acad. Polit. Sci. (life), Met. Mus. Art, Army Ordnance Assn., Nat. Geog. Soc., Nat. Rifle Assn., U.S. Revolver Assn.; mem. Am. Inst. C.P.A.'s, N.Y. State Soc. C.P.A.'s, Albert Gallatin Assos. Clubs: Harmonie (N.Y.C.); Palm Beach Country, Poinciana (Palm Beach, Fla.); Friars. Home: 203 S Lake Trail Palm Beach FL 33480

LEIDINGER, WILLIAM JOHN, city mgr.; b. Chgo., Feb. 1, 1940; s. Arthur George and Anna (Choisek) L.; B.A., Loras Coll., Dubuque, Iowa, 1962; M.A., State U. Iowa, 1963; m. Karen Aldinger, Sept. 1, 1962; children—Michael, Steven. Adminstrv. asst. to city mgr. Park Forest (Ill.), 1963-65; asst. to city mgr. Alexandria (Va.), 1965-71; asst. city mgr. Richmond (Va.), 1971-72, city mgr., 1972—; instr. Purdue U., No. Va. Community Coll.; guest lectr. U. Richmond, mem. bd. assos.; guest lectr. Va. Commonwealth U. Mem. Internat. City Mgmt. Assn. (chmn. labor/mgmt. relations com. 1974-75), Nat. League Cities, Va. Municipal League, Am. Soc. Pub. Adminstrn. Roman Catholic. Office: 900 E Broad St Richmond VA 23219*

LEIDNER, HAROLD EDWARD, lawyer; b. Cleve., Aug. 23, 1937; s. Nathan Nelson and Therese Loretta (Burdine) L.; A.B., Cornell U., 1959; LL.B., Western Res. U., 1963; m. Barbara Ann Weinberger, Dec. 15, 1965; children—Kenneth Jason, Andrew Mitchell. Admitted to Ohio bar, 1963, since practiced in Cleve.; prin. Fuerst, Leidner, Dougherty & Kasdan Co., 1968-79; asso. firm Benesch, Friedlander, Coplan & Aronoff, 1979—. Trustee, New Cleve. Opera Co. Mem. Am., Ohio, Cleve. bar assns., Am. Arbitration Assn. Republican. Clubs: Cornell; Commerce (Cleve.); Curzon House (London, Eng.). Law editor: Webster's New World Dictionary of the American Language, 1970. Home: 2709 Belvoir Blvd Shaker Heights OH 44122 Office: 1100 Citizens Bldg Cleveland OH 44114

LEIFER, CALVIN, oral and exptl. pathologist; b. N.Y.C., Mar. 4, 1929; s. Julius Kalman and Esther (Gisser) L.; B.A., N.Y. U., 1950, D.D.S., 1954; Ph.D. (Nat. Inst. Dental Research fellow), State U., N.Y., Buffalo, 1971; m. Judith Loeb, Sept. 11, 1963; children—Dory Ethan, Amira Karin. Gen. practice dentistry, New Haven, 1957-65; asso. prof. pathology Temple U., Phila., 1970-78, prof., 1978—; practice dentistry specializing in periodontics, Abington, Pa., 1974—. Mem. Cheltenham Sch. Bd. 4 yr. high sch. study com. Served to capt. USAF, 1954-56. Nat. Inst. Dental Research grantee, 1972-75; Am. Cancer Soc. grantee, 1976. Mem. Internat. Assn. Dental Research,

Am. Assn. for Dental Research, AAAS, Am. Acad. Oral Pathology, N.Y. Acad. Scis. Jewish. Contbr. articles to profl. jours. Home: 103 Waverly Rd Wyncote PA 19095 Office: 3223 N Broad St Philadelphia PA 19140

LEIFERMAN, IRWIN HAMILTON, indsl. and investment exec.; b. Chgo., Jan. 8, 1907; s. Beril and Ida (Rosenbaum) L.; student Crane Jr. Coll., 1923, Northwestern U., 1924-29; m. Silvia Weiner, Apr. 20, 1947. Purchasing agt. Hamilton-Ross Corp., Chgo. and Kokomo, Ind., 1924-30; pres. Hamilton Industries Co., 1931-64, chmn. bd., 1964—; past pres. Leiferman Investment Co., now cons.; v.p. Comet Prodns., Inc. (TV), 1965—. Mem. industry com. Dept. Labor, 1940. Mem. advisory com. Brandeis U., 1961-62, life mem. bd.; asso. Cancer Research Found. U. Chgo., 1958; mem. Mt. Sinai Hosp., Chgo.; hon. com. Lowe's Gala, 1972; charter mem. WPBT, Channel 2, Miami; co-founder, pres. Silvia and Irwin H. Leiferman Found.; nat. bd. govs., greater Chgo. bd. govs. Bonds for Israel; founder Miami Med. Center, Greater Technion Israel Inst. Tech., 1972; founder Mt. Sinai Hosp., Miami Beach, Fla., 1969, recipient spl. award, 1972; trustee, life mem. Nathan Goldblatt Soc. Cancer Research; patron Royal Ballet Soc. Miami, Lowe's Mus. Miami, Greater Art Center Miami, Philharmonic Soc. Miami; patron Greater Miami Cultural Art Center, hon. gala com., 1972. Recipient spl. awards War Bond Program, Sec. Treasury, U.S. Dept. Labor. Mem. Chgo. Assn. Commerce and Industry, Ill. Mfrs. Assn., Ill. C. of C., Friends Lowes Mus., Am. Contract Bridge League, Jewish Home for Aged Mens Club, Bayshore Service Club. Jewish (mem. bd. temple). Mem. B'nai B'rith. Clubs: Brandeis U. (life); Executives, Covenant, International, Green Acres, Standard, Bryn Mawr Country (Chgo.); Bayshore Service, Runaway Bay, Jockey, Brickell Bay, Westview Country (Miami, Fla.). Home: 10155 Collins Avenue Apt 1404 Bal Harbour FL 33154 also Standard Club 320 S Plymouth Ct Chicago IL 60604 Office: 975 Arthur Godfrey Rd Miami Beach FL also 33 N LaSalle St Chicago IL 60602

LEIFERMAN, SILVIA WEINER (MRS. IRWIN H. LEIFERMAN), artist, civic worker, sculptress; b. Chgo.; d. Morris and Annah (Kaplan) Weiner; student U. Chgo., 1960-61; studied design and painting, Chgo., Mexico, Rome, Italy, Madrid, Spain, Provincetown, Mass.; m. Irwin H. Leiferman, Apr. 20, 1947. Exhibited one-woman shows Schram Galleries, Ft. Lauderdale, Fla., 1966, 67, D'Arcy Galleries, N.Y.C., 1964, Stevens Annex Bldg., Chgo., 1965, Miami (Fla.) Mus. Modern Art, 1966, 72, Contemporary Gallery, Palm Beach, Fla., 1966, Westview Country Club, 1968, Gallery 99, 1969; exhibited group shows Ricardo Restaurant Gallery, Chgo., 1961, 62, Bryn Mawr (Chgo.) Country Club, 1961, 62, Covenant Club Ill., Chgo., 1963, D'Arcy Galleries, 1965, Internat. Platform Assn., 1967, Miami Mus. Modern Art, 1967, Bacardi Gallery, 1967, Hollywood Mus. Art, 1968, Gallery 99, Miami, Lowe Art Mus., Crystal Ho. Gallery, Miami Beach, 1968; represented in numerous pvt. collections. Head Pres. Accessories by Silvia, Chgo., 1964; v.p., sec. Leiferman Investment Corp. Organizer, charter mem. women's div. Hebrew U. Chgo., 1947; organizer women's div. Edgewater Hosp., 1954; chairwoman spl. sales and spl. events greater Chgo. Com. for State of Israel; originator, organizer Ambassador's Ball, 1956, Presentation Ball, 1963; met. chmn. numerous spl. events Nat. Council Jewish Women, Nathan Goldblatt Soc. Cancer Research, Chgo., now life mem., trustee; chmn. numerous spl. events North Shore (Ill.) Combined Jewish Appeal; chmn. women's com. Salute to Med. Research City of Hope, 1959; founder Ballet Soc. of Miami. Bd. dirs. Jewish Children's Bur., North Shore Women's Aux., Mt. Sinai Hosp., Chgo., George and Ann Portes Cancer Prevention Center Chgo., Nat. Council Jewish Women, Fox River (Ill.) Sanitorium, Edgewater Hosp., Greater Chgo. Bonds for Israel, Orgn. of Rehab. and Tng., Brandeis U., Art Inst. Chgo., Miami Mus. Modern Art; co-founder, v.p. Silvia and Irwin Leiferman Found., donor Leiferman award auspices City of Hope; mem. pacesetter/trustee com. Greater Miami Jewish Fedn., 1976-77; founder Mt. Sinai Hosp. Greater Miami (Fla.); donor Michael Reese Hosp., 1978, Miami Heart Inst., 1979, St. Joseph Hosp., 1979, Mt. Sinai Med. Center, 1979. Recipient citations for def. bond sales U.S. Govt., for Presentation Ball State of Israel, 1965; Pro Mundi Beneficio Gold medal Brazilian Acad. Humanities, 1976; numerous awards Bonds for Israel, Combined Jewish Appeal North Shore Spl. Gifts; Keys to cities Met. Miami area; named Woman of Valor, State of Israel, 1963; donor award Miami Heart Inst. Fellow Royal Soc. Arts and Scis.; mem. Internat. Council Mus., 1st Ann. Cultural Conf. Chgo., Am. Fedn. Arts, Artist's Equity Assn., Fla. Poetry Soc., Miami Art Center, Miami Beach Opera Guild Com., Greater Miami Cultural Art Center, Guild Com. Greater Miami Cultural Art Center, Sculptors of Fla., Royal Acad. Arts, Internat. Platform Assn., Lowe Art Mus., Am. Contract Bridge League. Jewish religion (mem. bd.). Clubs: Standard, Bryn Mawr Country, Covenant, Green Acres, Internat., Boye, Whitehall, Key (Chgo.); Runaway Bay, Jockey, Westview Country (Miami Beach, Fla.); Brickell Bay. Address: 10155 Collins Avenue Apt 1404 Bal Harbour FL 33154 also Tree Studio 6 E Ontario St Chicago IL 60611

LEIGH, DONALD CHARLES, educator; b. Toronto, Ont., Can., Feb. 25, 1929; s. Ernest Albert and Reba Stanley (Kidd) L.; B.S. in Engring. Physics, U. Toronto, 1951; Ph.D. in Math., Cambridge U., 1954; m. Anne Patricia Stoicheff, Sept. 2, 1952; children—Katherine, Cynthia, Timothy. Came to U.S., 1954. Sr. aerophysics engr. Gen. Dynamics Corp., Ft. Worth, 1954-56; supr. tech. computations Curtiss-Wright Corp., Princeton, N.J., 1956-57; lectr., asst. prof. dept. mech. engring. Princeton, 1958-65, asso. prof. depts. engring. mechanics and math. U. Ky., Lexington, 1965-68, prof., 1968—, chmn. dept. engring. mechanics, 1972—. Athlone fellow Cambridge U., 1951-54. Mem. Soc. Rheology, Soc. for Natural Philosophy, ASME, Am. Acad. Mechanics, Sigma Xi. Presbyterian. Author: Nonlinear Continuum Mechanics, 1968. Contbr. articles to profl. jours. Home: 1509 Lakewood Dr Lexington KY 40502

LEIGH, MITCH, composer; b. Bklyn., Jan. 30, 1928; B.A., M.A., Yale; studied with Paul Hindemith. Founder, chmn. bd., creative dir. Music Makers, Inc., N.Y.C.; writer, producer radio-TV mus. commls. Recipient awards Am. TV Comml. Festival, Venice Internat. Advt. Film Festival. Composer: (incidental music Broadway plays) Too True to Be Good, Never Live Over a Pretzel Factory; (stage score) Man of LaMancha (N.Y. Drama Critics Circle award best mus. 1965-66). Address: Music Makers Inc 200 Central Park S New York NY 10019

LEIGH, MONROE, lawyer; b. South Boston, Va., July 15, 1919; s. Leander Faulkner and Elizabeth Edmunds (Monroe) L.; B.A., Hampden-Sydney Coll., 1940; LL.B., U. Va., 1947; m. Mary Gallaher Leigh, Apr. 15, 1951; children—Edward Monroe, Parker McCollester, Elizabeth Faulkner. Admitted to Va. bar, 1947, D.C. bar, 1948, U.S. Supreme Ct., 1950; asso. firm Covington, Burling, Rublee, Acheson & Shorb, 1947-51; mem. U.S. del. N. Atlantic Council, London and Paris, 1951-53; dep. asst. gen. counsel Dept. Def., 1953-55, asst. gen. counsel internat. affairs, 1955-59; partner firm Steptoe and Johnson, Washington, 1961-75, 77—; legal adviser Dept. State, 1975-77; lectr. U. Va. Law Sch., 1964-75, 78—; mem. Permanent Ct. of Arbitration, The Hague, 1975—. Served with USAAF, 1943-46. Recipient Superior Honor award Sec. of State, 1977. Mem. Am. Bar Assn., Internat. Law Assn., Am. Soc. Internat. Law, Council Fgn. Relations, Washington Inst. Fgn. Affairs, Am. Law Inst. Episcopalian. Clubs: Colonnade, Metropolitan, Chevy Chase. Contbr. articles to profl. jours. Home: 5205 Westwood Dr Washington DC 20016 Office: 1250 Connecticut Ave NW Washington DC 20036

LEIGH, THOMAS WATKINS, lawyer; b. Winnsboro, La., Apr. 8, 1903; s. Benjamin Watkins and Olive (Buckingham) L.; LL.B., La. State U., 1924; m. Louise Grisham, July 7, 1942. Admitted to La. bar, 1924; pvt. practice, 1924-29; mem. firm Theus, Grisham, Davis & Leigh, Monroe, La., 1929—. Dir. First Nat. Bank West Monroe. Mem. Gov. La. Spl. Commn. Study Needs Higher Edn. La., 1954-56; mem. Pub. Affairs Research Council; del. La. Constl. Conv., 1973; mem. Gov. La. Spl. Tidelands Adv. Com., 1964-72; chmn. La. Mineral Bd., 1966-72. Bd. dirs. Council for Better La.; mem. bd. suprs. La. State U., 1940-60, chmn., 1948-50. Served as lt. comdr. USNR, 1942-45. Fellow Am. Bar Found.; mem. Am. (ho. of dels. 1958—, bd. govs. 1975-78), La. (pres. 1954-55, gov.) bar assns., Am. Coll. Probate Attys., Am. Coll. Trial Lawyers, Am., La. (council, v.p.) law insts., Am. Judicature Soc., Order of Coif, Gamma Eta Gamma, Theta Xi. Episcopalian (vestryman). Clubs: Army and Navy (Washington); Boston, Pickwick (New Orleans). Home: 1401 S Grand St Monroe LA 71202 Office: 1303 Bancroft Circle Monroe LA 71203

LEIGH, WALTER HENRY, educator; b. Lake City, Mich., Apr. 16, 1912; s. Walter Byron and Edith Estella (Henry) L.; A.B., Greenville Coll., 1934; Ph.D., U. Ill., 1938; m. Anna Mae Mullet, Aug. 30, 1938; children—Linda Gay, Jeffrey Brian. Mem. biology staff Chgo. City Colls., 1938-43, 46-49; faculty U. Miami (Fla.), 1949—, prof. zoology, 1954—, chmn. dept., 1957—. Served to capt. USAAF, 1943-46. Mem. Am. Soc. Parasitologists, Am. Soc. Zoologists, Soc. Systematic Zoology, Assn. Tropical Biology, Phi Beta Kappa, Sigma Xi, Phi Kappa Phi. Spl. research parasitology, ecology helminth parasites. Home: 5211 Granada Blvd Coral Gables FL 33146

LEIGH, WILLIAM COLSTON, lecture and entertainment exec.; b. N.Y.C., Aug. 7, 1901; s. William Robinson and Anna (Seng) L.; student Columbia U. Extension; m. Ardis Neff, Aug. 20, 1946; 1 son, William Colston. Pres., W. Colston Leigh, Inc.; clients managed include Eleanor Roosevelt, Mrs. Indira Gandhi, Madame V.L. Pandit, Vincent Price, Art Buchwald, Abba Ebam, Alex Haley, Hume Cronym, Jessica Tandy, David Niven, Clement Attlee, Dr. Will Durant, Alvin Toffler, Patrice Munsel, Betsy Palmer, Celeste Holm, Arthur C. Clarke, Betty Furness, Grace Moore, Lawrence Tibbett, Alec Templeton, others in concert, theatre and entertainment field. Collector, authority Am., English antiques. Episcopalian. Home: 26 Edgerstoune Rd Princeton NJ 08540 Office: 6 E 45th St New York NY 10017*

LEIGHTEN, EDWARD HENRY, publisher; b. Montclair, N.J., June 22, 1914; s. Jack and Mariette G. (Ackerman) L.; B.S. in Optics, U. Rochester, 1937; m. Alice Celia Bowne, Aug. 31, 1940; children—Judith (Mrs. Harvey L. Slade), Jeanne Elizabeth. Engr., Universal Camera Corp., N.Y.C., 1938-39; mem. editorial staff Photo Technique and Product Engring. mags. McGraw-Hill Pub. Co., N.Y.C., 1939-42; tech. editor U.S. Camera mag., N.Y.C., 1946-47; editor, pub. Photo Devels. (now Photo Mktg.) mag. Master Photo Dealers Assn., Jackson, Mich., 1947-52; editor Flow mag., Flow Quar. mag. and Flow Directory, Indsl. Pub. Co., Cleve., 1952-56, exec. editor, 1956-60; with Cahners Pub. Co., Boston, 1960—, pub. Modern Materials Handling mag., 1960—, v.p., 1966—, v.p., group pub. Modern Materials Handling and Traffic Mgmt. mags., 1974—; cons. materials handling systems. Mem. Westlake (Ohio) Sch. Bd., 1958-60, Westlake Library Bd., 1958-60. Served as lt. USNR, 1942-46. Recipient Honor award for contbns. to materials handling edn. Internat. Material Mgmt. Soc. Mem. Material Handling Inst., Caster and Floor Truck Mfrs. Assn., Nat. Wooden Pallet and Container Assn., Internat. Material Mgmt. Soc. (cert. profl. in material handling and material mgmt.), Material Handling Equipment Dealers Assn., Nat. Council Phys. Distbn. Mgmt., Bus./Profl. Advt. Assn. (cert. bus. communicator), Theta Chi. Home: 531 Riverview Dr Chatham MA 02633 Office: 221 Columbus Ave Boston MA 02116. *Full, clear, and honest communication among people—in social, industrial, professional and commercial endeavors—is essential to our social, economic, and political growth. To be a good communicator is to be a catalyst for progress in all aspects of life. Opportunities for good communicators abound, but relatively few persons are aware of them early enough in their careers. Too many who have writing abilities or aspirations think only in terms of news or literary careers. Whatever profession, trade or technology a person may choose, training in communications will enhance his development and speed his progress.*

LEIGHTON, DAVID KELLER, SR., clergyman; b. Edgewood, Pa., June 22, 1922; s. Frank Kingsley and Irene (Keller) L.; B.S., Northwestern U., 1947; D.D., Va. Theol. Sem., 1969; m. Carolyn Ruth Smith, Jan. 18, 1945; children—Charlotte, David Keller, Nancy Elizabeth (Mrs. Harold Otto Koenig). Personnel interviewer Ohio Rubber Co., Willoughby, 1947-50; asst. supr. employment Fisher Body div. Gen. Motors Corp., Pitts. plant, 1950-54; ordained priest Episcopal Ch., 1955; curate Calvary Episcopal Ch., Pitts., 1955-56; rector St. Andrews Episcopal Ch., Pitts., 1956-59; rector Ch. of Holy Nativity, Balt., 1959-63; tchr. sacred studies St. Paul Schs., Brooklandville, Md., 1960-63; archdeacon Episcopal Diocese Md., Balt., 1964-68, bishop coadjutor, 1968-72, bishop, 1972—. Vice pres. Diocesan Council Md., 1964-72, pres., 1972—; v.p. Cathedral chpt. Md., 1968—. Chmn. bd. Hannah More Acad., Reisterstown, Md., 1968-74; bd. dirs. Md. Council Chs., St. Timothy's Sch., Stevenson, Md., Ch. Mission of Help, Balt.; bd. dirs. Ch. Home and Hosp., Balt., v.p., 1972—; bd. mem. U. Balt. Served with USAAF, 1942-45; ETO. Mem. Engring. Soc. Balt., Cum Laude Soc. Balt., St. Andrews Soc. Home: 3601 N Charles St Baltimore MD 21218 Office: 105 W Monument St Baltimore MD 21201

LEIGHTON, DAVID STRUAN ROBERTSON, univ. adminstr.; b. Regina, Sask., Can., Feb. 20, 1928; s. Gordon Ernest and Mary Haskins (Robertson) L.; B.A., Queen's U., Kingston, Ont., 1950; M.B.A., Harvard, 1953, D.B.A., 1956; LL.D., U. Windsor, 1972; m. Margaret Helen House, Aug. 25, 1951; children—Douglas, Bruce, Katharine, Jennifer, Andrew. Editor, Canadian Press, 1950-51; research asso. Harvard, 1953-55, vis. prof., 1974; asst. prof., asso. prof., prof. U. Western Ont., 1955-70; dir. Banff (Alta.) Centre, 1970—; dir. Gulf Can. Ltd., GSW Ltd., Standard Brands Ltd., Canadian Appliance Mfg. Co. Ltd., Rio Algom Ltd., Lomex Mines, John Wiley & Sons Ltd. Chmn., Canadian Consumer Council, 1968-70; bd. govs. North-South Inst., Glenbow-Alta. Inst., So. Alta. Opera Assn., Mktg. Sci. Inst. George F. Baker scholar Harvard U.; recipient Alta. Achievement award, 1978. Mem. Am. Mktg. Assn. (past pres.). Author: (with McNair, Brown and England) Problems in Marketing, 1957; (with E.J. Fox) Marketing in Canada, 1958; (with Donald H. Thain) Canadian Problems in Marketing, 1959, 66, 72; (with Donald H. Thain and C.B. Johnston) How Industry Buys (Media-Scope award as best indsl. market research of 1960), 1959; (with Wilding and Wilson) The Distribution of Packaged Consumer Goods: An Annotated Bibliography, 1963; International Marketing: Text and Cases, 1965; (with Donald Thompson) Canadian Marketing: Problems and Prospect, 1973; (with Kenneth Simmonds) Case Problems in Marketing, 1973. Editor-in-chief Business Quar., 1958-61. Home: 101 St Julien Rd Banff AB Canada

LEIGHTON, GEORGE NEVES, judge; b. New Bedford, Mass., Oct. 22, 1912; s. Antonio N. and Anna Sylvia (Garcia) Leitao; A.B., Howard U., 1940; LL.B., Harvard, 1946; LL.D., Elmhurst Coll., 1964, John Marshall Law Sch., 1973, Southeastern Mass. U., 1975, New Eng. U. Sch. Law, 1978; m. Virginia Berry Quivers, June 21, 1942; children—Virginia Anne, Barbara Elaine. Admitted to Mass. bar, 1946, Ill. bar, 1947, U.S. Supreme Ct. bar, 1958; partner Moore, Ming & Leighton, Chgo., 1951-59, McCoy, Ming & Leighton, Chgo., 1959-64; judge Circuit Ct. Cook County Ill. Appellate Ct., 1st Dist., 1969-76; U.S. dist. judge No. Dist. Ill., 1976—. Mem. council sect. legal edn. and admissions to bar Am. Bar Assn., chmn. council, 1976; adj. prof. John Marshall Law Sch., Chgo.; commr., mem. character and fitness com. for 1st Appellate Dist., Supreme Ct. Ill., 1955-63, chmn. character and fitness com., 1961-62; mem. joint com. for revision jud. article Ill. and Chgo. bar assns., 1959-62, joint com. for revision Ill. Criminal Code, 1959-63; chmn. Ill. adv. com. U.S. Commn. on Civil Rights, 1964; mem. pub. rev. bd. UAW, AFL-CIO, 1961-70. Asst. atty. gen. State of Ill., 1950-51; pres. 3d Ward Regular Democratic Orgn., Cook County, Ill., 1951-53, v.p. 21st Ward, 1964. Bd. dirs. United Ch. Bd. for Homeland Ministries, United Ch. of Christ, Grant Hosp., Chgo. Served from 2d lt. to capt., inf. AUS, 1942-45. Decorated Bronze Star. Recipient Civil Liberties award Ill. div. ACLU, 1961; named Chicagoan of Year in Law and Judiciary, Jr. Assn. Commerce and Industry, 1964. Fellow Am. Bar Found.; mem. Howard U. Chgo. Alumni Club (chmn. bd. dirs.), John Howard Assn. (dir.), Chgo., Ill. bar assns., N.A.A.C.P. (chmn. legal redress com. Chgo. br.), Nat. Harvard Law Sch. Assn. (council), Phi Beta Kappa. Contbr. articles to legal jours. Home: 8400 S Prairie Ave Chicago IL 60619 Office: Dirksen Fed Bldg 219 S Dearborn Chicago IL 60604

LEIGHTON, GERTRUDE CATHERINE KERR, lawyer, educator; b. Belfast, Ireland, Dec. 9, 1914; d. Archibald O. and Gertrude (Hamilton) Leighton; brought to U.S., 1915, naturalized, 1918; A.B., Bryn Mawr Coll., 1938; LL.B., Yale, 1945, postgrad. in law (fellow), 1947-49. Lectr., Barnard Coll., N.Y.C., 1940-42; admitted to N.Y. State bar, 1947; with firm Carter, Ledyard & Milburn, N.Y.C., 1945-47; vis. lectr. law Yale, 1949-50; asst. prof. polit. sci. Bryn Mawr (Pa.) Coll., 1950-55, asso. prof., 1955-64, prof., 1964—, chmn. dept., 1963-65, 68-71. Fund for Advancement Edn. fellow, 1953-54, Rockefeller Found. fellow, 1957-58; lectr. law U. Pa. Law Sch., Phila., 1959-61, vis. asso. research prof. law and psychiatry, 1961-65. Mem. Am. Bar Assn., Am. Polit. Sci. Assn., Am. Soc. Internat. Law, Am. Assn. U. Profs., Bryn Mawr Alumnae Assn., Law and Society Assn. Episcopalian. Contbr. articles to legal jours. Home: Hollow Rd PO Box 146 Radnor PA 19087 Office: Bryn Mawr Coll Bryn Mawr PA 19010

LEIGHTON, JOHN J., lawyer; b. N.Y.C., June 14, 1911; B.A., Lehigh U., 1931; student Columbia Law Sch., 1931-32; LL.B., Bklyn. Law Sch., 1934; m. Martha J. Warren, Jan. 22, 1943; children—Christopher Warren, Thomas Keith. Admitted to N.Y. bar, 1935; sr. mem. firm Townley & Updike, N.Y.C. Served to lt. col. AUS, World War II. Clubs: Metropolitan, India House (N.Y.C.). Home: Chestnut Ridge Rd Mt Kisco NY 10549 also 203 E 72d St New York NY 10021 Office: 405 Lexington Ave New York NY 10017

LEIGHTON, JOSEPH, pathologist; b. N.Y.C., Dec. 13, 1921; A.B., Columbia U., 1942; M.D., L.I. Coll. Medicine, Bklyn., 1946; m. Rosalind Weinberger, Dec. 15, 1946; children—Daniel A., Edith R. Intern, Mt. Sinai Hosp., N.Y.C., 1946-47; resident in pathology Mass. Gen. Hosp., Boston, 1948-49, USPHS Hosp., Balt., 1950; research pathologist Nat. Cancer Inst., Bethesda, Md., 1951-56; mem. faculty dept. pathology U. Pitts. Sch. Medicine, 1956-70; prof., chmn. dept. pathology Med. Coll. Pa., Phila., 1971—. Served with USPHS, 1948-56. Eleanor Roosevelt Cancer Research fellow, 1970-71. Mem. Am. Assn. Cancer Research, Tissue Culture Assn., Am. Assn. Pathologists, Internat. Acad. Pathology. Author: The Spread of Cancer, 1967. Home: 1201 Waverly Rd Gladwyne PA 19035 Office: 3300 Henry Ave Philadelphia PA 19129

LEIGHTON, MARGARET CARVER, author; b. Oberlin, Ohio, Dec. 20, 1896; d. Thomas Nixon and Flora Frazee (Kirkendall) Carver; student pub. schs., Cambridge, Mass., Lycée Fenelon, Paris, France, Villa Rogivue, Switzerland; A.B., Radcliffe Coll.; m. James Herbert Leighton, May 5, 1921 (dec. Feb. 1935); children—James Herbert, Mary (Mrs. Carson F. Thomson), Thomas Carver, Sylvia (Mrs. Douglas Wikle). Former mem. bd. edn., Westfield, N.J. Served in Army Sch. of Nursing, World War I. Mem. Writers' Guild (Calif.), Authors League Am., P.E.N. Republican. Author: Junior High School Plays, 1938, The Secret of the Old House, 1941, Twelve Bright Trumpets (pub. in Eng. as The Conqueror), 1942; The Secret of the Closed Gate, 1944; The Singing Cave, 1945 (Jr. Lit. Guild selection, also received silver medal Commonwealth Club Calif.), 1946; Judith of France, 1948; Sword and the Compass, 1951; The Secret of Bucky Moran, 1952; The Story of Florence Nightingale, 1952; The Story of General Custer, 1954; Who Rides By, 1955; Comanche of the Seventh, 1957; The Secret of Smuggler's Cove, 1959; Journey for a Princess, 1960; Bride of Glory, 1962; Voyage to Coromandel, 1965; The Canyon Castaways, 1966; A Hole in the Hedge, 1968; Cleopatra, 1969; The Other Island, 1971; Shelley's Mary, 1973. Contbr. to Child Life, American Girl, Portal, Target, Classmate, Girls Today, Boys Today, also anthologies and sch. readers. Address: 1053 20th St Santa Monica CA 90403

LEIGHTON, ROBERT BENJAMIN, physicist, educator; b. Detroit, Sept. 10, 1919; s. George B. and Olga (Homrig) L.; B.S., Calif. Inst. Tech., 1941, M.S., 1944, Ph.D., 1947; m. Alice M. Winger, July 31, 1943 (div. 1974); children—Ralph, Alan; m. 2d, Margaret L. Lauritsen, Jan. 7, 1977. Asst. prof. Calif. Inst. Tech., Pasadena, 1949-53, asso. prof., 1953-59, prof. physics, 1959—, chmn. div. physics, math., astronomy, 1970-75. Prin. investigator TV Expt. Mariner 4, 1964, Mariners 6 and 7, 1969; co-investigator TV Expt. Mariner 9, 1971. Mem. Am. Phys. Soc., Am. Astron. Soc., Nat. Acad. Sci., Am. Acad. Arts and Scis. Author: Principles of Modern Physics, 1959; (with others) The Feynman Lectures on Physics, 1964. Office: Calif Inst Tech Pasadena CA 91125

LEIGON, RALPH ARTHUR, union ofcl.; b. Vaughan, N.Mex., Sept. 7, 1918; s. Grover G. and Sally Rachel (Cousins) L.; student pub. schs., Tucumcari, N.Mex.; m. Ruby Evelyn Morrow, Aug. 31, 1940; children—Marcia, Richard. Bus. mgr. Internat. Brotherhood Elec. Workers, Local Union 357, Las Vegas, 1950-69, mem. internat. exec. council ten Western states, Washington, 1960-76, sec. internat. exec. council, 1974-76, internat. sec., 1976—; pres. Nev. State AFL-CIO, 1958-63. Mem. Nev. Employment Security Adv. Bd., 1955-70, Nev. Gov.'s Com. on Indsl. Devel., 1958-69; mem. Nev. Bd. Edn., 1969-72; mem. Democratic House and Senate Council. Served with USN, 1943-46. Baptist. Clubs: Masons, Reston Golf and Country. Home: 2281 Double Eagle Ct Reston VA 22091 Office: 1125 15th St NW Washington DC 20005*

LEIK, ROBERT K., sociologist; b. Dubuque, Iowa, Nov. 26, 1930; s. Charles H. and Miriam J. (Doane) L.; B.S., U. Oreg., 1952; M.A., U. Wis., 1957, Ph.D., 1960; m. Sheila A. Selfors, July 28, 1969. From asst. prof. to prof. sociology U. Wash., Seattle, 1959-73; prof. U. Mass., Amherst, 1973-75; dir. Minn. Family Study Center, also prof. sociology U. Minn., Mpls., 1975—; vis. prof. U. Bergen (Norway),

1970-71, U. Alta. (Can.), summer 1971. Served with U.S. Army, 1953-55. Mem. Am. Sociol. Assn., Nat. Council Family Relations, AAAS, Pacific Sociol. Assn., Midwest Sociol. Soc. Author: Methods, Logic and Research of Sociology, 1972; co-author: Mathematical Sociology, 1975; contbr. articles to profl. jours. Office: 1014 Social Sci Bldg Univ Minn Minneapolis MN 55455

LEIMKUHLER, FERDINAND FRANCIS, educator; b. Balt., Dec. 31, 1928; s. Ferdinand Frank and Louise (Kimmel) L.; B.S. cum laude, Loyola Coll., Balt., 1950; B.Engring., Johns Hopkins, 1952, D.Engring. with distinction, 1962; m. Natalie Therese Morin, July 4, 1956; children—Kristin, Margaret, Jeanne, Benedict, Thomas, Ernest. Indsl. engr. E.I. DuPont de Nemours & Co., Inc., 1950-57; research engr. Johns Hopkins, 1957-61; prof. indsl. engring. Purdue U., 1961—, head Sch. Indsl. Engring., 1969-74; vis. prof. U. Calif. at Berkeley, 1968-69; vis. prof. (Fulbright-Hayes sr. lectr.) U. Ljubljana, Yugoslavia, 1974-75; cons. in field. Served with AUS, 1952-54. Mem. Am. Inst. Indsl. Engrs., Operations Research Soc. Am., Inst. Mgmt. Scis., Am. Soc. Engring. Edn., Sigma Xi, Alpha Sigma Nu, Tau Beta Pi. Office: Grissom Hall Purdue Univ Lafayette IN 47907

LEIN, ALLEN, univ. dean, physiologist; b. N.Y.C., Apr. 15, 1913; s. Benjamin and Nina (Elinson) L.; student U. Chgo., 1935; B.A., U. Calif. at Los Angeles, 1935, M.A., 1938; Ph.D., 1940; Muellhaupt scholar physiology, Ohio State U., 1940-41; m. Teresa LaFratta, Nov. 29, 1941; children—Laura, David. Instr. surg. research Ohio State U., 1941-42, research asso. aviation medicine War Research Program, 1942-43; asst. prof. physiology Vanderbilt U. Med. Sch., 1946-47; asst. prof. physiology Northwestern U. Sch. Medicine, 1947-52, asso. prof. physiology, 1952-53, Abbott asso. prof. physiology, 1953-61, prof., 1961-68, dir. student affairs, 1960-64, asst. dean, 1964-68, asst. dean Grad. Sch., 1966-68; asso. dean Sch. Medicine, prof. medicine U. Calif. at San Diego, 1968-73, prof. reproductive medicine, 1973—, asso. dean for grad. studies-health scis., 1974-77, dir. health professions honors program, 1979—; vis. prof. chemistry Calif. Inst. Tech., 1954-55; cons. VA Research Hosp., Chgo., 1964-68; adv. com. office sci. personnel Nat. Acad. Scis., 1969-73; Rockefeller Found. vis. scholar Bellagio Study and Conf. Center, 1977. Served to capt. USAAF, 1943-46; aviation physiologist, chief dept. biophysics Air Force Sch. Aviation Medicine. Guggenheim fellow biochem. research Collège de France, 1958-59. Fellow AAAS; mem. Soc. Exptl. Biology and Medicine, Am. Physiol. Soc., Endocrine Soc., Am. Soc. Biol. Scis., Sigma Xi. Author: The Cycling Female: Her Menstrual Rhythm, 1979; contbr. articles to sci. jours. Home: 8653 Dunaway Dr La Jolla CA 92037

LEIN, CHARLES D., univ. pres.; b. Sioux Falls, S.D., Nov. 2, 1941; s. Harold D. and Willa E. Lein; B.S., Augustana Coll., Sioux Falls, 1963; M.S., U. Wyo., 1964, Ed.D., 1970; m. Susan E. Buckingham, June 30, 1962; children—Kent, Keith, Steven, Greg. Pres., Treasure State Mgmt. Cons., Bozeman, Mont., 1968-70; teaching asst. U. Wyo., 1963-64, 66-68; v.p., dir. student housing, dir. placement, dir. counseling, instr. Nat. Coll. Bus., Rapid City, S.D., 1964-66; asst. prof. commerce Mont. State U., Bozeman, 1968-70; asso. prof. bus., chmn. dept. bus. adminstrn. Weber State Coll., Ogden, Utah, 1970-73; prof., dean Sch. Bus., Boise (Idaho) State U., 1973-77; pres., prof. mgmt. U. S.D., Vermillion, pres. U. S.D., Springfield, 1977—. Bd. dirs. Black Hills Playhouse, W.H. Over Mus.; chmn. bd. trustees U. Mid-Am., Lincoln, Nebr., 1978—; bd. dirs. Karl E. Mundt Hist. and Ednl. Found., Madison, S.D.; chmn. S.D. Bd. Regents Council of pres., 1978-79; lay rep. Public Broadcasting Service, Washington; mem. small bus. adminstrn. Sioux Falls Adv. Council, 1978-80; pres. Idaho Research Found., 1975-76; chmn. public employees div. United Way, 1976-77; bd. dirs. Ada County chpt. Am. Cancer Soc., 1975-77. Mem. Idaho Council Econ. Edn., Am. Assn. Univ. Adminstrs., Acad. Mgmt., Phi Delta Kappa, Kappa Delta Kappa, Delta Sigma Pi, Gamma Lambda Sigma, Pi Sigma Epsilon. Lutheran. Contbr. articles to profl. jours. Home: 1028 Valley View Dr Vermillion SD 57069 Office: U South Dakota Vermillion SD 57069

LEIN, JOHN NAVE, obstetrician, gynecologist, univ. adminstr.; b. Spokane, Wash., Oct. 25, 1926; s. Nave George and Bonnie L.; B.S., U. Idaho, 1951; M.D., U. Wash., 1955; m. Claire Cramer, Sept. 9, 1951; children—Michael, Patrick. Rotating intern Ind. U. Med. Center, 1955-56, resident in ob-gyn, 1956-60; practice medicine specializing in ob-gyn, Spokane, 1960-64; asst. prof. ob-gyn U. Wash., 1964-69, asso. prof., 1969-77, prof., 1977—, dir. continuing med. edn., 1964—, asst. dean Sch. Medicine, 1964-68, asso. dean, 1968—, legis. liaison health scis., 1972—, asst. dir. nat. govt. relations, 1979—; mem. staff Sacred Heart Hosp., Spokane, Univ. Hosp., Seattle, Harborview Med. Center, Seattle; mem. NIH Task Force on Prevention, Control, and Edn. in Respiratory Diseases, 1976-77; mem. nat. adv. council Nat. Health Service Corps, 1979—; mem. Liaison Com. Continuing Med. Edn., 1978—; speaker in field; Wash./Alaska Regional Med. Program grantee, producer numerous audiovisuals and video cassettes, 1969-71; dir. Gen. Telephone of N.W., Lincoln Mut. Bank, Lincoln First Fed. Savs. and Loan Assn. Bd. dirs. Seattle-King County Conv. and Vis. Bur., 1974—. Served with USN, 1944-45. Recipient 1st Pl. Nat. Biocommunications award, 1970. Diplomate Am. Bd. Obstetricians and Gynecologists. Mem. AMA, Assn. Am. Med. Colls., Wash. State Med. Assn., King County Med. Soc. Home: 23205 Main St Redmond WA 98052 Office: U Wash Sch Medicine Dept Ob-Gyn Seattle WA 98195

LEIN, MALCOLM EMIL, architect; b. Havre, Mont., July 19, 1913; s. Emil A. and Ruth (Fredeen) L.; student U. Wis., 1930; B.Arch., U. Minn., 1936; m. Miriam Balliet Bend, Apr. 13, 1939; children—Eric Manning, Kristin Anker, R. Kurt Harrison. Asst. head constrn. dept. F.W. Woolworth Co., Dist. Office, Mpls., 1936-41; pvt. practice architecture and design, St. Paul, 1946—; dir. Minn. Mus. of Art, St. Paul, 1947-77, pres., 1973-79; pres. Design Cons., Inc., St. Paul, 1949—, Mid-West Credit Corp., St. Paul, 1959—, Desconi Corp. Served to col. C.E., AUS, 1941-46; CBI. Mem. Am. Assn. Mus., Am. Fedn. Art, Archives Am. Art, Res. Officers Assn., Air Force Assn. Home: 361 Summit Ave Saint Paul MN 55102 Office: 305 St Peter St Saint Paul MN 55102

LEINBACH, FREDERICK SWAVELY, paper mfr.; b. Jonestown, Pa., Mar. 28, 1910; s. Henry Jerome and Mary (Swavely) L.; B.S., Lafayette Coll., Easton, Pa., 1931; postgrad. edn. U. Pa., 1932-33; m. Pauline V. Dotterer, Dec. 25, 1931; children—Linda Jay, Michael Swavely. Instr. sci. Swavely Sch., Manassas, Va., 1931-34; with Riegel Paper Corp., 1934—, asst. to sales mgr., 1948-50, sec., 1950-55, v.p., asst. gen. sales mgr., 1955-57, exec. v.p., 1957-59, pres., 1959-68, chief exec. officer, 1962-68, dir., 1952-71; mem. governing com. U.S. Philips Trust; dir. N.Am. Philips Corp., Rexham Corp. Asst. dir. containers div. WPB, 1942-43. Mem. Am Paper and Pulp Assn. (exec. com. v.p. 1961-65), Am. Paper Inst., Pulp, Paper and Paperboard Export Assn. (bd. govs., pres. 1964-66), Packaging Inst. (pres., dir., gen. tech. chmn. 1951-53). Clubs: University, Sky, (N.Y.C.). Home: 313 Gull Road Ocean City NJ 08226 Office: 350 Fifth Ave New York City NY 10001

LEINSDORF, ERICH, orch. condr.; b. Vienna, Austria, Feb. 4, 1912; s. Ludwig Julius and Charlotte (Loebl) L.; came to U.S. 1937, naturalized, 1942; ed. Vienna; Mus.D. (hon.), Baldwin-Wallace Coll., Berea, Ohio, 1945, Rutgers U., 1952; hon. degree Williams Coll., 1966, Columbia, 1967; m. Anne Frohnknecht, Aug. 3, 1939 (div.); children—David, Gregor, Joshua, Hester, Jennifer; m. 2d, Vera Graf. Asst. condr. Salzburg Festival, 1934-37; condr. Met. Opera until 1943, Cleve. Orch., 1943; music dir. Philharmonic Orch., Rochester, 1947-56; dir. N.Y.C. Center Opera, 1956, Met. Opera, 1957-62; music dir. Boston Symphony Orch., 1962-69; guest appearances with maj. orchs. in U.S., Europe, including Phila., Los Angeles, St. Louis, New Orleans, Mpls., Concertgebouw Amsterdam, Israel Philharmonic, San Francisco Opera, Bayreuth, Holland and Prague festival, London BBC, London Symphony, Orchestre de Paris, Cleve. Orch., Chgo. Symphony, Berlin Philharmonic, N.Y. Philharmonic, Vienna Symphony. Past mem. Corp. for Pub. Broadcasting; past mem. exec. com. John F. Kennedy Center for Performing Arts. Fellow Am. Acad. Arts and Scis. Author: Cadenza (autobiography). Contbr. articles to Atlantic Monthly, Sat. Rev., N.Y. Times, High Fidelity Publ. transcriptions of Brahms Chorale Preludes. Records for RCA Victor, Westminster. Columbia, Decca (London), E.M.I. Office: care Nancy Dodds 209 E 56th St New York City NY 10022

LEINSTER, COLIN RONALD, author, former mag. editor; b. Tynemouth, Eng., Dec. 19, 1939; s. Ronald Styan and Sheila Mary (Wright) L.; came to U.S., 1964; student London Poly. Sch. Journalism, 1961-64; m. Emily Banks, July 28, 1972. Reporter, West London Press, 1961-64, Cleve. Plain Dealer, 1964-65, New Orleans States-Item, 1965-66; Vietnam corr. Life mag., 1967-69, Midwest Bur. chief, 1970-71, asso. editor, 1971-72; free-lance writer, 1972-75; staff writer Free Enterprise mag., N.Y.C., 1975-77; contbg. editor Time-Life Books; editorial cons. Manpower Devel. Research Corp., N.Y.C.; text editor Tree Communications. Author: (novel) The Heritage of Michael Flaherty. Home: 600 West End Ave New York NY 10024 Office: 1212 Ave of Americas New York NY 10036

LEINWAND, GERALD, coll. pres.; b. Bklyn., Aug. 27, 1921; s. Louis and Rose (Simonoff) L.; B.A., N.Y. U., 1941, M.S., 1942, Ph.D., 1962; M.A., Columbia U., 1945; m. Selma Fienberg, Aug. 26, 1945; children—Roberta Leinwand Opper, Adrienne. With Rosetta Electric Co., N.Y.C., 1937-41; exec. trainee Abraham & Strauss, N.Y.C., 1941-42; tchr. social studies, public schs., N.Y.C., 1942-45, Bennington, Vt., 1945-51; owner, operator furniture retail bus., 1952-63; TV tchr. Sta.-WNDT, 1962-63; asst. prof. edn. CCNY, 1963-65, asso. prof., 1967-71, asst. dean, 1967-68; prof., dean Sch. Edn., Bernard M. Baruch Coll., City U. N.Y., 1968-77; pres. Oreg. Coll. Edn., 1977—; cons. in field; bd. dirs. N.Y.C. Council on Econ. Edn., Oreg. Council Econ. Edn.; mem. Coll. Pres.'s Group Studying Higher Edn. in Egypt and Greece, 1978. Bd. govs. YMCA, N.Y.C., 1977—. Recipient Founders' Day award N.Y. U., 1962. Mem. Nat. Council Social Studies, Am. Assn. Higher Edn., Assn. Curriculum Devel., N.Y. Soc. Exptl. Study Edn., Am. Hist. Assn. Author: The Pageant of World History; The Pageant of American History; Problems of American Society; (with Dan Feins) Teaching History and the Social Sciences; contbr. numerous articles on social scis. to Social Edn., Clearing House, Urban Rev. Social Action. Home: 395 College St S Monmouth OR 97361 Office: 345 Monmouth Ave N Monmouth OR 97361

LEIPER, HARPER, photographer; b. Malvern, Ark., Mar. 26, 1916; s. Samuel Harper and Annie (Nail) L.; student Rice U., 1934-36, U. Tex., 1938-40; M.Photography, Profl. Photographers Am., 1955, Profl. Photography Assn. Am., 1965; m. Frances Ann Wright, Dec. 22, 1944; children—Bill, James, Mary, Robert; m. 2d, Bennie Ross Lindley, Jan. 21, 1961; 1 son, David Lee. Founder, propr. Harper Leiper Studios, comml. photography, Houston, 1945—; originator comml. photography class Winona (Ind.) Sch. Photography, summer 1956, tchr., 1956, 58, 60, 62, 64. An originator, author, 1957, since chmn. nat. qualification program profl. photographers; 1st pres. Photog. Arts and Sci. Found., 1965. Mem. Houston Profl. Photographers Guild (a founder, pres. 1953), Profl. Photographers Am. (comml. dir. 1956-62, pres. 1965), Southwestern (pres. 1961, Nat. award 1961, 58), Tex. (pres. 1956), profl. photographers assns., Am. Soc. Photographers (pres. 1974). Home: 466 Gingham St Houston TX 77024 Office: 2800 West Dallas St Houston TX 77019

LEIPPER, DALE FREDERICK, educator, phys. oceanographer; b. Salem, Ohio, Sept. 8, 1914; s. Robert and Myrtle (Cost) L.; B.S. in Edn., Wittenberg Coll., 1937, D.Sc., 1968; M.A., Ohio State U., 1939; postgrad. U. Cal. at Los Angeles, 1939-40; Ph.D., Scripps Instn. Oceanography, 1950; m. Virginia Alma Harrison, May 14, 1942; children—Diane Louise, Janet Elizabeth, Bryan Robert, Anita Dale. Tchr. city schs., San Diego, 1940-41; research oceanographer, tchr. Scripps Instn. Oceanography, U. Calif., 1945-49; mem. faculty dept. oceanography and meteorology Tex. A & M U., 1949-68, head dept., 1949-64, prof., 1964-68; prof. Naval Postgrad. Sch., Monterey, Calif., 1968—, chmn. dept. oceanography, 1968-79; supr. research program NSF, Internat. Geophys. Year, Office Naval Research; mem. tech. panel oceanography, exec. vice chmn. meteorology panel U.S. Nat. Com. Internat. Geophys. Year; chmn. com. marine scis. So. Regional Edn. Bd., 1952-56; acting asso. dir. Tex. A & M U. Research Found., 1953-54. Served as capt. USAAF, 1941-45; weather officer, oceanographer. Mem. Am. Meteorol. Soc., Am. Geophys. Union, Am. Soc. Limnology and Oceanography (pres. 1957-58), Tex. (pres. 1955), Nat. (panel chmn. 1959-64) acads. sci., Marine Tech. Soc., Am. Soc. Oceanography (pres. 1967-68), Sigma Xi, Phi Kappa Phi. Rotarian. Home: 11532 Hidden Hills Rd Salinas CA 93908 Office: Dept Oceanography Naval Postgrad Sch Monterey CA 93940

LEIS, PHILIP EDWARD, anthropologist; b. Newburgh, N.Y., Oct. 19, 1931; s. Louis and Sarah (Cohen) L.; B.A., Antioch Coll., 1954; Ph.D., Northwestern U., 1962; m. Marida Hollos, Apr. 15, 1977; children by previous marriage—Mark Samuel, Rachel Beth. Lectr. anthropology Nat. Coll. Edn., Evanston, Ill., summer 1960; instr., then asst. prof. Iowa State U., Ames, 1960-62; successively asst. prof., asso. prof., prof. Brown U., Providence, 1962—, dir. anthropology, 1967-70, chmn. dept., 1970-76. Mem. African Studies Assn., Am. Ethnol. Soc., Am. Anthrop. Assn., Royal Anthrop. Inst., Sigma Xi. Author: Enculturation and Socialization in an Ijaw Village, 1972; co-editor: Ethnic Encounters, 1977. Home: 117 Terrace Ave Riverside RI 02915 Office: Dept Anthropology Brown U Providence RI 02912

LEISER, ERNEST STERN, TV news producer; b. Phila., Feb. 26, 1921; s. Monroe Felsenthal and Gertrude (Stern) L.; A.B., U. Chgo., 1941; m. Caroline Thomas Camp, Oct. 26, 1946; children—Nancy, Shelley, Nicholas. Reporter City News Bur. Chgo., 1941; asst. picture editor Chgo. Herald-Am., 1941-42, 46; corr. Overseas News Agy., 1947-52; successively corr., producer, dir. TV news, exec. producer CBS News, N.Y.C., 1953-72, sr. producer, producer bicentennial coverage, spl. reports, 1975—; exec. producer ABC News, N.Y.C., 1972-75. Served with AUS, 1942-46. Decorated Bronze Star medal; Croix de Guerre. Recipient Sigma Delta Chi award TV reporting, 1956; Peabody awards TV reporting and producing, 1956, 77; Ohio State awards, 1969, 77; Nat. Acad. TV Arts and Scis. award, 1968-69, 69-70, 70-71. Author: This is Germany, 1950. Contbr. articles to mags. Home: College Ave South Nyack NY 10960

LEISH, KENNETH WILLIAM, pub. co. exec.; b. Cambridge, Mass., Dec. 31, 1936; s. Frank and Lillian (Kargir) L.; A.B. magna cum laude, Harvard, 1958; M.S. in Journalism, Columbia, 1959; m. Barbara Lynn Ackerman, Nov. 27, 1966; children—Matthew, Emily, Adam. Interviewer, Oral History Office, Columbia, 1960; free lance drama reviewer Variety, 1961-66; editor Am. Heritage Pub. Co., Inc., N.Y.C., 1961-69, v.p., gen. mgr. book div., 1971-77; editor in chief Am. Heritage Press, 1970-71; mgr. large-format paperbacks Bantam Books Inc., N.Y.C., 1977—. Served with AUS, 1959-60. Club: Harvard (N.Y.C.). Author: The White House, 1972; A History of the Cinema, 1974. Editor in charge The American Heritage History of the Presidents and the Presidency, 1968. Home: 3 Vermont Ave White Plains NY 10606 Office: 666 Fifth Ave New York City NY 10019

LEISS, JAMES ELROY, physicist, govt. ofcl.; b. Youngstown, Ohio, June 2, 1924; s. Paul E. and Virginia C. (Bailey) L.; B.S., Case Inst. Tech., 1948; Ph.D., U. Ill., 1955; m. Wilma May Dindore, June 30, 1945; children—Paul, Judith, James, Susan. Mem. research staff dept. physics U. Ill., 1950-54; with Nat. Bur. Standards, 1954-79, dir. Center for Radiation Research, 1972-79; asso. dir. for high energy and nuclear physics Dept. Energy, Washington, 1979—. Served with U.S. Army, 1942-46. Recipient Gold medal Dept. Commerce. Mem. Am. Phys. Soc., AAAS, Sigma Xi. Contbr. articles to profl. jours. Home: 13013 Chestnut Oak Dr Gaithersburg MD 20760 Office: J-309-GTN Dept Energy Washington DC 20545

LEISURE, PETER KEETON, lawyer; b. N.Y.C., Mar. 21, 1929; s. George S. and Lucille E. (Pelouze) L.; B.A., Yale U., 1952; LL.B., U. Va., 1958; m. Kathleen Blair, Feb. 27, 1960; children—Lucille, Mary Blair, Kathleen. Admitted to N.Y. bar, 1959, U.S. Supreme Ct. bar, 1966; asso. firm Breed, Abbott & Morgan, 1958-61; asst. U.S. atty. So. Dist. N.Y., 1962-66; partner firm Curtis, Mallet-Prevost, Colt & Mosle, 1967-78, Whitman & Ransom, N.Y.C., 1978—; lectr. Practising Law Inst., 1968-70. Bd. dirs. Retarded Infants Services, 1968-78, pres., 1971-75; bd. dirs. Community Council of Greater N.Y., 1972-79, Youth Consultation Services, 1971-78; trustee Ch. Club of N.Y., 1973—. Fellow Am. Bar Found., Am. Coll. Trial Lawyers, Am. Law Inst.; mem. Am., N.Y. State, City of N.Y. bar assns., Fed. Bar Council (trustee, v.p. 1973-78). Contbr. articles to legal jours. Home: 1185 Park Ave New York NY 10028 Office: 522 Fifth Ave New York NY 10036

LEISY, JAMES FRANKLIN, publisher; b. Normal, Ill., Mar. 21, 1927; s. Ernest Erwin and Elva (Krehbiel) L.; B.B.A., So. Meth. U., 1949; m. Emily Ruth McQueen, June 8, 1949; children—James Franklin, Scot, Rebecca. Field rep. Prentice-Hall, Inc., N.Y.C., 1949-52, asso. editor, 1952-54; editor Allyn & Bacon, Inc., Boston, 1954-56; exec. editor Wadsworth Pub. Co., Inc., San Francisco, 1956-59, v.p., 1959-60, pres., 1960-77, chmn., chief exec. officer, 1977—, dir., 1962—; chmn. Prindle, Weber & Schmidt, Inc.; dir. San Francisco Mag., Inc., Internat. Thomson Orgn., Inc., Dickenson Pub. Co., Inc., Baron Data Systems, Inc. Cons. Vols. for Internat. Tech. Assistance; trombonist, mus. dir. T. Ford and the Model A's Roadhouse Band, 1966—. Bd. dirs. Bethel Coll.; bd. dirs., mem. exec. com. Calif. Council for Econ. Edn., 1968-71; mem. deans council Sch. Bus. Calif. State U., San Jose; mem. Nat. UN Day Com., 1978. Served with USNR, 1945-46. Named to Career Hall of Fame, So. Meth. U., 1968. Mem. Young President's Orgn. (dir. 1970-73), ASCAP, So. Meth. U. Alumni Assn. (dir. 1965-70), Chief Execs. Forum, World Business Council, Phi Eta Sigma, Alpha Phi Omega, Alpha Kappa Psi (nat. chmn. song com. 1963-71), Kappa Alpha. Club: Bohemian. Author: Abingdon Song Kit, 1957; Let's All Sing, 1958; Songs for Swinging Housemothers, 1960; Songs for Singin', 1961; Songs for Pickin' and Singin', 1962; Beer Bust Song Book, 1963; Hootenanny Tonight, 1964; Folk Song Fest, 1964; Folk Song Abecedary, 1966; Alpha Kappa Psi Sings, 1967; The Good Times Songbook, 1974; Scrooge, The Christmas Musical, 1978. Composer several popular songs including An Old Beer Bottle, Please Tell Me Why, A Personal Friend of Mine, A Little Old Lady in Tennis Shoes, Isn't This a Lovely Christmas. Office: 10 Davis Dr Belmont CA 94002

LEITERMAN, RICHARD MARK, film maker; b. Dome Mines, Ont., Can., Apr. 7, 1935; s. Douglas McGregor and Moynette (Stone) L.; grad. U. B.C., 1955; m. Margaret June Mansell, Nov. 10, 1960; children—Mark Julien, Rachel. Free-lance cinematographer, 1962—; cameraman films for NBC, ABC, CBS, NET, PBS, BBC, W. German TV; dir. photography nine Canadian feature films. Can. Council grantee, 1972, 75. Mem. Royal Canadian Acad. Arts. Home and Office: 31 Kendal Ave Toronto ON M5R 1L5 Canada

LEITH, CARLTON JAMES, educator, geologist; b. Madison, Wis., Sept. 24, 1919; s. Benjamin Donald and Edna (Elkinton) L.; B.A., U. Wis., 1940, M.A., 1941; Ph.D., U. Calif. at Berkeley, 1947; m. Marian B. Pollensky, June 8, 1941; children—Carol (Mrs. James W. Lee), Ronnie Sue. Mineral economist U.S. Bur. Mines, 1942-43; instr., then asst. prof. Ind. U., 1947-49; geologist U.S. Corps Engrs., 1949-51; with Standard Oil Co. Cal., 1951-60, Holmes & Narver, Inc., cons. engrs., 1960-61; faculty N.C. State U., Raleigh, 1961—, prof. geology, 1965—, head dept. geoscis., 1967—. Served with USNR, 1943-46. Mem. AAAS, Am. Assn. Petroleum Geologists, Am. Geophys. Union, Assn. Profl. Geol. Scientists, Geol. Soc. Am., Nat. Assn. Geology Tchrs., Soc. Econ. Paleontologists and Mineralogists. Home: Route 8 Box 202 Raleigh NC 27612

LEITH, CECIL ELDON, JR., mathematician; b. Boston, Jan. 31, 1923; s. Cecil Eldon and Elizabeth (Benedict) L.; A.B., U. Calif. at Berkeley, 1943, Ph.D., 1957; m. Mary Louise Henry, July 18, 1942; children—Ann, John, Paul. Exptl. physicist Lawrence Radiation Lab., Berkeley, 1946-52, theoretical physicist, Livermore, Calif., 1952-68; sr. scientist Nat. Center for Atmospheric Research, Boulder, Colo., 1968—, div. dir., 1977—; Symons Meml. lectr. Royal Meteorol. Soc., London, 1978; mem. Internat. Commn. Dynamic Meteorology; chmn. com. on atmospheric scis. NRC; mem. joint organizing com. Global Atmospheric Research Program, World Meteorol. Orgn. and Internat. Council Sci. Unions. Served with AUS, 1944-46. Recipient Meisinger award Am. Meteorol. Soc., 1967. Fellow Am. Phys. Soc., Am. Meteorol. Soc. Home: 320 Hollyberry Ln Boulder CO 80303 Office: Nat Center for Atmospheric Research PO Box 3000 Boulder CO 80307

LEITH, EMMETT NORMAN, educator, elec. engr.; b. Detroit, Mar. 12, 1927; s. Albert Donald and Dorothy Marie (Emmett) L.; B.S., Wayne State U., 1950, M.S., 1952, Ph.D., 1978; m. Lois June Neswold, Feb. 17, 1956; children—Kim Ellen, Pam Elizabeth. Mem. research staff U. Mich., 1952—, prof. elec. engring., 1968—, chief scientist Willow Run Labs., 1970—; cons. several indsl. corps. Served with USNR, 1945-46. Recipient Gordon Meml. award S.P.I.E., 1965; citation Am. Soc. Mag. Photographers, 1966; Achievement award U.S. Camera and Travel mag., 1967; Excellence of Paper award Soc. Motion Picture and TV Engrs., 1967; Daedalion award, 1968; Stuart Ballantine medal Franklin Inst., 1969; Distinguished Faculty Achievement award U. Mich., 1973; Alumni award Wayne State U., 1974; cited by Nobel Prize Commn. for contbns. to holography, 1971; Holley medal ASME, 1976; named Man of Year, Indsl. Research mag., 1966. Fellow Optical Soc. Am. (Wood medal 1975), IEEE (Liebmann award 1967; Inventor of Year award 1976), mem. Sigma Xi, Sigma Pi Sigma. Contbr. books, profl. jours. Patentee in field. First demonstrated (with colleague) capability of holography to form high-quality 3-dimensional image. Home: 51325 Murray Hill Canton

MI 48187 Office: Univ Mich Inst Sci and Tech PO Box 618 Ann Arbor MI 48107

LEITH, JOHN HADDON, clergyman, educator; b. Due West, S.C., Sept. 10, 1919; s. William H. and Lucy Ann (Haddon) L.; A.B., Erskine Coll., 1940, D.D. (hon.), 1972; B.D., Columbia Theol. Sem., 1943; M.A., Vanderbilt U., 1946; Ph.D., Yale U., 1949; D.D. (hon.), Davidson Coll., 1978; m. Ann Caroline White, Sept. 2, 1943; children—Henry White, Caroline Haddon. Ordained to ministry Presbyterian Ch., 1943; pastor chs. in Nashville and Auburn, Ala., 1944-59; Pemberton prof. theology Union Theol. Sem., Richmond, Va., 1959—; vis. prof. Columbia Theol. Sem., Eckerd Coll., New Coll. at U. Edinburgh; adj. prof. Va. Commonwealth U.; mem. adv. interim com. to revise book of ch. order Presbyn. Ch. U.S., 1955-61, mem. com. brief statement of faith, 1960-62, chmn. com. revision of chpt. 3 of Confession of Faith, mem. permanent nominating com. gen. assembly, 1972-75; chmn. bd. Presbyn. Survey, 1961-70; bd. dirs. Presbyn. Outlook Mag., 1962—; moderator Presbyn. Synod N.C., 1977-78. Trustee, Erskine Coll. Kent fellow, 1946-48; Folger Library fellow, 1964; grantee Advanced Religious Studies Found., 1974. Author: Creeds of the Churches, 1963, rev., 1973; The Church, A Believing Fellowship, 1965, rev., 1980; Assembly at Westminster, 1973; Greenville Church, The Story of a People, 1973; The Reformed Tradition, A Way of Being the Christian Community, 1977. Home: 1230 Rennie Ave Richmond VA 23227 Office: 3401 Brook Rd Richmond VA 23227

LEITH, RODERICK GORDON, airlines exec.; b. Bklyn., July 3, 1928; s. John William and Justina (MacIntosh) L.; B.B.A., City Coll. N.Y., 1955; M.B.A., N.Y. U., 1958; m. Grace Andersen, Aug. 15, 1954; children—Gayle, Nancy, Tracy. Asst. v.p. First Western Bank, Los Angeles, 1965-68; dir. comml. info. systems Western Air Lines, Inc., Los Angeles, 1968-70, v.p., controller, 1970—; lectr. Am. Inst. Banking, 1966-67. Mem. steering com. productivity Calif. Inst. Tech.; mem. advisory council Sch. Bus. and Econs. Calif. State U., Los Angeles. Served with AUS, 1950-52. Mem. Financial Execs. Inst., Am. Econ. Assn., Am. Accounting Assn. Home: Placentia CA 92670 Office: Western Air Lines Inc 6060 Avion Dr Los Angeles CA 90009

LEITH, ROYAL WILLIS, JR., investment banker; b. Boston, Mar. 4, 1929; s. Royal Willis and Katherine (Dunham) L.; student Dexter Sch., 1938-41, Milton Acad., 1942-46, Bowdoin Coll., 1950; m. Barbara Ann Bell, June 23, 1951; children—Royal Willis III, John Allen II and Alexander King (twins). With Burgess & Leith, Boston, 1950-75; sr. v.p., dir. Tucker, Anthony & R.L. Day Inc.; dir. Sage Labs., Inc.; trustee Dedham Instn. for Savs. Vice pres. Boston Stock Exchange, 1963-64, gov., 1962—, pres., 1964-65, chmn. bd. govs., 1965-69. Mem. Westwood Republican Town Com., 1953-58. Trustee Noble and Greenough Sch., Thoracic Found. Mem. Securities Industry Assn., Boston Investment Club, Marshall St. Hist. Soc. Mem. 1st Parish United Ch. Clubs: Somerset; Bowdoin (Boston); Dedham Country and Polo; Vintage Sports Car Clubs Am. (dir.); Bugatti Owners Club, Ltd. (London, Eng.), Am. Bugatti; Little Cranberry Island Yacht (Marblehead). Home: 115 Common St Dedham MA 02026 Office: 1 Beacon St Boston MA 02108

LEITH, W(ILLIAM) GORDON, farmer coop. exec.; b. Fond du Lac County, Wis., June 8, 1916; s. Ray H. and Clementina (Dalglish) L.; student Oshkosh State Tchrs. Coll., 1934-35; B.S., U. Wis., 1938; M.S., U. Calif. at Berkeley, 1939; m. Lillia Bounous, Feb. 1, 1943; 1 dau., Suzette E. With FCA, 1939-41; economist Nat. Council Farmer Coops., 1946-49, bd. dirs., 1960—, v.p., 1971-72, pres., 1973-74, chmn. bd., 1974-75; with Farmland Industries, Inc., Kansas City, Mo., 1949—, sec., 1961—, v.p., 1967—, also officer, dir. subsidiaries; chmn. bd. Farmland Foods, 1969—; pres. Farmland Agriservices, 1969—. Bd. dirs. Found. Am. Agr., Agrl. Coop. Devel. Internat.; mem. U.S. Dept. Agr. Tech. Advisory Com. Livestock and Livestock Products for Multilateral Trade Negotiations; mem. agrl. econs. research adv. com. Dept. Agr., 1964. Served with USNR, 1942-46. Mem. Am. Farm Econ. Assn., Am. Mktg. Assn., Alpha Zeta. Home: 4908 W 64th St Prairie Village KS 66208 Office: 3315 North Oak Trafficway Kansas City MO 64116

LEITMAN, HAROLD NORMAN, corp. exec.; b. Everett, Mass., Feb. 22, 1918; s. Max and Leah (Mogul) L.; grad. U. Fla., 1939; m. Shirley Bloom, Dec. 23, 1945; children—Valerie, Daniel. Pres., TT Systems Corp. Trustee, Beth Israel Hosp., N.Y.C. Mem. Young Pres.'s Orgn. Clubs: Advt.; City Athletic. Office: 9 E 37th St New York City NY 10016

LEITNER, ALFRED, educator, math. physicist; b. Vienna, Austria, Nov. 3, 1921; s. Philipp and Lona (Machlup) L.; came to U.S., 1938, naturalized, 1944; B.A., U. Buffalo, 1944; M.S., Yale, 1945, Ph.D., 1948; m. Marzia O'Neil, Nov. 24, 1948; children—Kathleen, Deborah, David. Research asso. Courant Inst. Math. Scis., N.Y.U., 1947-51; from asst. prof. to prof. physics Mich. State U., 1951-67; prof. physics Rensselaer Poly. Inst., 1967—; research asso. Harvard, 1965-66; cons. Harvard project physics, 1966-68. Guggenheim fellow, 1958-59; Deutscher Akademischer Austauschdienst fellow, 1977. Fellow Am. Phys. Soc.; mem. Assn. Physics Tchrs., Phi Beta Kappa, Sigma Xi. Author papers on theory spl. functions, boundary value problems, antennas, history of sci., teaching. Producer ednl. films: Liquid Helium, 1963; Superconductivity, 1966; Project Physics film loops, 1965-68; Dispersion, 1973; Fraunhofer (2 films), 1974. Home: 15 Fairlawn Ave Rensselaer NY 12144 Office: Dept Physics and Astronomy Rensselaer Poly Inst Troy NY 12181

LEITSTEIN, ROBERT, retail store exec., b. Yonkers, N.Y., Jan. 27, 1937; B.A., Hobart Coll., 1958. With Bloomingdales, N.Y.C., 1960-68; v.p. Neiman-Marcus, Dallas, 1968-76; pres. Robert Leitstein Assos., Dallas, 1976-78, Gump's, San Francisco, 1979—. Home: 30 Miller Pl San Francisco CA 94108 Office: Gump's 250 Post St San Francisco CA 94108

LEITZELL, TERRY LEE, govt. ofcl.; b. Williamsport, Pa., Apr. 15, 1942; s. Ernest Richard and Inez Mae (Taylor) L.; A.B., Cornell U., 1964; J.D., U. Pa., 1967; m. Lucy Acker Emmerich, June 18, 1966; children—Thomas Addison, Charles Taylor. Admitted to D.C. bar, 1967; consular officer Dept. State, Bombay, India, 1968-70, atty.-adv. for oceans affairs, Dept. State, Washington, 1970-77, chief U.S. negotiator UN law of sea negotiations, Geneva, also N.Y.C., 1974-77; asst. adminstr. for fisheries and dir. Nat. Marine Fisheries Service, NOAA, Dept. Commerce, Washington, 1978—. Mem. D.C. Bar Assn., Am. Soc. Internat. Law, Democrat. Home: 4432 Windom Pl NW Washington DC 20016 Office: 3300 Whitehaven Pkwy Washington DC 20235

LEJA, JAN, educator; b. Grodzisko, May 27, 1918; s. Jozef and Aniela (Pawlik) L.; student Royal Sch. Mines, 1945; B.S., U. London, 1945; Dipl. Ing., U. Sch. Mining and Metallurgy, Krakow, Poland, 1947; Ph.D., Cambridge U., Eng., 1954; Dr. h.c., U.M. Curie-Sklodowska, Lublin, Poland, 1976; m. Annabel Mary Mountford, Apr. 10, 1947; children—Nela, Kate, Mark, Clare Leja Ashdown, Gabrielle, John. Mill supt., reduction officer S.W. Africa Co., London, 1947-49 and Grootfontein (S.W. Africa), 1949-52; postdoctorate fellow colloid sci. Cambridge U., 1954-57; asst. prof., asso. prof., prof. U. Alta., 1957-65; prof. dept. mineral engring. U. B.C., Vancouver, 1965—; cons. Syncrude Can. Ltd., 1959-69. Fellow chem. Inst. Can., Inst. Mining and Metallurgy (London); mem. Am. Chem. Soc., Am. Inst. Mining and Metall. Engrs., Canadian Inst. Mining and Metallurgy, N.A.C.E.

LEJA, STANISLAW, educator; b. Grodzisko, Poland, Jan. 3, 1912; s. Jozef and Aniela (Pawlik) L.; M.A., Jan. Kazimierz U., Lwow, Poland, 1938; Ph.D., Cornell U., 1957; m. Weronika Pietrzak, Aug. 15, 1964; children—Janusz T., Stanislaw, Elizabeth P., Teresa P., Pawel P. Came to U.S., 1951, naturalized, 1956. Asst. math. Jan. Kazimierz U., Lwow, 1937-39, Polytechnika, Lwow, 1939-40; tchr. schs. in Palestine and Eng., 1945-51; prof. Western Mich. U., Kalamazoo, 1957—. Served with Polish Army, 1942-45. Mem. Am. Math. Soc., Math. Assn., Sigma Xi. Home: 931 Oakland Dr Kalamazoo MI 49008

LE JEUNE, FRANCIS ERNEST, JR., otolaryngologist; b. New Orleans, Jan. 3, 1929; s. Francis Ernest and Anna Lynne (Dodds) LeJ.; B.S., Tulane U., 1950, M.D., 1953; m. Ena Kay Hudson, Dec. 21, 1963; children—Francis III, Baltzer, Katherine, Ann. Intern, Charity Hosp., La., New Orleans, 1953-54; resident U. Iowa Hosps., Iowa City, 1954-57; mem. staff dept. otolaryngology Ochsner Clinic, New Orleans, 1959—, chmn. dept., 1965—; clin. prof. dept. otolaryngology Tulane U. Sch. Medicine, New Orleans, 1977—. Served with USAF, 1957-59. Mem. A.C.S., Am. Laryngol., Rhinol. and Otol. Soc., Am. Broncho-Esophagological Soc. Clubs: So. Yacht, Boston, Pendennis (New Orleans). Home: 334 Garden Rd New Orleans LA 70123 Office: 1514 Jefferson Hwy Jefferson LA 70121

LEJEUNE, MICHAEL LEONARD, banking ofcl.; b. Manchester, Eng., Mar. 22, 1918; s. Francis Arnold and Gladys (Brown) L.; came to U.S., 1924, naturalized 1953; B.A., Yale, 1940, postgrad. Grad. Sch., 1941; m. Margaret Werden Wilson, Feb. 15, 1947; children—Gordon Peter, Simon Michael Werden, Sarah Diana. Tchr., St. Paul's Sch., Concord, N.H., 1941; with IBRD, 1946—, asst. dir. ops. Europe, Africa, Australasia, 1957-63, asst. dir. ops. Far East, 1963-64, dir. adminstrn., 1964-67, dir. Middle East and N. Africa, 1967-68, Europe, Middle East, N. Africa, 1968-69, Eastern Africa, 1970-74; exec. sec. Consultative Group on Internat. Agrl. Research, 1974—. Mem. bd. govs. Beauvoir Sch., Wash., 1959-66, chmn., 1963-65; trustee Potomac Sch., McLean, Va., 1962-68. Served to capt. Kings Royal Rifle Corps, Brit. Army, 1942-46. Club: Metropolitan (Washington). Home: 626 Chain Bridge Rd McLean VA 22101 Office: 1818 H Street NW Washington DC 20433

LEJINS, PETER PIERRE, criminologist, sociologist, educator; b. Moscow, Russia, Jan. 20, 1909; s. Peter P. and Olga (Makarova) L.; M.Philosophy, U. Latvia, 1930, LL.M., 1933; postgrad. U. Paris, 1934; Ph.D. (Rockefeller fellow), U. Chgo., 1938; m. Nora Muller, June 6, 1937. Came to U.S., 1940, naturalized, 1944. Chair criminal law U. Latvia, 1938-40; prof. sociology U. Md., College Park, 1941—, acting dept. chmn., 1944-46, 61, dir. Inst. Criminal Justice and Criminology, 1969—; chmn. bd. dirs. Nat. Criminal Justice Ednl. Devel. Consortium, 1975-76; cons. area human resources USAF, 1951—; lectr. delinquency and crime Frederick A. Moran Meml. Inst., summers 1956, 57, 63. Mem. exec. com. Correctional Service Assos., 1947-50, Com. for Am. Participation in 2d Internat. Congress Criminology, Paris, 1950; mem. U.S. delegation 12th Internat. Penal and Penitentiary Congress, The Hague, 1950, 1st UN Congress for Prevention Crime and Treatment Delinquents, Geneva, 1955, 2d Congress, London, Eng., 1960; mem. U.S. delegation 3d UN Congress for Prevention Crime and Treatment of Offenders, Stockholm, 1965, 4th Congress, Kyoto, 1970, 5th Congress, Geneva, 1975; U.S. corr. to UN in social def. matters, 1965-76; vice chmn. bd. Joint Commn. on Manpower and Tng. in Corrections, 1964-70; U.S. rep. Internat. Penal and Penitentiary Found., 1974—; mem. Task Force Commd. to Study Correctional System; mem. Joint Commn. on Mental Illness and Health, 1956-57; chmn. cons. com. Uniform Crime Reporting, FBI, 1957-58; mem. bd. Criminal Justice Assn., Washington; pres. bd. Md. Prisoners Aid Assn., 1957-60; chmn. Joint Baltic Am. Com., 1961-62, 66; exec. com. corrections sect. United Community Services, Washington; mem. Md. Gov.'s Commn. Prevention and Treatment Juvenile Offenders; mem. exec. bd. profl. council, council research, trustee Nat. Council Crime and Delinquency, 1968-71, also mem. Md. Council; chmn. adv. bd. Md. Children's Center, 1959-65, chmn. research com., adv. council Inst. Criminological Research, Dept. Corrections, D.C.; chmn. adv. bd., mem. governing bd. Patuxent Inst. Defective Delinquents; chmn. subcom. on instns. task force on correction Gov.'s Crime Commn., 1968-70; mem. research and devel. task force Nat. Adv. Commn. Criminal Justice Standards and Goals, Law Enforcement Assistance Adminstrn., 1972-74, Phase II, 1974-76, chmn., 1974-76; vis. prof. Kuwait U., 1973; pres. Am. Assn. Doctoral Programs in Criminal Justice and Criminology, 1976—. Chmn. Social Survey Com., 1946-47, Community Chest Planning Council, 1949-57 (both Prince Georges County, Md.); dir. Health and Welfare Council Nat. Capitol area, 1st v.p. Prince Georges County Regional Com.; bd. dirs. Washington Action for Youth, United Planning Orgn., Am. Found., 1977—; chmn. D.C. Commrs. Com. on Youth Opportunity; pres. bd. dirs. Oscar Freire Inst., Sao Paolo, Brazil, 1974-77. Fellow Washington Acad. Sci., Internat. Centre Comparative Criminology; mem. Am. Correctional Assn. (dir., mem. exec. com., chmn. com. on research and planning, pres. 1962-63, chmn. research council), Am. (past pres. D.C.), Eastern, So. sociol. socs., Soc. Advancement Criminology, Nat. Probation Assn., Internat. Soc. Criminology (pres. sci. commn. 1973—), AAUP, Latvian Frat. Assn. (past pres.), Am. Latvian Assn. (pres. 1951-70, now hon. pres.), Free World Latvian Fedn (pres. 1956-70), Phi Kappa Phi, Omicron Delta Kappa, Alpha Kappa Delta. Rotarian. Clubs: Cosmos (Washington); Faculty (U. Md.) (College Park); Lettonia (past pres.). Chief editor Jour. Research in Crime and Delinquency, 1968-69. Contbr. articles to profl. jours. and encys. Home: 7114 Eversfield Dr College Heights Estates MD 20782

LEKACHMAN, ROBERT, educator, economist; b. N.Y.C., May 12, 1920; s. Samuel and Jennie (Kominsky) L.; A.B., Columbia, 1942, Ph.D., 1949; m. Eva Leona Woodbrey, June 11, 1948. Mem. faculty Barnard Coll., 1947-65; prof. econs., chmn. dept. State U. N.Y. at Stony Brook, 1965-68; distinguished prof. econs. Lehman Coll., City U. N.Y., 1973—; cons. Fund for Republic, Rockefeller Found., 20th Century Found. Adviser to Com. on Econ. Devel. Bd. dirs. Suffolk County chpt. ACLU, 1966—, mem. nat. ch.-state and acad. freedom coms., 1963-65, mem. equality com., 1972—. Founding mem. Riverside (N.Y.) Democrats, 1956. Served with AUS, 1942-45. Rockefeller fellow, 1962; recipient Blue Bear award Barnard student body, 1965. Liberal Arts fellow Harvard Law Sch., 1968-69; Guggenheim fellow, 1972-73. Mem. Am. Econ. Assn., AAUP, N.A.A.C.P., League Indsl. Democracy, Phi Beta Kappa. Club: Century Assn. Author: A History of Economic Ideas, 1959; The Age of Keynes, 1966; National Income and the Public Welfare, 1972; Inflation—The Permanent Problem of Boom and Bust, 1973; Economists at Bay, 1976. Columnist for Dissent; mem. editorial bd. Challenge, New Leader, Civil Liberties Rev., Christianity and Crisis. Home: 600 W 115th St New York City NY 10025

LEKAKIS, MICHAEL NICHOLAS, sculptor; b. N.Y.C., Mar. 1, 1907; s. Nicholas and Sophia (Ritsos) L. Exhibited one-man shows Whitney Mus. Am. Art, 1973, Dayton (Ohio) Art Mus., 1968; represented in permanent collections: Mus. Modern Art, Whitney Mus., Guggenheim Mus., Phila. Mus. Fine Art, Vassar Coll. Mus., Portland (Oreg.) Mus., Dayton (Ohio) Mus., Hartford (Conn.) Mus., Mus. Israel, Pinakothiki Mus., Athens, Greece, U. Nebr. Art Mus., Lincoln, Weatherspoon Art Gallery, U. N.C. at Greensboro, also numerous pvt. collections. Served with USAAF, 1942-45. Home: 345 W 29th St New York NY 10001 Office: 57 W 28th St New York NY 10001

LE KASHMAN, RAYMOND, mgmt. cons. co. exec.; b. N.Y.C., July 22, 1919; s. Nat and Gertrude Le K.; B.A. cum laude, Lafayette Coll., 1939; m. Beatrice Burke, July 1, 1949; children—John, Carol, Robin. With R.H. Macy & Co., Inc., N.Y.C., 1939-52; mgr. mktg. R. M. Hollingshead, Inc., Camden, N.J., 1952-55; partner, v.p. Booz, Allen & Hamilton, N.Y.C. and Zurich, 1955-66; pres. Knight & Gladieux, Co., N.Y.C., 1967-68; v.p. ITT, N.Y.C., 1969-70; pres. Calculon Corp. (formerly Auerbach Assos. Inc.), Phila., 1970—. Served with USAAF, 1942-45. Decorated air medal with 6 oak leaf clusters. Mem. Inst. Nav. Club: Sky (N.Y.C.). Home: 1 Little Fox Ln Westport CT 06880 Office: 121 N Broad St Philadelphia PA 19107

LELAND, AUSTIN PORTER, publisher; b. St. Louis, Jan. 31, 1907; s. Frederick Austin and Henrietta (Brolaski) L.; A.B., Princeton, 1928; m. Dorothy Lund, Apr. 24, 1935; children—Mary Talbot (Mrs. John Peters MacCarthy), Irene Austin (Mrs. Joseph H. Barzantny). With investment firm, 1928-31; sec.-treas. Sta. List Pub. Co., St. Louis, 1931-39, pres., 1939—; foreman Fed. Grand Jury for Eastern dist. Mo., 1952-53. Alumni trustee Princeton, 1950-54, hon. mem. alumni council, 1950—, pres. class 1928, 1963-68, mem. exec. com., 1968—; chmn. bd. Mary Inst. (country day sch. for girls), 1947-49; v.p. bd. trustees St. Louis Country Day Sch., 1960-62; trustee Nat. Trust Historic Preservation, also chmn. pub. affairs com., trustee nominating com.; trustee Jefferson Nat. Expansion Meml. Assn. Recipient Distinguished Service award for preservation Landmarks Assn. St. Louis, 1974. Mem. AIA (hon. asso. St. Louis chpt.), Def. Orientation Conf. Assn. (dir.), Landmarks Assn. St. Louis (chmn. Old Post Office landmark com.). Clubs: Traffic (N.Y.C.); Traffic, Princeton (past pres., chmn. Princeton schs. and scholarship com.), Noonday, Press, St. Louis Country, University (St. Louis); University Cottage (Princeton, N.J.); Princeton (N.Y.C.); Belvedere (trustee) (Charlevoix, Mich.); Nassau (Princeton). Died Jan. 24, 1975. Home: 35 Pointer Ln Ladue MO 63124

LELAND, DAVID DALE, bldg. products mfg. and distbn. co. exec.; b. Austin, Minn., July 26, 1935; s. P.C. and Leona May L.; B.S. in Forestry, U. Wash., Seattle, 1958; Program for Mgmt. Devel., Harvard U., 1969; m. Maralee Brown, June 9, 1961; children—David Mark, Todd Dale, Reid Hall. With Simpson Timber Co., 1959-76, v.p., mgr. Calif. ops., 1972-76; exec. v.p. bldg. products group S.W. Forest Industries Inc., Phoenix, 1976—. Served with USMCR, 1959. Home: 5119 E Arcadia Ln Phoenix AZ 85018 Office: 3443 N Central Ave Phoenix AZ 85011

LELAND, GEORGE THOMAS (MICKEY), congressman; b. Lubbock, Tex., Nov. 27, 1944; s. George Thomas and Alice Rains (Lewis) L.; B.S. in Pharmacy, Tex. So. U., 1970. Instr. clin. pharmacy Tex. So. U., 1970-71; mem. Tex. Ho. of Reps., 1973-78, vice chmn. public welfare subcom., 1975-76, mem. appropriations com., legis. budget bd., 1977-78; mem. 96th Congress from 18th Tex. Dist., freshman whip; co-chmn. Nat. Black-Hispanic Democratic Coalition, 1978—. Mem. Democratic Nat. Com., 1976—; mem. Tex. Democratic Black Caucus. Home: Houston TX Office: 1207 Longworth House Office Bldg Washington DC 20515

LELAND, LAWRENCE, ins. co. exec.; b. B.C., Can., Nov. 13, 1915; A.B., Earlham Coll. Asst. supt. agys. Am. United Life Ins. Co., 1948-58, agy. v.p., 1958-67, dir., 1962-67; sr. v.p., mem. operating com. Nat. Life Ins. Co., Montpelier, Vt., 1967-72, exec. v.p., 1972—, also dir.; dir. Nat. Life Investment Mgmt. Co., Inc.; pres., dir. Equity Service, Inc.; pres., dir. Adminstrv. Services, Inc. Trustee, Earlham Coll., 1958-67. C.L.U. Mem. Gen. Agts. and Mgrs. Assn., Central Vt., Lafayette (Ind.) (past pres.) life underwriters assns., Ind. Leaders Club. Clubs: Masons, Meridian Hills Country. Home: 12 Westwood Dr Montpelier VT 05602 Office: Nat Life Ins Co Nat Life Dr Montpelier VT 05602

LELAND, SARA (SALLY HARRINGTON), ballet dancer; b. Melrose, Mass., Aug. 2, 1941; studied with E. Virginia Williams, Robert Joffrey, also Sch. Am. Ballet. Debut with New Eng. Civic Ballet; appeared N.Y. City Opera, 1959; mem. Joffrey Ballet, 1959-60; mem. N.Y. City Ballet, 1960—, soloist, 1963-72, prin. dancer, 1972—; guest performances Boston Ballet, Boston Opera Co., Andre Eglevsky Co.; assisted Jerome Robbins in staging Dances at a Gathering, London; staged George Balanchine's Stars and Stripes for Boston Ballet and his Allegro Brillante for Dance Theater Harlem.*

LELAND, TIMOTHY, editor; b. Boston, Sept. 24, 1937; s. Oliver Stevens and Frances Chamberlain (Ayres) L.; A.B. cum laude, Harvard, 1960; M.S. with honors, Columbia Sch. Journalism, 1961; m. Natasha Bourso, Sept. 26, 1964; children—Christian Bourso, London Chamberlain. Med. editor Boston Herald, 1963-64; sci. editor Boston Globe, 1965-66, State House bur. chief, 1966-67, asst. city editor, 1968-69, investigative reporter, 1970-71, asst. mng. editor, 1972, mng. editor (Sunday), 1976—. Recipient Am. Polit. Sci. award, 1968; Pulitzer prize for investigative reporting, 1972, Sigma Delta Chi award for civic service (reporting), 1972, award for pub. service A.P. Mng. Editors, 1974; Sevellon Brown award, 1974. U.S.-South African Leader Exchange Program traveling grantee, 1969; Internat. fellow, Columbia, 1961. Mem. Noble and Greenough Grads. Assn. (exec. com. 1972-74), Am. Assn. Sunday and Feature Editors (pres. 1979-80). Club: Harvard (Boston). Home: 220 Dorset St Waban MA 02168 Office: Boston Globe 135 Morrissey Blvd Boston MA 02107

LELCHUK, ALAN, author, educator; b. Bklyn., Sept. 15, 1938; s. Harry and Belle (Simon) L.; B.A., Bklyn. Coll., 1960; M.A., Stanford, 1963, Ph.D., 1965; student U. London, 1963-64. Writer-in-residence, Brandeis U., 1966—; guest Mishkenot Sha'Ananim, Jerusalem, 1976-77. Yaddo and MacDowell Colony fellow, 1968-69. Guggenheim fellow, 1976-77. Mem. Authors Guild, P.E.N. Author: American Mischief, 1973; Miriam at Thirty-four, 1974; Shrinking, 1978. Asso. editor: Modern Occasions, 1970-72. Contbr. fiction, criticism to lit. mags. Home: RFD 2 Canaan NH 03741 Office: Dept English Brandeis U Waltham MA 02154

LELE, JAYANT KHANDERAO, educator; b. Sinnar, India, May 25, 1935; s. Khanderao Balwant and Laxmibai (Phanse) L.; B.A. with honours, U. Poona (India), 1956, M.A. in Sociology, 1958; Ph.D. in Sociology, Cornell U., 1964; m. Dorothy J. Lele, 1973; children—Ilson, Abhijeet J., Amod J. Came to Can., 1965. Instr. Cornell U., 1964-65; mem. faculty dept. polit. sci. Queen's U., Kingston, Ont., Can., 1965—, asso. prof., 1968-69, prof., 1969—, head dept. sociology, 1969—. Mem. Canadian Com. Internat. Scholarly Relations, 1967—. Jr. fellow Am. Inst. Indian Studies; mem. Indian Inst. Pub. Adminstrn. (life), Am. Sociol. Assn., Canadian Sociology-Anthropology Assn., Canadian Assn. S. Asian Studies (pres.). Author: Local Government in India, 1965. Home: 283 Victoria St Kingston ON Canada

LELE, PADMAKAR PRATAP, physician, educator; b. Chanda, India, Nov. 9, 1927; s. Pratap Vasudev and Indira (Prabhudesai) L.; came to U.S., 1958; M.D., Seth G.S. Med. Coll., 1950; D.Phil., Oxford (Eng.) U., 1955; m. Carla Maria Tophoff, Jan. 23, 1959; children—Martin, Malcolm. Intern K.E.M. Hosp., Bombay, India, 1950-51, resident, 1951-52; lectr. Oxford U., 1952-57; vis. scientist NIH, Bethesda, Md., 1958-59; tech. dir. med. acoustics research group and asst. neurophysiologist Mass. Gen. Hosp., Boston, 1959-69; asso. prof. medicine Mass. Inst. Tech., Cambridge, 1969-71, prof., 1972—; cons. in field. Fellow Acoustical Soc. Am.; mem. IEEE, Am. Physiol Soc., Physiol. Soc. Great Britain, Am. Inst. Ultrasound in Medicine (governing bd. 1973-76). Club: Winchester Boat. Asso. editor Ultrasound in Medicine and Biology, 1973—. Contbr. articles to med. jours. Home: 21 Squire Rd Winchester MA 01890 Office: Room 26-023 Mass Inst Tech Cambridge MA 02139

LELYVELD, ARTHUR JOSEPH, rabbi; b. N.Y.C., Feb. 6, 1913; s. Edward Joseph and Dora (Cohen) L.; A.B., Columbia, 1933; M. Hebrew Letters, Hebrew Union Coll., Cin., 1939, Edward L. Heinsheimer fellow, 1939-41; D.D. honoris causa, Hebrew Union Coll.-Jewish Inst. Religion, 1955; m. Toby Bookholtz, Dec. 26, 1933 (div.); children—Joseph Salem, David Simon, Michael Stephen; m. 2d, Teela Stovsky, Dec. 5, 1964; children—Benjamin, Robin Beth. Rabbi, Congregation B'nai Israel, Hamilton, Ohio, 1939-41, Temple Israel, Omaha, 1941-44; pres. Jewish Peace Fellowship, 1941-43; exec. dir. Com. Unity for Palestine, 1944-46, nat. vice chmn., 1944-48; asso. nat. dir. B'nai B'rith Hillel Founds., N.Y.C., 1946-47, nat. dir., 1948-56; exec. v.p. Am.-Israel Cultural Found., 1956-58; rabbi Fairmount Temple, Cleve., 1958—. Sec. Joint Rabbinical Com. Conscientious Objectors, 1941-46; Am. vice chmn. World U. Service, 1955-65; nat. pres. Am. Jewish Congress, 1966-72, hon. pres., 1972—; mem. publs. com. Jewish Publ. Soc.; Goldenson lectr. Hebrew Union Coll.-Jewish Inst. Religion, 1973. Am. Chmn. Omaha Fair Employment Practice Council, 1942-44; pub. panel chmn. WLB 1944; exec. com. Nat. Hillel Commn.; gen. chmn. Cleve. Jewish Welfare Fund, 1963; trustee Martin Luther King Center for Social Change. Mem. N.A.A.C.P. (hon. exec. com. Cleve. br.), Central Conf. Am. Rabbis (exec. bd., nat. v.p. 1973-75, pres. 1975—), Synagogue Council Am. (nat. v.p. 1975-79, nat. pres. 1979—), Am. Jewish League Israel (nat. v.p.), Nacoms, Phi Beta Kappa, Beta Sigma Rho. Mem. B'nai B'rith. Author: Atheism is Dead, 1968 (paperback edit. 1970); contbg. author: Religion in the State University, Jewish Heritage Reader; Censorship: For or Against; Punishment: For or Against; Population Control: For or Against. Contbr. Universal Jewish Ency., periodicals. Home: 13800 Shaker Blvd Cleveland OH 44120 Office: 23737 Fairmount Blvd Cleveland OH 44122

LEMAISTRE, CHARLES AUBREY, univ. chancellor, physician; b. Lockhart, Ala., Feb. 10, 1924; s. John Wesley and Edith (McLeod) LeM.; B.A., U. Ala., 1944; M.D., Cornell U., 1947; m. Joyce Trapp, June 3, 1952; children—Charles F., William Sidney, Joyce Anne, Helen Jean. Intern, then resident medicine N.Y. Hosp., 1947-49; research fellow infectious diseases Cornell U. Med. Coll., 1949-51, mem. faculty, 1951-54, asst. prof. medicine, 1953-54; mem. faculty Emory U. Sch. Medicine, 1954-59, prof. preventive medicine, chmn. dept., 1957-59; prof. medicine U. Tex. Southwestern Med. Sch., 1959-66, asso. dean, 1965-66; vice chancellor health affairs U. Tex. System, Austin, 1966-68, exec. vice chancellor, 1968-69, dep. chancellor, 1969-70, chancellor, 1971—, pres. Cancer Center; cons. epidemiology Communicable Disease Center, USPHS, 1953—; cons. medicine VA, 1954-59, area med. cons. Atlanta area, 1958-59; vis. staff physician Grady Meml. Hosp., Atlanta, 1954-59, Emory U. Hosp., 1954-59, Parkland Meml. Hosp., Dallas, 1959-66; med. dir. Woodlawn Hosp., Dallas, 1959-65. Mem. Surgeon Gen. Adv. Com. Smoking and Health, 1963-64; mem. AMA-Edn. Research Found. com. research tobacco and health, 1964-66; chmn. Gov. Tex. Com. Tb Eradication, 1963-64; cons. internal medicine Baylor U. Med. Center, Dallas, 1962—, St. Paul Hosp., Dallas, 1966—; cons. div. hosp. and med. facilities USPHS, 1966—; mem. N.Y.C. Task Force on Tb, 1967; cons. Bur. Health and Manpower, HEW, 1967—, mem. grad. med. edn. nat. adv. com. Health Resources Adminstrn., 1977—; mem. tobacco and cancer com. Am. Cancer Soc., Inc., 1977; mem. Tex. Legislature Dept. Health, Edn. and Welfare, 1967—; mem. Tex. Legislature Com. on Organ Transplantation, 1968—, Commn. Non-Traditional Study, 1971-73; mem. President's Commn. White House Fellows, 1971; chmn. subcom. on diversity and pluralism Nat. Council on Ednl. Research, 1973-75; bd. dirs. Assn. Tex. Colls. and Univs., 1974-75; mem. devel. council United Negro Coll. Fund, 1974—; mem. nat. adv. council Inst. for Services to Edn., 1974—; mem. exec. com. Assn. Am. Univs., 1974—; mem. Austin Coll. Devel. Commn., 1977—; Project HOPE com. on Health Policy, 1977. Chmn. steering com. Presbyn. Physicians for Fgn. Missions, 1960-62; mem. Ministers Cons. Clinic, Dallas, 1960-62; mem. bd. commrs. Nat. Commn. on Accrediting, 1973-76; mem. adv. council Austin Symphony Orch. 1973—; mem. joint task force on continuing competence in pharmacy Am. Pharm. Assn.-Am. Assn. Colls. in Pharmacy, 1973-74. Bd. dirs. Ga. Tb Assn., 1955-59; bd. dirs. Tex. div. Am. Cancer Soc., 197—, med. and scientific com. 1974-75, chmn. study com. on tobacco and cancer, 1976—, pub. edn. com. 1976—, exec. com. 1977—; bd. dirs. Damon Runyon-Walter Winchell Cancer Fund; trustee Biol. Humanics Found., Dallas, 1973—; chmn. health manpower com. Assn. Am. Univs., 1975—; sec. Council So. Univs., Inc., 1976—, pres., 1977—. Mem. Am. (v.p. 1964-65), So. (pres. 1963-64) thoracic socs., Nat. Tb Assn., Am., Tex., Ga. med. assns., Central Soc. Clin. Research, Dallas County Med. Soc., Dallas Clin. Soc., Alpha Omega Alpha. Presbyterian (deacon). Contbr. med. jours. Contbg. author: A Textbook of Medicine, 10 and 11th edits., 1963; Pharmacology in Medicine, 1958. Translating author: The Tubercle Bacillus, 1955. Editorial bd. Am. Rev. Respiratory Diseases, 1955-58. Home: 1909 Hill Oaks Ct Austin TX 78703 Office: University of Texas System 601 Colorado St Austin TX 78701

LEMAN, PAUL HENRI, former aluminum co. exec.; b. Montreal, Que., Can., Aug. 6, 1915; s. Beaudry J.B. and Caroline (Beique) L.; B.A., St. Mary's Coll., Montreal, 1934; LL.L., U. Montreal, 1937; postgrad. bus. adminstrn. Harvard, 1937-38; m. Jeannine Prud'homme, May 19, 1939; children—Denise, Jacques, Nicole, Marc, Claire. Admitted to Que. bar, 1937; with Alcan Aluminum Ltd., 1969-79, vice-chmn., 1977-79; ret., 1979; dir. Bell Can., Crédit Foncier Franco-Can. Mem. Can. Royal Commn. Banking and Finance, 1962-64. Mem. Conf. Bd. Home: 445 Saint Joseph Blvd W #93 Outremont Montreal PQ H2V 2P8 Canada Office: 1 Place Ville Marie Montreal PQ H3C 3H2 Canada

LEMANN, THOMAS BERTHELOT, lawyer; b. New Orleans, Jan. 3, 1926; s. Monte M. and Nettie E. (Hyman) L.; A.B. summa cum laude, Harvard U., 1949, LL.B., 1952; M.C.L., Tulane U., 1953; m. Barbara M. London, Apr. 14, 1951; children—Nicholas B., Nancy E. Admitted to La. bar, 1953, since practiced in New Orleans; asso. firm Monroe & Lemann, 1953-58, partner, 1958—; dir. B. Lemann & Bro., Mermentau Mineral & Land Co., Lastarmco, Inc., Royal St. Corp., Ingram Corp. Mem. council La. State Law Inst., mem. Community Property Revision adv. com., mem. UCCC adv. com., sec. trust adv. com.; mem. adv. bd. Tulane Law Sch.; chmn. Mayor's Cultural Resources Com., 1970-75; pres. Arts Council Greater New Orleans, 1975—; mem. vis. com. art museums Harvard U. Trustee Metairie Park Country Day Sch., 1956-71, pres., 1967-70; trustee New Orleans Philharmonic Symphony Soc., 1956-78, Flint-Goodridge Hosp., 1960-70; trustee La. Civil Service League, pres., 1974-76. Served with AUS, 1944-46; PTO. Mem. Am., La. (bd. govs. 1977-78), New Orleans bar assns., Assn. Bar City N.Y., Am. Law Inst., Soc. Bartolus, Phi Beta Kappa. Jewish. Clubs: New Orleans Country, Wyvern (New Orleans); Harvard (N.Y.C.). Contbr. articles to profl. publs. Home: 6020 Garfield St New Orleans LA 70118 Office: 1424 Whitney Bank Bldg New Orleans LA 70130

LEMAY, JACQUES, lawyer; b. Quebec City, Que., Can., July 10, 1940; s. Gerard and Jacqueline (Lachance) LeM.; B.A., Que. Sem., 1959; LL.L., Laval U., 1962, postgrad. U. Toronto, 1964; D.E.S., 1965. Called to bar, Que., 1963; practice in Quebec City, 1964—; mem. firm Prevost, Gagne, Flynn, Chouinard & Jacques, 1964-67; partner Flynn, Rivard, Jacques, Cimon, Lessard & LeMay, 1968—; legal adviser Societe des Ajusteurs d'Assurance, 1969. Mem. Societe des Etudes Juridiques (pres. 1969). Club: Cercle Universitaire (Que.). Home: 2760 Silencieuse Ste Foy PQ G1W 2E7 Canada Office: 2 Chauveau Ave Quebec PQ Canada

LEMAY, WILLIAM EDWARD, medical products co. exec.; b. Lancaster, Ky., June 5, 1924; s. Milton Randel and Ina (Hurt) LeM.; B.S., Otterbein Coll., 1948, Ph.D., 1974; M.S., U. Colo., 1949; m. Helen Rose Hilt, June 30, 1945; children—Helen Bernice, Connie Ann. Chemist, Protective Treatment, Inc., Dayton, Ohio, 1949-52; pres. Ohio Sealer & Chem. Corp., Dayton, 1952-67; pres. Dayton Flexible Products Co. div. Baxter Labs. Inc., 1967—; dir. Three Centuries, Inc. Trustee Otterbein Coll.; bd. dirs. City Mission, Dayton. Served with USAAF, 1942-46. Decorated Air medal. Mem. Am. Chem. Soc., Soc. Plastic Engrs., Engrs. Club Dayton. Patentee plastic gloves, process equipment. Home: 4849 Wilkerson Ln Waynesville OH 45068 Office: 2210 Arbor Blvd Dayton OH 45439

LEMBERGER, AUGUST PAUL, educator; b. Milw., Jan. 25, 1926; s. Max N. and Celia (Gehl) L.; B.S., U. Wis., 1948, Ph.D., 1952; m. Charlyne A. Young, June 30, 1947; children—Michael, Mary, Thomas, Terrence, Ann, Kathryn, Peter. Sr. chemist Merck & Co., Inc., Rahway, N.J., 1952-53; asst. prof. U. Wis. Sch. Pharmacy, 1953-57, asso. prof., 1957-63, prof. pharmacy, 1963-69; prof. pharmacy, dean U. Ill. Coll. Pharmacy, Chgo., 1969—. Sec., Wis. Pharmacy Internship Bd., 1965-69; conf. dir. Nat. Indsl. Pharm. Research Conf., 1966-69; mem. Am. Council on Pharm. Edn., 1978—. Served to 1st lt. AUS, 1944-46. Recipient Kiekhofer Meml. Teaching award U. Wis., 1957, citation of merit, 1977; Distinguished Pharmacist award Wis. Pharm. Assn., 1969. Fellow AAAS, Am. Found. for Pharm. Edn., Acad. Pharm. Scis.; mem. Am., Ill. pharm assns., AAAS, Am. Assn. Colls. of Pharmacy (past com. chmn., exec. com. 1971-74, chmn. council of deans 1975-77, chmn. sect. tchrs. of pharmacy Conf. Tchrs.), Acad. Pharm. Scis. (v.p. 1976-77), Am. Pharm. Assn. (judicial bd. 1976-79), Sigma Xi, Rho Chi (v.p. 1979—), Phi Eta Sigma. Home: 334 Shady Dr Palatine IL 60067 Office: 833 S Wood St Chicago IL 60612

LEMBERGER, LOUIS, pharmacologist, physician; b. Monticello, N.Y., May 8, 1937; s. Max and Ida (Seigel) L.; B.S. magna cum laude, Bklyn. Coll. Pharmacy, L.I. U., 1960; Ph.D. in Pharmacology, Albert Einstein Coll. Medicine, 1964, M.D., 1968; m. Myrna Sue Diamond, 1959; children—Harriet Felice, Margo Beth. Pharmacy intern VA Regional Office, Newark, summer 1960; postdoctoral fellow Albert Einstein Coll. Medicine, 1964-68; intern in medicine Met. Hosp. Center, N.Y. Med. Coll., N.Y.C., 1968-69; research asso. NIH, Bethesda, Md., 1969-71; practice medicine specializing in clin. pharmacology, Bethesda, 1969-71, Indpls., 1971—; clin. pharmacologist Lilly Lab. for Clin. Research, Eli Lilly & Co., Indpls., 1971-75, chief clin. pharmacology, 1975-78, dir. clin. pharmacology, 1978—; asst. prof. pharmacology Ind. U., 1972-73, asst. prof. medicine, 1972-73, asso. prof. pharmacology, 1973-77, asso. prof. medicine, 1973-77, prof. pharmacology, 1977—, prof. medicine, prof. psychiatry, 1977—, mem. grad. faculty, 1975—; adj. prof. clin. pharmacology, Ohio State U., 1975—; physician Wishard Meml. Hosp., 1976—; cons. U.S. Nat. Commn. on Marijuana and Drug Abuse, 1971-73, Can. Commn. Inquiry into Non-Med. Use Drugs, 1971-73; guest lectr. various univs., 1968—. Post adviser Crossroads of Am. council Boy Scouts Am., 1972-77. Served with USPHS, 1969-71. Fellow A.C.P., N.Y. Acad. Scis., Am. Coll. Neuropsychopharmacology; mem. Am. Soc. Pharmacology and Exptl. Therapeutics (com. div. clin. pharmacology 1972-78, chmn. com. 1978—), AAAS, Am. Soc. Clin. Pharmacology and Therapeutics (chmn. sect. neuropsychopharmacology 1973—, chmn. fin. com. 1976—, dir. 1975—), Am. Soc. Clin. Investigation, Collegium Internat. Neuro-Psychopharmacologicum, Am. Fedn. Clin. Research, Central Soc. Clin. Research, Soc. Neuroscis., Sigma Xi, Alpha Omega Alpha, Rho Chi. Jewish. Author: (with A. Rubin) Physiologic Disposition of Drugs of Abuse, 1976; contbr. numerous articles on biochemistry and pharmacology to sci. jours.; editorial bd. Excerpta Medica, 1972—, Clin. Pharmacology and Therapeutics, 1976—, Psychopharmacology, 1975—, Pharmacology, Internat. Jour. Exptl. and Clin. Pharmacology, 1978—. Office: Lilly Lab Clin Research Wishard Meml Hosp Indianapolis IN 46202

LEMCKE, NORMAN ROHDE, lawyer; b. N.Y.C., Dec. 3, 1894; s. Albert William and Dora (Rohde) L.; B.S., Amherst Coll., 1917; LL.B., N.Y. Law Sch., 1924, J.D., 1970; m. Elizabeth Bouteiller, Sept. 3, 1918 (dec.); 1 son, Norman Rohde. Admitted to N.J. bar, 1924; asso. firm Smith & Slingerland, Newark, 1924-27; with Prudential Ins. Co. of Am., 1927, br. office atty., Montreal, 1927-28, regional appraiser, supr., Newark, 1928-34, mgr. regional office, Phila., 1934-35, N.Y.C., 1935-37, supr. West Coast, 1937-44, East Coast, 1944, asst. sec., Newark, 1944-46, gen. mgr., 1946-47, v.p., 1962-63; ret., 1963; mem. firm Eisner & Lemcke, Newark, 1964-68; dir. govt. sponsored Housing Enterprises Can., 1945-47. Served as ensign USN, 1917-19. Mem. Am., N.J. State bar assns., Phi Beta Kappa, Alpha Delta Phi, Delta Theta Phi. Methodist. Address: 5 W Main St Brookside NJ 07926

LEMCOE, M. MARSHALL, civil engr.; b. St. Louis, Apr. 3, 1921; s. Louis and Bertha (Hiller) L.; B.S. in Civil Engring., Washington U., St. Louis, 1943, M.S. in Civil Engring., 1949; Ph.D. in Civil Engring., U. Ill., 1957; m. Sept. 6, 1951 (dec.); children—David, Margaret. Mgr. sect. strength analysis S.W. Research Inst., San Antonio, 1951-61; sr. tech. adviser, mgr. exptl. mechanics group Atomics Internat., Canoga Park, Calif., 1961-70; sr. research scientist, tech. adviser Battelle Meml. Inst., Columbus, Ohio, 1970—; lectr. in engring. mechanics Franklin U., Columbus, 1972-75. Served with USAAF, World War II. Recipient War Production award War Production Bd., 1945; Indsl. Research Mag. IR-100 award, 1976. Mem. Soc. Experiment Stress Analysis (chmn. pressure vessel research com. subcom. on plastic fatigue strength), Sigma Xi. Papers reviewer Exptl. Mechs. Jour.; contbr. numerous articles to profl. jours. Home: 2700 Fishinger Rd Upper Arlington OH 43221 Office: 505 King Ave Columbus OH 43201

LEMELIN, ROGER, newspaper publisher; b. Quebec, Que., Can., Apr. 7, 1919; s. Joseph and Florida (Dumontier) L.; hon. degree Laurentian U., Sudbury, Ont., 1976; m. Valeda Lavigueur, Oct. 27, 1945; children—Pierre, Jacques, Diane and Andre (twins), Sylvie. Journalist, Time and Fortune mags., from 1948; creator TV series The Plouffe Family, in Can.; pres. DuBuisson Prodns., from 1960; pres., pub. French daily La Presse, Montreal, 1972—. Guggenheim Found. fellow; Rockefeller Found. fellow. Mem. Royal Soc. Can., Acad. Goncourt, Can. News Hall Fame. Clubs: Mt. Royal, St. Denis (Montreal); Garrison (Quebec). Author: The Town Below, 1944, The Plouffe Family, 1949, Fantaisies sur les peches capitaux, 1949, In Quest of Splendor, 1952; also articles, revs.

LE MELLE, WILBERT JOHN, ambassador; b. New Iberia, La., Nov. 11, 1931; s. Eloi Sabas and Therese (Francis) Le M.; B.A., Notre Dame Sem., New Orleans, 1955, M.A., 1956; Ph.D. in Internat. Studies, U. Denver, 1963; LL.D. (hon.), Cuttington Univ. Coll., Liberia, 1978; m. Yvonne Tauriac, 1958; children—Patrice, Wilbert John, Gerald, Edward. Asst. prof. history and philosophy Grambling (La.) Coll., 1956-61; teaching fellow, then research asst. internat. relations U. Denver, 1961-63; mem. corr. faculty polit. sci. U. Minn., 1962-64; asst. prof. govt. and research assn. Center Devel. Research, African studies program Boston U., 1963-65; with Ford Found., 1965-77, rep. E. Africa, 1970-73, rep. N.Africa, 1973-76, dep. head Middle East and Africa program, 1976-77; Am. ambassador to Kenya and Seychelles, 1977—; cons. in field. Served with U.S. Army, 1957-59. Social Sci. Found. fellow, 1961-63, grantee, 1963. Mem. Am. Polit. Sci. Assn., Council Fgn. Relations. Democrat. Roman Catholic. Author: Bibliographie Selective des Livres, Articles et Documentations Traitant le Suget des Problems Administratives Africains, 1964; co-author: Readings on African Administration, 1964; The Black College: A Strategy for Relevancy, 1969; contbr. to profl. publs. Address: Am Embassy Box 1 APO New York NY 09675

LEMESH, NICHOLAS THOMAS, designer, filmmaker; b. McKees Rocks, Pa., May 21, 1946; s. Nicholas and Sophie (Nowak) L.; B.F.A. with honors, Carnegie-Mellon U., 1968; M.F.A., N.Y. U., 1971. Asst. program dir. Kingsley Assn., Pitts., 1968-70; art dir. William Sloane House YMCA, N.Y.C., 1969-71; graphic designer Kahn Assos., N.Y.C., 1971; adminstrv. asst. Grad. Inst. Film and TV, N.Y. U., 1971-72; film producer Grey Advt., N.Y.C., 1972—. Youth rep. League of Red Cross Socs. to UN; nat. gov. Nat. ARC, 1970-77; U.S. rep. Internat. Red Cross Conf., Geneva, 1969. Recipient Internat. Distinguished Service award for humanitarian service Macalester Coll., 1970. Mem. Nat. Inst. Social Scis., Broadcast Advt. Producers Soc. Am. Democrat. Mem. Byzantine Cath. Ch. Home: 240 E 35th St New York NY 10016 Office: 777 3d Ave New York NY 10017

LE MESSURIER, WILLIAM JAMES, structural engr.; b. Pontiac, Mich., June 12, 1926; s. William James and Bertha Emma (Sherman) LeM.; A.B. cum laude, Harvard Coll., 1947; S.M., M.I.T., 1953; m. Dorothy Wright Judd, June 20, 1953; children—Claire Elizabeth, Irene Louise, Peter Wright. Asst. prof. structural design M.I.T., 1951-56; asso. prof. Harvard U., 1956-61, lectr., 1973—; partner Goldberg, LeMessurier Assos., Structural Engrs., Boston, 1952-61; pres. LeMessurier Assos., Inc., Structural Engrs., Boston, 1961-69, Cambridge, Mass., 1969-73; chmn. Sippican Cons. Internat., Inc., Cambridge, 1973—; mem. adv. bd. Div. Constrn. VA, 1963-68; mem. Nat. Com. Housing Tech., 1969-70; mem. Cambridge Experimentation Rev. Bd., 1977. Recipient Allied Professions medal AIA, 1968; registered profl. engr., Mass., N.Y., Tenn., Colo., D.C. Fellow Am. Concrete Inst.; mem. ASCE, Nat. Acad. Engring. Episcopalian. Club: Met. (N.Y.C.). Structural engr. for: Boston City Hall, 1968; Dallas-Ft. Worth Airport, 1973; Nat. Air and Space Museum, Washington, 1976; Johns-Manville Hdqrs., Denver, 1977; Citicorp Center, N.Y.C., 1977; Fed. Res. Bank, Boston, 1978. Office: 1033 Massachusetts Ave Cambridge MA 02138

LEMIEUX, HENRY FISHER, constrn. co. exec.; b. Greenville, Miss., Aug. 20, 1926; s. Frederic Alexander and Elizabeth (Fisher) LeM.; B.E. in Elec. Engring., Tulane U., 1946, B.S. in Civil Engring., 1949; m. Marjorie Elizabeth Hunter, May 7, 1954; children—Michelle E., Jolie M., Babette A., Henry Fisher. Engr., field supt. Raymond Internat., Inc., 1949-51, dist. mgr., New Orleans, 1951-57, asst. v.p., New Orleans, N.Y.C., London, Eng., 1957-65, dir., N.Y.C., 1965—; v.p., gen. mgr. Raymond Concrete Pile div., 1965-68, pres., 1968-78, chief exec. officer, 1970—, chmn. bd., 1976—; also officer, dir. subs. cos.; dir. Tex. Commerce Bancshares, Inc., Houston, Hughes Tool Co., Houston, Home Oil Co. Ltd., Calgary. Mem. adv. bd. Tulane U. Engring. Sch., Tulane U. Grad. Sch. Bus. Adminstrn., also mem. pres.'s council; mem. adv. bd. U. Houston Bus. Sch.; mem. So. regional adv. bd. Inst. Internat. Edn. Served to lt. (j.g.) USNR, 1944-46. Registered profl. engr., Fla., La., N.Y. Mem. ASCE, ASTM, Moles, Beavers, Newcomen Soc. N.A., Pan Am. Soc. U.S., Tulane U. Alumni Assn. (dir.), Houston C. of C. (dir., exec. com.). Episcopalian. Clubs: Plimsoll, So. Yacht (New Orleans); Ramada, River Oaks Country, Houston, University (Houston); Sky (N.Y.C.); Ocean Reef (Key Largo). Address: PO Box 27456 Houston TX 77027

LEMKE, CARLTON EDWARD, mathematician, educator; b. Buffalo, Oct. 11, 1920; s. Carl and Estelle (Yuhnke) L.; B.A. magna cum laude, U. Buffalo, 1949; M.S., Carnegie Inst. Tech., 1951, Ph.D., 1953; m. Martha C. Harris, Feb. 5, 1948 (dec. Feb. 1976); children—Paul S., Susan M. With Gen. Electric Co., 1954-55, RCA, 1955-56; mem. faculty Rensselaer Poly. Inst., 1956—, prof. math., 1963—, now Ford Found. prof. math.; cons. to industry, 1963-70. Served with AUS, 1940-45. Co-recipient John von Neumann Theory prize Inst. Mgmt. Scis.-Ops. Research Soc. Am., 1978. Mem. Soc. Indsl. and Applied Math., Inst. Mgmt. Scis., Math. Programming Soc., Math. Assn. Am., Ops. Research Soc. Am. Asso. editor Jour. Inst. Mgmt. Scis., 1967—, Jour. Computer and Systems Scis., 1967—, Jour. Math. Programming, Jour. Math. Operations Research. Spl. research math. programming and game theory. Home: 10 Burke Dr Troy NY 12180

LEMLICH, ROBERT, educator; b. Bklyn., Aug. 22, 1926; s. Marcus S. and Mary (Marcus) L.; B.Chem. Engring. summa cum laude, N.Y. U., 1948; M.Chem. Engring., Poly. Inst. Bklyn., 1951; Ph.D., U. Cin., 1954; m. Elizabeth Ann Murphy, Jan. 31, 1976. Research chem. engr. Allied Chem. & Dye Corp., 1948-49; mem. faculty U. Cin., 1952—, prof. chem. engring., 1962—, fellow Grad. Sch., 1971—, chmn. fellows Grad. Sch., 1976-78, Research Corp. grantee, 1954-55, NSF grantee, 1956-59, 73, 77—, NIH grantee, 1959-69, P & G grantee, 1976-77; Fulbright lectr., Israel, 1958-59, Argentina, 1966; researcher, cons. in field. Served with USNR, 1944-46. Registered profl. engr., N.Y., Ohio. Recipient Sigma Xi award distinguished research U. Cin., 1969. Fellow AAAS; mem. Am. Inst. Chem. Engrs. (named Chem. Engr. of Yr. 1979), Am. Chem. Soc., Am. Soc. Engring. Edn., Sigma Xi, Tau Beta Pi, Phi Lambda Upsilon. Editor: Adsorptive Bubble Separation Techniques, 1972; editor, originator Jour. Chem. Engring. Edn., 1962-65. Home: 346 Bonnie Leslie Dr Bellevue KY 41073

LEMMON, ALLAN HAZLETT, ins. co. exec.; b. Kingston, Ont., Can., July 26, 1908; s. Allan and Martha Violet (Hazlett) L.; B.A., Queen's U., Kingston, 1929; m. Eleanor Margaret Scott, June 6, 1935; 1 son, 1 dau. With Can. Life Assurance Co., Toronto, Ont., 1928—, asst. treas., 1940-46, treas., 1946-53, v.p., treas., 1953-63, exec. v.p., treas., 1963, pres., 1964-73, chmn. bd., 1973—, also dir.; v.p., dir. Nat. Trust Co. Ltd. Clubs: Granite, Toronto, York, York Downs Golf and Country; Mt. Royal (Montreal). Home: 19 Country Ln Willowdale

ON M2L 1E1 Canada Office: 330 University Ave Toronto ON M5G 1R8 Canada

LEMMON, JACK, actor; b. Boston, Feb. 8, 1925; s. John Uhler, Jr. and Mildred LaRue (Noel) L.; grad. Phillips Andover Acad., 1943; B.S., B.A., Harvard, 1947; m. Cynthia Boyd Stone, May 7, 1950; 1 son, Christopher; m. 2d, Felicia Farr, Aug. 17, 1962; 1 dau., Courtney. Appeared in summer stock, 1940-48; radio, TV shows, 1948-52, including TV series That Wonderful Guy, 1950, summer replacement on Toni Twin Time, 1950, TV series The Adlibbers, 1951, Couple Next Door, 1951-52, Heaven for Betsy, 1952; pres. Jalem Prodns., N.Y.C., 1952—; appeared on Broadway in Room Service, 1953, Face of A Hero, 1960, Tribute (Broadway Drama Guild award), 1979; other stage appearances Idiot's Delight, 1970, Juno and the Paycock, 1975; appeared in films It Should Happen to You, Three for the Show, Phffft, My Sister Eileen, Mister Roberts (Acad. award best supporting actor), It Happened to Jane, You Can't Run Away From It, Fire Down Below, Cowboy, Operation Madball, Bell Book and Candle, Miss Casy Jones, Some Like It Hot, Apartment, The Wackiest Ship in the Army, Notorious Landlady, Irma La Douce, Under The Yum Yum Tree, Days of Wine and Roses, Good Neighbor Sam, How to Murder Your Wife, The Great Race, The Fortune Cookie, Luv, The Odd Couple, The April Fools, The Out-of-Towners, The War Between Men and Women, 1972, Avanti, 1972, Save the Tiger (Acad. award best actor), 1973, The Front Page, 1974, The Prisoner of 2d Avenue, 1975, Alex & the Gypsy, 1976, Airport, 1977, The Gentleman Tramp, 1977, The China Syndrome, 1978; dir. film Kotch, 1971; appeared on TV in The Entertainer (Emmy award nomination), 1975, 'S Wonderful, 'S Marvelous, 'S Gershwin (Emmy award), 1972. Served as ensign USNR, 1945-46. Clubs: Hasty Pudding (pres. 1945-46), Delphic (v.p. 1945-46), Dramatic (v.p. 1945) (Harvard); Players (N.Y.C.). Address: care Jalem Prodns 141 El Camino Suite 201 Beverly Hills CA 90212

LEMON, FRANK RAYMOND, physician, educator; b. San Bernardino, Calif., Oct. 16, 1917; s. Harry C. and Cora Alice (Taylor) L.; student La Sierra Coll., 1942-45; M.D., Loma Linda U., 1950; M.P.H., Tulane U., 1955; m. E. Marie La Pointe, May 26, 1940; children—Lynda (Mrs. David Snyder), Corali (Mrs. William Charles Stone), Taylor, Lowell. Intern, U.S. Marine Hosp., San Francisco, 1949-50; resident Contra Costa County Hosp., Martinez, Cal., 1950-51, VA Hosp., Long Beach, Calif., 1964-65; practice medicine, Antioch, Calif. and Greybull, Wyo., 1950-53, specializing in internal medicine, Santa Ana and Westminster, Calif., 1966-68; mem. staff Westminster Community Hosp., 1966-68; A.B. Chandler Med. Center, Lexington, Ky., 1968—; mem. faculty Loma Linda U., 1953-68, asst. prof. tropical and preventive medicine, 1953-59, asso. prof., 1959-68; clin. prof. medicine Coll. Medicine U. Ky., Lexington, 1968—, prof. community medicine, 1968—, asso. dean continuing edn. Coll. Medicine, 1968-72, asso. dean. extramural affairs, 1972—; asso. chief staff VA Hosp., Lexington; dist. med. cons., div. vocational rehab. Dept. Edn. Cal., 1962-68; chmn. subcom. vital and health statistics, U.S. Indian and Alaskan natives, U.S. Com. on Vital and Health Statistics, 1964-68. Served as asst. surgeon USPHS, 1949-50. Fellow A.C.P., Am. Coll. Preventive Medicine; Am. Pub. Health Assn.; mem. AMA, Soc. Tchrs. Preventive Medicine, Am. Soc. Internal Medicine, Am. Acad. Family Medicine (hon.), Delta Omega. Mem. Ch. Seventh-day Adventist (lay elder). Contbr. articles to profl. jours. Epidemiologic investigations of cardiovascular and pulmonary diseases in spl. populations. Home: 3200 Cornwall Dr Lexington KY 40503

LEMON, HENRY MARTYN, physician, educator; b. Chgo., Dec. 23, 1915; s. Harvey Brace and Louise (Birkhoff) L.; B.S., U. Chgo., 1938; M.D. cum laude, Harvard U., 1940; m. Harriet Tuxbury Qua, May 3, 1941; children—Elizabeth Anne Lemon Carr, Harvey Brace, Stanley Moncrief, David Tuxbury, Jennifer Jane Lemon Dewitt; m. 2d, Dorothy Campbell, May 28, 1976. Intern, Billings Hosp., Chgo., 1940-41, asst. resident medicine, 1941-42; asst. dept. medicine U. Chgo., 1942-43; chief med. resident Univ. Hosp., Boston, 1946-48; instr. medicine Boston U., 1946-48, asst. prof. medicine, 1948-54, asso. prof., 1954-61; dir. Eugene C. Eppley Cancer Inst., U. Nebr. Coll. Medicine, Omaha, 1961-68, prof. internal Medicine, 1961—; cons. internal medicine VA, Boston, Omaha, 1950—; bd. dirs. Mass., Nebr. divs. Am. Cancer Soc. Served to capt. M.C., U.S. Army, 1943-46; col. USAR ret. Recipient Disting. Ser. award U. Chgo. Med. Alumni, 1952, award of merit (3) AMA Sci. Exhibits, 1957, 1962, 1965, Disting. Teaching award U. Nebr. Med. Center, 1976; diplomate Am. Bd. Internal Medicine, Am. Bd. Med. Oncology. Fellow A.C.P.; mem. AMA, Am. Assn. Cancer Research, Am. Soc. Clin. Oncology, Endocrine Soc., Soc. Surg. Oncology, Central Soc. Clin. Research, Res. Officers Assn. Republican. Unitarian. Club: Rotary. Research in air-borne infection, Cytodiagnosis Pancreatic cancer, transplantation human cancer to hamsters, estrogen imbalance in breast cancer, endocrine and chemotherapy cancer, reduction toxicity in cancer chemotherapy, estriol prevention breast cancer, carcinogenesis breast, leukemia and lymphoma. Home: 10805 Poppleton Ave Omaha NE 68144 Office: Dept Internal Medicine U Nebr Omaha NE 68105

LEMON, JAMES THOMAS, educator; b. West Lorne, Ont., Can., July 2, 1929; s. Victor Earl and Grace Florence (Sharratt) L.; B.A., U. Western Ont., 1955; M.S., U. Wis., 1961, Ph.D., 1964; B.D., Yale, 1958; m. Carolyn J. Miller, Sept. 13, 1958; children—Margaret, Janet, Catherine. Ordained to ministry United Ch. Canada, 1958; minister United Ch. Can., Iron Bridge, Ont., 1958-60; asst. prof. geography U. Calif. at Los Angeles, 1964-67; asst. prof. U. Toronto, 1967-68, asso. prof., 1968-74, prof., 1974—, past dir. community living program Innis Coll., 1975-78. Chmn. Annex Ratepayer's Assn., Toronto, 1970-72, Confedn. Resident and Ratepayer Assns., Toronto, 1973; sch. trustee City of Toronto, 1977-78; dir. Social Planning Council Met. Toronto, 1976—. Can. Council grantee, 1962-63, 68-69, 74; Guggenheim fellow, 1974-75; recipient Beveridge award for best book on Am. history Am. Hist. Assn., 1972. Mem. Social Sci. Hist. Assn., Canadian Assn. Geographers, Assn. Am. Geographers, Canadian Assn. Am. Studies, New Democrat. Author: The Best Poor Man's Country: A Geographical Study of Early Southeastern Pennsylvania, 1972. Home: 78 Walmer Rd Toronto ON Canada

LEMON, MEADOWLARK, profl. basketball player; b. Wilmington, N.C., Apr. 25, 1932; s. Meadow and Maime (Nesbitts) L.; grad. high sch.; m. Willie Maultsby (div.); children—George, Beverly, Donna, Robin, Jonathan. With Harlem Globetrotters, 1954-78; appeared in TV series Hello Larry, 1979. Served with U.S. Army, 1952-54. Address: 30 Rockefeller Plaza New York NY 10020*

LEMON, ROBERT GRANVILLE, former profl. baseball mgr.; b. San Bernardino, Calif., Sept. 22, 1920; s. Earl and Ruth Edith (West) L.; student pub. schs.; m. Jane Howard McGee, Jan. 14, 1944; children—Jeffrey, James, Jerry. Mgr., Chgo. White Sox Profl. Baseball Team, 1977-78, N.Y. Yankees, 1978-79. Served with USNR, 1942-45. Named to Baseball Hall of Fame, 1976; Am. League Mgr. of Yr., 1978. Club: Elks.

LEMOND, ALAN ROY, editor; b. Evansville, Ind., Feb. 27, 1938; s. Jesse R. and Dorothy E. (Taylor) LeM.; B.A. in English, Oakland City (Ind.) U., 1965; m. Mary A. Hirsch, July 19, 1969; children—Lisa Anne, Nicole Christina. Copywriter, Esquire mag., 1965-67; from asso. editor to editor Cavalier mag., 1967-70; pres. New Earth, Inc., editorial cons. and packaging, N.Y.C., 1970—, Sweet Sulphur Springs, Inc., Velpen, Ind., 1978—; exec. editor Celebrity mag., 1975—. Served with AUS, 1961-63. Co-author: Mug Shots, 1972; Ralph Nader: A Man and a Movement, 1972; No Place to Hide, 1975; The Mark Spitz Complete Book of Swimming, 1976; Men's Hair: The Long and Short of It, 1979; author: Bravo Baryshnikov, 1978; co-founder, editor Your Land mag., 1972; editor Nostalgia Illustrated mag., 1974-75. Address: Box 65 Velpen IN 47590

LEMONICK, AARON, physicist, educator; b. Phila., Feb. 2, 1923; s. Samuel and Mary (Ferman) L.; B.A., U. Pa., 1950: M.A., Princeton, 1952, Ph.D., 1954; m. Eleanor Leah Drutt, Feb. 12, 1950; children—Michael Drutt, David Morris. Asst. prof. physics Haverford (Pa.) Coll., 1954-57, asso. prof., 1957-61, chmn. dept. physics, 1957-61; asso. prof. physics Princeton, 1961-64, prof., 1964—, asso. chmn. dept. physics, 1967-69, dean grad. sch., 1969-73, dean faculty, 1973—, asso. dir. Princeton-Pa. Accelerator, 1961-67, v.p. Princeton U. Press, 1973—. Fellow Am. Phys. Soc.; mem. Am. Assn. Physics Tchrs., AAUP, AAAS, Phi Beta Kappa, Sigma Xi. Home: Joseph Henry House Nassau St Princeton NJ 08540

LEMONT, GEORGE WILLIAM, comic artist; b. Santa Barbara, Calif., Mar. 5, 1922; s. George William and Lauretta Anita (Duff) L.; grad. high sch.; m. Tosca Corrine Amati, May 12, 1958. Lighting designer Peerless Electric, San Francisco, 1946-49; radio and TV performer various stas., San Francisco, 1950-61; syndicated comic artist NEA, San Francisco, 1961-72, United Feature Syndicate, San Francisco, 1973—; creative cons. Gross, Pera & Reid, Advt. Served with USAF, 1943-46. Recipient No. Calif. Acad. TV Arts and Scis. Emmy award for best children's TV show, 1951, best male performer, 1954. Mem. Nat. Cartoonists Soc. Democrat. Roman Catholic. Home and Office: 108 Palm Ave San Francisco CA 94118

LEMOS, RAMON MARCELINO, educator; b. Mobile, Ala., July 7, 1927; s. Marcelino and Marie Louise (Moore) L.; B.A., U. Ala., 1951; M.A., Duke, 1953, Ph.D., 1955; Fulbright scholar U. London (Eng.), 1955-56; m. Mamie Lou McCrory, Dec. 26, 1951; children—Noah Marcelino, William Ramon, Christopher Tait, John Paul. Mem. faculty U. Miami, 1956—, prof. philosophy, 1967—, chmn. dept., 1971—. Served with USMC, 1945-49. Named Outstanding Tchr., U. Miami, 1968. Mem. Am. Cath. Philos. Assn. (Fla. pres. 1971, 79), Fla. Philos. Assn. (pres. 1963), Phi Beta Kappa, Phi Kappa Phi. Author: Experience, Mind, and Value, 1969; Rousseau's Political Philosophy, 1977; Hobbes and Locke: Power and Consent, 1978. Home: 6960 SW 82d Ct Miami FL 33143

LEMP, FRANK MARCUS, shoe co. exec.; b. Boston, Sept. 8, 1928; s. Frank R. and Katheryne L.; B.A., Amherst Coll., 1950; m. Judith Hill, June 22, 1951; children—Ann, Mark C., F. Richard and William (twins). With Brown Shoe Co., St. Louis, 1953—, v.p., gen. sales mgr., 1969-73, sr. v.p. women's mktg., 1973-78, exec. v.p., 1978—; dir. Medserco., St. Louis. Bd. dirs. YMCA, St. Louis. Served with U.S. Army, 1950-52. Fulbright scholar. Mem. Am. Footwear Industries Am. (chmn. mktg. com.), 210 Assn. Republican. Clubs: Univ., N.Y. Athletic. Home: 101 S Rock Hill Rd Saint Louis MO 63119 Office: 8399 Maryland Ave Saint Louis MO 63105

LEMPERT, RICHARD OWEN, lawyer, educator; b. Hartford, Conn., June 2, 1942; s. Philip Leonard and Mary (Steinberg) L.; A.B., Oberlin Coll., 1964; J.D., U. Mich., 1968, Ph.D. in Sociology, 1971; m. Cynthia Ruth Willey, Sept. 10, 1967; 1 dau., Leah Rose. Asst. prof. law U. Mich., Ann Arbor, 1968-72, asso. prof., 1972-74, prof., 1974—; mem. adv. panel for law and social sci. div. NSF, 1976-79, mem. exec. com. of adv. com. for social sci., 1979; admitted to Mich. bar, 1978. Mem. State Bar Mich., Am. Sociol. Assn., Law and Soc. Assn. (trustee 1977-80, exec. com. 1979-80), Am. Judicature Soc. (programs com. 1976-79), Soc. Am. Law Tchrs., Phi Kappa Phi, Phi Beta Kappa. Author: (with Stephen Saltzburg) A Modern Approach to Evidence, 1977; editorial bd. Law and Soc. Rev., 1972-77, Evaluation Rev., 1979—; contbr. articles to profl. jours. Home: 325 Orchard Hills Dr Ann Arbor MI 48104 Office: Hutchins Hall Univ Mich Law Sch Ann Arbor MI 48109

LENABURG, ALVIN EDWARD, coop. exchange exec.; b. Bessie, Okla., Jan. 7, 1915; s. Rinehold and Katherine (Miller) L.; student John Brown U., 1938-40; m. Holly Ann Bucy, Oct. 15, 1944; children—Holly K., Brenda L., Melinda S. Leader, Civilian Conservation Corps, 1936-38; farm reporter Agr. Stabilization Conservation Service, 1935; v.p. Union Equity Coop. Exchange, Enid, Okla., 1970—, also v.p. adminstrv. services, treas.; engaged in farming, 1932-36. Served with U.S. Army, 1941-45. Decorated Bronze Star, Combat Inf. badge. Democrat. Club: Rotary. Address: 1902 E Maple St Enid OK 73701

LENAGH, THOMAS HUGH, found. exec.; b. Lawrence, Mass., Nov. 1, 1918; s. Frank Albert and Bethia M. (Coulter) L.; B.A., Williams Coll., 1941; postgrad. Sch. Advanced Studies, Washington, 1946; LL.B., Columbia, 1948; m. Leila Semple Fellner, Sept. 1, 1951; children—Madeleine, Katherine, Thomas C., Jessie. Admitted to Conn. bar, 1948; practice in Westport and Norwalk, 1948-49; investment analyst for investment firms, 1949-60; with Ford Found., 1960—, asst. treas., 1962-64, treas., 1964-76, fin. advisor, 1977-78; fin. v.p. Aspen Inst., N.Y.C., 1978—; adv. dir. New Perspective Fund; dir. U.S. Life Corp., Adams Express Co.; dir. North Penn R.R. Co., CML Group, Inc., MLAM Funds, SCI Systems, Inc.; adv. dir. Brazilian Investments, S.A.; trustee Central Savs. Bank. Trustee, chmn. bd. YWCA, N.Y., 1974—. Served USNR, 1941-46, 51-54; ret. capt. Res. Mem. N.Y. Soc. (pres. 1964-65), Inst. Chartered Financial Analysts (CFA), Financial Analysts Fedn. (pres. 1966-67), Phillips Andover Acad. Alumni Assn. (council 1965-68), Zeta Psi. Club: Downtown Athletic (N.Y.C.). Office: Aspen Inst 717 Fifth Ave New York City NY 10022

LENAHAN, EDWARD PATRICK, publishing co. exec.; b. Evanston, Ill., June 25, 1925; s. Edward Patrick and Emma Catherine (O'Shea) L.; A.B., Harvard, 1950; LL.D., Seattle U., 1975; m. Lois Elaine Alm, Sept. 6, 1952; children—Kathryn Crowley, Elizabeth O'Shea, Timothy Egan, Nancy Carpenter. Trainee, Asso. Mdsg. Corp., N.Y.C., 1950-51; mortgage banker J. Halperin & Co., N.Y.C., 1951-55; with Fortune mag., N.Y.C., 1955-70, 73—, advt. dir., 1969-70, publisher, 1973—; gen. mgr. Life mag., 1971-73; v.p. Time Inc., N.Y.C., 1973—, treas., 1975-78; pub. Fortune, 1979—. Served with USNR, 1943-46. Clubs: Harvard (N.Y.C.); Creek. Home: 10 The Knolls Locust Valley NY 11560 Office: Time and Life Bldg Rockefeller Center New York NY 10020

LENARD, ANDREW, educator; b. Balmazujvaros, Hungary, July, 18, 1927; s. Lawrence and Priscilla (Baron) L.; came to U.S., 1947, naturalized, 1952; B.A., U. Ia., 1949; Ph.D., 1953; m. Eva Veronica Kelemen, June 11, 1953; children—George Lawrence, Dorothy Claire. Research asso. Columbia, 1955-57; research staff mem. Plasma Physics Lab., Princeton, 1957-66; mem. Inst. for Advanced Study, 1965-66, 72-73; prof. math. physics Ind. U., 1966—; vis. mem. I.H.E.S., France, 1979-80. Served with AUS, 1953-55. Mem. Am. Phys. Soc., Am. Math. Soc. Contbr. articles to physics and math. jours. Home: 1205 Collinswood Dr Bloomington IN 47401

LENARDON, ROBERT JOSEPH, educator; b. Fort William, Ont., Can., Sept. 8, 1928; s. Louis and Nina (Boffa) L.; B.A. with 1st class honors in Latin, U. B.C. (Can.), 1949; M.A. in Classics, U. Cin., 1950, Ph.D., 1954. Came to U.S., 1949. Instr. Greek and Latin, Columbia, 1954-57; asst. prof. classics U. Wash., Seattle, 1957-59; mem. faculty dept. classics Ohio State U., Columbus, 1959—, asso. prof., 1963-69, prof., dir. grad. studies, 1969—; vis. prof. U. B.C., summers 1960, 61, 66, N.Y. U., 1973. Taft scholar and fellow, 1950-54; vis. fellow Corpus Christi Coll., Cambridge (Eng.) U., 1971. Mem. Am. Philol. Assn., Archeol. Inst. Am., Classical Assn. Middle West and South, Ohio Classical Assn., AAUP. Author: (with Mark P.O. Morford) Classical Mythology, 1971; The Saga of Themistocles, 1977. Book rev. editor Classical Jour., 1961-68. Home: 47 W 3d Ave Columbus OH 43202

LENCHUK, PAUL, JR., assn. exec.; b. Poland, Jan. 19, 1923 (parents Am. citizens); s. Paul and Julia (Zowta) L.; B.S., Bucknell U., 1947; m. Helen E. Meseroll, Aug. 16, 1947; children—Paul Pearson, Eve Ann, Donna Lee. Asst. exec. dir. Boys Club of N.Y.C., 1947-49; sales promotion mgr. Statis. Tabulating Co., N.Y.C., 1949-50; mgr. C. & A. Brennickmeyer, N.Y.C., 1950-54; exec. dir. Fla. Concrete and Products Assn., Winter Park, 1955-68; exec. dir. Nat. Concrete Masonry Assn., Arlington, Va., 1968-71, pres., 1971—. Chmn. bd. adjustments, Winter Park, 1964-67. Served with USNR, 1943-46. Recipient Grand award for mgmt. achievement Am. Soc. Assn. Execs., 1972. Mem. Am. (dir. 1962-65), Fla. (pres. 1961), socs. assns. execs., Am. Mgmt. Assn., Internat. Concrete Block Commn. (chmn. 1977—), Internat. Precast Assn. (exec. com.). Club: Washington Golf and Country (Arlington). Author: Concrete Products Manual, 1958, rev. edit., 1967; Getting Things Done Through Other People, 1973. Contbr. articles to assn. jours. Home: 1181 Daleview Dr McLean VA 22102 Office: 2302 Horsepen Rd Herndon VA 22070

LENCZOWSKI, GEORGE, educator; b. St. Petersburg, Russia, Feb. 2, 1915; s. George Kwiryn and Halina (Drewnowski) L.; came to U.S., 1945, naturalized, 1951; LL.M., U. Warsaw (Poland), 1936; Diploma Civil Law, U. Paris (France), 1936; J.S.D., U. Lille (France), 1937; m. Bronislawa Szylkiewicz, Mar. 19, 1943; children—John, Hubert. With Polish Fgn. Service, 1938-45; research fellow Sch. Advanced Internat. Studies, Johns Hopkins, 1945-46; from instr. to asso. prof. polit. sci. Hamilton Coll., Clinton, N.Y., 1946-52; from asso. prof. to prof. polit. sci. U. Calif. at Berkeley, 1952—. Vis. prof. Oxford (Eng.) U., 1958; dir. Mid East Research Project, Am. Enterprise Inst. for Pub. Policy Research, 1968-75. Bd. govs. Am. Research Inst. in Turkey, 1964—, Middle East Inst., Washington, 1973—; mem. adv. bd. Am. Enterprise Inst. for Pub. Policy Research, 1969—; trustee Coll. Prep. Sch., Berkeley, 1970—. Served with Polish Brigade, Brit. Army, 1941-42. Ford Found. fellow, 1952-53; Rockefeller Found. fellow, 1960. Mem. Am. Polit. Sci. Assn., Middle East Studies Assn., Polish Inst. Arts and Scis. in Am., San Francisco Com. on Fgn. Relations (steering com. 1973—). Clubs: Faculty, Bohemian (San Francisco). Author: Russia and the West in Iran, 1949; Oil and State in the Middle East, 1960; The Middle East in World Affairs, 1962; Soviet Advances in the Middle East, 1972. Editor: United States Interests in the Middle East, 1968; The Political Awakening in the Middle East, 1970; Political Elites in the Middle East, 1975; Iran under the Pahlavis, 1978. Mem. editorial bd. Western Polit. Quar., 1962-64, Jour. or Politics, 1969-72. Home: 2957 Avalon Ave Berkeley CA 94705

LENDRUM, JAMES THOBURN, architect; b. Oxford, N.Y., Jan. 21, 1907; s. Frederick Alexander and Mary Emma (Crist) L.; student Ohio Wesleyan U., 1925-26; B. Arch., U. Mich., 1930; M.Arch., U. Ill., 1946; m. Dorothea Lombard, Sept. 8, 1931; children—Peter Alexander, Nancy Caroline. Partner George E. Ramey & Co., Champaign, Ill., 1934-43; mem. firm Lendrum & Pusey, archtl. cons., 1955-58; mem. faculty gen. engring. drawing U. Ill., also dir. small homes council, prof. architecture; chief mission Archtl. Edn. Cons., Ford Found., Pakistan, 1957; prof. architecture U. Fla., 1957-69, head dept. architecture, 1957-67; housing cons. HHFA, 1950; v.p., dir. Environs, Inc., Phoenix; mem. firm Peter Lendrum & Assos., Phoenix, 1969—. Mem. archtl. standards adv. com. FHA, 1954-66; mem. bldg. research adv. bd. Nat. Acad. Scis., 1954-66; asst. dir. Bur. Archtl. and Community Research, 1955-67; mem.-at-large Internat. Council for Bldg. Research Studies and Documentation, Rotterdam; dir. Fla. Found. for Advancement Bldg., Inc. Registered architect, Ill., Fla., Pa., Ariz., Calif. Fellow A.I.A.; mem. Archtl. Assn. London, Fla. Assn. Architects (dir.), Alpha Rho Chi, Tau Sigma Delta. Methodist. Kiwanian (Gainesville). Author: (with F.M. Porter) Architectural Projections; also articles. Cons. House and Home. Home: 1233 E Escondido Dr Phoenix AZ 85014 Office: 3820 N 3d St Phoenix AZ 85012

LENEHAN, WILLIAM THURMAN, educator; b. Winnsboro, Tex., May 25, 1930; s. William Allen and Syble (Thurman) L.; B.A., U. Okla., 1955, Ph.D., 1963; m. Angelena Frensley, Aug. 23, 1962; 1 dau., Roma Eileen. Mem. faculty dept. English, U. Wis., Madison, 1962—, prof., 1970—, chmn. dept., 1977—. Served with USAF, 1950-53. Mem. MLA, Nat. Council Tchrs. English, Conf. Coll. Composition and Communication, AAUP. Methodist. Author: (with Wilma Ebbett) The Writer's Reader, 1967; contbr. articles to profl. jours. Office: 600 N Park St Madison WI 53706

LENFANT, CLAUDE JEAN-MARIE, physician, govt. ofcl.; b. Paris, Oct. 12, 1928; s. Robert and Jeanine (Leclerc) L.; came to U.S., 1960, naturalized, 1965; B.S., U. Rennes (France), 1948; M.D., U. Paris, 1956; children—Philipe, Bernard, Martine Lenfant Wayman, Brigitte Lenfant Martin, Christine Lenfant Duke. Intern, Hopitaux Assistance Publique, Paris; resident Hopital Rotschild, Paris; asst. prof. physiology U. Lille (France), 1959-60; from clin. instr. to prof. medicine physiology and biophysics U. Wash. Med. Sch., 1961-72; with Nat. Heart, Lung and Blood Inst. NIH, Bethesda, Md., 1970—, asso. dir. lung programs, 1970-72, dir. div. lung diseases, 1972—. Mem. Assn. Am. Physicians, French, Am. physiol. socs., N.Y. Acad. Scis., Undersea Med. Soc., Am. Soc. Clin. Investigation, Assn. Am. Physicians. Chief editor Lung Biology in Health and Disease; asso. editor Jour. Applied Physiology, 1976—, Am. Jour. Medicine, 1979—; mem. editorial bd. Undersea Biomed. Research, 1973-75, Respiration Physiology, 1971-75, Am. Jour. Physiology, 1971-75, Am. Rev. Respiratory Disease, 1974—. Home: 13201 Glen Rd Gaithersburg MD 20760 Office: 5333 Westbard Ave Bethesda MD 20014

LENG, SHAO CHUAN, educator; b. Chengtu, China, Feb. 14, 1921; s. Yin Tung and Nan (Chen) L.; B.A., Nat. Central U. China, 1943; M.A., Yale, 1948; Ph.D., U. Pa., 1950; m. Alice Li, Dec. 12, 1944 (dec. 1968); 1 son, David; m. 2d, Nora Yen, June 14, 1970. Came to U.S., 1945, naturalized, 1953. Lectr. U. Pa., 1949-50; from lectr. to prof. U. Va., Charlottesville, 1950-72, Doherty Found. prof. govt. and fgn. affairs, 1972—, chmn. com. Asian studies, 1965-68, 74—; Fulbright lectr. Doshisha (Japan) U., 1956-57; adviser Union Research Inst., Hong Kong, 1961; vis. scholar Harvard, 1962; research asso. Duke U. Rule of Law Research Center, 1964-66. Cons., Research Analysis Corp., 1968-71, HEW, 1978; research asso. Harvard Law Sch., 1968-69; Social Sci. Research Council grantee, 1956; research fellow Social Sci. Research Council-Am. Council

Learned Socs., 1961-62, 68-69; Fulbright Research scholar, Hong Kong and Taiwan, 1977. Mem. Am. Polit. Sci. Assn., Am. Soc. Internat. Law, Assn. Asian Studies. Author: Japan and Communist China, 1959; (with Norman D. Palmer) Sun Yat-sen and Communism, 1961; (with others) Sovereignty within the Law, 1965; Justice in Communist China, 1968. Editor: (with Hungdah Chiu) Law in Chinese Foreign Policy, 1972; Post-Mao China and U.S.-China Trade, 1977; cons. editor Asian Forum, 1974—, World Affairs, 1975—. Home: 217 Highview Ln Charlottesville VA 22901

LENGEMANN, FREDERICK WILLIAM, scientist, educator; b. N.Y.C., Apr. 8, 1925; s. Peter and Dorathea Johanna (Wolter) L.; student N.Y. State Sch. Agr., Farmingdale, 1942-43; B.S. with distinction, Cornell U., 1950, M.Nutrition Sci., 1951; Ph.D., U. Wis., 1954; m. J. Joan Doremus, Dec. 23, 1950; children—Frederick William Jr., David Munson. Research asso. U. Tenn.-AEC Agrl. Research Program, Oak Ridge, 1954-55; asst. prof. dept. chemistry U. Tenn. Med. Sch., Memphis, 1955-59; prof. dept. phys. biology N.Y. State Coll. Vet. Medicine, Cornell U., 1959—. Biochemist div. biology and medicine AEC, 1962-63; cons. FAO-IAEA, Vienna, Austria, 1966-67, 76-77, Fed. Radiation Council, 1968-70; IAEA expert U. Nacional Agraria, Peru, 1978. Mem. planning bd. Town of Dryden (N.Y.), 1963-68. Served with USNR, 1943-46. Decorated Air medal with 3 stars. Fellow AAAS; mem. Council Agrl. Sci. and Tech., Am. Dairy Sci. Assn., Am. Nutrition Soc., Fed. Am. Socs. for Exptl. Biology, Nat., N.Y. State Christmas tree growers assns., Sigma Xi, Phi Kappa Phi. Contbr. articles to profl. jours. Home: RD 1 Freeville NY 13068 Office: Dept Physical Biology NY State Coll Vet Medicine Cornell U Ithaca NY 14853

L'ENGLE, MADELEINE (MRS. HUGH FRANKLIN), author; N.Y.C., Nov. 29, 1918; d. Charles Wadsworth and Madeleine (Barnett) Camp; A.B., Smith Coll., 1941; postgrad. New Sch., 1941-42, Columbia, 1960-61; m. Hugh Franklin, Jan. 26, 1946; children—Josephine Franklin Jones, Maria Franklin Bion. Tchr. St. Hilda's and St. Hugh's Sch., 1960—; mem. faculty U. Ind., 1965-66, 71; writer-in-residence Ohio State U., 1970, U. Rochester, 1972, Wheaton Coll., 1976—, Cathedral St. John the Divine, N.Y.C., 1965—. Pres., Crosswicks Found. Recipient Newbery medal, 1963, Sequoyah award, 1965, runner-up award Hans Christian Andersen Internat. award, 1965, Lewis Carroll Shelf award, 1965, Austrian State Lit. award, 1969, Bishop's Cross, 1970, U. South Miss. medal, 1978. Mem. Authors Guild (mem. council, mem. membership com.), Authors League (mem. council), Writers Guild Am., Colonial Dames. Mem. Anglican Ch. Author: The Small Rain, 1945; Ilsa, 1946; Camilla Dickinson, 1951; A Winter's Love, 1957; And Both Were Young, 1949; Meet the Austins, 1960; A Wrinkle in Time, 1962; The Moon by Night, 1963; The 24 Days Before Christmas, 1964; The Arm of the Starfish, 1965; The Love Letters, 1966; The Journey with Jonah, 1967; The Young Unicorns, 1968; Dance in The Desert, 1969; Lines Scribbled on an Envelope, 1969; The Other Side of the Sun, 1971; A Circle of Quiet, 1972; A Wind in the Door, 1973; The Summer of the Great-grandmother, 1974; Dragons on the Waters, 1976; The Irrational Season, 1977; A Swiftly Tilting Planet, 1978; The Weather of the Heart, 1978; Ladder of Angels, 1979; A Ring of Endless Light, 1980. Collection of papers at Wheaton Coll. Home: Crosswicks Goshen CT 06756 Office: care Farrar Straus & Giroux Inc 19 Union Sq W New York NY 10003. *Over the years I've worked out a philosophy of failure which I find extraordinarily liberating. If I'm not free to fail, I'm not free to take risks, and everything in life that's worth doing involves a willingness to take a risk and involves the risk of failure. Each time I start a new book I am risking failure. Although I have had 25 books published, there are at least 6 full unpublished books which have failed, but which have been necessary for the book which then gets published. The same thing is true in all human relationships. Unless I'm willing to open myself up to risk and to being hurt, then I'm closing myself off to love and friendship.*

LENGYEL, BELA ADALBERT, physicist, educator; b. Budapest, Hungary, Oct. 5, 1910; s. Alexander and Irene (Gonda) L.; Ph.D. in Math., Pazmany U., Budapest, 1935; research fellow Harvard, 1935-36; m. 2d, Birgit Holmquist, Dec. 29, 1962; children—Judith Ann, Thomas Edward. Asst. in math. U. Tech. Scis., Budapest, 1931-34; asst. actuary, Budapest, 1936-37; asst. statistician, Worcester, Mass., 1938-39; instr. math. Rensselaer Poly. Inst., 1939-42; instr. physics Coll. City N.Y., 1942-43; asst. prof. U. Rochester, 1943-46; physicist Naval Research Lab., 1946-52; sr. staff physicist research labs. Hughes Aircraft Co., 1952-63, asso. head atomic physics dept., research labs., 1958-59; vis. asso. prof. engring. U. Calif. at Los Angeles, 1957; prof., chmn. dept. physics Calif. State U., Northridge, 1963-70, prof., 1970-77, prof. emeritus, 1977—; guest prof. U. Lund and Chalmers Tech. U., Sweden, 1971-72. Mem. Am. Math. Soc., Am. Phys. Soc., Inst. Electronic Engrs., Sigma Xi. Club: Sierra (Los Angeles). Author: Lasers, 1962, 2d edit., 1971; Introduction to Laser Physics, 1965. Home: 11748 Kiowa Ave Los Angeles CA 90049

LENGYEL, CORNEL ADAM, author; b. Fairfield, Conn., Jan. 1, 1915; s. Elmer Alexander and Mary Elizabeth (Bismarck) L.; ed. pub. schs.; m. Teresa Delaney Murphy, July 10, 1933; children—Jerome Benedict, Paul Joel, Michael Sebastian, Cornelia (Mrs. Charles Burke). Editor, supr. Fed. Research Project, San Francisco, 1938-41; music critic The Coast, San Francisco, 1937-41; shipwright, personnel officer Kaiser Shipyard, Richmond, Calif., 1942-44; mgr. Forty-Nine Theatre, Georgetown, Calif., 1946-50; editor W.H. Freeman Co., San Francisco, 1952-54; founder, exec. editor Dragon's Teeth Press, Georgetown, 1969—; vis. prof., lectr. English lit. Sacramento State Coll., 1962-63; writer-in-residence Hamline U., St. Paul, 1968-69; guest lectr. Mass. Inst. Tech., 1969. Served with U.S. Merchant Marine, 1944-45. Recipient 1st prize Poetry Soc. Va., 1951, 1st prize Maritime Poetry Awards, 1945, Albert M. Bender award in lit., 1945, Maxwell Anderson award drama, 1950, Di Castagnola award Poetry Soc. Am., 1971; Internat. Who's Who in Poetry award, 1972; Huntington Hartford Found. resident fellow, 1951, 64; MacDowell Colony resident fellow, 1967; Ossabaw Island Found. fellow, 1968; Nat. Endowment for Arts fellow, 1976-77. Mem. Modern Lang. Assn., AAUP, PEN, Poetry Soc. Am., Poetry Soc. Eng. Author: Thirty Pieces, 1933; The World's My Village, 1936; Jonah Fugitive, 1937; The Shadow Trap, 1939; The Atom Clock, 1950; The Last Shelter, 1954; American Testament, 1956; Four Days in July, 1958, Benedict Arnold, 1960; Presidents of the United States, 1961; Ethan Allen, 1962; Will of Stratford, 1963; Jesus the Galilean, 1966; The Declaration of Independence, 1968; Four Dozen Songs, 1970; The Lookout's Letter, 1971; The Creative Self, 1971; (plays) The Case of Benedict Arnold, 1975, Doctor Franklin, 1976; The Master Plan, 1978. Contbr. to anthologies The Golden Year, 1960; The Britannica Library of Great American Writing, 1961; The Menorah Treasury, 1964; Interpretation for Our Time, 1966. Address: Adam's Acres Georgetown CA 95634. *Knowing the shortness of his lease on earth, the poet must decide what he can do with his portion of time. Not what he would, but what he can and must do. The modern artist, caught in an existential cage, is impelled to act as if the choices he made were both free and inevitable. His task as an artist is the transmutation of time, and he knows that the purchase price of anything valuable in life is usually life itself. The writer who values time will not turn out a page which robs his reader of a portion of time, however small, without giving him in exchange a taste of eternity, however transient.*

LENGYEL, PETER, educator; b. Budapest, Hungary, May 24, 1929; s. Michael and Alice (Köszeg) L.; diploma chem. engring. Budapest Tech. U., 1951; Ph.D. in Biochemistry, N.Y. U., 1962; m. Suzanna Kadar, Dec. 5, 1956; children—Carole, Michael. Came to U.S., 1956, naturalized, 1962. Asst. prof. dept. biochemistry N.Y. U. Sch. Medicine, 1963; NIH spl. fellow Institut Pasteur, Service de Biochimie Cellulaire, Paris, France, 1963-64; asso. prof. dept. molecular biophysics and biochemistry Yale, 1965-69, prof. molecular biophysics and biochemistry, 1969—. Mem. Am. Soc. Biol. Chemists, Am. Chem. Soc., Sigma Xi. Research and publ. on nucleic acids, protein synthesis, animal viruses and the interferon system. Home: 29 Dogwood Circle Woodbridge CT 06525 Office: Box 1937 Yale Station Yale University New Haven CT 06520

LENHER, SAMUEL, chem. mfg. exec.; b. Madison, Wis., June 19, 1905; s. Victor and May (Blood) L.; B.A., U. Wis., 1924, D.Sc., 1959; Ph.D., U. London, 1926; D.Sc., U. Del., 1961; m. Irene Kirkland, Dec. 14, 1929; children—John K., Ann B. (Mrs. A.L. Robinson, Jr.), George V. Internat. Edn. Bd. fellow Berlin, 1927; NRC fellow U. Calif., 1928; with E. I. duPont de Nemours & Co., Wilmington, Del., 1929-78, successively research chemist, tech. adviser organic chems. dept., supt. develop. Chambers works, mgr. Chambers works, asst. gen. mgr. organic chems. div., 1929-55. v.p., dir. mem. exec. com., 1955-70, dir., 1955-78; commr. Farmers Bank of State of Del., 1976—; dir. Polychrome Corp. Mem. sec.'s cons. med. research and edn. HEW, 1957-58, adv. com. for Pub. Health Service personnel study, 1961, sec.'s task force environmental health and related problems, 1966-67; mem. gen. tech. adv. com. Office Coal Research, Dept. Interior, 1960-66; mem. research mgmt. adv. panel com. sci. and astronautics U.S. Ho. Reps., 1964-75; patent adv. com. U.S. Patent Office, 1965-68; mem. summer study on space applications Nat. Acad. Scis.-NASA, 1968; pres. Welfare Council Del., Inc.; adv. council Patent, Trademark and Copyright Research Inst., George Washington U., 1965-70. Bd. mgrs. Wistar Inst. Anatomy and Biology, 1959-71, v.p., 1961-71; lifetime trustee Johns Hopkins, 1959-77, fellow bd., 1977; trustee Tower Hill Sch., 1948-66, Wis. Alumni Research Found., 1957—; trustee U. Del., 1963—, chmn., 1972—; trustee Johns Hopkins Hosp., 1967-77; trustee, mem. corp. Marine Biol. Lab., Woods Hole, 1967-76; trustee U. Del. Research Found., 1954-75, pres., 1955-66; dir., mem. exec. com. United Community Fund No. Del., Inc., 1956-73, pres., 1968-70. Fellow Univ. Coll., London, 1966. Fellow N.Y. Acad. Scis.; mem. U.S. C. of C. (council trends and perspective 1966-70), Synthetic Organic Chem. Mfgs. Assn. U.S. (pres. 1955), Am. Chem. Soc., Soc. Chem. Industry (vice chmn. Am. sect. 1963, chmn. 1964), Am. Inst. Chem. Engrs., Am. Philos. Soc., Confrerie des Chevaliers du Tastevin, A.A.A.S., Am. Inst. Chemists. Unitarian. Clubs: Wilmington, Wilmington Country (dir. 1965-73); Quill and Grill; Greenville Country. Home: 50 Cokesburg Village Hockessin DE 19707 also Vineyard Haven MA 02568 Office: PO Box 3771 Greenville DE 19807

LENHOFF, HOWARD MAER, educator; b. North Adams, Mass., Jan. 27, 1929; s. Charles and Goldy Sarah (Rubin) L.; B.A., Coe Coll., 1950, D.Sc. (hon.), 1976; Ph.D., Johns Hopkins, 1955; m. Sylvia Grossman, June 20, 1954; children—Gloria, Bernard. USPHS fellow Loomis Lab., Greenwich, Conn., 1954-56; vis. lectr. Howard U., Washington, 1957-58; postdoctoral fellow Carnegie Instn., Washington, 1958; investigator Howard Hughes Med. Inst., Miami, 1958-63; prof. biology, dir. Lab. for Quantitative Biology, U. Miami, Coral Gables, 1963-69; prof. biol. scis. U. Calif. at Irvine, 1969—, dir. marine biology program, 1969-73, asso. dean biol. scis., 1969-70, dean grad. div., 1970-73; vis. scientist Weizmann Inst. Sci., Rehovot, Israel, 1968-69; vis. prof. chem. engring., Rothschild fellow Israel Inst. Tech., 1973-74; vis. prof. Hebrew U., Jerusalem, spring 1970, fall 1971, 77-78; dir. Nelson Research & Devel. Co., Irvine. Mem. sci. adv. bd. Orange Empire council Boy Scouts Am., 1971-73; vice chmn. So. Calif. div. Am. Assn. Profs. for Peace in Middle East, 1972—; v.p. bd. dirs. Am. Assn. for Ethiopian Jews, 1973-78, pres., 1978—; bd. govs. Israel Bonds Orange County, Calif., 1974—; bd. dirs. Dade County Heart Assn., Miami, 1958-61; pres. Hillel Council of Orange County, 1976-78; nat. chmn. faculty div. State of Israel Bonds, 1976. Served to 1st lt. USAF, 1956-58. Recipient Career Development award USPHS, 1965-69; Alumni award for community service U. Calif., Irvine, 1977. Louis Lipsky fellow, 1968-69. Fellow A.A.A.S.; mem. Am. Chem. Soc., Am. Biophys. Soc., Am. Soc. Cell Biologists, Am. Soc. Biol. Chemists, Soc. Gen. Physiogists, Soc. Growth and Devel., So. Calif. Technion Soc. (dir. 1976), Phi Beta Kappa, Sigma Xi, Phi Kappa Phi. Editor: Biology of Hydra, 1961; Hydra, 1969; Experimental Coelenterate Biology, 1972; Coelenterate Biology—Review and Perspectives, 1974; mem. editorial bd. Jour. Solid Phase Biochemistry, 1976—. Home: 304 Robin Hood Ln Costa Mesa CA 92627 Office: School Biological Sciences Univ California Irvine CA 92717

LENIHAN, JOSEPH LEO, r.r. exec.; b. Louisville, Aug. 31, 1920; s. Joseph L. and Josephine Frances (Kelly) L.; J.D. magna cum laude, U. Louisville, 1947. Admitted to Ky. bar, 1942, U.S. Supreme Ct. bar, 1957; with Louisville & Nashville R.R., Louisville, 1939—, gen. counsel, 1965—, v.p., 1973—, also dir.; dir. Seaboard Coast Line R.R. Co.; instr. law U. Louisville, 1948-50. Bd. dirs. U. Louisville Law Alumni Found., 1965—, treas., 1965-72, pres., 1972-73; bd. dirs. Cerebral Palsy Sch. Louisville, 1973—, sec., 1977, v.p., 1979; pres. adv. bd. St. James Parish Roman Catholic Ch., 1972-73, vice chmn. parish council, 1974-75, mem. council, 1977-79. Served to capt. U.S. Army, 1942-46. Mem. Am., Ky., Louisville bar assns. Democrat. Clubs: Pendennis, Wranglers (pres. 1974-75), Rotary (pres. 1974-75), Law. Home: 1718 Sulgrave Rd Louisville KY 40205 Office: 908 W Broadway Louisville KY 40201. *For a modest success and a pleasant life, the ingredients seem to be integrity, competence, diligence, and a pleasant disposition.*

LENKOSKI, LEO DOUGLAS, physician, educator; b. Northampton, Mass., May 13, 1925; s. Leo L. and Mary Agnes (Lee) L.; A.B., Harvard, 1948, spl. student, 1948-49; M.D., Western Res. U., 1953; grad. Cleve. Psychoanalytic Inst., 1964; m. Jeannette Teare, July 12, 1952; children—Jan Ellen, Mark Teare, Lisa Marie, Joanne Lee. Intern, Univ. Hosps., Cleve., 1953-54, resident in psychiatry, 1956-57, dir. psychiatry, 1970—; asst. resident in psychiatry Yale, 1954-56; teaching fellow Case Western Res. U., 1957-60, instr. to prof. psychiatry, 1960—; cons. Cleve. Center on Alcoholism, DePaul Maternity and Infant Home, St. Ann's Hosp., Def. Dept., Cleve. VA Hosp., Psychiat. Edn. br. NIMH; mem. Cuyahoga County Mental Health and Retardation Bd., 1967—, Health Planning and Devel. Commn., 1967-73, Ohio Mental Health and Retardation Commn., 1976—. Bd. dirs. Glen Oaks Sch., Hough-Norwood Health Center, Neighborhood Counseling Service. Served to 1st lt. USAAF, 1943-46. Decorated D.F.C., Air medal with oak leaf cluster. Career Tchr. grantee NIMH, 1958-60. Fellow Am. Psychiat. Assn., Am. Coll. Psychiatrists, Am. Coll. Psychoanalysts; mem. Ohio Psychiat. Assn. (pres. 1974—), Am. Psychoanalytic Assn., A.A.A.S., Assn. Am. Med. Colls., Cleve. Acad. Medicine, Ohio Med. Assn., Pasteur Club, Am. Assn. Chairmen Depts. Psychiatry (pres. 1978-79), Alpha Omega Alpha. Contbr. articles to profl. jours. Home: 3157 Kingsley St Shaker Heights OH 44122 Office: 2040 Abington Rd Cleveland OH 44106

LENNA, REGINALD ALEXANDER, mfg. co. exec.; b. Jamestown, N.Y., Dec. 3, 1912; s. Oscar Anrep and Hilda Marie (Nordstrom) L.; B.S., Lehigh U., 1936; m. 2d, Elizabeth Lyons, Apr. 9, 1961; 1 son by previous marriage, James Austin (dec.). With Blackstone Corp., Jamestown, 1936—, successively asst. sales mgr., works mgr., v.p., v.p. and gen. mgr., pres., gen. mgr., 1951-67, pres., chief exec. officer, 1967—; pres. Blackstone Indsl. Products, Ltd., Stratford, Ont., Can.; dir. Struthers Wells Corp., Bankers Trust of Western N.Y., Unigard Ins. Group, Blackstone Ultrasonics Inc. Mem. Am. Legion. Baptist. Elk. Home: 86 E Terrace Ave Lakewood NY 14750 Office: 1111 Allen St Jamestown NY 14701

LENNARZ, WILLIAM JOSEPH, research biologist, educator; b. N.Y.C., Sept. 28, 1934; s. William and Louise (Richter) L.; B.S., Pa. State U., 1956; Ph.D., U. Ill., 1959; research fellow, Harvard, 1959-62; m. Roberta S. Lozensky, June 16, 1956 (div. June 1973); children—William, Matthew, David; m. 2d, Sheila Jackson, July 13, 1973. Mem. faculty Johns Hopkins Sch. Medicine, 1962—, asso. prof. biochemistry, 1966-70, prof., 1971—; cons. NIH. Clayton Found. scholar, 1962-64; Lederle Faculty awardee, 1965-67; recipient Distinguished Young Scientist award Md., 1967. Mem. Am. Chem. Soc., Am. Soc. Biol. Chemists, Am. Soc. Microbiology, Sigma Xi, Phi Kappa Phi, Alpha Chi Sigma. Editorial bd. Jour. Biol. Chemistry, Jour. Membrane Biology, Biochemica et Biophysica Acta, Archives of Biochemistry and Biophysics, Biochemistry. Research biochemistry of cell surfaces and of fertilization. Home: 227 Newburg Ave Catonsville MD 21228 Office: 725 N Wolfe St Baltimore MD 21205

LENNON, JOHN ONO (FORMERLY JOHN WINSTON LENNON), singer, songwriter, musician; b. Liverpool, Eng., Oct. 9, 1940; s. Alfred and Julia (Stanley) L.; student Allerton Coll., Liverpool Art Coll.; m. Cynthia Powell, 1962; m. 2d, Yoko Ono, 1969; 1 son, 1 stepdau. Founder musical group The Quarreymen, 1955; appeared with various groups until forming The Beatles, 1960; appeared and recorded with the Beatles until 1970; played in Hamburg, W. Ger., 1960, 61, 62, Liverpool, 1960, 61; toured Scotland, Sweden, U.K., 1963; world tours, 1964, 65, 66; formed Apple Corp., Ltd., Beatles mgmt. co., 1968; solo artist since 1968; recording with Yoko Ono, 1968-69, Plastic Ono Band, 1969—, now U.S. resident; U.S. album releases include: (with the Beatles) Meet the Beatles, 1964, Beatles 2d Album, 1964, A Hard Day's Night, 1964, Something New, 1964, Beatles, '65, 1965, Early Beatles, 1965, Beatles VI, 1965, Help, 1965, Rubber Soul, 1965, Yesterday... and Today, 1966, Revolver, 1966, Sgt. Pepper's Lonely Hearts Club Band, 1967, Magical Mystery Tour, 1967, Abbey Road, 1968, Beatles, 1968, Yellow Submarine, 1969, Hey Jude, 1970, Let It Be, 1970; (with Yoko Ono) Two Virgins, 1968, Life with the Lions, 1969, Wedding Album, 1969; (with Plastic Ono Band) Live Peace in Toronto, 1969, John Lennon/Plastic Ono Band, 1970, Imagine, 1971, Some Time in New York City, 1972, Mind Games, 1973, Walls and Bridges, 1974, Rock n' Roll, 1975, Shaved Fish, 1975; composer songs: (with Paul McCartney) I Want to Hold Your Hand, She Loves You, Can't Buy Me Love, A Hard Day's Night, Help, In My Life, Ticket to Ride, Get Back, Hey Jude, If I Fell, others; (solo) Instant Karma, Give Peace a Chance, Mother, Imagine, Mind Games, Cold Turkey, Whatever Gets You Through the Night, Stand By Me, Woman's the Nigger of the World, Attica State, others; films include: (with the Beatles) A Hard Day's Night, 1964, Help, 1965, Magical Mystery Tour, 1967, Yellow Submarine, 1968, Let it Be, 1970; appeared in film How I Won the War, 1967. Decorated Order Brit. Empire; recipient Acad. award, 1970; Grammy award, 1964, 66, 67, 70, 72; numerous Gold Record and Gold Album awards. Author: In His Own Write, 1964; A Spaniard in the Works, 1965; Lennon Remembers, 1972. Office: care Press Relations Capitol Records 1370 Ave of the Americas New York NY 10019•

LENNON, JOSEPH LUKE, coll. ofcl.; b. Providence, Sept. 21, 1919; s. John Joseph and Marjorie (McCabe) L.; A.B., Providence Coll., 1940; S.T.B., Immaculate Conception Coll., 1946; M.A., U. Notre Dame, 1950, Ph.D., 1953; LL.D., Bradford Durfee Coll. Tech., 1963. Ordained priest Roman Cath. Ch., 1947; instr. U. Notre Dame, 1948-50; mem. edn. dept. Providence Coll., 1950- 51, 53-56, asst. dean men, 1953, dean of men, 1954-56, dean of coll., 1956-68, v.p. community affairs, 1968—; dir. Tchrs. Guild of Thomistic Inst., 1953-56; dir. Pennywise Shop. Mem. adv. council Citizens Ednl. Freedom; adv. bd. Perceptional Edn. and Research Center; co-chmn. Easter Seals, 1968; arbitrator R.I. Bd. Labor; adv. com. Mental Retardation R.I.; chmn. Nat. Library Week, R.I., 1962; mem. R.I. Adv. Com. Vocational Edn.; ann. lectr. Psychology and Everyday Life, WJAR-TV, 1960-75; mem. Gov. R.I. Com. to Study R.I. State Inst. at Howard; chmn. speaker's bur. United Fund Campaign, 1971; coordinator Civil Rights Affirmative Action Program, 1970-78; mem. Com. Future Jurisprudence in R.I.; com. clergy renewal Diocese Providence; mem. Com. for CROP-Community Hunger Appeal of Ch. World Service, 1974-75; mem. subcom. on family law Gov.'s Commn. on Jurisprudence of Future; mem. membership com. Cancer Control Bd. R.I., 1977; mem. Gov.'s Commn. on Consumer's Council, 1977; mem. Gov.'s Leadership Conf. on Citizen Participation. Bd. dirs. Blue Cross and Physicians Service, Progress for Providence, R.I. Legal Services, Fed. Hill House, Handgun Alert, Vols. in R.I. Schs., Meeting St. Sch., Big Sisters, R.I. Easter Seal, Blackstone Valley Surgicare; bd. dirs. R.I. Heart Assn., chmn. 1975 Heart Fund campaign; trustee R.I. chpt. Leukemia Soc. Am.; adv. bd. Parents Without Partners; bd. govs. John E. Fogarty Found., Irish Scholarship Found.; bd. dirs., trustee Big Sisters Assn., R.I.; bd. dirs. Diabetes Assn. R.I.; adv. bd. St. Joseph's Merged Hosps.; mem. corp. R.I. Hosp.; mem. adv. council Quirk Inst.; mem. Spl. Legis. Commn. Created on Catastrophic Health Ins., 1979—. Recipient Seal of Approval, R.I. Automobile Dealers Assn., 1978. Mem. Nat. Cath. Edn. Assn., Am. Cath. Sociol. Soc., Nat. Soc. Study Edn., Am. Philosophers Edn. Assn., New Eng. Ednl. Assn., New Eng. Guidance and Personnel Assn., Greater Providence Epilepsy Assn., Nat. Soc. Study Edn., Am. Arbitration Assn., Alpha Epsilon Delta, Delta Epsilon Sigma (pres. 1966-69). Author: The Role of Experience in the Acquisition of Scientific Knowledge, 1952; The Dean Speaks, 1958; College is for Knowledge, 1959, rev. as 30 Ways to Get Ahead at College, 1964. Home: Providence Coll River and Eaton Sts Providence RI 02918

LENNON, SISTER MARY ISIDORE, hosp. adminstr.; b. Kilkenny, Ireland; d. John and Brigid (Phelan) Lennon; B.S. in Nursing, St. Louis U., 1933, M.A., 1934, M.S.W., 1949. Came to U.S., 1925, naturalized, 1934. Supr. med. and surg. depts. St. John's Mercy Hosp., St. Louis, 1928-39, dir. nurses, 1939-45, supr. outpatient dept., 1945-61, dir. social service dept., 1949-61, asst. adminstr., 1961-64, mem. com. edn. and research, 1961—, pres. bd. trustees, adminstr., 1964—. Bd. govs. Cath. Charities of St. Louis, 1940—, mem. com. adoption, 1953—, com. care aging, 1960—; provincial adv. bd. Sisters of Mercy of Union, St. Louis, generalate commn. on health and welfare; mem. corporate bd. St. Louis Blue Cross, 1964—; mem. Mo. Bd. Nurse Examiners, 1966; bd. dirs., chmn. pub. relations com. St. Elizabeth's Hosp., Granite City, Ill.; mem. gen. assembly Greater St. Louis Health Systems Agy. Mem. Nat. League for Nurses, Mo. Assn. Social Welfare (com. aging), Nat. Conf. Cath. Charities, Hosp. Assn.

Met. St. Louis (dir., pub. relations com.), Acad. Certified Social Workers, Royal Soc. Promotion Health, St. Louis League Nursing, Am. Cath. Sociol. Soc., Am. Coll. Hosp. Administrs., Am. (com. library services 1966), Mo., Cath. hosp. assns., C. of C. Greater St. Louis. Author: Professional Adjustments for Students of Nursing, 1946; Sociology and Social Problems in Nursing, 1951; Mother Catherine McAuley, A Great Social Worker, 1951; Teaching in the Out-Patient Department, 1954; The Holy Sacrifice of the Mass and Prayers for Shut-Ins, 1954; Milestones of Mercy, 1957; My Daily Reminder, 1963; St. John's Mercy: A Milestone of Medical Progress in St. Louis, 1871-1971, 1972; Prayers and Reflections for Patients and Personnel in Burn Centers, 1977. Contbr. articles to profl. jours. Address: 615 S New Balias Rd St Louis MO 63141

LENNON, ROGER THOMAS, pub. co. exec.; b. N.Y.C., May 18, 1916; s. Martin J. and Mary Ann (O'Dea) L.; A.B., Fordham U., 1935, M.A., 1937; Ph.D., Tchrs. Coll., Columbia, 1952; m. Eleanor P. Mooney, Aug. 12, 1942; children—Roger, Brendan, Peter, Eleanor, Alice, Terence, Michael, Kevin. Test editor World Book Co., Yonkers, N.Y., 1937-42; chief placement and testing, civilian personnel Air Materiel Command USAF, Wright Field, Ohio, 1942-46; dir. test dept. Harcourt, Brace & World, Inc., N.Y.C., 1948-70; sr. v.p., dir. Harcourt Brace Jovanovich, Inc., N.Y.C., 1962-78, pres. Psychol. Corp., N.Y.C., 1971-75, chmn., dir., 1970-78. Mem. N.Y. State Adv. Council on Psychology, 1957-67. Fellow Am. Psychol. Assn.; mem. Am. Ednl. Research Assn., Am. Personnel and Guidance Assn., Nat. Council on Measurement in Edn. (bd. editors jour. 1965-68, pres. 1980), Am. Cath. Psychol. Assn. (pres. 1969-70), Sigma Xi, Phi Delta Kappa. Author: Otis-Lennon Mental Ability Tests, intelligence test series, 1967, also articles. Home: 83 Hawthorn Pl Briarcliff NY 10510 Office: 757 3d Ave New York NY 10017

LENNOX, DONALD D(UANE), office equipment co. exec.; b. Pitts., Dec. 3, 1918; s. Edward George and Sarah B. (Knight) L.; B.S. with honors, U. Pitts., 1947; m. Jane Armstrong, June 11, 1949; children—Donald D., J. Gordon. With Ford Motor Co., 1950-69; with Xerox Corp., 1969—, corp. v.p. and sr. v.p. info. tech. group, Rochester, N.Y., 1972-73, sr. v.p., sr. staff officer, Stamford, Conn., 1973-79, group v.p. and pres. info. system group, Rochester, 1979—, also dir.; dir. Sybron Corp., Rochester Telephone Corp., Schlegel Corp.; v.p. Rochester Indsl. Mgmr. Council. Vice chmn. bd. trustee St. John Fisher Coll.; trustee St. Ann's Home, Rochester; vice chmn. Allendale Columbia Sch., Rochester. Served with AC, USN, 1942-45; Decorated D.F.C. with 2 gold stars, Air medal with 4 gold stars. C.P.A., Pa. Mem. Rochester Area C. of C. (pres. 1979), Order of Artus, Soc. Automotive Engrs., Beta Gamma Sigma. Republican. Clubs: Country of Rochester, Genesee Valley. Home: 7 Old Landmark Dr Rochester NY 14618 Office: Xerox Sq Rochester NY 14644. *What modest success I have enjoyed is the result of hard work and dedication to the success of the organization public or private. Rarely is one's contribution to the success of the organization not recognized or rewarded.*

LENON, RICHARD ALLEN, corp. exec.; b. Lansing, Mich., Aug. 4, 1920; s. Theo and Elizabeth (Amon) L.; B.A., Western Mich. Coll., 1941; postgrad. Northwestern U., 1941-42; m. Helen Johnson, Sept. 13, 1941; children—Richard Allen, Pamela A., Lisa A. Mgr. finance div. Montgomery Ward & Co., Chgo., 1947-56; v.p. finance Westinghouse Air Brake Co., 1963-67, treas., 1965-67; v.p., treas. Internat. Minerals & Chem. Corp., Skokie, Ill., 1956-63, group v.p. finance and adminstrn., 1967-68, exec. v.p., 1968-70, pres., 1970-78, chmn., 1977—; dir. Am. Standard Co., Bankers Trust Co., Fed. Paper Bd. Co., The Signal Cos., Inc. Served to lt. comdr. USNR, 1942-47. Clubs: University, Glen View (Chgo.); Economic (N.Y.C.). Home: 803 Solar Ln Glenview IL 60025 Office: Internat Minerals & Chemical Corp 2315 Sanders Rd Northbrook IL 60062

LENS, SIDNEY, writer; b. Newark, Jan. 28, 1912; ed. pub. schs., N.Y.C.; m. Shirley Ruben, 1946. Dir. local 329, United Service Employees Union, AFL-CIO, 1941-66; lectr. fgn. affairs and labor U. Chgo., Roosevelt U., De Paul U., U. Ill., numerous others; columnist Nat. Cath. Reporter. Candidate for Congress, 2d Ill. Dist., 1962, Ill. Legislature, 1964. Bd. dirs. Chgo. Council Fgn. Relations; co-chmn. Nat. Com. To End War in Vietnam, New Mblzn. Com. to End War in Vietnam; chmn. Justice, Action and Peace in Latin Am. Recipient Patron Saints award Midland Authors, 1970; chmn. Impeach Nixon Com., 1973—; chmn. Inst. Social Studies; mem. steering com. Moblzn. for Survival. Fellow Inst. for Policy Studies (asso.). Author: Left, Right and Center, 1949; The Counterfeit Revolution, 1952; A World in Revolution, 1956; The Crisis of American Labor, 1959; Working Men, 1960; Africa Awakening Giant, 1962; The Futile Crusade, 1964; A Country Is Born, 1964; Radicalism in America, 1966; What Unions Do, 1968; Poverty: America's Enduring Paradox, 1969; The Military Industrial Complex, 1970; The Forging of the American Empire, 1972; The Labor Wars, 1973; Poverty: Yesterday and Today, 1973; The Promise and Pitfalls of Revolution, 1974; The Day Before Doomsday, 1977. Editor Liberation mag.; contbg. editor The Progressive. Contbr. to mags., newspapers, newspaper syndicates. Home: 990 Lake Shore Dr Chicago IL 60611

LENSEN, GEORGE ALEXANDER, historian, educator; b. Berlin, Germany, Nov. 5, 1923; s. Alexander and Charlotte (Baruchson) L.; came to U.S., 1939, naturalized, 1943; A.B., Columbia, 1947, M.A., 1948, Ph.D., 1951; divorced; children—Karen Meng-mei, Kristin Chung-Mei; m. 2d, Rumiya Shahbey Lensen, Aug. 17, 1969. Mem. faculty Fla. State U., 1949—, prof. history, 1959—; vis. prof. Columbia U., summers 1962-63; pres. Diplomatic Press, Inc., 1966—. Served to 1st lt. AUS, 1943-46. Grantee Social Sci. Research Council, 1957-58, Am. Philos. Soc., 1958, 61, 67, Am. Council Learned Socs. and Social Sci. Research Council, 1959, 61, Ford Found., 1975-78; Fulbright research scholar Hokkaido (Japan) U., 1953-54; postdoctoral researcher Leningrad (USSR) State U., 1961; sr. fellow Nat. Endowment Humanities, 1967-68; sr. scholar exchange Am. Council Learned Socs.-Acad. Sci. USSR, 1973, 74. Author: Report from Hokkaido: The Remains of Russian Culture in Northern Japan, 1954; Russia's Japan Expedition of 1852 to 1855, 1955; The Russian Push Toward Japan: Russo-Japanese Relations 1697-1875, 1959; The World Beyond Europe: An Introduction to the History of Africa, India, Southeast Asia and the Far East, 2d edit., 1966; The Soviet Union: An Introduction, 1967; The Russo-Chinese War, 1967; Japanese Recognition of the USSR: Soviet-Japanese Relations, 1921-30, 1970; Faces of Japan: A Photographic Study, 1968; April in Russia: A Photographic Study, 1970; The Strange Neutrality: Soviet Japanese Relations during The Second World War, 1972; The Damned Inheritance: The Soviet Union and the Manchurian Crises, 1924-35, 1974; Balance of Intrigue: International Rivalry in Korea and Manchuria 1884-1899, 2 vols., 1979; co-author: The Meaning of Yalta: Big Three Diplomacy and the New Balance of Power, 1966. Editor: Revelations of a Russian Diplomat: The Memoirs of Dmitrii I. Abrikossow, 1964; Russia's Eastward Expansion, 1964; Korea and Manchuria between Russia and Japan, 1895-1904: The Observations of Sir Ernest Satow, 1968; The d'Anethan Dispatches from Japan 1894-1910: The Observations of Baron Albert d'Anethan, 1967; Trading under Sail off Japan 1860-1899: The Recollections of Captain John Baxter Will, Sailing Master and Pilot, 1968; (handbook) Japanese Diplomatic and Consular Officials in Russia, 1968; (handbook) Russian Diplomatic and Consular Officials in East Asia, 1968; War and Revolution: Excerpts from the Letters and Diaries of the Countess Olga Poutiatine, 1971; Japanese Foreign Policy on the Eve of the Pacific War: A Soviet View by Leonid N. Kutakov, 1972; Balance of Intrigue: International Rivalry in Korea and Manchuria, 1884-1889, 1980. Home: 1001 Lasswade Dr Tallahassee FL 32312 Died Jan. 5, 1979.

LENSKI, GERHARD EMMANUEL, sociologist; b. Washington, Aug. 13, 1924; s. Gerhard Emmanuel and Christine Katharine (Umhau) L.; B.A., Yale U., 1947, Ph.D., 1950; m. Jean Virginia Cappelmann, Aug. 14, 1948; children—Jean, Robert, Katherine, Richard. Instr. to asso. prof. U. Mich., 1950-63; prof. sociology U. N.C., Chapel Hill, 1963-73, alumni distinguished prof., 1973—, chmn. dept. sociology, 1969-72. Served with USAAF, 1943-45. Guggenheim fellow, 1972-73. Fellow Am. Acad. Arts and Scis.; mem. Am. Sociol. Assn. (v.p. 1970-71), So. Sociol. Soc. (pres. 1977-78). Author: The Religious Factor, 1961; Power and Privilege, 1966; (with Jean Lenski) Human Societies, 1970. Home: 404 Westwood Dr Chapel Hill NC 27514

LENT, BERKELEY, justice; b. Los Angeles, Sept. 22, 1921; s. Oscar Paul and Patricia Lucile (Berkeley) L.; student Reed Coll., 1941, 46-47, Occidental Coll., Los Angeles, 1944-45; J.D., Willamette U., 1950; m. Joan Kay Burnett, Dec. 27, 1968; children—Patricia Brandt, Deirdre Lutjen, Eric, Terry. Asso. editor Bancroft-Whitney Law Pub. Co., San Francisco, 1950; admitted to Oreg. bar, 1950; with Office Gen. Counsel, Bonneville Power Adminstrn., Portland, Oreg., 1950-51, 52-53; individual practice law, Coos Bay, Oreg., 1951-52; asso. firm Peterson & Pozzi, Portland, 1952-53; partner firm Lent, York, Paulson & Bullock and predecessor firms, Portland, 1953-70; individual practice law, Portland, 1970-71; judge Circuit Ct. Multnomah County, 1971-77; asso. justice Oreg. Supreme Ct., Salem, 1977—. Mem. Oreg. Ho. of Reps., 1957-65, minority whip, 1965; mem. Oreg. Senate, 1967-71, majority leader, 1971. Served with USNR, 1942-45. Mem. VFW. Democrat. Club: Elks. Home: 3644 Mulvehill Ct N Salem OR 97303 Office: Oreg Supreme Ct Salem OR 97310

LENT, DONALD RAYMOND, artist; b. Marblehead, Mass., Dec. 28, 1933; s. Jesse Goodwin and Bessie May (Osborne) L.; B.A., U. Calif. at Santa Barbara, 1959; B.F.A. (Woodrow Wilson Nat. fellow), Yale U., 1960, M.F.A., 1963; m. Lynda Sue Litchfield, Aug. 19, 1973; children—Jesse Litchfield, Charlotte Fuller; children by previous marriage—Michael Paul, Jennifer Anne. Asso. prof. art U. Calif. at Santa Barbara, 1961-70; Dana prof. art, chmn. art dept. Bates Coll., Lewiston, Me., 1970—. Exhibited one-man shows, group shows. Served with U.S. Army, 1952-55. Artist: The Heat Lightning (book of etchings), 1967. Home: 10 Ware St Lewiston ME 04240

LENT, GEORGE EIDT, ret. economist; b. Glens Falls, N.Y., July 8, 1912; s. George Washington and Alice Louise (Myers) L.; B.S. in Bus. Administrn., Rensselaer Poly. Inst., 1934, M.B.A., 1935; Ph.D., Columbia U., 1947; m. Charlotte C. Kuhl, July 12, 1941; children—Peter de Ryck, Thomas Henry. Accountant, Arthur Andersen & Co., C.P.A.'s, N.Y.C., 1935-36; instr. econs. Rennsselear Poly. Inst., 1936-37; accountant Scovell, Wellington & Co., C.P.A.'s, N.Y.C., 1937-39; asst. prof. econs. U. Vt., 1941-42; economist Treasury Dept., 1942-43, Army Dept., 1943-44; asso. prof. econs. U. N.C., 1946-49; research asso. Nat. Bur. Econ. Research, 1949-50; asst. dir. research Treasury Dept., 1950-56; economist Def. Dept., 1957; prof. bus. econs. Amos Tuck Sch., Dartmouth, 1957-62; chief Fiscal Mission to Ecuador, OAS, 1962-63; chief bus. taxation staff Treasury Dept., 1963-64; asst. dir. fiscal affairs dept. IMF, Washington, 1964-74, sr. adviser, 1974-77, cons., 1977—; chief Fiscal Mission to Uruguay, OAS, 1963; vis. prof. finance Mass. Inst. Tech., 1960; Served to 1st lt. USAAF, 1944-46. Mem. Am. Econ. Assn., Nat. Tax Assn., Holland Soc. N.Y., Am. Numis. Soc., Internat. Numis. Soc. Conglist. Author: The Impact of the Undistributed Profits Tax, 1948; The Ownership of Tax Exempt Securities, 1955; also articles, reports. Home: 9522 Linden Ave Bethesda MD 20014

LENT, NORMAN FREDERICK, JR., congressman; b. Oceanside, N.Y., Mar. 23, 1931; s. Norman Frederick and Ellen (Bain) L.; B.A., Hofstra U., 1952; LL.B., Cornell U., 1957; children—Norman Frederick 3d, Barbara Anne, Thomas Benjamin. Admitted to N.Y. bar, 1957, Fla. bar, 1976; asso. police judge, East Rockaway, N.Y., 1958-60; confidential law sec. to N.Y. State Supreme Ct., 1960-62; mem. N.Y. State Senate, 1963-70, chmn. joint legislative com. public health, 1966-70; mem. 92d-96th Congresses from 4th Dist. N.Y. Republican exec. leader, East Rockaway, 1968-70. Trustee Franklin Gen. Hosp., Oceanside. Served with USNR, 1952-54. Recipient George Estabrook Disting. Service award Hofstra U., 1967, Israeli Prime Minister's medal, 1977. Mem. Am., Nassau County bar assns. Home: 48 Plymouth Rd East Rockaway NY 11518 Office: US Ho of Reps Washington DC 20515

LENTHALL, FRANKLYN, theatre mus. curator; b. Nanticoke, Pa., July 14, 1919; s. Samuel Franklyn and Lena (Fraunfelter) L.; student Cornell U., 1942-44, Am. Acad. Dramatic Arts, 1946. Appeared in profl. theatre, 1937-51; featured in movies, including Carnegie Hall, Portrait of Jenny, West Point Story, Naked City; producer, dir. with Lenthall Players, 1951-58; producer, owner, dir. Boothbay (Maine) Playhouse and Theatre Mus., 1957-74; curator Boothbay Theatre Mus. Mem. faculty Am. Acad. Dramatic Arts, 1949-54, Am. Theatre Wing, 1958-59. Mem. exec. bd. Theatre Library Assn., Lincoln Center, N.Y.C., 1966-70; mem. Maine Commn. on Arts and Humanities, 1967—; theatre cons., 1968—; lectr. on theatre; dir. off-Broadway prodn. Hello and Goodby (Athol Fugard), N.Y.C., 1977; theatre historian. Served with CIC, AUS, 1942-44. Mem. Drama League N.Y. (adv. bd. 1959—), Lincoln County Cultural and Hist. Assn. (trustee 1973-77), Boothbay C. of C. (dir. 1963-70). Methodist (lay Preacher). Contbr. articles on theatre to various publs; contbg. author: Autographs and Manuscripts: A Collector's Manuel, 1978. Address: Boothbay Theatre Museum Corey Ln Boothbay ME 04537. *Only in recent years have I learned to really appreciate and understand William Blake's lines from his poem ETERNITY: "He who binds to himself a joy Does the winged life destroy; But he who kisses the joy as it flies Lives in eternity's sunrise." Every day of my life I am more fully aware of the importance of the ARTS AND THE HUMANITIES in the lives of all of us. . .in the life of this great country. For too long they have been neglected.*

LENTS, JOHN ELDON, steel and shipbuilding co. exec.; b. Peck, Idaho, July 1, 1917; s. John Henry and Florence May (Parks) L.; student Kinman Bus. U., 1936-37; m. Marjorie June Hibbard, May 12, 1946; children—Michael, Sally. Clk. to office mgr. Consol. Builders, Inc., Grand Coulee, Wash., 1938-41; adminstrv. mgr. Oreg. Shipbuilding Co., Kaiser Co., Mill City, Oreg., 1942-52; adminstrv. mgr. Kaiser Engrs., Hanford, Wash., 1952-54, adminstrv. mgr., Cooma, NSW-Australia, 1954-57, staff analyst, Oakland, Calif., 1958; controller, asst. sec., asst. treas. Nat. Steel & Shipbuilding Co., San Diego, 1959-74, v.p., 1974—. Mem. exec. com. San Diego County Efficiency Study, 1969-70; mem. budget panel United Community Services, 1966-70. Mason, Elk. Home: 6960 Caminito Curva San Diego CA 92119 Office: 28th and Harbor Dr San Diego CA 92112

LENTZ, HAROLD HERBERT, coll. pres.; b. Nevada, Iowa, June 11, 1910; s. Rev. John Nelson and Ida Vera (Bowes) L.; A.B., Wittenberg Coll., 1932, LL.D., 1952; B.D., Hamma Div. Sch., 1935; A.M., Oberlin Coll., 1939; Ph.D., Yale, 1943; L.H.D. (hon.), Carroll Coll., 1975; m. Mary Eleanor Selby, June 15, 1935; children—Julia Edythe, Thomas William. Pastor Trinity Luth. Ch., Ashland, Ohio, 1935-52; mem. faculty Carthage Coll., Kenosha, Wis., 1952—, pres., 1952-76, pres. emeritus, 1976—; lectr. Internat. Luther Acad., Germany. Mem. bd. social missions United Luth. Ch. Am., 1945-52, pres., 1950-52; mem. div. student service Nat. Luth. Council, 1952-64; chmn. commn. evangelism Luth. Ch. Am., 1965-69; mem. U.S. adv. com. Luth. World Fedn., 1967—. Bd. dirs. Wittenberg Coll., 1944-51, Johnson Found., Fritsch Charitable Found. Mem. Wis. C. of C. (dir. 1965-69), Coll. Conf. Ill.-Wis. (pres. 1965-74), Tau Kappa Alpha, Pi Delta Epsilon, Pi Kappa Alpha (nat. chaplain 1966-69), Blue Key. Kiwanian. Clubs: University, Lake Shore (Chgo.); Racine Country. Author: Centennial History of Wittenberg College, 1945; Reformation Crossroads, 1958; The Miracle of Carthage, 1975. Home: 800 Springwood Dr Port Richey FL 33568 Office: Carthage Coll Kenosha WI 53140. *There are four factors that have contributed strongly to my progress in life. First is the principle of honesty and truthfulness so that people have learned I can be trusted. Second, it was my ideal to be of service to others and to live a worthwhile life, rather than one devoted to self-service. The third factor was the conviction reached early in life that an ability to write and speak well is essential to success in life. Finally, the value of getting as much education as possible was grasped in my early years, leading to the attainment to an earned doctorate. Added to all of these is the thought that common sense is a vital necessity to any achievement in life.*

LENTZ, JAMES EUGENE, banker; b. Indpls., Jan. 4, 1918; s. Frank E. and Eurene (Thomson) L.; student Purdue U., 1936-37, Ind. U. extension at Indpls., 1937-40; m. Carrie Beck, Nov. 20, 1947; children—William D., J. Richard. With Ind. Nat. Bank, Indpls., 1937—, sr. v.p. charge nat. accounts div. 1964-73 (on leave 1973-76), 77—; econ. devel. cons. State of Ind., 1973-76. Pres. Indpls. Econ. Devel. Commn.; bd. dirs. Big Bros. Greater Indpls., 1970—, pres., 1977, chmn. long range planning and budget com.; treas. First Meridian Heights Presbyn. Ch., 1968—, pres. Meml. Endowment Fund, mem. session, chmn. property and fin. com.; pres. Indpls. Economic Devel. Commn.; mem. Ind. Area Devel. Council; spl. asst. to lt. gov. Ind. for economic devel.; bd. dirs. Ind. Community Devel. Soc.; mem. Indpls. Citizens' Advisory Com. Air Quality; mem. Overall Economic Devel. Plan Com.; mem. planning and zoning legis. advisory com. Indpls. Met. Devel. Dept., mem. subcom. Capital Formation Group Joint Economic Devel. Task Force. Served with F.A., AUS, 1942-45; PTO. Decorated Bronze Star medal. Clubs: Columbia, Highland Golf and Country (Indpls.). Home: 7432 N Audubon Rd Indianapolis IN 46250 Office: 1 Indiana Sq Indianapolis IN 46266

LENTZ, LESLIE LAWRENCE, investment analyst; b. San Antonio, Aug. 5, 1901; s. Joseph G. and Rose (Finck) L.; student U. Va., 1919-21; LL.B., U. Tex., 1925; m. Cornelia Colby Cave, Dec. 29, 1930; children—Cornelia Colby (Mrs. Ernest L. Brown III), Leslie Lawrence. Admitted to Tex. bar, 1925; atty. Central Power & Light Co., San Antonio and Corpus Christi, Tex., 1926-34; with Merrill Lynch Pierce Fenner & Smith and predecessor cos., 1935-41; formed Lentz, Shaughnessy & Farquhar, 1941; sr. mng. partner Lentz, Newton & Co. (now Eppler, Guerin & Turner), San Antonio, 1947-71, now cons. Past mem. Pres.'s Com. for Trinity U., 1953. Served from capt. to maj. AUS, 1942-46. Mem. Order of Alamo, Beta Theta Pi, Phi Delta Phi. Roman Catholic. Clubs: San Antonio Country, Argyle (San Antonio). Home: 151 Park Hill Dr San Antonio TX 78212 Office: 214 NE Loop 410 PO Box 32768 San Antonio TX 78284. *Developed the philosophy many years ago always to do the right thing for its own sake; not because of possible recognition or rewards, nor fear of punishment. That honesty per se is insufficient - true moral integrity is the essential attribute.*

LENTZ, ROBERT HENRY, lawyer; b. Lake Huntington, N.Y., Dec. 9, 1924; s. Henry Bernard and Mary (Mahony) L.; student U. Ky., 1943; B.E.E. magna cum laude, Poly. Inst. Bklyn., 1951; J.D., Loyola U. at Los Angeles, 1956; children—Joanne, Kevin, Robert. Admitted to Calif. bar, 1956; sr. v.p., gen. counsel Litton Industries, Inc., Beverly Hills, Calif., 1954—; past dir. Redcor Corp.; past chmn. bd. Topaz Industries. Served with AUS, 1943-46. Mem. State Bar Calif. (panelist for continuing edn. of bar on corp. law 1973-75, mem. corp. law com. of corp. and bus. law sect. 1978—), Am. Arbitration Assn. (Los Angeles adv. council 1968—), Los Angeles County (exec. com. corp. law sect. 1971), Am. bar assns., Los Angeles Patent Law Assn., Licensing Execs. Soc., Eta Kappa Nu, Tau Beta Pi. Home: 10450 Wilshire Blvd Los Angeles CA 90024 Office: 360 N Crescent Dr Beverly Hills CA 90210

LENZ, HENRY PAUL, ins. co. exec.; b. N.Y.C., Nov. 24, 1925; s. Ernest and Margaret (Schick) L.; A.B., U. N.C., 1946; M.B.A., Coll. Ins., 1974; m. Norma M. Kull, Jan. 25, 1958; children—Susan, Scott, Theresa. Underwriter, U.S. Casualty Co., N.Y.C., 1948-55; underwriting mgr. Mass. Bonding & Ins. Co., N.Y.C., 1955-60; with Home Ins. Co., N.Y.C., 1960—, sr. v.p., 1972-75, exec. v.p., 1975—; pres., dir. Home Indemnity Co., Home Ins. Co. Ind., Home Ins. Co. Ill., City Ins. Co., Home Group Risk Mgmt.; chmn. bd. Seaboard Surety Co., Scott Wetzel Services Inc.; chmn., pres. City Ins. Co. (U.K.) Ltd., Home Reins. Co.; dir. Thico Plan, Inc., Thico Fin., Inc., Tower Hill Ins. Co. Served with USNR, 1944-47, 52-53. Decorated Army Commendation medal. Mem. Soc. C.P.C.U.'s, Phi Beta Kappa, Sigma Nu. Home: 21 Audubon Ct Short Hills NJ 07078 Office: 59 Maiden Ln New York NY 10038

LENZ, KAY, actress; b. Los Angeles, Mar. 4, 1953; d. Ted and Kay Lenz; student public schs., Van Nuys, Calif.; m. David Cassidy, Apr. 3, 1977. Appeared in television films A Summer Without Boys, 1973, Unwed Father, 1974, The Underground Man, 1974, The FBI Story: Alvan Karpus, Public Enemy Number One, 1974, Journey from Darkness, 1975; appeared on television shows Love Story, Gunsmoke, Medical Center, Kodiak, McCloud, Nakia, Cannon, Petrocelli, Rich Man, Poor Man, Jigsaw John; appeared in motion pictures Breezy, 1973, White Line Fever, 1975, The Great Scout and Cathouse Thursday, 1976, Moving Violation, 1976. Recipient Golden Apple nomination, 1973, Hollywood Fgn. Press nomination, 1973, Emmy award, 1974-75, Emmy nomination, 1975-76. Address: care Compass Mgmt Inc 211 S Beverly Dr Beverly Hills CA 90212

LENZINI, ARTHUR LEE, dentist; b. Denver, June 16, 1927; s. Joseph Peter and Josephine (Herzog) L.; student Centralia Jr. Coll., 1946-47, So. Ill. U., 1947-48; D.D.S., St. Louis U., 1952; m. Clementine Marco, June 21, 1948; children—Marc Joseph, Paul Arthur, John Gerard, Matthew Clement, Jane Elizabeth. Practice dentistry, Herrin, Ill., 1952—; mem. adv. bd. Dental Hygiene Sch., So. Ill. U.; mem. adv. bd. HEW; chmn. staff dental sect. Herrin Hosp.; treas. RABCO, Inc. Pres. 24th Congl. Dist. Conservative Caucus; mem. Belleville Cath. Diocesan Resource Bd., 1976; bd. mem. St. Mary's Cath. Sch., 1968-71. Served with U.S. Army, 1956-57. Mem. So. Ill. Dental Soc. (pres. 1962-63), Ill. Dental Soc. (councilman 1968-71), ADA (council on nat. bds.), Herrin C. of C. (dir.), Internat. Coll. Dentists, Pierre Fauchard Acad., Little Egypt Dental Research

Group. Clubs: Herrin Lions (past pres., sec., dir.), Elks, K.C. Home: Rural Route 1 Box 735 Herrin IL 62948 Office: 121 N 13th St Herrin IL 62948

LEON, BRUNO, architect, educator; b. Van Houten, N.Mex., Feb. 18, 1924; s. Giovanni and Rose (Cunico) L.; student Wayne State U., 1942, U. Detroit, 1945-48; B.Arch., N.C. State Coll., 1953; m. Louise Dal-Bo, Sept. 4, 1948; children—Mark Jon, John Anthony, Lisa Rose. Head design staff Fuller Research Found., Raleigh, N.C., 1954-55; archtl. designer I.M. Pei & Assos., N.Y.C. 1955-56; instr. Mass. Inst. Tech., 1956-59; designer Catalano & Belluschi, architects, Cambridge, Mass., 1958-59; asst. prof. U. Ill. at Urbana, 1959-61; dean Sch. Architecture, U. Detroit, 1961—; pvt. practice architecture, 1956—; pres. Bruno Leon Assos., Inc.; v.p. Trigon Enterprises Ltd., Mesilla, N.Mex. Served with USAAF, 1943-45. Registered architect, Mich., N.C., Mass., N.Y., N.Mex. Fellow AIA (dir. Detroit 1963-64); mem. Mich. Soc. Architects, Assn. Collegiate Schs. Architecture. Address: 9260 Anderson Rd Grosse Ile MI 48138. *I believe the integral quality of the human spirit to be the ability to dream rather than to rationalize.*

LEON, EDWARD J., lawyer; b. Chgo., Nov. 4, 1899; s. Murad and Susan (Tann) L.; student Columbia, 1920; LL.B., N.Y.U., 1923; m. Helen Hall, Sept. 5, 1970; 1 son, Richard Hall. Admitted to Conn. bar, 1923, N.Y. bar, 1925, D.C. bar, 1943, U.S. Supreme Ct., 1943; mem. firm. Leon, Weill and Mahony, and predecessors, N.Y.C., 1945—. Prin. officer Bd. Economic Warfare, Washington, 1942-43. Pres., dir. Children's Blood Found.; bd. dirs. Talisman Found.; trustee Pop Warner Football Scholars. Mem. Am. Soc. Internat. Law, Am. Judicature Soc., Am. Bar Assn., New York County lawyers Assn. Clubs: New York Athletic; Winged Foot Golf. Home: 122 E 76th St New York NY 10021 Office: 405 Lexington Ave New York NY 10016

LEON, LEONARD, diversified industry corp. exec.; b. Chgo., Oct. 13, 1923; s. Harry and Rachel Leon; student Tulane U., 1939-41; B.S., Tex. A&M U., 1947; postgrad. Harvard U. Advanced Mgmt. Program, 1972; m. Dora Rose Bernstein, July 31, 1943; children—Barbara, Roy, Jack. With Halliburton Co., 1948—, exec. v.p. services div., Duncan, Okla., 1969—, also dir. Served to 1st lt. USAAF, 1943-46. Decorated Air medal with 4 oak leaf clusters; registered profl. engr., Tex., Okla. Mem. Nat. Soc. Profl. Engrs., Okla. Soc. Profl. Engrs. (Outstanding Engr. in Mgmt. award 1975), Soc. Petroleum Engrs., Am. Petroleum Inst., Mid-Continent Oil and Gas Assn. Clubs: Houston, Elks. Home: 904 Hillcrest Dr Duncan OK 73533 Office: Halliburton Co 1013 Bois D'Arc Duncan OK 73533

LEON, TANIA JUSTINA, composer, music dir., pianist; b. Havana, Cuba, May 14, 1944; d. Oscar and Dora (Ferran) Leon; came to U.S., 1967; B.A. in Piano and Theory, Peyrellade Conservatory Music, Havana, 1963; M.A. in Music Edn., Nat. Conservatory Music, Havana, 1964; B.A. in Acctg., U. Havana, 1965; B.S. in Composition, N.Y. U., 1971, M.S., 1973, postgrad., 1973—. Piano soloist, Cuba, 1964-67; music dir. TV, Havana, 1965-66; piano soloist N.Y. Coll. of Music Orch., N.Y.C., 1967, N.Y. U. Orch., N.Y.C., 1969, Buffalo Symphony Orch., 1973; staff pianist, condr. Dance Theatre of Harlem, N.Y.C., 1968—, music dir., 1970-78, founder Dance Theatre of Harlem Orch., 1975, founder concert series Meet the Performer, 1977, music dir. Dance in Am. Spl. Sta. WNET-TV; guest condr. Genova (Italy) Symphony Orch., 1972, Juilliard Orch., Spoletto Festival, 1971, Symphony New World, 1974, Royal Ballet Orch., 1974, 76, BBC Orch., 1974, 76, Halle Orch., 1974, Buffalo Philharmonic Orch., 1975, Concert Orch. of L.I., 1979, Sadler's Well's Orch., 1979, London Universal Symphony, 1979, Composer's Forum, 1979; royal command performer London Palladium, 1974, 76, Concert Orch. L.I., 1976; concert pianist Sta WNYC-FM, 1968-70; conductor coordinator Music by Black Composers Series, Bklyn. Philharmonia, 1978-79; mus. dir. The Whiz, 1977, 78, Death, Destruction and Detroit; apptd. music dir. Intar Theatre, N.Y.C.; condr., mus. dir. Godspell, N.Y. U., 1978, Carmencita, 1978, The Whiz, 1978; composer: Haiku (ballet music), 1974; Tones (piano concerto), 1970; Sailor's Boat (score for musical), 1974; Dougla (African ballet), 1974; La Ramera de la Cueva (score for musical), 1974; Namiac Poems (voice, chorus and orch.), 1975; Spiritual Suite (2 sopranos, chorus and mixed ensemble with narrator), 1976; Concerto Criollo (concerto for piano, 8 timpanies and orch.), 1976; Pet's Suite (for flute and piano); I Got Ovah (for soprano, piano and percussion, based on poems by Carolyn M. Rodgers); panelist N.Y. State Council on the Arts, Nat. Endowment for the Arts. Recipient Young Composers prize Nat. Council Arts, Havana, 1966; Alvin Johnson award Am. Council Emigres in the Profession, 1971; Cintas award in composition, 1974-75, 78-79 Nat. Endowment for Arts fellow, 1975; also commd. for compositions. Mem. ASCAP (Composers award 1977-79), French Soc. Composers, Am. Fedn. Musicians, Center New Music, Am. Music Center, Internat. Artists Alliance, Am. Women Composers. Home: 35-20 Leverick St Apt B430 New York NY 11372 Office: Dance Theatre Harlem 466 W 152d St New York NY 10031

LEONARD, ALLAN LANGDON, JR., realtor; b. Los Angeles, May 26, 1915; s. Allan Langdon and Olive (Trask) L.; B.S., The Citadel, 1936; postgrad. George Washington U., 1963, 64; grad. Advanced Mgmt. Program, Harvard, 1964; m. Susan Clemson, Nov. 11, 1938; children—Allan Langdon III, Janet Leonard Atkins, Virginia Leonard Kishbauch. Commd. 2d lt. U.S. Army, 1940, advanced through grades to brig. gen., 1966; mil attache, Germany, 1953-56; U.S. del. SEATO, 1961; comdg. gen. U.S. Army Element, Alaskan Command, 1966-68; retired, 1970; v.p. Trask-Pacific Corp., Los Angeles, 1959—; sec. Clemson Devel. Corp., Los Angeles, 1971—. Volunteer, A.R.C., 1969—. Decorated D.S.M., Silver Star, Legion of Merit, Bronze Star (2). Mem. SR, Assn. U.S. Army, Episcopalian. Clubs: Army-Navy Country (Washington); Rancho Santa Fe Tennis. Home: 1620 San Pablo Dr Lake San Marcos CA 92069 Office: 11661 San Vicente Blvd Los Angeles CA 90049

LEONARD, BOB, profl. basketball club exec.; b. July 17, 1932; student Ind. U.; m. Nancy Leonard. Profl. basketball player Mpls. Lakers (later Los Angeles Lakers), 1957-61; profl. basketball player Chgo. Zyphers (later Balt. Zephyrs), 1961-62, player-coach, 1962-63, head coach, 1963-64; coach Ind. Pacers, Indpls., 1968-76, gen. mgr., 1976—. Named Coach of Year Am. Basketball Assn., 1970. Office: Indiana Pacers Market Sq Center Bldg 151 N Delaware St Indianapolis IN 46204

LEONARD, DAVID HENRY, TV broadcasting exec.; b. Missoula, Mont., Mar. 20, 1933; s. Robert Walter and Helen Louise (Henderson) L.; student Reed Coll., 1951; B.S., Iowa State U., 1956; M.A., Mich. State U., 1963; m. Mary Elizabeth Peterson, Dec. 28, 1957; children—Julie Ann, Peter David, Christopher Jay. Instr. telecommunicative arts Iowa State U., Ames, 1959-60; network program mgr. Oreg. Ednl. Broadcasting, Portland, 1960-65; exec. dir. Ednl. TV Stas. Program Service, Bloomington, Ind., 1965-69; gen. mgr. Pa. Pub. TV Network, Hershey, 1969-79. Served with U.S. Army, 1956-58. Mem. Nat. Assn. Ednl. Broadcasters. Democrat. Unitarian. Home: 1324 E Chocolate Ave Hershey PA 17033

LEONARD, DONALD LEE, clergyman, ch. ofcl.; b. New Salem, N.D., Sept. 3, 1915; s. John Calvin and Goldie (Lee) L.; A.B., Washington U., 1937; B.D., McCormick Theol. Sem., 1940, M.Div., 1970; M.A., Tex. Christian U., 1941; Ph.D., Yale, 1953; m. Ruth Pendleton, July 17, 1940; children—Donald Lee, Carolyn Jean. Ordained to ministry Presbyn. Ch. U.S.A., 1940; asso. minister First Congl. Ch., West Haven, Conn., 1941-43, Chevy Chase Presbyn. Ch., Washington, 1943-47, First Presbyn. Ch., Portland, Oreg., 1947-53; asso. editor for curriculum materials Bd. Christian Edn., United Presbyn. Ch. U.S.A., 1953-55, exec. editor, 1955-73; coordinator planning, studies and guidelines Vocation Agy., U.P. Ch., 1973-76, coordinator personnel planning and adminstrn., 1976—, also compensation coordinator Gen. Assembly Agys., 1973—. Mem. program bd., dept. ednl. devel. Nat. Council Chs.; pres. bd. mgrs. Presbyn. Distbn. Service, 1968-72; treas. Instroteach Inc. Mem. Nat. Ch. and Synagogue Library Assn. (pres.), Assn. Supervision and Curriculum Devel., Am. Acad. Religion, Adminstrv. Mgmt. Soc., Religious (dir.), Adult edn. assns., Am. Ednl. Research Assn., Soc. Ednl. Communications and Tech., Nat. Soc. Programmed Instrn., Am. Assn. Sch. Adminstrs., Nat. Assn. Ch. Bus. Adminstrs., Sigma Phi Epsilon, Delta Sigma Rho. Author: Toward a More Efficient Church, sect. VIII, 1941; Fundamentalistic Christian Education, 1953. Editor: The Christian Educator, 1957-62; mem. editorial bd. Religious Edn., 1958-79. Home: 31 Locust Rd Morton PA 19070 Office: 420 Interchurch Center 475 Riverside Dr New York NY 10027

LEONARD, EASON HARRIS, architect; b. El Reno, Okla., June 5, 1920; s. Carl Van Every and Zadeth Amy (Dutcher) L.; B.Arch., Okla. State U., 1943; m. Jeanne A. Mason, Nov. 1945 (dec. Sept. 1965); children—Bruce, Craig; m. 2d, Jeanne A. Burton, June 21, 1970. Asso., William Lescaze, Architect, N.Y.C., 1947-49, Chauncey W. Riley, Architect, N.Y.C., 1949, 1953; asso. I.M. Pei, N.Y.C., 1953-55, mng. partner, 1955—. Mem. Fifth Ave. Assn., 1970—. Served with C.E., U.S. Army, 1943-46. Fellow AIA; mem. Archtl. Registration Council U.K., Royal Inst. Brit. Architects (corporate mem.), Archtl. League, N.Y. Bldg. Congress, Nat. Council Archtl. Registration Bds., Singapore Register of Architects. Republican. Methodist. Clubs: Met., Sleepy Hollow Country. Major works include: Nat. Airlines Terminal at John F. Kennedy Airport; Dallas Municipal Adminstrn. Center; Mile High Center, Denver. Home: 975 Park Ave Apt 10-C New York NY 10028 Office: 600 Madison Ave 9th Floor New York NY 10022

LEONARD, EUGENE ALBERT, banker; b. St. Louis, Aug. 27, 1935; s. Albert Hiram and Mary (Crowson) L.; B.S., U. Mo., 1957, M.S., 1958, Ph.D., 1962; postgrad. Stonier Grad. Sch. Banking, Rutgers U., 1964-66; m. Mary Ann Sampson, Aug. 31, 1956; children—Charles, James, Susan. Instr. agrl. econs. U. Mo. at Columbia, 1959-60; with Fed. Res. Bank St. Louis, 1961-77, v.p., mgr., Memphis br., 1967-70, sr. v.p., 1970-71, 1st v.p., 1971-77; on loan to bd. govs. FRS as asst. sec., Washington, 1970-71; sr. v.p. Merc. Bancorp. Inc., St. Louis, 1977—; instr. econs. Central States Sch. Banking, 1962-69, Ill. Bankers Sch., 1962-74, Sch. Banking South, 1970—; instr. econs. Stonier Grad. Sch. Banking, 1975—, bd. regents, 1978—; adj. asso. prof. econs. Memphis State U., 1969-70. Bd. dirs. Logos Sch., St. Louis, 1977—. Mem. Gamma Sigma Delta, Kappa Sigma. Unitarian. Home: 30 Portland Pl Saint Louis MO 63108 Office: Mercantile Tower Saint Louis MO 63166

LEONARD, GEORGE ADAMS, lawyer, supermarket exec.; b. Clinton, Iowa, June 16, 1924; s. George Tod and Lola (Follett) L.; student Western Res. U., 1942-43; A.B., U. Mich., 1948, J.D., 1951; m. Ella Viola Converse, Nov. 5, 1948; children—Carolyn, George, Craig, Julie. Admitted to Mich. bar, 1951, Ohio bar, 1956; asso. firm Slyfield, Hartman, Reitz & Tait, Detroit, 1951-56; asst. sec. Kroger Co., Cin., 1958-66, gen. counsel, 1966—, v.p., sec., 1970—; dir. Gleaner Lite Ins. Soc., Am. Druggists Ins. Co. Chmn., North Star dist. Boy Scouts Am., Cin., 1966. Bd. dirs., mem. exec. com. Cin. chpt. ARC. Served with USAAF, 1942-45; ETO. Decorated D.F.C., Air medal with four oak leaf clusters. Mem. Am., Ohio, Cin. bar assns., State Bar Mich. Home: 10307 Crestwind Circle Cincinnati OH 45242 Office: 1014 Vine St Cincinnati OH 45201

LEONARD, GEORGE EDMUND, savs. and loan assn. exec.; b. Brookline, Mass., Sept. 1, 1912; s. George E. Leonard and Theresa (Carroll) L.; A.B., Columbia, 1935; m. Evelyn S. Fairbank, May 18, 1951; children—George E., Marsha Ann; 1 stepson, Leigh C. Fairbank III. With First Fed. Savs. of Phoenix, 1936-52, 60—, pres., 1961-63, pres., chmn. bd., 1963-73, chmn. bd., chief exec. officer, 1973—, also dir.; pres. San Diego Fed. Savs., 1952-54; financial v.p. Coast Fed. Savs., Los Angeles, 1954-56, Great Western Savs., Los Angeles, 1957-60; dir. Fed. Home Loan Bank, San Francisco, 1964, 67-72, vice chmn., 1969-71; dir. MGIC Investment Corp., MGIC. Mem. fed. adv. council Fed. Home Loan Bank Bd., 1965—; adv. council on govt. sect. for savs. and loan assns. Treasury Dept. Mem. Phoenix Com. of Forty; pres. Phoenix United Fund, 1975, 76; chmn. bd. dirs. Barrows Neurol. Inst., 1975; mem. exec. com., treas. Ariz. Heart Inst. Found., Jr. Achievement Met. Phoenix, 1964-66, Goodwill Industries Phoenix, 1966-69; chmn. dean's adv. council Coll. Bus. Adminstrn., Ariz. State U., 1975; pres. bd. trustees Camelback Mental Health Found. Served to lt. USNR, 1942-46. Mem. U.S., Ariz. (pres. 1964) savs. and loans leagues, Nat. League Insured Savs. Assns. (bd. govs. 1946-52, pres. 1964-65), U.S. League Insured Savs. (dir., exec. com.), Newcomen Soc., Navy League, Beta Theta Pi, Beta Gamma Sigma (hon.). Republican. Episcopalian. Clubs: Phoenix Country, Kiwanis (bd. dirs., pres.), Paradise Valley Country, Arizona (Phoenix). Home: 77 E Missouri St Apt 18 Phoenix AZ 85012 Office: PO Box 2263 Phoenix AZ 85002

LEONARD, HENRY SIGGINS, JR., educator; b. Needham, Mass., Oct. 12, 1930; s. Henry Siggins and Priscilla Lermond (Packard) L.; student Duke, 1948-49; B.S. with high honor, Mich. State U., 1952; A.M., Harvard U., 1953, Ph.D., 1958; m. Eva Maria Bendix, Sept. 4, 1954; 1 son, Henry Alan. Teaching fellow Harvard, 1954-56; asst. prof. math. Carnegie-Mellon U., 1958-64; asso. prof., 1964-68; prof. math. No. Ill. U., 1968—, asst. chmn. dept. math. scis., 1975-78; vis. asso. prof. math. U. Ill., 1967-68; vis. fellow dept. math. Yale, 1973-74. George C. Shattuck fellow and William Caspar Graustein Meml. fellow Harvard, 1953-54; prin. investigator NSF grants, 1960-70. Mem. Am. Math. Soc., Math. Assn. Am., Sigma Xi. Contbr. articles to profl. jours. Home: 121 Park Ave DeKalb IL 60115

LEONARD, HUGH (JOHN KEYES BYRNE), playwright; b. Dublin, Ireland, Nov. 9, 1926; student Presentation Coll. (Ireland), 1941-45; m. Paule Jacquet, 1955; 1 dau. Civil servant, Dublin, 1945-59; TV script editor, Manchester, Eng., 1961-63; free-lance writer, London, 1963-70; lit. editor Abbey Theatre, Dublin, 1976-77; author numerous plays, including: The Big Birthday, 1956, A Walk on the Water, 1960, Stephen D, 1962, The Saints Go Cycling In, 1965, The Au Pair Man, 1968, Da, 1973, Thieves, 1973, Irishmen, 1975, A Life, 1977; author numerous English TV plays, TV series and screenplays; author autobiography: The Bully and the Chap, 1979. Recipient Italia prize, 1967; Writer's Guild of Gt. Britain award, 1967; Tony award, 1978. Office: Killiney Heath Killiney County Dublin Ireland*

LEONARD, HUGH RANDOLPH, banker; b. Sutherland, Va., Mar. 26, 1922; s. Hugh and Annie Field (Sutherland) L.; B.A., Va. Poly. Inst., 1943; grad. Stonier Grad. Sch. Banking, Rutgers U., 1962; m. Jean Jennings Owen, Jan. 29, 1943; children—Hugh Randolph, Peggy Jean. With So. State Coop., 1946-48; with Nat. Cash Register Corp., 1948-50; with First Nat. Exchange Bank, Roanoke, Va., 1953—, sr. v.p., 1972-78, exec. officer-loans/trust 1978—, also chmn. sr. loan com., sec. exec. com.; past dir. Nat. Theatre Corp.; instr. Grad. Sch. Consumer Banking. Bd. dirs. Roanoke Symphony Soc., 1968-71; treas., bd. dirs. United Fund Roanoke Valley, 1965-68; trustee Grad. Sch. Consumer Banking, 1975-78. Served to capt. AUS, 1943-46, 51-52. Mem. Scabbard and Blade, Alpha Zeta. Home: 3116 Circle Dr SW Roanoke VA 24018 Office: 201 S Jefferson St Roanoke VA 24018

LEONARD, IRVING ALBERT, educator; b. New Haven, Dec. 1, 1896; s. Henry Austin and Lillian May (Phelps) L.; Ph.B., Yale. 1918; A.M., U. Cal., 1925, Ph.D., 1928; m. Dorothea Hope Taggart, June 5, 1921; children—David Phelps, Dorothea Irving. U.S. postal censor (Spanish), 1918; jr. exec. Pacific Comml. Co., N.Y.C., Manila Cebu and Iloilo, P.I., 1919-21; prof. U. Philippines, Los Baños, 1921-22; tchr. Spanish, Petaluma (Calif.) High Sch., 1922-23; successively grad. asst., instr., asst. prof. Spanish, U. Calif. at Berkeley, 1923-37; asst. dir. humanities Rockefeller Found., 1937-40; prof. history and Spanish, Brown U., 1940-42; prof. Spanish Am. lit. U. Mich., 1942-49, chmn. dept. Romance langs., 1945-51, prof. Spanish Am. lit. and history, 1949-62, Domingo Faustino Sarmiento U. prof. Spanish Am. history and lit., 1962-65, Henry Russell lectr., 1963; Fulbright prof. Oxford U., 1952. Am. del. Inter-Am. Conf. Coms. Intellectual Coop., Santiago, Chile, 1939; mem. com. on study teaching materials on inter Am. subjects Am. Council Edn., 1943; com. fellowships and grants Am. Council Learned Socs., 1944. Recipient Diploma de Honor, Academia Mexicana; Am. Council Learned Socs. traveling fellow., 1930-31; Guggenheim fellow, 1936. Fellow Hispanic Soc. Am.; mem. Am. Assn. Tchrs. Spanish, Research Club U. Mich. Author books including: Books of the Brave, 1949; Baroque Times in Old Mexico (Herbert E. Bolton Meml. award), 1959; Colonial Travelers in Latin America, 1972. Editor, translator books in field; asso editor: Handbook of Latin American Studies, 1935-65; Hispanic American Historical Review, 1941-47, 54—; Revista Hispánica Moderna, 1940—. Revista de Filologiá Hispanica, 1940—. Home: 18 Sycamore Knolls South Hadley MA 01075. *True success in all aspects of life is best achieved through recognizing that each and every person has potentialities best realized by stressing interdependence and cooperation rather than setting them at odds through competition.*

LEONARD, JAMES FULTON, diplomat; b. Osborne, Pa., May 30, 1920; s. James F. and Margaret (Trimble) L.; B.S. in Engring., Princeton U., 1942; postgrad. U. Paris, George Washington U., Harvard U., Columbia U.; m. Eleanor M. Hanson, Dec. 28, 1948; children—A.L. Thompson, Cynthia, Valerie, Diana, Carolyn, Pamela. Joined U.S. Fgn. Service, 1948; served in Damascus, Moscow, Paris, Taipei, Washington; asst. dir. ACDA, 1969-73; U.S. rep. Geneva Disarmament Conf., 1969-71; v.p. UN Assn./U.S.A., N.Y.C., 1973, pres., 1974-77; dep. permanent rep. of U.S. to UN, 1977-79; dep. spl. rep. to Middle East Peace Negotiations, 1979—. Served to capt., C.E., U.S. Army, 1942-46. Recipient Superior Service award Dept. State, 1967. Home: Arlington Towers Arlington VA Office: State Dept (SSN) Washington DC 20520

LEONARD, JAMES JOSEPH, physician, educator; b. Schenectady, June 17, 1924; s. James Joseph and Helena (Flood) L.; M.D., Georgetown U., 1950; m. Helen Louise Mitchell, Oct. 24, 1953; children—James Joseph, W. Jeffrey, Paul Mitchell, Kathleen Marie. Intern medicine Georgetown U. Hosp., 1950-51, jr. asst. resident, 1951-52, fellow cardiology, 1953-54; asst. resident medicine Boston City Hosp., 1952-53; resident pulmonary diseases D.C. Gen. Hosp., 1954-55, med. officer, 1955-56; instr. medicine Georgetown U. Med. Sch., 1955-56, Duke Med. Center, 1956-57; asst. prof. medicine, dir. div. cardiology Georgetown U. service D.C. Gen. Hosp., 1957-59; asst. prof. medicine U. Tex. Med. Br., Galveston, 1959-62; asso. prof. medicine Ohio State U. Med. Sch., 1962-63; dir. div. cardiology U. Pitts. Med. Sch., 1963-70, asso. prof. medicine, 1963-67, prof. medicine, 1967-77, acting chmn. dept., 1970, chmn. dept., 1971-77; prof., chmn. dept. medicine Uniformed Services U. of Health Scis., 1977—. Mem. So. Soc. Clin. Investigation, Central Soc. Clin. Research, Assn. Am. Physicians, Assn. Profs. Medicine, Assn. U. Cardiologists. Home: 3200 Farmington Dr Chevy Chase MD 20015

LEONARD, JERRIS, lawyer; b. Chgo., Jan. 17, 1931; s. Jerris G. and Jean Marie (Reville) L.; B.S., Marquette U., 1952, J.D., 1955; m. Mariellen C. Mathie, Aug. 22, 1953; children—Mary Alice, Jerris G., John E., Kathleen Ann, Francis X., Daniel J. Admitted to Wis. bar, 1955, D.C. bar, 1973; practice in Milw., 1955-69; mem. firm Michael, Best & Friedrich, 1964-69; asst. atty. gen. civil rights div. Dept. Justice, Washington, 1969-71, adminstr. Law Enforcement Assistance Adminstrn., 1971-73; partner Leonard Cohen & Gettings, Washington, 1973—. Mem. Wis. Assembly from Milwaukee County, 1957-61; mem. Wis. Senate, 1961-69, senate majority leader, 1967-69; pres. Wis. Agys. Bldg. Corp., 1963-69; chmn. Wis. Legislative Council, 1967-69; Republican candidate for U.S. Senate, 1968. Named 1 of 5 Outstanding Young Men, Wis. Jaycees, 1965. Mem. Am., Wis., Milw., D.C., Fed. bar assns., Am. Trial Lawyers Assn., Am. Judicature Soc., Nat. Lawyers Club, Alpha Sigma Nu. Home: 5109 Manning Pl NW Washington DC 20016 Office: 1700 Pennsylvania Ave NW Washington DC 20006

LEONARD, JOANNE, photographer, educator; b. Los Angeles, 1940; B.A., U. Calif. at Berkeley, 1962; postgrad. San Francisco State Coll., 1963-64. One-person shows: M.H. De Young Mus., San Francisco, 1968, Hopkins Center, Dartmouth, 1968, Seligman Gallery, Seattle, 1969, Wall St. Gallery, Spokane, Wash., 1973, San Francisco Art Inst., 1974, Bristol (Eng.) Poly. Art Gallery, 1975, Davis Art Gallery at Stephens Coll., 1977; group shows include: Focus Gallery, San Francisco, 1967-74, George Eastman House, Rochester, N.Y., 1969-70, Oakland (Calif.) Mus., 1971, Pasadena Art Mus., 1970, U. Calif. Mus., Berkeley, 1971, N.Y. Mus. Contemporary Crafts, 1971-72, San Francisco Mus. Art, 1971 and 1975, Light Gallery, N.Y.C., 1972, Laguna Beach (Calif.) Mus. Art, 1973, Balt. Mus. Art, 1973, Hansen Fuller Gallery, San Francisco, 1975, Seattle Art Mus., 1976, Stanford U. Mus., 1976, Green St. Gallery, N.Y.C., 1977, Whitney Mus. Art, N.Y.C., 1978; represented in permanent collections: U.S. State Dept., Am. Arts Documentation Centre, Exeter, Eng., San Francisco Mus. Art, Internat. Mus. Photography, Rochester, N.Y., Stanford U. Mus., also numerous pvt. collections; instr. photography San Francisco Art Inst., 1973-75, Mills Coll., Oakland, Calif., 1975—; asst. prof. photography numerous colls. and art schs., 1970—, U. Mich. Sch. Art, Ann Arbor, 1978—. Recipient award Life Mag. Internat. Photography Competition, 1970, Phelan award, 1971; Nat. Endowment for Arts photosurvey grantee, 1977. Office: Sch Art U Mich Ann Arbor MI

LEONARD, JOHN H., advt. exec.; b. N.Y.C., June 28, 1922; s. Frederick H. and Florence (Kiechlin) L.; B.S., N.Y. U., 1942, M.B.A. 1951; m. Marjorie Jane Haslun, Oct. 19, 1946; children—John Kiechlin, Janet Ann. Advt. mgr. Autographic Register Co., 1946-47; promotion mgr. Macfadden Pub. Co., 1947-50; successively copywriter, account exec., v.p. and account supr. Batten, Barton,

Durstine & Osborn, 1950-64; with Doyle Dane Bernbach, Inc., N.Y.C., 1964—, group sr. v.p., 1972—, dir., 1975—; lectr. Grad. Sch. Bus., N.Y. U., 1959-61. Vice pres. Am. Lutheran Publicity Bur. Bd. dirs. Am. Bible Soc.; trustee Wartburg Orphans Farm Home. Served with USAAF, 1943-46. Recipient Alumni Meritorious Service award N.Y. U., 1969. Mem. N.Y. U. Grad. Sch. Bus. Alumni Assn. (pres.), N.Y. U. Commerce Alumni Assn. (pres. 1979-80), Alpha Delta Sigma. Clubs: New York Univ. (chmn. bd.) (N.Y.C.); Pelham (N.Y.) Country; Ponte Vedra (Fla.) Country. Home: 93 Beverly Rd New Rochelle NY 10804 Office: 437 Madison Ave New York City NY 10022

LEONARD, JOHN WALTER, ret. petroleum co. exec.; b. Washington, Pa., Jan. 30, 1904; s. John Walter and Caroline (McCollum) L.; student Culver (Ind.) Mil. Acad.; B.S., U. Pitts., 1927; m. Ruth Snellenberger, Mar. 22, 1940; children—John Walter III, William McCollum, Caroline Marie, Linda L., Dorothy J. Treas. S.Am. Oil Co., Pitts., 1926-27; mgr. Big Horn Petroleum Co., Cody, Wyo., 1927-29; treas. Motembo Basin Petroleum Co., Havana, Cuba, 1930-48; pres. Meridian Drilling Co., Inc., Oklahoma City, 1950-59; chmn. bd. Leonard Refineries, Inc., Alma, Mich., 1937-70, Leonard Crude Oil Co., 1956-68; pres. Rowmor Corp., 1934-47, Leonard Oil, Inc., 1947-71; past chmn. bd., chief exec. officer Am. Security Bank; dir. Peoples Banking Corp. Mem. Small Bus. Adv. Council, 1954-67. Chmn. bd., exec. com. Mich. Accident Fund; past bd. dirs. Mt. Pleasant Community Hosp. Mem. Ind. Petroleum Assn. Am. (past v.p., past mem. exec. com.), Oil and Gas Assn. Mich. (past pres., now hon. bd. dirs.), Sigma Alpha Epsilon. Methodist. Elk. Clubs: Detroit Athletic, Detroit. Home: 1113 Kent Dr Mount Pleasant MI 48858 Office: 119 E Broadway Mount Pleasant MI 48858

LEONARD, NELSON JORDAN, educator; b. Newark, Sept. 1, 1916; s. Harvey Nelson and Olga Pauline (Jordan) L.; B.S. in Chemistry, Lehigh U., 1937, Sc.D., 1963; B.Sc., Oxford (Eng.) U., 1940; Ph.D., Columbia, 1942; m. Louise Cornelie Vermey, May 10, 1947; children—Kenneth Jan, Marcia Louise, James Nelson, David Anthony. Fellow and asst. chemistry U. Ill., Urbana, 1942-43, instr., 1943-44, asso., 1944-45, 46-47, asst. prof., 1947-49, asso. prof., 1950-52, prof. organic chemistry, 1952—, head div. organic chemistry, 1954-63, prof. chemistry, also Center for Advanced Study, 1968—, prof. biochemistry, 1973—. Investigator antimalarial program Com. Med. Research, OSRD, 1944-46; sci. cons. and spl. investigator Field Intelligence Agy. Tech., U.S. Army and Dept. Commerce, 1945-46; mem. Canadian Nat. Research Council, summer 1950; Swiss-Am. Found. lectr., 1953, 70; vis. lectr. U. Calif. at Los Angeles, summer 1953; Reilly lectr. U. Notre Dame, 1962, Stieglitz lectr. Chgo. sect. Am. Chem. Soc., 1962; Robert A. Welch Found. lectr., 1964; distinguished vis. lectr. U. Calif. at Davis, 1975; vis. lectr. Polish Acad. Scis., 1976; B.R. Baker Meml. lectr. U. Calif., Santa Barbara, 1976; Ritter Meml. lectr. Miami U., Oxford, Ohio; Werner E. Bachman Meml. lectr. U. Mich., Ann Arbor, 1977; vis. prof. Japan Soc. for Promotion of Sci., 1978; Arapahoe lectr. U. Colo., 1979; mem. program com. in basic scis. Arthur P. Sloan, Jr. Found., 1961-66; Philips lectr. Haverford, 1971; Baker lectr., Groningen, Netherlands, 1972; FMC lectr. Princeton, 1973; ednl. adv. bd. Guggenheim Found., 1969—, mem. com. of selection, 1977—. Recipient Am. Chem. Soc. award, 1963; medal Synthetic Organic Chem. Mfrs., 1970; Rockefeller Found. fellow, 1950; Guggenheim Meml. fellow, 1959, 67. Fellow Am. Acad. Arts and Scis.; mem. Polish Acad. Scis. (fgn.), Ill. Acad. Sci. (hon.), Gesellschaft Deutscher Chemiker, Nat. Acad. Scis., Am. Chem. Soc. (Edgar Fahs Smith award and lectureship Phila. sect. 1975, Centennial lectr. 1976), Am. Soc. Biol. Chemists, AAAS, Chem. Soc. London, Swiss Chem. Soc., Am.-Can. Soc. Plant Physiologists, Am. Soc. for Photobiology, Inter-Am. Photochem. Soc., Phi Beta Kappa, Phi Lambda Upsilon (hon.), Tau Beta Pi, Alpha Chi Sigma. Editor: Organic Syntheses, 1951-58, mem. adv. bd., 1958—, bd. dirs., 1969—, v.p., 1976—; editorial bd. Jour. Organic Chemistry, 1957-61, Jour. Am. Chem. Soc., 1960-72; adv. bd. Biochemistry, 1973-78; contbr. articles to profl. jours. Home: 606 W Indiana Ave Urbana IL 61801

LEONARD, RICHARD, journalist; b. N.Y.C., May 23, 1921; s. Richard B. and Stella (Hart) L.; B.A., U. Wis., 1947; m. Barbara Klausner, July 11, 1948; children—Laurie, Lisa. Reporter, Milw. Jour., 1947, picture editor, 1948, with Madison (Wis.) bur., 1949-50, state desk, 1951-52, state editor, 1953-62, mng. editor, 1962-66, editor, v.p. Jour. Co., 1967—; mem. Pulitzer Prize Adv. Bd. Served with AUS, 1942-46; ETO, PTO. Mem. Am. Soc. Newspaper Editors, Internat. Press. Inst. (dir. Am. com.), Inter-Am. Press Assn., Milw. Press Club (pres. 1965), Sigma Delta Chi (pres. Milw. chpt. 1962, regional dir. 1970 nat. treas. 1973, nat. sec. 1974, nat. pres. 1976). Home: 330 E Beaumont Ave Whitefish Bay WI 53217 Office: 333 W State St Milwaukee WI 53201

LEONARD, RICHARD GHEEN, devel. banker; b. Phila., May 27, 1912; s. Richard Dunlop and Jessie (Haines) L.; grad. William Penn Charter Sch., 1930; B.S. in Econs., Wharton Sch., U. Pa., 1934; m. Patricia Dermody, Mar. 3, 1951; 1 dau., Hope Kirk. Market analyst Atlantic Refining Co., 1934-42; chief fgn. exchange control Mil. Govt. Germany, 1946-48; U.S. mem. Allied Bank Commn., Frankfurt, Germany, 1948-50; dir. finance div. U.S. High Commn., Bonn, Germany, 1950-52; officer, adviser Govt. Devel. Bank P.R., 1956-59; cons. internat. projects Nat. Indsl. Conf. Bd., 1964-65; adviser Somali Devel. Bank, Mogadicio, Somalia, 1965-70; financial adviser Kenya Indsl. Promotion and Devel. Center, 1971-72; sr. indsl. adviser Ministry Industry, Mines and Tourism, Swaziland, 1972-75; Interport lectr. World Campus Afloat, 1974; lectr. Wharton Grad. Sch. Fin., U. Pa., 1976-77; cons. Overseas Pvt. Investment Corp., Washington, 1975—; lang. trainer for refugees Nationalities Service Center, Phila., 1978-79. Mem. West Germany Trade and Payments delegations, Eng., France, Italy, Netherlands, Greece, Switzerland, Sweden; del. W. Germany to Work Bank Meeting, Paris; vol. devel. div. Grad. Hosp. Phila., 1978-79. Served with AUS, 1942-46. Mem. Mil. Order Fgn. Wars, Phi Kappa Psi. Clubs: Rittenhouse (Phila.); Karen (Nairobi); Connanicut (Jamestown, R.I.). Author articles in field. Home: PO Box 292 Jamestown RI 02835 also 1917 Spruce St Philadelphia PA 19103

LEONARD, RICHARD MANNING, lawyer; b. Elyria, Ohio, Oct. 22, 1908; s. Charles M. and Donna Rae (Russell) L.; J.D., U. Calif. at Berkeley, 1932; m. Doris Frances Corcoran, July 14, 1934; children—Frances (Mrs. Richard Best), Elizabeth. Admitted to Calif. bar, 1933, U.S. Supreme Ct. bar, 1941; chief atty. Regional Agrl. Credit Corp., 1932-38; gen. practice law, San Francisco, 1938-42, 46-55; partner firm Leonard & Dole, San Francisco, 1955—; dir. Varian Assos., Palo Alto, Calif., 1948-74, past sec.; dir. Western Gold and Platinum Co., 1955-79, Granger Assos., Palo Alto, 1956—, also other corps. Active in conservation projects, 1930—; mem. Calif. Scenic Hwy. Commn. 1963-69, Calif. Redwood Parks Commn., 1969—; participant White House Conf. Natural Beauty, 1965; founder, pres. Conservation Law Soc. Am., Sierra Club Found.; founder, trustee Trustees for Conservation; founder, sec. Am. Conservation Films, Varian Found., Forest Genetics Research Found.; vice chmn. commn. on legislation Internat. Union for Conservation Nature, 1963-69; bd. dirs. Save-the-Redwoods League, 1954—, v.p., 1966-75, pres., 1975—; bd. dirs. Sierra Club, 1938-73, pres., 1953-55, hon. pres., 1976—; bd. dirs. Wilderness Soc., 1948—, v.p., 1962-63. Served from 1st lt. to maj. AUS, 1942-46; CBI. Decorated Bronze Star; recipient award Calif. Conservation Council, 1950, Izaak Walton League Am., 1954; Am. Motors Conservation award, 1964; Albright award Am. Scenic and Hist. Preservation Soc., 1972; John Muir award, 1973. Author: Belaying the Leader, 1946. Contbr. Mannual of Ski Mountaineering, Going Light with Backpack and Burro, Climbers Guide to Yosemite Valley and Sierra Nevada; also articles to tech. jours. Organized difficult rock climbing as sci. and sport in Western Am., 1932; made 1st ascents Cathedral Spires, 1934, Sawtooth Ridge, 1933, Leonard's Minaret, 1932. Home: 980 Keeler Ave Berkeley CA 94708 Office: 220 Bush St Suite 1500 San Francisco CA 94104

LEONARD, RODNEY EDWIN, nutrition inst. exec.; b. Eureka, Kans., Dec. 7, 1929; s. Clarence Eugene and Muriel Frances (Barnard) L.; B.S. in Econs., Kans. State U., 1951; postgrad. in Journalism, U. Minn., 1953-55; m. Elizabeth Karin Berg, June 13, 1955; children—Karin and Jane (twins), John Arthur. Reporter, Mpls. Tribune, 1955-56; product information Minn. Mining and Mfg. Co., 1956-58; press sec. to Gov. Freeman of Minn., 1958-61; asst. to sec. agr. for press relations, 1961-66, dep. asst. sec. agr., 1966-67; adminstr. Consumer and Marketing Service, U.S. Dept. Agr., Washington, 1968-69, cons., 1969—; exec. dir. Community Nutrition Inst., Washington, 1970-77, 79—; dep. dir. U.S. Office Consumer Affairs, Washington, 1977—. Mem. Sigma Delta Chi, Kappa Tau Alpha. Mem. Minn. Democratic Farmer Labor Party. Presbyn. Home: 5710 Kingswood Rd Bethesda MD 20014 Office: 1146 19th St NW Washington DC 20036

LEONARD, ROY JUNIOR, educator; b. Central Square, N.Y., Aug. 17, 1929; s. Roy Jackson and Margaret Elizabeth (Keller) L.; B.S., Clarkson Coll. Tech., 1952; M.S., U. Conn., 1954; postgrad. Mich. State U., 1954-55; Ph.D., Iowa State U., 1958; m. Edith Campbell Gilmore; children—Robert J., Constance J. Asst. prof. civil engring. U. Del., 1957-59; asso. prof. Lehigh U., 1959-65; spl. projects engr. Dames and Moore, geotech. cons., N.Y.C., 1965; prof. civil engring. U. Kans., Lawrence, 1965—; cons. in field. NSF fellow, 1963-65; registered profl. engr., N.Y., Pa., Kans., Mo. Fellow ASCE; mem. Assn. Engring. Geologists, Soc. Mining Engrs., Am. Soc. Engring. Edn., Chi Epsilon. Episcopalian. Home: Route 4 Box 241 Lawrence KS 66044

LEONARD, SHELDON, TV producer-dir.; b. N.Y.C., Feb. 22, 1907; s. Frank and Anna (Levitt) Bershad; B.A., Syracuse U., 1929; m. Frances Bober, June 28, 1931; children—Andrea (Mrs. Alexander S. Urbach), Stephen W. Actor numerous Broadway plays, 1930-39; motion picture appearances include Guys and Dolls, Pocketful of Miracles, Tortilla Flats, Another Thin Man, Tall, Dark and Handsome; radio roles with Jack Benny, Bob Hope, Phil Harris, others; producer-dir. TV shows Danny Thomas, Andy Griffith, Dick Van Dyke, Gomer Pyle, USMC, I Spy, others; star TV series Big Eddie, 1975; pres. T. & L. Prodns.; partner, officer Mayberry Prodns., Calvada Prodns., Sheldon Leonard Enterprises; guest prof. Syracuse U. Recipient Emmy award for best TV direction, 1957, 61, best comedy producer, 1970, 74, Christopher award, 1955, Golden Globe award, 1972, Sylvania award, 1973; Man of Year awards Nat. Assn. Radio Announcers, Profl. Mgrs. Guild, B'nai B'rith; Arents medal Syracuse U., 1967; Spl. Achievement award NAACP, 1968; Spl. Tribute award Nat. Collegiate Athletic Assn., 1969; Letterman of Distinction award Varsity Club, Syracuse U., 1971. Mem. Am. Acad. TV Arts and Scis. (v.p., trustee), Dirs. Guild Am. (nat. trustee, bd. govs., v.p.), Acad. Motion Picture Arts and Scis., Phi Kappa Phi. Author screen scripts: Mountains of Mink, Tiger Bait, Checkmate, others, 1948-57. Home: 1141 Loma Vista Dr Beverly Hills CA 90210 Office: Sheldon Leonard Prodns 315 S Beverly Dr Beverly Hills CA.
A man must be at peace with himself.

LEONARD, VINCENT M., bishop; b. Pa., Dec. 11, 1908; student Duquesne U., St. Vincent Sem. Ordained priest Roman Catholic Ch., 1935; Cath. chaplain Allegheny County Home and Woodville State Mental Hosp.; vicar gen. Diocese of Pitts., 1959; consecrated titular bishop of Arsacal and aux. bishop of Pitts., 1964, bishop, 1969—. Address: 111 Blvd of Allies Pittsburgh PA 15222*

LEONARD, WALTER JEWELL, univ. pres.; b. Alma, Ga., Oct. 3, 1929; s. Francis A. and Rachel (Kirkland) L.; student Savannah State Coll., 1947-50, Morehouse Coll., 1959-60, Atlanta U. Sch. Bus. Adminstrn., 1961-62; J.D., Howard U., 1968; student Advanced Mgmt. Program, Harvard U., 1977; m. Betty Earline Singleton, June 16, 1951; children—Anthony Carlton, Angela Michele. Asst. dean, lectr. Howard U. Law Sch., Washington, 1968-69; asst. dean Harvard U. Law Sch., Cambridge, Mass., 1969-71, also dir. admissions and financial aid, 1969-71, spl. asst. to pres., 1971-77; pres. Fisk U., Nashville, 1977—; propr., mgr. Leonard Land Co., Atlanta, 1962-65; cons. to Ford Found., 1969-71; hearing examiner OEO, Atlanta, 1969-70; vis. prof. law U. Calif. at Davis, summer, 1971, 72; mem. scholarship selection com. Nieman Found. Mem. citizens adv. and planning com. Unity Bank and Trust Co., Boston; mem. Fund for Peace, N.Y.C. Bd. dirs. Law Sch. Admissions Council, Princeton U.; trustee United Way of Boston, 1974, United Way of Nashville, Carleton Coll., Northfield, Minn., Nat. Urban League; bd. visitors U.S. Naval Acad.; mem. Nat. Ins. Adv. Council. Served with USCG, 1945-46. Recipient Outstanding Achievement in the Field of Law award Savannah NAACP, 1969; Distinguished Service award Fund for Peace, 1968; Melnea A. Cass Community award Boston YWCA, 1977; New Eng. Tribute dinner, 1977; Paul Robeson award Black Am. Law Students Assn., 1977; Frederick Douglass Pub. Service award Greater Boston YMCA, 1977, others. Mem. Assn. Am. Univs. (com. on affirmative action and equal pay), AAUP, Am. (commn. on a Nat. Inst. of Justice), Nat. (president's award 1972) bar assns., Assn. Am. Law Schs. (chmn. sect. on minority groups 1971-74), Nat. Urban League of Eastern Mass. (dir. 1975—), Internat. Assn. Y's Men's Club, Harvard Law Sch. Assn., Howard U. Law Sch. Alumni Assn. Author: Black Lawyers, 1976; contbr. articles on higher edn. to various publs. Home: 1604 Jackson St Nashville TN 37208 Office: Fisk University Nashville TN 37203

LEONARD, WALTER RAYMOND, biologist; b. Scott County, Va., July 5, 1923; s. Homer Stanley and Minnie Eunice (Neal) L.; B.A., Tusculum Coll., Greeneville, Tenn., 1946; M.A., Vanderbilt U., 1947, Ph.D., 1949; m. Alice Ann McCaskill, Sept. 1, 1951; children—Leslie Ann, Walter Raymond. Mem. faculty Wofford Coll., Spartanburg, S.C., 1949—, John M. Reeves prof. biology, 1954—; dir. diet control program Behavior Evaluation Center, Spartanburg, 1975—. Mem. research and allocations com. Am. Heart Fund of S.C. Served with USAAF, 1942-43. Walter Raymond Leonard scholarship created Wofford Coll., 1973. Mem. AAAS, S.C. Acad. Sci., S.C. Biologists Assn. (1st pres. 1971-72), Scabbard and Blade (hon.), Lambda Chi Alpha. Democrat. Methodist. Research on cell metabolism. Home: 110 Pinetree Circle Spartanburg SC 29302 Office: Wofford Coll N Church St Spartanburg SC 29301

LEONARD, WILL ERNEST, JR., lawyer; b. Shreveport, La., Jan. 18, 1935; s. Will Ernest and Nellie (Kenner) L.; B.A., Tulane U., 1956, LL.B., 1958; LL.M., Harvard, 1966; m. Maureen Laniak; children—Will Ernest III, Sherry Elizabeth, Robert Scott, Stephen Michael, Christopher Anthony, Colleen Mary, Leigh Alison. Admitted to La. bar, 1958, D.C. bar, 1963, U.S. Supreme Ct. bar; announcer sta. WVUE-TV, New Orleans, 1958-60; legislative asst. to U.S. Senator Russell B. Long, 1960-65; profl. staff mem. com. finance U.S. Senate, 1966-68; mem. Internat. Trade Commn. (formerly U.S. Tariff Commn.), 1968-77, chmn., 1975-76; Congl. staff fellow Am. Polit. Sci. Assn., 1965-66. Home: 5901 Gloster Rd Bethesda MD 20016 Office: 1629 K St NW Suite 1100 Washington DC 20006

LEONARD, WILLIAM AUGUSTUS, II, (Bill), broadcast news exec.; b. N.Y.C., Apr. 9, 1916; s. James G. and Ruth (Leonard) Moses; A.B., Dartmouth, 1937; children—William Augustus III, Andrew H., Nicolas D., James M., Oliver L.; m. 2d, Norma Wallace, May 11, 1957; stepchildren—Peter Jon, Christopher Wallace. Reporter, Bridgeport (Conn.) Post-Telegram, 1937-40; radio researcher Newell-Emmett Advt., N.Y.C., 1940-41; with CBS, Inc., N.Y.C., 1945—, programs include This is New York (radio), 1945-57, Eye on New York (TV), 1950-61, 6 O'Clock Report (TV), 1952-56, Voice of Am. Let's Find Out (radio), 1955-59, (radio), 1957-59, CBS news corr., 1959-64, exec. producer CBS News election unit, 1962-64, v.p. programming CBS News, 1965-72, sr. v.p., 1972-75, v.p. CBS, Inc., Washington, 1975-78, pres. CBS News, 1979—; dir. Nat. Assn. Broadcasters, 1976-78, AP, 1979—; producer, narrator Trujillo: Portrait of a Dictator, 1959, The Beat Majority, 1960, The Case of the Boston Electra, 1961, Robert Moses: The Man Who Built New York, 1963, The Education of George Waruhiu, 1964. Served from ensign to lt. comdr. USNR, 1941-45. Recipient Albert Lasker award for med. journalism, 1956; Ed Stout award for best Latin Am. reporting, 1960. Author: (with Andrew Hepburn) This is New York Guide, 1955. Home: 2411 California St Washington DC 20008 Office: CBS News 524 W 57th St New York NY 10019

LEONARD, WILLIAM NORRIS, economist, educator; b. Pitts., Dec. 13, 1912; s. Burt Hayes and Mabel Etta (Norris) L.; A.B., U. Va., 1936; M.A., U. Tex., 1938; Ph.D. (fellow), Columbia, 1945; m. Elizabeth Flora Waugh, Aug. 24, 1939; children—Virginia Leonard Ewing, John Waugh. Oil field worker Devonian Oil Co., Tulsa, 1930-32; instr., later asst. prof. econ. U. Conn., 1939-42; indsl. analyst, transp. officer WPB, 1942-45; asst. coordinator planning Trans-World Airlines, Kansas City, Mo., 1945-46; asso. prof., chmn. dept. econ. Rutgers U., 1946-49; prof. econ., head dept. econ. and commerce Pa. State Coll., 1949-53; chmn. dept. econ. and div. social sci. Hofstra U., Hempstead, N.Y., 1953-59, asst. pres., 1965-66; Fulbright prof., Haiti, 1974; prof., chmn. dept. econs. H. Lehman Coll., City U. N.Y., 1974-78; Disting. lectr. econs. U. South Fla., Tampa, 1978—; cons. FTC, 1968, Senate Antitrust and Monopoly Subcom., 1969—. Pres. Fed. R.R. Progress, 1953-56. Planning commr. Nassau County, 1962, chmn., 1963-65. Bd. dirs. L.I. Assn., Nassau-Suffolk YMCA. Mem. AAUP, Am., N.Y. State (pres. 1972-73), Eastern (dir. 1974—) econ. assns., Raven Soc., Phi Beta Kappa. Author: Business Size, Market Power and Public Policy, 1969; also articles. Home: 4425 Vieux Carre Circle Lutz FL 33549 Office: U South Fla Tampa FL 33620

LEONARDI, C. (LEO) WILLIAM, investment co. exec.; b. Sfax, Tunisia, May 27, 1925; s. William Joseph and Beatrice May (Frost) L.; ed. Durham (Eng.) U.; m. Dec. 21, 1973; children—Jane Frances Leonardi Reynolds, Stephen. Supr., George A. Touche & Co., London, 1951-54; sec.-treas. Maple Leaf Services, Ottawa, Ont., Can., 1955-59; gen. mgr. H.K. Porter (Can.) Ltd., Acton, Ont., 1959-60; treas. Trafalgar Investment Ltd., 1960-64; v.p., treas. Glengair Group after 1964; pres. Venezuelan Power Co. Ltd., 1964-74; mng. dir. Capital Diversified Ltd., 1964-74; now exec. v.p. fin. Jannock Ltd. (a continuing co. of Glengair), Toronto, Ont.; dir. ITL Industries Ltd., Westeel-Rosco Ltd. Served with RAF, 1943-47. Fellow Inst. Chartered Accts. of Eng. and Wales; mem. Inst. Chartered Accts. Ont., Fin. Exec. Inst., Conf. Bd. in Can., Council Fin. Execs. Roman Catholic. Home: 2323 Confederation Pkwy Apt 608 Mississauga ON L5B 1R6 Canada Office: PO Box 43 Toronto Dominion Centre Toronto ON M5K 1B7 Canada

LEONDES, CORNELIUS THOMAS, educator; b. Phila., July 21, 1927; s. Thomas and Calypso (Bezer) L.; B.S., U. Pa., 1949, M.S., 1951, Ph.D., 1954; m. Nancy Lyle Rinehart, Nov. 27, 1952; children—Gregory Philip, Geoffrey Thomas. Research asso., lectr. U. Pa., 1949-54; asso. engr. IBM Corp., 1954-55; prof. engring. U. Calif. at Los Angeles, 1955—, head information systems div., 1966-68, chmn. controls Ph.D. field, 1956—. Adviser to govt. Fellow I.E.E.E.; mem. Sigma Xi, Eta Kappa Nu, Tau Beta Pi, Sigma Tau, Pi Mu Epsilon. Co-author and/or editor 20 books, also numerous articles. Home: 175 Ashdale Pl Los Angeles CA 90049 Office: Engring Sch Univ Calif Los Angeles CA 90024

LEONE, CHARLES ABNER, immunologist, educator, univ. ofcl.; b. Camden, N.J., July 13, 1918; s. Charles and Hilda (Barnett) L.; B.S., Rutgers U., 1940, M.S., 1942, Ph.D., 1949; m. Madelyn Ann Danner, Nov. 20, 1941; children—C. Timothy, Patricia Ann, Dennis Alan. Instr. zoology Rutgers U., 1945-49; from asst. prof. to prof. zoology U. Kans., 1949-68, asso. prof. radiol. biology, 1952-56; prof. biology, dean Grad. Sch., Bowling Green (Ohio) State U., 1968-71, vice provost research and Grad. Sch., 1971-75; v.p.-provost U. Ark., Fayetteville, 1975-79; v.p. research and grad. programs U. Ark. System, 1979—; research asso. Argonne (Ill.) Nat. Lab., 1954-55. Served from 2d lt. to maj., inf., AUS, World War II. Decorated Bronze Star with oak leaf cluster, Purple Heart; recipient bd. regents citation Charles A. Leone Labs. Immunobiology U. Kans., 1968; bd. trustees citation Bowling Green State U. Fellow AAAS, N.Y. Acad. Scis.; mem. Am. Assn. Immunologists. Author: Ionizing Radiations and Immune Processes, 1962; Taxonomic Biochemistry on Serology, 1964. Contbr. numerous articles to profl. jours. Home: 700 Overcrest Fayetteville AR 72701

LEONE, FRED CHARLES, assn. exec.; b. N.Y.C., Aug. 3, 1922; s. Salvatore and Anna (Regalbuto) L.; B.A., Manhattan Coll.; M.S., Georgetown U., 1943; Ph.D., Purdue U., 1949; m. D. Elizabeth Spencer, Oct. 15, 1945; children—Charles, Elizabeth, Peter, Francis, Joseph, Lawrence, Lucille. Instr., Purdue U., 1943-44, 46-49; from asst. prof. to prof. Case Inst. Tech., 1949-66, acting head dept. math., 1963-65; Faculty fellow dept. statistics U. Calif. at Berkeley, 1962-63; prof. statistics, prof. indsl. and mgmt. engring. U. Iowa, 1966-73; exec. dir. Am. Statis. Assn., Washington, 1973—. Fulbright prof. U. Sao Paulo (Brazil), 1968-69. Trustee Goodrich Settlement, Cleve. Served with USNR, 1943-45; PTO. Fellow Am. Statis. Assn. (bd. dirs. 1972—sec.-treas. 1973—, exec. dir. 1973—, sect. chmn.), Am. Soc. Quality Control (com. chmn.), AAAS; mem. Bernoulli Soc. (council 1979—, chmn. com.), Internat. Statistics Inst., Biometrics Soc., Inst. Math. Statistics (com. chmn.), Inter-Am. Statis. Inst. Author: (with N.L. Johnson) Statistics and Experimental Design in Engineering and the Physical Sciences, 1977. Editor: Technometrics, 1963-68; N.Am. editor Internat. Jour. Statis. Theory and Methodology Abstracts, 1969-73. Contbr. articles to profl. jours. Home: 5915 16th St NW Washington DC 20011 Office: 806 15th St NW Washington DC 20005

LEONE, WILLIAM CHARLES, business cons.; b. Pitts., May 3, 1924; s. Joseph and Fortuna (Sammarco) L.; B.S., Carnegie Inst. Tech., 1944, M.S., 1948, D.Sc., 1952; m. Sara Jane Hollenback, Aug. 26, 1950; children—William Charles, David M., Patricia Ann, Mary Jane. Asst. prof. engring. Carnegie Inst. Tech., Pitts., 1946-53; div.

mgr. Indsl. Systems div. Hughes Aircraft, Los Angeles, 1953-59; v.p., gen. mgr., dir. Rheem Califone, Los Angeles, 1960, Rheem Electronics, Los Angeles, 1960-68; group v.p. Rheem Mfg. Co., 1968-71, exec. v.p., N.Y.C., 1971-72, pres., 1972—, also dir.; pres. City Investing Co. Internat., Inc., 1973-76; pres., chief exec. officer, dir. Farah Mfg. Co., El Paso, Tex., 1976-77; bus. cons., 1977-79; acting vice chmn. McCulloch Oil Corp., Los Angeles, 1979—, also dir.; dir. Arrowsmith Corp.; Datapoint Corp. Served to lt. (j.g.) USNR, 1944-46. Mem. ASME, IEEE, Am. Inst. Aeros. and Astronautics. Home: 2209 Chelsea Rd Palos Verdes Estates CA 90274

LEONETT, ANTHONY ARTHUR, banker; b. Summit, N.J., Jan. 4, 1929; s. Joseph J. and Margaret (DiGuglielmo) L.; B.S., Seton Hall U., 1950; certificate, Am. Inst. Banking, 1956; postgrad. U. Wis., 1962; m. Ann Marino, Oct. 6, 1974; 1 son by previous marriage, Anthony Arthur. Mgmt. tng. First Nat. Bank & Trust Co., Summit, 1950-56; v.p., auditor Nat. State Bank, Elizabeth, N.J., 1956—; instr. principles of auditing and bank operations Am. Inst. Banking. Served with U.S. Army, 1951-53. Recipient Irving Grabiel award for outstanding leadership in banking, 1979. Mem. Am. Inst. Banking (dir. chpt.), Bank Adminstrn. Inst. (N.J. state dir., 1977-79, pres. N.J. chpt., dist. dir. 1979—). Republican. Roman Catholic. K.C. Club: Minisink (Chatham). Home: 102 N Hillside Ave Chatham NJ 07928 Office: 68 Broad St Elizabeth NJ 07207

LEONHARDT, WILLIAM STROUP, chem. mfg. co. exec.; b. Phila., Feb. 14, 1916; s. Philip Carl and Eva (Stroup) L.; B.S., N.Y. U., 1940; m. Evelyn Frances Payne, Nov. 10, 1939; children—Lynne (Mrs. Allan Toth), Geraldine, William, Janet (Mrs. Thomas Small). Clk., Mfrs. Trust Co.; jr. accountant U.S. Rubber Co., Price Waterhouse & Co.; jr. accountant, auditor Comml. Solvents Corp., 1941-55, budget dir., treas., 1955-58, financial v.p., treas., 1959-67, financial v.p., 1967-72, exec. v.p., 1972-73, pres., 1973—, mem. exec. com.; exec. v.p., dir., Internat. Minerals & Chems. Corp., 1975-76; chmn. IMC Chem. Group; vice chmn. bd., chief fin. officer Reynolds Metals Co., 1979—, also dir.; dir. Royal Bank of Can. Trust Co.; pres., dir. Istituto Chemioterapico Italiano, S.p.A. (Milan), Indsl. Kern Espanola S.A. (Barcelona). Mem. Alpha Kappa Psi. Home: 3000 S Ocean Blvd Boca Raton FL 33432 Office: 6601 W Broad St Richmond VA 23261

LEONTIEF, WASSILY, economist; b. Leningrad, Russia, Aug. 5, 1906; s. Wassily and Eugenia (Bekker) L.; student U. Leningrad, 1921-25 (grad. Learned Economist); Ph.D., U. Berlin, 1928; Ph.D. honoris causa, U. Bruxelles (Belgium), 1962, U. York (Eng.), 1967, U. Louvain, 1971, U. Paris, 1972, U. Pa., 1976, U. Lancaster (Eng.), 1976; m. Estelle Helena Marks, Dec. 25, 1932; 1 dau., Svetlana Eugenia Alpers. Research economist Institut Fûr Weltwirtschaft, U. Kiel (Germany), 1927-28, 30; econ. adviser to Chinese govt., Nanking, 1929; with Nat. Bur. Econ. Research, N.Y.C., 1931; instr. econs. Harvard, 1931, asst. prof., 1933-39, asso. prof., 1939-46, prof., 1946-75, dir. econ. project, 1948-72; Henry Lee prof. econs., 1953-75; prof. econs., dir. Inst. Econ. Analysis, N.Y. U., 1975—; cons. Dept. Labor, 1941-47, OSS, 1943-45, UN, 1961-62, Dept. Commerce, 1966—. Decorated officer Order Cherubim (U. Pisa), 1953, Legion of Honor, 1967 (France); recipient Bernhard-Harms prize econs., West Germany, 1970, Nobel prize in econs., 1973. Guggenheim fellow, 1940, 50. Fellow Soc. Fellows Harvard (sr. fellow, chmn. 1964-75), Econometric Soc., Royal Statis. Assn. (hon.), Inst. de France (corr.); mem. Am. Philos. Soc., Am. Acad. Arts and Scis., Internat. Statis. Inst., Am. Econ. Assn., Am. Statis. Assn., Royal Econ. Soc., Japan Econ. Research Center (hon.), Brit. Acad. (corr.), French Acad. Scis. (corr.), Nat. Acad. Scis., Royal Irish Acad. (hon.), Brit. Assn. Advancement Sci. (pres. Sect. F 1976). Mem. Greek Orthodox Ch. Author: The Structure of the American Economy, 1919-29, 2d edit., 1976; Studies in the Structure of the American Economy, 1953, 2d edit., 1977; Input-Output Economics, 1966; Collected Essays, 1966; Theories, Facts and Policies, 1977; The Future of the World Economy, 1977. Contbr. articles to sci. jours. and periodicals U.S. and abroad. Home: New York NY 10011 summer West Burke VT 05871 Office: Inst Econ Analysis NY U 8 Washington Pl Washington Sq New York NY 10003

LEOPOLD, ESTELLA BERGERE, botanist, educator; b. Madison, Wis., Jan. 8, 1927; d. Aldo and Estella (Bergere) Leopold; Ph.B., U. Wis., 1948; M.S., U. Calif., Berkeley, 1950; Ph.D., Yale, 1955. Asst. physiology and embryology Genetics Expt. Sta., Smith Coll., 1951-52; asst. biologist, then asst. animal ecology Yale U., 1952-54; botanist, paleontology and stratigraphy br. U.S. Geol. Survey, 1955-76; adj. prof. biology U. Colo., 1967-76; dir. Quaternary Research Center, prof. botany and forest research U. Wash., Seattle, 1976—. Co-recipient Conservationist of Year award Nat. Wildlife Fedn., 1969; travel grantee NSF, Spain, 1957, Poland, 1961, Eng., 1977. Mem. Nat. Acad. Scis. (environ. studies bd. 1976-79), Ecol. Soc. Am., Internat. Quaternary Assn. U.S. Nat. Com., Am. Quaternary Assn., Bot. Soc. Am., Inst. Ecology (dir.). Home: 5608 17th St NE Seattle WA 98105 Office: Quaternary Research Center Univ Wash Seattle WA 98195

LEOPOLD, IRVING HENRY, physician, medical educator; b. Phila., Apr. 19, 1915; s. Abraham and Dora (Schlow) L.; student Pa. State U., 1934; M.D., U. Pa., 1938, D.Sc., 1943; m. Eunice Robinson, June 24, 1937; children—Ellen Robinson, John. Intern Hosp. U. Pa., 1938-40; fellow, instr. ophthalmology Hosp. U. Pa., also U. Pa. Med. Sch., 1940-45, asso., 1945-54; research investigator chem. warfare OSRD, 1941-45; mem. faculty U. Pa. Grad. Sch. Medicine, 1946-64, successively asso., asst. prof., asso. prof., 1946-55, prof., head dept. ophthalmology, 1955-64, chief dept. ophthalmology Grad. Hosp., 1955-61; dir. research Wills Eye Hosp., 1949-64, attending surgeon, 1952-64, med. dir., 1961-64, cons. surgeon, 1965—; chmn. sci. adv. com. Allergan Pharms., 1974, exec. v.p., 1975; prof., chmn. dept. ophthalmology Mt. Sinai Sch. Medicine, 1965—; dir. dept. ophthalmology Mt. Sinai Hosp., N.Y.C., 1964-75; prof., chmn. dept. ophthalmology U. Calif. at Irvine, 1975—; clin. prof. ophthalmolgy Coll. Phys. and Surg., Columbia, 1964-66; cons. ophthalmologist St. Joseph's Hosp., 1959—, Albert Einstein Med. Center, 1959—; Proctor lectr. U. Calif., 1962; Gifford Meml. lectr., Chgo., 1967; Edwin B. Dunphy lectr. Harvard, 1968, Walter Wright lectr. U. Toronto, 1969; Richardson Cross lectr. Royal Soc. Medicine, 1970; Doyne Meml. lectr. Ophthal. Soc. U.K., 1971; DeSchweinitz Meml. lectr., Phila., 1972; Jules Stein lectr. U. Calif., Los Angeles, 1974; Bedell lectr., Phila., 1975; Edwin B. Dunphy lectr. Harvard, 1975; cons. Chem. Warfare Service, U.S. Army, 1948-52, surgeon gen. USPHS, 1953—, FDA, HEW, 1963. Chmn. ophthalmology panel U.S. Pharmacopeia, 1960-70, mem. revision panel, 1970—; chmn. panel drug efficacy in ophthalmology Nat. Acad. Scis.-NRC, 1966-67; mem. tng. grants com. USPHS, 1952-58, mem. spl. sensory study sect. research record diseases and blindness, 1954-58; mem. field investigating com. Nat. Inst. Neurol. Diseases and Blindness, 1959-61, mem. neurd. project com., 1961-63, chmn. vision research tng. com., 1967-68. Trustee Seeing Eye Guide. Recipient Zentmayer award, 1945, 49; honor award Am. Acad. Ophthalmology, 1955; Edward Lorenzo Holmes citation and award, 1957; Friedenwald medal Assn. Research Ophthalmology, 1960. Diplomate Am. Bd. Ophthalmology (chmn. bd. 1971-72, chmn. visual scis. study sect. 1968-70, subcom. impaired vision and blindness 1967-69, task force on ocular pharmacology, 1967-69, cons. 1975-79). Mem. N.Y. Acad. Medicine, Am. Ophthal. Soc. (Verhoeff Meml. lectr. 1973, Lucien Howe medal 1974), N.Y. Ophthal. Soc., Am. Acad. Ophthalmology and Otolaryngology (chmn. drug com. ophthalmology 1963-74; Edward Jackson Meml. lectr. 1965), Assn. Research Ophthalmology (trustee, chmn.), Nat. Soc. Prevention Blindness (dir., v.p., exec. com.), A.C.S., AAAS, Art Alliance Phila., John Morgan Soc., Coll. Physicians Phila., Am. Diabetes Assn., A.M.A. (chmn. residency rev. com. ophthalmology 1970-72), N.Y. Acad. Sci., Pan Am. Assn. Ophthalmology, Pan Pacific Surg. Assn., N.Y. State, N.Y. County, Philadelphia County med. socs., Calif., Orange County med. assns., Sigma Xi, Alpha Omega Alpha. Clubs: Medical Biochemist, Vesper, Alpha (Phila.); Newport Beach Tennis, Big Canyon Country, Balboa Bay (Newport Beach, Calif.); Century Country, Princeton (N.Y.C.). Editor in chief: Survey of Ophthalmology, 1958-62, cons. editor, 1962—; editorial bd. Am. Jour. Diabetes, 1956-73, Investigative Ophthalmology, 1961-74, Am. Jour. Ophthalmology, 1965—. Home: 1484 Galaxy Dr Newport Beach CA 92660 Office: Dept Ophthalmology Calif Coll Medicine U Cal Irvine CA 92717

LEOPOLD, LUNA BERGERE, hydraulic engr., educator; b. Albuquerque, Oct. 8, 1915; s. Aldo and Estella (Bergere) L.; B.S., U. Wis., 1936; M.S., U. Calif. at Los Angeles, 1944; Ph.D., Harvard, 1950; D.Geography (hon.), U. Ottawa, 1969; D.Sc. (hon.), Iowa Wesleyan Coll., 1971; m. Barbara Beck Nelson, 1973; children—Bruce Carl, Madelyn Dennette. With Soil Conservation Service, 1938-41, U.S. Engrs. Office, 1941-42, U.S. Bur. Reclamation, 1946; head meterorologist Pineapple Research Inst. of Hawaii, 1946-49; hydraulic engr. U.S. Geol. Survey, 1950-71, chief hydrologist, 1957-66, sr. research hydrologist, 1966-71; prof. geology U. Calif. at Berkeley, 1973—. Served as capt. air weather service USAAF, 1942-46. Recipient Distinguished Service award Dept. of Interior, 1958; Kirk Bryan award Geol. Soc. Am., 1958; Veth medal Royal Netherlands Geog. Soc., 1963; Cullum Geog. medal Am. Geog. Soc., 1968; Rockefeller Pub. Service award, 1971. Mem. ASCE, Nat. Acad. Scis. (Warren prize), Geol. Soc. Am. (pres. 1972), Am. Geophys. Union, Am. Acad. Arts and Scis., Am. Philos. Soc., Sigma Xi, Tau Beta Pi, Phi Kappa Phi, Chi Epsilon. Club: Cosmos (Washington). Author: (with Thomas Maddock, Jr.) The Flood Control Controversy, 1954; Fluvial Processes in Geomorphology, 1964; Water, 1974; (with Thomas Dunne) Water in Environmental Planning, 1978; also tech. papers. Home: 400 Vermont Ave Berkeley CA 94707

LEOPOLD, RICHARD WILLIAM, educator; b. N.Y.C., Jan. 6, 1912; s. Harry and Ethel A. (Kimmelstiel) L.; A.B. with highest honors, Princeton, 1933; A.M., Harvard, 1934, Ph.D., 1938. Instr. history Harvard, 1937-40, asst. prof., 1940-48; asso. prof. history Northwestern U., 1948-53, prof., 1953-63, William Smith Mason prof. Am. history, 1963—, acting chmn. dept., 1954, 62, chmn., 1966-69; Albert Shaw lectr. Johns Hopkins, 1963; mem. Inst. Advanced Study, Princeton, 1960-61. Mem. hist. adv. com. Dept. Army, Dept. State, Navy Dept., AEC, Library of Congress, Nat. Archives Adv. Council, U.S. Marine Corps. Bd. dirs. Harry S. Truman Library Inst. Served from ensign to lt. USNR, 1942-46. Predoctoral field fellow Social Sci. Research Council, 1935-36; recipient John H. Dunning prize Am. Hist. Assn., 1940. Mem. Am., So. hist. assns., Mass. Hist. Soc. (corr. mem.), Orgn. Am. Historians (pres. 1976-77), Soc. for Historians of Am. Fgn. Relations (pres. 1970), Social Sci. Research Council, Phi Beta Kappa. Club: Cosmos (Washington). Author: Robert Dale Owen: A Biography, 1940; Elihu Root and the Conservative Tradition, 1954; The Growth of American Foreign Policy, 1962. Editor and contbr.: (with Arthur S. Link) Problems in American History, 3d edit., 1966, 4th edit., 1972; contbg. author: Change and Continuity in Twentieth-Century America, 1964; Interpreting American History, 1970; Pearl Harbor as History, 1973; The Future of History, 1977; The Korean War: A 25-Year Perspective, 1977; also articles in profl. jours. Home: 734 Noyes St Evanston IL 60201

LEOPOLD, ROBERT LIVINGSTON, physician, educator; b. Phila., Oct. 5, 1922; s. Simon Stein and Loraine (Livingston) L.; A.B., Harvard, 1944; M.D., U. Pa., 1946; postgrad. Phila. Psychoanalytic Inst., 1949-55; m. Edith Abelmann, Sept. 17, 1944; children—David A., Donald R., William S. Intern, resident neurology Grad. Hosp., U. Pa., 1946-50; fellow psychiatry Inst. Pa. Hosp., 1950-51, Hosp. U. Pa., 1951-52; practice medicine specializing in psychiatry, psychoanalysis, neurology, Phila., 1952-67; dir. West Phila. Community Mental Health Consortium, 1967-72; mem. staff Hosp. U. Pa., Grad. Hosp., Inst. Pa. Hosp., Phila. Psychiat. Center; prof. community psychiatry and community medicine U. Pa., 1968—, chmn. dept. community medicine, 1971-76; sr. psychiat. cons. Peace Corps, Washington, 1961-67; psychiat. cons. Am. Friends Service Com., Phila., 1954—. Bd. dirs. Eagleville Hosp., Emergency Care Research Found., Magee Meml. Rehab. Center. Served with AUS, 1943-46. Fellow Am. Psychiat. Assn., Am. Orthopsychiat. Assn.; mem. A.M.A., Pa., Phila. County med. socs., Am. Psychoanalytic Assn., Internat. Psychoanalytical Assn., Phila. Coll. Physicians, Group Advancement Psychiatry, Am. Pub. Health Assn. Home: 1900 Rittenhouse Sq Philadelphia PA 19103 Office: Dept Psychiatry 189 Gibson Hosp U Pa Philadelphia PA 19104

LEPAGE, WILBUR REED, educator; b. Kearny, N.J., Nov. 16, 1911; s. Wilbur Nicholas and Gertrude Elizabeth (Reedt) LeP.; E.E., Cornell U., 1933, Ph.D., 1941; M.S. in Physics, U. Rochester, 1939; m. Eveline Marie Jacobsen, June 9, 1936; 1 dau., Margaret Ann. Instr. engring. U. Rochester, 1933-38; grad. student, teaching asst. Cornell U., 1939-41; mem. staff advanced devel. lab. RCA, 1941; physicist radiation lab. Johns Hopkins, 1942-45; sr. research engr. Stromberg Carlson Co., 1946; prof. elec. engring. Syracuse U., 1947—, chmn. dept., 1956-74; initiated ann. Sagamore Conf. Elec. Engring. Edn., 1952; cons. to Signal Corps. U.S. Army, 1953; ednl. cons. UNESCO, 1967; guest lectr. Rumanian Assn. Scientists, 1977; mem. Nat. Com. on Elec. Engring. Films, 1964-71. Trustee Electronic Engring. Found., 1959-64. Fellow I.E.E.E. (chmn. com. basic scis. 1955-56), Am. Soc. Engring. Edn. (chmn. com. grad. study elec. engring. 1962-64), N.Y. Acad. Scis., AAUP, Sigma Xi. Author: Analysis Alternating Current Circuits, 1952; (with S. Seely) General Network Analysis 1952; Complex Variables and The Laplace Transform for Engineers, 1961; (with N. Balabanian) Electrical Science, Book I, 1970, Book II, 1972; Applied APL Programming, 1978. Home: 217 DeWitt Rd Syracuse NY 13214

LEPAWSKY, ALBERT, educator; b. Chgo., Feb. 16, 1908; s. Morris and Rose (Devin) L.; Ph.B., U. Chgo., 1927, Ph.D., 1931; European fellow Social Sci. Research Council, 1933-34; vis. fellow U. Hamburg (Germany), 1933, London (Eng.) Sch. Econs. and Polit. Sci., 1933-34, U. Berlin (Germany), 1934; m. Rosalind Almond, Apr. 17, 1935; children—Martha (Mrs. John Barker), Michael, Susan (Mrs. Saul Rosenstriech), Lucy (Mrs. Anthony Di Bianca). Successively instr., research asst., research asso., lectr. dept. polit. sci. U. Chgo., 1930-42; research dir. law dept. City of Chgo., 1935-36; asst. dir. Pub. Adminstrn. Clearing House, 1936-38; dir. Fedn. Tax Adminstrs., 1938-41, Inst. Pub. Service, U. Chgo., 1941-42; prof. pub. adminstrn. and polit. sci. U. Ala., also ednl. dir. So. Regional Tng. Program, 1945-52; prof. polit. sci. U. Calif. at Berkeley, 1953-75, prof. emeritus, 1976—; vis. prof. polit. sci. U. B.C., 1960-62; vis. scholar Inst. War and Peace Studies, Columbia U., 1971; scholar-in-residence Rockefeller Found. European Study Center, 1977; cons. fed., state, regional, local and UN agencies. Mem. Chgo. Plan Commn., 1940-42. Served from capt. to lt. col., USAAF, 1942-45. Mem. Am. (v.p. 1956-57), Western (pres. 1963-64) polit. sci. assns., Calif. Conservation Council (pres. 1958-60), Phi Beta Kappa. Democrat. Jewish. Address: 2570 Cedar St Berkeley CA 94708. *As a professor and practitioner of politics and administration, I am told by students and colleagues that my work has certain characteristics. First, I treat not only the specialized subject involved but I stress the general setting and surrounding circumstances. Secondly, I deal with people not merely as members of a class or an organization, but as unique individuals. If this characterization of me is correct, then it is a product of some lessons I have experienced in this technological and hierarchical world of ours. The perimeter is as crucial as the center and the person is as precious as the system.*

LE PELLEY, GUERNSEY, editorial cartoonist, writer; b. Chgo., May 14, 1910; s. Franklin and Ardria (Miner) LeP.; student Principia Coll., 1928-29, also Chgo. Art Inst., Evanston (Ill.) Acad. Fine Art, Northwestern U., Northeastern U.; B.A., Harvard; m. Maxine Gillis, Sept. 10, 1938; children—Lynn, Richard. Free-lance writer and artist, 1932—; author off-Broadway plays including Love is Too Much Trouble, 1946, To Blush Unseen, 1951, Absolutely Murder, 1954; writer Highland Park (Ill.) Press, 1930-33, radio sta. WFAA, Dallas, 1933-34; author daily comic strip Tubby, Christian Sci. Monitor, 1935—, editorial cartoonist, 1961—. Co-founder Sharon (Conn.) Playhouse, 1946. Served with USAAF, World War II. Mem. Assn. Am. Editorial Cartoonists (past adv. bd.), Nat. Cartoonists Soc., Aircraft Owners and Pilots Assn. Home: Sharon CT also 100 Memorial Dr Cambridge MA 02142 Office: 1 Norway St Boston MA 02115

LEPORE, ALBERT, educator; b. San Diego, Apr. 13, 1920; s. Louis and Jeanne (Robin) L.; B.A., San Diego State Coll., 1942; M.A., Columbia Tchrs. Coll., 1949; Ph.D., Columbia U., 1960; m. Margaret Alice Ashby, Dec. 28, 1947; children—Jeanne Robin, Lawrence Raymond. Tchr., San Diego pub. schs., 1946-48; mem. faculty San Francisco State Coll., 1951-59; prof. psychology Calif. State Coll., Hayward, 1959—, dean instrn., dean faculty, 1962-69, prof. edn. Pres. Alameda County Mental Health Assn., 1968-70; mem. Comprehensive Health Planning Council Alameda County. Adv. bd. St. Rose Hosp., also pres. bd. trustees; pres., trustee Hayward Unified Sch. Dist. Served to capt. AUS, 1942-46; ETO. Decorated Silver Star. Mem. Am. Psychol. Assn., A.A.A.S., Am. Ednl. Research Assn., Phi Delta Kappa, Kappa Delta Pi. Home: 2614 Lancaster Rd Hayward CA 94542

LEPORE, MICHAEL JOSEPH, physician; b. N.Y.C., May 8, 1910; s. Joseph and Florence (Melucci) L.; B.S., N.Y. U., 1929; M.S., U. Rochester, 1931, M.D. with honor, 1934; m. Ardean Clough Everett, Sept. 18, 1937; 1 son, Frederick Everett. Intern, Duke Hosp., asst. resident in medicine, 1934-37; fellow in medicine Yale U., 1935-36; asst. in medicine Columbia U., 1937-46, instr., 1946-52, asso. medicine, 1952-56, asst. clin. prof. medicine, 1956-63; practice medicine specializing in internal medicine and gastroenterology, 1937—; cons. in field; dir. Upjohn Gastrointestinal service Roosevelt Hosp., 1962-66, St. Vincent's Hosp. and Med. Center, 1966-75; mem. staffs Englewood (N.J.) Hosp., St. John's Riverside Hosp., Yonkers, N.Y.; attending physician St. Vincent's Hosp. and Med. Center, N.Y.C., Univ. Hosp., Bellevue Hosp. Center; asso. prof. clin. medicine Sch. Medicine, N.Y. U., 1968-70, prof., 1971—. Pres. Upjohn Gastrointestinal Found., 1962-79; mem. pres.'s leadership council U. Rochester. Served as lt. col. M.C., AUS, 1942-46. Decorated Army Commendation medal; diplomate Am. Bd. Internal Medicine. Fellow A.C.P., N.Y. Acad. Scis., N.Y. Acad. Medicine; mem. AMA, Am. Gastroenterol. Assn., N.Y. Gastroenterol. Assn., Physiol. Soc. Phila., AAAS, Royal Soc. Medicine, Alpha Omega Alpha, Sigma Xi. Contbr. articles to med. jours. Home: 80 N Woodland St Englewood NJ 07631 Office: 550 Park Ave New York NY 10021

LEPOW, IRWIN HOWARD, immunologist; b. N.Y.C., Sept. 2, 1923; s. Herman and Mollie (Rutchik) L.; B.S., Pa. State U., 1942; Ph.D., Case Western Res. U., 1951, M.D., 1958; m. Martha Josephine Lipson, Feb. 7, 1958; children—Lauren Ethel, David Andrew, Daniel Joseph. From instr. to prof. Case Western Res. U. Sch. Medicine, 1951-67; prof., head dept pathology U. Conn. Health Center, 1967-73, prof., head dept. medicine, 1973-78; pres. Sterling-Winthrop Research Inst., Rensselaer, N.Y., 1978—; chmn. allergy and immunology study sect. NIH, 1970-73; adv. mem. commn. immunization Armed Forces Epidemiol. Bd., 1969-74; chmn. research com. Conn. Heart Assn., 1970-72; chmn. Conn. Commn. Medicolegal Investigations, 1969-71. Trustee Trudeau Inst. Served with USAAF, 1943-45. Recipient Distinguished Alumnus award Case Western Res. U., 1968; Research career award NIH, 1962-67, grantee for research, 1955-78. Fellow A.C.P.; mem. Am. Assn. Immunologists (council 1974—, pres. 1979—), Am. Soc. Clin. Investigation, Am. Soc. Exptl. Pathology, Fedn. Am. Socs. for Exptl. Biology (v.p. 1979—), Infectious Diseases Soc. Am., Assn. Am. Physicians. Contbr. articles to profl. jours. Home: 73 Bentwood Ct Albany NY 12203 Office: Sterling-Winthrop Research Inst Rensselaer NY 12144

LEPPARD, RAYMOND JOHN, conductor; b. London, Aug. 11, 1927; came to U.S., 1976; s. Albert Victor and Bertha May (Beck) L.; M.A., U. Cambridge (Eng.), 1955; D.Litt. (hon.), U. Bath (Eng.), 1973. Fellow, Trinity Coll., univ. lectr. in music U. Cambridge, 1958-68; musical dir. English Chamber Orch., London, 1959-77; prin. condr. BBC No. Symphony Orch., Manchester, Eng., 1972-80; condr. symphony orchs. in Am. and Europe and Met. Opera, N.Y.C., Santa Fe Opera, San Francisco Opera, Convent Garden, Gyndebourne, Paris Opera. Decorated commendatore Della Republica Italiana. Rec. artist. Home: 1045 Park Ave New York NY 10028

LEPPER, MARK HUMMER, physician; b. Washington, June 12, 1917; s. Henry Albert and Georgianna (Hummer) L.; A.B., George Washington U., 1938, M.D., 1941; Sc.D., Rush U., 1973; m. Joyce Mae Sullivan, June 7, 1941; children—Mark Roger, Joyce Hummer. Intern Sibley Meml. Hosp., Washington, 1941-42; fellow medicine George Washington U., 1942-43, clin. instr. medicine, 1946-48, asso. medicine, 1949-50; asst. resident medicine Gallinger Municipal Hosp., Washington, 1943-44; pvt. practice, Washington, 1946-48; cons. internal medicine Walter Reed Gen. Hosp., Washington, 1948-50; med. supt. Municipal Contagious Diseases Hosp., Chgo., 1950-52; asso. prof. medicine charge preventive medicine U. Ill. Med. Sch., Chgo., 1952-55, prof. preventive medicine, head dept., 1955-66, prof. preventive medicine, 1966-71; exec. v.p. profl. and acad. affairs Presbyn. St. Luke's Hosp., Chgo., 1966-70; exec. v.p. profl. and acad. affairs Rush-Presbyn.-St. Lukes Med. Center, also dean Rush Med. Coll., Chgo., 1970-73; coordinator health services, dir. Comprehensive Health Planning Agy. Ill., 1973-76; v.p. for program evaluation Rush Med. Center, Chgo., 1976—, prof. medicine, 1970—. Served from 1st lt. to maj. M.C., AUS, 1944-46. Diplomate Am. Bd. Internal Medicine. Fellow A.C.P.; mem. A.M.A., Am. Fedn. Clin. Research, Central Soc. Clin. Research, Am. Soc. Clin. Investigation, Assn. Am. Physicians, Central Research Club, Chgo. Soc. Internal Medicine, Am. Pub. Health Assn., N.Y. Acad. Sci., Ill. Pub. Health Assn., Phi Beta Kappa, Sigma Xi. Home: 327 Hampton St Hinsdale IL 60521 Office: 1753 W Congress Pkwy Chicago IL 60612

LEPS, THOMAS MACMASTER, civil engr.; b. Keyser, W.Va., Dec. 3, 1914; s. Thomas Davis and Grace (King) L.; B.A., Stanford, 1936; M.S., Mass. Inst. Tech., 1939; m. Catherine Mary Sacksteder, June 22, 1940; 1 son, Timothy. Chief civil engr. So. Calif. Edison Co., Los Angeles, 1946-61; chief engr. Shannon & Wilson Co., Seattle, 1961-63; cons. civil engr., U.S. and abroad, Atherton, Calif., 1963—. Served with USN, 1943-46. Recipient certificate of Appreciation, Calif. Dept. Water Resources, 1971. Fellow ASCE (certificate of appreciation 1961); mem. U.S. Com. on Large Dams (exec. com. 1977—), Nat. Acad. Engring., Engrs. Club San Francisco, Phi Beta Kappa, Tau Beta Pi. Presbyterian. Contbr. articles to profl. jours. Address: 177 Watkins Ave Atherton CA 94025

LERCH, RICHARD HEAPHY, lawyer; b. Balt., Oct. 8, 1924; s. Charles Sebastian and Marguerite Mary (Mullen) L.; A.B. magna cum laude, Loyola Coll., Balt., 1947; LL.B., U. Md., 1949; m. Marie Therese Logan, Feb. 11, 1950; children—Marie L., Elizabeth L., Ellen C. Admitted to Md. bar, 1948, since practiced in Balt.; partner Lerch & Huesman, 1959—. Pres., Jr. Bar Assn., 1960. Served with AUS, 1944-46, 51-52. Mem. Am., Md., Balt. bar assns., Internat. Assn. Ins. Counsel. Democrat. Roman Catholic. Home: 5906 Meadowood Rd Baltimore MD 21212 Office: 504 Maryland Trust Bldg Baltimore MD 21202

LERMAN, ALBERT, advt. agy. exec.; b. Chgo., June 24, 1936; s. David and Mary (Oseas) L.; B. J. (7 scholarships), Northwestern U., 1958; m. Phyllis Carpenter, June 28, 1959; children—Dawn, April. Sr. writer Playboy Mag., Chgo., 1958-59; promotion mgr. Helene Curtis Co., Chgo., 1959-61; pres. Lerman Assos., Chgo., 1961-63; creative dir., group head Arthur Meyerhoff Assos., Chgo., 1963-64; v.p., creative dir. Leo Burnett Co., advt., Chgo., 1964-72; exec. v.p., creative dir. McCann-Erickson & Marschalk Co., advt., N.Y.C., 1972-77; pres., creative dir. Lerman & Van Leeuwen Advt. Agy., N.Y.C., 1977-78; sr. v.p., creative adv. to pres. Foote Cone & Belding, N.Y.C., 1978—; mem. faculty Columbia Coll., 1959-60. Recipient Outdoor Advt. Inst. award, 1969, Golden Lion award Cannes Film Festival, 1970, Silver medal N.Y. Art Dirs. Club, 1978; named Copywriter of Yr., Chgo. Copywriter's Club, 1968. Mem. Friars Club, Atrium Club, Chgo. Copywriter's Club, African Travel Assn., Sigma Delta Chi. Created advt. campaigns, including: Schlitz Man of Sea/Gusto, Fly The Friendly Skies of United; introduced Taster's Choice Coffee in U.S.; author: The Happy Cooker, 1977; subject of chpt. in Lifestyle and Psychographics, 1974; writer numerous popular songs. Office: care Foote Cone & Belding 200 Park Ave New York NY 10017

LERNER, AARON BUNSEN, educator, physician; b. Mpls., Sept. 21, 1920; s. Morris and Lena (Schneider) L.; B.A. cum laude, U. Minn., 1941, M.S., 1942, Ph.D., M.D., 1945; m. Marguerite Rush, June 21, 1945; children—Peter, Michael, Ethan, Seth. Asst. prof. dermatology U. Mich., 1949-52; asso. prof. dermatology U. Oreg. Med. Sch., 1952-55; mem. faculty Yale Med. Sch., 1955—, prof. dermatology, 1957—, head sect., 1955—. Served with M.C., U.S. Army, 1946-48. Recipient Thomas F. Andrews undergrad. award research U. Minn., 1941; postdoctorate fellow Am. Cancer Soc., Western Res. U., 1948-49. Mem. Nat. Acad. Scis., Am. Soc. Biol. Chemists, Am. Acad. Dermatology, New Eng. Dermatology Assn., Sigma Xi, Phi Lambda Upsilon, Alpha Omega Alpha. Home: Old Mill Rd Woodbridge CT 06525 Office: Medical Sch Yale Univ New Haven CT 06510

LERNER, ABBA PTACHYA, economist; b. Bessarabia, Russia, 1903; came to U.S., 1937, naturalized, 1949; s. Morris Isaac and Sofie (Buchman) L.; B.Sc. in Econs., U. London, 1932, Ph.D. in Econs., 1943; m. Alice Sendak, 1929; children—Lionel John, Marion; m. 2d, Daliah Goldfarb, 1960. Instr., London Sch. Econs., 1935-39; asst. prof. U. Kansas City, 1940-42; prof. New Sch. Social Research, N.Y.C., 1942-47, Roosevelt U., Chgo., 1947-59, Mich. State U., 1959-65; prof. U. Calif. at Berkeley, 1965-71; distinguished prof. econs. Queens Coll., City U. N.Y., 1971-78, Fla. State U., 1978—; vis. prof. Columbia U., U. Va., Amherst Coll., Hebrew U. Jerusalem, Johns Hopkins U., U. Hawaii, U. Calif. at Los Angeles, U. Tel Aviv, U. Rio de Janeiro, Fla. State U.; cons. RAND Corp., 1949, Econ. Commn. for Europe, Geneva, 1950-51, Inst. Mediterranean Affairs, N.Y.C., 1958-59; econ. adviser Govt. Israel, Jerusalem, 1953-55; adviser to treasury Govt. of Israel and Bank of Israel, 1955-56. Leon fellow, 1934-35; Rockefeller fellow, 1937-39; Center for Advanced Study in Behavioral Scis. fellow, 1960-61; NSF grantee, 1975-76; fellow Villa Serbelloni, Rockefeller Found., 1976. Fellow Am. Econ. Assn. (past v.p.), Econometric Soc., London Sch. Econs. (hon.); mem. Nat. Acad. Scis. Pres., Univ. Centers for Rational Alternatives, 1975-77. Author: Economics of Control, 1944; Economics of Employment, 1951; Essays in Economic Analysis, 1953; Everybody's Business, 1962; Flation, 1973; others; contbr. articles to profl. jours., Ency. Brit. Home: 1903 Angel's Hollow Tallahassee FL 32308 Office: Dept Econs Fla State U Tallahassee FL 32306

LERNER, ABRAM, museum dir., artist; b. N.Y.C., Apr. 11, 1913; s. Hyman and Sarah (Becker) L.; B.A., N.Y. U., 1935; student Ednl. Alliance, Art Students League, Bklyn. Mus.; m. Pauline Hanenberg, Oct. 7, 1940; 1 dau., Aline. Asso. dir. A.C.A. Gallery and Artist's Gallery, N.Y.C., 1945-57; curator Joseph H. Hirshhorn Collection, N.Y.C., 1957-66; dir. Joseph H. Hirshhorn Mus. and Sculpture Garden, Smithsonian Instn., Washington, 1967—; one man show Davis Gallery, N.Y.C., 1958; group shows include: A.C.A. Gallery, Peridot Gallery, Bklyn.-Mus., Pa. Acad., Davis Gallery; represented in pvt. collections. Adv. bd. Archives Am. Art, 1970—. Contbr. to mags., mus. catalogues. Office: Hirshhorn Museum and Sculpture Garden Smithsonian Instn Washington DC 20560

LERNER, ALAN BURTON, lawyer; b. N.Y.C., Nov. 17, 1930; s. Samuel A. and Helen (Zisfein) L.; B.B.A., Coll. City N.Y., 1951; LL.B., Yale U., 1954; m. Elisabeth Waltraud Bruttel, July 5, 1959; children—Raissa, Anthony, Jessica, James. Admitted to N.Y. bar, 1954; asso. firm Chadbourne, Parke, Whiteside & Wolff, N.Y.C., 1956-60; with legal dept. C.I.T. Fin. Corp., N.Y.C., 1960—, gen. counsel, sec., 1976—, v.p., 1977—; cons. Fed. Res. Bd., 1973, Nat. Conf. Commrs. on Uniform State Laws, 1966-68. Served with AUS, 1954-56. Mem. Am., D.C. bar assns., Assn. Bar City N.Y., Law Forum-Nat. Consumer Fin. Assn., Assn. Comml. Fin. Attys. Home: 101 Brookside Dr Greenwich CT 06830 Office: 650 Madison Ave New York City NY 10022

LERNER, ALAN JAY, playwright, lyricist; b. N.Y.C., Aug. 31, 1918; B.S., Harvard U., 1940. Broadway mus. plays include: (with Frederick Loewe) What's Up?, 1943, The Day Before Spring, 1945, Brigadoon (N.Y. Drama Critic's Circle award), 1947, Paint Your Wagon, 1951, My Fair Lady (N.Y. Drama Critic's Circle award, Donaldson award, Antoinette Perry award), 1956, Camelot, 1960, (with Kurt Weill) Love Life, 1948, (with Burton Lane) On a Clear Day You Can See Forever (Grammy award), 1965, (with Andre Previn) Coco, 1969, (with Frederick Loewe) Gigi (Antoinette Perry award for best score), 1973; (with Leonard Bernstein) 1600 Pennsylvania Avenue, 1976, (with Burton Lane) Carmelina, 1979; screen plays include: Royal Wedding, 1951, An American in Paris (Best screenplay Oscar, Screenwriters Guild award), 1951, Gigi (Motion Picture Acad. award, Screenwriters Guild award), 1958, My Fair Lady, 1964, Camelot, 1968, (also producer) Paint Your Wagon, 1969, On a Clear Day You Can See Forever, 1970, The Little Prince, 1974. Bd. govs. Nat. Hosp. for Speech Disorders, N.Y. Osteo. Hosp. Named to Songwriter's Hall of Fame, 1971. Mem. Dramatists Guild Am. (pres. 1958-63), Shaw Soc. Clubs: Players, Lambs. Address: 424 Madison Ave New York NY 10017

LERNER, ALBERT MARTIN, physician; b. St. Louis, Sept. 3, 1929; s. Bernard and Sarah L.; B.A., Washington U., St. Louis, 1950, M.D., 1954; m. Helen Saperstein, June, 1966; children—Joshua, Emily, Joel, Elizabeth. Intern, Barnes Hosp., St. Louis, 1954-55, sr. asst. resident, 1958-59; asst. resident Boston City Hosp., 1957-58; sr. asst. surgeon, lab. investigator Nat. Inst. Allergy and Infectious Diseases, 1955-57; research fellow in medicine Thorndike Meml. Lab., Boston City Hosp. and Harvard Med. Sch., 1959-62; fellow Med. Found. Greater Boston, Inc., 1960-63; research asso. dept. biology Mass. Inst. Tech., 1962-63; asso. prof. medicine, chief div. infectious diseases Wayne State U. Sch. Medicine, 1963-67, asso. in microbiology, 1963—, asso. in pathology, 1964—; prof. pro-tem dept. medicine William Beaumont Army Med. Center, El Paso, Tex., 1974; chief infectious diseases Detroit Gen. Hosp., 1963-73, asso. in medicine, 1963-65, in pathology, 1964-65, dir. bacteriology lab., 1964-69, clin. cons., 1969—, mem. attending staff in medicine, 1965-67, cons. pathology, 1965—, sr. mem. attending staff, 1967—; cons. in infectious diseases VA Hosps.; chief dept. medicine Hutzel Hosp., Detroit, 1970—; mem. cons. staff dept. pediatric medicine Children's Hosp. Mich., 1971—; mem. ad hoc advisory com. Antiviral Substances Program, Nat. Inst. Allergy and Infectious Diseases, 1971; external reviewer for research grants Med. Research Council Can., 1973; invited lectr. Johann Wolfgang Goethe U., Oberusel, Germany, 1974; mem. advisory com. Fedn. Am. Socs. Exptl. Biology. Served with USPHS, 1955-57. Recipient Staff award Sr. Class Wayne State U. Sch. Medicine, 1974; diplomate Am. Bd. Internal Medicine. Fellow A.C.P. (govs. advisory com. Mich. 1974—, chmn. com. conuing edn. Mich. chpt. 1976—), Am. Coll. Clin. Pharmacology; mem. Am. Soc. Microbiology, N.Y. Acad. Scis., Am. Fedn. Clin. Research (pres. Ann Arbor-Detroit-Toledo-Lansing chpt. 1967-68), Infectious Diseases Soc. Am., Central Soc. Clin. Research, Am. Soc. Clin. Investigation, Am. Assn. Immunologists Soc. Exptl. Biology and Medicine, Am. Pub. Health Assn., Detroit Med. Club, Wayne County Med. Soc. (chmn. med. sect. 1970-72), Am. Assn. Physicians, Mich. Found. Infectious Diseases (pres. 1976), Pan Am. Med. Assn. (life), Probus Club Detroit (5th Ann. award for acad. achievement 1967), Phi Lambda Kappa (award for outstanding contbn. to research, teaching and acad. medicine 1969). Asso. sci. editor Mich. Medicine, 1968-70; contbr. articles to profl. jours. Office: 4707 Saint Antoine St Detroit MI 48201

LERNER, DANIEL, social scientist, educator; b. N.Y.C., Nov. 3, 1917; s. Louis and Yetta (Swiger) L.; A.B., N.Y.U., 1938, M.A., 1939, Ph.D., 1948; m. Jean Weinstein, May 16, 1947; children—Louise, Thomas, Amy. Instr. modern European history and lit., 1939-42; European rep. Library of Congress Mission, 1946-47; exec. sec. and research dir. internat. studies project, 1947-53; acting prof. sociology Stanford, 1951-53; vis. prof. sociology Columbia, 1951; prof. sociology Mass. Inst. Tech., 1953—, Ford prof. sociology and internat. communications, 1958—, chmn. polit. and social sci. dept., 1963- 64; dir. Institut de Recherches Sociales, Paris, France, 1955-65; vis. prof. U. Paris (Sorbonne). Served to capt. AUS, 1942-46; chief editor intelligence br. Psychol. Warfare Div., SHAEF; chief intelligence Info. Control Div., Office of Mil. Govt. U.S. Decorated Bronze Star, Purple Heart; Palmes Academiques, officier d'Academie (France). Fellow Conf. Sci., Philosophy and Religion; mem. Am. Sociol. Soc., Am. Polit. Sci. Assn., World, Am. assns. pub. opinion research, Am. Psychol. Assn. Author: Psychological Warfare Against Nazi Germany, 1949; Propaganda in War and Crisis, 1951; (with H.D. Laswell) The Policy Sciences, 1951; The Nazi Elite, 1951; (with Raymond Aron) LaQuerelle de 1a CED, 1956; France Defeats E.D.C., 1957; The Passing of Traditional Society, 1958; The Human Meaning of the Social Sciences, 1959; Evidence and Inference, 1960; Quantity and Quality, 1961; Parts and Wholes, 1963; Cause and Effect, 1965; (with H.D. Lasswell) World Revolutionary Elites, 1965; (with Wilbur Schramm) Communication and Change in the Developing Countries, 1967; (with Morton Gorden) Euratlantica; Changing Perspectives of The European Elites, 1969; (with Wilbur Schramm) Communications and Change: The Last Ten Years-and the Next, 1976; Values and Development: Appraising Asian Experience, 1976; (with L.M. Nelson) Communication Research-A Half-Century Appraisal, 1977, Propaganda and Communication in World History, 3 vols., 1979; editor: M.I.T. Studies in Comparative Politics, 1965-75. Home: 232 Northrop Pl Santa Cruz CA 95060. *I hope that America will achieve what Athens dreamed of—the effective meeting of minds between men of knowledge and men of power—thereby making world peace the law of life on our planet.*

LERNER, DONALD MICHAEL, lawyer; b. Cin., July 20, 1935; s. Oscar Arthur and Frieda Rose (Fox) L.; B.S. cum laude, Miami U., Oxford, Ohio, 1957; LL.B., Yale U., 1960; m. Saundra Lee Butler, Dec. 16, 1974; children—Marcia Elaine, Kenneth Crowner, David Adam. Admitted to Ohio bar, 1960, Fla. bar, 1979, practiced in Cin., 1960—; partner, prin. firm Lerner, Sampson & Rothfuss Co., L.P.A., and predecessors, 1975—; dir. U.S. Precision Lens, Inc., Midwest Woodworking, Inc., Lomark Discount Drugs. Mem. Ohio Bar Assn., Cin. Bar Assn., Fla. Bar Assn. Home: 3663 Grovedale Pl Cincinnati OH 45208 Office: 700 Tri-State Bldg Cincinnati OH 45202 also 2500 N University Dr Suite 2 Fort Lauderdale FL

LERNER, ELIEZER, banker; b. Rowno, Poland, Jan. 19, 1916; s. Eliahu M. and Feiga (Kriwin) L.; grad. high sch., 1934; m. Lea Berkowsky, Aug. 20, 1940; children—Abraham I., Zipora (Mrs. Daniel Bursuk). Immigrated to Israel, 1935. With Union Bank Israel (formerly Palestine Corp.), Tel Aviv, 1935-71, dep. gen. mgr., 1967-71; exec. v.p. 1st Israel Bank (name now Bank Leumi Trust Co. N.Y.), N.Y.C., 1971-72, pres., 1972-78, sr. exec. officer-regional mgmt. Western Hemisphere, 1978—. Club: Manhattan (N.Y.C.). Home: 250 E 65th St New York City NY 10021 Office: 562 Fifth Ave New York City NY 10036

LERNER, EUGENE MAX, economist; b. Milw., Oct. 19, 1928; s. Hyman M. and Dorothy (Buchler) L.; B.A., U. Wis., 1949, M.A., 1950; Ph.D., U. Chgo., 1954; m. Janet Ruth Weiss, July 1, 1951; children—Susan, Laura, Dean. With Fed. Res. Bank Chgo., 1957-58; mem. faculty Coll. City N.Y., 1959-63, N.Y.U., 1963-66; mem. faculty Northwestern U., 1966—, prof. finance, 1966—. Mem. Am. Econ. Assn., Am. Finance Assn. Author: Readings In Financial Analysis, 1963; A Theory of Financial Analysis, 1967; Managerial Finance—A Systems Approach, 1971. Home: 823 Ingleside Pl Evanston IL 60201

LERNER, HARRY, lawyer, corp. exec.; b. Easton, Pa., Jan. 24, 1939; s. Albert I. and Shirley (Kraus) L.; B.A., Cornell U., 1960; J.D., N.Y. U., 1963; m. Sherryl Adrienne Blumin, Nov. 18, 1962; 1 dau., Michelle Hope. Admitted to N.Y. State bar, 1963, N.J. bar, 1966; asso. firm Otterbourg, Steindler, Houston & Rosen, N.Y.C., 1964-65; asso. firm Robert Greenberg, West New York, N.J., 1965-67; asst. house counsel Ronson Corp., Bridgewater, N.J., 1967-71; asst. to gen. counsel, 1971-75, sec., corp. counsel, 1975—. Served with U.S. Army, 1963-64. Mem. N.J. Bar Assn., Am. Soc. Corp. Secs., Zeta Beta Tau. Office: One Ronson Rd Bridgewater NJ 08807

LERNER, HARRY JONAS, publishing co. exec.; b. Mpls., Mar. 5, 1932; s. Morris and Lena (Liederschneider) L.; student U. Mich., 1952, Hebrew U., Jerusalem, 1953-54; B.A., U. Minn., 1957; m. Sharon Ruth Goldman, June 21, 1961; children—Adam Morris, Mia Carol, Daniel Aryeh, Leah Anne. Founder, Lerner Publs. Co., Mpls., 1959, pres., chief exec. officer, pub., 1959—; founder Muscle Bound Bindery, Inc., 1967, pres., chief exec. officer, 1967—; founder Carolrhoda Books, Inc., 1969, v.p., gen. mgr., 1969—; bd. visitors U. Minn. Press; del. White House Conf. on Library and Info. Services, 1979. Chmn. North Loop Bus. Assn., Mpls., 1972—, Minn. Book Pubs. Roundtable, 1974—. Bd. dirs., library dir. Jewish Community Center; bd. dirs. Fgn. Policy Assn. Minn., 1970-71. Served with AUS, 1954-56; ETO. Recipient Brotherhood award NCCJ, 1961, also numerous graphic arts awards. Mem. Mpls. Inst. Art, Walker Art Center, A.C.L.U., Delta Tau Kappa. Mem. Democratic Farmer Labor Party. Club: Daybreakers Breakfast (Mpls.). Home: 2215 N Willow Ln Minneapolis MN 55416 Office: 241 1st Ave N Minneapolis MN 55401

LERNER, LOUIS ABRAHAM, former ambassador, newspaper pub.; b. Chgo., June 12, 1935; s. Leo Alfred and Deana (Duskin) L.; student U. Chgo., 1951-54; Scandinavian seminars, Copenhagen, 1956-57; B.A., Roosevelt U., 1960; m. Susan Winchester, July 22, 1957; children—Lucy Alix, Jane Chelsea. Reporter North Town News, Chgo., 1954-56; corr. Accredited Home Newspapers Am., Chgo., Copenhagen, 1956-58; exec. Lerner Home Newspapers, Chgo., 1959-77, pub., 1969-77; U.S. ambassador to Norway, 1977-79; pres. Lerner Suburban Communications, 1970-77; dir. Myers Pub. Co., Lincoln-Belmont Pub. Co. Commr. Nat. Commn. on Libraries and Info. Scis., 1972-77; mem. Ill. Adv. Com. on State Library, 1969-77. Mem. citizen's bd. Catholic Interracial Council, 1964-69, Walker Art Center., Mpls., 1969-77, Chgo. Mus. Contemporary Art, 1965, Stedjelik Mus., Amsterdam, 1960; bd. dirs. Surburban Newspapers Am., Chgo. Better Bus. Bur., Chgo. Pub. Library, also v.p.; bd. dirs. Lyric Opera Guild; mem. Nat. UN Day Com., 1972-74. Recipient Service award Accredited Home Newspapers Am., 1960. Mem. North Town C. of C. (dir. 1963-65), Am. Acad. Polit. and Social Sci., ALA, Sigma Delta Chi. Democrat. Clubs: Headline, Econ., City (bd. govs. 1966-69) (Chgo.). Home: 442 W Wellington Chicago IL 60657 Office: 7519 N Ashland Ave Chicago IL 60626 also Dept State 2201 C St NW Washington DC 20520

LERNER, LOUIS C., corp. exec.; b. Boston, 1910; ed. State Tchrs. Coll., 1933. Pres., dir. Lerner & Co., Boca Raton, Fla.; pres., treas. Victoria Investment Co., Ltd., Halifax, N.S.; chmn. bd., chmn. exec. com. George E. Keith Co., Brockton, Mass.; chmn. bd., pres. Marina Industries, Squantum, Mass., Ofcl. Industries, Inc., N.Y.C.; dir. Coplay Cement Mfg. Co. Address: 315 Golf View Dr Boca Raton FL 33432

LERNER, MARTIN, mus. curator; b. N.Y.C., Nov. 14, 1936; s. Joseph and Rose (Kolberg) L.; B.A., Bklyn. Coll., 1959; postgrad. Inst. Fine Arts, N.Y. U., 1961-65; m. Roberta M. Rubenstein, Feb. 26, 1968; children—Benjamin Louis, Seth Laurence, Jocelyn Ann. Asst. prof. U. Calif., Santa Barbara, 1965-66; asst. curator Oriental art Cleve. Mus. Art, 1966-72; asst. prof. Case Western Res. U., 1968-72; vice chmn. charge Far Eastern art Met. Mus. Art, N.Y.C., 1972-75, curator Indian and S.E. Asian art, 1978—; cons. in field. Served with U.S. Army, 1959-61. Author: Bronze Sculpture from Asia, 1975; Blue and White: Early Japanese Export Ware, 1978; contbr. articles to profl. jours. Home: Giglio Ct Croton-on-Hudson NY 10520 Office: Met Mus of Art Fifth Ave at 82d St New York NY 10028

LERNER, MARVIN NORRIS, food co. exec.; b. Phila., Apr. 18, 1924; s. Abraham and Mae (Markowitz) L.; student Temple U., 1940-42; m. Joyce Altman, Nov. 6, 1949; children—Deborah, Patricia. Pres., Lerner Markets, Phila., 1947-57; dir. store operations Bargain City, 1957-59, dir. produce operations N.Y. br. Food Fair Stores, 1959-61, chain supr. discount operations, 1961-63, zone mgr. discount food operations, 1963-65, staff v.p. Pantry Pride supermarkets, 1974-76, exec. v.p., 1976-78, pres., 1978—, v.p. parent co. Food Fair, 1978—, sr. v.p., chief operating officer, 1978—; v.p. sales and ops. The Bohack Corp., Bklyn., 1965-69, exec. v.p., 1969-74, pres., chief exec. officer, 1974, also dir.; pres., chief exec. officer El-D Corp., Bala Cynwyd, Pa., 1979—. Mem. Roslyn Landmark Soc. Served to 1st lt., inf., AUS, 1942-47. Mem. N.Y. Food Mchts. Assn. (bd. dirs.). Home: 130 Cherry Ln Wynnewood PA 19096 Office: 3175 John F Kennedy Blvd Philadelphia PA

LERNER, MAX, author, lectr.; b. Minsk, Russia, Dec. 20, 1902; s. Benjamin and Bessie (Podel) L.; brought to U.S., 1907; A.B., Yale, 1923, student law, 1923-24; A.M., Washington U., St. Louis, 1925; Ph.D., Robert Brookings Grad. Sch. Econs. and Govt., Washington, 1927; m. Anita Marburg, July 20, 1928 (div. 1940); children—Constance, Pamela (dec.), Joanna; m. 2d, Edna Albers, Aug. 16, 1941; children—Michael, Stephen, Adam. Asst. editor Ency. Social Scis., 1927, later mng. editor; mem. social sci. faculty Sarah Lawrence Coll., 1932-35; chmn. faculty Wellesley Summer Inst., 1933-35; dir. consumers' div. Nat. Emergency Council, 1934; lectr. govt. Harvard, 1935-36, prof. govt. summer school, 1939-41; editor The Nation, 1936-38; prof. polit. sci. Williams Coll., 1938-43; radio commentator; editorial dir. PM, 1943-48; columnist N.Y. Star, 1948-49; prof. Am. civilization Brandeis U., 1949-73, dean Grad. Sch., 1954-56; world-wide syndicated columnist N.Y. Post and Los Angeles Times Syndicate, 1949—; Ford Found prof. Am. civilization Sch. Internat. Studies, U. Delhi, India, 1959-60; prof. human behavior Grad. Sch. Human Behavior, U.S. Internat. U., San Diego, 1974—. Ford Found. grantee European civilization study, 1962-63. Mem. N.E.A. (ednl. policies commn.). Author: It Is Later Than You Think, rev. edit., 1943; Ideas Are Weapons, 1939; Ideas for the Ice Age, 1941; The Mind and Faith of Justice Holmes, 1943; Public Journal, 1945; The Portable Veblen, 1948; Actions and Passions, 1949; America as a Civilization, 1957; The Unfinished Country, 1959; The Essential Works of John Stuart Mill, 1961; The Age of Overkill, 1962; Education and a Radical Humanism, 1962; Tocqueville and American Civilzation, 1969; Values in Education, 1976. Co-editor: Tocqueville, Democracy in America, 1966. Home: 25 East End Ave New York City NY 10028. *I have believed in love and work, and their linkage. I have believed that we are neither angels nor devils, but humans, with clusters of potentials in both directions. I am neither an optimist nor pessimist, but a possibilist.*

LERNER, NATHAN BERNARD, artist; b. Chgo., Mar. 15, 1913; s. Louis Alexander and Ida Lerner; student Nat. Acad. Art, Chgo., 1931, Art Inst. Chgo., 1933-34; B.S., Sch. Design in Chgo., 1941; m. Kiyoko Asai, July 1, 1968; children—Michael John, Amy Elizabeth. Head of photo workshop Sch. of Design in Chgo., 1941-43; head of product design workshop, dean of faculty and students Inst. of Design, Chgo., 1945-49, ednl. dir., 1946-47; prof. U. Ill., Chgo., 1967-72; pres. Lerner Design Assos., 1949-72; one man exhbns. include: Chgo. Mus. Sci. and Industry, 1974, Bauhaus Archives, Berlin, 1975, Pentax Gallery, Tokyo, 1976, Harry Lunn Gallery, Washington, 1977, Frumkin Gallery, Chgo., 1977, G.R. Hawkins Gallery, Los Angeles, 1977, represented in permanent collections Art Inst. Chgo., Mus. Modern

Art, N.Y.C., Mus. Modern Art, Paris, Bibliotheque National, Paris, Eastman House, Rochester, Bauhaus Archive, Berlio, Mpls. Art Inst., Mus. Contemporary Art, Chgo., Nihon U., Tokyo, Seattle Mus. Art, Monterey (Calif.) Inst. Art, Amon Carter Mus., Fort Worth. Ill. Arts Council grantee, 1977-78. Mem. Artists Guild Chgo., Art Inst. Chgo. Alumni Assn. Patentee in field. Address: 849 W Webster Chicago IL 60614

LERNER, WARREN, historian; b. Boston, July 16, 1929; s. Max and Rebecca (Rudnick) L.; B.S., Boston U., 1952; M.A. and cert. of Russian Inst. Columbia U., 1954, Ph.D. (Am. Council Learned Socs.-Social Service Research Council fgn. area fellow), 1961; m. Francine Sandra Pickow, Aug. 16, 1959; children—Suzanne Rachel, Amy Florence, Daniel Joseph. Asst. prof. history Roosevelt U., 1959-61; asst. prof. Duke U., 1961-65, asso. prof., 1965-72, prof., 1972—; cons. Nat. Endowment for Humanities, 1974—. Served with U.S. Army, 1954-56. Am. Philos. Soc. fellow, 1972; Nat. Endowment for Humanities sr. fellow, 1974-75. Mem. Conf. Slavic and East European History (exec. council 1978—), So. Conf. Slavic Studies. Jewish. Author: Karl Radek: The Last Internationalist, 1970; Editor: The Development of Soviet Foreign Policy, 1973; (with Clifford M. Foust) The Soviet World in Flux, 1967; contbr. articles to profl. jours.; internat. editorial bd. Studies in Comparative Communism, 1973—. Office: Dept History Duke U Durham NC 27706

LEROY, DAVID HENRY, lawyer, state atty. gen.; b. Seattle, Aug. 16, 1947; s. Harold David and Lela Fay (Palmer) L.; B.S., U. Idaho, 1969, J.D., 1971; M.Law, N.Y. U., 1972; m. Helen LaVonne Transue, Aug. 5, 1972. Admitted to Idaho bar, 1971, N.Y. State bar, 1973, U.S. Supreme Ct. bar, 1976; law clk. Idaho 4th Dist. Ct., Boise, 1969: legal asst. Boise Cascade Corp., 1970; asso. firm Rothblatt, Rothblatt, Seijas & Peskin, N.Y.C., 1971-73; dep. prosecutor Ada County Prosecutor's Office, Boise, 1973-74, pros. atty., 1974-78; atty. gen. State of Idaho, Boise, 1978—. Mem. State Task Force on Child Abuse, 1975; mem. Ada County Council on Alcoholism, 1976; del. Republican Nat. Conv., 1976; bd. dirs. United Fund, 1975-80; legal counsel Young Republicans, 1974-77. Mem. Nat. Dist. Atty.'s Assn., Idaho Prosecutors Assn., Am. Trial Lawyers Assn., Idaho Trial Lawyers Assn., Nat. Assn. Atty.'s Gen., Idaho Bar Assn., Omicron Sigma, Sigma Alpha Epsilon. Presbyterian. Home: 2305 Claremont Dr Boise ID 83702 Office: Statehouse Rm 210 Boise ID 83720

LEROY, HAROLD M., artist; b. N.Y.C., Dec. 12, 1905; s. Charles J. and Miriam (Raphael) Levy; student Columbia U., 1924-26, Bklyn. Mus. Art Sch., 1959-65, Art Students League, N.Y.C., summers 1961-62; pupil of Hans Hofmann, 1958; m. Irene F. Bloom, Oct. 30, 1927; children—Zelda Leroy Scholnick, Albert Ralphael. One-man exhbns. include Mattawan (N.J.) Art Gallery, 1966, Ella Lerner Galleries, N.Y.C., 1968, Gallery Royal, Bklyn., 1970, 72, Plainview (N.Y.) Public Library, 1972, Lexington Art Gallery, N.Y.C., 1976, Randall Gallery, N.Y.C., 1979; group exhbns. include Audubon Artists Nat. Acad., 1970-73, Les Artistes de l'Ecole Francaise, Paris, 1969, 70, Donnell Arts Library, N.Y.C., 1968, Va. State Coll., Petersburg, 1969, U. Mich., Ann Arbor, 1969, L.I. U., 1971, SUNY, Alfred, 1976, Cayuga Mus. History and Art, Auburn, N.Y., 1976, George Washington Carver Mus., Tuskegee, Ala., 1976; N.Y. U., 1979, U.S. Customs House, 1979, Bklyn. Mus., 1979, Lincoln Center, N.Y.C., 1977, 78, 79; represented in permanent collections: Butler Inst. Am. Art, Indpls., Mint Mus., Chrysler Mus., Miami (Fla.) Mus. Modern Art, Mus. Modern Art, London, Ont., Safed (Israel) Mus., Slater Meml. Mus., Norwich, Conn., Smithsonian Instn.; designer Charles J. Levy Co., 1927-28; designer costumes for Ziegfield Follies, 1929; writer, illustrator Hollywood Filmograph, 1931-32, Hollywood Screen World, 1932-44; contbr. Illustrated Milliner, 1929-32. Reporter, editor Midwood Manor News, civic assns., Bklyn., 1922-24. Recipient Gold medal Accademia Internazionale, 1973, award Nat. Arts Club, 1976, Benezit, Paris, 1976, Am. Vets. Soc. Artists, 1979. Mem. Am. Soc. Contemporary Artists (pres. 1979—), Artists Equity Assn. (dir. 1967-79), Group Three Artists (v.p.) 1969-74), Met. Painters and Sculptors (dir. 1973-74). Author: The Role of the American Artists in the Bicentennial Year, 1976; also articles. Pioneer in metaltone painting. . *My goal always has been to give back a part of the great store of beauty I've enjoyed in our world.*

LEROY, L. DAVID, journalist; b. Tignall, Ga., Jan. 2, 1920; s. Lansing Burrows and Glennie (David) LeR.; A.B., U. Ga., 1941; m. Mary Margaret Pridgeon, Sept. 2, 1945; children—David Charles, Gregory Alan. Mem. nat. staff V.F.W., Washington, 1947-48; copyscript writer Gardner Advt. Co., Washington, 1948-49; mng. editor Air Force Times, 1950-53; with U.S. News & World Report, 1953-70, news editor, 1953-64, mem. Capitol Hill staff, 1964-70; publs. dir. Republican Congl. Com., 1970-74, pub. relations dir., 1974-76; exec. dir. Nat. Press Found., 1977—. Active local Boy Scouts Am. Served with AUS, 1941-46. Decorated Purple Heart. Mem. Nat. Press Club (pres. 1967, bd. govs., chmn. bd. govs.), Nat. Rifle Assn., Sigma Delta Chi. Presbyn. (elder). Club: Fairfax Rod and Gun. Author: Gerald Ford—Untold Story, 1974; The Outdoorsman's Guide to Government Surplus, 1978; co-author: Building and Repairing Canoes and Kayaks, 1978. Editor: Nat. Press Club Record, 1960. Contbr. articles to mil. mags. Home: 4404 N 36th St Arlington VA 22207

LE ROY, MERVYN, motion picture producer; b. San Francisco, Oct. 15, 1900; s. Harry and Edna (Armer) Le R.; ed. pub. schs.; m. Doris Warner, Jan. 2, 1933; children—Warner Lewis, Linda Mervyn; m. 2d, Kathryn Spiegel, 1946. Began career as actor, 1912; asst. cameraman, 1919-20; directed motion pictures Little Caesar, I am a Fugitive from a Chain Gang, Tugboat Annie, Anthony Adverse, others; producer, dir. Warner Bros. Studios, 1936-38, Metro-Goldwyn-Mayer Studios, 1938—; organized own prodn. co. Arrowhead Prodns., Burbank, Calif., 1944; produced Stand Up and Fight, Wizard of Oz, Babes in Arms, Blossoms in the Dust, 1941, Random Harvest, 1942, Madame Curie, Thirty Seconds Over Tokyo, Without Reservations, Little Women, Any Number Can Play, 1949, East Side, West Side, 1950, Quo Vadis, 1951, Lovely to Look At, Million Dollar Mermaid, 1952; produced, directed No Time for Sergeants, 1958, The FBI Story, 1959, Wake Me When It's Over, 1960, Gypsy, 1962, Mary-Mary, 1964, Moment to Moment, 1965. Recipient Oscar for direction of The House I Live In, 1945; Victoire du Cinema Francais award, 1954; Irving Thalberg award, 1975; Club: Hollywood Turf (pres.). Author: Mervyn Le Roy: Take One, 1974. Address: 9200 Sunset Blvd Los Angeles CA 90069*

LEROY, ROBERT PIERRE, hotel exec.; b. Jersey City, Aug. 22, 1924; s. Elie Pierre and Helen (Wright) L.; student Loyola U., Los Angeles; m. Florence Simmons, June 15, 1957; children—Patria Anne, Robert David. Exec. with Hilton Hotels Corp., 1952-61; with Pick Hotels Corp., 1961-75; with Hotel div. IDS Properties, Inc., Mpls., 1976-77; v.p., gen. mgr. The Drake, Chgo., 1977—. Mem. Businessmen for Loyola U., Chgo., 1961—. Served with USNR, 1942-46. Recipient Hall of Fame Hospitality Industry award, 1969; named Mr. Gourmet, 1969. Mem. Internat. Wine and Food Soc. (Chgo. and London), Post Grad. Wine Coll., Connoisseurs Internat., Culinary Inst. Am. (dir.). Home: The Drake Apt 952 140 E Walton Pl Chicago IL 60611

LERRIGO, FRANK CHARLES, lawyer; b. Topeka, May 23, 1906; s. Charles H. and Annabel (Barry) L.; A.B., Stanford, 1928, LL.B., 1931; m. Margaret Craig Adams, June 30, 1937 (dec. Mar. 1968); children—Thomas Wayne, William C.; m. 2d, Margaret Crawford Marrs, Sept. 25, 1970. Admitted to Calif. bar, 1931; practiced in Fresno, 1935—; legal adviser Calif. Commr. of Corps., 1932-34; atty. Fed. Intermediate Credit Bank, 1934-35; of counsel Lerrigo, Thuesen, Walters, Nibler & Hedrick, 1977—; U.S. commr., 1936-70; fed. magistrate, 1971-77. Partner Varni Assos., investments. Chmn. legal seminar agrl. financing Calif. Bankers Assn., 1970. Chmn. Boy Scout Fund Drive, 1970. Pres. Reeves Lake Land Co.; bd. advisers Fresno Community Hosp. Recipient Silver Beaver award Boy Scouts Am., 1973. Mem. Am., Calif., Fresno County (past sec.) bar assns., Kappa Sigma. Conglist. Mason (32 deg., Shriner). Clubs: Fresno County Sportsman's (dir., past pres.), Shaver Lake Fishing (past pres.), Sunnyside Country (Fresno). Home: 1831 S Claremont St Fresno CA 93727 Office: Security Bank Bldg Fresno CA 93721

LERUDE, WARREN LESLIE, newspaper publisher; b. Reno, Oct. 29, 1937; s. Leslie Raymond and Ione (Lundy) L.; B.A. in Journalism, U. Nev., 1961; m. Janet Lagomarsino, Aug. 24, 1961; children—Eric Warren, Christopher Mario, Leslie Ann. Reporter, AP, Las Vegas, Reno, San Diego, Los Angeles, 1961-63; reporter Reno Evening Gazette, Nev. State Jour., 1963-65, news editor, 1965-68, mng. editor, 1968-72, exec. editor, 1972-77, pub., 1977—; Pulitzer prize juror, 1973, 74, 76; writer, editing lectr. Am. Press Inst.; chmn. Nat. Freedom of Info. Served with USN, 1967-69. Co-recipient Pulitzer prize in journalism for editorial writing, 1977. Mem. AP Mng. Editors Assn. (dir.), Am. Soc. Newspaper Editors, Am. Newspaper Pubs. Assn., Calif.-Nev. AP News Execs. Council (past chmn.), Nev. Press Assn. (pres. 1979—), Sigma Delta Chi. Mem. Christian Ch. Clubs: Lions; Elks. Home: 3825 N Folsom Dr Reno NV 89509 Office: 401 W 2d St Reno NV 89504. *The job of journalism in modern society not only to inform but to enlighten, with reason, through vigorous editorial writing.*

LESAR, HIRAM HENRY, lawyer, educator; b. Thebes, Ill., May 8, 1912; s. Jacob L. and Missouri Mabel (Keith) L.; A.B., U. Ill., 1934, J.D., 1936; J.S.D., Yale, 1938; m. Rosalee Berry, July 11, 1937; children—James Hiram, Albert Keith, Byron Lee. Admitted to Ill. bar, 1937, Mo. bar, 1954, U.S. Supreme Ct., 1960; asst. prof. law U. Kans., 1937-40, asso. prof., 1940-42; sr., prin. atty. bd. legal examiners U.S. CSC, 1942-44; asso. prof. law U. Mo., 1946-48, prof., 1948-57; prof. law Washington U., St. Louis, 1957-72, dean Sch. Law, 1960-72; dean, prof. law So. Ill. U., 1972—, interim pres. univ., 1974, acting pres., 1979—; vis. prof. law U. Ill., summer 1947, Ind. U., summer 1952, U. So. Calif., summer 1959, U. N.C., summer 1961, N.Y. U., summer 1965. Bd. dirs. Legal Aid Soc. St. Louis and St. Louis County, 1960-72, pres., 1966-67; mem. Human Relations Commn. University City, Mo., 1966-71, chmn., 1966, 67; mem. Fed. Mediation and Conciliation Service, other arbitration panels. Served from lt. (j.g.) to lt. comdr. USNR, 1944-46. Fellow Am. Bar Found.; mem. Am. Arbitration Assn., Am. Law Inst. Am., Fed., Mo., Ill., St. Louis bar assns., Am. Acad. Polit. and Social Sci., Am. Judicature Soc., AAUP, Phi Beta Kappa, Order of Coif, Phi Kappa Phi. Baptist. Mason (K.T.). Clubs: University (St. Louis); Nat. Lawyers (Washington); Yale (Chgo.); Jackson Country. Author: Landlord and Tenant, 1957. Contbr. to Am. Law of Property, 1952, supplement, 1977, also Dictionary Am. History, Ency. Brit. Home: 11 Hillcrest Dr Carbondale IL 62901

LESCAZE, LEE ADRIEN, journalist; b. N.Y.C., Dec. 8, 1938; s. William Edmond and Mary (Hughes) L.; A.B., Harvard, 1960; m. Rebecca Giraud Hughes, Mar. 25, 1967; children—Alexandra Hughes, Miranda Mary, Adrien William. With Washington Post, 1963—, asst. fgn. editor, 1965-67, Saigon corr., 1967-68, Hong Kong corr., 1970-73, fgn. editor, 1973-74, nat. editor, 1975-77, N.Y. corr., 1977—. Home: 209 E 48th St New York City NY 10017 Office: 1150 15th St Washington DC 20071

LESCH, GEORGE HENRY, mfg. co. exec.; b. Washburn, Ill., Oct. 10, 1909; s. William and Cora (Held) L.; B.S. with honours, U. Ill., 1931; LL.D., Syracuse U., 1964; m. Esther Barrett, Aug. 16, 1935; children—Elizabeth (Mrs. Arthur Ramee), Georgette (Mrs. Mark Copeland). With Arthur Anderson & Co., C.P.A.'s, Chgo., 1931-32; with Colgate Palmolive Co., 1932—, beginning as mem. fgn. dept., successively mem. European auditing staff, treas. Colgate-Palmolive S.A., pres., v.p. Colgate Palmolive Internat. charge sales and advt. U.K. and Europe, 1932-57, pres. Colgate Palmolive Internat., 1957-60, also dir.; pres., chief exec. officer Colgate-Palmolive Co., 1960-61, chmn. bd., pres., 1961-70, chmn. bd., 1970-75; dir. Bank N.Y., Amstar Corp., F.W. Woolworth Co., Uniroyal, Inc., Anchor Hocking Inc. Decorated comdr. Order Merit (Italy). Club: Candlewood Lake (Conn.). Home: 2817 Casey Key Rd Nokomis FL 33555

LESCH, JAMES RICHARD, mfg. co. exec.; b. Apache, Okla., July 13, 1921; s. Emil W. and Rose (Stenger) L.; B.S. in Mech. Engring., U. Okla., 1946; m. Zelma Lee Meeks, Sept. 10, 1942; children—James Richard, Jack Wayne, Terry Alan, Steven Andrew. With Hughes Tool Co., Houston, 1946—, v.p. product planning and adminstrn. services, 1962-68, dir., 1964—, sr. v.p., gen. mgr., 1968-72, pres., chief operating officer, 1972-79, pres., chief exec. officer, 1979—; dir., officer Hughes Tool Co. S.A.C.I.F.I., Hughes Tool Co., Ltd., Hughes Tool Co., Australia, Hughes Tool Co. de Mexico, Hughes Tool Co., C.A. (Venezuela), J.-Hughes Inc., dir. Raymond Internat.; adv. dir. Tex. Commerce Bank. Trustee United Fund, Houston and Harris County Tex. Trustee South Tex. Coll. Law; engring. found. adv. council U. Tex. at Austin; bd. dirs. Gulf Coast div. Tex. Soc. Prevention Blindness; nat. adv. bd. Goodwill Industries Am.; Houston area chmn. U.S. Savs. Bond Indsl. Payroll Savs. Com., 1978; exec. com. Center Internat. Bus. Served with U.S. Army, 1942-45. Named to U. Okla. Engring. Hall of Fame, 1971. Mem. Petroleum Equipment Suppliers Assn. (pres. 1979), Am. Petroleum Inst., Tex. Mid-Continent Oil and Gas Assn. (exec. com.), Internat. Assn. Drilling Contractors, Nat. Ocean Ind. Assn., Houston Dist. Export Council, Nomads, Houston C. of C. (dir. 1968—, chmn. 1977-78), Jr. Achievement of S.E. Tex. (pres. 1973-74). Methodist. Clubs: Masons, Houston Met. Racquet, 25 Yr. of Petroleum Industry, Petroleum, Houston, Lakeside Country (Houston). Home: 12210 Broken Bough Houston TX 77024 Office: PO Box 2539 Houston TX 77001

LESESNE, JOAB MAULDIN, JR., coll. pres.; b. Greenville, S.C., June 21, 1937; s. Joab Mauldin and Henrietta (Fennell) L.; B.A., Erskine Coll., 1959; M.A., U. S.C., 1961, Ph.D., 1967; m. Ruth Orborne, Feb. 1, 1958; children—Julia Ruth, Maryrose Lyle, Joab Mauldin III, Henry Herbert. Instr. U. S.C.-Coastal Carolina br., Conway, 1960-62; mem. faculty Wofford Coll., 1964—, dean coll., 1970-72, pres., 1972—; past pres. S.C. Assn. Colls. and Univs.; chmn. S.C. Tuition Grants Commn., 1972; mem. S.C. Commn. on Archives and History. Mem. S.C. Hist. Assn. (past pres.), S.C. N.G., Young Presidents Orgn. Methodist. Author: History of Erskine College, 1967. Home: 148 Wofford Campus Spartanburg SC 29303

LESH, JANET ROUNTREE, astrophysicist; b. Chgo., Aug. 14, 1937; d. Ernest Alonzo and Frances Careta (Vogel) Rountree; A.B., Cornell U., 1958; postgrad. U. Paris, 1958-60; Ph.D., U. Chgo., 1967; m. J. Harold Lesh, Apr. 19, 1960 (div. 1971); 1 dau., Kathryn Frances; m. 2d, Morris L. Aizenman, June 24, 1977. Sci. officer Leiden (Netherlands) Obs., 1968-70; astronomer adjoint Meudon (France) Obs., 1970-71; vis. fellow U. Colo., 1971-72; research astronomer, lectr. astronomy U. Denver, 1972—, dir. obs. ops., 1974—; NASA-NRC sr. resident research asso. Goddard Space Flight Center, 1977-79; phys. scientist Dept. Air Force, 1979—. Fulbright fellow, 1958-60. Mem. Internat. Astron. Union (commn. mem.), Am. Astron. Soc., Royal Astron. Soc., Phi Beta Kappa, Sigma Xi, Phi Kappa Phi. English lang. editor, translator Astronomy and Astrophysics: A European Jour., 1969-71. Contbr. numerous articles to profl. publs.; translator books from French, numerous articles from French and German. Home: 5912 Gloster Rd Bethesda MD 20016

LE SHAN, LAWRENCE L., psychologist; b. N.Y.C., Sept. 8, 1920; s. Julius and Rose Vivian (Rosenbaum) Le S.; B.S., Coll. William and Mary, 1942; M.A., U. Nebr., 1943; Ph.D., U. Chgo., 1954; m. Eda Joan Grossman, 1944; 1 dau., Wendy Jean. Instr., asst. prof. psychology, then asso. prof. Roosevelt U.; faculty Pace Coll., New Sch. for Social Research, Mills Coll., Union Theol. Sem.; chief dept. psychology Trafalgar Hosp. and Inst. Applied Biology, N.Y.C., 1952-64, dir. project on psychosomatic medicine, 1952-64, chief investigator project on parapsychology, 1964—. Served with U.S. Army, 1943-46, 49-51. Mem. Fedn. Am. Scientists, Am. Psychol. Assn., Am. Soc. Psychical Research, Assn. Humanistic Psychology, Parapsychology Assn. Author: (with others) Counselling the Dying, 1964; The Medium, the Mystic and the Physicist, 1975; How to Meditate (Christopher award), 1975; Alternate Realities, 1977; You Can Fight for Your Life, 1977. Office: 29 W 75th St New York City NY 10023

LE SHANA, DAVID CHARLES, coll. pres.; b. Lucknow, India, Nov. 15, 1932; s. Newman John and Gwendolyn Beatrice (White) Le S.; came to U.S., 1949, naturalized, 1958; A.B., Taylor U., Upland, Ind., 1953; A.M. in Edn., Ball State U., 1959; Ph.D., U. So. Calif., 1967; m. Rebecca Ann Swander, June 8, 1951; children—Deborah Lynn, James David, Catherine Ann, Christine Joy. Ordained to ministry Friends Ch., 1953; pastor Ypsilanti (Mich.) Friends Ch., 1953-54; dir. pub. relations, chaplain Taylor U., 1954-61; pastor 1st Friends Ch., Long Beach, Calif., 1961-67; mem. staff George Fox Coll., Newberg, Oreg., 1967—, pres., 1969—; bd. dirs. Council Advancement Small Colls., 1971—, chmn., 1976-78; chmn. commn. higher edn. Nat. Assn. Evangelicals, 1973-75, Oreg. Ind. Colls. Assn., 1971-72; mem. So. Calif. Radio and TV Commn., 1963-67; mem. fact-finding group to Bangladesh, 1972. Mem. adv. bd. Oriental Missionary Soc.; bd. dirs. Oreg. Ind. Coll. Found., 1969—, George Tex Coll. Found., 1971—, Herbert Hoover Found. Oreg., 1975—; bd. govs. Associated Christian Colls. Oreg., 1969-79. Recipient Alumni Service award Taylor U., 1961, Chamber of Achievement award, 1978; Tchr. of Yr. award Ball State U., 1978. Rotarian (bd. dirs. Newberg). Author: Quakers in California, 1969. Rec. album Songs of Discipleship, 1965. Home: 410 N College St Newberg OR 97132

LESHER, DEAN STANLEY, publisher; b. Williamsport, Md., Aug. 7, 1902; s. David Thomas and Margaret Elliot (Prosser) L.; B.A., magna cum laude, U. Md., 1924; LL.B., Harvard, 1926; m. Kathryn E. Crowder, 1929 (dec. Mar. 1971); children—Dean Stanley, Melinda Kay, Cynthia Ann; m. 2d, Margaret L. Ryan, Apr. 2, 1973; stepchildren—Patricia, Wendi, Jill, Roxanne. Admitted to Mo. bar, 1926, practiced in Kansas City, 1926-40; newspaper pub., Nebr., 1938-41, Calif., 1941—; pub. Merced Sun-Star, Madera Tribune, Antioch Ledger, Concord Transcript, Contra Costa Times, Pitts. Post Dispatch, Pleasanton Times, plus 16 weeklies; pres., dir. seven newspaper pub. cos., also radio sta. KBAR, Burley, Idaho. Past chmn. Calif. Mental Health Bd.; active numerous civic orgns. Bd. dirs. Better Bus. Bur., Oakland Mus., Children's Hosp. of East Bay Found., Bay Area Council; past bd. dirs. Calif. Safety Council, Commn. on Crime and Delinquency, Oakland Symphony Assn., Oakland Mus.; trustee Calif. State Univs. and Colls.; past gov. Calif. Community Colls. Recipient numerous journalistic awards; named Calif. Pub. of Yr., 1977. Mem. Calif. Newspaper Publishers Assn. (dir.), Suburban Newspapers Am. (dir.), Walnut Creek C. of C., Phi Delta Theta, Sigma Delta Chi, Theta Kappa Phi, Phi Kappa Phi. Republican. Mason, Rotarian (past dist. gov.). Clubs: Commonwealth, San Francisco Press, Harvard, Concord Century (v.p.); Round Hill Country. Home: Seven Oaks Circle Orinda CA 94563 Office: 2640 Shadelands Dr Walnut Creek CA 94596. *Self-fulfillment is the greatest attainment in life; helping others to attain this carries its own satisfaction.*

LESHER, DONALD MILES, lawyer; b. Middleport, Ohio, May 29, 1915; s. Miles Mosser and Edith Katherine (McMaster) L.; B.A., Colo. U., 1937; LL.B., Okla. U., 1940; m. Josephine Kirkmeyer, May 31, 1942; children—Donna J. Lesher Pinder, Karen A. Lesher Mariea, Lorraine C. Lesher Boyd; m. 2d, Barbara Jean Johnson, Feb. 20, 1963. Admitted to Colo. bar, 1941, since practiced in Denver; partner firm Knight & Lesher, 1953-58, Lesher, Schmidt & Van Cise, 1958-64, Lesher & Gregg, 1964-72; individual practice law, 1972—; dir. First S & L Shares, Inc., Majestic Savs. & Loan Assn.; instr. real estate law Westminster Law Sch., Denver U., 1955-59. Mem. Colo. Gen. Assembly, 1943-47. Served with USN, 1940-41. Mem. Am., Colo. (trustee 1948-51, v.p. 1954-55, award of merit 1958, chmn. real estate sect. 1962-64), Denver bar assns., Sigma Chi. Republican. Roman Catholic. Club: Denver Athletic. Home: 3243 S Adams Way Denver CO 80210 Office: 500 Boston Bldg Denver CO 80202

LESHER, JOHN LEE, JR., mgmt. cons. co. exec.; b. Harrisburg, Pa., Feb. 7, 1934; s. John Lee and Mary Alice (Watkeys) L.; B.A. cum laude, Williams Coll., 1956; M.B.A., Harvard U., 1958; m. Nancy Smith, July 11, 1970; children by previous marriage—John David, James Elam, Andrew Gwynne. Budget dir., asst. sec. The Barden Corp., Danbury, Conn., 1958-61; cons. Booz, Allen & Hamilton Inc., N.Y.C., 1962-64, asso., 1964-66, v.p., 1966-76, pres., 1976—. Vice chmn. fund raising com. Am. Mus. Natural History; mem. fund raising com. Phillips Exeter Acad. Clubs: Harvard Bus. Sch., Williams, Bedens Brook Country, Watch Hill Yacht (Princeton, N.J.); Misquamicut (Watch Hill, R.I.); Round Hill (Greenwich, Conn.). Office: 245 Park Ave New York City NY 10017

LESHER, RICHARD LEE, assn. exec.; b. Doylesburg, Pa., Oct. 28, 1933; s. Richard E. and Rosalie Orabelle (Meredith) L.; B.B.A., U. Pitts., 1958; M.S., Pa. State U., 1960; D.B.A., Ind. U., 1963; children—Douglas Allen, Laurie Lynn, Betsy Lee, Craig Collin. Asst. prof. coll. Commerce and Adminstrn., Ohio State U., 1963-64; cons. NASA, Washington, 1964-65, dep. asst. adminstr., 1965-66, asst. adminstr., 1966-69; bus. and mgmt. cons., Washington, 1969-71; pres. Nat. Center for Resource Recovery, Washington, 1971-75; pres. C. of C. of U.S., Washington, 1975—; dir. Union 1st Nat. Bank Washington, Nat. Center for Resource Recovery. Bd. dirs. Nat. Minority Purchasing Council, U.S.-USSR Trade and Econ. Council, Found. for Econ. Bus. Studies of Ind. U. Served with U.S. Army, 1954-56. Mem. Am. Soc. Assn. Execs., Am. C. of C. Execs. (dir.), So. Assn. C. of C. Execs., Washington Soc. Assn. Execs., Internat. Platform Assn., Am. Historic and Cultural Soc. (dir.), Phi Alpha Kappa, Beta Gamma Sigma. Club: Bethesda Country. Author syndicated newspaper column. Office: US C of C 1615 H St NW Washington DC 20062

LESHER, ROBERT OVERTON, lawyer; b. Phoenix, Apr. 6, 1921; s. Charles Zaner and Alice Marguerite (Heckman) L.; B.A., U. Ariz., 1942, LL.B., 1949; children—Stephen Harrison, Janet Kay. Admitted to Ariz. bar, 1949; atty. A. T.&Santa Fe Ry., 1949-54; pvt. practice, Tucson, 1954—; partner firm Lesher, Kimble & Rucker, 1960—; adj. prof. law U. Ariz. Law Sch., 1954—; mem. Supreme Ct. Ariz., 1960. Served with AUS, 1942-46, 50-52. Diplomate Am. Bd. Trial Advocates. Fellow Am. Coll. Trial Lawyers; mem. Am. Law Inst., Internat. Assn. Ins. Counsel. Republican. Clubs: Tucson Country, Skyline Country. Home: 510 N Dodge Blvd Tucson AZ 85716 Office: 3773 E Broadway Tucson AZ 85716

LESHNER, ZANE, fast food co. exec., lawyer; b. Niagara Falls, N.Y., May 7, 1942; s. Alex and Ethel (Freeman) L.; B.S. in Econs., Western Mich. U., 1965; J.D., Memphis State U., 1968; m. Dorothy Lynne Green, Feb. 4, 1965; children—Amy Loren, Wendy Nicole. Admitted to Tenn. bar, 1968, Fla. bar, 1974; corp. atty. W.R. Grace & Co., Memphis, 1968-72; exec. v.p., gen. counsel, asst. sec. Burger King Corp., Miami, Fla., 1972—. Chmn. subcom. on edn. S. Fla. Coordinating Council, 1979. Mem. Am. Bar Assn., Internat. Franchising Assn., Corp. Counsel Assn. Dade County. Office: 7360 N Kendall Dr Miami FL 33156

LESIKAR, RAYMOND VINCENT, educator; b. Rogers, Tex., June 29, 1922; s. Vince E. and Albina J. (Stanislaw) L.; B.B.A., U. Tex., 1947, M.B.A., 1948, Ph.D., 1954; m. Lu Clay Allen, July 7, 1945; children—Patricia (Mrs. Stephen Dale King), Raymond Vincent. With Douglas Aircraft Co., 1941-42, Sears, Roebuck & Co., 1947; instr. Tex. Christian U., 1948-49; asst. prof. U. Tex., 1949-54; faculty La. State U., Baton Rouge, 1954-77, prof. bus. adminstrn., 1959—, chmn. dept. mgmt., 1959-77, dean Coll. Bus. Adminstrn., 1963-64, 72-73, prof. emeritus, 1977—; adj. prof. U. Tex., Austin, 1977-79; prof., chmn. dept. behavioral sci. N. Tex. State U., Denton, 1979—; cons. in field. Served with AUS, 1943-46. Fellow Am. Bus. Communication Assn. (pres. 1961); mem. S.W. Social Sci. Assn. (pres. 1967), Acad. Mgmt., Internat. Communication Assn., Internat. Soc. Gen. Semantics, Beta Gamma Sigma, Phi Kappa Phi, Sigma Iota Epsilon. Rotarian. Club: Denton Country Author: Business Communication: Theory and Application, 1968, 2d edit., 1972, 3d edit., 1976, 4th edit., 1980; Report Writing for Business, 5th edit., 1973; Introduction to Business: A Societal Approach, 1972, 3d edit., 1979; Productive Business Writing, 1959; Business Report Writing, 1957; How to Write Reports, 1974; Basic Business Communication, 1979; contbr. articles to profl. jours. Home: Route 1 Argyle TX 76226

LESKO, HARRY JOSEPH, transportation co. exec.; b. Cleve., Dec. 6, 1920; s. Theodore Prokop and Bertha Barbara (Trojack) L.; B.B.A., Cleve. State U., 1956; m. Evelyn Martha Culley, Feb. 3, 1945; children—Harry Richard, Larry J., Garry E., Mark J., John M. Schedule analyst Cleve. Ry. System, 1938-40; pres., dir. Greyhound Lines, Inc., Phoenix, 1940—; pres. Atlantic Greyhound Lines of Va., Inc.; v.p. Gelco Bus Leasing Co., 1979—; pres. Trailways, Inc., Dallas, 1979—; dir. Southeastern Stages, Inc., Atlanta, N.Mex. Transp. Co., Roswell, KG Lines, Tulsa, Okla. Transp. Co., Lubbock, Tex., Jefferson Lines Inc., Mpls., Kerrville Bus. Co. (Tex.). Served to capt. USMC, 1942-46. Mem. Am. Bus. Assn. (dir.). Republican. Roman Catholic. Club: Paradise Valley Country. Office: 111 W Clarendon St Phoenix AZ 85077

LESKO, LEONARD HENRY, educator, Egyptologist; b. Chgo., Aug. 14, 1938; s. Matthew Edward and Josephine Bernice (Jaszczak) L.; B.A., Loyola U., Chgo., 1961, M.A., 1964; Ph.D., U. Chgo., 1969; m. Barbara Jadwiga Switalski, Dec. 29, 1966. Tchr., Quigley Prep. Sem. South, Chgo., 1961-64; Egyptologist, epigrapher, epigraphic survey Oriental Inst., U. Chgo., Luxor, Egypt, 1964-65; acting instr. U. Calif. at Berkeley, 1966-67, acting asst. prof., 1967-68, asst. prof., 1968-72, asso. prof., 1972-77, prof. Egyptology, 1977—, dir. Center Nr. Eastern Studies, 1973-75, chmn. dept., 1975-77, 79—, chmn. grad. program in ancient history and archeology, 1978-79. Nat. Endowment for Humanities fellow, 1970-71, grantee, 1975-79; recipient award computer oriented research in humanities Am. Council Learned Socs., 1973. Mem. Am. Research Center in Egypt (gov. 1973-75), Am. Oriental Soc., Archeol. Inst. Am. (pres. San Francisco chpt. 1976-78), Am. Philol. Assn., Egypt Expln. Soc., Found. Egyptologique Reine Elisabeth. Author: The Ancient Egyptian Book of Two Ways, 1972; Glossary of the Late Ramesside Letters, 1975; King Tut's Wine Cellar, 1977; Index of the Spells on Egyptian Middle Kingdom Coffins and Related Documents, 1979. Contbr. articles to profl. publs. and encys. Home: PO Box 907 Orinda CA 94563 Office: Dept Near Eastern Studies U Calif Berkeley CA 94720

LESLIE, CHARLES MILLER, educator; b. Lake Village, Ark., Nov. 8, 1923; s. James Lester and Ona (Waller) L.; Ph.B., U. Chgo., 1949, M.A., 1950, Ph.D., 1959; m. Zelda Solda, Sept. 7, 1946; children—Mario, Almira, Sam. Instr., U. Minn., 1954-56; from asst. prof. to asso. prof. Pomona Coll., 1956-65; prof. anthropology N.Y. U., 1967-76, chmn. dept. anthropology, 1967-71; prof. Center for Sci. and Culture, U. Del., 1976—. Served with USAAF, 1943-45. Fellow Am. Anthrop. Assn., Royal Anthrop. Inst., Southwestern Anthrop. Assn. (pres. 1961-62), N.Y. Acad. Sci., A.A.A.S., Asian Studies Assn., Latin Am. Studies Assn. Author: Now We Are Civilized, 1960; Anthropology of Folk Religion, 1960; Asian Medical Systems, 1976; editor: Social Sci. and Medicine, 1976—; (book series) Comparative Studies of Health Systems and Medical Care, 1977—. Home: 32 W 4th St New Castle DE 19720

LESLIE, DONALD SPENCE, JR., paper co. exec.; b. Mpls., June 5, 1925; s. Donald Spence and Dorothy (Rogers) L.; grad. Hotchkiss Sch., 1943; B.A. in Econs., Princeton, 1947; M.B.A., Harvard, 1953; m. Miriam Bennett, June 25, 1953; children—Bennett, Michael, Cynthia. With Weyerhaeuser Timber Co., 1949-51, Gulf Oil Co., 1953-56; with Hammermill Paper Co., 1956—, v.p., treas., 1963-67, v.p. finance, 1967-69, sr. v.p., 1969-70, dir., 1962—, exec. v.p., 1970—; dir. First Nat. Bank Pa., Erie, Lord Corp., Erie. Trustee, Gannon Coll., Hamot Med. Center, Erie; bd. overseers Sch. Engring., U. Pitts. Clubs: Aviation, Kahkwa, Erie (Erie); Princeton (N.Y.C.). Home: 4848 Wolf Rd Erie PA 16505 Office: PO Box 1440 Erie PA 16533

LESLIE, EUGENE V., physician; b. Buffalo, Feb. 20, 1927; s. William and Jeannie (Donald) L.; B.S., U. Buffalo, 1949, M.D., 1951. Intern, E.J. Meyer Meml. Hosp., Buffalo, 1951-52, resident in surgery, 1952-53, resident in radiology, 1953-56; NIH fellow in neuroradiology Queens Sq., London, 1956-57; neuroradiologist E.J. Meyer Meml. Hosp. (name changed to Erie County Med. Center), 1957-63, asso. dir. radiology, 1963-72, dir. radiology, 1972—; clin. asst. prof. radiology SUNY, Buffalo, 1957-63, clin. asso. prof., 1963-72, clin. prof., chmn. dept., 1972—. Served with U.S. Army, 1944-45. Fellow Am. Coll. Radiology; mem. Erie County Med. Soc., Med. Soc. State N.Y., AMA, Soc. Nuclear Medicine, Am. Soc. Neuroradiology (past sec.), Assn. Univ. Radiologists, Alpha Omega Alpha. Clubs: Buffalo Curling, Buffalo Canoe, Buffalo Yacht. Contbr. articles to profl. jours. Home: 260 Forestview Dr Williamsville NY 14221 Office: SUNY Sch of Medicine Dept Radiology Buffalo NY 14214

LESLIE, GERALD RONNELL, educator; b. Columbus, Ohio, Apr. 16, 1925; s. Robert Miles and Nellie (Wittkugle) L.; B.A. in Sociology, Ohio State U., 1948, M.A., 1949, Ph.D., 1951; m. Elizabeth Mae McLaughlin, Sept, 22, 1962; children—Robert, Kathleen, Brian, Robert Miles II, Pamela. Mem. faculty Purdue U., 1950-63, prof. sociology, 1957-63; prof. sociology, head dept. Okla. State U., 1963-67; prof., chmn. dept. sociology U. Fla., 1967-77; vis. prof. U. N.C. at Chapel Hill, 1953-54, Columbia Tchrs. Coll., 1956-57, U. Calif. at Berkeley, summer 1959. Served with AUS, 1943-46. Mem. Am. Sociol. Assn., A.A.U.P., Soc. Study Social Problems, Nat. Council Family Relations, Am. Assn. Marriage Counselors, Phi Beta Kappa. Author: The Sociology of Social Problems, 6th edit., 1978; The Family in Social Context, 1979; Studies in the Sociology of Social Problems, 1975; Order and Change, 1976; Marriage in a Changing World, 1977. Home: 2015 NW 27th St Gainesville FL 32605

LESLIE, HENRY ARTHUR, banker; b. Troy, Ala., Oct. 15, 1921; s. James B. and Alice (Minchener) L.; B.S., U. Ala., 1942, J.D., 1948; J.S.D., Yale, 1959; grad. Sch. Banking, Rutgers U., 1964; m. Anita Doyle, Apr. 5, 1943; children—Anita Lucinda (Mrs. David Miller), Henry Arthur. Admitted to Ala. bar, 1948; asst. prof. bus. law U. Ala., 1948-50, 52-54, prof. law, asst. dean Sch. Law, 1954-59; v.p. trust officer BIrmingham Trust Nat. Bank (Ala.), 1959-64; sr. v.p., trust officer Union Bank & Trust Co., Montgomery, Ala., 1964-73, sr. v.p., 1973-76, exec. v.p., 1976-78, pres., chief exec. officer, 1978—, dir., 1973—. State chmn. Radio Free Europe Fund, 1973; pres. Children's Center of Montgomery, 1971; atty. Water Improvement Commn. of Ala., 1971-75; mem. Ala. Bd. Bar Examiners. Chmn. bd. dirs. Ala. Bankers Found.; bd. dirs. Pike County Mus. Served to capt. AUS, 1942-46; to lt. col. J.A.G. Corps, Res. Decorated Bronze Star. Mem. Fed., Am., Ala., Montgomery bar assns., Am., Ala. (trust div. pres. 1963-65) bankers assns., Farrah Order Jurisprudence (pres. 1973), Newcomen Soc. N.Am., Montgomery C. of C. (dir.), Delta Sigma Pi, Phi Delta Phi, Omicron Delta Kappa, Pi Kappa Phi. Episcopalian (sr. warden). Kiwanian. Clubs: Maxwell Officers, Montgomery Country, Capital City. Contbr. articles to profl. jours. Home: 3332 Boxwood Dr Montgomery AL 36111 Office: Union Bank & Trust Co Montgomery AL 36104

LESLIE, JACQUES ROBERT, JR., journalist; b. Los Angeles, Mar. 12, 1947; s. Jacques Robert and Aleen (Wetstein) L.; B.A., Yale, 1968. Tchr., New Asia Coll., Chinese U., Hong Kong, 1968-70; free-lance journalist, Washington, 1970-71; fgn. corr. Los Angeles Times, Saigon, 1972-73, Phnom-Penh, 1973, Washington, 1974, chief New Delhi (India) bur., 1974-75, Madrid, 1975-76, chief Hong Kong bur., 1976-77; freelance journalist, 1977—. Recipient Best Fgn. Corr. award Sigma Delta Chi, 1973, citation reporting Overseas Press Club, 1973. Home: 10530 Edgely Pl Los Angeles CA 90024

LESLIE, JAMES HILL, paper co. exec.; b. Mpls., Feb. 27, 1930; s. Frank Paul and Ruth (Hill) L.; B.A., Princeton U., 1952; postgrad. Sloan Sch., M.I.T., 1954-55; m. Carol Van Camp, Mar. 23, 1972; children—Laura, Kate, James. With Leslie Paper Co., Mpls., 1955—, v.p., 1960-66, pres., 1966—; dir. Oil Republic Ins. Co., Minn. Title Fin. Corp; trustee F&M Savs. Bank. Served to lt. USN, 1952-54. Mem. Young Presidents Orgn. Club: Mpls., Boca Grande, Useppa Island. Office: PO Box 1351 Minneapolis MN 55440

LESLIE, JOHN C., aviation cons.; b. July 21, 1905; s. John and Bessie May (McAfee) L.; B.S., Princeton, 1926; B.S., Mass. Inst. Tech., 1928, M.S. (Alfred P. Sloan, Jr. fellow), 1943; m. Jean Savage, May 23, 1929; children—Pauline Leslie Lange, John, Peter, Susan Leslie Abu-Haidar. Asso. with Fokker Aircraft Corp., 1928-29; asst. to chief engr. Pan Am. Airways, Inc., 1929, asst. to div. engr., 1930-34, div. engr. Pacific div. developing engring. technique transocean flight, 1935-38, operations mgr. Pacific div., 1938-41, mgr. Atlantic div., 1941-45, v.p. Atlantic div., 1945-46, v.p., 1946, adminstrv. v.p., 1950-59, v.p., also asst. to pres., 1959-64, v.p., asst. to chmn., 1964-68, sr. v.p. internat. affairs, 1968-70, dir., 1950-70; sr. asso. R. Dixon Speas Assos., 1970-76. Mem. exec. com. Internat. Air Transp. Assn., 1947-70. Served to lt. comdr. USNR. Decorated comdr. Order Orange-Nassau; comdr. Nat. Order Ivory Coast. Fellow Am. Inst. Aeros. and Astronautics, Royal Aero. Soc. Clubs: Am. Yacht (Rye, N.Y.); Mill Reef (Antigua). Home: Mill Reef Club Saint John's Antigua West Indies Office: Pan Am Bldg New York City NY 10017

LESLIE, JOHN ETHELBERT, investment banker; b. Vienna, Austria, Oct. 13, 1910; s. Julius and Valerie (Lawetzky) L.; Dr. Jur., U. Vienna, 1932; diploma Consular Acad. Polit. Sci. and Econs., Vienna, 1934; M.S., Columbia, 1942; m. Evelyn Ottinger Goetz, Mar. 28, 1940. Came to U.S., 1938, naturalized, 1944. Sec. to judges Fed. Law Cts. Austria, 1934-36; pvt. practice, Vienna, 1936-38; sr. auditor Arthur Anderson & Co., C.P.A.'s, N.Y.C., 1941-46; prin. R.G. Rankin & Co., tax consultants, N.Y.C., 1946-55; with Bache & Co., Inc. (name now Bache Halsey Stuart-Shields Inc.), N.Y.C., 1955—, chmn. bd. dirs., 1969-76, chmn. exec. com., 1968-69, chief exec. officer, 1970-77; chmn. bd. Bache Group Inc., 1969-78; chmn. policy com. Bache Group and Bache Halsey Stuart Shields, 1978—; dir. Banom Corp.; pres., dir. 920 Fifth Ave. Corp.; mem. adv. com. on internat. capital markets N.Y. Stock Exchange, chmn., 1973-75, also mem. com. on access; hon. consul gen. Austria in N.Y.C., 1965—. Trustee, Inst. Internat. Edn.; pres., dir. Bache Corp. Found.; bd. dirs. Econ. Devel. Council N.Y., Beekman Downtown Hosp., H.L. Bache Found.; mem. adv. council internat. affairs Sch. Internat. Affairs, Columbia U.; mem. adv. bd. Leeds Castle Found. Decorated cruz Vermelha de Dedicacao (Portugal); Gt. Badge of Honor, comdr. 1st class Order Merit, Gt. Gold Cross Honor with star (Austria); Golden Order of Merit (Vienna); officer Nat. Order Merit (France); officer's cross Order of Merit (W.Ger.); recipient certificate appreciation City N.Y. Mem. Securities Industry Assn. (dir., bd. govs.), Council Fgn. Relations, Soc. Fgn. Consuls in N.Y.C., chambers commerce in N.Y.C. of Austria (pres., dir.), Belgium, France, Germany, Gt. Britain, Italy, The Netherlands, Spain, N.Y. Chamber Commerce and Industry (dir.), France-Am. Soc. (dir.), Alumni Assn. Sch. Bus. Columbia, Am. Fgn. Service Assn., Am. Soc. Internat. Law, Fgn. Policy Assn. (dir.), UN Assn.-U.S.A. (vice-chmn., gov.), Newcomen Soc. N.Am., Pilgrims of U.S. Clubs: Union, Econ., Bond, Paris-Am., Wall St., 25 Limited Luncheon (N.Y.C.); Piping Rock. Home: 920 Fifth Ave New York NY 10021 Office: Bache Plaza 100 Gold St New York NY 10038

LESLIE, JOHN HAMPTON, corp. exec.; b. Evanston, Ill., June 28, 1914; s. John W. and Alma (Bertles) L.; B.S., Harvard, 1937; m. Virginia Andersen, Aug. 5, 1950; children—James Woodworth, Victoria Hall. Design engr. Signode Corp. (formerly Signode Steel Strapping Co.), Chgo., 1937-41, v.p. engring. and research, 1946-49, pres., 1949-62, chmn. bd., 1962—; chief engr. South-Wind div. Stewart Warner Corp., 1941-46; dir. Detroit & Can. Tunnel Corp., Union Spl. Corp., Chgo., Ill. Power Co., Decatur. Trustee, Village of Winnetka (Ill.), 1955-59; mem. Winnetka Bd. Edn., 1963-69; trustee Signode Found., Inc., Skokie Valley Community Hosp., 1958-69, Northwestern U.; bd. dirs. Evanston Hosp. Clubs: Commercial, Mid-America, University (Chgo.); Indian Hill (Winnetka, Ill.). Home: 909 Sheridan Rd Winnetka IL 60093 Office: 3600 W Lake Ave Glenview IL 60025

LESLIE, JOHN WALTER, ednl. cons.; b. Norfolk, Va., Sept. 18, 1929; s. John Walter and Ella Arden (Squires) L.; B.A., Coll. William and Mary, 1952; student Mich. State U., 1957-58, U. Oreg., 1962-64; M.A., Am. U., 1968; m. Audrey May Munford, Apr. 9, 1957. From copy boy to sports reporter Norfolk Virginian-Pilot, 1944-49; sports reporter Newport News (Va.) Daily Press, 1950-52, asst. sports editor, 1956-57; asst. news editor Mich. State U., 1957-58; asso. dir. Ketchum, Inc., 1958-60; dir. devel. and pub. relations Lewis and Clark Coll., 1960-63; exec. v.p. Am. Coll. Pub. Relations Assn., 1963-74; pres. Instl. Advancement Consultants, Inc., also sr. v.p. Brakeley, John Price Jones, Inc., N.Y.C., 1974—. Served to 1st lt. USAF, 1952-56. Author: Focus on Understanding and Support: A Study in College Management, 1969; Seeking the Competitive Dollar, 1971; also articles. Home: 5410 Connecticut Ave NW Washington DC 20015 Office: 1100 17 St NW Washington DC 20036

LESLIE, JOHN WILLIAM, govt. ofcl.; b. Indpls., Nov. 22, 1923; s. John Edward and Catherine (Harris) L.; student U.S. Naval Acad., 1943-44, George Washington U., 1949, Indsl. Coll. Armed Forces, 1956; m. Joan Williams, Dec. 26, 1970; 1 dau. by previous marriage, Catherine Alexandra. Dep. excise adminstr. Ind., 1946-47; pvt. pub. relations bus., 1947-49; dir. pub. relations Ind. Dept. Vets. Affairs, 1949; press officer Dept. Labor, 1949-51, acting asst. dir. info., 1951-52, asst. dir., 1952-56, dep. dir., 1956-59, dir., 1959—. Mem., dir. pub. relations D.C. Com. Employment Physically Handicapped, 1952-53; trustee Washington chpt. Leukemia Soc. Am., 1976—. Served with U.S. Navy and USNR, 1941-46. Recipient commendation President's Com. Employment Physically Handicapped, 1954; Distinguished Service award Dept. Labor, 1962; citation outstanding service Navy Dept., 1964; Presdl. citation, 1966; Merit award Internat. Labor Press Assn., 1969; Distinguished Career Service award Dept. Labor, 1973; Communications award Ga. chpt. Pub. Relations Soc. Am., 1972; Sec. Labor's Recognition award, 1974. Mem. English Speaking Union, Brit. Embassy Players. Episcopalian. Club: Nat. Broadcasters. Home: 627 I St SW Washington DC 20024 Office: Dept of Labor 200 Constitution Ave NW Washington DC 20210

LESLIE, ROBERT WENDELL, bus. exec.; b. Lincoln, Nebr., Jan. 28, 1933; s. Oliver Wendell and Hazel Rosetta (Barnett) L.; B.A., Nebr. Wesleyan Coll., 1957; M.A., U. Nebr., 1960; m. Janet, June 5, 1957; children—Steven, David, Mark. Tchr., coach schs. in Nebr. and Calif., 1957-66; with Jostens Inc., Mpls., 1966—, v.p. sales, then v.p., div. mgr., 1971-72, pres., 1977—. Active Little League. Served with USNR, 1953-55. Republican. Presbyterian. Address: Jostens Inc 5501 Normal Center Dr Minneapolis MN 55437

LESLIE, ROYAL CONRAD, commodity market analyst; b. Springfield, Ohio, Sept. 3, 1923; s. Royal Conrad and Emily (Messenger) L.; B.S. in Bus. Adminstrn., Miami U., Oxford, Ohio, 1947; m. Cynthia Adams, Apr. 9, 1949; children—Bruce Alan, Lynda Ann, Elizabeth. Stock broker Merrill Lynch Pierce Fenner & Smith, Columbus, Ohio, 1949-55; commodity analyst F.I. DuPont & Co., Chgo., 1955-60, Bache & Co., Chgo., 1960-65; partner, commodity analyst Lamson Bros. & Co., Chgo., 1965-69, Mayer-Gelbort-Leslie, Inc., Chgo., 1970-75; pres. Leslie Analytical Orgn., Inc., Chgo., 1975—; adviser Thomson McKinnon Securities Inc.; mem. Chgo. Bd. Trade; monthly U.S. crop estimates distributed worldwide. Served to 1st lt., pilot, USAAF, 1943-45. Decorated Air medal with 2 oak leaf clusters, Bronze Star with 3 oak leaf clusters. Presbyterian. Author: Guide for Successful Trading, Stocks, Commodities and Gold, 1969. Office: 141 W Jackson Blvd Chicago IL 60604. *Each of us has the choice: we must make money work for us—or we must work for money.*

LESLIE, SEYMOUR MARVIN, recorded musical products co. exec.; b. N.Y.C., Dec. 16, 1922; s. Harry and Fay (Goldstein) L.; E.E., Syracuse U., 1945; grad. Advanced Mgmt. Program, Harvard U., 1961; L.H.D., Hofstra U., 1974; m. Barbara Miller, Mar. 30, 1947; children—Ellen, Jane, Carol. Sales mgr. Voco, Inc., N.Y.C., 1946-52; founder Pickwick Internat., Inc., Woodbury, N.Y., 1953, chmn. bd., pres., 1953-77; chmn. Leslie Group, Inc., 1977—; mem. adv. bd. Mfrs. Hanover Trust Co. Active Boy Scouts Am., 1947-50; mem. corp. adv. council Syracuse U.; mem. council Hofstra U.; bd. govs. Anti Defamation League, 1960—; v.p. Am. Med. Center, Denver; bd. dirs. L.I. Assn. Served to sgt. U.S. Army, 1942-46; PTO. Recipient Presdl. award Nat. Assn. Record Merchandisers, 1976, Distinguished Service award, 1977, Outstanding Arendts Alumnus award Syracuse U., 1978. Mem. ASCAP, Record Industry Assn. Am. (profl. group). Clubs: B'nai B'rith, Friars, Harvard, Harvard Bus. Sch. Home: 810 Channel Rd Woodmere NY 11598 Office: 1370 Ave of Americas New York NY 10019

LESLIE, WILLIAM, JR., cons. actuary; b. Berkeley, Calif., Oct. 2, 1918; s. William Leslie and Rose (Barker) L.; A.B., Princeton, 1940; m. Georgie Ann Burke, Apr. 29, 1942; children—Meredith (Mrs. Robert A. Welch), Karen (Mrs. Dean Brian McKay), William III, David. With actuarial div. Nat. Bur. Casualty Underwriters, N.Y.C., 1941-46, gen. mgr., 1958-64; supt. spl. risks dept. Royal-Globe Ins. Cos., N.Y.C., 1947-50; asst. mgr. Nat. Council Compensation Ins., 1950-55, gen. mgr., 1955-57; sec., actuary Continental Ins. Cos., 1957-58, v.p., actuary, 1964-78; exec. v.p., dir. subs. INSCO Systems Corp., 1978-79, v.p. parent co. Continental Corp., v.p. Tillinghast, Nelson & Warren, Inc., 1979—. Bd. dirs. Community Welfare Fund of Bronxville, Inc., 1959-61, pres., 1960. Served from ensign to lt., aviator, USNR, 1942-46. Fellow Casualty Actuarial Soc. (pres. 1960-61). Episcopalian (dept. finance Diocese N.Y. 1956-61). Home: 12024 Caminito Campana San Diego CA 92128 Office: 660 Newport Center Dr Newport Beach CA 92660

LESLIE, WILLIAM CAIRNS, metall. engr.; b. Dundee, Scotland, Jan. 6, 1920; came to U.S., 1925, naturalized, 1940; B.Metall. Engring., Ohio State U., 1947, M.Sc., 1948, Ph.D., 1949; m. Florence M. Hall, 1948; 1 dau. Metallurgist, U.S. Steel Research Lab., Kearny, N.J., 1949-53; asso. dir. staff research and devel. Thompson Products, Inc., Cleve., 1953-54; with U.S. Steel Corp., Monroeville, Pa., 1954-73, mgr. phys. metallurgy E.C. Bain Lab. for Fundamental Research, 1963-73; prof. materials engring. U. Mich., 1973—; adj. prof. metallurgy Bklyn. Poly. Inst., 1952-53; Battelle vis. prof. metallurgy Ohio State U., 1964-65; vis. prof. U. Melbourne (Australia), 1979; Am. Soc. Metals and AIME rep. to EJC Metric Council and Am. Nat. Metric Council, 1971—; mem. ship research com. NRC, 1978—; Garofalo lectr. Northwestern U., 1977; U.S. rep. Internat. Conf. Strength of Metals and Alloys, 1973—; mem. Charles Hatchett award panel Metals Soc. Gt. Britain, 1978—; cons. in field; mem. adv. com. div. metals and ceramics Oak Ridge Nat. Lab., 1974-75; mem. com. on basic research, advisor to Army Research Office, Durham, N.C., 1973-78; mem. ad hoc com. on non-magnetic structural steels Nat. Materials Adv. Bd., 1973-74. Served to 1st lt. C.E., U.S. Army, 1943-46. Named Disting. Alumnus, Ohio State U. Coll. Engring., 1967. Fellow Am. Soc. Metals (chmn. publs. com. 1966-67, mem. metals sci. div. council 1970-75, Pitts. chpt. Andrew Carnegie lectr. 1970, Edward DeMille Campbell lectr. 1971, Phila. chpt. Albert Sauveur lectr. 1975, Cleve. chpt. Zay Jeffries lectr. 1975); mem. Metals Soc. Gt. Britain, Iron and Steel Inst. Japan, AIME (v.p. and dir. 1975, Krumb lectr. 1967), AAAS, Metal Sci. Club N.Y., Am. Soc. Engring. Edn., Metall Soc. (chmn. Inst. of Metals div. 1971-72, dir. 1971-72), Sigma Xi, Tau Beta Pi. Contbr. articles to profl. jours.; patentee in field. Office: U Mich Dept Materials and Metall Engring Ann Arbor MI 48109

LESLY, PHILIP, pub. relations counsel; b. Chgo., May 29, 1918; B.S. magna cum laude, Northwestern U., 1940; m. Ruth Edwards, Oct. 17, 1940 (div. 1971); 1 son, Craig. Asst. news editor Chgo. Herald & Examiner, 1935-37; copywriter advt. dept. Sears, Roebuck & Co., Chgo., 1940-41; asst. dir. publicity Northwestern U., 1941-42; account exec. Theodore R. Sills & Co., pub. relations, Chgo., 1942, v.p., 1943, exec. v.p., 1945; dir. pub. relations Ziff-Davis Pub. Co., 1945-46; exec. v.p. Harry Coleman & Co., pub. relations, 1947-49; pres. Philip Lesly Co., pub. relations, Chgo., 1949—; lectr. pub. relations, pub. opinion to bus. and sch. groups. Recipient Gold Anvil award Public Relations Soc. Am., 1979; voted leading active practitioner Pub. Relations Reporter, 1978. Mem. Internat. Pub. Relations Assn., Pub. Relations Soc. Am., Phi Beta Kappa. Club: Mid-America (Chgo.). Co-author: Public Relations: Principles and Procedures, 1945; Everything and The Kitchen Sink, 1955. Author: The People Factor, 1974; Selections from Managing the Human Climate, 1979; (How We Discommunicate, 1979; (bimonthly) Managing the Human Climate; also articles in U.S., Brit. mags. and trade publs. Editor: Public Relations in Action, 1947; Public Relations Handbook, 3d rev. edit., 1967; Lesly's Public Relations Handbook, 1971, rev. edit., 1978. Home: 155 Harbor Dr Chicago IL 60601 Office: 130 E Randolph St Chicago IL 60601. *One should stand out by focusing on those talents and skills that others cannot demonstrate, rather than by competing with the crowd.*

LESNER, SAMUEL JOEL, critic; b. Chgo., Feb. 16, 1909; s. Jacob and Syma (Jenkins) L.; student Am. Conservatory Music, 1929-33; m. Esther M. Malkin, Apr. 6, 1941; children—Roberta L. (Mrs. Charles B. Bernstein), Judy Sue (Mrs. Robert Holstein). Library asst. Chgo. Daily News, 1928-41, music-nightlife reviewer, 1941-44, movie critic, 1945-71, nightlife reviewer, 1971-77; free-lance writer, tchr. baroque music, 1977—. Recipient Dirs. Guild Am. award for outstanding motion picture criticism, 1966. Home: 9230 Bennett Ave Chicago IL 60617 Office: 401 N Wabash Ave Chicago IL 60611

LESNIK, MAX, mag. editor; b. Vueltas, Cuba, Sept. 8, 1930; s. Samuel and Maria Teresa (Menendez) L.; came to U.S., 1961; B.A., U. Havana, 1953; m. Miriam Alvarez, Dec. 29, 1955; children—Miriam, Vivian. Radio commentator Cadena Oriental de Radio Network, Havana, 1953-57; columnist Bohemia mag., Havana, 1951-61, Miami corr., 1961-64; program producer radio sta. WMIE, Miami, 1965-67; pub., editor Replica mag., Replica newspaper, pres. Replica Pub. Inc., Miami, 1967—. Nat. coordinator Cuban People's party, 1950-56. Home: 5530 Sardina St Coral Gables FL 33146 Office: 2994 NW 7th St Miami FL 33125

LESOURD, FRANCIS ANCIL, lawyer; b. Seattle, June 22, 1908; s. Charles Lawson and Edna Blanche (Ball) LeS.; LL.B., U. Wash., 1932; m. Elizabeth Burgess Roberts, Feb. 18, 1935 (dec. 1979); children—Peter Charles, Christopher Roberts. Admitted to Wash. bar, 1932; asso. Chadwick, Chadwick & Mills, Seattle, 1932-33; atty. PWA, Washington, 1933-34; spl. asst. to atty. gen. tax div. Dept. Justice, Washington, 1934-37; asso. William Stanley, Washington, 1937-38; pvt. practice, Seattle, also regional atty. lands div. Dept. Justice, 1938-40; partner LeSourd, Patten, Fleming, Hartung & Emory, and predecessors, Seattle, 1941—; lectr. taxation and constl. law U. Wash., Washington Coll. Law; sec., dir. Bryant Corp., Seattle. Former Wash. State rep., nat. adv. bd. Council Pub. Lands; mem. Seattle Municipal Civil Service Commn., 1945-50; commr. Housing Authority Seattle, 1939-41. Ednl. dir. Wash. Democratic Central Com., 1954; mem. Wash. Dem. Finance Com., 1955-56. Mem. Am., Wash., Seattle bar assns., Seattle Opera Assn. (past pres.), Order of Coif, Phi Beta Kappa. Rotarian. Clubs: Rainier, Washington Athletic, Corinthian Yacht (Seattle). Home: 3143 W Laurelhurst Dr NE Seattle WA 98105 Office: 3900 Seattle 1st Nat Bank Bldg Seattle WA 98154

L'ESPERANCE, WILFORD LOUIS, economist, educator; b. N.Y.C., Dec. 9, 1930; A.B., Columbia Coll., 1951; M.S., Columbia U., 1952; Ph.D., U. Mich., 1963; m. Barbara Manochio, May 4, 1957 (d. Jan. 1977); children—Annette, Suzanne, Claire, Wilford. Math. analyst Ordnance Corps., U.S. Army Guided Missile Devel. Div., Huntsville, Ala., 1953-55; lectr. Ind. U., 1956-60; mktg. research analyst Gen. Electric Co., N.Y.C., Ft. Wayne, Ind., 1952-53, 55-60, cons., 1965; research asst. dept. econs. U. Mich., 1961-63; economist Bur. Comml. Fisheries, Dept. Interior, Ann Arbor, Mich., 1962-63, cons., Sandusky, Ohio, 1963-65; asst. prof. econs. Ohio State U., 1963-66, asso. prof., 1966-70, prof., 1970—, instr. exec. devel. program div. continuing edn., 1970-75; pres. M.W. Econometrics, Inc., Columbus, Ohio, 1973-79; cons. in field; mem. Ohio Gov.'s Task Force on Lake Erie Fishery, 1973-74, Population Study Group, Environ. Health Com., Office Comprehensive Health Planning, Ohio Dept. Health, 1973-76; mem. panel econ. adviser for John Glenn, Ohio Democratic candidate for U.S. Senate, 1974; mem. tech. adv. group Columbus Mayor's Econ. Devel. Council, 1975. Dept. Interior Bur. Comml. Fisheries grantee, 1963-64; Coll. Research Com., Coll. Commerce and Adminstrn. grantee, 1965-66; Ohio Dept. Devel. grantee, 1967-68; Coll. Research Com., Coll. Social and Behavioral Scis. grantee, 1969, 76. Mem. Am. Econ. Assn., Am. Statis. Assn. (pres. Columbus chpt. 1968), Econometric Soc., Regional Sci. Assn., Ohio Acad. Sci., AAUP, N.Y. State Soc. Cin., Ohio, Worthington hist. socs. Club: Hoover Yacht. Author: (with others) Columbus Area Economy-Structure and Growth, 1950-1985, 1966; Modern Statistics for Business and Economics, 1971; The Structure and Control of a State Economy, 1979; asso. editor Jour. Regional Sci., 1978—; contbr. articles on econs. to profl. jours. Home: 296 Acton Rd Columbus OH 43214 Office: Ohio State U 1775 S College Rd Columbus OH 43210

LESS, CLIFFORD MICHAEL, meat packing co. exec.; b. Monticello, Iowa, Sept. 19, 1934; s. Frank W. and Monica A. (May) L.; B.A. with honors, Loras Coll., 1956; J.D. with honors, U. Iowa, 1958; m. Geraldine, Sept. 7, 1957; children—Mike, Sue, Diane, Jerry. Admitted to Iowa bar, 1958; practiced law, Dubuque, Iowa, 1958-71; with subs. Cities Service Co., 1972-74; v.p., corp. counsel, sec. Dubuque Packing Co., 1974—, also dir., dir. subs. cos.; pres. Cascade Mchts. Assn., 1964. Mem. Am., Iowa, Dubuque County bar assns., Am. Meat Inst. (legal com.). Roman Catholic. Home: 2970 Arbor Oaks Ct Dubuque IA 52001 Office: 701 E 16th St Dubuque IA 52001

LESSARD, MARCEL, Can. govt. ofcl. Mem. Parliament from Lac St. Jean (Que.), former minister regional econ. expansion. Mem. Liberal Party.

LESSARD, PIERRE HENRI, food distbr.; b. Quebec City, Que., Can., Feb. 13, 1942; s. Maurice and Jacqueline (Lacasse) L.; B.A., Laval U., 1961, M.Sc.C., L.Sc.C., 1964; M.B.A., Harvard, 1967; m. Andree Dupuis, June 11, 1966; children—Pierre Philippe, Stephanie. Auditor, Touche-Ross & Partners, Montreal, Que., 1964-65; asst. to pres. Denault Ltée, Sherbrooke, Que., 1967-68, also treas., controller; treas., controller Provigo, Inc., Montreal, 1970-71, v.p. finance and adminstrn., 1972-76, pres., chief operating officer, 1976—, mem. exec. com., 1976—, also dir.; dir. M. Loeb, Ltd., Horne & Pitfield Foods Ltd., Market Wholesale Grocery Co., Nat. Drug & Chem. Co. Can. Ltd., Provigo (Montreal), Inc., Provigo (Sherbrooke) Inc., Provigo (Saguenay) Ltée, Provigo (Ottawa) Inc., Provifruit Inc., Provi-Soir Inc., Marché Aux Vraies Aubaines Inc., Aubaines Alimentaires Ltée, Denault Investments, Inc., AVA Warehouse Market Ltd., Provi-Viande Inc., Jato Inc., Le Marché à Go-Go Inc. Mem. Que. Inst. Chartered Accountants, Montreal Bd. Trade, Harvard Bus. Sch. Montreal. Home: 371 Lethbridge Ville Mont-Royal PQ H3P 1E6 Canada Office: 800 W Dorchester Blvd Montreal PQ H3B 1Y2 Canada

LESSARD, RAYMOND W., bishop, Roman Catholic Ch. Ordained priest, 1956, consecrated bishop, 1973; bishop diocese of Savannah, Ga., 1973—. Office: 225 Abercorn St PO Box 8789 Savannah GA 31412

LESSELLS, GERALD ALAN, chem. co. exec.; b. Wallasey, Eng., Aug. 5, 1926; s. Horace Alan and Elsie (Escott) L.; came to U.S., 1928, naturalized, 1936; B.S. in Chem. Engring. Practice, Mass. Inst. Tech., 1950; m. Mary Joline Reddan, June 11, 1950; children—Glenn Alan, Eric Michael, Douglas Bruce. Devel. engr. Mathieson Chem. Corp., Niagara Falls, N.Y., 1950-55; sr. devel. engr. Olin Mathieson Chem. Corp., Brandenburg, Ky., 1955-57; research supr. U.S. Indsl Chem. Co., Cin., 1957-61, group leader, Tuscola, Ill., 1961-65; mgr. process devel. Mobil Chem. Co., Edison, N.J., 1965-69; tech. dir., ink div. J.M. Huber Corp., Edison, 1969—. Cons., Community Action Tng. Inst. of N.J., 1968; vice chmn. research com. Nat. Printing Ink Research Inst., 1972-73; mem. ednl. council M.I.T., 1962—; life mem. NAACP, 1955—; chmn. Decatur (Ill.) Human Relations Commn., 1964-65; chmn. budget com. New Brunswick, Urban League, 1966-68; mem. Citizens Adv. Com. to Mayor of Edison, chmn. pub. info. com., 1967-68. Served with AUS, 1944-46. Registered profl. engr., Ohio, Ill. Fellow Am. Inst. Chem. Engrs. (nat. dir. 1973-75, Service to Soc. award 1974, minority affairs coordinator 1975—), Am. Chem. Soc. Reviewer, Indsl. and Engring. Chemistry, 1959-66. Contbr. articles to profl. jours. Patentee in field, 1963-69. Home: 30 Chandler Rd Edison NJ 08817 Office: Thornall St Edison NJ 08817

LESSELYOUNG, NICHOLAS JACOB, III, lawyer, pub. utility exec.; b. Chilton, Wis., Nov. 25, 1917; s. Nicholas Jacob and Veronica Louise (Rank) L.; LL.B., J.D., Marquette U., 1942; m. Emily J. Diedrich, June 5, 1941; children—Stephen John, John Blair, Claire Ann. Admitted to Wis. bar, 1942; individual practice law, Fond du Lac, Wis., 1946-55; mem. Pub. Service Commn. of Wis., Madison, 1955-58; partner firm Rieser Stafford Lesselyoung & Rosenbaum, Madison, 1958-60; v.p., gen. counsel, sec. Wis. Gas Co., Milw., 1960—. Mem. Wis. Ho. of Reps., 1950-55; mem. lay adv. bd. to Archbishop William E. Cousins, 1967—, chmn., 1973-77; bd. govs. Mt. Mary Coll., Milw., 1973—. Served with USN, 1943-46. Mem. Am., Wis., Milwaukee County, Fed. Energy bar assns., Wis. Assn. Mfrs., Am., Midwest gas assns. Republican. Roman Catholic. Clubs: University (Milw.); Ozaukee Country. Home: 929 W Shaker Circle Mequon WI 53092 Office: 626 E Wisconsin Ave Milwaukee WI 53202

LESSENBERRY, D. D., educator; b. Ky., Sept. 7, 1896; s. James David and Martha (Sanders) L.; B.S., Duquesne U., 1928; A.M., N.Y.U., 1934; LL.D., Westminister Coll., 1943; m. Elona J. Spence, Aug. 28, 1926 (dec. June 1933); m. 2d, Bess McC. Dahlinger, Dec. 26, 1945 (dec. Jan. 1973). Tchr., Allegheny High Sch., Pitts., 1919-27; prin. Allegheny Eve. High Sch., 1923-29, Bus. High Sch., Pitts., 1929-30; dir. courses bus. edn. U. Pitts., 1930-55, prof. edn., 1930-62, prof. edn. emeritus, 1962—. Bd. dirs. Western Pa. Sch. Blind Children. Recipient John Robert Gregg award, 1955. Mem. Nat. Bus. Tchrs. Fedn. (pres. 1935), Eastern Bus. Tchrs. Assn. (bd. dirs. 1930-35; pres. 1944), Internat., Nat., Tri-State (pres. 1942) bus. edn. assns., Phi Delta Kappa, Kappa Phi Kappa, Delta Delta Lambda, Delta Pi Epsilon (pres., 1941-42), Phi Eta Sigma. Clubs: Duquesne, Golf (Pitts.). Author: College Typewriting, coll. edit., 1930-42, 7th edit. (with S.J. Wanous and C. H. Duncan), 1964-65, 8th edit., 1969, 9th edit., 1976; 20th Century Typewriting, complete, 1927, 33, 4th edit., 1942, 6th edit. (with T.J. Crawford) 1952, 8th edit. (with Crawford and Erickson), 1962, 9th edit. (with Crawford and Erickson), 1967, 10th edit. (with others), 1971; (with others) Century Typewriting 21, 2d edit., 1977. Home: Route 1 Box 176D Cave City KY 42127

LESSER, EDWARD ARNOLD, bank exec.; b. N.Y.C., Feb. 2, 1934; s. Arnold A. and Dorothy B. (Stillwell) L.; B.S., Wharton Sch. U. Pa., 1955; m. Mary M. Maxwell, June 9, 1956; children—James Edward, Elizabeth Ann, Carol Jean. With Bankers Trust Co., N.Y.C., 1955—, sr. v.p. in charge of banking ops., 1971-74, exec. v.p. in charge banking ops and computer systems devel., 1974-77, exec. v.p. in charge of trust and investment, 1977—. Office: 280 Park Ave New York City NY 11694

LESSER, GERALD S., educator; b. Jamaica, N.Y., Aug. 22, 1926; s. Nathan and Esther (Lacks) L.; B.A., Columbia, 1947, M.A., 1948; Ph.D., Yale, 1952; M.A. (hon), Harvard, 1963; m. Stella Scharf, Aug. 15, 1953; children—Julie, Nina, Theodore. Research psychologist N.Y. State Brain Research Assn., 1948-49; postdoctoral fellow Yale Child Study Center, 1952-54; asst. prof. Adelphi Coll., 1954-56; asso. prof. Hunter Coll. of City U. N.Y., 1956-63; prof. edn. and devel. psychology Harvard, 1963-66, Charles Bigelow prof. edn. and devel. psychology, 1966—, dir. lab. human devel., 1963—. Chmn. bd. advisers and cons. Children's TV Workshop, 1968—. Mem. Am. Psychol. Assn., Sigma Xi. Home: 12 Tower Rd Lexington MA 02173 Office: Larsen Hall Harvard U Cambridge MA 02138

LESSER, SOL, motion picture exec.; b. Spokane, Feb. 17, 1890; D.F.A., U. Redlands, 1973; M.Film Scis., U. So. Calif.; children—Mrs. Marjorie Fasman, Julian. Co-founder Fox West Coast theatres (name now Mann Theatres), later becoming producer; became exec. charge feature prodn. R.K.O. Radio, 1941; creator Sol Lesser Prodns., Inc., 1945; founder Standard Theatres, Inc., 1947, Prin. Theater Corp. Am., Prin. Mgmt. Co., Prin. Securities Corp.; producer numerous feature pictures including 11 Tarzan features, Stage Door Canteen, Our Town, The Red House, Oliver Twist, Kon-Tiki. Prof. creative motion picture, profl. TV prodn. Sch. Cinema, U. So. Calif. Bd. dirs. Motion Picture and TV Relief Fund, Permanent Charities Com. Motion Picture Industry, Palm Springs Desert Mus.; founder-mem. Los Angeles County Mus. Art, Los Angeles Music Center. Recipient Jean Hersholt Motion Picture Acad. humanitarian award, 1960, also Oscar award for Kon-Tiki; Silver platter Sch. Performing Arts, U. So. Calif., 1973; named Patriarch of Theatre Industry, Nat. Assn. Theatre Owners, 1976. Clubs: Hillcrest Country; Tamarisk Country (Palm Springs, Calif.). Home: Wilshire Terrace 10375 Wilshire Blvd Los Angeles CA 90024 Office: 333 S Beverly Dr Beverly Hills CA 90212

LESSING, DORIS (MAY), writer; b. Kermanshah, Persia, Oct. 22, 1919; d. Alfred Cook and Emily Maude (McVeagh) Tayler; ed. in So. Rhodesia; m. Frank Charles Wisdom, 1939 (div. 1943); m. 2d, Gottfried Anton Nicholas Lessing, 1945 (div. 1949); children—John W., Jean W., Peter L. Author novels: The Grass is Singing, 1950, Children of Violence, 5 vols., 1951-69, Retreat to Innocence, 1953, The Golden Notebook, 1962, Briefing For a Descent Into Hell, 1971, The Summer Before the Dark, 1973, The Memoirs of a Survivor, 1975, Shikasta, 1979; short novels: Five, 1953; short stories: The Habit of Loving, 1958, A Man and Two Women, 1964, African Stories, 1965, The Temptation of Jack Orkney and Other Stories, 1972, The Story of a Non-Marrying Man, 1972, Collected African Stories, 1973; (play) Play with a Tiger, 1962; (essays) A Small Personal Voice, 1974; (poetry) Fourteen Poems, 1959; also author newspaper reports. Recipient Somerset Maugham award, 1954, Prix Medici, 1976. Mem. Nat. Inst. Arts and Letters. Address: care Curtis Brown 1 Craven Hill London W2 3EP England*

LESSITER, FRANK DONALD, editor; b. Pontiac, Mich., Oct. 5, 1939; s. Milon John and Donalda Belle (Taylor) L.; B.S. in Dairy Sci., Mich. State U., 1961, postgrad. in Advt., 1962-65; m. Pamela Ann Fuzak, Nov. 23, 1963; children—Deborah, Susan, Michael, Kelly. Info. specialist Mich. Coop. Extension Service, East Lansing, 1962-65; exec. editor Agrl. Pubs., Milw., 1965-68; editor Nat. Livestock Producer mag., Chgo., 1969-72; with Reiman Publs., Milw., 1972—, editor No-Till Farmer, 1972—, v.p., editor Nat. Livestock Producer, 1974-78, editor Farm Bldg. News, 1977—; exec. v.p. Reiman Assos. Named Farm Mag. Editor of Year, Dekalb AgResearch Program, 1972, Newsletter Editor of Year, Newsletter Clearing House, 1973, Best Farm Mktg. Writer, CIBA-Ceigy Awards Program, 1976, Farm Mag. Writer of Yr., 1977. Mem. Nat. Press Photographers Assn., Nat. Agrl. Mktg. Assn., Am. Agrl. Editors Assn. (Photographer of Year 1975). Author: (with Pamela Ann Fuzak Lessiter) Agricultural Travel Guide, 1971; Horsepower, 1977; contbg. author: Commodity Yearbook, 1972, 75. Home: 16000 Choctaw Trail Brookfield WI 53005 Office: 733 N Van Buren Milwaukee WI 53202

LESSLER, RICHARD SIGMUND, advt. agy. exec.; b. Lynbrook, N.Y., Aug. 26, 1924; s. William S. and Minnie (Gold) L.; B.A. in Exptl. Psychology, U. N.C., 1943; M.B.A., Columbia, 1948; postgrad. N.Y. U., 1948-52; m. Evelyn Sobotka, Aug. 31, 1952; children—Michael Jay, Jonathan Peter, Daniel Stephen. Research asso. CBS, 1948-49; with Dancer-Fitzgerald-Sample, Inc., 1949-55; with Grey Advt., Inc., 1955-72, chmn. bd., 1967-72, also dir., mem. exec. com., chmn. mgmt. com.; vice chmn. bd., chief operating officer U.S., chmn. exec. com. McCann-Erickson, Inc., N.Y.C., 1972-79; vice chmn. bd., chmn. ops. com. The Interpublic Group Cos., Inc., N.Y.C., 1979—. Served to lt. USNR, World War II. Mem. Phi Beta Kappa, Beta Gamma Sigma. Author: (with Brown and Weilbacher) Advertising Media, 1957; (with Nugent Wedding) Advertising Management, 1962. Home: 7 Hawthorne Ln Westport CT 06880 Office: 485 Lexington Ave New York NY 10017

LESTER, ANTALO DAVID, govt. ofcl.; b. Claremore, Okla., Sept. 25, 1941; s. Andrew Moses and Evelyn Virginia (Deer) L.; B.A., Brigham Young U., 1967; m. Henrietta Mildred Chestnut, Aug. 18, 1967; 1 son, Eric Wilben. Sect. head Calif. Fed. Savs., Los Angeles, 1967-68; econ. devel. specialist Nat. Congress Am. Indians, Washington, 1969-70; pres. United Indian Devel. Ann., Los Angeles, 1970-78; commr. adminstrn. for Native Ams. and chmn. Intra-Dept. Co cil on Indian Affairs, HEW, Washington, 1978—; mem. Los Angeles County Native Am. Indian Commn., 1977-78; mem. Nat. Adv. Council for Minority Bus., Nat. Council Indian Opportunity. Human relations commr. City of Los Angeles, 1975-78. Mem. Nat. Congress Am. Indians, Ams. for Indian Opportunity, Am. Indian Scholarships. Mormon. Office: 200 Independence Ave SW Washington DC 20201

LESTER, BARNETT BENJAMIN, editor, fgn. affairs officer; b. Toronto, Can., Aug. 7, 1912; s. Louis and Lena (Rubenstein) L; brought to U.S., 1917; student Cleve. Coll., Western Res. U., 1933; A.B., Oberlin Coll., 1934; student Oberlin Coll., 1930-34, 34-35, Nat. Inst. Pub. Affairs, Washington, 1935-36, Syracuse U., 1935-36, Acad. Internat. Law, The Hague, 1936; fellow Fletcher Sch. Law and Diplomacy, 1935-36; student Fgn. Service Inst., 1952, 56; m. Rita Constance Hatcher, May 31, 1943 (dec.); m. 2d, Claudette Yvonne Gionet, Apr. 19, 1970. Mem. staff various newspapers Cleve. area, 1928-33; feature writer Boston Sunday Post, 1935-38; mng. editor, later editor Exclusive Features Syndicate, Boston, 1936-38; asso. editor The Writer mag., Boston, 1936-38; info. officer Dept. Justice, 1938-41, asst. dir. feature div. Office Inter-Am. Affairs, 1941-45, info. publicist Dept. State, 1945; pub. relations exec. Al Paul Lefton Co., Inc., Phila., 1945-46, info. specialist, chief motion pictures, acting chief audio-visual sect. USPHS, Office Surgeon Gen., 1947-48; info. specialist Fed. Security Agy., 1948-49, chief editorial and prodn. sect. Nat. Heart Inst., info. specialist, sci. reports br. NIH, 1949-52, pub. info. chief, 1950; review officer Dept. State, 1952-61, supervisory publs. editor, 1961-63, editor-writer, 1963-73, pub. info. officer, 1973—, asso. editor Newsletter, 1977—, acting editor, 1978-79, fgn. service res. officer, 1965-73, assigned to policy and pub. info. affairs program, 1962-67, Newsletter and Info. Office, Office Dir. Gen. Fgn. Service, 1967—. Career counselor Oberlin Coll., 1940—. Recipient War Service award Co-ordinator Inter-Am. Affairs, 1945, Meritorious Honor Group award Dept. State, 1967, 40 Year Service award, 1979, Excellent Performance award, 1979, Spl. Achievement award, 1979; Bicentennial award Am. Revolution Bicentennial Adminstrn., 1977. Mem. Am. Fgn. Service Assn., Am. Polit. Sci. Assn., Am. Acad. Polit. and Social Sci., Acad. Polit. Sci., Diplomatic and Consular Officers Ret., Fed. Editors Assn. (Blue Pencil award 1975), Nat. Assn. Govt. Communicators, Internat. Platform Assn., Center for Study of Presidency. Clubs: Inter., Nat. Press, American Foreign Service (Washington). Author: (with others) The Writer's Handbook, 1936. Home: 2507 N Lincoln St Arlington VA 22207 Office: US Dept State Washington DC 20520

LESTER, CHARLES TURNER, univ. adminstr.; b. Covington, Ga., Nov. 10, 1911; s. Richard P. and Estelle P. (Rush) L.; A.B., Emory U., 1932, M.A., 1934; Ph.D., Pa. State U., 1941; m. Marlyn E. Tate, June 23, 1936; children—Charles Turner, James George III. High sch. sci. tchr., 1934-35; instr. chemistry Emory U., 1935-39; research chemist Am. Cyanamid Corp., 1941-42; mem. faculty Emory U., 1942—, prof. chemistry, 1950—, chmn. dept., 1954-57, dean Grad. Sch., 1957-79, v.p. grad. studies, 1970-73, v.p. arts and scis., 1973-79, acting dean Emory Coll., 1973-74, exec. v.p., dean faculties, 1979—. Vice chmn. Ocean Sci. Center, Atlantic Commn., 1967-72; mem. Ga. Sci. and Tech. Commn., 1963-72; mem. exec. com. Council Grad. Schs., 1965-68, chmn. elect. 1972, chmn., 1973, chmn. com. computer matching of fellowship awards, 1967-70; chief grad. acad. br. U.S. Office Edn., 1969-70. Bd. dirs. Oak Ridge Asso. Univs., 1962-65, mem. council, 1958-62, 72—; bd. dirs. Southeastern Edn. Lab., Atlanta, 1966-70, Atlanta Speech Sch., 1965-74; trustee Reinhardt Coll., 1966-76, Huntingdon Coll., 1968—; mem. exec. com. So. Conf. Grad. Schs., 1972-75; chmn. exec. com. Inter Univ. Urban Coop., 1973, chmn., 1973—; acting dir. Inst. Liberal Arts, 1976-77. Recipient Herty medal contbn. chemistry in Southeast, 1965. Mem. Am. Chem. Soc. (chmn. Ga. 1949), Am. Inst. Chemists (chmn. Piedmont chpt. 1958; honor scroll Piedmont chpt. 1970), Phi Beta Kappa, Sigma Xi, Omicron Delta Kappa, Phi Kappa Phi, Kappa Phi Kappa, Alpha Chi Sigma, Phi Lambda Upsilon. Methodist. Contbr. articles to profl. jours. Patentee in field. Home: 281 Chelsea Circle Decatur GA 30030 Office: Emory Univ Atlanta GA 30322

LESTER, EDWARD, lawyer; b. Hope, Ark., Nov. 18, 1921; s. Chester D. and Mary (White) L.; A.B., Hendrix Coll., 1943; LL.D., U. Ark., 1949; m. Mary Evelyn Markham, June 12, 1944; children—James Edward, Vernon Markham. Admitted to Ark. bar, 1949; partner firm Wright, Lindsey, Jennings, Lester & Shults, Little

Rock, 1950-65, Lester & Shults, Little Rock, 1965—. Pres. Ark. Conf. Local Bar Assns., 1960-61; vice chmn. Ark. Turnpike Authority. Mem. Ark. Ho. of Reps., 1949. Chmn. bd. trustees Hendrix Coll. Mem. Am., Ark. bar assns., Am. Judicature Soc. Home: 3 Pinnacle Dr Little Rock AR 72205 Office: Worthen Bank Bldg Little Rock AR 72201

LESTER, GARNER MCCONNICO, utility exec.; b. Jackson, Miss., June 17, 1897; s. John Wallace and Willie (Hoover) L.; B.S., Millsaps Coll., 1919; m. Elizabeth Wilkins, Mar. 10, 1926; children—Elizabeth McConnico (Mrs. Charles H. Foster, Jr.), Garner Wallace. Auditor, treas. Hiawatha Mfg. Co., Jackson, 1919-30; sec., mgr. Miss. Ginning and Mfg. Co., Jackson, 1930-37; owner, mgr. G. M. Lester & Co., cotton products, Jackson, 1937—; v.p. Hinds County Water Co., Jackson, 1927-33, pres., 1933—; dir. Deposit Guaranty Bank & Trust Co., Jackson. Bd. dirs. Nat. Tax Equality Assn., 1943-48, pres., 1948-63, chmn. bd., 1963—; organizer, 1st pres. Nat. Cotton Ginners Assn., 1933; bd. dirs. Nat. Cotton Council Am., 1941-57. Pres. Jackson YMCA, 1928; exec. com. Andrew Jackson council Boy Scouts Am., 1957—. Served with U.S. Army, World War I. Recipient Silver Beaver award Boy Scouts Am. Mem. Am. Water Works Assn., Water Pollution Control Fedn. (dir.), Jackson C. of C. (dir.), Am. Legion, Pi Kappa Alpha, Omicron Delta Kappa. Methodist (supt. Sunday sch.). Rotarian (past pres.). Club: Capital City (Jackson). Home: 2115 Terry Rd Jackson MS 39204 Office: PO Box 8127 Jackson MS 39204. *My mother taught me when a boy that if you knew how to work you would always be happy. I have found this to be true. I have also found that production means progress and that people mean problems. Another thought that has helped me is that, "Warm sympathy is often expressed by cold cash." Certainly, hard work, respect for old-fashioned honesty and for God's laws bring happiness.*

LESTER, HOWARD MILTON, lawyer; b. N.Y.C., Jan. 21, 1927; s. Harry and Fay (Aaron) L.; B.A., Bklyn. Coll., 1949; LL.B., Yale U., 1952; m. Patricia Barbara Briger, Mar. 6, 1956; children—Peter Bruce, Pamela Robin, Prescott Evan. Admitted to N.Y. bar, 1953, since practiced in N.Y.C.; former mem. firm Emile Z. Berman and A. Harold Frost; now mem. firm Lester, Schwab, Katz & Dwyer; lectr. Practicing Law Inst., 1962—. Chmn. joint conf. com. on calendar congestion and related problems 1st and 2d Jud. Depts., 1971-74. Trustee Buckley Country Day Sch., East Hills, N.Y., 1971-75. Served with U.S. Army, 1945-47. Mem. Am., N.Y. State (lectr.; chmn. exec. com. trial lawyer sect. 1972-73), Nassau County bar assns., Assn. Bar City of N.Y., Fedn. Ins. Counsel (v.p. 1967-68, gov. 1968—, pres. 1972-73, chmn. bd. 1973-74), Bklyn.-Manhattan Trial Lawyers (pres. 1971), N.Y. County Lawyers Assn., Def. Research Inst. (dir. 1972-77), Def. Assn. City of N.Y., Am. Arbitration Assn. (law com. 1977—), Internat. Assn. Ins. Counsel, U.S. C. of C. (steering com. product liability task force 1977—). Clubs: Glen Oaks, Yale (N.Y.C.); Sands Point Bath and Tennis; Corbey Court (New Haven). Contbr. articles profl. jours. Home: 14 Shorewood Dr Sands Point NY 11050 Office: 77 Water St New York City NY 10005

LESTER, JULIUS B., author; b. St. Louis, Jan. 27, 1939; s. W.D. and Julia (Smith) L.; B.A., Fisk U., 1960; m. Alida Carolyn Fechner; children—Jody Simone, Malcolm Coltrane, David Julius. Profl. musician and singer, recording for Vanguard Records; folklorist and writer; dir. Newport Folk Festival, 1966-68; now prof. Afro-Am. studies U. Mass., Amherst. Author: (with Pete Seeger) The 12-String Guitar as Played by Leadbelly, 1965; Look Out, Whitey, Black Power's Gon' Get Your Mama, 1968; To Be a Slave, 1968 (Newberry Honor book 1968); Black Folktales, 1969; Revolutionary Notes, 1969; Search for the New Land, 1970; The Knee-High Man and Other Tales, 1972; Long Journey Home: Stories from Black History, 1972 (Nat. Book Award finalist 1972); Two Love Stories, 1972; Who I Am, 1974; All Is Well, 1976. Editor: Seventh Son: The Thoughts and Writings of W.E.B. DuBois, vol. 1 and 2, 1971; asso. editor Sing Out, 1964-69; contbg. editor Broadside of New York, 1964-70; contbr. essays to N.Y. Times Book Rev. and Op-Ed Page, Rolling Stone, Essence, Katallagete, others. Address: 600 Station Rd Amherst MA 01002. *The older I become, the greater the mystery of my life. I think I see my life as journey into mystery, in awe and fear, with joy and apprehension. Whatever my accomplishments, my life is more than and other than, and finally, best expressed by the silence of winter snow, prairie skies, or a feathered serpent. To be as true and eloquent as a drop of water hanging from a twig—that is my ideal.*

LESTER, MALCOLM, educator; b. Georgetown, Ga., Dec. 9, 1924; s. Malcolm Nicholson and Emmie (Bledsoe) L.; A.B., Mercer U., 1945; M.A., U. Va., 1946, Ph.D., 1954; Fulbright scholar U. London (Eng.), 1949-50; m. Pauline Hardeman Domingos, July 7, 1956; 1 dau., Pauline Malcolm (dec.). Instr. history Mercer U., Macon, Ga., 1946-47, asst. prof., 1947-50, asso. prof., 1950-54, prof., 1954-59, dean Coll. Liberal Arts, 1955-59; prof. history Davidson (N.C.) Coll., 1959—, Charles A. Dana prof. history, 1977—, chmn. history dept., 1962—. Recipient Algernon Sydney Sullivan award Mercer U., 1945. Fellow Royal Hist. Soc. (Eng.); mem. Am., So. hist. assns., Orgn. Am. Historians, Nat. Trust (Eng.), Hist. Assn. Eng., Conf. Brit. Studies, AAUP, Soc. Nautical Research (Eng.), English Speaking Union, Raven Soc., Phi Beta Kappa (senator United chpts. 1976—), Omicron Delta Kappa. Presbyn. (elder 1964—, moderator Mecklenburg Presbytery 1974). Club: Colonnade (U. Va.). Author: Anthony Merry Redivivus: A Reappraisal of the British Minister to the United States, 1803-6, 1978; contbr. book revs. to various hist. jours. Home: 228 Roundway Down Davidson NC 28036

LESTER, RICHARD, film dir.; b. Jan. 19, 1932; s. Elliott and Ella (Young) L.; B.S., U. Pa.; m. Deirdre Vivian Smith, 1956; 2 children. TV dir. CBS, 1951-54; dir. TV Goon Shows, 1956; directed Running, Jumping and Standing Still Film (Acad. award nomination, 1st prize San Francisco Festival, 1960); dir. feature films It's Trad, Dad, 1962, Mouse on the Moon, 1963, A Hard Day's Night, 1964, The Knack, (Grand Prix, Cannes Film Festival), 1964, Help, (Best Film award, Best Dir. award Rio de Janeiro Festival), 1965, A Funny Thing Happened on the Way to the Forum, 1966, How I Won the War, 1967, Petulia, 1968, The Bed-Sitting Room, (Ghandi Peace prize, Berlin Festival 1969), 1969, The Three Musketeers, 1973, Juggernaut (Best Dir., Teheran Festival), 1974, The Four Musketeers, 1975, Royal Flash, 1975, Robin and Marian, 1976, The Ritz, 1976, Butch and Sundance—The Early Days, 1978, Cuba, 1979. Address: River Ln Petersham Surrey England

LESTER, RICHARD GARRISON, radiologist, educator; b. N.Y.C., Oct. 24, 1925; s. L. I. and Pauline (Smolan) L.; A.B., Princeton, 1946; M.D., Columbia, 1948; m. Marion Louise Kurtz, Jan. 17, 1949; children—Elizabeth P., Andrew W. Intern N.Y.C. Hosp., 1948-49, asst. resident medicine, 1949-50; asst. resident radiology Stanford Hosp., 1950-51, 53-54; from instr. to asso. prof. radiology U. Minn., 1954-61; prof. radiology, chmn. dept. Med. Coll. Va., 1961-65, Duke Sch. Medicine, 1965-76; prof. radiology U. Tex. Med. Sch., Houston, 1976—, chmn. dept., 1977—. Trustee Meharry Med. Coll., Nashville, 1975—. Served to capt. USAF, 1951-53. Fellow Am. Coll. Radiology, Am. Coll. Chest Physicians; mem. Assn. Univ. Radiologists, Am. Roentgen Ray Soc., Soc. Pediatric Radiology, Radiol. Soc. N.Am. (dir. 1976—). Mem. United Ch. of Christ (deacon). Author: (with others) Congenital Heart Disease, 1965; also numerous articles. Home: 4443 Mt Vernon St Houston TX 77006

LESTER, ROBERT CARLTON, educator; b. Lead, S.D., Feb. 1, 1933; s. Odell and Mary Olivia (Martin) L.; B.A., U. Mont., 1955; B.D., Yale U., 1958, M.A., 1959, Ph.D., 1963; m. Donna Helen Larson, Apr. 15, 1954; children—Paul E., Charles F., R. Timothy. Asst. prof., then asso. prof. Am. U., 1962-70; vis. prof. Cornell U., 1968-69; mem. faculty U. Colo., Boulder, 1970—, prof. religious studies, 1972—; vis. lectr. Dept. State, monthly 1963-70; mem. faculty Humanities Inst., Nat. Endowment Humanities, 1979. Ford Found. fellow, 1960-62; Fulbright Hays fellow, summer 1967, 74-75; Faculty fellow U. Colo., 1974-75. Mem. Am. Acad. Religion, Assn. Asian Studies, Soc. Values in Higher Edn., Phi Delta Phi. Author: Theravada Buddhism in Southeast Asia, 1973, Ramanuja on the Yoga, 1975, Srivacana Bhushana of Pillai Lokacharya, 1979. Office: Religious Studies Dept Univ Colo Boulder CO 80309

LESTER, ROBERT LEONARD, educator; b. New Haven, Aug. 21, 1929; s. Asher and Esther (Rubin) Alperowitz; B.S., Yale, 1951; Ph.D., Calif. Inst. Tech., 1956; m. Elizabeth Land, June 11, 1954; children—Henry Asher, Ellen Martha. Research fellow, Inst. Enzyme Research U. Wis., Madison, 1956-60; vis. research biologist U. Calif. at San Diego, 1969-70; prof. biochemistry Coll. Medicine U. Ky., Lexington, 1960—, chmn. dept. biochemistry, 1974—. NIH grantee, 1961—. Mem. Am. Soc. Biol. Chemists, Am. Chem. Soc., Am. Soc. Microbiology, A.A.A.S., Fedn. Am. Scientists, Sigma Xi. Editorial bd. Jour. Biol. Chemistry, 1966-71, Jour. Bacteriology, 1972—. Contbr. articles to profl. jours. Home: 318 Jesselin Dr Lexington KY 40503

LESTER, VIRGINIA LAUDANO, coll. adminstr.; b. Phila., Jan. 5, 1931; d. Edmund Francis and Emily Beatrice (Downes) Laudano; B.A., Pa. State U., 1952; M.Ed., Temple U., 1955; Ph.D., Union Grad. Sch., 1972; children—Pamela Lester, Valerie Lester. Tchr. pub. schs., Abington, Pa., 1952-55, Greenfield Center, N.Y., 1956; instr. edn. dept. Skidmore Coll., Saratoga Springs, N.Y., 1962-64, dir. ednl. research, 1967-72, asst. to the pres., 1968-72; asst. dir. Capitol Dist. Regional Supplementary Edn. Center, Albany, N.Y., 1966-67; asso. dean, asst. prof. state-wide programs Empire State Coll., State U. N.Y., Saratoga Springs, 1973-75, sr. asso. dean, asso. prof., 1975-76, acting dean state-wide programs, 1976; mem. cons. core faculty Union Grad. Sch., Union for Experimenting Colls. and Univs., Cin., 1975—; vis. faculty fellow Harvard U. Grad. Sch. Edn., 1976; pres., prof. interdisciplinary studies Mary Baldwin Coll., Staunton, Va., 1976—; cons. in field. Dir. So. Bankshares, 1977; bd. dirs. Council Advancement of Small Colls.; mem. com. on criminal sexual assault Va. State Crime Commn., 1976; v.p. Costume Collection, Inc., 1971-73; v.p. Warren, Washington, Saratoga Counties Planned Parenthood, 1972-74, bd. dirs., 1970-74; mem. Saratoga Springs Housing Bd. Appeals, 1966-76; bd. dirs. Nat. Center Higher Edn. Mgmt. Systems, Nat. Urban League, 1979—. Mem. Am. Assn. Higher Edn., Am. Acad. Polit. and Social Scis., Va. Found. Ind. Colls. (trustee), Va. Council Ind. Colls., Am. Council on Edn. (commn. on women in higher edn. 1977-80, Nat. Assn. Ind. Colls. and Univs. (dir.), Assn. Va. Colls. (sec.-treas. 1978-79, v.p. 1979-80, dir.), Pi Lambda Theta, Pi Gamma Mu, Chimes. Mem. Soc. of Friends. Home: 240 Kable St Staunton VA 24401 Office: Mary Baldwin Coll Staunton VA 24401. *I believe, not unlike many successful women in my generation, that I accepted each new opportunity as a gift of which to make the most. If I had been born three decades later I would aspire to create my own opportunities.*

LESTER, WILBUR RUFUS, lawyer, educator; b. Burns Township, Ill., Dec. 9, 1915; s. Rufus and Hattie (Brown) L.; B.A., Monmouth Coll., 1936; J.D., Northwestern Sch. Law, 1939; LL.M., Harvard, 1940; m. Ethel Singer McWilliam, Aug. 23, 1941; children—Byron McWilliam, Cynthia Mary, Roberta Ann, Marcia Aileen. Admitted to Ill. bar, 1940, U.S. Supreme Ct. bar, 1943, Ohio bar, 1955; law clk. to judge Ct. of Appeals, D.C., 1940-42; atty. Dept. Justice, 1942-43; atty., cons. Office of Econ. Stblzn., 1943-45; asst. atty., cons. Office War Moblzn. and Reconversion, 1945; asst. to Sec. of Treas., 1945-46; asso. firm Covington & Burling, 1946-54; vis. prof. law U. Ark., summer 1957; Northwestern U., 1958-59; prof. law U. Cin., 1954—, Rufus King prof. constl. law, 1967—. Mem. central com. Hamilton County Democratic Party, 1964-76, mem. steering com., 1966—. Recipient Dillwyn F. Ratcliff award AAUP, 1973; Goldman award for excellence in teaching, 1978. Mem. AAUP (pres. Cin. chpt. 1966-68, pres. Ohio Conf. 1970-71), Am. Judicature Soc. Unitarian. Home: 1517 Hollywood Ave Cincinnati OH 45224 Office: College of Law U Cincinnati Cincinnati OH 45221

LESTER, WILLIAM DALE, architect, engring. co. exec.; b. Mayfield, Ky., Oct. 29, 1922; s. Paul and Lottie Pearl Hawes L.; student Allegheny Coll., 1943-44, Murray State U., 1946-47; B.S. in Civil Engring., U. Ky., 1949; m. Carolyn Ray, Mar. 16, 1948; children—Dale, Paul. Supr. constrn. Ky. Dept. Hwys., Paducah, 1949-51; area engr. F.H. McGraw & Co., Paducah, 1951-53; structural supr. Giffels & Vallet, Portsmouth, Ohio, 1953-55; structural designer Rust Engrs., Birmingham, Ala., 1955-56; v.p., prodn. mgr. Watson & Co., Tampa, Fla., 1956-76, pres., 1976-78, vice chmn., 1978—. Cub scout master Boy Scouts Am., 1959; maj. United Fund, 1961. Served with USAAF, 1943-45. Fellow Fla. Engring. Soc.; mem. Nat. Soc. Profl. Engrs., ASCE. Baptist. Clubs: Kiwanis (dir. 1956-60); Rotary (dir. 1961—); Palma Ceia Golf and Country. Home: 3208 Morrison St Tampa FL 33609 Office: 3010 Azeele St Tampa FL 33609

LESUEUR, CHARLES ROBIN, librarian; b. Sarnia, Ont., Can., June 8, 1923, s. Norman Lisle and Janie Brenda (Turle) LeS.; B.A., U. Toronto, 1950, B.Social Work, 1951; M.L.S., Columbia, 1959. Came to U.S., 1955, naturalized, 1963. Lab. technician Imperial Oil Refinery, Sarnia, 1945-46; social worker Toronto Children's Aid Soc., 1951-53; wage and salary adminstr. Canadian Gen. Electric Co., 1953-55; engring. librarian N.Y.U., 1955-60; reference librarian Engring. Socs. Library, N.Y.C., 1960-61; engring. and sci. librarian N.Y.U., 1961-68; librarian Stevens Inst. Tech., 1968-72, Rockefeller U., N.Y.C., 1972-77, Harvard U. Med. Sch., 1977—. Served to lt. Royal Canadian Navy, 1941-45. Mem. Am., Med., NE, Mass. library assns., Am. Soc. Info. Sci., Columbia Sch. Library Service Alumni Assn. (dir. 1967-70, pres. 1971-72), Alumni Fedn. Columbia, Delta Upsilon. Home: 20 Chapel St Brookline MA 02146 Office: Francis A Countway Library 10 Shattuck St Boston MA 02115

LETHBRIDGE, FRANCIS DONALD, architect; b. Hackensack, N.J., Oct. 5, 1920; s. Berry B. and Florence A. (Lapham) L.; student Stevens Inst. Tech., 1937-40, Yale Sch. Architecture, 1945-46; m. Mary Jane Christopher, June 21, 1947; children—Catherine B. (Mrs. Robert G. Daniel, Jr.), Mary P., Christopher B., Margaret F. Partner archtl. firm Keyes, Smith, Satterlee & Lethbridge, Washington, 1951-55, Keyes, Lethbridge & Condon, Washington, 1956-75, Francis D. Lethbridge & Assos., Washington, 1975—; prin. works include Pine Spring Community, Fairfax County, Va., 1951-54, Potomac Overlook, 1955-58, U.S. Chancery, Lima, Peru, 1957, Forest Industries Bldg., Washington, 1961, Carderock Springs Community, Montgomery County, Md., 1963-65, Unitarian Ch., River Road, Md., 1964, master plan Arlington Nat. Cemetery, 1966-68, Ft. Lincoln New Town, 1968; mem. fgn. bldgs. archtl. rev. panel U.S. State Dept., 1977—; mem. archtl. adv. panel Fed. Res. Bd., 1979—. Mem. Potomac Planning Task Force, 1965-67; bd. advisers Nat. Trust for Hist. Preservation, 1969-71; mem. Joint Com. Landmarks Nat. Capital, 1964—, chmn., 1964-73. Trustee Nantucket Preservation Inst., 1972—. Served as officer, pilot USNR, 1942-45. Decorated D.F.C., Air medal; recipient Design Merit award AIA, 1955, 66, 1st honor award, 1966, Potomac Valley Chpt. Archtl. award, 1956, 58, 60, 62, 64, 66, 68, 70, 72, 74, 76, joint award of honor AIA-Nat. Assn. Home Builders, 1960; award in architecture Washington Bd. Trade, 1953, 55, 61, 63, 65, 67, 69, 71, 73. Fellow AIA (pres. Washington Met. chpt. 1964, v.p. 1969-70, pres. AIA found. 1971-73); mem. Soc. Archtl. Historians. Club: Cosmos (Washington). Co-author: Guide to the Architecture of Washington, D.C. Home: 2319 Bancroft Pl NW Washington DC 20008 also 48 Orange St Nantucket MA 02554 Office: 1326 18th St NW Washington DC 20036

LETICHE, JOHN MARION, economist, educator; b. Uman, Kiev, Russia, Nov. 11, 1918; s. Leon and Mary (Grossman) L.; B.A., McGill U., 1940, M.A., 1941; Ph.D. in Econs., U. Chgo., 1951; m. Emily Kuyper, Nov. 17, 1945; 1 son, Hugo K. Came to U.S., 1941, naturalized, 1949. Rockefeller fellow Council Fgn. Relations, N.Y.C., 1945-46; Smith-Mundt vis. prof. U. Aarhus and U. Copenhagen (Denmark), 1951-52; spl. tech. econ. adv. UN ECA, Africa, 1961-62; prof. U. Calif. at Berkeley, 1960—; cons. AID, U.S. depts. State, Labor, HUD and Treasury, 1962—; emissary to Japan and Korea, Dept. State, 1971; cons. Econ. Council Can., 1972—; lectr., Stockholm, Paris, Uppsala, Hamburg, Kiel, Oxford (Eng.), 1973, Joint Session Calif. Legislature, 1975. Recipient certificate merit Ency. Brit., Inst. World Affairs, Internat. Legal Center, U. Mich.; Adam Smith medal U. Verona, 1977; Guggenheim fellow, 1956-57. Mem. Am. Econ. Assn. (nominating com. 1968-69), Econometric Soc., Royal Econ. Soc., African Studies Assn., Am. Soc. Internat. Law (bd. 1969—72). Author: Reciprocal Trade Agreements in the World Economy, 1948, in Japanese, 1951; System or Theory of the Trade of the World, 2d edit., 1957; Balance of Payments and Economic Growth, 2d edit., 1976; A History of Russian Economic Thought, 2d edit., 1977; The Key Problems of Economic Reconstruction and Development in Nigeria, 1970; Dependent Monetary Systems and Economic Development, 1974; Lessons of the Oil Crisis, 1977; Gains from Trade, 1979; contbr. articles to encys., congl. coms. and profl. jours. Home: 968 Grizzly Peak Berkeley CA 94708

LETOFSKY, IRVIN MYLES, editor; b. Fargo, N.D., Apr. 26, 1931; s. Jacob and Jennie (Dervin) L.; student Yankton Coll., 1948-49, N.D. Agrl. Coll., 1949-50; Ph.B., U. N.D., 1954; postgrad. San Francisco State Coll., 1956; m. Briam Anna Zoccola, Nov. 2, 1978; children—Laurie, Paul, Polly, Cara. Sports editor Bismarck (N.D.) Tribune, 1957-58; reporter St. Paul Pioneer Press, 1958-63; asst. city editor Mpls. Tribune, 1963-76; editor Calendar sect. Los Angeles Times, 1976—. Served with U.S. Army, 1954-56. Recipient numerous Page One award Newspaper Guild Twin Cities, 1963-70. Office: Times Mirror Sq Los Angeles CA 90053

LETOURNEAU, JEAN-PAUL, assn. exec.; b. St.-Hyacinthe, Que., Can., May 4, 1930; s. Eugene and Annette (Deslandes) L.; Counsellor in Indsl. Relations, U. Montreal (Que.), 1953; cert. c. of c. adminstrn. U. Syracuse, 1962; cert. advanced mgmt. U.S. C. of C., 1965; m. Claire Paquin, Sept. 26, 1956. Mcpl. sec. Mont St.-Hilaire, Que., 1950-53; personnel mgr. Dupuis Freres, mail order house, 1953; editor Jeune Commerce, weekly tabloid, Fedn. Que. Jr. C's of C., 1953; sec. gen. Montreal Jr. C. of C., 1953-56; asst. gen. mgr. Province Que. C. of C., Montreal, 1956-59, gen. mgr., 1959-71, exec. v.p., 1971—. Mem. C. of C. Execs. Can., Corp. Counsellors in Indsl. Relations of Que., Inst. Assn. Execs. (can.), Am. C. of C. Execs. Roman Catholic. Club: St.-Denis. Author: Quebec, The Price of Independence, 1969. Home: 452 Tailhandier St-Bruno PQ J3V 4V2 Canada Office: 500 Saint Francois-Xavier St Montreal PQ H2Y 2T6 Canada. *Liberty is priceless; but liberty imposes responsibility, and if one is not responsible he will lose his liberty.*

LETOURNEAU, RICHARD HOWARD, coll. pres.; b. Stockton, Calif., Jan. 3, 1925; s. Robert G. and Evelyn (Peterson) LeT.; student Wheaton Coll., 1946, LeTourneau Coll., 1956; B.S., Tex. A. and M. U., 1958, M.S., 1961; Ph.D., Okla. State U., 1970; m. Louise Marion Jensen, Feb. 8, 1947; children—Robert Gilmore, Caleb Roy, Linda Louise, Liela Lynn. Gen. mgr. Miss. div. R.G. LeTourneau, Inc., Longview, Tex., 1949-52, v.p. prodn., 1952-57, exec. v.p., 1966, pres., 1966-71; sr. v.p. Marathon Mfg. Co., Houston, 1971-72, dir., 1971-76; pres. Mosley Machinery Co., Waco, Tex., 1972-73; v.p. LeTourneau Found., 1973-75; mem. Tex. Indsl. Commn., 1959-66; adminstrv. v.p. LeTourneau Coll., 1958-62, pres., 1962-68, 75—, chmn. bd. trustees, 1968-75. Past pres. LeTourneau Found. Served with C.E., AUS, 1944-46; PTO. Mem. Sigma Xi, Phi Kappa Phi, Tau Beta Pi, Alpha Pi Mu. Author: Management Plus, 1973; Keeping Your Cool in a World of Tension, 1975; Success Without Succeeding, 1976; Success Without Compromise, 1977. Home: NL-21 Lake Cherokee Longview TX 75603 Office: PO Box 7001 Longview TX 75602. *As a successful industrialist, educator and author, I have found that life is more than mind and body. Everyone, to have a joyous and truly successful life must also trust Jesus Christ as Lord for a spiritual dimension and overall balance in life. With this element missing, regardless of the profession followed, life will be hollow and meaningless, and an eternity of regret is certain.*

LETSINGER, ROBERT LEWIS, chemist, educator; b. Bloomfield, Ind., July 31, 1921; s. Reed A. and Etna (Phillips) L.; student Ind. U., 1939-41; B.S., Mass. Inst. Tech., 1943, Ph.D., 1945; m. Dorothy C. Thompson, Feb. 6, 1943; children—Louise, Reed, Sue. Asso., Mass. Inst. Tech., 1945-46; research chemist Tenn. Eastman Corp., 1946; faculty Northwestern U., 1946—, prof. chemistry, 1959—, chmn. dept., 1972-75. Mem. med. and organic chemistry fellowship panel NIH, 1966-69, medicinal chem. A study sect., 1971-75. Guggenheim fellow, 1956; JSPS fellow, Japan, 1978. Mem. Am. Chem. Soc. (bd. editors jour. 1969-72), A.A.A.S., Sigma Xi. Contbr. articles to profl. jours. Home: 316 3d St Wilmette IL 60091 Office: Northwestern U Chemistry Dept Tech Inst Evanston IL 60201

LETSON, JOHN WALTER, educator; b. Jasper, Ala., Oct. 22, 1911; s. Jesse Walter and Eugenia (Benton) L.; B.S., Auburn U., 1932; M.A., Columbia, 1942, Ed.D., 1949; LL.D. (hon.), Emory U., 1969; m. Sara Agnes Wilkes, Aug. 8, 1936; children—Judy (Mrs. James White), James F., Peggy (Mrs. William Thompson), Alan, Debbie. Tchr. pub. high schs., Siluria and Coffeeville, Ala., 1932-36; prin. Coffeeville High Sch., 1936-41, Tuskegee (Ala.) High Sch., 1942-44; supt. pub. schs., Bessemer, Ala., 1949-57, Chattanooga, 1957-60, Atlanta, 1960-73; dean sch. edn. Valdosta (Ga.) State Coll., 1973-78, prof. sch. adminstrn., 1978—; area dir. Nat. Youth Adminstrn., Montgomery, Ala., 1941-42; asst. dir. div. adminstrn. and finance Ala. Dept. Edn., 1946-49; vis. prof. U. Fla., summers 1954-56, Florence (Ala.) State Coll., 1957. Mem. Ga. Sci. and Tech. Commn., 1964-72, Phi Delta Kappa. Commn. Edn. and Human Rights, 1964-67; mem. Nat. Council on Humanities, 1966-67, Nat. Adv. Com. Vocational Edn., 1966-67, 69-72; mem. adv. com. Nat. Instructional TV Center, 1966-72; mem. adv. com. Edn. Digest, ETS Tchr. Exam.; mem. subcom. urban disadvantaged Com. for Econ. Devel.; bd. dirs. Teaching Film Custodians, 1967-73. Mem. Fulton County Bd. Health, 1960-73; trustee Joint Council Econ. Edn., 1965-71, Atlanta United Way, 1962-73; bd. dirs. Jr. Achievement Greater Atlanta, 1962-73, Atlanta YMCA, 1962-73, Atlanta Boys Club, 1970-73. Served as lt. USNR, 1944-46. Recipient Distinguished Library Service award for sch. adminstrs. Am. Assn. Sch. Librarians, 1972; Dept. Army outstanding civilian service medal; named distinguished prof. Nat. Acad. Sch. Execs., 1973. Mem. NEA (past dir., chmn. budget com.), Ga. Edn. Assn., Am. Assn. Sch. Adminstrs. (v.p. 1968, chmn. fed. policy com. 1969), So. Assn. Colls. and Schs., Newcomen Soc. N. Am., Horace Mann League, Cleve. Conf., Chattanooga (dir.), Bessemer (past pres.) chambers commerce, Kappa Phi Kappa, Phi Delta Kappa, Kappa Delta Pi. Methodist. Rotarian (pres. schoolmasters 1966, recipient Armin Maier award Atlanta). Clubs: Commerce, Capital City (Atlanta). Home: 92 Laurel Dr NE Atlanta GA 30342 Office: Valdosta State Coll Sch Edn Valdosta GA 31601

LETT, AUSTIN SHERWOOD, JR., mfg. co. exec.; b. Milw., June 5, 1941; s. Austin Sherwood and Kathyleen Blackburn (Sims) L.; B.S., U.S. Naval Acad., 1963; M.B.A., U. Mich., 1971; m. Lyla Louise Strauch, July 26, 1971. Commd. ensign U.S. Navy, 1963, advanced through grades to lt. comdr.; resigned, 1971; finance officer First Nat. Bank Chgo., 1971-74; treas. McGraw-Edison Co., Elgin, Ill., 1974—. Decorated Bronze Star, Navy Commendation medal. Republican. Episcopalian. Home: 238 Hillside Rd Barrington IL 60010 Office: 333 W River Rd Elgin IL 60120

LETTON, ALVA HAMBLIN, surgeon; b. Tampa, Fla., May 23, 1916; s. James Hervey and Minerva (Hamblin) L.; student U. Tampa, 1933-35, U. Fla., 1935-37; M.D., Emory U., 1941; m. Roberta Rogers, Oct. 7, 1938; children—Robert Hamblin, Alice Roberta. Intern Ga. Baptist Hosp., Atlanta, 1941-42, resident, 1942-43; practice medicine specializing gen. surgery (oncology), Atlanta, 1946—; chief staff, attending surgeon Ga. Bapt. Hosp., 1965-73; dir. breast cancer demonstration project Bapt. Med. Center; cons. Cobb Gen., Grady Meml., Scottish Rite hosps. Chmn. cancer task force Ga. Regional Med. Program, 1966-71; mem. Ga. Sci. and Tech. Com., 1964-70; active Am. Cancer Soc., 1949—, nat. chmn. pub. edn., 1965-68, nat. chmn. service com., 1968-69, nat. chmn. med. and sci. com., 1969-70, v.p., nat. pres.-elect, 1970-71, nat. pres., 1971-72; pres. Atlanta Med. Center, 1965—, Atlanta Health Evaluation Center, 1973—; mem. Gov.'s Sci. Adv. Council, 1972-75; mem. U.S. nat. com. Nat. Acad. Scis., 1976-79; bd. judges Criss Award; dir. IPA of Ga. Med. Plan; mem. Ethicon Gen. Surg. Adv. Panel, 1975—. mem. cancer control rehab. adv. com. Nat. Cancer Inst., 1975-79; Served with M.C., USNR, 1943-46. Recipient Aven Citizenship award Fulton County Med. Soc., 1960; Honor Alumnus award Emory U., 1973; Hardman award Med. Assn. Ga., 1973; highest award John Muir Med. Film Festival, 1978; diplomate Am. Bd. Surgery. Fellow A.C.S.; mem. Ewing Soc., Southeastern Surg. Congress (sec.-dir. 1960—), So. Surg. Assn., Soc. Nuclear Medicine, Am. Thyroid Assn. Baptist (deacon). Clubs: Capital City (Atlanta); University Yacht (Flowery Branch, Ga.). Chmn. editorial bd. Oncology Times; contbr. articles to profl. jours., films. Home: 3384 Rilman Rd NW Atlanta GA 30327 Office: 315 Boulevard NE Atlanta GA 30312

LETTON, HARRY PIKE, JR., utility exec.; b. Chgo., 1915; grad. U. Nebr., 1935; LL.M., Harvard, 1938. With Pacific Lighting Companies, 1951—, pres., chief exec. officer So. Calif. Gas Co., 1972—. Home: 1364 Wembley Rd San Marino CA 91108 Office: 810 S Flower St Los Angeles CA 90051

LETTVIN, THEODORE, concert pianist; b. Chgo., Oct. 29, 1926; s. Solomon and Fannie (Naktin) L.; Mus. B., Curtis Inst. Music, 1949; postgrad. U. Pa.; m. Joan Rorimer; children—Rory, Ellen, David. First appeared as concert pianist, 1931; solo debut with Chgo. Symphony Orch., 1939; solo, orchestral appearances include Boston Symphony Orch., N.Y. Philharmonic, Phila. Orch., Cleve. Orch., Chgo. Orch., Washington Nat. Symphony, Pitts. Symphony, Seattle Symphony, Mpls. Symphony, Atlanta Symphony, other Am. orchs., also European orchs.; radio appearance Bell Telephone Hour, 1948; debut Ravinia Festival, 1951; apprentice condr. William Steinberg, Buffalo Symphony Orch., 1950-51; concertized throughout U.S., Can., Europe, Africa, 1952—; recent concert appearances, Pitts., Cin., Atlanta, Boston, N.Y.C., Phila., Chgo., Cleve., Mpls. and numerous European orchs., Chautauqua, Ravinia, Interlochen and New Coll. Summer festivals, Town Hall, Alice Tully Hall concerts in N.Y.C.; TV performances include Firestone Hour, Chgo. Theatre of the Air, Boston Symphony Orch.; concert tours, Europe, 1952, 55, 58, 60, 62—, Israel, 1973, Africa and Japan, 1974; asst. artist Marlboro Music Festival, 1963; vis. lectr. U. Colo., 1956-57; head piano dept. Cleve. Music Sch. Settlement, 1957-68; prof. piano New Eng. Conservatory Music, Boston, 1968-77; prof. piano U. Mich. Sch. Music, Ann Arbor, 1977—; concerts, tchr. master classes U. S.E. Mass., summer 1973; mem. faculty Chamber Music Sch., U. Maine, Orono. Winner contest Soc. Am. Musicians 1933; recipient Naumberg award, 1948, Michaels meml. award, 1949; prize winner Belgian Internat. Music Competition, 1952. Mem. Am. Fedn. Musicians, Am. Guild Mus. Artists, A.A.U.P. (exec. com.), Music Tchrs. Nat. Assn., Am. Liszt Soc. Home: Bradford NH 03221 also 265 Parklake Ave Ann Arbor MI 48103 Office: Moore Bldg Sch Music U Mich Ann Arbor MI 48109

LETZLER, HARRY, sugar refining co. exec.; b. Balt., Jan. 25, 1915; s. Simon and Tena (Rosenzweig) L.; B.S., N.Y. U., 1935; M.B.A., Harvard, 1938; m. Shirley A. Zahner, Jan. 30, 1949; children—Stephen H., Patricia A., Jeffrey T., Jonathan R. With Nat. Sugar Refining Co., N.Y.C., 1938—, comptroller, 1960-68, v.p., comptroller, 1968-75, exec. v.p., treas., 1975—. Served to capt. AUS, 1941-46, 51-52. Mem. Fin. Execs. Inst. Clubs: Harvard Bus. Sch. (N.Y.C.); Village Bath and Tennis (Manhasset). Home: 86 Pickwick Rd Manhasset NY 11030 Office: 405 Lexington Ave New York City NY 10001

LEUBERT, ALFRED OTTO PAUL, internat. business cons.; b. N.Y.C., Dec. 7, 1922; s. Paul T. and Josephine (Haaga) L.; B.S., Fordham U., 1946; student Dartmouth, 1943; M.B.A., N.Y. U., 1950; m. Celestine Capka, July 22, 1944 (div. 1977); children—Eloise Ann (Mrs. Kevin B. Cronin), Susan Beth (Mrs. Stephen E. Melvin); m. 2d, Hope Sherman Drapkin, June 4, 1978. Account mgr. J.K. Lasser & Co., N.Y.C., 1948-52; controller Vision, Inc., N.Y.C., 1952-53; with Old Town Corp., 1953-58, controller, 1953-54, sec., controller, 1954-56, sec.-treas., 1956-57, v.p., treas., 1957-58, dir. subsidiaries Old Town Internat. Corp., Old Town Ribbon & Carbon Co., Inc. (Mass. and Calif.), 1955-58; v.p., controller Willcox & Gibbs, Inc., N.Y.C., 1958-59, v.p., treas., 1959-65, pres., dir., chief exec. officer, 1966-76; founder, pub., pres. Leubert's Compendium of Bus., Fin. and Econ. Barometers, 1978—; dir. Lane Office Equipment Inc., N.Y.C., 1960-76, Chyron Corp., S.R.C. Labs., Inc., Tectra Industries Inc.; instr. accountancy Pace Coll., 1955-57. Bd. dirs. United Fund of Manhasset, 1963-69, pres., 1964-65; bd. dirs. Actor's Studio, 1972-76; adv. bd. St. Anthony's Guidance Clinic, 1967-69. Served to 1st lt., inf. USMCR, 1943-46. Decorated Bronze Star; recipient Humanitarian award Hebrew Acad., N.Y.C., 1971. Mem. Nat. Assn. Accountants, Catholic Accountants Guild, Am. Inst. C.P.A.'s, N.Y. State Soc. C.P.A.'s, Financial Execs. Inst., Fordham U. Alumni Assn., Am. Arbitration Assn. (nat. panel arbitrators), Newcomen Soc. N.Am. Clubs: New York Univ., N.Y. Athletic (N.Y.C.).

LEUCHTENBURG, WILLIAM EDWARD, educator, historian; b. N.Y.C., Sept. 28, 1922; s. William Henry and Lauretta Cecilia (McNamara) L.; B.A., Cornell U., 1943; M.A., Columbia U., 1944, Ph.D., 1951; M.A., Oxford U.; m. Jean McIntire, Dec. 21, 1948; children—Thomas, Christopher, Joshua. Cartographer, U.S. Geol. Survey, 1942-43, Queens County dir., state youth dir. Liberal Party, 1943-44; asst. editor Am. Labor Conf. for Internat. Affairs, 1945; New Eng. field rep. Nat. Council for Permanent FEPC, 1945-46; nat. field rep., Mass. state dir. Ams. for Democratic Action, 1947-49, N.Y. State chmn., 1957-58; instr. N.Y. U., 1947; instr., then asst. prof. Smith Coll., 1949-51; asst. prof. Harvard, 1951-52; mem. faculty polit. sci. Columbia U., 1952—, asso. chmn. dept. history, 1958-61, 67-70, 74-75, DeWitt Clinton prof., 1971—; vis. prof. Salzburg Seminar Am. Studies, summer 1956; Harmsworth prof. Oxford (Eng.) U., 1971-72; elections analyst NBC, 1962, 64, 68, 72; adviser Social Security Adminstrn., 1964—; cons. Oxford U. Press, Ford Found., 1965-66, House Judiciary Com., 1975; mem. Nat. Study Commn. Records and Documents of Fed. Ofcls., 1975-77. County committeeman Democratic Party, 1953-55. Adv. com. on oral history John F. Kennedy Meml. Library, 1965—; adv. editorial bd. Franklin D. Roosevelt Library, 1971-76. Served with AUS, 1943. Fellow Center Advanced Study in Behaviorial Scis., Stanford, 1961-62; sr. fellow Nat. Endowment for Humanities, 1968-69, Nat. Humanities Center, 1978-79; Guggenheim fellow, 1975-76; fellow Queen's Coll., Oxford. Fellow Am. Acad. Arts and Scis.; mem. Orgn. Am. Historians (exec. bd. 1968-71), Am., So. hist. assns., Soc. Am. Historians (pres. 1978—), Mass. Hist. Soc. (corr.), P.E.N., Phi Beta Kappa. Club: Century Assn. (N.Y.C.). Author: Flood Control Politics, 1953; The Perils of Prosperity, 1958; Franklin D. Roosevelt and the New Deal, 1963 (Francis Parkman prize 1964, Bancroft prize 1964); New Deal and Global War, 1964; The Great Age of Change, 1964; A Troubled Feast, 1973; co-author: The Growth of the American Republic, 1969; The Unfinished Century, 1973; A Concise History of the American Republic, 1977; contbg. author: Times of Trial, 1958; Change and Continuity in Twentieth-Century America, 1964; An American Primer, 1966; Institutions in Modern America, 1967; The Comparative Approach to American History, 1968; Essays on the New Deal, 1968; The Great Depression, 1969; Interpreting American History, 1970; History of American Presidential Elections, 1971; The Columbia History of the World, 1972; Arab and American Cultures, 1977; Have We Overcome?, 1979; others. Editor: Theodore Roosevelt, The New Nationalism, 1961; Walter Lippmann, Drift and Mastery, 1961; Woodrow Wilson, The New Freedom, 1961; Franklin D. Roosevelt: A Profile, 1967; The New Deal: A Documentary History, 1968. Mem. editorial bd. Columbia U. Forum, 1960-64, Twentieth Century America, An Ency. of the Am. Constitution; co-editor Prentice-Hall Classics in History Series, Harper Am. Perspectives Series; editor Contemporary Am. History series, Columbia U. Press; mem. editorial adv. bd. Polit. Sci. Quar., Notable Am. Women; adv. bd. America: History and Life. Home: 86 Buena Vista Dr Dobbs Ferry NY 10522 Office: Columbia U New York NY 10027

LEUNG, SO WAH, educator; b. China, Nov. 2, 1918; s. Chuk Ping and Sue (Gom) L.; D.D.S., McGill U., 1943; B.S., 1945; Ph.D., U. Rochester, 1950; m. Ming Ren Chen, Aug. 17, 1957; 1 son, Kenneth Walter. Fellow in dentistry U. Rochester, 1944-50, asso. prof., 1950-52, prof., head dept. physiology, 1952-61; dir. grad. edn. U. Pitts. Sch. Dentistry, 1956-61; prof. oral biology U. Calif., Los Angeles, 1961-62; prof. oral biology U. B.C. Faculty Dentistry, Vancouver, 1962—, dean, 1962-77. Sci. cons. Johnson & Johnson, 1950-58, Colgate-Palmolive, 1958-66, Lever Bros., 1963-65; mem. Nat. Acad. Sci.-NRC, 1957-61, dental study sect. NIH, 1959-63; test constructor Nat. Bd. Dental Examiners, 1960-66; asso. Com. on Dental Research, NRC of Can., 1963-68; mem. Nat. Examining Bd. Can., 1965-71, chmn. com. of examiners, 1967-71. Bd. dirs. Charles Kent Scholarship and Charitable Found.; chmn. bd. Vancouver Chinese Cultural Centre, 1975—. Recipient Gold medal Montreal Dental Club, 1943, Centennial medal Govt. of Can., 1967. Fellow A.A.A.S. (councillor), Internat., Am. colls. dentists, Royal Coll. Dentists of Can.; mem. Canadian Dental Assn. (council on edn. 1964-67), Internat. Assn. for Dental Research (councillor 1967-73), Assn. Canadian Faculties of Dentistry (chmn. research com. 1968-70, pres. 1970-72), Sigma Xi, Omicron Kappa Upsilon. Contbr. articles to profl. jours. Home: 4883 College Highroad Vancouver BC Canada

LEV, DANIEL SAUL, polit. scientist; b. Youngstown, Ohio, Oct. 23, 1933; s. Louis and Bessie (Gessen) L.; B.A., Miami U., Oxford, Ohio, 1955; Ph.D., Cornell U., 1964; m. Arlene C. Offenhender, Mar. 22, 1958; children—Claire Ellen, Louis Benjamin George. Asst. prof. polit. sci. U. Calif. at Berkeley, 1965-70; asso. prof. U. Wash., Seattle, 1970-73, prof., 1974—. Mem. Am. Polit. Sci. Assn., Assn. Asian Studies. Author: The Transition to Guided Democracy in Indonesia, 1966; Islamic Courts in Indonesia, 1972; asso. editor Jour. Asian Studies, 1979—. Office: Polit Sci Dept U Wash Seattle WA 98195

LEVA, MARX, lawyer; b. Selma, Ala., Apr. 4, 1915; s. Leo and Fannie Rose (Gusdorf) L.; B.S., U. Ala., 1937, LL.D., 1978; LL.B., Harvard U., 1940; m. Shirley Pearlman, Oct. 31, 1942; children—Leo Marx, Lloyd Leva Plaine. Admitted to Ala. bar, 1940, U.S. Supreme Ct. bar, 1946, D.C. bar, 1950; note editor Harvard Law Rev., 1939, overseer, 1950-55; law clk. to Justice Hugo Black, U.S. Supreme Ct., 1940; sr. atty. O.P.A., 1941; acting regional atty. for Mich. and Ohio, WPB, 1942; counsel to fiscal dir. of Navy, 1946; spl. asst. to sec. of navy, 1947; spl. asst. and gen. counsel to Sec. Def., 1947-49; asst. sec. of def. (legal and legis.), 1949-51; partner firm Fowler, Leva, Hawes & Symington, 1951-67, Leva, Hawes, Symington, Martin & Oppenheimer, 1967—. Chmn. civilian-mil. review panel for spl. com. U.S. Senate, 1957; mem. Pres.'s Commn. to Rev. Fgn. Aid, 1958-59, Pres.'s Com. on Def. Establishment, 1960-61. Served with amphibious forces USNR, 1942-45; ETO, MTO. Selected Outstanding Young Man In Govt., Washington Jr. C. of C., 1949; decorated Bronze Star with combat distinguishing device. Home: 7115 Bradley Blvd Bethesda MD 20034 Office: 815 Connecticut Ave NW Washington DC 20006

LEVACK, ARTHUR PAUL, educator; b. Boston, Dec. 16, 1909; s. Arthur Joseph and Marie Agnes (St Onge) L.; B.A. magna cum laude, Harvard, 1932, M.A., 1934, Ph.D., 1941; m. Helen Gertrude O'Brien, Aug. 28, 1939; children—Ann Marie, Brian Paul. Teaching fellow Amherst Coll., 1935-36; instr. Fordham U., 1936-42, asst. prof., 1942-47, asso. prof., 1947-67, prof. 1967-69, emeritus, 1969—, chmn. dept. history, 1950-65, dean summer session, 1965-78. Mem. Am. Hist. Assn., Am. Cath. Hist. Assn. (pres. 1951), U.S. Cath. Hist. Soc. (pres. 1952-53). Republican. Roman Catholic. Author: (with R.J.S. Hoffman) Burke's Politics, 1949; (with A.I. Abell) A History of the United States, 1951. Contbr. to Ency. Americana, also articles to profl. jours. Home: 219 Bronx River Rd Yonkers NY 10704 Office: Fordham U Bronx NY 10458

LEVAL, PIERRE NELSON, judge; b. N.Y.C., Sept. 4, 1936; s. Fernand and Beatrice (Reiter) L.; B.A. cum laude, Harvard U., 1959, J.D. magna cum laude, 1963; m. Susana Torruella, July 26, 1973; 1 dau., India Luisa. Admitted to N.Y. State bar, 1964, U.S. Ct. Appeals 2d Circuit bar, 1964, U.S. Dist. Ct. bar for So. Dist. N.Y., 1966; law clk. to Hon. Henry J. Friendly, U.S. Ct. Appeals, 1963-64; asst. U.S. atty. So. Dist. N.Y., 1964-68, chief appellate atty., 1967-68; asso. firm Cleary, Gottlieb, Steen & Hamilton, N.Y.C., 1969-74; partner firm, 1973-75; 1st asst. dist. atty. Office of Dist. Atty., N.Y. County, 1975-76, chief asst. dist. atty., 1976-77; U.S. dist. judge So. Dist. N.Y., N.Y.C., 1978—. Served with U.S. Army, 1959. Mem. Am. Law Inst., Assn. Bar City N.Y., N.Y. County Lawyers Assn. Office: US Courthouse Foley Sq New York City NY 10007

LE VAN, C. J., army officer; b. Kansas City, Mo., Feb. 13, 1923; s. Carl J. and Rose Marie (Johnson) Le V.; B.G.E., U. Nebr., 1958; M.S., George Washington U., 1965; grad. Command and Gen. Staff Coll., 1955, War Coll., 1965; m. Mary Ann Bradshaw, Sept. 11, 1946. Commd. 2d lt. U.S. Army, 1942, advanced through grades to lt. gen., 1976; participant New Guinea campaign, 1943-44, occupation of Japan, 1946-49; comdr. air def. arty. units, Korea, 1953-54, Germany, 1965-67, Korea, 1969-70, U.S., 1970-71; mem. Army Gen. Staff, 1958-64; with Office Sec. Army, 1967; dir. Air Def. OACSFOR, Dept. Army, 1968-70; spl. asst. to Sec. of Army, comdg. gen. 32d AADCOM, Europe, 1971-73; comdr. U.S. Army Air Def. Center, Fort Bliss, Tex., 1973-76; dir. ops. Office Joint Chiefs Staff, Washington, 1976-78; mem. corp. staff R & D Assos., Arlington, Va., 1978—. Former mem. exec. bd. Transatlantic Council; chmn. Flussberg dist. Boy Scouts Am., 1971—; bd. dirs. United Fund El Paso, Armed Services Y-USO; trustee German Am. Inst., Saarbrucken, 1971—. Dir. at large S.W. Sun Carnival Assn. Decorated Def. D.S.M., Legion of Merit (5), Army Commendation medal (4), UN medal, Korean Nat. Security medal; Pace award, 1963. Lutheran. Clubs: Masons; mem. Grand Lodge of Tex., Rotary, Lions. Home: Arlington VA Office: Corp Staff R & D Assos Arlington VA 22209

LEVANDOWSKI, DONALD WILLIAM, geologist; b. Stockett, Mont., Dec. 20, 1927; s. Anthony and Ann (Hudak) L.; B.S., Mont. Coll. Mineral Sci. and Tech., 1950; M.S., U. Mich., 1952, Ph.D. (Phoenix Meml. fellow), 1956; m. Martha Mary Midlik, June 4, 1955; children—Mari Ann, Laura Joan. Research geologist Chevron Oil Field Research Co., La Habra, Calif., 1955-64; adminstrv. asst. to mgr. exploration research, 1964-65; geophysicist Standard Oil of Calif., La Habra, 1965-67; asst. party chief Dept. Natural Resources, Quebec, Que., summer 1969; asso. prof. dept. geoscis. Purdue U., West Lafayette, Ind., 1967-75, asso. head dept. geoscis., 1970-76, prof., 1975—, acting head, 1976-78, head, 1978—. Registered profl. engr., Mont. Fellow Geol. Soc. Am., Geol. Assn. Can.; mem. Am. Assn. Petroleum Geologists, Assn. Profl. Geol. Scientists (certified), Am. Soc. Photogrammetry, Sigma Xi, Phi Kappa Phi. Republican. Roman Catholic. Contbr. tech. articles to profl. jours. Home: 3711 Capilano Dr West Lafayette IN 47906 Office: Dept Geosciences Purdue U West Lafayette IN 47907

LEVARIE, SIEGMUND, musician, educator; b. Austria, July 24, 1914; student Northwestern U., 1932-33; condr.'s diploma New Vienna Conservatory, 1935; Ph.D. summa cum laude, U. Vienna, 1938; m. Norma Cohn, 1945; 1 dau., Janet. Came to U.S., 1932, naturalized, 1942. Faculty dept. music U. Chgo., 1938-52, founder, dir. Collegium Musicum, 1938, condr. univ. orch., dir. univ. concerts, 1938-52, faculty grad. courses, 1946-52; dean Chgo. Mus. Coll., 1952-54; exec. dir. Fromm Music Found., 1952-54, dir., 1954-57; prof. music Bklyn. Coll., 1954—, chmn. dept., 1954-62; condr. Bklyn. Community Symphony Orch., 1954-58. Served as capt., adj. gen. dept., AUS, 1941-46. Mem. Am. Musicol. Soc. Author: Mozart's Le Nozze di Figaro: A Critical Analysis, 1952; Fundamentals of Harmony, 1954; Guillaume de Machaut, 1954; Musical Italy Revisited, 1963; (with Ernst Levy) Tone: A Study in Musical Acoustics, 1968; A Dictionary of Musical Morphology, 1980; editor: Lucy Van-Jung Page: Recollections of Pupils and Friends, 1977; author articles, revs. Home: 624 3d St Brooklyn NY 11215

LEVATINO, ANTHONY SAMUEL, bank exec.; b. Independence, La., Sept. 26, 1940; s. Sam J. and Corinne M. L.; B.A., Tex. Tech. U., 1965; m. Maryneil Louise Ward, Aug. 21, 1965; children—Steven, Michael, Paul. With Lubbock Nat. Bank (Tex.), 1965-71; with First Nat. Bank, Dallas, 1971-76, sr. v.p., mgr. dept. real estate Houston Nat. Bank, 1977-78, exec. v.p., div. mgr. over comml., retail and real estate dept., 1978, exec. v.p., div. head, 1979—; instr., counselor Southwestern Grad. Sch. Banking, So. Methodist U. Served with USCGR. Mem. Soc. Real Estate Appraisers, Robert Morris Assos., Am. Mgmt. Assn., Tex. Bankers Assn., Tex. Mortgage Bankers Assn., Kappa Sigma Alumni. Democrat. Roman Catholic. Clubs: Houston, Houstonian, K.C. Office: PO Box 299001 Houston TX 77299

LEVATO, JOSEPH ANTHONY, mfg. co. exec.; b. Morristown, N.J., Mar. 3, 1941; s. Anthony Joseph and Julia Marie (Compoli) L.; B.S. in Acctg., U. Dayton, 1962; m. Diane Claire Schlichting, Oct. 16, 1965; children—Joseph Anthony, Kristin Mary, Thomas Scott. With U.S. Industries, Inc., N.Y.C., 1968—, controller-acctg., 1974-77, v.p., asst. to vice chmn., 1977-78, sr. v.p., corp. controller, 1978—; dir. Health Industries, Inc., USI Credit Corp. Served with N.G., 1963-69. Club: Spring Brook Country. Office: 250 Park Ave New York NY 10017

LÉVECQUE, MARCEL AMÉDÉE, mfg. co. exec.; b. Paris, July 15, 1922; s. Anatole Louis and Marguerite Adéle (Robineau) L.; Engring. degree Conservatoire National des Arts et Métiers, 1945; m. Régine Louise Lardeux, Mar. 11, 1944; children—Aliette, Jean-Luc, Marc. Asst. dir. metals lab. Laboratoire du Bâtiment et des Travaux Publics, Paris, 1941-42; asst. to tech. dir. Manufacture Nationale de Porcelaine de Sèvres (France), 1942-44, chief chemist, 1944-47; research engr. L'Office National d'Etudes et de Recherches Aéronautiques, Paris, 1947-50; research engr. Saint-Gobain Industries, Neuilly-sur-Seine, France, 1950-52, head research group, 1952-56, dir. devel. dept. for glasses, 1956-60, dir. research and devel. dept. of plate glass div., 1960-63, tech. mgr. Société d'Etude pour le Développement de la Fibre de Verre, 1963-68, tech. and research and devel. dir. of insulation, strand and asbestos-cement div., 1969-76; sr. v.p., chief technology CertainTeed Corp., Valley Forge, Pa., 1976-77, exec. v.p., 1977-78, pres., chief exec. officer, 1978—, chief of technology, 1977-78, chmn. operating com., 1978—, also dir. Recipient Prix du Cercle Republicain, 1945, Prix de la Société d'Encouragement pour l'Industrie et le Commerce, 1957; decorated chevalier du Mérite Industriel et Commercial, 1962, chevalier du Mérite National, 1974; prix de l'Energie, 1975. Patentee fiber glass insulation (30). Office: PO Box 860 Valley Forge PA 19482

LEVEE, JOHN HARRISON, artist, designer; b. Los Angeles, Apr. 4, 1924; s. Michael Charles and Roze L.; B.A., UCLA, 1948; postgrad. New Sch. Social Research, N.Y.C., 1949, Acad. Julian, 1950; m. Claude Marie, Dec. 19, 1964. One-man shows Konig Galerie, Geneva, 1971, Andre Emmerich Gallery, N.Y.C., 1957-59, 62, 66, Gimpel Fils, London, 1958, 60, 66, Galerie de France, 1961, 62, 64, 69, Nora Gallery, Jerusalem, Haifa (Israel) Mus. Art, Moose Gallery, Toronto, 1963, Phoenix Mus. Art, 1964, U. Ill. Krannert Art Mus., 1965, Tel Aviv (Israel) Mus., 1969, Margo Leavin Gallery, Los Angeles, 1970, Galerie la Toabis, Paris, 1975, Palm Springs (Calif.) Mus., 1978, Mus. Nice, France, 1980; group shows: Salon de Mai, Paris, 1954, Salon des Realités Nouvelles, 1954—, Carnegie Internat., 1955, 58, Washington's Corcoran Gallery of Art, 1956, 58, Mus. Modern Art N.Y.C., 1957, Whitney Mus., 1957-59, 65, Arts Club Chgo., 1958, Guggenheim Mus., 1966, others; vis. prof. art U. Ill., 1965, N.Y. U., 1967-68, U. So. Calif., 1971; many archtl. projects, France, U.S.A. Served with USAAF, 1944-46. Ford grantee, 1969; Tamarind fellow, Los Angeles, 1969; recipient prizes including

Watercolor Assn. Ann., 1955, 56, Commonwealth of Va. Biann. Purchase award, 1966, grand prix Woolmark Found., 1974-75, gran prix Biennale de Paris, 1969. Jewish. Home: 119 rue Notre Dame des Champs Paris 6 France

LEVEN, BORIS, motion picture art dir., designer; b. Moscow; s. Israel and Zinaida (Narkirier) L.; came to U.S., 1927, naturalized, 1939; B.Arch., U. So. Calif., 1932; certificate Beaux Arts Inst. Design, 1933; m. Vera Glooshkoff, Feb. 8, 1948. Sketch artist, designer Paramount Studios, 1933-35; travelled, painted abroad, 1935-36; art. dir. 20th Century Fox, 1937-38, 41-42, 45-46; free lance art dir., 1939-41; art dir. Universal Internat. Pictures, 1947-48; free lance art dir., prodn. designer, Los Angeles, 1948—; travelled, sketched in Europe, 1955-56, in Europe and Russia, 1959-60, 68, 70; exhibited water colors and paintings in pvt. collections; art dir. numerous motion pictures including Alexander's Ragtime Band, 1938, Hello, Frisco Hello, 1942, I Wonder Who's Kissing Her Now, 1946, Criscross, 1948, Sudden Fear, 1952, The Star, 1952, Silver Chalice, 1955, Giant, 1956, Anatomy of a Murder, 1959, West Side Story, 1961, Two for the Seesaw, 1962, The Sound of Music, 1964, The Sand Pebbles, 1965, Star, 1968, The Andromeda Strain, 1971, Jonathan Livingston Seagull, 1973, New York, New York!, 1977, The Last Waltz, 1978. Served with USAAF, 1942-45. Recipient 1st Emerson prize, 1932; 1st prize Beaux Arts Ball Program, 1932, Am. Inst. Steel Constrn., 1932, Nat. Scarab Travelling Sketch Competition, 1933; Photoplay mag. medal for Giant, 1956; 1st prize art direction Am. Inst. Decorators for The Senator Was Indiscreet, 1947; nominated for Acad. award in art direction for Alexander's Ragtime Band, Shanghai Gesture, Giant, West Side Story, The Sound of Music, The Sand Pebbles, Star, The Andromeda Strain; recipient Acad. award in art direction for West Side Story, 1961. Mem. Soc. Motion Picture Art Dirs., Acad. Motion Picture Arts and Scis., Scull and Dagger, Delta Phi Delta, Tau Sigma Delta. Address: 527 Hanley Pl Los Angeles CA 90049. *In my work I have always tried to achieve the greatest simplicity, both in form and style. And in my life and my relations with other human beings, I have always tried to be as honest with them as I am with myself.*

LEVEN, CHARLES LOUIS, educator; b. Chgo., May 2, 1928; s. Elie H. and Ruth (Reinach) R.; student Ill. Inst. Tech., 1945-46, U. Ill., 1947; B.S., Northwestern U., 1950, M.A., 1957, Ph.D., 1958; m. Dorothy Wish, Dec. 31, 1970; children—Ronald L., Robert M., Carol E., Philip W., Alice S. Economist, Fed. Res. Bank of Chgo., 1950-56; asst. prof. Iowa State U., 1957-59, U. Pa., 1959-62; asso. prof. U. Pitts., 1962-65; prof., dir. Inst. Urban and Regional Studies, Washington U., St. Louis, 1965—, chmn. dept. econs., 1975—; cons. P.R. Planning Bd., U. Alaska, U.S. Corps Army Engrs., Rand Corp. Served with USNR, 1945-56. Ford Found. fellow, 1956; grantee Social Sci. Research Council, 1960, Com. Urban Econ., 1965, NSF, 1968, 73, Merc. Bancorp., 1976, HUD, 1978. Mem. Am. Econ. Assn., Regional Sci. Assn. (pres. 1964-65), Western Regional Sci. Assn. (pres. 1974-75). Author: Theory and Method of Income and Product Accounts for Metropolitan Areas, 1963; Development Benefits of Water Resource Investment, 1969; An Analytical Framework for Regional Development Policy, 1970; Neighborhood Change, 1976; The Mature Metropolis, 1978. Office: Box 1208 Washington Univ Saint Louis MO 63130. *Achievement is satisfying, but especially so when one can win without others losing. At the same time, it appears unnecessary to be a failure to prove one's sincerity.*

LEVENE, SAM, actor; b. Russia, Aug. 28, 1905; s. Harry and Beth S. (Weiner) Levine; came to U.S., 1907, naturalized, 1937; student Am. Acad. Dramatic Arts, 1925-27, U. S.C., summer 1940; m. Constance Hoffman, 1953 (div.); 1 son, Joseph Kenneth. First Broadway appearance in Wall Street, 1927; other starring roles include Jarnegan, 1928, Street Scene, 1929, This Man's Town, 1930, Wonder Boy, 1931, Dinner At Eight, 1932, Yellow Jack, 1934, Spring Song, 1934, Three Men on a Horse (also USO, movies, radio and TV), 1935, 69, Room Service, 1937, Margin for Error, 1939, Grand Guignol Plays, 1943, Sound of Hunting, 1945, Light up the Sky, 1948, 71, Guys and Dolls, 1940 (also London and Las Vegas), The Matchmaker (London), 1954, Hot Corner, 1956, Fair Game, 1957, Make a Million, 1958, Heart Break House, 1959, The Good Soup, 1959, The Devil's Advocate, 1961, Let it Ride, 1961, Seidman and Son, 1962, Cafe Crown, 1964, Last Analysis, 1965, Nathan Weinstein's Daughter, 1966, The Impossible Years, 1966, Don't Drink the Water, 1968, Paris is Out, 1970, Light Up the Sky, 1970, 74, 75, A Dream out of Time, 1970, The Sunshine Boys, 1972, 73, 74, 75, Dreyfus, 1976, The Royal Family, 1976-77, The Merchant, 1977, The Prince of Grand Street, 1978, The Good-bye People, 1978; Goodnight Grandpa, 1979.

LEVENSON, ALAN IRA, physician, educator; b. Boston, July 25, 1935; s. Jacob Maurice and Frances Ethel (Biller) L.; A.B., Harvard, 1957, M.D., 1961, M.P.H., 1965; m. Myra Beatrice Katzen, June 12, 1960; children—Jonathan, Nancy. Intern U. Hosp., Ann Arbor, Mich., 1961-62; resident psychiatry Mass. Mental Health Center, Boston, 1962-65; staff psychiatrist NIMH, Chevy Chase, Md., 1965-66, dir. div. mental health service programs, 1967-69; prof., head dept. psychiatry U. Ariz. Coll. Medicine, Tucson, 1969—; pres. Palo Verde Mental Health Services, Tucson, 1971—; mem. staff Palo Verde Hosp., Tucson Med. Center, U. Hosp., Tucson. Bd. dirs. Tucson Urban League, 1971-78, Pima Council on Aging, 1976—. Served with USPHS, 1965-69. Diplomate Am. Bd. Psychiatry and Neurology. Fellow Am. Psychiat. Assn., Am. Coll. Psychiatrists, Am. Pub. Health Assn.; mem. Group for Advancement of Psychiatry. Author: The Community Mental Health Center: Strategies and Programs, 1972. Contbr. papers and articles to psychiat. jours. Office: Ariz Health Scis Center Tucson AZ 85724

LEVENSON, ALBERT MURRAY, economist, educator; b. Bklyn., May 23, 1931; s. Benjamin and Nettie (Reitzes) L.; B.A., Coll. City N.Y., 1953; Ph.D., Columbia, 1959; m. Evelyn Mittleman, July 4, 1954; children—Ira Seth, Beth Marcia. Asst. prof. econs. Hofstra U., Hempstead, N.Y., 1958-61; asst. prof. econs. Queens Coll., City U. N.Y., Flushing, 1961-67, asso. prof., 1967-70, prof. econs., 1970—, asso. dean faculty, 1970-78, acting chmn. dept. econs., 1969-70. Research cons. Hofstra U. Center for Bus. and Urban Research, 1967-71. Ford Found. fellow, 1958-59, at Inst. Basic Math., 1961-62. Mem. Am. Econ. Assn., Phi Beta Kappa, Pi Gamma Mu, Sigma Alpha. Author: Manpower Supply and Demand in Nassau-Suffolk, 1965-75, 1970; (with William Hamovitch) Projected Employment and Occupation Mix, Nassau-Suffolk, 1968; (with Babette Solon) Essential Price Theory, 1970. Contbr. articles to profl. jours. Home: 338 Church Ave Woodmere NY 11598

LEVENSON, JACOB CLAVNER, educator; b. Boston, Oct. 1, 1922; s. Joseph Mayer and Frances (Hahn) L.; A.B., Harvard, 1943, Ph.D., 1951; m. Charlotte Elizabeth Getz, June 6, 1946; children—Anne Berthe, Jill Mayer, Paul Getz. Tutor in history and lit. Harvard, 1946-50, vis. lectr. English and gen. edn., 1951-52; instr. English, U. Conn., 1950-54; asst. prof. to prof. English, U. Minn., 1954-67; Edgar Allan Poe prof. English, U. Va., Charlottesville, 1967—, chmn. dept., 1971-74; faculty Salzburg (Austria) Seminar in Am. Studies, 1947, 49; Mem. Com. of Cons., Notable Am. Women, 1607-1950, 63-72. Served with AUS, 1943-45. Decorated Bronze Star medal; Guggenheim fellow, 1958-59; Am. Council Learned Socs. fellow, 1961-62; recipient Am. Philos. Soc. Penrose grant, 1956, E. Harris Harbison award for distinguished teaching Danforth Found., 1966. Mem. Modern Lang. Assn., Am. Studies Assn., Signet Soc., English Inst., Phi Beta Kappa. Author: The Mind and Art of Henry Adams, 1957; Editor: (Mark Twain) Life on the Mississippi, 1967; Discussions of Hamlet, 1960; hist. and critical introductions The Works of Stephen Crane, II-V, VII, 1969-76. Mem. editorial bd. Am. Quarterly, 1964-70, Va. Quarterly Rev., 1968—, New Literary History, 1969—. Contbr. articles to profl. jours. Home: 1100 Free State Rd Charlottesville VA 22901

LEVENSON, ROBERT HAROLD, advt. agy. exec.; b. Bronx, N.Y., Nov. 23, 1929; s. William and Frieda L.; B.A., N.Y. U., 1950, M.A., 1951; m. Kathe T. Mooslie, Dec. 31, 1975; children—Keith, Seth. Copywriter, Doyle Dane Bernbach Internat. Inc., N.Y.C., 1959-68, copy chief, sr. v.p., 1968-72, exec. v.p. creative, 1972-74, vice chmn. creative, 1974—, also dir., 1970—. Served as 1st lt. USAF, 1954-56. Elected to Copywriters Hall of Fame, 1972. Office: Doyle Dane Bernbach Internat Inc 437 Madison Ave New York NY 10022

LEVENSON, SAMUEL, humorist; b. N.Y.C., Dec. 28, 1911; s. Hyman and Rebecca (Fishelman) L.; B.A., Bklyn. Coll., 1934, D.H.L., 1976; M.A., Columbia, 1938; L.H.D., St. Francis Coll., 1973; D.H.L., St. John's U., 1978; m. Esther Levine, Dec. 27, 1936; children—Conrad, Emily. Tchr., Abraham Lincoln High Sch., Bklyn., S.J. Tilden High Sch., Bklyn., 1934-46; comedian radio, theatre, TV, 1946—; star Sam Levenson Show, CBS, 1951; moderator Two for the Money, 1955-56; guest star Ed Sullivan Show; panelist This is Show Business, 1951-54; also Match Game, To Tell The Truth; also several guest appearaces. Bd. dirs. League Sch. Seriously Disturbed Children. Recipient citation of honor N.Y. U. Jewish Culture Found., 1952; citation Anti-Defamation League of B'nai B'rith, 1956; Meritorious Service award Nat. Press Club, 1957; medal of honor Nat. Acad. TV Arts and Scis., 1961; Disting. Service award City of N.Y., 1973; Cultural award State of Israel, 1975; award of merit Lotus Club, 1975; Man of Distinction award S. Shore Child Guidance Assn., L.I., N.Y., 1977, others. Mem. B'nai B'rith (dist. bd. govs.). Author: Everything but Money; Sex and the Single Child, 1969; In One Era and Out the Other, 1973; You Can Say That Again, Sam, 1975; A Time for Innocence, 1976; You Don't Have to be Who's Who to Know What's What, 1979. Address: 156 Beach 147 St Neponsit NY 11694

LEVENSON, SEYMOUR, educator; b. N.Y.C., Nov. 12, 1919; s. Samuel Falk and Lena (Miller) L.; B.B.A., Coll. City N.Y., 1942; grad. Indsl. Coll. Armed Forces, 1966; m. Marilyn Carroll Greenspoon, May 2, 1953; children—Gail Catherine, Jenifer Falk. Engaged in pvt. bus., 1939-40, as accountant, 1940-42; joined U.S. Fgn. Service, 1945; assigned Marseille, France, 1945-47, Nanking, China, 1947-49, Athens, Greece, 1950-52, State Dept., 1952-54, Brussels, Belgium, 1954-59, Monrovia, Liberia, 1959-61; exec. dir. Bur. Security and Consular Affairs, State Dept., 1962-66, Bur. Latin Am. Affairs, 1966-67; counselor embassy for adminstrn., Caracas, Venezuela, 1967-71; with State Dept., 1971-76; asst. prof. Capitol Inst. Tech., 1976—. Served with AUS, 1942-45; ETO. Mem. Am. Fgn. Service Assn., City Coll. Alumni Assn., Am. Soc. Public Adminstrn., Washington Performing Arts Soc., Alumni Assn. Indsl. Coll. of Armed Forces. Home: 9619 Alta Vista Terr Bethesda MD 20014 Office: Capitol Inst Tech Kensington MD 20795

LEVENSTEIN, ROBERT, real estate and mfg. co. exec.; b. N.Y.C., Aug. 13, 1926; s. Jules and Mollie (Jarvis) L.; B.S., St. Lawrence U., 1948; postgrad. Harvard, 1948; m. Martha Morrison, May 18, 1956; children—Margaret, Anne. Mgr. prodn. Ender Mfg. Co., N.Y.C., 1949-51; mgr. marketing Lightolier Inc., Jersey City, 1951-61; pres. Silvray-Litecraft Corp., Passaic, N.J., 1961-64; with Philips Industries, Dayton, Ohio, 1965-76, pres., 1968-76, also dir.; chief operating officer, dir. Kaufman and Broad, Inc., Los Angeles, 1976-77, pres., 1977—; dir. Manufactured Housing Inst.; mem. Calif. Housing Task Force, 1977-78. Served with USNR, 1944-46. Home: 1892 Linda Flora Dr Los Angeles CA 90024 Office: 10801 National Blvd Los Angeles CA 90064

LEVENTHAL, CARL M., physician, govt. ofcl.; b. N.Y.C., July 28, 1933; s. Isidor and Anna (Semmel) L.; A.B. cum laude, Harvard U., 1954; M.D., U. Rochester (N.Y.), 1959; m. Brigid Penelope Gray, Feb. 4, 1962; children—George Leon, Sarah Elizabeth, Dinah Susan, James Gray. Fellow in anatomy U. Rochester, 1956-57; intern, then asst. resident in medicine Johns Hopkins Hosp., 1959-61; asst. resident, then resident in neurology Mass. Gen. Hosp., Boston, 1961-64; commd. officer USPHS, 1963—, asst. surgeon gen., 1979—; asso. neuropathologist Nat. Inst. Neurol. Diseases and Blindness, 1964-66; neurologist Nat. Cancer Inst., 1966-68; asst. to dep. dir. sci., 1968-73, acting dep. dir. sci. NIH, 1973-74; dep. dir. bur. drugs FDA, Rockville, Md., 1974-77; dep. dir. Nat. Inst. Arthritis, Metabolism and Digestive Disorders, 1977—; asst. clin. prof. neurology Georgetown U. Med. Sch., 1966—. Decorated Commendation medal USPHS, 1970, Meritorious Service medal, 1974, 77. Diplomate Am. Bd. Psychiatry and Neurology. Fellow Am. Acad. Neurology; mem. Am. Assn. Neuropathologists, Alpha Omega Alpha. Home: 9254 Old Annapolis Rd Columbia MD 21045 Office: NIAMDD NIH Bethesda MD 20205

LEVENTHAL, HAROLD, talent mgr., producer; b. Ellenville, N.Y., May 24, 1919; s. Samuel and Sarah L.; student pub. schs., N.Y.C.; m. Natalie Buxbaum, May 2, 1954; children—Debra, Judith. Talent mgr., producer, 1950—; pres., prin. Harold Leventhal Mgmt., Inc., N.Y.C., 1950—; mgr. performers including Pete Seeger, Judy Collins, Arlo Guthrie, Theo Bikel, The Weavers, Alan Arkin; producer Broadway and Off-Broadway shows; co-producer United Artists' film Bound for Glory, 1976; asso. producer Alice's Restaurant, 1969; co-owner Sanga Music Co., Fall River Music Co. Served with Signal Corps, U.S. Army, World War II; CBI. Jewish. Office: 250 W 57th St New York NY 10019

LEVENTHAL, HOWARD, educator; b. Bklyn., Dec. 7, 1931; s. Elias and Mildred (Turetsky) L.; B.S., Queens Coll., City U. N.Y., 1952; M.A., U. N.C., 1954, Ph.D., 1956; m. Elaine A. Silverman, June 6, 1954; children—Edith Ann, Sharan Gale. Social psychologist USPHS, Washington, 1956-58; asst. prof. Yale, 1958-64, asso. prof., 1964-67; prof. psychology U. Wis.-Madison, 1967—. Cons., rev. panel mem. NIH, 1967-69, mem. arterio sclerosis research centers adv. com. Nat. Heart and Lung Inst., 1972-74; adv. editor psychology Markam Pub. Co., Chgo., 1971-73, Rand McNally Pub. Co., Chgo., 1973-75; mem. research adv. com. Feeling Good, Children's Television Workshop, 1973-74. Served from lt. (j.g.) to lt. USPHS, 1956-58. Grantee, NIH, 1959-70, NSF, 1960-62, 1970—, Robert Woods Johnson Found., 1973-76. Fellow Am. Psychol. Assn., A.A.A.S.; mem. Acad. Behavioral Medicine Research. Cons. editor Jour. Personality and Social Psychology, 1967-70, Personality: An Internat. Jour., 1970-72; editorial bd. Jour. Exptl. Social Psychology, 1974—. Home: 5938 S Hill Dr Madison WI 53705

LEVENTHAL, ROBERT STANLEY, beverage and chems. mfg. co. exec.; b. Cambridge, Mass., Jan. 8, 1927; s. Harold A. and Matilda (Goldwyn) L.; A.B., Harvard U., 1948, M.B.A., 1956; children by previous marriage—Jeffrey Nelson, Daniel Philip. Commd. ensign USN, 1948, advanced through grades to comdr., 1964; supply officer Naval Support Activity, Da Nang, Vietnam, 1965-66; with Office of Sec. of Def., Washington, 1966-68; ret., 1968; exec. asst. to chmn., dir. supply and distbn. Amerada Hess Corp., Woodbridge, N.J., 1968-71; exec. v.p. Engelhard Industries, Murray Hill, N.J., sr. v.p. Engelhard Minerals and Chems. Corp., N.Y.C., 1971-75; sr. v.p. Beker Industries Corp., Greenwich, Conn., 1975-77; pres., chief exec. officer, chief operating officer Publicker Industries Inc., Phila., 1977—, also. dir. Decorated Legion of Merit with gold star. Office: 777 W Putnam Ave Greenwich CT 06830

LEVEQUE, WILLIAM JUDSON, mathematician, educator, assn. exec.; b. Boulder, Colo., Aug. 9, 1923; s. Earl Mehlum and Doris (Roberts) LeV.; B.A. summa cum laude, U. Colo., 1944; M.A., Cornell U., 1945, Ph.D., 1947; m. Ann Thuma, May 8, 1970; 1 son by previous marriage, Randall John. Benjamin Peirce instr. Harvard, 1947-49; faculty math. U. Mich., 1949-70, prof., 1960-70, chmn., 1967-70; prof. Claremont (Calif.) Grad. Sch., 1970-77; exec. dir. Am. Math. Soc., 1977—; Chmn., Conf. Bd. Math. Scis., 1973-74. Fulbright research scholar, 1951-52; Alfred P. Sloan research fellow, 1957-60. Fellow AAAS; mem. Am. Math. Soc., Math. Assn. Am. Author: Topics in Number Theory, 2 vols., 1956; Elementary Theory of Numbers, 1962; Reviews in Number Theory, 6 vols., 1974; Fundamentals of Number Theory, 1977. Exec. editor Math. Revs., 1965-66. Contbr. articles to profl. jours. Home: 176 Cole Ave Providence RI 02906

LEVEQUE, WILLIAM JUDSON, mathematician, assn. exec.; b. Boulder, Colo., Aug. 9, 1923; s. Earl Mehlum and Doris (Roberts) LeV.; B.A. summa cum laude, U. Colo., 1944; M.A., Cornell U., 1945, Ph.D., 1947; m. Ann Thuma, May 8, 1970; 1 son by previous marriage, Randall John. Benjamin Peirce instr. Harvard, 1947-49; faculty math. U. Mich., 1949-70, prof., 1960-70, chmn., 1967-70; prof. Claremont (Cal.) Grad. Sch., 1970-77; exec. dir. Am. Math. Soc., 1977—. Chmn., Conf. Bd. Math. Scis., 1973-74. Fulbright research scholar, 1951-52; Alfred P. Sloan research fellow, 1957-60. Mem. Am. Math. Soc., Math. Assn. Am., London Math. Soc., AAAS. Author: Topics in Number Theory, 2 vols., 1956; Elementary Theory of Numbers, 1962; Reviews in Number Theory, 6 vols., 1974; Fundamentals of Number Theory, 1977. Exec. editor Math. Revs., 1965-66. Contbr. articles to profl. jours. Home: 176 Cole Ave Providence RI 02906 Office: Am Math Soc PO Box 6248 Providence RI 02940

LEVER, WALTER FREDERICK, physician, educator; b. Erfurt, Germany, Dec. 13, 1909; s. Alexander and Edith (Hirschberg) L.; student U. Heidelberg (Germany), 1928-30; M.D., U. Leipzig (Germany), 1934; m. Frances Broughton, Sept. 28, 1940 (div. 1969); children—Joan (Mrs. Harold H. Woollard III), Susan (Mrs. Thomas Barber); m. 2d, Gundula Schaumburg, May 10, 1971; children—Insa Bettina, Mark Alexander. Came to U.S., 1935, naturalized, 1941. Intern Cologne (Germany) U. Hosp., 1934-35, St. John's Hosp., Bklyn., 1936; resident dermatology Mass. Gen. Hosp., Boston, 1936-38, research fellow, 1938-44; from asst. to asst. clin. prof. dermatology Harvard Med. Sch., 1944-59, lectr., 1959-76; prof. dermatology Tufts U. Med. Sch, 1959-75, prof. emeritus, 1975—, chmn. dept., 1961-75, acting chmn., 1975-78; lectr. dermatology Boston U. Med. Sch., 1978—; dir. dermatology service Boston City Hosp., 1961-74; dermatologist-in-chief New Eng. Med. Center Hosps., 1959-78, asso. staff mem., 1978—; bd. consultation Mass. Gen. Hosp., 1959-76, hon. dermatologist, 1976—; cons. Robert Breck Brigham Hosp., 1949-76; prin. investigator lipid metabolism USPHS, 1951-65, electron microscopy, 1962-75; mem. gen. medicine study sect. NIH, 1959-63; Dohi lectr., Japan, 1963; Pritzker lectr. U. Toronto, 1976; Novy lectr. U. Calif., Davis, 1977. Diplomate Am. Bd. Dermatology (spl. competence certification in dermatopathology). Fellow Am. Acad. Dermatology (past dir.); mem. Soc. Investigative Dermatology (past dir., past pres.), New Eng. Dermatol. Soc., Am. Soc. Dermatopathology (past pres.), Am. Dermatol. Assn.; hon. mem. Pacific Dermatol. Assn., Austrian, Brit., Danish, Dutch, Finnish, French, German, Greek, Indian, Italian, Japanese, Polish, Uruguayan, Venezuelan, Yugoslav dermatol. socs. Lutheran. Author: Histopathology of the Skin, 5th edit., 1975; Pemphigus and Pemphigoid, 1965; (with Ken Hashimoto) Appendage Tumors of the Skin, 1969. Mem. editorial bd. Archives of Dermatology, 1963-72. Home: 51 Lincoln House Point Swampscott MA 01907 Office: 280 Washington St Brighton MA 02135

LEVERE, RICHARD CRAIG, elec. co. exec.; b. Bklyn., June 18, 1927; s. Chester Wallace and Beulah Elizabeth (Craig) LeV.; B.E.E., Poly. Inst. Bklyn., 1950; m. Marilyn Florence Harms, Mar. 8, 1952; children—Craig Williams, James Gordon, Elizabeth Grace. With Holophane div. Johns-Manville Sales Corp., Denver, 1950—, mgr. application engring., 1958-62, mgr. Light and Vision Inst., 1962-63, 66-72, mgr. engring. and tech. services, 1970-78, market mgr., 1978—; instr. illumination engring. Poly. Inst. Bklyn., 1969—; guest lectr. illumination Pratt Inst. Served with AUS, 1945-47. Fellow Illuminating Engring. Soc. (chmn. L.I. chpt. 1972). Presbyterian (elder 1950-51, 63-66, 67-68, 76—). Mason. Contbr. articles to tech. jours. Office: Ken-Caryl Ranch PO Box 5108 Denver CO 80217

LEVERENZ, OSCAR TAYLOR, accountant; b. Milw., May 15, 1919; s. Oscar and Mary E. (Taylor) L.; B.A., U. Wis., 1940; postgrad. Northwestern U., 1946-47; m. Marjorie Jean Peterson, Jan. 17, 1942; 1 son, Richard T. (dec.). Mem. staff Arthur Andersen & Co., Chgo., 1945-51, audit mgr., Dallas, 1951-56, partner charge Ft. Worth office, 1962-66, dir. Western U.S. ops., 1966-70, mng. partner Denver office, 1970-77; ret., 1977; sec., treas., dir. Republic Natural Gas Co., Dallas, 1956-61. Trustee Mt. Airy Found. Served to lt. USNR, 1941-45. C.P.A., Tex. Mem. Am. Inst. C.P.A.'s, Fin. Execs. Inst., Am. Accounting Assn., Phi Kappa Sigma. Clubs: Rotary; Fayetteville (Ark.) Country. Home: 2425 Boston Mountain View Fayetteville AR 72701 also Whippoorwill Ranch Huntsville AR

LEVERETT, MILES CORRINGTON, nuclear engr.; b. Danville, Ill., Dec. 18, 1910; s. Warren H. and Joanna (Corrington) L.; B.S., Kan. State Coll., 1931; M.S., U. Okla., 1932; Sc.D., Mass. Inst. Tech., 1938; m. Nancy Walker, Oct. 18, 1938. Asst. chemist Marathon Paper Mills Co., Menasha, Wis., 1932, Phillips Petroleum Co., Barlesville, Okla., 1933; sr. research engr. Humble Oil & Refining Co., Houston, 1938-42, research asso., 1948-49; dir. tech. div. Clinton Labs., 1942-48; tech. dir. nuclear energy for propulsion of aircraft project Fairchild Engine and Airplane Corp., 1949-51; engr., mgr. aircraft nuclear propulsion project Gen. Electric Co. 1951, then mgr. devel. labs. aircraft nuclear propulsion dept., then cons. engr. Hanford atomic products operation Gen. Electric Co., Richland, Wash., mgr. engring, N-Reactor dept., then mgr. nuclear safety appraisal; now cons. Fellow Am. Nuclear Soc. (pres. 1960-61); mem. Am. Phys. Soc., Am. Inst. Chem. Engrs., Am. Inst. Mining and Metall. Engrs., Inst. Aero. Scis. Home and office: 15233 Via Pinto Monte Sereno CA 95030

LEVERTOV, DENISE, poet; b. Ilford, Essex, Eng., Oct. 24, 1923; d. Paul Philip and Beatrice A. (Spooner-Jones) Levertoff; ed. privately; Litt.D., Colby Coll., 1970, U. Cin., 1973; m. Mitchell Goodman, Dec. 2, 1947 (div. 1975); 1 son, Nikolai. Came to U.S., 1948, naturalized, 1955. Tchr. craft of poetry Poetry Center, YMHA, N.Y.C., 1964; vis. lectr. Drew U., 1965, Coll. City N.Y., 1965, Vassar Coll., 1966-67, U. Calif. at Berkeley, 1969; vis. prof. Mass. Inst. Tech., 1969-70; scholar

Radcliffe Inst. Ind. Study, 1964-65, 65-66; artist-in-residence Kirkland Coll., 1970-71; Elliston lectr. U. Cin., spring 1973; vis. prof. Tufts U., 1973-74, 74-75, prof., 1975—. Guggenheim fellow, 1962; recipient Nat. Inst. Arts and Letters award, 1965, Longview award, 1961, Bess Hokins, Inez Boulton and Morton Dauwen Zabel prizes Poetry mag. Author: The Double Image, 1946; Here and Now, 1957; Overland to the Islands, 1958; With Eyes at the Back of Our Heads, 1960; The Jacob's Ladder, 1962; O Taste and See, 1964; The Sorrow Dance, 1967; Relearning the Alphabet, 1970; To Stay Alive, 1971; Footprints, 1972; The Poet in the World, 1974; The Freeing of the Dust, 1975; Life in the Forest, 1978; Collected Earlier Poems, 1940-1960, 1979. Translator: Selected Poems of Guillevic, 1969. Address: care New Directions 333 6th Ave New York City NY 10014

LÉVESQUE, CHARLES-HENRI, bishop; b. St-André de Kamouraska, Que., Can., Dec. 29, 1921; s. Alexis and Atala (Garneau) L.; B.A., Ste-Anne-de-la Pocatiere, 1944; B.Ph., Laval U., 1945, L.Th., 1949; D.D.C., Angelicum, Rome, 1955. Ordained priest Roman Catholic Ch., 1948; head discipline, tchr. history and letters College Ste-Amme-de-la-Pocatière, 1949-51; sec., master ceremonies Bishopric Ste. Anne, 1951; chancellor Diocese Ste. Anne, 1956, hon. canon, 1956, titular canon, 1957, secret chamberlain, 1960, aux. bishop Ste-Anne-de-la-Pocatière, 1965-68, bishop, 1968—. Mem. episcopal com. Office Catéchèse du Quebec; mem. com. des priorités Assembleé des Eveques du Que.; pres. Com. to Broadcast Liturg. Celebrations; co-pres. episcopal com. liturgy Conf. des Eveques catholiques du Can.; mem. Internat. Francophone Com. for Liturg. Translations. Decorated chevalier l'Order équestre du St. Sépulcre, K.C. (4 deg.). Home and office: 1200 4th Ave La Pocatière PQ G0R 1Z0 Canada*

LEVESQUE, J. LOUIS, corp. exec.; b. Nouvelle, Que., Can., Apr. 13, 1911; s. Jean and Mary (Greene) L.; ed. Gaspe Coll., St. Dunstan's U., Charlottetown, P.E.I.; D.C.Sc., St. Joseph U., Memramcook, N.B., 1952; Dr. Polit. Econs., Sacred Heart U., Bathurst, N.B., 1957, also U. Montreal; LL.D., St. Dunstan's U.; D.C.Sc., Laval U.; D.C.L., U. Moncton (N.B.); m. Jeanne Brisson, May, 1938; children—Andree, Suzanne, Pierre-Louis. With Provincial Bank of Can., Moncton, N.B., 1934-41; founder, 1941, Credit Interprovincial; chmn. bd. Levesque, Beaubien Inc., Indsl. Life Ins. Co.; pres. Le Crédit Interprovincial Incorporée; v.p. Gen. Trust of Can.; dir. Librairie Beauchemin Ltee., Windsor Raceway Holdings Ltd., L'Equitable Compagnie d'Assurances Générales, Hilton-Can. Ltd., Tropical Park Inc.; trustee Ont. Jockey Club Ltd. Bd. dirs. Miami Heart Inst., also Research Fund. Decorated Order of Can.; comdr. Order St. Gregory the Great; knight of magistral grace Sovereign and Mil. Order Malta. Clubs: Jockey of Can.; Indian Creek Country (Miami, Fla.). Home: 3465 Redpath St Montreal PQ Canada Office: 1245 Sherbrooke St W Suite 1205 Montreal PQ H3G 1G2 Canada

LEVESQUE, LOUIS, bishop; b. Amqui, Que., Can., May 27, 1908; s. Philippe and Catherine (Beaulieu) L.; B.A., Laval U., 1928, Ph.L., 1930, Th.D., 1932; S.S.L., Bib. Inst., Rome and Jerusalem, 1935. Ordained priest Roman Cath. Ch., 1932; tchr. holy scripture, Rimouski, Que., 1936-51; bishop of Hearst, Ont., 1952-64; archbishop of Rimouski, 1964-73. Chmn. Canadian Cath. Conf., 1965-67; mem. Congregation Bishops, Rome, 1968-73. Mem. Cath. Bibl. Assn. Am. Home: 57 Hotel de Ville Mont-Joli PQ G5H 1W9 Canada

LEVESQUE, RENE, Québec govt. ofcl.; b. New Carlisle, Que., Can., Aug. 24, 19[illegible]2; s. Dominique and Diane Dionne (Pineault) L.; student Laval U. Formerly radio announcer, war. corr. Am. Forces, Europe, 1944-45, Korea, CBC, 1952, chief French Network News Services, 1952-56; free-lance radio and TV commentator, Montreal, Qué.; mem. Qué. Legislature for Montreal-Laurier, 1960-70; minister pub. works and hydraulic works Province of Qué., Québec City, 1960-61, minister natural resources, 1961-66, minister family and social welfare, 1965-66; mem. Qué. Legislature from Taillon riding, 1976—; Prime Minister Qué., 1976—. Founder, Que. Sovereignty Assn., 1967; pres. Parti Québecois Author: Option Québec, 1968; La Passion du Québec, 1978. Address: Parliament Bldgs Québec PQ Canada also care Parti Québecois 8790 Ave du Parc Montreal PQ Canada

LEVESQUE, RENE JULES ALBERT, physicist, univ. adminstr.; b. St. Alexis, Que., Can., Oct. 30, 1926; s. Albert and Elmina Louisa (Veuilleux) L.; B.Sc., Sir George Williams U., 1952; Ph.D., Northwestern U., 1957; m. Alice Farnsworth, Apr. 6, 1956 (div.); children—Marc, Michel, Andre. Research asso. U. Md., 1957-59; asst. prof. U. Montreal, 1959-64, asso. prof., 1964-67, prof., 1967—, dir. nuclear physics lab., 1965-69, chmn. dept. physics, 1968-73, vice dean arts and scis., 1973-75, dean, 1975-78, v.p. research, 1978—; mem. advisory com. ING project Atomic Energy of Canada Ltd., 1966-69; mem. advisory bd. physics NRC Canada, 1972-74, pres. nuclear physics grant selection, 1973, mem. adv. bd. on TRIUMF, 1979—; v.p. Commn. Higher Studies Que. Ministry Edn., 1976-77; v.p. bd. dirs. Can.-France-Hawaii Telescope Corp., 1979-80; pres. permanent research com. Conf. Rectors and Prins. Que. Univs., 1979-80. Pres., Mouvement Laïc de langue française, 1961. Mem. Can. Assn. Physicists (pres. 1976-77), U. Montreal Faculty Assn. (pres. 1971), Fedn. Que. Faculty Assn. (pres. 1971-72), Interciencia Assn. (v.p. bd. dirs. 1979-80), Assn. Sci., Engring. and Technol. Community Can. (v.p. 1979-80). Home: 3250 Forest Hill St #1704 Montreal PQ H3V 1C8 Canada Office: Faculte Arts Sciences CP 6128 2900 Univ Montreal Montreal PQ Canada

LEVEY, GERRIT, chemist, educator; b. Friesland, Wis., Jan. 9, 1924; s. John G. and Bessie (Alsum) L.; A.B., Hope Coll., Holland, Mich., 1946; Ph.D., U. Wis., 1949; m. Mary Ryland Belt, Dec. 27, 1952; children—Christopher Gerrit, Douglas John, Bryan Osborn. Mem. faculty Berea (Ky.) Coll., 1949—, prof. chemistry, 1958—, also chmn. dept.; sabbatical leaves for study and research at Mass. Inst. Tech., U. Leeds (Eng.), Argonne Nat. Lab.; summer research appointments Brown U., U. Wis. Served with AUS, 1943-44. Recipient Seabury award for excellence in teaching Berea Coll., 1962. Mem. Am. Chem. Soc., Ky. Acad. Sci. (sec. 1957-64), South Central Assn. Chemists, Sigma Xi, Phi Lambda Upsilon. Contbr. articles to profl. jours. Home: 107 Van Winkle Grove Berea KY 40404

LEVI, ALBERT WILLIAM, educator; b. Indpls., June 19, 1911; s. Albert William and Stella (Levi) L.; A.B., Dartmouth, 1932; M.A., U. Chgo., 1933, Ph.D., 1935; children by previous marriage—Estelle (Mrs. Sasha (Weitman), Michael, David; m. Ute Schweitzer, May 2, 1966; children—Lawrence, Susannah. Mem. faculty Dartmouth, 1935-41, U. Chgo., 1941-45, Black Mountain Coll., 1945-50, U. Graz (Austria), 1951, U. Vienna (Austria), 1952; mem. faculty Washington U., St. Louis, 1952—, David May Distinguished Univ. Prof. humanities, 1965—. Mem. Nat. Council Humanities, 1966-72. Mem. Phi Beta Kappa. Author: Rational Belief, 1941; General Education in the Social Studies, 1948; Varieties of Experience, 1957; Philosophy and the Modern World (first Ralph Waldo Emerson award Phi Beta Kappa 1960), 1959; Literature, Philosophy and the Imagination, 1962; Humanism and Politics, 1969; The Humanities Today, 1970; Philosophy as Social Expression, 1974. Home: 7008 Waterman Ave St Louis MO 63130

LEVI, EDWARD HIRSCH, former atty. gen. U.S.; b. Chgo., June 26, 1911; s. Gerson B. and Elsa B. (Hirsch) L; Ph.B., U. Chgo., 1932, J.D., 1935, (hon.) L.H.D.; J.S.D. (Sterling fellow 1935-36), Yale U., 1938; LL.D., U. Mich., 1959, U. Calif. at Santa Cruz, Jewish Theol. Sem. Am., U. Iowa, Brandeis U., Lake Forest Coll., U. Pa., Dropsie U., Columbia, Yeshiva U., U. Rochester, U. Toronto, Yale, U. Notre Dame, Denison U., U. Nebr., U. Miami, Boston Coll., Brigham Young U.; L.H.D., Hebrew Union Coll., DePaul U., Loyola U., Kenyon Coll., Bard Coll., Beloit Coll.; D.C.L., N.Y. U.; m. Kate Sulzberger, June 4, 1946; children—John, David, Michael. Admitted to Ill. bar, U.S. Supreme Ct. bar, 1945; asst. prof. U. Chgo. Law Sch., 1936-40, prof. law, 1945-75, dean, 1950-62, provost univ., 1962-68, univ. pres., 1968-75, pres. emeritus, 1975—, Karl Llewellyn Distinguished Service prof. (on leave), from 1975, Glen A. Lloyd distinguished service prof., 1977—; atty. gen. U.S., 1975-77; Thomas Guest prof. U. Colo., summer 1960; Herman Phleger vis. prof. Stanford Law Sch., 1978; spl. asst. to atty. gen. U.S., Washington, 1940-45; 1st asst. war div. Dept. Justice, 1943, 1st asst. antitrust div., 1944-45; chmn. interdeptl. com. on monopolies and cartels, 1944; counsel Fedn. Atomic Scientists with respect to Atomic Energy Act, 1946; counsel subcom. on monopoly power Judiciary Com., 81st Congress, 1950; trustee Aerospace Corp. Mem. research adv. bd. Com. Econ. Devel., 1951-54; bd. Social Sci. Research Council, 1959-62, Council Legal Edn. and Profl. Responsibility, 1968-74; mem. Citizens Commn. Grad. Med. Edn., 1963-66, Commn. Founds. and Pvt. Philanthropy, 1969-70, Pres.'s Task Force Priorities in Higher Edn., 1969-70, Sloan Commn. Cable Communications, 1970, Nat. Commn. on Productivity, 1970-75, Nat. Council on Humanities, 1974-75. Hon. trustee U. Chgo., trustee Internat. Legal Center, 1966-75, Woodrow Wilson Nat. Fellowship Found., 1972-75, 77-79, Inst. Psychoanalysis Chgo., 1961-75, Urban Inst., 1968-75, Mus. Sci. and Industry, 1971-75, Russell Sage Found., 1971-75, Aspen Inst. Humanistic Studies, 1970-75, 77-79, Inst. Internat. Edn. (hon.), 1969; public dir. Chgo. Bd. Trade, 1977—; bd. overseers U. Pa., 1978—; chmn. bd. Nat. Humanities Center, 1979—; bd. dirs. MacArthur Found., 1979—. Decorated Legion of Honor (France). Fellow Am. Acad. Arts and Scis., Am. Bar Found.; mem. Am. Philos. Soc., Am., Ill., Chgo. bar assns., Am. Law Inst. (council), Am. Judicature Soc., Phi Beta Kappa, Order of Coif. Clubs: Century (N.Y.C.); Chgo., Comml., Quadrangle, Mid-Am. (Chgo.); Columbia Yacht; Cosmos (Washington). Author: Introduction to Legal Reasoning, 1949; Four Talks on Legal Education, 1952; Point of View, 1969; editor: Gilbert's Collier on Bankruptcy (with J. W. Moore), 1936; Elements of the Law (with R. S. Steffen), 1950. Office: 1116 E 59th St Chicago IL 60637

LEVI, HERBERT WALTER, biologist, educator; b. Frankfurt, Germany, Jan. 3, 1921; s. Ludwig and Irma (Hochschild) L.; came to U.S., 1938, naturalized, 1945; student Art Students League, N.Y.C., 1938-39; B.S., U. Conn., 1946; M.S., U. Wis., 1947, Ph.D., 1949; m. Lorna Rose, June 13, 1949; 1 dau., Frances. Instr., then asst. prof. to asso. prof. zoology, extension div. U. Wis., 1949-56; asst. curator arachnology Museum Comparative Zoology, Harvard, 1956-57, asso. curator, 1957-66, curator, 1966—, prof. biology Harvard, 1970—, Agassiz prof. zoology, 1972—; sec. Rocky Mountain Biol. Lab., 1959-65; vis. prof. Hebrew U., Jerusalem, 1975; bd. govs. Nature Conservatory, 1956-62; v.p. Centre International de Documentation Arachnologique, 1965-68. Mem. Am. Soc. Zoologists, Soc. Study Evolution, Soc. Systematic Zoology (councillor 1967-69), Am. Micros. Soc. (bd. reviewers 1973—), Am. Arachnol. Soc. (bd. editors 1974—, dir. 1975—, pres. 1979—), Am. Ecol. Soc., Wildlife Soc., Am. Ornithol. Union, Assn. Systematics Collections (council nat. systematic collections and resources 1975—), Wilderness Soc. Author: Spiders and Their Kin, 1968; numerous articles. Translator, editor: (Kaestner) Invertebrate Zoology, 3 vols. Home: Wheeler Rd Pepperell MA 01463 Office: Museum Comparative Zoology Harvard U Cambridge MA 02138

LEVI, ISAAC, educator; b. N.Y.C., June 30, 1930; s. Eliezer Asher and Eva (Lunenfeld) L.; B.A., N.Y. U., 1951; student Jewish Theol. Sem., 1947-52; M.A., Columbia, 1953, Ph.D., 1957; m. Judith S. Rubins, Dec. 25, 1951; children—Jonathan Abram, David Isser. Part-time instr. Rutgers U., 1954-56; lectr. Coll. City N.Y., 1956-57, asst. prof. philosophy, 1962-64; asst. prof. philosophy Western Res. U., 1957-62, asso. prof., 1964-67, prof., 1967-70, chmn. dept., 1968-70; prof. philosophy Columbia, 1970—, chmn. dept., 1973-76. Fulbright scholar, 1966-67; Guggenheim fellow, 1966-67; vis. scholar Corpus Christi Coll., Cambridge U., 1973. Mem. Am. Philos. Assn., Philosophy of Sci. Assn., Brit. Soc. Philosophy of Sci., AAUP, Phi Beta Kappa, Pi Mu Epsilon. Democrat. Author: Gambling with Truth, 1967; The Enterprise of Knowledge, 1980; also articles. Home: 25 Claremont Ave New York NY 10027

LEVI, JULIAN HIRSCH, lawyer; b. Chgo., July 25, 1909; s. Gerson Baruch and Elsa (Hirsch) L.; Ph.B. with honors, U. Chgo., 1929, J.D. cum laude, 1931; LL.D. (hon.), John Marshall Law Sch., Chgo., Lake Forest (Ill.) Coll., 1967; m. Marjorie Reynolds, Sept. 16, 1938; children—William Gerson, Kay Levi Pomeranz. Admitted to Ill. bar, 1931; partner firm Wilhartz & Hirsch, Chgo., 1931-46; officer Reynolds Pen Co., also Reynolds Printasign Co., Chgo., 1946-52; exec. dir. S.E. Chgo. Commn., 1952—; prof. urban studies U. Chgo., 1962—; vis. prof. Hastings Coll. Law, U. Calif., San Francisco, 1978-79, 79-80; dir. Hyatt Corp., 1977-79, Elsinor Corp., 1979—. Chmn. Chgo. Plan Commn., 1973-79; sec. Am. Council Edn., 1971-72; vice chmn. White House Task Force Cities, 1967; adv. to architect of Capitol, Washington, 1976—; trustee Michael Reese Hosp., Chgo., 1967—. Recipient Rockefeller Public Service award Princeton U., 1977. Mem. Am. Bar Assn., Am. Soc. Planning Ofcls., Chgo. Bar Assn. Jewish. Clubs: Tavern, Arts, Quadrangle (Chgo.). Author: Municipal and Institution Relations in Boston, 1964, Financing Education and the Effect of Tax Laws, 1975; chmn. editorial adv. bd. Coll. and Univ. Reporter, Urban Affairs Reporter. Office: 1400 E 53d St Chicago IL 60615

LEVI, KURT, banker; b. Wiesbaden, Germany, May 20, 1910; s. Josef and Martha (Kahn) L.; LL.B., U. Frankfurt (Germany), 1931; m. Ruth Neumann, Feb. 17, 1938; 1 son, Peter. Came to U.S., 1937, naturalized, 1942. Mdse. mgr. Consol. Retail Stores, Kansas City, Mo., 1937-55; with United Mo. Bank, Kansas City, 1956—, sr. v.p., 1971—. Gen. and area chmn. Kansas City (Mo.) United campaign, 1962; chmn. finance com. Camp Fire Girls Am., 1964; chmn. Kansas City Mayor's Prayer Breakfast Club, 1968; gen. chmn. Greater Kansas City Bonds for Israel, 1959; chmn. Greater Kansas City Conf. Soviet Jewry, 1966; vice chmn., mem. exec. bd. Community Relations Bur., 1972; pres. Heart Am. chpt. Religious Zionists Am., 1971. Bd. govs. Jewish Fedn. and Council Kansas City, 1972-79. Mem. Kansas City C. of C. Jewish (pres., chmn. bd. synagogue). Kiwanian (v.p. Kansas City Downtown club 1955, Legion of Honor); mem. B'nai B'rith (dist. pres. 1975-76). Home: 1019 W 66th Terr Kansas City MO 64113 Office: PO Box 226 Kansas City MO 64141

LEVI, ROBERT HENRY, dept. store exec., banker; b. Balt., Mar. 27, 1915; s. Abraham H. and Regina (Ottenheimer) L.; A.B., Johns Hopkins, 1936; m. Ryda Hecht, Oct. 18, 1939; children—Sandra Jean, Alexander Hecht, Richard Hecht. Salesman, The Hecht Co., dept. store, Washington, 1941-42, floor mgr., 1942, budget dir., 1945-46, asst. mgr., 1947-49; v.p. The Hecht Co., 1948; exec. v.p. charge corp. affairs, asst. mng. dir. The Hecht Co. Balt. stores, 1950-51, 1st exec. v.p., 1951-55, pres., 1955—, gen. mgr. Washington area, 1957-59; v.p., mem. exec., finance coms. May Dept. Stores Co., 1959-68, still dir.; dir. Savs. Bank Balt.; chmn. exec. com., dir. Merc.-Safe Deposit & Trust Co., 1968-70, vice chmn. bd., 1970—; dir. Hittman Assos., Am. Gen. Ins. Co., Fidelity & Deposit Co. Md. Mem. finance com., bd. dirs. Asso. Jewish Charities; bd. dirs. Jr. Achievement Met. Balt., Fed City Council, Washington; chmn. Greater Balt. Com.; dir. Urban Coalition; vice chmn., dir. Washington Downtown Progress; mem. Urban Renewal Council, Washington; chmn. Downtown Policy Com., D.C.; trustee, past pres. Sinai Hosp.; trustee Johns Hopkins Hosp., Balt.; trustee Goucher Coll., Johns Hopkins U.; mem. adv. com. Am. U. Sch. Bus. Adminstrn., Washington, Fight-Blight Fund, Green Spring Valley Planning Council; founder, chmn. bd. Balt. Community Found. Served to lt. USCGR, 1942-45. Named to Hall of Fame, Balt. City Coll.; decorated comdr. Oder Merit (Italian Republic); named Man of Year Washington, 1966. Mem. Nat. Retail Mchts. Assn. N.Y. (dir.), Am. Retail Fedn. (pres. 1965-67). Clubs: Center, Maryland, Suburban (Balt.). Home: 10801 Greenspring Ave Lutherville MD 21093 Office: Mercantile-Safe Deposit & Trust Co Room 805 2 Hopkins Plaza Baltimore MD 21203

LE VIEN, JOHN DOUGLAS (JACK), motion picture/TV producer, dir., author; b. N.Y.C., July 18, 1918; s. Christopher Luke and Rose Jeanette Le Vien; div. News editor Pathé News, 1946-57; ind. motion picture and TV dir. and producer, 1958—; producer TV series Valiant Years, 1959-60; exec. producer film Black Fox (Acad. award), 1962; producer and dir. (films) Finest Hours, 1963-64, A King's Story, 1965, Churchill Centenary, 1974, (TV shows) Other World of Winston Churchill, 1964, The Gathering Storm, 1973, The Amazing Voyage of Daffodil and Daisy, 1974, Cicero, 1975, Where the Lotus Fell, 1976, Flames Over the Sahara, 1977, Children of the Lotus, 1978, Churchill and His Generals, 1979; pres., exec. producer Le Vien Internat. Prodns. Ltd., N.Y.C., 1958—; chmn. bd., exec. producer Le Vien Films Ltd., London, Eng., 1963—; pres. Fits Travel (London) Ltd., 1978—, TCA Travel Corp. Am. Inc. Served to col. AUS, World War II; ETO; col. Res. Decorated Legion of Merit, Bronze Star; Legion of Honor, Croix de Guerre (France). Mem. Brit. Acad. Film & Television Arts. Club: Overseas Press (N.Y.C.). Author: The Valiant Years, 1961; The Finest Hours, 1964; The Duchess of Windsor, 1979. Home: 15 Chesterfield Hill London W1 England

LEVIN, ALAN M., TV journalist; b. Bklyn., Feb. 28, 1926; s. Herman and Shirley (Levinstein) L.; B.A., Wesleyan U., Middleton, Conn., 1946; m. Hannah Alexander, Oct. 30, 1948; children—Marc, Nicole, Danielle, Juliet. Reporter, columnist Plainfield (N.J.) Courier News, 1957-60; statehouse corr. AP, Trenton, N.J., 1960-61; writer N.Y. Post, 1961-63; press sec. Sen. Harrison Williams, Washington, 1963-64; news producer, writer WABC-TV, N.Y.C., 1965-67; documentary film maker NET, N.Y.C., 1968-69; documentary film maker, pub. affairs, news writer, dir., producer WNET-TV, N.Y.C., 1969—. Served with AUS, 1944-46. Recipient Emmy award for Sleep: The Fantastic Third of Your Life, 1967; Dupont-Columbia award for best TV reporting Defense and Domestic Needs: Contest for Tomorrow, 1968-69; George Polk Meml. award for Who Invited US?, 1970. Home: 88 Claremont Ave Maplewood NJ 07040 Office: 356 W 58th St New York City NY 10019

LEVIN, BENJAMIN, lawyer; b. Boston, Dec. 22, 1899; s. Harry and Anna (Mintz) L.; A.B., Trinity Coll., 1920; LL.B., Harvard, 1923; m. Charlotte I. Dane, Dec. 16, 1928 (dec.); children—Philip Dane, Ira D., Charles R.; m. 2d, Lillian H. Cohan, Nov. 15, 1973. Admitted to Mass. bar, 1923, Conn. bar, 1924; practice in Boston, 1923—; partner firm Mintz, Levin, Cohn, Glovsky and Popeo, and predecessors, 1965—. Mem. Mass. Commn. Adoption, 1946-48; mem. com. social services to families and individuals Boston United Community Services, 1959-69, mem. pub. relations com., 1959—; mem. com. pub. welfare Combined Jewish Philanthropies, Boston, 1961-70, trustee, 1952—; chmn. Com. Services to Unmarried Parents and Children, Boston, 1960-70; mem. nat. adv. com. Nat. Council on Illegitimacy, 1967-70; mem. com. services to mil. families Met. Boston chpt. A.R.C., 1965-69; adv. com. Crittendon Hastings House, 1969—. Bd. dirs. Mass. Soc. Prevention Cruelty to Children, 1958-74; trustee Found. for Character Edn., 1955-76. Mem. Am., Mass., Boston bar assns., Phi Beta Kappa. Jewish (trustee temple 1958-61). Mason. Club: Belmont (Mass.) Country; Harvard. Home: 209 Commonwealth Ave Apt 3-A Chestnut Hill MA 02167 Office: 1 Center Plaza Boston MA 02108

LEVIN, BERTRAM, physician, educator; b. Chgo., May 2, 1920; s. Max and Rose (Tenenbaum) L.; B.S., Central YMCA Coll., 1941; M.D., U. Ill., 1944; m. Lucille Marian Rusky, May 28, 1950; children—Elliot Marc, Karen Ruth, Diane Rebecca. Intern, Michael Reese Hosp., Chgo., 1945, resident radiology, 1948-50; Nat. Heart Inst. trainee U. Minn., 1952-53, clin. instr. radiology Med. Sch., 1952-53; clin. asst. prof. radiology Chgo. Med. Sch., 1955-61, asso. prof., 1961-69; prof. radiology Pritzker Sch. Medicine, U. Chgo., 1969—; dir. dept. diagnostic roentgenology Michael Reese Hosp. and Med Center, Chgo., 1954—; vis. prof. radiology Hebrew U.-Hadassah Med. Sch., Jerusalem, 1975-76. Pres. dist. council Chgo. Bd. Edn., 1970-71. Bd. dirs. Council Jewish Elderly, Drexel Home Aged, Bernard Horwich Jewish Community Center, Midwest region Jewish Welfare Bd. Served from 1st lt. to capt., AUS, 1945-47. Diplomate Am. Bd. Radiology. Fellow Chgo. Roentgen Soc., Am. Coll. Radiology; mem. Radiol. Soc. N.Am., Interam. Radiol. Soc., Inst. Medicine Chgo., N.Y. Acad. Scis., A.A.A.S., Assn. U. Radiologists. Mem. B'nai B'rith. Home: 7424 N Talman Chicago IL 60645 Office: 2929 S Ellis Ave Chicago IL 60616

LEVIN, CARL, pub. relations exec.; b. Ringgold, La.; student Coll. City N.Y., 1930-33; m. Doris Wechsler; m. 2d, Sonia Atlas, Oct. 13, 1958; children—Judith Friedman, Richard, Virginia Vinick, Alan Schwartzbach. Corr. Coll. City N.Y. for N.Y. Herald Tribune, 1930-34, staff reporter, 1934-43, Washington corr., 1943-45, 46-50, war and fgn. corr., Europe, 1945-46; free lance mag. writer, 1942-50; Washington mgr. William H. Weintraub & Co., advt. and pub. relations, 1950-52; charge Washington activities Schenley Industries, Inc., 1952-62, v.p., 1955-62; v.p. Schenley Distillers, Inc., 1955-62; dir. pub. support Trade Expansion Act, White House, 1962; pres. Carl Levin Assos., Inc., 1962-67; v.p., gen. mgr. Burson-Marsteller, Washington, 1968-72, v.p., sr. cons., 1972—; dir. Nat. Black News Service. Mem. Nat. Small Bus. Adv. Council, 1964-68. Active in founding Am.-Israel Soc. Bd. dirs. Interracial Council Bus. Opportunity, 1972-75; trustee Opera Soc. Washington, 1965-70, Fords Theater Soc., Washington, 1975—; co-chmn. Citizens Com. Opera, Washington, 1963. Mem. Pub. Relations Soc. Am., Sigma Delta Chi. Clubs: National Press, International (Washington); Lotos (N.Y.C.). Collaborator books on journalism, postwar security investigations; contbr. to nat. mags. Home: 2801 New Mexico Ave NW Washington DC 20007 Office: 1800 M St NW Washington DC 20006

LEVIN, CARL, U.S. senator; b. Detroit, June 28, 1934; B.A., Swarthmore Coll., 1956; J.D., Harvard U., 1959; m. Barbara Halpern, 1961; children—Kate, Laura, Erica. Mem. firm Grossman, Hyman & Grossman, Detroit, 1959-64; asst. atty. gen., gen. counsel Mich. CRC, 1964-67; chief appellate defender for city of Detroit, 1968-69; mem. firm Schlussel, Lifton, Simon, Rands & Kaufman, 1971-73, Jaafe,

Snider, Raitt, Garratt & Heuser, 1978-79; mem. City Council Detroit, 1970-73, pres., 1974-77; mem. U.S. Senate from Mich., 1979—; past instr. Wayne State U., U. Detroit. Mem. adv. bd. United Found.; mem. adv. com. ACLU of Mich.; bd. dirs. Internat. Inst. of Detroit; mem. regional adv. council Anti-Defamation League of B'nai B'rith. Mem. Am. Bar Assn., Mich. Bar Assn., Detroit Bar Assn. Democrat. Office: 3327 Dirksen Senate Office Bldg Washington DC 20510

LEVIN, CHARLES LEONARD, state justice; b. Detroit, Apr. 28, 1926; s. Theodore and Rhoda (Katzin) L.; B.A., U. Mich., 1947, LL.B., 1947; m. Patricia Joyce Oppenheim, Feb. 21, 1956; children—Arthur, Amy, Fredrick. Admitted to Mich. bar, 1947, N.Y. bar, 1949, U.S. Supreme Ct. bar, 1953, D.C. bar, 1954; practiced in N.Y.C., 1948-50, Detroit, 1950-66, partner firm Levin, Levin, Garvett & Dill, Detroit, 1951-66; judge Mich. Ct. Appeals, Detroit, 1966-73; justice Mich. Supreme Ct., 1973—; mem. Mich. Law Revision Commn., 1966. Trustee Marygrove Coll., 1971-77, chmn., 1971-74; mem. vis. coms. to Law Schs., U. Mich., U. Chgo., Wayne State U. Mem. Am. Law Inst. Home: 18280 Fairway Dr Detroit MI 48221 Office: 1008 Travelers Tower Southfield MI 48076

LEVIN, DAVID, educator; b. York, Pa., Nov. 21, 1924; s. Louis and Rose (Braufman) L.; A.B., Harvard, 1947, A.M., 1949, Ph.D., 1955; m. Patricia Marker, July 12, 1945; children—David, Rebecca. Instr. to prof. English, Stanford, 1952-71; Commonwealth prof. English, U. Va., Charlottesville, 1971—; Charles Warren research fellow Harvard, 1976-77. Mem. exec. bd. No. Calif., ACLU, 1966-71, Central Va. chpt., 1972-75. Served with USAAF, 1943-46. Fulbright Exchange lectr., 1956-57; fellow Center for Advanced Study in Behavioral Scis., 1962-63; sr. fellow Nat. Endowment for Humanities, 1968-69; Center for Advanced Studies, U. Va., 1971-74. Mem. Modern Lang. Assn., Am. Studies Assn., AAUP, NAACP. Author: What Happened in Salem?, 1952; History as Romantic Art, 1959; In Defense of Historical Literature, 1967; Cotton Mather, 1978; mem. editorial bd. Am. Quar., 1969-72; Am. Literature, 1970-73; Clio, 1971—. Home: Route 2 Box 399 Charlottesville VA 22901

LEVIN, GILBERT VICTOR, research co. exec.; b. Balt., Apr. 23, 1924; s. Henry I. and Lillian R. (Richman) L.; B.E., Johns Hopkins U., 1947, M.S., 1948, Ph.D., 1963; m. M. Karen Salisbury, Oct. 25, 1953; children—Ron L., Henry L., Carol Y. With Md. State Dept. Health, 1948-50, Calif. Dept. Health, 1950-51, D.C. Dept. Pub. Health, 1951-55; v.p. Resources Research, Inc., Washington, 1955-63; dir. life systems div. Hazleton Labs., Inc., Reston, Va., 1963-67; pres., chmn. bd. Biospherics Inc., Rockville, Md., 1967—. Experimenter Mariner 9 mission NASA, 1971, Viking Mission Labeled Release Life Detection expt., 1976. Served with U.S. Maritime Service, 1944-46. Recipient Pub. Service medal NASA, 1977. Fellow Am. Pub. Health Assn.; mem. AAAS (Newcomb Cleveland prize 1977), Am. Water Works Assn., Water Pollution Control Fedn., N.Y. Acad. Scis., Marine Tech. Soc., ASCE. Club: Cosmos. Patentee in field; inventor PhoStrip process for wastewater phosphate removal. Contbr. articles to profl. jours. Editorial bd. Bio Science, 1960-63. Home: 3180 Harness Creek Rd Annapolis MD 21403 Office: 4928 Wyaconda Rd Rockville MD 20852. *Man's ability to accumulate information through learning and to pass it on to his descendents frees his generations from endless repetition. He may hope to understand the universe and his place in it. The road to that ultimate goal is science. Most of all else is fashion.*

LEVIN, HAROLD ARTHUR, coll. ofcl.; b. N.Y.C., Oct. 9, 1918; s. Milton H. and Rachel (Cooperman) L.; A.B., N.Y. U., 1940; Alfred P. Sloan Found. fellow, U. Denver, 1940-42, M.S., 1947; postgrad. Georgetown U., 1946-48, George Washington U., 1951-52; m. Toby Poizner, Apr. 30, 1942; children—Jordan R., Erica. Personnel officer Office Emergency Mgmt., 1942-43; fgn. affairs officer Dept. State, 1946-49; requirements cons. ECA, Mission to Korea, 1949-50; internat. economist ECA, 1950-51; fgn. requirements specialist Def. Prodn. Adminstrn., 1951-53; control programs dir. East-West trade ICA, 1953-57; staff State Dept., U.S. mission to NATO and European Regional Orgns., Paris, 1957-61; dep. U.S. rep. to European Regional Trade Com., 1957-58, chief U.S. del. Internat. East-West trade coms., also dir. Office Security Trade Controls, 1958-61; chief internat. bus. practices div. Dept. State, 1961-67, AID ofcl., 1967-74, chief internat. trade div., 1967-68, acting dir. Office Commodity Import Programs, 1968-69, Bur. for Vietnam, chief Laos desk, 1969-72, dir. Office Laos Affairs, 1972-74; asst. v.p. for internat. affairs, research and planning div. Pharm. Mfrs. Assn., 1974-75; lectr. bus. adminstrn. and econs. Montgomery (Md.) Coll., 1975—; coordinator grad. programs Columbia Campus, Loyola Coll., 1976—; cons. Russel Sage Found., 1955; vis. scholar Georgetown U., 1973-74. Served to lt. USNR, 1943-46. Mem. Am. Fgn. Service Assn., Am. Soc. Pub. Adminstrn., Govtl. Research Assn., Phi Beta Kappa. Club: International (Washington). Contbr. articles to profl. jours. Home: 1601 Oaklawn Ct Silver Spring MD 20903 Office: Grad Div Loyola College American City Bldg Columbia MD 21044

LEVIN, HARRY, educator, univ. dean; b. Balt., Mar. 3, 1925; s. Morris and Bessie (Wolfe) L.; student Johns Hopkins, 1942-43; B.A., U. Md., 1948; M.A., U. Mich., 1949, Ph.D., 1951; m. Deborah B. Stern, Dec. 25, 1946; children—Diane Lynn, David Stern, Rebecca Lee. Postdoctoral fellow Harvard, 1950-51, asst. prof., research asso. Lab. Human Devel., 1951-55; vis. asso. prof. summers Stanford, 1955, 58; mem. faculty Cornell U., 1955—, prof. child devel. and psychology, 1961—, chmn. dept. psychology, 1966—, William R. Kenan, Jr. prof. psychology, 1967—, dean Coll. Arts and Scis., 1974-78; vis. scientist Harvard-Florence (Italy) project; vis. prof. psychology Mass. Inst. Tech., 1973; vis. prof. psychology and edn. Harvard U., 1978-79; cons. to govt. and industry, 1959—; chmn. psychology panel Com. Internat. Exchange Persons, 1963-66. Trustee Histadrut Israel Am. Cultural Exchange Inst.; vis. com. Harvard. Served with AUS, 1944-46. Social Sci. Research Council fellow, 1950-51; USPHS fellow, 1961-62. Fellow Am. Psychol. Assn.; mem. Am. Ednl. Research Assn., A.A.A.S., Phi Beta Kappa, Sigma Xi. Author: (with others) Patterns of Child Rearing, 1956; (with J.P. Williams) Basic Studies in Reading, 1970; (with E.J. Gibson) The Psychology of Reading, 1975; The Eye-Voice Span, 1979. Home: 1608 Hanshaw Rd Ithaca NY 14850

LEVIN, HARRY (TUCHMAN), educator, writer; b. Mpls., July 18, 1912; s. Isadore Henry and Beatrice (Tuchman) L.; A.B., Harvard, 1933; student U. Paris, 1934; mem. Soc. Fellows, jr. fellow, Harvard, 1934-39, sr. fellow, 1947-66; Litt. D., Syracuse U., 1952; LL.D. (hon.), St. Andrews, 1962; L.H.D. (hon.), Union Coll., 1968, Clarkson Coll., 1970; Dr. honoris causa, U. Paris-Sorbonne, 1973; m. Elena Ivanovna Zarudnaya, June 21, 1939; 1 dau., Marina (Mrs. J.R. Frederiksen). Instr., tutor in English, Harvard, 1939-44, asso. prof., 1944-48, prof. English and comparative lit., 1954-60, chmn. dept. comparative lit., 1946-51, 53-54, 61, 62-69, 77-78, chmn. div. modern langs., 1951-52, 55-61, Irving Babbitt prof. comparative lit., 1960—; lectr. Lowell Lectrs., 1952, Salzburg Seminar, 1953, Gauss seminars Princeton, 1961; exchange prof. U. Paris, 1953; vis. prof. Tokyo U., 1955; Mrs. William Beckman prof. U. Calif. at Berkeley, 1957; Alexander lectr. U. Toronto, 1958; Patten lectr. Ind. U., 1967; overseas fellow Churchill Coll., Cambridge U., 1967; vis. fellow All Souls Coll., Oxford (Eng.) U., 1974. Chmn. English Inst., 1957. Trustee Cambridge Drama Festival. Guggenheim fellow, 1943-44; recipient award Am. Acad. Arts and Letters; Am. Council Learned Soc. award distinguished scholarship in humanities, 1962; decorated chevalier Legion Honor; Huntington Library fellow, 1966. Fellow Am. Acad. Arts and Scis.; mem. Soc. Fellows (acting chmn. 1964-65), Nat. Inst. Arts and Letters, Internat. Assn. U. Profs. English, Internat. P.E.N. Club, Modern Lang. Assn., Am. Philos. Soc., Internat. (v.p. 1963-67), Am. (pres. 1965-68) comparative lit. assns., Modern Humanities Research Assn. (pres. 1976), Royal Netherlands Acad. Arts and Scis., Phi Beta Kappa. Club: Harvard (N.Y.C.). Author: The Broken Column: A Study in Romantic Hellenism, 1931; James Joyce: A Critical Introduction, 1941; The Overreacher: A Study of Christopher Marlowe, 1952; Symbolism and Fiction, 1956; Contexts of Criticism, 1957; The Power of Blackness: Hawthorne, Poe, Melville, 1958; The Question of Hamlet, 1959; The Gates of Horn: A Study of Five French Realists, 1963; Refractions: Essays in Comparative Literature, 1966; The Myth of the Golden Age in the Renaissance, 1969; Grounds for Comparison, 1972; Shakespeare and the Revolution of the Times, 1976. Editor: Selected Works of Ben Jonson, 1938; A Satire Against Mankind and Other Poems by the Earl of Rochester, 1942; The Portable James Joyce, 1945; Perspectives of Criticism, 1950; Shakespeare's Coriolanus, 1956; Hawthorne's Scarlet Letter, 1960; Shakespeare's Comedy of Errors, 1965; Veins of Humor, 1972; (with others) Riverside Shakespeare, 1974; editorial bd. Comparative Lit., Jour. History Ideas, Shakespeare Quar., Harvard English Studies. Contbr. criticisms to periodicals. Home: 14 Kirkland Pl Cambridge MA 02138 Office: 400 Boylston Hall Harvard U Cambridge MA 02138

LEVIN, HERMAN, theatrical producer; b. Phila., Dec. 1, 1907; s. Abraham and Jennie (Goldfin) L.; student U. Pa., 1925, Dickinson Sch. Law, Carlisle, Pa., 1926, St. John's U. Law Sch., 1931-35; m. 2d, Dawn McInerney, Apr. 16, 1956 (div.); m. 3d, Victoria Steiner (div.); 1 dau. by previous marriage, Gabrielle. Admitted to N.Y. bar, 1935; practice in N.Y.C., 1935-46; theatrical producer, 1946—; producer (with Melvyn Douglas) Call Me Mister, 1946, (with Oliver Smith) No Exit, 1947, Richard III, 1948, Gentlemen Prefer Blondes, 1949, Bless You All, 1950 (both with Oliver Smith), My Fair Lady, 1956, The Girl Who Came to Supper, 1963; The Great White Hope, 1968, Lovely Ladies, Kind Gentlemen, 1970, Tricks, 1973, revival My Fair Lady, 1975; dir. Bowline Corp., Bala-Cynwyd, Pa., Vesper Corp., Bala-Cynwyd. Pres., League N.Y. Theatres, 1955-57, Ind. Booking Offices, Inc., 1957-58. Club: Coffee House. Office: 424 Madison Ave New York NY 10017

LEVIN, IRA, author, playwright; b. N.Y.C., Aug. 27, 1929; s. Charles and Beatrice (Schlansky) L.; student Drake U., Des Moines, 1946-48; A.B., N.Y. U., 1950; m. Gabrielle Aronsohn, Aug. 20, 1960 (div. 1968); children—Adam, Jared, Nicholas; m. 2d, Phyllis Finkel, Aug. 26, 1979. Freelance writer, 1950—; author: A Kiss Before Dying, 1953, Rosemary's Baby, 1967, This Perfect Day, 1970, The Stepford Wives, 1972, The Boys from Brazil, 1976; playwright: No Time for Sergeants, 1955, Interlock, 1958, Critic's Choice, 1960, General Seeger, 1962, Drat! the Cat, 1965, Dr. Cook's Garden, 1967, Veronica's Room, 1973, Deathtrap, 1978, Break a Leg, 1979. Served with U.S. Army, 1953-55. Recipient Edgar Allan Poe award, 1954. Office: care Harold Ober Assos 40 E 49th St New York NY 10017

LEVIN, IRVING HERBERT, motion picture producer, basketball team owner; b. Chgo., Sept. 8, 1921; s. Isador and Ida Ann (Michael) L.; B.A., U. Ill., 1943; m. Michelle Metzger Howser, July 12, 1975; children—Donna Sue Liederman, Lon Allen, Sindee Dale, Jana Howser, Jill Howser. Pres., chief operating officer Nat. Gen. Corp., 1969-72; pres. Levin-Schulman Prodns., Ltd., Los Angeles, 1975—, Group L Prodns., San Diego Clippers Basketball Club; Trustee Am. Friends of Hebrew U. Served with USAAF, World War II. Decorated D.F.C., Air medal; named Motion Picture Pioneer of Yr., 1970. Mem. Nat. Basketball Assn. (chmn. bd. govs. 1977-79), Acad. Motion Picture Arts and Scis. Jewish. Clubs: 100 of Mass., Friars. Office: 9911 W Pico Blvd Los Angeles CA 90035 also 3500 Sports Arena Blvd San Diego CA 92110

LEVIN, JACOB JOSEPH, mathematician, educator; b. N.Y.C., Dec. 21, 1926; s. David and Rose (Kaplan) L.; B.E.E., Coll. City N.Y., 1949; Ph.D., Mass. Inst. Tech., 1953; m. Avis Harriet Ofstrock, Sept. 7, 1952; children—Debra F., Kenneth E., Claire B. Instr. math. Purdue U., 1953-55; lectr. Mass. Inst. Tech., 1955-56; staff mem. Lincoln Lab. of Mass. Inst. Tech., 1956-63; prof. math. U. Wis., 1963—; vis. prof. U. B.C., Vancouver, Can., 1977-78. Served with AUS, 1945-46. NSF sr. postdoctoral fellow, 1970-71. Mem. Am. Math. Soc., Soc. Indsl. and Applied Math., Sigma Xi. Contbr. articles to profl. jours. Home: 1110 Frisch Rd Madison WI 53711

LEVIN, MARTIN PAUL, pub. co. exec.; b. Phila., Dec. 20, 1918; s. Harry and Sarah (Haimon) L.; B.S., Temple U., 1950, postgrad. (personnel Council fellow), 1950; m. Marcia Obrasky, Apr. 2, 1939; children—Jeremy Carl, Wendy (Mrs. Pedro Sanchez), Hugh Lauter. Adminstrv. officer U.S. War Dept., 1940-44, VA, 1945-50; sr. v.p. Grosset & Dunlap, Inc., N.Y.C., 1950-66; pres. book pub. div. Times Mirror Co., N.Y.C., 1966—; chmn. bd. New Am. Library, Inc.; dir. New English Library, Ltd., C.V. Mosby Co., Year Book Med. Pubs., Harry N. Abrams, Inc., New Australian Library. Cons. Ford Found., India, 1957-58; mem. Pres.'s Working Com. on Books and Publs. Abroad; mem. exec. com. Center for the Book, Library of Congress; chmn. Franklin Book Programs; dir. Book Industry Research Council. Trustee William Alanson White Inst. Served with AUS, 1944-45. Mem. Assn. Am. Pubs. (dir., exec. com., mem. del. to USSR 1976, mem. del. to Peoples Republic of China 1979), Am. Book Pubs. Council (dir.). Clubs: Publishers Lunch, Friars. Author: Prepared Handbook of Advertising and Promotion Abroad, 1965. Home: 221 Kirby Ln Rye NY 10580 Office: 280 Park Ave New York City NY 10017

LEVIN, MEYER, writer; b. Chgo., Oct. 8, 1905; s. Joseph and Goldie (Levin) L.; Ph.B., U. Chgo., 1924; m. Mable Schamp Foy (div. 1944); 1 son, Jonathan; m. 2d, Tereska Szwarc, Mar. 25, 1948; children—Gabriel, Mikael, Dominique. Asst. editor Esquire and Coronet mags., 1934-38; film critic, writer-dir. OWI, 1942-43; war corr. Overseas News Agy., Europe, 1944-45; writer, producer Palestine feature film My Father's House, 1945; writer, dir., producer The Illegals, Europe, 1946; tchr. marionette theatre prodn. New Sch. Social Research, N.Y.C., 1932. Author: Reporter, 1929; Frankie and Johnny, 1930; Yehuda, 1931; The New Bridge, 1933; The Golden Mountain, 1934, republished as Classic Hassidic Tales, 1975; The Old Bunch, 1936; Citizens, 1940; My Father's House, 1946; In Search, 1950; Compulsion, 1956 (also as 3 act play 1959); Eva, 1959; (with T.K. Kurzband) Story of the Jewish Way of Life, 1959; The Fanatic, 1964; The Stronghold, 1965; Gore & Igor, 1968; Israel Haggadah for Passover, 1970; (with T.K. Kurzband) Story of the Synagogue; The Settlers, 1972; The Story of Israel, 1972; Beginnings in Jewish Philosophy, 1974; The Obsession, 1974; The Spell of Time, 1974; The Harvest, 1978. Address: Behrman House 1261 Broadway New York NY 10011

LEVIN, NATHAN WILLIS, investment cons., mgr.; b. Joliet, Ill., Oct. 10, 1904; s. Ben and Ida (Grossman) L.; Ph.B., U. Chgo., 1926; LL.D., New Sch. Social Research, 1964; m. Ethel Gordon, Mar. 16, 1928 (dec. Aug. 1935); children—Joan (Mrs. Russel Kirsch), Marion (Mrs. Nathan W. Gottfried (dec.); m. 2d, Pam Schorr, Apr. 2, 1941; children—Nina S., Robert N. With Union Trust Co., Chgo., 1926-27; instr. econs. and accounting State Coll. Wash., 1928; fellow econs. U. Chgo., 1929; financial asst. to Julius Rosenwald, 1929-32; asst. to Lessing J. Rosenwald in adminstrn. estate Julius Rosenwald, 1932-37; comptroller Julius Rosenwald Fund, 1929-48; investment cons., mgr., 1937—. Pres., treas., dir. Fortnightly Corp., 1948-70, Internat. Devel. Services, Inc., 1955-69; pres. Reporter Mag., 1948-68; pres., dir. Clarksburg & Fairmont (W.Va.) TV Cable Corp., 1955-67, No. W.Va. Broadcasting Co., 1963-76; chmn. Pantheon Books, Inc., 1948-62; chmn., dir. Oil Shale Corp. (now Tosco Corp.), 1957-70, vice chmn., 1970-78; chmn., dir. Starwood Corp., 1959-60; vice-chmn., dir. Pavelle Corp., 1964-72; v.p., dir. Chek-Chart Corp., 1955-70, Technol. Investors Corp., 1960-63; chmn. finance com., dir. Sci. Am., Inc., 1946—; dir. Exmet Corp., Liberia Corp. Mem. investment com. Mus. Modern Art, 1946—; treas. N.Y. Fund for Children, 1948-70; mem. adv. com. on mgmt. Dept. State, 1965; pub. mem. Fgn. Service Inspection Corp., Dept. State, Africa, 1965; mem. Internat. Service Corp., Ethiopia, 1971. Trustee New Sch. Social Research, 1942—, chmn. bd. trustees, 1960-63, acting pres., 1960-61, chmn. exec. com., 1964—; trustee Mus. Sci. and Industry, Chgo., 1930—, Adele R. Levy Fund, 1960-68, Hall of Sci., N.Y.C., 1969-78; trustee, chmn. exec. com. Internat. Inst. Rural Reconstrn., 1967—. C.P.A., Ill. Mem. Am. Inst. C.P.A.'s, Pub. Mem.'s Assn. of Dept. State (v.p., dir. 1965), Phi Beta Kappa. Clubs: Tavern, Quadrangle (Chgo.); Century (Purchase, N.Y.). Home: Crow Hill Rd Mt Kisco NY 10549 Office: 870 UN Plaza New York City NY 10017

LEVIN, NORMAN GORDON, JR., educator; b. Boston, Apr. 24, 1935; s. Norman Gordon and Evelyn (Richmond) L.; B.A., Yale, 1956; Ph.D., Harvard, 1967; m. Elayne L. Elashoff, Mar. 20, 1960; children—Kenneth Howard, Joanna Dale. Teaching fellow Harvard, 1959-63; mem. faculty Amherst Coll., 1964—, asso. prof. history, 1969-75, prof., 1975—. Author: Woodrow Wilson and World Politics (Bancroft prize Am. history 1968), 1968. Editor: Woodrow Wilson and the Paris Peace Conference, 1972; The Zionist Movement in Palestine and World Politics, 1880-1918, 1974. Home: 27 Woodside Ave Amherst MA 01002

LEVIN, RICHARD DONALD, architect; b. Cleve., Sept. 5, 1926; s. Harry B. and Rose C. L.; B.Arch., Ohio State U., 1951; m. Gail B. Ruslander, May 17, 1959; children—Geoffrey, Claudia, Douglas. Asso., Outcalt-Guenther Assos., Cleve., 1951-55, Victor Gruen Assos., Los Angeles, 1956-59; founder, pres. Richard Levin Assos. Inc., Architects, Dayton, Ohio, 1960-78; pres. Levin Porter Smith Inc., Architecture, Planning, Interior Design, Dayton, 1979—; mem. adv. com. Sch. Architecture, Ohio State U.; guest. lectr., critic at univs. Pres. bd. trustees Dayton Sr. Citizens Center, 1963-68, 78—; bd. dirs. Dayton Art Inst., 1968-78, chmn. bd. coll. art, 1973-76; trsutee Dayton Museum Natural History, 1974-78; bd. dirs. Downtown Dayton Assn., 1977—. Served with inf. U.S. Army, 1944-46. Fellow AIA (nat. com. on design 1976—, pres. Dayton chpt. 1967-68); mem. Architects Soc. Ohio (trustee 1967-70). Jewish. Designs include: Madden Hills Library, Dayton (AIA-ALA Archtl. Excellence award 1970), Homestead Fed. Savs., Dayton (Inst. Steel Constrn. and Architects Soc. Ohio Honor awards 1974), Miamisburg (Ohio) Civic Center (Architects Soc. Ohio award 1974), Model Neighborhood Community Center, Dayton, 1975, Wright State U. Med. Scis. Bldg. (Architects Soc. Ohio Honor award 1977), Good Samaritan Hosp. and Health Center, Dayton (Architects Soc. Ohio Honor award 1977, Dept. Nat. Health and Welfare Can. recognition as outstanding example of New Generation interstitial space hosp. 1979), Troy (Ohio) Library (AIA-ALA Archtl. Excellence award 1978), Maggie McKnight Apts., Xenia, Ohio, 1978. Home: 3445 Zephyr Dr Dayton OH 45414 Office: 24 N Jefferson St Dayton OH 45402

LEVIN, RICHARD LOUIS, educator; b. Buffalo, Aug. 31, 1922; s. Bernard and Meta (Block) L.; B.A., U. Chgo., 1943, M.A., 1947, Ph.D., 1957; m. Muriel Abrams, June 22, 1952; children—David, Daniel. Mem. faculty U. Chgo., 1949-57, asst. prof. English, 1953-57; prof. English, State U. N.Y. at Stony Brook, 1957—, acting chmn. English dept., 1960-63, 65-66. Mem. adv. bd. World Center for Shakespeare Studies. Served to lt. (j.g.) USNR, 1943-46; ETO. Recipient Explicator award, 1971; Am. Council Learned Socs. fellow, 1963-64; research fellow State U. N.Y., 1961, 65-68, 71, 73; Nat. Endowment for Humanities sr. fellow, 1974; Guggenheim fellow, 1978-79. Mem. Modern Lang. Assn. (mem. adv. com. publs.), Shakespeare Assn. Am. (trustee), Malone Soc., Internat. Shakespeare Assn., AAUP, Joseph Crabtree Found. Democrat. Jewish. Author, cons. in field. Editor: Tragedy: Plays, Theory and Criticism, 1960; The Question of Socrates, 1961; Tragedy Alternate, 1965; (Thomas Middleton) Michaelmas Term, 1966; The Multiple Plot in English Renaissance Drama, 1971; New Readings vs. Old Plays: Recent Trends in the Reinterpretation of English Renaissance Drama, 1979. Home: 26 Sparks St Huntington Station NY 11746 Office: Humanities Bldg State Univ New York Stony Brook NY 11794

LEVIN, ROBERT DANIEL, lawyer; b. N.Y.C., Feb. 27, 1930; s. Moses H. and Esther (Walzer) L.; A.B., Rutgers U., 1951; J.D., Columbia, 1954; m. Gladys Schoen, Apr. 8, 1954; children—Jeffrey, Donna. Admitted to N.Y. bar, 1954, since practiced in N.Y.C.; with firm Demov, Morris, Levin & Shein, 1954—, sr. partner, 1963—. Mem. N.Y. State Bar Assn., Bar Assn. City N.Y. (state legislation and real property law com.), Phi Beta Kappa, Phi Alpha Delta. Co-editor: N.Y. Law Jour. Realty Law Digest. Home: 12 Varian Ln Scarsdale NY 10583 Office: 40 W 57th St New York City NY 10019

LEVIN, ROBERT JOSEPH, retail grocery chain store exec.; b. Everett, Mass., Mar. 19, 1928; s. Edward A. and Rose E. Levin; B.A. cum laude, U. Wis., 1948; m. Carrol Silverman, June 21, 1948; children—Richard J., Cathy Levin Shuman. From dir. store ops. and purchasing to pres., treas. C.B. Perkins Tobacco Co., Boston, 1948-73, co. merged with Stop & Shop, Boston, 1971, v.p., then pres. Medi Mart div. Stop & Shop, 1971-75, group v.p. Stop & Shop Cos., Inc., Boston, 1975-79, sr. v.p., 1979—, also dir. Mem. Nat. Mass Retailing Inst. (dir.), U. Wis. Found. Jewish. Home: 65 Grove St Wellesley MA 02181 Office: 1776 Heritage Dr North Quincy MA 02171 also Box 369 Boston MA 02101

LEVIN, RUBEN, editor; b. Warsaw, Poland, Aug. 2, 1902; s. Benjamin D. and Ida (Gochlik) L.; brought to U.S., 1904, naturalized, 1917; B.A., U. Wis., 1930; m. Bertha G. Greenberg, June 7, 1931; children—David A., Jonathan H. Reporter, copyreader on various dailies, 1924-38; writer Labor Newspaper, 1938—, mgr., 1953—, editor, 1953—. Recipient Achievement awards U. Wis. Journalism Sch., Sidney Hillman Found., Internat. Labor Press Assn., Eugene V. Debs Found.; named Dean of U.S. Labor Editors, Eugene Debs Found./Internat. Labor Press Assn. Mem. Indsl. Relations Research Assn., Assn. R.R. Editors (pres.), Am. Newspaper Guild. Democrat. Jewish. Contbr. articles to profl. jours., Grolier-Americana Ann. Ency. Yearbook. Home: 2712 Blaine Dr Chevy Chase MD 20015 Office: 400 1st St NW Washington DC 20001

LEVIN, SIMON ASHER, mathematician, ecologist; b. Balt., Apr. 22, 1941; s. Theodore S. and Clara G. L.; B.A. in Math., Johns Hopkins U., 1961; Ph.D. in Math. (NSF fellow), U. Md., 1964; m.

Carole Lotte Leiffer, Aug. 4, 1964; children—Jacob, Rachel. Teaching asst. U. Md., 1961-62, research asso., 1964, visitor, 1968; NSF fellow U. Calif., Berkeley, 1964-65; asst. prof. math. Cornell U., 1965-70, asso. prof. applied math., ecology, theoretical and applied math., 1971-77, prof. applied math. and ecology, 1977—, chmn. sect. ecology and systematics div. biol. scis., 1974-79; vis. scholar U. Wash., 1973-74; vis. scientist Weizmann Inst., Rehovot, Israel, 1977, 80; hon. prof. U. B.C., 1979-80; chmn. Am. Math. Soc./Soc. Indsl. and Applied Maths. Com. on Maths. in Life Scis., 1973-79; mem. core panel on math. in biol. scis., program com. Internat. Congress Mathematicians, 1977-78; co-convenor Biomath. Conf., Oberwolfach, W. Ger., 1978; mem. adv. com. div. environ. scis. Oak Ridge Nat. Lab., 1978-81; vice chmn. math. Com. Concerned Scientists, N.Y.C., 1979—. Guggenheim fellow, 1979-80; Mem. Ecol. Soc. Am. (chmn. Mercer awards subcom. 1976, mem. council 1975-77), Soc. Indsl. and Applied Math. (mem. council 1977-79, council exec. com. 1978-79, council rep. to bd. trustees 1978-79, mng. editor Jour. Applied Math. 1975-79), AAAS, Am. Inst. Biol. Scis., Am. Math. Soc., Am. Soc. Naturalists, Brit. Ecol. Soc., Soc. Study Evolution, U.S. Com. for Israel Environment, Sigma Xi. Jewish. Editor: Lectures on Mathematics in the Life Sciences, vols. 7-12, 1974-79; Ecosystem Analysis and Prediction, 1974; (with R. H. Whittaker) Niche: Theory and Application, 1975; Studies in Mathematical Biology, 2 vols., 1978; editor: Ecology and Ecol. Monographs, 1975-77, Jour. Math. Biology, 1976—; mng. editor Biomath., 1976—, Lecture Notes in Biomath., 1973—; asso. editor Theoretical Population Biology, 1976—; editorial bd. Evolutionary Theory, 1976—, Discrete Applied Math., 1978-80; also various other editorial positions. Home: 115 Pine Tree Rd Ithaca NY 14850 Office: Ecology and Systematics Lab Cornell U Ithaca NY 14853

LEVIN, WILLIAM COHN, physician, educator; b. Waco, Tex., Mar. 2, 1917; s. Samuel P. and Jeanette (Cohn) L.; B.A., U. Tex., 1938, M.D., 1941; m. Edna Seinsheimer, June 23, 1941; children—Gerry Lee (Mrs. Eugene Hornstein), Carol Lynn. Intern Michael Reese Hosp., Chgo., 1941-42; resident John Sealy Hosp., Galveston, Tex., 1942-44; mem. staff U. Tex. Med. Br. Hosps., Galveston, 1944—, asso. prof. internal medicine, 1948-65, prof., 1965—, now Warmoth prof. hematology; pres. U. Tex. Med. Br., 1974—; past chmn., past mem. cancer clin. investigation rev. com. Nat. Cancer Inst. Exec. com., mem. nat. bd. Union Am. Hebrew Congregations; trustee Houston-Galveston Psychoanalytic Found., 1975—, Menil Found., 1976—. Recipient Nicholas and Katherine Leone award for adminstrv. excellence, 1977. Diplomate Am. Bd. Internal Medicine. Fellow A.C.P., Internat. Soc. Hematology; mem. Am. Fedn. Clin. Research, Central Soc. Clin. Research, Am. Soc. Hematology, Phi Beta Kappa, Sigma Xi, Alpha Omega Alpha. Home: 1301 Harbor View Dr Galveston TX 77550 Office: 816 Strand St Galveston TX 77550

LEVINE, AARON, city planner; b. Phila., July 16, 1917; s. Harry and Sophia (Raditz) L.; student U. Pa., 1937-40, B.S. in Landscape Architecture, 1951; student U. Calif., 1940-41; M.S. in Govt. Adminstrn., U. Pa., 1951; m. Beatrice Blass, May 16, 1958; children—Karen Levine Porreca, Lisa. Sr. planner Phila. City Planning Commn., 1946-51; area planner Housing and Home Fin. Agy., Washington, 1952; exec. dir. Phila. Citizens Council on City Planning, 1952-62; pres. Oahu Devel. Conf., Honolulu, 1962—; cons. and lectr. in field. Vice pres. Honolulu Symphony, 1966, Friends of Iolani Palace, 1966-74; bd. dirs. Hawaii Visitors Bur., 1970. Served with U.S. Army, 1943-45. Fellow Am. Soc. Landscape Architects; mem. Am. Soc. Planning Ofcls. (pres. 1967-68), AIA (hon.), Am. Planning Assn., Nat. Assn. Housing and Redevel. Ofcls., Internat. Fedn. Housing and Planning. Unitarian. Contbr. articles to profl. jours. Home: 1519 Kalaniwai Pl Honolulu HI 96821 Office: 119 Merchant St Honolulu HI 96813

LEVINE, ARNOLD MILTON, telephone co. engr.; b. Preston, Conn., Aug. 15, 1916; s. Samuel and Florence (Clark) L.; M.S. in Elec. Engring., U. Iowa, 1940; D.Sc. (hon.), Tri-State Coll., 1960; m. Bernice Eleanor Levich, Aug. 31, 1941; children—Mark Jeffrey, Michael Norman, Kevin Lawrence. Head, sound dept. CBS, 1940-42; with ITT, 1942—, beginning as engr. asst., successively engr., sr. engr., sr. project engr., dept. head, div. head, lab. head, lab. dir., 1942-58, v.p. missile and space systems, 1958-62, v.p. communications, 1962-64, v.p. aerospace, 1964-71; v.p., tech. dir. ITT Gilfillan, 1971-74, sr. scientist, 1974—. Active Boy Scouts Am. Named San Fernando Valley Engr. of Year. Fellow I.E.E.E., Inst. Advancement Engring.; mem. Am. Astronautical Soc. (dir.), Am. Inst. Aeros. and Astronautics (dir.), Am. Mgmt. Assn., Am. Ordnance Assn., Am. Rocket Soc., Inst. Nav., Am. Radio Relay League. Lion. Home: 10828 Fullbright Ave Chatsworth CA 91311 Office: 7821 Onion Ave Van Nuys CA 91409

LEVINE, BERNARD, mfg. co. exec.; b. N.Y.C., July 8, 1924; s. Louis and Rebekah (Cohen) L.; B.E.E., Cooper Union, 1944; M.E.E., N.Y.U., 1949; m. Ann Bluman, June 23, 1946; children—Jerome, Linda. Patent engr. AEC, 1949; v.p. Norden-Ketay Corp., N.Y.C., 1945-49, 49-58; gen. mgr. Ketay dept. Norden div. United Aircraft Corp., 1958-59; chmn. bd. Vernitron Corp., Great Neck, N.Y., 1959-70, vice chmn. bd., chmn. exec. com., chief finanical officer, 1970—; dir. Sun Gold Industries N.Y., Inc. Chmn. alumni devel. com. Cooper Union, 1969—, trustee, 1970—; donor Martin Luther King Jr. meml. scholarships U. Notre Dame, 1968—, mem. adv. council Coll. Engring., 1968—; pres. Malverne Jewish Center, 1976—. Recipient Cooper medal, 1944. Sr. mem. I.E.E.E.; mem. Peter Cooper Soc. (chmn.). Jewish religion. Club: Chemists (N.Y.C.). Patentee in field. Home: 2 Drake St Malverne NY 11565 Office: 175 Community Dr Great Neck NY 11021

LEVINE, DANIEL, historian; b. N.Y.C., Dec. 31, 1934; s. Morris Simeon and Margaret (Hirsch) L.; B.A. in History, Antioch Coll., 1956; Ph.D. in History (Woodrow Wilson fellow, Social Sci Research Council fellow), Northwestern U., 1961; m. Susan Rose, July 29, 1954; children—Timothy, Karen. Asst. prof. history Earlham Coll., 1960-63; asst. prof. Bowdoin Coll., 1963-66, asso. prof., 1966-72, prof, 1972—, Thomas Bracket Reed prof. history and polit. sci., 1974—; Fulbright lectr., Denmark, 1969-70; mem. jury Ralph Waldo Emerson prize Phi Beta Kappa, 1973-74. Guggenheim fellow, 1972-73. Mem. Am. Hist. Assn., Orgn. Am. Historians, AAUP, Social Welfare History Group (v.p. 1975—). Democrat. Author: Varieties of Reform Thought, 1964; Jane Addams and the Liberal Tradition, 1971; contrbr. articles to profl. jours; editorial bd. Explorations in Entrepreneurial History, 1962-70. Home: 3118 Mere Point Rd Brunswick ME 04011 Office: History Dept Bowdoin Coll Brunswick ME 04011

LEVINE, DAVID, artist; b. Bklyn., Dec. 20, 1926; s. Harry L.; B.F.A., Temple U., 1949, B.S. in Edn., 1949; postgrad. Hans Hoffman Sch. Paintings, 1950; children—Matthew, Eve. Exhibited one man shows: Forum Gallery, N.Y.C., 1966—, Ga. Mus. Art, 1968, Calif. Palace Legion of Honor, 1968-69, 71-72, Wesleyan U., 1970, Bklyn. Mus., 1971, Princeton U., 1972, Galerie Yves Lambert, Paris, 1972, Yale U., 1973, Hirshhorn Mus. and Sculpture Garden, Washington, 1976, Galerie Claude Bernard, 1979; represented by Forum Gallery. Served with U.S. Army, 1945-46. Recipient Tiffany award, 1955, Isaac N. Maynard prize, 1958, Julius Hallgarten prize, 1960, Thomas B. Clark prize, 1962, George Polk award, 1965, Childe Hassom Purchase prize, 1972, Benjamin Altman prize, 1973; Guggenheim fellow, 1967. Mem. NAD, Century Assn. Author: The Man From M.A.L.I.C.E., 1966; Pens and Needles, 1969; No Know Survivors, 1970; The Arts of David Levine, 1978. Address: c/o Forum Gallery 1018 Madison Ave New York City NY 10021

LEVINE, DAVID LAWRENCE, educator; b. N.Y.C., Aug. 30, 1919; s. Harold D. and Caroline (Leibowitz) L.; B.S., in Social Scis., Coll. City N.Y., 1941; M.S.W., U. Pa., 1943; Ph.D., U. Minn., 1953; m. Laura Ann Kaplan, June 5, 1942; children—Edwin Alfred, Deborah Janet, Elizabeth Phylis, Helen Dorothy. Visitor, intake worker Assn. Jewish Children, Phila., 1943-45; asst. to dir. Bklyn. Jewish Child Care Council, 1945-47; supr. children's services Jewish Family and Children's Services, Mpls., 1947-51; instr. family life edn. U. Minn., 1949-53, instr. Sch. Social Work, 1952-53; from asst. prof. to prof. Sch. Social Welfare, Fla. State U., 1953-67, chmn. dept. social work, 1965-67; asso. dean Sch. Social Work, Syracuse U., 1967-68; prof. social work Faculty Gerontology, U. Ga., Athens, 1968—; research asso. community mental health Harvard Sch. Pub. Health, 1959-60; cons. Operation Headstart, U. Miami (Fla.), 1965-67, cons. Geriatric Clinic, 1955. Pres. Leon County (Fla.) Mental Health Assn., 1961-63; chmn. Leon County Community Action Com., 1966; mem. bd. Fla. Assn. Mental Health, 1965-67; chmn. Twin Cities group Vocat. Guidance Assn., 1951; chmn. community planning and devel. com. Athens Community Council, 1969—; cons. Ga. State Commn. on Aging, 1969-70; chmn. Univ. Council on Gerontology, 1970-74; Ga. del. White House Conf. on Aging, 1971; v.p. Nat. Inter-Faith Coalition on Aging, 1972-73, chmn. edn. and research com., mem. research team Social Work Manpower Study; pres. Athens-Clarke County Community Coordinated Child Care, 1973; cons. Inst. for Creative Devel., Union Am. Hebrew Congregations, 1974-77; chmn. com. on licensing Ga. State Conf. on Social Welfare, 1975—; chmn. Title XX Planning Council, Dist. 10, Ga. Dept. Human Resources, 1976—, State 1st v.p., 1979—; co-dir. Livingston Found. Seminars on Humanistic Mgmt. in Health Care, U. Ga., chmn. student affairs U. Council, 1978-79; program adviser Campus-Free Coll., Washington. Fellow Am. Orthopsychiat. Assn., Gerontol. Soc.; mem. Acad. Certified Social Workers, Nat. Assn. Social Workers (Ga. council 1975-76). Address: 189 Colonial Dr Athens GA 30601

LEVINE, DONALD NATHAN, sociologist, educator; b. New Castle, Pa., June 16, 1931; s. Abe and Rose (Gusky) L.; A.B., U. Chgo., 1950, M.A., 1954, Ph.D., 1957; postgrad. U. Frankfurt (Germany), 1952-53; m. Ruth Weinstein, Aug. 26, 1967; children—Theodore, William, Rachel. Asst. prof. sociology U. Chgo., 1962-65, asso. prof., 1965-73, prof., 1973—; cons. on Ethiopian affairs to U.S. Govt. Recipient Quantrell award U. Chgo., 1971. Mem. Internat. Soc. Comparative Study Civilization, Am. Sociol. Assn. Jewish. Author: Wax and Gold: Tradition and Innovation in Ethiopian Culture, 1965; Georg Simmel on Individuality and Social Forms, 1971; Greater Ethiopia: The Evolution of a Multiethnic Society, 1974. Office: 1126 E 59th St Chicago IL 60637

LEVINE, EDWIN BURTON, educator; b. Chgo., Nov. 11, 1920; s. Benjamin and Bertha (Kauffman) L.; A.B., U. Chgo., 1949, A.M., 1950, Ph.D., 1953; m. Myra Estrin, Apr. 22, 1944; children—William Alan, Patricia Ann. Instr. classics U. Nebr., 1951-52; instr., then asst. prof. Wayne State U., 1955-60; instr. Detroit Bd. Edn., 1960-61, New Trier High Sch., Winnetka, Ill., 1962-64; vis. lectr. U. Ill. at Chgo. Circle, 1964-65, mem. faculty, 1965—, prof. classics, 1968—, head dept., 1969-74. Served with AUS, 1943-46. Fellow AAAS; mem. Am. Philol. Assn., Soc. for History Medicine, Archaeol. Inst. Am., Chgo. Classical Club (pres. 1967-69). Author: Introduction to Classical Greek, 1968. Prin. compiler: Follett World-Wide Latin-English Dictionary, 1968; Hippocrates, 1971; Landor's Latin Poetry, 1968. Home: 550 Sheridan Sq Evanston IL 60202 Office: 601 S Morgan St Chicago IL 60680

LEVINE, GEORGE RICHARD, univ. dean; b. Boston, Aug. 5, 1929; s. Jacob U. and Rose Lillian (Margolis) L.; B.A., Tufts Coll., Medford, Mass., 1951; M.A., Columbia, 1952, Ph.D., 1961; m. Joan Adler, June 8, 1958 (div. 1977); children—David, Michael; m. 2d, Linda Rashman, Apr. 17, 1977. Lectr. English, Columbia, 1956-58; instr. Northwestern U., 1959-63; mem. faculty State U. N.Y., Buffalo, 1963—, prof. English, 1970—, dean faculty arts and letters, 1975—. Chmn. bd. dirs. Youth Orch. Found., Buffalo, 1974-75; trustee Buffalo Chamber Music Soc. Served with AUS, 1952-54. Univ. fellow Columbia, 1958-59; Faculty Research fellow State U. N.Y., 1966, 67; Fulbright lectr., W. Ger., 1969-70; recipient Chancellor's award excellence in teaching State U. N.Y., Buffalo, 1973-74. Mem. Modern Lang. Assn., Am. Soc. 18th Century Studies. Jewish. Clubs: Adirondack Mountain, Foothills Trail. Author: Henry Fielding and The Dry Mock, 1967; also articles. Home: 388 Parker Ave Buffalo NY 14216 Office: Office Dean State Univ NY 810 Clemens Hall Buffalo NY 14260

LEVINE, HAROLD, advt. agy. exec.; b. Glen Cove, N.Y., Sept. 4, 1921; s. Jack and Lillian (Goldstein) L.; student Coll. City N.Y., 1938-41, N.Y. U., 1945-46; m. Sue Marsh, Dec. 29, 1946; children—Jay, Rita. Dir. advt. Griffon Cutlery Co., 1950-52; with Mervin & Jesse Levine Advt. Agy., N.Y.C., 1952-71, pres., 1968-77; pres. Levine, Huntley, Schmidt Advt. Agy., 1972-78; chmn. bd. Levine, Huntley, Schmidt, Plapler & Beaver, Inc., N.Y.C., 1978—; lectr. advt. L.I. U., 1948-58. Pres. Freeport Citizens Adv. Com. for Edn., 1964-66; trustee Freeport Hist. Soc., 1965-67; elected mem. Freeport Bd. Edn., 1967, v.p., 1969-70, pres., 1970-74, 76—. Served with AUS, 1942-44. Mem. Am. Assn. Advt. Agys. (chmn. N.Y. council 1978—), Alpha Delta Sigma. Home: 63 Cross Hwy Westport CT 06880 Office: 250 Park Ave New York NY 10020. *I have tried to maintain a healthy balance between my corporate life, personal life and community life. A successful man serves his family, his business and his community.*

LEVINE, HERBERT SAMUEL, educator; b. N.Y.C., Dec. 12, 1928; s. Hyman C. and Bertha H. (Shalit) L.; A.B., Harvard, 1950, A.M., 1952, Ph.D., 1961; m. Helene Jaffe, Jan. 25, 1953; children—Jonathan, Jan, Judith. Asst. prof., asso. prof., prof. U. Pa., Phila., 1960—, chmn. grad. group econs., 1970-73; vis. prof. Princeton, 1962, Harvard, 1963-64, Columbia, 1965, 66, 74, London Sch. Econs., 1968-69; trustee, mem. exec. com. Nat. Council Soviet and East European Research, 1978—; cons. Stanford Research Inst., Dept. State. Chmn. Am. Council Learned Socs.-Social Sci. Research Council joint com. Soviet studies, 1971-77. Bd. dirs. Ardwood Civic Assn. Served with U.S. Army, 1952-54. Recipient Wells prize Harvard, 1963, Distinguished Teaching award U. Pa., 1965; Ford fellow, 1958-59, Fulbright-Hays fellow, 1968-69, Am. Council Learned Socs. fellow, 1969, Russian Inst., Columbia fellow, 1973-74. Mem. Assn. Study Soviet Type Economies (exec. sec. 1961-67), Assn. Comparative Econ. Studies (exec. com. 1970-73). Co-author: Modernization of Japan and Russia, 1975. Co-editor: Mathematics and Computers in Soviet Economic Planning, 1967. Home: 178 Lakeside Rd Ardmore PA 19003 Office: Dept Econs U Pa Philadelphia PA 19104

LEVINE, HOWARD ARNOLD, judge; b. Mar. 4, 1932; B.A., Yale U., 1953; LL.B., 1956; m. Barbara Joan Segall, July 25, 1954; children—Neil Louis, Ruth Ellen, James Robert. Admitted to N.Y. bar, 1956; asst. in instruction, research asso. in criminal law Yale Law Sch., 1956-57; asso. firm Hughes, Hubbard, Blair, Reed, N.Y.C., 1957-59; practiced in Schenectady, 1959-70; asst. dist. atty. Schenectady County (N.Y.) 1961-66, dist. atty., 1967-70; judge Schenectady County Family Ct., 1971—; acting judge Schenectady County Ct., 1971—; Adminstr. judge family cts. N.Y. State 4th Jud. Dist.; vis. lectr. Albany Law Sch.; mem. N.Y. Gov.'s Panel on Juvenile Violence; mem. N.Y. State Temp. Commn. on Child Welfare, N.Y. State Temporary Commn. on Recodification of Family Ct. Act, N.Y. State Juvenile Justice Adv. Bd.; mem. ind. rev. bd. N.Y. State Div. for Youth; mem. rules and adv. com. on family ct. N.Y. State Jud. Conf. Bd. dirs. Schnecatady County Child Guildance Center, Carver Community Center Freedom Forum of Schnectady. Mem. Am. Law Inst., N.Y. State Bar Assn. (chmn. spl. com. on juvenile justice), Assn. Family Ct. Judges of State N.Y. (pres. 1979-80). Contbr. articles to law revs. Home: 1312 Rowe Rd Schenectady NY 12309 Office: County Bldg 620 State St Schenectady NY 12307

LEVINE, IRVING RASKIN, news commentator, author; b. Pawtucket, R.I.; s. Joseph and Emma (Raskin) L.; B.S., Brown U., 1944, L.H.D., 1969; M.S., Columbia, 1947; L.H.D., Bryant Coll., 1974; m. Nancy Cartmell Jones, July 12, 1957; children—Jeffrey, Daniel Rome, Jennifer Jones. Began career as reporter and rewriter Providence Jour., 1940-43; fgn. news editor Internat. News Service, 1947-48, chief Vienna (Austria) bur., 1948-50; with NBC, 1950—, war corr., Korea, 1950-52, chief corr., Moscow, 1955-59, Rome, 1959-67, 68-70, London, 1967-68, Washington, 1971—; spl. writer London Times, 1955-59; covered assignments in China, Czechoslovakia, Bulgaria, Poland, Japan, Viet Nam, Formosa, Thailand, Eng., France, Germany, Switzerland, Algeria, Congo, Israel, Turkey, Greece, Yugoslavia, Union of S.Africa, Denmark, Sweden, Ireland; lectr., 1953—. Recipient award for best radio-TV reporting from abroad Overseas Press Club, 1956; award for outstanding radio network broadcasting Nat. Headliners Club, 1957, Martin R. Gainsbrugh award for best econ. reporting, 1978; named one of 10 outstanding young men U.S. Jr. C. of C., 1956; 50th Anniversary award Columbia Sch. Journalism, 1963; Emmy award, 1966; named to R.I. Hall of Fame, 1972. Mem. Council on Fgn. Relations (fellowship 1952-53), Phi Beta Kappa. Club: Cosmos. Author: Main Street, USSR, 1959; Travel Guide to Russia, 1960; Main Street, Italy, 1963; The New Worker in Soviet Russia, 1973. Contbr. articles to nat. mags. Office: 4001 Nebraska Ave NW Washington DC 20016

LEVINE, JACK, food co. exec.; s. Ansel and Tillie (Held) L.; children—Judith, Dorothy, Trudy. With Steinberg Inc., Montreal, 1929—, v.p., gen. mgr. Que. div., then exec. v.p., 1965-77, pres., 1977—, also dir.; pres. Steinberg Food Co. Ltd., 1975—; dir. Phenix Flour Co. Ltd.; hon. lectr. McGill U. Bus. Sch. Bd. dirs. Niagper Inst. Recipient Golden Pencil award Can. Food Industry, Prime Minister Israel award. Mem. Personnel Assn. Jewish. Club: Masons. Home: 636 Algonquin Ave Town of Mount Royal PQ H3R 1E1 Canada Office: 1500 Atwater Ave Montreal PQ Canada

LEVINE, JACK, artist; b. Boston, Jan. 3, 1915; s. Samuel and Mary (Grinker) L.; studied with Dr. Denman W. Ross, Ph.D., 1929-31; A.F.D., Colby, 1956; m. Ruth Gikow; 1 dau., Susanna. One-man shows: Downtown Gallery, N.Y.C., 1938; Artists, 1942 Exhbn., Mus. Modern Art, N.Y.C., 1943; exhibited in group shows at Jeu de Paume, Paris, 1938; Carnegie Internat. exhbns., 1938, 39, 40; Artists for Victory, Met. Mus., N.Y.C., 1942; retrospective at Jewish Mus., N.Y.C., 1978-79; represented in permanent collections Mus. Modern Art, Met. Mus. Art, N.Y.C., William Hayes Fogg Mus., Harvard, Addison Gallery, Andover, Mass., Museum of the Vatican. Served with AUS, 1942-45. Recipient 2d purchase prize Artists for Victory Exhbn., Met. Mus., 1942. Mem. Nat. Inst. Arts and Letters, Nat. Acad. Arts and Letters, Am. Acad. Arts and Scis. Home: 68 Morton St New York City NY 10014

LEVINE, JAMES, condr.; b. Cin., June 23, 1943; student piano with Rosina Lhevinne, Juilliard Sch., Rudolf Serkin, Marlboro Festival. Asst. condr. Cleve. Orch., 1964-70, also piano soloist; now music dir. Met. Opera, N.Y.C and Ravinia Festival, Highland Park, Ill.; guest condr. and piano soloist with orchs. Chgo., Boston, Phila., N.Y., London, Berlin, Vienna; ann. appearances at Salzburg Festival; condr. numerous operatic recordings including premiere Grammophone recs. Verdi's Giovanna D'Arco and I Vespri Siciliani; symphonic recordings include complete Brahms symphonies with Chgo. Symphony, Schumann symphonies with Phila. Orch. Office: Met Opera New York NY 10023

LEVINE, JEROME, psychiatrist; b. N.Y.C., July 10, 1934; s. Abraham and Sadie (Glowatz) L.; B.A., U. Buffalo, 1954, M.D., 1958; children—Ross W., Lynn R. Intern, then psychiat. resident E.J. Meyer Meml. Hosp., Buffalo, 1958-61; sr. psychiat. resident St. Elizabeth's Hosp., Washington, 1961-62; staff psychiatrist USPHS Hosp., Lexington, Ky., 1962-64; research psychiatrist, asst. chief psychopharmacology research br. NIMH, 1964-67, chief of br., 1967—; instr. psychiatry Johns Hopkins Med. Sch., 1964-72; vis. prof. U. Pisa (Italy), 1977. Mem. Am. Psychopath. Assn., Am. Psychiat. Assn. (Hofheimer Research prize 1970), Am. Coll. Neuropsychopharmacology, Collegium Internationale Neuropsychopharmacologicum. Author books and papers on psychotomimetic drugs, drug metabolism, drug evaluation. Home: Apt 307 118 Monroe St Rockville MD 20850 Office: 5600 Fishers Ln Rockville MD 20857

LEVINE, JOSEPH, orch. condr.; b. Phila., Aug. 14, 1912; s. Harry and Sophia (Raditz) L.; Mus.B. in Conducting and Piano, Curtis Inst. Music, Phila., 1937; pupil Fritz Reiner and Artur Rodzinski in conducting, of Josef Hofmann in piano, of Wanda Landowska in harpsichord; m. Mary Thomas, Feb. 16, 1945; children—Stephen, David. Mem. faculty Curtis Inst., 1933-40; asst. condr. Phila. Grand Opera Co., 1938-40; founder, condr. New Center of Music Orch., Phila., 1940-43, Chamber Opera Soc., Phila., 1946-50; pianist Phila. Orch., 1940-43, 46-50; condr. USAAF Tactical Air Center Symphonette, 1943-45; piano accompanist with Joseph Szigeti, 1946-50; music dir., condr. Co-Opera Co., Phila., 1947-50, Am. Ballet Theatre, N.Y.C., 1950-58, Omaha Symphony Orch., 1958-69; faculty Cornish Sch. Allied Arts, Seattle, 1969-73, 76-79, mem. Cornish Trio, 1969-73; music dir. Omaha Civic Opera Soc., 1961-69, Omaha Starlight Theatre, 1961; fgn. tours. under auspices cultural exchange program State Dept., 1950-58; asso. condr. Seattle Symphony Orch., 1969-73, Hawaii Opera Theatre and Honolulu Symphony Orch., 1973-76; music dir., condr. Bremerton Symphony, 1979—; recorded ballet scores for Capitol Records, 1952-57; Am. condr. Royal Ballet Eng., 1963-65. Recipient citations Omaha C. of C., 1960, Dana Coll., 1961, Creighton U., 1962; Key to City Omaha, 1961; Mercian medal Coll. St. Mary, 1967. Rotarian. Author articles. Home: 2917 W Eaton St Seattle WA 98199

LEVINE, JOSEPH EDWARD, motion picture producer; b. Boston, Sept. 9, 1905; L.H.D. (hon.), Emerson Coll., 1968; m. Rosalie Harrison, 1939; 2 children. Motion pictures include Jack the Ripper,

1960, Hercules, 1959, Hercules Unchained, 1960, Bocaccio '70, 1962, The Sky Above-The Mud Below, 1960, Two Women, 1961, The Conjugal Bed, 1963, 8 1/2, 1963, Divorce-Italian Style, 1962, Marriage Italian Style, 1964, The Easy Life, Yesterday, Today and Tomorrow, 1964, The Carpetbaggers, 1964, Harlow, 1965, Zulu, 1964, Casanova '70, 1965, Darling, 1965, Woman Times Seven, 1967, The Graduate, 1967, The Producers, 1968, The Lion in Winter, 1968, Arruza, 1972, Thumb Tripping, 1972, They Call me Trinity, 1972, The Ruling Class, 1972, Carnal Knowledge, 1971, Day of the Dolphin, 1973, A Bridge Too Far, 1977, Magic, 1978; theater owner. New Haven; nat. distbr. movies, 1943—; formerly pres. Avco Embassy Pictures, now chmn. Joe E. Levine Presents, Inc. Office: care Joseph E Levine Presents Inc 227 Park Ave New York NY 10017*

LEVINE, JOSHUA, lawyer; b. N.Y.C., 1916; B.S.S., Coll. City N.Y., 1939; LL.B., N.Y. U., 1938; m. Selene Davidson; children—Judith, Beth, Linda. Admitted to N.Y. bar, 1939; mem. firm Davis & Gilbert, N.Y.C.; dir. Esquire Radio and Electronics Inc., 1960-70, sec., 1960—; dir. Weight Watchers Internat., Inc., 1968-70. Lectr. Practising Law Inst. div. gen. edn. and extension services N.Y. U. Mem. Am., N.Y. State bar assns. Jewish (founder, pres. synagogue 1961-63, hon. pres. 1963-77). Contr. chpt. Advt. and the Law to Bus. Mgmt. Handbook (J.K. Lasser). Home: 720 Milton Rd Rye NY 10580 Office: 850 3d Ave New York City NY 10022

LEVINE, LAURENCE WILLIAM, lawyer; b. N.Y.C., Apr. 9, 1931; s. Robert L. and Molly (Brunner) L.; B.A., Union Coll., 1952; LL.B., Harvard, 1955. Admitted to N.Y. State bar, 1958; Teaching fellow Def. Studies Program Harvard, 1955; aide to Adlai Stevenson, N.Y.C., 1956; office mgr. N.Y. com. Stevenson, Kefauver, Wagner, 1956; admitted to N.Y. bar, 1958; partner firm Walsh & Levine, N.Y.C., 1958—; sec.-treas. Kabuki Japanese Restaurant, N.Y.C., 1958—; counsel N.E. Airlines, N.Y.C., 1958-67, Brit. Eagle Airlines, 1963-69, Aerolineas Argentinas, 1960—, Banco de la Nacion Argentina, N.Y.C., 1972, Banco de Intercambio Regional Argentina, 1977—; partner San Francisco Mdse. Mart, Westbury Hotel, San Francisco, Kaanapoli Hotel, Hawaii; dir. N.Y. Venture Fund, N.Y.C., Pan Australian Fund; adv. bd. Banco de Intercambio Regional; public mem. Blue Cross/Blue Shield. Sec., N.Y. Com. for Dem. Votes, 1962-63. Mem. Assn. Bar City N.Y., N.Y. County Lawyers, Argentine-Am. C. of C. (dir.). Clubs: Downtown Athletic, Georgetown, Harvard, World Trade Center. Author: Gullibles Travels Thru Harvard, 1955; contbr. to East-Europe mag., 1969, Cambio Mag., Harvard Law Sch. Bull., N.Y. Times, Argentine newspapers, Rev. of River Plate, U.S.-China Relations, 1972. Home: 1435 Redford St Apt 12B Stamford CT 06905 Office: 60 Wall Tower 70 Pine St New York NY 10005

LEVINE, LAWRENCE STEVEN, lawyer; b. Bklyn., Mar. 30, 1934; s. Harry and Bess (Feiner) L.; A.B., Colgate U., 1955; LL.B., Yale, 1958; m. Linda Robbins, June 16, 1957; children—Lauren Victoria, Audrey Elizabeth, Hilary Anne. Admitted to N.Y. State bar, 1958, U.S. Supreme Ct. bar, 1973; asst. U.S. atty. Eastern Dist. N.Y., U.S. Dept. Justice, N.Y.C., 1958-62; asso. firm Kronish & Lieb, N.Y.C., 1962-63; mem. firm Beldock Levine & Hoffman, N.Y.C., 1964—; dir., mem. exec. com. Phila. Fury, N.Am. Soccer League; dir. various firms. Trustee Riverdale Country Sch., Associated YM-YWHA's Greater N.Y., Harry Levine Meml. Found. Mem. Fed. Bar Assn., N.Y. County Lawyers Assn., N.Y. State Dist. Attys. Assn., N.Y. Civil Liberties Union (cooperating counsel). Democrat. Jewish. Club: Yale (N.Y.C.). Home: 122 E 76th St New York NY 10021 Office: 565 Fifth Ave New York NY 10017

LEVINE, LES, artist; b. Dublin, Ireland, Oct. 6, 1935; s. Charles and Muriel (MacMahon) L.; came to U.S., 1964; student Central Sch. Arts and Crafts, London, 1953-56; m. Catherine Kazuko Kanai, Aug. 26, 1973; 1 son, Sean. Artist-in-residence Aspen Inst. Humanistic Studies, 1967-69; asst. prof. art N.Y. U., 1971-73, N.S. Coll. Art and Design, 1972-73; asso. editor Arts Mag., N.Y.C., 1973-74; asso. prof. art William Paterson Coll., Wayne, N.J., 1974-76, U. Ill., Chgo., 1975-76; one-man shows include: Internat. Cultureel Centrum, Antwerp, Belgium, 1978, Albright-Knox Gallery, Buffalo, 1977, Wadsworth Atheneum, Hartford, Conn., 1976, Adler Castillo, Caracas, Venezuela, 1975, Galeria Schema, Florence, Italy, 1974, Isaacs Gallery, Toronto, Ont., 1973, Finch Coll. Mus. Art, N.Y.C., 1972; group shows include: Canadian Sculpture Biennale (1st prize sculpture), 1967, Tokyo Biennale, 1974, Sao Paulo Biennale, 1975, Sydney (Australia) Biennale, 1976; U.S. rep. Documenta, Kassel, W. Ger., 1977; pres. Mus. Mott Art, Inc., 1970—. Fellow Nat. Endowment for Arts, 1974. Organizer Jimmy Carter Collection, Ga. Mus. Art, Athens, 1977. Author: Culture Hero, 1969; Media the Bio-Tech Rehearsal for Leaving the Body. Home and Office: 20 E 20th St New York NY 10003

LEVINE, LOWELL J., dentist; b. N.Y.C., Dec. 19, 1937; s. Nathan and Nettie (Fuchs) L.; B.A., Hobart Coll., 1959; D.D.S., N.Y. U., 1963; m. Barbara Ann Nadel, June 30, 1962; children—Matthew Steven, Brandon Howard. Pvt. practice of dentistry, Flushing, N.Y., 1965-76; clin. asst. prof. operative dentistry N.Y. U. Coll. Dentistry, N.Y.C., 1965-76, clin. asso. prof. behavioral scis., 1976—, clin. asso. prof. forensic medicine Sch. Medicine, 1965—; cons. in forensic odontology Office Chief Med. Examiner, City N.Y.; chief forensic odontologist Office of Med. Examiner Nassau County (N.Y.); guest lectr. Armed Forces Inst. Pathology, homicide investigators course and sex crimes investigators course N.Y.C. Police Dept., Nat. Death Investigation Seminar, Central Mo. State U., Medico Legal Seminar, New Eng. Conf. Police Adminstrs., Med. U. S.C., 1976, U. Md. Sch. Dentistry, 1976, U. Calif. at San Francisco, 1976, St. Francis Coll., Bklyn., 1976; lectr. forensic dentistry Continuing Edn. div. Brookdale Dental Center, N.Y. U.; tchr. med. and dental malpractice Practising Law Inst. Program chmn. 8th, 9th, 10th, 11th ann. Symposia Forensic Scis.; trustee Forensic Scis. Found., 1977—; adv. bd. Milton Helpern Internat. Center Forensic Scis., Wichita State U.; med. adv. bd. Andrew Menchell Infant Survival Found. Served from ensign to comdr. USNR. Diplomate Am. Bd. Forensic Odontology (dir.). Mem. N.Y. State, Queens County dental socs., ADA, Am. Acad. Forensic Scis. (chmn. odontology sect., exec. com. 1974-76, v.p. 1977-78), Forensic Sci. Soc. (London), Soc. Med. Jurisprudence, Am. Soc. Forensic Odontology, Indian Acad. Forensic Medicine, Naval Res. Assn. Editorial bd. Internat. Microfilm Jour. Legal Medicine, Jour. Forensic Scis. Home: 2 Rigger Ct Huntington Station NY 11746 Office: 42-47 Union St Flushing NY 11355. *It has been a great privilege to have met so many good people deeply concerned with justice for all.*

LEVINE, MARTIN, lawyer, educator; b. N.Y.C., June 1, 1939; s. Samuel J. and Ruth (Blumenstein) L.; A.B. summa cum laude, Brandeis U., 1960; J.D. with honors, Yale U., 1963; postgrad. U. Wis., 1967, U. Denver, 1970, Los Angeles Psychoanalytic Inst., 1971—, Nat. Inst. Trial Advocacy, 1975; m. Martha Lyon, Sept. 10, 1978. Admitted to Calif. bar, 1975, D.C. bar, 1964, also U.S. Supreme Ct.; law clk. Judge J. Skelly Wright, U.S. Ct. of Appeals, 1963-64; asst. prof. law U. So. Calif., Los Angeles, 1964-66, asso. prof., 1966-68, prof., 1969—, prof. psychiatry, 1978—, exec. dir. Inst. on Curriculum Reform and Clin. Edn., 1969-70, spl. asst. to univ. v.p., 1973, v.p. faculty senate, 1973-74, counselor univ. counseling center, 1975—; vis. prof. law Columbia U., 1968-69; vis. prof. social sci. U. Calif., San Diego, 1967, 71, 77, 78; adj. professor psychiatry and behavioral sci. Med. Sch., George Washington U., 1976—; mem. faculty Law Teaching Clinic, Assn. Am. Law Schs., 1969; sr. dep. Fed. Pub. Defender Office, Los Angeles, 1971-72, spl. dep., 1972-73; mem. faculty Nat. Sheriffs Inst., 1973-75; spl. counsel Ball, Hunt, Hart, Brown & Baerwitz, Los Angeles, 1975-76; gen. counsel Constitutional Rights subcom. U.S. Senate, 1976-77; asst. to chaplain Brandeis U., 1958-60; cons. Pres.'s Crime Commn., Peace Corps, ACTION, OEO, NSF, Calif. State Bar Com. Bar Examiners, others. Mem. jud. processes task force Los Angeles County Advisory Bd. on Criminal Justice, 1970-72; past exec. dir., pres., chmn. bd. Western Center on Law and Poverty; prin. investigator, coordinator Nat. Sr. Citizens Law Center, 1973-77, v.p., 1977—; mem. exec. com. of bd. Los Angeles Neighborhood Legal Services Soc., 1965-70; chmn. supervising com. Inst. on Law and Urban Problems, 1970-72; mem. steering com. of bd. Criminal Justice Council of Los Angeles County, 1969-72; chmn. univ. council U. So. Calif., 1973-74; mem. Los Angeles Dist. Atty.'s Community Advisory Council, 1976—; resource person crime and law enforcement Democratic Nat. Platform Com., 1976; bd. dirs. Anna Freud Found., Los Angeles, 1977—; mem. exec. com. legal services sect. State Bar Calif., 1977—; chmn. bd. trustees U. San Fernando Valley Coll. Law, 1978—. Recipient Perez prize for best article Yale U., 1973, award for outstanding service U. So. Calif., 1974; Louis D. Brandeis Hon. scholar in social sci., 1960, Woodrow Wilson Nat. fellow in sociology, 1960-61, Yale Law Nat. scholar, 1961-62; Council Legal Edn. for Profl. Responsibility fellow, 1971-72; named one of One Hundred Outstanding Young Leaders in Am. Higher Edn., Change Mag., 1978. Fellow Am. Sociol. Assn.; mem. Calif., D.C., Los Angeles County (past mem. exec. com. human rights sect.) bar assns., Nat. Legal Aid and Defender Assn., Law and Soc. Assn., Am. Psychology-Law Assn., Council for Psychoanalytic Edn., Am. Psychoanalytic Assn. (affiliate), Order of Coif, Phi Beta Kappa. Democrat. Jewish. Author: Property As An Idea and a Process, rev. edit., 1975; The Current Status of Juvenile Law, 1971. Bd. editors Yale Law Jour., 1961-63. Contbr. articles profl. jours. Office: T2751 Glendower Rd Los Angeles CA 90027

LEVINE, MARTIN DAVID, educator; b. Montreal, Que., Can., Mar. 30, 1938; s. Max and Ethel (Tauber) L.; B.Eng., McGill U., Montreal, 1960, M.Eng., 1963; Ph.D., Imperial Coll., U. London, 1965, also diploma; m. Deborah Tiger, June 6, 1961; children—Jonathan, Barbara. Part-time lectr. Imperial Coll., 1963-64; mem. faculty McGill U., 1965—, prof., 1977—; mem. tech. staff Jet Propulsion Lab., Pasadena, Calif., 1972-73; vis. prof. Hebrew U., Jerusalem, 1979-80; Can. rep. IAPR; cons. med. info. processing, image processing. Fellow Am. Soc. Engring. Edn.-Ford Found., 1972-73. Sr. mem. IEEE; mem. Computer Soc., Assn. Computing Machinery, Pattern Recognition Soc., Order Engrs. Que., Can. Soc. Computational Studies Intelligence. Jewish. Author, editor in field. Office: Dept Elec Engring McGill Univ 3480 University St Montreal PQ H3A 2A7 Canada

LEVINE, MICHAEL ELIAS, educator; b. N.Y.C., Apr. 8, 1941; s. Morris and Sara (Meltzer) L.; B.A., Reed Coll., Portland, Oreg., 1962; LL.B., Yale U., 1965; m. Carol June Stover, June 2, 1967; children—Sara Rebecca, Anna Rachel. Atty., CAB, Washington, 1965-66; spl. asst. Task Force Econ. Growth and Opportunity, 1966-67; law and econs. fellow U. Chgo. Law Sch., 1967-68; mem. faculty U. So. Calif. Law Center, 1968—, prof. law, 1972—; vis. prof. Duke U., 1972-73; Henry R. Luce prof. law and social change in tech. soc. Calif. Inst. Tech., Pasadena, 1973—, on leave, 1978; dir. Bur. Pricing and Domestic Aviation, CAB, 1978—; trustee Center Law in Pub. Interest, 1971-76; acad. visitor London Sch. Econs. and Polit. Sci., 1977; cons. to Commonwealth of P.R., 1974, U.S. Senate Subcom. on Adminstrv. Practice and Procedure, 1974-75, Calif. State Energy Commn., 1976, others. Mem. Assn. Am. Law Schs. (exec. council sect. antitrust and econ. regulation 1974—). Author articles air transp. regulation, theories of legal process behavior. Home: 1550 Arroyo View Dr Pasadena CA 91103 Office: Calif Inst Tech Pasadena CA 91125 also U So Calif Law Center Los Angeles CA 90007

LEVINE, MYRON, educator; b. Bklyn., July 28, 1926; s. Irving and Sarah (Perr) L.; B.A., Bklyn. Coll., 1947; Ph.D. (AEC fellow), Ind. U., 1952; m. Barbara Ruth Kohn, Feb. 4, 1950; children—Peter Arthur, Sura. Research asso. bacteriology U. Ill., Urbana, 1954-56; asst., then asso. biologist Brookhaven Nat. Lab., Upton, N.Y., 1956-61; vis. asso. prof. zoology U. Calif. at Los Angeles, 1960; asso. prof. human genetics U. Mich., Ann Arbor, 1961-67, prof., 1967—; tchr., cons. in field; vis. scientist Imperial Cancer Research Fund, London, 1973-74. Am. Cancer Soc. fellow Johns Hopkins U., 1952-54; Commonwealth Fund fellow for vis. scientists Inst. Molecular Biology, U. Geneva, 1966-67. Mem. Genetics Soc. Am., Am. Soc. Microbiology, Am. Inst. Biol. Scis., A.A.U.P., Sigma Xi. Editor Jour. Virology, 1972-77. Home: 356 Hilldale Dr Ann Arbor MI 48105

LEVINE, NAOMI BRONHEIM, univ. ofcl.; b. N.Y.C., Apr. 15, 1923; d. Nathan and Malvina (Mermelstein) Bronheim; B.A., Hunter Coll., 1941; LL.B., Columbia, 1946, J.D., 1970; m. Leonard Levine, Apr. 11, 1948; 1 dau., Joan. Admitted to N.Y. bar, 1946; with firm Scaadrett, Tuttle & Chalaire, N.Y.C., 1946-48, Charles Gottleib, N.Y.C., 1948-50; with Am. Jewish Congress, 1950-78, exec. dir., 1972-78; v.p. for external affairs N.Y. U., N.Y.C., 1978—; asst. prof. law and police sci. John Jay Coll., N.Y.C., 1969-73, L.I. U., 1965-69. Bd. dirs. Interracial Council Bus. Opportunities. Recipient Constl. Law prize Hunter Coll., 1944, named to Hall of Fame, 1972. Author: Ocean Hill Brownsville, Schools in Crisis, 1969; The Jewish Poor-an American Awakening, 1974. Mem. staff Columbia Law Rev., 1945-46. Home: 37 Washington Sq W New York NY 10011 Office: 70 Washington Sq S New York NY 10012

LEVINE, NORMAN DION, educator; b. Boston, Nov. 30, 1912; s. Max and Adele (Daen) L.; B.S., Iowa State U., 1933; Ph.D., U. Calif. at Berkeley, 1937; m. Helen Marie Saxon, Mar. 2, 1935. Asst. dept. zoology U. Calif., Berkeley, 1933-37; from asst. to prof. parasitology U. Ill. Coll. Vet. Medicine, Urbana, 1937—, dir. Center for Human Ecology, 1968-74. Chmn. tropical medicine and parasitology study sect. NIH, 1965-69, ad hoc com. on health sci. achievement award program, 1965, animal resources adv. com., 1971-75. Served to maj. AUS, 1942-46. Decorated Bronze Star. Recipient various research, tng. grants from NIH, NSF. Mem. Am. Micros. Soc. (hon., pres. 1968-69), Soc. Protozoologists (pres. 1959-60, exec. com. 1960—, hon.), Am. Soc. Profl. Biologists (pres. 1966-68), Ill. Acad. Sci. (pres. 1966-67), A.A.A.S. (council 1963-66, 69), Am. Soc. Parasitologists (pres.-elect 1979), Am. Bd. Microbiology (gov. bd. 1959-64), Phi Sigma (hon.). Author: Protozoan Parasites of Domestic Animals and of Man, 1961, rev., 1973; Nematode Parasites of Domestic Animals and of Man, 1968; Coccidian Parasites of Rodents, 1965; Coccidian Parasites of Ruminants, 1970; Textbook of Veterinary Parasitology, 1978; editor: Malaria in the Interior Valley of North America, 1964; Natural Nidality of Transmissible Diseases, 1966; Natural Nidality of Diseases, 1968; Animal Ecology, 1972; Human Ecology, 1975; Jour. Protozoology, 1965-71. Home: 702 LaSell Dr Champaign IL 61820 Office: Coll Vet Medicine U Ill Urbana IL 61801. *We can never loaf. Life is too short and the days are not long enough to learn all that we should. When I was very young I thought that I could know everything worth knowing. Now I'm afraid that I don't know my own restricted subject as well as I'd like. I suppose that it's the same with everyone else. It doesn't matter how good one is, he can always be better. But there is always the opposite view. Does keeping busy make me any happier than I would be if I simply lay under a tree and contemplated the clouds?*

LEVINE, NORMAN GENE, ins. co. exec.; b. N.Y.C., Sept. 14, 1926; s. Harris J. and Dorothy S. (Podolsky) L.; student U. Wis.-Madison, 1943-48; m. Sandra Leibow, Dec. 11, 1969; children from previous marriage—Linda (Mrs. James Pfeiffer), Danny, Donald. Agt. Aetna Life Ins. Co., N.Y.C., 1948-56, supr., 1956-59, gen. agt., 1959-75; pres. Norman G. Levine & Assos., reps. in No. Calif. for Mut. Benefit Life Ins. Co., San Francisco, 1975—; speaker in field; past div. v.p. Million Dollar Round Table; chmn. Life Underwriter Tng. Council, N.Y.C., 1955-57. Committeeman Bronx council Boy Scouts Am., 1948-55. Served with AUS, 1944-46; ETO. Recipient Julian Myrick award Gen. Agts. and Mgrs. Conf., 1969. Past mem. bd. dirs. Calif. Law Enforcement Needs Com. Mem. N.Y.C. (pres. 1967-68), N.Y. State (pres. 1968-69) assns. life underwriters, Nat. Assn. Life Underwriters (pres. 1974-75, dir. polit. action com. 1967-69), N.Y.C. Life Mgrs. Assn. (pres. 1974-75), Assn. Advanced Life Underwriters, Am. Soc. C.L.U.'s, Golden Key Soc. of Life Underwriters, Linnaean Soc., San Francisco C. of C., Audubon Soc., Am. Israel Friendship League (trustee). Mem. Order B'nai Zion (pres. 1964-67). Author: Yes You Can; How To Build a $1,000,000 Agency in Five Years or Less; editor bi-weekly news report Probe. Contbr. numerous articles to profl. jours. Author tapes on ins., mgmt., photography, Americanism. Home: 251 Crest Rd Woodside CA 94062 Office: 1 California St San Francisco CA 94111. *Profit and concern for people are not mutually exclusive and, in fact, people working in a synergistic relationship produce greater profit and general well-being. Democracy with all its problems is still clearly the best of all available methods of government; capitalism and free enterprise create the competition and reward that best challenge the human mind and body; and freedom to "stand tall" and be oneself with faith, integrity and dignity are the basis for one's conscience and a guide for society's morality.*

LEVINE, PHILIP, immunohematologist, geneticist, biomed. scientist; b. Russia, Aug. 10, 1900; s. Morris and Fay (Zirulick) L.; came to U.S., 1908, naturalized, 1917; B.S., Coll. City N.Y., 1919; M.D., Cornell U., 1923, M.A., 1925; Sc.D., Mich. State U., 1967; m. Hilda Lillian Perlmutter, May 1, 1938 (dec.); children—Phyllis Ann (Mrs. Harvey Klein), Mark Armin, Paul Karl (dec.), Victor Raphael. Asst., later asso. Rockefeller Inst. Med. Research, 1925-32; mem. faculty U. Wis. Med. Sch., 1932-35; bacteriologist, serologist Newark Beth Israel Hosp., 1935-44; dir. immunohematology div. Ortho Research Found., Raritan, N.J., 1944, now cons. Ortho Diagnostics, Ortho Pharm.; vis. investigator Meml. Sloan Kettering Inst. Cancer Research, 1976—; vis. fellow Faculty of Medicine, Cornell U., 1978; cons. Nassau Hosp., Mineola, N.Y.; hon. life mem. profl. staff Center for Immunology, State U. N.Y. at Buffalo, 1974—; Gehrman lectr. U. Ill. Coll. Medicine, 1975—; McNeal lectr., 1979. Recipient Passano Found. award, 1951, 1st Franz Oehlecker award and gold medal German Soc. Blood Transfusion, 1964, Joseph P. Kennedy Jr. Internat. award, 1965, Edward J. Ill award Acad. Medicine N.J., 1966, Clement von Pirquet gold medal VII Forum on Allergy, 1966, Mead Johnson award, 1942, Ward Burdick award, 1946, Lasker award, 1946, Phi Lambda Kappa Grand award, 1947, Karl Landsteiner award, 1956, Townsend Harris award, 1956, award merit Netherlands Red Cross, 1959, Gold medal award Norwegian Soc. Immunohematologists, Allan award Am. Soc. Human Genetics, Melvyn H. Motolinsky Research Found. award Rutgers Med. Sch., McNeill award N.J. Hosp. Assn., 1979. Fellow A.C.P., Royal Coll. Physicians, Explorers Club; mem. Nat. Acad. Sci., N.Y. Acad. Medicine, Am. Genetic Assn., Am. Assn. Immunologists, Soc. Exptl. Biology and Medicine, Med. Soc. State NJ., Am. Assn. Human Genetics (pres. 1969-70), N.Y. Acad. Scis. (hon. life), Harvey Soc., Norwegian Soc. Immunohematology (hon.), Sigma Xi. Jewish. Clubs: Lotos, Cosmos. Author numerous publs. original exptl. work on human blood groups, transfusions; author of laws in N.J. and Wis. on blood tests in paternity dispute. Discovered (with Dr. Landsteiner) blood factors M, N and P (M and N useful in paternity and bastardy cases); elaborated methods of studying bacteriophage; described causes of diseases of newborn (erythroblastosis fetalis); discovered human Rh blood factor and phenomenon of isoimmunization through pregnancy; described several other new blood antigens; discovered cause of anemia in Rh null individual; showed asso. blood group antigens in malignancies and that high-titer antibodies specific for these antigens specifically cytotoxic for such malignant tissues; described a normal antibody in normal human sera, the Forssman antibody as related to aging, cancer and other immune complex diseases. Mem. adv. bd. Vox Sanguinis; editorial bd. Transfusion. Home: Lotos Club 5 E 66th St New York NY 10021 Office: Ortho Research Found Raritan NJ 08869

LEVINE, PHILIP, univ. dean; b. Lawrence, Mass., Sept. 8, 1922; s. Samuel and Jennie (Derdak) L.; A.B., Harvard, 1946, A.M., 1948, Ph.D., 1952; m. Dinnie Moseson, June 19, 1955; children—Jared Elliott, Harlan Alcon. Instr., asst. prof. classics Harvard, 1952-59; asso. prof. classical langs. U. Tex. at Austin, 1959-61; asso. prof., prof. classics U. Calif. at Los Angeles, 1961—, dean div. humanities, 1965—. Mem. rev. com., sr. fellowship program Nat. Endowment for Humanities, 1966-70. Bd. govs. U. Judaism, 1968—. Served with AUS, 1943-46. Sheldon fellow, Italy; Guggenheim fellow; Fulbright Research grantee; recipient Bromberg Humanities award; decorated Cavaliere dell' Ordine Al Merito della Repubblica Italiana. Mem. Am. Philol. Assn. (dir. 1968-70), Mediaeval Acad. Am. (exec. council 1969-72), Renaissance Soc. Am., Modern Lang. Assn., Philol. Assn. Pacific Coast (chmn. gen. lit. 1964-65), Phi Beta Kappa. Author: Lo Scriptorium Vercellese da S. Eusebio ad Attone, 1958; St. Augustine, City of God, Books 12-15, 1966. Editor: Latin lt. sect. Twayne World Author Series, 1964—; adv. editor U. Calif. Publs. in Classical Studies, 1963-72; asso. editor U. Calif. Studies in Classical Antiquity, 1967-75, sr. co-editor, 1975—. Home: 224 S Almont Dr Beverly Hills CA 90211 Office: Dept Classics U Calif Los Angeles CA 90024

LEVINE, PHILIP, educator, poet; b. Detroit, Jan. 10, 1928; s. A. Harry and Esther Gertrude (Priscol) L.; B.A., Wayne State U., 1950, A.M., 1955; M.F.A., U. Iowa, 1957, studied with John Berryman, 1954; m. Frances Artley, July 14, 1954; children—Mark, John, Teddy. Instr., U. Iowa, 1955-57; instr. Calif. State U., Fresno, 1958—, prof. English, 1969—; Elliston lectr. poetry U. Cin.; poet-in-residence Vassar Coll., Nat. U. Australia; tchr. Princeton U., Columbia U., U. Calif., Berkeley. Active anti-Vietnam war movement. Recipient Joseph Henry Jackson award San Francisco Found., 1961, The Chaplebrook Found. award, 1968, Frank O'Hara Meml. prize, 1972; AAAL award, 1973; named outstanding lectr. Calif. State U., Fresno, 1971, outstanding prof. Calif. State U. System, 1972; Harriet Monroe Meml. prize for poetry; Lenore Marshall award for best Am. book of poems, 1976; Guggenheim fellow, 1973-74; Nat. Endowment for Arts grantee. Author: On the Edge, 1963; Not This Pig, 1968; Pili's Wall, 1971; Red Dust, 1971; They Feed They Lion, 1972; 1933, 1974; On The Edge & Over, 1976; The Names of the Lost, 1976; 7 Years from Somewhere, 1979; Ashes, 1979. Editor: (with E. Trejo) Tarumba, The Selected Poems of Jaime Sabines. Home: 4549 N Van Ness Fresno CA 93704. *My hope is to write poetry for people for whom there are no poems.*

LEVINE, RACHMIEL, physician, educator; b. Poland, Aug. 26, 1910; s. Solomon and Bessie (Benzion) L.; B.A., McGill U., 1932, M.D., 1936; m. Anne Gussack, Mar. 4, 1943; children—Judith Ann, Daniel Saul. Came to U.S., 1936, naturalized, 1944. Intern, then resident Michael Reese Hosp., Chgo., 1936-38, research fellow, 1939, dir. dept. metabolism, 1942-60, chmn. dept. madicine, 1952-60, dir. med. edn., 1952-60; professorial lectr. physiology U. Chgo., 1945-60; prof., chmn. dept. medicine N.Y. Med. Coll., 1960-71; exec. med. dir. City of Hope Med. Center, Duarte, Calif., 1971-78, dir. research, 1978—. Active United Jewish Appeal, Chgo., 1959-60. Cons. NSF, 1956-59, mem. bd. found. fund psychiat. research, 1958-61. Jakobaeus lectr. Karolinska Inst., Stockholm, 1963. Fellow Am. Acad. Arts and Scis.; mem. Am. Physiol. Soc., Endocrine Soc. (Upjohn award 1957), A.C.P., Assn. Am. Physicians, N.Y. Acad. Medicine, Chgo. Inst. Medicine, Am. Diabetes Assn. (Banting medal 1961; council 1958, pres. 1964-65), Internat. Diabetes Assn. (pres. 1967-70, hon. pres. 1970—), Harvey Soc. (pres. 1967-68). Contbr. numerous articles to profl. jours. Home: 2024 Canyon Rd Arcadia CA 91006 Office: City of Hope Med Center Duarte CA 91010

LEVINE, RAPHAEL DAVID, educator; b. Alexandria, Egypt, Mar. 29, 1938; s. Chaim S. and Sofia (Greenberg) L.; brought to U.S., 1939; M.Sc., Hebrew U., Jerusalem, Israel, 1959; Ph.D., Nottingham (Eng.) U., 1964; D.Phil., Oxford (Eng.) U., 1966; m. Gillah T. Ephraty, June 13, 1962; 1 dau., Ornah T. Vis. asst. prof. U. Wis., 1966-68; prof. theoretical chemistry Hebrew U., Jerusalem, 1969—; Battelle prof. chemistry and prof. math. Ohio State U., Columbus, 1970-74; Brittingham vis. prof. U. Wis., 1973; adj. prof. U. Tex., Austin, 1974—; Arthur D. Little lectr. M.I.T., 1978. Served with AUS, 1960-62. Ramsay Meml. fellow, 1964-66, Alfred P. Sloan fellow, 1970-72; recipient ann. award Internat. Acad. Quantum Molecular Sci., 1968, Landau prize, 1972; Israel prize in Exact Scis., 1974; Weizmann prize, 1979. Mem. Israel Chem. Soc. (chmn. div. chem. physics and theoretical chemistry), Am. Phys. Soc. Author: Quantum Mechanics of Molecular Rate Processes, 1969; Molecular Reaction Dynamics, 1974. Mem. editorial bds. several well known scientific jours. Contbr. articles to profl. jours. Home: 18 Shahar St Jerusalem Israel Office: Room 6-227 Mass Inst Tech Cambridge MA 02139

LEVINE, ROBERT, chemist, educator; b. Boston, July 30, 1919; s. Louis Harry and Sarah (Heller) L.; B.A., Dartmouth, 1940, M.A., 1942; Ph.D., Duke, 1945; m. Dorothy Clair Meltzer, Aug. 6, 1950; children—Ruth Marcia, Barbara Susan, David Joel. Chemist, Mathieson Chem. Corp., Niagara Falls, N.Y., 1945-46; from instr. to asso. prof. chemistry U. Pitts., 1946-59, prof. chemistry, 1959—; cons. to industry; editor-at-large Marcel Dekker, book publishers. Bd. dirs. Hebrew Inst. Pitts., Community Day Sch., Pitts. Mem. Am. Chem. Soc., AAUP, Pitts. Chemists Club, N.Y. Acad. Scis., Sigma Xi, Phi Lambda Upsilon. Jewish. Club: B'nai B'rith (pres. lodge). Editorial bd. Jour. Heterocyclic Chemistry. Contbr. numerous articles to profl. jours. Home: 5734 Woodmont St Pittsburgh PA 15217

LEVINE, ROBERT ARTHUR, economist, policy analyst; b. Bklyn., July 7, 1930; s. Isaac Bert and Jessie Sue (Palevsky) L.; B.A., Harvard U., 1950, M.A., 1951; Ph.D., Yale U., 1957; m. Esther Carol Knudsen, Mar. 2, 1953; children—David Knudsen, Peter Kemmerer, Joseph Karl. Economist, Rand Corp., 1957-61, sr. economist, 1962-65, 69-73; research asso. Harvard U. Center Internat. Affairs, 1961-62; asst. dir. for research, plans, programs and evaluation OEO, Washington, 1966-69; pres. N.Y.C.-Rand Inst., 1973-75; dep. dir. Congl. Budget Office, Washington, 1975-79; v.p. System Devel. Corp., Santa Monica, Calif., 1979—; sr. fellow Nat. Security Studies Program, UCLA, 1964-65; vis. prof. public policy Stanford U. Grad. Sch. Bus., 1972. Served with USN, 1951-54. Ford Found. grantee, 1969; German Marshall Fund grantee, 1979. Mem. Am. Econ. Assn., Inst. Strategic Studies. Clubs: Fed. City, Beverly Glen Democratic. Author: The Arms Debate, 1963; The Poor Ye Need Not Have With You, 1971; Public Plann.ng: Failure and Redirection, 1972. Home: 10321 Chrysanthemum Ln Los Angeles CA 90024 Office: System Devel Corp 2500 Colorado Ave Santa Monica CA 90406

LEVINE, ROBERT JOHN, physician, educator; b. N.Y.C., Dec. 29, 1934; s. Benjamin Bernard and Ruth Florence (Schwartz) L.; student Duke, 1951-54; M.D. with distinction, George Washington U., 1958; children—John Graham, Elizabeth Hurt. Med. house officer Peter Bent Brigham Hosp., Boston, 1958-59, asst. resident medicine, 1959-60; clin. asso. Nat. Heart Inst., Bethesda, Md., 1960-62, investigator, 1963-64; chief med. resident VA Hosp., West Haven, Conn., 1962-63, clin. investigator, 1964-66, attending physician, 1966—; instr. medicine Yale, 1962-63, instr. medicine and pharmacology, 1964-65, asst. prof. medicine and pharmacology, 1965-68, chief sect. clin. pharmacology, 1966-74, asso. prof., 1968-73, prof. medicine, lectr. pharmacology, 1973—, dir. physician's asso. program, 1973-75, clin. asst. medicine Yale-New Haven Med. Center, 1964-65, asst. attending physician, 1965-68, attending physician, 1968—; mem. Conn. Adv. Com. on Foods and Drugs, 1967—, sec., 1969-71, chmn., 1971-73; mem. com. myocardial infarction Nat. Heart and Lung Inst., 1969-72, mem. lipid metabolism adv. com., 1977-79; mem. blue ribbon panel on behavior modification drugs for sch. age children HEW, 1971; mem. div. med. scis. NRC, 1971-74; mem. rev. com. drug abuse research center NIMH, 1972; cons. Nat. Commn. for Protection of Human Subjects of Biomed. and Behavioral Research, 1974-78; chmn. award com. Nellie Westerman prize for Research in Ethics, 1975-79. Bd. dirs. Medicine in the Pub. Interest, Inc., 1976—. Served with USPHS, 1960-64. Multiple Research grantee. Fellow A.C.P., Am. Coll. Cardiology, Hastings Center Inst. of Soc., Ethics and Life Scis.; mem. Am. Soc. Clin. Investigation, Am. Soc. Clin. Pharmacology and Therapeutics, Am. Fedn. Clin. Research (nat. council 1967-76, exec. com. 1971-76), Am. Soc. Pharmacology and Exptl. Therapeutics (exec. com. 1974-77), AAAS, Histamine Club, Sigma Xi, Alpha Omega Alpha. Hon. adv. editorial bd. Biochem. Pharmacology, 1968—, asso. editor, 1969-74; editor Clin. Research, 1971-76; editorial bd. Internat. Ency. Pharmacology and Therapeutics, 1974—, Forum on Medicine, 1977—; editor IRB: A Review of Human Subjects Research, 1978—; editorial adv. bd. Jour. Family Practice, 1975—. Contbr. numerous articles to profl. jours. Home: 23 Eld St New Haven CT 06511 Office: Sch Medicine Yale U 333 Cedar St New Haven CT 06510

LEVINE, ROBERT SIDNEY, chem. engr.; b. Des Moines, June 4, 1921; s. George Julius and Betty (Dennen) L.; B.S. in Chem. Engring., Iowa State U., 1943; S.M. (Standard Oil Co. Ohio fellow 1947-48), M.I.T., 1946, Sc.D., 1949; m. Sharon Lorraine White; children—George, Gail, Tamara, Michelle, James. With Rocketdyne div. Rockwell Internat. Co., 1948-66; asso. research dir. NASA, 1966-74; chief liquid rocket tech. Nat. Bur. Standards, 1974—, chief fire sci. div. Center Fire Research, 1975—; mem. faculty UCLA, 1970-74, George Washington U., 1977; pres. Combustion Inst., 1974-78. Named Engr. of Year, Los Angeles sect. Am. Inst. Chem. Engrs., 1961. Mem. Am. Chem. Soc., AIAA, Nat. Fire Prevention Assn. Author papers in field. Home: 19017 Threshing Pl Gaithersburg MD 20760 Office: Nat Bur Standards Washington DC 20234

LEVINE, RUTH ROTHENBERG, educator; b. N.Y.C.; d. Jacob and Jeannette (Bandel) Rothenberg; B.A. magna cum laude, Hunter Coll., 1938; M.A., Columbia, 1939; Ph.D., Tufts U., 1955; m. Martin J. Levine, June 21, 1953. Asst. prof. Tufts U. Sch. Medicine, 1955-58; asst. prof. pharmacology Sch. Medicine, Boston U., 1958-61, asso. prof., 1961-65, prof., 1965—, univ. prof., 1972—, chmn. div. med. and dental scis. Grad. Sch., 1964—; mem. sci. adv. bd. U.S. EPA. Fellow AAAS; mem. Am. Soc. Pharmacology and Exptl. Therapeutics (sec.-treas. 1975-76), Biophys. Soc., Am. Chem. Soc., Am. Pharm. Assn., Acad. Scis., Phi Beta Kappa, Sigma Xi. Home: 212 Crafts Rd Chestnut Hill MA 02167 Office: Boston U Div Med and Dental Scis Boston MA 02118

LEVINE, SAMUEL GALE, educator; b. Malden, Mass., Nov. 1, 1928; s. Hyman Michael and Anna (Plotnick) L.; B.S., Tufts U., 1950; Ph.D., Harvard, 1954; m. Pearl Zelda Halperin, June 21, 1953; children—Cynthia, Amy, Beth, Kenneth. With Research Lab., U.S. Dept. Agr., Phila., 1956-60; with Natural Products Lab., Research Triangle Inst., Durham, N.C., 1960-64, cons., 1964—; mem. faculty N.C. State U., Raleigh, 1964—, prof. chemistry, 1967—. Served with AUS, 1954-56. Weizmann Sr. Postdoctoral fellow, 1971. Mem. Am. Chem. Soc., Phi Beta Kappa, Sigma Xi. Democrat. Jewish. Research in chemistry of natural products, especially steroids, conformational effects in cyclic and spirocyclic systems. Home: 1609 Ward St Durham NC 27707

LEVINE, SANFORD NORMAN, housing prodn. co. exec.; b. Chgo., Jan. 26, 1932; s. John and Celia (Rosenberg) L.; student Purdue U., 1950-51; B.S. in Mech. Engring., Wayne State U., 1956; m. Marsha Nancy Glass, Feb. 5, 1956. Program mgr. RCA, Van Nuys, Calif., 1956-62, 63-66; program mgr. Northrop Corp., Newbury Park, Calif., 1962-63; corp. v.p. Kaufman & Broad, Inc., Los Angeles, 1966-69, sr. v.p., 1969—, dir., 1977—; pres., dir. subsidiary co. Nation-Wide Cablevision, Inc., 1966-72; chmn., chief exec. officer Kaufman & Broad Home Systems, Inc., Los Angeles, 1973—. Served with USAF, 1951-52. Home: 809 S Bundy Dr Los Angeles CA 90049 Office: 10801 National Blvd Los Angeles CA 90064

LEVINE, SAUL, govt. ofcl.; b. Passaic, N.J., July 1, 1923; s. Abraham and Bella (Ellis) L.; B.S., U.S. Naval Acad., 1945; B.S. in Electronics, Mass. Inst. Tech., 1949; M.S. in Nuclear Engring., 1955; m. Sylvia Cynthia, June 6, 1945; children—Judith Barbara, David Paul, Robert Alter, Michael Hirsch. Commd. ensign U.S. Navy, 1945; submarine service, 1946-53; project officer U.S. Naval Reactors in charge nuclear power plant for U.S.S. Enterprise, 1955-58; chief system design sect. nav. br. Spl. Projects Office for Polaris missile system, 1958-62; ret., 1962; asst. dir. reactor tech. reactor licensing div. AEC, 1962-70, asst. dir. Office Environ. Affairs, Washington, 1970-73, project staff dir. reactor safety study, 1972-75, dep. dir. div. reactor safety research, 1973-75; dep. dir. Nuclear Regulatory Commn., Office of Nuclear Regulatory Research, 1975, dir., 1976—; lectr. nuclear safety Mass. Inst. Tech., summers, 1967—; U.S. AEC del. to UN Conf. on Environ., Stockholm, 1972; vice chmn. Com. on Safety of Nuclear Installations, OECD, 1977—. Recipient Disting. Service award AEC, 1975. Mem. Am. Nuclear Soc. Home: 9910 Fernwood Rd Bethesda MD 20034 Office: Office Nuclear Regulatory Research 1717 H St NW Washington DC 20555

LEVINE, SOL, sociologist, educator; b. Greenwood, Miss., Apr. 3, 1922; s. Samuel and Gussie (Kozlove) L.; B.A., Queens Coll., 1942; M.A., N.Y. U., 1948, Ph.D., 1953; m. Alice S. Gordon, July 15, 1963; children—Andrea, Pamela, Joshua. Instr. sociology Univ. Heights Coll., N.Y. U., 1951-53; asso. Sch. Pub. Health, Harvard, 1956-57, asst. prof., 1957-61, asso. prof., 1961-63, dir. social sci. program, 1963-66; prof., dir. div. behavioral scis. Johns Hopkins U., Balt., 1966-67, prof. social relations, 1966-72, prof. behavioral scis., 1966-72, chmn. dept. behavioral scis., 1967-72; dir. univ. profs. program Boston U., 1973-76, univ. prof. sociology and community medicine, 1973—, chmn. dept. sociology, 1976-79; cons. in field. Served with U.S. Army, 1942-45. Mem. Am. Pub. Health Assn., Am. Sociol. Assn. (chmn. med. sociology sect. 1968-69), Eastern Sociol. Assn., Soc. for Study of Social Problems, Inst. Medicine-Nat. Acad. Scis. Author: (with Odin Anderson and Gerald Gordon) Non-Group Enrollment for Health Insurance, 1957; (with Sydney H. Croog) The Heart Patient Recovers, 1978; editor: (with Howard Freeman and Leo Reeder) Handbook of Medical Sociology, 1963; (with others) The Dying Patient, 1970; (with Norman Scotch) Social Stress, 1970; (with Howard Freeman and Leo Reeder) Handbook of Medical Sociology, 2d edit., 1972, 3d edit., 1978. Home: 43 Salisbury Rd Brookline MA 02146 Office: 745 Commonwealth Ave Boston MA 02215

LEVINE, STUART GEORGE, educator; b. N.Y.C., May 25, 1932; s. Max and Jean (Berens) L.; A.B., Harvard U., 1954, M.A., Brown U., 1956, Ph.D., 1958; m. Susan F. Matthews, June 6, 1962; children—Rebecca, Aaron, Allen. Teaching fellow Brown U., 1956-57; instr. in English, U. Kans., Lawrence, 1958-61, asst. prof., 1961-64, asso. prof. Am. studies, 1964-66, prof., 1966—, founder, chmn. dept. Am. Studies, 1963-70; vis. prof. various univs.; Fulbright prof. U. La Plata (Argentina), 1962, U. Costa Rica, 1965, 67, Nat. Autonomous U. Mexico, 1972; scholar in residence U. Ariz., 1972-73; profl. concert musician, 1955-58, 73—; dir. Nat. Endowment Humanities Summer Seminar for Coll. Tchrs., 1978, also cons. panels. Regional chmn. Harvard Coll. Fund. Recipient Anisfield Wolf award (with others) Saturday Rev., 1968, citation NCCJ, 1969. Mem. Am. Studies Assn. (exec. com. nat. meeting 1965-66, publs. com. nat. meeting 1965-66), Midcontinent Am. Studies Assn. (exec. and editorial bds. 1960—), MLA, Am. Fedn. Musicians. Editor-in-chief: American Studies, 1960—. (With Susan F. Levine) The Short Fiction of Edgar Poe: An Annotated Edition, 1976; author: (with N. O. Lurie) The American Indian Today, 1968, Caffin's The Story of American Painting, 1970; Edgar Poe, Seer, and Craftsman, 1972. Home: 1846 Barker Ave Lawrence KS 66044. *When pressed to do what is right and really should be done, surprising number of Americans will, even with sacrifice. I see now that I have been allowed to do whatever useful things I have, because people who are supposed to be cynical—publishers, administrators, officials—did, in fact, respond idealistically when shown the values involved and the good to be done. Such behavior seems a key to national culture (my specialty); I read our history largely as the application of certain values to ever broader areas, and see our discontents as healthy signs that our standards keep getting higher.*

LEVINE, SUMNER NORTON, indsl. and materials engr., educator; b. Boston, Sept. 5, 1923; s. Frank and Lillian (Gold) L.; B.S., Brown U., 1946; Ph.D., U. Wis., 1949; postgrad. Mass. Inst. Tech., 1956; m. Caroline Gassner, Nov. 27, 1952; 1 dau., Joanne. Instr., U. Chgo., 1949-50; sr. research fellow Columbia, 1950-54; dir. research labs. VA, East Orange, N.J., 1954-56; adv. scientist comml. atom power div. Westinghouse Electric Co., Pitts., 1956; dir. chemistry Metallurgy and Materials Labs., also staff adv. engr. Gen. Engring. Labs., Am. Machine & Foundry Co., Greenwich, Conn., 1956-58; sect. head, materials and advanced electronic devices RCA, 1958-61; chmn. materials scis. dept., prof. engring. State U. N.Y. at Stony Brook, 1961—, also prof. and dir. grad. program in indsl. adminstrn.; dir. urban research, vis. prof. City U. N.Y. Grad. Center, 1967-68; Danforth vis. lectr., 1968-69; vis. prof. Yale Sch. Orgn. and Mgmt., 1976; prof. fin. Coll. Urban and Policy Scis., SUNY at Stony Brook, 1978—; cons. to industry. Recipient award for distinguished contbn. to biomed. materials research, 1973. Mem. I.E.E.E., Am. Chem. Soc., Am. Soc. Metals, Electrochem. Soc., Operations Research Soc. Am., Inst. Mgmt. Scis., Fgn. Policy Assn., N.Y. Acad. Scis. (chmn. conf. materials in biomed. engring. 1966, chmn. colloquia socioecon. planning 1966-68), Am. Soc. for Artificial Internal Organs, Soc. for Biomaterials (dir. 1974-76), N.Y. Soc. Security Analysts, Mus. Modern Art, Met. Mus. of Art, Sigma Xi. Author textbooks, profl. articles. Editor: Financial Analysts Handbook, 1975; Investment Manager's Handbook; Business Almanac, 1976, 77, 78, 79, 80; editor-in-chief Jour. Biomed. Materials Research, 1966-78, Jour. Socio-Economic Planning Scis., 1966; Advances in Biomed. Engring. and Med. Physics, 1966; editorial adviser Ocean Engring. Office: State Univ New York Long Island Center Stony Brook NY 11790

LEVINE, SUZANNE BRAUN, mag. editor; b. N.Y.C., June 21, 1941; d. Imre and Esther (Bernson) Braun; B.A. with honors, Radcliffe Coll., 1963; m. Robert F. Levine, Apr. 2, 1967. Reporter, Seattle mag., 1963-65; reporter, researcher Time/Life Books, N.Y.C., 1965-67; features editor Mademoiselle, N.Y.C., 1967-68, McCalls mag., N.Y.C., 1968-69; free lance writer, 1970; mng. editor Sexual Behavior mag., 1971-72, MS. mag., N.Y.C., 1972—. Bd. dirs. Women's Action Alliance. Mem. Am. Soc. Mag. Editors (exec. com.), Women's Media Group (exec. com.). Co-editor: The Decade of Women, 1980. Office: 370 Lexington Ave New York NY 10017

LEVINGER, JOSEPH SOLOMON, physicist, educator; b. N.Y.C., Nov. 14, 1921; s. Lee J. and Elma (Ehrlich) L.; B.S., U. Chgo., 1941, M.S., 1944; Ph.D., Cornell U., 1948; m. Gloria Edwards, Aug. 14, 1943; children—Sam, Laurie, Louis, Joe. Physicist, Metall. Lab., U. Chgo., 1942-44, Franklin Inst., Phila., 1945; instr. Cornell U., 1948-51, vis. prof., 1961-64; from asst. prof. to prof. La. State U., 1951-61; prof. physics Rensselaer Poly. Inst., 1964—; Fulbright fellow, asso. prof. U. Paris—Sud, 1972-73. Guggenheim fellow, 1957-58. Fellow Am. Phys. Soc. Author: Nuclear Photo-disintegration, 1961; Secrets of the Nucleus, 1967; The Two and Three Body Problem, 1974. Home: Red Mill Rd Rensselaer NY 12144 Office: Physics Dept Rensselaer Poly Inst Troy NY 12181

LEVINS, RICHARD, educator; b. N.Y.C., June 1, 1930; s. Ruben and Ruth (Sackman) L.; A.B., Cornell, 1951; Ph.D., Columbia, 1965; m. Rosario Morales, June 10, 1950; children—Aurora, Ricardo, Alejandro. Farmer, P.R., 1951-56; research asso. U. Rochester (N.Y.), 1960-61; asso. prof. biology U. P.R., 1961-66; asso. prof. biology and math. biology U. Chgo., 1967-68, prof., 1969-75; John Rock prof. population sci. Harvard Sch. Pub. Health, 1975—; vis. lectr. univs. Yale, Havana, Utah, Hanoi. Mem. sci. adv. council natural resources P.R. Dept. Pub. Works, 1970-72. Coffee region organizer P.R. Communist party, 1952-54; mem. Partido Socialista Puertorriqueño. Mem. Sci. for the People, Am. Acad. Arts and Sci., Sci. for Vietnam. Author: Evolution in Changing Environments, 1968. Editorial bd. La Escalera, 1965—, Am. Naturalist, 1968-71, Theoretical Population Biology, 1970—. Home: 107 Amory St Cambridge MA 02139. *Understand the world in order to change it, and in changing it get to understand it better.*

LEVINSKY, NORMAN GEORGE, physician, educator; b. Boston, Apr. 27, 1929; s. Harry and Gertrude (Kipperman) L.; A.B. summa cum laude, Harvard U., 1950, M.D. cum laude, 1954; m. Elena Sartori, June 17, 1956; children—Harold, Andrew, Nancy. Intern, Beth Israel Hosp., Boston, 1954-55, resident, 1955-56; commd. med. officer USPHS. 1956; clin. asso. Nat. Heart Inst., Bethesda, Md., 1956-58; NIH fellow Boston U. Med. Center, 1958-60; practice medicine, specializing in internal medicine and nephrology, Boston, 1960—; chief of medicine Boston City Hosp., 1968-72; physician-in-chief, dir. Evans dept. clin. research Univ. Hosp., Boston, 1972—; asst. prof., asso. prof. medicine Boston U., 1960-68, Wesselhoeft prof., 1968-72, Wade prof. medicine, 1972—. Mem. drug efficacy panel NRC. Diplomate Am. Bd. Internal Medicine, mem. nephrology test com., 1971-76. Mem. Am. Fedn. for Clin. Research, Am. Soc. for Clin. Investigation, Assn. Am. Physicians, Am. Physiol. Soc., Am. Soc. Nephrology, Phi Beta Kappa, Alpha Omega Alpha. Club: Interurban. Editor: (with R.W. Wilkins) Medicine: Essentials of Clinical Practice, 1978. Contbr. chpts. to books, sci. articles to med. jours. Home: 20 Kenwood Ave Newton MA 02159 Office: 75 E Newton St Boston MA 02118

LEVINSON, AARON PHILLIP, steel co. exec.; b. Pitts., Nov. 20, 1914; s. Samuel M. and Rose (Reuben) L.; student U. Pitts., 1932-33, Carnegie-Mellon Inst., 1934-35, Duquesne U., 1937-39; Harvard, 1956; LL.D., Point Park Coll., 1978; m. Sonia Zaludkowski, Aug. 28, 1938; children—F. James, Eleanor (Mrs. Jeffrey Scott Peris). Constrn. worker Rust Engring. Co., Washington, 1933; with Levinson Steel Co., Pitts., 1934—, gen. sales mgr., 1941-46, exec. v.p., 1946-50, pres., 1950-75, chmn. bd., 1975—; past pres. Levco Automotive Products Co.; dir. Autoclave Engrs., Inc., Erie, Pa., JML Trading Corp., N.Y.C., Auxier-Scott Supply Co., Okla. Conducted seminar for Alliance for Progress, AID, Venezuela, 1962. Bd. dirs., past chmn. bd. Housing Authority Pitts.; past pres. Pitts. chpt. Steel Service Center Inst.; past chmn., now mem. met. adv. bd. Anti-Defamation League; bd. dirs. United Jewish Fedn.; bd. dirs. Western Pa. Safety Council, Duquesne U., Pitts. Council for Internat. Visitors, Pitts. History and Landmarks Found., Urban League, Pitts. Jewish Community Center, Pitts. Pub. Theater; chmn. South Side Hosp., Montefiore Hosp.; past bd. dirs. Pa. Assn. for Blind, United Fund, Vocat. Rehab. Center, Pitts. chpt. Am. Jewish Com., Hosp. Planning Assn. Pitts., Point Park Coll., Sta. WQED; life mem., past dir. NAACP; bd. dirs., past pres. Am. Technion Soc.; life trustee, v.p. James & Rachel Levinson Found.; mem. adv. bd. Home for Crippled Children, Hillel Acad. Named One of Pitts. Hundred Leaders of Tomorrow, Time mag., 1953; recipient Herbert Lehman award, Emanual Specter award; Brotherhood award NCCJ, 1976; Albert Einstein award Am. Technion Soc., 1979. Mem. Am. Inst. Steel Constrn., Am. Mgmt. Assn., Pres.'s Assn., Chief Execs. Forum, Engrs. Soc. Western Pa., Pitts. C. of C., Steel Service Center Inst. Democrat. Jewish. Mem. B'nai B'rith (past pres. Pitts. chpt.). Clubs: Allegheny, Standard, Concordia, Pitts. Athletic Assn., Pittsburgh Press. Home: 5438 Forbes Ave Pittsburgh PA 15217 Office: PO Box 1617 Pittsburgh PA 15230. *Success to me is achieving one's full potential by living honestly, unselfishly and with convictions. These are some of the principles for which I strive: excellence in every undertaking; to know the true meaning of friendship; to respect the dignity of each individual; to know my own strengths and limitations; to be able to face my problems and to deal with them forcefully, no matter how difficult or how painful; to have firm convicions and yet to keep an open mind to ideas which may be different from mine.*

LEVINSON, DAVID LESTER, TV producer; b. Chgo., Aug. 4, 1939; s. Sidney O. and Tessie (Solomon) L.; student U. Chgo., 1957; B.Journalism, U. Mo., 1960, M.A., 1961; m. Marlene Asher, Nov. 2, 1961; children—Sidney, Melissa, Amy. With Universal Studios, Universal City, Cal., 1962—; producer The Bold Ones, 1972; pilot devel., 1973; co-producer TV series Charlie's Angels. Recipient Emmy for best series The Senator, 1970-71. Mem. Writers' Guild of Am., West. Democrat. Jewish. Office: Universal Studios Universal City CA 91608*

LEVINSON, HARRY, psychologist, educator; b. Port Jervis, N.Y., Jan. 16, 1922; s. David and Gussie (Nudell) L.; B.S., Kans. State Tchrs. Coll., 1943, M.S., 1946; Ph.D., U. Kans., 1952; m. Roberta Freiman, Jan. 11, 1946 (div. June 1972); children—Marc Richard,

Kathy, Anne, Brian Thomas. Coordinator profl. edn. Topeka State Hosp., 1950-53, psychologist, 1954-55; dir. div. indsl. mental health Menninger Found., Topeka, 1955-68; Thomas Henry Carroll-Ford Found. distinguished vis. prof. Harvard Grad. Sch. Bus., Boston, 1968-72; adj. prof. Coll. Bus. Administrn., Boston U., 1972-74; lectr. Harvard Med. Sch., 1972—; adj. prof. Pace U., 1972—; mem. Am. Bd. Profl. Psychology, 1972—, chmn., 1978—. Pres., Levinson Inst.; chmn. Kans. adv. com. U.S. Civil Rights Commn., 1962-68; chmn. Topeka Human Relations Commn., 1967-68. Served with F.A., AUS, 1944-46. Recipient Distinguished Alumnus award Kans. State Tchrs. Coll., 1968. Fellow Am. Psychol. Assn.; mem. A.A.A.S., Am. Sociol. Assn., Indsl. Relations Research Assn. Author: Emotional Health In the World of Work, 1964; Executive Stress, 1970; The Exceptional Executive (McKinsey Found. and Acad. Mgmt. awards, James A. Hamilton Hosp. Adminstrs. Book award), 1968; Organizational Diagnosis, 1971; The Great Jackass Fallacy, 1973. Home: 225 Brattle St Cambridge MA 02138

LEVINSON, LAWRENCE EDWARD, corp. exec., lawyer; b. N.Y.C., Aug. 25, 1930; s. Samuel Keever and Sara Lee (Tarvin) L.; B.A. magna cum laude, Syracuse U., 1952; LL.B., Harvard U., 1955; m. Fredrica Helene Sideman, Aug. 30, 1959; children—Elizabeth, Suzanne. Admitted to N.Y. bar, 1957; atty. Office Sec. Air Force, Washington, 1957-63; spl. assignments Office Sec. Def., Washington, 1963-65; dep. counsel to Pres. U.S., Washington, 1965-69; sr. v.p. Gulf & Western Industries, N.Y.C., 1969—; dir. Famous Players Canadien Corp., Paramount Pictures Corp. Mem. Nat. Council on Health Planning and Devel., Washington, 1978—. Served with Judge Adv. Div., U.S. Army, 1955-57. Mem. Phi Beta Kappa. Home: 531 Emerson Teaneck NJ 07666 Office: Gulf & Western Industries One Gulf & Western Plaza New York NY 10023

LEVINSON, RICHARD LEIGHTON, writer, producer; b. Phila., Aug. 7, 1934; s. William and Georgia Francis (Harbert) L.; B.S. in Econs., U. Pa., 1956; m. Rosanna Huffman, Apr. 20, 1968; 1 dau., Christine Leighton. Free-lance TV writer, 1959-66; author: (play) (with William Link) Prescription: Murder, 1962; (novel) (with William Link) Fineman, 1972; writer-producer Universal Studios, Universal City, Calif., 1966-77; co-pres. Richard Levinson/William Link Prodns., Los Angeles, 1978—; chmn. playwrights com. Actors' Studio West, 1965-68. Served with U.S. Army, 1957-58. Recipient Image award NAACP, 1970, Golden Globe award Hollywood Fgn. Press Assn., 1972, George Foster Peabody award, 1974, Edgar Alan Poe award Mystery Writers Am., 1979. Mem. Acad. TV Art and Scis. (Emmy award 1970, 72), Caucus for Writers, Producers and Dirs. (steering com. 1976-77), Writers Guild Am. (award 1972). Author numerous short stories, TV and film scripts, book revs. Home and Office: 215 S Cliffwood Ave Los Angeles CA 90049

LEVINSON, ROBERT ALAN, textile co. exec.; b. Balt., July 25, 1925; s. Louis and Frieda (Kellert) L.; A.B., Dartmouth U., 1946; M.B.A., Amos Tuck Sch. Bus. Adminstrn., 1946; postgrad. London Sch. Econs., 1946-47; m. Patricia S. Schulte, Apr. 23, 1954; children—Margot, Andrew, John. With Burlington Industries, N.Y.C., 1949-51; v.p., dir. Bangor Punta, Inc., N.Y.C., 1964-68; chmn. bd. Duplan Corp., N.Y.C., 1968—; dir. Sheldon Petroleum Co., Peabody Galion Corp. Chmn. Bklyn. Mus.; trustee Jewish Family Service, N.Y.C. Served with USNR, 1943-45, 52-54. Home: 1035 Fifth Ave New York City NY 10028 Office: 1430 Broadway New York City NY 10018

LEVINTHAL, ELLIOTT CHARLES, physicist; b. Bklyn., Apr. 13, 1922; s. Fred and Rose (Raiben) L.; B.A., Columbia Coll., 1942; M.S., Mass. Inst. Tech., 1943; Ph.D., Stanford U., 1949; m. Rhoda Arons, June 4, 1944; children—David, Judith, Michael, Daniel. Project engr. Sperry Gyroscope Co., N.Y.C., 1943-46; research asso. nuclear physics Stanford U., 1946-48; research physicist Varian Assos., Palo Alto, Calif., 1949-50, research dir., bd. dirs., 1950-52; chief engr. Century Electronics, Palo Alto, 1952-53; pres. Levinthal Electronics, Palo Alto, 1953-61; sr. scientist, dir. Instrumentation Research Lab., dept. genetics Stanford U. Sch. Medicine, 1961-74, asso. dean for research affairs, 1970-73, adj. prof. genetics, 1974—, dir. Instrumentation Research Lab., 1974—; bd. dirs. Diasonics, Inc., Palo Alto; cons. NASA, HEW. Recipient NASA Pub. Service medal, 1977. Mem. AAAS, Am. Phys. Soc., IEEE, Optical Soc. Am., Biomedical Engrng. Soc., Sigma Xi. Democrat. Jewish. Home: 59 Sutherland Dr Atherton CA 94025 Office: Dept Genetics Stanford U Med Sch Stanford CA 94305

LEVINTHAL, ISRAEL HERBERT, rabbi; b. Vilna, Russia, Feb. 12, 1888; s. Rabbi Bernard L. and Minna (Kleinberg) L.; A.B., Columbia, 1908, M.A., 1910; Rabbi, Jewish Theol. Sem. of Am., 1910, D.H.L., 1920, D.D. (hon.), 1940; J.D., N.Y.U., 1914; D.J.T. (hon.) Jewish Inst. of Religion, 1948; m. May R. Bogdanoff, Aug. 12, 1908; children—Helen Hadassah Lyons, Lazar E. Rabbi Temple B'nai Sholom, Bklyn., 1910-15, Temple Petach Tikvah, Bklyn., 1915-19, Bklyn. Jewish Center, 1919—. Founder and dir. Inst. Jewish Studies for Adults. Mem. adv. com. burial survey Met. Life Ins. Co., 1926-28. Lectr. in homiletics Jewish Theol. Sem., 1937-38, vis. prof. homiletics, 1948-62; mem. adv. council Jewish Information Bur.; mem. exec. council United Synagogue of Am.; hon. chmn. Bklyn. region Zionist Orgn. of Am.; trustee Israel Matz Found. for Hebrew Writers; chmn. bd. sponsors Hadoar (Hebrew weekly); mem. N.Y. Bd. of Jewish Ministers; nat. chmn. Jerusalem Synagogue Center Campaign, 1928-30; nat. chmn. Com. for Advancement of Hebrew Culture; mem. council Jewish Agy. for Palestine, 1929-33; mem. Brooklyn Citizen's Com. for Racial and Religious Amity; pres. Bklyn. Jewish Community Council, 1940-44, hon. pres., 1944—; bd. dirs. Bklyn. chpt. A.R.C. Del. of United Synagogue of Am., N.Y. Bd. of Jewish Ministers and Bklyn. Jewish Center, at dedication of Hebrew U. in Jerusalem. Mem. exec. com. Bklyn. Tb and Health Assn. of Bklyn. Bur. of Charities. Mem. Am. Schs. of Oriental Research, Jewish Acad. of Arts and Scis., Am. Acad. Jewish Research, Rabbinical Assembly of Am. (pres. 1930-32), Bklyn. Jewish Ministers Assn. (1st pres. 1929-31). Mem. Joint Prayer Book Commn. of Rabbinical Assembly and United Synagogue of Am. Winner Curtis medal (oratorical), Columbia, 1908. Club: The Judaeans. Author: The Jewish Law of Agency, 1923; Steering or Drifting Which?, 1928. Compiler: Song and Praise for Sabbath Eve (with Israel Goldfarb), 1920; Judaism-An Analysis and an Interpretation, 1935, Yiddish translation 1949; A New World Is Born, 1943; The Hour of Destiny, 1949; Point of View-An Analysis of American Judaism, 1958; Judaism Speaks to the Modern World, 1963; Selected Sermons in Hebrew, 1968; The Message of Israel, 1973. Contbr. articles to Jewish Quarterly Rev., etc. Home: 120 Rose Hill Ave New Rochelle NY 10804 Office: 667 Eastern Pkwy Brooklyn NY 11213

LEVIS, LARRY PATRICK, poet; b. Fresno, Calif., Sept. 30, 1946; s. William Kent and Carol (Mayo) L.; B.A., Fresno State Coll., 1968; M.A., Syracuse (N.Y.) U., 1970; Ph.D., U. Iowa, 1974; m. Marcia Ann Southwick, Mar. 8, 1975; 1 son, Nicholas. Teaching asst. Syracuse U., 1969-70; part-time instr. English, Fresno State Coll., 1970; lectr. Calif. State U., Los Angeles, 1970-72; teaching/writing fellow U. Iowa, 1972-74; asst. prof. English, U. Mo., Columbia, 1974—; field faculty adviser Goddard Coll., Plainfield, Vt., 1973; poet-in-residence Iowa Poets in Schs., 1973; author: Wrecking Crew, 1972; The Afterlife, 1977. Cornelia Carhart Ward fellow, 1968; fellow Nat. Endowment Arts, 1973; summer research grantee U. Mo., 1974, 79; recipient U.S. award Internat. Poetry Forum, 1971; Lamont Poetry prize, 1976. Mem. Acad. Am. Poets, Modern Lang. Assn. Home: 1024 Crestland Ave Columbia MO 65201 Office: English Dept Univ Missouri Columbia MO 65201

LEVISON, ROBERT HENRY, architect; b. Toronto, Ont., Can., Apr. 1, 1915 (parents Am. citizens); s. E. Hartley and Violet Jane Mae (Maxwell) L.; B.S. in Architecture, U. Fla., 1937; m. Roberta Stern Mason, Feb. 11, 1940; children—Barbara Ann (Mrs. Jack R. Stewart), Charles Ronald, Carol Sue (Mrs. Dion G. Dillon). Architect with Roy W. Wakeling, Clearwater, Fla., 1937-39, V.J. Elmore Stores, Inc., Ga., 1939-42; practice in Clearwarter, 1947—; partner firm Wakeling, Levison, Williams & Walker, 1947-71; v.p. Mudano Assos., Architects, Inc., 1971—. Chmn. Clearwater Planning and Zoning Bd., 1948-60, Contractors Exam. Bd., 1948—; pres. Pinellas County United Fund, 1966-67; dist. chmn. Boy Scouts Am., 1957; mem. Clearwater Com. 100; mem. Clearwater Housing Authority, 1969-76, chmn., 1973-78. Served to maj. AUS, 1941-46, to lt. col. Res. ret. Decorated Bronze Star, Purple Heart; recipient Disting. Alumni award U. Fla., 1978. Fellow A.I.A. (pres. Fla. central chpt. 1957-59, Fla. chpt. 1961-63, nat. dir. Fla. region 1963-66; recipient Edward C. Kemper award 1967, Gold Medal award Fla. chpt. 1971, Honor medal Fla. Central chpt. 1974), Clearwater C. of C. (gov.). Episcopalian. Office: 1189 NE Cleveland St Clearwater FL 33515

LEVIT, BERT WILLIAM, lawyer; b. San Francisco, Feb. 16, 1903; s. Morris and Fannie (Jacobs) L.; A.B. magna cum laude, Stanford, 1924, J.D., 1925; m. Thelma Clumeck, May 10, 1928 (dec. 1970); children—Victor Bert, Roger Clumeck; m. 2d, Edith I. Garland, Oct. 4, 1972. Admitted to Calif. bar, 1925; sr. partner firm Long & Levit, San Francisco and Los Angeles, 1927—, gen. counsel, 1977—; lectr. Stanford Law Sch., 1932-45. Spl. asst. to U.S. atty. gen., Washington, 1925-26; chief asst. dist. atty. San Francisco, 1944-45; chief dep. atty. gen. Calif., 1951; dir. finance State of Calif., 1959. Commr. edn. San Francisco pub. schs., 1948-58; charter mem. Calif. Law Revision Com., 1953-58, Calif. Scholarship Com., 1955-58; Calif. del. White House Conf. on Edn., 1955; pres. Calif. Sch. Bds. Assn., 1956-57; chmn. Gov.'s Com. on Calif. Govtl. Reorgn., 1959-60; pub. mem. Calif. Coordinating Council for Higher Edn., 1962-67. Pres. San Francisco br. Am. Cancer Soc., 1968-70, bd. dirs. Calif. div., 1971-74, recipient Pres.'s Gold award, 1978; legal counsel San Francisco Conservatory Music, 1971—, bd. dirs., 1971-77; bd. govs. Internat. Ins. Seminars, 1976—. Fellow Am. Coll. Trial Lawyers; mem. World Assn. Lawyers (founding mem.), Order of Coif, Phi Beta Kappa, Delta Sigma Rho. Clubs: Bankers, San Francisco Comml. Home: 20 Montecito Rd San Rafael CA 94901 Office: 465 California St San Francisco CA 94104

LEVIT, EDITHE JUDITH, physician; b. Wilkes-Barre, Pa., Nov. 29, 1926; B.S. in Biology, Bucknell U., 1946; M.D., Woman's Med. Coll. of Pa., 1951; D.M.S., Med. Coll. Pa., 1978; m. Samuel M. Levit, Mar. 2, 1952; children—Harry M., David B. Grad. asst. in psychology Bucknell U., 1946-47; intern Phila. Gen. Hosp., 1951-52, fellow in endocrinology, 1952-53, clin. instr., asso. in endocrinology, 1953-57, dir. med. edn., 1957-61, cons. med. edn., 1961-65; asst. dir. Nat. Bd. Med. Examiners, Phila., 1961-67, asso. dir., sec. bd., 1967-75, v.p., sec. bd., 1975-77, pres., dir., 1977—; cons. to certifying exam. com. Am. Bd. Internal Medicine, 1964-71, Am. Bd. Neurosurgery, 1964-72; evaluation cons. Given Inst. Pathobiology, 1974-75, Law Sch. Admissions Council, 1974; mem. adv. com. on fgn. med. grads. Inst. Medicine, Nat. Acad. Scis., 1974-76, mem., 1977—; cons. on women in medicine Josiah Macy, Jr. Found., 1976. Bd. dirs. Phila. Gen. Hosp. Found., 1964-70; chmn. profl. adv. com. Phila. Council for Internat. Visitors, 1958-61, bd. dirs., 1966-72, vice chmn. INTERMED adv. com., 1971-74. Recipient award for outstanding contbns. in field of med. edn. Commonwealth Com. of Woman's Med. Coll., 1970; Alumni award Bucknell U., 1978. Master A.C.P.; fellow Coll. Physicians of Phila.; mem. A.M.A., Pa., Phila. County (bd. censors) med. socs., Assn. Am. Med. Colls., AAUW (award to outstanding grad. Woman's Med. Coll. 1951), Alpha Omega Alpha, Phi Sigma. Contbr. articles to profl. jours. Home: 1910 Spruce St Philadelphia PA 19103 Office: 3930 Chestnut St Philadelphia PA 19104

LEVIT, GEORGE E., food mktg. cons.; b. Houston, May 6, 1929; s. Joe and Dora (Freedman) L.; B.B.A. cum laude, U. Tex., 1950; children—Laurie Jean, Cathy Rose, Nancy Ann, Stephen Fredrick. Vice pres. Grocers Supply Co., Inc., Houston, 1950-77, Concept Mktg. Corp., Houston, 1977—. Bd. dirs. Houston Goodwill Industries, Bays Harbor Found., Lighthouse for Blind; trustee Cenikor Found. Home: 2100 Tanglewilde St Apt 459 Houston TX 77063 Office: 2537 S Gessner Houston TX 77063

LEVIT, VICTOR BERT, lawyer, fgn. rep., civic worker; b. Singapore, Apr. 21, 1930 (parents Am. citizens); s. Bert W. and Thelma (Clumeck) L.; A.B. in Polit. Sci. with great distinction, Stanford, 1950, LL.B., 1952; m. Sherry Lynn Chamove, Feb. 25, 1962; children—Carson, Victoria. Admitted to Calif. bar, 1953; mem. firm Long & Levit, San Francisco and Los Angeles, 1953-55, partner, 1955—, mng. partner, 1971—; asso. and gen. legal counsel U.S. Jr. C. of C., 1959-61; legal counsel for consul gen. Ethiopia for San Francisco, 1964-71, hon. consul for Ethiopia, 1971-76; guest lectr. Stanford Law Sch., 1958—, Haile Selassie I Univ. Law Sch., 1972-76. Mem. Los Angeles Consular Corps, 1971-77; mem. San Francisco Consular Corps, 1971-77, vice dean, 1975-76. Grader Calif. Bar Exam., 1956-61; del. San Francisco Municipal Conf., 1955-63, vice chmn., 1960, chmn., 1961-63; campaign chmn. San Francisco Aid Retarded Children, 1960; mem. nat. com. Stanford Law Sch. Fund, 1959—; mem. Mayor's Osaka-San Francisco Affiliation Com., 1959-65, Mayor's Com. for Municipal Mgmt., 1961-64. Pres. San Francisco Young Republicans, 1955; mem. San Francisco Rep. Country Central Com., 1956-63; asso. mem. Calif. Rep. Central Com., 1956-63, 70-72; campaign chmn. San Francisco Assemblyman John Busterud, 1960. Bd. dirs. San Francisco Comml. Club, 1967-70, San Francisco Planning and Urban Renewal Assn., 1959-60, Nat. Found. Infantile Paralysis, 1958, Red Shield Youth Assn., Salvation Army, San Francisco, 1960-70; bd. dirs. NCCJ, San Francisco, 1959—, chmn. No. Calif., 1962-64, 68-70, mem. nat. bd. dirs., 1964-75; bd. dirs. San Francisco Tb and Health Assn., 1962-70, treas., 1964, pres., 1965-67; bd. dirs. San Francisco Assn. Mental Health, 1964-73, pres., 1968-71; mem. com. Nat. Assn. Mental Health, 1969-71; trustee United Bay Area Crusade, 1966-74, Ins. Forum San Francisco; bd. visitors Stanford Law Sch., 1969-75; mem. adv. bd. Jr. League San Francisco, 1971-75. Named Outstanding Young Man San Francisco mng. editors San Francisco newspapers, 1960, One of Five Outstanding Young Men, Calif., 1961. Mem. Am. (chmn. profl. liability com. for sect. gen. practice 1979—), San Francisco (chmn. ins. com. 1962, 73, chmn. charter flight com. 1962-66) bar assns., Consular Law Soc., Am. Arbitration Assn. (arbitrator), World Assn. Lawyers (chmn. parliamentary law com. 1976—), San Francisco Jr. (dir. 1959, pres. 1958), U.S. Jr. (exec. com. 1959-61) chambers commerce, Jr. Chamber Internat. (life, senator), Calif. Scholarship Fedn., U.S. (labor com. 1974-76), San Francisco (dir.) chambers commerce, Phi Beta Kappa, Order of Coif, Pi Sigma Alpha. Clubs: Commercial (dir.) (San Francisco); Commonwealth (quar. chmn.); California Tennis; Tiburon Peninsula; Concordia. Author: Legal Malpractice in California, 1974; Legal Malpractice, 1977. Note editor Stanford Law Rev., 1952-53; legal editor Underwriters' Report, 1963—. Contbr. articles to legal jours. Home: 45 Beach Rd Belvedere CA 94920 Office: 465 California St San Francisco CA 94104

LEVITAN, DAVID M(AURICE), lawyer; b. Tver, Lithuania, Dec. 25, 1915 (parents Am. citizens); B.S., Northwestern U., 1936, M.A., 1937; Ph.D., U. Chgo., 1940; J.D., Columbia U., 1948. Admitted to N.Y. State bar, 1948, U.S. Supreme Ct. bar, 1953; individual practice, N.Y.C., 1948-66; partner firm Hahn, Hessen, Margolis & Ryan, N.Y.C., 1966—; adj. prof. public law Columbia U. Law Sch., 1946-63, John Jay Coll. Criminal Justice, City U. N.Y., 1966-75; adj. prof. polit. sci., Post Coll., 1964-66; adj. prof. law Cardozo Sch. Law, 1978—. Mem. Nassau County (N.Y.) Welfare Bd., 1965-69. Mem. Am. Bar Assn., Am. Polit. Sci. Assn., Am. Soc. Internat. Law, N.Y. State Bar Assn., Assn. Bar City N.Y. Contbr. articles to legal jours. Home: 250 Scudders Ln Roslyn Harbor NY 11576 Office: Hahn Heese et al 350 Fifth Ave New York NY 10001

LEVITAN, SAR A., economist, educator; b. Shiauliai, Lithuania, Sept. 14, 1914; s. Osher N. and Yocheved (Rapoport) L.; came to U.S., 1931, naturalized, 1935; B.S., Coll. City N.Y., 1937; M.A., Columbia, 1939, Ph.D., 1949; m. Brita Ann Buchard, Oct. 15, 1946. Asso. prof. econs. State U. N.Y., Plattsburgh, 1946-51; pub. mem. rev. and appeals Wage Stblzn. Bd., Washington, 1951-53; specialist labor and econ. devel. Congl. Research Service, Library of Congress, 1954-60; dep. dir. Presdl. R.R. Commn., 1961; faculty George Washington U., Washington, 1962-63, 67—, dir. Center Social Policy Studies, research prof. econs., 1962-63, 67—; sr. economist W.E. Upjohn Inst., Washington, 1964-67; cons. in field. Mem. Nat. Council Employment Policy, 1967—, chmn., 1973—; chmn. Nat. Commn. on Employment and Unemployment Statistics, 1977—. Served to capt. AUS, 1942-46. Ford Found. grantee, 1962, 67—. Mem. Am. Econ. Assn., Am. Arbitration Assn. (labor panel), Fed. Mediation and Conciliation Service (labor panel), Indsl. Labor Relations Research Assn., Am. Mgmt. Assn. Author or co-author: Federal Aid to Depressed Areas, 1964; Federal Training and Work Programs in the Sixties, 1969; The Great Society's Poor Law: A New Approach to Poverty, 1969; Blue-Collar Workers, 1970; Big Brother's Indian Programs — With Reservations, 1970; Human Resources and Labor Markets, 1972, 76; Work and Welfare Go Together, 1972; Programs in Aid of the Poor for the 1970's, 1973, 76; Work Is Here to Stay, Alas, 1973; Swords Into Plowshares: Our GI Bill, 1973; Old Wars Remain Unfinished: The Veterans Benefit System, 1973; The Emergency Employment Act: The PEP Generation, 1974; Employment and Earnings Inadequacy, 1974; The Quest for a Federal Manpower Partnership, 1974; Still A Dream: The Changing Status of Blacks Since 1960, 1975; Indian Giving: Federal Programs for Native Americans, 1975; Minorities in the United States, 1975; Child Care and ABCs Too, 1975; The Promise of Greatness, 1976; Too Little But Not Too Late: Federal Aid to Lagging Areas, 1976; The Job Corps, 1976; Jobs for the Disabled, 1977; Shorter Hours, Shorter Weeks: Spreading the Work to Reduce Unemployment, 1977; Warriors at Work: The Volunteer Armed Force, 1977; More than Subsistence: Minimum Wages for the Working Poor, 1979; Evaluating Federal Social Programs: An Uncertain Art, 1979. Office: 2000 K St NW Suite 454 Washington DC 20006

LEVITAS, ELLIOTT H., congressman; b. Atlanta, Dec. 26, 1930; B.A., J.D., Emory U.; M.A. in Law (Rhodes scholar), Oxford (Eng.) U.; postgrad. U. Mich.; m. Barbara Hillman; children—Karen, Susan, Kevin. Admitted to Ga., U.S. Supreme Ct. bars; practice law, Atlanta, 1955—; mem. Ga. Ho. of Reps., 1965-74, chmn. Standing House Com. on Community Affairs, founder, mem. steering com. Caucus on Urban Legislation, chmn. MARTA Watchdog com.; mem. 94th-96th Congresses from 4th Ga. Dist., mem. Pub. Works and Transp. com., Govt. Ops. com.; lectr. law Law Sch., Emory U. Active Emory U. council Boy Scouts Am.; bd. dirs. Atlanta Jewish Community Center, Atlanta Jewish Welfare Fund. Served as lt. USAF, capt. USAF Res. Recipient Ga. Congressional Service award, Key Citizen award Ga. Municipal Assn.; two medals of distinction Am. Security Council; Guardian Small Bus. awards (2) Nat. Fedn. Ind. Bus.; Sam Beber Distinguished A.Z.A. of B'nai Brith Alumnus award, 1977; Watchdog of Treasury award Nat. Assn. Businessmen. Mem. Am., Ga., Atlanta bar assns., DeKalb C. of C., Emory Law Alumni Assn. (past pres.). Clubs: Lawyers, Commerce (Atlanta). Office: 329 Cannon House Office Bldg Washington DC 20515

LEVITINE, GEORGE, educator; b. Kharkoff, Russia, Mar. 17, 1916; s. Joseph J. and Maria (Arlozorof) L.; P.C.B., U. Paris, 1938; M.A., Boston U., 1946; Ph.D. (Edward R. Bacon scholar), Harvard, 1952; m. Eda Mezer, Dec. 2, 1944; children—Elizabeth (Mrs. Michael Bucuvalas), Annette, Denise. Came to U.S., 1942, naturalized, 1943. Instr. to prof. art Boston U. 1949-64; faculty Harvard U. Extension, 1959-64; prof., chmn. art dept. U. Md., College Park, 1964—. Mem. Gov.'s Council of Arts, 1967—; com. mem. Balt. Mus. Art, 1968—. Served with French Army, 1939-41; to 2d lt. AUS, 1942-45. Am. Council Learned Socs. grantee, 1961; Am. Philos. Soc. grantee, 1974, 78; Nat. Endowment for Humanities fellow Inst. for Advanced Study, Princeton, N.J., 1977-78. Mem. Coll. Art Assn., Am. Soc. Aesthetics, Nat. Soc. Lit. and the Arts. Author: The Sculpture of Falconet, 1972; The Dawn of Bohemianism: The "Barbu" Rebellion and Primitivism in Neoclassical France, 1978; Girondet-Trioson: An Iconographical Study, 1978; guest editor Comparative Literature Studies, 1968; rev. editor Art Jour., 1971—; editor-in-chief publs. U. Md. Art Gallery, 1967—. Contbr. articles to profl. jours. Home: 420 Pershing Dr Silver Spring MD 20910 Office: Art Dept U Md College Park MD 20740

LEVITON, ALAN EDWARD, museum curator; b. N.Y.C., Jan. 11, 1930; s. David and Charlotte (Weber) L.; A.B., Stanford, 1949, M.A., 1953, Ph.D., 1960; student Columbia U., summers 1947, 48, 53, N.Y. U., 1948, U. Nebr., 1954; m. Gladys Ann Robertson, June 30, 1952; children—David A., Charlotte A. Asst. curator herpetology Calif. Acad. Scis., San Francisco, 1957-60, asso. curator, 1960-61, chmn., curator, 1962—; asso. curator zool. collections Stanford, 1962-63, lectr. biol. sci., 1963-70; professorial lectr. Golden Gate U., 1953-63; adj. prof. biol. sci. San Francisco State U., 1967—. Am. Philos. Soc. grantee, 1960; NSF grantee, 1960-61, 77-79; Belvedere Sci. Fund grantee, 1958-59, 1962. Fellow Calif. Acad. Scis., AAAS (council 1976—, sec.-treas. Pacific div. 1975—), Explorers Club; mem. Am. Soc. Ichthyologists and Herpetologists (bd. govs. 1960—), Soc. Systematic Zoology (sec.-treas. Pacific sect. 1970-72), Herpetologists League (pres. 1961-62), Aircraft Owners and Pilots Assn., Soc. Vertebrate Paleontologists, Sigma Xi. Author: North American Amphibians and Reptiles, 1972. Contbr. numerous articles to sci., profl. jours. Home: 571 Kingsley Ave Palo Alto CA 94301 Office: Calif Acad Scis Golden Gate Park San Francisco CA 94118

LEVITON, HAROLD I., wiring devices co. exec.; b. Bklyn., Aug. 24, 1917; s. Isidor and Lena (Heymann) L.; B.B.A., U. Miami, 1939; LL.D. (hon.), Beaver Coll., 1979; m. Shirley Isacowitz, Jan. 30, 1941; children—Pat, Adrienne, Elizabeth. With Leviton Mfg. Co., Little Neck, N.Y., 1939—, v.p. purchasing, 1962-65, pres., chief exec. officer, 1965—. Chmn. Bd. Appeals Hewlett Harbor (N.Y.); acting mayor Village of Hewlett Harbor; chmn. bd., pres. United Jewish Y's of Long Island; trustee Bklyn. Jewish Hosp.; asso. trustee L.I. Jewish Hosp. Med. Center; v.p. Five Towns Community Chest; v.p.

Woodmere Acad. Recipient Humanitarian award Albert Einstein Coll. Medicine, 1976; Torch of Liberty award Anti-Defamation League, 1979. Mem. Nat. Elec. Mfrs. Assn. (bd. govs.). Clubs: Woodmere (N.Y.); Unity (Bklyn.). Home: 1312 Club Dr Hewlett Harbor NY 11557 Office: 59-25 Little Neck Pkwy Little Neck NY 11362

LEVITT, AARON LOUIS, home furnishings co. exec.; b. Des Moines, Jan. 4, 1916; s. Thomas I. and Jennie (Davidson) L.; B.A., Cornell U., 1937; m. Louise Gold, Mar. 15, 1949; children—Thomas William, James Nathan, Jean Evelyn. Asst. to furniture buyer Boutell Bros. Inc. subsidiary Davidson Boutell Co., Mpls., 1937-38, mgr. Davidson Boutell furniture dept. in J.C. Penney Co., Omaha, 1938-41, v.p., gen. mgr. Davidsons Furniture Co., Inc., Omaha, 1946-55, v.p. Davidson-Boutell Co. and subsidiary Duff & Repp, Inc., Kansas City, Mo., 1955-58, pres., 1958-66, pres. Duff & Repp, Inc. (Davidson-Boutell and subsidiaries acquired by Am. Nat. Stores 1966), 1966-71, chmn. bd. Duff & Repp, Inc., also v.p. corporate devel. Am. Nat. Stores, Inc., St. Louis, 1969-71; pres., owner Edward Keith, Inc., interior decorating and home furnishings store; dir. Columbia Union Nat. Bank and Trust Co., Kansas City, Mo., First Am. Financial Co., Kansas City, Mo.; dir. Credit Bur. Greater Kansas City, Inc., pres., 1968-69. Cons. Mayo's Home Furnishings, Inc., Scottsdale, Ariz., dir., 1974—. Past chmn. Omaha chpt. A.R.C.; past nat. v.p. fund campaign A.R.C.; past pres. Omaha Jaycees; chmn. Kansas City Pub. Solicitations Commn., 1967-72; bd. dirs., mem. exec. com. Starlight Theatre Assn., v.p., 1977—; mem. Kansas City Sister City Commn., Soc. Fellows Nelson Gallery Found., Civic Council Greater Kansas City; past dir. Greater Kansas City C. of C. Bd. dirs. Greater Kansas City chpt. A.R.C., chmn., 1973; bd. dirs. Memorah Med. Center, Mo. Mansion Preservation, Inc., 1975—, pres., 1976; bd. dirs. U. Mo. at Kansas City Assos., v.p. 1970-71, pres., 1972, trustee, 1971—, vice chmn. for devel., 1975, chmn., 1977—; trustee Kansas City Philharmonic Assn., Midwest Research Inst., Kansas City; bd. adv. trustees Citizens Bond Com., Kansas City; bd. dirs. Rockhurst Coll. Hon. Dir. Assn.; hon. trustee Kansas City Art Inst. Served to maj. AUS, 1941-46; PTO. Decorated Air medal, Bronze Star. Mem. Nat. Home Furnishings Assn. (pres. 1968, dir. 1961—, chmn. 1969—), Am. Royal Assn. (gov.), Mchts. Assn. (bd. dirs. 1975—), Zeta Beta Tau. Jewish. Rotarian. Clubs: River, Kansas City, Carriage, Oakwood Country. Home: 820 W 65th St Kansas City MO 64113 Office: 4646 Belleview Ave Kansas City MO 64112

LEVITT, ARTHUR, JR., banker; b. Bklyn., Feb. 3, 1931; s. Arthur and Dorothy (Wolff) L.; B.A., Williams Coll., 1952; m. Marylin Blauner, June 12, 1955; children—Arthur III, Lauri. Asst. promotion dir. Time, Inc., N.Y.C., 1954-59; v.p., dir. Oppenheimer Industries, Inc., Kansas City, Mo., 1959-61; pres. Shearson Hayden Stone Inc., N.Y.C., 1961-77; trustee East N.Y. Savs. Bank, N.Y.C.; gov. Am. Stock Exchange, chmn., chief exec. officer, 1978—; spl. cons. for edn. Mayor, N.Y.C., 1963-64. Mem. N.Y. State Council Arts, 1968—; del. N.Y. State Constl. Conv., 1967; trustee Community Service Soc.; chmn. bd. Poly Prep Country Day Sch. Served with USAF, 1952-54; maj. Res. Mem. Sierra Club, Phi Beta Kappa, Phi Sigma Kappa. Clubs: Adirondack Mountain, Century Country, India House, Bond, Economic, Century Assn. Office: American Stock Exchange Inc 86 Trinity Pl New York NY 10006

LEVITT, IRVING FRANCIS, business exec.; b. Braddock, Pa., July 3, 1915; s. Charles and Frances (Goretsky) L.; B.S. (hon.) in journalism, U. Mich., 1936; m. Florence Chaikin, Oct. 10, 1937; children—Robert Bruce, Linda Ann (Mrs. Stanley Ehrenpreis). Advt. mgr. feature writer Braddock (Pa.) Free Press, 1936-37; advt. mgr. Levitt Bros. Furniture Stores, 1936-38, partner, exec. adminstr. stores in Braddock, Vandergrift and New Kensington, Pa., 1938-55; exec. asst., v.p. Levinson Steel Co., Pitts., 1942-44; real estate, indsl. devel., 1938—; pres. Lepar, Inc., 1950—; pres., chmn. bd. Union Screw & Mfg. Co., Pitts.; chmn. bd. Investment Capitol Corp., Pitts., 1955—, Radix Orgn., Inc., N.Y.; pres. Kirwan Heights Land Co., King Land Co. (Ind.), Blawnox Realty Co.; chmn. bd. Apollo Industries, Inc., 1959-68; chmn. bd., dir. Apollo Internat. Corp.; pres., dir. Apollo-Peru S.A., Oakland Investment Corp., Pitts.; v.p., dir. Apollo Indsl., Inc., Apollo Investment Co., Pitts.; sr. v.p. Parker-Levitt Corp., Sarasota, Fla., Marble Island, Inc. (Vt.); partner Oliver-Smithfield Venture, Pitts., Nineteen Hundred Group Ltd., Sarasota; dir. Comml. Bank & Trust Co., Pitts. Nuclear Materials & Equipment Corp., Ednl. Audio Visual, Inc., N.Y., London; chmn. bd., dir. Lido Beach Devel. Co., Inc., Sarasota, Fla.; partner Pine Run Devel., Inc., Sarasota, Fla. Mem. Pitts. Bd. Realtors, New Kensington Indsl. Devel. Corp., Smaller Mfrs. Council. Bd. dirs. Massanutten Mil. Acad., Woodstock, Va., United Jewish Fedn. Finance, Pitts., Irene Kaufman Settlement Bd.; trustee Levitt Found. Pitts., Rodef Shalom Temple, Pitts. Mem. Nat. Sales Exec. Club (dir. 1952—), Am. Jewish Com., Chautauqua Soc. Clubs: Westmoreland Country (v.p. 1948—) (Export, Pa.); Marco Polo (N.Y.C.); Standard (dir.), Pitts. Athletic Assn. (Pitts.); Belfry New Century (London). Home: Longboat Key FL 33548 Office: Law and Finance Bldg Pittsburgh PA 15219 also 1900 Main St Sarasota FL 33577

LEVITT, ISRAEL MONROE, astronomer; b. Phila., Dec. 19, 1908; s. Joseph and Jennie (Marriner) L.; B.S. in Mech. Engring., Drexel U., 1932, D.Sc., 1958; A.M., U. Pa., 1937, Ph.D., 1948; D.Sc., Temple U., 1958, Phila. Coll. Pharmacy and Sci., 1963; m. Alice Gross, July 3, 1937; children—Peter Leighton, Nancy Ellen. Astronomer, Fels Planetarium of The Franklin Inst., Phila., 1934-39, asst. asso. dir., 1939-49, dir., 1949-72, v.p. inst., 1970-72; exec. dir. Phila. Mayor's Sci. and Tech. Adv. Council, 1972—; sr. lectr. astronomy U. Pa., 1977; astronomer The Flower Obs., 1946-48. Dir. Sci. Council, 1953—; sci. cons. to City of Phila., 1956-63. Chmn. Air Pollution Control Bd. of Phila., 1965—; bd. dirs. Univ. City Sci. Center, Cardiovascular Inst. of Hahnemann Hosp. Received USN Ordnance Devel. award, 1945; Henry Grier Bryant gold medal Geog. Soc. Phila., 1962; Joseph Priestley award Spring Garden Inst., Phila., 1963; Writing award Aviation/Space Writers Assn., 1965; Samuel S. Fels medal award, 1970. Fellow Brit. Interplanetary Soc., Am. Astron. Soc. (bd. govs., sci. adv. council), Am. Technion Soc.; mem. Am. Inst. Aeros. and Astronautics, Rittenhouse Astron. Soc. (past pres.), A.A.A.S., Aviation Writers Assn., Nat. Assn. Sci. Writers, Pi Tau Sigma. Club: Explorers. Author: Precision Laboratory Manual, 1932; (with Roy K. Marshall) Star Maps for Beginners, 1942; Space Traveler's Guide to Mars, 1956; Target for Tomorrow, 1959; (with Dandridge M. Cole) Exploring The Secrets of Space, 1963; Beyond the Known Universe, 1974; articles in jours., mags. on sci. subjects; author internationally syndicated column for Gen. Features. Inventor oxygen mask, pulse counting photoelectric photometer (with William Blitzstein). Home: 3900 Ford Rd Apt 7-0 Philadelphia PA 19131 Office: 428 City Hall Annex Philadelphia PA 19107

LEVITT, LEROY PAUL, psychiatrist; b. Plymouth, Pa., Jan. 8, 1918; s. Samuel and Paula (Goldstein) L.; B.S., Pa. State U., 1939; M.D., Chgo. Med. Sch., 1943; postgrad. Inst. Psychoanalysis, Chgo., 1950-59; div.; children—Steven C., Susan M., Jeremy W., Sara H.; m. 2d, Jane A. Glaim, Apr. 7, 1971. Intern, Beth David Hosp., N.Y.C., 1943; resident Elgin (Ill.) State Hosp., 1947-49; practice medicine, specializing in psychiatry and psychoanalysis, Chgo., 1949—; prof. psychiatry Chgo. Med. Sch., 1949-76, dean, 1966-73; dir. Ill. Dept. Mental Health, 1973-76; v.p. Mt. Sinai Hosp. Med. Center, Chgo., 1976—; prof. psychiatry Rush Med. Coll., 1976—; cons. Blue Cross-Blue Shield, 1977—, Nat. Council Aging, Ill. Psychiat. Inst. Mem. Mayor's Commn. on Aging, 1955—; pres. Chgo. Bd. Health, 1979—. Bd. dirs. Med. Center YMCA, Med. Careers Council; bd. govs. Inst. of Medicine of Chgo. Med. Soc. Served to capt. M.C., AUS, 1944-46. Named Prof. of Year, Chgo. Med. Sch., 1964; Tchr. of Year, Ill. Psychiat. Inst., 1966; Chicagoan of Yr. in Medicine, 1970. WHO fellow, Europe, 1970. Diplomate Am. Bd. Psychiatry and Neurology. Fellow Am. Psychiat. Assn. (life), Am. Acad. Psychoanalysis, Am., Internat. psychoanalytic assns., Ill. Psychiat. Soc. (pres.), Chgo. Inst. Medicine, Am. Coll. Psychiatrists, Am. Coll. Psychoanalysts, Sigma Xi, Alpha Omega Alpha, Phi Lambda Kappa (Gold medal sci. award). Home: 1520 N Dearborn Pkwy Chicago IL 60610 Office: Mt Sinai Hospital Med Center Chicago IL 60608

LEVITT, MORTIMER, merchant; b. N.Y.C., Feb. 28, 1907; s. Samuel and Mamie (Koenigsberg) L.; self ed.; m. Anne Fleisher, Jan. 21, 1937 (div. Nov. 1939); m. 2d, Anne Marie Gratzinger, June 18, 1948; children—Elizabeth Anne, Peter Eduard. Founder, pres. The Custom Shops, Inc., Sportswear by Peter, Morley Shirt Co., Inc., Leonardo Neckwear, Inc., Mortimer Levitt Gallery; producer The Concept (off-Broadway play), motion pictures The Concept, Who Said I Can't Ride a Rainbow?, The Dutchman, Marco Polo; producer Chamber Theatre series Manhattan Theatre Club. Mem. Mayor's Com. Drug Addiction. Chmn. ex-officio Daytop Village; chmn. bd. Young Concert Artists Inc. Bd. dirs. Lincoln Center Film Soc. Club: Windham Mountain. Home: 10 E 82d St New York City NY 10028 Office: 716 Fifth Ave New York City NY 10019. *Success in business is not for the greedy. On the contrary, lasting success is the result of giving more without charging more; and the possibilities are infinite.*

LEVITT, RICHARD SANDER, consumer finance co. exec.; b. Des Moines, May 8, 1930; s. Ellis Isaac and Nelle (Seff) L.; B.A., U. Iowa, 1952, J.D., 1954; m. Jeanne Strauss, July 2, 1952; children—Randall, Mark, Beth, Jay. With Dial Corp., Des Moines, 1954—, now pres., dir., mem. exec. com.; dir. Meredith Corp., Iowa-Des Moines Nat. Bank, City Center Corp., Equitable of Iowa Variable Annuity Account A, Civic Center Corp. Mem. Des Moines Art Center Acquisition Com.; mem. adv. council of credit research com. Purdue U.; bd. dirs. YMCA, Iowa Methodist Med. Center, Simpson Coll., Greater Des Moines Com., Des Moines Center Sci. and Industry Found., U. Iowa Found. Mem. Nat. Consumer Finance Assn. Democrat. Jewish. Clubs: Wakonda; Embassy; Des Moines; Standard (Chgo.). Home: 5300 Woodland Ave Des Moines IA 50312 Office: 207 9th St Des Moines IA 50307

LEVITT, SEYMOUR HERBERT, physician, educator; b. Chgo., July 18, 1928; s. Nathan E. and Margaret (Chizever) L.; B.A., U. Colo., 1950, M.D., 1954; m. Phillis Jeanne Martin, Oct. 31, 1952; children—Mary Jeanne, Jennifer Gaye, Scott Hayden. Intern, Phila. Gen. Hosp., 1954-55; resident in radiology U. Calif. at San Francisco Med. Center, 1957-61; instr. radiation therapy U. Mich., Ann Arbor, 1961-62, U. Rochester (N.Y.), 1962-63; asso. prof. radiology U. Okla., Oklahoma City, 1963-66; prof. radiology, chmn. div. radiotherapy Med. Coll. Va., Richmond, 1966-70; prof., head dept. therapeutic radiology U. Minn., Mpls., 1970—; cons. in field. Exec. bd. Am. Joint Com. for End Result Reporting and Cancer Staging; com. radiation oncology studies Nat. Cancer Inst. Diplomate Am. Bd. Radiology (trustee). Served with M.C., AUS, 1955-57. Fellow Am. Coll. Radiology; mem. Am. Radium Soc., Radiol. Soc. N. Am., Am. Assn. Cancer Research, Am. Cancer Soc. (pres. Minn. div. 1979-80), Am. Roentgen Ray Soc., Soc. Chmn. Acad. Radiation Oncology Programs (pres. 1974-76), Soc. Nuclear Medicine, Am. Soc. Clin. Oncology, Am. Soc. Therapeutic Radiologists (exec. bd. 74-78, pres. 1978-79), Phi Beta Kappa, Sigma Xi, Alpha Omega Alpha. Home: 6413 Cherokee Trail Minneapolis MN 55435 Office: U Minn Hosp PO Box 494 Minneapolis MN 55455

LEVITT, THEODORE, educator; b. Vollmerz, Germany, Mar. 1, 1925; came to U.S., 1935, naturalized, 1940; s. Boris and Recha (Gruenebaum) L.; B.A., Antioch Coll., 1949; Ph.D. in Econs., Ohio State U., 1951; m. Joan Levy, Aug. 1, 1948; children—John M., Frances B., Kathryn L., Laura C., Peter K. Mem. faculty Grad. Sch. Bus. Adminstrn., Harvard U., 1959—, prof. bus. adminstrn., 1964—; dir. Rob Roy, Inc., GCA Corp.; cons. in field. Served with U.S. Army, 1943-45. Recipient Charles Coolidge Parlin award as Mktg. Man of Year, 1970; George Gallup award for Mktg. Excellence, 1976; Paul D. Converse award Am. Mktg. Assn., 1978; award for outstanding bus. book offyear Acad. Mgmt., 1962. Author: Innovation in Marketing, 1962; Industrial Purchasing Behavior: A Study in Communications Effects, 1965; The Marketing Mode: Pathways to Corporate Growth, 1969; The Third Sector: New Tactics for a Responsive Society, 1973; Marketing for Business Growth, 1976; co-author: Marketing: A Contemporary Analysis, 1964. Contbr. articles to profl. jours. Home: Belmont MA 02178 Office: Harvard Bus Sch Boston MA 02163

LEVITT, WILLIAM JAIRD, builder; b. Bklyn., Feb. 11, 1907; s. Abraham and Pauline (Biederman) L.; D.C.S., St. John's U.; L.H.D., Yeshiva U.; Ph.D., Bar Ilan U.; m. Rhoda Kirshner, Nov. 16, 1929; children—William Jaird, James R.; m. 2d, Alice Kenny, Jan., 1959; m. 3d, Simone Korchin, Nov. 1969. Founder-chmn. Levitt & Sons, Inc.; chmn. bd. William J. Levitt, Inc., Levitt Industries, Inc., Internat. Community Corp. Bd. overseers Albert Einstein Coll. Medicine; bd. dirs. Am. Health Found.; trustee North Shore U. Hosp.; pres. Levitt Found. Served as lt. USNR, 1942-45; PTO. Recipient Frank P. Brown medal Franklin Inst. Pa., 1965. Office: Greenvale NY 11548

LEVITZ, RALPH, furniture co. exec.; b. Lebanon, Pa., Nov. 25, 1912; s. Richard B. and Sarah (Smeyne) L.; B.S., U. Pa., 1933; m. Esther M. Daniels, Feb. 19, 1949; 1 son, Philip A. Chmn. bd. dirs., past chief exec. officer Levitz Furniture Corp., Miami, Fla., 1936—; dir. Pan Am. Bank of Miami. Active United Jewish Appeal. Clubs: Brookside Country of Pottstown, Pa. (gov. 1959-65); Kings Bay Country, Jockey (Miami). Office: Levitz Furniture Corp 1370 NW 167th St Miami FL 33169*

LEVOVITZ, PESACH ZECHARIAH, rabbi; b. Poland, Sept. 15, 1922; s. Reuben and Leah Zlate (Kustanowitz) L.; came to U.S., 1923; B.A., Yeshivah U., 1942; rabbi, Mesivtha Tifereth Jerusalem Rabbinical Sem., 1943; m. Bluma D. Feder, Feb. 5, 1945 (dec. 1970); children—Sivya, Yaakov; m. 2d, Eleanore Herman Klugmann, 1972; children—Maurice, Danny, Renee, Jackie. Rabbi, Congregation Sons of Israel, Lakewood, N.J., 1944—; founder, 1945, since dean Bezalel Day Sch. Pres., Rabbinical Council Am., 1966-68, chmn. commn. on internat. affairs, 1972; mem. exec. com. Synagogue Council Am., 1953—; standing com. Conf. European Rabbis and Asso. Rabbis, 1964—; steering com. World Conf. Ashkenazi and Sephardi Synagogues; vice chmn. rabbinic cabinet Bonds for Israel, 1972; chaplain Lakewood Police Dept., 1950—; vis. chaplain Naval Air Sta., Lakehurst, N.J., 1945—; nat. chmn. ann. conv. Rabbinical of Am., 1971; v.p. Religious Zionists Am., 1974; nat. chmn. Vaad Haroshi Religious Zionists Am., 1975. Mem. adv. bd. Lakewood Housing Council, Nat. Community Relations Adv. Council, United Jewish Appeal. Mem. N.J. Drug Utilization Council. Recipient Revel Meml. award in religion and religious edn. Yeshivah Coll. Alumni Assn., 1967; award for outstanding rabbinic leadership Union of Orthodox Jewish Congregations Am., 1969; chief Rabbi Issas Halevi Herzog Torah Fellowship award Religious Zionists Am., 1972, chmn. nat. conv., 1974. Mem. Conf. Presidents Nat. Jewish Orgns., Am. Conf. Soviet Jewry. Home: 631 8th St Lakewood NJ 08701 Office: Congregation Sons of Israel Madison Ave at 6th St Lakewood NJ 08701

LEVY, BENJAMIN HIRSCH, lawyer; b. Savannah, Ga., Aug. 24, 1912; s. Arthur B. and Regena (Waterman) L.; B.S., U. Va., 1932; J.D., Harvard, 1935; m. Marion C. Abrahams, Aug. 7, 1940; children—Joan (Mrs. Gary M. Levy), Benjamin Hirsch. Admitted to Ga. bar, 1935, since practiced in Savannah; asso. Bright & Brennen, 1935-40; asso. Abrahams, Bouhan, Atkinson & Lawrence 1945-49; partner Bouhan, Williams & Levy, 1949—; dir. Solomons Co., Levy's of Savannah, Inc., Habersham Shopping, Inc., Chatham Orthopedic Assos., P.C., Alexander Bros. Co., Surgery Assos., P.C., Topp Cola Internat. Inc. Pres., Chatham County Bd. Edn., 1951-52; chmn. Savannah chpt. Am. Council for Judaism, 1954—; trustee Ga. Hist. Soc. Endowment Fund; mem. nat. exec. com. Am. Jewish Hist. Soc.; curator Ga. Hist. Soc. Served to lt. col. USAAF, 1940-45. Mem. Mil. Order World Wars (past chpt. comdr.). Jewish (pres. congregation). Rotarian (pres. 1962-63). Home: 3001 Atlantic Ave Savannah GA 31405 Office: PO Box 2139 Savannah GA 31402

LEVY, CAROL, editor; b. Lynn, Mass., Apr. 13, 1931; d. Samuel and Helen (Alpers) Levy; B.A., Syracuse U., 1952. Mem. staff The Reporter mag., 1952-53, True mag., 1953-54; with spl. services U.S. Army, 1954-56; mem. staff Forbes mag., 1957-61; research editor Dun's Rev., N.Y.C., 1961-62, sr. editor, 1963-69, asst. mng. editor, 1969-71, mng. editor, 1971—. Home: 10 Downing St New York City NY 10014 Office: 666 Fifth Ave New York City NY 10019

LEVY, CHARLES, JR., business exec.; b. Chgo., Apr. 27, 1913; s. Charles and Bertha (Friend) L.; student Wharton Sch., U. Pa., 1931-35; m. Ruth Doctoroff, Oct. 15, 1939; 1 dau., Barbara. Chmn. bd. dirs. Charles Levy Circulating Co., Chgo., 1961—. Bd. dirs. Jewish Fedn. Chgo., Michael Reese Hosp., Chgo., Park View Home, Temple Sholom, Mt. Sinai Med. Research, Lincoln Park Zool. Soc. Served with AUS, 1942-46. Decorated Bronze Star. Mem. Periodical Inst., Mid-Am. Periodical Assn., Council Periodical Distbrs. Clubs: Standard, Bryn Mawr Country, Carleton, Mid-Am. Office: 1200 N Branch St Chicago IL 60622

LEVY, DAVID, lawyer; b. Atlanta, July 7, 1937; s. Meyer and Elsie (Reisman) L.; B.A., Emory U., 1959, LL.B., 1961; LL.M., Georgetown U., 1964; m. Karen Shaw, Sept. 8, 1963; children—Jeffrey Mark, Robert William, Danielle Beth, Margo Shaw. Admitted to Ga. bar, 1961; atty. SEC, Washington, 1961-65; asso., partner Arnstein, Gluck, Weitzenfeld & Minow, Chgo., 1965-71; partner Kaler, Karesh & Frankel, Atlanta, 1971-73; v.p., sec., counsel Nat. Service Industries, Inc., Atlanta, 1973—. Mem. Am., Ga. bar assns. Home: 835 Overhill Ct NW Atlanta GA 30328 Office: 1180 Peachtree St NE Atlanta GA 30309

LEVY, DAVID, broadcasting exec.; b. Phila., Jan. 2; s. Benjamin and Lillian (Potash) L.; B.S. in Econs., Wharton Sch., U. Pa., 1934, M.B.A., 1935; m. Lucile Alva Wilds, July 25, 1941; children—Lance, Linda. With Young & Rubicam, Inc., N.Y.C., 1938-59, v.p., asso. dir. radio-TV dept., 1958-59; v.p. charge network programs and talent NBC, 1959-61; exec. producer Goodson-Todman Prodns., West Coast, 1968-69; exec. v.p., dir. Golden Orange Broadcasting Co., Anaheim, Calif.; exec. producer Double Life of Henry Phyffe, 1965; exec. producer, creator The Addams Family, 1964-66, The Pruitts of Southampton, 1966-67 (all ABC-TV) for Filmways TV Prodns.; exec. v.p. charge TV activities Four Star Internat., Inc., 1970-72; producer World Premier Sarge, exec. producer TV series Universal Studios for NBC, 1971-72; producer Paramount TV, 1972-73; creator, creative cons. TV series Addams Family for Hanna-Barbera Prodns. for NBC, 1973-74; creative cons. Name That Tune, Ralph Edwards Prodns., 1974-80; pres. Wilshire Prodns., Inc.; past mem. faculty Calif. State U., Northridge, 1973-77. Dir. radio and TV for Citizens for Eisenhower-Nixon, 1956; prod. 3-network program for closing Republican campaign broadcast, Four More Years. Served as lt. USNR, 1944-46; cons. Sec. Treasury, 1945-46; chief radio sect. war finance div. Treasury Dept. Mem. A.S.C.A.P., Acad. TV Arts and Scis., Writers Guild, Producers Guild Am. (sec., dir.), Hollywood Radio-TV Soc. (pres. 1969-70), Caucus Producers, Writers and Dirs. (sec., mem. steering com., exec. dir. 1979). Author: (novels) The Chameleons, 1964, reissued as The Network Jungle, 1976; The Gods of Foxcroft, 1970; also author, producer TV dramas and motion pictures; contbr. short stories to popular mags. Office: 214 1/2 S Spalding Dr Beverly Hills CA 90212

LEVY, DAVID ALFRED, physician, scientist; b. Washington, Aug. 27, 1930; s. Stanley A. and Blanche B. (Berman) L.; B.S., U. Md., 1952, M.D., 1954; m. Bette A. Davis, July 15, 1951; children—Jill, William, Stanley. Intern, resident in medicine U. Hosp., Balt., 1954-59; physician VA Hosp., Balt., 1961-62; fellow dept. microbiology Johns Hopkins U. Sch. Medicine, 1962-66, asst. prof. radiol. sci. Sch. Hygiene and Pub. Health, 1966-68, asso. prof., 1968-71, prof. radiol. sci. and epidemiology, 1972-73, prof. biochemistry and epidemiology, 1973—; mem. active staff Good Samaritan Hosp.; mem. courtesy staff Johns Hopkins Hosp.; mem. FDA Panel on Rev. of Allergenic Extracts, 1975—; mem. allergy and immunology rev. com. Nat. Inst. Allergy and Infectious Diseases, 1975-77. Served with U.S. Army, 1959-61. Diplomate Am. Bd. Internal Medicine, Am. Bd. Allergy and Clin. Immunology. Fellow Am. Acad. Allergy; mem. Md. Thoracic Soc., AAAS, Am. Assn. Immunologists, Soc. Exptl. Biology and Medicine, Am. Fedn. Clin. Research, Md. Soc. Allergy, Sigma Xi. Editorial bd. Clin. Immunology and Immunopathology, 1971-76; contbr. articles to med. jours. Office: 615 N Wolfe St Baltimore MD 21205

LEVY, DAVID C., coll. adminstr.; b. N.Y.C., Apr. 10, 1938; s. Edgar W. and Lucille (Corcos) L.; B.A., Columbia Coll., 1968; M.A., N.Y. U., 1967, Ph.D., 1979; m. Janet R. Meyer, June 7, 1959; children—Jessica Anne, Thomas William. Asst. dir. admissions Parsons Sch. Design, N.Y.C., 1961-62, dir. admissions, 1962-67, v.p., 1967-70, dean, chief adminstrv. officer, 1970—, exec. dean, 1979—, exec. dean, chief adminstrv. officer Otis Inst. of Parsons Sch. Design, Los Angeles, 1979—. Home: 159 S Mountain Rd New City NY 10956 Office: 66 Fifth Ave New York NY 10011

LEVY, EDWARD CHARLES, JR., mfg. co. exec.; b. Detroit, Nov. 14, 1931; s. Edward Charles and Pauline (Birndorf) L.; S.B., Mass. Inst. Tech., 1952; m. Julie Ruth Honigman, July 11, 1955; children—Ellen, Barbara, Carol. With Edward C. Levy Co., Detroit, 1952—, v.p. operations and engring., 1957-63, exec. v.p., 1963-70, pres., 1970—. Bd. dirs. Edward C. Levy Found., Mich. Cancer Found.; trustee Detroit Inst. Tech. Mem. Am. Concrete Inst., ASTM, Engring. Soc. Detroit. Jewish. Clubs: Renaissance Standard (Detroit); Franklin Hills Country (Franklin, Mich.). Office: 8800 Dix Ave Detroit MI 48209

LEVY, GEORGE HAROLD, publisher; b. N.Y.C., Apr. 8, 1924; s. Abraham Benjamin and Sybil (Rosenberg) L.; B.A., Hofstra Coll., 1950; m. Joan Helen Liebowitz, June 24, 1950; children—Richard,

David, Robin. Pres., Maco Pub. Co., Inc., N.Y.C., 1952—, Kingsbridge Communications, 1977—. Served with Signal Corps, AUS, 1942-46; PTO. Mem. Kensington Civic Orgn., United Jewish Appeal. Clubs: Masons (32 deg.), Shriners. Home: 30-A Arleigh Rd Great Neck NY 11021 Office: 535 Fifth Ave New York NY 10017

LEVY, GERALD JOSEPH, retail chain store exec.; b. N.Y.C., Mar. 14, 1927; s. Benjamin and Lillian (Weiss) L.; B.B.A., Pace Coll., 1952; M.B.A., Coll. City N.Y., 1956; m. Francine J. Rauchman, Nov. 11, 1951; children—David, Debra, Jessica. Expense controller Abraham & Straus, N.Y.C., 1956-60; budget dir. R.H. Macy, N.Y.C., 1960-64; controller Popular Club Plan, Inc., Passaic, N.J., 1964-65; v.p., treas., dir. Bond Stores Inc., N.Y.C., 1965-68; exec. v.p Barney's, Inc., N.Y.C., 1968-69; v.p. adminstrn., treas. Universal Edn. Corp., N.Y.C., 1969-70; v.p. finance and adminstrn. Miller Wohl Co. Inc., N.Y.C., 1970-78, also dir.; exec. v.p. Outlet Corp., Providence, 1978—. Active Boy Scouts Am., March of Dimes. Served with AUS, 1945-46. Mem. N.Y. Met. Controllers Assn. Home: 32 Rainbow Pond Dr Walpole MA 02081 Office: 176 Weybosset St Providence RI 02903

LEVY, GERHARD, pharmacologist; b. Wollin, Germany, Feb. 12, 1928; s. Gotthold and Eliesabeth (Luebeck) L.; came to U.S., 1948, naturalized, 1953; B.S., U. Calif. at San Francisco, 1955, Pharm.D., 1958; Dr. honoris causa, Uppsala (Sweden) U., 1975, Phila. Coll. Pharmacy and Sci., 1979; m. Rosalyn Mincer, June 8, 1958; children—David, Marc, Sharon. Asst. prof. pharmacy U. Buffalo, 1958-60; asso. prof. pharmacy State U. N.Y. at Buffalo, 1960-64, prof. biopharmaceutics, 1964-72, distinguished prof. pharmaceutics, 1972—, chmn. dept. pharmaceutics, 1966-70; vis. prof. Hebrew U., Jerusalem; cons. WHO, 1966, Bur. Drugs Adv. Panel System, FDA, 1971-74; mem. com. on problems of drug safety NRC, 1971-75; mem. pharmacol.-toxicol. com. NIH, 1971-75. Served with AUS, 1950-51. Recipient Ebert prize, 1969, Am. Pharm. Assn. Research Achievement award, 1969, McKeen Cattell award Am. Coll. Clin. Pharmacology, 1978, Host-Madsen medal Internat. Pharm. Fedn., 1978; named Alumnus of Year, U. Calif. Sch. Pharmacy Alumni Assn., 1970. Fellow Am. Pharm. Assn., Acad. Pharm. Scis., AAAS; mem. Inst. Medicine of Nat. Acad. Scis., Am. Chem. Soc., Am. Soc. Exptl. Pharmacology and Therapeutics, Soc. Exptl. Biology and Medicine. Mem. editorial bd. Jour. Pharm. Sci., 1970-75, Clin. Pharmacology and Therapeutics, 1969—, Internat. Jour. Clin. Pharmacology, 1968—, Drug Metabolism and Disposition, 1973—; contbr. articles to profl. jours. Home: 169 Surrey Run Williamsville NY 14221 Office: Sch Pharmacy State U NY Amherst NY 14260

LEVY, HAROLD ROCHELLE, govt. ofcl.; b. Trenton, N.J., Dec. 25, 1919; s. C. Harold and Margaret (Rochelle) L.; A.B., Washington and Lee U., 1942; m. Bonnie Angelo, Aug. 19, 1950; 1 son, Charles Christopher. Reporter, Trenton State Gazette, 1940-41; telegraph editor Winston-Salem Jour., 1946-50, Sunday editor Winston-Salem Jour. and Sentinel, 1950-53; spl. writer Newsday, 1953-55, Washington corr., 1955-62; asst. to sec. health, edn. and welfare, 1962-68; spl. asst. to chmn. Urban Coalition, 1968-70; asst. to chmn. Common Cause, 1970; spl. asst. to Senator Adlai E. Stevenson, 1970—. Served to capt., inf., AUS, 1942-46. Mem. Sigma Delta Chi, Omicron Delta Kappa, Phi Kappa Psi. Club: Federal City (Washington); Edgemoor (Bethesda, Md.). Home: 5401 Edgemoor Ln Bethesda MD 20014 Office: US Senate Washington DC 20510

LEVY, JACK I., lawyer, bus. exec.; b. Brownsville, Pa., Aug. 22, 1910; s. Morris and Belle (Wise) L.; A.B., U. Mich., 1931, J.D., 1934; m. Hariet Mindich, June 11, 1943; children—Margaret J. (Mrs. Castro), James B. Admitted to Ill., D.C. bars, 1935; with U.S. Dept. Agr., 1934-35; asso. Sonnenschein, Levinson, Carlin, Nath & Rosenthal, Chgo., 1935-47, partner, 1948-59; v.p. law and finance, dir. Gen. Am. Transp. Corp., Chgo., 1963-66, v.p. law, dir., 1966-69, sr. v.p., 1969-71, exec. v.p., 1971-78, sr. v.p., 1978—. Served from pvt. to capt. USAAF, 1942-45. Mem. Am., Ill., Chgo. bar assns., Order of Coif. Home: 1335 N Astor St Chicago IL 60610 Office: 120 Riverside Plaza Chicago IL 60606

LEVY, JAY RICHARD, communications exec.; b. N.Y.C., May 6, 1942; s. Paul and Lena (Finkel) L.; B.A., Adelphi U., 1963; m. Diane Sokol, July 14, 1966; children—Jill Kara, Allison Kim. Pres., Radio Pulsebeat News, 1960-65, Black Audio Network, 1970—, Trans World Communications, 1970—, Black Press Service, 1973— (all N.Y.C.). Mem. Radio-TV News Dirs. Assn., Sigma Delta Chi. Club: Deadline. Home: 85-15 Main St Briarwood NY 11435 Office: 166 Madison Ave New York NY 10016

LEVY, JOHN DAVID, health care products mfg. co. exec.; b. St. Louis, Nov. 4, 1918; s. Mont M. and Elma (Linz) L.; M.A., Yale U., 1939; M.B.A., Harvard U., 1941; m. Sally Seasongood, July 10, 1944; children—John David, Diane Levy Jacobson, Mont S. Advt. mgr. Angelica Uniform Co., 1955, v.p. sales, v.p. mktg., exec. v.p., to 1968; exec. v.p. Angelica Corp., St. Louis, 1968-72, pres., 1972-76, vice chmn. bd., 1976—, also dir. Served with U.S. Army, 1941-46. Clubs: Westwood Country, St. Louis, Stadium. Home: 816 S Hanley St Apt 16B Saint Louis MO 63105 Office: 10176 Corporate Sq Dr Saint Louis MO 63132

LEVY, JOSEPH, lawyer; b. N.Y.C., June 9, 1928; s. Morris Joseph and Dora (Cohen) L.; B.B.A. cum laude, Coll. City N.Y., 1950; LL.B. cum laude, N.Y. U., 1954; m. Gertrud C. Roeder, Jan. 20, 1967; children—Diana N., Susan R. Admitted to N.Y. bar, 1955, D.C. bar, 1968; asso. Parker, Chapin and Flattau, N.Y.C., 1954-62; partner firm Rivkin, Sherman & Levy, and predecessors, N.Y.C., 1962—. Sec., dir. Horizons Communications Corp., Quad Typographers, Inc.; sec. Savin Bus. Machines Corp., On-Line Systems, Inc., Lambda Tech., Inc. Served to capt. AUS, 1951-53. Home: 254 University Way Paramus NJ 07652 Office: 750 3d Ave New York City NY 10017

LEVY, KENNETH, educator; b. N.Y.C., Feb. 26, 1927; s. Meyer and Sylvia (Licht) L.; A.B., Queens Coll., 1947; M.F.A., Princeton, 1949, Ph.D., 1955; m. Clara Brooks Emmons, Jan. 25, 1956; children—Robert Brooks, Helen Gardner. Instr. music Princeton, 1952-54; asst. prof. Brandeis U., 1954-58, asso. prof., 1958-64, Frederick R. Mann prof. music, 1964-66, chmn. dept. music, 1958-65; prof. music Princeton, 1966—, chmn. dept., 1967-70. Served with USNR, 1945-46. Recipient Fulbright award, France, 1950-51, Italy, 1962-63; Guggenheim fellow, 1955-56; Am. Council Learned Socs. fellow, 1970-71. Mem. Am. Musicol. Soc., Societe Francaise de Musicologie, U.S. Nat. Com. for Byzantine Studies, Medieval Acad. Am. Asso. editor: Anthologie de la Chanson Parisienne au Seizieme Siecle, 1953. Editorial bd. Jour. Am. Musicol. Soc., 1963-75, Monumenta Musicae Byzantinae, 1968—, Grove's Dictionary, 6th edit. Contbr. articles to profl. jours. Address: Music Dept Princeton Univ Princeton NJ 08540

LEVY, KURT LEOPOLD, educator; b. Berlin, July 10, 1917; s. Anton and Toni (Moses) L.; B.A., U. Toronto, 1945, M.A., 1946, Ph.D., 1954; m. Enid Jane Gourlay, June 6, 1947; children—Leslie, Judy, Andy, Bruce, John. Mem. faculty dept. Spanish and Portuguese U. Toronto, 1950—, prof., 1965—, chmn. Latin Am. studies program, and Latin Am. studies com., 1965-70, chmn. dept. Spanish and Portuguese, 1978—; vis. prof. Universidad del Valle, Cali, Colombia, 1971-73. Nat. Research Council Can. fellow, 1950; Can. Council sr. fellow, 1964; Rockefeller Found. grantee, 1971-73. Mem. MLA, Am. Assn. Tchrs. Spanish and Portuguese, Internat. Inst. Latin Am. Lit., Am. Council Teaching of Fgn. Langs., Can. Assn. Hispanists, Internat. Assn. Hispanists. Author books in field including: Vida y obras de Tomas Carrasquilla, 1958; El ensayo y la critica en Iberoamerica, 1970. Home: 11 Rathnally Ave Toronto ON M4V 2M2 Canada Office: 21 Sussex Ave Toronto ON M5S 1A1 Canada

LEVY, LEON, investment co. exec.; b. N.Y.C., Sept. 13, 1925; s. Jerome and Sadie (Samuelson) L.; m. Roxanne Wruble, Dec. 13, 1959. Chmn. bd. Oppenheimer Holdings Inc., N.Y.C., 1951—; pres. Oppenheimer Fund, Inc., 1964—, Oppenheimer A.I.M. Fund, Inc., 1969—, Oppenheimer Time Fund, Inc., 1971—, Oppenheimer Spl. Fund, Inc., 1972—, Oppenheimer Monetary Bridge, Inc., 1973—, Oppenheimer Tax-Free Bond Fund, Inc., 1976—, Oppenheimer Option Income Fund, Inc., 1977—; chmn. bd. Oppenheimer Mgmt. Corp., 1969—; dir. Big Bear Stores, Reliable Stores, Automatic Service Co., Shirley of Atlanta, Havatampa; lectr. Coll. City N.Y., 1952-59; mem. adv. com. Encounter mag. Bd. dirs. Freedom House, Municipal Art Soc. N.Y., Internat. Found. for Art Research; trustee N.Y. U. Inst. Fine Arts. Served with AUS, 1945-46. Home: 983 Park Ave New York NY 10028 Office: 1 New York Plaza New York NY 10004

LEVY, LEONARD WILLIAMS, educator, author; b. Toronto, Ont., Can., Apr. 9, 1923 (parents Am. citizens); s. Albert and Rae (Williams) L.; B.S., Columbia, 1947, M.A., 1948, Ph.D. (Univ. fellow), 1951; m. Elyse Gitlow, Oct. 21, 1944; children—Wendy Ellen, Leslie Anne. Research asst. Columbia, 1950-51; instr., asst. prof., asso. prof., prof. Brandeis U., Waltham, Mass., 1951-70, first incumbent Earl Warren chair constl. history, 1957-70, dean Grad. Sch. Arts and Scis., 1958-63, dean faculty arts and scis., 1963-66; Andrew W. Mellon prof. humanities, history, chmn. grad. faculty history Claremont (Calif.) Grad. Sch., 1970—; Gaspar Brown lectr. Boston U., 1972; Elliott lectr. U. So. Calif. Law Sch., 1972; Hugo Black lectr. U. Ala., 1976; Bicentennial lectr. City of St. Louis, 1976. Mem. nat. bd. Commn. on Law and Social Action, Am. Jewish Congress; mem. U.S. Bicentennial Commn. Am. Revolution, 1966-68; mem. exec. council Inst. for Early Am. History and Culture; mem. nat. adv. council ACLU; Pulitzer prize juror, chmn. biog. jury, 1974, history jury, 1976; adv. bd. The John Marshall Papers. Served with AUS, 1943-46. Recipient Sigma Delta Chi prize for journalism history, 1961; Frank Luther Mott prize Kappa Tau Alpha, 1961; Pulitzer prize for history, 1969; Commonwealth Club prize for non-fiction, 1975. Guggenheim fellow, 1957-58; Center For Study Liberty in Am. fellow Harvard, 1961-62; Am. Bar Found. fellow, 1973-74, Nat. Endowment for Humanities sr. fellow, 1974. Mem. Am. Hist. Assn. (Littleton-Griswald com. legal history), Orgn. Am. Historians, Am. Soc. Legal History (dir.), Am. Antiquarian Soc., Soc. Am. Historians, Inst. Early Am. History and Culture (exec. council), Kappa Delta Pi. Democrat. Author: The Law of the Commonwealth and Chief Justice Shaw, 1957; Legacy of Suppression; Freedom of Speech and Press in Early American History, 1960; Jefferson and Civil Liberties; The Darker Side, 1963; Origins of the Fifth Amendment, 1968 (Pulitzer Prize in history 1969); Judgments: Essays on American Constitutional History, 1972; Against The Law: The Nixon Court and Criminal Justice, 1974. Editor: Major Crises in American History, 1962; The American Political Process, 1963; The Presidency, 1964; The Congress, 1964; The Judiciary, 1964; Parties and Pressure Groups, 1964; Freedom of the Press from Zenger to Jefferson, 1966; American Constitutional Law, 1966; Judicial Review and the Supreme Court, 1967; Freedom and Reform, 1967; Essays on The Making of the Constitution, 1969, The Fourteenth Amendment and the Bill of Rights, 1970; The Supreme Court Under Earl Warren, 1972; Jim Crow in Boston, 1974; Essays on the Early Republic, 1974; Blasphemy in Massachusetts, 1974. Gen. editor Am. Heritage Series, Documentary History of Western Civilization, Two Centuries of American Life Series, Bicentennial History of the American Revolution. Contbr. articles to profl. jours. Home: 820 N Cambridge Ave Claremont CA 91711

LEVY, LOUIS, chess master; b. N.Y.C., Feb. 10, 1921; s. Victor and Sarah (Caffina) L.; B.S., N.Y. U., 1941; m. Gloria Alice Cressy, Jan. 21, 1972. Engaged in car washing business, 1947-66; chess and bridge player, 1939—. Bd. dirs. N.J. Bridge League, 1969-73. Served with USAAF, 1942-46. Named U.S. Internat. Master, Am. Contract Bridge League, 1972; U.S. Nat. Open chess co-champion, 1972; Empire City chess champion, 1968. Mem. Marshall, Manhattan chess clubs, Am. Contract Bridge League. Address: 12317 Ridge Circle Los Angeles CA 90049

LEVY, MICHAEL RICHARD, publishing co. exec.; b. Dallas, May 17, 1946; s. Harry Aaron and Florence (Friedman) L.; B.S., U. Pa., 1968; J.D., U. Tex., 1972; m. Rebecca Gloria Schulman, Jan. 19, 1969; children—Anne Rachel, Tobin Janel and Mara Elizabeth (twins). Admitted to Tex. bar, 1972; pres. Mediatex Communications Corp., Austin, Tex., 1972—; founder, pub. Tex. Monthly mag., 1973—. Mem. State Bar Tex., Mag. Pubs. Assn., Headliners Club. Club: Citadel. Home: PO Box 146 Austin TX 78767 Office: PO Box 1569 Austin TX 78767

LEVY, MILTON LINCOLN, retail trade exec.; b. Boston, Feb. 12, 1915; s. Hyman J. and Lillian (Shapiro) L.; A.B. cum laude, Harvard, 1936, M.B.A., 1938; m. Shirley Feldberg, Jan. 6, 1946; children—John F., Steven D. Buyer, John Irving Shoe Co., Boston, 1939-45; dist. mgr. New Eng. Trading Corp., Framingham, Mass., 1946-56; sr. v.p., mem. exec. com. Zayre Corp., Framingham, 1956—. Fellow, Brandeis U.; mem. Am. Jewish Com. Trustee Beth Israel Hosp.; trustee, v.p. Hebrew Rehab. Center for Aged. Club: B'nai B'rith. Home: 30 Scotch Pine Rd Weston MA 02193 Office: Zayre Corp Framingham MA 01701

LEVY, NORMAN B., psychiatrist; b. N.Y.C., May 28, 1931; s. Barnett Theodore and Lena (Gulnick) L.; B.A. cum laude, N.Y. U., 1952; M.D., State U. N.Y., 1956; m. Lya Weiss, Mar. 9, 1958 (dec.); children—Karen, Susan, Joanne; m. 2d, Carol Lois Spiegel, Dec. 26, 1970, 1 son, Robert Barnett. Intern, Maimonides Med. Center, Bklyn., 1956-57; resident physician in medicine U. Pitts.-Presby. Hosp., 1957-58; resident in psychiatry Kings County Hosp. Center, Bklyn., 1960-63; instr. psychiatry State U. N.Y. Downstate Med. Center Coll. Medicine, Bklyn., 1963-67, asst. prof., 1967-73, asso. prof., 1973-79, prof., 1979-80, presiding officer faculty Coll. Medicine, 1974-76, asso. dir. med-psychiat. liaison service, 1972-80, dir., 1980—; prof. psychiatry, medicine, surgery N.Y. Med. Coll., 1980—. vis. prof. psychiatry and medicine So. Ill. U. Sch. Medicine, 1975; coordinator 1st Internat. Conf. Psychol. Factors in Hemodialysis and Transplantation, 1978. cons. NIMH. Served to capt. M.C., USAF, 1958-60. Diplomate Am. Bd. Psychiatry and Neurology (examiner). Fellow Am. Psychiat. Assn., A.C.P., Internat. Coll. Psychosomatic Medicine, Am. Assn. Psychoanalytic Physicians; mem. Am. Psychosomatic Soc., AAAS, N.Y. Acad. Scis., Psychonephrology Inst. (pres. 1978—), Assn. Acad. Psychiatry, Assn. Applied Psychoanalysis, Internat. Soc. Nephrology, Am. Soc. Nephrology, Am. Assn. Artificial Internal Organs, Soc. Liaison Psychiatry (dir.), Phi Beta Kappa, Sigma Xi. Editor: Living or Dying: Adaptation to Hemodialysis, 1974; Psychological Factors in Hemodialysis and Transplantation, 1980; Changing Role of Males in Society, 1980. Contbr. articles to jours., chpts. to textbooks in field of psychosomatic medicine, psychol. adaptation to hemodialysis and transplantation, death and dying, problems of spouses of psychoanalytic candidates, changing roles of males in soc. Asso. editor Gen. Hosp. Psychiatry, 1978—, Internat. Jour. Psychiatry in Medicine, 1977-78; mem. editorial bd. Jour. Dialysis, 1975—, Dialysis and Transplantation, 1977—. Home: 169 Westminster Rd Brooklyn NY 11218 Office: Dept Psychiatry NY Med Coll Valhalla NY 10595

LEVY, ROBERT, editor; b. N.Y.C., Oct. 1, 1926; s. Mack and Reggy (Steinbrecher) L.; B.S., City Coll. N.Y., 1949; m. Corinne Schlissel, Apr. 26, 1953; children—Randall Mark, Meredith Robin. Sr. editor Tide mag., N.Y.C., 1950-53; contbg. editor Time mag., N.Y.C., 1953-55; sr. editor Forbes mag., N.Y.C., 1955-59; v.p. Manning Pub. Relations Firm, N.Y.C., 1960-63; dir. pub. relations Elgin Watch Co., N.Y.C., 1963-64; sr. asso. Ruder & Finn, N.Y.C., 1965; sr. editor Dun's Review, N.Y.C., 1966—. Served with USAAF, World War II. Recipient citation Lincoln U. Sch. Journalism for significant contbn. to better human relations, 1952. Mem. N.Y. Financial Writers Assn. Home: 42 Wedgewood Dr Westbury NY 11590 Office: 666 Fifth Ave New York City NY 10019

LEVY, ROBERT ISAAC, physician; b. Bronx, N.Y., May 3, 1937; s. George Gerson and Sarah (Levinson) L.; B.A. with high honors and distinction, Cornell U., 1957; M.D. cum laude, Yale U., 1961; m. Ellen Marie Feis, 1958; children—Andrew, Joanne, Karen, Patricia. Intern, then asst. resident in medicine Yale-New Haven Med. Center, 1961-63; clin. asso. molecular diseases Nat. Heart and Lung Inst., Bethesda, Md., 1963-66; chief resident Nat. Heart, Lung and Blood Inst., Bethesda, 1965-66, attending physician molecular disease br., 1965—, head sect. lipoproteins, 1966—, dep. clin. dir. inst., 1968-69, chief clin. services molecular diseases br., 1969-73, chief lipid metabolism br., 1970-74, dir. div. heart and vascular diseases, 1973-75, dir. inst., 1975—; attending physician Georgetown U. med. div. D.C. Gen. Hosp., 1966-68; spl. cons. anti-lipid drugs FDA. Served as surgeon USPHS, 1963-66. Recipient Kees Thesis prize Yale U., 1961; Arthur S. Flemming award, 1975; Superior Service award HEW, 1975. Mem. Am. Heart Assn. (mem.-at-large exec. com. council basic sci.), Am. Inst. Nutrition, Am. Fedn. Clin. Research, N.Y. Acad. Scis., Am. Soc. Clin. Nutrition, Am. Soc. Clin. Investigation, Am. Coll. Cardiology, Am. Soc. Clin. Pharmacology and Therapeutics, Phi Beta Kappa, Sigma Xi, Alpha Omega Alpha, Alpha Epsilon Delta, Phi Kappa Phi. Contbr. profl. jours. Editor Jour. Lipid Research, 1972—, Circulation, 1974-76. Home: 8806 Daimler Ct Potomac MD 20854 Office: Nat Heart Lung and Blood Inst Bldg 31 Room 5A52 Bethesda MD 20014

LEVY, ROBERT JOSEPH, lawyer, educator; b. Phila., June 27, 1931; B.A., Kenyon Coll., 1952, J.D., U. Pa., 1957; m. Roberta K. Levy; children—Valerie R., Jonathan B., Joshua M. Admitted to D.C. bar, 1957, Minn. bar, 1966; trial atty. Dept. Justice, Washington, 1957-59; prof. law U. Minn., Mpls., 1959—; Ida Beam prof. law U. Iowa, 1978. Fellow Center Advanced Study in the Behavioral Scis., 1967-68. Author: (with Caleb Foote and Frank Sander) Cases and Materials on Family Law, 1966, rev. edit., 1976; (with Thomas Lewis and Peter Martin) Cases on Social Welfare and the Individual, 1970. Office: Law Sch U Minn Minneapolis MN 55422

LEVY, ROBERT PALEY, race track exec.; b. Phila., Mar. 30, 1931; s. Leon and Blanche (Paley) L.; B.A., U. Pa., 1952; m. Rochelle Feldman, June 4, 1955; children—Kathryn, Wendy, Robert Paley, Angela, Michael. Vice pres., treas. Del. River Terminal & Warehouse Co., Phila., 1954-63; pres. DRT Industries, Inc., Phila., 1963—; pres. Atlantic City Race Course, 1966—; owner Cisley Stable, Phila., 1955—; mgr. Blanche P. Levy (formerly Jaclyn) Stable, Phila., 1953—. Founder, pres. Little Quakers, 1953; trustee U. Pa.; bd. overseers William Penn Charter Sch., Police Athletic League, Phila. Recipient John B. Kelly Athletic award John B. Kelly Found.; Service to Youth award Pa. Sports Hall of Fame, 1974, inducted into Phila. chpt., 1979; Alumni Award of Merit Penn Charter Alumni Soc., 1977; Man of Yr. award Jockey Agts. Benevolent Assn., 1977; Disting. Am. award Phila. chpt. Nat. Football Found. and Hall of Fame, 1979. Mem. Thoroughbred Racing Assn. (dir.). Clubs: Boca Rio Golf; Bala Golf; Squires Golf; Ocean Reef. Home: 842 Muirfield Rd Bryn Mawr PA 19010 Office: 1212 Pennwalt Bldg Philadelphia PA 19102

LEVY, S. WILLIAM, dermatologist; b. San Francisco, Sept. 28, 1920; s. Joseph and Dora (Taylor) L.; B.S., Sch. Pharmacy, U. Calif., 1943, M.D., San Francisco, 1949; m. Elisabeth Rellstab, Mar. 17, 1974; children—Davis Lewis, Ann Louise. Practice medicine specializing in dermatology, San Francisco; research dermatologist Biomechanics Lab., U. Calif., San Francisco; mem. staff Children's Hosp., Adult Med. Center; cons. to hosps.; central med. adv. Calif. Blue Shield, San Francisco; clin. prof. dermatology U. Calif.; cons. in field. Served with USN, 1943-46. Recipient Lehn and Fink Gold Medal award. Fellow Am. Acad. Dermatology (Gold medal); mem. San Francisco Dermatol. Soc. (pres.), Pacific Dermatologic Assn. (v.p.), AMA, Calif. Med. Assn. (sci. council 1977-80), San Francisco Med. Soc. Author: Skin Problems of the Amputee, 1979. Home: 3838 California St Apt 801 San Francisco CA 94118 Office: 450 Sutter St Suite 2001 San Francisco CA 94108

LEVY, SIDNEY JAY, psychologist, educator; b. St. Louis, May 29, 1921; s. Jacob and Kate (Rosen) L.; Ph.B., U. Chgo., 1946, M.A., 1948, Ph.D., 1956; m. Bobette Adler, Aug. 29, 1953; children—Joyce, Bruce. Staff psychologist Social Research, Inc., Chgo., 1948, dir. psychol. research, 1952—; research asso. psychiatry Billings Hosp., Chgo., 1951; prof. marketing Northwestern U., 1962, prof. behavioral sci. in mgmt., 1970—. Served with USAAF, 1942-44. Mem. Am. Psychol. Assn., Am. Marketing Assn. (v.p. marketing edn. Chgo. chpt. 1967). Author: Living with Television, 1962; Promotion: Behavioral View, 1967; Promotional Behavior, 1970; Marketing, Society and Conflict, 1975; Marketplace Behavior-Its Meaning for Management, 1978. Home: 945 Sheridan Rd Evanston IL 60202

LEVY, SOLOMON E., philosopher; b. N.Y.C., Apr. 13, 1921; s. Ezra and Elisa (Cohen) L.; A.B. in Physics, Bklyn. Coll., 1942; Ph.D. in Philosophy, U. So. Calif., 1954; m. Patricia Lynne McCoy, Sept. 4, 1967. Electronics engr. Nat. Union Radio Corp., Newark, 1942-45; Fulbright research grantee U. Madras (India), 1951-52; mem. faculty U. Mo., Kansas City, 1956—, prof. philosophy, 1966—. Served with AUS, 1946-47. Mem. Am. Philos. Assn., AAUP, History of Sci. Soc., Philosophy of Sci. Soc. Contbr. articles to profl. jours. Home: 8756 Chestnut Circle Kansas City MO 64114

LEVY, STANLEY HERBERT, lawyer; b. Phila., Apr. 4, 1922; s. Max and Rose (Cohen) L.; B.A., Cornell U., 1943; LL.B., Harvard, 1949, J.D., 1968; m. Gloria Kamber, Dec. 20, 1953; children—Steven M., Peter B. Admitted to N.Y. State bar, 1949, also Supreme Ct. U.S., U.S. Dist. Ct. for Eastern and So. Dists. N.Y., U.S. Treasury Dept. bars; practiced in N.Y.C., 1949—. Mem. Republican Town Com., Scarsdale, 1963-65. Mem. com. religious affairs Fedn. Jewish Philanthropies of N.Y.; trustee Ednl. Alliance, Jewish Community Center, White Plains, N.Y. Served to 1st lt. F.A., AUS, 1943-47. Mem. Assn. Bar City N.Y. Clubs: Harvard, Cornell (N.Y.C.); Quaker Ridge Golf, Boulder Brook Riding (Scarsdale); White Plains Flying, Chevalier de Confrerie des Chevaliers du Tastevin, Commanderie de

Bordeaux. Home: 7 Leatherstocking Ln Scarsdale NY 10583 Office: 645 Fifth Ave New York City NY 10022

LEVY, STEPHEN RAYMOND, cons., research and devel. co. exec.; b. Everett, Mass., May 4, 1940; s. Robert George and Lillian (Berfield) L.; B.B.A., U. Mass., 1962; m. Sandra Helen Rosen, Aug. 26, 1961; children—Phillip, Susan. Pres., chief exec. officer, dir. Bolt Beranek & Newman, Inc., Cambridge, Mass.; dir. Telenet Communications Corp., Washington. Served with AUS, 1963-66. Decorated Army Commendation medal. Mem. Assn. for Computing Machinery, Nat. Contract Mgrs. Assn., Fin. Execs. Inst. Home: 39 Lafayette Dr Sudbury MA 01776 Office: 50 Moulton St Cambridge MA 02138

LEVY, WALTER JAMES, oil cons.; b. Hamburg, Germany, Mar. 21, 1911; s. Moses and Bertha (Lindenberger) L.; student U. Heidelberg, 1929-30, U. Berlin, 1930-31, U. Kiel, 1931-32; m. Augusta Sondheimer, Apr. 11, 1942; children—Robert Alan, Susan Clementine. Asst. to editor Petroleum Press Bur., London, Eng., 1936-41; free lance economist, N.Y.C., 1941-42; chief petroleum sect. OSS, Washington, 1942-45; asst. office intelligence research Dept. State, 1945-48, cons., also Pres. com. fgn. aid, 1948; chief oil br. ECA, 1948-49, cons., 1949-51; econ. cons., 1949—, NSRB, 1950; pres. Materials Policy Commn., 1951; cons. policy planning staff Dept. State, 1952-53, ICA, 1956-57, cons. office Under Sec. and Asst. Secs., 1960—, Office Civil and Def. Moblzn., 1960, European Econ. Community, 1970; fgn. econ. adviser Socony-Vacuum Oil Co., 1948; adviser to Mr. Harriman on mission to Iran, 1951. Petroleum adviser U.S. del. Council Fgn. Ministers meeting 1947; mem. U.S. del. of Austrian Treaty Commn., 1947; mem. State Dept. del. for oil discussions with U.K., 1946; mem. U.S. del. trade discussion with Sweden, 1945; mem. U.S. world programming group on petroleum, 1945; mem. enemy oil com. Joint Chiefs Staff, 1943-45; oil adviser to spl. emissary of Pres. Kennedy to Pres. of Indonesia, 1963. Mem. adv. council to Sch. Advanced Internat. Studies Johns Hopkins U. Recipient spl. plaque in grateful appreciation for invaluable contbr. to welfare U.S., Sec. State, 1968; decorated Dato Setia haila Jasa, Sultan Brunei, 1968; Order of Taj, Iran, 1969; hon. companion Order St. Michael and St. George (Eng.); President's certificate of merit. Mem. Council on Fgn. Relations. Contbr. articles to profl. publs. Home: 300 Central Park W New York NY 10024 also Westport CT 06880 Office: 30 Rockefeller Plaza New York NY 10020

LEVY, WILLARD LINZ, vocational apparel co. exec.; b. St. Louis, June 8, 1914; s. Mont M. and Elma (Linz) L.; ed. U. Pa., 1936; m. Alice Rudolph, Aug. 7, 1964; children—Elma Levy Sachar, Jill Levy Petzall. With Angelica Corp. (formerly Angelica Uniform Co.), St. Louis, 1934—, pres., 1946-73, 76—, chmn. bd., chief exec. officer, 1973—, also dir.; dir. First Nat. Bank St. Louis. Mem. St. Louis Joint Bd. Health and Hosps.; mem. president's council St. Louis U., gen. chmn. for 1978 Danforth Challenge campaign; nat. exec. bd., past nat. v.p. Am. Jewish Com. Bd. dirs. Jewish Hosp. St. Louis, St. Louis Symphony; trustee St. Louis Art Mus.; life dir., past pres. Jewish Fedn. St. Louis; bd. dirs. United Fund Greater St. Louis; adv. bd. St. Louis Minority Econ. Devel. Agy. Recipient Human Relations award Am. Jewish Com., 1968; named hon. col. Mo. Mem. Eliot Soc. of Washington U., Washington U. Faculty Center. Clubs: Westwood Country, Stadium, St. Louis, Press, Nooday (St. Louis); Cat Cay (Bahamas); Palm Bay (Miami, Fla.); Ocean Reef (Key Largo, Fla.). Home: 21 Spoede Ln Creve Coeur MO 63141 Office: Suite 100 10176 Corporate Sq St Louis MO 63132. *The World belongs to those who care.*

LEW, ALLEN YUEN, architect; b. Fresno, Calif., Nov. 6, 1912; s. Lew and Lena (Wong) Yuen; B.Arch., U. Calif. at Berkeley, 1935; m. Lillie Lee, Feb. 8, 1939; children—Audrey Hee, Donna Leong, Michael Lew. Asso. Ernst J. Kump, 1938-40; designer Douglas Aircraft Co., 1940-41, Lambert & Lew COnstrn. Co., 1943-51; architect Allen Lew Assos., 1952-75; prin. Allen Lew Assos., 1975; pres. Allen Y. Lew & William E. Patnaude, Inc., Architects & Planners, Fresno; cons. architect Calif. State U. at Fresno, 1967-78. Mem. Fresno City Planning Commn., 1957-59, Fresno City Redevel. Agy., 1960-61. Fellow AIA (pres., dir. San Joaquin chpt. 1955-57; treas. Calif. council 1958, 59; numerous awards San Joaquin chpt.). Club: Rotary (Fresno-West). Main works include: Fresno Air Terminal, Fresno Mcpl. Service Center, Confucius Ch., Sanger Library, Calif. State U. Student Union. Home: 1752 W Browning St Fresno CA 93711 Office: 1050 S St Fresno CA 93721

LEWAN, ROLAND, JR., savs. and loan assn. exec.; b. Newark, Mar. 7, 1930; s. Roland L. and Dorothy (McCance) L.; B.S., Upsala Coll., 1951; postgrad. Am. Savs. and Loan Inst., 1960, Ind. U. Grad. Sch. Savs. and Loan, 1964; m. Lois Edwards, Aug. 17, 1957; children—Roland III, Lori Ann. Asst. v.p. Yorke Savs. and Loan Assn., Newark, 1955-59; v.p. Investors Savs. and Loan Assn., Millburn, N.J., 1959-64, sr. v.p., 1964-72, pres., 1972—. Pres. Millburn-Short Hills Scholastic Boosters, 1971-73; former mem. council Short Hills Assn., 1971; former trustee N.J. Coll. Fund Assn., Inc., Summit, 1975. Served with AUS, 1951-53. Mem. Central Corp. Savs. and Loan Assns. (dir.), U.S. League Savs. Assns., Essex County Savs. League Sales Execs. Club No. N.J. Clubs: Masons (32 deg.); Baltusrol Golf (Springfield, N.J.). Home: Young's Rd New Vernon NJ 07976 Office: 249 Millburn Ave Millburn NJ 07041

LEWENSTEIN, MORRIS ROBERT, educator; b. Duluth, Minn., Oct. 30, 1923; s. Samuel and Gertrude (Flint) L.; student Itasca Jr. Coll., Colraine, Minn., 1940-42; B.A., U. Chgo., 1944, M.A., 1947; Ph.D., U. Ill., 1953; m. Ida Joyce Jenkins, Aug. 17, 1958; children—Jay, Daniel. Tchr. Momence (Ill.) High Sch., 1944-46, Joliet (Ill.) High Sch., 1947-50, U. Ill. High Sch., 1952-53; instr. San Francisco State Coll. (name changed to Calif. State U. at San Francisco), 1953-55, asst. prof., 1955-59, asso. prof., 1959-63, prof., 1963—, chmn. dept. social sci., 1959-69, exec. sec. acad. senate, 1969-71; co-founder Calif. Council Social Studies. Mem. Am. Acad. Polit. and Social Sci., Phi Beta Kappa, Phi Delta Kappa. Author: (with Edith Starratt) Our American Government Today, rev. edit., 1965; Teaching Social Studies in Junior and Senior High Schools, 1963. Home: 3029 Rivera Dr Burlingame CA 94010 Office: Social Sci Dept San Francisco State Univ San Francisco CA 94132. *I try to take from the past what is useful, but also to invent and experiment with new ideas and techniques in those areas where traditional patterns and practices fail to satisfy real needs.*

LEWENTHAL, REEVES, SR., oil exec.; b. Rockford, Ill., June 17, 1909; s. Harry Reeves and Bella Broad (Petigorski) L.; student Slade Sch., London, Eng., 1928; extension course, U. Mich., 1926-27; m. Elinor Davidson, Feb. 17, 1932 (div.); 1 dau., Lana; m. 2d, Concetta Marie Citrano, May 14, 1971; 1 son, Reeves. Newspaper reporter, 1928; dir. pub. relations Nat. Acad., 1929-34, Beaux Arts Inst., 1930-31, Municipal Art Soc., N.Y.C., 1930-33, Soc. Am. Etchers, 1929-34, Allied Artists Am., 1929-34; pres. Asso. Am. Artists, 1934-44, chm. bd., 1944-58; pres. United Printers and Pub., Inc., 1958-60, Apollo Petroleum Corp., N.Y.C.; chmn. bd. Ray Resources Corp., Allegheny and Western Energy Corp. Mem. N.Y.C. Com. Adult Edn., 1935-37; mem. art adv. com. War Dept., 1942; expert cons. for art to chief of engrs., U.S. Army, 1942. Recipient Gold medal for contbn. to Am. art Nat. Commn. to Advance Am. Art, 1932; Gold medal and Diplome de Merite, Union Francaise Des Inventeurs, 1954; De La Croix de Lorraine, L'Ordre Chevalier (France), 1954; Diplome and Croix d'Honneur (commandeur) Academie Nationale de Republique Francaise, 1954; Croix d'Honneur, 2d Class (France), 1954. Mem. Crystal Collectors' Soc. (sec.), Am. Inst. Graphic Art, Acad. Polit. Sci., Republique Francaise Nationale Artistique et Litteraire. Author: Work for Artists. Home: 1625 SE 10th Ave Fort Lauderdale FL 33316 Office: 100 Park Ave New York NY

LEWERT, ROBERT MURDOCH, microbiologist, educator; b. Scranton, Pa., Sept. 30, 1919; s. Philip John and Nell (Bertholf) L.; B.S., U. Mich., 1941; M.S., Lehigh U., 1943; Sc.D., Johns Hopkins, 1948; m. Evelyn P. Allen, Feb. 19, 1948; children—Philip Allen, Barbara Joan. Instr. biology Lehigh U., 1941-43, Hobart and William Smith Colls., Geneva, N.Y., 1943-44; instr. dept. bacteriology and parasitology U. Chgo., 1948-52, asst. prof., 1952-56, asso. prof. microbiology, 1957-61, prof., 1961—. Vis. prof. parasitology U. Philippines Inst. Hygiene, 1961, 63-66; mem. com. on parasitic diseases Armed Forces Epidemiological Bd., 1955-73; cons. to surgeon gen. Dept. Army, 1956-75; cons. on parasitic diseases Hines (Ill.) VA Hosp., 1975—; mem. tropical medicine and parasitology study sect. USPHS, 1965-69, allergy and infectious diseases tng. grant com., 1969-73. Served with USNR, 1944-46. Fulbright fellow, 1961; Guggenheim fellow, 1961. Diplomate in parasitology Am. Bd. Microbiologists. Mem. Am. Acad. Microbiology, Am. Soc. Parasitologists, Am. Soc. Tropical Medicine and Hygiene, A.A.A.S., Royal Soc. Tropical Medicine and Hygiene, N.Y. Acad. Scis., Nippon Bijitsu Token Hozon Kyokai (life), Japanese Sword Soc. of U.S. (chmn. 1977—), Sigma Xi. Mem. editorial bd. Jour. Parasitology, 1958-64, Abstracts of Bioanalytic Tech., 1959-63, Jour. Infectious Disease, Am. Jour. Epidemiology, Am. Jour. Tropical Medicine and Hygiene. Research on immunity to schistosomiasis, histochem. and cytochem. studies on invasiveness of parasites, biochemistry of host-parasite relationships. Home: 5534 S Blackstone Ave Chicago IL 60637 Office: 920 E 58th St Chicago IL 60637

LEWICKI, ANN MARIA, radiologist; b. Kowel, Poland, Aug. 25, 1932; d. Marjan and Anna Grete (Meyer) L.; came to U.S., 1952, naturalized, 1956; A.B. cum laude, Albion Coll., 1956; M.D., Wayne State U., 1959; M.P.H., Harvard U., 1976. Intern, D.C. Gen. Hosp., 1959-60; resident in radiology Wayne State Affiliated Hosps., Detroit, 1960-63; staff radiologist William Beaumont Hosp., Royal Oak, Mich., 1963-64; instr. radiology Stanford U., 1964-67, asst. prof. radiology, 1967; asso. radiology Harvard U., 1967-70, asst. prof. radiology, 1970-74, asso. prof., 1974-76; asso. prof. George Washington U. Med. Center, 1975-76, prof., 1976—. Diplomate Am. Bd. Radiology. Mem. Am. Roentgen Ray Soc., D.C. Med. Soc., Soc. Gastrointestinal Radiologists, Am. Coll. Radiology, Radiol. Soc. N.Am., Am. Med. Women's Assn., AMA, Am. Public Health Assn., AAAS, NOW. Home: 2801 New Mexico Ave NW Washington DC 20007 Office: 901 23d St Washington DC 20037

LEWIN, GEORGE FOREST, ins. co. exec.; b. Plainfield, N.H., Oct. 25, 1916; s. George Forest and Maude (Walsh) L.; A.B., Middlebury Coll., 1940; LL.B., J.D., Georgetown U., 1951; m. Barbara DeFord, May 26, 1943. Claims adjuster Liberty Mut. Ins. Co., 1940-41; exec. trainee Provident Mut. Life Ins. Co., 1941-43; asst. Washington rep. Anthracite Coal Industry, 1943-45; asst. traffic mgr. Aircraft Industries Assn., 1945-47; with Govt. Employees Ins. Co., Washington, 1947-73, v.p., sec., 1963-70, sr. v.p., 1970-73; v.p. Govt. Employees Life Ins. Co., Govt. Employees Ins. Co., Govt. Employees Financial Corp., 1974-76; sec. Criterion Ins. Co., 1964-70, exec. v.p., 1973-74, pres., 1974—, also dir. Trustee Kimball Union Acad., Meriden, N.H., 1977—. Mem. Am., Va. bar assns., Newcomen Soc., Phi Alpha Delta, Kappa Delta Rho. Republican. Methodist. Home: 5225 Connecticut Ave NW Washington DC 20015 Office: 5260 Western Ave NW Washington DC 20015

LEWIN, LEONARD CASE, writer; b. N.Y.C., Oct. 2, 1916; s. M.G. and Eva (Case) L.; A.B., Harvard U., 1936; children—Michael Z., Julie E. Author: A Treasury of American Political Humor, 1964; Report from Iron Mountain, 1967; Triage, 1972; also criticism, commentary, satire (pseudonym L.L. Case). Address: Box 112 Stonington CT 06378

LEWIN, PHILIP MARTIN, banker; b. Chgo., Jan. 15, 1935; s. Lewis Birkwood and Sadie Z. (Edelstein) L.; B.S., Northwestern U., 1956; m. Judith Ann Langert, Mar. 1, 1958; children—Stanton, Stephanie. With Continental Ill. Nat. Bank and Trust Co., Chgo., 1956—, asst. cashier, 1960-66, 2d. v.p., 1966-69, v.p., 1969-70, head new bus. task force, 1970-75; pres., chief exec. officer Drovers Nat. Bank, 1975-76; pres., chief operating officer Exchange Nat. Bank, Chgo., 1976—; vice-chmn. Am.-Israel Bank, Tel Aviv, 1977—. Asst. treas. Ill. div. Am. Cancer Soc., 1966-69, treas., 1970-75, vice chmn., 1975-77, chmn., 1977—. Bd. dirs. Hebrew Theol. Coll., 1968-69; nat. del., bd. dirs. Am. Cancer Soc. Served with AUS, 1957. Mem. Am. Israel C. of C. (dir. 1960—). Home: 720 Oakton St Evanston IL 60202 Office: Exchange Nat Bank 130 S LaSalle St Chicago IL 60690

LEWIN, WALTER H(ENDRIK) G(USTAV), physicist; b. The Hague, Holland, Jan. 29, 1936; s. Walter S. and Pieternella J. (Van der Tang) L.; came to U.S., 1966; Ph.D. in Physics, U. Delft (Holland), 1965. Instr., Libanon Lyceum, Rotterdam and U. Delft, Holland, 1960-66; asst. prof. physics M.I.T., 1966-68, asso. prof., 1968-74, prof., 1974—. Recipient medal for exceptional sci. achievement NASA, 1978. Mem. Am. Phys. Soc., Am. Astron. Soc., Internat. Astron. Union. Research and publs. in high energy astrophysics, x-ray astronomy; collaboration with artists. Office: MIT 37-627 Cambridge MA 02139

LEWINE, RICHARD, composer; b. N.Y.C., July 28, 1910; s. Irving and Jane (Weinberg) L.; student music Columbia; m. Mary Haas, Sept. 29, 1945 (dec. Dec. 1968); children—Peter Emmett, Cornelia Mary.; m. 2d, Elizabeth Craig Rivers, Nov. 27, 1970. Composer mus. scores theatrical prodns. Naughty-Naught, The Fireman's Flame, The Girl From Wyoming, 1938-40, Broadway Revue, Make Mine Manhattan, 1948, Ziegfeld Follies, 1956, The Girls Against the Boys, 1959; producer Noel Coward-Mary Martin Show, 1955, Rodgers and Hammerstein's Cinderella, 1957, Cole Porter's Aladdin, 1958; exec. producer N.Y. Philharmonic Young People's Concerts with Leonard Bernstein, 1957-61; dir. spl. projects CBS-TV, 1957-61; producer ABC TV show Hootenanny, 1963-64; producer CBS show My Name Is Barbra; producer-composer film The Days of Wilfred Owen, 1966; producer Rodgers & Hart Today, ABC-TV, 1967, Pinocchio, NBC-TV, 1968; co-author theatrical prodn. Rodgers and Hart, 1975. Served with Signal Corps., AUS, 1942-46. Recipient award Screen Producers Guild, 1965; Nat. TV Acad. award, 1965. Mem. Authors League Am., A.S.C.A.P., Dramatists Guild Council, Dramatists Guild (v.p.), Authors League Fund (treas.), Dramatists Guild Fund (sec.). Club: The Coffee House (N.Y.C.). Author: (with Alfred Simon) Ency. of Theatre Music; Songs of the American Theater, 1973; contbg. author: Playwrights, Composers, Lyricists, On Theater, 1974. Address: 352 E 69th St New York City NY 10021

LEWINE, ROBERT F., broadcasting co. exec.; b. N.Y.C., Apr. 16, 1913; s. Irving I. and Jane (Weinberg) L.; B.A., Swarthmore Coll., 1934; m. Lucille Litwin, May 18, 1938; 1 son, Robert W. Vice pres. operations Cine-TV Studios, Inc., 1945-47; dir. radio and TV, Hirshon-Garfield, Inc., advt., 1949-52; Eastern program dir. ABC, 1953-54, nat. program dir., 1954-55, v.p. programming and talent, 1955-56; v.p. night time programs TV network NBC, N.Y.C., 1957, v.p. nat. programs TV network, 1958-59; v.p. charge programs CBS Films, Inc., 1959-62; v.p. programs Hollywood, CBS TV Network, 1962-64; exec. v.p. Creative Mgmt. Assos., Ltd., 1964-65; v.p. charge prodn. Warner Bros. TV, Burbank, Calif., 1965-68; pres., chief exec. officer Nat. Acad. TV Arts and Scis., Beverly Hills, Calif., 1970-76; sr. cons. NBC TV Network, Burbank, 1977—; chmn. bd. Riverside Broadcasting Co., Los Angeles, 1977—. Trustee, Am. Women in Radio and TV Soc. Found., Columbia Coll., Los Angeles; pres. TV Arts and Scis. Found., 1964—, Film and TV Study Center, Los Angeles; bd. dirs. Paw Soc.; mem. internat. adv. council Population Inst. Served as lt. USNR, 1942-45. Mem. Nat. Acad. TV Arts and Scis. (pres. N.Y. chpt. 1958-59, 1st nat. v.p. 1958-59, gov. 1954-62, pres. 1961-63, chmn. membership com. 1960). Club: Quaker Ridge (N.Y.) Golf (dir. 1953-55). Home: 9360 Readcrest Dr Beverly Hills CA 90210 Office: 4605 Lankershim Blvd North Hollywood CA 91602

LEWINE, SIDNEY, hosp. adminstr.; b. Atlantic City, Mar. 31, 1915; s. Oscar and Yetta (Liberman) L.; B.A., U. Pa., 1935, M.A., 1936, grad. fellow, 1937-39; m. Lenore Gittelman, Feb. 27, 1937; children—David, Mark, Barbara. Psychologist, Jewish Vocat. Service, Cleve., 1939-41, dir., 1944-50; asst. dir. Employment and Vocat. Bur., Phila., 1941-43; chief manpower utilization div. War Manpower Commn. region III, Phila., 1943-44; asst. dir. Mt. Sinai Hosp., Cleve., 1950-52, dir., 1952-77, cons., 1978—; chmn. hosp. adv. com. Blue Cross N.E. Ohio, 1965-69; mem. admistrv. bd. Council of Teaching Hosps. of Am. Assn. Med. Colls., 1969-76, chmn., 1974-75; mem. joint com. Am. Hosp. Assn. and Am. Nurses Assn., 1971-75; chmn. adv. council Ohio State Nurse Bd., 1972-74; mem. Ohio Gov.'s Commn. on Malpractice, 1976-77. Mem. health industry wage and salary com. Cost of Living Council, 1973. Fellow Am. Coll. Hosp. Adminstrs.; mem. Am. (chmn. com. personnel adminstrn. 1959-61, vice chmn. council profl. practice 1964-66, chmn. bd. com. labor relations policy 1972; dir. Center for Urban Hosps. 1978—), Greater Cleve. (pres. 1969-72), Ohio (pres. 1964-65) hosp. assns., Cleve. Psychol. Assn. (pres. 1947-49), N.E. Ohio Vocat. Guidance Assn. (pres. 1949-50). Home: 23250 S Woodland Rd Cleveland OH 44122 Office: Mount Sinai Hosp University Circle Cleveland OH 44106

LEWINSOHN, JOANN, fgn. service officer; b. Oklahoma City, Mar. 26, 1931; d. Milton and H. Maree (Myer) L.; A.B., Stanford U., 1952; M.A., Johns Hopkins Sch. Advanced Internat. Studies, 1954; postgrad. Rangoon U., 1955, U. Philippines, 1957. Adminstrv. asst. Cambodian Embassy, 1958-59; pub. affairs trainee USIA, 1959; jr. officer trainee Phnom Penh, 1959, pub. affairs asst., 1960; asst. cultural officer Djakarta, 1961; lang. tng. Agy. Cambodian, 1963-64; press-publs. officer Phnom Penh, 1964, acting pub. affairs officer, 1965; press-publs. officer, Manila, 1965-66; agy. desk officer for Philippines, Indonesia, Burma, 1967; fgn. affairs officer, 1968-69; pub. affairs officer USIA, dir. USIS, Kuala Lumpur, 1970-72; dir. USIS, Stockholm, 1972-75; dep. asst. dir. for Europe, USIA, Washington, 1975-77, dir. for Europe, 1977-78; dir. for Europe Internat. Communication Agy., 1978—. Home: 2816 P St NW Washington DC 20007 Office: ICA 1750 Pennsylvania Ave NW Washington DC 20547

LEWIS, AL, actor, dir., educator; b. N.Y.C., Apr. 30, 1923; s. Alexander and Ida (Nedal) Meister; grad. Oswego State Tchrs. Coll., 1944; M.A., Columbia U., 1947, Ph.D., 1952; student Actors Workshop, 1947-55; m. Marge Domowitz, Nov. 1, 1956; children—David, Theodore, Paul. Stage appearances include Ice Man Cometh, 1956; TV appearances include Car 54 Where Are You?, The Munsters; films include They Shoot Horses. Lectr. black history in Am. Mem. AFTRA, Actors Equity Assn., Screen Actors Guild, Am. Guild Mus. Artists. Home: 14755 Hartsook St Van Nuys CA 91403 Office: 35 W 92d St New York City NY 10025

LEWIS, ALEXANDER, JR., oil co. exec.; b. Danville, Pa., July 21, 1916; s. Alexander and Elizabeth (Mason) L.; B.S., Ursinus Coll., 1938; M.S., U. Pa., 1940; Ph.D., U. Pitts., 1951; m. Alice Kabakjian, May 1, 1942; children—Alexander III, Dennis James, Brady Mason. Chemist refinery tech. div. Gulf Oil Corp., Phila., 1938-42, chief product devel. engr., Pitts., 1951-54, mgr. chem. marketing, petro-chem. dept., 1954-58, mgr. petrochems. dept., 1958—, v.p., 1960-64, sr. v.p., 1964—; pres. Internat. Trade and Tech., 1978—. Mem. Pa. Gov.'s Sci. Adv. Com., 1965—, Pa. State Com. for Nuclear Energy Devel. and Radiation Control, 1969—, Pa. State Bd. Edn., 1969—; pres. Gulf Oil Found., 1973; v.p. World Petroleum Congresses, London, 1975. Trustee Ursinus Coll., 1972, Point Park Coll., 1973; bd. regents Georgetown U.; bd. dirs. St. Clair Meml. Hosp., Pitts., Internat. Mgmt. and Devel. Inst., Washington. Fellow Mellon Inst. Indsl. Research, 1946-51. Served to lt. USNR, 1942-46. Mem. Am. Chem. Soc., Am. Petroleum Inst., Soc. Automotive Engrs., A.A.A.S., Pitts. Chemists Club, Sigma Psi, Phi Lambda Upsilon. Clubs: Duquesne, University, Downtown, Longue Vue (Pitts.); Frosty Valley Country (Danville, Pa.). Home: 807 Valleyview Rd Pittsburgh PA 15243 Office: Gulf Bldg Pittsburgh PA 15219

LEWIS, ALLAN, educator, author, dir., actor; b. N.Y.C., June 30, 1905; s. Barnett and Rebecca (Ehrlich) L.; student Townsend Harris Hall, 1919-22; B.A., Coll. City N.Y., 1927; M.A., Columbia, 1929; postgrad. New Sch. Social Research, 1936-39; Ph.D., Stanford, 1941; Dr. Modern Letters, Nat. U. Mexico, 1956; m. Brooke Waring, June 24, 1944; children—Anita Sorel, Lanny. Program dir. Keystone Broadcasting System, 1939-41; chmn. theatre dept. Bennington Coll., 1948-50; prof. theatre history Nat. U. Mexico, 1950-58; dir. Am. Shakespeare Festival Theatre, exec. dir. New Dramatists Com., 1959-61; chmn. drama dept. Briarcliff Coll., 1962-65; Littlefield prof. Shakespearean studies U. Bridgeport (Conn.), 1965-76, dir. Shakespeare Inst., 1965-75; vis. lectr. New Sch. Social Research; drama critic New Haven Register; resource participant Aspen Inst. for Humanities; fellow Folger Library. Served with AUS, 1942-46; CBI. Mem. Internat. Shakespeare Conf. (Eng.), Am. Theatre Assn., A.A.U.P., Modern Lang. Assn., Internat. Assn. U. Profs. English, World Shakespeare Assn. Author: El Teatro Moderno, 1957; The Contemporary Theatre, 1965; American Plays and Playwrights, 1967; Ionesco, 1971; The Contemporary Shakespeare, 1980. Translator: Five Mexican Painters, 1957. Contbr. articles to lit. jours. Home: 4 Elwil Dr Westport CT 06880

LEWIS, ANDREW LINDSAY, JR., financial and mgmt. cons.; b. Phila., Nov. 3, 1931; s. Andrew Lindsay and Lucille (Bricker) L.; B.S., Haverford (Pa.) Coll., 1953; M.B.A., Harvard, 1955; postgrad. Mass. Inst. Tech., 1968; m. Marilyn S. Stoughton, June 1, 1950; children—Karen Stoughton Sacks, Russell Shepherd, Andrew Lindsay IV. Foreman, job supt., prodn. mgr., dir. Henkels & McCoy, Inc., Blue Bell, Pa., 1955-60; dir. marketing, v.p. sales, dir. Am. Olean Tile Co., Inc. div. Nat. Gypsum Co., Lansdale, Pa., 1960-68; v.p., asst. to chmn. Nat. Gypsum Co., Buffalo, 1969-70; chmn. Simplex Wire & Cable Co., Boston, 1970-72; pres., chief exec. officer Snelling & Snelling, Inc., 1970-74; with Lewis & Assos., Financial and Mgmt. Consultants, Plymouth Meeting, Pa., 1974—; dir. Wawa, Inc., Henkels & McCoy, Inc., Tamaqua Wire & Cable Co., Provident Nat. Corp., Provident Nat. Bank, Phila. Suburban Water Co., Colman Co., Inc., Confer-Smith, Inc.; trustee Reading Co., 1971-77. Chmn.

Tri-Twp. Indsl. Devel. Com., Montgomery County, 1960; v.p., mem. exec. bd. North Penn United Fund, 1960-68, chmn., 1964. Orgn. chmn. Dick Schweicker for Congress Com., 1960; Pa. state committeeman 24th Senatorial Dist., 1964-66, 70-73; Republican county chmn. Montgomery County, Pa., 1965-68; del. Rep. Nat. Conv., 1968, 72; chmn. Schweiker for Senator Com., 1968; mem. finance com. Montgomery County Rep. Com., 1969; chmn. Rep. Finance Com. Pa., 1971-73; Rep. candidate for gov., 1974; Rep. nat. committeeman for Pa., 1976—; mem. exec. bd. Valley Forge council Boy Scouts Am. Clubs: Phila., Union League, Phila. Aviation Country (Phila.); Saucon Valley Country (Bethlehem, Pa.). Home: RD 1 Schwenksville PA 19473 Office: 1 Plymouth Meeting Plymouth Meeting PA 19462

LEWIS, ANTHONY, newspaper columnist; b. N.Y.C., Mar. 27, 1927; s. Kassel and Sylvia (Surut) L.; A.B., Harvard U., 1948; m. Linda Rannells, July 8, 1951; children—Eliza, David, Mia. Deskman, Sunday dept. N.Y. Times, 1948-52; staff Democratic Nat. Com., 1952; reporter Washington Daily News, 1952-55; reporter Washington bur. N.Y. Times, 1955-64, chief London bur., 1965-72; editorial columnist, 1969—. Bd. dirs. Grenville Clark Fund, Dartmouth Coll. Recipient Heywood Broun award, 1955, Pulitzer prize for nat. reporting, 1955, 63. Nieman fellow, 1956-57. Clubs: Garrick (London); Tavern (Boston). Author: Gideon's Trumpet (award as best fact-crime book Mystery Writers Am.), 1964; Portrait of a Decade: The Second American Revolution, 1964. Contbr. articles to profl. jours. Address: NY Times 84 State St Boston MA 02109

LEWIS, ARCHIBALD ROSS, educator; b. Bronxville, N.Y., Aug. 25, 1914; s. Burdett Gibson and Pearl Merriam (Archibald) L.; A.B., Princeton, 1936, M.A., 1939, Ph.D., 1940; m. Elizabeth Z. Cutler, Dec. 27, 1954; children—David Adelbert, Allyson Cutler. Adj. prof. history U. S.C., 1940-42, asso. prof., 1947-48, prof., 1948-51; Fulbright research scholar in Belgium, 1950-51; asso. prof. history U. Tex., 1951-55, prof. history, chmn. dept., 1955-59, 63-69; prof. history U. Mass., Amherst, 1969—; co-dir. Munson-Maritime Inst., Mystic Seaport, 1959-61. Fulbright prof. UAR, 1964-65; sec.-gen. 2d Internat. Congress Historians U.S. and Mexico, 1958. Served to maj. AUS, 1942-46. Decorated Bronze Star medal; Croix de Guerre (France). Ford Found. fellow in Europe, 1954-55; Am. Council Learned Socs. fellow, 1959-60. Fellow Middle East Studies Assn., Royal Hist. Soc., Mediaeval Acad. Am. (councillor 1970—); mem. New Eng. Medieval Conf. (sec. 1974—), Am. Hist. Assn., Phi Beta Kappa. Presbyn. Club: Town and Gown (Austin). Author: Naval Power and Trade in the Mediterranean, 1951; The Northern Seas, 1958; (with T. McGann) The New World Looks at its History, 1963; The Development of Southern French and Catalan Society; Emerging Medieval Europe; Aspects of The Renaissance, 1967; The High Middle Ages, 1970; The Islamic World and the West, 1970; Knights and Samurai, 1974; The Sea and Medieval Civilizations, 1978. Address: Dept History U Mass Amherst MA 01002

LEWIS, ARTHUR DEE, corp. exec.; b. Greenville, Tex., Sept. 13, 1918; s. Carl Hamilton and Maxie (Curtis) L.; student U. Tex., 1935-41, Advanced Mgmt. Program, Harvard, 1952; Sc.D., Clarkson Coll. Tech.; m. Hildegard Bair, Dec. 7, 1946; children—Gregory Scott, Kimberly Kealani. With Am. Airlines, 1941-55, beginning as cargo research analyst, successively supr. spl. projects, mgr. econ. analysis br., dir. econ. planning div., 1941-54, asst. v.p. planning, 1954-55; exec. v.p. Hawaiian Airlines, 1955, pres., dir., chief exec. officer, 1955-64; sr. v.p., gen. mgr., dir. Eastern Air Lines, 1964-67, pres., chief operating officer, dir., 1967-69; gen. partner F. Smithers & Co., 1969—, chmn., pres., chief exec. officer, 1969-73; chmn., chief exec. officer U.S. Ry. Assn., 1974-77; pres., dir. Am. Bus Assn., 1977—; organizer Consol. Ry. Corp.; organizer Nat. Ry. Passenger Corp.; dir. Riegel Paper Corp., Rexham Corp., Bank of Commerce, Iroquois Brands Ltd., Bankers Security Life Ins. Soc., Irvin Industries, C. Brewer & Co., Bishop Trust Co., Internat. Bank, Washington; cons. airline moblzn., transp. div. Nat. Security Resources Bd., Korean War; cons. Def. Air Transp. Adminstrn., 1951-55, Dept. Transp., 1969. Bd. regents U. Hawaii; bd. govs. Pacific and Asian Affairs Council, Iolani Sch. Boys; bd. dirs. Hawaii Visitors Bur.; chmn., trustee Clarkson Coll. Tech. Mem. Am. Mgmt. Assn. (dir., mem. exec. com.), Honolulu C. of C. (dir. 1958-59), Young Presidents Orgn., World Bus. Council (pres., dir. 1973—), Conquistadores del Cielo (dir.). Clubs: Links, River, Woodway, Sky (N.Y.C.); Burning Tree (Bethesda, Md.); Met. (Washington). Home: 9900 Meriden Rd Potomac MD 20854 Office: 1025 Connecticut Ave NW Washington DC 20036

LEWIS, BEN WILLIAM, economist, educator, cons.; b. Mt. Pleasant, Mich., Nov. 5, 1900; s. William Edward and Bertha Louise (Kinney) L.; student Central Mich. Teachers Coll., 1918-19; A.B., U. Mich., 1922, A.M., 1923, Ph.D., 1926, student Law Sch., 1929-30; student Harvard Law Sch., 1927-28; LL.B., Western Reserve, 1934; LL.D., Oberlin Coll., 1969; m. Gertrude Mae Dodds, Sept. 7, 1923; children—Harriet Patricia, John Francis. Instr. econ., U. Mich., 1922-25; asst. prof. econ., Oberlin (Ohio) Coll., 1925-28, asso. prof., 1928-36, prof., 1936-67, prof. emeritus, 1967—, chmn. dept., 1951-65; program adviser Ford Found., 1967-71; summer tchr. U. Chgo., 1931, 37, U. Mich., 1946, 48, 1951-58; Columbia, 1947, U. Calif., 1949, U. Minn., 1950, Pomona Coll., 1952, U. Colo., 1959; vis. distinguished prof. Va. Commonwealth U., spring 1975; part time mem. staff Brookings Instn., 1938-39; staff U.S. Labor Dept., summer 1939; chief econ. consumer div., U.S. Dept. Interior, 1940, chief econ. consumer div., Nat. Def. Adv. Commn., 1940 41; price exec., asst. to dep. adminstr. for prices, dir. indsl. mfg. div. O.P.A., 1941-43; chief distbn. div., Relief and Rehabilitation, 1943; sec. distbn. com. 1st USRRA Conf., 1943; chief indsl. orgn. sect., Fgn. Econ. Adminstrn., 1944; chief patent contracts sect., Office of Alien Property Custodian, 1944. Served as code supervisor and rep. on adv. council. Consumers Adv. Bd., Nat. Recovery Adminstrn., 1934-35; cons. Ford Found. Mem. Oberlin City Council, 1947-55. Mem. Fulbright Screening Com. Econs., 1952-57; trustee Joint Council on Economic Education, v.p., 1963-69. Mem. AAUP, Am. (v.p. 1957), Midwest (pres. 1959-60) econ. assns., Tchrs. Ins. and Annuity Assn. (trustee 1964-68), Am. Acad. Arts and Scis., Phi Beta Kappa. Clubs: City (Oberlin); Cosmos (Washington). Mem. com. on personnel, Social Sci. Research Council, 1941-44. Author: Price and Prodn. Control in Great Britain, 1937; British Planning and Nationalization, 1952; chapters in Government and Economic Life, Volume II, 1940, Readings in the Social Control of Industry, 1942, Economic Problems of Latin America, 1944; A Cartel Policy for the United Nations, 1945; American Thought, 1947; The Changing American Economy, 1967. Mem. bd. editors Am. Econ. Rev., 1941-43. Contbr. econ. and legal periodicals, lit. mags. Home: 68 S Professor St Oberlin OH 44074

LEWIS, BENJAMIN MORGAN, librarian; b. Buffalo, Jan. 8, 1920; s. Harry Fletcher and Mildred (Judd) L.; student Wesleyan U., Middletown, Conn., 1937-38; B.A., Ohio Wesleyan U., 1941; A.M. in History, U. Mich., 1947, M.A. in Library Sci., 1950, Ph.D., 1956; m. Lois Maujer, Sept. 10, 1942; children—Gary, Robert, Nancy. Asst. librarian Eastern Ill. State Coll., 1951-55; librarian Hamline U., 1955-64, Denison U., 1964-66; librarian Ohio Wesleyan, 1966—. Mem. Phi Delta Theta. Compiler: A Register of Editors, Printers and Publishers of American Magazines, 1741-1810, 1957; A Guide to Engravings in American Magazines, 1741-1810, 1959; An Introduction to American Magazines, 1800-1810, 1961. Home: 40 Hillside Dr Delaware OH 43015

LEWIS, BERNARD, historian; b. London, May 31, 1916; came to U.S., 1974; s. Harry and Jane (Levy) L.; B.A. with 1st class honors, U. London, 1936, Ph.D., 1939; Diplome des Etudes Semitiques, U. Paris, 1937; LL.D., Hebrew U., Jerusalem, 1973, Tel Aviv U., 1979; children—Melanie, Michael. Prof. history of Near and Middle East, Sch. Oriental and African Studies, U. London, 1949-74; Cleveland E. Dodge prof. Near Eastern Studies, Princeton U., 1974—; mem. Inst. Advanced Study, Princeton, N.J. Served with Brit. Army, 1940-41. Recipient Citation of Honor, Turkish Ministry of Culture, 1973, Harvey prize Technion Israel Inst. Tech., 1978. Fellow Brit. Acad.; mem. Royal Asiatic Soc., Royal Hist. Soc., Royal Inst. Internat. Affairs, Am. Hist. Assn., Am. Oriental Soc., Am. Philos. Soc., Turkish Hist. Soc. (hon.), Institut d'Egypte (corr.). Club: Athenaeum. Author numerous books, the most recent being: Islam from the Prophet Muhammad to the Capture of Constantinople, 2 vols., 1974. Office: Princeton U Dept Near Eastern Studies Princeton NJ 08540

LEWIS, BOYD DE WOLF, editor, writer; b. Boston, Aug. 18, 1905; s. Harry Braddock and Margaret De Wolf (Wade) L.; student Boston U., 1923-27; m. Hazel Reviere Bestick, Sept. 1, 1929; children—David De Wolf, Patricia Ann. Reporter, editor and bur. mgr. U.P. Assns., 1927-45; war corr. with Canadian, Brit. and Am. forces, 1944-45, 1 of 3 Am. press reps. at German surrender, Rheims, France, 1945; European news mgr. U.P., 1945; exec. editor Newspaper Enterprise Assn., N.Y.C., 1945—, v.p., 1949-63, pres., 1963-72. Vice pres. pub. info. Nat. Safety Council, 1949-57; pub. The World Almanac, 1966-72. Sec. bd. Wolf Trap Found., 1975-76; cons. Naples (Fla.) Inst. Clubs: Dutch Treat, Nat. Press. Address: 9319 Old Court House Rd Vienna VA 22180

LEWIS, CARL CHANDLER, JR., telephone co. exec.; b. Akron, Ohio, Mar. 26, 1920; s. Carl Chandler and Lulu (Gibson) L.; B.S., U. Akron, 1942; M.B.A., Harvard, 1943; m. Marjorie Inama, Oct. 26, 1943; children—Nancy Lynn (Mrs. Donald W. LaFond), Craig Thomas. Accountant, Ohio Bell Telephone Co., Cleve., 1946-54, chief statistician, 1962-63, asst. comptroller, 1967-68, v.p., comptroller, 1968—; data processing mgr. Am. Tel. & Tel., 1954-62. Mem. Greater Cleve. Growth Assn., Citizens League Greater Cleve. Served to capt. AUS, 1943-46. Mem. Akron U., Harvard alumni assns., Financial Execs. Inst., Beta Delta Psi. Home: 10728 Partridge Trail Brecksville OH 44141 Office: 100 Erieview Plaza Cleveland OH 44114

LEWIS, CARY BLACKBURN, JR., accountant, lawyer, educator; b. Chgo., Sept. 13, 1921; s. Cary Blackburn and Bertha (Mosley) L.; A.B., U. Ill., 1942; M.B.A., U. Chgo., 1947; J.D., DePaul U., 1966; Advanced Mgmt. certificate Harvard, 1971; m. Eleanor Taylor, Feb. 28, 1943; 1 dau., Cheryl (Mrs. Walker Beverly IV); m. 2d, Mary Lewis, Dec., 1970; 1 son, Cary Blackburn III. Asst. prof. accounting Ky. State Coll., Frankfort, 1947-50; asso. prof. So. U., Baton Rouge, 1950-51; sr. auditor M.T. Washington, C.P.A.'s, Chgo., 1951-53; auditor Collier-Lewis Realty Co., 1953-65; auditor A.A. Rayner & Sons, 1960-66; tchr. Chgo. Pub. Schs., 1951-57; asso. prof. law, accounting Chgo. Tchrs. Coll., 1957-65, budget coordinator, 1966-67; asso. prof. law, accounting Ill. Tchrs. Coll., 1965-67, Chgo. State Coll., 1967-70; prof. Chgo. State U., 1970—, spl. asst. to v.p., 1976—. C.P.A., Chgo., 1950—; lawyer, Chgo., 1966—. Budgetary cons. Office Econ. Opportunity; ednl. cons. to HEW; auditing cons. to Dept. Labor; mgmt. cons. to Black Econ. Union, 1969—; chmn. edn. adv. com. N.A.A.C.P., 1966—. Served to 2d lt. AC, AUS, 1942-54. Recipient Wisdom award of Honor, 1971. C.P.A., Ill. Mem. Am., Ill., Chgo. bar assns., Am. Assn. Accountants, A.A.U.P., Am. Bus. Law Assn., Am. Judicature Soc., World Wide Acad. Scholars, Am. Inst. C.P.A.'s. Club: Chgo. City. Author: How to Take an Inventory, 1948; Directory of Negro Business of Baton Rouge, La., 1950. Contbr. Bus. Men's Guide, 1971. Home: 18252 S California Ave Homewood IL 60430. *Tenacity, diligence, integrity, positive thought, thanks to the almighty, always do your best, mental and physical recreation, respect for the dignity of people, equity, and love of family.*

LEWIS, CEYLON SMITH, JR., physician; b. Muskogee, Okla., July 19, 1920; s. Ceylon Smith and Glenn (Ellis) L.; B.A., Washington U., 1942, M.D., 1945; m. Marguerite Dearmont, Dec. 20, 1943; children—Sarah Lee Lewis Lorenz, Ceylon Smith, Carol D. Lewis Kast. Intern, Salt Lake Gen. Hosp., Salt Lake City, 1945-46, fellow in cardiovascular disease, 1950-51; resident in internal medicine VA Hosp., Salt Lake City, 1948-50; practice medicine specializing in internal medicine and cardiology, Tulsa, 1951—; mem. staff St. John's Hosp., Tulsa, 1952—, chief of staff, 1963, chmn. dept. medicine, 1970-71, mem. teaching staff, 1952—; cons. in internal medicine and cardiology Indian Health Service Claremore (Okla.) Indian Hosp., 1956—; vis. staff Hillcrest Med. Center, Tulsa, 1953—; vis. staff St. Francis Hosp., Tulsa, 1963—; vis. staff Univ. Hosp., Oklahoma City, 1973—; med. dir. St. John's Med. Center, Tulsa, 1976-78; asst. clin. prof. medicine Okla. U., 1970-74, asso. clin. prof., 1975-76; clin. prof. U. Okla., Tulsa Med. Coll., 1976—; adj. clin. prof. med. scis. U. Tulsa Coll. Nursing, 1978—; mem. Residency Rev. Com. Internal Medicine, 1979—; mem. State Health Coordinating Council, 1977—; bd. commrs. Joint Commn. Accreditation Hosps., 1979—; mem. Okla. Physician Manpower Tng. Commn., 1975—, vice—chmn., 1979. Trustee, Coll. Ozarks, 1962-72, chmn., 1964-66; bd. dirs. United Way, Tulsa, 1973—, St. John Med. Center, Tulsa, 1975—; bd. dirs. Okla. Found. Peer Rev., 1973—, treas., 1973—; pres. Tulsa Med. Edn. Found., Inc., 1973-77; elder 1st Presbyterian Ch., Tulsa, 1959—; chmn. joint com. on health affairs United Presby. Ch. in U.S.A., 1969-72; pres. Presbyn. Med. Mission Fund, Inc., Woodville, Tex., 1973—. Served with M.C. AUS, 1946-48. Diplomate Am. Bd. Internal Medicine, bd. govs., 1976—. Fellow A.C.P. (chmn. bd. govs. 1978-79), Am. Coll. Cardiology, Am. Coll. Chest Physicians; mem. Tulsa County Med. Soc. (pres. 1971), Okla. Med. Assn. (pres. 1977-78), AMA, Am. Fedn. Clin. Research, Okla. Soc. Internal Medicine (pres. 1971-72), Am. Soc. Internal Medicine, Tulsa County Heart Assn. (dir. 1952-74, pres. 1956-57), Okla. Heart Assn. (dir. 1952—, pres. 1959-60), Am. Heart Assn. (fellow council clin. cardiology, v.p. 1974-75). Clubs: So. Hills Country, Tulsa. Contbr. articles to profl. jours. Office: 1705 E 19th St Tulsa OK 74104

LEWIS, CHARLES EDWIN, physician, educator; b. Kansas City, Dec. 28, 1928; s. Claude Herbert and Maudie Friels (Holaday) L.; student U. Kans., 1948-49; M.D., Harvard, 1953; M.S., U. Cin., 1957, Sc.D., 1959; m. Mary Ann Gurera, Dec. 27, 1963; children—Kevin Neil, David Bradford, Matthew Clinton, Karen Carleen. Intern, resident U. Kans. Hosp., 1953-54; trainee USPHS, 1956-58; fellow occupational health Eastman Kodak Co., 1958-59; asst. clin. prof. edpidemiology Baylor U. Sch. Medicine, 1960-61; asso. prof. medicine U. Kans. Med. Sch., 1961-62, prof., chmn. dept. preventive medicine, 1962-69; coordinator Kan. Regional Med. Program, 1967-69; prof. social medicine Harvard Med. Sch., 1969-70; prof. pub. health, head div. health adminstrn. U. Calif. Med. Sch., Los Angeles, 1970-72, prof. medicine, head div. gen. internal medicine and health services research, 1972—, prof. nursing Sch. Nursing, 1973—, dir. Health Services Research Center, 1976—; cons. to industry; mem. Nat. Bd. Med. Examiners, 1964-68; health services research study sect. USPHS, 1968—; mem. U.S. Com. Health and Vital Statistics, 1968-72; mem. Kans. Comprehensive Health Planning Council, 1968-69; mem. adv. bd. Hosp. Research and Edn. Trust, 1972-75. Bd. dirs. Kans. Cancer Soc., 1968-69, Florence Crittenden Home, Kansas City, 1968-69, vis. Nurse Assn. Los Angeles, 1972—. Served to capt. USAF, 1954-56. Recipient Ginsberg prize medicine U. Kans., 1954. Fellow Am. Pub. Health Assn., Acad. Occupational Medicine; mem. Internat. Epidemiology Soc., Assn. Tchrs. Preventive Medicine (pres. 1969-70, Inst. of Medicine of Nat. Acad. Scis. Contbr. articles to profl. Jours. Home: 221 Burlingame St Los Angeles CA 90049

LEWIS, CHARLES JOHN, grain, feed and chem co. exec.; b. Park River, N.D., May 20, 1927; s. William Henry and Hazel Elizabeth (Ramsey) L.; Asso. Sci., N.D. Sch. Forestry, 1950; B.S., Utah State U., 1952; M.S., Iowa State U., 1954, Ph.D., 1956; m. Norma McLaughlin, Aug. 5, 1950; children—Patrick Jay, Susan Lee. Nutritionist, Kent Foods, Inc., Muscatine, Iowa, 1956, dir. nutrition and research, 1957, v.p., from 1958, exec. v.p., dir. corp. research and devel., 1968—, also mem. exec. com., dir.; head, animal sci. dept. S.D. State U., Brookings. 1967-68; exec. v.p., dir. corp. research and devel., mem. exec. com., dir. Grain Processing Corp., Muscatine, 1968—; mem. exec. com., dir. Nat. Feed Ingredients. Bd. dirs. Agrl. Research Council. Served with USMCR, 1947-48. Recipient Man of Year award Nat. Feed Ingredients Assn., 1976. Mem. number profl. socs. Home: 7 Colony Dr Muscatine IA 52761 Office: 1600 Oregon St Muscatine IA 52761

LEWIS, CHARLES W., lawyer; b. Danville, Va., Aug. 19, 1904; s. William Baskerville and Maggie (Watkins) L.; A.B., Va. Mil. Inst., 1924; postgrad. Washington and Lee U. Law Sch., 1924-26; LL.B., Yale U., 1927; m. Ida Maria Bonzi, Dec. 8, 1937; children—Charles W., Maria Lewis Phillips. Capt., instr. English and mil. sci. Va. Mil. Inst., 1924-26; admitted to Va. bar, 1926, N.Y. bar 1928; practiced in N.Y.C., 1927—; partner Townsend & Lewis, 1935-52, sr. partner, 1952-73; a mng. partner Thacher, Proffitt & Wood, 1973-76, counsel, 1977—; dir. Gen. Am. Oil Co. of Tex., 1959-79, dir. emeritus, 1979—. Bd. visitors Va. Mil. Inst., 1960-64, trustee Found., 1955-79; trustee Brick Presbyn. Ch., N.Y.C., 1973-79, pres. bd. trustees, 1976-79. Mem. Am., N.Y. State bar assns., Assn. Bar City N.Y., The Virginians (N.Y.) (gov. 1963-64), Va. Mil. Inst. Alumni Assn. (pres. N.Y. chpt. 1951-52), Kappa Alpha (pres. alumni chpt. N.Y. 1934-35), S.A.R., Soc. Colonial Wars, Phi Delta Phi. Clubs: University, Down Town Assn., Squadron A, (N.Y.C.); Country of Fairfield, Fairfield County Hunt (Conn.); Masons; Hillsboro, Ponte Vedra (Fla.). Home: Greenfield Hill Fairfield CT 06430 Office: 40 Wall St New York NY 10005

LEWIS, CHARLES WILLIAM, JR., physician; b. Greensboro, N.C., May 13, 1921; s. Charles William and Ida (Hodgkin) L.; B.S., Guilford Coll., 1942; M.D., Duke, 1945; m. Gene Harlow, Nov. 10, 1945; children—Charles William III, Allan McDonald, Lloyd Arthur, Richard Harlow. Commd. ensign M.C., USN, 1943, advanced through grades to capt., 1960; sr. med. officer U.S.S. Orion, 1946-48, Naval Hosp., Pensacola, 1948-50; resident urology Naval Hosp., San Diego, 1950-53; chief urology naval hosps., Guam, 1953-54, Jacksonville, Fla., 1955-58, St. Albans, N.Y., 1958-66; M.C. detail officer, 1966-69; comdg. officer Naval Hosp., Jacksonville, 1969—72; dep. dir. Navy Regional Med. Center, Portsmouth, Va., 1972-73; chief urology U. Hosp. of Jacksonville, 1973—; asst. prof. U. Fla. Sch. Medicine, 1973—. Mem. Mayor's Health Adv. Bd., Jacksonville, 1969-72. Bd. dirs. Mental Health Clinic Duval County (Fla.), pres., 1979. Decorated Navy Commendation medal, Meritorious Service medal. Mem. A.M.A., Am. Urol. Assn., Duval County Med. Soc. (v.p. 1979), Fla. Urol. Soc., Nu Sigma Nu, Alpha Omega Alpha. Home: 4835 Raggedy Point Rd Orange Park FL 32073

LEWIS, CHESTER MILTON, pub. co. exec.; b. Oyster Bay, L.I., N.Y., Jan. 12, 1914; s. Harry Scudder and Mabel Cornelia (Hauser) L.; student Columbia Coll., 1934; m. Isabelle Joan Finch, June 2, 1945; 1 dau., Holly Finch. With N.Y. Times Library, N.Y.C., 1933—, asst. mgr. morgue, 1945-46, library supr., 1946-47, chief librarian, 1947-64, gen. services mgr., 1964-69, dir. archives, 1969-79, dir. oral history programs, 1970-79, med. adminstr., 1972-79, Idea award program adminstr., 1976-79, curator Mus. of Printed Word, 1976-79, cons., historian emeritus, 1979—; lectr., Grad. Sch. Library Sci., Pratt Inst., N.Y.C., 1956-58; vis. lectr. Grad. Sch. Bus. Adminstrn., Cornell U., 1959-60; cons. microphotography and library operations; dir. Microfilming Corp. Am., 1962-72. Mem. info. services com. Welfare Council, N.Y.C., 1950-53; v.p., treas. Rolling Wood Assn., 1950-51. Chmn. adv. council Grad Sch. Library Sci. C.W. Post Coll., 1966-69; mem. adv. com. Edward R. Murrow Meml. Library, 1966—; mem. N.Y. State Adv. Com. on Newspaper Preservation, 1974—. Recipient Jack K. Burness Meml. award for distinguished librarianship, 1965; named Hon. Alumnus Alumni, Assn. Sch. Library Sci. Columbia, 1956. Fellow Nat. Microfilm Assn.; mem. Spl. Libraries Assn. (chmn. newspaper div. 1964, award merit 1972, 2d v.p. 1952-53, 1st v.p. 1954-55, pres. 1955-56, chmn. hdqrs. salary rev. com. 1956-57, chmn. promotion techniques com. 1956-59, exec. bd. 1956-57, chmn. awards com. 1957-68, rep. Am. Standard Assn. com. on photo duplicating documents 1960-66, chmn. copyright law revision com. 1960-71, rep. joint libraries com. on copyright 1960-69, internat. mgmt. congress com. 1962-64, profl. cons. 1960—, alt. del. Council for Internat. Progress in Mgmt. 1963-66), A.L.A. (com. library standards microfilm 1961-64), Council Nat. Library Assns., Oral History Assn. (mem. com. on evaluation 1976-77, adviser oral history programs 1977, mem. nominating com. 1977-79, com. on copyright and legal agreements 1978—, com. on evaluations and standards 1978—, cons. 1978—), Soc. Am. Archivists, Beta Phi Mu. Co-author: Microrecording-Industrial and Library Applications, 1956. Editor: Special Libraries—How to Plan and Equip Them.; mem. editorial bd. Am. Documentation, 1962-71; contbr. bus. and profl. periodicals. Home: 18 Beacon Hill Rd Port Washington NY 11050 Office: 229 W 43d St New York NY 10036

LEWIS, CLAUDE, JR., shoe co. exec.; b. Jefferson City, Mo., Aug. 21, 1924; s. Claude and Opal Mae (Fowler) L.; A.B., Central Meth. Coll., Fayette, Mo., 1949; postgrad. U. Mo., 1949-50; m. Aletha Avonell Harrison, Oct. 16, 1943; 1 son, Gregory Lee. Office mgr. Brown Shoe Co., Moberly, Mo., 1950, dept. supr., St. Louis, 1954-58; asst. gen. supt. Kinney Shoe Corp., Carlisle, Pa., 1959-62, gen. supt., 1962-65, dir. purchasing, 1965-68, v.p. mfg. div., 1968, pres. mfg. div., 1969-74, corp. exec. v.p., 1974—, also dir., mem. exec. com.; dir. Farmers Trust Co.; dir., v.p. Kinney Shoe Corp. Can., Ltd. Bd. dirs., exec. com. Carlisle (Pa.) Hosp. Served with AUS, 1942-46, 50-52. Mem. Am. Footwear Industries Assn. (dir., mem. exec. com.). Republican. Methodist. Clubs: Masons (32 deg.), N.Y. Athletic, Carlisle Country; Officers (Army War Coll., Carlisle, Pa.) (Naval Depot, Mechanicsburg, Pa.). Home: 627 Belvedere St Carlisle PA 17013 Office: Kinney Shoe Corp 1275 Ritner Hwy Carlisle PA 17013

LEWIS, CLAUDE AUBREY, journalist, editor; b. N.Y.C., Dec. 14, 1936; s. Robert G. and Hazel L. (Perkinson) L.; B.A. in English, CCNY, 1958; m. Beverly Irene McKelvey, Mar. 13, 1937; children—Pamela Irene, Bryan Aubrey, Craig Elliott, Beverley Claudette. Reporter, Newsweek Mag., N.Y.C., 1953-63; spl. writer N.Y. Herald Tribune, 1963-64; reporter writer NBC-TV, Phila., 1965-66, Westinghouse Broadcasting, Phila., 1966-67; columnist Phila. Bull., 1967—, asso. editor, 1975—; mem. faculty journalism Temple U., Phila., 1975-79, Columbia U., N.Y.C., 1973-74, Villanova

(Pa.) U., 1974-76; mem. Tony Awards Com., 1977-78; served as Pulitzer Prize juror, 1976-77; tchr. English, Alternative Day Sch., North Philadelphia, 1972. Recipient numerous awards including: Gold Typewriter award, 1963, 71, Meritorious Service award Lincoln U., 1975, Donaldson award Pa. Med. Soc. Mem. Assn. of Black Journalists (co-founder, dir. 1974-79), Sigma Delta Chi. Author: (biography) Adam Clayton Powell, Jr., 1960, Muhammad Ali, 1963, Dr. Ralph Bunche, 1969, Benjamin Banneker, 1973; contbg. author: New York City in Crisis, 1964. Address: Philadelphia Bulletin 30th and Market St Philadelphia PA 19101

LEWIS, CLYDE A., lawyer; b. Hoquiam, Wash., June 20, 1913; s. J.D. Clyde and Loretta C. (Adelsperger) L.; A.B., U. Notre Dame, 1934; J.D., Harvard U., 1939; m. Helen M. Judge, Sept. 22, 1936; children—Clyde A., John E. Admitted to N.Y. bar, 1940; mem. Jerry, Lewis, Wylie, & Lyon, and predecessor firms, Plattsburg. Dir. Dominion Lime, Ltd. Comdr. in chief V.F.W., 1949-50, also served as sr. and jr. vice comdr. in chief, mem. nat. legis. com. Served to maj. USAAF, 1942-45. Decorated D.F.C. with 2 oak leaf clusters, Air medal with 4 oak leaf clusters; Croix de Guerre (France); decorated knight of Malta. Mem. Am. Legion, Am., N.Y. State bar assns., Notre Dame, Harvard alumni assns., U.S. Strategic Inst., Am. Security Council, Def. Orientation Conf. Assn. Republican. Roman Catholic. K.C., Elk. Home: 4 Lighthouse Ln Plattsburg NY 12901 Office: 53 Court St Plattsburg NY 12901

LEWIS, DALE KENTON, lawyer; b. Woodland, Kans., June 20, 1937; s. W. Homer and L. Fern Lewis; B.A., State U. Iowa, 1959; J.D., Colo. U., 1962; m. Constance L. Coover, Dec. 27, 1958; children—James W., Bari Lynn, Brad Kenton. Admitted to Colo. bar, 1962, Ind. bar, 1968; mem. firm Lewis & Ausenhus, Loveland, Colo., 1962-67; with Eli Lilly and Co., 1967—, gen. counsel Elanco Products Co., 1969-77, gen. counsel, sec. Elizabeth Arden, Inc., 1977—. Mem. Am. Bar Assn., Order of the Coif. Episcopalian. Office: 307 E McCarty St Indianapolis IN 46285

LEWIS, DANIEL CURTIS, JR., paper co. exec.; b. Suffolk, Va., Aug. 26, 1918; s. Daniel Curtis and Frances (Rawls) L.; A.B. cum laude, Washington and Lee U., 1942; M.B.A. with distinction, Harvard, 1948, D.C.S., 1954; m. Elizabeth Shirley Baer, June 5, 1948; children—Lawrence S., Clifford R., Robert D. Jr. staff accountant Lybrand Ross Bros. & Montgomery, Boston, 1948-49; asst. prof. commerce Washington and Lee U., 1949-52; research asso. bus. adminstrn. Grad. Sch. Bus. Adminstrn., Harvard, 1952-54; asst. to pres. Lynchburg Foundry Co. (Va.), 1954-56, controller, 1956-60, sec., asst. treas., 1960-63; asst. sec. Woodward Iron Co., Birmingham and Lynchburg, 1961-63; asst. to pres. Chesapeake Corp. Va., West Point, 1963-66, v.p. adminstrn., 1966—, also dir.; pres. Chesapeake Bay Plywood Corp., 1967—, also dir.; sec. Greenlife Products Co., 1969—, also dir.; dir. York River Oyster Research Corp., Cands Lumber Co. Chmn., Lynchburg Citizens Sch. Study Commn., 1960-61; mem. Va. Commn. State and Local Revenues, Expenditures and Related Matters, 1962-63, Va. Commn. Higher Edn., 1964-65; mem. West Point Sch. Bd., 1964-76, chmn., 1965-76; mem. Va. Bd. Community Colls., 1966-76, vice chmn., 1970-71, chmn., 1971-76; mem. West Point Bi-racial Com., 1968—, Va. Pub. Telecommunications Council, 1972-76. Bd. dirs. Lynchburg chpt. ARC, 1956-59, West Point Improvement Assn., 1964-67; bd. dirs. Lynchburg Guidance Center, 1956-59, pres., 1958-59; bd. dirs. United Fund Lynchburg, 1959-61, v.p., 1960-61; treas. Va. Found. Ind. Colls., 1957-63, trustee, 1966—; trustee Va. Episcopal Sch., 1960-66, Williamsburg Community Hosp., 1967-70; pres. bd. dirs. Ednl. Found. for Community Colls. Va., 1968-76; dir. sponsors Sch. Bus. Adminstrn., Coll. William and Mary, 1970—; bd. dirs. Va. Found. Humanities and Pub. Policy, 1978—. Served with USNR, 1942-46. Mem. Financial Execs. Inst., Newcomen Soc. N.Am., So. Forest Inst. (pres. 1971). Episcopalian. (vestryman, layreader). Clubs: Harvard of Va.; West Point Country (dir.); Ware River Yacht. Home: Tanager Ct West Point VA 23181 Office: Chesapeake Corp West Point VA 23181. *Each individual has been created with talents—some more or less than others. However, each individual is the steward of these talents and has an obligation to utilize them to the betterment of man. My principles, ideals, goals, and standards of conduct emanate from this tenet. Any success which I may have achieved is attributable to the implementation of this tenet.*

LEWIS, DANIEL E., choreographer; b. N.Y.C., July 12, 1944; s. Jerome and Louise L.; diploma Juilliard Sch., 1966. Dancer, asst. Jose Limon Dance Co., 1962-72, artistic dir., 1972-73; dir. Daniel Lewis Dance Repertory Co., N.Y.C., 1973—; choreographer Huston Grand Opera, 1978, Dallas Civic Opera, 1976; dir. dance programs Royal Swedish Ballet, Alvin Ailey Dance Co., Batsheva Dance Co., Royal Danish Ballet, Am. Ballet Theater; mem. faculty Juilliard Sch., 1967—; dir. dance programs Lincoln Center student programs. Nat. Endowment Arts fellow, 1973. Mem. Am. Guild Mus. Artists, Soc. Stage Dirs. and Choreographers. Home: 260 W 22d St New York NY 10011 Office: 32 Jones St New York NY 10014

LEWIS, DARRELL L., mcht.; b. Mason City, Iowa, Nov. 20, 1931; s. Milton Loren and Blanche Ione (Wilson) L.; grad. high sch.; m. Mary Jo Bahnsen, Oct. 22, 1950; children—John L., Lonnette Ann, Sherri Jo. With Osco Drug, Inc. subsidiary Jewel Cos., Inc., 1949-62, with Jewel Turn-Style 1962, pres. Turn-Style Family Centers, Franklin Park, Ill., 1967-75; v.p. store and sales devel. Osco Drug Inc., 1975—; pres. D.L. Lewis Drug Co. Inc., 1978—. Home: 229 Sherwood Dr Wood Dale IL 60191 Office: 367 E Potter St Wood Dale IL 60191

LEWIS, DAVID JAMES, psychiatrist; b. Montreal, Que., Can., May 28, 1920; s. David Sclater and Evelyn Doris (Ross) L.; B.A., McGill U., Montreal, 1941; M.D., U. Toronto (Ont., Can.), 1950; m. Catherine Jefferson Lewis, Dec. 20, 1949; children—David Wilson Ross, Anne Sclater, Peter James, Naomi Catherine, Jane A. Squier, Reporter, Ottawa (Ont.) Jour., 1939-41; intern Toronto Gen. Hosp., 1950-51; asst. resident Johns Hopkins Hosp., 1952-54, Maudsley Hosp., London, 1954; asst. psychiatrist St. Michael's Hosp., Toronto, 1956-65; to asst. prof. U. Toronto, 1956-65; asst. psychiatrist Royal Victoria Hosp., Toronto, 1965-66, sr. psychiatrist, 1966-72; clin. dir. Allan Meml. Inst., Toronto, 1966-71; asso. prof. psychiatry, coordinator postgrad. edn. in psychiatry McGill U., 1965-72; prof. U. Calgary (Alta., Can.), 1971—; physician Foothills Hosp. Psychiatry, Calgary, 1971—; cons. Mineral Springs Hosp., Banff, Alta., 1972-78. Gov. Royal Humane Soc. Served to lt. comdr. Royal Can. Navy, 1941-45. Recipient testimonial Royal Humane Soc., 1944. Fellow Royal Coll. Physicians Can., Am. Psychiat. Assn.; mem. Royal Coll. Psychiatry, Can. Med. Assn., Royal Soc. Medicine, Am. Group Psychotherapy Assn., Canadian Psychiat. Assn., Alta. Psychiat. Assn., Nu Sigma Nu. Clubs: Alpine (Canmore, Alta.); U. Calgary Faculty. Home: Serendip Rural Route 1 Calgary AB T2P 2G4 Canada Office: Foothills Hosp 16th Ave and 29th St Calgary AB T2N 2T9 Canada

LEWIS, DAVID KELLOGG, philosopher, educator; b. Oberlin, Ohio, Sept. 28, 1941; s. John Donald and Ewart (Kellogg) L.; B.A., Swarthmore Coll., 1962; M.A., Harvard U., 1964, Ph.D., 1967; m. Stephanie Robinson, Sept. 5, 1965. Asst. prof. philosophy UCLA, 1966-70; mem. faculty Princeton, 1970—, prof. philosophy, 1973—; cons. Hudson Inst., 1962-75; Fulbright lectr., Australia, 1971; Fulbright research fellow, N.Z., 1976. Recipient Matchette prize for philos. writing, 1972. Mem. AAUP. Author: Convention: A Philosophical Study, 1969; Counterfactuals, 1973. Office: Dept Philosophy Princeton Univ Princeton NJ 08544

LEWIS, DAVID LANIER, educator; b. Bethalto, Ill., Apr. 5, 1927; s. Donald F. and Edith (Jinkinson) L.; B.S., U. Ill., 1948; M.S., Boston U., 1955; M.A., U. Mich., 1956, Ph.D., 1959; postgrad. (Fulbright scholar) London Sch. Econs., 1956-57; m. Florence Yuri Tanaka, Apr. 5, 1953; children—Kim, Leilani, Sumiko, Lance. Reporter, Edwardsville (Ill.) Intelligencer, 1948; bur. chief, state editor Alton (Ill.) Telegraph, 1948-50; editor employee publs. St. Louis Lincoln-Mercury Plant, 1950-51; press relations rep. Borden Co., N.Y.C., 1952, Ford Motor Co., Dearborn, Mich., 1952-55; pub. relations exec. Gen. Motors Corp., Detroit, 1959-65; asso. prof. bus. history U. Mich., Ann Arbor, 1965-68, prof., 1968—. Cons. indsl. properties, div. history Mich. Dept. State, 1973—; coordinator oral history program Pub. Relations Found. for Research and Edn. Trustee, Nat. Automotive History Collection, Detroit; mem. exec. com. U. Mich. Press. Served with USNR, 1945-46. Mem. Econ. History Assn., Mich., Ill. hist. socs., Soc. Automotive Historians (dir.), Am. Hist. Assn. Author: The Public Image of Henry Ford: An American Folk Hero and His Company, 1976. Asso. editor Model A News, Cars & Parts; feature editor Bulb Horn; mem. editorial bd. Mich. Quar. Rev.; contbg. editor Horseless Carriage Gazette, Model T Times, V-8 Times, Old Car Illustrated. Home: 2588 Hawthorn St Ann Arbor MI 48104

LEWIS, DAVID SLOAN, JR., aircraft co. exec.; b. North Augusta, S.C., July 6, 1917; s. David S. and Reuben (Walton) L.; student U. S.C., 1934-37; B.S. in Aero. Engring., Ga. Inst. Tech., 1939; m. Dorothy Sharpe, Dec. 20, 1941; children—Susan, David Sloan III, Robert, Andrew. Aerodynamicist, Glenn L. Martin Co., Balt., 1939-46; chief aerodynamics McDonnell Aircraft Corp., St. Louis, 1946-52, chief preliminary design, 1952-55, mgr. sales, 1955-56, mgr. projects, 1956-57, v.p. project mgmt., 1957-59, sr. v.p. ops., 1960-61, exec. v.p. 1961-62, pres., 1962-67; pres. McDonnell-Douglas Co., also chmn. Douglas Aircraft Co. div., 1967-70; chmn., chief exec. officer Gen. Dynamics Corp., 1970—; dir. Ralston Purina Co., St. Louis, BankAm. Corp., San Francisco. Alderman, Ferguson, Mo., 1951-54. Trustee, Washington U., St. Louis. Fellow Am. Inst. Aeros. and Astronautics. Episcopalian. Home: 10045 Litzsinger Rd St Louis MO 63124 Office: Pierre Laclede Center St Louis MO 63105

LEWIS, DAVID THOMAS, Judge; b. Salt Lake City, Apr. 25, 1912; s. Thomas David and Ettie (Ellerbeck) L.; B.A., U. Utah, 1934, LL.B., 1937, LL.D., 1971; m. Marie Stewart, Sept. 10, 1938; children—Kent, David, Frank. Admitted to Utah bar, 1938; practiced Salt Lake City, 1938-50; state dist. judge, 1950-56; U.S. circuit judge 10th Circuit, 1956—, chief judge, 1970-77, sr. judge, 1977—. Chmn., Circuit Chief Judges Conf., 1974-75. Mem. Utah Legislature, 1947-48. Served with criminal investigation div. AUS, 1944-45. Mem. Am., Fed., Utah bar assns., Maritime Law Assn., Order of Coif, Phi Delta Phi. Club: Salt Lake Country. Home: 1333 Emigration Circle Salt Lake City UT 84108 Office: Fed Bldg Salt Lake City UT 84138

LEWIS, DELBERT RAY, broadcasting exec.; b. Wilmington, Calif., June 9, 1926; s. Clarence Alma and Gerladine Naomi (Gorham) L.; B.S. in Civil Engring., U. Ariz., 1951; m. Jewell McFarland, June 16, 1951; children—Kara Lynne, William Craig, John David, Leah Louise, Delbert Ray. Project engr. for engring. research and devel. labs., Ft. Belvoir, Va., 1950-53; owner, operator farms, Florence and Coolidge, Ariz., 1953—; a founder, part-owner, dir. sta. KTVK-TV, Phoenix, 1953—, pres., 1976—. Pres., Florence Flood Control Bd., 1955—; bd. dirs. local Boy Scouts Am., 1962-72; mem. Florence Sch. Bd., 1965-72, pres., 1967-70. Served with USNR, 1944-46; PTO. Democrat. Presbyterian. Clubs: Florence-Coolidge Rotary (past pres.), U. Ariz. Alumni (pres. Florence-Coolidge chpt. 1960-64), Shriners. Home: 807 W Roosevelt St Coolidge AZ 85228 Office: 3435 N 16th St Phoenix AZ 85016

LEWIS, DONALD JOSEPH, educator; b. Waterloo, Iowa, July 22, 1922; s. Joseph George and Gesine (Kettwig) L.; B.A., U. Calif. at Los Angeles, 1947, M.A., 1948; Ph.D., U. So. Calif., 1950; m. Nan Agricola, Aug. 23, 1953; children—Mark A., Treyenn A. Asst. prof. Northwestern U., 1951-57; asso. prof. then prof. La. State U., 1959-61; prof. psychology, chmn. dept. Rutgers U., New Brunswick, N.J., 1962-68; prof., chmn. dept. psychology U. So. Calif., 1968-72, dean social scis. and communication, 1972-76, prof. psychiatry, 1976—, sr. research scientist Social Scis. Research Inst., 1976—, also chmn. dept. psychology. Bd. dirs. San Pedro and Peninsula Hosp., Jack Kramer Tennis Club. Mem. Am., Western psychol. assns., A.A.A.S. Author: Science of Psychology, 1963; also numerous articles. Home: 2112 Mt Shasta Dr San Pedro CA 90732 Office: U So Calif Los Angeles CA 90007

LEWIS, DONALD S., fin. cons.; b. Bay City, Mich., Dec. 16, 1927; s. Raymond P. and Marjorie M. (Snover) L.; B.B.A., U. Mich., 1951, M.B.A., 1952; children—Jeffrey, Sharon, Brian, Annette. Partner Arthur Andersen & Co., 1961-64; sr. v.p. finance, dir. Foote, Cone & Belding Communications, Inc., 1964-71; pres., chief exec. officer FAS Internat., Inc., Westport, Conn., 1971-74; sr. v.p., dir. Playboy Enterprises, Inc., Chgo., 1974-78; fin. cons., 1978—. Served with AUS, 1946-47. Mem. Am. Inst. C.P.A.'s, Financial Execs. Inst. Clubs: Chgo. Yacht, U. Mich. (Chgo.). Office: Walnut St Cos Cob CT 06807

LEWIS, DUDLEY CUSHMAN, lawyer; b. Honolulu, Mar. 26, 1909; s. Abraham and Alice Hall (Jones) L.; A.B., Harvard, 1930, LL.B., 1934; m. Elizabeth Sullivan Seymour, June 28, 1932; children—Peter Cushman, Leilani. Admitted to Hawaii bar, 1935, since practiced in Honolulu; partner Lewis, Buck & Saunders, 1946-66, Lewis, Saunders & Sharpless, 1966-68, Lewis, Saunders & Key, 1969-71; of counsel Damon, Key, Char & Bocken, 1971. Dir. Hawaiian Electric Co., Inc., C. Brewer & Co., Ltd., First Hawaiian Bank, 1st Hawaiian, Inc., Hawaii Thrift & Loan; trustee S.M. Damon Estate. Dep. atty. gen. Hawaii, 1935-36, 45-46. Served from lt. (j.g.) to comdr., USNR, 1941-46. Mem. Internat. Game Fish Assn. (trustee, v.p.), Am. Bar Assn., Bar Assn. Hawaii (past pres.). Clubs: Oahu Country, Pacific (Honolulu); Pacific Union (San Francisco); Butte Lodge Outing (Colusa, Calif.). Home: 3939 Old Pali Rd Honolulu HI 96817 Office: 810 Richards St Honolulu HI 96813. *My credo is and has been: integrity, fidelity, honesty, industry.*

LEWIS, EDITH PATTON, editor; b. Phila., Aug. 27, 1914; d. William Harrison and Anna May (Issertell) Patton; B.A., Smith Coll., 1935; M.Nursing, Western Res. U., 1939; m. Leon Phillips Lewis, Jan. 10, 1948. With Am. Jour. of Nursing Co., N.Y.C., 1945—, editor Am. Jour. Nursing, 1957-59, Nursing Research, 1953-57, Nursing Outlook, 1970—; cons. in field. Recipient Distinguished Alumnus award Frances Payne Bolton Sch. Nursing, Case Western Res. U., 1975. Fellow Am. Acad. Nursing; mem. Am. Nurses Assn., Nat. League Nursing, Sigma Theta Tau. Author: Nurse: Careers Within a Career, 1963. Home: Palmer St Extension Norwich CT 06360 Office: Nursing Outlook 10 Columbus Circle New York City NY 10019

LEWIS, EDWARD, publisher; b. Bronx, N.Y., May 15, 1940; s. George and Jewell (Spencer) Clark; B.A., U. N.Mex., 1964, M.A., 1966; postgrad. N.Y. U., 1966-69. Lectr. for Peace Corps at U. N.M., 1963; adminstrv. analyst City Mgr.'s Office, Albuquerque, 1964-65; financial analyst First Nat. City Bank, N.Y.C., 1966-69; pub. Essence mag., N.Y.C., 1969—; dir. Freedom Nat. Bank, N.Y.C. Bd. dirs. Vol. Urban Cons. Group, Black Council on Africa, Fund for New Horizons for Retarded, Inc., 21st Century Found., Rheeland Found., Negro Ensemble N.Y.C., Sch. Vol. Program, trustee Coty. Recipient Decision Maker award Nat. Assn. Media Women, 1975; Nat. ICBO award for minority businessman of yr., 1979; named Businessman of Year, Blackfrica Promotions, Inc., 1974. Mem. 100 Black Men, Inc., Uptown C. of C., N.Y.C. Chamber Commerce and Industry. Office: 1500 Broadway New York NY 10036

LEWIS, EDWARD EARL, publisher; b. Royal Oak, Mich., Mar. 9, 1926; s. Arthur Earl and Rose Martha (Gerboth) L.; B.S., Ball State U., 1959; m. Jean Elizabeth Sanborn, Sept. 23, 1952; children—Steven Edward, Jon Richard, Brian Arthur. Newspaper reporter Star, Muncie, Ind., 1944-46, Statesman, Salem, Ore., 1946-48; editor Jour. Gas City, Inc., 1949-51, Argus, Brighton, Mich., 1953-55; writer Chrysler Corp., Detroit, 1955-58; pub. relations exec. Wyandotte Chems. (Mich.), 1958-61; advt. mgr. Gelman Instrument Co., Ann Arbor, Mich., 1962-66, founder pub. subsidiary, 1966, v.p., gen. mgr., 1966-68, pres., gen. mgr., 1968-71; owner, pres., treas. Ann Arbor Sci. Pubs., Inc., 1971—. Instr., Cleary Coll., Ypsilanti, Mich., 1964. Mem. Bd. Edn., Chelsea, Mich., 1968-70. Served with USNR, 1943-44. Mem. Indsl. Editors Assn. Detroit (pres.), Internat. Council Indsl. Editors. Mason. Club: Chelsea Rod and Gun. Home: 314 E Middle St Chelsea MI 48118 Office: 230 Collingwood St Drawer 1425 Ann Arbor MI 48106

LEWIS, EDWARD GREY, lawyer; b. Atlantic City, Sept. 27, 1937; s. John Connell and Ella Perrin (Grey) L.; A.B., Princeton, 1959; LL.B., U. Pa., 1963; m. Carolyn Groves; 1 dau., Leslie Groves; 1 dau. by previous marriage, Amy T. Admitted to D.C. bar, 1964; asst. U.S. atty. D.C., 1966-68; dep. asst. atty. gen. Civil Div., Dept. Justice, Washington, 1970-73; gen. counsel Dept. Navy, Washington, 1973-77; of counsel firm Morgan, Lewis & Bockius, Washington, 1977—. Served to capt., arty., U.S. Army, 1959-60. Home: 408 Duke St Alexandria VA 22314 Office: 1800 M St NW Washington DC 20350

LEWIS, EDWARD SHAKESPEAR, educator; b. Platte City, Mo., Aug. 17, 1901; s. William Talifero and Belle Zora (Caldwell) L.; Ph.B., U. Chgo., 1925; A.M., U. Pa., 1939; Ph.D., N.Y. U., 1961; LL.D., U. Cin., 1970; m. Mary Cecil Miller, June 5, 1926; children—Raphael, Carol (Mrs. Thomas Matthew). Prof. history Fla. A. & M. Coll., Tallahassee, 1925-27; exec. dir. Kansas City (Mo.) Urban League, 1927-31; dir. Balt. Urban League, 1931-42; exec. dir. N.Y.C. Urban League, 1942-63; prof. coop. edn. Borough of Manhattan Community Coll., N.Y.C., 1964—, dir. coop. edn. programs, 1964-70, dean coop. edn., 1971-78, dean emeritus, 1978—. Mem. Pres.'s Consumer Advisory Council, 1963-64; mem. advisory bd. on social welfare, N.Y.C., 1968—. Bd. dirs. Consumer-Farmer Found., Fedn. of Protestant Welfare Agys.; life mem., bd. dirs. Fresh Air Fund, 1960—; mem. Consumer Advisory Council Pres. Kennedy, Pres. Johnson. Named Man of Year, Balt. Afro-Am. Newspapers, 1941; recipient merit award Commonwealth of P.R., 1954; Bronze medal City of N.Y., 1963. Mem. Nat. Coop. Edn. Assn. (pres. 1971-72), Kappa Alpha Psi. Mason. Club: Frontiers (Balt.). Contbr. articles to profl. jours. Home: 100 La Salle St New York NY 10027

LEWIS, EDWARD SHELDON, educator; b. Berkeley, Calif., May 7, 1920; s. Gilbert Newton and Mary (Sheldon) L.; B.S., U. Calif. at Berkeley, 1940; M.A., Harvard, 1947, Ph.D., 1947; m. Fofo Catsinas, Dec. 21, 1955; children—Richard Peter, Gregory Gilbert. NRC postdoctoral fellow U. Calif. at Los Angeles, 1947-48; asst. prof., asso. prof., prof. chemistry Rice U., Houston, 1948—, chmn. dept. chemistry, 1963-67. Vis. prof. U. Southampton (Eng.), 1957, Phys. Chem. Lab., Oxford (Eng.) U., 1967-68, U. Kent, Canterbury, Eng., 1977. Served with USNR, 1944-46. Guggenheim fellow, 1968. Fellow Royal Irish Acad.; mem. Am. Chem. Soc., Chem. Soc. (London), Phi Beta Kappa, Sigma Xi, Phi Lambda Upsilon. Contbr. articles to profl. jours. Editor: Investigation of Rates and Mechanisms of Reactions, 1974. Home: 5651 Chevy Chase Houston TX 77056

LEWIS, EDWARD VAN VLIET, naval architect, educator; b. East Hampton, N.Y., Jan. 6, 1914; s. Edward R. and Susan C. (Van Vliet) L.; B.A., Neb. Wesleyan U., 1935; student U. Glasgow (Scotland), 1935-36; M.S., Stevens Inst. Tech., 1955; m. Adelyn C. Sar, Sept. 9, 1939; children—Edward A., Pamela F. From jr. architect to asst. head design George G. Sharp, naval architect, N.Y.C., 1936-51; head ship div. Davidson Lab., Stevens Inst. Tech., Hoboken, N.J., 1951-61, research prof., 1959-61; research prof. naval architecture, dir. research Webb Inst. Naval Architecture, Glen Cove, N.Y., 1961-78; dir. Center Maritime Studies, 1967-78; vis. research prof. U.S. Naval Acad., Annapolis, 1979—. Tech. adviser Am. Bur. Shipping, 1970-78. Registered profl. engr., N.Y. Fellow Soc. Naval Architects and Marine Engrs. (hon. v.p.; Linnard prize 1955, Davidson medal 1966), Royal Instn. Naval Architects, Internat. Ship Structures Congress, Sigma Xi, Phi Kappa Phi. Unitarian. Co-author: Ships, 1965; editor revised edit. Principles of Naval Architecture, 1979—; contbr. articles to profl. jours., chpts. to books. Inventor ship for high rough-water speed. Home and office: 97 Plymouth Dr N Glen Head NY 11545

LEWIS, EMANUEL P., banker; b. Balt., May 3, 1903; s. Joseph and Bertha (Westheimer) L.; student pub. schs.; m. Frances Donner, Feb. 14, 1934; children—Richard Arthur, Susan Donner. Credit mgr. James Talcott, Inc., N.Y.C., 1929, dir., 1936, v.p., 1938-56, exec. v.p., 1956-58; pres., dir. Shapiro Bros. Factors Corp., 1958-69; pres. Shapiro Factors div. Chase Manhattan Bank, N.A., 1954-71; mng. dir. Slavenburg Corp. subsidiary N.V. Slavenburgs Bank, 1972—; dir. 1200 Corp.; former dir. Interstate Dept. Stores, Inc. Mem. N.Y. Credit Men's Assn., Nat. Fedn. Textiles, Am. Arbitration Assn. Republican. Jewish. Clubs: Harmonie, The 475, City Athletic (N.Y.C.). Home: 21 E 87th St New York City NY 10028 Office: 1 Penn Plaza 250 W 34th St New York City NY 10001

LEWIS, EMANUEL RAYMOND, writer, librarian; b. Oakland, Calif., Nov. 30, 1928; s. Jacob A. and Rose (Grossman) L.; B.A., U. Calif., Berkeley, 1951, M.A., 1953; Ph.D., U. Oreg., 1962; m. Joan R. Wilson, Feb. 7, 1954; 1 son, Joseph J.; m. 2d, Eleanor M. Gamarsh, Aug. 24, 1967. Asst. prof. psychology Oreg. Coll. Edn., 1961-62, Oreg. State U., 1962-67; project mgr. System Devel. Corp., Falls Church, Va., 1968-69; vis. postdoctoral research asso. in Am. history Smithsonian Instn., Washington, 1969-70; chief historian, dir. research Contract Archeology, Alexandria, Va., 1971-73; librarian U.S. Ho. of Reps., Washington, 1973—. Served with M.I., U.S. Army, 1954-56. NIMH research fellow, 1960. Author: Seacoast Fortifications of the United States, 1970, 79; editor: The Educational Information Center, 1969. Office: B-18 Cannon House Office Bldg Washington DC 20515

LEWIS, FLORA, journalist; b. Los Angeles; d. Benjamin and Pauline (Kallin) Lewis; B.A., U. Calif. at Los Angeles, 1941; M.S., Columbia, 1942; m. Sydney Gruson, Aug. 17, 1945 (div.); children—Kerry,

Sheila, Lindsey. Reporter, Los Angeles Times, 1941, A.P., N.Y., Washington, London, 1942-46; free lance or contract for Observer, Economist, Financial Times, France-soir, Time Mag., N.Y. Times Mag., London, Warsaw, Berlin, Hague, Mexico City, Tel Aviv, 1946-54, Prague, Warsaw, 1956-58; editor McGraw-Hill, N.Y.C., 1955; bur. chief Washington Post, Bonn, London, N.Y.C., 1958-66; syndicated columnist Newsday, Paris, N.Y.C., 1967-72; bur. chief N.Y. Times, Paris, 1972—, European diplomatic corr., 1976—; Arthur D. Morse fellow in communications and society Aspen Inst. for Humanistic Studies, 1977. Recipient awards for best interpretation fgn. affairs, 1956, best reporting fgn. affairs 1960 Overseas Press Club, Columbia Journalism Sch. 50th Anniversary Honor award, 1963; award for disting. diplomatic reporting George Washington U. Sch. Fgn. Service, 1978. Mem. Phi Beta Kappa. Author: Case History of Hope, 1958, Red Pawn, 1964, One of Our H-Bombs is Missing, 1967. Contbr. to anthologies, books, mags. Office: NY Times Foreign News Desk 229 W 43d St New York NY 10036 also NY Times 3 Rue Scribe Paris 9e France

LEWIS, FLOYD WALLACE, electric utility exec.; b. Lincoln County, Miss., Sept. 23, 1925; s. Thomas Cassidy and Lizzie (Lofton) L.; B.B.A., Tulane U., 1945, LL.B., 1949; m. Jimmie Etoile Slawson, Dec. 27, 1949; children—Floyd Wallace, Gail, Julie, Ann, Carol, Michael Paul. Admitted to La. bar, 1949; with New Orleans Pub. Service Inc., 1949-62, v.p., chief financial officer, 1960-62; v.p. Ark. Power & Light Co., Little Rock, 1962-63, sr. v.p., 1963-67; exec. v.p., dir. La. Power & Light Co., New Orleans, 1967-68, pres., 1968-70, chief exec. officer, 1968-71, chmn. bd., 1970-72; pres. Middle South Utilities, Inc., 1970-79, chmn. bd., 1979—, also dir., chief exec. officer, 1972—; pres., dir. Middle South Services, Inc., New Orleans, 1970-75, chmn., 1975—, chief exec. officer, 1972—; pres., dir. Middle South Energy, Inc., 1974—; chmn. bd. System Fuels, Inc., 1972—; dir. New Orleans br. Fed. Res. Bank, 1974-75, chmn., 1975; dir. Fed. Res. Bank of Atlanta, Breeder Reactor Corp., New Orleans Pub. Service Inc., Ark. Power and Light Co., Ark.-Mo. Power Co., La. Power & Light Co., Miss. Power and Light Co. Mem. adv. com. Elec. Cos. Advt. Program, 1969-72, chmn., 1970-71; mem. electric utility advisory com. to Fed. Energy Adminstrn., 1975-76; chmn. Edison Electric Inst., 1976-77, mem. exec. com., 1974-78; mem. exec. com. Assn. Edison Illuminating Cos., 1973—; dir. Electric Power Research Inst., 1977—, chmn., 1979—; dir. Am. Nuclear Energy Council. Mem. exec. bd. New Orleans area council Boy Scouts Am., 1967—, v.p., 1970-74, pres., 1975-76, mem. regional exec. com., 1968—; v.p. Com. for a Better La., 1975-76, sr. v.p., 1976-77, pres., 1977-78; vice chmn. campaign United Fund, New Orleans, 1970, chmn., 1971. Bd. dirs. New Orleans Symphony Soc., 1974-75, Pub. Affairs Research Council of La.; pres. New Orleans Bapt. Sem. Found., 1973-76; trustee New Orleans Baptist Theol. Sem. 1954-62, 1968-78, v.p., 1970-78; bd. adminstrs. Tulane U., 1973—; bd. visitors Tulane U., 1968-71, gov. Med. Center, 1969-73, vice chmn., 1969-71, chmn. alumni adv. council Grad. Sch. Bus., 1970-73, recipient Outstanding Alumni award, 1970; v.p. Internat. House, 1970; trustee Com. Econ. Devel., 1972—, Gulf South Research Inst.; mem. bd. Ochsner Med. Found., 1976—, mem. exec. com., 1977—. Served to ensign USNR, 1945-46. Recipient Silver Beaver, Silver Antelope Boy Scouts Am. Mem. Am., La. bar assns., Tulane Alumni Assn. (exec. com., treas. 1970), New Orleans Area C. of C. (v.p. 1970, dir. 1970-73, 78), Order of Coif, Beta Gamma Sigma, Omicron Delta Kappa, Beta Theta Pi, Phi Delta Phi. Baptist (deacon). Home: 5557 Berkley Dr New Orleans LA 70114 Office: 225 Baronne St New Orleans LA 70161

LEWIS, FRANK HARLAN, univ. dean; b. Redlands, Calif., Jan. 8, 1919; s. Frank Hooker and Mary Elizabeth (Smith) L.; A.A., San Bernardino Valley Coll., 1937; B.A., U. Calif. at Los Angeles, 1941, M.A., 1942, Ph.D., 1946; postgrad. Calif. Inst. Tech., 1942-44; m. Margaret Ruth Ensign, Aug. 2, 1945; children—Donald Austin, Frank Murray; m. 2d, Ann Gibbons, Dec. 23, 1968. Mem. faculty U. Calif. at Los Angeles, 1946—, prof. botany, 1956—, systematist expt. sta., 1956-62, chmn. dept., 1959-62, dean div. life scis., 1962—. Cons. genetics NSF, 1958-61, specialized biol. facilities, 1963-68. Trustee Graeme Joseph Revolving Scholarship Fund. NRC fellow John Innes Hort. Instn., London, Eng., 1947-48; Guggenheim fellow, 1954-55. Fellow AAAS (council mem. 1974-76), Calif. Acad. Sci.; mem. Bot. Soc. Am. (pres. Pacific div. 1959, Merit award 1972), Soc. Study Evolution (pres. 1961), Internat. Orgn. Plant Biosystematists (exec. com. 1961—, v.p. 1964-69, pres. 1969-75), Am. Soc. Naturalists (pres. 1971), Am. Soc. Plant Taxonomists (pres. 1969), Internat. Soc. Plant Taxonomists, Phi Beta Kappa, Sigma Xi. Bd. editors Evolution, 1951-53, editor, 1972-74; bd. editors Am. Jour. Botany, 1964-66, Am. Naturalist, 1965-67, 77-79; chmn. bd. editors U. Calif. publs. in botany, 1958-62. Home: 14280 Sunset Blvd Pacific Palisades CA 90272

LEWIS, FRANK RUSSELL, banker; b. Birmingham, Ala., May 8, 1925; s. James Eugene and Margaret Louise (Russell) L.; student Samford U., 1946-48; student U. Ala., 1948-50; m. Shella Shelton, June 17, 1950; 1 dau., Leesa June. Credit mgr. Kessler's, Inc., Birmingham, 1950-52; collection mgr. Sears, Roebuck & Co., Birmingham, 1952-59; credit mgr. Bromberg's Inc., Birmingham, 1959; with Birmingham Trust Nat. Bank, 1959—, now exec. v.p., security officer; exec. v.p. So. Bancorp. Ala. dir. So. Data Services, Inc. Pres., Birmingham Children's Theatre, 1976-78, bd. dirs., 1978—; pres. Greater Birmingham Arts Alliance. Served with USNR, 1943-46. Named Boss of Year, Credit Women Birmingham Club, 1968. Mem. Delta Chi. Republican. Baptist (deacon). Clubs: Exchange, Monday Morning Quarterback, Vestavia Country, The Club, Inc., Relay House (Birmingham). Home: 3750 River Oaks Ln Birmingham AL 35223 Office: 112 N 20th St Birmingham AL 35290

LEWIS, GENE DALE, historian, educator; b. Globe, Ariz., Feb. 20, 1931; s. Abner E. and May J. (Hyatt) L.; B.A., Ariz. State U., 1951, M.A., 1952; Ph.D., U. Ill., 1957; m. Dottie Ladd Bidlingmeyer, Aug. 3, 1963. Lectr., Ariz. State U., 1953, So. Ill. U., 1957-58; vis. asso. prof. history U. Ill., Urbana, 1965, Case-Western Res. U., Cleve., 1966; prof. history U. Cin., 1958—, sr. v.p., provost, 1973-76. Recipient Barbour award for excellence U. Cin., 1969; Nat. award Omicron Delta Kappa, 1968. Mem. AAUP, So., Am. hist. assns., Orgn. Am. Historians. Author: Charles Ellet Jr., Engineer as Individualist, 1968. Home: 444 Rawson Wood Ln Cincinnati OH 45220 Office: Dept History U Cin Cincinnati OH 45221

LEWIS, GEORGE KNOWLTON, educator; b. Waltham, Mass., Jan. 11, 1923; s. George W. and Alice (Merrill) L.; A.B., Harvard, 1944, A.M., Ph.D., 1956; m. Shirley Peakes, Dec. 31, 1942; children—Martha S., Pamela W., Peter G. Mem. faculty Boston U., 1950—, asso. prof., 1957-63, prof. geography, 1964—; cons. aerial photography, photo interpretation; analyst location studies in retail location; lectr. Wellesley Coll., Harvard Sch. Design. Selectman, Town of Wayland (Mass.), 1960-67. Founder, bd. dirs. Sudbury Valley Trustees, Inc. Served with USNR, 1943-45, 51-52. Decorated Order of Simon Bolívar (Venezuela). Mem. Assn. Am. Geographers, Am. Geog. Soc. Research and publ. on cities and tributary areas. Home: 182 Concord Rd Wayland MA 01778 Office: 48 Cummington St Boston MA 02215

LEWIS, GEORGE RUSSEL, librarian; b. Webster County, Miss., July 15, 1929; s. John Terry and Martha (Shaffer) L.; grad. Clarke Meml. Coll., 1950; B.A. with honors, Miss. Coll., 1952; M.S. in Library Sci., La. State U., 1956; postgrad. Baylor U., 1957; M.L.S., Fla. State U., 1973, Ph.D., 1975; m. Bobbie Jean McClain, Nov. 26, 1952; children—Karen Denise, Michael Keith. Tchr. English, Forest City (Miss.) Schs., 1952-54; grad. asst. La. State U. Library, 1954-56; asst. pub. service librarian, then cataloger Baylor U. Library, 1956-58; head circulation dept. Auburn U. Library, 1958-62; head librarian Ky. So. Coll., Louisville, 1962-63; dir. libraries Miss. State U., 1963—. Mem. Miss. Library Commn. Mem. ALA (council 1976—), (Miss. membership chmn.), Miss., Southeastern library assns., Assn. Coll. and Research Libraries, Phi Kappa Phi, Phi Delta Kappa. Baptist. Club: Rotary. Home: PO Box 723 Mississippi State MS 39762

LEWIS, GEORGE STEPHEN, architect; b. Boston, Dec. 7, 1908; s. William Joseph and Florence Ann (Whitehead) L.; cert. M.I.T., 1926; grad. (Harvard scholar) Boston Archtl. Sch., 1931; cert. Boston U., 1939; grad. Archtl. Sch., Harvard, 1932, Command and Gen. Staff Coll., 1956, U.S. Army C.E. Sch., 1957, Indsl. Coll. of Armed Forces, 1963. Architect with Maginnis & Walsh, Boston, 1925-31; profl. practice, Boston, 1928 41; head architect firm Lewis, Spering & Rogers, Boston, 1941-47; prin. architect George Stephen Lewis & Assos., Boston, 1947—; chief architect Pub. Works Dept., U.S. Navy, Boston, 1953-65. Mem. Nat. Fed. Agencies Com., 1969, Civic Design Com., 1965-67; participant AIA-HUD Assisted Housing Seminar, 1972, AIA-Cons. Engrs. Council-Profl. Engrs. in Pvt. Practice Conf. Profl. Liability Service, 1972, 75, Cons. Engrs. Council Conf. Occupational, Safety and Health Adminstrn., 1972, 74, Nat. Seminar Architects-Engrs. Firms on Contracts and Programs, New Orleans, 1971; rep. Nat. Architects-Engrs. Pub. Affairs Conf., Washington, 1972-76; mem. N.E. regional council AIA Conf. Nat. and Regional Planning, Ethics and Bus., 1942-78; mem. archtl.-engring. firms contract bd. Boston Naval Shipyard, 1971-73. Served with AUS, 1943-46. Created knight, France, 1961; recipient Great Silver medal of Paris, 1962; Harvard scholar Boston Archtl. Center, 1931; Rotch Travelling fellow architecture, 1933-35; award of honor, mem. Hall of Fame, Wisdom Soc., 1970; citation Nat. Found. Arts and Humanities. Mem. AIA (nat. legis. minuteman 1968-79, del. nat. convs. 1946-71, ofcl. recorder 1979), Constrn. Specifications Inst. (chmn. publicity com. Boston chpt. 1974-75, chpt. dir. 1978-80, del. N.E. region 1 conf. 1976, 78, pres.'s cert. Boston chpt. 1977), Boston Soc. Architects (profl. practices com. 1974-79), Order Lafayette (nat. v.p., dir., historian 1958-79), Fed. Profl. Assn., Archtl. Assn. London, Greater Boston C. of C., Inst. Contemporary Art, UN Assn. (charter), Mil. Order World Wars (exec. com. 1973-79), Res. Officers Assn. (nominating com., army council chpt. 4 1974-77). Clubs: Harvard, Mass. Republican. Prin. works include: Renovation State Capitol, Mass., 1948-51; Renovation Admiral's Residence, Boston Naval Shipyard, 1959-60; San. Bldg., Nahant, Mass., 1948-49; Lodgen's Supermarket, Roslindale, Mass., 1948; modern residences Boston Housing Authority, 1947-48; (with John A. McPherson) design Ch. of Annunciation, Danvers, Mass., 1936-37. Contbr. numerous articles to profl. jours., newspapers. Address: 1376 Commonwealth Ave Suite 21 Boston MA 02134 Office: 294 Washington St Boston MA 02108. *My objectives have been reached by: having a conscious interest in activities of our life and education that will be beneficial; taking part when possible in regular and special activities influencing the profession of architecture, its advancement and business progress and actions; making friends with the press and our governmental representatives and senators, writing to them information and news that will benefit our nation and communities; taking the opportunity to travel broadly to appreciate the national and international natural resources of our world and to create better relations amongst our peoples by doing so; taking continued interest in the security of the U.S. by participating in each of our civilian-military organizations and their programs.*

LEWIS, GEORGE WITHROW, automobile distbg. co. exec.; b. Berwyn, Ill., May 13, 1929; s. George Edward and Katherine (Withrow) L.; A.B., Princeton, 1951; M.B.A., Harvard, 1955; m. Ellen Freer Baker, Sept. 14, 1963; children—George Baker, Martha Freer. With Ford Motor Co., 1955-62; cons. McKinsey & Co., N.Y.C., 1962-64; pres. Rolls-Royce Motors Internat. U.S.A. and Europe, Lyndhurst, N.J., 1965—; chmn. Park Ward Motors, N.Y.C.; alt. dir. Moto-Equipos, S.A., (Mexico City, Mexico). Served to 1st lt., arty. AUS, 1952-53; Korea. Episcopalian (vestryman). Clubs: Reform (London); Metropolitan, Princeton (N.Y.C.); Plainfield (N.J.) Country. Home: 50 Century Ln Watchung NJ 07060 Office: Lyndhurst Corp Center Lyndhurst NJ 07071

LEWIS, GLENN ALUN, artist; b. Chemainus, B.C., Can., Oct. 26, 1935; s. Rhys Thomas and Phyllis (Ramsey) L.; grad. with honors Vancouver Sch. Art, 1958; postgrad. in edn. U. B.C., 1958-59. Ceramic apprentice with Bernard Leach, St. Ives, Eng., 1961-63; instr. ceramics Faculty of Edn., U. B.C., Vancouver, 1964-67, instr. fine arts dept., 1971-74; vis. prof. Alfred U., N.Y. State Coll. Ceramics, 1970-71; program coordinator Western Front Soc., Vancouver, 1973—; works include mural Nat. Sci. Library, Ottawa, Ont., Can., 1973. Can. Council grantee, 1967, 70, 76. Mem. Royal Hort. Soc., Garden History Soc. Address: 303 E 8th Ave Vancouver BC V5T 1S1 Canada

LEWIS, GOLDY SARAH, real estate developer, corp. exec.; b. West Selkirk, Man., Can., June 15, 1921; came to U.S., 1923, naturalized, 1935; d. David and Rose (Dwor) Kimmel; B.S., UCLA, 1943; postgrad. U. So. Calif., 1944-45; m. Ralph Milton Lewis, June 12, 1941; children—Richard Alan, Robert Edward, Roger Gordon, Randall Wayne. Pvt. practice acctg., Los Angeles, 1945-55; law office mgr., Los Angeles, 1953-55; dir., exec. v.p. Lewis Homes, Upland, Calif., 1955—; dir., exec. v.p. Lewis Construction Co., Upland, 1959—, Lewis Bldg. Co., Inc., Las Vegas, 1960—, Republic Sales Co., Inc., 1956—, Kimmel Enterprises, Inc., 1959—; mng. partner Lewis Homes of Calif., 1973—, Lewis Homes of Nev., 1972—, Western Properties, 1972—, Foothill Investment Co., 1971—, Republic Mgmt. Co., 1978—. Mem. Dean's Council UCLA Grad. Sch. Architecture and Urban Planning; mem. UCLA Found., Chancellor's Assos. Recipient 1st award of distinction Am. Builder mag., 1963. Mem. Nat. Assn. Home Builders, Bldg. Industry Assn. So. Calif., Internat. Council Shopping Centers, Urban Land Inst., AAUW. Contbr. articles to mags., jours. Home: 2120 Vallejo Way Upland CA 91786 Office: PO Box 670 Upland CA 91786

LEWIS, HAL GRAHAM, educator; b. Greensboro, Ga., Apr. 16, 1909; s. Edward Lloyd and Lillian (Boswell) L.; A.B., U. Ga., 1930; M.A. in Edn., U. Fla., 1938; student Columbia Tchrs. Coll., 1941-44; Ph.D., Columbia, 1951; m. Mary Godwin, Sept. 5, 1936; children—Gray, Mary Elizabeth. Tchr., Hollywood, Fla., 1931-36; supervising tchr. P.K. Yonge Lab. Sch., U. Fla., 1936-41; state supr. adult edn. WPA, 1941; instr. edn. Adelphi Coll., Garden City, N.Y., 1942-44; prof. edn. U. Fla., 1944-48, 49—, head dept. founds. of edn., 1949-55, 61-64, 69-78, distinguished service prof., 1976-78, emeritus, 1978—; vis. prof. edn. Fresno State Coll., Univs. I., Rutgers, Hawaii; edn. specialist Mil. Govt. Germany, 1948-49. Mem. Phi Beta Kappa, Kappa Delta Pi. Home: 1230 SW 9th Rd Gainesville FL 32601. *Do the best you can with what you have to improve conditions that are around you.*

LEWIS, HAROLD GREGG, economist, educator; b. Homer, Mich., May 9, 1914; s. Clayton Arthur and Florence (Gregg) L.; student Port Huron Jr. Coll., 1932-34; A.B., U. Chgo., 1936, Ph.D., 1947; m. Julia Catherine Elliott, Dec. 14, 1938; children—Peter Elliott, John Gregg, Scott Porter. Instr. econs. U. Chgo., 1939-43, asst. prof., 1945-49, asso. prof., 1949-57, prof., 1957-75; prof. econs. Duke, 1975—; asst. dir. wage stblzn. WLB, 1943-45. Served with USAAF, 1945. Mem. Am. Econ. Assn., Phi Beta Kappa. Author: Unionism and Relative Wages in the United States, 1963. Contbr. articles to profl. jours. Home: 102 Longwood Pl Chapel Hill NC 27514

LEWIS, HAROLD WALTER, univ. ofcl.; b. Keene, N.H., May 7, 1917; s. Hiram Edwin and Lena (Ashton) L.; B.S. Middlebury (Vt.) Coll., 1938; M.A., U. Buffalo, 1940; Ph.D., Duke, 1950; m. Mary Anne O'Rourke, June 1, 1946; children—Barbara, Richard. Physicist, Naval Ordnance Lab., also Bur. Ordnance, 1941-46; mem. faculty Duke, Durham, N.C.) 1949—, prof. physics, 1959—, dean arts and scis., 1963-69, vice provost, 1963—, dean faculty, 1969—. Fellow Am. Phys. Soc.; mem. Am. Assn. Physics Tchrs. Spl. research on nuclear physics. Home: 1708 Woodburn Rd Durham NC 27705

LEWIS, HAROLD WARREN, educator; b. N.Y.C., Oct. 1, 1923; B.A., N.Y. U., 1943; Ph.D., U. Calif., Berkeley, 1948; m. Mary Rosso, July 25, 1947; children—Nina, Roger. Mem. Inst. for Advanced Study, Princeton, 1947-48, 50-51; mem. faculty U. Calif., Berkeley, 1948-50; with Bell Telephone Labs., Murray Hill, N.J., 1951-56; mem. faculty U. Wis. at Madison, 1956-64, Princeton, 1961-62; prof. physics U. Calif. at Santa Barbara, 1964—. Served with USNR, 1944-46. Home: 4162 Cresta Ave Santa Barbara CA 93110

LEWIS, HARRY ARTHUR, hosp. exec.; b. Akron, Ohio, Oct. 25, 1919; s. Charles Antsel and Ethelyn Louise (Peterson) L.; student Los Angeles Pacific Coll., 1939-40, U. Calif. Extension, Berkeley, 1957-63, Cornell U., 1964, U. of Pacific, 1968-69; m. Ella Jane Broomfield, Nov. 16, 1940; children—Karen Lewis, Susan (Mrs. James Johnson). Service and supply officer Stockton (Calif.) State Hosp., 1953-59, hosp. bus. adminstr., 1959-70; hosp. adminstr. Stockton and Met. State hosps., 1970—; now exec. dir. Lanterman State Hosp. Former trustee Los Angeles Pacific Coll. Served with AUS, 1942-45. Mem. Am. Coll. Hosp. Adminstrs. Office: 3530 W Pomona Blvd Pomona CA 91766

LEWIS, HARVEY SHELTON, educator; b. Jackson, Miss., Aug. 6, 1938; s. Willie Fred and Mozelle (Peden) L.; B.S., Miss. State U., 1961; M.B.A., U. Ark., 1963, Ph.D., 1966; grad. Sch. Banking South, La. State U., 1969, Sr. Bank Officers Sch., Harvard, 1973; m. Di Ann Bartee, June 2, 1961; children—Jon Brian, Lauri Ann, Heather Ann. Mem. faculty Miss. State U., Mississippi State, 1965-73, asso. prof. fin., 1966-68, prof., head dept. fin. and ins., 1968-73; prof. econs. and banking, head chair banking U. Miss., University, 1974-77, chmn. senate of faculty, 1978; dir., mem. faculty Miss. Sch. Banking, 1974-77, vice chancellor, prof. econs. and banking, 1977—. Partner Mid-South Cons. and Research Assos., Starkville, Miss., 1965-73; instr. Am. Inst. Banking, Corinth, Tupelo and Starkville, 1968-73; mem. faculty Sch. Banking of South, La. State U.. 1970-77, Ark. Sch. Banking, 1975-77; vis. prof. finance U. Ark. European Grad. Programs, 1973. Bd. dirs. Sand Water Creek Water Pollution Control Assn., Wesley Found. Miss. State U., 1969-73, U. Miss., 1974-77; mem. bd. pensions North Miss. Conf., United Meth. Ch., 1977—. Recipient Outstanding Tchr. award U. Miss., 1977. Mem. Miss. Econ. Council, East Miss. Council (charter mem.), Ozark Econ. Assn. (pres. 1967-68), Am., So. fin. assns., Bank Mktg. and Pub. Relations Assn., Fin. Execs. Inst., Newcomen Soc. N. Am. (Miss. com.), Oxford-Lafayette County C. of C., Blue Key, Omicron Delta Kappa, Alpha Kappa Psi, Beta Gamma Sigma, Pi Sigma Epsilon, Lambda Chi Alpha. Methodist (adminstrv. bd., council on ministries, fin. com.). Lion (pres. Starkville 1972-73, v.p. Oxford 1975-76). Contbr. articles to profl. jours. Home: 221 Carol Ln Oxford MS 38655 Office: Lyceum Bldg U of Miss University MS 38677

LEWIS, HELEN PHELPS HOYT, assn. exec.; b. Lakewood, N.J., Dec. 27, 1902; d. John Sherman and Ethel Phelps (Stokes) Hoyt; A.B., Bryn Mawr (Pa.) Coll., 1923; M.A., Union Theol. Sem. of Columbia U., 1925; m. Byron Stookey, May 11, 1929 (dec. Oct. 20, 1966); children—John Hoyt, Lyman Brumbaugh, Byron; m. 2d, Robert James Lewis, Aug. 5, 1971. Bd. mgrs. Christodora Settlement House, N.Y.C., 1927-38, 1st v.p., 1929-38; nat. bd. YWCA, 1927-30; mem. women's adv. council N.Y. Bot. Garden, 1952—; mem. nursing com. Columbia Presbyn. Med. Center, N.Y.C., 1944-54, trustee, 1969-78, hon. trustee, 1978—; mem. women's aux. Neurol. Inst., N.Y.C., 1939—, chmn., 1949-54; mem. women's exec. com., chmn. com. hosp. auxs. United Hosp. Fund, 1951-64, vice chmn. women's campaign com., 1961-62, chmn. women's subcom. distbn., 1963-65, vice chmn. women's exec. com., 1963-64. Mem. Colonial Dames Am. (dir. 1951-56, chmn. scholarship com. 1949-51, pres.-gen. 1953-56), Daus. Cincinnati. Presbyterian. Clubs: Darien (Conn.) Garden (pres. 1935-38); Millbrook Garden (past pres.); Garden Club Am.; Colony (gov. 1954-76, sec. 1956-59, sec., v.p. 1969-71, pres. 1972-76, chmn. membership com. 1956-71) (N.Y.C). Republican. Address: 580 Park Ave New York NY 10021

LEWIS, HENRY, condr.; b. 1932; ed. (music scholarship) U. So. Calif.; m. Marilyn Horne. Double-bass player with Los Angeles Philharmonic, later asso. condr. for 3 years; founder Los Angeles Chamber Orch., 1958; music dir. Los Angeles Opera Co., 1965-68; condr. N.J. Symphony, Newark, 1968 76; former condr. Met. Opera; condr. ballet-cantata, Gershwiniana, La Scala opera house, Milan, 1965; guest condr. maj. world orchs. Served with U.S. Army as condr. 7th Army Symphony, 1950's.*

LEWIS, HENRY WILKINS, univ. adminstr., lawyer, educator; b. Jackson, N.C., Nov. 7, 1916; s. Edmund Wilkins and Jane Crichton (Williams) L.; A.B., U. N.C., 1937; J.D., Harvard, 1940. Admitted to N.C. bar, 1940; practice in Jackson, 1940-41; mem. staff Inst. of Govt., U. N.C., 1946-51, research prof. pub. law and govt., 1951-57, prof., 1957-73, acting v.p. U. N.C., 1968-69, dir. Inst. Govt., 1973-78, Kenan prof. pub. law and govt., 1975-78, emeritus, 1978—; v.p. Wilkins Texas Corp., Brodnax, Va., 1967—, also dir.; counsel N.C. Elections Laws Commn., 1967, N.C. Commn. for Study Local and Ad Valorem Tax Structure, 1970, N.C. Commn. for Study Property Tax Exemptions and Classifications, 1973; mem. N.C. Criminal Justice Tng. and Standards Council, 1973-78, N.C. Criminal Justice Edn. and Tng. System Council, 1973-78, N.C. Commn. on Productivity in State Govt., 1976-77. Mem. adv. bd. N.C. State Art Soc., 1962-63; mem. Com. for Restoration St. John's Ch., Williamsboro, N.C., 1950-79; mem. adv. bd. Ackland Art Center, U. N.C., 1957-78. Trustee Va. Episcopal Sch. Served to capt. AUS, 1941-46. Mem. Lincoln's Inn Soc., N.C. Bar Assn., N.C. Lit. and Hist. Assn. (v.p. 1972-75), N.C. Collectors (pres. 1965-66), Roanoke-Chowan Group (convenor 1962-65), Order of Gimghouls, Phi Beta Kappa, Alpha Tau Omega. Episcopalian (parish conv. del. 1948, 50-51, 63-64, 66-69, 71, 74-75, 78; mem. diocesan standing com. 1957-64, 65-68, 69-72, 73-76, dep. Gen. Conv. 1967, 69, 70, 76, 79). Author: Property Tax Collection in North Carolina, 1951, rev. edit., 1957; The General Assembly of North Carolina: Organization and Procedure, 1952; Legislative Committees in North Carolina, 1952; Basic Legal Problems in the Taxation of Property, 1958; (with Robert G. Byrd) In Rem Property

Tax Foreclosure, 1959; An Introduction to County Government, 1963, rev. edit., 1968; Primary and General Election Law and Procedure, 11 edits., latest 1968; Property Tax Exemptions and Classifications, 1970; The Property Tax: An Introduction, 1972, rev. edits., 1975, 78. Contbr. articles to profl. jours. Home: 407 North St Chapel Hill NC 27514

LEWIS, HERMAN WILLIAN, geneticist; b. Chgo., July 10, 1923; s. Jacob and Mary (Weiss) L.; B.S., U. Ill., 1947, M.S., 1949; Ph.D., U. Calif. at Berkeley, 1952; m. Helen Simon, Dec. 29, 1942; children—David, Miriam. Prof. genetics Mass. Inst. Tech., 1954-61; dir. genetic biology program NSF, Washington, 1962-66, head cellular biology sect., 1966-77, sr. scientist for recombinant DNA activities, 1977—. Served with AUS, 1943-45. USPHS postdoctoral fellow, 1952-54; research grantee, 1954-62; recipient Mendel medal Czechoslovakian Acad. Scis., 1965; Outstanding Service award Genetic Soc. Am., 1979. Mem. Genetics Soc. Am., Am. Soc. Cel. Biology, Am. Soc. Human Genetics, Biophys. Soc., Sigma Xi. Author research papers. Home: 5325 Chevy Chase Pkwy Washington DC 20015 Office: 1800 G St Washington DC 20550. *Be impatient with ignorance, but be patient with the ignorant.*

LEWIS, IRVING JAMES, educator; b. Boston, July 9, 1918; s. Harry and Sarah (Bloomberg) L.; A.B., Harvard U., 1939; A.M., U. Chgo., 1940; m. Rose Helen Greenwald, June 15, 1941; children—Deborah Ann, Amy Rebecca, William David. With U.S. Govt., 1942-70, dep. chief internat. div. Bur. Budget, 1955-57, 59-65, dept. head Intergovtl. Com. European Migration, Geneva, 1957-59, chief health and welfare div. Bur. Budget, 1965-67, dep. asst. dir. Bur., 1967-68, dep. adminstr. health services and mental health adminstrn. HEW, 1968-70; prof. community health Albert Einstein Coll. Medicine, Bronx, N.Y., 1970—. Served with CIC, AUS, 1943-46. Brookings fellow, 1941; WHO fellow, 1977; recipient Exceptional Service award Bur. Budget, 1964; Ann. Career Service award Nat. Civil Service League, 1969. Fellow N.Y. Acad. Medicine (asso.); mem. Am. Soc. Pub. Adminstrs., Am. Pub. Health Assn., Med. Health and Research Assn. (v.p.), Assn. Am. Med. Colls., Am. Vets. Com. (pres. Washington 1949), Inst. Medicine, Nat. Acad. Scis. Jewish (pres. temple). Club: Harvard (N.Y.C.). Home: 262 Monterey Ave Pelham NY 10803 Office: Albert Einstein Coll Medicine Bronx NY 10641

LEWIS, JACK (CECIL PAUL), editor, publisher; b. North English, Iowa, Nov. 13, 1924; s. Cecil Howell and Winifred (Warner) L.; B.A., State U. Iowa, 1949; children—Dana Claudia, Brandon Paul. Publicist savs. bonds U.S. Treasury Dept., Des Moines, 1948-49; reporter Santa Ana (Calif.) Register, 1949-50; motion picture writer Monogram Pictures, 1950; reporter Daily Pilot, Costa Mesa, Calif., 1956-57; editor Challenge Pub., North Hollywood, Calif., 1957-60; pres. Gallant Pub. Co. Inc., 1960—; pres. Charger Prodns. Inc., Capistrano Beach, Calif., 1971—, editor Gun World, 1960—. Served to lt. col. USMCR, 1942-46, 50-56, 58, 70. Decorated Bronze Star, Air medal (3). Mem. Writers Guild Am., U.S. Marine Corps Combat Corrs. Assn. (pres. 1970-71, 73-74, chmn. bd. dirs. 1972-78), Sigma Nu, Sigma Delta Chi. Republican. Author 8 novels, 12 other books, 11 TV shows, 7 motion pictures; contbr. articles to mags. Home: 2701 Calle de Comercio San Clemente CA 92672 Office: 34249 Camino Capistrano Capistrano Beach CA 92624

LEWIS, JAMES ELDON, health care exec.; b. Pontiac, Mich., Jan. 5, 1938; s. Wilbert Arthur and Mary Helen (Eatwell) L.; B.S., Eastern Mich. U., 1961; M.A., U. Ga., 1963, Ph.D., 1966; m. Rachel Ann Allen, Aug. 18, 1963; children—James Eldon, Sara Ann. Asst. prof. geography La. State U., 1966-69, U. Va., 1969-73; v.p. Enviro-Med, Inc., Washington, 1973-74; sr. profl. asso. Inst. Medicine, Nat. Acad. Scis., 1975-77; interim dean, then dean U. Okla. Med. Coll., Tulsa, 1977-78; dir. U. Okla. Health Sci. Center, Washington, 1978-79; v.p. CDP Assos., Inc., Rockville, Md., 1979, pres. Health Resources Devel. Group, 1979—; cons. in field. Alumni Found. fellow U. Ga., 1964-66. Author reports, papers in field. Home: 1052 Leigh Mill Rd Great Falls VA 22066

LEWIS, JAMES KIRTLEY, banker; b. N.Y.C., Feb. 14, 1926; s. Kirtley Bowen and Margaret (Carpenter) L.; B.A., St. Lawrence U., 1946; postgrad. Stonier Grad. Sch. Banking, 1956; m. Mary Blight Biddle, June 27, 1959; children—Diana T., Thomas K., Mary Biddle. With Chem. Bank N.Y. Trust Co., 1946-52; asst. cashier Central Trust Co., Cin., 1952-56, asst. v.p., 1956-58, v.p., 1958-69, sr. v.p., 1969-74, exec. v.p., 1974—; dir. Begley Drug Co., Richmond, Ky. Am. Controlled Industries, Inc., Jung Products, Inc., Valley Industries, Inc., Hamilton Tool Co. Vice chmn., trustee Cin. Council on World Affairs, Cin. Zoo, Children's Protective Agy. Home: 3530 Bayard Dr Cincinnati OH 45208 Office: Central Trust Co Cincinnati OH 45202

LEWIS, JAMES MOSE, agrl. coop. exec.; b. Mt. Sterling, Ky., June 8, 1918; s. Charles Hawkins and Mary (Lane) L.; student Ohio State U., 1938-39; m. Marjorie Crites, June 16, 1943; children—James C., Richard C. Holstein cattle breeder, Hamilton, Ohio, 1920—; dir. Ohio Farm Bur. Fedn., also Ohio Farm Bur. Coop., 1950-60; mem. Agrl. Stblzn. Com. Ohio, 1957-58; v.p. Ohio Farm Bur. Coop. Assn., 1955-58, pres., 1958—; pres. Ohio Holstein Assn., 1958—; dir. Coop. League U.S.A., United Coops., Coop. Mills, Nationwide Mut. Ins. Co., Nationwide Corp., 1972—; pres. Ohio Purebred Dairy Cattle Assn., 1960—; chmn. gen. Nationwide Ins. Co., 1965—; dir. Nat. Holstein-Friesian Assn. Am.; chmn. bd. Nationwide Consumer Services, 1971—, Nationwide Mut. Fire Ins. Co., 1974—. Mem. Fairfield Twp. Farm Bur., Ohio Expn. Com., Grange. Methodist. Address: 9400 Keplar Ford Rd Orient OH 43146

LEWIS, JAMES PITCHER, paper mfg. co. exec.; b. Beaver Falls, N.Y., Aug. 28, 1917; s. Harry S. and Mary (Pitcher) L.; student Williams Coll., 1935-39; m. Lorraine Ellis, Apr. 23, 1941; children—Jay Purdy, Lawrence Ellis, William Pitcher. With J.P. Lewis Co., 1939—, v.p., 1946-50, pres., 1950—. Trustee emeritus Clarkson Coll. Tech., Deerfield Acad. Served with USCGR, 1942-44. Home: The Moorings 905 Bowline Dr Vero Beach FL 32960

LEWIS, JAMES WOODROW, state chief justice; b. Darlington County, S.C., Mar. 8, 1912; s. W. J. and Mary Aletha (Bryant) L.; A.B., U. S.C., 1932; m. Alice Lee, Dec. 26, 1936; 1 dau., Barbara (Mrs. Olin D. Haynes). Admitted to S.C. bar, 1935; mem. S.C. Hwy. Commn., 1936-40; mem. S.C. Ho. of Reps. from Darlington County, 1935-36, 43-45; judge 4th Jud. Circuit S.C., 1945-61; asso. justice Supreme Ct. S.C., 1961-75, chief justice, 1975—. Address: PO Box 53 Darlington SC 29532

LEWIS, JERRY, comedian; b. 1926; ed. Irvington (N.J.) High Sch.; m. Patti Palmer, 1944; children—Gary, Ronnie, Scotty, Chris, Anthony, Joseph. Began as entertainer with record routine at Catskill (N.Y.) hotel; formed comedy team with Dean Martin, 1946-56; performed as a single, 1956—; films include Delicate Delinquent, 1957; including Sad Sack, 1957; Rockabye Baby, 1958; Geisha Boy, 1958; Don't Give Up the Ship, 1958; Visit to a Small Planet, 1959; Bellboy, 1960; Cinderfella, 1960; Ladies Man, Errand Boy, It's Only Money, The Nutty Professor, The Patsy, Disorderly Orderly, Don't Raise the Bridge, Lower the River, also Hook, Line and Sinker, Big Mouth, Boeing, Boeing, Three on a Couch, Which Way to the Front. Prof. cinema U. So. Calif.; pres. Jerry Lewis Prodns., Jerry Lewis Films Inc., P.J. Prodns., Inc., Patti Enterprises. Nat. chmn. Muscular Dystrophy Assn. Mem. Screen Producers Guild, Screen Dirs. Guild, Screen Writers Guild. Office: Jerry Lewis Films Suite 830 1888 Century Park E Los Angeles CA 90067

LEWIS, JERRY, U.S. congressman; b. Oct. 21, 1934; B.A., UCLA, 1956. Life ins. underwriter; field rep. for former U.S. Rep. Jerry Pettis; mem. Calif. State Assembly, 1968-78, vice chmn. rules com., chmn. subcom. on air quality; mem. 96th Congress from 37th Calif. dist. Mem. San Bernardino Sch. Bd. Named One of Outstanding Young Men, Calif. Jaycees, 1970. Office: 327 Cannon House Office Bldg Washington DC 20515

LEWIS, JESSICA HELEN (MRS. JACK D. MYERS), physician, educator; b. Harpswell, Maine, Oct. 26, 1917; d. Warren Harmon and Margaret (Reed) Lewis; A.B., Goucher Coll., 1938; M.D., Johns Hopkins, 1942; m. Jack D. Myers, Aug. 31, 1946; children—Judith Duane (dec.), John Lewis, Jessica Reed, Elizabeth Read, Margaret Anne. USPHS Research fellow U. N.C., 1947-48, research asso. dept. physiology, 1948-55; asso. dept. medicine Duke Med. Sch., 1951-55; research asso. dept. medicine U. Pitts., 1955-58, faculty, 1958—, research asso. prof., 1965-70, prof. medicine, 1970—; dir. research Central Blood Bank Pitts., 1969—, v.p., 1974—; dir. Hemophilia Center Western Pa., 1973—. Mem. Am. Physiol. Soc., Am. Soc. Clin. Investigation, Am. Fedn. Clin. Research, Soc. for Exptl. Biol. Medicine, Internat., Am. socs. hematology, Sigma Xi. Research, numerous publs. on mechanism blood coagulation, fibrinolysis, hemorrhagic and thrombotic diseases. Home: 2689 Oak Hill Dr Allison Park PA 15101 Office: Dept Medicine U Pitts Pittsburgh PA 15261 also Central Blood Bank Pitts 812 Fifth Ave Pittsburgh PA 15219

LEWIS, JOHN CLARK, JR., mfg. co. exec.; b. Livingston, Mont., Oct. 15, 1935; s. John Clark and Louise A. (Anderson) L.; B.S., Fresno (Calif.) State U., 1957; m. Carolyn Jean Keesling, Sept. 4, 1960; children—Robert, Anne, James. With Service Bur. Corp., Calif., 1960-70, Computer Scis. Corp., El Segundo, Calif., 1970; with Xerox Corp., El Segundo, 1970-77, pres. bus. systems div., 1977; pres. Amdahl Corp., Sunnyvale, Calif., 1977—. Served with USNR, 1957-60. Roman Catholic. Address: 13864 Yerba Santa Ct Saratoga CA 95070

LEWIS, JOHN GIDEON, JR., assn. exec.; b. Natchitoches, La., Dec. 9, 1903; s. John Gideon and Virginia (Thompson) L.; B.A., Fisk U., 1923; Ph.D. in Humanities, Central State Coll., Wilberforce, Ohio, 1961; m. Amelia Jones, Oct. 27, 1933. Farmer, Natchitoches, La., 1923-37; grand master of Prince Hall Masons for La., Baton Rouge, 1941—; sovereign grand comdr. Scottish Rite Masonry So. jurisdiction Prince Hall Affiliation, Baton Rouge, 1961—. Bd. dirs. Baranco-Clark YMCA, Baton Rouge, 1960-64, Flint Goodridge Hosp. of Dillard U., Legal Def. and Ednl. Fund NAACP. Recipient Equal Opportunity award Urban League, 1961, Grand Band of Star of Africa Republica of Liberia, 1972; named one of 100 Most Influential Blacks in Am., Ebony Mag., 1972-74. Mem. Smithsonian Assos., La. Edn. Assn. (life), NAACP, Alpha Phi Alpha, Sigma Pi Phi. Democrat. Baptist (trustee, treas. 1947-75). Mason, Odd Fellow. Home: 1605 Harding Blvd Baton Rouge LA 70807 Office: 1335 North Blvd Baton Rouge LA 70802. *I have tried to live so that no one will regret having done me a favor.*

LEWIS, JOHN PRIOR, economist, educator; b. Albany, N.Y., Mar. 18, 1921; s. Leon Ray and Grace (Prior) L.; student St. Andrews U. (Scotland), 1939-40; A.B., Union Coll., Schenectady, 1941; M.Pub. Adminstrn., Harvard, 1943, Ph.D. in Polit. Economy and Govt., 1950; D.C.L., Union Coll., 1970; m. June Estelle Ryan, July 12, 1946; children—Betsy Prior, Sally Eastman, Amanda Barnum. Instr., asst. prof. econs. and govt. Union Coll., Schenectady, 1946-50; mem. staff, asst. to chmn. Council Econ. Advisers, Exec. Office of Pres., Washington, 1950-53; cons. UN Korean Reconstrn. Agy., Pusan, Korea, 1953; asso. prof. Ind. U., 1953-56, prof. bus. econs. and pub. policy, 1956-64, distinguished service prof. bus. econs. and pub. policy, 1964, chmn. dept., 1961-63; mem. Council Econ. Advisers, Exec. Office of Pres., Washington, 1963-64; minister-dir. USAID mission to India, 1964-69; dean Woodrow Wilson Sch. Pub. Affairs, 1969-74, prof. econs. and internat. affairs Princeton, 1969—, on leave, 1979—; chmn. devel. assistance com. OECD, Paris, 1979—. Sr. staff mem. in India, Brookings Instn., Washington, 1959-60; mem. UN Com. on Devel. Planning, 1970—, rapporteur, 1972-78. Served to lt. USNR, 1943-46: PTO. Author: Reconstruction and Development in South Korea, 1955; Business Conditions Analysis, 1959, 2d edit. (with R.C. Turner), 1967; Quiet Crisis in India: Economic Development and American Policy, 1962; (with Ishan Kapur) The World Bank Group, Multilateral Aid, and the 1970's 1973. Home: 16 Villa Said 75116 Paris France

LEWIS, JOHN WILSON, polit. scientist; b. King County, Wash., Nov. 16, 1930; s. Albert Lloyd and Clara (Lewis) Seeman; A.B. with highest honors, UCLA, 1953, M.A., 1958, Ph.D., 1962; m. Jacquelyn Clark, June 19, 1954; children—Cynthia, Stephen, Amy. Asst. prof. govt. Cornell U., 1961-64, asso. prof., 1964-68; prof. polit. sci. Stanford U., 1968—, William Haas prof. Chinese politics, 1972—; chmn. joint com. on contemporary China, Social Sci. Research Council-Am. Council Learned Socs., 1976-79; bd. dirs. Nat. Com. on U.S.-China Relations; cons. Senate Select Com. on Intelligence; dir. N.E. U.S. Forum on Internat. Policy, Stanford U.; dir. arms control and disarmament program Stanford U.; chmn. com. advanced study in China Com. Scholarly Communication with People's Republic of China. Served with USN, 1954-57. Mem. Assn. Asian Studies, Am. Polit. Sci. Assn., Council on Fgn. Relations. Author: Leadership in Communist China, 1963; Major Doctrines of Communist China, 1964; co-author: The United States in Vietnam, 1967; Modernization by Design, 1969. Editor: The City in Communist China, 1971; Party Leadership and Revolutionary Power in China, 1970; Peasant Rebellion and Communist Revolution in Asia, 1974. Contbr. to Congress and Arms Control, 1978; China's Quest for Independence, 1979, others. Mem. editorial bds. China Quar., Internat. Security, Survey, Chinese Law and Govt. Negotiated first univ. discussion arms control and internat. security matters Chinese People's Inst. Fgn. Affairs, 1978; negotiated first univ. tng. and exchange agreement People's Republic of China, 1978. Home: 541 San Juan St Stanford CA 94305 Office: Dept Polit Sci Stanford U Stanford CA 94305

LEWIS, JORDAN DAVID, internat. bus. exec.; b. Chgo., Aug. 9, 1937; s. Murray Robert and Ruth (Weinstein) L.; B.S.Engring. in Physics, U. Mich., 1960, B.S.Engring. in Math., 1960, M.S.Engring. in Nuclear Engring. (fellow), 1963, M.S.Engring. in Info. Systems, 1963, Ph.D. in Thermonuclear Physics, 1966; m. Lynn Lopata, Sept. 20, 1964; children—Matthew Michael, Katherine Anne. Instr. physics U. Mich. at Dearborn, 1962-64, research asst., 1964-66; with Battelle Devel. Corp., Columbus, Ohio, 1966-72, asst. mgr. devel. dept., 1968-70, mgr. gen. operations, 1970-72; dir. applied tech. programs Batelle Columbus Labs., Columbus, 1972; dir. exptl. tech. incentives program Nat. Bur. Standards, Washington, 1973-77; exec. dir. A.T. Internat., Washington, 1977—, U.S. del. to OECD, Paris; expert witness on tech., economics and pub. policy before Congl. coms.; adviser on technol. change and econ. growth to fgn. govts. and internat. orgns.; adv. on product, market and bus. devel. to corps.; keynote speaker various internat. confs. on tech. and econ. growth; chmn. Fed. Task Force on Energy Intensive Products, 1975. Co-chmn. Columbus Outdoor Summer Concerts, 1968-70; chmn. bd. dirs. Columbus Inner-City Econ. Devel. Corp., 1969-71. AEC fellow, 1964-66. Fellow AAAS (mem. council; chmn. indsl. sci. sect. 1975); mem. Acad. Contemporary Problems, Inst. Pub. Adminstrn., Sigma Xi. Editor: (with Lynn L. Lewis) Industrial Approaches to Urban Problems, 1972. Contbr. articles to profl. jours. Home: 3707 33d Pl NW Washington DC 20008

LEWIS, L(EO) RHODES, educator; b. Emporia, Kans., Nov. 27, 1919; s. Edwin James and Mabel (Rhodes) L.; Mus.B., Baker U., 1941; M.S., Kans. State U., 1949; Ph.D., Ia. U., 1956; m. Roberta Palmquist, Dec. 25, 1942; children—Gavin Rhodes, Trevor Robert, Scott Rhys, Lisa Ellen. Supr. music Swink (Colo.) pub. schs., 1948; instr. Kans. State U., Manhattan, 1948-49; prof. Eastern Oreg. Coll., LaGrande, 1949-63; prof. U. Wis. at Eau Claire, 1963—, chmn. dept. music, 1963-73. Mus. dir., condr. Am. Community Symphony Orch., European and Far East concert tours, 1961, 63, 65, 68, 69, 71; mus. dir. 1st Luth. Ch., Eau Claire, 1964-76. Mem. exec. com. Wis. Arts Council, 1966-73. Served with USN, 1941-48. Decorated Croix de Commandeur, French Legion Honor, 1961. Named Outstanding alumni Kans. State U., 1960. Mem. Young Audiences Wis. (v.p. 1967-75, exec. dir. 1975-78), Wis. Symphony Orch. Assn. (pres. 1966-68), Am. Symphony Orch. League (dir. 1956-59), Music Educators Nat. Conf., Nat. Assn. Am. Composers and Condrs., Wis. Music Educators Assn., Am. Fedn. Musicians, Phi Mu Alpha Sinfonia, Phi Delta Kappa, Delta Tau Delta. Presbyn. (elder). Lion (dist. gov. 1972-73, dir. Wis. Lions found. 1974-79), Elk. Home: Box 101-471 Roosevelt St Eau Claire WI 54701

LEWIS, MATTHEW, JR., newspaperman; b. McDonald, Pa., Mar. 8, 1930; s. Matthew and Alzenia Temperance (Heath) L.; student Howard U., 1947, U. Pitts., 1948; m. Jeannine Wells, July 13, 1974; children by previous marriages—Charlene, Matthew Marvin, Kevin. Instr. audio-visual dept. Morgan State Coll., Balt., 1957-65; news, then mag. photographer Washington Post, 1965-76, asst. mng. editor photography, 1976—. Served with USN, 1949-52. Recipient Pulitzer prize feature photography, 1975. Mem. White House News Photographers Assn., Nat. Press photographers assns. Home: 18740 Tanterra Way Brookeville MD 20729 Office: 1150 15th St NW Washington DC 20071

LEWIS, MEL (MELVIN SOKOLOFF), musician; b. Buffalo, May 10, 1929; s. Samuel and Mildred (Brown) S.; student pub. schs., Buffalo; m. Doris J. Sutphin, Dec. 25, 1952; children—Anita Lynn, Lori Ellen, Donna Jeanne. Drummer with orchs. of Boyd Raeburn, 1948, Alvino Ray, 1948, Ray Anthony, 1949, 53-54, Tex Beneke, 1950-53, Stan Kenton, 1954-57; freelance recording, Hollywood, Calif., 1957-59; appeared with ABC Studios, Hollywood, 1959-60, Gerry Mulligan Orch., 1960, Dizzy Gillespie, 1961, NBC Studios, Hollywood, 1961-62, Benny Goodman, 1962; with Thad Jones-Mel Lewis Orch., 1965—, leader, 1979—; bandleader, tchr. New Eng. Conservatory-William Patterson State Coll. Recipient Russian Allstars Jazz Poll award as best drummer, 1962, Downbeat Critics Best Drummer award, 1963, Downbeat awards as best band, 1966, 72—, Readers Poll awards, 1973—, Jazz Forum awards, 1975—, Swing Jour. awards, 1975, 76, Playboy Allstars Poll award, 1975. Mem. Am. Fedn. Musicians, Nat. Acad. Rec. Arts and Scis. Democrat. Jewish. Office: care Willard Alexander Inc 660 Madison Ave New York NY 10021

LEWIS, MORRIS, JR., wholesale and retail grocery exec.; b. Lexington, Miss., Apr. 19, 1911; s. Morris and Julia (Herrman) L.; B.S. in Econs., U. Pa., 1932; m. Frederica Lantor, Nov. 21, 1933; children—Morris III, Julia (Mrs. Gerald W. Miller). With Lewis Grocer Co., Indianola, Miss., 1932—, pres, 1937-69, chmn. bd., 1969—; pres. Sunflower Stores, Indianola, 1948-69, chmn. bd., 1969—; v.p., dir. Super Valu Stores, Inc, Hopkins, Minn., 1965-70, chmn. bd., 1970-76, chmn. exec. com., 1976—, dir., 1976—; chmn. audit com., mem. exec. com., dir. 1st Miss. Corp., Jackson, dir. Peoples Bank of Indianola, W.E. Walker Stores, Inc., Jackson, First Miss Inc., Ft. Madison, Iowa; dir., mem. exec. com. Columbus & Greenville R.R. Mem. Nat. council Boy Scouts Am., also dir., past pres. Delta council; trustee Millsaps Coll., Jackson. Served to maj. AUS, World War II. Named Indianola Citizen of Year, Indianola C. of C., 1954. Mem. Nat.-Am. Wholesale Grocers Assn. (past nat. pres., past chmn. bd.), Miss. C. of C. (past pres.). Rotarian (past pres.). Home: One Arbor Ln Indianola MS 38751 Office: Hwy 49W Indianola MS 38751

LEWIS, NORMAN, educator, author; b. N.Y.C., Dec. 30, 1912; s. Herman and Deborah (Nevins) L.; B.A., City Coll. N.Y., 1939; M.A., Columbia, 1941; m. Mary Goldstein, July 28, 1934; children—Margery, Debra. Instr., lectr. City U. N.Y., 1943-52; asso. prof. English, N.Y.U., 1955-64; instr. Compton (Calif.) Coll., summers 1962-64, U. Calif. at Los Angeles extension, 1962-69; prof. English, Rio Hondo Coll., Whittier, Calif., 1964—, chmn. communications dept., 1964-75. Author: (with Wilfred Funk) Thirty Days to a More Powerful Vocabulary, 1942, rev., 1970; Power with Words, 1943; How to Read Better and Faster, 1944, rev. edit., 1978; The Lewis English Refresher and Vocabulary Builder, 1945; Better English, 1948; Word Power Made Easy, 1949, rev. edit., 1978; The Rapid Vocabulary Builder, 1951; How to Get More Out of Your Reading, 1951; Twenty Days to Better Spelling, 1953; The New Roget's Thesaurus in Dictionary Form, 1961, rev. edit., 1978; Dictionary of Correct Spelling, 1962; Correct Spelling Made Easy, 1963; Dictionary of Modern Pronunciation, 1963; New Guide to Word Power, 1963; The New Power with Words, 1964; Thirty Days to Better English, 1964; The Modern Thesaurus of Synonyms, 1965; RSVP-Reading, Spelling, Vocabulary, Pronunciation, elementary texts I-III, 1966, coll. edit., 1977; See, Say, and Write!, Books I and II, 1973; Instant Spelling Power, 1976; R.S.V.P. for College English Power, Book II, 1978, Book III, 1979; also numerous articles in nat. mags.

LEWIS, OREN RITTER, judge; b. Seymour, Ind., Oct. 7, 1902; s. Jno M. and Emma A. (Crabb) L.; student Hanover Coll., 1924; LL.B., George Washington U., 1939; m. Grace M. Wells, Aug. 12, 1925; children—Oren Ritter, Robert Wells. Circulation mgr. Washington Times Herald, 1926-33; with various Hearst newspapers, 1933-39; owner, pub. Alexandria-Arlington-Fairfax Jours., 1940-61; admitted to Va. bar, 1939; practiced in Arlington County, 1939-60; judge U.S. Dist. Ct., Eastern Dist. Va., Alexandria, 1960—. County and dist. chmn. Republican Party, 1932-58. Served with USN, World War I. Mem. Am. Bar Assn., Va. Bar Assn., Arlington County Bar Assn. (pres.), Jud. Council U.S., Nat. Lawyers Club. Clubs: Masons (32 deg.); Shriners; Kiwanis (pres., lt. gov.); Washington Golf and Country. Home: 3409 N Albemarle St Arlington VA 22207 Office: US Dist Ct Alexandria VA 22313

LEWIS, ORME, lawyer; b. Phoenix, Jan. 7, 1903; s. Ernest W. and Ethel (Orme) L.; ed. Stanford, 1920-21; LL.B., George Washington U., 1926; m. Barbara C. Smith; 1 son, Orme. Admitted to Ariz. bar, 1926, Calif. bar, 1931, U.S. Supreme Ct. bar, 1955, D.C. bar, 1969; practiced in Phoenix, 1926—; now mem. Lewis and Roca; asst. sec.

Dept. Interior, 1953-55; mem. 9th Ariz. State Legislature. U.S. rep. GATT, 1955. Fellow Am. Bar Assn. Clubs: Arizona, Paradise Valley (Phoenix); Metropolitan, Capitol Hill (Washington). Home: 97 Mountain Shadows W Scottsdale AZ 85253 Office: 100 W Washington Phoenix AZ 85003

LEWIS, PERRY JOSHUA, investment banker; b. San Antonio, Feb. 11, 1938; s. Perry Joshua and Zeline L. L.; B.A., Princeton U., 1959; m. Memrie Taylor Mosier, May 12, 1962; children—Perry Joshua, IV, Memrie Fraser. Registered rep. Lee Higginson Corp., N.Y.C., 1960-63; comml. project mgr. Parsons & Whittemore, Inc., N.Y.C., 1964-67; sr. v.p., mgr. corp. fin. div. Smith Barney, Harris Upham & Co. Inc., N.Y.C., 1967—; dir. Combined Ins. Co. Am., Chgo. Bd. dirs. 55th St. Dance Theater Found., Inc., N.Y.; bd. dirs. Lake-Cook Theatre Fod., Lake Forest, Ill., 1973—, chmn., 1973-77. Served with U.S. Army, 1959-60, 61-62. Clubs: Knickerbocker of N.Y., Econ. of Chgo. Home: 167 Zaccheus Mead Ln Greenwich CT 06830 Office: Smith Barney Harris Upham & Co Inc 1345 Ave of Americas New York NY 10019

LEWIS, PETER BENJAMIN, ins. co. exec.; b. Cleve., Nov. 11, 1933; s. Joseph M. and Helen (Rosenfeld) L.; A.B., Princeton U., 1955; m. June 19, 1955: children—Ivy, Jonathan, Adam. With Progressive Ins. Cos., 1955—, pres., chief exec. officer Progressive Casualty Ins. Co., The Progressive Corp., Mayfield Village, Ohio, 1965-79, chmn. bd., chief exec. officer, 1979—. Trustee, Greater Cleve. Growth Assn., Hillcrest Hosp., 1977-78. Mem. Young Pres.'s Orgn., Soc. C.P.C.U.'s (pres. Cleve. chpt.). Clubs: Cleve. Racquet, Oakwood, Union. Office: 6300 Wilson Mills Rd Mayfield Village OH 44143

LEWIS, PETER CUSHMAN, electric co. exec.; b. Cleve., June 9, 1934; s. Dudley C. and Elizabeth (Seymour) L.; student Deerfield Acad., 1950-52; B.A., Williams Coll., 1956; LL.B., U. Va., 1962; m. Mary Louise Earthrowl, Dec. 22, 1956; children—Peter Cushman, Kimberly, Geoffrey Seymour. Admitted to Hawaii bar, 1962; practice in Honolulu, 1962-68; dep. atty. gen. State of Hawaii, 1962-68; asst. sec. Hawaiian Electric Co., Honolulu, 1968, sec., 1968—, asst. treas., 1971-74, treas., 1974-75, asst. v.p., 1975-77, v.p., adminstrn., sec., 1977—; per diem dist. judge Honolulu, 1970—. Del., asst. sec. Constl. Conv. Hawaii, 1968, del., 1978. Served to 1st lt. USAF, 1956-59. Mem. Am. (past mem. exec. council young lawyers sect.), Hawaii (sec. young lawyers sect., past pres.) bar assns., Am., Hawaii socs. corporate secs., Hawaii Econ. Assn., Hawaiian Ednl. Council, Delta Kappa Epsilon, Phi Alpha Delta. Democrat. Clubs: Hawaii Big Game Fishing (past pres.), Pacific. Home: 3929 Old Pali Rd Honolulu HI 96817 Office: PO Box 2750 Honolulu HI 96840

LEWIS, PHILIP, edn. co. exec.; b. Chgo., Oct. 23, 1913; s. Solomon and Fannie (Margolis) L.; B.S., DePaul U., Chgo., 1937, M.A., 1939; Ed.D., Columbia Tchrs. Coll., 1951; m. Geraldine Gisela Lawenda, Sept. 1, 1947; 1 dau., Linda Susan. Chmn. dept. edn. Chgo. Tchrs. Coll., also asst. prin., tchr. South Shore High Sch., Chgo., 1940-51; prin. Herman Felsenthal Elementary Sch., Chgo., 1955-57; dir. Bur. Instructional Materials, Chgo. Pub. Schs., 1957-63, dir. Bur. Research Devel. and Spl. Projects, 1963-67; pres. Instructional Dynamics Inc., Chgo., 1967—; nat. cons. TV and instructional techniques, 1955—. Chmn. adv. com. U.S. Office Edn., Title VII, 1964-67. Served to lt. comdr. USNR, 1942-45. Mem. Soc. Programmed and Automated Learning (pres. 1960—), NEA (v.p. dept. audiovisual instrn., chmn. commn. on tech. standards dept. audiovisual instrn. 1965—), Nat. Assn. Ednl. Broadcasters, Am. Legion, Council for Ednl. Facilities Planners (editorial adv. bd. 1972—), Ill. C. of C. (mem. edn. com. 1970—), Chgo. Assn. Commerce and Industry (chmn. edn. com. 1970—), Nat. Audio-Visual Assn. (profl devel. bd. 1969-76, chmn.), Phi Delta Kappa. Mason (32 deg., Shriner), Rotarian. Club: Chicago Press. Author: Educational Television Guidebook for Electronics Industries Association, 1961; also numerous articles. Editorial bd. Nation's Schs. and Colls.; multimedia tech. editor T.H.E. Jour., Tech. Horizons in Edn.; cons. Jour. Ednl. Tech. and Communications; producer ednl., multimedia, tng. and mental health and human devel. materials, Who's Who in Bus. and Fin. Home: 2 E Oak St Apt 3201 Chicago IL 60611 Office: 666 N Lake Shore Dr Chicago IL 60611

LEWIS, PHILLIP ALBERT, coll. dean; b. Indpls., Feb. 11, 1921; s. C.A. and Elizabeth (Martin) L.; B.S., Aurora Coll., 1942; postgrad. Ill. Inst. Tech., 1947-49; M.S., Okla. State U., 1954, Ph.D., 1956; m. JoAnn Steiner, June 17, 1944; children—Bradley G., Linda S., Paul A., Johnson A. (dec.), Scott P., DeAnn E. Instr. chemistry and math. Duluth (Minn.) Jr. Coll., 1946; asst. prof. chemistry Aurora (Ill.) Coll., 1946-47, 47-49, U. Kansas City (Mo.), 1954-56; sr. chemist Midwest Research Inst., 1956-59; prof., chmn. chemistry dept. Iowa Wesleyan Coll., Mt. Pleasant, 1959-64; prof. chemistry Hastings (Nebr.) Coll., 1965-68; prof. chemistry, coll. dean Westminster Coll., New Wilmington, Pa., 1968—; vis. lectr. Nat. Coll., Kansas City, Mo., William Jewell Coll., U. Kansas City; Fulbright lectr. Meerut Coll., Agra U. Meerut, Uttar Pradesh, India, 1964-65; program mgr. NSF, 1977; vis. scientist Iowa Acad. Sci., 1960-64, Nebr. Acad., 1965-68. Mem. exec. council Moraine Trails council Boy Scouts Am., 1970. Served with Signal Corps, AUS, 1942-46. Mem. Am. Chem. Soc., AAAS, Pa. Assn. Academic Deans, Am. Conf. Academic Deans, Eastern Assn. Coll. Deans and Advisers Students, Research Soc. Am., Sigma Xi, Phi Lambda Upsilon. Methodist. Club: Rotary. Home: 139 Beechwood Rd New Wilmington PA 16142

LEWIS, PHILLIP HAROLD, mus. curator; b. Chgo., July 31, 1922; s. Bernard and Sonia (Pimstein) L.; B.F.A., Art Inst. Chgo., 1947; M.A., U. Chgo., 1953, Ph.D., 1966; postgrad. (Fulbright ednl. grant) Australian Nat. U., Canberra, 1953-54; m. Sally Leah Rappaport, Aug. 25, 1949; children—David Bernard, Betty Alice and Emily Ruth (twins). Conducted field research project on primitive art of New Ireland, 1953-54, 70; designed and installed anthrop., geol., hist. exhbns. in Grout Hist. Mus., Waterloo, Ia., 1955; asst. curator primitive art Field Mus. Natural History, Chgo., 1957-59, asso. curator, 1960, curator, 1961-67, curator primitive art and Melanesian ethnology, 1968—, chmn. dept. anthropology, 1975—. Served with USAAF, 1942-45. Fellow Royal Anthrop. Inst. Gt. Britain and Ireland, Am. Anthrop. Assn. Home: 1118 Main St Evanston IL 60202 Office: Field Mus Natural History Roosevelt Rd and Lake Shore Dr Chicago IL 60605

LEWIS, RALPH MILTON, real estate developer, acct., lawyer, corp. exec.; b. Johnstown, Pa., Nov. 9, 1919; s. Morris and Sarah (Galfond) L.; A.A., Los Angeles City Coll., 1939; B.S., UCLA, 1941; postgrad. U. So. Calif., 1945-48; m. Goldy Sarah Kimmel, June 12, 1941; children—Richard Alan, Robert Edward, Roger Gordon, Randall Wayne. Pvt. practice acctg., Los Angeles, 1945-55; admitted to Calif. bar, 1952; practice law, Los Angeles, 1953-55; founder Lewis Homes, 1957; chmn. bd. Lewis Construction Co., Upland, Calif., 1959—, Lewis Bldg. Co., Las Vegas, 1960—, Republic Sales Co., Inc., Upland, 1956—; dir., v.p. Kimmel Enterprises, Inc., 1959—; mng. partner Lewis Homes of Calif., 1973—, Lewis Homes of Nev., 1972—, Western Properties, Upland, 1972—, Foothill Investment Co., Las Vegas, 1971—, Republic Mgmt. Co., Upland, 1978—; instr. U. So. Calif., UCLA, Los Angeles City Coll., 1948-54, Dooley Law Rev. Course, 1953-54; guest lectr. numerous colls., univs. Mem., com. chmn. Calif. Commn. of Housing and Community Devel., 1965-67; mem. Calif. Gov.'s Task Force on the Home Bldg. and Construction Industry, 1967; pres. Bd. of Edn., Citrust Community Coll. Dist., Azusa, Calif., 1969, 73, mem., 1967-73; mem. Citizens Planning Council, Los Angeles County Regional Planning Commn., 1972-73; mem. UCLA Found. Chancellor's Assos.; mem. dean's council UCLA Grad. Sch. Architecture and Urban Planning. Recipient Humanitarian award NCCJ, 1979; Builder of Year award Bldg. Industry Assn. So. Calif., 1970. Mem. Am. Bar Assn., Calif. Soc. C.P.A.'s, Nat. Assn. Home Builders (dir.), Calif. Bldg. Industry Assn. (dir., chmn. affordable housing task force 1978-80), Bldg. Industry Assn. So. Calif. (past treas., pres., dir.). Contbr. articles to mags., jours. Home: 2120 Vallejo Way Upland CA 91786 Office: PO Box 670 Upland CA 91786

LEWIS, RAMSEY EMANUEL, JR., pianist, composer; b. Chgo., May 27, 1935; s. Ramsey Emanuel and Pauline (Richards) L.; student Chgo. Music Coll., 1947-54, U. Ill., 1953-54, De Paul U., 1954-55; m. Geraldine Taylor, Apr. 7, 1954; children—Vita Denise, Ramsey Emanuel III, Marcus Kevin, Dawn, Kendall. Mgr. record dept. Hudson-Ross, Inc., Chgo., 1954-56; organizer Ramsey Lewis Trio, 1956; now solo artist; 1st profl. appearance, Chgo., 1957, appeared N.Y.C., 1958—, San Francisco, 1962; played Randall's Island Jazz Festival, N.Y.C., 1959, Saugatuck (Mich.) Jazz Festival, 1960, Newport (R.I.) Jazz Festival, 1961, 63; also jazz concerts of various univs., 1961; toured with Free Sounds of 1963; appeared in film Save the Children, 1973; numerous TV performances; rec. artist Columbia Records; recipient Grammy award for The In Crowd, 1965, Hold It Right There, 1966, Hang on Sloopy, 1973; albums include Another Voyage, 1970, The Piano Player, 1970, Then Changes, 1970, Back To The Roots, 1971, Upendo Ni Pomojos, 1972, Funky Serenity; composer Fantasia for Drums, Look-a-Here, Sound of Christmas, Sound of Spring, others; organizer Rams' L Prodns., Inc., Chgo., 1966, Ramsel Pub. Co., Chgo., 1966. Address: care Cavallo-Ruffalo Mgmt 9885 Charleville Blvd Beverly Hills CA 90212*

LEWIS, RICHARD ALAN, real estate developer; b. Torrance, Calif., Jan. 14, 1944; s. Ralph Milton and Goldy Sarah (Kimmel) L.; B.A., Claremont Men's Coll., 1965; children—Jennifer Ann, David Richard. Mgmt. trainee Lewis Homes, Upland, Calif., 1965-67, asst. v.p., 1967-70, v.p., 1970-74, pres., 1974—; pres. Lewis Constrn. Co., Inc., Upland, 1974—; mem. faculty Mt. San Antonio Coll.; lectr., speaker at numerous trade assn. and civic meetings. Mem. Upland Bldg. Codes Appeals Bd. 1978—. Served with Air N.G., 1965-71. Lic. real estate broker, lic. gen. bldg. contractor, Calif. Mem. Homebuilders Council, Sales and Mktg. Council, Bldg. Industry Assn. (v.p. Baldy View chpt. 1972-73, 74-75, pres. 1973-74). Republican. Home: 1873 N Euclid Upland CA 91786 Office: PO Box 670 Upland CA 91786

LEWIS, RICHARD BURTON, educator; b. Mountain View, Calif., Feb. 8, 1906; s. William M. and Daisy R. (Peter) L.; A.B., Pacific Union Coll., 1927; A.M., U. So. Calif., 1937; Ph.D., Stanford U., 1949; m. Virginia R. Dail, Aug. 21, 1932; children—Richard Burton, Mary Anne (Mrs. David R. Victorino). Prin., San Diego Acad., 1927-35, Pacific Union Coll. Prep. Sch., Angwin, Calif., 1935-38; asst. prof. speech Walla Walla (Wash.) Coll., 1938-45; prof. English, Pacific Union Coll., 1945-55; book editor, prodn. mgr. Chapel Records, Pacific Press Pub. Assn., Mountain View, 1955-61; acad. dean La Sierra (Calif.) Coll., 1961-67; prof. English, Loma Linda U., Riverside, 1967—. Prof., Seventh-Day Adventists Theol. Sem., Washington, summer 1943. Mem. Modern Lang. Assn., Milton Soc. Author: Streams of Light, The History of the Pacific Press, 1958; The Protestant Dilemma, 1961; Ignatius and the Lord's Day, 1968. Home: 5226 Peacock Ln Riverside CA 92505

LEWIS, RICHARD CLAYTON, artist; b. Roswell, N.Mex., Apr. 21, 1908; s. Richard Welbourne and Lillian Lupton (Johnston) L.; B.F.A., Okla. State U., 1934; art student Chouinard Art Inst., Am. Acad.; m. Elizabeth Ann Morgan, Aug. 24, 1940; children—Elizabeth Clayton, Alice Morgan, Nancy Lee, Laura Northlich. Pres., Comml. Art Studio, Chgo., 1940-58; partner Telepix, TV comml. prodn., Chgo., 1948-58; Midwest producer MGM, 1958-60, Desilu Inc., 1960-62, Paramount, 1962-64 (all Chgo.); artist specializing in Am. city scenes, lectr., 1968—. Mem. Winnetka (Ill.) Park Bd., 1947-55. Mem. Artist Guild Chgo., Nat. Soc. Watercolor Artists, Chgo. Press Club, Beta Theta Pi. Presbyterian. Composer songs. Originator children's games. Patentee various products. Address: 2710 Grand Ave San Diego CA 92109

LEWIS, RICHARD STANLEY, editor, author; b. Pitts., Jan. 8, 1916; s. S. Morton and Mary L. (Lefstein) L.; B.A., Pa. State U., 1937; m. Louise G. Silberstein, June 8, 1938; children—Jonathan, David. Reporter, Cleve. Press, 1937-38; rewrite man, drama critic Indpls. Times, 1938-43, reporter, city editor, 1946-49; reporter St. Louis Star-Times, 1949-51; mem. staff Chgo. Sun-Times, 1951-68, sci. editor, 1967-68; mng. editor Bull. Atomic Scientists, Chgo., 1968-70, editor, 1971-74. Writing cons. earth sci. curriculum project NSF, summers 1964-65. Served with AUS, 1943-46: ETO. Mem. Authors Guild, Authors League Am. Club: Nat. Press (Washington). Author: The Other Child, rev. edit., 1960; A Continent for Science, 1965; Appointment on The Moon, 1968, rev. edit., 1969; The Nuclear Power Rebellion, 1972; The Voyages of Apollo, 1974; From Vinland to Mars: 1000 Years of Exploration, 1976; The Other Child Grows Up, 1977. Editor: Man on the Moon, 1969; Alamagordo Plus 25 Years, 1970; Frozen Future, 1972; The Energy Crisis, 1972; The Environmental Revolution, 1973. Home: 1401 S Magnolia Dr Indialantic FL 32903

LEWIS, ROBERT GEORGE, orgn. exec., cons; b. Baker, Mont., June 5, 1919; s. George A. and Edith (Johnson) L.; A.B., U. Wis., 1942; m. Martha Barron Wells, June 6, 1942; children—Eric Robert, Sarah Varnum (Mrs. David Lasker), Martha Dustin (Mrs. Irwin Bitter), Peter Garrett. Editor Wis. REA News, also pub. relations dir. Wis. Electric Coop., Madison, 1946-51; editor Washington Newsletter, Nat. Farmers Union, Washington, 1952-57, now nat. sec., econ. counsel; adminstrv. asst. Sen. William Proxmire, 1957-59; agr. coordinator Exec. Office, State Wis., 1959-60; dep. adminstr. commodity operations, Agrl. Stablzn. and Conservation Service, also v.p. CCC, 1961-64; adminstr. Rural Community Devel. Service, Dept. Agr., 1965-67; cons. to AID, 1967; pvt. trade and econs. cons., 1968—. Exec. com. Electric Consumers Info. Com., Washington, 1952-57; U.S. del. Internat. Wheat Council, Haymarket House, London. Agrl. adviser Sen. Kefauver, candidate for v.p., 1956; sec. adv. council com. agr. Nat. Democratic Com., 1960; dir. nat. hdqrs. Farmers for Kennedy and Johnson Com., Washington, 1960. Served to 1st lt. AUS, 1942-45. Decorated D.S.C., Bronze Star medal; Croix de Guerre with etoile d'argent (France). Contbr. articles to jours. Home: Blue Mounds WI 53517 also 3512 Porter St NW Washington DC 20016 Office: 1012-14th St NW Washington DC 20005

LEWIS, ROBERT JAMES, investment banker; b. Macomb, Ill., Feb. 23, 1899; s. Robert E. and Addie (Applegate) L.; A.B., Yale U., 1921; m. Ellen James Evans, Dec. 5, 1925 (dec.); children—Ellen (Mrs. Lewis Parisot), Robert E., Peter (dec.); m. 2d, Helen Hoyt Stookey, Aug. 5, 1971. Supr. credit investigations Bankers Trust Co., 1921-24; sales mgr. Graham, Parsons & Co., 1924-31; partner Estabrook & Co., 1931-68; ltd. partner Clark, Dodge & Co., Inc., 1968-74. Bd. govs. N.Y. Stock Exchange, 1960-66. Bd. dirs. Third St. Music Sch. Settlement. Served as seaman USN, World War I; to lt. comdr. USNR, World War II. Mem. Assn. Stock Exchange Firms (pres. 1958), Euthanasia Soc. (treas.). Presbyterian. Clubs: Down Town Assn., Bond (pres. 1956), Links, University, Fairfield Country, Pilgrims. Home: 580 Park Ave New York NY 10021

LEWIS, ROBERT LAWRENCE, lawyer; b. N.Y.C., Sept. 25, 1919; s. Isador and Sadie (Holzinger) L.; A.B., Hamilton Coll., 1940; LL.B., Case Western Res. U., 1948; m. Frieda Friedman, Nov. 24, 1940 (dec. 1961); children—Brian S., Paul E., David N.; m. 2d, Joanne Marcia Waxman, June 16, 1963; children—Pavia S., Eraclea S. With firm Ulmer, Berne, Laronge, Glickman & Curtis, Cleve., 1948—, partner, 1956—; prof. law, dir. grad. div. Cleve.-Marshall Law Sch. (now Cleve. State U.), 1948-58; dir. Banner Industries, Inc., Cleve., 1968—. Cons., evaluator North Central Assn. Colls. and Schs. Mem. Cleve. Area Arts Council, 1971-73; pres. Fairmount Center for Creative and Performing Arts, 1973-75; trustee, chmn. bd. Cuyahoga Community Coll.; trustee Cuyahoga Community Coll. Found., Playhouse Sq. Found., Cleve., Council for Interinstnl. Leadership, Pace Assn., New Orgn. for Visual Arts; bd. dirs. Assn. Governing Bds. Univs. and Colls.; bd. advisers Cleve. Ballet; trustee, v.p. New Cleve. Opera Co. Served to 1st lt., arty. and ordnance corps, AUS, 1942-46; NATOUSA. Decorated Legion of Merit, Exec. Order Ohio Commodore, Phi Beta Kappa. Home: 2115 Elandon Dr Cleveland Heights OH 44106 Office: 900 Bond Court Bldg Cleveland OH 44114. *There is neither a standard nor a uniform set of qualities which best fits one to be a member of society, and anyone who contends to the contrary, may be equated with the infamous and mythical Procrustes. I for one prefer the preservation of individuality. No one of us should be fitted to the bed of Procrustes. I prefer that we shall all survive; and each of us shall then be the richer for the survival of the other.*

LEWIS, ROBERT MILLER, vet. pathologist; b. Flushing, N.Y., May 20, 1937; s. W. Wilson and Dorothy (Miller) L.; D.V.M., Wash. State U., 1961; m. Sandra Shurtleff, Dec. 27, 1958; children—Jon Robert, Karin Anne. Intern, Angell Meml. Animal Hosp., Boston, 1961-62, research asso. in pathology, 1962-65, asso. pathologist, 1965-67, affiliate in medicine, 1968-75; research fellow dept. pathology Harvard U. Med. Sch., 1962-65, asst. in pathology, 1965-68, clin. asst. in pathology, 1968-76; fellow dept. hematology New Eng. Med. Center Hosp., Boston, summer 1963, cons. dept. surg. research, 1962-65, mem. spl. sci. staff, 1966-75, chief vet. service, 1970-75; instr. in surgery Tufts U. Sch. Medicine, 1965-66, sr. instr., 1966-67, asst. prof. surgery, 1967-71, dir. lab. animal scis., 1969-75, asso. prof., 1971-75; prof. pathology, chmn. dept. pathology N.Y. State Coll. Vet. Medicine, Cornell U., 1975—. Recipient Mary Mitchell award Angell Meml. Hosp., 1961; Dept. Agr. grantee, 1977-79; NIH grantee, 1978-79; lic. veterinarian, Wash., Oreg., Mass. Mem. New Eng. Pathology Soc., AVMA, Am. Coll. Vet. Pathologists (diplomate), Internat. Acad. Pathology, Am. Assn. Lab. Animal Scis., New Eng. Colloquy Comparative Pathologists, AAAS, N.Y. Acad. Scis., Sigma Xi, Phi Zeta. Contbr. numerous articles to profl. publs. Home: 10 Sunnyslope St Ithaca NY 14850 Office: Dept Pathology NY State Coll Vet Medicine Cornell U Ithaca NY 14853

LEWIS, ROBERT RICHARDS, JR., physicist; b. New Haven, Mar. 7, 1927; s. Robert Richards and Lela (Hoyt) L.; B.S. in Physics and Math., U. Mich., 1950, M.S., 1952, Ph.D., 1954; m. Gertrude G. Baumberger, June 17, 1950; children—Natalie Gail Lewis McClure, Susan G., Laura Helen, Robert Russell. Asst. prof. physics U. Notre Dame, 1954-56; mem. Inst. Advanced Study, 1956-58; mem. faculty U. Mich., 1959—, now prof. physics. Served with USN, 1945-46. Mem. Am. Phys. Soc., Nat. Audubon Soc. Research, publs. on weak interactions in nuclear and atomic physics. Office: Dept Physics U Mich Ann Arbor MI 48109

LEWIS, ROGER, investment co. exec.; b. Los Angeles, Jan. 11, 1912; s. Clarence V. and Charlotte (Gibbons) L.; A.B., Stanford U., 1934; m. Elly Thummler, Mar. 8, 1938; children—Ronald, Gail (Mrs. Joseph G. Tobin), Pamela (Mrs. Robert E. Casey). Dir. materiel, later asst. sales mgr. Lockheed Aircraft Corp., 1934-47; v.p. Canadair, Ltd., Montreal, Can., 1947-50; v.p. Curtiss-Wright Corp., 1950-53; asst. sec. air force, 1953-55; exec. v.p., dir. Pan Am. World Airways, 1955-62; chmn., pres. Gen. Dynamics Corp., 1962-70, pres., 1970-71; pres., chmn. Nat. Railroad Passenger Corp., 1971-75; sr. v.p. corp. fin. Hornblower, Weeks, Noyes & Trask Inc., 1975-78, also dir.; cons. Loeb Rhoades Hornblower; dir. Bunker-Ramo Corp., Granger Assos. Bd. dirs. Nat. Alliance Businessmen, Nat. Indsl. Conf. Bd. Trustee Stanford. Recipient Medal of Freedom, 1955. Fellow Am. Inst. Aeros. and Astronautics; mem. Sigma Nu. Clubs: Links, University (N.Y.C.); Metropolitan (Washington); Bohemian (San Francisco). Office: 14 Wall St New York NY 10005

LEWIS, SAMUEL WINFIELD, ambassador; b. Houston, Oct. 1, 1930; s. Samuel Winfield and Sue Roselle (Hurley) L.; B.A. magna cum laude, Yale, 1952; M.A., Johns Hopkins, 1954; m. Sallie Kate Smoot, June 20, 1953; children—Pamela Gracelle, Richard Winfield. Exec. asst. Am. Trucking Assn., Washington. 1953-54; fgn. service officer Dept. State, Washington, 1954—; consular officer, Naples, 1954-55; consul, Florence, 1955-59; officer-in-charge Italian affairs, Washington, 1959-61; spl. asst. to under sec. state, Washington, 1961-63; dep. asst. dir. US AID Mission to Brazil, Rio de Janeiro, 1964-66; dep. dir. Office Brazil Affairs, Washington, 1967-68; sr. staff mem. for Latin Am. Affairs, Nat. Security Council, White House, Washington, 1968-69; spl. asst. for policy planning Bur. Inter-Am. Affairs, Washington, 1969; spl. asst. to dir. gen. Fgn. Service, 1970-71; dep. chief Mission and counselor embassy, Kabul, Afghanistan, 1971-74; dep. dir. policy planning staff Dept. State, 1974-75, asst. sec. state for internat. orgn., 1975-77; U.S. ambassador to Israel, 1977—. Recipient William A. Jump award for outstanding service in pub. adminstrn., 1967; Meritorious Honor award Dept. State, 1967, AID, 1967; Pres.' Mgmt. Improvement certificate, 1971; Distinguished Honor award, 1977. Vis. fellow, Princeton, 1963-64. Mem. Council on Fgn. Relations, Phi Beta Kappa. Episcopalian. Home: Am Ambassador's Residence Herzelia Pituach Tel Aviv Israel Office: American Embassy Tel Aviv Israel

LEWIS, SHARI, ventriloquist, puppeteer; b. N.Y.C., Jan. 17, 1934; d. Abraham B. and Ann (Ritz) Hurwitz; student Columbia; m. Jeremy Tarcher, Mar. 15, 1958; 1 dau., Mallory. Recorded LP records, Fun in Shariland, Hi Kids, Shari in Storyland; star weekly NBC-TV show The Shari Lewis Show; star weekly TV show BBC, London, 1969-73, weekly TV show for ind. network in Gt. Britain, 1970; writer, producer, star NBC spl. A Picture of Us, 1971; command performance, London, 1970, 73, 78. Mem. nat. bd. dirs. Girl Scouts U.S.; internat. bd. dirs. Boy Scouts Am.; past pres. Am. Center Films for Children. Winner TV Emmy awards for best local program and outstanding female personality, 1957, for best children's show and outstanding female personality, 1958, 59, as outstanding children's entertainer, 1972-73; Peabody award, 1960; Monte Carlo Internat. TV award, 1961; Radio-TV Mirror award, 1960. Author: Shari Lewis Puppet Book; Fun for the Kids; Folding Paper Puppets; Folding Paper Toys; Dear Shari; Folding Paper Mask; Mcgraw Hill Headstart books (4); Making Easy Puppets; Be Nimble, Be Quick; Tell-It Make-It Book; Magic for Non-Magicians; The Kids-Only Club Book; How Kids Can Really Make Money; Toystore-in-a-Book; Impossible Unless You Know How; Spooky Stuff. Address: care SLS

Entertainment Enterprises Inc 6464 Sunset Blvd Los Angeles CA 90028

LEWIS, SHERMAN RICHARD, JR., investmet banker; b. Ottawa, Ill., Dec. 11, 1936; s. Sherman Richard and Audrey Julia (Rusteen) L.; A.B., Northwestern U., 1958; M.B.A., U. Chgo., 1964; m. Dorothy Marie Downie, Sept. 9, 1967; children—Thomas, Catherine, Elizabeth, Michael. With investment dept. Am. Nat. Bank & Trust Co., Chgo., 1961-64; v.p. Halsey, Stuart & Co., N.Y.C., 1964-70, v.p. in charge N.Y. corp. fin. dept., 1970-73; v.p. C.J. Lawrence & Sons, N.Y.C., 1970; partner Loeb, Rhoades & Co., N.Y.C., 1974-76, partner in charge corp. fin. dept., 1975-76, exec. v.p., dir., 1976-77, pres., co-chief exec. officer, 1977-78; vice chmn., co-chief exec. officer Loeb Rhoades, Hornblower & Co., N.Y.C., 1978-79; pres. Shearson Loeb Rhoades, Inc., N.Y.C., 1979—. Served as commd. officer USMC, 1958-61. Mem. N.Y. Soc. Security Analysts. Clubs: Bond, India House, Ridgewood Country, University. Home: 623 Belmont Rd Ridgewood NJ 07450 Office: Shearson Loeb Rhoades Inc 14 Wall St New York NY 10005

LEWIS, STEPHEN RICHMOND, JR., economist; b. Englewood, N.J., Feb. 11, 1939; s. Stephen Richmond and Esther (Magan) L.; B.A., Williams Coll., 1960; M.A., Stanford U., 1962, Ph.D., 1963; m. Gayle Elizabeth Foster, June 24, 1961; children—Virginia Rebecca, Deborah Elizabeth, Mark Stephen. Instr., Stanford U., 1962-63; research advisor Pakistan Inst. Devel. Econs., Karachi, 1963-65; asst. prof. econs. Harvard U., 1965-66; asst. prof. econs. Williams Coll., 1966-68, asso. prof., 1968-73, prof., 1973-76, Herbert H. Lehman prof., 1976—, provost of coll., 1968-71, 73-77; vis. sr. research fellow Inst. Devel. Studies, Nairobi, Kenya, 1971-73; econ. cons. to Ministry of Finance and Devel. Planning, Govt. of Botswana, 1977-79; cons. econs. Ford Found., World Bank, Orgn. Econ. Coop. and Devel., Govts. of Kenya, Philippines, Botswana. Danforth Found. fellow, 1960-63; Ford Found. dissertation fellow, 1962-63. Mem. Nat. Tax Assn., Am. Econ. Assn., Phi Beta Kappa. Author: Economic Policy and Industrial Growth in Pakistan, 1969; Pakistan: Industrialization and Trade Policy, 1970; Taxation for Development, 1979; (with others) Relative Price Changes and Industrialization in Pakistan, 1967. Contbr. chpts. in books, articles profl. jours. Address: 410 Petersburg Rd Williamstown MA 02167

LEWIS, STUART MILTON, editor; b. Rochester, N.Y., Mar. 25, 1929; s. Milton W. and Jean (Mashke) L.; B.S. in Physics, Poly Inst. Bklyn., 1953; m. Helen J. Hayes, Nov. 20, 1949; children—Yvette, Peter, Eric. Test engr. Sperry Gyroscope Co., Great Neck, N.Y., 1953-56; asst. mng. editor Transmission and Distbn. mag., Cleworth Pub. Co., Cos Cob, Conn., 1956-57, mng. editor, 1957-58, exec. editor, 1958—, v.p., 1969—, editor, 1970—; operator weather sta. Stamford (Conn.) Mus. and Nature Center, 1958—. Served with USMC, 1946-48. Mem. IEEE, Am. Meteorol. Soc. Unitarian-Universalist (pres. local soc.). Home: 56 Crooked Trail Rowayton CT 06853 Office: 1 River Rd Cos Cob CT 06807

LEWIS, SYDNEY, retail co. exec.; b. Richmond, Va., Oct. 24, 1919; s. Julius Beryl and Dora (Lewis) L.; B.A., Washington and Lee U., 1940, postgrad. in law, 1940-42; postgrad. bus. adminstrn., Harvard, 1942-43, in law, George Washington U., 1946; m. Frances Aaronson, Sept. 3, 1942; children—Sydney Jr., Andrew Marc, Susan (Mrs. Dixon Butler). Admitted to Va. bar, 1942, D.C. bar, 1947; v.p. New Standard Pub. Co. Inc., Richmond, 1947-58, pres., 1958—, also dir.; founding pres., chmn. Best Products Co. Inc., Richmond, 1951—, also dir. Pres. Richmond Jewish Community Council, 1953—. Trustee Washington and Lee U., Lexington, Va., Va. Union Univ., Richmond, Hirshorn Mus., Washington, 1976—, Inst. Contemporary Art, Phila., 1975—, Sch. Visual Arts, Boston U., 1976—, Va. Environ. Endowment Fund, Va. Found. for Humanities and Public Policy. mem. bd. assos. U. Richmond. Recipient nat. honoree award Beta Gamma Sigma, 1976. Club: Lakeside Country. Home: 2601 Monument Ave Richmond VA 23220 Office PO Box 26303 Richmond VA 23260

LEWIS, WALTER DAVID, historian; b. Towanda, Pa., June 24, 1931; s. Gordon Cleon and Eleanor Esther (Tobias) L.; B.A. cum laude, Pa. State U., 1952; M.A., 1954; Ph.D., Cornell U., 1961; m. Carolyn Wyatt Brown, June 12, 1954; children—Daniel Kent, Virginia Lorraine, Nancy Ellyn. Instr. public speaking Hamilton Coll., Clinton, N.Y., 1954-57; fellowship coordinator Eleutherian Mill-Hagley Found., Wilmington, Del., also lectr. history U. Del., 1959-65; asso. prof. history SUNY at Buffalo, 1965-71, prof., 1971; Hudson prof. history and engring. Auburn (Ala.) U., 1971—, dir. univ. project tech., human values and So. future, 1974-79. Sr. fellow in Am. civilization Cornell U., 1958-59; grantee Nat. Endowment for Humanities, 1973-79, Delta Air Lines Found., 1973-79, Eleutherian Mills Hist. Library, 1970-73; post-doctoral fellow Nat. Humanities Inst., U. Chgo., 1978-79; exec. co-producer documentary film About Us: A Deep South Portrait, 1977. Mem. Soc. History Tech. (adv. com., Leonardo da Vinci prize com.), Bus. History Conf., Lexington Group Transp. Historians, Phi Beta Kappa. Episcopalian. Author: From Newgate to Dannemora: The Rise of the Penitentiary in New York, 1965; Iron and Steel in America, 1976; co-author: Delta: The History of an Airline, 1979; contbg. author: The Professions in America, 1965; Technology in Western Civilization, 1967; The Development of an American Culture, 1969; Notable American Women, 1971, Co-editor: Economic Change in the Civil War Era, 1965; The Southern Mystique: Technology and Human Values in a Changing Region, 1977. Contbr. articles to profl. jours. Office: 7030 Haley Center Auburn U Auburn AL 36830. *My profession is thinking and writing about the past, with occasional speculations about the future; but my personal goal is to live history as joyfully as possible in the present—the eternal NOW.*

LEWIS, WELBOURNE WALKER, JR., lawyer; b. Lewisburg, Tenn., Jan. 11, 1915; s. Welbourne Walker and Jessie (Culbertson) L.; A.B., Dartmouth, 1936; LL.B., Harvard, 1939; m. 3d, Esther Phillips, July 26, 1975; children by previous marriage—Welbourne Walker III, H. Hunter, Berton B. Admitted to Ohio bar, 1939, since practiced in Dayton; asso. Smith, Schnacke & Compton, 1939-45; mem. firm Smith & Schnacke, from 1945, now of counsel; chmn. Master Consol., Inc., 1950-67; sec. Mead Corp., Dayton, 1952-64, gen. counsel, 1958-75, dir., 1959-75; dir. Dayton Aircraft Products, Inc., Vulcan Tool Co.; chmn. bd. Lion Uniform, Inc., Queen City Leasing Corp., Gem City Leasing, Inc., Advanced Telecom Systems, Inc., Delta Fin. Systems Corp.; vice chmn. bd., dir. Greater Miami Investment Service, Inc. Bd. dirs. Dayton dept. A.R.C.; former trustee Dayton Pvt. Sch. Found. Mem. Am., Ohio, Dayton bar assns., Dayton Council World Affairs (dir.), Phi Beta Kappa, Delta Tau Delta, Delta Sigma Rho. Episcopalian (trustee, mem. planning com. Diocese So. Ohio). Clubs: Dayton, Moraine Country, Dartmouth (Dayton). Home: 765 Winding Way Kettering OH 45419 Office: 2000 Courthouse Plaza NE 10 W 2d St Dayton OH 45402

LEWIS, WILBUR H., ednl. mgmt. cons.; b. Belmont, Ohio, Sept. 16, 1930; s. Charles W. and Lily B. (Dunfee) L.; student Miami U., Oxford, Ohio, 1948-51; B.S.B.A., Ohio State U., 1953; M.Ed., Ohio U., 1961, Ph.D., 1964; m. Jean E. Lewis, Aug. 22, 1958; children—David, Deretta, Denise, Dawn, Darrin. Tchr. pub. schs., Scioto County, Ohio, 1957; tchr., adminstr. public schs., Belmont County, Ohio, 1958-60; prin. high sch., adminstrv. asst. to supt. public schs., Athens, Ohio, 1961-64; asst. supt., 1966-67; grad. asst. Ohio U., 1960-61, asst. prof., 1964-66; prin. high sch. public schs., Wilmington, Ohio, 1967-68; with Parma (Ohio) City Schs., 1968-77, asso. supt., 1972-75, supt., 1970-72, 75-77; supt. Tucson Unified Sch. Dist., 1977-79; cons. ednl. mgmt., Tucson, 1979—; adv., Nigeria, 1964-66; vice chmn. nat. adv. council Edn. Disadvantaged Children, 1972-79. Planning div. United Way, Tucson, 1978—; bd. dirs. Jr. Achievement, Tucson, 1978—, Christ Presbyterian Ch., Tucson, 1978—. Served with U.S. Army, 1954-56. Recipient numerous civic awards for community service; Kettering Found. fellow, 1970. Mem. Am. Assn. Sch. Adminstrs., Buckeye Assn. Sch. Adminstrs., Ariz. Sch. Adminstrs., Phi Delta Kappa, Lambda Chi Alpha, Sigma Phi Epsilon. Clubs: Rotary Tucson Rod and Gun (Tucson); Masons, Shriners (Wheeling, W.Va.). Research in organizational devel., adminstrv. behavior patterns, tchr. job satisfaction, student achievement. Home and Office: 7552 E Knollwood Circle Tucson AZ 85715. *To achieve one must aspire. To aspire one must dream. But if dreams and aspirations are to become achievements one must persevere. The perseverance necessary to turn dreams and aspirations into achievements has always been made easier for me knowing that children and youth were the benefactors of my efforts.*

LEWIS, WILLARD DEMING, univ. pres.; b. Augusta, Ga., Jan. 6, 1915; s. Willard and Constance (Deming) L.; A.B., Harvard U., 1935, A.M., 1939, Ph.D., 1941; B.A., Oxford (Eng.) U., 1938, M.A., 1945; L.H.D., Moravian Coll.; LL.D., Lafayette Coll., Rutgers U., Muhlenberg Coll., Hahnemann Med. Coll.; D.Sc., Med. Coll. Pa.; D.Eng., Lehigh U.; m. Marian Carter Chapman, Nov. 1, 1941 (dec. July 1965); children—Caroline Carter (Mrs. Ross Canterbury), Constance Carter (Mrs. Edward LaMonte), Linda Deming, Catherine Doten (Mrs. Owen Floody), Marian Chapman; m. 2d, Emmeline Hoffman, Oct. 22, 1966. Asso. with Bell Telephone Labs., Inc., 1941-62, exec. dir. research communications systems, 1958-62; a founder, mng. dir. systems study center Bellcomm., Inc., 1962-64; pres. Lehigh U., Bethlehem, Pa., 1964—; dir. Bethlehem Steel Co., Pa. Power & Light Co., Fairchild Industries, Fischer-Porter Co.; mem. Polaris Communications Com., 1958-63, Def. Industry Adv. Com., 1962-63; mem. Naval Research Adv. Com., 1964-69, chmn., 1967-69; mem. Def. Sci. Bd., 1967-69; chmn. Pa. Bd. Edn., 1968-73, Pa. Commn. Ind. Colls. and Univs., 1976-77; chmn. Assn. of Ind. Engring. Colls., 1968-70; mem. NRC, 1973-74. Mem. sch. bd., Little Silver, N.J., 1949-50; mem. overseers com. to visit div. engring. and applied sci., Harvard, 1954-66; mem. council Harvard Found. Advanced Study and Research, 1959-64, chmn., 1961-62. Fellow IEEE, AAAS; mem. Am. Phys. Soc., Am. Assn. Rhodes Scholars, Harvard Engring. Soc., Nat. Acad. Engring. (council 1972—, exec. com. 1973—), Delta Upsilon. Clubs: University (N.Y.C.); Cosmos (Washington); Saucon Valley Country (Bethlehem, Pa.). Patentee in field. Home: President's House Lehigh Univ Campus 28 Bethlehem PA 18015

LEWIS, WILLIAM, tenor; b. Tulsa, Nov. 23, 1935; student Karl Kritz, Ft. Worth, Arthur Faguy-Cote, Ft. Worth, Max Klein, N.Y.C., Susan Seton, N.Y.C., Hulda and Luigi Rossini, N.Y.C.; m. Daphne Lewis; 3 children. Operatic debut in Gianni Schicchi, Ft. Worth Opera Assn., 1953; appeared with maj. cos., including Spoleto (Italy) Festival, Can. Opera Co., Toronto, Ont., Cin. Opera Assn., Dallas Civic Opera Co., Ft. Worth Opera Assn., Hawaii Opera Theatre, Milw. Florentine Opera Co., N.J. State Opera Co., N.Y.C. Opera, Pitts. Opera, San Francisco Opera Co., Santa Fe Opera; now resident mem. Met. Opera Assn. Winner Met. Opera Nat. Council Auditions, 1953; recipient award Nat. Assn. Tchrs. Singing, 1953. Office: care Met Opera Guild Inc 1865 Broadway New York NY 10023*

LEWIS, WILLIAM ARTHUR, economist; b. St. Lucia, B.W.I., Jan. 23, 1915; s. George and Ida (Barton) L.; student St. Mary's Coll., St. Lucia, 1924-29; B.Com., London Sch. Econs., 1937, Ph.D., 1940; M.A. (hon.), Manchester U., 1951, D.Sc., 1973; L.H.D., Columbia U., 1954, Boston U., 1972; LL.D., U. Toronto, 1959, Williams Coll., 1959, U. Wales, 1960, U. Bristol, 1961, U. Dakar, 1962, U. Leicester, 1964, Rutgers U., 1965, U. Brussels, 1968, The Open U., 1974; Litt.D., U. West Indies, 1966, U. Lagos, 1974, Northwestern U., 1979; hon. fellow London Sch. Econs., 1959, Weizmann Inst., 1962; m. Gladys Isabel Jacobs, May 5, 1947; children—Elizabeth Anne, Barbara Jean. Asst. lectr., then lectr., reader London Sch. Econs., 1938-48; Stanley Jevons prof. polit. economy U. Manchester, 1948-59; prin., vice chancelor U. West Indies, 1959-63; prof. econs., internat. affairs Princeton U., 1963—; prin. Bd. Trade, then Colonial Office U.K., 1943-44; mem. Colonial Econ. Adv. Council U.K., 1945-49; dir. Colonial Devel. Corp. U.K., 1950-52; mem. Deptl. Com. on Fuel and Power U.K., 1951-52; econ. adviser Prime Minister of Ghana, 1957-58; dep. mng. dir. UN Spl. Fund, 1959-60; spl. adviser Prime Minister West Indies, 1961-62; dir. Indsl. Devel. Corp., Jamaica, 1962-63; dir. Central Bank of Jamaica, 1961-62; pres. Caribbean Devel. Bank, 1970-73; chancellor U. Guyana, 1967-73. Mem. econ. adv. council NAACP, 1978—. Decorated Knight Bachelor, 1963; co-recipient Nobel prize in econs., 1979. Corr. fellow Brit. Acad.; mem. Am. Philos. Soc., Royal Econ. Soc. (council 1949-58), Manchester Statis. Soc. (pres. 1956), Econ. Soc. Ghana (pres. 1958), Am. Econ. Assn. (v.p. 1965, Distinguished fellow 1969); hon. fgn. mem. Am. Acad. Arts and Scis. Author: Economic Problems of Today, 1940; The Principles of Economic Planning, 1949; The Economics of Overhead Costs, 1949; Economic Survey, 1919-39, 1950; The Theory of Economic Growth, 1955; Politics in West Africa, 1965; Development Planning, 1966; Reflections on the Economic Growth of Nigeria, 1967; Some Aspects of Economic Development, 1969; The Evolution of the International Economic Order, 1978; Growth and Fluctuations 1870-1913, 1978; editor: Tropical Development, 1970. Address: Woodrow Wilson School Princeton U Princeton NJ 08540

LEWIS, WILLIAM EDWARD, ins. co. exec.; b. Indpls., Aug. 7, 1920; s. Frank Charles and Dema (Fleck) L.; student Purdue U., 1939-41; B.S., U. Mich., 1944; m. Betty Ann Eversole, Dec. 1, 1951; children—James B., Margaret A. With Lincoln Nat. Life Ins. Co., Ft. Wayne, Ind., 1944—, asst. actuary, 1952-57, asso. actuary, 1957-60, 2d v.p., controller, 1960-65, v.p., controller, 1965-71, sr. v.p., 1971—. Fellow Soc. Actuaries. Home: 6207 Millhollow Ln Fort Wayne IN 46815 Office: 1300 S Clinton St Fort Wayne IN 46801

LEWIS, WILLIAM WALKER, govt. ofcl.; b. Roanoke, Va., Mar. 29, 1942; s. William Walker and Nancy Katherine (Phipps) L.; B.S. with honors in Physics, Va. Polytechnic Inst., 1963; Ph.D. in Theoretical Physics, Oxford U., 1966; m. Jutta Maria Schwarzkopf, Dec. 27, 1966; children—Christopher William, Monica Gisela. Mem. staff Office of Asst. Sec. for Systems Analysis, Dept. Def., Washington, 1966-69; asso. provost for resource planning, lectr. public and internat. affairs Princeton U., 1969-71; dir. office of analytical studies U. Calif., Berkeley, 1971-73; sr. ops. officer World Bank, 1973-77; prin. dep. asst. sec. for program analysis and evaluation Dept. Def., Washington, 1977-79; asst. sec. policy and evaluation Dept. Energy, Washington, 1979—. Rhodes scholar, 1963-66. Office: Forrestal Bldg Washington DC 20585

LEWIS, WILMARTH SHELDON, author, editor; b. Alameda, Calif., Nov. 14, 1895; s. Azro Nathaniel and Miranda (Sheldon) L.; student Thacher Sch., 1910-14; B.A., Yale, 1918, hon. M.A., 1937, LL.D., 1965; Litt.D., Brown U., 1945, U. Rochester, 1946, Nat. U. Ireland, 1957, U. Del., 1961, U. Cambridge (Eng.), 1962, U. Melbourne, 1972; L.H.D., Trinity Coll., 1950, Bucknell U., 1958; LL.D., U. Hartford, 1972; m. Annie Burr Auchincloss, Jan. 25, 1928 (dec. 1959). Asso. Yale U. Press, 1920-22; research asso. Yale, 1933-38; chief info. div. OSS, 1941-43. Chmn. John Carter Brown Library Assos., 1944-47, mem. bd. mgmt.; chmn. Yale Library Assos., 1933-45; hon. fellow Pierpont Morgan Library; trustee Inst. Advanced Study, Watkinson Library, Hartford, Redwood Library, Newport, Thacher Sch. Ojai (Calif.), Henry F. DuPont Mus., Winterthur, Historic Deerfield (Mass.), John F. Kennedy Library; mem. Nat. Portrait Gallery Commn., Nat. Collection Fine Arts; founder chmn. librarians council Library of Congress, 1942-46. Served as 2d lt., 144th F.A., U.S. Army, 1917-19. Fellow Yale, 1938-64. Recipient Yale medal, 1965, Donald F. Hyde award Princeton, 1968; Gleeson Library Assos. medal U. San Francisco, 1969; Benjamin Franklin gold medal Royal Soc. Arts, 1975; Nathan Hale award Yale Club Hartford, 1975; Nat. Portrait Gallery gold medal, 1978. Fellow Am. Philos. Soc., Am. Acad. Arts and Scis., Royal Soc. Lit.; mem. Soc. Colonial Wars, Soc. Cin (hon.), Soc. Antiquaries, Royal Soc. Arts, Holland Soc. N.Y., Phi Beta Kappa (hon.), Beta Theta Pi, Scroll and Key. Clubs: Pacific Union (San Francisco); Athenaeum (London); Century, Grolier, Yale (N.Y.C.); Tavern (Boston); Metropolitan (Washington). Author: Tutor's Lane, 1922; Three Tours Through London in the Years 1748, 1776 and 1797 (Colver lectures Brown U.), 1941; The Yale Collections, 1946; Collector's Progress, 1951; Horace Walpole's Library (Sandars lectures Cambridge U.), 1957; Horace Walpole (Mellon lectures), 1960; One Man's Education, 1967; See For Yourself, 1971; Read As You Please, 1977; Rescuing Horace Walpole, 1978. Editor: A Selection of Letters of Horace Walpole, 1926, 1951, 73; Horace Walpole's Fugitive Verses, 1931; Private Charity in England, 1947-57 (with Ralph M. Williams), 1938; Yale edition Horace Walpole's Correspondence, 39 vols., 1937-73. Contbr. Atlantic Monthly, Am. Scholar, Va. Quar., Yale Rev., other mags. Home: Farmington CT 06032 Died Oct. 7, 1979.

LEWIS, WILSON D., banker; b. Indiana, Pa., July 17, 1908; s. I. Earl and Mary Belle (Shields) L.; A.B., Pa. State U., 1930; m. Anna B. Davis, Sept. 13, 1930; 1 dau., Elizabeth S. Lewis Wengert. Examiner, Pa. State Banking Dept., 1930-35; with Dauphin Deposit Bank & Trust Co., Harrisburg, Pa., 1935—, v.p., 1954-66, sr. v.p., 1966-70, pres., 1970-74, chief exec. officer, 1972—, chmn. bd., chmn. exec. com., 1974—; chmn. bd., chief exec. officer Dauphin Deposit Bank & Trust Co.; dir. Millers Mut. Ins. Co., AMP Inc., Pamcor, Inc., Stabler Cos., Inc., Union Quarries, Inc., M. Harvey Taylor & Son, Inc., Munster Summerhill Coal Co. Bd. dirs., mem. exec. com. Harrisburg Area Indsl. Devel. Corp.; bd. dirs., v.p. Polyclinic Med. Center; bd. dirs. Presbyn. Homes, Found. for Ind. Colls., Inc., James T. Hambay Found. Mem. Am. Inst. Banking (past pres. Harrisburg chpt.), C. of C. Greater Harrisburg Area (pres. 1966), Lancaster, York Area, Greater West Shore Area chambers commerce, Pa. State Alumni Assn., Kappa Sigma. Clubs: Jesters, Masons, Shriners; Country of Harrisburg, Blue Mountain Golf; Lafayette (York); Hamilton (Lancaster); Tuesday (Harrisburg); Surf (Miami, Fla.). Home: 3794 Dawn Mar St Lenker Manor Harrisburg PA 17111 Office: 213 Market St Harrisburg PA 17101

LEWITZKY, BELLA, choreographer; b. Los Angeles, Jan. 13, 1916; d. Joseph and Nina (Ossman) L.; student San Bernardino Valley (Calif.) Jr. Coll., 1933-34; m. Newell Taylor Reynolds, June 22, 1940; 1 dau., Nora Elizabeth. Co-founder, co-dir. Dance Theatre, Los Angeles, 1946-50; founder, dir. Dance Assos., Los Angeles, 1951-55; founder, 1966, since artistic dir. Bella Lewitzky Dance Co., Los Angeles; chmn. contemporary dance dept. U. So. Calif., Idyllwild, 1956-72, adv. panel, 1972—; founder Sch. Dance, Calif. Inst. Arts, 1969, dean, 1969-72; vice chmn. dance adv. panel Nat. Endowment Arts, 1974-77, mem. artists-in-schs. adv. panel, 1974-75; mem. Nat. Adv. Bd. Young Audiences, 1974—, Joint Commn. Dance and Theater Accreditation, 1979—; com. mem. Am. chpt. Internat. Dance Council of UNESCO, 1974—; bd. dirs. Am. Arts Alliance, 1977—, Arts, Edn. and Americans, 1978—; trustee Calif. Assn. Dance Cos., 1976-81; choreographer, 1948—. Recipient ann. award Dance mag., 1978, Dir.'s award Calif. Dance Educators Assn., 1978; grantee Mellon Found., 1975, Guggenheim Found., 1977-78, Nat. Endowment Arts, 1969—. Author articles in field. Address: 3594 Multiview Dr Los Angeles CA 90068. *Dance is communicative of personal, emotive knowledge—of sensory information common to all. The feel of the wind, the exhilaration of clear space, the headiness of an enormous height, the marvel of human power, one's personal worth—can take shape and be illuminated in dance. How wonderful to work at something you love! How remarkable to be given the opportunity to utilize one's whole being, one's physical knowledge, intellectual capacity, imagination, creativity. How good to practice this and know that it will not engage you in mass murders of warfare; it will not destroy our environment. It is capable of healing, celebrating, and sharing human resources. My philosophy is predicated on the belief that choreography is the taskmaster of us all. In each work, I attempt to discover again the truth of that statement.*

LEWONTIN, RICHARD CHARLES, educator; b. N.Y.C., Mar. 29, 1929; s. Max and Lillian (Wilson) L.; A.B., Harvard, 1951; M.A., Columbia, 1952, Ph.D., 1954; m. Mary Jane Christianson, Apr. 10, 1947; children—David John, Stephen Paul, James Peter, Timothy Andrew. Asst. prof. N.C. State U., 1954-58; from asst. prof. biology to prof. U. Rochester, 1958-64; prof. zoology and math. biology U. Chgo., 1964-73, asso. dean biol. scis., 1966-69, Louis Block prof. biol. scis., 1969-73; Alexander Agassiz prof. zoology Harvard, 1973—. Fellow Am. Acad. Arts and Scis., A.A.A.S.; mem. Am. Eugenics Soc. (bd. dirs. 1966—), Soc. Study Evolution (past pres.). Editor: Am. Naturalist, 1964-70. Mailing Address: Marlboro VT 05344

LEWYN, THOMAS MARK, lawyer; b. N.Y.C., July 2, 1930; s. Oswald and Agnes (Maas) L.; B.A., Stanford, 1952, postgrad., 1952-54; LL.B., Columbia, 1955; m. Ann Salfeld, July 15, 1955; children—Alfred Thomas, Mark Henry. Admitted to N.Y. bar, 1957, since practiced in N.Y.C.; asso. Simpson, Thacher & Bartlett, 1957-64, partner, 1965-75, sr. partner, 1976—. Sec., dir. Paramount Pictures Corp.; dir. Cinema Internat. Corp.; counsel Gulf & Western Industries, Inc. Served to 1st lt., F.A., AUS, 1955-57. Mem. Assn. Bar City N.Y., Am., N.Y. State bar assns. Contbr. articles to profl. jours. Home: 911 Park Ave New York NY 10021 Office: 1 Battery Plaza New York NY 10004

LEWYT, ALEXANDER MILTON, investment exec.; b. N.Y.C., Dec. 31, 1908; s. Arthur and Frieda (Blum) L.; student Bklyn. Poly. Inst., 1924-27, N.Y.U., 1927-30, Pratt Inst., 1930-33; m. Elisabeth Deval. Dir., Budd Corp., Phila. Pres. North Shore Animal League, Port Washington, N.Y. Bd. dirs. Chartres (France) S.P.C.A. Recipient Horatio Alger award Am. Schs. and Colls. Assn., 1950; N.Y.U. Marketing award, 1950; U. Louisville Distinguished Leadership award, 1950, Advt. Club of Louisville, 1951; award Ordnance Dept., War Dept., 1946; award of Merit for civic work, 1951; award for outstanding work in aid of handicapped children N.Y. Philanthropic League, 1951; citation Printers' Ink, outstanding advertiser, merchandiser, 1951-53; Youth Oscar award Youth United, 1952; decorated Legion of Honor (France). Mem. Confrerie des Chevaliers du Tastevin (officier commandeur), Commanderie de Bordeaux (commandeur), Tau Beta Pi (hon.). Clubs: Paris American. Co-author: America's Twelve Master Salesmen. Inventor Lewyt vacuum cleaner. Home: 431 E 52d St New York City NY 10022 also Sands Point NY 11050 and Chartres France Office: 660 Madison Ave New York City NY 10021

LEY, ALLYN BRYSON, physician, educator; b. Springfield, Mass., Dec. 5, 1918; s. Leo L. and Lovira J. (Tait) L.; A.B., Dartmouth, 1939, student Med. Sch., 1938-40; M.D., Columbia, 1942; m. Sydney Barr, Oct. 30, 1943 (dec. Sept. 1965); children—S. Bryson, David P., Christopher W., R.G. Douglas; m. 2d, Barbara Goble, Nov. 24, 1967; children—F. Bradford, Marcy. Intern N.Y. Postgrad. Hosp., 1942-43, N.Y. Hosp., 1946-47; resident N.Y. Hosp., 1947-48, Meml. Center, N.Y.C., 1948-49; research fellow Thorndike Meml. Lab., Harvard Med. Sch., 1949-51; mem. faculty Cornell U. Med. Coll., N.Y.C., 1951—, prof. medicine, 1963-71, prof. clin. medicine, 1971—, prof. clin. and preventive medicine Cornell U., Ithaca, N.Y., 1971—, dir. health services, 1971—, dir. hematology and blood bank labs. Meml. Center, 1951-63, mem. med. bd., 1957-63; mem. med. bd. N.Y. Hosp., 1963-69, dir. ambulatory services, 1963-69; chief staff S.S. Hope, 1969-70. Served as officer, M.C., USNR, 1943-46. Damon Runyon Com. on Growth fellow, 1949-51. Fellow A.C.P.; mem. Am. Assn. Blood Banks (bd. dirs. 1958-60), Am. Soc. Hematology, Am. Fedn. Clin. Research, A.A.A.S., N.Y. Acad. Medicine, Tompkins County Med. Soc., Am. Coll. Health Assn., Harvey Soc. Democrat. Presbyn. Clubs: Cornell Golf, Ithaca Yacht, Ithaca Paddle Tennis. Home: 110 Highland Ave Ithaca NY 14850 Office: 10 Central Ave Ithaca NY 14853

LEY, HERBERT LEONARD, JR., med. cons.; b. Columbus, Ohio, Sept. 7, 1923; s. Herbert Leonard and Laura (Spencer) L.; M.D., Harvard U., 1946, M.P.H., 1951. Commd. 1st lt., M.C., U.S. Army, 1947, advanced through grades to lt. col., 1955; resigned, 1958; prof. microbiology George Washington U. Sch. Medicine, 1958-61; civil service with U.S. Army Research Office, 1961-63; asso. prof. epidemiology and microbiology Harvard Sch. Pub. Health, 1963-66; dir. Bur. Medicine, FDA, 1966-68, commr. food and drugs, 1968-69; cons. to food and drug industry, 1969—. Decorated Bronze Star. Fellow Am. Coll. Preventive Medicine; mem. Am. Acad. Microbiology. Contbr. sci. articles to profl. jours., chpts to med. texts. Office: 1160 Rockville Pike Suite 208 PO Box 2047 Rockville MD 20852

LEY, KATHERINE LOUISE, educator; b. Prairie du Sac, Wis., Dec. 6, 1919; d. Ivan Herman and G. Louise (Conger) Ley; B.S., U. Wis., 1941; M.S., UCLA, 1947; Ph.D., U. Iowa, 1960. Tchr. pub. schs., Platteville, Wis., 1941-43; instr. Iowa State Coll., Ames, 1943-45; instr., asst. prof., asso. prof. U. Colo., Boulder, 1946-61; asso. prof. U. Mich., Ann Arbor, 1961-66; vis. prof. U. So. Calif., Los Angeles, summer, 1959, U. Wash., Seattle, summer 1961, U. N.C., 1971, Tex. Women's U., 1973; Distinguished vis. prof. U. Bridgeport (Conn.), 1974, Bowling Green State U., 1978; prof., chmn. women's phys. edn. dept. State U. N.Y., Coll. at Cortland, 1966-78; prof., chmn., athletic dir. Capital U., Columbus, Ohio, 1978—. Cons. Ednl. Testing Service, Princeton, N.J., 1968—; chmn. Nat. Com. on Standards for Girls and Women's Sports, 1954-56; mem. governing council U.S. Track and Field Fedn., 1962-65; U.S. Gymnastics Fedn., 1962; 1st chmn. Commn. on Intercollegiate Athletics for Women, 1966-69; bd. cons. U.S. Olympic Com., 1969—. Recipient merit award Eastern Assn. Phys. Edn. Coll. Women, 1974, Assn. Intercollegiate Athletics for Women, 1979; M. Gladys Scott award U. Iowa, 1975; Varsity C Faculty award, 1979; Honor Fellow award Nat. Assn. Girls and Women in Sport, 1979. Mem. AAHPER (life, v.p. 1961, mem. exec. council phys. edn. div. 1972, pres. 1974—, honor award Eastern dist. 1976), Nat. Assn. Phys. Edn. Coll. Women, Am. Acad. Phys. Edn., Am. Coll. Sports Medicine, Nat. Found. for Health, Phys. Edn. and Recreation, Phi Kappa Phi, Delta Kappa Gamma. Mem. Order Eastern Star. Co-author: Team and Individual Sports for Women, 1955. Editor, cons. Addison Wesley Pub. Co., Reading, Mass. Contbr. articles to profl. jours. Office: Capital U Columbus OH 43209

LEYDEN, DONALD ELLIOTT, chemist; b. Gadsden, Ala., June 26, 1938; s. Elliott Hampton and Vivian Ione (Buckner) L.; B.S., Kent State U., Ohio, 1960; M.S., Emory U., 1961, Ph.D., 1964; m. Alice Jane Trowbridge, June 10, 1961; children—Mary Dawn, Sean Michael. Faculty, U. Ga., Athens, 1965-76; Phillipson prof. environ. and mining chemistry U. Denver, 1976—. NIH grantee 1965-68; NSF grantee, 1970—; Phillip Morris Tobacco Co. grantee, 1973-74. Mem. Am. Chem. Soc., Soc. for Applied Spectroscopy. Editorial adv. bd. Analytica Chimica Acta, 1977—, Internat. Jour. Environ. Analytical Chemistry, 1977—. Contbr. articles in field to profl. jours. Home: 7234 S Harrison Way Littleton CO 80122 Office: Dept Chemistry U Denver Denver CO 80208

LEYDEN, NORMAN FOWLER, conductor, arranger; b. Springfield, Mass., Oct. 17, 1917; s. James Alexander and Constance (Fowler) L.; B.A., Yale U., 1938, Mus.B., 1939; M.A., Tchrs. Coll., Columbia U., 1965, Ed.D., 1968; m. Alice Wells, Mar. 28, 1942; children—Robert, Constance. Arranger, Glenn Miller Army Air Force Band, Eng. and France, 1944-45; chief arranger Tex Beneke-Glenn Miller Orch., 1945-48; artists and repertoire staff Victor Records, N.Y.C., 1951-52; mus. dir. for Arthur Godfrey, CBS, N.Y.C., 1956-59; mus. dir. for Gordon MacRae, 1962-67; freelance arranger and condr., 1949-68; asst. prof. music Portland (Oreg.) State U., 1970-75; founding condr. Westchester Youth Symphony, White Plains, N.Y., 1957-68, condr. Oreg. Symphony Pops, 1971—, Seattle Symphony Pops, 1973—; asso. condr. Oreg. Symphony, 1974—; guest condr. Minn. Orch., 1975—, Denver Symphony, 1977—, Spokane Symphony, 1975—, Phoenix Symphony, 1977, San Francisco Symphony, 1977—, Chgo. Grant Park Symphony, 1977—, Boston Pops, 1978. Served with USAAF, 1941-45. Mem. Am. Fedn. Musicians, Am. Symphony Orch. League. Composer: Concerto for Trombones, 1959; Secret River, 1961; Serenade for String Orchestra, 1965; (ballet) The Secret River. Home: 2635 SW Montgomery Dr Portland OR 97201 Office: care Oregon Symphony 1119 SW Park Ave Portland OR 97205

LEYDORF, FREDERICK LEROY, lawyer; b. Toledo, June 13, 1930; s. Loftin Herman and Dorothy DeRoyal (Cramer) L.; student U. Toledo, 1948-49; B.B.A., U. Mich., 1953; J.D., UCLA, 1958; m. Mary MacKenzie Malcolm, Mar. 28, 1953; children—Robert Malcolm, William Frederick, Katherine Ann, Thomas Richard, Deborah Mary. Admitted to Calif. bar, 1959; asso. firm Hammack & Pugh, Los Angeles, 1959-61; partner Willis, Butler, Sheifly, Leydorf & Grant, Los Angeles, 1961—; lectr., cons. Calif. Continuing Edn. of Bar, 1965—. Chmn. pub. adminstr.-pub. guardian adv. commn. Los Angeles County Bd. Suprs., 1972-73; bd. dirs. J.W. and Ida M. Jameson Found., 1967—. Served to lt. USNR, 1953-55. Cert. specialist in taxation law, Calif. Mem. Los Angeles County Bar Found. (pres. 1977-79), Am., Los Angeles County (trustee 1973-75) bar assns., State Bar Calif. (chmn. conf. dels. 1977, mem. exec. com. estate planning, trust and probate sect. 1979—), Western Pension Confs., Am. Coll. Probate Counsel, Internat. Acad. Estate and Trust Law (v.p. U.S. 1978—), Life Ins. and Trust Council Los Angeles, Los Angeles World Affairs Council, Phi Delta Phi, Phi Delta Theta. Republican. Lutheran. Clubs: Chancery, Jonathan (Los Angeles); Annandale Golf, Flintridge Riding (Pasadena). Contbg. author: California Non-Profit Corporations, 1969. Contbr. articles to profl. jours. Home: 2165 El Molino Pl San Marino CA 91108 Office: 606 S Olive St Los Angeles CA 90014

LEYERLE, JOHN FRANK, univ. adminstr.; b. Syracuse, N.Y., Nov. 18, 1926; came to Can., 1959, naturalized, 1979; s. Frank John and Margarita Emily (Leland) L.; B.S., U.S. Naval Acad., 1949; B.A., Oxford (Eng.) U., 1958, M.A., 1962; Ph.D., Harvard U., 1977; D.Litt. (hon.), Western Mich. U., 1972; m. Mary Ellen Parry, June 21, 1950; children—Eve Parry, Christopher Bennett, Sarah Blake, Andrew Geoffrey Bessinger. Lectr. dept. English U. Toronto (Ont., Can.), 1959-61, asst. prof. English, 1961-64, asso. prof., 1964-66, prof., 1966—, dir. Centre for Medieval Studies, 1966-76, dean Sch. Grad. Studies, 1978—. Fulbright fellow Magdalen Coll. Oxford U., 1954-56; Connaught sr. fellow in humanities, 1978-79. Fellow Mediaeval Acad. Am.; mem. MLA, Assn. Can. Univ. Tchrs. English. Contbr. numerous articles to profl. publs.; editor: Computers and Old English Concordances, 1971; Chivalric Literature, 1980; Chaucer: A Select Bibliography, 1980; chmn. editorial bd. Speculum Anniversary Monographs, 1975—; gen. editor Toronto Medieval Bibliographies, 1967—; editorial bd. Dictionary of The Middle Ages, 1977—. Home: 31 South Dr Toronto ON M4W 1R2 Canada Office: U Toronto 65 St George St Toronto ON M5S 1A1 Canada. *I have tried to make innovative and responsible contributions to my community of associates and colleagues a major goal. The most effective contributions I have made in administrative work, in scholarship, and in teaching have all been based, plumb and level, on creative use of past traditions involving disciplined knowledge, hard work, and individual initiative. I see myself as an innovative traditionalist.*

LEYH, GEORGE FRANCIS, assn. exec.; b. Utica, N.Y., Oct. 1, 1931; s. George Robert and Mary Kathleen (Haley) L.; B.C.E., Cornell U., 1954, M.S. (Univ. fellow), 1956; m. Mary Alice Mosher, Sept. 17, 1955; children—Timothy George, Kristin Ann. Structural engr. Eckerlin and Klepper, Syracuse, N.Y., 1956-59; asso. dir. engring. Martin Marietta Corp., Chgo., 1959-63; structural engr. Portland Cement Assn., Chgo., 1963-67; dir. mktg. Concrete Reinforcing Steel Inst., Chgo., 1967-75; exec. dir. Am. Concrete Inst., Detroit, 1975—, editor jour., 1975—. Mem. Planning Commn., Streamwood, Ill., 1960-68; chmn. Lake Bluff (Ill.) Citizens Com. for Conservation, 1972. Recipient Bloem Disting. Service award Am. Concrete Inst., 1972. Mem. ASCE, Am. Soc. Assn. Execs., Am. Mgmt. Assn., Nat. Inst. Bldg. Scis., Am. Ry. Engring. Assn., Phi Kappa Phi. Clubs: North Star Sail, Lake Bluff Yacht (dir. 1969-74, commodore 1973). Home: 1327 Lone Pine Rd Bloomfield Hills MI 48013 Office: Am Concrete Inst 22400 W Seven Mile Rd Detroit MI 48219

LEYMASTER, GLEN R., assn. exec.; b. Aurora, Nebr., Aug. 17, 1915; s. Leslie and Frances (Wertman) L.; A.B., U. Nebr., 1938; M.D., Harvard, 1942; M.P.H., Johns Hopkins U., 1950; m. Margaret Hendricks, June 20, 1942; children—Mark H., Mary Beth, Lynn F. Intern, asst. resident, resident Harvard Med. Service, Boston City Hosp., 1942-44; mem. faculty Johns Hopkins Med. Sch., 1944-48, instr., asst. prof. bacteriology Sch. Pub. Health and Hygiene, 1946-48; asso. prof. pub. health, instr. medicine U. Utah Sch. Medicine, 1948-50, prof., head dept., preventive medicine, asst. prof. medicine, also dir. univ. health service, 1950-60; adviser med. edn.- preventive medicine ICA, Bangkok, Thailand, 1956-58; asso. sec. council med. edn. and hosps. AMA, Chgo., 1960-63, dir. dept. undergrad. med. edn., 1970-75; exec. dir. Am. Bd. Med. Spltys., Evanston, Ill., 1975—; pres., dean Women's Med. Coll. Pa., 1964-70. Mem. Am., Ill., Chgo. med. assns., Inst. Medicine Chgo., Phi Beta Kappa, Sigma Xi, Alpha Omega Alpha. Contbr. articles in field to profl. jours. Home: 1155 Michigan Ave Wilmette IL 60091 Office: 1603 Orrington Ave Evanston IL 60201

LEZAK, SIDNEY IRVING, U.S. atty.; b. Chgo., Nov. 8, 1924; s. Manny and Celia (Weiner) L.; student Northwestern U., 1941-42; Ph.B., U. Chgo., 1946, J.D., 1949; m. Muriel Elaine Deutsch, June 26, 1949; children—Anne, David, Miriam. Admitted to Oreg. bar, 1949; pvt. practice, Portland, 1949-61; partner firm Bailey, Lezak, Swink & Gates, Portland, 1954-61; U.S. atty. Dist. of Oreg., 1961—. Mem. cabinet U. Chgo.; bd. govs. World Affairs Council Oreg., Nature Conservancy, Oreg.; bd. overseers Lewis & Clark Coll. Served to 1st lt. navigator, USAAF, World War II. Decorated D.F.C., Air medal. Mem. Am., Fed. (pres. Oreg. br. 1962-63, chmn. council on adminstrn. justice), Oreg., Multnomah County bar assns., Am. Judicature Soc. Jewish. Clubs: City (gov., pres. 1972), Multnomah (Portland). Contbr. articles to legal publs. Home: 1811 SW Boundary St Portland OR 97201 Office: PO Box 71 US Courthouse Portland OR 97207

LHAMON, GEORGE MARION, mfg. co. exec.; b. Los Angeles, Mar. 3, 1917; s. Ruskin Marion and Mary (Taylor) L.; B.S., U.S. Naval Acad., 1939; J.D., George Washington U., 1949; m. Mary Bruce Taylor, May 31, 1941; children—Frederic T., Judith A., Joel D. Commd. 2d lt. USMC, 1939, advanced through grades to lt. col., 1947; served in Iceland and S. Pacific, World War II, resigned, 1954; admitted to D.C. bar, 1949, Va. bar, 1949, Wash. bar, 1954, also U.S. Supreme Ct.; with Pacific Car and Foundry Co. (now called PACCAR Inc.), Bellevue, Wash., 1954—, v.p., treas., 1964-72, v.p. internat. finance, 1972—, also treas., pres. subsidiary finance cos., 1972—. Trustee Wash. Research Council, World Affairs Council Seattle. Decorated Silver Star medal. Mem. Marine Corps Res. Officers Assn., Order of Coif. Home: 6518 Parkpoint Way NE Seattle WA 98115 Office: Box 1518 Bellevue WA 98004

LHAMON, WILLIAM TAYLOR, psychiatrist, educator; b. Washington, June 11, 1915; s. Ruskin Marion and Mary Stella (Taylor) L.; A.B., Stanford, 1936, M.D., 1940; m. Dorothy Elizabeth Kearton, Apr. 11, 1942; children—William Taylor, Deborah Ann, Emily Newell, Martha Louise, Sarah Tucker. Instr. psychiatry Cornell U. Med. Coll., N.Y.C., 1947-48; asso. clin. prof. U. Pa., Phila., 1948-54; prof. psychiatry, chmn. dept. Baylor U. Med. Coll., 1954-62; dir. Houston State Psychiat. Inst., 1958-62; psychiatrist-in-chief Jefferson Davis Hosp., Houston, 1954-62; Barklie McKee Henry prof. psychiatry Cornell U. Med. Coll., also psychiatrist-in-chief N.Y. Hosp. and dir. Payne Whitney Clinic, 1962-74; prof. psychiatry Cornell U., 1962—, also med. dir. Westchester div. N.Y. Hosp., 1974-75. Fellow Am. Psychiat. Assn.; mem. Phila. Coll. Physicians, N.Y. Acad. Scis. Office: New York Hosp Westchester Div White Plains NY 10605

L'HEUREUX, JOHN CLARKE, educator; b. South Hadley, Mass., Oct. 26, 1934; s. Wilfred Joseph and Mildred (Clarke) L'H.; A.B., Weston Coll., 1959, Ph.L., 1960; M.A., Boston Coll., 1963; S.T.L., Woodstock Coll., 1967; student Harvard U., 1967-68; m. Joan Ann Polston, June 26, 1971. Ordained priest Roman Catholic Ch., 1966, laicized, 1971; writer in residence Georgetown U., 1964-65, Regis Coll., 1968-69; staff editor The Atlantic, 1968-69, contbg. editor, 1969—; vis. prof. Am. lit. Hamline U., 1971, Tufts Coll., 1971-72; vis. asst. prof. Harvard U., 1973; asso. prof. English, Stanford U., 1973—. Author: Quick as Dandelions, 1964; Rubrics for a Revolution, 1967; Picnic in Babylon, 1967; One Eye and a Measuring Rod, 1968; No Place for Hiding, 1971; Tight White Collar, 1972; The Clang Birds, 1972; Family Affairs, 1974; Jessica Fayer, 1976; Desires, 1980. Office: English Dept Stanford Stanford CA 94305

LHOTKA, JOHN FRANCIS, physician, educator; b. Butte, Mont., May 13, 1921; s. John Francis and Mary (Backowske) L.; B.A., U. Mont., 1942; M.S. in Anatomy, Northwestern U., 1948, M.B., 1949, M.D., 1951, Ph.D., 1953; m. Lois Katherine Clysdale, Sept. 21, 1951. Asst. in anatomy Northwestern U., 1947-50, Stain Commn. fellow, summer 1953; asst. prof. anatomy U. Okla. Med. Sch., 1951-55, asso. prof., 1955-69, prof. anatomical scis., 1969—. Active in humis. field, especially medieval coinage of Western Europe. Served to 1st lt. CWS, USAAF, 1942-46; PTO. Recipient 4 Heath medals, Medal of Merit, Farran Zerbe award, initial Newell award Am. Numis. Assn., Donat Cross 1st class Order St. Lazarus of Jerusalem. Fellow Am. (life; patron), Royal (life), Swiss (life), Spanish numis. socs., Am. Geriatric Soc., Internat. Acad. Pathology, Royal Soc. Health, London, Am. Inst. Chemists, Augustan Soc.; mem. Am. Numis. Assn. (life), Am. Philatelic Soc. (life), Philatelic Found., Okla. Acad. Sci. (sr.), Okla. State Hist. Soc. (life), Am. Soc. Herpatologists and Ichthyologists, Co. Mil. Historians, Orders and Medals Soc. Am., Brit. Mus. Soc., Metro. Mus. (N.Y.), Oriental Inst. Chgo., Nat. Rifle Assn. (life endowment), Am. Def. Preparedness Assn. (life), Am. Assn. Anatomists, Histochem. Soc., Am. Soc. Zoology, Biol. Stain Commn., Am. Security Council, Soc. for Exptl. Biology and Medicine, Am. Chem. Soc., Archeol. Inst. Am., E. African Wildlife Soc. (life), Nat. Wildlife Fedn., Am. Soc. Mil. Insignia Collectors, Tokens and Medals Soc., Sigma Xi, Phi Sigma. Club: Oklahoma City Petroleum. Author monographs: Introduction to East Roman Coinage, 1957; Medieval Bracteates, 1958; Medieval French Feudal Coinage, 1966; (with P.K. Anderson) Survey of Medieval Iberian Coinages, 1963; also articles in field histochemistry. Office: U Okla Health Center PO Box 26901 Oklahoma City OK 73190

LI, CHOH HAO, biochemist, endocrinologist; b. Canton, China, Apr. 21, 1913; s. Kan-chi Li and Mewching Tsui; B.S., U. Nanking, 1933; Ph.D., U. Calif. at Berkeley, 1938; M.D. (hon.), Cath. U. of Chile, 1962; LL.D., Chinese U., Hong Kong, 1970; D.Sc., U. Pacific, 1971, Marquette U., 1971, St. Peter's Coll., 1971; hon. doctor, Uppsala U., 1977; D.Sc., U. San Francisco, 1978, L.I. U., 1979; m. Annie Lu, Oct. 1, 1938; children—Wei-i Li, Ann-si Li, Eva Li. Came to U.S., 1935, naturalized, 1955. Instr. chemistry U. Nanking, 1933-35; research asso. U. Calif. at Berkeley, 1938-44, asst. prof. exptl. biology, 1944-47, asso. prof., 1947-49, prof. biochemistry, prof. exptl. endocrinology dir. Hormone Research Lab., Berkeley and San Francisco, 1950—. Mem. acad. adv. bd. Chinese U., Hong Kong, 1963—; adv. bd. Chem. Research Center, Nat. Taiwan U., 1964—; vis. scientist Children's Cancer Research Found., Boston, 1955, 63-73; co-chmn. Internat. Symposium on Growth Hormone, Milan, Italy, 1967, Internat. Symposium on Protein and Polypeptide Hormones, Leige, Belgium, 1968; hon. pres. Internat. Symposium on Gonadotropins, Bangalore, India, 1973; chmn. Internat. Symposium on Proteins, Taipei, 1978, Internat. Symposium Growth Hormones and other Biologically Active Peptides, Milan, Italy, 1979; vis. prof. U. Montreal, 1948, Nat. Taiwan U., 1958, Chinese U. Hong Kong, 1967, Marquette U., 1973. Recipient numerous honors, including Ciba award in endocrinology, 1947, Francis Emory Septennial prize Am. Acad. Arts and Scis., 1955, Albert Lasker award for basic med. research, 1962, Golden Plate award Am. Acad. Achievement, 1964, Univ. medal, Liege, Belgium, 1968; Sci. Achievement award AMA, 1970; Nat. award Am. Cancer Soc., 1971; Nicholas Andry award Assn. Bone and Joint Surgeons, 1972; Lewis prize Am. Philos. Soc., 1977; Nichols medal Am. Chem. Soc., 1979; Sci. award Academia Santa Chicra, Genoa, 1979. Faculty Research lectr. U. Calif., San Francisco, 1962-63, Evan lectr., 1976; ann. lectr. Japanese Endocrine Soc., 1965; Pres. Marcos lectr., Manila, Philippines, 1967; Lasker award lectr. Salk Inst., 1969; Nord lectr. Fordham U., 1972. Guggenheim fellow, 1948. Fellow Am. Acad. Arts and Scis., AAAS, N.Y. Acad. Sci., Am. Inst. Chemists; mem. Am. Chem. Soc. (Calif. sect. award 1951), Am. Soc. Biol. Chemists, Am. Soc. Zoologists, Endocrine Soc., Biochem. Soc. London, Soc. Exptl. Biol. Medicine; hon. mem. Harvey Soc., Argentina Soc. Endocrinological Metabolism Biol. Soc. Chile, Academia Sinica (Republic of China, Hu Shih meml. lectr. 1967), Nat. Acad. Scis.; fgn. mem. Chilean Acad. Scis., Israel Biochem. Soc. Co-editor: Methods in Medical Research, vol. 3, 1950, Perspectives in the Biochemistry of Large Molecules, Supplement 1, 1962; sect. editor Chem. Abstracts, 1960-63; co-asso. editor Internat. Jour. Peptide and Protein Research, 1969-76, editor-in-chief, 1976—; mem. editorial advisory bd. Family Health, 1969—, Biopolymers, 1979—; editorial bd. Current Topics in Exptl. Endocrinology, 1969—, Archives Biochem. Biophysics, 1979—; editor Hormonal Proteins and Peptides, 1973—, Versatility of Proteins, 1979. Home: 901 Arlington Ave Berkeley CA 94707

LI, NORMAN CHUNG, educator; b. Foochow, China, Jan. 13, 1913; s. Pel Ting and Chiu Tuan (Lin) L.; came to U.S., 1930, naturalized, 1955; B.S. cum laude, Kenyon Coll., 1933; M.S., U. Mich., 1934; Ph.D., U. Wis., 1936; m. Hazel Chou, Mar. 30, 1937; children—Peter, Paul, John, Mary, Eunice. Prof., Anhwei (China) U., 1936-38; lectr. Yenching U., Peiping, China, 1938-40; asso. prof. Fu Jen U., Pelping, 1940-45, prof., 1946; asst. prof. chemistry St. Louis U., 1946-48, asso. prof., 1948-52; prof. chemistry Duquesne U., Pitts., 1952—, Distinguished Service prof., named outstanding scholar, 1978—; cons. Argonne (Ill.) Nat. Lab.; vis. scientist NIH; mem. advisory com. Biomed. Facility Mellon Inst., Nat. Taiwan U. Grantee NSF, NIH, AEC. Fellow AAAS, Am. Inst. Chemists, Sigma Xi. Roman Catholic. Contbr. articles to profl. jours. Home: 5563 Beacon St Pittsburgh PA 15217

LI, PETER JOSEPH TA, publisher; b. Hong Kong, July 8, 1938; s. Norman C. and Hazel (Chow) L.; came to U.S., 1946, naturalized, 1958; B.A., Duquesne U., 1961; m. Anna M. Abmayr, May 22, 1965; children—Lisa Ann, Susan Ann. Advt. mgr. Sewickley Herald Pub. Co., Sewickley, Pa., 1960-62; dir. advt. Pitts. Courier Pub. Co., 1962-63; pub. dir. George A. Pflaum, Pub., Dayton, Ohio, 1963-71; pres., pub. Peter Li, Inc., Dayton, 1971—; cons. NEA, 1973—. Exec. adv. bd. U.S. Congressional Rep., Charles Whalen, Jr., Ohio, 1976—. Named Outstanding Grad. in Journalism, Duquesne U., 1961. Mem. Nat. Audiovisual Assn. (bd. dirs. 1977—, chmn. religious council), Nat. Sch. Supply and Equipment Assn. (bd. dirs. 1977—), Cath. Audiovisual Educators Assn. (bd. dirs. 1971—), Nat. Cath. Ednl. Exhibitors (bd. dirs. 1971—), Nat. Office Products Assn., Assn. Media Producers, Christian Booksellers Assn., Am. Assn. Media Educators in Religion, Cath. Library Vols. Am. (dir.), Nat. Ch. Goods Assn., Cath. Press Assn. Pub., Today's Cath. Tchr., 1971—, Catechist, 1976—, Ednl. Dealer mags., 1976—. Home: 1490 Lynnfield Dr Dayton OH 45429 Office: 2451 E River Rd Dayton OH 45438

LI, TIEN-YI, educator; b. Juyang, Honan, China, Mar. 14, 1915; s. Kuei-hsin and Hsin (Li) L.; came to U.S., 1945, naturalized, 1961; B.A., Nankai (China) U., 1937; M.A. in History, Yale U., 1946, Ph.D., 1950; m. Julia Wen-yu Liu, Sept. 14, 1963; 1 son, Norman. Mem. faculty Yale U., 1951-69, prof. Chinese lit. and culture, 1962-69; lectr. Far Eastern history Smith Coll., 1951, U. Hawaii, 1963; vis. prof. history and Chinese lang. and lit. Ind. U., 1960-61, sec., editor Tsing Hua Jour. Chinese Studies, 1955—; asso. univ. seminar modern China, Columbia, 1957—; dir., editor Far Eastern Publs., Yale, 1960-69; Mershon prof. Chinese lit. and history Ohio State U., Columbus,

1969—, chmn. dept., 1971-75; vis. prof. Chinese history, dir. Inst. Chinese Studies, Chinese U. of Hong Kong, 1976-77. Fellow Branford Coll., Yale, 1958-69; corr. research fellow Academia Sinica, 1964—; hon. research fellow China Acad., 1967—. Mem. Am. Hist. Assn., Am. Oriental Soc., Assn. Asian Studies, Chinese Lang. Tchrs. Assn. Author: Woodrow Wilson's China Policy, 1913-1917, 1952; P'o-an ching-ch'i, 2 vols., 1967; Chinese Fiction: A Bibliography of Books and Articles in Chinese and English, 1968; Chinese Historical Literature, 1977. Home: 4532 Kipling Rd Columbus OH 43220

LI, TING YI, educator; b. Peking, China, Dec. 19, 1918; s. Chien-Sen and Chun-shu (Hsia) L.; B.S., Nat. Central U. (China), 1940; Aero. Engr., Calif. Inst. Tech., 1947, Ph.D., 1950; m. Tsun Hwei Chu, Jan. 16, 1949; children—Marinda, Maria, Martha, Jason. Came to U.S., 1945, naturalized, 1955. Research engr. Nat. Bur. Aero. Research, China, 1940-44; engr. Chinese Air Force Office, Washington, 1945-50; research engr. Calif. Inst. Tech., 1950-52, sr. research engr., 1952-55; asst. prof. Rensselaer Poly. Inst., 1955-56, asso. prof., 1956-59, prof., 1959-62, dir. hypersonic research, 1960-62; prof. U. Cin., 1962-65; prof. Ohio State U., Columbus, 1965—. Cons. in field. Recipient 1st research award Chinese Inst. Aero. Engrs., 1948. Asso. fellow Am. Inst. Aero. and Astronautics; mem. Am. Rocket Soc. (sr.), Am. Inst. Physics, Am. Soc. Engring. Edn., Sigma Xi. Contbr. articles to profl. jours. Home: 3966 Fairlington Dr Columbus OH 43220

LIACOS, PAUL JULIAN, justice Mass. Supreme Ct.; b. Peabody, Mass., Nov. 20, 1929; s. James A. and Pitsa K. (Karis) L.; A.B. magna cum laude, Boston U. Coll. Liberal Arts, 1950; LL.B. magna cum laude, Boston U., 1952; LL.M., Harvard U., 1953; diploma Air Command and Staff Sch., 1954; m. Maureen G. McKean, Oct. 6, 1954; children—James P., Diana M., Mark C., Gregory A. Admitted to Mass. bar, 1952; partner firm Liacos and Liacos, Peabody, Mass., 1952-76; prof. law Boston U., 1952-76, adj. prof. law, 1976—; Distinguished lectr. on law U.S. Mil. Acad., West Point, N.Y., 1972; lectr. Suffolk U. Sch. Law, 1978-79; cons. to atty. gen. Mass. on staffing and personnel, 1974-75; lectr. on criminal evidence Boston Police Acad., 1963-64; reporter New Eng. Conf. on Def. of the Indigent, Harvard Law Sch., 1963; reader and cons. on legal manuscripts Little, Brown & Co., Boston, 1968-76; editorial cons. Warren, Gorham & Lamont, 1968-69; asso. justice Mass. Supreme Jud. Ct., 1976—; mem. steering com. Lawyers Com. for Civil Rights under Law, Boston, 1969-72. Trustee exec. com. Chamberlayne Sch. and Jr. Coll., Boston, 1972-74; hon. trustee Deree-Pierce Colls., Athens, Greece, 1976—. Served with USAF, 1953-56. Named Man of Year, Law Sch., 1952; recipient Man of Year award Alpha Omega, 1977; named mem. Colleguum Distinguished Alumni Boston U. Coll. Liberal Arts, 1974. Mem. Am., Mass. (criminal law com. 1964-66), Essex County, Peabody bar assns., Am. Judicature Soc., Assn. Trial Lawyers Am. (editor 1968-73), Harvard Law Sch Assn., Boston U. Law Sch. Alumni Assn. (Silver Shingle award 1977), Phi Beta Kappa. Democrat. Mem. Greek Orthodox Ch. Author: Handbook of Massachusetts Evidence, 1967; contbr. articles in field to legal jours.; book rev. editor Boston U. Law Rev., 1952. Home: 30 Sparrow Ln Peabody MA 01960 Office: 1300 New Courthouse Pemberton Sq Boston MA 02108

LIACOURAS, PETER JAMES, univ. adminstr., lawyer; b. Phila., Apr. 9, 1931; s. James Peter and Stella (Lagakos) L.; student Coll. William and Mary, 1950-51; B.S., Drexel U., 1953; J.D., U. Pa., 1956; M.A., Fletcher Sch. Law and Diplomacy, 1958; LL.M., Harvard U., 1959; postgrad. (Sterling fellow) Yale U. Law Sch., 1964-65; m. Anne Locke Myers, Sept. 5, 1959; children—Lisa Ann, James Peter, Stephen Myers, Gregory Locke. Admitted to Pa. bar, 1957; atty. Defender Assn. Phila., 1956-57, 59; research asso. Duke U. Law Sch. Rule of Law Research Center, 1959-63; asst. prof. law Temple U., 1963-65, asso. prof., 1965-67, prof., 1967—, dean Sch. Law, 1972—; spl. dist. atty., Phila., 1969, 70; chmn. Select Commn. on Pa. Bar Exam. Procedures, 1970; co-chmn. sect. legal edn. World Peace Through Law Center, 1973-74; chmn. confidentiality com. Pa. Gov.'s Justice Commn., 1974-78; lectr. law schs., India, 1967, Rome, 1974, 75, Ghana, 1975, Hebrew U., Jerusalem, 1975, 76, 77, 78, 79, Greece, 1977, 78, 79; cons. internat. law. Recipient Human Rights award Nat. Conv. Women in Law, 1976, Ann. Human Relations award Am. Jewish Com., Phila., 1978. Mem. Am. Bar Assn. (task force for improvement legal edn. or profl. opportunities for disadvantaged 1978—), Pa. Bar Assn., Phila. Bar Assn., Phila. Com. Fgn. Relations. Democrat. Greek Orthodox. Author: The International Court of Justice, 2 vols., 1962; contbr. numerous articles to law jours., 1957—. Home: 305 Righters Mill Rd Gladwyne PA 19035 Office: 1719 N Broad St Philadelphia PA 19122

LIBASSI, FRANK PETER, lawyer, govt. ofcl.; b. N.Y.C., Apr. 20, 1930; s. Frank G. and Mary (Marino) L.; B.A. cum laude with honors in Polit. Sci., Colgate U., 1951; LL.B., Yale U., 1954; m. Mary Frances Steen, July 10, 1954; children—Thomas, Timothy, Jennifer. Admitted to N.Y. bar, 1955; enforcement atty. N.Y. State Housing and Rent Commn., 1954-56; regional dir. N.Y. State Commn. on Human Rights, Albany, 1956-62; dep. staff dir. U.S. Commn. on Civil Rights, 1962-66; spl. asst. to sec., dir. office for civil rights HEW, Washington, 1966-68; exec. v.p. The Urban Coalition, Washington, 1968-71; v.p. Am. City Corp., Columbia, Md., 1971-72; pres., chief exec. officer Greater Hartford Process Inc. (Greater Hartford Community Devel. Corp.), 1971-77; gen. counsel HEW, Washington, 1977-79; partner firm Verner, Liipfert, Bernhard and McPherson, 1979—; vis. lectr. Anderson Coll., Chatham Coll., Goddard Coll., Ohio Wesleyan U., 1974-76; adj. faculty Grad. Sch. Bus. and Pub. Adminstrn., U. Hartford, 1976-77; mem. Urban Land Inst., 1971—; adv. bd. Bur. Nat. Affairs Housing and Community Devel. Reporter, 1972-77; incorporator Inst. Living, 1973—, Hartford Hosp., 1973—. Mem. adv. com. Democratic Nat. Com., 1974—. Recipient Superior Performance award U.S. Commn. on Civil Rights, 1963, Meritorious Service award, 1965; Sec.'s spl. citation, 1967, Distinguished Service award HEW, 1968. Woodrow Wilson sr. fellow, 1973—. Mem. Am., Fed., N.Y. State bar assns. Clubs: Hartford. Author: The Negro in the Armed Forces, 1963; Family Housing and the Negro Serviceman, 1963; Equal Opportunity in Farm Programs, 1965; Revitalizing Central City Investment, 1977. Home: 580 J Mountain Rd West Hartford CT 06117 Office: 1660 L St NW Suite 1100 Washington DC 20036 also 100 Constitution Plaza 12th Floor Hartford CT 06103

LIBBIN, EPHRAM, dept. store exec.; b. Hartford, Conn., June 22, 1918; s. Jacob and Lena (Falkoff) L.; student Bentley Coll., 1947; m. Edith M. Pasternack, June 29, 1947; children—Ira L., Jerome E., Martin R. With Henry Silverman & Co., C.P.A.'s, Worcester, Mass., 1947-60; comptroller Ames Dept. Stores, Inc., Rocky Hill, Conn., 1960-66, asst. treas., 1966-72, v.p., treas., 1972—, dir., 1966—. Vice pres., dir. Beth Hillel Synagogue, 1975-77. Served with AUS, 1941-44. Mem. New Eng. Controllers Assn., Jewish War Vets. Club: K.P. Home: 94 Northbrook Dr West Hartford CT 06117 Office: 2418 Main St Rocky Hill CT 06067

LIBBY, LEONA MARSHALL (MRS. WILLARD LIBBY), physicist; b. LaGrange, Ill., Aug. 9, 1919; d. Weightstill and Mary (Holderness) Woods; B.S., U. Chgo., 1938, Ph.D., 1943; m. John Marshall, July 3, 1943; m. 2d, Willard Libby, Dec. 1966. Research fellow U. Chgo., 1939-42, 46-48, research asso. Metall. Lab., 1942-46, Inst. Nuclear Studies, 1948-53, asst. prof., 1953-60; asso. prof. N.Y. U., 1960-62, prof., 1962-63; prof. physics U. Colo., Boulder, 1963; mem. staff RAND Corp., Santa Monica, Cal., 1963-70; mem. staff R & D Assos., Santa Monica, 1970—; physicist Hanford Engring. Works, 1944-46. Vis. scientist Brookhaven Nat. Lab., 1958—; vis. prof. Engring. Sch., U. Cal. at Los Angeles, adj. prof., 1973; cons. Los Alamos Nat. Lab.; fellow Inst. for Advanced Study, Princeton, N.J., 1957-58. Fellow Am. Phys. Soc., Royal Geog. Soc. Asso. editor Phys. Rev., 1960-62. Home: 129 Ocean Way Santa Monica CA 90402 Office: U Calif Engineering Sch Los Angeles CA 90024

LIBBY, WILLARD FRANK, educator, chemist; b. Grand Valley, Colo., Dec. 17, 1908; s. Ora Edward and Eva May (Rivers) L.; B.S., U. Calif., 1931, Ph.D., 1933; Sc.D., Wesleyan U., 1955, Syracuse U., 1957, Trinity Coll., U. Dublin, 1957, Carnegie Inst. Tech., 1959, Georgetown U., 1962, Manhattan Coll., 1963, U. Newcastle-Upon-Tyne (Eng.), 1965, Gustavus Adolphus Coll., 1970, U. South Fla., 1975, U. Colo., 1977; m. Leonor Hickey, Aug. 9, 1940 (div. 1966); children—Janet Eva, Susan Charlotte; m. 2d, Leona Woods Marshall, 1966. Instr. chemistry U. Calif., 1933, asst. prof., 1938, asso. prof., 1945; chemist Columbia War Research Div. (S.A.M. Labs.), 1941-45; prof. chemistry Inst. Nuclear Studies and dept. chemistry U. Chgo., 1945-59; prof. chemistry UCLA, 1959—, dir. Inst. Geophysics and Planetary Physics, 1962—; research asso. Geophys. Lab., Carnegie Instn. Washington, 1954-59; spl. vis. prof. chemistry, physics, astrophysics and aero-engring. U. Colo., 1967-70; spl. vis. prof. chemistry U. South Fla., Tampa, 1972; dir. Sci. Research Instrument Corp., Hedge Fund Am., Summit Capital Fund. Inc., Nuclear Systems, Inc., Research Cottrell, Inc., W.F. Libby Labs., Douglas Aircraft Co., Data Design Labs.; mem. acad. adv. bd. RAND Corp., 1968-77. Mem. com. sr. responsible reviewers AEC, 1945-52, mem. gen. adv. com., 1950-54, 60-62, mem. Plowshare adv. com., 1959-72, mem. AEC, 1954-59; mem. Calif. Air Resources Bd., 1967-72; mem. com. selection Guggenheim Meml. Found., 1959-77; mem. Pres.'s Task Force Air Pollution, 1969-70, U.S./Japan Com. Sci. Cooperation, 1970-73; mem. vis. com. Jet Propulsion Lab., 1968-72; sci. adviser State of Idaho, 1969-72; mem. Calif. Gov.'s Earthquake Council, 1972—. Bd. dirs., pres. Isotope Found. Recipient Research Corp. award, 1951; Chandler medal Columbia, 1954; Am. Chem. Soc. award, 1956; Remsen Meml. lecture award, 1955; City Coll. N.Y. Bicentennial lecture award, 1956; Elliott Cresson medal Franklin Inst., 1957; Williard Gibbs medal, 1958; Albert Einstein award, 1959; Priestly award Dickinson Coll., 1959; Nobel prize for chemistry, 1960; Day medal Geol. Soc. Am., 1961; Calif. Alumnus of Year award, 1963; Gold medal Am. Inst. Chemists, 1970. Guggenheim fellow, 1941-42, 51, 59. Fellow Am. Nuclear Soc., Am. Inst. Chemists, Brit. Acad. (corr.); mem. Am. Philos. Soc., Am. Acad. Arts and Scis., Nat. Acad. Scis., Heidelberg Acad. Sci., AAAS, Am. Phys. Soc., Am. Inst. Chem. Engrs., Am. Chem. Soc., Am. Geophys. Union, Am. Inst. Aeros. and Astronautics, Bolivian Soc. Anthropology, Berkeley Fellows (charter), Geochem. Soc., Geol. Soc. Am., Royal Swedish Acad. Sci., Phi Beta Kappa, Sigma Xi, Pi Mu Epsilon, Alpha Chi Sigma, Phi Lambda Upsilon. Clubs: Explorers; Cosmos (Washington); Metropolitan, Century Assn. (N.Y.C.). Author: Radiocarbon Dating, 1955. Editorial bd. Science, 1962-70, Space Life Scis., 1970—, Sci. of Total Environment, 1973—, Environ. Geology, 1973—; editorial adv. bd. Indsl. Research, 1967-73. Contbr. articles to chem. jours. Home: 129 Ocean Way Santa Monica CA 90402

LIBERACE (WLAD ZIU VALENTINO LIBERACE), pianist, concert artist, composer; b. West Allis, Wis., May 16, 1919; s. Salvatore and Frances Liberace; student Wis. Coll. Music. Soloist, Chgo. Symphony Orch. in Milw.; entertainer, Milw., 1940-45; TV debut Sta. KLAC, Los Angeles, 1952; weekly TV show on film, after 1952; concert tours, 1953; appeared Carnegie Hall, 1953, Madison Square Garden, 1954; recorded for Columbia Records, Coral Records; starred in motion picture Sincerely Yours, 1955; appeared in film The Loved One, 1965. Recipient Emmy awards (2); named Entertainer of Year, 1973. Mem. ASCAP, Nat. Acad. Rec. Arts and Scis. Author: Liberace Cooks, 1970; Liberace, 1973. Home: Las Vegas NV 89119 Office: 4993 Wilbur St Las Vegas NV 89119

LIBERATORE, NICHOLAS ALFRED, diversified co. exec.; b. N.Y.C., June 19, 1916; s. Alexander and Angelina (Laspagnoletta) L.; M.A., Fairfield U.; m. Jean Talbot MacAdam, June 6, 1943 (div.); children—Virginia, George, Nicholas, Elliott, Mark; m. 2d, Marianne Westpalm van Hoorn Jewett, Feb. 10, 1973. Vice pres. Ebasco Internat. Co., N.Y.C., 1956-58; pres. Raymond Concrete Pile Co. Am., N.Y.C., 1958-59; chmn. operating com. Brown-Raymond-Walsh, Madrid, Spain, 1959-62; v.p. Raymond Internat. Inc., N.Y.C., 1962-65; v.p., then sr. v.p., pres. internat. Group Lone Star Industries, Inc., Greenwich, Conn., 1965-74; sr. v.p. Ebasco Services Inc., N.Y.C., 1974-77; exec. v.p. Genstar Ltd., San Francisco, 1977—; Served to capt., C.E., AUS, 1943-46. Decorated Bronze Star medal, Army Commendation medal; Cross of Isabel the Catholic (Spain). Mem. Pan-Am. Soc. (hon. pres., dir.). Club: Economic (N.Y.C.). Home: 1100 Sacramento St San Francisco CA 94108 Office: 3 Embarcadero Center Suite 2500 San Francisco CA 94111

LIBERMAN, ALEXANDER, artist, editor; b. Kiev, Russia, Sept. 4, 1912; came to U.S., 1941, naturalized, 1946; s. Simon and Henriette (Pascar) L.; student in architecture Ecole des Beaux Arts, Paris, 1930; m. Tatiana Yacovleff Du Plessix, Nov. 4, 1942, 1 stepdau., Francine Du Plessix Gray. Art dir., mng. editor Vu Paris, 1931-36; art dir. Vogue mag. Conde Nast Publs., N.Y.C., 1941-43, art dir. Conde Nast Publs., 1943—, editorial dir., 1962—; exhibited Mus. Modern Art, 1959, retrospective painting and sculpture exhibit Corcoran Gallery Art, Washington, 1970; sculptor works Covenant, U. Pa., 1975, Symbol, Rockford, Ill., 1978. Decorated chevalier Legion of Honor (France). Club: Century Assn. (N.Y.C.). Editor books, including: The Artist in His Studio, 1960; Greece Gods and Art, 1968. Home: 173 E 70th St New York NY 10021 Office: Conde Nast Publs Inc 350 Madison Ave New York NY 10017

LIBERMAN, ALVIN MEYER, psychologist; b. St. Joseph, Mo., May 10, 1917; s. Max and Lotte (Korbholz) L.; A.B., U. Mo., 1938, M.A., 1939; Ph.D., Yale U., 1942; m. Isabelle Yoffe, June 1, 1941; children—Mark Yoffe, Michael Charles, Sarah Ivy. Mem. faculty U. Conn., Storrs, 1949—, prof. psychology, 1950—; adj. prof. linguistics Yale U., 1968—; pres., dir. research Haskins Labs., New Haven, 1975—. Guggenheim fellow, 1964-65. Fellow Am. Acad. Arts and Scis.; mem. Nat. Acad. Scis., Soc. Exptl. Psychologists, Acoustical Soc. Am., Am. Psychol. Assn. Contbr. articles to profl. jours. Address: 614 Storrs Rd Mansfield Center CT 06250

LIBERMAN, LEE MARVIN, utility exec.; b. Salt Lake City, July 12, 1921; s. Benjamin L. and Sylvia (Goldflam) L.; B.S. in Chem. Engring., Yale, 1942; m. Jeanne Hirsch, Oct. 19, 1946; children—Alise, James, Celia. With Laclede Gas Co., St. Louis, 1945—, exec. v.p., 1968-70, pres., 1970—, chief exec. officer, 1974—, chmn., 1976—, also dir.; dir. Boatmen's Bancshares, Boatmen's Nat. Bank, Angelica Corp., Valley Industries, Inc. Mem. Civic Progress, Inc., Regional Commerce and Growth Assn.; past pres. Family and Childrens Service St. Louis. Bd. dirs. Art and Edn. Council, St. Louis Symphony Orch.; exec. com. United Way; trustee Washington U.; past chmn. bd. Jewish Hosp. Served with USAAF, 1944-45. Registered profl. engr., Mo. Mem. Nat. Soc. Profl. Engrs., Mo. C. of C. Club: Yale (trustee, St. Louis). Home: 11703 Tarrytown Dr Creve Coeur MO 63141 Office: 720 Olive St St Louis MO 63101

LIBERMAN, MYRON MANDELL, educator; b. N.Y.C., Oct. 3, 1921; s. Morton J. and Jane (Schatz) L.; A.B., Lafayette Coll., 1943; M.A., N.Y. U., 1946; m. Mathilda Nahra, Mar. 28, 1958; children—Noah James, Alexander Mikhail. Instr. dept. English, Wayne State U., Detroit, 1957-60; Oakes Ames prof. English lit. Grinnell (Iowa) Coll., 1960—. Mem. Modern Lang. Assn., Newberry Library Assn. Author: A Preface to Literary Analysis, 1964; The Practice of Criticism, 1966; A Modern Lexicon of Literary Terms, 1968; Maggot and Worm and Eight Other Stories, 1969; Katherine Anne Porter's Fiction, 1971. Home: 1315 Broad St Grinnell IA 50112 Office: Carnegie Hall Park St Grinnell IA 50112

LIBERTO, JOSEPH SALVATORE, banker; b. Balt., Apr. 26, 1929; s. Cosimo and Anna (Serio) L.; student Balt. City Coll., 1945-47; certificate accounting Balt. Coll. Commerce, 1949; grad. Nat. Assn. Bank Auditors and Comptrollers Sch. Banking, U. Wis., 1968; m. Mary Jane Colandro, May 20, 1962; children—Joseph C., Grace Ann. With Union Trust Co. Md., Balt., 1954—, auditor, 1963—, asst. v.p., security officer, 1979—. Served with AUS, 1951-53; Japan. Mem. Bank Adminstrn. Inst. (pres. Balt. 1968—), Inst. Internal Auditors. Home: 5609 Biddison Ave Baltimore MD 21206 Office: Union Trust Co Md Baltimore and St Paul Sts Baltimore MD 21203

LIBIN, PAUL, theatre exec., producer; b. Chgo., Dec. 12, 1930; s. Ely L.; student U. Ill.; B.F.A., Columbia U., 1956; m. Florence Rowe, Sept. 25, 1957; children—Charles, Claire, Andrea. Producer numerous plays, including The Crucible, 1958, Six Characters in Search of an Author, 1963, Royal Hunt of the Sun, 1965; mng. dir. Circle in the Sq. Theatre, N.Y.C., 1965—; co-producer numerous plays, including Uncle Vanya, 1973, The Iceman Cometh, 1973, Death of a Salesman, 1975, The Lady from the Sea, 1976, The Night of the Iguana, 1976, The Club, 1976, Tartuffe, 1977; owner, operator Martinique Theatre, N.Y.C. Served with U.S. Army, 1953-55. Recipient Obie award for The Club, Village Voice, 1977; Tony award, 1976. Mem. League Off Broadway Theatres and Producers (pres.), League N.Y. Theatres and Producers (bd. govs.). Office: Circle in the Square 1633 Broadway New York NY 10019

LIBOFF, RICHARD LAWRENCE, physicist; b. N.Y.C., Dec 30, 1931; s. William and Sarah (Mell) L.; A.B., Bklyn. Coll., 1953; Ph.D., N.Y. U., 1961; m. Myra Blatt, July 4, 1954; children—David, Lisa. Asst. prof. physics N.Y. U., 1961-63; prof. applied physics and elec. engring. Cornell U., 1964—; prin. investigator Air Force Office Sci. Research, 1978—. Served with Chem. Corps, U.S. Army, 1953-55. Recipient Founders Day cert. N.Y. U., 1961; Solvay fellow, 1972. Fellow Am. Phys. Soc.; mem. Sigma Xi. Author: Introduction to the Theory of Kinetic Equations, 1969, 79, Russian edit., 1974; Introductory Quantum Mechanics, 1979. Office: Phillips Hall Cornell U Ithaca NY 14853

LIBSCH, JOSEPH FRANCIS, educator; b. Rockville, Conn., May 7, 1918; s. Joseph J. and Martha (Lipke) L.; S.B., M.I.T., 1940, S.M., 1941, Sc.D., 1941; m. Eleanor Richmond Say, Sept. 20, 1941; children—Karl David, Lawrence Russell, Thomas Alan. Mem. faculty Lehigh U., 1946—, prof. metallurgy, 1954—, Alcoa prof., 1967—, chmn. dept. metallurgy and materials sci., 1960-69, head Materials Research Center, 1962-69, v.p. research, 1969—. Cons. metallurgist Lepel High Frequency Labs., 1945—; materials cons. Smith Kline French Labs., 1956-73; mem. Pa. Gov.'s Sci. Advisory Com., 1972—. Mem. corp. Lancaster (Pa.) Theol. Sem., 1961-73, 78—; bd. dirs. Pa. Sci. and Engring. Found., 1972, 76—; pres., bd. dirs. Am. Soc. for Metals Found. for Edn. and Research, 1974-78. Served to capt., ordnance dept. AUS, 1941-45. Mem. Am. Soc. for Metals (award teaching metallurgy 1954, nat. trustee 1968-70, v.p. 1973, pres. 1974, trustee 1973-75), Am. Inst. Mining, Metall. and Petroleum Engrs., Inst. Metals, Am. Soc. Engring. Edn., ASTM, Sigma Xi, Tau Beta Pi. Mem. United Ch. Christ (elder). Contbr. articles to profl. jours. Home: 3410 Mountainview Circle Bethlehem PA 18017

LICHINE, ALEXIS, wine grower, bus. exec., author; b. Moscow, Russia, Dec. 3, 1913; s. Alexander and Alice L.; student Ecole Alsacienne, also Cours de Droit Internat., Paris, France; B.S. in Econs., U. Pa., 1933; m. Arlene Dahl, Dec. 23, 1965 (div. 1968); children (by previous marriage)—Alexandra, Alexis. Came to U.S., 1934, naturalized, 1938. Dir. several wine importing cos. N.Y. until 1942; wine importer, N.Y.C., 1946-68; propr. Chateau Prieuré-Lichine, Margaux; v.p., dir., cons. Somerset Wine Co., Inc., N.Y.; former co-propr. Chateau Lascombes, Margaux (Gironde), France; former pres. Hedges & Butler Imports, Ltd., N.Y.C., 1965-68; founder, past dir. Alexis Lichine & Co., Bordeaux, France; past pres. Jacks Bay and Cotton Garden Devel. Corp., V.I.; dir. Marbella Beach Hotel S.A., Marbella Costa Del Sol Spain, Celulose de Angola S.A.; founder Baie de Marigot Land Devel. Corp., St. Martin, W.I.; Organizer ann. art exhbn. La Vigne et Le Vin, Margaux, 1961-71. Served to maj. AUS, 1942-46. Decorated officier Legion of Honor, Medaille Reconnaissance Francaise, Croix de Guerre with 3 palms, (France); Bronze Star medal (U.S.); comdr. Ouissam Alaouite (Morocco); comdr. Nicham Iftikar (Tunisia); officer Order Leopold of Belgium. Mem. Academie du Vin de Bordeaux, Jurade de St. Emilion (officer), Commanderie de Bordeaux (officer). Mem. Am. Soc. French Legion of Honor (dir.). Author: Wines of France, rev. edit., 1970; New Encyclopedia of Wines and Spirits, rev. edit., 1977-79; Alexis Lichine's Guide to the Wines and Vineyards of France, 1979. Contbr. articles to nat. mags. U.S., France. Record album The Joy of Wine, 1968, reproduced, 1973. Home: 998 Fifth Ave New York NY 10028

LICHSTEIN, HERMAN CARLTON, microbiologist, educator; b. N.Y.C., Jan. 14, 1918; s. Siegfried W. and Luba (Berson) L.; A.B., N.Y. U., 1939, M.S. in Pub. Health, U. Mich., 1940, Sc.D. in Bacteriology, 1943; m. Shirley Riback, Jan. 24, 1942; children—Michael, Peter. Instr., U. Wis., 1943-46; asso. prof., then prof. U. Tenn., 1947-50; asso. prof., then prof. U. Minn., 1950-61; prof. microbiology, dir. dept. U. Cin. Coll. Medicine, 1961-78, dir. grad. studies microbiology, 1962-78, prof. microbiology, 1961—; mem. Linacre Coll., Oxford U., 1976; mem. microbiology tng. com. NIH, 1963-66, microbiology fellowships com., 1966-70; mem. sci. faculty fellowship panel NSF, 1960-63; mem. Gov. Minn. Com. Edn. Exceptional Child, 1956-57. Bd. dirs. Walnut Hills (Ohio) High Sch. Assn., 1964-66. NRC fellow Cornell U., 1946-47; fellow U. Cin. Grad. Sch. 1965. Diplomate Am. Bd. Microbiology. Fellow AAAS, Am. Acad. Microbiology (gov. 1972-75, chmn. 1973); mem. Am. Soc. Microbiology, Am. Soc. Biol. Chemists, Soc. Gen. Microbiology, Assn. Med. Sch. Microbiology Chairmen (council 1970-72, trustee 1974-77), Soc. Exptl. Biology and Medicine, Am. Inst. Biol. Scis., Sigma Xi (pres. Cin. chpt. 1971-73), Phi Kappa Phi, Pi Kappa Epsilon. Author: (with Evelyn Oginsky) Experimental Microbial Physiology, 1965; also articles. Home: 3800 Middleton Ave Cincinnati OH 45220 Office: Medical Science Bldg Univ Cin Coll Medicine Cincinnati OH 45267

LICHSTEIN, JACOB, physician; b. Phila., July 4, 1908; s. Solomon and Clara (Barmash) L.; student (Mayor's competitive scholar) Phila. Coll. Art, 1925, U. Pa. (Mayor's competitive scholar), 1925-28; M.D., Jefferson Med. Coll., 1932; m. Lilyan Cohen, Dec. 1939 (div. 1966);

children—Henry Alan, Gabrielle; m. 2d, Mary McDonnell, Feb. 5, 1975 (div. 1976). Rotating resident Albert Einstein Med. Center, Phila., 1932-34, attending staff med. div., 1936-42, attending gastrointestinal clinic, 1936-41; contract surgeon Civilian Conservation Corps, Galeton, Pa., 1934-35; pvt. practice medicine, Phila., 1935-42, specializing in internal medicine and gastroenterology, Los Angeles, 1946—; demonstrator pathology Jefferson Med. Coll., Phila., 1936-40; attending staff Cedars of Lebanon Hosp., 1947-76, Los Angeles County Hosp., 1946-66, emeritus, 1966—; mem. staff Los Angeles County Hosp. Unit II, 1964-67, Temple Hosp., 1948-75, Union Health Center, 1956-58, Mt. Sinai Hosp., 1966—; attending specialist gastroenterology Wadsworth VA Gen. Hosp., 1963—; cons. Midway Hosp., Los Angeles, 1970-75, Westside Hosp., Los Angeles, 1970-75; emeritus physician Cedars-Sinai Med. Center, Los Angeles, 1976—; instr. medicine U. So. Calif. Med. Sch., 1946-52, asst. prof. clin. medicine, 1952-64, postgrad. lectr. gastroenterology, 1947-53; asso. clin. prof. medicine UCLA Sch. Medicine, 1975-77, asst. clin. prof. U. Calif. at Los Angeles Center for Health Scis., 1967—; med. dir. Gay-Henry Gastrointestinal Research Found., Los Angeles, 1957—; med. cons. county, state and fed. agencies. Mem. Pan-Am. Cytology Union, 1952-61. Vice pres. bd. Players Prodn. Co., Inc., Los Angeles; producer-dir. Beards and Belles, 1937-40. Served to 1st lt., M.C., Civilian Conservation Corps, 1934-35, to maj. AUS, 1942-46: ETO. Recipient grants clin. research gastroenterology, 1952—. Diplomate Am. Bd. Internal Medicine (sub-specialty gastroenterology). Fellow A.C.P., Am. Coll. Gastroenterology (1st prize sci. exhibit 1959), Am. Geriatrics Soc; mem. Am. Gastroent. Assn. (sr.), AMA, Calif., Los Angeles Bowling Green Assn., Los Angeles County med. socs., So. Calif. Soc. Gastroenterology (pres. 1965), Am. Fedn. Clin. Research (sr.), Am., Calif., Los Angeles socs. internal medicine, AAAS, So. Calif. Soc. Gastrointestinal Endoscopy, N.Y. Acad. Scis., ANTA (pres. So. Calif. chpt. 1967, prodn. head Free Shakespeare in the Parks program Los Angeles). Democrat. Mason (32). Club: Hollywood Comedy. Contbr. numerous articles to profl. jours. Pvt. book, art collector. Address: 3870 Latrobe St Los Angeles CA 90031

LICHT, FRANK, former gov of R.I., lawyer; b. Providence, Mar. 3, 1916; s. Jacob and Rose (Kassed) L.; A.B., Brown U., 1938, LL.D., 1975; LL.B., Harvard, 1941; LL.D., St. Francis Coll., Biddeford, Maine, 1969, Yeshiva U., 1970, R.I. Coll., 1971, U. R.I., 1971; L.H.D., Hebrew Union Coll., 1971, Suffolk U., 1971; LL.H., Our Lady of Providence Sem., 1973; m. Dorothy Shirley Krauss, June 16, 1946; children—Beth Ellen (Mrs. John Laramee), Carol Ann (Mrs. Dennis Kanin), Judith Joan. Admitted to R.I. bar, 1942, also U.S. Supreme Ct.; law clk. 1st U.S. Circuit Ct. Appeals, Boston, 1942-43; partner Letts & Quinn, Providence, 1943-56, Letts, Quinn & Licht, Providence, 1973—; asso. justice R.I. Superior Ct., 1956-68. Lectr., Bryant Coll., Providence, 1958-64, Nat. Conf. Trial Ct. Judges Coll., Reno, 1967; teaching fellow Harvard U. Inst. of Politics, 1972-73. Vice pres. bd. Gen. Jewish Com. Providence, 1960-66; pres. bd. Gen. Jewish Com. R.I., 1967-68; co-chmn. So. New Eng. Conf. Christians and Jews, 1959-68; chmn. Chapin Hosp. Commn., Providence, 1967; pres., dir. R.I. Council Community Services. Mem. R.I. Senate from Providence, 1949-56; gov. R.I., 1969-73. Trustee, bd. dirs. Butler Hosp., Providence; bd. dirs. Providence Human Relations Commn.; exec. com. Nat. Govs. Conf., 1971. Recipient Lehman award for R.I., 1965; named Man of Year, Providence Sunday Jour., 1969; recipient Herbert H. Lehman Ethics award Jewish Theol. Sem. Am., 1969; Herbert H. Lehman citation Nat. Info. Bur. for Jewish Life, Inc., 1970; hon. fellow Hebrew U., Jerusalem, 1969; Ford Found. grantee. Mem. Am., R.I. bar assns., Nat. Conf. Trial Ct. Judges (exec. com.), Phi Beta Kappa, Delta Sigma Rho. Jewish (v.p. temple). Contbr. articles to profl. jours. Home: 640 Elmgrove Ave Providence RI 02906 Office: 1616 Hospital Trust Tower Providence RI 02903

LICHT, FRED STEPHEN, art historian and archaeologist; b. June 9, 1928; B.A. in Comparative Lit., U. Wis., 1949; Ph.D. in Art History and Archaeology insigni cum laude, U. Basel (Switzerland), 1952; m. Meg Monay Licht; children—Matthew, Daniel, Sabina. Spl. fellow in humanities Princeton U., 1955, instr. Greek, 1955-57; asso. prof. Williams Coll., 1957-62; Fulbright postdoctoral fellow, Florence, Italy, 1962; prof. Brown U., 1965-68, chmn. dept., 1968; dir. Fla. State U. Study Center in Florence, 1968-78; dir. Art Museum, Princeton U., 1978—, prof. art history and archaeology, 1979—; Clark Art Inst. chair art history, Williamstown, Mass., 1974. Decorated grande officiale Republic of Italy. Mem. Phi Beta Kappa. Author: Die Landschaft in den Werken von Nicolas Poussin, 1955; Sculpture of the 19th and 20th Centuries, 1967; Goya in Perspective, 1973; Goya in a Modern Key, 1979; contbr. articles to profl. publs. Home: 35 University Pl Princeton NJ 08540 Office: Art Museum Princeton U Princeton NJ 08540

LICHT, JENNIFER MCCONNELL, mus. art curator; b. London, Eng., June 11, 1940; d. John J. Wickham and Ethel Whitehead (Connor) McConnell; diploma U. Paris, 1959, U. Perugia, 1961; M.A., Columbia U., 1977, now postgrad. doctoral program; m. Ira Richard Licht, Sept. 1963. Curator Mus. of Modern Art, N.Y.C., 1963-76, dir. exhbns., lectr. 20th century art, 1975. U.S. Commr. 8e Biennale de Paris, 1973. Guggenheim fellow, 1971; pres.'s fellow Columbia U., 1977. Book editor Art Jour., 1978—; contbr. articles on contemporary art to profl. publs. Office: Columbia U New York NY 10027

LICHT, PAUL, zoologist; b. St. Louis, Mar. 12, 1938; s. Harry and Betty L.; B.A., Washington U., St. Louis, 1959; Ph.D., U. Mich., 1964; m. Barbara Margaret Morrison, June 30, 1963; children Andrew Stephen, Rachael Margaret, Carolyn Ann. Asst. prof. zoology U. Calif., Berkeley, 1964-68, asso. prof., 1968-72, prof., 1972—, chmn. dept. zoology, 1977—. Fellow AAAS; mem. Soc. for Biology Reprodn., Soc. Ichthyology and Herpetology, Am. Inst. Biol. Sci. Research, numerous publs. in field, 1964—; editor McGraw Hill Book Series, 1967—; mem. editorial and adv. bds. Gen. Comparative Endocrinology, 1978—. Office: Dept Zoology U Calif Berkeley CA 94720

LICHT, SIDNEY, physician; b. N.Y.C., Apr. 18, 1907; s. Herman Selig and Julia (Frank) L.; B.S., City Coll. N.Y., 1927; M.D., N.Y.U., 1931; m. Elizabeth Schweitzer, Mar. 16, 1937; children—Vera Hermine, Phyllis Roxanne, Jeffrey Louis. Intern, Mt. Sinai Hosp., N.Y.C., 1931-32, Sea View Hosp., N.Y.C., 1932-33, Beth Israel Hosp., N.Y.C., 1933-35; practice medicine, 1935—, N.Y.C., 1935-42; mem. staff VA Hosp., Boston, 1946, VA Hosp., West Haven, Conn.; cons. phys. medicine Gaylord Hosp., Wallingford, Conn., 1961—; cons. Beth Israel Hosp., 1967, Inst. Crippled and Disabled, 1967, Montefiore Hosp. (all N.Y.C.); asst. clin. prof. med. Yale Med. Sch., 1955-64; prof. med. lit. U. Miami, 1975—. Served with AUS, 1942-46. Recipient Krusen award, 1974. Hon. mem. Argentine, Brit., Canadian, Danish, French, German, Italian and Polish socs. phys. medicine, Argentine Assn. Kinesiology, Canadian Occupational Therapy Assn., Asian-Pacific League Phys. Medicine and Rehab.; mem. Am. Soc. Med. Hydrology (pres. 1962-65), Am. Congress Rehab. Medicine (pres. 1967-68), Internat. Rehab. Med. Assn. (sec. 1968-70), Internat. Congress Phys. Medicine (v.p. 1968). Club: City Athletic (N.Y.C.). Author: Music in Medicine, 1946; Occupational Therapy Source Book, 1947; co-author: Occupational Therapy, 1950; Physical Medicine in General Practice, 1952; Electrodiagnosis and Electromyography, 1956; Therapeutic Heat, 1958; Therapeutic Exercise, 1958; Therapeutic Electricity and Ultraviolet Radiation, 1959; Massage Manipulation and Traction, 1960; World Directory of Physical Medicine Specialists, 1960; Medical Hydrology, 1965; Medical Climatology, 1964; Orthotics Etcetera, 1966; Rehabilitation and Medicine, 1968; Arthritis and Rehabilitation, 1969; Stroke and Its Rehabilitation, 1974. Emeritus editor Am. Jour. Phys. Medicine; editor Occupational Therapy and Rehab., 1947-51. Address: 700 Biltmore Way Coral Gables FL 33134

LICHTEN, WILLIAM LEWIS, physicist; b. Phila., Mar. 5, 1928; s. Harold and Goldie (Rosenbaum) L.; B.A., Swarthmore Coll., 1949; M.S., U. Chgo., 1953, Ph.D., 1956; M.A. (hon.), Yale U., 1964; m. Susan Lurie, June 18, 1950; children—Michael, Stephen, Julia. NSF postdoctoral fellow and research staff physicist Columbia U., 1956-58; asst. prof. U. Chgo., 1958-63, asso. prof., 1963-64; prof. physics Yale U., 1964-75, prof. physics and engring. and applied sci., 1975—. Sloan Found. fellow, 1959-65; NSF grantee, 1959—; HEW grantee, 1969-71. Fellow Am. Phys. Soc.; mem. Nat. Assn. Metric Edn. (dir.), Am. Assn. Physics Tchrs. Author: Ideas in Physics, 1973; also articles. Home: 785 Forest Rd New Haven CT 06515 Office: Becton Center 15 Prospect St Yale U New Haven CT 06520

LICHTENBERG, DON BERNETT, educator; b. Passaic, N.J., July 2, 1928; s. Milton and Ida (Krulewitz) L.; B.A., N.Y. U., 1950; M.S., U. Ill., 1951, Ph.D., 1955; m. Rita Kalter, Jan. 10, 1954; children—Naomi, Rebecca. Research asso. Ind. U., Bloomington, 1955-57, asso. prof., 1963-66, prof. physics, 1966—; asst. prof. Mich. State U., 1958-61, asso. prof., 1961-63; physicist Stanford Linear Accelerator Center, 1962-63; Vis. prof. U. Hamburg (Germany), 1957-58, Tel-Aviv U., 1967-68, Imperial Coll., London, 1971; vis. sr. fellow Oxford U., 1979-80. Fellow Am. Phys. Soc., Phi Beta Kappa, Sigma Xi. Author: Meson and Baryon Spectroscopy, 1965; (with K. Johnson, J. Schwinger, S. Weinberg) Particles and Field Theory, 1965; Unitary Symmetry and Elementary Particles, 1970, 2d edit., 1978; also numerous articles. Home: 715 S Fess Ave Bloomington IN 47401

LICHTENBERG, MARGARET KLEE, editor; b. N.Y.C., Nov. 19, 1941; d. Lawrence and Shirley Jane (Wicksman) Klee; B.A., U. Mich., 1963; student Harvard Grad. Sch., 1963; m. James Lester Lichtenberg, Mar. 31, 1963; children—Gregory Lawrence, Amanda Zoe. Writer, free-lance critic, 1961—; book rev. editor New Woman mag., 1972-73; asso. editor children's books Parents Mag. Press, 1974; editor, rights dir. Books for Young People, Frederick Warne & Co., N.Y.C., 1975-78; sr. editor Simon & Schuster, N.Y.C., 1979—. Bd. dirs. Children's Book Council. Recipient Avery Hopwood award (2) in drama and fiction, 1962, (2) in drama and poetry, 1963; Coll. Fiction Contest award Mademoiselle mag., 1963. Woodrow Wilson fellow, 1963. Mem. Women's Nat. Book Assn. (pres. N.Y. chpt.). Author articles, stories, poetry, revs. in mags., newspapers, anthologies. Home: 712 Washington St New York NY 10014 Office: 1230 Ave of Americas New York NY 10020

LICHTENBERGER, HAROLD V., engr.; b. Decatur, Ill., Apr. 22, 1920; s. James Floyd and Velma (Lutes) L.; A.B., James Millikin U., 1942; m. Alice Large, Aug. 15, 1943; children—Ann, Jane, Lynn, Jack, Chris. Physics research, engring., engring. devel. Metall. Lab., Argonne Nat. Lab., 1942-56, devel. nuclear reactor, heavy water moderated reactor, reactor to produce elec. power, boiling reactor; v.p. Gen. Nuclear Engring. Corp., 1956-61; asst. div. dir., mgr. mfg. nuclear div. Combustion Engring., Inc., 1961-74, v.p. mfg., nuclear power systems, 1974-75, v.p. nuclear fuel, nuclear power systems, 1975—. Fellow Am. Nuclear Soc. Home: 34 Fox Den Rd West Simsbury CT 06092 Office: PO Box 500 Windsor CT 06095

LICHTENSTEIN, LAWRENCE MARK, physician; b. Washington, May 31, 1934; s. Samuel and Lillian (Colodny) L.; M.D., U. Chgo., 1960; Ph.D., Johns Hopkins U., 1965; m. Carolyn Eggert, June 15, 1956; children—Elizabeth, Joshua, Rebekah. Intern, Johns Hopkins Hosp., 1960-61; resident in medicine, 1965-66; asst. prof. medicine Johns Hopkins U. Sch. Medicine, 1966-70, asso. prof., 1970-75, prof., 1975—. Diplomate Am. Bd. Allergy and Immunology. Fellow A.C.P., Am. Acad. Allergy; mem. Am. Assn. Immunology, Am. Fedn. Clin. Research, Am. Soc. Clin. Investigation, Am. Soc. Exptl. Pathology, Collegium Internat. Allergologicum, ASPET. Democrat. Jewish. Mem. editorial bds. Jour. Immunology, Jour. of Allergy and Clin. Immunology, Internat. Archives of Allergy and Applied Immunology, Immunopharmacology. Contbr. articles to profl. jours. Home: 1600 The Terraces Baltimore MD 21209 Office: Good Samaritan Hosp 5601 Loch Raven Blvd Baltimore MD 21239

LICHTENSTEIN, ROY, artist; b. N.Y.C., Oct. 27, 1923; s. Milton and Beatrice (Werner) L.; B.F.A., Ohio State U., 1946, M.F.A., 1949; m. Isabel Wilson, June 12, 1949 (div.); children—David, Mitchell; m. 2d, Dorothy Herzka, Nov. 1, 1968. Instr., Ohio State U., 1946-51; asst. prof. N.Y. State U., Oswego, 1957-60, Douglass Coll., Rutgers U., 1960-63; pop art and other themes derived from comic strip techniques; one-man shows include Leo Castelli Gallery, N.Y.C., 1962, 63, 65, 67, 71, 72, 73, 74, 75, 77, 79, Galerie Illeana Sornabend, Paris, 1963, 65, 70, 75, Venice Biennale, 1966, Pasadena (Calif.) Art Mus., 1967, Mpls. Walker Art Center, Tate Gallery London, 1967, Stedelick Mus., Amsterdam, 1967, Guggenheim Mus., N.Y.C., 1969, Nelson Gallery, Kansas City, Mo., 1969, Mus. Contemporary Art, Chgo., 1970, Galerie Beyeler, Basel, Switzerland, 1973, Centre National D'Art Contemporain, Paris, 1975, Seattle Art Mus., 1976; exhibited in group shows Sidney Janis Gallery, N.Y.C., Whitney Mus. Am. Art, Nat. Collection Fine Art, Washington, 1966, others; created outside wall for Circarama of N.Y. State Pavilion, N.Y. World's Fair, 1963, billboard for Expo 67, Montreal. Served with AUS, 1943-46. Home: PO Box 1369 Southampton NY 11968

LICHTENSTEIN, STEPHEN FRANK, lawyer, bus. exec.; b. Balt., Apr. 24, 1931; s. Sidney and Edith (Alterman) L.; A.B., Washington and Lee U., 1953; LL.B., N.Y. U., 1956; m. Carole D. Goldstein, Aug. 3, 1958; children—Lee, Holly, Paul, Matthew. Admitted to Va. bar, 1956, N.J. bar, 1957, U.S. Supreme Ct. bar, 1963; sr. partner firm Coleman, Lichtenstein & Segal, Trenton, 1961-76; dep. atty. gen. of N.J., 1958-61; v.p., sec., gen. counsel Lenox, Inc., Trenton, N.J., 1976—; hearing examiner N.J. Div. on Civil Rights, 1963-72. Mem. Mercer County Ethics Com., 1969-71; bd. dirs. Mercer County Legal Aid Soc., 1969-74; chmn. N.J. Clean Air Council, 1968-70, mem., 1970-72; trustee Princeton Day Sch., 1977—. Mem. Am., N.J., Mercer County (trustee 1972—) bar assns., Am. Judicature Soc., Am. Soc. Corporate Secs., Phi Beta Kappa, Omicron Delta Kappa. Office: Lenox Inc Old Princeton Pike Lawrenceville NJ 08648

LICHTER, EDWARD ARTHUR, physician, educator; b. Chgo., June 5, 1928; s. Joseph and Eva (Wise) L.; Ph.B., U. Chgo., 1947; B.S., Roosevelt U., 1949; M.S., U. Ill., 1951, M.D., 1955; m. Charlotte Sells, Sept. 6, 1952; children—Michael, Jay. Intern, Fitzsimons Army Hosp., Denver, 1955-56; resident internal medicine U. Ill., Chgo., 1958-61, asso. prof. preventive medicine and community health Med. Center, 1966-69, prof., dept. head preventive medicine and community health, 1969—, prof., dept. head health care services, 1972-79, prof. community health scis., 1979—; practice medicine specializing in internal medicine and preventive medicine, Chgo., 1966—. Fellow in immunology NIH, 1961-63, USPHS officer, mem. staff immunology, 1963-66. Served with AUS, 1955-58. Mem. Am. Pub. Health Assn., Central Soc. for Clin. Research, Chgo. Heart Assn., Chgo. Health Systems Agency, Consumers Health Group, Alpha Omega Alpha. Home: 1310 Maple St Evanston IL 60201 Office: 835 S Wolcott St Chicago IL 60612

LICHTERMAN, MARTIN, educator; b. N.Y.C., July 18, 1918; s. Joseph Aaron and Esther S. (Schacknowitz) L.; B.S., Harvard U., 1939, A.M., 1947; Ph.D., Columbia U., 1952; m. Charlotte Rottenberg, Oct. 7, 1945; children—Joshua David, Andrew Marc. Instr., Rutgers U., Newark, 1948-51; instr., lectr. Princeton U., 1953-55, mem. research staff Center for Research on World Polit. Instns., 1951-53; asst. prof. M.I.T., 1955-60; dir. research to gov. Mass., 1959-60; exec. sec., dir. New Eng. Bd. Higher Edn., Winchester, Mass., 1961-66; dean Center Humanities and Social Scis. Union Coll., Schenectady, 1966-71, acting dean faculty, 1971-72, dean faculty, 1972-76, prof. history, 1966-76, distinguished prof. history and higher edn., 1976-78; dean Empire State Coll./SUNY L.I. Regional Center, Old Westbury, 1978—; cons. 20th Century Fund, N.Y.C., 1955-57; mem. Mass. Bd. Collegiate Authority, 1961-66; vice chmn. bd. Mass. Com. Children and Youth, 1963-66, mem. exec. bd., 1961-66; adv. bd. Civil Liberties Mass., 1963-66; chmn. bd. New Eng. Council Advancement Sch. Adminstrn., 1961-63; vice chmn. Capital Dist. Civil Liberties Union, 1966-67; chmn. Freedom's Forum, Inc., 1970-71, Schnectady Renewals, Inc., 1972-76. Mem. Am. Hist. Assn., Orgn. Am. Historians. Author: (with others) Political Community in the North Atlantic Area; To the Yalu and Back. Contbr. articles to profl. jours. Home: 68 Southdown Rd Huntington NY 11743 Office: Empire State Coll-LI Regional Center at Old Westbury PO Box 130 Trainor House 223 Store Hill Rd Old Westbury NY 11568

LICHTIN, J. LEON, pharmacist; b. Phila., Mar. 5, 1924; s. Aaron and Rosa (Rosenberg) L.; B.S. in Pharmacy, Phila. Coll. Pharmacy and Sci., 1944, M.S. in Pharmacy, 1947; Ph.D. in Pharmacy, Ohio State U., 1950; m. Beverly I. Cohen, Aug. 6, 1950; children—Benjamin Lloyd, Alan Eli. Asst. prof. pharmacy U. Cin., 1950-51, asso. prof., 1951-64, prof., 1964—, Andrew Jergens prof. pharmacy, 1971—; cons. in cosmetic sci. Past pres. No. Hills Synagogue, Cin. Fellow Soc. Cosmetic Chemists; mem. Am. Pharm. Assn., Am. Colls. of Pharmacy Assn., AAAS, Sigma Xi, Rho Chi. Contbr. articles in field to pharm. jours.; patentee in field; composer string music. Home: 801 Cloverview Ave Cincinnati OH 45231 Office: 208 Wherry Hall Coll Pharmacy U Cin Cincinnati OH 45267

LICHTIN, NORMAN NAHUM, educator; b. Newark, Aug. 10, 1922; s. James Jechiel and Clara (Greenspan) L.; B.S., Antioch Coll., 1944; M.S., Purdue U., 1945; Ph.D., Harvard, 1948; m. Phyllis Selma Wasserman, May 30, 1947; children—Harold Hirsh, Sara Marjorie, Daniel Albert. Faculty, Boston U., 1947—, prof. chemistry, 1961—, Univ. prof., 1973—, chmn. dept. chemistry, 1973—. Vis. chemist Brookhaven Nat. Lab., Upton, N.Y., 1957-58, research collaborator, 1958-70; guest scientist Weizmann Inst. Sci., Rehovoth, Israel, 1962-63; vis. prof. Hebrew U., Jerusalem, 1962-63, 70-71, 75, 76. NSF fellow, 1962-63. Fellow AAAS, Am. Inst. Chemists; mem. Am. Chem. Soc., Radiation Research Soc., Internat. Solar Energy Soc., Electrochem. Soc., AAUP, Sigma Xi, Phi Beta Kappa (hon.). Asso. editor Solar Energy, 1976—. Research, publs. on mechanisms of chem. reactions including reaction of atomic nitrogen with organic compounds, the influence of high energy radiation on organic compounds, photochem. conversion solar energy, ionization processes and ionic reactions in solutions in liquid sulfur dioxide. Home: 195 Morton St Newton Centre MA 02159 Office: 685 Commonwealth Ave Boston MA 02215

LICHTWARDT, RICHARD DONALD, govt. ofcl.; b. Helena, Mont., Jan. 27, 1931; s. Bartley Henry and Edna Currie (Day) L.; B.B.A. with honors, U. Tex., 1960; M.B.A., Syracuse U., 1964; m. Dorothy Lawrence, July 14, 1971; children by previous marriage—Richard Donald, Brian R., Sandra G. Enlisted man U.S. Air Force, 1951-53, commd. 2d lt., 1953, advanced through grades to lt. col., 1969; staff supply officer, Korea, Okinawa and Tex., 1953-58; base supply officer, Libya, 1960-63; dir. logistics plans USAF Acad., Colo., 1964-68; staff logistics officer, Thailand, 1968-69, Hdqrs., Washington, 1969-72, ret., 1972; program analyst FCC, Washington, 1972-74, asst. chief Field Ops. Bur., 1974—, exec. dir., 1974—. Home: 3224 Amberley Ln Fairfax VA 22031 Office: Office of Exec Dir FCC 1919 M St NW Washington DC 20554

LICHTY, GEORGE M., cartoonist; b. Chgo., May 16, 1905; s. Julius and Ella (Hirsch) Lichtenstein; student Chgo. Art Inst., 1924-25; A.B., U. Mich., 1929; m. Eleanor Louise Fretter, Jan. 5, 1931; children—Linda Louise, Susan Emory. Sports cartoonist Chgo. Daily Times, 1930-32, created feature Grin and Bear It, 1932, syndicated by United Features Syndicate, N.Y.C., 1934-40, Chgo. Sun-Times, 1947-67, Field Newspaper Syndicate, Chgo., 1967—. Mem. Nat. Cartoonists Soc. Democrat. Clubs: Press, Bohemian (San Francisco). Home: 6519 Meadowridge Dr Santa Rosa CA 95405 Office: Field Newspaper Syndicate 401 N Wabash Ave Chicago IL 60611

LICK, WILBERT JAMES, educator; b. Cleve., June 12, 1933; s. Fred and Hulda (Sunntag) L.; B.A.E., Rensselaer Poly. Inst., 1955, M.A.E., 1957, Ph.D., 1958; m. Margaret Miller, Apr. 7, 1965; children—James, Sarah. Asst. prof. Harvard, 1959-66; sr. research fellow Calif. Inst. Tech., 1966-67; mem. faculty Case Western Res. U., 1967-79, prof. earth scis., 1970-79, chmn. dept., 1973-76; prof. mech. engring. U. Calif., Santa Barbara, 1979—. Home: 1236 Camino Meleno Santa Barbara CA 93111 Office: Dept Mech and Environ Engring U Calif Santa Barbara CA 93106

LICKLE, WILLIAM CAUFFIEL, banker; b. Wilmington, Del., Aug. 2, 1929; s. Charles Harold and Hazel (Cauffiel) L.; B.A., U. Va., 1951, LL.B., 1953; m. Renee Carpenter Kitchell, Nov. 24, 1950; children—Sydney Cauffiel Lindley, Garrison duPont, Ashley Morgan, Kemble Carpenter. Admitted to Va. bar, 1953; registered rep. Laird & Co., Inc., Wilmington, Del., 1953-55; v.p., dir. Niront & Co., realtors, Wilmington, 1955-56; partner Wheelock & Lickle, realtors, Greenville, Del., 1956-57; rep. Laird, Bissell & Meeds, Inc., Wilmington, 1957-73, v.p., 1962-65, sec., dir., 1965—, exec. v.p., 1967-68, pres., 1968-69, chmn. exec. com., 1969, chmn. bd., 1970-73; sr. v.p., dir. Dean Witter & Co. Inc., 1973-77; vice chmn. bd. Del. Trust Co., 1977—; dir. Bessemer Trust Co. N.J., Bessemer Trust Co. Fla.; vice chmn. Fair Hill Races, 1975—. Commr. New Castle County (Del.) Airport, 1964-67, New Castle County Transp. Commn., 1967-69; spl. gifts chmn. Am. Cancer Soc., 1968; treas. Del. Republican Com., 1964-68. Bd. dirs., treas., chmn. finance com. Wilmington Med. Center, 1965—; bd. dirs. Del. Mus. Natural History, 1974—, Boys Club Wilmington, nat. com. of The Added Dimension for Choate Sch., Easter Seal Soc. Del., Fair Hill, Inc.; bd. dirs., past v.p., founder Better Bus. Bur. Del., 1966-72; bd. dirs., treas. Blue Cross-Blue Shield Del., 1963-68; trustee Thomas Jefferson U., 1971-78; chmn. fin. com. Del. Cancer Network, 1975-77; steward Nat. Steeplechase and Hunt Assn., 1977—. Mem. Am., Va. bar assns., Kappa Alpha, Phi Alpha Delta. Clubs: Wilmington, Wilmington Country; Vicmead Hunt (Greenville, Del.); Bath and Tennis (Palm Beach, Fla.). Home: Box 3793 Greenville DE 19807 Office: Del Trust Co Wilmington DE 19899

LIDBETTER, WARD PRITCHARD, mfg. co. exec.; b. W. Allis, Wis., Aug. 24, 1915; s. John Walter and Ada Mary (Jones) L.; B.A., Beloit (Wis.) Coll., 1937; m. Virginia Ruth Crowell, Apr. 12, 1947; children—Virginia, Gordon, John. With Rockford Products Corp. (Ill.), 1941—, pres., 1965—; dir. Am. Nat. Bank of Rockford, Colonial Bank of Rockford, No. Ill. Gas, Aurora, J.L. Clark Mfg. Co., Rockford. Bd. govs. Indsl. Fasteners Inst., 1966—; pres. Swedish Am. Hosp., Rockford, 1972-74, trustee, 1956—; pres. Rockford Community Trust, 1971-77; trustee Rockford Coll., 1965—; bd. corporators Ill. Hosp. and Health Service, Inc., 1965—. Recipient Spl. Alumni award Beloit Coll., 1968. Republican. Congregationalist. Clubs: Victory Tennis, Forest Hills Country, Pyramid, Masons, Shriners, Jesters. Home: 2509 Westbrook Dr Rockford IL 61107 Office: 707 Harrison Ave Rockford IL 61101

LIDDELL, DONALD MACY, JR., ret. investment counsellor; b. Elizabeth, N.J., Mar. 11, 1907; s. Donald M. and Edith (Stabler) L.; B.S., Princeton, 1928; grad. student Am. Inst. Banking, N.Y. U.; m. Jane Hawley Hawkes, Mar. 30, 1940; children—Jane Liddell Bass, Donald Roger Brooke. Statistician, Banker's Trust Co., N.Y.C., 1928-29, White, Weld & Co., 1929-33; security analyst Fidelity Union Trust Co., Newark, 1935-40; v.p., dir. Templeton, Dobbrow & Vance, Inc., 1946-51, exec. v.p., 1951-60, chmn. bd., 1960-74; dir. 930 Park Ave. Corp., Nat. State Bank of Elizabeth. Bd. dirs. N.Y. Sch. Interior Design, Smoke, Fire and Burn Inst. Served as Res. officer U.S. Army, 1933-35; lt. col. AUS, 1940-45, finance officer Eastern Def. Command, 1944-45. Mem. Soc. Colonial Wars (treas.-gen. 1969-78), Mil. Order Loyal Legion (comdr.-in-chief 1961-62), S.R., Mil. Order Fgn. Wars, Order Colonial Lords of Manors in Am. (treas. 1969—, pres. 1972-75). Republican. Episcopalian. Clubs: Down Town Assn., Union, Badminton, University, Church, Pilgrims of U.S. (N.Y.C.); Englewood, Englewood Field, Hillsboro. Contbr. articles to profl. publs. Home: 181 Linden Ave Englewood NJ 07631 also 930 Park Ave New York NY 10028

LIDDELL, JAMES WOODLAN, contracting co. exec.; b. Ft. Worth, Oct. 26, 1918; s. Jamerson W. and Mary Alicia (Brown) L.; B.S. in Indsl. Engring., Northwestern U., 1940; m. Marion Young, Apr. 10, 1943; children—Lynn, William Kirk. Salesman, Harrisburg, Pa., Detroit, commodity mgr., dept. mgr. Armstrong Cork Co., Lancaster, Pa., 1940-58; pres. Armstrong Contracting & Supply Co., Lancaster, 1958-69; pres. AC and S Corp., Lancaster, 1969—, also dir.; dir. Nat. Central Bank, Educators Mut. Life Ins. Co., Watt and Shand. Trustee, Lancaster Gen. Hosp. Served from ensign to lt. comdr., USNR, World War II. Decorated Silver Star medal, Bronze Star medal, Purple Heart. Republican. Presbyn. Clubs: Lancaster Country, Hamilton. Seaview Country. Home: RD 1 Box 151 Pequea PA 17565 Office: 120 N Lime St Lancaster PA 17603

LIDDELL, LEON MORRIS, educator, librarian; b. Gainesville, Tex., July 21, 1914; s. Thomas Leon and Minnie Mae (Morris) L.; B.A., U. Tex., 1937, J.D., 1937; B.L.S., U. Chgo., 1946; postgrad. Columbia U., 1948. Admitted to Tex. bar, 1937; practiced in Gainesville, 1938-39; with claims dept. Hartford Accident & Indemnity Co., 1937-38, Pacific Mut. Life Ins. Co., 1939-41; asst. prof. law, law librarian U. Conn., 1946-47; asst. prof. law U. Minn., 1949-50, asso. prof., 1950-54, prof. law, 1954-60, law librarian, 1949-60; prof. law, law librarian U. Chgo., 1960-74, prof. law, law librarian emeritus, 1974—; prof. law, law librarian Northwestern U. Law Sch., 1974—. Served from 2d lt. to maj. AUS, 1941-46. Mem. Am. Bar Assn., Am., Chgo (past pres.) assns. law libraries, Spl. Libraries Assn. Mason. Home: 880 Lake Shore Dr Chicago IL 60611

LIDDICOAT, RICHARD THOMAS, JR., inst. exec.; b. Kearsarge, Mich., Mar. 2, 1918; s. Richard Thomas and Carmen (Williams) L.; B.S. in Geology, U. Mich., M.S. in Mineralogy, 1940; grad. gemologist Gemological Inst. Am., 1941; M.S. in Meteorology, Calif. Inst. Tech., 1944; m. Mary Imogene Hibbard, Sept. 21, 1939. With Gemological Inst. Am., Los Angeles, 1940-42, 46—, asst. dir., 1950-52, exec. dir., 1952—, pres., 1970—, editor Gem and Gemology, 1952—. Supr. ednl. sessions ann. conclaves Am. Gem Soc., 1948—; hon. certified gemologist, 1947; hon. research staff Los Angeles Mus. Natural History, 1968—; U.S. del. Internat. Gem Conf., 1960, 64, 66, 68, 70, 72, 75, 77, 79; del. President's Conf. Small Bus., 1957. Fellow Mineral. Soc. Am., Geol. Soc. Am., AAAS, Am. Gem Soc (Shipley award 1976); mem. Sigma Xi, Sigma Gamma Epsilon. Author: Handbook of Gem Identification, 10th edit., 1975; (with others) The Diamond Dictionary, 1960, 2d edit., 1977; (with Copeland) Jewelers Manual, 2d edit., 1967; numerous articles. Contbr. to Ency. Americana, Ency. Sci. and Tech., Ency. Brit., Jr. Species of tourmaline group called Liddicoatite in his honor. Home: 1484 Allenford Ave Los Angeles CA 90049 Office: 1660 Stewart St Santa Monica CA 90404

LIDDLE, ALAN CURTIS, architect; b. Tacoma, Mar. 10, 1922; s. Abram Dix and Myrtle (Maytum) L.; B.Arch., U. Wash., 1948; postgrad. Eidgenoissche Technische Hochschule, Zurich, Switzerland, 1950-51. Asst. prof. architecture U. Wash., 1954-55; prin. Liddle & Jones, Tacoma, 1957-67; prin. Alan Liddle, architects, Tacoma, 1967—; architect oceanography bldgs U. Wash., 1967, Tacoma Art Mus., 1971, Charles Wright Acad., Tacoma, 1962, Pacific Nat. Bank Wash., Auburn, 1965. Pres. bd. Allied Arts Tacoma, 1963-64, Civic Arts Commn. Tacoma-Pierce County, 1969; commr. Wash. Arts Commn., 1971. Bd. dirs. Tacoma Art Mus., Tacoma Zool. Soc., Tacoma Philharmonic, Inc. Served with AUS, 1943-46. Fellow A.I.A. (pres. S.W. Wash. chpt. 1967-68); mem. Wash. Hist. Soc., U. Wash. Alumni Assn. (all life). Home: 12735 Gravelly Lake Dr SW Tacoma WA 98499 Office: 703 Pacific Ave Tacoma WA 98402

LIDDLE, GRANT WINDER, physician, educator; b. American Fork, Utah, June 27, 1921; s. Parley H. and Elizabeth (Winder) L.; B.S., U. Utah, 1943; M.D., U. Calif. at San Francisco, 1948; m. Victoria Ragin; children—Kathryn (Mrs. James C. Wallwork), Annette, Rodger, Robert, Patricia. Intern in internal medicine U. Calif. Hosp., 1948-49, asst. resident, 1949-51; research fellow metabolic unit U. Calif. at San Francisco, 1951-53; instr. medicine U. Calif. Sch. Medicine, San Francisco, 1953; surgeon sect. clin. endocrinology Nat. Heart Inst., 1953-56; asso. prof. medicine, chief endocrine service Vanderbilt U. Sch. Medicine, 1956-61, prof., 1961—, chmn. dept. medicine, 1968—. Mem. endocrinology study sect. USPHS, 1958-62, chmn. diabetes and metabolism tng. grants com., 1963-66, mem. Nat. Adv. Arthritis and Metabolic Diseases Council, 1967-71; investigator selection com. VA, 1970-74. Served with AUS, 1943-46. Recipient Sir Henry Hallett Dale medal Soc. Endocrinology (Gt. Britain), 1973. Fellow A.C.P. (John Phillips Meml. award 1977); mem. Assn. Am. Physicians, Endocrine Soc. (council 1962-65, 70-75; pres. 1973-74; Upjohn award 1962, Distinguished Leadership award 1971), Am. (sec.-treas. 1963-66, pres. 1966-67), So. (council 1963-64, 66-67, pres. 1965-66, Founder's medal 1977) socs. clin. investigation, Internat. Soc. Endocrinology (chmn. exec. com. 1968—, pres. 1976—), Assn. Profs. Med. (pres. 1977—). Contbr. articles to profl. jours. Home: 770 Norwood Dr Nashville TN 37204

LIDE, THEODORE ELLIS, JR., textile co. exec.; b. Darlington, S.C., May 13, 1926; s. Theodore Ellis and Elizabeth (DeVane) L.; B.S., U.S. Naval Acad., 1949; postgrad. U. N.C., 1961-62; m. Ruth Rose Zapp, June 4, 1949; children—Theodore Ellis, Meredith Ann, Michael Edmund. Commd. ensign USN, 1949, advanced through grades to lt., 1953, ret., 1954; indsl. engr. Steel Heddle Mfg. Co., Greenville, S.C., 1954-56; with Burlington Madison Yarn Co. div. Burlington Industries (N.C.), 1956-75, exec. v.p. mfg., corporate dir. purchasing, 1975—; dir. Madison br. Northwestern Bank. Commr. Madison Housing Authority, 1967-72; bd. dirs. Annie Penn Meml. Hosp., Reidsville, N.C., Piedmont Health Systems Agy., Greensboro, N.C., 1977—; bd. govs. ARC, 1969-72. Mem. Pi Kappa Alpha. Methodist. Club: Deep Springs Country (Madison). Home: 111 Cassandra Rd Madison NC 27025

LIDICKER, WILLIAM ZANDER, JR., zoologist; b. Evanston, Ill., Aug. 19, 1932; s. William Zander and Frida (Schroeter) L.; B.S., Cornell U., 1953; M.S., U. Ill., 1954, Ph.D., 1957; m. Naomi Ishino, Aug. 18, 1956; children—Jeffrey Roger, Kenneth Paul. Instr. zoology, asst. curator mammals U. Calif., Berkeley, 1957-59, asst. prof., asst. curator, 1959-65, asso. prof., asso. curator, 1965-69, asso. dir. Mus. Vertebrate Zoology, 1968—, acting dir., 1974-75, prof. zoology, curator mammals, 1969—. Bd. dirs. No. Calif. Com. for Environ. Info., 1971—. Fellow AAAS, Calif. Acad. Scis.; mem. Am. Soc. Mammalogists (dir., 2d v.p. 1974-76, pres. 1976-78), Am. Soc. Naturalists, others. Club: Berkeley Folk Dancers (pres. 1969). Contbr. articles to profl. jours. Office: Mus of Vertebrate Zoology U Calif Berkeley CA 94720

LIDOW, ERIC, elec. parts mfg. co. exec.; b. Vilnius, Lithuania, Dec. 22, 1912; s. Leon and Rachel (Schwartz) L.; M. Elec. Engring., Technische Hochschule, Berlin, Germany, 1937; m. Judith Margolis, July 2, 1939 (div. 1952); 1 son, Alan; m. 2d, Elizabeth Hay, Oct. 1952; children—Derek Balfour, Alexander. Came to U.S., 1937, naturalized, 1941. Elec. engr. Super Electric Co., Berlin, Germany, 1937; elec. devel. engr. Emby Products Cal., 1939-41; co-founder, v.p. Selenium Corp. Am., 1941-46; with Internat. Rectifier Corp., El Segundo, Calif., 1946—, now pres., chmn. bd., also dir. corp. and domestic and fgn. subsidiaries. Mem. Assos. Calif. Inst. Tech. Bd. dirs. Lidow Found.; trustee City of Hope, Los Angeles County Mus. Art. Sr. mem. IEEE; mem. Am. Technion Soc. (v.p.). Patentee in semiconductors. Home: 454 Cuesta Way Los Angeles CA 90024 Office: 9220 Sunset Blvd Los Angeles CA 90069

LIDSKY, LAWRENCE MARK, nuclear engr.; b. N.Y.C., Oct. 15, 1935; s. Harry Aaron and Ada (Marks) L.; B.Engring. Physics, Cornell U., 1958; Ph.D., Mass. Inst. Tech., 1962; m. Judith Suzanne Lockser, Aug. 31, 1958; children—Loren Phillip, Jane Elizabeth, David Benjamin. Ford postdoctoral fellow Mass. Inst. Tech., 1962-63, mem. faculty, 1963—, prof. nuclear engring., 1976—, also asso. dir. Plasma Fusion Center; pres. TFG, Inc. Mem. Am. Phys. Soc. Democrat. Editor, Jour. Fusion Energy; author papers on plasma physics, fission-fusion symbiosis, fusion reactor tech. Home: 215 Highland Ave Newtonville MA 02160 Office: 38-174 Mass Inst Tech Cambridge MA 02139. *It is necessary, although not always sufficient, to leave matters a little better than they were before one's arrival. One can always do more but should never do less.*

LIDSTONE, HERRICK KENLEY, lawyer; b. Bellingham, Wash., Apr. 2, 1921; s. Herrick K. and Jean (Richardson) L.; student State U. Iowa, 1938-39; A.B., Harvard U., 1942, LL.B., 1948; m. Marcia E. Drake, Dec. 17, 1942; children—Herrick Kenley, Rosalind Grace, Christopher Drake. Admitted to N.Y. bar, 1949, Colo. bar, 1978; practiced in N.Y.C., 1949-77; partner Battle, Fowler, Lidstone, Jaffin, Pierce & Kheel, 1960-77, of counsel, 1978—; prof. law N.Y. Law Sch., 1950-53; vis. prof. law U. Colo. Law Sch., Boulder, 1978—; asst. dir. Harvard Law Sch. Internat. Program Taxation, 1953-57; instr. law U. Va., 1957-58; lectr. Practising Law Inst., 1949—, also various law insts. and panels; UN adviser taxation Chile, 1954-57, pvt. adviser 1957-61; U.S. Point 4 adviser taxation El Salvador, 1955; panelist tax reform Ho. Reps. Ways and Means Com., 1973. Chmn. adv. com. Pelham (N.Y.) Recreation Commn., 1965-67; trustee Sapelo Island Research Found., 1967-77. Served to capt. AUS, 1942-45. Mem. Am. Bar Assn. (chmn. sect. taxation coms. legis. drafting 1959-62, agr. 1966-69), Assn. Bar City N.Y., Tax Club N.Y.C., Greater Denver Tax Counsel Assn., Beta Theta Pi. Episcopalian. Club: Harvard (N.Y.C.). Author: The Federal Estate Tax, 1952; Tax Administration in Underdeveloped Countries, 1956; Taxation in Chile, 1954; Taxation in El Salvador, 1955; also articles; co-author: Taxation of Farmers, 1979; gen. editor, co-author: Guide for Artists and Organizations, 1979. Home: 1200 Bellaire St Broomfield CO 80020 Office: 2600 Colorado Nat Bldg Denver CO 80202

LIDTKE, VERNON LEROY, educator; b. Avon, S.D., May 4, 1930; s. Albert William and Aganeta (Boese) L.; B.A., U. Oreg., 1952, M.A., 1955; Ph.D., U. Calif., Berkeley, 1962; m. Doris Eileen Keefe, Apr. 21, 1951. Tchr. high sch., Riddle, Oreg., 1953-55; instr. social sci. U. Calif., Berkeley, 1960-62; asst. prof. history Mich. State U., 1962-66, asso. prof., 1966-68; vis. asst. prof. U. Calif., Berkeley, 1963; asso. prof. Johns Hopkins U., 1968-73, prof., 1973—, chmn. dept. history, 1975—. Fulbright research fellow, 1959-60, 66-67; Nat. Endowment Humanities fellow, 1969-70. Mem. Am. Hist. Assn., AAUP, Conf. Group for Central European History (officer 1973—), Conf. Group German Politics (officer 1975—). Club: Johns Hopkins. Author: The Outlawed Party: Social Democracy in Germany, 1878-1890, 1966; editorial bd. Jour. Modern History, 1973-76; contbr. articles to profl. jours. Home: 4806 Wilmslow Rd Baltimore MD 21210 Office: Dept History Johns Hopkins U Baltimore MD 21218

LIEB, ELLIOTT HERSHEL, physicist, mathematician, educator; b. Boston, July 31, 1932; s. Sinclair M. and Clara (Rosenstein) L.; B.Sc., M.I.T., 1953; Ph.D., U. Birmingham (Eng.), 1956; D.Sc.h.c., U. Copenhagen, 1979; m. Christiane Fellbaum; children—Alexander, Gregory. With IBM Corp., 1960-63; sr. lectr. Fourah Bay Coll., Sierra Leone, 1961; mem. faculty Yeshiva U., 1963-66, Northeastern U., 1966-68, M.I.T.; 1968-75 prof. physics, 1963-68, prof. math., 1968-73, prof. math. and physics, 1973—; prof. math. and physics Princeton U., 1975—. Recipient Boris Pregel award chem. physics N.Y. Acad. Scis., 1970; Dannie Heineman prize for mathematical physics Am. Inst. Physics and Am. Phys. Soc., 1978. Fellow Am. Phys. Soc.; mem. Austrian Acad. Scis. Author: (with D.C. Mattis) Mathematical Physics in One Dimension, 1966; (with B. Simon and A. Wightman) Studies in Mathematical Physics; also articles. Office: Physics Dept Jadwin Hall Princeton U PO Box 708 Princeton NJ 08544

LIEB, IRWIN CHESTER, educator; b. Newark, Nov. 9, 1925; s. Moses Lewis and Gussie (Krytzer) L.; A.B., Princeton, 1947; A.M., Cornell U., Ithaca, N.Y., 1949; Ph.D., Yale, 1953; m. Martha Isabel Simonson, Aug. 23, 1960 (div.); children—Michael Adam, Gordon Nichols. Instr., then asst. prof. philosophy Yale, 1953-59; prof. philosophy Conn. Coll., 1959-63, U. Tex., Austin, 1963—, asso. grad. dean, 1973-75, v.p., dean grad. studies, 1975—. Mem. exec. com. Assn. Grad. Schs., Council Grad. Schs. Served with USNR, 1943-45. Morse traveling fellow, 1956; fellow Am. Council Learned Socs., 1964. Mem. Am. Philos. Assn., Metaphys. Soc. (councillor 1968-70), Philosophy Edn. Soc. (dir.). Author: Peirce's Letters, 1953; Experience, Existence and the Good, 1961; The Four Faces of Man, 1970; also monographs, articles. Home: 4612 Shoal Creek Blvd Austin TX 78756

LIEBELT, ROBERT ARTHUR, physician, educator; b. Chgo., Feb. 3, 1927; s. Arthur H. and Helen (Madej) L.; B.S., Loyola U., Chgo., 1950; M.S., Wash. State U., 1952; Ph.D. with honors Baylor U., 1957, M.D. with honors, 1958; m. Annabel Glockler, June 26, 1954; children—Ralph, Laurie, Erica, Nancy. Research asst. Wash. State U., 1950-52; instr. anatomy Baylor U. Coll. Medicine, 1956-58, asst. prof., 1958-59, asso. prof., 1959-60, prof., chmn. dept. anatomy, 1960-71; asso. dean for curriculum Med. Coll. Ga., Augusta, 1971-72, provost, 1972-74, also prof. exptl. medicine, prof. dept. cell and molecular biology, until 1974; charter dean, prof. anatomy Northeastern Ohio Univs. Coll. Medicine, Rootstown, 1974-79, provost, dean, 1979—. Vis. prof. oncology Okayama (Japan) U., 1961; pres. Anatomical Bd. Tex., 1968-72; participant White House Conf. Food, Nutrition and Health. Served with USNR, 1944-46. Named Outstanding Naval Air Reservist, 1948; Outstanding Basic Sci. Tchr., Baylor U., 1964, 65, 67, 69, 70, 71; Outstanding Faculty Alumni award Baylor U., 1971. Fellow A.A.A.S.; mem. Am. Assn. Cancer Research, Am. Assn. Anatomists, Soc. Exptl. Pathology, Aerospace, Undersea med. socs., Tex. Acad. Sci. (v.p.), Am. Assn. Cancer Research (pres. S.W. sect.), Alpha Omega Alpha. Home: 1972 Pineview Dr Kent OH 44240

LIEBENOW, ROBERT C., assn. exec.; b. Aberdeen, S.D., Sept. 13, 1922; s. Albert C. and Leta V. (Foot) L.; student No. State Tchrs. Coll., Aberdeen, 1940-42; J.D., U. S.D., 1946; m. Patricia Marie Stoddard, Nov. 10, 1946; children—Ann M., Charles R., Jane A., Paul J., Martha J. Admitted to Ill. bar, 1948, D.C. bar, 1969; lawyer First Nat. Bank, Chgo., 1946-52; asst. sec. Bd. Trade, City of Chgo., 1952, sec., 1953-55, exec. sec., 1955, pres., 1956-65; pres. Corn Refiners Assn., Inc., 1965—. Named One of Ten Outstanding Young Men, U.S. Jr. C. of C. 1956. Mem. Phi Delta Theta Alumni Assn. Clubs: National Press, Congressional Country, University (Washington); Union League, Economic (Chgo.). Home: 1217 Colonial Rd McLean VA 22101 Office: 1001 Connecticut Ave NW Suite 1022 Washington DC 20036

LIEBENOW, ROBERT C., assn. exec.; b. Aberdeen, S.D., Sept. 13, 1922; s. Albert C. and Leta V. (Foot) L.; student No. State Tchrs. Coll., Aberdeen, 1940-42; J.D., U. S.D., 1946; m. Patricia Marie Stoddard, Nov. 10, 1946; children—Ann M., Charles R., Jane A., Paul J., Martha J. Admitted to Ill. bar, 1948, D.C. bar, 1969; lawyer First Nat. Bank, Chgo., 1946-52; asst. sec. Bd. Trade, City of Chgo., 1952, sec., 1953-55, exec. sec., 1955, pres., 1956-65; pres. Corn Refiners Assn., Inc., 1965—. Named One of Ten Outstanding Young Men, U.S. Jr. C. of C. 1956. Mem. Phi Delta Theta Alumni Assn. Clubs: National Press, Congressional Country, University (Washington); Union League, Economic (Chgo.). Home: 1217 Colonial Rd McLean VA 22101 Office: 1001 Connecticut Ave NW Suite 1022 Washington DC 20036

LIEBER, CHARLES DONALD, publisher; b. Scheveningen, Netherlands, Jan. 30, 1921; s. Edmund Z. and Gabrielle (Lifczis) L.; student U. Brussels, 1938-40; B.A., New Sch. for Social Research, 1948; m. Miriam Levin, July 17, 1960; children—John Nathan, James Edmund, George Theodore, Anne Gabrielle. Came to U.S., 1941, naturalized, 1944. With H. Bittner & Co., Pubs., N.Y.C., 1947-49; with Alfred A. Knopf, Inc., 1949-52; dir. coll. dept. Random House, N.Y.C., 1952-64; pub. Atherton Press, N.Y.C., 1964-67; pres. Atherton Press, Inc., N.Y.C., 1967-70; v.p. Aldine-Atherton, Inc., N.Y.C., Chgo., 1971-72; pres. Lieber-Atherton, Inc., N.Y.C., 1972—. Chmn. West Side Jewish Community Council, Manhattan. Served to lt. AUS, 1942-46; CBI. Mem. Am. Polit. Sci. Assn., Am. Sociol. Assn., Am. Hist. Assn., Coll. Pubs. Group (chmn. 1965-66). Author: (with A.D. Murphy) Great Events of World History, 1964. Home: 389 West End Ave New York NY 10024 Office: 1841 Broadway New York NY 10023

LIEBER, CHARLES SAUL, physician, educator; b. Antwerp, Belgium, Feb. 13, 1931; s. Isaac and Lea (Maj) L.; candidate in natural and med. sci. U. Brussels, 1951; M.D., 1955; m. M.A. Leo; children—Colette, Daniel, Lea, Samuel. Came to U.S., 1958, naturalized, 1966. Intern, resident U. Hosp., Brugmann, Brussels, Belgium, 1954-56, research fellow med. found. Queen Elizabeth, 1956-58; research fellow Thorndike Meml. Lab., Harvard Med. Sch., 1958-60, instr., 1961, asso., 1962; asso. prof. medicine Cornell U., 1963-68; dir. liver disease and nutrition unit Bellevue Hosp., N.Y.C., 1963-68; chief sect. liver disease and nutrition VA Hosp., Bronx, N.Y., 1968—; prof. medicine Mt. Sinai Sch. Medicine, 1969—, prof. pathology, 1976—, dir. Alcohol Research Center, 1977—; asso. vis. physician Cornell Med. div. Bellevue, Meml., James Ewing hosps., 1964-69; Am. Coll. Gastroenterology disting. lectr., 1978; Henry Baker lectr., 1979. Recipient award of Belgian Govt. for research on gastric secretion, 1956; Research Career Devel. award NIH, USPHS, 1964-68, E.M. Jellinek Meml. award, 1976; A. Boudreau award Laval U., 1977; W.S. Middleton award, 1977. Mem. Assn. Am. Physicians, N.Y. Gastroent. Assn. (pres. 1974-75), Am. Soc. Biol. Chemistry, A.C.P., Am. Inst. Nutrition, Am. Med. Soc. Alcohol (pres. 1974-77), Am. Soc. Clin. Nutrition (McCollum award 1973, pres. 1975-76), Am. Soc. Clin. Investigation, Am. Soc. Pharmacol. Exptl. Therapy, Am. Gastroent. Assn. (Distinguished Achievement award 1973), AAAS, Am. Assn. Study Liver Diseases, Am. Oil Chem. Soc. Home: 6 Johnson Ave Englewood Cliffs NJ 07632 Office: 130 W Kingsbridge Rd Bronx NY 10468

LIEBER, DAVID LEO, univ. pres.; b. Stryj, Poland, Feb. 20, 1925; s. Max and Gussie (Jarmush) L.; came to U.S., 1927, naturalized, 1936; B.A., City Coll. N.Y., 1944; B.Hebrew Lit., Jewish Theol. Sem. Am., 1944, M.Hebrew Lit., 1948, D. Hebrew Lit., 1951; M.A., Columbia, 1947; postgrad. U. Wash., 1954-55, U. Calif. at Los Angeles, 1961-63; m. Esther Kobre, June 10, 1945; children—Michael, Daniel Deborah, Susan. Rabbi, 1948, Sinai Temple, Los Angeles, 1950-54; dir. B'nai B'rith Hillel, Seattle, Cambridge, 1954-56; dean students U. Judaism, Los Angeles, 1956-63, pres., Samuel A. Fryer prof. Bible, 1963—. Lectr. Hebrew U. Calif. at Los Angeles, 1957—; vice chancellor Jewish Theol. Sem., 1972—; mem. exec. council Rabbinical Assembly, 1966-69; vice chmn. Am. Jewish Com., Los Angeles, 1972—. Served to lt. USAF, 1951-53. Mem. Assn. Profs. Jewish Studies (dir. 1970-71), Phi Beta Kappa. Mem. editorial bd. Conservative Judaism, 1968-70. Home: 305 El Camino Dr Beverly Hills CA 90212 Office: 15600 Mulholland Dr Los Angeles CA 90024

LIEBERMAN, GERALD J., educator; b. N.Y.C., Dec. 31, 1925; s. Joseph and Ida (Margolis) L.; B.S. in Mech. Engring., Cooper Union, 1948; A.M. in Math. Statistics, Columbia, 1949; Ph.D., Stanford, 1953; m. Helen Herbert, Oct. 27, 1950; children—Janet, Joanne, Michael, Diana. Math. statistician Nat. Bur. Standards, 1949-50; mem. faculty Stanford, 1953—, prof. statistics and indsl. engring., 1959-67, prof. statistics and operations research, 1967—, chmn. dept. operations research, 1967-75, asso. dean Sch. Humanities and Scis., 1975-77, acting v.p. and provost, 1979, vice provost, dean research, 1977—; cons. to govt. and industry, 1953—. Fellow Am. Statis. Assn., Inst. Math. Statistics, Am. Soc. Quality Control (Shewhart medal 1972), AAAS; mem. Inst. Mgmt. Sci. (pres.-elect 1979-80), Ops. Research Soc. Am., Sigma Xi, Pi Tau Sigma. Author: (with A. H. Bowker) Engineering Statistics, 1959, 2d edit., 1972; (with F.S.

Hillier) Introduction to Operations Research, 1967, 2d edit., 1974. Home: 811 San Francisco Terr Stanford CA 94305

LIEBERMAN, HENRY RICHARD, journalist, editor; b. St. Louis, Nov. 24, 1916; s. Joseph M. and Golda (Spector) L.; A.B., Columbia, 1937, M.A., 1950; m. Kathryn Gwenith Martin, June 11, 1949; children—Peter Martin, Linda Susan. Reporter, Washington corr. newspaper PM, N.Y.C., 1940-42; editor fgn. news bur. OWI, 1942-44, chief news editor China, 1945; staff reporter N.Y. Times, 1937-40, fgn. corr., China, 1945-49 S.E. Asia, India, Pakistan, 50-57, asst. to fgn. editor 1957-60, asst. news editor, 1960-65, sci. news coordinator, 1965-69, dir. sci. and edn. news, 1969-74, dir. sci., 1974-75, asst. to exec. editor, 1975—. Mem. Council on Fgn. Relations (fellow 1949-50), I.E.E.E. (sr.), Phi Beta Kappa. Home: 3 Medford Ln Scarsdale NY 10583 Office: 229 W 43d St New York City NY 10036

LIEBERMAN, LAURENCE J., poet, educator; b. Detroit, Feb. 16, 1935; s. Nathan and Anita (Cohen) L.; B.A., U. Mich., 1956, M.A. in English, 1958; postgrad. U. Calif. at Berkeley; m. Bernice Clair Braun, June 17, 1956; children—Carla, Deborah, Isaac. Prof. English, Coll. V.I., 1964-68; prof. English and creative writing U. Ill., Urbana, 1968—. U. Ill. Center for Advanced Study Creative Writing fellow, Japan, 1971-72. Recipient award for Best Poems of 1968, Nat. Endowment for Arts, 1969. Author: The Unblinding, 1968; The Achievement of James Dickey, 1969; The Osprey Suicides, 1973—; Unassigned Frequencies: American Poetry in Review (1964-77), 1977; God's Measurements, 1980. Poetry editor poetry books program U. Ill. Press, 1970—; regular poetry reviewer Yale Rev. Contbr. poetry to lit. jours., popular mags. Office: English Dept U Ill Urbana IL 61801

LIEBERMAN, LEONARD, supermarket exec.; b. Elizabeth, N.J., Jan. 23, 1929; s. Joseph Harry and Bessie (Bernstein) L.; B.A., Yale U., 1950; J.D., Columbia U., 1953; grad. Advanced Mgmt. Program, Harvard U., 1970; children—Elizabeth Susan, Nancy Ellen, Anne Judith. Admitted to N.J. bar, 1954; asso., then partner firms in Newark and Orange, 1954-65; v.p., gen. counsel, dir. Supermarkets Operating Co., Union, N.J., 1963-66; v.p., gen. counsel Supermarkets Gen. Corp., Woodbridge, N.J., 1966-69, sr. v.p., 1969—, chmn. Pathmark div., 1977-79, exec. asst. to pres., 1979—, also dir., mem. exec. com. dir. Quantronix Corp., 1969-79; instr. Am. Inst. Banking, 1954-55; mem. Food Industry Joint Com. Data Transmission Networks, 1977—. . Trustee Jewish Counseling and Service Agy. Essex County, 1968-73, Greater Newark Better Bus. Bur., 1968-69, Jewish Community Fedn. Met. N.J., 1974-77; trustee Newark Beth Israel Med. Center, Newark, 1971—, treas., 1972-73, pres., 1973-78. Recipient Justice Louis D. Brandeis Humanitarian award N.J. region Zionist Orgn. Am., 1977. Mem. Food Mktg. Inst. Club: Harvard (N.Y.C.). Office: 301 Blair Rd Woodbridge NJ 07095

LIEBERMAN, LEONARD, physician; b. Milw., June 16, 1920; s. Morris and Rachel (Klieger) L.; B.S., Marquette U., 1940, M.D., 1944; m. Barbara Altfeld, Mar. 25, 1951; children—Deborah Lynn, Marsha Beth. Intern, Milw. County Gen. Hosp., 1944-45, resident internal medicine, 1945-50, now mem. attending staff; practice medicine specializing in internal medicine, Milw., 1950—; physician South div. Milw. County Mental Health Center, 1950-53, acting clin. dir., 1955-61, med. dir., 1961—; clin. instr. Med. Sch., Marquette U., 1955—. Mem. Citizens Adv. Com. on Community Day Care Centers for Mentally Handicapped, 1964-66; team capt. Milw. Jewish Welfare Fund, 1965. Served to capt., M.C., AUS, 1953-55. Mem. A.M.A., Am. Psychiat. Assn., Assn. Mental Hosp. Supts., Nat. Rehab. Assn., Mental Health Soc., Orgn. for Rehab. Tng. Fedn. Mem. B'nai B'rith. Asst. editor Skin Manifestations of Internal Disorders, 1947. Contbr. articles to profl. jours. Home: 4415 N Wildwood Ave Milwaukee WI 53211 Office: 9035 Watertown Plank Rd Milwaukee WI 53226

LIEBERMAN, PHILIP, linguist; b. Bklyn., Oct. 25, 1934; s. Harry Israel and Miriam (Mendelson) L.; B.S. in Elec. Engring. M.I.T., M.S. in Elec. Engring., 1958, Ph.D. in Linguistics, 1966; m. Marcia Mazo Rubinstein, June 2, 1957; children—Benjamin David, Daniel Eric. Research scientist Air Force Cambridge (Mass.) Research Labs., 1958-66; asso. prof. linguistics and elec. engring. U. Conn., 1967-69, prof. linguistics, 1969-74, mem. research staff Haskins Labs., 1967-74; prof. linguistics Brown U., 1974—, chmn. dept. linguistics, 1975-78. Served with USAF, 1958-62. Recipient award for contbn. to speech sci. Am. Speech and Hearing Assn., 1975; NIH grantee, 1975—. Fellow Am. Anthropol. Assn.; mem. Acoustical Soc. Am., Am. Assn. Phys. Anthropologists, Linguistic Soc. Am., AAAS, Soc. Forensic Analysis Speech. Club: Swiss Alpine. Author: Intonation, Perception and Language, 1966; The Speech of Primates, 1972; On the Origins of Language, An Introduction to the Evolution of Speech, 1975; Speech Physiology and Acoustic Phonetics, 1978; patentee method for acoustic detection of pathologic larynges, method for acoustic bullet detection. Home: 141 Elton St Providence RI 02906 Office: Box E Dept Linguistics Brown U Providence RI 02912

LIEBERMAN, SEYMOUR, educator; b. N.Y.C., Dec. 1, 1916; s. Samuel D. and Sadie (Levin) L.; B.S., Bklyn. Coll., 1936; M.S., U. Ill., 1937; Ph.D. (Rockefeller scholar 1939-41), Stanford, 1941; Traveling fellow U. Basle (Switzerland), Eidgenoess. Tech. Hochschule, Zurich, Switzerland, 1946-47; m. Sandra Spar, June 5, 1944; 1 son, Paul B. Chemist, Schering Corp., 1938-39; spl. research asso. Harvard, 1941-45; asso. mem. Sloan-Kettering Inst., 1945-50; mem. faculty Columbia Coll. Phys. and Surg., N.Y.C., 1950—, prof. biochemistry, 1962—, Mem. subcom. human applications radioactive materials N.Y.C. Health Dept. Pfizer traveling fellow McGill U., 1968; Syntex lectr. Mexican Endocrine Soc. 1970; mem. Am. Cancer Soc. panel steroids, 1945-49, hormones 1949-50, com. pathogenesis of cancer, 1957-60; mem. endocrine study sect. NIH, 1959-63, chmn., 1963-65, mem. gen. clin. research centers, 1967-71; Mem. med. adv. com. Population Council, 1961-73; mem. endocrinology panel Cancer Chemotherapy Nat. Service Center, 1958-62; cons. WHO human reprodn. unit, 1972-74; cons. Ford Found., 1974—. Recipient Distinguished Alumnus award Bklyn. Coll., 1971. Fellow N.Y. Acad. Scis., Nat. Acad. Scis.; mem. Am. Soc. Biol. Chemists, Am. Chem. Soc., Internat. Soc. Endocrinology (U.S. del. central com.), Endocrine Soc. (Ciba award 1952, Koch award 1970; council 1970-73; pres. 1974-75), Harvey Soc. asso. editor Jour. Clin. Endocrinology and Metabolism, 1963-67, editorial bd., 1958-63, 68-70; editorial bd. Jour. Biol. Chemistry, 1975—. Contbr. articles to profl. jours. Home: 32-22 163d St Flushing NY 11358 Office: 630 W 168th St New York NY 10032

LIEBERMAN, WILLIAM S., museum curator; b. Paris, France, Feb. 14, 1924; (parents Am. citizens); s. Max and Bertha M. (Slattery) L.; B.A. with high honors, Swarthmore Coll., 1943; postgrad. Harvard, 1943-45. Staff dept. exhbns. and publs. Mus. Modern Art, N.Y.C., 1943, asst. to Alfred H. Barr, Jr., 1945-49, asso. curator prints, 1949-53, curator prints, 1953-59, curator drawings and prints, 1959-66, dir. drawings and prints, 1966-67, curator painting and sculpture, 1967-69, dir. painting and sculpture, 1969-71, dir. drawings, 1971—; dir. print exhbns., Paris, London, Yugoslavia. Juror Internat. Graphic Arts Soc., also 3d and 4th Internat. Biennial Exhbn. Prints, Tokyo; mem. adv. bd. Pratt Contemporaries Graphic Art Centre; trustee Cosmopolitan Arts Found.; adviser William and Noma Copley Found.; mem. dance com. Library and Mus. of Performing Arts, Lincoln Center; mem. exhbn. com. Japan Soc., Center for Inter-Am. Relations. Decorated chevalier l'Ordrel des Arts et des Lettres (France). Mem. Am. Fedn. Arts (trustee), Print Council Am. (dir.). Club: Century Assn., Grolier (N.Y.C.); Turf (London). Author monographs on modern artists. Contbr. articles art publs. Address: 11 W 53d St New York City NY 10019

LIEBERSON, STANLEY, sociologist, educator; b. Montreal, Que., Can., Apr. 20, 1933; s. Jack and Ida (Cohen) L.; student Bklyn. Coll., 1950-52; M.A., U. Chgo., 1958, Ph.D., 1960; m. Patricia Ellen Beard, 1960; children—Rebecca, David, Miriam, Rachel. Asso. dir. Iowa Urban Community Research Center, U. Iowa, 1959-61, instr., asst. prof. sociology, 1959-61; asst. prof. sociology U. Wis., 1961-63, asso. prof., 1963-66, prof., 1966-67; prof. sociology U. Wash., 1967-71, dir. Center Studies Demography and Ecology, 1968-71; prof. sociology U. Chgo., 1971-74, asso. dir. Population Research Center, 1971-74; prof. sociology U. Ariz., Tucson, 1974—, head dept., 1976-79; vis. prof. Stanford U., summer 1970; Claude Bissell disting. vis. prof. U. Toronto, 1979-80; mem. com. on sociolinguistics Social Sci. Research Council, 1964-70; mem. sociology panel NSF, 1978—. Recipient Colver Rosenberger Ednl. prize, 1960; Guggenheim fellow, 1972-73. Mem. Am. Sociol. Assn., Population Assn. Am. (dir. 1969-72), Internat. Population Union, Sociol. Research Assn. (exec. com. 1976—, pres.-elect). Author: (with others) Metropolis and Region, 1960; Ethnic Patterns in American Cities, 1963. Editor: Explorations in Sociolinguistics, 1967; (with Beverly Duncan) Metropolis and Region in Transition, 1970; Language and Ethnic Relations in Canada, 1970; A Piece of the Pie; asso. editor Social Problems, 1965-67; Sociol. Methods and Research, 1971—; editorial cons. Sociol. Inquiry, 1965-67; adv. editor Am. Jour. Sociology, 1969-74; editorial bd. Lang. in Society, 1972-74, Internat. Jour. Sociology of Lang., 1974—, Canadian Jour. Sociology, 1975—; advisory council Sociol. Abstracts, 1972-73. Home: 3520 N Prescott Pl Tucson AZ 85715

LIEBERT, JOHN GRANVILLE, govt. ofcl., lawyer; b. Coffeyville, Kans., June 25, 1915; s. Frank J. and Helen Ely (Reardin) L.; Ph.B., Creighton U., 1935, LL.B., 1937; LL.M., Cath. U. Am., 1938; grad. Naval Sch. for Mil. Govt., Princeton U., 1945, Army Civil Affairs Sch., Stanford U., 1945; m. Margaret Ann Kinsler, Oct. 5, 1940; children—Mary Margaret, Carolyn Ann. Admitted to Nebr. bar, 1937, D.C. bar, 1948, U.S. Supreme Ct. bar, 1964; atty. Dept. Agr., 1938-42; chief econ. controls br. Supreme Comdr. Allied Powers, Tokyo, 1945-47; pvt. practice law, Washington, 1947-51; pres. United Overseas Corp., 1950-52; spl. asst. to adminstr. (Emissary to Republic South Korea), exec. asst. to dep. adminstr. Def. Minerals Procurement Adminstrn., 1951-53; spl. asst. to asst. sec. for mineral resources Dept. Interior, 1953-60; U.S. rep. OEEC Energy Com., Paris, 1957-60; head U.S. del. energy experts to Econ. Commn. Europe, Geneva, 1958; atty. Office Gen. Counsel, U.S. Dept. Agr., 1961-69, adminstrv. law judge, 1969—; chmn. United Overseas Corp.; dir. Raven Products, Inc. Dir. Rehab. Com. for Cath. Church in Japan, 1947-50; dir. Philosophy Edn. Soc., 1975—. Served as lt., amphibious forces, USNR, 1942-45. Decorated knight comdr. Order St. Sylvester, 1948. Mem. Am. (exec. com. conf. adminstrv. law judges 1972—, chmn. 1976), Nebr. bar assns., Fed. Adminstrv. Law Judges Conf. (exec. com. 1969-73), Am. Judicature Soc., John Carroll Soc. Club. Home: 7503 Clarendon Rd Bethesda MD 20014 Office: US Dept Agr Washington DC 20006

LIEBESKIND, HERBERT, educator; b. N.Y.C., Nov. 24, 1921; s. Irving and Irene (Bauman) L.; B.A., N.Y. U., 1941; m. Ruth Feldman, Sept. 5, 1943; children—Jan M., Nina S. Teaching fellow N.Y. U., 1941-43, asst. instr., 1943-45; instr. Cooper Union, N.Y.C., 1945-48, asst. prof., 1948-59, asso. prof., 1959-66, prof. chemistry, 1966—, asst. dean, 1968-70, dir. admissions, registrar, 1970-72, dean admissions and records, 1972—. Vis. lectr. Stevens Inst. Tech., 1953-55; vis. asso. prof. Yeshiva U., 1961-62. Pres. Bay Terrace Jewish Center, Bayside, N.Y., 1964-65. Mem. N.Y. Acad. Scis., Am. Chem. Soc., A.A.A.S., Am. Soc. Engring. Edn., AAUP, Chemistry Tchrs. Club N.Y. (pres. 1961-62; Oscar R. Foster award 1969), Phi Beta Kappa, Phi Lambda Upsilon. Mem. B'nai B'rith (bd. dirs. Bay Terrace Lodge). Contbr. Ency. Americana. Home: 212-19 16th Ave Bayside NY 11360 Office: Cooper Union Cooper Sq New York City NY 10003

LIEBLEIN, SEYMOUR, mech. engr.; b. N.Y.C., June 17, 1923; s. David and Rose (Brandstein) L.; B.M.E., Coll. City N.Y., 1944; M.S. in Aero. Engring., Case. Inst. Tech., 1952. Research engr. axial-flow compressors NACA, Cleve., 1944-57; supervisory research engr. Space Power Systems, NASA, Cleve., 1957-65, supervisory research engr. VTOL Propulsion Systems, 1965-72, tech. asst. to chief V/STOL and Noise div., 1972-76; mgr. Tech. Report Services, Rocky River, Ohio, 1976—. Recipient NACA exceptional service medal, 1957. Asso. fellow Am. Inst. Aeros. and Astronautics (Goddard award 1967); mem. ASME (ann. award gas turbine div. 1961). Contbr. articles to profl. jours. Home: 3400 Wooster Rd Apt 320 Rocky River OH 44116

LIEBMAN, LANCE MALCOLM, lawyer; b. Newark, Sept. 11, 1941; s. Roy and Barbara (Trilinsky) L.; B.A., Yale U., 1962; M.A., Cambridge U., 1964; LL.B., Harvard U., 1967; m. Carol Bensinger, June 28, 1964; children—Jeffrey, Benjamin. Admitted to D.C. bar, 1968, Mass. bar, 1976; asst. to Mayor Lindsay, N.Y.C., 1968-70; asst. prof. law Harvard U., 1970-76, prof., 1976—. Successor trustee Yale Corp. Home: 86 Sargent St Newton MA 02158 Office: Langdell Hall Harvard U Law Sch Cambridge MA 02138

LIEBMAN, MILTON, publisher, journalist; b. Bklyn., Oct. 23, 1928; s. Abraham and Zelda (Shapiro) L.; student City U. N.Y., 1946-51; m. Mary Jane Isabel Ladin, Feb. 20, 1964; children—Jessica Zoe, Katherine M. Pub. relations exec. Med. and Pharm. Info. Bur., 1953-54, 58-59, William Douglas McAdams, 1954-58; dept. editor Med. News, 1959-61; mng. editor Med. World News, N.Y.C., 1961-66; pub. Hosp. Practice mag., N.Y.C., 1966—; v.p., dir. HP Pub. Co., Inc.; pres. Assn. Ind. Clin. Publs., Inc. Served with U.S. Army Res., 1951-53. Mem. Nat. Assn. Sci. Writers, Am. Med. Writers Assn., Am. Pub. Health Assn., AAAS. Clubs: Pharm. Advt. of N.Y., Midwest Pharm. Advt. (Chgo.). Home: 280 Riverside Dr New York NY 10025 Office: 575 Lexington Ave New York NY 10022

LIEBMANN, GEORGE WILLIAM, lawyer; b. N.Y.C., June 20, 1939; s. William B. and Margaret (Hirschman) L.; A.B., Dartmouth Coll., 1960; J.D., U. Chgo., 1963; m. Anne-Lise Grimstad, Apr. 29, 1967; children—Pamela Dione, George William, Franklin Alexander. With Chaucer Head Book Shop, Inc., N.Y.C., 1958-59; admitted to Md. bar, 1964, Ill. bar, 1964; law clk. to Chief Judge Frederick W. Brune, Ct. Appeals Md., 1963-64; asst. atty. gen. State of Md., Balt., 1967-69; asso. firm Frank, Bernstein, Conaway and Goldman, Balt., 1964-67, partner, 1970-79; exec. asst. to Gov. Md., Annapolis, 1979—; lectr. in law U. Md. Law Sch., 1977-78; asst. reporter Md. Commn. on Criminal Law and Procedure, 1965-70; reporter Md. Joint Com. on Revision Replevin Laws, 1972; mem. Gov.'s Commn. to Revise Annotated Code Md., 1974—. Served with USAR, 1965. Mem. Am. Law Inst., Fed. Jud. Conf. of 4th Circuit, Am. Bar Assn., Md. Bar Assn. (chmn. sect. jud. adminstrn. 1975-77), Library Co. of Balt. Bar (dir. 1967—, pres. 1975-77), Bar Assn. Balt. City. Democrat. Episcopalian. Author: Maryland District Court Law and Practice, 2 vols., 1976; contbr. articles to law jours.; mng. editor U. Chgo. Law Rev., 1962-63. Home: 122 Taplow Rd Baltimore MD 21212 Office: State House Annapolis MD 21404

LIEBOWITZ, HAROLD, univ. dean; b. Bklyn., June 25, 1924; s. Samuel and Sarah (Kaplan) L.; B. in Aero. Engring., Poly. Inst. Bklyn., 1944, M. in Aero. Engring., 1946, D. in Aero. Engring. 1948; m. Marilyn Iris Lampert, June 24, 1951; children—Alisa Lynn, Jay, Jill Denice. With Office Naval Research, 1948-60; asst. dean Grad. Sch., exec. dir. engring. expt. sta. U. Colo. at Boulder, 1960-61, also vis. prof. aero. engring.; head structural mechs. br. Office Naval Research, 1961-68, dir. Navy programs in solid propellant mechanics, 1962-68; dean Sch. Engring. and Applied Sci., George Washington U., Washington, 1968—; research prof. Cath. U., Washington, 1962-68. Cons., Office Naval Research, 1960—, Reynolds Metals Co., 1968—, Pergamon Press, 1968—, Acad. Press, 1968—; mem. Israeli-Am. Materials Adv. Group, 1970—; sci. adviser Congl. Ad Hoc Com. on Environ. Quality, 1969—; co-dir. Joint Inst. for Advancement Flight Scis. NASA-Langley Research Center, Hampton, Va., 1971. Recipient Outstanding award Office Naval Research, 1961, Research Accomplishment Superior award, 1961; Superior Civilian Service award USN, 1965, 67; Commendation Outstanding Contbns. sec. navy, 1966. Fellow AAAS, AIAA, Am. Soc. Metals; mem. Soc. Engring. Scis. (past pres.), Sci. Research Soc. Am., Am. Technion Soc. (dir.), Am. Acad. Mechanics (founder, pres.), Internat. Coop. Fracture Inst. (founder, v.p.), Engrs. Council for Profl. Devel., Nat. Acad. Engring. (home sec.), Sigma Xi, Tau Beta Pi, Sigma Gamma Tau, Sigma Tau. Editor: Advanced Treatise on Fracture, 7 vols., 1969-72; founder, editor-in-chief Internat. Jour. Computers and Structures, 1971—; founder, editor Internat. Jour. Engring. Fracture Mechanics, 1968—. Contbr. articles to profl. jours. Home: 9112 LeVelle Dr Chevy Chase MD 20015 Office: 725 23d St NW Washington DC 20052

LIEDERMAN, AL, editorial cartoonist; b. Rochester, N.Y., Sept. 26, 1911; s. Samuel and Eva (Buff) L.; m. Lee Kleinman, Mar. 8, 1937; children—Carole, Russell. Former editorial cartoonist Rochester Eve. Jour., Syracuse (N.Y.) Jour. and Am., N.Y. Post, then L.I. Press; cartoons syndicated by Rothco Cartoons Inc. Recipient Page One award N.Y. Newspaper Guild; award Nat. Found. Hwy. Safety, 1972, 74. Mem. Soc. Editorial Cartoonists, Nat. Cartoonist Soc. Baseball Writers Assn., Am. Artists and Writers Asso. Creator of All Stars, syndicated cartoon panel, 1956; cartoons rep. Syracuse U. Archives, Albert T. Reid Cartoon Collection, U. Kans. Author: Li'l Leaguer, 1960. Home: 1700 St Johns Ave Merrick NY 11566 Office: 92-20 168th St Jamaica NY 11433

LIEDHOLM, CARL EDWARD, educator; b. Long Beach, Calif., July 22, 1940; s. George Edward and Marian (Folts) L.; B.A., Pomona Coll., 1961; Ph.D., U. Mich., 1965; m. Margaret Edith Osgood, Nov. 29, 1963; children—Kathleen Elizabeth, Erik Alken. Adviser, acting dir. Econ. Devel. Inst., U. Nigeria, Enugu, 1965-67; asst. prof. econs. Mich. State U., East Lansing, 1967-69, chmn. econs. dept., 1969-74, prof. econs., 1972—, dir. Off-farm Employment Project, 1977—; cons. in field. NDEA fellow, 1961-65; Yale U. vis. fellow, 1974; Sussex (U.K.) U. vis. fellow, 1975; chmn. selection com. Internat. Doctoral Research Fellowship Program for Africa, Social Sci. Research Council, 1977-78. Fellow African Studies Assn.; mem. Am. Econs. Assn., Nigeria, Royal econ. socs., Phi Beta Kappa. Club: Calif. Cello. Author; Growth and Development of Nigerian Economy (with Carl Eicher), 1970; The Indian Iron and Steel Industry: An Analysis of Comparative Advantage, 1972. Home: 830 Wildwood Dr East Lansing MI 48823

LIEDTKE, JOHN HUGH, petroleum co. exec.; b. Tulsa, Feb. 10, 1922; B.A., Amherst Coll., 1942; postgrad. Harvard Grad. Sch., Bus. Adminstrn., 1943; LL.B., U. Tex., 1947; m. Betty Lyn; children—Karen, Kristin, John Hugh, Blake, Kathryn. Chmn., chief exec. officer Pennzoil Co., Houston, Pennzoil United, Inc. (formerly United Gas Corp.); dir. Elk Refining Co., Penn Grade Assn., 1st Nat. Bank Midland (Tex.), Capital Nat. Bank, Houston. Trustee Houston United Fund, Kincaid Sch., Houston, Rice U., Baylor Coll. Medicine, U.S. Naval Acad. Found.; bd. dirs. Meth. Hosp., Houston. Mem. Tex. Mid-Continent Oil and Gas Assn. (dir.), Nat. Petroleum Refiners Assn. (dir.), Am. Petroleum Inst. (dir.), Nat. Petroleum Council (dir.), Ind. Petroleum Assn. Am. (dir.), Beta Theta Pi, Phi Alpha Delta. Clubs: Houston Country, Ramada, Pennhills, Bradford (Pa.) Country; Rolling Rock (Ligonier, Pa.), Racquet (Midland); Calgary (Alta., Can.) Petroleum. Office: Pennzoil Pl 900 SE Tower Houston TX 77001*

LIEDTKE, JOHN HUGH, petroleum co. exec.; b. Tulsa, Feb. 10, 1922; B.A., Amherst Coll., 1942; postgrad. Harvard Grad. Sch., Bus. Adminstrn., 1943; LL.B., U. Tex., 1947; m. Betty Lyn; children—Karen, Kristin, John Hugh, Blake, Kathryn. Chmn., chief exec. officer Pennzoil Co., Houston. Trustee Houston United Fund, Kinkaid Sch., Houston, Rice U., Baylor Coll. Medicine, U.S. Naval Acad. Found., Lawrence Acad.; council overseers Jesse H. Jones Grad. Sch. Adminstrn. Rice U. Mem. Tex. Mid-Continent Oil and Gas Assn. (dir.), Am. Petroleum Inst. (dir.), Nat. Petroleum Council (dir.), Houston C. of C. (dir.), Beta Theta Pi, Phi Alpha Delta. Clubs: Houston Country, Ramada, Pennhills, Bradford (Pa.) Country; Rolling Rock (Ligonier, Pa.), Racquet (Midland); Calgary (Alta., Can.) Petroleum. Office: Pennzoil Pl 700 Milam Houston TX 77002

LIEF, HAROLD ISAIAH, psychiatrist; b. N.Y.C., Dec. 29, 1917; s. Jacob F. and Mollie (Filler) L.; B.A., U. Mich., 1938; M.D., N.Y. U., 1942; certificate in psychoanalysis Columbia Coll. Physicians and Surgeons, 1950; M.A. (hon.), U. Pa., 1971; m. Myrtis A. Brumfield, Mar. 3, 1961; Caleb B., Frederick V., Oliver F.; children from previous marriage—Polly Lief Goldberg, Jonathan F. Intern, Queens Gen. Hosp., Jamaica, N.Y., 1942-43; resident psychiatry L.I. Coll. Medicine, 1946-48; pvt. practice psychiatry, N.Y.C., 1948-51; asst. physician Presbyn. Hosp., N.Y.C., 1949-51; asst. prof. Tulane U., New Orleans, 1951-54, asso. prof., 1954-60, prof. psychiatry, 1960-67; prof. psychiatry, dir. div. family study U. Pa., Phila., 1967—, dir. Marriage Council of Phila. and Center for Study of Sex. Edn. in Medicine, 1968—; mem. staff U. Pa. Hosp., 1967—. Mem. La. State Commn. Civil Rights, 1958-67. Served to maj. M.C., U.S. Army, 1943-46. Commonwealth Fund fellow, 1963-64. Fellow Phila. Coll. Physicians, Am. Psychiat. Assn. (life), N.Y. Acad. Scis., AAAS, Acad. Psychoanalysis (charter, past pres.), Am. Coll. Psychiatry (founding), Am. Coll. Psychoanalysis (charter); mem. Am. Assn. Marriage and Family Counselors, Sex Information and Edn. Council U.S. (past pres.), Am. Psychopathol. Assn., Group Advancement Psychiatry, Am. Orthopsychiat. Assn., Am. Soc. Adolescent Psychiatry, Am. Psychosomatic Soc., Internat. Acad. Sex Research, Soc. Sci. Study of Sex, Am. Soc. Sex Educators, Counselors and Therapists, Soc. Sex Therapists and Researchers, Am. Assn. Planned Parenthood Physicians, Sigma Xi, Alpha Omega Alpha, Phi Eta Sigma, Phi Kappa Phi. Club: Germantown Cricket (Phila.). Author: (with Daniel and William Thompson) The Eighth Generation, 1960. Editor: (with Victor and Nina Lief) Psychological Basis of Medical Practice, 1963; Medical Aspects of Human Sexuality, 1976; (with Arno Karlen) Sex Education in Medicine, 1976. Contbr. numerous articles to publs. Home: 101 S Buck Ln Haverford PA 19041 Office:

School of Medicine University of Pennsylvania 4025 Chestnut St Philadelphia PA 19104

LIEF, LEONARD, coll. pres.; b. N.Y.C., June 14, 1924; s. Aaron and Tillie (Newman) L.; A.B., N.Y. U., 1946; M.A., Columbia U., 1947; Ph.D., Syracuse U., 1953; m. Ruth Ann Haring, June 21, 1954; 1 dau., Madelon. Instr. English, Syracuse U., 1947-52; instr. Wayne U., 1953-55; instr. Hunter Coll., 1955-61, asst. prof., 1961-65, asso. prof., 1965-67, prof., 1968—, chmn. English dept., 1965-67; provost Hunter-in-the-Bronx, 1967; pres. Herbert H. Lehman Coll., City U. N.Y., 1968—. Bd. mgrs. N.Y. Bot. Garden; bd. dirs. Fordham Redevel. Corp. Served with AUS, 1943-45. Mem. Council of Pres.'s City U. N.Y., Regents Coordinating Council, Phi Beta Kappa. Club: Century Assn. Author: (with David Hawke) American Colloquy, 1963; (with Myron Matlaw) Story and Critic, 1963; The New Conservatives, 1967; (with James Light) The Modern Age, 1969, 72, 76. Home: 681 W 231st St Bronx NY 10463 Office: Herbert H Lehman Coll The City U NY Bronx NY 10468

LIEM, CHANNING, educator; b. Ulyul, Korea, Oct. 30, 1909; s. Posung and Posun (Yu) L.; B.S., Lafayette Coll., 1934; M.A., Princeton, 1943, Ph.D., 1945; m. Popai Lee, Jan. 29, 1940; children—Edith (Mrs. Young Jo Sul), G. Ramsay, Paul L. Postdoctoral fellow Yale, 1954-55; dir. Korean Ch. and Inst., N.Y.C., 1936-41; cons. Far Eastern affairs U.S. Office Censorship and War Information, N.Y.C., 1942-45; instr. Princeton, 1946-48; Korean affairs adviser U.S. Mil. Gov. in Korea, Seoul, 1948-49; prof. polit. sci. Chatham Coll., 1949-60; prof. polit. sci. State U. N.Y. Coll. of New Paltz, also chmn., prof. polit. sci. Asian studies, prof. emeritus, 1978—; ambassador Republic Korea to UN, 1960-61; spl. envoy to Republic Korea to Southwestern African Republics, Cameroun, Dahomey, Congo, Ivory Coast, Togo, Ghana, Senegal, 1961; adviser Nat. Com. for Def. Democratic Rights, Republic Korea, 1972—. Trustee Korean Edn. Found. Am., 1944-55. Recipient Humanitarian award Nat. Achievement Clubs, 1953; Ford faculty fellowship Chatham Coll., 1954-55; citation for meritorious service Republic Korea, 1961. Mem. Am. Polit. Sci. Assn., Internat. Mark Twain Soc. (hon.), Union Overseas Koreans for Democracy and Unification (sr. chmn.). Club: Princeton (N.Y.C.). Author: America's Gift to Korea: Life of Philip Jaisohn, 1952; Civilization of East Asia, 1973. Contbr. articles to profl. publs. Editor: Voice of the Korean People. Home: 252 Old Kingston Rd New Paltz NY 12561. *The guideline for my life is simple and not new. It consists of the following: Be guided by noble ideas rather than persons who profess to represent the ideals; and Try hard to faithfully personify those ideals which I cherish by practice.*

LIEM, KAREL FREDERIK, biologist, educator; b. Jogya, Java, Indonesia, Nov. 24, 1935; s. Soen Ging and Maria Carolina (Bader) L.; came to U.S., 1964; B.Sc., U. Indonesia, 1957, M.Sc. cum laude, 1958; Ph.D., U. Ill., 1961; A.M. (hon.), Harvard, 1972; m. Hetty Khouw, Sept. 4, 1965; children—Karel Frederik, Erika Elise. Asst. prof. U. Leiden (Netherlands), 1962-64; asst. prof., then asso. prof. U. Ill., Urbana, 1964-72; asst. curator, then asso. curator of anatomy Field Museum Natural History, Chgo., 1966-72; Henry Bryant Bigelow prof. biology, curator ichthyology Harvard, 1972—. Mem. vis. com. New Eng. Aquarium; trustee Cohasset (Mass.) Marine Biol. Lab.; mem. com. Latimeria, Nat. Acad. Scis. Guggenheim fellow, 1970. Fellow Linnean Soc.; mem. Am. Soc. Ichthyologists and Herpetologists, Am. Soc. Zoologists, Zool. Soc. London (sci. fellow), Soc. Study Evolution. Editor: Copeia, 1974; asso. editor jour. morphology, 1974—. Home: 40 Woodside Dr Sudbury MA 01776 Office: Museum Comparative Zoology Harvard Univ Cambridge MA 02138

LIEN, JESSE RUDOLPH, communications and electronics co. exec.; b. Portland, Oreg., Nov. 15, 1917; s. Rudolph Cornelius and Maude (Glazner) L.; B.A. in Physics, Reed Coll., 1942; postgrad. Mass. Inst. Tech., 1942; M.A., Boston U., 1953; m. Wilma Mae Richard, Aug. 9, 1941; children—Gregory Richard, Kevin Jesse. Communications engr. Northwestern Electric Co., Portland, 1941-42; mem. tech. staff Radiation Lab., Mass. Inst. Tech., Cambridge, 1942-45; research engr. Nav. Research Lab., Washington, 1945-46; asst. chief air research div., chief ionospheric rocket sounding sect. USAF Cambridge Research Center, Bedford, Mass., 1946-53; with Sylvania Electric Products Inc. (name changed to GTE Sylvania Inc. 1971), Mountain View, Calif. and Waltham, Mass., 1953—, v.p., gen. mgr. West div., 1960-69, sr. v.p., gen. mgr. electronic systems group 1969-77; pres. GTE Labs. and v.p. engring. GTE Products, Stamford, Conn., 1977—; cons. govt. agys., 1946-71; mem. San Francisco Bay Area Health Facilities Council, 1966-70, gov. San Francisco Bay Area Council, 1965-70. Trustee, Gordon Coll., Wenham, Mass., 1972—. Mem. N.Y. Acad. Scis., IEEE, AAAS, Am. Astronom. Soc., Am. Inst. Aero. and Astronautics, Am. Radio Relay League, Am. Mgmt. Assn., Electronic Industries Assn. (past chmn. bd. dirs. govtl. div.), Assn. U.S. Army, Research Soc. Am., Western Electronics Mfrs. Assn. (past bd. dirs.), Nation Security Indsl. Assn. (chmn. bd. trustees). Contbr. books, articles, chpts. to profl. jours. Patentee in field. Home: Wahackme Ln New Canaan CT 06840 Office: One Stamford Forum Stamford CT 06904

LIENER, IRVIN ERNEST, educator; b. Pitts., June 27, 1919; s. Max and Esther (Mayer) L.; B.S., Mass. Inst. Tech., 1941; Ph.D., U. So. Calif., 1949; m. Dorothy Joan Claysmith, June 13, 1945; children—Sally Ann, Wendy Roberta. Faculty, U. Minn., St. Paul, 1949—, prof. dept. biochemistry, 1957—; Wellcome vis. prof. nutrition Wash. State U., 1979. Served with AUS, 1942-46. Recipient Spencer award for outstanding achievement in agrl. chemistry, 1976. Wellcome Trust travel grantee, 1967; research grantee USPHS, USDA, NSF; Guggenheim fellow, 1957. Mem. Am. Soc. Biol. Chemists, Am. Inst. Nutrition, Venezuelan Assn. Advancement Sci. (hon.), Phi Beta Kappa, Sigma Xi, Phi Kappa Phi. Author: Organic and Biological Chemistry, 1966. Editor: Toxic Constituents of Plant Foodstuffs, 1969; Toxic Constituents of Animal Food Stuffs, 1974. Contbr. articles to profl. jours. Home: 3086 N Oxford St St Paul MN 55113

LIENERT, ROBERT MARCELLUS, magazine editor; b. Inland, Nebr., Apr. 26, 1926; s. Charles Theodore and Mary Elizabeth (Samson) L.; B.A., U. Nebr., 1946; M.S. in Journalism, Northwestern U., 1947; m. Audrey Jean Gagnon, Jan. 8, 1949; children—Paul, Jean, Charles, Thomas, Anthony. Night sports editor, reporter, copy editor Nebr. State Jour., Lincoln, 1946; copy editor Detroit Free Press, 1947-53; with Automotive News mag., Detroit, 1953—, news editor, 1962-66, mng. editor, 1966-74, editor, 1974—, also editor at large AutoWeek mag., Reno. Mem. zoning bd. review, New Baltimore, Mich., 1973—, mem. library commn., 1976—. Home: 52155 Base St New Baltimore MI 48047 Office: 965 E Jefferson St Detroit MI 48207

LIEPMANN, KLAUS, condr., violinist, educator; b. Kiel, Germany, Feb. 3, 1907; s. Moritz and Helene (Robert) L.; ed. Acad. Music, Cologne, Germany, 1925-29; m. Olga Christine Mylord, July 1, 1933; 1 dau., Lise. Came to U.S., 1933, naturalized, 1940. Mem. Cologne String Quartet, 1930-33; dir. chamber music Fieldston Sch., Ethical Culture Soc., 1933-35; condr. Yale Symphony Orch., 1935-39; instr. Yale Sch. Music, 1939-44; music adviser 1st Service Command U.S. Army, 1945; dir. music Thayer Acad., also head, music dept. Beaver Country Day Sch., 1946-47; mem. faculty, dir. music, condr. choral soc., Mass. Inst. Tech., 1947-72, prof. music, 1956—, chmn. music sect., 1961-72, sr. lectr., emeritus dir., 1972—; lectr. extension courses Harvard, 1956-76; vis. prof. Worcester Poly. Inst., 1975—. Author: The Language of Music, 1953. Home: PO Box 147 Westport Point MA 02791

LIEPOLD, ROBERT BRUCE, telecommunications co. exec.; b. Chgo., Oct. 4, 1925; s. Albin J. and Jeannette H. (Hussander) L.; B.S.E.E., U. Wis., 1946; m. Mary Jane Gerrity, Dec. 29, 1964; 1 son, John. Vice pres. mktg. Automatic Electric Co., Northlake, Ill., 1947-68; pres. United Bus. Communications, Kansas City, Mo., 1969-74; cons. telecommunications, St. Louis, 1974-78; exec. v.p. United Telecommunications, Kansas City, Mo., 1978—. Served with USN, 1943-46, 52-54. Mem. IEEE, Telephone Pioneers, U.S. Ind. Telephone Assn., Elec. Industries Assn. Office: PO Box 11315 Plaza Sta Kansas City MO 64112

LIERMAN, JAMES DARWIN, pharm. co. exec.; b. Champaign, Ill., 1916; s. John W. and Jennie (Rhodes) L.; B.S., U. Ill., 1939; m. Isabel Parks, Aug. 1, 1941; children—James C., David P. With Johnson & Johnson, 1940-69, began as salesman, successively dir. indsl. div., product dir., dir. hosp. merchandising, dir. hosp. div., 1940-68, v.p., 1968-69; corporate exec. v.p., chmn. mgmt. com. C.R. Bard, Inc., Murray Hill, N.J., 1969—, also dir. Served as maj., AUS, 1941-45. Decorated Presdl. citation, Silver Star medal, Bronze Star medal. Clubs: Echo Lake Country (Westfield, N.J.); Turtle Creek (Fla.); Wildcat Cliffs (Highlands, N.C.). Home: 76 Turtle Creek Dr Tequesta FL 33458

LIETZ, FRED EDGAR, orgn. exec.; b. Buckley, Ill, Dec. 20, 1916; s. Fred William and Minnie (Weber) L.; B.S. in Edn., Concordia Tchrs. Coll., 1939; postgrad. No. Ill. State Tchrs. Coll., 1942-43, Northwestern U., 1945; LL.D., Concordia Tchrs. Coll., Seward, Nebr., 1978; m. Vera Emma Rissman, Oct. 4, 1940; children—Gene Ellen, Sue Ellen, June Elaine. Tchr., prin. Immanuel Luth. Sch., Hickley, Ill., 1939-44; tchr., prin., sch. adminstr. Peace Luth. Sch., Saginaw, Mich., 1944-57; exec. sec. ch. extension dept. Mo. Synod, Luth. Ch., St. Louis, 1957—. Pres. council on Ch. Planning and Architecture, 1973. Pres. West Canterbury Assn., Affton, Mo., 1962-63, 72-73, speaker ch. bldg. and financing. Mem. Nat. Council Chs. Christ U.S.A. (exec. com.). Contbr. articles to profl. jours. Home: 10015 Coventry Ln St Louis MO 63123 Office: 500 N Broadway St Louis MO 63102

LIETZKE, MILTON HENRY, educator; b. Syracuse, N.Y., Nov. 23, 1920; s. Henry Robert and Emma (Gutknecht) L.; B.A., Colgate U., 1942; M.S., U. Wis., 1944, Ph.D., 1949; m. Marjorie Helen Padrutt, May 31, 1943; children—Kathryn Ann, Milton Henry, Carol Lynn; m. 2d, Eleanor Jean Hawkins, May 29, 1965; adopted children—Susan Lucinda, Mary Lindl. Lab. supr. Tenn. Eastman Corp., Oak Ridge, 1944-47; group leader chemistry div. Oak Ridge Nat. Lab., 1949—; prof. chemistry U. Tenn., Knoxville, 1964—. Bd. dirs. Oak Ridge Festival, 1962-64. Fellow N.Y. Acad. Scis.; mem. Am. Chem. Soc., Sci. Research Soc. Am., Tenn. Acad. Sci., Alpha Chi Sigma. Contbr. numerous articles and reports to profl. jours. Home: 4165 Towanda Trail Knoxville TN 37919 Office: Dept Chemistry U Tenn Knoxville TN 37916

LIEUALLEN, ROY ELWAYNE, state ofcl.; b. Weston, Oreg., Aug. 12, 1916; s. Roy W. and Viola (Brown) L.; B.S., Pacific U., Forest Grove, Oreg., 1940, L.H.D., 1959; M.S., U. Oreg., 1947; Ed.D., Stanford, 1955; LL.D., Willamette U., Salem., Oreg., 1963; m. Barbara E. Wales, Feb. 20, 1943; children—Douglas W., Scott E., Barbara E., Margaret A. Tchr. Pilot Rock (Oreg.) High Sch., 1940-42, 46; registrar Oreg. Coll. Edn., Monmouth, 1946-55, adminstr.-in-charge, 1955, pres., 1955-62; chancellor Oreg. State System Higher Edn., 1962—. Oreg. commr. Western Interstate Commn. Higher Edn.; commr. Edn. Compact of the States. Bd. dirs. Oreg. Mus. Sci. and Industry. Served from ensign to lt. (s.g.) USNR, 1942-45. Mem. Blue Key, Phi Delta Kappa. Democrat. Methodist. Office: P O Box 3175 Eugene OR 97403

LIEUWEN, EDWIN, historian, educator; b. Harrison, S.D., Feb. 8, 1923; s. John and Hannah (Muilenberg) L.; A.B., U. Calif. at Berkeley, 1947, M.A., 1948, Ph.D., 1951; m. Marian Rachel Whitehead, Apr. 11, 1947; children—John Neal, Peter Edwin, Andrew Lee, James Earl, Catherine Ann. Instr. history U. Calif. at Los Angeles, 1951-52; vis. asst. prof. history U. Calif. at Berkeley, 1954-55; with U.S. Govt. Service, 1952-53, 55-57; prof. history U. N.Mex., 1957—, chmn. dept., 1957-67, faculty research lectr., 1965. Doherty fellow, Venezuela, 1950-51; Fulbright lectr. U. Utrecht, 1953-54; fellow Council Fgn. Relations, 1957-58. Served to lt. (j.g.) USNR, 1943-46. Mem. Am. Hist. Assn. Author: Petroleum in Venezuela, 1955; Arms and Politics in Latin America, 2d edit., 1961; Presidents vs. Generals, 1964; Venezuela, 2d edit., 1965; The United States and Latin America, 1965; Mexican Militarism, 1968; The Cuban Revolution, 1971. Home: 2504 Harold Pl NE Albuquerque NM 87106

LIFFERS, WILLIAM ALBERT, chem. co. exec.; b. Union City, N.J., Jan. 12, 1929; s. William F. and Gertrude (Wildemann) L.; B.S. in Bus. Adminstrn., Seton Hall U., 1953; m. Mary Rafferty, Sept. 5, 1953; children—Steven, Linda, Wendy. With Am. Cyanamid Co., Wayne, N.J., 1953—, v.p. Cyanamid Internat., 1972-74, pres. Cyanamid Americas/Far East, 1974-76, corp. v.p., 1976-77, sr. v.p., dir., 1977-78, vice chmn., 1978—. Served with Finance Corps, U.S. Army, 1951-53. Office: American Cyanamid Co Berdan Ave Wayne NJ 07470

LIFLAND, WILLIAM THOMAS, lawyer: b. Jersey City, Nov. 15, 1928; B.S., Yale U., 1949; LL.B., Harvard U., 1952. Admitted to D.C. bar, 1952, N.Y. bar, 1956, N.J. bar, 1965; with Office Gen. Counsel, USAF, 1952-54; law clk. to Justice Harlan, U.S. Supreme Ct., Washington, 1955; asso. firm Cahill, Gordon & Reindel, N.Y.C., 1955—, partner, 1965—, asso. Paris office, 1958-60. Mem. Am. Bar Assn. (chmn. civil practice and procedure com. antitrust law sect. 1970-72, mem. sect. council 1975—, mem. commn. on law and economy 1975—), N.Y. State Bar Assn. (chmn. antitrust law sect. 1973-74). Pres., Harvard Law Rev., 1951-52; contbr. articles to profl. jours.; author monthly column N.Y. Law Jour. Home: 138 Wilson Rd Princeton NJ 08540 Office: 80 Pine St New York NY 10005

LIFTON, DONALD BRIAN, lawyer; b. Detroit, June 16, 1939; s. Maurice W. and Bert (Olanosky) L.; student Oberlin Coll.; J.D., Detroit Coll. Law, 1968; m. Susan Gayle Grossman, Sept. 13, 1964; children—Katherine Elizabeth, Robert Abraham. Admitted to Mich. bar, 1968; asso. firm Sugar, Schwartz & Silver, Detroit, 1968-70; partner firm Schlussel, Lifton, Simon, Rands & Kaufman, Detroit, 1970—. Served to 1st lt. AUS, 1964. Mem. Am., Mich., Detroit bar assns. Clubs: Knollwood Country, Detroit Economic, Renaissance. Office: 500 NBS Financial Center 29201 Telegraph Rd Southfield MI 48076

LIFTON, ROBERT JAY, psychiatrist; b. N.Y.C., May 16, 1926; s. Harold A. and Ciel (Roth) L.; student Cornell U., Ithaca, N.Y., 1942-44; M.D., N.Y. Med. Coll., 1948, D.H.L., 1977; D.Sc. (hon.), Lawrence U., 1971, Merrimack Coll., 1973; D.H.L., Wilmington Coll., 1975; m. Betty Jean Kirschner, Mar. 1, 1952; children—Kenneth Jay, Karen. Intern, Jewish Hosp., Bklyn., 1948-49; resident psychiatry State U. N.Y. Downstate Med. Center, 1949-51; mem. faculty Washington Sch. Psychiatry, 1954-55; research asso. psychiatry, also asso. East Asian studies Harvard U., 1956-61; Found.'s Fund for research psychiatry asso. prof. Yale Med. Sch., 1961-67, research prof., 1967—; cons. behavioral scis. study sect. NIMH, 1962-64, com. invasion of privacy N.Y. State Bar Assn., 1963-64, Columbia seminars modern Japan and Oriental thought and religion, 1965—. Organizer Redress group IAEA, Vienna, 1975. Served to capt. USAF, 1951-53. Recipient Pub. Service award N.Y. Soc. Clin. Psychologists, Alumni medal N.Y. Med. Coll., 1970, Karen Horney lectr. award, 1972, Distinguished Service award Soc. Adolescent Psychiatry, 1972, Mt. Airy Found. Gold medal, 1973; Gay lectr. Harvard Med. Sch., 1976. Fellow Am. Acad. Arts and Scis., Am. Psychiat. Assn.; mem. Assn. Asian Studies, AAAS, Group Study Psychohist. Process (coordinator), Fedn. Am. Scientists, Soc. Psychol. Study of Social Issues. Author: Thought Reform and the Psychology of Totalism: A Study of Brainwashing in China, 1961; Revolutionary Immorality: Mao Tse-Tung and the Chinese Cultural Revolution, 1968; Death in Life: Survivors of Hiroshima (Nat. Book award, Van Wyck Brooks award), 1968; History and Human Survival, 1970; Boundaries: Psychological Man in Revolution, 1970; Home from the War: Vietnam Veterans—Neither Victims Nor Executioners, 1973; (with Eric Olson) Living and Dying, 1974; The Life of the Self, 1976; (with Shuichi Kato and Michael Reich) Six Lives/Six Deaths: Portraits from Modern Japan, 1978; The Broken Connection: Death and the Continuity of Life, 1979; (humorous cartoons) Birds, 1969, Psycho Birds, 1979; editor: Woman in America, 1965; America and the Asian Revolutions, 1970; (with R.A. Falk and G. Kolko) Crimes of War, 1971; (with Eric Olson) Explorations in Psychohistory: The Wellfleet Papers, 1975. Office: 25 Park St New Haven CT 06519

LIFTON, ROBERT KENNETH, investment co. exec.; b. N.Y.C., Jan. 9, 1928; s. Benjamin and Anna (Pike) L.; B.B.A. magna cum laude, Coll. City N.Y., 1948; LL.B., Yale, 1951; m. Loretta J. Silver, Sept. 5, 1954; children—Elizabeth Gail, Karen Grace. Admitted to N.Y. bar, 1952; asso. atty. Kaye, Scholer, Fierman, Hays & Handler, N.Y.C., 1955-56; asst. to pres. Glickman Corp., N.Y.C., 1956-57; pres. Robert K. Lifton, Inc., N.Y.C., 1957-61; chmn. bd. Terminal Tower Co., Inc., Cleve., 1959-63; pres. Transcontinental Investing Corp., N.Y.C., 1961-69, chmn. bd., 1969-72; partner Venture Assos., 1972; mem. faculty Columbia Law Sch., 1973—, Yale Law Sch., 1973—. Guest lectr. Practicing Law inst., Yale Law Sch., Pace Inst., N.Y. U.; founder Nat. Exec. Conf. Washington Inc.; trustee Modern Mortgage Investors, 1973—. Mem. McGovern econ. advisory com., 1972-73; chmn. parents com. Barnard Coll., 1976-78; mem. com. of the collection Whitney Mus., 1976—; trustee Yale Law Sch. Fund, 1974—. Served to lt. (j.g.) USNR: Korea. Mem. Order of Coif. Club: Yale (N.Y.C.). Author: Practical Real Estate: Legal Tax and Business Strategies, 1978. Contbr. articles to profl. jours., handbooks. Home: 983 Park Ave New York NY 10028 Office: 600 Third Ave New York NY 10017

LIFTON, WALTER M., educator; b. Bklyn., Nov. 2, 1918; s. Samuel S. and Sarah G. (Berman) L.; B.A., Bklyn. Coll., 1942; M.A., N.Y. U., 1947, Ph.D., 1950; m. Ruth S. Knoppow, Oct. 1, 1940; children—Hazel Miriam Lifton Kroesser, Robert William. Sr. vocat. appraiser Vets. Guidance Center, Hunter Coll., 1946-48; psychologist, research div. N.Y. U., 1948-50; asso. prof. edn., guidance and counseling U. Ill., 1950-59; dir. guidance publs. and services Sci. Research Assos., Chgo., 1959-63; coordinator pupil personnel services Rochester (N.Y.) City Sch. Dist., 1964-70; prof. edn. dept. counseling psychology and student devel. SUNY, Albany, 1970—; vis. prof., lectr. guidance and counseling 34 colls. and univs.; cons. in field; mem. White House Conf. on Children and Youth, 1969-70, cons. Title III ESEA project Knox County, Tenn., 1967; interim dir. Action for a Better Community, Rochester, 1964-65, Center for Coop. Action in Urban Edn., Rochester, 1966. Served with AUS, 1942-46. Mem. Nat. Assn. Pupil Personnel Adminstrs. (pres. 1970), Nat. Vocat. Guidance Assn., Assn. for Specialist in Group Work (sec. 1976—, pres. 1980-81). Author: Keys to Vocational Decisions, 1964; Working With Groups, 2d edit., 1966; Educating for Tomorrow—The Role of Media, Career Devel. and Society, 1970; Groups—Facilitating Individual Growth and Societal Change, 1972; (film) Just Like a Family, 1979; contbr. articles to profl. jours. Home: 106 Greenleaf Dr Newtonville NY 12128 Office: State U NY 1400 Washington Ave Albany NY 12222. *As a person in the mental health field my focus has been increasingly concerned with prevention rather than remediation, and with helping people shape their environments not just adjust to their status quo.*

LIGERTWOOD, JOHN ROSS, ch. exec.; b. Calgary, Alta., Can., Aug. 9, 1927; s. John Charles Murray and Florence Edna (Ross) L.; Chartered Accountant, U. Man., 1954; m. Mary Eleanor Cunningham, July 7, 1962; children—Barbara Anne, Mary Elizabeth, David Alan Napier. Auditor, Peat, Marwick, Mitchell & Co., C.P.A.'s, 1943-55; treas. Gen. Synod, Anglican Ch. of Can., Toronto, Ont., 1955—. Treas. Anglican Found. Can., Missionary Soc., Anglican Ch. of Can. Mem. Bd. Trade Met. Toronto. Home: 47 Sagebrush Ln Don Mills ON Canada Office: 600 Jarvis St Toronto ON Canada

LIGETT, WALDO BUFORD, inst. adminstr.; b. Middletown, Ohio, Nov. 2, 1916; s. Waldo Buford and Mabel Louise (Berkley) L.; B.S., Antioch Coll., 1939; M.S., Purdue U., 1941, Ph.D., 1944, D.Sc. (hon.), 1965; grad. Advanced Mgmt. Program, Harvard, 1967; m. Ann Elizabeth Hartwell, Aug. 29, 1940; children—Robert A., John D., Michael T., Steven D., Daniel L. Chemist, Eastman Kodak Co., Rochester, N.Y., 1935-38; research supr. Ethyl Corp., Detroit, 1944-51, asst. dir. chem., 1951-52, asso. dir. chem., 1952-62, dir. research and devel., 1962-63; v.p. Celanese Chem. Co., Corpus Christi, Tex., 1963-64, v.p. tech. and mfg., 1964-66; tech. dir. Celanese Corp., N.Y.C., 1966-67, v.p., 1967-72; v.p. Franklin Inst., Phila., 1973—, pres. Franklin Research Center, 1975—; dir. Franklin-Hahnemann Inst., 1974—. Fellow Am. Inst. Chemists; mem. Am. Chem. Soc., AAAS, Indsl. Research Inst., Research Soc. Am., N.Y. Assn. Research Dirs., Am. Nuclear Soc., Atomic Indsl. Forum. Patentee in field. Home: 2 Blackwell Pl Philadelphia PA 19147 Office: Benjamin Franklin Pkwy at 20th St Philadelphia PA 19103

LIGGETT, DARWIN SLIGAR, ins. co. exec.; b. York, Nebr., Feb. 7, 1916; s. Wilbur G. and Grace (Cooley) L.; B.S. in Bus. Adminstrn., U. Nebr., 1937; postgrad. U. So. Calif., 1955; m. Marilou Williams, Aug. 11, 1938; children—Cheryl S. (Mrs. Eric D. McCaleb), Richard D., Scott G. Group rep. Aetna Life Ins. Co., 1937-48; regional group rep. Mass. Mut. Life, Detroit, 1948-50; v.p. R.C. Wilson Agy., Detroit, 1950-51; regional group mgr. Pacific Mut. Life Ins. Co., 1951-52, asst. sec. group, Los Angeles, 1952-55, asst. v.p., 1955-60, v.p., 1960-70, sr. v.p., 1970-76, sr. v.p., exec. officer, 1976—; chmn., chief exec. officer PM Life Ins. Co., Armonk, N.Y.; pres. Pacific Cons. Corp., Newport Beach, Calif.; dir. Pacific Equity Sales Co., Newport Beach, Western Health Mgmt. Corp., Los Angeles. Past pres. bd. trustees Morningside Hosp., Los Angeles; vice chmn. bd. dirs. Luth. Hosp. Soc. So. Calif.; mem. Calif. Citizens Commn. on Tort Reform. Served to lt. (j.g.) USNR, 1942-46. Mem. Health Ins. Assn. Am. (past dir.), Calif. Taxpayers Assn. (dir.), Assn. for Calif. Tort Reform (dir., sec.-treas.). Sigma Nu. Republican. Presbyterian. Clubs: Town Hall (Los Angeles); Big Canyon Country (Newport Beach). Home: 5582

Kingsford Terr Irvine CA 92715 Office: Pacific Mut Life Ins Co 700 Newport Center Dr Newport Beach CA 92663

LIGGETT, THOMAS JACKSON, theol. sem. pres.; b. Nashville, May 27, 1919; s. Thomas Jackson and Lola Cleveland (Ballentine) L.; A.B., Transylvania U., 1940; M.Div., Lexington Theol. Sem., 1944; postgrad. Union Theol. Sem. and Columbia, 1950-52; LL.D., Interamerican U., 1965, Culver-Stockton Coll., 1959, Butler U., 1975; D.H.L., Transylvania U., 1969; D.D., Eureka Coll., 1971; m. Virginia Corrine Moore, Aug. 12, 1941; children—Thomas Milton, Margaret Ann (Mrs. William David Herod). Ordained to ministry Christian Ch., 1940; pastor in Danville, Ky., 1943-45; missionary, Argentina, 1946-57; prof. Union Theol. Sem., Buenos Aires, 1948-57; pres. Evang. Sem. of P.R., 1957-65; exec. sec. for Latin Am., Christian Ch., 1965-67, chmn. div. world mission, 1967-68, pres. United Christian Missionary Soc., 1968-74; pres. Christian Theol. Sem., Indpls., 1974—. Del., World Council Chs. assembly in Uppsala, 1968, adviser assembly, Nairobi, Kenya, 1975; mem. governing bd. Nat. Council Chs., 1969-75. Co-chmn. McGovern Task Force on Fgn. Policy in Latin Am., 1972. Democratic precinct committeeman, 1970-72. Mem. Disciples of Christ Hist. Soc. (life), Theta Phi. Author: Where Tomorrow Struggles to be Born, 1970. Editor: Cuadernos Teologicos, 1954-55. Home: 445 Blue Ridge Rd Indianapolis IN 46208 Office: 1000 W 42d St Indianapolis IN 46208

LIGGETT, WILLIAM N., banker; b. Ripley, Ohio, Apr. 29, 1917; s. J. N. and Ida (Montgomery) L.; B.S., Miami U., Oxford, Ohio, 1939, LL.D., 1974—; grad. U. Wis. Sch. Banking, 1950; m. Marjorie Lloyd, May 15, 1940; children—William Reese, Lloyd N., Ann, Jane. Asst. cashier Citizens Nat. Bank, Ripley, 1940; past field sec. Ohio Bankers Assn.; with 1st Nat. Bank Cin., 1948—, v.p., 1949-64, exec. v.p., 1964-68. pres., chief exec. officer, 1968-72, chmn. bd., chief exec. officer, 1972—, also dir.; chmn., chief exec. officer 1st Nat. Cin. Corp., 1974—; examiner FDIC, 1942-48; dir. Cin. br. Fed. Res. Bank of Cleve., Dayton Malleable, Inc., Cin. Gas & Electric Co., Coca Cola Bottling Corp.; Midland Co., Lodge & Shipley Co., Morris Bean & Co., Wilson Freight Co., Hennegan Co., Schauer Mfg. Co. Served to lt. (j.g.) USNR, 1944-46. Mem. Am. (v.p. Ohio 1955), Ohio (treas. 1958-59, v.p. 1979-80) bankers assns., Newcomen Soc. N. Am. Home: 2555 Observatory Ave Cincinnati OH 45208 Office: 1st Nat Bank 4th and Walnut Sts Cincinnati OH 45202

LIGGIO, CARL DONALD, lawyer; b. N.Y.C., Sept. 5, 1943; A.B., Georgetown U., 1963; J.D., N.Y. U., 1967. Admitted to N.Y. State bar, 1967, D.C. bar, 1967; cons. firm Arent, Fox, Kintner, Plotkin & Kahn, Washington, 1968-69; asso. firm White & Case, N.Y.C., 1969-72; gen. counsel Arthur Young & Co., N.Y.C., 1972—. Mem. Am., N.Y. State, D.C. bar assns., Assn. Bar City N.Y. Contbr. articles to legal and bus. jours. Home: 11 E 86th St New York NY 10028 Office: 277 Park Ave New York NY 10017

LIGHT, ARTHUR HEATH, clergyman; s. Alexander Heath and Mary Watkins (Nelson) L.; B.A., Hampden-Sydney Coll., 1951; M.Div., Va. Theol. Sem., 1954, D.Div., 1970; D.Div., St. Paul's Coll., 1979; m. Sarah Ann Jones, June 12, 1954; children—William Alexander, Philip Nelson, John Page, Sarah Heath. Ordained to ministry as priest Episcopal Ch., 1955; rector West Mecklenburg Cure, Boydton, Va., 1954-58, Christ Ch., Elizabeth City, N.C., 1958-63, St. Marys Ch., Kinston, N.C., 1963-67, Christ and St. Luke's Ch., Norfolk, Va., 1967-79; bishop Diocese of Southwestern Va., Roanoke, 1979—. Bd. dirs. United Communities Fund, 1969—, Norfolk Seamen's Friends Soc., 1969—, Tidewater Assembly on Family Life, 1970—, Friends of Juvenile Ct., 1975—, Va. Inst. Pastoral Care, 1971-72, Va. Council Chs.; mem. bio-med. ethics com. Eastern Va. Med. Sch., 1973—; trustee Va. Epis. Sch., Lynchburg, Epis. High Sch., Alexandria, Va. Theol. Sem., Alexandria, Boys' Home, Covington, Stuart Hall Sch., Staunton, St. Paul's Coll., Lawrenceville. Democrat. Home: 2524 Wycliffe Ave Roanoke VA 24014 Office: 1000 1st St SW Roanoke VA 24009

LIGHT, GARY LYLE, transp. corp. exec.; b. St. Johns, Mich., July 20, 1937; s. Edward and Margaret L.; B.S., Ferris State Coll., 1962; m. Janet K. Henning, June 16, 1962; children—Paul, Mark, Michael. Audit mgr. Arthur Andersen & Co., Los Angeles/Indpls., 1962-69; asst. controller Stanray Corp., Chgo., 1969-71; audit mgr. Arthur Andersen & Co., Indpls., 1971-73; exec. v.p. Mayflower Corp., Indpls., 1973—. Served with USN, 1955-58. C.P.A. Mem. Am. Inst. C.P.A.'s, Fin. Execs. Inst. Club: Kiwanis. Home: 3460 Briar Pl Carmel IN 46032 Office: Mayflower Corp 9998 N Michigan Rd Carmel IN 46032

LIGHT, JAMES FOREST, univ. dean; b. Memphis, Nov. 5, 1921; s. Luther and Lois Ginevra (Billings) L.; B.A., U. Chgo., 1945, M.A., 1947; Ph.D., Syracuse U., 1953; m. Norma Rowena Neal, Mar. 8, 1948 (dec. 1959); children—Sheldon Neal, Matthew Forest, Jama Rowena; m. 2d, Amy Marcella Wolf, Dec. 20, 1959. Instr. U. Ky., 1947-48, Syracuse U., 1948-53; asso. prof. Radford Coll., 1953-56; asst. prof. Ind. State U., 1956-59, asso. prof., 1959-61, prof., 1961-65; Bernhard prof., chmn. dept. English, U. Bridgeport, 1965-71; dean Sch. of Humanities of Calif. State U., Fresno, 1971-72; dean of faculties Lehman Coll. of City U. N.Y., 1972-73, provost, 1973-79; dean Coll. Liberal Arts, So. Ill. U., Carbondale, 1979—; Fulbright prof. Keele U., Eng., 1963-64; vis. prof. City U. N.Y., summers 1966-69. Fellow Found. Econ. Edn., Yaddo Writers and Artists Colony. Mem. Modern Lang. Assn., AAUP, Nat. Council Tchrs. English, Ind. Coll. English Assn. (pres. 1962-63), New Eng. Coll. English Assn. (dir. 1969-71). Democrat. Author: Nathanael West: an Interpretive Study, rev. edit., 1971; John William DeForest, 1965; J.D. Salinger, 1967. Editor: The Modern Age, 3d rev. edit., 1976; Studies in All the Kings Men, 1971. Contbr. articles to profl. jours. Home: 900 Skyline Dr Carbondale IL 62901

LIGHT, KENNETH B., mfg. co. exec.; b. N.Y.C., June 2, 1932; s. Max and Mollie (Schein) Lichtenholtz; B.S., N.Y. U., 1954, LL.B. cum laude, 1957; M.B.A., U. Chgo., 1976; m. Judith Klein, May 28, 1961; children—Corey, Randi Beth, Allison. Admitted to N.Y. bar, 1957; partner firm Light & Light, Bklyn., 1958-61; asst. sec. Gen. Bronze Corp., Garden City, N.Y., 1961-69; sec., gen. counsel Allied Products Corp., Chgo., 1969-76, v.p., gen. counsel, 1976-79, sr. v.p., 1979—; dir. Aurora Corp. Ill., Chgo. Mem. Chgo. Bar Assn., N.Y.C. (v.p. 1967-69), Am. (dir. 1967-68) subcontractors assns., Chgo. Assn. Commerce and Industry. Home: 1825 Cavell Ave Highland Park IL 60035 Office: 10 S Riverside Plaza Chicago IL 60606

LIGHT, KENNETH FREEMAN, coll. adminstr.; b. Detroit, Jan. 22, 1922; s. Delbert Bertram and Hilma (Stolt) L.; B.S., U. Ill., 1949; M.A., Mich. State U., 1952, Ph.D., 1967; m. Shirley Claire Bower, Jan. 7, 1944; children—Karen Christine, Kevin Harold, Brian Curtis. Instr. mech. engring. dept. Mich. Tech. U., 1956-60, asso. prof., coordinator for tech. edn., 1960-65; vice chancellor for acad. affairs, v.p. for acad. affairs Lake Superior State Coll. of Mich. Tech. U., Sault Ste. Marie, Mich., 1965-76; pres. Oreg. Inst. Tech., Klamath Falls, 1976—. Pres. Upper Peninsula Health Edn. Corp., 1975-76; mem. Mich. Manpower Commn., 1973-74, Career and Vocat. Edn. Adv. Council, 1977—, Oreg. Manpower Commn., 1978—. Served with USAF, 1942-45. Mem. AAUP, Am. Soc. Engring. Edn., Am. Soc. Mil. Engrs., Phi Delta Kappa. Club: Rotary. Home: 1895 Park Klamath Falls OR 97601

LIGHT, (MARVIN) LAWRENCE, advt. agy. exec.; b. Montreal, Que., Can., June 12, 1941; s. Louis and Celia L.; B.S., McGill U., Montreal, 1962; M.A., Ohio State U., 1965, Ph.D., 1967; m. Joyce Wax, June 18, 1966; children—Laura, Michelle. Exec. v.p. Batten Barton Durstine & Osborn Inc., N.Y.C. Mem. Am. Mktg. Assn., Am. Psychol. Assn. Home: 11 Gatefield Dr Greenwich CT 06830 Office: 383 Madison Ave New York NY 10017

LIGHT, MURRAY BENJAMIN, newspaper editor; b. Bklyn., Oct. 14, 1926; s. Paul and Rose (Liatsk) L.; B.S., Bklyn. Coll., 1948; M.S. in Journalism, Northwestern U., 1949; m. Joan M. Cottrell; children—Lee (Mrs. John Scott Monier), Laura Jo, Jeffrey Eugene. Coll. stringer Bklyn. Eagle, 1946-48; copy editor New York Wold-Telegram, 1949; with Buffalo Evening News, 1949—, news editor, 1962-69, mng. editor for news, 1969—, editor, v.p., 1979—; Upstate chmn. New York Fair Trial Free Press Conf. Mem. bus. adv. bd. Nat. Alliance Businessmen, 1970-72; bd. dirs. Better Bus. Bur.; mem. parents bd. Bryn Mawr (Pa.) Coll., 1976-77; trustee Nichols Sch., Buffalo. Served with AUS, World War II; PTO. Mem. N.Y. State Soc. Newspaper Editors (pres. 1977), N.Y. State Pubs. Assn. (chmn. awards com.), Am. Soc. Newspaper Editors, A.P. Mng. Editors Assn., Frontier Press Club, Sigma Delta Chi, Kappa Tau Alpha. Home: 25 Oakland Pl Buffalo NY 14222 Office: Buffalo Evening News 1 News Plaza Buffalo NY 14240

LIGHT, WALTER FREDERICK, telecommunications co. exec.; b. Cobalt, Ont., Can., June 24, 1923; s. Herbert and Rosetta Elizabeth (Hoffman) L.; B.Sc. with honours, Queen's U., 1949; m. Margaret Anne Wylie Miller, July 8, 1950; children—Elizabeth Jean, Janice Catherine. Exec. v.p. operations Bell Can., Montreal, Que., 1970-74; pres., dir. No. Telecom Ltd., Montreal, 1974-79, pres., chief exec. officer, 1979—; dir. Royal Bank of Can., Hudson's Bay Oil and Gas Co. Ltd., Genstar Ltd. Bd. dirs. Canadian Exec. Service Overseas; bd. govs. Assos. Carleton U.; trustee Queen's U.; bd. govs. Montreal Museum Fine Arts. Served with RCAF, 1942-45. Fellow Engring. Inst. Can.; mem. Corp. Profl. Engrs. Que., Assn. Profl. Engrs. Ont., Elec. Mfrs. Club, C.D. Howe Research Inst. Clubs; Mount Royal, Forest and Stream, Masons. Home: 5 Normandy Dr Montreal PQ H3R 3H7 Canada Office: 1600 Dorchester Blvd W Montreal PQ H3H 1R1 Canada

LIGHTFOOT, EDWIN NIBLOCK, JR., chem. engr.; b. Milw., Sept. 25, 1925; s. Edwin Niblock and Harriett Anna (Grimm) L.; B.Ch.Ed., Cornell U., 1947, Ph.D. in Chem. Engring., 1951; m. Lila Smith, June 9, 1949; children—Theodore Ann, Edwin James, Nancy Lila, Robert William, David Thomas. Chem. engr. Gen. Foods, Hoboken, N.J., 1947, Charles Pfizer & Sons, Bklyn., 1950-53; asst. prof. biochem. engring. U. Wis., Madison, 1950-53, asso. prof. chem. engring., 1953-57, prof., 1957—; cons., lectr. in field; Fulbright research scholar Norwegian Tech. U., 1962; vis. prof. Tunghai U. and Chinese Petroleum Co., Taiwan, 1964, Stanford U., summer 1971, Danish Tech. U., 1971; Erskine fellow U. Canterbury, Christ Church, N.Z., 1972. Mem. Am. Inst. Chem. Engrs. (William H. Walker award 1975), Am. Chem. Soc., Nat. Acad. Engring., Sigma Xi, Alpha Chi Sigma. Author: (with others) Transport Phenomena, 1960; Transport Phenomena and Living Systems, 1974; contbr. numerous articles to profl. jours.; patentee in field. Office: 1415 Johnson Dr Madison WI 53706

LIGHTFOOT, GORDON MEREDITH, singer, songwriter; b. Orillia, Ont., Can., Nov. 17, 1938; s. Gordon Meredith and Jessie Vick (Trill) M.; student Westlake Coll. Music, Los Angeles, 1958; divorced; children—Fred, Ingrid. Singer, songwriter, 1959—; compositions include Early Morning Rain, 1965, Canadian Railroad Trilogy, 1967, If You Could Read My Mind, 1970, Sundown, 1974, Carefree Highway, 1974, The Wreck of the Edmund Fitzgerald, 1976, Race Among the Ruins, 1976. Decorated Order Can., 1970; named Top Folksinger, Juno Gold Leaf Awards, 1965, 66, 68, 69, 73, 74, 75, 76, 77, Top Male Vocalist, 1967, 70, 71, 72, 74, Composer of Year, 1972, 76; recipient awards for songs ASCAP, 71, 74, 76, 77; Pop Record of Year award Music Operators Am., 1974; Vanier award Canadian Jaycees, 1977; numerous Gold albums, Can., U.S., Australia; Platinum album for Sundown; Gold record for Sundown. Office: 350 Davenport Rd Toronto ON M5R 1K8 Canada

LIGHTNER, JERRY PRESTON, assn. exec.; b. St. Edward, Nebr., May 14, 1929; s. George Fox and Marion Viola (Preston) L.; B.S., Nebr. State Coll., Wayne, 1952; M.A., U. No. Colo., Greeley, 1954, Ed.D., 1970; m. Ardyce Stevens, Sept. 13, 1953 (div. 1966); children—Jon T., Jean M.; m. 2d, Magdalena de Kock, Feb. 8, 1969. Tchr. biology Utica (Nebr.) High Sch., 1952-53, Great Falls (Mont.) High Sch., 1954-64; exec. dir. Nat. Assn. Biology Tchrs., Inc., Washington, 1965-78; writer, cons., mem. gov. bd. Biol. Scis. Curriculum Study, Boulder, Colo. NSF fellow, U. S.D., 1958-59, Ind. U. grantee, 1964. Fellow AAAS (council 1968-78); life mem. Nat. Sci. Tchrs. Assn., Nat., Mont. edn. assns., U.S. Tennis Assn.; mem. Am. Inst. Biol. Scis., Nat. Assn. Research Sci. Teaching. Mng. editor Am. Biology Tchr., 1965-78; editor NABT News and Views, 1967-78; Am. editor Jour. Biol. Edn., 1974-79. Home: Route 1 Box 100 Aldie VA 22001

LIGHTSTONE, MARILYN, actress; b. Montreal, Que., Can., June 28, 1940; d. Manuel and Sophie (Shulman) Lightstone; B.A., McGill U., 1962; grad. Nat. Theatre Sch., 1965. Appeared in (films) Lies My Father Told Me (Best Actress award Canadian Film awards), 1976, In Praise of Older Women (Best Supporting Actress award Canadian Film awards), 1977; (plays) Miss Margarida (English lang. premiere), 1976; The Dybbuk, Mark Taper Forum (Los Angeles Drama Critics award), Los Angeles, 1975, Mary Queen of Scots, Charlottetown Festival, N.B., Can., 1974, King Lear, Lincoln Center, N.Y.C., 1972, The Seagull, Stratford Festival, Ont., 1968, Electra, St. Lawrence Centre, Toronto, Yard of the Sun, 1970, Billy the Kid, Stratford Festival, Ont., Mary and Joseph, Lorimar, 1979, Refugees, drama, opera, 1979; performer numerous TV shows, including The Adventurers, Man Alive, Witness to Yesterday, also radio and TV commls. Home: 15 Olympus Ave Toronto ON Canada Office: care Moses Znaimer 99 Queen St E Toronto ON M5C 2M1 Canada

LIGUTTI, LUIGI GINO, clergyman; b. Romans, Udine, Italy, Mar. 21, 1895; s. Spiridione and Theresa (Ciriani) L.; came to U.S., 1912, naturalized, 1918; A.B., St. Ambrose Coll., Davenport, Ia., 1914, LL.D., 1938; S.T.B., St. Mary's Sem., Balt., 1917; A.M., Cath. U. Am., 1918, LL.D., 1968; LL.D., Loyola U., New Orleans, 1947, St. Francis Xavier U., Antigonish, N.S., 1957, Drake U., 1964, Drew U., 1972. Ordained priest, Roman Catholic Ch., 1919; tchr. Dowling Coll., Des Moines, 1918-20; pastor, Woodbine, Ia., 1920-26, Granger, 1926-41; exec. sec. Nat. Catholic Rural Life Conf., Des Moines, 1941-49, exec. dir., 1949-58; dir. internat. affairs Nat. Cath. Rural Life Conf., Vatican City, 1958—. Cons. 2d Vatican Council, Commn. Lay Apostolate, mem. Pontifical Commn. for Justice of Peace; pres. Agrimission, 1971—. Apptd. ofcl. Permanent Observer for the Holy See with FAO, UN, 1949—; del. FAO convs. Recipient Nat. Peace award Cath. Assn. Internat. Peace; subject FAO-UN Agricola medal, 1978. Mem. Am. Acad. Polit. and Social Sci., Cath. Sociol. Soc., Friends of the Land. K.C. Author: Rural Roads to Security (with Reverend John C. Rawe, S.J.), 1939. Contbr. to Commweal, America, and other mags. Apptd. Domestic Prelate, 1939; canon St. Mary Major's Basilica in Rome; protonotary apostolic. Address: Palazzo San Calisto Vatican City Europe also 3801 Grand Ave Des Moines IA 50312

LIJINSKY, WILLIAM, biochemist; b. Dublin, Ireland, Oct. 19, 1928; s. Morris and Rebacca (Hershman) L.; came to U.S., 1951; B.Sc. with honours, U. Liverpool (Eng.), 1949, Ph.D., 1951; m. Rosalie K. Elespuru, June 10, 1973; 1 dau. by previous marriage, Sharon Anne. Asst. prof., then asso. prof. Chgo. Med. Sch., 1955-68; prof. biochemistry U. Nebr. Med. Sch., Omaha, 1968-71; group leader carcinogenesis program Oak Ridge Nat. Lab., 1971-76; dir. chem. carcinogenesis program Frederick (Md.) Cancer Research Center, 1976—. Mem. Biochem. Soc., Am. Chem. Soc., Am. Assn. Cancer Research, Am. Soc. Biol. Chemists, Environmental Mutagen Soc., Soc. Occupational and Environ. Health, Sigma Xi. Author research papers, revs. Home: Route 5 Box 311 Frederick MD 21701 Office: Frederick Cancer Research Center Frederick MD 21701

LIKELY, WADSWORTH, assn. exec., public relations cons.; b. N.Y.C., June 20, 1917; s. David Stanley and Gail (Rogers) L.; ed. Antioch Coll., New Sch. for Social Research m. Audrey R. Armstrong, June 30, 1973. Sci. writer Sci. Service, Inc., Washington, 1949-53; staff writer Am. Chem. Soc. News Service, 1960; writer N.Y. Herald Tribune, 1960; public info. cons. Internat. Rescue Com., 1961; medicine editor Newsweek, 1961-62; asso. editor, then mng. editor Nuclear Industry, monthly mag. Atomic Indsl. Forum, 1962-63, mng. editor, 1963-68; public relations adviser; chmn. N.Y. State Atomic and Space Devel. Authority, 1968-70; dir. public relations N.Y. Acad. Scis., 1970-73; public relations cons., N.Y.C., 1973—; exec. dir. Nat. Assn. Sci. Writers, Inc., pub. newsletter, 1978—. Served with U.S. Army, 1940-45, 53-59. Decorated Purple Heart. Mem. Am. Veterans Com. (a founder). Democrat. Address: 200 E 36th St New York NY 10016

LIKENS, GENE ELDEN, ecologist; b. Pierceton, Ind., Jan. 6, 1935; s. Benjamin and Josephine (Garner) L.; B.S., Manchester (Ind.) Coll., 1957, D.Sc. (hon.), 1979; M.S., U. Wis., 1959, Ph.D., 1962; children—Kathy, Gregory, Leslie. Asst. zoology Manchester Coll., 1955-57; grad. teaching asst. U. Wis., 1957-59, vis. lectr., 1963; instr. zoology, Dartmouth Coll., 1961, instr. biol. scis., 1963, asst. prof., then asso. prof., 1963-69; mem. faculty Cornell U., 1969—, prof. ecology, 1972—; vis. prof. Center Advanced Research, also dept. environ. scis. U. Va., Charlottesville, 1978-79; lectr. Williams Summer Inst. Coll. Tchrs., 1966, 67, Drew Summer Inst. Coll. Tchrs., 1968, Cornell U. Alumni Assn., 1978; Paul C. Lemon ecology lectr. SUNY, Albany, 1978; chmn. New Eng. div. task force conservation aquatic ecosystems U.S. Internat. Biol. Program, 1966-67; vis. asso. ecologist Brookhaven Nat. Lab., 1968; cons. in field, mem. numerous govt. and sci. panels, participant numerous confs. Recipient Conservation award Am. Motors Corp., 1969; NATO sr. fellow, 1969; Guggenheim fellow, 1972-73; grantee NSF. Fellow AAAS; mem. Ecol. Soc. Am. (chmn. study com. 1971-74, v.p. 1978-79), Am. Soc. Limnology and Oceanography (pres. 1976-77), Am. Acad. Arts and Scis., Am. Polar Soc., Explorers Club, Freshwater Biol. Assn., Internat. Assn. Gt. Lakes Research, Internat. Water Resources Assn. (charter), Soc. Internat. Limnologiae (nat. rep.), Sigma Xi, Gamma Alpha, Phi Sigma. Methodist. Author books and papers in field. Home: 112 Crest Ln Ithaca NY 14850 Office: 221 Langmuir Lab Cornell Univ Ithaca NY 14850

LIKER, ALAN DONALD, lawyer; b. Bklyn., Nov. 13, 1937; s. Jack and Goldi (Waldman) L.; B.B.A., Coll. City N.Y., 1959; LL.B., N.Y. U., 1961, LL.M., 1962; m. Gail Waltman, June 5, 1960; children—Harley, Renee Ester, Elisa. Admitted to Calif. bar, 1968; teaching fellow Harvard Law Sch. Internat. Program in Taxation, 1962-64; prof. law U. N.Mex. Sch. Law, 1964-66, U. Calif. Law Sch., Los Angeles, 1966-67; prof. law U. So. Calif. Law Sch., 1967-68, asst. dir. Tax Inst., 1968, chmn. panel taxation Calif. Continuing Edn. of Bar, also chmn. panel recent devel. in tax practice; partner firm Nelson, Liker & Merrifield, 1970-76; prin. Xerox Devel. Corp., 1976—; legal cons. U.S. Treasury Dept., 1964-66. Bd. dirs. Hillel Hebrew Acad. Kennison fellow grad. tax program N.Y. U., 1962. Mem. Am., Los Angeles County bar assns., State Bar Calif. Jewish. Author: (with H. Schwartz) The Widow's Election, 1967; New Horizons in the Taxation of Trusts, 1968. Home: 10560 Wyton Dr Westwood CA 90024 Office: 9200 Sunset Blvd Los Angeles CA 90069

LIKERT, RENSIS, social scientist, educator; b. Cheyenne, Wyo., Aug. 5, 1903; s. George Herbert and Cornelia A. (Zonne) L.; A.B., U. Mich., 1926; Ph.D., Columbia U., 1932; Dr. Honoris Causa, U. Tilburg (Netherlands) 1967; m. Jane Gibson, Aug. 31, 1928; children—Elizabeth Jane (Mrs. Martin David), Patricia Anne (Mrs. James E. Pohlman). Instr., N.Y. U., later asst. prof.; head research dept. Life Ins. Sales Research Bur.; head div. program surveys B.A.E., Dept. Agr.; dir. morale div. U.S. Strategic Bombing Survey, dir. Survey Research Center, U. Mich., 1946-49, dir. Inst. for Social Research, 1949-70, dir. emeritus, 1971—, prof. psychology and sociology emeritus; chmn. bd. Rensis Likert Asso., Inc., 1971—. Recipient Medal of Freedom, 1946; Paul D. Converse award Marketing Symposium, U. Ill., 1955; James A. Hamilton Hosp. Adminstrs. award, 1961; Publs. award Orgn. Devel. Council, 1962; McKinsey Found. Book award Am. Acad. Mgmt., 1962; Warner W. Stockberger award Soc. Personnel Adminstrn., 1963; Distinguished Faculty Achievement award U. Mich., 1963; Human Relations award Soc. for Advancement Mgmt., 1967; award for profl. achievement Am. Bd. Examiners in Profl. Psychology, 1968; Outstanding Achievement award Am. Soc. for Tng. and Devel., 1969; Exceptionally Distinguished Achievement award Am. Assn. for Pub. Opinion Research, 1973. Fellow Am. Psychol. Assn. (dir. 1950-53); mem. Am. Statis. Assn. (v.p. 1953-55, pres. 1958); mem. Acad. Mgmt., Am. Sociol. Assn., Internat. Soc. Polit. Psychology, Internat. Assn. Applied Psychology, Am. Soc. Pub. Adminstrn., AAAS, Nat. Acad. Pub. Adminstrn., Inst. Mgmt. Scis., Sigma Xi, Phi Kappa Phi, Tau Beta Pi. Author: (with Gardner Murphy) Public Opinion and the Individual, 1938; Morale and Agency Management, 1940; New Patterns of Management, 1961; The Human Organization; Its Management and Value, 1967; (with Jane Gibson Likert) New Ways of Managing Conflict, 1976. Editor: (with S.P. Hayes) Some Applications of Behaviorial Research, 1957. Contbr. articles to jours. Home: 860 Mokulua Dr Kailua HI 96734 Office: 630 City Center Bldg Ann Arbor MI 48108

LIKINS, PETER WILLIAM, educator; b. Tracy, Calif., July 4, 1936; s. Ennis Blaine and Dorothy Louise (Medlin) L.; B.S. in C.E., Stanford, 1957, Ph.D. in Engring. Mechanics, 1965; S.M. in C.E., Mass. Inst. Tech., 1958; m. Patricia Ruth Kitsmiller, Dec. 18, 1955; children—Teresa, Lora, Paul, Linda, Krista, John. Devel. engr. Jet Propulsion Lab., Pasadena, Calif., 1958-60; asst. prof. engring. U. Calif., Los Angeles, 1964-69, asso. prof., 1969-72, prof., 1972-76, asst. dean, 1974-75, asso. dean, 1975-76; dean engring. and applied sci. Columbia, 1976—. Engring. cons. U.S. and fgn. corps. and govt. agys., 1965—. Ford Found. fellow, 1970-72. Fellow Am. Inst. Aeros. and Astronautics (asso.); mem. ASME, Am. Soc. Engring. Edn., Phi Beta Kappa, Sigma Xi, Tau Beta Pi. Author: Elements of Engineering

Mechanics, 1973. Contbr. articles to profl. jours. Home: 49 Oak Ave Park Ridge NJ 07656 Office: 510 Seeley Mudd Bldg Columbia U New York City NY 10027

LIKOFF, WILLIAM, cardiologist, coll. and hosp. adminstr.; b. Phila., Feb. 5, 1912; s. Morris Aaron and Goldie (Sklaroff) L.; B.A., Darmouth Coll., 1933; M.D., Hahnemann Med. Coll., 1938; m. Mariell Jessup Moore, Oct. 22, 1978; children—Jane Ellen Likoff Yudis, Joy Likoff Kantor. Intern, Mt. Sinai Hosp., Phila., 1938-39, resident in pathology, 1939-40, in internal medicine, 1940-42; resident in cardiology Peter Bent Brigham Hosp., Boston, 1942-43; practice medicine specializing in cardiology, Phila., 1947—; asst. prof. medicine Hahnemann Med. Coll. and Hosp., to 1946, asso. prof., 1946-51, prof., 1951-64, pres., chief exec. officer, 1977—, mem. staff; Wilson-Myers lectr. Mich. Heart Assn., 1977; Ann. lectr. Am. Heart Assn./Southeastern Pa., 1978. Served with U.S. Army, 1943-46. Recipient Ann. Gold medal Phi Lambda Kappa, 1979, Father Clarence E. Shaffrey, S.D. award St. Joseph U., 1979; William Likoff Alumni Lectureship established by Alumni Assn. Hahnemann Med. Coll. and Hosp., 1978. Fellow Am. Coll. Cardiology (Disting.; pres. 1967-68, editor-in-chief extended learning program 1977—), Am. Coll. Chest Physicians; mem. Pa. Heart Assn., Am. Acad. Scis., Pa. Med. Soc., Heart Assn. Southeastern Pa. (pres. 1965-66), Phila. Acad. Cardiology (founding physician 1978). Jewish. Clubs: Locust, Hahnemann. Author books, the most recent being: (with others) Your Heart, 1972, Protegez Votre Coeur Elsevier Sequola, 1975; editorial bd. Am. Heart Jour., 1970-74; cons. editor Clin. Trends in Cardiology, 1977—. Office: 230 N Broad St Philadelphia PA 19102

LILHOLT, HAROLD CARL, consumer product co. exec.; b. Honesdale, Pa., Sept. 9, 1930; s. Harold Luther and Margaret Jeanette (Myers) L.; B.S., Syracuse U., 1955; M.B.A., Kent State U., 1961; m. Clare Jeanette Willey, June 11, 1955; children—Patricia, Paul, David. Fin. dir. Europe, B.F. Goodrich Co., The Hague, Netherlands, 1955-67; exec. v.p., treas. Oneida, Ltd. (N.Y.), 1967—, also dir.; dir. Camden Wire Co., Leavens; mem. adv. bd., mem. internat. adv. council Lincoln Banks, 1978-79. Vice chmn. bd. govs. Oneida City Hosp., 1976-79; mem. Central N.Y. State Health Systems Agy., 1978-79. Served with U.S. Army, 1948-51. Republican. Presbyterian. Clubs: DAV, Am. Legion. Home: 158 Fairview Ave Oneida NY 13421 Office: Oneida Ltd Kenwood Ave Oneida NY 13421

LILIENFELD, ABRAHAM MORRIS, epidemiologist, educator; b. N.Y.C., Nov. 13, 1920; s. Joel and Eugenia (Kugler) L.; A.B., Johns Hopkins, 1941, M.P.H., 1949; M.D., U. Md., 1944, Sc.D. (hon.), 1975; m. Lorraine Zemil, July 18, 1943; children—Julia, Saul, David. Intern, resident obstetrics Luth. Hosp., Balt., 1944-46; asso. pub. health physician N.Y. Dept. Health, 1949-50; dir. So. health dist. Balt. Dept. Health, 1949-52; asst. prof. epidemiology Johns Hopkins, 1952-54, prof. chronic diseases, chmn. dept., 1958-70, prof., chmn. dept. epidemiology, 1970-75, univ. distinguished service prof., 1975—; dir. gamma globulin evaluation center USPHS, 1952; chief dept. statistics and epidemiology Roswell Park Meml. Inst., 1954-58. Mem. Nat. Advisory Heart Council, 1962-66; chmn. NIH joint council subcom. on cerebrovascular disease, 1966-68; research adv. council Am. Cancer Soc., 1965-70; staff dir. President's Commn. Heart Disease Cancer and Stroke, 1964-67; chmn. adv. council preventive medicine Md. Dept. Health, 1964-68. Trustee Md. Heart Assn.; exec. bd. Md. div. Am. Cancer Soc., 1964-70; trustee Balt. Hebrew Coll., 1973—, chmn., 1974-77. Recipient Bronfman award pub. health achievement Am. Pub. Health Assn., 1968; John Snow award for contbns. to epidemiology, 1975; Research Career award NIH, 1962. Fellow Am. Pub. Health Assn., Am. Coll. Preventive Medicine, Am. Statis. Assn.; mem. Am. Epidemiol. Soc. (pres. 1970-71), AAAS, Soc. Epidemiol. Research, Inst. Medicine of Nat. Acad. Scis. Bd. overseers Am. Jour. Epidemiology; bd. editors Postgrad. Medicine, Preventive Medicine. Home: 3203 Old Post Dr Pikesville MD 21208

LILIENFIELD, LAWRENCE SPENCER, physiologist; b. Bklyn., May 5, 1927; s. Henry Jacob and Lee (Markman) L.; B.S., Villanova U., 1945; M.D., Georgetown U., 1949, M.S., 1954, Ph.D., 1956; m. Eleanor Marion Russ, Oct. 22, 1950; children—Jan, Adele, Lisa. Intern, Georgetown U. Hosp., 1949-50, resident in internal medicine, 1952-54; instr. medicine Georgetown U., Washington, 1954-58, asst. prof., 1958-61, asso. prof., 1961-64, prof., chmn. dept. physiology and biophysics, 1964—; cons. in field. Bd. dirs., chmn. research Washington Heart Assn.; mem. med. adv. bd. Am. Heart Assn. Served with USNR, 1944-46, USAF, 1950-52. USPHS Research Career award, 1963. Diplomate Am. Bd. Internal Medicine. Fellow A.C.P.; mem. Am. Soc. Clin. Investigation, Am. Physiol. Soc., Am. Heart Assn., Biophys. Soc., Soc. Exptl. Biology and Medicine, Am. Fedn. Clin. Research, Alpha Omega Alpha. Contbr. articles to profl. jours.; editorial bd. Am. Jour. Physiology, 1963-73. Home: 6304 Maiden Ln Bethesda MD 20034 Office: Georgetown U 3900 Reservoir Rd NE Washington DC 20007

LILIENTHAL, ALFRED M., author, editor; b. N.Y.C., Dec. 15, 1915; s. Herbert and Lottye (Kohn) L.; B.A., Cornell U., Ithaca, N.Y., 1934; LL.B., Columbia U., 1938, J.D., 1969. Admitted to N.Y. bar, 1938; with Bennet, House & Couts, N.Y.C., 1939-41, State Dept., 1942-43, 45-48; cons. U.S. del. UN San Francisco Conf., 1945; adminstrv. practice, 1947-50; editor, pub. Middle East Perspective, monthly newsletter; lectr. on Middle East at numerous colls. throughout U.S. and fgn. countries, 1951—; frequent guest TV and radio news commentator on Middle East devels., 1960-75; lectr. cultural symposium United Arab Emirates, Libya and Lebanon; polit. columnist daily Al Qabas, Kuwait, 1976-77; accredited corr. to UN; chmn. Coalition On the Middle East. Pres., Republican First Voters League, 1940; Fusion Party candidate for N.Y.C. Council, 1941; leader fight against Communist controlled Am. Youth Congress, 1941. Served with AUS, 1943-45. Club: Cornell of N.Y. Author: Which Way to World Government, 1949; What Price Israel?, 1954; There Goes the Middle East, 1957; Studies in Twentieth Century Diplomacy, 1959; The Other Side of the Coin, 1965; The Zionist Connection, 1978; contbr. to book Zionism-The Dream and the Reality, 1974; also numerous mag. articles and syndicated newspieces. Office: 850 7th Ave New York City NY 10019

LILIENTHAL, DAVID ELI, bus. cons., writer; b. Morton, Ill., July 8, 1899; s. Leo and Minna (Rosenak) L.; A.B., DePauw U., 1920, LL.D., 1945; LL.B., Harvard, 1923; LL.D., Lehigh U., 1949, Mich. State Coll., 1949, Boston U., 1952, Universidad de los Andes, Columbia, 1954, U. Calif. at Los Angeles, 1964, Ind. U., 1965; Dr. Pub. Adminstrn., U. Ill., 1967; m. Helen Marian Lamb, Sept. 4, 1923; children—Nancy Alice (Mrs. Bromberger), David Eli Jr. Admitted to Ill. bar, 1923; practice law, Chgo., 1923-31; mem. Wis. Pub. Service Commn., 1931-33; dir. TVA, 1933-41, chmn. 1941-46; chmn. A.E.C., 1946-50; chmn. bd., chief exec. officer Devel. and Resources Corp., 1955-79; adviser pres. Republic Colombia, 1954, co-chmn. Joint Postwar Devel. Group, Vietnam, 1967-70 chmn. U.S. State Dept. bd. cons. Internat. Control Atomic Energy, 1946; mem. Council Fgn. Relations. Trustee Twentieth Century Fund, Com. Econ. Devel. Recipient Progressive Farmer award, 1945; Cath. Com. South award, 1946; Freedom award, 1949; Pub. Welfare medal Nat. Acad. Sci., 1951; comendador de la Orden el Sol del Peru, 1964; comendador Orden de Rio Branco (Brazil), 1972. Mem. Am. Acad. Arts and Sci., Am. Philos. Soc., Authors Guild, Phi Beta Kappa. Club: Century (N.Y.C.). Author: TVA: Democracy on the March, 1944; This I Do Believe, 1949; Big Business A New Era, 1953; The Multinational Corporation, 1960; Change, Hope, and the Bomb, 1963; Journals of David E. Lilienthal, Vols. I and II, 1964, Volume III, 1966, Vol. IV, 1969, Vol. V, 1971, Vol. VI, 1976; Management: A Humanist Art, 1967. Home: 88 Battle Rd Princeton NJ 08540 Office: 1230 Ave of Americas New York NY 10020

LILIENTHAL, JAMES RICHARD, engr.; b. N.Y.C., Aug. 14, 1916; s. August Beekman and Mathilda (Schreiner) L.; student Coll. City N.Y., 1933-34; B.S. in Naval Architecture and Marine Engring., Webb. Inst. Naval Architecture, 1938; m. Elizabeth Haworth, May 27, 1944; children—Marguerite, Richard B., James H., Ann E. Chief engr. Stability Meter Corp., N.Y.C., 1938-40; product engr. Sperry Gyroscope Co., N.Y.C., 1940-47; group leader Los Alamos Sci. Lab., 1947-67, asst. div. leader, 1967-77. Mem. Los Alamos Town Council, 1948-49; mem. bd. assos. St. John's Coll., Santa Fe, 1966-72. Chmn. bd. trustees Mesa Pub. Library, Los Alamos, 1953-55. Registered profl. engr., N.Y., N.Mex. Fellow Am. Nuclear Soc. (nat. v.p., pres. 1972-73, past dir.); mem. N.Y. Acad. Scis. (emeritus). Home: 1964 Juniper St Los Alamos NM 87544

LILJEGREN, FRANK SIGFRID, artist, art assn. ofcl.; b. N.Y.C., Feb. 23, 1930; s. Josef Sigfrid and Ester (Davidsson) L.; student Art Students League, N.Y.C., 1950-55; m. Donna Kathryn Hallam, Oct. 12, 1957. Exhibited at Suffolk Mus., Stonybrook, N.Y., Springfield (Mass.) Mus., Marion Kugler McNay Art Inst., San Antonio, Philbrook Mus., Tulsa, N.A.D., N.Y.C., New Britain (Conn.) Mus. Am. Art; represented in permanent collections Art Students League, Manhattan Savs. Bank, N.Y.C., Am. Ednl. Pubs. Inst., N.Y.C., New Britain Mus. Am. Art. Instr. painting, drawing, composition Westchester County Center, White Plains, N.Y., 1967-77, Art Students League, 1974-75, Wassenberg Art Center, Van Wert, Ohio, 1977—; corr. sec. Allied Artists Am., N.Y.C., 1967, exhbn. chmn., 1968—, pres., 1970-72, also dir. Served with AUS, 1951. Recipient numerous awards for still life oil paintings. Mem. Fine Arts Fedn. N.Y., Art Students League (life), Acad. Artists Assn., Council Am. Artists Socs., Artists Fellowship. Club: Salmagundi. Office: 203 S Cherry St Van Wert OH 45891. *The best advice I could give young artists is to first learn their craft to the fullest so that they can then be free to express themselves in what ever style and medium they then choose to work. Last but not least, they should have self-respect and great love for what they are doing.*

LILL, GORDON GRIGSBY, phys. scientist; b. Mt. Hope, Kans., Feb. 23, 1918; s. Percy Eugene and Helen Elizabeth (Bottomly) L.; B.S., Kans. State Coll., 1940, M.S., 1946; student U. Calif. at Berkeley, 1946-47; D.Sc. (hon.), U. Miami, 1964; m. Mildred Adams, Apr. 30, 1943; children—Candace Ann, Christopher Grigsby. Asst. chief geol. party Kans. State Hwy. Commn., 1941; head geophysics br. Office Naval Research, 1947-59, earth sci. adviser, 1960-61; sr. sci. adviser Lockheed Aircraft Corp., 1961-62, 66-70, corporate research adviser, 1962-64, dir. Project Mohole, 1964-66, sr. sci. advisor, 1966-70; dep. dir. Nat. Ocean Survey, Dept. Commerce, 1970-79. Cons. com. geography and geophysics Research Devel. Bd., Nat. Mil. Establishment, 1947-53; pvt. geol. research U.S. Nat. Mus.; mem. Bikini Sci. Resurvey, 1947; mineral. survey, Liberia, West Africa, 1949-50; mem. Brussels meeting Comitè Spl. d'lannee Geophysique Internationale, 1955, Moscow, 1958; chmn. tech. panel oceanography Internat. Geophys. Year, 1957-58; mem. AMSOC com. Nat. Acad. Scis.-NCR; vice chmn. Calif. Adv. Commn. on Marine and Coastal Resources, 1968-70. Bd. dirs. Oceanographic Fund, 1968-70. Served as lt. comdr. USNR, 1941-45. Recipient Distinguished Service award Kans. State U., 1957. Fellow AAAS, Geol. Soc. Am.; mem. Am. Geophys. Union, Phi Kappa Phi, Sigma Gamma Epsilon. Club: Cosmos. Contbr. sci. articles to profl. jours. Home: 9606 Hillridge Dr Kensington MD 20795

LILLEHEI, CLARENCE WALTON, surgeon; b. Mpls., Oct. 23, 1918; s. Clarence Ingewald and Elizabeth Lillian (Walton) L.; B.S., U. Minn., 1939, M.D., 1942, M.S. in Physiology, 1951, Ph.D. in Surgery, 1951; Dr. Medicinae h.c., U. Oslo, 1976; m. Katherine Ruth Lindberg, Dec. 31, 1946; children—Kimberle Rae (Mrs. Allen Loken), Craig Walton, Kevin Owen, Clark William. Instr. dept. surgery U. Minn. Med. Sch., 1949-51, asso. prof. surgery, 1951-56, prof. surgery, 1956-67; chmn. dept. surgery Cornell U. Med. Center, N.Y.C., 1967-74, Lewis Atterbury Stimson prof. surgery Med. Coll., 1967-74; surgeon-in chief N.Y. Hosp., N.Y.C., 1967-70; pvt. practice medicine, 1942—, specializing gen., thoracic and cardiovascular surgery, 1945—. Served lt. col. M.C., AUS, 1942-46. Recipient Theobald-Smith award A.A.A.S., 1951; 1st prize Am. Coll. Coll. Chest Physicians, 1952; Lasker award, 1955; Ida. B. Gould award A.A.A.S., 1957; Hektoen Gold medal A.M.A., 1957; Oscar B. Hunter award Am. Therapeutic Soc., 1958; Purdue Frederick Med. Achievement Travel award Internat. Consul for Health, 1958; Malcom F. Rogers Meml. award Wis. Heart Assn., 1962; Cummings Humanitarian award Am. Coll. Cardiology, 1963, Gairdner Found. Internat. award, 1963; Honor award Stevens Inst. Tech., 1967; Gold Plate award Am. Acad. Achievement, 1968; decorated Officer Order of Leopold (Belgium). Diplomate Am. Bd. Surgery, 1951, Am. Bd. Thoracic Surgery, 1954. Fellow A.C.S., Am. Coll. Chest Physicians, Am. Coll. Cardiology (pres. 1966-67), Am. Coll. Angiology, Am. Heart Assn., Halsted Soc., Internat. Soc. Surgery, Allen O. Whipple Surg. Soc., Pan Am. Med. Soc., Royal Soc. Medicine (Gt. Britain), Soc. Thoracic Surgery; mem. AMA (Billings silver medal 1972), Am. Surg. Assn., Am. Assn. Thoracic Surgery, Soc. U. Surgeons, Soc. Exptl. Biology and Medicine, A.A.A.S., Internat. Cardiovascular Soc., Soc. Vascular Surgery, Sigma Xi. Home: 73 Otis Ln Saint Paul MN 55104

LILLEHEI, RICHARD CARLTON, surgeon, med. researcher, educator; b. Mpls., Dec. 10, 1927; s. Clarence I. and Elizabeth L. (Walton) L.; B.A. magna cum laude, U. Minn., 1948, B.S., 1949, M.D., 1951, Ph.D., 1960; m. Betty Jeanne Larsen, Dec. 20, 1952; children—Richard Carlton, Theodore J., John C., James L. Intern, Hennepin County Gen. Hosp., Mpls., 1951-52; resident surgeon U. Minn. Health Scis. Center, Mpls., 1952-54, 56-59, resident cardiovascular surgeon, 1959-60, asst. prof. surgery, 1960-62, asso. prof., 1962-66, prof., 1966—. Served as capt. M.C., AUS, 1954-56. Recipient Hektoen gold medal AMA, 1964, Irving S. Cutter gold medal Phi Rho Sigma, 1976; named Man of Year, Minn. Jr. C. of C., 1962. Mem. Phi Beta Kappa, Sigma Xi, Alpha Omega Alpha. Contbr. articles to profl. jours., chpts. in books. Finished Boston Marathon, 1972-79. Home: 1814 Oliver Ave S Minneapolis MN 55405

LILLER, WILLIAM, educator; b. Phila., Apr. 1, 1927; s. Carroll K. and Catherine (Dellinger) L.; A.B., Harvard U., 1949; M.A., U. Mich., 1951, Ph.D., 1953; m. Lorraine Dundas, Apr. 6, 1951 (div. 1958); 1 dau., Tamara Kay; m. 2d, Martha Hazen, June 20, 1959; children—John Avery, Hilary Webb. Supt. Harvard Meteor Expdn., Las Cruces, N.Mex., 1952-53; from instr. to asso. prof. astronomy U. Mich., 1953-60; prof. astronomy Harvard and Radcliffe Coll., 1960-62, Robert Wheeler Willson prof. applied astronomy, 1962—, chmn. dept. astronomy, 1960-66, master Adams House, Harvard, 1968-73. Guggenheim fellow, 1964-65. Served with USNR, 1945-46. Mem. Internat. Astron. Union, Am. Astron. Soc. (chmn. com. astron. motion pictures 1960-64, councillor 1962-65), Royal Astron. Soc., Am. Acad. Arts and Sci., Astron. Soc. Pacific. Editor: Space Astrophysics, 1961. Office: Harvard Coll Observatory 60 Gordon St Cambridge MA 02138

LILLEVANG, OMAR JOHANSEN, civil engr.; b. Los Angeles, Sept. 8, 1914; s. Gunnar Johansen and Nina (Christiansen) L.; A.A., Los Angeles Jr. Coll., 1935; B.S., U. Calif., Berkeley, 1937, postgrad., 1950-51; m. D. Miriam Guest, Sept. 10, 1939; children—Ralph Glen, Carol Ellen. Topographic surveyor Calif. Hwy. Commn., 1937; asst. engr. Coachella Valley County (Calif.) Water and Stormwater Dist., 1938; harbor constrn. engr., 1939-40; cantonment design and constrn. engr., 1941; constrn. engr. dams, aqueduct, tunnel, pump plants, 1942; water resources analyst, 1943; with Leeds, Hill, Barnard and Jewett, Cons. Engrs., and successors, Los Angeles, 1938-43, 46-61, supervising engr., 1950-61; v.p., dir. Leeds, Hill & Jewett Inc.-Cons. Engrs., Los Angeles, 1961-64; cons. civil engring., especially for harbors, rivers, lakes, seas, coastal processes, Los Angeles, 1964—; mem. advisory panel for shore erosion protection, U.S. Army Chief Engrs. Trustee, chmn. bldg. com. Plymouth Congregational Ch. of Whittier, Calif. Served with USN, 1943-46. Registered profl. engr., Alaska, Calif., Hawaii, N.J., Oreg., Utah, Wash., Wis. Fellow ASCE (mem. task groups), Am. Cons. Engrs. Council; mem. Am. Shore Beach Preservation Assn. (dir.), Permanent Internat. Assn. Navigation Congresses, Am. Assn. Port Authorities, Soc. Am. Mil. Engrs., U.S. Power Squadron. Club: Rotary Internat. Contbr. articles to profl. jours. including Shore & Beach mag. Home: 14318 Eastridge Dr Whittier CA 90602 Office: 13601 Whittier Blvd Suite 400 Whittier CA 90605

LILLEY, ROBERT FRANCIS, textile co. exec.; b. Mass., May 29, 1939; s. John F. and Helen M. (Mahoney) L.; B.S., Northeastern U., 1962; M.B.A., Boston Coll., 1967; grad. advanced mgmt. program Harvard U., 1977; m. Nancy C. Latshaw, Aug. 4, 1962; children—Robert, Michael, Kathleen. Systems analyst Ratheon Co., 1962-64; with Am. Thread Co., Stamford, Conn., 1964—, gen. corp. controller, 1975-78, v.p., sec., treas., 1978-79, pres., chief exec. officer, 1979—; dir. Atcot Corp., Calico USA Ltd. Dir., Northeastern U. Mem. Am. Textile Mfrs. Assn., N.C. Textile Assn. (dir.). Home: 22 Red Fox Ln Trumbull CT 06611 Office: High Ridge Park Stamford CT 06905

LILLEY, THEODORE ROBERT, assn. exec.; b. Paterson, N.J., Jan. 11, 1923; s. Ernest Raymond and Antoinette Eleanor (Hartmann) L.; B.A. cum laude, N.Y. U., 1946; M.B.A., Columbia U., 1948; m. Marguerite Anne Gallman, Jan. 27, 1951; children—Cheryl Anne, Wayne Robert, Ross Warren. With Standard Oil Co. (N.J.), 1948-64, investment mgr., 1956-62, fin. mgr., 1962-64; asst. treas. Esso Internat. Inc., 1964-69; v.p. Tchr. Ins. and Annuity Assn. and Coll. Retirement Equities Fund, 1969-72; exec. dir. Fin. Analysts Fedn., N.Y.C., 1972-73, pres., 1973—; mem. advisory council Fin. Acctg. Standards Bd., 1976. Mem. bd. nat. missions United Presbyn. Ch. U.S.A., 1966-72, mem. United Presbyn. Found., 1972—. Bd. dirs. Near East Found., 1970—; trustee Ramapo Coll. Served to 1st lt. inf. AUS, 1943-46; ETO. Decorated Bronze Star, Purple Heart. Chartered financial analyst. Mem. Phi Beta Kappa, Phi Lambda Upsilon, Beta Gamma Sigma. Home: 26 Thatcher Rd Tenafly NJ 07670 Office: 1633 Broadway New York NY 10019

LILLEY, TOM, orgn. exec.; b. Bluefield, W.Va., Aug. 13, 1912; s. Charles Ellis and Minnie Alice (Holland) L.; B.A., Harvard, 1934, M.B.A., 1936; m. Nancy Clegg, Dec. 27, 1936; children—Anne, Cynthia, Susan. Indsl. dept. Lehman Bros., N.Y.C., 1936-40; staff Burlington Mills, Greensboro, N.C., 1941-42; asso. prof., asst. dir. research Harvard Bus. Sch., 1942-48; successively mem. controller's office Ford div., product planning mgr., asst. gen. mgr. internat. div. Ford Motor Co., v.p. internat. staff, 1948-65; dir. Export-Import Bank of U.S., 1965-72; treas. Population Crisis Com., Washington, 1974—; dir. Huyck Corp. Past mem. Internat. Road Fedn., Nat. Fgn. Trade Council, Nat. Export Expansion Council, U.S. Council Internat. C. of C. (trustee). Presbyn. Home: 1522 34th St NW Washington DC 20007 Office: Population Crisis Com 1120 19th St NW Suite 550 Washington DC 20036

LILLIE, BEATRICE (LADY PEEL), actress; b. Toronto, Ont., Can., May 29, 1894; d. John and Lucie (Shaw) Lillie; ed. St. Agnes Coll., Belleville, Ont.; m. Sir Robert Peel (dec. 1934); 1 son, Robert (killed while with Royal Navy in Far East, 1942). Made first stage appearance in Not Likely, London, Eng., 1914; first N.Y. appearance at Times Square Theatre in Andre Charlot's Revue of 1924; has appeared in many plays in London and N.Y.; plays in N.Y. include Charlot's Revue of 1926, Oh, Please, 1926, She's My Baby, 1928, This Year of Grace, 1928, The Third Little Show, 1931, Too True To Be Good by George Bernard Shaw, 1932, Walk a Little Faster, 1932, At Home Abroad, 1935, The Show is On, 1936, Set to Music, 1939, Seven Lively Arts, 1944, Inside U.S.A., 1948-49, An Evening with Beatrice Lillie, 1952-53, Golden Jubilee edit. Ziegfeld Follies, 1957, High Spirits, 1964-65. Motion pictures: Exit Smiling, 1926, Doctor Rhythm, 1938, On Approval, 1943, Around the World in 80 days, 1955, Thoroughly Modern Millie, 1967, many others; numerous radio and TV appearances; during World War II entertained allied troops in England, Europe, Middle East and North Africa. Decorated by Gen. Charles de Gaulle; awarded African Star; other war citations and service ribbons; Donaldson award of 1944-45; 1948 citation by Nat. Conf. of Christians and Jews; citation as Greatest Comedienne of All Time, Am. Fedn. Women's Philanthropies, 1953; Spl. Antoinette Perry award for distinguished contbn. to theatre, 1953; Sarah Siddons award, 1954, Outer Circle award, 1964. Author: (autobiography) Every Other Inch a Lady, 1972. Address: case S Medina 61 Broadway New York NY 10006*

LILLIE, JOHN MITCHELL, salt co. exec.; b. Chgo., Feb. 2, 1937; s. Walter Theodore and Mary Ann (Hatch) L.; B.S., Stanford, 1959, M.S., M.B.A., 1962-64; m. Daryl Lee Harvey, Sept. 1, 1967; children—Alissa Ann, Theodore Perry. Various positions including dir. systems devel., also asst. to pres. Boise Cascade Corp., 1964-68; v.p., chief financial officer Arcata Nat. Corp., Menlo Park, Calif., 1968-70, exec. v.p., chief operating officer, 1970-72; pres., chief exec. officer Leslie Salt Co., Newark, Calif., 1972-79; exec. v.p. Lucky Stores Inc., Dublin, Calif., 1979—; dir. Spectra Physics Inc. Mem. Beta Theta Pi, Tau Beta Pi. Office: 6300 Clark Ave Dublin CA 94566

LILLIENSTEIN, MAXWELL JULIUS, lawyer; b. Bklyn., Dec. 18, 1927; s. Benjamin and Lillian (Camporeale) L.; B. Social Scis. cum laude, Coll. City N.Y., 1949; LL.B., Columbia, 1952; m. Janet Newman, June 23, 1951; children—Steven, Robert, Carol. Admitted to N.Y. bar, 1952; partner Friedberg, Blue & Rich, N.Y.C., 1958-63, Rich, Krinsly, Katz, Lillienstein, N.Y.C., 1963—; gen. counsel Am. Booksellers Assn. Pres. Maxwell Fund, 1967-72; dir. numerous corps.; investment adviser. Pres. Ardsley (N.Y.) Democratic Club, Westchester County, 1966-67, mem. exec. bd., 1966-70; Westchester County Dem. committeeman; trustee Village of Ardsley, 1968-71, village atty., 1971-79. Chmn. Ardsley (N.Y.) Library Com., 1967-68; mem. Ardsley Narcotics Guidance Council, 1971-78. Served with AC, AUS, 1946-47. Contbr. numerous articles to mags. and newspapers. Home: 7 Rest Ave Ardsley NY 10502 Office: Rich Krinsly Katz Lillienstein 99 Park Ave New York NY 10016

LILLY, DORIS, author; b. Los Angeles, Dec. 26, 1930; d. Otto William and Edith Marie (Humphries) Lilly; grad. high sch. Soc. columnist N.Y. Post, 1958-68; gossip columnist WPIX, N.Y.C., 1974-77; syndicated gossip columnist McNaught Sydicate, 1977—. Author: How to Marry A Millionaire, 1951; How to Make Love in Five Languages, 1964; Those Fabulous Greeks: Onassis, Niarchos and Livanos, 1970; Glamour Girl, 1977. Contbr. to maj. nat. mags., including McCall's, Ladies Home Jour., Harpers Bazaar, Cosmopolitan, Photoplay. Address: 150 E 69th St New York NY 10021*

LILLY, HUGH TUCKER, engring. and constrn. co. exec.; b. Abilene, Tex., Feb. 11, 1928; s. Dennis Q. and Valtye Lee (Tucker) L.; B.S. in Elec. Engring., U. Tex., 1950; m. Laura Mai Hightowa, Oct. 18, 1952. From engr. to project mgr. Brown & Root, Inc., 1950-67; with Mid-Valley, Inc., Houston, 1968—, v.p., 1971-74, sr. v.p., 1974—, also dir. Served with AUS, 1945-47. Methodist. Home: 4811 O'Meara St Houston TX 77035 Office: 2002 S Weyside St PO Box 2634 Houston TX 77001

LILLY, JAMES ALEXANDER, constrn. co. exec.; b. Bluefield, W.Va., Sept. 1, 1918; s. Clifford Abraham and Eva Acre (Dinwiddie) L.; Engr., Bluefield Coll., 1938; B.S. in Mech. Engring., Va. Poly. Inst. and State U., Blacksburg, 1940; children—James Alexander, Pamela, Robert Clifton, Anne Martha. Engr., Ingersoll Rand Co., N.Y.C., 1940-42; engr., gen. supr. George M. Brewster & Son Co., Bogota, N.J., 1945-49; engr. W.S. Bellow Constrn. Co., Houston, 1949-50; engr., supt. McKenzie Constrn. Co., San Antonio, 1950-54; project mgr. Whittle Constrn. Co., Dallas, 1954-59; with Morrison-Knudsen Co., Inc., Boise, Idaho, 1959—, gen. mgr., Vietnam, 1965-68, v.p., gen. mgr. Morrison-Knudsen Internat. Co., Inc., 1968-71, v.p. spl. div., 1971-72, v.p. domestic ops., 1972-73, exec. v.p. domestic ops., 1973-76, exec. v.p. N. Am. ops., 1976—, also dir.; pres., chief exec. officer, dir. M-K Nat. Corp.; v.p., dir.; Canadian Rescon Ltd., North Western Dredging Co. Ltd., No. Constrn. Co. Ltd., High Rock Mining Co., Ltd., Emkay Fin. Co., Inc.; dir. Internat. Engring. Co., Inc. Served with USMCR, 1942-45. Decorated Air medal with oak leaf clusters, D.F.C. with stars. Mem. Alaska Pipeline Builders Assn., AAAS, ASCE, Soc. Am. Mil. Engrs., ASME, Am. Inst. Chem. Engrs., Soc. Chem. Engrs., Am. Underground-Space Assn., Am. Wind Energy Assn., Assn. Energy Engrs., Am. Inst. Metall. Engrs., Am. Nuclear Soc., Brit. Tunnelling Soc., Internat. Platform Assn., Internat. Tech. Inst., Newcomen Soc. in N.Am., Soc. Mining Engrs., Sunsat Energy Council, The Moles (trustee), Beavers (dir.), Tau Beta Pi, Pi Tau Sigma. Episcopalian. Club: Hillcrest Country. Home: 3001 S Roosevelt St Boise ID 83705 Office: 1 Morrison-Knudsen Plaza Boise ID 83729

LILLY, JAMES EPLING, corp. fin. exec.; b. Normal, Ky., Oct. 4, 1915; s. William Webster and Hattie Glenn (Epling) L.; student Concord State Coll., 1932-33, exec. program Columbia U., 1970; m. Opal Elizabeth Anderson, May 4, 1937; children—Kay Lilly Cox, Franklin Brice. Adminstrv. posts U.S. Forest Service, Ky., 1934-38, U.S. C.E., Ind., Ill. and Ky., 1938-43, 46-52; successively chief auditor, budget mgr., asst. controller, asst. treas., treas. Brown & Williamson Tobacco Corp., Louisville, 1952-79; dir. fin. adminstrn. Brown & Williamson Industries, Inc., Louisville, 1979—; treas. Gimbel Bros., Inc., 1979—. Pres., bd. dirs. Louisville-Jefferson County Youth Orch.; pres. Louisville Deaf Oral Sch., 1977-79; bd. trustees Meth. Evang. Hosp. Found., 1977—, exec. com., 1979—; treas. City of Northfield (Ky.). Served with AUS, 1943-46; ETO, PTO. Cert. internal auditor, Ky. Mem. Fin. Execs. Inst. (dir., pres. Louisville chpt. 1977-79), Hon. Order Ky. Cols. Methodist. Clubs: Masons, Kiwanis. Home: 6102 Stannye Dr Louisville KY 40222 Office: 2000 Citizens Plaza Louisville KY 40202

LILLY, JOHN CUNNINGHAM, med. scientist, author; b. St. Paul, Jan. 6, 1915; s. Richard Coyle and Rachel (Cunningham) L.; B.Sc., Calif. Inst. Tech., 1938; student Dartmouth Med. Sch.; M.D., U. Pa., 1942; m. Antonietta Ficorotta, 1975; children—John, Charles, Cynthia, Pamela, Nina. Mem. faculty U. Pa., 1942-56, fellow in biophysics E. R. Johnson Found. Med. Physics, 1942-46, asso., 1946-49, asst. prof. biophysics, 1949-52, asso. prof. med. physics, 1952-56, also asso. prof. exptl. neurology dept. neurology and Grad. Sch. Medicine, 1952-56; chief cortical integration sect. Lab. of Neurophysiology NIMH and Nat. Inst. Neurol. Disease and Blindness, 1953-58; established Communication Research Inst., St. Thomas, V.I., 1959; chmn. neurol. div. Md. Psychiat. Research Center, 1968; Hixon lectr. Calif. Inst. Tech., 1952; Mayo Found. lectr., 1952; Colloquium lectr. Harvard U., 1954; John Kershman Meml. lectr., 1961; prof. medicine U. Miami Med. Sch., 1960; also lectr. numerous univs., learned socs. Condr. war research for com. on med. research OSRD-USAF, 1942-46 (Effective Service award 1945); fellowship bd. Nat. Inst. Mental Health, 1954-57; sci. adv. com. for grad. schs. NIH, 1954; mem. bioscis. adv. panel Office Sci. Research, USAF Research and Devel. Command, 1958, 61, sci. adv. bd., 1958-63. Recipient John Clark Research prize, 1943; grantees NIH, 1946-69, Office Naval Research, NSF, NASA, 1962; fellow Center for Advanced Study Behavioral Scis., 1969-70; resident asso. Esalen Inst., 1969-71. Fellow AAAS, N.Y. Acad. Scis.; mem. Am. Physiol. Soc. (steering com. on neurophysiology 1953-56), Am. Electroencephalographic Soc., IEEE, Biophys. Soc. (charter), Acoustical Soc. Am., Assn. Research in Nervous and Mental Diseases, Sigma Xi, Alpha Mu Pi Omega. Author: Man and Dolphin, 1961, The Mind of the Dolphin, 1967; Programming and Metaprogramming in the Human Biocomputer, Theory and Experiments, 1972; The Center of the Cyclone, 1972; Simulations of God: the Science of Belief, 1974; The Deep Self: Isolation Tank Relaxation, 1976; The Scientist: a Novel autobiography, 1978; Communication Between Man and Dolphin: The Possibility of Talking with Other Species, 1978; also sci. papers pub. in jours.; co-author: The Dolphin in History, 1963; (with Antoniette Lilly) The Dyadic Cyclone. Address: Human/Dolphin Found and Human Software Inc Box 4172 Malibu CA 90265. *My life is devoted to exploration of inner and outer realities; this means a thorough self-review frequently, conducted with candor and discipline derived from medical, scientific, psychoanalytic and research training over the years. I have resumed scientific and engineering research on human-dolphin communication. My goal is to break the interspecies communication barrier with microprocessors and minicomputers.*

LILLY, JOHN RICHARD, fin. cons.; b. St. Paul, Aug. 15, 1928; s. Richard J. and Katherine (Kaye) L.; A.B., U. Neb., 1950; J.D., Georgetown U., 1955; m. Marcella K. Seymour, June 21, 1958; children—Marcella K., John Richard. Admitted to bar; sr. fin. analyst, internat. staff Ford Motor Co., Dearborn, Mich., 1956-60; asst. to treas. Overseas Chem. div. W. R. Grace & Co., Boston, 1960-61, Singer Co., N.Y.C., 1961-63; treas. Richardson-Merrell, Inc., N.Y.C., 1964-72; sr. v.p. fin. US Industries Inc., N.Y.C., 1972-77; v.p., chief fin. officer Food Fair, Inc., Phila., 1977-79; pres. J.R. Lilly Assos., Inc., Greenwich, Conn., 1979—. Served to 1st lt. AUS, 1951-53. Decorated Bronze Star medal. Mem. Am. Mgmt. Assn. (fin. council), Delta Theta Chi, Sigma Chi. Clubs: Treasurers, Union League (N.Y.C.); Riverside Yacht. Home: 20 Owenoke Way Riverside CT 06878

LILLY, THOMAS GERALD, lawyer; b. Belzoni, Miss., Sept. 17, 1933; s. Sale Trice and Margaret Evelyn (Butt) L.; B.B.A., Tulane U., 1955; LL.B., U. Miss., 1960, J.D., 1968; m. Constance Ray Holland, Dec. 29, 1962; children—Thomas Gerald, William Holland, Carolyn Ray. Admitted to Miss. bar, 1960; asso. firm Stovall & Price, Corinth, Miss., 1960-62; asst. U.S. atty. No. Dist. Miss., Oxford, 1962-66; asso. firm Wise Carter Child Steen & Caraway and predecessor, Jackson, Miss., 1966-67, partner, 1967—. Served with USNR, 1955-58. Decorated Navy Commendation medal. Mem. Fed. Bar Assn. (2d v.p. 1977-78, pres. 1979-80), Am. Bar Assn., Hinds County (Miss.) Bar Assn., Miss. State Bar, Omicron Delta Kappa, Phi Delta Phi. Methodist. Clubs: Army and Navy, Nat. Lawyers (gov.) (Washington). Home: 4408 Deer Creek Dr Jackson MS 39211 Office: PO Box 651 925 Electric Bldg Jackson MS 39205

LILLY, WILLIAM ELDRIDGE, govt. ofcl.; b. Liberty, Tex., Aug. 25, 1921; s. Lawrence C. and Maude (McKinney) L.; A.B., U. Calif. at Berkeley, 1950, grad. student, 1950-51; m. Blanche Elizabeth Bromert, Jan. 18, 1944; children—Lizbeth Kristine, William Michael. Program analyst Naval Ordnance Test Sta., China Lake, Calif., 1950-52; head estimates and analysis Naval Bur. Ordnance, Washington, 1952-54; dep. budget officer Nat. Bur. Standards, 1954-56; asst. dir. plans and programs Navy Polaris program, 1956-60; with NASA, 1960—, asst. adminstr. for adminstrn., 1967-72, comptroller, 1972—. Pres. Arlington County (Va.) Youth Orgn., 1966-69. Served with USN, 1940-46. Recipient Exceptional Service medal NASA, 1966, 69, Distinguished Service medal, 1973; Career Service award Nat. Civil Service League, 1978. Mem. Phi Beta Kappa, Pi Sigma Alpha. Home: 2762 S Ives St Arlington VA 22206 Office: 400 Maryland Ave SW Washington DC 20456

LIM, HENRY CHOL, chem. engr.; b. Seoul, Korea, Oct. 24, 1935; s. Kwang Un and Chang Soon (Kim) L.; came to U.S., 1953, naturalized, 1969; B.S., Okla. State U., 1957; M.S.E., U. Mich., 1959; Ph.D., Northwestern U., 1966; m. Sun Boo Lee, Dec. 11, 1959; children—David, Carol, Michael. Research asst. U. Mich. Research Inst., 1957-59; research engr. Pfizer Inc., Groton, Conn., 1959-63; asst. prof. chem. engring. Purdue U., Lafayette, Ind., 1966-70, asso. prof., 1970-74, prof., 1974—; cons. in field. Mem. Am. Inst. Chem. Engrs., Am. Chem. Soc., AAUP, Inst. Food Technologists, Sigma Xi, Phi Kappa Phi, Phi Lambda Upsilon. Author: Biological Wastewater Treatment: Theory and Applications, 1980. Home: 100 Spinning Wheel Ct West Lafayette IN 47906 Office: Sch of Chem Engring Purdue U West Lafayette IN 47907

LIMBACH, WALTER F., constrn. co. exec.; b. Pitts., June 17, 1924; s. Emil and Sarah (Zuckerman) L.; B.S., Lehigh U., 1947; children—Elsa, Kurt; m. Sarah Z. Minard, June 16, 1976. With Limbach Co., Pitts., 1947—, v.p., 1955-57, pres., 1957—, dir., 1955—; dir. Contractors Mut. Assn., Washington, 1971—, vice chmn., 1973-78, chmn., 1978—. Bd. dirs. Hill House Assn., Pitts., v.p., 1968-73; bd. dirs. Allegheny Vocat. Rehab. Center, Pitts., 1975—. Served with USNR, 1943-46. Mem. Sheet Metal and Air Conditioning Contractors Nat. Assn. (pres. 1958-59). Home: 5200 Pembroke Pl Pittsburgh PA 15232 Office: 1441 Four Gateway Center Pittsburgh PA 15222

LIMBAUGH, RUSH HUDSON, lawyer; b. nr. Sedgewickville, Mo., Sept. 27, 1891; s. Joseph Headley and Susan Frances (Presnell) L.; student Cape Girardeau (Mo.) Normal Sch., 1907-08, 09-12; A.B., U. Mo., 1916; m. Bee Seabaugh, Aug. 29, 1914 (dec.); children—Rush Hudson, Manley O., Stephen Nathaniel. Tchr. rural sch., Mo., 1908-09; admitted to Mo. bar, 1916, since practiced in Cape Girardeau; sr. mem. firm Limbaugh, Limbaugh & Russell and predecessor firm, 1946—; gen. counsel Colonial Fed. Savs. & Loan Assn., 1932-66; city counselor, Cape Girardeau, 1924-30; commr. St. Louis Ct. Appeals, 1935, Supreme Ct. Mo., 1950-51; Nelson Meml. lectr. U. Mo., 1955; Dept. State lectr., India, 1958. Served as rep. 56th Gen. Assembly, Mo., 1931-33; mem. Mo. Commn. Human Rights, 1965-73; adv. bd. Salvation Army; trustee Old McKendree Chapel (nat. Meth. Shrine). Recipient S.E. Mo. State Coll. Alumni award 1961; U. Mo. at Columbia award for distinguished service in law, 1964. Fellow Am. Bar. Found., Am. Coll. Trial Lawyers, Am. Coll. Probate Counsel; mem. Am. Soc. Internat. Law, Am. Judicature Soc., Am. Law Inst., Am. Bar Assn. (mem. council, sect. real property, probate and trust law, 1950-54, chmn. sect. 1954-55; mem. ho. dels. 1955-59; standing com. bill of rights 1959-66, chmn. com. 1960-61, 63-65), Inst. Jud. Adminstrn., Am. Soc. Legal History, Inter-Am. Bar Assn., Mo. Bar Found., Selden Soc., Mo. Bar (pres. 1955-56), State Hist. Soc. Mo. (trustee, past pres.), Cape Girardeau County Bar Assn. (pres. 1929-31), Order Coif (hon.), Scribes, Phi Delta Phi, Delta Sigma Rho. Republican. Methodist. Mason. Clubs: Missouri Athletic; Cape Girardeau Country, Cape Girardeau Executives, Rotary (pres. 1948-49). Author: Missouri Practice. Contbr. articles to profl. jours. Home: 635 Sylvan Ln Cape Girardeau MO 63701 Office: 2027 Broadway Cape Girardeau MO 63701

LIN, CHIA-CHIAO, mathematician; b. Foochow, China, July 7, 1916; s. Kai and Y.T. Lin; B.Sc., Nat. Tsing Hua U., 1937; M.A., U. Toronto, 1941; Ph.D., Calif. Inst. Tech., 1944; LL.D., Chinese U. Hong Kong, 1973; m. Shou-Ying Liang, 1946; 1 dau., Lillian. Asst. prof. Brown U., Providence, 1945-46, asso. prof., 1946-67; asso. prof. M.I.T., Boston, 1947-52, prof. applied math., 1953—, chmn. com. on applied math., dept. math., 1962-66, inst. prof., 1966—; hon. lectr. in field. Recipient Timoshenko medal ASME, 1975; Guggenheim fellow, 1953, 60; mem. Inst. for Advanced Study, Princeton, 1959-60, 65-66. Fellow Am. Acad. Arts and Scis., Inst. Aerospace Scis.; mem. Nat. Acad. Scis. (Com. on Support and Research in Math. Scis. Applied Math. and Numerical Analysis award 1976), Am. Astron. Soc., Am. Math. Soc., Am. Phys. Soc., Soc. for Indsl. and Applied Math. (pres. 1972-74, trustee 1978-80). Author: pamphlet On the Motion of Vortices in Two Dimensions, 1943, monograph The Theory of Hydrodynamic Stability, 1955, Statistical Theories of Turbulence, 1961, Hydrodynamics of Helium II, 1961, (with Frank H. Shu) Density Wave Theory of Spiral Structure, 1970, (with Lee A Segel) Mathematics Applied to Deterministic Problems in the Natural Sciences, 1974. Office: Dept Math MIT Cambridge MA 02139

LIN, EDMUND CHI CHIEN, microbiologist; b. Peking, China, Oct. 28, 1928; s. Hsin Kwei and Chen Kwan (Pan) L.; came to U.S., 1949; student Nat. Peking U., 1949-50; A.B., U. Rochester, 1952; Ph.D., Harvard, 1957. Asst. prof. biol. chemistry Harvard Med. Sch., Boston, 1963-67, asso. prof. bacteriology and immunology, 1968, prof. microbiology and molecular genetics, 1969—, chmn. dept., 1973-75; vis. prof. bacteriology U. Calif. at Berkeley, 1972; mem. bd. sci. counselors, div. cancer biology and diagnosis Nat. Cancer Inst., 1979—. Guggenheim fellow, 1969; Ruby Boyer Miller fellow in med. research, 1972—; Fogarty Internat. scholar, 1977. Mem. editorial bd. Jour. Bacteriology, 1973-75, Jour. Biol. Chemistry, 1976—; contbr. numerous articles and revs. to profl. jours. Office: Dept Microbiology and Molecular Genetics Harvard Med School 25 Shattuck St Boston MA 02115

LIN, JOSEPH PEN-TZE, neuroradiologist, clin. adminstr., educator; b. Foochow, China, Nov. 25, 1932; came to U.S., 1959, naturalized, 1974; s. Tai Shui and Chin Sien L.; M.D., Nat. Taiwan U., 1957; m. Lillian Y. Hsu, Dec. 23, 1959; children—James S., Carol W., Julia W. Rotating intern Robert B. Green Meml. Hosp., San Antonio, 1959-60; resident in radiology Santa Rosa Med. Center, San Antonio, 1960-61, Bellevue Hosp. Center, N.Y.C., 1961-63; fellow in neuroradiology N.Y. U. Med. Center, N.Y.C., 1963-65; instr., radiology, 1965-67, asst. prof., 1967-70, asso. prof., 1970-74, prof., 1974—; dir. neuroradiology sect. Univ. Hosp., N.Y.C., 1974—. Diplomate Am. Bd. Radiology. Fellow Am. Coll. Radiology; mem. Am. Chinese Med. Soc. (pres. 1978). Contbr. articles on neuroradiology to med. jours. Home: 15 Oxford Rd New Rochelle NY 10804 Office: NY U Med Center 550 1st Ave New York NY 10016

LIN, TSUNG-YI, psychiatrist; b. Taiwan, Formosa, Sept. 19, 1920; s. Mou-Seng and Chai-Huan (Wang) L.; came to Can., 1973, naturalized, 1977; student Taihoku Coll., Taiwan, 1936-39; M.D., Tokyo Imperial U., 1943, D.Med. Sci., 1953; m. Mei-chen Lee, Apr. 8, 1946; children—Siong-chi, Leng-bun, Hiok-bun, Oat-bun, Tah-chi. Intern, Tokyo U. Hosp., 1943; resident in psychiatry Tokyo U., 1943-46; practice medicine specializing in psychiatry, Taipei, Taiwan, 1946-64, Ann Arbor, Mich., 1969-73, Vancouver, B.C., Can., 1973—; lectr. in psychiatry Nat. Taiwan U., 1947-52, asso. prof. psychiatry, 1952-56, chief dept. neurology and psychiatry, 1952-56, chmn. dept., 1956-67; prof., 1956-67; vis. prof. community mental health Sch. Pub. Health, prof. psychiatry Med. Sch. U. Mich., 1969-70, prof. community mental health, prof. psychiatry, 1970-73; prof. U. B.C. (Can.), Vancouver, 1973—, also mem. staff Health Sci. Centre Hosp.; expert adviser on mental health WHO, 1955-65, sr. med. officer, 1965-69, adviser on mental health research, 1969-79. Fellow Royal Coll. Physicians, Surgeons of Can., Am. Psychiat. Assn.; mem. World Fedn. Mental Health (pres. 1975-79), Am. Pub. Health Assn., Chinese Nat. Assn. Mental Hygiene, Japanese Psychiat. Assn., Formosa Med. Assn., Chinese (pres. 1954-65), Philippines socs. for neurology, psychiatry, Internat. Epidemiol. Soc. Editorial bd. Formosan Med. Jour., 1958-64, Psychiatry, 1973. Home: 6287 MacDonald St Vancouver BC V6N 1E7 Canada Office: Dept Psychiatry Health Scis Centre Hosp U BC Vancouver BC V6T 2A1 Canada

LIN, TUNG YEN, civil engr., educator; b. Foochow, China, Nov. 14, 1911; s. Ting Chang and Feng Yi (Kuo) L.; B.S. in Civil Engring., Tangshan Coll., Chiaotung U., 1931; M.S., U. Calif. at Berkeley, 1933; LL.D., Chinese U. Hong Kong, 1972; m. Margaret Kao, July 20, 1941; children—Paul, Verna. Came to U.S., 1946, naturalized, 1951. Chief bridge engr., chief design engr. Chinese Govt. Rys., 1933-46; asst., then asso. prof. U. Calif., 1946-55, prof., 1955-76, chmn. div. structural engring., 1960-63, dir. structural lab., 1960-63; chmn. bd. T.Y. Lin Internat., cons. engrs., 1953—, Inter-Continental Peace Bridge, Inc., 1968—; cons. to State of Calif., Def. Dept., also to industry; chmn. World Conf. Prestressed Concrete, 1957, Western Conf. Prestressed Concrete Bldgs., 1960. Recipient Berkeley citation award, 1976; NRC Quarter-Century award, 1977. Mem. ASCE (life; Wellington award, Howard medal), Nat. Acad. Engring., Academia Sinica, Internat. Fedn. Prestressing (Freyssinet medal), Am. Concrete Inst. (hon.), Prestressed Concrete Inst. (medal of honor). Author: Design of Prestressed Concrete Structures, 1955, rev. edit., 1963; (with B. Bresler, Jack Scalzi) Design of Steel Structures, rev. edit., 1968. Contbr. articles to profl. jours. Home: 8701 Don Carol Dr El Cerrito CA 94530 Office: 315 Bay St San Francisco CA 94133. *Fear incites fear; complex breeds complex. If one learns to control one's own fear and complex, and at the same time understands those of others, one will have gone a long way toward success and happiness.*

LIN, Y.K., educator; b. Foochow, Fukien, China, Oct. 30, 1923; s. Fa Been and Chi Ying (Cheng) L.; came to U.S., 1954, naturalized, 1964; B.S., Amoy U., 1946; M.S., Stanford U., 1955, Ph.D., 1957; m. Ying-yuh June Wang, Mar. 29, 1952; children—Jane, Della, Lucia, Winifred. Tchr., Amoy U., China, 1946-48, Imperial Coll. Engring., Ethiopia, 1957-58; engr. Vertol Aircraft Corp., Morton, Pa., 1956-57; research engr. Boeing Co., Renton, Wash., 1958-60; asst. prof. U. Ill., Urbana, 1960-62, asso. prof., 1962-65, prof. aero. and astron. engring., 1965—; vis. prof. mech. engring. M.I.T., 1967-68; sr. vis. fellow Inst. Sound and Vibration Research, U. Southampton (Eng.), 1976; cons. Gen. Motors Corp., Boeing Co., Gen. Dynamics Corp., TRW Corp. Sr. postdoctoral fellow NSF, 1967-68. Fellow Am. Acad. Mechanics, Acoustical Soc. Am., AIAA (asso.); mem. Sigma Xi. Author: Probabilistic Theory of Structural Dynamics, 1967. Contbr. articles to profl. jours. Home: 1909 Woodfield Rd Champaign IL 61820 Office: Aero and Astronautical Engring Dept U Ill Urbana IL 61801

LINCK, LAWRENCE J., mgmt. counselor; b. Detroit, Aug. 14, 1908; s. Frank J. and Beulah Maude (Osborne) L.; Ph.B., Northwestern, 1938, M.S., 1941; LL.D., Bradley U., 1951; m. Barbara Christina Krippner, Sept. 4, 1929 (dec. Apr. 1973); children—Gale Jo (Mrs. G.A. Partoyan), Lawrence Jefferson; m. 2d, Elisabeth Brittain Regnery, Dec. 11, 1974 (div. Feb. 1978). Dept. head, personnel mgmt. Postal-Telegraph Cable Co., Chgo., 1929-35; pvt. personnel cons., 1935-41; dir. Chgo. Syphillis Control Project, 1937-39; spl. cons. USPHS, 1937-39; lectr. psychology Northwestern U., 1937-39; exec. dir. Ill. Commn. Handicapped Children, 1940-45; dir. div. services for crippled children U. Ill., 1941-45; instr. social adminstrn. Loyola U., 1943-45; instr. pub. adminstrn. U. Ill. Coll. Medicine, 1943-50; exec. dir., sec. Nat. Soc. Crippled Children and Adults, 1945-56, trustee-at-large, 1956-63; pres. Lawrence J. Linck and Co., 1956—; mgmt. counselor Health and Rehab., Brazil, 1957—. Cons. adminstrn. Community Planning, HEW, 1957—; exec. v.p. Nat. Assn. Mental Health, 1959-60; mem. nat. adv. com. maternal and child health, crippled children's services U.S. Children's Bur., 1943-51; mem. Nat. Commn. on Children and Youth, 1946-51; mem. com. on community rehab. centers Baruch Com. on Phys. Medicine, 1943-51; mem. exec. com. Pres.'s Com. on Employment of Handicapped; mem., sec. bd. dirs. Riveredge Hosp.; v.p. Brain Research Found. U. Chgo.; bd. dirs., exec. com. Nat. Health Council, 1950-56; chmn., pres. bd. dirs. Robert Crown Center for Health Edn. Recipient Chgo. Distinguished Service award U.S. Jr. C. of C., 1938; award of merit Northwestern Alumni Assn., 1947; citation for distinguished leadership Nat. Soc. Crippled Children and Adults, 1949. Mem. Internat. Soc. Rehab. of Disabled (exec. council 1945-68, chmn. 8th World Congress Rehab. 1960, treas.), Assn. Rehab. Centers (hon.). Rotarian (v.p. Chgo. 1963-64). Clubs: University, Literary (Chgo.); Hinsdale (Ill.) Golf; Oak Brook (Ill.) Polo. Editor: Crippled Child mag., 1945-56. Author, lectr. Home: PO Box 374 Hinsdale IL 60521 Office: 21 Salt Creek Ln Hinsdale IL 60521. *To do the good, the just, the fair, the considerate; to love, to respect, to appreciate, to praise, to learn, to believe in the worth of all mankind and to use one's gifts for peace and understanding.*

LINCOLN, C(HARLES) ERIC, sociologist, educator, author; b. Athens, Ala., June 23, 1924; s. Less and Mattie (Sowell) L.; A.B., Lemoyne Coll., 1947; A.M., Fisk U., 1954; postgrad. law U. Chgo., 1948-49, B.D., 1956; M.Ed., Boston U., 1960, Ph.D., 1960; LL.D., Carlton Coll., 1968; L.H.D., St. Michael's, 1970; m. Lucy Cook, July 1, 1961; children—Hilary Anne, Less Charles II; children by previous marriage—Cecil Eric, Joyce Elaine. Pastor, John Calvin Presbyn. Ch., Nashville, 1953-54; asst. personnel dean Fisk U., Nashville, 1953-54; asst. prof. religion and philosophy Clark Coll., 1954-60, asso. prof. social philosophy, 1960-61, prof. social relations, 1961-65, asst. to pres., 1960-63; prof. sociology Portland (Ore.) State U., 1965-67; prof. sociology and religion Union Theol. Sem., N.Y.C., 1965-73; adj. prof. sociology Vassar Coll., 1969-70; adj. prof. religion Columbia U., 1965-73; adj. prof. religion Vanderbilt U., 1973-76; prof. sociology and religion, chmn. dept. religious studies Fisk U., Nashville, 1973-76; prof. religion Duke U., Durham, N.C., 1976—; lectr. in residence Dartmouth, 1962, vis. prof. social relations, 1963; intern in coll. adminstrn. Brown U., 1964-65; resident fellow Hope Coll., Brown U., 1964-65; resident chaplain Sch. Theology, Boston U., 1958-59, dir. Panel of Americans, 1958-60, adj. prof. Human Relations Center, 1963-65; lectr. Harvard, Yale, univs. Madrid (Spain), Oslo (Norway), Edinburgh (Scotland), London (Eng.) Sch. Econs., Shiraz, Abu Dhabi and Oman, 1964; others; external assessor univs. of Ghana, 1975; cons. research Office Edn.; rep. Dept. State at internat. seminar on Am. Negro Freedom Movement, Paris, France, 1965; participant Internat. Conf. on Color, Copenhagen, Denmark, 1965; founding pres. Black Acad. Arts and Letters; bd. advisers Martin Luther King Meml. Trustee Boston U.; former asso. dir. Am. Forum for African Study; bd. dirs. African Student Aid Fund; vis. prof. Queens Coll., 1972. Served with USNR, 1944-45. Crusade fellow, 1957; John Hay Whitney fellow, 1957-58, Eli Lilly fellow, 1958; Human Relations fellow, 1959, 60; Fund for Advancement Edn. grantee, 1964; Lilly Endowment grantee, 1976, 78. Fellow Am. Acad. Arts and Scis.; mem. Soc. of Psychol. Study Social Issues, AAUP, N.Y. Acad. Scis., N.E.A., Nat. Social Sci. Assn., Assn. for Study Negro Life and History, Am., So. sociol. assns., Am. Psychol. Assn., Soc. Sci. Study Religion, Kappa Alpha Psi. Mason (33 deg.). Author: The Black Muslims in America, 1961, 2d edit., 1973; 1961; My Face is Black, 1964; The Negro Pilgrimage in America, 1967; Sounds of the Struggle, 1967, Is Anybody Listening?, 1968; The Black Americans, 1969; A Profile of Martin Luther King, 1969; The Black Experience in Religion, 1974; The Black Church since Frazier, 1974. Gen. editor C. Eric Lincoln Series in Black Religion. Contbr. articles Ency. Brit., World Book Ency., Ency. Americana, N.Y. Times, books, periodicals. Home: Kumasi Hill Route 1 Box 271-N Hillsborough NC 27278 Office: 227 Gray Bldg Duke U Durham NC 27706

LINCOLN, FRANKLIN BENJAMIN, JR., lawyer; b. Bklyn., Jan. 18, 1908; s. Franklin Benjamin and Anna (Ellensberg) L.; A.B., Colgate U., 1931, LL.D. (hon.), 1960; J.D., Columbia, 1934; m. Helen C. Benz, Oct. 8, 1938; children—Carol Concors, Franklin Benjamin III. Admitted to N.Y. bar, 1934, D.C. bar, 1960, U.S. Supreme Ct. bar, 1944; with Sullivan & Cromwell, N.Y.C., 1934-41, Lundgren, Lincoln & McDaniel, N.Y.C., 1941-59; prin. analyst Hdqrs. Army Service Forces, Washington, 1943; civilian counsel to fiscal dir. Dept. Navy, 1944-45; asst. sec. def., 1959-61; pres. Monroe Internat., Inc., 1961-64; v.p. Litton Industries, Inc., 1961-64; partner Seward & Kissel, 1964-66; sr. partner Mudge, Rose, Guthrie & Alexander, 1966—; v.p., dir. Cypress Communications Corp., 1965-69; dir., chmn. exec. com. Shelter Resources Corp., 1968-70; dir. Pacific Tin Consol. Corp., ITEL Corp., Barnes Engring. Co., 1958-59, 61-62. Advisory bd. Nat. Council for Gifted; Pres. Nixon's rep. in 1968-69 Transition; mem. Pres.' Fgn. Intelligence Advisory Bd., 1969-73. Trustee, chmn. bd. Colgate U.; bd. dirs. World Bd. of Trade, 1973-75; bd. dirs., chmn. Fed. Home Loan Bank Bd. N.Y. Served to lt. USNR, 1943-44. Recipient Distinguished Pub. Service medal Def. Dept., 1961. Mem. Am., N.Y. State bar assns., Assn. Bar City N.Y., Phi Beta Kappa, Delta Upsilon, Delta Sigma Rho, Phi Delta Phi. Republican. Christian Scientist. Clubs: Down Town Assn. (N.Y.C.); Metropolitan (Washington); Canoe Brook Country (Summit, N.J.). Author: Presidential Transition, 1968-1969. Home: 22 Roland Dr Short Hills NJ 07078 Office: 20 Broad St New York City NY 10005

LINCOLN, J(EANNETTE) VIRGINIA, physicist; b. Ames, Iowa, Sept. 7, 1915; d. Rush B. and Jeannette (Bartholomew) L.; B.A. in Physics, Wellesley Coll., 1936; M.S. in Household Equipment, Iowa State U., 1938, research fellow, 1936-37. Grad. asst. Iowa State U., Ames, 1937-38, instr. household equipment, 1938-42; physicist Nat. Bur. Standards, Washington, 1942-54, Boulder, Colo., 1954-65, sect. chief Radio Warning Services, 1959-65; chief Aeronomy and Space Data Center, ESSA Research Labs., 1966-70; chief World Data Center A for Solar-Terrestrial Physics, Environ. Data and Info. Service, NOAA, Boulder, 1970—; sec. for World Days, Internat. Ursigram and World Days Service, 1961—; U.S. del. to internat. radio consultive com. for study group 6 Ionospheric Propagation Meetings, 1962—; reporter Internat. Assn. Geomagnetism and Aeronomy, 1963-66; sec. Ionospheric Network adv. group Internat. Union Radio Sci., 1969-72, vice chmn., 1972—; mem. Internat. Astron. U. Commn. Solar Activity, 1973. Recipient Gold medal distinguished service Dept. Commerce, 1973. Fellow AAAS; mem. Internat. Assn. Geomagnetism and Aeronomy, Am. Geophys. Union, Am. Astron. Soc., Soc. Women Engrs. (chmn. Denver sect. 1973-74, sect. rep. 1974-75), AAUW, Assn. Fed. Profl. and Adminstrv. Women of Denver (chmn. 1971-72), P.E.O. (chpt. pres. 1957-58), Sigma Xi. Republican. Episcopalian. Club: Soroptimist (pres. Boulder br. 1960-61). Co-author sunspot number prediction method; editor, compiler solar-terrestrial physics data. Home: 2005 Alpine Dr Boulder CO 80302 Office: Nat Oceanic and Atmospheric Adminstrn Boulder CO 80302

LIND, CHESTER CARL, banker; b. Firesteel, S.D., Aug. 4, 1918; s. Carl L. and Dorothy (Kiehl) L.; student U. S.D., 1940, No. State Coll. Sch. Banking, U. Wis., 1951; m. Marie C. Decker, June 4, 1941; children—Karen (Mrs. Darrel Pederson), James, Stephen, John. With Dewey County Bank, Timber Lake, S.D., 1935, 1st Nat. Bank, Aberdeen, S.D., 1935-66, asst. v.p., 1947-50, v.p., 1950-54, exec. v.p., dir., 1954, pres., dir., 1954-66; exec. v.p. First Am. Nat. Bank, Duluth, Minn., 1966-68, pres., dir., 1968-75; exec. v.p. N.W. Bancorp., Mpls., 1975-79, pres., chief exec. officer, 1979—; tchr. bank mgmt. Minn. Sch. Banking, St. Olaf Coll. Chmn. S.D. Indsl. Expansion Agy., 1963-64, Nat. Alliance Businessmen, Dulugh, Superior, Wis., 1970; past v.p. bd. dirs. Upper Midwest Devel. Council. Served to maj. AUS, 1941-46. Decorated Bronze Star medal; named Outstanding Young Man, Aberdeen Jaycees, 1949, Boss of Year, 1956. Mem. Minn. Bankers Assn. (mem. council), Duluth C. of C. (past pres.). Clubs: Masons, Shriners, Elks, Mpls. Home: 8441 Irwin Rd Bloomington MN 55437 Office: 1200 NW Bank Bldg Minneapolis MN 55480

LIND, DAVID ARTHUR, educator; b. Seattle, Sept. 12, 1918; s. John Arthur and Hilda Katrina (Erickson) L.; B.S., U. Wash., 1940; M.S., Calif. Inst. Tech., 1943, Ph.D., 1948; m. Mary Frances Dungan, Oct. 25, 1945; children—Catherine, Margaret, John, Christopher. Jr. aerodynamist Boeing Air plane Co., 1942-43; physicist Applied Physics Lab., U. Wash., 1943-45; research fellow Calif. Inst. Tech., 1948-50; Guggenheim fellow Nobel Inst. Physics, Stockholm, Sweden, 1950-51; asst. prof. U. Wis.-Madison, 1951-56; mem. faculty U. Colo., 1956—, prof. physics, 1959—, chmn. dept. physics and astrophysics, 1974-78; physicist AEC, 1969-70; cons., vis. staff mem. Los Alamos Sci. Lab., 1964—. Fellow Am. Phys. Soc.; mem. Am. Assn. Physics Tchrs., Phi Beta Kappa, Sigma Xi. Democrat. Mem. United Ch. Christ. Club: Colo. Mountain (Denver). Home: 920 Jasmine Circle Boulder CO 80302

LIND, LEVI ROBERT, author; b. Trenton, N.J., July 29, 1906; s. John Edward and Lydia (Nieminen) L.; B.A., U. Ill., 1929, M.A., 1932, Ph.D., 1936; m. Elena Marchant y Riquelme, Aug. 25, 1929; 1 dau., Rosa Elena (Mrs. D.C. Fuchs). Asst. prof., asso. prof. classics Wabash Coll., Crawfordsville, Ind., 1929-40; successively asst. prof., asso. prof., prof., Univ. Distinguished prof. classics U. Kans., Lawrence, 1940—, chmn. dept., 1940-64. Vis. research prof. history medicine U. Calif. at Los Angeles, summer 1959, U. Ill., summer 1937, 45; sec. Am. Com. on Medieval Latin Dictionary, UAI, 1937-41; U. Kans. rep. to adv. council Am. Acad. in Rome; pres. Central Labor Union, AFL, Lawrence, 1948-49. Fulbright research grantee, Rome, Italy, 1954-55; NIH grantee in history of medicine, 1960-63; Am. Council Learned Socs. fellow, 1940. Mem. Am. Philol. Assn., Classical Assn. Middle West and South, Medieval Acad. Am., History of Sci. Soc., Phi Beta Kappa (com. qualifications united chpts. 1955-61). Club: Discussion. Author: Medieval Latin Studies: Their Nature and Possibilities, 1941; The Vita Sancti Malchi of Reginald of Canterbury: a critical edition, 1942; The Epitome of Andreas Vesalius, 1949; Lyric Poetry of the Italian Renaissance: an Anthology With Verse Translations, 1954; Ten Greek Plays in Contemporary Translations, 1957; Latin Poetry in Verse Translation, 1957; Ecclesiale by Alexander of Villa Dei, 1958; Berengario da Carpi, A Short Introduction to Anatomy, 1959; Vergil's Aeneid, 1963; Aldrovandi on Chickens: The Ornithology of Ulisse Aldrovandi (1600), 1963; Epitaph for Poets and Other Poems, 1966; Twentieth Century Italian Poetry: a Bilingual Anthology, 1974; Johann Wolfgang von Goethe, Roman Elegies and Venetian Epigrams, 1974; Studies in Pre-Vesalian Anatomy, 1975; Ovid, Tristia, 1975; André Chenier, Elegies and Camille, 1978. Editor: Problemata Varia Anatomica, 1968. Home: 1714 Indiana St Lawrence KS 66044

LIND, MARSHALL LEE, state ofcl.; b. Appleton, Wis., June 1, 1936; s. Darwin F. and Elsie R. (Blohm) L.; B.S., U. Wis., 1958; M.Ed., U. Mont., 1965; Ph.D., Northwestern U., 1969; m. Lois Ann Zimmerman, Nov. 22, 1958; children—Peter, Elizabeth, Jeffry. Jr. high sch. tchr., Bunduel, Wis., 1959-61; tchr., adminstr. Bur. Indian Affairs, Alaska, 1961-67; supt. Kodiak Island (Alaska) Borough Sch. Dist., 1969-71; commr. edn. State of Alaska, Juneau, 1971—; vis. prof. Northwestern U. Mem. Nat. Adv. Council for Adult Edn., 1975—; bd. dirs. Council of Chief State Sch. Officers, N.W. Regional Ednl. Lab. Served with U.S. Army, 1958-59. Mem. Am. Assn. Sch. Adminstrs., NEA, Phi Delta Kappa. Methodist. Rotarian. Home: 1765 Evergreen Ave Juneau AK 99801 Office: Pouch F Juneau AK 99801

LINDAUER, JOHN HOWARD, business exec.; b. Montclair, N.J., Nov. 20, 1937; s. John Howard and Louise (Platts) L.; B.S., Ariz. State U., 1960; Ph.D. in Econs., Okla. State U., 1964; m. Jacqueline Shelly, Sept. 2, 1960; children—Susan, John Howard. Asst. prof. econs. Occidental Coll., Los Angeles, 1964-66; asso. prof. Claremont (Calif.) Men's Coll. and Grad. Sch., 1966-70, prof., chmn. econs., 1970-74; dean Coll. Bus., Murray (Ky.) State U., 1974-76; chancellor U. Alaska, Anchorage, 1976-78; commr. Alaska Pipeline, 1978; pres., chief exec. officer Alaska Industry and Energy Corp., 1978—; dir. various cos.; cons. econ. policy and devel. U.S. Congress, 1966—; co-founder, vice chmn. Group Against Smog Pollution, 1968—; pres. So. Calif. Econ. Assn., 1974; cons. econ. policy state legislatures; Fulbright prof., India, 1972, vis. prof. U. Sussex (Eng.), 1972-73; cons. econ. U.S. corps.; mem. Air Force Adv. Bd. Served with AUS, 1955-57. Mem. Am. Econ. Assn. Author: Macroeconomics, 1968, 71, 76; Economics: The Modern View, 1977; Land Taxation and the Indian Economic Development, 1979; editor: Macroeconomic Readings; contbr. articles to profl. jours. Home: 393 Geneva Pl Anchorage AK 99504

LINDBERG, CHARLES DAVID, lawyer; b. Moline, Ill., Sept. 11, 1928; s. Victor Samuel and Alice Christine (Johnson) L.; A.B., Augustana Coll., Rock Island, Ill., 1950; LL.B., Yale U., 1953; m. Marian J. Wagner, June 14, 1953; children—Christine, Breta, John, Eric. Admitted to Ohio bar, 1953, since practiced in Cin.; asso. firm Taft, Stettinius & Hollister, 1953-61, partner, 1961—; dir. Taft Broadcasting Co., Cin. Reds Profl. Baseball Team, Coca-Cola Bottling Cin., Arga Co., Cup Vending Co. Ohio, J.J. Gillespie, Inc.; corp. sec. Taft Broadcasting Co., Xomox Corp., Family Leisure Centers, Inc., Good Samaritan Hosp. Cin. Bd. dirs. Augustana Coll., 1978—; pres. Cin. Bd. Edn., 1971, 74, Zion Lutheran Ch., Cin., 1966-69; vice chmn. policy com. Hamilton County Republican Party, 1978-79; trustee Greater Cin. Center Econ. Edn., 1976—; chmn. Better Neighborhood Sch. Com., Cin., 1975—; chmn. law firm div. Cin. United Appeal, 1976; chmn. local govt. com. Cin. C. of C., 1977. Mem. Am. Bar Assn., Ohio Bar Assn., Cin. Bar Assn. Clubs: Queen City, Queen City Optimists, Commonwealth, Cin. Country. Bd. editors Nat. Law Jour. Home: 1559 Moon Valley Rd Cincinnati OH 45230 Office: 600 Dixie Terminal Bldg Cincinnati OH 45202

LINDBERG, HOWARD AVERY, physician; b. Chgo., May 30, 1910; s. Fritz A. and Ella C. (Carlson) L.; B.S., Northwestern U., 1931, M.D. 1935, M.S. 1936; m. Joan S. Streeter, Nov. 24, 1938; children—Suzanne (Mrs. John Schneiter), Nancy (Mrs. Robert D. Brinkerhoff), Jean (Mrs. Mark Shelton). Fellow, researcher internal medicine Northwestern U., Med. Sch., Chgo., 1938-40, asso. prof. medicine, 1948-74, prof. preventive and community medicine, 1974—, chief cardiovascular renal clinic, 1957-62; dir. Ill. Pneumonia Control Program, 1938-40; attending staff Northwestern Meml. Hosp. (formerly Passavant Hosp.), Chgo., 1941, chief staff, 1956; med. dir. Jewel Companies, Inc., A.C. Nielsen Co., Health Evaluation Programs, Inc.; med. cons. Benefit Trust Ins. Co., Chgo., Burlington-No., Inc.; med. dir. Amsted Industries, Inc. regional cons. internal medicine Surgeon Gen. Mem. of steering com. Bd. govs., 2d v.p. Chgo. Heart Assn.; investigator Nat. Diet and Heart Study, 1964—. Bd. dirs. Chgo. chpt. ARC. Served to lt. col., M.C., AUS, 1942-45. Fellow A.C.P., Am. Coll. Cardiology; mem. AMA, Am. Heart Assn., Central Soc. Clin. Investigation, Am. Fedn. Clin. Research, Am. Soc. Internal Medicine, Chgo. Soc. Internal Medicine, N.Y. Acad. Sci., Am. Legion (med. dir. Health Evaluation programs 1978), Sigma Xi, Sigma Alpha Epsilon, Phi Rho Sigma. Presbyn. Author: Handbook on Treatment of Pneumonia, 1939. Contbr. articles med. jours. Home: 1112 Greenwood Ave Wilmette IL 60091 Office: 720 N Michigan Ave Chicago IL 60611

LINDBERG, JEAN MELVILLE, cons. co. exec.; b. N.Y.C., Aug. 27, 1918; student Am. Inst. Banking, 1937-39, Columbia, 1946-47; grad. Rutgers U. Grad. Sch. Banking, 1957, Advanced Mgmt. Program, Harvard, 1961; m. Patricia E. Ryan, Aug. 7, 1943; 1 dau., Marian E. With Chase Manhattan Bank, N.Y.C., 1937-73, sr. v.p., 1965-73; vice chmn. Chase Investors Mgmt. Corp. N.Y., 1973-78; v.p. Buck Cons., Inc., 1978—; dir. Chase Manhattan Executor and Trustee Corp. Ltd., London, Eng. Treas., Am. Pension Conf., 1956-61. Pres., Bd. Edn., Central Sch. Dist. 3, Oyster Bay, N.Y., 1962-65. Bd. dirs., treas. Greater N.Y. council Girl Scouts U.S.A., 1965—. Served to capt. AUS, 1941-46. Mem. Am., N.Y. State (chmn. employees benefit fund com. 1965-73) bankers assns., Corp. Fiduciaries Assn. N.Y., U.S. C. of C. (pvt. pension plans com. 1965-73), Vets. 7th Regt. N.Y. N.G. Clubs: Economic (N.Y.C.); North Hempstead Country (Port Washington, N.Y.). Home: 25 Woodland Rd Roslyn NY 11576 Office: 2 Pennsylvania Plaza New York NY 10001

LINDBERG, WILLIAM J., judge; b. Minot, N.D., Dec. 17, 1904; s. Carl and Elizabeth (Beran) L.; B.A., LL.B., Gonzaga Law Sch., 1927; LL.M., Georgetown U., 1928; m. Josephine Byrd Poe, July 24, 1937; children—Josephine Poe, Elizabeth Beran, William J., John F. Admitted to Wash. bar, 1927; clk. Senator C.C. Dill, Washington, 1928; asso. law firm Cannon, McKevitt & Frazer, Spokane, 1928-33; prof. law Gonzaga Law Sch., 1928-33; sec. Wash. State Senate, 1933; asst. atty. gen., Olympia, 1933-34; mem. Wash. State Liquor Control Bd., 1934-41; individual practice law, Olympia, 1941-44, Seattle, 1944-51; apptd. U.S. Dist. Judge for Eastern and Western dists. Wash., 1951-61; chief judge Western Dist. Wash., 1959-71, sr. judge (ret.), 1971—. Dist. Ct. rep. 9th Circuit to U.S. Jud. Conf., 1960-63. Mem. Am., Wash. State, Seattle bar assns. Office: 407 US Courthouse Seattle WA 98104*

LINDBERGH, ANNE SPENCER MORROW (MRS. CHARLES AUGUSTUS LINDBERGH), author; b. 1906; d. Dwight Whitney and Elizabeth Reeve (Cutter) Morrow; grad. Miss Chapin's Sch., N.Y.C.; grad. Smith Coll., Northampton, Mass., 1928, M.A. (hon.), 1935; m. Charles Augustus Lindbergh, May 27, 1929 (dec. 1974); children—Charles Augustus (dec.), Jon Morrow, Land Morrow, Anne Spencer, Scott Morrow, Reeve Morrow. Recipient two prizes for lit. work Smith Coll.; cross of honor (for part in survey of trans-Atlantic air route) U.S. Flag Assn., 1933; Hubbard gold medal (for work as co-pilot and radio operator in flight of 40,000 miles over five continents Nat. Geog. Soc., 1934. Author: North to the Orient, 1935; Listen, the Wind, 1938; The Wave of the Future, 1940; The Steep Ascent, 1944; Gift from the Sea, 1955; Unicorn and Other Poems; Dearly Beloved, 1962; Earth Shine, 1969; Bring me a Unicorn, 1972; Hour of Gold, Hour of Lead, 1973; Locked Rooms and Open Doors, 1974; The Flower and the Nettle, 1976. Address: Scott's Cove Darien CT 06820

LINDE, HANS ARTHUR, justice Oreg. Supreme Ct.; b. Berlin, Germany, Apr. 15, 1924; s. Bruno C. and Luise (Rosenhain) L.; came to U.S., 1939, naturalized, 1943; B.A., Reed Coll., 1947; J.D., U. Calif., Berkeley, 1950; m. Helen Tucker, Aug. 13, 1945; children—Lisa, David Tucker. Admitted to Oreg. bar, 1951; law clk. U.S. Supreme Ct. Justice William O. Douglas, 1950-51; atty. Office of Legal Adviser, Dept. State, 1951-53; individual practice law, Portland, Oreg., 1953-54; legis. asst. U.S. Sen. Richard L. Neuberger, 1955-58; asso. prof., prof. U. Oreg. Law Sch., 1959-76; justice Oreg. Supreme Ct., Salem, 1977—; Fulbright lectr. Freiburg U., 1967-68, Hamburg U., 1975-76; cons. U.S. ACDA, Dept. Def., 1962-76; mem. Adminstrv. Conf. U.S., 1978—. Mem. Oreg. Constl. Revision Commn., 1961-62. Served with U.S. Army, 1943-46. Mem. Am., Oreg. bar assns., Am. Law Inst., Order of Coif, Phi Beta Kappa. Author: (with George Bunn) Legislative and Administrative Processes, 1976. Home: 2545 Birds Hill Dr S Salem OR 97302 Office: Oreg Supreme Ct Salem OR 97310

LINDE, SHIRLEY MOTTER, author, publishing co. exec.; b. Cin., Mar. 22, 1929; d. Park Owen and Helen (Eberhardt) Motter; B.S., U. Cin., 1951; M.S., U. Mich., 1953; m. Douglas W. Linde, 1954 (div. 1967); children—Scott, Robert. Successively chief Chgo. bur. Med. News, Med. Tribune, Tele-Med, Inc., dir. Lake Lotawana Writers Conf., research chemist Andrew Jergens Co., research asst. U. Cin. Med. Sch., research fellow U. Mich. Med. Sch., asst. editor Jour. Internat. Coll. Surgeons, med. copy editor Year Book Pubs., chief info. services Northwestern U. Med. and Dental Schs., asso. editor Together mag. Methodist Pub. House; pres. Pavilion Pub. Co., N.Y.C., Med-Assist, Inc.; writer-editor Collins Assos. Pub.; lectr. Columbia U.; dir. Commando Contractors, Inc. Mem. Nat. Assn. Sci. Writers (exec. com.), Am. Med. Writers Assn. (v.p., sec., Outstanding Service award 1972), AAAS, Authors League. Author: The Big Ditch-Story of the Suez Canal, 1962; Total Rehabilitation of Epileptics, 1962; Heart Attacks That Aren't, 1966; Airline Stewardess Handbook, 1968; Modern Woman's Medical Dictionary, 1968; Cosmetic Surgery-What It Can Do For You, 1971; Emergency Family First Aid Guide, 1971; Sickle Cell-A Complete Guide to Prevention and Treatment, 1972; (with Arthur Michele) Orthotherapy, 1971; (with Howard G. Rapaport) The Complete Allergy Guide, 1970; The Sleep Book, 1974; (with Frank Finnerty, Jr.) High Blood Pressure, 1975; (with Gideon Panter) Now That You've Had Your Baby, 1976; (with Robert Atkins) Superenergy Diet, 1977; Shirley Linde's Whole Health Catalogue, 1978; How To Beat a Bad Back, 1979; editor: Radioactivity in Man, 1961; Science and the Public, 1962; Response of the Nervous System to Ionizing Radiation, 1962; Medical Science in the News, 1965; contbr. articles to profl. publs. Home: Box 4196 Treasure Cay Abaco Bahamas

LINDEE, ROBERT GRANT, found. exec.; b. Denver, Oct. 11, 1927; s. Arthur Victor and Miriam A. (Grant) L.; B.A., U. Colo., 1950; m. Marjorie Anne Frame, Feb. 21, 1952; children—Grant R., Mark T., Anne M. Exec. asst. to v.p. for med. affairs U. Colo. Med. Center, Denver, 1960-63; asst. to pres. Affiliated Hosp. Center, Boston, 1963-65; asso. dean for adminstrn. Stanford U. Sch. Medicine, 1965-72, v.p., asso. dir. Center for Advanced Studies in Behavioral Scis., 1979—, Henry J. Kaiser Family Found., Palo Alto, Calif., 1972—; adminstrv. cons. NIH, 1963—; exec. dir. Sun Valley Forum on Nat. Health, Inc., 1972—; dir. Inst. for Med. Research, 1973—; dir. Lancet Med. Industries, 1973—; dir. Orinoco Found., 1975—; dir. Sensory Aids Found., 1976—. Deacon Menlo Park Presbyn. Ch., 1971-73, trustee, 1976—. Served with U.S. Army, 1953-55. Mem. Assn. Am. Med. Colls. Clubs: Stanford Faculty, Stanford Golf. Home: 14414 Liddicoat Circle Los Altos Hills CA 94022 Office: 202 Junipero Serra Blvd Stanford CA 94305

LINDELL, EDWARD ALBERT, coll. pres.; b. Denver, Nov. 30, 1928; s. Edward Gustaf and Estelle (Lundin) L.; B.A., U. Denver, 1950, M.A., 1956, Ed.D., 1960, L.H.D. (hon.), 1975; Litt.D. (hon.), Tusculum Coll., 1979; m. Patricia Clare Eckert, Sept. 2, 1965; children—Edward Paul, Erik Adam. Tchr., N. Denver High Sch., 1952-61; asst. dean Coll. Arts and Scis., U. Denver, 1961-65, dean, 1965-75; pres. Gustavus Adolphus Coll., St. Peter, Minn., 1975—. Mem. exec. bd. Rocky Mountain Synod Lutheran Ch. Am., 1968—, also pres. bd. coll. edn. and ch. vocations. Trustee Midland Luth. Coll., Fremont, Nebr., Kans. Wesleyan U., Colo. Assn. Ind. Colls. and Univs., Luth. Med. Center, Wheatridge, Colo., Luth. Sch. Theology, Chgo., 1975—, St. John's U., Minn., 1978—; bd. dirs. Pacific Luth. Theol. Sem., 1978—, Loretto Heights Coll., Colo., 1978—, Swedish Council Am., 1978—; exec. bd. Luth. Council U.S.A., v.p., 1975—. Named Outstanding Faculty Mem., Coll. Arts and Scis., U. Denver, 1964; decorated knight King of Sweden, 1976. Mem. Swedish Pioneer Hist. Soc. (dir. 1979—), Phi Beta Kappa. Home: President's Residence Gustavus Adolphus College St Peter MN 56082

LINDEMANN, CARL, JR., broadcasting co. exec.; b. Hackensack, N.J., Dec. 15, 1922; s. Carl and Dorothy (O'Connor) L.; grad. Phillips Exeter Acad., 1940; S.B., Mass. Inst. Tech., 1947; m. Marguerite Darmour Williams, Apr. 8, 1951; children—Catherine Darmour, Sarah C., Frances C., Mary A., Carl III. With Foote, Cone & Belding, 1947; with NBC, 1948—, v.p. NBC-TV, 1959—, v.p. program sales, 1960-77, charge daytime programs TV network, 1957-77, v.p. programs Calif. nat. programs, 1960-77, v.p. spl. projects, news, 1962-64, v.p. sports, 1963-77, cons. N.Y. Olympic Project, 1977; exec. producer Nat. Hockey League Network, 1977-78; v.p. programs CBS Sports, 1978—. Mem. nat. council Boy Scouts Am. Mem. vis. com. Mass. Inst. Tech. Served to 1st lt. AUS, 1942-46. Clubs: Greenwich Country; Chebeague Country. Home: 7 Gracie Sq New York NY 10028 also Chebeague Island ME 04107 Office: CBS 51 W 52d St New York City NY 10019

LINDEMANN, OSCAR CURTIS, banker; b. Bartlett, Tex., July 19, 1922; s. Edwin E. and Thecla (Schawe) L.; B.B.A., U. Tex., 1947, M.B.A., 1948; m. Martha Menn, Mar. 19, 1944; children—Richard, Merrianne, Carol Beth. Instr. banking and finance U. Tex., 1948-51; with Tex. Bank & Trust Co., Dallas, 1951-77, pres., 1965-71, chmn., 1971—, also dir., mem. exec. com.; with United Nat. Bank, Dallas, 1977-78; vice chmn. Nat. Bank Commerce, Dallas, 1978—. Mem. Circle Ten Boy Scout Found.; vice chmn. spl. gifts div. Dallas Baptist Coll. Devel. Fund; mem. Dallas Crime Commn.; mem. investment com. Am. Lutheran Ch., Mpls., 1960—; bd. dirs., treas. Dallas County chpt. ARC; bd. dirs. Dallas County United Fund, 1966-71; bd. dirs., treas. Dallas Citizens Council; bd. dirs. Dallas Summer Musicals, Dallas Zool. Soc.; trustee Southwestern Med. Found.; bd. devel. Presbyn. Hosp.; pres. Dallas Clearing House Assn., 1969; adv. council U. Tex. Coll. Bus. Adminstrn. Found. Mem. Am. (governing council and research), Tex. (pres. 1971-72) bankers assns., Robert Morris Assos., U. Tex. Ex-students Assn. (exec. council). Clubs: Salesmanship; City (dir., treas.), Northwood (bd. govs.); Preston Trail Golf. Home: 5105 Royal Crest Dallas TX 75229 Office: Nat Bank Commerce Dallas TX 75221

LINDEMER, LAWRENCE BOYD, lawyer, utility exec., former state Supreme Ct. justice; b. Syracuse, N.Y., Aug. 21, 1921; s. George F. and Altamae (Reimers) L.; student Taft Sch., 1939, Hamilton Coll., 1939-41; A.B., U. Mich., 1943, LL.B., 1948; m. Rebecca Mead Gale, Dec. 31, 1940; children—Lawrence Boyd, David G. Commr.'s asst., commn. on orgn. Exec. Br. Govt., Hoover Comm., 1953-55; admitted to Mich. bar, 1948, since practiced in Stockbridge and Lansing; asst. pros. atty., Ingham County, 1949-51; partner Foster, Lindemer, Swift & Collins and predecessor firm, 1955-75; justice Mich. Supreme Ct., Lansing, 1975-76; v.p., gen. counsel Consumers Power Co. Mem. Mich. Ho. of Reps., 1951-52; Republican state chmn., 1957-61; mem. Rep. Nat. Com., 1957-61; Rep. candidate atty. gen. Mich., 1966. Regent U. Mich., 1968-75. Served with USAAF, 1943-45. Mem. Am., Ingham County bar assns., State Bar Mich. (commr. 1963-70). Presbyterian (elder). Home: 424 Morton St Stockbridge MI 49285 Office: Consumers Power Co 212 W Michigan Ave Jackson MI 49201

LINDEN, HAL, actor, singer; b. Bronx, N.Y., Mar. 20, 1931; s. Charles and Frances (Rosen) Lipshitz; B.B.A., Coll. City N.Y., 1952; student Am. Theatre Wing, N.Y.C., 1954-55; student acting Paul Mann, 1956-60, Lloyd Richards, 1962-63; student voice Lou McCollogh, 1953-56, John Mace, 1958-64; m. Frances Martin, Apr. 13, 1958; children—Amelia Christine, Jennifer Dru, Nora Kathryn, Ian Martin. Saxophone player and singer; played with bands of Sammy Kaye, Bobby Sherwood and Boyd Raeburn; stage debut in Wonderful Town, Cape Cod Melody Tent, Hyannis, Mass., 1955; N.Y. stage debut as understudy to Sydney Chaplain in Bells are Ringing, 1956, then took over lead; other stage appearances include: On a Clear Day, Wildcat, Something More!, Subways are for Sleeping, Ilya Darling, The Apple Tree, The Education of HYMAN KAPLAN, The Rothschilds (Tony award 1971), Three Men on a Horse, Pajama Game; appeared in film Bells are Ringing, 1959; TV series Barney Miller, 1975—; host children's series Animals Animals Animals; narrator series Saga of the Western World, 1963-64; film When You Comin' Back, Red Ryder?, 1979. Served in U.S. Army, 1952-54. Mem. Actors Equity, Screen Actors Guild, AFTRA, AGVA, Am. Fedn. Musicians. Office: care ABC 41-51 Prospect Ave Hollywood CA 90027*

LINDEN, HENRY ROBERT, chem. engring. research exec.; b. Vienna, Austria, Feb. 21, 1922; s. Fred and Edith (Lermer) L.; came to U.S., 1939, naturalized, 1945; B.S., Ga. Sch. Tech., 1944; M.Chem. Engring., Poly. Inst. Bklyn., 1947; Ph.D., Ill. Inst. Tech., 1952; m. Natalie Govedarica, 1967; children by previous marriage—Robert, Debra. Chem. engr. Socony Vacuum Labs., 1944-47; with Inst. of Gas Tech., 1947-78, various research mgmt. positions, 1947-61, dir., 1961-69, exec. v.p., dir., 1969-74, pres., trustee, 1974-78; research asso. prof. Ill. Inst. Tech., 1954-62, adj. prof., 1962-78, research prof. chem. engring., prof. gas engring., 1978—; chief operating officer Gas Devels. Corp., 1965-73, chief exec. officer, 1973-78, also dir.; pres., dir. Gas Research Inst., 1976—; dir. So. Natural Resources, Inc., Reynolds Metals Co. Trustee Argonne Univs. Assn.; bd. dirs. Ams. for Energy Independence. Recipient award of merit, operating sect. Am. Gas Assn., Disting. Service award Am. Gas Assn.; Walton Clark Medal Franklin Inst., Bunsen-Pettenkofer-Ehrentafel medal Deutscher Verein des Gas- und Wasserfaches. Fellow Am. Inst. Chem. Engrs., Inst. of Fuel; mem. Am. Chem. Soc. (recipient H.H. Storch award; chmn. div. fuel chemistry 1967, councilor 1969-77), Nat. Acad. Engring. Author tech. articles. Holder U.S. and fgn. patents in fuel tech. Home: 1515 N Astor St Chicago IL 60610 Office: 10 W 35th St Chicago IL 60616

LINDEN, JANINE M., advt. agy. exec.; b. N.Y.C., Oct 2, 1946; d. Moses Fortune and Emma (Leo) Mager; B.A., U. Pa., 1968; m. Peter Linden, July 19, 1972. Asst. buyer Bloomingdale's, N.Y.C., 1968-69; fashion credits editor Harper's Bazaar, N.Y.C., 1969-72; asso. dir. pub. relations Cotton, Inc., N.Y.C., 1972-73; press officer Harrods Ltd., London, 1973-74; project mgr. J.C. Penney Co., Inc., N.Y.C., 1974-75; dir. pub. relations Kenyon & Eckhardt, Inc., N.Y.C., 1975-77; v.p. corp. communications Compton Advt., Inc., 1977—. Mem. Advt. Women N.Y., Public Relations Soc. Am., Pub. Club London. Home: 433 E 51st St New York NY 10022 Office: Compton Advt Inc 625 Madison Ave New York NY 10022

LINDENBERGER, HERBERT SAMUEL, author, educator; b. Los Angeles, Apr. 4, 1929; s. Hermann and Celia (Weinkrantz) L.; B.A., Antioch Coll., Yellow Springs, Ohio, 1951; Ph.D., U. Wash., Seattle, 1955; m. Claire Flaherty, June 14, 1961; children—Michael James, Elizabeth Celia. From instr. to prof. English and comparative lit. U. Calif., Riverside, 1954-66; prof. German and English, chmn. program comparative lit. Washington U., St. Louis, 1966-69; Avalon Found. prof. humanities, chmn. program comparative lit. Stanford U., 1969—. Fulbright scholar, Austria, 1952-53; Guggenheim fellow, 1968-69; Nat. Endowment Humanities fellow, 1975-76. Mem. Modern Lang. Assn., Am. Comparative Lit. Assn. Author: On Wordsworth's Prelude, 1963; Georg Büchner, 1964; Lear and Cordelia at Home (play), 1968; Georg Trakl, 1971; Historical Drama: The Relation of Literature and Reality, 1975; Saul's Fall: A Critical Fiction, 1979. Home: 901 Wing Pl Stanford CA 94305 Office: Comparative Lit Stanford Univ Stanford CA 94305

LINDENFELD, PETER, educator; b. Vienna, Austria, Mar. 10, 1925; s. Bela and Elda (Lachs) L.; student U. Man. (Can.), 1942-43; B.A.Sc., U.B.C. (Can.), 1946, M.A. Sc., 1948; Ph.D., Columbia U., 1954; m. Lore Kadden, May 31, 1953; children—Thomas, Naomi. Came to U.S., 1948, naturalized, 1957. Vis. lectr. Drew U., Madison, N.J., 1952-53; instr. Rutgers U., 1953-55, asst. prof. physics, 1955-61, asso. prof., 1961-66, prof., 1966—; cons. summer inst. AID, Tirupati, India, 1955; regional counselor N.J. Am. Inst. Physics, 1963-71; dir. NSF In-service Insts. High Sch. Tchrs., 1964-66. Rutgers Research Council fellow and guest scientist Faculté des Sciences U. Paris-Sud, Orsay, France, 1970-71. Fellow Am. Phys. Soc.; mem. Am. Assn. Physics Tchrs. (hon. mem. N.J. sect.), AAUP. Contbr. articles to profl. jours. Home: 121 Harris Rd Princeton NJ 08540 Office: Dept Physics Rutgers U New Brunswick NJ 08903

LINDER, ALLAN DAVID, biologist, educator; b. Grand Island, Nebr., Sept. 27, 1925; s. J. Harold and Catherine (Heins) L.; B.S., U. Nebr., 1951; M.S., Okla. State U., 1952, Ph.D., 1956; m. Mary A. Matern, Aug. 20, 1949; 1 dau., Jo Anne. Asst. prof. zoology U. Wichita, 1956-59, U. So. Ill., 1959-60; asso. prof. zoology Idaho State U., 1960-66, prof. zoology, 1966—, chmn. dept. biology, 1965-75, asst. dean Coll. Liberal Arts, 1966-70, 76-78. Served with USNR, 1943-46. Mem. Idaho Acad. Sci., Soc. for Study Amphibians and Reptiles, Am. Soc. Ichthyologists and Herpetolgists, Soc. Vertebrate Paleontology, Sigma Xi. Home: 101 Dartmouth St Pocatello ID 83201

LINDER, ALLEN JAMES, judge; b. Hamburg, Ark., July 23, 1921; s. Allen Jefferson and Fannie Gray (Moseley) L.; LL.B., Ark. Law Sch., Little Rock, 1946; m. June Evelyn Thach, Apr. 22, 1943; children—Jo Evelyn, Carolyn Jeanne. Admitted to Ark. bar, 1946; practiced in Hamburg, 1946-61, Little Rock, 1970-74; pvt. practice, 1946-61; pros. atty. 10th Jud. Dist. Ark., 1951-60; mcpl. judge, Hamburg, 1961-62; gen. counsel Nat. Investors Group Ins. Cos., 1961-70; now judge Ashley County Juvenile Ct. Del., Democratic Nat. Conv., 1952, 56, 64, 68, 72; bd. dirs., trustee, past chmn. Ark. Bapt. Med. Center, Little Rock, Meml. Hosp., North Little Rock. Served with AUS, 1942-46. Baptist. Clubs: Masons (32 deg.), Shriners, Rotary. Home 214 E Jackson Ave Hamburg AR 71646 Office: 208 E Lincoln St Hamburg AR 71646

LINDER, BRUNO, chemist, educator; b. Sniatyn, Poland, Sept. 3, 1924; s. Elias and Feiga (Kleinman) L.; B.S., Upsala Coll., 1948; M.S., Ohio U., 1950; Ph.D., UCLA, 1955; m. Cecelia Fahn, Feb. 14, 1953; children—William H., Diane T., Richard A., Nancy M., Carolyn B. Asst. research chemist, engring. dept. UCLA, 1955; research asso. U. Wis. Naval Research Lab., 1955-57; asst. prof. Fla. State U., 1957-61, asso. prof., 1961-65, prof. chemistry, 1965—, chmn. chem. physics program, 1971-73, 75—; research participant Oak Ridge Nat. Lab., summers 1958, 59, 61; vis. asso. prof. U. Wis., summer 1964, U. Amsterdam, 1964-65; vis. prof. Hebrew U. of Jerusalem, 1973. Guggenheim fellow, 1964-65. Mem. Am. Chem. Soc. (sect. chmn. 1964, 78—), Am. Phys. Soc., Southeastern Theoretical Chemistry Assn. (founder, chmn. 1969-72, program chmn. 1974-76), Sigma Xi, Phi Lambda Upsilon, Phi Mu Alpha. Home: 2226 Demeron Rd Tallahassee FL 32303

LINDER, FORREST EDWARD, educator; b. Waltham, Mass., Nov. 21, 1906; s. Gustaf Ferdinand and Lillian (Domville) L.; B.A., State U. Ia., 1930, M.A., 1931, Ph.D., 1932; m. Gretchen Alma Otto, Dec. 21, 1931; children—Gordon Forrest, Louise Alma. Asso. biostatistician Worcester (Mass.) State Hosp., 1932-35; asst. chief div. vital statistics Bur. Census, 1935-44; chief demographic and social statistics UN, 1946-56; dir. Nat. Center Health Statistics, 1956-67; vis. prof. U. N.C., 1966, prof. biostatistics Sch. Pub. Health, 1967-77. Cons. Ford Found., 1962—; adviser WHO, 1957—; pres. Internat. Inst. for Vital Registration and Statistics, 1974—. Served to comdr. USNR, 1944-46. Recipient Distinguished Service award HEW, 1966; Bronfman prize Am. Pub. Health Assn., 1967. Mem. Am. Pub. Health Assn., Am. Statis. Assn., Internat. Statis. Inst., Sigma Xi. Club: Cosmos (Washington). Author: Manual de Estadistica Vital, 1942; Vital Statistics Rate in the United States, 1900-1940, 1943; also articles. Home: 15115 Vantage Hill Rd Silver Spring MD 20906

LINDER, HAROLD F., fin. cons.; b. Bklyn., Sept. 13, 1900; s. William and Florence (Strauss) L.; student Columbia U., 1917-19; LL.D., U. Pa., 1972; m. Bertha Rubin, Oct. 5, 1930; children—Prudence Linder Steiner, Susan. Mfg. bus. positions, 1919-25; joined in forming Cornell, Linder & Co., indsl. mgmt. and reorgns., 1925-33; partner Carl M. Loeb, Rhoades & Co., security and commodity brokerage, banking, 1933-38; extensively engaged in philanthropic work, 1938-42, 45-48; various corp. directorships, 1938-61; pres. Gen. Am. Investors Co. Inc., 1948-55; dep. asst. sec. of state for econ. affairs Dept. State, Washington, 1951, asst. sec., 1952-53; pres., chmn. Export-Import Bank, Washington, 1961-68; U.S. ambassador to Can., Ottawa, Ont., 1968-69; trustee Inst. Advanced Study, Princeton, N.J., 1949—, chmn. bd., 1969-72, emeritus, 1972—; cons. Internat. Fin. Corp., World Bank Group, 1970-76; mem. bd. overseers Faculty of Arts and Scis., U. Pa.; mem. adv. council Faculty Internat. Affairs, Columbia U. Mem. council Sch. Advanced Internat. Studies, Johns Hopkins U., Washington; mem. fin. com. Smithsonian Inst. Served as comdr. USNR, 1942-45. Benjamin Franklin fellow Royal Soc. Arts; mem. Council on Fgn. Relations, AAAS (fin. com.). Clubs: Cosmos (Washington); Recess (N.Y.C.); Century Assn.; White's (London). Office: 40 Wall St New York NY 10005

LINDER, ISHAM WISEMAN, govt. ofcl., former naval officer; b. Jacksonville, Ill., Feb. 14, 1924; s. Isham Doyle and Mary Grace (Wiseman) L.; B.S., U.S. Naval Acad., 1946; M.S., U.S. Naval Postgrad. Sch., 1956; B.S. in Elec. Engring., Mass. Inst. Tech., 1949; Ph.D. in Engring. Sci., U. Calif., Berkeley, 1960; m. Ann Fisher, Sept. 21, 1948; children—Bruce, Susan, Nancy, David, Mary. Commd. ensign U.S. Navy, 1946, designated naval aviator, 1950, advanced through grades to rear adm., 1971; comdr. U.S.S. Cleveland, 1968-69, U.S.S. Intrepid, 1970-71; naval nuclear power supr., 1966; supt. Naval Postgrad. Sch., Monterey, Calif., 1974-78; ret., 1978; dir. Def. Test and Evaluation Office Sec. Def., Washington, 1978—. Mem. Sigma Xi, Tau Beta Pi. Address: 420 N Saint Asaph St Alexandria VA 22314

LINDER, JAMES BENJAMIN, naval officer; b. Osceola, Iowa, Oct. 13, 1925; s. Merlyn Dewey and Gracia Irene (McKay) L.; student U. Kans., 1943; B.S., U.S. Naval Acad., 1949; grad. Naval War Coll., 1960; postgrad. George Washington U., 1962-64; m. Patricia Joy Weir, June 9, 1949; children—Jamey, Jeffrey, Benjamin. Served as enlisted man U.S. Navy, 1943-45, commd. ensign, 1949, advanced through grades to rear admiral, 1974; pilot Fighter Squadron 112, Korea, 1951-54; ops. officer Attack Squadron 172, 1959-60; aide to chief naval personnel, Washington, 1963-64; exec. officer Attack Squadron 76, 1974-75; comdg. officer Spirits of 76, S.E. Asia, 1965-66; comdr. Attack Carrier Air Wing 15, 1967, U.S.S. Coral Sea, 1967-68; pilot, Vietnam, 1965-68; exec. asst. to asst. sec. navy for manpower and res. affairs, 1969; comdr. U.S.S. Sylvania, 1971; comdg. officer U.S.S. Forrestal, 1972; dir. naval adminstrn. Office of Chief Naval Ops., Dept. Navy, 1973-74; comdr. Carrier Group 4, Norfolk, Va., 1975-77; comdr. U.S. Taiwan Def. Command, Republic China, 1977-79. Decorated Navy Cross, Silver Star (4), D.F.C. (7), Legion of Merit (3), Air Medal (24). Mem. Naval Acad. Alumni, U.S. Naval Inst., Assn. Naval Aviation Inc., V.F.W. Clubs: Masons, Kiwanis, Am. U., Rotary. Home: 2632 S Kings Rd Virginia Beach VA 23452 Office: CINCLANT Fleet care CODE 01 Norfolk VA 23511

LINDEROTH, ROGER STANLEY, mfg. co. exec.; b. Harvard, Ill., Nov. 21, 1923; s. Stanley V. and Ada G. (Seaver) L.; student Beloit Coll.; m. M. Joanne Yust, Dec. 30, 1948; children—Coni, Karen, Chris. With Amerock Corp., Rockford, Ill., 1948—, exec. v.p., 1967-73, pres., 1973-79, chmn. bd., 1979—; corp. v.p. Anchor Hocking Corp., 1975—; dir. Am. Nat. Bank & Trust Co., Rockford, Liberty Mut. Ins. Co.-Midwest, Arkwright Boston Ins. Co.-Midwest. Trustee, Swedish Am. Hosp., Rockford. Served with USAAF, 1943-45. Mem. Am. Hardware Mfrs. Assn., Nat. Kitchen Cabinet Assn. Home: PO Box 5851 Rockford IL 61125 Office: 4000A Auburn St Rockford IL 61101

LINDESMITH, ALFRED RAY, educator; b. Owatonna, Minn., Aug. 3, 1905; s. David Ray and Louise (Priebe) L.; B.A., Carleton Coll., 1927; M.A., Columbia Tchrs. Coll., 1930; Ph.D. in Sociology, U. Chgo., 1936; m. Gertrude Louise Augusta Wollaeger, June 21, 1930; 1 dau., Karen. Mem. faculty Ind. U., 1936—, prof. sociology, 1955—, Univ. prof. sociology, 1965—, emeritus, 1975—; vis. asso. prof. U. So. Calif., 1950-51; sr. research fellow U. Chgo. Law Sch., 1956-57; Fulbright grantee to India, 1952-53; cons. in drug problems. Mem. Ind. Citizens Council Crime and Delinquency, 1965—; del. White House Conf. Drug Abuse, 1962. Served to 1st lt. USAAF, 1943-45. Recipient Sutherland award Am. Soc. Criminology, 1970. Mem. Am., North Central sociol. assns., AAUP (pres. Ind. U. chpt. 1965-66), Soc. Study Social Problems (pres. 1959-60), Nat. Assn. Prevention Addiction to Narcotics (advisory and editorial bds.), Phi Beta Kappa. Author: Opiate Addiction, 1947; (with others) Anomie and Deviant Behavior, 1964; (with Dr. A. Strauss) Social Psychology, 1949; The Addict and the Law, 1965. Editor or co-editor: The Sutherland Papers. 1956; Drug Addiction: Crime or Disease, 1961; Addiction and Opiates, 1968. Home: 515 S Rose Ave Bloomington IN 47401

LINDFORS, VIVECA, actress; b. Uppsala, Sweden; d. Torsten and Karin (Dymling) L.; grad. Gymnasium, Stockholm; m. George Tabori, July 4, 1954; children—John, Lena, Kristoffer. Came to U.S., 1946, naturalized, 1950. Joined Royal Drama Theatre, Sweden, 1938; appeared in plays in Sweden including Twelfth Night, 1945, Bloodwedding, 1944, French Without Tears, 1942; Swedish films include: Think if I Marry the Minister, 1940, Anna Lans, 1941, The Two Brothers, 1941, In Death's Waiting Room, 1942; plays in the U.S. include: I've Got Sixpence, 1953, Anastasia (Drama League award), 1954, An Eve With Will Shakespeare, 1953, Miss Julie, 1955, King Lear, 1955, Brecht on Brecht, 1961, I Am A Woman (co-producer, co-arranger, actress), Mother Courage, 1970, Dance of Death, 1971, Theatre of Space and Touring, 1973; toured in Far Country, coll. readings, 1964; films in U.S. include: Night Unto Night, 1947, Don Juan, 1947, No Sad Songs for You, 1948, Four Men in a Jeep (Berlin Film Festival award), 1948, Run for Cover, 1953, Captain Dreyfus, 1956, Weddings and Babies, 1956, No Exit (Berlin Festival Silver Bear award), 1960, Affair of the Skin, 1962, Sylvia, 1964, Brainstorm, 1965, The Stronger, The Jewish Wife, An Actor Works, The Way We Were, 1972, Welcome to LA, 1975, Tabu, 1975, The Wedding, 1977, Girlfriend, 1978; TV appearances include: The Bridge of San Luis Rey, 1958, The Idiot, 1958, Defenders, 1963, Naked City, 1963, Ben Casey, 1964, The Nurses, 1964, other weekly shows; theatre prodns. I Am A Woman, My Mother, My Son; prod. Strolling Players for coll. tours, 1966-69; Artistic dir., founder Berkshire Theatre Festival; founder Berkshire Children's Theatre. Address: care Bret Adams Ltd 36 E 61st St New York NY 10021

LINDGREN, BERNARD WILLIAM, educator; b. Mpls., May 13, 1924; s. Carl E. and Lillian W. (Benson) L.; B.A., U. Minn., 1943, M.A., 1947, Ph.D., 1949; m. S. Louise Rippel, Mar. 31, 1945; children—Carol (Mrs. William G.E. Jacobs), Barbara (Mrs. David L. Wolf), Nancy. Instr., Mass. Inst. Tech., 1949-51; mathematician Mpls. Honeywell Co., 1951-53; faculty U. Minn., Mpls., 1953—, prof. statistics, 1968—, chmn. dept., 1963-73. Cons. to industry. Served to lt. (j.g.) USNR, 1944-46. NSF sci. faculty fellow, 1959-60. Fellow Am. Statis. Assn.; mem. Inst. Math. Statistics, Phi Beta Kappa, Sigma Xi. Author: Statistical Theory, 3d edit., 1976; Elements of Decision Theory, 1971; Basic Ideas of Statisitcs, 1975; (with G.W. McElrath and D.A. Berry) Introduction to Probability and Statistics, 4th edit., 1978. Home: 1860 Noble Dr Golden Valley MN 55422

LINDGREN, RAYMOND ELMER, educator; b. Kansas City, Kans., Feb. 10, 1913; s. Charles Victor and Hannah (Carlson) L.; A.B., U. Calif. at Los Angeles, 1935, M.A., 1940, Ph.D., 1943; m. Genevieve Juanita Anderson, June 7, 1940; children—Karen Suzanne, John Eric, Diane Victoria. Instr., asst. prof. Occidental Coll., 1942-45, asso. prof. history, 1954-57, chmn. dept. history, 1956-61; asst. prof., then asso. prof. history Vanderbilt U., 1945-49, asso. prof., 1951-52; vis. lectr. Scandinavian area studies U. Minn., 1949-50, U. Wis., 1952-54; prof. history, dean Calif. State U. at Long Beach, 1961-66, acad. v.p., 1966-67, prof. history, 1969—; resident dir. Calif. State Colls. Internat. Programs, Uppsala, prof. history, 1967-69; NATO vis. prof. U. Oslo, 1967. Fulbright scholar to Norway, 1950-51; Gustaf V fellow Am. Scandinavian Found., 1951. Past dir. and pres. So. Calif. chpt. Am. Scandinavian Found. Decorated knight 1st class Order of North Star (Sweden). Mem. Am. Hist. Assn., Danish, Swedish, Norwegian hist. socs., Phi Kappa Phi, Phi Alpha Theta, Phi Delta Kappa. Lutheran. Author: (with Floyd Cave) Origins and Consequences of World War II, 1948; (with K. Deutsch, others) Political Community and the North Atlantic Area, 1957; Norway-Sweden: Union, Disunion and Scandinavian Integration, 1959. Address: Calif State U Long Beach CA 90840

LINDGREN, RICHARD THOMAS, constrn. machinery co. exec.; b. Two Harbors, Minn., Apr. 5, 1927; s. Arvid John and Agnes (Sellman) L.; student Virginia (Minn.) Jr. Coll., 1947; B.B.A., U. Minn., 1949; M.B.A., Harvard, 1951-53; LL.D., Buena Vista Coll., 1970; m. Lois Irene Nelson, June 17, 1950; children—Douglas John, Danna Carol. With Ford Motor Co., Dearborn, Mich., 1953-71, dir. mktg. ops., 1970-71; group v.p. Allis-Chalmers Co., Milw., 1971-73; exec. v.p. Mead Corp., Dayton, Ohio, 1973-75; pres. Koehring Co., Milw., 1975-76, chmn., 1976—; chmn. bd. ROTEK Inc.; dir. KYNOS S.A., Madrid, Spain, Wick Bldg. Systems, Madison, Wis.; vice chmn. dist. export council U.S. Dept. Commerce, 1974-75. Trustee Buena Vista Coll., 1962-70; bd. dirs. Luth. Social Services of Wis. and Upper Mich., Curtis R. Froedert Meml. Hosp., Milw. Served with AUS, 1945-46; ETO. Mem. Soc. Automotive Engrs., Constrn. Industry Mfrs. Assn. (dir.). Lutheran. Home: 16620 Mary Cliff Brookfield WI 53005 Office: Koehring Co 200 Executive Dr Brookfield WI 53005

LINDH, PATRICIA SULLIVAN, govt. ofcl.; b. Toledo, Oct, 2, 1928; d. Lawrence Walsh and Lillian Winifred (Devlin) Sullivan; B.A., Trinity Coll., Washington, 1950, LL.D., 1975; LL.D., Walsh Coll., Canton, Ohio, 1975; m. H. Robert Lindh, Jr., Nov. 12, 1955; children—Sheila, Deborah, Robert. Adoption case worker Catholic Charities, Chgo., 1954-55; editor Singapore Am. Newspaper, 1957-62; spl. asst. to counsellor to Pres., 1974, spl. asst. to Pres., 1975-76; dep. asst. sec. state for ednl. and cultural affairs Dept. State, 1976-78; v.p., dir. corp. communications Bank Am., Los Angeles, 1978—. Vice pres. Arts Council, Found. for Hist. La., 1973-74; trustee Calif. Hosp. Med. Center; bd. dirs. Children's Bur. Los Angeles, Nat. Fedn. Rep. Women; mem. adv. panel Assn. Jr. Leagues, 1979—. Republican state vice chairwoman La., 1970-74; v.p. Women in Politics: Goals Congress of Baton Rouge, 1971; Rep. nat. committeewoman, La., 1974. Bd. dirs. Jr. League of Baton Rouge, 1969, Baton Rouge Civic Symphony, 1971; trustee La. Arts and Sci. Center, 1970-73. Mem. AAUW. Roman Catholic. Home: 3278 Wilshire Blvd Apt 602 Los Angeles CA 90010

LINDHEIM, RICHARD DAVID, producer; b. N.Y.C., May 28, 1939; s. Gilbert R. and Pearl (Gruskin) L.; B.S., U. Redlands, 1961; postgrad U. So. Calif., 1963; m. Dec. 22, 1963; children—Susan

Patricia, David Howard. Adminstrv. asst. story dept. CBS, 1963-69; project dir. entertainment testing ASI Market Research, Los Angeles, 1964-69; v.p. program research NBC, Burbank, Calif., 1969-77, v.p. dramatic programs, 1977-79; producer Universal TV, Universal City, Calif., 1979—; asst. prof. Calif. State U.; sr. lectr. U. So. Calif.; lectr. UCLA; reviewer Nat. Endowment for Humanities. Mem. Acad. TV Arts and Scis., Producers Guild Am., Writers Guild Am., Nat. Assn. Rail Passengers. Democrat. Jewish. Contbr. articles to profl. jours. Office: 100 Universal Plaza Universal City CA 91608. *In this sophisticated society there are fewer and fewer opportunities for the individual. Technology has made most tasks too complex for one man. As a result the ability to work with other people and to provide leadership and management to groups of people has become vital. The key ingredients are communication, respect for others, and a feeling of belonging, while working in a relaxed, casual environment, where the leader is responsible and receptive.*

LINDHOLM, CARL EDWARD, electronics co. exec.; b. N.Y.C., Mar. 8, 1929; s. Carl Edward and Elsie (Krone) L.; B.S., Webb Inst., N.Y.C., 1950; M.S. in Indsl. Engring., N.Y. U., 1952, M.B.A., 1954; m. Louise MacDonald; children—Jeffrey, Julia, Claire. With Motorola Inc., 1967—, v.p., dir. corp. staff, then sr. v.p., dir. corp. staff, Schaumburg, Ill., 1974-75, sr. v.p., gen. mgr. automotive products div., 1975-78, sr. v.p., gen. mgr. automotive and display systems group, 1978—. Served with USNR, 1955-58. Address: Motorola Inc 1299 E Algonquin Rd Schaumburg IL 60196

LINDHOLM, DWIGHT HENRY, lawyer; b. Blackduck, Minn., May 27, 1930; s. Henry Nathanial and Viola Eudora (Gummert) L.; student Macalester Coll., 1948-49; B.B.A., U. Minn., 1951, LL.B., 1954; postgrad. Mexico City Coll. (now U. of Ams.), 1956-57; m. Loretta Catherine Brown, Aug. 29, 1958; children—Douglas Dwight, Dionne Louise, Jeanne Marie, Philip Clayton, Kathleen Anne. Admitted to Minn. bar, 1954, Calif. bar, 1958; practice law, 1958-65; partner firm Lindholm & Johnson, Los Angeles, 1965-69, 72—, Cotter, Lindholm & Johnson, Los Angeles, 1969-72; individual practice law, Los Angeles, 1972—. Mem. Calif. Republican Central Com., 1962-63, Los Angeles Republican County Central Com., 1962-66. Bd. dirs. Family Service Los Angeles, 1964-70, v.p., 1968-70; bd. dirs. Wilshire YMCA, 1976-77; trustee Westlake Girls Sch., 1978. Served as capt. JAG Corps, USAF, 1954-56. Recipient Presdl. award Los Angeles Jr. C. of C., 1959. Mem. Am., Calif., Los Angeles County bar assns., Lawyers Club Los Angeles, Los Angeles Trial Lawyers Assn., Delta Sigma Pi, Delta Sigma Rho, Delta Theta Phi (state chancellor 1972-73). Presbyterian (elder 1962—, dir. 1972-75, treas. 1972). Clubs: Masons, Shrine, Rotary (dir. 1975-78), Anacapa Yacht, Calif. Home: 255 S Rossmore Ave Los Angeles CA 90004 Office: 3701 Wilshire Blvd Suite 700 Los Angeles CA 90010

LINDHOLM, JOHN VICTOR, ch. ofcl.; b. Kane, Pa., Dec. 29, 1934; s. John Edwin and Mary (Nord) L.; B.B.A., Upsala Coll., 1956; postgrad. N.Y. U., 1960-66; m. Ann Christine Lundquist, Apr. 27, 1957; children—Scott Benjamin, Kristine Ann, John Edwin. Loan officer Irving Trust Co., N.Y.C., 1960-61; treas., sec. for fin. bd. World Missions Lutheran Ch. Am., N.Y.C., 1961-69, coordinator spl. services, 1969-72, exec. dir. Office for Research and Planning, 1972-74; pres., exec. dir. EOPI, 1974—; dir. fin. Guideposts Assos. Inc., 1975—; v.p. Stock in Trade, Sherman, Conn., 1979—; mem. adv. com. county trust region Bank of N.Y., Brewster, 1978—. Treas., Putnam Alliance, 1978—; trustee Bethel Meth. Home, 1978—; mem. Sherman Planning and Zoning Commn., 1979—. Served to lt. USNR, 1956-59. Mem. Paradise Falls Lutheran Assn. (dir. 1969-72). Lutheran. Club: Carmel Rotary (dir.). Author: Program Planning and Budgeting for the Churches, 1971; Reporting System for Non-Profit Organizations, 1974. Home: Taber Rd Quaker Ridge Sherman CT 06784 Office: Seminary Hill Carmel NY 10512

LINDHOLM, RICHARD WADSWORTH, educator; b. Mankato, Minn., June 11, 1914; s. Theodore E. and Elizabeth S. (Swanson) L.; B.A., Gustavus Adolphus Coll., 1935; M.A., U. Minn., 1938; Ph.D., U. Tex., 1942; m. Mary M. Trunko, Sept. 11, 1948; 1 son, Richard Theodore. Tchr., Souris (N.D.) Jr. High Sch., 1935, Worthington (Minn.) High Sch., 1938-39; mem. Minn. Income Study, 1939-40; instr. Coll. St. Thomas, 1940-41, U. Tex., 1941- 42; asst. prof. Tex. A. and M. Coll., 1942, Ohio State U., 1946-48; asso. prof. Mich. State U., 1948-50, prof., 1950-58; dean Coll. Bus. Adminstrn., U. Oreg., 1958-71, founder, dean Grad. Sch. Mgmt. and Bus., 1967-71, prof. finance, 1971—. Fiscal economist Fed. Res. Bd., 1950-51, 64-65; econ. cons. 1st Nat. Bank of Oreg., 1961-69; mem. Mich. Employment Com., 1954; sr. tax adviser, cons. econ. devel. ICA, Saigon, Viet-Nam, 1955-57; bus. tax cons. Mich. Legislature tax study, 1958; coordinator econ. adv. group in Korea, 1959-61; nat. com. Taxation, Resources and Econ. Devel.; tax com. to increase exports Dept. Commerce, 1965—; tax adviser Australian Govt., 1969, Gov. of Oreg., 1970-71. Cons. U.S. Dept. State, 1972-75, Dept. Planning, Istanbul, Turkey, 1974, U.S. Com. Ways and Means, 1975; tax adviser, Philippines, 1977. Chmn. Chinju-Eugene Sister City Com., 1961. Mem. Oreg. Econ. Adv. Com., 1966—. Served from pvt. to capt. AUS, 1942-45; ETO. Decorated 5 battle stars. Fulbright lectr., Pakistan, 1952; Lincoln Inst. Land Policy grantee, 1976, 77. Mem. Am. (pres. 1976), Western econ. assns., Nat. (dir. 1967-70), Western tax assns., Asia Soc., Pi Beta Delta, Beta Gamma Sigma (distinguished scholar 1975-76), Pi Gamma Mu. Author: The Corporate Franchise as the Basis of Taxation, 1944; Taxation in Ohio, 1946; Public Finance of Air Transportation, 1948; Introduction to Fiscal Policy, 2d edit., 1955; (with others) Public Finance and Fiscal Policy, 2d edit., 1958; Money and Banking, 3d edit., 1969; Money and Finance, 1951; Taxation of the Trucking Industry, 1951; Principles of Money and Banking, 1954; Money and Banking and Economic Development in Free Viet-Nam, 1957; (sr. author) Our American Economy, 1958, 4th edit., 1970; (with others) The Tax Systems of Michigan with Recommendations, 1958; Economic Development Policy, 1964; A Description and Analysis of Oregon's Fiscal System, 1971; Editor, contbr. Viet-Nam: The First Five Years, 1959; Property Taxation U.S.A., 1967; Property Taxation and the Finance of Education, 1974; A Business Approach to Taxation, 1966; Business Taxation Notes, 1967; Taxation of Timber Resources, 1973; New Tax Directions for the United States, 1975; Value Added Tax, 1976; Property Tax Reform, 1977; Money Management and Institutions, 1978; Financ and Management of State and Local Government, 1979; contbr. articles to profl. jours. Home: 2520 Fairmount Blvd Eugene OR 97403

LINDHOLM, WILLIAM LAWRENCE, ret. telephone co. exec.; b. Mountain Grove, Mo., May 27, 1914; s. Lawrence E. and Elizabeth (Mitchell) L.; student U. Ala., 1933-34; B.A. in Bus. Adminstrn., U. Mo., 1936; LL.D., Bethany Coll., 1972; m. Eleanor Lane Davis, June 16, 1939; 1 son, Robert Kenneth. With Southwestern Bell Telephone Co., 1936-65, gen. mgr. S. Tex. area, Houston, 1959-63, v.p. for Tex., Dallas, 1963-65; pres., chief exec. officer Chesapeake & Potomac Telephone Cos., 1965-70; exec. v.p. Am. Tel. & Tel. Co., N.Y.C., 1970-72, vice chmn. bd., 1972-76, pres., 1976-77; dir. Shell Oil Co., Tex. Instruments, Austin Bancshares. Methodist. Home: 112 Firebird Austin TX 78734

LINDLEY, AUDRA, actress; b. Los Angeles, Sept. 24, 1925; d. Bert and Bessie (Fisher) L.; children—John, Elizabeth, Alice, William, Bert. Appeared in leading roles in Broadway plays, including: Take Her She's Mine, 1962, A Case of Libel, 1964, Spofford, 1968; summer theatre appearance: The Chic Life, Westport, Conn. (Straw Hat award), 1970; appeared in numerous live TV dramas, 1950's, including Kraft Show, Robert Montgomery Presents, Playhouse 90; TV series: Bridget Loves Bernie, 1972, Fay, 1975, Doc, 1974, Three's Company, 1976-78, Another World (as Liz Mathews), 1964-69, The Ropers (as Helen Roper), 1979—; TV movie: Pearl, 1978; movies: Taking Off, 1970, The Heartbreak Kid, 1972, When Ya Coming Back Red Ryder, 1979; guest appearances on various TV shows. Mem. Screen Actors Guild, AFTRA, Actors Equity. Democrat. Office: care ABC Press Relations 1330 Ave of Americas New York NY 10019

LINDLEY, DENTON RAY, clergyman, coll. adminstr.; b. May, Tex., May 27, 1905; s. Calvin Denton and Maud (Brown) L.; student Johnson Bible Coll., 1922-23; A.B., Phillips U., 1926; B.D., Brite Coll. of the Bible, Tex. Christian U., 1941, D.Litt., 1967; B.D., magna cum laude, Yale U., 1941; M.A., 1943, Ph.D., 1947; LL.D., Atlantic Christian Coll., 1956; L.H.D., William Woods Coll., 1972; D.D., Culver-Stockton Coll., 1974; m. Maybon Marie Torrey, Mar. 17, 1926; children—Gene Ray, Neil Everett. Pastor Central Christian Ch., Weatherford, Tex., 1928-30, First Christian Ch., Big Spring, Tex., 1930-33, St. Charles Av. Christian Ch., New Orleans, 1933-37; pres. La. Christian Missionary Soc., 1934- 36; editor, Louisiana Christian, 1933-37; pastor Central Christian Ch., San Antonio, 1937-40; pres. Tex. Christian Ministers' Inst., 1938; dean Young Peoples Summer Confs. of Disciples of Christ, 1935-46; lectr. Businessmen's Bible Class, San Antonio, 1938-40; head dept. Christian ministries, Brite Coll. of The Bible, Tex. Christian U., 1941-47, dean, 1947-50, v.p., 1953-58, exec. v.p., 1958, pres., 1959-62; pres. Atlantic Christian Coll., Wilson, N.C., 1950-53; pres. U. of Americas, 1962-71, chancellor, 1971—. Vice pres. Internat. Conv. Disciples of Christ, 1950-52; chmn. bd. higher edn., Disciples of Christ, 1952-53; del. World Conf. on Faith and Order, Lund, Sweden, 1952. Mem. exec. com. N.C. Coll. Conf., 1952-53; exec. com., unified promotion Disciples of Christ, 1952-53; panel of scholars Disciples of Christ, 1955—; mem. commn. ministerial placement, Christian Chs., 1958—; trustee Tex. Bd. Christian Chs., 1958-60. Dir. Sem. State Bank, Ft. Worth. Mem. Religious Edn. Assn., S.W. Bibl. Inst., Intersem. Assn., Tex. Council Ch. related Colls. (pres. 1961-62), Am. C. of C. (dir.), Am. Soc. of Mexico (dir.), Mexican-N.Am. Cultural Inst. (dir.), So. Assn. Colls. (commn. on Latin Am. relations). Mason. Clubs: University; Rotary. Author: Alexander Campbell-Herald of Religious Liberty, 1948; Calling a Minster, 1950; Apostle of Freedom, 1957; (with others) The Faith of Tradition, 1963; also articles on religious subjects. Home and office: 142 Paradise Valley W Columbia TX 77486

LINDLEY, JAMES GUNN, banker; b. Greensboro, N.C., June 13, 1931; s. Paul Cameron and Helen Marie (Gunn) L.; B.S. in Bus. Adminstrn., U. N.C., 1953; M.B.A. in Fin., N.Y. U., 1960; m. Jane Kennedy, Dec. 3, 1954; children—James Gunn, Patricia Van, Julia Anne. Sr. v.p. Mfrs. Hanover Trust Co., N.Y.C., 1953-75; pres., chief exec. officer Bankshares of N.C. and Bank of N.C., N.A., Raleigh, 1975-79, S.C. Nat. Bank, Columbia, 1979—; pres. S.C. Nat. Corp., 1979—. Served to capt. USNR, 1953-57. Office: PO Box 168 Columbia SC 29202

LINDLEY, JOHN MARSHALL, soup co. exec.; b. Hamilton, Ont., Can., Dec. 12, 1930; s. Robert M. and Janet I. (Marshall) L.; B.S. in Agr., U. Guelph (Ont.); m. Joan V. Stiles, Nov. 3, 1956; children—Stephen, Douglas, Jane. County agt. Ont. Dept. Agr., 1953-55; with Campbell Soup Co. Ltd., Toronto, Ont., 1955-71, pres., 1966-71; pres. Campbell Soups Internat., Europe, 1971-75, 1975—; v.p. Campbell Soup Co., Camden, N.J. Bd. govs. U. Guelph, 1969-71, Queensway Hosp., Toronto, 1968-71. Mem. U. Guelph Alumni Assn., World Affairs Council, Agrl. Inst. Can., Union League. Episcopalian. Clubs: Nat., Masons. Office: Campbell Pl Camden NJ 08101*

LINDMAN, ERICK LEROY, educator; b. Seattle, May 26, 1909; s. Erik Herman and Beda (Carlson) L.; A.B., Whitman Coll., 1931; Ph.D., U. Wash., 1948; m. Blanche Anna Ashton, July 7, 1934; children—Erick LeRoy, Valerie Ann, Alan Ashton. High sch. tchr. Seattle pub. schs., 1934-41; dir. research, dep. supt. schs. Wash., 1941-49; chief sch. finance sect., dir. sch. adminstrn. br. U.S. Office Edn., Washington, 1949-52; prof. edn., chmn. dept. George Peabody Coll. Tchrs., 1952-59; prof. edn., Sch. Edn., U. Calif. at Los Angeles, 1959—, acting dean Sch. Edn., 1966-67; cons. ednl. finance, 1952—. Mem. N.E.A. (chmn. com. ednl. finance 1962-65), Am. Ednl. Research Assn., Am. Assn. Sch. Adminstrn., Phi Beta Kappa. Author: (with Edgar Morphet) Public School Finance Programs in the Forty Eight States, 1950; The Federal Government and the Pub. Schs., 1966; Dilemmas of School Finance, 1974. Home: 14119 Village 14 Camarillo CA 93010 Office: Grad Sch Edn U Calif Los Angeles CA 90024. *A problem is not solved when its origins have been described nor when its scapegoats have been selected, but only after a promising course of action has been identified.*

LINDNER, CARL H., diversified financial holding co. exec.; b. Dayton, 1919. Chmn. bd., pres. Gt. Am. Ins. Co., Cin.; pub. Cin. Enquirer; chmn. bd. Provident Bank, Cin., Hunter Savs. Assn., Cin., United Liberty Life Ins. Co.; partner United Dairy Farmers Investment Co., Cin.; dir. United Brands, Combined Communications, Fairmont Foods. Home: 8555 Shawnee Run Rd Cincinnati OH 45243 Office: 1 E 4th St Cincinnati OH 45202

LINDNER, KENNETH EDWARD, state ofcl.; b. LaCrosse, Wis., Nov. 29, 1922; s. Henry B. and Cora (Ward) L.; B.S., Wis. State U., 1949; M.A., U. Ia., 1953; Ph.D., 1966; m. Ila M. Jacobson, Feb. 28, 1947; children—Diane, Charles, Barbara, Nancy, John, Sara. High sch. chemistry tchr. Black River Falls, Wis., 1949-55; prof. chemistry Wis. State U., LaCrosse, 1956-67; head acad. affairs Wis. State U. System, Madison, 1967-70; chancellor U. Wis.-LaCrosse, 1971-79; chmn. Council Chancellors U. Wis. System, 1978-79; sec. Wis. State Dept. Adminstrn., 1979—; cons. radiation chemistry Dairyland Power Coop., LaCrosse Boiling Water Reactor, 1966-67; cons. radiation safety Gunderson Clinic, Luth. Hosp., LaCrosse, 1966-67; cons-examiner N. Central Assn. Colls. and Secondary Schs., 1972—, commr., 1976—. Served with AUS, 1942-45. Mem. Internat. Radiation Protection Soc., Am. Chem. Soc., Health Physics Soc. Home: 6639 Chestnut Circle Windsor WI 53598

LINDNER, ROBERT DAVID, financial co. exec.; b. Dayton, O., Aug. 5, 1920; s. Carl Henry and Clara (Serrer) L.; grad. high sch.; m. Betty Ruth Johnston, Mar. 29, 1947; children—Robert David, Jeffrey Scott, Alan Bradford, David Clark. With Am. Financial Corp., Cin., 1959—, former v.p., vice chmn. bd., now sr. v.p., vice chmn. bd. Partner, United Dairy Farmers, Cin., 1940—. Trustee No. Bapt. Theol. Sem. Served with U.S. Army, 1942-45. Mason. Home: 6950 Given Rd Cincinnati OH 45243 Office: 3955 Montgomery Rd Cincinnati OH 45212

LINDON, JOHN ARNOLD, psychiatrist, psychoanalyst; b. Chgo., Mar. 11, 1924; s. Albert and Rose L.; M.D., U. Louisville, 1948; Ph.D., So. Calif. Psychoanalytic Inst., 1977; m. Ruth N. Blumenson, May 22, 1953 (dec. 1971); children—Julie Helen, Mark Lincoln; m. 2d, Marilyn Becker, June 4, 1973. Intern, Cedars of Lebanon Hosp., Los Angeles, 1948-49; resident Brentwood Neuropsychiat. Center, 1949-52; psychoanalytic tng. Inst. Psychoanalytic Medicine So. Calif. (now So. Calif. Psychoanalytic Inst.), 1950-55, both Los Angeles, mem. faculty, 1958—; pvt. practice psychiatry and psychoanalysis, Beverly Hills, Los Angeles, 1951—; instr. Coll. Med. Evangelists, 1952-53; asst. clin. prof. psychiatry U. So. Calif., 1960-68; asso. clin. prof. psychiatry Med. Sch. U. Calif. at Los Angeles, 1968—, also asso. vis. psychiatrist univ. hosp. and clinics; cons. Calif. Dept. Mental Hygiene, Los Angeles, 1957-72, Calif. Dept. Correction, 1962—; sr. cons. Met. State Hosp., Norwalk, Calif., 1957-72; pres. Psychiat. Research Found., 1958—. Served with AUS, 1942-46. Diplomate Am. Bd. Psychiatry and Neurology, Nat. Bd. Med. Examiners. Fellow Am. Psychiat. Assn.; mem. AAAS, Am., So. Calif. (past v.p.), Internat. (clin. essay prize 1957) psychoanalytic assns., Am., Calif., Los Angeles County med. assns., UCLA Med. Soc., Fedn. Am. Scientists, Am. Soc. for Adolescent Psychiatry, So. Calif. Psychoanalytic Inst. (supervising and tng. analyst, also trustee 1960-63, 68-74, sec.-treas. 1971-74, chmn. 1978—, pres. 1978—), So. Calif. Psychiat. Soc. Author numerous books, also articles profl. jours. Editor-in-chief Psychoanalytic Forum, 1965—; contbg. editor Ann. Survey of Psychoanalysis, 1959—. Office: 10921 Wilshire Blvd Los Angeles CA 90024

LINDOW, JOHN WESLEY, banker; b. Detroit, June 28, 1910; s. Wesley and Ida Anna (Oetjen) L.; A.B., Wayne U., 1931; M.A., George Washington U., 1940; m. Eleanor Niemetta, Aug. 2, 1940; children—John Frederick, Eric Anthony. Economist, FCA, 1934; economist Treasury Dept., 1934-47, asst. dir. research and statistics, 1944-47; with Irving Trust Co., N.Y.C., 1947-75, v.p. charge econs. dept., 1947-55, v.p., head investment adminstrn. div., 1955-68, sec., 1959-70, sr. v.p., 1961-66, exec. v.p., 1966-75; exec. v.p. Charter N.Y. Corp., 1966-70, vice chmn., 1970-72, pres., 1972-75, also dir.; chmn. bd. First Capital Inc., 1975—; former mem. faculty Stonier Grad. Sch. Banking, Rutgers U.; mem. adv. com. banking Bur. Budget; com. tax policies econ. growth. Nat. Bur. Econ. Research; mem. adv. com. to supt. banks N.Y. State, 1973-74, trustee Banking Research Fund; bd. dirs., mem. exec. com., chmn. research com. Assn. Bank Holding Cos.; occasional cons. Fed. Home Loan Bank Bd. and Sec. of Treasury. Recipient Alumni award Wayne U., 1953. Mem. Phi Beta Kappa. Author: Inside the Money Market, 1972; co-author: Determining the Business Outlook, 1954; author articles in field. Home: 23 Bellows Ln Manhasset NY 11030 Office: 1800 M St NW Suite 900 Washington DC 20036

LINDQUIST, CLARENCE BERNHART, govt. ednl. adminstr.; b. Superior, Wis., Dec. 21, 1913; s. Gust and Hannah (Berentson) L.; B.E., U. Wis., 1937, M. Philosophy, 1939, Ph.D., 1941; m. Helen Jane Conroy, Dec. 29, 1941; children—Clarence Conroy, Thomas Ward, James Raymond, Robert Michael, Mary Lenore. Instr. U.S. Naval Acad., Annapolis, Md., 1941-42, asst. prof., 1945-46; mem. faculty U. Minn., Duluth, 1946-57, adminstrv. asst. to provost, 1949-51, prof., head math. and engring., 1951-57; program and research specialist U.S. Office Edn., Washington, 1957—, chief higher edn. personnel tng. programs, bur. postsecondary edn., 1974-76, program mgr. domestic mining and mineral fuel conservation fellowship program, 1976—; cons. Conf. Bd. Math. Scis., NSF. Served to lt. comdr. USNR, 1942-45. U. Wis. Alumni fellow. Mem. AAAS, NEA, Am. Math. Soc., Math. Assn. Am., Ret. Officers Assn., Sigma Xi. Lutheran. Author: Mathematics in Colleges and Universities, 1965; Recent Trends in Soviet Scientific and Technical Education, 1964; Soviet Education Programs, 1960; Aspects of Undergraduate Training in the Mathematical Sciences, 1969; NDEA Fellowships for College Teaching, 1971; also articles in profl. jours. Home: 6008 Utah Ave NW Washington DC 20015 Office: 400 Maryland Ave SW Washington DC 20202

LINDQUIST, RAYMOND IRVING, clergyman; b. Sumner, Nebr., Apr. 14, 1907; s. Rev. Elmer H. and Esther (Nyberg) L.; student Kearney State Coll., 1925; A.B., Wheaton Coll., Ill., 1929; student Columbia Law Sch., 1929-30; A.M., Princeton U., 1933; Th.B. (Hugh Davies prize homiletics; Erdman prize Bible; Zwemer fellow Comparative Religions), Princeton Sem., 1933; D.D., Cumberland U., 1939; LL.D., Bloomfield Coll., N.J., 1957, Eastern Coll., 1977; L.H.D., U. Calif., 1963; m. Ella Sofield, Sept. 16, 1930; children—Ray Irving, Ruth Elizabeth Lindquist McCalmont. Ordained to ministry Presbyn. Ch., 1934; dir. religious edn. Third Presbyn. Ch., Newark, 1931-34; minister Old First Presbyn. Ch., Orange, N.J., 1934-53, Hollywood First Presbyn. Ch., 1953-71; vis. prof. homiletics Bloomfield Sem., N.J., 1945-53; lectr. Princeton Sem., Pittcairn-Crabbe, Pitts., USAF, Israel, Germany, Johnston Island, UCLA, U. So. Calif., Pentagon, Northwestern U. Pres. bd. nat. missions United Presbyn. Ch., 1955-62, gen. council, 1955-62; v.p. Templeton Found. Bd. dirs. Presbyn. Ministers Fund, Phila., Presbyn. Med. Center, Hollywood, Calif., Met. YMCA, Los Angeles; trustee Princeton Theol. Sem. Mem. Phi Kappa Delta. Clubs: Rotary, Los Angeles Country (Los Angeles); Symposium (Princeton); Glen Lake, Sunset Rock (Sparta, N.J.); Shadow Mountain (Palm Desert, Calif.). Author: Notes for Living. Home: 74237 Old Prospector Trail Palm Desert CA 92260 Office: 568 B Ave Sevilla Laguna Hills CA 92653. *Faith is not jumping to conclusions; it is concluding to jump.*

LINDQUIST, RICHARD FREDERICK, fin. co. exec.; b. Chgo., Dec. 25, 1923; s. Alexander G. and Alta (Lishness) L.; B.S. with honors, U. Ill., 1948; m. Catherine W. Neumann, Aug. 12, 1946 (div.); children—Jeffrey S., Nancy A.; m. 2d, Joan G. Hayden. Mgr., Arthur Andersen & Co., C.P.A.'s, Ill., Tex., Okla., 1948-54; dir., sec., treas. Gibraltar Oil Co., Oklahoma City, 1954-56; fin. and adminstrv. v.p. Curtiss Candy Co., Chgo., 1957-59; comptroller Assos. Corp. of N.Am., N.Y.C., 1959-69, v.p., 1972, sr. v.p., 1972, exec. v.p., 1973—; exec. v.p. Assos. First Capital Corp., N.Y.C., 1975—. Bd. dirs., mem. exec. com. Civic Center Found., South Bend, Ind., 1975-76. Served with AUS, World War II. Mem. Fin. Execs. Inst. (dir. 1973-76). Home: 5411 Royal Crest Dr Dallas TX 75229 Office: Assos Corp NAm (Tex) PO Box 222822 Dallas TX 75222

LINDQUIST, ROBERT STEWART, banker; b. Lansing, Mich., Dec. 27, 1922; s. Alfred John and Dagny Constance (Hanson) L.; student Mich. State U., 1942-43; A.B., U. Mich., 1950; student Advanced Mgmt. Program, Harvard, 1972; m. 2d, Peggy Miller Clark, Aug. 9, 1977; 2 daus., 4 stepsons. With China Office, UNRRA, 1946-47, Internat. Refugee Orgn. in Germany and Switzerland, 1948-49; joined U.S. Fgn. Service, 1952; asst. attache embassy, Damascus, Syria, 1952-53; attache embassy, Jidda, Saudi Arabia, 1953-54; Chinese lang. student embassy, Taipei, Republic China, 1956-58; 2d sec. embassy, Djakarta, Indonesia, 1958-59; consul, prin. officer, Medan, Indonesia, 1959-60; officer charge Indonesian affairs State Dept., 1960-62; assigned sr. seminar fgn. policy State Dept., 1962-63; counselor polit. affairs embassy, Taipei, Taiwan, 1963-66; country dir. Australia, New Zealand and Pacific Islands, State Dept., 1966-68; counselor embassy, dep. chief mission embassy, Kuala Lumpur, Malaysia, 1968-71; counselor of embassy, Bangkok, Thailand, 1971-72; asst. dir. for mgmt. Fgn. Service Inst., Dept. of State, Washington, 1973-75; ret., 1975; v.p.-area mgr. for Asia, Internat. Fin. Services div. Chase Manhattan Bank, Hong Kong, 1976—. Served to 1st lt. USMCR, 1943-46, 51-52; PTO. Home: Flint Hill VA 22627 Office: Chase Manhattan Bank GPO Box 104 Hong Kong

LINDSAY, BRYAN EUGENE, educator, writer; b. Bklyn., Sept. 19, 1931; s. Eugene Fenton and Evelyn (Moore) L.; B.A., Troy (Ala.) State Coll., 1956; M.A., George Peabody Coll. Tchrs., 1962, Ph.D., 1966; m. Mary Ray Moore; children—Eric Evan, Alyson, Christy, Tracey, Jason Moore. Choral and stage band dir. Choctawatchee High Sch., Shalimar, Fla., 1956-61; chmn. dept. humanities, dir. music Okaloosa-Walton Jr. Coll., Valparaiso, Fla., 1965-69; chmn. gen. studies humanities program, prof. humanities Eastern Ky. U., Richmond, 1969-72; mem. staff Center Humanities, Converse Coll., Spartanburg, S.C., 1972-76; asso. prof. U.S.C., Spartanburg, 1976—; specialist, workshop gifted and talented, gifted program devel. sect. Ill. Dept. Edn., 1970—. Served with USAF, 1951-54. NDEA fellow, 1961-64; Guidance and Counseling Inst. fellow, 1960; Mem. ASCAP (Composers award 1963, 64, 65), Nat. Acad. Rec. Arts and Scis., Nat. Assn. Jazz Educators (div. coordinator 1972-74), Nat. Assn. Humanities Edn. (pres. 1976-78, exec. sec. 1978—), Am. Film Inst., S.C. Music Educators Assn., Music Educators Nat. Conf., World Poetry Soc., World Future Soc. Author poems. composer music. Home: 109 Greenbriar Rd Spartanburg SC 29302 Office: Sch Humanities and Scis U SC Spartanburg SC 29303

LINDSAY, CHARLES JOSEPH, banker; b. Bklyn., Mar. 21, 1924; s. George Patrick and Evelyn (Roth) L.; student U. Mo., 1943; grad. Am. Savs. and Loan Inst., 1947, Savs. and Loan Grad. Sch., Ind. U.; Profl. Studies in Bus. Adminstrn. Degree with high distinction, Pace U., 1973; m. Marie A. Faraone, Jan. 19, 1947; children—George, Charles, Mary Ann. With Serial Fed. Savs. & Loan Assn., N.Y.C., 1947—, successively teller, supr., asst. v.p., asst. sec., sec., v.p. and sec., sr. v.p. and dir., pres., 1965—. Mem. faculty, bd. govs. Savs. and Loan Inst.; gov. for N.Y. State, Nat. League Savs. Assns. Mem. Pres.' advisory council Fairfield U. Served with USAAF, World War II. Decorated Air medal with cluster. Recipient Alumnus of Year award Pace U., 1975. Mem. N.Y. Fin. Advertisers, State League Savs. Assn. (dir.), Nat. League Savs. Assns. (exec. com., dir.), Alumni Assn. Pace U. (pres. 1977—, dir.). Clubs: Aspetuck Country (Weston, Conn.); Richmond County Country (S.I., N.Y.). Home: Winter Leaves 4 Lilac Ln Weston CT 06883 Office: 140 William St New York NY 10038

LINDSAY, CHARLES ROGERS, III, ret. chem. mfr.; b. Chgo., July 10, 1903; s. Charles Rogers, Jr. and Dorothea (Gilman) L.; grad. St. Albans Sch., Washington.; A.B., Williams Coll., 1925; m. Isabella Woods Walsh, May 15, 1926; children—Dorothea Gilman (Mrs. Jurgen W. Heberle), Katherine Bingham. Vice pres., dir. Lindsay Chem. Co., West Chicago, Ill., 1926-37, chmn. bd., pres., 1937-58; v.p., dir. Am. Potash & Chem. Corp., Los Angeles, 1958-68. Mem. personnel security bd. AEC, 1950-70. Precinct committeeman Republican Party, St. Charles, Ill., 1954—, presdl. elector for Ill., 1956; chmn. St. Charles Rep. Central Com., 1966-70. Mem. exec. com. County Bd. Kane County, Ill., 1972—; mem. exec. com. Kane County Forest Preserve, 1972—. Adv. bd. Salvation Army; trustee Delnor Hosp., St. Charles, Ill. Mem. Masters Fox Hounds Assn. Am., Sigma Phi Soc. Congregationalist. Clubs: Chevy Chase (Washington); Williams (N.Y.C.); University, Tavern, (Chgo.); Mill Reef (Antigua, B.W.I.); Dunham Woods Riding, Wayne-DuPage Hunt (master fox hounds 1935-45) (Wayne, Ill.). Home: 34 W 856 Country Club Rd St Charles IL 60174

LINDSAY, DALE RICHARD, research adminstr.; b. Bunker Hill, Kans., Aug. 9, 1913; s. Charles Edwin and Iva (Missimer) L.; A.B., U. Kans., 1937, M.A., 1938; Ph.D., Iowa State Coll., 1943; m. Sybil Anne McCoy, June 6, 1937; children—Martha Lou Lindsay McKay, Judith Anne Lindsay Clapp, Patricia Dale. Entomologist, Dept. Agr., summers 1937-39; teaching fellow, instr., research asso. Iowa State Coll., 1938-43; commd. officer USPHS, 1943—, scientist dir., 1955; assigned malaria control in war areas, 1943-45; entomologist charge operations Communicable Disease Center Activies, Pharr, Tex., 1945-48; chief Thomasville (Ga.) field sta., 1948-53; chief program evaluation sect., div. research grants NIH, 1953-55, asst. chief div., 1955-60, chief div., 1960-63; dep. to gen. dir. Mass. Gen. Hosp., Boston, 1963-65; spl. asst. to chancellor health scis. U. Calif. at Davis, 1965-67, asst. chancellor research and health scis., 1968-69; asso. commr. sci. FDA, 1969-71; asso. dir. med. and allied health edn. Duke U., 1971-75; asst. dir. for sci. coordination Nat. Center for Toxicol. Research, Jefferson, Ark., 1975-76; adj. prof. medicine U. Ark. Med. Sch., 1975-76; asso. dept. family and community medicine U. Ariz., 1977—. Agrl. bd. Nat. Acad. Sci.-NRC, 1970-73; mem. exec. com., public trustee Nutrition Found., 1972, Environ. and Agrl. Found., 1974—; chmn. sci. adv. bd. Nat. Center for Toxicol. Research, 1972-74. Fellow AAAS, Am. Public Health Assn.; mem. Entomol. Soc. Am. (gov. bd. 1958-62), Soc. Tropical Medicine and Hygiene, Commd. Officer Assn. USPHS (treas. nat. exec. com. 1959-61), Assn. Am. Med. Schs., Sigma Xi, Phi Kappa Phi, Gamma Sigma Delta.

LINDSAY, DAVID BREED, JR., editor, publisher; b. Fayetteville, N.C., Dec. 25, 1922; s. David Breed and Helen Carter (Dodson) L.; B.S., Purdue U., 1947; m. Elizabeth Hotchkiss Girvin, June 19, 1944; children—David G. B., Robert A., Ann C., Edward H. Reporter/photographer Marion (Ind.) Chronicle, 1947-48; gen. mgr. Sarasota (Fla.) Herald Tribune, 1948-55, pres., editor, 1955—; pres. Cavalier Aircraft Corp., 1955-70; designer, test pilot Enforcer Aircraft; cons. Piper Aircraft Corp. Founder, trustee New Coll., Sarasota, 1950-75. Served with U.S. Army, 1943-46. Decorated Army Commendation medal. Mem. Am. Newspaper Pubs. Assn. (dir.), Am. Newspaper Pubs. Assn. Found. (pres.), Inter Am. Press Assn. (dir.), Soc. Exptl. Test Pilots. Episcopalian. Clubs: Met. (Washington); Old Capital (Monterey, Calif.); Univ. (Sarasota). Inventor various aircraft systems, including Enforcer Aircraft. Office: PO Box 1719 Sarasota FL 33578

LINDSAY, DENNIS JOHN, lawyer; b. Winnipeg, Man., Can., Mar. 22, 1918; s. Robert Kenneth and Sadi (Gombriche) L.; came to U.S., 1919, naturalized, 1941; student Ridley Coll. (Can.), 1930-34; B.A., Oberlin Coll., 1938; J.D., U. Mich., 1941; m. Elizabeth D. Carpenter, Nov. 11, 1943; children—Elizabeth A., James Niles, Patricia, Susan. Admitted to Mich. bar, 1941, N.Y. bar, 1945, Oreg. bar, 1948; atty. Dept. Interior, 1941-43; asso. firm Cahill, Gordon, Zachry & Reindel, N.Y.C., 1943-48; dep. dist. atty., Portland, Oreg., 1948-50; partner Krause, Evans, & Lindsay and successor firms, Portland, 1950-67; sr. partner Lindsay, Nahstoll, Hart, Neil & Weigler, Portland, 1967—. Mem. Port of Portland Commn., 1957-69, pres., 1958-60, 65, 68-69; mem. City of Portland Devel. Commn., 1974—. Mem. Am., Multnomah County bar assns., Oreg. State Bar (chmn. various coms.), Maritime Law Assn., Am. Judicature Soc., Propeller Club U.S. Democrat. Episcopalian. Home: 11050 SW Riverside Dr Portland OR 97219 Office: Carriage House 1331 SW Broadway Portland OR 97201

LINDSAY, DONALD PARKER, savs. bank exec.; b. Spokane, Aug. 31, 1915; s. Alexander John and Alice Maude (Kelly) L.; student U. Wash., 1934-35; m. Patricia Lally, Oct. 2, 1940; children—Karen, Bridget, Monica. With Lincoln Mut. Savs. Bank, Spokane, 1935—, pres., 1962—; dir. First Nat. Bank, Spokane; pres. Mut. Savs. Banks Wash. Chmn. United Red Feather drive, Spokane, 1952; past pres. Spokane Philharmonic; trustee Spokane Unltd.; past trustee Mcpl. League Spokane; past chmn. Champagne Ball Charities. Served from pvt. to 1st lt. USAAF, 1942-46. Mem. Wash. Savs. League (past pres.), Nat. Assn. Mut. Savs. Banks (dir.), Soc. Residential Appraisers (past pres.), Spokane C. of C. (trustee). Clubs: University (past pres.); Spokane Country (past pres.); The Spokane. Home: E 1306 Rockwood Blvd Spokane WA 99203 Office: W 818 Riverside Ave Spokane WA 99201

LINDSAY, FRANKLIN ANTHONY, corp. exec.; b. Kenton, Ohio, Mar. 12, 1916; s. Harry Wyatt and Ruth (Andrews) L.; A.B., Stanford, 1938; postgrad. Harvard, 1946; m. Margot Coffin, Dec. 17, 1948; children—Catherine, Alison, John Franklin. With Columbia div. U.S. Steel Corp., 1938-39; exec. asst. to Bernard Baruch, U.S. delegation UN Atomic Energy Commn., 1946; cons. Ho. of Reps. Select (Herter) Com. on Fgn. Aid, 1947-48, ECA, Paris; rep. to exec. com. OEEC, 1948-49; with CIA, 1949-53; with pub. affairs program Ford Found., 1953-56; prin. McKinsey & Co., Inc., N.Y.C., 1956-61; exec. v.p., dir. Itek Corp., Lexington, Mass., 1961-62, pres., dir., 1962-75, chmn. bd., 1975—. Research asso. Inst. Politics, Harvard, 1967-71; cons. 2d Hoover Commn., 1954, The White House, 1955; mem. Rockefeller Spl. Studies Panel Econ. Policy, 1956, Gaither Com. Nat. Security Policy, 1957; asst. staff dir. President's Com. World Econ. Policy, 1958; mem. President Elect's Task Force on Disarmament, 1960; dir. Com. for Nat. Trade Policy, 1956-71; adv. council dept. econs. Princeton, 1961-64; trustee Bennington Coll., 1963-73; chmn. bd. trustees Edn. Devel. Center, 1967-73; mem. vis. com. dept. econs. Harvard, 1976—; mem. President's Adv. Com. on Trade Negotiations, 1976—; bd. dirs. Nat. Bur. Econ. Research, 1976—; mem. advisory council Gas Research Inst., 1977—; vice chmn. energy and raw materials, bus. and industry advisory com. OECD, 1977; bd. dirs. Corp. Public/Pvt. Ventures, 1978—; mem. advisory bd. Public Agenda Found., 1978—, mem. Nat. Research Council Commn. Sociotech. Systems, 1978—; bd. dirs. Resources for the Future, 1978—. Served to lt. col. AUS, 1940-45, with guerrilla forces, Europe (OSS), 1944-45, chief U.S. Mil. Mission to Yugoslavia, 1945. Decorated Legion of Merit. Mem. Nat. Planning Assn. (vice chmn. com. arms control 1959-62), Council Fgn. Relations, Inst. Strategic Studies (London), Com. for Econ. Devel. (trustee 1967—, vice chmn. 1974—, chmn. research and policy com. 1976—), UN Assn. U.S.A. (gov. 1968-75), Canadian-Am. Com., Hudson Inst. (pub. mem.), Phi Beta Kappa, Tau Beta Pi. Club: Century Assn. Author: New Techniques of Mgmt. Decision Making, 1958; also articles on nat. and fgn. policy. Home: Lincoln MA 01773 Office: Itek Corp Lexington MA 02173

LINDSAY, GEORGE CARROLL, museum dir.; b. Cochranville, Pa., Sept. 28, 1928; s. J. George and M. Elizabeth (Copeland) L.; B.A., Franklin and Marshall Coll., 1950; student Dickinson Sch. Law, 1950-53; M.A. (Wintherthur fellow early Am. culture 1953-55), U. Del., 1955; m. Mary-Edythe Shelley, June 27, 1953. Asst. to dir. Henry Francis du Pont Wintherthur (Del.) Mus., 1955-56; asst. curator ethnology Smithsonian Instn., 1956-57, asso. curator cultural history, 1957-58, curator mus. service, 1958-66; dir. mus. services N.Y. State Mus., 1966—; lectr. early Am. decorative arts and architecture; cons. in field. Vice pres. Alexandria (Va.) Assn., 1961-62, pres., 1962-63, bd. dirs., 1963-66; bd. dirs. Greater Washington Ednl. TV Assn., 1964-66, mem. programming com., 1965-66; bd. dirs. No. Va. Fine Arts Assn., 1964-66, Mus. Audio-Visual Applications Group, 1962-70; mem. com. furnishing ofcl. reception room State Dept., 1960-75. Bd. dirs. Menands (N.Y.) Pub. Library, 1970—, Albany Symphony Orch., 1969-72. Mem. Am. Assn. Mus. (council 1969-72, v.p. 1970-71, chmn. profl. relations com. 1974—), N.Y. State Assn. Museums (sec. 1968-77, pres. 1977-79), St. Andrews Soc. Mem. Soc. Friends. Clubs: Brunswick Sportsman's (Cropseyville, N.Y.), Fort Orange (Albany). Home: 30 Brookside Ave Albany NY 12204 Office: NY State Mus Cultural Edn Center Albany NY 12230

LINDSAY, GEORGE CLAYTON, editor; b. Springfield, Ill., June 24, 1912; s. George and Margaret (Liddell) L.; B.S., U. Ill., 1933; m. Hazel Damaris Cook, June 19, 1935; 1 son, George Clayton, Jr. Asst. editor Mechanization-The Mag. of Modern Coal, 1939-43, asso. editor, 1943-46, editorial bd., 1946-47, editor, 1948-55; co-editor Mechannual-The Book of Mechanization Progress, 1939-46, editor, 1947-55; editorial bd. Utilization, 1947-55; editor Rock Products, Maclean-Hunter Pub. Corp., 1956-59; editor Concrete Products, 1956-57, asso. mgr., 1957-59; editorial dir. Rock Products and Concrete Products, 1959-64; editorial dir. Rock Products, Coal Mining and Processing and Metal Mining and Processing, 1964-65; gen. mgr., pub. Coal Mining and Processing, 1965—; v.p. Gorresens, Inc., 1966—. Served to lt. USNR, 1944-46. Mem. Am. Inst. Mining, Metall. and Petroleum Engrs., Ill. Mining Inst., Assn. Indsl. Advertisers. Republican. Baptist. Club: Rolling Green Country (Arlington Heights, Ill.). Home: 2515 Farrell Ave Park Ridge IL 60068 Office: 300 W Adams St Chicago IL 60606

LINDSAY, GEORGE EDMUND, museum dir.; b. Pomona, Calif., Aug. 17, 1916; s. Charles Wesley and Alice (Foster) L.; student San Diego State Coll., 1936-39; B.A., Stanford, 1951, Ph.D., 1956; m. Geraldine Kendrick Morris, 1972. Dir. Desert Bot. Gardes, Phoenix, 1939-40, San Diego Natural History Mus., 1956-63, Calif. Acad. Scis., San Francisco, 1963—; spl. research taxonomy desert plants, Cactaceae of Baja Calif., Mexico. Served to capt. USAAF, 1943-46. Decorated Air medal with 3 clusters, Bronze Star. Fellow San Diego Soc. Natural History, Zool. Soc. San Diego, Calif. Acad. Scis., A.A.A.S., Cactus and Succulent Soc. Home: 3675 Washington St San Francisco CA 94118 Office: Calif Acad Scis San Francisco CA 94118

LINDSAY, JOHN VLIET, former mayor, former congressman, author, lawyer; b. N.Y.C., Nov. 24, 1921; s. George Nelson and Eleanor (Vliet) L.; grad. St. Paul's Sch., Concord, N.H., 1940; B.A., Yale U., 1944, LL.B., 1948; LL.D., Harvard U., 1969; LL.D. (hon.), Williams Coll., 1968; m. Mary Harrison, June 18, 1949; children—Katharine, Margaret, Anne, John Vliet. Admitted to N.Y. State bar, 1949, Fed. bar So. Dist. N.Y., 1950, U.S. Supreme Ct. bar, 1955, D.C. bar, 1958; mem. firm Webster & Sheffield, N.Y.C., 1953-60, 74—; exec. asst. to U.S. atty. gen., 1955-56; mem. 86th-89th congresses from 17th Dist. N.Y.; mayor N.Y.C., 1965-73. Commentator on TV. Served as lt. USNR, 1943-46. Mem. Assn. Bar City N.Y., Am., N.Y. bar assns. Episcopalian. Author: Journey Into Politics, 1966; The City, 1970; The Edge, 1976.

LINDSAY, ROBERT, physicist; b. New Haven, Mar. 3, 1924; s. Robert Bruce and Rachel (Easterbrooks) L.; B.S., Brown U., 1947; M.A., Rice U., 1949, Ph.D., 1951; m. Charlotte Rose Melton, May 3, 1952; children—Nancy Carolyn, William Melton, Ann Elizabeth. Physicist, Nat. Bur. Standards, Washington, 1951-53, summer 1955; asst. prof. physics So. Meth. U., Dallas, 1953-56; asst. prof. physics Trinity Coll., Hartford, Conn., 1956-59, asso. prof., 1959-65, prof., 1965—, Brownell-Jarvis prof. natural philosophy and physics, 1978—. Served to 1st. lt. USAAF, 1943-46. Mem. Am. Phys. Soc., Am. Assn. Physics Tchrs., AAUP, Sci. Research Soc., Am., Sigma Xi. Editor: Early Concepts of Energy in Atomic Physics, 1979. Contbr. articles to profl. jours. Home: 62 Midwell Rd Wethersfield CT 06109 Office: Physics Dept Trinity Coll Hartford CT 06106

LINDSAY, ROBERT, educator; b. Durham, N.C., Nov. 27, 1924; s. Albert and Emily Frances (Sheridan) L.; B.A., U. Wis., 1953, M.A., 1954; Ph.D., U. Minn., 1965; m. Mary Anne Phillips, Jan. 3, 1950; children—Phillips S., Nancy B. Reporter, commentator, news dir. WKOW, UPI, WIBA, WHA-TV, Madison, Wis., 1947-50, 54-57; faculty U. Wis., Madison, 1952-57, vis. prof., 1959-65; faculty U. Minn., Mpls., 1957—, prof. mass communication and internat. relations, 1971—. Sr. program specialist for space communication UNESCO, Paris, France, 1968 -69; lectr. univs. and journalism tng. centers Belgium, Bolivia, Brazil, Ecuador, France, Mex., Hong Kong, Thailand, Malaysia, Singapore, U.K., others; U.S. Dept. State specialist Latin Am., S.E. Asia, Africa, Middle East, 1965-78; chmn. Internat. Communication Devel. Council, Midwest Univs. Consortium for Internat. Activities, 1970-72; news service U. Wis., U.S. Navy Journalist Sch., Great Lakes, Ill., Def. Info. Sch., Ft. Slocum, N.Y. Mem. Citizens adv. com. Twin City Area Ednl. TV Corp., 1975-77. Served with USMC, 1941-45, 50-52, capt. Res. ret. Found. for Public Relations Research and Edn. fellow, 1959, 67; Office Internat. Programs grantee, 1971; U. Minn. research grantee, 1967. Recipient Ariel award Mpls. Citizens Com. on Public Edn., 1960, Mem. Inst. Internat. Communications, Internat. Assn. for Mass Communication Research, Internat. Communication Assn., Internat. Studies Assn., Internat. Press Inst., Institut Internat. de Droit Spatial, Soc. for Internat. Devel., World Future Soc., Brit. Inst. for Internat. and Comparative Law, Centre d'Etude des Consequences Generales de Grandes Techniques Nouvelles, Canadian Inst. Internat. Affairs, Communication Assn. Pacific, Asian Mass Communication Research and Info. Centre, Inter-Am. Assn. Broadcasters, Inter-Am. Press Assn., Latin Am. Studies Assn., Am. Soc. Internat. Law, AAAS, Fgn. Policy Assn., Soc. Profl. Journalists, Radio-TV News Dirs. Assn., Inst. of Journalists (London), Ret. Officers Assn., Internat. Platform Assn., Am. Soc. 18th Century Studies, Kappa Tau Alpha. Clubs: Geneva Press (Switzerland); Minn. Press, Univ. Author: This High Name, 1956. Contbr. articles to profl. and scholarly jours. Home: 11 Hillside Ct Saint Paul MN 55108 Office: 111 Murphy Hall U Minn Minneapolis MN 55455

LINDSAY, ROBERT BLAKE THEODORE (TED), hockey coach; b. Renfrew, Ont., Can., July 29, 1925. Hockey player Detroit Red Wings, 1944-57, 64-65, coach and gen. mgr., 1977—; player Chgo. Black Hawks, 1957-60; sportscaster NBC-TV, 1972-73. Named to Hockey Hall of Fame, 1966. Office: Detroit Red Wings 5920 Grand River Detroit MI 48208*

LINDSAY, ROBERT BRUCE, physicist, educator, editor; b. New Bedford, Mass., Jan. 1, 1900; s. Robert and Eleanora Elizabeth (Leuchsenring) L.; A.B., Brown U., 1920, M.S., 1920, D.Sc. (hon.), 1978; Ph.D., Mass. Inst. Tech., 1924; Ed.D. (hon.), R.I. Coll. Edn., 1959; Sc.D. (hon.), Southeastern Mass. Technol. Inst., 1968; m. Rachel Tupper Easterbrooks, July 29, 1922; children—Robert, Evelyn Tupper (Mrs. Richard C. Roberts). Inst. physics Mass. Inst. Tech., 1920-22; fellow Am.-Scandinavian Found. Copenhagen, 1922-23; instr. physics Yale, 1923-27, asst. prof., 1927-30; asso. prof. theoretical physics, Brown U., 1930-36, Hazard prof. physics 1936—, prof. emeritus physics, 1971—, chmn. dept., 1934-54; dean grad. sch., 1954-66, dir. Ultrasonics Lab., 1946-63; vis. prof. physics, Poly. Inst. Bklyn., 1932-41. Dir. phys. research Div. Phys. War Research, Duke U., 1942-43. Lectr., U.S. Navy Electronics Lab., San. Diego, summer, 1946, 1949; cons. Bur. of Ships, U.S. Navy Dept., 1944-47; chmn. governing board New Eng. Sch. Sci. Council, 1947-50; dir. Research Analysis group at Brown U. for research in underwater sound 1948-54; sci. adviser U.S. Naval War Coll., 1952-54; mem. div. phys. scis. NRC, 1953-57; chmn. phys. adv. com. Nat. Bur. Standards, 1957-60; regional counsellor for R.I. Am. Inst. Physics Program, 1961-62, exec. com. governing bd., 1959-71; mem. vis. scientists program Am. Inst. Physics; cons. research and devel. Asst. Sec. Def., 1954-57; U.S. Mem. Internat Commn. on Acoustics, 1963-69; cons. on physics instrn. U.S. Naval Acad., 1969-70. Pres. Assn. Grad. Schs. in Assn. Am. Univs., 1965-66. Served with USNR, World War I. Fellow Brit. Inst. Acoustics (hon.), AAAS (v.p., chmn. sect. B 1959, sect L 1968), Am. Phys. Soc. (chmn. New Eng. sect. 1935-36, mem. council 1943-46), Am. Acad. Arts and Scis. (v.p. 1957-59), Acoustical Soc. Am. (v.p. 1951-52, pres. 1956-57, gold medal 1963); mem. Soc. of Rheology, Am. Inst. Physics (gov. bd. 1956-71), Am. Assn. Phys. Tchrs. (mem. exec. com. 1945-47, distinguished service award 1963), Am. Math. Soc., Philosophy of Sci. Assn. (gov. bd. 1958-59), History of Sci. Soc., New Eng. Conf. Grad. Edn. (pres. 1961-62), Phi Beta Kappa, Sigma Xi (nat. lectr. 1967-68, Bicentennial lectr. 1975-77). Author: (with G.W. Stewart) Acoustics, 1930; (with H. Margenau) Foundations of Physics, 1936; Physical Statistics, 1941; Physical Mechanics, 1933; Concepts and Methods of Theoretical Physics, 1951; Mechanical Radiation, 1960; The Role of Science in Civilization, 1963; The Nature of Physics, 1968; Lord Rayleigh—The Man and His Work, 1970; Basic Concepts of Physics, 1971; Julius Robert Mayer—Prophet of Energy, 1973; Acoustics, Its Historical and Philosophical Development, 1973; Physical Acoustics, 1974; Energy-Early Historical Development of the Concept, 1975; Applications of Energy: Nineteenth Century, 1976; The Control of Energy, 1977; also articles in field. Editor-in-chief Acoustical Soc. Am., 1957—; editor jour., 1957—; editor: Sound, Its Uses and Control, 1962-63; gen. editor Benchmark Series in Acoustics, 1971—; co-editor Benchmark Series on Energy, 1974—; editorial bd. Founds. of Physics, 1970—. Club: Faculty. Home: 91 Indian Ave Portsmouth RI 02871. *I am not sure that I understand just what success in life is. Perhaps personal satisfaction is more meaningful. Concerning this about all I can say is that I have enjoyed the work in my chosen profession and have done my best to help others help themselves. I have also tried to follow the thermodynamic imperative, that is, to consume as much entropy as possible in order to fight, in a humble way, the inexorable increase in entropy implicit in the second law of thermodynamics and guaranteed as the ultimate end of our universe. Though we cannot hope really to SAVE AMERICA FROM ENTROPY (as the car stickers have it) each of us has a moral obligation to fight the second law in our lives as best we can.*

LINDSAY, ROBERT VAN CLEEF, banker; b. N.Y.C., Jan. 1, 1926; s. George N. and Eleanor (Vliet) L.; B.A., Yale U., 1949; m. Nancy A. Dalley, Apr. 29, 1950; children—Cameron, Dorothy A., Robert D. With J.P. Morgan & Co., 1949—, asst. treas., asst. v.p., 1949-60; v.p. Morgan Guaranty Trust Co., 1960-69, sr. v.p., 1969-76, exec. v.p., 1976—, chmn. exec. com., 1978—; dir. St. Joe Minerals Corp., Chubb Corp. Bd. dirs. N.Y. Philharmonic Symphony Soc., 1966-73, 77—; trustee Cooper Union, 1967-73. Served with U.S. Mcht. Marine, 1943-45. Mem. Soc. for Prevention Cruelty to Animals (bd. mgrs. 1962-72), L.I. Biol. Assn. (dir. 1953-73), Phi Beta Kappa, Chi Psi. Episcopalian. Clubs: Links, Leash. Home: Box 296 Altamont Rd Millbrook NY 12545 Office: 23 Wall St New York NY 10015

LINDSAY, RUSSELL FRANCIS, mfg. exec.; b. Shrewsbury, Mass., Mar. 6, 1926; s. Foster Joseph and Antoinette (Cartier) L.; student Worcester Jr. Coll., 1946-48, Newark Coll. Engring., 1953-56; m. Harriett McCauley, Sept. 12, 1974; children—James, John, Kathleen, Maureen. Draftsman, Springfield (Ill.) Boiler Co., 1948-51, Riley Stoker Co., Worcester, Mass., 1951-53; chief engr. Edgemoor Iron Works, Wilmington, Del., 1956-58; sales engr. Zurn Emergy div. Zurn Industries, Inc., Erie, Pa., 1958-60, sales mgr., 1960-62, v.p. mktg., gen. mgr., 1962-66; group v.p. Zurn Industries, Inc., 1966-70, exec. v.p., 1974—, also dir.; dir. Robert Irsay Co., Chgo., Vulcan Mfg. Co., Cin. Corporator St. Vincent Health Center, Erie. Served with USAF, 1944-46. Mem. ASME, Am. Boiler Mfrs. Assn., Cooling Tower Inst. Clubs: Kaukwa Country, Clearwater Yacht, Erie, Univ. Home: 155 W 41st St Erie PA 16508 Office: One Zurn Pl Box 2000 Erie PA 16512

LINDSAY, WILLIAM KERR, surgeon; b. Vancouver, B.C., Can., Sept. 3, 1920; s. James Arthur and Lottie Mary (Early) L.; M.D., U. Toronto, 1945, B.S., 1949, M.S., 1959; m. Frances Beatrice Ferris, Feb. 15, 1945; children—William Arthur, Barbara Susanne, Katherine Mary, Anne Louise. Intern, Toronto Gen. Hosp.; resident Montreal Gen. Hosp., 1951-52, Baylor U. Hosp., 1952-53; practice medicine, specializing in surgery, Toronto, 1953—; staff surgeon to chief div. plastic surgery Hosp. for Sick Children, 1952-58, project dir. Research Inst., 1954—; faculty dept. surgery U. Toronto Faculty of Medicine, 1953—, prof., 1968—, chmn. interhospital com. for plastic surgery, 1965—. Chmn. med. dental staff com. Ont. Crippled Childrens Center, 1958-63. Served with M.C., Royal Canadian Army, 1943-46; to lt. Royal Canadian Navy, 1946-47. Fellow Royal Coll. Surgeons Can., A.C.S.; mem. Am. Assn. Plastic Surgeons (pres. 1970-71), Canadian Soc. Plastic Surgeons (pres.), Ont. Soc. for Crippled Children (chmn. med. adv. com. 1957-65), Am. Soc. Plastic and Reconstructive Surgeons Am. Soc. Surgery of the Hand, Am. Cleft Palate Assn. Home: 44 Clarendon Ave Toronto ON M4V 1J1 Canada Office: 555 University Ave Toronto ON M5G 1X8 Canada

LINDSELL, HAROLD, clergyman, educator, editor; b. N.Y.C., Dec. 22, 1913; s. Leonard Anthony and Ella Briggs (Harris) L.; B.S., Wheaton Coll., 1938; M.A., U. Calif., 1939, Ph.D., N.Y. U., 1942; D.D., Fuller Theol. Sem., 1964; m. Marion Joanne Bolinder, June 12, 1943; children—Judith Ann (Mrs. William C. Wood), Joanne (Mrs. Robert Webber), Nancy J. (Mrs. Daniel Sharp), John H. Prof. history, missions, registrar Columbia Bible Coll., 1942-44; ordained to ministry Baptist Ch., 1944; prof. missions, asso. prof. ch. history No. Bapt. Theol. Sem., 1944-47, prof., 1947-51, registrar, 1947-50, dean, 1950-51; dean faculty, prof. missions Fuller Theol. Sem., 1951-61, v.p., prof. missions, 1961-64; asso. editor Christianity Today, 1964-67, editor, 1968-78, emeritus, 1978—; prof. Bible, Wheaton (Ill.) Coll., 1967-68. Trustee emeritus Westmont Coll., Wheaton Coll., Luther Rice Sem., Outreach; chmn. Gordon Conwell Theol. Sem. Mem. Tournament Roses, Nat. Assn. Bibl. Instr., Am. Hist. Assn., Am. Soc. Ch. History, Nat., Greater Washington (pres. 1966-67) assns. evangelicals, Am. Acad. Polit. and Social Scis., Evang. Theol. Soc. (pres. 1970-71), Pi Gamma Mu, Pi Kappa Delta, Alpha Gamma Omega. Republican. Club: Cosmos (Washington). Author: Abundantly Above, 1944; The Thing Appointed, 1949; A Christian Philosophy of Missions, 1949; Park Street Prophet, 1951; (with C. J. Woodbridge) Handbook of Christian Truth, 1953; Missionary Principles and Practice, 1955; The Morning Altar, 1956; Daily Bible Readings from the Revised Standard Version, 1957; Christianity and the Cults, 1963; Harper Study Bible (rev. standard version), 1964; When You Pray, 1969; The World the Flesh and the Devil, 1973; The Battle for the Bible, 1976; The Bible in the Balance, 1979; also articles. Editor: The Church's Worldwide Mission, 1966. Home and Office: 25 W 426 Hevern Dr Wheaton IL 60187. *My life has been undergirded by the Hebrew-Christian life and world view as found in the Bible, whose central personage is Jesus Christ. My ethical principles and standards for personal conduct are taken from the Bible and particularly from Jesus' Sermon on the Mount. Success must be measured not in terms of status, wealth, popularity, or position; it must be measured by how closely a man lives up to the highest ideals of life and how unblemished his character is.*

LINDSEY, DAVID, educator; b. Waldwick, N.J., Dec. 1, 1914; s. Frederick Brooks and Mary (Krichbaum) L.; student Amherst Coll., 1932-33; B.A., Cornell U., 1936; M.A., Pa. State U., 1938; Ph.D., U. Chgo., 1950; m. Suzanne Rossini, Dec. 1968; 1 son by previous marriage David Scott. Tchr. high schs., N.J., 1936-43; edn. sec. Am. Friends Service Com., 1943-45; asso. prof. history Baldwin-Wallace Coll., 1946-55; vis. asso. prof. Oberlin Coll., 1955-56; prof. history Calif. State U. at Los Angeles, 1956—, chmn. dept., 1964-66; vis. prof. Western Res. U., summer 1962; Fulbright prof. U. Athens (Greece), 1962-63, U. Madrid, 1968-69, U. Md. (overseas), 1969-70. Mem. Am. Hist. Assn., Orgn. Am. Historians, Soc. Am. Historians, Am. Name Soc., AAUP, History Guild So. Calif. Author: Ohio's Western Reserve, 1955; Sunset Cox, Irrepressible Democrat, 1959; Abraham Lincoln and Jefferson Davis, 1960; Andrew Jackson and Henry Clay, 1963; Andrew Jackson and John. C. Calhoun, 1973; Americans in Conflict: The Civil War and Reconstruction, 1974; Nineteenth Century American Utopias, 1976. Home: 173 Bay Shore Ave Long Beach CA 90803 Office: 5151 State University Dr Los Angeles CA 90032

LINDSEY, HENRY CARLTON, educator; b. Coushatta, La., Jan. 3, 1918; s. Benjamin Dennis and Vallie (Snead) L.; B.A., Ouachita Coll., 1948; M.A., La. State U., 1951; Ph.D., U. Denver, 1962; m. Evelyn Natille Pierce, Dec. 27, 1947; children—John Bryan, Lovie Denise, Mark Pierce. Instr. Ouachita U., Arkadelphia, Ark., 1952-53; chmn. drama dept. Howard Coll., Birmingham, Ala., 1953-56; edn. specialist USAF Air U., 1956-58; chmn. speech dept. Georgetown (Ky.) Coll., 1958-61; dir. extension Kans. State Coll., Emporia, 1961-63; chmn. drama dept. Baylor U., 1963-64; acad. v.p. Ouachita U., 1964-69; chmn. speech dept. Miss. State Coll. Women, 1969-70; acad. v.p. Howard Payne Coll., Brownwood, Tex., 1970-74; edn. specialist Community Coll. of Air Force, pres. Internat. Cons. Agy., San Antonio, 1974—; edn. cons. Kans. State Coll., 1968, 69, Western Ky. State U., 1975. Served with AUS, 1942-45; ETO; lt. col. USAF Res. Decorated Bronze Star with oak leaf cluster. Fellow Internat. Inst. Arts and Letters; mem. Speech Assn. Am., Theta Xi, Theta Alpha Phi. Baptist (deacon). Club: Rotary. Author: (plays) The Inner Light, 1947; Grey Harvest, 1951; Call Me Penny, 1952; Forver Judy, 1953; Mr. Sweeney's Conversion, 1954; Curfew, 1956. Asso. editor Players Mag., 1953-56. Drama, book reviewer Birmingham (Ala.) News, 1963-65. Contbr. to profl. jours. and mags. Home: 318 Westwind Circle San Antonio TX 78239

LINDSEY, JAMES RUSSELL, educator; b. Tifton, Ga., Dec. 6, 1933; s. Eulen Russell and Eula M. (Jones) L.; B.S., U. Ga., 1956, D.V.M. cum laude, 1957; M.S., 1961; m. Elizabeth Anne Fort, May 31, 1958; children—James Russell, Leigh Ann, Sephen Fort, Amy Faith. Instr. vet. parasitology Auburn (Ala.) U., 1957-59, asst. prof., 1959-61; fellow pathology Johns Hopkins, 1961-63, instr. lab. animal medicine, instr. pathology, 1964-65, asst. prof. lab. animal medicine, asst. prof. pathology Sch. Medicine, 1965-67; asso. prof. pathology U. Ala. Med. Center, Birmingham, 1969—, prof. comparative medicine, 1968—, chmn. dept. comparative medicine, 1968-75; chief research in lab. animal medicine Birmingham VA Hosp., 1969—. Mem. animal resources adv. com. NIH, 1972-76. Recipient Charles River award, 1979. Diplomate Am. Coll. Lab. Animal Medicine (pres. 1970-71), Am. Coll. Vet. Pathologists. Mem. Sigma Xi, Phi Sigma, Phi Kappa Phi, Alpha Zeta, Phi Zeta. Contbr. articles to tech. jours. Research in comparative pathology, lab. animal diseases complicating research. Home: 3644 Oakdale Rd Birmingham AL 35223

LINDSEY, JOHN HORACE, ins. co. exec., museum ofcl.; b. Waxahachie, Tex., July 28, 1922; s. Harry E. and Marie (Smith) L.; B.A., Tex. A. and M. U., 1944; m. Sara Houstoun, Aug. 30, 1946; children—Edwin H., David C. With Employers Casualty Co., 1947-53; propr. Lindsey Ins. Agy., Houston, 1953—; dir. So. Nat. Bank, Houston. Vice pres. Houston Mus. Fine Arts; pres. Alley Theatre; bd. dirs. South Tex. Coll. Law, Tex. A. and M. U. Research Found. Served to 1st lt. AUS, 1943-46. Home: 5568 Candlewood St Houston TX 77056 Office: So Nat Bank Bldg Houston TX 77002

LINDSEY, JOHN MORTON, airline exec.; b. Peekskill, N.Y., Jan. 8, 1930; s. Morton Cole and Blodwyn (Price) L.; A.B., Duke, 1951; LL.B., U. Denver, 1957; m. Doris Marie Restein, Sept. 9, 1951; children—Linda, Gail, Jill, Lisa. Admitted to Colo. bar, 1958; atty. CAB, Washington, 1958-63; asst. sec. Nat. Airlines, Miami, Fla., 1963-64, sec., 1964-70, asso. gen. counsel, 1970-75, sec., 1970—, gen. counsel, 1975—. Served to lt. (j.g.) USNR, 1951-55; capt. Res. Methodist. Home: 7271 S W 128th St Miami FL 33156 Office: PO Box 592055 AMF Miami FL 33159

LINDSEY, ROBERT SOURS, lawyer; b. Dixon, S.D., May 1, 1913; s. Albert Samuel and Ferne (Sours) L.; A.B., Washington U., St. Louis, 1936, LL.B., 1936; m. Grace Edith Grimme, Mar. 6, 1943; children—Carol Jeanne (Mrs. James C. Brandt), Bruce Robert. Admitted to Mo. bar, 1936, Ark. bar, 1943; practice in St. Louis, 1936-43, Little Rock, 1943—; partner firm Wright, Lindsey & Jennings, 1946—. Sec., dir. Ferncliff, Inc., 1945-66. Bd. dirs. Presbyn. Village, Inc., 1962-66, 70-76, 78—, pres., 1972-74; bd. dirs. Met. YMCA, 1962-68, pres., 1965-66; bd. dirs. Presbyn. Found. Ark., Inc., 1962-71, pres., 1966-67; bd. dirs. Ark. Assn. Mental Health, 1960-69, treas., 1963-65; mem. Ark. Merit System Council, 1967-76, chmn., 1968-69; trustee Ark. Law Sch., Austin Presbyn. Theol. Sem., 1971-77, Ark. Found. Asso. Colls., 1975—. Fellow Am. Bar Found.; mem. Am., Ark. (chmn. exec. com. 1965-66, exec. council 1976-77, Outstanding Lawyer award 1969), Pulaski County (pres. 1972-73) bar assns., Internat. Assn. Ins. Counsel, Am. Judicature Soc., Am. Counsel Assn., Phi Delta Phi. Presbyn. Clubs: Little Rock, Exchange, Pleasant Valley Country, Capital. Home: 20 E Palisades Dr Little Rock AR 72207 Office: Worthen Bank Bldg Little Rock AR 72201

LINDSLEY, DAN LESLIE, JR., geneticist; b. Evanston, Ill., Oct. 13, 1925; s. Dan Leslie and Ruth Christine (Hubbard) L.; student U. Tex., 1943-45, Med. Sch., U. Ark., 1945-46; A.B., U. Mo., 1947, M.A., 1949; Ph.D., Calif. Inst. Tech., 1952; m. Lois Jean Whistler, Aug. 26, 1947; children—Kathleen Ann, Dale Edward, Jennifer Joyce, Dan Arthur. Biologist, Oak Ridge Nat. Lab., 1954-67; prof. biology U. Calif. at San Diego, La Jolla, 1967—. Served in USNR, 1943-45. Mem. Am. Assn. Arts and Scis., Nat. Acad. Scis., Genetics Soc. Am. Author: (with E.H. Grell) Genetic Variations of Drosophila melanogaster, 1968. Home: 2611 Inyaha Ln La Jolla CA 92037 Office: Dept Biology U Calif at San Diego La Jolla CA 92093

LINDSLEY, DONALD BENJAMIN, physiol. psychologist, educator; b. Brownhelm, Ohio, Dec. 23, 1907; s. Benjamin Kent and Mattie Elizabeth (Jenne) L.; A.B., Wittenberg Coll. (now U.), 1929, D.Sc., 1959; A.M., U. Iowa, 1930, Ph.D., 1932; Sc.D., Brown U., 1958, Trinity Coll., Hartford, Conn., 1965; D.Sc., Loyola U. Chgo., 1969; Ph.D. (hon.), Johannes Gutenberg U., Mainz, W.Ger., 1977; m. Ellen Ford, Aug. 16, 1933; children—David Ford, Margaret, Robert Kent, Sara Ellen. Instr. psychology U. Ill., 1932-33; NRC fellow Harvard U. Med. Sch., 1933-35; research asso. Western Res. U. Med. Sch., 1935-38; asst. prof. psychology Brown U., also dir. psychol. and neurophysiol. lab. Bradley Hosp., 1938-46; dir. war research project on radar operation Yale, OSRD, Nat. Def. Research Com., Camp Murphy and Boca Raton AFB, Fla., 1943-45; prof. psychology Northwestern U., 1946-51; prof. psychology, physiology, psychiatry and pediatrics UCLA, 1951-77, prof. emeritus, 1977—; mem. Brain Research Inst., 1961—) chmn. dept. psychology, 1959-62; William James lectr. Harvard, 1958; Univ. Research lectr. U. Calif. at Los Angeles, 1959; Walter B. Pillsbury lectr. psychology Cornell U., 1963. Mem. sci. adv. bd. USAF, 1947-49; undersea warfare com. NRC, 1951-64; cons. NSF, 1952-54; mem. mental health study sect. NIMH, 1953-57, neurol. study sect. Nat. Inst. Neurol. Diseases and Blindness, 1958-62; chmn. behavioral scis. tng. com. Nat. Inst. Gen. Med. Scis., 1966-69; mem. behavioral biology adv. panel AIBS-NASA; mem. space sci. bd. Nat. Acad. Scis., 1967-70; mem. com. space medicine, 1969-71; mem. Calif. Legis. Assembly Sci. and Tech. Council, 1970-71. Awarded Presdl. Cert. of Merit (for war work), 1948; Guggenheim fellow, Europe, 1959; Distinguished Sci. Achievement award Calif. Psychol. Assn., 1977. Mem. Nat. Acad. Scis. (chmn. com. long duration missions in space, 1967-72, mem. space sci. board), Am. Psychol. Assn. (Distinguished Sci. Contbn. award 1959), Am. Physiol. Soc., Soc. Exptl. Psychologists, Am. Electroencephalographic Soc. (pres. 1964-65), AAAS (v.p. 1954, chmn. sect. J 1977), Midwest Psychol. Assn. (pres. 1952), Am. Acad. Cerebral Palsy, Western Soc. Electroencephalography (hon. mem. with great distinction; pres. 1957), Western Psychol. Assn. (pres. 1959-60), Am. Acad. Arts and Scis., Internat. Brain Research Orgn. (treas. 1967-71), Soc. Neuroscis. (Donald B. Lindsley prize in behavioral neurosci. established in his name), Sigma Xi, Alpha Omega Alpha, Gamma Alpha, Phi Gamma Delta. Conglist. Cons. editor Jour. Exptl. Psychology, 1947-68, Jour. Comparative and Physiol. Psychology, 1952-62, Jour. Personality, 1958-62; editorial bd. Internat. Jour. Physiol. and Behav., 1965—, Exptl. Brain Research, 1965-76, Developmental Psychobiology, 1968—. Contbr. numerous articles on physiol. psychology, neurosci., brain and behavior to sci. jours., also numerous chpts. in books. Home: 471 23d St Santa Monica CA 90402 Office: Dept Psychology U Calif Los Angeles CA 90024

LINDSTROM, ERNEST ALGOT, lawyer; b. Marion, N.D., Aug. 25, 1931; s. Carl E. and Mabel S. (Brox) L.; student Concordia Coll., Moorhead, Minn., 1949-51; B.S., U. N.D., 1953; LL.B., U. Minn., 1957; m. Jeanne E. Turnquist, Dec. 30, 1960; children—Monica, Mark, Eric, Paul, Kristin. Admitted to Minn. bar, 1957, since practiced in Mpls.; spl. municipal judge, Richfield, Minn., 1962-64; lectr. U. Minn., 1963-65; mem. Minn. Ho. of Reps., 1967-74, majority leader; mem. firm Ernest A. Lindstrom Ltd. C.P.A., Minn. Mem. Am., Minn., Hennepin County bar assns. Home: 7406 Freemont Ave S Richfield MN 55423 Office: 7600 Parklawn Ave Minneapolis MN 55435

LINDSTROM, KENNETH ALBERT, banker; b. Chgo., Oct. 1, 1927; s. Olaf Albert and Judith K. (Johnson) L.; student Duluth Jr. Coll., 1945-46, 47-48; B.B.A., U. Minn., 1950; m. Charlotte Anne Fuller, May 19, 1956; children—Thomas, Mary. Mgr., Price Waterhouse & Co., Chgo., 1950-66; v.p., comptroller Nat. Blvd. Bank Chgo., 1966-71, v.p., comptroller, sec., 1972-73, v.p., 1973-76, cashier, sec., 1973—, sr. v.p., 1976—. Served with AUS, 1946-47. C.P.A., Ill. Mem. Am. Inst. C.P.A.'s, Ill. Soc. C.P.A.'s. Club: Economic (Chgo.). Home: 1116 Arbor Ln Glenview IL 60025 Office: 410 N Michigan Ave Chicago IL 60611

LINDSTROM, RALPH EMIL, fgn. service officer; b. Anoka, Minn., Apr. 10, 1925; s. Peter and Edith B. (Nelson) L.; A.B. cum laude, Harvard U., 1950; postgrad. Princeton U., 1959-60, Brown U., 1969-70; m. Gloria Marie Fessler, Mar. 20, 1948; children—Karen Ann, Christine Marie, Cynthia Lee. Commd. fgn. service officer Dept. State, 1952; polit. officer Am. embassy, Kabul, Afghanistan, 1952-54, Paris, 1954-57, Am. Consulate-Gen., Hong Kong, 1957-59; intelligence specialist Dept. State, Washington, 1960-62; econ. officer Am. embassy, Moscow, 1963-65; chief internat. payments div. Dept. State, 1965-67; econ. counselor Am. embassy, Moscow, 1967-69; chief arms transfer div. ACDA, 1970-73; dep. chief mission Am. embassy, Nairobi, Kenya, 1973-77; consulgen., Dhahran, Saudi Arabia, 1978—. Served with U.S. Army, 1943-44, USN, 1944-46. Address: American Consulate General Dhahran APO New York NY 09616

LINDUSKA, JOSEPH PAUL, biologist, assn. exec.; b. Butte, Mont., July 25, 1913; s. Joseph and Helen (Nettik) L.; student Mont. Sch. Mines, 1932-35; B.A., U. Mont., 1936, M.A., 1939; Ph.D., Mich. State U., 1949; m. Lilian Ruth Hopkins, Aug. 7, 1936; children—Joanne Ruth (Mrs. Kent S. Price), James J. Entomologist, bur. entomol. and plant quarantine U.S. Dept. Agr., 1937-40, 42-45; game biologist Mich. Dept. Conservation, 1941-42, 46; wildlife biologist U.S. Fish and Wildlife Service, 1947-48, asst. chief wildlife research, Washington, 1948-50, chief br. game mgmt., 1950-56; dir. pub. relations and wildlife mgmt. Remington Arms Co., 1956-66; asso. dir. U.S. Bur. Sport Fisheries and Wildlife, Washington, 1966-73, sr. scientist, 1973-74; v.p. for sci. Nat. Audubon Soc., Washington, 1974-78. Past pres. Wildlife Soc. Mem. Outdoor Writers Assn. Am., Internat. Assn. Game, Fish and Conservation Commrs., Am. Fisheries Soc., Soil Conservation Soc. Clubs: Cosmos, Biologists Field (Washington). Contbr. articles to outdoor mags. Home and Office: 220 Richards Dr Chestertown MD 21620

LINDZEN, RICHARD SIEGMUND, meteorologist; b. Webster, Mass., Feb. 8, 1940; s. Abe and Sara (Blachman) L.; A.B., Harvard U., 1960, S.M., 1961, Ph.D., 1964; m. Nadine Lucie Kalougine, Apr. 7, 1965; children—Eric, Nathaniel. Research asso. U. Wash., Seattle, 1964-65, U. Oslo, 1965-66; with Nat. Center Atmospheric Research, Boulder, Colo., 1966-68; mem. faculty U. Chgo., 1968-72; prof. meteorology Harvard U., 1972—; Lady Davis vis. prof. Hebrew U., 1979; cons. Naval Research Labs., NASA, others. Recipient Macelwane award Am. Geophys. Union, 1968. Fellow Am. Meteorol. Soc. (Meisinger award 1969; councillor 1972-75), Nat. Acad. Scis., Am. Acad. Arts and Scis. Jewish. Co-author: Atmospheric Tides; contbr. to profl. jours. Home: 301 Lake Ave Newton MA 02161 Office: Pierce Hall Harvard Univ Cambridge MA 02138

LINDZEY, GARDNER, educator, psychologist; b. Wilmington, Del., Nov. 27, 1920; s. James and Marguerite (Shotwell) L.; A.B., Pa. State U., 1943, M.S., 1945; Ph.D., Harvard U., 1949; m. Andrea Lewis, Nov. 28, 1944; children—Jeffrey, Leslie, Gardner, David, Jonathan. Research analyst OSRD, 1944-45; instr. psychology Pa. State U., 1945; head guidance center, lectr., psychology Western Res. U., 1945-46; teaching fellow Harvard U., 1946-47, research fellow, 1947-49, research asso., asst. prof., 1949-53, lectr., chmn. psychol. clinic staff, 1953-56, prof., chmn. dept., 1972-73; prof. psychology Syracuse U., 1956-57, U. Minn., 1957-64; prof. psychology U. Tex., 1964-72, chmn., 1964-68, v.p. acad. affairs, 1968-70, v.p. ad interim, 1971, v.p., dean Grad. Studies, prof. psychology, 1973-75; dir. Center for Advanced Study in Behavioral Scis., Stanford, Calif., 1975—. Mem. psychopharmacology study sect. NIMH, 1958-62, mem. program-project com., 1963-67, mem. adv. com. on extramural research, 1968-71; mem. com. faculty research fellowships Social Sci. Research Council, 1960-63, bd. dirs., 1962-76, mem. com. problems and policy, 1963-70, 72-76, chmn., 1965-70, mem. exec. com. 1970-75, chmn., 1971-75, mem. com. genetics and behavior, 1961-67, chmn., 1961-65; mem. com. biol. bases social behavior, 1967—; mem. com. work and personality in middle years 1972-77; mem. sociology and social psychology panel NSF, 1965-68, mem. spl. commn. social scis., 1968-69, mem. advisory com. research, 1974—, mem. Waterman award com., 1976—; mem. exec. com., assembly behavioral and social sci. Nat. Acad. Sci.-NRC, 1970—, mem. com. life sci. and pub. policy, 1968-74, mem. panel nat. needs for biomed. and behavioral research personnel, 1974—, mem. com. social sci. in NSF, 1975—, mem. Inst. Medicine, 1975—; mem. com. on drug abuse Office Sci. and Tech., 1962-63; mem. Presdl. Com. Nat. Medal Sci., 1966-69; bd. dirs. Found.'s Fund Research in Psychiatry, 1967-70; bd. dirs. Am. Psychol. Found., 1968-76, v.p., 1971-73, pres., 1974-76. Fellow, Center Advanced Study Behavioral Scis., Stanford, 1955-56, 63-64, 71-72, Inst. Medicine, 1975—. Fellow Am. Psychol. Assn. (dir., 1962-68, 70-74, mem. publs. bd. 1956-59, 70-73, chmn. 1958-59, mem. council of reps. 1959-67, 68-74, pres. div. social and personality psychology 1963-64, mem. policy and planning 1975, 78; 1964-66, pres. assn. 1966-67, mem. council of editors 1968-73, chmn. com. sci. award 1968-69, pres. div. gen. psychology, 1970-71), Am. Acad. Arts and Scis., Am. Philos. Soc., AAAS, Am. Sociol. Assn.; mem. Am. Eugenics Soc. (dir. 1962-70), Soc. Social Biology (dir. 1972—, pres. 1978—), Am. Psychol. Assn. (dir. ins. trust 1973—), Univs. Research Assn. (dir. 1968-71), Assn. Univ. for Research Astronomy (dir. 1973-75). Club: Cosmos. Author: (with Hall) Theories of Personality, 1957, 70, 78; (with Allport and Vernon) Study of Values, 1951, 60; Projective Techniques and Cross-Cultural Research, 1961; (with J.C. Loehlin and J.N. Spuhler) Race Differences in Intelligence, 1975; (with C.S. Hall and R.F. Thompson) Psychology, 1975; also articles. Editor: Handbook of Social Psychology, Vols. 1 and 2, 1954, Vols. 1-5, 1969; Assessment of Human Motives, 1958; Contemporary Psychology, 1967-73; History of Psychology in Autobiography, Vol. 6, 1974; asso. editor Psychol. Abstracts, 1960-62, Ency. Social Scis., 1962-67; co-editor Century Psychology Series, 1960-74, Theories of Personality; Primary Sources and Research, 1965, History of Psychology in Autobiography, Vol. V, 1968, Behavioral Genetics: Methods and Research, 1969, Contributions to Behavior-Genetic Analysis, 1970. Home: 890 Robb Rd Palo Alto CA 94306

LINE, LESLIE DALE, assn. exec., editor; b. Sparta, Mich., June 24, 1935; s. John Jacob and Hazel (Light) L.; student Aquinas Coll., 1953-56; m. Lois Anne Anderson, June 3, 1961; children—Michael John, Heather Lynette. Photographer, reporter Birmingham (Mich.) Eccentric, 1957-58; chief photographer Midland (Mich.) Daily News, 1958-63, conservation editor, 1958-65, wire editor, 1964-65; editor Audubon Mag., Nat. Audubon Soc., N.Y.C., 1966—, v.p. for publs., 1975—; President's fellow R.I. Sch. Design, 1978. Mem. environ. adv. com. Fed. Energy Adminstrn., 1974-77. Mem. continuing edn. adv. com. Dobbs Ferry (N.Y.), 1975-77. Author: Seasons, 1973; The Sea Has Wings, 1973; Dining on a Sunbeam, 1973; Mystery of the Everglades, 1972; The Floor of the Forest, 1974; Puffin Island, 1971; The Milkweed and its World of Animals, 1976; The Land of the Giant Tortoise, 1978; editor: The Pleasure of Birds, 1975; What We Save Now, 1973; This Good Earth, 1974; The Pleasure of Animals, 1976; The Audubon Society Book of Birds, 1976, of Wild Animals, 1977, of Wild Flowers, 1978, of Marine Life, 1979. Office: 950 3d Ave New York NY 10022

LINEBERRY, ROBERT LEON, polit. scientist; b. Oklahoma City, May 4, 1942; s. John and Julia (Flemming) L.; B.A., U. Okla., 1964; Ph.D., U. N.C., Chapel Hill, 1968; m. Nita Ann Ray, Sept. 5, 1964; children—Mary Nicole, Robert Keith. Asst. prof., then asso. prof. govt. U. Tex., Austin, 1967-74; mem. faculty Northwestern U., 1974—, prof. polit. sci. and urban affairs, 1976—. Research grantee NSF, 1969, 74, Law Enforcement Assistance Adminstrn., 1978. Mem. Am. Polit. Sci. Assn., Policy Studies Orgn., Midwest Polit. Sci. Assn., Southwestern Social Sci. Assn. Democrat. Author: Equality and Urban Policy, 1977, American Public Policy, 1977; co-author: Urban Politics and Public Policy, 3d edit., 1978; co-editor: The New Urban Politics, 1976. Office: Dept Polit Sci Northwestern Univ Evanston IL 60201

LINEHAN, JOHN ANDREW, ambassador; b. Mass., July 20, 1924; A.B., Boston U., 1948; B.S., Georgetown U., 1949; M.S., Auburn U., 1971; m. Janice Rowley. Clk. Dept. State, Washington, 1950-52, fgn. affairs officer, 1952, consular officer, Paris, 1952-56, Quebec, Que., Can., 1956-58; personnel officer, Washington, 1958-60, internat.

relations officer, 1961-62, prin. officer, Adelaide, Australia, 1962-67; supervisory polit. officer, Monrovia, Liberia, 1967-70; detailed to Air War Coll., 1970-71; dep. dir. for So. African Affairs, Dept. State, Washington, 1971-73, dir. pub. affairs African Bur., 1973-75, Minister-Counselor (DCM) Accra, 1975-77, ambassador to Sierra Leone, 1977—. Served with AUS, 1943-45. Office: Freetown State Dept Washington DC 20520

LINEHAN, KATHLEEN MARY, govt. ofcl.; b. Bryn Mawr, Pa., Sept. 23, 1950; d. John Joseph Fitzhenry and Katherine Miller L.; B.A. with high honors, U. Md., 1972; M.A., George Washington U., 1975; J.D., George Mason U., 1980. Legis. asst. to Congressman Mendel Davis, 1973-74; legis. specialist, office of congl. affairs FEA, Washington, 1974-76, spl. asst. to adminstr., 1977; spl. asst. to dep. sec. Dept. Energy, Washington, 1977—. Mem. Phi Kappa Phi, Pi Sigma Alpha. Office: Dept Energy 1000 Independence Ave SW Washington DC 20585

LINEN, EDWIN K., ship repair exec.; b. Orange, N.J., June 15, 1914; s. George M. and Isabel (Kearsing) L.; grad. East Orange (N.J.) High Sch.; m. Mildred Loughman Oct. 26, 1940 (div. 1965); children—Sister Barbara, Adrienne (Mrs. May), Judith, E. Kevin, Robert; m. 2d, Camille Cribari Voigt, Aug. 8, 1966. With Todd Shipyards Corp., N.Y.C., 1932—, sec. to pres., asst. corp. sec., 1940-53, corp. sec., 1953-79, also dir. Mem. Am. Soc. Corp. Secs., Soc. Naval Architects and Marine Engrs. (affiliate). Clubs: Whitehall, Westchester Country, Propeller (bd. govs.) (N.Y.C.). Home: 60 Priscilla Ln Port Chester NY 10573 Office: One State St Plaza New York NY 10004

LINFORD, HENRY BLOOD, educator; b. Logan, Utah, Apr. 23, 1911; s. James Henry, Jr. and Mary Hooper (Blood) L.; B.S., Utah State Agrl. Coll., 1931; M.S., Wash. State Coll., 1933, Ph.D., 1936; postgrad. Columbia, 1936-37; m. Rebecca Marian Ririe, Sept. 4, 1936; children—Henry Larry, Marian, Alan Kenneth. Research chemist Am. Smelting & Refining Co., Perth Amboy, N.J., 1937-41; instr. chem. engring. Columbia, 1941-46, asst. prof., 1946-49, asso. prof., 1949-52, prof. chem. engring., 1952-76, prof. emeritus, 1976—; asst. to pres. Polychrome Corp., Yonkers, N.Y., 1976—, acting dir. research and devel., 1977-78, dir. research and devel., 1978—; electrochem. cons., 1941—. Recipient Acheson medal Electrochem. Soc., 1960, Sci. Achievement award Am. Electroplaters Soc., 1967, Great Tchr. award Soc. Older Grads. Columbia, 1968; Harold C. Urey award Phi Lambda Upsilon, 1977; Distinguished Service award Utah State U., 1978. Fellow N.Y. Acad. Sci., Am. Inst. Chemists; hon. mem. Electrochem. Soc. (sec. 1949-59, pres. 1961-62); mem. Am. Inst. Chem. Engrs., Am. Chem. Soc., Am. Electroplaters Soc. (bd. dirs. 1966-69), Nat. Assn. Corrosion Engrs. Home: 5 Laurence Ct Closter NJ 07624 Office: Columbia U New York NY 10027

LING, CYRIL CURTIS, ednl. orgn. exec.; b. Detroit, Jan. 28, 1936; s. Robert Harold and Marie Magdalen (Guilloz) L.; B.S., Wayne State U., 1957, M.B.A., 1958; D.Bus.Adminstrn., Ind. U., 1962; m. Kathryn Ruth Wrolstad, June 16, 1974; children by previous marriage—Robin Kyle, Renee Hollis, Roslyn Elaine. Teaching fellow Wayne State U., Detroit, 1957-58; teaching asso. in mgmt. Ind. U., 1958-59, faculty lectr., 1959-60; asst. prof. mgmt. U. Cin., 1960-63, asso. prof. mgmt., 1963-66; asso. prof. bus. adminstrn., dir. mgmt. center U. Richmond (Va.), 1966-67; mng. dir. Am. Assn. Collegiate Schs. Bus., St. Louis, 1967-71, exec. v.p., 1971-76; sr. v.p. Bank Adminstrn. Inst., Park Ridge, Ill., 1976—; cons., trainer to bus., hosps., govt. agys. Mem. U.S. Nat. Commn. for UNESCO, 1974-76; nat. adv. council SBA. Trustee Joint Council on Econ. Edn., 1974-76; mem. vis. com. Lehigh U. Mem. Psi Chi, Omicron Delta Kappa, Sigma Iota Epsilon, Beta Gamma Sigma. Mason (Shriner). Author: The Management of Personnel Relations: History and Origins, 1965. Former editor AACSB Bull. Home: 831 W Wellington St Chicago IL 60657. *The highest reward for a man's toil is not what he gets for it, but what he becomes by it.*

LING, FREDERICK FONGSUN, educator; b. Tsingtao, China, Jan. 2, 1927; s. Frank Fengchi and Helen (Wong) L.; B.S. in Civil Engring., St. John's U., Shanghai, 1947; B.S. in Mech. Engring., Bucknell U., 1949; M.S., Carnegie-Mellon U., 1951, Sc.D., 1954; m. Linda Kwok, Feb. 20, 1954; children—Erica Helen, Alfred Frank, Arthur Theodoric. Came to U.S., 1947, naturalized, 1962. Engr., Kwan, Chu & Young, cons. engrs., Shanghai, 1947, Loftus Engring. Corp., Pitts., 1951; asst. prof. math. Carnegie-Mellon U., 1954-56; asst. prof. Rensselaer Poly. Inst., Troy, N.Y., 1956-58, asso. prof., 1958-63, prof., 1963-73, William Howard Hart prof. rational and tech. mechanics, 1973—, chmn. dept. mechanics, 1967-74, chmn. dept. mech. engring., aero. engring. and mechanics, 1974—; vis. prof. U. Leads (Eng.), 1970-71. Cons., S.W. Research Inst., Gen. Electric Co., Mitre Corp., Alco Products, Inc., Mech. Tech., Inc., Wear Scis., Inc. NSF sr. fellow, 1970. Fellow Am. Soc. Lubrication Engrs. (Nat. award 1977), ASME (v.p. research 1977—), Am. Acad. Mechanics; mem. Nat. Acad. Engring., AAAS, N.Y. Acad. Scis., Soc. Engring. Sci., Am. Phys. Soc., Gordon Research Conf. on Friction, Lubrication and Wear (chmn. 1970), Sigma Xi, Tau Beta Pi, Pi Mu Epsilon, Pi Tau Sigma. Contbr. articles to profl. jours. Home: 30 Mellon Ave Troy NY 12180

LING, JAMES J., financial cons.; b. Hugo, Okla.; s. Henry William and Mary (Jones) L.; student St. John's Coll. Prep. Sch., Shreveport. Founder, chief exec. officer Ling-Temco-Vought, Inc. (now LTV Corp.), 1957-70; pres. Matrix, Inc., pvt. investments, Dallas, dir. Dallas Cowboys Football Club. Bd. dirs. Dallas Theatre Center; bd. dirs., mem. council Cotton Bowl Council; mem. Hudson Inst.; former trustee So. Methodist U., Tex. Tech. U., St. Mark's Sch. Tex.; mem. vis. coms. Inst.; elec. engring. M.I.T., 1967-72; pres.'s council Calif. Inst. Tech., 1968-71. Served with USNR, World War II; PTO. Knight of Malta. Club: Brook Hollow Country. Home: 5432 Bent Tree Dr Dallas TX 75248 Office: 4835 LBJ Freeway Dallas TX 75234

LING, JOSEPH TSO-TI, mfg. co. exec.; b. Peking, China, June 10, 1919; came to U.S., 1948, naturalized, 1963; s. Ping Sun and Chong Hung (Lee) L.; B.C.E., Hangchow Christian Coll., Shanghai, China, 1944; M.S. in Civil Engring., U. Minn., 1950, Ph.D. in San. Engring., 1952; m. Rose Hsu, Feb. 1, 1944; children—Lois Ling Olson, Rosa-Mai Ling Ahlgren, Louis, Lorraine. Civil engr. Nanking-Shanghai R.R. System, 1944-47; research asst. san. engring., U. Minn., 1948-52; sr. staff san. engr. Gen. Mills, Inc., Mpls., 1953-55; dir. dept. san. engring. research Ministry Municipal Constrn., Peking, 1956-57; prof. civil engring. Bapt. U., Hong Kong, 1958-59; head dept. water and san. engring. Minn. Mining & Mfg. Co., St. Paul, 1960-66, mgr. environ. and civil engring., 1967-70, dir. environ. engring. and pollution control, 1970-74, v.p. environ. engring. and pollution control, 1975—. Adv. mem. on air pollution Minn. Bd. Health, 1964-66; mem. Minn. Gov.'s Adv. Com. on Air Resources, 1966-67; mem. adv. panel on environ. pollution U.S. C. of C., 1966-71; mem. chem. indsl. com., adv. to Ohio River Valley Water Sanitation Commn., 1962-76; mem. environ. quality panel Electronic Industries Assn., 1971—; mem. environ. quality com. NAM, 1965—; mem. Pres.'s Adv. Bd. on Air Quality, 1974-75; vice chmn. environ. com. U.S. Bur. and Industry Adv. Com. to OECD, 1975—; mem. adv. subcom. on environ., health and safety regulations Pres.'s Domestic Policy Rev. of Indsl. Innovation, 1978-79; adv. panel tech. innovation and health, safety and environ. regulation Office Tech. Assessment of U.S. Congress, 1978—; exec. com. engring. assembly NRC, 1977—, also environ. studies bd. Commn. Natural Resources, 1977—; mem. staff services subcom. of environ. com. Bus. Roundtable, 1975—; mem. environ. com. U.S. Council, Internat. C. of C., 1978—; adv. com. on research applications policy NSF, 1976—. Trustee Belwin Outdoor Lab., St. Paul; bd. dirs. Fresh Water Biol. Found., Northwest Area Found., St. Paul Area YMCA, Midwest China Study Center, Minn. Environ. Sci. Found. Woodrow Wilson Sr. fellow, 1975—; registered profl. engr., Minn., Ala., N.J., Okla., W.Va., N.Y., Ill., Ind., Pa., Mich. Fellow ASCE; mem. Nat. Acad. Engring., Am. Acad. Environ. Engrs., Minn. Assn. Commerce and Industry, Am. Water Works Assn., Air Pollution Control Assn. (dir.), Mfg. Chemists Assn., Water Pollution Control Fedn. Club: Rainbow (Mpls.). Contbr. articles to profl. jours. Home: 2090 Arcade St Saint Paul MN 55109 Office: Minn Mining & Mfg Co Box 33331 900 Bush Ave Saint Paul MN 55133. *There must be a goal in any stage of one's life. It must be high enough to offer a challenge. One should not wait for the opportunity but create the opportunity to achieve that goal.*

LINGAFELTER, EDWARD CLAY, JR., educator; b. Toledo, Mar. 28, 1914; s. Edward Clay and Winifred (Jordan) L.; B.S., U. Calif. at Berkeley, 1935, Ph.D., 1939; m. Roberta Crowe Kneedler, Apr. 30, 1938; children—Robert Edward, Thomas Edward, James Edward, Richard Edward, Daniel Edward. Mem. faculty U. Wash., Seattle, 1939—, prof. chemistry, 1952—, asso. dean Grad. Sch., 1960-68. Mem. Am. Chem. Soc., Am. Crystallography Assn. (pres. 1974), A.A.A.S., Assn. Italian Cristallografia. Research and publs. on solutions, molecular structures of paraffin-chain and coordination compounds. Home: 5323 27th Ave NE Seattle WA 98105

LINGEMAN, RICHARD ROBERTS, editor, writer; b. Crawfordsville, Ind., Jan. 2, 1931; s. Byron Newton and Vera Frances (Spencer) L.; B.A., Haverford Coll., 1953; postgrad. Yale U. Law Sch., 1956-58, Columbia U. Grad. Sch. Comparative Lit., 1958-60; m. Anthea Judy Nicholson, Apr. 3, 1965; 1 dau., Jenifer Kate. Exec. editor Monocle mag., N.Y.C., 1960-69; asso. editor, columnist N.Y. Times Book Review, 1969-78; exec. editor The Nation, N.Y.C., 1978—. Served with U.S. Army, 1953-56. Mem. Authors Guild (council), P.E.N. (exec. bd.), N.Y. Hist. Soc., Phi Beta Kappa. Author: Drugs from A to Z, 1969; Don't You Know There's A War On?, 1971; Small Town America, 1980. Office: 72 Fifth Ave New York NY 10011

LINGL, FRIEDRICH ALBERT, psychiatrist; b. Munich, Germany, Apr. 4, 1927; s. Friedrich Hugo and Marie Luise (Lindner) L.; M.D., Ludwig-Maxim U., Munich, 1952; m. Leonore E. Trautner, Nov. 15, 1955; children—Herbert F., Angelika M. Came to U.S., 1957, naturalized, 1962. Intern Edward W. Sparrow Hosp., 1957-58; resident internal medicine City Hosp., Augsburg, Germany, 1953-54; resident psychiatry Columbus (Ohio) State Hosp., 1958-61; supt. Hawthornden State Hosp., Northfield, Ohio, 1963-66; dir. Cleve. Psychiat. Inst., 1966-72; pvt. practice, 1972—; med. dir. Windsor Hosp., 1976—; asst. clin. prof. Case Western Res. U., 1970—. Diplomate Am. Bd. Psychiatry and Neurology. Fellow Am. Psychiat. Assn.; mem. A.M.A., Ohio Med. Assn., Ohio Psychiat. Assn., Am. Assn. Med. Supts., Gerontology Soc., Cleve. Psychiat. Soc. Contbr. articles to med. jours. Address: 40 Farwood Dr Chagrin Falls OH 44022 Office: 6801 Mayfield Rd Cleveland OH 44124

LINGOES, JAMES CHARLES, educator, psychologist; b. Boston, July 27, 1923; s. James Charles and Estelle Gladys (Bruce) L.; student San Francisco Jr. Coll., 1938-40; B.A., U. Calif., Berkeley, 1949; postgrad. Coll. Pacific, 1950-51; Ph.D., Mich. State U., 1960; m. Julia Gibson, Oct. 18, 1944; children—Michael Anthony, Melanie Vanessa. Asst. prof. dept. psychology U. Mich., 1960-64, asso. prof., 1964-74, prof., research scientist, 1974—; vis. asso. prof. U. Calif., Berkeley, 1966-67. Served with AUS, 1941-45. NSF grantee, 1965-73. Mem. Am. Psychol. Assn., Soc. Multivariate Exptl. Psychologists, Psychometric Soc., AAUP, Sigma Xi. Contbr. articles to profl. jours. Home: 2664 Lowell Rd Ann Arbor MI 48103 Office: Dept Psychology U Mich Ann Arbor MI 48109

LINK, ARTHUR A., gov. N.D.; b. Alexander, N.D., May 24, 1914; ed. N.D. State U.; m. Grace Johnson; 5 sons, 1 dau. Mem. N.D. House of Reps., 1947-71, speaker, 1965; mem. 92d Congress from 2d Dist. N.D., 1970-72; gov. N.D., 1973—. Chmn., N.D. Adv. Council for Vocat. Edn., 1969-71; past mem. Randolph Twp. Bd., McKenzie County Welfare Bd.; chmn. agr. com. Nat. Govs. Assn.; past chmn. Midwestern Govs. Conf.; past state co-chmn. Old West Regional Commn.; active N.D.'s Nonpartisan League Bd. dirs. Williston U. Center Found. former chmn. resolutions com. ann. meetings Farmers Union Grain Terminal Assn.; former mem. bd. dirs. McKenzie County Hist. Soc., Lewis and Clark Trial Mus.; former mem. Alexander Sch. Bd. Charter mem. Nat. Cowboy Hall Fame. Democrat. Lutheran (past council pres., past supt. Sunday sch.). Lion (past pres. Alexander club). Home: Alexander ND 58831 Office: Office of Governor State Capitol Bismarck ND 58501

LINK, ARTHUR ERNEST, educator; b. Montgomery, Ala., Mar. 14, 1920; s. Ernest Arthur and Dorothy (Williams) L.; B.A., U. Calif. at Berkeley, 1947, M.A., 1948, Ph.D. (U. Cal. fellow 1952-54), 1957; postgrad. (Fulbright fellow) Yenching U. (China), 1948-50; 1 adopted son, Vance Hua-hsin. Asst. prof. Chinese and East Asian thought U. Mich., Ann Arbor, 1957-61, asso. prof., 1961-63; prof. religious studies U. B.C. (Can.), Vancouver, 1964—; Fulbright scholar Academia Sinica, Taiwan, 1960-62; vis. prof. U. Wis., Madison, 1968. Served with USAAF, 1942-45. Decorated Air medal. Am. Philos. Soc. research fellow, 1962; Can. Council research scholar, 1967-68, 70-71. Mem. Am. Oriental Soc., Assn. Asian Studies (exec. com. Buddhist studies 1968—). Phi Beta Kappa, Alpha Mu Gamma. Contbr. articles to Oriental and religious jours. Home 5051 Howe Sound Ln Vancouver BC Canada

LINK, ARTHUR STANLEY, educator; b. New Market, Va., Aug. 8, 1920; s. John William and Helen Elizabeth (Link) L.; A.B. with highest honors, U. N.C., 1941, Ph.D., 1945; postgrad. Columbia, 1944-45; M.A., Oxford (Eng.) U., 1958; Litt.D., Bucknell U., 1961, U. N.C., 1962; L.H.D., Washington Coll., 1962; Litt.D., Washington and Lee U., 1965; H.H.D. (hon.), Davidson Coll., 1965; m. Margaret McDowell Douglas, June 2, 1945; children—Arthur Stanley, James Douglas, Margaret McDowell, William Allen. Instr., N.C. State Coll., 1943-44; instr. Princeton, 1945-48, asst. prof., 1948-49, mem. Inst. Advanced Study, 1949, 54-55; asso. prof. Northwestern U., 1949-54, prof., 1954-60; prof. Princeton, 1960-65, Edwards prof. Am. history, 1965-76, George H. Davis '86 prof. Am. history, 1976—; Albert Shaw lectr. Johns Hopkins, 1956; Harmsworth prof. Am. history Oxford U., 1958-59; Commonwealth Fund lectr. U. London, 1977. Mem. Nat. Hist. Publs. Commn., 1968-72. Bd. trustees Westminster (Pa.) Coll. Guggenheim fellow, 1950-51. Recipient Bancroft prize for biography, 1957, 61; hon. fellow Jagellonian U., Crocow, Poland. Fellow Am. Acad. Arts and Scis., Soc. Am. Historians; mem. Am. Philos. Soc., Am. Hist. Assn., So. Hist. Assn. (v.p. 1967-68, pres. 1968-69), Orgn. Am. Historians, Nat. Council Chs. (v.p. 1963-66), Mass. Hist. Soc. (corr.), Assn. Documentary Editors (pres. 1978-79), Phi Beta Kappa. Author: Wilson: The Road to the White House, 1947; (with R. W. Leopold and Stanley Coben) Problems in American History, 1972; Woodrow Wilson and the Progressive Era, 1954; (with William B. Catton) American Epoch, 1980; Wilson: The New Freedom, 1956; Wilson the Diplomatist, 1957; Wilson: The Struggle for Neutrality, 1914-15, 1960; La Politica de los Estados Unidas en America Latina, 1960; (with D.S. Muzzey) Our American Republic, 1963, Our Country's History, 1964; Woodrow Wilson, A Brief Biography, 1963; Wilson: Confusions and Crises, 1915-1916, 1964; Wilson: Campaigns for Progressivism and Peace, 1916-17, 1965; editor (with R.W. Patrick) Writing Southern History, 1967; The Growth of American Democracy, 1968; Woodrow Wilson, A Profile, 1968; The Impact of World War I, 1969; (with W.M. Leary, Jr.) The Diplomacy of World Power: The United States, 1889-1920, 1970; (with Stanley Coben) The Democratic Heritage: A History of the United States, 1971; The Higher Realism of Woodrow Wilson and Other Essays, 1970; Woodrow Wilson: Revolution, War, and Peace, 1979; editor-in-chief; Papers of Woodrow Wilson, 32 vols., 1966-79; mem. bd. editors Jour. So. History, 1955-58, 63-66, Jour. Am. History, 1967-70. Contbr. articles to popular and profl. jours. Home: 133 Mt Lucas Rd Princeton NJ 08540. *I have no thoughts on life that do not stem from my Christian faith. I believe that God created me to be a loving, caring person to do His work in the world. I also believe that He called me to my vocation of teacher and scholar.*

LINK, DAVID MERRILL, govt. ofcl.; b. N.Y.C., Feb. 5, 1930; s. Frederick George and Eleanore Sarah (Merrill) L.; B.S., Mass. Inst. Tech., 1952; M.S., U. Ill., 1953; M.B.A., Harvard U., 1960; m. Shirley G. Crane, Jan. 21, 1956; children—Susan C., David F. With Melpar, Inc., Boston, 1957-58, Hewlett Packard Corp., Palo Alto, Calif., 1960-61, Gen. Tech. Corp., Torrance, Calif., 1961-63, Hewlett Packard Corp., Waltham, Mass., 1963-69, Sterling Inst., Boston, 1969-70; with FDA, Rockville, Md., 1970—, dir. Bur. Med. Devices, 1974; instr. Boston Coll. Grad. Sch. Bus. Adminstrn., 1970. Served with USAF, 1952-57. Mem. Assn. Advancement Med. Instrumentation, Sigma Xi. Home: 11825 Hunting Ridge Rd Potomac MD 20854 Office: 8757 Georgia Ave Silver Spring MD 20910

LINK, EDWIN ALBERT, aviation exec., inventor; b. Huntington, Ind., July 26, 1904; s. Edwin A. and Katherine (Martin) L.; student pub. schs., Binghamton, N.Y. and Lindsley Inst.; D.C.S. (hon.), Tufts U., 1952; D.E. (hon.), Coll. Osteo. Medicine and Surgery, 1964; LL.D., Hamilton Coll., 1964; D.Sc. (hon.), Syracuse U., 1966, Fla. Inst. Tech., 1970; m. Marion Clayton, June 6, 1931; children—William Martin, Edwin Clayton (dec.). Aviator, 1927—; pres., founder Link Aviation, Inc., Binghamton, N.Y., 1935-53; pres. Gen. Precision Equipment Corp., 1958-59, dir.; pres. Marine Sci. Center, Ft. Pierce, Fla.; dir., cons. Link div. Singer Co.; dir. emeritus U.S. Air, Inc. Founder Link Found., 1953; gov. Flight Safety Found., 1953-61; mem. naval research adv. com. Lab. Adv. Bd. for Undersea Warfare, 1968-76; mem. Presdl. Task Force on Oceanography, 1969. Hon. trustee Woods Hole Oceanographic Instn.; bd. dirs., trustee Harbor Br. Found., Inc. Recipient Potts medal Franklin Inst., 1945; Wakefield medal Royal Aero. Soc., 1947; exceptional service medal U.S. Air Force; Frank G. Brewer trophy, 1957; Flight Safety Found. Aviation Week award, 1958; Nat. Aviation Club award of achievement, 1963; Elisha Kent Kane gold medal Geog. Soc. Phila., 1965; NOGI award for sci. Underwater Soc. Am., 1965; Centennial medal Syracuse U., 1970; Matthew Fontaine Maury medal for oceanographic achievement Smithsonian Instn., 1971; Gold medal award Internat. Oceanographic Found., 1974; named to Ox 5 Club Aviation Hall Fame, 1972, Aviation Hall of Fame, Dayton, Ohio, 1976. Fellow Am. Inst. Aeros. and Astronautics (de Flores award 1967); mem. Acad. Aeronautics (trustee emeritus), Inst. Nav. (past pres.), Nat. Geog. Soc. Clubs: Binghamton, Wings (N.Y.); Nat. Aviation (Washington); Riomar (Vero Beach, Fla.); Yacht. Author: (with P.V.H. Weems) Simplified Celestial Navigation, 1940. Inventor Link Aviation Trainers; developer diver lock out small submarines, other underwater ocean engring. products.

LINK, MAE MILLS (MRS. S. GORDDEN LINK), space medicine historian and cons.; b. Corbin, Ky., May 14, 1915; d. William Speed and Florence (Estes) Mills; B.S., George Peabody Coll. for Tchrs., 1936; M.A., Vanderbilt U., 1937; Ph.D., Am. U., 1951; grad. Air War Coll., 1965; m. S. Gordden Link, Jan. 11, 1936. Instr. social sci. Oglethorpe U., 1938-39; instr. English, Drury Coll., 1940-41; asso. dir. edn. Ga. Warm Springs Found., 1941-42; mil. historian Hdqrs. Army Air Forces, 1943-45, Office Mil. History, Dept. of Army, 1945-51; spl. asst. to surgeon gen., sr. med. historian U.S. Air Force, Washington, 1951-62; cons. in documentation and space medicine historian NASA, Washington, 1962-64, coordinator documentation, life scis. historian, 1964-70; research asso. Ohio State U. Found., 1970-72. Mem. exec. com. Orgn. for Advancement Coll. Teaching. Trustee, dir. history fellows Amos R. Koontz Meml. Found. Recipient Meritorious Service award U.S. Air Force, 1955, Ann. Outstanding Performance awards, 1956-62, Outstanding Alumna award Sue Bennett Coll., 1977. Fellow Am. Med. Writers Assn. (past dir. Middle Atlantic region); mem. Aerospace Med. Assn., Air Force Hist. Found. (charter), Internat. Congress History Medicine, Societe International d'Histoire de la Medecine. Republican. Episcopalian. Clubs: Garden of Va.; Nat. Space. Author: Medical Support of the Army Air Forces in World War II, 1955; Annual Reports of the U.S. Air Force Medical Service, 1949-62; Space Medicine in Project Mercury, 1965; (with others) (USA/USSR Joint Publ.) Foundations of Space Biology and Medicine, 1976. Editor: U.S. Air Force Med. Service Digest, 1957-62. Contbr. to Ency. Brit., Funk & Wagnalls New Ency. Collier's Ency., profl. jours. Home: Dellbrook Riverton VA 22651 Office: Koontz Center for Advanced Studies Riverton VA. *The desire to reconcile scientific and philosophical truth led to my formal education in the discipline of historical research and writing. The challenge of man's oldest dream—to learn the secret of the universe—led me to concentrate upon aerospace medical research and the related Space sciences. Perhaps our children's children or theirs will ultimately glimpse the truths that thus far have eluded earthbound man.*

LINK, MARILYN CALMES, found. exec.; b. Glendale, Calif., Feb. 20, 1924; d. Edwin Albert and Marie (Calmes) Link; student Syracuse U., 1942-44, Stephens Coll., 1945; B.S., N.Y. U., 1946; M.S., U. Ill., 1949; postgrad. Columbia U., 1952-53. Staff asst. edn. div. Link Aviation, Binghamton, N.Y., 1946-48; tchr. elementary sch., Milburn, N.J., 1949-51; exec. pilot Wood-Mosaic Co., Louisville, 1952-53; instr. U. Nebr. at Lincoln, 1951-53; exec. sec. Link Found., Binghamton, N.Y., 1954—, dir. Fla. First Nat. Bank, Vero Beach; adminstrv. asst. Gen. Precision Equipment, N.Y.C., 1958-61; spl. asst. pub. relations Mohawk Airlines, N.Y.C., 1961-72; mgr. sales devel. Hughes Airwest Airlines, Eastern region, 1972-78; adviser Dept. Def., 1973; collaborator Nat. Air and Space Mus., Smithsonian Inst., 1954-59. Trustee Link Found., 1970—; sec., trustee Atlantic Found., Lawrenceville, N.J., 1973—; trustee, mng. dir. Harbor Branch Found., 1973—; bd. dirs. Woods Hole Oceanographic Inst., 1978—; bd. curators Stephens Coll., 1971-74. Recipient U. Aviation Assn. award. 1962, Frank B. Brewer Trophy, Nat. Aero. Assns., 1963, Lady Hay Drummond-Hay Trophy, Women's Internat. Aero. Assn., 1965. Office: Box 6398 Lawrenceville NJ 08648

LINK, MAX EUGENE, chem. co. exec.; b. St. Gallen, Switzerland, Sept. 26, 1940; came to U.S., 1978; s. Eugene Anton and Anna J. (Juen) L.; Ph.D. in Econs., U. St. Gallen, 1970. Head dept. econs. Latin Am. Inst., U. St. Gallen, 1969-71; with dept. econ. affairs

Sandoz Ltd., Basle, Switzerland, 1971-76; mem. exec. com. charge econ. policy Swiss Soc. Chem. Industry, 1976-77; exec. v.p. fin. Sandoz, Inc., East Hanover, N.J., 1977—. Author papers in field. Home: Claridge II Apt 9KW Verona NJ 07044 Office: Sandoz Inc Route 10 East Hanover NJ 07936

LINK, RICHARD MEBOLDT, investment banker; b. Bklyn., July 27, 1913; s. Charles Christian and Anna (Meboldt) L.; student Columbia, 1930-35; B.S., U. So. Cal., 1936; m. Clara Cornell Tomlin, Dec. 26, 1936; children—Charles David, Laura Ann. Security analyst William R. Staats & Co., Los Angeles, 1936-40; mgr. security analysis Bankamerica Co., San Francisco, 1940-42; regional rationing statistician OPA, San Francisco 1942-43; analyst U.S. Navy Price Adjustment Bd., San Francisco, 1943-45; with Blyth & Co., Inc., Los Angeles, 1945-72, v.p., 1955-72, dir., 1959-72, sr. v.p., mem. exec. com., 1962-72; dir. Purex Corp. Lectr. finance extension div. U. Calif. at Los Angeles, 1946-51. Clubs: California (Los Angeles); Annandale Golf (Pasadena). Home: 555 S San Rafael Ave Pasadena CA 91105

LINK, ROGER PAUL, veterinarian, educator; b. Woodbine, Iowa, Jan. 24, 1910; s. Walter George and Jennie (Fornia) L.; D.V.M., Iowa State U., 1934; student U. Chgo., 1934; M.S., Kans. State U., Manhattan, 1938; Ph.D., U. Ill., 1951; m. Marjorie Haines, Apr. 16, 1938; 1 son, Ronald Charles. Instr. physiology and pharmacology Mich. State U., 1934-35; instr., then asst. prof. vet. physiology Kans. State U., 1935-45; instr. Northwestern U. Med. Sch., 1946; mem. faculty U. Ill., 1946—, prof. vet. physiology and pharmacology, 1955—, head dept., 1961—; vis. prof. vet. pharmacology Chas. Pfizer & Co., 1955. Cons. div. health manpower, Bur. Health Manpower, Dept. Health, Edn. and Welfare; chmn. revision com. vet. drugs Nat. Formulary, 1960-65; mem. U.S. Pharmacopeia Conv., 1960-70, 75—; adv. bd. Morris Animal Found. Active Little League, Babe Ruth Baseball. Mem. Am. (chmn. council biol. and therapeutic agts. 1961-62, pres. 1972, mem. council on edn. 1975), Ill. (pres. 1966, recipient service award 1968) vet. med. assns., Am. Chem. Soc., Sigma Xi, Phi Kappa Phi, Gamma Sigma Delta, Phi Zeta, Phi Sigma, Sigma Phi Epsilon. Methodist. Home: 1708 Pleasant St Urbana IL 61801

LINK, S. GORDDEN, educator, poet; b. Chgo., Apr. 9, 1907; s. Joseph S. and Florence (Tannenholtz) L.; B.S., N.Y. U., 1929, A.M., 1930; M.Ed., Harvard, 1932; Ph.D., George Peabody Coll. for Tchrs., 1938; postgrad. Yale, 1931, Columbia, 1935, George Washington U., 1956, Washington Sch. of Psychiatry, 1958; m. Mae Mills, Jan. 11, 1936. Faculty, Limestone Coll., 1930-34; vis. prof. Northeastern U., 1932-33; lectr. George Peabody Coll. for Tchrs., 1934-38; asst. pastor McKendree Meth. Ch., Nashville, 1937-38; prof., chaplain Oglethorpe U., 1938-39; vis. prof. St. Lawrence U., 1939-40; dir. tng., personnel Microstat Corp., 1941-42; cons. tng. within industry programs WPB, 1941-42; dir. writing workshop McCoy Coll., Johns Hopkins, 1947-51; cons. office Chief of Staff, U.S. Army, 1948-49; chmn. div. humanities Anne Arundel Community Coll., Severna Park, Md., 1962-64, prof. English, poet in residence, 1962-66; writer-in-residence, dir. liberal arts Southeastern U., Washington, 1966-71; emeritus dir. liberal arts, writer in residence, 1971—; professorial lectr. grad. div. Loyola Coll., Balt., 1962-64; cons. various fed. agys., 1950-54; lectr. univs. Calcutta, New Delhi, Nanking, Shanghai, others; exec. dir. Orgn. for Advancement Coll. Teaching, 1964-73, pres., 1973—; pres. Center for Advanced Studies, Amos R. Koontz Meml. Found., Dellbrook campus, Riverton, Va.; writer in residence Shenandoah Coll. and Conservatory Music, 1971—; dir. Dellbrook-Shenandoah Coll. Writers' Conf., 1969—. Chmn., Univ. Press Fund; nat. adv. bd. Am. Security Council. Chmn. bd. trustees Amos R. Koontz Meml. Found.; chmn. bd. govs. Shenandoah Valley Acad. Lit., 1976—. Served from 2d lt. to maj. M.I. AUS, 1942-47; lt. col. ret. Decorated Army Commendation medal with oak leaf cluster, Bronze Star, Army-Navy Air Force medal 1st class (China); Spl. Breast Order Yun Hui with rosette, Breast Order Pau Tang with rosette (China). Fellow Am. Assn. Social Psychiatry (Merrill Moore award 1960); mem. Latin Am. Inst. Washington (past pres.), Poetry Soc. Am. (Lola Ridge award 1948, James Joyce award 1971, Christopher Morley Meml. award 1976, v.p. 1978—), Poetry Soc. Ga., New Eng. Poetry Club, Baker St. Irregulars, Mil. Order World Wars, Ret. Officers Assn., Shelley Soc. N.Y. (hon.). Republican. Methodist. Club: Army and Navy (Washington). Author: One Small Unwilling Captain — A Study of the Japanese Mind, 1937; The German Prisoner of War, 1944; The Engineers in the Pacific, 1947; Pocket Guide to Germany, 1951, Three Poems for Now, 1953, 58, 72; Personal Journal for Yesterday, Now and Tomorrow Maybe: Poems 1943-1978, 1980; The Bakers Dozen You Asked For, 1980. Contbr. to poetry anthologies. Poetry recorded Permanent Collection Modern Poetry, Library of Congress, 1961, 73. Home: Dellbrook Riverton VA 22651 Office: Center for Advanced Studies Dellbrook Campus Riverton VA 22651. *No one lives forever, but I have the rest of my life for fashioning special keys that will open the doors of young minds to vistas they would never else have known.*

LINKE, WILLIAM FINAN, chem. co. research exec.; b. Ravena, N.Y., Aug. 4, 1924; s. Martin and Grace Evelyn (Finan) L.; B.S. (N.Y. State Regent's scholar), Coll. City N.Y., 1945; M.S., N.Y. U., 1946, Ph.D., 1948; m. Ruth Ann Renz, Apr. 14, 1949; children—William Finan, Robert Christopher, Jennifer Ann. Instr. chemistry N.Y. U., 1948-52, asst. prof. chemistry, 1952-57; with Am. Cyanamid Co., Stamford, Conn., 1957—, dir. divisional research div. indsl. chems. div., 1970-71, dir. Stamford research lab., 1972—. Mem. mayor's advisory coms. City of Stamford, 1972-75, fire commr., 1976—; chmn. Stamford Democratic Town Party, 1972. Recipient Am. Inst. Chemists award, 1945. Mem. Am. Chem. Soc., TAPPI, Sigma Xi, Phi Lambda Upsilon. Author: Qualitative Analysis, 1952; editor solubilities monographs Am. Chem. Soc., 1952, 58, 60; contbr. articles to chem. analytical texts and profl. jours.; patentee in field. Home: 75 Ridgecrest Rd Stamford CT 06903 Office: 1936 W Main St Stamford CT 06904

LINKLETTER, ARTHUR GORDON, radio and TV broadcaster; b. Moose Jaw, Sask., Can., July 17, 1912; s. Fulton John and Mary (Metzler) L.; A.B., San Diego State Coll., 1934; m. Lois Foerster, Nov. 25, 1935; children—Jack, Dawn, Robert, Sharon, Diane (dec.). Program dir. sta. KGB, San Diego, 1934; program dir. Calif. Internat. Expn., San Diego, 1935; radio dir. Tex. Centennial Expn., Dallas, 1936; San Francisco World's Fair, 1937-39; author Cavalcade of Golden West (theme spectacle), 1940; author and co-producer Cavalcade of Am. (theme spectacle), 1941; pres. Linkletter Prodns., writer, producer, star in West Coast radio shows, 1940-55; partner, co-owner John Guedel Radio Prodns.; former star, writer People Are Funny, NBC-TV and radio; Art Linkletter's House Party, CBS-TV and radio; chmn. bd. Linkletter Enterprises; owner Art Linkletter Oil Enterprises; dir. MGM, Mc Moran Oil, Western Airlines, Inc., Nat. Liberty Ins. Co. Nat. bd. dirs. Goodwill Industries. Recipient numerous awards. Author: People Are Funny, 1953; Kids Say The Darndest Things, 1957; The Secret World of Kids, 1959; Confessions of a Happy Man, 1961; Kids Still Say The Darndest Things, 1961; A Child's Garden of Misinformation, 1965; I Wish I'd Said That, 1968; Linkletter Down Under, 1969; Oops, 1969; Drugs at My Door Step, 1973; Women Are My Favorite People, 1974; How to be a Super Salesman, 1974; Yes, You Can!, 1979. Address: 8530 Wilshire Blvd Beverly Hills CA 90211

LINMAN, JAMES WILLIAM, physician, educator; b. Monmouth, Ill., July 20, 1924; s. Chester E. and Ruth L. (Pearson) L.; B.S., U. Ill., 1945, M.D., 1947; m. Frances Firth, Aug. 31, 1946; children—John, Jean, James, Jeffrey. Intern, resident internal medicine U. Mich., 1947-51, fellow in hematology, 1951-52; 54-56, asst. prof. internal medicine Med. Sch., 1955-56; chief hematology sect. VA Research Hosp. Chgo., asso. prof. medicine Northwestern U. Med. Sch., 1956-65; prof. internal medicine Mayo Grad. Sch. Medicine, U. Minn., cons. hematology and head spl. hematology sect. Mayo Clinic-Found., Rochester, Minn., 1965-72; prof. medicine, dir. Osgood Leukemia Center, U. Oreg. Health Sci. Center, Portland, 1972-79, head hematology div., 1976-78; prof. medicine U. Hawaii, Honolulu, 1979—. Served with USAF, 1952-54. Recipient Tchr. of Year award Mayo Fellows Assn., 1970. Mem. Am. Soc. Clin. Investigation, Central Soc. Clin. Research, Am., Internat. socs. hematology, A.C.P., Soc. Exptl. Biology and Medicine, Western Assn. Physicians, Western Soc. Clin. Research, Pacific Interurban Clin. Club, Sigma Xi, Alpha Omega Alpha, Phi Kappa Phi. Author: Principles of Hematology, 1966; Factors Controlling Erythropoiesis, 1960; The Leukemias, 1971; Hematology, 1975. Contbr. articles to profl. jours. Home: 2130 Pililani Pl Honolulu HI 96822 Office: John A Burns Sch Medicine U Hawaii 1356 Lusitana St Honolulu HI 96813

LINN, EDWARD ALLEN, writer; b. Boston, Nov. 14, 1922; s. Hyman and Gertrude (Ober) L.; B.S. in Journalism, Boston U., 1950; m. Ruth Goldberg, June 12, 1949; children—Michael, David, Hildy. With USIS, Washington, 1951-52; asst. editor Macfadden Publs., 1952-53; free-lance writer, 1953-63; contbg. editor Sat. Eve. Post, 1964-68. Named Mag. Sportswriter of Year, Nat. Sportscasters and Sportswriters Assn., 1963. Mem. Authors Guild. Author: Veeck-as in Wreck, 1962; The Last Loud Roar, 1964; The Hustler's Handbook, 1965; Koufax, 1966; Masque of Honor, 1969; Thirty Tons a Day, 1972; The Adversaries, 1973; Big Julie of Vegas, 1974; Out of the Fire, 1975; Nice Guys Finish Last, 1975; Where The Money Was, 1976; Inside the Yankees, The Championship Season, 1978. Address: 46 Marilyn Blvd Plainview NY 11803

LINN, JAMES HERBERT, banking exec.; b. Jacksonville, Fla., Nov. 22, 1925; s. Herbert P. and Evelyn Lucile (Gore) L.; B.A. in Econs., U. Mo., Kansas City, 1950; m. Betty J. Thatcher, Oct. 22, 1949; children—David, Donald, Charles, Craig, Jill. From mgmt. trainee to sr. loan officer Commerce Bank of Kansas City div. Commerce Bancshares, Inc., now exec. v.p. Commerce Bancshares, Inc.; dir. Commerce Mortgage Co., CBI Ins. Co. Trustee, Sci. Pioneers, Inc. Served with inf. U.S. Army, 1944-46. Mem. Robert Morris Assos., Kansas City C. of C. Club: Univ. Home: 10261 Rosewood Overland Park KS 66207 Office: 720 Main St Kansas City MO 64105

LINNA, TIMO JUHANI, immunologist, researcher, educator; b. Tavastkyro, Finland, Mar. 16, 1937; came to U.S., 1968, naturalized, 1973; foster son Gustaf Lennart and Anne-Marie (Forsstrom) Ackell; M.B., U. Uppsala (Sweden), 1959, M.D., 1965, Ph.D., 1967; m. Rhoda Margareta Popova, May 20, 1961; children—Alexander, Fredrik, Maria. Intern, resident hosps. in Sweden; practice medicine hosps. and clinic in Sweden; asst. prof. histology U. Uppsala, 1967-71; asst. prof. microbiology and immunology Temple U., Phila., 1970-71, dir. lab. clin. immunology hosps., 1970-72, adviser clin. immunology, 1972—, asso. prof. microbiology, immunology Temple U., Phila., 1971-78, prof., 1978—; immunology cons. UNDP/World Bank/WHO Spl. Program for Research and Tng. in Tropical Diseases, WHO, Geneva, 1978-79; mem. sci. adv. council Internat. Inst. Immunology Tng. and Research, Amsterdam, Netherlands, USPHS Internat. postdoctoral research fellow, 1968-70; spl. research fellow U. Minn., 1970; Eleanor Roosevelt Am. Cancer Soc. fellow, 1976; grantee Swedish Med. Research Council, 1969-71, NIH, 1972—. Mem. Am. Assn. Cancer Research, Am. Assn. Immunologists (chmn. edn. com.), Am. Assn. Pathologists, Am. Soc. Microbiology, Internat. Soc. Exptl. Hematology, Internat. Soc. Lymphology, N.Y. Acad. Scis., Reticuloendothelial Soc., Royal Lymphatic Soc. Uppsala, Scandinavian Soc. Immunology, Soc. Swedish Physicians, Swedish Med. Assn. Lutheran. Author books, contbr. articles to profl. publs. Home: 1927 Birchwood Ct Cherry Hill NJ 08003 Office: 3400 N Broad St Philadelphia PA 19140

LINNELL, ALBERT PAUL, educator; b. Canby, Minn., June 30, 1922; s. Edward Payson and Pearl (Huston) L.; B.A., Coll. of Wooster, 1944; Ph.D., Harvard, 1950; M.A., Amherst Coll., 1962; m. Mildred Jane Elliott, May 24, 1944; children—Carol Anne, Paul Huston, John Andrew, Barbara Marie, James Scott. Instr., Amherst Coll., 1949-51, asst. prof., 1951-54, asso. prof., 1954-62, prof. astronomy, 1962-66; prof., chmn. astronomy dept. Mich. State U., East Lansing, 1966-76; instl. rep. Mass. Inst. Tech. Computer Center, 1960-63. Served to 1st lt., Signal Corps, AUS, 1942-46. Mem. Am. Astron. Soc., A.A.A.S., Assn. Univs. Research Astronomy (dir.-at-large 1962-65), Internat. Astron. Union, Phi Beta Kappa, Sigma Xi. Contbr. articles to profl. jours. Home: 1918 Yuma Trail Okemos MI 48864

LINNELL, ROBERT DALE, moving and storage co. exec.; b. Salt Lake City, Aug. 31, 1932; s. Robert D. and Ruby Florence (Meyers) L.; student acctg. U. Utah, 1959-60, Brigham Young U., Provo, Utah, 1962; m. Lois Athay, July 18, 1958; children—Lori, Randy, Brad, Mike, Roger. Controller, Salt Lake Union Stockyards, 1959-60; v.p. fin. Baileys Moving & Storage Co., Salt Lake City, 1963-70, pres., 1971—; dir. Allied Van Lines, 1975—, mem. exec. com., 1978—. Mem. Bountiful (Utah) City Council, 1979—. Served with USN, 1952-56; Korea. Mem. Nat. Furniture Warehousemen's Assn., Am. Mover's Conf., Salt Lake City C. of C. Republican. Mormon. Club: Rotary. Home: 2415 Claremont Dr Bountiful UT 84010 Office: 640 N Main St North Salt Lake City UT 84054

LINNELL, ROBERT HARTLEY, univ. exec.; b. Kalkaska, Mich., Aug. 15, 1922; s. Earl Dean and Constance (Hartley) L.; B.S., U. N.H., 1944, M.S., 1948; Ph.D., U. Rochester, 1950; m. Myrle Elizabeth Talbot, June 17, 1950; children—Charlene LeGro, Lloyd Robert, Randa Ruth, Dean Maxfield. Asst. instr. U. N.H., 1942-44, instr., 1947; asst. prof. chemistry Am., U., Beirut, 1950-52, asso. prof., chmn. chemistry dept., 1952-55; v.p. Tizon Chem. Corp., Flemington, N.J., 1955-58; asso. prof. chemistry U. Vt., 1958-61; dir. Scott Research Labs., Plumsteadville, Pa., 1961-62; program dir. for phys. chemistry NSF, 1962-65, planning asso., 1965-67, program mgr. for departmental sci. devel., 1967-69; dean Coll. Letters, Arts and Scis., U. So. Calif., Los Angeles, 1969-70, dir. Office Instl. Studies, 1970—; cons. Reheis Corp., 1958-61, Coll. Chemistry Cons. Service, 1970—, EPA, Lake Erie Environment Program. Served with USNR, 1944-46. Recipient Outstanding Achievement award Coll. Tech., U. N.H., 1969. Fellow A.A.A.S.; mem. Am. Chem. Soc. (program chmn. Washington 1968, program chmn. div. chem. edn. 1971), Am. Assn. for Higher Edn., Assn. for Instl. Research, Am. Acad. Polit. and Social Sci. Author: Air Pollution, 1973; Hydrogen Bonding, 1971; Graduate Student Support and Manpower Resources in Graduate Science Education, 1968. Contbr. articles to profl. jours. Patentee in chemistry field. Home: 2716 Severance St Los Angeles CA 90007 Office: Office Instl Studies U So Calif Los Angeles CA 90007

LINNENBURGER, RALPH LEROY, magazine art exec.; b. Keokuk, Iowa, Aug. 31, 1917; s. Albert Phillip and Sarah Ellen (Wharton) L.; student Denver Art Inst., 1946-47, Am. Acad. Art, 1947-49; m. Marian Christine Wirtz, Nov. 29, 1944; children—Bruce Edward, Christine Ellen. Art editor Popular Mechanics mag., Chgo., 1949-57; art dir. Today's Health, Am. Med. News, JAMA, MD's Wife, Prism, also 10 splty. jours. for A.M.A., Chgo., 1958—. Served with AUS, 1941-44. Recipient numerous art awards; 33 pub. and art awards for Prism mag., 1974, 5 in 1975. Home: 22 W 440 Teakwood Dr Glen Ellyn IL 60137 Office: 535 N Dearborn St Chicago IL 60610

LINOWES, DAVID FRANCIS, corp. exec., educator; b. N.J., Mar. 16, 1917; B.S. (with honors), U. Ill., 1941; m. Dorothy Lee Wolf, Mar. 24, 1946; children—Joanne Gail, Richard Gary, Susan Joyce, Jonathan Scott. Founder, partner Leopold & Linowes, C.P.A.'s, Washington, 1946-62, cons. sr. partner, 1962—; partner S.D. Leidesdorf & Co., C.P.A.'s, N.Y.C., 1963-65, Laventhol & Horwath, 1965-75; chmn. bd. dirs. Perpetual Investment Co., Mickleberry Corp., 1970-73; dir., chmn. finance com. Horn & Hardart Co., 1971-77; dir., chmn. audit com. Piper Aircraft, 1972-77; dir. Saturday Rev./World Mag., Inc., 1972-77, Chris Craft Industries, Inc.; cons. DATA Internat. Assistance Corps., 1962-68, U.S. Dept. State, UN, Sec. HEW; chmn. Fed. Privacy Protection Commn., Washington, 1975-77; adj. prof. Southeastern U., 1948-53; adj. prof. mgmt. N.Y. U., 1965-73; Distinguished Arthur Young Prof. U. Ill., 1973-74, Harold Boeschenstein prof. polit. economy and pub. policy, 1976—. Chmn. profl. adv. com. U. Ill., chmn. internat. adv. com. Tel Aviv U.; headed U.S. State Dept. Mission to Turkey, 1967, to India, 1970, Pakistan, 1968, Greece, 1971. Trustee Boy's Club Greater Washington, 1955-62, Am. Inst. Found., 1962-68; Asso. YM-YWHA's Greater N.Y.; bd. dirs. NCCJ, N.Y.C. Vice chmn. Charities Advisory Com. of D.C., 1958-62; chmn. nat. men's com. for integrity in industry, mem. bus. advisory com. Religion in Am. Life, Inc.; chmn. nat. council U.S. People for UN. Served to 1st lt. Signal Corps, AUS, 1942-46. Recipient 1970 Human Relations award Am. Jewish Com. C.P.A., D.C., N.Y. Mem. Am. Inst. C.P.A.'s (v.p. 1962-63, exec. com. 1961-67, chmn. com. on federally assisted programs, chmn. budget and finance com. 1962-63, 1964-67, trial bd., chmn. 1973-76), D.C. Inst. C.P.A.'S (pres. 1956-57), N.Y. Soc. C.P.A.'s, Conf. Bd. U.S. (del. 1960-62), Com. for Econ. Devel., N.Y.C. C. of C. and Industry (council 1965-72; exec. com.; chmn. city affairs com.), Acad. Polit. Sci., UN Assn. N.Y. State (adv. council), U. Ill. Found. (dir.), Phi Kappa Phi (nat. dir.), Beta Alpha Psi (hon.), Beta Gamma Sigma, Phi Alpha Chi. Jewish (trustee temple). Clubs: Nat. Capital Democratic (founding); Scarsdale Golf; Army-Navy, Federal City (Washington); University, Harmonie, Pinnacle (N.Y.C.). Author: Managing Growth Through Acquisition, 1968; Strategies For Survival-Socio-Economic Management, 1973; The Corporate Conscience, 1974; Personal Privacy in an Information Society. Contbr. articles to profl. jours. Home: 9 Wayside Ln Scarsdale NY 10583 also 2208 Fletcher St Urbana IL 61801 Office: 919 3d Ave New York NY 10022 also 308 Lincoln Hall U Ill Urbana IL 61801. *Time is life itself. Never spill a drop of it; for to do so would be to lose the only thing in this world that can never be recaptured. Use every hour to develop and nourish mind or body in your youth; to recharge and nourish the understanding of mind and strength of body in middle age.*

LINOWITZ, SOL MYRON, lawyer, diplomat; b. Trenton, N.J., Dec. 7, 1913; s. Joseph and Rose (Oglenskye) L.; A.B., Hamilton Coll., 1935; J.D., Cornell U., 1938; LL.D., Allegheny Coll., Amherst U., Bucknell U., Babson Inst., Colgate U., Curry Coll., Elmira Coll., Georgetown U., Hamilton Coll., Ithaca Coll., Oberlin U., St. John Fisher Coll., St. Lawrence U., Washington U., St. Louis, Marietta Coll., Notre Dame U., U. Pacific, Pratt Inst., Roosevelt U., U. Mich., U. Mo., Syracuse U.; L.H.D., Am. U., Yeshiva U., Marietta Coll., U. Judaism, Wooster Coll.; m. Evelyn Zimmerman, Sept. 3, 1939; children—Anne, June, Jan, Ronni. Admitted to N.Y. bar, 1938; asst. gen. counsel OPA, Washington, 1942-44; partner firm Sutherland, Linowitz & Williams, 1946-58, Harris, Beach, Keating, Wilcox & Linowitz, Rochester, N.Y., 1958-66; chmn. Nat. Urban Coalition, 1970—; chmn. bd., chmn. exec. com., gen. counsel Xerox Corp., 1958-66; chmn. bd., chief exec. officer Xerox Internat., 1966; dir. Time Inc., Pan Am. World Airways, Inc.; trustee Mut. Life Ins. Co. N.Y.; sr. partner Coudert Bros., 1969—; ambassador to OAS, 1966-69; co-negotiator Panama Canal treaties, 1977-78; spl. Middle East negotiator for Pres. Carter, 1979—. Pres. Fed. City Council, 1974-78; chmn. Pres.'s Commn. World Hunger, 1978—; mem. Commn. on Critical Choices for Americans. Trustee Hamilton Coll., Am. Jewish Com., Cornell U., Johns Hopkins U., Am. Assembly, Salk Inst.; dir., co-founder Internat. Exec. Service Corps; chmn. State Dept. Adv. Com. on Internat. Orgns., 1963-66; chmn. Nat. Council Fgn. Policy Assn.; chmn. bd. dirs. Jewish Theol. Sem. Served to lt. USNR, 1944-46. Fellow Am. Acad. Arts and Scis.; mem. Am. (pres. N.Y. State), Rochester (pres. 1952) assns. for UN, Rochester C. of C. (pres. 1958), Am., N.Y., Rochester (v.p. 1949-50) bar assns., Am. Assn. UN (dir.), Council on Fgn. Relations, Trilateral Commn., Order of Coif, Phi Beta Kappa, Phi Kappa Phi. Author: This Troubled Urban World. Contbr. articles to profl. jours. Home: 2325 Wyoming Ave NW Washington DC 20008 Office: 1 Farragut Sq S Washington DC 20006

LINSALATA, FRANK NATALE, mfg. co. exec.; b. Akron, Ohio, Dec. 29, 1942; s. Thomas and Agnes (Quattrocchi) L.; B.S., Case Inst. Tech., 1963; M.B.A., Harvard, 1965; postgrad. Cleve. Marshall Law Sch., 1968-69. Asst. to pres. Midland-Ross Corp., Cleve., 1965-66, plant supr., 1966-68, dir. financial planning 1969-70, controller, 1970-71, v.p.-controller, 1971-73, v.p. fin., 1973-77, group v.p., 1977—; dir. Midland-Ross of Can. Ltd., Girling Midland-Ross Ltd. Mem. Greater Cleve. Growth Assn. Mem. Financial Execs. Inst., Blue Key, Beta Theta Pi, Tau Beta Pi. Republican. Clubs: Harvard, Harvard Business School, Union, Lakeside Yacht, Canterbury Country, Mid-Day (Cleve.). Author: (with others) Marketing Your Bank Computer Services Profitably, 1965. Home: 20851 Edgecliff Dr Euclid OH 44123 Office: 20600 Chagrin Blvd Cleveland OH 44122

LINSCHITZ, HENRY, educator, chemist; b. N.Y.C., Aug. 18, 1919; s. Joseph and Mindel (Margulies) L.; B.S., Coll. City N.Y., 1940; M.A., Duke U., 1941, Ph.D., 1946; m. Suzanne Ruth Hodes, Aug. 28, 1964; 1 son, Joseph Martin. Mem. research staff Explosives Research Lab., Bruceton, Pa., 1943; sect. leader Los Alamos Lab., 1943-46; research fellow Inst. Nuclear Studies, U. Chgo., 1946-48; from asst. prof. to asso. prof. Syracuse U., 1948-57; prof. chemistry Brandeis U., 1957—; vis. scientist Brookhaven Nat. Lab., 1955-56; Fulbright vis. prof. Hebrew U., 1961. Mem. adv. com. space biology NASA, 1959; mem. study sect. biophys. chemistry NIH, 1962- 66; mem. com. photobiology Nat. Acad. Scis., 1965—. Guggenheim fellow Weizmann Inst., Rehovot, Israel, 1971-72. Fellow Am. Acad. Arts and Scis.; mem. Am. Chem. Soc., AAAS. Spl. research photochemistry, photobiology, chem. kinetics. Home: 35 Riverside Dr Waltham MA 02154

LINSE, EUGENE W., educator. Prof., Concordia Coll., St. Paul. Chmn. Commn. on Social Concerns Luth. Ch.-Mo. Synod, adminstr. housing concerns, 1968-69; pres. Citizens for Ednl. Freedom, 1972—; exec. dir. Lutherans for Life, 1978—. Address: Concordia Coll Dept Social Sci St Paul MN 55104. *Where change in our social order is to be achieved, it will occur only as a consequence of our dedicated, persistent, and unflagging efforts. Where it does not occur, ours is the obligation to redouble our efforts.*

LINSKY, LEONARD, educator; b. Chgo., Nov. 13, 1922; s. Harry and Beatrice (Urist) L.; B.A., U. Calif., Berkeley, 1943, M.A., 1947, Ph.D., 1948; m. Joan Ogden Gregg, Jan. 23, 1947; children—Harry, Bernard. Faculty, U. Ill., 1948-67; prof. philosophy U. Chgo., 1967—, chmn. dept., 1968-74; vis. prof. U. Wis., 1951, U. Mich., 1956, U. Amsterdam, 1960-61, U. Chgo., 1964, 66; Bar Hillel meml. lectr. Tel Aviv U., 1978. Recipient medal U. Liege (Belgium), 1961. Mem. Am. Philos. Assn. (pres. Western div. 1976-77). Author: Referring, 1967; Names and Descriptions, 1977. Editor: Semantics and the Philosophy of Language, 1952; Reference and Modality, 1971. Home: 1413 E 57th St Chicago IL 60637

LINSLEY, EARLE GORTON, entomologist, educator; b. Oakland, Calif., May 1, 1910; s. Earle Garfield and Marguerite (Vesper) L.; B.S., U. Calif., 1932, M.S., 1933, Ph.D., 1938; Guggenheim fellow Am. Mus. Natural History, 1947-48; m. Juanita Murdoch, Aug. 22, 1935; children—Joan, James Murdoch. Asst. dept. entomology and parasitology U. Calif. at Berkeley, 1933-35, teaching asst., 1935-37, instr., 1939-43, asst. prof., 1943-49, asso. prof., 1949-53, prof., 1953-74, prof. emeritus, 1974—; chmn. dept. entomology and parasitology, 1951-59, dean College Agr. Sci., 1960-73; asso. quarantine entomologist Calif. Dept. Agr., 1938; jr. entomologist Agrl. Expt. Sta., Calif., 1939-43, asst. entomologist, 1943-49, asso. entomologist, 1949-53, entomologist, 1953—, asst. dir., 1960-62, asso. dir., 1962-73; research prof. Miller Inst. Basic Research Sci., 1959-60; research asso. Coleoptera, Calif. Acad. Sci, 1939—; collaborator Dept. Interior, 1953-55; sec. Am. Com. Entomol. Nomenclature, 1944-48; cons. NSF, 1967-68. Mem. Galápagos Internat. Sci. Project, 1964; mem. agrl. sci. planning com. Orgn. Tropical Studies, 1968-71; mem. com. insect pests NRC-Nat. Acad. Sci., 1963-69. Recipient Berkeley citation U. Cal., 1973; Centennial medal Calif. Agrl. Expt. Sta., 1975. Fellow Calif. Acad. Sci. (Fellows award 1973), AAAS; mem. Entomol. Soc. Am. (hon. mem. v.p. 1948, pres. 1952), Calif. C. of C. (agri. com. 1967-73), Pacific Coast (honored mem.; sec. 1934-38, 40-42, pres. 1938-40), Canadian, Kans. entomol. socs., Ecol. Soc. Am., So. Calif. Acad. Sci., Am., Western socs. naturalists, Soc. Study Evolution, Western Assn. Agrl. Expt. Sta. Dirs. (exec. com. bd. dirs. 1961-71), Soc. Systematic Zoology, Am. Forestry Assn., Soc. Study Coleoptera, Sigma Xi, Alpha Zeta, Phi Sigma, Gamma Alpha, Phi Mu Delta. Club: Commonwealth. Author: (with Mayr and Usinger) Methods and Principles of Systematic Zoology, 1953; also papers on insect taxonomy, biology and anthecology. Editor Pan-Pacific Entomologist, 1943-50. Home: 290 Alvarado Rd Berkeley CA 94705

LINTNER, JOHN, educator, economist; b. Lone Elm, Kans., Feb. 9, 1916; s. John Virgil and Pearl (Daily) L.; A.B., U. Kans., 1939, M.A., 1940; M.A., Harvard U., 1942, Ph.D., 1946; m. Sylvia Chace, June 17, 1944 (dec.); children—John Howland, Nancy Chace Molvig; m. 2d, Eleanor J. Hodges, June 8, 1963; 1 stepson, Allan Hodges. Instr., U. Kans., 1939-40; staff Nat. Bur. Econ. Research, 1941; teaching fellow Harvard U., 1941-42, faculty Grad. Sch. Bus. Adminstrn., 1945—, prof. bus. adminstrn., 1956-64, Gund prof. econs. and bus. adminstrn., 1964—. Dir. U.S. & Fgn. Securities Corp.; trustee, dir. Chase of Boston Mut. Funds, 1975—; trustee Cambridge Savs. Bank, 1950—. Cons. govt. agencies, pvt. founds., bus. firms; sr. cons. to Sec. of Treasury, 1975-78; asso. editor, mem. exec. com. Review of Economics and Statistics, 1950—. Fellow Am. Acad. Arts and Scis., Econometric Soc.; mem. Am. Econ. Assn., Am. Fin. Assn. (pres. 1974), AAAS, Soc. of Fellows (Harvard), Phi Beta Kappa. Author: (with J. K. Butters) Effect of Federal Taxes on Growing Enterprises, 1945; Mutual Savings Banks in the Savings and Mortgage Markets, 1948; Corporate Profits in Perspective, 1950; (with J. K. Butters and W. L. Cary) Effect of Taxation on Corporate Mergers, 1951. Asso. editor Jour. Fin. Econs., 1973-79; contbr. articles to profl. and bus. jours. Home: 50 Tyler Rd Belmont MA 02178 Office: Harvard Bus Sch Boston MA 02163

LINTON, CALVIN DARLINGTON, educator, coll. dean; b. Kensington, Md., June 11, 1914; s. Irwin Helfenstein and Helen Pauline (Grier) L.; student Erskine Coll., S.C., 1931-32; A.B., George Washington U., 1935; A.M., Johns Hopkins, 1939, Ph.D., 1940; m. Jeanne Elting LeFevre, Aug. 1, 1951. Lecture reporter, instr. stenotyping Temple Bus. Sch., Washington, 1935-36; instr. English, Wheaton Coll., Ill., summer 1938, Johns Hopkins, 1939-40; asso. prof., chmn. English dept. Queens Coll., N.C., 1940-41; asst. prof. English, George Washington U., 1945-46, asso. prof., 1946-48, prof. English lit., 1948—, asst. dean Columbian Coll., 1949-56, asso. dean, 1956-57, dean, 1957—; lectr. lit. subjects WGMS, Washington, 1953-54; lectr. in renaissance intellectual history Inst. Renaissance Studies Folger Shakespeare Library, Washington, 1971. Cons. various govt. agys. in report writing. Vice chmn. Commn. Instns. Higher Edn., Middle States Assn., 1968-72. Trustee Am. Coll. in Paris, 1975-79. Served as lt. (j.g.), Office Sec. of Navy, 1941-43; lt. comdr. Minecraft Tng. Center, Norfolk, Va., 1943-45. Mem. Modern Lang. Assn., Coll. English Assn., Modern Humanities Research Assn. (Am. chmn. 1960-63, Am. sec. 1963—), Conf. on Christianity and Lit. (pres. 1964-66), Am. Conf. Acad. Deans, Eastern Assn. Coll. Deans and Advisers of Students (exec. com. 1963-65, pres. 1966-67), Internat. Assn. U. Profs. English, Lit. Soc. Washington (pres. 1973—). Presbyn. Clubs: Tudor and Stuart (Johns Hopkins); Cosmos (pres. 1973) (Washington). Author: Report Construction and Analysis (U.S. Map Service), 1953; How to Write Reports, 1954; Effective Writing, 1958; also articles in lit. field. Editor-at-large Christianity Today, 1974—; editor Bicentennial Almanac, 1975; The American Almanac, 1977. Home: 5216 Farrington Rd Washington DC 20016

LINTON, FREDERICK M., mgmt. cons. firm exec.; b. Stanton, Mich., 1932; B.A., Mich. State U., 1959, M.A., 1960; m. Peggy Jensen, May 27, 1954; children—Michael, Melinda, Margaret. Tchr., San Diego, 1960-66; with AMCORD, Inc., 1966-69, Peat, Marwick & Mitchel, Los Angeles, 1969-70; sr. v.p. Shareholders Capital Corp., Los Angeles, 1970-72; pres., chief exec. officer Boyden Assos. Inc., N.Y.C. and Los Angeles, 1972-74; pres., chmn. Delta Group Inc., Newport Beach, Calif., 1974—. Dir Irvine Indsl. League. Bd. dirs. U. Calif. at Irvine Indsl. Assn. Mem. Calif. Council Econ. Edn. (pres., trustee), Newcomen Soc. N.Am., Town Hall Calif., World Affairs Council, Internat. Club Los Angeles. Home: 2706 Vista Umbrosa Newport Beach CA 92660 Office: 369 San Miguel Suite 180 Newport Beach CA 92660

LINTON, MARGARET REYNOLDS, publisher; b. S.C., July 31; d. Andrew and Louise (Gaskin) Reynolds; m. Amos Linton, May 15, 1950 (dec.); 1 son, Gary Leo. Operator Linton Funeral Home; sec.-treas. Black Broadcasting Coalition; publisher, editor Critique Publ. Asso., Youngstown; producer, host weekly TV show One Woman's World sta. WYTV, Youngstown. Founder Broadway Theatre League; chmn. Fashion Fair; mem. N.A.A.C.P. Hostess Johnson-Humphrey Inaugural; sec. Citizens for Kennedy; mem. Youngstown Human Relations Commn.; mem. panel Dem. Nat. Com. Bd. dirs. MacGuffey Manor, Inc. convalescent home, Housing Opportunities, Inc. low cost housing, Urban League, Cancer Soc., Children's Service. Named B'nai B'rith Woman of Year, 1961. Mem. Am. Assn. Workers for Blind, Am. Assn. Instrs. for Blind, O. Negro Bus. and Profl. Women (1st gov.), Buckeye Funeral Dirs., Nat. Assn. Fashion and Accessory Designers. Elk. Club: Bridge. Home and office: 632 Belmont Ave Youngstown OH 44502

LINTON, ROBERT EDWARD, investment banker; b. N.Y.C., May 19, 1925; s. Adolph B. and Helen (Hirshon) L.; m. Margot R. Tishman, June 19, 1952; children—Roberta Helen, Thomas Norman, Jeffrey Robert, Elizabeth Marie. With Drexel Burnham Lambert Inc., N.Y.C., 1946—, sr. exec. v.p., dir., 1972-77, pres., dir., chief exec. officer, 1977—. Served to 2d lt. USAAF, 1943-45. Mem. Nat. Assn. Securities Dealers (chmn. corp. fin. com., dir., mem. exec. com.). N.Y. Soc. Security Analysts. Club: Century Country (Purchase, N.Y.). Home: Purchase Ln Rye NY 10580 Office: 60 Broad St New York NY 10004

LINTON, RODNEY CURTIS, banker; b. Dearborn, Mich., Feb. 20, 1925; s. Ronald Curtis and Helene (Simpson) L.; A.B., U. Mich., 1948, LL.B., 1952; m. Patricia F. Stansell, Dec. 7, 1951. Admitted to Mich. bar, 1952; mgr. community relations Chrysler Corp., Detroit, 1952-61; sr. v.p., cashier Nat. Bank Detroit, 1961—. Served with USMCR, 1943-46, 51-52. Mem. Mich. Bar Assn., VFW. Episcopalian. Clubs: Detroit Athletic, Dearborn Country. Home: 10 Amherst Ln Dearborn MI 48120 Office: Box 116 Woodward at Fort St Detroit MI 48232

LINTON, ROY NATHAN, graphic arts co. exec.; b. Jamestown, Ohio, Jan. 22, 1918; s. Lindley Vanniman and Pearl Candice (Jackson) L.; A.B., Cedarville Coll., 1938; postgrad. Ohio State U., 1938-40; m. Joyce Sandra Phillips, Dec. 11, 1945; children—Michael, Philip. Tchr. math. Blanchester (Ohio) High Sch., 1938-41; with Standard Register Co., Dayton, 1947—, v.p. ops., 1971-72, exec. v.p., 1972-77, pres., 1977—, also dir. Trustee Miami Valley Hosp., Dayton. Served to maj., field arty., AUS, 1941-46. Mem. Data Processing Mgmt. Assn., Nat. Assn. Accountants, C. of C., Sales and Mktg. Execs Internat., Toastmasters Club. Republican. Mason, Rotarian. Clubs: Executives (Chgo.); Dayton, Dayton Racquet, City (Dayton). Home: 6116 Old Spanish Trail Dayton OH 45459 Office: 626 Albany St Dayton OH 45401

LINVILL, JOHN GRIMES, educator; b. Kansas City, Mo., Aug. 8, 1919; s. Thomas G. and Emma (Crayne) L.; A.B., William Jewell Coll., 1941; S.B., Mass. Inst. Tech., 1943, S.M., 1945, Sc.D., 1949; Dr. Applied Sci., U. Louvain (Belgium), 1966; m. Marjorie Webber, Dec. 28, 1943; children—Gregory Thomas, Candace Sue. Asst. prof. elec. engring. Mass. Inst. Tech., 1949-51; mem. tech. staff Bell Telephone Labs., 1951-55; asso. prof. elec. engring. Stanford, 1955-57, prof., dir. solid-state electronics lab., 1957-64, prof., chmn. dept. elec. engring., 1964—; co-founder, dir. Telesensory Systems, Inc.; dir. Spectra-Physics, Inc. Recipient citation for achievement William Jewell Coll., 1963. Fellow IEEE (Edn. medal 1976); mem. Nat. Acad. Engring., Am. Acad. Arts and Scis. Author: (with J.F. Gibbons) Transistors and Active Circuits, 1961; Models of Transistors and Diodes, 1963. Inventor Optacon, reading aid for blind. Home: 30 Holden Ct Portola Valley CA 94025 Office: Dept Elec Engring Stanford U Stanford CA 94305

LINVILL, WILLIAM KIRBY, elec. engr.; b. Kansas City, Mo., Aug. 8, 1919; s. Thomas Grimes and Emma Kirby (Crayne) L.; A.B. in Math. and Physics, William Jewell Coll., 1941; A.B./S.M. Elec. Engring., M.I.T., 1945, Sc.D. in Elec. Engring., 1949; m. Bessie Blythe Burkhardt, June 28, 1949; m. Bessie Blythe Burkhardt, June 28, 1942; children—Barbara, Mary Lou, Thomas, Anne, Carl. Asst. prof. elec. engring. M.I.T., 1949-53, asso. prof., 1953-56; project leader Inst. Def. Analysis, Pentagon, Washington, 1956-58; sr. staff mem. electronics Rand Corp., Santa Monica, Calif., 1958-60; prof. elec. engring. Stanford U., 1960-64, chmn., prof. Inst. in Engring.-Econ. Systems, 1964-67, now prof., chmn. dept. engring. econ. systems; Battelle fellow, Columbus, Ohio, 1971-72; mem. vis. com. Nat. Bur. Standards, Dept. Commerce; mem. adv. com. on space and terrestrial applications NASA; mem. Westinghouse Electronics Research Adv. Council, Pitts.; vis. prof. elec. engring. U. Tex., Austin. Fellow IEEE; mem. Nat. Acad. Engring., AAAS. Democrat. Home: 105 Shawnee Pass Portola Valley CA 94025 Office: Dept Engring-Econ Systems Stanford U Stanford CA 94305

LINVILLE, LARRY LAVON, actor; b. Ojai, Calif., Sept. 29, 1939; s. Harry Lavon and Fay Pauline (Kennedy) L.; student U. Colo., 1957-59, Royal Acad. Dramatic Arts, 1959-61; married; 1 dau., Kelly Leigh. Mem. various repertory theatres, 1961-68; Broadway appearance in More Stately Mansions, 1968; film appearances in Kotch, 1972; TV role in M-A-S-H., 1971-77; TV appearance Grandpa Goes to Washington, 1978. Mem. Actor's Equity Assn., AFTRA, Screen Actor's Guild, Writer's Guild Am. Author: (film) Ragwing, 1975. Designer, builder LTB-1 exptl. tailless sailplane. *Trust only those who tell you what you should hear, not those who tell you what you want to hear.*

LINVILLE, THOMAS MERRIAM, engr.; b. Washington, Mar. 3, 1904; s. Thomas and Clara (Merriam) L.; E.E., U. Va., 1926; grad. advanced mgmt. program Harvard U., 1950, mod. engring. program U. Calif. at Los Angeles, 1960; m. Eleanor Priest, Nov. 25, 1939; children—Eleanor, Thomas Priest, Edward Dwight. Various govt. positions, 1918-26; with Gen. Electric Co., 1926-66, beginning with Advanced Engring. Program to 1931, successively in engring. dept. chmn. rotating machines product com., chmn. rotating machines devel. com., staff asst. to mgr. engring., mgr. engring. edn., mgmt. consultation div., mgr. exec. devel. dept., 1926-53, mgr. research operation dept., 1953-64, mgr. research application dept., research services, 1964-66; chief exec. Linville Co., Engrs., Research & Devel., 1966—; mem. USN tech. missions Pearl Harbor, 1942, Europe, 1945; mem. NRC, 1960-68. Chmn., Schenectady City Planning Commn., 1951; pres. N.Y. State Citizens Com. for Pub. Schs., 1952-53; mem. Gov.'s Council Advancement Research and Devel. N.Y. State, 1960—; pres. Schenectady Mus., 1964-69; chmn. Community Chest, 1964; chmn. Devel. Council for Sci., Rensselaer Poly. Inst., 1960-67; vis. com. Norwich U., 1970—, Clarkson Inst. Tech., 1959-65; pres. Mohawk-Hudson council ETV-WMHT Channel 17, 1966-70; bd. dirs. Sunnyview Hosp.; pres. Schenectady Indsl. Devel. Corp., 1967-69. Served to lt. USNR, 1940-42. Recipient Charles A. Coffin award, USN Certificate of Commendation; Schenectady Profl. Engrs. Soc. Engr.-of-Year award, 1960. Fellow IEEE (past dir.), ASME, AAAS; mem. Nat. (pres. 1966-67), N.Y. State (pres. 1954-55), socs. profl. engrs., Am. Soc. Engring. Edn., Engrs. Joint Council (dir. 1954-59), Am. Acad. Polit. and Social Sci., N.Y. Acad. Scis., Schenectady C. of C. (past dir., v.p.), Raven Soc., Tau Beta Pi (eminent mem., nat. pres. 1974-76), Theta Tau, Delta Upsilon. Unitarian (pres. 1940-45). Clubs: Rotary, Mohawk, Mohawk Golf. Contbr. articles to jours. Address: 1147 Wendell Ave Schenectady NY 12308. *God and my parents gave me the will to live gracefully and graciously, to love the rocks and rills, the woods and temple hills, to find my richest rewards in my wife and children, to seek richer goals as well as money, to think first and speak later, to search for the roots of problems, to conceive and synthesize, to be helpful, never to obstruct, to enthuse and inspire, not to act or speak in anger, to treasure and use humor, to be industrious and honest, to turn savings into property, to be grateful, to seek justice, liberty, and culture for all. Thus I have lived fully and richly.*

LION, DONOR, govt. ofcl.; b. N.Y.C., May 3, 1924; s. David and Anna (Holstein) L.; A.B., Harvard U., 1945, Ph.D., 1954; M.A., U. Buffalo, 1948; m. Linda Haverberg, Sept. 29, 1978; children—Ann, Amy. Teaching fellow, instr. econs. U. Buffalo, also Millard Fillmore Coll.; 1946-48; teaching fellow econs. Harvard U., 1948-51; economist Pres.'s Materials Policy Commn., 1951, Nat. Security Resources Bd., 1952; program dir. MSA, 1952-54; econs. cons. Robert R. Nathan Assos., 1954-57; mgmt. cons. Booz, Allen & Hamilton, 1957-62; asst. dir. AID mission to Brazil, also dir. N.E. program, Brazil, 1963-67; asso. asst. adminstr., program coordinator AID, 1967-68; consul gen., N.E. Brazil, 1968-71; mem. Sr. Seminar in Fgn. Policy, 1971-72; dir. MRSD, Bur. Latin Am., AID, Washington, 1972-75, asso. asst. adminstr. DR, 1975-76, dep. asst. adminstr. Bur. Latin Am., 1976-77, dir. AID mission to Jamaica, 1977—. Address: Agy Internat Devel Washington DC 20523

LION, PAUL MICHEL, III, transp. engr.; b. Washington, Dec. 7, 1934; s. Paul Miller and Anna Louise (Chandler) L.; B.S., U.S. Mil. Acad., 1956; M.A., M.S.E. in Aero. Engring., Princeton U., 1963, Ph.D., 1965; m. Jane Sanford, June 16, 1956; children—David, James, Thomas, William. Engr., Applied Physics Lab., Silver Spring, Md., 1960-61; research asst. Princeton U., 1961, postdoctoral fellow, 1965-66, with dept. aerospace and mech. sci., 1966-73, dept. civil engring., 1973—, engr., 1966—, asst. prof. transp., 1966-70, asso. prof., 1970-74, prof., 1974-79; dir. ops. and cost analysis U.S. Ry. Assn., Washington, 1977—; cons. in field; mem. Transp. Research Bd. Served with arty. U.S. Army, 1956-59; Germany. Mem. ASCE, Ops. Research Soc. Am., IEEE. Contbr. articles to profl. publs. Home: 7012 Hamel Hill Ct McLean VA 22101 Office: L'Enfant Plaza N Washington DC 20595

LIONNI, LEO, designer, painter, sculptor; b. Amsterdam, Holland, May 5, 1910; s. Louis and Elizabeth (Grossouw) L.; student U. Zurich, 1928-30; Ph.D., U. Genoa, Italy, 1935; m. Nora Maffi, Dec. 23, 1931; children—Louis, Paul. Came to U.S., 1939, naturalized, 1945. Freelance writer, designer, painter, 1930-39; with N. W. Ayer & Son, Inc., Phila., 1939-47; art dir. Fortune, 1949—; design dir. Olivetti Corp. of Am., 1949—; exhibited Norlyst Gallery, N.Y., 1947, Print Club of Phila., 1948, Mus. Modern Art, N.Y.C., 1954; one-man show Worcester (Mass.) Mus., 1958, Portland Mus., Phila. Art Alliance, 1959, Naviglio, Milano, Italy, 1963, Obelisco, Rome, 1964, Ariete, Milano, 1966, Milione, Milano, 1972, I Portici, Torino, Italy, Biennale di Venezia, Linea 70, Verona, Italy, Vicolo, Genova, Italy, 1973, Klingspor Mus., Offenbach, Germany, 1974, Baukunst Galerie, Cologne, Germany, 1974, 78, Galleria CIAK, Rome, Italy, 1975, Galleria dell'Oca, Rome, 1976, Staempfli Gallery, N.Y.C., 1977, 79, Mus. Castelvecchio, Verona, 1978, Frankfurter Galerie, Frankfurt, W. Ger., 1979. Named Art Dir. of year 1955 Nat. Soc. Art Dirs.; named to Art Dir.'s Hall Fame, 1974; recipient Gold medal Architecture Archtl. League, 1956, Illustrated Book award German Govt., 1965, Golden Apple award 1st Internat. Biennial, Bratislava; George Miller lectr. Ill., 1967. Mem. Am. Inst. Graphic Arts (pres.), Artists Equity, Authors League Am., Alliance Graphique Internationale. Author: Little Blue and Little Yellow, 1959; Inch by Inch, 1960; On My Beach, 1961; Swimmy, 1963; Tico, 1964; Frederick, 1967; The Alphabet Tree, 1968; The Biggest House in the World, 1968; Alexander and The Wind-up Mouse, 1969; Fish is Fish, 1970; Theodore and the Talking Mushroom, 1971; Il Taccuino di Leo Lionni, 1972; The Greentail Mouse, 1973; A Color of His Own, 1974; In the Rabbitgarden, 1975; Pezzettino, 1976; A Parallel Botany, 1977; I Want To Stay Here, 1977; Geraldine, The Music-Mouse, 1979; editor: Print, 1955-57, Panorama, 1964-65. Home: San Bernardo Lavagna Italy also Porcignano Radda in Chianti Italy

LIPETZ, MILTON EDWARD, univ. adminstr.; b. Bklyn., Mar. 10, 1930; s. Samuel Phillip and Goldie Rebecca (Lipetz) L.; B.A., N.Y. U., 1951; M.A., Bklyn. Coll., 1953; Ph.D., Ohio State U., 1958; m. Marilyn Altman, Apr. 6, 1952; children—Bruce David, Valerie Ellin. Research asso. Ohio State U., Columbus, 1958; asst. prof. psychology U. Colo., Boulder, 1958-63, asso. prof., 1963-67, prof., 1967—, dean Grad. Sch., 1973-79, vice chancellor for research, 1974-79, vice chancellor for acad. affairs, dean of faculties, 1979—. Diplomate Am. Bd. Profl. Psychology. Mem. Am., Colo. psychol. assns. Cons. editor Jour. Personality and Social Psychology, 1973-76. Contbr. articles to profl. jours. Home: Boulder Heights Boulder CO 80302 Office: Vice Chancellor for Acad Affairs U Colo Boulder CO 80302

LIPFORD, ROCQUE EDWARD, corp. exec., lawyer; b. Monroe, Mich., Aug. 16, 1938; s. Frank G. and Mary A. (Mastromarco) L.; B.S., U. Mich., 1960, M.S., 1961, J.D., 1964; m. Marcia A. Griffin, Aug. 5, 1966; children—Lisa, Rocque Edward, Jennifer, Katherine. Instr. mech. engring. U. Mich., 1961-63; admitted to Mich. bar, 1964; atty. Miller, Canfield, Paddock & Stone, Detroit, 1965-66; asst. gen. counsel Monroe Auto Equipment Co., 1966-70, gen. counsel, 1970-72, v.p., gen. counsel, 1973—; v.p., gen. counsel Tenneco Automotive, 1977—; partner firm Miller, Canfield, Paddock & Stone, Detroit, 1978—; dir. Monroe Auto Equipment Co. of Can. Ltd. Mem. Mich., Ohio bar assns., Tau Beta Pi, Pi Tau Sigma. Clubs: North Cape Yacht, Monroe Golf and Country. Home: 471 Hollywood Ave Monroe MI 48161 Office: 1426 E 1st St Monroe MI 48161

LIPHAM, JAMES MAURICE, educator; b. Fyffe, Ala., Aug. 10, 1927; s. William Herbert and Ava Frances (Gilley) L.; A.A., Tenn. Wesleyan Coll., 1948; B.S., U. Ga., 1951, M.Ed., 1953; Ph.D., U. Chgo., 1960; m. Charlotte Kight, June 10, 1956; children—Mary Elizabeth, William James. Tchr. Tifton (Ga.) High Sch., 1953-55, Upper Arlington (Ohio) High Sch., 1955-56; supt. schs., DeGraff, Ohio, 1956-58; staff asso. U. Chgo., 1958-60; prof. ednl. adminstrn. U. Wis., 1960—; vis. lectr. Boston U., 1969; cons. Wis. pub. schs., 1960—. Served with AUS, 1946-48, 51-52. Mem. N.E.A., Wis. Edn. Assn., Wis. Assn. Sch. Adminstrs., Am. Ednl. Research Assn., Phi Beta Kappa, Phi Kappa Phi, Phi Delta Kappa, Kappa Delta Pi, Gamma Sigma Epsilon. Baptist. Mason, Kiwanian. Author: Administrative Theory as a Guide to Action, 1960; Educational Administration as a Social Process, 1968; The Principalship: Foundations and Functions, 1974; The Principal and Individually Guided Education, 1976. Asso. editor School Review, 1959-60, Administrator's Notebook, 1959-60. Contbr. articles profl. jours. Home: 63i8 Old Sauk Rd Madison WI 53705

LIPINSKY DE ORLOV, LINO SIGISMONDO, artist; b. Rome, Italy, Jan. 14, 1908; s. Sigismondo and Elinita K. (Burgess) L.; ed. in Rome and Munich, 1914-19; studied under father at Brit. Acad. Arts, Rome, 1922-25; grad. Royal Acad. Arts, Rome, 1937; m. Leah S. Penner, Oct. 1, 1943; children—Lino S.M., Lucian C.M. Came to U.S., 1940, naturalized, 1945. Painter, etcher, mus. curator, historian; head exhibits design dept. Mus. City N.Y., 1959-67; curator history John Jay Homestead, N.Y. State Parks and Recreation Div. for Hist. Preservation, Katonah, 1967—; mem. art admissions com. Huntington Hartford Found., 1962-65; dir. ann. Winter Antiques Show, N.Y., 1957-60, Garibaldi-Meucci Meml. Mus., S.I., N.Y., 1956—; art cons. Italian embassy, Washington, also consulate gen. Italy in N.Y.C.; works exhibited fgn. countries, N.A.D., Art Inst. Chgo., Met. Mus. Art, Albright Art Gallery, Cleve. Mus. Art, Detroit Mus. Art, many other cities and mus.; one-man shows include Palazzetto Venezia, Rome, 1928, Boston Symphony Hall, 1941, Jr. League Gallery, Boston, 1941; Knoedler Gallery, N.Y.C., 1945; Avery Hall, Columbia, 1955, Cosmos Club, Washington, 1955, Smithsonian Inst., U.S. Nat. Mus., 1955, Galleria Costa, Palma de Mallorca, Spain, 1955, numerous pvt. galleries; represented permanent collections Mus. City N.Y., Library Congress, Met. Mus., N.Y. Pub. Library, Columbia, Detroit Inst. Arts, Gabinetto delle Stampe, Rome, Galleria Nazionale d'Arte Moderna, Rome, numerous other museums and pvt. collections; executed mural for the banquet hall, Palace of Maharaja of Indore, 1947, several ch. murals, 1942-48, Diorama: Verrazzano's Discovery of New York Bay in 1524, 1955, circular mural: View of New Amsterdam in 1660, Mus. City. N.Y., 1965; designed mus. exhibit N.Y. World's Fair, 1964-65, Bedford Hist. Soc. Mus., 1970. Mem. Bedford (N.Y.) Tricentennial Commn., 1980. Served with Italian Army, 1936, U.S. intelligence div. 6th Service Command, OSS, World War II. Awarded numerous prizes, including Silver medal of Ministero dell'Educazione Nazionale, Rome, 1928, 31; diplome d'Honneur, silver medal Expn. de Budapest, 1936; Diplome de Grand Prix, gold medal, Diplome d'Honneur, Paris Expn. Internationale, 1937; Chgo. Soc. Etchers, 1941, 50; Soc. Am. Etchers, 1942; Joseph Pennell prize Library of Congress, 1942; Detroit Inst. Arts, 1943; Guild Hall, Easthampton, N.Y., 1946; Kosciuszko Found., N.Y., 1948; decorated officer Order of Merit Rep. of Italy, 1958; recipient Gold medal and certificate of merit Order Sons of Italy in Am., 1961, L.L. Huttleston Staff award State N.Y. Council on Parks and Recreation, 1974; Hist. Tomahawk award Westchester County Hist. Soc., 1979. Mem. Soc. Am. Graphic Artists, Audubon Artists (chmn. exhbn. com. 1952), Chgo. Soc. Etchers, United Scenic Artists, Am. Assn. Museums, Comitato Nazionale Per le Onoranze a Giovanni Da Verrazzano, Gruppo Romano Incisori Artisti, Internat. Platform Assn., Nat. Soc. Lit. and Arts, Bedford Farmers' Club, N.Y. State Assn. Mus., Knights Mark Twain, N.Y. State Employees Assn., Bedford Hist. Soc. Author: Pocket Anatomy in Color for Artists, 1947; Giovanni Da Verrazzano, The Discoverer of New York Bay, 1524, 1958; Contbg. author numerous art and hist. books. Contbr. articles to profl. jours. Home: John Jay Homestead Katonah NY 10536

LIPKA, DAVID H., food co. exec.; b. Bklyn., Nov. 14, 1929; s. Charles and Leonie Viola Lipka; B.A., Bklyn. Coll., 1954; student N.Y. U. Sch. Bus.; m. Lillian Wissner, Feb. 14, 1954; children—Andrew, Wendy, Suzanne. With DCA Food Industries, 1955—, v.p. ops., 1969-72, pres. DCA Co. div., 1972-78, pres., chief exec. officer DCA Food Industries Inc., N.Y.C., 1978—. Bd. dirs. Am. Inst. Baking, Karen Horney Clinic. Served with U.S. Army, 1951-53. Mem. Am. Baking Assn. (Privy Council), Inst. Food Technologists, Am. Mgmt. Assn., Nat. Indsl. Conf. Bd. Club: Mill River (Old Brookville, N.Y.). Patentee food processing. Home: 19 Oakwood Circle Roslyn NY 11576 Office: 919 3d Ave New York NY 10022

LIPKIN, MACK, JR., physician, researcher, educator; b. N.Y.C., May 17, 1943; s. Mack and Carol H. (Fraenkel) L.; A.B. magna cum laude, Harvard, 1965, M.D., 1970. Intern, resident in internal medicine U. N.C., Chapel Hill, 1970-72; resident, fellow in medicine and psychiatry Strong Meml. Hosp., U. Rochester (N.Y.), 1972-74, asst. prof. medicine and psychiatry U. Rochester, 1974—; mem. med. group Genesee Valley Group Health Assn., Rochester, 1973—; med. dir. Threshold, Rochester, 1973-77; vis. research fellow Rockefeller Found. Mem. AAAS, Am. Psychosomatic Soc., Soc. Research and Edn. Primary Care Internal Medicine, Phi Beta Kappa. Co-editor: Cellular Neurophysiology, 1972, Genetic Responsibility: On Choosing Our Children's Genes, 1974. Home: 29 Westmoreland Dr Rochester NY 14620 Office: Rockefeller Found 1133 Ave of Americas New York NY 10036

LIPKIN, MARTIN, physician, scientist; b. N.Y.C., Apr. 30, 1926; s. Samuel S. and Celia (Greenfield) L.; A.B., N.Y. U., 1946, M.D., 1950; m. Joan Schulein, Feb. 16, 1958; children—Richard, Steve. Fellow, Cornell U. Med. Coll., 1952; practice medicine specializing in internal medicine, gastroenterology and neoplastic diseases, N.Y.C.; mem. staff N.Y. Hosp., Meml. Hosp. for Cancer and Allied Diseases; asso. prof. medicine Cornell Med. Coll., N.Y.C., 1963-78, prof. medicine, 1978—, prof. Grad. Sch. Med. Scis., 1978—; asso. mem. Meml. Sloan Kettering Cancer Center, 1973—. Served as officer USN, 1953-55. Recipient NIH career devel. award, 1962-71; Albert F.R. Andresen lectureship N.Y. State Med. Soc., 1971—; diplomate Nat. Bd. Med. Examiners. Fellow A.C.P.; mem. Med. Soc. State of N.Y. (chmn. sect. gastroenterology and colon and rectal surgery 1974-75, exec. com. Nat. Large Bowel Cancer Project 1974-76, asso. chmn. sci. program com. 1977—), Digestive Diseases Soc. (founding), Internat. Soc. Investigative Gastroenterology (founding), Am. Soc. Clin. Investigation, Am. Physiol. Soc., Am. Assn. Cancer Research, Am. Gastroenterol. Assn., Soc. for Exptl. Biology and Medicine, Am. Soc. Exptl. Pathology, Harvey Soc. Clubs: Griffis, Fairview, Cornell (N.Y.). Mem. editorial bd. Bioscis. Communications, Cell and Tissue Kinetics, others; editor Gastrointestinal Tract Cancer, 1978; contbr. articles to sci., Nature, Jour. Clin. Investigation, Exptl. Cell Research, other profl. jours. Office: 1275 York Ave New York NY 10021

LIPKIN, SEYMOUR, pianist, conductor; b. Detroit, May 14, 1927; s. Ezra and Leah (Vidaver) L.; Mus. B., Curtis Inst. Music, 1947; studied piano with David Saperton, 1938-41, Rudolf Serkin, Mieczyslaw Horszowski, 1941-47, conducting with Serge Koussevitzky, Berkshire Music Center, 1946, 48, 49; m. Catherine Lee Bing, Dec. 27, 1961; 1 son, Jonathan Michael. Debut with Detroit Civic Orch., 1937; apprentice condr. to George Szell, Cleve. Orch., 1947-48; appearances as pianist other orchs. including Boston Symphony in Tanglewood; ann. tours including soloist Buffalo and Nat. Symphony; soloist, asst. condr. N.Y. Philharmonic tour, Europe and Russia, 1959; conducting debut Detroit Symphony, 1944; co-condr. Curtis Inst. Orch., 1952-53; asst. condr. Goldovsky Opera Co. on tour, 1953; condr. N.Y.C. Opera Co., 1958; one of three asst. condrs. New York Philharmonic, 1959-60; mus. dir. Teaneck (N.J.) Symphony, 1961-70, L.I. Symphony, 1963-79, Scarboro (N.Y.) Chamber Orch., 1964-65; music dir. N.Y. City Center Joffrey Ballet, 1966-68, prin. guest condr., 1968-72, music dir., 1972-79; mem. faculty Manhattan Sch. Music, 1965-70, 72—; mem. piano faculty Curtis Inst. Music, 1969—; faculty music dept. Marymount Coll., Tarrytown, N.Y., 1963-72, chmn. music dept., 1968-71; condr. Bklyn. Coll. Orch., 1973-74. Recipient 1st prize Rachmaninoff piano competition, 1948; Ford Found. award to commn. and perform concerto by Harold Shapero, 1959. Mem. Am. Guild Mus. Artists, Am. Fedn. Musicians. Home: 420 West End Ave New York NY 10024

LIPMAN, DAVID, editor; b. Springfield, Mo., Feb. 13, 1931; s. Benjamin and Rose (Mack) L.; B.J., U. Mo., 1953; m. Marilyn Lee Vittert, Dec. 10, 1961; children—Gay Ilene, Benjamin Alan. Sports editor Jefferson City (Mo.) Post-Tribune, 1953, Springfield Daily News, 1953-54; gen. assignment reporter Springfield Leader and Press, 1956-57; reporter, copy editor Kansas City (Mo.) Star, 1957-60; sports reporter St. Louis Post-Dispatch, 1960-66, asst. sports editor, 1966-68, news editor, 1968-71, asst. mng. editor, 1971-78, mng. editor, 1979—; guest lectr. Am. Press Inst., Columbia Journalism Sch., 1967-70. Bd. dirs. Mid-Am. Press Inst., 1973—, chmn., 1975-77; bd. dirs. Mid-Am. Newspaper Conf., 1973-75; trustee United Hebrew Congregation, 1975-77. Served to 1st lt. USAF, 1954-56. Mem. Football Writers Assn. Am. (bd. dirs. 1968), Sigma Delta Chi (pres. St. Louis chpt. 1976-77), Kappa Tau Alpha, Omicron Delta Kappa. Jewish. Author: Maybe I'll Pitch Forever, 1962; Mr. Baseball, The Story of Branch Rickey, 1966; Ken Boyer, 1967; Joe Namath, 1968; co-author: The Speed King, The Story of Bob Hayes, 1971, Bob Gibson Pitching Ace, 1975, Jim Hart Underrated Quarterback, 1977. Office: 900 N 12th Blvd St Louis MO 63101

LIPMAN, HOWARD WALDMAN, securities co. exec.; b. Albany, N.Y., July 11, 1905; s. Isac and Fanny (Waldman) L.; art student, Europe, 1925-29; m. Jean Herzberg, Nov. 11, 1932; 1 son, Peter W. With J.S. Bache, N.Y.C., 1929-39; partner Neuberger & Berman, N.Y.C., 1939—, mng. partner, 1955-73; now ltd. partner. Vice pres. Wilton (Conn.) Library, 1945-55, pres., 1956-57. Trustee Archives Am. Art, Smithsonian Instn., 1956—, pres., 1971-74; trustee Whitney Mus. Am. Art, N.Y.C., 1968—, pres., 1974—, chmn. bd., 1977; trustee Phoenix Art Mus. Clubs: Century Assn., Board Room (N.Y.C.); Aspetuck Valley (Conn.) Country; Desert Forest Golf (Carefree, Ariz.). Pres., Howard and Jean Lipman Found., collection Am. sculpture owned by and circulated through Whitney Mus. Am. Art. Home: 25 Sutton Pl S New York NY 10022 Office: 522 Fifth Ave New York NY 10036

LIPMAN, IRA ACKERMAN, security services co. exec.; b. Little Rock, Nov. 15, 1940; s. Mark and Belle (Ackerman) L.; student Ohio Wesleyan U., 1958-60; LL.D. (hon.), John Marshall U., 1970; m. Barbara Ellen Kelly Couch, July 5, 1970; children—Gustave K., Joshua S, M Benjamin. Salesman, exec. Mark Lipman Service Inc., Memphis, 1960-63; v.p. Guardsmark, Inc., Memphis, 1963-66, pres., 1966—, chmn. bd., 1968—; Entrepreneurial fellow Memphis State U., 1976; bd. dirs. Nat. Council on Crime and Delinquency, 1975, exec. com., 1976, chmn. fin. com., treas., 1978-79; mem. environ. security com. of pvt. security adv. council Law Enforcement Assistance Adminstrn., 1975-76. Shelby County chmn. U.S. Savs. Bonds, 1976; mem. pres.'s council Memphis State U., 1975—; met. chmn. Nat. Alliance of Businessmen, Memphis, 1970-71, Union of Am. Hebrew Congregations Task Force, 1979—; mem. young leadership cabinet United Jewish Appeal, 1973—; mem. exec. bd. Chickasaw council Boy Scouts Am., 1978—; bd. dirs. Tenn. Ind. Coll. Fund, 1977-79, mem. exec. com., 1978—; trustee Memphis Acad. Arts, 1977—. Mem. Internat. Assn. Chiefs Police, Am. Soc. Criminology, Internat. Soc. for Criminology, Am. Soc. Indsl. Security (cert. protection profl.). Clubs: B'nai B'rith, Ridgeway Country, Racquet, Summit, Delta, Petroleum, Economic. Author: How To Protect Yourself from Crime, 1975. Contbr. articles to numerous jours., mags. and newspapers. Home: 4490 Park Ave Memphis TN 38117 also 58 W 58th St New York NY 10019 Office: 22 S 2d St Memphis TN 38103 also 40 W 57th St New York NY 10019

LIPMANN, FRITZ (ALBERT), biochemist; b. Koenigsberg, Germany, June 12, 1899; s. Leopold and Gertrud (Lachmanski) L.; student U. Koenigsberg, 1917-22, U. Munich, 1919; M.D., U. Berlin, 1924, Ph.D., 1928; M.D. (hon.), U. Marseilles, 1947, U. Copenhagen, 1972; M.A. (hon.), Harvard, 1949; D.Sc. (hon.), U. Chgo., 1953, U. Paris, 1966, Harvard, 1967, Rockefeller U., 1971; L.H.D., Brandeis U., 1959, Yeshiva U., 1964; m. Elfreda M. Hall, June 23, 1931; 1 son, Stephen. Came to U.S., 1939, naturalized, 1944. Research asst. Prof. Meyerhof's Lab., Kaiser Wilhelm Inst., Berlin and Heidelberg, 1927-30; Dr. A Fischer's Lab., Berlin, 1930-31; Rockefeller fellow Rockefeller Inst. Med. Research, N.Y.C., 1931-32; research asso. Biol. Inst. Carlsberg Found., Copenhagen, Denmark, 1932-39, dept. biochemistry Med. Sch. Cornell U., 1939-41; research chemist, head biochem. research lab. Mass. Gen. Hosp., Boston, 1941-57; prof. biol. chemistry Med. Sch. Harvard, 1949-57; prof. Rockefeller U., 1957—. Recipient Carl Neuberg medal, 1948; Mead Johnson & Co. award for outstanding work on Vitamin B-complex, 1948; Nobel prize for medicine and physiology, 1953; Nat. Medal Sci., 1966. Fellow N.Y. Acad. Sci., Danish Royal Acad. Scis.; fgn. mem. Royal Soc.; mem. Nat. Acad. Scis., Am. Chem. Soc., Am. Soc. Microbiology, Biochem. Soc., A.A.A.S., Am. Soc. Biol. Chemists, Harvey Soc., Am. Philos. Soc. Author: Wanderings of a Biochemist, 1971. Author sci. papers. Home: 201 E 17th St New York City NY 10003 also RD 2 Box 347 Rhinebeck NY 12572 Office: Rockefeller University New York City NY 10021

LIPNICK, ELTON STANLEY, lawyer; b. Galveston, Tex., Oct. 3, 1934; s. Paul and Fannie (Hochman) L.; B.B.A., U. Tex., 1955; LL.B., S. Tex. Coll. Law, 1962; children—David, Amy. Field agt., dist. conferee IRS, Houston, 1959-64; admitted to Tex. bar, 1962; atty. Lipnick & Gordon Co., Houston, 1964—; lectr. taxation S. Tex. Coll. Law, 1966-69. Trustee, pres. S. Tex. Law Jour. Served with AUS, 1957-58. Mem. Mensa, Beta Alpha Psi, Beta Gamma Sigma. Jewish. Club: Westwood Country. Contbr. articles to profl. jours. Home: 11611 Windy Ln Houston TX 77024 Office: 1921 Bank of the Southwest Bldg Houston TX 77002

LIPPARD, STEPHEN JAMES, chemist, educator; b. Pitts., Oct. 12, 1940; s. Alvin I. and Ruth (Green) L.; B.A., Haverford Coll., 1962; Ph.D. (NSF fellow) Mass. Inst. Tech., 1965; m. Judith Ann Drezner, Aug. 16, 1964; children—Andrew (dec.), Joshua, Alexander. Postdoctoral research asso. chemistry Mass. Inst. Tech., Cambridge, 1965-66; asst. prof. chemistry Columbia, N.Y.C., 1966-69, asso. prof., 1969-72, prof., 1972—; mem. study sect. medicinal chemistry NIH, 1973-77. Coach, Demarest Borough Soccer Team, 1975—. Alfred P. Sloan fellow, 1968-70; Guggenheim fellow, 1972; recipient Tchr.-Scholar award Camille and Henry Dreyfus Found., 1971-76; sr. internat. fellow John E. Fogarty Internat. Center, 1979. Mem. Am. Chem. Soc., AAAS, Am. Crystallographic Assn., Chem. Soc. (London), Biophys. Soc., Phi Beta Kappa. Editor Progress in Inorganic Chemistry, 1967—; contbr. articles to profl. jours. Home: 168 Donnybrook Dr Demarest NJ 07627 Office: Box 611 Havemeyer Columbia U New York City NY 10027

LIPPE, IRVIN S., internat. labor affairs cons., ret. fgn. service officer; b. Zanesville, Ohio, Feb. 11, 1915; s. Samuel and Ann (Greenberg) Lipsky; A.B., U. Ill., 1938; m. Bernice Nan Feldman, Sept. 13, 1937; children—Stuart Harris, Michael Justin, Laurel Rachel. Editor, dir. pub. relations Brotherhood R.R. Trainmen, 1946-55; labor attache Am. embassy, Havana, Cuba, 1951-53; consul, labor officer Am. consulate gen., Singapore, 1955-57; 1st sec., labor attache Am. embassy, Brussels, 1957-60; labor adviser Bur. European Affairs, Dept. State, Washington, 1960-62; 1st sec., labor attache U.S. mission to UN, Geneva, Switzerland, 1962-65; labor attache Am. embassy, Paris, France, 1965-69; labor attache, polit. officer Am. embassy, London, Eng., 1969-73; detailed as spl. asst. and internat. adviser to Fed. Mediation and Conciliation Service, Washington, 1973; dir. for UNESCO affairs Bur. Internat. Orgns., Dept. State, Washington, 1973-75; dir. pub. information UN liaison office ILO, N.Y.C., 1975-78. Home and Office: RD 2 Carversville Rd Doylestown PA 18901

LIPPE, MELVIN KARL, lawyer; b. Chgo., Oct. 21, 1933; s. Melvin M. and Myrtle (Karlsberg) L.; B.S., Northwestern U., 1955, J.D., 1958; grad. certificate Grad. Sch. Banking, U. Wis., 1965; certificate Sr. Bank Officers Seminar, Harvard, 1966; children—Suzanne, Michael S., Deanna; m. 2d, Sandra M. Bauer, Jan. 5, 1974. Admitted to Ill. bar, 1958; asso. D'Ancona, Pflaum, Wyatt & Riskind, Chgo., 1958-61; asst. to chmn. bd. Exchange Nat. Bank of Chgo., 1961-62, asst. v.p., 1962-64, v.p., 1964-66, sr. v.p., sec. to bd. dirs., 1966-69, exec. v.p., dir., 1969-74, vice chmn. bd., 1974-76, also dir.; exec. v.p., dir. Exchange Internat. Corp., 1972-74; vice chmn. bd., dir. Am.-Israel Bank, Ltd., 1974-76; partner firm Antonow & Fink, Chgo., 1977—; instr. Ill. Inst. Tech., 1960-63. Treas. Chgo. chpt. Am. Jewish Com., 1974-78. Bd. dirs., v.p. Jewish Community Centers Chgo.; bd. dirs. Young Men's Jewish Council, Chgo., pres., 1971. Served with Ill. N.G., 1959. C.P.A. Mem. Am., Ill., Chgo. bar assns., Am. Jewish Com., Phi Epsilon Pi, Tau Epsilon Rho, Beta Gamma Sigma. Jewish. Clubs: Standard (Chgo.). Office: 111 E Wacker Dr Chicago IL 60601

LIPPER, KENNETH, investment banking co. exec.; b. N.Y.C., June 19, 1941; s. George and Sally L.; B.A., Columbia U., 1962; J.D., Harvard U., 1965; LL.M. in Civil Law System, N.Y. U., 1966; postgrad. Faculte de Droit et Economiqes, Paris, 1967; m. Evelyn R. Gruss, June 12, 1966; children—Joanna Helene, Daniella, Tamara, Julia. Admitted to N.Y. bar, 1965; asso. firm Fried, Frank, Harris, Shriver & Jacobson, N.Y.C., 1967-68; dir. industry policy Office of Fgn. Direct Investment, Washington, 1968-69; gen. partner Lehman Bros., N.Y.C., 1969-75; partner Salomon Bros., N.Y.C., 1976—; pres. Martini & Rossi Corp., 1977—; adj. prof. Sch. Internat. Affairs Columbia U., 1976—. Ford Found. grantee, 1965-67. Mem. Council on Fgn. Relations, Phi Beta Kappa. Clubs: Univ., Mid-Atlantic. Author: Cartels Are No Solution, 1978; Financial Aspects of Foreign Investment in the United States, 1979. Home: 1095 Park Ave New York NY 10028 Office: 1 New York Plaza New York NY 10028

LIPPERT, ALBERT, health service exec.; b. Bklyn., Apr. 23, 1925; s. Hyman and Becky (Shapiro) L.; B.B.A., Coll. City N.Y., 1949; m. Felice Sally Mark, June 21, 1953; children—Keith Lawrence, Randy Seth. Asst. buyer Goldrings, 1949-51; buyer, mdse. mgr. Mangel Stores Corp., 1951-67; v.p. Weight Watchers Internat., Inc., Manhasset, N.Y., 1967-68, chmn. bd.. pres., 1968-79, chmn. bd., chief exec. officer, 1979—; treas., dir. W.W. Twentyfirst Corp. 1st v.p. City of Hope; active Mr. and Mrs. League, Grand St. Boys Club. Served with AUS, 1943-46; ETO. Named man of year, N.Y. Council Civic Affairs, 1968. K.P. Home: Sousa Dr Sands Point NY 11050 Office: 800 Community Dr Manhasset NY 11030

LIPPINCOTT, BARTON HIRST, publisher; b. Jamestown, R.I., July 26, 1925; s. Bertram and Elsie DuPuy Graham (Hirst) L.; B.S., Yale U., 1946; m. Beatrice Woolsey Bronson, Sept. 17, 1950 (div. 1969); m. 2d Carol Helms Earle, July 14, 1972; children—Louise Woolsey, Deborah Wharton, Frances Bronson, Elizabeth Barton. Sales clk. Bumpus Book Store, London, 1947; with J.B. Lippincott Co., 1947—, pres., Phila., 1978—. Served with USN, 1943-46. Mem. Assn. Am. Pubs. (dir.), St. Anthony Frat. Clubs: Phila. Cricket, Phila., Conanicut Yacht. Office: JB Lippincott Co East Washington Sq Philadelphia PA 19105

LIPPINCOTT, BENJAMIN EVANS, polit. scientist; b. Alexandria, Ind., Nov. 26, 1902; s. Jason Evans and Laura (d'Isay) L.; B.S., Yale, 1925; student Brasemose, Oxford, Eng., 1926; Ph.D., London Sch. Econs. and Polit. Sci., U. London, 1930; m. Gertrude Lawton, June 22, 1934. Instr. polit. sci. U. Minn., 1929-32, asst. prof., 1932-39, asso. prof., 1939-42, prof., 1946-71; vis. prof. Stanford, 1953; guest lectr. U. Mich., 1958, Yale Law Sch., 1966; lectr. Johns Hopkins, 1957, vis. prof., 1966-68. Chmn. tng. guidance staff 2655th A.R.C., Mpls., 1955-59, adviser to comdr., 1960; mem. nat. ednl. adv. com. Consumer's Union. Liaison officer USAF Acad., 1959-62, coordinator Minn., 1961-62, ret., 1962; mem. ROTC Panel, Res. Forces Policy Bd., Dept. Def., 1961-68; trustee Walker Art Center, 1939-41. Commd. 1st lt. AC, AUS, 1942, lt. col., 1946, col. USAF Res., 1952; historian 13th Air Force, S. and S.W. Pacific, 1944-45. Decorated Legion of Merit. Mem. Royal Inst. Philosophy, A.A.U.P. (pres. U. Minn. chpt. 1960-61), Internat. Polit. Sci. Assn. (rep. Am. assn. at internat. congress Rome 1958), Am. Soc. Polit. and Legal Philosophy (first v.p. 1960-61), Midwest Polit. Sci. Assn., Am. Polit. Sci. Assn. (chmn. research com. on polit. theory 1941-42; established award polit. theory 1975), Am. Acad. Polit. and Social Sci., Social Sci. Research Council (civil liberties com. 1941-43), St. Elmo Soc. Aurelian Honor Soc., Am. Fedn. Tchrs. (pres. U. Minn. chpt. 1938-39), Minn. Civil Liberties Union (chmn. acad. freedom com. 1965-67), Am. Peace Soc. (dir. 1972—), Center for Study of Presidency (bd. editors 1974—). Clubs: 39ers (U. Minn.); Skylight (Mpls.); Eastward Ho (Cape Cod). Author: Victorian Critics of Democracy, 1938; From Fiji Through the Philippines with the Thirteenth Air Force, 1947; Democracy's Dilemma; The Totalitarian Party in Free Society, 1965. Editor, contbr.: Govt. Control of the Economic Order, 1935, Lange and Taylor, On the Economic Theory of Socialism, 1938 (trans. into 7 langs.); History Thirteenth Air Force (AAF Archives), 1944-45. Contbr.: Contemporary Political Science, 1950; Soviet Total War, 1956. Contbr. articles to profl. jours. Home: 252 Bedford St SE Minneapolis MN 55414

LIPPINCOTT, JOSEPH WHARTON, JR., publisher; b. Bethayres, Pa., Oct. 2, 1914; s. Joseph Wharton and Elizabeth Schuyler (Mills) L.; student St. Paul's Sch., 1928-33, Princeton, 1933-37; m. Josephine Drexel Henry, 1937 (div.); 1 dau., Elizabeth Seton; m. 2d, Marie Louise Beck, Dec. 8, 1950; 1 son, Joseph Wharton III. With J.B. Lippincott Co., Phila., 1937-78, dir., 1940-78, sec., 1942-46, exec. v.p., 1953-58, pres., 1958-78, chmn. bd., 1974-78; sec. Med. Sci., Inc., 1956-68; v.p., dir. A.J. Holman Co., 1962-73, chmn. bd., 1973-78; dir. Harper & Row Pubs., Inc. Trustee Ludington Pub. Library, Free Library Phila.; bd. dirs. Am. Ednl. Pubs. Inst., 1967-70, U. Pa. Press, 1971-76, Urban Libraries Council, 1978—. Served with Am. Field Service, 1943-45. Mem. Am. Book Pubs. Council (dir. 1962-65), Booksellers Assn. Phila. (dir. 1960-66, pres. 1964-65), ALA (council 1968-72), Hist. Soc. Pa. (dir. 1966-78), Netherlands Soc. Phila., Pa. Soc. Sons of Revolution. Clubs: Down Town, Franklin Inn, Wilderness (Phila.); Merion Cricket (Haverford); Field (Sarasota, Fla.); Princeton (N.Y.C.). Home: 2409 Casey Key Rd Nokomis FL 33555

LIPPINCOTT, SARAH LEE, astronomer; b. Phila., Oct. 26, 1920; d. George E. and Sarah (Evans) Lippincott; student Swarthmore Coll., 1938-39, M.A., 1950; B.A., U. Pa., 1942; D.Sc., Villanova U., 1973. Research asst. Sproul Obs., Swarthmore (Pa.) Coll., 1941-50, research asso., 1951-72, dir., 1972—, prof., 1977—. Mem. Savoy Opera Co., Phila., 1947—; bd. mgrs. Societe de Bienfaisance de Philadelphie, 1966-69. Recipient achievement award Kappa Kappa Gamma, 1966; Distinguished Daus. of Pa. award, 1976; Fulbright fellow Paris, 1953-54. Mem. Rittenhouse, Am. (lectr. 1961—) astronom. socs., Internat. Astron. Union (v.p. commn. 26 1970-73, pres. 1973-76), Sigma Xi (nat. lectr. 1971-73). Author: (with Joseph M. Joseph) Point to the Stars, 1963, 3d edit., 1977; (with Laurence Lafore) Philadelphia, the Unexpected City, 1965. Contbr. articles to profl. jours. Office: Sproul Observatory Swarthmore Coll Swarthmore PA 19081

LIPPINCOTT, WALTER HEULINGS, JR., publishing co. exec.; b. Phila., Jan. 16, 1939; s. Walter Heulings and Helen B. (Howe) L.; A.B., Princeton U., 1960; m. Caroline Seebohm, June 8, 1974; 1 dau., Sophie. With Morgan Guaranty Trust Co., N.Y.C., 1960-63; coll. traveler Harper & Row Pubs., 1963-65, editor, 1965-70, editor-in-chief, coll. dept., 1970-74; editorial dir. Cambridge Univ. Press, N.Y.C., 1974—. Bd. dirs. Met. Opera Guild, Am. Friends of Aldeburgh Festival. Club: N.Y. Racquet and Tennis. Home: 322 Central Park W New York NY 10025 Office: 32 E 57th St New York NY 10022

LIPPINCOTT, WILLIAM THOMAS, educator, chemist; b. Balt., Apr. 4, 1924; s. William Thomas and Marie (Petry) L.; B.S., Capital U., 1948, Sc.D., 1974; Ph.D. (DuPont Teaching fellow), Ohio State U., 1954; m. Shirley Sue Epperson, Jan. 1, 1953; children—William Thomas III, David B., Loralee L. Faculty, Capital U., 1948-53, asst. prof., 1951-53; asst. prof. Mich. State U., 1954-57; asso. prof. U. Fla., 1957-61; prof. chemistry Ohio State U., Columbus, 1961-73, vice chmn. chemistry, 1964-66; prof. chemistry U. Ariz., Tucson, 1973—. Mem. Adv. Council on Coll. Chemistry, 1964-67. Recipient Coll. Tchr. award Mfg. Chemists' Assn., 1966. Mem. Am. Chem. Soc. (award in chem. edn., 1975), AAAS (mem. coop. com. on teaching sci. and math. 1962-65), Sigma Xi, Phi Lambda Upsilon, Alpha Chi Sigma. Author: (with others) Chemistry, A Study of Matter, 3d edit., 1977; (with others) Chemistry: Patterns and Properties, 1971; also articles. Editor: Jour. Chem. Edn., 1967-79. Research on rates and mechanisms autoxidation, organometallic compounds, ednl. methods. Home: 3822 N Calle Hondonada Tucson AZ 85715

LIPPITT, GORDON LESLIE, educator; b. Fergus Falls, Minn., Aug. 20, 1920; s. Walter Otis and Lois (Garvey) L.; B.S., Springfield Coll., 1942; B.D., Yale, 1945; M.A., U. Nebr., 1947; Ph.D., Am. U., 1959; Litt.D. (hon.), Springfield Coll., 1971; m. Phyllis Eleanor Parker, June 6, 1942; children—Anne Lippitt Rarich, Mary Lippitt Burner, Constance Lippitt Ridgway. Dir. Indsl. Fedn., New Haven, 1942-46; exec. dir. U. Nebr. YMCA, 1946-49; asst. prof. psychology Union Coll., 1949-50; program dir. Midcentury White House Conf. on Children and Youth, 1950; dir. edn., tng. European Productivity Program, Mut. Security Agy., 1951-52; program dir. Nat. Tng. Labs., N.E.A., 1952-59; dir. Center Behavioral Scis., George Washington U., 1959-65, prof. behavioral scis., 1960—; vis. scholar U. Calif. at Los Angeles, 1967. Pres. Leadership Resources, Inc., 1960-67, chmn. bd., 1967-69; pres. Project Assos., Inc.; chmn. bd. Glenwood Manor Farms, Orgn. Renewal, Inc., Internat. Consultants Found.; dir. Petroleum Exploration & Devel. Funds, Inc., 1968-70. Mem. nat. community affairs com. nat. bd. YMCA, 1965-70; chmn. Nat. Youth Gov.'s Com., 1966-68. Mem. organizational adv. com. Democratic Nat. Com., 1958-60. Bd. dirs. Washington YMCA; trustee Nat. Research Fund; bd. mem. Am. Soc. Tng. and Devel., 1965-67, regional v.p., 1968, pres., 1969. Recipient Outstanding Civilian Service medal Dept. Army, 1962; Rufus Jones lectr., 1966; Leadership award Hillsdale Coll., 1970; YMCA Century club award, 1974-76. Diplomate Am. Bd. Profl. Psychology. Fellow Inst. Applied Behavioral Scis.; mem. Am. Psychol. Assn., Am. Soc. Pub. Adminstrn., AAUP, NEA, Acad. Mgmt., Soc. Study Social Issues, Soc. Personnel Adminstrn. (exec. com. 1966-67, chmn. div. 1976), Am. Soc. Tng. and Devel. (pres. 1969, Torch award 1975), Pi Gamma Mu, Phi Delta Kappa, Psi Chi. Methodist. Author: Leader Looks at Group Effectiveness, 1962; Quest for Dialogue, 1966; Organization Renewal, 1969; co-author: Optimizing Human Resource Development, 1971; Visualizing Change, 1973; Consulting Process in Action, 1978. Editor: New Trends in Political Education, 1959; Leadership in Action, 1955; co-editor Handbook on Management Development and Training, 1975; co-editor Helping Across Cultures, 1978. Monthly guest columnist for mag. Nation's Cities, 1967, Tng. Dirs. Jour., 1969. Contbr. articles to profl. jours. Home: 5605 Lamar Rd Washington DC 20016. *In my search for quality of life, it has become apparent that the support of colleagues, family, and those you serve are essential. Effective leadership is a performing art, combining scientific knowledge with professional competence. I am still learning.*

LIPPMAN, MONROE, educator; b. Virginia, Minn., Dec. 10, 1905; s. Benjamin M. and Anne (Margulis) L.; A.B., U. Mich., 1926, M.A., 1929, Ph.D., 1937; m. Ruth Harriet Weeding, June 25, 1930. Instr., dir. theatre S.W. Tex. State Tchrs. Coll., 1929-30, asst. prof., 1930-32, asso. prof., 1932-35; teaching fellow U. Mich., 1935-37; instr., dir. theatre Tulane U., 1937- 38, asst. prof., 1938-41, head dept. theatre and speech, 1940-67, asso. prof., 1941-47, prof., 1947-67; prof. theatre, head dept. drama and cinema N.Y.U., 1967-70; prof. theatre, chmn. dept. U. Calif. at Riverside, 1970-73, prof. emeritus, 1973—; vis. prof. U. Tex., summer 1932, Mt. Holyoke Coll., summer 1940, U. Mich., summers 1945, 50, 53, U. Minn., summer 1947, 63, U. Denver, summer 1959, U. Wash., 1977; vis. artist Hamline U., 1974. Exec. dir. Le Petit Theatre du Vieux Carre, New Orleans, 1946-53; mem. drama panel Cultural Exchange Program, State Dept., 1965-70; cons. theatre program Nat. Endowment for Arts, 1973-74. Guggenheim fellow, 1956; recipient Ford Found. travel and study grant, 1965. Fellow Am. Ednl. Theatre Assn. (pres. 1950; award 1975); mem. ANTA (bd. dirs. 1950, 53, 55, 57-62), Am. Soc. Theatre Research, Nat. Coll. Players (pres. 1946, 47), Nat. Theatre Conf. (bd. trustees 1953-55, 65-67), S.W. Theatre Conf. (pres. 1954), Theatre Library Assn. (bd. dirs. 1967-70), AAUP (pres. Tulane U. chpt. 1961), Pi Kappa Delta, Omicron Delta Kappa. Democrat. Club: Players (N.Y.C.). Contbr. articles to profl. jours. Dir. over 130 theatrical prodns. Address: Dept Theatre Univ Calif Riverside CA 92507. *It's been fun. I'd hate to pontificate about it.*

LIPPMAN, THOMAS WOODLEY, fgn. corr.; b. N.Y.C., Oct. 28, 1940; s. Bertram and Marie Abigail Gallagher L.; A.B., Columbia U., 1961; m. Sidney Jane Coffin, Apr. 22, 1967; children—Jessica, Elizabeth, Steven. Reporter Phila. Inquirer, 1965-66; reporter, Washington Post, 1966-70, editor, 1970-72, fgn. corr., 1972—; lectr. in field. Vis. prof. journalism Am. U. Cairo, 1975-76. Home: 3925 McKinley St NW Washington DC 20015 Office: Washington Post PO Box 2040 Cairo Egypt

LIPPMAN, WILLIAM JENNINGS, investment co. exec.; b. N.Y.C., Feb. 13, 1925; s. Henry J. and Fanny (Schapira) L.; B.B.A. cum laude, Coll. City N.Y., 1947; M.B.A., N.Y.U., 1957; m. Doris Kaplan, July 11, 1948; children—Howard Mark, Deborah Ellen. Marketing mgr. Pavelle Color, Inc., N.Y.C., 1947-50; sales mgr. Terminal Home Sales Corp., N.Y.C., 1950-55; div. mgr. King Merritt & Co., Inc., Englewood, N.J., 1955-60; pres., dir. William Jennings & Co., Inc., Ft. Lee, N.J., 1960—; pres., dir. Pilgrim Fund, Inc., Pilgrim Mgmt. Corp., Fort Lee, Magnavest Corp., Magna-Cap Fund, Inc., Magna Income Trust. Mem. faculty Fairleigh Dickinson U. Sch. Bus. Adminstrn., 1957-69. Bd. govs. Investment Co. Inst. Mem. Nat. Assn. Securities Dealers (investment cos. com.). Contbg. author Investment Dealer Digest. Home: 881 E Lawn Dr Teaneck NJ 07666 Office: 185 Cross St Fort Lee NJ 07024

LIPPOLD, RICHARD, sculptor; b. Milw., May 3, 1915; s. Adolph and Elsa (Schmidt) L.; student U. Chgo., 1934-37; B.F.A., Art Inst. Chgo., 1937; D.F.A. (hon.), Ripon Coll., 1968; m. Louise Greuel, Aug. 24, 1940; children—Lisa, Tiana, Ero. Tchr. Layton Sch. Art, Milw., 1940-41, U. Mich., 1941-44, Goddard Coll., 1945-47; head art sect. Trenton (N.J.) Jr. Coll., 1948-52; prof. Hunter Coll., N.Y.C., 1952-67. Works exhibited Inst. Arts, Detroit, 1946-47, St. Louis City Mus., 1946, Toronto (Ont.) Mus., 1947, Whitney Mus., N.Y.C., 1947, 49, 51-53, 76, Calif. Palace Legion of Honor, San Francisco, 1948, Fundacao de Arte Moderne, Sao Paulo, Brazil, 1948, Mus. Modern Art, N.Y.C., 1951-53, 63, Tate Gallery, London, 1953, Musée d'Art Moderne, Paris, 1955, Nat. Collection Fine Arts, Washington, 1976, Nat. Air and Space Mus., Washington, 1976; one-man shows Willard Gallery, N.Y.C., 1947-48, 50, 53, 62, 68, 73, Arts Club, Chgo., Layton Art Gallery, Milw., 1953; represented in collections Addison Gallery Am. Art, Andover, Mass., Fogg Mus., Harvard U., Wadsworth Atheneum, Hartford, Mus. Modern Art, Whitney Mus., N.Y.C., Newark Mus., Met. Mus. Art, N.Y.C., Detroit Art Inst., Des Moines Art Inst., Brooks Gallery, Memphis, Mobile (Ala.) Art Mus., Museé de Vin, Pavillac, France, Munson-Williams-Proctor Inst., Utica, N.Y., Va. Mus. Fine Arts, Milw. Art Center, Yale U. Art Gallery, others, also pvt. collections U.S. and Europe; commns. include Inland Steel Bldg., Chgo., 1958, Portsmouth (R.I.) Priory Ch., 1960, Pan Am Bldg., N.Y.C., 1961, Avery Fisher Hall, Lincoln Center, N.Y.C., 1961, Jesse Jones Hall, Houston, 1965, St. Mary's Cathedral, San Francisco, 1967, Christian Sci. Center, Boston, 1974, Hyatt Regency Atlanta, 1975, others; commns. include Fairlane Plaza, Dearborn, Mich., 1975, 115 foot stainless steel sculpture on mall in front Air and Space Mus., Washington, 1976, King's Retiring Room, Riyadh, Saudi Arabia, 1977, Columbia (S.C.) Mall, 1977, airport and casino, Kish Island, Iran, 1978. Recipient Third prize Internat. Sculpture Competition, Inst. Contemporary Arts, London, 1953; Creative Arts award, Brandeis U., 1958; silver medal Archtl. League N.Y., 1960; Honor award Municipal Art Soc. N.Y., 1963; Fine Arts medal AIA, 1970. Mem. Nat. Inst. Arts and Letters (v.p. 1966). Address: Willard Gallery 29 E 72d St New York NY 10016

LIPSCHITZ, CHAIM URE, rabbi; b. Jerusalem, Aug. 10, 1912; s. Moses (Grand Rabbi) and Chaya (Lichtman); student in Israel, 1930-38; student Dropsie Coll., Phila., 1940; D.D. (hon.), St. Andrews Coll., London, Eng., 1958, Philathea Coll., London, Ont., Can., 1965; m. Rivkah Bernstein, Apr., 1936; children—Beatrice, Bina, Sarah, Zionah. Rabbi, 1938; served with Am. consul-gen. in Israel, 1936-38; dir. Congregation Chevra Machzikai Hadaath of Phila., 1938-50; condr. daily, weekly radio program, Phila., 1940-41; founder, exec. dir., prin. Beth Jacob Sch. for Girls, Phila., 1946-50; asso. Jewish Morning Jour., 1949-51; dir. Rabbinical Alliance Am., 1951-55; leader Congregation Ohev Sholom, Bklyn., 1951-60; conducts weekly radio program Yeshiva Quiz Kids, 1962- 64; program coordinator Yeshiva Trade Sch. Mem. Gov.'s Adv. Council of State Human Rights Commn.; pres. Nat. Info. for Jewish Life, 1960-72; sec. Joint Orthodox Chaplaincy Bd., 1954—. Del. World Conf. Orthodox Jews in Israel, 1955; charter mem. Met. Orthodox Bd. Rabbis; mem. Mayor Wagner's Com. Religious Leaders; mem. adv. council Joint Legislative Com. Met. and Regional Area Studies, State Human Rights. Mem. selective service N.Y.; adviser IRS; founder, pres. Jewish Speakers Bur. Am.; exec. dir. Community Service Bur. of Mesifta Torah Vodaath, 1951—; pres. Congress Against Religious Discrimination; chmn. bd. govs. Girls Coll. of Israel; v.p. Torah Hoadam Inst. Mem. Alumni Assn. Torah Vodaath (dir. 1952-53), Agudath Israel (founder, hon. pres. Phila. 1938, nat. exec. dir. 1951, pres. Bklyn. 1953-54, pres. Williamsburg 1958), Met. Bd. Orthodox Rabbis (presidium mem.), Nat. Sponsors Nat. Rev. (mem. com.); treas. Yeshiva Chai Olom, Jerusalem, 1965, Kupat Cholim L'Bnai Yeshivot, 1966, Yeshiva Leflaget Reuben of Jerusalem, 1966; exec. com. Communist Anti-Semitic Policy and Practice, 1967; trustee Feiga-Gory-Remetier Found., 1977. Mem. Internat. Conf. Weekly Newspaper Editors. Author: The Shiled of Israel, 1940; A Treatise on International Date Line in Relation to Jewish Law, 1956; co-author Rabbinical Alliance Torah and Sermon Manual, 1955. Editor: Thought of the Week (vol. of sermons), 1959, (weekly) The Jewish Press, 1959—; asso. editor (jour.) Kerem, 1959—; editor-in-chief Ency. Orthodox Biographies, 1977; contbg. editor various encys.; mem. adv. council Who's Who in Am. Contbr. to newspapers, profl. pubs. Home: 1692 17th Ave Brooklyn NY 11211. *Our Sages say "Virtue is the reward of virtue." Our goal is to strive for holiness of person in holiness of living.*

LIPSCOMB, EDWARD LOWNDES, pub. relations cons.; b. Hollandale, Miss., Sept. 27, 1906; s. Rev. Thomas Heber and Lutie (Scott) L.; A.B., U. Miss., 1927; m. Cornelia Loper, June 21, 1929; children—Cornelia Blanche, Martha Ethel, Lynda Lowndes. Asst. to prof. English, U. Miss., 1925-27; reporter, newscaster Gulf Coast Guide, Gulfport, Miss., 1927-31, mng. editor, 1931-36; dir. Miss. Advt. Commn., Jackson, 1936-39; dir. pub. relations and sales promotion Nat. Cotton Council, 1939-66, pub. relations and sales promotion counselor, 1966—; advt. cons. Cotton Producers Inst., 1962-70; chmn. pub. relations com. Eisenhower People-to-People Program, 1956-57. Mem. com. orgn. Internat. Pub. Relations Assn., 1953, pres., 1958-59; v.p. Agrl. Relations Council, 1953, pres., 1955; mem. adv. bd. Pub. Relations News, 1953-55, Advt. Fedn. Am. Award, 1953; mem. info. adv. com. U.S. Dept. Agr., 1953-54. Trustee, Found. Pub. Relations Research and Edn., 1954-59. Recipient Distinguished Service award, Pub. Relations Soc. Am., 1958; Pub. Relations News Ann. Achievement award, 1950, Freedoms Found. Honor medal for pub. addresses, 1950, 52, 53, 60. Mem. Pub. Relations Soc. Am. (pres. 1952), Textile Bag Mfrs. Assn. (advt. adv. com. 1944-56), Gulf Coast, Miss. (past sec.) press assns., S.A.R. (pres. Memphis chpt. 1962, pres. Tenn. 1963, nat. trustee 1963-64), Magna Charta Barons, Huguenot Soc., Soc. Ams. Royal Descent, Beta Theta Pi. Author: Grassroots Public Relations for Agriculture, 1950; Personal Practice of Freedom, 1952; Public Relations or Peasantry, 1960. Contbr. newspapers, mags. articles. Speaker before nat. agrl., profl. groups. Home: 94 N Goodlett Memphis TN 38117 Office: Box 12285 Memphis TN 38112

LIPSCOMB, PAUL ROGERS, orthopaedic surgeon, educator; b. Clio, S.C., Mar. 23, 1914; s. Paul Holmes and Mary Emma (Rogers) L.; B.S., U. S.C., 1935; M.D., Med. Coll. S.C., 1938; M.S. in Orthopaedic Surgery, Mayo Found., U. Minn., 1942; m. Phyllis M. Oesterreich, July 20, 1940; children—Susan Lovering, Paul Rogers. Intern, Cooper Hosp., Camden, N.J., 1938-39; asst. to staff orthopaedic surgery Mayo Clinic, 1941-43, staff asso., 1943-69, v.p. staff, 1963; cons. Methodist, St. Mary's hosps., 1943-69; mem. faculty Mayo Grad. Sch., U. Minn., 1944-69, prof. orthopaedic surgery, 1961-69, mem. univ. senate from Mayo Grad. Sch., 1963-67, past mem. grad. and admissions com. and joint com. Grad. Sch. U. Minn. and Mayo Grad. Sch.; prof., chmn. dept. orthopedic surgery Sch. of Medicine, U. Calif. at Davis, 1969—; hon. vis. prof. orthopedics U. Auckland (N.Z.), 1978. Diplomate Am. Bd. Orthopaedic Surgery (sec. 1968-71, pres. 1971-73). Mem. Am. Acad. Orthopaedic Surgery (chmn. com. sci. investigation 1955-56; chmn. instrl. course com., editor instrl. course lectures 1961-63, chmn. com. on arthritis 1970—), Orthopaedic Research Soc. (chmn. membership com., mem. exec. com. 1956), A.M.A. (chmn. orthopaedic sect. 1965), A.C.S., Am. Orthopaedic Assn. (pres. 1974-75), Western Orthopaedic Assn., Am. Soc. Surgery Hand, Clin. Orthopaedic Soc., Internat. Soc. Orthopaedic Surgery and Traumatology, Central, Internat. orthopaedic clubs, N.Z. Orthopedic Assn. (corr.), Sacramento County, Yolo County med. socs., Calif. Med. Assn., Sigma Xi, Alpha Omega Alpha. Methodist. Contbr. numerous articles to profl. jours. Home: 749 Sycamore Ln Davis CA 95616

LIPSCOMB, THOMAS HEBER, III, pub. co. exec.; b. Washington, Sept. 12, 1938; s. Thomas Heber and Louise Buchanan (Heiss) L.; B.A., Coll. William and Mary, 1961; M.A., Ind. U., 1965; m. Nancy Christina Unger, Nov. 4, 1967; children—Peter Scott, Adrienne Claire. Editor, Bobbs-Merrill Co., 1965-67, Stein & Day Pubs., 1967-69; sr. editor Prentice-Hall, Inc., 1969-70; exec. editor, editor-in-chief Dodd, Mead & Co., 1970-73; pres. Mason & Lipscomb Pubs., 1973-74; partner Hamilton Assos., 1974-76; pres. Quadrangle/N.Y. Times Book Co., 1976—. Lectr., N.Y.U. Center for Pub. and Graphics, 1972—. Mem. New York Republican County Com., 1971—. Mem. exec. bd. Am. Center of P.E.N.; trustee Robert Coll., Istanbul, Turkey; mem. panel of advisors George Polk Award. Served to lt. U.S. Army, 1961-64. Mem. Council on Fgn. Relations, Internat. Broadcast Inst., Mid-Atlantic Club. Episcopalian. Clubs: University, Players (N.Y.C.); Mashomack (Shelter Island, N.Y.); Metropolitan, Nat. Press (Washington). Home: 9 Sniffen Ct New York NY 10028 Office: 3 Park Ave New York NY 10016

LIPSCOMB, WILLIAM NUNN, JR., educator, phys. chemist; b. Cleve., Dec. 9, 1919; s. William Nunn and Edna Patterson (Porter) L.; B.S., U. Ky., 1941, D.Sc. (hon.), 1963; Ph.D., Calif. Inst. Tech., 1946; Dr.h.c., U. Munich, 1976; m. Mary Adele Sargent, May 20, 1944; children—Dorothy Jean, James Sargent. Phys. chemist OSRD, 1942-46; with U. Minn., 1946-59, successively asst. prof., asso. prof. and acting chief phys. chemistry div., prof. and chief phys. chemistry div., 1954-59; prof. chemistry, Harvard U., 1959-71, Abbott and James Lawrence prof., 1971—, chmn. dept. chemistry, 1962-65. Mem. U.S.A. Nat. Com. for Crystallography, 1954-59, 60-63, 65-67; chmn. program com. Fourth Internat. Congress of Crystallography, Montreal, 1957. Guggenheim fellow Oxford U., Eng., 1954-55, Cambridge U., Eng., 1973; NSF sr. postdoctoral fellow, 1965-66; Overseas fellow Churchill Coll., Cambridge, Eng., 1966; Robert Welch Found. lectr., 1966, 71, Howard U. distinguished lecture series, 1966; George Fisher Baker lectr. Cornell U., 1969; centenary lectr. Chem. Soc. (London), 1972; lectr. Weizmann Inst., Rehoveth, Israel, 1974; Evans award lectr. Ohio State U., 1974; Gilbert Newton Lewis Meml. lectr. U. Calif., Berkeley, 1974, also lectureships Mich. State U., 1975, U. Iowa, 1975, Ill. Inst. Tech., 1976, numerous others. Recipient Harrison Howe award in Chemistry, 1958; Distinguished Alumni Centennial award U. Ky., 1965; Distinguished Service in advancement inorganic chemistry Am. Chem. Soc., 1968; George Ledlie prize Harvard, 1971; Nobel prize in chemistry, 1976; Disting. Alumni award Calif. Inst. Tech., 1977. Fellow Am. Acad. Arts and Scis., Am. Phys. Soc.; mem. Am. Chem. Soc. (Peter Debye award phys. chemistry 1973, chmn. Minn. sect. 1949-50), Am. Crystallographic Assn. (pres. 1955), Nat. Acad. Sci., Netherlands Acad. Arts and Scis. (fgn.), Phi Beta Kappa, Sigma Xi, Alpha Chi Sigma, Phi Lambda Upsilon, Sigma Pi Sigma, Phi Mu Epsilon. Author: The Boron Hydrides, 1963; (with G.R. Eaton) NMR Studies of Boron Hydrides and Related Compounds, 1969. Contbr. articles to profl. jours. Asso. editor: Jour. Chemical Physics, 1955-57. Clarinetist, mem. Amateur Chamber Music Players. Home: 26 Woodfall Rd Belmont MA 02178 Office: Dept of Chemistry Harvard U Cambridge MA 02138

LIPSET, SEYMOUR MARTIN, sociologist, educator; b. N.Y.C., Mar. 18, 1922; s. Max and Lena (Lippman) L.; B.S., City Coll. N.Y., 1943, Ph.D., Columbia, 1949; M.A. honoris causa, Harvard, 1966; LL.D., Villanova U., 1973; m. Elsie Braun, Dec. 26, 1944; children—David, Daniel, Carola. Lectr., U. Toronto, 1946-48; asst. prof. U. Calif. at Berkeley, 1948-50; asst., then asso. prof. grad. faculty Columbia, 1950-56, asst. dir. Bur. Applied Social Research, 1954-56; prof. sociology U. Calif. at Berkeley, 1956-66, dir. Inst. Internat. Studies, 1962-66; vis. prof. social relations and govt. Harvard, 1965-66, prof. govt. and sociology, 1966—, exec. com. Center Internat. Affairs, 1966-75, George Markham prof., 1974-75; prof. polit. sci. and sociology, sr. fellow Hoover Instn., Stanford, 1975—; Henry Ford vis. research prof. Yale, 1960-61; Paley lectr. Hebrew U., 1973. Mem. Bd. Fgn. Scholarships, 1968-71. Nat. chmn. B'nai B'rith Hillel Found., 1975-79; asso. pres. Am. Profs. for Peace in Middle East, 1976-77, nat. pres., 1977—; co-chmn. Com. for Effective UNESCO, 1976—. Fellow Social Sci. Research Council, 1945-46, Center Advanced Study Behavioral Sci., 1955-56, 72-73; Gunnar Myrdal prize, 1970; Townsend Harris medal, 1971; Guggenheim Found. fellow, 1971-72; 125th Anniversary Alumni medal Coll. City N.Y., 1973. Fellow Am. Acad. Arts and Scis. (v.p. 1974-78), Nat. Acad. Sci., Nat. Acad. Edn., Am. Sociol. Assn. (council 1959-62, MacIver award 1962); mem. Am. (council 1975-77), Internat. polit. sci. assns., Internat. Soc. Polit. Psychology (pres. 1979-80), Internat. Sociol. Assn. (chmn. com. polit. sociology 1959-71), Finnish Acad. Sci. (hon.), AAAS (chmn. sect. on econ. and social sci. 1975-76). Club: Cosmos (Washington). Author: Agrarian Socialism, 1950; (with others) Union Democracy, 1956; (with R. Bendix) Social Mobility in Industrial Society, 1959; Political Man, 1960; The First New Nation, 1963; Revolution and Counter Revolution, 1968; (with Earl Raab) The Politics of Unreason, 1970; Rebellion in the University, 1972; (with Everett Ladd) Academics and the 1972 Election, 1973, Professors, Unions and American Higher Education, 1973, The Divided Academy, 1975; (with David Riesman) Education and Politics at Harvard, 1975; (with I.L. Horowitz) Dialogues on American Politics, 1978. Co-editor: Class, Status and Power, 1953; Labor and Trade Unionism, 1960; Sociology: The Progress of a Decade, 1961; Culture and Social Character, 1961; The Berkeley Student Revolt, 1965; Class, Status and Power in Comparative Perspective, 1966; Social Structure, Mobility and Economic Development, 1966; Elites in Latin America, 1967; Party Systems and Voter Alignments, 1967; Students in Revolt, 1969; Issues in Politics and Government, 1970; Failure of a Dream? Essays in the History of American Socialism, 1974; Public Opinion mag.; Polit. Psychology mag.; editor: Students and Politics, 1967; Politics and Social Science, 1969; Emerging Coalitions in American Politics, 1978; The Third Century, 1979; adv. editor: Comparative Politics; various jours. Home: 650 Gerona Rd Stanford CA 94305 Office: Herbert Hoover Meml Bldg Stanford U Stanford CA 94305

LIPSETT, MORTIMER BROADWIN, physician; b. N.Y.C., Feb. 20, 1921; s. Theodore and Gertrude (Broadwin) L.; A.B., U. Calif., 1943; M.S., U. So. Calif., 1947, M.D., 1951; m. Lois Friedman, Mar. 11, 1974; children—Roger, Edward. Research asso. U. So. Calif., 1947; intern Los Angeles County Hosp., 1951-52; resident in internal medicine Sawtelle VA Hosp., Los Angeles, 1952-54; USPHS fellow, asst. mem. Sloan-Kettering Inst., N.Y.C., 1954-57; mem. staff NIH, 1957-74, 76—, asso. sci. dir. intramural research, chief reprodn. research br. Nat. Inst. Child Health and Human Devel., 1970-74, asso. dir. clin. care, dir. Clin. Center, NIH, 1976—; dir. Cancer Center N.W. Ohio, Cleve., also prof. medicine Case Western Res. U. Med. Sch., 1974-76. Served with AUS, 1944-46. Decorated Bronze Star with oak leaf cluster; recipient Alfred P. Sloan award cancer research Sloan-Kettering Inst., 1955; Superior Service Honor award HEW, 1969. Diplomate Am. Bd. Internal Medicine. Fellow ACP; mem. Endocrine Soc. (sec.-treas. 1974-78, pres. 1979-80; Disting. Leadership award 1976), Internat. Soc. Endocrinology (sec.-gen. 1976—), AAAS, Am. Assn. Cancer Research, Am. Fedn. Clin. Research, Am. Soc. Andrology, Am. Soc. Clin. Investigation, Assn. Am. Physicians, Harvey Soc., Soc. Study Reprodn., German Endocrine Soc. (corr.). Home: 5204 W Cedar Ln Bethesda MD 20014 Office: Clinical Center NIH Bethesda MD 20205

LIPSEY, RICHARD GEORGE, economist, educator; b. Victoria, B.C., Can., Aug. 28, 1928; s. Richard Andrew and Faith Thirell (Ledingham) L.; B.A. with honours, U. B.C., 1950; M.A., U. Toronto, 1953; Ph.D., London Sch. Econs., 1958; m. Diana Louise Smart, Mar. 17, 1960; children—Mark Alexander (stepson), Mathew Richard, Joanna Louise, Claudia Amanda. Research asst. B.C. Dept. Trade and Industry, 1950-53; from asst. lectr. to prof. econs. London Sch. Econs., 1955-63; prof. econs., chmn. dept., dean Sch. Social Studies, U. Essex (Eng.), 1965-69; vis. prof. U. B.C., 1969-70, U. Colo., 1973-74; Irving Fisher vis. prof. Yale U., 1979-80; Sir Edward

Peacock prof. econs. Queen's U., Kingston, Ont., 1970—; dir. research into growth in U.K., Nat. Econ. Devel. Council U.K., 1961-63; mem. council and planning com. Nat. Inst. Econ. and Social Research U.K., 1962-69; mem. bd. Social Sci. Research Council U.K., 1966-69. Fellow Econometric Soc.; mem. Royal Econ. Soc. (council 1967-71), Econ. Study Soc. (chmn. 1965-69), Am. Econ. Assn., Can. Econ. Assn. (pres.-elect 1979-80). Author: An Introduction to Positive Economics, 5th edit., 1978; The Theory of Customs Unions: A General Equilibrium Analysis, 1971; co-author: An Introduction to a Mathematical Treatment of Economics, 3d edit., 1977; Economics, 5th edit., 1978; Mathematical Economics, 1976. Editor: Rev. Econ. Studies, 1962-64. Office: Dept Economics Queen's Univ Kingston ON K7L 3N6 Canada

LIPSEY, ROBERT EDWARD, economist, educator; b. N.Y.C., Aug. 14, 1926; s. Meyer Aaron and Anna (Weinstein) L.; B.A., Columbia, 1944, M.A., 1946, Ph.D., 1961; m. Sally Irene Rothstein, Nov. 24, 1948; children—Marion, Carol, Eleanor. Research asst. Nat. Bur. Econ. Research, N.Y.C., 1945-53, research asso., 1953-60, sr. research staff, 1960—, v.p. research, 1970-75, dir. internat. studies, 1975-78, dir. N.Y. Office, 1978—; lectr. econs. Columbia, 1961-64; prof. econs. Queens Coll. City U. N.Y., 1967—; cons. Dept. Commerce, Fed. Res. Bd.; mem. Pres.'s Adv. Bd. Internat. Investment, 1977-78. Fellow Am. Statis. Assn.; mem. Am. Econ. Assn., Econometric Soc., Conf. on Research in Income and Wealth, Internat. Assn. for Research in Income and Wealth. Author: Price and Quantity Trends in the Foreign Trade of the U.S., 1963; (with Raymond W. Goldsmith) Studies in the National Balance Sheet of the U.S., 1963; (with Doris Preston) Source Book of Statistics Relating to Construction, 1966; (with Irving B. Kravis) Price Competitiveness in World Trade, 1971; (with Phillip Cagan) Financial Effects of Inflation, 1978. Contbr. articles to profl. jours. Home: 149-01 32d Ave Flushing NY 11354 Office: 15-19 W 4th St New York NY 10012

LIPSHIE, JOSEPH, apparel mfg. co. exec.; b. Bklyn., Sept. 16, 1911; s. Arthur and Rose Hannah (Knopfer) L.; A.B., Syracuse (N.Y.) U., 1932; m. Mildred Lee Wright, Mar. 5, 1942; children—Arthur Bruce, Mary Jane, Samuel David. With Salant Corp., N.Y.C., 1935—, pres., chief exec. officer, 1965-74, chmn. bd., 1974-75, chmn. exec. com., 1976—; dir. Am. Gen. Mut. Funds, Houston, Hollowform, Inc., Woodland Hills, Calif., Child Health Centers Am., Jackson, Tenn. Bd. dirs. West Tenn. council Boy Scouts Am., United Way, Jackson. Served with USCGR, 1942-45. Mem. Am. Apparel Mfrs. Assn. (dir., v.p. East coast), Am. Apparel Edn. Found. (v.p.), Tau Epsilon Phi. Democrat. Jewish. Club: Shriners. Home: 647 N Russell Rd Jackson TN 38301 Office: 330 Fifth Ave New York City NY 10001

LIPSHUTZ, ROBERT JEROME, lawyer, former govt. ofcl.; b. Atlanta, Dec. 27, 1921; s. Allen A. and Edith (Gavronski) L.; J.D., U. Ga., 1943; m. Barbara Sorelle Levin, Feb. 16, 1950 (dec.); children—Randall M., Judith Ann, Wendy Jean, Debbie Sue; m. 2d, Betty Beck Rosenberg, Feb. 10, 1973; step-children—Robert, Nancy Fay. Admitted to Ga. bar, 1943; practice in Atlanta, 1947-77, 79—; partner firm Haas Holland Lipshutz Livison & Gilbert, 1979—; counsel to Pres. U.S., Washington, 1977-79. Former vice chmn. Ga. Bd. Human Resources; pres. Roxboro Valley Assn. Treas., Jimmy Carter Presdl. Campaign Com., chmn. Nat. Dem. Telethon, 1973. Served to capt. AUS, 1943-46. Mem. Am., Ga., Atlanta bar assns., Atlanta Lawyers Club, Atlanta. Jewish (past pres. temple). Mem. B'nai B'rith (past pres.). Home: 5270 New London Trace NW Atlanta GA 30327 Office: Suite 2300 Harris Tower Peachtree Center Atlanta GA 30303

LIPSHY, BEN ALLEN, corp. exec.; b. Ft. Worth, Oct. 3, 1910; s. Julius and Sarah Ethel (Korman) L.; grad. high sch.; m. Udys Weinstein, Sept. 7, 1931; children—Joy (Mrs. Lawrence Burk), Barbara (Mrs. Alan Marcus), Bruce Arlen. With Zale Corp., Dallas, 1926—, store mgr., Amarillo, Tex., 1934-40, supr. group stores, 1940-51, treas., 1951-57, pres., 1957-71, chmn. bd., 1971—, also dir.; dir. Republic Nat. of Tex. Corp., Dallas. Mem. Dallas Crime Commn., Dallas Citizens Council; mem. Jewish Welfare Fedn. Dallas. Bd. dirs. Dallas Community Coll. Dist. Found., Southwestern Med. Found., Dallas Alliance, World Trade Center, State Fair Tex., Tex. Retail Found., Better Bus. Bur., Callier Speech and Hearing Center, Dallas, St. Paul Hosp.; trustee Nat. Jewish Hosp. Denver. Jewish (bd. dirs. temple). Mason (Shriner). Club: Columbian Country. Home: 6335 W Northwest Hwy Dallas TX 75225 Office: 3000 Diamond Park Dallas TX 75247

LIPSIG, HARRY H., lawyer; b. Poland, Dec. 26, 1901; s. David and Rose Lipsig; LL.B., Bklyn. Law Sch., 1926; m. Mildred Slonim, Sept. 14, 1924. Admitted to U.S. Supreme Ct. bar, N.Y. State bar; formerly mem. faculty N.Y. Law Sch.; now sr. partner firm Lipsig, Sullivan, Mollen & Liapakis, P.C., N.Y.C.; lectr. in field. Pres. Public Awareness Soc. (formerly Inst. of Asia and Africa). Recipient Outstanding Leadership recognition Internat. Acad. Estates Attys., 1960, award Anti-Defamation League Appeal, 1971. Fellow Internat. Acad. Trial Attys. (former dir.); mem. N.Y. State Trial Lawyers Assn. (Law Day award 1979; dir.), Assn. Trial Lawyers City N.Y. (dir.), N.Y. Criminal and Civil Cts. Bar Assn. (dir.), Internat. Bar Assn., Am. Bar Assn., Am. Assn. Trial Lawyers, Fed. Bar Council, N.Y. State Bar Assn., Assn. Bar City N.Y., N.Y. County Lawyers Assn., Met. Trial Lawyers Assn., Bklyn.-Manhattan Trial Lawyers Assn., Bronx Bar Assn., Bronx Women's Bar Assn., Bklyn. Bar Assn., Bklyn. Women's Bar Assn., N.Y. Women's Bar Assn., Bklyn. Trial Lawyers Assn., Puerto Rican Bar Assn., N.Y. Criminal Bar Assn., Queens Women's Bar Assn., Kings County Criminal Bar Assn. Contbr. articles to profl. jours. Home: 860 UN Plaza New York NY 10017 Office: 100 Church St New York NY 10007

LIPSITT, LEWIS PAEFF, educator; b. New Bedford, Mass., June 28, 1929; s. Joseph and Anna Naomi (Paeff) L.; B.A., U. Chgo., 1950; M.S., U. Mass., 1952; Ph.D., U. Iowa, 1957; m. Edna Brill Duchin, June 8, 1952; children—Mark, Ann. Instr. dept. psychology Brown U., Providence, 1957, asst. prof., 1958-61, asso. prof., 1961-66, prof., 1966—, dir. Child Study Center, 1967—. Mem. Gov.'s Adv. Commn. on Mental Retardation, 1963-66; cons. NIH; mem. edn. task force Model Cities Program, Providence, 1969-71; fellow Stanford Center for Advanced Study in Behavioral Scis., 1979-80. Bd. dirs. Providence Child Guidance Clinic, 1960-63; trustee Butler Hosp., Providence. Served with USAF, 1952-54. USPHS Spl. Research fellow, 1966, Guggenheim fellow, 1972-73, USPHS fellow, 1973. Fellow Am. Psychol. Assn. (exec. com. div. developmental psychology 1967-70; pres.-elect 1979-80, pres. 1980-81), AAAS; mem. Soc. for Research Child Devel., AAUP. Co-author: Child Development, 1979. Editor: Research Readings in Child Psychology, 1963; Experimental Child Psychology, 1971; co-editor: Advances in Child Development and Behavior. Contbr. articles to profl. jours. Home: 63 Boylston Ave Providence RI 02906

LIPSKY, SANFORD, educator, chemist; b. N.Y.C., Jan. 24, 1930; s. Sol H. and Shirley (Seitz) L.; A.B., Syracuse U., 1950; M.S., U. Chgo., 1952, Ph.D., 1954; m. Janet Barbara Grassi, July 3, 1960 (div. Oct. 1970); children—Jessica K., Jennifer J. Research asso. radiation lab. U. Notre Dame, 1954-57; asst. prof. chemistry N.Y. U., 1957-59; faculty U. Minn., 1959—, prof. chemistry, 1967—. Recipient U. Notre Dame Centennial Sci. Award Honor, 1965. Mem. Am. Phys. Soc., Am. Chem. Soc., Radiation Research Soc., Faraday Soc., Phi Beta Kappa. Asso. editor Radiation Research. Home: 303 5th Ave SE Minneapolis MN 55414

LIPSON, HARRY AARON, JR., educator; b. Wilkes Barre, Pa., Mar. 10, 1919; s. Harry Aaron and Irma (Lowenstein) L.; B.S., U. Ala., 1939; M.B.A., Northwestern U., 1941; Ph.D., U. Pa., 1955; m. Miriam Lipson, July 5, 1948 (dec. Oct. 1971); children—Harry Aaron III, Carolyn Miriam; m. 2d, Adele Bloch, Aug. 27, 1972; children by previous marriage—Jeannie, Martha (Bear). Instr. econs. U. Ala., 1941-43, asst. prof. marketing, 1948-53, asso. prof., 1953-57, prof., 1957-60, prof., head dept. marketing, 1960-69, prof. marketing, 1970-73, U. Bd. Visitors research prof., 1973—; instr. Pa. Area Coll., 1946-48. Sr. cons. Harry A. Lipson & Assos., 1948— vis. prof. Ashridge Mgmt. Coll., fall 1972. Pres., Tuscaloosa Federated Charities, 1950, 68-69; mem. Black Warrior council Boy Scouts Am., 1964-69. Served with USAAF, 1943-46. Recipient Morris L. Mayer Outstanding Tchr. award, 1970. Mem. Am., So. (pres. 1969-70) marketing assns., Am. Econ. Assn., AAUP, Beta Gamma Sigma, Alpha Kappa Psi, Chi Alpha Phi, Pi Sigma Epsilon. Jewish (pres. temple 1962-64). Mem. B'nai B'rith (past pres. Tuscaloosa). Sr. author: Introduction to Marketing: An Administrative Approach, 1971; Decision Exercises in Marketing, 1971; Cases in Marketing: An Administrative Approach, 1971; Marketing Fundamentals, 1974. Bd. editors: Jour. of Marketing, 1960-76. Contbr. articles to profl. jours. Home: 2825 Montclair Rd Tuscaloosa AL 35404 Office: Box 5021 University AL 35486

LIPSON, LEON SAMUEL, legal educator; b. Chelsea, Mass., Aug. 4, 1921; s. Max and Cecilia (Zetzel) L.; A.B., Harvard U., 1941, M.A., 1943, LL.B., 1950; M.A., Yale, 1960; m. Dorothy Ann Rapoport, June 28, 1949; children—James Ezra, Abigail, Michael Aaron. Announcer, news editor radio sta. WCOP, Boston, 1943-44; analyst Fgn. Econ. Adminstrn., 1944-45; policy and liaison officer restitution br., econ. div. Office Mil. Govt. U.S., Berlin, Germany, 1946-47; admitted to N.Y. and D.C. bars, 1951; asso. firm Cleary, Gottlieb, Friendly & Ball, N.Y.C. and Washington, 1950-56; asso. prof. law Yale, 1957-60, prof., 1960—, asso. provost Yale, 1965-68, fellow Trumbull Coll.; fellow Center Advanced Study Behavioral Sci., 1968-69, dir. Inst. Socialist Law, 1975—; adv. U.S. mission to UN, 1959; mem. adv. bd. Rand Grad. Inst., 1977—; mem. Internat. Research and Exchanges Bd., 1973-74. Bd. dirs. Social Sci. Research Council, 1970-78, exec. com., 1971-78, chmn., 1974-78. Rockefeller Found. fellow, Bellagio, Italy, 1978. Mem. Am. Bar Assn. (chmn. com. Soviet law 1957-59, reporter com. law outer space 1958-60), Internat. Law Assn. (chmn. air and space law com. Am. br. 1961-65), Am. Soc. Internat. Law. Author: (with N. deB. Katzenbach) Report on the Law of Outer Space, 1961. Contbr. books, legal periodicals. Home: 8 St Ronan Terr New Haven CT 06511

LIPSON, PAUL S., lawyer; b. N.Y.C., Nov. 1, 1915; s. Joshua and Goldie (Meisel) L.; B.A., City Coll., N.Y., 1935; LL.B., Columbia, 1938; m. Marcia S. Segerman, Feb. 7, 1970; children—Carol Lipson Wilson, Richard J. Admitted to N.Y. bar, 1938, since practiced in N.Y.C.; partner firm Blum, Haimoff, Gersen, Lipson & Szabad, 1968—. Chmn. law com. Soc. Ethical Culture, City N.Y., 1968—, v.p., 1960—; chmn. law com. Am. Ethical Union, 1976—; trustee Ethical Culture, 1960—. Served with AUS, 1943-45. Decorated Bronze Star. Mem. Am. Bar Assn., Assn. Bar City N.Y. Editor Columbia Law Rev., 1937-38. Home: 137 E 36th St New York City NY 10016 Office: 270 Madison Ave New York City NY 10016

LIPTON, CHARLES, pub. relations exec.; b. N.Y.C., May 11, 1928; s. Jack B. and Bertha (Lesser) L.; A.B., Harvard U., 1948; m. Audrey Williams, Nov. 11, 1951; children—Susan, Jack. Market researcher Cecil & Presbury, Inc., N.Y.C., 1948-49; spl. events dir. 20th Century Fox Film Corp., N.Y.C., 1949-52; account exec. Ruder & Finn, Inc., N.Y.C., 1953-58, v.p., 1958-63, sr. v.p., 1963-69, chmn. bd., 1969—; guest lectr. Boston U., 1967-68. Mem. council Center for Vocat. Arts, Norwalk, Conn., 1966-74; trustee Norwalk Jewish Center, 1966-70, Temple Shalom, Norwalk, 1970—, Nat. Emphysema Soc., 1972—; treas., mem. exec. com. Norwalk Symphony Soc., 1972—; chmn. parents council Washington U., St. Louis, 1976-77, trustee, 1977—; mem. Com. for Corporate Support of Pvt. Univs. Mem. Am. Mgmt. Assn., Nat. Investor Relations Inst. Clubs: Harvard, Midday (N.Y.C.); Harvard Varsity. Home: 18 Douglas Dr Norwalk CT 06850 Office: 110 E 59th St New York City NY 10022

LIPTON, JOAN ELAINE, advt. agy. exec.; b. N.Y.C., July 12, 1930; B.A., Barnard Coll., 1949; 1 son, David Dean. With Young & Rubicam, Inc., advt. agy., N.Y.C., 1949-52, Robert W. Orr & Assos., advt. agy., N.Y.C., 1952-57, Benton & Bowles, Inc., advt. agy., N.Y.C., 1957-64; asso. dir. Benton & Bowles, Ltd., London, Eng., 1964-68; with McCann-Erickson, Inc., advt. agy., N.Y.C., 1968—, v.p., 1970-79, sr. v.p., creative dir., 1979—. Bd. dirs. Advt. Women N.Y. Found., Inc.; mem. Bus. Council for the UN Decade for Women, 1977-78. Named Woman of Yr., Am. Advt. Fedn., 1974; recipient Honors award Ohio U. Sch. Journalism, 1976; Matrix award, 1979; YWCA award for women achievers, 1979. Mem. Advt. Women N.Y. (1st v.p. 1975-76, v.p. Found. 1977-78), Women in Communications (pres. N.Y. chpt. 1974-76, named Nat. Headliner 1976). Office: McCann-Erickson Inc 485 Lexington Ave New York NY 10017

LIPTON, MARTHA, mezzo-soprano; b. N.Y.C., Apr. 6, 1913; d. Leon and Estelle (Laiken) Lipton; student on fellowship at Juilliard Grad. Sch., grad. 1940. Guest soloist, Voice of Firestone, radio program, May 29, 1940, New Friends of Music, Feb. 1940, Pitts. Symphony, Mar. 1940; made personal appearances throughout the country, 1939-41, Town Hall Recital, Mar. 1941, opera debut, New Opera Co., New York, Cosi Fan Tutti, Mozart, Mar. 1941, Pique Dame, Tchaikowsky, 1942, Met. Opera Assn. (N.Y.C.) debut, Nov. 1944, Teatro Municipal (Rio de Janeiro) debut, July 1946, 3 appearances with NBC orchestra, 1943; appearances since 1950 include: Concert Town Hall, N.Y.C., Vienna State Opera. Paris Opera, Met. Opera, N.Y. Philharmonic Orch., Phila. Orch., Boston Symphony Orch., Chgo. Symphonies; prof. music Ind. U., 1960—. Winner Schuber Meml. Young Artists Contest (Nat. Fedn. Music Clubs) consisting of $1500 award and concert tour of country; MacDowell Club Young Artist award; hon. mem. Delta Omicron. Address: Ind U Music Sch Bloomington IN 47401

LIPTON, MARTIN, lawyer; b. N.J., June 22, 1931; s. Samuel D. and Fannie L.; B.S. in Econs., U. Pa., 1952; LL.B., N.Y. U., 1955; m. Eric H. Steinberger, Mar. 25, 1978. Partner firm Wachtell Lipton Rosen & Katz, N.Y.C.; adj. prof. law N.Y. U. Office: 299 Park Ave New York NY 10017

LIPTON, MORRIS ABRAHAM, research psychiatrist; b. N.Y.C., Dec. 27, 1915; s. Theodore and Rose (Latt) Lipschitz; B.S., City Coll. N.Y., 1935; Ph.M., U. Wis., 1937, Ph.D., 1939; M.D. with high honors, U. Chgo., 1948; m. Barbara Steiner, Dec. 28, 1940; children—Judith Eve, Susan Victoria, David Mark. Research asst. U. Wis., Madison, 1937-39, research fellow biochemistry, 1939-40; research asso., instr. U. Chgo., 1940-41, instr. dept. physiology, 1941-45, sr. research chemist, 1941-45, research asso., instr. dept. medicine, 1945-46; intern, Michael Reese Hosp., Chgo., 1948-49; resident and fellow in psychiatry U. Chgo., 1949-51, part-time resident in medicine and instr. psychiatry, 1951-52, instr. and resident in medicine, 1952-53, asst. prof. medicine and psychiatry, 1953-54; asst. prof. medicine Northwestern U., Evanston, Ill., 1954-59; chief investigative medicine service and chief psychosomatic service VA Research Hosp., Chgo., 1954-56, asst. dir. profl. services for research, 1956-59; research asso. Chgo. Inst. Psychoanalysis, 1954-59; vis. prof. U. Buenos Aires, 1958; asso. prof. psychiatry and dir. research devel. U. N.C., Chapel Hill, 1959-63, prof. psychiatry and dir. research devel., 1963-70, chmn. dept. psychiatry, 1970-73, prof. dept. biochemistry, 1973—, Sarah Graham Kenan Distinguished prof. of psychiatry, 1972—; vis. scientist Nat. Heart Inst., Lab. of Clin. Biochemistry, Bethesda, Md., 1965-66; dir. biol. scis. research center U. N.C. Child Devel. Research Inst., 1965—; cons. NIH, 1965-69, FDA, Bur. of Drugs, 1973—, NIMH, 1972—, VA Med. Research Career Devel. Com., 1975—; scientific cons. N.C. Alcoholism Research Authority, 1974—. Mem. N.C. Multiversity task force on univ.-state dept. of mental health resources, needs and collaborative opportunities, 1972—; mem. N.C. Found. for Mental Health Research; chmn. Nat. Advisory Com. on Hyperkinesis and Food Additives, 1975—; mem. Presdl. Commn. on Obscenity and Pornography, 1968-70, many others. Recipient NIMH Research Career Devel. Award, Grade II, 1962-67; diplomate Am. Bd. Psychiatry and Neurology, Am. Bd. Internal Medicine. Fellow Am. Coll. Neuropsychopharmacology, Am. Coll. Psychiatrists, A.C.P., Am. Psychiat. Assn.; mem. AAUP, Soc. for Exptl. Biology and Medicine, Am. Soc. Biol. Chemists, Am. Psychosomatic Soc., Am. Fedn. for Clin. Research, N.Y. Acad. Sci., Soc. for Psychiat. Research, Soc. for Exptl. Biology and Medicine, So. Soc. for Clin. Investigation, Am. Psychopath. Assn., Soc. for Neurosci., Am. Assn. of Med. Colls., Sigma Xi, Phi Lambda Upsilon, Alpha Omega Alpha. Cons. editor Neuropharmacology and Psychopharmacology, 1969-70; editorial bd. Am. Jour. Psychiatry, 1970—, Psychopharmacology Communications, 1974—, Neuropsychobiology, 1974—; editorial advisory bd. N.C. Jour. Mental Health, 1975—, Ann. Rev. Psychiat. Drug Treatment, 1973—; contbr. numerous articles in field to profl. jours. Home: 2004 Lakeshore Dr Chapel Hill NC 27514 Office: Rm 210 BSRC U NC Chapel Hill NC 27514

LIQUORI, MARTIN WILLIAM, JR., athlete, business exec.; b. Montclair, N.J., Sept. 11, 1949; s. Martin William and Sara Ann (Tosone) L.; B.S., Villanova U., 1972; postgrad. U. Fla., 1973-75; m. Carol Ann Jones, Oct. 16, 1971. Master of ceremonies I.T.A. ProTrack, Los Angeles, 1971-73; commentator ABC-TV, N.Y.C., 1971—; pres. Athletic Attic, Inc., Gainesville, Fla., 1972—; designer, promotional dir. Brooks Shoe Co., Hanover, Pa., 1974—; pres. Marty Liquori Sportswear Inc.; v.p. Athletic Lady. Club: Athletic Attic. Home: 5904 NW 57th Way Gainesville FL 32605 Office: 2300 SW 34th St Gainesville FL 32605. *Lucky is the man who discovers his talents early in life—more fortunate is he who has the maturity to develop those talents.*

LIS, EDWARD FRANCIS, pediatrician; b. Chgo., Apr. 1, 1918; s. Stephen and Stephanie L.; student DePaul U., 1936-37; B.S., M.D., U. Ill.; m. Sonne Nadine Kowalsen, Apr. 3, 1944; children—Jeffrey Warren, James Bryan. Pvt. practice, Park Forest, Ill., 1949-51; faculty U. Ill. Coll. Medicine, 1951—, now prof. pediatrics, also dir. div. services crippled children, 1959—; dir. center handicapped children Research and Ednl. Hosp., U. Ill., 1955—. Chmn. research adv. com. Children's Bur., HEW, 1964-67; mem. Ill. Commn. Children. Served to capt. AUS, 1944-46. Fellow Am. Acad. Pediatrics, Am. Pub. Health Assn.; mem. Sigma Xi. Contbr. to profl. jours. Home: 3003 Balmoral St Flossmoor IL 60422 Office: 840 S Wood St Chicago IL 60612

LISANBY, JAMES WALKER, naval officer; b. Princeton, Ky., Jan. 31, 1928; s. Alvin and Rebecca L.; B.S. in Elec. Engring., U.S. Naval Acad., 1950; Engrs. Degree in Naval Architecture, M.I.T., 1953-56; student Program for Mgmt. Devel., Harvard U., 1967; m. Gladys Elnora Kemp, Nov. 18, 1951; children—Elizabeth Ann, Sarah Hollingsworth. Commd. ensign U.S. Navy, 1950, advanced through grades to rear adm., 1977; ship supt. Charleston Naval Shipyard, 1956-59; main propulsion asst. U.S.S. Antietam (CVS 36), 1959-61; asst. for ship materials, staff, comdr.-in-chief Atlantic Fleet, 1961-63; asst. for new constrn. (cruisers and destroyers) Naval Ship Systems Command, Dept. Navy, Washington, 1963-65, head procurement and prodn. br., fast deployment logistic ship project office, 1965-68, exec. asst. to comdr., 1969-70; dir. indsl. engring. office of asst. sec. of navy, (installations and logistics), 1968-69; supr. shipbldg., Pascagoula, Miss., 1970-73, asst. for ship design, office chief naval ops., 1973-74; project mgr. LHA class amphibious assault ships, 1974-77; comdr. Naval Ship Engring. Center, Navy Dept., Washington, 1977-79; dep. comdr. ship design and integration Naval Sea Systems Command, Dept. Navy, Washington, 1979—. Recipient Engr. of Yr. award Soc. Mfg. Engrs., 1979. Mem. Am. Soc. Naval Engrs. (nat. v.p. 1979—), Soc. Naval Architects and Marine Engrs., Sigma Xi, Tau Beta Pi. Office: Dep Comdr for Ship Design and Integration Naval Sea Systems Command Washington DC 20362

LISCHER, LUDWIG FREDERICK, utility co. exec.; b. Darmstadt, Germany, Mar. 1, 1915; s. Ludwig J. and Paula (Stahlecker) L.; came to U.S., 1923, naturalized, 1933; B.S. in Elec. Engring., Purdue U., 1937, D.Eng. (hon.), 1976; m. Helen Lucille Rentz, Oct. 1, 1938; 1 dau., Linda Sue. With Commonwealth Edison Co., Chgo., 1937—, v.p. charge engring., research and tech. activities, 1964—; mem. various tech. adv. coms. to fed. agys. and Edison Electric Inst.; mem. research adv. com. Electric Power Research Inst. Bd. dirs. Chgo. Engring. and Sci. Center; trustee Ill. Inst. Tech. Served to lt. col., AUS and USAAF, 1941-45. Registered profl. engr., Ill. Fellow IEEE; mem. ASME, Nat. Acad. Engring., Am. Nuclear Soc., Tau Beta Pi, Eta Kappa Nu. Contbr. articles to profl. jours. Home: 124 W Willow St Lombard IL 60148 Office: 1 First Nat Plaza Chicago IL 60690

LISENSKY, ROBERT PAUL, univ. ofcl.; b. Pitts., Dec. 5, 1928; s. Albert Edward and Gertrude Elizabeth (Wittlinger) L.; B.A. cum laude, W.Va. Wesleyan Coll., 1951; S.T.B. magna cum laude, Boston U., 1954, Ph.D., 1960; m. Mary Agatha Herrick, Aug. 18, 1951; children—George, Joan, Carol. Asso. prof., chmn. dept. sociology and anthropology MacMurray Coll., 1958-64; acad. dean, prof. sociology, v.p. acad. affairs Albion Coll., 1964-67; v.p. acad. affairs prof. sociology Ohio Wesleyan U., 1967-73; pres. Willamette U., Salem, Oreg., 1973—; cons. Pub. Housing Adminstrn. for Scott and Green Counties, Ill., 1960-62, Ill. Sch. for Deaf, 1963-65, Clarke Sch. for Deaf, Northampton, Mass., 1967-69, HEW, Rochester, N.Y., 1970; co-dir. GLCA Faculty Seminar, Yugoslavia, summer 1970, dir., summer 1971; examiner N. Central Assn. Colls. and Secondary Schs.; bd. dirs. NCHEMS, 1976—, pres.-elect, 1979-80. Mem. Am. Sociol. Assn., Nat. Assn. Schs. and Colls. United Meth. Ch. (pres. 1979-80), Oreg. Ind. Coll. Assn. Rotarian. Clubs: University. Contbr. articles to profl. jours. Home: 325 Lincoln Ave Salem OR 97302

LISH, GORDON JAY, editor; b. Hewlett, N.Y., Feb. 11, 1934; s. Philip and Regina (Deutsch) L.; grad. Phillips Acad., 1952; B.A. cum laude, U. Ariz., 1959; postgrad. San Francisco State Coll., 1960; m. Loretta Frances Fokes, Nov. 7, 1956 (div. May 1967); children—Jennifer, Rebecca, Ethan; m. 2d, Barbara Works, May 30, 1969; 1 son, Atticus. Broadcaster stas. KPDN, Tex., WELI, New Haven, WVNJ, N.Y.C., 1960-63; instr. English, Mills High Sch. and

Coll. San Mateo, Calif., 1961-63, editorial dir. Genesis West, 1961-65; editor-in-chief, dir. linguistic studies Behavioral Research Labs., Menlo Park, Calif., 1963-66; with Ednl. Devel. Corp., Palo Alto, 1966-69; fiction editor Esquire mag., N.Y.C., 1969-77; with Alfred A. Knopf, Inc., 1977—; lectr. Yale, 1973-74, guest fellow, 1974-78; author fiction and non-fiction under several pen-names. Pres. Chrysalis West Found., 1962—. Recipient award distinguished editing in fiction Am. Soc. Mag. Editors, 1971, Columbia Grad. Sch. Journalism award for distinguished editing in fiction, 1971, in non-fiction, 1975. Author: English Grammar, 1964; The Gabbernot, 1965; Why Work, 1966; A Man's Work, 1967; New Sounds in American Fiction, 1969; Secrets High and Low, 1979. Editor: The Secret Life of Our Times, 1973; All Our Secrets Are the Same, 1976; Chrysalis Rev., 1959-61; Gordon Lish/McGraw-Hill Books, 1974—. Office: 201 E 50th St New York NY 10022

LISI, UGO JOSEPH, banker; b. West New York, N.J., Feb. 2, 1918; s. Felix and Mary (Baldassarre) L.; B.A. in Econs., Drew U., 1940; postgrad. N.Y. U. Sch. Bus. Adminstrn., 1946, Stonier Grad. Sch. Banking, 1949; m. Mary Elizabeth Story, Mar. 4, 1943; children—Robert J., Joan Ellen. With First Nat. Bank, Union City, N.J., 1940-47; asst. sec., br. mgr. Hudson Trust Co., Union City, 1947-56; with Banco de Ponce, 1956—, sr. v.p. charge N.Y. ops., 1968-75; dir. Commerce, Labor and Industry Kings County, N.Y., Coalition Venture Corp., N.Y.C., Bancap, N.Y.C.; resident adviser Banco Popular Espanol, Madrid, 1976. Mem. adv. bd. Manhattan Community Coll., 1968—; mem. Palisades Interstate Park Commn., 1976. Bd. dirs. Aspira of Am., Amanece, N.Y.C., Inst. Fgn. Bankers N.Y., Urban Coalition N.Y., Rand Inst. N.Y.; trustee YWCA, N.Y.C., N. Hudson (N.J.) Salvation Army, 1956; commr. Palisades Interstate Park Commn., 1977—; trustee Doricua U., N.Y.C., 1976. Served to lt. col. AUS, 1941-45. Mem. Bankers Assn. Fgn. Trade, N.Y. Credit Men Assn., Fgn. Bankers Inst., Am. Canoe Assn. (vice commodore Atlantic div. 1964), P.R. C. of C. in N.Y.C. (dir.), Am. Arbitration Assn. (dir., mem. exec. com.). Contbr. articles to profl. jours. Home: 226 N Central Ave Ramsey NJ 07446 Office: 1221 Ave of Americas New York NY 10029

LISK, ROBERT DOUGLAS, educator; b. Pembroke, Ont., Can., Nov. 10, 1934; s. Robert Leslie and Elsie (Yandt) L.; B.A., Queen's U., 1957; A.M., Harvard, 1959, Ph.D., 1960. Came to U.S., 1961. Mem. faculty Princeton, 1960—, instr. biology, 1960-62, asst. prof., 1962-65, asso. prof., 1965-70, prof., 1970—. Mem. adv. panel Regulatory Biology NSF, 1972-75. Fellow AAAS; mem. Am. Assn. Anatomists, Am. Soc. Physiologists, Am. Soc. Zoologists, Animal Behavior Soc., Endocrine Soc., Internat. Brain Research Orgn., Soc. Study Reprodn. Editorial bd. Am. Jour. Physiology, 1968-71, Jour. Applied Physiology, 1968-71, Jour. Exptl. Zoology, 1971-75, Neuroendocrinology, 1966-75; Biology of Reproduction, 1974—. Contbr. articles on neural regulation reprodn. to profl. jours. Home: 12 E Stanworth Dr Princeton NJ 08540

LISKA, GEORGE, educator, author; b. Pardubice, Czechoslovakia, June 30, 1922; s. Bedrich and Karla (Slezakova) L.; Dr.Jr., Charles U., Prague, Czechoslovakia, 1948; Ph.D. in Polit. Sci., Harvard U., 1955; m. Suzy Colombier, June 30, 1962; children—Ian Pierre, Anne Fernande. Came to U.S., 1949, naturalized, 1957. Sec. to sec. gen. Czechoslovak Ministry Fgn. Affairs, 1946-48; exec. asst. Council Free Czechoslovakia, Washington, 1949-52; asst. prof. polit. sci. U. Chgo., 1958-61; prof. polit. sci. Johns Hopkins U. and Sch. Advanced Internat. Studies, Washington, also research asso. Washington Center Fgn. Policy Research, 1964—. Recipient Sumner prize Harvard, 1955. Author: International Equilibrium, 1957; The New Statecraft, 1960; Nations in Alliance, 1962; Europe Ascendant, 1964; Imperial America, 1967; War and Order, 1968; (with Robert E. Osgood and others) America and the World, 1970, Retreat From Empire?, 1973; States in Evolution, 1973; Beyond Kissinger, 1975; Quest for Equilibrium, 1977; Career of Empire, 1978. Office: 1740 Massachusetts Ave NW Washington DC 20036

LISKAMM, WILLIAM HUGO, architect, urban planner; b. N.Y.C., Sept. 10, 1931; s. William J. and Johanne (Herz) L.; B.Arch., Pratt Inst., 1954; Fulbright scholar, Technische Hochschule, Stuttgart, Germany, 1954-55; M.Arch., Harvard, 1956; divorced; children—Erika, Thea, Fiona. Project architect maj. archtl. and urban planning programs, Calif. and N.Y., 1958-63; exec. v.p. Okamoto & Liskamm, Inc., planners and architects, San Francisco, 1963-71; ind. archtl. and urban planning cons., 1971-74; pres. William H. Liskamm, AIA, AIP, Inc., 1974—; dir. planning Woodward-Clyde Consultants, San Francisco, 1978—; architect and environ. planning cons., 1980—; cons. architect U. Calif. at Santa Barbara, 1971—, Environmental Impact of New Town, San Mateo, 1973-75, Golden Gate Transp. Corridor Program, San Francisco, 1973-75, Impact of High Rise Devel., Dept. Housing and Urban Devel., 1973; asst. prof. dept. architecture Coll. Environ. Design, U. Calif. at Berkeley, 1963-69, lectr., 1975—, vice chmn., 1965-67, lectr., 1975-78; vis. sr. lectr. U. Coll., London, 1967-68; cons. Regional Ocean Coastline Plan—Assn. Bay Area Govts., 1972—, appearance and design element Calif. Coastal Zone Plan, Calif. Coastal Zone Conservation Commn., 1974, citizens participation element Shelby Farms Planning Program, Memphis, 1975—; cons. devel. comprehensive planning methodology USAF, Washington; cons. environ. performance evaluation selected BART stas. San Francisco Bay Area; cons. transp. services for elderly and handicapped Marin County (Calif.); chmn. bd. Archtl. Found. No. Calif. Chmn. design rev. bd. San Francisco Bay Conservation and Devel. Commn., State of Calif. Served to 1st lt. C.E., AUS, 1956-58. Recipient awards for profl. projects HUD; Am. Inst. Planners award for San Francisco Urban Design Plan, 1972. Wheelwright fellow Harvard, 1967-68, Nat. Endowment for Arts grantee. Mem. AIA (coll. of fellows), Am. Inst. Planners, Am. Arbitration Assn., Nat. Council Archtl. Registration Bds. Club: Harvard (San Francisco). Address: 19 Olive Ave San Rafael CA 94901

LISLE-CANNON, RICHMOND, financial cons.; b. N.Y.C., Feb. 18, 1914; s. Edward William and Edith Lisle (McCurley) Cannon; student Lincoln Meml. U., 1934-37; m. Cherry Pinckard Clark, Aug. 4, 1961; 1 son, Anthony; stepchildren—Eastburn Clark, Galen Pinckard Clark. Engr., Atlantic Metal Products Co., Reliance Bronze & Steel Co., to 1939; gen. mgr. Comolite Corp., Long Island City, N.Y., 1939-47; asst. to pres. Bijur Lubricating Corp., Rochelle Park, N.Y., 1947-53; pres. L.H. Wright Co., Inc., N.Y.C., La Jolla, Calif., 1953-63; founder Anglo-Am. Stamp Co., Ltd., chmn. bd.; founder, dir. Hydrovoil Transit Corp., Tobaccoles Smokes Corp., Internat. Philatelic Corp., Arab World Financial Adv. Service; founder, pres., dir. Sovereign Am. Arts Corp., N.Y.C.; partner A.L. Williamson & Co., Inc., N.J. Mem. Order First Families Va., Soc. Colonial Wars, U.S. Mil. Order Loyal Legion, S.R., Magna Charta Barons, N.Y. Colonial Order Acorn, SAR, St. George Soc., Soc. War of 1812, Vets. Corps Arty. Republican. Mason. Clubs: Meadow (Southampton, N.Y.), Am. Curson, Clermont (London, Eng.); British Luncheon, Church, Nat. Steeple Chase; Tuxedo, St. Anthony (N.Y.C.); Schloss Mittersill (Salzburg, Austria); Anabels, Chelsea Arts, Guards (London); Newport (R.I.) Reading Room, Newport Country. Pub., Yachting Monthly, 1957-60. Address: 130 E 62d St New York NY 10021 also 27 Eaton Sq London SW 1 England also Beacon Rock Harrison Ave Newport RI

LISSIM, SIMON, painter, designer; b. Kiev, Russia, Oct. 24, 1900; s. Michel and Anna Maria (Schorr) L.; student Art Sch. of Alexander Monko; grad. Naoumenko Sch., 1919; student Sorbonne, Ecole du Louvre; m. Irene Zalchoupine, 1925 (dec. 1945); m. 2d, Dorothea Howson Waples, January 25, 1946. Came to U.S., 1941, naturalized, 1946. Stage designer Theatre de l'Oeuvre, 1923, Theatre de L'Atelier, Theatre National de l'Opera Comique, Theatre des Nouveautes, Paris, 1931, Theatre Michel, Theatre Antoine, 1932; head art edn. project N.Y. Pub. Library, N.Y.C., 1942-66; faculty French Lycee, N.Y.C., 1943-49, Horace Mann-Lincoln High Sch., Columbia; faculty Coll. City N.Y., 1944, art supr. adult edn. program, 1945-47, asst. prof. art, 1947-54, asso. prof., 1954-60, prof., 1960-71, prof. emeritus, 1971, asst. dir. evening session charge adult edn. program, 1948-50, asst. dir. Sch. Gen. Studies, div. adult edn., 1950-64; faculty French Summer Sch., McGill U., 1949; works include painting, stage designs, ceramics, gouaches, china; works permanently exhibited N.Y. Pub. Library, Bklyn. Mus. Art, Hyde Park Library, Met. Mus. of Art, Boston Mus. Fine Arts, Fogg Mus. Art, Cleve. Mus. Fine Arts, Santa Barbara Mus. Art, Cooper Mus., Columbus (Ohio) Gallery Fine Arts, Fla. So. Coll., Va. Mus. Art, Phila. Mus. Art, Victoria and Albert Mus., London, Eng., Shakespeare Meml. Mus., Stratford-on-Avon, Eng., Nat. Gallery of Can., Ottawa, Musee Nat. du Jeu de Paume, France, Nat. Collection Fine Arts, Washington, Calif. Palace Legion Honor, San Francisco, others, museums in Eng., France, Prague, Holland, Austria, Can., Denmark, Switzerland, Italy, Portugal, Spain, Belgium, Latvia, Norway; traveling exhbn. The World of Simon Lissim, Internat. Exhbns. Found., 1979-80; illustrator several books; has given over 80 one-man shows in various countries. Chmn. nat. selection com. Fulbright awards in painting, sculpture, graphic arts, 1956. Served as vol. French Army, World War II. Recipient silver medal Internat. Exhbn., Paris, 1925, gold medal, Barcelona, 1929; two grand Diplome d'honneur, Paris, 1937. Hon. fellow Am.-Scandinavian Found. U.S.A.; mem. Royal Soc. Arts (v.p. council), Société du Salon d'Automme, Société des Artistes Decorateurs (Paris), Royal Acad. Fine Arts St. George (Barcelona, Spain) (hon. corr.), AAUP, Coll. Art Assn., Am., Theatre Library Assn. Am., Royal Soc. Miniature Painters (hon.), Audubon Artists. Club: Century (N.Y.C.). Contbr. articles to books, periodicals. Home: 3100 Binnacle Dr Naples FL 33940

LISSITZYN, OLIVER JAMES, lawyer, educator; b. Moscow, Russia, Mar. 21, 1912; s. James John and Anastasia (Ivanoff) L.; brought to U.S., 1923, naturalized, 1931; A.B., Columbia, 1933, LL.B., 1935, Ph.D., 1942; m. Elizabeth Tilton Hyde, Feb. 22, 1944; 1 son, Lawrence Hyde. Admitted to N.Y. bar, 1936, since practiced in N.Y.C.; asst. reporter neutrality Harvard Research Internat. Law, 1937-39; research fellow Council Fgn. Relations, N.Y.C., 1939-40; spl. asst. Carnegie Endowment Internat. Peace, 1940-41; analyst, chief sect. OSS, 1941-43; asst. prof. pub. law Columbia, 1946-55, asso. prof., 1955-63, prof., 1963-79, Hamilton Fish prof. internat. and diplomacy, 1979—; lectr. U.S. Naval War Coll., 1955-65, Hague Acad. Internat. Law, summer 1968; Charles H. Stockton prof. internat. law U.S. Naval War Coll., 1969-70; legal analyst Am. Airlines, Inc., 1946-48; asso. Aviation Adv. Service, N.Y.C., to study fgn. airline subsidies for U.S. Senate com. interstate and fgn. commerce, 1951. Served from 1st lt. to capt., AUS, 1943-46. Mem. Am. Soc. Internat. Law (exec. council 1950-53), Am. Bar Assn., Internat. Law Assn. (exec. com. Am. br. 1954-77, hon. v.p. 1977—). Author: (with A.S. Keller and F.J. Mann) Creation of Rights of Sovereignty Through Symbolic Acts 1400-1800, 1938; International Air Transport and National Policy, 1942; The International Court of Justice, 1951; Nacionalidad de la Propiedad y Control de las Lineas en Derecho Internacional Aereo (pamphlet), 1951; International Law Today and Tomorrow, 1965; (with W.G. Friedmann and R.C. Pugh) Cases and Materials on International Law, 1969. Home: 35 Claremont Ave New York NY 10027

LIST, EUGENE, pianist; b. Calif., 1921; ed. Los Angeles and Phila.; studied with Olga Samaroff, Phila. Conservatory of Music and Juilliard Sch. N.Y.C. Began pub. appearances as pianist in early years; profl. debut with Phila. Symphony Orch. under Leopold Stokowski; N.Y. debut with N.Y. Philharmonic under Otto Klemperer; has appeared as guest with leading orchs. and in recitals throughout U.S. and abroad; also played over radio; currently performs with Vermont Festival Players. Mailing address: care Nat Artists Mgmt 165 W 46th St New York NY 10036*

LIST, ROBERT FRANK, gov. Nev.; b. Visalia, Calif., Sept. 1, 1936; s. Franklin Way and Alice A. (Dove) L.; B.S., Utah State U., 1959; J.D., Hastings Coll. Law, San Francisco, 1962; m. Kathryn Sue Geary, July 1, 1962; children—Suzanne Kathryn, Franklin Mark, Michelle Alice. Admitted to Nev. bar, 1962; practice in Carson City, 1962-66; dist. atty. Carson City, 1966-70; atty. gen. Nev., 1970-79, gov., 1979—; mem. Nev. Crime Commn., 1968—; mem. Commn. for Rev. Nat. Policy toward Gambling, 1972—. Chmn. Nev. Young Republicans, 1963-64; nat. vice chmn. Young Republicans, 1967-68; del. Rep. Nat. Conv., 1968, 72, 76; bd. dirs. Am. Council Young Polit. Leaders, 1972—; bd. visitors U.S. Air Force Acad. Mem. Nat. Assn. Atty. Gens. (exec. com. 1971—, chmn. Western region 1972-73, 75-76), Am., Nev. bar assns., Utah State U., U. Cal. (pres. Sierra Nev. chpt. 1970-72) alumni assns., Sigma Alpha Epsilon, Phi Alpha Delta. Elk, Rotarian. Club: Prospectors of Reno. Office: Office of Gov Capitol Bldg Carson City NV 89710

LIST, ROLAND, meteorologist; b. Frauenfeld, Switzerland, Feb. 21, 1929; came to Can., 1963; s. August Joseph and Anna (Kaufmann) L.; Dipl. Phys. Eidgenössische Technische Hochschule, Zurich, Switzerland, 1952, Dr. sc. nat., 1960; m. Gertrud K. Egli, Apr. 14, 1956; children—Beat R., Claudia G. Head hail sect. Swiss Fed. Inst. for Snow and Avalanche Research, Davos, 1952-63; prof. physics U. Toronto (Ont., Can.), 1963—, asso. chmn. dept. physics, 1969-73; chmn. exec. com. panel of experts on weather modification World Meteorol. Orgn., Geneva, 1970—; vis. prof. Swiss Fedn. Inst. Tech., Zurich, summer 1974; dir. Univ. Corp. Atmospheric Research, Boulder, 1974-77; mem. sci. council space shuttle program U.S. Univ. Space Research Assn., Houston, 1978—. Recipient Sesqui-Centennial medal Leningrad (USSR) U., 1970, Patterson medal Meteor. Service of Can., 1978; adminstr. NRC Can. devel. grant for atmospheric dynamics, 1974-79. Fellow Royal Soc. Can.; mem. Can. Acad. Sci., Am. Meterol. Soc., Can. Assn. Physicists, Can. Geophys. Union, Can. Meteorol. and Oceanic Soc., Am. Geophys. Union, Royal Meterol. Soc., Swiss Phys. Soc., Gesellschaft Ehemaliger Studierender der ETH. Contbr. numerous articles on exptl. and theoretical atmospheric physics, especially on formation of precipitation, cloud dynamics, weather modification and societal and climatic impact to profl. publs. Home: 58 Olsen Dr Don Mills ON M3A 3J3 Canada Office: Dept Physics U Toronto Toronto ON M5S 1A7 Canada

LISTER, LOUIS, psychotherapist, economist, sociologist; b. N.Y.C., Dec. 6, 1914; s. Morris and Rose (Smithberg) L.; B.S., Coll. City N.Y., 1938; M.A., Columbia, 1940, Ph.D., 1960; m. Jeanne Lampert, Jan. 15, 1939. Chief coal br. ECA, 1948-51; U.S. del. to NATO, OEEC, Paris. Econ. Commn. Europe, Geneva, 1951-53; research dir. 20th Century Fund, 1955; research prof. New Sch. for Social Research, 1961—; dir. project in govt. energy policies in U.S. for Resources for Future, Inc., 1961—; pvt. practice psychotherapy; prof. sociology Columbia U., Hunter Coll., Yeshiva U. Fellow Am. Assn. Marital and Family Therapists (asso.). Author: Europe's Coal and Steel Community, an Experiment in Economic Union, 1960. Home: 165 W 91st St New York NY 10024

LISTER, ROBERT HILL, archeologist, educator; b. Las Vegas, N.Mex., Aug. 7, 1915; s. Frank Hiram and Bye (Hill) L.; B.A., U. N.Mex., 1937, M.A., 1938; M.A., Harvard, 1947, Ph.D., 1950; m. Florence Ellen Cline, July 24, 1942; children—Frank Cline, Gary Givhan. Anthropologist, specializing Am. archeology, U. Colo., 1947-70; with dept. anthropology U. N.Mex., Albuquerque, 1971—; archaeol. excavations in Am. S.W., Mexico and Nubia. Served to maj. AUS, 1941-46. Mem. Am. Anthrop. Assn., Soc. Am. Archaeology, Soc. Hist. Archaeology. Home: PO Box 712 Corrales NM 87048 Office: Dept Anthropology U NMex Albuquerque NM 87131

LISTER, THOMAS MOSIE, composer, lyricist, pub. co. exec., clergyman; b. Empire, Ga., Sept. 8, 1921; s. Willis Waller and Orena Pearl (Holland) L.; attended Rennsalaer Poly. Inst., 1944-45, Middle Ga. Coll., 1945-46, U. South Fla., 1968; m. Jewel Wylene Whitten, June 2, 1946; children—Brenda (Mrs. James Milton Vann), Barbara (Mrs. David Miller Williams). Composer, lyricist numerous gospel songs, 1940—; singer, Tampa, Fla., and Atlanta, 1941, 46-47; founder, pres. Mosie Lister Publs., Atlanta, 1952-56, Tampa, 1956—; affiliate for performance and synchronization rights SESAC, Inc., 1955—; affiliate Lillenas Pub. Co., Kansas City, Mo., 1969—, also cons. and dir.; ordained to ministry Baptist Ch., 1975; choral dir. Served with USNR, 1942-45. Named Bapt. Layman of Year for Tampa, 1971; inducted into Gospel Hall of Fame, 1976; recipient Humanist award Sesac, Inc., 1976; Mosie Lister Day named in his honor, Tampa, 1974. Mem. Gospel Music Assn. (dir. 1970-71), Fla. Bapt. Ministers of Music Assn. (hon. life). Democrat. Compiler song collections, hymnbooks, and others. Arranger religious music for choral groups and ensembles; songs include How Long Has It Been?, Where No One Stands Alone, Then I Met the Master, 'Til the Storm Passes By, His Grace Is Sufficient for Me, I'm Feeling Fine; contbg. arranger profl. singing groups; studied privately at Tampa U., 1958-63. Address: PO Box 270182 Tampa FL 33688

LISTON, MARY FRANCES, educator; b. N.Y.C., Dec. 17, 1920; d. Michael Joseph and Ellen Theresa (Shaughnessy) Liston; B.S., Coll. Mt. St. Vincent, 1944; M.S., Catholic U. Am., 1945; Ed.D., Columbia, 1962. Dir. psychiat. nursing and edn. Nat. League for Nursing, N.Y.C., 1958-66; prof. Sch. Nursing, Cath. U. Am., Washington, 1966—, dean, 1966-73; spl. assignment Imperial Med. Center, Tehran, Iran, 1975-78; dep. dir. for program affairs Nat. League for Nursing, N.Y.C., 1978—. Mem. Sigma Theta Tau. Home: 182 Garth Rd Scarsdale NY 10583 Office: 10 Columbus Circle New York NY 10019

LITCHFIELD, JOHN THOMAS, JR., physician; b. Mpls., Aug. 29, 1912; s. John Thomas and Agnes A. (LeDuc) L.; B.S., U. Minn., 1935, M.B., 1936, M.D., 1937; m. Ann E. Sliwka, Oct. 16, 1937; children—John Thomas III, Barbara Ann. Instr. dept. pharmacology and exptl. therapeutics Johns Hopkins Med. Sch., 1937-43; asst. prof. dept. pharmacology U. Minn., 1943-45; group leader, asst. dir., then dir. pharm. research chemotherapy div. Stamford Research Labs., Am. Cyanamid Co., 1945-54; dir. exptl. therapeutics research sect. Lederle Labs. div., 1955-63, dir. research, 1963-68; cons. Nat. Library Medicine and U.S. Dept. Agr., 1969-70; dir. extramural and clin. research Bur. Drugs FDA, 1970-71; med. asso. Kremers-Urban Co. Mem. Commn. on Drug Safety; cons. to council on drugs A.M.A., Nat. Library Medicine, U.S. Dept. Agr. Fellow N.Y. Acad. Scis., A.A.A.S.; mem. Soc. Toxicology, Am. Soc. Pharmacology and Exptl. Therapeutics, Soc. Exptl. Biology and Medicine, Canadian Assn. for Research in Toxicology, N.Y. State Soc. Med. Research, Drug Information Assn., Sigma Xi. Address: Hardscrabble Heathsville VA 22473

LITFIN, RICHARD ALBERT, press news orgn. exec.; b. The Dalles, Oreg., Sept. 9, 1918; s. Bernard R. and Alberta (Knappenberger) L.; B.J., U. Mo., 1940; m. Marie Foley, June 28, 1944; children—Maria Eschen, Mercedes Zingmark, Regina Cochran, Angela, Thomas, Anthony. With U.P.I., 1940—, bur. mgr., Olympia, Wash., 1946-47, Pacific Northwest bus. rep., 1946-52, San Francisco rep., 1953-54, bus. mgr. Pacific div., 1954-56, div. mgr., 1956-75, v.p. western region, 1976—. Midshipman, Northwestern U., 1940, commd. ensign USN, 1941; assigned Battleship Idaho, 1941; after flight tng., assigned Fighting 12, U.S.S. Saratoga, S. Pacific, 1942; inactive status 1946—. Bd. fellows, mem. pres.'s adv. com. U. Santa Clara; mem. com. for art Stanford U.; mem. de Saissett Art Mus.-U. Santa Clara. Decorated D.F.C., Air Medal with stars. Mem. SAR, U.S. Hist. Soc., Sigma Delta Chi, Alpha Delta Sigma, Sigma Alpha Epsilon. Republican. Roman Catholic. Clubs: Press, Commonwealth (San Francisco). Home: 1790 Oak Ave Menlo Park CA 94025 Office: UPI Fox Plaza San Francisco CA 94103

LITHERLAND, ALBERT EDWARD, educator; b. Wallasey, Eng., Mar. 12, 1928; s. Albert and Ethel (Clement) L.; came to Can., 1953, naturalized, 1964; B.Sc., U. Liverpool (Eng.), 1949, Ph.D., 1955; m. Anne Allen, May 12, 1956; children—Jane Elizabeth, Rosamund Mary. Rutherford scholar Atomic Energy of Can., Chalk River, Ont., 1953-55, sci. officer, 1955-66; prof. physics U. Toronto, 1966—. Recipient Rutherford medal, Inst. Physics, London, 1974. Fellow Royal Soc. Can., Royal Soc. London; mem. Can. Assn. Physicists (Gold medal for achievement in physics 1971), Am. Phys. Soc. Contbr. articles in field to profl. jours. Home: 3 Hawthorn Gardens Toronto ON M4W 1P4 Canada Office: 60 Saint George St Toronto ON M5S 1A7 Canada

LITKE, ARTHUR LUDWIG, govt. ofcl.; b. Torrington, Conn., Apr. 4, 1922; s. Gustav and Julia (Weiman) L.; B.S. in Econs., Trinity Coll., 1944; M.B.A., U. Pa., 1947; grad. Advanced Mgmt. Program, Harvard U., 1961; student George Washington U., 1949-51; m. Stephanie Eleanore Lojewski, June 9, 1951; children—Arthur Lawrence, Suzanne Elizabeth. With GAO, 1946-64, asso. dir. civil accounting and auditing div., 1963-64; chief accountant, chief Office Accounting and Fin., FPC (FERC), 1964-73; mem. Fin. Acctg. Standards Bd., 1973-78; asso. adminstr. for econ. and regulatory adminstrn. Dept. Energy, Washington, 1978; cons. to comptroller gen. of U.S., GAO, 1978—; mem. teaching staff econs. dept. Cath. U. Am., 1966-67; professorial lectr. accounting Sch. Govt. and Bus. Adminstrn., George Washington U., 1967-73. Bd. dirs. Potomac Swimming and Recreation Assn., 1958-72; adv. bd. Conn. State Opera Assn., 1973-78. Recipient Meritorious Service award GAO, 1959; Meritorious Service award FPC, 1969, Distinguished Service award, 1973; Distinguished Leadership award Assn. Govt. Accountants, 1969; Robert W. King Meml. gold medal, 1975; C.P.A., N.C. Mem. Am. Inst. C.P.A.'s (com. on auditing procedure 1967-70, ethics com. 1971-73), Nat. Assn. Accountants (Washington chpt. William H. Churchill Meml. award 1966, 71), Washington, N.Y. socs. security analysts, Assn. Govt. Accountants (research chmn. 1964-65, grants chmn. 1965-67, chmn. fed. fin. mgmt. standards bd. 1968-71, fgn. affairs 1979—, ethics bd. 1978— nat. pres. 1972-73, dir. Washington chpt. 1969-72), Accounting Research Assn., Am. Arbitration Assn., Nat. Soc. Rate of Return Analysts, Am. Accountants Assn., Potomac C. of C. (dir. 1972-73), Nat. Economists Club, Pi Kappa Alpha.

Lutheran (council). Contbr. articles to profl. jours. Home: 1422 Lady Bird Dr McLean VA 22101 Office: GAO Washington DC

LITMAN, BERNARD, elec. engr.; b. N.Y.C., Oct. 26, 1920; s. Nathan and Gussie (Friedman) L.; B.S. in Elec. Engring., Columbia U., 1941, Ph.D., 1949; M.S., U. Pitts., 1943; m. Ellen Ann Kaufman, Feb. 27, 1949; children—Barbara, Richard. Design engr. energy equipment Westinghouse Electric Co., Pitts., 1941-47; with AMBAC Industries div. United Tech. Corp., Garden City, N.Y., 1949—, tech. dir. guidance equipment Atlas inter-continental missile, 1962-63, chief engr. systems devel. and research, 1964—; Westinghouse lectr. U. Pitts., 1944; lectr. Adelphi U., Garden City. William Petit Trobridge fellow, 1948. Asso. fellow Am. Inst. Aeros. and Astronautics (Achievement award L.I. sect. 1966); mem. IEEE (sr.), Am. Automatic Control Council, N.Y.-N.J. Trail Conf., Sigma Xi. Jewish. Co-author: Gyroscopics, 1961; author, patentee rotary amplifiers, axial motors, gravity pendulums, inductors, 2 axis accellerometers, ballistic missile safety devices, gyro attenuators, thrust retainers. Home: 2857 Morgan Dr Wantagh NY 11793 Office: AMBAC Industries Roosevelt Field Garden City NY 11530

LITMAN, ROSLYN MARGOLIS, lawyer; b. N.Y.C., Sept. 30, 1928; d. Harry and Dorothy (Perlow) Margolis; B.A., U. Pitts., 1949, J.D., 1952; m. S. David Litman, Nov. 22, 1950; children—Jessica, Hannah, Harry. Admitted to Pa. bar, 1952, since practiced in Pitts.; partner firm Litman, Litman, Harris & Specter, 1952; adj. prof. U. Pitts. Law Sch., 1958—; permanent del. Conf. U.S. Circuit Ct. Appeals for 3d Circuit. Chmn., Pitts. Pub. Parking Authority, 1970-74; bd. dirs. Pa. Bar Inst., 1979—. Mem. Pa. (bd. govs. 1976-79), Allegheny County (pres. 1975) bar assns., Allegheny County Acad. Trial Lawyers (charter). Home: 1047 Negley Ave S Pittsburgh PA 15217 Office: 1701 Grant Bldg Pittsburgh PA 15219

LITSCHGI, ALBERT BYRNE, lawyer; b. Charleston, S.C., Dec. 31, 1920; s. Albert William and Mary Catherine (Byrne) L.; B.B.A., U. Fla., 1941; J.D., Harvard U., 1948; m. Mary Elaine Herring, Sept. 13, 1952. Admitted to Fla. bar, 1948, D.C. bar, 1950; atty. Office Gen. Counsel, Treasury Dept., Washington, 1949-52; legis. asst. to U.S. senator, 1952; mem. firm Hedrick & Lane, Washington, 1953-60, Coles, Himes & Litschgi, Tampa, Fla., 1960-62, Shackleford, Farrior, Stallings & Evans, 1962—; chmn. SGL Industries, Inc., 1976—; incorporator, dir. Communications Satellite Corp., 1962-64; mem. Fla. Jud. Council, 1965-68; mem. U.S. Internal Revenue Commn. Adv. Group, 1967-68. Mem. Harvard Law Sch. Assn. (nat. council 1956-61), Am. Bar Assn. (chmn. excise and miscellaneous tax com. tax sect. 1956-59), Fla. Bar, Bar Assn. D.C. Home: 1903 Wykagyl St Tampa FL 33609 Office: 1st Florida Tower Tampa FL 33602

LITSKY, WARREN, educator; b. Worcester, Mass., June 10, 1924; s. Joseph and Esther (Kreplick) L.; A.B., Clark U., 1945; M.S., U. Mass., 1948; Ph.D., Mich. State U., 1951; postdoctoral fellow Fla. State U., 1965-66; m. Bertha Mead Yanis, Aug. 27, 1965. Instr. Mich. State U., 1951; mem. faculty U. Mass., Amherst, 1951—, prof. microbiology, 1956—, Commonwealth prof., 1961—, chmn. dept. environ. scis., 1972—, dir. Inst. Agrl. and Indsl. Microbiology, 1962—, dir. Tech. Guidance Center Indsl. Environmental Control, 1968-73; affiliate prof. biology Clark U., 1967—; vis. lectr. Am. U., 1968-69; pres. Environmental Mgmt., Inc., 1968-77; cons. Fed. Water Pollution Control Adminstrn., 1961-69, EPA, 1969—, div. hosp. and med. facilities USPHS, 1967—, NRC, 1965-69, 76—, numerous corps.; mem. adv. council Mass. Water Resources Research Center, 1964-73; mem. Spl. Commn. to Study Reuse Solid Waste, 1970-73; mem. adv. com. environmental impact statements Lower Pioneer Valley Planning Commn., 1970-74; research adviser Walden U., Naples, Fla., 1975—; dir. Rush-Hampton Industries, Longwood, Fla.; mem. tech. adv. com. sewage treatment and related facilities Town of Amherst, 1973-75; mem. U.S. Com. Israel Environment, 1973—; mem. Mass. Commn. Nuclear Safety, 1974-76. Recipient Sayer prize microbiology Mich. State U., 1951; Distinguished Service award Fitchburg (Mass.) Jr. C. of C., 1954; Editorial award Jour. Hosp. Mgmt., 1968; Outstanding Prof. award Stockbridge Sch., U. Mass., 1975; citation for sci. rev. EPA, 1977; Disting. Tchr. award U. Mass., 1979; named Man of Yr., B'nai B'rith, 1959. Diplomate Am. Acad. Sanitarians. Fellow Am. Pub. Health Assn. (editor lab. sect. newsletter 1969-76, mem. council lab. sect. 1971-74, chmn. sect. 1975-76, Difco best paper award 1977), Royal Soc. Health, AAAS, Am. Acad. Microbiology; mem. Am. Soc. Microbiology (pres. Conn. Valley br. 1970-71, gov. council 1972-75), Soc. Indsl. Microbiology (editor newsletter 1963-66), Soc. Applied Microbiology (Eng.), Water Pollution Control Fedn., Nat. Environ. Health Assn., Sigma Xi, Phi Tau Sigma (hon.), Phi Kappa Phi (hon.). Mason (Shriner). Co-author: Industrial Microbiology, 1976. Mem. editorial bd. Applied Microbiology, 1961-76, Industrials Lacteas, 1967-71, Health Lab. Sci., 1970-74; contbg. editor Jour. Environmental Health, 1970—; adv. editorial bd. Nations Health, 1972-75; co-editor 6 Procs. Contbr. articles to profl. jours. Patentee in field. Home: 9 Kettle Pond Rd Amherst MA 01002 Office: Marshall Hall U Mass Amherst MA 01003

LITT, MITCHELL, chem. engr., educator; b. Bklyn., Oct. 11, 1932; s. Saul and Mollie (Steinbaum) L.; A.B., Columbia, 1953, B.S. in Engring., 1954, M.S., 1956, D.Engring. Sci., 1961; m. Zelda Sheila Levine, Sept. 6, 1955; children—Ellen Beth, Steven Eric. Research engr. Esso Research and Engring. Co., 1958-61; faculty U. Pa., 1961—, asso. prof. chem. engring., 1965-72, prof., 1972—, prof. bioengring., 1977—; vis. prof. environ. medicine Duke, 1971-72; spl. research biorheology transp. processes, chemically reacting systems, med. aspects engring. Mem. Am. Inst. Chem. Engrs.; mem. Am. Soc. Engring. Edn., Am. Chem. Soc., Biomed. Engring. Soc., Internat. Soc. Biorheology, Phi Beta Kappa, Sigma Xi, Tau Beta Pi, Phi Lambda Upsilon, Theta Tau. Co-editor: Rheology of Biological Systems, 1973. Contbr. articles to profl. engrs. Home: 28 Barnwell Dr Willingboro NJ 08046 Office: Univ Pennsylvania Philadelphia PA 19104

LITT, NAHUM, lawyer; b. Balt., Aug. 3, 1935; s. Harry and Reva L. (Naiman) L.; A.B., Cornell U., 1956; LL.B., Columbia U., 1959; m. Judith A. Holzman, June 26, 1961; 1 dau., Marcia. Admitted to Md. bar, 1956, D.C. bar, 1969; atty. Office proceedings, ICC, Washington, 1960-65, appellate trial lawyer Gen. Consul's Office, 1965-70; hearing examiner Fed. Energy Regulatory Agy., 1970-77; chief adminstrv. law judge CAB, Washington, 1977-79; chief adminstrv. law judge Dept. Labor, Washington, 1979—. Mem. Fed. Adminstrv. Law Judges Conf. (pres. 1977), Am. Bar Assn., Fed. Bar Assn. Club: Cosmos. Home: 4956 Sentinel Dr Bethesda MD 20016 Office: 1111 20th St NW Suite 700 Washington DC

LITTAUER, RAPHAEL MAX, educator; b. Leipzig, Germany, Nov. 28, 1925; s. Paul Julius and Margarete (Stehr) L.; B.A., U. Cambridge (Eng.), 1946, Ph.D., 1950; m. Salome Alexandra Kroch, 1950; children—Celia Ruth, Benjamin Marc. Came to U.S., 1950, naturalized, 1956. Research asst. Cavendish Lab., Cambridge, Eng., 1945-50; research asso. Gen. Electric Research Lab., Schenectady, 1954-55; research asso. Cornell U., 1950-54, research asso. prof. physics, 1955-62, research prof., 1962-65, prof., 1965—, chmn. dept. physics, 1974-77; cons. Lansing Research Corp., 1966-67. Mem. Am. Phys. Soc. Author: (with R.R. Wilson) Accelerators, 1960, Pulse Electronics, 1965. Home: 1417 Slaterville Rd Ithaca NY 14850

LITTELL, FRANKLIN HAMLIN, educator; b. Syracuse, N.Y., June 20, 1917; s. Clair F. and Lena Augusta (Hamlin) L.; B.A., Cornell Coll., 1937, D.D., 1953; B.D., Union Theol. Sem., 1940; Ph.D., Yale, 1946; Dr. Theology, U. Marburg, 1957; Litt.D., Thiel Coll., 1968; D.H.L., Widener Coll., 1969, Hebrew Union Coll., 1975, Gratz Coll., 1977; m. Harriet Davidson Lewis, June 15, 1939; children—Jennith, Karen, Miriam, Stephen. Chief Protestant adviser to U.S. High Commr., other service in Germany, 1949-51, 53-58; dir. Lane Hall, U. Mich., 1944-49; prof. Chgo. Theol. Sem., 1962-69; prof. religion Temple U., 1969—; Walker-Ames prof. U. Wash., 1976. Corr. faculty mem. Inst. Contemporary Jewry, Hebrew U., 1973—; cons. NCCJ, 1958—; vice chmn. Center for Reformation Research, 1964-77; nat. chmn. Inst. for Am. Democracy, 1966-69, sr. scholar, 1969-76; pres. Christians Concerned for Israel, 1971-78, Nat. Leadership Conf. for Israel, 1978—; founder, chmn. ecumenical com. Deutscher Evangelischer Kirchentag, 1953-58; co-founder, cons. Assn. Coordination Univ. Religious Affairs, 1959—. Decorated Grosse Verdienstkreuz (Fed. Republic Germany). Mem. European Assn. Evang. Acads. (co-founder), Phi Beta Kappa, Phi Beta Kappa Assos. Clubs: Yale; George Town. Author: The Anabaptist View of the Church: an Introduction to Sectarian Protestantism (recipient Brewer award Am. Society Ch. History), 1952, rev. 1958, 64; From State Church to Pluralism, 1962, rev. 1970. Editor: Reformation Studies, 1962. Co-editor: Weltkirchenlexikon: Handbuch der Oekumene, 1960; The German Church Struggle and the Holocaust, 1974; The Crucifixion of the Jews, 1975; The Macmillan Atlas History of Christianity, 1976. Office: Temple Univ Philadelphia PA 19122

LITTELL, GALE PATTERSON, telephone co. exec.; b. Pekin, Ind., Oct. 6, 1917; s. Harold Crawford and Ethel Vanita (Whitson) L.; A.B., Ind. U., 1938; m. Justine Delores Davis, Dec. 20, 1945; children—Jane Ann (Mrs. Philip Meyer), John Harold. Sunday editor Indpls. Star, 1948-52; with Ind. Bell Telephone Co., 1952-61, gen. mgr. comml. dept., 1960-61; v.p. pub. relations N.J. Bell Telephone Co., 1961-63, v.p. met. area, 1963-66, v.p. revenue and bus. research, 1966-71; asst. v.p. AT & T Co., 1971-75; v.p. pub. relations So. Bell Telephone Co., 1975—. Served to maj., 101st Airborne Div., AUS, World War II. Mem. Sigma Delta Chi. Methodist. Clubs: Commerce, Cherokee Town and Country. Home: 5398 Trowbridge Dr Dunwoody GA 30338 Office: Hurt Bldg Atlanta GA 30301

LITTELL, JAMES ELMER, lawyer; b. Allegan, Mich., Aug. 28, 1902; s. James Elmer and Belle M. (White) L.; student Kalamazoo Coll., 1920-22; A.B., U. Mich., 1930; legal edn. U. Mich.; m. Clara Jane Clute, Sept. 10, 1933 (dec. Apr. 1976); 1 dau., Nancy Jane (Mrs. Ronald D. Wick). Admitted to Mich. bar, 1931; practiced in Detroit, 1931—; partner Hesse & Littell, 1936-45, Poole, Littell & Sutherland, 1945-76; of counsel firm Butzel, Long, Gust & Van Zile, 1976—; dir., sec. Poole Broadcasting Co., Flint, Mich., 1964-76. Mem. Am., Mich., Detroit bar assns., Am. Judicature Soc., Pi Kappa Delta, Sigma Alpha Epsilon. Republican. Baptist. Clubs: Detroit, Meadowbrook Country (Northville, Mich.); Glen Lake Yacht (Glen Arbor, Mich.); Huron River Hunting and Fishing (Farmington, Mich.). Home: 46920 W Seven Mile Rd Northville MI 48167 Office: First National Bldg Detroit MI 48226

LITTELL, NORMAN MATHER, lawyer; b. Indpls., Sept. 8, 1899; s. Dr. Joseph and Clara (Munger) L.; A.B., Wabash Coll., 1921; B.A., Christ Ch. Coll., Oxford, Eng. (Rhodes Scholar), 1924; M.A., Oxford U., Eng.; postgrad. Harvard Law Sch., 1925; LL.B., U. Washington, 1929; m. Katherine Maher, June 14, 1930; children—Katherine M., Norman Mather. Fgn. corr. Phila. Pub. Ledger, League of Nations, Geneva, 1923; admitted to Wash. State bar, 1929, asso. U.S. Supreme Ct., 1933; law firm Bogle, Bogle & Gates, Seattle, 1929-34; spl. asst. U.S. atty. gen. and asst. solicitor Dept. Interior, representing Adminstr. Petroleum Code and Pacific Coast Petroleum Agy. in N.W. states, 1934-35; partner law firm Evans, McLaren & Littell, Seattle, 1936-39; asst. atty. gen. U.S. in charge Pub. Lands Div., 1939-44; in gen. corp. and internat. law practice, Washington, 1944—. Organizer, exec. sec. Nat. Com. Against Nazi Persecution of Minorities, 1941-44; organizer, 1st pres. Am. Youth Hostels; testified before Congl. coms. in aid of fgn. investments, 1948-51; author guarantees sect. for pvt. investments abroad in Marshall Plan, E.C.A. Act; fgn. law cons. U.S. State Dept. at various times, Taiwan, June, 1960, Turkey, June 1961, co-author Fgn. Investment Encouragement Law of The Republic of China, Taiwan, 1960; gen. counsel, claims atty. Navajo Tribe Indians, 1947-67. Mem. Am. (past chmn. com. on fgn. econ. cooperation, com. on internat. finance, subcom. on subsidiaries in fgn. trade, mem. com. internat. trade and investment 1962-64), Internat. (chmn. sect. internat. econ. cooperation 1949-54), Fed., Inter-Am., Md., D.C., bar assns., Am. Soc. Internat. Law, Internat. C. of C. (com. on econ. devel. and fgn. investments 1951-53), Oxford Soc. Washington (sec.), Beta Theta Pi. Contbr. articles, papers on fgn. investment law to profl. jours. Home: Homeport Mason's Beach Deale MD 20751 Office: 1826 Jefferson Pl NW Washington DC 20036

LITTELL, WALLACE WILLIAM, govt. ofcl.; b. Meadville, Pa., Feb. 10, 1922; s. Clair Francis and Lena Augusta (Hamlin) L.; B.A., Cornell Coll., Mt. Vernon, Iowa, 1947; M.A., certificate Russian Inst., Columbia, 1949; student Heidelberg (Germany) U., 1949-50, Goettingen (Germany) U., 1951-52, Columbia, 1955-56; m. Betty Gay Paris, June 4, 1948; children—David, Linda, Harriet, Julie, Andrea. With U.S. Forest Service, 1944-46, 47, 48, UNRRA, Poland and Greece, 1946; cultural affairs adviser, Darmstadt, Germany, 1949, Hanover, Germany, 1950-53; editor Ost-Probleme, USIS publ., Bonn, Germany, 1953-55; cultural attache Am. embassy, Moscow, 1956-58; fgn. affairs officer USIA, Washington, 1958-59, 60-61; dir. policy and research Am. Nat. Exhbn., Moscow, 1959-60; 1st sec., chief press and cultural sect. embassy, Warsaw, Poland, 1961-65; dep. asst. dir. Soviet Union and Eastern Europe, USIA, 1965-68, asst. dir. Soviet Union and Eastern Europe, 1968-69; counselor embassy for pub. affairs CPAO, Belgrade, Yugoslavia, 1970-74; pub. affairs officer Am. embassy, Berlin, East Germany, 1975-76; assigned to Sr. Seminar in Fgn. Policy, Dept. State, 1976-77; chief Program Evaluation Staff, USIA, 1977-78; counselor embassy for press and culture Am. embassy, Moscow, 1978—. Recipient Meritorious Service award USIA, 1958, Am. Nat. Exhbn. Moscow, 1959. Mem. Phi Beta Kappa. Home: 8512 Pelham Rd Bethesda MD 20034 Office: Am Embassy Moscow Dept State Washington DC 20520

LITTIG, LAWRENCE WILLIAM, psychologist, educator; b. Madison, Wis., June 30, 1927; s. Lawrence Victor and Elsie Louise (Rosanske) L.; B.S., U. Wis., 1950, M.S., 1955; Ph.D., U. Mich., 1959; m. Iris Mark, June 15, 1957; children—Eve Alexandra, Amy Victoria, Sharon Elizabeth. Asst. prof. psychology U. Buffalo, 1959-62; asst. program dir. instl. programs NSF, Washington, 1962-63; social psychologist W.E. Upjohn Inst. Employment Research, Washington, 1963-65; prof. social psychology Howard U., Washington, 1965—; Fulbright prof. U. Nottingham, 1961-62; vis. scholar U. London, 1971-72; cons. Brookings Instn., 1968-70, Dept. Labor, 1968-70; vis. prof. U. Wis., 1970. U.S. Office Edn. grantee, 1965-70; NIMH research grantee, 1968-69; NSF research grantee, 1961-62, Nat. Inst. Child Health and Human Devel. grantee, 1971-73. Fellow Am. Psychol. Assn., Soc. Psychol. Study Social Issues; mem. AAAS, Am. Sociol. Assn., Psychonomic Assn., Brit. Psychol. Soc., Sigma Xi. Cons. editor Jour. Cross Cultural Psychology, 1969-74. Clubs: Cosmos (Washington); Yacht Club (Annapolis, Md.); Amateur Fencing (London). Home: 7011 Meadow Ln Chevy Chase MD 20015 Office: Dept Psychology Howard U Washington DC 20059

LITTLE, ALAN BRIAN, obstetrician, gynecologist; b. Montreal, Que., Can., Mar. 11, 1925; s. Herbert Melville and Mary Lizette (Campbell) L.; came to U.S., 1951, naturalized, 1959; B.A., McGill U., 1948, M.D., C.M., 1950; m. Nancy Alison Campbell, Aug. 20, 1949; children—Michael C. (dec.), Susan MacF. and Deborah MacF. (twins), Catherine E., Jane A., Mary L. Intern, Montreal Gen. Hosp., 1950-51; resident Boston Lying-in and Free Hosp. for Women, 1951-55, asst. obstetrician, asso. obstetrician and gynecologist, 1955-65; teaching fellow, asst. prof. Harvard Med. Sch., 1952-65; prof. obstetrics and gynecology to Arthur H. Bill prof. obstetrics and gynecology, dir. dept. reproductive biology Case Western Res. U. Sch. Medicine, Cleve., 1965—; dir. dept. obstetrics and gynecology Univ. Hosps., Cleve.; mem. com. on population research Nat. Inst. Child Health and Human Devel. Served with RCAF, 1943-45. Fellow Am., Royal colls. surgeons, Am. Coll. Obstetricians and Gynecologists; mem. AMA, Endocrine Soc., Am. Gynecol. Soc., Am., Central assns. obstetrics and gynecology, Assn. Profs. Obstetrics and Gynecology, Soc. Gynecol. Investigation. Author: (with B. Tenney) Clinical Obstetrics, 1962. Editor: (with others) Gynecology and Obstetrics-Health Care for Women, 1975. Contbr. articles profl. jours. Office: 2065 Adelbert Rd Cleveland OH 44106

LITTLE, BERNARD HAROLD, elec. equipment mfg. co. exec.; b. Pitts., Oct. 19, 1921; s. Robert E. and Irene (Jamison) L.; student Robert Morris Jr. Coll., 1947-49; children—Dorothy, Michele, Richard. With Ernst & Ernst, C.P.A.'s, 1949-59, mgr., 1957-59; with Ohio Brass Co., Mansfield, 1959—, v.p. finance, 1967—, sec.-treas., 1961—. Chmn. bd. dirs. Tax Council, Inc., Washington. Served with USAAF, 1943-47. C.P.A., Pa. Mem. Ohio Mfg. Assn. (trustee, v.p.). Home: PO Box 1481 Mansfield OH 44901 Office: 380 N Main St Mansfield OH 44902

LITTLE, C(HARLES) EDWARD, SR., broadcasting exec.; b. Norfolk, Va., June 22, 1923; s. Cecil Abernathy and Minnie Elizabeth (Mock) L.; student Duke, 1942-46; B.Ed., U. Miami (Fla.), 1950; m. Marie Frances Griswold, Jan. 29, 1946; children—C. Edward, Stephen G., Betsy Marie, Lynda Suzanne. Profl. baseball player minor league teams N.Y. Yankees, Norfolk, 1946, Kansas City, Mo., 1947, Augusta, Ga., 1947, Newark, 1948-49, Syracuse, N.Y., 1950, Miami, 1951-54; dir. sales Sportservice, Inc., winters 1946-54; account exec. sta. WITV-TV, Miami, 1954-55, v.p., gen. mgr., 1955-57; dir. promotion Miami Marlins Baseball Team, 1957; gen. mgr. sta. WGMA, Hollywood, Fla., 1958-65, pres., gen. mgr., 1966-71; v.p., gen. mgr. sta. KBTR, Denver, 1965-66; pres. Mut. Broadcasting System, Inc., 1972-78, pres. Mut. Black Network, 1972-75, exec. v.p., 1976. Mem. Pres.'s Com. on Employment of Handicapped, 1973. Served as lt. USMC. Mem. Nat. Assn. Broadcasters (dir.), Hwy. Users Fedn. (dir.), Advt. Council (dir.), Radio Advt. Bur. (dir.), Radio and TV Corrs. Assn., Internat. Radio and TV Soc. Methodist. Clubs: Nat. Broadcasters, St. Andrews Golf, Emerald Hills Golf, Mt. Glen Country, Grandfather Golf and Country. Home and office: PO Box 479 Mt Glen Golf and Country Club Estates Newland NC 28657

LITTLE, CARL MAURICE, performing arts adminstr.; b. Campbellton, N.B., Can., Mar. 17, 1924; s. George Everett and Ada (Boucher) L.; B.Sc., Dalhousie U., Halifax, N.S., Can., 1945, Licentiate of Music, 1945, Diploma Engring., 1944; Asso., Royal Coll. Music, London, 1952; Licentiate, Royal Acad. Music, London, 1952; m. Frances R. Corner, Aug. 27, 1949; children—Christine, Geoffrey, Jennifer, Stephen; m. 2d, Barbara Wolfond, Dec. 8, 1978. Tchr. music public schs., Outremont, Que., Can., 1949-50; pvt. tchr. music, Montreal, Que., 1946-59, Toronto, Ont., 1959-70; pianist, 1945-52; producer music CBC Radio, Montreal, 1952-59, Toronto, 1959-65, nat. network supr. serious music, Toronto, 1965-75; mgr. Nat. Arts Centre Orch., Ottawa, 1975-78: co-founder, pres. Little Gallery of the Arts, Ottawa, 1979—. Mem. Can. Conf. of Arts, Can. Music Council, Can. Amateur Musicians Assn. (dir.; co-founder); Ont. Choral Fedn., Nat. Arts Centre Orch. Assn. Club: Ottawa Athletic. Instrumental in founding and adminstrn. of CBC competitions, CBC music projects and programs. Address: 151 Bay St Suite 902 Ottawa ON K1R 7T2 Canada

LITTLE, CLEAVON JAKE, actor; b. Chickasha, Okla., June 1, 1939; s. Malchi and de Etta (Jones) L.; B.A., San Diego Coll., 1965; postgrad. Am. Acad. Dramatic Arts, 1965-67. Actor, appearing in plays MacBird, 1967, Hamlet, 1967, Scuba Duba, 1967-68, Jimmy Shine, 1968-69, Someone's Comin' Hungry, 1969, Ofay Watcher, 1969, Purlie, 1970, Narrow Road To The Deep North, 1972, The Charlatan, 1974, All Over Town, 1974, The Poison Tree, 1976, Same Time Next Year, 1977, Sly Fox, 1978; TV appearance in Temperature's Rising, 1972, Felony Squad, All in The Family, The Homecoming, The Day The Earth Moved, Bros. Grimm, 1977; appeared in films Blazing Saddles, 1974, Greased Lightning, 1977, FM, 1978, Scavenger Hunt, 1979. Recipient Tony award for best actor in a musical, 1969-70, N.Y. Critic Poll award, 1970, Drama Desk Award, 1970, F. and M. Schaefer Brewing Co. award, 1970 NAACP Image award, 1976. Office: care Perry Potkin & Co 9200 Sunset Blvd 607 Los Angeles CA 90069

LITTLE, DENNIS GAGE, diversified elec. mfg. co. exec.; b. Cambridge, Mass., June 22, 1935; s. Thomas Wolcott and Margaret (deRonge) L.; A.B., Harvard, 1956, M.B.A. with distinction, 1961; m. Susan Gay Walker, May 11, 1957; children—Heather Gage, Jennifer Wolcott. With J.P. Stevens & Co., Inc., 1961-67, asst. to financial v.p., 1961-67; treas. Gen. Cable Corp., 1967—, v.p., 1969-78, v.p. indsl. relations, 1975-78, sr. v.p., chief fin. officer, 1978—, also dir. Served with USNR, 1956-59. Mem. Financial Execs. Inst. Clubs: University (N.Y.C.); Bedford (N.Y.) Golf and Tennis; Owl (Cambridge, Mass.). Home: 300 Erskine Rd Stamford CT 06903 Office: 500 W Putnam Ave Greenwich CT 06830

LITTLE, EDWARD SOUTHARD, govt. ofcl.; b. Toledo, July 20, 1918; s. Herbert Woodruff and Sara Marie (Southard) L.; A.B., Swarthmore Coll., 1939; M.A., Fletcher Sch. Law and Diplomacy, 1940; Ph.D., Am. U., 1959; m. Marian Elizabeth McCarty, Oct. 17, 1941. With U.S. Dept. Agr., 1940-42, OPA, 1946-47; staff Dept. of State, 1947—; with ICA, economist U.S. Operations Mission to Spain, 1954-56; economist div. econ. devel., 1956-57, officer in charge Caribbean affairs, 1957-58, dep. dir. Office Caribbean and Mexican Affairs, 1958-59, counselor of embassy, Quito, Ecuador, 1959-61; dep. exec. sec. Dept. State, 1962-63; spl. asst. to sec. of state, 1963-65; assigned Nat. War Coll., 1965-66; counselor of embassy, Bern, Switzerland, 1966-69; country dir. for North Coast affairs Bur. Inter-Am. Affairs, 1969-73, acting coordinator for Cuban affairs, 1973-74; Am. ambassador to Chad, 1974-76; assigned to Intelligence Community Staff, 1976-78, sr. fgn. service insp., 1978-79; ret., 1979; part-time expert insp. Served from ensign to lt. USNR, 1942-46, now comdr. Res. ret. Mem. U.S. Naval Inst., Phi Kappa Psi. Club: Belle Haven Country (Alexandria, Va.). Home: 2105 Forest Hill Rd Alexandria VA 22307

LITTLE, ELBERT LUTHER, JR., dendrologist, botanist; b. Fort Smith, Ark., Oct. 15, 1907; s. Elbert L. and Josephine (Conner) L.; B.A., U. Okla., 1927, B.S., 1932; M.S., Ph.D., U. Chgo., 1929;

postgrad. U. Mich., 1927, Utah State U., 1928; m. Ruby Rema Rice, Aug. 14, 1943; children—Gordon Rice, Melvin Weaver, Alice Conner. Botanist, Okla. Div. Forestry, 1930, 77-78; asst. prof. biology Southwestern Okla. State U., 1930-33; from asst. to asso. forest ecologist Forest Service, U.S. Dept. Agr., Tucson, 1934-42, dendrologist, Washington, 1942-67, chief dendrologist, 1967-76; botanist Fgn. Econ. Adminstrn., Bogotá, Colombia, 1943-45; prodn. specialist U.S. Comml. Co., Mexico, 1945; prof. dendrology Universidad de Los Andes, Mérida, Venezuela, 1953-54, 60; botanist U. Md., Guyana, 1955; cons. UN Mission, Costa Rica, 1964-65, 67, Ecuador, 1965, 75, Nicaragua, 1971; vis. prof. biology Va. Poly. Inst. State U., 1966-67; prof. U. D.C., 1979; collaborator U.S. Nat. Mus. Natural History, Smithsonian Instn., 1965-76, research asso., 1976—. Recipient Superior Service award U.S. Dept. Agr. 1960, Distinguished Service award, 1973. Fellow Soc. Am. Foresters, AAAS, Washington Acad. Scis., Okla. Acad. Sci.; mem. Am. Inst. Biol. Scis. (gov. bd. 1956-60), Bot. Soc. Am., Internat., Am. socs. plant taxonomists, Ecol. Soc. Am., Phi Beta Kappa, Sigma Xi, Phi Sigma, Beta Beta Beta. Author: Checklist of United States Trees; Common Trees of Puerto Rico and the Virgin Islands; Arboles Comunes de Esmeraldas (Ecuador); Atlas of United States Trees; Alaska Trees and Shrubs; Common Forest Trees of Hawaii; Audubon Society Field Guide to North American Trees; also tech. articles. Home: 924 20th St S Arlington VA 22202 Office: Dept Botany Smithsonian Instn Washington DC 20560

LITTLE, GRETCHEN DOHM, ret. librarian; b. High Bridge, N.J., Nov. 7, 1913; d. James L. and Gretchen B. (Dohm) Little; A.B., Duke, 1936; B.S. in L.S., Drexel Inst. Tech., 1949. Asst. Librarian devel. dept. Uniroyal, 1936-37; tech. librarian Mead Corp., 1937-43, ICI Americas Inc. (formerly Atlas Chem. Industries), 1943-78; now cons. in field. Mem. AAAS, Am. Chem. Soc., Spl. Libraries Assn. (v.p. 1953-54, pres. 1954-55, chmn. sci.-tech. div.; chmn. 50th anniversary conv., elected to Hall of Fame 1979). Address: 1600 Sunset Ln Wilmington DE 19810

LITTLE, JACK DENVER, research co. exec.; b. Madison, Ill., Feb. 8, 1929; s. Denver Cecil and Fay L.; B.A., Westminster Coll.; postgrad. UCLA, U. Utah; grad. Advanced Mgmt. Program, Harvard Bus. Sch.; m. Lydia Arlene Garry, June 2, 1951; children—Susan Orban, Kimberly Daley. Data reduction engr. Sperry Corp., 1952-54; head computer sci. team Rand Corp., 1954-62; with Planning Research Corp., Washington, 1962—, pres. PRC Info. Scis. Co., PRC Data Services Co., subs. cos., exec. v.p. Planning Research Corp., pres. PRC Internat. Served with USNR, 1946-48. Office: 1850 K St NW Washington DC 20006

LITTLE, JAMES MAXWELL, educator; b. Commerce, Ga., Dec. 16, 1910; s. Claude and Cora (Quillian) L.; A.B., Emory U., 1932, M.S., 1933; Ph.D., Vanderbilt U., 1941; m. Louise Toepel, Aug. 20, 1934 (dec. Mar. 1978); children—Paul G., Nancy C., John M.; m. 2d, Emily Angell, Mar. 30, 1979. Asst. in physiology Emory U. Med. Sch., 1933-35; instr. biochemistry Vanderbilt U., 1936-41; mem. faculty Bowman Gray Sch. Medicine, Wake Forest U., Winston-Salem, N.C., 1941—, asst. dean, 1957-60, prof. pharmacology, chmn. dept., asso. physiology, 1963-73, prof. pharmacology, asso. physiology, 1973—. Charter mem., pres. Piedmont Craftsmen, Inc., 1963-71; bd. dirs. N.C. League Creative Arts and Crafts, 1975—. Fellow AAAS; mem. Am. Physiol. Soc., Soc. Exptl. Biology and Medicine, Am. Soc. Pharmacology and Exptl. Therapeutics, Am., N.C. (Bronze and Silver medallion 1970), Forsyth County heart assns., Phi Beta Kappa, Sigma Xi. Presbyn. (elder). Author: An Introduction to the Experimental Method, 1961. Contbr. articles to profl. jours. Home: 3100 Buena Vista Rd Winston-Salem NC 27106

LITTLE, JAMES REICHARD, dentist; b. St. Paul, Jan. 13, 1920; s. Joseph Monroe and Elizabeth (Reichard) L.; D.D.S., U. Minn., 1943; m. Janet Mae Coates, Sept. 4, 1943; children—John Coates, Laura Elizabeth. Practice gen. dentistry, St. Paul, 1946—; cons. Central Regional Testing Agency. Bd. dirs. St. Paul Area Health Council. Served to maj. Dental Corps, AUS, 1943-46. Fellow Am. (pres. Minn. sect. 1965), Internat. colls. dentists; mem. Am. (spl. cons., council on Nat. Bd. Examiners), Minn. dental assns., St. Paul Dist. Dental Soc. (exec. council), Minn. Acad. Restorative Dentistry, U. Minn. Dental Alumni Assn. (pres. 1963), Minn. State Bd. Dentistry, Am. Assn. Dental Schs. (spl. cons.), Am. Assn. Dental Examiners, Exec. Council (pres. 1974-75), U. Minn. Century Club (dir. 1975-79), St. Paul Jr. C. of C., Sigma Alpha Epsilon. Republican. Unitarian. Clubs: Masons, Rotary, Town and Country. Home: 1870 Eagle Redge D Saint Paul MN 55118 Office: 1371 W 7th St Saint Paul MN 55102

LITTLE, JOHN DUTTON CONANT, mgmt. scientist, educator; b. Boston, Feb. 1, 1928; s. John Dutton and Margaret (Jones) L.; S.B. in Physics, Mass. Inst. Tech., 1948, Ph.D., 1955; m. Elizabeth Davenport Alden, Sept. 12, 1953; children—John Norris, Sarah Alden, Thomas Dunham Conant, Ruel Davenport. Engr., Gen. Electric Co., Schenectady, 1949-50; asst. prof. operations research Case-Western Res. U., 1957-60, asso. prof., 1960-62; research asst. Mass. Inst. Tech., 1951-54, asso. prof. mgmt., 1962-67, prof., 1967-78, George M. Bunker prof. mgmt., 1978—; dir. Ops. Research Center, 1969-76; head mgmt. sci. group Sloan Sch. Mgmt., 1972—; chmn. bd. dirs. Mgmt. Decision Systems, Inc., 1967—. Cons. operations research indsl. govtl. orgns., 1958—. Served with AUS, 1955-56. Fellow A.A.A.S.; mem. Operations Research Soc. Am. (council 1970-73, pres. 1979-80), Inst. Mgmt. Scis. (v.p. 1976-79), Am. Mktg. Assn., Sigma Xi. Asso. editor Mgmt. Sci., 1967-71. Contbr. articles to profl. jours. Research on math. programming, queuing theory, marketing, traffic control, on-line decision models. Home: Conant Rd RD 1 Lincoln MA 01773 Office: Sloan Sch Mgmt Mass Inst Tech Cambridge MA 02139

LITTLE, JOHN RUSSELL, univ. adminstr.; b. Aberdeen, Wash., May 29, 1904; s. Harry Drew and Grace (Garfield) L.; B.S., Colo. State U., 1928, M.S., 1934; Ed.D., U. Colo., 1948; m. Lois Alberta Powell, June 5, 1928; children—John Russell, Jean (Mrs. Raymond Elliott). Elementary tchr., Akron, Colo., 1924-26; prin. Center (Colo.) Sch., 1928-33, supt., 1934-41; supt. schs., Arvada, Colo., 1941-47; asst. prof., student counsellor U. Colo., 1947-48, asst. dir. admissions, 1949-50, asso. prof., dir. admissions and records, 1950-55, prof., dean summer sessions, 1955-65, prof., asso. dean faculties, 1965-72, acting dean Coll. Arts and Scis., 1959-61, sec. univ., sec. bd. regents, 1967-70, editor Sch. and U. Rev., 1970-72, dean, prof. emeritus, 1972—, pres. ret. faculty, 1979; cons. on scholarships Boettcher Found., 1952—; cons. summer session studies U.S. Office Edn., 1959-65; dir. studies for establishment univ. br. centers in Colo., 1961—. Mem. Am. Assn. Jr. Colls., Higher Edn. Assn., Am. Assn. Collegiate Registrars and Admissions Officers (chmn. com. on internat. scholarships 1952-56, chmn. nat. convention com. 1955), Boulder C. of C., Colo.-Wyo. Assn. Collegiate Registrars and Adminstrn. Officers (past pres.), Assn. Deans U. Summer Sessions (pres. 1959, sec. 1960), Rocky Mountain Assn. Summer Session Dirs. (chmn. 1958), Nat., Colo. edn. assns., Am., Colo. assns. sch. adminstrs., AAUP, Am. Assn. U. Summer Sch. Adminstrs. (recorder 1964-69, pres. 1968), North Central Conf. of Summer Schs. (pres. 1963-64, pres. emeritus), Phi Delta Kappa, Kappa Kappa Psi, Alpha Gamma Rho. Republican. Presbyn. Rotarian, Mason (32 deg.). Club: University. Author: State Responsibility for Public Education and Application to Colorado, 1948. Co-author, editor: University of Colorado Report on Expansion of Higher Education in Colorado, 1961; prin. co-author, editor: Year Around Operation in American Universities, 1963; Revision of the Laws of the Regents of the University of Colorado, 1968. Contbr. articles to profl. jours. Home: 815 7th St Boulder CO 80302. *Giving the best of which I have been mentally and physically capable in each task attempted; maintaining high sensitivity to the needs and responsibilities of people; appreciation of beauty in all forms and adherence to Christian principles as I understand them-these have been and remain my guidelines.*

LITTLE, JOSEPH ALEXANDER, pediatrician; b. Bessemer, Ala., Mar. 16, 1918; s. Joseph Alexander and Kathleen W. (Vann) L.; A.B., Vanderbilt U., 1940, M.D., 1943; m. Sarah Goodpasture, Aug. 2, 1941; children—Sarah Marsh, Susan McLaughlin, Joseph Alexander. Intern, Vanderbilt Univ. Hosp., Nashville, 1943, 46-47; resident Children's Hosp., Cin., 1947-48; practice medicine, specializing in pediatrics, Cin., 1948-49, Louisville, 1949-62, Nashville, 1962-70, Shreveport, La., 1970—; pediatrician-in-chief Children's Hosp. Louisville, 1956-62; instr. pediatrics U. Cin. Sch. Medicine, 1948-49; asst. to prof. U. Louisville Sch. Medicine, 1949-62; asso. prof. pediatrics Vanderbilt U. Sch. Medicine, 1962-70; prof., head dept. pediatrics La. State U. Med. Center Sch. Medicine, 1970—. Pres., Caddo-Bossier Day Care Assn., 1972-74. Mem. Am. Acad. Pediatrics (chmn. Ky. 1959-62), Am. Pediatric Soc., Am. Heart Assn. (pres. La.), Alpha Omega Alpha, Omicron Delta Kappa. Episcopalian. Home: 445 McCormick St Shreveport LA 71104 Office: PO Box 33932 Shreveport LA 71130

LITTLE, LARRY CHATMON, football player; b. Groveland, Ga., Nov. 2, 1945; s. George C. and Ida Mae (Haynes) L.; B.A., Bethune Cookman Coll., 1967; Sc.D. (hon.), Biscayne Coll., 1972. Offensive lineman San Diego Chargers, 1967-68, Miami Dolphins, Miami, Fla., 1969—; tchr. Dade County Sch. Bd., 1969-70. Vice pres., dir. Larry Little's Gold Coast Summer Camp, Inc., Miami, 1970—; mem. Gov.'s Com. on Human Relations, 1973-74; atty. gen. com. on drug abuse, 1973-74; active Boys' Club Miami, 1970—, Archie Stone Sports Found., 1970—, Nat. Center for Voluntary Action, Heart Assn. Greater Miami, 1973-74. Named King of Day, Variety Club, 1972; Citizen of Year, Omega Psi Phi, 1971, Frontier Club, 1971; named Profl. Athlete of Year, Dade Jr. Coll., 1971; named All Offensive Lineman of Year, Nat. Football League, 1970-73, Am. Football League, 1971-73; Forrest Gregg award Offensive Lineman of Year in Nat. Football League, 1972; All Pro, 1971, 72, 73, 74, 75. Mem. Bicentennial Patriots Orgn., Urban League Dade County, Nat. Football League Players Assn. Democrat. Baptist. Office: 330 Biscayne Blvd Bldg Miami FL 33132*

LITTLE, LOYD HARRY, JR., author; b. Hickory, N.C., Sept. 12, 1940; s. Loyd Harry and Rebecca Lillian (Bailey) L.; B.A. in Journalism (Hickory Daily Record scholar), U. N.C., 1962, postgrad., 1967-68; m. Drena Edwards, Dec. 23, 1963. Editor, Lumbee weekly newspaper, Pembroke, N.C., 1966; med. reporter Winston-Salem (N.C.) Jour., 1967-69; bus. editor Raleigh (N.C.) News and Observer, 1969; editor Carolina Fin. Times, Raleigh, 1970-75; spl. projects editor Durham (N.C.) Morning Herald, 1976—; tchr. creative writing courses U. N.C., 1976. Chmn., Orange Grove Precinct Republican Party, 1972—. Served with Green Berets, U.S. Army, 1962-65. Decorated Commendation medal, Combat Inf. badge, Combat Med. badge, Vietnamese Bronze Star medal. Mem. PEN. Club: Chez Hickory. Author: Parthian Shot (Ernest Hemingway award), 1975; In the Village of the Man, 1978. Home: Route 3 Box 91 Hillsborough NC 27278 Office: Durham Morning Herald Durham NC 27703

LITTLE, RICHARD CARUTHERS, actor; b. Ottawa, Ont., Can., Nov. 26, 1938; s. Lawrence Peniston and Elizabeth Maud (Wilson) L.; ed. Lisgar Collegiate, Ottawa, 1953-57; student drama Ottawa Little Theatre, 1950-60; m. Jeanne E. Worden, Oct. 16, 1971. First TV appearance in U.S. on Judy Garland Show, 1964; appearances films, TV, night clubs; host TV series The Rich Little Show, 1975-76. Winner Entertainer of Year award, 1974. Office: care Jerry Goldstein Goldstein Co Inc 9200 Sunset Blvd Suite 913 Los Angeles CA 90069

LITTLE, ROBERT ANDREWS, architect, designer; b. Brookline, Mass., Sept. 9, 1915; s. Clarence Cook and Katherine Day (Andrews) L.; A.B., cum laude, Harvard U., 1937, M.Arch., 1939; m. Ann Murphy Halle, Dec. 27, 1940; children—Sam Robertson, Revere Little. Designer, G.H. Perkins, Cambridge, Mass., 1939-41; architect U.S. Navy, Washington, 1941-43, ops. analyst Air Staff Intelligence, Washington, 1943-45; prin. Robert A. Little & Assos., Cleve., 1946-58, 67-69; partner Little & Dalton, Cleve., 1958-67; dir. design Dalton-Dalton-Little-Newport, Cleve., 1969-78; owner Robert A. Little, Design and Architecture, 1978—; tchr., lectr. Harvard, U. Pa., Carnegie Inst. Tech., U. Mich., Smith Coll., U. Notre Dame, Kent State U.; exhibited art and graphics in Cleve., Phila., Boston. Trustee Cleve. Mus. Sci., 1952-56, Cleve. Inst. Music, 1956-58; mem. Cleve. Fine Arts Com. Served with U.S. Army, 1940. Fellow AIA (pres. Cleve. chpt. 1966-68, nat. and state design awards), Harvard Sch. of Design Alumni Assn. (past pres., internat. dir. of devel.). Works include Air Force Mus., Dayton, Ohio, Supreme Ct. and Tower, Columbus, Ohio. Home: 5 Pepper Ridge Rd Cleveland OH 44124 Office: Cleveland OH. *As a child, I drew pictures all the time—and they were my current ideal—a face I thought pretty, a massive locomotive, a pine tree against the sea, or a castle in the sky. As an adult Designer and Artist, too, I have spent my whole life dreaming of beauty, and trying to create it—and, of course, never fully succeeding. But the great satisfaction has not been the results, but rather the breathless moments of the search itself, and the boundless horizons of the dream.*

LITTLE, ROBERT COLBY, physiologist, educator; b. Norwalk, Ohio, June 2, 1920; s. Edwin Robert and Eleanor Thresher (Colby) L.; A.B., Denison U., 1942; M.D., Western Res. U., 1944, M.S., 1948; m. Claire Campbell Means, Jan. 20, 1945; children—William C., Edwin C. Intern Grace Hosp., Detroit, 1944-45; USPHS postdoctoral research fellow Western Res. U., 1948-49; resident internal medicine Crile VA Hosp., Cleve., 1949-50; asst. prof. physiology, then asso. prof. physiology and medicine U. Tenn. Sch. Medicine, 1950-54; research participant Oak Ridge Inst. Nuclear Studies, 1952; dir. clin. research Mead Johnson & Co., 1954-57; lectr. medicine U. Louisville, 1955-57; dir. cardio pulmonary labs. Scott Sherwood and Brindley Found., Temple, Tex., 1957-59; prof. physiology, asst. prof. medicine Seton Hall Coll. Medicine and Dentistry, 1957-64; prof. physiology, chmn. dept., also asst. prof. medicine Ohio State U. Sch. Medicine, 1964-73; prof. physiology, chmn. dept., prof. medicine Med. Coll. Ga. Sch. Medicine, Augusta, 1973—. Cons. in field. Served to capt. M.C., AUS, 1945-47. Mem. Am. Physiol. Soc., So. Soc. Clin. Investigation, Am. Heart Assn., Assn. Chmn. Depts. Physiology, Soc. Exptl. Biology and Medicine, Am. Fedn. Clin. Research, Sigma Xi, Sigma Chi, Alpha Kappa Kappa. Author: Physiology of the Heart and Circulation, 1977; editor: Physiology of Atrial Pacemakers and Conductive Tissues, 1980; contbr. articles to profl. jours. Home: 44 Plantation Hills Dr Evans GA 30809

LITTLE, ROBERT NARVAEZ, JR., educator; b. Houston, Mar. 11, 1913; s. Robert Narvaez and Lillian (Kinney) L.; student U. Tex. at Austin, 1929-32; B.A., Rice, 1935, M.A., 1942, Ph.D., 1943; m. Betty Jo Browning, June 1, 1942; children—Scott Robert, Emily Browning. Asst. seismologist Shell Oil Co., Houston, 1936-40; asst. prof. physics U. Oreg., Eugene, 1943-44; research scientist, airborne fire control systems U. Tex. at Austin, 1944-46, asst. prof. physics, 1946-50, asso. prof., 1950-53; chief nuclear physics Gen. Dynamics, Fort Worth, 1953-55; prof. physics and edn. U. Tex. at Austin, 1955—. Cons. Los Alamos Sci. Lab., 1949-51, Sandia Corp., 1955-56, Bendix Corp., 1955-56, Tex. Nuclear Corp., 1956-58, Kaman Nuclear Corp., 1956, Inst. Pedagogico, Caracas, Venezuela, 1969-70, Univ. Valle, Guatemala, 1969—; pvt. practice cons., Austin, 1951—. Mem. commn. coll. physics Am. Assn. Physics Tchrs., 1962-66; U. Tex. rep. Council Oak Ridge Asso. Univs., 1955-73; adviser (Consejo Superior Universitario Centro Americano, C.Am., 1965-69; dir. NSF grants U. Tex., 1958, 60, 64-71; mem. mission to evaluate multinat. physics projects OAS. Fellow Tex. Acad. Sci., Am. Physics Soc., Am. Inst. Physics (bd. govs. 1969-72); mem. Am. Assn. Physics Tchrs. (pres. 1970-71), Groupe Internat. de Recherche Sur L'enseignement de la Physique, Sociedad Centro Americana de Fisica, Sociedad Costarricense De Fisica, Sigma Xi, Sigma Pi Sigma. Home: 3928 Balcones Dr Austin TX 78731

LITTLE, ROBERT WILLIAM, mech. engr., educator; b. Oklahoma City, Feb. 25, 1933; s. Harry Glenn and Mary Evelyn (Miller) L.; B.S. in Mech. Engring., Duke, 1955; M.S., U. Wis.-Madison, 1959, Ph.D., 1962; children—Deborah, Catherine, Colleen, Jennifer, Karen. Design engr. Allis Chalmers Mfg. Co., Milw., 1955-57; instr. mech. engring. Marquette U., 1957-59; instr. U. Wis., 1959-62, asst. prof., 1962-63; asst. prof. Okla. State U., 1963-65; prof. Mich. State U., 1965—, chmn. dept. mech. engring., 1972-77, chmn. dept. biomechanics, 1977—. Cons. A. C. Electronics Co., Ford Motor Co., CBS Research Lab., B. F. Goodrich Co.; lectr. AID, India, 1965. Vice pres. Okemos (Mich.) Sch. Bd., 1967-72; mem. Meridian Twp. (Mich.) Charter Commn., 1969-70; mem. Meridian Twp. Zoning Bd. Appeals, 1969-71. NSF grantee, 1964-69, 79; recipient award for excellence in instrn. engring. students Western Electric Co., 1970-71; NIH grantee, 1973-75, 79—. Mem. Soc. Engring. Sci., Am. Soc. Biomechanics, Sigma Xi, Pi Tau Sigma, Tau Beta Pi. Author: Elasticity, 1973. Contbr. articles to profl. jours. Home: 2402 Hulett Rd Okemos MI 48864 Office: Dept of Biomechanics Mich State U East Lansing MI 48824

LITTLE, ROYAL, investment co. exec.; b. Wakefield, Mass., Mar. 1, 1896; student Harvard, 1919; m. Augusta Willoughby Ellis, Sept. 10, 1932 (div. 1959); children—Augusta Willoughby, Arthur Dehon. Chmn. bd. Lonsdale Enterprises, Inc., fin. cons.; ret. chmn., dir. Amtel, Inc.; cons., past chmn. bd. Indian Head Mills, Inc.; founder, past chmn. bd. Textron Inc.; dir. Cleve. Metal Abrasive, Inc., Greenville Tube Co., MD Pneumatics, Inc., Old Fox Chem. Co., Wood Flong Corp., SW Tube Co. Trustee, v.p. Mus. Sci., Boston. Home: Nassau Bahamas Office: 40 Westminster St Providence RI 02903

LITTLE, WALTER FRANCIS, JR., publishing co. exec.; b. Leland, Miss., Aug. 14, 1927; s. Walter Francis and Josephine (Bailey) L.; student N.C. U., 1944-45; B.A., Washington and Lee U., 1949; m. Beverly Lynn Cox, Aug. 3, 1958; children—Walter Francis III, Vicki Lynn. Tri-state editor Delta-Democrat Times, Greenville, Miss., 1950-51; asst. mgr. Delta Council, Stoneville, Miss., 1951-55; advt. mgr. Yazoo City (Miss.) Herald, 1955-56; pres. Little Publs. Inc., Memphis, 1957—, founder, pub. Cotton Farming mag., 1957—, Rice Farming mag., 1967—, Cotton Applicator mag., 1971—, Midwest Farmer File, 1979—. Served with AUS, 1945-46. Mem. Nat. Agri-Mktg. Assn. (pres. chpt. 1970-71). Presbyn. (deacon). Home: 6366 Old Orchard Cove Memphis TN 38138 Office: 6263 Poplar Ave Memphis TN 38138

LITTLE, WILLIAM ARTHUR, physicist, educator; b. South Africa, Nov. 17, 1930; s. William Henry and Margaret (Macleod) L.; Ph.D., Rhodes U., S. Africa, 1953, Glasgow (Scotland) U., 1957; m. Annie W. Smith, July 15, 1955; children—Lucy Claire, Linda Susan, Jonathan William. Came to U.S., 1958, naturalized, 1964. Faculty, Stanford, 1958—, prof. physics, 1965—. Cons. to industry, 1960—. NRC Can. posdoctoral fellow; Vancouver, Can., 1956-58; Sloan Found. fellow, 1959-63, Fellow Am. Phys. Soc. Spl. Research low temperature physics, superconductivity, neural network theory. Home: 15 Crescent Dr Palo Alto CA 94301 Office: Physics Dept Stanford Univ Stanford CA 94305

LITTLE, WILLIAM FREDERICK, educator; b. Hickory, N.C., Nov. 11, 1929; s. William H. and Mary (Sheely) L.; B.S., Lenoir Rhyne Coll., 1950; M.A., U. N.C., 1952, Ph.D. (Morehead scholar), 1954; m. Edna Dell Hoyle, July 19, 1958; 1 dau., Teresa Dell. Postdoctoral research Univ. Coll., London, 1954-55; instr. Reed Coll., 1955-56; faculty U. N.C., Chapel Hill, 1956—, prof., 1965—, chmn., 1965-70, vice chancellor devel. and pub. service, 1973-78, univ. disting. prof., 1977—; exec. com. of bd. govs., cons. Research Triangle Inst.; v.p. Triangle Univs. Center for Advanced Studies, Inc., 1975—. Mem. Gov's Sci. Adv. Com., 1962-64; chmn. central selection com. Morehead Found., 1968—; bd. dirs. N.C. Bd. Sci. and Tech.; trustee Lenoir Rhyne Coll., 1965-68. Mem. Am. Chem. Soc. (past chmn. N.C. sect.), AAAS, Sigma Xi. Democrat. Lutheran. Contbr. articles to profl. jours. Home: 201 Markham Dr Chapel Hill NC 27514

LITTLEFAIR, DUNCAN ELLIOT, clergyman; b. Toronto, Ont., Can., Oct. 4, 1912; B.A., McMaster U., 1934, B.D., 1936; student U. Basle (Switzerland), U. Tubingen (Germany), 1938-39; Ph.D., U. Chgo., 1940; m. Gertrude M. Baokes, Dec. 31, 1939; children—Margo (Mrs. Clarence Wilbur), Wendy, Candi (Mrs. William Reese), Christopher and Alan (twins). Came to U.S., 1936, naturalized, 1942. Ordained to ministry Baptist Ch., 1940; minister Kenilworth (Ill.) Union Ch., 1940-44, Fountain St. Bapt. Ch., Grand Rapids, Mich., 1944. Speaker, Chgo. Sunday Evening Club. Author: A Primer for Modern Man, 1955; The Glory Within You, 1973; Sin Comes of Age, 1975. Home: 5225 Buttrick Rd SE Route 1 Alto MI 49302 Office: 24 Fountain St NE Grand Rapids MI 49502

LITTLEFIELD, DAVID JOSEPH, educator; b. Tupper Lake, N.Y., Aug. 22, 1928; s. James Herbert and Grace (Hayes) L.; A.B., Spring Hill Coll., Mobile, 1951; M.A., Yale, 1953, Ph.D. in English, 1961; vis. fellow Classics, Princeton, 1965-66; m. Jean Alice Johnston, Aug. 25, 1953; children—James Patrick, David Joseph, Thomas Mark, Christopher Johnston. Mem. faculty Middlebury (Vt.) Coll., 1953—, prof. English, 1969—, dir. Freshman English, 1966-68, dir. Braitmayer Teaching Fellow Program, 1967-69, chmn. div. humanities, 1967-70, chmn. dept. English and drama, 1971-74, Old Dominion Found. prof., 1969-70, Philip Battell Stewart and Frances Cowles Stewart prof. English, 1971—; cons. Kinney Nat. Service Corp., 1968; cons.-panelist media program div. pub. programs Nat. Endowment for Humanities, 1975—, fellow Stanford, summer 1975; vis. prof. Antioch Sch. Law, Washington, summer 1976, fall 1978. Mem. Vt. Council on Humanities and Pub. Issues, 1972—, chmn., 1972-76; mem. Am. Acad. Arts and Scis. adv. com. to WNET/Channel 13 Liberty Series, 1974-75. Served with USAF, 1951-52. Mem. Modern Lang. Assn., Am. Philol. Assn., Classical

Assn. New Eng. Editor: Twentieth Interpretations of the Frogs; faculty book rev., Books of Merit, 1964-69. Home: RD 2 Middlebury VT 05753 Office: Munroe Hall Middlebury Coll Middlebury VT 05753

LITTLEFIELD, EDMUND WATTIS, mining co. exec.; b. Ogden, Utah, Apr. 16, 1914; s. Edmond Arthur and Marguerite (Wattis) L.; B.A. with great distinction, Stanford, 1936, M.B.A., 1938; m. Jeannik Mequet, June 14, 1945; children—Edmund Wattis, Jacques Mequet, Denise Renee. With Standard Oil Co. of Calif., 1938-41, Golden State Co., Ltd., 1946-50; v.p., treas. Utah Internat. Inc. (formerly Utah Constrn. & Mining Co.), San Francisco, 1951-56, exec. com., dir., 1951—, exec. v.p., 1956, gen. mgr., 1958—, pres., 1961—, chmn. bd., 1971—, chief exec. officer, 1971-78, chmn. exec. com., 1978—, dir., 1979—, officer, dir. various subsidiaries; chmn. SRI Internat.; dir. Wells Fargo & Co., Federated Dept. Stores, So. Pacific Co., Del Monte Corp., Indsl. Indemnity Co., Gen. Electric Co.; mem. internat. adv. bd. Pan Am. Mem. Bus. Council. Trustee San Francisco Bay Area Council; bd. dirs. Center for Advanced Study in Behavioral Scis. Served as lt. (j.g.) USNR, 1941-43; spl. asst. to dep. adminstr. Petroleum Adminstrn. for War, 1943-45. Recipient Ernest C. Arbuckle award Stanford Bus. Sch. Assn., 1970, Golden Beaver award, 1970, Bldg. Industry Achievement award, 1972, Harvard Bus. Statesman award, 1974. Mem. San Francisco C. of C. (pres. 1956), Am. Inst. Mining, Metall. and Petroleum Engrs., Conf. Bd., Phi Beta Kappa, Chi Psi. Clubs: Burlingame (Calif.) Country; Pacific Union, Stock Exchange (dir.), San Francisco Golf (San Francisco); Augusta National Golf; The Links; Pauma Valley Country, Eldorado Country; Bohemian, Cypress Point (Pebble Beach, Calif.). Home: 405 Chapin Ln Burlingame CA 94010 Office: 550 California St San Francisco CA 94104

LITTLEFIELD, JOHN WALLEY, geneticist, univ. adminstr., pediatrician; b. Providence, Dec. 3, 1925; s. Ivory and Mary Russell (Walley) L.; M.D., Harvard U., 1947; m. Elizabeth Legge, Nov. 11, 1950; children—Peter P., John W., Elizabeth L. Intern, Mass. Gen. Hosp., Boston, 1947-48, resident in medicine, 1948-50, staff 1956-74, chief genetics unit children's service, 1966-73; asso. in medicine Harvard U. Med. Sch., 1956-62, asst. prof. medicine, 1962-66, asst. prof. pediatrics, 1966-69, prof. pediatrics, 1970-73; prof., chmn. dept. pediatrics Johns Hopkins U. Sch. Medicine, Balt., 1974—, pediatrician-in-chief Johns Hopkins U. Hosp., 1974—. Served with USNR, 1952-54. Guggenheim fellow, 1965-66. Diplomate Am. Bd. Internal Medicine. Mem. Am. Acad. Arts and Scis., Nat. Acad. Scis., Am. Soc. Biol. Chemists, Am. Soc. Clin. Investigation, Tissue Culture Assn., Soc. Pediatric Research, Am. Soc. Human Genetics, Am. Pediatric Soc., Am. Acad. Pediatrics, Assn. Am. Physicians, Phi Beta Kappa, Alpha Omega Alpha. Author: Variation, Senescence and Neoplasia in Cultured Somatic Cells, 1976. Home: 304 Golf Course Rd Owings Mills MD 21117 Office: Children's Medical and Surgical Center 2-116 Johns Hopkins Hosp Baltimore MD 21205

LITTLEFIELD, PAUL DAMON, mgmt. cons.; b. Cambridge, Mass., June 8, 1920; s. W. Joseph and Sally Pastorius (Damon) L.; A.B., Harvard, 1942, M.B.A. with distinction (Baker scholar), 1948; m. Emmy Farnsworth Neiley, June 19, 1943; children—Diane Neiley (Mrs. Richard P. Berry, Jr.), Elizabeth Damon (Mrs. Thomas Lehman), Paul Damon. Asso. with Freeport Minerals Co., N.Y.C., 1948-50, 52-62, treas., 1956-62; v.p. finance, treas. Arthur D. Little, Inc., Cambridge, 1962-73, sr. v.p., chief fin. officer, 1973—; asst. to pres. Coty, Inc., 1950-52; dir. Cambridge Trust Co., Courier Corp., Lowell, Mass. Trustee, New Eng. Med. Center Hosp., Boston, Old Sturbridge Village. Served to lt. comdr. USNR, 1942-45. Mem. Harvard Bus. Sch. Assn. Boston (past pres.), Financial Execs. Inst. Clubs: Annisquam (Mass.) Yacht (past gov.); Harvard, Treasurer's, Forecaster's (N.Y.C.); Weston (Mass.) Golf; Union (Boston). Home: 223 Aspen Circle Lincoln MA 01773 Office: Acorn Park Cambridge MA 02140

LITTLEFIELD, ROBERT CRANDALL, savs. and loan exec.; b. Monterey, Calif., Jan. 18, 1930; s. Glenn Crandall and Mary (Hill) L.; A.A., Monterey Peninsula Coll., 1950; student Stanford, 1951; B.A., San Jose State Coll., 1953; m. Mary Ortman, Feb. 28, 1954 (dec.); 1 dau., Susan Marie; m. 2d, Patricia R. Hodgson, Oct. 24, 1976. Pres., dir. Monterey Savs. and Loan Assn., 1948—; pres., dir. First Monterey Co., 1954—; pres., dir. Bessemer Oil Co., 1948—. Sec.-treas., dir. United Fund Monterey Peninsula, 1955-75; vice chmn. Monterey City Planning Commn., 1961-72; bd. dirs. Monterey History and Art Assn., 1970—; trustee Eskaton Monterey Hosp., 1977—. Served with AUS, 1951-53. Named Young Man of Year, Jr. C. of C., 1961. Mem. Monterey Peninsula C. of C. (treas., dir. 1955—, named citizen of year 1977), Calif. Savs. and Loan League (dir. 1976—). Republican. Methodist (treas.). Elk, Kiwanian (treas.). Home: 134 Littlefield Rd Monterey CA 93940 Office: PO Drawer M Monterey CA 93940 also 449 Alvarado St Monterey CA 93940

LITTLEFORD, WILLIAM DONALDSON, publisher; b. Ft. Thomas, Ky., Aug. 4, 1914; s. Roger Seiter and Marjorie (Donaldson) L.; student U. Cin.; grad. Advanced Mgmt. Program, Harvard, 1951; m. Mariana Weber, May 8, 1936 (dec. Feb. 1958); children—Anne, Michael; m. 2d, Marian Hastings, Aug. 20, 1958; children—Joseph M. Towne, Marian Towne. With Billboard Pub. Inc., Cin., 1934—, gen. mgr., 1943-58, pres., 1958-76, chmn. bd., 1976—, also dir.; dir. Littleford Bros., Inc., Donaldson Art Sign Co. Dir. Advt. Council, 1963—; dir. Asso. Bus. Publs., Inc., 1957-62, chmn. bd., 1960-61; bd. dirs. Audit Bur. Circulations, 1959-67, Mag. Pubs. Assn., 1967—, Second Class Mail Publs., 1962-70, Am. Bus. Press, 1965-68, 70-76, Pensord Press Ltd., Wales, U.K., 1969—, United Color Press, Dayton, Ohio, 1970—, Red Tag News Publs., Inc., 1971-77. Mem. Beta Theta Pi. Episcopalian (vestryman 1966-69). Clubs: Creek (Locust Valley, N.Y.); University (Cin.); Harvard (N.Y.C.). Home: 18 Glenwood Rd Roslyn Harbor NY 11576 Office: 1515 Broadway New York City NY 10036

LITTLEJOHN, ANGUS CHISHOLM, banker; b. Marshall, Tex., Oct. 23, 1916; s. Angus C. and Regina (Scully) L.; student Dartmouth, 1935-37; LL.B., U. Va., 1941; m. Mercedes Daly, Sept. 28, 1946; children—Angus Chisholm, Mercedes Guevara, Robert Duncan. Admitted to Va. bar, 1941; mng. partner Littlejohn e Cia, and predecessor, investment advisers, Rio de Janeiro and Sao Paulo, Brazil, 1946-64; co-founder Solidor, Inc., 1951, Tudor Ltd., 1953, Anhanguera Corp., 1955, Constanta, Inc., 1960; mng. dir. internat. div. U.S. Trust Co., N.Y.C., 1964-66; pres. Deltec Securities Corp., N.Y.C., 1966-68, also dir.; pres. U.S. Trust Co., Internat. Corp., N.Y.C., 1969-74; dep. chmn. Carbomin Internat. Corp. and ICM Group of Cos., 1976—, also dir.; dir. Leckie Smokeless Coal Co., ICM Mo., G & W Carbomin Cole Co., ICM Steel Corp., Exchange Nat. Bank Chgo., Republic Mgmt. Corp., Brazilian Mining and Dredging Co. Bd. dirs. Am. C. of C., Brazil and Sao Paulo, 1952-60. Served as officer USNR, 1942-45. Clubs: Recess, University, River (N.Y.C.). Home: 850 Park Ave New York NY 10021 Office: 25 Broadway New York NY 10021

LITTLEJOHN, CAMERON BRUCE, state justice; b. Pacolet, S.C., July 22, 1913; s. Cameron and Lady Sara (Warmoth) L.; A.B., Wofford Coll., Spartanburg, S.C., 1925, LL.D., 1968; LL.B., U. S.C., 1936, J.D., 1970; m. Inell Smith, Feb. 7, 1942 (dec. 1962); children—Inell (Mrs. Dan L. Allen III), Cameron Bruce. Admitted to S.C. bar, 1936; practice in Spartanburg, 1936-43, 46-49; circuit judge, 1949-67; justice Supreme Ct. S.C., 1967—; permanent mem. 4th U.S. Ct. Appeals Jud. Conf., 1966—. Mem. S.C. Ho. Reps., 1937-43, 47-49, speaker, 1947-49; del. county, state and nat. Democrat convs. Trustee North Greenville Jr. Coll., 1962-67; alumni bd. dirs. Wofford Coll., 1966-68. Served to 1st lt. AUS, 1943-46. Mem. Appellate Judges Conf., Am. Legion, Forty and Eight, V.F.W., Civitan Club, Blue Key. Editorial staff Trial Judges Jour., 1963-67. Home: 450 Connecticut Ave Spartanburg SC 29302

LITTLEJOHN, OLIVER MARSILIUS, coll. dean; b. Cowpens, S.C., Sept. 29, 1924; s. Thomas C. and Lillie Kate (Coveney) L.; B.S. in Chemistry, U. S.C., 1948, B.S. in Pharmacy cum laude, 1949; M.S. in Pharmacy, U. Fla., 1951, Ph.D., 1953; m. Beverly Sue Seastrunk, Dec. 18, 1948; children—Daniel Oliver, Susan Katherine. Instr. pharmacy U. S.C., 1948-49; pharmacist Smith Drug Store, Spartanburg, S.C., 1949-50; grad. asst. U. Fla., 1952-53; asst. prof. pharmacy, head dept. So. Coll. Pharmacy, 1953-56; prof. pharmacy, head dept. U. Ky., 1956-57; dean, prof. pharmacy So. Sch. Pharmacy, Mercer U., 1957—. Del. U.S. Pharmacopeial Conv., 1960, 70, 75. Served with inf., AUS, 1943-46; ETO. Decorated Bronze Star, Purple Heart, Combat Inf. badge. Fellow Am. Found. Pharm. Edn.; mem. Am., Ga. pharm. assns., Am. Assn. Colls. Pharmacy, Sigma Xi, Omicron Delta Kappa, Rho Chi, Gamma Sigma Epsilon, Phi Sigma. Baptist (deacon). Contbr. articles to profl. jours. Home: 6485 Bridgewood Valley Rd NW Atlanta GA 30328

LITTLER, GENE ALEC, profl. golfer; b. San Diego, Calif., July 21, 1930; s. Stanley Fred and Dorothy (Paul) L.; student San Diego State Coll.; m. Shirley Mae Warren, Jan. 5, 1951; children—Curt Michael, Suzanne. Golf pro winner Nat. Jr. Championship, 1948, Nat. Amateur Championship, 1953, U.S. Open, 1961, Canadian Open, 1965, Tournament of Champions, 1955, 56, 57, World Series of Golf, 1966; mem. U.S. Ryder Cup Team, 61, 63, 65, 67, 69, 71, 75. Served with USN, 1951-54. Home: La Jolla CA 92037 Office: US Golf Assn Far Hills NJ 07931

LITTLER, MARK DUNHAM, accountant; b. Mackinaw, Ill., Sept. 3, 1911; s. Sherman Henry and Mabel (Dunham) L.; B.S., U. Ill., 1933; m. Edith Elaine Uhrenholdt, Aug. 11, 1960; children—Richard, Barbara, Beverly. With Arthur Andersen & Co., C.P.A.'s, 1933-74, resident partner, London, 1945-48, N.Y.C., 1948-52, mng. partner Detroit office, 1952-70, sr. partner, 1970-74; sec.-treas. Longton Hall Galleries, Inc., 1974—. Pres. Detroit Council Chs., 1959-61, Friends Detroit Pub. Library, 1958-60; mem. Gov. Mich. Task Force Expenditure Mgmt., 1963-66, chmn., 1965-66; vice chmn. Commn. on Fed. Paperwork, 1975-77; mem. Detroit Commn. Community Relations, 1962-65; bd. dirs. Detroit Symphony Orch., 1960-73, Detroit Grand Opera Assn., 1959-73, Boulevard Gen. Hosp., 1963-68, United Community Services Detroit, 1962-64, Jr. Achievement Southeastern Mich., 1962-72, Mich. Children's Aid Soc., 1958-63, Greater Detroit Area Hosp. Council, 1964-73, United Found., 1969-72, Hutzel Hosp., 1968-72, New Detroit, 1970-73, Emmet County United Way, 1978—. Named Layman of Year, Detroit Council Chs., 1962. C.P.A., Mich. Mem. Am. Inst. C.P.A.'s, Mich. Assn. C.P.A.'s. Presbyterian. Clubs: Detroit Country, Detroit Athletic. Home: 117 Howard St Petoskey MI 49770

LITTLETON, HARVEY KLINE, artist; b. Corning, N.Y., June 14, 1922; s. Jesse Talbot and Bessie (Cook) L.; student U. Mich., 1939-42, B.Design, 1947; M.F.A., Cranbrook Acad. Art, 1951; m. Bess Toyo Tamura, Sept. 6, 1947; children—Carol Louise Littleton Shay, Thomas Harvey, Kathryn Tamra (dec.), Maurine Bess, John Christopher. Instr. ceramics Toledo Mus. Art, 1949-51; prof. art U. Wis., Madison, 1951-77, chmn. dept., 1964-67, 69-71, prof. emeritus, 1977—; recent one- and two-man exhbns. include: Lee Nordness Galleries, N.Y.C., 1969-70, Wright Art Center, Beloit, Wis., 1972, Maison de Culture, Liege, Belgium, 1974, J & L Lobmeyr, Vienna, 1974, Brooks Meml. Art Gallery, Memphis, 1975, Contemporary Art Glass Gallery, N.Y.C., 1977, 78, 79; represented in permanent collections: Victoria and Albert Mus., London, museums in Germany, Holland, Switzerland, Belgium, Austria and Czechoslovakia, also Met. Mus. Art, N.Y.C., Mus. Modern Art, N.Y.C., Corning Mus. of Glass, Toledo Mus. Art, Detroit Art Inst., Milw. Art Center, Smithsonian Instn., Washington, U. Mich., U. Ill., Ohio State U., U. Nebr., U. Ariz., numerous other pub. and pvt. collections. Mem. Sch. Bd. Joint Dist. 3, Verona, Wis., 1961-64. Served with Signal Corps, U.S. Army, 1942-45; ETO. Toledo Mus. Art research grantee, 1962; Louis Comfort Tiffany Found. grantee, 1970-71; Corning Glass Works grantee, 1974; U. Wis. research grantee, 1954, 57, 62, 73, 75; Nat. Endowment for Arts grantee, 1978-79. Fellow Am. Crafts Council (trustee 1957, 61-64, trustee emeritus); mem. Nat. Council for Edn. in Ceramic Arts (hon.), Glass Art Soc. (hon. life), Beta Theta Pi. Democrat. Author: Glass Blowing—A Search for Form, 1971. Home: Route 1 Box 843 Spruce Pine NC 28777

LITTLETON, ISAAC THOMAS, III, librarian; b. Hartsville, Tenn., Jan. 28, 1921; s. Isaac Thomas and Bessie (Lowe) L.; A.B., U. N.C., 1943; M.A., U. Tenn., 1950; M.S. in L.S., U. Ill., 1951, Ph.D., 1968; m. Dorothy Young, Aug. 12, 1949; children—Sally Lowe, Thomas Young, Elizabeth. Tng. officer VA, 1946-47, head circulation dept., 1951-53; asst. to librarian U. N.C. Library, 1953-58; with D.H. Hill Library, N.C. State U., Raleigh, 1959—, dir., 1967—; instr. Peabody Library Sch., summer 1958; cons. in field, 1959—. Served to lt. (j.g.) USNR, 1943-46. Council on Library Resources fellow, 1976-77. Mem. ALA, N.C. (2d v.p. 1972-74, exec. bd. 1974-78), Southeastern (treas. 1959-60, exec. bd. 1974-78) library assns., Spl. Libraries Assn., Assn. Southeastern Research Libraries (chmn. 1971-72), Southeastern Library Network (dir. 1973-74), Beta Phi Mu, Phi Kappa Phi. Author: Bibliographic Organization and Use of the Literature of Agricultural Economics, 1967; State Systems of Higher Education and Libraries, 1977. Editor: North Carolina Union List of Scientific Serials. 1965-67. Home: 4813 Brookhaven Dr Raleigh NC 27612

LITTLEWOOD, DOUGLAS BURDEN, business brokerage exec.; b. Buffalo, Sept. 24, 1922; s. Frank and G. Joan (Burden) L.; B.S. in Mech. Engring., Rensselaer Poly. Inst., 1945; M.B.A., Harvard, 1947; m. Jevene Hope Baker, July 2, 1949; children—Douglas Baker, Dean Houston, Laurie Lee. Sales engr. Otis Elevator Co., 1948-49; asst. to sec. Nat Gypsum Co., Buffalo, 1949-52, sec., 1952-67; investment banker Hornblower & Weeks, 1967-68; pres. Littlewood Assos., Inc., Valuvest, Inc., 1968—. Pres. Greater Niagara Frontier council Boy Scouts Am.; active Buffalo YMCA, United Fund. Bd. dirs., treas. Western N.Y. Traffic Safety Council; bd. dirs., chmn. adv. bd. Salvation Army, NCCJ; bd. dirs., v.p. N.E. region Boy Scouts Am., recipient Silver Beaver, 1965, Silver Antelope, 1978, Disting. Eagle, 1979. Served to lt. (j.g.) USNR, 1943-46. Mem. Buffalo Jr. (past dir., chmn. bd.), Buffalo chambers commerce, Am. Soc. Corporate Secs. Clubs: Buffalo City, Buffalo Canoe (past commodore), Saturn, Buffalo Country. Home: 22 Dawnbrook Ln Buffalo NY 14221 Office: 2204 Main Place Tower Buffalo NY 14202. *If you truly believe you are happy and successful then, and only then, you truly are.*

LITTLEWOOD, GEORGE, publisher, editor; b. Barrow-in-Furness, Eng., Feb. 3, 1917; s. George Francis and Jane Elizabeth (Wilkinson) L.; came to U.S., 1921, naturalized, 1943; student Columbia U. Sch. Gen. Studies, 1951-56; m. Evelyn Lucia Lindner, June 19, 1942; children—George Frederic, Deborah Mary. Mktg. dir. Indl. Press, Inc., N.Y.C., 1965-72; v.p. Gordon Publs.; pub. Metalworking Digest, Mining/Processing Equipment, Morristown, N.J., 1972—. Welfare dir. Kinnelon, N.J., 1965-71; v.p. Fayson Lakes Assn., 1960, 64; sec. Zoning Bd., Cresskill, N.J., 1953-56. Served with AUS, 1942-45. Republican. Presbyn. Home: 4 Heather Terr Kinnelon NJ 07405 Office: 20 Community Pl Morristown NJ 07960

LITTMAN, EARL, advt. and pub. relations co. exec.; b. N.Y.C., Jan. 29, 1927; B.S.A., N.Y. U., 1948; m. Natalie Jacobson, Dec. 21, 1948; children—Erica Littman Humphrey, Bonnie Littman Likover, Michael. With George N. Kahn Co., N.Y.C., 1948-50, Jones & Brown Inc., Pitts., 1950-55; pres., dir. advt. and pub. relations Goodwin, Dannenbaum, Littman & Wingfield, Inc., Houston, 1955—; dir. Benito Advt. Agy., Tampa, Fla. Trustee Tex. So. U. Found. Mem. Affiliated Advt. Agys. Internat. (past pres.). Home: 210 Pine Hollow Houston TX 77056 Office: 7676 Woodway Houston TX 77027

LITTMAN, HOWARD, educator; b. Bklyn., Apr. 22, 1927; s. Morris and Gertrude (Goldberg) L.; B.Chem.Engring., Cornell U., 1951; Ph.D., Yale, 1956; m. Arline F. Caruso, July 3, 1955; children—Susan Joy, Vicki Kim, Paul William. Asst., then asso. prof. Syracuse U., 1955-65; on leave to Brookhaven Nat. Lab., summer 1957, Argonne Nat. Lab., 1957-59; faculty Rensselaer Poly. Inst., Troy, N.Y., 1965—, prof. chem. engring., 1967—, chmn. faculty council, 1975-76; vis. prof. Imperial Coll., London, Eng., 1971-72; Fulbright lectr. U. Belgrade, Yugoslavia, 1972. A founder Onondaga Hill Free Library, 1961, trustee, 1961-65, pres., 1965; a founder Onondaga Library System, 1962, trustee, 1962-65, v.p., 1965; trustee Capital Dist. Library Council, 1969-75, pres., 1970, 73. Served with USN, 1945-46. IREX grantee U. Belgrade, summer 1973. Mem. Am. Inst. Chem. Engrs., Am. Chem. Soc., Sigma Xi. Contbr. articles to profl. jours. Home: 7 Tulip Tree Ln Schenectady NY 12309 Office: Rensselaer Poly Inst Troy NY 12181

LITTMAN, LYNNE, film dir.; b. N.Y.C., June 26, 1941; d. Carl and Yetta (Abler) L.; B.A., Sarah Lawrence Coll., 1962; student The Sorbonne, Paris, France, 1960-61; m. Taylor Hackford, May 7, 1977; 1 son, Alexander Littman; 1 stepson, Rio Hackford. Researcher for CBS News, 1965; asso. producer Nat. Ednl. TV, 1966-69; dir. NIMH film series on drug abuse UCLA Media Center, 1970; producer, dir. documentary films, news and public affairs series KCET Community TV So. Calif., 1971-77; dir. WNET Ind. Filmmakers Series, 1979; co-producer, dir. TV spl. Rick Nelson, It's All Right Now, 1978 films include: Number Our Days (Acad. award Best Documentary Short), 1977, Till Death Do Us Part (CPB award), 1976, In the Matter of Kenneth (Los Angeles Emmy award), 1974, Wanted: Operadoras (Los Angeles Emmy award), 1974, Women in Waiting, 1975. Recipient numerous awards, including Los Angeles Press Club award, 1977, San Francisco Internat. Film Festival award, 1977, Corp. for Public Broadcasting award, 1977, Los Angeles Emmy award, 1972, 73, 74, 77; Columbia/Dupont Journalism award, 1977; Ford Found. grantee, 1978. Mem. Writers Guild, AFTRA, Dirs. Guild Am., Women in Film.

LITTMAN, RICHARD ANTON, psychologist, educator; b. N.Y.C., May 8, 1919; s. Joseph and Sarah (Feinberg) L.; A.B., George Washington U., 1943; postgrad. Ind. U., 1943- 44; Ph.D., Ohio State U., 1948; m. Isabelle Cohen, Mar. 17, 1941; children—David, Barbara, Daniel, Rebecca. Faculty, U. Oreg., 1948—, prof. psychology, 1959—, chmn. dept., 1963-68, vice provost acad. planning and resources, 1971-73. Vis. scientist Nat. Inst. Mental Health, 1958-59. Sr. postdoctoral fellow NSF, U. Paris, 1966-67; sr. fellow Nat. Endowment for Humanities, 1973-74. Mem. Am., Western, psychol. assns., Soc. Research and Child Devel., Psychonomics Soc., Am. Assn. U. Profs., History Sci. Soc., Am. Philos. Assn., Sigma Xi. Contbr. articles to profl. jours. Home: 3625 Glen Oak Dr Eugene OR 97405 Office: Dept of Psychology University of Oreg Eugene OR 97403

LITTNER, NER, psychoanalyst; b. Toronto, Ont., Can., Nov. 17, 1915; s. Mayer and Emma (Dlugash) L.; B.A. in Biol. and Med. Scis., U. Toronto, 1937, A.D.A., 1939, M.D., 1940; m. Zelda Louise Friedman, June 30, 1947 (div. May 1966); 1 dau., Edith. Came to U.S., 1947, naturalized, 1952. Intern, St. Vincents Hosp., Los Angeles, 1940-41; resident White Meml. Hosp., Los Angeles, 1941-42, Chgo. State Hosp., 1947-49, Ill. Neuropsychiat. Inst., Chgo., 1948, Chgo. Municipal Ct. Psychiat. Inst., 1948, U. Ill. Hosps., Chgo., 1949; fellow Ill. Inst. Juvenile Research, Chgo., 1949-51, Chgo. Inst. Psychoanalysis, 1949-54; practice medicine specializing in psychiatry, psychoanalysis children and adults, Chgo., 1954—; faculty Chgo. Inst. Psychoanalysis, 1957—, supr., 1953—, lectr., 1953—, adv. com. child care course, 1955—, clin. asso. clinic, 1956—, dir. child therapy program, 1961—, dir. extension div., 1968-74; lectr. in psychiatry U. Ind. Sch. Social Work, 1952-54; clin. asst. prof. psychiatry U. Ill. Coll. Medicine, 1957-61; lectr. psychiatry U. Chgo. Sch. Social Service Adminstrn., 1958-61, 69-74, Smith Coll. Sch. Social Work, 1962-68; psychiat. cons. Chgo. Nursery and Half-Orphan Asylum, 1951-54, Jewish Childrens Bur., Chgo., 1953-56, 75-76, Cath. Youth Orgn. Child Guidance Clinic, Chgo., 1954, Ill. Childrens Home and Aid Soc. Chgo., 1954-68. Mem. Motion Picture Appeal Bd. Chgo., 1962—; mem. Gov. Ill. Adv. Council, 1970-72; tech. cons. group for Ill. activities White House Conf. Children and Youth, 1970; chmn. adv. com. child psychiatry services Ill. Dept. Mental Health, 1962-65, mem., 1965-68; parent and child center planning com. Chgo. Com. Urban Opportunity, 1969-70; mem. Ill. Mental Health Planning Bd., 1965-66; curriculum com. Council Social Work Edn., 1963-65; mem. Project Straight Dope, 1970-71; v.p. Citizens Com. for Battered Children, 1973-77. Adv. com. Ill. div. Am. Civil Liberties Union, 1968—. Bd. dirs. Hull House's Jane Addams Center, 1965-69, Big Bros. Assn. Chgo., 1966—, Mary Meyer Sch., 1966-69. Served to maj. M.C., Canadian Army, 1942-46. Recipient Edith L. Lauer award Child Welfare League Am., 1959. Diplomate Am. Bd. Psychiatry and Neurology. Mem. Mental Health Soc. Greater Chgo. (chmn. com. unmet needs), Am. Psychiat. Assn. (chmn. com. psychiat. social work), Chgo. Council Child Psychiatry (chmn. legislative com., pres. 1966-67), Ill. Psychiat. Soc. (chmn. com. psychiat. social work, mem. legislative com.), Am. Psychoanalytic Assn. (chmn. com. on extension divs., mem. com. on affiliated socs.), Chgo. Psychoanalytic Soc. (mem. membership, edn. coms.), Am. Orthopsychiat. Assn., Acad. Child Psychiatry (cons. on adolescence, on by-laws), A.M.A., Ill., Chgo. med. socs., Am. Assn. Child Psychoanalysis. Lectr. in field. Contbr. articles to profl. jours. Research field childrens psychosomatic illnesses. Home: 155 Harbor Dr Chicago IL 60601 Office: 180 N Michigan Ave Chicago IL 60601

LITTON, WILLARD WARREN, mfg. co. exec.; b. Cambridge, Ill., Sept. 14, 1920; s. Merle Wells and Natalia (Zatterberg) L.; B.S. in Indsl. Engring., Washington U., St. Louis, 1951; M.B.A., U. So. Calif., 1962; m. Betty Jean Ewing, May 24, 1947; children—Vicki Jo, Wendy Gay. Division accountant Interpace Co., Los Angeles, 1954-56; with Whittaker Corp., Los Angeles, 1956-68, 72—, div. controller, 1960-68, adminstr., 1972-75, div. v.p., 1975—; treas. Tasker

Industries, Los Angeles, 1968-72; dir., sec. Valencia Highlands, Inc., 1965—. Served to 1st lt. USAAF, 1943-47. Registered profl. engr., Calif. Mem. Am. Inst. Indsl. Engrs., Disabled Officers Assn., Sigma Xi, Tau Beta Pi, Pi Mu Epsilon, Alpha Pi Mu, Sigma Phi Epsilon. Home: 18161 Ludlow St Northridge CA 91326 Office: 22116 Soledad Canyon Rd Saugus CA 91350

LITZ, ARTHUR WALTON, JR., educator; b. Nashville, Oct. 31, 1929; s. Arthur Walton and Lucile (Courtney) L.; A.B., Princeton, 1951; D.Phil. (Rhodes scholar), Oxford (Eng.) U., 1954; m. Marian Ann Weller, Feb. 2, 1958; children—Katharine, Andrew, Victoria, Emily. Instr., Princeton, 1956-58; lectr. Columbia, 1957-58; mem. faculty Princeton, 1958—, prof. English lit., 1968—, chmn. English dept., 1974—. Vis. prof. Bryn Mawr Coll., Swarthmore Coll., Temple U.; mem. editorial bd. Princeton U. Press, 1967-71. Served with AUS, 1954-56. Fellow Am. Council Learned Socs., 1960-61; sr. fellow Nat. Endowment for Humanities, 1974-75. Recipient E. Harris Harbison award for gifted teaching, 1972. Author: The Art of James Joyce, 1961; Modern American Fiction: Essays in Criticism, 1963; Jane Austen, 1965; James Joyce, 1966; James Joyce's Dubliners, 1969; The Poetic Development of Wallace Stevens, 1972; Eliot in His Time, 1973; Major American Short Stories, 1975; Scribner Quarto of Modern Literature, 1977. Home: 187 Prospect St Princeton NJ 08540

LITZINGER, BOYD, educator; b. Johnstown, Pa., Apr. 2, 1929; s. B. A. and Sara (Ignoffo) L.; student St. Francis Coll. (Pa.), 1947-49; B.A., U. S.C., 1951, M.A., 1952; Ph.D., U. Tenn., 1956; m. Maria Antonia Letro, June 10, 1961; children—Michael Boyd, Gretchen Maria. Instr. English, Tex. Technol. Coll., 1956-57; asst. prof. U. S.C., 1957-59; asst. prof. St. Bonaventure (N.Y.) U., 1959, asso. prof., 1960-65, prof., 1965—, asst. dean., 1967-69, dean arts and scis., 1969-74; vis. prof. U. Tenn., 1961-62, U. Wis., summer 1965. Mem. AAUP (charter pres. 1965-66), Modern Lang. Assn., New Eng. Modern Lang. Assn., N.E. Regional Assn. Acad. Adminstrs. (sec.-treas. 1967-68), Delta Sigma Phi, Delta Epsilon Sigma (v.p. 1968-70, pres. 1971-74, exec. com. 1974—). Roman Catholic. Author: Time's Revenges, 1964; (with K.L. Knickerbocker) The Browning Critics, 1965; (with D. Smalley) Browning: The Critical Heritage, 1970; Robert Browning's Letters to the Lehmanns, 1975; (novel) Watch It, Dr. Adrian, 1977. Mem. editorial bd. Victorian Poetry, 1963—, Cithara, 1960—, Studies in Browning and His Circle. Contbr. articles to profl. jours. Home: 214 White Oak Dr Allegany NY 14706 Office: St Bonaventure U St Bonaventure NY 14778

LITZSINGER, PAUL RICHARD, pub. co. exec.; b. Clayton, Mo., Jan. 8, 1932; s. Melvin Paul and Catherine (Mooney) L.; B.S., U. Mo., 1954; m. Dona Lucy Follett, July 10, 1954; children—Mark, Robin, Heidi, Shawn, Todd. With Follett Corp., Chgo., 1957—, retail stores supr., 1962-66, pres. retail stores div., 1966-76, pres. corp., 1977—. Area dir. United Crusade; bd. dirs. Hinsdale Community House. Served With USAF, 1954-57. Mem. Nat. Assn. Coll. Stores (dir., 1971-73), Nat. Assn. Colls. Stores Corp. (pres. 1974-75, trustee), Am. Assn. Pubs., Fla. Assn. Coll. Stores, Nat. Assn. Aux. Enterprise Dirs., Nat. Assn. Bus. Mgrs., Nat. Assn. Coll. and Univ. Bus. Officers, Nat. Assn. Jr. Colls. Presbyterian. Clubs: Knollwood Golf, Oak Park Racquet. Home: 1650 Greenbay Rd Lake Bluff IL 60044 Office: 1000 W Washington Blvd Chicago IL 60607

LIU, BEDE, elec. engr.; b. Shanghai, China, Sept. 25, 1934; s. Henry and Shan (Yao) L.; came to U.S., 1954, naturalized, 1960; B.S. in Elec. Engring., Nat. Taiwan U., 1954; M.E.E., Poly. Inst. Bklyn., 1956, D.E.E., 1960; m. Maria Agatha Sang, Jan. 31, 1959; 1 dau., Beatrice Agatha. Equipment engr. Western Electric Co., N.Y.C., 1954-56; intermediate engr. A.B. DuMont Lab., Clifton, N.J., summer 1956; mem. tech. staff Bell Telephone Labs., Murray Hill, N.J., 1959-62, summers 1957, 58, 66; mem. faculty Princeton U., 1962—, prof. elec. engring., 1969—; vis. prof. Nat. Taiwan U., 1970-71, U. Calif., Berkeley, 1971. Fellow IEEE. Co-author: Digital Signal Processing, 1976. Editor: Digital Filters and the Fast Fourier Transform, 1975. Home: 248 Hartley Ave Princeton NJ 08540 Office: Dept Elec Engring Princeton Univ Princeton NJ 08540

LIU, BEN-CHIEH, economist; b. Chungking, China, Nov. 17, 1938; s. Pei-juang and Chung-su L.; came to U.S., 1965, naturalized, 1973; B.A., Nat. Taiwan U., 1961; M.A., Meml. U. Nfld., 1965; M.A., Washington U., St. Louis, 1968, Ph.D., 1971; m. Jill Jyh-huey, Oct. 2, 1965; children—Tina Won-ting, Roger Won-jung, Milton Won-ming. Economist, Chinese Air Force and Central Customs, Taiwan, 1961-63; resource economist Canadian Land Inventory and Forest Services, Nfld., 1963-65; research project dir. St. Louis Regional Indsl. Devel. Corp., 1968-72; prin. econs. Midwest Research Inst., Kansas City, Mo., 1972—; vis. prof. econs. U. Mo., 1970—; cons. UN, NSF. Recipient research study award Am. Indsl. Devel. Council, 1969. U.S. Econ. Devel. Adminstrn. fellow, 1967-68; Korean Govt. scholar, 1962-63, World U. Services scholar, 1963-65. Fellow Am. Statis. Assn. (com. mem.); mem. Am. Econ. Assn., Econometric Soc., Royal Econ. Soc., Internat. Statis. Instn., Assn. for Social Econs. (com. mem.), Tax Inst. Am. Author: Interindustrial Structure Analysis: An Input-Output Study for St. Louis Region, 1968; The Quality of Life in the United States, 1970; Rating, Index and Statistics, 1973; Quality of Life Indicators in U.S. Metropolitan Areas, 1975; Physical and Economic Damage Functions for Air Pollutants by Receptors, 1976; mem. editorial bd. Am. Jour. Econs. and Sociology, Internat. Jour. Math. Social Sci.; contbr. articles to profl. jours. Home: 10500 W 53d St Shawnee KS 66203 Office: 425 Volker Blvd Kansas City MO 64110. *The joy of living may temporarily rest on present or past glory, but it is the immersion in planning for the future—the living ahead of one's time—which ensures permanently the flourishing of the joy of life. In a commonwealth society, happiness does not come from doing what we like to do, but from liking what we have to do!*

LIU, BENJAMIN YOUNG-HWAI, educator; b. Shanghai, China, Aug. 15, 1934; s. Wilson Wan-su and Dorothy Pao-ning (Cheng) L.; student Nat. Taiwan U., 1951-54; B.S. in Mech. Engring., U. Nebr., 1956; Ph.D., U. Minn., 1960; m. Helen Hai-ling Cheng, June 14, 1958; 1 son, Lawrence A.S. Asso. engr. Honeywell Co., Mpls., 1956; research asst., instr. U. Minn., 1956-60, asst. prof., 1960-67, asso. prof., 1967-69, prof., 1969—. Dir. Particle Tech. Lab., 1973—; vis. prof. U. Paris, 1968-69. Guggenheim fellow, 1968-69. Mem. ASME, Am. Soc. Heating, Refrigeration and Air Conditioning Engrs., Solar Energy Soc., Am. Soc. Engring. Edn., Air Pollution Control Assn., Chinese Am. Assn. Minn. (pres. 1971-72). Unitarian. Contbg. author: Aerosol Science, 1966. Editor: Fine Particles, 1976; Application of Solar Energy for Heating and Cooling Buildings, 1977. Contbr. articles to Ency. Chem. Tech. Patentee in field. Home: 1 N Deep Lake Rd St Paul MN 55110

LIU, JAMES JO-YÜ, educator; b. Peking, China, Apr. 14, 1926; s. Yu-hsin and Pao-ling (Yen) L.; B.A., Fu Jen U. (China), 1948; postgrad. Tsing Hua U. (China), 1948, Oxford U. (Eng.), 1950-51; M.A., U. Bristol (Eng.), 1952; m. Claire Magdalen Morris, Nov. 30, 1957 (div. 1974); 1 dau., Sarah Meiwen. Came to U.S., 1961, naturalized, 1974. Lectr. Chinese, London (Eng.) U., 1951-56; lectr. Hong Kong U., 1956-59; asso. prof. English, New Asia Coll., Hong Kong, 1959-61; asst. prof. Chinese, U. Hawaii, Honolulu, 1961-64; vis. asso. prof. U. Pitts., 1964-65; asso. prof. U.Chgo., 1965-67; prof. Chinese, Stanford, 1967—, courtesy prof. comparative lit., 1977—, chmn. dept. Asian langs., 1969-75. External examiner to U. Bristol, 1953, U. London, 1958, Chinese U. Hong Kong, 1968-69; cons. Nat. Endowment for Humanities, 1973—, dir. Summer Seminar for Coll. Tchrs., 1976; mem. adv. screening com. in Chinese studies Council Internat. Exchange of Scholars, 1974-77. Guggenheim fellow, 1971; Am. Council Learned Socs. grantee, 1972; Nat. Endowment for Humanities fellow, 1978-79. Mem. Assn. Asian Studies, Am. Oriental Soc. Author: The Art of Chinese Poetry, 1962; The Chinese Knight Errant, 1967; The Poetry of Li Shang-yin, 1969; Major Lyricists of the Northern Sung, 1974; Chinese Theories of Literature, 1975; Essentials of Chinese Literary Art, 1979, others. Editor: Jour. Hong Kong br. Royal Asiatic Soc., 1960-61. Home: 914 Mears Ct Stanford CA 94305

LIU VI-CHENG, educator; b. Wu-ching, China, Sept. 1, 1917; s. Bi-Ching and Shu-Fung (Keng) L.; B.S., Chiao Tung U., 1940; M.S., U. Mich., 1947, Ph.D., 1951; m. Hsi-Yen Wang, Mar. 1, 1947. Came to U.S., 1946, naturalized, 1973. Instr., Tsing-Hua U., Kunming, 1940-46; research engr. Engring. Research Inst., U. Mich., Ann Arbor, 1951-59, prof. aerospace engring., 1959—; cons. NASA, 1964-65. Ministry of Edn. China research fellow, 1946-49; NASA research grantee, 1964—. Research in rarefied gas dynamics, ionospheric physics, space physics. Home: 2104 Vinewood Blvd Ann Arbor MI 48104

LIVE, ISRAEL, microbiologist, educator; b. Zakrzewce, Austria, Apr. 26, 1907; s. Herman and Rose (Nagelberg) L.; V.M.D., U. Pa., 1934, A.M., 1936, Ph.D., 1940; m. Anna Harris, Nov. 25, 1936; children—Theodore Ross, David Harris. Came to U.S., 1928, naturalized, 1934. Faculty U. Pa., 1934—, successively asst. pathology, instr., asso., asst. prof., asst. prof. bacteriology, asso. prof., 1934-53, prof. microbiology, 1953—, chmn. dept., 1953-64; expert for com. on brucellosis WHO, UN; mem. com. on brucellosis research Nat. Acad. Scis.-NRC. Diplomate Am. Bd. Microbiology. Fellow Am. Coll. Vet. Microbioloby (charter), A.A.A.S., Am. Acad. Microbiology; mem. AVMA, Soc. Am. Bacteriologists, Am. Pub. Health Orgn., Am. Assn. Immunologists, U.S. Livestock San. Assn., Assn. Research Workers Animal Diseases in N. Am., World Assn. Vet. Microbiologists, Immunologists and Specialists in Infectious Diseases. Contbr. to The Staphylococci, 1972. Home: 2414 Bryn Mawr Ave Philadelphia PA 19131

LIVELY, EDWIN LOWE, educator; b. Fairmont, W.Va., Aug. 14, 1920; s. E.L. and Lucy (Ross) L.; A.B. in Edn., Fairmont State Coll., 1940; M.A. in Sociology, Ohio State U., 1946, Ph.D., 1959; m. Virginia Isabelle Reed, Aug. 25, 1940; children—Lynellen, Gerianne (Mrs. Michael Green), Edwin L. II. Tchr. high sch., Farmington, W.Va., 1940-42; instr. Kent State U., 1947-53, asst. prof., 1953-58, asso. prof., 1958-63; prof. sociology, chmn. dept. Akron U., 1963-68, dean grad. studies and research, 1968-75, prof., 1975-78; lectr. Labor and Edn. Service, Ohio State U., 1966-68; cons. Ohio Youth Commn., Akron Urban Renewal, Akron Community Action Council, Akron Community Relations Commn., Canton (Ohio) Bd. Edn. Pres., Greater Akron Area Council Alcoholism, 1969-71; chmn. Akron Commn. Civil Disorders, 1968-69; pres. United Community Council, 1972-74; bd. dirs. Goals for Greater Akron Area, 1974—. Served with USAAF, 1942-45. Decorated Air medal with five oak leaf clusters. Swift fellow, 1963; grantee Esso Edn. Found., 1966, div. adult and vocational research Dept. Health, Edn. and Welfare, 1967, Ohio Bd. Regents, 1967, Ohio Dept. Health, 1968. Fellow Am. Sociol. Assn.; mem. Ohio Valley Sociol. Soc. (bd. dirs. 1964-68), Nat. Council Family Relations, Summit County Mental Health Assn. (pres. 1965-67). Mason. Contbg. editor Dynamic Urban Sociology, 1954; guest editor Sociol. Focus, 1970. Home: 5540 Tamberlane 216 Palm Beach Gardens FL 33410

LIVELY, MICHAEL ERIC, financial co. exec.; b. Seattle, Nov. 13, 1923; s. Daniel O'Connor and Erna (Lazda) L.; B.B.A., So. Meth. U., 1949; m. Sheila Sanders, Feb. 17, 1973; children—Sarah, Jennifer. With Am. Express Co., 1949—, gen. mgr. credit card div., 1958-61, v.p., Switzerland, 1962-65, sr. v.p., then pres. Travelers Cheque div., N.Y.C., 1966—. Served to capt. AUS, 1942-46. Home: Buckfield Ln Greenwich CT 06830 Office: Am Express Plaza New York City NY 10004

LIVELY, PIERCE, fed. judge; b. Louisville, Aug. 17, 1921; s. Henry Thad and Ruby Durrett (Keating) L.; A.B., Centre Coll., Ky., 1943; LL.B., U. Va., 1948; m. Amelia Harrington, May 25, 1946; children—Susan, Katherine, Thad. Admitted to Ky. bar, 1948; individual practice law, Danville, Ky., 1949-57; mem. firm Lively and Rodes, Danville, 1957-72; U.S. Circuit Ct. judge 6th Circuit Ct., Appeals, Cin., 1972—. Mem. Ky. Commn. on Economy and Efficiency in Govt., 1963-65, Ky. Jud. Advisory Com., 1972. Trustee Centre Coll. Served with USNR, 1943-46. Mem. Am. Bar Assn., Am. Judicature Soc., Order of Coif, Raven Soc., Phi Beta Kappa, Omicron Delta Kappa. Presbyterian. Formerly mem. editorial bd. Va. Law Rev. Home: 530 Dogwood Dr Danville KY 40422 Office: Fed Bldg Danville KY 40422 also Room 812 US Courthouse Cincinnati OH 45202

LIVERMORE, JOSEPH MCMASTER, lawyer, univ. dean; b. Portland, Oreg., Feb. 5, 1937; s. Ernest R. and Frances (McMaster) L.; A.B., Dartmouth, 1958; LL.B., Stanford, 1961; m. Elaine Dufort, Mar. 18, 1966; 1 son, Caleb. Admitted to Calif. bar, 1962, Minn. bar, 1968, Ariz. bar, 1974; asso. firm Brobeck, Phleger & Harrison, San Francisco, 1961, 64-65; prof. law U. Minn., Mpls., 1965-73; asst. U.S. atty., Mpls., 1971-72; dean Coll. Law, U. Ariz., Tucson, 1973-77, prof. law, 1977—. Served with JAG Corps, AUS, 1962-63. Mem. Ariz., Minn., Am. bar assns., State Bar Calif., Order of Coif, Phi Beta Kappa. Home: 2216 E 5th St Tucson AZ 85719 Office: U of Ariz Coll of Law Tucson AZ 85721

LIVERSAGE, RICHARD ALBERT, zoologist, educator; b. Fitchburg, Mass., July 8, 1925; s. Rodney Marcellus and Hazel Mildred (Huntting) L.; B.A., Marlboro Coll., 1951; A.M., Amherst Coll., 1953; A.M., Princeton, 1957, Ph.D., 1958; m. June Patricia Krebs, June 19, 1954; children—John Walter, Robert Richard, James Keith, Ross Andrew. Fellow Bowdoin Coll., Brunswick, Maine, 1953-54; instr. Amherst Coll., 1954-55, Princeton, 1958-60; mem. faculty U. Toronto, 1960—, prof. zoology, 1969—, grad. sec. dept., 1975-77, asso. chmn. grad. affairs dept., 1978—. Investigator, Huntsman Marine Lab., St. Andrews, N.B., Can., 1968—. Served as flight engr. USAAF, 1943-45. Decorated. Mem. Am. Soc. Zoologists, Soc. Devel. Biology, Can. Soc. Zoologists, Royal Canadian Inst. Author research publns. in vivo and in vitro studies on role of nerves and endocrine secretions in amphibian and fish appendage regeneration. Home: 30 Almond Ave Thornhill ON L3T 1L1 Canada Office: Ramsay Wright Zool Lab Univ Toronto Toronto ON M5S 1A1 Canada

LIVESAY, JACKSON EDWARD, ret. radiologist, educator; b. Mont., Jan. 13, 1914; s. David Edward and Harriet (Craig) L.; B.A., Cornell Coll., Mt. Vernon, Ia., 1935; M.D., U. Ia., 1938; m. Jean Elizabeth Anderson, June 29, 1940; children—Richard Wyman, Lois Ellen, Donald Edward, Charles Jackson. Intern, then resident Hurley Hosp., Flint, Mich., 1938-40; fellow radiology Jefferson Hosp., Phila., 1940-42; pvt. practice, Flint, 1943—; chief staff St. Joseph Hosp., Flint, 1961-79, chief radiology, 1952-79; asso. clin. prof. Coll. Human Medicine, Mich. State U.; cons. radiologist Buick and A.C. Spark Plug Indsl. Hosps. Fellow Am. Coll. Radiology (pres. 1966-67); mem. A.M.A., Mich. Med. Soc. (Pres.'s award 1966), Radiol. Soc. N. Am., Am., Detroit (pres.) Roentgen ray socs. Home: 702 Blanchard Dr Flint MI 48503

LIVEZEY, WILLIAM EDMUND, historian, educator; b. Barnesville, Ohio, Aug. 11, 1903; s. Charles and Elizabeth (Smith) L.; A.B., Earlham Coll., 1927; M.A., Haverford Coll., 1928; certificate L'Institut Universitaire de Hautes Etudes Internationales, Geneva, Switzerland, 1930-31; Ph.D., Ohio State U., 1937; m. Martha Ann Taylor, June 24, 1935; children—Kathleen Ann, Wilberta Mae, Elnora Beth, Lorinda Sue. Tchr. Friends Boarding Sch., Barnesville, Ohio, 1928-30, 31-34; grad. asst. Ohio State U., 1936-37; faculty dept. history U. Okla., 1937—, prof., 1950—, acting chmn. dept. history, 1953, acting dean Coll. Arts and Scis., 1953-54, dean, 1954-65, dean emeritus, 1965—, Regents prof., 1965-73, emeritus, 1973—. Biddle traveling fellow, Europe, 1930-31; fellow Fund for Advancement Edn., 1951-52. Recipient John H. Dunning award Am. Hist. Assn., 1948. Mem. Phi Beta Kappa. Presbyn. Author: Mahan on Sea Power, 1947; (with Garel A. Grunder) The Philippines and the United States, 1951. Home: 630 S Lahoma Norman OK 73069

LIVICK, MALCOLM HARRIS, sch. adminstr.; b. Staunton, Va., Apr. 5, 1929; s. Arthur Crawford and Sallie (Harris) L.; student Hampden Sydney Coll., 1947-48; B.S., U. Va., 1951; M.Ed., Madison Coll., 1965; m. Linda Moorman Roller, July 21, 1956; children—Malcolm Harris, Charles Roller, Linda Lee, Todd Stephenson, Taylor Crawford. Instr., coach Augusta Mil. Acad., 1955-56; instr. Norfolk (Va.) pub. schs., 1956-57; underwriter Mutual of N.Y., Norfolk, 1957-58; coach, asst. prin. Augusta Mil. Acad., Fort Defiance, Va., 1958-66, supt., 1966—; Dir. First Commonwealth Corp. Chmn., Upper Valley Regional Park Authority, 1969-78. Trustee King's Daus. Hosp., Staunton, Massanetta Springs. Served with USAF, 1951-55. Mem. Va. Mil. Schs. League (pres. 1966-68), Va. Assn. Prep. Schs. (exec. com. 1967—, pres. 1971-72), Nat., Va. assns. secondary sch. prins. Presbyn. (deacon 1963-65, elder 1965—). Kiwanian (pres. 1970-71, lt. gov. elect 1971, gov. 1979—). Address: Augusta Mil Acad PO Box 100 Fort Defiance VA 24437

LIVIDINI, XAVIER SAVERIO, hotel exec.; b. Detroit, Aug. 8, 1929; s. Aurelio and Zelia Lividini; B.S. in Bus. Mgmt., Fordham U., 1951; grad. Arden House Advancemen Mgmt. course, Columbia U., 1966; m. Diana Lusardi, Nov. 14, 1954; children—Debra, Xavier, Jacqueline. Room clk., conv. mgr. Statler Hilton Hotel, N.Y.C., 1953-59; dir. sales and catering Biltmore Hotel, N.Y.C., 1959-61; gen. sales mgr. N.Y. Hilton Hotel, 1961-65; dir. sales Waldorf Astoria Hotel, N.Y.C., 1965-69; asst. v.p., dir. sales Eastern div. sales Hilton Hotels Corp., 1969-71; gen. mgr. Hotel New Yorker, 1971-72; mgr. Statler Hilton Hotel, N.Y.C., 1972-73; gen. mgr. Flamingo Hotel, Las Vegas, 1973-74; v.p., gen. mgr. Statler Hilton Hotel, 1974—, also asst. v.p. Hilton Hotels Corp. Served with USMCR, 1951-53; Korea. Mem. Am. (dir. Nev. chpt. 1973-74), N.Y. State hotel-motel assns., N.Y.C. Hotel Assn., N.Y.C. Conv. and Visitors Bur. (dir.), N.Y.C. Hotel Sales Mgmt. Assn. (past pres.), Internat. Hotel Sales Assn. (bd. govs. 1969-73). Roman Catholic. Home: 401 7th Ave New York City NY 10001 Office: Statler Hilton 401 7th Ave New York City NY 10001

LIVINGOOD, CLARENCE S., dermatologist; b. Elverson, Pa., Aug. 7, 1911; s. Clarence A. and Eliza (Zerr) L.; B.S., Ursinus Coll., 1932; M.D., U. Pa., 1936; m. Louise Sinclair Woelpper, Oct. 24, 1947; children—Wilson, Louise S., Clarence, Susan, Elizabeth. Intern, then resident dermatology Hosp. U. Pa., 1936-41; asst. prof. dermatology U. Pa. Med. Sch., 1946-48, Grad. Sch., 1946-49; chief dermatology Children's Hosp. Pa., 1946-48; prof., chmn. dept. dermatology Jefferson Med. Sch., Phila., 1948-49; prof., chmn. dept. dermatology U. Tex. Sch. Medicine, 1949-53; chmn. dermatology dept. Henry Ford Hosp., Detroit, 1953-76, chmn. emeritus, 1976—; team physician Detroit Tigers baseball club; clin. prof. dermatology U. Mich. Sch. Medicine; mem. com. on cut. diseases AFEB, 1956-72; chief cons. dermatology VA, 1953-59. Sec.-gen. XII Internat. Congress of Dermatology, 1962; exec. com. Am. Bd. Med. Specialties, 1974-76; mem. AMA residency rev. com. for dermatology, 1957-67; adv. com. Nat. Disease and Therapeutic Index, 1974—; bd. dirs., treas. Council Med. Splty. Socs., 1976—, mem. liaison com. on grad. med. edn., 1978—. Trustee Dermatology Found., 1965-71, ECFMG, 1975—. Served to lt. col. M.C., AUS, 1942-46. Decorated Bronze Star, Legion of Merit. Diplomate Am. Bd. Dermatology (exec. dir. 1968—). Fellow Am. Acad. Dermatology (dir., past pres.; Gold medal 1975), A.C.P.; mem. AMA (ho. of dels., chmn. sect. dermatology 1958), Soc. Investigative Dermatology (past pres.), Am. Dermatol. Assn. (past pres., dir. 1964-68), Coll. Physicians Phila., Pacific (hon.), Phila., Detroit (past pres.) dermatol. socs., Mich. Med. Soc. (jud. council, ho. dels. 1974—), Med. Cons. Soc. World War II, Assn. Mil. Dermatologists, Detroit Acad. Medicine, Assn. Maj. League Team Physicians, Assn. Dermatology Argentina (corr.), N.Y. Acad. Scis. (internat. congress dermatology); hon. mem. Danish Soc., Indian Assn. Dermatologists, Brit., Yugoslavian, Israel dermatol. socs. Clubs: Grosse Pointe; Witenagemote; Detroit Boat. Author: (with D.M. Pillsbury, M.B. Sulzberger) Manual of Dermatology; editorial bd. AMA Archives of Dermatology, Excerpta Medica, Conn's Current Therapy, Jour. Geriatrics; contbr. articles to med. jours. Home: 345 University Pl Grosse Pointe MI 48230 Office: Henry Ford Hosp Detroit MI 48202

LIVINGSTON, ALAN W., former entertainment co. exec.; b. McDonald, Pa.; s. Maurice and Rose (Wachtel) L.; B.S., Wharton Sch. U. Pa., 1940; m. Elaine Osterweil, Oct. 23, 1943; children—Peter, Laurie; m. 2d, Nancy Olson, Sept. 1, 1962; 1 son, Christopher. Exec. v.p. charge artists and repertoire Capitol Records, Inc., 1946-56, pres., 1960-68, chmn. bd., 1968; pres. Capitol Industries, 1968; pres., chmn. Mediarts, Inc., 1969-76; pres. entertainment group 20th Century-Fox Film Corp., Beverly Hills, Calif., 1976-79; v.p. NBC, 1956-60; dir. Bob Hope Enterprises, Figaro, Inc., Elec. & Mus. Industries, Ltd. Britain, Technicolor, Inc. Mem. A.S.C.A.P., Acad. Motion Picture Arts and Scis., Acad. TV Arts and Scis., Record Industry Assn. Am. (dir.). Home: 945 N Alpine Dr Beverly Hills CA 90210

LIVINGSTON, BOYNTON PARKER, lawyer; b. Washington, Mar. 15, 1913; s. Ozias Boynton and Bertha (Parker) L.; student U. Va., 1936; J.D., George Washington U., 1940; m. Katherine Fenwick, Feb. 14, 1942; 1 son, Boynton Parker. Admitted to D.C. bar, 1940; atty., D.C., 1940-42; mem. firm Mason, Fenwick & Lawrence, Washington, 1946—, sr. partner, 1956—. Mem. Bar Assn. D.C. (bd. dirs. 1962-63, chmn. patent, trademark and copywright sect. 1962-63), Am. Bar Assn. (chmn. trademark div. 1960-61), Am. Patent Law Assn. (sec. 1956-58, bd. mgrs. 1961-63), Judge Advs. Assn. (chmn. patent and trademark com. 1950-61), Inter-Am. Bar Assn. Rotarian. Clubs: Washington Golf and Country, Internat. (Washington); Farmington (Va.) Country. Home: 2300 N Quantico St Arlington VA 22205 Office: 1730 Rhode Island Ave NW Washington DC 20036

LIVINGSTON, DAVID GLENN, banker; b. Van Wert, Ohio, Oct. 28, 1933; s. Glenn Herbert and Helen Ida (Gilliland) L.; A.B. in Econs., U. Mich., 1956, M.B.A., 1956; m. Joyce Bricker, Aug. 28, 1955; children—Laura Ann, Linda Joy, David B., Douglas G. Sr.

credit analyst, adminstrv. asst. No. Trust Co., Chgo., 1956-59; br. adminstrn. and credit supr. United Calif. Bank, San Francisco, 1959-62; asst. v.p. Bank of N.Mex., Albuquerque, 1962, v.p., 1962-65, sr. v.p., 1965-68, exec. v.p., 1968-70; chmn. bd. First Nat. Bank Albuquerque, 1970-75; pres. David Livingston & Assos., Inc., 1975—, N.Mex.-Pacific Investment Corp., 1979—. Hon. dir. Chaparral council Girl Scouts U.S.A., 1970—; bd. dirs. Albuquerque YMCA (also pres.); trustee Albuquerque Acad. Mem. Kappa Sigma. Presbyn. Clubs: Albuquerque Country, Petroleum, Tennis (Albuquerque). Home: 1730 Lafayette Dr NE Albuquerque NM 87106 Office: Rio Grande Valley Bank Bldg Suite 205 501 Trjeras NW PO Box 25803 Albuquerque NM 87102

LIVINGSTON, ELLIS N., educator; b. Iberia, Mo., Nov. 27, 1920; s. Frank P. and Ethel (Waite) L.; A.A., Iberia Jr. Coll., 1940; B.A., Knox Coll., 1942; Ph.D., U. Minn., 1953; m. Edith Nixdorf, Feb. 16, 1946; children—Lydia J. Livingston Walters, Franklin E., Mary R. Livingston Retsinas, Thomas W., Anthony J., Martha. Mem. faculty history dept. U. Minn., Duluth, 1949—, prof. Am. history, 1963—. Served as officer USMCR, 1942-45. Decorated Bronze Star. Mem. Orgn. Am. Historians, NAACP, Phi Beta Kappa, Phi Alpha Theta. Democrat. Mem. United Ch. of Christ. Home: 2431 E 6th St Duluth MN 55812

LIVINGSTON, FREDERICK RICHARD, lawyer; b. Newark, Nov. 26, 1912; s. Charles L. and Lillian (Gika) L.; LL.B., Rutgers U., 1936; m. Gertrude B. Sonn, Jan. 1, 1938; 1 dau., Lucie. Admitted to N.J. bar, 1937, N.Y. bar, 1949; atty., trial examiner NLRB, 1939-43; spl. rep. to U.S. sec. labor, 1945-47; sr. partner firm Kaye, Scholer, Fierman, Hays & Handler, N.Y.C., 1947—; adj. prof. Grad. Sch. Bus., Columbia U.; mem. Presdl. Adv. Com. Fed. Pay; chmn. Presdl. Emergency Bd. Ry. Labor Act; cons., spl. mediator labor-ry. disputes; mem. Armour Automation Com. lectr. in field. Trustee Com. Young Audiences; bd. dirs., mem. exec. com. Work in Am. Inst. Recipient award merit Dept. Labor, 1972. Mem. Am., Fed., N.Y. State bar assns., Assn. Bar City N.Y., Nat. Acad. Arbitrators, Am. Arbitration Assn. (mem. exec. com.), Indsl. Relations Research Assn. (counsel). Home: 1016 Fifth Ave New York NY 10028 Office: 425 Park Ave New York NY 10022

LIVINGSTON, J. A., economist; b. N.Y.C., Feb. 10, 1905; s. Solomon Joseph and Maud (Stern) L.; A.B., U. Mich., 1925; Litt.D., Temple U., 1966; m. Rosalie L. Frenger, Sept. 16, 1927; 1 dau., Patricia (Mrs. Mathew Herban III). Newspaper reporter, 1925-30; exec. editor N.Y. Daily Investment News, 1931-34; pub. utility editor Financial World, 1935; economist Bus. Week, 1935-42, W.P.B. and Office War Moblzn. and Reconversion, 1942-45; began column Bus. Outlook, now syndicated U.S., Can., 1945; financial editor Phila. Record, 1946; bus. columnist Washington Post, 1947; financial editor Phila. Bull., 1948-67; econ. columnist Phila. Bull., 1968-72, Phila. Inquirer, 1972—. Broadcaster, WCAU radio sta., Phila., 1962-64; prof. econs. Temple U., 1971-72. Mem. intensive review com. sec. commerce to analyze program U.S. Bur. Census. Recipient Loeb Mag. award, 1958; Loeb Newspaper award, 1960, 71, 76; citation for excellence in Journalism Temple U., 1960; best bus. reporting from abroad award Overseas Press Club, 1962, 65, 75; Pulitzer prize for internat. reporting, 1965; Merit award Poor Richard Club, 1965; INGAA-U. Mo. Journalism awards, 1966, 67, 68; Outstanding Achievement award U. Mich., 1964, Sesquicentennial award, 1967, Distinguished Service award, 1976; Heroism award Phila. Police Dept., 1967; 1st Hentz award for financial journalism, 1967; three John Hancock awards for excellence for syndicated and news service writers, 1967, 68, 74; Nat. Assn. Investment Clubs award, 1970; 1st Gerald Loeb Meml. award U. Calif. at Los Angeles, 1974, 1st John Hancock Permanent Recognition award for excellence in financial journalism, 1974; 1st pl. media award Amos Tuck Sch., Dartmouth Coll., 1978, 79. Fellow Nat. Assn. Bus. Economists; mem. Am. Econ. Assn., Am. Statis. Assn., Fin. Analysts Phila., Soc. Am. Bus. and Econ. Writers (1st pres. 1964), Am. Assn. for Advancement Slavic Studies, Art Alliance, Sigma Delta Chi. Clubs: Cosmos (Washington); Sunday Breakfast, Franklin Inn, Urban (Phila.). Author: Reconversion-The Job Ahead, 1944; The American Stockholder, 1958, rev. edit., 1963; newspaper series: America's Stake in the British Crisis, 1949; The Soviet Challenge, 1956; The Kennedy Crash, 1962; The Common Market, 1962; The Powerful Pull of the Dollar, 1964; Gold and the Dollar, 1966; The Great Society and the Stock Market, 1966; Economic Consequences of Vietnam, 1968; Gold vs. the Dollar, 1968; Money-A New Epoch, 1969; The British Economy—Human Race Against Ruin, 1974; The Second Battle of Britain, 1975; Great Britain in Adversity, 1977; The Decline of the Dollar: An American Tragedy, 1978; South Africa: In the Throes of Change, 1978; contbr. to Ency. Social Scis., Compton's Ency., also nat. publs. and learned jours. Home: 2110 Delancey Pl Philadelphia PA 19103 also Tinicum PA 18947 Office: Phila Inquirer Philadelphia PA 19101

LIVINGSTON, J. STERLING, mgmt. cons., educator; b. Salt Lake City, June 7, 1916; s. Julius Edward and Lucille (Scott) L.; B.B.A. cum laude, U. So. Calif., 1938; M.B.A., Harvard U., 1940, D.C.S., 1948; m. Ruth Elizabeth Flume, Feb. 6, 1943; children—Lucille Scott, Sterling Chistopher, Matthew Steele, Florence. Research asst. Grad. Sch. Bus. Administrn., Harvard U., 1940, asst. prof., 1946-48, asso. prof., 1948-50, prof., 1956-71; spl. asst. to asst. atty. gen. Thurman Arnold, cons. to chmn. WPB, 1941-42; dir. Harbridge House, Inc., mgmt. cons., 1949-63, pres., 1949-61, chmn., 1961-63; pres., dir. Mgmt. Systems Corp., Cambridge, 1960-65; mng. partner Peat, Marwick, Livingston & Co., 1965-67; pres. Sterling Inst., Washington, 1967—, Tech. Fund P.R., Inc., 1961-64; v.p., treas. pres. Mining Research Corp., 1950-56, dir., 1951-56. Bd. dirs. Nat. Security Indsl. Assn. Served as comdr. Supply Corps, USNR, 1942-46. Recipient Ann. Merit award Armed Forces Mgmt. Assn., 1962; McKinsey award Harvard Bus. Rev., 1971. Mem. Phi Kappa Tau. Clubs: Harvard (N.Y.C.); Harvard Bus. Sch. (Boston). Author: (with R.T. Davis) Cases in Sales Management; contbr. articles to profl. jours. Home: 1121 Crandon Blvd Key Biscayne FL 33149 Office: 700 Dodge Center 1010 Wisconsin Ave NW Washington DC 20007

LIVINGSTON, JAMES ARCHIBALD, JR., life ins. co. exec.; b. Macon, Ga., Aug. 8, 1918; s. James Archibald and Hazel (Wiley) L.; A.B., U. Mich., 1939, M.B.A., 1940; m. Margaret Gresham, July 15, 1947; children—Mary Margaret, James Archibald III, Katherine, Elizabeth. With Met. Life Ins. Co., 1939-40, Nat. Life & Accident Ins. Co., Nashville, 1940-44; with Liberty Nat. Life Ins. Co., Birmingham, Ala., 1944—, chief actuary, 1965—, v.p., 1960-73, sr. v.p. in charge ins. operations, dir., 1973—; dir. Liberty Nat. Fire Ins. Co., Brown Service Funeral Homes Co. Pres., Jefferson Tb Sanatorium Soc., 1965, Birmingham br. English Speaking Union, 1967; bd. dirs. Lake Shore Hosp., 1979. Served with USNR, World War II. Fellow Soc. Actuaries; mem. Internat. Soc. Actuaries, Am. Acad. Actuaries, Southeastern Actuaries Club (past pres.), St. Andrews Soc. Middle South. Club: Rotary (dir. 1976-78). Home: 12 Country Club Rd Birmingham AL 35213 Office: 301 S 20th St Birmingham AL 35202

LIVINGSTON, JAMES CRAIG, educator; b. Grand Rapids, Mich., July 12, 1930; s. Leo A. and Olive (Osterhaven) L.; B.A., Kenyon Coll., 1952; M.Div., Union Theol. Sem., 1956; Ph.D., Columbia U., 1965; m. Jacqueline Ouellette, Sept. 4, 1954; children—Sarah Elizabeth, Susannah Craig. Tutor Union Theol. Sem., N.Y.C.,1960-63; asst. prof. religion So. Methodist U., Dallas, 1963-68; asso. prof., chmn. dept. religion Coll. of William and Mary, Williamsburg, Va., 1968-72, prof. religion, 1973—, dean undergrad. program, 1973-78; vis. fellow Clare Hall Cambridge U., Eng., 1967-68. Am. Council Learned Socs. fellow, 1972-73; Nat. Endowment for Humanities fellow, 1979-80. Mem. Am. Acad. Religion, Nineteenth Century Theology Group. Democrat. Episcopalian. Author: Modern Christian Thought, 1971; The Ethics of Belief, 1974. Editor: Literature and Dogma, Matthew Arnold, 1970. Home: 105 Cove Rd Williamsburg VA 23185

LIVINGSTON, JAY, composer; b. McDonald, Pa., Mar. 28, 1915; s. Maurice and Rose (Wachtel) L.; B.A., U. Pa., 1937; m. Lynne Gordon, Mar. 19, 1947; children—Travilyn, Tammy. With Paramount Pictures, 1945-55; writer songs for over 100 motion pictures, including G'Bye Now, To Each His Own, Silver Bells, Buttons and Bows, Golden Earrings, Mona Lisa, Que Será Sera, Tammy, Dear Heart, Wish Me a Rainbow, Never Let Me Go, others; songs, spl. material Olsen and Johnson Broadway shows, Hellzapoppin, Sons O' Fun; writer score Oh Captain, Broadway, 1958, Let It Ride, Broadway, 1961; 2 songs in Sugar Babies, Broadway, 1979; writer TV theme songs including Bonanza, Mister Ed, To Rome with Love. Recipient 3 Acad. award Oscars for songs; elected to Songwriters Hall of Fame, 1973. Mem. Acad. TV Arts and Scis., A.S.C.A.P., Acad. Motion Picture Arts and Scis. (exec. bd.), Nat. Acad. Rec. Arts and Scis. (gov.), Composers and Lyricists Guild Am. (exec. bd.), Am. Guild Authors and Composers, AFTRA, Dramatist's Guild. Mailing Address: care ASCAP 1 Lincoln Plaza New York NY 10023

LIVINGSTON, JOHNSTON R., mfg. co. exec.; b. Foochow, China, Dec. 18, 1923 (parents U.S. citizens); s. Henry Walter V and Alice (Moorehead) L.; B.S. with honors in Engring., Yale, 1947; M.B.A. with distinction (Baker scholar), Harvard, 1949; m. Caroline Johnson, Aug. 17, 1946 (dec.); children—Henry, Ann, Jane, David; m. 2d, Patricia Karolchuck, Sept. 4, 1965. With Mpls.-Honeywell Regulator Co., 1949-55; with Whirlpool Corp., 1956-66, v.p. until 1966; v.p. Redman Industries, Dallas, 1966-67; dir. Constrn. Tech., Inc., Dallas, 1967—, chmn. bd., pres., Denver, 1974—; pres. Marcor Housing Systems, Inc., Denver, 1971-74. Former mem. industry adv. com. Nat. Housing Center; dir., past pres. Nat. Home Improvement Council; pres. Denver Symphony Assn., 1977—. Served with USAAF, 1943-46. Mem. Sigma Xi, Tau Beta Pi. Home: 869 Vine St Denver CO 80206 Office: 5070 Oakland St Denver CO 80239

LIVINGSTON, MOLLIE PARNIS, designer; b. N.Y.C.; d. Abraham and Sarah Parnis; m. Leon Jay Livingston, June 26, 1930; 1 son, Robert Lewis. Sec.-treas. Parnis Livingston, Inc.; pres. Mollie Parnis Co., Mollie Parnis Boutique, Mollie Parnis at Home. Designer cadet nurses uniform. Founder, Dress Up Your Neighborhood competitions, N.Y.C., Jerusalem, Israel. Home: 812 Park Ave New York City NY 10021 Office: 530 7th Ave New York City NY 10018

LIVINGSTON, PATRICK MURRAY, editor; b. Pitts., Oct. 16, 1920; s. John and Sarah Ann (Malloy) L.; B.A., St. Francis Coll., Loretto, Pa., 1941; LL.B., J.D., Duquesne U.; m. Eileen Hamilton, Nov. 24, 1962; children—Linda Maureen, Patricia Michele, James L. Hamilton III (stepson). Publicity dir. Pitts. Steelers, 1942-48; sports writer, sports editor Pitts. Press Co., 1949—. Elector, Profl. Football Hall of Fame. Bd. dirs. Scoreboard Fund. Served to lt. USNR, 1942-46. Recipient Keystone award Pa. Newspaper Pubs. Assn., 1977; Dick McCann award Pro Football Writers Assn. Am. Mem. Pitts. Press Club (dir. 1968—). Club: Rolling Hills Country. Author: Pro Football Handbook, 1961. Home: 7200 Baptist Rd Bethel Park PA 15102 Office: 34 Blvd of the Allies Pittsburgh PA 15230

LIVINGSTON, R(USSELL) LYNN, advt. agy. exec.; b. Beloit, Wis., Jan. 7, 1940; s. Russell Gust and Francis Mercedes (Higgens) L.; B.A. in Communications, U. So. Calif., 1962; m. Patricia Jane Stiles, Nov. 26, 1966; children—Douglas Scott, Mark Lynn, Kelly Lynn. Advt./pub. relations mgr. Hibak Records Co., Hollywood, Calif., 1967; advt. asst. Beckman Instruments Co., Fullerton, Calif., 1968; advt./mktg. dir. Coleman Systems, Irvine Calif., 1969-71; owner, operator Livingston & Assos., Fountain Valley, Calif., 1971-72; copywriter Cochrane Chase & Co. (name changed to Cochrane Chase, Livingston & Co. 1979), Newport Beach, Calif., 1972-73, v.p., 1973-76, pres., 1976—, also dir. Served to lt. USN, 1962-66; Vietman. Decorated Navy Commendation medal; recipient Pheonix Service award Huntington Park (Calif.), 1958. Mem. Western States Advt. Assn., Am. Advt. Fedn., Am. Assn. Advt. Agys., Mut. Advt. Agy. Assn. PubliMondial, Am. Mktg. Assn., Bus. and Profl. Advt. Assn. (v.p. local chpt.), Phi Kappa Tau. Republican. Roman Catholic. Club: Santiago Canyon Tennis. Contbg. author/editor: THe Marketing Problem Solver, 1974. Office: 660 Newport Center Dr Suite 1000 Newport Beach CA 92663

LIVINGSTON, ROBERT BURR, neuroscientist, educator; b. Boston, Oct. 9, 1918; s. William Kenneth and Ruth Forbes (Brown) L.; A.B., Stanford, 1940, M.D., 1944; m. Mandana Beckner, Dec. 21, 1954; children—Louise, Dana, Justyn. Intern, asst. resident internal medicine Stanford Hosp., 1943-44; instr. physiology Yale Sch. Medicine, 1946-48, asst. prof., 1950-52; research asst. psychiatry Harvard Med. Sch., 1947-48; NRC sr. fellow neurology Inst. Physiology, Geneva, Switzerland, 1948-49; Wilhelm Gruber fellow neurophysiology, Switzerland, France, Eng., 1949-50; exec. asst. to pres. Nat. Acad. Scis.-NRC, 1951-52; asso. prof. physiology and anatomy U. Calif. at Los Angeles, 1952-56, prof., 1956-57; dir. basic research NIMH and Nat. Inst. Neurol. Diseases and Blindness, 1956-61, chief neurobiology lab. NIMH, 1960-65; prof. dept. neuroscis. U. Calif. at San Diego Sch. Medicine, 1965—, chmn. dept., 1965-70; Gast prof. U. Zurich, Switzerland, 1971-72. cons. NRC, VA, NASA, HEW; asso. neuroscis. research program Mass. Inst. Tech., 1963-76, hon. asso., 1976—. Bd. dirs. Foundations' Fund for Research in Psychiatry, 1954-57; bd. incorporators Jour. History of Medicine and Allied Scis. Served to lt. (j.g.) M.C., USNR, 1944-46. Decorated Bronze Star. Fellow A.A.A.S. (chmn. commn. sci. edn. 1968-71), Am. Acad. Arts and Scis.; mem. Am. Physiol. Soc., Am. Assn. Anatomists, Am. Neurol. Assn., Am. Acad. Neurology, Assn. for Research in Nervous and Mental Diseases, Am. Assn. Neurol. Surgeons. Adv. editorial bd. Jour. Neurophysiology, 1959-65; editorial bd. Internat. Jour. Psychobiology, 1970—; cons. editor Jour. Neurosci. Research, 1975—. Home: 7818 Camino Noguera San Diego CA 92122

LIVINGSTON, ROBERT EDWARD, lawyer; b. Orlando, Fla., Mar. 11, 1938; s. Howard Gordon and Eula Frances (Adams) L.; A.B., Davidson Coll., 1960; LL.B., Harvard U., 1963; m. Helen Williams John, Oct. 26, 1968; children—James Thomas, John Charles. Admitted to Fla. bar, 1963, D.C. bar, 1977; asso. firm Mershon Sawyer Johnston Dunwody & Cole, Miami, Fla., 1963-68, partner, 1968-77; partner firm Mahoney Hadlow & Adams, Miami, 1977—. Mem. Dade County Bar Assn. (pres. 1979-80), Fla. Bar Assn., Am. Bar Assn., (del. 1979—), Am. Law Inst. Democrat. Presbyterian. Clubs: Rod and Reel, Univ. Home: 4680 SW 74th St Miami FL 33143 Office: 1401 First Fed Bldg Miami FL 33131

LIVINGSTON, ROBERT LINLITHGOW, JR., Congressman; b. Colorado Springs, Colo., Apr. 30, 1943; s. Robert L. and Dorothy (Godwin) L.; B.A. in Econs., Tulane U., 1967, J.D., 1968; postgrad. Loyola Inst. Politics, 1973; m. Bonnie Robichaux, Sept. 13, 1965; children—Robert Linlithgow, III, Richard Godwin, David Barkley. Admitted to La. bar, 1968; partner firm Livingston & Powers, New Orleans, 1976-77; asst. U.S. atty., dep. chief Criminal Div., 1970-73; chief spl. prosecutor, chief Armed Roberty Div., Orleans Parish Dist. Atty.'s Office, 1974-75; chief prosecutor organized crime unit La. Atty. Gen.'s Office, 1975-76; mem. 95th and 96th Congresses from 1st La. Dist. Mem. nat. adv. bd. Young Ams. for Freedom, Citizens Com. for Right to Keep and Bear Arms. Served with USN, 1961-63. Named Outstanding Asst. U.S. Atty., 1973. Mem. Am., Fed., La., New Orleans bar assns., Navy League, Am. Legion. Republican. Episcopalian. Clubs: Masons; Young Mens Business. Home: 701 Patterson St New Orleans LA 70114 Office: 1233 Longworth House Office Bldg Washington DC 20515

LIVINGSTON, ROBERT LOUIS, chemist, educator; b. Ada, Ohio, Nov. 15, 1918; s. Ralph and Ruth (Sink) L.; B.S., Ohio State U., 1939; M.S., U. Mich., 1941, Ph.D., 1943; m. Virginia Capron, May 30, 1943 (div. 1973); children—Douglas, Roy, Margaret, Bruce; m. 2d, Jean Moriarty, Aug. 25, 1979. Asso. chemist Naval Research Lab., Ann Arbor, Mich., 1944-46; faculty Purdue U., Lafayette, Ind., 1946—, prof. chemistry, 1954—, asst. dept. head, 1960-68, dir. NSF-URP Program, 1969-72. Cons. Coll. Entrance Exam. Bd., 1972—. Recipient Standard Oil Teaching award, 1968. Mem. Am. Chem. Soc. (sec. div. chem. edn. 1963-68, mem. exec. com. 1968-71), Sigma Xi, Phi Lambda Upsilon, Phi Delta Kappa, Phi Eta Sigma, Gamma Alpha. Author: (with F.D. Martin) Lecture Notebook and Recitation Questions, General Chemistry, pub. annually 1952-64. Contbr. to profl. jours. Research on molecular structure of gaseous molecules by electron diffraction. Home: 1816 Ravinia Rd West Lafayette IN 47906 Office: Dept Chemistry Purdue U Lafayette IN 47907

LIVINGSTON, WILLIAM HENRY, JR., architect; b. Phila., Dec. 22, 1921; s. William Henry and Lillian Meyers (Jackson) L.; B.Arch., U. Pa., 1947; m. Joan Holleyman, Dec. 21, 1946; children—William Henry, Frederic Holleyman, Holly, John Barry, Robert Alan. Draftsman, Davis Dunlap & Carver, Phila., 1946-48; project architect Harbeson Hough Livingston & Larson, Phila., 1948-60; partner H2L2 Architects/Planners, Phila.,1961—; sec.-treas. H2L2 Design, Inc., 1977—. Mem. vestry St. Mary's Episcopal Ch., Ardmore, Pa., 1958-64; scoutmaster Ardmore Troop 98, Valley Forge council Boy Scouts Am., 1961-63; bd. dirs. Nationalities Service Center of Phila., 1966-76, pres., 1970-72, dir. emeritus, 1976—; mem. standing com. United Way S.E. Pa., 1976—. Served with C.E., U.S. Army, 1943-45; ETO. Recipient Warren Powers Laird medal U. Pa., 1942, Brooke Bronze medal, 1947; Order of Arrow award Valley Forge Boy Scouts Am., 1962. Mem. AIA (dir. Phila. chpt.), Constrn. Specification Inst., Phila. Art Alliance, Tau Sigma Delta, Sigma Alpha Epsilon. Republican. Club: Union League (Phila.). Archtl. designer: Fed. Res. Bd. Martin Bldg., Washington, 1974. Home: 749 King of Prussia Rd Radnor PA 19087 Office: 1500 Architects Bldg 117 S 17th St Philadelphia PA 19103

LIVINGSTON, WILLIAM SAMUEL, educator; b. Ironton, Ohio, July 1, 1920; s. Samuel G. and Bata (Elkins) L.; B.A., Ohio State U., 1943, M.A., 1943; Ph.D., Yale, 1950; m. Lana Sanor, July 10, 1943; children—Stephen Sanor, David Duncan. Asst. prof. U. Tex., Austin, 1949-54, asso. prof., 1954-61, prof. govt., 1961—, chmn. dept. govt., 1965-69, asst. dean Grad. Sch., 1954-58, chmn. grad. Assembly, 1965-68, chmn. faculty senate, 1973-79, chmn. dept. comparative studies, 1978-79; vice chancellor acad. programs U. Tex. System, 1969-71, v.p., dean grad. studies, 1979—; vis. prof. Yale, 1955-56, Duke, 1960-61. Mem. Internat. Council on Future of Univ. Served to 1st lt. FA, AUS, 1943-45. Decorated Bronze Star, Purple Heart. Recipient Teaching Excellence award, 1959; Ford Found. fellow, 1952-53, Guggenheim fellow, 1959-60; USIS lectr. in U.K. and India, 1977. Mem. Am. (com. on sci. information exchange 1969-72, exec. council and adminstrv. com. 1972-74, chmn. nominating com. 1973-74, 78-79), So. (exec. council 1964-67, pres. 1974-75), Southwestern (pres. 1973-74), Brit., Canadian polit. sci. assns., Hansard Soc. (London), Austin Soc. for Pub. Adminstrn. (pres. 1973-74), Southwestern Social Sci. Assn. (v.p. 1975-76, pres. 1977-78), Phi Beta Kappa, Omicron Delta Kappa, Phi Gamma Delta, Pi Sigma Alpha (nat. council 1976—, nat. pres.-elect 1978-80). Author: Federalism and Constitutional Change, 1956. Contbg. author: World Pressures on American Foreign Policy, 1962; Teaching Political Science, 1965; Federalism: Infinite Variety in Theory and Practice, 1968. Editor: A Prospect of Liberal Democracy, 1979; co-editor: Australia, New Zealand and the Pacific Islands Since the First World War, 1979. Editor, contbr. author: Federalism in the Commonwealth, 1963. Book rev. editor Jour. Politics, 1965-68, editor-in-chief, 1968-72. Mem. editorial bd. Polit. Sci. Quar., Publius: Jour. of Federalism; chmn. bd. editors P.S. Home: 3203 Greenlee Dr Austin TX 78703

LIVINGSTONE, FRANK BROWN, anthropologist, educator; b. Winchester, Mass., Dec. 8, 1928; s. Guy Philip and Margery Stuart (Brown) L.; A.B., Harvard U., 1950; Ph.D., U. Mich., 1957; m. Carol Southworth Ludington, Aug. 13, 1960; 1 dau., Amy Fenner. Research asso. Liberian Inst. Tropical Medicine, 1955-56, 57-58; asst. prof. anthropology U. Mich., Ann Arbor, 1959-63, asso. prof., 1963-68, prof., 1968—; cons. in field. Constable, Ann Arbor Twp., 1963-65. Served with U.S. Army, 1951-53. NSF fellow, 1957-59. Recipient Martin Luther King award So. Christian Leadership Conf., 1972. Mem. Am. Anthrop. Assn., Am. Soc. Human Genetics, Am. Assn. Phys. Anthropologists. Author: Abnormal Hemoglobins in Human Populations, 1967. Contbr. articles to profl. jours. Home: 471 Rock Creek Dr Ann Arbor MI 48104 Office: Dept Anthropology University Michigan Ann Arbor MI 48109

LIVINGSTONE, JOHN LESLIE, acct., bus. economist, educator; b. Johannesburg, S.Africa, Aug. 29, 1932; s. Philip and Jenny (Smulian) L.; B.Com., U. Witwatersrand, S.Africa, 1956; M.B.A., Stanford U., 1963, Ph.D., 1966; m. Trudy Dorothy Zweig, Aug. 7, 1977; Budget dir. Edgars Stores Ltd., S. Africa, 1958-61; asso. prof. Ohio State U., Columbus, 1966-69, Arthur Young Disting. prof., 1970-73; Fuller E. Callaway prof. Ga. Inst. Tech., Atlanta, 1973-78; partner, dir. tech. services Coopers & Lybrand, N.Y.C., 1979—; prin. Mgmt. Analysis Center, Inc., Cambridge, Mass., 1975-78; cons. FPC, SEC, HEW, also maj. corps. Mem. exec. bd. Ga. Inst. Tech., 1976—. Chartered acct. Mem. Am. Acctg. Assn., Nat. Assn. Accts., Stanford U. Alumni Assn., Beta Gamma Sigma. Author 7 books including: Accounting for Changing Prices: Replacement Cost and General Price Level Adjustments, 1976; Modern Accounting Systems: Design and Installation, 1975; contbr. articles to profl. jours.; asso. editor Decision Scis., 1973—; mem. editorial bd. The Acctg. Rev., 1969-72, 76—, Acctg., Orgns. and Soc., 1975—. Office: Coopers & Lybrand 1251 Ave of Americas New York NY 10020

LIVINGSTONE, RAY(MOND) S., business cons.; b. Pitts., Feb. 12, 1907; s. Maurice M. and Ella Marie (Villatte) L.; student Case Inst. Tech., 1924-27, D.Eng. (hon.), 1954; m. Sylvia Flora, May 5, 1934; children—Raymond S., Barbara Anne Aguirre. With TRW Inc. (formerly Thompson Products, Inc.), 1929-66, dir. personnel,

1934-42, other spl. assignments in selling and mfg., v.p. indsl. and govt. relations, 1942-66; vis. prof. Fla. Atlantic U., Boca Raton, 1966—; cons. Harris Corp., Cleve., 1966-72; dir. Prodn. Machinery Corp., 1960-76. Mgmt. mem. Nat. Labor-Mgmt. Manpower Adv. Com. Past pres. Cleve. Community Chest, Cleve. Welfare Fedn., Case Alumni Assn., Cleve. Personnel Assn. Trustee Am. Enterprise Inst., 1962-78, Community Chest Greater Cleve. (life), Euclid Glenville Hosp. (life); exec. adv. com. Fla. Atlantic U.; vice chmn. Civil Service Bd., Boca Raton, 1975—. Mem. Econ. Round Table Boca Raton, Aerospace Industries Assn. (past nat. chmn. indsl. relations com.), Personnel Round Table. Mason (33 deg., Shriner). Club: Royal Palm Yacht and Country (Boca Raton, Fla.). Home: 282 Fan Palm Rd Boca Raton FL 33432

LIVSEY, WILLIAM JAMES, JR., army officer; b. Clarkston, Ga., June 8, 1931; s. William James and Erma Louise (Brand) L.; B.S. in Phys. Edn. and Biology, North Ga. Coll., 1952; M.S. in Psychology, Vanderbilt U., 1964; postgrad. Command and Gen. Staff Coll., 1961-62, Armed Forces Staff Coll., 1966-67, U.S. Army War Coll., 1968-69; m. Bena Sue Burns, Oct. 4, 1952; children—David and William James III (twins), John, Timothy. Commd. 2d lt. U.S. Army, 1952, advanced through grades to maj. gen., 1977; served in Korean War, 1952; co. comdr. 30th Inf. Regt., Ft. Benning, Ga., 1953-54, instr. Inf. Sch., 1954-57; staff officer/co. comdr. 2d Bn., 36th Inf. Regt., 1958-60; aide-de-camp to Comdg. Gen., 3d Armored Div., Germany, 1960-61; instr. U.S. Mil. Acad., 1964-66; comdr. 2d Bn., 35th Inf., 4th Inf. Div., Vietnam, 1967-68; served in Office of Chief of Staff, Research and Devel., Washington, 1969-71; comdr. 2d Brigade, 4th Inf. Div., Ft. Carson, Colo., 1971-72; exec. officer, sr. aide to Chief of Staff of Army, 1972-74; asst. div. comdr. 4th Inf. Div., 1974-76; chief of staff I Corps, Republic of Korea, Camp Redcloud, 1976; comdg. gen. U.S. Army Inf. Center, Ft. Benning, 1977-79; comdg. gen. 8th Inf. Div. (Mechanized), W. Ger., 1979—. Decorated Silver Star, D.F.C., Bronze Star, Legion of Merit with 3 oak leaf clusters, Army Commendation medal with 2 oak leaf clusters, Air medal with 10 oak leaf clusters. Mem. Assn. U.S. Army, 4th Inf. Div. Assn. Club: Rotary. Home: 5658 Mannheimer Strasse Bad Kreuznach Fed Republic of Germany Office: HHC 8th Inf Div APO NY 09111

LIZARDI, MANUEL, banker; b. Celaya, Guanajuato, Mexico, Jan. 8, 1913; s. Fernando and Teresa (Albarran) L.; student Colegio Frances Morelos, Mexico, 1933; grad. U. Nexico, 1940; m. Guadalupe Calderon, Dec. 5, 1953; children—Manuel, Javier, Teresa, Francisco, Fernando, Maria Guadalupe. With Banco Nacional de Mexico, S.A., 1936—, asst. head legal dept., 1953-57, head legal dept., 1957-67, sub dir., 1968, dir., v.p., chief counsel, 1968-78, sec., alt. mem. bd. dirs., 1978—; of counsel firm Goodrich, Dalton, Little and Riquelme, 1978—; prof. comml. law and corps. Escuela Libre de Derecho. Mem. Barra Mexicana Colegio de Abogados, Socio Supernumerario of Academia de Jurisprudencia y Legislacion. Home: 335 Brisa St Mexico DF20 Mexico Office: 44 Isabel la Catolica Mexico DF 1 Mexico. *Man was made to work as the bird was made to fly.*

LJUNGDAHL, LARS GERHARD, educator; b. Stockholm, Sweden, Aug. 5, 1926; s. Karl Axel Gerhard and Ruth Elisabeth (Soderlund) L.; B.S., Stockholm Tech. Inst., 1945; Ph.D., Case Western Res. U., 1964; m. Britt-Marie Swahn, Aug. 28, 1949; children—Ann-Sofie Elisabeth, Lars Per-Olof. Came to U.S., 1958, naturalized, 1969. Research technologist Karolinska Institut, Stockholm, 1943-46; research chemist Stockholm Brewery Co., 1947-58; sr. instr. Case Western Res. U., Cleve., 1964-66, asst. prof., 1967; asst. prof. U. Ga., Athens, 1967-69, asso. prof. biochemistry and microbiology, 1969-75, prof., 1975—. Recipient Sr. U.S. Scientist award research and teaching Alexander von Humboldt-Stiftung, Gottingen, Germany, 1974-75. Research grantee NIH, NSF, Dept. Engery. Mem. Am. Soc. Biol. Chemists, Am. Soc. Microbiology, Am. Chem. Soc., AAAS, N.Y. Acad. Sci., Biochem. Soc. (U.K.), Swedish Chem. Soc., Sigma Xi. Contbr. articles to profl. jours. Home: 250 Hancock Ln Athens GA 30605

LLAND, MICHAEL, ballet dancer; b. Bishopsville, S.C., 1925. Debut in Song of Norway, Broadway, 1944; dancer Teatro Mcpl., Rio de Janeiro, from 1945; soloist, then prin. dancer Am. Ballet Theatre, N.Y.C., until 1968; ballet master Houston Ballet, 1968-71, Am. Ballet Theatre, 1971—. Address: care Am Ballet Theatre 888 7th Ave New York NY 10019*

LLEWELLYN, JAMES BRUCE, govt. ofcl.; b. Bronx, N.Y., July pres. Overseas Pvt. Investment Corp., Washington, 1978—; 16, 1927; s. Charles W. and Nessa F. (Lopez) L.; B.S., City Coll. N.Y., 1955; LL.B., N.Y. Law Sch., 1960; postgrad. Columbia Grad. Sch. Bus., 1956, N.Y. U. Sch. Pub. Adminstrn., 1961; LL.D., Wagner Coll., 1978; m. Jacqueline Brown, Nov. 7, 1965; children—Christina Lisa, Alexandra Maria. Owner, mgr. H.A.T. Corp., 1959-65; exec. dir. Upper Manhattan Small Bus. Devel. Corp., N.Y.C., 1965; regional dir. U.S. SBA, N.Y.C., 1965-66; exec. dir. N.Y. Small Bus. Devel. Center, Inc., N.Y.C., 1966-67; dep. commr. dept. rent and housing maintenance Housing and Devel. Adminstrn., N.Y.C., 1967-69; pres. Fedco Foods Corp., Bronx, N.Y., 1969-78; chmn., dir. Freedom Nat. Bank, 1973-76; pres. Overseas Pvt. Investment Corp.. Washington, 1978—. Past pres. One Hundred Black Men, Inc.; past co-chmn. Interracial Council Bus. Opportunity; pres. Riverpoint Towers Coop. Assn.; bd. dirs. Tb Assn. N.Y., N.Y. Urban Coalition; chmn. bd. dirs. Coalition Venture Capital Corp.; bd. dirs. S. Bronx Overall Econ. Devel.; v.p., bd. dirs. Fedn. Protestant Welfare Agencies; bd. dirs. Children's TV Workshop. Served as officer U.S. Army, 1944-48. Mem. NAACP, Urban League. Episcopalian. Office: Overseas Pvt Investment Corp 1129 20th St NW Washington DC 20527

LLEWELLYN, JOHN ANTHONY, educator; b. Cardiff, Wales, Apr. 22, 1933; s. John and Morella (Roberts) L.; B.S.C., Univ. Coll., Cardiff, 1955, Ph.D., 1958; m. Valerie Mya Davies-Jones, 1957; children—Gareth, Sian, Cerl. Came to U.S., 1960, naturalized, 1966. Fellow NRC of Can., 1958-60; research asso. Fla. State U., Tallahassee, 1960-61, Inst. Molecular Biophysics, 1961-62, asst. prof. chemistry, 1962-64, asso. prof. Sch. Engring. Sci., 1964-72, dean Sch. Engring. Sci., 1970-72; prof. dept. energy conversion Coll. Engring. U. South Fla., Tampa, 1972—. Scientist astronaut, 1967-68; dir. Racon Corp. Coordinator, Scientist in the Sea Project, 1973; aquanaut Nat. Oceanographic Atmospheric Adminstrn., 1976. Mem. Royal Inst. Chemistry, Am. Inst. Aeros. and Astronautics, Radiation Research Soc., Sigma Xi, Omicron Delta Kappa. Home: 3010 St Charles Dr Tampa FL 33618

LLEWELLYN, RALPH ALVIN, educator; b. Detroit, June 27, 1933; s. Ralph A. and Mary (Green) L.; B.S. in Chem. Engring. with high honors, Rose-Hulman Inst. Tech., 1955; Ph.D. in Physics, Purdue U., 1962; m. Laura Diane Alsop, June 12, 1955; children—Mark Jeffrey, Rita Annette, Lisa Suzanne, Eric Matthew. Mem. faculty Rose-Hulman Inst. Tech., Terre Haute, Ind., 1961-70, asso. prof., 1964-68, prof., 1968-70, chmn. dept. physics, 1969-70; prof., chmn. dept. Ind. State U., Terre Haute, 1970-72, 74; exec. sec. Energy Bd. Nat. Acad. Scis., Washington, 1972-74. Vis. prof. Rensselaer Poly. Inst., Troy, N.Y., 1964; cons. Commn. on Coll. Physics, 1967-69, NSF, 1965-66; mem. Ind. Lt. Gov.'s Sci. Adv. Council, 1974—; mem. Ind. Gov.'s Energy Extension Service Adv. Bd. Trustee Merom (Ind.) Inst. NSF Coop. fellow, 1959-60. Fellow Ind. Acad. Sci. (chmn. physics div. 1969-70, Speaker of Yr. award 1975, pres.-elect 1980); Am. Council Edn. Academic Adminstrn. Internship Program; mem. AAAS, Am. Phys. Soc., Am. Assn. Physics Tchrs. (pres. Ind.), Am. Soc. Oceanography, AAUP, Internat. Assn. Great Lakes Research. Asso. editor: Phys. Rev. Letters. contbr. articles to profl. jours. Producer instructional films and TV. Home: Rural Route 16 Box 209 Brazil IN 47834 Office: Dept Physics Ind State U Terre Haute IN 47809

LLEWELLYN, WILLIAM ALFRED, book publisher; b. Welling, Eng., Nov. 25, 1934; s. William and Brenda Ivy (Popely) L.; came to U.S., 1967; m. Annette McFadzean, Jan. 18, 1963; children—Lee Anne, Stephanie Kim. Advt. dir. Ency. Brit., Can., 1966-67; asst. to pres. Ency. Brit., Inc., Chgo., 1968; mng. dir. Ency. Brit., Geneva, Switzerland, 1968-71; pres., pub. G.&C. Merriam Co., Springfield, Mass., 1972—, also dir.; dir. W. Llewellyn & Co., Ltd., Bickley, Eng. Served with RAF, 1952-54. Address: 47 Federal St Springfield MA 01101

LLEWELLYN-THOMAS, EDWARD, physician; b. Salisbury, Eng., Dec. 15, 1917; s. Hugh and Beatrice Caroline (Carre) L.; B.S.c., U. London (Eng.), 1950; M.D., McGill U., 1955; m. Ellen Wise Buford, Sept. 25, 1947; children—Caroline, Roland, Edward Jr. Engr., BBC, London, 1935-39; controller Tellecommunications, Singapore, 1945-50; research asso. dept. psychiatry Cornell U. Med. Sch., 1956-60; physician scientist Def. Research Bd. Can., Toronto, Ont., 1958-61; prof. pharmacology U. Toronto, 1961—, also asso. dean medicine. Served to capt. Brit. Army, 1939-45. Fellow Royal Soc. Can., Inst. Elec. Engrs.; mem. Human Factors Assn. Can. (pres. 1969-70). Club: Univ. Home: 67 Balliol St Toronto ON M45 1C2 Canada Office: Faculty Medicine U Toronto Toronto ON Canada

LLOYD, ALBERT LAWRENCE, JR., educator; b. Evanston, Ill., Aug. 10, 1930; A.B., George Washington U., 1951, M.A., 1954, Ph.D., 1957; married; 1 child. Asso. in German, George Washington U., 1954-57; mem. faculty U. Pa., 1957—, prof. German, 1970—, chmn. dept., 1972—; nat. advisory bd. Jr. Yr. in Munich and Freiburg Program, 1962—. Grantee Am. Philos. Soc., 1966; Nat. Endowment for Humanities grantee, 1978—. Mem. Inst. Deutsche Sprache, Modern Lang. Assn., Linguistic Soc. Am., Am. Assn. Tchrs. German, Mediaeval Acad. Am., Phi Beta Kappa. Author: The Manuscripts and Fragments of Notker's Psalter, 1958; Der Münchener Psalter des 14 Jahrhunderts: Eine Auswahl zusammen mit den entsprechenden Teilen von Notkers Psalter herausgegeben, 1969; also articles; co-author: Deutsch und Deutschland heute, 1967. Address: 745 Williams Bldg Univ Pa Philadelphia PA 19104

LLOYD, ARTHUR YOUNG, ret. state ofcl., farmer, educator; b. Lisman, Ky., Jan. 12, 1908; s. Arthur Lee and Susan Mabel (Young) L.; A.B., Western Ky. State U., 1926; M.A., Vanderbilt U., 1929, Ph.D., 1934; postgrad. Ind. U., summer 1928, George Peabody Coll. Tchrs., summer 1930; grad. Army Command and Gen. Staff Sch., 1957; m. Lucy B. Simms, Nov. 27, 1941 (dec.); 1 dau., Elizabeth (Mrs. Brereton C. Jones). Prin., Webster County High Sch., Wheatcroft, Ky., 1926-28; instr. polit. sci. Vanderbilt U., 1929-31; asso. prof. history and polit. sci. Morehead State Tchrs. Coll., 1931-34, prof., head dept., 1934-36; dir. pub. assistance Ky. Dept. Welfare, 1936-42, commr. dept., 1947-48; dir. Legislative Research Commn. Ky., 1948-56; v.p., mng. dir. Burley and Dark Tobacco Export Assn., Inc., Washington, 1957-59; exec. dir. Nat. Cigar Leaf Tobacco Assn., Inc., Washington, 1957-59; joined U.S. Army Res., 1927; served to col., active duty, 1942-46; transferred to Ky. N.G., 1959; maj. gen. N.G. U.S., 1960; ret. as maj. gen. AUS, 1968; adj. gen. Ky., 1959-67; dir. civil def. Ky., 1959-68, chmn Ky. Disabled Ex-Service Mens Bd., 1960-68; adminstr. Ky. Vets. Bonus, 1960- 67; chairman Ky. U.S.O., 1960-68; state dir. Ky.'s Emergency Resource Planning Com., 1962-68; operator tobacco and livestock farm, Woodford County, Ky., 1941—. Lectr. pub. welfare adminstrn. U. Ky., Lexington, 1968-70; lectr. polit. sci. Eastern Ky. U., 1973-78, acting chmn. polit. sci. dept., 1974-75. Pres., Nat. Legislative Service Conf., 1953-54; mem. Gov. Ky. Personnel and Policy Com., 1950-55; Ky. del. Midcentury White House Conf., 1950. Mem. Ky. Partners of Alliance with Ecuador, 1966-67. Trustee Midway Coll., 1948-74. Decorated Legion of Merit, Bronze Star. Mem. Council State Govts. (bd. mgrs. 1952-57, 59-75), So. Hist. Assn., Ky. Farm Bur. Fedn. (pres. Woodford County 1951-54), Ky. Welfare Assn., Ky. Hist. Soc. (life, v.p. 1976—), N.G. Assn. U.S. (chmn. pub. relations com. 1962, mem. exec. council 1964-69), Am. Soc. Pub. Adminstrn. (pres. Ky. 1950-51), Am. Legion, V.F.W., Nat. Aberdeen-Angus Breeders Assn., Adjs. Gen. Assn. U.S. (pres. 1966-67), Ret. Officers Assn. (regional rep. 1971-75, pres. Ky. council of chpts. 1976-78). Democrat. Baptist. Clubs: Filson (life, Louisville); Rotary; Lexington Polo, Lafayette, Civil War Round Table, Spindletop Hall (Lexington). Author: The Slavery Controversy, 1939; Kentucky Government, 1980. Home: 200 Shriners Ln Lexington KY 40502 Office: Airdrie Farms Midway KY 40347. *God has been good to me by providing that I be born to educated, religious parents, who lived by the moral code in which they believed and whose lives have been a continuous inspiration to acquire knowledge and to help others less fortunate. Over the years, many outstanding people—teachers, leaders in government, business and the military services, and even the young people that, from time to time, I have endeavored to instruct—have contributed materially to whatever little success I have managed to achieve.*

LLOYD, DAVID PIERCE CARADOC, physiologist; b. Auburn, Ala., Sept. 22, 1911; s. Francis Ernest and Mary Elizabeth (Hart) L.; B.Sc., McGill U., 1932; B.A. (Rhodes scholar), Oxford U. (Eng.), 1936, Dr. Philosophy, 1938, D.Sc., 1961, M.A., 1964; D.Sc. (hon.), Rockefeller U., 1978; m. Kathleen Mansfield Elliott, Mar. 20, 1937; children—Marion Gwenellen, Owen H.T., Evan E.M.; m. 2d, Cynthia Meynell, Nov. 17, 1957. Deptl. demonstrator physiology Oxford U., 1935-36; asst., asso. dept. med. research U. Toronto, 1936-39; with Rockefeller U. Med. Research, 1939-43, 46, mem., 1949—, prof., 1957-71; hon. research fellow U. Coll. London (Eng.), 1970—; asst. prof. physiology Yale, 1943-45; Johnston lectr. U. Minn., 1948; James Arthur lectr. Am. Mus. Natural History, 1958; mem. study sect. and coms. Nat. Inst. Neurol. Diseases and Blindness. Mem. adv. com. Nat. Found. Infantile Paralysis, 1947-59; trustee Internat. Poliomyelitis Congress, 1948—. Recipient Reeve prize medicine U. Toronto, 1939. Mem. Nat. Acad. Sci., Am. Physiol. Soc., Physiol. Soc. Gt. Britain, AAAS, Assn. Research Nervous and Mental Diseases, Harvey Soc. Contbr. chpt. Howell's Textbook of Physiology, rev. edit. 1946, 49, 55, Annotations Reflex Activity of the Spinal Cord, 1972. Author articles on neurophysiology. Home: New Cottage Greatham Pulborough Sussex RH20 2ES England

LLOYD, DONALD PARKINSON, food co. exec.; b. Ogden, Utah, Sept. 21, 1905; s. Charles E. and Lucy (Parkinson) L.; B.A., Brigham Young U., 1928; postgrad. Georgetown U., 1929-30; m. Helen Carroll, June 27, 1928; children—Donald C., Jon C., William H., Lynette. Comml. agt. U.S. Dept. Commerce, Washington, 1929-30, Salt Lake City, 1931-32; sec.-mgr. Utah Retail Grocers Assn., 1933-40; mgr. Asso. Food Stores, Inc., Salt Lake City, 1940-72, pres., 1966-72; past pres. Coop. Food Distbrs. Am.; past pres. Pacific Merc. Co.; past gov. Universal Products Code; pres., gen. mgr. Merchants, Inc., 1956-78; dir. Animal Nutrition Co., Am. Protectors Ins. Co. Mem. Trade Mission to S. Africa, U.S. Govt., 1957. Bd. dirs. Utah Symphony Orch., Washington Mormon Temple Visitors Center. Recipient U. Utah award for outstanding bus. achievement, 1961; Salesman of Year award Utah Sales Marketing Execs., 1967; Outstanding Service award Utah Food Industry, 1970. Republican. Mem. Ch. of Jesus Christ of Latter-day Saints. Clubs: Alta, National Asparagus (hon.). Home: 2045 E 13th S Salt Lake City UT 84108 Office: 9900 Stoneybrook Dr Kensington MD

LLOYD, DOUGLAS SEWARD, state ofcl.; b. Bklyn., Oct. 16, 1939; s. Heber Hughes and Virginia Seward (Chamberlin) L.; A.B. in Chemistry, Duke U., 1961, M.D., 1971; postgrad. Old Dominion U., 1965-67; M.P.H. in Health Planning, U. N.C., 1971. Intern pediatrics Duke U., Durham, N.C., 1971-72, clin. scholar, 1972, resident in family practice, 1972-73; commr. health Conn. Dept. Health, 1973—; lectr. Yale U., Conn., 1973—. Bd. dirs. Conn. Med. Inst., 1975—. Served with USNR, 1961. Recipient Lange Publ. award, 1971. Mem. Am. Pub. Health Assn., AMA, Conn. State Med. Soc., Hartford County Med. Assn. Contbr. articles to profl. jours. Home: 300 Russell Rd Wethersfield CT 06109 Office: 79 Elm St Hartford CT 06115

LLOYD, EDMUND SHERMAN, retail exec.; b. Bloomingburg, N.Y., Feb. 12, 1912; s. Thomas Lloyd and Mercedes (Andrews) L.; B.S. in Bus. Adminstrn., U. Pa., 1935; m. Zita Maier, Dec. 19, 1964; children—Tom, James, Zita, Linda, Harold, Sue Pace, Jeff, Joseph. Founder, Lloyd's Shopping Centers, Inc., Middletown, N.Y., 1935, now chmn. bd. Mem. Middletown Fire Dept., Middletown Bd. Edn.; chmn. Middletown Republican Party. Mem. Food Mktg. Inst., N.Y. State Food Mchts. Assn., Middletown Indsl. Devel. Corp., Middletown C. of C. Club: Middletown Lions. Office: Lloyd's Shopping Centers Inc Box 730 Route 211 E Middletown NY 10940

LLOYD, FRANCIS VERNON, JR., educator; b. York Harbor, Maine, June 19, 1908; s. Francis Vernon and Mary Emlen (Lowell) L.; B.A., Stanford, 1933; certificate d'Instruction, Alliance Francaise, Paris, France, 1934; postgrad New Coll., Oxford (Eng.) U., 1934-35; M.Ed., Harvard, 1949; postgrad. Washington U., St. Louis, 1957; m. Elisabeth Boardman, Dec. 28, 1933; children—Francis Vernon III, Malcolm, Boardman, Mary Emlen Lowell. Tchr. English, head lower sch., dir. studies, vice rector St. Paul's Sch., Concord, N.H., 1935-57; lectr. Harvard Sch. Edn., 1950; supt. Clayton (Mo.) Sch. Dist., 1957-63; dir. U. Chgo. Lab. Schs., 1963-70; professorial lectr. U. Chgo., 1963-70; dir. Ednl. Consultants, South Yarmouth, Mass., 1970-78. Lectr., U. Va., 1968, U. Mich., 1968-70. Mem. Concord Bd. Edn., 1950-57; reader in English, Coll. Entrance Exam. Bd., 1936-43; v.p. New Eng. Assn. Colls. and Secondary Schs., 1955-57; mem. Nat. Adv. Council Modern Lang. Project, 1960-65; chmn. scholarship com. Headline Club, Chgo., 1965-70, Wingspread, Chgo., 1970; trustee Webster Coll., 1967—, Eaglebrook Sch., 1965-75, Berkshire Sch., 1976—, Cape Cod Acad., 1978—. Del. 4th Soviet-Am. Citizens Conf., Leningrad, 1964; hon. guest Australian Ind. Sch. Assn., 1967. Mem. Am. Assn. Sch. Adminstrs.; life mem. N.E.A., Headmasters Assn., Phi Delta Kappa, Sigma Delta Chi. Clubs: Harvard (N.Y.C., Boston). Author. Forward to Teach, 1967. Contbr. articles to profl. jours. Collaborator: Preparation of Teachers of Secondary Schools, 1958. Columnist: N.A.I.S. Bull.-An Apple For, 1967-73. Home: Box 38 222 Pleasant St South Yarmouth MA 02664

LLOYD, FREDRIC REYNOLDS, pharm. co. exec.; b. Wilkes Barre, Pa., Sept. 25, 1923; s. John Stanley and Edith May (Reynolds) L.; B.S., Purdue U., 1944, Ph.D., 1949; m. Beverly Jeanne Brand, May 19, 1945; children—Beverly Christine, Carolyn Reynolds. With Eli Lilly & Co., Indpls., 1949-64, asst. dir. chem. mfg., 1956-64, v.p. European ops. Eli Lilly Internat., 1965-72, v.p. production ops. div. Eli Lilly & Co., Indpls., 1973—. Mem. Ind. Lt. Gov.'s Sci. Adv. Com., 1973—. Served with USNR, 1943-45. Recipient Distinguished Engring. Alumnus award Purdue U., 1973. Mem. Am. Inst. Chem. Engrs., Am. Chem. Soc., Nat. Assn. Profl. Engrs., Sigma Xi, Phi Kappa Psi. Episcopalian. Club: Woodstock, Masons. Home: 402 Westwood Rd Indianapolis IN 46240 Office: 307 E McCarty St Indianapolis IN 46225. *There is always a way to solve every business problem by the objective application of solid technical and human principles.*

LLOYD, GARY ARTHUR, orgn. exec.; b. Hatfield, Ind., July 27, 1934; s. Roscoe C. and Margaret (Dawson) L.; B.A., Northwestern U., 1955; M.S.W., Tulane U., 1961, Ph.D., 1965. Social worker U.S. Army Consultation Service, Ft. Benning, Ga., 1957-58; social worker La. Bur. Child Welfare, New Orleans, 1959-60; social worker Charity Hosp. La., New Orleans, 1961-62; mem. faculty Tulane U. Sch. Social Work, 1964-73; prof., chmn. community orgn. and social planning, dean Grad. Sch. Social Work, U. Houston, 1973-77; vis. prof. San Jose State U., 1978; mem. Commn. on Accreditation, Council on Social Work Edn., 1976—, exec. dir., 1979—. Mem. Orleans Parish Welfare Bd., 1970-73, Community Relations Council, 1968-70, Gov.'s Com. on Goals for La., 1970-71, Mayor's Task Force on Juvenile Delinquency, 1972-73. Served with AUS, 1957-58. Fellow Am. Acad. Mental Health Adminstrn. (charter); mem. Nat. Assn. Social Workers (dir. S.E. La. chpt. 1966-69), Community Services Council, Internat. Assn. Schs. Social Work (dir. 1979—), Tex. United Community Services, Acad. Certified Social Workers, Soc. Gen. Systems Research, Assn. Marriage and Family Therapists, Am. Group Psychotherapy Assn., Council Social Work Edn., Am. Pub. Health Assn., AAUP. Democrat. Episcopalian. Author: Charities, Settlements and Social Work, 1971; Current Trends in Social Work Practice, 1972; The Culture and Politics of Social Work, 1978; editor: Readings in Social Work Practice, 1970; contbr. articles to profl. jours. Home: 294 W 4th St New York NY 10014

LLOYD, HERMON, architect; b. Houston, Oct. 9, 1909; s. Hermon Franklin and Ethel (Pearce) L.; B.A., B.S. in Architecture, Rice Inst., 1931; m. Alma Owen, July 15, 1933 (dec.); children—Hermon, Darden. Pvt. practice architecture, Houston, 1933—; partner Lloyd, Jones & Brewer, 1977—; prin. works include Rice U. Stadium, 1950, new music hall for City Houston, 1956, Fannin Bank Bldg., 1962, Harris County Domed Stadium, 1963, Am. Gen. Center, 1965, Hofheinz Pavillion, U. Houston, 1971, Enco Bldg., 1973, Greenway Plaza, 1974, Allen Center, 1978. Fellow AIA; mem. Tex. Soc. Architects, 1973, Greenway Plaza, 1974. Fellow A. I.A.; mem. Tex. Soc. Architects, Houston C. of C. Clubs: Houston, Plaza. Home: 2009 Chilton St Houston TX 77019 Office: 802 Lovett Blvd Houston TX 77006

LLOYD, HUGH ADAMS, lawyer; b. Pine Apple, Ala., Oct. 5, 1918; s. James Adams and Kate (Compton) L.; student Oglethorpe U., 1936-37; A.B., U. Ala., 1941, LL.B., 1942; m. Lydia Douglas, Sept. 18, 1942; children—Kathryn Adams (Mrs. Harlan G. Allen, Jr.), Sally Douglas (Mrs. Charles Proctor), Elizabeth Anne, Hugh Adams. Adjudicator, VA, Montgomery, Ala., 1946-47; admitted to Ala. bar, 1942, also U.S. Supreme Ct.; partner firm Lloyd, & Dinning & Boggs, Demopolis, Ala., 1947—. Dir. Robertson Banking Co., Demopolis, Allen Capital Enterprises, Atlanta, Robertson Bank's Ins. Agy. Active Boy Scouts Am.; chmn. Demopolis Indsl. Devel. Com., 1970; mem. Regional Com. Juvenile Delinquency, 1970. Chmn. Marengo County Devel. Bd., 1972-73; mem. Demopolis City Council, 1974. Served with AUS, 1943-45. Decorated Bronze Star; recipient Silver Beaver award Boy Scouts Am., 1972. Mem. Am. Judicature Soc., Am., Ala., 17th Jud. Circuit (pres.) bar assns., Demopolis C. of C. (pres.). Baptist (chmn. ch. bd. deacons). Kiwanian (dist. gov. 1967, chmn. internat. com. Key clubs 1969, internat. com. on boys and girls work 1972). Clubs: Kiwanis (dist. chmn. laws and regulations com. Ala. dist. 1979), Demopolis Country (pres. 1967-68). Home: 1408 Colony Rd Demopolis AL 36732 Office: 305 N Walnut Ave PO Drawer Z Demopolis AL 36732

LLOYD, JIM, congressman; b. Helena, Mont., July 27, 1922; s. Robert and Marie (Lunders) L.; B.A., Stanford U., 1958; M.A., U. So. Calif., 1966; m. Jacqueline Jane Vaughan, Nov. 27, 1948; 1 son, Brian Patrick. Commd. officer U.S. Navy, 1942-63; dir. pub. relations Aerojet Gen., So. Calif., 1963-65; owner, operator Lloyds Pub. Relations and Advt., 1966-74; mem. 94th-96th Congresses from 35th Calif. Dist. Tchr. Mt. San Antonio Coll., 1970-73. Pres. Friends Ontario (Calif.) Internat. Airport, 1973-74; mem. So. Calif. Aviation Council, 1972-74. Pres. Covina (Calif.) Democratic Club, 1964-66; mem. Dem. County Central Com., 1966-68, State Central Com., 1968-72; councilman, West Covina, Calif., 1968-74, mayor, 1973-74. Office: 222 Cannon House Office Bldg Washington DC 20515

LLOYD, JOHN A., life ins. co. exec.; b. Jackson, Ohio, Oct. 17, 1901; s. Homer A. and Cora (Miller) L., D.S.C. (hon.), U. Cin., 1967; m. Lillian Freund, May 29, 1926; children—John A., Elizabeth (Mrs. Norman H. Ulmer). Mng. editor Portsmouth (Ohio) Morning Sun, 1920-29; advt. and pub. bus., Portsmouth, 1929-33; v.p., dir. Union Central Life Ins. Co., Cin., 1943, pres., 1956-73, chmn., 1973-76, chmn. bd., 1976-77; pres. Lloyd & Co.; dir. Central Trust Co., Central Bancorp., Cin. Gas & Electric Co. Ohio supt. ins., 1939, 41, 43. Mem. Ohio Senate, 1931-36. Trustee Cin. Symphony Orch. 1946-56; chmn. Friends Symphony Orch. Mem. St. David's Soc. Cin. (chmn.), Ohio Assn. Ins. Agts. (past exec. sec.), Ohio Hist. Soc. (trustee), A.P. Editors Ohio (pres. 1929), Cin. C. of C. (pres., dir. 1951-53). Mason (33 deg.), Lion (dist. gov. 1931-32, internat. bd. dirs. 1932-35). Clubs: Columbus; Bankers, Queen City, Cin. Country, Hamilton (Cin.). Home: 420 Oak Rd Glendale OH 45246 Office: 16 Village Sq Cincinnati OH 45246

LLOYD, JOHN HENRY, JR., r.r. ofcl.; b. Glasgow, Mont., July 27, 1917; s. John Henry and Edith Mae (Wright) Lloyd; student No. Mont. Coll., 1935-37; B.S., U. Pa., 1942; m. Dorothy Pauline Rigg, Sept. 17, 1944; children—Edith, John, Robert, Joseph. Railroad officer G.N. Ry., 1935-50; trainmaster, asst. supt., supt., asst. gen mgr. Rock Island Lines, 1950-56; gen. mgr. Alaska R.R., 1956-58; gen. supt. motive power Rock Island Ry., 1958-60, asst. v.p., 1960, v.p. operations, 1961; v.p. ops. M.P. R.R., 1961-68, exec. v.p., 1968-72, pres., 1972—, vice chmn., chief exec. officer, 1978—. Served as lt. USNR, 1942-45. Mem. Phi Delta Theta. Episcopalian. Mason. Clubs: Missouri Athletic, Old Warson Country, Union League, Media, University. Home: 5 Indian Creek Ln Saint Louis MO 63131 Office: Mo-Pacific Bldg Saint Louis MO 63103

LLOYD, LEWIS EWAN, univ. adminstr.; b. Montreal, Que., Can., Feb. 3, 1924; B.Sc., McGill U., 1948, M.Sc., 1950, Ph.D., 1952; m. Pauline M. Sharpe, June 3, 1950; children—David, Nancy, Robert, James. Research asso. Cornell U., Ithaca, N.Y., 1952-53; asst. prof. nutrition McGill U., Macdonald Coll., Que., Can., 1953-56, asso. prof., 1956-60, prof. animal sci., chmn. dept., 1960-67, dean Faculty of Agr., vice prin., 1977—; dir. Sch. Home Econs., U. Man., Winnipeg, 1967-70, dean Faculty Home Econs., 1970-77. Bd. dirs. Age and Opportunity Centre, Winnipeg, 1968-76. Served with Can. Army, 1943-46. Underwood fellow Rowett Research Inst., Aberdeen, Scotland, 1958-59. Mem. Can., U.K. nutrition socs., Can. Inst. Food Sci. and Tech., Am. Inst. Nutrition, Can. Dietetic Assn., Can. Assn. Gerontology. Clubs: Summerlea Golf and Country, Golf. Author: Fundamentals of Nutrition, 1958, 2d edit., 1978. Home: 21048 Lakeshore Rd Ste Anne de Bellevue PQ H9X 1S2 Canada Office: Box 238 MacDonald Coll PQ H9X 1C0 Canada

LLOYD, MARION MUSSER, civic worker; b. Muscatine, Iowa, Sept. 11, 1910; d. Clifton R. and Margaret (Kulp) Musser; A.B., Vassar Coll., 1932; D.H.L., Maryville (Tenn.) Coll., 1959, Lake Forest (Ill.) Coll., 1974; LL.D., Grinnell (Iowa) Coll., 1973; m. Glen A. Lloyd, Nov. 15, 1940 (dec. 1975); children—Megan Lloyd Hill, Mary J. Estrin, Ann Baldwin (dec.), John Musser. Trustee Vassar Coll., 1956-67, mem. exec. com., 1964—; trustee Am. U. in Cairo (Egypt), 1954-67; trustee Ravinia (Ill.) Festival Assn., 1962—, chmn. bd., 1971-75; mem. women's bd. U. Chgo., 1955—; mem. Goodman Theatre Com., 1972-75; bd. dirs. Gen. Service Found., 1949—, Forest Fund, 1955—; trustee U. Chgo., 1975—. Dir. Lake Forest Book Store, Inc. (Ill.), 1958-65. Mem. bd. Deerfield Shields (Ill.) Women's Republican Club, 1948-54; mem. Rep. Central Com. for 13th Congl. Dist. Ill., 1952-54. Trustee Community Music Assn., Lake Forest, Ill., Chgo. Ednl. TV Assn., Chgo. Orchestral Assn.; mem. adv. bd. Planned Parenthood Chgo., 1975—. Clubs: Cosmopolitan (N.Y.C.); Friday, Onwentsia, Vassar (Chgo.). Address: Route 1 Box 32 St Mary's Rd Libertyville IL 60048

LLOYD, MORRIS, investment banker; b. Ardmore, Pa., Apr. 20, 1913; s. Stacy B. and Eleanor B. (Morris) L.; B.A., Princeton U., 1936; m. Hope Starr, Oct. 3, 1936; children—Morris, Thomas, Mary Lloyd Barlow, David, John S., Hope Lloyd Yates. With Drexel & Co. (name changed to Drexel Burnham Lambert, Inc.), Phila., 1936—, exec. v.p., 19—; trustee Phila. Savs. Fund Soc., 1966—. Trustee, officer Chestnut Hill Hosp., 1939—. Mem. Am. Philos. Soc. (councillor, mem. fin. com.). Republican. Episcopalian. Clubs: Phila., Racquet, Sunnybrook Golf, Mid Ocean, Princeton (N.Y.C.). Home: 1777 Willow Grove Ave Philadelphia PA 19118 Office: 1500 Walnut St Philadelphia PA 19102

LLOYD, NORMAN, musician, found. exec.; b. Pottsville, Pa., Nov. 8, 1909; s. David and Annie Sarah (Holstein) L.; B.S., N.Y. U., 1932, M.A., 1936; Mus.D., Phila. Conservatory Music, 1963, New Eng. Conservatory, 1965, Peabody Inst., 1973; grad. piano study with Abbey Whiteside; study in music composition with Vincent Jones, Aaron Copland; m. Ruth Dorothy Rohrbacher, Apr. 10, 1933; children—David Walter, Alex. Instr., Ernest Williams Band Sch., 1935-37; lectr. N.Y. U., 1936-45; faculty Sarah Lawrence Coll., 1936-46, condr. chorus, 1945-49; dir. edn. Juilliard Sch. Music, 1946-49, faculty, 1949-63; dean Oberlin Coll. Conservatory Music, 1963-65; dir. arts program Rockefeller Found., 1965-72, cons., 1973-75; cons. Nat. Assn. Schs. Music, 1973-76, Mary Flagler Cary Charity Trust, 1974—; composer, condr. dance scores for Martha Graham, 1935, Hanya Holm, 1937, Doris Humphrey, 1941-46, 49, Jose Limon, 1949; composer, condr. numerous music scores for exptl. and documentary films OWI, Internat. Film Found., Shirley Clarke-Halcyon Films, Mus. Modern Art, others; compositions include Song for Summer's End, 1951, Nocturne for Voices, 1953, 3 Pieces for Violin and Piano, 1957, A Walt Whitman Overture for Band, 1962, Sonata for Piano, 1963, Three Scenes from Memory, 1963, Episodes for Piano, 1964; Rememories for Wind Orchestra, 1974. Mem. vis. com. humanities Mass. Inst. Tech., 1973-75; vis. com. arts Tufts U., 1976—; bd. dirs. Nat. Music Council. Mem. ASCAP, Am. Fedn. Musicians, Pi Kappa Lambda. Compiled: (with M. Boni) Fireside Book of Folk Songs, 1947, Fireside Book of American Songs, 1952, Fireside Book of Love Songs, 1954, Favorite Christmas Carols, 1957, Songs of the Gilded Age, 1960; (with Arnold Fish) Fundamentals of Sight Singing, 1963 (with Ruth Lloyd) The American Heritage Songbook, 1969; Creative Keyboard Musicianship, 1975. Author: Golden Ency. of Music, 1968. Home: 82 Richmond Hill Rd Greenwich CT 06830

LLOYD, R. MCALLISTER, banker, found. exec.; b. N.Y.C., Jan. 12, 1898; s. Robert McAllister and Jennet Maitland (Belknap) L.; A.B., Harvard, 1919; LL.D., Lawrence Coll., 1960, Juniata Coll., 1961, Yale, 1963, N.Y.U., 1963; m. Isabel Goodwin, Oct. 8, 1921; children—Mary Remsen (Mrs. Frederic L. Steele), Robert McAllister, Eleanor (Mrs. William L. Helm, Jr.). Clk., Nat. City Bank N.Y., 1919-20; asst. trust officer N.Y. Trust Co., 1920-30; asst. v.p. Bank of N.Y., 1930-36, v.p., 1936-45; pres., chmn. Tchrs. Ins. & Annuity Assn. Am., 1945-57, chmn., 1957-62, trustee, 1945-68; pres., chmn. Coll. Retirement Equities Fund, 1952-57, chmn., 1957-62, trustee, 1952-68; chmn., trustee Grant Found., 1946—. Mem. investments com. UN, 1952-72, chmn., 1962-72; mem. N.Y. State Commn. on Pensions, 1954-56, on Ednl. Finances, 1954-55; adv. council Fed. Social Security Financing, 1957-58. One-man exhbns. watercolors Lyman Allyn Mus., New London, Conn., 1974, Harkness House Gallery, N.Y.C., 1977. Mem. Royal Commn. on Freeport, Bahamas, 1969-70. Trustee N.Y. Hist. Soc. Served with Ambulance Corps, ARC, France, 1917; as lt., inf. U.S. Army, 1918; mem. N.Y. N.G., 1919-23. Mem. Soc. Cin. in N.J., St. David's Soc., St. Andrews Soc., Loyal Legion, Am. Geog. Soc. Republican. Presbyn. Clubs: Century Assn., Harvard (N.Y.C.). Home: 1115 Weed St New Canaan CT 06840 also 164 E 72d St New York NY 10021 Office: Grant Found 130 E 59th St New York NY 10022

LLOYD, RALPH WALDO, coll. pres. emeritus; b. Friendsville, Tenn., Oct. 6, 1892; s. Henry Baldwin and Maud (Jones) L.; B.A., Maryville (Tenn.) Coll., 1915, D.D., 1929; B.D., McCormick Theol. Sem., 1924; LL.D., Centre Coll., 1940, U. Chattanooga, 1953; Litt.D., Lake Forest Coll., 1954, Westminster Coll., 1955; L.H.D., Lincoln Meml. U., 1955; S.T.D., Blackburn Coll., 1955; Pd.D., Monmouth Coll., 1961; m. Margaret Anderson Bell, June 21, 1917; children—John Vernon, Hal Baldwin, Ruth Bell (Mrs. Frank A. Kramer), Louise Margaret (Mrs. James E. Palm). Instr., athletic coach Westminster Coll. Salt Lake City, 1915-17, asst. to pres. 1918-19; with Fulton Sylphon Mfg. Co., Knoxville, Tenn., 1920-21; ordained to ministry Presbyn. Ch., U.S.A., 1923; supply First Presbyn. Ch., Ossian, Ind., 1922-23; pastor First Ch., Murphysboro, Ill., 1924-26, Edgewood Ch., Pitts., 1926-30; pres. Maryville Coll., 1930-61, now pres. emeritus; moderator Presbytery of Cairo, Ill., 1926, Presbytery of Union, 1932-33, Synod of Mid-South, 1944-46; gen. council Presbyn. Synod Tenn., 1931-40, chmn., 1940-42. Mem. permanent commn. inter ch. relations Presbyn. Ch. U.S.A., 1938-58, chmn., 1941-58, moderator gen. assembly, 1954-55; mem. Presbyn. Ch. U.S.A. deputation to China, 1946; chmn. com. lay edn. Presbyn. Council on Theol. Edn., 1943-48; mem. commn. on ecumenical mission and relations United Presbyn. Ch. U.S.A., 1958-60; mem. So. area bd. YMCA 1939-54; Nat. Council Commn. Student Work. 1939-42, chmn. So. area, 1942-45, pres. So. area council, 1946-48; Am. sec. World Alliance Presbyn. and Ref. Chs., 1951-59, pres., 1959-64; mem. central com. World Council Chs., 1951-61; gen. bd. Nat. Council Chs., 1950-60. Pres. Affiliated Ind. Colls. Tenn., Inc., 1958-61; mem. Nat. Conf. Ch. Related Colls., 1937-45, v.p., 1937, pres., 1938; pres. Pan-Presbyn. Coll. Union, 1938; pres. Presbyn. Coll. Union, 1943, Tenn. Coll. Assn., 1942-43; mem. commn. insts. higher edn. So. Assn. Colls. and Secondary Schs., 1940-47; del. Presbyn. Ch. in U.S.A., World Council Chs., Amsterdam, 1948, Evanston, 1954, New Delhi, 1961. Served as 1st lt., F.A., U.S. Army, 1917-18. Author Maryville College-A History of 150 Years, 1969; Westminster United Presbyterian Church (Bradenton, Fla.)—A History of 50 Years, 1974; articles and addresses pub. in various ednl. and religious jours. Address: 5916 Riverview Blvd Bradenton FL 33505

LLOYD, TREVOR, geographer, assn. exec.; b. London, Eng., May 4, 1906; s. Jonathan and Mary (Gordge) L.; student Sidcot Sch., Somerset, Eng., 1920-24; B.Sc., U. Bristol, Eng., 1929, D.Sc., 1949; Ph.D., Clark U., Worcester, Mass., 1940; M.A. (hon.), Dartmouth, 1944; LL.D., U. Windsor (Can.), 1973; m. Joan Glassco, 1936 (div. 1966); children—Mona Jean, Hugh Glassco; m. 2d, Beryl Chadwick, 1966 (dec. 1966). Pres., Nat. Union Students of Gt. Britain, 1930-31; leader Brit. Debating team to Can. and U.S., 1930; geography specialist Winnipeg (Can.) Pub. Schs., 1931-38; asst. prof. geography Carleton Coll., 1942; asst. prof. geography Dartmouth, 1942-44, prof., 1944-59, chmn. dept. geography, 1946-52; prof. human geography McGill U., Montreal, Que., Can., 1959-77, prof. emeritus, 1977—, chmn., 1962-66, dir. geography Summer Sch., 1963-65, mem. univ. senate, 1968-72, dir. U. Centre for No. Research, 1973-77; exec. dir. Assn. Canadian Univs. for No. Studies, Ottawa, 1977—; vis. lectr. geography summer schs., U. Man., Rochester, McGill, Dalhousie, U. B.C.; vis. prof. Stockholm Sch. Econs., 1967; sr. research asst. Wartime Information Bd., Ottawa, 1943; His Majesty's consul for Can. in Greenland, 1944-45; 1st chief Geog. Bur. Can. Govt., 1947-48; project officer Royal Commn. Govt. Orgn., 1961-62; geog. field work throughout Europe and N.Am., particularly Arctic Can. and Greenland, Lapland, Brit. Isles, Eastern Europe, Western USSR, Siberia, Andes of Bolivia and Peru, French West Africa; geog. cons. on resources and adminstrn. of Arctic and Antarctic. Bd. govs. Canadian-Scandinavian Found., 1973—, pres., 1976-77. Decorated Can. Centennial medal, Royal Jubilee medal; research grantee Rockefeller Found., 1947, Carnegie Corp., 1933, 49, 51, Can. Council, 1960, 67, 70, 73, Nuffield Found., 1967. Fellow Royal, Am. geog. socs., Royal Soc. Can., Social Scis. Research Council Can., Arctic Inst. N.Am. (gov. 1949-50, 59-64, 66-69, chmn. 1967-69), AAAS (sect. chmn. 1965); mem. Canadian Inst. Internat. Affairs, Greenland Soc., Assn. Am. Geographers, Canadian Assn. Geographers (pres. 1957-58, Distinguished Service award 1977), New Eng. Geog. Conf. (pres. 1953), Royal Soc. Tchrs. (London), Inst. Current World Affairs N.Y. (gov., vice chmn. 1966, chmn. 1974), McGill Assn. Univ. Tchrs. (pres. 1969-71), Geog. Soc. Finland (hon.). Mem. Soc. of Friends. Author: Sky-Highways-Geography from the Air, 1945; Canada and Her Neighbors, 1947, 65; Southern Lands, 1961; Canada et les Voisins, 1953, 67; Lands of Europe and Asia, 1956, 64; A Geographer's World, 1968. Editor: Arctic, 1947-49. Contbr. numerous tech. papers on Arctic Can., Greenland, Lapland, and on ednl. aspects of geography. Home: 120 Wurtemburg St Apt 2 Ottawa ON K1A 8M3 Canada Office: 130 Albert St Suite 1208 Ottawa ON K1P 5G4 Canada

LLOYD-JONES, DONALD J., airline exec.; b. N.Y.C., May 25, 1931; s. Silas and Esther (McDonald) L.- J.; B.A., Swarthmore Coll., 1952; M.B.A., Columbia, 1954, Ph.D., 1960; m. Beverly L. Miller, June 12, 1954; children—Anne, Susan, Donald M., Lisa. Instr., Columbia, 1952-62; sr. analyst transp. and econs. Am. Airlines, N.Y.C., 1957-62, dir. econ. research, 1962-65, asst. v.p. econ. research, 1965-66, v.p. corporate planning, 1966-69, sr. v.p., finance, 1969-72, sr. v.p. operations, 1972—, also dir.; dir. SGL Industries, Inc. Airline chmn. Community Service Soc. N.Y., 1959-70; mem. bd. mgrs. Swarthmore Coll., 1970—. Nat. Acad. Scis. fellow, 1956-57. Mem. Am. Statis. Assn., Beta Gamma Sigma. Club: Dallas Petroleum. Home: 200 Washington Ave Dobbs Ferry NY 10522 Office: PO Box 61616 DFW Airport TX 75261

LO, ARTHUR WU-NIEN, engring. educator; b. Shanghai, China, May 21, 1916; s. Liang-Kan and Shou-Pan (Heng) L.; came to U.S., 1945, naturalized, 1957; B.S., Yenching U., 1938; M.A., Oberlin Coll., 1946; Ph.D., U. Ill., 1949; m. Elizabeth H. Shen, Aug. 24, 1950; children—Katherine E., James A. Mem. tech. staff RCA Research Labs., 1951-60; mgr. advanced devel., data systems div. IBM Corp., 1960-62, mgr. exploratory devel., components div., 1962-64; prof. elec. engring. Princeton U., 1964—. Cons. in field, 1964—; spl. research digital electronics and computer systems. Fellow IEEE; mem. Sigma Xi, Eta Kappa Nu, Pi Mu Epsilon. Author: Transistor Electronics, 1955; Introduction to Digital Electronics, 1967; also papers in field. Patentee in field. Home: 102 Maclean Circle Princeton NJ 08540

LO, IRVING YUCHENG, educator; b. Foochow, China, Sept. 19, 1922; s. Lo Mien-hou and Hsiu-chih (Wu) L.; B.A. summa cum laude, St. John's U., Shanghai, China, 1945; M.A., Harvard U., 1949; Ph.D., U. Wis., 1954; m. Lena Woo-lih Dunn, Aug. 11, 1945; 1 son, Adrian Hsiang-yung. Research asst. U. Wis., 1950-52; instr. English, Stillman Coll., Tuscaloosa, Ala., 1952-53, prof. English, chmn. dept. English and div. humanities; asst. prof. English, Western Mich. U., Kalamazoo, 1957-61, asso. prof., 1961-64; asso. prof. dept. Oriental studies U. Iowa, 1964-67, acting chmn., 1965-66; asso. prof. East Asian langs. and lit. Ind. U., 1967-71, prof., 1971—, chmn. dept., 1974—; vis. prof. Stanford U., 1971-72. Fulbright-Hayes fellow, 1966-67. Mem. Modern Lang. Assn., Assn. Asian Studies, Am. Oriental Soc. Mem. editorial bd. Lit. East and West; author 2 books; editor Translation from Chinese Literature series Ind. U. Press; contbr. articles to profl. jours. Home: 2219 Sussex Dr Bloomington IN 47401 Office: East Asian Langs and Culture Dept Ind U Bloomington IN 47401

LO, RONALD PING WONG, banker; b. Hong Kong, Apr. 9, 1936; s. Robert Ka Fatt and Esther Ming Fung (Ching) L.; B.C.S., Melbourne (Australia) U., 1961; m. Carol Rosemary Dyason, June 11, 1965; children—Howard Brenden, Collin Harvard. Tchr. Chao Yang Chinese Sch., Singapore, 1955-56; accounts auditor Wilson, Bishop & Henderson, Melbourne, Australia, 1959; tchr. Niddrie high sch., Essenden, Australia, 1961-62; marketing mgr. Harper Gilfillan Ltd., Singapore and Malaysia, 1963-71; 1st sec. Singapore embassy, Washington, 1971-74; v.p., internat. dept. Republic Nat. Bank Dallas, 1974-79; v.p., group head for eastern hemisphere, div. internat. devel. Merc. Trust Co. N.A., St. Louis, 1979—. Cons. mem. Internat. Research Affiliate, Singapore, 1964. Rep. Asia Pacific group of countries Interim Communications Satellite Com. of INTELSAT, 1972, also bd. govs. Mem. Banking Inst. Australasia. Presbyterian. Home: 4 Foxcliff Ct Manchester MO 63011

LOACH, PAUL ALLEN, biochemist, biophysicist, educator; b. Findlay, Ohio, July 18, 1934; s. Leland Oris and Dorothy Elizabeth (Davis) L.; B.S., U. Akron, 1957; Ph.D. (NIH fellow), Yale, 1961; m. Patricia Ann Johnson, Dec. 28, 1957; children—Mark, Eric, Jennifer. Research asso. Nat. Acad. Scis.-NRC postdoctoral fellow U. Calif. at Berkeley, 1961-63; asst. prof. chemistry Northwestern U., 1963-68, asso. prof., 1968-73, prof., 1973-74, prof. biochemistry and molecular biology, and chemistry, 1974—. Cons. Argonne (Ill.) Nat. Lab. Recipient C.P. award U. Akron, 1957, Research Career Devel. award USPHS, 1971-76. Mem. Am. Soc. Biol. Chemists, Am. Chem. Soc., AAAS, Biophys. Soc., Am. Soc. Photobiology. Conglist. (Man of Year award 1969-71, chmn. ch. council 1974-75). Asso. editor Photochemistry and Photobiology, 1973—, Biophysics of Structure and Mechanism, 1973—. Contbr. articles, revs. to profl. jours.

LOADER, JAY GORDON, utility co. exec.; b. Plainfield, N.J., Aug. 3, 1923; s. Carl and Madalyn (Wright) L.; B.S., U. Ala., 1951; m. Joan Merrell, Aug. 19, 1965; children—Patricia Kay, Michael Jay, Sandra Lee, Gigi Ann. Auditor Arthur Andersen & Co., Atlanta, 1951-55; with Fla. Power Corp., St. Petersburg, Fla., 1955—, asst. sec., asst. treas., 1960-67, sec.-treas., 1967—; dir. Fla. Nat. Bank at St. Petersburg. Mem. fin. com. Edison Electric Inst. Served with AUS, 1943-44. C.P.A., Ga. Mem. Am. Inst. C.P.A.'s, Fla. Soc. C.P.A.'s, Am. Soc. Corporate Secs., Fin. Analysts Soc. Central Fla., U. Ala. Alumni Assn., Phi Eta Sigma, Beta Gamma Sigma, Beta Alpha Psi. Clubs: Bath (Redington Beach); Yacht (St. Petersburg); Treasure Island Tennis and Yacht. Home: 10212 Tarpon Dr Treasure Island St Petersburg FL 33706 Office: 3201 34th St S St Petersburg FL 33711

LOAR, PEGGY ANN WAHL, museum ofcl.; b. Cin., May 14, 1948; d. Jerome Vincent and Elizabeth Ann (Ranz) Wahl; B.A., U. Cin., 1970, M.A., 1971; m. Kenton J. Loar, Sept. 5, 1970. Teaching asst. U. Cin., 1970-71; asst. curator in charge edn., acting curator Indpls. Museum of Art, 1971-72, asso. curator in charge edn., acting curator, 1972-73, curator edn., 1973—, asst. to dir., 1976—, organizer exhibit Ind. Stoneware, 1974; program dir. Inst. Mus. Services/HEW, Washington, 1978-79, asst. dir., 1979—; lectr. art appreciation Ind. U.-Purdue U., Indpls., 1972-75. Chmn. membership subcom and exec. com. Ind. Com. for Humanities, 1972—, vice chmn. com., 1976-78; mem. adv. panel Ind. Arts Commn., 1974—; mem. Ind. Supt.'s Adv. Com. for Arts in Edn., 1975—; bd. dirs. Ind. Alliance for Arts in Edn., Hosp. Audiences, 1973—, Mus. Edn. Roundtable, Washington. Mem. Coll. Art Assn., Am. Assn. Museums, Ind. Film Council, Indpls. Art League Found., Nat. Art Edn. Assn., Am. Film Inst. Home: 1536 15th St NW Washington DC 20005 Office: Inst Mus Services 200 Independence Ave SW Washington DC 20201

LOBANOV-ROSTOVSKY, OLEG, symphony orch. dir.; b. San Francisco, July 12, 1934; s. Andrei and Grace S. (Pope) Lobanov-R.; B.A., U. Mich., 1956; m. Susan Waters, Sept. 8, 1979; children—Christopher, Nicholas. Community concert rep. Columbia Artists Mgmt. Inc., 1958-59; mgr. Columbus (Ohio) Symphony Orch., 1959-62, Hartford (Conn.) Symphony Orch., 1962-65; Balt. Symphony, 1965-69; program officer div. humanities and arts Ford Found., 1969-75; exec. dir. Denver Symphony Orch., 1975-76; mng. dir. Nat. Symphony Orch., Washington, 1977—; mem. orch. panel Nat. Endowment Arts; past mem. bd. dirs. Am. Symphony Orch. League. Address: Nat Symphony Orch Kennedy Center Washington DC 20566

LOBB, RODMOND KENNETH, aero. engr.; b. Edmonton, Alta., Can., Feb. 10, 1925; naturalized U.S. citizen, 1956; s. Rodmond and Edith Kathleen (Badger) L.; B.S. in Engring. Physics, U. Alta., 1947; M.S. in Aero. Engring., 1948; Ph.D. in Aero. Engring., U. Toronto, 1950; m. Anne Palsat, Dec. 24, 1947; children—Doris A., Barbara A. Chief aerodynamics dept. Naval Ordnance Lab., White Oak, Md., 1957-61, aeroballistics program chief, 1961-66, asso. tech. dir., head aero and hydroballistics, 1966-74; tech. dir. Naval Air Devel. Center, Warminister, Pa., 1974—; lectr. U. Md., Cath. U. Am. Recipient Superior Civilian Services award Dept. Navy, 1968. Fellow AIAA. Home: 336 E Casals Pl Ambler PA 19002 Office: Naval Air Devel Center Warminster PA 18974

LOBDELL, FRANK, artist; b. Kansas City, Mo., 1921; studied St. Paul Sch. Art, 1938-39, with Cameron Booth, Calif. Sch. Fine Arts, 1947-50, Academie de la Grande Chaumiere, Paris, France, 1950-51; m. Ann Morency, 1952; children—Frank Saxton, Judson Earle. One man shows Lucien Labaudt Gallery, 1949, Martha Jackson Gallery, 1958, 60, 63, 72, 74, de Young Meml. Mus., San Francisco, 1959,

Ferus Gallery, 1962, Pasadena Art Mus., 1961, San Francisco Mus. Art, 1969, Benador Gallerie, Geneva, Switzerland, 1964, Gallerie Anderson-Mayer, Paris, 1965; retrospective show Pasadena Art Mus. and Stanford Mus., 1966; exhibited group Shows Salon du Mai, Paris, 1950, III Sao Paulo Biennial, 1955, Waddington Gallery, London, 1961, Whitney Mus. Am. Art, 1962-63, 72, Guggenheim Mus., N.Y.C., 1964, Vancouver (Can.) Print Internat., 1967, Pasadena Art Mus., 1969, Van Abbemuseum, Eindhoven, Holland, 1970; Corcoran Gallery Art, Washington, 1971, U. Ill., 1974; represented in permanent collections Pasadena Art Mus., San Francisco Mus. Art, Oakland Mus. Art, Los Angeles County Mus., others. Tchr., Calif. Sch. Fine Arts, 1957-65; prof. art Stanford, 1965—. Served with AUS, 1942-46. Recipient Nealie Sullivan award, 1960. Home: 340 Palo Alto Ave Palo Alto CA 94301

LOBDELL, LEIGHTON MANSFIELD, ins. co. exec.; b. N.Y.C., Sept. 27, 1927; s. Leighton and Ruth A. (Adams) L.; A.B., U. Va., 1952; m. Phyllis B. Scott, Apr. 5, 1952; children—Shelley A., Lanier S., Leighton D., Kimberly, Andrew A. Trust adminstr. U.S. Trust Co., N.Y.C., 1952-54; with Continental Ins. Co., 1954—, v.p., treas., N.Y.C., 1969—; v.p., treas. Continental Corp., N.Y.C., 1968—; treas. Continental Found.; dir. Afco Credit Corp. and affiliates; trustee Ind. Savs. Bank, Bklyn. Bd. dirs. N.J. Jr. C. of C., 1961-62. Served with AUS, 1946-48. Mem. N.Y. Soc. Security Analysts. Clubs: Seabright (N.J.) Lawn Tennis and Cricket, Seabright Beach; Church (N.Y.C.). Home: One Shrewsbury Dr Apt 2A Rumson NJ 07760 Office: 80 Maiden Ln New York NY 10038

LOBDELL, ROBERT CHARLES, newspaper exec.; b. Mankato, Minn., Jan. 1, 1926; s. Darwin Norman and Hilda Cecelia (Peterson) L.; A.B., Stanford U., 1948, LL.B., 1950; m. Nancy Marion Lower, July 12, 1952; children—Teresa M., Robert John, William Scott, James Marston. Admitted to Calif. bar, 1951, U.S. Supreme Ct., 1964; Atty. legal dept. Bank of Am., Los Angeles, 1951-52; atty., corporate officer Youngstown Sheet and Tube Co., 1952-65; asst. gen. counsel, asst. sec. Times Mirror Co., 1965-70, v.p., asst. sec., 1970—; v.p., gen. counsel Los Angeles Times, 1970—; sec., trustee Pfaffinger Found., sec., trustee Los Angeles Times Fund. Gov. Stanford Assos.; bd. dirs. Los Angeles County Bar Found. Mem. Am., Calif., Los Angeles County bar assns., Am. Soc. Corporate Secs, Beta Theta Pi. Club: University. Home: 925 Hillside Dr Long Beach CA 90815 Office: Times Mirror Sq Los Angeles CA 90053

LOBECK, CHARLES CHAMPLIN, educator; b. New Rochelle, N.Y., May 20, 1926; s. Charles Champlin and Jeanne Louise (Weiss) L.; A.B., Hobart Coll., 1948; M.D., U. Rochester, 1952; m. Isabelle Emerson, Feb. 6, 1954; children—Charles C., Anne C., Sarah E., Jane M. Intern, Grace-New Haven Community Hosp., 1953; resident Strong Meml. Hosp., 1953-55, instr. pediatrics, 1955—; sr. instr. pediatrics U. Rochester Med. Sch., 1958; former mem. faculty U. Wis. Med. Sch., Madison, prof. pediatrics, chmn. dept., 1964-74, asso. dean, 1974-76; now dean Sch. Medicine, U. Mo., Columbia. Cons. NIH; mem. gen. med. and sci. adv. council Nat. Cystic Fibrosis Research Found.; trustee Nat. Cystic Fibrosis Found. Served with USAAF, 1944-46. NIH, grantee 1958—. Fellow Am. Acad. Pediatrics; mem. Am. Pediatric Soc., Soc. Pediatric Research, Midwest Soc. Pediatric Research (pres. 1972). Office: U Mo Columbia Sch Medicine 807 Stadium Rd Columbia MO 65212

LOBEL, ARNOLD STARK, author, illustrator; b. Los Angeles, May 22, 1933; s. Joseph and Lucille Harriet (Stark) L.; B.F.A., Pratt Inst., 1955; m. Anita, Apr. 16, 1955; children—Adrianne, Adam. Author, illustrator children's books: Zoo for Mister Muster, 1962, Prince Bertram the Red, 1963, Holiday for Mister Muster, 1963, Giant John, 1964, Lucille, 1964, Martha the Movie Mouse, 1966, Great Blueness and Other Predicaments, 1968, Small Pig, 1969, Frog and Toad Are Friends, 1970, Ice-Cream Cone Coot and Other Rare Birds, 1971, On the Day Peter Stuyvesant Sailed into Town, 1971, Mouse Tales, 1972, Frog and Toad Together, 1972, The Man Who Took the Indoors Out, 1974, Owl at Home, 1975, Frog and Toad All Year, 1976, Mouse Soup, 1977, Gregory Griggs and the Nursery Rhyme People, 1978; Days With Frog and Toad, 1979; Fables, 1980. Recipient Caldecott Honor award, 1970-71, Newberry Honor award, 1972, Christopher award, 1971-76; Nat. Book awards finalist, 1970, 71, 75. Mem. Authors Guild. Address: care Harper & Row Inc 10 E 53d St New York NY 10022

LO BELLO, NINO, author, journalist; b. Bklyn., Sept. 8, 1921; s. Joseph and Rosalie (Moscarelli) Lo B.; B.A., Queens Coll., N.Y.C., 1947; M.A., N.Y. U., 1948; m. Irene Helen Rooney, Feb. 22, 1948; children—Susan, Thomas. Reporter and columnist Ridgewood (N.Y.) Times, 1946-50; instr. sociology U. Kans., 1950-55; Rome corr. Bus. Week mag., 1959-62, N.Y. Jour. Commerce, 1962-64; Vienna corr. 103 U.S. and Canadian dailies, 1964—; vis. prof. sociology Denison U., Ohio, spring 1956; vis. prof. journalism U. Alaska, summer 1974. Served in USAF, 1942-46. Recipient Goldener Rathausmann award for Outstanding Fgn. Reporting, Vienna, 1974; named Alumnus of Year, Grover Cleveland High Sch., Queens, N.Y., 1977. Mem. Overseas Press Club Am., Am. Soc. Journalists and Authors, Fgn. Press Club Vienna. Club: Loyalty of Vienna. Author: The Vatican Empire (N.Y. Times Best Seller List), 1969; Vatican, U.S.A., 1972; The Vatican's Wealth, 1971; contbr. articles to mags. and jours. Home: 78 Walnut St Winsted CT 06098 Office: 8 Bankgasse Vienna Austria 1010

LOBER, DONALD WARRING, JR., real estate exec.; b. Weston, Mo., Jan. 7, 1921; s. Donald W. and Ammie (Layton) L.; student Mo. Valley Coll., 1939-40, U. Mo., 1941; m. Helen Frances Brownsberger, Mar. 27, 1942; children—James, Susan, Charles, Nancy, Linda, John. With U.S. Savs. and Loan League, Chgo., 1946; investment officer First Fed. Savs., Chgo., 1947-48; partner Lober Motor Co., Liberty, Mo., 1949-50; investment officer Home Savs. Assn., Kansas City, 1951-55; exec. v.p. Mid-Am. Fire & Marine Ins. Co., Kansas City, 1956-57, Charles F. Curry Real Estate Co., Kansas City, 1958-61; exec. v.p. Home Savs. Assn., Kansas City, 1962-71, pres., 1971-76; now in comml. real estate. Served to capt. USAAF, World War II; ETO. Democrat. Baptist. Mason (Shriner). Home: 7914 W Country Club Dr Overland Park KS 66212 Office: 10310 State Line Leawood KS 66206

LOBER, PAUL HALLAM, educator; b. Mpls., Sept. 25, 1919; s. Harold A. and Minnie (Toraason) L.; B.S., U. Minn., 1942, M.D., 1944, Ph.D. in Pathology, 1951. Intern, resident Hennepin County Gen. Hosp., 1944-46; fellow dept. pathology U. Minn., Mpls., 1948-51, faculty Med. Sch., 1951—, prof. pathology, 1963—; surg. pathologist Univ. Hosps., Mpls., 1951-74, Northwestern Hosp., Mpls., 1974—. Served to capt. AUS, 1946-48. Fellow Coll. Am. Pathologists; mem. AMA, Am. Soc. Clin. Pathologists, Internat. Acad. Pathology, Am. Assn. Pathologists, Am. Soc. Cytology, N.Y. Acad. Scis., Alpha Omega Alpha. Home: 5800 View Ln Edina MN 55436 Office: Pathology Dept Northwestern Hosp 810 E 27th St Minneapolis MN 55407

LOBIANCO, TONY, actor; b. N.Y.C., Oct. 19, 1936. Founder Triangle Theater, 1963; Broadway debut in The Office, 1966; other Broadway appearances include: Royal Hunt of the Sun, Rose Tattoo, The Goodbye People; off-Broadway appearances include: Oh Dad, Poor Dad, Zoo Story, Tartuffe, Yankees 3, Detroit O (Obie award 1976); films include: The French Connection, The Seven-Ups, The Honeymoon Killers, F.I.S.T., Bloodbrothers; TV appearances include: Hidden Faces, Love of Life, Police Story, The Story of Jacob and Joseph. Office: care Paul Kohner Michael Levy Agy 9169 Sunset Blvd Hollywood CA 90069*

LOBITZ, WALTER CHARLES, JR., physician, educator; b. Cin., Dec. 13, 1911; s. Walter Charles and Elsa (Spangenberg) L.; student Brown U., 1930-31; B.Sc., U. Cin., 1939, M.B., 1940, M.D., 1941; M.Sc., U. Minn., 1945; M.A. (hon.), Dartmouth, 1958; LL.D., Hokkaido U., 1976; m. Caroline Elizabeth Rockwell, July 11, 1942; children—Walter Charles III, John Rockwell, Susan Hastings. Intern, Cin. Gen. Hosp., 1940, resident medicine, 1941; fellow Mayo Found., 1942-45; 1st asst. Mayo Clinic, 1945-47; chmn. sect. dermatology Hitchcock Clinic, Hanover, N.H., 1947-59, bd. dirs., 1955; faculty Dartmouth Med. Sch., 1947-59, prof. dermatology, 1957-59; prof. dermatology, head div. U. Oreg. Med. Sch., 1959-69, chmn. dept., 1969-77; prof. U. Oreg. Health Scis. Center. Area cons. VA, 1949-59; mem. commn. cutaneous diseases Armed Forces Epidemiologic Bd., 1955—; cons., mem. gen. med. study sect. USPHS, 1961-65; mem. grant rev. com. United Health Found., 1964-65; cons. dermatology tng. grants com. Nat. Inst. Arthritis and Metabolic Diseases, 1966-70; cons. VA Hosp., U. Oreg. Med. Sch., 1959—; civilian cons. to surg. gen. USAF, 1969—; U.S. Air Force-Nat. cons. to Surgeon Gen., 1970. Trustee Dermatology Found., Med. Research Found. Oreg., 1972, exec. com., 1972—, v.p., 1975-76, pres., 1977-78; music adv. com. Oreg. Symphony Orch., 1970-73; mem. Oreg. Ballet Council, 1974; bd. govs. Hitchcock Hosp., 1955; trustee Hitchcock Found., 1958-59, exec. com. 1958-59. Dohi Meml. lectr. Japanese Dermatol. Assn., 1964; lectr. U. Copenhagen, Denmark, 1969, 74. Recipient Outstanding Achievement award U. Minn., 1964. Diplomate Am. Bd. Dermatology (bd. dirs. 1955-64, pres. 1962). Fellow A.C.P., A.M.A., Am. Acad. Dermatology (bd. dirs. 1958-61, 66-69, pres. 1969), Phila. Coll. Physicians (hon.); mem. Am. Dermatol. Assn. (bd. dirs. 1962-67, pres. 1972), Soc. Investigative Dermatology (v.p. 1952, bd. dirs. 1953-58, pres. 1957, hon. mem.), N.H., Multnomah County, Oreg., Japanese (hon.) med. socs., N.Y. Acad. Scis., A.A.A.S., Pacific N.W. (pres. 1971), Pacific, Israeli (hon.) dermatol. assns., Northwest Soc. Clin. Research, Oreg. Dermatol. Soc. (pres. 1969), Portland Acad. Medicine, Am. Fedn. Clin. Research, Pacific Interurban Clin. Club (councillor 1971), Internat. Soc. Tropical Dermatology, Sigma Xi, Pi Kappa Epsilon, Alpha Omega Alpha; hon. mem. Soc. Venezolana de Dermatologia and Leprologia, French Soc. Dermatology, Brit. Assn. Dermatology, Assn. parala Investigacion Dermatologica (Venezuela), Soc. Dermatol. Danicae, Italian, Japan, Hokkaido, Sapporo derm. socs. Presbyn. Author numerous articles in field. Co-editor: The Epidermis; editorial bd. Jour. Investigative Dermatology, 1958-61, Excerpta of Medicine, 1961-78; mem. editorial bd. Archives Dermatology, 1960-77, chief editor, 1963-68. Home: 2211 SW First Ave Portland OR 97201

LOBNER, KNEELAND HARKNESS, lawyer; b. Sacramento, Feb. 2, 1919; s. Leo Kneeland and Laura (Roberts) L.; A.A., Sacramento City Coll., 1939; J.D., Hastings Coll. Law, 1944; m. Adele Frances Ohe, Dec. 20, 1941; children—Breton K., Robert K., Susan. A. Lobner Schroeder. Admitted to Calif. bar, 1946, U.S. Supreme Ct. bar, 1960; atty. City of Auburn, Calif., 1946-47; asso. firm K.D. Robinson, Auburn, 1946-47; dep. dist. atty. Sacramento County, 1947-49; atty. Calif. Automobile Assn., Sacramento, 1949-52; partner firm Lobner and Bull, Sacramento, 1958—. Councilman, City of Sacramento, 1957-62, vice mayor, 1962; mem. Sacramento Met. Adv. Com., 1957-59, Sacramento Redevel. Agy., 1964-73, chmn., 1970-72; mem. Sacramento Estate Planning Council, 1960—; mem. Sacramento County Republican Central Com., 1955-57, Calif. Rep. Central Com., 1962-68; bd. dirs. Am. Cancer Soc., Sacramento, 1956-64, pres., 1963-64; bd. dirs. Calif. Mus. Assn., 1968-73, pres., 1969-71; bd. dirs. Am. Heart Assn., Sacramento, 1958-68; bd. govs. Hastings Law Coll., 1960—, pres., 1966; pres. Hastings 1066 Found., 1976; bd. dirs. Sacramento Symphony Found. Served with AUS, 1944-46. Recipient Outstanding Alumnus award Hastings Coll. Law, 1976. Fellow Am. Coll. Probate Counsel; mem. Am. Bd. Trial Advocates (advocate), Am., Sacramento County (pres. 1973) bar assns., State Bar Calif., Am. Judicature Soc., Better Bus. Bur. Sacramento (pres. 1967), Sacramento Zool. Soc. (pres. 1965), Am. Legion, Sacramento County Bar Council. Clubs: Del Paso Country, Elks. Office: 717 20th St Sacramento CA 95814

LOBSENZ, AMELIA, public relations co. exec.; b. Greensboro, N.C.; d. Leo and Florence (Scheer) Freitag; B.A., Agnes Scott Coll., 1944; m. Harry Abrahams, Aug. 17, 1957; children—Michael, Kay. Dir. mag. dept. Edward Gottlieb & Assos., N.Y.C., 1952-56; pres. Lobsenz Public Relations Co., N.Y.C., 1956-75; chmn. bd., chief exec. officer Lobsenz-Stevens Inc., N.Y.C., 1975-79; lectr. in field. Recipient award for best article on ins. Mag. Writers, 1974; named to Acad. Women Achievers, YWCA, 1978. Mem. Am. Soc. Journalists and Authors, Am. Med. Writers Assn., Am. Women in Radio and TV, Nat. Assn. Sci. Writers, Public Relations Soc. Am. (Pres.'s award for outstanding service 1975, 78, dir. N.Y. chpt. 1971-79, chmn. nat. com. on public relations for public relations 1977-79), Publicity Club N.Y., Publicity Club Chgo. Clubs: Windham Mountain, Racquet Club of Old Westbury (N.Y.). Author: Kay Everett Calls CQ, 1951 (Jr. Lit. Guild Selection); Kay Everett Works DX, 1952; contbr. articles to mags. Office: Two Park Ave New York NY 10016

LOCALIO, ARTHUR, surgeon, educator; b. N.Y.C., Oct. 4, 1911;; s. Joseph and Carmella (Franco) L.; A.B., Cornell U., 1932; M.D., U. Rochester, 1936; D.Sc., Columbia, 1942; m. Ruth Virginia Adkins, July 14, 1945; children—William Hale, Susan Emily, Arthur Russell, David Charles. Intern pathology N.Y. U. Hosp., 1936-37, intern medicine, 1937-38, asst. resident in surgery, 1938-40, sr. resident, 1940-42, asst. surgeon, 1945-47, asst. attending surgeon, 1947-49, asso. attending surgeon, 1949-52, attending surgeon, 1952—; clin. asst. vis. surgeon 4th surg. div. Bellevue Hosp., N.Y.C., 1945-46, asst. vis. surgeon, 1946-48, asso. vis. surgeon, 1948-52, vis. surgeon, 1952—; practice medicine specializing in surgery, N.Y.C., 1945—; instr. surgery Columbia Postgrad. Med. Sch., N.Y.C., 1945-48, asst. prof., 1948-49; asst. prof. surgery N.Y. U. Schs. Medicine, N.Y.C., 1949-50, asso. prof., 1950-53, prof., 1953—, Johnson and Johnson Distinguished prof. surgery, 1972—; cons. in surgery Riverview Hosp., Red Bank, N.J., 1952—, Monmouth Meml. Hosp., Long Branch, N.J., 1952—, St. Barnabas Hosp., N.Y.C., 1958—, VA Hosp., N.Y.C., Wyckoff Heights Hosp., Bklyn., N.Y. Infirmary, N.Y.C., Booth Meml. Hosp., Flushing, N.Y., Brookhaven Meml. Hosp., Patchogue, N.Y. Served from capt. to lt. col. M.C., AUS, 1942-45; PTO. Diplomate Am. Bd. Surgery. Mem. Am., N.Y. gastroent. assns., A.C.S., A.M.A., Am. Assn. for Surgery of Trauma, Soc. for Surgery Alimentary Tract, N.Y. Acad. Medicine (trustee 1971—), N.Y. Acad. Scis., N.Y. Cancer Soc., N.Y. Soc. Colon and Rectal Surgeons, Pan Am. (N.Am. chmn. sect. gen. surgery 1972—), N.Y. County, N.Y. State med. socs., Sociedad Colombiana de Cirujanos, Societe Internationale de Chirurgie, N.Y., B.C. surg. socs., Transplantation Soc., Am. Surg. Assn., Sigma Xi. Contbr. articles to med. jours. Home: 2 Beekman Pl New York NY 10022 Office: NY U Sch Medicine 530 1st Ave New York NY 10016

LOCHER, RALPH S., justice Ohio Supreme Ct.; b. Moreni, Romania, July 24, 1915; s. Ephraim and Natalie (Voigt) L.; B.A. with honors, Bluffton Coll., 1936; LL.B., Case Western Res. U., 1939; m. Eleanor Worthington, June 18, 1939; 1 dau., Virginia Lynn. Admitted to Ohio bar, 1939; former sec. to Gov. Ohio; former law dir. City of Cleve.; former mayor Cleve.; judge Ohio Ct. Common Pleas Cuyahoga County, 1969-72, Cuyahoga County Ct. Probate Div., 1973-77; justice Supreme Ct. Ohio, 1977—. Mem. Am. Bar Assn., Bar Assn. Greater Cleve., Cuyahoga County Bar Assn. Democrat. Office: State Office Tower 30 E Broad St Columbus OH 43215*

LOCHER, RICHARD EARL, editorial cartoonist; b. Dubuque, Iowa, June 4, 1929; s. Joseph John and Lucille (Jungk) L.; student Loras Coll., 1948, Chgo. Acad. Fine Arts, 1949-51; B.F.A., Art Center, Los Angeles, 1954, postgrad., 1955-56; m. Mary Therese Cosgrove, June 15, 1957; children—Stephen Robert, John Joseph, Jana Lynne. Asst. writer, artist Buck Rogers Comic Strip, 1954-57, Dick Tracy Comic Strip, 1957-61, Martin Aerospace Co., Denver, 1962-63; art dir. Hansen Co., Chgo., N.Y.C., 1963-68; founder, pres. Novamark Corp., Chgo., 1968-72; editorial cartoonist Chgo. Tribune, 1972—; cons. McDonalds Corp., Oakbrook, Ill.; tchr. art at local high schs. and colls. Served with USAF, 1951-53. Recipient Dragonslayer award U.S. Indsl. Council, 1976, 77, 78; runner-up Overseas Press Club award, 1978. Mem. Assn. Am. Editorial Cartoonists. Author: Dick Locher Draws Fire, 1980. Patentee, Poker Face device to play poker without cards. Home: 921 Heatherton St Naperville IL 60540 Office: Chgo Tribune 435 N Michigan Ave Chicago IL 60611. *It is vitally important to strive for excellence, and to provide that goal with Clear direction, desire and energy. It is only more important to maintain friendships and help others achieve excellence.*

LOCHHEAD, DOUGLAS GRANT, librarian, educator; b. Guelph, Ont., Can., Mar. 25, 1922; s. Allan Grant and Helen Louise (Van Wart) L.; B.A. in Sociology and Psychology, McGill U., Montreal, Que., Can., 1943, B.L.S., 1951; M.A. in English, U. Toronto (Ont.), 1947; m. Jean St. Clair Beckwith, Sept. 17, 1949; children—Sara Louise, Mary Elizabeth. Advt. and newspaper work, Toronto and Ottawa, Ont., 1947-50; chief librarian Victoria (B.C., Can.) Coll., 1951-52, lectr. sociology, 1951-52; librarian Cornell U., Ithaca, N.Y., 1952-53; prof., univ. librarian Dalhousie U., Halifax, N.S., Can., 1953-60; dir. libraries, asst. prof. English, York U., Toronto, 1960-63; librarian Massey Coll., U. Toronto, 1963-75, spl. lectr. grad. dept. English, 1964-65, prof. English in bibliography, palaeography, Canadian poetry, 1965-75, asso. instr. faculty library sci., fellow Massey Coll., 1965-75, asso. fellow, 1975—; Davidson prof., dir. Can. studies program Centre for Can. Studies, Mt. Allison U., Sackville, N.B., Can., 1975—. Served to lt. arty., inf., Can. Army, 1943-45. Fellow Royal Soc. Can.; mem. Bibliog. Soc. Can. (pres. 1974-76), Quadrats (founder, joint jost), League Canadian Poets (vice chmn. 1968-72), bibliog. socs. Am., London, U. Va., Oxford (Eng.) Bibliog. Soc. Author: The Heart is Fire, 1959; It is All Around, 1960; Millwood Road Poems, 1970; Prayers in a Field, 1974; The Full Furnace: Collected Poems, 1975; High Marsh Road, 1979. Editor: (with Raymond Souster) Made in Canada: an anthology of Contemporary Canadian Poetry, 1970; 100 Poems of Nineteenth Century Canada, 1974; gen. editor Literature of Canada Series, Poetry and Prose in Retrospect, 1972—; Toronto Reprint Library of Canadian Prose and Poetry, 50 vols., 1973-78. Home: PO Box 1108 7 Quarry Ln Sackville NB E0A 3C0 Canada

LO CHIANO, ROCCO, natural gas co. exec.; b. Kansas City, Mo., Jan. 24, 1925; s. Anthony and Leona (Mangiarcina) LoC.; B.S. in Mech. Engring., Iowa State U., 1944; m. Sally Norman, Aug. 2, 1975; children—Steve, Mark, Nancy. Resident engr. Panhandle Eastern Pipeline Co., Kansas City, Mo., 1946-50; sr. engr. Trunk Line Gas Co., Houston, 1950-53; asst. chief engr. Interstate Gas Co., Houston, 1953-59; v.p. Gulf Interstate Engring. Co., Houston, 1959-64; with No. Natural Gas Co., Omaha, 1964—, v.p. engring. div., 1966, group v.p. corp. engring. and research, 1975—, dir. subs.; v.p., dir. No. Petrochem. Co. Served with USNR, 1944-46. Mem. Am. Gas Assn. Home: 11802 Washington Circle Omaha NE 68137 Office: 2223 Dodge St Omaha NE 68102

LOCHMILLER, RODNEY GLEN, trucking co. exec.; b. Ainsworth, Nebr., Oct. 5, 1921; s. Herbert M. and Edith (Smith) L.; student Am. U., Biarritz, France, 1945, Denver U., 1946, also profl. courses; m. Mary M. Frauen, Oct. 6, 1941; children—Roxann Lochmiller Varzeas, Kurtis L. With Pacific Intermountain Express, Denver, Oakland, Calif., and Portland, Oreg., 1941-59, dist. mgr., Portland, 1958-59; gen. mgr. Western Produce Express, Portland, 1959-60; terminal mgr. Transcon Lines, Los Angeles, 1960-62; v.p., operating services div. Navajo Freight Lines, Denver, 1963-67, sr. v.p., 1970-75, pres., 1975—, also dir.; v.p. ops., dir. Thurston Motor Lines, Charlotte, N.C., 1967-69; dir. ops. Valley Cooperstate, Los Angeles, 1969-70. Served with U.S. Army, 1942-46. Mem. Western Operators Assn. (dir. 1973—), Terminal Ops. Council, N. Mex., Colo. (3d v.p., mem. exec. com.) motor carriers assns., Western Trucking Employers (dir. 1974), Am. Trucking Assn., AIM (mem. pres.'s council 1974-75), Delta Nu Alpha, also traffic clubs. Republican. Presbyterian. Clubs: Masons, Shriners, Elks. Home: 4570 E Yale St #701 Denver CO 80222 Office: 1205 S Platte River Dr Denver CO 80223

LOCK, RICHARD WILLIAM, packaging co. exec.; b. N.Y.C., Oct. 5, 1931; s. Albert and Catherine Dorothy (Magnus) L.; B.S., Rutgers U., 1953; M.B.A., N.Y. U., 1958; m. Elizabeth Louise Kenney, Nov. 2, 1957; children—Albert, Dorothy, John. Acct., Gen. Electric Co., 1953-54, Union Carbide Co., N.Y.C., 1956-58; div. controller St. Regis Paper Co., Houston, 1959-62; treas. Owens-Illinois, Inc., Toledo, 1962—. Chmn. adv. bd. Toledo Salvation Army, 1974-77; pres. Toledo Area Govtl. Research Assn., 1978-79. Served with USAF, 1954-56. Mem. Fin. Execs. Inst., Am. Soc. Corp. Secs., Phi Beta Kappa. Republican. Lutheran. Club: Toledo. Home: 6110 Jeffrey Ln Sylvania OH 43560 Office: PO Box 1035 Toledo OH 43666

LOCKARD, WALTER DUANE, educator, polit. scientist; b. Owings, W.Va., Nov. 26, 1921; s. J. Clyde and Virgie (Walters) L.; student Fairmont (W.Va.) Tchrs. Coll., 1939-41, W.Va., U., 1941-42; B.A., Yale, 1947, M.A., 1948, Ph.D., 1952; m. Beverly L. White, July 6, 1942; children—Linda L., Janet F., Leslie K. Instr., Wesleyan U., Middletown, Conn., 1950-51; faculty Conn. Coll., New London, 1951-61; faculty Princeton, 1961—, prof. polit. sci., 1964—, chmn. dept. politics, 1969-72; vis. lectr. Yale, 1960-61; Fulbright-Hayes prof. U. Kent, Eng., 1972-73. Mem. Conn. Senate, 1955-57; del. N.J. Constl. Conv., 1966. Served to capt. USAAF, 1942-46; ETO. Decorated Air medals (five). Ford faculty fellow, 1954-55; Social Sci. Research fellow, 1960-61, 62-63. Mem. Am. Polit. Sci. Assn., AAUP. Author: New England State Politics, 1959; The Politics of State and Local Government, 1963; The New Jersey Governor, 1964; Toward Equal Opportunity, 1968; The Perverted Priorities of American Politics, 1971. Home: 72 Western Way Princeton NJ 08540

LOCKARD, WILLIAM KIRBY, architect; b. Cobden, Ill., July 24, 1929; s. Melvin Clarence and Zella (Mangold) L.; B.S. in Architecture, U. Ill., 1952; M.Arch., M.I.T., 1962; m. Peggy Lou Hamilton, Dec. 9, 1972; children—Rita Gail, Melvin Scott, William Brodie. Architect-in-tng. Scholer, Sakeller & Fuller, Tucson, 1954-59; chief designer Friedman & Jobusch, Tucson, 1959-61; asst. prof.

architecture U. Ariz., 1962-65, asso. prof., 1966-67, prof., 1968—; vis. lectr. to univs., colls.; condr. design graphics workshops, 1975-78; vis. prof. Esquela Mexicana de Arquitectura, Universidad La Salle, Mexico City, 1977; mem. Tucson Planning and Zoning Commn., 1971-73, chmn., 1972. Served to 1st lt. Armored Div., U.S. Army, 1952-54. Recipient 3d prize Biscayne West Nat. Design Competition for Urban Housing, Miami, Fla., 1976, Creative Teaching award U. Ariz., 1976. Fellow AIA. Author: Drawing as a Means to Architecture, 1968; Design Drawing Experiences, 1973; Design Drawing, 1974; designer Dove of Peace Lutheran Ch., Tucson, 1966 (AIA Regional award of merit 1969). Home: 2901 E Mabel St Tucson AZ 85716

LOCKE, BARRY M(YLES), state ofcl.; b. Boston, Dec. 21, 1930; B.S., Boston U., 1953; m. Ann Boggio, Oct. 21, 1956; children—Vanessa, Valerie, Alison. Editor, Three Rivers (Mich.) Daily Newspaper, 1956-57; Vt. bur. mgr. UPI, 1957-61; exec. adminstr. to gov. Vt., 1961-63; New Eng. public info. dir. IRS, 1963-64; chief press sec. to gov. Mass., Boston, 1964-69; spl. asst. to sec. Transp., Washington, 1969-72; spl. asst. to adminstr. Law Enforcement Assistance Adminstrn. and dir. public affairs White House Energy Policy Office, 1972-73; prin. Smith and Locke Assos., Inc., transp. mgmt. cons., Washington, 1974-77; exec. dir. Bi-State Devel. Agy., St. Louis, 1977-78; sec. transp. and constrn. Commonwealth of Mass., Boston, 1979—; guest lectr. Boston U., Am. U.; bd. dirs. Ill. Public Transit Assn., 1978-79, Ill. Public Airports Assn., 1978-79. Bd. dirs. Loretto-Hilton Repertory Theatre, St. Louis, 1978-79; mem. Mass. Ednl. TV Commn., 1965-68, Mass. CD Communications Commn., 1965-68; mem. adv. devel. council Emerson Coll., 1966-68. Served with U.S. Army, 1953-55. Recipient cert. merit UPI, 1960, medal for outstanding service sec. Transp., 1972. Office: Exec Office Transp and Constrn Mass Boston MA 02108

LOCKE, CHARLES STANLEY, mfg. co. exec.; b. Laurel, Miss., Mar. 5, 1929; s. R. C. and Florence (Parker) L.; B.B.A., U. Miss., 1952, M.S., 1955; m. Nora Fulkerson, Mar. 15, 1952; children—Cathy, Stanley, Lauren, Pamela. With Corvey Engring. Co., Inc., Washington, 1952, Price Waterhouse & Co., C.P.A.'s, New Orleans, 1955-58, Westvaco, Inc., 1958-64; controller A.E. Staley Mfg. Co., 1964-69; v.p. Brown Co., Pasadena, Calif., 1969-73, also dir., mem. exec. com.; sr. v.p. Allen Group Inc., Melville, N.Y., 1973-75; v.p. fin. dir. Morton-Norwich Products, Inc., Chgo., 1975—. Served with AUS, 1952-54. Mem. Nat. Assn. Accountants, Financial Execs. Inst., Beta Alpha Psi. Methodist. Home: 1504 N Waukegan Rd Lake Forest IL 60045 Office: Morton-Norwich Products Inc 110 N Wacker Dr Chicago IL 60606

LOCKE, EDITH RAYMOND, editor; b. Vienna, Austria, Aug. 3, 1921; d. Herman and Dora (Hochberg) Laub; student Bklyn. Coll., 1940-42, City Coll. N.Y., 1942-45; m. A. Ralph Locke, Jr., May 29, 1963; 1 dau., Katherine Dee. Came to U.S., 1939, naturalized, 1944. Asst. to advt. dir. Harper's Bazaar, N.Y.C., 1945-46, asso. mdse. editor Jr. Bazaar, 1946-48; fashion dir. Abbott Kimball Advt. Agy., N.Y.C., 1948-49; asso. fashion editor Mademoiselle mag., N.Y.C., 1949-59, fashion editor, 1959-67, exec. editor, 1967-72, editor-in-chief, 1972—. Mem. Am. Fashion Critics Coty award jury. Mem. Am. Soc. Mag. Editors, Fashion Group (pres. 1972-73). Author: The Red Door, 1965. Office: 350 Madison Ave New York NY 10017

LOCKE, EDWIN ALLEN, JR., club exec.; b. Boston, June 8, 1910; s. Edwin Allen and Elizabeth (Ferguson) L.; grad. Phillips Acad., Exeter, N.H., 1928; A.B., cum laude, Harvard, 1932; m. Dorothy Q. Clark, June 16, 1934 (div.); children—Elizabeth Eliane, Edwin Allen III, Benjamin Clark; m. 2d, Karin Marsh, 1952; 1 son, Jonathan Winston. Asso., Chase Nat. Bank, N.Y.C., 1932-33, Paris br., 1933-35, London br., 1935-36, N.Y.C., 1936-40, v.p., 1947-51; Office Coordinator Purchases, adv. commn. to Council Nat. Def., 1940-41; asst. dep. dir. priorities div. Office Prodn. Mgmt., 1941; dep. chief staff officer Supply Priorities and Allocation Bd., 1941-42; asst. to chmn. WPB, 1942-44; exec. asst. to personal rep. of Pres., 1944-45, personal rep. of Pres., 1945-47; also spl. asst. to pres., 1946-47; spl. rep. Sec. State, ambassador to Near East, 1951-53; exec. asst. to pres. Union Tank Car Co., Chgo., 1953-54, exec. v.p., 1954-55, pres., dir., 1955-63; pres., chief exec. officer Modern Homes Constrn. Co., Valdosta, Ga., 1963-67, Coastal Products Corp., Blountstown, Fla., 1964-67; pres., chief exec. officer Am. Paper Inst., N.Y.C., 1967-77, Econ. Club of N.Y., 1977—; chmn., dir. Fed. Home Loan Bank of Chgo., 1956-63; dir. Nat. Am. Ins. Co. N.Y., Stuyvesant Life Ins. Co. Mem. Presdl. Survey Mission to Liberia and Tunisia, 1963; mem. adv. com. on internat. bus. problems Dept. State, 1962-67. Trustee China Med. Bd. Clubs: Chicago; Harvard, Racquet and Tennis (N.Y.C.); Metropolitan (Washington). Office: 522 Fifth Ave New York City NY 10036

LOCKE, EDWIN ALLEN, III, psychologist, educator; b. N.Y.C., May 15, 1938; s. Edwin Allen and Dorothy (Clark) L.; B.A., Harvard U., 1960; M.A., Cornell U., 1962, Ph.D., 1964; m. Anne Hassard, June 13, 1968. Asso. research scientist Am. Inst. Research, 1964-66, research scientist, 1966-70; asst. prof. psychology U. Md., College Park, 1967-69, asso. prof., 1969-70, asso. prof. bus. adminstrn., mgmt. and psychology, 1970-73, prof., 1973—. Office Naval Research grantee, 1964, 79; NIMH grantee, 1967. Fellow Am. Psychol. Assn.; mem. Acad. Mgmt., N.Y. Acad. Scis. Author: A Guide to Effective Study, 1975; cons. editor Jour. Applied Psychology, 1972—; contbr. articles to profl. jours. Home: 2659 Carrollton Rd Annapolis MD 21403 Office: Coll Bus and Mgmt U Md College Park MD 20742. *The most important literary/philosophical influence in my life has been Ayn Rand. Her philosophy of Objectivism demonstrates that man's highest purpose in the achievement of his own happiness and that reason is his only means to achieve it. Her novels, which portray man as an heroic being, are an inspiration to every man to achieve the best within him.*

LOCKE, JACK LAMBOURNE, astronomer; b. Brantford, Ont., Can., May 1, 1921; s. Joseph Thomas and Mabel Caroline (Lambourne) L.; B.A. in Math. and Physics, U. Toronto (Ont.), 1946, M.A. in Physics, 1947, Ph.D. in Physics, 1949; m. Edith Joyce Moxon, May 24, 1946; children—John Andrew, Marion Jane. Astronomer, Dominion Obs., Ottawa, Ont., 1949-55, chief of stellar physics div., 1955-66; officer-in-charge Dominion Radio Astrophys. Obs., Penticton, B.C., Can., 1959-62; asso. dir. div. radio and elec. engring. NRC Can., Ottawa, 1969-75, dir. Herzberg Inst. Astrophysics, 1975—. Served with Royal Can. Navy, 1942-45. Co-recipient Rumford premium Am. Acad. Arts and Sci. Fellow Royal Soc. Can.; mem. Am. Astron. Soc., Can. Astron. Soc., Royal Astron. Soc. Can., Inst. Radio and Electronics Engrs. Home: 2150 Braeside Ave Ottawa ON K1H 7J5 Canada Office: Herzberg Inst Astrophysics NRC Can Ottawa ON K1A 0R6 Canada

LOCKE, JOHN ROBINSON, lawyer; b. San Antonio, Feb. 10, 1894; s. Jonathan and Brent (Robinson) L.; LL.B., U. Va., 1915; postgrad. U. Tex., 1915-16; m. Grace Walker, Oct. 25, 1921; children—Grace W. (Mrs. F. Barton Harvey, Jr.), John Robinson. Admitted to Tex. bar, 1916; with Templeton, Brooks, Napier & Brown, 1916-25, Brewer & Locke, 1925-26, Kelso, Locke & Lepick, and predecessors, San Antonio, 1927-72, Groce, Locke & Hebdon, 1972—; pres. San Antonio Joint Stock Land Bank, 1940-48; dir. Frost Nat. Bank. Vice pres. San Antonio Bd. Edn., 1938-44; mem. San Antonio Water Bd., 1954-57; mem. San Antonio Pub. Service Bd., 1964-74, chmn., 1970-74. Served as 1st lt. F.A., U.S. Army, 1917-19. Mem. Am., Tex. bar assns. Club: San Antonio Country. Home: 138 E Gramercy St San Antonio TX 78212 Office: Frost Bank Tower San Antonio TX 78205

LOCKE, LOUIS GLENN, educator; b. Woodstock, Va., May 3, 1912; s. Thomas Glenn and Turah (Funk) L.; A.B., Bridgewater Coll., 1933; A.M., George Washington U., 1934; A.M. (Dexter travelling fellow, Univ. fellow), Harvard U., 1937, Ph.D., 1938; Ford Found. fellow Harvard and Yale U., 1953-54; m. Jeanette Wolfe, Sept. 3, 1940; children—Sarah Anne (Mrs. Walter D. Clark, Jr.), Elizabeth Louise. Acting prof. English, U. N.B. (Can.), 1938-39; asst. prof. English, Mary Washington Coll., U. Va., 1939-43; head English dept. 20th USAAF Coll. Tng. Detachment, 1943-44; asso. prof. Southwestern U., 1944-47; prof. Mary Baldwin Coll., 1947-56; chmn. dept. English, Madison Coll., Harrisonburg, Va., 1956-67, dir. div. humanities, 1956-69, dean Sch. Humanities, 1969-72, James Madison distinguished prof., 1972-77, emeritus, 1977—; vis. summer prof. Pa. State U., 1948, U. N.Mex., 1950; dir. Nat. Bank Woodstock, 1961-68; dir. Va. Nat. Bank, Woodstock, 1969—, chmn. bd., 1973—. Bd. dirs. James Madison Univ. Found., 1969—; bd. dirs., sec. Explicator Lit. Found., 1969—. Mem. Modern Lang. Assn. Am., Nat. Council Tchrs. English, S. Atlantic Modern Lang. Assn., Conf. Coll. Composition and Communication, English Inst., Coll. English Assn., Omicron Delta Kappa, Tau Kappa Alpha. Episcopalian. Author: (with others) Literature of Western Civilization, 2 vols., 1952; (with George Arms) Symposium, 1954; Tillotson: A Study in Seventeenth-Century Literature, 1954; University Readings, 1961; (with Harris Wilson) The University Handbook, 2d edit., 1966; (with others) Toward Liberal Education, 5th edit., 1967; Introduction to Literature, 5th edit., 1967; Readings for Liberal Education, 5th edit., 1967; (with others) TLE Six: Options for the 1970's, 1972; (with others) The Writer's World: Readings for College Composition, 1978. Exec. editor, co-founder The Explicator, 1942—. Home: 474 Ott St Harrisonburg VA 22801

LOCKE, NORTON, hotel mgmt. and constrn. co. exec.; b. Mpls., May 22, 1927; s. Ben and Harriet (Markus) L.; B.S., U. Wis., 1951; M.B.A., Mich. State U., 1957; m. Peggy Jane Smith, Nov. 6, 1959; children—Alexandria, Jonina, Elizabeth, Victoria. Corp. dir. food and beverage Kahler Corp., Rochester, Minn., 1970; gen. mgr., chief exec. officer Carolando Corp., Orlando, Fla., 1971-74, also dir.; gen. mgr. Radisson Muehlebach Hotel, Kansas City, Radisson Cadillac Hotel, Detroit, 1974-79; v.p., gen. mgr. White Co. Hospitality Div., Merrillville, Ind., 1979—; faculty Vallencia Coll., 1971-74. Bd. dirs. U. Minn. Tech. Coll., 1970-75, Am. Hotel and Motel Assn. Sch., 1975-79, Detroit Conv. and Visitors Bur. Served with inf., AUS, 1944-46. Mem. Internat. Food Service Execs. Assn. (dir. 1971-74), Am. Hotel and Motel Assn., Am. Chefs Assn., Mich. and Ind. Hotel Assn., Nat. Restaurant Assn., Hotel Sales Mgrs. Assn., Am. Fisheries Inst. (dir. 1970-71). Republican. Clubs: Masons; Shriners; Rotary; SKAL Internat.; Toastmasters Internat. Home: 4292 Park Pl Lake of Four Seasons IN 46307 Office: 3528 Windsor Pl Crown Point IN 46307

LOCKE, RICHARD VAN DE SANDE, investment banker; b. Flushing, N.Y., Apr. 17, 1937; s. Homer F. and Ruth E. (Rosenlund) L.; B.S., Bucknell U., 1958. With Kidder, Peabody & Co., investment bankers, N.Y.C., 1958-64; gen. partner Eastman, Dillon, Union Securities & Co., Inc., N.Y.C., 1964-72; exec. v.p., dir. Blyth Eastman Dillon & Co., Inc., N.Y.C., 1972-75, E.F. Hutton & Co., N.Y.C., 1975—; mem. N.Y., Am. stock exchanges. Served to 1st lt. U.S. Army, 1958-59, 61-62. Mem. N.Y.C. C. of C., Mcpl. Forum N.Y., Mcpl. Fin. Officers Assn., Internat. Bridge, Turnpike and Tunnel Assn., Am. Public Power Assn., Mcpl. Forum Washington, Mcpl. Bond Club N.Y., Soc. Am. Musicians, Antique Automobile Club Am., Lambda Chi Alpha, Theta Alpha Pi. Clubs: Am., Internat. Brotherhood magicians, India House, The Club, City Midday; Beacon Hill (N.J.); Lake Naomi (Pocono Pines, Pa.); Inner Circle (London). Home: 234 W 10th St New York NY 10014 Office: One Battery Park Plaza New York NY 10004

LOCKE, SONDRA, actress; b. Shelbyville, Tenn., May 28, 1947; d. Alfred Taylor and Pauline (Bayne) L.; student Middle Tenn. State U.; m. Gordon Leigh Anderson, Sept. 25, 1967. Appeared in films: The Heart is a Lonely Hunter, 1968, Run Shadow Run, 1969, Willard, 1970, The Daughter (Reflection of Fear), 1971, The Second Coming of Suzanne, 1972, Death Game, 1973, The Outlaw Josey Wales, 1975, Wishbone Cutter, 1976, The Gauntlet, 1977, Every Which Way But Loose, 1978, Bronco Billy, 1979. Office: care William Morris Agy Inc 151 El Camino Beverly Hills CA 90212

LOCKE, WALTER MICHAEL, naval officer; b. Berkeley, Calif., Apr. 11, 1930; s. Walter Anthony and Alice Marie (Heafey) L.; B.S., U.S. Naval Acad., 1952; M.S. in Elec. Engring., U.S. Naval Postgrad. Sch., 1960; m. Rosemary Ann O'Keefe, Aug. 4, 1956; children—Walter Michael, Thomas Tobias, Mary Alice. Commd. ensign U.S. Navy, 1952, advanced through grades to rear adm., 1978; designated naval aviator, 1954; project mgr. Tomahawk cruise missile Naval Air Systems Command, 1972-76; dir. joint cruise missiles project Dept. Def., Washington, 1977—. Mem. Assn. for Unmanned Vehicle Systems (trustee), U.S. Naval Acad. Alumni Assn. Office: Joint Cruise Missiles Project Navy Dept Washington DC 20360

LOCKE, WENDELL VERNON, architect; b. Douglas, Kans., Aug. 19, 1924; s. Noel Corbet and Francis Meryl (McNutt) L.; B.A., Okla. State U., 1950, B.Arch., 1953; m. Thyra June Shattuck, Nov. 27, 1947; children—Diane Adele Miller, Jeanne Sharon Millican, Anita Sue Haftek, Betty Karen; m. 2d, Wilburta Cartwright Arnold, Dec. 20, 1975. Pres., Locke Wright Foster, Inc., Architects and Planner, Oklahoma City, 1962—; guest lectr. U. Okla., 1964—; spl. cons. George Peabody Coll. Tchrs., 1974. Bd. govs. Okla. State U. Devel. Found., 1974—. Served with U.S. Army, World War II. Fellow AIA (pres. Okla. chpt. 1978, chmn. nat. com. on architecture for edn. 1975); mem. Council Ednl. Facility Planners Internat. (bd. dirs. 1975-78, pres.-elect. 1979). Home: Route 13 Box 122A Oklahoma City OK 73132 Office: 5700 N Portland Suite 301 Oklahoma City OK 73112

LOCKETT, AUBREY LEE, farmer, investor; b. Wilbarger County, Tex., July 31, 1901; s. Frank S. and Ida (Lowe) L.; student Bowie Comml. Coll., 1918, Tyler Comml. Coll., 1919; m. Jewell Nowlin, May 28, 1924; 1 dau., Linda Lee (Mrs. Ben Archer). Owner, mgr. Aubrey L. Lockett Gins, Vernon, Tex., 1920-76; pres., gen. mgr. Lockett Seed Co., Vernon, 1947-68, chmn. bd., 1968-76; mng. partner Lockett Farms, Vernon, 1934—; pres. Waggoner Nat. Bank, Vernon, 1943-50, chmn. bd., 1950-60, hon. chmn. bd., 1960—; pres., treas. Lockett Farms, Inc., 1976—. Treas. Nat. Cotton Council Am., 1955-62, v.p., 1962-63, pres., 1964, chmn. bd., 1965; treas. Oscar Johnson Cotton Found., 1955-69, chmn. bd., 1968-70; treas. Found. Cotton Research and Edn., 1955-57, pres., 1968-70; mem. cotton and cottonseed research and marketing adv. com. Dept. Agr., 1951-62; sec. Santa Rosa Roundup and Livestock Assn., 1946-69. Trustee Tex. 4-H Youth Devel. Council, 1964—; mem. Baylor U. Devel. Council, 1967-78; trustee Hardin-Simmons U., 1975—, High Plains Research Found., 1971—. Named Tex. Cotton Ginner of Year, 1959, Nat. Cotton Ginner of Year, 1959, Man of Year in Tex. Agr., Tex. County Agrl. Agts. Assn., 1974; recipient Man of Yr. in S.W. Agr. award Progressive Farmer, 1968, Knapp Porter award Tex. Agrl. Extension Service, Tex. A. and M. U., 1972, Tex. County Agrl. Agts. Assn. Man of Year award, 1974. Mem. Nat. (bd. dirs.; charter mem.), Tex. (hon. adviser, pres. 1936-38) cotton ginners assns., Tex. Planting Seed Breeders Assn., So. Seedmen's Assn., Nat. Council Comml. Plant Breeders (charter), Okla. Cotton Ginners Assn. (asso.), Cotton Producers Inst. (charter trustee), Vernon, W. Tex., U.S. chambers commerce. Baptist. Rotarian, Mason (32 deg., Shriner, Jester, life). Home: 2222 Powell St Vernon TX 76384 Office: 2222-A Powell St Vernon TX 76384

LOCKEY, STEPHEN DANIEL, physician; b. East Pikeland Twp., Pa., Apr. 29, 1904; s. Stephen and Elizabeth (Demeter) L.; B.S., Franklin and Marshall Coll., Lancaster, Pa., 1928; M.D., Temple U., 1932; m. Anna Bair Funk, Nov. 30, 1933; children—Doris Anne Lockey Bock, Stephen Daniel, Richard Funk, James Edward. Rotating intern Lancaster Gen. Hosp., 1932-33, founder, chief dept. allergy, 1935-70, chief emeritus, 1970—, founder, chief dept. inhalation therapy and ventilation studies, 1952-55, asso. chief, 1955-70; gen. practice medicine, East Petersburg, Pa., 1933-45, specializing in allergy, Lancaster, 1945—; mem. staff, allergist St. Joseph Hosp., Lancaster. Cons. allergist Community Meml. Hosp., West Grove, Pa.; allergist Student Infirmary, Franklin and Marshall Coll.; cons. in allergy Armstrong Cork Co., Lancaster, 1940-50, De Walt, Inc., Lancaster, 1940-45, B.F. Goodrich Rubber Co., Oaks, Pa., 1940-50; lectr. U. Tex., Southwestern Sch. Medicine, Dallas, 1969-72. Vice pres., co-founder Citizens Scholarship Found. of Lancaster County, 1963, bd. dirs., 1963—, pres., 1964; pres. Allergy Found. of Lancaster County; bd. dirs. Lancaster County Council for Sr. Citizens, Phoebe-Devitt Homes for Aged, United Ch. of Christ, 1963-72, Salvation Army; mem. exec. bd. United Ch. of Christ Retirement Homes, 1962-64, Boy Scouts Am. and Girl Scouts Am., Lancaster County; mem. parents com. Ursinus Coll., Collegeville, Pa. Recipient awards Pa. Allergy Assn., 1949, 58, Pa. Med. Soc., 1962, 66, AMA, 1969, 73; award for outstanding contbns. to allergy and medicine Am. Coll. Allergists, 1970; Jonathan Forman award Soc. Clin. Ecology, 1974; Abraham Lincoln award, 1974; Alumni citation Franklin and Marshall Coll., 1979. Diplomate Am. Bd. Clin. Immunology and Allergy. Fellow Am. Assn. Clin. Immunology and Allergy, Am. Coll. Allergists (past 2d v.p., chmn. sect. tech. 1944-80, Disting. Service award 1976, award of merit 1977); mem. Am., Pan Am. (lectr.) med. assns., Pa. Allergy Assn. (past pres., life mem., past chmn. bd. regents), Pa. (chmn. splty. sect. in allergy), Lancaster City and County (trustee) med. socs., Soc. for Clin. Ecology, Am. Assn. Med. Writers, Internat. Assn. Allergology, Am. Med. Writers Assn. Clubs: Elks, Kiwanis, Hamilton, Temple U. Alumni of Lancaster County (pres. 1965-66). Contbr. articles to profl. jours. Home: 1911 Millersville Pike Lancaster PA 17603 Office: 60 N West End Ave Lancaster PA 17603. *Lord, show Thy healing Power in me, so that I may use it: to comfort the sick and the disturbed; to disturb those who are too comfortable, in behalf of others.*

LOCKHART, JAMES ANTHONY, securities dealer; b. Toronto, Ont., Can., May 16, 1930; s. James Watson and Beatrice Alma (Corsan) L.; Licenciate, Trinity Coll., U. London (Eng.), 1951; m. Valerie Hammett, Sept. 27, 1958; children—James Percy, Peter Burritt, Clare Louise. With research dept. Dominion Securities Corp., Toronto, 1952-53, br. mgr., Victoria, B.C., 1954-55, v.p., dep. mgr., London, 1956-65, v.p., dep. mgr., dir., N.Y.C., 1965-67; v.p., dir. Model Roland & Co., N.Y.C., 1968-74; v.p. Shields Model Roland, Inc., N.Y.C., 1974-76, Lazard Frères & Co., N.Y.C., 1977-78; asso. C&R Pastor, N.Y.C., 1978—; dir. Assn. Internat. Bond Dealers, Zurich, Switzerland. Mem. exec. council Morris-Sussex council Boy Scouts Am., 1967—. Mem. Canadian Soc. N.Y. (v.p. 1971-76). Mason. Clubs: India House (N.Y.C.); Savile (London). Home: 73 Van Houten Ave Chatham NJ 07928 Office: 405 Park Ave New York NY 10022

LOCKHART, JAMES BLAKELY, car rental co. exec.; b. N.Y.C., May 27, 1936; s. Edgar L. and Margaret Evelyn (Blakely) L.; B.S., Boston U., 1956, J.D., 1959; m. Ruth Douglas, Oct. 30, 1976; 1 son, Marc Blakely. Admitted to S.C. bar, 1959, Ill. bar, 1963; sr. partner Rivers, Lockhart, Clayter & Lawrence, Chgo., 1965-71; sr. v.p. legal affairs, sec., dir. Budget Rent-a-Car Corp., Chgo., 1972-79; v.p. public affairs Transam. Corp., San Francisco, 1979—; chmn. bd. Chgo. Community Ventures, Inc., 1975-79; dir. Budget Rent-a-Car Internat., Inc. Mem. men's council Art Inst. Chgo., 1970-72. Vice pres., bd. dirs. Lawrence Hall Sch. for Boys; bd. dirs., v.p. mem. exec. com. Bd. Episcopal Charities. Served to capt., JAG Corps, AUS, 1960-63. Recipient WBEE Radio Community Service award, 1973. Mem. Car and Truck Rental and Leasing Assn. Am. (dir.), Internat. Franchise Assn. (dir.), Am., Ill., S.C. bar assns., Kappa Alpha Psi. Episcopalian. Club: Masons. Home: 392 Springfield Pl Moraga CA 94556 Office: 600 Montgomery St San Francisco CA 94111

LOCKHART, JOHN MALLORY, mgmt. cons.; b. Mellen, Wis., May 17, 1911; s. Carl Wright and Gladys (Gale) L.; B.S., Northwestern U., 1931; C.P.A., U. Ill., 1934; J.D., Chgo.-Kent Coll. Law, 1938; m. Judith Anne Wood, Feb. 26, 1938; children—Wood Alexander, Gale, Thomas. Teaching fellow Northwestern U., 1931; asst. v.p. Welsh, Davis & Co., investment bankers, Chgo., 1935-41; treas. Transcontinental & Western Air, Inc., Kansas City, Mo., 1941-47; exec. v.p., gen. mgr. TACA Airways, S.A., 1944-45; v.p., dir. The Kroger Co., 1947-71, exec. v.p., 1961-71; pres. Kroger Family Center Stores, 1969-71, Lockhart Co., mgmt. cons., 1971—; v.p. corporate finance Gradison & Co., 1973—; chmn. bd., chief exec. officer Ohio Real Estate Investment Co., Ohio Real Estate Equity Corp., 1974-76; dir. Alexander's Inc., N.Y.C., Employers Mut. Cos., Des Moines, Witt Co., Anchor Galvanizing Corp.; chmn. bd. Autotronics Systems, Inc., 1976-78, Fred S. James & Co.; dir. Vectra Internat., Inc. Chmn., Hamilton County Hosp. Commn.; mem. adv. bd. Greater Cin. Airport. Clubs: Queen City, Bankers, Hyde Park Golf and Country, Commercial, Cincinnati Country (Cin.); Conquistadores del Cielo. Home: 2770 Walsh Rd Cincinnati OH 45208 Office: 580 Bldg Cincinnati OH 45202

LOCKHART, JUNE, actress; d. Gene and Kathleen Lockhart; children—Anne, June Elizabeth. Motion pictures include All This and Heaven, Too., Sergeant York, Miss Annie Rooney, Meet Me In St. Louis, Son of Lassie, White Cliffs of Dover, Keep Your Powder Dry, Bury Me Dead, T-Men, It's A Joke, Son, Time Limit; also TV appearances including series Lassie, Lost in Space, Petticoat Junction; theatre appearances 40 Carats, Butterflies Are Free, Best of Friends, No Sex Please, We're British. Recipient Tony award for Love or Money; named Woman of Year in Drama, A.P., 1948. Address: care Contemporary Artists 132 Lasky Dr Beverly Hills CA 90212*

LOCKHART, VANCE ELVIS, found. exec.; b. Morgan County, Ind., Oct. 7, 1920; s. Charles B. and Mary (Jones) L.; B.S., Purdue U., 1944. Dir. pub. relations, advt. and mktg. research Ind. Farm Bur. Coop., 1946-59; exec. dir. Am. Mktg. Assn., Chgo., 1959-64; gen. mgr. Am. Soc. Assn. Execs., 1964-76; staff dir. Nat. Assn. Expn. Mgrs., 1970-74; sr. v.p. Arthritis Found., Atlanta, 1976—. Served from ensign to lt., USNR, 1943-46; comdr. Res. Mem. Internat. Mktg. Fedn. (sec. 1962-65), Alpha Zeta. Clubs: Chgo. Advt., Press. Home: 734 E Paces Ferry Rd Atlanta GA 30305 Office: 3400 Peachtree Rd Atlanta GA 30326

LOCKHART, WILLIAM RAYMOND, educator; b. Carlisle, Ind., Nov. 25, 1925; s. William E. and Jewell (Johnson) L.; A.B., Ind. State Tchrs. Coll., 1949; M.S., Purdue U., 1951, Ph.D., 1954; m. Barbara Powers, Aug. 2, 1947; children—Laurence L., Thomas R., Alan K., Sally Ann. Research fellow Purdue U., 1951-53; postdoctoral fellow U. Chgo., 1953-54; asst. prof. bacteriology Iowa State U. Sci. and Tech., 1954-58, asso. prof., 1958-60, prof., 1960—, chmn. dept. bacteriology, 1960-74. Trustee Am. Type Culture Collection, 1966-74. Served with AUS, 1944-46; PTO. Fellow Am. Acad. Microbiology; mem. Am. Soc. Microbiology (pres. N.C. br. 1965), Soc. Gen. Microbiology, Sigma Xi. Sect. editor Biol. Abstracts, 1956—; editorial bd. Applied Microbiology, 1963-65, Jour. Bacteriology, 1965-72. Address: 2606 Northwood St Ames IA 50010

LOCKHEAD, GREGORY ROGER, educator; b. Boston, Aug. 8, 1931; s. John Roger and Ester Mae (Bixby) L.; B.S., Tufts U., 1958; Ph.D., Johns Hopkins, 1965; m. Jeanne Marie Hutchinson, June 8, 1957; children—Diane, Elaine, John. Psychologist research staff IBM Research, Yorktown Heights, N.Y., 1958-61; research asso., instr. Johns Hopkins, 1961-65; asst. prof. psychology Duke, 1965-68, asso. prof., 1968-71, prof., 1971—. Cons. in human engring. Served with USNR, 1951-55. NSF grantee, 1966-69, 79—; USPHS grantee, 1963-69, 70—. Mem. Psychonomic Soc., Am. Psychol. Assn., Sigma Xi. Lion. Cons. editor Perception and Psychophysics. Contbr. articles to profl. jours., chpts. to books. Home: 101 Emerald Circle Durham NC 27707 Office: Dept Psychology Duke Univ Durham NC 27706

LOCKLIN, WILBERT EDWIN, coll. pres.; b. Washington, Apr. 2, 1920; s. Wilbert Edwin and Margaret Mae (Franklin) L.; B.S., Johns Hopkins, 1942; LL.D., George Williams Coll., 1966; m. Olga Maria Osterwald, June 28, 1947; children—Kenneth, Patricia, Randall. Vice-pres. Nat. Bur. Pvt. Schs., N.Y.C., 1947-49; account exec. Reuel Estill & Co., N.Y.C., 1949-51; asst. dir. admissions Johns Hopkins, 1945-47, asst. to pres., 1955-65; v.p. Johns Hopkins Fund, 1960-65; pres. Springfield (Mass.) Coll., 1965—. Dir. Valley Bank and Trust Co. Mem. exec. com. Assn. Ind. Colls. and Univs. in Mass.; founding mem. Cooperating Colls. of Greater Springfield. Bd. dirs. Springfield Symphony Orch. Served with USAAF, 1942-45. Clubs: Colony, Longmeadow Country (Springfield); University (N.Y.C.). Home: 425 Alden Springfield MA 01109

LOCKMILLER, DAVID ALEXANDER, lawyer, educator; b. Athens, Tenn., Aug. 30, 1906; s. George Franklin and Lotta May (Ulrey) L.; B.Ph., Emory U., 1927, A.M., 1928, LL.D., 1954; J.D., Cumberland U., 1929, LL.D., 1940; Ph.D., U. N.C., 1935; postgrad. summers Oxford U., Eng., 1937, U. Chgo., 1940, U. Paris, 1952; Litt.D., U. Chattanooga, 1960; L.H.D., Am. U., 1961, Tenn. Wesleyan Coll., 1962; m. Alma Elizabeth Russell, Sept. 23, 1930; children—Franklin Russell, Carlotta Elizabeth Lockmiller Tillman. Admitted to bars Ohio, Mo., Okla., Ark., N.C., Tenn., Supreme Ct. U.S.; practiced in Monett, Mo., 1929-33; research asst. Inst. for Research in Social Sci., U. N.C., 1934-35; instr. history, polit. sci. N.C. State U., 1935-36, asst. prof., 1936-38, asso. prof. 1938-41, prof., head dept., 1940-42; pres. U. Chattanooga, 1942-59, Ohio Wesleyan U., 1959-61; exec. dir. Nat. Home Study Council, Washington, 1961-72; edn. cons., 1972—. Vis. prof. Am. history Emory U., summer 1938, N.C. Coll., Durham, summer 1941; vis. prof. geography Meredith Coll., 1941-42; 1st vice chmn. Am. Council on Edn., 1952-53. Mem. exec. com. N.C. Hist. Highway Markers, 1935-42, Nat. Mental Health Council USPHS; def. adv. com. edn. Armed Forces; mem. Pres.'s Commn. to Argentina Sesquicentennial, 1960. Past mem. U. Senate Meth. Ch. State dept. rep. to colls. and univs. Far East, 1953. Hon. trustee U. Chattanooga Found. Rockefeller Found. Travel grantee to Brit. univs., 1956. Recipient Chattanooga Man of Year Award, 1953; Hon. alumnus N.C. State U., 1940; NTL Home Study Council Man of Year award, 1969; Distinguished Service award United Schs. Bus., 1972; Spl. Achievement award Nat. Assn. Trade and Tech. Schs., 1972; named to NTL Home Study Council Hall of Fame. Fellow Am. Scandinavian Found.; mem. Assn. Am. Colls. (pres. 1960-61), So. U. Conf. (exec. sec. 1956-59), Assn. Urban Univs. (past pres.), Internat. Conf. on Correspondence Edn., Chattanooga Bar Assn., Chattanooga Exec. Club (ex-pres.), S.A.R., Am. Hist. Assn., Tenn. Coll. Assn. (pres. 1948-49), So. Assn. of Colls. and Secondary Schs. (v.p. 1953), Am. Polit. Sci. Assn., So. Hist. Assn., Bar Assn. Ohio, Am. Mil. Inst., Conf. on Latin Am. Studies, State Lit. and Hist. Assn. N.C., Newcomen Soc., Sovereign Order St. John of Jerusalem-Knights of Malta, Phi Beta Kappa, Phi Kappa Phi, Omicron Delta Kappa, Blue Key, Phi Delta Phi, Pi Gamma Mu, Pi Delta Epsilon, Tau Kappa Alpha, Sigma Chi, Alpha Pi Omega, Delta Sigma Rho, Alpha Beta Kappa (founder, pres.). Republican. Methodist. Mason (K.T., Shriner). Rotarian (past Chattanooga pres., dist. gov.), Kiwanian (hon.). Clubs: Torch International, Cosmos (Washington). Author: Magoon in Cuba, A History of the Second Intervention, 1906-09, 1938, 69; Sir William Blackstone, 1938, 70; History of N.C. State College of Agriculture and Engineering, 1889-1939, 1939; The Consolidation of the University of North Carolina, 1942; General Enoch H. Crowder: Father of Selective Service, 1955; Scholars on Parade, 1969. Contbr. to hist., ednl. jours., encys. Home: Box 1372 Sedona AZ 86336

LOCKRIDGE, ERNEST HUGH, educator, author; b. Bloomington, Ind., Nov. 28, 1938; s. Ross Franklin, Jr. and Vernice (Baker) L.; A.B., Ind. U., 1960; M.A. (Woodrow Wilson fellow), Yale, 1961, Ph.D., 1964; m. Rebecca Anne Bryant, Aug. 27, 1960; children—Laurel, Ellen, Sarah. Instr., Yale, 1963-66, asst. prof., 1966-70, lectr., 1970-71; asso. prof. English dept. Ohio State U., Columbus, 1971-76, prof., 1976—. Fellow Center for Advanced Study, U. Ill., 1969-70. Mem. Phi Beta Kappa, Phi Gamma Delta. Author: (novels) Hartspring Blows His Mind, 1968; Prince Elmo's Fire, 1974; Flying Elbows, 1975; (criticism) Twentieth-Century Interpretations of the Great Gatsby, 1968. Home: 45 W Weisheimer St Columbus OH 43214

LOCKTON, JOHN DUDLEY, JR., lawyer, investment co. exec.; b. Schenectady, Aug. 14, 1937; s. John Dudley and Alice (Hanson) L.; grad. Deerfield Acad., 1955; B.A., Yale, 1959; LL.B., Harvard, 1962; m. Maryann Rogers Von Ulmer, Dec. 30, 1959. Admitted to N.Y. bar, 1963; atty. White & Case, N.Y.C., 1962; sec., counsel Reuben H. Donnelley Corp., N.Y.C., 1968; exec. v.p. Funk & Wagnalls, 1974; pres. Moody's Investors Service, N.Y.C., 1976, Dun & Bradstreet Internat., Ltd., N.Y.C., 1979—. Mem. Phi Beta Kappa. Clubs: Round Hill (Greenwich, Conn.); Wentworth (Virginia Waters, Eng.). Home: Old Bedford Rd Greenwich CT 06830 Office: 99 Church St New York NY 10017

LOCKWOOD, AUGUST GRAHAM, editor; b. Bklyn., Oct. 5, 1917; s. August and Estelle (Graham) L.; m. Marjorie McElfresh, Sept. 2, 1938; children—Linda, Karen, Janet. Reporter, L.I. Press, Jamaica, N.Y., 1937-47, night editor, 1947-60, city editor, 1960-67, news editor, 1967-68; mng. editor Jersey Journal, Jersey City, 1968-70, editor, 1970—. Lectr. journalism Queens Coll., Flushing, N.Y., 1960-67. Served with USNR, 1944-45. Mem. Am. Soc. Newspaper Editors, N.J. Press Assn. Roman Catholic. Author: How to Finish Your Attic and Basement Yourself, 1953. Contbr. articles to popular mags. Home: Scotch Plains NJ 07076 Office: 30 Journal Sq Jersey City NJ 07306

LOCKWOOD, GARY, actor; b. Van Nuys, Calif., 1937. Former stuntman, now actor films and TV; film appearances include Tall Story, Splendor in the Grass, 1961, Wild in the Country, 1962, 2001: A Space Odyssey, 1968, The Model Shop, 1969, They Came to Rob Las Vegas, 1969, The Body, 1971, Stand Up and Be Counted, 1972; TV appearances include Follow the Sun, 1961, The Lieutenant, 1963, also TV movies. Address: care Agy for Performing Arts 9000 Sunset Blvd Suite 315 Los Angeles CA 90069*

LOCKWOOD, JOHN ALEXANDER, physicist, educator; b. Easton, Pa., July 12, 1919; s. Harold John and Elizabeth (Van Campen) L.; A.B., Dartmouth, 1941; M.S., Lafayette Coll., 1943; Ph.D., Yale, 1948; m. Jean Elizabeth Manville, Mar. 28, 1942; children—Heidi, Nancy, Jane. Faculty U. N.H., 1948—, prof. physics, 1959—, chmn. dept., 1962-65, asst. dean Grad. Sch., 1973-74, asso. dir. research, 1974—; spl. research cosmic ray time variations, neutron and gamma-ray measurements. Fellow Am. Phys. Soc.; mem. Am. Assn. Physics Tchrs., A.A.A.S., Am. Geophys. Union, Sigma Xi. Contbr. articles to profl. jours. Home: 6 Valentine Hill Rd Durham NH 03824

LOCKWOOD, LEE, financier; b. Waco, Tex., Nov. 11, 1900; s. James H. and Gussie (Doss) L.; student U. Tex., 1918-22; LL.D., Baylor U.; m. Marie Coates, Oct. 3, 1923; children—Ann Marie (Mrs. Duncan C. Howard), Laurine Lockwood Dosher. Chmn., Waco Mortgage Co., First Waco Co., Inc., Waco Savs. & Loan Assn.; owner Waco Lumber Co.; vice chairman Farm & Home Savs. Assn.; dir. Citizens Nat. Bank Waco, Merc. Nat. Bank Dallas. Past chmn. Commn. Higher Edn. Tex.; mem. Tex. com. on church and state Baylor U. Del. Democratic Nat. Conv., 1940, 44, 48, 52. Pres. Masonic Home and Sch. Tex., 1951-60; chmn. emeritus Scottish Rite Found. Tex., Scottish Rite Ednl. Assn. Tex., Scottish Rite Hosp., Dallas; bd. dirs. Community Chest, Waco, Waco Boys Club, Waco Growth Found.; dir. George Washington Nat. Meml. Assn.; bd. regents U. Tex., 1953-59; trustee Freedoms Found., Valley Forge. Recipient George Washington award. Mem. Waco C. of C., S.A.R. (gold citizenship medal Tex. chpt.), Soc. Colonial Wars. Mason (33 deg.; past dep. grand comdr., mem. emeritus Supreme Council); mem. Order De Molay (past grand master), Order Red Cross of Constantine (past grand sovereign). Home: 5000 Lockwood Dr Waco TX 76710 Office: 1227 N Valley Mills Dr Waco TX 76710

LOCKWOOD, LEE JONATHAN, photographer, author; b. N.Y.C., May 4, 1932; s. Arthur H. and Ruth J. (Edinberg) L.; B.A., Boston U., 1954; postgrad. Columbia, 1956-59; m. Joyce Greenfield, June 14, 1964; children— Andrew William, Gillian. U.S. corr. Bunte Illustrierte, 1959-61; staff photographer Black Star Agy., 1961—; editor Contemporary Photographer Quar., 1963-66; Rockefeller artist-in-residence sta. WGBH-TV, Boston, 1967-68; lectr. photojournalism Boston U., 1974-76. Served with AUS, 1954-56. Recipient award best fgn. reporting Overseas Press Club, 1967. Mem. Author's Guild, Assn. Heliographers, Am. Soc. Mag. Photographers. Author: Castro's Cuba, Cuba's Fidel, 1967; Conversation with Eldridge Cleaver/Algiers, 1969; (with Father Daniel Berrigan) Absurd Convictions, Modest Hopes, 1972; producer TV documentary The Holy Outlaw, 1970; photographs and articles in nat. mags. Office: Black Star Agy 450 Park Ave S New York City NY 10016

LOCKWOOD, LEWIS HENRY, music historian, educator; b. N.Y.C., Dec. 16, 1930; s. Gerald and Madeline (Wartell) L.; B.A., Queens Coll., 1952; M.F.A., Princeton, 1955, Ph.D., 1960; m. Doris Hoffman, Dec. 26, 1953; children—Alison, Daniel. Mem. faculty Princeton, 1958—, instr., 1958-59, asst. prof., 1959-65, asso. prof., 1965-68, prof. music, 1968—, dept. chmn., 1970-73, 78—, Robert Schirmer prof. music, 1973—; vis. mem. Inst. for Advanced Study, 1977-78. Served with AUS, 1956-58. Recipient Fulbright award for study in Italy, 1955-56; Nat. Endowment for Humanities sr. fellow, 1973-74; Guggenheim Found. fellow, 1977-78. Fellow Am. Council Learned Socs., 1968-69; mem. Am. (del. to Am. Council Learned Socs. 1966-67, v.p. 1970-72; Alfred Einstein award 1971), Internat. musicol. socs., Renaissance Soc. Am. Author: The Counter-Reformation and the Masses of Vincenzo Ruffo, 1970. Editor-in-Chief Jour. of Am. Musicol. Soc., 1963-66; cons. editor: The New Grove Dictionary of Music and Musicians. Contbr. articles on Renaissance music and Beethoven to profl. jours. Address: Dept Music Princeton Univ Princeton NJ 08540

LOCKWOOD, LOUISE FIELD (MRS. WILLARD A. LOCKWOOD), editor; b. Bryn Mawr, Pa., Oct. 18, 1923; d. William Thompson and Andree (Berthault) Field; B.A., Bryn Mawr Coll., 1945; postgrad. Coll. City N.Y., 1947-49; m. Willard A. Lockwood, June 7, 1947; children—Andree, Rachel, Winthrop. Psychologist, Brearley Sch., N.Y.C., 1947-51; asso. editor Choice mag., Middletown, Conn., 1964—. Bd. dirs. League Women Voters, 1962-65. Home: 36 Mansfield Terr Middletown CT 06457 Office: 100 Riverview Center Middletown CT 06457

LOCKWOOD, NORMAND, composer, educator; b. N.Y.C., Mar. 19, 1906; s. Samuel Pierson and Angelina (Normand-Smith) L.; student U. Mich. Sch. Music, 1921-24; studied orchestration with Ottorino Respighi, Rome, 1924-25, composition with Nadia Boulanger, Paris, 1925-28, 32; Mus. D., Berea Coll., 1973; m. Dorothy Sanders, Sept. 21, 1926; children—Deborah, Angeline-Rose, Hedwig-Marie. Asst. prof. theory composition Oberlin Coll., 1932-37, asso. prof., 1937-45; Guggenheim fellow, 1943-44, 44-45; faculty Union Theol. Sem. Sch. Sacred Music, 1945—; head dept. theory, composition Westminster Choir Coll., 1948-50; chmn. Yaddo Music Period, Saratoga Springs, N.Y., 1945; lectr. music Columbia Coll., 1945-48, Columbia, 1945—, Queens Coll., 1950-51; staff Composers' Conf., MIddlebury, Vt., 1948; prof., head dept. music Trinity U., 1953-55; vis. prof. theory and composition U. Oreg., 1957-58, U. Hawaii, 1960-61; composer-in-residence U. Denver, 1961—, asso. prof. 1968-74, prof. emeritus, 1974—; guest composer, lectr., condr. at Composers' Forum, N.Y.C., Internat. Soc. Contemporary Music U. Ill., Conn. Coll., Woman's Coll. U. N.C., Western Res. U., Symposium Contemporary Am. Music, U. Tex., Ill. Wesleyan U., others. Recipient Rome prize Am. Acad. in Rome, 1929-32, Swift prize, 1934, World's Fair prize, 1939, Nat. Inst. Arts and Letters award; Ernest Bloch award United Temple Chorus, 1947; Publ. award Soc. Pub. Am. Music, 1947; commissioned Alice M. Ditson, 1944, Elizabeth Sprague Coolidge, 1941, Ind. U., 1951, Broadcast Music Inc., Univ. Mus. Soc. U. Mich., Am. Guild Organists, Mass for Children and Orch. (Children's Chorale, Denver), 1976, Four Excursions for Four Basses (Alaska Festival of Music), 1977, 2d Concerto for Organ and Brasses (Marilyn Mason), 1977, also commns. churches, orchs., univs. U.S. Mem. Nat. Assn. Am. Composers and Condrs., Am. Composers. Alliance, Phi Mu Alpha Sinfonia. Composer, arranger, transcriber religious, choral music. Address: Am Composers Alliance 170 W 74th St New York City NY 10023

LOCKWOOD, RALPH HAROLD, banker; b. Columbus, Ohio, Apr. 17, 1929; s. Grace Hardman; student Ohio State U., 1959-61; m. Ruth Ellen Buchman, June 24, 1950; children—Kathy Ellen, Jeffrey Allen. With Huntington Nat. Bank, Columbus, sr. v.p. charge data processing. Served with USMCR, 1952-54. Mem. Am. (exec. com. ops.-automation div. 1975—, chmn. research and planning com. 1975—, co-chmn. nat. ops. and automation conf. 1976), Ohio (chmn. ops. and automation com. 1975-77) bankers assns. Baptist. Address: 2361 Morse Rd Columbus OH 43229

LOCKWOOD, RHODES GREENE, lawyer; b. Buchanan, Va., Nov. 26, 1919; s. Rhodes G. and Violet (Bennett) L.; B.A., Williams Coll., 1941; postgrad U. Va., 1941-42, Va. Poly. Inst., 1946-47; LL.B., Harvard U., 1949; m. Mary Hitchcock, Jan. 22, 1949; children—Mary Howland, Rhodes G., Faith B., Rebecca Ingersoll. Admitted to Mass. bar, 1949; asso. firm Choate, Hall & Stewart, Boston, 1949-59, partner, 1959—. Sec., TMCA Found., Inc., Boston; sec., trustee Peter Bent Brigham Hosp., Boston, Univ. Hosp., Boston; vice chmn. Wellesley (Mass.) Sch. Com., 1966, chmn., 1967-69. Served with USNR, 1942-52. Mem. Mass. Bar Assn., Boston Bar Assn., Am. Law Inst., Am. Soc. Hosp. Attys., Mass. Hosp. Assn., Harvard U. Law Sch. Alumni Assn. Democrat. Home: 11 Windsor Rd Wellesley Hills MA 02181 Office: 60 State St Boston MA 02109

LOCKWOOD, RICHARD ALLEN, physician, health sci. centers adminstr.; b. Los Angeles, Nov. 14, 1924; s. Harry Boyne and Pauline (Winsten) L.; M.D., Johns Hopkins U., 1947; children—John, Bruce, Paula, Kimberly. Intern in pathology Strong Meml. Hosp., U. Rochester, 1947-48; intern in surgery Johns Hopkins Hosp., Balt., 1948-49; resident in surgery Wadsworth VA Hosp., Los Angeles, 1949-50, resident in proctology, 1953-55; practice medicine specializing in proctology, Los Angeles, 1955-64; project dir. med. edn. study U. Hawaii, Honolulu, 1964-66; dir. hosps. and clinics U. Calif. at San Diego, 1966-71, also dean for continuing edn. and health manpower, 1971-73; dir. programming and facilities devel. Med. Centers, Tex. Tech. U. Sch. Medicine, 1973-74, prof. surgery, 1973—, v.p. Health Scis. Centers, 1974—. Served with USNR, 1950-52. Mem. Assn. Acad. Health Centers, Tex. Med. Assn. (cons. council on med. edn. and hosps. 1975—), Lubbock-Crosby-Garza Counties med. socs. Author: Atlas of Anorectal Surgery, 1964. Home: 4908 19th St Lubbock TX 79407 Office: TTUHSC Lubbock TX 79430

LOCKWOOD, ROBERT WILLIAM, utility co. exec.; b. Orange, N.J., July 3, 1927; s. Alfred E. and Anna R. (Greer) L.; M.E., Stevens Inst. Tech., 1951; m. Elaine Gundlach, June 25, 1949; children—Robert William, Richard B., Craig G. With Public Service Electric & Gas Co., Newark, 1951—, gen. mgr. environ. affairs, 1973-74, v.p. corp. services, 1974-77, sr. v.p. adminstrn., 1977—. Mem. Union County (N.J.) Regional Bd. Edn., 1965-68; mem. Clark Twp. (N.J.) Bd. Edn., 1955-63, pres., 1962-63; chmn. civic div. United Way Campaign, N.J., 1977; trustee Boys' Clubs Newark, 1963—, pres., 1973-74, chmn. bd., 1975-76, 79—. Served with USN, 1945-46. Recipient Atkins award N.J. Sci. Tchrs. Assn., 1974; Man and Boy award Boys' Clubs Newark, 1975. Mem. Nat. Assn. Purchasing Mgrs. (hon. mem. Public Utility Buyers Group). Clubs: Plainfield Country, Essex. Home: 180 Central Ave New Providence NJ 07974 Office: 80 Park Pl Newark NJ 07102

LOCKWOOD, THEODORE DAVIDGE, coll. pres.; b. Hanover, N.H., Dec. 5, 1924; s. Harold John and Elizabeth (Van Campen) L.; B.A., Trinity Coll., 1948; M.A., Princeton, 1950, Ph.D., 1952; L.H.D., Concord Coll., 1968; LL.D., Union Coll., 1968, U. Hartford, 1969; L.H.D., Wesleyan U., Middletown, Conn., 1970; m. Elizabeth Anne White, Apr. 13, 1944; children—Tamara Jane Lockwood Quinn, Richard Davidge, Mavis Ferens, Serena Katherine. Instr. great issues Dartmouth, 1952-53; asst. prof. history Juniata Coll., Huntingdon, Pa., 1953-55, Mass. Inst. Tech., 1955-60; dean faculty Concord Coll., Athens, W.Va., 1960-64; provost, dean faculty Union Coll., Schenectady, 1964-68; pres. Trinity Coll., Hartford, Conn., 1968—. Dir. Conn. Gen. Ins. Corp., 1973—. Chmn. Greater Hartford Consortium for Higher Edn., 1972—. Bd. dirs. Vols. Internat. Tech. Assistance, 1965—, chmn., 1966-71. Bd. fellows Trinity Coll., 1962-64, bd. trustees, 1964—; corporator Hartford Hosp., 1968—, Hartford Pub. Library, 1969—; bd. dirs. Inst. for Living, 1969—, Edn. Commn. of States, 1969-71, Am. Council on Edn., 1977—; trustee Northwood Sch., Lake Placid, N.Y., 1969-78; dir. adv. council Audubon Soc. Expdn. Inst., 1978—. Served with U.S. Army, 1943-45. Belgian-Am. Fellow, 1959. Mem. Assn. Am. Colls. (dir. 1973-78, chmn. 1976-77), Greater Hartford C. of C. (dir. 1977—), Phi Beta Kappa, Pi Gamma Mu. Unitarian. Author: Mountaineers, 1945; Studies in European Socialism, 1960; Our Mutual Concern: The Role of the Independent College, 1968. Address: Trinity Coll Hartford CT 06106

LOCKWOOD, WILLARD ATKINSON, publisher; b. Washington, Mar. 4, 1924; s. Hanford Nichols and Anna Lillian Atkinson L.; B.A., Wesleyan U., 1945; postgrad. Art Students League N.Y.C., 1949-50; m. Marie Louise Field, June 7, 1947 (div. 1979); children—Andree, Rachel, Winthrop; m. 2d, Eleanor Bloch, 1979. Mem. staff book design, prodn. various pubs. N.Y.C., 1947-51; asso. art editor U. Okla. Press, Norman, 1951-53, art editor, 1953-55; asst. mng. editor Charles E. Merrill Books, Middletown, Conn., 1955-57; dir. Wesleyan U. Press, Middletown, 1957—; dir. City Savs. Bank Middletown. Treas. Assn. Am. Univ. Presses, 1970-72, pres., 1976-77. Mem. Middletown Commn. on Arts, 1972-75; corporator Middlesex Meml. Hosp. Mem. Columbiad Club Conn., Publishers Lunch Club (N.Y.C.), Phi Beta Kappa. Democrat. Rotarian. Contbr. articles to profl. publs. Home: 236 Ridgefield Dr Middletown CT 06457 Office: Wesleyan U Press Middletown CT 06457

LODER, DWIGHT ELLSWORTH, bishop; b. Waverly, Nebr., July 8, 1914; s. William and Alice C. (Snyder) L.; A.B., U. Nebr., 1936; S.T.B., Boston U., 1939; D.D. (hon.), Hamline U., 1951, Garrett Theol. Sem., 1955, Albion Coll., 1968; D.S.T., Dickinson Coll., 1966; L.H.D., Willamette Coll., 1966; LL.D., Baldwin-Wallace Coll., 1976, Ohio No. U., 1979; m. Mildred Ethyl Shay, Sept. 17, 1939; children—Ruth Ann Loder Burnecke, William, David, Asso. pastor 1st Congl. Ch., Stoneham, Mass., 1937-39; ordained to ministry Meth. Ch., 1939; pastor, North Towanda, Pa., 1939-41, Blossburg, 1941-47; minister Hennepin Ave. Ch., Mpls., 1947-55; pres. Garrett Theol. Sem., Evanston, Ill., 1955-64; consecrated bishop Meth. Ch., 1964; assigned Mich. area, 1964, Ohio West area, 1976—; mem. Central N.Y. Conf., 1939-47, Minn. Conf., 1947-57, Rock River Ann. Conf., 1947-64; lectr. 8th ann. Ministers' Convocation So. Calif., 1956, N. Am. Faith and Order Study Conf. World Council Chs., 1957; Glide lectr. Glide Sch. Evangelism, San Francisco, 1960; Fondren lectr. So. Meth. U., Dallas, 1965; Willson lectr. Lon Morris Coll., Jacksonville, Tex., 1967; del. World Meth. Convocation Theol. Edn., 1961, Gen. Conf. Meth. Ch., 1960, 64; del. N. Central Jurisdictional Conf., 1960, 64, Rock River Ann. Conf., 1957-64; rep. theol. edn. on ministerial exchange World Meth. Council, 1959—, pres. Am. sect., 1977—; mem. univ. senate Meth. Ch., 1963-64, commn. chaplains, 1966-72, pres. nat. bd. missions, 1968-72, mem. bd. publs., 1972—; pres.-elect Council of Bishops, 1973-74, pres., 1974-75; commd. to study episcopacy and dist. superintendancy, 1972-76, to study ministry, 1972-76. Mem. Mich. Gov.'s Crime Commn., 1966-69, Mich. Officers State Compensation Com., 1968-76. Trustee Ohio No. U., Ohio

Wesleyan U., Baldwin-Wallace Coll., Otterbein Coll., Mt. Union Coll., United Meth. Children's Home, Riverside Meth. Hosp., Bethesda Hosp., Meth. Home on College Hill, Wesley Glen Retirement Center. Recipient Distinguished Alumnus award Boston U. Sch. Theology, 1964. Mem. Am. Assn. Theol. Schs., Assn. Meth. Theol. Schs. (pres. 1960), Chgo. Ch. Fedn., Chgo., Evanston ministerial assns., Chgo. Theol. Faculties Union (pres. 1961), Commn. Ecumenical Consultation, N. Central Jurisdictional Commn. Higher Edn., Alpha Kappa Psi (hon.). Mason (Shriner). Clubs: Ohio State U. Faculty, Columbus Athletic. Home: 787 Tweed Ct Worthington OH 43085 Office: 471 E Broad St Columbus OH 43215

LODER, WALTER MORGAN, ret. constrn. co. exec.; b. Newton, Kans., Apr. 7, 1917; s. Winfield Ross and Daisy (Guinn) L.; B.S., U. Kans., 1940; M.B.A., U. So. Calif., 1945; certificate Alexander Hamilton Inst., 1967; m. Edna Mae Fox, Jan. 21, 1950; children—Lance Morgan, Lori. Partner, Bing & Loder, Beverly Hills, Calif., 1946-49; treas., controller Pacific Electric Contractors, Inc., Anchorage, 1949-53; tax cons. Costello & Miller, Boise, Idaho, 1953-56; fgn. bus. mgr., dir. auditing Morrison-Knudsen Co., Inc., Boise, 1956-70, treas., 1970-73; owner Walt Loder Co., Boise, 1973—. Chmn. Boise chpt. ARC, Boise Philharmonic Assn. C.P.A., Cal. Mem. Financial Execs. Inst., Am. Mgmt. Assn., Phi Delta Theta. Episcopalian. Mason, Rotarian. Clubs: Hillcrest Country, Arid (Boise). Home: 3701 Crescent Rim Dr Boise ID 83704

LODGE, HENRY CABOT, former senator, former govt. ofcl., author, lectr.; b. Nahant, Mass., July 5, 1902; s. George Cabot and Mathilda Elizabeth Frelinghuysen (Davis) L.; g.s. of late U.S. Sen. Henry Cabot Lodge; grad. Middlesex Mass. Sch., 1920; A.B., Harvard, 1924; LL.B., Northeastern U., 1938; D.C.L., Bishop's U., 1953; LL.D., Clark U., Norwich U., 1951, Hamilton Coll., Franklin and Marshall Coll., Boston U., 1953, Harvard, 1954, N.Y. U., Fordham U., Rensselaer Polytechnic Inst., 1955, Lehigh University, U. Pa., 1956, also Williams Coll., Union Coll., Boston Coll., Princeton, Adelphi U., Columbia, U. N.H., Notre Dame U., U. Mass., Am. U.; Docteur es Lettres, Laval Univ., m. Emily Sears, July 1, 1926; children—George Cabot, Henry Sears. With Boston Evening Transcript 1923, N.Y. Herald Tribune, 1924; mem. Mass. Gen. Court, 1933-36; elected to U.S. Senate from Mass., 1936, for term ending 1943; reelected, 1942, resigned to go into U.S. Army; reelected Nov. 5, 1946, for term ending Jan. 1953; U.S. rep. UN, 1953-60; director gen. The Atlantic Inst., 1961-62; U.S. ambassador to South Viet Nam, 1963-64, 65-67, ambassador at large, 1967-68; ambassador to Germany, 1968-69; personal rep. to head U.S. delegation to Vietnam Peace Talks, Paris 1969; spl. envoy to visit Vatican, 1970-77; vis. prof. Gordon Coll., 1977; Chmn. Presdl. Commn. for Observance of UN 25th Anniversary, 1970-71; mem. nat. council Salvation Army, 1976; campaign mgr. for nomination Gen. Dwight D. Eisenhower, 1952; nominated for v.p. Republican Party, 1960; bd. overseers Harvard. Active Res. Officer from 1925; maj. U.S.A., with 1st Am. Tank Detachment in Brit. 8th Army, Libya, 1942, Italy 1944; lt. col., So. France, Rhine and So. Germany, 1944-45; ret. maj. gen. Res. Decorated Bronze Star, Legion of Merit medal, 6 battle stars; Legion of Honor, Croix de Guerre (with palm) (France); Chevalier's cross Order of Polonia Restituta; Humane Order African Redemption (Liberia); Grand Cross of Merit (Malta); Nat. Order (Republic Viet Nam); recipient Distinguished Honor award State Dept.; Sylvanus Thayer medal West Point; Pres. Eisenhower's Gold Medal; unanimously thanked by U.S. Senate for Vietnam service, 1967. others. Author: The Storm Has Many Eyes, 1973; As It Was, 1976. First senator since Civil War to resign to enter U.S. Army. Address: 275 Hale St Beverly MA 01915. *Thomas Jefferson said that the most important single qualification for worldly "success" was good humor. I would rate physical stamina and a good clear head equally high. Nor can a full life (which surely must be included in any truthful definition of "success") be lived without ideals. The nation should be inspired by the ideals of the Declaration of Independence and of the Preamble to the Constitution; the individual, by the teachings of religion.*

LODGE, HOWARD THOMAS, JR., ret. banker; b. Bryn Mawr, Pa., Feb. 11, 1914; s. Howard Thomas and Emma Irene (Darwood) L.; B.S. in Econs., Haverford Coll., 1936; certificate Stonier Grad. Sch. Banking, Rutgers U., 1949; m. Frances Lois Rinehart, Oct. 25, 1939; children—Thomas Russell, Howard Rinehart. With Fidelity Bank, Phila., and predecessors, 1939-79, v.p., 1956-71, sr. v.p., 1971-79. Vice chmn. Main Line dist. Boy Scouts Am., 1964—. Bd. mgrs. Central YMCA of Phila., 1965—, chmn., 1974-75. Served to lt. (j.g.) USNR, 1943-46; PTO. Mem. Robert Morris Assos., Phila. Ret. Bank Officers Club, Stonier Grad. Sch. Banking Assn., World Affairs Council Phila. Republican. Presbyn. Club: Anglers (Phila.). Home: 114 Airdale Rd Rosemont PA 19010

LODWICK, GWILYM SAVAGE, educator; b. Mystic, Iowa, Aug. 30, 1917; s. Gwylim S. and Lucy A. (Fuller) L.; student Drake U., 1934-35; B.S., State U. Iowa, 1942, M.D., 1943; m. Maria Antonia De Brito Barata; children from previous marriage—Gwilym Savage III, Philip Galligan, Malcolm Kerr, Terry Ann. Resident pathology State U. Iowa, 1947-48, resident radiology, 1948-50; fellow, sr. fellow radiologic and orthopedic pathology Armed Forces Inst. Pathology, 1951; asst., then asso. prof. State U. Iowa Med. Sch., 1951-56; prof. radiology, chmn. dept. U. Mo. at Columbia Med. Sch., 1956-78, research prof. radiology, 1978—, prof. bioengring., 1969—, acting dean, 1959, asso. dean, 1959-64; cons. in field; vis. prof. Keio U. Sch. Medicine, Tokyo, 1974—. Mem. radiology tng. com. Nat. Inst. Gen. Med. Scis., NIH, 1966-70; com. radiology Nat. Acad. Scis.-NRC, 1970; chmn. com. computers Am. Coll. Radiology, 1965, Internat. Commn. Radiol. Edn. and Information, 1969—; cons. to health care tech. div. Nat. Center for Health Services, Research and Devel., 1971—; dir. Mid-Am. Bone Tumor Diagnostic Center and Registry, 1971—; adv. com. mem. NIH Biomed. Image Processing Grant Jet Propulsion Lab., 1969-73; nat. chmn. MUMPS Users Group, 1973-75; mem. radiation study sect. div. research grants NIH, 1976-79, mem. study sect. on diagnostic radiology and nuclear medicine div. research grants, 1979—. Served to maj. AUS, 1943-46. Decorated Sakari Mustakallio medal (Finland); named Most Disting. Alumnus in Radiology, State U. Ia. Centennial, 1970; recipient Sigma Xi Research award U. Mo., Columbia, 1972, Gold medal XIII Internat. Conf. Radiology, Madrid, 1973. Fellow A.M.A. (radiology rev. bd. council med. edn., council rep. on residency rev. com. for radiology 1969-74); mem. Am. Coll. Radiology, European Soc. Radiology (European steering com. on computers), Radiol. Soc. N.Am. (3d v.p. 1974-75), Assn. U. Radiologists, Mo. Radiol. Soc. (1st pres. 1961-62), Alpha Omega Alpha; hon. mem. Portuguese Soc. Radiology and Nuclear Medicine, Tex. Radiol. Soc., Ind. Roentgen Soc., Phila. Roentgen Ray Soc., Finnish Radiol. Soc. (hon.). Author: Tumors of Bones and Joints, others; also articles. Adv. editorial bd. Radiology, 1965—, Current/Clin. Practice, 1972—; mem. editorial bd. Jour. Med. Systems, 1976—, Radiol. Sci. Update div. Biomedia, Inc., 1975—; mem. cons. editorial bd. Skeletal Radiology, 1977—, Contemporary Diagnostic Radiology, 1978—. Home: 911 LaGrange Columbia MO 65201

LOE, JOSEPH SPARKMAN, transp. exec.; b. Agua Dulce, Tex., Sept. 19, 1914; s. John Joseph and Lela (Sparkman) L.; student various trade sch. safety and mgmt. courses, 1950-75; m. Ruth Ann Brown, Sept. 25, 1937; children—Lynda, James. Salesman, Bordens Co., Phoenix, 1933-41; fireman Atchison Topeka & the Santa Fe R.R., Winslow, Ariz., 1941-43; with Phoenix Transit (formerly Met. Line and Valley Transit Lines), 1943—, asst. mgr., 1965-70, mgr., 1970—. Mem. Am. Public Transit Assn. (dir.), Phoenix C. of C., Valley Forward Assn., Scottsdale (Ariz.) C. of C., Hotel Motel Sales Assn., Innkeepers Assn. Republican. Clubs: Pinewood Country, Masons, Shriners. Home: 7003 N 14th Ave Phoenix AZ 85021 Office: 101 N 1st Ave Phoenix AZ 85003

LOEB, CARL M., JR., metallurgist; b. St. Louis, Aug. 10, 1904; s. Carl M. and Adeline (Moses) L.; B.S., Princeton, 1926; M.S., Mass. Inst. Tech., 1928; m. Lucille H. S. Schamberg, Jan. 30, 1929; children—Constance Margaret (Mrs. Cohn), Carl M. III, Peter Kenneth. Metall. work Central Alloy Steel Corp., Canton, O., 1928-29, Anaconda Copper Mining Co. (Mont.), 1929-32; with Amax Inc. (formerly Climax Molybdenum Co.), Detroit, 1932—, dist. metallurgist, N.Y.C., 1933-37, v.p. in charge devel., publicity, 1937-54, dir., 1948—, mem. exec. com., 1960—, chmn., 1975-77; ltd. partner Loeb, Rhoades & Co., 1955-76; Chmn. com. on correctional and protectional care, also mem. exec. com. N.Y. State com. 1960 White House Conf. Children and Youth; mem. tech. assistance com. White House Conf., 1970; pres. Community Council Greater N.Y., 1956-60, chmn., 1960-62; trustee Nat. Council on Crime and Delinquency, 1963—, v.p., 1966-67, pres., 1967-72, vice chmn., 1972—; chmn. N.Y.C. Bd. Correction, 1957-61; past v.p. Nat. Jewish Welfare Bd.; mem. commn. on correctional facilities and services, Am. Bar Assn., 1970-76; cons. Commn. on Rev. of Nat. Policy toward Gambling, 1975-76. Bd. dirs. Day Care and Child Devel. Council Am., 1962-70. Mem. corp. devel. com. Mass. Inst. Tech., 1966—. Mem. S.A.R. Republican. Clubs: LaQuinta (Calif.) Country; Engineers, Princeton (N.Y.C.); Century Country (White Plains, N.Y.); Tower (Princeton). Home: Khakum Dr Greenwich CT 06830 Office: 501 E 87th St New York City NY 10028

LOEB, CHARLES EDWARD, mag. publisher; b. Phila., Apr. 3, 1914; s. Harry and Anna (Burwell) L.; A.B., Lafayette Coll., Easton, Pa., 1936; m. Helen Smethers, Aug. 13, 1958; children—Margaret, Thomas, Melissa, Scott. Sales trainee Whitehead Metal Products Co., 1936-37; with Cue Pub. Co., Inc., N.Y.C., 1937—, mng. editor, 1941-44, bus. mgr., 1946-58, v.p., pub., 1958—; dir. Theatre, Inc., Bedside Network. Dir. N.Y. Bd. Trade. Chmn. Arts and Bus. Council, N.Y.C., 1973—; sec.-treas. Conv. and Visitors Bur., 1973—; v.p. Muscular Dystrophy Assn., 1971-74. Served with AUS, 1944-46. Decorated Army Commendation medal. Clubs: Friars; Dutch Treat. Home: 37 Plymouth Rd Summit NJ 07901 Office: 545 Madison Ave New York City NY 10022

LOEB, DIANE SPIELER, mezzo soprano; b. Ottawa, Can., May 7, 1945; d. Bertram Isaac and Blanche Druke (Spieler) L.; B.A., U. Toronto, 1966, M.A., 1969; m. John McClelland, May 15, 1970. Debuts include: Faust, Toronto, 1974, Magic Flute, Ottawa, 1975, Cosi Fan Tutte, France, 1977, La Cenerentola, Germany, 1977; appeared with Can. Opera Co., Munster Opera Co., Aachen Opera Co., W. Ger.; appeared with symphony orchs. of Ottawa, Hamilton, Ont., Can., Edmonton, Festival of Albi, France. Recipient 1st prize Concours International de la Melodie Francaise, Paris, 1971; regional finalist Met. Nat. Auditions, 1974. Mem. Assn. Can. Radio and Television Artists, Can. Actors Equity Assn. Office: care Hart/Murdock Artists Mgmt 191 College St Toronto ON Canada

LOEB, JOHN LANGELOTH, banker, broker; b. St. Louis, Nov. 11, 1902; s. Carl Morris and Adeline (Moses) L.; student Dartmouth, 1920-21; S.B. cum laude, Harvard U., 1924, LL.D., 1971; m. Frances Lehman, Nov. 18, 1926; children—Judith H. (Mrs. Marco Chiara), John Langecloth, Ann Loeb Bronfman, Arthur Lehman, Deborah Loeb Brice. With Am. Metal Co., Pitts. office, 1924-26, N.Y. office, 1926-28; with Wertheim & Co., 1929-30; partner Loeb, Rhoades & Co., Inc., N.Y.C., 1931-55, sr. partner, 1955-77, chmn., 1977—; chmn. fin. com. Loeb, Rhoades, Hornblower & Co., 1978—; dir. Dome Petroleum Ltd., Toronto, Ont.; gov. N.Y. Stock Exchange, 1951-54; adv. com. on internat. bus. problems State Dept., 1967-69, 70—. Served with Treasury Dept., Office War Mblzn., Washington, 1942-44. Hon. trustee Montefiore Hosp.; chmn., chief exec. officer Jacob and Valeria Langeloth Found.; bd. overseers Harvard U., 1962-68; hon. gov. N.Y. Hosp.; trustee, chmn. Inst. Fine Arts, N.Y. U. Mem. Council Fgn. Relations, C. of C., SAR, Newcomen Soc. Clubs: Recess, Economic, City Midday, Sky (N.Y.C.); Century Country (White Plains); Harvard (Boston, N.Y.C.); Stanwich (Greenwich, Conn.); East Hill (Nassau); Regency; Lyford Cay. Home: 730 Park Ave New York NY 10021 Office: 42 Wall St New York NY 10005

LOEB, JOHN LANGELOTH, JR., investment banker; b. N.Y.C., May 2, 1930; s. John Langeloth and Frances (Lehman) L.; grad. Hotchkiss Sch., 1948; A.B. cum laude, Harvard, 1952, M.B.A., 1954; children—Nicholas, Alexandra. With Loeb, Rhoades & Co., N.Y.C., 1956—, gen. partner, mem. mgmt. com., 1959-73, mng. partner, pres., 1971-73, ltd. partner, 1973—; chmn. bd. Holly Sugar Co., Colo., 1969-71. Spl. adviser environ. matters to Gov. Nelson A. Rockefeller, 1967-73; chmn. Gov. N.Y. Council Environ. Advisers, 1970-75. Trustee Montefiore Hosp. and Med. Center, Museum City N.Y., Winston Churchill Found., John and Frances L. Loeb Found.; mem. vis. com. of bd. overseers to visit Grad. Sch. Bus. Adminstrn. and dept. govt. Harvard. Served as 1st lt. USAF, 1954-56. Clubs: Recess, City Midday. (N.Y.C.); Century; Sleepy Hollow (Westchester, N.Y.); Buck's, Brooks's (London, Eng.); Royal Swedish Yacht (Stockholm); Lyford Cay (Nassau). Home: Ridgeleigh Anderson Hill Rd Purchase NY 10577 Office: Loeb Rhoades & Co 375 Park Ave New York NY 10022

LOEB, PETER KENNETH, investment banker; b. N.Y.C., Apr. 8, 1936; s. Carl M. and Lucille H. (Schamberg) L.; B.A., Yale, 1958; M.B.A., Columbia, 1961; children—Peter Kenneth, Karen Elizabeth, James Matthew. With Shearson Loeb Rhoades, N.Y.C., now mng. dir.; dir. Design Works Bedford-Stuyvesant; mem. com. on securities Am. Stock Exchange. Asso., Lincoln Center for Performing Arts, Inc.; mem. Mus. Modern Art, Met. Mus. Art, Philharmonic Symphony Soc. N.Y.; mem. Wall St. com. N.Y. Urban Coalition, 1969-71; chmn. tournament marshal com. Westchester Golf Classic; vice chmn. Pacesetter com. Greater N.Y. council Boy Scouts Am., 1966-67. Mem. exec. bd. new leadership div. Fedn. Jewish Philanthropies, 1963-64; mem. adv. bd. Atoms Track Club-Bedford-Stuyvesant; bd. dirs., pres. N.Y.C. Baseball Fedn.; trustee Columbia U., Allen-Stevenson Sch., Beekman Downtown Hosp.; vice chmn. nat. devel. bd. Columbia U., mem. adv. council Bus. Sch., 1976—. Recipient Distinguished Service award N.Y.C. Baseball Fedn., 1976; Alumni medal for conspicuous service Columbia U., 1975, Bus. Sch., 1976. Mem. Securities Traders Assn. N.Y., Investment Assn. N.Y. (exec. bd. 1969, adv. counsel), Securities Industry Assn. (governing council 1977-79), Nat. Assn. Security Dealers (dist. 12 com.), Columbia Grad. Sch. Bus. Alumni Assn. (dir., pres. 1971-74), Columbia U. Alumni Fedn. (dir. 1971-74), S.A.R. Clubs: City Midday, Bond, Century Country (dir. 1973-77), Madison Square Garden, Doubles. Home: 50 E 77th St New York NY 10021 Office: 14 Wall St New York NY 10005

LOEB, VIRGIL, JR., physician; b. St. Louis, Sept. 21, 1921; s. Virgil and Therese (Meltzer) L.; student Swarthmore Coll., 1938-41; M.D., Washington U., St. Louis, 1944; m. Lenore Harlow, Sept. 8, 1950; children—Katherine Loeb Barksdale, Elizabeth Loeb McCane, David, Mark. Intern, Barnes and Jewish hosps., St. Louis, 1944-45; resident in internal medicine, research fellow in hematology Washington U. and Barnes Hosp., 1947-52; med. faculty, 1951—, prof. clin. medicine, 1978—, clin. research and cons. practice med. oncology, hematology, 1951—, dir. Central Diagnostic Labs., Barnes Hosp., 1952-68; staff numerous hosps., 1951—; cons. Nat. Cancer Inst., 1966—; chmn. cancer clin. investigation rev. com. Nat. Cancer Inst., 1966-69, mem. diagnostic research adv. com., 1972-75; mem. nat. adv. coms. Am. Cancer Soc., 1969—. Mem. oncology merit rev. bd. VA, 1971-75; bd. dirs. Nat. and Mo. div. Am. Cancer Soc., St. Louis Blue Cross and Blue Shield; trustee John Burroughs Sch., 1966-69. Served with M.C., AUS, 1945-47. Diplomate Am. Bd. Internal Medicine. Fellow A.C.P.; mem. Central Soc. Clin. Research, Inst. Medicine of Nat. Acad. Sci., Am. Assn. Cancer Research, Am. Soc. Clin., Oncology, Am. Fedn. Clin. Research, Internat. Soc. Hematology, Am. Soc. Hematology, St. Louis Soc. Internal Medicine (pres. 1974), Sigma Xi, Alpha Omega Alpha. Contbg. author books, contbr. articles to profl. publs. Home: 24 Deerfield Rd Saint Louis MO 63124 Office: 3102 Queeny Tower Barnes Hosp Plaza Saint Louis MO 63110

LOEB, WILLIAM, publisher; b. Washington, Dec. 26, 1905; s. William and Katharine W. (Dorr) L.; A.B., Williams Coll., 1927; postgrad. Harvard Law Sch., 1929-31; m. Nackey Scripps, July 15, 1952; children—Edith, Elizabeth. Pres., publisher Saint Albans (Vt.) Daily Messenger, 1941—, Vt. Sunday News, 1942-62, Manchester Union Leader, 1946—, N.H. Sunday News, 1948—, publisher Haverhill (Mass.) Jour., 1957-65, Conn. Sunday Herald, 1964-74, Merrimack Valley Pub. Co., 1962. Bd. dirs. Am. China Policy Assn., pres., 1941-43; chmn. Council Profit Sharing Industries, 1949-52. Trustee Lahey Clinic, Boston. Decorated comdr. Cross Polonia Restituta; Knight of Malta. Mem. Nat. Rifle Assn. (dir.), Zeta Psi. Baptist. Clubs: Seawanhaka Corinthian Yacht (Oyster Bay, L.I., N.Y.); Harvard (Boston); Prospectors (Reno). Home: Nevada Star Ranch 6995 Franktown Rd Carson City NV 89701

LOEBBECKE, ERNEST JAMES, ret. ins. co. exec.; b. Chico, Calif., Jan. 31, 1911; s. Ernst Frederick and Mary (Kratzer) L.; student U. San Francisco, 1928-30, Southwestern U., 1930-32; LL.D., Loyola U., Los Angeles; D.B.A. (hon.), U. San Francisco; m. Anna E. Davis, Aug. 27, 1932; children—Mary A., Robert E. Office mgr. Craig & Strachan, C.P.A.'s, Los Angeles, 1930-33; treas. Title Guarantee & Trust Co., Los Angeles, 1934- 43; owner, opr. Ernest J. Loebbecke, C.P.A., Los Angeles, 1943-45; v.p., gen. mgr. Los Angeles Towel Service Co., 1945-47; treas. Title Ins. and Trust Co., Los Angeles, 1947-55, pres., 1955-63, chmn. bd., 1963-72; pres. TI Corp. (Calif.), 1968-72, chmn. bd., 1972-76, chief exec. officer, 1968-76, now dir.; dir. Am. Express Co., Title Ins. & Trust Co., Pioneer Nat. Title Ins. Co., Knudsen Creamery Co., Los Angeles, Fireman's Fund Ins. Co., Transmix Corp., IT Corp. Mem. exec. com. Boy Scouts Am., Los Angeles; mem. Mayor's Com. Human Relations, Los Angeles; pres. Los Angeles Welfare Fedn., 1957-60; mem. adv. com. Calif. Mus. Sci. and Industry, Los Angeles; campaign chmn. Los Angeles Community Chest, 1960- 61; founding and hon. pres. United Way, Inc. Regent, mem. pres.'s adv. council U. San Francisco; trustee Harvey Mudd Coll. C.P.A., Calif. Mem. Am. Title Assn. (past pres.), Calif. Land Title Assn. (past pres.), Calif. Soc. C.P.A.'s, Calif. Ins. Fedn. (dir.), U.S. (v.p., dir.), Calif. (pres. 1969-70), Los Angeles (past v.p., dir.) chambers commerce, Home Bldrs. Inst., Town Hall. Mason. Clubs: Twilight, Sunset, California (Los Angeles); Pacific Union (San Francisco); Annandale Golf (Pasadena, Calif.). Home: 3472 Yorkshire Rd Pasadena CA 91107 Office: 700 Wilshire Blvd Los Angeles CA 90017

LOEBER, RICHARD HAROLD, ins. co. exec.; b. Schenectady, N.Y., Mar. 4, 1931; s. David and Katherine (Daumn) L.; B.S. in Mathematics, Union Coll., 1953; m. Patricia Dion, July 1, 1951; children—Lawrence, Pamela. With Aetna Life Ins. Co., Hartford, Conn., 1953—, various positions, now v.p., actuary group div.; dir. Aetna Casualty & Surety Co. Am., Conn. Health Reinsurance Assn., Nat. Fund for Med. Edn. Fellow Soc. Actuaries, Am. Acad. Actuaries. Club: Golf of Avon. Home: 150 Winding Ln Avon CT 06001 Office: 151 Farmington Ave Hartford CT 06115

LOEBL, ERNEST MOSHE, educator, univ. dean; b. Vienna, Austria, July 30, 1923; s. Heinrich and Therese (Weiner) L.; M.Sc., Hebrew U., 1946; Ph.D., Columbia, 1952; m. Suzanne Bamberger, Mar. 15, 1950; children—Judith H., David A. Came to U.S., 1947, naturalized, 1955. Mem. faculty Poly. Inst. N.Y., 1952—, prof. phys. chemistry, 1963—; dean natural scis. and math. Yeshiva U., N.Y.C., 1980—; cons., lectr. in field. NSF sci. faculty fellow Uppsala U., Oxford U., 1963-64; vis. scientist Sheffield U., 1971, Hebrew U., 1973. Mem. Am. Chem. Soc., Am. Phys. Soc., AAAS, AAUP (chpt. chmn. 1968), Sigma Xi (chpt. v.p. 1979), Phi Lambda Upsilon. Author: Group Theory, Vol. I, 1968, Vol. II, 1971, Vol. III, 1975. Editor: Physical Chemistry Monograph Series, 1966; Current Chemical Concepts Series, 1968. Home: 788 Riverside Dr New York NY 10032 Office: 333 Jay St Brooklyn NY 11201

LOEBL, SUZANNE BAMBERGER, author, editor; b. Hannover, Germany; d. Hugo and Margaret (Schwarzhaupt) Bamberger; came to U.S., 1946, naturalized, 1951; student Lycée de Forest, Brussels, 1938-42, Institut Meurice Chimie, Brussels, 1944-46, Columbia, 1946-48; m. Ernest M. Loebl, Mar. 15, 1950; children—Judith Hannah, David Albert. Research asst. Sloane-Kettering Inst. for Cancer Research, N.Y.C., 1948-52, N.Y. U., 1952-54; freelance tech. writer and translator, 1958—; sci. editor N.Y. Heart Assn., N.Y.C., 1969-71; sci. editor Arthritis Found., N.Y.C., 1971-77. Mem. community bd. Columbia-Presbyterian Hosp., 1979—. Advanced Sci. Writing fellow Columbia, 1968-69. Recipient Matrix award N.Y. Women in Communications, 1974. Mem. Nat. Assn. Sci. Writers, Am. Soc. Journalists and Authors. Author: Fighting the Unseen: The Story of Viruses, 1967; Exploring the Mind: Man's Search for Mental Health, 1968; Conception, Contraception, A New Look, 1974; The Nurses' Drug Handbook, 1977; (with Albert Decker) Why Can't We Have a Baby, 1978. Home and Office: 788 Riverside Dr New York NY 10032

LOEBLICH, HELEN NINA TAPPAN, paleontologist, educator; b. Norman, Okla., Oct. 12, 1917; d. Frank Girard and Mary (Jenks) Tappan; B.S., U. Okla., 1937, M.S., 1939; Ph.D., U. Chgo., 1942; m. Alfred Richard Loeblich, Jr., June 18, 1939; children—Alfred Richard III, Karen Elizabeth Loeblich McClelland, Judith Anne Loeblich Covey, Daryl Louise Loeblich Ford. Instr. geology Tulane U., 1942-43; geologist U.S. Geol. Survey, 1943-45, 47-59; mem. faculty U. Calif. at Los Angeles, 1958—, prof. geology, 1966—, vice chmn. dept. geology, 1973-75; research asso. Smithsonian Instn., 1954-57; asso. editor Cushman Found. Foraminiferal Research, 1950-51. Guggenheim fellow, 1953-54. Fellow Geol. Soc. Am. (councilor 1979—); mem. Paleontol. Soc., Soc. Protozoologists, Phycological Soc. Am., AAUP, Soc. Econ. Paleontologists and Mineralogists (councilor for paleontology 1975-77, hon. mem. 1978—), Internat. Phycological Soc., Internat. Paleontological Assn., Marine Biol. Assn.

LUNDE, FINN, psychiatrist; b. Tolga, Norway, Jan. 12, 1928; s. Sindre and Ingeborg (Haug) L.; M.D., Oslo U., 1952; m. Beverly Jean Fenton, Oct. 6, 1956 (dec. Sept. 1978); children—Halvor, Anne Marie; m. 2d, Lois Lowden, June 23, 1979. Came to U.S., 1956, naturalized, 1959. Intern Luth. Hosp., LaCrosse, Wis., 1952-53; jr. asst. resident psychiatry Montreal (Que.) Gen. Hosp., 1955-56; resident U. Hosp. Coll. Medicine, U. Nebr., 1956-58, asst. instr. neurology and psychiatry, 1958-60, instr., 1960-63, asst. prof., 1963-65; practice medicine, Fergus Falls, Minn., 1953, specializing in psychiatry, Ingleside, Neb., 1958-65; staff physician Fergus Falls State Hosp., 1953; psychiatrist Hastings (Neb.) State Hosp., 1958-60, clin. dir., 1960-62, supt., 1962-65; chief profl. edn. De Witt State Hosp., Auburn, Calif., 1965-67, asso. med. dir., 1967-72. Bd. dirs. Community Chest, ARC. Served to capt. M.C., Norwegian Army, 1954-55. Diplomate Am. Bd. Psychiatry and Neurology. Fellow Am. Psychiat. Assn.; mem. AMA, Norwegian, Calif. (alternate del.) med. assns., Placer-Nevada County Med. Soc. (pres. 1974), Assn. Am. Med. Colls., Assn. Med. Supts. Mental Hosps. Lutheran. Rotarian. Club: Auburn Valley Golf and Country. Contbr. articles med. jours. Address: 402 Sunrise Ave Roseville CA 95678

LUNDE, FRITHJOF MARTIN, architect, planner; b. Risor, Norway, Feb. 7, 1921; s. Frithjof and Amalie Magdalena (Ellingsen) L.; B.Arch., Pratt U., 1947; m. Janet Yvonne Govia, Aug. 10, 1962; children—Eric Frithjof, Gale Edith (dec.), Lars Elling, Martine Lorraine Amalie. Staff architect, N.Y.C., 1947-49; chief office Lorimer & Rose, Architects and Engrs., N.Y.C., 1949-55; partner Warner Burns Toan Lunde, Architects, N.Y.C., 1956-71, sr. mng. partner, 1971—; pres. TEG Internat., Ltd., N.Y.C., 1971-77; pres. Townland Mktg. and Devel. Corp., N.Y.C.; mem. task group, chmn. study program work group Hudson Basin Project, 1975-76. Tourism cons. Central Bank of Dominican Republic. Served to capt. USAAC, 1943-45. Decorated D.F.C., Air medal. Fellow AIA (nat. chmn. com. on regional devel. and natural resources 1977, mem. energy task force 1972-73); mem. ASCE (environ. impact assessment research council). Home: Lundegaard Watch Hill Rd Peekskill NY 10566 Office: 724 Fifth Ave New York NY 10019

LUNDEBERG, PHILIP KARL, museum curator; b. Mpls., June 14, 1923; s. Olav Knutson and Vivian Juliet (Boraas) L.; B.A. summa cum laude, Duke, 1944, M.A., 1947; Ph.D. (Austin fellow 1949), Harvard, 1954; m. Eleanore Lillian Berntson, July 18, 1953; 1 son, Karl Fredrik. Asst. to historian U.S. Naval ops. in World War II, Navy Dept., 1950-53; asst. prof. history St. Olaf Coll., 1953-55, U.S. Naval Acad., 1955-59; asso. curator naval history Nat. Mus. History and Tech., Smithsonian Instn., 1959-61, curator of naval history, 1961—. Chmn. Internat. Congress Maritime Museums, 1972-75; v.p. U.S. Commn. on Mil. History, 1975-79; sec. Internat. Commn. Mus. Security, 1975-79; pres. Council Am. Maritime Museums, 1976-78. Served with USNR, 1943-46, 50-52, comdr. Res. Decorated Bronze Star, Purple Heart; recipient Bronze medal Internat. Commn. Mil. History, 1975. Fellow Am. Mil. Inst. (Moncado prize 1964, v.p. 1968-71, pres. 1971-73); mem. Am. Assn. Museums, Am. Hist. Assn., AAUP, Naval Hist. Found., Nat. Trust for Historic Preservation (maritime preservation com. 1975-79), Soc. Hist. Tech., Phi Beta Kappa. Author: Samuel Colt's Submarine Battery, 1974; co-author: Sea Power: A Naval History, 1960. Editor: Bibliographie de L'Histoire des Grandes Routes Maritimes: Etats-Unis D'Amérique, 1970. Home: 1107 Croton Dr Alexandria VA 22308 Office: Nat Museum of History and Tech Smithsonian Inst Washington DC 20560

LUNDELIUS, ERNEST LUTHER, JR., vertebrate paleontologist, educator; b. Austin, Tex., Dec. 2, 1927; s. Ernest Luther and Hazel (Halton) L.; B.S. in Geology, U. Tex., 1950; Ph.D. in Paleozoology, U. Chgo., 1954; m. Judith Weiser, Sept. 28, 1953; children—Jennifer, Rolf Eric. Postdoctoral research fellow Calif. Inst. Tech., 1956-57; mem. faculty U. Tex., Austin, 1957—, prof. vertebrate paleontology, 1969— John Andrew Wilson prof. vertebrate paleontology, 1978—. Served with AUS, 1946-47. Home: 7310 Running Rope Dr Austin TX 78731 Office: Dept Geol Scis Univ Tex Austin TX 78712

LUNDELL, CYRUS LONGWORTH, scientist, exec.; b. Austin, Tex., Nov. 5, 1907; s. John Cyrus and Ruth Marie (Karling) L.; A.B., So. Methodist U., 1932; student Columbia, 1929; A.M., U. Mich., 1934, Ph.D., 1936; m. Amelia Anderson, Jan. 15, 1931; children—Jon Richard, Karen Dianne. Asst. physiologist Tropical Plant Research Found., 1928-30; asst. bot. gardens U. Mich., 1932-35, asst. curator herbarium, 1935-39, curator, 1939-43; research asso. Carnegie Inst. of Washington, 1933-41; research prof. botany So. Methodist U., 1941-43, prof. botany, dir. Inst. Technology and Plant Industry, 1943-46, prof. botany, dir. univ. herbarium, 1946-48; field technician Rubber Reserve Co., 1943; prodn. specialist Fgn. Econ. Adminstrn., 1943; exec. v.p., dir., chief scientist, head Hoblitzelle Agrl. Lab., Tex. Research Found., 1946-72; dir. plant scis. lab. U. Tex. at Dallas, 1972—, prof. plant scis., 1972-75, prof. botany and environ. scis., 1975-78, prof. emeritus, 1978—; adj. prof. botany U. Tex. at Austin, 1972—; dir., botanist U. Mich., Carnegie Instn. Washington expdns. to Mex. and C. Am., 1933-38; discoverer, explorer Mayan cities of Calakmul, 1931, Polol, 1933. Recipient Distinguished Alumnus award So. Meth. U., 1954; Advancement of Tex. Agr. and Rural Life award Assn. Tex. Soil and Water Conservation Dists., 1966; Distinguished Service award State Assn. Young Farmers Tex., 1967; award of Merit Dallas So. Meml. Assn., 1973; The Chancellor's Council U. Tex. System, 1973. Fellow A.A.A.S., Texas Acad. Sci. (hon. life); mem. Am. Soc. Plant Taxonomists, Cal. Bot. Soc., Sigma Xi, Phi Kappa Phi. Author: Agricultural Research at Renner, 1944-1966, 1967; Flora of Texas, 3 vols.; editor Wrightia, A Botanical Jour.; contbr. 180 articles to profl. jours. Home: 7043 Desco Dr Dallas TX 75225 Office: Univ Tex at Dallas Box 688 Richardson TX 75080

LUNDEN, LAURENCE RAYMOND, educator; b. Watertown, S.D., Apr. 5, 1907; s. Hans and Gertrude Bertine (Peterson) L.; B.A., Grinnell Coll., 1929; postgrad. U. Minn., 1929-34; LL.D., Luther Coll., 1940; m. Anne Elizabeth Stub, June 21, 1941 (dec. Oct. 1967); children—Laurence Raymond, John Peter. Instr. Sch. Bus. Adminstrn., U. Minn., 1929-39. asso. prof., 1939-57, prof., 1957—, also editor Financial and Investment Rev., 1932-43, investment counsel bd. regents, 1936-46, asst. comptroller, 1941-43, asst. sec. bd. regents, 1941-52, comptroller, 1943-59, treas. bd. regents, 1952-59, v.p., 1959-72, sec. bd. regents, 1959—; faculty, mem. adminstrv. com. Grad. Sch. Banking, U. Wis., 1944—; trustee Farmers & Mechanics Savs. Bank. Mem. neurology program project com. NIH; cons. tng. contracts USAAF, 1941-42; gov.'s adv. com. on state trust funds, 1946-63; mem. Little Hoover Commn. State Minn., 1952; cons. NSF, 1965—. Trustee Luther Coll., 1940-52; bd. dirs., exec. com. North Star Research and Devel. Inst.; trustee, chmn. budget com. Argonne Univs. Assn., 1966-70, cons., 1970—; dir. U. Minn. Found.; trustee Fairview Hosp. Mem. Central Assn. Coll. and Univ. Bus. Officers (treas., v.p., pres. 1947-52), Nat. Fedn. Assns. Coll. and Univ. Bus. Officers (dir., v.p. 1953—), Am. Council Edn. (chmn. com. taxation and fiscal reporting 1949-57), Assn. Land-Grant Colls. and Univs., Nat. Assn. State Univs., Midwestern Univs. Research Assn. (dir., sec. 1954—, pres. 1965-71), Am. Econ. Assn., Norwegian-American Hist. Assn., Phi Beta Kappa, Sigma Delta Chi, Alpha Kappa Psi. Clubs: University, Athletic (Mpls.). Author: A Type Study of American Banking (with R. A. Stevenson, others), 1934. Contbr. articles profl. publs. Home: 3700 48th Ave S Minneapolis MN 55406

LUNDEN, SAMUEL EUGENE, architect; b. Chgo., July 14, 1897; s. Albert Axel and Christina Eugenia (Erickson) L.; student Calif. Inst. Tech., Pasadena, 1918; B.Arch., Mass. Inst. Tech., 1921; m. Leila Burton Allen, Mar. 13, 1925; children—Alice Marie, Robert Allen, Ardelle Leila. Mem. Am. Students Reconstrn. Unit, Verdun, France, 1921; traveled and studied architecture in Europe, 1921, 51, 61, 68; asso. with office Cram & Ferguson, Boston, 1921-27; commenced practice of architecture in 1928; partner Samuel E. Lunden-Joseph L. Johnson, architects, Los Angeles, 1960-78; cons. architect Lyon Assos., Inc., Los Angeles, 1978—; projects include Pacific Coast Stock Exchange; Edward L. Doheny Meml. Library; cons. architect Allan Hancock Found., residence halls U. So. Calif.; architect Hosp. Good Samaritan Med. Center, Los Angeles, 1943-73; City Hall South Los Angeles, 1954, (co-architect) Rd. Dept. Adminstrn. Bldg., Vets. Meml. Regional County Park, County Los Angeles; master plan Temple Urban Renewal Project, Los Angeles 1958, Las Palmas Sch. Girls, Probation Dept. County Los Angeles, 1959, (co-architect) Harbor Police Sta., City Los Angeles, 1961, Western Fed. Bldg., complete modernization, 1964; cons. architect VA Hosp., Phoenix, 1948; master plans and design sch. bldgs. S. Bay Union High Sch. Dist., Van Nuys High Sch., North Valley Occupational Center, Los Angeles Unified Sch. Dist.; co-architect Univ. Center, Calif. State U. at Fullerton; mem. planning commn. Manhattan Beach, 1942-43. Bd. govs. Town Hall Calif., 1955-60, 62-68, pres., 1965; vice chmn. Citizens Traffic, Transp. Com., Los Angeles Area, 1954-55; mem. Am. Arbitration Assn., 1953—, Los Angeles adv. council, 1967-75. Recipient first prize Am. Hosp. Assn. competition for design small community hosp., 1945; certificate merit So. Calif. chpt. AIA; Town Hall award, 1960; hon. sec. Mass. Inst. Tech., Alumni Assn., mem. alumni fund bd., 1967-70, mem. corp. devel. com., 1965—, corp. leadership award, 1976, Beaver award; Kemper award AIA, 1963. Fellow AIA (v.p. 1945-47; pres. So. Calif. chpt. 1942-43, dir. Calif. council 1965); mem. Los Angeles Area C. of C. Clubs: M.I.T. of So. Calif. (pres. 1955); Assos. (U. So. Calif.); California (Los Angeles). Author: Community Development Through an Exposition for Los Angeles, 1944. Inventor conductive pad and system for discharging static charges for hosp. operating rooms. Home: 6205 Via Colinita Rancho Palos Verdes CA 90274 Office: 606 S Olive St Suite 701 Los Angeles CA 90014

LUNDGREN, LAWRENCE WILLIAM, educator; b. Attleboro, Mass., Mar. 17, 1932; s. Lawrence William and Hope Minerva (Baker) L.; A.B., Brown U., 1953; Ph.D., Yale, 1958; m. Marjorie Curtis Hay, Mar. 13, 1954 (div. 1975); children—Gary William, Julie Ann. Instr. dept. geol. scis. U. Rochester (N.Y.), 1956-58, asst. prof., 1958-63, asso. prof., 1963-67, prof., 1967—, acting chmn. dept., 1963-64, 69-70, chmn., 1971-74, 76—; NSF faculty fellow Johns Hopkins U., 1976, U.S. Geol. Survey, 1977, geologist Conn. Geol. and Natural History Survey, 1956—. Bd. dirs. Rochester Com. for Sci. Information. Shell, NSF, Fulbright lectr. U. Oulu (Finland), 1967-68. Mem. Geol., Soc. Am., Sigma Xi. Home: 176 Canterbury Rd Rochester NY 14607

LUNDGREN, ROBERT WAYNE, utility exec.; b. Omaha, Oct. 4, 1917; s. Cornelius and Elin Lundgren; B.S. in Elec. Engring., Mass. Inst. Tech., 1940; m. Barbara J. Long, Feb. 25, 1945; children—Sharon Ann, Sandra Jane, Suzanne. With Detroit Edison Co., formerly v.p. purchases and real estate, now exec. v.p. adminstrn.; dir. Edison Illuminating Co., Midwest Energy Resources Co., St. Clair Energy Co. Bd. dirs. Mich. Electric Assn., Citizens Research Council, League Handicapped, Detroit Goodwill Industries. Served with USNR, 1942-46. Mem. Greater Detroit C. of C., Nat. Assn. Purchasing Mgmt., Pub. Utility Buyers Group, Purchasing Roundtable, Detroit Econ. Club. Presbyn. Clubs: Detroit Athletic, Forest Lake Country. Home: 661 S Hill Rd Bloomfield Hills MI 48013 Office: 2000 2d St Detroit MI 48226

LUNDIN, OSCAR ALEXIS, corp. exec.; b. Detroit, Nov. 10, 1910; s. August and Christina (Nelson) L.; A.B. in Bus. Adminstrn., U. Mich., 1932; m. Elizabeth Randolph Hutchison, Oct. 12, 1940; children—David Oscar, Susan Elizabeth (Mrs. Ralph Thomas Jr.). With Gen. Motors Corp., 1933-75, comptroller Allison div., Indpls., 1954-60, treas. corp., Detroit, 1960-66, v.p. charge staff 1968-70, mem. adminstrn. com., 1968-75, exec. v.p. finance, 1970-74, dir., mem. finance and exec. coms., 1970-75, vice chmn., 1974-75; pres., Gen. Motors Acceptance Corp., 1966-68, dir., 1966-75; chmn. bd. Motors Ins. Corp., 1966-68, dir., 1962-75; dir. Detroit Bank and Trust, 1975—, CPC Internat., Inc., 1975—, Consol. Rail Corp., 1976—. Mem. Theta Xi. Clubs: Bloomfield Hills (Mich.) Country; Detroit, Recess (Detroit); University (N.Y.C.); Ocean Club (Ocean Ridge); Country of Fla. (Delray Beach). Home: 191 Marblehead Dr Bloomfield Hills MI 48013

LUNDINE, STANLEY NELSON, congressman, lawyer; b. Jamestown, N.Y., Feb. 4, 1939; m. Karol Anne Ludwig; children—John Ludwig, Mark Andrew. Mayor of Jamestown, 1969-76; mem. 95th Congress from 39th N.Y. Dist., mem. banking, fin. and urban affairs coms., sci. and tech. com., select com. on aging. Office: 430 Cannon Bldg Washington DC 20515

LUNDQUIST, CARL HAROLD, coll. pres.; b. Elgin, Ill., Nov. 16, 1916; s. Henry and Esther (Gustafson) L.; B.A., Sioux Falls Coll., 1939; B.D., Bethel Theol. Sem., 1943; Th.M., Eastern Bapt. Theol. Sem., 1946; D.D., No. Bapt. Theol. Sem., 1957, Th.D., 1960; m. Nancy Mae Zimmerman, Sept. 15, 1942; children—Carole (Mrs. James Spickelmier), Eugene, Jill (Mrs. James Anderson), Susan. Ordained to ministry Bapt. Ch., 1944; pastor Elim Bapt. Ch., Chgo., 1943-53; pres. Bethel Coll. and Sem., St. Paul, 1954—. Mem. exec. com., treas. Minn. Pvt. Coll. Fund. 1971; sec. Minn. Pvt. Coll. Council, 1971; exec. com. Christian Coll. Coalition, chmn. commn. on ch. life Bapt. World Alliance; mem. exec. com. Bapt. World Alliance; adv. bd. Am. Behavioral Labs., Youth Gospel Crusade, chmn. Consortium Minn. Sem. Pres.'s; trustee Bapt. Hosp. Fund, St. Paul, James Jerome Hill Reference Library; bd. dirs. Youth Leadership-Minn., Council for Advancement of Small Colls., Met. Hosp. Center. Mem. NEA, Nat. Assn. Evangs. (v.p. exec. com., chmn. commn. on higher edn., now pres.), Sem. Profs. in Practical Fields, Speech Assn. Clubs: Rotary, Minnesota. Home: 1900 Asbury Ave St Paul MN 55113

LUNDQUIST, CHARLES ARTHUR, govt. ofcl.; b. Webster, S.D., Mar. 26, 1928; s. Arthur Reynald and Olive Esther (Parks) L.; B.S., S.D. State U., 1949, D.Sc., 1979; Ph.D., U. Kans., 1953; m. Patricia Jean Richardson, Nov. 28, 1951; children—Clara Lee, Dawn Elizabeth, Frances Johanna, Eric Arthur, Gary Lars. Asst. prof. engring. research Pa. State U., 1953-54; sect. chief U.S. Army Ballistic Missile Agy., Huntsville, Ala., 1956-60; br. chief NASA-Marshall Space Flight Center, Huntsville, 1960-62, dir. Space Scis. Lab., 1973—; asst. dir. sci. Smithsonian Astrophys. Obs., Cambridge, Mass., 1962-73; asso. Harvard Coll. Obs., 1962-73. Trustee Huntsville Symphony Orch. Served with U.S. Army, 1954-56. Recipient Exceptional Sci. Achievement medal NASA, 1971; Hermann Oberth award AIAA, 1978. Mem. AAAS, N.Y. Acad. Scis., Am. Geophys. Union, Am. Astron. Soc. Editor: (with G. Weis) Smithsonian Institution Standard Earth, 1966; The Physics and Astronomy of Space Science, 1966. Home: 214 Jones Valley Dr SW Huntsville AL 35802 Office: Space Sci Lab George C Marshall Space Flight Center AL 35812

LUNDQUIST, CLARENCE THEODORE, lawyer; b. Chgo., Jan. 3, 1909; s. Frank and Bessie (Larson) l.; student Northwestern U., 1927-29, Grad. Sch. Bus., 1932-35; B.S. in Commerce, U. Ill., 1932; J.D., Georgetown U., 1944; m. Edith M. Otte, July 9, 1938; 1 dau., Donna Fey Collins. Statistician, Bur. Labor Statistics, Dept. Labor, 1935-38, investigatigator, adminstrv. ofcl. wage and hour div., 1938-42, 46-49; dep. dir. legislative program Office Sec. Def., 1949-55; dep. adminstr. wage and hour and pub. contracts div. Dept. Labor 1955-58, adminstr., 1958-69; with law firm McDermott & Russell, 1969-75; adminstr. code of ethics Direct Selling Assn., 1971-74; arbitrator, 1970—. admitted to D.C. bar, 1945. U.S. Del. ILO, Geneva, Switzerland, 1957, 68. Served from 2d lt. to lt. col. AUS, 1942-46. Clubs: Congl. Country (Bethesda, Md.); Boca Raton (Fla.) Hotel and Club. Home: 4990 Sentinel Dr Sumner MD 20016 also Boca Raton FL 33432

LUNDQUIST, JAMES H., lawyer; b. Chgo., Mar. 24, 1931; s. Harold L. and Beatrice E. (Anderson) L.; A.B., Millikin U., 1952; J.D., John Marshall Law Sch., 1954; m. Beverly J. Williams, Nov. 26, 1955; children—John Redfield, Ann Tecla. Admitted to Ill. bar, 1954, N.Y., D.C. bar, 1961, U.S. Supreme Ct. bar, 1963; practice in Chgo., 1954-55, 57-60; partner firm Barnes, Richardson & Colburn, N.Y.C., D.C. and Chgo., 1960—; lectr. in field. Chmn., Nassau County Task Force on Aging, 1964-66; mem. Nassau County Mental Health Bd., 1965-70; bd. dirs. Nassau County chpt. NCCJ, 1965-77; corp. mem. Community Service Soc. N.Y.C., 1970-78; trustee Methodist Ch., Port Washington, N.Y. Served to lt. AUS, 1955-56. Recipient Merit award John Marshall Law Sch., 1974. Mem. Am. (chmn. standing com. customs law 1967-73), N.Y., D.C., Fed. bar assns., Assn. Bar City N.Y. (fed. legislation com. 1970-73), Assn. Customs Bar (pres. 1978—), John Marshall Law Sch. Alumni Assn., Sigma Alpha Epsilon. Democrat. Clubs: Union League (N.Y.C.); Univ. (Washington); Manhasset Bay Yacht. Author: Guide to Import and Export Procedure, 1975. Contbr. articles to profl. jours. Home: Sands Point NY Office: 475 Park Ave S New York NY 10016 also 1819 H St NW Washington DC 20006

LUNDVALL, BRUCE GILBERT, recording co. exec.; b. Englewood, N.J., Sept. 13, 1935; s. Howard Leonard and Florence Matilda (MacNeille) L.; B.S., Bucknell U.; m. Katherine Abel, Nov. 26, 1960; children—Eric, Tor, Kurt. Mem. media dept. Doherty, Clifford, Steers and Shenfield, Advt., 1957-58; mgmt. trainee Columbia Records, 1961-62, product mgr. popular albums, 1963-65, dir. product mgmt., 1965-67, v.p. merchandising, 1967-70, v.p. mktg., 1970-74; v.p., gen. mgr. CBS Records, N.Y.C., 1974-76, pres., 1976—. Bd. deacons, bd. trustees Emmanual Ch.; bd. dirs. N.Y. chpt. Am. Cancer Soc., bd. advisers Black Music Assn. Served with U.S. Army. Recipient Leukemia research Humanitarian award T. J. Martell Found., 1977; Humanitarian award Music Industry chpt. City of Hope, 1979; Trendsetter award Billboard mag., 1979, others. Mem. Nat. Assn. Record Merchandisers (bd. advisors), Rec. Industry Assn. Am. (chmn. bd. 1979—), Nat. Assn. Recording Arts and Scis. (bd. dirs.), Country Music Assn. (bd. govs.), Nat. Assn. Jazz Educators (bd. advisers). Republican. Club: Toastmasters Internat. Home: 345 Crescent Ave Wyckoff NJ 07481 Office: 51 W 52d St New York City NY

LUNDY, DANIEL FRANCIS, communications co. exec.; b. N.Y.C., Nov. 29, 1930; s. Daniel M. and Josephine Elizabeth (Corcoran) L.; B.S., Fordham U., 1952; J.D., St. John's U., N.Y.C., 1958; m. Janet M. Taylor, Dec. 27, 1952; children—Daniel Thomas, Joanne, Mary Elizabeth, Susan Teresa. Admitted to N.Y. bar, 1959, D.C. bar, 1970, N.J. bar, 1971; corp. tax dir. Merck & Co., Inc., 1964-70; tax atty. Shanley & Fisher, Esqs., Newark, 1970-72; partner Coopers & Lybrand, C.P.A.'s, N.Y.C., 1973-76; v.p., dir. taxes ITT, N.Y.C., 1976—. Served with AUS, 1952-54. C.P.A. Mem. Am. Inst. C.P.A.'s, Internat. Fiscal Assn. Contbr. to profl. jours. Home: 424 Colonial Ave Westfield NJ 07090 Office: 320 Park Ave New York NY 10022

LUNDY, HERBERT FRANCIS, ret. newspaper editor; b. Blaine, Wash., Feb. 8, 1907; s. John Stanton and Anna Melissa (Furness) L.; B.S., U. Oreg., 1928; m. Josephine Evalin Sheldon, Oct. 26, 1929; children—Michael David, Judith Ann (Mrs. Charles U. Vaughan) (dec.), John Roger. Reporter, editor Tillamook (Oreg.) Herald, 1928-29, Eugene (Oreg.) Register, 1929-30, Medford (Oreg.) Daily News, 1931-32; staff writer U.P.I., Portland, Oreg. and San Francisco, 1932-36; with The Oregonian, Portland, 1936-77, reporter, polit. writer, editorial writer, asso. editor, 1945-56, editor editorial page, 1956-77. Mem. adv. council Bonneville Power Adminstrn.; mem. Oreg. Fish and Wildlife Commn. Mem. Am. Soc. Newspaper Editors, Izaak Walton League, Nat. Wildlife Fedn. (dir.), Sigma Delta Chi. Home: 13150 SW Fielding Rd Lake Oswego OR 97034

LUNDY, JOSEPH EDWARD, automobile co. exec.; b. Clarion, Iowa, Jan. 6, 1915; s. Vern E. and Mary L. (Chambers) L.; B.A., State U. Iowa, 1936; fellow, Princeton, 1936-39. Mem. econs. faculty Princeton, 1940-42; with Ford Motor Co., Dearborn, Mich., 1946—, beginning as planning ofcl., successively dir. fin. planning and analysis, asst. controller charge financial analysis, gen. asst. controller, 1946-57, treas., 1957-61, v.p., controller, 1961-62, v.p. finance, 1962-67, exec. v.p., 1967-79, now dir. and vice-chmn. fin. com. Served from pvt. to maj., USAAF, 1943-45; dir. research and analysis Office Statis. Control, Hdqrs. USAAF, 1945. Decorated Legion of Merit. Mem. Phi Beta Kappa, Delta Upsilon. Clubs: Detroit Princeton, Detroit. Roman Catholic. Home: 7 Brookwood Ln Dearborn MI 48120 Office: Ford Motor Co American Rd Dearborn MI 48121

LUNGER, IRVIN EUGENE, univ. pres., clergyman; b. Williamsport, Pa., June 28, 1912; s. George Lee and Mabel Clara (Griggs) L.; A.B. magna cum laude, Bethany Coll., 1934, Litt.D., 1959; B.D., U. Chgo., 1935, A.M., 1936, Ph.D., 1938; postgrad. U. Munich (Germany), 1936-37; L.H.D., U. Ala., 1965; Litt.D., Eastern Ky. U., 1974; m. Eleanor Jeanne Zink, Feb. 10, 1939 (dec. Aug. 1955); children—Susan Ann (Mrs. Lee C. Brown) (dec.), Kathryn Elizabeth (Mrs. Bob Willis); m. 2d, Kay Walsh Ritchey, June 19, 1957; foster son, Owsley Ritchey. Ordained to ministry Disciples of Christ Ch., 1932; minister Christian Ch., Morristown, O., 1930-34, University Ch. Disciples of Christ, Chgo., 1939-55; prof. religion, dean Morrison Chapel, Transylvania U., Lexington, Ky., 1955-56, acad. dean, 1956-57, pres., 1957-76, pres. emeritus, 1976—; pres., dir. Bd. Higher Edn., Disciples of Christ, 1963-64. Pres. bd. dirs. Henry Clay Found., Lexington, 1968—; chmn. exec. com. Ky. Ind. Coll. Found., 1967-68; Ky. chmn. Rhodes Scholarship Selection Com., 1960-67; mem. Gov.'s Commn. Higher Edn. (Ky.), 1964-69; mem. Lexington-Fayette Found., 1960—; chmn. bd. dirs. Living Arts and Sci. Center, Inc., 1968-69; bd. dirs. Edni. Adv. and Reference Corp., N.Y.C., 1965-70, United Fund, 1959-65, pres., 1962-64; chmn. bd. dirs. Lexington Pub. Library, 1966-70; bd. dirs. Fund for Advancement of Edn. and Research, U. Ky. Med. Center, 1974—. Named Ky. col., 1959. Mem. Council Ind. Ky. Colls. and Univs. (pres. 1966, 68), Conf. Ch.-Related Colls. of South (pres. 1970), Omicron Delta Kappa, Tau Kappa Alpha, Beta Theta Pi. Democrat. Rotarian (hon.), Kiwanian (hon.). Clubs: Informal, Lafayette (Lexington); Idle Hour Country. Contbr. to Faith of the Free, 1940. Home: Herrington Woods Route 1 Harrodsburg KY 40330

LUNGHINO, DONALD JOSEPH, chem. co. exec., lawyer; b. Rochester, N.Y., Mar. 16, 1921; s. Donatus L. and Mary G. (Devito) L.; A.B., Columbia, 1942, LL.B., 1948; m. Anne Wilbor, Sept. 9, 1950; children—David, Steven, Derek. Admitted to N.Y. State bar, 1948; asso. firms Ehrich, Royall, Wheeler & Holland, Paul, Weiss, Goldberg, Rifkind, Wharton & Garrison, Davis, Polk, Wardwell, Sunderland & Kiendl (all N.Y.C.), 1948-56; corporate and tax atty. Lever Bros. Co., N.Y.C., 1956-68, asst. sec., corporate affairs counsel, 1968-70, sec., asso. gen. counsel, 1970-74, sec., gen. counsel, 1974-77, v.p., sec., gen. counsel, 1977—; v.p., treas., gen. counsel Unilever U.S., Inc., N.Y.C., 1978—. Dep. moderator Westport (Conn.) Town Meeting, 1968-73, moderator, 1973-77. Trustee, Mid-Fairfield (Conn.) County Youth Mus., 1968-73. Served to lt., USNR, World War II; ETO MTO, PTO. Mem. Am., N.Y. State bar assns., Assn. Bar City N.Y. Home: One Cockenoe Dr Westport CT 06880 Office: 390 Park Ave New York City NY 10022

LUNGREN, DANIEL EDWARD, congressman; b. Long Beach, Calif., Sept. 22, 1946; s. John Charles and Lorain Kathleen (Youngberg) L.; A.B. cum laude, Notre Dame U., 1968; postgrad. U. So. Calif. Law Sch., 1968-69; J.D., Georgetown U., 1971; m. Barbara Kolls, Aug. 2, 1969; children—Jeffrey Edward, Kelly Christine, Kathleen Marie. Admitted to Calif. bar, 1972; staff asst. Sen. George Murphy, Sen. William Brock, 1969-71; spl. asst. to co-chmn. Republican Nat. Com., dir. spl. programs Rep. Nat. Com., 1971-72; asso. firm Ball, Hunt, Hart, Brown & Baerwitz, Long Beach, 1971-78, partner, 1978; mem. 96th Congress from 34th Calif. Dist. Mem. Rep. State Central Com. Calif., 1974—; co-chmn. Nat. Congressional Council, 1977-78; bd. dirs. Long Beach chpt. ARC, Boy's Club. Recipient Good Samaritan award Los Angeles Council Mormon Chs., 1976. Mem. Am. Bar Assn., Los Angeles County Bar Assn., Long Beach County Bar Assn. Republican. Roman Catholic. Office: 5514 Britton Dr Long Beach CA 90815 and 1313 Longworth House Office Bldg Washington DC 20515

LUNIN, MARTIN, educator; b. N.Y.C., Aug. 31, 1917; s. Samuel and Sadie (Malk) L.; B.S., Okla. A. and M. Coll., 1938; D.D.S., Washington U., St. Louis, 1950; M.P.H., Columbia, 1952; m. Lois Helene Frumkin, June 22, 1947. Instr., then asst. prof. Columbia Coll. Physicians and Surgeons, 1952-58; asso. prof. U. Tex. dental br., 1958-64, prof., head dept. pathology, 1964; asst. dean U. Md. Sch. Dentistry, 1968-71, asso. dean, 1971-76; pvt. practice, N.Y.C., 1950-58. Served to capt. AUS, 1941-46. Fellow Am. Acad. Oral Pathology, AAAS; mem. Am. Dental Assn., AAUP, Am. Assn. Cancer Edn., Internat. Assn. Dental Research. Home: 28 Olmsted Green Baltimore MD 21210

LUNN, JOHN ALECK, company dir.; b. Ft. Collins, Colo., Sept. 6, 1894; s. John Gordon and Kate Eugenia (Wentz) L.; B.S., Colo. State U., 1915, M.S., 1921, D.Sc. (hon.), 1956; B.S., Harvard, 1917; S.B., Mass. Inst. Tech., 1917; m. Susan Elizabeth Williams, Feb. 4, 1926 (dec.); children—Jean Williams, John Gordon. Research in refrigeration, Cambridge, Mass., 1919-23; factory mgr. Nat. Refrigerating Co., Boston, 1923-26; sales engr. Winchester Repeating Arms Co., 1926-29; with Dewey & Almy Chem. Co., Cambridge, 1929-50, v.p., 1950; v.p., dir. mfg. and dir. Kendall Co., Boston, 1950-60, cons., 1960-75; hon. dir. Jamesbury Corp., Adage, Inc.; mem. corp. Cambridge Savs. Bank. Mem. Cambridge Redevel. Authority, 1958-70; group leader with FIAT investigation, German Chem. Industry, 1946. Pres. emeritus trustees Franklin Found. and Inst. Served as 2d lt. C.E., to capt. C.W.S., U.S. Army, 1917-19; AEF. Mem. Am. Soc. M.E. (life), Alumni Assn. Mass. Inst. Tech. (pres. 1950-51), Mass. Iota Tau Assn. (dir.), Sigma Alpha Epsilon, Theta Tau. Mason. Clubs: The Country (Brookline, Mass.); Mass. Inst. Tech. Faculty, Harvard, Cambridge (Cambridge); Army and Navy (Washington). Contbr. articles to trade and tech. publs. Home: 37 Larch Rd Cambridge MA 02138

LUNN, ROBERT JOSEPH, army officer; b. Spring Valley, Ill., Sept. 1, 1927; s. Thomas and Marcella Chirella L.; B.S., U.S. Military Acad., 1950; B.S., M.S., U. Ariz., 1961; m. Louise Marie Herrmann, Apr. 4, 1951; children—Robin Louise, Robert Julian, Sean Thomas. Commd. 2d lt., U.S. Army, 1950, advanced through grades to maj. gen., 1976; dep. comdg. gen. 32d Army Air Def. Command, Germany, 1971-74; comdg. gen., Fort Bliss, Tex., 1974-77; dir. devel. U.S. Army Devel. and Readiness Command, Alexandria, Va., 1977-79; asst. dep. chief of staff for research devel. acquisition, Dept. Army, Washington, 1979—. Decorated 2 Legion of Merit, others. Home: 7910 Claudia Dr Oxon Hill MD 20021 Office: Office of Dep Chief of Staff for Research Devel and Acquisition Dept Army Washington DC 20310

LUNN, ROYSTON CHARLES, automobile co. exec.; b. Richmond, Surrey, Eng., June 26, 1925; came to U.S., 1958, naturalized, 1963; s. Ernest Frederick and Ida May (Winslet) L.; student Leeds (Eng.) U., 1949-50, Birmingham (Eng.) U., 1952-53; grad. in Mech. and Aero. Engring., Kingston (Eng.) Coll., 1954; m. Jeanie Mary Darby, June 21, 1947; children—Nicola, Patrice. Toolmaker apprentice H.E.M. Ltd., Hook, Eng., 1939-43; designer AC Cars, Thames Ditton, Eng., 1946-47; asst. chief designer Aston Martin Ltd., Feltham, Eng., 1947-49; chief designer Jowett Motor Co., Bradford, Eng., 1949-54; product research mgr. Ford of Eng., Birmingham, 1954-56, product planning mgr., 1956-58; advanced vehicle supr. Ford Motor Co., Dearborn, Mich., 1958-60, advanced vehicle mgr., 1960-63, spl. vehicle mgr., 1963-68; exec. v.p. KarKraft, Inc., Detroit, 1968-71; dir. Jeep engring. Am. Motors Corp., Detroit, 1971-78, v.p. product engr., 1978—. Served with RAF, 1943-44. Mem. Inst. Mech. Engrs. (Gt. Britain), Soc. Automotive Engrs. Home: 3970 Penberton Ln Ann Arbor MI 48105 Office: 14250 Plymouth Rd Detroit MI 48154

LUNNEY, GLYNN STEPHEN, govt. ofcl.; b. Old Forge, Pa., Nov. 27, 1936; s. William John and Helen Rita (Glynn) L.; student U. Scranton, 1953-55, LL.D. (hon.), 1971; B.S. in Aero. Engring., U. Detroit, 1958; m. Marilyn Jean Kurtz, Apr. 30, 1960; children—Jenifer, Glynn, Shawn, Bryan. With NASA, 1955—, chief Apollo Spacecraft office, tech. dir. Apollo-Soyuz 3 test project, now mgr. shuttle payload integration and devel. program. Recipient Exceptional Service medal NASA, 1968, 69, Outstanding Performance award, 1967, Sustained Superior Performance award, 1964, Group Achievement award, 1962, 67, 68, 68, Distinguished Service medal, 1971, 75; Lawrence Sperry award Am. Inst. Aeronautics and Astronautics, 1970; Arthur S. Flemming award, 1975; Louis W. Hill Space Transp. award, 1976; Spl. Achievement award NASA, 1978; Allan D. Emil Meml. award, 1978. Mem. AIAA, Am. Astronautical Soc., Pi Tau Sigma, Tau Beta Pi. Home: 6 Queen's Ln Friendswood TX 77546 Office: NASA Johnson Space Center Houston TX 77058

LUNNON, BETTY SHEEHAN, librarian; b. Montgomery, Ala., May 29, 1908; d. Merrill Ashurst and Martha Tula (Guice) Sheehan; A.B., George Washington U., 1936; M.A. in L.S., Appalachian State U., N.C., 1959; m. David D. White, Nov. 27, 1927 (div. 1936); m. 2d, James Lunnon, May 13, 1939 (dec. 1954); 1 dau., Penelope Anne (Mrs. Darrell F. Fleeger). Tchr., librarian Seale, Hayneville and Dadeville, Ala., 1927-31; social case worker Coosa County, Ala., 1931-33; statis. cataloger div. social research WPA, 1934-36; librarian Edison Sr. High Sch., Miami, Fla., 1936-42, Fairlawn Elementary Sch., Miami, 1952-54; asst. prof. library sci. U. Miami, summers, eves. 1960-67; supr. Dade County Sch. Libraries, Miami, 1954-68; supr. libraries, dept. edn. Pago Pago, Am. Samoa, 1968-73; librarian Cushman Pvt. Sch., Miami, 1973—; also library cons. Dir. Book Selection Workshop, Drexel Inst., summer 1964; cons. Materials Workshop, Jacksonville (Ala.) U., spring 1968; mem. library com. Field Enterprises Corp., 1964-68. Recipient Britannica award for sch. library devel., 1965; Theta Sigma Phi (Miami) Headliner award, 1965. Mem. A.L.A., Fla. (pres. 1961-62), Hawaiian library assns., N.E.A., Fla. Sch. Library Assn. (pres. 1956), Am. Assn. Sch. Librarians (dir. 1962-64, chmn. supervisors sect. 1965), Quota Internat. (pres. Coral Gables 1965, lt. gov. 27th dist. 1966), Delta Kappa Gamma, Kappa Delta Pi. Author: Jacarézinho Vadico, 1948; also short stories, articles. Co-editor Books for Boys and Girls, 1955-68. Home: 1002 Granada Blvd Coral Gables FL 33134 Office: Cushman Sch Library 592 NE 60th St Miami FL 33137

LUNT, HORACE GRAY, linguist, educator; b. Colorado Springs, Colo., Sept. 12, 1918; s. Horace Fletcher and Irene (Jewett) L.; A.B., Harvard U., 1941; M.A., U. Calif., Berkeley, 1942; postgrad. Charles U., Prague, Czechoslovakia, 1946-47; Ph.D. (Rockefeller fellow), Columbia U., 1950; m. Sally Herman, June 2, 1963; children—Elizabeth, Catherine. Lectr. in Serbo-Croatian, Columbia U., 1948-49; asst. prof. Slavic langs. and lit. Harvard U., 1949-54, asso. prof., 1954-60, prof., 1960—, Samuel H. Cross prof. Slavic langs. and lits., 1965—, chmn. dept. Slavic langs. and lits., 1959-73, 75-76, mem. exec. com. Russian Research Center, 1970—, Ukrainian Research Inst., 1974—. Served with U.S. Army, 1942-45. Guggenheim fellow, 1960-61. Mem. Macedonian Acad. Arts and Scis. (corr.), Linguistic Soc. Am., Assn. Am. Tchrs. Slavic and European Langs., Am. Assn. Advancement Slavic Studies. Author: Grammar of the Macedonian Literary Language, 1952; Old Church Slavonic Grammar, 1955, 6th, rev. edit., 1974; Fundamentals of Russian, 1958, 2d rev. edit., 1968; Progressive Palatalization of Common Slavic, 1979; editor Harvard Slavic Studies, 1953-70. Home: 75 Bradford Rd Weston MA 02193 Office: Boylston 301 Harvard U Cambridge MA 02138

LUNT, OWEN RAYNAL, educator, biologist; b. El Paso, Tex., Apr. 8, 1921; s. Owen and Velma (Jackson) L.; B.A. in Chemistry, 1947; Ph.D. in Agronomy, 1951; m. Helen Hickman, Aug. 8, 1953; children—David, Carol, Janet. Mem. faculty U. Calif. at Los Angeles, 1951—, prof. plant nutrition, 1964—, acting chmn. dept. biophysics, 1965-70, dir. Lab. Nuclear Medicine and Radiation Biology, 1968—. Served with USN 1944-46. Fellow Am. Soc. Agronomy, Soil Sci. Soc. Am.; mem. Am. Soc. Plant Physiologists, Internat. Soc. Soil Sci., AAAS, Am. Nuclear Soc. (Los Angeles chpt.), Sigma Xi. Republican. Mem. Ch. Jesus Christ of Latter-day Saints. Research in soil chemistry, fertility, plant physiology. Home: 1200 Roberto Ln Los Angeles CA 90024 Office: 900 Veteran Ave Los Angeles CA 90024

LUONGO, ALFRED L., judge; b. Phila., Aug. 17, 1920; s. Daniel A. and Innocenza (Godio) L.; B.S. in Econs., U. Pa., 1941, LL.B., 1947; m. Dorothy West, Mar. 2, 1946; children—Stephen, Cecilia. Admitted to Pa. bar, 1948; law clk. Ct. Common Pleas, Philadelphia County, 1948-49, U.S. Dist. Ct. Eastern Dist. Pa., 1949-52, 53; asst. U.S. atty. Eastern Dist. Pa., 1952-53; with firm Blank, Rudenko, Klaus & Rome, Phila., 1953, partner, 1954-61; judge U.S. Dist. Ct., Eastern Dist. Pa., 1961—. Trustee, Community Coll. Phila., 1964-70. Served with AUS, 1942-46. Decorated Bronze Star. Mem. Am., Pa., Phila. bar assns., Justinian Soc., St. Thomas More Soc., Am. Legion, VFW, Order Sons of Italy in Am. Home: 3929 Henry Ave Philadelphia PA 19129 Office: US Court House Philadelphia PA 19106

LUONGO, C. PAUL, pub. relations agy. exec.; b. Winchester, Mass., Dec. 31, 1930; s. Carmine and Carmela (Gilberti) L.; grad. Cambridge Sch. Radio-TV, 1955; diploma Bentley Coll., 1951; B.S./B.A., Suffolk U., 1955; M.B.A., Babson Coll., 1956; Asso. Applied Soc. (hon.), Grahm Jr. Coll., 1970. Jr. exec. Raytheon Co., Lexington, Mass., 1956-59; account exec. Young & Rubicam, Inc., 1959-62; v.p. Copley Advt. Agy., Boston, 1962-64; pres., C. Paul Luongo Co., Boston, 1964—; TV personality America's Best!; also appearances Merv Griffin Show, Tomorrow Show, NBC-TV, TV-radio shows in Can. Served with AUS, 1952-54. Mem. Bostonian Soc. Club: N.Y. Athletic. Creator America's Best!; author syndicated newspaper-mag. features Communications Today, Pub. Relations Today. Home: Copley Square Boston MA 02116 Office: 441 Stuart St Boston MA 02116. *I believe in the work ethic, integrity and the maximum utilization of time for work and recreational activities. I loathe prejudice in any form, dishonesty and indolent people.*

LUPER, HAROLD LEE, educator; b. Oporto, Portugal, Dec. 21, 1924 (parents Am. citizens); s. Albert W. and Fannie (Hawkins) L.; A.B., Western Mich. Coll., 1949; M.A., Ohio State U., 1950, Ph.D., 1954, m. Mary Leatherwood, Jan. 24, 1944; children—John Stephen, Sally Ann, Robert Louis. Grad. asst. Speech and Hearing Clinic, Ohio State U., 1949-50, instr. speech, 1951-54; asst. prof. speech Central Mich. Coll., 1950-51; asst. prof., then asso. prof. U. Ga., 1954-63; prof., head dept. audiology and speech pathology U. Tenn., 1963—, dir. Hearing and Speech Center, 1966-73. Mem. Am. (v.p. adminstrn. 1971-73, legislative councillor 1969-70), Tenn. (pres. 1966-67) speech and hearing assns. Author: (with Robert L. Mulder) Stuttering: Therapy for Children, 1964; also articles. Home: 7705 Sabre Dr Knoxville TN 37919

LUPER, ORAL LEON, oil co. exec.; b. Paden, Okla., June 15, 1914; s. Thomas M. and Alma C. (Kern) L.; B.S. in Accounting, U. Okla., 1936; student Northwestern U., 1938; m. Muriel H. Leverett, Nov. 22, 1938; children—Barbara L. Hoek, Candice L. DePauw. With Exxon Co., U.S.A., Houston, 1946—, supr. methods and procedures staff, asst. gen. auditor, gen. auditor, asst. to controller, asst. controller, 1946-53, controller, 1953-62, gen. mgr. Eastern Esso region, 1962-64, exec. asst. to pres., exec. asst. to chmn. bd. Exxon Corp., N.Y.C., 1964-65, dir. Exxon Co., U.S.A., 1965-67, v.p., dir., 1967-73, sr. v.p., mem. mgmt. com., 1973-79. Pres., trustee Fin. Execs. Research Found.; bd. dirs. Houston Symphony Soc. Served to lt. col. AUS, 1941-46. Decorated Legion of Merit, Commendation of Merit. C.P.A., N.Y., Tex. Mem. Am. Inst. C.P.A.'s (past dir., past mem. accounting principles bd.), Accounting Research Assn. (past trustee), Fin. Execs. Inst. (past pres. Houston, dir., mem. exec. com.), Tex. Soc. C.P.A.'s (past pres. Houston), Tex. Assn. Bus. (dir.-at-large), Am. Petroleum Inst., Beta Gamma Sigma. Methodist. Clubs: Houston, Petroleum, River Oaks Country, Houstonian (Houston). Home: 11107 Meadowick Dr Houston TX 77024

LUPINO, IDA, actress, movie dir.; b. London, Eng., Feb. 4, 1918; d. Stanley and Constance (O'Shay) Lupino; m. Louis Hayward, 1938 (div.); m. 2d, Howard Duff, Oct. 1951; 1 dau., Bridget Marelia. Motion pictures include Escape Me Never, 1947, The Sea Wolfe, 1941, Lust for Gold, 1949, Sea Devils, 1937, Moontide, 1942, Woman in Hiding, 1950, They Drive by Night, 1940, The Gay Desparados, 1936, Hollywood Canteen, 1944, Forever and a Day, 1943, Ladies in Retirement, 1941, Thank Your Lucky Stars, 1943, Life Begins at Eight Thirty, 1942, Adventure of Sherlock Holmes, 1939, The Light that Failed, 1940, Lady and the Mob, 1939, Lone Wolf Spy Hunt, 1939, High Sierra, 1941, The Hard Way, 1942, Out of the Fog, 1941, In Our Time, 1944, Pillow to Post, 1945, Devotion, 1946, The Man I Love, 1947, Deep Valley, 1947, Road House, 1948, On Dangerous Ground, 1951, Beware, My Lovely, 1952, Jennifer, 1953, The Bigamist, 1953, Private Hell 36, 1954, Women's Prison, 1955, Big Knife, 1955, While the City Sleeps, 1956, Junior Bonner, 1972, The Devil's Rain, 1975, The Food of the Gods, 1976; TV series Mr. Adams and Eve, 1956-58; now producer and dir. Office: care Michael Karg Agy Beverly Hills CA

LUPONE, PATTI, actress; b. Northport, L.I., N.Y., Apr. 21, 1949; d. Orlando Joseph and Angela Louise (Patti) DuP.; B.F.A., The Juilliard Sch., 1972. Off-Broadway productions include: The School for Scandal, The Lower Depths, Stage Directions, The Woods; appeared in Broadway productions: The Time of Your Life, The Three Sisters, The Robber Bridegroom, The Water Engine, The Beggar's Opera, Next Time I'll Sing to You; Star Broadway play Evita, 1979—. Office: care Evita Company 1270 Ave of the Americas New York NY 10020

LUPTON, CHARLES HAMILTON, JR., educator, pathologist; b. Norfolk, Va., July 17, 1919; s. Charles Hamilton and Susan Elizabeth (Watson) L.; B.A., U. Va., 1942, M.D., 1944; m. Mary Elizabeth Rand, May 26, 1945; children—Charles Hamilton III, William Kenan, Susan Lynne. Rotating intern U.S. Naval Hosp., Portsmouth, Va., 1944-45; surg. intern Duke Hosp., 1946-47; successively resident pathology, instr., then asst. prof. pathology U. Va. Med. Sch., 1947-53; asso. prof. pathology Med. Coll. Ala., 1955-60; acting chmn. dept. pathology U. Ala. Med. Center, 1960-61, prof., chmn. dept., 1961-74, prof. pathology, 1974—. Served with USNR, 1945-46, 53-55. Mem. Coll. Am. Pathologists, AMA, AAAS, Jefferson County Med. Soc., Ala. Assn. Pathologists, Internat. Acad. Pathologists, Nat. Assn. Med. Examiners, Am. Assn. Pathologists, Am. Soc. Clin. Pathologists, Am. Assn. Med. Colls., N.Y. Acad. Scis., U. Va. Med. Alumni Assn. (pres. 1978-79), Am. Acad. Forensic Scis. Home: 3652 Rockhill Rd Birmingham AL 35223

LUPU, RADU, pianist; b. Galati, Romania, Nov. 30, 1945; s. Meir and Ana (Gabor) L.; attended Conservatoire Tchaikovsky, Moscow, USSR, 1962-69; m. Elizabeth Nilson, 1971. London debut, 1969, Berlin, 1971; U.S. debut with Cleve. Orch. in N.Y.C.; appearances with worldwide maj. orchs., including: Berlin Philharmonic, Israel Philharmonic, Orch de Paris, Concertgebonn, N.Y. Philharmonic, Phila., Chgo. Symphony Orch., Cleve.; rec. artist Decca Records. Recipient 1st prize Van Cliburn Internat. Piano Competition, 1966, Enescu Competition, 1967, Leeds Internat. Piano Competition, 1969.

LURIA, SALVADOR EDWARD, biologist; b. Turin, Italy, Aug. 13, 1912; s. David and Ester (Sacerdote) L.; M.D., U. Torino (Italy), 1935; m. Zella Hurwitz, Apr. 18, 1945; 1 son, Daniel. Came to U.S., 1940, naturalized, 1947. Research fellow Curie Lab., Inst. of Radium, Paris, France, 1938-40; research asst. surg. bacteriology Columbia, 1940-42; successively instr., asst. prof., asso. prof. bacteriology Ind. U., 1943-50; prof. bacteriology U. Ill., 1950-59; prof. microbiology Mass. Inst. Tech., 1959-64, Sedgwick prof. biology, 1964—, Inst. prof., 1970—, dir. center cancer research, 1972—; non-resident fellow Salk Inst. Biol. Studies, 1965—; lectr. biophysics U. Colo., 1950; Jesup lectr. zoology Columbia, 1950; Nieuwland lectr. biology U. Notre Dame, 1959; Dyer lectr. NIH, 1963; with OSRD, Carnegie Instn., Washington, 1945-46. Guggenheim fellow Vanderbilt U. and Princeton, 1942-43, Pasteur Inst., Paris, 1963-64. Co-recipient Nobel prize for medicine, 1969. Mem. Am. Philos. Soc., Am. Soc. Microbiology (pres. 1967-68), Nat. Acad. Scis., Am. Acad. Arts and Scis., AAAS, Soc. Gen. Microbiology, Genetics Soc. Am., AAUP, Sigma Xi. Asso. editor Jour. Bacteriology, 1950-55; editor Virology, 1955—; sect. editor Biol. Abstracts, 1958-62; editorial bd. Exptl. Cell Research Jour., 1948—; adv. bd. Jour. Molecular Biology, 1958-64; hon. editorial adv. bd. Jour. Photochemistry and Photobiology, 1961—. Office: Dept Biology Mass Inst Tech Cambridge MA 02139*

LURIA, SYDNEY AARON, lawyer; b. N.Y.C., Feb. 2, 1908; s. Philip and Rebecca (Isaacson) L.; A.B., Coll. City N.Y., 1929; LL.B., Harvard, 1934; m. Lucille Rubinstein, Sept. 1, 1943; children—Paula Luria (Mrs. William F. Caplan), Philip. Admitted to N.Y. bar, 1934; asso. firm Carb, Luria, Glassner, Cook & Kufeld, N.Y.C., 1934-38, partner, 1938—, sr. partner, 1963—. Dir. Cushman & Wakefield, Inc., L. Luria & Son, Inc. Bd. govs., v.p. Real Estate Bd. N.Y., trustee Bettina and Leone J. Peters Found., PEF Israel Endowment Funds, Guidance Center, Max and Rosa Gold Found., Philharmonic Symphony Soc., Westchester, N.Y. Served with USAAF, 1942-46. Mem. Am. Bar Assn., Bar Assn. City N.Y., N.Y. County Lawyers Assn. Home: 150 East End Ave New York NY 10028 Office: 529 Fifth Ave New York NY 10017

LURIE, ALISON, author; b. Chgo., Sept. 3, 1936; A.B., Radcliffe Coll., 1947; children—John, Jeremy, Joshua. Lectr. English, Cornell U., 1969-73, adj. asso. prof., 1973, asso. prof., 1976-79, prof., 1979—; author: V.R. Lang: a Memoir, 1959; Love and Friendship, 1962; Nowhere City, 1965; Imaginary Friends, 1967; Real People, 1969; The War Between the Tates, 1974; Only Children, 1979. Recipient award in lit. Am. Acad. Arts and Letters, 1978. Yaddo Found. fellow, 1963, 64, 66; Guggenheim fellow, 1965; Rockefeller Found. fellow, 1967. Address: Dept English Cornell Univ Ithaca NY 14850

LURIE, ALVIN DAVID, lawyer; b. N.Y.C., Apr. 16, 1923; s. Samuel and Rose L.; A.B., Cornell U., 1943, LL.B., 1944; m. Marian Weinberg, Aug. 21, 1944; children—James, Jean, Margery, Jonathan. Admitted to N.Y. bar, 1944, D.C. bar, 1978; asso. and partner various N.Y.C. law firms, 1944-74, including Lurie & Rubin, 1961-68, Aranow, Brodsky, Bohlinger & Einhorn, 1968-74; asst. commr. for employee plans and exempt orgns. IRS, Washington, 1975-78; partner firm Chadbourne, Parke, Whiteside & Wolff, N.Y.C., 1978—. Mem. Am. Bar Assn., Fed. Bar Assn., N.Y. State Bar Assn., Assn. Bar City N.Y., Am. Law Inst. Contbr. articles to law revs., tax jours. Office: 30 Rockefeller Plaza New York NY 10020. *Though I enjoy spates of tennis, and Broadway plays, and good food, and chamber music, I have no real hobbies, enjoying my work more than any of these. Hard work, in intensive spurts, then broken by doses of the former pleasures, is my formula. But the work must be varied, permitting application of different skills in constantly changing, creative ways. But one thing more is needed: readiness to seize the moment; for only in that way will new opportunities come, with new achievements and recurrent gratification.*

LURIE, HAROLD, educator; b. Durban, South Africa, Mar. 28, 1924; s. Samuel Isaac and Dora (Mitchell) L.; B.Sc., U. Natal (South Africa), 1945, M.Sc., 1946; Ph.D., Calif. Inst. Tech., 1950; m. Patricia Elkin, Mar. 26, 1959 (div. 1978); children—Diana Isabel, David Andrew. Came to U.S., 1946, naturalized, 1952. Lectr. aeros. Calif. Inst. Tech., 1948-50, asst. prof. applied mechanics, 1953-56, asso. prof., 1956-64, prof. engring. sci. 1964-70, asso. dean grad. studies, 1964-70; dir. research and devel. New Eng. Electric System, 1971-79; dean of engring. Poly. Inst. N.Y., Bklyn., 1979—; cons., 1978—; acting dir. Advanced Systems dept. Electric Power Research Inst., 1974-75; cons. Yankee Atomic Electric Co., 1970-71; head weapons effectiveness group RAND Corp., 1950-52; sr. devel. engr. Oak Ridge Nat. Lab., 1956-57. Office: 333 Jay St Brooklyn NY 11201

LURIE, MELVIN, educator, economist; b. Cambridge, Mass., July 3, 1923; s. Samuel and Sadye (Goldberg) L.; student Boston U., 1941-43; B.A., Pa. State U., 1948; M.A., U. Chgo., 1951, Ph.D., 1958; m. Lois Irma Cone, June 5, 1955; children—Jonathan Adam, Robert James, Alexander David, Susannah Beth. Wage analyst U.S. Wage Stblzn. Bd., 1951-53; instr. U. Conn., Storrs, 1954-60; asst. prof. U. R.I., 1960-62, asso. prof., 1963-66; vis. asso. prof. Wesleyan U., Middletown, Conn., 1962-63; prof. U. Wis.-Milw., 1966—, chmn. dept. econs., 1968-72, 77-78, asso. dean Coll. Letters and Sci., 1972-76, spl. asst. to dean, 1976-77. Econ. cons. Served with AUS, 1943-46. Ford Found. Summer faculty fellow Yale, 1958, Harvard, 1964; grantee research U. Calif. at Berkeley 1964, U. Chgo., 1965, U.S. Commn. on Rural Poverty, 1967; mem. U. Chgo. Alumni Cabinet, 1976—. Mem. Asso. Appraisers of Earning Capacity (adv. bd. 1968-70), Am. Econ. Assn., Indsl. Relations Research Assn., Am. Soc. Econometric Appraisers (exec. bd. dirs. 1968-70). Editor: R.I. Bus. Quar., 1963-66. Contbr. articles to profl., other jours. Home: 3032 N Summit Ave Milwaukee WI 53211

LURIE, NANCY OESTREICH, anthropologist; b. Milw., Jan. 29, 1924; d. Carl Ralph and Rayline (Danielson) Oestreich; B.A., U. Wis., 1945; M.A., U. Chgo., 1947; Ph.D., Northwestern U., 1952; LL.D., Northland Coll., 1976; m. Edward Lurie, 1951 (div. 1963). Instr. U. Wis.-Milw., 1947-49, 51-53, asst. prof., 1961-63, prof., 1963-72, chmn. anthropology dept., 1967-70; curator anthropology Milw. Pub. Museum, 1972—; lectr. U. Mich., 1956-61, cons. expert witness for attys. representing tribal clients before U.S. Indian Claims Commn., 1957-64. Recipient (with co-editor) Anisfield-Wolf award for best scholarly book in intergroup relations, The American Indian Today, 1968. Fellow AAAS, Am. Anthrop. Assn. (exec. bd. 1977—); mem. Am. Ethnol. Soc., Soc. Applied Anthropology, Central States Anthrop. Soc. (pres. 1967), Sigma Xi. Editor, translator: Mountain Wolf Woman, The Autobiography of a Winnebago Woman, 1961. Home: 3342 N Gordon Pl Milwaukee WI 53212

LURIE, RANAN RAYMOND, polit. analyst, polit. cartoonist, artist, lectr.; b. Port Said, Egypt, May 26, 1932; s. Joseph and Rose (Same) L. (parents Israeli citizens); student Herzelia Coll., Tel Aviv, Israel, 1949, Jerusalem Art Coll., 1951; m. Tamar Fletcher, Feb. 26, 1958; children—Rod, Barry, Daphne, Danielle. Came to U.S., 1968, naturalized, 1974; corr. Maariv Daily, 1950-52; features editor Hador Daily, 1953-54; staff polit. cartoonist Yedioth Aharonot Daily, 1955-66; 22 one-man shows Israel, Can., U.S., 1960-75, including Expo 67, Can., Dominion Gallery, Montreal, Que., Can., Lim Galley, Tel Aviv, 1965, Overseas Press Club, N.Y.C., 1962, 64, 75, U.S. Senate, Washington; exhibited numerous group shows including Smithsonian Instn., 1972; polit. cartoonist Life Mag., N.Y.C., 1968-73; contbr. N.Y. Times, 1970-72; contbg. editor, polit. cartoonist Newsweek Internat., 1974-76; editor, polit. cartoonist Vision Mag. of South Am., 1974-76; syndicated United Features Syndicate, 1971-73; syndicated nationally by Los Angeles Times, also internationally by N.Y. Times to over 260 newspapers, 1973-75; syndicated nationally by King Features Syndicate, internationally by Editors Press Syndicate (345 newspapers), 1975—; lectr. polit. cartooning U. Hawaii; univ. lectr. in fine arts, polit. cartoon and polit. analysis Am. Program Bur., Boston. Served as maj. inf. Israeli Army Res., 1948-67. Recipient highest Israeli journalism award, 1954; U.S. Headliners award, 1972; named Outstanding Editorial Cartoonist of Nat. Cartoonist Soc., 1971, 72, 73, 74, 75, 76, 77, 78; Salon award Montreal Cartoon, 1971; N.Y. Front Page award, 1972, 74, 77; certificate of merit U.S. Publ. Designers, 1974. Mem. Nat. Cartoonist Soc. Am., Assn. Editorial Cartoonists, Sigma Delta Chi. Clubs: Overseas Press; Friars. Author: Among the Suns, Lurie's Best Cartoons, Nixon Rated Cartoons, Pardon Me, Mr. President, 1973, rev. edit., 1974. Creator The Expandable Painting, 1969. Cartoons used as guidelines in several encys., polit. sci. books. Home: Baldwin Farms North Greenwich CT 06830. *The moment of truth will come when the cartoonist gauges the margin of time from the day he drew the cartoon. Then he can see how clearly or unclearly he has evaluated the situation through his work. Eventually, the simple facts and reality always win. Then it becomes apparent that wishful thinking is meaningless and the capacity to evaluate the project and even predict the events that are happening will eventually cement the professional status and integrity of the cartoonist.*

LURIE, WILLIAM L., paper co. exec.; b. Latrobe, Pa., Feb. 8, 1931; s. Samuel C. and Josephine M. (Adams) L.; B.S., Northwestern U., 1952, M.B.A. with distinction, 1954, J.D., 1955; m. Rita F. Mandel, Aug. 31, 1952; children—Ellen, Lynn, Jay. Admitted to Mich. bar, 1955, Ill. bar, 1955, N.Y. bar, 1956; with Gen. Electric Co., various locations, 1955-69, v.p., gen. mgr. internat. support div., 1969-72, v.p. internat. strategic planning, 1972-74; v.p., gen. counsel Internat. Paper Co., N.Y.C., 1974-76, v.p. external affairs, 1976, exec. v.p. diversified bus., gen. counsel, 1976—; lectr. in field. Mem. computer sci. and engring. bd. Nat. Acad. Sci., 1968-70; mem. industry adv. council Overseas Pvt. Investment Corp., 1971-73. Mem. Fgn. Policy Assn. (dir.), Brit.-Am. C. of C. (dir.), Order of Coif, Beta Gamma Sigma. Office: 220 E 42d St New York City NY 10017

LURTON, H. WILLIAM, corp. exec.; b. Greenwich, Conn., Sept. 18, 1929; s. William Pearl and Elizabeth (McDow) L.; B.A., Principia Coll., 1951; m. Cynthia Oakes, Apr. 9, 1955; children—Scott, Carrie, Nancy, Jennifer. Vice pres., gen. mgr. Jostens/Am. Yearbook Co., 1969-70; exec. v.p., chief operating officer, dir. Jostens, Inc., Mpls., 1970-71, pres., 1971—, chief exec. officer, 1972—, chmn. bd., 1975—; dir. Munsingwear, Deluxe Check Printers, First Trust Co., St. Paul. Bd. dirs. Mpls. YMCA. Served with USMC, 1951-53. Christian Scientist. Clubs: Wayzata (Minn.) Country; Minneapolis. Home: 3300 Fox St Long Lake MN 55356 Office: 5501 Norman Center Dr Minneapolis MN 55437

LUSH, GERSON HARRISON, cons.; b. Phila., May 2, 1912; s. Max and Anna Leah (Harrison) L.; student George Washington U., U. Md.; m. Claire Werchow, Nov. 25, 1937; children—Lee M., Anne, Susan. Reporter, newswriter Phila. Inquirer, 1933-40, chief Harrisburg (Pa.) bur., 1940-50; corr., contbr. N.Y. Times, Life and Time mags., Pitts. Press, Erie (Pa.) Times, 1940-50; adminstrv. asst. to U.S. Senator Duff, 1951-57; Washington dir. Office U.S. Commr. Gen., Brussels World's Fair, 1957-59; U.S. fgn. service res. officer, 1959-77; spl. asst. to dep. asst. sec. state for budget and finance, 1959-60; spl. asst. to asst. sec. state for adminstrn., 1960-65; dir. policy and pub. info. affairs program Office Dep. Under Sec. State for Adminstrn., Dept. State, 1965-72; dir. newsletter and info. Office Dir. Gen., U.S. Fgn. Service, 1972-77; govt. cons., 1977-78; pub. affairs cons., adviser state and nat. polit. campaigns, 1952, 54, 56; pres. Pa. Legis. Corrs. Assn., 1949-50. Mem. Nat. Assn. Govt. Communicators, U.S. Senate Assn. Adminstrv. Assts. and Secs. Club: Nat. Press (Washington). Editor: Dept State Newsletter, 1961-77. Contbr. to Ency. Brit. Yearbook, 1959. Home: 3305 Runnymede Pl NW Washington DC 20015

LUSH, JAY LAURENCE, research worker; b. Shambaugh., Iowa, Jan. 3, 1896; s. Henry and Mary Eliza (Pritchard) L.; B.S., Kans. State Agrl. Coll., Manhattan, Kans., 1916, M.S., 1918; Ph.D., U. Wis., 1921; Dr. Agr., Agrl. Coll. Sweden, U. Giessen, 1957, Royal Danish Vet. and Agrl. Coll., 1958; LL.D., Mich. State U., 1964; D.Sc., U. Ill., 1969, Kans. State U., 1970, U. Wis., 1970, Swiss Fed. Inst. Tech., 1971, Agrl. U. Norway, 1975; m. Adaline Lincoln, Dec. 20, 1923; children—Mary Elizabeth, David Alan. Research in animal genetics Tex. Agrl. Exptl. Sta., 1921-29, prof. animal breeding Iowa State Coll., 1930—; temp. duty U.S. Dept. State in Gt. Britain and with Council for Sci. and Indsl. Research in Australia, 1948. Guest lectr. Advanced Sch. Agr. and Vet. Medicine, Vicosa, Brazil, 1941, FAO Center, New Delhi, India, 1954; lectr. INTA, Argentina, 1966-67. NRC fellow in Denmark, 1934. Commd. 2d lt. AS U.S. Army, 1919. Recipient First Morrison award Am. Soc. Animal Prodn. 1946, Borden award for research dairy prodn., 1958, von Nathusius medal, 1960, U.S. Nat. Medal Sci., 1968, prize for agr. Wolf Found., 1979. Fellow Royal Soc. Edinburgh (hon.); mem. Am. Soc. Naturalists, Genetics Soc. Am., Am. Soc. Animal Sci., Nat. Acad. Sci., Sigma Xi. Presbyterian. Mason. Author: Animal Breeding Plans, 1945. Home: 3226 Oakland St Ames IA 50010

LUSK, WILLIAM EDWARD, real estate, oil co. exec.; b. Medicine Lodge, Kans., May 16, 1916; s. William Edward and Teresa (Rhoades) L.; B.S. in Edn., A.B. in Econs., Ft. Hays State Coll., 1939; student Washburn U., 1936; postgrad. Kans. U., 1940-41; m. Anita Ballard, Feb. 1, 1942; children—William Edward, Janet Kathryn and James Raymond (twins). Tchr., Protection (Kans.) High Sch., 1939-41; mgr. real estate dept. Wheeler, Kelly & Hagny Investment Co., Wichita, Kans., 1946-63; co-founder, exec. v.p., treas., dir. Clinton Oil Co., Wichita, 1963-73; pres. Lusk Real Estate Co., 1963—, Lusk Investment Co., 1973—. Pres., Wichita Real Estate Bd., 1961. Founder, Lusk Found., 1968, William E. Lusk Scholarship, Ft. Hays State Coll., 1969; bd. dirs. Jr. Achievement Wichita. Served with USNR, 1942-46; comdr. Res. Named Kans. Realtor of Year, Kans. Assn. Real Estate Bds., 1962; recipient Alumni Achievement award Ft. Hays Kan. State Coll., 1971. Mem. VFW, Sojourners, Res. Officers Assn., Naval Res. Officers Assn., Navy League, Phi Alpha Delta, Alpha Kappa Psi (hon.). Methodist (bd. dirs. 1965-70, fin. chmn. 1969—). Mason (32 deg.). Clubs: Wichita Country, Wichita (dir. 1969-72, pres. 1972), McConnell AFB Officers. Home: 6 W Parkway N Wichita KS 67206 Office: 207 S Broadway Wichita KS 67202. *In business and personal relationships I have found strength in times of adversity and self-control in times of success by forming the habit of calling to mind this guideline: Things are never as good as they seem to be on the day they look good-nor are things as bad as they seem to be on the day they appear bad.*

LUSKIN, BERT L., lawyer, arbitrator; b. Syracuse, N.Y., Sept. 28, 1911; s. Hyman and Kate (Goren) L.; J.D., DePaul U., 1932; m. Ruth Katz, Dec. 25, 1938; children—Allan T., Robert D. Admitted to Ill. bar, 1933, since practiced in Chgo.; arbitrator, 1943—. Guest lectr. arbitration and labor law numerous univs.; mem. arbitration panel Fed. Mediation and Conciliation Service, Am. Arbitration Assn.; permanent arbitrator under collective bargaining agreement numerous cos., unions. Pub. panel mem. 6th regional WLB, 1943-45. Bd. dirs., past pres. Found. Emotionally Disturbed Children; past v.p. Midwest adv. bd. Am. Med. Center. Mem. Nat. Acad. Arbitrators (past pres.), Decalogue Soc. Lawyers, Indsl. Relations Research Assn., Am., Ill., Chgo. bar assns. Club: City (Chgo.). Home: 76 Indian Tree Dr Highland Park IL 60035 Office: 134 N LaSalle St Chicago IL 60602

LUSKY, LOUIS, legal educator; b. Columbus, Ohio, May 15, 1915; s. Leonard Morris and Amy (Kleeman) L.; B.A., U. Louisville, 1935; LL.B., Columbia, 1937; m. Ruth Agnes Anderson, Aug. 31, 1946; children—Mary Hibbard, John Anderson; 1 son by previous marriage, Peter Joris. Admitted to N.Y. bar, 1938, Ky. bar, 1947; law clk. to Supreme Ct. Justice Harlan F. Stone, 1937-38; asso. firm Root, Clark, Buckner & Ballantine, N.Y.C., 1938-42, 44-45; civilian mem. ops. analysis sect. 8th Air Force, 1943-44; with legal div. U.S. Mil. Govt. Germany, 1945-46; partner firm Wyatt & Grafton, Louisville, 1947-51; pvt. practice, Louisville, 1952-63; prof. law Columbia Law Sch., 1963—, Betts prof. law, 1979—. Mem. ACLU (nat. com. 1963-67, nat. bd. 1967-70), Am. Law Inst., Am. Bar Assn., Bar Assn. City N.Y. Author: (with others) Southern Justice, 1965; By What Right?, 1975. Home: 623 Eastbrook Rd Ridgewood NJ 07450 Office: 435 W 116th St New York NY 10027

LUSS, DAN, chem. engr., educator; b. Tel Aviv, Israel, May 5, 1938; s. Manfred and Gertrude (Weinstein) L.; B.S., Technion Inst. Tech., Haifa, Israel, 1960, M.Sc., 1963; Ph.D., U. Minn., 1966; m. Amalia Rubin, Sept. 4, 1966; children—Michal, Noya, Limor. Came to U.S., 1963, naturalized, 1973. Asst. prof. chem. engring., U. Minn., Mpls., 1966-67; asst. prof. chem. engring. U. Houston, 1967-69, asso. prof., 1969-72, prof., 1972—, chmn. dept., 1975—; cons. to several chem. cos. Registered profl. engr., Tex. Mem. Am. Inst. Chem. Engrs. (Allan P. Colburn award 1973, Profl. Progress award 1979, mem. editorial bd. jour.), Am. Chem. Soc. (Honor scroll award of indsl. engring. chemistry div. 1967), Am. Soc. Engring. Edn. (Curtis McGraw award 1977). Mem. editorial bd. Catalysis Revs.; Sci. and Engring. Home: 6242 Paisley St Houston TX 77096

LUSSIER, CHARLES A., found. exec.; b. Montreal, Que., Can., Aug. 18, 1920; LL.L., U. Montreal, 1945; m. Monique Lortie, Sept. 14, 1953; children—Sylvain, Hubert, Caroline, Sophie. Dir., La Maison des Etudiants Canadiens at Cité de Paris, 1957-61; del. gen. Del. Generale du Quebec, Paris, 1961-65; asst. dep. minister Dept. Citizenship and Immigration, Ottawa, 1965-67, spl. adviser Dept. Energy, Mines and Resources, 1967-68; asst. under sec. State, 1968-70; mem. Pub. Service Commn. Can., 1970-76; dir. The Can. Council, Ottawa, 1976—; prof. U. Ottawa, 1974-76. Mem. Inst. Pub. Adminstrn. Can., Canadian Council Christians and Jews (dir.), Institut France-Canada (dir.), Centre de récherches en relations humaines U. Montreal (dir.), Alliance Française d'Ottawa (past v.p.). Roman Catholic. Home: 211 River Rd Ottawa ON K1L 8B5 Canada Office: 255 Albert St Ottawa ON K1P 5V8 Canada

LUSSIER, JEAN-PAUL, educator; b. Montreal, Que., Can., Sept. 17, 1917; s. Eugene and Parmelia (Gauthier) L.; B.A., U. Montreal, 1938, D.D.S., 1942, M.S., 1952; Ph.D., U. Calif. at San Francisco, 1959; D.S.C. (hon.), McGill U., 1972; m. Juliette Laurin, May 4, 1943; children—Louis, Renee (Mrs. Stanley Brecknock), Josee, Anne (Mrs. Gilles Morin), Pierre, Helene (Mrs. A. Black), Andre. Mem. U. Montreal faculty medicine, dept. physiology, 1946-52, 54-57, mem. faculty dentistry, 1957-62, 79—, dean, 1962-79, chmn. health scis. coordinating com., 1979—; research fellow U. Calif. at San Francisco, 1952-54; cons. WHO, 1972—. Recipient award Am. Acad. Dental Medicine, 1958, award Alpha Omega, 1962. Fellow Am. Coll. Dentists, Internat. Coll. Dentists, Royal Coll. Dentists; mem. Fedn. Dentaire Internationale, Que. Health Research Council. Home: 3507 Vendome St Montreal PQ H4A 3M6 Canada

LUSTED, LEE BROWNING, radiologist; b. Mason City, Iowa, May 22, 1922; s. George Charles and Maude (Browning) L.; B.A., Cornell Coll., 1943, D.Sc., 1963; M.D., Harvard U., 1950; m. Winifred Chamberlin, Aug. 24, 1943; children—Lee Browning II, Hugh S. Intern, Mass. Meml. Hosp., Boston, 1950-51; resident in radiology U. Calif., San Francisco, 1951-54, asst. prof., 1954-56; asst. radiologist NIH, Bethesda, Md., 1956-58; asso. prof. radiology U. Rochester (N.Y.), 1958-62, prof. biomed. engring., 1960-62; prof. radiology U. Oreg., Portland, 1962-68; prof., chmn. dept. radiology Stritch Sch. Medicine, Loyola U., Maywood, Ill., 1968-69; prof., vice chmn. dept. radiology U. Chgo., 1969-78; clin. prof. U. Calif., San Diego, 1978—; clin. mem. Scripps Clinic & Research Found., La Jolla, Calif., 1978—. Trustee Cornell Coll. Fellow Am. Coll. Radiology (chmn. efficacy studies 1971—), Soc. Med. Decision Making (sec.-treas. 1979—), N.Y. Acad. Sci., AAAS, IEEE, Radiol. Soc. Am. (Meml. Fund lectr.). Author: Prime, 1967; Introduction to Medical Decision Making, 1968; Atlas of Roentgenographic Measurement, 4th edit., 1978; editor Med. Decision Making, 1979—. Contbr. articles to sci. jours. Home and Office: PO Box 2209 Rancho Santa Fe CA 92067

LUSTER, GEORGE ORCHARD, ednl. adminstr. b. Pitts., Mar. 20, 1921; s. James W. and Gertrude (Orchard) L.; B.S. with honors, U. Pitts., 1949; C.P.A., Pa., 1951; m. Edith A. Townsend, May 3, 1946; children—Thomas, Carolea, Patricia. Accountant, Am. Inst. Research, Pitts., 1948-49; mgr. Price Waterhouse & Co., C.P.A.'s, Pitts., 1949-59; treas., asst. sec. Mellon Inst., Pitts., 1959-67; treas. Carnegie-Mellon U., 1967—; asst. sec., asst. treas., supervising com. Bellefield Boiler Plant, Pitts., 1962-71; treas., asst. sec. MPC Corp., Pitts., 1963—. Instr., Robert Morris Sch., 1955-59, U. Pitts., 1959. Bd. dirs. Central Blood Bank, Pitts., 1973—. Served with USAAF, 1943-46. Mem. Fin. Execs. Inst., Am., Pa. insts. C.P.A.'s, Air Pollution Control Assn. (treas. 1966—), Wesley Inst., Alpha Kappa Psi, Beta Gamma Sigma. Republican. Methodist. Club: Valley Brook Country. Home: 2319 Caswell Dr Bethel Park PA 15102 Office: 5000 Forbes Ave Pittsburgh PA 15213

LUSTIG, HARRY, coll. dean, physicist; b. Vienna, Austria, Sept. 23, 1925; s. Hans and Hedwig (Faltitschek) L.; came to U.S., 1939, naturalized, 1944; B.S., Coll. City N.Y., 1948; M.S. (fellow), U. Ill., 1949, Ph.D., 1953; m. Judith Louise Hirshfield, Sept. 20, 1953 (dec. July 1975); children—Lawrence John, Nicholas Daniel. Teaching asst. U. Ill., 1949-51, research asst., 1951-53; mem. faculty Coll. City N.Y., 1953—, prof. physics, 1967—, chmn. dept., 1965-70, exec. officer physics doctoral program, 1968-71, asso. dean for sci., 1972-75, dean Coll. Liberal Arts and Sci., 1973-74, dean of sci., 1975—. Prin. scientist Nuclear Devel. Corp. Am., 1955-60; vis. research asst. prof. U. Ill., 1959-60; Fulbright prof. Univ. Coll., Dublin, Ireland, 1964-65; vis. scholar Stanford, summer 1963; vis. prof. U. Colo., summer 1966, U. Wash., summer 1967, 69. Sec., Univs. Com. on Problems of War and Peace of Greater N.Y., 1962-64, chmn., 1965-67; sr. officer UNESCO, 1970-72, cons., 1972-75, 79; cons. U.S. Internat. Communications Agy, 1975. Served with AUS, 1944-46. Fellow N.Y. Acad. Scis.; mem. Am. Phys. Soc., Am. Assn. Physics Tchrs., Phi Beta Kappa, Sigma Xi (chmn. Coll. City N.Y. 1963-64). Contbr. articles to profl. jours. Home: 501 E 79th St New York NY 10021

LUSTIG, ROBERT T., profl. football team exec. Mem. mgmt. staff Buffalo Bills, formerly recruiter, now gen. mgr., v.p., dir. Address: care Buffalo Bills One Bills Dr Orchard Park NY 14127*

LUSZTIG, PETER ALFRED, univ. adminstr., educator; b. Budapest, Hungary, May 12, 1930; s. Alfred Peter and Susan (Szabo) L.; B.Com., U. B.C. (Can.), Vancouver, 1954; M.B.A., U. Western Ont. (Can.), London, 1955; Ph.D. (Ford Found. faculty dissertation fellow), Stanford U., 1964; m. Penny Bicknell, Aug. 26, 1961; children—Michael, Cameron, Carrie. Asst. to comptroller B.C. Electric, Vancouver, 1955-57; instr. fin. U. B.C., 1957-60, asst. prof. fin., 1962-64, asso. prof., 1964-68, prof., 1968—, dean Faculty Commerce, 1977—, Killam sr. research fellow, 1968-69, mem. univ. senate, 1976—; vis. prof. IMEDE, Switzerland, 1973-74; vis. prof. London Grad. Sch. Bus. Studies, 1968-69; bd. govs. Inst. Can. Bankers, 1978—. Mem. Am. Fin. Assn., Council Deans, Fin. Mgmt. Assn. Lutheran. Clubs: Univ. of Vancouver, Arbutus. Author: Report of the Royal Commission on Automobile Insurance, 2 vols., 1968; Financial Management in a Canadian Setting, 2d rev. edit., 1978. Office: Faculty Commerce and Bus Adminstrn U BC Vancouver BC V6T 1W5 Canada

LUTER, JOHN, newsman, educator; b. Knoxville, Tenn., Jan. 17, 1919; s. John Thomas and Bertha Mae (Carver) L.; B.A., St. Mary's U., Tex., 1939, postgrad. Coll. Law, 1939-42; fellow Time Inc., Sch. Advanced Internat. Studies, Washington, 1945; m. Mary Hickey, 1948 (dec.); 1 dau., Linda; m. 2d, Yvonne Spiegelberg, 1966 (div. 1971); m. 3d, Nan Hoyt Lawrence, 1974. Reporter, San Antonio Light, 1939-42, Washington Star, 1942-44; corr. Washington bur. Time mag., 1944-45, war corr. in Pacific, 1945; fgn. corr. Time and Life mags., Southeast Asia, 1945-46, Japan, 1946-47, Israel, 1948-49, Italy, 1949-54; asst. editor internat. edit. Life mag., 1954-56; reporter, writer CBS News, 1957-58; asso. editor Newsweek mag., 1958-61; radio news commentator stas. WQXR and QXR-FM Network, 1960-61; coordinator advanced internat. reporting program Columbia Grad. Sch. Journalism, 1961-72, dir. Maria Moors Cabot Prize Program, 1961-74; mem. profl. staff Bank St. Coll. Edn., 1973-74; prof., dir. journalism U. Hawaii, Honolulu, 1974—. Chmn. internat. relations com. N.Y.C. Protestant Council, 1968-71; chmn. adv. screening com. communications Sr. Fulbright Program, 1970-73; trustee Overseas Press Club Found., 1962-72, chmn., 1964-65; bd. dirs. UN Assn. N.Y., 1973-74; vice chmn. Honolulu Community Media Council, 1978-80. Mem. Assn. Edn. Journalism, Am. Soc. Journalism Sch. Adminstrs., World Affairs Forum Hawaii, Japan-Am. Soc. Hawaii, Sigma Delta Chi (mem. chpt. exec. council 1966-69). Clubs: Overseas Press (pres. N.Y.C. 1960-62); Honolulu Press, Outrigger Canoe. Adv. editor Columbia Journalism Rev., 1961-72. Home: 2442 Halekoa Dr Honolulu HI 96821 Office: 208 Crawford Hall U Hawaii 2550 Campus Rd Honolulu HI 96822

LUTES, DONALD HENRY, architect; b. San Diego, Mar. 7, 1926; s. Charles McKinley and Helen (Bjoraker) L.; B.Arch., U. Oreg., 1950; m. Donnie Wageman, Aug. 14, 1949; children—Laura Jo, Gail Eileen, Dana Charles. Pvt. archtl. practice, Springfield, Oreg., 1956-58; partner with John Amundson, Springfield, 1958-70; pres. Lutes & Amundson, Springfield, 1970-72; partner Lutes, Masarie & Sanetel, 1973—. Cons. prof. architecture U. Oreg., 1964-66. Chmn., Springfield Planning Commn., 1956-64, Urban Design and Devel. Corp. 1968-70, Eugene Non-Profit Housing, Inc., 1970. Chmn., Springfield United Appeal, 1959. Served to 1st lt. AUS, 1943-46, 51-52. Decorated Bronze Star. Named Jr. 1st citizen Springfield C. of C., 1957, 1st citizen, 1968. Fellow AIA (chmn. urban design com. 1966, chmn. nominating com. 1968); mem. Theta Chi. Rotarian. Architect: Springfield Pub. Library, 1957, Mt. Hood Community Coll., 1965—, Shoppers Paradise Expt. in Downtown Revitalization, 1957. Home: 778 Crest Ln Springfield OR 97477 Office: 417 N A St Springfield OR 97477

LUTEY, JOHN KENT, ret. govt. ofcl.; b. Butte, Mont., Sept. 19, 1902; s. William John and Martha Louise (Williams) L.; grad. Mt. Hermon Sch., 1920; student Wharton Sch. of U. Pa., 1920-24; m. Agnes Theresa Sakal, Sept. 28, 1949; children—Iona Teresa, Vanessa Louise. With Henningsen Produce Co., Fed. Inc., U.S.A., Shanghai, China, 1925-40; founder, pres., dir. Kibon S.A., Sao Paulo and Rio de Janeiro, Brazil, 1940-62; dir. div. industry AID, Brazil, 1964-66; spl. ambassador of Iceland for inauguration Pres. Kubitschek of Brazil, 1956. Bd. dirs. Inst. Brazil-U.S., 1956-58. Pres. Strangers Hosp., Rio de Janeiro, 1950-51. Hon. consul of Iceland in Brazil, 1949-56, hon. consul gen., 1956-62; decorated knight comdr. Order Falcon, 1953, grand knight, 1956 (Iceland). Mem. Am. C. of C. for Brazil (pres. 1951, permanent dir. 1952—), Am. Soc. Rio de Janeiro (pres. 1948). Methodist. Clubs: Univ. Pennsylvania (N.Y.C.); Scarsdale (N.Y.)

Golf; Little (Delray Beach, Fla.). Home: Seagate Manor 400 Seasage Dr Delray Beach FL 33444

LUTHER, CLARK EDWARD, airline co. exec.; b. Hooper, Nebr., Dec. 8, 1924; s. Ernest M. and Marguerite (Cullamore) L.; B.S., U. Md., 1947, M.B.A., 1954; A.M.P., Harvard U., 1963; m. Barbara L. Price, May 30, 1947; children—Scott, Donna, Susan. Trainee, Gen. Electric Co., Schenectady, N.Y., 1947-48; statistician Western Md. R.R., Balt., 1948; with Capital Airlines Co., Washington, 1948-61, capt., 1952-61, dir. flight ops., 1960-61; flight capt., mgr. flying United Air Lines, Denver and Chgo., 1961-66, regional mgr. flight ops., 1966-71, v.p. system personnel, Chgo., 1971-75, sr. v.p. personnel and indsl. relations, 1975, sr. v.p. flight ops., 1976—. Mem. exec. bd. N.W. Suburban council Boy Scouts Am., 1972—. Served with USAAF, 1942-45. Decorated D.F.C., Air medal with 4 oak leaf clusters. Mem. Air Transport Assn. (ops. com.), Internat. Air Transport Assn. (tech. com.), Phi Kappa Phi, Alpha Tau Omega, Beta Gamma Sigma. Clubs: Masons, Shriners. Home: 715 W Maple St Arlington Heights IL 60005 Office: PO Box 66100 Chicago IL 60666

LUTHER, HERBERT ADESLA, educator; b. Eldred, Pa., Jan. 3, 1910; A.B., U. Pitts., 1934; M.S., U. Iowa, 1935, Ph.D. in Math., 1937; married; 3 children. Mathematician, Westinghouse Research Labs., Pa., 1945-46; from instr to asso. prof. math. Tex. A&M U., 1937-47, prof., 1947-76, prof. emeritus, 1976—, also head dept. NASA research grantee, 1965-66. Mem. Am. Math. Assn., Am. Math. Soc. Office: Dept Math Tex A&M U College Station TX 77843

LUTHER, JAMES HOWARD, pharm. co. exec.; b. West New York, N.J., Jan. 27, 1928; s. James Howard and Margaret Mary (Leyden) L.; A.B. magna cum laude, Fordham U., 1948, J.D. cum laude, 1951; m. Frances Audrey Lynch, July 14, 1951; children—David Gerard, Stephanie Lynch. Admitted to N.Y. bar, 1951; asso. firm Donovan, Leisure, Newton & Irvine, N.Y.C., 1951-55; with Sterling Drug Inc., N.Y.C., 1955—, v.p., 1968-78, gen. counsel, 1976—, sr. v.p., 1978—, also dir. Mem. Am. Bar Assn., Proprietary Assn. (v.p., dir. 1972—). Roman Catholic. Home: 1175 York Ave New York NY 10021 Office: 90 Park Ave New York NY 10016

LUTKEN, DONALD C., utility co. exec; b. Jackson, Miss., Mar. 26, 1924; s. Peter Koch and Erma (Curry) L.; student Miss. State U.; B.S., U.S. Naval Acad., 1946; m. Melissa Turner, June 11, 1946; children—Melissa (Mrs. Hugo Newcomb, Jr.), Isabel Poteat (Mrs. W.L. Eggart), Donald C., Lucie T. (Mrs. David Morgan). Edwin Poteat. With Miss. Power & Light Co., 1949—, exec. v.p. operations, 1969-70, pres., 1970—, chief exec. officer, 1971—; dir. Middle South Utilities, Inc., Miss. Power & Light Co., Unifirst Fed. Savs. & Loan Assn., Southeastern Electric Exchange, Southwest Power Pool. Miss. chmn. payroll U.S. Savs. Bond div. Treasury Dept. Mem. exec. bd. Andrew Jackson council Boy Scouts Am., v.p. S.E. region Area IV. Trustee Belhaven Coll., So. Research Inst., Miss. Found. Ind. Colls.; bd. dirs. Miss. Art Assn., Central Miss. Growth Found., YMCA. Served with USNR, 1946-49. Mem. Jackson C. of C., Jackson Symphony League, Newcomen Soc., Miss. State U. Alumni Found., Nat. Assn. Electric Cos., Miss. Soc. Profl. Engrs., ASME, IEEE, Edison Electric Inst., Miss. Mfrs. Assn., Miss. Econ. Assn., Miss. Hist. Soc. Presbyn. (past deacon). Rotarian. Clubs: Jackson Country, University, Capital City Petroleum (Jackson). Home: Route 2 Box 250 Sub Rosa Jackson MS 39209 Office: PO Box 1640 Jackson MS 39209

LUTNICKI, VICTOR A., ins. co. exec.; b. Chgo., Dec. 20, 1914; s. Anthony E. and Anna (Angel) L.; B.A., Northwestern U., 1936, J.D., 1939; grad. Advanced Mgmt. Program, Harvard U., 1953; m. Harriet Howe, Feb. 4, 1940; children—Anne, Robert, William. Admitted to Ill. bar, 1939, Mass. bar, 1946; asst. counsel Am. Life Conv., 1938- 42, 46; asso. counsel John Hancock Mut. Life Ins. Co., Boston, 1946-52, 2d v.p., 1952-56, counsel, 2d v.p., 1954-56, v.p., gen. solicitor, 1956-57, v.p. in charge group ins. ops., mem. exec. com., 1957-61, sr. v.p., 1961-67, exec. v.p., 1967—, dir., 1966—; chmn. bd. John Hancock Internat. Services, S.A.; dir. mem. exec. and fin. com. Maritime Life (Caribbean) Ltd.; dir. Arthur D. Little Mgmt. Edn. Inst., Inc., Maritime Life Ins. Co., Halifax, N.S., Can., Flagstaff Corp. Participant Aspen (Colo.) Inst. Humanistic Studies, 1960, moderator, 1961; corporator Mus. of Sci., Boston; bd. dirs. Am. Mgmt. Assn.; pres. bd. DeCordova and Dana Mus.; alumni regent Northwestern U.; chmn. bd. trustees Andover Newton Theol. Sch. Served to lt. comdr., aviation, USNR, 1942-46. Decorated Air medal. Mem. Am. Bar Assn. (ho. dels.), Assn. Life Ins. Counsel, Phi Beta Kappa. Mem. United Ch. Christ (moderator). Clubs: Univ. (N.Y.C.); Algonquin, Appalachian Mountain. Contbr. articles to profl. publs. Home: Bedford Rd Lincoln MA 01773 Office: 200 Berkeley St Boston MA 02116

LUTON, JOHNSTON EDWARD, ret. govt. ofcl.; b. Corinth, Miss., Sept. 9, 1910; s. Johnston E. and Olga (Schoolar) L.; A.B., Union U., Jackson, Tenn., 1932; postgrad. Am. U., 1948-50, Am. Mgmt. Assn., N.Y.C., 1957; m. Mary J. Harper, Aug. 31, 1935. Bus. mgr. soil conservation service U.S. Dept. Agr., Tenn., Ky. and Ind., 1935-43, asst. chief div. fiscal mgmt. Office Budget and Fin., Washington, 1946-50; chief mgmt. improvement br. GSA, Washington, 1950-53; asst. gen. sec. adminstrn. Nat. Council Chs. Christ, N.Y.C., 1953-57; asst. dir. adminstrn. NSF, Washington, 1957-61; mgmt. cons., 1961-62; dir. orgn. and mgmt. policy staff GSA, 1962-67, dir. mgmt. systems staff, 1967-72, dir. Office Mgmt. Services, 1972-74. Mem. Sigma Alpha Epsilon. Methodist. Club: Belle Haven Country. Home: 1907 Belfield Rd Alexandria VA 22307. *For a while integrity seemed to be in danger of becoming extinct in our society. But I sense it is returning among the new generation. We should help these young people nourish it until it becomes one of the outstanding characteristics of our great country.*

LUTTINGER, JOAQUIN MAZDAK, physicist, educator; b. N.Y.C., Dec. 2, 1923; s. Paul and Shirley (Levy) L.; S.B., Mass. Inst. Tech., 1944, Ph.D., 1947; m. Abigail Thomas, Sept. 17, 1970; 1 dau., Catherine; stepchildren—Sarah, Jennifer, Ralph. Swiss-Am. exchange fellow Swiss Fed. Inst. Tech., Zurich, 1947-48, Nat. Research fellow, 1948-49; Jewitt fellow Inst. for Advanced Study, Princeton, N.J., 1949-50; asst. prof. physics U. Wis., 1950-51, asso. prof., 1951-53; asso. prof. U. Mich., Ann Arbor, 1953-57; prof. U. Pa., Phila., 1958-60; prof. Columbia U., N.Y.C., 1960—, chmn. dept. physics, 1977—; cons. in field. Served with Signal Corps, U.S. Army, 1944-46. NRC fellow Ecole Normale Superieure, Paris, 1957-58, Rockefeller U., 1967-68; Guggenheim fellow, Rockefeller U., 1975-76. Fellow Am. Phys. Soc.; mem. Nat. Acad. Scis. Contbr. numerous articles to profl. jours. Home: 29 Claremont Ave New York NY 10027 Office: Dept Physics Columbia U New York City NY 10027

LUTWAK, LEO, physician, educator; b. N.Y.C., Mar. 27, 1928; s. Herman and Charlotte (Safirstein) L.; B.S., Coll. City N.Y., 1945; M.S., U. Wis., 1946; Ph.D., U. Mich., 1950; M.D., Yale U., 1956; m. Cecile Kroshinsky, Dec. 23, 1950 (dec. 1976); children—Mark Steven, Diane Ellen, Paul Jonathan, Jean Rachel, Robert Ira; m. 2d, Victoria Jones, 1976; 1 son, David Morris. Biochemist, Brookhaven Nat. Lab., 1950-52, dept. surgery Yale, 1952-56; intern medicine Duke Hosp., 1956-57; clin. asso. NIH, 1957-59, sr. investigator, 1960-63; resident medicine USPHS Hosp., San Francisco, 1959-60; asst. clin. prof. medicine Georgetown U., 1961-63; Jamison prof. clin. nutrition, prof. univ. health services, also dir. clin. nutrition unit Cornell U., 1963-72; prof. medicine U. Calif. at Los Angeles Med. Sch., also prof. nutrition Sch. Pub. Health, 1972-76; chief sect. endocrinology, nutrition and metabolism VA Hosp., Sepulveda, Calif., 1972-76; chmn. dept. medicine Akron (Ohio) City Hosp., 1976-78; prof. medicine, prof. and program dir. nutritional scis. NE Ohio Univs. Coll. Medicine, 1976—; adj. prof. Akron U., 1977—; NRC sr. research fellow Ames Research Lab., NASA, Calif., 1970-71; vis. prof. medicine Stanford Med. Sch., 1970-71; spl. research endocrinology, bone physiology, obesity; cons. adv. panel NIH, 1964-68, Gerontol. Soc., 1964; cons. NASA, 1964—, Tompkins County Hosp., 1963-72. Pres., Ithaca Assn. Jewish Studies, 1964. Fellow Am. Inst. Chemists, Am. Coll. Nutrition, A.C.P.; mem. Soc. Exptl. Biology and Medicine, AAAS, Am. Fedn. Clin. Research, Am. Bd. Nutrition (dir.), Am. Inst. Nutrition, Am. Physiol. Soc., Am., Akron (dir. 1976—) diabetes assns., Am. Soc. Clin. Nutrition, Western Soc. Clin. Research, Endocrine Soc., N.Y. Acad. Scis., Phi Beta Kappa, Sigma Xi, Phi Lambda Upsilon. Author articles in field. Home: 1211 Oak Knoll Dr Akron OH 44313 Office: 400 Wabash Ave Akron OH 44308

LUTY, FRITZ WILHELM, physicist, educator; b. Essen, Germany, Apr. 12, 1928; s. Wilhelm and Charlotte (Hartenstein) L.; came to U.S., 1965; Diplom Physicist, U. Gottingen, Germany, 1953; Dr. rer.nat., U. Stuttgart, Germany, 1956; m. Uta Scheil, Aug. 26, 1960; children—Markus, Christoph. Dozent physics U. Stuttgart, 1961; vis. prof. U. Sao Paulo, 1962; vis. asso. prof. U. Ill., 1963; prof. physics U. Utah, Salt Lake City, 1965—; vis. prof. Technische Hochschule, Munich, 1971. USAF Offices for Sci. Research grantee, 1966-70, NSF grantee, 1972—. Fellow Japanese Soc. for Advancement Sci., Am. Phys. Soc.; mem. German Phys. Soc. Contbr. articles to profl. jours. Home: 1506 Kristianna Circle Salt Lake City UT 84103

LUTZ, ADELINE LOUISE, museum ofcl.; b. Lincoln, Ill., Sept. 16, 1907; d. Edward Chamberlin and Annette Chamberlain (Bates) L.; A.B., Sweet Briar Coll., 1929. Mem. staff Art Inst. Chgo., 1930—, adminstrv. asst., 1955-57, asst. sec., 1957-63, sec., 1963-78; cons., 1978—, life trustee, 1979. Sec., Midway Apt. Bldg. Corp., Chgo., 1964-71; Newberry Library asso; mem. women's bd. U. Chgo., 1962—, Women's Coll. Bd., Chgo., 1933-34. Mem. Am. Assn. Museums, Soc. Mayflower Descs., Library Soc. U. Chgo., Huguenot Soc. Ill., Sweet Briar Alumnae Assn. Club: Arts (Chgo.). Home: 1534 E 59th St Chicago IL 60637

LUTZ, CARL FREIHEIT, ednl. adminstr., state ofcl.; b. Lansing, Mich., Dec. 8, 1934; s. Paul and Edmunda (Freiheit) L.; B.S. in Metallurgy, Mich. State U., 1956; M.S., Carnegie Inst. Tech., 1957, Ph.D., 1959; postgrad. student Max Planck Inst. Physics, 1959-60; m. Vivian Ericson, Aug. 18, 1959; children—Timothy Paul, Elizabeth. Asst. prof. USAF Acad., 1960-63; sr. engr. Rockwell-Standard Corp., Detroit, 1963-66, Kaiser Aluminum Co., Spokane, 1966-67; v.p., dean engring. S.D. Sch. Mines and Tech., Rapid City, 1967-74; dep. commr. higher edn. State of Ind., Indpls., 1974-79; v.p. Ind. Vocat.-Tech. Coll., Mishawaka, 1979—. Served with USAF, 1960-63. Mem. Am. Soc. Engring. Edn., Am. Inst. Mining, Metall. and Petroleum Engrs., Am. Soc. Metals, Soc. Research Adminstrs., Sigma Xi, Delta Sigma Phi.

LUTZ, HARTWELL BORDEN, lawyer, judge; b. Montgomery, Ala., July 28, 1932; s. James Penrose and Edna Gray (Borden) L.; B.S. in Law, U. Ala., 1954, J.D., 1956; m. Jonnie F.; children—John Hartwell, James Martin, Robert Gray. Admitted to Ala. bar, 1956, practiced in Huntsville, 1960-78; mem. firm Lutz, Fay and Foley. Mem. Ala. Ho. of Reps., 1970-78; judge Ala. Dist. Ct., Huntsville, 1978—. Served to capt. AUS, 1957-60. Recipient Madison County Jaycees Good Govt. award, 1974, 76; named Hardest Working Rep. Ala. Capitol Press Corps, 1975. Mem. Ala., Huntsville-Madison County bar assns., Am. Judicature Soc. Clubs: Kiwanis, Elks. Home: 1409 Dale Circle Huntsville AL 35801 Office: Madison County Court House Huntsville AL 35801

LUTZ, NORMAN EMIL, metal products co. exec.; b. Racine, Wis., June 15, 1915; s. Emil C. and Emilie H. (Gunderson) L.; m. Grace Beales, Apr. 5, 1941; children—Janet, Susan (Mrs. William R. Kenyon), James. Mgr., Certified Grocers Coop., Kenosha, Wis., 1939-42; chmn., chief exec. officer, dir. Snap-on Tools Corp., Kenosha, 1945—; v.p., dir. Snap-On Inter-Ams., Ltd.; dir. Kelsey Welding & Supply Corp.; dir. Brown Nat. Bank, Kenosha, Frost Co. Treas., Kenosha County Republican Party, 1968. Vice pres. Kenosha United Fund. Bd. dirs., past pres. Christian Youth Council; bd. dirs. Kenosha County chpt. ARC, Wis. Found. for Ind. Colls.; trustee Carthage Coll. Served with USNR, 1942-45. Mem. Wis. Mfrs. and Commerce Assn. (dir.), Kenosha Mfrs. Assn. Methodist. Elk, Rotarian. Home: 523 78th St Kenosha WI 53140 Office: 8028 28th Ave Kenosha WI 53140

LUTZ, RAYMOND PRICE, educator; b. Oak Park, Ill., Feb. 27, 1936; s. Raymond Price and Sibyl Elizabeth (Haralson) L.; B.S. in Mech. Engring., U. N.Mex., 1958, M.B.A., 1962; Ph.D., Iowa State U., 1964; m. Nancy Marie Cole, Aug. 22, 1958. With Sandia Corp., Albuquerque, summers 1958-63; instr. mech. engring. U. N.Mex., 1958-62; asst. to asso. prof. indsl. engring. N.Mex. State U., 1964-68; prof. head indsl. engring. U. Okla., 1968-73; prof., acting dean Sch. Mgmt., U. Tex. at Dallas, 1973-76, dean Sch. Mgmt., 1976-78, exec. dean grad. studies and research, 1979—; cons. Bell Telephone Labs., Tex. Instruments, Kennecott Corp., City of Dallas, Oklahoma City, U.S. Army, USAF, U.S. Dept. Transp., Los Angeles and Seattle public schs. Registered profl. engr., N.Mex., Okla. Fellow AAAS, Am. Inst. Indsl. Engrs. (v.p. industry and mgmt. divs., trustee, dir. engring. economy div., systems engring. group); mem. Am. Soc. Engring. Edn. (Eugene L. Grant award 1972, chmn. enging. economy div.), Ops. Research Soc. Am., Inst. Mgmt. Sci. Editor, asso. editor for manuscripts Engring. Economist, 1971-77; editor-in-chief: Handbook of Finance, Accounting and Economics. Home: 10275 Hollow Way Dallas TX 75229

LUTZ, ROBERT ANTHONY, motor mfg. co. exec.; b. Zurich, Switzerland, Feb. 12, 1932; s. Robert H. and Marguerite Gertrude Louise (Schmid) L.; grad. Ecole Superieure de Commerce du Canton de Vaud; B.S., U. Calif., also M.B.A.; m. Heide Marie Schmid, 1980; children from previous marriage—Jacqueline Louise, Carolyn Jeanne, Catherine Ann, Alexandra Bettina. With Swiss Mgmt. Devel. Inst., 1962-63, Gen. Motors Corp., N.Y.C., 1963-65; with Opel, Germany, 1965-66, bd. mem., 1969-71; with Bavarian Motor Works, 1972-74, Ford Motor Co./Ford Werke A.G., Germany, 1974-76; v.p. truck ops., corporate v.p. Ford of Europe, 1976-77, pres., 1977-79, chmn., 1979—. Served to capt. USMC, 1954-59. Kaiser Found. grantee, 1962. Home: Compass Green High St Stock Essex England Office: Ford of Europe Inc Eagle Way Brentwood Essex England

LUTZ, WILBUR MASSER, hosp. adminstr., psychiatrist; b. Reading, Pa., Jan. 4, 1915; s. Jesse Ruth and Elizabeth Marks (Masser) L.; A.B. cum laude, Princeton, 1937; M.D., U. Pa., 1941; m. Charlotte Ann Bricker, May 5, 1941; children—Suzanne Louise (Mrs. Robert G. Dodge), Karlotta Ann (Mrs. Richard W. Bartholomew), Gretchen Ann (Mrs. Jeffrey Winston), Karen Louise (Mrs. Stephen Ytterberg), Louise Ann. Intern, Reading Hosp., 1941-42; fellow psychiatry Pa. Hosp., 1942-43, Grad. Sch. Medicine, U. Pa., 1946-47; clin. dir. Wernersville (Pa.) State Hosp., 1948-65, asst. supt., 1965-69, dir., 1969—. Trustee Berks County Mental Health Assn., Berks County Council on Alcoholism. Served to sr. asst. surgeon USPHS, 1943-46. Diplomate Am. Bd. Psychiatry and Neurology. Fellow Pa. Psychiat. Soc., Am. Psychiat. Assn., AAAS; mem. South Heidelberg Chowder and Marching Soc. (pres.). Contbr. articles to profl. jours. Address: Wernersville PA 19565

LUTZKY, SEYMOUR EZEKIEL, educator; b. N.Y.C., May 31, 1920; s. Morris and Bessie (Anachowitz) L.; B.J., A.B., U. Mo., 1942; M.A., State U. Iowa, 1948, Ph.D., 1951; m. Doris Elaine Thomas, July 30, 1945; children—Dina, Deborah. Instr., U. Iowa, 1948-51; vis. prof. Oreg. Coll., Monmouth, 1951; editor, tchr. Dept. Def., Washington, 1952-58; with Library of Congress Washington, 1959-60; prof., chmn. dept. Am. studies, U. Hawaii, 1961—; dir. Asia-Am. program East-West Center, Honolulu, 1964-69. Served to 1st lt. AUS, 1942-46. Decorated 4 Battle Stars, Purple Heart. Mem. Am. Studies Assn., Am. Hist. Assn., Orgn. Am. Historians, AAUP. Home: 3233 Woodlawn Dr Honolulu HI 96822

LUUS, REIN, chem. engr., educator; b. Tartu, Estonia, Mar. 8, 1939; s. Edgar and Aili (Prakson) L.; came to Can., 1949, naturalized, 1955; B.A., M.A. in Sci., U. Toronto, 1962; A.M., Princeton U., 1963, Ph.D., 1964; m. Taina Hilkka Inkeri Jaakola, June 17, 1973. Fellow in chem. engring. Princeton U., 1964-65; asst. prof. chem. engring. U. Toronto, Ont., 1965-68, asso. prof., 1968-74, prof., 1974—; dir. Chem. Engring. Research Cons. Ltd., Toronto, Ont., Can., 1966—; cons. in field. Nat. Research Council of Can. sr. fellow Steel Co. Canada 1972-73. Recipient E.W. R. Steacie prize NRC Can., 1976. Fellow Chem. Inst. Can.; mem. Can. Soc. for Chem. Engring., Assn. Profl. Engrs. Ont., Sigma Xi. Lutheran. Clubs: Royal Canadian Yacht, Hart House Squash. Author: (with L. Lapidus) Optimal Control of Engineering Processes, 1967. Home: 3 Terrington Ct Don Mills ON M3B 2J9 Canada Office: Dept Chemical Engineering University Toronto Toronto ON M5S 1A4 Canada. *Through conscientious and continuous effort, the intellectual ability of a person can be substantially improved. A positive attitude is just as important as the ability to tackle a challenging problem. Life is beautiful if lived in an appreciative manner.*

LUVISI, LEE, concert pianist; b. Louisville, Dec. 12, 1937; student Curtis Inst. Music, 1952-57; m. Nina Hussey, June 20, 1959; 1 son, Brian. Mem. faculty Curtis Inst. Music, 1957-62; artist in residence, chmn. piano dept. U. Louisville Sch. Music. Office: School of Music Univ Louisville Louisville KY 40222

LUX, JOHN H., corp. exec.; b. Logansport, Ind., Feb. 3, 1918; s. Carl Harrison and Mary Emma (Dunn) L.; B.S., Purdue U., 1939; Ph.D., 1942; m. Betty F. Passow, Aug. 27, 1940; children—John Ernst, Courtney Rae; m. 2d, Bernice Weitzel Brown, 1965; m. 3d, Linda Merrill Brown, Mar. 2, 1978; children—Julia Elizabeth, Jenifyr Claire. Asst. dir. research and devel. The Neville Co., 1943-46; v.p., cons. Atomic Basic Chems., 1946-47; dir. research Witco Chem. Co., 1947-50; mgr. new product devel. Gen. Electric Co., 1950-52; v.p. Shea Chem. Co., 1952-55; pres., dir. Haveg Industries, Inc., Wilmington, Del., 1955-66, Haveg Corp., Tourlux Mgmt. Corp., P.R.; chmn. bd. Hemisphere Products Corp., P.R., Reinhold Enging. & Plastics Co., Norwalk, Calif., Am. Super-Temperatures Wires Co.; pres. Ametek, Inc., 1966-69, chmn. bd., chief exec. officer, 1969—. Mem. Am. Inst. Chem. Engrs., Am. Chem. Soc., Am. Inst. Aeros. and Astronautics, Franklin Inst., AAAS, Comml. Chem. Devel. Assn., Chemists Club, Sigma Xi, Phi Lambda Upsilon. Clubs: Metropolitan, Catalyst. Home: Regency Towers Apt 6-B Las Vegas NV Office: 410 Park Ave 21st Floor New York City NY 10022

LUXEMBURG, WILHELMUS ANTHONIUS JOSEPHUS, educator; b. Delft, Netherlands, Apr. 11, 1929; s. Everardus H. and Digna (Van Kranendonk) L.; B.A., U. Leiden (Netherlands), 1950, M.A., 1953; Ph.D., Delft Inst. Tech., 1955; m. Geetruida Zappeij, Aug. 2, 1955; children—Ronald P., Jacqueline T. Postdoctoral fellow NRC Can., 1955-56; mem. faculty U. Toronto, 1956-58; faculty Calif. Inst. Tech., Pasadena, 1958—, prof. math., 1962—, exec. dir. for math., 1970—; cons. Burroughs Corp., Pasadena, 1963-64. Mem. Am., Dutch math. socs., Math. Assn. Am., Canadian Math. Congress, Soc. for Indsl. and Applied Math., Royal Acad. Scis. Amsterdam. Research and publs. on theory of integration, spaces of measurable functions, ordinary differential equations, numerical analysis, topological linear spaces, Boolean algebras, axiomatic set theory, theory of Riesz spaces, non-standard analysis. Home: 817 S El Molino Ave Pasadena CA 91106

LUXENBERG, MALCOLM NEUWAHL, ophthalmologist; b. Philipsburg, Pa., July 29, 1935; s. Maurice and Henrietta (Neuwahl) L.; student Tulane U., 1953-56; M.D., U. Miami (Fla.), 1960; m. Sandra Diane Rosen, June 16, 1957; children—Steven Neuwahl, Cathy Ann. Intern, Cin. Gen. Hosp., 1960-61; resident in neurology U. Vt. Affiliated Hosps., Burlington, 1961-63; resident in opthalmology Bascom Palmer Eye Inst., U. Miami-Jackson Meml. Hosp., Miami, Fla., 1963-66; asst. prof. ophthalmology Coll. Medicine, U. Iowa, Iowa City, 1968-70; chief ophthalmology service VA Hosp., Iowa City, 1968-70; practice medicine specializing in ophthalmology, West Palm Beach, Fla., 1970-72; prof., chmn. dept. ophthalmology Med. Coll. Ga., Augusta, 1972—; clin. asst. prof. ophthalmology Bascom Palmer Eye Inst., Sch. Medicine, U. Miami, 1971-72; cons. ophthalmology VA Hosp., Augusta, 1972—. Sr. surgeon USPHS, 1966-68. Diplomate Am. Bd. Ophthalmology. Mem. AMA, Am. Acad. Ophthalmology, Am. Ophthalmol. Soc., Assn. Research in Vision and Ophthalmology, Assn. Univ. Profs. in Ophthalmology, Ga. Soc. Ophthalmology, Med. Assn. Ga., Richmond County Med. Soc. Home: 512 Scotts Way Augusta GA 30909 Office: Dept Ophthalmology Med Coll Georgia Augusta GA 30912

LUZINSKI, GREGORY MICHAEL, profl. baseball player; b. Chgo., Nov. 22, 1950. Profl. baseball player minor leagues, Huron, Raleigh-Durham, Reading, Eugene, 1968-71; with Phila. Phillies, 1971—. Named Eastern League Player of Year, 1970; named to Sporting News Nat. League All-Star Team, 1975, 77; named to Nat. League All-Star team, 1975, 76, 77, 78. Office: care Philadelphia Phillies PO Box 7575 Philadelphia PA 19101

LYALL, KATHARINE C(ULBERT), research economist; b. Lancaster, Pa., Apr. 26, 1941; d. John D. and Eleanor G. L., B.A. in Econs., Cornell U., 1963, Ph.D. in Econs., 1969; M.B.A., N.Y. U., 1965. Economist, Chase Manhattan Bank, N.Y.C., 1963-65; asst. prof. econs. Syracuse U., 1969-72; prof. econs. Johns Hopkins U., 1972-77; dep. asst. sec. for econs. Office Econ. Affairs, HUD, Washington, 1977-79; v.p. Council on Applied Social Research. Recipient award for Balt., Metro Center Policy Com., 1977. Mem. Am. Econ. Assn., Evaluation Research Soc., Phi Beta Kappa. Author: Reforming Public Welfare, 1976; Microeconomic Issues of the 70's, 1978. Home: 117 Cross Keys Rd Baltimore MD 21210 Office: Center for Met Planning and Research Shriver Hall Johns Hopkins U Baltimore MD 21218

LYCHE, IVER, business exec.; b. Oslo, Norway, Oct. 17, 1923; s. Einar and Helga (Aaby) L.; came to U.S., 1946; B.S., U. Calif., 1948, M.B.A., 1949; m. Joan Shuman, Feb. 10, 1950; children—Helga,

Karen, Sylvia, Iver. Salesman, Fibreboard Products, San Francisco, 1950-53; pres. Shuman, Agnew & Co., San Francisco, 1963—, chmn. bd., 1968—; mng. dir. Morgan Stanley & Co., 1977—; dir. Overseas Shipping Co., Am. Potato Co. Chmn. bd. Pacific Med. Center. Served with Royal Norwegian Air Force, 1942-45. Mem. Norwegian-Am. C. of C. (pres.). Clubs: Pacific Union, Bohemian, San Francisco Golf (San Francisco); Burlingame Country (pres.). Home: 101 New Place Rd Hillsborough CA 94010 Office: 650 California St San Francisco CA 94108

LYDECKER, RICHARD ACKERMAN, ins. co. exec.; b. East Orange, N.J., Apr. 26, 1917; s. Frederick A. and Mary (Carpenter) L.; A.B. Princeton, 1938; m. Gertrude McC. Marsh, June 15, 1939; children—Richard Ackerman, Susan Couthouy, Mary Carpenter. Asst. sec. Providence Washington Ins. Co., 1950-53; sec. Gt. Am. Ins. Co., N.Y.C., 1953-56, v.p., 1956-65, exec. v.p., 1965-68, pres., 1968-70; sr. v.p., dir. U.S. Fire Ins. Co., North River Fire Ins. Co., Westchester Fire Ins. Co., Internat. Ins. Co. Served to lt. USNR, 1942-46. Mem. Holland Soc. N.Y. Episcopalian. Club: Roxiticus Golf. Home: RFD Box 60A Childs Rd Basking Ridge NJ 07920 Office: PO Box 2387 Morristown NJ 07960

LYDICK, LAWRENCE TUPPER, judge; b. San Diego, June 22, 1916; s. Roy Telling and Geneva (Lydick) L.; A.B., Stanford, 1938, LL.B. (Crothers law scholar), 1942; postgrad. (Sigma Nu exchange scholar), U. Freiburg (Germany), 1938-39, Harvard, 1943, Mass. Inst. Tech., 1943-44; m. Gretta Grant, Aug. 7, 1938; children—Gretta Grant, Lawrence Tupper; m. 2d, Martha Martinez, Oct. 1969; 1 son, Chip. Admitted to Calif. bar, 1946, since practiced in Los Angeles; dir. disputes div. 10th region Nat. War Labor Bd., San Francisco, 1942-43; asst. to pres., gen. counsel U.S. Grant Export-Import, Ltd., Los Angeles, 1946-48; asso. Adams, Duque & Hazeltine, Los Angeles, 1948-53, partner, 1953-71; U.S. dist. ct. judge Central Dist. Calif., 1971—. Served from ensign to lt. USNR, 1943-46. Mem. Am., Calif., Los Angeles bar assns., Sigma Nu. Republican. Congregationalist. Clubs: Commonwealth (San Francisco); Town Hall. Home: 549 Camino Verde South Pasadena CA 91030 Office: US Court House Los Angeles CA 90012

LYDMAN, JACK WILSON, cons., former ambassador; b. N.Y.C., Feb. 6, 1914; A.B., Bard Coll., 1936, LL.D., 1973; postgrad. Columbia, 1937-40; diploma U. Hamburg (Germany), 1935; L.H.D., Baldwin-Wallace Coll., 1978; m. Josefa Cummings, Sept. 14, 1946. Teaching fellow Columbia, 1937; instr. Bard Coll., 1938-42; with War Dept., 1942-45; div. chief U.S. Strategic Bombing Survey, 1945-46; fgn. affairs officer State Dept., 1946-55; joined U.S. Fgn. Service, 1955; dep. dir. Research Service Center SEATO, Bangkok, Thailand, 1956; consul, Surabaya and Portuguese Timor, 1958-60; counselor econ. affairs, Djakarta, 1960-62; assigned Sr. Seminar Fgn. Policy, Washington, 1962-63; counselor embassy, Canberra, Australia, 1963-64, charge d'affaires, 1964-65; minister—counselor, dep. chief mission to Indonesia, 1966-69; U.S. ambassador to Malaysia, 1969-73; cons., 1973—. Home: 2815 Q St NW Washington DC 20007

LYDOLPH, PAUL EDWARD, educator; b. Bonaparte, Iowa, Jan. 4, 1924; s. Guy W. and Pauline (Ruschke) L.; B.A., U. Iowa, 1948; M.S., U. Wis., 1951, Ph.D., 1955; student Harvard, 1944, Mass. Inst. Tech., 1945, U. Calif. at Los Angeles, 1956, U. Calif. at Berkeley, 1956-57; m. Mary J. Klahn, Dec. 17, 1966; children by previous marriage—Edward, Donald, Paul, Thomas, Andrew. Tchr. math. Pisgah (Iowa) Pub. Sch., 1946-47, Packwood (Iowa) Pub. Sch., 1947-49; asst. prof., then asso. prof. Los Angeles State Coll., 1952-59; mem. faculty U. Wis. at Milw., 1959—, prof. geography, 1962—, chmn. dept., 1963-69, 71-72. Lectr., U. Hawaii, summer 1965, Oxford U., Stockholm Sch. Econs., 1970; C.I.C. Exchange prof. U. Mich., Ann Arbor, 1977, U. Iowa, Iowa City, 1978; Smithsonian Instn. tour dir. to USSR, 1976, 77, 78, 79. Served with USAAF, 1943-47. Ford Found. fellow, 1956-57. Author: Geography of the USSR, 3d edit., 1977; Climates of the USSR, Vol. 7, World Survey of Climatology, 1977; Geography of the USSR: Topical Analysis, 1979; also articles. Home: Box 323 Route 2 Elkhart Lake WI 53020 Office: Dept Geography Univ Wis-Milw Milwaukee WI 53201

LYET, JEAN PAUL, diversified mfg. co. exec.; b. Phila., May 6, 1917; s. Louis F. and Elizabeth (Fortune) L.; grad. U. Pa. Sch. Accounts and Fin., 1941; m. Dorothy Lillian Storz, Sept. 29, 1945. Pub. accountant Ernst & Ernst, C.P.A.'s, Reading, Pa., 1940-43; with New Holland (Pa.) div. Sperry Rand Corp., and predecessor, 1943—, v.p., sec.-treas., 1947-67, v.p., gen. mgr. N. Am. div., 1967-69, pres. New Holland div., 1969—; asst. treas. Sperry Rand Corp., 1955-67, v.p., 1970, exec. v.p., 1970-71, pres., 1971-72, chmn. bd., chief exec. officer, 1972—, dir., 1970—; dir. Armstrong Cork Co., Continental Group, Mfrs. Hanover Corp., Mfrs. Hanover Trust Co., NL Industries, Hershey Trust Co., Eastman Kodak. Mem. Pres.'s Export Council, Bus. Council, Emergency Com. for Am. Trade. Nat. chmn. Religion in Am. Life; bd. mgrs. Hershey Indsl. Sch.; trustee U. Pa., Lancaster Country Day Sch., Elizabethtown Coll. Mem. Machinery and Allied Products Inst. (exec. com.). Episcopalian (vestryman 1955—). Clubs: Lancaster Country, Hamilton (Lancaster); Blind Brook (Port Chester, N.Y.); River, Links, Economic (N.Y.C.); Siwanoy (Bronxville, N.Y.). Office: 1290 Ave of Americas New York NY 10019

LYFORD, JOSEPH PHILIP, educator; b. Chgo., Aug. 4, 1918; s. Philip and Ruth (Pray) L.; grad. Phillips Acad., Andover, Mass., 1937; A.B. with honors, Harvard, 1941; m. Margaretta Jean Thomas, Feb. 16, 1963; children—Amy Jean, Joseph Philip. Reporter, Boston Post, 1938-41, Internat. News Service, 1946-47; asst. editor New Republic, 1947-48; press sec. to Gov. Bowles of Conn., 1949-50; exec. sec. to Senator Benton of Conn., 1950; European corr. Hartford (Conn.) Times, 1951; dir. staff Pub. Edn. Assn., N.Y.C., 1953-55; exec. Fund for Republic, 1955-66; prof. journalism U. Calif. at Berkeley, 1966—. Cons., Center Study Democratic Instns., Santa Barbara, Calif., 1966—, Pub. Broadcast Lab., N.Y.C., 1968, subcom. exec. reorgn. U.S. Senate, 1966. Mem. bd. edn. Dist. 5, N.Y.C. 1964-66. Chmn. Democratic Town Com., Westport, Conn., 1950-52; Dem. candidate for Congress, 1952, 54. Pres., Fund For Peace, N.Y.C., 1969-71, trustee, 1969—; trustee Center for Def. Info., Washington. Served to lt. USNR, 1941-46. Recipient Sidney Hillman Found. award in lit., 1967. Mem. Council Fgn. Relations. Conglist. Club: Coffee House (N.Y.C.). Author: Candidate, The Agreeable Autocracies, 1961; The Talk in Vandalia, 1963; The Airtight Cage, 1966; also articles. Home: 216 Crestview Dr Orinda CA 94563 Office: Evans Hall Univ California Berkeley CA 94720

LYGHT, CHARLES EVERARD, physician; b. Hamilton, Ont., Can., July 26, 1901; s. George Albert and Florence (Pountney) L.; M.D., C.M., Queens U., Kingston, Ont., 1926; m. Mona Havergal Kerruish, June 29, 1927; 1 dau., Mona Mary (Mrs. Perry E. Massey, Jr.). Came to U.S., 1927, naturalized, 1934. Advanced from instr. to asso. prof. clin. medicine U. Wis., 1927-36, dir. dept. student health, 1931-36; dir. Coll. Health Service, prof. health and phys. edn. Carleton Coll., Northfield, Minn., 1936-42; dir. health edn. Nat. Tb Assn., 1942-47; with Merck & Co., Inc., Rahway, N.J., 1947-66, mgr. med. lit. dept., 1947-50, asso. med. dir. med. div., 1950-56; dir. med. communications Merck Sharp and Dohme Research Labs., 1956-66; editor in chief Merck Manual Diagnosis and Therapy, 1948-66, editor Seminar Report, 1956-61; now engaged in med. writing and editing; pharm. cons. Recipient Distinguished Service award Am. Med. Writers Assn., 1961. Fellow A.C.P., Am. Geriatrics Soc. (pres., Thewlis award 1972, editor-in-chief jour. 1973—), Am. Coll. Chest Physicians, Am. Pub. Health Assn., Am. Med. Writers Assn. (pres.), Royal Soc. Health; mem. AMA, Pharm. Mfrs. Assn. (chmn. med. sect. 1956-58), Fla. Med. Assn., Marion County Med. Soc., Am. Thoracic Soc., Am. Soc. Clin. Pharmacology and Therapeutics, Assn. Med. Dirs. (pres.), AAAS, Nat. Conf. Tb Workers, Sigma Xi, Alpha Kappa Kappa. Presbyterian. Republican. Elk. Editorial bd. Current Therapeutic Research. Address: Turban 5802 Shell Point Village Fort Myers FL 33908. *Hard work, soft answers, faith in God, respect for people and pride in this country.*

LYKE, JAMES PATTERSON, bishop; b. Chgo., Feb. 18, 1939; A.B. in Philosophy, Quincy Coll., 1963; M.Div. in Theology, St. Joseph Sem., Teutopolis, Ill., 1967; postgrad. Union Grad. Sch., Yellow Springs, Ohio, 1977. Joined Order of Friars Minor, Roman Catholic Ch., 1959, ordained priest, 1966, consecrated bishop, 1979; tchr. religion Padua Franciscan High Sch., Parma, Ohio, 1966-67; adminstr. Father Bertrand Elem. Sch., Memphis, 1968-69; pastor St. Thomas Ch., Memphis, 1969-77; pastor Ch. of St. Benedict the Black, dir. Newman Center, Grambling (La.) State U., 1977-79; aux. bishop of Cleve., Episcopal vicar for urban region Diocese of Cleve., 1979—. Mem. Clergy and Laity Concerned, Nat. Conf. Black Churchmen, Urban League, So. Poverty Law Center, Assn. for Study Afro-Am. Life and History (founding mem. Memphis br.), Nat. Conf. Cath. Bishops, Nat. Black Cath. Clergy Caucus (pres. 1977-79). Clubs: Knights of St. Peter Claver, K.C. Home and Office: Diocese of Cleve-The Cath Center 1021 Superior Ave Cleveland OH 44114

LYKES, JOSEPH T., JR., steamship co. exec.; b. New Rochelle, N.Y., Nov. 14, 1918; grad. Washington and Lee U., 1941; m. Marjorie Carrere; children—Joseph T. III, Margaret, Leslie, Mary, Catherine, Howell Tyson II, Christopher, William, Thompson. With Lykes Bros. Steamship Co., pres., 1962-65, vice chmn., 1965-67, chmn. 1967-69; chmn., chief exec. officer Lykes Corp., 1969—; officer, dir. subs. cos.; dir. Whitney Nat. Bank, New Orleans S.S. Assn.; mem. internat. adv. bd. Chem. Bank N.Y. Trustee Washington and Lee U.; former bd. dirs., exec. com. Internat. House. Served with USNR, World War II. Mem. U.S. C. of C. (fgn. policy com.), Nat. Export Expansion Council, Greater New Orleans C. of C. (past dir.). Clubs: New Orleans Country, Pickwick, Boston. Office: Lykes Center 300 Poydras St New Orleans LA 70130*

LYKOS, PETER GEORGE, educator, scientist; b. Chgo., Jan. 22, 1927; s. George Peter and Theodora (Psimoulis) L.; B.S., Northwestern U., 1950; Ph.D., Carnegie Inst. Tech., 1955; m. Marie Nina Shumicki, July 2, 1950; children—George, Kristina, Andrew. Prof. chemistry Ill. Inst. Tech., 1955—, dir. computation center and computer sci. dept., 1963-71; cons. solid state sci. Argonne Nat. Lab., 1958-66; cons. radiation therapy Michael Reese Hosp., Chgo., 1966-71; head computer impact on soc. NSF, 1971-73. Pres. Four Pi, Inc., Oak Park, Ill., 1966—; chmn. com. on computers in chemistry, chemistry div. Nat. Acad. Scis.-NRC; dir. Assn. Media-based Continuing Engring. Edn. Bd. dirs. Interactive Instrnl. TV, 1976-78, Oak Park Public Library, 1976—. Served with USNR, 1944-46. Mem. Am. Chem. Soc. (chmn. edn. com. Chgo., co-dir. Operation Interface I, chmn. div. computers in chemistry, mem. com. on profl. tng., adv. bd. Chemistry and Engring. News), Assn. Computing Machinery (chmn. Chgo., nat. lectr., chmn. spl. interest group on computers and soc., liaison to Am. Fedn. Info. Processing Socs. 1976-78), Sigma Xi, Alpha Chi Sigma, Phi Sigma. Author tech. articles. Home: 316 N Ridgeland Ave Oak Park IL 60302 Office: Ill Inst Tech Chicago IL 60616

LYKOUDIS, PAUL S., educator; b. Preveza, Greece, Dec. 3, 1926; s. Savvas Paul and Loukia (Miliaressis) L.; came to U.S., 1953, naturalized, 1964; Mech. and Elec. Engring. degree, Nat. Tech. U. Athens (Greece), 1950; M.S. in Mech. Engring., Purdue U., 1954, Ph.D., 1956; m. Maria Komis, Nov. 26, 1953; 1 son, Michael. Mem. faculty Purdue U., 1956—, prof. aeros., astronautics and engring. scis., 1960-73, prof., head sch. nuclear engring., 1973—, dir. Aerospace Scis. Lab., 1968-73. Vis. prof. aero. engring. Cornell U., 1960-61; cons. RAND Corp., 1960—, Argonne Nat. Lab., 1974—. Grantee NSF, 1960—. Asso. fellow Am. Inst. Aeros. and Astronautics (former asso. editor jour.); mem. Am. Phys. Soc., Am. Astron. Soc., Am. Nuclear Soc., Sigma Xi. Contbr. numerous papers in field of heat transfer, fluid mechanics, magneto-fluid-mechanics, astrophysics, and fluid mechanics of physiol. systems. Home: 222 E Navajo West Lafayette IN 47906 Office: Sch Nuclear Engring Purdue Lafayette IN 47907

LYLE, JAMES ALBERT, educator; b. Lexington, Ky., Sept. 19, 1916; s. James Maxwell and Alice (Johns) L.; B.S. cum laude, U. Ky., 1940; M.S., N.C. State U., 1946; Ph.D., U. Minn., 1953; m. Dora Matthews, July 11, 1948; 1 son, James Albert. Jr. plant pathologist U. Hawaii, Honolulu, 1946-47; asst. plant pathologist Auburn (Ala.) U., 1947-53, asso. plant pathologist, 1953-54, head botany and plant pathology, 1954-70, prof., head dept. botany and microbiology, 1970—. Mem. Ala. Acad. Sci., Am. Inst. Biol. Scis., Am. Phytopath. Soc., Am. Peanut Research and Edn. Assn., Ala. Pesticide Inst., Phi Beta Kappa, Sigma Xi, Phi Epsilon Phi, Phi Kappa Phi, Gamma Sigma Delta, Gamma Alpha. Baptist. Mason (32 deg., Shriner). Home: 241 Singleton St Auburn AL 36830

LYLE, ROBERT EDWARD, JR., chemist; b. Atlanta, Jan. 26, 1926; s. Robert Edward and Adaline (Cason) L.; B.A., Emory U., 1945, M.S., 1946; Ph.D., U. Wis., 1949; m. Gloria Gilbert, Aug. 28, 1947. Asst. prof. Oberlin Coll., 1949-51; mem. faculty U. N.H., Durham, 1951-76, prof. chemistry, 1957-76; prof., chmn. dept. chemistry N. Tex. State U., Denton 1977-79; v.p. div. chemistry and chem. engring. S.W. Research Inst., San Antonio, 1979—; cons. Arthur D. Little, Cambridge, Mass., 1963-72, Sharps Assos., 1970-75, Stohler Isotope Chems., Inc., 1975—; guest, vis. scientist NIH, Bethesda, Md., 1958-59; NSF vis. scientist, 1962—; vis. prof. chemistry U. Va., 1973-74, U. Grenoble (France), 1976; adj. prof. chemistry Bowdoin Coll., 1975-77; USPHS fellow Oxford U., Eng., 1965—. Recipient Honor Scroll award Mass. chpt. Am. Inst. Chemists, 1971. Mem. Am. Chem. Soc. (council 1965-77, council rep. medicinal chemistry 1978—, nominations and elections com. 1970-74, com. on coms. 1974-77, cons. coll. chemistry Cons. Service 1971-76), Chem. Soc. (London), AAAS, Phi Beta Kappa, Sigma Xi. Editorial adv. bd. Current Abstract Chemistry, 1973—. Research, publs. on molecular nature of heterocyclic compounds with particular emphasis on pharmacol., conformation, reductions and molecular rearrangements. Home: 12814 Kings Forest San Antonio TX 76230

LYLE, ROBERT SIMPSON, educator; b. Newark, May 22, 1907; s. Herbert Cecil and Winona (Cort) L.; A.B., Dartmouth, 1929; Ed.M., Cornell U., 1940; m. Lelia D. Scott, June 25, 1932 (dec. Mar. 1949); m. 2d, Carolyn Jean Nice, Aug. 19, 1950; children—Robert Simpson, Catherine Jean. Tchr. Latin and English, athletic coach St. Georges Sch., Newport, R.I., 1929-30; head Latin dept., athletic coach Peddie Sch., Hightstown, N.J., 1930-34; head Latin dept., asst. to headmaster, athletic coach Sidwell Friends Sch., Washington, 1934-42, headmaster, 1949-61; headmaster Hockaday Sch., Dallas, 1961-71, St. Andrews Sch., Tyler, Tex., 1971-73, St. James Sch., Texarkana, Tex., 1974-75; tchr. Latin, Greenhill Sch., Dallas, 1975-76; ednl. cons., 1976—. Eastern rep. Odyssey Press, N.Y.C., 1947-48. Served to lt. comdr. USNR, 1942-47, 48-49. Mem. Country Day Sch. Headmasters Assn. (treas.), Ind. Schs. Assn. SW (past pres.), Headmasters Assn., Ind. Schs. Assn. Washington (past pres.), Ednl. Records Bur. (trustee), Nat. Assn. Ind. Schs. (dir.), Fed. Schoolmen Club Washington, Sigma Chi, Phi Delta Kappa. Mem. Soc. of Friends. Rotarian. Club: Washington Classical (past v.p.). Address: 5906 Del Roy Dr Dallas TX 75230

LYLES, WILLIAM GORDON, architect; b. Whitmire, S.C., Oct. 23, 1913; s. John Thomas and Maggie (Livingston) L.; B.S. in Architecture, Clemson U., 1934; m. Louise Stork, Jan. 15, 1937; children—William Gordon, Robert Thomas. Archtl. apprentice various architects, 1934-37; founder, pres., chmn. bd. Lyles, Bissett, Carlisle & Wolff, Inc., Columbia, Spartanburg, Florence, Greensboro, Alexandria, Richmond, Rockville, 1947-74; founder, chmn., pres. William G. Lyles, Inc., cons., 1976—. Founder, 1st. chmn. Columbia-Richland County Indsl. Devel. Commn., 1958-61, Columbia Community Relations Council, 1963-75, Clemson Archtl. Found., 1955—; founding mem. Richland County Historic Commn., 1975—; trustee United Community Services, 1968-72, Columbia Town Theater, 1973-77; mem. S.C. State Devel. Bd., 1973-77; mem. council Ebeneezer Lutheran Ch., 1954-57, 60-64, 66-70, mem. emeritus, 1977—; founder, chmn. Associated Investments, 1950—; mem. bd. Bankers Trust S.C., 1960-75, Bank of Commerce, Prosperity, S.C., 1952-74. Served to col. C.E., U.S. Army, 1941-45. Decorated Legion of Merit. Recipient numerous awards and citations for design excellence. Fellow ASCE, AIA (chmn. nat. govt. affairs com. 1965-70; vice-chmn., founding mem. COFPAES 1968-71); mem. Columbia C. of C. (dir. 1958-62, 70-72), Newcomen Soc., Blue Key. Clubs: Cosmos (Washington); Forest Lake Country, Palmetto, Summit (Columbia). Contbr. articles to profl. jours. Important works include Central Library U. S.C., S.C. State Capitol Complex Office Bldgs., Bankers Trust Bldg., U. S.C. Coliseum, Clemson U. Library, Rutledge Bldg., Eisenhower Meml. Hosp., Ft. Gordon, U. S.C. Humanities Center, numerous other ednl., comml., govtl., med. and mil. facilities. Home: The Heritage 1829 Senate St Columbia SC 29201

LYMAN, CHARLES PEIRSON, comparative physiologist; b. Brookline, Mass., Sept. 23, 1912; s. Henry and Elizabeth (Cabot) L.; A.B., Harvard U., 1936, A.M., 1939, Ph.D., 1942; m. Jane Hunnewell Cheever, June 21, 1941; children—Charles Peirson, Jane Sargent, Theodore, David Russell, Elizabeth Anne. Asst. curator mammals Mus. Comparative Zoology, Harvard U., Cambridge, Mass., 1945-51, asso. curator mammals, 1951-56, research asso., 1956-58, curator in mammalogy, 1968—; curator Warren Anat. Mus., Harvard Med. Sch., Boston, 1970—; asso. Harvard Med. Sch., 1949-60, asst. prof. anatomy, 1960-67, asso. prof. anatomy, 1967-76, prof. biology, 1976—; mem. NIH Study Sect., 1965-69; mem. nat. adv. bd. Biotron, 1965-75; mem. standing com. Trustees Public Reservations; trustee Mass. Soc. Promoting Agr. Served to maj. USAF, 1942-45. NSF grantee, 1960—; NIH grantee, 1955-76. Fellow AAAS; mem. Am. Zool. Soc., Am. Physiol. Soc., Am. Soc. Mammalogists, Am. Acad. Arts and Sci., Sigma Xi. Republican. Unitarian. Clubs: Harvard, Tavern, Dedham Country and Polo. Contbr. articles, mostly on hibernation in mammals and reactions of mammals to environ. extremes, to profl. jours. Home: 105 Elm St Canton MA 02021 Office: Harvard U Mus Comparative Zoology Cambridge MA 02138

LYMAN, HENRY, pub.; b. Boston, Oct. 30, 1915; s. Henry and Elizabeth (Cabot) L.; A.B. cum laude, Harvard, 1937; m. Marjorie Borum, June 27, 1953. News reporter Cape Cod Colonial, Hyannis, Mass., 1937-38; reporter Athol (Mass.) Daily News, 1938-40; editor Open Road Pub. Co., Boston, 1946-48; pub. Salt Water Sportsman, 1948—; exec. dir. Fund for Preservation of Wildlife, Natural Areas, Boston, 1971-76, dir., 1979—; dir. Samuel Cabot Inc., 1974—, Harvard Mag., 1955-77. Mem. Mass. Commn. Ocean Mgmt., 1963-73, Mass. Marine Fisheries Adv. Com., 1967-76; mem. marine fisheries adv. com. U.S. Dept. of Commerce, 1971-74; chmn. Canton (Mass.) Conservation Commn., 1965-70, New Eng. Regional Fisheries Mgmt. Council, 1976-79; cons. govtl. marine fisheries agys. Vice pres. Thompson Acad., Boston, 1970-76; bd. dirs. Nat. Coalition Marine Conservation, 1974—, Boston Harbor Assos., 1973-76, Internat. Atlantic Salmon Found., 1978—; bd. dirs. New Eng. Aquarium Inc., 1961-79, chmn. bd., 1976-79, trustee, 1979—; bd. dirs. Found. for Reproductive Research, 1965-71. Served with USNR, 1940-46, to comdr., 1952-53. Mem. N.E. Outdoor Writers Assn., Outdoor Writers Assn. Am. Clubs: Harvard, Tavern. Author: Bluefishing, 1955; (with Frank Woolner) The Complete Book of Striped Bass Fishing, 1959; Tackle Talk, 1971, The Complete Book of Weakfishing; Successful Bluefishing, 1974. Office: Salt Water Sportsman 10 High St Boston MA 02110

LYMAN, MARGARET MORNER (PEGGY), dancer; b. Cin., June 28, 1950; d. James Louis and Annie Earlene (Weeks) Morner; student U. Cin., 1968; m., Aug. 29, 1970. Soloist, Cin. Ballet Co., 1964-68, N.Y.C. Opera Ballet, 1969, Radio City Music Hall Ballet Co., N.Y.C., 1970, Contemporary Dance Theater, Cin., 1970-71; mem. chorus Broadway production Sugar, 1971-73; prin. dancer Martha Graham Dance Co., N.Y.C., 1973—, TV spl. Graham's Dance in Am., 1976; artistic dir. Peggy Lyman Dance Co., Cin., 1977—; artist in residence, dir. dance div. No. Ky. U., Highland Heights; guest artist, dance tchr. Des Moines Civic Ballet, All-State Fine Arts Program, Lincoln, Nebr.; guest tchr. Harbinger Dance Co., Detroit; chmn. performing arts panel Comprehensive Employment and Tng. Act, Cin. Mem. Am. Guild Mus. Artists. Home: 231 E 76th St New York NY 10021 Office: Martha Graham Dance Co 316 E 63d St New York NY 10021

LYMAN, RICHARD RANDALL, lawyer; b. Toledo, Apr. 21, 1916; s. Carroll Sanford and Myrtle (Bach) L.; A.B., Oberlin Coll., 1938; LL.B., U. Mich., 1940; m. Marijean Ryan, Sept. 7, 1940; children-Judith Lyman O'Brien, Susan Jean (Mrs. Ronald Andryc), Robert Carroll. Admitted to Ohio bar, 1941, D.C. bar, 1971; since practiced in Toledo; partner firm Mulholland, Hickey, Lyman, McCormick, Fisher & Hickey, and predecessor, 1953—; counsel Ry. Labor Execs. Assn., Ry. Employees Dept. AFL-CIO; counsel for employees in cases before state and fed. cts. ICC, Nat. Mediation Bd., Presdl. Emergency Bds. Mem. Am., Ohio, Lucas County, Toledo, D.C. bar assns. Unitarian. Clubs: Toledo Yacht; Bayview Yacht (Detroit). Home: 425 Forest Dr Rossford OH 43460 Office: Nat Bank Bldg Toledo OH 43604

LYMAN, RICHARD WALL, univ. pres., historian; b. Phila., Oct. 18, 1923; s. Charles M. and Aglae (Wall) L.; B.A., Swarthmore Coll., 1947, LL.D., 1974; M.A., Harvard, 1948, Ph.D., 1954; Fulbright fellow London (Eng.) Sch. Econs., 1951-52; LL.D., Washington U., St. Louis, 1971, Mills Coll., 1972, Yale, 1975; L.H.D., U. Rochester, 1975; m. Elizabeth D. Schauffler, Aug. 20, 1947; children—Jennifer P., Holly S., Christopher M., Timothy R. Teaching fellow, tutor Harvard, 1949-51; instr. Swarthmore Coll., 1952-53; instr., then asst. prof. Washington U., St. Louis, 1953-58; mem. faculty Stanford, 1958—, prof. history, 1962—, asso. dean Sch. Humanities and Scis., 1964-66, v.p., provost, 1967-70, pres. of univ., 1970—; spl. corr. The Economist, London, 1953—; hon. fellow London Sch. Econs., 1978—. Mem. Nat. Council on Humanities, 1976—; chmn. Commn.

on Humanities, 1978—; trustee Rockefeller Found., 1976—, Carnegie Found. Advancement of Teaching, 1976—; bd. dirs. Nat. Assn. Ind. Colls. and Univs., 1976-77; chmn. exec. com. Assn. Am. Univs., 1978-79. Served with USAAF, 1943-46. Decorated officier Legion of Honor; Guggenheim fellow, 1959-60. Fellow Royal Hist. Soc.; mem. Am. Acad. Arts and Scis., Am. Hist. Assn., Conf. Brit. Studies, Soc. Study Labour History (London), Phi Beta Kappa. Author: The First Labour Government, 1957. Editor: (with Lewis W. Spitz) Major Crises in Western Civilization, 1965. Mem. editorial bd. Jour. Modern History, 1958-61. Home: 623 Mirada Stanford CA 94305

LYMAN, WILLIAM WELLES, JR., architect; b. New London, Conn., Aug. 31, 1916; s. William Welles and Gladys Estelle (Latimer) L.; B.Arch., U. Mich., 1939; M.Arch., Harvard U., 1940; children by previous marriage—Cheryl, Steven, Philip, Susan, Donna, Patricia; m. 2d, Joan Evelyn Dalrymple Hanson, Sept. 27, 1970. With various archtl. offices, including Gropius & Breuer, Cambridge, Mass., 1941, Coolidge, Shepley, Bulfinch & Abbot, Boston, 1941, Carl Koch, Belmont, Mass., 1941-42, Hugh Stubbins, Cambridge, 1942, Saarinen Saarinen & Swanson, Bloomfield Hills, Mich., 1946, Skidmore Owings & Merrill, N.Y.C., 1946-47; asso. Charles Burchard, Cambridge, Mass., 1947-53, Smith Hinchman & Grylls, Detroit, 1953-56, Swanson Assos., Bloomfield Hills, Mich., 1956-59, Smith & Smith, Royal, Mich., 1959-62; partner Jickling & Lyman Architects (name later changed to Jickling Lyman & Powell Assos. Inc.), Birmingham, Mich., 1962—, now pres.; instr. Harvard U. Grad. Sch. Design, 1947-53. Chmn. citizens' elementary curriculum study com. Birmingham Public Schs., 1962-63; bd. dirs. Birmingham Teen Center, 1965-67, Birmingham Community House, 1967-70, Birmingham Hist. Soc., 1967-70; chmn. hist. dist. study com. City of Birmingham, 1975-77. Served with USCG, 1942-46. George Booth traveling fellow, 1940-41. Fellow AIA; mem. Mich. Soc. Architects (dir. 1967-71, pres. 1970). Contbr. articles to profl. jours.; designer Bentley Hist. Library, U. Mich., 1973, Gerald R. Ford Library, U. Mich., 1980. Office: 909 Haynes St Birmingham MI 48011

LYNCH, BEN E., banker; b. 1922; student No. Mont. Coll.; B.A., U. Wash., 1947; married. With Rainier Nat. Bank, Seattle, 1947—, v.p., gen. auditor, 1976—. Office: PO Box 3966 Seattle WA 98124

LYNCH, BENJAMIN LEO, educator, oral surgeon; b. Omaha, Dec. 29, 1923; s. William Patrick and Mary (Rauber) L.; B.S.D., Creighton U., 1945, D.D.S., 1947, A.M., 1953; fellow U. Tex., 1947-48; M.S.D., Northwestern U., 1954; m. Colleen D. Cook Nov. 10, 1956; children—Kathleen Ann, Mary Elizabeth, Patrick, George, Martha, Estelle. Asst. instr. oral surgery Creighton U., 1948-50, instr., 1950-52, asst. prof., 1952-53, dean Sch. Dentistry, 1954-61, asso. prof. oral surgery and dir. dept., 1954-55, dir. oral surgery dept., 1960-67, also coordinator grad. and postgrad. programs; chief oral surgeon Douglas County Hosp., Omaha, 1951-63; pres. dental staff Children's Meml. Hosp., Omaha, 1952, 59, co-founder cleft palate team, 1959, prof. oral surgery, 1957—; chmn. dept. dentistry Bergan-Mercy Hosp., Omaha, 1963-68; mem. exec. com., head dental staff Luth. Hosp., 1963-66; bd. dirs. Nebr. Dental Service Corp., 1972-78, pres., 1974-78; treas. Children's Meml. Hosp. Med.-dental staff, 1979-80. Mem. Omaha-Douglas County Health Bd., 1966-68, v.p., 1967, pres., 1968; exec. com. Nebr. div. Am. Cancer Soc., 1963-67. Bd. dirs. Nebr. Blue Cross, 1968—, exec. com., 1973—. Served at Walter Reed U.S. Army Med. Center, 1955-57, lectr. Sch. Medicine, 1957-58. Diplomate Am. Bd. Oral Surgeons. Fellow Am. Coll. Dentists (Nebr. chpt. pres. 1973-74); mem. Am., Midwest, Nebr. (founder 1957, pres. 1961) socs. oral surgeons, Nebr. Dental Soc. (trustee 1964-66, chmn. Hall Fame com. 1973-76, mem. nomination com. 1973-76, chmn. program com. 1969, chmn. history and necrology com. 1974-76), Omaha Dist. (pres. 1963-64, chmn. peer rev. com. 1974-76) dental socs., Am. Coll. Oral-Maxillofacial Surgeons (founding mem.), Nebr. Soc. Dental Anesthesiology (founder, 1st pres.), Alpha Sigma Nu, Omicron Kappa Epsilon, Delta Sigma Delta. Club: Optimists. Home: 509 S Happy Hollow Blvd Omaha NE 68106 Office: 8601 W Dodge Rd Omaha NE 68114

LYNCH, BEVERLY PFEIFER, librarian; b. Fargo, N.D., Dec. 27, 1935; d. Joseph B. and Nellie K. (Bailey) Pfeifer; B.S., N.D. State U., 1957; M.S., U. Ill., 1959; Ph.D., U. Wis., 1972; m. John A. Lynch, Aug. 24, 1968. Librarian, Marquette U., 1959-60, 62-63; exchange librarian Plymouth (Eng.) Pub. Library, 1960-61; asst. head serials div. Yale U. Library, 1963-65, head, 1965-68; vis. lectr. U. Wis., Madison, 1970-71, U. Chgo., 1975; exec. sec. Assn. Coll. and Research Libraries, 1972-76; univ. librarian U. Ill., Chgo. Circle, 1977—; vis. prof. U. Tex., Austin, 1978. Home: 1859 N 68th St Milwaukee WI 53213 Office: PO Box 8198 Chicago IL 60680

LYNCH, CHARLES ALLEN, food co. exec.; b. Denver, Sept. 7, 1927; s. Laurence J. and Louanna (Robertson) L.; B.S., Yale U., 1950; m. Linda Bennet, June 14, 1952; children—Charles A., Tara O'Hara, Casey Alexander. With E.I. duPont de Nemours & Co., Inc., Wilmington, Del., 1950-69, dir. mktg., 1965-69; corp. v.p. SCOA Industries, Columbus, Ohio, 1969-72; corp. exec. v.p. W.R. Grace & Co., N.Y.C., 1972-78, also mem. rotating bd.; pres., chief exec. officer Saga Corp., Menlo Park, Calif., 1978—. Bd. dirs. San Francisco YMCA, Bay Area Council; trustee San Francisco Ballet, Hill Sch., formerly chmn. bd. trustees Am. Footwear Inst.; mem. Joslin Diabetes Found.; nat. trustee YMCA. Served with USNR, 1945. Mem. Nat. Restaurant Assn. (dir.), Am. Footwear Industries Assn. (past dir.). Republican. Clubs: Wilmington Country; Yale (N.Y.C.); Internat. Lawn Tennis; Ponte Vedra (Fla.) Beach and Tennis; Coral Beach and Tennis (Bermuda). Home: 180 Magnolia Dr Atherton CA 94025 Office: 1 Saga Ln Menlo Park CA 94025

LYNCH, CORWIN JAMES, JR., fast food co. exec.; b. Chgo., June 27, 1934; s. Corwin J. and Margaret L.; B.S. in Psychology, Ill. Inst. Tech., 1957; postgrad. U. Colo., 1958; children—Beth, Terry, Kevin, Tim, Sean, Brian. Exec. v.p. McDonald's Corp., 1960-73; pres., chief exec. officer A & W, 1975-77; v.p., mng. dir. internat. Burger King Corp., Miami, Fla., 1977-78, exec. v.p., mng. dir. internat., 1978—. Served with U.S. Army, 1957-58. Mem. Internat. Franchise Assn., Nat. Restaurant Assn. Office: 7360 N Kendall Dr Miami FL 33156

LYNCH, CREIGHTON BROOKS, investment co. exec.; b. Henderson, Tex., July 9, 1917; s. George Hugh and Gladys W. (Everett) L.; m. Dixie Lee Shaw, Nov. 14, 1942; children—Michael C., Jana B. Field supr. Acceptance Finance Co., St. Louis, 1945-54; div. mgr., sr. v.p., exec. v.p., pres., chmn. bd. Southwestern Investment Co., Amarillo, Tex., 1954—. Served with USN, 1941-45. Mem. Calif. (dir.), N.Mex. (dir.), Ariz. (dir.) loan and finance assns., Nat. (dir.), Tex. (pres.) consumers finance assns. Republican. Office: PO Box 871 Amarillo TX 79101

LYNCH, DALE L., supermarket chain exec.; b. Long Beach, Calif., 1921; student Long Beach City Coll., Los Angeles State Coll. With Safeway Stores, Inc., Oakland, Calif., 1940—, v.p., mgr. Seattle retail div., 1972-75, v.p., mgr. N.W. region, 1975-76, v.p. adminstrn., 1976-77, pres., 1977—, also dir. Office: 201 Fourth St Oakland CA 94660*

LYNCH, DAVID WILLIAM, educator, physicist; b. Rochester, N.Y., July 14, 1932; s. William J. and Eleanor (Fouratt) L.; B.S., Rensselaer Poly. Inst., 1954; M.S., U. Ill., 1955, Ph.D., 1958; m. Joan N. Hill, Aug. 29, 1954; children—Jean Louise, Richard William, David Allan. Asst. prof. physics Iowa State U., 1959-63, asso. prof., 1963-66, prof., 1966—; on leave at U. Hamburg (Germany) and U. Rome (Italy), 1968-69; sr. physicist, sect. chief Ames Lab. of Dept. of Energy; Fulbright scholar, U. Pavia (Italy), 1958-59; vis. prof. U. Hamburg, summer 1974. Fellow Am. Phys. Soc.; mem. Optical Soc. Am., AAAS. Research on solid state physics. Home: 3315 Ross Rd Ames IA 50010

LYNCH, DONALD EUGENE, ins. co. exec.; b. McLean, Ill., Jan. 19, 1925; s. Clarence Ernest and Lorena Beatrice (Hancock) L.; Ph.B., Ill. Wesleyan Coll., 1950; m. Marjorie June Zoller, Aug. 11, 1946; children—Donn Steven, Lesle Kathlene. Underwriter, State Farm Life Ins. Co., Bloomington, Ill., 1950-53, underwriting mgr., Phila., 1953-58, asst. to underwriting v.p., 1958-59; chief underwriter IDS Life Ins. Co., Mpls., 1959-64, v.p. underwriting, 1964-70, exec. v.p. ins. ops., 1970—. Served with USMC, 1943-46; PTO. Club: Optimists. Office: IDS Life Ins Co IDS Tower Minneapolis MN 55402

LYNCH, EDWARD MICHAEL, labor union ofcl.; b. Brockport, N.Y., Oct. 1, 1920; s. Joseph R. and Ida M. (Ritchlin) L.; student parochial and pub. schs., Rochester, N.Y.; m. Gloria Jeanne Mangano, Nov. 25, 1978. Broadcast technician WHEC, Rochester, N.Y., 1946-52; local pres. Nat. Assn. Broadcast Employees and Technicians, 1947-52, regional dir., Buffalo, 1952-68, network coordinator, Bethesda, Md., 1968—, internat. pres., 1971—. Served with Signal Corps, AUS, 1943-46. Office: 7101 Wisconsin Ave Bethesda MD 20014

LYNCH, EDWARD STEPHEN, corp. exec.; b. Holyoke, Mass., Oct. 5, 1911; s. Edward Joseph and Katherine Veronica (Moriarty) L.; A.B., Amherst Coll., 1931; M.A., Harvard U., 1934, Ph.D., 1936; m. Anna Azzariti, Aug. 3, 1946; children—Julia M., Edward G., Robert G., Stephen G. Instr. econs. Princeton, 1935-38; asst. prof. econs. Iowa State Coll., 1938-41; chief economist IBRD, Washington, 1946-48; chief economist, acting exec. v.p. Export-Import Bank Washington, 1948-59; v.p. overseas cos. Westinghouse Internat., 1960-66; v.p., treas. ITT Europe, Inc., Brussels, Belgium, 1966—, v.p. ITT Corp., 1973-76; cons., economist Sogen Swiss Internat. Corp., N.Y.C., 1977—; consultore Prefecture of Econ. Affairs of the Holy See, Vatican City, 1979—. Served with AUS, 1943-45. Mem. Am. Econs. Assn., Council on Fgn. Relations, Phi Beta Kappa. Home: Via Ximenes No 7 Rome Italy Office: Via Rubens 38 Rome Italy 00197

LYNCH, FRANK WILLIAM, aerospace co. exec.; b. San Francisco, Nov. 26, 1921; s. James Garfield and Med (Kelly) L.; A.B., Stanford U., 1943, postgrad., 1946-48; m. Marilyn Leona Hopwood, June 24, 1950; children—Kathyn Leona, Molly Louise. Research engr. Boeing Airplane Co., Seattle, 1948-50; with Northrop Corp., Hawthorn, Calif., 1950-57, Los Angeles, 1959—, sr. v.p. ops. corp. hdqrs., 1974-78, sr. v.p. and group exec. Tactical Systems Group, 1978—; div. v.p. engring. Lear-Siegler Corp. Anaheim, Calif., 1957-59. Served with AC, U.S. Army, 1942-46. Mem.IEEE, AIAA, Assn. U.S. Army, Am. Def. Preparedness Assn., Mchts. and Mfrs. Assn. Los Angeles (dir.). Club: Balboa Yacht (Newport Beach, Calif.). Home: 1933 Altura Dr Corona Del Mar CA 92625 Office: 1800 Century Park E Los Angeles CA 90067

LYNCH, FREDERICK, JR., banker; b. N.Y.C., Sept. 24, 1914; s. Frederick and Maude (Dutton) L.; ed. Colgate U., 1936; m. Janet Spurrier, Nov. 30, 1936; children—Holly Reid Lynch Hilborn, Frederick III. Mgr., Western Union Telegraph Co., N.Y.C., 1936-42; dir. indsl. relations ABC, 1942- 50; with Central Nat. Bank Cleve., 1950-79, sr. v.p. corporate relations and public affairs, 1973-79; adminstrv. v.p. George S. Voinovich, Inc., Cleve., 1979—; faculty N.Y. U., 1946. Mem. bd. Ohio Info. Com., dir. 21st dist., 1966-69; mem. personnel adv. com. Cleve. Welfare Fedn., 1960-71; mem. exec. com. Cleve. chpt. ARC, 1958-69, chmn., 1962-64; exec. bd. Greater Cleve. council Boy Scouts Am., 1971-76, Cleve. Jr. Achievement, 1969-74; bd. dirs. Cleve.-Cuyahoga County Port Authority, 1975, Regional Transit Authority-Cleve.; v.p., trustee Am. Cancer Soc., Urban League Cleve. Mem. Am. Mgmt. Assn., Greater Cleve. Growth Assn., Ohio Bankers Assn. (pub. affairs com. Cleve.), Am. Inst. Banking, Phi Kappa Psi. Republican. Clubs: Country, Clevelander (Cleve.); Catawba Island (Port Clinton, Ohio). Home: 11720 Edgewater Dr Lakewood OH 44107 Office: 1224 Huron Mall Bldg Cleveland OH 44115

LYNCH, GERALD JOHN, mfg. co. exec.; b. Detroit, Feb. 22, 1906; s. Patrick John and Julia (O'Meara) L.; A.B., Wayne U., 1929, M.A., 1935; J.D., U. Detroit, 1933; D.B.A. (hon.), U. Dayton; m. Mary Romaine Livernois, July 20, 1937; children—Terence, Rose Mary (Mrs. Norman S. Mitchell), Laura Lee (Mrs. Martin J. Foley), Gerald John, Julie Anne. Admitted to Mich. bar, 1933; practice in Detroit, 1933-42; dir. war contract adminstrn. dept. Fisher Body div. Gen. Motors Corp., 1942-46; dir. war contract adminstrn. dept., exec. asst. controller, dir. Washington office, exec. asst. to group exec. tractor and internat. group, dir. Office Def. Products and Govtl. Relations, Ford Motor Co., 1946-56, pres. subsidiary Aeronutronic Systems, Inc., 1956-59, v.p., gen. mgr. aeronutronic div., 1959-62, group v.p. def. products, 1960-62; chmn. bd. Menasco Mfg. Co., 1962—; group v.p., dir. Colt Industries Inc.; dir. Lloyds Bank Calif., Los Angeles. Trustee Calif. Museum Found. bd. dirs. United Way, Los Angeles. Clubs: Metropolitan (Washington); California (Los Angeles); Annandale (Pasadena); Century II (Ft. Worth). Home: 920 Avondale Rd San Marino CA 91108 Office: 805 S San Fernando Blvd Burbank CA 91510

LYNCH, GERALD WELDON, clin. psychologist; b. N.Y.C., Mar. 24, 1937; s. Edward Dewey and Alice Margaret (Weldon) L.; B.S., Fordham Coll., 1958; Ph.D., N.Y. U., 1968; m. Eleanor Gay Sherry, Dec. 5, 1970; children—Timothy, Elizabeth. Tech. employment rep. Bell Telephone Labs., N.Y.C., 1958-63; psychologist VA Hosp., N.Y., Palo Alto, Calif., 1964-68; asst. prof. psychology John Jay Coll. Criminal Justice, N.Y.C., 1967-71, dir. student activities, 1968-70, asso. prof., 1971-74, prof., 1974—, dean students, 1968-71, v.p., 1971-76, pres., 1976—. Trustee, N.Y.C. Police Found.; bd. dirs. Research Found. City Univ.; chmn. N.Y. State Gambling Study Panel, 1979; mem. N.Y. State Crime Control Planning Bd., 1979—. Recipient Criminal Justice award N.Y. State Bar Assn., 1977; Disting. Alumni award in edn. Fordham Coll. Alumni Assn., 1978. Mem. Acad. Criminal Justice Scis., Am. Acad. Profl. Law Enforcement (dir.), Am. Soc. Criminology, Am. Assn. Univ. Adminstrs., AAAS, Am. Psychol. Assn. Democrat. Roman Catholic. Club: Bridgehampton. Contbr. articles to profl. jours. Home: 540 E 20th St New York NY 10009 Office: 444 W 56th St New York NY 10019

LYNCH, HENRY THOMSON, med. educator; b. Lawrence, Mass., Jan. 4, 1928; s. Henry F. and Eleanor (Thomson) L.; B.S., Okla., 1951; M.A., Denver U., 1952; M.D., U. Tex., Galveston, 1960; m. Jane Smith, Nov. 9, 1951; children—Patrick, Kathleen, Ann. Intern, St. Mary's Hosp., Evansville, Ind., 1960; resident U. Nebr. Sch. Medicine, 1961-64, sr. clin. cancer trainee, 1964-66; practice medicine specializing in internal medicine, Omaha, 1967—; asst. prof. medicine U. Tex. M.D. Anderson Hosp., Houston, 1966-67; asso. prof. Creighton U. Sch. Medicine, Omaha, 1967-70, prof., chmn. dept. preventive medicine and pub. health, 1970—. Served with USNR, 1944-46. Mem. Am. Soc. Human Genetic, Am. Soc. Clin. Oncology, Am. Assn. Cancer Research, Alpha Omega Alpha. Author: Hereditary Factors in Carcinoma, 1967; Dynamic Genetic Counseling for Clinicians, 1969; Cancer and You, 1971; Skin, Heredity and Malignant Neoplasms, 1973; Cancer Genetics, 1975; also numerous sci. articles. Home: 9406 Douglas St Omaha NE 68114

LYNCH, JOHN BROWN, plastic surgeon; b. Akron, Ohio, Feb. 5, 1929; s. John A. and Eloise L.; student Vanderbilt U., 1946-49; M.D., U. Tenn., 1952; m. Jean Crane, July 2, 1950; children—John Brown, Margaret Frances Lynch Calahan. Rotating intern John Gaston Hosp., Memphis, Tenn., 1953-54; resident in gen. surgery U. Tex. Med. Br., Galveston, 1956-59, resident in plastic surgery, 1959-62, instr., 1962, asst. prof. surgery, 1962-67, asso. prof., 1967-72, prof., 1972-73; prof., plastic surgery, chmn. dept. plastic surgery Vanderbilt U. Med. Center, 1973—. Served as capt. USAF, 1954-56. Diplomate Am. Bd. Plastic Surgery (chmn.). Fellow A.C.S.; mem. Singleton Surg. Soc. (sec.-treas. 1968-72), AMA, Am. Soc. Plastic and Reconstructive Surgeons (Ednl. Found.), Am. Assn. Plastic Surgeons, Plastic Surgery Research Council, Am. Cleft Palate Assn., Am. Burn Assn., Soc. Head and Neck Surgeons, Internat. Burn Assn., Pan Am. Med. Assn., Am. Cancer Soc. (pres. Galveston County, Tex., Chpt. 1968), So. Med. Assn. (chmn. sect. plastic surgery, 1972-73), Tenn. med. Assn., Nashville Acad. Medicine, Tenn. Soc. Plastic Surgeons, Southeastern Soc. Plastic Surgeons, Southeastern Surg. Soc., H. William Scott, Jr., Soc., Nashville Surg. Soc., Am. Soc. Maxillofacial Surgeons, So. Surg. Assn., Am. Surg. Assn., Sigma Xi. Contbr. numerous articles to med. publs.; editor: (with S. R. Lewis) Symposium on the Treatment of Burns, 1973. Home: 2312 Valley Brook Rd Nashville TN 37215 Office: Room S-2221 Vanderbilt Hosp Nashville TN 37232

LYNCH, JOHN ELLSWORTH, hosp. adminstr.; b. Fargo, N.D., June 8, 1935; s. John Joseph and Mary Louise (Paulson) L.; B.S. in Bus. Adminstrn., U. N.D., 1959; M.B.A., U. Mo., 1969; m. Beth Margaret Pallas, July 14, 1956; children—John Ellsworth, Michael, Kevin. Fin. mgr. U.S. Steel Corp., Chgo., 1959-63; controller Decatur (Ill.) and Macon County Hosp., 1963-65; asst. exec. dir. Research Hosp. and Med. Center, Kansas City, Mo., 1965-70; chief exec. officer N.C. Baptist Hosps., Winston-Salem, 1970—; chmn. fin. com. Winston-Salem Savs. & Loan Assn.; dir. Winston-Salem Savs. & Loan Assn.; trustee, mem. exec. com. N.C. Blue Cross/Blue Shield. Mem. exec. com. Forsyth County chpt. ARC; mem. Forsyth County Bd. Health; mem.-at-large, chmn. state health facilities plan devel. com. N.C. Statewide Health Coordinating Council; bd. dirs. Amos Cottage; trustee Piedmont Assn. Industries. Served with AUS, 1954-57. Mem. Am. Coll. Hosp. Adminstrs., N.C. Hosp. Assn. (trustee), Beta Gamma Sigma, Beta Alpha Psi. Republican. Baptist. Club: Rotary. Home: 430 Staffordshire St Winston-Salem NC 27104 Office: 300 S Hawthorne Rd Winston-Salem NC 27103

LYNCH, JOHN F., oil co. exec.; b. Catawissa, Mo., Jan. 22, 1912; s. John Galvin and Leatha (McNaughton) L.; student Washington U., St. Louis, 1928-33; m. Josephine Blanche Short, June 1, 1939 (dec. May 1974); children—Alice Ann (Mrs. William I. Wyatt, Jr.), Mary Kathryn. Mem. prodn. and natural gasoline and refining depts. Shamrock Oil & Gas Corp., Amarillo, Tex., 1937-39, asst. supt. ops., 1939; refinery supt. Fletcher Oil Co., Los Angeles, 1939-42, mgr. Calif. ops., 1944; mgr. cycling ops. La Gloria Corp., Corpus Christi, Tex., 1944-46, v.p., 1946, pres., 1947-54; pres., dir. La Gloria Oil & Gas Co., 1954-71; v.p., dir. Gt. So. Chem. Corp., 1950-62; sr. v.p., dir. Tex. Eastern Transmission Corp., 1957-71, mem. finance com., dir., 1971—; dir. Corpus Christi State Nat. Bank, So. Nat. Bank Houston. Mem. Gulf Coast council Boy Scouts Am., 1947-58, v.p., fin. chmn., 1948-55, regional dir., 1953, mem. exec. com. Houston area, 1959—, pres. Sam Houston area council, 1960-62, mem. nat. exec. bd. and chmn. region 9 exec. com., 1964—. Pres. bd. dirs. Lower Nueces River Water Supply Dist., 1952-58. Chmn. bd. dirs. Tex. Coll. of Arts and Industries, 1952-67; bd. dirs. South Tex. Coll. Law, Episcopal Radio TV Found., St. Stephen's Episcopal Sch., Austin, St. Luke's Episcopal Hosp., Houston, So. Meth. U., Washington U., Westminster Coll., Fulton, Mo., Kinkaid Sch., Houston. Mem. Ind. Natural Gas Assn. Am. (dir., vice chmn. producers div. 1959—), Natural Gas Assn. Am. (pres. 1951-52), Mid-Continent Oil and Gas Assn. (exec. com.), Tex. Ind. Royalty Owners Assn. (dir.), Am. Petroleum Inst. (dir., gen. com. div. prodn., past mem. nat. oil policy com.), Am. Gas Assn. (gas industry devel. com. 1959—), Ind. Petroleum Assn. Am. (past mem. natural gas com.). Clubs: Sportsmen's of Texas, Inc. (pres. 1959-60); Kings Men, Corpus Christi Country; River Oaks Country, Petroleum, Ramada (Houston). Home: 3711 San Felipe Rd Houston TX 77027 Office: Southern Nat Bank Bldg Houston TX 77002

LYNCH, JOHN FRANCIS, newsman; b. La Moure, N.D., Sept. 17, 1917; s. William David and Ana (Cruden) L.; B.S., N.D. State U., 1940; m. Barbara Ruth Washburn, Feb. 2, 1951; children—Amanda Ruth, William Dana. Printer's devil LaMoure Chronicle (N.D.), 1934-35; reporter Fargo (N.D.) Forum and WDAY, Inc., 1940- 43; reporter-editor Midwest burs. U.P.I., 1943-51; TV newswriter-producer NBC, 1951-58; dir. pub. affairs CBS, 1959-60; with ABC News, 1960—, Washington bur. chief, 1965-75, dir. polit. unit, 1975—; producer radio TV pool Presdl. Inauguration 1965, Gemini V; Internat. broadcast pool Apollo II moon walk. Mem. Radio-TV Corrs. Assn. (pres. 1967-68). Home: 111 Haddon Pl Upper Montclair NJ 07043 Office: 1330 Ave of Americas New York City NY 10019

LYNCH, KEVIN ANDREW, city planner, educator; b. Chgo., Jan. 7, 1918; s. James Joseph and Laura (Healy) L.; student Yale, 1935-37; apprenticeship with F.L. Wright, 1937-39; student Rensselaer Poly. Inst., 1940; B.City Planning, Mass. Inst. Tech., 1947; Dr.-Ing., U. Stuttgart, 1978; m. Anne Macklin Borders, June 7, 1941; children—David, Laura, Catherine, Peter. With Schweikher, Elting and Lamb, architects, Chgo., 1940-41; asst. dir. Dept. City Planning, Greensboro, N.C., 1947-48; instr. to prof. city planning Mass. Inst. Tech., Cambridge, 1948-78; partner Carr Lynch Assos., environ. design, 1977—; cons. Boston, Cleve., Balt., Los Angeles, Mpls., P.R., San Salvador, Columbia, Md., Venezuela, Town Gay Head, Mass., UNESCO, Vineyard Open Land Found., Martha's Vineyard, Mass., Dallas, San Diego, Ottawa, Ont., Can., Fez, Morocco, Washington, Lewiston, Maine, Massport, Boston. Chmn., Watertown Planning Bd., 1962-65. Trustee Palfrey St. Sch., Watertown, 1964-70. Served with C.E., AUS, 1941-46. Decorated Bronze Star; recipient 50th Anniversary award Am. Inst. Planners, 1967; Allied Professions medal AIA, 1974. Author: The Image of the City, 1960; Site Planning, 1962, 72; (with others) The View From the Road, 1964; What Time Is This Place, 1972; managing the Sense of a Region, 1976; Growing Up in Cities, 1977. Home: 85 Russell Ave Watertown MA 02172 Office: Carr Lynch Assos 45 Hancock St Cambridge MA 02139

LYNCH, MARTIN ANDREW, air cargo and leasing co. exec.; b. Chgo., Oct. 5, 1937; s. George Irwin and Cecilia Veronica (Corley) L.; B.S., De Paul U., 1962; m. Shirley Ann McKee, Oct. 20, 1962; children—Kathleen Marie, Kevin Michael, Karen Ann, Daniel Patrick, Michelle Eileen. Audit mgr. Price Waterhouse Co., Chgo., 1962-69; asst. to pres. Scot Lad Foods, Chgo., 1969-70; v.p. fin.

N.Am. Car Corp., Chgo., 1970—, dir., 1972—; v.p. fin. Tiger Internat. Inc., Los Angeles, 1976—. Served with USMC, 1957-58. C.P.A. Mem. Fin. Execs. Inst., Am. Inst. C.P.A.'s, Ill. Assn. C.P.A.'s. Roman Catholic. Clubs: Metropolitan (Chgo.); Northridge Tennis. Office: 1888 Century Park E Los Angeles CA 90067

LYNCH, RAY JOSEPH, gas pipeline co. exec.; b. Chgo., Oct. 10, 1922; s. Rollin John and Eva (Schoeller) L.; B.S. in Commerce, U. Ill., 1948; C.P.A.; m. Leila Mariotti, June 11, 1949; children—Dawn, Mary Joy, Tim, Cheryl, Jane, Martha, Christopher, John, Robert. With Arthur Andersen & Co., C.P.A.'s, Chgo., 1948-53, Mich. Wis. Pipe Line Co., Detroit, 1953—, treas. 1960—, v.p., 1962—, exec. v.p., 1969-73, pres., 1973—, dir. Mich. Wis., its parent Am. Natural Resources Co. and affiliate Gt. Lakes Gas Transmission Co., also Mich. Nat. Bank Detroit. Bd. dirs. Boysville of Mich. Served as pilot USAAF, World War II. Mem. Am. Gas Assn., Interstate Natural Gas Assn. Home: 529 Ballantyne Rd Grosse Pointe Shores MI 48236 Office: 1 Woodward Ave Detroit MI 48226

LYNCH, ROBERT JOHN, architect; b. Boston; s. Clement F. and Eleanor M. (Brooks) L.; B.A., U. Notre Dame, 1949, B.Arch., 1953, B. Archtl. Engring., 1953; m. Diana M. Hoover, 1960; children—Stephen, Kathryn, Susan. Prin., Robert J. Lynch, archtl. engring. firm specializing in archtl. needs of physically handicapped, Malden, Mass., 1965—; cons. on accessibility to physically handicapped Nat. Park Service, Urban Mass Transp. Adminstrn.; co-founder Nat. Center for Barrier-Free Environment. Fellow AIA; mem. Boston Soc. Architects. Author Access 76, project dir. Easter Seal Soc. Mass. Home: 37 Old Brook Circle Melrose MA 02176 Office: 440 Pleasant St Malden MA 02148

LYNCH, ROBERT MERRILL, bus. exec.; b. Wilmington, Del., Jan. 24, 1919; s. William Saxton and Margaret (Murray) L.; B.A. in Econs., Lehigh U., 1942; m. Janet Tee, Dec. 26, 1942; children—Peter Earle, Robert Saxton, Susan Murray. With Internat. Freighting Corp., N.Y.C., 1942-47, Shipping Enterprises Corp., N.Y.C., 1947-48; mgr. shipping dept. A. Johnson & Co., Inc., N.Y.C., 1948-53, exec. v.p., 1953-55, pres., 1955—, also dir.; dir. Parkson Corp., C.H. Sprague & Son Co., Axel Johnson Corp., Ingersoll Steel Co., Axel Johnson Industries Ltd. Served as 1st lt. USAAF, 1943-46. Decorated Order of Vasa (Sweden). Mem. Soc. Naval Architects and Marine Engrs., Swedish-Am. C. of C. (dir.). Clubs: Met., N.Y. Athletic, Pelham Country, Essex Yacht. Home: Riverside Ave Old Saybrook CT 06475 Office: 110 E 59th St New York City NY 10022

LYNCH, ROBERT R(ICHARD), ins. co. exec.; b. Newark, July 23, 1929; s. Joseph P. and Anna T. (Daly) L.; B.S., Seton Hall U., 1949; M.B.A., N.Y. U., 1954; m. Tonia Sauerwein, June 21, 1952; children—Roberta, Maureen, Matthew, Janice, Justin, Robert. Mgr. organizational planning Merck & Co., Rahway, N.J., 1950-65; dir. manpower devel. Aetna Life & Casualty Co., Hartford, Conn., 1965-68; 2d v.p. personnel Penn Mut. Life Ins. Co., Phila., 1968-72, v.p. adminstrn., 1972-76, sr. v.p., 1976—. Trustee, Pierce Jr. Coll. Mem. Am. Soc. C.L.U.'s. Roman Catholic. Club: Haddonfield Democratic. Office: 530 Walnut St Philadelphia PA 19172

LYNCH, THOMAS FRANCIS, archeologist, educator; b. Mpls., Feb. 25, 1938; s. Francis Watson and Viola Eugenie (White) L.; B.A., Cornell U., 1960; M.A., U. Chgo., 1962, Ph.D., 1967; m. Barbara Amy Deutsch, Feb. 4, 1961; children—Elizabeth Ann, Jean Margaret, Julia Frances. Archeologist, Ida. State U. Mus., Pocatello, 1963-64; instr. to prof. and chmn. anthropology dept. Cornell U., Ithaca, N.Y., 1964—, dir. Cornell Intercollege Program in Archeology, 1971-74, 75—. Recipient NSF and other research grants for archeol. excavations in Peru, Chile and Ecuador, 1964-76. Fellow AAAS, Explorers Club; mem. Soc. for Am. Archeology, Prehistoric Soc. Gt. Britain, Am. Quaternary Assn., Inst. Andean Research (dir. 1976-79), Centro de Estudios Andinos Cuzco (cons. mem.), Phi Beta Kappa. Contbr. articles to profl. jours.

LYNCH, THOMAS PATRICK, army officer; b. Janesville, Minn., Mar. 3, 1927; s. Thomas Phillip and Sybella Magdeline (Breuer) L.; student U. Louisville, 1958-59, U. Hawaii, 1962, U. Md., 1964-65; grad. U.S. Army Armor Sch., 1956, Army Command and Gen. Staff Coll., 1964, U.S. Army War Coll., 1969; m. Carol Lee Newbill, Dec. 20, 1950; children—Michael Thomas, Maureen Lucille, Theresa Ann, Molly Lee, Susan Elaine. Served with U.S. Army, 1945-52; commd. 2d lt., 1952, advanced through grades to maj. gen., 1978; platoon leader Korean War; served in various command and staff assignments, 1952-66; comdr. inf. bn., Vietnam, 1966-67; comdr. 2d Brigade, 1st Armored div. U.S. Army Europe, Erlangen, W. Ger., 1973-75; comdr. 7th Army Tng. Command, Grafenwelter, W. Ger., 1975-78; comdg. gen. U.S. Army Armor Center and Sch., Ft. Knox, Ky., 1978—. Mem. exec. bd. Old Ky. Home council Boy Scouts Am., 1978—; mem. community adv. bd. Sta.-WKPC-TV, Louisville, 1979—. Decorated Silver Star, Legion of Merit, Meritorious Service medal with oak leaf cluster, Bronze Star medal with oak leaf cluster and valor device, Air medal with 5 oak leaf clusters, U.S. Presdl. citation (U.S.); comdr. Order of Merit (W. Ger.). Mem. Assn. U.S. Army, U.S. Armor Assn. (v.p.), Am. Def. Preparedness Assn. Roman Catholic. Home: Quarters One Fort Knox KY 40121 Office: Comdg Gen US Army Armor Center and Fort Knox Fort Knox KY 40121. *My life has been guided by a belief in a philosophy which is expressed in the following: God, grant me the serenity to accept the things I cannot change; courage to change the things I can; and the wisdom to know the difference.*

LYNCH, THOMAS PETER, securities exec.; b. N.Y.C., May 3, 1924; s. Michael Joseph and Margaret Mary (Fitzgerald) L.; student Syracuse U., 1943-44; B.B.A., Baruch Coll., 1947; m. Madeleine D'Eufemia, June 3, 1950; children—Francine, Richard. Acct., Deloitte, Haskins & Sells, N.Y.C., 1947-56; partner Bache & Co., N.Y.C., 1956-61; v.p. E. F. Hutton Group Inc., N.Y.C., 1962-67, sr. v.p., 1967-72, exec. v.p., 1972—, also dir.; pres., dir. cash Res. Mgmt. Inc. Served with U.S. Army, 1943-46. Decorated Bronze Star. Mem. Am. Inst. C.P.A.'s, Fin. Execs. Inst. Clubs: Broad St., Canoe Brook Country Office: 1 Battery Park Plaza New York NY 10004

LYNCH, VINCENT DE PAUL, educator; b. Niagara Falls, N.Y., May 27, 1927; s. Arthur John and Phoebe (Tooker) L.; B.S., Niagara U., 1950; B.S. in Pharmacy, St. John's U., 1954; M.S., U. Conn., 1956, Ph.D., 1959; m. Vivian Tamburrino, Aug. 21, 1954; children—Michael, Stephen, Richard, Laura Anne. Mem. faculty St. John's U., Jamaica, N.Y., 1961—, chmn. dept. pharmacognosy, pharmacology and allied scis., 1961-73, prof., 1966—, dir. div. toxicology, 1969—, chmn. dept. pharm. scis., 1973—. Cons. N.Y. State Legislature Subcom. on Drug Abuse, 1969—, N.Y. State Narcotic Addiction Control Commn., 1969—. Served with USNR, 1944-46. Mem. Am. Assn. Colls. Pharmacy, Internat. Soc. Psychoneuroendocrinology, Internat. Narcotics Officers Enforcement Assn., Soc. Forensic Toxicology, Sigma Xi, Rho Chi. Research and publs. on drug abuse, alcohol and marijuana. Home: 200 Laurel Ln Laurel Hollow NY 11791 Office: Dept Pharm Scis St John's Univ Jamaica NY 11432

LYNCH, WILLIAM BRENNAN, JR., lawyer; b. Monmouth, Ill., Mar. 5, 1926; s. William Brennan and Mildred Maureen (Wimp) L.; B.A., Monmouth Coll., 1949; J.D., U. Mich., 1952; children—Jeanne, William Brennan III, Katherine. Admitted to Calif. bar, 1953, Wis. bar, 1959, U.S. Supreme Ct. bar, 1964; advanced underwriting atty. Northwestern Mut. Life Ins. Co., Milw., 1954-57; counsel Seefurth-McGiveran, ins. cons., Milw., 1957-61; mem. firm Lynch, Nelson & Seligmann, Los Angeles, 1961—. Pres. Estate Counselor's Forum, 1967-68. Served with USNR, 1944-46. Mem. Am., Calif., Los Angeles bar assns., Los Angeles Ins. and Trust Council. Democrat. Roman Catholic. Home: 13920 Old Harbor Ln Marina del Rey CA 90291 Office: 626 Wilshire Blvd Los Angeles CA 90017

LYNCH, WILLIAM MARK, wire and cable co. exec.; b. Mahanoy City, Pa., Aug. 5, 1921; s. William E. and Margaret B. (Burke) L.; B.E.E., Villanova U., 1942; grad. Advanced Mgmt. Program, Harvard U., 1972; m. Doris Gustavson, Apr. 20, 1946. Mgr. mfg. circuit protective devel. Gen. Electric Co., Plainville, Conn., 1958-64, gen. mgr. radio receiver dept., Utica, N.Y., 1964-68, mgr. overseas sourcing, Syracuse, N.Y., 1968-69; v.p. ops. Insilco Corp., 1969-77; exec. v.p. Times Fiber Communications, Inc., pres. Times Wire & Cable Div., Wallingford, Conn., 1977—. Bd. dirs. YMCA, 1965-68; trustee ch., 1948-53, United Fund, 1967-68, New Haven Symphony Orch., 1979-80. Mem. AIEE, Am. Soc. Profl. Engrs. Republican. Clubs: New Haven Country, Masons, Shriners. Office: Times Wire & Cable 358 Hall Ave Wallingford CT 06492

LYNCH, WILLIAM WALKER, savs. and loan assn. exec.; b. Washington, Sept. 18, 1926; s. Talbott and Gertrude (Farrell) L.; A.B., George Washington U., 1950; m. Barbara Van Sant, Apr. 21, 1951; children—John S., William Walker, Franklin P., Mark F. Vice pres., treas., dir. Met. Mortgage Co., Washington, 1950-55; dir., mem. exec. com. Prog. Fed. Savs. & Loan Assn., Washington, 1953-58; v.p., treas., dir. Anderson & Co., Inc., Washington, 1953-59; with First Fed. Savs. & Loan Assn., West Palm Beach, Fla., 1959—, exec. v.p., 1966—. Mem. tournament com. 53d Profl. Golfers Assn. Championship, 1971; mem. tournament com. 19th World Cup Internat. Golf Assn., Palm Beach Gardens, Fla., 1971. Treas. Herbert Hoover Dike Dedication com., 1960, Asst. treas. Fla. Kennedy-Johnson campaign, 1960. Bd. dirs. Am. Cancer Soc., 1967-69, local Community Chest, 1962-64. Served with USNR, 1944-46. Mem. U.S. Savs. and Loan League (mem. investments and mortgage lending com. 1974—), West Palm Beach C. of C. (dir. 1970), Pi Kappa Alpha. Democrat. Roman Catholic. Clubs: West Palm Beach Kiwanis (dir. 1961, v.p. 1970-71, pres. 1971-72); North Palm Beach Country; Old Guard Soc. of Palm Beach Golfers. Home: 1032 Country Club Dr North Palm Beach FL 33403 Office: First Federal Savings & Loan Assn 215 S Olive Ave West Palm Beach FL 33401

LYNCH, WILLIAM WALMSLEY, JR., educator; b. Jerome, Ariz., Dec. 30, 1921; s. William W. and Miriam (Hatch) L.; B.A., Williams Coll., 1943; M.A., Yale U., 1948, Ph.D., 1950; m. Violet Dobson Cook, Jan. 11, 1944; children—Alexandra McAlpine, Suzanne Dobson. Econ. analyst Bd. Econ. Warfare, 1943; instr. Greenwood Sch., Ruxton, Md., 1946-47, New Haven State Tchrs. Coll., 1949-50, U. N.H., 1950-52; mem. faculty Ind. U., Bloomington, 1952—, prof. ednl. psychology, 1962—, chmn. dept., 1958-68, asso. dean faculties, 1978—; sr. researcher Center for Innovation in Teaching Handicapped, 1969—; Fulbright lectr. U. Amsterdam (Netherlands), 1960-61; Kennedy Found. vis. prof. George Peabody Coll., 1963-64; vis. prof. U. So. Calif., summer 1967; U. Calif. at Los Angeles, summer 1967. Served with AUS, 1944-46; ETO. Mem. Am. Psychol. Assn., Am. Ednl. Research Assn., Am. Assn. Mental Deficiency, AAUP, Phi Beta Kappa. Unitarian-Universalist. (chmn. bd. dirs. 1967-68). Author monographs. Home: 2611 Fairoaks Ln Bloomington IN 47401

LYNCH-STAUNTON, FRANK C., Can. provincial ofcl.; b. Pincher Creek, Alta., Can., Mar. 8, 1905; student engring. U. Alta., 1923-27; m. Monica Adam, Sept. 21, 1929 (dec. Sept. 1976); children—Betty Lowe, Marina Field, Hugh. Formerly with Imperial Oil Co.; founding mem. and dir. Community Auction Sales; former councillor Mcpl. Dist. Pincher Creek; now lt. gov. Province Alta., Edmonton; mem. Govt. House Bd., 1978-79. Senator, U. Lethbridge; mem. Can. Council, 1959-65; bd. dirs. Glenbow Found., 1974-79. Served to maj. Can. Militia and Army Res., 1934-42. Office: Office of Lt Gov Legis Bldg Edmonton AB T5K 2B6 Canada

LYNDE, PAUL EDWARD, actor, comedian; b. Mt. Vernon, Ohio, June 13, 1926; s. Hoy C. and Sylvia (Bell) L.; B.S., Northwestern U., 1948. Appeared night clubs, 1950—; theatre debut Happy Birthday, Corning (N.Y.) Summer Theatre, 1951; Broadway debut New Faces of '56; other theatre appearances include: Anything Goes, Dream Girl, Show Boat, A Streetcar Named Desire, Irene, Panama Hattie, Visit to a Small Planet, Desk Set, Season in the Sun, Dig We Must, Once More With Feeling, Bye Bye Birdie; film appearances include: New Faces, 1954, Bye Bye Birdie, 1963, Under the Yum-Yum Tree, 1963, Son of Flubber, 1963, For Those Who Think Young, 1964, Send Me No Flowers, 1964, The Glass Bottom Boat, 1965, Beach Blanket Bingo, 1965, How Sweet It Is, 1968, Hugo the Hippo, 1978, Rabbit Test, 1978, The Villain, 1979; appeared in TV series: Bewitched, Hollywood Squares, 1966—, The Paul Lynde Show, 1972-73, Temperatures Rising, 1974; TV movies: Gidget Grows Up, 1969, Gidget Gets Married, 1972; host TV variety hour Paul Lynde Comedy Hour, 1975; numerous other TV appearances. Mem. AFTRA, Acad. Motion Picture Arts and Scis., Screen Actors Guild, Actors Equity Assn., Phi Kappa Sigma, Deru frat. Office: care Press Dept NBC 30 Rockefeller Plaza New York NY 10020*

LYNDE, STAN, cartoonist, artist; b. Billings, Mont., Sept. 23, 1931; s. Myron Wayne and Eleanor Della (Graf) L.; student U. Mont., 1949-51, Sch. Visual Arts N.Y.C., 1957-58; m. Sandra J. Dunning, Feb. 1952 (div. 1956); children—Shannon K., Michael Casey; m. 2d, Jane P. Quinn, June 1958 (div. 1967); 1 adopted son, Matthew Stephan; m. 3d, Sidne Norine Henderson, Apr. 13, 1968; 1 son, Taylor Justaad; adopted children—Mark Arnold, Richard Lewis. Reporter, Wall St. Jour., 1956-58; cartoonist, creator Rick O'Shay comic strip, syndicated by Chgo. Tribune and N.Y. News Syndicate, 1958-77; creator Latigo comic strip syndicated by Field Newspaper Syndicate, 1979—. Dep. U.S. marshal, Mont., 1969-77. Served with USNR, 1951-55. Recipient public service awards Girl Scouts, Boy Scouts, Forest Service and others; Inkpot award for achievement in comic art, 1977; hon. mem. Crow tribe. Mem. Nat. Cartoonists Soc., Comics Council, Mont. Peace Officers Assn. (life), Sigma Chi. Democrat. Baptist. Home: Red Lodge MT 59068

LYNDON, MAYNARD, architect; b. Howell, Mich., Sept. 6, 1907; s. Roy J. and Alethea (Hill) L.; B.S., U. Mich., 1928; m. Joyce Earley, 1962; children—Donlyn, Maynard, Jo. Architect, Dept. Interior, Washington, 1933-35, Lyndon & Smith, Detroit, 1935-42; pvt. practice architecture, Los Angeles, 1942-72; archtl. research, Europe, 1972—; principal Lyndon Design Counsellors, London; exhibited Am. Pavillion Internat. Exposition, Paris, 1935, Royal Soc. Brit. Architects, 1937, Am. Fedn. Arts, Washington, 1938, Trois Siecles d'aus Stats-Unis, Museo du Jeu de Paume, Paris, 1938, Fifth Pan-Am. Congress Architecture, Uruguay, 1940, Archtl. League, N.Y.C., 1941, Mus. Modern Art, N.Y.C., 1942; critic Coll. of Architecture, U. So. Calif.; design cons. U. Md., 1965. Mem. archtl. commn. Claremont Coll. Mem. Los Angeles County Bd. Appeals, 1960-64. Recipient 1st prize nat. competition edn. bldgs. Northville Sch., 1937, 2d prize Beecher High Sch., 1940, Silver Medal, diploma 5th Pan-Am. Congress Architects, 3d prize nat. competition for store-front design, 1942; nat. award merit AIA, 1939, 50, 51; honor awards So. Calif. AIA, 1954 (2), 1957, 66; certificate Nat. Council Registration Bds., 1969. Registered architect, U.K. Fellow AIA (pres. Calif. chpt. 1959); mem. Calif. Council Architects (exec. adminstrv. com. 1960). Architect: Tenth Ch., 28th Ch. of Christ, Scientist, Los Angeles, 1954, 72; Bunche Hall, U. Calif. at Los Angeles, 1964; physics research labs. and lecture hall U. Calif. at Riverside, 1965; adminstrn. tower Calif. State U., Los Angeles, 1969; also pub. schs., Ojai, Monrovia, Vista, Malibu, Calif. Address: Rheinpromenade 12 Rheinheim 7891 Küssaberg Germany

LYNDS, BEVERLY TURNER, astronomer; b. Shreveport, La., Aug. 19, 1929; d. Homer Emory and Nettie Lee (Robertson) Turner; B.S., Centenary Coll., 1949; postgrad. Tulane U., 1949-50; Ph.D., U. Calif., Berkeley, 1955; m. Clarence Roger Lynds, June 19, 1954; 1 dau., Susan Elizabeth. Research asso. U. Calif., 1955-58; research asso. Nat. Radio Astronomy Obs., Green Bank, W.Va., 1959-60; asst. prof. astronomy U. Ariz., 1961-65, asso. prof., 1965-71; asso. astronomer, asst. to dir. Kitt Peak Nat. Obs., Tucson, 1971-75, astronomer, asst. dir., 1976-77, astronomer, 1977—. Mem. Internat. Astron. Union, Am. Astron. Soc. (councillor), AAAS (chmn. sect. D). Author: (with others) Elementary Astronomy, 1959; editor: Dark Nebulae, 1971. Office: PO Box 26732 Tucson AZ 85726. *Knowing that there are many ways of making a contribution to the world we live in and choosing to use the opportunities available can result in a personal satisfaction which is the best form of success.*

LYNE, AUSTIN FRANCIS, bus. exec.; b. Newton, Mass., Jan. 7, 1927; s. Daniel Joseph and Susan Markham O'Brien L.; B.A., Harvard U., 1948; postgrad. U. Geneva, 1948-49; m. Ann Blair, Nov. 27, 1954; children—Austin Francis, Jane Markham, Elizabeth Morgan, James Blair, Michael Davitt, Stephen Christopher. Store clk. 1st Nat. Stores Inc., Somerville, Mass., 1949-50, mgmt. trainee, 1950; warehouse supr., 1950, buyer, 1950-64, sales promotion mgr., 1964-67, advt. mgr., 1967, v.p. sales devel., 1968-73, sr. v.p. services, 1973-76; mgmt. cons., 1976-77; pres. The Good Sport, Inc., Cohasset, Mass., 1977—; dir. Mass. Bay Investment Corp. Coach Belmont Youth Hockey Assn., 1963—. Mem. Concord (Mass.) Republican Town Com., 1964—, treas., 1967-74. Alumni council Boston Latin Sch., 1976—. Bd. dirs. Internat. Friendship League, Elizabeth Peabody Settlement House, 1961-67; trustee Fenn Sch., 1972-78, Belmont Hill Sch., 1972-73. Corporator Robert B. Brigham Hosp., 1971. Served with USNR, 1945-46. Mem. Sorrento Village Improvement Assn. Clubs: Harvard in Concord (pres. 1965-67), Concord Country, Megunticook Rod and Gun, Harvard Varsity. Home: 121 Sudbury Rd Concord MA 01742 Office: 166 Cushing Hwy Cohasset MA 02025

LYNES, (JOSEPH) RUSSELL, (JR.), editor, author; b. Great Barrington, Mass., Dec. 2, 1910; s. Joseph Russell and Adelaide (Sparkman) L.; student Cathedral Choir Sch., N.Y., 1920-25, Berkshire Sch., Sheffield, Mass., 1925-28; B.A., Yale U., 1932; D.F.A. (hon.), Union Coll., Schenectady; L.H.D., Md. Inst., 1973; Litt.D., North Adam State Coll., 1977; m. Mildred Akin, May 30, 1934; children—George Platt II, Elizabeth Russell. With Harper & Bros., pubs., 1932-36; dir. publs. Vassar Coll., Poughkeepsie, N.Y., 1936-37; asst. prin. Shipley Sch., Bryn Mawr, Pa., 1937-40, prin., 1940-44; asst. chief, civilian tng. br. Army Service Forces, War Dept., Washington, 1942-44; asst. editor Harper's Mag., 1944-47, mng. editor, 1947-67, contbg. editor, 1967—. Mem. Landmarks Preservation Commn., N.Y.C., 1962-68, Art Commn., N.Y.C., 1971-73. Asso. fellow Berkeley Coll., Yale U.; mem. Humanities Com., Whitney Found.; trustee N.Y. Hist. Soc., Am. Acad. in Rome; pres. bd. trustees Archives of Am. Art, 1966-71, McDowell Colony, 1969-73; mem. council Cooper-Hewitt Mus.; mem. vis. com. for Am. art Met. Mus. Fellow Soc. Am. Historians; Benjamin Franklin fellow Royal Soc. Arts; mem. Authors League Am., Soc. Archtl. Historians, Zeta Psi. Episcopalian. Club: Century (N.Y.C.). Author: Highbrow, Lowbrow, Middlebrow, 1949; Snobs, 1950; Guests, 1951; The Tastemakers, 1954; A Surfeit of Honey, 1957; Cadwallader, 1959; The Domesticated Americans, 1963; Confessions of a Dilettante, 1966; The Art-Makers of 19th Century America, 1970; Good Old Modern, 1973. Contbg. editor Harper's Mag., Art in Am., 1969-71. Contbr. articles, stories, essays to mags. Home and office: 427 E 84th St New York NY 10028

LYNETT, GEORGE VINCENT, newspaper pub.; b. Scranton, Pa., Dec. 1, 1943; s. Edward James and Jean Marie (O'Hara) L.; A.B. in English, Coll. of Holy Cross, 1965; M.B.A., U. Scranton, 1971; J.D., Georgetown U., 1978; m. Patricia Brady, June 4, 1966; children—Sheila Ellen, George Vincent, James Brady. Co-pub., Scranton Times and Sunday Times, 1967—; mem. firm Haggerty, McDonnell & O'Brien, Scranton, 1978—; dir. 3d Nat. Bank and Trust Co., Scranton. Co-chmn., United Way of Lackawanna County, 1972; chmn. Lackawanna County Cancer Crusade, 1969; pres. Allied Services for Handicapped, 1973-75; trustee U. Scranton, 1970-76. Served with USNR, 1965-67. Mem. Lackawanna Bar Assn., Pa. Bar Assn., Pa. Newspaper Pubs. Assn., Am. Newspaper Pubs. Assn. Democrat. Roman Catholic. Club: Scranton Country. Home: 1750 N Washington Ave Scranton PA 18509 Office: Scranton Times Co Penn Ave and Spruce St Scranton PA 18501

LYNETT, LAWRENCE WILSON, mfg. co. exec.; b. N.Y.C., Sept. 11, 1921; s. James Degge and Lillian (Lonquist) L.; B.B.A., Manhattan Coll., 1943; m. Mary C. McCarthy, Mar. 25, 1945; 1 dau., Michele. With IBM Corp., 1946—, mgr. adminstrv. research, 1966—; asso. adminstrv. mgmt. Simmons Coll., 1966—. Mem. Nat. Adv. Com. for Bus. Edn. Curriculum Devel., 1973—. Served to lt. USNR, World War II; PTO. Decorated Navy Commendation ribbon; Presdl. Commendation for devel. adminstrv. mgmt. program for U.S. Govt. Mgrs., 1966. Mem. Adminstrv. Mgmt. Soc. (internat. pres. 1966-67; Diamond Mgmt. key 1963, Internat. Mgmt. award 1967), Office Execs. Assn. N.Y. (pres. 1960-61; Leadership award 1961), Am. Mgmt. Assn. (v.p. gen. services div., dir. 1975—). Chmn. editorial bd. Impact, 1977—. Home: Putnam Green Greenwich CT 06830 also Carefree AZ 85331 Office: IBM Corp Old Orchard Rd Armonk NY 10504. *The most effective way to cope with change is to help create it.*

LYNETT, WILLIAM RUDDY, pub., broadcasting cos. exec.; b. Scranton, Pa., Jan. 18, 1947; s. Edward James and Jean O'Hara L.; B.S., U. Scranton, 1972; m. Linda Lee Kehrli, Jan. 27, 1968; children—Scott, Jennifer. Co-pub. Scranton Times, 1966—; v.p., chief exec. officer Shamrock Devel. Corp., 1971—; pres. Towanda Daily Rev., 1977—. Bd. dirs. Community Med. Center, Scranton; chmn. Mayor's Library Fund Drive, 1974; chmn. spl. gifts div. Heart Fund, 1975. Mem. Nat. Assn. Broadcasters, Pa. Assn. Broadcasters, Am. Newspaper Pubs. Assn., Pa. Newspaper Pubs. Assn. Democrat. Roman Catholic. Clubs: Scranton Country, Elks, K.C. Home: 1601 Monroe Ave Dunmore PA 18509 Office: 149 Penn Ave Scranton PA 18501

LYNG, RICHARD EDMUND, trade assn. exec.; b. San Francisco, June 29, 1918; s. Edmund John and Sarah Cecilia (McGrath) L.; Ph.B. cum laude, U. Notre Dame, 1940; m. Bethyl Ball, June 25, 1944; children—Jeanette (Mrs. Gary Robinson), Marilyn (Mrs. Daniel O'Connell). With Ed J. Lyng Co., Modesto, Cal., 1945-66, pres.,

1949-66; dir. Cal. Dept. Agr., 1967-69; asst. sec. Dept. Agr., Washington, 1969-73; pres. Am. Meat Inst., Washington, 1973—; dir. Commodity Credit Corp., 1969-73, Nat. Livestock and Meat Bd., 1973-76, Tri-Valley Growers; bd. govs. Refrigeration Research Found., 1974-77; mem. adv. bd. Chgo. Merc. Exchange; chmn. food and kindred products adv. com. Commerce Dept.; chmn. U.S. Child Nutrition Adv. Com., 1971-73; mem. animal health com. Nat. Acad. Sci. Chmn., Stanislaus County (Calif.) Republican Central Com., 1961-62; dir. agr. div. Pres. Ford Com., 1976. Mem. agribus. adv. bd. U. Santa Clara; trustee Farm Found. Served with AUS, 1941-45. Mem. C. of C. U.S. (food and agr. com.). Roman Catholic. Rotarian. Clubs: Washington Golf and Country; Capitol Hill, Commonwealth. Home: 4058 41st St North Arlington VA 22207 Office: PO Box 3556 Washington DC 20007

LYNLEY, CAROL ANN, actress; b. N.Y.C., Feb. 13, 1942; d. Cyril and Frances (Felch) Jones; 1 dau. by previous marriage, Jill Victoria. TV appearances include: Goodyear Playhouse, 1956, Alfred Hitchcock Presents, 1957, Dupont Show of Month, 1957, G.E. Theatre, 1958, 59, 59, Pursuit, 1958, Shirley Temple's Story Book, 1958, Laf Hit, 1962, Alcoa Premiere, 1962, Virginian, 1962, Dick Powell Theatre, 1963, Bob Hope Chrysler Theatre, 1965, 66, Run for Your Life, 1966, Man from U.N.C.L.E., 1967, Invaders, 1967, Journey to Unknown, 1968, Big Valley, 1968, Shadow on the Land, 1968, The Smugglers, 1968, It Takes a Thief, 1969, The Immortal, 1969, 70, Bold Ones, 1970, Most Deadly Game, 1970, Weekend of Terror, 1970, Mannix, 1971, Cable Car Mystery, 1971, Night Stalker, 1972, Night Gallery, 1972, Sixth Sense, 1972, Quincy, 1976, Police Woman, 1976; numerous movies, including: Holiday for Lovers, 1959, Blue Denim, 1959, Return to Peyton Place, 1961, The Cardinal, 1963, Under the Yum Yum Tree, 1964, Harlow, 1965, Bunny Lake is Missing, 1965, The Shuttered Room, 1966, Danger Route, 1968, The Maltese Bippy, 1969, Norwood, 1970. Office: care Agy for Performing Arts 9000 Sunset Blvd Suite 315 Los Angeles CA 90069*

LYNN, ARTHUR DELLERT, JR., educator, economist; b. Portsmouth, Ohio, Nov. 12, 1921; s. Arthur Dellert and Helen B. (Willis) L.; student Va. Mil. Inst., 1938-39, U.S. Naval Acad., 1939; B.A., Ohio State U., 1941, M.A. in Econs., 1943, J.D., 1948, Ph.D. in Econs., 1951; postgrad. Law Sch., U. Mich., 1968-70; m. Pauline Judith Wardlow, Dec. 29, 1943; children—Pamela Wardlow, Constance Karen, Deborah Joanne, Patricia Diane. Mem. faculty Ohio State U., 1941—, prof. econs., 1961—, asso. dean Coll. Commerce and Adminstrn., 1962-65, asso. dean faculties, 1965-70, lectr. Coll. Law, 1961-67, adj. prof. law, 1967—, prof. pub. adminstrn., 1969—, lectr. exec. devel. program, 1958-71, acting dir. div. pub. adminstrn., summers 1973, 74, acting dir. Sch. Pub. Adminstrn., summer 1975. Vis. prof. econs. Ohio Wesleyan U., 1958-59, U. Calif.-Berkeley, summer, 1972; admitted to Ohio bar, 1948, U.S. Supreme Ct., 1966; mem. firm Lynn & Lynn, Portsmouth, 1949-50. Mem. Gov. Ohio Econ. Research Council, 1966-70. Trustee Griffith Meml. Found. Ins. Edn.; chmn. external econs. adv. com. Marietta Coll., 1975-79. Served to 1st lt. F.A., AUS, 1942-46. Mem. Am. (chmn. com. state and local taxes sect. taxation 1961-63), Ohio, Columbus bar assns., Am., Midwest, Royal econs. assns., AAUP, Nat. Tax Assn. (chmn. com. model property tax assessment and equalization methods and procedures 1961-65, mem. exec. com. 1965-73, v.p., pres. 1969-70), Tax Inst. (adv. council 1960-63), Nat. Tax Assn.-Tax Inst. Am. (sec. 1975—), Am. Arbitration Assn. (nat. panel), AAAS, Acad. Mgmt., Ohio Council Econ. Edn. (dir. 1964-74), Com. on Taxation, Resources, and Econ. Devel. (chmn. 1979—), Internat. Fiscal Assn., Inst. Internat. des Finances Publiques, Internat. Assn. Assessing Officers (edn. adv. com.), Omicron Delta Epsilon, Beta Theta Pi, Phi Delta Phi, Beta Gamma Sigma, Pi Sigma Alpha. Episcopalian. Rotarian. Clubs: Faculty, Athletic, Torch (Columbus). Editor: The Property Tax and Its Administration, 1970; Property Taxation, Land Use and Public Policy, 1976. Editorial adv. bd. Tax Bramble Bush, 1959-70; asso. editor Nat. Tax Jour., 1971—. Office: 1775 S College Rd Columbus OH 43210

LYNN, BRUCE GREINER, lawyer; s. Harry and Anna G. L.; B.A., Ohio State U., 1938; J.D., Harvard U., 1941; m. Mary Cornelia Evans, Sept. 7, 1940; children—Connie Lynn Moelk, Anne C. Lynn Schofield, Bruce Greiner, Douglas E. Admitted to Ohio bar, 1941; partner firm Bricker & Eckler, Columbus, Ohio; mem. exec. com. Commn. on Interprofl. Edn. and Practice. Fellow Am. Coll. Trial Lawyers (chmn. Ohio com.); mem. Ohio State Bar Found., Am. Bar Found., Columbus Bar Assn. (pres. 1956-57), Ohio Bar Assn. (exec. com. 1966-69). Home: 6677 Merwin Rd Worthington OH 43085 Office: 100 E Broad St Columbus OH 43215

LYNN, CHESTER BERNARD, indsl. distbn. co. exec.; b. Niagara Falls, N.Y., June 3, 1914; s. Ralph Bell and Stella Frances (Connors) L.; B.A. magna cum laude, John Carroll U., 1936; m. Marian Rose Paskert, May 2, 1942; children—Michael Ralph, Mary Ann, Patricia Ann. Sales corr. Linde Air Products Co., Cleve., 1936-42; sales mgr. Cleve. Ignition Co., 1946-54, asst. to pres., 1949-54; dir. sales tng. Premier Indsl. Corp., Cleve., 1954-58, sales adminstrv. mgr., 1956-58; with Lawson Products, Inc., Chgo., 1958—, exec. v.p. sales, 1965-74, pres., 1974-77, chmn. bd., 1977—, chief exec. officer, 1977—, mem. exec. com., 1977—, also dir. and dir. various subs's. Served to capt. AC, U.S. Army, 1942-46, to maj. USAF, 1950-52; PTO, ETO. Mem. Sales Mktg. Execs. Club Chgo., Execs. Club Chgo., Am. Mgmt. Assn. Republican. Roman Catholic. Club: Mission Hills Country. Home: 3851 N Mission Hills Rd Northbrook IL 60062 Office: 1666 E Touhy Ave Des Plaines IL 60018. *Whatever your age, keep your mind open for fresh ideas. As long as you're "green", you'll grow. When you ripen, you'll fall off the tree.*

LYNN, DONALD JUSTIN, lawyer; b. Youngstown, Ohio, Jan. 9, 1891; s. Emery Francis and Harriet Belle (Crooks) L.; A.B. cum laude, Harvard, 1913, LL.B., 1916; m. Frances Viola Manson, June 10, 1918; children—Lesley Frances (Mrs. Richard H. Weichsel), Frances Harriet. Admitted to Ohio bar, 1917, since practiced in Youngstown; asso. Harrington, Huxley & Smith and predecessor firms, 1916-32, partner, 1932-77; counsel RFC, Washington, 1933-34; chmn. bd. Blue Cross Eastern Ohio, Inc.; dir. emeritus Union Nat. Bank. Trustee, sec.-treas. Youngstown Hosp. Assn.; trustee, v.p. Belmont Park Cemetery Assn. Lt. col. Ohio N.G., 1941-47; col. Ohio Def. Corps., comdg. 3d area Ohio, 1949-56, brig. gen., comdr. 2d Brigade, 1956-59. Mem. Am., Ohio., Mahoning County bar assns., Am. Legion, SAR, Mahoning Valley Hist. Soc. (trustee, v.p.), Alpha Sigma Phi, Phi Kappa Epsilon. Presbyn. (clk., elder). Rotarian. Clubs: Youngstown, Youngstown Country. Home: 2356 5th Ave Youngstown OH 44504

LYNN, EDWARD EARL, business exec., lawyer; b. Coldwater, Kans., Mar. 27, 1918; s. Earl Lee and Edna (Lovejoy) L.; B.S., U. Ill., 1942, J.D., 1947; m. Mary Helen Melvin, June 6, 1942; children—Susan Lynn Williams, Betsy Ruth. Admitted to Ill. bar, 1947, Ohio bar, 1961, Mo. bar, 1972; practice in Chgo., 1947-57; partner firm Johnston, Thompson, Raymond, Mayer & Jenner (name now Jenner & Block), Chgo., 1956-57; exec. v.p. personnel and indsl. relations Fairbanks, Morse & Co., Chgo., 1957-61; asst. gen. counsel Youngstown Sheet & Tube Co. (Ohio), 1961-67, asst. sec., 1962-67, gen. counsel, sec., 1967-71, dir., mem. exec. com., 1969-71; v.p., chief legal officer, mem. exec. com., dir. Lykes-Youngstown Corp., 1969-71; dir. Lykes Bros. S.S. Co., Inc., Lykes-Youngstown Fin. Corp., 1969-71; v.p., gen. counsel Gen. Dynamic Corp., St. Louis, 1971—, also dir. Trustee, sec. St. Louis Children's Hosp.; trustee MacMurray Coll., Jacksonville, Ill. Mem. Am., Mo. bar assns., Ohio Mfrs. Assn. (trustee 1967-71), Order of Coif, Phi Kappa Phi, Beta Gamma Sigma. Presbyterian. Clubs: St. Louis, Old Warson Country (St. Louis); Legal (Chgo.). Home: 9 Radnor Rd Saint Louis MO 63131 Office: Gen Dynamic Corp Pierre Laclede Center Saint Louis MO 63105

LYNN, FREDRIC MICHAEL, profl. baseball player; b. Chgo., Feb. 3, 1952; s. Fredric Elwood and Marie Elizabeth (Marshall) L.; student U. So. Calif., 1971-73; m. Diane May Minkle, Feb. 9, 1974; children—Jason Andrew, Jennifer Andrea. Center fielder Boston Red Sox, 1973—. Named Am. League Batting Champion, 1979; mem. Am. League All-star team, 1975-79; named Most Valuable Player and Rookie of Year Am. League, 1975; recipient Rawlings Gold Glove award, 1975, 78, 79; Seagrams Seven Crowns of Sports award, 1979. Mem. Major League Baseball Players Assn. Republican. Lutheran. Office: 24 Yawkee Way Boston MA 02115

LYNN, HENRY SHARPE, investment banker; b. Pitts., July 16, 1907; s. Albert M. and Ethel (Sharpe) L.; A.B., Princeton, 1928; M.B.A., Harvard, 1930; m. Fariss Gambrill, Feb. 4, 1942; children—Henry Sharpe, George Gambrill. Clk., salesman Sterne, Agee & Leach, Inc., Birmingham, Ala., 1930-40, partner, 1951-63, v.p., treas., dir., 1963-67, pres., 1967-76, chmn. exec. com., 1976—; asst. v.p., v.p. Birmingham Trust Nat. Bank, 1940-51. Mem. N.Y. Stock Exchange. Past v.p., bd. dirs. Jefferson County Coordinating Council; past vice chmn. bd. Jefferson County Health Council; past bd. dirs. Jefferson Family Counselling Assn.; past pres. and trustee Jefferson Tb Sanatorium. Served from lt. (j.g.) to lt. comdr., USNR, 1942-45. Mem. S.R., Soc. Colonial Wars. Republican. Episcopalian (vestry). Clubs: Mountain Brook, Birmingham Country, Relay House, Downtown, Shoal Creek (Birmingham); Boston (New Orleans); Princeton, Racquet and Tennis (N.Y.). Home: 2878 Shook Hill Rd Birmingham AL 35223 Office: 1500 First Nat So Natural Bldg Birmingham AL 35203

LYNN, JAMES THOMAS, lawyer; b. Cleve., Feb. 27, 1927; s. Fredrick Robert and Dorthea Estelle (Petersen) L.; A.B. summa cum laude, Western Res. U., 1948; LL.B. magna cum laude, Harvard U., 1951; m. Joan Miller, June 5, 1954; children—Marjorie, Peter, Sarah. Admitted to Ohio bar, 1951; asso. firm Jones, Day, Cockley & Reavis, Cleve., 1951-59, partner, 1960-69; gen. counsel U.S. Dept. Commerce, Washington, 1969-71, under sec., 1971-73; counsellor to the Pres. for community devel., Washington, 1973; sec. HUD, Washington, 1973-75; dir. Office of Mgmt. and Budget, Washington, 1975-77; partner firm Jones, Day, Reavis & Pogue, Washington, 1977—; dir. Aetna Life & Casualty Co. Pres. Fed. City Council, Washington, 1978—; gen. counsel Rep. Nat. Com., 1979—; trustee Case Western Res. U., 1978—. Served with USN, 1945-46. Mem. Am. Bar Assn., Fed. Bar Assn., Ohio Bar Assn., Cleve. Bar Assn., Council Fgn. Relations. Episcopalian. Office: 1735 Eye St NW Washington DC 20006

LYNN, JANET (JANET LYNN NOWICKI), profl. figure skater; b. Chgo., Apr. 6, 1953; d. Florian Walter and Ethelyne (Gehrke) Nowicki; student Rockford (Ill.) Coll., 1972. Figure skater, 1955—; profl. skater, 1973—; mem. Ice Follies, 1972—; U.S. Nat. Ladies Figure Skating champion, 1969-73; Olympic and World Bronze medallist, 1972; World Ladies Figure Skating Silver medalist, 1973. Performed ice show to raise money for Shriners Hosps. Crippled Children and Burn Research Insts., 1973; mem. speakers bur. Fellowship Christian Athletes, 1970—. Home: 4215 Marsh Ave Rockford IL 61111. *I have found that I want to do what is right for the Glory of God in Christ. As in anything, skating has been a challenge. I have tried to meet each challenge in my skating only with love for what I was doing instead of a selfish desire only to win.*

LYNN, JOSEPH HENRY, ednl. adminstr.; b. Sacramento, Apr. 29, 1920; s. Henry Michael and Martha Elnore (Zimmerman) L.; B.A., U. Mich., 1942; M.A., U. Calif. at Berkeley, 1947; M.A., Calif. State U., Sacramento, 1967; m. Carole Wetherbee, Dec. 28, 1943; children—Richard, Philip, Suzanne, Patrick. Prin. pub. schs. Sacramento, 1961-66; asst. supt. bus., 1972-73, supt. schs., 1974—. Active United Crusade, Cath. Welfare Bur., Easter Seal Soc. Served with USAAF, 1942-45. Decorated D.F.C., Air medal with 3 oak leaf clusters. Mem. Assn. Am. Sch. Adminstrs., Assn. Calif. Sch. Adminstrs. Democrat. Roman Catholic. Clubs: Rotary, Serra. Home: 2685 11th Ave Sacramento CA 95818

LYNN, KENNETH SCHUYLER, educator; b. Cleve., June 17, 1923; s. Ernest Lee and Edna (Marcey) L.; A.B., Harvard, 1947, A.M., 1950, Ph.D., 1954; m. Valerie Ann Roemer, Sept. 23, 1948; children—Andrew Schuyler, Elisabeth, Sophia. Mem. faculty Harvard, 1954-68, prof. English, 1963-68, chmn. Am. civilization program, 1960-61, 64-68; prof. Am. studies Fed. City Coll., 1968-69; prof. history Johns Hopkins, Balt., 1969—; vis. prof. U. Madrid (Spain), 1963-64; Phi Beta Kappa vis. scholar, 1976-77. Served with USAAF, 1943-46. Mem. Mass. Hist. Soc., Am. Hist. Assn., Am. Studies Assn., Modern Lang. Assn. Author: Dream of Success, 1955; Mark Twain and Southwestern Humor, 1959; William Dean Howells . . An American Life, 1971; Visions of America, 1973; A Divided People, 1977. Editor: The Comic Tradition in America, 1958: The American Society, 1963; World In a Glass, 1966. Gen. editor Houghton Mifflin Riverside Lit. Series, 1962—; asso. editor Daedalus, 1962-68, New Eng. Quar., 1963—. Home: 1709 Hoban Rd NW Washington DC 20007

LYNN, LAURENCE EDWIN, JR., educator; b. Long Beach, Calif., June 10, 1937; s. Laurence Edwin and Marjorie Louise (Hart) L.; A.B., U. Calif., 1959; Ph.D. (Ford Found. fellow), Yale, 1966; div.; children—Stephen Louis, Daniel Laurence, Diana Jane, Julia Suzanne; m. 2d, Patricia Ramsey Lynn. Dep. asst. sec. def. (OASD/SA), Dept. Def., Washington, 1965-69; asst. for program analysis Nat. Security Council, Washington, 1969-70; asso. prof. bus. Stanford Grad. Sch. Bus., 1970-71; asst. sec. planning and evaluation HEW, Washington, 1971-73; asst. sec. program devel. and budget U.S. Dept. Interior, Washington, 1973-74; sr. fellow Brookings Instn., 1974-75; prof. pub. policy John Fitzgerald Kennedy Sch. of Govt., Harvard, 1975—. Served to 1st lt. AUS, 1963-65. Recipient Sec. Def. Meritorious Civilian Service medal, Presdl. Certificate of Distinguished Achievement. Mem. Am. Econ. Assn., U. Calif. Alumni Assn., Council on Fgn. Relations, Phi Beta Kappa. Contbr. articles profl. jours. Home: 38 Witches Spring Rd RFD 3 Milford NH 03055 Office: JF Kennedy Sch Govt Harvard Cambridge MA 02138

LYNN, LORETTA WEBB (MRS. OLIVER LYNN, JR.), singer; b. Butcher Hollow, Ky., Apr. 14, 1935; d. Ted and Clara (Butcher) Webb; student pub. schs.; m. Oliver V. Lynn, Jr., Jan. 10, 1948; children—Betty Sue Lynn Markworth, Jack Benny, Clara Lynn Lyell, Ernest Ray, Peggy, Patsy. Country vocalist with MCA records, 1961—; numerous gold albums; sec.-treas. Loretta Lynn Enterprises; v.p. United Talent, Inc.; hon. chmn. bd. Loretta Lynn Western Stores. Hon. rep. United Giver's Fund, 1971. Named Country Music Assn. Female Vocalist of Year, 1967, 72, 73, Entertainer of Year, 1972; named Top Duet of 1972, 73, 74, 75; Grammy award, 1971; Am. Music award, 1978. Recorded 1st album to be certified gold by a country female vocalist. Author: Coal Miner's Daughter, 1976. Office: 1511 Sigler St Nashville TN 37203*

LYNN, MICHAEL EDWARD, III, profl. football team exec.; b. Scranton, Pa., May 18, 1936; s. Robert Norman and Gertrude (Smith) L.; student Pace U.; m. Jorja Swaney, July 12, 1967; children—Louisa, Robert, Michael Edward IV, Lucia. Mgr., Dixiemart-Corondolet, Inc., Memphis, 1965-67; pres. Mid South Sports, Inc., Memphis, 1967-74; v.p., gen. mgr. Minn. Vikings Profl. Football Team, 1974—; founder East-West All Am. Basketball Game, 1968, Mid South Prodn. Co., 1970; chief exec. officer Memphis Am. Basketball Team, 1970. Founder Morris County Theatre League and Hightstown Little Theatre Group, 1961. Served with AUS, 1955-58. Roman Catholic.*

LYNN, OTIS CLYDE, army officer; b. Flynn's Lick, Tenn., Feb. 14, 1927; s. Dillard A. and Jennie Sue (Pruett) L.; student Vanderbilt U., 1944-45; B.G.E., U. Omaha, 1963; M.A., George Washington U., 1968; m. Jacque Gilbert, Mar. 17, 1946; children—Clyde Gilbert, Gary Jackson. Commd. 2d lt., U.S. Army, 1946, advanced through grades to maj. gen., 1972; mem. Office Joint Chiefs of Staff, Pentagon, 1969; chief of staff 2d Div., Korea, 1970; comdr. 1st Brigade 2d div., Korea, 1971; asst. div. comdr. 101st Div., Fort Campbell, Ky., 1974; chief of staff XVIII Airborne Corps, Fort Bragg, N.C., 1975; chief of staff U.S. Forces, Japan, 1975-78; comdg. gen. 25th Inf. Div., Schofield Barracks, Hawaii, 1978—. Decorated Silver Star with two oak leaf clusters, Legion of Merit, Bronze Star, Air Medal, Purple Heart. Mem. Assn. of U.S. Army. Mem. Ch. of Christ. Home: 227 General Loop Schofield Barracks HI 96786 Office: Comdg Gen 25th Inf Div Schofield Barracks HI 96857

LYNN, ROBERT ATHAN, univ. dean; b. Oak Park, Ill., Nov. 11, 1930; s. Harvey Leroy and Mabel (Brian) L.; B.S., Maryville Coll., 1951; M.S., U. Tenn., 1955; Ph.D., U. Ill., 1958; m. Naomi Burgos, Aug. 28, 1954; children—Mary Louise, Nancy Ruth, Judith Mae, Jo-an Ellen. From instr. to prof. Maryville Coll., 1955-64; asso. prof. econs. and bus. U. Mo. at Columbia, 1964-67, prof., 1967-68; resident dir. Whiteman AFB Grad. Program Bus., 1966-68; dean Coll. Bus. Adminstrn., Kan. State U., 1968—; comml. cons. radio sta. KSEW, Sitka, Alaska, 1961. Served with AUS, 1952-53; Korea. Ford fellow, 1956-58. Mem. Am. Mktg. Assn., Am., Midwest, So. econ. assns. Democrat. Rotarian. Author: Basic Economic Principles, 1965, 70, 74; Price Policies and Marketing Management, 1967; Marketing Principles and Market Action, 1969; also articles. Home: 1324 N 8th St Manhattan KS 66502

LYNN, ROBERT WOOD, educator; b. Wheatland, Wyo., Apr. 3, 1925; s. William McGregor and Janet (Reid) L.; A.B., Princeton U., 1948; B.D., Yale U., 1952; Th.D., Union Theol. Sem., N.Y.C., 1962; m. Katharine Mitchell Wuerth, Mar. 8, 1952; children—Thomas Taylor, Janet MacGregor, Elizabeth Mitchell, Sarah McKee. Ordained to ministry Presbyn. Ch., 1952; asst. minister Montview Presbyn. Ch., Denver, 1952-59; mem. faculty Union Theol. Sem., N.Y.C., 1959-75, dean Auburn program, 1960—, prof., 1965-75; v.p. Lilly Endowment, Inc., 1976—; vis. prof. Drew U., Andover Newton Theol. Sch., Fordham U., Tchrs. Coll. Columbia U. Served with AUS, 1943-44. Woodrow Wilson fellow, 1948-49; Presbyn. Grad. fellow, 1959-60. Author: Protestant Strategies in Education; co-author The Big Little School; also articles. Home: 6154 Forest View Dr Indianapolis IN 46208

LYNN, THOMAS NEIL, JR., physician, med. educator; b. Ft. Worth, Tex., Feb. 14, 1930; s. Thomas Neil and Florence Van Zandt (Jennings) L.; B.S., U. Okla., 1951, M.D., 1955; m. Virginia Carolyn Harsh, July 26, 1952; children—Thomas Neil, Leslie Elizabeth, Kathryn Barry. Intern Barnes Hosp., St. Louis, 1955-56, resident, 1956-57; clin. asso Nat. Heart Inst. NIH, Bethesda, Md., 1957-59; chief resident medicine U. Okla. Hosps., 1959-61; med. staff U. Hosps. and Clinics, 1970-72; staff Okla. Children's Meml. Hosp., Presbyn. Hosp., VA Hosp., Oklahoma City; instr. community health Okla. Med. Center, 1961—, asst. prof., 1961-63, asso. prof., 1963-67, prof., chmn. dept., 1970—, acting dean U. Okla. Coll. Medicine, 1974-76, dean, 1976—. Mem. governing bd. Okla. Physician Manpower Tng. Commn., Ambulatory Health Care Consortium, Inc.; mem. Okla. Bd. Medicolegal Examiners. Diplomate Am. Bd. Internal Medicine, Am. Bd. Preventive Medicine. Fellow Am. Coll. Preventive Medicine; mem. Am. Fedn. Clin. Research, Assn. Am. Med. Colls., AAAS, Assn. Tchrs. Preventive Medicine, AMA, Okla. Med. Assn., Oklahoma County Med. Soc. (trustee), Okla. Acad. Family Physicians, Am. Acad. Family Physicians. Sigma Xi, Alpha Omega Alpha, Phi Sigma, Alpha Tau Omega. Presbyn. Contbr. articles to profl. jours. Home: 3136 Pine Ridge Rd Oklahoma City OK 73120. *Individuals should live their life and conduct their affairs such that all succeeding generations will be benefitted and be glad that these people lived.*

LYNN, WALTER ROYAL, engr., ednl. adminstr.; b. N.Y.C., Oct. 1, 1928; s. Norman and Gussie (Gdalin) L.; B.S., U. Miami, 1950; M.S., U. N.C., 1955; Ph.D., Northwestern U., 1963; m. Barbara Lee Campbell, June 3, 1960; children—Michael Drew. Land surveyor Ehly Constrn. Co., Miami, Fla., 1950-51; chief party Rader Engring. Co., Miami, 1951; supt. sewage treatment, lectr. civil engring. U. Miami, 1951-53, asst. prof. mech. engring., 1954-55; asst. prof. civil engring., 1955-57, research asst. prof. marine lab., 1957-58, asso. prof. civil and indsl. engring., 1959-61; dir. research Ralph B. Carter Co., 1957-58; asso. prof. san. engring. Cornell U., Ithaca, N.Y., 1961-64, prof. civil and environ. engring., 1964—, dir. Center Environ. Quality Mgmt., 1966-76, dir. Sch. Civil and Environ. Engring., 1970-78, adj. prof. pub. health Med. Coll., 1971—; mem. spl. adv. commn. solid wastes NRC, 1968-76; com. to rev. Washington met. water supply study Nat. Acad. Engring., 1976—; cons. WHO, 1969—, Rockefeller Found., 1976—, SEARO, 1978. Chmn., Ithaca Mayor's Citizens Adv. Com., 1964-65, Ithaca Urban Renewal Agy., 1965-68. Served with AUS, 1946-48. Registered profl. engr., N.Y. State; registered land surveyor, Fla. Fellow ASCE; mem. AAAS, Inst. Mgmt. Sci., Ops. Research Soc. Am., Nat. Acad. Engrs. Mex. (corr.), Sigma Xi, Phi Kappa Phi. Editor: (with A. Charnes) Mathematical Analysis of Decision Problems in Ecology, 1975; asso. editor Jour. Ops. Research, 1968-76, Jour. Environ. Econs. and Mgmt. Contbr. chpt. to Human Ecology and Public Health, 1969. Home: 102 Iroquois Pl Ithaca NY 14850

LYNN, WILBERT, greeting card co. exec.; b. Berwick, Pa., Aug. 2, 1927; s. Wilbert G. and Hazel (Levan) L.; B.B.A., Pace U., 1950; m. Margaret T. Ferguson, July 1, 1951; children—Craig, Sharon. Auditor, Seidman & Seidman, N.Y.C., 1950-58; controller Union Bldg. & Investment Co., Passaic, N.J., 1958-59; in various auditing positions Curtiss Wright Corp., Woodridge, N.J., 1959-62; controller Hayden Pub. Co., N.Y.C., 1962-63; ops. controller Gen. Foods Corp. Post Div., Battlecreek, Mich., 1963-65; exec. v.p. corp., pres. Rust Greetings div. Rust Craft Greeting Cards, Inc., Dedham, Mass., 1965—. Pres. Woodland Acres Community Assn., Westwood, Mass., 1970; troop com. chmn. Boy Scouts Am., 1974-75. Served with USN, 19—. C.P.A., N.J. Episcopalian. Club: Masons (Ridgewood, N.J.). Home: 165 Alder Rd Westwood MA 02090 Office: Rust Craft Park Dedham MA 02026

LYNN, WILLIAM HARCOURT, advt. agy. exec.; b. N.Y.C., Feb. 17, 1931; s. William Harcourt and Helen (Martin) L.; B.A., U. Toronto (Ont., Can.), 1953; m. Gay Stirling, July 30, 1960; children—William Harcourt, III, Margaret Stirling. Vice pres. Batten, Barton, Durstine & Osborne Inc., N.Y.C.; exec. v.p. Am. Nat. Enterprises Inc., Salt Lake City; now sr. v.p. corp. Ketchum MacLeod & Grove Inc., N.Y.C. Vice pres., bd. dirs., mem. exec. com. U.S. Yacht Racing Union; mem. U.S. Olympic Yachting Com. Mem. Am. Advt. Agy. Assn. (vice chmn. broadcast council), Internat. Radio/TV Soc. (TV council), Nat. Assn. TV Program Execs. Clubs: N.Y. Yacht, Am. Yacht, Hopetown Harbor Sailing. Home: 64 Halls Ln Rye NY 10580 Office: 90 Park Ave New York NY 10016

LYNN, WILLIAM SANFORD, JR., pulmonologist; b. Clarendon, Va., June 14, 1922; s. William Sanford and Lois (Law) L.; M.D., Columbia U., 1946; m. Nov. 29, 1947; children—David, Peter, Melanie, Leslie. Intern, Duke U. Hosp., Durham, N.C.; resident Duke U. Hosp. and U. Pa., Phila.; instr. in biochemistry U. Pa., 1952-55; asst. prof. Duke U., 1956, asso. prof., to 1964, prof. medicine and biochemistry, 1964—. Served with U.S. Army, 1941-46. Markle scholar, 1955-59. Mem. Am. Soc. Biochemistry, Soc. Clin. Investigations, Am. Thoracic Soc. Democrat. Baptist. Contbr. numerous articles to profl. jours. Office: Duke U Durham NC 27710

LYNN, YEN-MOW, educator; b. Shanghai, China, Jan. 17, 1935; came to U.S., 1956, naturalized, 1969; s. Thuinli and Pao-Chiung (Tcheng) L.; B.S., Nat. Taiwan U., 1955; M.S., Calif. Inst. Tech., 1957, Ph.D., 1961; m. Helen Han, Sept. 5, 1964; children—Edward, Kirk, Genevieve. Asst., then asso. research scientist Courant Inst. Math. Scis., N.Y. U., 1960-64; asso. prof. Ill. Inst. Tech., 1964-67; asso. prof., then prof. math. U. Md., Baltimore County, 1967—, chmn. dept. math., 1976—; sr. resident research asso. Nat. Acad. Scis.-NRC, NASA Ames Research Center, summers 1966, 67; cons. NASA Ames Research Center, 1966, U.S. Army Ballistic Research Lab., 1969-75. Mem. Am. Math. Soc., Soc. Indsl. and Applied Math., Math. Assn. Am., Am. Phys. Soc., Am. Geophys. Union, AAAS. Contbr. articles to profl. jours. Office: 5401 Wilkens Ave Baltimore MD 21228

LYNNE, SEYBOURN HARRIS, judge; b. Decatur, Ala., July 25, 1907; s. Seybourn Arthur and Annie Leigh (Harris) L.; B.S., Ala. Polytechnic Inst., 1927; LL.B., U. Ala., 1930, LL.D., 1973; m. Katherine Donaldson Brandau, June 16, 1937; 1 dau., Katherine Roberta. Admitted to Ala. bar, 1930; gen. practice law, Decatur, Ala., 1930-34; judge Morgan (Ala.) County Ct., 1934-41, 8th Jud. Circuit Ct. Ala., 1941-42, U.S. Dist. Ct. No. Dist. Ala., 1946—, chief judge, 1953-73, sr. judge, 1973—. Served to lt. col., JAGC, U.S. Army, 1942-46. Decorated Bronze Star; named to Ala. Acad. Honor, 1978. Mem. Ala., Am. bar assns., Blue Key, Scabbard and Blade, Pi Kappa Alpha, Phi Kappa Phi, Phi Delta Phi, Omicron Delta Kappa, Alpha Phi Epsilon. Democrat. Baptist. Kiwanian (dist. gov. Ala. dist. 1938). Clubs: Birmingham Country, Univ. of Ala. A. Home: 3323 Briarcliff Rd Birmingham AL 35223 Office: Federal Bldg Birmingham AL 35203

LYNTON, ERNEST ALBERT, physicist, univ. ofcl.; b. Berlin, Germany, July 17, 1926; s. Arthur J. and Lizzie (Kiefe) Lowenstein; came to U.S., 1941, naturalized, 1945; B.S., Carnegie Inst. Tech., 1947, M.S., 1948; Ph.D., Yale, 1951; m. Carla Ellen Kaufmann, Aug. 4, 1953; children—David Michael, Eric Daniel. AEC postdoctoral fellow U. Leiden (Holland), 1951-52; faculty Rutgers U., 1952-74, prof. physics, 1962-74, dean Livingston Coll., 1965-73; sr. v.p. acad. affairs, Commonwealth prof. physics U. Mass., 1974—; vis. prof., Fulbright fellow U. Grenoble (France), 1959-60; cons. NSF, 1965-70; Ford Found., 1973. Mem. Commn. on Higher Edn. Middle States Assn., 1972-74; adv. bd. Princeton Sch. Architecture, 1971—; vis. com. Case Western Res. U., 1972-78. Pres., Princeton (N.J.) Jewish Center, 1964-66. Bd. dirs. Princeton Assn. Human Rights, 1962-65, Mercer County chpt. ACLU, 1966-70. Served with AUS, 1944-46. Fellow Am. Phys. Soc.; mem. AAUP, Sigma Xi. Author: Superconductivity, 3d edit., 1968 (translated into French, Russian, German); also articles. Home: 14 Allerton St Brookline MA 02146 Office: U Mass 250 Stuart St Boston MA 02116

LYNTON, HAROLD S., lawyer; b. N.Y.C., Nov. 2, 1909; A.B. magna cum laude, Yale, 1929; LL.B. cum laude, Harvard, 1932. Admitted to N.Y. bar, 1933, U.S. Supreme Ct. bar, 1947; now mem. firm Shea & Gould; dir., adv. bd. mem. Collier Cos., Naples, Fla. Served with AUS, 1943-45. Mem. Am., N.Y. State bar assns., Assn. Bar City N.Y., New York County Lawyers Assn. Phi Beta Kappa. Office: 330 Madison Ave New York NY 10017

LYON, BRYCE DALE, educator, historian; b. Bellevue, Ohio, Apr. 22, 1920; s. E. Paul and Florence (Gundrum) L.; A.B., Baldwin-Wallace Coll., 1942; Ph.D., Cornell U., 1949; Pd.D. (hon.), 1972; m. Mary Elizabeth Lewis, June 3, 1944; children—Geoffrey P., Jacqueline M. Asst. prof. history U. Colo., 1949-51, Harvard, 1951-56; asso. prof. U. Ill. at Urbana, 1956-59; prof. U. Calif. at Berkeley, 1959-65; Barnaby and Mary Critchfield Keeney prof. history Brown U., 1965—, chmn. history dept., 1968—. Served with AUS and USAAF, 1942-46. Fellow Royal Hist. Soc., Am. Acad. Arts and Scis., Medieval Acad. Am.; mem. Econ. History Assn., Am. Hist. Assn., Conf. Brit. Studies. Author: Medieval Institutions, 1954; From Fief to Indenture, 1957; A History of the World, 1960; Constitutional and Legal History of Medieval England, 1960; Medieval History, 4th rev. edit., 1962; The High Middle Ages, 1964; The Middle Ages in Recent Historical Thought, 2d edit., 1965; Medieval Finance, 1967; The Origins of the Middle Ages, 1971; Henri Pirenne: A Biographical and Intellectual Study, 1974; The Journal de querre of Henri Pireene, 1976; Studies of West European Medieval Institutions, 1978. Home: 41 Laurel Ave Providence RI 02906

LYON, CECIL BURTON, internat. orgn. ofcl.; b. S.I., N.Y., Nov. 8, 1903; s. Edmund Burton and Emily (Vyse) L.; A.B., Harvard U., 1927; m. Elizabeth Sturgis Grew, Oct. 7, 1933; children—Alice E. Lyon Thompson, Lilla Cabot Lyon Girodias. Investment banker, N.Y.C., 1927-31; vice consul U.S. fgn. service, Havana, Cuba, 1931, Hong Kong, 1932; 3d sec. embassy, Tokyo, 1933, Peiping, China, 1933-38; 3d and 2d sec., Santiago, Chile, 1938-42; with Dept. State, 1942-44; 1st sec., Cairo, 1944-46; spl. asst. to asst. sec. of state for polit. affairs, 1947-48; counselor of embassy, Warsaw, Poland, 1948-50; assigned Nat. War Coll., 1950-51; dep. comdt. office U.S. High Commr. for Germany, Berlin, 1951-54; dir. office German affairs, State Dept., 1954-55, dep. asst. sec. of state Inter-Am. Affairs, 1955-56; U.S. ambassador to Chile, 1956-58, Sri Lanka, 1964-67; minister to France, 1958-64; v.p. Internat. Rescue Com. Hon. bd. dirs. Henry St. Settlement, N.Y.C., Harris Found., Hancock, N.H. Roman Catholic. Clubs: Met., Alibi (Washington); Harvard, Brook (N.Y.C.). Home: Hancock NH 03449 Office: Internat Rescue Com 386 Park Ave S New York NY 10016

LYON, CHARLES STUART, lawyer; b. Atlanta, N.Y., Nov. 24, 1916; s. Hyatt H. and Laura B. (Cotton) L.; A.B., Swarthmore Coll., 1937; LL.B., Columbia U., 1941; m. Isabel Logan, Nov. 27, 1943; children—Charles Brooks, Jonathan Winslow, Emily Morgan. Admitted to Pa. bar, 1942, N.Y. State bar, 1943, U.S. Supreme Ct. bar, 1952; asso. firm Morgan, Lewis & Bockius, Phila., 1941-42, Alvord & Alvord, N.Y.C., 1942-46; trial atty., dep. chief counsel prosecution of war crimes, Nuremberg, 1946-48; partner firm Skadden, Arps, Slate & Lyon, 1948-51; asst. counsel, chief counsel King subcom. Ways and Means Com., Ho. of Reps., 1951-52; asst. atty. gen. tax div. Dept. Justice, 1952-53; partner firm Spence & Hotchkiss, N.Y.C., 1953-54; practiced in N.Y.C., 1954—; lectr. fed. taxation N.Y. U., 1955-56, prof. law, 1956—. Mem. Am. Bar Assn. Presbyterian. Contbr. articles to profl. jours. Home: 20 W 16th St New York NY 10011

LYON, DAVID NATHANIEL, educator; b. Altoona, Kans., Apr. 15, 1919; s. George Granville and Lola (Kemp) L.; A.B., U. Mo., 1940, M.A., 1942; Ph.D., U. Calif. at Berkeley, 1948; m. M. Bernece Bailey, 1942; children—Ellen Louise, John Clark. Research asso. U. Calif. at Berkeley, 1948-52, research chemist, 1953-58, research chem. engr., 1958, prof. chem. engring., 1965—, asst. dean Coll. Chemistry, 1969-72. Vis. mem. tech. staff Bell Telephone Labs., 1963-64; cons. low temperature engring. and processes, 1954—. Pres., Giauque Sci. Papers Found., 1966—. Mem. Am. Chem. Soc., Am. Inst. Chem. Engrs., AAAS, N.Y. Acad. Scis., Sigma Xi, Phi Beta Kappa. Home: 1103 Sutter St Berkeley CA 94707

LYON, ELIJAH WILSON, coll. pres. emeritus, historian; b. Heidelberg, Miss., June 6, 1904; s. Rufus and Willia (Wilson) L.; B.A., U. Miss., 1925; B.A. (Rhodes scholar), Oxford (Eng.) U., 1927, B. Litt. (Rhodes scholar), 1928; Ph.D., U. Chgo., 1932; LL.D., Colgate U., 1945, U. Calif., 1958, Grinnell Coll., 1966, Clarement Men's Coll., 1967, Coll. Idaho, 1967; D.Litt., Occidental Coll., 1947, U. Redlands, 1968; L.H.D., Trinity Coll., 1955, Claremont Grad. Sch., 1968, Hamilton Coll., 1974, Pomona Coll., 1974; m. Carolyn M. Bartel, Aug. 26, 1933; children—Elizabeth (Mrs. Julian Pierce Webb), John Wilson. Asst. prof. La. Poly. Inst., 1928-29; from asst. prof. to prof. history Colgate U., 1929-41; pres. Pomona Coll., Claremont, Calif., 1941-69, now pres. emeritus. Chmn. bd. Adam H. Bartel Co., Richmond, Ind. Tchr. summer sch. Syracuse U., 1935-36, U. Rochester, 1940, U. Mo., 1941; chmn. commn. on coll. students Am. Council Edn., 1957-58, chmn. commn. on lang. and area centers, 1960-61, mem. commn. on fed. relations, 1960-63, mem. overseas liaison com., 1962-68; mem. Nat. Commn. on Accrediting, 1957-60; mem. Pacific Regional Com. for Marshall scholarships, 1960-66; mem. vis. com. on coll. U. Chgo. Mem. Cal. Spl. Crime Study Commn. on Organized Crime, 1951-52. Trustee Pacific Sch. Religion, Pomona Coll. (hon.), Latin Am. scholarship program of Am. Univs., 1968-71, John Randolph Haynes and Dora Haynes Found., Inst. Internat. Edn. (hon.); bd. dirs. Th. R. Knudsen and Valley M. Knudsen Found. Recipient Alumni medal U. Chgo., 1967, award Am. Acad. Achievement, 1968; named to Hall of Fame, U. Miss., 1975; decorated hon. comdr. Order Brit. Empire. Grantee Social Sci. Research Council, 1937. Mem. Western Coll. Assn. (pres. 1943-44), Am. Council Learned Socs. (Pacific Coast com. on humanities 1947-58), Am., So. hist. assns., Orgn. Am. Historians, La., Miss., So. Calif. hist. socs., Council Fgn. Relations, Town Hall, Phi Beta Kappa, Beta Theta Pi. Conglist. Clubs: California, University (Los Angeles); University (Pasadena). Author: Louisiana in French Diplomacy (1759-1804), 1934, rev. edit., 74; The Man Who Sold Louisiana, The Life of François Barbé-Marbois, 1942, revised edit., 74; The History of Pomona Coll., 1977. Editor: The History of Louisiana by François Barbé-Marbois, 1977; bd. editors Jour. Modern History, 1943-46. Contbr essays and critical revs. to hist. and coll. jours. Editor: The Am. Oxonian, 1956-62. Home: 534 W 12th St Claremont CA 91711

LYON, EUGENE DAVISSON, dentist; b. Balt., Apr. 22, 1913; s. Guy Orval and Gladys (Davisson) L.; A.B., Johns Hopkins, 1933; D.D.S., U. Md., 1938; M.S., U. Minn., 1942; m. Doris Eleanor Miller, June 17, 1939; children—Elizabeth Gale, Wendy Louise. Intern Johns Hopkins Hosp., 1938-39, asso. dental surgeon in charge, 1946-50, dental surgeon in charge, 1950—; asst. prof. dental surgery Johns Hopkins Sch. Medicine, Balt., 1965—; fellow dental surgery Mayo Clinic, 1939-42. Served as maj., Dental Corps, AUS, 1942-45. Diplomate Am. Bd. Oral Surgery. Mem. Am. Coll. Dentists, ADA, Balt. City Dental Soc. (pres. 1959-60), Am., Mid-Atlantic (pres. 1954) socs. oral surgeons, Johns Hopkins Med. and Chirurg. Soc., Alumni Assn. Mayo Found. Med. Edn. and Research, Psi Omega, Omicron Kappa Upsilon, Sigma Phi Epsilon. Methodist. Home: 5710 Stony Run Dr Baltimore MD 21210 Office: 200 Towsontown Blvd Baltimore MD 21204

LYON, FRED WILLIAM, news agency exec.; b. Atlanta, Mar. 7, 1929; s. Fred William and Gladys (Perry) L.; B.B.A., Ga. State U., 1959; m. 2d, Deborah Lane, Sept. 5, 1977; children by previous marriage—Anne Elizabeth, William Scott. With United Press Internat., 1944—, mgr. newspictures Atlanta Bur., 1957-62, So. div., 1962-69; gen. mgr. newspictures, N.Y.C., 1970-72, v.p. newspictures, 1972—. Served with U.S. Army, 1950-52. Mem. Nat. Press Photographers Assn., Sigma Delta Chi. Democrat. Lutheran. Home: 207 Coachlight Sq Montrose NY 10548 Office: 220 E 42d St New York City NY 10017

LYON, FREDERICK CHARLES, freight co. exec.; b. Salmon, Idaho, Dec. 5, 1939; s. C. Walker and Grace M. (Larsen) L.; B.S. in Bus., U. Idaho, 1962, J.D., 1964; m. Diana L. Burns, Sept. 26, 1964; children—Julie, Michael. Pros. atty. Lemhi County (Idaho), 1964-67; corp. counsel Garrett Freightlines, Inc., Pocatello, Idaho, 1967—, v.p., sec., 1970—, gen. counsel, 1978—. Mem. Phi Alpha Delta, Alpha Kappa Psi, Beta Theta Pi. Clubs: Pocatello Golf and Country, Masons, Elks. Office: Garrett Freightlines Inc 2055 Garrett Way Pocatello ID 83201

LYON, GEORGE MARSHALL, sr. ret. physician; b. Union City, Pa., Feb. 8, 1895; s. Marshall Allen and Harriet Bell (Law) L.; tchr. tng. Marshall Coll., Huntington, W.Va., 1909-13; B.S., Denison U., 1916, D.Sc. (hon.), 1956; M.D., Johns Hopkins, 1920; m. Virginia Sutherland, June 24, 1922 (dec. June 1926); children—Virgina (Mrs. B. McCraw), Natalie (Mrs. E.J. Olmi, Jr.), Elizabeth (Mrs. J. Miller, Jr.); m. 2d, Theeta Carrington Searcy, July 29, 1927; 1 son, George Marshall. Resident house officer Harriet Lane Home, Johns Hopkins Hosp., 1919-21; pediatrician Holzer, Huntington Meml., St. Mary's hosps., 1921-42; dir. sch. health and sch. health edn. program Cabell County pub. schs., 1933-39; lectr. clin. grad. confs., Va., 1934, 35, W.Va., 1936, 37, Miss., 1938; cons. nuclear medicine VA Hosp., Miami, 1967—. Chmn., W.Va. White Ho. Conf. Child Health and Protection, 1933; ofcl. del. U.S. Govt. to 7th Pan-Am. Congress on the Child, Mexico City, 1935; adv. com. on maternal and child health Children's Bur., Dept. Labor, 1936-42; mem. joint com. health problems in edn. NEA-AMA, 1940-50 (chmn. 1949); spl. asst. atomic medicine Office Chief Med. Dir. and chief radioisotope sect. VA, 1947-52, asst. chief med. dir. research and edn., 1952-56; dir. VA Hosp., 1956-64; tech. adviser and cons. numerous govtl. and pvt. orgns. including NSRB, USN; safety officer and rep. surgeon gen. staff CJTF-ONE (Bikini Tests), 1946-47. Commd. lt. comdr. M.C. USNR, 1935, comdr., 1940, capt., 1942; chem. warfare offioer, staff comdr. U.S. Naval Forces in Europe, 1942-44; safety officer liquid thermal diffusion plant Navy Yard, Phila., 1944-46; chief div. atomic def. USN Bur. Medicine and Surgery, 1947. Decorated USN Legion of Merit with gold star, Bronze Star with combat V. Recipient Exceptional Service award VA, 1956. Fellow Am. Acad. Pediatrics Am. Coll. Nuclear Medicine (hon.); mem. Radiation Research Soc., AMA, Am. Pediatric Soc. Republican. Presbyn. Mason. Author numerous articles in field. Determined minimal lethal concentration of mustard gas for Chem. Warfare Service, U.S. Army, 1918. Address: 1400 Dale Ln Delray Beach FL 33444. *A wonderful widowed mother, father having died when I was six years old. Inspiring and helpful teachers at Marshall College, Denison University, and Johns Hopkins Medical School. (Many of the latter university have had a lifelong influence—personal as well as professional.) Exceptional opportunities for involvement in a golden age of medicine and in military service.*

LYON, GEORGE ROBERT, advt. exec.; b. N.Y.C., Feb. 13, 1923; s. Gordon and Gladys (Dempsey) L.; student Coll. City N.Y., 1943, Syracuse U., 1943; m. Jacqueline Jacobson, Apr. 27, 1950; children—Maureen, Patrice, Dana Jean. With advt. dept. Sterling Drug Co., 1939-43; v.p. Fuller & Smith & Ross, 1947-66; chmn. Conahay & Lyon, Inc., N.Y.C., 1965—. Bd. dirs. Adoption and Childrens Services of Westchester. Served with AUS, 1943-46. Mem. Am. Assn. Advt. Agys. (gov. Eastern region). Conglist. Club: Scarsdale Golf. Home: 15 Whig Rd Scarsdale NY 10583 Office: 380 Madison Ave New York NY 10017

LYON, HARVEY WILLIAM, dentist; b. Chgo., May 20, 1920; s. Harvey Cady and Christina (Brown) L.; B.S., Marquette U., 1942, D.D.S., 1945; M.S., Georgetown U., 1951, Ph.D., 1956; m. Margaret Ann Siggelkow, Apr. 26, 1946; children—Mark, Leslie, Karin. Commd. lt. (j.g.) Dental Corps, USN, 1943, advanced through grades to capt., 1960; ret., 1965; dir. clin. research, also sec. Council Dental Research, ADA, Chgo., 1965-79; cons., 1979—; cons. U.S. Naval Dental Research Inst., 1966—; research asso. Northwestern U. Dental Sch., 1968-76; mem. exec. com., div. med. scis. NRC, 1968-76. Fellow Am. Coll. Dentists, AAAS (council); mem. ADA, Fedn. Dentaire Internat. (research cons., editorial bd.), Electron Microprobe Soc. Am., European Soc. Caries Research, Internat. Assn. Dental Research, Odontographic Soc. Chgo., Alpha Chi, Psi Omega. Republican. Club: Dad's (Glenbrook, Ill.). Contbr. articles to profl. jours. Home and Office: 788 Taylor Ln Stoughton WI 53589

LYON, JAMES BURROUGHS, lawyer; b. N.Y.C., May 11, 1930; s. Francis Murray and Edith May (Strong) L.; B.A., Amherst Coll., 1952; LL.B., Yale U., 1955. Admitted to Conn. bar, 1955, U.S. Tax Ct. bar, 1970; asst. football coach Yale U., 1953-55; asso. firm Murtha, Cullina, Richter and Pinney and predecessor, Hartford, Conn., 1956-61, partner, 1961—; mem. adv. com., lectr. and session leader N.Y. U. Inst. on Fed. Taxation, 1973—. Trustee, Kingswood-Oxford Sch., West Hartford, Conn., 1961—, chmn. bd. trustees, 1975-78; trustee Old Sturbridge Vill. (Mass.), 1974—; trustee Wadsworth Atheneum, 1968—, v.p. 1973—. Recipient medal for eminent service Amherst Coll., 1967. Mem. Greater Hartford C. of C. (co-chmn. sports and recreation com.), Hartford County Bar Assn., Conn. Bar Assn. (lectr. continuing legal edn. programs 1963—), Am. Bar Assn., Assn. Bar City N.Y., Conn. Bar Found. (dir. 1975—), Phi Beta Kappa. Republican. Roman Catholic. Clubs: Hartford, Hartford Golf, Univ. (pres. 1976-78), Tennis (Hartford); Yale, Union (N.Y.C.); Limestone Trout (East Canaan, Conn.); Dauntless (Essex, Conn.). Home: 25 Bishop Rd West Hartford CT 06119 Office: 101 Pearl St Hartford CT 06103

LYON, JOHN DAVID, lawyer, oil co. exec.; b. Tulsa, Feb. 16, 1937; s. Buford Carl and Mary Louise (Cochrane) L.; B.A., U. Chgo., 1955; J.D., Harvard, 1960; m. Melinda Frances Mitchell, June 16, 1972. Admitted to N.Y. bar, 1962, Calif. bar, 1974; asso. firm Paul, Weiss, Rifkind, Wharton & Garrison, N.Y.C., 1961-65; with Tosco Corp., 1965—, v.p., gen. counsel, 1970-75, exec. v.p., Los Angeles, 1975—, also dir.; pres. Lion Oil Co., 1976-77. Mem. Assn. Bar City N.Y., Los Angeles County Bar Assn. Democrat. Office: 10100 Santa Monica Blvd Los Angeles CA 90067

LYON, RICHARD HAROLD, educator, physicist; b. Evansville, Ind., Aug. 24, 1929; s. Chester Clyde and Gertrude (Schucker) L.; A.B., Evansville Coll., 1952; Ph.D. in Physics (Owens-Corning fellow), Mass. Inst. Tech., 1955; D.Eng., U. Evansville, 1976; m. Jean Wheaton; children—Katherine Ruth, Geoffrey Cleveland, Suzanne Marie. Mem. research staff Mass. Inst. Tech., 1955-56, lectr. mech. engring., 1963-69, prof. mech. engring., 1970—; asst. prof. elec. engring. U. Minn., 1956-59; NSF postdoctoral fellow U. Manchester (Eng.), 1959-60; sr. scientist Bolt, Beranek & Newman, Cambridge, 1960-66, v.p., 1966-70; chmn. Cambridge Collaborative, Inc., 1972; v.p. Grozier Pub., Inc., 1972; pres. Grozier Tech. Systems, 1976. Bd. dirs. Boston Light Opera, Ltd., 1975. Fellow Acoustical Soc. Am. (asso. editor Jour. 1967-74, exec. council 1976-79); mem. Sigma Xi, Sigma Pi Sigma. Author: Transportation Noise, 1974; Theory and Applications of Statistical Energy Analysis, 1975. Research, publs. in fields of nonlinear random oscillations, energy transfer in complex structures, sound transmission in marine and aerospace vehicles, bldg. acoustics, environ. noise. Home: 60 Prentiss Ln Belmont MA 02178 Office: Room 3-366 Mass Inst Tech Cambridge MA 02139

LYON, ROGER ADRIAN, banker; b. Phillipsburg, N.J., June 28, 1927; s. Howard Suydam and Mildred (Derry) L.; B.A., Princeton, 1950; M.B.A., Rutgers U., 1954, postgrad. Stonier Grad. Sch. Banking, 1959; m. Mary Woodford, June 17, 1950; children—Nancy Carol, Roger Adrian. With Chase Nat. Bank (now Chase Manhattan Bank), N.Y.C., 1950-76, ofcl. staff, 1954-76, sr. v.p. bank portfolio group, 1969-72, exec. v.p. instl. banking dept., 1972-76; exec. v.p. Chase Manhattan Corp., 1972-76; pres. Valley Nat. Bank, Phoenix, 1976—; mem. adv. bd. Mountain Bell, 1979; instr. Stonier Grad. Sch. Banking, 1960-72. Pres. East Jersey Bd. Proprs., 1972-76; chmn. Phoenix Pvt. Industry Council, 1979; met. Phoenix chmn. Nat. Alliance of Bus., 1979; trustee Nat. YMCA, 1964-76, mem. adminstrv. com., exec. com. fin. and budget, 1966-76, nat. treas., 1973-76; bd. dirs. Heard Mus. Served with USMCR, 1945-46, 51, 52. Mem. Am. Bankers Assn. (chmn. corr. bank div. 1973-75, treas. 1975-77). Author: Commercial Bank Investment Portfolio Management, 1960. Home: 4434 Clearwater Pkwy Paradise Valley AZ 85253 Office: Valley Nat Bank PO Box 71 Phoenix AZ 85001

LYON, SCOTT CALVIN, economist, govt. ofcl.; b. Columbus, Ohio, Aug. 18, 1912; s. Clarence Calvin and Anna Luella (Scott) L.; B.Ch.E., Ohio State U., 1934; postgrad., Mass. Inst. Tech., 1936-38, Russian Inst., Columbia, 1947-48; m. Nancy Otis Wilson, June 5, 1948; children—David Laurence, Peter Scott, Stephen Otis. Chem. engr. Standard Oil Co. N.J., 1934-36; fgn. service officer Dept. of State, serving Lisbon, Horta, Sao Vicente, Antwerp, Brussels, Mexico City, Vladivostok, Moscow, Bad Nauheim, Munich and Washington, from 1940, acting chief Soviet orbit staff USIA, 1955-57, pub. affairs advisor Office Eastern European Affairs, Dept. State, Washington, 1957-58, dep. dir. East-West contacts staff, 1958-59; prin. econ. officer, Consulate Gen., São Paulo, Brazil, 1959-62, dep. prin. officer, from 1962; internat. economist Office Trade Policy, Dept. Treasury, Washington, 1974—. Served as lt. F.A. Res., U.S. Army, 1933-42. Mem. Sigma Nu, Tau Beta Pi, Phi Lambda Upsilon. Address: 13 Oxford St Chevy Chase MD 20015

LYON, STERLING RUFUS, premier Man. (Can.); b. Windsor, Ont., Can., Jan. 30, 1927; s. David Rufus and Ella Mae (Cuthbert) L.; B.A., U. Winnipeg, 1948; LL.B., U. Man., 1953; m. Barbara Jean Mayers, Sept. 26, 1953; children—Nancy, Andrea, Peter, Jennifer, Jonathan. Admitted to Man. bar, 1953; crown atty., dept. atty. gen. Man.,

1953-57; partner firm Bowles, Christie & Lyon, 1957-58; mem. Man. Legis. Assembly, 1958-69; atty. gen. Man., 1958-63, minister of municipal affairs, 1960-61, of pub. utilities, 1961-63, of mines and natural resources, 1963-66, of tourism and recreation, 1966-68, commr. No. affairs, 1966-68; leader Progressive Conservative Party, 1975—; mem. Man. Legis. Assembly from Souris-Killarney, 1976-77, for Charleswood, 1977; premier of Man., 1977—; chmn. econ. devel. com. Cabinet; chmn. 1st Canadian Conf. on Pollution, Montreal, 1966; pres. Can. Council Resource Ministers, 1965-66; del. Hague Conf. on Pvt. Internat. Law, 1968. Former trustee Wildlife Found. Man., N.Am. Wildlife Found.; bd. regents U. Winnipeg. Served in RCAF Res., 1950-53. Recipient U. Winnipeg Alumni Assn. Jubilee award, 1973; created Queen's Counsel, 1960. Mem. Law Soc. Man., Canadian., Man. bar assns. Mem. United Ch. Can. Club: Winnipeg Trap and Skeet. Office: Office of Premier Legislative Bldg Winnipeg MB R3C 0V8 Canada*

LYON, WALDO KAMPMEIER, physicist; b. Los Angeles, May 19, 1914; s. Charles R. and Anna (Kampmeier) L.; A.B., U. Calif. at Los Angeles, 1936, M.A., 1937, Ph.D., 1941; m. Virginia Louise Backus, Aug. 28, 1937; children—Lorraine Mae, Russell Roy. Research physicist, head submarine and Arctic research br. U.S. Naval Electronics Lab., 1941-66, sr. scientist wave measurement group Bikini Atom Bomb Test, 1946, submarine physicist USN-Byrd Antarctic Expdn., 1946, chief sci. Joint U.S.-Canadian Beaufort Sea Sci. Expdns., 1950-54, chief scientist Arctic submarine research, 1964—, dir. Arctic Submarine Lab., 1966—; lectr., physicist U. Calif. at Los Angeles, 1948-49; sr. scientist 1st submarine polar transit Arctic Ocean, U.S.S. Nautilus, 1958 1st winter North Pole transit U.S.S. Skate, 1959, 1st transpolar N.W. passage, U.S.S. Sea Dragon, 1960, sr. scientist 1st dual submarine North Pole expdn., 1962; chief scientist North Pole Submarine Expdns. by Queenfish, 1967, Whale, 1969, Hammer-head, 1971, Hawkbill, 1973, Bluefish, 1975, Gurnard, 1976, Flying Fish, 1977, Pintado, 1978, Archerfish, 1979. Recipient Disting. Civilian Service award U. S. Navy, 1955, 58, Dept. Def., 1956, President's Distinguished Federal Civilian Service award, 1962; Edward Dickson U. Calif. at Los Angeles Alumnus award, 1963; Gold medal award Am. Soc. Naval Engrs., 1959. Fellow Am. Phys. Soc., Arctic Inst. N.Am., Acoustical Soc. Am., AAAS; mem. Am. Soc. Naval Engrs. (hon. life), Am. Geophys. Union, Brit. Glaciological Soc., Am. Badminton Assn. (pres. 1966-68), Nat. (com. polar research), N.Y. (life) acads. scis., Sigma Xi. Home: 1330 Alexandria Dr San Diego CA 92107 Office: Arctic Submarine Lab Naval Ocean Systems Center San Diego CA 92152

LYONS, CHAMP, JR., lawyer; b. Boston, Dec. 6, 1940; A.B., Harvard U., 1962; LL.B., U. Ala., 1965; m. Emily Lee Oswalt, 1967; children—Emily Olive, Champ III. Admitted to Ala. bar, 1965, U.S. Supreme Ct. bar, 1973; law clk. U.S. Dist. Ct., Mobile, Ala., 1965-67; asso. firm Capell, Howard, Knabe & Cobbs, Montgomery, Ala., 1967-70, partner firm, 1970-76; partner firm Coale, Helmsing, Lyons & Sims, Mobile, 1976—; mem. advisory commn. on civil procedure Ala. Supreme Ct., 1971—. Mem. Am., Ala. bar assns., Am., Ala. law insts., Farrah Law Soc. Author: Alabama Practice, 1973; contbr. articles to law jours. Home: 229 Ridgelawn Dr E Mobile AL 36608 Office: 2750 1st Nat Bank Bldg PO Box 2767 Mobile AL 36601

LYONS, CHARLES A., JR., univ. chancellor; b. Conetoe, N.C., Apr. 5, 1926; student Columbia, summer 1948; A.B., Shaw U., Raleigh, N.C., 1949; M.A., Ohio State U., 1954, Ph.D., 1957; postgrad. Johns Hopkins, summer 1952, Gokhale Inst. Politics and Econs., India, 1954-55, Harvard, 1962; m. Rosa Dance; children—Sheila, Brenda, Charles Herbert. Tchr. English and social studies Raleigh Pub. Schs., 1949-50; teaching grad. asst. dept. polit. sci. Ohio State U., 1951-56; asso. prof. polit. sci. Grambling (La.) Coll., 1956-59; prof. polit. sci. and history Elizabeth City (N.C.) State Coll., 1959-62, dean of coll., 1959-62; exec. sec. N.C. Tchrs. Assn., Raleigh, 1962-64; dir. admissions Howard U., Washington, 1964-69; pres. Fayetteville (N.C.) State U., 1969-72, chancellor, 1972—. Cons., Commn. on Instructional Tech., Washington, 1968, Josiah Macy, Jr. Found. Conf., Washington, 1968; mem. TACTICS, Positive Futures, Inst. on Policy Commn., Washington, Internat. Service to Edn., N.Y.C.; pres. Nat. Assn. for Equal Opportunity in Higher Edn., 1974—. Chmn. edn. com. Grambling Fed. Credit Union; charter mem. Civil Improvement Com., Grambling, 1956-59; chmn. coll. sect. Pasquotank United Fund Campaign, Elizabeth City; chmn. negro community sect. Cancer Fund Drive, Elizabeth City, 1959-62; sec.-treas. Pasquotank County br. NAACP, Elizabeth City, 1959-62, mem. exec. com. Raleigh br., 1962-64; chmn. Citizens Coordinating Com. for Equal Opportunity in Pub. Accommodations and Employment, Raleigh; vice chmn. Mayor's Community Relations Com., Raleigh, 1962-64; chmn. sch. and community relations com. Project OPEN; mem. S.E. Community Edn. Planning Council, Washington, 1964-69. Pres., chmn. bd. dirs. Investment Research Orgn., Inc.; vice-chmn. bd. trustees Opportunity Project for Edn. NOW. Served with AUS. Recipient Fulbright travel research grant to India, 1954, Alumni Achievement award Ohio State U., 1974. Mem. Am., Middle States assns. collegiate registrars and admissions officers, Assn. Coll. Admissions Counselors, Am. Polit. Sci. Assn., NEA, Assn. for Study Negro Life and History, Am. Assn. State Colls. and Univs., Fayetteville Area C. of C., Alpha Kappa Mu, Sigma Rho Sigma, Pi Sigma Alpha, Phi Alpha Theta. Baptist. Club: Civitan (Fayetteville). Editor jour. and newsletter N.C. Tchrs. Assn., 1962-64. Address: Fayetteville State U Fayetteville NC 28301

LYONS, CLIFFORD PIERSON, educator; b. Chgo., Oct. 5, 1904; s. Charles and Ina (Pierson) L.; A.B., Cornell Coll., Mt. Vernon, Iowa, 1925, Litt.D., 1953; postgrad. U. Chgo., summers 1927-29; Ph.D., Johns Hopkins U., 1932; m. Gladys M. Hart, Sept. 4, 1928. Instr. English, speech, athletics, secondary schs., Berea (Ky.) Coll., 1925-28; prin. acad. Lincoln Meml. U. Harrogate, Tenn., 1928-29; instr. English, Johns Hopkins, 1930-36; prof. English, head dept. U. Fla., 1936-46, chmn. div. lang. and lit., 1939-46; prof. English, U. N.C., 1946-61, Kenan prof. English, 1961-74, prof. emeritus, 1974—, head dept. English, 1946-52, dean Coll. Arts and Scis., 1951-54, sec. faculty, 1966-69. Mem. English lit. com. Selection Fulbright Fellowships, 1954-57. Served as lt. comdr. USNR 1942-45. Mem. Modern Lang. Assn. Am. (exec. council 1953-56), Southeastern Renaissance Conf. (pres. 1964), Coll. English Assn., AAUP, Assn. U. Profs., South Atlantic Modern Lang. Assn. (pres. 1939), Phi Beta Kappa, Phi Gamma Delta. Democrat. Episcopalian (sr. warden, pres. Durham-Orange County council). Clubs: Tudor and Stuart (Johns Hopkins); Chapel Hill Golf and Country. Co-founder, asso. editor ELH, Jour. English Literary History, 1934-54; asso. editor South Atlantic Bull., 1939-50; editorial bd. Studies in Philology, 1950-73. Contbr. articles, revs. to prof. jours. Home: 716 Greenwood Rd Chapel Hill NC 27514 Office: Dept English U NC Chapel Hill NC 27514

LYONS, DANIEL EDWARD, diversified co. exec.; b. Los Angeles, Apr. 19, 1928; s. Edward James and Ethel (Coldwater) L.; B.B.A., Loyola U. (Calif.), 1950; M.B.A., U. So. Calif., 1952; m. Evelyn Marie Zamboni, Feb. 4, 1951; children—Robert Patrick, Mary Colleen, Daniel Christopher, Thomas Peter, Edward Charles, Joseph Michael. Vice-pres., treas. Huddle Enterprises, Los Angeles, 1959-61, v.p. Marnel Devel. Co., San Diego, 1961-63; mgr. investments Litton Industries Inc., Los Angeles, 1963-66; v.p. fin. City Investing Co., Beverly Hills, Calif., 1966-72, exec. v.p., chief fin. officer, N.Y.C., 1972—, also dir.; dir. GDV, Inc., Armada Corp., Korn/Ferry Internat. Served with USMCR, 1946-48. Home: 320 The Strand Manhattan Beach CA 90266 Office: 9100 Wilshire Blvd Beverly Hills CA 90212

LYONS, DAVID BARRY, educator; b. N.Y.C., Feb. 6, 1935; s. Joseph and Betty (Janower) L.; student Cooper Union, 1952-54, 56-57; B.A., Bklyn. Coll., 1960; M.A. (Gen. Electric Found. fellow), Harvard U., 1963, PH.D. (Woodrow Wilson dissertation fellow), 1963; postgrad. Oxford (Eng.) U., 1963-64; m. Sandra Yetta Nemiroff, Dec. 18, 1955; children—Matthew, Emily, Jeremy. Asst. prof. philosophy Cornell U., Ithaca, N.Y., 1964-67, asso. prof., 1967-71, prof. philosophy, 1971—, chmn. dept. philosophy, 1978—, prof. law, 1979—. Recipient Clark award Cornell U., 1976; Woodrow Wilson hon. fellow, 1960-61; Knox traveling fellow, 1963-64; Guggenheim fellow, 1970-71; Soc. for Humanities fellow, 1972-73; Nat. Endowment for Humanities fellow, 1977-78. Mem. Am. Philos. Assn., Am. Assn. Polit. and Legal Philosophy, Soc. Philosophy and Public Affairs, Aristotelian Soc. Author: Forms and Limits of Utilitarianism, 1965; In the Interest of the Governed, 1973; Rights, 1978; editor Philos. Rev., 1968-70, 73-75. Home: 309 Mitchell St Ithaca NY 14850 Office: Dept Philosophy Cornell U Ithaca NY 14853

LYONS, DENNIS GERALD, lawyer; b. Passaic, N.J., Nov. 20, 1931; s. Denis A.G. and Agnes C. (Dyt) L.; A.B., Holy Cross Coll., 1952; J.D., Harvard U., 1955; children—Andrew, Sarah, Tessa. Admitted to D.C. bar, 1955, N.Y. bar, 1956, U.S. Supreme Ct., 1960; law clk. U.S. Supreme Ct., Washington, 1958-60; asso. firm Arnold & Porter, Washington, 1960-62, partner, 1963—; v.p., gen. counsel, dir. Gulf United Corp., Jacksonville, Fla., 1968—; asst. sec. Braniff Airways, Dallas, 1966-77; trustee GMR Properties, Boston. Served with USAF, 1955-58. Mem. Am. Law Inst., Am. Bar Assn. Pres., Harvard Law Rev., 1954-55. Home: 2500 Virginia Ave NW Washington DC 20037 Office: 1229 19th St NW Washington DC 20036

LYONS, ELLIS, lawyer; b. Scranton, Pa., Mar. 24, 1915; s. Charles and Anna (Abrams) L.; student U. Scranton, 1933-34; A.B. (Coll. scholar), Oberlin Coll., 1936; J.D. (Univ. fellow), Northwestern U., 1939; m. Anita Chester, June 18, 1952; children—Charles, Cathy. Admitted to D.C. bar,1939, U.S. Supreme Ct., 1946; atty. Dept. Justice, 1940-43, spl. asst. to U.S. Atty. Gen., 1945-50, chief legal cons. Dept. Justice, 1950-53; acting asst. atty. gen. U.S., 1952-53; partner firm Perlman, Lyons and Emmerglick and predecessors, Washington, 1953-65, Volpe, Boskey and Lyons, Washington, 1965—; inst. in bus. law Am. U., 1963-66; gen. counsel Am. Optometric Assn., Conf. Am. Renting and Leasing Assn.; gen. counsel, sec. Am. Automotive Leasing Assn., Am. Assn. Equipment Lessors. Served to lt. USCG, 1943-45. Mem. D.C. Bar, Bar Assn. D.C., Fed. Bar Assn., Am. Bar Assn., Am. Law Inst., Phi Beta Kappa, Tau Epsilon Rho. Jewish. Home: 4101 Blackthorn St Chevy Chase MD 20015 Office: Suite 602 918 16th St NW Washington DC 20006

LYONS, FRANCIS JOSEPH, banker; b. Phila., Nov. 3, 1921; s. John Thomas and Cecilia Catherine (Regan) L.; B.S., Georgetown U., 1950; LL.B., 1962; m. Rose Jordan, Nov. 28, 1953; children—Francis X., Mark J., Mary C. With Riggs Nat. Bank, Washington, 1950—, v.p., 1968-72, sr. v.p., trust officer 1972-77, exec. v.p., 1977—; mem. Washington Bd. Trade, 1965—. Treas., trustee Religious Edn. Found., Washington. Served with AUS, 1942-44. Decorated Bronze Star, Purple Heart. Mem. D.C. Bankers Assn. (chmn. fiduciaries 1971-72), Washington Soc. Investment Analysts, Va. Bar Assn. Roman Catholic. K.C., Clubs: Washington Golf and Country, Metropolitan, 1925 F Street. Home: 602 Upham Pl Vienna VA 22180 Office: 800 17th St NW Washington DC 20013

LYONS, FREDERICK WILLIAM, JR., pharm. co. exec.; b. Youngstown, Ohio, Nov. 7, 1935; s. Frederick William and Edith (Barnes) L.; B.S., U. Mich., 1957; M.B.A., Harvard U., 1959; m. Carol Lee deBruin, Aug. 30, 1957; children—Linda Kay, Stephen Frederick. Div. mgr. cost accounting and purchasing Alcon Labs., Inc., Fort Worth, 1959-61, salesman, 1961-62; dir. mktg. Conal Pharms., Inc., Chgo., 1962-64, gen. mgr., 1964-65, v.p., gen. mgr., 1965-70; v.p., gen. mgr. Marion Labs., Inc., Kansas City, Mo., 1970-72, sr. v.p., dir., pres. Pharm div., 1972-74, exec. v.p., dir., 1974-77, pres., chief operating officer, dir., 1977—; dir. Commerce Bank of Kansas City, N.A. Mem. nat. adv. council Ariz. Heart Inst. Mem. Pharm. Mfrs. Assn. (dir.), ACT Found., Rho Chi, Phi Kappa Phi, Phi Gamma Delta. Home: 5740 State Line Shawnee Mission KS 66208 Office: 10236 Bunker Ridge Rd Kansas City MO 64137

LYONS, GENE MARTIN, educator, polit. scientist; b. Revere, Mass., Feb. 29, 1924; s. Abraham M. and Mary (Karger) L.; B.A., Tufts Coll., 1947; license en Scis. Politiques, Inst. Internat. Studies, Geneva, Switzerland, 1949; Ph.D., Columbia, 1958; m. Micheline Pohl, Sept. 5, 1951; children—Catherine Anne, Daniel Eugene, Mark Lucien. Mgmt. officer Internat. Refugee Orgn., Geneva, 1948-52; budget and adminstrv. officer UN Korean Reconstrn. Agy., 1952-56; mem. faculty Dartmouth, 1957—, prof. govt., 1965—, dir. Pub. Affairs Center, 1961-66, 73-75, asso. dean faculty social scis., 1974-78; vis. lectr. Sch. Mgmt. Mass. Inst. Tech., 1961-70. Exec. sec. adv. com. govt. program behavioral scis. Nat. Acad. Scis., 1966-68; dir. dept. social scis. UNESCO, 1970-72, mem. U.S. Nat. Commn., 1975-80, vice chmn., 1977-78, adv. U.S. del. UNESCO 19th Gen. Conf., 1976, 20th Gen. Conf., 1978, U.S. rep. to European Conf., 1977. Served with AUS, 1943-46. Mem. Am. Polit. Sci. Assn., Internat. Studies Assn., AAUP. Author: Military Policy and Economic Aid: The Korean Case, 1961; (with J.W. Masland) Education and Military Leadership, 1959; (with L. Morton) Schools For Strategy, 1965; The Uneasy Partnership, 1969. Editor: Social Research and Public Politics, 1975. Editor, contbr. America: Purpose and Power, 1965; Social Science and the Federal Government, 1971. Home: Main St Norwich VT 05055 Office: Silsby Hall Dartmouth Coll Hanover NH 03755

LYONS, GEORGE SAGE, lawyer, oil jobber, former state legislator; b. Mobile, Ala., Oct. 1, 1936; s. Mark, Jr. and Ruth (Kelly) L.; B.A. in Econs., Washington and Lee U., Lexington, Va., 1958; LL.B., U. Ala., 1960; m. Elsie Crain, Feb. 5, 1960; children-George Sage, Amelia C. Admitted to Ala. bar, 1960; practice in Mobile, 1962—; partner Lyons, Pipes & Cook, 1962—; mem. Ala. Ho. of Reps., 1969-75, speaker ho., 1971-75; pres., treas. dir. Crain Oil Co., Inc., Guntersville, Ala.; dir. First Bancgroup Ala., Inc., Jordan Industries, Inc., 1st Nat. Bank Mobile; mem. exec. com. Ala. Petroleum Council; mem. Tenn-Tombigbee Waterway Devel. Authority, 1966-70; chmn. Ala. Commn. on Higher Edn., 1971-78. Served to capt., JAGC, U.S. Army, 1960-62. Decorated Army Commendation medal. Mem. Am., Ala., Mobile County bar assns., Mid-Continent Oil and Gas Assn. (dir. Ala.-Miss. div.), Maritime Law Assn. U.S., Omicron Delta Kappa, Phi Delta Phi. Episcopalian. Home: 107 Carmel Dr E Mobile AL 36608 Office: 2 N Royal St Mobile AL 36601

LYONS, HAROLD ALOYSIUS, physician, educator; b. Bklyn., Sept. 14, 1913; s. Harry A. and Louise (de Tourreil) L.; B.S. cum laude, St. John's U., 1935; M.D., L.I. Coll. Medicine, 1940; m. Rita M. Wood, Mar. 9, 1940; children—Harold Aloysius, Frances Louis, Gail Jean, Robert Louis, Margaret Alida Marie, George Christopher, J. Lawrence, Anne Marie. Intern, L.I. Coll. Hosp., 1939-40, Bklyn. Hosp., 1940-41; resident U.S. Naval Hosp., St. Albans, 1945-48; instr. internal medicine Downstate Med. Center, SUNY, Bklyn., 1948-49; dir. pulmonary disease div. King County Hosp. Center, and Downstate Med. Center, Univ. Hosp., Bklyn., 1953—; instr. L.I. Coll. Medicine, 1948-49, asst. prof., 1949-50; asst. prof. Georgetown U. Coll. Medicine, Washington, 1950-51; asso. prof. SUNY Coll. Medicine, 1953-59, prof., 1959—; vis. prof. Cath. U. Chile, Santiago, 1967, Nat. Def. Center and Nat. U. Sch. Medicine, Taipei, Taiwan, 1965, U.S. Army Hosp., El Paso, 1971, Brown U. Sch. Medicine, 1974; cons. Bklyn. Hosp., 1953—, U.S. Naval Hosp., St. Albans, N.Y., 1958-73, Mercy Hosp., Rockville Center, N.Y., 1957—, VA Hosp., Bklyn., also Brookdale Med. Center; sr. cons. USPHS Hosp., S.I.; med. examiner FAA; med. adv. cons. U.S. Public Health Social Welfare, 1964—; ofcl. examiner Am. Bd. Internal Medicine. Former chmn. com. pulmonary diseases regional med. program Nassau and Suffolk counties; mem. com. pulmonary disease regional med. program Met. N.Y.; mem. internat. adv. com. Aspen Lung Conf. Served to comdr. M.C., USNR, 1941-53. Decorated Air medal; recipient Achievements award Am. Acad. Angiology, 1966; diplomate Am. Bd. Internal Medicine, Pan Am. Med. Assn. Fellow Am. Coll. Chest Physicians (mem. gov.'s com., com. postgrad. courses), A.C.P., N.Y. Acad. Medicine, N.Y. Acad. Scis., Chilean Tb Soc. (hon.); mem. Med. Research Soc. (Gt. Britain), Harvey Soc., Am. Nuclear Soc., AMA, N.Y. Med. Soc., Kings County Med. Soc., Am. Heart Assn., N.Y. Heart Assn., Am. Thoracic Soc., N.Y. Thoracic Soc. (past pres.), Internat. Soc. Cardiovascular Diseases, Am. Fedn. Clin. Research, Am. Assn. Med. Colls., Bklyn. Soc. Internal Medicine (past pres.), Bklyn. Thoracic Soc. (past pres.), Bklyn. Lung Assn. (v.p.), Am. Physiol. Soc., AAAS, Aerospace Med. Assn., IEEE, Soc. Biomed. Engring. (charter), Sigma Xi, Alpha Omega Alpha. Editor: Vascular Diseases of Lung. Home: Harbor Rd Sands Point NY 11050 Office: 450 Clarkson Ave Brooklyn NY 11203

LYONS, J(AMES) AUSTIN, JR., ins. co. exec.; b. N.Y.C., July 26, 1922; s. J. Austin and Virginia (Malia) L.; student Holy Cross Coll., 1940-42, Fordham Coll., 1942-43; LL.B., Columbia U., 1948; m. Carol Lou Reid, July 21, 1956; children—J. Austin, Louise. Admitted to N.Y. bar, 1949; with Met. Life Ins. Co., N.Y.C., 1949—, v.p., asso. gen. counsel, 1975, gen. counsel, sec., 1976, sr. v.p., gen. counsel, 1977—; dir. Met. Property & Casualty Co., Met. Ins. & Annuity Co., Met. Reins. Co. Served with USAAF, 1943-46. Mem. Am. Bar Assn., Assn. Life Ins. Counsel. Club: Whippoorwill (Armonk, N.Y.). Home: 77 Cross Ridge Rd Chappaqua NY 10514 Office: 1 Madison Ave New York NY 10010

LYONS, JAMES ALOYSIUS, JR., naval officer; b. Jersey City, Sept. 28, 1927; s. James Aloysius and Marion F. (Bach) L.; B.S., U.S. Naval Acad., 1952; student command and staff course Naval War Coll., 1963-64, Nat. War Coll., 1970-71; m. Renee Wilcox Chevalier, Apr. 10, 1954; children—Michele, Yvonne, James Aloysius, III. Commd. ensign, U.S. Navy, 1952, advanced through grades to rear adm., 1978; served at sea aboard 6th fleet flagship U.S.S. Salem, 1952-59; exec. officer U.S.S. Miller, 1959-61; antisubmarine warfare and weapons officer cruiser-destroyer Flottilla Four, 1961-63; dir. Navy plans, strategic plans div. Office of Chief of Naval Ops., Washington, 1964-66; comdr. U.S.S. Charles S. Sperry, 1966-68; exec. asst. and sr. aide to dep. chief of naval ops. for plans and policy, 1971-74; comdr. guided missile cruiser U.S.S. Richmond K. Turner, 1974-75; chief of staff Carrier Group Four, 1975-76; sr. asst. on Joint Chiefs of Staff Matters, div. strategy, plans and policy, Office Chief Naval Ops., Washington, 1976-78; dep. dir. strategic plans and policy div. Office Chief of Naval Ops., 1978; asst. dep. for polit. mil. affairs Directorate Orgn. Joint Chiefs of Staff, Washington, 1978-79, dir. polit.-mil. affairs, 1979—, U.S. rep. arms limitation talks with USSR, Helsinki, 1978, Mexico City, 1978. Decorated Legion of Merit, Meritorious Service medal with gold star, Navy Commendation medal with gold star, Navy Achievement medal. Mem. U.S. Naval Acad. Alumni Assn., U.S. Naval Acad. Athletic Assn. Roman Catholic. Home: 903 Banbury Ct McLean VA 22101 Office: Dept Def Orgn Joint Chiefs of Staff Pentagon Washington DC 20301

LYONS, JAMES DAVID, bus. services exec.; b. Chgo., Jan. 6, 1935; s. Fred L. and Agnes C. (Brown) L.; student U. Ill., 1953-54; B.S., Rutgers U., 1956; m. Mary Lou Fisher, July 21, 1956; children—David, James, Dennis, Deborah. With A.C. Nielsen Co., Northbrook, Ill., 1958—, beginning as mgmt. trainee, successively methods analyst, analysis dept. mgr., account exec., v.p., product mgr., 1971-74, exec. v.p., 1974-77, gen. mgr. media research div., 1974-77, dir., 1975—, pres., chief exec. officer Media Research Services Group, 1977—. Served with AUS, 1955-57. Mem. Am. Mgmt. Assn., Am. Mktg. Assn. Clubs: Univ. (N.Y.C.); Mich. Shores (Wilmette, Ill.). Home: 416 Woodstock Ave Kenilworth IL 60043 Office: Nielsen Plaza Northbrook IL 60062

LYONS, JERRY LEE, mech. engr., engring. research exec.; b. St. Louis, Apr. 2, 1939; s. Ferd H. and Edna T. Lyons; B.S. in Mech. Engring., Okla. Inst. Tech., 1964. Project engr. Harris Mfg. Co., St. Louis, 1964-70, Essex Cryogenics Industries, St. Louis, 1970-73; mgr. engring. research Chemetron Corp., St. Louis, 1973-77; instr. fluid controls Extension div. Wis. U., 1977—; pres. Yankee Ingenuity, Inc., St. Louis, 1973—; adj. prof. engring. fluid power dept. Bradley U., Peoria, Ill., 1977—; gen. mgr. engring. research and devel. Essex Fluid Controls div. Essex Industries, Inc., St. Louis, 1977—. Served with USAF, 1957-62. Registered profl. engr., Mo. Mem. Soc. Mfg. Engrs. (chmn. Mo. registration com. 1975—), ASME, Nat. Soc. Profl. Engrs., Mo. Soc. Profl. Engrs., St. Louis Soc. Mfg. Engrs. (chmn. edn. com. 1979-80, chmn. profl. devel., registration and cert. com. 1975-79), Instrument Soc. Am. (mem. control valve stability com. 1978—), St. Louis Engrs. Club (award of merit 1977), Am. Security Council (committeeman 1976—), Nat. Fluid Power Assn. (mem. com. on pressure ratings 1975-77). Author: Home Study Series Course on Actuators and Accessories, 1977; The Valve Designers Handbook, 1977; The Lyons' Encyclopedia of Valves, 1975; The Designers Handbook of Pressure Sensing Devices, 1979; Special Process Applications, 1980; contbr. articles to profl. jours. Lutheran. Home: 7535 Harlan Walk Saint Louis MO 63123 Office: 8213 Gravois Ave Saint Louis MO 63123

LYONS, JOHN BARTHOLOMEW, educator; b. Quincy, Mass., Nov. 22, 1916; s. Lawrence W. and Anna G. (Reardon) L.; A.B., Harvard, 1938, A.M., 1939, Ph.D., 1942; m. Mary P. Johnson, Nov. 4, 1945; children—Rosemary, Elisabeth, John, Barbara, Diana. With U.S. Geol. Survey, 1941—; asst. prof. geology Dartmouth, 1946-52, prof. geology, 1952—. Served as capt. USAAF, 1942-45. Fellow Geol. Soc. Am., Phi Beta Kappa, Sigma Xi. Contbr. sci. jours. Home: 4 Read Rd Hanover NH 03755

LYONS, JOHN H., union ofcl.; b. Cleve., Oct. 29, 1919; s. John H. and Elizabeth M. (Sexton) L.; B.M.E., Mo. Sch. Mines, 1942; m. Dorothy Ann Boyen, Apr. 15, 1944; children—Cheryl Ann Lyons Lawbaugh, Joanne. With Gen. Bronze Corp., N.Y.C., 1946-54; mem. Internat. Assn. Bridge, Structural and Ornamental Iron Workers, 1937—, rep., 1954—, gen. organizer, 1954-58, gen. v.p., 1959-61, pres., 1961—; v.p. bldg. and constrn. trades dept. AFL-CIO, 1961—, v.p. metal trades dept., 1961—, v.p. AFL-CIO, 1967—, mem. internal disputes panel 1961—; mem. adv. com. White House Conf. on Balanced Nat. Growth and Econ. Devel., 1978; mem. citizens adv. com Pres.'s Com. Juvenile Delinquency, 1962—; adv. council Bur.

Employment Security, 1962—; mem. Taft-Hartley Labor-Mgmt. Panel 1963—; chmn. labor adv. com. Pres.'s Com. Equal Employment Opportunity, 1964—; mem. Nat. Manpower Adv. Com., 1963—, Nat. Commn. Urban Problems, 1967—. Bd. dirs. Boys Town Mo., 1966—. Served with USAAF, 1943-46. Home: 9012 Congressional Ct Potomac MD 20854 Office: 1750 New York Ave NW Washington DC 20006

LYONS, JOHN W(INSHIP), govt. adminstr., chemist; b. Reading, Mass., Nov. 5, 1930; A.B. in Chemistry, Harvard U., 1952; A.M. in Phys. Chemistry, Washington U., St. Louis, 1963, Ph.D. in Phys. Chemistry, 1964. With Monsanto Co., 1955-73, group leader, sect. mgr. research dept., inorganic chems. div., 1962-69, mgr. comml. devel., head fire safety center, 1969-73; mem. ad hoc panel on fire research Nat. Bur. Standards, Washington, 1971-73, dir. Center for Fire Research, 1973-77, dir. Inst. Applied Tech., 1977-78, dir. Nat. Engring. Lab., 1978—; chmn. Products Research Com., trust which adminstrs. fire research funds, 1974-79; bd. dirs. Nat. Fire Protection Assn., 1978—; vis. lectr. various univs.; co-chmn. U.S.-Japan Natural Resources Panel on Fire Research, 1975-78. Served with U.S. Army, 1953-54. Recipient Gold medal Dept. Commerce, 1977, Pres.'s Mgmt. Improvement award White House, 1978. Fellow AAAS; mem. Am. Chem. Soc. (chmn. St. Louis sect. 1971-72), Sigma Xi. Author: Viscosity and Flow Measurement, 1963; The Chemistry and Uses of Fire Retardants, 1970; contbr. numerous articles to profl. publs. Office: Nat Engring Lab Nat Bur Standards Washington DC 20234

LYONS, JOSEPH NORMAN, ins. exec.; b. Boston, Sept. 5, 1901; s. George Alfred and Alice Antoinette (Sheehan) L.; grad. Boston Latin Sch., 1917; m. Helen Mary O'Karski, June 27, 1942; children—Joseph Norman, Christie Ann, Mary Candace. With John Paulding Meade Co., ins., Boston, 1917-34; founder, pres. Cushing, Lyons, Inc., Boston, 1934—; founder Am. Ednl. Ins. Fund, 1960—; organizer Pilgram Ins. Co., 1960. Trustee Mass. Regional Arthritis and Rheumatism Found. Mem. Boston Bd. Fire Underwriters, Mass. Brokers Assn. (past dir.), Bostonian Soc. Clubs: Arundel Beach, Cape Arundel Golf. Home: 11 Beechcroft Rd Newton MA 02158 Office: 89 Broad St Boston MA 02110

LYONS, M. ARNOLD, lawyer; b. Mpls., June 3, 1911; s. S. Harry and Sarah (Shoenberger) Labovitz; B.A., U. Minn., 1932, J.D., 1934; m. Vera Nissenson, Dec. 22, 1935; children—David J., Barbara E. (Mrs. Herbert J. Buirge), Lisa. Admitted to Minn. bar, 1934, U.S. Dist. Ct. bar, 1935, also U.S. Supreme Ct., others; practice in Mpls., 1934-41, 41—; mem. firm Robins, Davis & Lyons, Mpls., 1941—; dir. Barton Contracting Co., Comml. Aggregates, Inc.; adj. prof. law, trusts and estates U. Minn. Law Sch.; prof. law Hamline U., St. Paul. Chmn. Minn. chpt. Bonds for Israel; co-chmn. initial gifts div. Mpls. Fedn. for Jewish Service, 1965. Sustaining mem. World Peace Through Law Center. Recipient Sholom award State Israel Bonds, 1972; Distinguished Service award United Synagogue Am., 1972; named Prof. of Yr., Student Bar Assn. Hamline U., 1978. Mem. Am. (chmn. Minn. membership com., sect. taxation), Minn., Hennepin County bar assns., Am. Arbitration Assn. (nat. panel), Am. Judicature Soc., U. Minn. Alumni Assn. (life). Jewish (pres. synagogue, chmn. capital bldg. fund). Mason (Shriner), Odd Fellow. Club: University of Minn. Alumni (Mpls.). Top law sch. grad. named M. Arnold Lyons scholar in his honor at Hamline U. Home: 4001 Basswood Rd Minneapolis MN 55416 Office: 33 S 5th St Minneapolis MN 55402

LYONS, THOMAS (JAMES), retail co. exec.; b. San Francisco, Oct. 4, 1928; s. John Michael and Margaret Katherine (Hanrahan) L.; B.S. (Phelan scholar), U. Santa Clara, 1950; m. Mary Lou Pilakowski, Aug. 26, 1950; children—Kathleen, Pamela, Timothy, Mary Ellen, Erin, Kevin. With J.C. Penney Co. Inc., 1950—, dir. domestic and internat. devel., N.Y.C., 1976-78, dir. public affairs, 1978, dir. spl. bus. ops., 1979—, v.p., 1974—; dir. J.C. Penney Casualty Ins. Co., J.C. Penney Life Ins. Co., J.C. Penney Europe, Inc. Served with U.S. Army, 1950-52. Mem. Nat. Retail Mchts. Assn., Nat. Retail Mchts. Assn. Internat. Republican. Roman Catholic. Club: Rotary. Office: 1301 Ave of Americas New York NY 10019

LYONS, THOMAS WILLIAM, clergyman; b. Washington, Sept. 26, 1923; s. Thomas William and Nora (Bagley) L.; student St. Charles Coll., 1937-43; A.B., St. Mary's Sem., Balt., 1945, S.T.B., 1946, postgrad., 1946-48. Ordained priest Roman Catholic Ch., 1948; served at St. John the Evangelist Ch., Silver Spring, Md., 1948-49, St. Matthew's Cathedral, Washington, 1949-53; dir. Mackin High Sch., Washington, 1953-57; asst. dir. edn. archdiocese Washington, 1954-64, dir., 1964-73, sec. for Christian edn., 1973-75; pastor St. Francis de Sales Ch., Washington, 1963-66, St. Thomas Apostle Ch., Washington, 1966-76; consecrated bishop; aux. bishop Washington, 1974—. Chmn., Archdiocesan Commn. on Sacred Music, 1966-70. Mem. Nat. Cath. Ednl. Assn. (v.p. 1965-69), Assn. Cath. Sch. Supts. (chmn. 1968-70). Home: 2665 Woodley Rd NW Washington DC 20008 Office: 1721 Rhode Island Ave NW Washington DC 20036

LYONS, WILLIAM ALOYSIUS, utility exec.; b. Bklyn., May 29, 1908; s. Samuel J. and Anna (McAuliffe) L.; student N.Y. U., 1928, Fordham U., 1929, Harvard Advanced Mgmt. Program, 1954; m. Fern N. Kels, Aug. 18, 1934; children—Anna Clare Lyons Corkery, Nona Marie Lyons Livingston. Accountant, Utility Mgmt. Corp., 1929-34, asst. to comptroller, 1934-40, asst. to pres., 1940-41; comptroller NYPA-NJ Utilities Co., 1941-44; asst. to pres. N.Y. State Electric & Gas Corp., Binghamton, 1944-51, v.p., 1951-62, exec. v.p., 1962-66, pres., 1966-73, chmn. bd., chief exec. officer, 1973-77, dir., chmn. exec. and fin. com., 1977—; chmn. Empire Power Resources Inc.; dir. Utilities Mut. Ins. Co., Raymond Corp., Greene, Gt. Am. Industries, Inc. Dir. allocations br. WPB, Office of War Utilities, 1942-44. Mem. N.Y. State Energy Research and Devel. Authority; vice chmn. N.Y. State Econ. Devel. Bd.; trustee, chmn. exec. com. Ithaca Coll. Clubs: Sky (N.Y.C.); Binghamton City and Country. Home: 152 Riverside Dr Binghamton NY 13905 Office: NY State Electric & Gas Corp 4500 Vestal Pkwy E Binghamton NY 13902

LYSAUGHT, J. DONALD, lawyer; b. Kansas City, Kans., Dec. 7, 1923; s. Michael Clarence and Minnie (Hill) L.; A.B., U. Kans., 1948, LL.B., 1949; m. Jeen Lois Hunter, Dec. 15, 1945; children—Nancy Jeen, J. Donald, Deborah Geralyn, Wendy Lynn, Jeffrey Patrick, Victoria Anne. Admitted to Kans. bar, 1949, since practiced in Kansas City; partner firm Stanley, Schroeder, Weeks, Thomas & Lysaught, 1955-68; mem. firm Weeks, Thomas, Lysaught & Mustain, Chartered, 1969—; served as judge pro tem Dist. Ct. Wyandotte County, Kans., 1953. Served with AUS, World War II. Decorated Army Commendation ribbon with cluster. Mem. Kans. Res. Officers Assn. (judge adv. 1954), Order of Coif, Phi Delta Phi, Alpha Tau Omega. Home: 4409 W 64th St Prairie Village KS 66208 Office: Capitol Federal Bldg Overland Park KS 66207

LYSINGER, REX JACKSON, gas distbn. co. exec.; b. Pitts., Aug. 14, 1937; s. W. Mark and Clare Ann (Long) L.; B.S. in Indsl. Engring., U. Pitts., 1959; m. Jodene Elizabeth Scott, Sept. 19, 1958; children—Teri Jo, Beth Ann, Rex Jay, Holly Sue. Engr., staff asst. E. Ohio Gas Co., Cleve., 1959-64, asst. dist. supt., 1964-65; v.p., engr., cons., mgr. Stone & Webster, N.Y.C., 1965-74, v.p., Houston, 1974-75; v.p. corporate planning Ala. Gas Corp., Birmingham, 1975-77, pres., dir., 1977—; dir. Alagasco Energy Co., Inc., Birmingham, 1977—. Bd. dirs. Met. Devel. Bd. Birmingham, 1978, Nat. Alliance of Bus., 1978. Served with USAR, 1960-61. Mem. Am., So. (dir. 1978—) gas assns. Clubs: Downtown, Relay House, Mountain Brook Swim and Tennis, Rotary. Home: 4925 Stone Mill Rd Mountain Brook AL 35223 Office: 1918 1st Ave N Birmingham AL 35295

LYSTAD, MARY HANEMANN (MRS. ROBERT LYSTAD), sociologist, author; b. New Orleans, Apr. 11, 1928; d. James and Mary (Douglass) Hanemann; A.B. cum laude, Newcomb Coll., 1949; M.A., Columbia, 1951; Ph.D., Tulane U., 1955; m. Robert Lystad, June 20, 1953; children—Lisa Douglass, Anne Hanemann, Mary Lunde, Robert Douglass, James Hanemann. Postdoctoral fellow social psychology S.E. La. Hosp., Mandeville, 1955-57; field research social psychology, Ghana, 1957-58, South Africa and Swaziland, 1968; chief sociologist Collaborative Child Devel. Project, Charity Hosp. La., New Orleans, 1958-61; cons. spl. operations research office Am. U., Washington, 1962; feature writer African div. Voice Am., Washington, 1964-73; program analyst NIMH, Washington, 1968-72, spl. asst. to dir. div. spl. mental health programs, 1973-78, asso. dir. for planning and coordination div. spl. mental health programs, 1978—; cons. on youth Nat. Goals Research Staff, White House, Washington, 1969-70. Fellow Am. Sociol. Assn. Author: Millicent the Monster, 1968; Social Aspects of Alienation, 1969; Jennifer Takes Over P.S. 94, 1972; James the Jaguar, 1972; As They See It: Changing Values of College Youth, 1972; That New Boy, 1973; Halloween Parade, 1973; Violence at Home, 1974; A Child's World As Seen in His Stories and Drawings, 1974; From Dr. Mather to Dr. Seuss: 200 Years of American Books for Children, 1979. Home: 4900 Scarsdale Rd Washington DC 20016 Office: 5600 Fishers Ln Rockville MD 20852

LYSTAD, ROBERT ARTHUR, educator; b. Milw., Aug. 10, 1920; s. Arthur Frederick and Lulu Marion (Lunde) L.; B.A., U. Wis., 1941; B.D., Drew Theol. Sem., 1944; Ph.D. in Anthropology, Northwestern U., 1951; m. Anita E. Firing, June 11, 1945 (dec. 1952); m. 2d, Mary Agnes Hanemann, June 20, 1953; children—Lisa Douglass, Anne Hanemann, Mary Lunde, Robert Douglass, James Hanemann. Prof. anthropology Tulane U., 1951-61, head dept. sociology and anthropology Newcomb Coll. of Univ., 1959-61; asso. prof. African studies Sch. Advanced Internat. Studies, Johns Hopkins, 1961-64, prof., 1964—; cons. Voice Am., various depts. U.S. govt., 1961—; dir. Carnegie Endowment Found. and Rockefeller Found. seminars in diplomacy, 1961-77. Del. to Anglo-Am. Parliamentary Confs. on Africa, 1965-77, Confs. of African and Am. Reps., 1973, 75, dir. confs., 1978—. Mem. Ohio Conf. Methodist Ch., 1944-73. Fellow Social Sci. Research Council, Gold Coast and Ivory Coast, 1949-50; grantee Carnegie Corp., Ghana, 1957-58. Mem. Am. Anthrop. Assn., African Studies Assn. Author: The Ashanti: A Proud People, 1958; also articles in field. Editor: The African World: A Survey of Social Research, 1965. Home: 4900 Scarsdale Rd Washington DC 20016

LYSYK, KENNETH MARTIN, lawyer, univ. adminstr.; b. Weyburn, Sask., Can., July 1, 1934; s. Michael and Anna (Maradyn) L.; B.A., McGill U., 1954; LL.B., U. Sask., 1957; B.C.L., Oxford U., 1960; m. Patricia Kinnon, Oct. 2, 1959; children—Joanne, Karen, Stephanie. Lectr. U. B.C., 1960-62, asst. prof., 1962-65, asso. prof., 1965-68, prof., 1968-69; admitted to Sask. bar, B.C. bar, Yukon bar; apptd. Queen's counsel, 1973; adviser Constl. Rev. sect. Privy Council Office, Govt. of Can., Ottawa, 1969-70; prof. Faculty of Law U. Toronto, 1970-72; dep. atty. gen. Govt. of Sask., Regina, 1972-76; dean Law Sch., U. B.C., Vancouver, 1976—; dir. Potash Corp. of Sask., 1975—. Chmn. Alaska Hwy. Pipeline Inquiry, 1977. Mem. Can. Bar Assn., Can. Assn. Law Tchrs. Home: 6950 Yew St Vancouver BC Canada Office: Faculty of Law U BC Vancouver BC Canada

LYTHCOTT, GEORGE IGNATIUS, physician, govt. adminstr.; b. N.Y.C., Apr. 29, 1918; s. George Ignatius and Evelyn (Wilson) L.; B.Sc., Bates Coll., 1939; M.D., Boston U., 1943; m. Jean Snookes, Jan., 1966; children—Ngina Lythcott Darden, George, Michael, Stephen, Julie. Intern, Boston City Hosp., 1943-44, resident in pediatrics, 1944-46; regional dir. West Africa Smallpox Eradication Program, Center for Disease Control, Atlanta, 1966-69; asso. dean for urban and community health affairs, prof. pediatrics Columbia U. Coll. Physicians and Surgeons, 1969-74; asso. vice chancellor for health scis., prof. pediatrics U. Wis., Madison, 1974-77, Edward Jenner prof. internat. health, 1977; adminstr. Health Services Adminstrn., asst. surgeon gen. USPHS, HEW, Rockville, Md., 1977—; mem. exec. com., public trustee Nutrition Found.; alt. U.S. del. UNICEF, 1978—; team leader Nat. Acad. Sci. Inst. Medicine del. to Peoples Republic China, 1978; trustee Africare; bd. dirs. Council Fgn. Relations; clin. prof. pediatrics and child health Howard U. Served as capt., M.C., USAF, 1953-55. Recipient Centennial Alumni citation Boston U., 1973, Meritorious Honor award AID, 1971. Mem. Assn. Am. Med. Colls. (task force on minority student opportunities in medicine). Author: Black Related Diseases, 1975. Office: 5600 Fishers Ln Room 14-05 Rockville MD 20857

LYTLE, ANDREW NELSON, author, editor; b. Murfreesboro, Tenn., Dec. 26, 1902; s. Robert Logan and Lillie Belle (Nelson) L.; A.B., Vanderbilt U., 1925; student Baker's 47 Workshop, Yale Sch. of Drama, 1927-28; Litt.D. (hon.), Kenyon Coll., 1965, U. Fla., 1970, U. South, 1973; m. Edna Langdon Barker, June 20, 1938; children—Pamela, Katharine Anne, Lillie Langdon. Prof. history U. of South, also mng. editor Sewanee Rev., 1942-43, prof. English, editor Sewanee Rev., 1961-73, ret., 1973. Lectr., U. Iowa Sch. Writing, 1946, lectr., acting head, 1947; lectr. creative writing U. Fla., 1948-61; leader humanities div. internat. seminar Harvard, summer 1954; tchr. Vanderbilt U., Nashville, spring 1974, U. Ky., Lexington, 1976. Guggenheim fellow for creative work in fiction, 1940-41, 41-42, 60-61; Kenyon Rev. fellow for fiction, 1956. Recipient Nat. Found. Arts and Humanities award, 1966-67; Brown fellow U. of South, fall 1978. Mem. Assn. Little Mags. Am. (officer), So. Acad. Letters, Arts and Scis., Council Lit. Mags., Phi Beta Kappa, Kappa Alpha (Southern). Episcopalian. Author several books 1930—; latest titles, The Velvet Horn, 1957; A Novel, Novella and Four Stories, 1958; the Hero With the Private Parts, 1966; A Wake for the Living, a family chronicle, 1975. Editor: Craft and Vision: The Best Fiction from the Sewanee Review, 1971. Contbr. articles, verse, fiction to various publs. Home: Monteagle SS Assembly Monteagle TN 37356

LYTLE, CHARLES HEINZ, retail store exec.; b. Pitts., Feb. 3, 1930; s. Harry and Rebecca (Heinz) L.; A.B., Lafayette Coll., 1953; postgrad. Harvard Bus. Sch., 1975; m. Elizabeth Ann Frampton, Oct. 6, 1962; children—Charles John, Christopher Heinz. With G.C. Murphy Co., 1953—, asst. dir. personnel, McKeesport, Pa., 1969-73, asst. v.p. personnel, 1973-75, v.p. personnel, 1975-78, exec. v.p. ops., 1978-79, pres., chief operating officer, 1979—. Mem. bus. adv. bd. Grad. Sch. Bus., Ohio U., U. Pitts.; bd. dirs. McKeesport Neighborhood Ministry, Pitts.-Allegheny County chpt. ARC. Served with U.S. Army, 1953-55. Mem. Assn. Gen. Mdse. Chains, Pitts. Personnel Assn., Chi Phi. Presbyterian. Clubs: Univ., Duquesne. Home: 3377 Cochise Dr Pittsburgh PA 15241 Office: 531 5th Ave McKeesport PA 15132

LYTLE, RICHARD, artist; b. Albany, N.Y., Feb. 14, 1935; s. Ralph Dudley and Mary (Putnam) L.; student Cooper Union, 1952-55; B.F.A., Yale, 1957, M.F.A., 1960; m. Berit Ore, June 16, 1959; children—Mara, Claudia, Dorian. Instr. Yale Sch. Art and Architecture, 1960-63; tchr. Yale-Norfolk Summer Sch., 1960, 61, 63, dir., 1976, 77; dean Silvermine Coll. of Art, 1963-65; asso. prof. Yale, 1966—, asso. dean Sch. Art, 1975-77; one man shows: Borgenicht Gallery, N.Y.C., 1961, 63, 64, 66, 68, 72, Cortland Coll., 1968, U. Hartford, 1970, U. Conn., 1973, De Cordova Mus., 1974, Marilyn Pearl Gallery, N.Y.C., 1977, 79, Trinity Coll., 1977; group shows include Art in Am., 1959, 16 Americans, 1959, Seattle World's Fair Exhbn., 1962, Young New Eng. Painters Traveling Exhibit, 1969, Artists Abroad, Inst. Internat. Edn., 1969; represented in permanent collections Mus. Modern Art, Yale Art Gallery, Columbia Internat. House, Johnson Collection, Cin. Art Mus., Chase Manhattan Bank Citicorp, Am. Tel. & Tel., Albrecht Art Gallery; 160 ft. wall relief on exterior campus center Fairfield (Conn.) U. Mem. Oxford (Conn.) Bd. Fin., 1966-68. Fulbright grantee, Florence, Italy, 1958-59. Address: Sperry Rd Woodbridge CT 06525

LYTLE, WILLIAM EBEN, lawyer; b. Geneva, N.Y., Oct. 26, 1905; s. Claude C. and Louise (Eshenour) L.; A.B. summa cum laude, Hobart Coll., 1926; LL.B., Harvard, 1929; m. Emily Phillips Payson, Aug. 29, 1932; children—Valerie Page Lytle Gunning, John Reading, Bruce Phillips. Admitted to N.Y. bar, 1929, since practiced in Buffalo; partner Phillips, Lytle, Hitchcock, Blaine & Huber, 1946-75, counsel, 1975—. Former mem. N.Y. State Probation Commn.; bd. dirs. James H. Cummings Found.; formerly chancellor Prostestant Episcopal Diocese Western N.Y. Fellow Am. Bar Found., Am. Coll. Probate Counsel; mem. N.Y. State, Erie County bar assns., Buffalo Hist. Soc., Phi Beta Kappa, Kappa Alpha. Clubs: Buffalo, Mid-Day. Home: 16 Berkley Pl Buffalo NY 14209 Office: 3400 Marine Midland Center Buffalo NY 14203

MA, MICHAEL, violinist; b. Vienna, Austria, Mar. 13, 1946; s. James and Shu-Hsien M.; came to U.S., naturalized, 1971; student New Sch. of Music, Curtis Inst. Music, Phila., 1961-69; m. Margaret Higham; 1 dau., C. Michelle. Violinist, New Art String Quartet, 1967-76; concertmaster Lake George Opera Co., 1969, Lancaster and York (Pa.) Opera Co., 1969-74, Goldovsky Opera Co., 1969, Mostovoy Concerto Soloists of Phila., 1970-76, Santa Fe (N.Mex.) Opera Orch.; asst. concertmaster N.C. Symphony, Raleigh; concertmaster N.C. Chamber Orch. Omega.

MAAS, DUANE HARRIS, distilling co. exec.; b. Tilleda, Wis., Aug. 26, 1927; s. John William and Adela (Giessel) M.; B.S., U. Wis., 1951; m. Sonja Johnson, Mar. 11, 1950; children—Jon Kermit, Duane Arthur, Thomas Ervin. With Shell Chem. Corp., 1951-59; plant mgr. Fleischmann Distilling Corp., Owensboro, Ky., 1959-63, Plainfield, Ill., 1963-65; asst. to v.p. Barton Distilling Co., Chgo., 1965-68, exec. asst. to pres., 1968, v.p. adminstrn., 1968; v.p., gen. mgr. Barton Brands, Inc., Chgo., 1968—72; pres. Leaf Confectionery div. W.R. Grace, Chgo., 1972-74; v.p., gen. mgr. Morand Bros. Inc., Chgo., 1974—; v.p., sec.-treas. Marketing Directions Inc., Chgo., 1974—; pres. Associated Wine Producers, Inc., 1979—; past pres. Barton Distilling (Can.), Ltd.; past dir. Barton Distilling (Scotland), Ltd., Barton Distillers Europe, Barton Internat., Ltd. Sec.-treas. Plainfield Twp. Park Dist., 1967-70; chmn. Plainfield Planning and Zoning Commn., 1965-70. Served with USAAF, 1945-47. Mem. Am. Mgmt. Assn., Ill. C. of C., Wis. Alumni Assn. Lutheran. Home: 65 E Scott St Chicago IL 60610 Office: 2555 S Leavitt St Chicago IL 60608

MAAS, MICHAEL, architect; b. N.Y.C., June 16, 1931; s. Carl and Madeleine (Fellheimer) M.; B.Arch., Rensselaer Poly. Inst., 1954; m. Jane Ann Brown, Aug. 31, 1957; children—Katherine Ann, Jennifer Ann. Designer, Fellheimer and Wagner, architects, N.Y.C., 1957-59; designer Voorhees, Walker, Smith, Smith and Haines, architects, N.Y.C., 1959-60, project architect, 1960-63; project mgr. Smith, Haines, Lundberg and Waehler, N.Y.C., 1963-72; sr. asso. Haines, Lunberg & Waehler, N.Y.C., 1971-72, partner, 1972-75, mng. partner, 1975—. Design critic N.Y. Sch. Interior Decoration, 1960-61. Chmn. archtl. adv. com. Rensselaer Poly. Inst., 1973-75. Bd. dirs. Emerson Sch., N.Y.C. Served to capt. USMCR, 1954-57. Mem. A.I.A. (dir. N.Y. chpt.), Nat. Council Archtl. Bds., N.Y. Bldg. Congress (v.p.), Delta Kappa Epsilon (pres. alumni council Psi Omega chpt. 1962-64). Clubs: Westhampton (N.Y.) Country, Westhampton Mallet, Pine Valley Golf; Winged Foot Golf; Union League. Home: 1155 Park Ave New York NY 10028 Office: 2 Park Ave New York NY 10016

MAAS, PETER, writer; b. N.Y.C., June 27, 1929; s. Carl and Madeleine (Fellheimer) M.; B.A., Duke U., 1949; postgrad. The Sorbonne, Paris, 1950; m. Audrey Gellen, Apr. 4, 1962 (dec. July 1975); 1 son, John Michael. Asso. editor Collier's mag., 1954-56; sr. editor Look mag., 1959-61; contbg. writer Sat. Evening Post, 1961-66; cons. Curtis Pub. Co., 1966-67; contbg. editor New York mag., 1968-71; free-lance contbr. nat. mags., newspapers, 1954—; spl. cons. David Brinkley's Jour., NBC-TV, 1961-62; author: The Rescuer, 1967; The Valachi Papers, 1969; Serpico, 1973; King of the Gypsies, 1975; Made in America, 1979; works included in anthology. Served with USNR, 1952-54. Mem. P.E.N. Am. Center. Roman Catholic. Office: care Internat Creative Mgmt 40 W 57th St New York NY 10019

MAAS, WERNER KARL, educator; b. Kaiserslautern, Germany, Apr. 27, 1921; s. Albert and Esther (Meyer) M.; came to U.S., 1936, naturalized, 1945; A.B., Harvard, 1943; Ph.D., Columbia, 1948; m. Renata Diringer, Oct. 15, 1960; children—Peter, Andrew, Helen. Postdoctoral fellow Cal. Inst. Tech., Pasadena, 1946-48; commd. officer USPHS, Tb Research Lab., Cornell U. Sch., N.Y.C., 1948-54; asst. prof. pharmacology N.Y. U., 1954-57, asso. prof. microbiology, 1957-63, prof., 1963—, chmn. dept. basic med. scis., 1974—. USPHS Career grantee, 1962—. Mem. Am. Soc. Biol. Chemists, Genetics Soc. Am., Am. Soc. Microbiology. Home: 86 Villard Ave Hastings on Hudson NY 10706 Office: 550 1st Ave New York City NY 10016

MAASS, ARTHUR, educator; b. Balt., July 24, 1917; s. Arthur Leopold and Selma (Rosenhelm) M.; A.B., Johns Hopkins, 1939; M.P.A., Harvard, 1941, Ph.D., 1949. Adminstrv. asst. Bur. Budget, 1939-40; intern. Nat. Inst. Pub. Affairs, 1939-40; research technician Nat. Resources Planning Bd., 1941-42; budget analyst Dept. Navy, 1946; water resources analyst Natural Resources Task Force, Hoover Commn., 1948; faculty Harvard, 1949—, prof. govt., 1959-67, Frank G. Thomson prof. govt., 1967—, chmn. dept., 1963-67, sec. Grad. Sch. Pub. Adminstrn., 1954-59. Cons. Office Dir. Budget, 1949, Office Sec. Interior, 1950-52, Pres.'s Materials Policy Commn., 1951-52, TVA, 1952, C.E., 1961—, Bur. Reclamation, 1971; dir. survey unit conservation and devel. Conn. Little Hoover Commn., 1949-50; dir. survey unit conservation agys. Mass. Little Hoover Commn., 1950-51; vis. prof. polit. sci. U. Calif. at Berkeley, 1951, U. P.R., 1955. Served to lt. comdr. USNR, 1942-46. Guggenheim fellow, 1955; Fulbright research fellow, Spain, 1960-61; Faculty research fellow Social Sci. Research Council, 1961. Author: Muddy Waters, The Army Engineers and the Nation's Rivers, 1951; co-author: Area and Power, 1959; Design of Water-Resource Systems: New Techniques for Relating Economic Objectives, Engineering Analysis and Governmental Planning, 1962; . . . and the Desert Shall Rejoice: Conflict, Growth and Justice in Arid Environments, 1978; contbr.

articles to profl. jours. Clubs: Cosmos (Washington); Harvard (N.Y.C.). Home: 63 Atlantic Ave Boston MA 02110 Office: Littauer Center Harvard Cambridge MA 02138

MAASS, RICHARD, investment exec.; b. Balt., May 20, 1919; s. Arthur L. and Selma (Rosenheim) M.; B.S., N.Y. U., 1949; m. Dolly Kern Lederer, Apr. 4, 1943; children—Douglas Owen, Richard Andrew. Partner, Reredel Assos., White Plains, N.Y., 1945—; dir. Airtronics, Inc. Pres., Urban League of Westchester County, N.Y., 1952-58, Sr. Personnel Employment Com., 1965-67, White Plains (N.Y.) United Way, 1969, Am. Jewish Com., N.Y.C., 1977-79; mayor City of White Plains, 1974; mem. White Plains Urban Renewal Agy., 1974—; historian Westchester County, 1979—; chmn. Nat. Conf. on Soviet Jewry, 1971-73. Served with USN, 1941-45. Democrat. Jewish. Clubs: Grolier (N.Y.C.); Fed. City (Washington). Home: 3 Murchison Pl White Plains NY 10605 Office: PO Box 270 White Plains NY 10602

MAASS, WILLIAM GEORGE, publisher; b. Chgo., Sept. 16, 1925: s. George and Lillian (Miller) M.; B.S., Purdue U., 1948; m. Jeanne Hodek, Feb. 12, 1949; children—Christie Ann, Jeffery Alan, Karen Ann. Dist. mgr. Conn. area Conover-Mast Purchasing Directory, 1948; Chgo. rep. Constrn. Equipment, C-M Publs., Inc., 1949-51, bus. mgr. former Aviation Age mag., now Space/Aeronautics, 1951-53, pub., 1953—, pub. Instnl. Feeding and Housing, 1956—; v.p. Conover-Mast Publs., Inc., 1955-65; v.p. corporate devel. Cahners Pub. Co., Inc., Boston, 1965-68; pres., founder Tech. Communication Inc., 1968—; chmn. bd. Center Mgmt. Communication, N.Y.C., 1976—; sr. v.p. Hayden Pubs. Co., Rochelle Park, N.J.; creator, pub. Internat. Sci. and Tech., 1962; founder The Innovation Group, 1969; pres. Exec. VideoForum Inc., 1972; pub. Electronic Design mag. Club: Union League. Home: Woodlanes Rd Harrison NY 10528 Office: Hayden Pub Co Rochelle Park NJ 07662

MAAZEL, LORIN, conductor, violinist; b. Paris, France, Mar. 6, 1930 (parents Am. citizens); s. Lincoln and Marie (Varencove) M.; Mus. D. (hon.), U. Pitts., 1968; H.H.D., Beaver Coll., 1973; m. Israela Margalit, Sept. 29, 1969; children—Ilann Sean, Fiona. Debut as conductor, 1953; condr. festivals in Edinburgh (Scotland), Bayreuth (Germany) and Salzburg (Austria), 1960-70; world tours include Japan, Far East, Asia, Europe, Latin Am., Australia, USSR; artistic dir. Deutsche Oper Berlin 1965-71; mus. dir. Radio Symphony Orch., Berlin, 1965-75; music dir. Cleve. Orch., 1972—; prin. guest condr. New Philharmonia Orch., London, 1976—, Radio France, Paris; mgr., artistic dir. Vienna State Opera, 1979. recording of Cleve. Orch., Vienna Philharmonic for London Records, Deutsche Grammophon, Berliner Philharmonie, Angel Records, New Philharmonia, CBS. Office: Cleve Orchestra Severance Hall Cleveland OH 44106

MABBS, EDWARD CARL, mfg. co. exec.; b. St. Louis, Sept. 8, 1921; s. Ralph I. and Anna (Renner) M.; B.S. in Mech. Engring., Cornell U., 1943; m. Margaret E. von Paulsen, Oct. 16, 1943; children—Susan, Carl, Kenneth, Meg. With Linde div. Union Carbide Corp., Newark, also Essington, Pa., Tonawanda, N.Y., 1946-55; plant mgr. Wright Hoist div. Acco., York, Pa., 1955-62; group v.p. Am. Chain & Cable Co., Bridgeport, Conn., 1962-68, exec. v.p., dir., 1968-71; pres., chief exec. officer, dir. Esterline Corp., N.Y.C., 1971—72; pres. Indsl. Components group Rockwell Internat. Corp., Pitts., 1972-75; pres., chief exec. officer, dir. Incom Internat. Inc., Pitts., 1975—; dir. L.B. Foster Co., Pitts. Trustee, Point Park Coll. exec. bd. Pomperaug council Boy Scouts Am. Registered profl. engr. Mem. Internat. Materials Mgmt. Soc. (dir.), Am. Prodn. and Inventory Control Soc. (dir.), Bridgeport C. of C. (past dir.), Material Handling Inst. (past pres.). Home: 343 Fox Chapel Rd Pittsburgh PA 15238 Office: 415 Holiday Dr Pittsburgh PA 15220

MABEE, CARLETON, educator; b. Shanghai, China, Dec. 25, 1914; s. Fred Carleton and Miriam (Bentley) M.; A.B., Bates Coll., 1936; M.A. (Perkins scholar), Columbia U., 1938, Ph.D., 1942; m. Norma Dierking, Dec. 20, 1945; children—Timothy I., Susan (Mrs. Paul Newhouse). Instr. history Swarthmore (Pa.) Coll., 1944; tutor Olivet (Mich.) Coll., 1947-49; asst. prof. liberal studies Clarkson Coll. Tech., Potsdam, N.Y., 1949-51, asso. prof., 1951-55, prof., 1955-61; dir. social studies div. Delta Coll., University Center, Mich., 1961-64; prof., chmn. dept. humanities and social scis. Rose Poly. Inst., Terre Haute, Ind., 1964-65; prof. history State U. Coll. at New Paltz, N.Y., 1965—, chmn. dept., 1969-73; participant in numerous projects for Am. Friends Service Com., 1941-47, 53, 63. Recipient Pulitzer prize, 1944, Bergstein award excellence teaching Delta Coll., 1963, Anisfield-Wolf award race relations, 1971; research grantee Research Found. State U. N.Y., 1965, 67, 68, Am. Philos. Soc., 1970, Nat. Inst. Edn., 1973-76; Fulbright prof. Keio U., Tokyo, Japan, 1953-54. Mem. N.Y. State, N.Y.C., L.I. hist. assns., Phi Beta Kappa, Delta Sigma Rho. Author: The American Leonardo, A Life of Samuel F.B. Morse, 2d edit., 1969; The Seaway Story, 1961; Black Freedom: The Nonviolent Abolitionists from 1830 through the Civil War, 1970; also articles; editor: (with James A. Fletcher) A Quaker Speaks from the Black Experience: The Life and Selected Writings of Barrington Dunbar, 1979; Black Education in New York State: From Colonial to Modern Times, 1979. Home: RFD Gardiner NY 12525 Office: History Dept State Univ Coll New Paltz NY 12562

MABLEY, JACK, newspaper columnist; b. Binghamton, N.Y., Oct. 26, 1915; s. Clarence Ware and Mabelle (Howe) M.; B.S., U. Ill., 1938; m. Frances Habeck, Aug. 29, 1940; children—Jill, Ann, Pat, Robert. With Chgo. Daily News, 1938-61, reporter, writer, columnist, 1957-61; columnist Chgo.'s Am., 1961-69, asst. mng. editor, 1966-69; asso. editor Chgo. Today, 1969-73; columnist Chgo. Today, Chgo. Tribune, 1973-74, Chgo. Tribune, 1974—. Lectr. journalism Northwestern U., 1949-50. Pres., Village of Glenview, Ill., 1957-61, Skokie Valley Community Hosp., Skokie, Ill., 1977—. Served from ensign to lt. USNR, 1941-45. Recipient Media award Nat. Assn. for Retarded Citizens, 1977. Home: 2275 Winnetka Rd Glenview IL 60025 Office: Chgo Tribune 435 N Michigan Ave Chicago IL 60611

MABLEY, THOMAS, advt. agy. exec.; b. Newton, Kans., June 5, 1933; s. Thomas and Clara (Batjer) M.; student U. Pa. Sch. of Fine Arts, 1952-54; A.B., Wabash Coll., 1957; m. Cary Marvel, Dec. 2, 1961 (div.); children—Winifred Marvel, Jennifer Batuer. Asst. advt. dir. Structural Clay Products Inst., Washington, 1957-62; advt. dir. Home Mfrs. Assn., Washington, 1962-63; sr. copywriter Manchester Orgns., advt., Washington, 1963-64; creative dir. Washington office J. Walter Thompson Co., 1964-68, sr. v.p., creative supr., mem. creative bd., N.Y.C., 1968—; guest lectr. on advt. copywriting. Recipient numerous advt. industry awards for creative work. Episcopalian. Club: St. Elmo (Phila.). Author: The Marines Are Looking For A Few Good Men.*

MABON, JOHN SCOTT, former publisher; b. Yonkers, N.Y., Dec. 26, 1909; s. Arthur Frederick and Elizabeth Prescott (Noyes) M.; B.A., Columbia, 1931; m. Inés Camprubí, Aug. 7, 1936; 1 son, Ferdy. Engaged in real estate and transp. bus., N.Y.C., 1932-34; asst. editor D. Appleton Century Co., Inc., N.Y.C., 1935-38; free-lance reviewer and pub.'s reader, 1938; asso. editor Alfred A. Knopf, Inc., N.Y.C., 1940-41; dir. Atlantic Monthly Press, Boston, 1942-44; asso. editor Ladies Home Jour., Phila., 1945-46; v.p., editor Peoples Book Club, N.Y.C., 1947-52; v.p. La Prensa, N.Y.C., 1952-60; asso. dir. U. Mich. Press, Ann Arbor, 1965-72, 74-75, acting dir., 1972-74. Bd. dirs. Merc. Library Assn., 1948-65. Mem. Delta Psi. Clubs: P.E.N.; Princeton (N.Y.C.). Contbr. book revs. to Saturday Rev., N.Y. Herald-Tribune. Home: 5 Martin Dale Greenwich CT 06830

MABRY, HARRY COOPER, lawyer; b. Carlisle County (Ky.), Feb. 16, 1895; s. Jesse J. and Onie (Nance) M.; grad. summa cum laude, Southwestern Coll., 1916; LL.B., Yale, 1923, J.D., 1971; m. LaVerne Dages, June 30, 1930; children—Dorothy (Mrs. Frank W. Chambers), Marjorie (Mrs. James R. Howard), Elizabeth (Mrs. Ron Rhodes). Admitted to Calif. bar, 1924, also Supreme Ct. bar; since practiced in Los Angeles; former counsel Boulder Dam project, Boulder Dam power line, Mono Basin Water Devel.; local counsel Mfrs. Trust Co., N.Y.C.; spl. counsel Supt. Banks of Calif.; atty. for heirs of Lady Mendl, Don Lee, Jacob H. Wood, Lupe Velez, Jesse E. Anderson, Theodore Kosloff, William Cornell Greene, Mary Greene Wiswall, Michael O'Donnell, Frank Wilkins, others; supt. Moorewood pub. schs., 1913-15. Regional rep. Yale Law Sch., 1928-36, chmn. Yale Class Reunion, 1938, 63, 68, 73; mem. Yale Univ. Alumni Bd. 1968—, Yale Law Sch. Grad. Bd., 1957—; Yale class secretary, 1962—; bd. govs. Yale Publishing Assn., 1933-38. Served as 1st lt. U.S. Army, World War I; aviator; Named hon. Indian chief Pacific Internat. Expn., San Diego, 1936; hon. col. staff Gov. of N.Mex., 1950. Mem. Am. (mem. resolutions com. 21 years, chmn. 1963-64), Los Angeles County bar assns., Am. Coll. Probate Counsel (founder, pres. 1949), Am. Judicature Soc., Chancery Club Am. (pres. 1929-30), Am. Legion (comdr. Los Angeles post 1938-39), S.A.R. (pres. Los Angeles 1942-50), Calif. Jr. C. of C. (pres. 1929-30), A.S.C.A.P., Soc. Authors and Composers Mexico, Los Angeles World Affairs Council, Book and Gavel (Yale), Phi Alpha Delta, Pi Kappa Delta, Tau Kappa Epsilon. Mason, Scottish Rite, Shriner. Clubs: Yale of Southern Calif. (pres. 1934-36); Los Angeles Athletic, Greater Los Angeles Press. Author: Road to Yale; Romance and Results in the Development of Water and Power Resources of Los Angeles; Americanism and the Great American, Will Rogers; The Spirit and the Sword; Decision; Just Barely; Will Contests; Oral Agreements to Provide By Will; Impossibilities in Estate Litigation, Apparent or Real; Disputing Indisputable Presumptions, Revoking Irrevocable Trusts, Breaking Unbreakable Wills and Enforcing Unenforceable Agreements; others. Lyricist, composer: Rainbow of Hawaii; Dear Old Western Home; A Smile Is Worth a Million; I Could Cry Over You; White Cristmas Snow; Alleluia; Back to Mexico; Calypso and Limbo; Yosemite; Catalina Isle; Los Angeles (City of the Angels); (music adaptation) Hail Southwestern Hail (lyrics), others. Home: 2226 N New Hampshire Ave Los Angeles CA 90027. *Motto: Faithful work and fervent prayer. Work: If we do our best, is that not all that Heaven will require, or man can expect? Endeavor: To labor faithfully, to think honestly, to speak truthfully, and to act justly. Goal: To love and be loved by God and man.*

MACADAM, RICHARD G., indsl. designer, automotive co. exec.; b. Wilmington, Del., May 23, 1930; s. John and Christine (Iszard) M.; student U. Del., 1948-49, Phila. Mus. Coll. Art, 1949-51, Pa. Acad. Fine Arts, 1951-54; D.Arts (hon.), Art Center Coll., Pasadena, Calif., 1977; children—Loch I., Heather. Designer, Packard Co., Detroit, 1954-56, Gen. Motors Co., Warren, Mich., 1956-57; with Chrysler Corp., Highland Park, Mich., 1957—, dir. design, 1972-74, v.p. for design, 1974—. Mem. Indsl. Designers Soc. Am., Engring. Soc. Detroit. Clubs: Grosse Pointe Yacht, Detroit Athletic. Office: 12000 Lynn Townsend Dr Highland Park MI 48231

MACADAM, WALTER KAVANAGH, cons. engr.; b. N.Y.C., Nov. 16, 1913; s. John Moore and Mary (Kavanagh) MacA.; B.S. and M.S. in Elec. Engring., Mass. Inst. Tech., 1937; m. Rilla Reed, Jan. 30, 1941; children—Ann (Mrs. Dennis P. Delorier), Marie (Mrs. Paul Hoffman), Clair (Mrs. Bruno Aimi), Daniel, David, Barbara. With AT&T, 1937-68, with long lines dept., 1951-53, 54-56, supt. engring, Distant Early Warning radar installation in Arctic for subsidiary, Western Electric Co. 1953-54, transmission engr. parent co., 1956-59, bldg. and equipment engr., 1959, asst. chief engr., 1959-60, v.p. def., 1960-68; v.p. engring. N.Y. Telephone Co., 1968-73; cons. engr., 1973—. Bd. dirs. United Engring. Trustees, 1965-73, pres., 1971; bd. dirs. N.Y. State Vehicle Polution Control Corp.; trustee Montshire Mus. Sci. Recipient Vail medal AT&T, 1937. Fellow IEEE (dir. 1963—, pres. 1967); mem. ASME, Nat. Soc. Profl. Engrs., Armed Forces Communications and Electronics Assn. (dir. 1968-72), Sigma Xi, Tau Beta Pi, Eta Kappa Nu. Club: K.C. (4 deg.). Home: 10 Rayton Rd Hanover NH 03755

MACALEER, RICHARD JAMES, info. systems co. exec.; b. Elizabeth, N.J., Jan. 29, 1934; s. William and Edna Sara (Green) M.; B.S.E. cum laude, Princeton U., 1955; m. L. Jean Ledbetter, Apr. 23, 1956; children—David, Cynthia, Scott. Systems analyst Hercules Chem. Co., Wilmington, Del., 1959-64; mktg. rep. IBM, Phila., 1964-68; chmn., pres. Shared Med. Systems Corp., King of Prussia, Pa., 1968—; dir. Nat. Central Bank, Lancaster, Pa. Served with USN, 1955-59. Office: 650 Park Ave King of Prussia PA 19406

MACALISTER, PAUL RITTER, designer; b. Camden, N.J., Oct. 15, 1901; s. Alexander and Sarah (Ritter) MacA.; student Pa. Mus. Sch. Indsl. Art, Pa. Acad. Fine Arts; grad. Ecole des Beaux Arts, France, 1924, Yale Sch. Fine Arts, 1926; m. Verner Peterson, June 7, 1926 (dec. 1979); 1 dau., Verner Peterson (dec.). Established MacAlister & Alvord, Inc., N.Y.C., 1926, pres., 1926-31; pres. Paul MacAlister, Inc., N.Y.C., 1931-42; established Permanent Exhbn. of Decorative Arts and Crafts, Inc., Rockefeller Center, pres., 1931-37, dir., 1937-40, dir. pvt. museum Americana Hayloft; designed interior George Vanderbilt home, Sands Point, L.I.; designer interior decorations for yachts owned by Clarence Mackay, Thomas Eastman, others; co-designer interior Rockefeller Model Apt., N.Y.C.; designer Capsule Gallery project; re-entered pvt. practice as pres. Paul MacAlister, Inc., executing interior and indsl. designs, 1940; dir. interior decoration, indsl. design Montgomery Ward, 1946-48; in pvt. practice interior design, style and color consultation to industry, 1948—; co-designer Astrosphere Celestial Globe, 1970; co-designer, mfg. Astrolabe Kit, 1974; Trilogy of Time Instruments Kit, 1976; co-designer, Handcrafted brass Macet Nocturnal ltd. edit., 1978: inventor Plan-A-Room; editor, producer pioneer television program on home decoration America Redecorates, NBC; on WGN-TV, in Plan-A-Room and Interior Decoration; WNBQ-NBC, Chgo., Rooms for Improvement, 1952-53; design, color cons. NBC Home Show. Prize winner Chgo. Tribune's Better Rooms for Better Living, nat. competition, 1948, serving as mem. jury of awards, 1949-51. Served as comdr. USNR, World War II; Recipient Dorothy Dawe award TV Field, 1955. Fellow Indsl. Designers' Inst. (nat. pres. 1950-51; founder design award 1951, chmn. award program 1951-55, 60; Silver medal 1956, citation of merit 1961), Royal Soc. Arts (life), Indsl. Designers Soc. Am.; mem. Beaux Arts Inst. Design, Early Am. Industries Assn., Mil. Order Fgn. Wars. Episcopalian. Club: Yale, Author: Display for Better Business, 1954. Midwest Editor Interior Design and Decoration, 1949-50. Producer: Decorama, color film. Address: Arden Shore Ln Box 157 Lake Bluff IL 60044. *To innovate within the framework of tradition is a concept I have held since my student days in architectural design.*

MACALLISTER, JACK ALFRED, telephone co. exec.; b. Humeston, Iowa, July 12, 1927; s. Maxwell A. and Opal E. (Caldwell) MacA.; B.Commerce, U. Iowa, 1950; student Iowa State Tchrs. Coll., Cedar Rapids, 1947-48; m. Marilyn Anderson, June 12, 1950; children—Steven, James, Sue. With Northwestern Bell Telephone Co., 1950-65, 67—, v.p. ops., Omaha, 1974-75, pres., 1965—; mem. staff AT&T, N.Y.C., 1965-67; dir. Northwest Bancorp., Mpls., U.S. Nat. Bank, Omaha, St. Paul Cos., Inc., Toro Co. Mem. cons. com. SAC; exec. com. econ. devel. council Omaha C. of C.; trustee Midwest Research Inst., Kansas City, Mo.; bd. dirs. Creighton U., Omaha, Creighton-Omaha Regional Health Care Corp. Served with USNR, 1945-46. Clubs: Omaha, Omaha Country; Plaza. Office: Northwestern Bell Telephone Co 100 S 19th St Omaha NE 68102*

MACARTHUR, DONALD MALCOLM, bus. exec.; b. Detroit, Jan. 7, 1931; s. Donald J. and Margaret (MacAulay) MacA.; B.Sc. with honors, St. Andrews (Scotland) U., 1954; Ph.D., Edinburgh (Scotland) U., 1957; m. Diana Taylor, Mar. 31, 1962; children—Elizabeth, Alexander. Mem. faculty U. Conn., 1957-58; with Melpar Inc., 1958-66, mgr. research center, 1964-66; dep. dir. research and tech. Office Sec. Def., 1966-70, cons., 1970-72; pres., chief exec. officer Enviro Control Inc., 1970—, also dir.; pres., chief exec. officer Dynamac Corp., 1975—; chmn. bd. Borriston Research Labs., Inc., 1976—, Consumer Dynamics, Inc., 1976—; cons. water pollution U.S. Dept. Interior, 1965. Trustee Nat. Grad. U., 1970-72. Fellow Am. Inst. Chemists; mem. N.Y. Acad. Scis., Am. Chem. Soc., AAAS., Nat. Assn. Life Sci. Industries (bd. dirs. 1979—). Author tech. articles. Home: 5313 Albemarle St Washington DC 20016 Office: One Central Plaza 11300 Rockville Pike Rockville MD 20852

MACARTHUR, GLORIA, poet; b. Washington, May 14, 1924; d. Emmet Carlyle and Genevieve (Walsh) Gudger; student Vassar Coll., 1942-43; B.A. cum laude, U. Minn., 1946; m. Colin MacArthur, Mar. 17, 1949; 1 son, Glen Cameron. Columnist, Mpls. Daily Times, 1946-48; reporter, page editor Palm Springs (Calif.) News, 1948-49. Recipient Conrad Aiken award Poetry Soc. Ga., 1963, Lucy B. McIntire award, 1968, Thomas Joseph Blackwell Meml. award, 1978; Harry Kovner Meml. Peace award Poetry Soc. Tex., 1964; William Marion Reedy award Poetry Soc. Am., 1966. Mem. poetry socs. Am., Ga., Delta Phi Lambda. Poetry included in anthologies Avalon Anthologies, 1957, 58, Poets of American Anthology, 1957, Epos Anthology, 1958, 75, The Poetry Society America Anthologies, The Golden Year, 1960, The Diamond Anthology, 1971; also in mags. Address: 9901 SW 67th Ave Miami FL 33156

MACARTHUR, JAMES, actor; b. Los Angeles, Dec. 8, 1937; adopted s. Charles MacArthur and Helen Hayes; children—Charles, Mary. Acting debut in The Corn is Green in summer stock, Olney, Md., 1945; appeared on Broadway in Invitation to a March, 1960; films include: The Young Stranger, 1957, The Light in the Forest, 1958, The Third Man on the Mountain, 1959, Kidnapped, 1960, The Swiss Family Robinson, 1960, The Interns, 1962, Spencer's Mountain, 1963, The Truth About Spring, 1965, The Bedford Incident, 1965, Ride Beyond Vengeance, 1966, The Love-Ins, 1967, Hang 'Em High, 1968, The Angry Breed, 1968; regular on TV series Hawaii Five-O, 1968-79; numerous other TV appearances. Office: care Contemporary-Korman Artists Ltd Contemporary Artists Bldg 132 Lasky Dr Beverly Hills CA 90212*

MACAULAY, HUGH HOLLEMAN, JR., educator; b. Seneca, S.C., May 17, 1924; s. Hugh Holleman and Josey (Dendy) M.; student U. Tenn., 1941-42; B.S., U. Ala., 1947, M.S., 1948: Ph.D. in Econs., Columbia, 1957; m. Mary Frances Beavers, Aug. 31, 1947; children—Hugh Holleman III, Mary Anne, Frances Beavers. Faculty, Clemson (S.C.) U., 1949—, prof. econs., 1957-65, Alumni prof. econs., 1965—, dean Grad. Sch., 1961-65; adj. scholar Am. Enterprise Inst.; vis. prof. econs. Tex. Tech U., 1972, Tex. A. and M. U., 1974, 77-78; lectr. econs. Columbia, 1955-56; fiscal economist tax analysis staff Treasury Dept., 1959-60. Mem. Am., So. econ. assns., Nat. Tax Assn. Presbyn. Author: Fringe Benefits and Their Federal Tax Treatment, 1959; (with others) The Pollution Problem, 1968, The Economics of Environmental Quality, 1972; (with T.B. Yandle) Environmental Use and the Market, 1977. Home: Box 72 Clemson SC 29631

MACAULEY, ROBIE MAYHEW, editor; b. Grand Rapids, Mich., May 31, 1919; s. George William and Emma (Hobart) M.; A.B., Kenyon Coll., 1941; M.F.A., State U. Iowa, 1950; postgrad U. London, 1964-65; m. Anne Draper, June 19, 1948; 1 son, Cameron; m. 2d, Pamela Painter, Aug. 9, 1979. Instr. English, Bard Coll., 1946-47, State U. Iowa, 1947-50; asst. prof. U. N.C., 1950-53; editor Kenyon Rev., 1959-66; sr. editor Playboy mag., Chgo., 1966-77, Houghton Mifflin Co., Boston, 1977—; lectr. for State Dept., Australia, 1962. Served with AUS, 1942-46. Guggenheim fellow, 1964; Fulbright research fellow, 1964-65. O'Henry Short Story winner, 1967. Mem. P.E.N. Episcopalian. Author: (novel) The Disguises of Love, 1952; (short stories) The End of Pity, 1957; (criticism) Technique in Fiction, 1964; (novel) A Secret History of Time to Come, 1979. Contbr. to N.Y. Times, Cosmopolitan, New Republic, Vogue, Esquire, Encounter, Partisan Rev., others. Office: Houghton Mifflin Co 2 Park St Boston MA 02107

MAC AVOY, PAUL WEBSTER, economist, educator; b. Haverhill, Mass., Apr. 21, 1934; s. Paul Everett and Louise Madeline (Webster) MacA.; A.B., Bates Coll., 1955, LL.D., 1976; M.A., Yale, 1956, Ph.D., 1960; m. Katherine Ann Manning, June 13, 1955; children—Libby, Matthew. Instr., Yale Coll., 1960; asst. prof. U. Chgo., 1961-63; asst. prof., asso. prof., prof. mgmt. Sloan Sch. Mgmt., Mass. Inst. Tech., Cambridge, 1963-74, Henry R. Luce prof. pub. policy, 1974-75; mem. Pres.'s Council Econ. Advisers, 1975-76; prof. econs. and mgmt. Yale U., 1976-78, Steinbach prof. orgn. and mgmt. and econs., 1979—; dir. Am. Cyanamid, Amax Corp. Trustee, Bates Coll. Author: Price Formation in Natural Gas Fields, 1962; Economic Strategy for Developing Nuclear Breeder Reactors, 1969; (with Stephen Breyer) Energy Regulation by the Federal Power Commission, 1974; (with R. Pindyck) The Economics of the Natural Gas Shortage, 1975; The Economics and Politics of International Commodity Agreements, 1977; The Regulated Industries, 1979; editor: Ford Administration Papers on Regulatory Reform, 8 vols., 1977-78. Home: 652 Nut Plains Rd Guilford CT 06437

MAC AVOY, THOMAS COLEMAN, glass mfg. co. exec.; b. Jamaica, N.Y., Apr. 24, 1928; s. Joseph V. and Edna M. MacA.; B.S. in Chemistry, Queens Coll., 1950; M.S. in Chemistry, St. John's U., 1952, D.Sc. (hon.), 1973; Ph.D. in Chemistry, U. Cin., 1952; m. Margaret M. Walsh, Dec. 27, 1952; children—Moira MacAvoy Brown, Ellen, Christopher, Neil. Chemist, Charles Pfizer & Co., Bklyn., 1957-60; mgr. electronics research Corning Glass Works (N.Y.), 1960-64, dir. phys. research, 1964-66, v.p. electronic products div., 1966-69, v.p. tech. products div., 1969-71, pres., 1971—, also dir.; dir. Quaker Oats Co. Trustee Corning Community Coll., Corning Found., Corning Mus. Glass; pres. N.E. region Boy Scouts Am. Served with USN, 1946; with USAF, 1952-53. Recipient Silver Antelope award Boy Scouts Am., 1976, Silver Beaver award, 1975. Mem. Am. Mgmt. Assn., Electrical Mfrs. Club, Greater Corning Area C. of C. Roman Catholic. Club: Univ. (N.Y.C.). Patentee in field;

contbr. articles to tech. jours. Office: Corning Glass Works Corning NY 14830*

MACBETH, ROBERT ALEXANDER LESLIE, physician, educator; b. Edmonton, Alta., Can., Aug. 26, 1920; s. Alfred William and Agnes (Lewis) M.; B.A., U. Alta., 1942, M.D., 1944; M.Sc., McGill U., 1947; m. Monique Elizabeth Filliol, Aug. 10, 1949; children—Michele Agnes (Mrs. Harold Gordon Cliff), Nicole Elizabeth, Danielle Monique, Joanne Leslie. Intern U. Alta. Hosp. and Royal Alexandra Hosp., Edmonton, 1943-45; resident Montreal Gen. Hosp. and Royal Victoria Hosp., Montreal, 1948-49, 51-52, Children's Meml. Hosp., Montreal, 1949-50, Brit. Postgrad. Med. Sch., Hosp., London, 1950-51; mem. faculty U. Alta. Med. Sch., 1953-75, prof. surgery, chmn. dept., 1960-75; asso. dean, prof. surgery Dalhousie U., St. John, N.B., 1975-77; exec. v.p. Can. Cancer Soc., 1977—; exec. dir. Nat. Cancer Inst. Can., 1977—. Served with M.C., Royal Canadian Army, 1943-46. Recipient Mosher medal, also Harrison prize, 1944. Nuffield overseas fellow, 1950-51; James IV surg. traveler, 1965. Mem. Canadian Med. Assn., Alta. Surg. Soc., Royal Coll. Phys. and Surg. Can., A.C.S., Canadian Assn. Clin. Surgeons, Edmonton Acad. Medicine, Canadian Soc. Clin. Investigation (council 1966-72), Canadian Assn. Gastroenterology, Am., Western surg. assns., Soc. Univ. Surgeons, Surg. Biology Club 11, Soc. Univ. Surg. Chmn., Assn. Am. Med. Colls., Am. Assn. History Medicine, James IV Assn. Contbr. articles to profl. jours. Home: 7 Gordon Rd Willowdale ON M2P 1E2 Canada Office: Suite 401 77 Bloor St W Toronto ON M5S 2V7 Canada

MACBRIDE, THOMAS JAMISON, U.S. judge; b. Sacramento, Mar. 25, 1914; s. Frank and Lotta Kirtley (Little) MacB.; A.B., U. Calif. at Berkeley, 1936, J.D., 1940; m. Martha Harrold, Nov. 7, 1947; children—Peter, Thomas Jamison, David, Laurie. Admitted to Calif. bar, 1940; dep. atty. gen. Calif., 1941-42; pvt. practice, Sacramento, 1946-61; U.S. dist. judge Eastern Dist. Calif., Sacramento, 1961-67, chief judge, 1967-79, sr. judge, 1979—. mem. U.S. Jud. Conf., 1975-78. Pres., Town Hall, Sacramento, 1952, N.E. area YMCA, Sacramento, 1960; mem. Nat. Commn. on Reform Fed. Criminal Laws, 1967-71. Mem. Calif. Legislature from Sacramento County, 1955-60. Bd. dirs. Sacramento YMCA. Served to lt. USNR. 1942-46. Mem. Am. Bar Assn., U. Calif. Alumni Assn. (v.p. 1955, 60), Kappa Sigma, Phi Delta Phi. Democrat. Mason (32 deg., Shriner, Jester), Rotarian (pres. 1966-67). Clubs: Sutter, University (pres. 1953), Comstock (pres. 1975-76); Senator Outing (sec.-treas.). Home: 1800 Rockwood Dr Sacramento CA 95825 Office: 2012 US Courthouse Sacramento CA 95814

MACCALLAN, W(ILLIAM) DAVID, investment co. exec.; b. London, Eng., Apr. 9, 1927; s. Arthur Ferguson and Hester McNeill (Boyd Carpenter) MacC.; came to U.S., 1950, naturalized, 1956; B.Sc., McGill U., Montreal, 1946, M.A., 1948; postgrad. Yale, 1950-52; m. Nancy Dawes Gillmor, Nov. 1, 1947; children—Christopher Daniel, Deirdre Hester. With Brit. and fgn. sect. investment dept. Sun Life Assurance Co. of Can., Montreal, 1947-50; investment research Bank of New York, 1953-55; security analyst Adams Express Co., N.Y.C. and Balt., 1955-69, v.p., 1969-71, chmn. bd., 1971—; chmn. bd. Petroleum & Resources Corp. Mem. Balt. Security Analysts Assn. Clubs: Sky, Economic, Yale (N.Y.C.); Center (Balt.). Home: 1217 Bolton St Baltimore MD 21217 Office: 201 N Charles St Baltimore MD 21201

MAC CALLUM, GERALD CUSHING, JR., educator; b. Spokane, Wash., June 16, 1925; s. Gerald Cushing and Grace C.D. (Hallahan) MacC.; student Wash. State Coll., 1946-48; B.A., U. Calif. at Berkeley, 1950, M.A., 1954, Ph.D., 1961; postgrad. (Fulbright scholar) Oxford U. (Eng.), 1958-59; m. Paulette Naomi Griffith, 1951 (dec. 1975); m. 2d, Susan Louise Feagin, 1977; 1 dau., Deborah Ellen. Instr., Cornell U., Ithaca, N.Y., 1959-61; asst. prof. U. Wis., Madison, 1961-65, asso. prof., 1966-69, prof. philosophy, 1969—, chmn. dept., 1970-72; vis. asso. prof. U. Wash., Seattle, 1965-66. Served with AUS, 1943-46. Am. Council Learned Socs. fellow, 1969-70. Mem. AAUP, Am. Soc. Polit. and Legal Philosophy, Council Polit. Studies, Am. Philos. Assn. (sec.-treas. western div. 1967-69, chmn. com. on status and future of profession 1973-76). Contbr. articles to profl. and legal jours. Home: 726 Copeland St Madison WI 53711 Office: U Wis Dept Philosophy Madison WI 53706

MACCAMPBELL, JAMES CURTIS, librarian; b. Plain City, Ohio, Oct. 17, 1916; s. Lloyd Zenas and Mary (McCullough) MacC.; B.A., Ohio Wesleyan U., 1939; M.A., Ohio State U., 1946, Ph.D., 1957; M.S., Simmons Coll., 1962; m. Barbara Barrett, May 9, 1942. Tchr. elementary and secondary sch., Delaware, Ohio, 1939-42; tchr.-prin. Springfield Twp. pub. schs., Lucas County, Ohio, 1942- 43; prin. Erie County pub. schs., Sandusky, O., 1942-43; elementary sch. supr. Painesville (Ohio) city schs., 1946-48; asst. dir. Univ. Sch., Kent State U., 1948-50; instr. edn. Ohio State U., 1950-52; dir. elementary schs. Cleveland Heights-University Heights City Sch. Dist., Cleve., 1952-57; prof. edn. U. Maine, 1957—, librarian, 1962—, chmn. dept. library service, 1966-76. Pres. Ohio Assn. Supervision and Curriculum Devel., 1949-51; chmn. Maine Library Adv. Commn., 1970-72; mem. Maine Library Commn., 1976—; mem. library adv. council to pub. printer GPO, 1975-78. Trustee Bangor-Brewer Tb Assn., 1968-76, pres., 1970-74. Mem. NEA, ALA, New Eng. Library Assn. (dir.), Am. Assn. U. Profs., Assn. Coll. and Research Libraries. Author articles, book revs. Editor: Readings in the Language Arts in the Elementary School, 1964; (with Eleanor Peck) Focus on Reading, 1965. Home: 12 Mainewood Ave Orono ME 04473. *As I grow older, I find myself growing more philosophical and greatly more optimistic about the improvability of mankind. The world, in spite of its chaotic aspects, is slowly becoming a better place, and young people—under the sympathetic and skillful tutelage of their elders—will continue to be the catalyst that can continue to improve the lives of all people everywhere.*

MAC CARTHY, JOHN PETERS, trust co. exec.; b. St. Louis, Apr. 6, 1933; s. John Donald and Ruth (Peters) Mac C.; A.B., Princeton U., 1954; LL.B., Harvard U., 1959; m. Talbot Leland, June 21, 1958; children—John Leland, Talbot Peters. Admitted to Mo. bar, 1959; partner Bryan Cave McPheeters & McRoberts, St. Louis, 1959-69; sec. 1st Union Co., bank holding co., St. Louis, 1969—, also dir.; sec. St. Louis Union Trust Co., 1969-72, exec. v.p., 1972-75, pres., 1975—, chief exec. officer, 1979—, also dir.; vice chmn. First Union Bancorp., St. Louis, 1979—; dir. KSH Inc., Ocean Drilling and Exploration Co., Miss. Lime Co. Trustee Washington U., St. Louis, 1972—, St. Louis Art Mus., 1976—, St. Louis Country Day Sch., 1973—. Served with USNR, 1954-56. Mem. Am. Bar Assn., St. Louis Bar Assn. Clubs: Noonday, Bogey, St. Louis Country. Home: 6 Robin Hill Ln Saint Louis MO 63124 Office: St Louis Union Trust Co 510 Locust St Saint Louis MO 63101

MACCARTY, COLLIN STEWART, neurosurgeon; b. Rochester, Minn., Sept. 20, 1915; s. William Carpenter and Helen M. (Collin) MacC.; A.B., Dartmouth, 1937; M.D. Johns Hopkins, 1940; M.S. in Neurosurgery (fellow 1941-44), Mayo Found., U. Minn., 1944; m. Margery Deal, June 15, 1940; children—Collin Stewart, Robert Lee, Helen Carpenter. Surg. house officer Johns Hopkins Hosp., 1940-41; mem. staff neurosurgery Mayo Clinic, 1946—, chmn. dept. neurosurgery, 1963-75, pres. med. staff, 1966; mem. faculty Mayo Found., U. Minn., 1947—, prof. neurol. surgery, 1961-73, asso. dir. for grad. edn., 1975-79, dir. for grad. edn., 1979—; prof. neurol. surgery Mayo Med. Sch., 1973—; vis. prof. Western Res. U., 1966, Johns Hopkins U., 1969, U. Okla., 1971, Ohio State U. Coll. Medicine, 1977; cons. neurosurgery Lackland AFB, 1971; cons. Surgeon Gen. U.S. Navy, 1977. Chmn., Mayo Centennial Com., 1960-64, also semicentennial Mayo Found. Med. Edn. and Research. Mem. adv. com. to dean Dartmouth Med. Sch., 1968-72, bd. overseers, 1973—, chmn. bd. overseers, 1977—; mem. adv. bd. medicine and surgery Dept. Navy, 1970. Served to lt. M.C., USNR, 1944-46. Diplomate Am. Bd. Neurol. Surgery (del.). Mem. Neurosurg. Soc. Am. (v.p. 1954, pres. 1959), A.C.S. (grad. edn. com. 1968-72), Am. Assn. Neurol. Surgeons (dir. 1965-73, v.p. 1965-66, pres. 1970-71, del. World Fedn. 1973, 77), World Fedn. Neurosurgery Soc. (sec. congress affairs 1965-69), Soc. Neurol. Surgeons (rep. to Am. Bd. Neurol. Surgery 1972—), AMA (mem. council med. edn. 1967-72), Minn. Med. Assn., Zumbro Valley Med. Soc., Neurosurg. Travel Club, Societa Italiana de Neurochirurgia (corr.), Egyptian Soc. Neurol. Surgeons (hon.), Sigma Xi. Club: Internat. Travellers. Author: The Surgical Treatment of Intracranial Meningiomas, 1961; (with Kernohan and Slooff) Primary Intramedullary Tumors of the Spinal Cord and Filum Terminale, 1964. Developed spinal cordectomy and selective spinal cordectomy, also surg. treatment sacrococcygeal chordomas. Home: 207 5th Ave SW Rochester MN 55901 Office: Mayo Clinic Rochester MN 55901

MACCOBY, ELEANOR EMMONS, educator; b. Tacoma, May 15, 1917; d. H. Eugene and Viva (Johnson) Emmons; student Reed Coll., 1934-35, 36-37; B.A., U. Wash., 1939; M.A., U. Mich., 1949, Ph.D., 1950; m. Nathan Maccoby, Sept. 16, 1938; children—Janice B. (Mrs. Douglass Carmichael), Sarah, Mark. Study dir., div. program surveys Dept. Agr., 1942-46, Survey Research Center, U. Mich., 1946-48, lectr. social relations Harvard, 1950-58; faculty Stanford U., 1958—, prof. psychology, 1958—, chmn. dept., 1973-76. Center for Advanced Study in Behavioral Sci. fellow, 1969-70. Fellow Am. Psychol. Assn. (div. pres. child psychology); mem. Soc. Research Child Devel. (gov. council 1963; pres.-elect 1979—), Western Psychol. Assn. (pres. 1974-75). Author: (with R.R. Sears, H. Levin) Patterns of Child Rearing, 1957; (with M. Zellner) Experiments in Primary Education, 1970; (with C.N. Jacklin) The Psychology of Sex Differences, 1974. Editor: Readings in Social Psychology, 1957; Development of Sex Differences, 1966. Contbr. articles to profl. jours. Home: 729 Mayfield Ave Stanford CA 94305

MACCOBY, NATHAN, communication psychologist, educator; b. London, Eng., Feb. 17, 1912; s. Moses Isaac and Ethel Leah (Fisher) M.; A.B., Reed Coll., 1933; A.M., U. Wash., 1938; Ph.D., U. Mich., 1950; m. Eleanor Emmons, Sept. 16, 1938; children—Janice B., Sarah B. (Mrs. Russell N. Hatch), Mark E. Instr. psychology Oreg. State Coll., 1939-40; examiner U.S. CSC, 1940-42; adminstrv. officer fuel rationing div. OPA, 1942-43, asst. chief, chief placement officer, 1945-47; research psychologist U.S. Army Info. and Edn. div., 1943-45; study dir. human relations and group orgn., survey research center U. Mich., 1947-49; dir. div. research. sch. pub. relations and communications Boston U., 1949-59, chmn. psychology dept., 1954-59, Earl Newsom prof. opinion research, 1949-54, prof. communication research 1955-59; vis. prof. psychology and communication-journalism, Stanford, 1958-59, prof. communication, 1959-77, James M. Peck prof. internat. communication, 1975-77, prof. emeritus, 1977—, acting dir. Inst. Communication Research, 1962-63, 69-70, dir., 1973—, acting exec. head dept. communication, 1963-64, chmn., 1970-71, staff com. fgn. affairs personnel, 1961-63, co-dir. heart disease prevention community studies program, 1972—; cons. Nat. Research Council, Nat. Heart, Lung and Blood Inst., NIH, Dept. State, Inst. Medicine; adv. council on edn. for health Am. Council Life Ins.; bd. dirs., cons. Center Consumer Health Edn. Fellow AAAS, Am. Psychol. Assn.; mem. Am. Assn. Pub. Opinion Research, Soc. Psychol. Study Social Issues (council mem. 1965-69, chmn. research grants-in-aid com. 1966-68), Internat. Communication Assn. (dir. 1972—, pres. 1974-75), Sigma XI. Asso. editor Jour. Communication; mem. editorial bd. Pub. Opinion Quar. Contbr. articles to profl. jours. Home: 729 Mayfield Ave Stanford CA 94305

MAC CORKLE, STUART ALEXANDER, author; b. Lexington, Va., Sept. 1, 1903; s. John Gold and Mattie Ella (Swink) MacC.; A.B., Washington and Lee U., 1924, LL.D., 1964; M.A., U. Va., 1928, Ph.D., Johns Hopkins, 1931; m. L. Lucile Emerson, Sept. 26, 1942. Instr. govt. U. Tex., 1930-31; asso. prof. govt. Southwestern Coll., 1931-32; instr. govt. U. Tex., 1932-34, asst. prof., 1934-37, asso. prof., dir. Bur. Municipal Research, 1937-41, prof., dir., 1941-50, prof., dir. Inst. Pub. Affairs, 1950-67; now pvt. cons. Chief adviser pub. adminstrn. Seoul Nat. U., 1958-60; Fulbright lectr. Coll. Europe, Bruges, Belgium, 1964; vis. ednl. counselor Nat. Inst. Pub. Affairs, 1941-42; lectr. Nat. U. Mexico, summer 1944, 68; mem. summer session staff U. Ill., 1946; spl. cons. USAAF, 1942. Prin. civilian mblzn. adviser Office of Civilian Def., 1942-43; chmn. Tex. Tax Commn., 1949; exec. dir. Tex. Economy Commn., 1951-52; mem. Austin City Council, 1949-51, 69-71, mayor pro tem, 1951-53, 69-71. Mem. Southwestern Social Sci. Assn. (sec.-treas. 1934-37), Am. Polit. Sci. Assn., Am. Soc. for Pub. Adminstrn., Internat. (hon. life), Tex. (hon. life) city mgrs. assns., Phi Beta Kappa, Pi Sigma Alpha, Kappa Sigma. Rotarian. Clubs: University (Washington); Headliners (Austin). Author: The American Recognition Policy Toward Mexico, 1933; Police and Allied Powers of Municipalities in Texas, 1938; Municipal Administration, 1942; American Municipal Government and Administration, 1948; (with Dick Smith) Texas Government, 1949, rev., 1974, 8th edit. (with Janice C. May), 1979; Austin's Three Forms of Government, 1973; Cities from Scratch, 1974; (with Dick Smith, Thomas P. Yoakum) Texas Civics, 1955. Editorial bd. Public Administration Rev., 1942-44. Contbr. articles to profl. Jours., newspapers. Home: 3719 Gilbert Austin TX 78703. *What little success I may have attained in life is largely due to two factors. First, my parents expected me to succeed. I have tried not to disappoint them. Second, back of all success there must be a willing capacity for hard work.*

MACCORQUODALE, KENNETH, psychologist, educator; b. Olivia, Minn., June 26, 1919; s. Alexander Ross and Hallie (Chambers) MacC.; B.A., U. Minn., 1941, M.A., 1942, Ph.D., 1946; m. Sally Sperling, July 9, 1976. From instr. to asso. prof. psychology U. Minn., Mpls., 1946-55, prof., 1955—, chmn. dept., 1960-64; vis. prof. U. Calif., Los Angeles, 1959, U. Calif., Riverside, 1964; cons., NIMH; mem. Dartmouth Conf. on Learning Theory, Social Sci. Research Council, 1951. Mem. sponsoring com. Am.-Scottish Found. Fellow Ford Found. Fund Advancement Edn., 1954-55, Minn. Center Philosophy Sci., 1955. Mem. N.Y. Acad. Scis., Am., Midwestern psychol. assns., Psychonomic Soc., AAAS, Sigma Xi. Co-author: Modern Learning Theory, 1954. Editor: Wiley Interscience Series in Behavior. Home: 1530 S 6th St Minneapolis MN 55455 Office: Psychology Dept Elliott Hall U Minn Minneapolis MN 55455

MAC COWATT, HASKELL PAWLING, broadcasting exec.; b. Plainfield, N.J., Apr. 15, 1931; s. Horace Haskell and Carolyn Fowler (Darby) MacC.; A.B., Colgate U., 1953; M.S. (Sloan fellow), Mass. Inst. Tech., 1973; m. Margaret Haydee Gentles, Apr. 23, 1960; children—Thomas Haskell, Nancy Wallace, Sally Pawling. Copywriter, Batten, Barton, Durstine & Osborn, 1956-60, account exec., 1960-62; asst. dir. advt. and sales promotion CBS TV Network, 1962-64; mgr. design CBS Inc., N.Y.C., 1964-66, dir. corporate info., 1966-69, dir. investor relations, 1969-73, v.p. investor relations, 1973-75, v.p., treas., 1975-77, v.p. adminstrn., 1977—. Bd. dirs. Colgate U. Alumni Corp. Served with U.S. Army, 1954-56. Office: 51 W 52d St New York City NY 10019

MACCRATE, ROBERT, lawyer; b. Bklyn., July 18, 1921; s. John and Flora (MacNicholl) MacC.; B.A., Haverford Coll., 1943; LL.B., Harvard U., 1948; m. Constance Trapp, May 4, 1946; children—Christopher Robert, Barbara Constance MacCrate Gatti, Thomas John. Admitted to N.Y. bar, 1949, U.S. Supreme Ct. bar, 1955, D.C. bar, 1965; asso. firm Sullivan & Cromwell, N.Y.C., 1948-51, 51-55, partner, 1956-59, 62—; law sec. to N.Y. Appelate Div. Presding Justice David W. Peck, 1951; counsel to N.Y. Gov. Nelson A. Rockefeller, 1959-62; spl. counsel to U.S. Army for Investigation Mylai incident, 1969-70; adv. Bata Shoe Orgn.; counsel N.Y. State Ct. on Judiciary, 1971; mem. jud. selection com. for fed. judgeships Senator Jacob K. Javits, 1972—; mem. jud. nominating com. N.Y. 2d Jud. Dept., 1975—; trustee Lawyers Com. for Civil Rights Under Law, 1976—; chmn. Fund for Modern Cts., 1978—. Bd. mgrs. Haverford Coll., 1971—. Served to lt. USNR, 1943-46. Fellow Am. Bar Found. (chmn. N.Y. state 1973—); mem. Am. Bar Assn. (del. 1972-78, N.Y. State del. 1979—), N.Y. State Bar Assn. (pres. 1972-73, del. 1972—), Assn. Bar City N.Y. (v.p. 1969-71, chmn. exec. com. 1968-69, chmn. library com. 1977—), N.Y. County Lawyers Assn., D.C. Bar Assn., Am. Coll. Trial Lawyers, Am. Soc. Internat. Law (exec. council 1975—), Union Internationale des Avocats, Acad. Polit. Sci. (dir. 1975—), Am. Acad. Polit. and Social Sci., Am. Judicature Soc. (pres. 1979—, dir. and mem. exec. com. 1974—), Practising Law Inst. (trustee and mem. exec. com. 1972—), Am. Law Inst. (exec. com. council 1975—), N.Y. Bar Found. (pres. 1976—), Phi Beta Kappa. Clubs: Century Assn., Recess, Univ. (N.Y.C.); Ft. Orange (Albany, N.Y.); Port Washington (N.Y.) Yacht. Contbr. articles to profl. jours. Home: 40 The Terrace Plandome NY 11030 Office: 125 Broad St New York NY 10004 also 1775 Pennsylvania Ave Washington DC 20006

MACCRIMMON, KENNETH ROBERT, ednl. adminstr., educator; b. Hamilton, Ont., Can., Dec. 28, 1937; s. Archibald Robert and Dorothy Anna (Williams) MacC.; B.S., UCLA, 1959, M.B.A., 1960, Ph.D., 1965; m. Marilyn L. Turner, Feb. 3, 1962; children—Karyn, Keith, Brian. Asst. prof. bus. adminstrn. Carnegie-Mellon U., 1964-68, asso. prof., 1968-70; prof. bus. adminstrn. U. B.C. (Can.), Vancouver, 1970—, asst. dean grad. studies, 1978—; cons. to industry. Can. Council sabbatical leave fellow, 1975-76; Social Scis. and Humanities research grantee, 1972—; Def. Research Bd. grantee, 1972-75; Industry, Trade and Commerce grantee, 1972-75. Mem. Econometric Soc., Am. Econ. Assn., Am. Polit. Sci. Assn., Can. Polit. Sci. Assn., Ops. Research Soc., Instl. Mgmt. Scis., Can. Assn. Univ. Tchrs. Contbr. articles on mgmt., econs, and psychology to profl. publs.; asso. editor Jour. Am. Statis. Assn., 1978—; INFORS, 1978—; editorial bd. Jour. Enterprise Mgmt., 1978—. Home: 4593 W 6th Ave Vancouver BC V6R 1V4 Canada Office: Faculty of Commerce U BC Vancouver BC V6T 1W5 Canada

MACCURDY, RAYMOND RALPH, JR., educator; b. Oklahoma City, May 12, 1916; s. Raymond R. and Ada May (Eastland) MacC.; B.A., La. State U., 1939; M.A., 1941; Ph.D., U. N.C., 1948; m. Blanche Hermine Wolf, June 2, 1939; children—George Grant II, William Douglas. Asso. prof. modern langs. U. Ga., 1948-49; asso. prof. modern langs. U. N.Mex., Albuquerque, 1949-53, prof., 1953—, chmn. dept. modern and classical langs., 1963-68. Nat. Def. Edn. Act. coordinator lang. Programs Am. Assn. Tchrs. Spanish and Portuguese, 1958-59. Served to maj. AUS, World War II; CBI. Julius Rosenwald fellow, 1941, 46; Fund for Advancement Edn. fellow, 1954-55; Fulbright research scholar, Spain, 1960-61, Mem. Rocky Mountain Modern Lang. Assn. (pres. 1957), Hispanic Soc. Am. Author: The Spanish Dialect in St. Bernard Parish, Louisiana, 1950; Francisco de Rojas Zorrilla and the Tragedy, 1958; Francisco de Rojas Zorilla, 1969. Editor: Rojas Zorrilla, Morir Pensando Matar, La Vida en el Ataud, 1961; Lucrecia y Tarquino, 1963; Numancia Cercada y Numancia destruida, 1977; Tirso de Molina, El Burlador de Sevilla, 1965; Del rey abajo, ninguno, 1970; Spanish Drama of the Golden Age-Twelve Plays, 1971; The Tragic Fall: Don Alvaro de Luna and Other Favorites in Spanish Golden Age Drama, 1978. Home: 1804 Newton Pl NE Albuquerque NM 87106

MACDANIEL, GIBBS, JR., financial exec.; b. San Antonio, Feb. 8, 1937; s. Gibbs and Virginia Morse (Paine) M.; B.A., U. Tex., Austin, 1958; M.A., Johns Hopkins U., 1962; m. Grace Nan Jennings, June 7, 1958; children—Gibbs, III, Shelley Grace. Asst. mgr. First Nat. City Bank, N.Y.C., Panama and Honduras, 1962-68; v.p., mgr. Houston Nat. Bank, 1968-75; treas. Raymond Internat. Inc., Houston, 1976-79; mng. asso. Korn/Ferry Internat., Houston, 1979—; dir. Galleria Bank, Houston. Served to lt. USNR, 1958-60. Mem. Fin. Execs. Inst., Houston World Trade Assn. (pres. 1974-76), Bankers Assn. Fgn. Trade (dir. 1975-76). Methodist. Club: Briar (Houston). Home: 2528 Reba Dr Houston TX 77019 Office: 1225 Galleria Tower East Houston TX 77056

MACDERMOT, GALT, composer; b. Montreal, Can., Dec. 19, 1928; s. Terrence and Elizabeth (Savage) MacD.; ed. Capetown (S. Africa) U.; m. Marlene Bruynzell; 4 children. Formerly ch. organist, then dance band musician; composer: African Waltz (Grammy award), 1961; Hair (Grammy award; Vernon Rice award, Drama Desk award), 1968; Two Gentlemen of Verona (Drama Desk award, Critics' Circle award), 1971-72; A Gun Play, 1971; Hairpieces; composer films: Cotton Comes to Harlem, 1970, Fortune and Men's Eyes, 1971, Rhinoceros, 1974; theatre music; Hamlet, 1967, Twelfth Night, 1969, Dude, 1972, The Maxi-Bar Tragedy, 1972-73, La Novella-A Puerto Rican Soap Opera, 1973, The Karl Marx Play, 1973, Straws in the Wind, 1974, others; composer: Mass in F, 1971, Take This Bread-A Mass in Our Time, 1975. Address: care ASCAP 1 Lincoln Plaza New York NY 10020*

MACDONALD, ALAN HUGH, librarian, univ. adminstr.; b. Ottawa, Ont., Can., Mar. 3, 1943; s. Vincent C. and Hilda C. (Durney) MacD.; B.A., Dalhousie U., Halifax N.S., 1963; B.L.S., U. Toronto (Ont.), 1964; m. Elizabeth McGonigal. With Dalhousie U., 1964-78, asst. univ. librarian, 1970-72, health sci. librarian, 1972-78, lectr. Sch. Library Services, 1969-78; dir. libraries U. Calgary (Alta., Can.), 1979—; librarian N.S. Barristers Soc., 1969-74; mem. adv. bd. Nat. Library Can., 1972-76, Health Scis. Resource Centre, Can. Inst. Sci. and Tech. Info., 1977-79. Pres. TELED, community media access orgn., Halifax, N.S., 1972-74. Council Library Resources fellow, 1975. Mem. Can. Library Assn. (treas. 1977-79, v.p., pres.-elect 1979-80), Atlantic Provinces Library Assn. (pres. 1977-78), Library Assn. Alta., Can. Health Library Assn. (treas. 1977-79), Can. Assn. Law Libraries, Library Assn. Australia (asso. 1977), N.Z. Library Assn., Foothills Library Assn., Can. Assn. Info Sci. (pres. 1979-80), Can. Assn. Univ. Tchrs. Office: 2920 24th Ave NW Calgary AB T2K 1N4 Canada

MACDONALD, BRIAN, choreographer; b. Montreal, Que., Can., May 14, 1928; s. Ian Ronald and Mabel (Lee) M.; B.A. in English, McGill U. (Can.), 1953; studied with Gerald Crevier, Elizabeth Leese,

Francoise Sullivan; student Martha Graham Sch.; m. Annette Weidersheim-Paul, Dec. 20, 1964. Music critic Montreal Herald, 1949-51; charter mem. corps. de ballet Nat. Ballet Can., Toronto, Ont., 1951-53; co-founder Montreal Ballet Theatre, 1956; vis. choreographer Royal Winnipeg (Man., Can.) Ballet, 1958, ofcl. choreographer, from 1959; dir. Royal Swedish Ballet, Stockholm, 1964-66, Norwegian Ballet, Oslo, 1964-66; founder Royal Swedish Ballet Festival, 1965; artistic dir. Harkness Ballet, 1967-68; artistic dir. Les Grands Ballet Canadiens, Montreal, from 1974, now resident choreographer; formerly mem. staff Banff Sch. Fine Arts; formerly dir. Nat. Theatre Sch.; has done choreography for Robert Joffrey Ballet, Banff Sch. Festival Ballet, others. Decorated medal of service of Order Can.; recipient Gold Star for best abstract ballet 2nd Paris Internat. Festival of Dance, 1964; King's scholar, Stockholm; Can. Council sr. arts fellow, 1958, 60-61. Office: care Les Grands Ballet Canadiens 5465 Queen Mary Rd Montreal PQ H3X 1V5 Canada*

MACDONALD, CALEB ALAN, frozen food co. exec.; b. Norwalk, Ohio, May 19, 1933; s. Julian Fairman and Ruth (Laylin) MacD.; B.S. in Hotel Mgmt., Cornell U., 1955; m. Marilyn Miller, Feb. 1, 1955; children—Mark Alan, Diane Laylin. With restaurant div. Stouffer Corp., 1955-62, with frozen foods div., 1962—, v.p., gen. mgr., Solon, Ohio, 1968-72, pres., 1972—; exec. v.p. Stouffer Corp.; chmn. food service adv. com., trustee Cleve. Soc. Blind. Mem. Am. Frozen Food Inst. (1st vice chmn., dir.), FACT (chmn. mktg. com.), Internat. Frozen Food Assn., Solon C. of C. (pres. 1972), Bluecoats. Republican. Episcopalian. Club: Country. Office: 5750 Harper Rd Solon OH 44139

MACDONALD, CYNTHIA LEE, poet, educator; b. N.Y.C., Feb. 2, 1928; d. Leonard C. and Dorothy Tim (Kiam) Lee; B.A., Bennington Coll., 1950; M.A., Sarah Lawrence Coll., 1970; children—Jennifer Tim, Scott Thurston. Teaching asst. Sarah Lawrence Coll., Bronxville, N.Y., 1969-70, asst. prof. Horace Gregory writing program, 1970-74, acting dean of studies, asso. prof., 1974-75; vis. prof. The Writing Seminars, Johns Hopkins U., Balt., 1975-76, prof., 1976-79; prof., dir. creative writing program dept. English, U. Houston, 1979—. Recipient award Am. Inst. Arts Letters, 1977; Nat. Endowment Arts grantee, 1973, 78; Rockefeller fellow Aspen Inst. for Humanistic Studies, 1978. Mem. Poetry Soc. Am., PEN. Author poetry: Amputations, 1972; Transplants, 1976; Pruning the Annuals, 1976; (W)holes, 1980. Office: Dept English University of Houston Houston TX 77004

MACDONALD, DANIEL JOSEPH, Can. govt. ofcl.; b. Bothwell, P.E.I., Can., July 23, 1918; s. Daniel Lauchlin and Elizabeth Margaret (Fisher) MacD.; student Bothwell schs.; m. Pauline Peters, Nov. 13, 1946; children—Blair, Heather, Gail, Daniel, Leo, Walter, Gloria. Engaged in farming, Bothwell, 1938-40, 45—; pres. local Coop. Assn., 1955-60; mem. Legis. Assembly for First Kings, 1962-72; minister of agr. and forestry, 1966-72; mem. Parliament for Cardigan, 1972—; minister vets. affairs, 1972—. Mem. South Lake Sch. Bd., 1960's. Served with Can. Army, 1940-45; Italy. Recipient Confedn. Centennial medal, 1973; hon. col. P.E.I. Regt. Mem. War Amputations Can., Royal Can. Legion (past br. pres.). Liberal. Roman Catholic. Clubs: Lions, K.C. Home: Bothwell PE C0A 2B0 Canada Office: Room 507 Confedn Bldg House of Commons Ottawa ON K1A 0X2 Canada

MACDONALD, DAVID ROBERT, lawyer; b. Chgo., Nov. 1, 1930; s. James Wear and Frances Esther (Wine) M.; B.S., Cornell U., 1952; J.D., U. Mich., 1955; m. Verna Joy Odell, Feb. 17, 1962; children—Martha, Emily, David, Rachel, Rebecca. Admitted to Ill. bar, 1955; practiced in Chgo., 1957-74; mem. firm Kirkland, Ellis, Hodson, Chaffetz & Masters, Chgo., 1957-62, partner, 1962; partner Baker & McKenzie, Chgo., 1962-74, 77—; asst. sec. of Treasury for enforcement, ops. and tariff affairs Dept. Treasury, Washington, 1974-76; undersec. of Navy, 1976-77; dir. Chgo. City Bank, Reed Nat. Corp.; mem. Chgo. Crime Commn., 1977—. Nat. chmn. U. Mich. Law Sch. Fund, 1977-78; mem. com. visitors U. Mich. Law Sch., 1962—. Served with AUS, 1955-57. Mem. Am., Ill., Chgo. bar assns., Chgo. Assn. Commerce and Industry (dir. 1977—). Club: Econ. (Chgo.). Home: 411 Sheridan Rd Winnetka IL 60093 Office: Room 2900 Prudential Plaza Chicago IL 60601

MACDONALD, DONALD ARTHUR, pub. co. exec.; b. Union City, N.J., Nov. 30, 1919; s. Richard A. and Marie (McDonald) M.; B.S. cum laude, N.Y. U., 1948, M.B.A., 1950; m. Ruth Moran, Dec. 21, 1942; children—Ronald A., Martha J., Marie C., Donald A., Charles A. Advt. sales rep. Wall Street Jour., Dow Jones & Co., Inc., N.Y.C., 1953-55, mgr. New Eng. and Canadian ter., 1955-58, Eastern advt. mgr., 1958-61, exec. advt. mgr., 1961-63, advt. dir. sales promotion and prodn. depts., 1963-67, v.p. advt. sales, 1970-74, sr. v.p., 1974—, mem. mgmt. com., 1967—; vice chmn. Dow Jones & Co. Inc., 1979—, also dir.; chmn. council judges Advt. Hall of Fame, 1972-78. Recipient Silver medal Advt. Club N.Y., 1965. Served to capt. AUS, 1942-46. Mem. Assn. Indsl. Advertisers, Am. Advt. Fedn. (dir. 1962—, past chmn.), Advt. Fedn. Am. (past gov. 2d dist., past chmn. joint commn., past chmn.), Advt. Council (dir.), N.Y. Advt. Club (dir.), Beta Gamma Sigma. Club: Downtown Athletic, Univ. (N.Y.C.); Rumson Country (N.J.). Home: 15 Buttonwood Ln Rumson NJ 07760 Office: 22 Cortlandt St New York NY 10007

MACDONALD, DONALD STOVEL, lawyer, former Canadian govt. ofcl.; b. Ottawa, Ont., Can., Mar. 1, 1932; s. Donald Angus and Marjorie (Stovel) M.; student Ashbury Coll., Ottawa; B.A., U. Toronto, 1951; grad. Osgoode Hall Sch., 1955; LL.M., Harvard, 1956; diploma internat. law Cambridge U., 1957; LL.D., St. Lawrence U.; D.Eng., Colo. Sch. Mines; m. Ruth Hutchison, Mar. 4, 1961; children—Leigh, Nikki, Althea, Sonja. Called to Ont. bar, 1955; asso. McCarthy & McCarthy, Toronto, 1957-62; M.P. for Toronto-Rosedale, 1962, reelected 1963, 65, 68, 72, 74; parliamentary sec. to Minister of Justice, 1963-65, to Minister of Finance, 1965, to Sec. of State for External Affairs, 1966-68, to Minister of Industry, 1968; apptd. minister without portfolio, 1968; pres. Privy Council and Govt. House Leader, 1968; minister of nat. def., Ottawa, 1970-72; minister energy, mines and resources, 1972-75; minister of finance, 1975-77; partner firm McCarthy & McCarthy, Toronto, 1977—; spl. lectr. U. Toronto Law Sch.; dir. Boise Cascade Corp., DuPont Can. Inc., Mfrs. Life Ins. Co., McDonnell Douglas Corp., Shell Can. Ltd.; mem. Can.-Am. com. Trilateral Commn. Mem. Delta Kappa Epsilon. Liberal. Baptist. Home: 29 Dunvegan Rd Toronto ON M4V 2P5 Canada Office: PO Box 48 Toronto Dominion Center Toronto ON Canada

MACDONALD, DWIGHT, author; b. N.Y.C., Mar. 24, 1906; s. Dwight and Alice (Hedges) M.; grad. Phillips Exeter Acad., 1924; B.A., Yale, 1928; Litt.D. (hon.), Wesleyan U., Middletown, Conn., 1964; m. Nancy Rodman, 1935 (div. 1950); children—Michael, Nicholas; m. 2d, Gloria Lanier, 1950; stepchildren—Day, Sabina. Staff writer Fortune, 1929-36; asso. editor Partisan Rev., 1937-43; editor and pub. Politics, 1944-49; staff writer New Yorker mag., 1951-71; movie critic Esquire mag., 1960-66; vis. prof. Northwestern U., 1956, Bard Coll., 1960, U. Tex. at Austin, 1966, U. Calif. at Santa Cruz, 1969, Hofstra U., 1969-70, U. Wis. at Milw., 1970, U. Mass. at Amherst, 1971, Yale, 1971, State U. N.Y. at Buffalo, 1973-74, John Jay Coll., 1974-76, U. Calif. at San Diego, 1977. Chmn. Spanish Refugee Aid, 1968—. Guggenheim fellow, 1966; fellow Ezra Stiles Coll., Yale, 1967—. Mem. Am. Acad. Arts and Scis., Am. Inst. Arts and Letters, Hedonists, Psi Upsilon. Author: Henry Wallace: The Man and the Myth, 1948; The Root is Man, 1953; The Ford Foundation, 1956; Against the American Grain: Essays on the Effects of Mass Culture, 1962; Dwight Macdonald on Movies, 1969; Politics Past, 1970; Discriminations: Essays & Afterthoughts, 1938-74; Editor: Parodies, an Anthology from Chaucer to Beerbohm-and After, 1960; Selected Poems of Edgar Allan Poe (with hist. and critical intro.), 1966; My Past & Thoughts An Annotated Abridgment of the Memoirs of Alexander Herzen, 1973. Home: Spring Close Ln East Hampton NY 11937 also 56 E 87th St New York NY 10028

MACDONALD, FLORA ISABEL, Can. govt. ofcl.; b. North Sydney, N.S., Can., June 3, 1926; d. George Frederick and Mary Isabel (Royle) MacD.; attended Empire Bus. Coll.; grad. Nat. Def. Coll., 1972; D.H.L. (hon.), Mt. St. Vincent U., 1979. Formerly in various secretarial positions; with Progressive Conservative Party Hdqrs., Ottawa, Ont., Can., 1956-65, exec. dir., 1960-65; adminstrv. officer, tutor dept. polit. studies Queen's U., 1966-72, also cons. Student Vo. Bur.; mem. Can. Parliament for Kingston and the Islands, Ont., 1972—, Progressive Conservative spokesman for Indian Affairs and No. Devel., 1972, for Housing and Urban Devel., 1974, chmn. Progressive Conservative Caucus Com. on Fed.-Provincial Relations, 1976, minister of state for external affairs, 1979—. Vice pres. Kingston and Islands Progressive Conservative Assn, 1962-72; nat. sec. Progressive Conservative Assn. of Can., 1966-69; exec. dir. Com. for Ind. Can., 1971; pres. Elizabeth Fry Soc. of Kingston, 1968-70; mem. fin. com. Hotel Dieu Hosp., 1969-71; co-chmn. Kingston Waterfront Com., 1971. Mem. Can. Inst. Fgn. Affairs (dir. 1969-73), Can. Polit. Sci. Assn. (dir. 1972-75), Can. Inst. Internat. Affairs, Can. Civil Liberties Assn. Mem. United Ch. of Canada. Office: House of Commons Ottawa ON K1A 0A6 Canada also Dept External Affairs Lester B Pearson Bldg 125 Sussex Dr Ottawa ON K1A 0G2 Canada*

MACDONALD, GEORGE CRAWFORD, investment banker; b. Toronto, Ont., Can., Dec. 9, 1914; s. George Harold and Florence (Crawford) MacD.; student St. Andrews Coll., Aurora, Ont., 1933; extension student U. Toronto, 1945-46; m. Elizabeth Ann Hodgeman, June 11, 1938; children—Peter George, Susan Elizabeth. With McLeod, Young, Weir Ltd., 1933—, exec. v.p., 1967-69, pres., 1969-75, chief exec. officer, 1969—, chmn., 1975—, also dir.; vice chmn., dir. McLead, Young, Weir, Inc., N.Y.C., 1954—; dir. Dilworth, Secord Meagher Ltd., Toronto, Traders Group Ltd., Toronto, Fulcrum Investments Co. Ltd. Bd. govs. Lakefield Coll. Sch.; trustee St. Andrew's Coll. Found. Served to lt. comdr. Royal Canadian Navy, 1941-45, Mem. Investment Bankers Assn. Am. (chmn. Canadian com. 1964, bd. govs. 1964-67). Clubs: St. James's, Badminton and Squash (Montreal); Metropolitan, Canadian (N.Y.C.); Toronto, Granite, Toronto Hunt, Lambton Golf and Country (Toronto); York. Home: 70 Montclair Ave PH2 Toronto ON M5P 1P7 Canada Office: Comml Union Tower PO Box 433 Toronto-Dominion Centre Toronto ON M5K 1M2 Canada

MAC DONALD, GORDON JAMES FRASER, geophysicist; b. Mexico City, July 30, 1929; s. Gordon and Josephine (Bennett) Mac D.; A.B. summa cum laude, Harvard U., 1950, A.M., 1952, Ph.D., 1954; m. Marcelline Kuglen (dec.); children—Gordon James, Maureen, Michael; m. 2d, Betty Ann Kipniss; 1 son, Bruce. Asst. prof. geology, geophysics Mass. Inst. Tech., 1954-55, asso. prof. geophysics, 1955-58; staff asso. geophysics lab. Carnegie Inst. Washington, 1955-63; cons. U.S. Geol. Survey, 1955-60; prof. geophysics U. Calif. at Los Angeles, 1958-68, dir. atmospheric research lab., 1960-66, asso. dir. Inst. Geophysics and Planetary Physics, 1960-68; v.p. research Inst. for Def. Analyses, 1966-67, exec. v.p., 1967-68, trustee, 1966-70; vice chancellor for research and grad. affairs U. Calif. at Santa Barbara, 1968-69, prof. physics and geophysics, 1968-69; mem. council on Environ. Quality, Washington, 1969-72; Henry R. Luce prof. environ. studies and policy, dir. environ. studies program Dartmouth, 1972—; trustee Mitre Corp., disting. vis. scholar, 1977-79, chief scientist, 1979—; cons. NASA, 1960-70, mem. lunar and planetary missions bd., 1967; mem. def. sci. bd. Dept. Def., 1966-70; cons. Dept. State, 1967-70; mem. Pres.'s Sci. Adv. Com., 1965-69; adv. panel on nuclear effects Office Tech. Assessment, 1975—. Fellow Am. Acad. Arts and Scis., AAAS; mem. Am. Math. Soc., Nat. Acad. Scis. (chmn. environmental studies bd. 1970, 72-73, chmn. commn. on natural resources 1973—), Am., Royal astron. socs., Am. Mineral. Soc., Am. Geophys. Union., Geochem. Soc. Am., Geol. Soc. Am., Am. Meteorol. Soc., Am. Philos. Soc., Seismol. Soc. Am., Soc. Indsl. and Applied Math., Council Fgn. Relations, Sigma Xi. Author: The Rotation of the Earth, 1960; co-author: Sound and Light Phenomena: A Study of Historical and Modern Occurrences, 1978. Contbr. articles to sci., tech. jours. Address: MITRE Corp 1820 Dolly Madison Blvd McLean VA 22102

MACDONALD, H. MALCOLM, educator; b. San Francisco, May 21, 1914; s. George Childs and Helena (Zaun) M.; B.A., U. San Francisco, 1935; M.A., Harvard, 1937, Ph.D. (Savage scholar), 1939. Instr., U. Tex., 1938, U.S. Naval Acad., 1945-46; asst. prof. U. Tex., Austin, 1946, asso. prof., 1946, prof., 1953—, chmn. dept., 1953-66, dean ad interim Coll. Arts and Scis., 1967, chmn. dept. govt., 1971-75, mil. coordinator Office Pres. U., 1948—. Johnson vis. prof. Pomona Coll. and Claremont Grad. Center, 1965; vis. prof. So. Meth. Sch. Law, 1963; vis. lectr. U. San Francisco, 1939. Mem. Sec. Navy Bd. Ednl. Policy, 1962-65, Bur. Naval Personnel Task Force Edn., 1964-66, Legislative Internship Com., Tex., 1964-69. Bd. dirs. Clan Donald Ednl. Trust. Served with USNR, 1941-45. Recipient Internat. Relations award St. Mary's U., 1966. Excellence in Teaching award U. Tex., 1958. Fellow Royal Econ. Soc.; mem. Am., Southwestern, So. polit. sci. assns., Southwestern Social Sci. Assn., Am. Soc. Polit. and Legal Philosophy, U.S. Naval Inst. Clubs: Army and Navy (Washington); Town and Gown (Austin). Author: (with Webb, Lewis, Straus) Readings in American Government, 5th edit., 1968; Readings in American National Government, 1964; The Intellectual in Politics, 1966. Book rev. editor Social Sci. Quar., 1946—. Contbr. articles to profl. jours. Home: 3518 Lakeland Dr Austin TX 78731

MACDONALD, J(OHN) TYLER P(ERINEAU), JR., advt. agency exec.; b. Atlanta, Mar. 25, 1924; s. John Tyler Perineau and Francis Marie (Bain) M.; B.A., U. So. Calif., 1946; m. Mary Lou Krouse, Apr. 18, 1969; children—Priscilla, John, Peter. Copywriter Hixson-Odonnell Inc., Los Angeles, 1946-56; exec. v.p. Hixson & Jorgensen Inc., Los Angeles, 1956-68, pres., 1968-70; chmn. N.W. Ayer/Jorgensen/Macdonald, Los Angeles, 1970—, exec. v.p., dir. NW Ayer ABH Internat., Inc., N.Y.C., 1971—, Chmn. Los Angeles Mayor's Econ. Advisory Council, 1975-78; chmn. planning and programming Los Angeles Bicentennial, 1978; mem. bd. council'rs U. So. Calif. Inst. Marine and Oceanographic Studies, 1978. Served with USMCR, 1944-45. Named Advt. Exec. of Year, Western States Advt. Agency Assn., 1973. Mem. Invest in America (dir.), Los Angeles Conv. Bur. (dir.), Los Angeles Area C. of C. (dir. 1973-80). Republican. Clubs: Newport Harbor Yacht (commodore), Back Bay (Newport Beach). Home: 19 Encore Ct Newport Beach CA 92663 also 241 Descanso Avalon Santa Catalina Island CA Office: 707 Wilshire Blvd Los Angeles CA 90017

MAC DONALD, JAMES GORDON, ins. exec.; b. N.Y.C., June 16, 1925; s. Daniel M. and Anne C. (Macdonald) MacD.; B.A., Hobart Coll., 1948; m. Imogene Williamson, Feb. 4, 1950; children—James Gordon, Patricia J., Nancy C. With Liberty Mut. Ins. Co., Newark, 1948-52; Mich. and N.Y. group supr. New York Life Ins. Co., 1952-56; group underwriter Tchrs. Ins. & Annuity Assn., Coll. Retirement Equity Fund, N.Y.C., 1956-58, group officer, 1958-60, asst. v.p., 1960-63, v.p., 1963-72, exec. v.p. adminstrn., 1972—. Trustee, Saugatuck Congl. Ch., 1974—, Coll. Retirement Equities Fund, 1978; trustee, pres. Tchrs., Ins. and Annuity Assn., 1979—. Served to lt. (j.g.) USN, 1943-47. Mem. Am. Pension Conf., Health Ins. Assn. Am., St. Andrews Soc. New York. Republican. Clubs: Patterson Country (dir. Fairfield, Conn.); Hobart, Williams (N.Y.C.). Home: 5 Ivy Knoll Westport CT 06880 Office: 730 3d Ave New York NY 10017

MACDONALD, JAMES ROSS, physicist, educator; b. Savannah, Ga., Feb. 27, 1923; s. John Elwood and Antonina Jones (Hansell) M.; B.A., Williams Coll., 1944; S.B., Mass. Inst. Tech., 1944, S.M., 1947; D.Phil. (Rhodes scholar) Oxford (Eng.) U., 1950, D.Sc., 1967; m. Margaret Milward Taylor, Aug. 3, 1946; children—Antonina Hansell, James Ross, William Taylor. Mem. staff Digital Computer Lab., Mass. Inst. Tech., 1946-47; physicist Armour Research Found., Chgo., 1950-52; asso. physicist Argonne Nat. Lab., 1952-53; with Tex. Instruments Inc., Dallas, 1953-74, v.p. corporate research and engring., 1968-73, v.p. corporate research and devel., 1973-74; dir. Simmonds Precision Products Inc., 1979—; William Rand Kenan Jr. prof. physics U. N.C., Chapel Hill, 1974—; adj. prof. biophysics U. Tex., Dallas, 1954-74; mem. solid state scis. panel NRC, 1965-73; mem. adv. com. for sci. edn. NSF, 1971-73; mem. vis. com. physics Mass. Inst. Tech., 1971-74. Mem. Dallas Radio Commn., 1967-71; mem. sci. adv. council Callier Hearing and Speech Center, Dallas, 1974-78; bd. dirs. League for Ednl. Advancement in Dallas, 1965-70. Fellow Am. Phys. Soc., IEEE (awards 1962, 74; asso. editor Transactions of Profl. Group on Audio 1961-66, Transactions on Audio and Electroacoustics 1966-73), AAAS; mem. Nat. Acad. Engring. (exec. com. assembly of engring. 1975-78, council 1971-74), Nat. Acad. Scis. (chmn. numerical data adv. bd. 1970-71, com. on motor vehicle emissions 1973-74), Am. Inst. Physics. (chmn. com. on profl. concerns 1976-78), Electrochem. Soc., Audio Engring. Soc., Phi Beta Kappa, Sigma Xi. Contbr. articles to profl. jours.; patentee in field. Home: 308 Laurel Hill Rd Chapel Hill NC 27514 Office: Dept Physics and Astronomy U NC Chapel Hill NC 27514

MACDONALD, JOHN DANN, author; b. Sharon, Pa., July 24, 1916; s. Eugene Andrew and Marguerite Grace (Dann) MacD.; student U. Pa., 1934-36; B.S., Syracuse U., 1938; M.B.A., Harvard Grad. Sch. Bus. Adminstrn., 1939; D.H.L. (hon.), Hobart and William Smith Colls., 1978; m. Dorothy Mary Prentiss, July 3, 1937; 1 son, Maynard John Prentiss. Author over 500 pieces of fiction, 65 novels, 1946—, including The Executioners, 1958; Please Write for Details, 1959; The End of the Night, 1960; A Flash of Green, 1962; A Key to the Suite (Grand prix de literateur policiere), 1964; The House Guests, 1965; The Last One Left, 1967; No Deadly Drug, 1968; The Turquoise Lament, 1973; The Dreadful Lemon Sky, 1975; Condominium, 1977; The Empty Copper Sea, 1978; The Green Ripper, 1979. Served to lt. col. AUS, 1940-46. Recipient Benjamin Franklin award for the best Am. short story, 1955; Pioneer medal Syracuse U., 1971; Edgar Grand Master award Mystery Writers Am., 1972. Mem. Mystery Writers Am. (pres. 1962), Authors Guild, P.E.N. Club. Home: Sarasota FL 33581

MACDONALD, JOHN WINCHESTER, educator, lawyer; b. Albany, N.Y., Mar. 29, 1905; s. John Winchester and Catherine C. (Burns) M.; A.B., A.M., J.D., Cornell U., 1921-26; grad. Army Indsl. Coll. (indsl. reconversion), 1944; LL.D., Canisius Coll., 1959; m. Mary Elizabeth Brown, Sept. 26, 1927; children—John Winchester, Mary (Mrs. O'Connell; dec.), Catherine (Mrs. Wigsten), Virginia (Mrs. Lindseth), Rita. Admitted N.Y. bar, 1926; asso. Hun Parker & Reilly, Albany, N.Y., 1926-27; clk. court of claims, State of N.Y., 1927-30; asst. prof. law, Cornell U., 1930-35, sec. Cornell Law Sch., 1932-35, prof. law, 1935—, Edwin H. Woodruff prof. law, 1960-73, emeritus, 1973—, acting prof. govt., 1951, faculty rep. bd. trustees, 1951-55, chmn. adminstrv. com., 1954-56; vis. prof. law Columbia, 1947, 52, N.Y.U., 1957; lectr. St. Lawrence U. Inst. Crime and Delinquency, 1951-58; gen. counsel, dir. Therm, Inc.; dir. other corps.; staff gen. counsel Asso. Gas & Electric Corp. in reorgn. 1942; spl. asst. U.S. Atty. Gen., 1942; dir. N.Y. Legislative Service, Inc. Research asso. N.Y. Commn. on Adminstrn. of Justice, 1932-33; exec. sec., dir. N.Y. State Law Revision Commn., 1934-56, commr., 1956—, chmn., 1958-73; del. N.Y. Constl. Conv., 1967, dir. com. on style and arrangement; vis. prof. St. Johns U., 1959; bd. visitors, Elmira (N.Y.) State Reformatory, 1942-47; del. from Cornell U. to N.Y. Joint Conf. on Legal Edn. Mem. Cornell Law Assn. (sec. 1932-35). Mem. Am. Acad. Polit. Sci., Scribes, Am. Judicature Soc., Am., N.Y. State, Tompkins County bar assns., Assn. Bar City N.Y., Am. Law Inst. (permanent editorial bd. uniform comml. code), Am. Assn. U. Profs., Cath. Commn. Intellectual and Cultural Affairs, John Henry Newman Soc., Phi Beta Kappa, Delta Sigma Rho, Order of the Coif. Democrat. K.C. (4 deg.). Roman Catholic. Clubs: Cornell (New York); Country; Yacht (Ithaca). Editor: vols. 1 and 2, N.Y. State Constitutional Convention Committee Reports, 1938 (with Horace E. Read) Cases and Materials on Legislation, 1947; (with Horace E. Read and Jefferson B. Fordham) Cases and Materials on Legislation, 2d edit., 1959, 3d edit. (with Read, Fordham and Pierce), 1973; (with Horace E. Read, Jefferson B. Fordham, William J. Pierce) Materials on Legislation, 3d Edit., 1973. Reports, Recommendations and Studies New York Law Revision Commission since 1934—. Co-editor (with Robert S. Stevens, Arthur E. Sutherland and Harrop A. Freeman) Materials on Introduction to Study of Law. Contbr. articles to profl. jours. Home: 15-D Strawberry Hill Ithaca NY 14850 Office: Myron Taylor Hall Ithaca NY 14850

MACDONALD, KENNETH, editor; b. Jefferson, Iowa, Sept. 3, 1905; s. William Arthur and Mabel (Swearingen) McD.; A.B., U. Iowa, 1926; m. Helen Inman, June 17, 1929; 1 son, Stephen. With Des Moines Register and Tribune, 1926—, successively reporter, copyreader, telegraph editor, city editor, mng. editor, exec. editor, v.p., 1946-76, editor, 1953-76, editorial chmn., 1976-77, chief operating officer, 1960-70, dir., 1940—. Bd. dirs. A.P., 1956-65, 1st v.p., 1963-65; adv. bd. Pulitzer prizes, 1958-70. Trustee Simpson Coll., chmn. bd., 1957-59; bd. dirs. Iowa Lutheran Hosp., Des Moines. Served as air combat intelligence officer USNR, World War II; PTO. Mem. Am. Soc. Newspaper Editors (dir. 1950-56, pres. 1955), Sigma Delta Chi. Mem. Episcopal Ch. Club: Des Moines. Home: 3412 Southern Hills Dr Des Moines IA 50321 Office: 715 Locust St Des Moines IA 50304

MACDONALD, KEVIN JOHN, artist; b. Washington, July 2, 1946; s. Lawrence and Frances Ellen (Quinn) MacD.; student Montgomery Coll., 1964-66; B.F.A., George Washington U., 1969; postgrad. Corcoran Sch. Art, 1969. Exhbns. include: Corcoran Gallery Art, Washington, 1974, 76, 79, Md. Biennial, Balt. Mus., 1976, 78, Phillips Collection, Washington, 1977, Lunn Gallery, Washington, 1976, 77, 79; represented in permanent collections: Met. Mus., N.Y.C., Corcoran Gallery, Phillips Collection. Address: 8207 Georgia Ave # 5 Silver Spring MD 20910

MAC DONALD, MALCOLM MURDOCH, editor, publisher; b. Uniontown, Pa., June 15, 1935; s. Morgan Bowman and Ruth (Newcomb) Greene Mac D.; B.A., Trinity Coll. (Conn.), 1957; m. Constance Emily Marsh, June 13, 1959; children—Randall Malcolm, Alison Margaret, Ellen Marsh. Coll. rep. Midwest D. Van Nostrand Co. Inc., Princeton, N.J., 1958-62, asso. sci. editor, 1962, sci. editor, 1963-68; sci. editor Van Nostrand Reinhold Co., N.Y.C., 1968-70; editor Pa. State U. Press, State College, Pa., 1970-72; chief editor U. N.C. Press, Chapel Hill, 1972—, asst. dir., 1975-76; asst. dir., editor U. Ga. Press, Athens, 1976-78; dir. U. Ala. Press, 1978—; co-prin. (with Constance M. MacDonald) Editorial Assos., cons. in field. Active Boy Scouts Am. Author: (With Cecil E. Johnson) Society and the Environment, 1971; (with Robert E. Davis) Chemistry and Society, 1972. Office: U Ala Press Box 2877 University AL 35486

MACDONALD, MARGARET MARY, banker; b. Pittston, Pa., July 7, 1920; d. John Joseph and Margaret Gertrude (McLaughlin) MacDonald; B.B.A. magna cum laude, St. John's U., 1953; M.B.A., N.Y. U., 1960; certificate Stonier Grad. Sch. Banking, Rutgers U., 1966. Pub. accountant S.D. Leidesdorf & Co., N.Y.C., 1953-57; accountant Talco Engring. Co., Hamden, Conn., 1957; with Empire Bank & Trust Co., 1950-53; with Bank of N.Y. (merger Empire Trust Co. into Bank of N.Y.), 1957-68, asst. auditor, 1960-68; v.p., controller 1st Empire Bank, N.Y.C., 1968-73; dep. auditor Mfrs. Hanover Trust Co., 1974-78; bank examiner Fed. Res. Bank, N.Y., 1979—. Active Omega, N.Y. U., 1960, treas., 1965-68. Recipient Baush & Lomb Sci. award, 1938. C.P.A., chartered bank auditor, N.Y.; cert. data processing auditor. Mem. Am. Inst. C.P.A.'s, N.Y. C.P.A.'s, Bank Adminstrn. Inst. (mem. exec. com. 1971, sec.-treas. 1973, nat. bd. regents chartered bank auditor program 1973-75). Home: 50 Fort Pl New York NY 10301

MACDONALD, MAXWELL DOUGLAS, newspaper exec.; b. Yorkton, Sask., Can., Aug. 9, 1920; s. Bannatyne and Margaret Charters (Love) M.; B.A., U. Western Ont., 1949; m. Kathleen Bulman Townend, July 25, 1950; children—Heather, Ellen, Douglas. With Sask. Star-Phoenix, 1947, 67-72, London (Ont.) Free Press, 1948-52, 55-67, Gran de Prairie (Alta.) Herald-Tribune, 1953-55; exec. v.p. Regina (Sask.) Leader-Post, 1972—. Served with Royal Canadian Navy, 1941-45. Mem. Canadian Press, Commonwealth Press Union, Internat. Press Inst., Am., Canadian daily newspaper pubs. assns., Canadian C. of C. Clubs: Assinabia; Wascana Golf and Country; Regina Curling. Home: 1336 Gryphon's Walk Regina SK S4S 6X1 Canada Office: 1964 Park St Regina SK S4P 3G4 Canada. *The most dramatic improvement in my life was the day I took my first honest look at myself. I was about 56 years old at the time and I've been amazed ever since what old dogs can learn.*

MACDONALD, PETER MCINTYRE, newspaper exec.; b. Glasgow, Scotland, May 3, 1916; s. Donald and Agnes (McIntyre) M.; student U. Kans., 1945-47; m. Barbara Laubengayer, Oct. 16, 1943; children—Heather M. Smith, Janet Martin. Came to U.S., 1945, naturalized, 1947. Promotion mgr. radio sta. KSAL, Salina, Kans., 1947-48; advt. mgr. Salina Jour., 1950-54, bus. mgr., 1954-56; v.p. Hutchinson (Kans.) News, 1956-61, pres., pub., 1962-65; pres., gen. mgr. Harris Enterprises, Inc., 1966-78, chmn., 1978—, pubs. Hutchinson News, Ottawa Herald, Garden City Telegram, Chanute Tribune, Salina Jour., Hays News, Olathe News (all Kans.), Burlington (Iowa) Hawkeye, Camarillo (Calif.) News, operators radio stas. KIUL, Garden City, KTOP, Topeka, KBUR, Burlington, WJOL, Joliet, Ill., KFKA, Greeley, Colo., KSEL, Lubbock, Tex.; dir. Dillon Cos., 1st Nat. Bank Hutchinson, Consol. Printing Co., Salina. Chmn. adv. bd. UPI, 1974-77. Mem. advisory com. U. Kans. Sch. Bus. Served from sgt. to squadron leader RAF, 1939-45. Mem. Hutchinson C. of C., Inland Daily Press Assn. (pres. 1969). Mason (Shriner, Jester). Clubs: Royal and Ancient Golf, Royal Highland Yacht. Home: 205 Kisiwa Pkwy Hutchinson KS 67501 Office: 300 W 2d St Hutchinson KS 67501

MACDONALD, RAY WOODWARD, corp. exec.; b. Chgo., Dec. 20, 1912; s. Alexander R. and Emma Christine (Woodward) M.; student U. Chgo. Sch. Bus. Adminstrn., 1935; D.Sc. in Indsl. Mgmt. (hon.), Lawrence Inst. Tech., Detroit; LL.D., Wayne State U., Union Coll.; m. Florence Shanahan, July 12, 1947; children—Thomas, James, Richard. With Burroughs Corp., Detroit, 1935—, beginning as salesman, successively staff export dept., asst. export mgr., export mgr., gen. mgr. internat. ops., v.p. internat. sales and service, 1935-57, v.p. charge internat. group, 1957-64, exec. v.p., 1964-66, pres., 1966-73, chmn. bd., 1973-77, chief exec. officer, 1967-77, hon. chmn. bd., 1978—, also dir.; dir. Crysler Corp., Detroit. Mem. Brit. N.Am. Com., Fgn. Policy Com. Bd. dirs. United Found., Detroit, New Detroit, Inc.; mem. vis. com. Harvard Bus. Sch. Mem. Internat. C. of C. (U.S. council). Clubs: Economic (past chmn. bd. dirs.), Detroit, Grosse Pointe; Links (N.Y.C.).

MACDONALD, REYNOLD COLEMAN, steel co. exec.; b. Billings, Mont., Oct. 7, 1918; s. Donald and Claudia (Reynolds) MacD.; student Los Angeles City Coll., 1936-37; m. Mary Helen Smith, Mar. 27, 1938; children—Glory, Darcy. Asst. gen. supt. Kaiser Steel Corp., Fontana, Calif., 1946-63; v.p. ops. Lone Star Steel Co. (Tex.), 1963-67; pres., dir. Interlake Steel Corp., Chgo., 1967-69, pres., chief exec. officer, 1969—; dir. Central Nat. Bank, ARA Services, Inc., Parker Hannifin Corp. Pres., Cucomonga (Calif.) Sch. Bd., 1961-63. Mem. Am. Iron and Steel Inst. (dir.), Assn. Iron and Steel Engrs. (pres. 1972, dir.), Chgo. Assn. Commerce and Industry (dir.), U.S. Auto Club (dir.). Club: Masons. Office: Interlake Steel Corp 310 S Michigan Ave Chicago IL 60604*

MACDONALD, RICHARD ANNIS, physician; b. Manistee, Mich., July 23, 1928; s. Robert R. and Julia (Graczyk) MacD.; A.B., Albion Coll., 1951; M.D., Boston U., 1954; m. Jean Marie McLaughlin, June 7, 1954; children—Linda Anne, Richard Annis, Marie Aran. Intern Boston City Hosp., 1954-55, resident pathology, 1955-59; mem. faculty Harvard Med. Sch., 1958-65, instr., 1959-60, asst. prof., 1962-65; prof. pathology Sch. Medicine U. Colo., 1966-69, Boston U. Med. Sch., 1969-70; prof. pathology, chmn. dept. pathology U. Mass. Med. Sch., Worcester, 1970-73; prof. pathology Boston U. Sch. Medicine, 1973—; chief pathology service Norwood (Mass.) Hosp., 1973—; asso. chief staff research and edn. Denver VA Hosp., 1968-69; chief lab. service, 1968-69; chief lab. service Boston VA Hosp., 1969-70. Mem. study sec. NIH, 1967-69; mem. evaluation com. on research and edn. VA, 1966-68. Served with USNR, 1943-45. Mem. AMA, Am. Soc. Exptl. Pathology, Internat. Acad. Pathology, Internat. Soc. Hematology, Mass. Med. Soc. New Eng. Soc. Pathology, Phi Beta Kappa. Author: Hemocrhromatosis and Hemosiderois, 1964; also articles. Home: 53 Bonad Rd West Newton MA 02165 Office: 800 Washington St Norwood MA 02062

MACDONALD, ROBERT MUNRO, educator; b. Glasgow, Scotland, July 9, 1923; s. Robert and Sidney (Wilson) M.; came to U.S., 1948; B.A., Yale, 1950, M.A., 1951, Ph.D., 1955; M.A. (hon.), Dartmouth, 1966; m. Mado Ruth Ambach, June 22, 1953; children—Laura Anne, Kevin Angus. Asst. prof. econs. U. Calif. at Los Angeles, 1953-56, Yale, 1956-59; faculty Amos Tuck Sch. Bus. Adminstrn., Dartmouth, 1959—, prof. bus. econs., 1965—. Served to sub-lt. Brit. Royal Navy, 1941-45. Mem. Am. Econ. Assn., Indsl. Relations Research Assn., AAUP, Phi Beta Kappa. Author: Collective Bargaining in the Automobile Industry, 1963. Contbr. to books, articles to profl. jours. Home: 19 Rip Rd Hanover NH 03755

MACDONALD, ROBERT RIGG, JR., museum ofcl.; b. Pitts., May 11, 1942; s. Robert Rigg and Ruth (Johnson) M.; B.A., U. Notre Dame, 1964, M.A., 1965; M.A., U. Pa., 1970; m. Catherine Ronan, Nov. 25, 1965; children—Matthew, Robert, Catherine. Asst. curator Smithsonian Instn., Washington, 1965; curator Mercer Mus., Doylestown, Pa., 1966-70; dir. New Haven Colony Hist. Soc., 1970-74, La. State Mus., New Orleans, 1974—; mem. mus. panel Nat. Historic Publs. and Record Commn., La. Com.; active Nat. Endowment for Humanities. Asso. fellow Berkeley Coll., Yale U., 1978; Hagley fellow U. Del., 1970-71; Univ. scholar U. Notre Dame, 1964-65. Mem. Am. Assn. State and Local History (council), Am. Assn. Museums, Nat. Trust for Historic Preservation, S.E. Mus. Conf. (council). Roman Catholic. Editor: New Haven Colony Furniture, 1973; Louisiana Images 1880-1920, 1975; Louisiana Black Heritage, 1977; Louisiana Portraitures, 1979. Home: 8008 Jeannette Pl New Orleans LA 70118 Office: 751 Chartres St New Orleans LA 70116

MACDONALD, ROBERT TAYLOR, newspaper exec.; Mt. Vernon, N.Y., Oct. 25, 1930; s. Joseph Taylor and Mary Gertrude (Broderick) MacD.; B.S., Yale, 1952; M.B.A., Wharton Sch. of U. Pa., 1958; m. Christiana Barbara Besch, June 25, 1960 (div. 1977); children—Gregory, Michael, Jennifer; m. 2d, Gillian S.T. Tripier, 1978. Pub., Mariner, monthly trade mag., 1956; bus. mgmt. cons., 1958-61; v.p., adminstrn., dir. N.Y. Herald Tribune, Inc., 1961-63, exec. v.p., 1963-66; pub. N.Y. Herald Tribune-Washington Post Internat., 1966-67, Internat. Herald Tribune, 1967-77; chmn. Hudson Research Europe, Ltd., 1977—; v.p. internat. ops., Washington Post Co., 1966-70, asst. to chmn., 1968-70. Bd. govs. Am. Hosp. of Paris. Served as lt. USNR, 1953-56. Mem. Fgn. Policy Assn., Am. C. of C. in Paris (dir.), Phi Gamma Delta. Clubs: Yale, Wharton MBA (dir., past pres.) (N.Y.C.); Apawamis (Rye, N.Y.); Stamford (Conn.) Yacht, Travelers (Paris). Home: West Cornwall CT 06796 Office: 444 Madison Ave New York NY 10022 also 54 rue de Varenne 75007 Paris France

MACDONALD, RODERICK, librarian; b. Mpls., Mar. 13, 1931; s. Roderick and Frances Ruth (Lawrence) Mac D.; B.A., Macalester Coll., 1953; M.A., U. Minn., 1959; m. Joanne Gaffney, Jan. 4, 1958; children—Maria Halliday, Roderick III, David, Louise. City librarian Free Pub. Library, Kaukauna, Wis., 1959-61; reference librarian, asst. prof. Macalester Coll., 1961-66; dir. Anoka County Library, Mpls., 1966-69, Pub. Library, Des Moines, 1969-78, Dakota County Library System, Burnsville, Minn., 1978—. Served with AUS, 1953-55. Mem. ALA, Iowa Library Assn. (legis. chmn. 1971), Minn. Library Assn. (pres. 1968). Democrat. Home: 2712 Teton Ct Burnsville MN 55337 Office: 1101 W County Rd 42 Burnsville MN 55337

MAC DONALD, STEWART FERGUSON, chemist; b. Toronto, Ont., Can., Aug. 17, 1913; s. Mervil and Margaret Stuart (MacGregor) MacD.; B.A., U. Toronto, 1936, M.A., 1937; Dr. rer. nat. (Gertrude Davis Exchange fellow), Technische Hochschule, Munich, Germany, 1939; m. Marian Katherine de Courcy O'Grady, Oct. 14, 1945; children—Peter, Lorna, Wanda, Constance, Sheila. Research asso. dept. med. research U. Toronto, 1939-40, asst. prof. chemistry, 1942-48; chemist Welland Chem. Works, 1940-42; research asso. Connaught Labs., 1944-45; with Univ. Chem. Lab., Cambridge (Eng.) U., 1948-52; sr. research officer NRC Can., Ottawa, Ont., 1952, prin. research officer div. pure chemistry, 1968, with div. biol. scis., 1968-78, ret., 1978. Welcome fellow, 1948-52. Fellow Royal Soc. Can.; mem. Am. Chem. Soc., Chem. Inst. Can. Contbr. articles to chem. jours.

MACDONALD, THOMAS COOK, JR., lawyer; b. Atlanta, Oct. 11, 1929; s. Thomas Cook and Mary (Morgan) MacD.; B.S. with high honors, U. Fla., 1951, LL.B. with high honors, 1953; m. Gay Anne Everiss; children—Margaret Anne, Thomas William. Admitted to Fla. bar, 1953; practiced in Tampa, 1953—; mem. firm Shackleford, Farrior, Stallings & Evans, 1953—; dir. Jim Walter Corp., Royal Trust Bank Tampa; legis. counsel Gov. of Fla., 1963; del. 5th Circuit Jud. Conf., 1970—. Mem. Fla. Student Scholarship and Loan Commn., 1963-67, Hillsborough County Pub. Edn. Study Commn., 1965; lic. lay reader Episcopal Ch., 1962—; mem. adv. bd. Tampa Bay Soccer Club, Inc.; bd. dirs. U. Fla. Found.; pres. U. Fla. Nat. Alumni Assn., 1973. Served to 1st lt., JAGD, USAF, 1953-55. Recipient Disting. Alumnus award U. Fla., 1976. Fellow Am. Coll. Trial Lawyers, Am. Bar Found.; mem. Am. Bar Assn. (com. on ethics and profl. responsibility 1970-76), Am. Law Inst., Fla. Bar (chmn. com. profl. ethics 1966-70, bd. govs. 1970-74, bar mem. Supreme Ct. com. on standards conduct governing judges 1976), Fla. West Coast Sports Assn. (sec.), Phi Kappa Phi, Phi Delta Phi, Fla. Blue Key, Kappa Alpha. Home: 1904 Holly Ln Tampa FL 33609 Office: PO Box 3324 Tampa FL 33601

MACDONALD, WALTER HOWARD, banker; b. Covington, Ky., Feb. 24, 1920; s. Lloyd A. and Martha (Otto) MacD.; certificate accounting U. Cin., 1950, B.S. in Commerce, 1963; grad. Rutgers U. Grad. Sch. Banking, 1958, Advanced Mgmt. Program Case Western Res. U., 1968; m. Patricia A. Moldstad, July 17, 1953; 1 son, John Roderick. With Fed. Res. Bank Cin., 1937-39, Newport Nat. Bank (Ky.), 1939-48, Deins Automobile Co., Cin., 1949-50; with Fed. Res. Bank Cleve., 1951—, 1st v.p., 1966—. Chmn. conf. 1st vice presidents Fed. Res. Banks, 1970, 77. Mem. Greater Cleve. Growth Assn., 1966—; trustee Cleve. Council on World Affairs, St. Luke's Hosp., Greater Cleve. Hosp. Assn. Served with USMCR, 1941-45. Mem. Am. Inst. Banking, Newcomen Soc. N.Am., Alpha Kappa Psi. Methodist. Home: 2707 Colchester Rd Cleveland Heights OH 44106 Office: PO Box 6387 Cleveland OH 44101

MACDONALD, WILLIAM LLOYD, educator, author; b. Putnam, Conn., July 12, 1921; s. William Lloyd and Susan (Elrod) MacD.; ed. Gov. Dummer Acad., 1938; A.B., Harvard, 1949, A.M., 1953, Ph.D., 1956; children—Noel, Nicholas. Lectr., Boston Archtl. Center, 1950-54; instr. Wheaton (Mass.) Coll., 1953-54 instr., then asso. prof. Yale, 1956-65; prof. archtl. history Smith Coll., 1965—, Sophia Smith prof., 1969-74, A.P. Brown prof., 1974—, chmn. art dept., 1971-73, 76; exec. sec. Byzantine Inst., 1950-54; vis. prof. Mass. Inst. Tech., 1966, Harvard, 1968, 69, 70, 72, Boston U., 1971, Trinity Coll., Rome, Italy, 1970, 72, U. Calif., Berkeley, 1979. Served with USAAF, 1942-45. Morse fellow Yale, 1962-63; recipient award Am. Council Learned Socs., 1959, 68, Am. Philos. Soc., 1962; Rome prize fellow Am. Acad. Rome, 1954-56. Mem. Soc. Archtl. Historians (past dir.), Soc. Libyan Studies, Soc. Promotion Roman Studies, Am. Assn. Archtl. Bibliographers, Archaeol. Inst. Am., Internat. Assn. Classical Archaeology. Author: Early Christian and Byzantine Architecture, 1962; The Architecture of the Roman Empire, I, 1965; Northampton Massachusetts Architecture and Buildings, 1975; The Pantheon-Design, Meaning and Progeny, 1976; Piranesi's Carceri, 1979; asso. editor Princeton Dictionary Classical Archaeology, 1976. Home: 25 Henshaw Ave Northampton MA 01060 Office: Art Dept Smith College Northampton MA 01063

MACDONELL, JAMES JOHNSON, govt. ofcl.; b. Calgary, Alta., Can., Sept. 13, 1915; s. Archibald Joseph and Lillian Catherine (Johnson) M.; m. Audrey Mary Grafton, May 15, 1941; 1 dau., Audrey Anne. Partner-in-charge mgmt. cons. services Price Waterhouse & Co., Montreal, Que., Can., 1945-68; sr. partner Price Waterhouse Assos., Montreal, 1968-73; auditor gen. Can., Ottawa, 1973—. Bd. dirs., hon. treas. St. Mary's Hosp., Montreal, 1966-73. Chartered Accountant, Que. Fellow Mgmt. Cons.'s Que., Chartered Accountants Ont.; founding mem. Can. Assn. Mgmt. Cons. (pres. 1965-66). Clubs: Mount Royal (Montreal); Rideau (Ottawa); Met. (N.Y.). Home: 195 Clearview Ave Ottawa ON K1Z 6S1 Canada Office: 240 Sparks St Ottawa ON K1A 0G6 Canada

MACDONNELL, ROBERT GEORGE, govt. ofcl.; b. Spokane, Wash., May 10, 1911; s. John Grant and Marguerite (Crane) MacD.; B.S., U.S. Mil. Acad., 1934; M.S. in Civil Engring., U. Calif. at Berkeley, 1938; grad. Army War Coll., 1952; m. Harriett Virginia Burks, Nov. 16, 1935; children—Robert Irwin, Richard Burks, Marguerite. Commd. 2d lt. U.S. Army, 1934, advanced through grades to maj. gen., 1962; served in New Guinea, So. Philippines, Leyte and Luzon, World War II; asso. prof. engring, U.S. Mil. Acad., 1947-51; assigned VII Corps, Germany, 1952-55; mem. faculty Army War Coll., 1955-56; asst. comdt. U.S. Army Engrs. Sch., 1956-58; div. engr. S. Pacific div., also pres. Calif. Debris Commn., 1958-61; dir. supply C.E., 1961-62, dir. civil works 1962-63, dep. chief engrs., 1963-67; chmn. U.S. Bd. Engrs. Rivers and Harbors, 1962-69; mem. staff U.S. Senate, 1969—; pres. U.S. Beach Erosion Bd., 1962-63. Chmn. Am. sect. Permanent Internat. Assn. Nav. Congresses, Brussels, 1962-63; pres. Mississippi River Commn., 1967-69; chmn. Red River Commn., 1967-69. Decorated Legion of Merit, D.S.M. (2), Bronze Star medal, Army Commendation ribbon. Registered profl. engr., La., Miss., Wash. Home: 1701 N Kent St Arlington VA 22209 Office: Old Senate Office Bldg Washington DC 20510

MACDOUGAL, GARY EDWARD, indsl. products mfg. co. exec.; b. Chgo., July 3, 1936; s. Thomas William and Lorna Lee (McDougall) MacD.; B.S. in Engring., UCLA, 1958; M.B.A., Harvard U., 1962; m. Julianne Laurel Maxwell, June 13, 1959; children—Gary Edward, Michael Scott. Cons., McKinsey & Co., N.Y.C., also Los Angeles, 1963-68, partner, 1968-69; chmn. bd., chief exec. officer Mark Controls Corp. (formerly Clayton Mark & Co.), Evanston, Ill., 1969—, also pres., 1971-76; dir. United Parcel Service Am., Inc., N.Y.C., Union Camp Corp., Wayne, N.J., Maremont Corp., Chgo.; dir., mem. exec. com. Sargent Welch Sci. Co., Skokie, Ill.; instr. UCLA, 1969. Asso., Northwestern U., Evanston; trustee UCLA Found. Served to lt. USNR, 1958-61. Mem. Kappa Sigma. Episcopalian. Clubs: Harvard of N.Y.; Econ. of Chgo., Harvard Bus. Sch. (Chgo.). Contbr. articles to profl. jours., chpts. to books. Home: 591 Plum Tree Rd Barrington Hills IL 60010 Office: 1900 Dempster St Evanston IL 60204. *Work hard and be considerate of and helpful to those you meet along the way. Inevitably their support is important for success. Luck helps too.*

MACDOUGALL, CURTIS DANIEL, educator, b. Fond du Lac, Wis., Feb. 11, 1903; s. Gilbert Thomas and Isabella (McCollum) M.; B.A., Ripon Coll., 1923; M.S., Northwestern U., 1926; Ph.D., U. Wis., 1933; Litt.D., Columbia Coll., Chgo., 1965; m. Genevieve Rockwood; children—Gordon Pier, Allan Kent, Lois Mae, Priscilla Ruth, Bonnie Maurine. Reporter, Daily Commonwealth, Fond du Lac, 1918; with Commonwealth-Reporter, 1918-23; spl. writer Two Rivers (Wis.) Chronicle, 1923-25; staff corr. Chgo. bur. U.P., 1926-27; head courses in journalism Lehigh U., Bethlehem, Pa., 1927-31; reporter St. Louis Star-Times, 1933-34; editor Evanston (Ill.) Daily News-Index, 1934-37; editor Nat. Almanac and Year Book, 1937-40, News Map of Week, 1938-39; state supr. Ill. Writers Project, 1939-42; editorial writer Chgo. Sun, 1942; prof. journalism Northwestern U., Evanston, Ill., 1942-71; Matters of Opinion, WBBM-CBS, 1972-75; columnist Chgo. Skyline, 1978—; editorial adviser Suburban Press Found., 1959-63. Past mem. bd. Chgo. Area Project; chmn., commr. Cook County Housing Authority, 1946-56; nat. adv. com. on acad. freedom ACLU. Recipient Outstanding Journalism Edn. award Sigma Delta Chi, So. Ill. U., 1972; Ball State U. Distinguished Service in Journalism award; alumni citation U. Wis., 1971, Ripon Coll., 1951. Fellow Am. Sociol. Assn.; mem. Am. Assn. Tchrs. Journalism (past pres.), Am. Assn. Pub. Opinion Research, Assn. Edn. Journalism, Phi Beta Kappa, Sigma Delta Chi (awards 1946, 53, 68), Alpha Kappa Delta, Tau Kappa Alpha, Pi Delta Epsilon, Pi Kappa Delta, Acacia. Author: Brown and White Manual, 1930; Reporting for Beginners, 1932; Teachers Manual, 1932; Interpretative Reporting, 1938, rev. 1948, 57, 63, 68, 72, 77; Hoaxes, 1940, rev., 1957; Newsroom Problems and Policies, 1941, rev., 1963; Covering the Courts, 1946; Understanding Public Opinion, 1952, rev. 1966; Greater Dead Than Alive, 1963; The Press and its Problems, 1964; Gideon's Army, 1965; Reporters Report Reporters, 1968; News Pictures Fit to Print, 1971; Principles of Editorial Writing, 1973. Contbr. to mags. Home: 537 Judson Ave Evanston IL 60202

MACDOUGALL, HARTLAND MOLSON, banker; b. Montreal, Que., Can., Jan. 28, 1931; s. Hartland Campbell and M. Dorothy (Molson) MacD.; ed. LeRosey, Switzerland, 1947-48, McGill U., 1949-53, Advanced Mgmt. Program, Harvard U.; m. Eve Gordon, Oct. 29, 1954; children—Cynthia, Wendy, Keith, Willa, Tania. With Bank Montreal, various locations, sr. v.p. Alta. div., 1968-69, sr. v.p. Ont. div., 1969-70, exec. v.p., Toronto, 1970-73, exec. v.p., Montreal, 1973-74, exec. v.p., dir., 1974—, gen. mgr. central ops., 1975-76, exec. v.p., gen. mgr. corp. banking, 1976—, also dir. Founding chmn. Heritage Can.; past bd. govs., past chmn. Council Can. Unity; hon. treas. Duke of Edinburgh Awards in Can.; mem. adv. council Faculty of Commerce, U. B.C.; gov. Olympic Trust; bd. dirs. Empire Club Found., St. Michaels Hosp.; senator Stratford Shakespearean Found. Clubs: Vancouver, Vancouver Lawn Tennis and Badminton; Ranchmen's (Calgary, Alta.); St. James, Montreal Indoor Tennis, Montreal Racket; York; Badminton and Racket, Toronto; Caledon Riding and Hunt; Caledon Ski; Queen's. Home: Belfountain ON L0N 1B0 Canada Office: 1st Bank Tower 1st Canadian Pl Toronto ON M5X 1A1 Canada

MACDOUGALL, IVER CAMERON, lawyer; b. Phila., Nov. 12, 1926; s. Iver Cameron and Edna (Gloeckner) M.; A.B., Yale U., 1949; LL.B., Harvard U., 1952; m. Terry Maunsell, Nov. 26, 1955; children—Bruce, Alison, Gordon. Admitted to Tenn. bar, 1952, Calif. bar, 1955, Wash. bar, 1979; asso. firm Stewart & Crownover, Nashville, 1952-53; with Stauffer Chem. Co., Westport, Conn., 1953—, v.p., 1968-78, sec., 1971-77, gen. counsel, 1977-78; individual practice law, Seattle, 1979—. Served with AUS, 1945-46. Mem. Am. Bar Assn., State Bar Calif., Wash. State Bar Assn., Bar Assn. City N.Y. Democrat. Club: Met. (Washington). Address: 10618 NE South Beach Rd Bainbridge Island WA 98110 Office: 120 Madrone Ln Winslow WA 98110

MACDOUGALL, RODERICK MARTIN, banker; b. N.Y.C., Mar. 27, 1926; s. Albert Edward and Ina M. (Brown) MacD.; B.A., Harvard U., 1951; m. Barbara Park, Oct. 31, 1952; children—Douglas E., Gordon P., Harriet H. and Susan B. (twins). Vice pres. Morgan Guaranty Trust Trust Co., N.Y.C., 1951-57; exec. v.p. Marine Midland Bank, Rochester, N.Y., 1967-68, pres., chief exec. officer, 1968-73; pres. New Eng. Mchts. Nat. Bank, Boston, 1974-76, pres., 1976-78, chief exec. officer, 1976—, chmn., 1978—; chmn., pres., dir. New Eng. Mchts. Co., Inc.; chmn., dir. New Eng. Enterprises Capital Corp., New Eng. Investment Services Corp., New Eng. Mchts.

Leasing Corp.; dir. New Eng. Mchts. Bank Internat., New Eng. Mchts. Realty Corp., EG&G, Inc., Arkwright-Boston, Mfrs. Mut. Ins. Co., New Eng. Mut. Life Ins. Co., Schlegel Mfg. Co. Trustee Boston Symphony Orch., Northeastern U., Boston; mem. corp. Babson Coll., Mass. Gen. Hosp., Mus. of Sci.; bd. dirs., v.p. Urban League Eastern Mass., United Way Mass. Bay. Served with USNR, 1943-46. Mem. Assn. Res. City Bankers, Mass. Bankers Assn., Greater Boston C. of C. (dir.). Clubs: Country (Brookline, Mass.); Somerset, Commercial, Merchants (Boston). Home: 120 Ridgeway Rd Weston MA 02193 Office: New Eng Mchts Nat Bank 28 State St Boston MA 02109

MAC DOWELL, WILLIAM DUNLAP, seed mfg. co. exec.; b. Bronxville, N.Y., Dec. 2, 1931; s. John Watson and Ruth Weld (Dunlap) MacD.; B.A., Oberlin Coll., 1953; M.B.A., Harvard U., 1955; m. Jane Kemmerer, July 3, 1954; children—Anne, W. Douglas, Edward W. Sales mgmt. Procter & Gamble Distbg., Boston, 1955-57, N.Y.C., 1957-59, Cin., 1960, Balt., 1960-62; mktg. mgr. J.H. Filbert Inc., Balt., 1963; mktg. and venture mgr. Gen. Foods Corp., White Plains, N.Y., 1963-70; pres., chief exec. officer W. Atlee Burpee Co., Warminster, Pa., 1970—, also dir.; dir. Luther Burbank Seed Co., James Vick's Inc., Fertl Inc. Mem. Am. Seed Trade Assn. (dir.), Pa. Hort. Soc. (dir.), Nat. Jr. Hort Assn. (dir.), Nat. Assn. Conservation Dists. Office: W Atlee Burpee Co 300 Park Ave Warminster PA 18974*

MACE, DAVID ROBERT, educator; b. Scotland, June 21, 1907; s. Joseph and Josephine (Reid) M.; B.Sc., U. London (Eng.), 1928; B.A., Cambridge (Eng.) U., 1930, M.A., 1933; Ph.D., U. Manchester (Eng.), 1942; LL.D., Alma Coll., 1977; D.S.S., Brigham Young U., 1977; m. Vera Chapman, July 26, 1933; children—Sheila (Mrs. Jagan M. Rao), Fiona (Mrs. John S. Patterson). Ordained to ministry Meth. Ch., 1933; minister in Eng., 1930-44; now mem. Soc. of Friends; marriage counselor, 1944—; a founder Nat. Marriage Guidance Council Gt. Britain, 1938, exec. dir., 1942-49, v.p., 1949—; prof. human relations Drew U., 1949-59; asso. prof. family study U. Pa. Sch. Medicine, staff cons. Marriage Council Phila., 1959-60; exec. dir. Am. Assn. Marriage Counselors, 1960-67; prof. family sociology Bowman Gray Sch. Medicine, Wake Forest U., Winston-Salem, N.C., 1967-77; field work in marriage guidance and family welfare in Africa, Asia, 1954, 58, 68, Australia, New Zealand and Asia, 1956, 67, Caribbean, S.Am., 1960, 61, Soviet Union, 1960. Pres., Nat. Council Family Relations, 1961-62; v.p. Internat. Union Family Orgns., 1961-70, chmn. internat. commn. marriage and marriage guidance, 1961-70; family life cons. World Council Chs., 1958-72; pres. Sex Info. and Edn. Council U.S., 1965-66, Assn. Couples for Marriage Enrichment, 1973—; sec. Groves Conf. on Marriage and Family, 1968-71. Recipient numerous awards latest including Distinguished Contbn. award Am. Assn. Marriage and Family Counselors, 1975, citation N.C. Family Life Council, 1975, award Nat. Council Family Relations, 1975, Man of Year award Forsyth County Mental Health Assn., 1975, award Assn. Couples Marriage Enrichment, 1976. Author: Does Sex Morality Matter?, 1942; Marriage Counselling, 1948; Marriage Crisis, 1948; Marriage, The Art of Lasting Love, 1952; Hebrew Marriage, 1953; Whom God Hath Joined, 1953; Success in Marriage, 1958; Youth Looks Toward Marriage, 1957; (with Mrs. Mace) Marriage East and West, 1960; (with Mrs. Mace) The Soviet Family, 1962; The Christian Response to the Sexual Revolution, 1970; Getting Ready for Marriage, 1972; Abortion: The Agonizing Decision, 1972; Sexual Difficulties in Marriage, 1972; (with Vera Mace) We Can Have Better Marriages—If We Really Want Them, 1974, Men, Women, and God, 1976, Marriage Enrichment in the Church, 1976, Towards Better Marriages, 1976, How to Have a Happy Marriage, 1976; also numerous articles. Home: PO Box 5182 Winston-Salem NC 27103 Office: Bowman Gray Medical Sch Winston-Salem NC 27103

MACE, DEAN TOLLE, educator; b. Neosho, Mo., May 21, 1922; s. Rector Tolle and Beatrice B.(Dunkeson) M.; B.A., Washington U., St. Louis, 1948; M.A., Columbia, 1949, Ph.D., 1952; m. Mary Ann Fitz-Hugh, June 24, 1950; children—Thomas Fitz-Hugh, Sarah Tolle. Instr. English, Washington U., 1950-52; faculty Vassar Coll., Poughkeepsie, N.Y., 1952—, prof. English, 1966—, chmn. dept., 1968—. Vis. reader English, U. York (Eng.), 1966-67. Served with inf. AUS, 1942-45. Vassar Coll. faculty fellow for research, 1959. Mem. Modern Lang. Assn., AAUP. Contbr. articles to profl. jours. Home: 168 College Ave Poughkeepsie NY 12601

MACEACHEN, ALLAN JOSEPH, Canadian govt. ofcl.; b. Inverness, N.S., Can., July 6, 1921; B.A., St. Francis Xavier U.; M.A., U. Toronto, 1946; student indsl. relations U. Chgo., Mass. Inst. Tech., 1951. Prof. econs. St. Francis Xavier U., 1946, head dept. social scis., 1948-51. Mem. Parliament for Inverness-Richmond, 1953-57, 62-68, for Cape Breton-Highlands-Canso, 1968—; minister labor, 1963-65, minister of nat. health and welfare, 1965-68, minister of manpower and immigration, 1968-70, pres. Privy Council, 1970-74, 76—, mem., 1974—, sec. state for external affairs, 1974-76, dep. prime minister, 1977—. Parliamentary observer 10th Gen. Assembly UN, 1955, alternate del. 22d session UN Econ. and Social Council, Geneva, 1956; leader Canadian delegation Commonwealth Parliamentary Conf., London, Eng., 1973; co-chmn. Conf. Internat. Econ. Cooperation, 1975—. Home: Rural Route 1 Whycocomagh NS Canada Office: House of Commons Ottawa ON Canada

MACER, DAN JOHNSTONE, hosp. adminstr.; b. Evansville, Ind., May 25, 1917; s. Clarence Guy and Ann (Johnstone) M.; B.S., Northwestern U., 1939, M.S. in Hosp. Adminstrn. with distinction, 1959; m. Eugenia Loretta Andrews, June 1, 1943; children—Eugenia Ann, Dan James. Chief hosp. ops. VA br. office, St. Paul, 1947-50; asst. mgr. VA hosps., Ft. Wayne, Ind., 1951, Kerrville, Tex., 1952, Augusta, Ga., 1952-56; mgr. VA Hosp., Sunmount, N.Y., 1956-58; dir. Va Research Hosp., Chgo., 1958-62; mem. hosp. adminstrn. faculty Northwestern U., 1959-61; dir. VA Hosps., Pitts., 1962-67; asst. vice chancellor health professions U. Pitts., 1968-71, prof. med. and hosp. adminstrn. U. Pitts. Grad. Sch. Pub. Health, 1962-71; prof. Coll. Health and Coll. Medicine, U. Okla., 1971—; dir. VA Hosps. and Clinics, Oklahoma City, 1971-76; dir. VA Med. Dist. 20 (Okla.-Ark.), 1971-76; lectr. George Washington U., 1961—; v.p. Hosp. Casualty Co., Oklahoma City, 1978—; pres. Dan J. Macer & Assos., Inc., cons. to health field; cons. nat. health profl. assns., indsl. corps., archtl. corps, health planners; cons. Health Services and Mental Health Adminstrn., HEW, 1968. Coordinator civil def. and disaster planning all hosps., Chgo. nr. North Side, 1961; chmn. welfare and planning council Savannah River Community Chest, Augusta, 1954-56; chmn. group 17 fed. sect., govt. div. United Fund Allegheny County, 1964-65; mem. Fed. Interagy. Bd. Dirs., 1964-68; sec. U. Pitts. Health Center, 1969-71; chmn. health com. Health and Welfare Assn. Alleghany County, 1970-71; chmn. devel. com. Northwestern U. Alumni Program in Hosp. Adminstrn.; chmn. adv. com. Regional Med. Program Western Pa., 1966-71; mem. steering com. Comprehensive Health Planning Western Pa.; dir. Am. States Regional Conf., 1971; vice chmn. procedures com., mem.-at-large exec. com. Okla. Regional Med. Program, 1971—; mem. Gov's Adv. Com. Comprehensive Health Planning, 1971—, Gov's Com. Employment of Handicapped, 1972, Pres.'s Com. Employment of Handicapped, 1962; chmn. VA chief med. dir.'s com. for evaluation and reorgn. VA health care delivery services, 1974—; chmn. planning com. for constrn. New Children's Meml. Hosp., 1974—; chmn. Gov.'s Ad Hoc Com on Fed.-State Planning, 1973—; mem. Gov.'s Health Scis. Center planning and adv. com., 1973—, State Health Planning Council, 1973—; chmn. Okla. Health Goals and Planning Priorities Com., 1973—. Bd. dirs. Comprehensive Health Planning Agy., Western Pa.; bd. dirs. Health Services Corp., 1969-71; trustee Okla. Council Health Careers and Manpower, 1976—. Examiner, Am. Coll. Hosp. Adminstrs. Served maj. Med. Adminstrv. Corps, AUS, 1941-46. Decorated Bronze Star, Purple Heart. Recipient citations VFW, 1959, Am. Legion, 1956, 58, DAV, 1964, Okla. Regional Med. Program, 1976, Okla. Gov.'s Office Health Planning, 1976; Laura G. Jackson award in recognition exceptional service in field of hosp. adminstrn., 1971. Fellow Am. Pub. Health Assn., Am. Coll. Hosp. Adminstrs.; mem. Am. Hosp. Assn. (mem. council med. edn. 1976—), Hosp. Assn. Pa. (vice chmn. med. relations 1965-66, chmn. rehab. com. 1965-66, vice chmn. council on profl. practices, dir.), Hosp. Council Western Pa., Assn. Am. Med. Colls. (exec. com. council teaching hosps.), Oklahoma City C. of C. (vice chmn. research and edn. div. 1975—), Northwestern U. Alumni Assn. (pres. Acacia chpt. 1961, hosp. adminstrn. chpt. 1962). Rotarian, Kiwanian. Clubs: Lake Shore (Chgo.); University (Pitts.); Twin Hills Golf and Country. Author articles in field. Home: 2925 Pelham Dr Oklahoma City OK 73120 Office: U Okla Health Scis Center PO Box 26901 Oklahoma City OK 73190

MACERA, SALVATORE, indsl. exec.; b. Cambridge, Mass., May 3, 1931; s. Benedetto and Anna (DeVellis) M.; B.B.A., Northeastern U., 1960; m. Josephine Guarnaccia (div.); children—Michael, Richard, Michelle; m. 2d, Daphne Lee. Financial analyst Ford Motor Co., 1955-58; v.p. finance and adminstrn. LFE Electronics div. Lab. for Electronics, Boston, 1958-63; v.p., chief financial officer Itek Corp., 1963-73, exec. v.p., 1973—, also dir.; dir. Harbor Nat. Bank, Boston. Mem. budget com. Financial Inst. Served with AUS. Mem. Nat. Security Indsl. Assn. (v.p. Boston). Home: 19 Union Wharf Boston MA 02109 Office: 10 Maguire Rd Lexington MA 02173

MACESICH, GEORGE, educator, economist, author; b. Cleve., May 27, 1927; s. Walter (Vaso) and Milka (Tepavac) M.; A.A., George Washington U., 1951, B.A., 1953, M.A., 1954; Ph.D., U. Chgo., 1958; m. Susana Sonia Svorkovich, Feb. 16, 1955; children—Maja Susana Radmila, Milka Milena Milica, George Milan Peter. Research asso. U. Chgo., 1956-58; research economist U.S. C. of C., Washington, 1958-59; dir. Fla. Council on Econ. Devel., Tallahassee, 1961-63; asst. prof. econs. Fla. State U., Tallahassee, 1959-61, asso. prof., 1961-63, prof. econs., 1963—, also dir. Center for Yugoslav-Am. Studies, Research and Exchanges, 1965—, mng. editor Slavic papers, 1967-74, Procs. and Reports, 1974—; prof. econs. Faculty Polit Sci., U. Belgrade (Yugoslavia, 1971—, prof. econs. Faculty Orgnl. Scis., 1972—; mem. nat. adv. council U. Montenegro (Yugoslavia), 1972—. Econ. cons. U.S. Dept. Commerce, 1961—. Served with USN, 1944-53. Mem. Am., So. (editorial bd. jour. 1961-63) econ. assns., Am. Statis. Assn., Am. Econ. History Assn. Mem. Serbian Orthodox Ch. Author: Commercial Banking and Regional Development, 1965; Yugoslavia: Theory and Practice of Development Planning, 1964; Statistical Abstracts for Florida, 1963; Money and the Canadian Economy, 1967; Economic Stability: A Comparative Analysis, 1973; Money in a European Common Market Setting, 1972; Monetary Theory and Policy: Theoretical and Empirical Issues, 1973; Financing Industrial and Regional Development: American Experience with the Small Business Administration, 1955-65, 1972; Monetary and Financial Organization for Growth and Stability: The U.S. and Yugoslavia, 1972; (with D. Dimitrijevic) Money and Finance in Contemporary Yugoslavia, 1973. Contbr. articles to profl. jours. Home: 2401 Delgado Dr Tallahassee FL 32304

MAC EWAN, DOUGLAS WILLIAM, physician, educator; b. Ottawa, Ont., Can., Nov. 11, 1924; s. James Urquhart and Eleanor (Smith) Mac E.; B.Sc., McGill U., 1948, M.D.C.M., 1952; m. Elizabeth Turner-Bone, June 23, 1951; children—Joanne, Elspeth, Eleanor, James. Intern, then resident Montreal Gen. Hosp., 1953-58; radiology teaching appointments McGill U., Montreal Childrens Hosp., 1958-63; asso. radiologist Montreal Gen. Hosp., 1963-65; prof., chmn. radiology U. Man., Winnipeg, 1966—, radiologist-in-chief Health Scis. Centre, 1966—. Chmn. McGill Grad. Soc., Winnipeg, 1976—. Served with RCAF, 1943-45. Fellow Royal Coll. Physicians and Surgeons (Can.), Am. Coll. Radiology; mem. Can. Assn. Radiologists, Radiol. Soc. N.Am. (treas. 1976—), Am. Coll. Radiology. Club: Winter (Winnipeg). Home: 30 Aldershot Blvd Winnipeg MB R3P 0C8 Canada Office: 700 William Ave Winnipeg MB Canada

MACEY, MORRIS WILLIAM, lawyer; b. Camilla, Ga., Dec. 25, 1922; s. Isadore and Freda (Berman) M.; A.B., U. Ga., 1946, LL.B., 1943; LL.M., Harvard, 1947; m. Dora Rosenfield, Dec. 28, 1950; children—Morris William, Jonathan Rosenfield, Rex Philip. Admitted to Ga. bar, 1943; practiced in Atlanta, 1947—; partner firm Macey & Zusmann; formerly instr. Emory U. Law Sch., U. Ga. Law Sch. Pres. Comml. Law League Am., 1966-67. Trustee Fisk U. Served with AUS, 1943-46. Mem. Internat., Am., Ga., Atlanta bar assns., Nat. Bankruptcy Conf., Nat. Conf. Commrs. on Uniform State Laws, Am. Law Inst., Phi Beta Kappa, Omicron Delta Kappa. Jewish (trustee Temple Sinai 1969-70). Mason (Shriner). Clubs: Lawyers, Harvard, Standard, Commerce (Atlanta). Asso. editor Comml. Law Jour. Home: 4175 Conway Valley Rd NW Atlanta GA 30327 Office: 1795 Peachtree Rd NE Atlanta GA 30309

MAC FADDEN, CHARLES ROSS, fisheries and seafood exec.; b. New Glasgow, N.S., Can., June 21, 1913; s. William Smith and Marion (MacPherson) MacF.; student Maritime Bus. Coll., 1931-33; m. Marian Louise Peart, July 19, 1947; children—David William Bruce, Heather Ann, Ian Ross. Accountant, Fed. Income Tax Dept., Halifax, N.S., 1939-45; chief accountant Nat. Sea Products Ltd., Halifax, 1945-61, sec.-treas., dir., 1961-65, v.p. finance, 1965-77, sr. v.p., 1977—, dir., mem. exec. com., 1967—; pres., dir. Mormac Investments, Ltd.; dir. Eaton-Bay Viking Fund Ltd., Eaton-Bay Commonwealth Fund Ltd., Eaton-Bay Venture Fund Ltd., Eaton-Bay Growth Fund Ltd., Eaton-Bay Internat. Fund Ltd., Eaton-Bay Leverage Fund Ltd., Eaton-Bay Dividend Fund Ltd., Lobster Hutch Ltd.; chmn. bd., pres. McDermaid Agys. Ltd., Mainland Investment Ltd.; dir. Can. Internat. Ins. Ltd. (Bermuda), Cambridge Reins. Ltd. (Bermuda), Hamilton Ins. Brokerage Ltd. (Bermuda); trustee Eaton Income Fund. Mem. Halifax Bd. Trade. Registered mgmt. accountant. Fellow Inst. Chartered Secs.; mem. N.S. Soc. Indsl. Accountants (past pres.), Soc. Mgmt. Accountants Can. (past pres., past nat. chmn. edn. com.). Clubs: Halifax; Saraguay; Ashburn Golf. Home: Indian Point Glen Haven Halifax County NS B0J 3J0 Canada Office: Duke St Towers Scotia Sq Halifax NS Canada

MACFADDEN, CLIFFORD HERBERT, educator; b. Salem, Mich., Jan. 30, 1908; s. James W. and Augusta (Bigg) MacF.; B.A., U. Mich., 1937, M.A., 1939, Ph.D., 1948; m. Alyce E. Keller, Oct. 6, 1934. Chief cartographic sect., mil. intelligence War Dept., 1942-46; faculty U. Calif. at Los Angeles, 1946—, prof. geography, 1958—, chmn. dept., 1961-66, fgn. student adviser, 1957-60, dir. U. Calif. Study Center, Chinese U., Hong Kong, 1972-74; prof. geography, chmn. dept. U. Ceylon, 1950-51, 53-56; Fulbright prof. U. Delhi Grad. Sch. Econs., 1960-61. Mem. Mich. Acad. Sci., Arts and Letters, Geog. Soc. India, Asia Soc., Explorers Club. Author textbooks, atlases, profl. papers econ. geography, geography So. Asia. Home: 14907 Bestor Blvd Pacific Palisades CA 90272 Office: 405 Hilgard Ave Los Angeles CA 90024

MAC FADYEN, JOHN A., JR., educator; b. Scranton, Pa., July 10, 1922; s. John A. and Jessie (Peck) MacF.; B.A., Williams Coll., 1948; M.S., Lehigh U., 1950; Ph.D., Columbia, 1962; m. Diane L. Beersmann, June 7, 1967; children—John A. III, Janet C., Jean G. Mem. faculty Williams Coll., 1952—, prof., 1967—, chmn. geology dept., 1968—; research asso. Mineral. Inst., Oslo; vis. scientist Royal Sch. Mines, Imperial Coll., London, 1979-80; cons. non-metallic econ. geology, also engring. geology; vis. prof. U. Aarhus (Denmark), 1972-73. Chmn. Williamstown (Mass.) Finance Com., 1962-63; vice chmn. Berkshire council Boy Scouts Am., 1963. Served with USNR, 1942-45. Mem. Geol. Soc. Am., Norsk Geologisk Forening, Sigma Phi, Sigma Xi. Republican. Episcopalian. Club: Wadawanuck. Home: Forest Rd Williamstown MA 01267 Mailing Address: 22 Burton Ct Franklin's Row London SW3 England

MAC FADYEN, JOHN HAYTER, architect; b. Duluth, Minn., Mar. 5, 1923; s. John Alfred and Grace (Spurbeck) MacF.; A.B., Princeton, 1946, M.F.A. in Architecture, 1949; m. Mary-Esther Edge, May 23, 1951; children—John Tevere, William Loyall, Luke Sewall, Camilla. With firm MacFadyen & Knowles, N.Y.C., MacFadyen/Devido, N.Y.C., 1969-78. Exec. dir. N.Y. State Council on Arts, 1961-64; pres. Asso. Councils Arts, 1970-73, bd. dirs., 1962—. Served with AUS, 1946-47. Fellow Am. Acad. in Rome; hon. mem. Buffalo Fine Arts Soc. Club: Coffee House. Prin. works include: Saratoga Performing Arts Center, Wolf Trap Farm Park, Robin Hood Dell. Home: Route 1 Box 167 Millbrook NY 12545 Office: 250 W 57th St New York NY 10019

MACFARLAN, DUNCAN, ins. co. exec.; b. Paterson, N.J., June 21, 1926; s. Donald and Adele (Haefeli) M.; B.A., Dartmouth Coll., 1947; m. Joan Mattucci, July 31, 1948; children—Duncan Andrew, Donald Dean, Joan Catherine. With Prudential Ins. Co. Am., 1947—, exec. dir. ordinary agys., Jacksonville, Fla., 1956-63, v.p., Mpls., 1963-65, Houston, 1965-67, sr. v.p., 1967-73, exec. v.p., Newark, 1973-79, pres. So.-Central ops., Jacksonville, 1979—; chmn. bd. Prudential's Gibraltar Fund. Chmn. nat. adv. bd. Nat. Assn. Retarded Citizens Research and Demonstration Inst.; mem. lay adv. bd. St. Vincent's Hosp., Jacksonville. Mem. Life Ins. Mktg. and Research Assn. (past chmn. bd.), Underwriter Tng. Council (past chmn.). Clubs: Channel, Ponte Vedra, Sawgrass, River, Ocean Reef. Office: Prudential Ins Co Prudential Dr Jacksonville FL 32231

MACFARLAND, LONSDALE PORTER, JR., lawyer; b. Sheffield, Ala., Jan. 23, 1911; s. Lonsdale Porter and Elizabeth (Crowe) MacF.; grad. Branham and Hughes Mil. Acad., Spring Hill, Tenn., 1927; B.S. in Civil Engring., Va. Mil. Inst., 1931; LL.B., Cumberland U., 1933; m. Perre Coleman Hutton, July 8, 1939; children—Perre Coleman, Lonsdale. Admitted to Tenn. bar, 1933, practiced in Lebanon, 1933-39, Columbia, 1946—; individual practice law, Columbia; gen. counsel Pub. Service Commn. Tenn., 1939-41. Pres. Middle Tenn. Bank of Columbia, 1939-70, chmn. bd., 1970—; organizer, pres. Caribbean Finance Co., San Juan, P.R., 1956-65. Mem. Presdl. Electoral Coll., 1948; chmn. bd. Maury County Hosp., Columbia, Tenn. Served from 1st lt. to col., 5th Armored Div., AUS, 1941-46. Decorated Legion of Merit, Bronze Star; Croix de Guerre (France); Croix de Guerre with palms (Luxembourg); Red Star (Russia). Mem. Tenn. (pres. 1958-59), Am. (ho. of dels. 1954-56) bar assns. Democrat. Presbyn. Clubs: Cumberland, Belle Meade Country (Nashville). Home: Pulaski Pike Columbia TN 38401 Office: Middle Tenn Bank Bldg Columbia TN 38401

MACFARLANE, ANDREW WALKER, editor, univ. dean; b. Toronto, Ont., Can., Feb. 18, 1928; s. Joseph Arthur and Marguerite (Walker) MacF.; student U. Sask. (Can.), 1945-46; B.A., U. Toronto, 1949; M.L.S., U. Western Ont., 1977; m. Nancy Elizabeth Claire Wallace, Feb. 21, 1959 (separated 1975); children—Jeanie Andreas, Catriona Flora. Office boy Canadian Press, Toronto, 1949; reporter Halifax (N.S., Can.) Chronicle Herald, 1949-51, Scottish Daily Express, Glasgow, 1951-53; subeditor London (Eng.) Evening Standard, 1953-55; copy editor, night editor, feature editor, gen. reporter, daily columnist, asst. to pub. Telegram, Toronto, 1955-64, mng. editor, corporate dir., 1964-69, dir. research and devel., 1969-71, exec. editor, 1971—; dir. Citizen's Inquiry br. Ministry Govt. Services, Province of Ont., 1971-72; chmn. dept., dean Grad. Sch. Journalism, U. Western Ont., 1973—. Co-chmn. Ont.-Que. Journalist Exchange; Bd. dirs. Canadian Medic-Alert, 1959; past bd. dirs. Met. Toronto Children's Aid Soc.; mem. advisory council Province of Ont. Medal Good Citizenship, 1976—. Recipient Bowater award, 1960; Nat. Newspaper award, 1958, 59. Southam fellow, 1961. Decorated knight comdr. Order St. Lazarus Jerusalem. Mem. Royal Canadian Mil. Inst., Canadian Mng. Editors Conf. (past dir.). Club: Toronto Men's Press, London City Press. Author: The Neverland of the Neglected Child, 1957. Office: U Western Ont Middlesex Coll London ON Canada

MACFARLANE, DAVID DIMLING, dept. store exec.; b. Du Bois, Pa., Nov. 28, 1905; s. Randolph Tillie and Myrtle (McAninch) MacF.; student Southwestern U., 1939, Loyola U., Chgo., 1940-41; m. Louella Bamberger, July 28, 1924; 1 son, Michael. With FEDCO/Inc., 1949—, pres., 1951—. Chmn., Community Relations Conf. So. Calif., 1959-60. Recipient Toastmaster Internat. award, 1940. Office: 14626 Titus St Van Nuys CA 91406*

MAC FARLANE, JOHN DEE, atty. gen. Colo.; b. Pueblo, Colo., Oct. 4, 1933; s. John Lincoln and Estamae (Lewis) MacF.; A.B. cum laude, Harvard U., 1955; LL.B., Stanford U., 1962; m. Janet Gertmenian, Dec. 28, 1962; children—Jennifer, John Lewis, Andrew Galt. Mgmt. analyst Hdqrs. USAF, Washington, 1955-57; admitted to Colo. bar; dep. dist. atty., Pueblo, 1962-64; individual practice law, Pueblo, 1965-70; chief dep. state pub. defender, Denver, 1971-74; atty. gen. Colo., Denver, 1975—. Mem. Colo. Ho. of Reps., 1965-68, Colo. Senate, 1969-70. Served with U.S. Army, 1957-59. Mem. Colo. Bar Assn., Nat. Assn. Attys. Gen. (pres. 1979-80). Democrat. Presbyterian. Bd. editors Stanford Law Rev., 1960-62, mng. editor, 1961-62. Home: 2080 Bellaire St Denver CO 80207 Office: 1525 Sherman St Denver CO 80203*

MACFARLANE, KILGORE, JR., banker; b. Seattle, Aug. 8, 1900; s. Walter K. and Blanche (Stetson) M.; Ph.B., Brown U., 1923; m. Elizabeth Kerr, June 10, 1926; children—Mrs. Barclay Martin, Mrs. J. L. Feininger, Mrs. W. Clarke. Vice pres., trust officer First Nat. Bank of Princeton, 1936-41; pres. trustee Schenectady Savs. Bank, 1941-58; past pres., trustee Buffalo Savs. Bank; dir. Savs. Bank Trust Co., N.Y.C.; chmn. finance com. United Bank of Phoenix (formerly Guaranty Bank of Phoenix); chmn. bd. 1st Security Bank; dir. Western Empire Life Ins. Co., Denver. Spl. asst. to gov. Ariz. for indsl. devel., 1961-65. Asst. nat. coordinator Nixon-Lodge, 1960. Bd. dirs. United Chest Appeal, Asso. Alumni Brown U., Brown Football Assn. Recipient citation Brown U., 1959, Andrew S. Joslin award, 1977, Brown Bear award, 1978. Mem. Nat. Savs. Bank Assn. (dir. 1954-60), Savs. Bank Assn. N.Y. (past pres., dir.), U.S. Golf Seniors, World Sr. Golf Assn., 200 Soc. Gentlemen Golfers, Alpha Delta Phi, Phi Delta Phi. Clubs: Paradise Valley Country (Scottsdale); Brown U. (pres.)

(Phoenix). Home: 6942 E Exeter Scottsdale AZ 85251 Office: care of United Bank 3550 N Central St Phoenix AZ 85012

MACFARLANE, MALCOLM HARRIS, educator; b. Brechin, Scotland, May 22, 1933; s. Malcolm P. and Mary (Harris) M.; M.A., U. Edinburgh (Scotland), 1955; Ph.D., U. Rochester, 1960; m. Eleanor Carman, May 30, 1957; children—Douglas, Kenneth, Sheila, Christine. Came to U.S., 1956. Research asso. Argonne (Ill.) Nat. Lab., 1959-60; asst. prof. physics U. Rochester, 1960-61; asso. physicist Argonne Nat. Lab., 1961-68, sr. physicist, 1968—; prof. physics U. Chgo., 1968—; vis. fellow All Souls Coll., Oxford (Eng.) U., 1966-67; cons. Ency. Brit. Guggenheim fellow physics, 1966-67. Fellow Am. Phys. Soc.; mem. Nuclear Physics sect. Am. Phys. Soc. (mem. exec. com. 1969-71). Contbr. articles of theoretical nuclear physics to profl. jours. Home: 514 Mark Ln Downers Grove IL 60515 Office: Physics div Argonne Nat Lab 9700 S Cass Ave Argonne IL 60439

MACFARLANE, ROBERT STETSON, JR., found. exec.; b. Seattle, Oct. 13, 1932; s. Robert Stetson and Irene Vivian (Clemens) M.; grad. Hotchkiss Sch., 1950; A.B. cum laude, Princeton, 1954; B.D., Princeton Theol. Sem., 1958; M.A., San Francisco State U., 1967; M.L.S., U. So. Calif., 1979; m. Janet Caroline Clayton, Aug. 13, 1958; children—Robert Stetson III, Duncan Clayton. Ordained to ministry Presbyn. Ch., 1960; asst. pastor First Presbyn. Ch., Burlingame, Cal., 1960-63, asso. pastor, 1963-66; asso. chmn. div. evangelism Bd. Nat. Missions, Presbyn. Ch. U.S.A., N.Y.C., 1967-72; pres. Found. Funds of Norton Simon, Inc., Los Angeles, 1972-78; mng. trustee Durfee Found., San Marino, Calif., 1978—; partner Found. Mgrs. Inc., Princeton, N.J., 1978—; pres. Los Angeles Inter-Found. Center, 1973-77. Mem. Nat. Presbyn. Health and Welfare Bd., 1968-71; mem. No. Calif. Homes of San Francisco, 1964-66, San Francisco bd. Fed. Home Loan Bank, 1975-78. Pres. bd. dirs. Pasadena Art Mus., 1974-77; cultural adviser Gallaudet Coll., Washington, 1977—. Republican. Presbyn. Co-author pamphlets including: How Does the Congregation Plan for Mission?; Guidelines for the Development of Local Church Clusters; Mission and Evangelism; Enlistment in Mission. Home: 16656 Linda Terr Pacific Palisades CA 90272 Office: Durfee Found 114 E Huntington Dr Suite F Alhambra CA 91801

MACGINITIE, WALTER HAROLD, psychologist; b. Carmel, Calif., Aug. 14, 1928; s. George Eber and Nettie Lorene (Murray) MacG.; B.A., U. Calif., Los Angeles, 1949; A.M., Stanford U., 1950; Ph.D., Columbia U., 1960; m. Ruth Olive Kilpatrick, Sept. 2, 1950; children—Mary Catherine, Laura Anne. Tchr., Long Beach (Calif.) Unified Sch. Dist. 1950, 1955-56; mem. faculty Columbia U. Tchrs. Coll., 1959—, prof. psychology and edn., 1970—; research asso. Lexington Sch. Deaf, N.Y.C., 1963-69. Served with USAF, 1950-54. Life mem. Calif. PTA; fellow Am. Psychol. Assn., AAAS, Nat. Conf. Research English, N.Y. Acad. Scis.; mem. Internat. Reading Assn. (pres. 1976-77). Co-author: Gates-MacGinitie Reading Tests, 1965, 78; Psychological Foundations of Education, 1968. Editor: Assessment Problems in Reading, 1972; co-editor: Verbal Behavior of the Deaf Child, 1969. Home: 132 High St Leonia NJ 07605 Office: Box 140 Teachers Coll Columbia Univ New York City NY 10027

MACGOWAN, CHARLES FREDERIC, chem. co. exec.; b. Rock Island, Ill., Nov. 24, 1918; s. Charles John and Clara (Ohge) MacG.; student Wright Jr. Coll., Chgo., 1936-37, North Park Coll., Chgo., 1938-39, Harvard, 1955-56; m. Shirley Esther Sutherland, Feb. 22, 1941; children—Lynn Merle, Charles John II. Partner, C.B. Isett Co., Chgo., 1946-49; indsl. engr. Graver Tank & Mfg. Co., East Chicago, Ind., 1949-50; asst. bus. mgr. Boilermakers Local 374 State Ind., 1950-54; internat. rep. Internat. Brotherhood Boilermakers, 1954-60; dir. Office Saline Water, U.S. Dept Interior, Washington, 1961-65, spl. asst. to sec., 1965-66; coordinator intergovtl. relations Fed. Water Pollution Control Adminstrn., 1966-67; govt. relations mgr. Dow Chem. Co., Washington, 1967—; cons. nuclear desalting Internat. Atomic Energy Agy. (Vienna, Austria); tech. cons. AFL-CIO. Chmn. Ind. Boiler and Pressure Vessel Bd., 1960-61. Mem. Am. Water Works Assn., Aircraft Owners and Pilots Assn., Md. Acad. Sci. Democrat. Methodist. Mason. Contbr. articles to profl. jours. Home: 661 Ad Hoc Rd Great Falls VA 22066 Office: 1800 M St NW Washington DC 20036

MAC GOWAN, MARY EUGENIA, lawyer; b. Turlock, Calif., Aug. 4, 1928; d. William Ray and Mary Bolling (Gilbert) Kern; A.B., U. Calif., Berkeley, 1950; J.D., U. Calif., San Francisco, 1953; m. Gordon Scott Millar, Jan. 2, 1970; 1 dau., Heather Mary. Admitted to Calif. bar; research atty. Supreme Ct. Calif., 1954, Calif. Ct. Appeals, 1955; partner firm MacGowan & MacGowan, Calif., 1956-68; individual practice law, San Francisco, 1968—. Bd. dirs. San Francisco Speech and Hearing Center, San Francisco Legal Aid Soc., J.A.C.K.I.E. Mem. Am., Calif., San Francisco bar assns., Queen's Bench. Clubs: San Francisco Lawyers, Forest Hill Garden. Home: 35 Lopez Ave San Francisco CA 94116 Office: 220 Bush St San Francisco CA 94104

MACGRAW, ALI, actress; b. Pound Ridge, N.Y., 1939; ed. Wellesley Coll.; m. 2d, Robert Evans, 1970 (div.); m. 3d, Steve McQueen, 1973 (div.). Previous to film career was editorial asst. Harper's Bazaar Mag., asst. to photographer Melvin Sokolsky; actress films including Goodbye, Columbus, 1969, Love Story, 1971, The Getaway, 1973, Convoy, 1978, Players, 1979. Office: 8899 Beverly Blvd Suite 501 Los Angeles CA 90048*

MACGREGOR, CLARK, co. exec.; b. Mpls., July 12, 1922; s. William Edwin and Edith (Clark) MacG.; grad. cum laude, Dartmouth, 1946; J.D., U. Minn., 1948; m. Barbara Porter Spicer, June 16, 1948; children—Susan Clark, Laurie Miller, Eleanor Martin. Admitted to Minn. bar, 1948, practiced in Mpls. until 1961; partner firm King & MacGregor, 1952-61; mem. 87th-91st Congress, 3d Dist. Minn., mem. jud. com., com. on banking and currency; counsel to Pres. for congl. affairs, 1971-72; Nixon campaign dir., 1972; v.p. United Technologies Corp., 1972—. Bd. dirs. Nat. Symphony Orch. Assn., Wolf Trap Found., Ford's Theatre; trustee Boys Clubs Am., Meridian House Internat. Served to 2d lt. AUS, 1942-45; CBI. Decorated Bronze Star, Legion of Merit. Mem. Nat. Security Indsl. Assn., Air Force Assn. (govt. adv. council), Assn. U.S. Army, Aero. Club Washington. Republican. Presbyn. Clubs: Burning Tree, Metropolitan, Chevy Chase. Home: 2834 Foxhall Rd NW Washington DC 20007 Office: 1125 15th St NW Washington DC 20005

MACGREGOR, GEORGE LESCHER, JR., banker; b. Dallas, Sept. 15, 1936; s. George Lescher and Jean (Edge) MacG.; B.B.A., U. Tex., 1958; m. Nancy Clement, Feb. 16, 1963; children—George Lescher III, Michael Fordtran. Asst. cashier First Nat. Bank in Dallas, 1960-64, asst. v.p., 1964-68; v.p. Nat. Bank of Commerce of Dallas, 1968-70, sr. v.p., 1970-73, exec. v.p., 1973—; pres., chief exec. officer Mountain Banks Ltd., Colorado Springs, 1974—; chief exec. officer Highfield Fin. (U.S.A.) Ltd., 1978—. Served with M.C., AUS, 1958-60. Mem. Am. Inst. Banking (hon.), Phi Gamma Delta. Episcopalian. Clubs: Dallas Country; Idlewild, Terpsichorean, Koon Kreek (Dallas). Home: 9 El Encanto Colorado Springs CO 80906 Office: 1736 Blake St Denver CO 80202

MACGREGOR, IAN KINLOCH, investment banker; b. Kinlochleven, Scotland, Sept. 12, 1912; s. Daniel and Grace Fraser (Maclean) MacG.; B.Sc. with honors, U. Glasgow, 1935; LL.D., Denver U., 1970; D.Eng., Mont. U., 1970; D.Sc., Angola U., 1970; LL.D., Strathclyde U., 1972; U. Wyo., 1973, U. Glasgow, 1978; m. Sibyl M. K. Spencer, Apr. 11, 1942; children—Ian Charles Spencer, Elizabeth Grace Bates. Vice-pres. Am. Metal Climax, 1957-65; exec. v.p. AMAX, 1965-66, pres., 1967-77, chmn. bd., 1969-77, chief exec. officer, 1967-77, dir., hon. chmn., 1977—; chmn. Alumax, 1974—; gen. partner Lazard Freres, Inc., N.Y.C.; dir. Am. Cyanamid, Brunswick Corp., Singer Corp., L.T.V. Corp., Brit. Leyland, Atlantic Assets; gov. N.Y. Ins. Exchange. Decorated chevalier Legion of Honor (France); recipient Rand gold medal Am. Inst. Mining, Metall. and Petroleum Engrs., 1978, Jackling gold medal Am. Inst. Mining, Metall. and Petroleum Engrs., 1978, Jackling gold medal Mining and Metall. Soc. Am., 1979. Fellow Aluminum Assn., Instn. Mining and Metallurgy (London); mem. Am. Mining Congress (chmn. 1974-77), U.S. Council Internat. C. of C. (chmn. 1973-76, past pres.), German Am. C. of C. (chmn. N.Y. 1979), Far East Am. Council (chmn. 1978-79), Europe-Businessmen's Council (chmn. 1977-78), U.S. Japan Businessmen's Council (mem. exec. com. 1976-79), Soc. Automotive Engrs., Brit. Inst. Mech. Engrs., Resources for the Future (dir.), Internat. Inst. for Environ. and Devel. (dir.), Trade Policy Research Centre (dir.). Clubs: University, Links, Brook, Sky (N.Y.C.); Metropolitan (Washington); Blind Brook, Indian Harbor, Bellehaven. Home: 2 Broad Rd Greenwich CT 06830 Office: Amax Center Greenwich CT 06830 also Lazard Freres 1 Rockefeller Plaza New York NY 10020

MAC GREGOR, JOHN BOYKO, painter; b. Dorking, Eng., Jan. 12, 1944; s. Wallace Robert and Joan Pearl (Barter) MacG.; came to Can., 1948, naturalized, 1971; student York (Eng.) Meml. Coll., Central Tech. Art Sch., Toronto, Ont., Can.; m. Melanie Anne Furse, Apr. 15, 1971; 1 dau., Katherine Olivia. Mem. faculty Artist's Workshop, Toronto, 1967, 75, 77, Ont. Coll. Art, Toronto, 1970-72, 75, York U., Toronto, 1971-73, New Sch., Toronto, 1972-75, Hart House, U. Toronto, 1976-77; dir. New Sch. of Art, Toronto, 1977—; one-man shows: Isaacs Gallery, Toronto, 1968, 70, 72, 73, 74, 75, 77, Hart House, U. Toronto, 1967, Chatham (Ont.) Gallery, 1972, Gallery III, Montreal, Que., Can., 1973, Victoria Playhouse, Petrolia, Ont., 1974, Gallery Graphics, Ottawa, Ont., 1975; group shows include: Trajectory, Paris, 1973, Mus. Modern Art, Museum d'art Moderne, Yugoslavia, 1972, Can. Artists, 1968, Nat. Gallery Can., Art Gallery Ont., 1970, Montreal Mus. Fine Art, Oreg. State U., 1976, U. Western Ont., 1976, Trent U., 1976; represented in permanent collections: Nat. Gallery Can., Ottawa, Art Gallery Ont., Owens Art Gallery, N.B., Can., U. Western Ont., London, Winnipeg (Man., Can.) Art Gallery, Rothman's Art Gallery, Stratford, Ont., London (Ont.) Public Library and Mus., Can. Council Art Bank, Ottawa, Ministry External Affairs, Ottawa, U. Guelph (Ont.), Windsor Art Gallery, also numerous pvt. collections. Can. Council grantee, 1967, 71, sr. grantee, 1974, 76; Can. Council Arts Bursary grantee, 1968, 69, 70, 72. Mem. Ch. Eng. Office: care Isaacs Gallery 832 Younge St Toronto ON M4W 2H1 Canada. *My art has changed from realism to non-representational. So much is a conflict—between introspective, intuitive expression and a technical approach; between deeply personal starting points and the need to translate this into something that can be collectively understood; between spontaneity and deliberation. My goal is to be able to go into myself, but without the self-destruction that this route caused so many of North America's Abstract Expressionists. This is the ultimate paradox—to maintain a certain naiveté while increasing my self-awareness.*

MACGREGOR, KENNETH ROBERT, ins. co. exec.; b. Ottawa, Ont., Can., July 21, 1906; s. Robert and Margaret (Goundrey) M.; B.Sc. in Mech. Engring., Queens U., 1929; m. Charlotte Jessie Donnelly, June 29, 1935; children—Jayne Ennis, Kenneth Robert. Lectr., Queens U., 1929-30; joined Fed. Dept. Ins., Ottawa, 1930, served in actuarial and exam. brs., later in adminstrn. br., supt. ins. with rank of dep. minister, 1953-64; pres. Mut. Life Assurance Co. of Can., 1964-73, chmn., 1973—; dir. Can. Trust Co., Econ. Mut. Ins. Co., Miss & Rouville Ins. Co. Trustee Queens U. Served as maj. Gov. Gen.'s Foot Guards, 1923-45; mem. Canadian Bisley Rifle Team, 1926-28; comdt., 1957. Fellow Soc. Actuaries (former gov., v.p.); mem. Dominion of Can. Rifle Assn. (life gov.), Canadian Life Ins. Assn. (pres. 1968-69). Presbyterian. Clubs: Rideau; Royal Ottawa Golf; Westmount Golf and Country; National; York; Balboa. Home: 125 John Blvd Waterloo ON Canada Office: 227 King St S Waterloo ON Canada

MACGREGOR, WALLACE, cons. mineral economist; author; b. N.Y.C., Nov. 27, 1917; s. Alexander and Isabelle (Bradley) M.; M.B.A., Harvard, 1947; m. Mabel Evans, Sept. 11, 1939; children—Joan W. (Mrs. Frank Marino), Barbara, Margaret, Catherine (Mrs. Paul A. Nancarrow). With Am. Export Lines, 1935-42; cons. engr. Coverdale & Colpitts, N.Y.C., 1947-50; asst. treas., then treas. Climax Molybdenum Co., N.Y.C., 1950-57, pres., 1960-66; v.p. Consol. Toronto Devel. Corp., 1958-59, Homestake Mining Co., 1959-60; v.p. Am. Metal Climax, Inc., N.Y.C., 1960-66; sr. exec. v.p., 1966-67, also dir.; v.p. Kaiser Aluminum & Chem. Corp., Oakland, Calif., 1967-69, exec. v.p., 1969-72; dir. New Caledonian Nickel Co., 1969-72, Placer Exploration, Ltd., 1969-72, Natomas Co., 1974—, Homestake Mining Co., 1977—; cons. mine fin. and orgn., 1973—. Mem. fin. com. Ednl. Testing Service, Princeton, N.J., 1954-67; dir. Inst. Ednl. Devel., 1965-67. Served with USNR, 1942-45; lt. comdr. Res. Mem. Am. Inst. Mining, Metall. and Petroleum Engrs., Mining and Metall. Soc. Am., Soc. Western Artists. Presbyn. Clubs: Mining, Harvard (N.Y.C.); Bohemian (San Francisco). Address: PO Box 66 Tiburon CA 94920

MACHEMER, ROBERT, ophthalmologist; b. Muenster, Germany, Mar. 16, 1933; came to U.S., 1966, naturalized, 1972; s. Helmut and Erna M.; student univs. Muenster, Freiburg (Germany), Vienna, Austria, 1953-59, med. diploma, 1959; m. Christine Haller, July 28, 1961; 1 dau., Ruth. Intern in surgery Poliklinik Sued, Halle, Germany, 1959, Krankenhaus Rodalben (Germany), 1960, 61. intern in ob-gyn, Gertraudenkrankenhaus, Berlin, 1960, intern in internal medicine Diakonissenhaus, Freiburg, 1960-61; Fellow in gen. pathology Univ. Inst. of Pathology, Freiburg, Germany, 1961-62; resident in ophthalmology Augenklinik der Universitaet Goettingen (Germany), 1962-65; sci. asst. U. Goettingen, 1962-68; Deutscher Akademischer Austauschdienst research fellow Bascom Palmer Eye Inst., U. Miami (Fla.), 1966-67, Nat. Council to combat Blindness research fellow, 1967-68, instr. ophthalmology 1968-70, asst. prof. ophthalmology, 1970-74, asso. prof., 1974-78, prof., 1978; prof., chmn. dept. ophthalmology Duke U. Eye Center, 1978—; mem. staff VA Hosp., Miami, 1969-78, chief sect. ophthalmology, 1969-71; mem. staff VA Hosp., Durham, N.C., 1978—; mem. policy adv. group, diabetic retinopathy vitrectomy study NIH, 1978. Recipient Hermann Wacker award Club Jules Gonin, 1972, Golden Eagle award for movies CINE, 1973, 74, 75, Gold medal 12th Internat. Congress Ophthalmology, Paris, 1974, award for services Am. Acad. Ophthalmology and Otolaryngology, 1977, Trustees award Research to Prevent Blindness, 1978; Research to Prevent Blindness Louis B. Mayer scholar, 1971; diplomate Am. Bd. Ophthalmology. Mem. Pan Am. Soc. Ophthalmic Microsurgery, Pan. Am. Assn. Ophthalmology, Am. Ophthalmol. Soc., Retina Soc., N.C. Med. Soc., Club Jules Gonin, Assn. Research in Vision and Ophthalmology. Author: (with T. Aaberg) Vitrectomy, 1979; contbr. numerous articles to med. publs. Office: Duke U Eye Center PO Box 3802 Durham NC 27710

MACHLE, EDWARD JOHNSTONE, educator; b. Canton, China, Sept. 29, 1918 (parents Am. citizens); s. Edward Charles and Jean (Mawson) M.; student Pacific Lutheran Jr. Coll., 1937; B.A., Whitworth Coll., 1939; B.D., San Francisco Theol. Sem. 1942, M.A., 1944; Ph.D., Columbia U., 1952; m. Neva Hull, Aug. 29, 1942; children—Stewart, Douglas, Kathi; m. 2d, Mary Lou Reynolds, Dec. 15, 1970; stepchildren—Rebecca, Richard, Harvey, Robin. Ordained to ministry Presbyn. Ch., 1942; minister in Concrete, Wash., 1942-43; asst. minister, San Francisco, 1943-44, Mineola, N.Y., 1944-46; instr. Columbia, 1946-47; asst. prof. U. Colo., 1947-53, asso. prof., 1953-63, prof., 1963—, chmn. dept., 1951-52, 56-58, 66-69; vis. lectr. U. Alta., summer 1960, Iliff Sch. Theology, 1962; in-parish research dir. San Francisco Theol. Sem.; dir. music St. Andrew Presbyn. Ch., Boulder, Colo., 1961-70; guest lectr. ch. music U. Colo. Sch. Music, 1950-65. Mem. Am. Fedn. Tchrs., Am. Phil. Assn., Assn. for Asian Studies, Soc. Asian and comparative Philosophy, Mt.-Plains Philosophy Conf., Am. Acad. Religion. Presbyn. Home: 789 15th St Boulder CO 80302

MACHLIN, MILTON ROBERT, editor, writer; b. N.Y.C., June 26, 1924; s. Morris Lewis and Lillie (Manevetz) M.; A.B., Brown U., 1948; Degre Avance, Sorbonne (Paris, France), 1949; m. Barbara Scadron Sheckley, June 11, 1959; 1 foster son, Jason Sheckley. Reporter, columnist Clifton (N.J.) Morning Leader, 1950-52; editor Service Americain AFP, news wire service, 1952; editor Magazine House, 1953-55, Hillman Periodicals, 1955-57; mng. editor Argosy mag., 1960—, editor, 1969—, dir. film div.; creative dir. Pelican Prodns., 1974. Served with AUS, 1942-45. Recipient Mystery Writers spl. award, 1976, Porgie award, 1977. Mem. Mystery Writers Am., Internat. Motor Press Assn. Club: Explorers. Author: Ninth Life, 1961; Private Hell of Hemingway, 1962; MacArthur—A Fighting Man, 1965; The Search for Michael Rockefeller, 1972; The Family Man, 1974; French Connection II, 1975; The Setup, 1975; Pipeline, 1976; Atlanta, 1979; The Complete UFO Book, 1979. Home: 27 Washington Sq N New York NY 10011 also Brinton Hill Salisbury CT 06068

MACHLUP, FRITZ, economist; b. Wiener Neustadt, Austria, Dec. 15, 1902; s. Berthold and Cecile (Hayman) M.; Dr. rer pol., U. Vienna, 1923; LL.D., Lawrence U., 1956, Lehigh U., 1967, La Salle Coll., 1968; Dr. Sc. Pol. h.c., U. Kiel, 1965; L.H.D., Case Inst. Tech., 1967; Dr. oecon. h.c., U. St. Gallen, 1972; m. Mitzi Herzog, Mar. 3, 1925; children—Stefan, Hanna. Came to U.S. 1933, naturalized 1940. Partner, dir. Timmersdorfer Holzstoff und Pappenfabrik Emerich Kren and Co., Vienna, 1922-33; partner, mng. dir. Ybbstaler Pappenfabriken Adolf Leitner und Bruder, Vienna, 1924-33; dir. First Hungarian Card Board Mfg. Corp., Budapest, 1924-48; mem. council Austrian Cardboard Cartel, Vienna, 1929-31; lectr. Volkshochschule, Vienna, 1929-33; research fellow Rockefeller Found., 1933-35; vis. lectr. Harvard, 1935, summer 1936, 38-39; Frank H. Goodyear prof. econs. U. Buffalo, 1935-47; Abram G. Hutzler prof. polit. economy Johns Hopkins, 1947-60; Walker prof. econs. and internat. finance, dir. internat. finance sect. Princeton, 1960-71; prof. econs. N.Y. U., 1971—. Vis. prof. Cornell U., 1937-38, Northwestern U., summer 1938, U. Calif., summer 1939, Stanford, summers 1940, 47, U. Mich., summer 1941, Am. U., 1943-46, Columbia, summer 1948, U. Calif. at Los Angeles, summer 1949, Kyoto U., Doshisha U., Japan, 1955, Osaka U., 1970, U. Melbourne, 1970, U. Vienna, 1973; chief div. research and statistics Office of Alien Property Custodian, Washington, 1943-46; cons. U.S. Treasury Dept., 1965-77; pres. Internat. Econ. Assn., 1971-74, hon. pres., 1974—. Decorated comdr. Star of Africa (Liberia); Gt. Silver Medal of Honor with star (Austria). Fellow Am. Acad. Arts Scis., AAAS.; mem. Am. Philos. Soc., Am. (bd. editors 1938-41, acting mng. editor 1944-45, pres. 1966), So. (pres. 1959-60) econ. assns., Royal Econ. Soc., AAUP, (1st v.p. 1960-62, pres. 1962-64), Nat. Acad. Edn., Nationalökonomische Gesellschaft, Vienna (treas., sec. 1927-33), Accademia Nazionale dei Lincei (fgn.), Phi Beta Kappa (hon.). Author books, 1925—, including: The Stock Market, Credit and Capital Formation, 1940; International Trade and the National Income Multiplier, 1943; The Basing Point System, 1949; The Political Economy of Monopoly, 1952; The Economics of Sellers' Competition, 1952; An Economic Review of the Patent System, 1958; Production and Distribution of Knowledge in the U.S., 1962; Essays on Economic Semantics, 1963; International Payments, Debts, and Gold, 1964; Involuntary Foreign Lending, 1965; Remaking the International Monetary System, 1968; Education and Economic Growth, 1970; The Alignment of Foreign-Exchange Rates, 1972; International Monetary Systems, 1975; Selected Economic Writings of Fritz Machlup, 1976; A History of Thought on Economic Integration, 1977; Methodology of Economics and Other Social Sciences, 1978; Information through the Printed Word: Books, Journals, Libraries, 3 vols., 1979. Home: 279 Ridgeview Rd Princeton NJ 08540

MACHOL, ROBERT E., systems analyst; b. N.Y.C., Oct. 16, 1917; s. Morris R. and Claudia (Engel) M.; B.A., Harvard, 1938; Ph.D. in Chemistry, U. Mich., 1957; m. Florence Guttman, Sept. 8, 1946; children—Margot E., Kennard D. Research engr., lectr. U. Mich., 1951-58; from asso. prof. to prof. elec. engring. Purdue U., 1958-61; v.p. systems Conductron Corp., Ann Arbor, Mich., 1961-64; prof. systems engring., head dept. U. Ill. at Chgo., 1964-67; prof. systems Grad. Sch. Mgmt., Northwestern U., 1967—; vis. scientist NASA-Ames Research Center, 1974-75; liaison scientist U.S. Office Naval Research, London, 1979—; cons. to govt. and industry; dir. TAD Products Corp., Markite Corp. Mem. Washtenaw County Met. Planning Commn., 1961-64. Served to lt. comdr. USNR, World War II. Mem. Ops. Research Soc. Am. (pres. 1971-72), Inst. Mgmt. Scis. Author: (with Harry H. Goode) System Engineering, 1957 (transl. into French, Japanese, Russian); Elementary Systems Mathematics, 1976; others. Editor: Information and Decision Processes, 1960; System Engineering Handbook, 1965; (with S.P. Ladary) Management Sciences in Sports, 1976; Optimal Strategies in Sports, 1977. Editor-in-chief TIMS Studies in Mgmt. Scis., 1977—. Home: 2020 Orrington Ave Evanston IL 60201 Office: Northwestern U Evanston IL 60201

MACHT, CAROL MALISOFF, mus. curator; b. N.Y.C.; d. Samuel S. and Bertha (Jacobus) Malisoff; B.A., Goucher Coll., 1940; M.A., Johns Hopkins, 1942, Ph.D. (univ. scholar), 1945; m. Martin B. Macht, Dec. 5, 1939; 1 dau., Ann E. Librarian, Enoch Pratt Free Library, Baltimore, 1942-45; librarian Cin. Pub. Library, 1945-46; curator decorative arts Cin. Art Mus., 1958-63, sr. curator, 1973—. Tchr., Cin. Art Acad., 1958-72, Jr. League Docent Program, Cin. 1962-73; organizer, lectr. decorative art series Cin. Art Mus., 1961—; chmn. visual arts com., vis. com. Sch. for Creative and Performing Arts, Cin., 1979—; sponsor Am. Friends of Attingham Summer Sch., 1977—; lectr. Victoria and Albert Mus., 1969, others; organizer various exhbns. Nat. Endowment for Arts Attingham fellow, 1974. Mem. Am. Victorian Soc. (dir. Ohio River Valley chpt. 1977—. Author: Classical Sources of Wedgwood Design, 1957; also articles. Home: 3939 Erie Ave Cincinnati OH 45208 Office: Cin Art Museum Eden Park Cincinnati OH 45202. *It has been important to me to be a listener as well as a doer. It is not important to talk but to do.*

MACHT, JOHN JOSEPH, specialty chain store exec.; b. Syracuse, N.Y., Dec. 26, 1936; s. Milton and Sylvia Pearl (Smith) M.: B.A., U. Mich., 1958; m. Gail Leichtman, Oct. 27, 1961; children—Hilary Ann, Timothy Andrew. Successively mdsg. mgr. Abraham & Straus, Bklyn.; sr. v.p. mdsg. Macy's, N.Y.C.; now pres., chief operating officer Ups 'n Downs, Inc., N.Y.C., also dir., mem. exec. com. Office: 461 8th Ave New York NY 10001

MACHT, ROBERT, retail co. exec.; b. Syracuse, N.Y., Aug. 26, 1918; s. Aaron and Belle Macht; B.A., Syracuse U., 1939; m. Dorothy G. Brenner, Mar. 14, 1950; children—Stephen S., Ellen B. With Dey Bros. & Co., Syracuse, 1939-55, v.p., gen. mdse. mgr., 1955; with Jordan Marsh-Fla., 1955, pres., 1958—; group mgr. Allied Stores Corp., 1961-63, v.p., 1963-68, sr. v.p., 1968-70, exec. v.p., 1970; vice chmn. bd. First Nat. Bank Miami, 1970; chmn. bd., dir. Southeast Services, Inc., also exec. v.p. Southeast Banking Corp., Miami, 1970-76; chmn. bd., pres., chief exec. officer Susan Crane, Inc., Dallas, 1976—. Trustee U. Miami. Clubs: Miami, Standard, Bankers, Kings Bay Yacht and Country (Miami). Home: 905 Alfonso Ave Coral Gables FL 33146 Office: 1000 Brickell Ave Miami FL 33131 also 8107 Chancellor Rd Dallas TX 75247

MACILVAINE, CHALMERS ACHESON, coal mining co. exec.; b. Bklyn., Oct. 25, 1921; s. James Andrew and Helen Marie (Acheson) MacI.; A.B., Stanford, 1943; m. Elizabeth Jean Babcock, Mar. 26, 1943; children—Judith Anne, Joseph Chad, Martha Elizabeth. With Kaiser Steel Corp., 1946-73, asst. controller, 1953-62, treas., 1962-70, v.p., 1967-70, v.p. finance and planning, 1970-73, also v.p., dir. subsidiaries; v.p. project financing group Bank of Am., San Francisco, 1973-74, sr. v.p., dep. head Asia div., 1974-77; sr. v.p.-fin. Peabody Coal Co., St. Louis, 1978—; pres. Bamerical Internat. Fin. Corp., 1973-74. Served to lt. (j.g.) USNR, 1943-46. Mem. Phi Beta Kappa, Sigma Chi. Clubs: Berkeley Tennis; Tokyo Lawn Tennis; Frontenac Tennis, Noonday, Mo. Athletic, St. Louis Amateur Athletic Assn. (St. Louis). Home: 650 S Price Rd Saint Louis MO 63102 Office: 301 N Memorial Dr Saint Louis MO 63102

MACINNES, HELEN (MRS. GILBERT HIGHET), author; b. Glasgow, Scotland, Oct. 7, 1907; d. Donald and Jessica (McDiarmid) MacInnes; M.A., Glasgow U., 1928; student U. Coll., London, 1930-31; m. Gilbert Highet, Sept. 22, 1932; 1 son, Gilbert Keith MacInnes. Came to U.S., 1937, naturalized, 1951. Recipient Wallace award Am.-Scottish Found., 1973. Presbyn. Author: Above Suspicion, 1941; Assignment in Brittany, 1942; While Still We Live, 1944; Horizon, 1946; Friends and Lovers, 1947; Rest and Be Thankful, 1949; Neither Five Nor Three, 1951; I and My True Love, 1953; Pray For A Brave Heart, 1955; North from Rome, 1958; Decision at Delphi, 1960; Assignment: Suspense, 1961; The Venetian Affair, 1963; Home is the Hunter, 1964; The Double Image, 1966; The Salzburg Connection, 1968; Message from Malaga, 1971; The Snare of the Hunter, 1974; Agent in Place, 1976; Prelude to Terror, 1978. Home: 15 Jefferys Ln East Hampton NY 11937

MAC INTOSH, ALVIN MACGREGOR, printing co. exec.; b. Trenton, N.S., Can., July 22, 1918; s. Robert Abbott and Margaret Annie (MacGregor) MacI.; certified gen. accountant, 1950; registered mgmt. accountant, 1951; m. Grace Jessie Murray, June 8, 1945; children—Ronald, Lynn, Terry. Asst. accountant Pickford & Black Ltd., Halifax, N.S., 1939-41, accountant, 1945-51; with Lawson & Jones, Ltd., Toronto and London, Ont., 1951—, sec.-treas., 1973—, dir., 1978—, also sec.-treas., dir. subs. cos. Served with RCAF, 1941-45. Mem. London C. of C., Certified Gen. Accountants Assn., Soc. Mgmt. Accountants. Progressive Conservative. Mem. United Ch. Can. Home: 65 Westmorland Pl London ON N6J 1T9 Canada Office: 395 Wellington Rd S London ON N6C 4P9 Canada

MAC INTOSH, FRANK CAMPBELL, educator, physiologist; b. Baddeck, N.S., Can., Dec. 24, 1909; s. Charles C. and Beenie (Matheson) MacI.; B.A., Dalhousie U., 1930, M.A., 1932, LL.D., 1976; Ph.D., McGill U., 1937; LL.D., U. Alta., 1964, Queen's U., 1965; M.D. (hon.), U. Ottawa, 1974; m. Mary Mac Lachlan Mac Kay, Dec. 14, 1938; children—Christine (Mrs. Andrew G. Lejtenyi), Barbara (Mrs. Joachim N.M. Hardt), Andrew, Janet (Mrs. Horst Intscher), Roderick. Mem. research staff Med. Research Council Gt. Britain, 1938-49; prof. physiology McGill U., 1949-78, chmn. dept. physiology, 1949-64. Treas., Internat. Union Physiol. Scis., 1962-68; mem. Med. Research Council Can., 1961-63, Sci. Council Can., 1966-71. Fellow Royal Soc. (London), Royal Soc. Can., N.Y. Acad. Scis.; mem. Canadian (pres. 1960-61), Am. physiol. socs., Physiol. Soc. Gt. Britain, Internat. Soc. Neurochemistry, Sigma Xi. Editor: Canadian Jour. Physiol. Pharmacology, 1968-72. Contbr. papers to profl. lit. Home: 145 Wolseley Ave Montreal West PQ Canada

MACINTOSH, WILLIAM JAMES, lawyer; b. Glens Falls, N.Y., May 12, 1901; s. Gershom Banker and Mattie May (Hood) MacI.; B.S., U. Pa., 1922, J.D., 1926; m. Elise Robinson McIlvaine, May 11, 1974. Instr., U. Pa., Wharton Sch., 1923-24, U. Pa. Law Sch., 1927-29; admitted to Pa. bar, 1926, since practiced in Phila.; asso. Morgan, Lewis & Bockius, 1926-30, mem. firm, 1931-43, 44—. Dir., mem. exec. com. Phila. Suburban Water Co.; dir. emeritus Am. Water Works Co.; dir. Better Materials Corp., Norcross, Inc.; gen. counsel, renegotiation div., War Dept., U.S. Govt., 1943-44; gen. counsel, War Contracts Price Adjustment Bd., 1944. Counsel, Rep. State Com. Pa., 1967—, pres. Pa. Electoral Coll., 1973. Chmn. bd. trustees Grundy Found. Trustee Ware Found. Mem. Am. Bar Assn. (ho. of dels. 1946, chmn. adminstrv. law sect. 1948, chmn. pub. utility law sect. 1964-65), Nat. Assn. Water Cos. (dir.), Fed. Power Bar Assn. (pres., 1951), Fed. Bar Assn., Am. Judicature Soc., Phi Gamma Delta, Beta Gamma Sigma, Order of the Coif. Republican. Home: 641 Black Rock Rd Bryn Mawr PA 19010 Office: Fidelity Bldg Philadelphia PA 19109

MACINTYRE, A(LFONSO) EVERETTE, lawyer; b. nr. Burlington, N.C., Feb. 3, 1901; s. William Seymour and Ella Mary (Clark) MacI.; A.B., U. N.C., 1926; LL.B., George Washington U., 1929; m. Reita Jane Lyons, Aug. 20, 1929; 1 son, Miles Everette. Admitted to N.C. bar, 1929, D.C. bar, 1930, U.S. Supreme Ct. bar, 1933, Va. bar, 1938; practiced in Washington, 1929—; atty. examiner, rev., sr. and prin. atty., chief div. antitrust trials Bur. Litigation, FTC, Washington, 1930-54, adviser on anti-monopoly cases 1954-55, commr., 1961-73; staff dir. select com. on small bus. U.S. Ho. Reps., Washington, 1955-57, gen. counsel, 1957-61; counsel to firm McKean, MacIntyre & Wilson, Washington, 1973—. Mem. Am., Fed. bar assns., Am. Acad. Polit. and Social Scis., Acad. Polit. Scis. (life). Club: Nat. Lawyers. Home: 1564 Colonial Terr Arlington VA 22209 Office: Suite 710 1900 L St NW Washington DC 20036. *During my tenure in office, I considered it my duty and obligation to have as my policy, the policy of my government based on the policy of the law, and to serve that policy with unswerving loyalty to my country. It was my idea that the proper course to follow in my work would be to understand the problems presented to me by other officials and other citizens, and I felt that I could do that better by objectively seeking and appraising all relevant factual information concerning such problems.*

MACINTYRE, ALASDAIR CHALMERS, educator; b. Glasgow, Scotland, Jan. 12, 1929; s. Eneas John and Margaret Emily (Chalmers) MacI.; B.A., Queen Mary Coll., U. London, 1949; M.A., Manchester U., 1951, Oxford U., 1961. Came to U.S., 1969. Lectr. Manchester (Eng.) U., 1951-57, Leeds (Eng.) U., 1957-61; research fellow Nuffield Coll. Oxford (Eng.) U., 1961-62; sr. fellow Council Humanities, Princeton, 1962-63; fellow Univ. Coll., Oxford U., 1963-66; prof. sociology U. Essex (Eng.), 1966-69; prof. history of ideas Brandeis U., Waltham, Mass., 1969-72; dean Coll. Liberal Arts Boston U., 1972-73, prof. philosophy and polit. sci., 1972—; Riddell lectr. U. Newcastle on Tyne (Eng.), 1964; Bampton lectr. Columbia, 1966. Mem. Nat. Council Diplomas in Art and Design, Britain, 1968-70, Nat. Humanities Faculty, 1971—. Hon. mem. Phi Beta Kappa. Author: Marxism and Christianity, 1953; The Unconscious, 1957; A Short History of Ethics, 1966; Against the Self-Images of the Age, 1971. Home: 40 Charles River Rd Watertown MA 02172 Office: Dept Philosophy Boston Univ Boston MA 02215

MACIOCE, THOMAS MATTHEW, lawyer, merchandising exec.; b. N.Y.C., Jan. 2, 1919; s. Anthony and Angelina (Vodola) M.; B.A., Columbia, 1939, LL.B., 1942; student N.Y. U. Sch. Finance, 1946-49; m. Francesca Paula Spinelli, June 25, 1944; 1 dau., Francesca Lee. Admitted to N.Y. bar, 1946, U.S. Supreme ct. bar, 1966; asst. sec. Flintkote Mines, Ltd., 1948; v.p., dir. Bloomsburg Mills, Inc., 1952-57; pres., dir. L.F. Dommerich & Co., 1957-60; corp. v.p. Allied Stores Corp., N.Y.C., 1960-69, sr. v.p., 1969-70, pres., 1970—, chief exec. officer, 1972—, also dir.; dir. Hercules Inc., Mfrs. Hanover Trust Co., ABC, Penn Central Corp. Trustee Columbia; chmn. Tax Found. Served to lt. comdr. USNR, World War II. Recipient Theodore Roosevelt Assn. Meml. award; Brainard Meml. prize, 1939; Brotherhood award NCCJ, 1971; Silver Jubilee award Nat. Jewish Hosp. of Denver; Fund for Higher Edn. award, 1977; Israel Prime Minister's award, 1977; Legion of Order of Merit award, Italy. Mem. Young Presidents Orgn., Acad. Polit. Sci. (treas., v.p., dir.). Knight of Malta. Home: Quaker Ridge Dr Brookville NY 11545 Office: 1114 Ave of Americas New York NY 10036

MACIVER, JOHN KENNETH, lawyer; b. Milw., Mar. 22, 1931; s. Wallace and Elizabeth (MacRae) MacI.; B.S., U. Wis., 1953, LL.B., 1955; m. Margaret J. Vail, Sept. 4, 1954; children—Douglas B., Carolyn V., Kenneth D., Laura E. Admitted to Wis. bar, 1955; mem. law firm Michael, Best & Friedrich, Milw., 1955—, partner, 1961—. Chmn. bd. dirs. Nat. Council on Alcoholism, 1971-73, pres., 1974-77; sec. Interagy. Com. Fed. Activities for Alcoholism, 1976-79; chmn. exec. com. nat. review bd. East West Center, Honolulu, 1971-78, vice chmn., bd. dirs., 1975-78; co-chmn. fund drive United Performing Arts Fund of Greater Milw., 1975, pres., 1978-79, bd. dirs., 1974—; bd. dirs., exec. com. Milw. Symphony Orch., 1968—, pres. elect, 1978-79; vice chmn. Wis. Knowles for Gov. Com., 1964, 66, 68; Wis. del. Republican Nat. Conv., 1968, 72; mem. Wis. Rep. Finance Com., 1969-73; chmn. Wis. Nixon for Pres. Com., 1968, 72, Wis. Olson for Gov. Com., 1970, Wis. Bush for Pres. campaign, 1979—. Recipient Silver Key award Nat. Council on Alcoholism, 1975, also Bronze Key award Milw. Council on Alcoholism. Mem. State Bar of Wis. (vice chmn. antitrust com. 1963-64, chmn. labor law sect. 1961-63). Clubs: Town, Milwaukee (Milw.). Home: 959 E Circle Dr Milwaukee WI 53217 Office: 250 E Wisconsin Ave Milwaukee WI 53202

MACIVER, LOREN, artist; b. N.Y.C., Feb. 2, 1909; d. Charles Augustus Paul and Julia (MacIver) Newman; student Art Students League, 1919; m. Lloyd Frankenberg. One-man shows East River Gallery, N.Y.C., 1938, Pierre Matisse Gallery, N.Y.C., 1940-44, 49, 56, 61, 66, 70, Mus. Modern Art Traveling Exhbn., 1941, Vassar Art Gallery, 1950, Wellesley Coll., 1951, Whitney Mus., 1953, Dallas Mus. Fine Arts, 1953, Venice Biennale, 1967, Musee des Beaux Arts, Lyons, France, 1968, Musee de l'Art Moderne de la Ville de Paris, 1968, Musee des Ponchettes, Nice, France, 1968; works exhibited Mus. of Modern Art, exhbn. Federal Art, 1937, Fantastic Art, Dada, Surrealism, 1938, Art In Our Time, 1939, selections from Mus. of Modern Art collection, various years, Fourteen Americans, 1946, exhbn. of Am. Art, Jeu de Paume, Paris, 1938, St. Louis Mus., Whitney Mus., Bklyn. Mus., Corcoran Art Gallery, State Dept. exhbn. sent to Europe, 1946, Tolouse Mus. Fine Arts, 1967; represented in permanent collections Mus. Modern Art, Met. Mus., Detroit Inst., Los Angeles, San Francisco, Newark museums, Addison Gallery, Whitney Mus., Wadsworth Atheneum, Smith Coll. Mus., Phillips Collection, Washington, Joseph Hirshhorn Collection, Washington, Williams Coll., Elliott Collection, others. Recipient first prize Corcoran Art Gallery, 1957; Ford Found. grantee, 1960; 1st prize Art Inst. Chgo., 1961, purchase prize Kranner Art Mus. of U. Ill., 1963, award Mark Rothko Found., 1972; Guggenheim fellow, 1976. Mem. Nat. Inst. Arts and Letters. Home: 61 Perry St New York NY 10014 Office: Pierce Matisse Gallery 57 E 57th St New York NY 10022

MACK, CLIFFORD GLENN, fin. exec.; b. Pitts., Feb. 23, 1927; s. Jay Ord and Willa June (Shupe) M.; B.B.A., U. Pitts., 1952; M.B.A., Temple U., 1955; children—Jeffrey, Cynthia, Marcia. Asst. treas. Air Products & Chems., Inc., Allentown, Pa., 1957-69; dir. internat. fin., asst. treas. Harris Corp., Cleve., 1969-75; treas. A.B. Dick Co., Chgo., 1975—; pres. A.B. Dick Realty Corp.; dir. Keystone Bldg. Maintenance Corp., Phila. Served with AUS, 1945-48. Mem. Fin. Execs. Inst. Contbg. author: Credit Management Handbook, 1955. Home: 453 Raintree Dr Glen Ellyn IL 60137 Office: 5700 W Touhy Ave Chicago IL 60648

MACK, EDWARD GIBSON, business exec.; b. Toronto, Ont., Can., Dec. 4, 1917; s. Edward Gibson and Marion Margaret (Ward) M.; grad. Pickering Coll., 1938; student Syracuse U., 1938-40, U. Pa., 1945-46; m. Ruth Harriet Davies, Aug. 3, 1940 (dec.); children—Edward D., Carol Mack Shaw, Susan Mack Vassel; m. 2d, Isolde Maderson, Sept. 30, 1978. Investment analyst trust dept. Syracuse Trust Co. (N.Y.), 1939-43; accountant Hurdman & Cranstoun, C.P.A.'s, Syracuse, 1943-44; asst. cashier Bank of Am., Los Angeles, 1946-48; from dist. sales mgr. to dir. mktg. and prodn. research Easy Washing Machine Corp., Syracuse, 1948-55; dir. research Avco Corp., Connersville, Ind., 1955-58; exec. sec. planning and policy bd. Aeronca Mfg. Corp., Middletown, Ohio, 1958-60; pres., dir. E.D.I., State College, Pa., 1960-62, Sherman Indsl. Electronics Inc., Eutectics Inc.; exec. Richards Musical Instruments, Inc., Elkhart, Ind., 1962-65; mgr. supply and distbn. plastic products Union Carbide Ltd., Lindsay, Ont., 1965-68; corp. sec. Dominion Dairies Ltd., Toronto, 1968-73, v.p., sec., 1973—; sec., dir. Sealtest (Can.) Ltd. Served with U.S. Army, World War II. Mem. Am. Mktg. Assn., Inst. Chartered Secs. and Adminstrs. (affiliate), Sigma Chi. Republican. Clubs: Elks, Toastmasters, Am. Legion. Home: 1647 Bathurst St Suite 2 Toronto ON M5P 3J6 Canada Office: 235 Walmer Rd Toronto ON M5R 2Y1 Canada

MACK, EDWARD JOHN, business exec.; b. Mooresville, N.C., Feb. 10, 1916; s. Side and Tabatha (Ikall) M.; B.S., Davidson Coll., 1937; M.B.A., Harvard, 1939; m. Lorraine Loriaux, Sept. 2, 1946; children—John Edward, Janice, Robin, Eric Geoffrey. Pub. accountant A.M. Pullen & Co., 1939-41; C.P.A., 1941; mgmt. cons. Griffenhagen & Asso., 1946-48; head audit dept. Burlington Mills Corp., 1948-51; controller Dan River Mills, Inc., 1952-55; sr. asst. controller Burlington Industries, Inc., Greensboro, N.C., 1955, controller, 1962-68, v.p., controller, 1968-72, sr. v.p., controller, 1972-73, sr. v.p., 1973-75, exec. v.p., 1975—, also dir.; regional dir. Mfrs. Hanover Bank; pres. Fin. Execs. Research Found., 1971-73. Trustee St. Andrews Presbyn. Coll., 1971—, chmn. bd. trustees, 1975—, chmn. bus. affairs com., 1974—, chmn. pres. search com., 1974; exec. bd. Gen. Greene council Boy Scouts Am.; bd. visitors Duke Grad. Sch. Bus. Adminstrn., 1974—, Davidson Coll., 1974—. Served as col. Fin. Corps, USAF, 1941-46. Mem. Am. Inst. Accountants, Fin. Execs. Inst. (area v.p. 1970-71, vice chmn. bd. 1973-74, chmn. bd. 1974-75). Home: 2323 Princess Ann St Greensboro NC 27408 Office: PO Box 21207 Greensboro NC 27420

MACK, EUGENE KEVIN, container mfg. co. exec.; b. Chgo., June 10, 1922; s. Victor E. and Cassie (Gorman) M.; student Northwestern U., 1940-42; m. Mary E. Schweank, Apr. 28, 1945; children—Karen Ann, James Dennis, Maureen Elizabeth. With Armstrong Paint & Varnish Works, Inc., Chgo., 1940—, v.p., 1960-65, pres., 1965—, also dir.; pres. J & S Steel Corp., Franklin Park, Ill., 1969—; chmn. bd. Armstrong Chemcon, Inc., until 1973; founder Container Sales Corp., 1974, pres., dir., 1974—; dir. Pacific Holding Corp., Los Angeles. Served as aviator USNR, 1942-45. Mem. Nat. Paint, Varnish and Lacquer Assn. (dir.). Clubs: La Grange Country, Chicago Athletic Assn. Home: 15 Stafford Ln Oak Brook IL 60521 Office: 1127 S Mannheim Rd Westchester IL 60153

MACK, IRVING, physician; b. Vilna, Poland, Apr. 15, 1919; s. Meilach and Rebecca (Zelcer) M.; came to U.S., 1921, naturalized, 1927; B.S., U. Chgo., 1939, M.D., 1942; m. Jean Charlotte Tarrant, Nov. 8, 1959 (dec. Nov. 1969); children—Melissa, Susan. Intern, Cook County Hosp., Chgo., 1942-43; sr. resident medicine Michael Reese Hosp., Chgo., 1944-45, sr. fellow dept. cardiovascular research, 1945-46, research asso. Cardiovascular Inst., 1946-59, chief Thursday chest clinic of hosp., 1952-73, sr. attending physician, 1973—; practice medicine, specializing in internal medicine, Chgo., 1946—; clin. asso. prof. medicine Chgo. Med. Sch., 1949-73; clin. prof. medicine Pritzker Sch. Medicine, U. Chgo., 1973—; cons. in field. Exec. com. Michael Reese Hosp., 1962-66, trustee hosp. and med. center. Recipient Freermedal, U. Chgo. Coll. Medicine, 1942. Diplomate Am. Bd. Internal Medicine with Subsplty. in pulmonary disease, Nat. Bd. Med. Examiners. Fellow A.C.P., Am. Coll. Chest Physicians (chmn. sect. electrocardiography 1953-59), Am. Coll. Cardiology; mem. Am. Fedn. Clin. Research, Am. Thoracic Soc., Am. Heart Assn., Am. Psychosomatic Soc., Am. Soc. Internal Medicine, Am. Assn. History Medicine, AMA, Phi Beta Kappa, Sigma Xi, Alpha Omega Alpha, other orgns. Contbr. articles med. jours. cardiac arrythmias, rheumatic heart disease, electrocardiography, pulmonary physiology, emphysema, Tb, related fields. Editorial bd. Cardiology, 1958-67. Home: 5490 S Shore Dr Chicago IL 60615 Office: 104 S Michigan Ave Chicago IL 60603

MACK, JEROME DAVID, banker; b. Albion, Mich., Nov. 6, 1920; s. Nate and Jennie (Solomon) M.; B.S., U. Calif. at Los Angeles, 1943; m. Joyce Rosenberg, Mar. 30, 1947; children—Barbara, Karen, Marilynn. Various positions as accountant, Calif., gen. contractor, Nev., prior to 1952; pres. 1st Bancorp., Riviera Hotel; v.p., treas. Continental Connector Corp.,; vice-chmn. bd. Valley Bank of Nev. (formerly Bank of Las Vegas), 1965—; dir. Pioneer Title Ins. Co., 4 Queens Hotel (all Las Vegas, Nev.). Mem. Nat. Conf. Christians and Jews, Nev. chmn., 1965, now mem. nat. bd. dirs.; adv. council S.W. Regional Lab. for Ednl. Research and Devel.; chmn. Nev. United Jewish Appeal, 1962-65; chmn. bd. Combined Las Vegas Jewish Appeal; chmn. Nev. Joint Def. Appeal, 1962-64; mem. nat council Am. Jewish Com.; mem. nat. campaign cabinet Israel Bonds and United Jewish Appeal; mem. panel U.S. Circuit Judge Nominating Commn. for 9th Dist. State finance chmn. Johnson-Humphrey Democratic Com., 1964; state coordinator, treas. U.S. Senator Howard W. Cannon; mem. nat. finance com. to elect Senator Henry M. Jackson Pres., 1972; chmn. Nev. Tax Commn. Trustee U. Nev. at Las Vegas Found., U. Calif. at Los Angeles; bd. overseers U. Judaism. Served with USAAF, 1942-45. Mem. Las Vegas C. of C. (dir.), Zeta Beta Tau. Jewish (pres. temple 1964-66). Office: Valley Bank of Nevada PO Box 15427 Las Vegas NV 89114

MACK, JOHN EDWARD, psychiatrist; b. N.Y.C., Oct. 4, 1929; s. Edward Clarence and Ruth (Prince) M.; B.A., Oberlin (Ohio) Coll., 1951; M.D., Harvard U., 1955; m. Sally Ann Stahl, July 12, 1959; children—Daniel, Kenneth, David Anthony. Intern, Mass. Gen. Hosp., Boston, 1955-56; resident in psychiatry Mass. Mental Health Center, Boston, 1956-59, chief resident day and night hosps., 1957-59; teaching fellow, then research fellow Harvard U. Med. Sch., 1956-59; cons. Mass. Div. Legal Medicine, 1958, VA day hosps., 1959; practice medicine specializing in psychiatry, Cambridge, Brookline, Mass., 1961; candidate in tng. Boston Psychoanalytic Soc. and Inst., 1961-67; sr. physician Mass. Mental Health Center, 1961, fellow child psychiatry, children's unit, 1961-63, staff psychiatrist, 1963—, staff visitor Service I, 1963-65, prin. psychiatrist, 1965, asso. dir. psychiatry, 1965-67, dir. research children's unit, 1967-70, coordinator Harvard U. Med. Sch. teaching children's unit, 1968-70; mem. staff div. legal medicine Roxbury (Mass.) Ct. Clinic, 1962-63; asst. in psychiatry Harvard U. Med. Sch., 1963-64, mem. faculty, 1964—, prof. psychiatry, 1972—, head dept., 1973-77; jr. vis. physician Cambridge (Mass.) City Hosp., 1967, sr. vis. physician, 1968-69, chief dept. psychiatry, 1969-76; cons. Univ. Health Services, Harvard U., 1972-75, also lectr. psychology and social relations; dir. edn. Cambridge-Somerville Mental Health and Retardation Center, 1975—; mem. faculty Boston Psychoanalytic Soc. and Inst., 1969—, mem. edn. com., 1975—. Served to capt. USAF, 1959-61. Recipient Felix and Helene Deutsch Sci. prize Boston Psychoanalytic Soc. and Inst., 1964; Harry S. Solomon award Mass. Mental Health Center, 1967; Pulitzer prize in biography for A Prince of Our Disorder: The Life of T.E. Lawrence, 1976. Diplomate Am. Bd. Psychiatry; cert. psychoanalysis and child psychoanalysis. Fellow Am. Psychiat. Assn.; mem. Mass., Norfolk County med. socs., Am. Group Psychotherapy Assn., New Eng. Council Child Psychiatry, Assn. Psychophysiol. Study Sleep, Group Advancement Psychiatry, Am. Psychoanalytic Assn., Am. Acad. Child Psychiatry, Boylston Soc., Alpha Omega Alpha. Author: Nightmares and Human Conflict, 1970; editor Borderline States in Psychiatry, 1975; contbr. to med. jours.

MACK, JOHN O., lawyer; b. Columbus, Ohio, May 10, 1932; s. Eugene Henry and Eunice (Genthner) M.; B.S. in Econs., U. Pa., 1954, LL.B. cum laude, 1961; m. Cristina Ann Iannone, 1967; children—John Whitney, Elizabeth Ann, Andrew Laughlin. Admitted to Calif. bar, 1962; asso. firm Pillsbury, Madison & Sutro, San Francisco 1961-63; asst. v.p., sec. Bank of Calif. N.A., San Francisco, 1963-75, v.p., sec., 1972-75; v.p., sec. BanCal Tri State Corp., 1972-75; practice law, San Francisco, 1976—; sr. mng. partner firm Cooke & Mack, San Francisco, 1978—; partner Red Hills Investment Co., 1979—. Bd. dirs., pres. Lone Mountain Children's Center, 1978—. Served to lt. USNR, 1954-58. Home: 2963 23d Ave San Francisco CA 94132 Office: 221 Pine St Suite 500 San Francisco CA 94104

MACK, JULIA COOPER, judge; b. Fayetteville, N.C., July 17, 1920; d. Dallas L. and Emily (McKay) Perry; B.S., Hampton Inst., 1940; LL.B., Howard U., 1951; m. Jerry S. Cooper, July 30, 1943; 1 dau., Cheryl; m. 2d, Clifford S. Mack, Nov. 21, 1957. Admitted to D.C. bar, 1952; legal cons. OPS, Washington, 1952-53; atty.-advisor office gen. counsel Gen. Services Adminstrn., 1953-54; trial appellate atty. criminal div. Dept. Justice, 1954-68; civil rights atty. Office Gen.

Counsel, Equal Employment Opportunity Commn., Washington, 1968-75, judge Ct. Appeals, Washington, 1975—. Mem. Am., Fed., Washington, Nat. bar assns. Home: 1610 Varnum St NW Washington DC 20011 Office: 500 Indiana Ave NW Washington DC 20001

MACK, RAYMOND FRANCIS, newspaper exec.; b. Aitkin, Minn., Sept. 5, 1912; s. Raymond Frederick and Bertha (Tuller) M.; student pub. schs., Va., Minn.; m. Betty Habes, Oct. 17, 1941; children—Patricia, Douglas. Country circulation mgr. Duluth (Minn.) Herald News Tribune, 1930-40, St. Paul Dispatch Pioneer Press, 1940-42; circulation mgr. Washington Daily News, 1942-58; advt. dir., 1958-59, bus. mgr., 1959-72, pres., 1968-72; asst. gen. bus. mgr. Scripps-Howard Newspapers, 1972—; spl. adviser to pres. Washington Star-News, 1972-75. Exec. bd. Nat. Capitol council Boy Scouts Am.; past bd. dirs. Nat. Capital Com., YMCA Davis Meml. Goodwill Industries; bd. dirs. Washington area chpt. Nat. Multiple Sclerosis Soc. Mem. Inter-State Circulation Mgrs. Assn. (past pres.), Internat. Circulation Mgrs. Assn. (past dir.), Washington Bd. Trade, Washington Conv. and Visitor's Bur. Clubs: Washington Advertising, Nat. Press, Columbia Country, Kiwanis (Washington). Home: 3706 Leland St Chevy Chase MD 20015 Office: 777 14th St NW Washington DC 20005

MACK, RAYMOND WRIGHT, ednl. adminstr.; b. Ashtabula, Ohio, July 15, 1927; s. Wright R. and Hazel E. (Card) M.; A.B. with honors, Baldwin-Wallace Coll., 1949; M.A., U. N.C., 1951, Ph.D., 1953; m. Barbara Leonard, Mar. 1948 (div. 1953); 1 son, Donald Gene; m. 2d, Elizabeth Ann Hunter, Oct. 16, 1953; children—Meredith Lou, Julia Glen, Margaret Kingsley. Asst. prof. sociology and anthropology U. Miss., 1953; faculty Northwestern U., 1953—, asso. prof. sociology, 1957-62, prof. sociology, 1962—, chmn. dept., 1959-67, dir. Center for Urban Affairs, 1968-71, v.p., dean of faculties, 1971-74, provost, 1974—; dir. program for Bell System execs., 1958-59. Fellow Am. Sociol. Assn. (mem. council 1966-69); mem. Soc. Study Social Problems (pres. 1969-70), Midwest Sociol. Soc. (pres. 1967), Alpha Kappa Delta (pres. 1967-68). Author: (with Freeman and Yellin) Social Mobility, 1957; (with Kimball Young) Sociology and Social Life, 1959; Transforming America, 1967; Editor: (with Kimball Young) Principles of Sociology; A Reader in Theory and Research, 1960; Race, Class and Power, 1963; Our Children's Burden, 1967. The American Sociologist, 1968-70; The Changing South, 1970; Prejudice and Race Relations, 1970. Home: 2233 Orrington Ave Evanston IL 60201

MACK, ROBERT EMMET, hosp. adminstr.; b. Morris, Ill., 1924; M.D., St. Louis U., 1948. Intern, St. Marys Hosp. Group, 1948-49, asst. physician; asst. resident, then resident internal medicine St. Louis U., 1949-52; asst. chief radioisope clinic Walter Reed Army Med. Center, 1954-56; chief med. service, chief radioisopte service St. Louis VA Hosp., 1956-61; vis. physician St. Louis City Hosp., 1957-61; chmn. dept. medicine Womans Hosp., Detroit, 1961-66; dir. Hutzel Hosp., Detroit, 1966-71, pres., 1971—; asst. prof. medicine St. Louis U., 1957-61; asso. prof. medicine Wayne State U., 1961-66, prof., 1966—, dir. admissions, 1978—. Diplomate Am. Bd. Internal Medicine. Fellow A.C.P., Am. Coll. Hosp. Adminstrs. Soc. Med. Adminstrs. Mem. AMA, Am. Fedn. Clin. Research, Central Soc. Clin. Research, Am. Endocrine Soc., Am. Physiol. Soc. Home: 3020 Westview Ct Bloomfield Hills MI 48013 Office: 4707 St Antoine Blvd Detroit MI 48201

MACK, RUTH P., economist; b. N.Y.C.; d. Julius and Clara (Rich) Prince; A.B., Barnard Coll.; M.A., Ph.D., Columbia, 1937; m. Edward C. Mack, 1932; children—Mary-Lee Ingbar, John E. Tchr., Hunter Coll., Coll. City N.Y., Columbia; adj. prof. Bernard Baruch Sch. Bus. Adminstrn., Coll. City N.Y.; mem. research staff Nat. Bur. Econ. Research, 1941-67; sr. mgmt. cons. econs. and fiscal problems, N.Y.C., 1958-60; dir. econ. studies Inst. Pub. Adminstrn., 1960—. Vis. prof. Yale, 1963-64, City Coll., City U. N.Y., 1965-67. Mem. adv. com. on consumer expenditure surveys Bur. Labor Statics, U.S. Dept. Labor, 1960-65. Mem. Am. Econ. Assn. (exec. com. 1955-57), Acad. Polit. Sci., Econometric Soc. Author: Controlling Retailers, a study of cooperation and control in the retail trade with spl. reference to N.R.A.; Flow of Business Funds and Consumer Purchasing Power; Taxing to Prevent Inflation (with Carl Shoup and Milton Friedman); Economics of Consumption in Survey of Contemporary Economics, vol. II; Consumption and Business Fluctuations: A Case Study of the Shoe, Leather, Hide Sequence; Information Expectations and Inventory Fluctuation, a study of materials, stock on hand and on order, 1967; (with Sumner Meyers) Outdoor Recreation in Measuring Benefits of Government Investments, 1965; (with Donald Shoup) Advance Land Acquisition by Local Governments, Benefit-Cost Analysis as an Aid to Policy, 1968; Planning on Uncertainty, Decision Making in Business and Government Administration, 1971; contbr. reports to govt. studies, chpts. to books and articles to profl. jours. Home: Wildcliff Rd New Rochelle NY 10805 Office: 55 W 44th St New York City NY 10036

MACK, THOMAS LEE, profl. football player, business exec.; b. Cleve., Nov. 1, 1943; s. Raymond James and Jean Roberta (Fischer) M.; B.S. in Mech. Engring., U. Mich., 1968; m. Anne Margaret Tollefson, July 2, 1966; children—Kristan Elizabeth, Kathryn Anne, Carolyn Ellen. Profl. football player Los Angeles Rams, 1966—; played in Pro-Bowl All Star Games, 1968, 76-79, All-NFL, 1967-68; engr., salesman Bechtel Power Corp., Norwalk, Calif., 1970—, now sr. bus. devel. rep. Los Angeles Power Div. Elder, San Marino Community Ch.-Presbyn.; bd. dirs. San Gabriel Community Ch.; chmn. Pro Nuclear Campaign, S. Orange County, 1976; bd. dirs. Boy Scouts Am. Served with Army N.G., 1966-72. Recipient cert. of esteem Dept. Def. Mem. Pacific Coast Elec. Assn., Los Angeles Electric Club, Ariz. Electric League. Republican. Clubs: San Gabriel Country; San Marino City. Office: 12400 E Imperial Hwy Norwalk CA 90650*

MACK, WALTER STAUNTON, corp. exec.; b. N.Y.C., Oct. 19, 1895; s. Walter Staunton and Alice (Ranger) M.; A.B., Harvard, 1917; m. 2d, Ruth J. Watkins, 1942; children—Walter III, Alice Ruth; children by previous marriage—Anthony Reckford, Florence Ann. Salesman, Bedford Mills, Inc., 1919; became pres., 1926; later v.p. Wm. B. Nichols & Co.; then v.p. Equity Corp., chmn. bd., dir. United Cigar-Whelan Stores Corp.; v.p. Phoenix Securities Corp., 1934, pres. 1938-51; chmn. bd., pres. Pepsi-Cola Co., 1951-56; became pres., chmn. bd. Nedicks, Inc., 1951; pres. C & C Super Corp., parent co. B/G Foods, Inc., Cantrell & Cochrane Corp., mfr. several soft drinks, including Super Cola; former chmn. bd., chief exec. officer Gt. Am. Industries, Inc.; pres., chmn. Rubatex Corp.; pres. Gt. Am. Minerals Corp.; chmn. Aminex Resources Corp., 1970—; chmn. Aminex Petroleum Ltd.; chmn. bd. King Cola Corp.; v.p., treas., dir. Polls Creek Coal Co., Leslie County, Ky., 1977—, Indian Head Mining Co., River Coal Co., Knott County, Ky., 1977—; dir. N.Y. Bd. Trade. Republican candidate N.Y. State Senate, 1932, treas. Rep. co. com. N.Y. State Senate, 1932; treas. Rep. co. com. N.Y.C., 1934-36; treas. Fusion Co. Com. for election Mayor La Guardia, 1937; chmn. Nat. Com. Reps. and Inds. for Johnson, 1964. Mem. Mayor's Adv. and Def. Coms.; vice chmn. Greater N.Y. Fund, 1941; dir. Queens C. of C., N.Y. World's Fair Com.; Manhattan counsel, mem. State Commn. Human Rights; dir. City Center Music and Drama; hon. chmn. Queens County Cancer Com., 1946, Queens Greater N.Y. Fund Com., 1946; chmn. Dewey-Warren Citizens Com., 1948. Trustee French and Polyclinic Hosp. Served as ensign USN, 1917-19. Mem. Litchfield Hunter Breeders Soc. (treas.). Jewish (trustee, treas. temple). Clubs: Jefferson Island, Harvard (N.Y.C.); Harvard (Boston); Sky; Ocean Country; Ariz. Country. Home: 530 E 72d St New York NY 10021 Office: 445 Park Ave New York NY 10022. *It is most important that a man in business should consider at all times his responsibility to the well-being of his employees and the general public. He should keep in close touch with them by personally entering into public affairs and community activities.*

MACK, WILLIAM PADEN, naval officer; b. Hillsboro, Ill., Aug. 6, 1915; s. Albert Roscoe and Mary Jo (Paden) M.; B.S., U.S. Naval Acad., 1937; grad. Nat. War Coll., 1956; M.A., George Washington U., 1964; m. Ruth George McMillin, Nov. 11, 1939; children—William Paden, Margaret Ellen. Commd. ensign U.S. Navy, 1937, advanced through grades to vice adm., 1970; comdr. U.S.S. Woodworth, 1944, U.S.S. R.B. Anderson, 1949, Destroyer Div. 22, 1956, Destroyer Squadron 28, 1960; became chief info. Navy Dept., 1963, then comdr. U.S. 7th Fleet, until 1972; supt. U.S. Naval Acad., 1972-75; pres. Carl Vinson Corp. Vice chmn. bd. Northlake (Ill.) Community Hosp.; pres. Navy Marine Corps Coast Guard Found.; bd. dirs. Human Resources Research Orgn.; trustee Naval Acad. Found.; mem. bd. control U.S. Naval Inst. Clubs: Nat. Press (Washington); Army Navy Country (bd. govs.) (Arlington, Va.); N.Y. Yacht. Author: Naval Officers Guide, 1958; also articles. Home: 3067 Rundelac Rd Annapolis MD 21403

MACKAL, ROY PAUL, educator, biochemist; b. Milw., Aug. 1, 1925; s. Roy Frank and Lilly (Fisher) M.; B.S., U. Chgo., 1949, Ph.D., 1953; m. Lillian Louise Olson, Mar. 13, 1969; 1 son by previous marriage, Paul Karl. Research Naval Research Lab., Bellevue, Washington, 1944-45; faculty U. Chgo., 1953—, asso. prof. biochemistry, 1964—, research asso. biology Office of Pres., 1974—; U.S. dir. Loch Ness Investigation Bur. Served with USNR, 1943-44, USMCR, 1944-46. Mem. Am. Soc. Biol. Chemists, Am. Soc. Phys. Anthropology, Soc. for Protection of Old Fishes, Sigma Xi, Phi Eta Sigma. Clubs: Adventurer's (Chgo.); Savages (London). Home: 9027 S Oakley Ave Chicago IL 60620. *Never allow fear of what others might think keep you from doing what you believe is right. Consider the advice of others, but rely on your own judgement.*

MACKALL, LAIDLER BOWIE, lawyer; b. Washington, Aug. 8, 1916; s. Laidler and Evelyn (Bowie) M.; A.B., Princeton U., 1938; postgrad. Georgetown U., 1938-40, J.D., 1946; m. Nancy M. Taylor, Aug. 28, 1942; children—Nancy Mackall Lurton, Christie Mackall Connard, Susan Mackall Smythe, Bruce Mackall Sloan; m. 2d, Prudence Robertson, July 26, 1978. Admitted to D.C. bar, 1947, ICC bar, 1951, U.S. Supreme Ct. bar, 1958; law clk. to chief judge of predecessor to D.C. Ct. Appeals, 1946-47; asso. firm Minor, Gatley & Drury, Washington, 1947-49; asso. firm Steptoe & Johnson, Washington, 1949-51, partner, 1952—; mem. D.C. Ct. Appeals Com. on Admissions, 1974-78; bd. mgrs. Nat. Conf. Bar Examiners, 1974-77. Served with USAAF, 1940-46, 51. Decorated Silver Star, D.F.C. with oak leaf cluster, Air medal with 5 oak leaf clusters. Fellow Am. Coll. Trial Lawyers; mem. Am. Bar Assn. (past vice chmn. standing com. aviation ins. law); D.C. Bar, Bar Assn. D.C. (past chmn. com. on negligence, motor vehicle and compensation law), Am. Law Inst., Nat. Assn. R.R. Trial Counsel, Barristers Club (v.p. 1964). Episcopalian. Clubs: Chevy Chase (Md.) Country; Princess Anne (Va.) County; Mid Ocean (Bermuda). Home: 6400 Brookville Rd Chevy Chase MD 20015 Office: 1250 Connecticut Ave NW Washington DC 20036

MACKASEY, BRYCE STUART, airline exec.; b. Quebec, Can., Aug. 25, 1921; s. Frank and Ann (Glover) M.; student McGill U., Loyola Coll.; LL.D., Sir George Williams U., 1970; m. Margaret O'Malley, Feb. 13, 1942; children—Brenda (Mrs. Len Savage), Bryan, Michael, Susan. Mem. Can. Ho. of Commons, 1962-76; minister of labour of the Crown, 1968-72; minister of manpower and immigration, 1972; minister without portfolio, 1972-74; postmaster gen., 1974-76; mem. Que. Nat. Assembly, from 1976; pres. Air Canada, 1978—. Office: Air Canada Place Ville Marie Montreal PQ H3B 3P7 Canada*

MACKAVEY, WILLIAM RAYMOND, psychologist; b. Detroit, Oct. 23, 1932; s. John and Pearl (Oprish) M.; B.A., Wayne State U., Detroit, 1954; M.A., Mich. State U., E. Lansing, 1956, Ph.D., 1959. NIMH postdoctoral fellow vision lab. Mich. State U., 1959-61; mem. faculty Boston U., 1961—, prof. exptl. psychology, 1970—, chmn. dept., 1979—. Mem. Am. Psychol. Assn., Eastern Psychol. Assn. Office: 64 Cummington St Boston MA 02215

MACKAY, JOHN ALEXANDER, clergyman, educator; b. Inverness, Scotland, May 17, 1889; s. Duncan and Isabelle (Macdonald) M.; came to U.S., 1932, naturalized, 1941; M.A. with 1st class honors in philosophy, U. Aberdeen (Scotland), 1912; B.D., Princeton Theol. Sem., 1915; postgrad. U. Madrid, 1915-16; D.Litt., U. Lima, Peru, 1918; U. Bonn, Germany, 1930; D.D., Princeton; LL.D., Ohio Wesleyan U., 1937, Albright Coll., 1938, Coll. of Wooster, 1952; D.D., Aberdeen U., 1939, Debrecen U., Hungary, 1939, Presbyn. Coll., Montreal, 1942, Serampore Coll., India, 1953; L.H.D., Boston U., 1939, Lafayette Coll., 1939; hon. fellow Stanford, 1941; m. Jane Logan Wells, Aug. 16, 1916; children—Isobel Elizabeth (Mrs. Bruce M. Metzger), Duncan Alexander Duff, Elena Florence (Mrs. Sherwood H. Reisner), Ruth (Mrs. Robert M. Russell). Prin., Anglo-Peruvian Coll., Lima, 1916-25; prof. philosophy Nat. U. Peru, 1925; lectr., writer under S.Am. Fedn. YMCA's, 1926-32; named lectr. numerous colls., sems., univs., 1932—; sec. Presbyn. Bd. Fgn. Missions, 1932-36; pres. Princeton Theol. Sem., prof. ecumenics, 1936-59, pres. emeritus; adj. prof. Hispanic thought Am. U., Washington, 1961-64; Joseph Cooke lectr. in Asia, 1961. Mem. adv. council, dept. philosophy Princeton, 1941-62. Pres. Am. Assn. Theol. Schs., 1948-50; mem. central com. World Council Chs., 1948-54; chmn. Internat. Missionary Council, 1947-59, hon. chmn., 1959-61; chmn. joint com. Internat. Missionary Council and World Council Chs., 1948-54, pres. Presbyn. Bd. Fgn. Missions, 1945-51; chmn. Commn. of Universal Ch. and World of Nations, Oxford Conf. on Ch., Community and State, 1937; moderator Gen. Assembly Presbyn. Ch. in U.S.A., 1953-54. Decorated comdr. Palmas Magisteriales (Peru); recipient Upper Room citation, 1954. Author numerous books in Spanish, English, 1927—, including Mas Yo OS Digo, 1927; El Sentido de la vida, 1931; The Other Spanish Christ, 1932; A Preface to Christian Theology, 1942; Christianity on the Frontier, 1950; Gods Order: The Ephesian Letter and this Present Time, 1953; The Presbyterian Way of Life, 1960; His Life and Our Life, 1964; Ecumenics: The Science of the Church Universal, 1964; Christian Reality and Appearance, 1969; Realidad e Idolatria, 1970. Editor: Theology Today, 1944-51, chmn. editorial council, 1951-59. Clubs: Cosmos (Washington); Nassau (Princeton). Home: Meadow Lakes Apt 39-09 Hightstown NJ 08520

MACKAY, JOHN ROSS, geographer; b. Tamsui, Taiwan, Dec. 31, 1915; s. George William and Jean (Ross) M.; B.A., Clark U., 1939; M.A., Boston U., 1941; Ph.D., U. Montreal (Que., Can.), 1949; Docteur de l'université (hon.), Ottawa U., 1972; m. Violet Anne Meekins, Feb. 19, 1944; children—Margaret Anne, Leslie Isabel. Asst. prof. geography McGill U., Montreal, 1946-49; prof. U. B.C. (Can.), Vancouver, 1949—; Disting. vis. prof. U. Wash., fall 1977. Served with Can. Army, 1941-46. Recipient Massey medal Royal Can. Geog. Soc., 1967; Centennial medal Govt. Can., 1967; Queen's Silver Jubilee medal, 1977. Mem. Can. Assn. Geographers (pres. 1953-54), Assn. Am. Geographers (pres. 1969), Royal Soc. Can. (Miller medal 1975), Arctic Inst. N. Am. (chmn. bd. govs. 1962-64), Geol. Soc. Am. Presbyterian. Research, numerous publs. on permafrost, ground ice, ice wedges and pingos, Can. Arctic. Office: Dept Geography U BC Vancouver BC V6T 1W5 Canada

MAC KAY, PIERRE ANTONY, educator; b. Toronto, 1933; came to U.S., 1948, naturalized, 1955; s. Louis Alexander and Constance Charlotte (Charlesworth) MacK.; B.A., Yale U., 1954; M.A., U. Calif., Berkeley, 1959, Ph.D., 1964; m. Theodora Stillwell, Dec. 30, 1963; children—Camilla Martha, Alexandra Constance. Instr. classics U. Oreg., 1957-58; lectr. Greek, Bryn Mawr Coll., 1963-64; mem. faculty dept. classics, dept. near Eastern langs. U. Wash., Seattle, 1966—, prof., 1976—; vis. mem. Inst. Advanced Study, 1973-74. Served with U.S. Army, 1954-56. Nat. Endowment Humanities grantee, 1971-72, 78-80; NSF grantee, 1975-76. Mem. Am. Sch. Classical Studies, Am. Research Center in Egypt, Brit. Inst. Archaeology, Mediaeval Acad. Am. Home: 5643 20th Ave NE Seattle WA 98105 Office: Dept Classics Univ of Wash Seattle WA 98195

MACKAY, WILLIAM BRYDON FRASER, educator; b. Winnipeg, Man., Can., May 21, 1914; s. Daniel Sayre and Catherine Agnes (Brydon) M.; B.Sc. in Elec. Engring., U. Man., 1938; B.Metall. Engring., U. Minn., 1940, M.S., 1947, Ph.D., 1953; m. Kathleen Hephzibah Griffiths, Nov. 22, 1941; children—Daniel Sutherland Campbell, William Alexander Fraser, John Campbell Fraser. Instr., then asst. prof. metallurgy U. Minn., 1946-56; chief metall. engr. Atlas Steels Ltd., 1956-60, mgr. research and devel., 1961-62; dir. research and tech. Atlas Titanium Ltd., 1962-63; mgr. applied research Atlas Steels Co., 1963-66; mem. faculty Queen's U., Kingston, Ont., 1966—, prof., metall. engring., 1966—, head dept. metall. engring., 1966-77, acting dean Faculty Applied Sci., 1976-77, asso. dean, 1978—; cons. in field. Asst. provincial commnr. Ont., Boy Scouts Can., 1964-66, mem. provincial council, 1969—. Served as lt. Canadian Army, 1939, to wing comdr. RCAF, 1940-46. Fellow Engring. Inst. Can., Am. Soc. Metals; mem. Metals Soc. Gt. Britain, Can. Soc. Mech. Engring., Assn. Profl. Engrs. Ont. Presbyn. (elder). Mason. Clubs: Queen's U. Faculty, Royal Military Coll. Can. (Kingston). Author, patentee in field. Home: Box 95 Ravensview Rural Route 1 Kingston ON K7L 4V1 Canada

MAC KAYE, WILLIAM ROSS, journalist; b. N.Y.C., June 1, 1934; s. Milton and Dorothy Cameron (Disney) Mac K.; A.B., Harvard U., 1955; postgrad. Gen. Theol. Sem., 1955-56; m. Mary Anne Garner, Sept. 1, 1956; children—Katharine Veta Kristin, Susannah Dorothy Aquin, Ian Thomas Garner, Alexander John Daniel, Amanda Hope Julie. Lay asst. St. Mary's Episcopal Ch., N.Y.C., 1956-57; reporter Mpls. Star, 1958-61; Washington corr. Houston Chronicle, 1961-66; religion editor Washington Post, 1966-75, asso. editor Washington Post Mag., 1975—. Trustee, Gen. Theol. Sem., 1972-78. Recipient Supple award for distinguished religious journalism Religion Newswriters Assn., 1968. Fellow Fund Theol. Edn., 1955-56; Congl. fellow Am. Polit. Sci. Assn., 1960-61; profl. journalism fellow Stanford U., 1974-75. Mem. Religion Newswriters Assn. Author: A New Coalition Takes Control, 1962; (with Ernest N. Harmon and Milton MacKaye) Combat Commander: The Autobiography of a Soldier, 1970. Home: 3819 Beecher St NW Washington DC 20007 Office: 1150 15th St NW Washington DC 20071

MACKEIGAN, IAN MALCOLM, Canadian justice; b. St. John, N.B., Can., Apr. 11, 1915; s. John Angus and Mabel (McAvity) MacK.; B.A. with gt. distinction, Dalhousie U., Halifax, N.S., Can., 1934, M.A. in Philosophy, 1935, LL.B., 1938, LL.D. (hon.), 1975; M.A. in Public Adminstrn., U. Toronto, 1939; m. Jean C. Geddes, May 30, 1942; children—John M., Robert G., Janet MacKeigan Ling. Called to N.S. bar, 1939, P.E.I. bar, 1970, created queen's counsel, 1954; practice law, Halifax, 1939-40, 50-73; dep. enforcement adminstr. Wartimes Prices and Trade Bd., Ottawa, Ont., Can., 1940-46; dep. commr. Combines Investigation Commn., Ottawa, 1946-50; chief justice N.S., adminstr. Govt. Province N.S., 1973—; chmn. Atlantic Devel. Bd., 1963-69; bd. govs. Public Archives N.S. Recipient Carswell prize Dalhousie U., 1938; Centennial medal, 1967; Jubilee medal, 1977. Fellow Am. Coll. Trial Lawyers, Found. Legal Research Can.; mem. Canadian Bar Assn. (exec. com.), N.S. Bar Assn. (pres. 1960-61), Phi Kappa Pi. Mem. United Ch. Can. Clubs: Saraquay, Waegwoltic, Ashburn Golf, Halifax. Home: 833 Marlborough Ave Halifax NS B3H 3G7 Canada Office: 1815 Lower Water St PO Box 2314 Halifax NS B3J 3C8 Canada

MACKENDRICK, LILIAN, artist; b. Bklyn., July 14, 1906; d. Joseph and Rebecca (Keila) Block; B.S., N.Y. U., 1928; m. David MacKendrick, Aug. 16, 1936. Exhibited in one-man shows at Mortimer Levitt Gallery, N.Y.C., 1949, 51, Galeria d'Arte Contemporanea, Bordighera, Italy, 1955, Ga. Mus. Art, Athens, 1955, Galerie Benezit, Paris, 1957, 56, 59, 65, Hirschl and Adler Galleries, N.Y.C., 1958, 60, 62, 64, 67, Main St. Gallery, Chgo., 1959, Galaxy Gallery, Phoenix, 1963, Volta Pl. Gallery, Washington, 1964, Hammer Galleries, N.Y.C., 1970, Jacob Guttmann Gallery, N.Y.C., 1976, Hurlburt Gallery, Greenwich, Conn., 1976, Palm Beach (Fla.) Galleries, 1978, others; exhibited in group shows Audubon Artists, N.Y.C., 1951, 53, Witte Mus. Art, San Antonio, 1952, N.Y. City Center, 1954, 55, Galerie 65, Cannes, France, 1959, others; represented in permanent collections at Mus. Fine Arts, Houston, Wadsworth Atheneum, Hartford, Conn., Walker Art Center, Mpls., Hirshhorn Mus. Art, Washington, Met. Mus. Art, N.Y.C., Brandeis U., Waltham, Mass., Israel Mus., Jerusalem, Museo de Arte de Ponce (P.R.), Radcliffe Inst. at Harvard, also pvt. collections. Recipient Gold medal Third Biennial of Am. Painting, Italy, 1955. Subject of numerous mag. articles. Home: 230 Central Park S New York NY 10019

MACKENDRICK, PAUL LACHLAN, educator; b. Taunton, Mass., Feb. 11, 1914; s. Ralph Fulton and Sarah (Harvey) M.; A.B. summa cum laude, Harvard, 1934, A.M., 1937, Ph.D., 1938; postgrad. Balliol Coll., Oxford, 1934-36; m. Dorothy Grace Lau, Mar. 17, 1945; children—Andrew Lachlan, Sarah Ann. Instr., Phillips Acad., 1938-41, Harvard, 1946; asst. prof. U. Wis., 1946-48, asso. prof., 1948-52, prof., 1952-75, Lily Ross Taylor prof., 1975—; prof. charge Sch. Classical Studies, Am. Acad. Rome, summers 1956-59; vis. prof. U. Colo., summer 1964; mem. Inst. for Advanced Study, Princeton, 1964-65; vis. prof. U. Ibadan, Nigeria, 1965-66; prof. charge Intercoll. Center for Classical Studies, Rome, 1973-74; Rockefeller scholar-in-residence Bellagio Center, Italy, 1977; vis. fellow Churchill Coll., Cambridge U., 1977-78; Phi Beta Kappa nat. lectr., 1970-71. Sec., dir. Am. Council Learned Socs., 1956-57, dir., 1960-63. Trustee Am. Acad. in Rome, 1966-72; bd. dirs. Nat. Humanities Faculty, 1968-71, chmn., 1969-70. Served to lt. USNR, 1941-45. Guggenheim fellow, 1957-58. Mem. Classical Assn. Middle West and South (pres. 1969-70), Am. Philol. Assn. (sec.-treas. 1954-56). Archeol. Inst. Am. Madison Soc. (pres. 1963), Phi Beta Kappa (pres. Wis. 1965-66). Club: Century Assn. (N.Y.C.). Author: (with Herbert M. Howe) Classics in Translation, 1952; (with V.M. Scramuzza) The Ancient World, 1958; The Roman Mind at Work, 1958; The Mute Stones Speak, 1960; The

Greek Stones Speak, 1962; Western Civilization, 1968; The Athenian Aristocracy, 399-31 B.C., 1969; The Iberian Stones Speak, 1969; Romans on the Rhine, 1970; Roman France, 1972; Dacian Stones Speak, 1975; North African Stones Speak, 1980. Home: 208 Bordner Dr Madison WI 53705

MACKENZIE, ALISTAIR MACINTOSH, food products co. exec.; b. Toronto, Ont., Can., May 29, 1929; s. Alexander and Jean Neilson (Climie) MacK.; B.A., U. Toronto, 1951; m. Julie Ann Murray, Oct. 1, 1954; children—Anne Elizabeth, Duncan Alexander. With Can. Packers Ltd., Toronto, 1951—, office mgr., 1957-60, gen. credit mgr., 1960-65, gen. office mgr., 1965-69, sec., 1969—. Mem. Canadian Creditmen's Assn. (gov. Ont. div. 1957), Canadian Credit Inst. Mem. United Ch. (elder 1977). Home: 146 The Kingsway Toronto ON M8X 2V3 Canada Office: 95 St Clair Ave W Toronto ON M4V 1P2 Canada

MACKENZIE, CHARLES SHERRARD, coll. pres.; b. Quincy, Mass., Aug. 21, 1924; s. Charles Sherrard and Dorothy (Eaton) MacK.; B.A., Gordon Coll., 1946; M.Div., Princeton Theol. Sem., 1949, Ph.D., 1955; student Boston U., 1942-43, Oxford U. (Eng.), 1965, U. Hamburg, 1968; m. Florence Evelyn Phelps Meyer, Aug. 28, 1964; 1 son, Robert Walter Meyer. Ordained to ministry Congl. Christian Ch., 1949; pastor Carversville (Pa.) Christian Ch., 1948-51; fellow faculty Princeton Theol. Sem., 1949-51, 53-54; pastor First Presbyn. Ch., Avenel, N.J., 1954-64, Broadway Presbyn. Ch., N.Y.C., 1964-67, First Presbyn. Ch., San Mateo, Calif., 1967-71; pres. Grove City (Pa.) Coll., 1971—. Mem. exec. com. Presbyns. United for Bibl. Concern. Mem. Human Relations Commn., San Mateo, 1968-70; mem. Indsl. Devel. Council, Grove City, 1972—. Served with USAF, 1951-53. Mem. Presbyn. Coll. Union, Am. Assn. Pres.'s Ind. Colls. and Univs. Republican. Clubs: Masons, Univ. Boston. Author: The Anguish and Joy of Pascal, 1973. Home: 350 Memorial Ave Grove City PA 16127

MACKENZIE, COSMO GLENN, scientist, educator; b. Balt., May 22, 1907; s. George Norbury and Mary (Forwood) M.; A.B., Johns Hopkins U., 1932, D.Sc., 1936; m. Julia Francis Buzz, Sept. 5, 1936; children—Thomas Brooke, Julia Anne Vernon. Research asso. biochemistry Johns Hopkins U. Sch. Hygiene and Pub. Health, 1936-38, asst. prof., 1938-42; research asso., asst. prof., asso. prof. Cornell U. Med. Sch., 1946-50; prof. U. Colo. Med. Sch., Denver, 1973-75, prof. emeritus, 1975—, chmn. dept. biochemistry, 1950-73, asso. investigator Webb-Waring Lung Inst., Med. Center, 1976—. Served from 1st lt. to capt. USAAF, 1942-46. Fellow N.Y. Acad. Scis., AAAS; mem. Am. Soc. Biol. Chemists, Inst. Nutrition, Am. Chem. Soc., Sigma Xi. Editor: Procs. Soc. for Exptl. Biology and Medicine, 1952-56, Jour. Nutrition, 1956-60. Discovered antidystrophic activity of Vitamin E, antithyroid drugs, pituitary-thyroid feedback, prolongation of consciousness by glucose at high altitude, prodn. one-carbon compounds in higher animals, role of albumin-bound fatty acids in fat accumulation in mammalian cells, role of pH in mammalian cell growth and fat content. Home: 1 Bellaire St Denver CO 80220

MACKENZIE, DONALD CAMPBELL, educator; b. Tain, Scotland, Nov. 11, 1919; s. Donald and Alice Annand (Murray) M.; grad. Phillips Exeter Acad., 1938; A.B., Princeton, 1942, M.A. (Woodrow Wilson, Westcott, Page fellow), 1948, Ph.D., 1949; m. Martha Ann Lauderdale, Dec. 28, 1967; children—Donald C., David M. Came to U.S., 1928, naturalized, 1935. Instr., lectr., asst. prof. classics, jr. fellow Council Humanities, Princeton, 1949-60; prof. classics, chmn. dept. fng. langs. Rice U., 1960-63; prof. classics Williams Coll., Williamstown, Mass., 1963-66, chmn., 1964-66; prof. classics U. Waterloo, Ont., Can., 1969—, acting chmn. dept. classics and Romance langs., 1970-71; vis. sr. mem. Wolfson Coll., Cambridge U., 1976-77. Served from pvt. to capt. USAAF, 1942-46. Mem. Am. Philol. Assn., Phi Beta Kappa. Club: Princeton U. Tower, Contbr. revs. to scholarly jours. Translator: Complete Works of Milton, vol. 4, 1966. Home: 68 William St W Waterloo ON Canada

MACKENZIE, DONALD MATTHEW, educator; b. Homewood, Ill., Oct. 1, 1911; s. Alick Martin and Margaret (Black) M.; A.B., Park Coll., Parkville, Mo., 1933, L.H.D., 1972; A.M., U. Chgo., 1937, Ph.D., 1955; LL.D., St. Francis Coll., Biddeford, Maine, 1967, Loyola U. Chgo., 1967; m. Ruth Yoakum, Dec. 26, 1937; children—Donald Matthew, Roderick Ian. Dir. student personnel Dakota Wesleyan U., Mitchell, S.D., 1937-41; tech. asst. Office Sec. Commn. on Colls. and Univs., North Central Assn. Colls. and Secondary Schs., Chgo., 1941-45; commn. examiner, cons., 1945—; registrar Frances Shimer Coll., Mt. Carroll, Ill., 1945-46; dean Blackburn Coll., Carlinville, Ill., 1946-56, acting pres., 1949; staff dir. Ill. Higher Edn. Commn. 1956-57; research asso. dept. edn. U. Chgo., 1957-60; asso. sec. Commn. on Colls. and Univs., N. Central Assn., 1957-60, asst. dir. leadership tng. project N. Central Assn., 1958-60; dean faculty Lindenwood Coll., St. Charles, Mo., 1960-62; asso. dir., study ch. related colls. and univs. Danforth Found., 1962-65; dir. instnl. study Park Coll., Parkville, Mo., 1965-66, pres., 1966-72; cons. Mo. Commn. on Higher Edn., 1972-73; exec. dir. Commn. on Future, Lutheran Ednl. Conf. N.Am., 1974; cons., Mo. Dept. Higher Edn., 1975. Recipient Distinguished Service award Park Coll. Alumni Assn., 1963. Mem. Nat. Soc. Study Edn., Am. Ednl. Research Assn., NEA, Phi Delta Kappa. Presbyn. (pres. Coll. Union 1970, elder). Author: (with M.M. Pattillo) Church Sponsored Higher Education. Home: 1055 Ridge Rd Homewood IL 60430

MACKENZIE, GEORGE ALLAN, Canadian air force officer; b. Kingston, Jamaica, Dec. 15, 1931; s. George Adam and Annette Louise (Maduro) MacK.; student Jamaica Coll., Kingston, 1944-48; m. Valerie Ann Marchand, June 30, 1971; children from previous marriage—Richard Michael, Barbara Wynne. Commd. flying officer Canadian Air Force, 1952, advanced through grades to lt. gen., 1978; comdr. Canadian Forces Air Command, Winnipeg, Man., 1978—. Decorated comdr. Order of Mil. Merit (Can.). Mem. United Services Inst. Can. (hon. v.p.), Canadian Corps Commissionaires (hon. gov.). Clubs: Rotary, Carleton (Winnipeg). Home: 205 Dromore Ave Winnipeg MB R3M 0H9 Canada Office: Air Command Hdqrs Canadian Forces Base Winnipeg Westwin MB R2R 0T0 Canada

MACKENZIE, GISELE, singer, actress; b. Winnipeg, Man., Can., Jan. 10, 1927; d. George Mackenzie and Marietta (Manseau) Lafleche; student Sacred Heart Sch., Winnipeg, 1933-41, Royal Conservatory Music, Toronto, 1941-49; m. Robert J. Shuttleworth, 1958 (div. 1966); children—MacKenzie Duffy, Gisele Melissa; m. 2d, Robert Francis Klein. Came to the U.S., 1951, naturalized, 1957. Singer, CBC networks, 1946-50; TV singer with Bob Crosby, CBS, Hollywood, with Mario Lanza, NBC, 1951-53; featured singer Your Hit Parade, NBC, N.Y.C., 1953-57; actress Kraft Theatre, Gen. Electric Theatre, Studio One, Jack Benny Show, Jack Parr Show, others; star Gisele MacKenzie Show, 1957-58; theatre appearances include King and I, Annie Get Your Gun, Gypsy, South Pacific, Sound of Music, Hello Dolly, Mame, Molly Brown. Hon. mayor Encino, Calif., 1962-63. Mem. Acad. TV Arts Scis. (dir. 1956-57).

MACKENZIE, GORDON BLAIR, automobile co. exec.; b. Kalamazoo, July 12, 1921; s. Clark W. and Madeleine A. MacK.; B.A., U. Mich., 1943, M.B.A., 1946; m. Marion W., Sept. 17, 1949; children—Gordon Blair, John, David. With Packard Motor Car Co., 1946-48; in retail automobile bus., 1952-54; with Ford Motor Co., 1954—, v.p. Ford of Europe, Essex, Eng., 1973—, v.p. sales ops. Ford Motor Co., 1973—. Served to capt. U.S. Army, 1943-46. Mem. Sigma Chi. Clubs: Pine Lake Country, Masons, Shriners. Office: Ford Motor Co 300 Renaissance Center Detroit MI 48243

MACKENZIE, JAMES WILLIAM, surgeon; b. Cleve., Oct. 17, 1925; s. William and Martha (Neiswonger) M.; B.S., U. Mich., 1948, M.D., 1951; m. Melinda Sprague, Sept. 1977; 1 son, Douglas. Instr. U. Mich., 1960-62; chief sect. thoracic and cardiovascular surgery U. Mo. Med. Center, 1962-69, asst. prof. surgery U. Mo., 1962-63, asso. prof., 1963-66, prof., 1966-69, asst. chmn., 1968; prof., chmn. dept. surgery Coll. Medicine and Dentistry N.J.-Rutgers Med. Sch., Piscataway, N.J., 1969—, dean, 1971-74. Served with USNR, 1953-55. Mem. AMA, Soc. Thoracic Surgeons, Am. Assn. for Thoracic Surgery, Central Surg. Assn., So. Thoracic Surgery Assn., A.C.S., Sigma Xi, Alpha Omega Alpha. Home: 174 Laurel Circle Princeton NJ 08540 Office: Coll Medicine and Dentistry NJ Med Sch PO Box 101 Piscataway NJ 08854

MACKENZIE, JOHN, corp. exec.; b. 1919; B.S., N.Y. U., 1948. Accountant, S.Am. Devel. Co., N.Y.C., 1938-41; financial comptroller French Oil Ind. Agy.-Groupment D'Archat des Carburants, N.Y., 1946-53; v.p., treas. George Hall Corp., 1954-56; asst. treas. Am. Petrofina, Inc., 1956-61, sec., 1961-64, v.p., sec., 1964-68, sr. v.p., sec., 1968—; pres., dir. Am. Petrofina Holding Co., Am. Petrofina Exploration Co. Norway; dir. Cosden Oil & Chem. Co., Dixie Lime & Stone Co. Mem. Belgium-Am. C. of C. (dir.). Address: Fina Plaza 8350 N Central Expressway Dallas TX 75206

MACKENZIE, JOHN DOUGLAS, educator; b. Hong Kong, Feb. 18, 1926; s. John and Hannah (Wong) MacK.; came to U.S., 1954, naturalized, 1963; B.Sc., U. London, 1952, Ph.D., 1954; m. Jennifer Russell, Oct. 2, 1954; children—Timothy John, Andrea Louise, Peter Neil. Research asst., lectr. Princeton U., 1954-56; ICI fellow Cambridge (Eng.) U., 1956-57; research scientist Gen. Electric Research Center, N.Y.C., 1957-63; prof. materials sci. Rensselaer Poly. Inst., 1963-69; prof. engring. U. Calif., Los Angeles, 1969—; U.S. rep. Internat. Glass Commn., 1964-71. Fellow Am. Ceramic Soc., Royal Inst. Chemistry; mem. Nat. Acad. Engring., Am. Phys. Soc., Electrochem. Soc., ASTM, Am. Chem. Soc., Soc. Glass Tech. Author books in field (6); editor Jour. Non-Crystalline Solids, 1968—. Patentee in field; contbr. articles to profl. jours. Office: 6532 Boelter Hall Univ of Calif Los Angeles CA 90024

MACKENZIE, JOHN PETTIBONE, journalist; b. Glen Ellyn, Ill., July 19, 1930; s. John W. P. and Elizabeth (Andersen) MacK.; B.A. in Am. Studies cum laude, Amherst Coll., 1952; postgrad. Harvard U. Law Sch., 1964-65; m. Amanda Fisk, Oct. 24, 1959 (div. 1977); children—Bradley John, Alice Fisk, Douglas Bain. Staff writer Washington Post, 1956-77, Supreme Ct. reporter, 1965-77; Walter E. Meyer vis. research prof. law N.Y. U., 1977-78; lectr. law SUNY Buffalo Law Sch., 1979; spl. contbr. to editorial page N.Y. Times, N.Y.C., 1977—. Served to lt. j.g. USN, 1952-55. Recipient Gavel award for legal reporting Am. Bar Assn., 1967. Clubs: Washington Press, Fed. City, Internat. of Washington. Author: The Appearance of Justice, 1974 (Am. Bar Assn. Gavel award 1975); contbr. articles to mags., law books, law revs. Home: 7-13 Washington Sq N New York NY 10003

MACKENZIE, KENNETH VICTOR, physicist; b. Brandon, Man., Can., Aug. 29, 1911; s. William Franklin and Allie Esther (Stinson) M.; came to U.S., 1923, naturalized, 1939; student Willamette U., 1930-33; B.S. in Math. and Physics, U. Wash., 1934, M.S. in Physics, 1936; m. Catherine Jane (Oleson) Morales, Oct. 18, 1968; children by previous marriage—Dorothy Kay Mighell, Robert Bruce, Kenneth Donald, Jessie Jean. Physicist, Oreg. State Hwy. Dept., 1936-41; head physicist Puget Sound Magnetic Survey Range, USN, Kingston, Wash., 1941-44; asso. physicist Applied Physics Lab., U. Wash., 1944-46; group leader, deep and shallow water propagation Navy Electronics Lab., San Diego, 1946-51; sect. head scattering and oceanography br., 1951-55, head shallow water acoustical process sect., 1955-61; exchange scientist Her Majesty's Underwater Weapons Establishment, Eng., 1961-62; chief scientist deep submergence program Navy Electronics Lab. 1962-67; sr. physicist acoustic propagation div. Undersea Surveillance and Ocean Sci. Dept., Naval Undersea Center (formerly Navy Electronics Lab.), 1967-73; sr. staff scientist, primary adviser sci. and engring. directorate staff U.S. Naval Oceanographic Office, Washington, 1973-76; sr. staff physicist Environ. Research Requirements Office, Naval Ocean Research and Devel. Activity, Bay St. Louis, Miss., 1976-79; prin. Mackenzie Marine Sci. Cons.'s, San Diego, 1979—; cons. allied govts. and def. industry. Fifty-one deep submergence dives including 12 aboard bathyscaphs Trieste I and II, 36 on Deepstar-4000; hon. committeeman Internat. Ocean Devel. Conf., Tokyo, 1971—; speaker Joint Oceanographic Assembly IUGG, Edinburgh, Scotland, 1976; week aboard nuclear research submarine NR-1. Recipient certificate for exceptional service Bur. Ordnance, 1945, certificate merit Office Sci. Research, 1945, Navy Electronics Lab award, 1960, Navy commendation for Trieste search and location of Thresher, 1963, Alumni citation Willamette U., 1969, Superior Achievement award Inst. Nav., 1971; Meritorious Civilian Service award USN, 1979; registered profl. engr., Oreg., Wash. Fellow Acoustical Soc. Am., Explorers Club, Marine Tech. Soc. (founding); mem. Am. Geophys. Union, Am. Oceanic Orgn., Am. Phys. Soc., Inst. Navigation (nat. marine chmn. 1965-66, Western regional councilor 1966-68, 73-75), Instrument Soc. Am. (nat. dir. marine scis. div. 1968-70), Navy League, Optical Soc. Am., St. Andrews Soc. (Scotland), Caledonian Soc., Sigma Xi. Contbr. numerous articles, book chpts. to profl. lit. Home: 430 San Antonio Ave San Diego CA 92106 Office: PO Box 80715 Midway Sta San Diego CA 92138

MAC KENZIE, NORMAN HUGH, educator; b. Salisbury, Rhodesia, Mar. 8, 1915; s. Thomas Hugh and Ruth Blanche (Huskisson) MacK.; B.A., Rhodes U., South Africa, 1934, M.A. 1935, Diploma in Edn., 1936; Ph.D. (Union scholar), U. London, 1940; m. Rita Mavis Hofmann, Aug. 14, 1948; children—Catherine, Ronald. Lectr. in English, Rhodes U., South Africa, 1937, U. Hong Kong, 1940-41, U. Melbourne (Australia), 1946-48; sr. lectr.-in-charge U. Natal (Durban), 1949-55; prof., head English dept. U. Coll., Rhodesia, 1955-65, dean Faculty Arts and Edn., 1957-60, 63-64; prof., head English dept. Laurentian U., Ont., Can., 1965-66; prof. English, Queen's U., Kingston, Ont., 1966—, dir. grad. studies in English, 1967-73, chmn. council grad. studies, 1971-73, chmn. editorial bd. Yeats Studies, 1972-74. Exec. Central Africa Drama League, 1959-65; mem. exec. com. Can. Irish Studies, 1968-73. Served with Hong Kong Vol. Def. Corps, 1940-45; prisoner of war China and Japan, 1941-45. Brit. Council scholar, 1954; Killam sr. fellow, 1979-80. Fellow Royal Soc. Can.; mem. English Assn. Rhodesia (pres. 1957-65), Rhodesia Drama Assn. (vice chmn. 1957-65), Hopkins Soc. (pres. 1972—), Yeats Soc. (life), Internat. Assn. U. Profs. English, MLA, Internat. Assn. for Study Anglo-Irish Lits. Author: South African Travel Literature in the 17th Century, 1955; The Outlook for English in Central Africa, 1960; Hopkins, 1968; editor (with W.H. Gardner) The Poems of Gerard Manley Hopkins, 1967, rev. edit., 1970; Poems by Hopkins, 1974; U. Natal Gazette, 1954-55; contbr. chpts. to Testing the English Proficiency of Foreign Students, 1961, English Studies Today-Third Series, 1963, Sphere History of English Literature, Vol. VI, 1970, Readings of the Wreck of the Deutschland, 1976, Festschrift for E.R. Seary, 1975, British and American Literature 1880-1920, 1976, Myth and Reality in Irish Literature, 1977; contbr. articles to Internat. Rev. Edn., Bull. Inst. Hist. Research, Times Lit. Supplement, The Month, Modern Lang. Quar., Queen's Quar., others. Home: 416 Windward Pl Kingston ON K7M 4E4 Canada

MACKENZIE, OSSIAN, ednl. cons.; b. Hampden, Me., July 26, 1907; s. L. Robert and Evangeline Marion (Taylor) MacK.; B.A., U. Mont., 1928; postgrad. Harvard, 1928-31; J.D., Fordham U., 1938; LL.D., Rider Coll., 1962; m. Kyle Habberton, June 16, 1934; 1 dau., Robin (Mrs. Lucien E. Ferster). Estate supr. Guaranty Trust Co. of N.Y., 1931-39; admitted to N.Y. bar, 1938; head state and local tax dept. Allied Chem. & Dye Corp., N.Y.C., 1939-43; head tax dept. West Penn Electric Co., N.Y.C., 1946-47; univ. devel. officer Columbia, 1947-50; asst. dean Grad. Sch. Bus., asst. to exec. dir. Am. Assembly, 1950-53; dean Coll. Bus. Adminstrn., Pa. State U., 1953-73, asst. to pres., 1956-57, v.p., 1957-58, ednl. cons., 1977—, prof. mgmt., chmn. dept. bus and econs. Rutgers U., Camden, N.J., 1973-77. Cons., Dept. of State, 1955-57, U. Costa Rica, 1964-65, Dept. of Health, Edn. and Welfare, 1967, Comptroller Gen. U.S., 1968-74, Ala. A. and M. U., 1968—, Esan U., Lima, Peru, 1971—; dir. Corr. Edn. Research Project, 1964-68. Served with USMCR, 1943-46. Recipient Disting. Alumnus award U. Mont., 1979. Mem. Middle Atlantic Assn. Colls. Bus. Adminstrn. (pres. 1961), Am. Assembly Collegiate Schs. Bus. (pres. 1973), Council for Profl. Edn. for Bus. (pres. 1962), Verband der Hochschullehrer fur Betriebsbswirtschaft, Beta Gamma Sigma (pres. 1966-70), Pi Gamma Mu, Sigma Delta Chi, Sigma Chi. Republican. Protestant. Mason. Clubs: Harvard (N.Y.C.); Pa. State Faculty. Author books, articles in field. Home: 327 Arbor Way State College PA 16801 Office: 801 L Bus Adminstrn Bldg Pa State U University Park PA 16802

MACKENZIE, RALPH SIDNEY, aerospace exec.; b. Bklyn., Aug. 29, 1934; s. George William and Evelyn Ruth (Fanning) MacK.; B.S. in Aero. Engring., U. Fla., 1955; m. Sara Lee Henderson, Nov. 12, 1976; children—Douglas, Kirk, Shirley, Kyle, Kristeen. Aerosystems engr. Gen. Dynamics, Fort Worth, 1955-63, group engr., project engr., 1963-72, project engr., v.p., program dir. Tomahawk Cruise Missile Programs, Convair div., San Diego, 1972—. Home: 5426 Avenida Fiesta La Jolla CA 92037 Office: 5001 Kearny Villa Rd San Diego CA 92138

MACKENZIE, RANSOM GILLET, banker; b. Watervliet, N.Y., Sept. 1, 1906; s. Charles H. and Emma H. (Herbert) MacK.; A.B., Syracuse U., 1929; grad. Rutgers U. Grad. Sch. Banking, 1941; m. Marjorie P. Smith, June 1, 1935. With Marine Midland Trust Co. Central N.Y., Syracuse, 1929—, v.p., trust officer, 1948-61, exec. v.p., 1961-64, pres., 1964-68, chmn. bd., 1968-71, also dir.; dir. Cambridge Filter Corp., Climax Corp., Mac-Law Tool & Aircraft Parts, Inc., Genimar Inc., Taylor Wine Co., Inc. Trustee Onondaga Community Coll.; mem. council Upstate Med. Center State U. N.Y. Bd. dirs., treas. Trustees Assn. Two Year Colls. State U. N.Y.; bd. dirs. local Boy Scouts Am., A.R.C., Rescue Mission, Syracuse, Met. Devel. Assn. Syracuse, United Cerebral Palsy and Handicapped Children's Assn. Syracuse. Named Outstanding Syracuse Businessman of Year in Banking and Finance, 1962; Outstanding Citizen award for Community Achievement, 1967. Mem. Am., N.Y. State bankers assns. Clubs: Century, Onondaga Golf and Country, University (Syracuse). Home: 35 The Orchard Fayetteville NY 13066 Office: 344 S Warren St Syracuse NY 13201

MACKENZIE, RICHARD STANLEY, educator; b. Detroit, Dec. 28, 1933; s. Stanley Alexander and Isabel (Willoughbe) M.; student Stanford, 1951-52; D.D.S., U. Mich., 1958, M.S., 1960; Ph.D., U. Pitts., 1965; m. Claire Grace Shepard, June 22, 1957; children—Douglas Alexander, Willow Ann. Head dental behavioral sci. dept. U. Pitts., 1965-68, dir. ednl. research in dentistry, 1966-69; dir. Office Dental Edn., U. Fla., Gainesville, 1969—; cons. USPHS, ADA, Central Office VA Hosps., Pan Am. Health Orgn. Mem. Citizen's for Mich., 1958-60. Recipient Career Devel. award USPHS, 1970. Mem. ADA, Internat. Assn. for Dental Research, Am. Psychol. Assn., Am. Ednl. Research Assn., Behavioral Scientists in Dental Research (pres. 1972), Sigma Xi, Phi Kappa Phi, Omicron Kappa Upsilon, Sigma Phi, Delta Sigma Delta. Editorial bd. Jour. Dental Edn., 1969-76. Home: 3715 SE 37th St Gainesville FL 32601

MACKERODT, FRED, public relations specialist; b. Bklyn., Sept. 17, 1938; s. Leroy and Margaret (Murphy) M.; student N.Y. U., 1958-59; m. Barbara Anne Balakier, Feb. 15, 1975. Freelance writer, photographer, N.Y.C. and Barcelona, Spain, 1968-73; editor Cars Mag., Popular Publs. Inc., N.Y.C., 1973-76; pres. Fred Mackerodt & Assos. pub. relations and publicity, N.Y.C., 1976—. Mem. Internat. Motor Press Assn. (dir. 1975—), Overseas Press Club, Publicity Club N.Y., N.Y. Zool. Soc. (aquarium field asso. 1971—). Contbr. articles to popular mags. Home and Office: 209 W 86th St Suite 901 New York NY 10024

MACKEY, GEORGE WHITELAW, educator, mathematician; b. St. Louis, Feb. 1, 1916; s. William Sturges and Dorothy Frances (Allison) M.; B.A., Rice Inst., 1938; A.M., Harvard U., 1939, Ph.D., 1942; M.A., Oxford, 1966; m. Alice Willard, Dec. 9, 1960; 1 dau., Ann Sturges Mackey. Instr. math. Ill. Inst. Tech., 1942-43; faculty instr. math. Harvard, 1943-46, asst. prof., 1946-48, asso. prof., 1948-56, prof. math., 1956-69, Landon T. Clay prof. math. and theoretical sci., 1969—; vis. prof. U. Chgo., summer 1955, UCLA, summer 1959, Tata Inst. Fundamental Research, Bombay, India, 1970-71; Walker Ames vis. prof. U. Wash., summer 1961; Eastman vis. prof. Oxford, 1966-67. Served as civilian, operational research sect. 8th Air Force, 1944, applied math. panel NDRC, 1945. Guggenheim fellow, 1949-50, 61-62, 70-71. Mem. Am. Math. Soc. (v.p. 1964-65, Steele prize 1974), Nat. Acad. Scis., Société Mathematique de France, Am. Philos. Soc., Am. Acad. Arts and Scis., Phi Beta Kappa, Sigma Xi. Author: Mathematical Foundations of Quantum Mechanics, 1963; Lectures on the Theory of Functions of a Complex Variable, 1967; Induced Representations and Quantum Mechanics, 1968; The Theory of Unitary Group Representations, 1976; Unitary Group Representations in Physics, Probability and Number Theory, 1978. Contbr. articles math. jours. Home: 25 Coolidge Hill Rd Cambridge MA 02138

MACKEY, HOWARD HAMILTON, SR., architect, planner, educator; b. Phila., Nov. 25, 1901; s. Henry Bardon and Anna (Wills) M.; B. Arch., U. Pa., 1924, M. Arch., 1937; m. Matilda Eleanor Kendricks, July 2, 1925; 1 son, Howard Hamilton. Tchr. architecture, design, urban planning and tropical architecture Howard U., 1924-73, acting head, dept. architecture, 1930-37, head, 1937-71, head program city planning, 1967-71, asso. dean Sch. Engring. and Architecture, 1964-65, founder, dean Sch. Architecture and City Planning, 1970-71; Asso. Building Research Adv. Bd., 1966—; registered architect, D.C., Md., Va., Pa., N.J.; in pvt. practice, Phila., Washington, 1935—; staff civil engring. dept. U. Md.; housing and town planning cons. to Brit. Guiana and Surinam, 1954-57; archtl. cons. U.S. GSA, 1971; U.S. del. Inter-Am. (Pan-Am.) Housing Conf., Bogota, Colombia, 1956; U.S. mem. planning com., speaker Town and Country Devel. Planning Conf., Trinidad, B.W.I., 1956; pioneered nat. exhibits by Negro architects, 1930; participated in Chgo. War Meml. Archtl. Competition, 1930; exhibited Chgo. Art Inst., 1930, Architects' Bldg., Phila., 1930, Howard U. Gallery of Art, 1931, Corcoran Gallery of Art, Washington, 1931-32, Art Center, N.Y.C., 1933, Archtl. League N.Y., N.Y. Pub. Library; traveling exhibit, Harmon Found., 1933; architect for Parkside Dwelling Housing Project, Washington, comml., residential, ch. bldgs.; cons. to embassies, Ghana, Nigeria and India, Washington. Active Jr. Police, Citizens' Corps, Teen-Age Center for Girls (all Washington); rep. Pleasant Plains Citizens Assn., Citizens' Council on Community Planning, Washington; mem. citizens adv. zoning com. D.C. Commrs.; Howard U. rep. 6th world congress Internat. Union Architects, London, 1961; archtl. design panel Balt. Community Renewal and Housing Agy., 1964-68; design adv. com. FHA honor awards in residential design, 1964; Howard U. rep. 8th World Congress Internat. Union Architects, Paris, 1965; mem. design adv. panel Dept. Housing and Community Devel., Balt., 1968-71; mem. D.C. Bd. Examiners and Registrars Architects, 1969-77, D.C. Bd. Zoning Adjustment, 1971-73; mem. joint com. Fine Arts Commn. and Nat. Capital Planning Commn. on Landmarks of Nation's Capital, 1970-73. Recipient Engring. and Archtl. Alumni Service award Howard U., 1961; Distinguished Service award Nat. Tech. Assn., 1961; donor Howard H. Mackey, Sr., Emergency Student Loan Fund, Howard U., 1974, Matilda Kendricks Mackey Meml. Student Loan Fund for Women, 1976; contbr. Howard H. Mackey, Sr., Papers, Documents and Memorabilia to Moorland-Spingarn Research Center, Howard U., 1975. Fellow AIA (coll. of fellows, del. 11th Pan Am. Congress Architects 1965); mem. Assn. Collegiate Schs. Architecture, Washington Bldg. Congress (gov., met. planning com.; transp. com.), Met. Washington Bd. Trade (community planning com.), Nat. Council for Advancement Negro in Architecture (trustee), Nat. Tech. Assn., Nat. Builders Assn., Am. Assn. U. Profs., Archtl. League N.Y., Omega Psi Phi, Tau Beta Pi, Tau Sigma Delta. Baptist. Photographs of work: Howard U. publs., Architecture as a Career, 1931; Progressive Architecture, 1944, 1950. Contbr. profl. publs. Home and Office: 4721 Colorado Ave NW Washington DC 20011. *Life, with its disappointments and frustrations, at best is a compromise-if you can't get what you want, want what you can get, and do something constructive and beneficial with it.*

MACKEY, JOHN ALEXANDER, fin. exec.; b. Cleve., Sept. 18, 1933; s. William Adolph and Helmi Maria (Lindholm) M.; B.S.C.E., U. Toledo, 1955; M.S., Purdue U., 1957; m. Norma K. Jones, Oct. 10, 1959; children—Kimberly Lynne, Kirk William. Mgr. mgmt. info. Mobil Oil Corp., N.Y.C., 1967; mgr. fin. analysis Far East region, 1968; dir. fin. analysis Lehigh Valley Industries, N.Y.C., 1968-73, asst. treas., 1973-77, treas., 1977—. Lutheran. Office: 200 E 42d St New York NY 10017

MACKEY, LEONARD BRUCE, diversified mfg. corp. exec.; b. Washington, Aug. 31, 1925; s. Stuart J. and Margaret B. (Browne) M.; B.E.E., Rensselaer Poly. Inst., 1945; J.D., George Washington U., 1950; m. Britta Beckhaus, Mar. 2, 1974; children—Leonard B., Cathleen C., Wendy F. Instr. elec. engring. Rensselaer Poly. Inst., Troy, N.Y., 1946-47; patent examiner U.S. Patent Office, Washington, 1947-50; admitted to N.Y. bar, 1954; atty. Gen. Electric Co., Schenectady and N.Y.C., 1953-60; dir. licensing, asst. sec. ITT, N.Y.C., 1960-73, v.p., gen. patent counsel, dir. licensing, 1973—. Mem. Recreation Commn., Rye, N.Y., 1966-67, Planning Commn., 1967-70, 72-75, city councilman, 1970-71. Served as ensign USNR, 1943-45, to lt., 1951-53. Mem. Am. Bar Assn., Am. Patent Law Assn. (bd. mgrs. 1968-70, 2d v.p. 1979), Licensing Execs. Soc. U.S.A. (pres. 1978), Eta Kappa Nu. Republican. Presbyterian. Clubs: Am. Yacht (sec. 1968-70), Masons. Home: ITT World Hdqrs 320 Park Ave New York NY 10022

MACKEY, LOUIS HENRY, educator; b. Sidney, Ohio, Sept. 24, 1926; s. Louis Henry and Clara Emma (Maurer) M.; B.A., Capital U., 1948; student Duke, 1948-50; M.A., Yale, 1953, Ph.D., 1954; m. Linda Kay Barabas, July 8, 1968; children—Stephen Louis, Thomas Adam, Jacob Louis, Eva Maria. Instr. philosophy Yale, 1953-55, asst. prof. (Morse fellow), 1955-59; asso. prof. philosophy Rice U., Houston, 1959-65, prof., 1965-67; prof. U. Tex., Austin, 1967—. Nat. Endowment for Humanities fellow, 1976-77. Episcopalian. Author: Kierkegaard: A Kind of Poet, 1971; contbr. articles to profl. jours. Home: 9824 Timber Ridge Pass Austin TX 78746 Office: 225 WAG U Tex Austin TX 78712

MACKEY, MAURICE CECIL, univ. pres.; b. Montgomery, Ala., Jan. 23, 1929; s. M. Cecil and Annie Laurie (Kimrey) M.; B.A., U. Ala., 1949, M.A., 1953, LL.B., 1958; Ph.D., U. Ill., 1955; postgrad. Harvard, 1958-59; m. Clare Siewert, Aug. 29, 1953; children—Carol, John, Ann. Asst. prof. econs. U. Ill., 1955-56; asso. prof. econs. U.S. Air Force Acad., 1956-57; admitted to Ala. bar, 1958; asst. prof. law U. Ala., 1958-62; with FAA, 1963-65, U.S. Dept. Commerce, 1965-67; asst. sec. U.S. Dept. Transp., 1967-69; exec. v.p., prof. law Fla. State U., Tallahassee, 1969-71; pres. U. South Fla., Tampa, 1971-76; pres., prof. law Tex. Tech U., Lubbock, 1976-79; pres., prof. econs. Mich. State U., East Lansing, 1979—; asst. counsel Subcom. on Antitrust and Monopoly, U.S. Senate, 1962-63; mem. adv. com. U.S. Coast Guard Acad. 1969-71; chmn. Fla. Gov.'s Adv. Com. on Transp., 1975, Nat. Boating Safety Adv. Council, 1975—; mem. adv. council NSF, 1978—; asso. China Council, 1979—. Bd. dirs. Gulf Ridge council Boy Scouts Am., Tampa United Fund; bd. dirs. Lubbock United Way. Served with USAF, 1956-57. Recipient Arthur S. Flemming award Washington Jaycees, 1967. Mem. Fla. Council 100, Tampa C. of C. (bd. govs.), Am. Assn. State Colls. and Univs. (pres., dir.), Artus, Phi Kappa Phi, Chi Alpha Phi. Office: President's Office Michigan State U East Lansing MI 48824

MACKEY, SHELDON ELIAS, clergyman; b. Bethlehem, Pa., Nov. 20, 1913; s. Elias and Pearl Elizabeth (Cunningham) M.; A.B., Moravian Coll., 1936; B.D., Lancaster Theol. Sem., 1939; D.D., Franklin and Marshall Coll., 1954; LL.D., Ursinus Coll., 1958; m. Marie Louise Dillinger, Sept. 20, 1939; children—Peter David, John Harry, Mary Susan, Timothy Andrew, Philip James. Ordained to ministry Evang. and Reformed Ch., 1939; pastor Pa. congregations, 1939-54; adminstrv. asst. to pres. Evang. and Reformed Ch., 1954-57, sec., 1957-78, also editor Yearbook, dir. correlation and sec. gen. council Gen. Synod; co-sec. United Church of Christ, also sec. exec. council, adminstrv. com., 1957-61, mem. finance and budget com., exec. sec. stewardship council, 1961-79. Bd. dirs. Ursinus Coll.; trustee Lancaster Theol. Sem. Mem. Nat. Council Chs. in U.S.A. (chmn. sect. stewardship and benevolence, mem. exec. com.). Club: Masons. Contbr. articles to religious publs. Home: 701 Worthington Dr Exton PA 19341 Office: 1505 Race St Philadelphia PA 19102. *At the heart of my life has been a deep concern for people. The investment of my life in and through the Christian Church has been focused on service. The impetus for such a focus derives from my understanding of the Christian faith. Whether as a pastor or as a church administrator my major effort has been toward the growth of people in their service to God and human kind.*

MACKEY, WILLARD CLYDE, JR., advt. exec.; b. Rockford, Ill., Oct. 18, 1922; s. Willard Clyde and Anna B. (Bertog) M.; B.A., Beloit (Wis.) Coll., 1947; m. Lois Eileen Wilson, Sept. 8, 1945; children—Barbara (Mrs. James Seagle, Jr.), William C., David. Copywriter, Howard H. Monk, Rockford, Ill., 1947-50; product advt. mgr. Swift & Co., Chgo., 1950-53; product mgr. Gen. Foods Corp., White Plains, N.Y., 1953-56; v.p., account supr. Sullivan, Stauffer, Colwell & Bayles, N.Y.C., 1956-63; sr. mgmt. officer McCann-Erickson, Inc., Atlanta, 1964-66; exec. v.p., dir. Marschalk Co., Inc., Atlanta, 1967; sr. v.p. Inter-pub. Group Cos., Inc., Atlanta, 1968; v.p., internat. dir. mktg. Coca-Cola Co., Atlanta, 1969-70; chmn. bd., chief exec. officer Marschalk Co., Inc., N.Y.C., 1970-75; pres. McCann-Erickson Worldwide, N.Y.C., 1975-78, vice-chmn. McCann-Erickson Worldwide, 1978—. Trustee, Episcopal Radio/TV Found., Beloit Coll. Served to 1st lt. USMCR, 1943-46. Decorated Silver Star, Purple Heart. Mem. Phi Kappa Psi. Clubs: Woodway Country (Darien, Conn.); New Canaan (Conn.) Country; Piedmont Driving, Peachtree Golf (Atlanta). Home: 1211 Smith Ridge Rd New Canaan CT 06840 Office: 485 Lexington Ave New York NY 10017

MACKEY, WILLIAM FRANCIS, educator; b. Winnipeg, Man., Can., Jan. 26, 1918; s. Thomas Clutterbuck and Margaret Emily (Kennedy) M.; B.A., U. Man., 1939; M.A., Laval U., 1942; A.M., Harvard, 1948; D. Litt., U. Geneva (Switzerland), 1965; m. Ilonka Schmidt, Sept. 2, 1949; children—Ilona, Ariane. Asst. prof. Laval U., Quebec, 1945-48, prof., 1955—, dir. Internat. Center for Research on Bilingualism, 1967-70; sr. lectr. U. London, 1948-50; vis. prof. U. Alta., 1958-59, U. Cal., 1966, U. Tex., San Antonio, 1974, U. Nice, 1975; cons. BBC, 1949-50, Intergovtl. Com. on European Migration, Geneva, 1955-59, Humanities Research Council, 1962-66, Sci. Council Can., 1967-68, U.S. Office Edn., 1968, Ford Found., 1970. Chief of mission UNESCO Lang. Seminar, Helsinki, 1962; chmn., organizer UNESCO Internat. Seminar on Description and Measurement of Bilingualism, Moncton, 1967; participant UNESCO Mission to the Seychelles, 1978. Mem. jury Quebec Lit. and Sci. awards, 1953-56, Can. Council Research Grants Com., 1969, Nat. Com. for Study Bilingual Edn., 1970, Fed. Commn. of Bilingual Dists., 1972-75; mem. Ind. Com. Lang. Tng. in Pub. Service Can., 1975-77. Served with Canadian Army. Recipient Jubilee medal Inst. Linguists (London), 1974. Ford Found. grantee, 1967; Can. Council grantee, 1968. Adair Meml. lectr. McGill U. Fellow Royal Soc. Can., Royal Acad. Belgium; mem. Société de linguistique de Paris, Permanent Internat. Com. Linguists, Linguistic Soc. Am., Internat. Phonetics Assn. Club: Cercle Universitaire de Québec. Author: Language Teaching Analysis, 1965; Bilingualism as a World Problem, 1967; Bilingual Education in a Binational School, 1971; Internat. Bibliography on Bilingualism, 1972; Bilinguisme et contact des langues, 1976; Bilingual Schools for a Bicultural Community, 1977; Le bilinguisme canadien, 1978. Gen. editor: Studies in Bilingual Education, The Multinational Society, Bilingualism in Early Childhood, Sociolinguistic Studies in Language Contact. Contbr. articles to profl. jours. Address: CIRB Pavillon Casault Cité Universitaire Université Laval PQ G1K 7P4 Canada

MACKEY, WILLIAM STURGES, JR., health care exec.; b. St. Louis, May 27, 1921; s. William Sturges and Dorothy Francis (Allison) M.; B.A., Rice U., 1943; M.B.A., U. Tex., 1950; m. Margaret Powell, Dec. 10, 1943; children—Dorothy (Mrs. Jean Claude Lurie), John Powell, James Wescott. Asso. prof. accounting Rice U., 1946-62; v.p., treas. Mandrel Industries, 1962-66; v.p. fin. Tex. Internat. Airlines, 1966-69; pres. Lifemark Corp., Houston, after 1969, now chmn., chief exec. officer; dir. So. Nat. Bank of Houston, Spaw-Glass, Inc. Served to 1st lt., USAAF, 1943-46. Mem. Am. Inst. C.P.A.'s, Tex. Soc. C.P.A.'s, Rice U. Council in Accounting, Houston Philos. Soc., Fedn. Am. Hosps. Episcopalian. Clubs: Houston, Houston City, Lakeside Country, Houstonian. Home: 2011 Albans St Houston TX 77005 Office: PO Box 3448 Houston TX 77001

MACKIE, FREDERICK DAVID, utility exec.; b. Ashland, Wis., Aug. 3, 1910; s. David and Johanna (Zilisch) M.; B.S. in Elec. Engring., U. Wis., 1933; m. Ruth Elizabeth Babcock, Aug. 27, 1937; children—Marilyn Ruth, Frederick D. With Madison Gas & Electric Co. (Wis.), 1934—, exec. v.p., 1964-66, pres., gen. mgr., 1966—, chmn. bd., 1976—, also dir. Recipient Disting. Service citation Coll. Engring., U. Wis., 1969. Registered profl. engr., Wis. Mem. I.E.E.E., Nat., Wis. socs. profl. engrs., Am. Gas Assn., Wis. Utilities Assn., Madison Tech. Club, Edison Electric Inst. Lutheran. Kiwanian. Club: Madison. Home: 58 Golf Course Rd Madison WI 53704 Office: 100 N Fairchild St Madison WI 53701

MAC KIE, FREDERICK JAMES, JR., architect; b. Cheyenne, Wyo., Aug. 13, 1905; s. Frederick James and Mayme A. (Buechner) MacK.; B.S. in Architecture, U. Tex., 1928; m. Lily Bess Voss, May 20, 1931 (dec. 1942); children—Gayle (Mrs. Robert H. Bynes), Paula Jean (Mrs. Michael J. O'Keefe), Frederick James III; m. 2d, Helen Louise Simpson Roberts, Nov. 13, 1944. Partner, MacKie and Kamrath, architects, Houston, 1937-77; mem. Tex. Bd. Archtl. Examiners, 1951-55, chmn., 1954; pres. Tex. Archtl. Found., 1961-62. Served to lt. col. AUS, 1942-46. Named adm. Tex. Navy, 1958. Fellow A.I.A. (pres. Houston 1947, nat. planning com. 1958-61); mem. Tex. Soc. Architects (pres. 1957), Phi Kappa Psi. Episcopalian. Club: Ironwood Country. Home: 73-537 Dalea Ln Palm Desert CA 92260

MACKIE, ROBERT GORDON, costume and fashion designer; b. Monterey Park, Calif., Mar. 24, 1940; s. Charles Robert and Mildred Agnes (Smith) M.; student Chouinard Art Inst., 1958-61; m. Marianne Wolford, Mar. 14, 1960 (div.); 1 son, Robin Gordon. Sketch for Jean Louis, 1962-63; mem. staff Edith Head, 1962-63; designer costumes for film Divorce, American Style, 1966; co-designer for films Funny Lady, 1975, Lady Sings the Blues, 1972; designer for TV shows Diahann Carroll Summer Show, 1976, Sonny and Cher Show, 1976-77, Cher, 1976, Of Three I Sing, 1972, Once Upon a Matrress, 1973, Sonny and Cher Comedy Hour, 1971, Carol Burnett Show, 1967-77, Diana Ross and The Supremes and The Temptations on Broadway, 1969, Fred Astaire Show, 1968, Carol Channing Presents the Seven Deadly Sins, 1968, Kismet, 1967, Carousel, 1967, Brigadoon, 1966, Alice Through the Looking Glass, 1967; also for various specials and nightclub acts; co-designer theatrical prodns. Lorelei, 1972, On The Town, 1971. Recipient Costume Designers Guild award, 1968; Emmy award, 1969, 76; co-recipient Emmy award, 1967. Democrat. Author: Dressing for Glamour, 1979. Address: 8636 Melrose Ave Los Angeles CA 90069*

MACKIMM, J(AMES) BRADLEY, publisher; b. Chgo., Oct. 5, 1932; s. Alexander George and Rose Mary (Bradley) MacK.; B.A., Denison U., 1954; m. Carol Ann Syvertsen, Dec. 27, 1955; children—Catherine, Leslie, Carrie. Dist. mgr. Penton Pub. Co., Cleve., 1957-58, Detroit, 1958-63, Chgo., 1964-65; dist. mgr. McGraw-Hill, Inc., Chgo., 1965-67, regional mgr., 1967, advt. sales mgr., N.Y.C., 1968-73, publisher med. jours., 1973-76, MD publications, 1976-78, Med. Recert. Assos., 1979—. Pres., Midland Parent Tchrs. Orgn., Rye, N.Y., 1972, Joseph Sears Parent Tchrs. Orgn., Kenilworth, Ill., 1967, Denison U. Alumni Council, 1974-76. Served to 1st lt. USAF, 1954. Clubs: Chicago Athletic Assn.; Manursing Island; Apawamis. Home: 62 Apawamis Ave Rye NY 10580 Office: 190 E Post Rd White Plains NY 10601

MACKIN, BERNARD JOHN, natural resource co. exec.; b. Dallas, Sept. 5, 1917; s. James Stephen and Martha (Dettmann) M.; B.B.A., U. Tex.; also LL.B.; m. Elizabeth Storie, July 12, 1946. Admitted to Tex. bar; asso. firm Baker & Botts, Houston, 1946-52, mem. firm, 1952-79, sr. mem., 1979; chmn. bd., chief exec. officer Zapata Corp., Houston, 1979—; dir. Tenneco Inc., Houston, Houston Nat. Bank. Served to maj., inf. U.S. Army, 1941-46. Decorated Bronze Star. Mem. Internat. Bar Assn., Am. Bar Assn., Tex. Bar Assn., various bus. and trade assns. Roman Catholic. Clubs: Houston Country, Tejas, Remada (Houston); Recess (N.Y.C.). Office: PO Box 4241 Houston TX 77001

MACKIN, COOPER RICHERSON, univ. dean; b. Selma, Ala., Apr. 26, 1933; s. Thomas R. and Muriel (Green) M.; B.A., Troy State Coll., 1956; M.A., Tulane U., 1958; Ph.D., Rice U., 1962; m. Catherine Barragy, Feb. 15, 1958; children—Michele, Patrick, Daniel. Instr., Tex. So. U., 1958-59; asst. prof. N. Tex. State U., Denton, 1962-63; asst. prof. U. New Orleans, 1963-66, asso. prof., 1966-70, prof. English, 1970—, chmn. dept., 1966-69, dean Coll. Liberal Arts, 1969—. Bd. dirs. New Orleans chpt. NCCJ, 1969-79. Served with AUS, 1953-55. Mem. Renaissance Soc. Am., Milton Soc. Am., S. Central Modern Lang. Assn. Author: William Styron, 1969. Contbr. articles on 17th century English lit. to profl. jours. Home: 18 Charlotte Dr New Orleans LA 70122

MACKIN, FRANCIS CHARLES, priest, univ. provost; b. Boston, Nov. 4, 1919; s. Jeremiah Joseph and Margaret Gertrude (Sullivan) M.; student Holy Cross Coll., 1942; Ph.L., Weston Coll., 1948; S.T.L., 1954; M.A., Boston Coll., 1951. Joined Soc. of Jesus, 1942; ordained priest Roman Catholic Ch., 1954; instr. theology Boston Coll., Chestnut Hill, Mass., 1955-56, asst. dean students, 1956-57, asst. dir. admissions, 1958-64, exec. asst. to pres., 1959-64; rector, headmaster Cranwell Sch., Lenox, Mass., 1964-70; provost Fordham U. at Lincoln Center, N.Y.C., 1970-79, v.p., Westchester, 1979—. Bd. dirs. N.Y. chpt. ARC; mem. adv. bd. African Student Aid Fund; trustee Loyola Sch.; mem. N.Y.C. adv. council Cornell U. Coop. Extension Program; active NCCJ; mem. Montserrat Nat. Trust. Mem. Am. Council on Edn., Nat. Cath. Ednl. Assn., Phi Delta Kappa. Home: Fordham U Bronx NY 10458 Office: Grad Center Fordham U in Westchester Tarrytown NY 10591

MACKINLAY, IAN, architect; b. San Francisco, Aug. 13, 1926; s. John B. and Ruth (Kroll) M.; B. Arch., U. Cal. at Berkeley, 1958; m. Ann Strong, Aug. 25, 1951; children—Jock, Katherine, Bruce, Clifton, Robert. Chief engr. European Exchange System, Nuremberg, Germany, 1951-57; instr. architecture U. Cal. at Berkeley, 1957-58; pres. Mackinlay/Winnacker/McNeil A.I.A. & Assos., Oakland, Cal., Honolulu and Agana, Guam, 1958—; prin. works include Syntex Interim Facilities, Palo Alto, Cal., 1968, Cornell U. Synchrotron Lab., 1968, Boreal Ridge Ski Lodge, Sierra Mountains, Cal., 1966. Served with USNR, 1945-46. Recipient Archtl. award excellence Am. Inst. Steel Constrn., 1968; 1st honor award Homes for Better Living, 1968, Design award Progressive Architecture mag., 1967; award of merit Western Homes Awards, 1967-68, honor award, 1965-66, award of merit, 1965-66; Mem. A.I.A. (chmn. Redwood Task Force Com. 1967-68, pub. relations com. San Francisco chpt. 1968; Nat. honor award 1967,68, Bay Area Honor award No. Cal. chpt. 1967), Soc. Archtl. Historians, Sierra Club, Planning and Conservation League, Am. Arbitration Assn., USSA (bd. dirs. 1968-69), Far West (1st v.p. 1968-69) ski assns. Office: 2333 Harrison St Oakland CA 94612

MAC KINNEY, ARCHIE ALLEN, JR., physician; b. St. Paul, Aug. 16, 1929; s. Archie Allen and Doris (Hoops) MacK.; B.A., Wheaton (Ill.) Coll., 1951; M.D., U. Rochester, 1955; m. Shirley Schaefer, Apr. 9, 1955; children—Julianne, Theodore, John. Intern, resident in medicine U. Wis. Hosp., 1955-59; clin. asso. NIH, 1959-61; clin. investigator VA, 1961-64; asst. prof. medicine U. Wis., Madison, 1964-68, asso. prof., 1968-74, prof., 1974—; chief hematology VA Hosp., Madison, 1964—, chief nuclear medicine, 1964-73, 78-79. Served with USPHS, 1959-61. Danforth asso., 1962. Mem. Am. Soc. Hematology, Am. Fedn. Clin. Research, Central Soc. Clin. Research. Republican. Baptist. Contbr. articles to med. jours. Home: 190 N Prospect Madison WI 53705 Office: 2500 Overlook Terr Madison WI 53705

MACKINNON, ALECK MACDONALD, chem-pharm. co. exec.; b. Phila., Dec. 2, 1924; s. George Aleck and Eleanor (Donaghy) MacK.; B.S. in Indsl. Engring., Pa. State U., 1948; M.B.A. in Corp. Finance, Wharton Sch. of U. Pa., 1954; m. Marion Louise Lewis, Aug. 21, 1948; children—Larry Donald, Janis Lee, Lynn Ann, Susan Beth. With Atlantic Refining Co., 1948-58; with Warner-Lambert Pharm. Co., 1958-67, treas., 1961-67; v.p. finance CIBA Corp., 1967-68, exec. v.p., 1968-70; v.p. CIBA-GEIGY Corp., 1970—, pres. pharms. div., 1977-79, pres. CIBA-GEIGY Corp., 1980—, also dir.; dir. Toms River Chem. Corp., Airwick Industries, Inc., Alza Corp, Summit Bancorp. Industry chmn. United Fund Morris County, 1960-61, mem. budget com., 1962, capital fund com., 1966-70, investment com., 1967-70. Trustee Morris County Soc. Crippled Children and Adults, 1966-68. Served to lt. (j.g.) USNR, 1943-46. Mem. Am. Mgmt. Assn. (financial planning council 1964-71, mem. pres.'s council 1972—), Assn. Corp. Growth (trustee 1964-67), Fin. Execs. Inst. (vice chmn. drug and cosmetic sect. 1964-66), Pharm. Mfrs. Assn. (vice chmn. fin. sect. 1967, bd. dirs. 1977—). Clubs: Country of Darien, Tokeneke. Home: 31 Old Farm Rd Darien CT 06820 Office: Ardsley NY 10502

MACKINNON, ALEXANDER DONALD, lawyer; b. Bushkill, Pa., Oct. 15, 1895; s. Alexander and Mary (Kennedy) MacK.; student Pa. State Coll., 1915-18, U. Mich. Law Sch., 1919-20; LL.B., Columbia, 1922; m. Helen Richardson Smith, Sept. 10, 1924; children—Nancy Jean (Mrs. Cecil H. London), Donna (Mrs. Floyd O. Flom). Admitted to N.Y. bar, 1923, since practiced in N.Y.C.; partner firm Milbank, Tweed, Hadley and McCloy, 1934—. Pres., James Founds., N.Y.C.; bd. visitors Columbia Law Sch. Mem. Am., N.Y. State bar assns., Assn. Bar City N.Y., Am. Coll. Trial Lawyers, Columbia Law Sch. Alumni Assn. (pres. 1959-60), N.Y. County Lawyers Assn. Clubs: Union, St. Andrew's Soc., Wall Street (N.Y.C.); Rock Spring (West Orange, N.J.); Morristown (N.J.). Home: 76 Burnett Terr West Orange NJ 07059 Office: 1 Chase Manhattan Plaza New York City NY 10005

MACKINNON, CYRUS LELAND, newspaper exec.; b. Eldorado, Kans., Aug. 16, 1916; s. Frederick Benjamin and Cecil Prescott (Leland) MacK.; B.A., Dartmouth, 1938; m. Helen Wigglesworth, Feb. 25, 1939; children—Stephen, Peter, Cecil, Anne. Gen. trainee Automatic Electric Co., Chgo., 1938-41; personnel dir. Sherwin-Williams Co., Chgo., 1941-46; gen. mgr. Franklin Assn., Chgo., 1946-55; mng. dir. Inst. Newspaper Operations (name later changed to Am. Newspaper Pubs. Assn. Research Inst.), Chgo., 1955-59; sales mgr., adminstr. R.R. Donnelley & Sons, Chgo., 1959-65; exec. v.p. Courier-Jour., Standard Gravure Corp., WHAS, Inc., 1965-75, pres. Courier-Jour. & Louisville Times, 1975—, exec.

v.p. Standard Gravure Corp.; v.p. WHAS Inc.; dir. Bowne & Co., Inc., 1977—, Nat. Pub. Radio, 1978—. Met. chmn. Nat. Alliance Businessmen 1968—. Chmn. bd. Action Now, Inc.; bd. dirs. Falls Region Health Council, 1968-73, Housing Now, Inc., Better Govt. Assn. Ill., 1954-59; trustee Nat. Found./March of Dimes, 1977—. Mem. Indsl. Relations Assn. Chgo. (dir., pres. 1946), So. Newspaper Pubs. Assn., Casque and Gauntlet Soc., Psi Upsilon. Rotarian. Clubs: Helium, Jefferson, Louisville Country, River Valley (Louisville). Home: 5803 Orion Rd Glenview KY 40025 Office: 525 W Broadway Louisville KY 40202

MAC KINNON, FRANK, educator; b. Charlottetown, P.E.I., Can., Apr. 24, 1919; s. Murdoch and Perle (Taylor) MacK.; B.A. with honors, McGill U., 1941; M.A., U. Toronto, 1942, Ph.D., 1950; LL.D. (hon.), U. N.B., 1950, Dalhousie U., 1964; m. Daphne Martin, Apr. 27, 1943; children—Philip, David, Peter, Pamela. Indsl. relations officer Dept. Labor, Ottawa, Can., 1942-45; lectr. polit. sci. U. Toronto, 1945-46; chmn. dept. polit. sci. Carleton U., Ottawa, 1946-49; prin. Prince of Wales Coll., Charlottetown, P.E.I., 1949-68; prof. polit. sci. U. Calgary (Alta., Can.), 1968—. Pres. Atlantic Provinces Econ. Council, 1957-59; mem. Can. Council, 1957-63. Decorated Order of Can. Mem. Can. Polit. Sci. Assn. (v.p. 1961-63), Inst. Pub. Adminstrn. Can. (pres. 1964-65), Can. Hist. Assn. Clubs: Canadian, Royal Overseas League (London). Author: The Politics of Education, 1960; Postures and Politics, 1973; The Crown in Canada, 1976; others. Home: 1130 Crescent Rd Calgary AB T2M 4A8 Canada Office: U Calgary Calgary AB Canada

MACKINNON, GEORGE E., U.S. judge; b. St. Paul, Apr. 22, 1906; s. James Alexander Wiley and Cora Blanche (Asselstine) MacK.; student U. Colo., 1923-24; LL.B., U. Minn., 1929; m. Elizabeth Valentine Davis, August 20, 1938; children—Catharine Alice, James Davis, Leonard Davis. Admitted to Minn. bar, 1929, U.S. Supreme Ct. bar; asst. gen. counsel Investors Syndicate, Mpls., 1929-42; engaged pvt. practice law, 1949-53, 58-61; elected mem. Minn. Ho. of Reps. from 29th dist., 1934, 36, 38, 40; mem. 80th Congress 1947-49, 3d Minn. Dist.; U.S. dist. atty. for Minn., 1953-58; spl. asst. to U.S. atty. gen., 1960; gen. counsel, v.p. Investors Mut. Funds, Mpls., 1961-69; judge U.S. Ct. Appeals for D.C. Circuit, 1969—; pres. judge U.S. Fgn. Intelligence Surveillance Ct. of Rev., 1979—. Republican nominee for Gov. of Minn., 1958. Served to comdr. U.S. Navy Air Force, 1942-46; Cited for meritorious service by comdr. Air Force U.S. Atlantic Fleet. Mem. Am., Minn., Hennepin County bar assns., Delta Tau Delta, Phi Delta Phi. Republican. Episcopalian. Clubs: Minneapolis; Lawyers (Washington); Masons (32 deg.). Author: Minn. State Reorganization Act, 1939; State Civil Service Law, 1939; Old Age Assistance Act, 1936. Home: 11333 Willowbrook Dr Potomac MD 20854 Office: US Court House Washington DC 20001

MAC KINNON, GREGORY ALOYSIUS, educator, clergyman; b. Antigonish, N.S., Can., June 16, 1925; s. William Francis and Mary Patricia (Chisholm) MacK.; B.A., St. Francis Xavier U., 1946; S.T.L., Ottawa U., 1960, S.T.D., Ph.D., 1964. Ordained priest Roman Catholic Ch., 1950; asso. pastor Mt. Carmel Parish, New Waterford, N.S., 1950-54; mem. staff St. Francis Xavier U., Antigonish, 1954-60, 63—, asso. dean arts, dir. summer sch., 1970-78, pres., vice chancellor, 1978—. Address: Office of Pres St Francis Xavier U Antigonish NS B2G 1C0 Canada

MACKLE, FRANCIS ELLIOTT, JR., home builder, community developer; b. Atlanta, July 23, 1916; s. Francis Elliott and Theresa Agnes (Roche) M.; B.S. in Engring., Vanderbilt U., 1938; m. Virginia Steward, Sept. 3, 1940; children—Francis Elliott III, Nancy Radcliffe. Joined Mackle Co., 1938, v.p., 1947-71, pres., 1971—; with Gen. Devel. Corp., 1954-61, pres., dir., 1958-61, chmn. bd., 1961; pres. Mackle Bros., Inc., 1962-63; pres., chief exec. officer, dir. Deltona Corp., 1963-79, chmn., chief exec. officer, 1979—; dir. Mut. of Omaha Ins. Co., W.R. Grace & Co., Companion Life Ins. Co., United Benefit Life Ins. Co. Adv. bd. FHA, 1961-62; pres. Fla. div. Horsemen's Benevolent and Protective Assn., 1964-65, nat. pres., 1964-69; mem. Inter-Am. Center Authority, 1966-69. Trustee United Fund Dade County, 1962-66, Mercy Hosp., 1971—; bd. lay trustees U. Notre Dame, 1964. Served as lt., C.E. Corps, USNR, World War II. Roman Catholic (chmn. diocesan devel. fund 1962). Home: 1410 W 25th St Sunset Island No 2 Miami Beach FL 33140 Office: 3250 SW 3d Ave Miami FL 33129

MACKLEM, MICHAEL KIRKPATRICK, publisher; b. Toronto, Ont., Can., July 12, 1928; s. Hedley Clark and Mary Eileen (Kirkpatrick) M.; B.A., U. Toronto, 1950; A.M. (Charles Scribner fellow), Princeton U., 1952, Ph.D. (Porter Ogden Jacobus fellow, Royal Soc. Can. fellow), 1954; m. Anne Woodburne Hardy, Dec. 30, 1950; children—Timothy Street, Nicholas Hardy. Instr., English, Yale U., New Haven, 1954-55; staff editor Ency. Canadiana, 1955-58; asst. to dir. Humanities Research Council of Can., 1958-60; gen. mgr. Oberon Press, Ottawa, Ont., 1966—; pres. Michael, Hardy, Ltd., Ottawa, 1972—. Can. Council fellow, 1964-65. Author: The Anatomy of the World: Relations Between Natural and Moral Law from Donne to Pope, 1958; God Have Mercy: The Life of John Fisher of Rochester, 1967; Cinderella, 1969; Voyages to New France 1615-1618, 1970; Voyages to New France 1599-1603, 1971; The Sleeping Beauty, 1973; Jacques The Woodcutter, 1977; Liberty and the Holy City, 1978. Home: 555 Maple Ln Ottawa ON K1M 0N7 Canada Office: Oberon Press 401a Inn of the Provinces Ottawa ON K1R 7S8 Canada

MACKLER, TINA, artist; b. London, Eng.; d. Leon and Ethel (Tischler) Mackler; student Arts Students League, N.Y.C., Indsl. Sch. Design, N.Y.C., New Sch., N.Y.C.; div.; 1 dau., Leonore Bloom. Tchr. art Nat. Acad. Ballet, N.Y.C., 1966-69; tchr. adults West Side YMCA, N.Y.C.; illustrator Informal Dictionary of Ballet, World Pub. Co.; co-author, illustrator To Dance, To Live; pub. Dance Horizons, 1977; one-person shows Alfred Valente Gallery, N.Y.C., 1967, Mus. Performing Arts, N.Y.C., 1973, Adelphi U., L.I., N.Y., 1975, Phila. Art Alliance, 1976, Jackson (Miss.) Mus. Art, 1978, Guild Gallery, N.Y.C., 1979; exhibited in group shows Alfredo Gallery, N.Y.C., 1964, 1966, Dutchess Hall Gallery, Poughkeepsie, N.Y., 1969, Wright/Hepburn/Webster Gallery, N.Y.C., 1960, 70, N.Y. Pub. Library, 1973, O'Keefe Centre, Ont., Can., 1974, Ball State U., 1974, N.A.D. annual, 1974, Audubon Artists Annual, 1975, Nat. Pastel Show, 1975, Commedia Dell Art Adelphi U., 1974, Guild Gallery, N.Y.C., 1978; works rep. in permanent collections Nat. Collection Fine Prints, Smithsonian Instn., Washington, Israel Mus., Jerusalem, La Jolla (Calif.) Mus., U. Wis. Mus., Circus World Mus., Baraboo, Wis., Fairleigh Dickinson U., Circus Hall of Fame Mus., Sarasota, Fla., Adelphi U., Mus. Performing Arts Lincoln Center, N.Y.C., Jackson (Miss.) Mus. Art, Original Print Collectors Group Ltd., also notable pvt. collections Am. and abroad; completed series of studies on Spanish dance and impressions of Spain for Spanish Ministry Info. and Tourism, 1976; rep. in Bordon Pub. Co.'s Master Draughtsman Series of Ballet Drawings along with Degas; original stone lithographs of Marcel Marceau, Margot Fonteyn and Rudolf Nureyev and numerous dance soloists N.Y. Times Mag., also nat. mags., 1975-78. Works shown on TV: Joe Franklin Show, 1979, NBC-TV preview Mus. Performing Arts, Lincoln Center, 1973, Channel 13 TV Art Auction, 1978, 79. Home: 25 Central Park W New York NY 10023.

I have long felt the influence which the arts exert on the minds and hearts of mankind. Believing, as I do, that the world today stands in need of spiritual truths, ideals and moral standards, it is my desire to reach out and set before the public some of the beauty and grandeur which reside in the human soul and expresses itself through that most primal art - the dance.

MACKLIN, GORDON STANLEY, assn. ofcl.; b. Cleve., May 13, 1928; s. Gordon Stanley and Evelyn B. (Cosline) M.; B.A., Brown U., 1950; m. Marilyn C. Michell, Aug. 18, 1951; children—Gordon Stanley III, Nancy Jean, Lisa Ann, Gary David. With McDonald & Co., Cleve., 1950-70, sales rep., Findlay, O., 1951-58, gen. partner, 1958-70, with syndicate and sales mgmt. dept., 1958-61, corporate finance dept., 1961-70, mem. exec. com., 1967-70; pres. Nat. Assn. of Securities Dealeas, Inc., 1970—; chmn. bd. Nat. Clearing Corp., 1970-76. Mem. Newcomen Soc., Delta Tau Delta. Methodist. Clubs: Burning Tree, Metropolitan, Congressional Country (Bethesda, Md.); George Town, Univ. (Washington); Univ. (N.Y.C.). Home: 8212 Burning Tree Rd Bethesda MD 20034 also St Andrews Club Apt 102 Delray Beach FL 33444 Office: 1735 K St NW Washington DC 20006

MACKMULL, JACK VINCENT, army officer; b. Dayton, Ohio, Dec. 1, 1927; s. Milford F. and Olivia A. (Mast) M.; B.S., U.S. Mil. Acad., 1950; grad. Command and Gen. Staff Coll., 1968; m. Beverly M. Boehm, June 17, 1950; children—Jack V., Stephen J., Kimberly A. Commd. 2d lt. U.S. Army, 1950, advanced through grades to maj. gen., 1977; chief, warrant officer br., Washington, 1966-67; comdr. 164th combat aviation group, Vietnam, 1968; comdg. gen. 1st. aviation brigade, Vietnam, 1972-73; dep. comdg. gen. AVSCOM, St. Louis, 1973-74; asst. div. comdr. 101st div., Fort Campbell, Ky., 1975-76; chief of staff 18th airborne corps, Ft. Bragg, N.C., 1976-77; comdg. gen. John F. Kennedy Center Mil. Assistance, comdt. U.S. Army Inst. Mil. Assistance, Ft. Bragg, 1977—. Decorated Legion of Merit with 4 oak leaf clusters, Silver Star, Bronze Star with oak leaf cluster, others. Mem. U.S. Army Spl. Forces Assn. (hon. pres.), Assn. U.S. Army, Assn. Grads. U.S. Mil. Acad. Home: 2 Dupont Plaza Fort Bragg NC 28307 Office: US Army John F Kennedy Center for Mil Assistance Fort Bragg NC 28307

MACKOWSKI, JOHN JOSEPH, ins. co. exec.; b. Westport, Mass., Feb. 1, 1926; s. John J. and Victoria K. (Skript) Mieczkowski; A.B., Duke, 1948; postgrad. Harvard Bus. Sch., 1970-71; m. Ruth Williams, Feb. 3, 1951; children—Martha, John Matthew, Daniel, Joan. With Ins. Co. of N.Am., Boston, Phila., Chgo., 1948-51; with Atlantic Mut. Ins. Co., N.Y.C., 1951—, now pres.; trustee-dir. Atlantic Mut. Centennial Ins. Cos. Trustee Coll. of Ins.; bd. dirs. Ins. Info. Inst., YMCA Greater N.Y.; bd. mgrs. Am. Bur. Shipping. Served to 1st lt. USMCR, 1943-46. Mem. Sigma Chi, Beta Lambda. Episcopalian. Clubs: Tokeneke (Darien, Conn.); Downtown Assn., Univ., Econ. (N.Y.). Home: 5 East Trail Darien CT 06820 Office: 45 Wall St New York City NY 10005

MACKSEY, RICHARD ALAN, educator; b. Glen Ridge, N.J., July 25, 1931; s. Kenneth William and Hazel Mae (Hennie) M.; student Princeton U., 1948-51, Oxford U., 1951; M.A., Johns Hopkins U., 1954, Ph.D., 1957; m. Catherine Deriseau Chance, Sept. 17, 1956; 1 son, Richard Alan Jr. instr. Johns Hopkins U., 1953-55; instr. English and classics Loyola U., 1956-57, asst. prof., 1957-58; asst. prof. Writing Seminars, Johns Hopkins U., 1958-64, asso. prof. humanistic studies, 1964-72, chmn. comparative lit. program, 1968—, prof. humanistic studies, dir. Humanities Center, 1973—; lectr. Balt. Mus. Art, 1964-65, 77—; dir. Bollingen Poetry Festivals, Theatre Hopkins, Film Workshop, Tantamount Films, Film Forum, Dialogue of the Arts, Friends of Johns Hopkins Library. Mem. Balt. Bicentennial Com., Md. Film Festival Com., Balt. Film Festival Com., Md. Com. on Adult Edn. Served to major USAR. Mem. Modern Lang. Assn., English Inst., South Atlantic Modern Lang. Assn., Am. Soc. Aesthetics, Coll. English Assn., AAUP, Mediaeval Academy, Renaissance Soc., Semiotic Soc. Am. (editorial bd.), Phi Beta Kappa, Lambda Iota Tau. Clubs: Grolier, Hamilton St., Bibliophiles, Tudor and Stuart (dir.). Author: La Lanterne magique, 1958, Florilegium anglicum, 1964 (poetry); The Structuralist Controversy, 1972; Velocities of Change, 1974; The Pioneer Century, 1976; and others. Editor Modern Lang. Notes, 1962—; Glyph: Johns Hopkins Textual Studies, 1977—; mem. editorial bds. various jours., Johns Hopkins Univ. Press. Home: 107 St Martin's Rd Baltimore MD 21218 Office: Humanities Center Johns Hopkins U Baltimore MD 21218

MACLAGAN, JOHN LYALL, petroleum co. exec.; b. Lethbridge, Alta., Can., Oct. 26, 1929; s. Frederick Alexander Lyall and Dora Ellen (Dean) M.; B.Commerce, U. Alta., 1952; m. Joan Lily Prince, July 15, 1965; 1 dau., Susan. Staff auditor Price Waterhouse & Co., Calgary, 1952-56; accountant Union Oil Co. of Calif., Alta., 1956-61; mgr. accounting Union Oil Co. of Can., Ltd., Calgary, 1961-72, treas., comptroller, 1972-75, v.p. fin., treas., 1975—. Chartered accountant, Alta. Mem. Canadian Inst. Chartered Accountants, Fin. Execs. Inst. Clubs: Calgary Petroleum, Earl Grey Golf. Home: 308 Roxborough Rd SW Calgary AB T2S 0R4 Canada Office: 335 8th Ave SW Calgary AB T2P 1C9 Canada

MACLAINE, ALLAN HUGH, educator; b. Montreal, Can., Oct. 24, 1924; B.A., McGill U., 1945; Ph.D. in English, Brown U., 1951. Instr. English, McGill U., 1946-47, Brown U., 1947-50, U. Mass., 1951-54; from asst. prof. to prof. Tex. Christian U., 1954-62; prof. English, U.R.I., 1962—, also dean div. univ. extension, 1967-71. Mem. Coll. English Assn. (pres. 1965, dir. 1961-66), Modern Lang. Assn. Author: Student's Comprehensive Guide to the Canterbury Tales, 1964; Robert Fergusson, 1965; also articles. Address: care Dept English Univ Rhode Island Kingston RI 02881

MACLAINE, SHIRLEY, actress; b. Richmond, Va., Apr. 24, 1934; d. Ira O. and Kathlyn (MacLean) Beatty; ed. high sch.; m. Steve Parker, Sept. 17, 1954; 1 dau., Stephanie Sachiko. Broadway plays include Me and Juliet, 1953, Pajama Game, 1954; actress movies The Touble With Harry, 1954, Artists and Models, 1954, Around the World in 80 Days, 1955-56, Hot Spell, 1957, The Matchmaker, 1957, The Sheepman, 1957, Some Came Running, 1958 (Fgn. Press award 1959), Ask Any Girl (Silver Bear award as best actress Internat. Berlin Film Festival), 1959, Career, 1959, Can-Can, 1959, The Apartment (Best Actress prize Venice Film Festival), 1959, Children's Hour, 1960, Two for the Seesaw, 1962, Irma La Douce, 1963, What A Way to Go and The Yellow Rolls Royce, 1964, John Goldfarb Please Come Home, 1965, Gambit and Woman Times Seven, 1967, The Bliss of Mrs. Blossom and Two Mules for Sister Sara, 1969, Desperate Characters, 1971, The Possession of Joel Delaney, 1972, The Turning Point, 1977, Being There, 1979; TV show Shirley's World, 1971-72. Author: Don't Fall Off the Mountain, 1970; The New Celebrity Cookbook, 1973; You Can Get There From Here, 1975; editor: McGovern: The Man and His Beliefs, 1972. Office: care Internat Creative Mgmt 8899 Beverly Blvd Los Angeles CA 90048*

MACLAMROC, JAMES GWALTNEY WESTWARREN, lawyer, financier, philanthropist; b. Greensboro, N.C.; s. James Robbins and Grace (West) MacL.; A.B., U. N.C.; J.D., Yale; m. Maxine Pugh, Jan. 19, 1954; children—Alan G. W., Brian G.W. Admitted to N.C. bar, also U.S. Supreme Ct. bar; practice law, Greensboro. Owner, developer Lamrocton residential subdiv., Greensboro; pres. Lamrocton Co., WKIX Broadcasting Co., Tri-Cities Broadcasting Co., Golden Strand Broadcasting Co. Mem. N.C. Hwy. Commn.; chmn. Greater Greensboro Planning Bd., Greater Greensboro Arterial Rds. Commn.; mem. standing com. history, scenario and title Greensboro Sesquicentennial Celebration Pageant, Guilford County com. N.C. Confederate Centennial Commn., Guilford County com. N.C. Am. Revolution Bicentennial Commn., Guilford County Bicentennial Commn.; chmn. finance and bldg. com., mem. exec. com. Carolina Charter Tercentenary Commn.; chmn. finance com. Historic Hillsborough Commn.; past mem. legislative com. N.C. Library Assn.; mem. nat. com., chmn. N.C. com. Yale Law Library Fund; county historian Guilford County. Trustee Dolley Madison Found., John M. Morehead Commn.; pres., trustee Greensboro Hist. Museum. Ky. col.; adm. N.C. Navy; donor MacLamroc Collection of Ancestral Family Portraits to N.C. Mus. Art, land for MacLamroc State Park nr. Greensboro. Mem. Am. (chmn. com. magistrates and traffic cts.), N.C. (past mem. exec. com., 1st v.p., chmn. com. justices peace), Greensboro bar assns., N.C. State Bar, Am. Judicature Soc., Am. Arbitration Assn. (nat. panel), Greensboro Council Social Agys., Greensboro Community Council, Greensboro C. of C. (dir., mem. exec. com., chmn. good rds. div.), Newcomen Soc., N.C. Soc. Local and County Historians (v.p., adv. com.), N.C. Lit. and Hist. Assn. (v.p., exec. com.), Historic Preservation Soc. N.C. (past v.p., Cannon cup 1958), Assn. Preservation Va. Antiquities, Va. Hist. Soc., Ulster-Scot Hist. Soc., N.C. Art Soc., Archael. Soc. N.C. (exec. com.), New Eng. Historic Geneal. Soc., Harleian Soc. (London, Eng.), Soc. Genealogists (Eng.), Scottish Geneal. Soc., English-Speaking Union, Pilgrims U.S., Order Crown Charlemagne, Order Three Crusades, Mil. Order Crusades, Baronial Order Magna Charta, Plantagenet Soc., Order Crown in Am., Nat. Soc. Ams. Royal Descent, Jamestowne Soc., Soc. Colonial Wars (1st gov. N.C.), Huguenot Soc., Soc. Descs. Colonial Clergy (chancellor), Order Ams. Armorial Ancestry, S.A.R. (past pres. N.C.), S.R., Soc. War 1812, Sons Confederate Vets. (comdr. N.C.), Nat. Trust Historic Preservation, N.C. Civil War Roundtable (dir., exec. com.), Sigma Chi, Phi Delta Phi. Episcopalian. Mason (Shriner), Kiwanian. Clubs: Greensboro Country, Merchants and Manufacturers (past v.p.), Executives, Sedgefield Country (Greensboro); Twin City (Winston-Salem, N.C.); Corbey Court (Yale); Yale (N.Y.C.). Contbr. to newspapers, mags., radio, TV. Inventor MacLamroc phonetic alphabet. Home: 191O Pembroke Rd Greensboro NC 27408 Office: 212 W Friendly Ave Greensboro NC 27401

MACLANE, SAUNDERS, mathematician, educator; b. Taftville, Conn., Aug. 4, 1909; s. Donald Bradford and Winifred (Saunders) MacL.; Ph.B., Yale, 1930; A.M., U. Chgo., 1931; D.Phil., Goettingen, Germany, 1934; D.Sc. (hon.), Purdue U., 1965, Yale, 1969, Coe Coll., 1973, U. Pa., 1977; LL.D., Glasgow U. (Scotland), 1971; m. Dorothy M. Jones, July 21, 1933; children—Margaret Ferguson, Cynthia M. Hay. Sterling Research fellow, Yale, 1933-34; Benjamin Peirce instr., Harvard, 1934-36; instr. Cornell U., 1936-37, U. Chgo., 1937-38; asst. prof. Harvard, 1938-41, asso. prof., 1941-46, prof. 1946-47; prof. math. U. Chgo., 1947-63, chmn. dept., 1952-58, Max Mason Distinguished Service prof. of math., 1963—; exec. com. mem. Internat. Math. Union, 1954-58; research mathematician Applied Math. Group, Columbia, 1943-44, dir., 1944-45. Mem. Nat. Sci. Bd., 1974—. John Simon Guggenheim fellow, 1947-48, 72-73. Awarded Chauvenet prize for mathematical exposition by Math. Assn. Am., 1941, Montclair Yale Cup, 1929. Mem. Am. Math. Soc. (v.p. 1946-47, council 1939-41, pres. 1973-74), Math. Assn. Am. (v.p. 1948-49, pres. 1950-52, Distinguished Service award 1975), Nat. Acad. Sci. (council 1958-61, 69-72, v.p. 1973—, chmn. editorial bd. procs. 1960-68), Royal Danish Acad. Scis. (fgn. mem.), Am. Philos. Soc. (mem. council 1960-63, v.p. 1968-71), Akademie der Wissenschaften (Heidelberg), Royal Soc. Edinburgh, Assn. for Symbolic Logic (exec. com. 1945-47), Am. Acad. Arts and Sci., Phi Beta Kappa, Sigma Xi. Conglist. Author: (with Garrett Birkhoff) Survey of Modern Algebra. 1942; Homology, 1963; (with Garrett Birkhoff) Algebra, 1967; Categories for the Working Mathematician, 1971. Editor bull. Am. Math. Soc., 1943-46, mng. editor, 1946-47; editor, Transactions Am. Math. Soc., 1949-54. Chmn. editl. com. Carus Math. Monographs, 1940-45. Contbr. sci. articles on math. to Bull. of Am. Math. Soc., Transactions of the Am. Math. Soc., Duke Math. Jour., Annals Math. Home: 5712 S Dorchester Ave Chicago IL 60637

MACLAREN, GRANT WOODWARD, merchant; b. Vancouver, B.C., Can., June 18, 1933; s. Grant Oswald and Elizabeth Eleanor (Sanders) MacL.; grad. U. B.C.; chartered accountant; m. Sherrill Maxwell, May 17, 1962; children—Nicola Eleanor, Michelle Maxwell, Grant Douglas, Monique Elizabeth. With Price Waterhouse Co., chartered accountants, Vancouver; with Woodward Dept. Stores Ltd., Vancouver, store mgr., now exec. v.p., also dir. Trustee Lester Pearson Coll. Pacific; bd. dirs., 1st v.p. B.C. Heart Found. Mem. Chartered Accountants Assn. Clubs: Vancouver Arbutus. Home: 1529 W 35th St Vancouver BC V6M 1H1 Canada Office: 101 W Hastings St Vancouver BC V6A 1N5 Canada

MACLAREN, ROY, publisher, mem. Parliament; b. Vancouver, B.C., Can., Oct. 26, 1934; s. Wilbur and Anne (Graham) MacL.; B.A., U. B.C., 1955; M.A., U. Cambridge (Eng.), 1957; postgrad. Harvard Grad. Sch. Bus. Adminstrn., 1974; m. Alethea Mitchell, June 25, 1959; children—Ian, Vanessa, Malcolm. Fgn. service officer Can. Diplomatic Service in Vietnam, Czechoslovakia, Switzerland, UN, 1957-69; dir. corporate pub. affairs Massey-Ferguson Ltd., Toronto, Ont., 1969-74; chmn., chief exec. officer Ogilvy & Mather (Can.), Toronto, 1974-76; pub. Canadian Bus. Mag.; pres. C.B. Media Ltd.; dir. Leigh Instruments. Spl. lectr. U. Toronto, 1970-76. Chmn. Canadian Govt. Task Force on Relations Between Govt. and Bus., 1976. Mem. Toronto Planning Bd., 1974-76; mem. Parliament of Can., 1979—. Bd. dirs. Can. Inst. Internat. Affairs, Canadian Inst. Pub. Affairs, Etobicoke Gen. Hosp. Clubs: Royal Can. Yacht, Rideau, University. Author: Canadians in Russia, 1918-19, 1976; Canadians on the Nile, 1882-1898, 1978. Contbr. articles to jours. Home: 425 Russell Hill Rd Toronto ON M5P 2S4 Canada Office: 56 The Esplanade Toronto ON M5E 1R5 Canada

MACLAUGHLIN, HARRY HUNTER, judge; b. Breckenridge, Minn., Aug. 9, 1927; s. Harry Hunter and Grace (Swank) MacL.; B.B.A. with distinction, U. Minn., 1949, LL.B., J.D., 1956; m. Mary Jean Shaffer, June 25, 1958; children—David, Douglas. Admitted to Minn. bar, 1956; law clk. to justice Minn. Supreme Ct.; practice in Mpls., 1956-72; asso. justice Minn. Supreme Ct., 1972-77; U.S. dist. judge Dist. of Minn., Mpls., 1977—; part-time instr. William Mitchell Coll. Law, St. Paul, 1958-63; lectr. U. Minn. Law Sch., 1973—. Mem. Mpls. Charter Commn., 1967-72, Minn. State Coll. Bd., 1971-72, Minn. Jud. Council, 1972; mem. nat. adv. council Small Bus. Adminstrn., 1967-69. Served with USNR, 1945-46. Mem. Am., Minn., Hennepin County bar assns., Am. Trial Lawyers Assn., Beta Gamma Sigma, Phi Delta Phi. Methodist. Bd. editors Minn. Law Rev., 1954-55. Home: 2301 Oliver Ave S Minneapolis MN 55405 Office: 609 US Courthouse 110 S 4th St Minneapolis MN 55401

MACLAUGHLIN, ROBERT STACY, mfg. co. exec.; b. Hartford, Conn., May 31, 1934; s. Harry B. and Esther (Anderson) MacL.; grad. Loomis Sch., 1952; B.A., Yale, 1956; m. Patricia Ellen Dolan, June 16, 1956; children—Kyle Ann, Stephen Burdett, Pamela Ellen. Mem. controller's staff Norton Co., Worcester, Mass., 1956-63; asst. treas.

Norton Internat., Inc., Worcester, 1963-66; controller, asst. treas., sec. subsidiary U.S. Stoneware, Inc., Akron, Ohio, 1966-68; controller Dennison Mfg. Co., Framingham, Mass., 1968-74, v.p., controller, 1974-75, fin. v.p., 1975—, also dir. Mem. Fin. Execs. Inst., Nat. Assn. Accountants. Club: New Bedford Yacht. Home: 147 Front St Marblehead MA 01945 Office: 275 Wyman St Waltham MA 02154

MAC LAURY, BRUCE KING, instn. exec.; b. Mount Kisco, N.Y., May 7, 1931; s. Bruce King and Edith Mae (Wills) MacL.; B.A., Princeton, 1953; M.A., Harvard, 1958, Ph.D., 1961; m. Virginia Doris Naef, Jan. 8, 1955; children—John, David. Successively mgr., v.p. fgn. dept. Fed. Res. Bank N.Y., N.Y.C., 1958-69; dep. under sec. for monetary affairs U.S. Treasury Dept., Washington, 1969-71; pres. Fed. Res. Bank of Mpls., 1971-77; pres. Brookings Instn., Washington, 1977—. Bd. dirs. Dayton Hudson Corp., 1977—. Trustee Joint Council Econ. Edn., 1978—, Com. for Econ. Devel., 1978—; mem. Council on Fgn. Relations, N.Y.C., 1962—; mem. Trilateral Commn., N.Y.C., 1974—. Served to lt. AUS, 1954-56. Recipient Exceptional Service award U.S. Treasury Dept., 1971. Mem. Am. Econ. Assn., Phi Beta Kappa. Club: Cosmos (Washington). Home: 955 Swinks Mill Rd McLean VA 22101 Office: 1775 Massachusetts Ave NW Washington DC 20036

MACLAY, DONALD MERLE, lawyer; b. Belleville, Pa., Feb. 16, 1934; s. Robert Barr and Grace Virginia (Royer) M.; A.B. magna cum laude, Grove City Coll., 1956; LL.B., U. Pa., 1961; m. Nancy Margaret Hixenbaugh, Sept. 13, 1958; children—Susan Jo, Timothy Dean. Admitted to D.C. bar, 1968, Pa. bar, 1970; commd. fgn. service officer State Dept., 1961; assigned Am. embassy, Cotonou, Dahomey, 1962-64, Am. Consulate Gen., Frankfurt, Germany, 1964-66, State Dept., Washington, 1966-69; dir. courses of study Am. Law Inst.-Am. Bar Assn. Com. on Continuing Profl. Edn., Phila., 1969—. Served with U.S. Army, 1956-58. Mem. Am. Law Inst., Am. Bar Assn., Pa. Bar Assn., Phila. Bar Assn. Republican. Presbyterian. Home: 936 Church Rd Springfield PA 19064 Office: 4025 Chestnut St Philadelphia PA 19104

MACLEAN, ALISTAIR, author; b. Scotland, 1922; ed. Glasgow U. Former tchr. jr. secondary sch., Rutherglen, Glasgow, Scotland; author, screenwriter, 1955—; books include: HMS Ulysses, 1955, The Guns of Navarone, 1957, South By Java Head, 1958, The Last Frontier, 1959, Night Without End, 1960, The Dark Crusader, 1961, Fear is the Key, 1961, The Golden Rendezvous, 1962, The Satan Bug, 1962, All About Lawrence of Arabia, 1962, Ice Station Zebra, 1963, When Eight Bells Toll, 1966, Where Eagles Dare, 1967, Force 10 from Navarone, 1968, Puppet on a Chain, 1969, Caravan to Vaccares, 1970, Bear Island, 1971, Captain Cook, 1972, The Way to Dusty Death, 1973, Breakheart Pass, 1974, Circus, 1975, The Golden Gate, 1976, Flood Tide, 1977, Seawitch, 1977, Goodbye California, 1978; screenplays include: Where Eagles Dare, Caravan to Vaccares, Deakin, When Eight Bells Toll, Breakheart Pass. Served with Royal Navy, World War II. Office: care William Collins Sons & Co Ltd 14 St James Pl London SW 1 England*

MACLEAN, DANIEL CRAWFORD, III, lawyer; b. N.Y.C., Sept. 15, 1942; s. Daniel Crawford and Elsie O. (Reeh) M.; A.B., Columbia U., 1964; Certificat, U. Paris, 1964; J.D., Georgetown U., 1967; m. Hildi Starstrom; 1 dau. by previous marriage—Lisa. Admitted to Conn. bar, 1967; atty. SEC, Washington, 1967-72; mem. firm Reavis & McGrath, N.Y.C., 1972-73; asso. gen. counsel Dreyfus Corp., N.Y.C., 1973-78, gen. counsel, sec., 1978—. Mem. Am., Conn. bar assns. Democrat. Episcopalian. Home: 22 Peach Hill Rd Darien CT 06820 Office: 767 Fifth Ave New York NY 10022

MAC LEAN, DONALD DREW, lawyer; b. Seattle, Oct. 11, 1923; s. James Matthew and Julia Agnes (Drew) MacL.; B.S., U.S. Merchant Marine Acad., 1943; B.S.L., U. Wash., 1949, J.D., 1950; m. Joan Mary Rogers, May 1, 1954; children—Jane, Margaret Mary, Mary Denise, Drew, James, Peter, Sarah Susan. Asst. to dean U. Wash. Sch. Law, 1950-52; practice law, Seattle, 1952-62; partner firm McMicken, Rupp & Schweppe, Seattle, 1959-62; gen. atty. Pacific N.W. Bell Telephone Co., Seattle, 1962-75, v.p., gen. counsel, sec., 1975—. Bd. dirs. Seattle Urban League, 1975—; trustee Pacific N.W. Indian Center, Mus. Native Am. Cultures, Spokane, 1976—, Matteo Ricci Coll., 1976—; v.p., bd. dirs. J. Homer Butler Found., 1975—; mem. vis. com. U. Wash. Law Sch.; commr. CSC, Clyde Hill, Wash., 1973—. Served with USNR, 1943-46. Recipient Bus. achievement award U.S. Merchant Marine Acad., 1963. Mem. Am. Bar Assn., Wash. State Bar Assn., Seattle-King County Bar Assn., Am. Judicature Soc., Mcpl. League. Roman Catholic. Clubs: Rainier, Harbor, Wash. Athletic, Central Park Tennis. Office: 1600 Bell Plaza Rm 3204 Seattle WA 98191

MACLEAN, DONALD ISIDORE, univ. pres., clergyman; b. Norwalk, Conn., Nov. 25, 1929; s. Chester M. and Irene A. (Paquette) MacL.; A.B., Boston Coll., 1953, M.A., 1959; Ph.L., Weston Coll., 1954; Ph.D., Catholic U. Am., 1958; postgrad. U. Innsbruck, Austria, 1958-62. Ordained priest Roman Catholic Ch., 1961; Alexander von Humboldt fellow, research asso. Inst. Phys. Chemistry, U. Goettingen, Germany, 1962-65; asst. prof. Boston Coll., 1966-70, asso. prof., 1970-73, dir. labs. dept. chemistry, 1967-71; prin. investigator Air Force Office Sci. Research, 1968-73; tech. dir., prin. investigator Boston Coll. Themis Program, Office Naval Research, 1969-74; v.p. acad. affairs, dean faculties Creighton U., Omaha, 1973-76; pres. St. Joseph's U., Phila., 1976—. Bd. dirs. Phila. Urban Coalition, 1976—, Am. Council Edn., 1978—; trustee St. Louis U., 1975—. Mem. AAAS, Am. Council Edn., Assn. Jesuit Colls. and Univs. (dir. 1979—), Combustion Inst., Union League, Acad. Scis. Phila., Phila. C. of C. (dir. 1978—), Sigma Xi, Alpha Sigma Nu. Address: City Ave at 54th St Philadelphia PA 19131

MACLEAN, GUY ROBERTSON, univ. adminstr.; b. Sydney, N.S., Can., Dec. 21, 1929; s. Charles Whitmore and Mary Malinda (Nicholson) MacL.; B.A., Dalhousie U., 1951, M.A., 1953; B.A. (Rhodes scholar), Oxford U., 1955, M.A., 1959; Ph.D., Duke, 1958; m. Mary Judith Hunter, June 29, 1963; children—Colin Hunter, Mary Jocelyn. Asst. prof. Dalhousie U., Halifax, N.S., 1957-61, asso. prof., 1961-65, prof., 1965—, dean of residence, 1961-63, acting chmn. dept. history, 1963-64, asst. dean Faculty Grad. Studies, 1965-66, dean, 1966-69, dean Faculty Arts and Sci., 1969-75, v.p. academic, 1974—; dean of men Kings Coll., 1957-61; lectr. U. Alta., 1963, N.S. Tech. Coll., 1965-66. Mem. Rhodes Scholarship Com., N.S.; mem. Maritime Provinces Higher Edn. Commn.; mem. Social Scis. and Humanities Research Council Can., 1978—; bd. dirs. Donner Canadian Found., Toronto; bd. govs. Coll. of Cape Breton; chmn. bd. dirs. Opera East. Served as 2d lt. Canadian Army, 1949-51. Recipient Centennial medal, 1967, Jubilee medal, 1978; Can. Council fellow, 1968-69. Mem. Canadian Hist. Assn. (exec. council 1967-68), Canadian Inst. Internat. Affairs (pres. Halifax 1965), Canadian Rhodes Scholar Assn., Nova Scotia Soccer Assn. (pres. 1976—). Mem. United Ch. of Can. Club: Waegwoltic. Editor introduction The Life and Times of A.T. Galt, 1966. Contbr. articles to profl. jours. Home: Marlborough Woods Halifax NS Canada

MACLEAN, HECTOR, banker, lawyer; b. Balt., Sept. 15, 1920; s. Angus W. and Margaret (French) MacL.; B.S., Davidson Coll., 1941; J.D., U. N.C., 1948; m. Lyl Francis Warwick, Dec. 18, 1944; 1 dau., Lyl M. Clinard. Admitted to N.C. bar, 1948; pvt. practice, 1948—; chmn. bd., chief exec. officer So. Nat. Bank N.C., So. Nat. Corp.; pres., dir. Lumberton Implement Co.; dir. N.C. Natural Gas Corp. Mayor of Lumberton, 1949-53; mem. N.C. Senate, 1961-71. Pres. Med. Found. N.C.; chmn. bd. N.C. Bicentennial Com. Served from lt. to capt. AUS, 1942-46. Decorated Bronze Star medal. Mem. Robeson County Hist. Soc. (past pres.), Lumberton C. of C., Am., N.C. bar assns., Sigma Alpha Epsilon, Omicron Delta Kappa, Phi Delta Phi. Clubs: Pinecrest Country (Lumberton); Country of N.C. (Pinehurst); Litchfield Country (Pawleys Island, S.C.). Home: 2101 Elm St Lumberton NC 28358 Office: 500 Chestnut St Lumberton NC 28358

MACLEAN, JOHN ALLAN, mfg. exec.; b. Maxton, N.C., Mar. 29, 1912; s. Sylvester Brown and Florence (Wooten) MacL.; B.S., U. N.C., 1933, M.S., 1936; D.Sc., Tri-State Coll., 1972; m. Gladys Wilkie, July 4, 1930; children—Jane Sherrill, Ann Wilkie. Instr. mech. engring. U. N.C., 1934-36; asst. prof. aero. engring. U. Notre Dame, 1936-40; successively sr. engr., quality mgr., asst. aircraft mgr., dir. indsl. relations, gen. mgr. automotive products Bendix products div. Bendix Aviation Corp., South Bend, Ind., 1940-57, asst. group exec., 1957-59; dir. Dodge Mfg. Corp. (merged with Reliance Electric Co. 1967 and now a div.), Mishawaka, Ind., 1956-67, pres., 1959-74; v.p., dir. Reliance Electric Co., 1967-74; dir. 1st Bank & Trust Co., South Bend, Ind. Bell Telephone Co., Aro Corp., Sibley Machine & Foundry Corp., No. Ind. Pub. Service Co., J.H. Fenner & Co., Hull, Eng. Mem. Ind. C. of C. (pres. 1970-71, dir.), Phi Beta Kappa, Tau Beta Pi. Presbyn. Contbr. articles aero. jours. Home: 1521 E Washington Ave South Bend IN 46617 Office: 325 JMS Bldg South Bend IN 46601

MAC LEAN, JOHN ANGUS, premier P.E.I. (Can.); b. Lewes, P.E.I., May 15, 1914; s. George Allen and Sarah Mac L.; student U. B.C. (Can.), Vancouver; B.Sc., Mt. Allison U., 1939, LL.D., 1958; m. Gwendolyn Esther Burwash, Oct. 29, 1952; children—Sarah Jean, Allan Duart, Mary Esther, Robert Angus. Mem. Can. House of Commons, Ottawa, Ont., 1951-76; mem. Privy Council Can., 1957—; minister of fisheries Govt. Can., 1957-63; mem. P.E.I. Legislature, 1977—; premier P.E.I., 1979—. Leader, Progressive Conservative Party of P.E.I., 1976—. Served with RCAF, 1939-47. Presbyterian. Office: Office of Premier Province House Charlottetown PE C1A 7N8 Canada*

MACLEAN, JOHN RONALD, lawyer; b. Pueblo, Colo., Jan. 19, 1938; s. John Ronald and Mary Victoria (Curlin) MacL.; student U. Okla., 1956; B.S., U.S. Mil. Acad., 1961; J.D., Vanderbilt U., 1967; m. Carol Jean Turner, Aug. 18, 1962; children—Leslie Carol, John Ronald. Admitted to Tex. bar, 1967; practicing atty. Turner & MacLean, Cleburne, Tex., 1964-67; county atty. Johnson County, Tex., 1967-76; dist. atty. 18th Jud. Dist. of Tex., 1976—. Pres. Johnson County United Fund, 1976. Served with AUS, 1961-64. Mem. Tex., Johnson County (pres. 1969) bar assns., Tex. Trial Lawyers Assn., Tex. Dist. and County Attys. Assn., Vanderbilt U. Law Sch. Bar Assn. (past pres.). Democrat. Methodist. Elk. Club: Exchange (Cleburne). Home: 1216 Westhill St Cleburne TX 76013 Office: PO Box 350 Cleburne TX 76031

MAC LEAN, LLOYD DOUGLAS, surgeon; b. Calgary, Alta., Can., June 24, 1924; s. Fred Hugh and Azilda (Trudel) MacL.; B.Sc. (Viscount Bennett scholar), U. Alta., 1946, M.D. (Viscount Bennett scholar), 1949; Ph.D., U. Minn., 1957; m. Eleanor Colle, June 30, 1954; children—Hugh, Charles, Ian, James, Martha. Resident, U. Minn. Hosp., Mpls., 1950-56; instr. dept. surgery U. Minn., Mpls., 1956-58, asst. prof. surgery, 1958-59, asso. prof., 1959-62; prof. McGill U., Montreal, Que., Can., 1962—, chmn. dept. surgery, 1968-73; surgeon-in-chief Ancker Hosp., St. Paul, 1957-62, Royal Victoria Hosp., Montreal, 1962—. Fellow Royal Soc. Can.; mem. Am. Surg. Assn., Soc. Univ. Surgeons, A.C.S., Central Surg. Assn., Am. Physiol. Soc., Am. Assn. Thoracic and Cardiovascular Surgery, Soc. Surgery of Alimentary Tract. Contbr. numerous articles on surgery, shock, host resistance and transplantation to profl. jours. Home: 5 Renfrew St Westmount PQ H3Y 2X3 Canada Office: 687 Pine St Montreal PQ H3A 1A1 Canada

MACLEAN, MALCOLM RODERICK, lawyer; b. Easthampton, N.Y., Sept. 14, 1919; s. Malcolm Roderick and Emily Marriott (Helm) M.; A.B., Yale U., 1941; LL.B., Harvard U., 1948; m. Frances Ravenel Grimball, Nov. 13, 1948; children—Nancy, John. Admitted to Ga. bar, 1948; mem. firm Hunter, Houlihan, Maclean, Exley, Dunn & Connerat and predecessors, Savannah, Ga., 1948—; dir. Savannah Bank & Trust Co.; asst. city atty. City of Savannah, 1955-57, alderman and mayor pro-tem, 1957-60, mayor, 1960-66; atty. Chat County (Ga.) Sch. Bd., 1970-72. Served to comdr. USNR, 1941-46, 50-52. Decorated Bronze Star. Mem. Am. Coll. Trial Lawyers, Am., Ga., Savannah bar assns., Nat. Assn. Ry. Trial Lawyers, Maritime Law Assn. Democrat. Episcopalian. Home: 412 E 45th St Savannah GA 31405 Office: PO Box 9848 Savannah GA 31402

MACLEAN, PAUL DONALD, ofcl. HEW; b. Phelps, N.Y., May 1, 1913; s. Charles Chalmers and Elizabeth (Dreyfus) MacL.; B.A., Yale U., 1935; postgrad. U. Edinburgh (Scotland), 1935-36; M.D. cum laude, Yale U., 1940; m. Alison Stokes, July 16, 1942; children—Paul, David, Alexander, James, Alison. Intern in medicine Johns Hopkins U., 1940-41; asst. resident medicine New Haven Hosp., Yale Sch. Medicine, 1941-42, research asst. pathology, 1942, asst. prof. physiology, 1949-51, asst. prof. psychiatry, physiology and neurology, 1951-53, asso. prof. physiology, 1956-57; clin. instr. medicine U. Wash. Med. Sch., Seattle, 1946-47; USPHS research fellow Harvard U. Med. Sch., also Mass. Gen. Hosp., 1947-49; dir. EEG lab. New Haven Hosp., 1951-52; asso. prof. psychiatry, physiology and neurology, attending physician Grace-New Haven Hosp., 1953-56; sr. postdoctoral fellow NSF dept. physiology U. Zurich, 1956-57; chief sect. limbic integration and behavior Lab. Neurophysiology Intramural Research, NIMH, USPHS, HEW, Bethesda, Md., 1957-71, chief lab. brain evolution and behavior, Intramural Research, Bethesda, Md., 1971—. Trustee L.S.B. Leakey Found. Served to maj. M.C., AUS, 1942-46; PTO. Recipient award for disting. research Assn. for Research in Nervous and Mental Disease, 1964; Salmon lectureship award, 1966; Superior Service award HEW, 1967; Hincks Meml. lectr., Ont.; Spl. award Am. Psychopathol. Assn., 1971; G. Burroughs Mider NIH Lectureship award, 1972; Karl Spencer Lashley award Am. Philos. Soc., 1972. Mem. Am. Electroencephalographic Soc., Am. Neurol. Assn., Am. Assn. History of Medicine, Am. Physiol. Soc., Am. Soc. Naturalists, Eastern Assn. Electroencephalgraphers, Am. Assn. Neurol. Surgeons, Soc. Neurosci., Am. Assn. Anatomists, Sigma Xi, Alpha Omega Alpha. Editorial bd. Jour. Nervous and Mental Disease. Home: 9916 Logan Dr Potomac MD 20854 Office: NIMH Lab Brain Evolution and Behavior 9000 Rockville Pike Bethesda MD 20205

MACLEAN, WILLIAM, ins. exec.; b. Manchester, Eng., Dec. 27, 1908; s. Robert and Eva (Epplestone) MacL.; student pub. schs. of Eng.; m. Shirley A. Durring, Sept. 12, 1932 (died 1949); 1 dau., Janet; m. 2d, Margaret Strickland, Aug. 20, 1953; 1 son, William. Came to U.S., 1921, naturalized, 1926. With Joseph Froggatt & Co., Inc., pub. accountants, N.Y. City, 1929-47; with Nat. Union Fire Ins. Co. of Pitts., 1947-69, dir., 1949—, v.p., 1951-56, pres., 1956-69. Pres. Friends of the Library of Collier County. Clubs: University; Royal Poinciana Golf; Naples Sailing and Yacht. Home: 6 Sabre Cay Naples FL 33940

MACLEAY, DONALD, lawyer; b. Tacoma, Dec. 27, 1908; s. Lachlan and Mabel (Nye) M.; student Hill Mil. Acad., Portland, Oreg., 1922-24, Phillips Acad., Andover, Mass., 1924-25; LL.B., U. Colo., 1931; m. Elizabeth Hall Fesser, Jan. 27, 1934; children—Donald, Linda Dewell, Murdo Lachlan. Admitted to Colo., Ill., D.C. bars, 1931-33; com. prevention, punishment of crime Chgo. Assn. Commerce, 1931-32; gen. practice of law, 1933—; with Esch, Kerr, Woolley, Taylor & Shipe, and successor firm Kerr, Shipe & Macleay, also Turney, Rives & Macleay; partner Macleay, Lynch, Bernhard & Gregg and predecessor firms, Washington, 1946—. Served to lt. USNR, 1943-45. Mem. Am., D.C., Maritime Adminstrv. bar assns., Am. Judicature Soc., Assn. ICC Practitioners, Maritime Law Assn. U.S., Phi Delta Phi, Chi Psi. Episcopalian. Clubs: University, Propeller (Washington); Belle Haven Country (Alexandria, Va.); Internat. House (New Orleans). Home: 1800 Edgehill Dr Belle Haven Alexandria VA 23307 Office: 1625 K St NW Washington DC 20006

MAC LEISH, ARCHIBALD, poet; b. Glencoe, Ill., May 7, 1892; s. Andrew and Martha (Hillard) Mac L.; A.B., Yale U., 1915, Litt.D. (hon.), 1939; LL.B., Harvard, 1919, Litt.D. (hon.), 1955; M.A. (hon.), Tufts Coll., 1932; Litt.D. (hon.), Wesleyan U., 1938, Colby Coll., 1938, U. Pa., 1941, U. Ill., 1946, Washington U., 1948, Columbia, 1954; L.H.D. (hon.), Dartmouth, 1940; LL.D., John Hopkins U., 1941, U. Calif., 1943, Queens U., Ont., 1948, Carleton Coll., 1956, Amherst Coll., 1963; Litt.D. (hon.), Rockford Coll., 1953, U. Pitts., 1959, Brandeis U., 1959; D.C.L. (hon.), Union Coll., 1941, U. P.R., 1953; L.H.D. (hon.), Princeton, 1965; D.H.L. (hon.), Williams Coll., 1942; m. Ada Hitchcock, June 21, 1916; children—Kenneth (dec.), Brewster Hitchcock (dec.), Mary Hillard, William Hitchcock. Rede lectr. Cambridge (Eng.) U., 1942; Boylston prof. Harvard, 1949-62; Simpson lectr. Amherst Coll., 1963-67; Librarian of Congress, 1939-44; also dir. U.S. Office Facts & Figures, 1941-42, asst. dir. OWI, 1942-43; asst. sec. state, 1944-45. Am. del. Conf. Allied Ministers of Edn., London, 1944; chmn. Am. delegation London Conf. to draw up constn. for UNESCO, 1945; chmn. Am. delegation 1st Gen. Conf. UNESCO, Paris, 1946; first Am. mem. exec. council UNESCO. Served from pvt. to capt. U.S. Army, 1917-19; overseas, France, 1917-18. Decorated comdr. Legion of Honor (France); Encomienda Order el Sol del Peru; recipient Bollingen prize in poetry, 1953, Nat. Book Award in poetry, 1953, Pulitzer prize in poetry, 1932, 53, Pulitzer prize in drama, 1959, Antoinette Perry award in drama, 1959, Presdl. Medal of Freedom, 1977, Nat. Medal for Lit., 1978, Gold medal for poetry Am. Acad., 1979. Mem. Am. Acad. Arts and Letters (pres. 1953-56). Clubs: Century (N.Y.C.); Tavern (Boston). Author: (verse) The Happy Marriage, 1924; The Pot of Earth, 1925; (verse play) Nobodaddy, 1925; (verse) Streets in the Moon, 1926; (verse) The Hamlet of A. MacLeish, 1928; (verse) New Found Land, 1930; (verse) Conquistador, 1932; (verse) Frescoes for Mr. Rockefeller's City, 1933; Collected Poems, 1924-33; Union Pacific, a ballet, 1934; Panic (verse play), 1935; Public Speech (verse), 1936; The Fall of the City (verse play for radio), 1937; Land of the Free (verse), 1938; Air Raid (verse play for radio), 1938; America Was Promises (verse), 1939; The Irresponsibles (prose), 1940; The American Cause (prose), 1941; A Time to Speak (prose), 1941; A Time To Act (prose), 1942; American Opinion and the War (prose), 1942; American Story (broadcasts), 1944; Act Five (verse), 1948; Poetry and Opinion (prose), 1950; Freedom is the Right to Choose (prose), 1951; Collected Poems, 1917-52; Songs for Eve (verse), 1954; J.B. (verse play), 1958; Poetry and Experience (prose), 1961; Eleanor Roosevelt Story (book), 1965 (motion picture 1965; Academy award 1966); Herakles (verse play), 1967; Magic Prison (libretto), 1967; An Evening's Journey to Conway Massachusetts (play), 1967; (prose) A Continuing Journey, 1968; (verse) The Wild Old Wicked Man and Other Poems, 1968; Scratch (prose play), 1971; The Human Season (selected poems), 1972; The Great American Fourth of July Parade (verse play for radio), 1975; New & Collected Poems, 1917-1976, 1976; (prose) Riders on the Earth, 1978. Address: Conway MA 01341

MAC LENNAN, DAVID HERMAN, biochemist; b. Swan River, Man., Can., July 3, 1937; s. Douglas Henry and Sigridur (Sigurdson) MacL.; B.S., Man. U., 1959; M.S., Purdue U., 1961, Ph.D., 1963; m. Linda Carol Vass, Aug. 18, 1965; children—Jeremy Douglas, Jonathan David. Postdoctoral fellow Inst. Enzyme Research, U. Wis., Madison, 1963-64, asst. prof., 1964-68; asso. prof. Banting and Best Dept. Med. Research U. Toronto (Ont., Can.), 1969-74, prof., 1974—, acting chmn., 1978—; mem. med. adv. bd. Muscular Dystrophy Assn. Can. Med. Research Council scholar, 1969-71; I.W. Killam Meml. scholar, 1977-78. Mem. Can. Biochem. Soc. (Ayerst award 1974), Am. Soc. Biol. Chemists. Contbr. articles in field to profl. jours.; mem. editorial bd. Jour. Biol. Chemistry. Home: 293 Lytton Blvd Toronto ON M5N 1R7 Canada Office: C H Best Inst 112 College St Toronto ON M5G 1L6 Canada

MACLENNAN, HUGH, author, educator; b. Glace Bay, N.S., Can., Mar. 20, 1907; s. Samuel J. and Katherine (McQuarrie) MacL.; ed. Halifax Acad.; B.A. (gov.-gen.'s Gold Medal, Rhodes scholar), Dalhousie U., 1928, LL.D., 1955; B.A., Oriel Coll., Oxford U., 1932; M.A., Ph.D., Princeton, 1935; D.Litt., Western Ont. U., 1952, Man. U., 1953, Waterloo Luth. U., 1961, Dalhousie U., Bishop's U., U. Toronto, U. B.C., McMaster U.; m. Dorothy Duncan, June 22, 1936 (dec. 1957); m. 2d, Frances Aline Walker, 1959. Prof. English dept. McGill U., Montreal, Que., Can., 1952—. Recipient gov.-gen's award for fiction, 1945, 48, 59, non-fiction, 1949-54; Lorne Pierce Gold medal Royal Soc. Can., 1952; Guggenheim fellow, 1943-44. Asso. fellow Royal Soc. Can., Royal Soc. Lit. (London). Clubs: Montreal Amateur Athletic Assn., McGill Faculty, North Hatley (Montreal). Author: Oxyrhunchus, 1935; Barometer Rising, 1941; Two Solitudes, 1945; The Precipice, 1958; Each Mans Son, 1951; Thirty and Three, 1954; The Watch that Ends the Night (Canadian gov.-gen. award for English fiction, 1959), 1959; Scotchman's Return and Other Essays, 1960; Seven Rivers of Canada, 1961; Return of the Sphinx, 1967; The Colour of Canada, 1967; Rivers of Canada, 1974; also articles to Sat. Rev. Lit., Vogue, Holiday, Macleans and other publs. Address: McGill U Montreal PQ Canada

MACLEOD, DONALD, clergyman, educator; b. Broughton, N.S., Can., Dec. 31, 1913; s. Donald Archibald and Anne (MacKenzie) M.; A.B., Dalhousie U., Halifax, N.S., 1934, M.A., 1935, LL.D., 1978; B.D. (E.F. Grant scholar), Pine Hill Div. Hall, Halifax, 1938, D.D., 1970; Th.D., U. Toronto, 1947; m. Norma Eliner Harper, Jan. 5, 1948 (dec. Mar. 1972); children—John Fraser, David Ainslie, Anne, Leslie. Teaching fellow dept. English, Dalhousie U., 1935-38; ordained to ministry Presbyn. Ch., 1938; minister First Ch., Louisburg, N.S., 1938-41; asso. minister, Bloor St. Ch., Toronto, 1941-45; sr. tutor Men's Residences Victoria Coll., Toronto, 1943-45; teaching fellow dept. homiletics Princeton Theol. Sem., 1946-47; asst. prof., 1947-53, asso. prof., 1953-61, prof., 1961—; lectr. Princeton Summer Inst. Theology, 1948—; vis. lectr. Westminster Choir Coll., 1952, 55-58; lectr. Gettysburg Sem., 1952, Jr. Pastors Sch., Reading Pa., 1954, Conf. on Evangelism, Whitby, Ont., 1957, Hampton (Va.) Inst., 1957, Union Sem., Richmond, Va., 1958, Crozier Sem., Chester, Pa., 1961, Ann. Pastors Conf. Am. Luth. Ch., Green Lake, Wis., 1966, Coll. Preachers, Nat. Cathedral Washington, 1967; lectr. continuing edn. Presbyn. Coll., Montreal, 1972—; Mullins lectr. So. Baptist Theol.

Sem., 1970; Kyes' lectr. Kirk in the Hills, Detroit, 1973; chmn. Synod Com. on Capital Ch., Trenton, N.J.; mem. coms. Christian edn., candidates and credentials, social edn. and action Presbytery New Brunswick; commr. Gen. Assembly United Presbyn. Ch., Oklahoma City, 1965; spl. preacher Princeton, Lehigh, Muhlenberg, Mt. Allison U. and Rutgers U. Chapels, Chgo. Sunday Evening Club, Am. Preacher Series Eaton Meml. Ch., Toronto, Chatauqua Evangelist, Riverside Ch., N.Y.C., Fifth Av. Presbyn Ch., N.Y.C., Nat. Presbyn. Ch., Washington, Preaching Mission McGuire AFB, Chaplains Seminars, USAF, 1967-68; adv. bd. Chapel of Princeton U. Fellow Am. Assn. Theol. Schs.; mem. Am. Assn. Theol. Profs. in Practical Fields (exec. com.), Ch. Service Soc. (past v.p.), Clan Macleod Soc. Am. (chaplain), Am. Acad. Homiletics (founder, pres.). Author: Word and Sacrament, 1960; Presbyterian Worship, 1965; Higher Reaches, 1971; Proclamation, 1975. Editor: Here Is My Method, 1952; Princeton Sem. Bull., 1956—. Translator Dynamics of Worship, 1967. Mem. editorial bd. Theology Today, 1948-61, Pulpit Preaching, 1970—. Am. corr. The United Church Observer, 1947-56, N.J. corr. The Christian Century, 1957-65. Contbr. articles profl. publs. Home: 48 Mercer St Princeton NJ 08540. *Too often we interpret the Boy Scouts' slogan "Be Prepared" as a caution against danger or disaster, but its thrust is largely positive. It implies being prepared for every opportunity. Never did I have any particular position in mind, but every door which has opened to me found me ready and equipped for it.*

MACLEOD, GAVIN, actor; b. Mt. Kisco, N.Y., Feb. 28; B.F.A., Ithaca Coll.; m. Patti Steele; children—Keith, David, Julie, Meghan; stepchildren—Tommy, Stephanie, Andrew. Regular on TV series McHale's Navy, 1962-64, The Mary Tyler Moore Show, 1970-77, The Love Boat, 1977—; other TV appearances include: To Catch a Thief, Hawaii Five-O, Run for Your Life, The Hollywood Squares, The Mike Douglas Show; TV movie Only with Married Men, 1974; films include: I Want to Live, 1958, Compulsion, 1959, Operation Petticoat, 1959, High Time, 1960, War Hunt, 1962, McHale's Navy, 1964, Sand Pebbles, 1966, Deathwatch, 1967, The Party, 1968, Kelly's Heroes, 1970; stage appearances: A Hatful of Rain, Middle of the Night, The Egg, An Evening of the Absurd, Lullabye, The Web and the Rock, Carousel, A Funny Thing Happened on the Way to the Forum, Gypsy, The Seven-Year Itch, Annie Get Your Gun. Served in USAF. Mem. AFTRA. Office: care ABC 1330 Ave of Americas New York NY 10019. *Simply, we are meant to be happy in life, not unhappy; we are meant to succeed in life, not fail; it's up to us!*

MACLEOD, ROBERT ANGUS, educator, microbiologist; b. Athabasca, Alta., Can., July 13, 1921; s. Norman John and Eleonora Pauline Bertha (Westerhoff) MacL.; B.A., U. B.C., 1943, M.A., 1945; Ph.D., U. Wis., 1949; m. Patricia Rose Marie Robertson, Sept. 1, 1948; children—Douglas John, Alexander Robert, Kathleen Mary (Mrs. Stephen Cook), David Gordon, Michael Norman, Susan Joan. Asst. prof. Queen's U., Kingston, Ont., 1949-53; sr. biochemist Fisheries Research Bd. Can., Vancouver, B.C., 1953-60; mem. faculty McGill U., Montreal, 1960—, prof. microbiology, 1964—, chmn. dept. MacDonald Campus, 1974—; cons. Def. Research Bd. Can., 1962-74. Fellow Royal Soc. Can. (Harrison prize 1960); mem. Canadian (award 1973), Am. socs. microbiologists, Am. Soc. Biol. Chemists. Roman Catholic. Author papers in field. Home: 448 Greenwood Dr Beaconsfield PQ Canada Office: Dept Microbiology MacDonald Campus McGill Univ Ste Anne de Bellevue PQ Canada

MACLEOD, ROBERT FREDRIC, editor, publisher; b. Chgo., Oct. 15, 1917; s. Ernest F. and Martha W. (Ruzicka) MacL.; B.A., Dartmouth Coll., 1939; children—Merrill, Robert Fredric, E. Jay, Ian. Advt. mgr. Town & Country mag., N.Y.C., 1949; v.p., pub. Harper's Bazaar, N.Y.C., 1950-55, 55-60; v.p., advt. dir. Hearst Mags., N.Y.C., 1960-62; pub. Seventeen mag., N.Y.C., 1962-63; v.p., dir. mktg. Subscription TV Inc., Santa Monica, Calif., 1963-64; editor, pub. Teen Mag., Los Angeles, 1965—; v.p. Petersen Pub. Co., Los Angeles, 1976—. Served to maj. USMC, 1941-46. Named to Football Hall of Fame, 1977. Club: Bel Air Country. Home: 110 Colony Dr Malibu CA 90265 Office: 8831 Sunset Blvd Los Angeles CA 90069

MACLEOD, WILLIAM JOHN, ednl. adminstr.; b. Everett, Mass., Sept. 25, 1917; s. Daniel and Margaret (Currie) MacL.; Th.B., Gordon Coll., 1938; M.A., Boston U., 1940; Ph.D., 1948, L.H.D., 1974; certificate Am. Sch. Classical Studies, Athens, Greece, 1963; Ford fellow U. Mich. Center Middle East Studies, 1965; m. Laura Irene Hall, June 15, 1946; children—Glen Gary, Bruce Alan, Bonnie Laurel. Asst. dir. Bur. of Appts. of Boston U., 1938-42, dir., coordinator religious activities, 1946-47; chmn. dept. philosophy, prof. Baldwin-Wallace Coll., 1948-69; chmn. div. humanities U. Me. at Portland, 1969-70, acting pres., 1970-71, v.p. for acad. affairs, 1971-75; dir. evaluation commn. on Instns. of Higher Edn. N.Eng. Assn. Schs. and Colls., 1976—; nat. exec. sec. Phi Sigma Tau, 1955-70. Andrew Mellon lectr. on State of the Arts, Great Britain, 1968. Served with AUS, 1942-46. Danforth grantee, 1960; recipient Strosacker award for distinguished teaching Baldwin-Wallace Coll., 1969. Mem. Am. Philos. Assn., Am. Assn. U. Profs., Phi Sigma Tau, Omicron Delta Kappa, Alpha Tau Omega. Author: Contagious Ideas and Dynamic Events. 1964. Editor: (with Dr. Zaki N. Mahmoud) Contemporary Islamic Philosophy; editor of Dialogue, 1955-70. Home: 8 Cabot Dr Nashua NH 03060 Office: 131 Middlesex Turnpike Burlington MA 01803

MACMAHON, CHARLES HUTCHINS, JR., architect; b. Ft. Seward, Alaska, June 6, 1918; s. Charles H. and Charlotte (Currie) MacM.; student Bowdoin Coll., 1936-37, U. Pa., 1937-38; B.Arch., U. Mich., 1942; m. Ethel Hayward Pearce, Nov. 14, 1942; children—Charles H. III, Charlotte (Mrs. Douglas E. Neumann). Dist. mgr. U.S. Gypsum Co., Chgo., 1947-52; gen. sales mgr. Spickelmeier Co., Indpls., 1952-55; with Smith, Tarapata, MacMahon, Inc., Birmingham, Mich., 1956-59; pres. Tarapata-MacMahon-Paulsen, Bloomfield Hills, Mich., 1959-73, cons., 1973—; pres. MacMahon-Cajacob Assos., DeLand, Fla., 1978—; dir. Allied Co. Inc., Venture Services Ltd., Alaska-Valdez Co.; works include Central Plaza, Canton, O., Gen. Motors Inst., Flint, Mich., Washtenaw Community Coll., Ann Arbor, Mich. Mem. Mich. Bd. Registration of Architects, Engrs. and Surveyors, 1964-68. Chmn. bd. trustees Bloomfield Twp. Zoning Bd. Appeals, 1968-69. Bd. dirs. Brookside Sch., Cranbrook, 1964-68, Shadybrook House, Mentor, O., 1969—; trustee Haven Hill Found., 1970—, Inst. for Advanced Pastoral Studies. Served as lt., USNR, 1942-45. Fellow A.I.A.; mem. Sch. Facilities Council (v.p., dir.), Mich. Soc. Architects (pres. 1962-64), Psi Upsilon. Episcopalian. Clubs: Halifax (Daytona Beach, Fla.); Deland Country, Lake Beresford Yacht (Fla.). Address: 115 S Boundary Ave DeLand FL 32720

MACMAHON, LLOYD FRANCIS, judge; b. Elmira, N.Y., Aug. 12, 1912; s. Frank A. and Edith (Newton) MacM.; student Syracuse U., 1932-34; A.B., Cornell U., 1936, LL.B., 1938; m. Margaret A. Daly, July 9, 1938; children—Patricia MacMahon Milano, Kathleen MacMahon Taylor, John, Theresa MacMahon Finneran. Admitted to N.Y. bar, 1939; asso. firm Donovan, Leisure, Newton, Lumbard & Irvine, N.Y.C, 1942-53; chief asst. U.S. atty. So Dist. N.Y., 1953-55, U.S. atty., 1955; partner firm Kramer, Marx, Greenlee, Backus & MacMahon, N.Y.C., 1955-57; individual practice, N.Y.C., 1958-59; U.S. dist. judge So. Dist. N.Y., 1959—. Served as lt. (j.g.) USNR, 1944-45. Mem. Am., Fed. bar assns., Phi Delta Phi. Home: 9 Odgen Ave White Plains NY 10605 Office: US Courthouse New York NY 10007

MACMANUS, YVONNE CRISTINA, editor; b. Los Angeles, Mar. 18, 1931; d. Daniel S. and Josefina Lydia (Pina) MacManus; student N.Y. U., U. London (Eng.), U. So. Cal. Asso. editor Bobbs-Merrill, N.Y.C., 1960-63; television producer Leo Burnett Ltd., London, 1965-66; editor-in-chief Leisure Books, Los Angeles, 1970-72; tchr. pub. course U. Cal. at Los Angeles Extension, 1972; owner YM Enterprises, Los Angeles, 1972—; sr. editor Major Books, 1975-77; co-pub., editor-in-chief Timely Books, New Milford, Conn., 1977—. Mem. Authors Guild. Author: With Fate Conspire, 1974; Bequeath Them No Tumbled House, 1977; Better Luck Elsewhere, 1976. Contbr. articles profl. publs. Address: care Timely Books PO Box 267 New Milford CT 06776

MACMASTER, DANIEL MILLER, mus. ofcl.; b. Chgo., Feb. 11, 1913; s. Daniel Howard and Charlotte Louise (Miller) MacM.; student Lakeside Press Tng. Sch., 1930-31, U. Chgo., 1931-34; L.H.D., Lincoln Coll., 1970; D.H.L., DePaul U., 1978; m. Sylvia Jane Hill, Feb. 22, 1935; children—Daniel Miller, Jane Irene (Mrs. Robert W. Lightoll). Mem. staff Mus. Sci. and Industry, Chgo., 1933—, acting dir., 1950, dir., 1951-72, pres., 1968-78, pres. emeritus, 1978—, trustee, 1968—; gen. mgr. Chgo. R.R. Fair, 1948-49. Mem. Homewood (Ill.) Bd. Edn., 1945-49, pres., 1948-49; mem. U. Ill. Citizens Adv. Com., 1945—; sec. Higher Edn. Commn. Ill., 1955-59; dir. Hyde Park Bank and Trust Co.; U.S. State Dept. specialist to Ireland, Germany, Sweden, 1963; dir. Floating Seminar to Greece, 1960; guest mus. cons. Fed. Republic Germany, 1961, Iran, 1973, 76, Hong Kong, Singapore, Chile and Peru, 1978. Mem. Nat. 4-H Service Com. Hon. dir. Chgo. Chamber Orch. Soc., pres. 1969-70; bd. dirs. Sears-Roebuck Found., 1970-73, Internat. Coll. Surgeons Hall of Fame; mem. citizens bd. U. Chgo., Lincoln Acad. Ill.; hon. trustee U. Chgo. Cancer Research Found.; trustee Adler Planetarium; dir. emeritus Monmouth Coll.; bd. govs. Chgo. Heart Assn., vice chmn., 1972-73; bd. commrs. Ill. Sesquicentennial, 1968. Decorated Golden Cross Royal Order Phoenix (Greece); Officer's Cross Polonia Restituta (Poland); Grand Badge of Honor (Austria), Grand Badge of Honor of Burgenland (Austria); Golden Badge of Honor (Vienna); Officer's Cross 1st class Order of Merit (Germany), Officer Order of Merit (Luxembourg); Order Cultural Merit (Poland); recipient Patriotic Civilian Service award U.S. Army, St. Andrews Soc. Citizen of Yr. award, 1978. Fellow Assn. Sci. and Tech. Centers; mem. Kappa Sigma. Clubs: Tavern, Quadrangle, Commercial. Author: (with others) Exploring the Mysteries of Physics and Chemistry, 1938. Book reviewer. Contbr. to newspapers, mags., encys. Home: 910 Bruce Ave Flossmoor IL 60422 Office: Museum of Science and Industry 57th St and South Lake Shore Dr Chicago IL 60637

MACMASTER, ROBERT ELLSWORTH, educator, historian; b. Winthrop, Mass., Oct. 10, 1919; s. Joseph Oscar and Ruby (Slocomb) MacM.; A.B., Harvard, 1941, A.M., 1948, Ph.D., 1952; m. Ann Elizabeth Lynch, Apr. 28, 1942; children—Angus Michael, Martha Ann, David Joseph. Mem. faculty Mass. Inst. Tech., 1952—, prof. history and lit., 1967—, chmn. history sect., 1970-72. Served with AUS, 1941-46. Mem. Am. Assn. Advancement Slavic Studies. Author: Danilevsky: A Russian Totalitarian Philosopher, 1967. Home: 461 Main St Hingham MA 02043 Office: Mass Inst Tech Cambridge MA 02139

MACMILLAN, DOUGLAS CLARK, naval architect; b. Dedham, Mass., July 15, 1912; s. James Duncan and Mary Grace (MacNeill) MacM.; B.S., Mass. Inst. Tech., 1934; m. Elizabeth Jane Smith, Sept. 9, 1939; children—Douglas Stuart, John Richard. Engrs., Fed. Shipbldg. & Dry Dock Co., Kearny, N.J., 1934-41; from chief marine engr. to tech. mgr. George G. Sharp, N.A., N.Y.C., 1941-51; pres. George G. Sharp, Inc., N.Y.C., 1951-69, chmn. bd., 1969-70; cons. naval architect, 1970—; asst. to gen. mgr., cons. Quincy Shipbldg. div. Gen. Dynamics Corp., 1972-77; bd. dirs. Atomic Indsl. Forum, 1965-67; mem. coms. Nat. Acad. Scis.-NRC; adv. coms. U.S. Navy, USCG. Past trustee St. Johns Guild, N.Y.C. Recipient Elmer A. Sperry medal ASME-Soc. Naval Architects and Marine Engrs.-Soc. Automotive Engrs.-IEEE-Am. Inst. Aeros. and Astronautics, 1969; Registered profl. engr., N.Y., N.J. Fellow Soc. Naval Architects and Marine Engrs. (hon. v.p.; David W. Taylor Gold medal 1969); mem. Nat. Acad. Engring., Am. Bur. Shipping, Am. Soc. Naval Engrs. Methodist. Author papers in field. Home: Box 834 Colony Dr East Orleans MA 02643

MACMILLAN, GARY DUANE, librarian; b. Posen, Mich., Sept. 25, 1932; s. William Duncan and Celia (Hubbard) MacM.; B.A. in Psychology, Kalamazoo Coll., 1953, B.A. in Sociology, 1954; A.M. in L.S., U. Mich., 1955. Librarian, Detroit Pub. Library, 1955-56, 58-61; head librarian Detroit Inst. Tech., 1961-65; librarian Cornell U., 1965; tech. adv. to library U. Liberia, Monrovia, 1965-67, head librarian, 1967-68; serials librarian, asst. acquisitions librarian Mich. State U., East Lansing, 1968-70; dir. libraries Rochester Inst. Tech., 1970—. Served with AUS, 1956-58. Mem. A.L.A. Compiler bibliography of documents pertaining to Liberia in U.S. Nat. Archives, 1842-1929. Home: 15 Chadbourne Rd Rochester NY 14618

MACMILLAN, JAMES MURDOCK, corp. med. exec., med. educator; b. Abingdon, Va., Aug. 12, 1912; s. Jason Leon and Nell Theresa (Rankin) MacM.; B.A., Coll. Wooster (O.), 1933; M.D., Western Res. U., 1937; m. Sara Wishart, June 22, 1935; children—David Wishart, James Murdock, Richard Elliott. Intern, Cleve. City Hosp., 1937-38; resident in internal medicine, gastroenterology Henry Ford Hosp., Detroit, 1938-42; practice medicine specializing in internal medicine and gastroenterology, Richmond, Va., 1946-56; corp. med. dir. Reynolds Metals Co., Richmond, 1956—; asst. clin. prof. medicine Health Scis. Div., Va. Commonwealth U., Richmond, 1946—. Mem. Richmond Area Community Council, 1950-65. Served to maj. M.C., AUS, 1942-46. Diplomate Am. Bd. Internal Medicine. Fellow A.C.P., Am. Gastroent. Assn., Am. Acad. Occupational Medicine (sec. 1972-74), Am. Occupational Med. Assn. (dir. 1975-78); mem. Am. Cancer Soc. (dir.), Va. Occupational Med. Assn. (pres.). Kiwanian. Clubs: Commonwealth, Indian Creek Yacht. Home: 9135-A Derbyshire Rd Richmond VA 23229 Office: 6601 W Broad St Richmond VA 23230

MACMILLAN, KENNETH, choreographer; b. Dec. 11, 1929; m. Deborah Williams, 1974. Resident choreographer Royal Ballet, London, until 1966; dir. ballet Deutsche Opera, West Berlin, 1966-70; dir. Royal Ballet, London, 1970-77, choreographer, 1977—. Maj. choreography includes Romeo and Juliet, Song of the Earth, Rite of Spring, Las Hermanas, The Invitation, Diversions, Baiser de la Fée, Danses concertants, Agon, Solitaire, Noctambules, House of Birds, Images of Love, The Seven Deadly Sins, Anastasia, Cain and Abel, Olympiad, Triad, Ballade, The Poltroon, Maonn, Elite Syncopations, The Four Seasons, Rituals. Office: c/o The Royal Ballet Royal Opera House Covent Garden London WC2 England*

MACMILLAN, WILLIAM HOOPER, univ. dean; b. Boston, Oct. 21, 1923; s. Alexander Stewart and Leslie (Hooper) M.; B.A., McGill U., 1948; Ph.D., Yale U., 1954; m. Anne Stearns, May 29, 1948; children—Leslie Jean, Robert Bruce, William Ian. Instr. pharmacology U. Vt. Coll. Medicine, 1954-55, asst. prof., 1955-59, asso. prof., 1959-64, chmn. dept. pharmacology, 1962-63, prof. pharmacology, 1964-76, dean Grad. Coll., 1963-69; research fellow USPHS, U. Oxford (Eng.), 1958-59; cons. New Eng. Assn. Schs. and Colls., 1967-71; Ford Found. project specialist, sci. adv. to Haile Sellassie I U., Addis Ababa. Ethiopia, 1969-71; dean Grad. Coll., U. Vt., 1971-76; dean Grad. Sch., prof. biology U. Ala., 1976—. Exec. com. African grad. fellowship program African-Am. Inst., N.Y.C., 1971—; chmn. com. on biomed. scis. Council of Grad. Schs., Washington, 1973-77; exec. com. Northeast Assn. Grad. Schs., 1975-76. Served as officer USNR, 1943-46. Mem. Am. Soc. Pharmacology and Exptl. Therapeutics, AAAS, N.Y. Acad. Sci., AAUP, Sigma Xi. Home: 123 Woodland Hills Tuscaloosa AL 35405

MACMILLAN, WILLIAM LEEDOM, JR., trade assn. mgmt. co. exec.; b. Phila., Nov. 11, 1913; s. William Leedom and Maude (White) MacM.; student Am. Inst. Banking, 1935; m. Eleanor Knowlton, Dec. 17, 1941; children—William Leedom III, Bruce K. Salesman, Megow Corp., Phila., 1938-41, sales mgr., 1947-48; salesman Xacto, Inc., N.Y.C., 1946-47; show mgr. World Hobby Expns., 1948-49; rep. hobby mgrs. Mfrs. Agt., 1949-55; exec. dir. Hobby Industry of Am., Inc., N.Y.C., 1956-66; owner Mgmt. Services, Ridgewood, N.J., 1966-67; exec. v.p. Multi Service Assos., Phila., 1967-69; owner Mgmt. Services, Moorestown, N.J., 1970-74, pres. MacMillan & Assos., 1974-78, chmn. bd., 1978—; pres. Wide World Travel Service, 1978—. Served from seaman to lt. (j.g.), USCGR, 1942-46. Mem. Am. (dir.), Phila. (past pres., life mem.), N.Y. (dir., pres. 1967—) socs. assn. execs., Inst. Assn. Mgmt. Cos. (dir., sec.-treas. 1976, pres.-elect 1979). Presbyterian. Clubs: Masons, Rotary. Home: 416 Edgemoor Dr Moorestown NJ 08057 Office: 59 E Main St Moorestown NJ 08057

MACMILLEN, WILLIAM CHARLES, JR., investment banker; b. Troy, N.Y., May 24, 1913; s. William C. and Anna C. (Dugan) MacM.; student William Coll., 1931-34; LL.B., Albany Law Sch., 1937; m. Barbara Christy Downing, Mar. 6, 1942; children—Paul Downing, Sally, Anita, William, Nancy. Partner firm MacMillen & Filley, 1939-41; asst. to chmn. Allegheny Corp., 1946; pres. Fedn. Ry. Progress, 1947-48, Eagle Lion Films, Inc., 1949-50, Chesapeake Industries, Inc., 1950-57, Colonial Trust Co., 1957-59; cons. Kuhn, Loeb & Co., 1960-61; chmn., dir. Lexington Internat., Inc., 1962; pres. Cosmos Am. Corp., 1963-64, Internat. Bus. Relations Corp., 1965-66, Tower Internat., Inc., 1967-68; pres., dir. William C. MacMillen & Co., Inc., 1969—; racehorse owner and breeder; dir. Colonial Surety Co., Comml. Alliance Corp. and subs., Republic Nat. Bank N.Y. and subs., Eutectic Welding Alloys Corp., Walter Reade Orgn., Inc., Producers Chem. Corp., Vanguard Internat. Aircargo, Inc., Compucom Systems Inc., Fin. Guaranty Ins. Co. Served as maj. USAAF, 1942-45. Decorated Legion of Merit. Mem. Mgmt. Execs. Soc. Clubs: Saratoga Golf, Rockaway Hunting, Turf and Field; Racquet and Tennis. Home: 254 Victoria Pl Lawrence NY 11559

MACMINN, ALEENE BARNES, journalist; b. Salt Lake City, Sept. 19, 1930; d. Harold S. and Allie J. (Rasmussen) Barnes; B.A. in Journalism, U. So. Calif., 1952; m. Fraser K. MacMinn, July 28, 1961; children—Margaret A., Gregor Geordie. Women's page reporter Glendale (Calif.) News Press, 1948-52, women's page writer Los Angeles Times, 1953-57, asst. family editor, 1957-60, asst. TV editor, 1960-65, exec. TV editor, 1965-69, asst. entertainment editor, 1969-72, TV Times editor, 1972-76, TV editor, 1976—; sr. lectr. Sch. of Journalism, U. So. Calif. Mem. Theta Sigma Phi, Alpha Gamma Delta. Office: Los Angeles Times Times-Mirror Sq Los Angeles CA 90053

MACMULLEN, RAMSAY, educator; b. N.Y.C., Mar. 3, 1928; s. Charles William and Margaret (Richmond) MacM.; A.B., Harvard, 1950, A.M., 1953, Ph.D., 1957; m. Edith Merriman Nye, Aug. 7, 1954; children—John A., Priscilla N., William R., Lucinda S. Instr., asst. prof. U. Oreg., 1956-61; asso. prof., prof. Brandeis U., 1961-67, chmn. dept. classics, 1965-66; prof. Yale, 1967—, chmn. dept. history, 1970-72. Recipient Porter prize Coll. Art Assn., 1964; Fulbright fellow, 1960-61; Guggenheim fellow, 1964; Princeton Inst. for Advanced Study fellow, 1964-65; Nat. Endowment for Humanities sr. fellow, 1974-75. Mem. Soc. for Promotion Roman Studies, Assn. Ancient Historians (pres. 1978—). Author: Soldier and Civilian in the Later Roman Empire, 1963; Enemies of the Roman Order, 1966; Constantine, 1969; Roman Social Relations, 1974; Roman Government's Response to Crisis, 1976. Home: 25 Long Hill Rd Clinton CT 06413 Office: Dept History Yale New Haven CT 06520

MACMURRAY, CHARLES GAYLORD, graphic designer; b. Waverly, Iowa, July 20, 1924; s. Michael G. and Edna (Prosser) MacM.; student Art Inst. Chgo., 1942, 46, 48, Inst. Design, 1953, U. Chgo., 1958, 59, 78—; m. Shirley Joan Westphal, Mar. 13, 1949; children—Bruce Kevin, Craig, Kristin Ann. Designer, Abbott Labs. Internat. Co., 1948-49; typographic designer, art dir. house publs. U.S. Gypsum Co., Inland Steel Corp., also Chrysler Corp., 1950-54; design mgr. for art studio, 1954-59; mgr. graphics and packaging, asso. partner Latham-Tyler-Jensen, Inc., Chgo., 1961-69; partner Charles MacMurray & Assos., 1969-73; pres. Charles MacMurray Design Inc., Chgo., 1973—; designer corp. identification programs, packaging, internat. exhbts. and museums, archtl. graphics. Mem. jury St. Paul Art Dirs. Exhbn., 1960, Memphis Art Dirs. Club, 1958, Artists Guild Chgo. exhbns., 1961; instr. Chgo. Sch. Profl. Arts, 1961—; work exhbt. mags., profl. publs.; mem. Design Conf., Aspen, Colo., 1957-59; mem. Internat. Council Graphic Design Assns., 1963—. Served with USAAF, 1943-46; ETO. Recipient award Type Directors N.Y., 1958; Trademarks U.S.A. Exhbn., Chgo., 1964, Chgo. 2, 3, 4 Exhbns.; mem. 27 Chgo. Designers, 1970—. Small arms instr. Nat. Rifle Assn., 1968—. Mem. Soc. Typographic Arts (dir. 1960-62, 64—, pres. 1963-66; awards 1960, 61, 63, 65, 66), Am. Inst. Graphic Arts, 27 Chgo. Designers. Office: 444 N Michigan Ave Chicago IL 60611

MACMURRAY, FREDERICK MARTIN, actor; b. Kankakee, Ill., Aug. 30, 1908; s. Frederick and Maleta (Martin) MacM.; student Carroll Coll., Waukesha, Wis., 1925-26; m. Lillian Lamont, June 20, 1936; m. 2d, June Haver, June 28, 1954. Played in orchs., Chgo. and Los Angeles, 1925-29; appeared in vaudeville, 1929-34, played in stage shows Three's a Crowd and Roberta, N.Y., 1934; in motion pictures, 1934—, including: The Egg and I, 1947, Miracle of the Bells, 1948, Don't Trust Your Husband, 1949, Family Honeymoon, 1949, The Caine Mutiny, 1953, The Far Horizons, 1954, Woman's World, 1954, Rains of Ranchipur, 1955, The Shaggy Dog, 1959, The Apartment, 1960, The Absent Minded Professor, 1961, Son of Flubber, 1963, Bon Voyage, 1962, Kisses for My President, 1964, Follow Me Boys, 1966, The Happiest Millionaire, 1967, The Swarm, 1978; star TV show My Three Sons, 1960-72, TV film Beyond the Bermuda Triangle, 1975. Home: 485 Halvern Dr Los Angeles CA 90049 Address: care Chasin-Park-Citron Agy 9255 Sunset Blvd Los Angeles CA 90069*

MAC NAMARA, DONAL EOIN JOSEPH, criminologist; b. N.Y.C., Aug. 13, 1916; s. Daniel Patrick and Rita F.V. (Chambers) Mac N.; B.S., Columbia U., 1939, M.Phil., 1948, M.Pub. Adminstrn., N.Y. U., 1946; m. Margaret Elizabeth Scott, July 30, 1953; 1 son, Brian Scott. Instr. polit. sci. Rutgers U., New Brunswick, N.J., 1948-49; asst. dir. Delinquency Control Inst. Los Angeles, 1949-50;

dir. law enforcement program U. So. Calif., 1949-50; vis. prof. U. Louisville, 1950-71, Fla. State U., Tallahassee, 1958, St. Lawrence U., Canton, N.Y., 1954, 56; chmn. Law Enforcement Insts., N.Y. U., 1950-57; coordinator police sci. programs Bklyn. Coll., 1954-57; with N.Y. Inst. Criminology, N.Y.C., 1950-63, asso. dean, 1955-56, dean, 1956-63; prof. criminology Center Corrections Tng., City U. N.Y., 1966-67, charge corrections programs John Jay Coll. Criminal Justice, 1965—, dir. summer session, Ireland, 1970. Mng. partner Flath-MacNamara Assos., N.Y.C., 1958-64; dir. Crime Show Consultants, N.Y.C., Traffic Mgmt. Survey Fund, Inc., N.Y.C.; Eastern regional dir. Character Underwriters, Inc., Los Angeles; vis. mem. faculty Hunter, Queens, Bklyn. colls., 1952-58; vis. lectr. criminology Brandeis U., Waltham, Mass., 1962; lectr. police adminstrn. State U. N.Y., 1966-67; lectr. penology City Coll., 1965-67; specialist police, correctional adminstrn. grad. progran tng. pub. adminstrn. State of N.Y., Albany, 1951-56; criminological cons. Am. Express Co., 1962-68; cons. Bergen County, N.J., 1967, N.J. Commn. Civil Disorders, 1967-68; vis. prof. criminology U. Utah, Salt Lake City, 1962; pres. League to Abolish Capital Punishment, 1958-70, chmn. bd., 1959—; col. aide-de-camp to commr. Ky. State Police, 1963; external assessor in police and pub. adminstrn. Republic of Ireland, 1975; vis. prof. Inst. Pub. Adminstrn., Dublin, 1974-75. Exec. v.p. Real Estate Bd., Bronx, N.Y., 1964-65. Served to maj. AUS, 1942-48. Recipient award of honor Internat. Assn. Women Police, 1960; Herbert A. Bloch award Am. Soc. Criminology, 1967. Fellow A.A.A.S. (chmn. sci. criminology sect., mem. council 1957—), Am. Acad. Criminalistics (presiding); mem. Internat. Police Officers Assn. (life), Am. Soc. Criminology (pres. 1960-64), Am. Sociol. Assn., Am. Acad. Polit. and Social Sci., Assn. Psychiat. Treatment Offenders (program coordinator 1954-58), Mil. Police Assn., Internat. Criminological Soc., Am. Assn. Criminologists (hon. life), Internat. Assn. Chiefs Police, Am. Correctional Assn., Internat. Juvenile Officers Assn., Better Bus. Bur., Am. Soc. Pub. Adminstrn., Am. Polit. Sci. Assn., Nat. Inst. Social and Behavioral Scis., Edn. Research Assn. (exec. dir. 1965-69), Nat. Police Officers Assn. Am. (research dir. 1963-67), Pi Sigma Alpha. Author: Problems of Sex Behavior, 1968; Perspectives on Correction, 1971; Corrections: Problems of Punishment and Rehabilitation, 1973; Police: Problems and Prospects, 1974; Criminal Justice, 1976; Sex, Crime and the Law, 1977; Incarceration: The Sociology of Imprisonment, 1978; also articles. Am. editor Excerpta Criminologica, 1965—; editor-in-chief Criminology: An Interdisciplinary Jour., 1975-78; asso. editor Internat. Jour. Criminology and Penology, Abstracts Police Sci., Jour. Corrective Psychiatry. Home: 206 Christie Heights Leonia NJ 07605 Office: 444 W 56th St New York NY 10019

MACNAMARA, JOHN, steel co. exec.; b. Hamilton, Ont., Can., Mar. 22, 1925; s. John Edward and Raechel (Watt) M.; B.Sc., McMaster U., 1947, M.Sc., 1949, Ph.D., 1951; m. Mary Jane Anne Walsh, Oct. 15, 1949; children—John Alexander, Dean Stafford, Peter MacEvery, Stephen Walsh. Research officer NRC, Hamilton, 1949-51; with Algoma Steel Corp., Ltd., Sault Ste. Marie, Ont., 1951—, successively asst. chief chemist, asst. supt., supt., div. supt., v.p. ops., 1951-73, exec. v.p., 1973-76, pres., chief exec. officer, 1976—; dir. Dominion Bridge Co., Montreal, Canadian Pacific Investments. Bd. dirs. Plummer Meml. Hosp. Mem. Am. Iron and Steel Inst. (dir.), Internat. Iron and Steel Inst. (dir.). Contbr. articles to profl. jours. Office: Algoma Steel Corp Ltd 503 Queen St E Sault Ste Marie ON P6A 5P2 Canada*

MACNAMARA, THOMAS EDWARD, physician, educator; b. Airdrie, Scotland, May 23, 1929; s. Edward Francis and Bridget Monica (Fawcett) M.; came to U.S., 1956, naturalized, 1962; student Paisley Tech. Coll., Glasgow U., 1947, M.B., Ch.B., 1952; m. Julia B. Caulfield, Sept. 22, 1956; children—Edward, Brian, Mary, Bridget, Anne. Intern Victoria Infirmary, Glasgow, 1953, Leith Hosp., Edinburgh, Bellsdyke Hosp., Larbert, 1954, St. Martins Hosp., Bath, 1954, Birmingham (Eng.) Accident Hosp., 1955; resident in anesthesiology Mass. Gen. Hosp., Boston, 1956; practice medicine specializing in anesthesia, Washington, 1957-59, 62—, Boston, 1960-62; mem. staff Georgetown U. Hosp., Mass. Gen. Hosp., Boston, Jefferson Meml. Hosp., Ranson, W.Va. Instr. anesthesia Georgetown U., 1957-60, prof., chmn. dept. anesthesia Med. Center, 1962—; chief anesthesiology NIH Clin. Center, Bethesda, Md., 1975—; asst. in anesthesia Mass. Gen. Hosp., Harvard Med. Sch., 1960-62; cons. VA Hosp., Washington, 1962—, Walter Reed Army Med. Center, Washington, Jefferson Meml. Hosp. Bd. dirs. Georgetown U. Fed. Credit Union; senator U. Faculty Senate, Georgetown U., 1967—, v.p., 1967-70, pres., 1973-75. Diplomate Am. Bd. Anesthesiology. Fellow Am. Coll. Anesthesiologists (asso. examiner 1966—); mem. Brit., Mass., D.C. med. socs., Am. Soc. Anesthesiologists, Royal Soc. Medicine, Soc. Acad. Anesthesia Chairmen, Soc. for Obstetrics Anesthesiology and Perinatology, A.A.U.P., Am. Assn. Regional Anesthesia, Internat. Assn. Study of Pain, Soc. Neurol. Anesthesia, Internat. Anesthesia Research Soc., Md.-D.C. Soc. Anesthesiology (pres. sect. II 1966-67). Editor: Surgical Digest, 1966-70, Clinical Therapeutics, 1976—. Home: 2736 N Nelson St Arlington VA 22207 Office: Dept Anesthesia Georgetown U Hosp 3800 Reservoir Rd NW Washington DC 20007

MACNAUGHT, J. WATSON, lawyer; b. Coleman, P.E.I., Can., June 19, 1904; s. Robert C. and Emily (Moreshead) MacN.; B.A., Dalhousie U., 1928, LL.B., 1930; m. Eva Palmer, May 11, 1932; children—John William, David Alexander. Called to Canadian bar, created King's counsel, 1942; law clk. Prince Edward Isle Legislative Assembly, 1935-41, clk. of assembly, 1941-45; crown prosecutor Prince County, 1942- 45; mem. Ho. of Commons, 1945-47, 63-65; Parliamentary asst. to minister fisheries, 1948-57; solicitor gen. Can., 1963-65; minister mines and tech. surveys, 1965; chmn. of Dominion Coal Bd., 1966-69; now mem. firm J. Watson & John W. MacNaught, P.E.I. Sec., P.E.I. br. Commonwealth Parliamentary Assn., 1941-45, del. conf., Wellington, New Zealand, 1950; adviser Canandian delegation Tokyo meeting, 1955; head Canadian delegation orgn. Internat. N. Pacific Fisheries Commn., Washington, 1953; Canadian rep. inauguration pres. of Mexico, 1964. Mem. Canadian Assn. Retarded Children, P.E.I., N.S. bar assns., Phi Delta Phi. Rotarian. Home: Summerside PE Canada Office: Suite 7 Smallman Bldg Summerside PE Canada

MACNAUGHTON, ALEXANDER DOUGLAS, educator; b. New Haven, July 10, 1913: s. Norman and Kathleen (Chalk) MacN.; B.A., Adrian Coll., 1934, D.H.L., 1979; M.S., U. Mich., 1938; postgrad., Harvard, 1940-4i; B.D., Yale, 1943; Ph.D., U. Chgo., 1956; m. Thelma Broadrick, May 19, 1944; children—N. George, Thomas D., John W., Jean K. Tchr., Otisville (Mich.) Pub. Schs., 1935-36; ordained to ministry Methodist Ch., 1943; minister to students Wesley Found., Ohio U., 1943-45; dir. Student Christian Found., So. Ill. U., 1945-48; pastor Meth. Ch., Hoytville, O., 1951-56; prof. religion Defiance (0.) Coll., 1956-61; prof. religion Adrian (Mich.) Coll., 1961—, chmn. dept. philosophy and religion, 1966-77. Bd. dirs. Mich. Intercollegiate Athletic Assn. Mem. Ohio Colls. Assn. (sec. religion sect. 1961-62), Am. Acad. Religion (sec. Midwest region 1971-72, membership chmn. 1972-73, v.p., program chmn. 1973-74, pres. 1975-76). Author: The Methodist Church in Michigan: The Twentieth Century, 1976. Home: 1218 Madison Dr Adrian MI 49221

MACNAUGHTON, ANGUS ATHOLE, diversified industry exec.; b. Montreal, Que., Can., July 15, 1931; s. Athole Austin and Emily Kidder (MacLean) MacN.; student Lower Can. Coll., Montreal, 1947-48, McGill U., 1949-54; m. Penelope Bower Lewis, Mar. 2, 1957; children—Gillian Heather, Angus Andrew. Auditor, Coopers & Lybrand, Montreal, 1949-55; accountant Genstar Ltd., Montreal, 1955, asst. treas., 1956-61, treas., 1961-64, v.p., 1964-70, exec. v.p., 1970-73, pres., 1973-76, vice chmn., chief exec. officer, 1976—; dir. Can. Pacific Investments Ltd., Dart Containerline Inc., Royal Trust Co., Can. Comml. Corp. Mem. Tax Execs. Inst. (past pres. Montreal chpt.), Que. Inst. Chartered Accountants. Clubs: Mount Royal; St. James. Home: 72 Sunnyside Ave Westmount PQ Canada Office: Suite 4105 1 Pl Ville Marie Montreal PQ Canada

MACNAUGHTON, DONALD SINCLAIR, hosp. supply co. exec.; b. Schenectady, July 14, 1917; s. William and Marion (Colquhoun) MacN.; A.B., Syracuse U., 1939, LL.B., 1948; m. Winifred Thomas, Apr. 10, 1941; children—Donald, David. Tchr. history Pulaski (N.Y.) Acad. and Central Sch., 1939-42; admitted to N.Y. bar, 1948; pvt. practice, Pulaski, 1948-54; dep. supt. ins. N.Y. State, 1954-55; with Prudential Ins. Co. Am., 1955-78, pres., chief exec. officer, 1969-70, chmn. bd., chief exec. officer, 1970-78, now dir.; chmn. bd., chief exec. officer Hosp. Corp. Am., Nashville, 1978—; dir. Exxon Corp., AT&T, Johnson & Johnson. Trustee Syracuse U.; bd. overseers Wharton Sch. Served as 1st lt. with AC, U.S. Army, 1942-46. Mem. Am. Bar Assn., Bus. Council. Clubs: Eastward Ho!, El Dorado, Links. Home: Nashville TN 37205 Office: HCA Park Plaza Nashville TN 37203

MACNAUGHTON, JAMES ROBERT, accountant; b. Fredericton, N.B., Can., Apr. 11, 1918; s. Herbert R. and Jennie (Gamble) MacN.; came to U.S., 1923, naturalized, 1942; B.B.A., U. Minn., 1941; m. Emilie Borgwald, Jan. 19, 1944; children—Carol, James, Ann. With Ernst & Ernst, C.P.A.'s, 1941—, partner, Des Moines, 1956-70, partner in charge Mid-Atlantic dist., Washington, 1970-78; cons., 1978—; adminstr. Sibley Meml. Hosp., Washington, 1979—; dir. Met. Washington Bd. of Trade. Pres., Jr. Achievement Des Moines, 1963-64; regional bd. mem. Midwest Jr. Achievement, 1964—; pres. Music Under the Stars, Des Moines, 1964—. Bd. dirs. Iowa Taxpayers Assn., 1965—, CIRAS, Salvation Army, Boys Home of Iowa. Served to lt. (j.g.) USCGR, 1942-45. C.P.A., Iowa, 6 other states. Mem. Am. Inst. C.P.A.'s, Iowa Soc. C.P.A.'s (pres. 1957-58), Des Moines C. of C. (dir.), Beta Gamma Sigma (hon.), Beta Alpha Psi (hon.). Episcopalian. Mason (Shriner, Jester), Rotarian. Clubs: Des Moines, Golf and Country (pres. 1960), Des Moines Wakonda (Des Moines); Internat. (Washington). Home: 9605 Weathered Oak Ct Bethesda MD 20034 Office: 1225 Connecticut Ave NW Washington DC 20036

MACNEE, (DANIEL) PATRICK, actor; b. London, Feb. 6, 1922; s. Daniel and Doratisea Mary (Henry) M.; student pvt. schs., Eng.; children—Rupert, Jenny. Appeared in the theatre, Eng., 1939-42, 46-52, Can. and U.S., 1952-60; appeared on TV series The Avengers, 1960-69; in TV movies: No Such Thing As A Vampire, Sherlock Holmes in New York, Matt Helm, Mister Jerico; TV guest appearances in Battlestar Gallactica, Night Gallery, Columbo, Great Mysteries, Diana. Served with Brit. Navy, 1942-46. Recipient Variety Artist award of Gt. Brit., 1963. Mem. Actors Equity, AFTRA, Screen Actors Guild, Assn. Can. TV and Radio Artists. Office: care Phil Gersh Agy Inc 222 N Canon Dr Beverly Hills CA 90210

MACNEIL, CORNELL HILL, baritone; b. Mpls., Sept. 24, 1922; s. Walter Hill and Harriette Belle (Cornell) MacN.; student Hartt Sch. Music, U. Hartford, 1944-45; m. Tania Rudensky, May 23, 1972; children by previous marriage—Walter Gavan, Mary Ellen, Dennis Michael, Susan, Katherine Mary. Appeared in Broadway plays Sweethearts, 1947, Where's Charley, 1949; debut in opera in The Consul, N.Y.C., 1950; N.Y.C. Opera debut Germont in La Traviata, 1953, La Scala debut as Charles V in Ernani, 1959, Met. Opera debut as Rigoletto in Rigoletto, 1959; appeared in leading opera houses Europe, N.Am. and S.Am.; recorded numerous albums. Named Alumnus of Year, Hartt Sch. Music, 1976. Mem. Am. Guild Musical Artists (pres. 1971-77). Office: care Columbia Arts Mgmt Inc 165 W 57th St New York NY 10019

MACNEIL, GRACE M. S. MCKITTRICK (MRS. DOUGLAS H. MACNEIL), civic worker; b. Natchez, Miss., Nov. 25, 1907; d. David Lawrence and Charlotte Linton (Surget) McKittrick; B.A., H. Sophie Newcomb Coll., Tulane U., 1929; m. Douglas H. MacNeil, Sept. 25, 1933 (dec. May 1963); children—Elizabeth C. (Mrs. William Franklin Boggess), Anne W.S. Plantation owner, operator, Miss., La., 1946—: owner Elms Ct., Natchez. Nat. staff mem. Girl Scouts U.S.A., 1930-39, dir., 1955—, chmn. nat. exec. com., 1960-69, v.p., 1960-69, pres., 1969-72; mem. world com. Girl Guides/Girl Scouts, 1972—; mem. N.J. Welfare Council, 1933-36; chmn. dental health com. Council Social Agys., Somerset County, Somerville, N.J., 1951-53; mem. Council Community Service, Princeton Day Schs., 1960-62; v.p. Council Nat. Orgns. for Children and Youth, 1960-63, mem. nat. adv. com., 1965-69. Dir. Family Service Agy., Princeton, N.J., 1948-52; trustee Miss Fines Sch., 1953-55, chmn. planning com., 1956-62; trustee Princeton Day Schs., 1960-64. Mem. English-Speaking Union (dir. 1960-65), UN Assn. Am. (dir. 1964-67), Pi Beta Phi. Clubs: Present Day (pres. Princeton 1951-53); Tulane University Alumni (dir. N.Y.C. 1959-63); Natchez Garden (dir. 1967—, pres. 1974—). Home: Elms Ct Box 284 Natchez MS 39120

MAC NEIL, JOSEPH NEIL, clergyman; b. Sydney, N.S., Can., Apr. 15, 1924; s. John Martin and Kate (Mac Lean) Mac N.; B.A., St. Francis Xavier U., Antigonish, N.S., 1944; postgrad. Holy Heart Sem., Halifax, N.S., 1944-48, U. Perugia, 1956, U. Chgo., 1964; J.C.D., U. St. Thomas, Rome, 1958. Ordained priest Roman Catholic Ch., 1948; pastor parishes in N.S., 1948-55; officialis Chancery Office, Antigonish, 1958-59; adminstrn. Diocese of Antigonish, 1959-60; rector Cathedral Antigonish, 1961; dir. extension dept. St. Francis Xavier U., Antigonish, 1961-69, v.p., 1962-69; bishop, St. John, N.B., Can., 1969-74; archbishop of Edmonton (Alta.), 1973—; chancellor U. St. Thomas, Fredericton, N.B., 1969-73. Vice chmn. N.S. Voluntary Econ. Planning Bd., 1965-69; exec. Atlantic Provinces Econ. Council, 1968-73, Can. Council Rural Devel., 1965-75; dir. Program and Planning Agy. N.S. Govt., 1969. Mem. Canadian Assn. Adult Edn. (past pres. N.S.), Canadian Assn. Dirs. Univ. Extension and Summer Schs. (past pres.), Inst. Research on Public Policy (founding mem.), Can. Conf. Cath. Bishops (v.p. 1977—). Address: 10044 113th St Edmonton AB T5K 1N8 Canada

MACNEIL, ROBERT BRECKENRIDGE WARE, broadcast journalist; b. Montreal, Que., Can., Jan. 19, 1931; s. Robert A.S. and Margaret Virginia (Oxner) MacN.; came to U.S., 1963: student Dalhousie U., 1949-51; B.A., Carleton U., 1955; L.H.D. (hon.), William Patterson Coll., 1977, Beaver Coll., 1979, Bates Coll., 1979; m. Rosemarie Anne Copland, 1956 (div. 1964); children—Catherine Anne, Ian B.; m. 2d, Jane J. Doherty, May 29, 1965; children—Alison N., William H. Radio actor CBC, Halifax, N.S., Can., 1950-52, radio/TV announcer, 1954-55: announcer Sta.-CJCH, Halifax, 1951-52; announcer, news writer Sta. CFRA, Ottawa, Ont., Can., 1952-54; sub-editor to filing editor Reuters News Agy., London, 1955-60; news corr. NBC, London, 1960-63, Washington, 1963-65, N.Y.C., 1965-67; corr. Panorama program BBC, London, 1967-71, 73-75; sr. corr. Nat. Public Affairs Center for TV, Washington, 1971-73; exec. editor, co-anchor MacNeil/Lehrer Report, Sta. -WNET-TV, N.Y.C., 1975—. Recipient awards, including George Foster Peabody award U. Ga., 1977; Dupont award Columbia Sch. Journalism, 1977; Emmy award, 1974. Mem. AFTRA, Assn. Radio and TV News Analysts, Writers Guild Am. Club: American Yacht (Rye, N.Y.). Author: The People Machine, The Influence of Television on American Politics, 1978. Office: WNET/13 356 W 58th St New York NY 10019

MACNEILL, ARTHUR EDSON, physician, sci. cons.; b. Waltham, Mass., July 14, 1912; s. Charles Alfred and Florence (Wright) MacN.; A.B., Harvard, 1933, M.D., 1937; grad. Army Sch. Aviation Medicine, 1942; m. Lydia Mae Rhoades, June 25, 1941; children—Marjorie Ann, Arthur Edson. Intern, Mary Hitchcock Meml. Hosp., Hanover, N.H., 1937-38; physician Health Service, Dartmouth, 1938-41, acting med. dir., 1945-46, instr. anatomy, sec., Med. Sch., 1944-46, research asso. physiol. scis., 1946-50; univ. physician U. Fla., Gainesville, 1946-47; cons. med. and biol. research Fgn. Service, U.S. Dept. State, 1950; dir. labs. U. Buffalo Chronic Disease Research Inst., 1950-56, lectr. medicine, 1951-57; asst. research prof. surgery, Buswell Research fellow U. Buffalo Sch. Medicine, 1957-61; asso. research prof. surgery State U. N.Y., Buffalo Sch. Medicine, 1961-64; research adviser Buffalo Children's Hosp., 1958-64; chief clin. investigative cons. Respirator Center, Buffalo, 1954-55; devel. blood dialyzer, blood pumps, blood flowmeters, blood rheometer, other devices for profl. treatment vital organs; private cons. in field; research staff, adj. med. bd. Buffalo Gen. Hosp., 1951-64, cons. surg. research staff, 1957-64, dir. dept. therapeutic engring., 1958-64; dir. Inst. for Therapeutic Engring., Sunapee, N.H., 1964-65; dir. Dialysis Research Inst., Sunapee, 1965—; research cons. therapeutic engring., 1964—; med. asso. Crotched Mountain Rehab. Center, Greenfield, N.H., 1967—. Served from 1st lt. to maj. M.C., USAAF, 1941-44; surgeon 72d Fighter Wing, 1943-44, staff surgeon, 1944; maj. Hon. Res., USAF, 1951—. Recipient Maj. Louis Livingston Seaman award Assn. Mil. Surgeons U.S., 1949; 1st award sci. research Med. Soc. State N.Y., 1953; Redway award Med. Soc. State N.Y., 1963. Mem. Instrument Soc. Am. (dir. med. and biol. div. 1956-57), A.M.A., N.H., Grafton County med. assns., Assn. Mil. Surgeons, A.A.A.S., N.Y. Acad. Scis., Am. Soc. Nephrology, Am., N.H. heart assns., N.H. Orthopedic Soc., Nat. Kidney Found., Sigma Xi. Methodist. Contbr. to profl. jours. Home: Garnet Hill Rd Sunapee NH 03782 Office: Box 334 Sunapee NH 03782

MAC NEILL, JAMES WILLIAM, govt. adminstr.; b. Sask., Can., Apr. 22, 1928; s. Leslie William and Helga Ingeborg (Nohlgren) MacN.; B.A., U. Sask., 1949, B.E. Mech., 1958; Diplome, U. Stockholm, 1951; m. Phyllis Beryl Ferguson, Nov. 30, 1953; children—Catherine Anne, Robin Lynne. Spl. adv. on constl. rev. Privy Council Office, Govt. Can., Ottawa, Ont., 1969-70; asst. sec. Can. Ministry of State for Urban Affairs, Ottawa, 1970-73, (permanent) sec., 1973-76; Can. AEP, Can. commr.-gen. UN Human Settlements Conf., Vancouver, B.C., 1975-78; dir. environ. directorate OECD, Paris, 1978—; cons. UN Environ. Program, 1977. Mem. Can. Inst. Public Adminstrn., Assn. Profl. Engrs. Ont., Assn. Profl. Engrs. Sask. Author: Environmental Management, 1971. Office: 2 rue Andre-Pascal Paris 75775 France

MACNEIL OF BARRA, IAN RODERICK, lawyer, educator; b. N.Y.C., June 20, 1929; s. Robert Lister and Kathleen Gertrude (Metcalf) M.; B.A. magna cum laude, U. Vt., 1950; J.D. magna cum laude, Harvard U., 1955; m. Nancy Carol Wilson, Mar. 29, 1952; children—Roderick, Jennifer, Duncan (dec.), Andrew. Admitted to N.H. bar, 1956; law clk. Hon. Peter Woodbury, 1955-56; asso. firm Sulloway, Hollis, Godfrey & Soden, Concord, N.H., 1956-59; mem. faculty Cornell U. Law Sch., Ithaca, N.Y., 1959-72, 74—, Ingersoll prof. law, 1976—; vis. prof. U. East Africa, 1965-67, Duke U., 1971-72; prof. law, mem. Inst. Advanced Studies, U. Va., 1972-74; vis. fellow Centre for Socio-legal Studies and Wolfson Coll., Oxford U., 1979; hon. vis. fellow faculty law U. Edinburgh, 1979; Rosenthal lectr. Northwestern U. Sch. Law, 1979. Served with U.S. Army, 1951-53. Guggenheim fellow, 1978-79; recipient Emil Brown Preventive Law prize, 1971. Fellow Royal Soc. Antiquities (Scotland); mem. Am. Law Inst., Am. Bar Assn., N.H. Bar Assn., Can. Assn. Law Tchrs., Soc. Public Tchrs. Law, Standing Council Scottish Chiefs. Club: Puffin's (Edinburgh). Author: Bankruptcy Law in East Africa, 1966; Contracts: Exchange Transactions and Relations, 2d edit., 1978. Home: 105 Devon Rd Ithaca NY 14850 and Kisimul Castle Isle of Barra Scotland Office: Cornell Law Sch Ithaca NY 14853

MACNELLY, JEFFREY KENNETH, cartoonist; b. N.Y.C., Sept. 17, 1947; s. Clarence Lamont and Ruth Ellen (Fox) M.; grad. Phillips Acad., 1965; student U. N.C., Chapel Hill, 1965-69; m. Marguerite Dewey Daniels, July 19, 1969; children—Jeffrey Kenneth, Frank Daniels. Cartoonist, staff artist Chapel Hill Weekly, 1969-70; cartoonist Richmond (Va.) News Leader, 1970—. Recipient Pulitzer prize for editorial cartoons, 1972. Office: 333 E Grace St Richmond VA 23219

MACNICHOL, EDWARD FORD, JR., biophysicist; b. Toledo, Oct. 24, 1918; s. Edward Ford and Adelaide (Foster) MacN.; A.B., Princeton, 1941; student U. Pa., 1946-48; Ph.D., Johns Hopkins, 1952; m. Anne Proctor Ayer, Sept. 7, 1940; children—Edward Ford III, Anne (Mrs. David A. Brownell). Staff mem. radiation lab. Mass. Inst. Tech., 1941-46; from instr. to prof. biophysics Johns Hopkins, 1952-68; research biophysicist, asst. dir. Marine Biol. Lab., Woods Hole, Mass., 1972-76, dir. Lab. Sensory Physiology, 1973—; prof. physiology Boston U. Med. Sch., 1973—; dir. Nat. Inst. Neurol. Diseases and Stroke, 1968-72, acting dir. Nat. Eye Inst., NIH, 1968-69. Mem. visual scis. study sect. NIH, 1963-66; mem. bd. sci. counsellors Nat. Inst. Neurol. Disease, and Blindness, 1965-68, chmn. 1968—; mem. U.S. Nat. Com. Photobiology, 1966-68; mem. U.S. Nat. Com. Pure and Applied Biophysics, 1966. Bd. dirs. Deafness Research Found., 1973—, sec., 1976-78. Recipient certificate of appreciation War Dept.-Navy Dept., 1947. Fellow IEEE (Engring. in Biology and Medicine prize award 1965; editor trans. biomed. engring. 1963-65); mem. AAAS, Am. Phys. Soc., Am. Physiol. Soc., Biophys. Soc., Soc. for Neurosci. Co-editor: Sensory Processes, 1978—. Research in neurophysiology of vision; design instrumentation biol. research. Home: 120 Racing Beach Ave Falmouth MA 02540 Office: Marine Biol Lab Woods Hole MA 02543

MACNIDER, JACK, cement co. exec.; b. Washington, Feb. 21, 1927; s. Hanford and Margaret Elizabeth (McAuley) MacN.; grad. Milton (Mass.) Acad., 1946; B.A., Harvard U., 1950, M.B.A. with distinction, 1952; m. Margaret Hansen, Sept. 9, 1950; 1 son, Charles Hanford. With U.S. Steel Corp., 1952-54; with Northwestern States Portland Cement Co., Mason City, Iowa, 1954—, v.p., asst. gen. mgr., 1959-60, pres., gen. mgr., 1960—, chmn. bd., 1979—, also dir.; dir. Portland Cement Assn., 1962—, chmn., 1974—; dir. First Nat. Bank Mason City; sec.-treas., pres., dir. Mason City Hotel Corp.; pres., dir. Indianhead Farms, Inc., 1976—; trustee Equitable Life Ins. Co. Iowa. Pres. N. Iowa Med. Center, 1974—. Trustee Beloit Coll., Midwest Research Inst., Kansas City, Mo., Iowa Natural Heritage Found., 1979—; hon. trustee Upper Iowa U., Fayette; pres. Iowa Coll. Found., 1962. Served with USMCR, 1944-45. Mem. NAM (dir. 1978—), Young Pres. Orgn., Portland Cement Assn. (chmn. bd. 1974-75, dir.), Iowa Mfrs. Assn. (chmn. 1971-72, dir.), Mason City C. of C. (pres.

1962), Am. Legion (past post comdr.). Republican. Conglist. Mason. Clubs: Euchre and Cycle, Mason City Country (Mason City); Minneapolis; University (Chgo.); Des Moines; Lost Tree (Fla.). Home: Box 623 Mason City IA 50401 Office: Box 1008 Mason City IA 50401

MACNUTT, GLENN GORDON, painter, illustrator; b. London, Ont., Can., Jan. 21, 1906; s. Gordon Ross and Ann Mary (Amirault) MacN.; student Sch. of Mus. Fine Arts, Boston, 1930-32, Mass. Sch. Art, Boston, 1924-28; m. Evelyn Louise Simpson, Oct. 12, 1935; children—Jean Ann, Glenn Stephen, Karen Louise. Came to U.S., 1922, naturalized, 1931. Exhibited Bklyn. Mus., 1939-41, Art Inst. Chgo., 1939-41, 42, Met. Mus., 1941-42, Pa. Acad. Fine Arts, 1942-52, Los Angeles Pub. Library, 1954; one man shows Guild Boston Artists, 1940-41, 43, Whistler House, 1942, Wellesley Coll., Doll and Richards Gallery, 1947; represented permanent collections Boston Mus. Fine Arts, New Britain (Conn.) Art Inst., Farnsworth Mus., Me., Harvard U., Wheaton Coll., Mass., Mather Sch., Boston, Frye Mus., Seattle. Recipient Richard Mitton award 1942, 55, 57; Herbert L. Pratt award Am. Watercolor Soc., 1956; award Concord Art Assn., 1953, Boston Soc. Watercolor Painters, 1954-56; Emily Lowe prize Allied Artists Am., 1960; Adolph and Clara Obrig prize N.A.D., 1963. Mem. Boston Soc. Watercolor Painters (v.p., sec.-treas., 1945-48), Guild Boston Artists (bd. mgrs.), Am. Watercolor Soc. (Grumbacher award 1965, E. Heiland award 1971, Ford Times award 1972), N.A.D., Allied Artists Am. (Emily Lowe award 1960, Frank Liljegren award 1972). Address: 129 Minot St Dorchester MA 02122

MACOMBER, ALLISON RUFUS, sculptor; b. Taunton, Mass., July 5, 1916; s. Allison Rufus and Rose Anne (Williams) M.; student Mass. Coll. Art, 1934-38; studied with Cyrus Dallin, 1934-38, Raymond Porter, 1934-38, Henry Kitson, 1937-40; m. Kathleen Mary Fripp, Oct. 2, 1944; children—Daphne Mary, Philip Allison. Designer, Radiation Lab., Mass. Inst. Tech., 1940-42; sculptor portraits, coins, medals, memls., archtl. works in bronze and stone throughout U.S., other countries; artist in residence Boston Coll., 1963-79; mem. Mass. State Senate Art Commn., 1975-79. Served with USAAF, 1942-45. Decorated D.F.C., Air medal with 4 oak leaf clusters. Mem. Fall River Art Assn. (hon.). Episcopalian. Home: Mulberry Cottage Segregansett MA 02773 Office: Barry Art Center Boston Coll Chestnut Hill MA 02167 Died 1979.

MACOMBER, JOHN D., chem. co. exec.; b. Rochester, N.Y., Jan. 13, 1928; s. William Butts and Elizabeth Currie (Ranlet) M.; grad. Phillips Andover Acad., 1946; B.A., Yale, 1950; M.B.A., Harvard, 1952; m. Caroline Morgan, Oct. 21, 1955; children—Janet Morgan, Elizabeth Currie, William Butts II. With McKinsey & Co., N.Y.C., France and Switzerland, 1954-73, mng. dir., Geneva, Switzerland, 1961-64, continental coordinator, Europe, 1964-68, dir., 1964-73; pres. Celanese Corp., N.Y.C., 1973—, chief exec. officer, 1977—; dir. Chase Manhattan Bank, R.J. Reynolds Industries, Inc., Bristol-Myers Co. Vice chmn. N.Y. Philharmonic Orch.; trustee Com. Econ. Devel., N.Y. Zool. Soc.; bd. dirs. Lincoln Center for Performing Arts, Center for Inter-Am. Relations. Served to 1st lt. USAF, 1952-53. Mem. Council on Fgn. Relations, Pilgrims U.S. Clubs: Links, River, Union, Harvard Bus. Sch. (N.Y.C.). Office: 1211 Ave of Americas New York NY 10036

MACOMBER, WILLIAM BUTTS, mus. exec.; b. Rochester, N.Y., Mar. 28, 1921; s. William Butts and Elizabeth Currie (Ranlet) M.; grad. Phillips Andover Acad., 1940; A.B., Yale, 1943, M.A., 1947; LL.B., Harvard, 1949; M.A., U. Chgo., 1951; m. Phyllis D. Bernau, Dec. 28, 1963. Lectr. govt. Boston U., 1947-49; with CIA, Washington, 1951-53; spl. asst. to spl. asst. to sec. for intelligence Dept. State, Washington, 1953-54; adminstrv. asst. to Sen. John Sherman Cooper, 1954; spl. asst. to under sec. of state Herbert Hoover, Jr., 1955, to sec. of state John Foster Dulles, 1955-57; asst. sec. of state for congl. relations, 1957-62; A.E. and P. to Jordan, 1961-64; asst. adminstr. AID, Washington, 1964-67; asst. sec. for congl. relations Dept. State, 1967-69, dep. under sec. of state for adminstrn., 1969-73; U.S. ambassador to Turkey, 1973-78; pres. Met. Mus. Art, N.Y.C., 1978—. Served as lt. USMC, 1943-46. Club: Genesee. Home: 993 Fifth Ave New York NY 10028 Office: Met Mus Art New York NY 10028

MACON, JOSEPH ALLSTON, judge; b. Wetumpka, Ala., July 17, 1917; s. Thomas Leonard and Mattie Janie (Sanford) M.; J.D., U. Ala., 1940; grad. Nat. Coll. State Trial Judges, 1968; m. Helen Etha Nix, Nov. 28, 1940; children—Joseph Allston, Thomas Leonard, Mary Helen. Admitted to Ala. bar, 1940, practiced in Wetumpka, 1940-42, 46-64; mem. firm Jones and Macon, 1946-64; dist. atty. 19th Jud. Circuit, Wetumpka, 1964-66, judge, 1966—. Dir. Citizens Bank. Served with AUS, 1942-46. Mem. Am., Ala., Elmore County, 19th Jud. Circuit (pres. 1958) bar assns., Ala., Continuing Legal Edn. circuit judges assns., Farrah Law Soc., Am. Judicature Soc., Elmore County Hist. Soc., Sigma Chi. Democrat. Baptist. Mason (Shriner), Lion. Home: 206 Tuskeena St Wetumpka AL 36092 Office: Courthouse Wetumpka AL 36092

MACON, SETH CRAVEN, ins. co. exec.; b. Climax, N.C., Mar. 22, 1919; s. Oren T. and Kate (Craven) M.; A.B., Guilford Coll., 1940; grad. Am. Coll. Life Underwriters, 1949; postgrad. Inst. Ins. Marketing, So. Methodist U., 1947, exec. program U. N.C., 1958; m. Hazel Lee Monsees, June 27, 1942; children—Carol Susan, Randall Seth. With Jefferson Standard Life Ins. Co., 1940—, v.p., asso. agy. mgr., 1964-67, v.p., agy. mgr., 1967-70, sr. v.p., dir., mem. finance com., 1970—; v.p. Jefferson-Pilot Corp., 1974—, also dir. Trustee Life Underwriters Tng. Council, 1974-76, Guilford Coll., 1969—. Served with USAAF, 1942-46. Recipient Disting. Alumnus award Guilford Coll., 1978. Mem. Life Ins. Marketing and Research Assn. (dir. 1974-78, chmn. 1976-77). Baptist (deacon 1960—, mem. finance com. 1960—). Rotarian (dir.). Clubs: Starmount Forest Country, Greensboro City (Greensboro). Author: Action in Recruiting, 1970; Recruiting—Today's Number One Priority in Agency Management, 1979. Home: 3803 Madison Ave Greensboro NC 27403 Office: PO Box 21008 Greensboro NC 27420

MACOVSKI, ALBERT, educator; b. N.Y.C., May 2, 1929; s. Philip and Rose (Winogrand) M.; B.E.E., City Coll. N.Y., 1950; M.E.E., Poly. Inst. Bklyn., 1953; Ph.D., Stanford U., 1968; m. Adelaide Paris, Aug. 5, 1950; children—Michael, Nancy. Mem. tech. staff RCA Labs., Princeton, N.J., 1950-57; asst. prof., then asso. prof. Poly. Inst. Bklyn., 1957-60; staff scientist Stanford Research Inst., Menlo Park, Calif., 1960-71; fellow U. Calif. Med. Center, San Francisco, 1971-72; prof. elec. engring. and radiology Stanford U., 1972—; cons. to industry. Recipient Achievement award RCA Labs., 1952, 54; award for color TV circuits Inst. Radio Engrs., 1958; NIH spl. fellow, 1971. Fellow IEEE (Zworykin award 1973), Optical Soc. Am.; mem. Am. Assn. Physicists in Medicine, Sigma Xi, Eta Kappa Nu. Jewish. Author, patentee in field. Home: 2505 Alpine Rd Menlo Park CA 94025 Office: Elec Engring Dept Stanford CA 94305

MACPHAIL, LELAND STANFORD, JR., baseball exec.; b. Nashville, Oct. 25, 1917; s. Leland Stanford and Inez (Thompson) MacP.; B.A., Swarthmore Coll., 1939; m. Jane Hamilton, Nov. 18, 1939; children—Leland Stanford, Alen H., Bruce T., Andrew B. With Kennett-Murray Co., Florence, S.C., 1939-40, Reading (Pa.) Baseball Club, 1941-42, Toronto (Ont.) Baseball Club, 1942-43; tchr. math. Deerfield (Mass.) Acad., 1943; gen. mgr. Kansas City (Mo.) Baseball Club, 1946-48; dir. player personnel N.Y. Yankees Baseball Club, 1949-58; gen. mgr. Balt. Orioles Baseball Club, 1959-66; pres. Balt. Baseball Club, Inc., 1960-66; exec. v.p., gen. mgr. N.Y. Yankees, 1966-73; pres. Am. League, 1973—. Served to lt. (j.g.) USNR, 1944-46. Named Major League Exec. of Year, 1966. Mem. Delta Upsilon. Office: 280 Park Ave Am League New York NY 10017*

MAC PHAIL, ROBERT WILLIAM, energy co. exec.; b. Pitts., June 28, 1923; s. Ian and Catherine Geisler (Engelman) MacP.; B.S. in Elec. Engring., U. Mich., 1953; m. Kitty Marie D'Eath, May 15, 1948; children—Brian Jackson, Robert Ian. Mgr. fleet test and devel. N.Am. Aviation Co., Los Angeles, 1954-58; gen. mgr. Kaiser Jeep Taubate, Brazil, 1958-69; exec. dir. Jari Industria e Commercio Brasileiro, Brazil, 1969-70; exec. v.p. ops., dir. Kaiser Resources, Ltd., Vancouver, B.C., Can., 1972—; instr. Owens State Tech. Coll., Perrysburgh, Ohio, 1971-72. Served with USAAF, 1942-45. Decorated D.F.C. with oak leaf cluster, Air medal; registered profl. engr., B.C.; certified comml. pilot. Home: PO Box 48748 Vancouver BC Canada Office: 1500 W Georgia St Vancouver BC V6G 2Z8 Canada

MACPHERSON, CRAWFORD BROUGH, polit. scientist; b. Toronto, Ont., Can., Nov. 18, 1911; s. Walter Ernest and Elsie Margaret (Adams) M.; B.A., U. Toronto, 1933; M.Sc., U. London, 1935, D.Sc., 1955; D.Litt. (hon.), Meml. U. Nfld., 1970; LL.D. (hon.), Queen's U., 1970, U. Western Ont., 1973; m. Kathleen Margaret Walker, Sept. 25, 1943; children—Susan Margaret, Stephen Denis, Sheila Jane. Lectr. polit. economy U. Toronto, 1935-42, 44-45, faculty, 1945—, asso. prof. polit. economy, 1951-56, prof. polit. sci., 1956—, Univ. prof., 1975—; acting prof. econ., polit. sci. U. N.B., 1942-43; exec. officer Wartime Info. Bd., Ottawa, Ont., 1943-44; vis. prof. Hebrew U., Jerusalem, 1972, Inst. Philosophy, Aarhus (Denmark) U., 1975. Nuffield Found. fellow, 1952-53, Can. Council sr. fellow, 1959-60, Churchill Coll., Cambridge U. fellow, 1967-68, Commonwealth U. interchange scholar, 1965, Inst. Advanced Studies, Australian Nat. U. fellow, 1973; decorated officer Order of Can. Fellow Royal Soc. Can., Royal Hist. Soc. (Eng.); mem. Internat. Polit. Sci. Assn. (exec. mem. 1950-58), Can. Polit. Sci. Assn. (pres. 1963-64), Conf. for Study Polit. Thought (chmn. 1972-74, 76-77), Can. Assn. Univ. Tchrs. (pres. 1968-69). Author: Democracy in Alberta - The Theory and Practice of a Quasi-Party System, 1953, 2d edit., 1962; The Political Theory of Possessive Individualism, Hobbes to Locke, 1962, transl.: German, 1967, Spanish, 1970, French, 1971, Italian, 1973, Portuguese, 1979; The Real World of Democracy (The Massey Lectures, 4th Series), 1965, English edit., 1976, U.S. edit., 1972, transls.: Japanese, 1967, German, 1967, Spanish, Swedish, 1968, Danish, 1970, French, 1976; Democratic Theory - Essays in Retrieval, 1973, transls.: German, 1977, Italian, Japanese, 1978; The Life and Times of Liberal Democracy, 1977, transls.: Italian, Japanese, Portuguese, 1979; editor: The Future of Canadian Federalism (with P.-A. Crepeau), 1965; Thomas Hobbes' Leviathan (with an Introduction and a Note on the Text), 1968; Property, Mainstream and Critical Positions (with chpts. 1, 12), 1978; Can. Govt. Series, 1961-75. Office: Dept Polit Economy U Toronto 100 Saint George St Toronto ON M5S 1A1 Canada

MAC PHERSON, DONALD WILLIAM, broadcasting co. exec.; b. Toronto, Ont., Can., Mar. 15, 1932; s. Robert and Elizabeth (Brown) MacP.; m. Barbara Joan Lawrey, Mar. 11, 1961; children—Alexandrina, Jaimie. Producer, dir. Can. Broadcasting Corp., Toronto, 1952-65; dir. prodn. Chetwynd Films, Toronto, 1965-67; exec. producer ETV Br. of Ont. Govt., 1967-68; dir. news and info. programming CTV Television Network, Toronto, 1968-71; regional dir. Can. Broadcasting Corp., Toronto, 1971-74, v.p., gen. mgr. English services div., 1974—.

MACPHERSON, DUNCAN IAN, cartoonist; b. Toronto, Ont., Can., Sept. 20, 1924; s. Alexander and Margaret (Matheson) M.; student Boston Museum Sch. Fine Art, 1947-48; Ont. Coll. Art, Toronto, 1949-51; m. Dorothy Blackhall; 1 son, Ian. Free lance editorial and advt. illustrator, 1949-59; polit. cartoonist Toronto Daily Star, 1959—. Served with RCAF, 1942-46. Recipient Nat. Press Club award, 1973, Molson award Can. Council, 1971, Nat. Newspaper awards for editorial cartooning 1959, 60, 62, 65, 70, 72, Royal Acad. Arts medal, 1966; named to Canadian News Hall of Fame, 1976. Fellow Ont. Coll. Art; mem. Am. Assn. Editorial Cartoonists, Royal Canadian Acad. Arts. Author: Reportage and Political Review, 1966, Macpherson's Canada, 1969, also numerous cartoon anns.; patentee illustration for TV; research on history Upper Can. Office: Toronto Daily Star Ltd One Yonge St Toronto ON M5E 1E6 Canada

MACPHERSON, HERBERT GRENFELL, nuclear engr.; b. Victorville, Calif., Nov. 2, 1911; s. Duncan William and Minnie Belle (Morrison) MacP.; student San Diego State Coll., 1928-31; A.B., U. Calif., Berkeley, 1932, Ph.D. in Physics, 1937; m. Janet Taylor Wolfenden, June 5, 1937; children—Janet Lynne, Robert Duncan. Research scientist Nat. Carbon Co., Cleve., 1937-50, asst. dir. research, 1950-56; dir. reactor programs Oak Ridge Nat. Lab., 1956-64, dep. dir., 1964-70; prof. nuclear engring. U. Tenn., 1970-76; acting dir. Inst. for Energy Analysis, Oak Ridge, 1974-75, cons., 1975—; cons. in field. Fellow Am. Phys. Soc., Am. Nuclear Soc.; mem. AAAS, Nat. Acad. Engrs., Phi Beta Kappa, Sigma Xi. Clubs: Cosmos, Oak Ridge Country. Editor: (with Lane and Maslan) Fluid Fuel Reactor, 1958; devel. nuclear grade graphite, 1941-50, molten salt reactor, 1956-65; assisted in founding Inst. Energy Analysis, 1974-75. Home: 102 Orchard Circle Oak Ridge TN 37830 Office: Oak Ridge Associated Univs PO Box 117 Oak Ridge TN 37830. *I have tried to understand the nature of my own mix of talents and to find a place where its application could make a positive contribution. This led me into the complex area of the development of nuclear power, where corrdination of disciplines and cooperation of participants are vital.*

MACPHERSON, JAMES LUSK, govt. ofcl.; b. Butte, Mont., Dec. 25, 1923; s. James Lusk and Mary Louise (Thibadeau) M.; B.A. with honors, U. Mont., 1948, M.A. in Econs., 1949; m. Dorothy Laura LeVasseur, Jan. 4, 1948; children—Sandra Lee, James Lusk, Laura Marie. Instr. econs. U. Mont., 1949-51; indsl. relations analyst 13th region Wage Stablzn. Bd., 1951-52; commr. Fed. Mediation and Concilation Service, Seattle, 1952-59, asst. regional dir., Chgo., 1959-60, regional dir., Cleve., 1960-75, Seattle, 1975—; exec. dir. Constrn. Industry Collective Bargaining Commn., Washington, 1969-70; public mem. Constrn. Industry Stablzn. Com., 1973-74. Mem. Indsl. Relations Research Assn. Home: 3556 W Howe St Seattle WA 98199 Office: 4th and Vine Bldg 2615 4th Ave Seattle WA 98121

MAC QUARRIE, (ELINOR) DIANE, librarian; b. Westville, N.S., Can., Oct. 6, 1936; d. Robert Hugh and Kathleen Muriel (Matheson) MacQ.; B.A., Acadia U., Wolfville, N.S., 1957; B.L.S., U. Toronto (Ont., Can.), 1960, M.L.S., 1974. Chief librarian Halifax Co uty (N.S.) Regional Library, 1964-67; supr. Public Libraries Province N.S., Halifax, 1967-73; chief librarian Halifax City Regional Library, 1974—. Mem. Can. Library Assn. (councillor 1969-72), ALA, Atlantic Provinces Library Assn., N.S. Library Assn. Club: Zonta (Halifax). Home: Apt 33 6080 Pepperell St Halifax NS B3H 2N7 Canada Office: 5381 Spring Garden Rd Halifax NS B3J 1E9 Canada

MACQUEEN, ANGUS JAMES, clergyman; b. Port Morien, N.S., Can., July 3, 1912; s. Duncan Archibald and Lillian Jane (Wadden) MacQ.; B.A. with honors, Mt. Allison U., Sackville, N.B., 1933, LL.D., 1959; B.D., Pine Hill Div. Hall, Halifax, N.S., 1938, D.D., 1958; LL.D., U. Western Ont., 1959; D.D., Victoria U., Toronto, Canada; m. Netta May MacFadyen, Oct. 28, 1936; children—Marian Janet (Mrs. Colin H.H. McNairn), Joan Elizabeth (Mrs. John F.T. Warren), Barbara Jane, Heather Margaret (Mrs. William B. Niven). Ordained to ministry, United Ch. of Can., 1935; pastor, Port Hawkesbury, N.S., 1936-39, Antigonish, N.S., 1939-42, St. John, N.B., 1942-46, Edmonton, Alta., 1946-51, First-St. Andrew's United Ch., London, Can., 1951-64, St. George's United Ch., Toronto, 1964—; chmn. bd. evangelism and social service United Ch. of Can., 1954-58, moderator gen. council, 1958-60, also mem. various coms.; chancellor Mt. Allison U. Ecumenical rep. to chs. U.S., Europe, Africa. Chmn. bd. dirs. United Ch. Observer. Author: Superman is An Idiot; The Ten Commandments; contbr. chpt. The Minister's Handbook, In Such an Age, others. contbr. articles to religious jours., Can., Britain, U.S. Home: 217 Lytton Blvd Toronto ON M4R 1L6 Canada Office: Lytton Blvd and Duplex Ave Toronto ON Canada

MACQUEEN, JAMES ROBERT, lawyer; b. Niles, O., May 25, 1917; s. Walter F. and Martha (Stephenson) MacQ.; A.B., Miami U., Oxford, O., 1939; LL.B., Western Res. U., 1942; postgrad. Case Sch. Applied Sci., Cleve., 1942, U. Chgo., 1942-43; m. Rebecca Anne Cavanaugh, June 12, 1943; children—Marianne, James Patrick, Douglas Fulton, John Cavanaugh. Admitted to Ohio bar, 1942; staff mem. Radiation Lab., Mass. Inst. Tech., 1943. Part-time instr. Youngstown (O.) Coll. 1947-49. City solicitor, Niles, 1960-61, 64-65. Served with AUS, 1943-45. Mem. Am., Ohio, Trumbull County bar assns., Sigma Nu, Sigma Pi Sigma, Phi Mu Alpha, Phi Delta Phi. Rotarian (pres. Niles 1951-52). Home: 919 John St Niles OH 44446 Office: Niles Bank Bldg Niles OH 44446

MACQUEEN, KENNETH H., broadcasting exec.; b. Detroit, May 21, 1932; s. Kenneth H. and Viola MacQ.; B.A. in Econs., Duke; m. Janet Dietrich, May 16, 1959; children—James, Lynette Ann, Karen. Sales exec. Katz Agy., Chgo., 1958-64; spot salesman, account exec. ABC-TV, Chgo., 1964; sales mgr. Sta. WXYZ-TV, Detroit, 1964-69; gen. mgr. WABC-TV, N.Y.C., 1969—; v.p. ABC. Mem. N.Y.C. Mayor's Council on Adoption; bd. dirs. Better Bus. Bur. Met. N.Y. Mem. Nat. Acad. TV Arts and Scis., N.Y. State Broadcasters Assn. (dir., v.p.), Internat. Radio and TV Soc. Club: Milbrook (Greenwich, Conn.). Home: 165-A Stanwich Rd Greenwich CT 06830 Office: 1330 Ave of Americas New York NY 10019

MAC QUEEN, ROBERT MOFFAT, solar physicist; b. Memphis, Mar. 28, 1938; s. Marion Leigh and Grace (Gilfillan) MacQ.; B.S., Southwestern U., Memphis, 1960; Ph.D., Johns Hopkins U., 1968; m. Caroline Gibbs, June 25, 1960; children—Andrew, Marjorie. Asst. prof. physics Southwestern U., Memphis, 1961-63; instr. physics and astronomy Goucher Coll., Towson, Md., 1964-66; sr. research scientist Nat. Center for Atmospheric Research, Boulder, Colo., 1967—, dir. high altitude obs., 1979—, prin. investigator NASA Apollo program, 1971-75, NASA Skylab program, 1970—; lectr. U. Colo., 1968—; mem. com. on space astronomy Nat. Acad. Scis., 1973-75, mem. com. on space physics, 1979—. Recipient NASA Exceptional Sci. Achievement medal, 1974. Mem. Am. Astron. Soc. (chmn. solar physics div. 1976-78), Optical Soc. Am., Am. Assn. Physics Tchrs. Home: 1366 Northridge Ct Boulder CO 80302 Office: Box 3000 Nat Center for Atmospheric Research Boulder CO 80307

MACRAE, CAMERON FARQUHAR, lawyer; b. Wilmington, N.C., Dec. 26, 1905; s. Cameron F. and Fairinda (Payne) MacR.; B.S. in Civil Engring., U. N.C., 1926; postgrad. Pitts. Sch. Accountancy, 1929-30; LL.B., N.Y. Law Sch., 1937; m. Jane B. Miller, Dec. 24, 1935; 1 son, Cameron Farquhar III. Pvt. practice civil engring., 1926-37; admitted to N.Y. bar, 1937, since practiced in N.Y.C. and Washington; partner Whitman, Ransom & Coulson, 1941-58; sr. partner LeBoeuf, Lamb, Leiby & MacRae, 1958—, pres. partner, 1976—. Dir., mem. exec. com. Orange & Rockland Utilities, Inc.; v.p. Hobe Sound Co., Hobe Sound Water Co.; dir. Rockland Electric Co. Trustee, hon. chmn. Clear Pool Camp, 1968—, pres. 1951-68; trustee N.C. Soc. N.Y., pres., 1958-60; trustee, chmn. Southampton (N.Y.) Hosp.; mem. nat. vis. council for health scis. faculties Columbia U.; cons. Task Force Water Resources and Power, 2d Hoover Comm., 1953-55; mem. energy fin. adv. com. Fed. Energy Adminstrn., 1976-78. Served as col. AUS, World War II. Decorated Legion of Merit. Mem. Am., Fed. Energy (pres. 1969-70), N.Y. State, N.Y.C., D.C. bar assns., Am. Law Inst., N.Y. Law Inst., Edison Elec. Inst. (chmn. legal com. 1973-75), Mayflower Soc., Pilgrims of U.S., Zeta Psi, Phi Delta Phi. Republican. Episcopalian. Clubs: Univ., Down Town Assn., Brook (N.Y.C.); Meadow, Southhampton Shinnecock Hills Golf (Southampton, L.I.) (gov.); Island (Hobe Sound, Fla.); Seminole Golf (Palm Beach, Fla.); Mill Reef (Antigua, W.I.). Contbr. articles profl. jours. Home: 200 E 66th St New York NY 10021 Office: 140 Broadway New York NY 10005

MAC RAE, DONALD ALEXANDER, educator; b. Halifax, N.S., Can., Feb. 19, 1916; s. Donald Alexander and Laura (Barnstead) Mac R.; B.A., U. Toronto (Ont., Can.), 1937; A.M., Harvard, 1940, Ph.D., 1943; m. Margaret Elizabeth Malcolm, Aug. 25, 1939; children—David M., Charles D., Andrew R. Mem. faculty U. Pa., 1941-42; instr. Cornell U., 1942-44; scientist Carbide & Carbon Chem. Corp., Oak Ridge, 1944-46; asst. prof. Case Inst. Tech., Cleve., 1946-53; asso. prof. U. Toronto, 1953-55, prof., 1955—, dir. David Dunlap Obs., 1965-78; dir. Can.-France-Hawaii Telescope Corp., 1974-79, Can. Corp. Univ. Space Sci., 1978—. Trustee Univs. Space Research Assn., 1969-76. Fellow Royal Soc. Can., Royal Astron. Soc.; mem. Am., Canadian astron. assns. Home: 427 Glencairn Ave Toronto ON M5N 1V4 Canada Office: 60 St George St Toronto ON Canada

MACRAE, DONALD POLLARD, book publisher; b. Phila., June 18, 1916; s. Durant L. and Rebecca (Anderson) M.; student Temple U., 1934-37; m. Ruth Kahl, Sept. 24, 1945; children—Heather, Laurie, Robin. With Macrae Smith Co., Phila., 1946—, v.p., 1953-61, v.p., editor-in-chief, 1961-62, pres., 1962—, also dir. Bd. dirs. Phila. Booksellers Assn., 1957; adv. bd. Phila. Book Clinic, 1948—. Pres. Haddonfield (N.J.) Friends of the Library, 1952-54; mem. Friends of Free Library, Phila., 1962—; bd. govs. Phila. Central YMCA Health Club, 1963-66. Served to 1st lt. USAAF, 1942-45. Decorated Air medal, Purple Heart medal. Mem. Assn. Am. Pubs. Republican. Episcopalian (vestry 1955-58). Club: Down Town (Phila.). Home: 30 Treaty Elms Lane Haddonfield NJ 08033 Office: 225 S 15th St Philadelphia PA 19102

MACRAE, DUNCAN, JR., educator, social scientist; b. Glen Ridge, N.J., Sept. 30, 1921; s. Duncan and Rebecca (Kyle) MacR.; A.B., Johns Hopkins, 1942; A.M., Harvard, 1943, Ph.D., 1950; m. Edith Judith Krugelis, June 24, 1950; 1 dau., Amy Frances. Mem. staff Radiation Lab., Mass. Inst. Tech., 1943-46; instr., then lectr. sociology Princeton, 1949-51; research asso. Lab. Social Relations, Harvard,

1951-53; asst. prof. sociology U. Cal. at Berkeley, 1953-57; mem. faculty U. Chgo., 1957-72, prof. polit. sci. and sociology, 1964-72; William Rand Kenan, Jr. prof. polit. sci. and sociology U. N.C., Chapel Hill, 1972—. Pres. Policy Studies Assn., 1974-75. Fulbright research scholar, France, 1956-57. Fellow AAAS, Am. Acad. Arts and Scis.; mem. Am. Polit. Sci. Assn., Am. Sociol. Assn., Am. Econ. Assn., Phi Beta Kappa. Author: Dimensions of Congressional Voting, 1958; Parliament, Parties and Society in France 1946-58, 1967; Issues and Parties in Legislative Voting, 1970; The Social Function of Social Science, 1976; (with James A. Wilde) Policy Analysis for Public Decisions, 1979. Editor: (with others) Electronic Instruments, 1948. Home: 737 Gimghoul Rd Chapel Hill NC 27514

MACRAE, EDITH KRUGELIS (MRS. DUNCAN MACRAE, JR.), biologist, educator; b. Waterbury, Conn., Jan. 24, 1919; d. Peter Charles and Ezabel (Natkevicius) Krugelis; B.S., Bates Coll., 1940; M.A., Columbia, 1941, Ph.D., 1946; m. Duncan MacRae, Jr., June 24, 1950; 1 dau., Amy Frances. Instr. zoology Vassar Coll., 1945-47; Donner Found., also Am. Cancer Soc. fellow Carlsberg Lab., Copenhagen, Denmark, 1947-49; research asso. Osborn Zool. Lab., Yale, 1949-51; instr. biology Mass. Inst. Tech., 1951-53; research zoologist U. Calif. at Berkeley, 1953-56; asst. prof. anatomy U. Ill., Chgo., 1957-64, asso. prof., 1964-66, prof., 1966-72, acting head and chmn., 1969-70; vis. prof. anatomy U. N.C., Chapel Hill, 1971-72, prof. anatomy, 1972—. Recipient Raymond B. Allen Instructorship award U. Ill. Med. Sch., 1964; CCB Excellence in Teaching award U. N.C. Med. Sch., 1976. Guggenheim fellow, 1964-65. Mem. A.A.A.S., Am. Soc. for Cell Biology, Electron Microscope Soc. Am., Am. Assn. Anatomists, Southeastern Electron Microscopy Soc. (pres. 1978-79), Am. Soc. Zoologists, N.Y. Acad. Scis., Phi Beta Kappa, Sigma Xi. Contbr. articles sci. jours. Home: 737 Gimghoul Rd Chapel Hill NC 27514

MAC RAE, GEORGE WINSOR, clergyman, educator; b. Lynn, Mass., July 27, 1928; s. George Roy and Katherine (MacDonald) MacR.; B.A., Boston Coll., 1953; M.A., Johns Hopkins U., 1957; S.T.L., Weston Coll., 1961; Ph.D., Cambridge U., 1966. Joined Soc. of Jesus, 1948; ordained priest, Roman Catholic Ch., 1960; instr. Fairfield (Conn.) Prep. Sch., 1954-56; prof. Weston Sch. of Theology, Cambridge, Mass., 1965-73; Stillman prof. Roman Catholic studies Harvard Div. Sch., 1973—. Trustee Fordham U., 1968-71, Coll. of Holy Cross, 1978—. Am. Council Learned Socs. fellow, 1972-73. Mem. Soc. Bibl. Lit. (exec. sec. 1973-76), Council on Study of Religion (vice-chmn. 1969-74, chmn. 1977—), Internat. Soc. New Testament Studies (mem. editorial bd. 1973-77), Cath. Bibl. Assn. (mem. editorial bd.). Club: Boston Ministers. Editor New Testament Abstracts, 1967-72. Editor several books. Home: 5 Fernald Dr Cambridge MA 02138 Office: Harvard Divinity Sch Cambridge MA 02138

MACRAE, GORDON, singer, actor; b. East Orange, N.J., Mar. 12, 1921; m. Sheila Stephens, May 21, 1941; children—Meredith, Heather, W. Gordon, Bruce; m. 2d, Elizabeth Lambert Schrafft, Sept. 25, 1967; 1 dau., Amanda. Child actor, radio, stock; stage appearance Three to Make Ready; juvenile soloist Ray Bolger Revue; appeared Millpond Playhouse, Roslyn, L.I.; motion pictures include Big Punch, 1948, Look for the Silver Lining, 1949, Backfire, 1949, Return of the Frontiersmen, 1950, Tea for Two, 1950, West Point Story, 1951, On Moonlight Bay, 1951, About Face, 1952, Desert Song, 1952, Three Sailors and a Girl, 1953, Oklahoma, 1955, Carousel, 1956, The Best Things in Life are Free, 1956; night club and TV appearances; rec. artist Capitol Records. Recipient Star of Season award March of Dimes, 1968. Office: PO Box 706 Pebble Beach CA 93953

MAC RAE, HERBERT FARQUHAR, coll. prin.; b. Middle River, N.S., Can., Mar. 30, 1926; s. Murdoch John and Jessie (Matheson) Mac R.; diploma N.S. Agrl. Coll., 1952; B.Sc., Macdonald Coll. McGill U., 1954, M.Sc., 1956, Ph.D., 1960; m. Mary Ruth Finlayson, Sept. 24, 1955; children—Roderick John, Elizabeth Anne, Christy Margaret, Mary Jean. Chemist, food and drug directorate Dept. Nat. Health and Welfare, Ottawa, Ont., 1960-61; mem. faculty Macdonald Coll. McGill U., 1961-72, asso. prof. animal sci., chmn. dept., 1967-70, prof., chmn. dept., 1970-72; prin. N.S. Agrl. Coll., Truro, 1972—. Mem. Agrl. Inst. Can., Can. Soc. Animal Sci., Sigma Xi. Club: Rotary. Home: 7 Hickman Dr Truro NS B2N 2Z2 Canada

MACRAE, JOHN, JR., publishing co. exec.; b. The Plains, Va., Dec. 17, 1898; s. John and Katherine (Green) M.; B.S., U. Va., 1919; m. Anne McCrory Hinton, Oct. 12, 1926; children—Pamela Anne (Mrs. E.L. Bermingham), Jill Allison (Mrs. John Witherbee), John III. Supr., U.S. Shipping Bd., 1921; with E.P. Dutton & Co., Inc., N.Y.C., 1928—, chmn. bd., pres., 1970—, also mem. exec. com. Served to capt. U.S. Army, 1917-19. Mem. Sigma Chi. Clubs: American Yacht; Field (Greenwich, Conn.); Nantucket (Mass.) Yacht; University. Author: Best From Yank. Home: The Chateau 2151 Gulf Shore Blvd Naples FL 33940 also 47 Cliff Rd Nantucket MA 02554 Office: 201 Park Ave S New York NY 10003

MACRAE, JOHN, III, editor, publisher; b. N.Y.C., Nov. 21, 1931; s. John, Jr. and Anne (Hinton) M.; A.B., Harvard U., 1954; m. Frances Arthur Cummins, May 18, 1957 (div. 1976); children—John Yancey, Elizabeth Hinton, Phebe Barber, Annabel Cummins. Engaged in sales and mktg. Owens-Corning Fiberglas Corp., 1957-60; with Harper & Row, 1960-67, exec. editor, dep. dir. trade complex, 1965-67; editor-in-chief, v.p., mng. dir. E.P. Dutton, 1968-69, pres., editor, 1969—; dir. Childcraft Corp.; mem. com. reading Am. Book Pubs. Council, 1968-69; mem. Van Wyck Brooks Lit. Award Com. Del., White House Conf. on Natural Beauty, 1965; co-dir. Hudson River Valley Conservation Commn.; mem. publs. com. Mus. Modern Art, 1978—; trustee Palisades (N.Y.) Free Library, 1966-70, pres., 1967-68; bd. dirs. Soc. Family of Man; trustee, bd. dirs. Roger Klein Award, Editorial, 1969—. Served with AUS, 1954-56. Mem. P.E.N. (mem. exec. bd., dir. transl. com.), Mid-Atlantic Conservation Council, Am. Mus. Natural History (vice chmn. pub. 1973-76), Assn. Am. Pubs. (internat. freedom to publish com. 1978—). Democrat. Clubs: Porcellian (Harvard); Century Assn. Office: EP Dutton Co 2 Park Ave New York NY 10016

MAC RAE, MARION BELL, archtl. and design historian; b. Apple Hill, Ont., Can., Apr. 30, 1921; d. John Donald and Hazel Ross (Carlyle) Mac R.; A.O.C.A., Ont. Coll. Art, Toronto, 1947; postgrad. U. Ill., 1951-54. Instr. design and museum research Ont. Coll. Art, 1949-79, instr. environ. design, 1977—; vis. lectr. dept. architecture U. Toronto, 1973-76, 77-78; mem. adv. com. on design Upper Can. Vill. Restoration, 1957-61; spl. asst. to design cons. Dundurn Castle Restoration, 1963-67. Mem. Soc. Archtl. Historians, Interior Designers of Ont. (asso.), Victorian Soc. (Eng.), Soc. Study Architecture in Can., Archtl. Conservancy of Ont. Liberal. Mem. United Ch. of Can. Author: (with Anthony Adamson) The Ancestral Roof, 1963, Hallowed Walls (Gov.-Gen's Lit. award), 1975; MacNab of Dundurn, 1971. Home: 80 Lawton Blvd Toronto ON M4V 2A2 Canada Office: Ont Coll Art 100 McCaul St Toronto ON M5T 1W1 Canada

MACRAE, SHEILA STEPHENS, entertainer; b. London, Sept. 24; d. Louis and Winifred (Baker) Stephens; m. Gordon MacRae, May 21, 1941; children—Meredith, Heather, Gar, Robert Bruce; m. 2d, Ron Wayne. Formerly appeared in roles with summer theatre, Roslyn, N.Y., then disc jockey, also radio actress; writer material for husband on TV and in nightclubs, now mem. act; appeared in TV series Jackie Gleason Show, 1966-70, Sheila MacRae Show, 1971; rec. artist Capitol records. Bd. dirs., a founder Share, Inc.*

MACRURY, KING, mgmt. counselor; b. Manchester, N.H., Oct. 14, 1915; s. Colin H. and Lauretta C. (Shea) MacR.; A.B., Rollins Coll., 1938; postgrad. St. Anselms Coll., L.I. Coll. Medicine, Princeton; 1 son, Colin C. Asst. personnel dir. Lily-Tulip Cup Corp., 1939; asst. dir. market research Ward Baking Co., 1940-41; staff mem. Nat. Indsl. Conf. Bd., 1941-43; cons. indsl. relations and orgn. planning McKinsey & Co., 1946-48; internal cons. Oxford Paper Co., 1949-50; installer, dir. indsl. relations Champion Internation Co., 1950-51; pvt. practice mgmt. counselor, 1951—; lectr. Indsl. Edn. Inst., 1962-68, Mgmt. Center, Cambridge, 1968-71, Dun & Bradstreet, 1979—, extension div. U. N.H., 1968—, extension program U. Maine, 1978—, also U. Bridgeport, extension program U. Conn.; coordinator mgmt. edn. extension div. U. Conn., 1964-68, Philippine Council Mgmt., 1969—, Econ. Devel. Found. Philippines, 1969—, Am. Metal Stamping Assn., 1969—; condr. mgmt. seminars for Asian Assn. Mgmt. Orgns. C.I.O.S., 1972. Mem. Indsl. Devel. Commn. Andover, 1957-58; manpower com. U.S. Dept. Labor Bus. Adv. Council, 1958-61. Served to lt. USNR, 1943-46. Mem. N.H. Dental Soc. (hon.). Author: Developing Your People Potential. Contbr. numerous articles in field to profl. jours. Office: Box 215 Rye NH 03870

MACSAI, JOHN, architect; b. Budapest, Hungary, May 20, 1926; s. Ferenc and Margit (Rosenfeld) Lusztig; came to U.S., 1947, naturalized, 1954; Baccalaureate summa cum laude, Kolcsey Gimnasium, Budapest, 1944; student Atelier Art Sch., Budapest, 1941-43, Poly. U., Budapest, 1945-47; B.Arch. magna cum laude, Miami U., Oxford, Ohio, 1949; m. Geraldine Marcus, May 7, 1950; children—Pamela, Aaron, Marian, Gwen. Archtl. designer Skidmore, Owings & Merrill, Chgo., Pace Assos., Chgo., Raymond Loewy Assos., Chgo., 1949-55; partner Hausner & Macsai, Chgo., 1955-71, Campbell & Macsai, Chgo., 1971-74; prin. John Macsai & Assos., Architects, Inc., Chgo., 1975—; prof. architecture U. Ill., Chgo. Circle, 1970—. Chmn. SE Council Integrated Communities, 1968-70. Recipient award citations Chgo. chpt. AIA. Fellow AIA. Jewish. Author: High Rise Apartment Buildings—A Design Primer, 1972; Housing, 1976; co-author: Designing Environments for the Aged, 1977. Works include Nat. Opinion Research Center, U. Chgo., 1967; High Energy Physics Bldg., U. Chgo., 1968; Social Services Center, U. Chgo., 1970; Harbor House, Malibu East apt. bldg., Chgo., 1972. Home: 1207 Judson Ave Evanston IL 60202 Office: John Macsai & Assos 168 N Michigan Ave Chicago IL 60601. *To find pleasure in everything; to drive hard in whatever I have to do; to avoid hurting people; to be able to see life's ironies; to laugh at anything, including myself.*

MACTAGGART, BARRY, chem. co. exec.; b. Kandos, N.S.W., Australia, Dec. 29, 1931; s. Malcolm Ian and Dorothy (Schroder) MacT.; m. Robin Margaret Wilson, Nov. 21, 1962; children—Susan, Ian, Cameron. Mgr., Peat Marwick Mitchell & Co., Sydney, Australia, 1949-58; with Pfizer Internat., N.Y.C., 1959—, traveling auditor, 1959-61, controller Asia, 1961-64, adminstrn. dir., 1964-68, pres., 1968-72, exec. v.p. Pfizer Internat., N.Y.C., 1972—, corporate v.p. Pfizer Inc., 1975—. Mem. Australian Soc. Chartered Accountants. Clubs: Milbrook; Hong Kong. Home: 41 Woodside Dr Greenwich CT 06830 Office: 235 E 42d St New York City NY 10017

MACURDY, JOHN EDWARD, basso; b. Detroit, Mar. 18, 1929; s. Blanchard Archibald and Dorathea Rosalie (Radtke) Mc Curdy; student Wayne State U., 1947; student of Avery Crew, Detroit, 1946; m. Justine May Votypka, Apr. 12, 1958; children—Allison Anne, John Blanchard. Mem. N.Y.C. Opera, 1959-62, Met. Opera, 1962—; appeared in U.S., Europe, including: San Francisco Opera, La Scala; appeared in world premieres: Mourning Becomes Electra, Met. Opera, 1967, Anthony and Cleopatra, Met. Opera, 1966, Wuthering Heights, Santa Fe Opera, 1958, Six Characters in Search of an Author, N.Y.C. Opera, 1959, Griffalkin, Tanglewood Festival, 1957; appeared in Am. premieres: Capriccio, Santa Fe Opera, 1958, Murder in the Cathedral, Empire State Music Festival, Bear Mountain Park, N.Y., 1959, Inspector General, N.Y.C. Opera, 1960; appeared with numerous orchs.; film Don Giovanni, 1979. Served with USAF, 1950-54. Recipient medal for artistic merit during Mich. Week, City of Detroit, 1969. Mem. Bohemians. Presbyterian. Club: Bohemian of San Francisco. Home: Tall Oaks Ct Stamford CT 06903 Office: Met Opera Lincoln Center New York NY 10023

MACVANE, JOHN FRANKLIN, news analyst; b. Portland, Maine, Apr. 29, 1912; s. William Leslie and Bertha (Achorn) MacV.; grad. Phillips Exeter Acad.; B.A., Williams Coll., 1933; B.Litt., Exeter Coll. Oxford U., 1936; m. Lucy Maxwell, Dec. 17, 1937 (div.); children—Ian (dec.), Myles Angus, Sara Ann Andrew, Matthew Chattan, Fiona Ellen; m. 2d, Henriette Butler Kidder, May 27, 1969. Reporter, ship news columnist Bklyn. Daily Eagle, 1935-36; reporter N.Y. Sun, 1936-38; sub-editor London Daily Express, 1938-39, Continental Daily Mail, Paris, 1939; corr. Exchange Telegraph Agy., Internat. News Service covering Fall of France; reporter, war corr. assigned Brit. Army, NBC, London, 1940-42, North African campaign Morocco-Algeria-Tunisia, 1942-43, Brit. and Am. Armies; covered Casablanca Conf., 1943; landed with 16th Inf. Regt. U.S. 1st Inf. Div., Normandy on D-Day; later U.S. 1st Army, 1944-45, French Deuxieme Div. Blindé Paris, 1944; UN corr. NBC covering UN Security Council, 1946. Berlin air lift, 1948, UN Gen. Assembly, Paris, 1948; producer, moderator weekly radio, TV panel United or Not show, ABC, 1950-52; with UN Gen. Assembly, Paris, 1951-52; UN corr. ABC 1953-78, Photo Communications Co., 1978—; writer-commentator documentary TV film series, Alaska: The New Frontier, for Nat. Ednl. Television, 1960. Decorated Purple Heart medal; chevalier Legion of Honor, 1947, Medaille de la France Libérée, 1948, officer, 1979 (France). Recipient Nat. Headliners award, 1947; Am. Assn. for UN award, 1960. Mem. Assn. Radio-TV News Analysts (pres. 1948-49, 55, 56, sec. 1954), St. Andrews Soc. N.Y., UN Corrs. Assn. (pres. 1964), Pilgrims of U.S., France-Am. Soc., Gargoyle Soc., Soc. of Silurians (gov.), Am. Soc. French Legion of Honor, France Am. Soc., Sigma Delta Chi, Sigma Phi (trustee Williams chpt. 1968-73). Clubs: Williams; Press (London, Eng.). Author: Journey into War, 1943; War and Diplomacy in North Africa, 1944; Embassy Extraordinary; The United States Mission to UN, 1961; On the Air in World War II, 1979. Home: 488 Pequot Ave Southport CT 06490 Office: Room 368 United Nations New York NY 10017

MAC VEIGH, JOSEPH GIBBS, ins. co. exec.; b. Chgo., Mar. 17, 1932; s. Francis Joseph and Adelaide Sarah (Sweeny) MacV.; B.S. in History, Xavier U., 1955; m. Margaret Ellen Bowyer, Apr. 28, 1956; children—Patrick, Margaret, Richard, Timothy, Elizabeth, Thomas, Christine. With Western & So. Life Ins. Co., Cin., 1958—, asst. dir. EDP systems, 1966-68, 2d v.p., asst. treas., 1968-75, v.p., treas., 1976—. Chmn., Community Action Commn., Cin., 1968-69; chmn. planning div. United Appeal/Community Chest, 1975-76; trustee Community Chest. Served with arty. U.S. Army, 1956-57. Roman Catholic. Home: 3478 Vista Terr Cincinnati OH 45208 Office: 400 Broadway Cincinnati OH 45202

MAC VICAR, MARGARET LOVE AGNES, materials scientist, educator; b. Hamilton, Ont., Can., Nov. 20, 1943; d. George Francis and Elizabeth Margaret (Thompson) MacVicar; came to U.S., 1946, naturalized, 1953; S.B. in Physics, Mass. Inst. Tech., 1964, Sc.D. in Metallurgy, 1967. Postdoctoral fellow Cavendish Lab., U. Cambridge, Eng., 1967-69, (NATO fellow, Marie Curie fellow; instr. physics M.I.T., Cambridge, 1969-70, asst. prof., 1970-74, asso. prof. physics, 1974-79, asso. prof. phys. sci., 1979—; Chancellor's Distinguished prof. U. Calif., Berkeley, 1979; cons. to univs., industry, non-profit orgns. Bd. dirs. Oral Edn. Center of So. Calif., Los Angeles; trustee Carnegie Found. for Advancement Teaching; mem. corp. and program com. Boston Mus. Sci.; mem. Carnegie Council on Policy Studies in Higher Edn. Recipient Class Of 1922 Career Devel. chair Mass. Inst. Tech., 1973-79, Most Significant Contribution to Edn. award, 1977; Young Faculty Research award Gen. Electric Found., 1976-79; Danforth Found. asso., 1972—. Mem. Am. Vacuum Soc., AAAS (nat. com. on sci. in promotion human welfare 1971-74), Am. Soc. Metals, Am. Women in Sci., Women in Sci. and Engring., Am. Soc. Metall. Engrs., Am. Phys. Soc., Sigma Xi. Patentee in field. Home: PO Box 304 Mass Inst Tech Br Cambridge MA 02139

MAC VICAR, ROBERT WILLIAM, univ. pres.; b. Princeton, Minn., Sept. 28, 1918; s. George William and Elizabeth (Brennan) MacV.; B.A., U. Wyo., 1939, LL.D., 1977; M.S., Okla. State U., 1940; Ph.D., U. Wis., 1946; m. Clarice Chambers, Dec. 23, 1948; children—Miriam J., John R. Asso. prof., prof. biochemistry Okla. State U., 1946-64, dean grad. sch., 1953-64, v.p. acad. affairs, 1957-64; v.p. acad. affairs So. Ill. U., 1964-68, chancellor So. Ill. U. at Carbondale, 1964-70; pres. Oreg. State U., Corvallis, 1970—; founding mem., bd. dirs. Central Ednl. Midwest Research Lab., chmn. exec. com., 1969-70. Served with U.S. Army, 1939-45. Rhodes scholar, 1939. Mem. Am. Soc. Biol. Chemists, Am. Chem. Soc., Am. Inst. Nutrition, Okla. Acad. Sci., Phi Beta Kappa, Sigma Xi, Phi Kappa Phi. Presbyterian. Club: Arlington (Portland). Home: 3520 NW Hayes Corvallis OR 97330 Office: Oreg State U Corvallis OR 97331

MACVITTIE, ROBERT WILLIAM, coll. pres.; b. Middletown, N.Y., Dec. 29, 1920; s. Mortimer, Jr. and Mary (Thompson) MacV.; B.Ed., State U. N.Y., Oneonta, 1944; M.A., N.Y. U., 1946. Ed.D., 1954; m. Margaret L. Cooper, July 15, 1944; children—Robert William II, Beth Ann, Geralyn Amy. Elementary tchr. Pine Plains (N.Y.) Central Sch., 1944; social sci. tchr. Meml. Jr. High Sch., Middletown, N.Y., 1944-48; supervising prin. Montowese Sch., North Haven, Conn., 1948-52, Ridge Rd. Sch., North Haven, 1952-53; prof. sch. adminstrn., prin. lab. sch. N.Y. State Coll. Tchrs., Buffalo, 1954-56; dir. div. elementary and secondary edn. State U. N.Y. Coll., Buffalo, 1956-58, dean coll., 1958-63, pres. State U. Coll., Geneseo, 1963-79, emeritus, 1979—. Mem. nat. com., regional adv. bd. Bank & Trust Co., Oneonta, N.Y. Mem. State U. N.Y. Commn. Univ. Purposes and Priorities; exec. com. Rochester Area Colls., Inc., 1972-79, State U. N.Y. Council Pres.'s, 1970-72, 76-78. Mem. citizens salary adv. com. Kenmore (N.Y.) Bd. edn., 1957; cons. sch. program evaluation team Tchrs. Coll., Temple U., 1956-57; mem. Livingston County Planning Bd., 1967-73, chmn., 1972-73; bd. dirs. Am. Assn. State Colls. and Univs., 1977-79. Mem. Am. Assn. Higher Edn., Am. Assn. Sch. Adminstrs., Am. Assn. U. Adminstrs. (pres. 1971-73, dir. 1977-79, gen. sec. 1979—), Am. Acad. Polit. and Social Scis., Livingston C. of C. (dir. 1970—), Phi Delta Kappa, Kappa Delta Pi. Club: Oneonta Country. Author: Handbook for Substitute Teachers, 3d edit., 1959; also numerous articles. Home: Stony Brook Gilbertsville NY 13776

MAC WATTERS, VIRGINIA, singer, actress; b. Phila.; d. Frederick-Kennedy and Idoleein (Hallowell) Mac W.; student (Zeckwer Hahn Phila. Musical Acad. scholar), Curtis Inst. Music, Phila., 1941-42; grad. Phila. Normal Sch.; m. Paul Abée, June 10, 1960. Singer leading role Broadway musical Rosalinda, 1942-44, Mr. Strauss Goes to Boston, 1945; leading roles, opera: San Francisco, 1944, N.Y.C. Center, 1946-50, Guatemala, El Salvador, C. Am., 1948; TV singer NBC Network, Menotti's Old Maid and the Thief, 1949, Would-be Gentleman, 1955; leading singer Met. Opera Co., coast-to-coast tour Die Fledermaus, 1951; Met. Opera, 1952-60; leading soprano Central City Opera Festival, Colo., 1952-56; concert singer symphony orchs., U.S., Can., S. Am.; opened N.Y. Empire State Music Festival, 1959; asso. prof. voice U. Ind., 1957-68, prof., 1968—. Recipient Mile award for performance as Zerbinetta in Richard Strauss opera, radio program Album Familiar Music, 1949; Disting. Teaching award Ind. U., 1979; Frederic Bachman Lieber Meml. award; leading soprano for reopening of Royal Opera House, Covent Garden, London, 1946-47. Mem. Nat. Fedn. of Music Clubs, Nat. Soc. Arts and Letters, Nat. Soc. Lit. and Arts, Soc. Am. Musicians, Nat. Assn. Tchrs. of Singing, Internat. Platform Assn., Sigma Alpha Iota. Club: Matinee Musical (Phila., Indpls.). Home: 3800 Arlington Rd Bloomington IN 47401 Office: Ind U Sch Music Bloomington IN 47401

MACWILLIAMS, JOHN J., ins. co. exec.; b. Syracuse, N.Y., Apr. 30, 1929; s. John J. and Marion (Klock) MacW.; B.A. in English, Hobart Coll., 1951; m. Lee Elliott, May 6, 1953; children—John J., William Brewster, Peter Huntington, Cameron Lee. With Aetna Life & Casualty Co., 1954-68, dir. internat. dept., 1966-68; pres. Colonial Penn Life Ins. Co., Phila., 1968-72, chmn. bd., 1968—; pres. Colonial Penn Ins. Co., Phila., 1969-72, chmn. bd., 1969—; chmn. bd., chief exec. officer Colonial Penn Group, Inc., Phila., 1969—; dir. Provident Nat. Bank; dir., mem. exec. com. Provident Nat. Corp. Mem. Mus. Assos., assos. com. Phila. Mus. Art; bd. dirs. World Affairs Council; trustee Drexel U.; bd. dirs., exec. com. Old Phila. Corp. Served to 1st lt. U.S. Army, 1951-53. Mem. Greater Phila. C. of C. (dir.). Clubs: Nat. Golf Links, U. N.Y.; Racquet (Phila.); Gulph Mills Golf; Philadelphia; Courts; Mill Reef; Merion Cricket; Quogue (L.I.) Field, Quogue Beach. Home: 1234 Country Club Rd Gladwyne PA 19035 Office: 5 Penn Center Plaza Philadelphia PA 19103

MACY, BILL (WILLIAM MACY GARBER), actor; b. Revere, Mass., May 18, 1922; grad. N.Y. U., 1954; m. Samantha Harper. Stage debut in walk-on role in The Jewish Wife; appeared in Antioch (Ohio) Shakespeare Festival; understudy for Walter Matthau in Once More With Feeling, Broadway, 1958; stage appearances include: The Threepenny Opera, 1959, The Balcony, 1960, America Hurrah, Interview and TV, all 1966, Cannibals, 1967, Guns of Carrar, 1968, Oh, Calcutta!, London and Broadway, 1969, Awake and Sing!, 1970, And Miss Reardon Drinks a Little, 1971; regular TV series Maude, 1972-78, Hanging In, 1979—; TV movies All Together Now, 1975, Death at Love House, 1976; film The Late Show, 1977. Mem. AFTRA. Office: care Creative Artists Inc 1888 Century Park E Suite 1400 Los Angeles CA 90067*

MACY, JOHN WILLIAMS, JR., govt. ofcl.; b. Chgo., Apr. 6, 1917; s. John Williams and Juliette (Shaw) M.; B.A., Wesleyan U., 1938; LL.D., Cornell Coll., Mt. Vernon, Iowa, 1963, Colgate U., 1965, Allegheny Coll., 1965, Eastern Ky. Coll., 1966, Dartmouth Coll., 1966, Wesleyan U., 1967, U. Del., 1967, Ind. State U., 1968, Ithaca Coll., 1969, St. John's U., 1969, Austin Coll., 1972; m. Joyce Hagen, Feb. 12, 1944; children—Thomas, Mary, Susan, Richard. Govt. intern Nat. Inst. Pub. Affairs, Washington, 1938-39; adminstrv. aide Social Security Bd., Washington, 1939-40; personnel specialist War Dept.,

Washington and Chgo., 1940-42, asst. dir. civilian personnel, Washington, 1942-43, 46-47; dir. orgn. and personnel AEC Los Alamos, 1947-51; spl. asst. under-sec. Army, Washington, 1951-53; exec. dir. CSC, Washington, 1953-58, chmn., 1961-69; exec. v.p. Wesleyan U., 1958-61, trustee, 1954-59, 61-74, vice chmn., 1969-74; pres. Corp. for Pub. Broadcasting, 1969-72; pres. Council Better Bus. Burs. Inc., 1973-74; pres. Devel. and Resources Corp., 1975-79; dir. Fed. Emergency Mgmt. Agy., Washington, 1979—; mem. Internat. Civil Service Adv. Bd., 1964-70. Bd. dirs. Inst. Ct. Mgmt., 1969-79; trustee Bennett Coll., 1970-73, Potomac Sch., Va., 1967-73, Expt. in Internat. Living, 1966-69; trustee Am. Film Inst., 1971-75, treas., 1974-75; bd. visitors George Mason U., 1973-79; bd. govs. Am. Stock Exchange, 1972-77, ARC, 1979—; bd. dirs. Cultural Resources, 1978-79. Served as capt. USAAF, 1943-46. Mem. Am. Soc. Pub. Adminstrn. (nat. pres. 1958-59), Phi Beta Kappa, Phi Nu Theta. Clubs: Army and Navy, Federal City, City Tavern (Washington); University, Century (N.Y.), Langley; Nantucket Yacht. Author: Public Service, 1971; (with W.R. Keast) Faculty Tenure, 1973; To Irrigate A Wasteland, 1974. Home: 1127 Langley Ln McLean VA 22101 Office: 1725 I St NW Washington DC 20472

MADAN, BAL KRISHNA, banker, economist; b. Sahowala, Punjab, India, July 13, 1911; s. Shiv Ram and Jamnadevi (Chhabra) M.; B.A. with honors, U. Punjab, 1931, M.A., 1933, Ph.D., 1937; m. Savitri Pahwa, Oct. 11, 1935; children—Pradeep, Dilip, Rajiv, Rakesh. Econ. adviser Govt. Punjab, 1940-41; dir. research Res. Bank India, 1941; alternate exec. dir. IMF, 1946, IBRD, 1947; exec. dir. IMF, 1948-50; with Res. Bank India, 1950-67, dep. gov., 1964-67, vice chmn. Indsl. Devel. Bank, 1964-67; exec. dir. IMF, Washington, 1967-71, chmn. Bonus Rev. Com., India, 1972-74, chmn. Mgmt. Devel. Inst., 1973—; del. numerous internat. confs.; sec. Indian del. UN Monetary and Financial Conf., Bretton Woods, 1944. Dep. sec. Tariff Bd. India, 1946-47; mem. Indian Finance Commn., 1951-53, Indian Taxation Enquiry Commn., 1953-54; mem. standing com. Indian Panel Econs., 1952-64; mem. Indian Foodgrains Enquiry Com., 1957, Com. Distbn. Incomes and Levels of Living, 1960-70, UN Expert Group on Spl. UN Fund for Econ. Devel., 1955; dir. Indsl. Finance Corp. India, 1960-64, Life Ins. Corp. India, 1964-67; mem. governing body Indian Investment Center, 1961-67, Sch. Internat. Studies, New Delhi, 1955-65, Nat. Council Applied Econ. Research, 1974—, Risk Capital Found., New Delhi, 1975-79, Nat. Inst. Pub. Fin. and Policy, 1976—; chmn. Wages, Incomes and Prices Com., 1964-66. Mem. Indian Soc. Agrl. Economists (pres. 1957), Indian Econ. Assn. (pres. 1961), Soc. Internat. Devel. Bombay (pres. 1962-66), Soc. Internat. Devel. Washington. Clubs: Cricket of India, United Services (Bombay); Delhi Gymkhana (New Delhi); Bretton Woods Recreation Center (Washington). Author: India and Imperial Preference—A Study in Commerical Policy, 1939; Aspects of Economic Development and Policy, 1964; The Real Wages of Industrial Labour in India, 1977; Report on a Study of Debt-Equity Ratio Norms, 1978. Home: B-100 Greater Kailash-I New Delhi 48 India Office: Management Development Institute F-45 South Extension (NDSE) Part-I Ring Rd New Delhi 110 049 India

MADDEN, CLIFFORD JOHN, computer co. exec.; b. Bessmer, Mich., Feb. 16, 1936; s. Boris and Mary Madden; B.S. in Bus. Adminstrn., Miami U., Oxford, Ohio, 1961; J.D., U. Mich., 1963; m. Mary E. Smaltz, Sept. 5, 1959; children—Todd, Derk. Admitted to Colo. bar, 1964, Wis. bar, 1965; asso. gen. counsel Security Life & Accident Co., Denver, 1963-65; v.p., gen. counsel Gateway Foods, Inc., LaCrosse, Wis., 1965-69; dir. internat. fin. Pillsbury Co., Mpls., 1969-72; v.p. fin. Rucker Co., Oakland, Calif., 1972-74; sr. v.p. fin., sec. Amdahl Corp., Sunnyvale, Calif., 1975—. Served with AUS, 1954-57. C.P.A., Wis. Mem. Am. Bar Assn., Am. Inst. C.P.A.'s, Phi Beta Kappa, Beta Gamma Sigma. Home: 835 Chiltern Rd Hillsborough CA 94010 Office: 1250 E Arques Ave Sunnyvale CA 94086. *Integrity must exist before success.*

MADDEN, DAVID, author; b. Knoxville, Tenn., July 25, 1933; s. James Helvy and Emily (Merritt) M.; B.S., U. Tenn., 1957; M.A., San Francisco State Coll., 1958; postgrad. Yale Drama Sch., 1959-60; m. Roberta Margaret Young, Sept. 6, 1956; 1 son, Blake Dana. Faculty, Appalachian State Tchrs. Coll., Boone, N.C., 1957-58, Centre Coll., Danville, Ky., 1960-62, U. Louisville, 1962-64, Kenyon Coll., Gambier, O., 1964-66, Ohio U., Athens, 1966-68; writer-in-residence La. State U., Baton Rouge, 1968—. Mem. adv. bd. Baton Rouge Arts Council. Served with AUS, 1953-55. Recipient Rockefeller grant in fiction, 1969. John Golden fellow in playwriting, 1959. Mem. Authors League, Asso. Writing Programs (bd.), Popular Culture Assn. (chmn.), Image Film Soc. Democrat. Author: (novels) Cassandra Singing, 1969, Bijou, 1974, The Suicides Wife, 1978, Pleasure Dome, 1979; (stories) The Shadow Knows (Nat. Council on Arts selection), 1970; (lit. criticism) Wright Morris, 1964, Poetic Image in Six Genres, 1969, James M. Cain, 1970. Asst. editor The Kenyon Rev., 1964-66. Editor: Remembering James Agee, 1974. Home: 614 Park Blvd Baton Rouge LA 70806

MADDEN, EDWARD HARRY, educator; b. Gary, Ind., May 18, 1925; s. Harry Albert and Amelia Dorothy (Schepper) M.; A.B., Oberlin Coll., 1946, A.M., 1947; Ph.D., U. Iowa, 1950; m. Marian Sue Canaday, Sept. 15, 1946; children—Kerry Arthur, Dennis William. Prof. philosophy U. Conn., 1950-59, San Jose State Coll., 1959-64, State U. N.Y. at Buffalo, 1964—; vis. prof. Brown U., 1954-55, Amherst Coll., 1962, U. Toronto, 1967, Am. U. Beirut (Lebanon), 1969-70; sr. research fellow Linacre Coll., Oxford U., 1978. Served with USNR, 1943-45. Recipient Am. Philos. Soc. research grant, 1961; Fulbright-Hays award, 1969-70. Mem. C.S. Peirce Soc. (pres. 1962-63, sec.-treas. 1960-61), Philosophy Sci. Assn. (editorial bd. jour.), Am. Council Learned Socs. (selection com.), Am. Philos. Assn. (co-chmn. com. publs.), Phi Kappa Phi. Author: Philosophical Problems Of Psychology, 1962; Chauncey Wright And The Foundations Of Pragmatism, 1963; Evil And The Concept Of God, 1968; Civil Disobedience And Moral Law, 1968; The Structure Of Scientific Thought, 1960; Causal Powers, 1975; Causing, Perceiving and Believing, 1975. Gen. editor Harvard U. Press, Source Books in History Sci. Cons. editor Jour. of History of Philosophy. Editorial bd. The Works of William James, The Works of C.S. Peirce. Home: 120 Brantwood Rd Buffalo NY 14226

MADDEN, FRANK AUGUSTUS, JR., lawyer, corp. exec.; b. Kansas City, Mo., Dec. 7, 1924; s. Frank Augustus and Helen (Gascon) M.; B.S.S., Georgetown U., 1949; LL.B., N.Y. Law Sch., 1957, J.D., 1956; m. Joan D. Mayne, June 19, 1954; children—Deborah, Pamela, Stephen. Admitted to N.Y., U.S. Supreme Ct. bars; spl. agt. FBI, Washington, N.Y.C., Chgo., 1950-58; mgr. housing dept. U.S. Carbide Corp., 1958-62; chief exec. officer Homequity, Inc., Wilton, Conn., 1962-64; chmn., chief exec. officer Holiday Homes Internat., Greenwich, Conn., 1974-78, Executrans, Inc., Northbrook, Ill., 1964—, Previews, Inc., 1973-78; dir. Trans-Exec. Corp., Exec-Van Systems. Fundraiser, Salisbury (Conn.) Sch., Georgetown U. Served with U.S. Army, 1943-45. Lic. real estate broker, N.Y., Conn., N.J., N.C. Mem. Am., Fed. bar assns., Bar Assn. City N.Y., Soc. Former Spl. Agts. FBI, Georgetown Alumni Assn., Nat. Assn. Real Estate Brokers. Clubs: Woodway Country (Darien, Conn.); Belle Haven (Greenwich). Home: 65 Lost District Dr New Canaan CT 06840 also 10747 N Military Trail Palm Beach Gardens FL Office: Greenwich Office Park Greenwich CT 06830

MADDEN, HENRY MILLER, educator; b. Oakland, Calif., June 17, 1912; s. Henry Joseph and Martha Ann (Miller) M.; A.B., Stanford, 1933; student U. Budapest, 1936-37; A.M., Columbia, 1944, Ph.D., 1948; B.L.S., U. Calif., 1947. Instr. history Stanford, 1937-42; acting asst. prof. history State U. Wash., 1948; ofcl. Internat. Refugee Orgn., Linz, Austria, 1948-49; univ. librarian Calif. State U., Fresno, 1949-79, adj. prof. bibliography, 1979—; Fulbright lectr., Austrian Nat. Library, 1953-54. Served as lt. comdr. U.S.N.R., 1942-46; sec. Tripartite Naval Commn., Berlin, Germany, 1945-46. Mem. Am. Hist. Assn., Calif. Library Assn. (past pres.), U.S. Naval Inst., A.L.A., Phi Beta Kappa. Club: Roxburghe (San Francisco). Author: Xantus, Hungarian Naturalist in the Pioneer West, 1949; German Travelers in California, 1958; From Kapuvár to California, 1893, 1979. Editor: California Librarian, 1963-66. Contbr. profl. publs. Home: 4687 Wishon Ave Fresno CA 93704

MADDEN, JOHN, former profl. football coach; b. Austin, Minn., 1936; B.S., Calif. Poly. U., 1959, M.A., 1961; m. Virginia Madden; children—Mike, Joe. Player, Phila. Eagles, NFL team, 1959; asst. coach Hancock Jr. Coll., Santa Maria, Calif., 1960-62, head coach, 1962-64; defensive coordinator Calif. State U. at San Diego, 1964-66; with Oakland Raiders Am. Football League (now Am. Football Conf., NFL team, 1967-79, linebacker coach, 1967-69, head coach, 1969-79; head coach Am. Football Conf. team NFL Pro Bowl, 1971, 73, 74, 75; head coach 6 Western div. Am. Football Conf. championship teams, Super Bowl champions, 1976. Named Coach of Year, Am. Football League, 1969. Home: Pleasanton CA

MADDEN, JOHN BECKWITH, banker; b. Bklyn., Jan. 22, 1919; s. John James and Rachel (Beckwith) M.; B.A., Yale, 1941; M.B.A., N.Y.U., 1949; m. Mary Audrey Ritter, June 18, 1950; children—Nancy Fiske, John Beckwith, Peter Fiske. With Brown Bros. Harriman & Co., N.Y.C., 1946—, gen. partner, 1955—, mng. partner, 1968—; dir. Mcht.-Sterling Corp., Freeport Minerals Co., Mcht. Properties, Inc., Bklyn. Union Gas Co., Fuel Resources Inc.; trustee Mut. Life Ins. Co. N.Y., Bklyn. Savs. Bank. Vice pres., trustee Boys' Club N.Y. Inc. Trustee Yale U.; mem. distbn. com. N.Y. Community Trust; bd. dirs. James Found. Served as capt. AUS, 1941-45. Mem. Assn. Res. City Bankers, Am. Inst. Banking (adv. com. N.Y. chpt.). Office: 59 Wall St New York NY 10005

MADDEN, KENNETH CROMWELL, state supt. edn.; b. Orbisonia, Pa., Sept. 20, 1917; s. Charles A. and Elsie (Cromwell) M.; B.S., Shippensburg (Pa.) Coll., 1939; M.A., U. N.C., 1946; Ed.D., Pa. State U., 1950; m. Mabel Alice Failes, Apr. 26, 1942; children—Margaret Adele, Kay Eileen, Kenneth Cromwell, Judith Marie. From tchr. to supervising prin. Orbisonia (Pa.) pub. schs., 1939-49; exec. asst. citizenship edn. project Columbia Tchrs. Coll., 1952; supt. Seaford (Del.) Spl. Sch. Dist., 1952-67; supt. pub. instrn., Del., 1967—; prof. U. Del. extension, 1964—. Chmn. Del. Bd. Edn. Sch. Bldg. Survey, 1955; pres. Delmarva Ednl. TV, 1960-62; regional dir. Asso. Pub. Sch. Systems (N.J., Pa., Del., Md.), 1962-64; chmn. Del. Bd. Edn. Staffing Plan for Del. Schs., 1962-64; rep. of Del. to Tri-State Instructional Broadcasting Council, 1963; pres. Del. Sch. Study Council, 1965-67. Served to maj. AUS, 1941-46; brig. gen. Del. N.G., 1969—. Decorated Bronze Star; recipient Conspicious Service medal Del., 1958; 1st winner Sussex County Distinguished Educator award, 1964; Pub. Service award V.F.W., 1956, Distinguished Alumnus award Shippensburg State Coll., 1972, Outstanding Educator award Del. Bus. Clubs, 1973, Freedom Found. Educators award, 1975. Mem. Nat., Del. (bd. dirs. 1956-60) edn. assns., Del. Chief Sch. Officers Assn. (pres. 1958), Vocational Indsl. Clubs Am. (hon. life mem.), Distributive Edn. Clubs Am. (hon. life mem.), Am. Legion (past post vice comdr.). Kiwanian (pres. Seaford 1961). Author articles in field. Home: 1 Beaver Dam Rd Seaford DE 19973 Office: PO Box 697 Dover DE 19901

MADDEN, MURDAUGH STUART, lawyer; b. Morgantown, W.Va., Feb. 26, 1922; s. Joseph Warren and Margaret (Liddell) M.; student Oberlin Coll., 1939-40; B.A., George Washington U., 1942; LL.B., J.D., Harvard, 1948; m. Eileen Dillon, June 17, 1978; children by previous marriage—Liddell Louise, Murdaugh Stuart, Michael Mann. Admitted to D.C. and Va. bars, 1948; asst. counsel Bur. Aero., 1948-50; pvt. practice, Washington, 1950—; sr. partner Shaw Pittman, Potts, Trowbridge & Madden, 1961-71; gen. counsel Humane Soc. U.S.; counsel embassy Saudi Arabia. Trustee Inst. for Study Nat. Behavior, Princeton N.J., Friends of India Com., Washington; v.p., mem. council World Fedn. for Protection Animals, Zurich, Internat. Soc. for Protection of Animals, London; bd. dirs. Nat. Assn. Advancement Humane Edn., Nat. Humane Edn. Center. Served with USAAF, 1942-45; ETO. Mem. Am. (past chmn. internat. and comparative law com. internat. transp.), D.C. (past dir., com. bar ethics revision), Va. bar assns., The Barristers, Am. Soc. Internat. Law, Harvard Law Sch. Assn., Oberlin Alumni Assn., Phi Sigma Kappa. Episcopalian. Clubs: Met., St. Albans Tennis (Washington); Columbia Country (Bethesda, Md.); Harvard of N.Y. Author: (with Sherman L. Cohn) The Legal Status and Problems of the American Abroad, 1966. Home: 2530 Queen Anne's Ln NW Washington DC 20037 Office: 2100 L St NW Washington DC 20037

MADDEN, RICHARD BLAINE, forest products co. exec.; b. Short Hills, N.J., Apr. 27, 1929; s. James L. and Irma (Twining) M.; B.S., Princeton, 1951; J.D., U. Mich., 1956; M.B.A., N.Y. U., 1959; m. Joan Fairbairn, May 24, 1958; children—John Richard, Lynn Marie, Kathryn Ann, Andrew Twining. Admitted to Mich. bar, 1956, N.Y. bar, 1958; gen. asst. treas.'s dept. Socony Mobil Oil Corp., N.Y.C., 1956-57, spl. asst., 1958-59, fin. rep., 1960; asst. to pres. Mobil Chem. Co., also dir. Mobil Chems. Ltd. of Eng., 1960-63; exec. v.p., gen. mgr. Kordite Corp., also v.p. Mobil Plastics, 1963-66, v.p. Mobil Chem. Co., N.Y.C., 1966-68, group v.p., 1968-70, asst. treas. Mobil Oil Corp., 1970-71; chmn. Mobil Oil Estates Ltd., 1970-71; pres., chmn., chief exec. officer Potlatch Corp., San Francisco, 1971—; dir. Pacific Gas and Electric Co., Del Monte Corp., AMFAC, Inc. From lectr. to adj. asso. prof. fin. N.Y. U., 1960-63. Bd. dirs., mem. exec. com. Am. Paper Inst.; trustee, exec. com. Am. Enterprise Inst., bd. govs., exec. com. San Francisco Symphony Assn.; bd. dirs. San Francisco Opera Assn. Served to lt (j.g.) USNR, 1951-54. Mem. N.Y., Mich. bar assns. Roman Catholic. Clubs: University (N.Y.C.); Pacific Union (San Francisco); Lagunitas (Ross, Calif.). Home: PO Box 1153 Ross CA 94957 Office: PO Box 3591 San Francisco CA 94119

MADDEN, WALES HENDRIX, JR., lawyer; b. Amarillo, Tex., Sept. 1, 1927; s. Wales Hendrix and Kathryn (Nash) M.; B.A., U. Tex., 1950, LL.B., 1952; m. Alma Faye Cowden, Nov. 8, 1952; children—Wales Hendrix III, Straughn. Admitted to Tex. bar, 1952, practiced in Amarillo; dir. First Nat. Bank of Amarillo, Mesa Petroleum Co., Nowlin Mfg. Co. Mem. Tex. Constnl. Revision Commn., 1973—. Mem. bd. regents Amarillo Coll., 1958-59; bd. regents U. Tex., 1959-65, also mem. univ. devel. bd.; mem. Tex. Coll. and Univ. System Coordinating Bd. 1964-69; mem. Amarillo Area Found., Cal Farley's Boys Ranch. Trustee Trinity U., San Antonio. Served with USNR. Named Outstanding Man of Amarillo, 1972; Disting. Alumnus, U. Tex., 1979. Mem. Am., Amarillo (pres. 1956) bar assns., Amarillo C. of C. (pres. 1968), State Bar Tex., State Jr. Bar Tex. (pres. 1956), Friar Soc., Phi Alpha Delta, Phi Delta Theta, Phi Eta Sigma, Pi Sigma Alpha. Presbyterian (elder). Home: 2701 Teckla St Amarillo TX 79106 Office: 700 W 9th St Amarillo TX 79101

MADDIN, ROBERT, educator; b. Hartford, Conn., Oct. 20, 1918; s. Isadore and Mae (Jacobs) M.; B.S., Purdue U., 1942; D.Engring., Yale, 1948; m. Odell E. Steinberg, July 9, 1945; children—Leslie Jeanne, Jill Andrea. Research fellow Yale, 1948-49; asst. prof. Johns Hopkins, 1949-52, asso. prof., 1952-55; vis. prof. U. Birmingham (Eng.), 1954-55, Oxford (Eng.) U., 1970; prof. U. Pa., 1955-56; prof., dir. Sch. Metallurgy and Materials Sci., 1957-72, Univ. prof. metallurgy, 1973—; lectr. univs. and mfg. plants, Eng., France, Germany, Israel, India, Japan. Served as lt. USAAF. World War II. Named Distinguished Engring. Alumnus, Purdue U., 1974. Fellow Am. Soc. Metals; mem. Yale Engring. Assos., Yale Metall. Assos., Am. Inst. Mining and Metall. Engrs. (chmn. publs. com., exec. com.), U. Birmingham Metall. Soc. (hon. life), Md. Inst. Metals (hon. dir.), Sigma Xi. Author: (with H. Kimura) Quench Hardening in Metals, 1971; also chpts. in books. Editor: Creep and Recovery. Editor-in-chief Materials Science and Engineering. Contbr. tech. articles profl. publs. Home: Penn Towers 1801 JF Kennedy Blvd Philadelphia PA 19103

MADDOCK, CHARLES SANFORD, lawyer, mfg. co. exec.; b. Utica, N.Y., May 6, 1911; s. Robert Alfred and Catherine (Roberts) M.; B.A., U. Colo., 1932; LL.B., Harvard, 1935; m. Rita Maher, Mar. 12, 1938; children—Robert A., Catherine E. Admitted to Mass. bar, 1935, Del. bar, 1946, also U.S. Supreme Ct.; asso. firm Gaston, Snow, Rice & Boyd, Boston, 1935-43; with Hercules, Inc., and predecessor, 1943-76, gen. counsel, 1955-76, dir., 1971-76; counsel Cooch & Taylor, Wilmington, Del., 1976—. Cons. lawyers services Am. Bar Assn. survey legal profession, 1948-50. Mem. planning commn., Newark, Del., 1951-53; pres. Travelers Aid Soc., Wilmington, Del., 1955-57, 64-65; mem. corp. Lesley Coll., Cambridge, Mass., 1937-42; mem. vis. com. Harvard Law Sch., 1955-62; mem. PLI Adv. Council of Corporate Law Depts., chmn., 1972—; mem. legal adv. com. N.A.M., M.C.A.; mem. adv. bd. Internat. and Comparative Law Center Southwestern Legal Found., vice chmn., 1973-76. Bd. dirs. Family Services No. Del., 1955-66; trustee Curran Found.; trustee Nursing Sch. Wilmington, 1977, pres., 1977—; trustee Wilmington Med. Center, 1977—. Mem. Am. (chmn. standing com. edn. about Communism 1967-69), Del. bar assns., Assn. Gen. Counsel (past pres.), Soc. Cincinnati (hon.), Pi Gamma Mu, Delta Sigma Rho, Beta Theta Pi. Episcopalian. Clubs: Wilmington Country: Greenville. Contbr. to profl. jours. Home: Greenville DE 19807 Office: 901 Market St Wilmington DE 19801

MADDOCKS, ROBERT ALLEN, mfg. co. exec.; b. Missouri Valley, Ia., Dec. 25, 1933; s. Clarence A. and Helen Louise (Unger) M.; B.S., Drake U., 1956, J.D., 1958; m. JoAnn Skaggs, June 2, 1956; children—Todd Duncan, Susan Colette, Amy Annette. Individual practice law, Clarion, Ia., 1958-67; atty. Massey Ferguson, Inc., Des Moines, 1967-68; div. gen. counsel, Akron, O., 1968-69; asst. sec., gen. counsel, dir. corporate relations Kellwood Co., St. Louis, 1970-73, sec., gen. counsel, 1973—, v.p., 1978—, also dir. subsidiaries. Sec., dir. Midwest Credit Corp. Wright County atty., Clarion, 1961-65. Trustee Maryville Coll., St. Louis, 1975-78; bd. dirs. Kellwood Found., 1975—. Mem. Am. Bar Assn., Inter-Am., Ia., Ohio, Mo. bar assns., Am. Trial Lawyers Assn., Nat. Corporate Secs. Assn., Comml. Law League, Licensing Execs. Soc., N.A.M. (corporate relations com.), Am. Apparel Mfrs. Assn. (legal com.), Canvas Products Assn. Internat. (chmn. law and legis. com., Labor Policy Assn. Home: 13456 Thornhill Dr Saint Louis MO 63131 Office: 600 Kellwood Pkwy Saint Louis MO 63124

MADDOX, ALVA HUGH, state justice; b. Andalusia, Ala., Apr. 17, 1930; s. Christopher Columbus and Audie Lodella (Freeman) M.; A.B. in Journalism, U. Ala., 1952, LL.B., 1957; m. Virginia Ann Roberts, June 14, 1958; children—Robert Hugh, Patricia Jane. With Florala News, 1947; cashier Treas.'s Office, U. Ala., 1948-52, 54-56; admitted to Ala. bar, 1957; law clk. Ct. of Appeals of Ala., Montgomery, 1957; atty., field examiner VA, Montgomery, 1958; law clk. U.S. Dist. Ct., Montgomery, 1959-60; practice law, Montgomery, 1961-64; asst. dist. atty. 15th Jud. Circuit, Montgomery, legal adviser Gov. George Wallace, 1965-67, Lurleen B. Wallace, 1967-68, Gov. Albert P. Brewer, 1968-69; circuit judge 15th Jud. Circuit, Montgomery, 1963; asso. justice Supreme Ct. Ala., Montgomery, 1969—; adj. prof. Troy State U., 1976—; prof. law Jones Law Inst., Montgomery, 1961-62, 76; mem. Jud. Planning Commn. Ala., Permanent Study Commn. Ala. Judiciary. Pres. youth legislature YMCA, 1978—, bd. dirs. Central br.; bd. dirs. Baptist Med. Center, Montgomery Baptist Hosp. Found. Served with USAF, 1952-54; col. Res. Mem. Am., Ala. bar assns., Am. Judicature Soc., Farrah Law Soc., Inst. Jud. Adminstrn., Ala. Law Inst., Arnold Air Soc., Pershing Rifles, Omicron Delta Kappa, Phi Alpha Delta, Sigma Delta Chi. Democrat. Baptist (deacon 1966—). Kiwanian (dir.). Club: Maxwell AFB Officers Open Mess (Montgomery). Author: Billy Boll Weevil—A Pest Becomes a Hero, 1976. Home: 3137 Hathaway Pl Montgomery AL 36111 Office: PO Box 218 Montgomery AL 36101. *A deep faith in God, the ability to get to the heart of a problem and decide what to do about it, and move on, profiting by any mistakes.*

MADDOX, DAN WAITE, credit corp. exec.; b. Easonville, Ala., June 9, 1909; s. William Notley and Minnie (Waite) M.; student Ga. Sch. Tech., 1925-29; m. Margaret Huffman, June 21, 1969; children—Judith E. Maddox Nebhut, Ellen King Maddox Christianson, James Notley. With Universal C.I.T. Corp., N.Y.C., 1930-41; founder, chief exec. officer Assos. Capital Corp., Nashville, 1943-74; chmn. Assos. Corp. N.Am., Dallas, 1974—, chief exec. officer, 1974-79; dir. Gulf & Western Industries, N.Y.C., Capital Life Ins. Co., Denver, Shoney's Inc., Nashville, Commerce Union Bank, Nashville, Assos. First Capital Corp. N.Y., Tenn. Valley Bankshares, Nashville. Mem. Tenn. Econ. Devel. Com., 1971—, Tenn. Agrl. and Indsl. Commn., 1972—; trustee African Wildlife Leadership Found., Washington; trustee Children's Mus., Nashville, 1959—, v.p., 1971-74; trustee Maddox Found., Nashville, Montgomery-Bell Acad., Nashville, 1972—. Recipient Weatherby award Shikar Safari Club Internat., 1967. Mem. East African Profl. Hunters Assn. Clubs: Mill Reef (Antiqua, W.I.); Explorers, Boone and Crockett (N.Y.C.); Belle Meade, Cumberland (Nashville). Office: Assos First Capital Corp 1 Gulf and Western Plaza New York NY 10023

MADDOX, JESSE CORDELL, coll. pres.; b. LaGrange, Ga., Dec. 30, 1931; s. Jesse Garland and Esther Ann (Palmer) M.; B.A., Furman U., 1954, LL.D., 1976; B.D., So. Baptist Theol. Sem., 1957, Miv.D., 1960; D.D., Baptist Coll. Charleston ton (S.C.), 1972; m. Brona Moorefield, Mar. 30, 1957; children—Jesse Cordell, Michael, Brian, Gayle. Ordained to ministry So. Bapt. Conv., 1950; asso. brotherhood dept. S.C. Bapt. Conv., 1957-61; dir. devel., asst. to pres. Furman U., Greenville, S.C., 1961-71; pres. Anderson (S.C.) Coll., 1972-77, Carson Newman Coll., Jefferson City, Tenn., 1977—. Served as chaplain U.S. Army, 1957-62. Mem. Nat. Council Jr. Colls. (pres. 1976), So. Assn. Ch. Related Colls. (v.p. 1979), Adv. Council Pvt. Colls. S.C. (chmn. 1975). Club: Jefferson City Rotary (pres. 1978-79). Home: Route 1 Jefferson City TN 37760 Office: Carson Newman Coll Russel St Jefferson City TN 37760

MADDOX, LESTER GARFIELD, Realtor, former gov. Ga.; b. Atlanta, Sept. 30, 1915; s. Dean G. and Flonnie Maddox; ed. coll. corr. courses; m. Virginia Cox; children—Linda Maddox Densmore, Lester, Virginia Louise, Larry. Engaged in real estate, grocery, restaurant and furniture business; gov. of Ga., 1967-71, lt. gov., 1971-75. Mem. Ga. C. of C., Travelers Protective Assn.; hon. mem. Ga. Sheriff's Assn. Peace Officers Assn., Justices of Peace and Constables Assn. Democrat. Baptist. Clubs: Masons, Shriners, Moose, Buckhead 50.*

MADDOX, ROBERT NOTT, chem. engr., educator; b. Winslow, Ark., Sept. 29, 1925; s. R.L. and Mabel (Nott) M.; student Iowa State Coll., 1944-45; B.S., U. Ark., 1948; M.S., U. Okla., 1950; Ph.D., Okla. State U., 1955; m. Paula Robinson, Oct. 6, 1951; children—Deirdre O'Neil, Robert Dozier. Mem. faculty Sch. Chem. Engring., Okla. State U., 1950-51, 52-58, prof., head dept., 1958-77, Leonard F. Sheerar prof., 1976—, dir. phys. properties lab., 1976—; design engr. process div. Black, Sivalls & Bryson, Inc., Oklahoma City, 1951-52; adminstrv. v.p., tech. dir. Fluid Properties Research, Inc.; chem. engring. cons. Served with USNR, 1944-45. Registered profl. engr., Okla. Fellow Am. Inst. Chem. Engrs. (chpt. pres. 1956-57); mem. Nat., Okla. (chpt. pres. 1961-62, dir. 1966-68, Engr. of Year 1972) socs. profl. engrs., Am. Soc. Engring. Edn., Am. Inst. Mining Engrs., Soc. Petroleum Engrs., Am. Chem. Soc. (treas. indsl. and engring. chemistry div. 1966-68, chmn. div. 1970, Stewart award 1971), Nat. Gas Processors Assn. (editorial adv. bd. engring. data book 1972—), Sigma Xi, Omega Chi Epsilon (nat. pres. 1968-70), Tau Beta Pi, Alpha Chi Sigma, Omicron Delta Kappa, Sigma Nu (high council 1966-70, regent 1972-74). Episcopalian (lay reader, vestryman). Clubs: Elks, Masons. Author numerous tech. papers. Home: 301 Orchard Ln Stillwater OK 74074

MADDUX, JAMES FREDERICK, psychiatrist, hosp. adminstr. b. Sycamore, Ga., Aug. 17, 1916; s. Creedt T. and Ida (Nussell) M.; M.D., Med. Coll. Ga., 1941; m. Agnes G. Griffin, July 29, 1945; children—James Michael, Frederick Taylor, John Stephen, Mary Bernadette. Resident in psychiatry USPHS Hosp., Ft. Worth, 1942-43, Colo. Psychopathic Hosp., Denver, 1946-48; health cons., region 6 HEW, 1948-54, chief mental health service, region 5, 1954-58; dep. med. officer charge USPHS Hosp., Lexington, Ky., 1958-62; chief NIMH Clin. Research Center, Ft. Worth, 1962-69; prof. psychiatry U. Tex. Health Sci. Center, San Antonio, 1969—. Pres. bd. Child Guidance Clinic Ft. Worth, 1964-65. Served to lt. comdr. USCG, 1943-46. Fellow A.M.A., Am. Psychiat. Assn., Am. Orthopsychiat. Assn. Author papers on mental health and drug dependence. Address: 7703 Floyd Curl Dr San Antonio TX 78284

MADEIRA, FRANCIS KING CAREY, educator, condr.; b. Jenkintown, Pa., Feb. 21, 1917; s. Percy Childs and Margaret (Carey) M.; grad. Avon Old Farms, 1934; student piano Julliard Grad. Sch., 1937-40, conducting, 1940-43; D.F.A. (hon.), Providence Coll., 1966; D.H.L., R.I. Coll., 1969; m. Jean E. Browning, June 17, 1947. Instr. music Brown U., 1943-46, asst. prof. music, 1946-56, asso. prof. music, 1956—; founder, condr. R.I. Philharm. Orch., 1945-78; concert pianist recitals and condr. concerts U.S. and Europe; also guest condr. U.S. and fgn. orchs.; world premiere Trilogy (JFK-MLK-RFK) (by Ron Nelson) with R.I. Philharmonic Orch., 1969. Recipient Gov.'s award for excellence in arts, 1972; John F. Kennedy award for service to community, 1978. Mem. Nat. Assn. Am. Composers and Condrs., Am. Symphony Orch. League (v.p. 1950-52). Home: North Waterboro ME 04061

MADEIRA, ROBERT LEHMAN, assn. exec.; b. Elizabethtown, Pa., Aug. 30, 1915; s. Isaac Titus and Elsie Hernley (Lehman) M.; student Juniata Coll., 1933-34; B.S. in Econs., Elizabethtown Coll., 1937; postgrad. Mpls. Honeywell Sch. Aero. Engring., U. Minn., 1945; m. Mary Elizabeth Evans, Feb. 5, 1938; children—Terry Madeira Harsney, Betsy Madeira Landre. Pianist, tchr., Elizabethtown, 1935-41; automobile salesman Packard Lancaster Co., Lancaster, Pa., 1937; owner, mgr. Conewago Foods, Elizabethtown, 1938-39; aircraft technician U.S. Air Force Middletown, Pa. and Columbia, S.C., 1941-42; project engr. Mpls. Honeywell, Chgo. and Mpls., 1942-45; mgr. Iceland, Inc., Elizabethtown, 1945-51; exec. sec. Nat. Frozen Food Locker Inst., Elizabethtown, 1951-55; exec. dir. Nat. Inst. Locker and Freezer Provisioners, Elizabethtown, 1955-73, Am. Assn. Meat Processors, Elizabethtown, 1973—. Chmn., Elizabethtown ARC, 1948-49, Elizabethtown Community Chest, 1952-53, Elizabethtown Park Dr., 1950; bd. dirs. Lancaster Com. of 100, 1953-57, Elizabethtown Music Found., 1951-57, Norlanco Med. Center, Elizabethtown, 1972-75; chmn. fund dr. Norlanco Med. Center, 1972-73. Recipient Man of Yr. award Nat. Inst. Locker and Freezer Provisioners, 1955; honor cert. Freedoms Found. at Valley Forge, 1976. Mem. Am. Soc. Assn. Execs. (Key award 1971, chartered assn. exec.), C. of C. U.S., Nat. Assn. Exhbn. Mgrs., Nat. Fedn. Ind. Bus., Ams. United for Separation of Ch. and State, Gideons Internat., Nat. Right-to-Work Com. Republican. Presbyterian. Home: 1001 S Locust St Elizabethtown PA 17022 Office: Am Assn Meat Processors 224 E High St Elizabethtown PA 17022

MADEY, RICHARD, physicist, educator; b. Bklyn., Feb. 23, 1922; s. Elia Doher and Dorothy Ann (Diab) M.; B.E.E. (Conn. Alumni scholar), Rensselaer Poly. Inst., 1942; Ph.D. in Physics, U. Calif. at Berkeley, 1952; m. Mary Lou Kirch, Sept. 8, 1951; children—Doren Louise, Diane Claire, Daryl Jane, Richard Kirk, Ronald Eliot, Randall Clarke. Elec. engr. Allen B. Dumont Labs., Passaic, N.J., 1934-44; physicist Lawrence Radiation Lab., Berkeley, 1947-53, guest scientist, 1971, 73, 77-79; asso. physicist Brookhaven Nat. Lab., Upton, L.I., N.Y., 1953-56, guest scientist, 1961, 74; scientist Republic Aviation Corp., Farmingdale, N.Y., 1956-58, sr. scientist, 1958-61, chief staff scientist modern physics, 1961-62, chief applied physics subdiv. of research div., 1964; prof. physics Clarkson Coll. Tech., Potsdam, N.Y., 1965-71, chmn. dept., 1965; prof. physics, chmn. dept. Kent (Ohio) State U., 1971—; cons. Ross Radio Corp., Berkeley, 1952-53, West Coast Electronics Lab., Willys Motor Co., Oakland, Calif., 1954-55, Kaiser Aircraft & Electronics Corp., Palo Alto, Calif., 1955-56, Health and Safety Lab., U.S. AEC, N.Y.C., 1965-75, ERDA, 1975-77, Dept. Energy, 1977—, Lawrence Berkeley Lab., 1978—, Ecol. Energy Systems, 1979; mem. Am. Inst. Biol. Scis. radiation biology adv. panel to NASA Office Life Scis., 1979—; guest scientist Nevis Cyclotron Lab., Columbia U., Irvington-on-the-Hudson, N.Y., 1955, 75, 77, Foster Radiation Lab., McGill U., Montreal, Que., Can., 1967, 68, NRC, Ottawa, Ont., Can., 1968, 69, 70, Nuclear Structure Lab., U. Rochester (N.Y.), 1970, Lawrence Berkeley Lab., 1971, 72, 77-79, Ind. U. Cyclotron Facility, Bloomington, 1975—, Cyclotron Lab., U. Md. at College Park, 1973, 74, 75, 78—; prin. investigator U.S. Air Force, 1963-75, AEC, 1967-75, ERDA, 1975-77, Dept. Energy, 1977—, NSF, 1971—, Nat. Cancer Inst., NIH, 1973—, NASA, 1974—; mem. site visit team and rev. panel Nat. Cancer Inst., 1979. Served from ensign to lt. (j.g.), USNR, 1944-46. Decorated Naval Ordnance Devel. award (U.S.); Letter Commendation (Brit. Admiralty); recipient Army-Navy "E" award, 1943; registered profl. engr., Calif. Fellow N.Y. Acad. Scis., AAAS; mem. Inst. Colloid and Surface Sci., IEEE, Ohio Acad. Scis., AAUP, Am. Geophys. Union, Am. Phys. Soc., Am. Nuclear Soc. (membership com. 1962-63; membership com. shielding, dosimetry div. 1964-65, nominating com. 1965-66, exec. com. 1963-65, treas. 1964-65; dir. N.Y. met. sect. 1960-61, spl. program chmn. 1960-62, sec. 1962-63, vice chmn. 1963, chmn. 1964, award 1965), Sigma Xi, Sigma Pi Sigma, Eta Kappa Nu, Pi Delta Epsilon. Author: (with Robert M. Winter) Modern Physics, 1971; contbr. numerous articles tech. lit. Patentee in field. Home: 5225 Cline Rd Brimfield OH 44240

MADGETT, NAOMI LONG, poet, publisher; b. Norfolk, Va., July 5, 1923; d. Clarence Marcellus and Maude Selena (Hilton) Long; B.A., Va. State Coll., 1945; M.Ed., Wayne State U., 1956, postgrad., 1967-68; postgrad. U. Detroit, 1961-62; m. Julian F. Witherspoon, Mar. 31, 1946 (div. Apr. 1949); 1 dau., Jill Witherspoon Boyer; m. 2d, William H. Madgett, July 29, 1954 (div. Dec. 1960); m. 3d, Leonard P. Andrews, Mar. 31, 1972. Reporter, copyreader Mich. Chronicle, Detroit, 1945-46; service rep. Mich. Bell Telephone Co., Detroit, 1948-54; tchr. high sch. English, Detroit Pub. Schs., 1955-65, 66-68; research asso. Oakland U., Rochester, Mich., 1965-66, mem. Ann. Writers Conf., 1968—; lectr. English, U. Mich., 1970-71; asso. prof. English, Eastern Mich. U., Ypsilanti, 1968-73. prof., 1973—; editor-pub. Lotus Press, 1974—; poet-in-residence Humanities Center, Richmond, Va., 1973. Mem. lit. adv. panel Mich. Council for The Arts, participant Artists in The Schs. program. Recipient Esther R. Beer Poetry award Nat. Writers Club, 1957, Distinguished English Tchr. of Year award, 1967; Mott fellow in English, 1965. Mem. Coll. Lang. Assn., Detroit Women Writers, Nat. Council Tchrs. of English, NAACP, Alpha Kappa Alpha. Mem. United Ch. of Christ. Author poetry Songs to a Phantom Nightingale (under name Naomi Cornelia Long), 1941; One and the Many, 1956; Star by Star, 1965, 70; Pink Ladies in the Afternoon, 1972; Exits and Entrances, 1978; textbook (with Ethel Tincher and Henry B. Maloney) Success in Language and Literature B, 1967. Home: 16886 Inverness Ave Detroit MI 48221 Office: English Dept Eastern Michigan University Ypsilanti MI 48197. *I have always seen, as the primary goal of my life, the expression of words, if only a few, that might live beyond me, outrank my personal existence, and carry some meaning and truth to future generations.*

MADIGAN, EDWARD R., congressman; b. Lincoln, Ill., Jan. 13, 1936; grad. Lincoln Coll., 1955, D.H.L., 1975; D.H.L., Millikin U., Ill. Wesleyan U.; m. Evelyn M. George, 1955; children—Kimberly, Kellie, Mary Beth. mem. Ill. Ho. of Reps., 1967-72; mem. 93d to 96th congresses from Ill. Recipient Outstanding Legislator award Ill. Assn. Sch. Supts., 1968, Outstanding Pub. Service award Lincoln Coll. Alumni Assn. Mem. Ill. Jaycees (past v.p.), Lincoln C. of C. Elk, Kiwanian. Office: 2457 Rayburn House Office Bldg Washington DC 20515

MADIGAN, JOSEPH EDWARD, food and chem. co. exec.; b. Bklyn., June 26, 1932; s. James Peter and Mary (Goldman) M.; B.B.A. cum laude, Baruch Sch., CUNY, 1958; M.B.A., N.Y. U., 1963; children— Kerri Ann, Kimberly Ann. Adminstrv. asst. Asso. Metals & Minerals Corp., 1961-63; financial analyst, fgn. exchange trader, corp. portfolio trader AMAX, Inc., 1963-65; mgr. corp. portfolio, dir. cash mgmt., asst. treas. Trans World Airlines, Inc., 1965-68; treas. Borden, Inc., 1968-76, v.p., treas., 1976—. Served with USN, 1951-55. Mem. Fin. Execs. Inst., Assn. for Corp. Growth, Am. Mgmt. Assn., Baruch Sch.-CUNY Alumni Assn., N.Y. U. Alumni Assn., Nat. Investor Relations Inst., N.Y. U. Finance Club, Internat. Platform Assn., Beta Gamma Sigma. Republican. Roman Catholic. Clubs: Manhattan, N.Y. U., Plandome Country. Home: 56 Abbey Rd Manhasset NY 11030 Office: 277 Park Ave New York NY 10017

MADIGAN, MICHAEL J., cons. engr.; b. Danbury, Conn., Dec. 6, 1894; s. Richard Michael and Josephine (Canty) M.; m. Sybil Stearns (dec.); 1 dau., Mary Jane. Pres. firm Madigan-Hyland, S.A.; chmn. bd. dirs., pres. Madigan-Hyland Co., Ltd.; asst. to under sec. of war, 1941-45. Cons. engr. for World Bank, 1947-49. Served with U.S. Army, World War I; overseas. Awarded Medal for Merit. Mem. ASCE (hon.), Inst. Cons. Engrs. Clubs: Cosmos (Washington); Union League (N.Y.C.). Home: Rock Island Farm Hinsdale NH 03451

MADIGAN, RICHARD ALLEN, museum dir.; b. Corning, N.Y., Oct. 29, 1937; s. Myles L. and Rebekah M. (Bacon) M.; A.B., Drew U., 1959; m. Mary Jean Smith, June 11, 1960 (div. 1975); children—Richard Allen, Dana Smith, Reese Jennings; m. 2d, Alice Sturrock, Sept. 6, 1975 (div. May 1978); m. 3d, Cara Montgomery, Aug. 5, 1978. Pub. contact rep. Corning Glass Center, 1959, supr. visitor relations, 1959-60; dir. Andrew Dickson White Mus. Art, Cornell U., 1960-63; asst. dir., asst. sec. Corcoran Gallery Art, Washington, 1963-67; dir. N. Tex. Museums Resources Council, 1967-68, Bklyn. Children's Mus., 1968-69; exec. dir. Wave Hill Center Environ. Studies, 1969-74; instr. anthropology dept. Lehman Coll., 1968-74; dir. Norton Gallery and Sch. Art, West Palm Beach Fla., 1974—; sec. Art Mus. of The Palm Beaches, Inc., 1974—; past instr. art dept. George Washington U.; v.p. Palm Beach Festival; lectr. Fgn. Service Inst., Dept. State. Bd. dirs. Fla. Theatre Festival, 1975—; trustee Greater Washington Ednl. Television Assn. (WETA-TV). Mem. Am. Assn. Museums (chmn. coll. and univ. museums sect. 1962-63), Museums Council N.Y.C. (chmn. 1970-71), Fla. Art Mus. Dirs. Assn. (pres. 1978-79), S.E. Museums Conf. (dir.). Address: 5656 Upland Way West Palm Beach FL 33409

MADISON, CHARLES A(LLAN), author, editor; b. near Kiev, Russia, Apr. 16, 1895; s. David and Pessie (Burakowsky) M.; came to U.S., 1906, naturalized, 1916; A.B., U. of Mich., 1921; A.M., Harvard, 1922; m. Edith Hellman, July 1, 1924; 1 dau., Jeppy (Mrs. Leonard Yarensky). Mechanic in automobile factories, Detroit, 1909-16; asst. book editor Am. Book Co., N.Y. City, 1922-24, coll. book editor Henry Holt and Co., 1924-50, mng. editor, 1950-62. Mem. Authors Guild, Phi Beta Kappa. Author: Critics and Crusaders, 1947, rev. edit., 1959; American Labor Leaders, 1950, rev. edit., 1962; Leaders and Liberals in 20th Century America, 1961; the Owl Among Colophons, 1966; Book Publishing in America, 1966; Yiddish Literature: Its Scope and Major Writers, 1968; Eminent American Jews, 1970; Irving to Irving: Author-Publisher Relations, 1974; Jewish Publishing in America, 1976. Co-author: American Radicals, 1957. Contbr. critical essays and revs. to leading periodicals. Home: 231 E 76th St New York City NY 10021 also 78 Mountain Rd West Redding CT 06896

MADISON, ROBERT P., architect; b. Cleve., July 28, 1923; s. Robert J. and Nettie (Brown) M.; student Howard U., 1940-43; B.Arch., Western Res. U., 1946-48; M.Arch., Harvard, 1952; m. Leatrice L. Branch, Apr. 16, 1949; children—Jeanne Marie, Juliette Branch. Mem. various archtl. firms, 1948-52; instr. Howard U., Washington, 1952-54; pres. Madison-Madison, internat. architects, engrs. and planners, Cleve., 1954—; dir. Indsl. Bank of Washington. Vis. prof. Howard U., 1961-62; lectr. Western Res. U., 1964-65; mem. U.S. architects del. Peoples Repub. China, 1974. Mem. tech. advisory com. Cleve. Bd. Edn., 1960—; mem. advisory com. Cleve. Urban Renewal, 1963—; mem. fine arts advisory com. to mayor Cleve.; mem. archtl. advisory council Cornell U. Trustee Case Western Res. U., Glen Oak Sch.; bd. dirs. Jr. Achievement Greater Cleve. Served to 1st lt., inf. AUS, 1943-46. Decorated Purple Heart. Fulbright fellow, 1952-53. Fellow A.I.A. (chpt. pres., nat. task force for creative econs. 1973); mem. Architects Soc. Ohio, Epsilon Delta Rho, Alpha Phi Alpha, Sigma Pi Phi. Club: City (Cleve.). Prin. works include: U.S. Embassy Dakar, Senegal, West Africa, 1966. Home: 2339 N Park Blvd Cleveland Heights OH 44106 Office: 1900 Euclid Ave Cleveland OH 44115

MADISON, THOMAS F., telephone co. exec.; b. Mpls., Feb. 25, 1936; s. Earl and Bernice Madison; B.S. in Aero. Engring., U. Minn., 1959; m. Marilyn Louise Johnson, June 22, 1957; children—Michael T., Mary A., Mark R. With Northwestern Bell Telephone Co., 1954—, ops. mgr. Met. St. Paul, until 1977, v.p., chief exec. officer S.D., 1977-79, v.p., chief exec. officer Minn., Mpls., 1979—. Bd. dirs. Kidney Found. Upper Midwest, Urban Coalition Mpls.; mem. Mpls. Met. Housing Corp.; trustee Mpls. Soc. Fine Arts. Mem. Minn. N.G., 1953-54. Mem. Mpls. C. of C. (dir.). Roman Catholic. Clubs: Mpls. Athletic, Minneapolis, Minikahda (Mpls.); Minneapolis (St. Paul). Address: 5212 Dundee Rd Minneapolis MN 55436 Office: 200 S5th St Minneapolis MN 55402

MADOW, LEO, physician, educator; b. Cleve., Oct. 18, 1915; s. Solomon Martin and Anna (Meyers) M.; A.B., Western Res. U., 1937, M.D., 1942; M.A., Ohio State U., 1938; m. Jean Antoinette Weisman, Apr. 16, 1942; children—Michael, Robert. Intern Phila. Gen. Hosp., 1942-43; resident Phila. Gen. Hosp., Jefferson Hosp., Inst. Pa. Hosp., 1943-46; practice medicine, specializing in psychiatry, Phila., 1948—; prof., chmn. dept. neurology Med. Coll. Pa., Phila., 1958-65, prof., chmn. dept. psychiatry and neurology, 1965-70, prof., chmn. dept. psychiatry, 1970—; tng. analyst, past pres. Phila. Psychoanalytic Inst.; past pres., mem. med. staff Inst. Pa. Hosp. Served to capt. AUS, 1944-46. Named Outstanding Educator of Am., 1972. Diplomate Am. Bd. Psychiatry and Neurology. Fellow Am. Psychiat. Assn., A.C.P., Am. Coll. Psychiatrists; mem. Am. Psychoanalytic Assn., Am. Neurol. Assn., Group for Advancement of Psychiatry (treas.), Am. Orthopsychiat. Assn., A.A.A.S., Phila. Psychoanalytic Soc. (past pres.), Phila. Psychiat. Soc. (past pres.), Alpha Omega Alpha, Phi Soc. Club: Sydenham Coterie. Author: Anger, 1972. Editor: Dreams, 1970; Sensory Deprivation, 1970; Psychomimetic Drugs, 1971; Integration of Child Psychiatry with Basic Residency Program, 1975. Home: 135 Sibley Rd Narberth PA 19072 Office: 3300 Henry Ave Philadelphia PA 19129

MADSEN, BRIGHAM DWAINE, educator; b. Magna, Utah, Oct. 21, 1914; s. Brigham and Lydia (Cushing) M.; B.A., U. Utah, 1938; M.A., U. Cal. at Berkeley, 1940, Ph.D., 1948; m. Betty McAllister, Aug. 11, 1939; children—Karen Madsen Loos, David B., Linda Madsen Dunning, Steven M. Prin., Grade Sch. and Jr. High Sch., Pingree, Ida., 1938-39; asso. prof. history Brigham Young U., Provo, Utah, 1948-54; pres., mgr. Madsen Bros. Constrn. Co., Salt Lake City, 1954-61; prof. history Utah State U., Logan, 1961-64; asst. dir. tng. Peace Corps, Washington, 1964-65; first dir. tng. Vols. in Service to Am., Washington, 1965; dean div. continuing edn. U. Utah, Salt Lake City, 1965-66, dep. acad. v.p., 1966-67, adminstrv. v.p., 1967-71, dir. libraries, 1971-73, prof. history, 1973—, chmn. dept. history, 1974-75. Served to 1st lt., inf., AUS, 1943-46. Mem. Phi Kappa Phi. Phi Alpha Theta. Mem. Ch. of Jesus Christ of Latter-day Saints. Author: Bannock of Idaho, 1958. Editor: The Now Generation, 1971; Letters of Long Ago, 1973. Home: 2181 Lincoln Lane Salt Lake City UT 84117

MADSEN, CHARLES CLIFFORD, coll. cons.; b. Luck, Wis., Feb. 13, 1908; s. Mads Peter and Ella (Johnson) M.; A.B., U. Minn., 1931; B.D., Trinity Theol. Sem., 1934; Th.D., Central Bapt. Theol. Sem. Kansas City, Kan., 1949; D.D. (hon.), Midland Lutheran Coll., 1965; L.D.H. (hon.), Dana Coll., 1971; m. Esther Johnson, June 12, 1934; children—Carol Sonya (Mrs. Ray Lee Dickson), Maurice Lowell. Ordained to ministry Luth. Ch., 1934; pastor Our Savior's Ch., Kansas City, Kan., 1934-42; prof. practical theol. Trinity Sem., Blair, Neb., 1946-56; dir. Christian activities Dana Coll., Blair, 1946—, chmn. Christianity dept., 1946-56, acting pres., 1956-57, pres., 1957-71, cons., 1971—. Mem. Neb. Higher Edn. Facilities Commn.; mem. Neb. Supreme Ct. Nominating Commn. Past pres. Neb. Ind. Coll. Found., Tri-State Coll. Conf. Served to lt. comdr. Chaplains Corps, USNR, World War II; capt., chaplain Res. (ret.). Decorated Knight Order of Dannebrog (Denmark). Mem. V.F.W., Neb. Assn. Colls. and Univs. (past pres.). Rotarian. Contbr. articles profl. jours. Home: 2519 College Dr Blair NE 68008

MADSEN, DONALD GEORGE, chem. co. exec.; b. Champaign, Ill., Oct. 29, 1923; s. George Swend and Frances Margaret (Spahr) M.; B.S. in Chemistry, Central YMCA Coll., Chgo., 1945; m. Rose Ann Ryan, Mar. 3, 1945; children—Sandra Karen, Christine Ryan. With Baxter Travenol Labs., Inc., Deerfield, Ill., 1946—, chemist, Morton Grove, 1946-49, mfg. startup, South Africa, 1949, plant mgr., Greenville, Ky., 1951-54, gen. mgr., Brussels, Belgium, 1954-60, plant mgr., Kingstree, S.C., 1960-67, dir. mfg., Morton Grove, 1970-71, pres. Wallerstein div., 1972-75, v.p. mfg. Travenol div., 1975—, v.p. corp. prodn., 1979—. Pres., Kingstree C. of C., 1964; mem. Northbrook (Ill.) Caucus Com., 1969. Served to 1st lt. USAAF, 1943-46. Mem. Am. Chem. Soc. Presbyn. Club: Exmoor Country (Highland Park, Ill.). Home: 1404 Linden Dr Northbrook IL 60062 Office: 1 Baxter Pkwy Deerfield IL 60015

MADSEN, H(ENRY) STEPHEN, lawyer; b. Momence, Ill., Feb. 5, 1924; s. Frederick and Christine (Landgren) M.; M.B.A., U. Chgo., 1948; LL.B., Yale U., 1951; m. Carol Ruth Olmstead, Dec. 30, 1967; children—Stephen Stewart, Christie Morgan, Kelly Ann. Admitted to Wash. bar, 1951, Ohio bar, 1953, U.S. Supreme Ct. bar, 1975; research asst. Wash. Water Power Co., Spokane, 1951; asso. firm Baker, Hostetler & Paterson, Cleve., 1952-59, partner, 1960—; chmn. bd. trustees Blue Cross Northeastern Ohio, 1972—; Danish consul for Ohio, 1973—. Served with AC, U.S. Army, 1943-46. Mem. Am. Coll. Trial Lawyers, Am. Law Inst., Am. Judicature Soc., Am. Bar Assn., Ohio Bar Assn., Cleve. Bar Assn. Clubs: Union of Cleve., Cleve. Athletic; Yale of N.Y.C. Office: 1956 Union Commerce Bldg Cleveland OH 44115

MADTES, RICHARD EASTMAN, educator; b. Youngstown, Ohio, Dec. 3, 1921; s. George Rummel and Katherine (Eastman) M.; B.A., Allegheny Coll., 1948; M.A., Cornell U., 1949; Ph.D., Columbia U., 1961; m. Elaine Hengen, Dec. 23, 1941; 1 dau., Barbara Lynn. Instr. English, State U. Coll. N.Y., New Paltz, 1949-55, asst. prof., 1955-57, asso. prof., 1957-62, asst. to pres., 1957-60; asso. prof. English, Allegheny Coll., Meadville, Pa., 1962-68, prof., 1968—, Eliza Kingsley Arter prof. English, 1969. Served with USAAF, 1942-45. Mem. Modern Lang. Assn., AAUP. Democrat. Home: 35 Cedarcrest Dr Meadville PA 16335 Office: Dept of English Allegheny College Meadville PA 16335

MADUZIA, EDWARD A., lawyer; b. Chgo., Apr. 5, 1941; s. Wells H. and Dorothy (Voss) S.; B.S., Northwestern U., 1963; J.D., U. Chgo., 1966; m. Sandra J. Brantley, May 23, 1970; children—Amber Monite, Donald Kenrick. Admitted to Ill. bar, 1966, U.S. Supreme Ct. bar, 1970; asso. mem. firm Thomas, Blass, Simpson & Tyler, Chgo., 1966-70, mem. firm, 1970-76; individual practice law, Chgo., 1976—; lectr. Loyola U., 1974—. Active Chgo. chpt. ARC, 1969—; mem. Library Renovation Com., 1977—. Recipient Outstanding Alumnus award Northwestern U., 1977. Mem. Am., Ill. bar assns., Judicature Soc. Democrat. Clubs: Rotary, Elks, Masons. Home: 4505 N Manor Chicago IL 60625

MAECHLING, CHARLES, JR., lawyer, cons.; b. N.Y.C., Apr. 18, 1920; s. Charles and Eugenie M.; B.A., Yale U., 1941; LL.B., U. Va., 1949; m. Janet Leighton, Sept. 2, 1944; children—Philip Leighton and Eugenie Elisabeth. Admitted to N.Y. bar, 1949, D.C. bar, 1957; asso. firm Sullivan & Cromwell, N.Y.C., 1949-51; atty. Office Sec. Air Force, 1951-52; mgr., counsel govt. relations dept. Electronics

Industries Assn., Washington, 1953-56; partner firm Shaw, Pittman, Potts & Maechling, 1956-61; dir. for internal def. Dept. State, Washington, 1961-63; spl. asst. to undersec. for polit. affairs, 1963-65, spl. asst. to ambassador-at-large, 1965-66; dep. gen. counsel NSF, 1966-71, spl. asst. to dir., 1972-74; prof. law U. Va., 1974-76; counsel firm Kirlin, Campbell & Keating, 1976—; legal adviser internat. matters Nat. Acad. Scis., 1972-74, mem. ocean policy com.; mem. law-of-sea and other adv. coms. Dept. State; gen. counsel Fairways Corp., 1959-61. Served to lt. comdr. USNR, 1941-46; mem. secretariat Joint Chiefs Staff, 1943-44, del. to Cairo Conf., 1943. Recipient Ross Essay award Am. Bar Assn., 1969. Clubs: City Tavern, Army-Navy (Washington); Greencroft (Charlottesville). Editor-in-chief Va. Law Rev., 1948-49. Contbr. articles to N.Y. Times, Washington Post, profl. and lit. jours. Home: 3403 Lowell St NW Washington DC 20016

MAECK, JOHN VAN SICKLEN, physician, educator; b. Shelburne, Vt., Mar. 10, 1914; s. Benjamin Harris and Hannah (Tracy) M.; B.S., U. Vt., 1936, M.D., 1939; m. Doris Ruth Wehrle, June 17, 1939; children—Sarah (Mrs. Albert C. Williams), Steven. Asst. clin. instr. pathology Yale Sch. Medicine, 1939-40; intern Lenox Hill Hosp., N.Y.C., 1940-42; resident Womans Hosp. N.Y., 1946-48; practice medicine, specializing in obstetrics and gynecology, Burlington, Vt., 1948—; instr. obstetrics and gynecology U. Vt. Coll. Medicine, 1948-49, asst. prof., 1950-52, asso. prof., 1952-56, prof., 1956—, cmn. dept., 1950-75, chief of service obstetrics and gynecology Mary Fletcher Hosp., 1950-66, De Goesbriand Meml. Hosp., 1964-66, Med. Center Hosp. Vt., 1967-75; cons. Porter Hosp., Middlebury, Vt., Moses Ludington Hosp., Ticonderoga, N.Y., Vt. State Hosp., Waterbury. Mem. test com. obstetrics and gynecology Nat. Bd. Med. Examiners; obstetrician-gynecologist Project HOPE, Colombo, Ceylon, 1968-69; vis. prof. gynecology and obstetrics Stanford, 1977. Mem. exec. com. Coll. Medicine, U. Vt., 1948-75, chmn. bldg. fund com., 1964, chmn. search com for dean Coll. Medicine, 1966. Mem. exec. bd. Community Chest, Planned Parenthood Vt. Served to maj., M.C., AUS, 1942-46. Diplomate Am. Bd. Obstetrics and Gynecology (dir., v.p.). Fellow A.C.S.; mem. Am. Gynecol. Soc. (council 1977-79), Am. Gynecol. Club (pres. 1979), Am. Coll. Obstetricians and Gynecologists (past sect. chmn.), New Eng. Obstetrical Soc. Am. Sterility Soc., Assn. Profs. Gynecology and Obstetrics (past mem. council), Am. Assn. Ob-Gyn (council 1977—), Assn. Am. Med. Colls., A.M.A., Vt., Chittenden County med. socs., Am. Cancer Soc. (pres. Vt. div.), Lake Champlain C. of C. (exec. bd.), Alpha Omega Alpha. Unitarian (trustee). Asso. editor Danforth Text Ob-Gyn, 2d, 3d, 4th edits. Contbr. articles to profl. jours. Home: South Forty Shelburne VT 05482 Office: Given Med Bldg Burlington VT 05401

MAEDEL, GEORGE FREDERICK, engr., educator; b. Bklyn., July 21, 1903; s. George and Nelda (Kushman) M.; A.B., Columbia, 1924, E.E., 1926; m. Nellie Morris, June 6, 1931 (dec.); children—Carol, Ruth. Engring. asst. N.Y. Edison Co., 1926- 27, N.Y. Telephone Co., 1927-31; pres. Audio Products Engring. Co., 1931-33; RCA Insts., Inc., N.Y.C., 1933-68, pres., 1953-65, chmn. acad. affairs com. 1965-68; prof. N.Y. Inst. Tech., 1968—; instr. eve. engring. sch. Columbia; instr. math. eve. session Pratt Inst., Bklyn.; owner Maedel Pub. House, Bklyn. Profl. engr., N.Y. Mem. IEEE, Am. Inst. Engring. Edn., Am. Soc. Engring. Edn. Mason. Author math. textbooks. Home: 593 E 38th St Brooklyn NY 11203

MAEHL, WILLIAM HENRY, JR., educator; b. Chicago Heights, Ill., June 13, 1930; s. William Henry and Marvel Lillian (Carlson) M.; B.A., U. Minn., 1950, M.A., 1951; postgrad (Fulbright fellow), King's Coll., U. Durham (Eng.), 1955-56; Ph.D., U. Chgo., 1957; m. Audrey Mae Ellsworth, Aug. 25, 1962; 1 dau., Christine Amanda. Asst. prof. Montclair (N.J.) State Coll., 1957-58; asst. prof. Washington Coll., Chestertown, Md., 1958-59; asst. prof. U. Okla., Norman, 1959-64, asso. prof., 1964-70, prof. English history, 1970—, dean Coll. Liberal Studies, 1976—, vice provost for continuing edn. and public service, 1979—; vis prof. U. Nebr., summer, 1965; vis. fellow Wolfson Coll. Oxford (Eng.) U., spring, 1975; fellow Salzburg Seminar in Am. Studies, 1976. Served with AUS, 1953-55. Leverhulme Research fellow, 1961-62; grantee Am. Philos. Soc., 1961-62, 67-68, 71, 76. Fellow Royal Hist. Soc.; mem. Am. Hist. Assn., Conf. on Brit. Studies, Soc. for Study Labour History, Econ. History Soc. Author: The Reform Bill of 1832, 1967; editor: R.G. Gammage, Chartist Reminiscences, 1979; also articles. Home: 2601 Meadowbrook Dr Norman OK 73069 Office: Room 111 1700 Asp Ave Norman OK 73037

MAEROFF, GENE IRVING, journalist; b. Cleve., Jan. 8, 1939; s. Harry B. and Charlotte (Szabo) M.; B.S., Ohio U., 1961; M.S., Boston U., 1962; children—Janine Amanda, Adam Jonathan, Rachel Judith. Teaching fellow Boston U., 1961-62; news bur. dir. R.I. Coll., 1962-64; religion editor Akron (O.) Beacon Jour., 1964-65; with Cleve. Plain Dealer, 1965-71, asso. editor, 1969-71; edn. writer N.Y. Times, N.Y.C., 1971—; contbr. mags. Trustee Jewish Family Service Assn., Ed Bang Journalism Scholarship Found. Recipient writing awards Press Club Cleve., A.P. Soc. Ohio, Edn. Writers Assn., AAUP, Internat. Reading Assn. Mem. Omicron Delta Kappa, Kappa Tau Alpha, Phi Sigma Delta. Author: (with others) The New York Times Guide to Suburban Public Schools, 1976; contbr. to The Human Encounter: Readings in Education, 1973; Alternative Education, 1976; Human Dynamics in Psychology and Education, 1977; Social Problems, 1978. Office: 229 W 43d St New York NY 10036

MAES, ROBERT ADAMSON, fin. found. exec.; b. New Orleans, Jan. 31, 1910; s. Urban and Sabina Gertrude (Adamson) M.; B.S., Yale U., 1931; postgrad. Harvard U. Sch. Bus., 1931-32; m. Virginia Orr, Nov. 29, 1963; children—Robert Adamson, Nancy Maes Aherne. With Union Transfer Co., Phila., 1932-33; overseer United Fruit Co., Guatemala, 1933-35; accountant Price Waterhouse & Co., C.P.A.'s, Phila., 1936-41; fin. cons., 1945-50; pres. Independence Found., Phila., 1950—, also dir.; dir. Discount Corp. N.Y., Greit Realty Trust. Trustee Franklin and Marshall Coll., Lancaster, Pa. Served to lt. USNR, 1942-45. C.P.A., Pa. Republican. Episcopalian. Clubs: Midday, Racquet (Phila.); Riverview (Albany, Ga.). Home: Box 166 Route 2 Glenmoore PA 19343 Office: 2500 Phila Nat Bank Bldg Philadelphia PA 19107

MAESTRONE, FRANK EUSEBIO, govt. ofcl.; b. Springfield, Mass., Dec. 20, 1922; s. John Battista and Margaret Carlotta (Villanova) M.; B.A., Yale, 1943; grad. Naval War Coll., 1963; m. Jo Colwell, Jan. 20, 1951; children—Mark, Anne. Joined U.S. Fgn. Service, 1948; assigned Vienna and Salzburg, Austria, 1948, 54, Hamburg, Germany, 1949, Khorramshahr, Iran, 1960, NATO, Paris, 1963, Brussels, 1968; dep. asst. sec. gen. NATO, Brussels, 1968-71; counselor of embassy for polit. affairs, Manila, Philippines, 1971-73; Dept. State adviser to pres. Naval War Coll., 1973; minister-counselor, Cairo, Egypt, 1974-76; ambassador to Kuwait, 1976—. Served with AUS, 1943-46. Named chevalier de Merite Agricole (France). Mem. Am. Fgn. Service Assn., Internat. Inst. Strategic Studies. Office: US Embassy PO Box 77 Safat Kuwait*

MAFFIE, MICHAEL OTIS, utility exec.; b. Los Angeles, Jan. 26, 1948; s. Cornelius Michael and Elaine Minie (Wack) M.; B.S. in Acctg., U. So. Calif., 1969, M.B.A. in Fin., 1970; m. Nickie Neville, Apr. 10, 1971; 1 dau., Wendy. Audit mgr. Arthur Andersen & Co., C.P.A.'s, Los Angeles, 1970-78; treas. Southwest Gas Corp., Las Vegas, 1978—. Address: 5241 Spring Mountain Rd Las Vegas NV 89114

MAFFIN, ROBERT WILLIAM, assn. exec.; b. Newton, Iowa, Sept. 27, 1926; s. Howard and Margaret E. (Dorman) M.; B.S., U. Oreg., 1955; m. Constance Whitaker, June 22, 1974; children—Stephen, Carolyn, Lesa. Dir. dept. urban renewal City of Tacoma, 1960-64; exec. dir. Redevel. Agy., Fresno, Calif., 1964-67; gen. dep. urgan renewal adminstrn. HUD, Washington, 1967-69; sr. v.p. Devel. Research Asso., Los Angeles and Washington, 1969-70; exec. dir. Nat. Assn. Housing and Redevel. Ofcls., Washington, 1970—; bd. dirs. Nat. Housing Conf., Nat. Acad. Code Adminstrn., Council for Internat. Urban Liaison, Found. for Coop. Housing, Back-To-the Cities, Inc. Served with USNR, 1944-46. Democrat. Co-author: Charting a Local Community Development Course, 1975. Home: 1324 Vermont Ave NW Washington DC 20005 Office: 2600 Virginia Ave NW Washington DC 20037

MAFFITT, THEODORE STUART, JR., architect; b. Palestine, Tex., Mar. 11, 1923; s. Theodore Stuart and Annie Jo M.; B.Arch., Tex. A&M U., 1948; m. Patricia J. Wheeler, June 3, 1947; children—Andrea and Angela (twins), Stuart, Anne, Allison. Partner Theo. S. & Theodore S. Maffitt Jr., AIA Architects, Palestine, 1948-58; practice architecture, Palestine, 1958-78; partner Ted Maffitt Assos.-Architects, Palestine, 1978—. Served to lt. col., inf., U.S. Army, 1942-46. Decorated Bronze Star. Fellow AIA (dir. 1979—); mem. Tex. Soc. Architects (Presdl. award 1976). Democrat. Home: 215 E Reagan St Palestine TX 75801 Office: 510 N Sycamore St Palestine TX 75801

MAFFRY, AUGUST, banker, economist; b. Macon, Mo., July 22, 1905; s. August Fritz and Jessie Fremont (Williams) M.; A.B., U. Mo., 1926, A.M., 1928, Ph.D., 1930; exchange student U. Tübingen, Germany, 1926-27; m. Alice Mary Henry, June 8, 1929; children—Alice Mary (Mrs. William Silas Talbot), August. Instr., U. Mo., 1929-30, Dartmouth, 1930-34; ofcl. U.S. Dept. of Commerce, 1935- 45; v.p., econ. adviser Export-Import Bank, Washington, 1945-47; v.p. Irving Trust Co., N.Y.C., 1948-61, sr. v.p., 1961-68; dep. gen. mgr. Internat. Comml. Bank Ltd., London, 1967-68. Sec. Am. sect. Mexican-Am. Commn. for Econ. Cooperation, 1943; tech. adviser U.S. delegation Internat. Monetary and Financial Conf., Bretton Woods, 1944; tech. officer Inter-Am. Conf. on Problems of War and Peace, Mexico City, 1945; tech. adviser, inaugural and 1st meetings Internat. Monetary Fund and Internat. Bank for Reconstrn. and Devel., Savannah, 1945, Washington, 1946; cons. ECA, 1948-68; Internat. Devel. adv. bd., 1950-51. Decorated Sitara-i-Quaid-i-Azam (Pakistan); comdr. Order of Merit (Italy); comdr. Order of Phoenix (Greece); Nat. Order of Merit (France). Mem. Council Fgn. Relations, Kappa Sigma, Phi Beta Kappa. Presbyn. Clubs: Metropolitan (Washington); University (N.Y.C.). Co-author: Process of Inflation in France, 1914-27, 1928. Contbr. numerous reports, pamphlets, articles to U.S. govt. publs. Home: 13800 Fairhill Rd Suite 210 Shaker Heights OH 44120

MAG, ARTHUR, lawyer; b. New Britain, Conn., Oct. 11, 1896; s. Nathan Elihu and Rebecca (Goldberg) M.; A.B., Yale, 1918, J.D., 1920; LL.D., U. Mo.-Kansas City, 1974; m. Selma Rothenberg, Nov. 7, 1925 (dec. Oct. 1930); children—Josephine Selma Randall, Helen Louise Wolcott; m. 2d, Charline Weil, Nov. 24, 1932. Admitted to Conn., Mo. bars, 1920, since practiced in Kansas City; with Stinson, Mag & Fizzell, 1924—; chmn. exec. com. Host Internat., Inc., Los Angeles; chmn. Schutte Lumber Co.; dir. Price Candy Co., Rival Mfg. Co., Marley Co., Hereford Redevel. Corp., First Nat. Bank of Kansas City, 1st Nat. Charter Corp., Standard Milling Co., L.B. Price Merc. Co., St. Louis. Gold, Inc., Denver, Helzberg's Diamond Shops, Z Bar Cattle Co. Pres. Greater Kansas City Mental Health Found., 1952-56; mem. nat. adv. council Mental Health, 1955-59; chmn. Greater Kansas City liaison com. Regional Med. Programs, 1952-66—; mem. Gov.'s Citizens Com. on Delinquency and Crime, 1966-68; mem. Mo. Com. for White House Conf. on Aging; mem. Mayor's Commn. on Civil Disorder, 1968; mem. Citizens Study Com. on Kansas City-Jackson County Health Services, 1968; co-chmn. Gov.'s Task Force on Role of Pvt. Higher Edn. in Mo., 1970. Hon. chmn. bd. dirs. Menorah Med. Center; mem. bd. curators Stephens Coll., 1967-72; trustee, v.p. Mo. Bar Found.; trustee U. Mo. at Kansas City, Frederic Ervine McIlvain Trust, Carrie J. Loose Fund, Harry Wilson Loose Fund, Sadie Danciger Trust, Edward F. Swinney Trust, Kansas City Assn. Trusts and Founds., Carl W. Allendoerfer Meml. Library Trust, Menninger Found., Topeka, Menorah Found. Med. Research; exec. com. Midwest Research Inst. Hon. mem. exec. com. Yale Law Sch. Assn. Served with USN, 1918, Recipient Pro Meritis award Rockhurst Coll., 1960; Mr. Kansas City award, 1964; Brotherhood citation Nat. Conf. Christians and Jews, 1965; Law Day award U. Mo. at Kansas City, 1966; Chancellor's medallion U. Mo. at Kansas City, 1965, Civic Service award Hebrew Acad. Kansas City, 1975, award Kansas City Mental Health Found., 1976. Hon. fellow Am. Coll. Hosp. Adminstrs.; mem. Am., Mo., Kansas City bar assns., Lawyers Assn. Kansas City, Assn. Bar City N.Y., Mo. Acad. Squires, Order of Coif, Delta Sigma Rho. Republican. Clubs: Yale (N.Y.C.); Kansas City, Oakwood Country (Kansas City); Reform (London, Eng.); Standard (Chgo.); Graduate (New Haven). Author: Trusteeship, 1948. Home: 5049 Wornall Rd Kansas City MO 64112 Office: 2100 TenMain Center PO Box 19251 Kansas City MO 64141

MAG, EDWARD ARNOLD, legal cons.; b. New Britain, Conn., Sept. 16, 1899; s. Nathan Elihu and Rebecca (Goldberg) M.; B.A., Yale, 1921, LL.B., 1923; m. Marian Spater, Jan. 30, 1940 (div. Aug. 1955); m. 2d, Mary C. Walker, Sept. 10, 1960. Admitted to Conn. bar, 1923, U.S. Supreme Ct. bar, 1936; asso. firm Rushmore, Bisbee & Stern, N.Y.C., 1923-24; practice in New Britain, 1924-34, 36-42; asst. litigation atty. NRA, Washington, 1935-36; asst. gen. counsel Lend-Lease Adminstrn., Washington, 1943, prin. rep., Cairo, Egypt, 1943-45; internat. law expert, chief of counsel br. U.S. Forces in Austria, 1946-47; legal attache Am. Legation, Budapest, Hungary, 1948-49, Vienna, Austria, 1950-51; econ. controls officer Am. embassy, Tokyo, 1952-54; 1st sec., consul Am. embassy, Rome, Italy, 1954-62; Am. agt. Italian-Am. Conciliation Commn., 1956-62; now cons. Am. and internat. law. Chmn. New Britain Pub. Housing Authority, 1938, 40-41. Mem. mgmt. com. Anglo-Am. Nursing Home, 1956-77; chmn. adv. bd. Temple U., Rome, 1968-77. Mem. adminstrv. tribunal Inst. for Unification Pvt. Internat. Law, Rome, 1972. Mem. Am. Soc. Internat. Law, Phi Beta Kappa. Clubs: Rome American, Rome Golf. Home: 201 Via Osuna PO Box 1736 Rancho Santa Fe CA 92067

MAGA, JOHN ANTHONY, cons. engr.; b. Forbes, Colo., Jan. 8, 1916; s. James and Louise (Franchetto) M.; B.S., U. Calif., 1938, M.S., 1953; m. Mary Y. Daba, May 6, 1944; children—Carol Ann, Richard J. San. engr. State of Calif., 1940-55; chief bur. air sanitation Calif. Dept. Pub. Health, 1955-68; exec. officer Cal. Air Resources Bd., Sacramento, 1968-73; dep. sec. Cal. Resources Agy., 1973-74; cons. engr., 1975—. Served as lt. USNR, 1942-45. Mem. Am. Air Pollution Control Assn. (past dir., S. Smith Griswold award), Water Pollution Control Assn. (past pres. Calif.), Chi Epsilon, Delta Omega. Contbr. articles to profl. jours. Home: 7023 13th St Sacramento CA 95831 Office: 7023 13th P St Sacramento CA 95814

MAGAD, SAMUEL, orch. concertmaster; b. Chgo., May 14, 1932; s. Herman and Doris (Walder) M.; Mus.B., De Paul U., 1955; student Paul Stassevitch; m. Miriam Seefor, Feb. 13, 1955; children—Debra, Carlen. Orch. violin soloist, beginning 1944; with Chgo. Symphony Orch., 1958—, asst. concertmaster, 1966-72, co-concertmaster, 1972—; concertmaster Grant Park Symphony Orch., 1970-71; dir., 1st violinist Chgo. Symphony Chamber Players; founder Chgo. Symphony Trio; prof. violin Northwestern U., Evanston, Ill., also 1st violinist Eckstein Quartet. Served with orch. AUS, 1955-58. Home: 1015 Edgebrook Glencoe IL 60022 Office: 220 S Michigan Ave Chicago IL 60604

MAGAFAN, ETHEL, artist; b. Chgo., Oct. 10, 1916; d. Peter J. and Julie (Bronick) Magafan; student Colorado Springs Fine Arts Center; m. Bruce Currie, June 30, 1946; 1 dau., Jenne Magafan. John Stacey scholar, 1947; Tiffany fellow, 1949; Fulbright grant recipient, 1951; painter of 8 murals including Social Security Bldg., Washington, Recorder of Deeds Bldg., Senate Chamber, South Denver Post Office, Fredericksburg (Va.) Nat. Mil. Park, 1978; paintings exhibited Carnegie Inst. Corcoran Gallery, Pa. Acad. Fine Arts, NAD, Met. Mus., Denver Art Mus., San Francisco Mus., N.Y. Exhbn., 1950-51, 53, 55, 56, 59, 61, 63, 66, 69, 70, 73; represented in permanent collections, including Springfield (Mo.) Art Mus., Provincetown Art Assn., Met. Mus. Art, Denver Art Mus., Del. Soc. Fine Arts, Des Moines Art Center, Norfolk, Columbia mus., Butler Inst. Art, others, also pvt. collections; guest artist in residence Syracuse U., 1976. Recipient Collectors Am. Art award, 1947, 48, Adele Hyde Morrison prize San Francisco Mus., 1950, hon. mention Am. Painting Today exhbn., Met Mus. Art, 1950, 1st Hallgarten prize NAD, 1951, Ida Wells Stroud award, Am. Watercolor Soc., 1955, purchase prize Nat. Exhbn. Contemporary Arts, 1956, Altman prize for landscape NAD, 1956, Hallmark Art award, 1952, Purchase award, Ball State Tchrs. Coll. Art Gallery, 1958, Columbia (S.C.) Mus., 1959, Portland (Maine) Mus., 1959, 1st award Albany Inst. Art, 1962, Benjamin Altman award NAD, 1964, 73, Andrew Carnegie prize, 1977, award Conn. Acad. Fine Arts, 1965, purchase award Watercolor U.S.A., Springfield Mus., 1966, Kirk Meml. award NAD, 1967, Berkshire Art Assn. award, 1966, 67, 68, 75, jurors prize Albany Inst. Art, 1969, Grumbacher award, 1970, 75, Hassam Fund purchase, 1970, Arches Paper award Am. Watercolor Soc., 1973, Zimmerman award Phila. Watercolor Soc., 1973; Pres.'s award Audubon Artists, 1974, Emily Lowe award, 1979, Stefan Hirsch Meml. award Audubon Artists Ann., 1976, award Rocky Mountain Nat. Watermedia Exhbn., 1976; Condec award Silvermine Guild Artists, 1978, award, 1979; Cooperstown Art Assn. award, 1978. Mem. NAD (2d v.p. 1975). Home: RFD Box 284 Woodstock NY 12498 Office: Midtown Galleries 11 E 57th St New York NY 10022

MAGARAM, PHILIP SIDNEY, lawyer; b. N.Y.C., July 29, 1937; s. Bernard and Ida (Weiss) M.; B.S. in Accounting with honors, U. Calif. at Los Angeles, 1958, LL.B., 1961; m. Marilyn Francine Tepper, Feb. 20, 1966; children—Justin Bernard, Jodi Camille. Admitted to Calif. bar, 1962; mem. firm Magaram, Riskin, Wayne & Minikes, P.C., Los Angeles, 1963—. Lectr. on taxation related subjects. Trustee, treas. Los Angeles County chpt. Leukemia Soc. Am., 1969; gov. So. Calif. Arthritis Found. Mem. Beverly Hills, Los Angeles, Century City (gov. 1974-76), Am. bar assns., State Bar Calif., Phi Alpha Delta (pres. chpt. 1961), Beta Gamma Sigma, Phi Eta Sigma, Tau Delta Phi. Contbg. author: Tax Ideas, 1968, 75. Contbr. articles to profl. jours. Home: 18041 Rodarte Way Encino CA 91316 Office: 1880 Century Park E Los Angeles CA 90067

MAGASANIK, BORIS, educator, microbiologist; b. Kharkoff, Russia, Dec. 19, 1919; s. Naum and Charlotte (Schreiber) M.; came to U.S., 1938, naturalized, 1942; student U. Vienna, 1937-38; B.S., Coll. City N.Y., 1941; postgrad. Pa. State Coll., 1941-42; Ph.D., Columbia, 1948; m. Adele Karp, Aug. 9, 1949. Tech. asst. Mt. Sinai Hosp., N.Y.C., 1939-41; asst. chemistry Columbia, 1946-47, W.J. Gies fellow biochemistry, 1947-48, research asst. biochemistry, 1948-49; Harold C. Ernst fellow bacteriology and immunology Harvard, 1949-51, asso., 1951-53, Markle scholar med. sci., 1951-56, tutor biochem. scis., 1952—, asst. prof. bacteriology and immunology, 1953-58, asso. prof., 1958-60; prof. microbiology Mass. Inst. Tech., 1960-77, head dept. biology, 1967-77, Jacqes Monod prof. microbiology, 1977—. Guggenheim fellow, 1959. Mem. Nat. Acad. Scis., Am. Acad. Arts and Scis., Am. Soc. Biol. Chemists, Am. Soc. Microbiology, Am. Chem. Soc., AAAS, Sigma Xi. Contbr. articles profl. jours. Editor: Jour. Molecular Biology, 1964-66, Biochem. and Biophys. Research Communications, 1964—, Jour. Biol. Chemistry, 1972-77. Home: 120 Collins Rd Waban MA 02168 Office: Mass Inst Tech Cambridge MA 02139

MAGAZINER, HENRY JONAS, architect; b. Phila., Sept. 13, 1911; s. Louis and Selma (Jonas) M.; B.Arch., U. Pa., 1936; m. Reba Henken, June 19, 1938; children—Ellen Louise (Mrs. Alan I. Widiss), Fred Thomas. Draftsman, Phila. City Planning Project, 1936-37; draftsman Louis Magaziner, Architect, Phila., 1937-39, architect, 1946-48; chief Architects' Squad, Day & Zimmermann, Inc., Burlington, Iowa, 1940-41; architect Albert Kahn, Architect, Detroit, 1942; designer Wright Aero. Corp., Wood Ridge, N.J., 1943-45; partner Louis & Henry Magaziner, Phila., 1948-56; architect, planner pvt. practice, 1956-72; regional hist. architect Mid-Atlantic Region, Nat. Park Service, Phila., 1972—. Archtl. adviser Phila. Hist. Commn., 1970-75, mem. archtl. com., 1970—, chmn. archtl. com., 1972-75. Mem. Council for Internat. Visitors. Vice pres. Phila. Health and Welfare Council, 1957-62, Phila. chpt. Victorian Soc. in Am., 1975; v.p. for city planning Germantown Community Council, 1957-62; bd. dirs. Downtown Children's (day care) Center, 1956-73, v.p., 1960-61; bd. dirs. Allens Lane Art Center, 1954-72, Neighborhood Centre of Phila., 1956-74, Hist. Soc. Pa., 1970-74, Chestnut Hill Hist. Soc., Germantown Hist. Soc., Stewardson Meml. Fellowship in Architecture, Friends of Laurel Hill Cemetery; bd. dirs. Maxwell Mansion Mus., pres., 1964-67. Fellow AIA (com. historic resources); mem. Assn. for Preservation Tech., Eastern Nat. Park and Monument Assn., Fellows in Am. Studies, Hist. Soc. Pa., Nat. Parks and Conservation Assn., Nat. Trust for Historic Preservation, Pa. Soc. Architects, Phila. Soc. for Preservation of Landmarks, Soc. Archtl. Historians (dir. 1977—), T-Square Atelier (pres. 1963-65), Victorian Soc. in Am., Am. Arbitration Assn. (arbitrator), Sierra Club, Phila. Art Alliance, Athenaeum of Phila., Print Club. Address: 732 Westview St Philadelphia PA 19119

MAGEE, DONAL F., physiologist; b. Aberdeen, June 4, 1924; M.A., B.M., B.Ch., Oxford (Eng.) U., 1948, D.M., 1972; Ph.D., U. Ill., 1952. Mem. faculty U. Wash., Seattle, 1952-65; mem. faculty Creighton U., Omaha, 1965—, now prof. physiology. Guggenheim fellow, 1959-60; Fogarty Internat. fellow, 1978-79. Mem. Am. Gastroenterol. Assn., Am. Physiol. Soc., Brit. Med. Assn., Am. Soc. Pharmacology and Exptl. Therapeutics, Soc. Exptl. Biology and Medicine. Home: 310 S 55th St Omaha NE 68132 Office: Dept Physiology Creighton Univ 2500 California St Omaha NE 68178

MAGEE, JOHN FRANCIS, research co. exec.; b. Bangor, Maine, Dec. 3, 1926; s. John Henry and Marie (Frawley) M.; A.B., Bowdoin Coll., 1946; M.S., U. Maine, 1952; M.B.A., Harvard U., 1948; m. Dorothy Elma Hundley, Nov. 19, 1949; children—Catherine Anne, John Hundley, Andrew Stephen. With Arthur D. Little, Inc.,

Cambridge, Mass., 1950—, v.p., 1961-72, pres., 1972—, chief exec. officer, 1974—, also dir.; dir. John Hancock Mut. Life Ins. Co., Boston, Houghton-Mifflin, Inc., Boston, New Eng. Mchts. Co., Boston. Trustee New Eng. Aquarium, Boston, Univ. Med. Center, Boston, Bowdoin Coll. Served with USNR, 1944-46. Mem. Ops. Research Soc. Am. (pres. 1966-67), Inst. Mgmt. Scis. (pres. 1971-72), Phi Beta Kappa, Phi Kappa Psi. Clubs: Concord (Mass.) Country (gov. 1971—); The Country (Brookline, Mass.); Somerset (Boston). Author: Physical Distribution Systems, 1967; Industrial Logistics: Analysis and Management of Physical Supply and Distribution Systems, 1968; (with D. M. Boodman) Production Planning and Inventory Control, 1968. Home: 51 Lewis Rd Concord MA 01742 Office: 25 Acorn Park Cambridge MA 02140

MAGEE, JOHN LAFAYETTE, educator; b. Franklinton, La., Oct. 28, 1914; s. John L. and Edith (Jenkins) M.; B.A., Miss. Coll., 1935; M.S., Vanderbilt U., 1936; Ph.D., U. Wis., 1939; m. Priscilla Williams, Jan. 1, 1948; children—Lawrence Edward, Linda Sue, John Bradley. NRC fellow Princeton, 1939-40, research asso., 1940-41; research chemist B.F. Goodrich Co., 1941-43; staff mem. Los Alamos Sci. Lab., 1943-45; group leader Naval Ordnance Test Sta., Calif., 1945-46; sr. scientist Argonne Nat. Lab., Chgo., 1946-48; faculty U. Notre Dame, 1948-77, asst. prof., 1948-49, asso. prof., 1949-53, prof., 1953-77, asso. dir. radiation lab., 1954-71, dir., 1971-75, chmn. chem. physics program, head chemistry dept., 1967-70; vis. sr. staff mem. Lawrence Berkeley Lab., 1976-77, sr. staff mem., 1977—. Observer atomic testing, Bikini, S. Pacific, 1946; project dir. Weapons Evaluation Group, Dept. Def., 1955-57. Trustee Argonne Univs. Assn., 1965-69. Mem. Am. Chem. Soc., Radiation Research Soc. (council mem. 1957-60, 66-69, pres. 1967-68), Am. Phys. Soc., AAUP (pres. Notre Dame chpt. 1959-61), AAAS, Faraday Soc., Sigma Xi. Co-editor; Comparative Effects of Radiation; Advances in Radiation Chemistry. Home: 6 Dorothy Pl Berkeley CA 94705

MAGEE, PAUL TERRY, molecular biologist; b. Los Angeles, Oct. 26, 1934; s. John Paul and Lois Lorene (Cowgill) M.; B.S., Yale U., 1959; Ph.D., U. Calif., Berkeley, 1964; m. Beatrice Buten, Aug. 6, 1964; children—Alexander John, Amos Hart. Am. Cancer Soc. postdoctoral fellow Lab. Enzymologie, Gif-sur-Yvette, France, 1964-66; mem. faculty Yale U., 1966-77, asst. prof. microbiology, 1966-72, asso. prof. microbiology and human genetics, 1972-75, asso. prof. human genetics, 1975-77, dean Trumbull Coll., 1969-72; prof. microbiology, chmn. dept. microbiology and public health Mich. State U., East Lansing, 1977—; mem. genetics adv. panel NSF, 1978-81; cons. Corning Glass Works, 1978—. Mem. Am. Soc. Biol. Chemists, Am. Soc. Microbiologists, AAAS, Genetics Soc. Am. Jewish. Editorial bd. Jour. Bacteriology, 1975—. Office: Dept Microbiology and Public Health Mich State Univ East Lansing MI 48824

MAGEE, PETER NOEL, pathologist; b. Sheffield, Yorkshire, Eng., Dec. 21, 1921; s. John Albert and Elsie May (Mould) M.; student Worksop Coll. Cambridge (Eng.) U., 1940-42; M.B., B.Chir., Univ. Coll. Hosp., London, 1945; m. Ines Verspyck, Dec. 15, 1951; children—Rosemary Anne, Michael John. House physician Univ. Coll. Hosp., Kent and Sussex Hosp., 1946-47; Graham scholar in pathology U. London, U. Coll. Hosp. Med. Sch., 1951-53; mem. sci. staff, toxicology research unit Med. Research Council Labs., Carshalton, Surrey, 1953-68; Philip Hill prof. exptl. biochemistry U. London at Courtauld Inst. Biochemistry, Middlesex Hosp. Med. Sch., 1967-75; dir. Fels Research Inst., Temple U. Med. Sch., Phila., 1975—. Mem. grand council Cancer Research Campaign of Gt. Britain, 1972—. Served with Med. Br., RAF, 1947-49. Recipient Johann Georg Zimmermann Sci. prize for cancer research Medizinische Hochschule, Hannover, 1975. Mem. Brit. Med. Assn., Am. Assn. Pathologists, Am. Assn. for Cancer Research, Pathol. Soc. Gt. Britain and Ireland, Biochemical Soc. (U.K.), Soc. Toxicology, Internat. Acad. Environmental Safety. Episcopalian. Clubs: Athenaeum (London). Contbr. sci. articles to profl. jours. Home: 1240 Morris Rd Wynnewood PA 19096 Office: 3420 N Broad St Philadelphia PA 19140

MAGEE, WARREN EGBERT, lawyer; b. Washington, Apr. 27, 1908; s. William D. and Maude M. (Marks) M.; LL.B., Washington Coll. Law, Am. U., 1930, LL.M., 1931; m. Sue Mayfield Wren, Apr. 9, 1930 (dec. 1945); children—Robert Warren, James Worthington, Dianne Yvonne; m. Leslie Y. Eisenhower, Dec. 7, 1960. Admitted to D.C., bar, 1930. spl. atty. U.S. Dept. Justice, 1935-38; asso. in pvt. law practice with Charles S. Baker, 1938-43; head firm of Magee & Bulow, 1955—; gen. counsel assns., ins. cos. and various corps; represented Baron Ernest von Weizaecker, German State Sec. and last German Ambassador to the Holy See at Nuremburg trials. Mem. Fed., Am., D.C. bar assns., A.A.A.S., Am. Judicature Soc., Nat. Geog. Soc., Fedn. Ins. Counsel. Clubs: University, Congressional Country, Touchdown, Queen Anne Country, Newcomers. Home: 5009 Newport Av Westgate MD 20016 also 3701 Bayshore Blvd Tampa FL Office: 1100 17th St NW Washington DC 20036

MAGEN, MYRON SHIMIN, osteo. physician, educator; b. Bklyn., Mar. 1, 1926; s. Barney and Gertrude Beatrice (Cohen) M.; D.O., Coll. Osteo. Medicine and Surgery, Des Moines, 1951; m. Ruth Sherman, July 6, 1952; children—Jed, Ned, Randy. Chmn. dept. pediatrics Detroit Osteo. Hosp., 1965-67; dean Mich. Coll. Osteo. Medicine, Pontiac, 1968-70; med. dir., dir. med. edn. Zieger-Botsford Hosps., Farmington, Mich., 1968-70; dean, prof. pediatrics Coll. Osteo. Medicine, Mich. State U., East Lansing, 1970—; cons. HEW, 1969—, Mich. Health Adv. Council, 1970—; mem. grad. med. edn. nat. adv. com. Sec. HEW, 1978—; mem. spl. med. adv. group VA, 1973 77. Mem. Am. Osteo. Assn., Mich. Assn. Osteo. Physicians and Surgeons, Sigma Sigma Phi. Served with USNR, 1943-45. Author publs. in field. Home: 1251 Farwood Dr East Lansing MI 48823. *Intellectual curiosity combined with an interest in people. The supposition that there are views other than one's own that have merit. The ability to view dissent as an expression of a position that may have more validity than orthodoxy. Honesty of expression.*

MAGER, ARTUR, aerospace co. exec.; b. Nieglowice, Poland, Sept. 21, 1919; s. Herman and Ella (Kornbluh) M.; came to U.S., 1939, naturalized, 1944; B.S., U. Mich., 1943; M.S., Case Inst. Tech., 1951; Ph.D., Calif. Inst. Tech., 1953; m. Phyllis Weisman, Aug. 19, 1942; 1 dau., Ilana G. Aero. research scientist NASA Lewis Labs., Cleve., 1946-51; research scientist Marquardt Corp., Van Nuys, Calif., 1954-60; dir. Nat. Engring. Sci. Co., Pasadena, Calif., 1960-61; dir. spacecraft scis. Aerospace Corp., El Segundo, 1961-64; gen. mgr. applied mechanics div., 1964-68, v.p., gen. mgr. engring. sci. ops., 1968-78, v.p. engring. group, 1978—; mem. BSD Re-entry Panel, 1961-63, NASA com. missile and space vehicle aerodynamics, 1963-65; mem. adv. com. AFML, 1971-72. Mem. alumni fund council Calif. Inst. Tech., 1972-74; mem. indsl. council West Coast U.; bd. councilors U. So. Calif. Sch. Engring.; mem. developmental disabilities bd. Area X, chmn., 1976-78; bd. dirs. Calif. Assn. for Retarded, 1972-74, recipient Golden Rule award, 1977; pres. Exceptional Children's Found., 1970-72. Recipient Distinguished Alumni award U. Mich., 1969; registered profl. engr., Ohio. Fellow Inst. Advanced Engring., Am. Inst. Aeros. and Astronautics (chmn. Los Angeles sect. 1967-68, dir. 1975-77, pres.-elect 1979); mem. AAAS, Gesellschaft Angewandte Mathematik Mechanik, Technion Soc., Am. Phys. Soc., ASME, Nat. Acad. Engring., Sigma Xi. Contbr. to profl. publs. Home: 1353 Woodruff Ave Los Angeles CA 90024 Office: 2350 E El Segundo Blvd El Segundo CA 90245 also Aerospace Corp PO Box 92957 Los Angeles CA 90009

MAGER, EZRA PASCAL, stock broker; b. N.Y.C., Nov. 1, 1941; s. Harold and Naomi (Levinson) M.; B.A., Cornell U., 1963; M.B.A., Harvard, 1966; m. Sarah Johnson, Mar. 25, 1964 (div.); 1 dau., Emma Rachel; m. 2d, Reeva Starkman, May 14, 1972; 1 dau., Camilla Elizabeth. Successively v.p., sr. v.p., exec. v.p. and dir. Seiden & DeCuevas, Inc., N.Y.C., 1966-73; exec. v.p., dir. Furman Selz Mager Dietz & Birney, Inc., N.Y.C., 1973—. Mem. Midwest Stock Exchange. Pres., Baron de Hirsch Fund. Mem. N.Y. Soc. Security Analysts, Alpha Delta Phi. Democrat. Club: Harvard (N.Y.C.). Home: 40 E 88th St New York NY 10028 Office: 110 Wall St New York NY 10005

MAGER, GERALD, former judge; b. Bklyn., June 1, 1934; s. Morris David and Adele (Lapter) M.; B.A., U. Miami, 1956, J.R.D., 1959; m. Naomi Himmelstein, Aug. 24, 1956; children—Marc Adam, Scott Alan, Russ Even, Seth Lee. Admitted to Fla. bar, 1959, to U.S. Supreme Ct. bar; asst. atty. gen. State of Fla., 1959-67; legal counsel to Gov. of Fla., 1967-70; judge 4th Dist. Ct. Appeal, West Palm Beach, Fla., 1970-77, chief judge, 1976-77, Chmn. Fla. Adv. Council Mental Retardation, 1965-67. Mem. Interstate Oil Compact Commn., 1967; mem., coordinator Law Enforcement Planning Council, 1970; mem. Fla. Jud. Council, 1970—. Bd. dirs. LaMoyne Art Found., 1966-68. Named outstanding young man of Am., Jaycees, 1968; recipient good govt. award, Tallahassee Jaycees, 1968, govtl. affairs state award, Fla. Jaycees, 1965, legis. service award Fla. Psychol. Assn., 1961. Mem. Am., Fla. (com. on jud. selection, tenure and compensation, chmn. com. on standards jud. conduct 1974-77, mem. jud. adminstrn. com., pub. affairs and media com. 1974-75, chmn. conf. Dist. Ct. Appeals judges 1976-77), Broward, Palm Beach, Orange and Brevard County bar assns., Am. Judicature Soc., Fla. Jud. Council, Am. Soc. Pub. Adminstrn., Gen. Alumni Assn. U. Miami, Tau Delta Phi (founder), Tau Epsilon Rho, Omicron Delta Kappa (hon.). Jewish (trustee, dir. temple). Elk, Lion, Kiwanian; mem. Woodmen of World. Club: Capital Toastmasters (Tallahassee). Home: 3105 Palm Aire Dr Pompano Beach FL 33060 Office: 2021 Tyler St Hollywood FL 33022

MAGGAL, MOSHE MORRIS, rabbi; b. Nagyecsed, Hungary, Mar. 16, 1908; s. David and Ester (Fulop) Gelberman; came to U.S., 1950, naturalized, 1960; B.A., Nat. Rabbinical Sem., Budapest, Hungary, 1933, Rabbinical degree, 1934; postgrad. U. Zurich, Switzerland, 1935, Hebrew U., Jerusalem, Israel, 1936; Ph.D. (hon.), Ben Franklin Acad., Washington, 1979; m. Rachel Delia Diamond, July 8, 1951; children—Davida Elizabeth, Michelle Judith, Elana Ilene. Rabbi Temple Meyer-David, Claremont, N.H., 1951-52, Temple Beth Aaron, Billings, Mont., 1952-54, Alhambra (Calif.) Jewish Center, 1955-57, Temple Beth Kodesh, Canoga Park, Calif., 1959-61, Congregation Ahavath Israel, Hollywood, Calif., 1966—; civilian chaplain USAAF Base, Great Falls, Mont., 1952-54. Editor, Hebrew weekly Iton Meyuhad, Tel Aviv, Israel, 1940-47; asso. editor Heritage newspaper, Los Angeles, 1958-60; lectr. Free Enterprise Speakers Bur., Coast Fed. Savs. & Loan Assn., 1971—. Pres., Beverly Hills Zionist Orgn., 1973—, exec. v.p. So. Pacific Region, 1973—; mem. Los Angeles-Eilat Sister City Com. Mem. Speakers Bur. of Com. for Re-election of Pres., 1972; hon. lt. col. New Spirit of 76 Found.; mem. nat. adv. bd. Ben Franklin Acad., Inst. for Advanced Studies. Served with Israel Def. Army, 1948-49. Recipient Nat. Sermon Contest award Spiritual Moblzn., 1952, citation Crusade for Freedom, 1952; named to Los Angeles Bicentennial Com. Speakers Bur. for Am. Revolution Bicentennial Adminstrn., 1975. Hon. sheriff Yellowstone County, Mont., 1954; hon. adviser to Cecil B. DeMille, The Ten Commandments movie, 1954. Mem. Nat. Jewish Info. Service (founder, pres. 1960—), Town Hall of Cal., World Affairs Council, Internat. Visitors Program. Democrat. Club: Greater Los Angeles Press. Author: Acres of Happiness, 1968. Editor: Voice of Judaism, 1960—. Home: 5174 W 8th St Los Angeles CA 90036

MAGGS, PETER BLOUNT, educator; b. Durham, N.C., July 24, 1936; s. Douglas Blount and Dorothy (Mackay) M.; A.B., Harvard U., 1957, J.D., 1961; postgrad. (exchange student) Leningrad (USSR) State U., 1961-62; m. Barbara Ann Widenor, Feb. 27, 1960; children—Bruce MacDowell, Gregory Eaton, Stephanie Ann, Katherine Ellen. Admitted to D.C. bar, 1962; research asso. Harvard Law Sch., 1963-64; asst. prof. law U. Ill., 1964-67, asso. prof., 1967-69, prof., 1969—; Fulbright research scholar, Yugoslavia, 1967; East-West Center fellow, 1972; Fulbright lectr. Moscow State U., 1977. Guggenheim fellow, 1979. Mem. Am. Bar Assn. (chmn. com. on Soviet law sect. internat. law 1976—), Am. Assn. Advancement Slavic Studies (parliamentarian 1977—), Assn. Am. Law Schs. (chmn. sect. comparative law 1977). Author: (with Harold J. Berman) Disarmament Inspection Under Soviet Law, 1961; (with others) The Soviet Legal System, 2d edit., 1969, 3d rev. edit., 1977; editor: (with others) Soviet Law Since Stalin, vol. 1., 1977, vol. 2, 1978, vol. 3, 1979; editor Soviet Statutes and Decisions, 1976—; reporter Uniform Simplification of Land Transfers Act; developer computer programs for legal edn.; designer talking computer terminal for blind. Office: U Ill Coll Law Champaign IL 61820

MAGILL, BRADFORD STEELE, lawyer; b. Washington, Apr. 14, 1909; s. Louis J. and Florence (McKeehan) M.; student U.S. Naval Acad., 1926-28; B.A., Yale, 1931; J.D., Harvard, 1934; m. Francesca McKenney, Sept. 20, 1940 (dec. Aug. 1974); children—B. Steele Jr., Louis C.; m. 2d, Ruth Sparkman Hill, June 11, 1977. Admitted to N.Y. bar, 1935, Conn. bar, 1972; practiced in N.Y.C. and Greenwich, Conn., 1935—; counsel firm Huber, Magill, Lawrence & Farrell, 1979—, Magill, Badger, Fisher, Cohen & Barnett, Greenwich, 1977-77. Mem., chmn. Greenwich Planning and Zoning Commn., 1961-72. Mem. Greenwich Republican Town Com., 1952-63. Served to lt. col. USAAF, 1942-45. Decorated Bronze Star. Mem. Am., N.Y. State, Conn., Greenwich bar assns., Greenwich C. of C. (dir. 1950-60, pres. 1953), Chi Psi. Episcopalian (vestryman). Home: 601 Sunset Rd Coral Gables FL 33146 Office: 99 Park Ave New York NY 10016 also 15 Sherwood Pl Greenwich CT 06830. *Nothing in life beats hard work, a sense of humor and the love of a wonderful woman.*

MAGILL, J(AMES) MARION, music educator; b. Due West, S.C., Dec. 12, 1921; s. John Thomas and Zula Lee (Presnell) M.; A.B., Erskine Coll., 1942; M.A., Columbia, 1952, Ed.D., 1957; m. Kirk Hunter, Mar. 31, 1943; children—Jane Hunter, James Marion (dec.). Tchr. pub. schs., Ware Shoals, S.C., 1942-44; dir. instrumental music Greenville (S.C.) City Sch., 1944-51; supr. music pub. schs., Anderson County, S.C., 1951-55; dir. music Greenville County (S.C.) Pub. Schs., 1955-63, pub. schs., Balt., 1963-70; prof. music edn. Columbia, 1970—. Instrumental and choral condr. state music festivals; condr. civic oratorios and orch., Anderson, S.C., 1962-73. Recipient Scroll of Honor for outstanding civic contbns. to arts Anderson Ind. Daily Mail Pubs., 1963, 1971, Pres.'s award in arts Balt. Arts Council, 1968. Mem. Music Educators Nat. Conf., Sinfonia, Phi Mu Alpha, Phi Delta Kappa. Presbyn. (deacon 1948, elder 1968-70). Kiwanian. Club: Torch Internat. Author: Guide for Music of the World's Great Composers, 1960. Recorded for Bowmar Recs., 1967-68. Home: 501 W 120th St New York City NY 10027

MAGILL, ROBERT FRANCIS, automobile co. exec.; b. Bloomington, Ind., Apr. 16, 1917; s. Alva Edison and Harriet Elizabeth (Rogers) M.; A.B., Ind. U., 1938; LL.B., Harvard U., 1941; m. Aileen, July 20, 1943; children—Robert Francis, Ann Magill Nahigian, Douglas, Thomas. Admitted to Ind. bar, 1941, D.C. bar, 1954; asst. tax legis. counsel Dept. Treasury, Washington, 1946-53, asst. head legal adv. staff, 1953-55; with Gen. Motors Corp., Detroit, 1955—, asst. treas., 1962-68, exec. in charge industry-govt. relations, 1968-71, v.p. in charge industry-govt. relations, 1971—. Bd. dirs. Mid-Am. Legal Found., Civic Searchlight, Civic Inc., Detroit Met. Indsl. Devel. Corp., Citizen's Research Council, Ford's Theatre Soc., Washington, Traffic Safety Assn. Detroit, Internat. Road Fedn. Served as lt. comdr. USN, 1942-45. Mem. Am., Fed. bar assns., Soc. Automotive Engrs., NAM (dir.), Mich. State (dir.), Greater Detroit (dir.) chambers of commerce, Council State Chambers (dir.), Mich. Mfrs. Assn. (dir.), Mich. Assn. Traffic Safety (pres.), Phi Beta Kappa. Clubs: Recess (Detroit); Oakland Hills Country (Birmingham, Mich.); Lawyers, Burning Tree, Internat. (Washington). Home: 1234 Willow Ln Birmingham MI 48009 Office: 13-135 Gen Motors Bldg Detroit MI 48202

MAGILL, SAMUEL HAYS, educator; b. Decatur, Ga., July 19, 1928; s. Orrin Rankin and Ellen Howe (Bell) M.; grad. Deerfield Acad., 1946; A.B., U. N.C., 1950; B.D., Yale U., 1953; Ph.D., Duke U., 1962; children—Samuel Hays, Katherine Williams, Sarah Suzanne. Ordained to ministry Congl. Christian Ch., 1953; gen. sec. Davidson Coll. YMCA, 1953-55; successively dir. student activities, asst. dean student affairs, part-time instr. religion U. N.C. at Chapel Hill, 1955- 59; chaplain Dickinson Coll., 1962-63, asst. prof. religion, 1962-66, asso. prof. religion, 1966-68, dean coll., 1963-68, Danforth Found. spl. grad. fellow, 1959-61; pres. Council Protestant Colls. and Univs., Washington, 1968-70; exec. asso., chief office acad. affairs Assn. Am. Colls., 1971-76; pres. Simon's Rock Early Coll., Great Barrington, Mass., 1976-79. Mem. United Bd. Coll. Devel. Fellow Soc. for Religion in Higher Edn. (dir.); mem. Am. Acad. Religion, AAUP (asso.), Delta Psi, Omicron Delta Kappa. Home: PO Box 187 South Egremont MA 01258

MAGINN, EDWARD JOSEPH, clergyman; b. Glasgow, Scotland, Jan. 4, 1897; s. Edward and Agnes (Keenan) M.; came to U.S., 1904, naturalized, 1917; student St. Mary's Acad., Glens Falls, N.Y., 1911-13, Holy Cross Coll., 1914-16, St. Joseph's Sem., Yonkers, N.Y., 1916-22. Ordained priest Roman Catholic Ch., 1922; chancellor Cath. Diocese of Albany, N.Y., 1924-36, vicar gen., 1936—; pastor Ch. of St. Vincent de Paul, Albany, N.Y., 1944-72; vice chancellor Coll. St. Rose, Albany, 1936—. Appointed Domestic Prelate by Pope Pius XI with title Rt. Rev. Monsignor, 1936; titular bishop of Curium and aux. bishop of Albany, N.Y., June, 1957; consecrated bishop, Sept., 1957; apostolic adminstr. Diocese of Albany, 1966-69, aux. bishop, 1969-72, titular bishop of curium, 1972—. Home: 900 Madison Ave Albany NY 12208

MAGINN, RAYMOND GRAHAM, utility exec.; b. St. Louis, Aug. 20, 1925; s. Raymond G. and Adeline (Kreutzer) M.; student Miss. Coll., 1943-45; B.S., U. S.C., 1946, Washington U., St. Louis, 1952; m. Violet D. Hicks, July 9, 1949; children—Pamela L., Michael J. With Arthur Andersen & Co., C.P.A.'s, St. Louis, 1952-60; pvt. practice as C.P.A., Quincy, Ill., 1960-63; with Central Ill. Light Co., 1963—, sec.-treas., 1968-72, controller, 1972—. Served with USNR, 1943-47. C.P.A., Ill. Mem. Am. Inst. C.P.A.'s, Ill. Soc. C.P.A.'s. Home: 306 W Stratford Dr Peoria IL 61614 Office: 300 Liberty St Peoria IL 61602

MAGINN, WALLACE ALLTON, utility exec.; b. West Orange, N.J., Feb. 26, 1925; s. Charles E. and Louise Helen (Osterstock) M.; B.S., U.S. Mcht. Marine Acad., 1945; B.S., N.Y. U., 1951; m. LaVerne Chappell, July 7, 1945; children—Cynthia, Stephen, Glenn. Accountant, Price, Waterhouse & Co., C.P.A.'s, N.Y.C., 1942-43, 45-49, Met. Opera, 1949-51; with Pub. Service Electric and Gas Co., Newark, 1951—, treas., 1972-75, v.p., treas., 1975—; dir. Nuclear Mut. Ltd., Hamilton, Bermuda, Nat. Bank N.J., New Brunswick. Trustee United Hosps. Newark, 1976—. Served with U.S. Maritime Service, 1943-45. Mem. Am. Gas Assn., Financial Execs. Inst. Presbyn. Clubs: Shrewsbury Sailing and Yacht, Bamm Hollow Country; Downtown (Newark). Office: 80 Park Pl Newark NJ 07101

MAGLICH, BOGDAN C., physicist; b. Yugoslavia; s. Cveta and Ivanka (Bingulac) M.; diploma physics U. Belgrade, 1951; M.S., U. Liverpool (Eng.), 1955; Ph.D., Mass. Inst. Tech., 1959; m. Elowyn Castle Westervelt, 1959 (div. 1969); children—Marko Castle, Ivanka Taylor; m. Sharon Bundy Chagnaud, 1970 (div. 1977); 1 dau., Roberta Cveta. Came to U.S., 1956, naturalized, 1967. Staff mem. Lawrence Berkeley Lab., 1959-62; dep. group leader Brit. group CERN European Orgn. Nuclear Research, Geneva, 1962-63, leader Swiss group, 1964-67; vis. prof. U. Pa., 1967-69; prof. physics, prin. investigator high energy physics Rutgers U., 1969-74; chmn. Migma Inst. High Energy Fusion, 1974—; pres., chmn. Fusion Energy Corp., Princeton, N.J., 1974—; dir. Nat. Computer Analysts, Princeton. Resident scientist UN-ILO Seminar Econ. Devel. East Africa, Kenya, 1967; lectr. Postdoctoral Sch. Physics, Yerevan, USSR, 1965, Internat. Sch. Majorana, Italy, 1969; mem. U.S. delegation Internat. Conf. High Energy Physics, Vienna, 1968, Kiev, 1970; spl. rep. of U.S. Pres. to Yugoslavia, 1976. Chmn. Yugoslav-Am. Bicentennial Com., 1975-76. Recipient White House citation, 1961; Bourgeois d'honneur de Lens, Switzerland, 1973; UNESCO fellow, 1957-58. Fellow Am. Phys. Soc.; mem. Ripon Soc. (bd. govs.), Sigma Xi. Clubs: Nassau, Mass. Inst. Tech. (N.Y. and Princeton). Discoverer omega-meson, 1961, missing-mass spectrometer, 1964, delta-meson, 1963, g-meson, S, T, U-mesons, 1965, precetron, 1969, migma-cell, 1972. Editor: Adventures in Experimental Physics. Patentee in field. Office: PO Box 2005 Princeton NJ 08540

MAGLIONE, RALPH JOHN, JR., ret. air force officer; b. Akron, Ohio, Dec. 11, 1926; s. Ralph John and Katherine (Lucricia) M.; student Dayton U., 1944-45, Ind. U., 1945; B.A. in Econs., U. Md., 1964; grad. Nat. War College, Washington, 1968; M.S. in Internat. Affairs, George Washington U., 1968; m. Caroline Barbara Stofcho, Sept. 18, 1948; 1 dau., Annette Patricia. Commd. 2d lt. USAF, 1950, advanced through grades to maj. gen., 1974; pilot 27th Fighter Escort Wing, 1950-59; flight comdr., ops. officer 81st Tactical Fighter Wing, 1959-62; action officer, officer assignments div. Office of Dep. Chief of Staff for Personnel, Washington, 1962-65; comdr., leader Thunderbird Aerial Demonstration Team, 1965-67; chief Ho. of Reps. Liaison Office, Office of Legis. Liaison, Office of Sec. Air Force, Washington, 1968-71; comdr. 3525th Pilot Tng. Wing, Williams AFB, Ariz., 1971-72; dir. personnel Mil. Assistance Command Vietnam, 1972-73; chief ops. and plans div. Def. Attache Office, Saigon, 1973-73; dir. legis. liaison Office of Sec. Air Force, Washington, 1974-77, ret., 1977; cons. legis. matters, aircraft design and sales, 1977—. Decorated D.S.M., Silver Star, Legion of Merit with oak leaf cluster, D.F.C. with oak leaf cluster, Air medal with 5 oak leaf clusters, Purple Heart; Oct. 4, 1966 designated Ralph Maglione Day by mayor Akron; named Ky. col., adm. Tex. Navy, hon. conch of Key West, commodore Nebr. Navy, Ark. traveler. Mem. Las Vegas Jr. C. of C. (hon.). Roman Catholic. Home and office: 8225 Buckspark Ln W Potomac MD 20854

MAGNER, GEORGE WILLIAM, univ. ofcl.; b. Harrissville, R.I., Jan. 22, 1927; s. Edmund H. and Cora (Tessier) M.; B.A., N.Mex. Highlands U., 1950; M.S.W., U. Conn., 1952; Ph.D., U. Chgo., 1961; m. Dolores Marie Jones, June 9, 1956; children—Christine Agnes, Laura Marie. Social work dir. Lima (Ohio) State Hosp., 1954-59; social service chief Ill. State Psychiat. Inst., Chgo., 1959-66; asso. prof. social work U. Ill., Chgo. Circle Campus, 1966-69, prof., 1969-78, asso. dir. Sch. Social Work, 1970-74, interim acad. vice chancellor, 1974-76; provost U. Houston Central Campus, 1978—; dir. Leadership Tng. Program in Mental Health, 1963-74. Served with U.S. Army, 1944-46. Recipient Disting. Alumni award U. Conn. Sch. Social Work, 1971; NIMH fellow, 1955-57. Mem. Nat. Assn. Social Workers, Council Social Work Edn. Democrat. Roman Catholic. Author: Supervision in Mental Health, 1968; contbr. articles to profl. jours.; editor: Leadership Training in Mental Health, 1970. Office: U Houston Houston TX 77004

MAGNIN, CYRIL, retail trade exec.; b. San Francisco, July 6, 1899; s. Joseph and Charlotte (Davis) M.; student U. Calif. 1919-22; LL.D., U. Pacific, 1967; Ph.D. in Fine Arts (hon.), U. San Francisco, 1978; m. Anna Smithline, Nov. 19, 1926 (dec. Nov. 1948); children—Donald, Ellen, Jerry. Former pres., now chmn. bd. Joseph Magnin Co., Inc., San Francisco; gen. partner Cyril Magnin Investments, Ltd.; dir. Spectrum Foods, Inc., Lilli Ann Corp. Chief protocol City and County San Francisco; v.p. Calif. Mus. Found.; mem. Asian Arts Com., Blyth Zellerbach Com. Bd. dirs. March of Dimes Nat. Found.; pres. Calif. Assn. A.C.T.; bd. govs. San Francisco Heart Assn.; bd. dirs., mem. exec. com. Fine Arts Mus. San Francisco; mem. exec. com. Asian Art Mus. San Francisco; trustee Am. Cancer Soc., San Francisco Opera Assn., Boys Town Italy; pres. bd. advs. Calif. Culinary Acad. Decorated Star of Solidarity (Italy); Legion of Honor (France); comdr. Brit. Empire; Cross of Order of Merit (Fed. Republic Germany); Order of Phoenix (Greece); comdr. Royal Order No. Star (Sweden); Order de Isabel La Catolica (Spain); recipient numerous awards including: Man of Yr. award NCCJ, 1962, Retailer of Yr. award, 1962; Disting. Citizens award City and County Los Angeles, 1965; San Franciscan award San Francisco Jr. C. of C., 1969; Bus. and Profl. award Nat. Asthma Center, 1978; Leadership award Fashion Inst. Design and Merchandising, 1978. Mem. UN Assn. San Francisco (life dir.), Greater San Francisco C. of C. (past pres., past chmn.). Mason (Shriner). Clubs: St. Francis Yacht, Villa Taverna, World Trade (dir.). Home: Mark Hopkins Hotel San Francisco CA 94106 Office: 59 Harrison St San Francisco CA 94105

MAGNIN, EDGAR FOGEL, rabbi; b. San Francisco, July 1, 1890; s. Sam and Lilly (Fogel) M.; A.B., U. Cin., 1913; B.H. and Rabbi, Hebrew Union Coll., 1914, D.D., 1945; L.H.D. (hon.), Calif. Coll. Medicine, 1944; S.T.D., U. So. Calif., 1956; LL.D., Wilberforce U., 1962, Pepperdine U., 1973; m. Evelyn Rosenthal. June 15, 1916; children—Henry David, Mae. Rabbi, Temple Israel, Stockton, Calif., 1914, Wilshire Blvd. Temple, Los Angeles, 1915—; lectr. history U. So. Calif., 1934-55; rep. Jewish Welfare Bd. So. Calif. during World War; v.p. Cedars of Lebanon Hosp.; bd. dirs. Cedars-Sinai Med. Center; mem. Central Conf. Am. Rabbis, Nat. Acad. Am. Lit., Los Angeles Rabbinical Assn., Los Angeles Philharm. Orch. Assn., Jewish Welfare Bd. (chmn.), Citizens Com. Adv. Bd. Los Angeles Bd. of Edn., C. of C., Nat. Econ. League (nat. council), Assn. Advancement Home Builders, Menorah Assn. (bd. govs.), Calif. Zoöl. Soc. (founder, life mem.), Pan Am. Fellowship, U.S. Flag Assn., Am. Joint Distbn. Commn. (nat. council), Protective Order Police of Calif., mem. adv. coms. several of these groups; mem. many nat., state and local civic and community groups for spl. purposes; active all religious, govtl., social, ednl. and cultural orgns., served or is serving as an officer of many, including, among others: United Service Orgns., Inc.. NCCJ, Nat. Council for Palestine, Crippled Children's Soc. of Los Angeles Co., France Forever Free French Movement in Am., citizens com. Conf. of Childhood and Youth in War Time, trustee Calif. Coll. Medicine, Welfare Fedn. Los Angeles, Am. Friends of Hebrew U., Los Angeles Area council Boy Scouts Am., Los Angeles Community Chest, Los Angeles County Tb and Health Assn., All-Year Club of So. Calif.; Hillel Found., Los Angeles Area; adminstrv. bd. Hebrew Union Coll., Jewish Inst. Religion, Com. Nat. Jewish Hosp. at Denver; bd. dirs. Thomas A. Dooley Found., Jewish Free Loan Assn., Los Angeles World Affairs Council; founding bd. mem. Hollywood Bowl, Community Chest; mem. adv. cabinet Western region Jewish Nat. Fund; gen. adv. com. Los Angeles County chpt. Muscular Dystrophy Assn. Am., Greater Los Angeles chpt. Nat. Safety Council; mem. adv. council Guide Dogs for Blind; sponsoring com. So. Calif. com. WHO; founding sponsor Friends of Libraries U. So. Calif.; mem. Los Angeles County Com. Affairs of Aging; mem. Los Angeles Forward City Govt. for Future; chaplain Beverly Hills council Navy League U.S., also life mem., God and Country award, 1977. Recipient 50 Yr. Service award Los Angeles chpt. ARC, 1977, award City of Los Angeles, 1977; Man of Yr. award Miracle Mile Lions, 1977; Ann. Spirit of Los Angeles award Los Angeles Hdqrs. City Assn.; Los Angeles Area USO Disting. Am. award; County of Los Angeles Disting. Service medal. Hon. mem. Soc. for History of Medicine of the Cedars of Lebanon Hosp. Republican. Clubs: Masons (33 deg., Shriner, past grand chaplain Grand lodge of Calif., Outstanding Mason of Yr. award). Rotary, B'nai B'rith (past grand pres. Dist. 4, life mem. gen. com., Man of Yr. award); Beverly Hills, Men's (Beverly Hills); Twenty, Breakfast, Hillcrest Country (Los Angeles); Faculty (U. So. Calif.); Hollywood Press, Friars, Marine Corps. Author: How to Live a Richer and Fuller Life. Contbr. articles to jours.; columnist Los Angeles Herald Examiner. Home: 615 N Walden Drive Beverly Hills CA 90210 Address: 3663 Wilshire Blvd Los Angeles CA 90010

MAGNUS, WILHELM, mathematician; b. Berlin, Germany, Feb. 5, 1907; s. Alfred and Paula (Kalkbrenner) M.; Ph.D., U. Frankfurt (Germany), 1931; m. Gertrud Remy, Aug. 5, 1939; children—Jutta, Bettina, Alfred. Came to U.S., 1948, naturalized, 1955. Lectr. U. Frankfurt, 1933-38; prof. U. Goettingen, 1947-48; research asso. Calif. Inst. Tech., 1948-50; prof. math. N.Y. U., 1950-73. now prof. emeritus; prof. N.Y. Poly. Inst., 1973—; spl. research group theory, spl. functions math. physics, diffraction problems, differential equations. Rockefeller fellow, 1934; Guggenheim fellow, 1969; Fulbright-Hays sr. research scholar, 1973-74. Mem. Goettingen Acad. Scis., Am. Math. Soc. Author books, articles in field. Home: 11 Lomond Pl New Rochelle NY 10804 Office: 251 Mercer St New York NY 10012

MAGNUSON, HAROLD JOSEPH, physician; b. Halstead, Kans., Mar. 31, 1913; s. Joseph Simeon and Margaret Ethel (Matson) M.; A.B., U. So. Calif., 1934, M.D., 1938, M.P.H., Johns Hopkins, 1942; m. Ruth Prusia, Feb. 16, 1935 (dec. 1941); children—Karen Margaret (Mrs. Thomas Mauro, Jr.), Ruth Ellen (Mrs. John Gilleland); m. 2d, Kathryne I. Bause, Dec. 20, 1941. Intern, Los Angeles County Gen. Hosp., 1937-39, research fellow A.C.P., 1939-40; instr. medicine U. So. Calif., 1939-41; commd. asst. surgeon USPHS, 1941, med. dir., 1952; instr. medicine Johns Hopkins, 1943-46; research prof. exptl. medicine U. N.C., 1946-55; chief div. occupational health USPHS, 1956-62; ret. 1962; prof. internal medicine U. Mich. Sch. Medicine, prof. indsl. health, 1962-76, prof. emeritus, 1976—, chmn. dept. U. Mich. Sch. Pub. Health, also dir. Inst. Indsl. Health, 1962-69, asso. dean Sch. Pub. Health, 1969-76. Mem. U.S. delegation ILO Conf., 1958, 59. Chmn. U.S. indsl. toxicology delegation to USSR, 1963. Diplomate Am. Bd. Preventive Medicine (mem. bd. 1964—, vice chmn. occupational medicine 1968). Fellow A.C.P., A.A.A.S., A.M.A. (chmn. sect. preventive medicine 1966, Hektoen bronze medal 1956), Am. Acad. Occupational Medicine, Am. Pub. Health Assn. (chmn. sect. occupational health 1966), Indsl. Med. Assn., Knudsen award 1970); mem. Soc. Clin. Investigation, Soc. Exptl. Biology and Medicine, Soc. Exptl. Pathology, Mich. Indsl. Med. Assn. (pres. 1965-66), Internat. Congress Indsl. Medicine (v.p. 1969), Rammazzini Soc., Phi Beta Kappa, Sigma Xi, Alpha Omega Alpha, Delta Omega. Club: Rancho Bernardo Mens Golf. Home: 12305 Fernando Dr San Diego CA 92128

MAGNUSON, KEITH ARLEN, profl. hockey player; b. Wadena, Sask., Can., Apr. 27, 1947; s. Joseph Carl and Birdie Pauline (Fransen) M.; came to U.S., 1964; B.B.A., U. Denver, 1969; m. Cynthia White; 1 son, Kevin. Profl. hockey player with Chgo. Blackhawks, 1969—. Salesman, T.W. Anderson Real Estate, Denver, 1969; mktg. rep. Joyce Seven-Up Bottling Co., Chgo., 1970-73, account exec., 1973—. Named 5th Best Defenseman in All-Star Team West Div., 1971, Sportsman of Year, City of Hope Med. Research, 1971. Author: (with Robert Bradford) None Against, 1973. Address: 1800 W Madison St Chicago IL 60612 also 4544 W Carroll St Chicago IL 60624*

MAGNUSON, RICHARD H., lawyer; b. Willmar, Minn., Aug. 12, 1925; s. William G. and Ruth E. M.; student Gustavus Adolphus Coll., 1946-48, U. Oreg., 1948; B.S. in Law, U. Minn., 1950, LL.B., J.D., 1952; m. Finette Love, June 10, 1952; children—Marcus R., Scott C., Finette E., Leif L. Admitted to Minn. bar, 1954; atty. Cenex, Inc., St. Paul, 1954-69; v.p., gen. counsel Land O'Lakes, Inc., Mpls., 1970—; dir. Group Health Plan, Inc., Mpls., 1960-70, pres., 1964-68, counsel, 1970—; lectr. Practising Law Inst., 1974-76; chmn. legal, tax and accounting com. Nat. Council Farmer Coops., 1970-72. Mem. Minn. Tax Commn., 1970-74, Minn. Environ. Quality Bd., 1974-78. Served with USN, 1943-46. Mem. Am., Minn., Mpls. bar assns. Democrat. Unitarian. Club: St. Paul Athletic. Home: 2141 Doswell Ave Saint Paul MN 55108 Office: 614 McKinley Pl Minneapolis MN 55413

MAGNUSON, ROBERT MARTIN, hosp. adminstr.; b. Chgo., June 28, 1927; s. Martin David and Adena Marie (Hallberg) M.; B.S. cum laude, Lake Forest (Ill.) Coll., 1951; M.B.A., Harvard U., 1955; m. Patricia Ann McNaughton, Dec. 30, 1960; children—Thomas Martin, Dana Caroline. Factory budget mgr., asst. budget dir. Zenith Radio Corp., Chgo., 1955-57; asst. adminstr., controller Meml. Hosp. of DuPage County, Elmhurst, Ill., 1957-64, asso. adminstr., 1964-66, exec. dir., 1966—; officer, dir. Chgo. Hosp. Council, 1970—; mem. hosp. adv. council Ill. Dept. Pub. Health, 1972-76; faculty preceptor U. Chgo. Program in Hosp. Adminstrn., 1971—, Northwestern U. Program in Hosp. and Health Sci. Adminstrn., 1972—; dir. DuPage County Community Nursing Service, 1964-67, Elmhurst Fed. Savs. & Loan Assn., 1971—. Served with USN, 1945-48, 51-52. Mem. Am. Coll. Hosp. Adminstrs., Ill. Hosp. Assn. (dist. pres. 1967-69), Inter-Hosp. Planning Assn. of Western Suburbs (pres., dir.). Republican. Club: Medinah (Ill.) Country. Office: 200 Berteau St Elmhurst IL 60126

MAGNUSON, WARREN GRANT, U.S. senator; b. Moorhead, Minn., Apr. 12, 1905; student U. N.D., N.D. State, 1923-24; LL.B., U. Wash., 1929; m. Jermaine Elliott Peralta, Oct. 4, 1964. Admitted to Wash. bar, 1929, and practiced in Wash. State; spl. prosecutor King County, 1931; mem. Wash. State Legislature, 1933-34; asst. U.S. dist. atty. 1934; pros. atty. King County, 1934-36; mem. 75th to 78th congresses from 1st Wash. Dist.; mem. U.S. Senate, 1944—, pres. pro tem., chmn. com. on appropriations. Del. from Seattle to State Constl. Conv., 1933; sec. Seattle Municipal League, 1930-31. Lt. comdr. U.S. Naval Res. Mem. Am. Legion, V.F.W., Theta Chi. Democrat. Lutheran. Clubs: Washington Athletic of Seattle; Burning Tree (Washington). Office: 127 Russell Bldg Washington DC 20510

MAGNUSON, WARREN ROGER, church ofcl.; b. Mpls., Dec. 5, 1921; s. Edwin John and Hulda (Smith) M.; A.A., Bethel Jr. Coll., 1942; B.A., U. Minn., 1946; B.D., Bethel Theol. Sem., 1946; hon. degree Judson Coll., Elgin, Ill., 1973; m. Margaret Linnea Johnson, June 9, 1944. Ordained to ministry Baptist Ch., 1946; pastor Immanuel Bapt. Ch., St. Paul, 1943-46, Washington Ave. Bapt. Ch., Ludington, Mich., 1947-50, 1st Bapt. Ch., Willmar, Minn., 1950-54, Central Bapt. Ch., St. Paul, 1954-69; gen. sec. Bapt. Gen. Conf., Chgo., 1969—. Moderator, Minn. Bapt. Conf., 1959, trustee, 1965-69; moderator Bapt. Gen. Conf., 1965, mem. bd. missions, 1965—. Mem. exec. com. Bapt. Joint Com. on Pub. Affairs, 1970—, chmn., 1970-72; mem. exec. com. Gen. Commn. on Chaplains and Armed Forces Personnel, 1969—, Bapt. World Alliance, 1970—. Bd. regents Bethel Coll. Mem. Nat. Assn. Evangelicals (adminstrv. council 1970—), Am. Bible Soc. (adv. council 1969—). Home: 1313 Landwehr Rd Northbrook IL 60062 Office: 1233 Central St Evanston IL 60201

MAGNUSSON, PAUL CHRISTOPHER, journalist; b. Washington, Sept. 7, 1947; s. Warren Douglas and Flora Elizabeth (Mesheau) M.; B.A., Randolph-Macon Coll., 1969; postgrad. Syracuse U., 1969-73. Reporter, news editor Fauquier Democrat, Warrenton, Va., 1972-74; columnist, reporter Martinsville (Va.) Bull., 1974-75; reporter Richmond (Va.) Mercury, 1975, Bergen Record, Hackensack, N.J., 1975-76, Detroit Free Press, 1976—; guest lectr. U. Mich., Mich. State U. Recipient awards Va. Press Assn., 1974, 75; 1st pl. enterprise reporting award Mich. Press Assn., 1978; 1st place investigative reporting and overall sweepstates award Mich., AP, 1978; Heywood Broun award Newspaper Guild, 1978; Mich. award of newspaper excellence UPI, 1979; Golden medallion for disting. pub. service Detroit Press Club Found., 1979. Mem. ACLU, Amnesty Internat. Home: 7718 E Jefferson St Detroit MI 48214 Office: Detroit Free Press 321 W Lafayette St Detroit MI 48226

MAGOON, JOHN HENRY, JR., airlines exec.; b. Honolulu, Dec. 2, 1915; s. John H. and Juliet (Carroll) M.; student U. Calif. at Berkeley, 1933-35; m. Adele Whitlock, Oct. 28, 1939; 1 dau., Sara. Pres., Hawaiian Linen Supply, Ltd., 1941-60; pres., dir. Hawaiian Securities & Realty, Ltd., Honolulu, 1955—; pres. Hawaiian Airlines, Inc., Honolulu, 1964—, also chmn. bd., chief exec. officer; dir. Hawaiian Trust Co., Ltd., Castle & Cooke, Inc., Magoon Bros., Ltd., Magoon Estate, Ltd., Magoon Devel. Corp., Magoon Land Corp., First Ins. Co. Hawaii, Ltd., Cox Broadcasting Corp., Atlanta; mem. adv. com. to bd. dirs. New Eng. Mut. Life Ins. Co., Boston. Mem. Territorial CSC, 1948-53; bd. govs. Iolani Sch.; pres. bd. trustees Kapiolani Hosp.; bd. dirs. Hawaii Visitors Bur. Mem. C. of C. Hawaii (dir.), Phi Kappa Psi. Clubs: Outrigger Canoe, Pacific, Oahu Country, Waialae Country, Diamond Head Tennis; Met. (Washington). Office: Hawaiian Airlines Inc Honolulu Internat Airport Honolulu HI 96820*

MAGOR, LOUIS ROLAND, symphony chorus dir.; b. Auburn, Nebr., May 16, 1945; s. John William and Eleanor Lucille (Niemann) M.; B.Mus. Edn., Northwestern U., 1967, Mus.M., 1974. Choral dir. Avoca Jr. High Sch., Wilmette, Ill., 1968-70; choral dir. Niles North High Sch., Skokie, Ill., 1970-73; dir. San Francisco Symphony Chorus, 1974—; founder The Louis Magor Singers; mem. faculty San Francisco Conservatory of Music, 1976-78, San Francisco State U., 1979—. Mem. Pi Kappa Lambda. Office: 107 War Memorial Veterans Bldg San Francisco CA 94102

MAGOUN, FRANCIS PEABODY, JR., educator; b. N.Y.C., Jan. 6, 1895; s. Francis Peabody and Jeanne Cassard (Bartholow) M.; prep. edn., St. Andrew's Sch., Concord, Mass., and Noble and Greenough Sch., Boston; A.B., Harvard, 1916, Ph.D., 1923; Trinity Coll., Cambridge, Eng., 1919; Ph.D. (hon.), Helsinki U., 1969; m. Margaret Boyden, June 30, 1926; children—Francis Peabody III, William Cowper Boyden, Margaret Boyden, Jean Bartholow. Instr. English, Harvard, 1919-20, 1923-27, asst. prof. English, 1927-30, asso. prof. comparative lit., 1930-37, prof. comparative lit., 1937-51, prof. English, 1951-61, now emeritus; Harvard exchange prof. to U. Paris and U. Strasbourg, 1931-32; spl. univ. lectr. U. London, 1951; Guggenheim fellow, 1955-56. Mng. editor of Speculum, a Jour. of Mediaeval Studies, 1926-30; editor Harvard Studies and Notes in Philology and Lit., 1934-35. Field service with Am. Ambulance Corps, France, 1916-17; cadet. later 2d lt. and lt. Royal Flying Corps., R.A.F., B.E.F., France, 1917-19. Awarded Mil. Cross (Brit.), 1918; Medaille de l'Universite de Strasbourg, 1932; comdr. Order of Lion of Finland, 1964. Fellow Mediaeval Acad. Am.; mem. Modern Lang. Assn. Am., Soc. Neophilogique de Helsinki, Kalevala Soc. Helsinki. Club: Faculty (Harvard University). Author: The Gests of King Alexander of Macedon, 1929. Rev. editor: The Founders of Eng., F.B. Gummere, 1930; History of Football from the Beginnings to 1871, 1938; Survivals in Old Norwegian (with H. M. Smyser), 1941; transl. and adapter (with H. Kökeritz) of Gösta Bergman, A Short History of the Swedish Language, 1975; Walter of Acquitaine (with H.M. Smyser), 1977; A Grouped Frequency World-List of Anglo-Saxon Poetry (with J. F. Madden), 1954; Anglo-Saxon Poems, 1969; Graded Finnish Readers 1-4 (with T. J. Heiskanen); Beowulf and Judith, 1962; The Vercelli Book Poems, 1965; A Chaucer Gazetter, 1961; Agricola's Gospel of Mark, 1967. Translator: (with A. H. Krappe) Grimm Brothers German Folk Tales, 1960; Eyvind of the Mountains (Sigurjonsson), 1961; The Kalevala (Lönnrot), 1963, The Old Kalevala, 1969; contbr. to Otfrid von Weissenburg, 1978; also articles to Am. and European philol. jours. Recipient hommage vol. Franciplegius: Medieval Studies in Honor of Francis Peabody Magoun, Jr., 1965. Home: 29 Reservoir St Cambridge MA 02138

MAGOVERN, FREDERICK JOHN, lawyer; b. Bklyn., Sept. 12, 1946; s. John Joseph and Grace E. (Poppe) M.; B.A., Manhattan Coll., 1968; J.D., Fordham U., 1971; m. Susan H. Kaiser, May 19, 1973. Admitted to N.Y. State bar, 1972; asso. firm Bodell & Gross, N.Y.C., 1973-75; partner firm Bodell, Gross & Magovern, N.Y.C., 1975, Bodell & Magovern, P.C., 1975-79; individual practice, 1979—. Mem. Am., Nassau County bar assns., Assn. Bar City N.Y., Catholic Lawyers Guild, N.Y. State Trial Lawyers Assn. Club: Unqua Corinthian Yacht. Mem. editorial bd. Nassau Lawyer, 1974-75. Home: 34 Chestnut St Garden City NY 11530 Office: 102 E 35th St New York NY 10016

MAGOWAN, ROBERT ANDERSON, corp. exec.; b. Chester, Pa., Sept. 19, 1903; s. Edward Thomas and Estelle (Smith) M.; B.S., Harvard U., 1927; LL.D., Widener Coll., 1960, Trinity Coll., 1963, m. Doris Merrill, June 15, 1935; children—Robert Anderson, Merrill L., Peter A., Stephen C., Mark E. Mdse. mgr. R.H. Macy & Co., 1927-34; v.p. N.W. Ayer & Son, 1934-35; v.p. Safeway Stores, Inc., San Francisco, 1935-38, chmn. exec. com., 1975—, chmn. bd., 1955—; chief exec., chmn. bd. Can. Safeway Ltd.; v.p. Merrill Lynch & Co., Inc., 1938-40; partner Merrill Lynch, Pierce, Fenner & Beane, 1940-55, ltd. partner, 1955—; former dir. R.H. Macy & Co., Bank of Calif., So. Pacific Co. (mem. exec. com.), Fibreboard Paper Products Corp., Caterpillar Tractor Co., Del Monte Properties, Inc.; dir. J.G. Boswell Co., Inc. Bd. dirs. Beekman Downtown Hosp., N.Y.C., 1953; trustee San Francisco Mus. Art, 1956; bd. dirs. San Francisco Opera; mem. exec. com. Bay Area Crusade. Served as lt. USNR, 1942-45. Decorated Knight Comdr. Order Brit. Empire; Knight Venerable Order Hosp. St. John of Jerusalem. Mem. Assn. Stock Exchange Firms (gov. 1948-55). Episcopalian (trustee). Clubs: Brook, River, Harvard (N.Y.C.; Nat. Golf, Shinnecock Hills Golf, Meadow, Southampton (Southampton, N.Y.); Bohemian, Burlingame Country, Pacific Union, San Francisco Golf (San Francisco); Cypress Point (Pebble Beach, Calif.); Everglades, Bath and Tennis, Seminole (Palm Beach, Fla.). Home: 2100 Washington St San Francisco CA 94109 Office: 4th and Jackson Sts Oakland CA 94660

MAGRATH, C. PETER, univ. pres.; b. N.Y.C., Apr. 23, 1933; s. Laurence Wilfrid and Guilia Maria (Dentice) M.; B.A summa cum laude, U. N.H., 1955; Ph.D., Cornell U., 1962; m. Diane Fay Skomars, Mar. 25, 1978; children—Valerie Ruth, Monette Fay. Mem. faculty Brown U., 1961-68, prof. polit. sci., 1967-68, asso. dean Grad. Sch., 1965-66; dean Coll. Arts and Sci., U. Nebr., Lincoln 1968-69, dean faculties, 1969-72, interim chancellor univ., 1971-72, prof. polit. sci., 1968-72, vice chancellor for acad. affairs, 1972; pres. State U. N.Y. at Binghamton, 1972-74, prof. polit. sci., 1972-74; pres. U. Minn., Mpls., 1974—. Served with AUS, 1955-57. Mem. Am., Midwest polit. sci. assns., Orgn. Am. Historians, Phi Beta Kappa, Phi Kappa Phi, Pi Gamma Mu, Pi Sigma Alpha, Kappa Tau Alpha. Author: Morrison R. Waite; The Triumph of Character, 1963; Yazoo: Law and Politics in the New Republic, The Case of Fletcher v. Peck, 1966; Constitutionalism and Politics: Conflict and Consensus, 1968; (with others) The American Democracy, 2d edit., 1973; (with others) Issues and Perspectives in American Government, 1971; also articles. Office: 202 Morrill Hall Minneapolis MN 55455. *True personal success cannot be measured by public acclaim, recognition, or status. It grows out of an ability to recognize right from wrong, and to maintain principles of fairness and understanding in all human relationships—regardless of one's role in life. In my case I have tried to fulfill this ideal; I have been willing to exercise leadership by asserting my judgements and views openly and directly on the educational and human issues that "came my way."*

MAGUIRE, ANDREW, congressman; b. Columbus, Ohio, Mar. 11, 1939; s. Bruce and Ruth Maguire; B.A., Oberlin Coll., 1961; Ph.D., Harvard U., 1966; 1 son, Jay. Adviser polit. and security affairs State Dept., also mem. U.S. del. UN Gen. Assembly, 1966-69; dir. devel. program City of Jamaica (N.Y.), 1969-72; cons. nat. affairs div. Ford Found, 1972-74; mem. 94th-95th Congresses from 7th N.J. Dist. Bd. dirs. Bergen-Passaic chpt. Nat. Multiple Sclerosis Soc., Bergen County chpt. NAACP. Danforth fellow, Woodrow Wilson fellow, Fgn. Area Tng. fellow. Recipient Achievement award Jamaica C. of C., 1970, Citizen of Year award Jewish War Vets. Dept. N.J., 1976. Democrat. Mem. UN Assn., Common Cause. Author: Toward Uhurn in Tanzania: The Politics of Participation, 1969. Office: 1112 Longworth House Office Bldg Washington DC 20515

MAGUIRE, BASSETT, botanist; b. Alabama City, Ala., Aug. 4, 1904; s. Charles T. and Rose (Bassett) M.; B.S., U. Ga., 1926; grad. student U. Pitts., 1926; Ph.D., Cornell U., 1938; m. Ruth Richards, 1926; children—Bassett, Grace (Mrs. Daniel N. MacLemore, Jr.); m. 2d, Celia Kramer, Mar. 25, 1951. High sch. tchr. sci. and biology, Athens, Ga., 1926-27; instr. botany U. Ga., 1927-29, Cornell U., 1929-31, 37-38; prof. Utah State U., 1931-43; curator, head curator N.Y. Bot. Garden, 1943—, Nathaniel Lord Britton distinguished sr. curator, 1961—, asst. dir., 1968-69, dir. botany, 1969-71, 73-75, dir. emeritus, sr. scientist, mem. bd. mgrs., 1971—; dir. botany Jardin Botánico Nacional, Santo Domingo, Dominican Republic; exec. dir. Orgn. for Flora Neotropica, 1964-75; aquatic botanist N.Y. State Conservation Dept., 1930-31, U.S. Bur. Fisheries, 1932, 34; ecologist, spl. agt. U.S. Conservation Service, Dept. Agr., 1934-35; adj. prof. botany Columbia, N.Y.C., 1961—, City U. N.Y.; non-resident prof. Utah State U.; discoverer (with John J. Wurdack) Serrania de la Neblina, mountain complex on Venezuelan-Brazilian frontier, 1953; bot. exploration N.Am., especially Rocky Mountains and Intermontane U.S., 1923-55; mem., leader, dir. numerous expdns. to tropical S.Am., including Roraima Formation (Lost Worlds) and Amazon Basin. Del., UNESCO, 1947, 64, FAO, 1961; dir. sci. N.Y. Bot. Garden, 1974—, also mem. corp.; founder, exec. dir. Orgn. for Flora Neotropica, 1964-76; cons. Jardin Botánico, Santo Domingo, Dominican Republic, Eli Lilly, Warner-Lambert, Tex. Instrument, Nat. Bulk Carriers. Mem. corp. N.Y. Bot. Garden; trustee Mary Cary Arboretum. Recipient Sarah Gildersleeve Fife Meml. award, 1952; David Livingstone centenary medal Am. Geog. Soc., 1965; grantee NSF, Am. Philos. Soc., Guggenheim Found., Explorers Club. Corr. mem. Royal Netherlands Bot. Soc. (hon.); hon. fellow Assn. for Tropical Biology (founder; pres. 1964-65); mem. Orgn. Tropical Studies (founder), Torrey Bot. Club (pres. 1963-64), N.Y. Acad. Scis., Sociedad Venezolana de Ciencias Naturales (hon.), Torrey Bot. Club (pres. 1963-64), AAAS, Bot. Soc. Am., Internat. Soc. Plant Taxonomy, Am. Soc. Plant Taxonomists, Orgn. Flora Neotropica (commn.), Soc. Bot. Dominicana (hon.), Am. Geog. Soc. (hon.), Newcomen Soc. (life), Academia de Ciencias de la Républica Dominicana (founder, mem. biology com.), El Patronato Jardín Botánico Nacional (Santo Domingo, Dominican Republic). Author articles, treatises on Western Am. botany, Neotropics vegetation and geography. Home: 120-24 Dreiser Loop Bronx NY 10475 also Quinta Najayo San Cristobal Dominican Republic Office: NY Botanical Garden Bronx New York NY 10458

MAGUIRE, JOHN DAVID, educator; b. Montgomery, Ala., Aug. 7, 1932; s. John Henry and Clyde (Merrill) M.; A.B. magna cum laude, Washington and Lee U., 1953, LL.D., 1979; Fulbright scholar, Edinburgh (Scotland) U., 1953-54; B.D. summa cum laude, Yale, 1956, Ph.D., 1960; postdoctoral research, Yale U. and U. Tübingen (Germany), 1964-65, Univ. of Calif. at Berkeley, 1968-69, Silliman U., Chinese U., Hong Kong, 1976-77; m. Lillian Louise Parrish, Aug. 29, 1953; children—Catherine Merrill, Mary Elizabeth, Anne King. Acting chaplain Washington and Lee Univ., 1952-53; acting dir. Internat. Student Center, New Haven, 1956-58; asst. in instrn. systematic theology Yale Div. Sch., 1958-59; mem. faculty Wesleyan U., Middletown, Conn., 1960-70, asso. provost, 1967-68; vis. lectr. Pacific School Religion, 1968-69; pres. State U. N.Y. Coll. at Old Westbury, 1970—. Mem. Conn. adv. com. U.S. Commn. Civil Rights, 1961-66; participant White House Conf. on Civil Rights, 1966; permanent trustee and dir. Martin Luther King Center for Social Change, Atlanta, 1968—; pres., bd. dirs. Nassau County Health and Welfare Council, 1971—; trustee L.I. Regional Advisory Council Higher Edn., United Bd. for Christian Edn. in Asia; adviser Danforth Fedn. Grad. Fellowship Selection, China Inst. Am. Recipient Julia A. Archibald High Scholarship award Yale Div. Sch., 1956; Day fellow Yale Grad. Sch., 1956-57, Kent fellow, 1957-60; Howard Found. postdoctoral fellow Brown U. Grad. Sch.. 1964-65; Fenn lectr., 7 Asian countries, 1977; recipient Conn. Prince Hall Masons' award outstanding contbs. human rights in Conn., 1965; E. Harris Harbison Gt. Tchr. prize Danforth Found., 1968. Mem. Soc. Religion Higher Edn. (bd. dirs. 1967—, pres.), Hazen Theol. Discussion Group, Phi Beta Kappa, Omicron Delta Kappa, Democrat. Author: The Dance of the Pilgrim: A Christian Style of Life for Today, 1967; also numerous articles. Home: 223 Store Hill Rd Old Westbury NY 11568

MAGUIRE, JOHN JOSEPH, archbishop; b. N.Y.C., Dec. 11, 1904; s. James and Ellen (Shea) M.; student Cathedral Coll., St. Joseph's Sem., Dunwoodie, Yonkers, N.Y.; LL.D., Fordham U., Manhattan Coll., 1961. Ordained priest Roman Catholic Ch., 1928; asst. St. Patrick's Ch., Manhattan; asst. chancellor Archdiocese of N.Y., 1940-45, vice chancellor, 1945-47, chancellor of Archdiocese, 1947-53, vicar gen., 1953-59; consecrated bishop, 1959; aux. bishop of N.Y., 1959-65; co-adjutor archbishop of N.Y., 1965—; titular bishop of Tabalta. Private chamberlian to Pope Pius XII, 1945—, domestic prelate, 1948—. Address: 460 Madison Ave New York NY 10022*

MAGUIRE, JOHN PATRICK, mfg. co. exec., lawyer; b. New Britain, Conn., Apr. 1, 1917; s. John Patrick and Edna Frances (Cashen) M.; student Holy Cross Coll., 1933-34; degree in bus. adminstrn. with distinction Babson Inst., 1936; A.B. cum laude, Princeton, 1941; LL.B., Yale, 1943; LL.D., St. Bonaventure U., 1970; m. Mary-Emily Jones, Sept. 8, 1945; children—Peter Dunbar, Joan Guilford. Admitted to Conn. bar, 1943, N.Y. bar, 1944; asso. firm Cravath, Swaine & Moore, and predecessor, N.Y.C., 1943-51, 52-54; v.p., dir. Forbes, Inc., also mng. editor Investors Adv. Inst., 1951-52; asst. counsel Gen. Dynamics Corp., 1954-60, sec., 1962—; sec., gen. counsel Tex. Butadiene & Chem. Corp., 1960-62. Bd. govs. N.Y. Young Republican Club, 1951-52; trustee John Burroughs Sch. Mem. Am. Bar Assn., Am. Soc. Corp. Secs., St. Louis Council World Affairs (trustee). Catholic. Clubs: Piping Rock (Locust Valley, L.I.); Univ., Princeton (St. Louis); Tiger Inn, Nassau (Princeton). Home: 38 Briarcliff St Saint Louis MO 63124 Office: Pierre Laclede Center Saint Louis MO 63105

MAGUIRE, JOSEPH F., bishop; b. Sept. 4, 1919; ed. Boston Coll., St. John's Sem., Boston. Ordained priest Roman Catholic Ch., 1945, named monsignor, 1964; successively asst. pastor St. Joseph Ch., Lynn, Mass., St. Anne Ch., Readville, Mass., Blessed Sacrament Ch., Jamaica Plain, Mass., St. Mary Ch., Milton, Mass.; sec. to Cardinal Cushing, Boston, 1962-70, to Archbishop Medeiros, 1970-71; consecrated titular bishop of Macteris and aux. bishop of Boston, 1972-76; apptd. coadjutor bishop of Spring, Mass., 1976-77, succeeded as bishop of Springfield, 1977—; archdiocesan cons., 1968—. Office: Convent of the Good Shepherd 280 Tinkham Rd Springfield MA 01129*

MAGUIRE, ROBERT ALAN, educator; b. Canton, Mass., June 21, 1930; s. Frederick William and Ruth Spalding (Plunkett) M.; A.B., Dartmouth Coll., 1951; M.A., certificate Russian Inst., Columbia U., 1953, Ph.D., 1961. Instr. Russian, Duke U., 1958-60; asst. prof. Russian, Dartmouth Coll., 1960-62; asst. prof. Russian lang. and lit. Columbia U., N.Y.C., 1962-66, asso. prof., 1966-70, prof., 1970—, chmn. dept. Slavic langs., 1977—; vis. lectr. Ind. U., 1961, 66, 69; vis. prof. U. Ill., 1976; vis. fellow St. Anthony's Coll., Oxford (Eng.) U., 1971-72; mem. adv. bd. Sr. Fulbright-Hays Program, 1971-74, Nat. Endowment for Humanities; sponsoring com. Leo Tolstoy Mus. and Research Library, 1979—. Served with U.S. Army, 1953-55. Guggenheim fellow, 1969-70, Am. Council Learned Socs. fellow, 1967, Ford Found. fellow, 1957-58. Mem. Am. Assn. Advancement of Slavic Studies (dir. 1977—), Am. Assn. Tchrs. Slavic and East European Langs., AAUP, MLA, Polish Inst. Arts and Scis., PEN, Kosciuszko Found. Author: Red Virgin Soil: Soviet Literature in the 1920's, 1968; Gogol from the Twentieth Century; Eleven Essays, 1974, and others; co-translator: Petersburg (Andrei Bely), 1978; The Survivor and Other Poems (Tadeusz Rozewicz), 1976; mem. editorial bd. Teaching Lang. through Lit., 1972-77, mng. editor, 1978—; mem. editorial bd. Slavic Rev., 1966-69, Polish Rev., 1979—; mem. editorial adv. bd. Princeton Essays in Literature, 1972-77; contbr. articles to profl. jours. Home: 560 Riverside Dr Apt 20-H New York NY 10027 Office: Dept Slavic Langs Columbia U New York NY 10027. *Emerson's idea that life is a "perfect whole" has guided me for years. Literature is the best record of man's attempts to grasp this whole.*

MAGUIRE, ROBERT EDWARD, pub. utility exec.; b. Somerville, Mass., Jan. 25, 1928; s. Hugh Edward and Alice Theresa (Garrity) M.; B.S. in Chem. Engring., Northeastern U., 1950; B.B.A. in Engring. and Mgmt., 1953; m. Leona Rosemarie Beaulieu, June 21, 1952; children—Lynne Marie, Steven Francis, Judith Anne, David Robert. Supt., Wachusett Gas Co., Leominster, Mass., 1954-58; gen. supt. Lawrence (Mass.) Gas Co., 1958-60, v.p., mgr., 1960-68; v.p., mgr. Mystic Valley Gas Co., Malden, Mass., 1968-70; v.p., regional exec. Mass. Electric Co., North Andover, 1970-71; v.p. New Eng. Power Service Co., Westboro, Mass., 1971-72; New Eng. Electric System, Westboro, 1972-75; exec. v.p. Eastern Utilities Assos., Boston, 1975—. Treas., Lawrence Red Cross, 1966-68; mem. budget com. Greater Lawrence United Fund, 1965-67. Recipient Paul Revere Leadership medal Greater Boston C. of C., 1962. Mem. Greater Lawrence (past pres., Distinguished Service award 1963), Malden (dir. 1969) chambers commerce, Electric Inst. (dir. 1972-75), Am., New Eng. gas assns. Club: Lanam (Andover). Home: 22 Ivy Ln Andover MA 01810 Office: 99 High St Boston MA 02110

MAGWOOD, JOHN MCLEAN, lawyer, orgn. ofcl.; b. Toronto, Ont., Can., Aug. 26, 1912; s. Samuel John Newton and Susannah Maud (McLean) M.; B.A., U. Toronto, 1933, M.A., 1937, LL.B., 1938; m. Doris Rose Johnston, June 18, 1938; children—Beverley Dawn (Mrs. Jamieson), Charles Johnston. Called to Ont. bar, 1936, apptd. Queen's counsel, 1956; practice in Toronto, 1936—; sr. partner firm Magwood, Frith, Pocock, Rogers & O'Callaghan, 1950—. Pres. nat. council YMCA's of Can., 1961-63, vice chmn. nat. bd. YMCA's of U.S.A., 1961-63, hon. v.p., life mem. nat. council; chmn. hon. govs. Toronto YMCA; past pres. Canadian Council for Internat. Cooperation, 1972—; chmn. bd., exec. com. Canadian Exec. Service Overseas, 1977—; trustee Lawrence Park Community Ch. Served to maj. Canadian Army, World War II; mentioned in dispatches. Decorated Can. Centennial medal, 1967, Queen Elizabeth Silver Jubilee medal, 1977. Mem. Canadian Bar Assn., York County Law Assn. (past pres.), Psi Upsilon (past pres.). Clubs: Osler Bluff Ski; Rosedale Golf; Badminton and Racquet, Strollers; University (Toronto). Home: 10 Avoca Ave Toronto ON M4T 2B7 Canada also Creemore ON L0M 1G0 Canada Office: 44 King St W Toronto ON M5H 1E2 Canada

MAGYAR, GABRIEL, cellist; b. Budapest, Hungary, Dec. 5, 1914; s. Samuel and Margaret (Wald) M.; bachelor's degree, Madach Imre Gymnazium, Budapest, 1932; student Nat. Sch. Music, Budapest, 1932; master's degree, Royal Hungarian Franz Liszt Conservatory, Budapest, 1936; m. Julie Dora, July 17, 1952. Came to U.S., 1949, naturalized, 1955. Concert cellist, Europe, 1932-41, S.Am., 1947-49, U.S., 1949—; first performance cello concert Darius Milhaud, Budapest, 1938; tchr., solo cellist, U.S., 1949-56; prof. cello and chamber music U. Okla., 1951-56; cellist Hungarian String Quartet, 1956-72; prof. cello and chamber music U. Ill., Urbana, 1973—; prof. chamber music Colby Coll., summers 1962-72, Banff Art Centre, summers 1972—; rec. artist for Deutsche Grammophon, Pathe, Marconi and Vox records. Recipient Grand Prix du Disque-Paris for Beethoven Quartets. Mem. Phi Mu Alpha Sinfonia (hon.). Home: 708 Dover Pl Champaign IL 61820 Office: care U Ill Urbana IL 61801

MAH, RICHARD SZE HAO, chem. educator; b. Shanghai, China, Dec. 16, 1934; s. Fabian Soh Pai and E. Shang (Chang) M.; came to U.S., 1961, naturalized, 1972; B.Sc., U. Birmingham, 1957; D.I.C., Ph.D. (Leverhulme student), Imperial Coll. Sci. and Tech., U. London, 1961; m. Shopin Stella Lee, Aug. 31, 1962; 1 son, Christopher. Jr. chem. engr. A.P.V. Co., Ltd., Crawley, Sussex, Eng., 1957-58; research fellow U. Minn., 1961-63; research engr. Union Carbide Corp. Tech. Center, South Charleston, W.Va., 1963-67; group head/sr. project analyst Esso Maths. & Systems, Inc., Florham Park, N.J., 1967-72; asso. prof. chem. engring. Northwestern U., Evanston, Ill., 1972-77, prof., 1977—; sec., trustee CACHE Corp., Cambridge, Mass.; cons. Argonne Nat. Lab., 1975-78. Mem. Am. Chem. Soc., Am. Inst. Chem. Engrs. (chmn. systems and process design com. 1978—), Am. Soc. Engring. Edn., Assn. Computing Machinery, Tau Beta Pi. Mem. United Ch. of Christ. Contbr. articles to profl. jours. Home: 1020 Burton Terr Glenview IL 60025 Office: Dept Chem Engring Northwestern U Evanston IL 60201. *Live every day as if it is our last. Each day of life is a marvelous gift of God. Let us count all our blessings and put to use every minute of our day and every resource of our life. Every morning let us marvel at the miraculous world which He has created for us. Every night let us thank God for giving us another day of fulfillment and go to sleep with the expectation of another great day of miracles for tomorrow.*

MAHAFFAY, WILLIAM EDWARD, mech. engr.; s. James W. and Ida (Hyink) M.; B.S., Northwestern U., 1933; m. Carolyn Dahlquist, Oct. 15, 1935; 1 son, John W. Various positions Internat. Harvester Co., 1935-42, plant engr. Refrigeration div., 1942-45, chief engr. advanced engring sect., 1945-51; exec. engr. Whirlpool Corp., St. Joseph, Mich., 1951-53, dir. engring. and research, 1953-56, v.p. engring. and research, 1956-65, group v.p., 1965-70. Dir. Robbins & Myers Inc., Dayton, Ohio, Ranco Inc., Columbus, O. Engring. cons.; adj. prof. U. Mich., 1970—; vis. prof. Purdue. Life regent Northwestern U.; tech. adv. com. Purdue U. Registered engr., Ind. Mem. Am. Soc. Heating, Refrigeration and Air-Conditioning Engrs., ASME, Acacia, Sci. Research Soc. Am., Northwestern U. Alumni Assn., Instrument Soc. Am., Tau Beta Pi, Pi Tau Sigma. Clubs: Union League (Chgo.); Paradise Valley Country (Scottsdale); Racquet (Dayton). Home: 86 Colonia Miramonte Scottsdale AZ 85253

MAHAFFEY, JOHN, profl. golfer; b. Kerrville, Tex., May 9, 1948; B.S. in Psychology, U. Houston, 1970; m. Susan Mahaffey. Nat. Coll. Athletic Assn. champion, 1970; prof., 1971—; winner Sahara Invitational, 1973, Pleasant Valley Classic, 1978, Profl. Golfers Assn. Championship, 1978, Bob Hope Desert Classic, 1979. Office: care Riverhill Country Club Kerrville TX 78028*

MAHAFFEY, MARYANN, city ofcl., social worker; b. Burlington, Iowa, Jan. 18, 1925; d. Kent and Nelle (Widener) Mahaffey; B.A., Cornell Coll., Mt. Vernon, Iowa, 1946; M.S.W., U. So. Calif., 1951; m. Herman Dooha, June 8, 1950; 1 dau., Susan Margaret. Recreation dir. Japanese Relocation Center, Poston, Ariz., 1945, Seattle YWCA, 1946-49, Girl Scouts Met. Detroit and Indpls., 1951-54, Merrill-Palmer Inst., Detroit, 1954-56, 69, United Cerebral Palsy Assn., Chgo., 1956-57, Brightmoor Community Center, 1959-63; program coordinator, social service dir. Detroit Foster Homes project Merrill-Palmer Inst., 1963-65; prof. social work Wayne State U., 1975—; mem. Detroit City Council, 1974—, pres. protem, 1978—; dep. chmn. White House Conf. on Families, 1979. Commr., Detroit Commn. on Children and Youth, 1968-71; exec. com. Urban Alliance, 1968-70; legislative rep., chmn. Mich. Social Work Council, 1965-68; conf. chmn. Nat. Confs. on Foster Care for Emotionally Disturbed Children, 1964-66; v.p. Detroit Fedn. Settlements, 1961-63; chmn. recreation and social services com. Youth Opportunity Council, Detroit, 1967-68; cons. Fedn. for Aid to Dependent Children, 1961-67; chmn. Detroit Mayor's Common Council Task Force on Hunger and Malnutrition, 1970-74; chmn. Gov.'s Nutrition Comm., 1973—. Exec. bd. 17th Dist. Democratic Party, 1969-74; mem. Mich. Dem. Central Com., 1972-74; spokeswoman Mich. Dem. Women's Caucus, 1971-73. Bd. dirs., personnel com. Met. Detroit YWCA, 1972-74; adv. com. Detroit Sexual Assault Center; bd. trustees Eastern Dist. Mich., U.S. Dist. Ct. Pre-Trial Service Agy.; bd. dirs. Group Health Services Orgn.; chmn. Better Health Care Coalition; mem. Mich. Statewide Health Coordinating Council; U.S. del. to Internat. Women's Year conf., Mexico City, 1975. Recipient award of merit Fedn. Aid Dependent Children, 1965, Alumni Achievement award Cornell Coll. Iowa, 1974, Citizenship award Local 22 UAW, 1975, Outstanding Leadership award Detroit chpt. Am. Soc. Women Accountants, 1975; named Detroit Social Worker of Year, 1974, Feminist of Year, Detroit NOW, 1974, One of 10 Most Influential Detroit Women, 1975. Fellow Am. Orthopsychiat. Assn.; mem. Nat. Assn. Social Workers (first woman pres. 1975-77), Nat. Conf. Social Welfare, Coalition Labor Union Women, YWCA, Am. Pub. Welfare Assn., Am. Soc. Pub. Adminstrs., Japanese Am. Citizens League, League Women Voters, Nat. Co. Negro Women (life), Acad. Certified Social Workers (charter), Nat. Women's Polit. Caucus (del. founding conv.), Mich. Women's Polit. Caucus, Am. Fedn. Tchrs., NAACP, ACLU, AAAS, AAUP, NOW, Women's Econ. Office: Detroit City Council Detroit MI 48223

MAHAN, ARCHIE IRVIN, research physicist; b. Portland, Maine, Sept. 1, 1909; s. A.E. and Harriett E. (Lockhart) M.; A.B. Friends U., 1931; student U. Kan., 1932; Ph.D., Johns Hopkins, 1940; m. Frances Ford Beck, Apr. 7, 1941; 1 son, Archie Harvin. Instr. physics Georgetown U., 1939-41; physicist, div. chief Naval Ordnance Lab., 1942-56; sr. and prin. physicist Applied Physics Lab., Johns Hopkins, 1956—; grad. sch. lectr. Georgetown U., 1955, 56; spl. research phys. and geometrical optics. Postdoctoral research program and rev. com. NRC. Recipient merit award Navy Dept., 1943, 50. Fellow Am. Phys. Soc., Optical Soc. Am. (treas. 1962—, bd. dirs. 1962—, asso. editor Jour. 1955—), A.A.A.S., Washington Acad. Scis.; mem. Am. Inst. Physics (bd. dirs. 1962—, exec. com. 1970), Washington Philos. Soc. (pres. 1953). Contbr. numerous articles to profl. jours. Home: 10 Millgrove Pl Ednor MD 20904 Office: Johns Hopkins Rd Laurel MD 20810

MAHAN, HAROLD DEAN, museum exec.; b. Ferndale, Mich., June 11, 1931; s. Elbert Verl and Jo Anna (Upton) M.; B.A., Wayne State U., 1954; M.S., U. Mich., 1957; Ph.D. (NSF fellow), Mich. State U., 1964; m. Mary Jane Gairdner, June 9, 1954; children—Michael, Eric, David, Christopher, Thomas. Instr. biology Central Mich. U., Mt. Pleasant, 1957-60, asst. prof., 1960-64, asso. prof., 1964-68, prof., 1968-73, dir. Center for Cultural and Natural History, 1970-72; dir. Cleve. Mus. Natural History, 1973—; pres. Environ. Enterprises, Inc., Mt. Pleasant; adj. prof. Case Western Res. U., 1973—; resident scientist Museo de Historio Natural, Cali, Colombia, 1968; pres. Midwest Museums Conf., 1974—; pres. Ohio Mus. Assns., 1976—. Mem. Airport Commn., Mt. Pleasant, 1965-68; pres. Mich. Audubon Soc., 1972-73; mem. Ohio Natural Areas Council, 1974—; trustee Shaker Lakes Regional Nature Center; corp. bd. Holden Arboretum; bd. dirs. Greater Cleve. Garden Center, Univ. Circle, Inst. Environ. Edn. Served with USAF, 1950-53. Recipient Louis Agassiz Fuertes Research award, 1957. Mem. Am. Ornithol. Union, Wilson Ornithol. Club, Animal Behavior Soc., Mich. Audubon Soc. (dir., pres.), Sigma Xi, Phi Kappa Phi, Phi Sigma, Phi Delta Kappa, Beta Beta Beta. Unitarian. Clubs: Cleve. Playhouse; Rowfant; Explorers (N.Y.C.). Author: (with George J. Wallace) An Introduction to Ornithology, 1975. Editor: The Jack Pine Warbler, 1965-71; nature columnist Cleve. Press, 1973-74; book rev. editor: Explorer Mag., 1974—, contbr. articles to profl. jours. Home: 28050 Gates Mills Blvd Pepper Pike OH 44124 Office: Cleve Mus Natural History Wade Oval University Circle Cleveland OH 44106

MAHANTHAPPA, KALYANA THIPPERUDRAIAH, educator, physicist; b. Hirehalli, Mysore, India, Oct. 29, 1934; s. Kalyana and Thippamma (Maddanappa) T.; B.Sc., Central Coll. Bangalore, India, 1954; M.Sc., Delhi U., 1956; Ph.D. (Faculty Arts and Scis. fellow), Harvard, 1961; m. Prameela Talkerappa, Oct. 30, 1961; children—Nagesh, Rudresh, Mahesh. Research asso. U. Cal. at Los Angeles, 1961-63; asst. prof. U. Pa., Phila., 1963-66; mem. Inst. Advanced Study, Princeton, N.J., 1964-65; asso. prof. physics U. Colo., Boulder, 1966-69, prof., 1969—, Faculty Research fellow, 1970-71. Cons. Aerojet-Gen., Los Angeles, 1962-63; dir. Summer Inst. Theoretical Physics, Boulder, 1968-69, NATO Advanced Study Inst. in Elem. Particles, 1979. Fellow Am. Phys. Soc.; mem. AAAS, Sigma Xi. Contbr. articles to profl. jours. Research theoretical high energy and elementary particle physics. Home 2865 Darley Ave Boulder CO 80303

MAHARD, RICHARD HAROLD, educator; b. Lawton, Mich., July 5, 1915; s. John William and Mary Luella (Klein) M.; A.B., Eastern Mich. U., 1935; M.A., Columbia, 1941, Ph.D., 1949; m. Marian Janet Neir, June 12, 1938. Instr. geography Eastern Mich. U., 1934-36; grad. asst. Columbia, 1938-41, vis. prof. geology, 1956; with U.S. Geol. Survey, 1946, 49; instr. geology, geography Denison U., 1941-49, asst. prof., 1949-51, asso. prof., 1951-55, prof., 1955—, chmn. dept., 1950-61; vis. prof. geography Stanford, 1952; vis. prof. geology U. Mich., 1958, Columbia, 1956, 61; vis. scholar in polit. geography London Sch. Econs. and Polit. Sci., 1953, 60. Served with AUS, 1945-46. Fellow Geol. Soc. Am., A.A.A.S. (sec. sect. E 1960-68, v.p. and chmn. sect. E 1969-70); mem. Assn. Am. Geographers, Am. Geog. Soc., Nat. Assn. Geology Tchrs. Home: 115 W Elm St PO Box 342 Granville OH 43023

MAHER, ADRIAN WILLIAM, lawyer; b. New Haven, Oct. 5, 1902; s. Edward J. and Mary F. (Mallon) M.; grad. Collegiate Prep. Sch., New Haven; J.D., Ohio No. Law Sch., 1926, LL.D., 1973; m. Rose Florence Dorgan, Dec. 31, 1928; children—Adrian W., James J., Kathleen (Mrs. John F. De-Pledge), Maureen L., Brian Paul, Kevin J. Admitted to Ohio bar, 1926, Conn. bar, 1928, U.S. Supreme Ct. bar; pros. atty. Stratford (Conn.) Municipal Ct., 1933-45; U.S. atty. Dist. of Conn., 1945-53; now practicing in Bridgeport, Conn., mem. firm Maher & Maher. Chmn. Stratford Rationing Bd., 1942-44. Chmn. Conn. Democratic Central Com., 1944-45. Trustee Cardinal Cushing Coll., 1962-72, Milford Acad. 1962-70. Fellow Am. Coll. Trial Lawyers; mem. Am., Conn., Fed., Bridgeport bar assns., Am. Judicature Soc. Democrat. Roman Catholic (trustee). Club: Algonquin (Conn.). Home: 25 Cartright St Bridgeport CT 06604 Office: 955 Main St PO Box 269 Bridgeport CT 06601

MAHER, BRENDAN ARNOLD, psychologist, editor; b. Widnes, Eng., Oct. 31, 1924; s. Thomas F. and Agnes (Power) M.; B.A. with honours, U. Manchester (Eng.), 1950; M.A., Ohio State U., 1951, Ph.D., 1954; student U. Ill. Med. Sch., 1952-53; A.M. (hon.), Harvard, 1972; m. Winifred Barbara Brown, Aug. 27, 1952; children—Rebecca, Thomas, Nicholas, Liam, Niall. Came to U.S., 1955. Psychologist Her Majesty's Prison, Wakefield, Eng., 1954-55; instr. Ohio State U., 1955-56; asst. prof. Northwestern U., 1956-58; asso. prof. La. State U., 1958-60; lectr. Harvard, 1960-64, chmn. Center Research Personality, 1962-64; prof. U. Wis., 1964-67; vis. fellow U. Copenhagen, 1966-67, vis. fellow and research scientist, 1979, prof. psychology Brandeis U., 1967-72, dean Grad. Sch., 1969-71, dean faculty, 1971-72; prof. Harvard, 1972—, chmn. dept. psychology and social relations, 1973-78; asso. psychologist McLean Hosp., Belmont, Mass., 1968-77, psychologist, 1977—; cons. in medicine Peter Bent Brigham Hosp., Boston, 1977—; cons. in psychology Mass. Gen. Hosp., 1977—. Served with Brit. Royal Navy, 1943-47. Diplomate Am. Bd. Examiners in Profl. Psychology. Fellow Am. Psychol. Assn., AAAS; mem. Am. Eastern, Brit. psychol. assns. Author: Principles of Psychopathology, 1966; Introduction to Research in Psychopathology, 1970; editor: Progress in Experimental Personality Research, 1964—; Jour. Cons. and Clin. Psychology, 1972-78; cons. editor Jour. Cons. Clin. Psychology, Jour. Abnormal Psychology, Contemporary Psychology, Behavior Therapy. Office: William James Hall Harvard U Cambridge MA 02138

MAHER, FRANK THOMAS, physician; b. East St. Louis, Ill., Sept. 23, 1909; s. Richard Patrick and Mabel (Holliday) M.; student Ill. Coll., Jacksonville, 1932-33; B.S. with high honors, U. Ill., 1937, M.S., 1938, Ph.D., 1941, M.D. with high honors, 1947; m. Lucille Marie Quirk, Nov. 15, 1941; 1 son, Terence James. Asst. prof. pharmacology U. Ill., 1943-47, prof. pharmacognosy and pharmacology, head dept., 1948-53; asst. dean pharmacy, 1949-53; Mayo Clinic research asso., 1947-48; cons. Mayo Clinic, asso. prof. pharmacology Mayo Found., U. Minn., 1953-63, prof. pharmacology, 1962—, prof. pharmacology and lab. medicine Mayo Med. Sch., 1972-74, ret., 1974. Del. to U.S. Pharmacopoeial Conv., Washington, 1950. Mem. A.M.A., Minn. Med. Assn., Am. Heart Assn., Internat. Soc. Nephrologists, Am. Soc. Nephrology, Soc. Nuclear Medicine, A.C.P., Soc. Exptl. Pathology, Sigma Xi, Alpha Omega Alpha, Rho Chi, Phi Beta Pi, Kappa Psi. Author monograph: The Reticulo-Endothelial System in Sulfonamide Activity, 1944. Home: 815 10th St SW Rochester MN 55901

MAHER, JOHN RICHARD, advt. agy. exec.; b. N.Y.C., Mar. 9, 1932; s. Edgar F. and Frances A. (O'Darwell) M.; A.B., U. Notre Dame, 1953; m. Marilyn R. Brink, Nov. 28, 1958; children—Molly Ann, Mary F., Kathleen M. Account supr. Benton & Bowles, N.Y.C., 1963-67; advt. dir. Continental Airlines, Los Angeles, 1967-69, asst. v.p. market service, 1969-71, v.p. market planning, 1971-74; sr. v.p., group account dir. J. Walter Thompson Co., N.Y.C., 1974-76, sr. v.p., gen. mgr., Washington, 1976—; asst. prof. Georgetown U.; mem. adv. com. Internat. Mgmt. Devel. Inst. Chmn. communications com. Alliance to Save Energy; bd. dirs. USO. Served with USN, 1953-56. Roman Catholic. Clubs: Aspetuck Valley Country, Regency Racquet. Office: 1156 15th St NW Washington DC 20005*

MAHER, LEO THOMAS, bishop; b. Mt. Union, Iowa, July 1, 1915; s. Thomas and Mary (Teberg) M.; ed. St. Joseph's Coll., Mountain View, Calif., also St. Patrick's Sem., Menlo Park, Calif. Ordained priest Roman Catholic Ch.; asst. pastor in San Francisco, 1944-47; sec. archbishop of San Francisco, 1947-61; chancellor Archdiocese San Francisco, 1956-62, dir. vocations, 1957-62, archdiocesan consultor, 1959-62; apptd. domestic prelate, 1954; bishop Santa Rosa, Calif., 1962-69; 3d bishop of San Diego, 1969—; prior Western Lieutenancy of Knights and Ladies of Holy Sepulchre. Bd. dirs. Soc. Propagation of Faith, Youth's Director, Cath. Youth Orgn.; chmn. bd. trustees U. San Diego. Del. Ecumenical Council, Rome, Italy, 1962, 63, 64, 65. Home: 2031 Sunset Blvd San Diego CA 92103 Office: Diocesan Office Alcala Park San Diego CA 92110

MAHER, LOUIS JAMES, JR., geologist, educator; b. Iowa City, Iowa, Dec. 18, 1933; s. Louis James and Edith Marie (Ham) M.; B.A., U. Iowa, 1955, M.S., 1959; Ph.D., U. Minn., 1961; m. Elizabeth Jane Crawford, June 7, 1956; children—Louis James, Robert Crawford, Barbara Ruth. Mem. faculty dept. geology and geophysics U. Wis.-Madison, 1962—, prof., 1970—. Served with U.S. Army, 1956-58. Danforth fellow, 1955-61; NSF fellow, 1959-61; NATO fellow, 1961-62. Fellow AAAS, Geol. Soc. Am.; mem. Am. Quaternary Assn., Ecol. Soc. Am., Wis. Acad. Sci., Arts and Letters, Sigma Xi. Episcopalian. Contbr. articles to profl. jours. Office: Dept Geology and Geophysics U Wis Madison WI 53706

MAHER, PATRICK JOSEPH, utility co. exec.; b. Dublin, Ireland, Apr. 20, 1936; s. Pierce Albeus and Mary (Brady) M.; came to U.S., 1946, naturalized, 1955; B.B.A. in Fin., Iona Coll., 1959; M.B.A. in Banking and Fin., N.Y. U., 1965; m. Catherine M. Sullivan, Oct. 13, 1962; children—Kathy, Kevin, Erin, Megan. With spl. devel. program Chase Manhattan Bank, N.Y.C., 1961-64, 2d v.p. fiduciary dept., 1964-68; asst. v.p. Nat. Comml. Bank, Albany, N.Y., 1968-70; chief sect. utility fin. N.Y. State Pub. Service Commn., Albany, 1970-74; v.p., chief fin. officer Washington Gas Light Co., 1974—. Served with USAR, 1960-61. Mem. Fin. Mgmt. Assn., Am. Gas Assn., Nat. Soc. Rate of Return Analysts. Roman Catholic. Club: N.Y. Athletic. Home: Route 2 Box 166-H Leesburg VA 22075 Office: 1100 H St NW Washington DC 20080

MAHER, PETER SUTTON, bank exec.; b. Boston, Apr. 8, 1944; s. Frank Barry and Josephine Virginia (Loveday) M.; B.A., Yale U., 1966; M.B.A., Harvard U., 1969; m. Martha Burke, 1966; children—Melissa, Meredith, Martha. With State St. Bank & Trust Co., Boston, 1970—, v.p., 1973-76, sr. v.p., treas., 1976-77, exec. v.p. comml. banking group State St. Boston Corp., 1978—, chmn. State St. Bank Boston Internat., 1977—; dir. Ky. Mortgage Co. Trustee, Roxbury (Mass.) Latin Sch., 1978—. Served with USCGR, 1966-72. Mem. Fin. Execs. Insts., Assn. Res. City Bankers. Home: 5 Russell Rd Duxbury MA 02332 Office: State St Bank & Trust Co 225 Franklin St Boston MA 02110

MAHER, ROBERT FRANCIS, anthropologist, educator; b. Eldora, Iowa, July 14, 1922; s. John Ralph and Alice (Anderson) M.; B.S., U. Wis., 1948, M.S., 1950, Ph.D., 1958; m. Lisa Erika Lellep, Jan. 7, 1957; children—Kevin, Mark, Michael, Eve. Sr. Fulbright research scholar U. Philippines, 1960-61; instr. U. Wis., Milw., 1953-54; instr. DePauw U., Greencastle, Ind., 1956-57; with dept. anthropology Western Mich. U., Kalamazoo, 1957—, prof., 1966—, chmn. dept., 1966-71, 73-74; research asso. Nat. Mus. Philippines, 1973, 76, 78. Served with AUS, 1942-46; ETO. Recipient Genevieve Gorst Herfurth award for publ. in social sci. U. Wis., 1961. Ford fellow, 1954-55, Knapp fellow, 1955-56. Mem. Am. Anthrop. Assn., Soc. for Am. Archeology, Central States Anthrop. Soc. (exec. bd. 1973-76, v.p. 1977, pres. 1979-80), Phi Kappa Phi. Author: New Men of Papua, 1961; (with Claude S. Phillips Jr.) Cultural Evolution of Asia and North Africa, 1973. Home: 3315 W Michigan Ave Kalamazoo MI 49007

MAHER, TRAFFORD PATRICK, educator; b. Platte Center, Neb., Mar. 17, 1914; s. Thomas M. and Edna Patrick (Smith) M.; student Creighton U., 1930-32; A.M., St. Louis U., 1939; postgrad. U. Minn., 1949; Ph.D., Catholic U. Am., 1952. Joined Soc. Jesus, 1932; ordained priest Roman Catholic Ch., 1946; tchr. Campion High Sch., Prarie du Chien, Wis., Regis High Sch., Denver, 1939-42, Creighton U. High Sch., Omaha, 1942-43, Cath. U. Am., 1943-57; dir. dept. edn. St. Louis U., 1957-68, trustee, 1963-67, dir. Human Relations Center, 1954-73, Fordyce House Conf. Center, 1973-75, affirmative action officer, 1975—. Ednl. cons. Nat. Conf. Christians and Jews, 1957—, trustee, 1972—; chmn. Mo. Commn. on Human Rights, 1958-61; chmn. Mo. adv. com. to Fed. Civil Rights Commn., 1962—; pres. Mo. Assn. Social Welfare. Adv. bd. Med. Schs. Eastern Va.; trustee Ednl. Found. of Licensed Practical Nurses; bd. dirs. Nat. Conf. Christians and Jews. Named Man of Year Internat. Frontiers, 1963. Mem. Social Health Assn. Mo. (v.p.), Nat. Social Health Assn. (dir.), Nat. Workshop Policy Commn. (dir., mem. exec. com.), Nat. Assn. Intergroup Edn. Ofcls. (dir.), Am. Personnel and Guidance Assn., Nat., Adult edn. assns., Assn. for Supervision and Curriculum Devel., Soc. for Study Social Problems, Am. Acad. Polit. and Social Scis. Author: Lest We Build on Sand, 1962; Urban Renewal and Social Renovation, 1963; Self-A Measurless Sea, 1966; Religious Education for a Lunar Age, 1972. Home: 221 N Grand Ave St Louis MO 63103. *As a person, a professional, a professor, and a Jesuit priest, my life has been motivated and guided by a neverending echo in my ear: "And the second law is like the first, one must love his neighbor as himself." Who is one's neighbor? Every fellow human being. A human being can communicate in a caring and healing manner in direct proportion to how he can love. Love is the answer! The state of love exists when one practically cares enough to want another to grow. Christ said: Love!. . . I've tried to incorporate these two realities into my life in seeking professionally—and as a priest—the total area of human relations: human rights and civil rights.*

MAHESH, VIRENDRA BUSHAN, endocrinologist; b. India, Apr. 25, 1932; s. Narinjan Prasad and Sobhagyawati; came to U.S., 1958, naturalized, 1968; B.Sc. with honors, Patna U., India, 1951; M.Sc. in Chemistry, Delhi U., India, 1953, Ph.D., 1955; D.Phil. in Biol. Sci., Oxford U., 1958; m. Sushila Kumari Aggarwal, June 29, 1955; children—Anita Rani, Vinit Kumar. James Hudson Brown Meml. fellow Yale U., 1958-59; asst. research prof. endocrinology Med. Coll. Ga., Augusta, 1959-63, asso. research prof. endocrinology, 1963-66, prof., 1966-70, Regents prof., 1970-79, Robert B. Greenblatt prof., 1979—, chmn. endocrinology, 1972—; dir. Center for Population Studies, 1971—; mem. reproductive biology study sect. NIH, 1977-81. Recipient Rubin award Am. Soc. Study of Sterility, 1963; Billings Silver medal, 1965; NIH research grantee, 1960—. Mem. Chem. Soc. (Eng.), Biochem. Soc. (Eng.), Endocrine Soc., Soc. Biol. Chemists, Soc. for Gynecologic Investigation, Internat. Soc. Neuroendocrinology, Soc. for Study Reproduction, Am. Physiol. Soc., Internat. Soc. Reproductive Medicine (pres. 1980—), Soc. Exptl. Biology and Medicine, Am. Fertility Soc., Am. Assn. Lab. Animal Sci., N.Y. Acad. Scis., AAUP, Sigma Xi. Contbr. articles to profl. jours., chpts. to books; mem. editorial bd. Steroids, 1963—, Jour. of Clin. Endocrinologic Metabolism, 1976-81; mem. adv. bd. Maturitas, 1977—. Office: Dept Endocrinology Medical College of Georgia Augusta GA 30912

MAHEY, JOHN ANDREW, museum dir.; b. DuBois, Pa., Mar. 30, 1932; s. Manasseh A. and Bernyce (Holdar) M.; student Columbia U., 1950-52; B.A., Pa. State U., 1959, M.A., 1962. Asst. dir. Peale Mus., Balt., 1964-69; dir. E.B. Crocker Art Gallery, 1969-72, Cummer Gallery of Art, 1972-75, Meml. Art Gallery of U. Rochester, 1975-79; chief curator Philbrook Art Center, Tulsa, 1979—. Served with USAF, 1952-57, 62-64. Fulbright scholar, 1962. Mem. Assn. Art Mus. Dirs., Am. Assn. Museums, Mus. Assn. N.Y. State, Arts Council of Rochester, Phi Beta Kappa, Phi Alpha Theta. Contbr. articles on artists to art his. jours.; author exhbn. catalogs. Home: 4160 S Rockford Pl Tulsa OK 74105

MAHIN, CHARLES BOYD, lawyer; b. Cheney, Kans., Jan. 13, 1908; s. Charles Albert and Amy Irene (McIntire) M.; A.B., Wichita State U., 1929; J.D., U. Chgo., 1935; m. Wanda Fern Spray, May 30, 1936; children—Charles Douglas, Linda Ruth Mahin Boundy. High sch. prin., Burrton, Kans., 1931-34; admitted to Ill. bar, 1936; partner firm Keck, Mahin & Cate, Chgo., 1950—; dir. Edward Hines Lumber Co., Clow Corp. Served to lt. col. USAAF, 1941-46. Decorated Legion of Merit. Mem. Am., Ill., Chgo., 7th Circuit bar assns., U.S. C. of C. (past chmn. secondary boycott subcom.), Order of Coif. Clubs: Hinsdale Golf (past pres., dir.); Sea Pines Plantation; Union League, Met. (Chgo.). Home: 735 Cleveland Rd Hinsdale IL 60521 Office: 8300 Sears Tower 233 S Wacker Dr Chicago IL 60606

MAHL, GEORGE FRANKLIN, educator, psychoanalyst, psychologist; b. Akron, Ohio, Nov. 27, 1917; s. Floyd Alexander and Margaret (Strecker) M.; A. B., Oberlin Coll., 1939, M.A., 1941; Ph.D., Yale, 1948; certificate Western New Eng. Inst. Psychoanalysis, 1962; m. Martha Jane Fenn, Jan. 10, 1944; 1 dau., Barbara Jessica. Asst. psychology Oberlin Coll., 1939-41; research asst. psychology Yale, 1941-42, mem. faculty, 1947—, prof. psychology 1964—; tchr. Western New Eng. Inst. Psychoanalysis, 1961—, pres., 1972-74. Served to 1st lt. AUS, 1942-46. Fellow Am. Psychol. Assn., A.A.A.S.; mem. Eastern Psychol. Assn., Western New Eng. Inst. Psychoanalysis, Western New Eng. Psychoanalytic Soc. Home: 106 Bayard Ave North Haven CT 06518 Office: 25 Park St New Haven CT 06519

MAHLER, HARRY BEZ, architect; b. Upper Montclair, N.J., Aug. 8, 1928; s. Harry A. and Pauline Marie (Bez) M.; B.Arch., Columbia, 1954, William K. Fellows fellow, 1954-55; m. Elizabeth Willett, Oct. 2, 1954; children—Debra, Steven, Suzanne. Successively draftsman, designer, chief designer, asso., partner for design The Grad Partnership, Newark, 1949—; adj. prof., curriculum coordinator design and drawing Pratt Inst.; adv. com., chmn. fee com. N.J. Sch. Architecture. Former commr., chmn. Montclair Redevel. Agy. Chmn. barrier free architecture com. Easter Seal Soc. N.J.; pres. N.J. Zool. Soc. Served with Signal Corps, U.S. Army, 1946-48. Recipient archtl. awards AIA, Illuminating Engrs. Soc., N.J. Soc. Architects, Bell System, Am. Concrete Inst., N.J. Bus. Mag. Fellow AIA; mem. AIA (pres. design com.), N.J. Soc. Architects, Beta Theta Pi. Methodist. Contbr. articles to profl. jours. Home: 214 Highland Ave Upper Montclair NJ 07043 Office: The Grad Partnership Gateway One Newark NJ 07102

MAHLER, HENRY RALPH, educator, biochemist; b. Vienna, Austria, Nov. 12, 1921; s. Hans and Elly (Schulhof) M.; came to U.S., 1938, naturalized, 1944; A.B., Swarthmore Coll., 1943; Ph.D., U. Calif. at Berkeley, 1948; m. Annemarie Ettinger, Feb. 2, 1948; children—Anthony J., Andrew M., Barbara A. Sr. chemist Tex. Research Found., 1948-49; research asso. U. Wis., Madison, 1949, 50, asst. prof., 1950-55; faculty Ind. U., Bloomington, 1955—, prof. chemistry, 1957-66, research prof., 1966; Rockefeller Found. Spl. fellow, vis. prof. U. Sao Paulo (Brazil), 1966—; vis. investigator Centre de Génétique Moléculaire, Gif-sur-Yvette, France, 1962-63, 69-70, 77; vis. prof. U. Paris, 1970, University Coll., London, 1976, U. Vienna, 1977; vis. investigator, mem. corp. Marine Biol. Lab., Woods Hole, Mass., 1960—. Mem. biochemistry study sect. NIH, 1967-71, mental retardation research tng. com., 1971-74. Recipient Research Career award NIH, USPHS, 1962—, NSF Travel award, 1955, 61. Mem. Am. Soc. Biol. Chemists, Biochem. Soc. (London, Eng.), AAAS, Am. Chem. Soc., Biophys. Soc., Soc. Cell Biology, Internat., Am. socs. neurochemistry, Sigma Xi. Author: (with E.H. Cordes) Biological Chemistry, 2d edit., 1971; Basic Biological Chemistry, 1968; also numerous articles. Mem.-editorial bd. Jour. of Neurochemistry, Jour. of Theoretical Biology, Plasmid. Research on isolation, modes action, biosynthesis respiratory enzymes, formation, integration in respiratory particles, control and mechanisms mitochondrial mutations, nucleic acids, role macromolecular synthesis in formation and modification of synapses. Home: 1880 Covenanter Dr Bloomington IN 47401

MAHLMANN, JOHN JAMES, assn. exec.; b. Washington, Jan. 21, 1942; s. Charles Victor and Mary Elizabeth (Deye) M.; B.F.A., Boston U., 1962, M.F.A., 1963; postgrad. U. Notre Dame, summer 1962; Ed.D., Pa. State U., 1970; m. Ning Ning Chang, Feb. 5, 1972; 1 son, Justin Geeng Ming. Grad. asst. Boston U., 1962-63, instr., supr. student tchrs., dir. masters degree candidates, 1964-66; grad. asst., research asst. Pa. State U., 1963-64, instr., 1966-67, dir. gallery, art edn. dept., 1966-67; asst. prof. Tex. Tech U., 1967-69, chmn. tenure and promotions com.; dir. publs., asst. exec. sec. Nat. Art Edn. Assn., Washington, 1969-71, exec. sec., 1971—, also tour dir. to Japan and Orient; instr. drawing Lubbock Art Assn.; asst. debate coach, asst. coordinator forensics Boston U.; exhibited at Boston U., Pa. State U., Harvard, Tex. Tech. U., Salem (Mass.) State Coll., Botolph Gallery, Boston, Inst. Contemporary Art, Boston, Barncellar Gallery, Orleans, Mass., State Gallery, State College, Pa., Halls Gallery, Lubbock, Lubbock Art Assn., Loft Gallery, San Antonio, Llano Estacado Art Assn., Hobbs, N.M., Purdue U., Cushing Gallery, Dallas, Religious Art Exhbn., Cranbrook Acad. Art, Bloomfield Hills, Mich., Upstairs Gallery, Arlington, Tex., S.W. Tex. State Coll., San Marcos. Mem. Nat. Art Edn. Assn., Am., Washington socs. assn. execs., Phi Delta Kappa. Editor: Art Education, 1970—, Art Teacher, 1971—. Contbr. articles to mags. Home: 11702 Indian Ridge Rd Reston VA 22070 Office: 1201 16th St NW Washington DC 20036

MAHLSTEDT, WALTER, ins. co. exec.; b. N.Y.C., Sept. 20, 1910; s. Frederick and Catherine (Buell) M.; student pub. schs. N.Y.C.; m. Catherine Hoffman, June 5, 1937; children—Frederick, Robert. With Tchrs. Ins. and Annuity Assn. Am., N.Y.C., 1929—, exec. v.p. investments, 1967-75, trustee, 1970—, chmn. finance com., 1972—; dir. Heitman Realty Fund, 1975-76; mem. investment adv. panel Pension Benefit Guaranty Corp., 1975—. Trustee, chmn. investment com. Devereux Found., Devon, Pa. Fellow Life Office Mgmt. Assn. Club: Hyannis Yacht (Mass.). Home: 160 W Clinton Ave Tenafly NJ 07670 Office: 730 3d Av New York NY 10017

MAHMOUD, ALY AHMED, educator; b. Cairo, Jan. 25, 1935; s. Ahmed Aly and Amina Mohammed (Rashwan) M.; came to U.S., 1960, naturalized, 1970; B.Sc. with distinction and honors (Nat. Honor student) Ain Shams U., Cairo, 1958; M.S., Purdue U., 1961, Ph.D., 1964; m. Lucinda Lou Keller, Dec. 20, 1962; children—Ramy, Samy. Instr. elec. engring. Ain Shams U., 1958-60; asst, prof. elec. engring. U. N.B., Fredericton, 1964; research engr. No. Electric Research and Devel. Lab., Ottawa, Ont., Can., summer 1964; asst. prof. elec. engring. U. Asyut (Egypt), 1964-66; sr. research elec. engr. Naval Civil Engring. Lab., Port Hueneme, Calif., 1968-69, summer 1970; asst. prof. elec. engring. U. Mo., Columbia, 1966-71, asso. prof., 1971-73, prof., 1973-76; prof. elec. engring., program mgr. Power Affiliates Research Program, supr. Power System Computer Service, Iowa State U., Ames, 1976--; with FPC, summer 1974; program mgr. NSF, 1975-76; cons. in field. Vice chmn. Water and Light Adv. Bd. City of Columbia, 1973—. Am. Friends of Middle East fellow, 1960-68. Mem. IEEE, Power Engring. Soc., Am. Phys. Soc., Egyptian Profl. Engring. Soc., Am. Soc. Engring. Edn., Sigma Xi, Tau Beta Pi, Eta Kappa Nu. Contbr. articles to profl. jours. Patentee in field. Home: 230 Trailridge Rd Ames IA 50010. *In this country there are outstanding opportunities for those who are willing to work hard to serve the society and their profession. I am thankful to be in the U.S. and to have found this type of opportunity.*

MAHON, ELDON BROOKS, U.S. judge; b. Loraine, Tex., Apr. 9, 1918; s. John Bryan and Nola May (Muns) M.; B.A., McMurry Coll., 1939; LL.B., U. Tex., 1942; m. Nova Lee Groom, June 1, 1941; children—Jana, Martha, Brad. Admitted to Tex. bar, 1942; law clk. Tex. Supreme Ct., 1945-46; county atty. Mitchell County, Tex., 1947; dist. atty. 32d Jud. Dist. Tex., 1948-60, dist. judge, 1960-63; v.p. Tex. Electric Service Co., Ft. Worth, 1963-64; practiced law, Abilene, Tex., 1964-68; U.S. atty. No. Dist. Tex., Ft. Worth, 1968; now judge U.S. Dist. Ct. for No. Tex., Ft. Worth. Pres. W. Tex. council Girl Scouts U.S.A., 1966-68. Trustee McMurry Coll. Served with USAAF, 1942-45. Named an outstanding Tex. prosecutor Tex. Law Enforcement Found., 1957. Mem. Am., Fed., Ft.-Worth-Tarrant County bar assns., Am. Judicature Assn., State Bar Tex. Methodist (past del. confs.). Home: 4167 Sarita St Fort Worth TX 76109 Office: US Dist Court 403 US Courthouse Fort Worth TX 76102*

MAHON, JAMES SAMUEL, lawyer; b. Eastland, Tex., Apr. 18, 1920; s. Ralph Dominic and Nora (Hefley) M.; B.B.A., U. Tex., 1943, J.D., 1948; m. Judy French, Jan. 20, 1962; children—Erin, Lorin, Kevin. Admitted to Tex. bar, 1948; asst. dist. atty., Dallas, 1949-50; atty. OPS, Dallas, 1951-53; pvt. practice, Dallas, 1953—; partner firm Mahon, Fitzgerald & Winston, 1970—; lectr. S.W. Inst. Grad. Studies in Banking, 1974—. Served with AUS, 1942-46. Mem. Am., Tex., Dallas bar assns. Democrat. Methodist. Home: 5515 Lobello St Dallas TX 75229 Office: 2430 One Main Pl Dallas TX 75250

MAHON, JOHN KEITH, educator; b. Ottumwa, Iowa, Feb. 8, 1912; s. John Keith and Ellen (Stoltz) M.; B.A., Swarthmore Coll., 1934; Ph.D., U. Calif. at Los Angeles, 1950; m. Enid Pasek, Feb. 28, 1948; 1 son, John Keith III. Sec., treas. Samuel Mahon Co., Ottumwa, 1934-42; civilian mil. historian Office Chief Mil. History, Dept. Army, 1951-54, acting chief organizational history and honors br., 1953-54; interim instr. Colo. A. and M. Coll., 1950, U.S. history U. Calif. at Los Angeles, 1950-51; asst. prof. U. Fla., Gainesville, 1954-60, asso. prof., 1960-66, prof., 1966—, acting chmn. dept. history, 1965-66, chmn., 1966-73, chmn. Faculty Seminar on Am. Civilization, 1965-66; chmn. symposium at Mission Nombre de Dios, St. Augustine, 1966; Harold K. Johnson vis. prof. mil. history U.S. Army Mil. History Inst., 1977-78; dir. Doris Duke project to record oral history of Indians of Southeast U.S. Mem. Fla. Antiquities Com., 1966. Trustee Am. Mil. Inst. Served to capt., F.A., AUS, 1942-46. Recipient Fla. Blue Key Distinguished Faculty award, 1965; U. Fla. research grantee, 1963, award Am. Philos. Soc., 1963, 67, award of merit Am. Assn. for State and Local History, 1968. Mem. Am. Mil. Inst. (trustee, bd. editors), Am., So. hist. assns., Orgn. Am. Historians, AAUP, Fla. Hist. Soc. (bd. editors, dir. 1973—), Phi Alpha Theta. Club: University (Washington). Author: Decade of Decision; History of Second Seminole War; History of the War of 1812, 1971. Contbr. articles profl. jours. Home: 4129 SW 2d Ave Gainesville FL 32601. *A historian must try to do justice to the figures of the past, inasmuch as they rarely receive justice while alive.*

MAHON, MALACHY THOMAS, legal educator; b. N.Y.C., Jan. 4, 1934; s. James and Alice (Rooney) M.; B.A., Manhattan Coll., 1954; J.D., Fordham U., 1960; m. Margaret Phyllis Kirwan, Jan. 25, 1958; children—Veronica, Laura, Malachy. Admitted to N.Y. bar, 1960; law clk. to Chief Magistrate John M. Murtagh, N.Y.C., 1959-60, U.S. Supreme Ct. Justice Tom C. Clark, 1960-61; asso. law firm Hale Russell & Stentzel, N.Y.C., 1961-62, Mudge Rose Guthrie & Alexander, N.Y.C., 1979—; prof. Fordham U. Law Sch., 1962-68; prof. law Hofstra U. Law Sch., 1968—, dean, 1968-73; vis. prof. U. Tex. Law Sch., 1973-74; exec. dir., spl. N.Y. State asst. atty. gen. Meyer Investigation Spl. Attica Prosecutor's Office, 1975. Chief counsel N.Y. Gov.'s Spl. Com. on Criminal Offenders, 1966. Served with AUS, 1954-56. Mem. Am. Law Inst., N.Y. State, Am. bar assns., Assn. of Bar of City N.Y., Inst. Judicial Adminstrn. Staff author Mental Illness, Due Process and the Criminal Defendant, 1968; monthly columnist N.Y. Law Jour., 1976-78. Home: 45 Thornwood Lane Roslyn Heights NY 11577 Office: Hofstra U Law Sch Hempstead NY 11550

MAHONEY, SISTER COLETTE, coll. pres., biologist; b. Jamaica, N.Y., July 19, 1926; d. Timothy and Lillian (Boylan) M.; B.S., Marymount Coll., 1949, LL.D. (hon.), 1973; M.S., Fordham U., 1952, Ph.D., 1961; H.H.D. (hon.), St. Francis de Sales, 1974. Joined Religious of Sacred Heart of Mary, 1945; tchr. biology Acad. Sacred Heart of Mary, N.Y.C., 1947-57, prin., 1965-67; instr. biology Marymount Coll., Arlington, Va., 1957-61, also chmn. sci. dept.; asso. prof. biology Marymount Coll., Tarrytown, N.Y., 1961-65; pres., trustee Marymount Manhattan Coll., N.Y.C., 1967—; dir. Dollar Savs. Bank, Manhattan Life Ins. Co., Jack Lenor Larsen, Inc.; mem. ex-officio steering council Good Housekeeping. Mem. Pres.'s Adv. Com. on Econ. Role of Women, 1973-74; mem. Regent's Regional Coordinating Council of N.Y.C., Women's Coll. Coalition; bd. advisers China Inst. in Am., Inc.; bd. dirs. Inst. for Mediation and Conflict Resolution, N.Y. Council Higher Edn., Council Higher Edn. N.Y.C., Marymount Secondary sch. N.Y., Yorkville Civic Council, Council for Career Planning, Inc.; pres. Women's Forum; trustee Coll. Boca Raton, Mt. St. Mary's Coll. Recipient Extraordinary Woman of Achievement award NCCJ, 1978; decorated cavaliere Order of Merit (Italy), 1978. Fellow AAUW; mem. Commn. on Religion in Higher Edn., Am. Inst. Biol. Scis., N.Y. Acad. Scis., N.Y. Bus. and Profl. Women's Assn., N.Y. State Legis. Inst. Contbr. articles on biology to sci. publs. Home: 221 E 71st St New York City NY 10021

MAHONEY, DAVID, corp. exec.; b. N.Y.C., May 17, 1923; s. David J. and Laurette (Cahill) M.; grad. LaSalle Mil. Acad., 1941; B.S., U. Pa., 1945; student Columbia, 1946-47; LL.D., Manhattan Coll.; m. Barbara A. Moore, May 12, 1951 (dec.); children—David Joseph III, Barbara; m. 2d, Hildegarde Ercklentz Merrill, June 24, 1978. Advt. v.p. Ruthrauff & Ryan, Inc., N.Y.C., 1949-51; founder, pres. David J. Mahoney, Inc., N.Y.C., 1951-56, also dir.; pres., dir. Good Humor Corp., 1956-61; exec. v.p., dir. Colgate Palmolive Co., 1961-66; pres., chief exec. officer Canada Dry Corp., 1966-68; pres. Norton Simon, Inc., 1968-69, pres., dir., chief exec. officer, 1969-77, chmn. bd., chief exec. officer, 1970—; dir. N.Y. Telephone Co. Chmn. Am. Revolution Bicentennial Commn., 1970. Chmn. bd. trustees Am. Health Found.; chmn. bd. dirs. Phoenix House, Charles A. Dana Found.; bd. dirs. Nat. Urban League; trustee Tuskegee Inst., U. Pa. Recipient Torch of Liberty award Anti-Defamation League, 1970, Patriot's award Congl. Medal of Honor Soc., 1972, Applause award Sales Exec. Club, 1973, U.S. Marines Leatherneck award, 1975, Corporate Leadership award Girl Scouts, 1976, Horatio Alger award, 1977, Nat. Brotherhood award NCCJ, 1979; named Man of Year Advt. Age, 1972, Man of Year Wharton Sch. Bus., 1972, Hon. mem. Boys Club N.Y. Alumni Assn., 1978. Mem. Young Pres.'s Orgn. Office: Norton Simon Inc 277 Park Ave New York NY 10017

MAHONEY, EDWARD MAURICE, mut. fund exec.; b. Cedar Rapids, Nebr., Jan. 7, 1930; s. Maurice J. and Anna Marie (Walla) M.; Ph.B., U. Notre Dame, 1952; m. Catherine Buechter, June 9, 1952; children—Kathy, Janie, Debbie, Patty, Terry, Sharon, Tim. With Fin. Programs, Inc., Denver, 1955-71, v.p., 1965-71; v.p. St. Paul Investors Co., Mpls., 1971-74, pres., 1974—, also dir.; pres., dir. St. Paul Securities, Inc., St. Paul Advisers, Inc. Served to lt. (j.g.) USNR, 1952-55. Mem. Sales Mktg. Execs. Roman Catholic. Clubs: Lafayette (gov.) (Mpls.); K.C. Home: 2760 Pheasant Rd Excelsior MN 55331 Office: Box 43284 Saint Paul MN 55164

MAHONEY, GERARD MICHAEL, univ. pres.; b. Bklyn., Feb. 23, 1933; s. Michael and Barbara (Schmitt) M.; B.A., Mary Immaculate Sem. and Coll., Northampton, Pa., 1957, postgrad., 1957-61; J.C.B., Catholic U. Am., 1962, J.C.L., 1963, J.C.D., 1964. Joined Congregation of Mission, Roman Catholic Ch., 1947, ordained priest, 1961; spiritual dir., prof. theology and canon law Sem. Our Lady of Angels, Albany, N.Y., 1964-66; dir. scholastics, prof. theology and canon law Mary Immaculate Sem. and Coll., 1966-69, part-time lectr., 1969-75; dir. novices St. Vincent's Sem., Phila., 1969-75; superior Vicentian Residence, Niagara Falls, N.Y., 1975-76, part-time lectr. Niagara (N.Y.) U., 1975-76, pres., chmn. trustees, 1976—; mem. provincial council Eastern province Congregation of Mission, 1970—, chmn. commn. formation and membership gen. assembly, 1974, superior gen. preparatory commn. gen. assembly, 1974; mem. med.-moral ethics com. Roman Cath. Diocese, also pro-syndal examiner; mem. Commn. Ind. Colls. and Univs. Task Force; chmn. Western N.Y. Consortium Higher Edn. Trustee Congregation of Mission of St. Vincent de Paul, Germantown, Pa., St. John's U., N.Y.C.; bd. dirs. Niagara Falls chpt. ARC; exec. bd. NCCJ. Address: Niagara Univ Niagara University NY 14109

MAHONEY, J. DANIEL, chmn. N.Y. State Conservative Party; b. Orange, N.J., Sept. 7, 1931; s. Daniel Vincent and Louisa (Dunbar) M.; B.A. magna cum laude, St. Bonaventure U., 1952; LL.B. (Kent scholar), Columbia U., 1955; m. Kathleen Mary O'Doherty, Oct. 22, 1955; children—John Daniel, Kieran Vincent, Francis Kirk, Mary Louisa, Eileen Ann, Elizabeth. Admitted to N.Y. State bar, 1960; asso. firm Simpson Thatcher & Bartlett, N.Y.C., 1958-62; partner firm Wormser, Keily, Alessandroni, Mahoney & McCann, N.Y.C., 1965-74; partner firm Windels, Manx, Davies & Ives, N.Y.C., 1974—; state chmn. N.Y. Conservative Party, 1962—; dir. Nat. Rev., Inc., N.Y.C., 1972—. Mem. nat. adv. bd. Young Ams. for Freedom, 1964—. Served to lt. (j.g.) USCGR, 1955-58. Roman Catholic. Author: Actions Speak Louder, The Story of the New York Conservative Party, 1967. Home: 264 Hardscrabble Rd Briarcliff Manor NY 10510 Office: 51 W 51st St New York NY 10019

MAHONEY, JAMES OWEN, educator, mural painter; b. Dallas, Oct. 16, 1907; s. James Owen and Lacy Edna (Braden) M.; B.A., So. Meth. U., 1929; B.F.A., Yale, 1932; fellow in painting Am. Acad. Rome, 1932-35. Mem. faculty Cornell U., 1939—, prof. art, 1954—, chmn. art dept., 1963-68; prin. mural commns. include Hall of State at Tex. Centennial Expn., Dallas, 1936; Hall of Judiciary, Fed. Bldg., also Communications Bldg., all at N.Y. World's Fair, 1938; presdl. suite Adolphus Hotel, Dallas, 1950; Shriver Hall at Johns Hopkins, 1957; altar piece All Saints Episcopal Ch., Chevy Chase, Md., 1958. Fairmont Hotel, Atlanta, 1974. Served to capt. USAAF, World War II; ETO. Recipient Prix de Rome, 1932. Mem. Nat. Soc. Mural Painters. Club: Century Assn. (N.Y.C.). Home: 45 Twin Glens Rd Ithaca NY 14850

MAHONEY, JAMES P., bishop; b. Saskatoon, Sask., Can., Dec. 7, 1927. Ordained priest Roman Catholic Ch., 1952; bishop Saskatoon, 1967—. Office: 106 5th Ave N Saskatoon SK S7K 2NT Canada*

MAHONEY, JOHN F., former coll. adminstr., pub. co. exec.; b. Detroit, May 19, 1929; s. James Frank and Rosine (Mulreney) M.; B.A., U. Detroit, 1950, M.A., 1952; Ph.D., U. N.C., 1956; children—Penelope (Mrs. Charles Goergen), Thomas, Brendan, Mildred. Instr. English, U. N.C., 1952-54; instr. Latin, Duke, 1954-56; asst., then asso. prof. Duquesne U., 1956-61; mem. faculty U. Detroit, 1961—, prof. English, chmn. dept., 1964-69, dean Coll. Arts and Scis., 1969-73; dean Walden U., Naples, Fla., 1973-74; v.p. acad. affairs William Paterson Coll., Wayne, N.J., 1974-79, dean Walden West, La Jolla, Calif., 1978-79; pres. VRI Pub., N.Y.C. and Los Angeles, U-P Laddi Pub. Co., Los Angeles; research dir. B.E.L.I., Redondo Beach, Calif. Columnist, also trustee Am. Grad. Commn. Democratic candidate for sch. bd., Bethel Park, Pa., 1956. Mem. Modern Lang. Assn. Am., Dante Soc. Am., Am. Assn. Higher Edn., Am. Conf. Acad. Deans. Author: Parousia, 1956. Editor: In Honor of U.T. Holmes, 1966; American Author and Critics series, 1959; The Insistent Present, 1970; New Poets, New Music, 1971; New Fiction, Non-Fiction, 1972. Home: 259 Manchester Ave Playa Del Rey CA 90291. *Chaucer remarked, through one of his Knights, that it was a curious, ironic world, wondering what man really did want from it—"now with his love, now in his colde grave/Allone, withouten any compaignye." Administrators all ought keep in mind that medieval version of the most historically uniform of human counsel: "In time, you won't be important, even if now it seems you are." As a balance, a Latin dictum says: Age Quod agis—hard to translate, but "do what you're doing" is close. There's a world yet to invent, but almost as much to learn that the millions before us knew.*

MAHONEY, MARGARET ELLERBE, found. exec.; b. Nashville, Oct. 24, 1924; d. Charles Hallam and Leslie Nelson (Savage) Mahoney; B.A. magna cum laude, Vanderbilt U., 1946. Fgn. affairs officer State Dept., Washington, 1946-53; exec. asso., asso. sec. Carnegie Corp., N.Y.C., 1953-72; v.p. Robert Wood Johnson Found., Princeton, N.J., 1972—; mem. com. on goals and priorities Nat. Bd. Med. Examiners, 1971-73; mem. com. for med. dept. M.I.T.; mem. bd. maternal, child and family health research NRC; vis. fellow Sch. Architecture and Urban Planning, Princeton, 1973—. Mem. Presdl. Task Force on Medicaid and Medicare, 1969-70, Med. Assistance Adv. Council, HEW, 1970-71, health industry adv. com. Phase IV, Cost of Living Council, 1973; adv. mem. Nat. Bur. Econ. Research; mem. task force on edn., tng. and devel. of profl. artists and arts educators Nat. Endowment for Arts; mem. overseers com. to visit univ. health services Harvard. Bd. dirs. Sun Valley Forum on Health, Inc., Nat. Research Inst. for the Arts; trustee Nat. Humanities Center, Dermatology Found., Found. Center; mem. vis. com. on edn. Phila. Mus. Art, 1978—; Mem. Inst. Medicine, AAAS, Council Fgn. Relations, Nat. Trust for Historic Preservation. Club: Cosmopolitan (N.Y.C.). Author: The Arts on Campus, 1970. Contbr. articles profl. publs. Office: Robert Wood Johnson Found PO Box 2316 Princeton NJ 08540

MAHONEY, MICHAEL ROBERT TAYLOR, art historian, educator; b. Worcester, Mass., Jan. 24, 1935; s. Michael J. and Mary (Taylor) M.; grad. Phillips Acad., 1953; B.A., Yale U., 1959; Ph.D., Courtauld Inst., U. London, 1965. Finley fellow Nat. Gallery Art, 1962-64; fellow Harvard Center Italian Studies, Villa I Tatti, 1963; museum curator Nat. Gallery Art, 1964-69, curator sculpture, 1967; prof. fine arts, chmn. dept. Trinity Coll., Hartford, Conn., 1969—, Genevieve Harlow Goodwin prof. fine arts, 1974—. Incorporator, Hartford Pub. Library, 1970—; elector Wadsworth Atheneum, Hartford, 1974—. Trustee Cesare Barbieri Found., Trinity Coll., 1977—. Club: The Club (Farmington, Conn.). Author: The Drawings of Salvator Rosa, 1977. Editor: National Gallery of Art Report and Studies in the History of Art, 1968-69. Address: 70 Lorraine St Hartford CT 06105 also Trinity Coll Hartford CT 06106

MAHONEY, RICHARD JOHN, diversified mfg. co. exec.; b. Springfield, Mass., Jan. 30, 1934; s. Maurice E. and Marion L. (Kennedy) M.; B.S. in Chemistry, U. Mass., 1955; m. Barbara M. Barnett, Jan. 26, 1957; children—Stephen, William, Robert. Sales trainee chem. div. U.S. Rubber Co., Naugatuck, Conn., 1955-56; field sales Alco Chem. Corp., New Eng., 1959-62; successively product devel. specialist various sales and tech. service positions, market mgr. new products div. Monsanto Co., 1962-67, div. sales dir. plastic products, Kenilworth, N.J., 1967-71, sales dir. agrl. div., St. Louis, 1971-72, dir. of sales, 1972-74, dir. ops. internat. Monsanto Agrl. Products Co., 1974, gen. mgr. overseas div., 1975, corp. v.p. and mng. dir., 1976, group v.p. and mng. dir. Monsanto Plastics & Resins Co., 1976-77, exec. v.p., 1977—, dir., 1979—; dir. First Nat. Bank St. Louis. Campaign chmn. Greater St. Louis Arts and Edn. Fund Drive, 1979; mem. adv. bd. St. John's Mercy Med. Center, 1979; mem. Chancellor's Council of U. Mo., St. Louis, 1979; mem. mktg. adv. bd. Columbia U., N.Y.C., 1978. Served to 1st lt. USAF, 1956-59. Mem. Chem. Mfrs. Assn. Club: Bellerive Country. Office: 800 N Lindbergh Blvd Saint Louis MO 63166

MAHONEY, THOMAS HENRY DONALD, educator, govt. ofcl.; b. Cambridge, Mass., Nov. 4, 1913; s. Thomas Henry, Jr. and Frances (Lucy) M.; A.B., Boston Coll., 1936, A.M., 1937; Ph.D., George Washington U., 1944; M.P.A., Harvard U., 1967; m. Phyllis Norton, July 14, 1951; children—Thomas Henry IV, Linda, David, Peter, Philip. Instr., Gonzaga Sch., Washington, 1937-39, Dunbarton Coll., Washington, 1938-39; instr., then asst. prof. history Boston Coll., 1939-44; asst. prof. history Holy Cross Coll., 1944-46; vis. lectr. history and govt. Smith Coll., 1944-45, Wellesley Coll., 1947-48; mem. faculty Mass. Inst. Tech., 1945—, prof. history, 1961—, chmn. sect. history, 1963-65, 73—; vis. prof. U. So. Calif., summer 1950; Lowell lectr., Boston, 1957; Carnegie fellow Harvard Law Sch., 1965-66; sec. elder affairs Commonwealth of Mass., 1979—; mem. ethnic com. U.S. Dept. Edn., 1979—; corporator, trustee Cambridgeport Savs. Bank. Mem. Cambridge Sch. Com., 1948-54; mem. Mass. Fulbright Com., 1953—, chmn., 1966-74; bd. dirs. Mass. Civic League, 1967—; state rep. Mass. Gen. Ct., 1971-78, chmn. energy com., 1977-78, chmn. ethics com., 1977-78. Trustee Cambridge Library, 1948-54, Mass. State Library, 1952-61; bd. dirs. Internat. Student Fedn.; mem. Cambridge City Council, 1964-72. Am. Council of Learned Socs. fellow, 1938, Guggenheim fellow, 1961-62. Fellow Royal Hist. Soc.; mem. Am., Am. Catholic (pres. 1957), Mass. hist. assns., Cath. Commn. Cultural and Intellectual Affairs, Conf. Brit. Studies, Nat. Conf. State Legislators (sci. and tech. com., intergovtl. relations com., mem. del. Peoples Republic of China 1976, 78). Clubs: Harvard (Boston); Oyster Harbors Golf, Weston Golf, Cambridge (Mass.). Author: Edmund Burke and Ireland, 1960; co-author: Readings in International Order, 1951; China, Japan and the Powers, 2d edit., 1960; The U.S. in World History, 3d edit., 1963; Edmund Burke: The Enlightenment and the Modern World, 1967; 1776, 1977. Editor: Burke's Reflections, 1955; Selected Writings and Speeches of Edmund Burke on America, 1964. Home: 86 Sparks St Cambridge MA 02138 also 47 Samoset Rd Sagamore Beach MA 02561

MAHONEY, TIMOTHY JOSEPH, ins. brokerage exec.; b. Newark, Nov. 24, 1937; s. Timothy J. and Sara H. (Healy) M.; B.A. in Econs., U. Notre Dame, 1959; m. Margaret F. Ward, Aug. 14, 1965; children—Timmy, Meg, Maura, Tara, Kevin. Account exec. Despard & Co., Inc., N.Y.C., 1960-65, asst. v.p., 1965-70; v.p. Fred S. James & Co. of N.Y., Inc., N.Y.C., 1970-75, exec. v.p., 1975-77, pres., chief exec. officer, 1977—; exec. v.p. Fred S. James & Co., 1979—, also dir. Office: 55 Water St New York NY 10041

MAHONEY, TOM (JOHN THOMAS), writer, editor; b. Dallas, Dec. 3, 1905; s. James Owen and Lacy (Braden) M.; B.J., U. Mo., 1927; m. Grace Dooley, 1930 (div.); 1 dau., Grace (Mrs. William Graves); m. 2d, Caroline Bird, Jan. 5, 1957; 1 son, John Thomas. With Dallas News, 1925-26; city editor El Paso Post, 1927-30; with UP, 1930-34; with Buffalo Times, 1934-36; editor Mechanix Illus., 1936-37; asso. editor, Look mag., 1937-39; with Gen. Electric Co., 1939-43; with overseas O.W.I., 1943; asso. editor Fortune mag., 1943-45; with Ben Sonnenberg, 1945-47, Young & Rubicam, Inc., 1948-56, Dudley-Anderson-Yutzy, 1956-68. Cons. ECA. Mem. Nat. Assn. Sci. Writers, Soc. Journalists and Authors, Authors League, P.E.N., Am. Philatelic Soc., Manuscript Soc. Am. Aviation Hist. Soc., AAAS, Psywar Soc., History of Sci. Soc., Dutchess County Hist. Soc., Sigma Delta Chi. Clubs: Overseas Press, Collectors, Nat. Press (Washington); Baker Street Irregulars. Author: (with L. Sloane) The Great Merchants, 1974; The Merchants of Life, 1959; The Story of George Romney, 1960; (with George Schuster) The Longest Auto Race, 1966; (with Barry Sadler) I'm a Lucky One, 1967; FDR, The Great Collector, 1980. Contbr. articles to leading mags. Home: 60 Gramercy Park New York City NY 10010 also 31 Sunrise Ln PO Box 3289 Poughkeepsie NY 12603

MAHONEY, WILLIAM GRATTAN, lawyer; b. Washington, Oct. 5, 1925; s. William Grattan and Gladys (Smith) M.; J.D., U. Notre Dame, 1950; m. Marian Antoinette Bock, Sept. 16, 1950; children—Mary Kathleen, Brian Charles, Sharon Anne, Kevin William, Eileen Patricia. Admitted to D.C. bar, 1950; with criminal div. Dept. Justice, 1950-52; asso., then partner firm Mulholland, Hickey & Lyman, Washington, 1952-70; partner firms Highsaw & Mahoney, 1970-76, Highsaw, Mahoney & Friedman, Washington, 1976—; lectr. AFL-CIO Studies Center. Mem. pastoral commn. Roman Cath. Archdiocese Washington, 1967-74, gen. chmn. project commitment, 1967-69; pres. Burnt Mills Manor Civic Assn., 1968-76. Served with USAAF, 1944-46. Mem. Am., D.C., Fed. bar assns., John Carroll Soc., Barristers. Clubs: Serra (pres. 1966-67), Touchdown (gov. 1971-73), University, Internat. (Washington). Home: 415 Neale Ave Silver Spring MD 20901 Office: 1050 17th St NW Washington DC 20036

MAHONEY, WILLIAM PATRICK, mfg. co. exec.; b. Chgo., Nov. 24, 1935; s. John C. and Mary C. Mahoney; B.S. in Indsl. Engring., Ill. Inst. Tech., 1957, M.B.A., 1961; m. Eileen C. Faxel, Apr. 19, 1958; children—Cathleen, Sharon, John, Kevin, Matthew. Mgmt. trainee FOMOCO, 1957-58; with Motorola Co., 1958-74, div. controller, 1972-74; v.p. fin. Kitchens of Sara Lee, Deerfield, Ill., 1974-77, pres., 1977—; instr. indsl. mgmt. Ill. Inst. Tech. Mem. Am. Inst. Indsl. Engrs. Roman Catholic. Office: Kitchens of Sara Lee 500 Waukegan Rd Deerfield IL 60015*

MAHONY, ROGER MICHAEL, bishop; b. Hollywood, Calif., Feb. 27, 1936; s. Victory James and Loretta Marie (Baron) M.; A.A., Our Lady of Queen of the Angels Sem., 1956; B.A., St. John's Sem. Coll., 1958, B.S.T., 1962; M.S.W., Catholic U. Am., 1964. Ordained priest Roman Catholic Ch., 1962; asst. pastor St. John's Cathedral, Fresno, Calif., 1962; in residence St. Genevieve's Parish, Fresno, 1964, adminstr., 1964-67, pastor, 1967-68; in residence St. John's Cathedral, Fresno, 1968-73, rector, 1973—; ordained bishop, 1975; titular bishop of Tamascani and aux. bishop of Fresno, 1975—; vicar gen. Diocese of Fresno, 1975—, chancellor, 1970—; diocesan dir. Cath. Charities and Social Service, Fresno, 1964-70; exec. dir. Cath. Welfare Bur., Fresno, 1964-70, Infant of Prague Adoption Service, 1964-70; chaplain St. Vincent de Paul Soc., Fresno, 1964-70; mem. faculty Fresno State U. extension div., 1965-67; sec. U.S. Cath. bishops ad hoc com. on farm labor Nat. Conf. Cath. Bishops, 1970-75; chmn. com. on pub. welfare and income maintenance Nat. Conf. Cath. Charities, 1969-70; bd. dirs. West Coast Regional Office of Bishops Com. for Spanish-Speaking, 1967-70: chmn. Calif. Assn. Cath. Charities Dirs., 1965-69; trustee St. Patrick's Sem., Archdiocese of San Francisco, 1974-75. Mem. Urban Coalition of Fresno, 1968-72; mem. Fresno County Econ. Opportunities Commn., 1964-65, Fresno County Alcoholic Rehab. Com., 1966-67; mem. Fresno City Charter Rev. Com., 1968-70, Mexican-Am. Council for Better Housing, 1968-72; mem. Redevel. Agy., City of Fresno, 1970-75; bd. dirs. Fresno Community Workshop, 1965-67; trustee St. Agnes Hosp., Fresno. Named chaplain to His Holiness Pope Paul VI, 1967; Young Man of Yr., Fresno Jr. C. of C., 1967. Mem. Canon Law Soc. Am., Nat. Assn. Social Workers. Home and office: PO Box 1668 Fresno CA 93717

MAHONY, WALTER BUTLER, JR., mag. editor; b. Scarborough, N.Y., Nov. 4, 1914; s. Walter Butler and Mary Murray (Butler) M.; grad. Deerfield Acad., 1932; A.B., Amherst Coll., 1936; student Yale Law Sch., also Grad. Sch., 1936-37; m. Marguerite duPont Lee, June 9, 1941; children—Barbara Lee Mahony Kent, Walter Butler III, Robert Murray. With Reader's Digest, 1937—, sr. editor, 1949-59, asst. mng. editor, 1959-65, mng. editor, v.p., 1965-73, exec. editor, v.p., 1973-76, dir., 1974-76, chief text editor, gen. books div., 1976—. Trustee Cisqua Sch., Chappaqua, N.Y., 1951-54, Emma Willard Sch., Troy, N.Y., 1959-62; bd. dirs. Boscobel Restoration, Inc., 1970—. Served to lt. comdr. USNR, 1940-45. Mem. Phi Beta Kappa, Delta Kappa Epsilon, Sigma Delta Chi. Conglist. (deacon 1956-59). Home: Hook Rd Bedford NY 10506 Office: Reader's Digest 750 3d Ave New York NY 10017

MAHOOD, STEPHEN CARROLL, lawyer, oil well drilling and pipeline constrn. co. exec.; b. Houston, Aug. 30, 1941; s. David Warren and Llewellyn Mahood; B.B.A., So. Meth. U., Dallas, 1963, J.D., 1966; m. Lelia Alice Moss, Jan. 25, 1964; children—Katherine Marie, Margaret Moss. Admitted to Tex. bar; with Houston Contracting Co., New Orleans, 1966-68, Nigeria, 1968-70; with Sedco Inc., Dallas, 1971—. Mem. Am. Tex., bar assns., Phi Delta Theta, Phi Alpha Delta. Republican. Presbyterian. Clubs: Dallas Country, Bent Tree Country (Dallas). Home: 3412 University St Dallas TX 75205 Office: 1901 N Akard St Dallas TX 75201

MAHOWALD, MARK EDWARD, educator; b. Albany, Minn., Dec. 1, 1931; s. Aloyis Peter and Cecilia Ann (Maus) M.; student Carnegie Mellon U., 1949-51; B.A., U. Minn., 1953, M.A., 1954, Ph.D., 1955; m. Zoemarie Graham, July 17, 1954; children—John, Mary, Katherine, Mark G., Paul. Sr. engr. Gen. Electric Co., Cin., 1956-57; asst. prof. math. Xavier U., Cin., 1957-59; asst. prof. Syracuse (N.Y.) U., 1959-63; prof. Northwestern U., Evanston, Ill., 1963—, chmn. dept. math., 1972-75. Served to 2nd lt., USMCR, 1955-56. Sloan fellow, 1964-66. Contbr. numerous articles on homotopy of spheres, related problems in algebraic topology. Home: 500 Greenleaf St Wilmette IL 60091 Office: 2033 Sheridan Rd Evanston IL 60201

MAHROUS, HAROUN, educator, elec. engr.; b. Fayoum, Egypt, Apr. 15, 1921; s. M.H. and Linda (Salib) M.; B.S. in Elec. Engring. with honors, Cairo U., 1943; D.Sc.Techn. in Elec. Engring., Swiss Fed. Inst. Tech., 1951; m. Graziella Tommasina, Aug. 9, 1951; 1 dau., Serenella. Came to U.S., 1954, naturalized, 1959. Asst. physics Cairo U., 1943-45; sr. lectr. elec. engring. Ibrahim (Egypt) U., 1951-54; asso. prof. elec. engring. Pratt Inst., 1954-56, prof., 1958—, chmn. dept., 1958-71, chmn. archtl., chem., indsl. and mech. engring. depts., 1973-75; asst. prof., then asso. prof. U. Ill., 1955-58, mem. ultramicrowave research group, 1956, 57; mem. power devel. group Bell Telephone Labs., summers 1958, 59, tech. staff, 1965, cons., 1966; mem. solid state memory div., cryogenics group IBM Corp., summer 1962, cons., 1963; program dir. engring. div. NSF, Washington, 1968; engring. cons. L.I. Lighting Co., summer 1970. Registered profl. engr., N.Y. State. Sr. mem. I.E.E.E.; mem. N.Y. Acad. Scis., Eta Kappa Nu, Tau Beta Pi. Author: Der Einfluss der Harmonischen auf den Anlauf der Synchronmaschinen, 1953; also tech. papers. Home: 365 Clinton Ave Brooklyn NY 11238

MAI, KLAUS LUDWIG, chem. co. exec.; b. Changsha, China, Mar. 7, 1930; s. Ludwig H. and Ilse (Behrend) M.; B.S. in Chem. Engring., Gonzaga U., Spokane, Wash., 1951; M.S., U. Wash., Seattle, 1952, Ph.D., 1954; m. Helen M. Martinchek, July 14, 1957; children—Martin, Michael, Mark, Matthew. With Shell Chem. Co., 1957-74, 77—, various overseas assignments, 1974-75, v.p., Houston, 1977—; v.p. transp. and supplies Shell Oil Co., 1976-77; chmn., pres. various subs. Shell Oil Co. Registered profl. engr., Wash. Mem. Am. Inst. Chem. Engrs., Soc. Chem. Industry, Chem. Mfrs. Assn., Soap and Detergents Assn. (dir. 1969-72), Sigma Xi, Tau Beta Pi. Clubs: Lakeside Country, Plaza (Houston). Contbr. articles to profl. publs. Office: PO Box 2463 Houston TX 77001

MAI, LUDWIG HUBERT, educator; b. Mannheim, Germany, Mar. 27, 1898; s. Hubert Chrysant and Anna Maria (Specht) M.; B.B.A., Coll. Econs. and Bus. Adminstr., Mannheim, 1920; M.A., Wolfgang Goethe U., Frankfurt, Germany, 1921, Dr. Rer. Pol., 1923; m. Ilse Behrend, Feb. 12, 1927; children—Veronica (Mrs. J. Ray Reynolds), Klaus L., Ursula (Mrs. Gordon A. White). Came to U.S., 1950. Instr., Coll. Bus. Adminstrn., Augsburg, Germany, 1921; mgr. DEFAG, China, 1923-45; lectr. Jr. Coll. Tientsin (China), 1945-49; mem. faculty St. Mary's U., San Antonio, 1950—, prof. econs., 1959—, dean Grad. Sch., 1959-68. Internat. trade cons. Southwest Research Inst.; dir. Inst. Internat. Relations, San Antonio; ednl. dir. Tex. Internat. Trade Assn. Mem. Am. Econ. Assn., Southwestern Social Sci. Assn., Royal Econ. Soc., Assn. Social Econs., Pi Gamma Mu, Omicron Delta Epsilon. Roman Catholic. Author: The Southwest Import and Export, 1956; Approach to Economics, 1960; Men and Ideas in Economics, 1975. Home: 343 Shadwell Dr San Antonio TX 78228

MAIBACH, BEN C., JR., bus. exec.; b. Bay City, Mich., 1920; Chmn., dir. Barton-Malow Co., Detroit; pres., dir. Cloverdale Equipment Co., Sarasota Chrysler-Plymouth, S-C-P Leasing Corp., Barton-Malow of Fla.; dir. Seven-Seven Corp., Asso. Gen. Ins. Co., Asso. Gen. Life Co., Mich. Mut. Liability Co. Trustee Barton-Malow Found., New Detroit; asst. sec., trustee Apostolic Christian Ch., Detroit; bd. dirs. S.E. Mich. chpt. ARC, United Found. Home: 14726 Fox St Detroit MI 48239 Office: PO Box 5200 Detroit MI 48235

MAICHEL, JOSEPH RAYMOND, lawyer, business exec.; b. Stanton, N.D., Nov. 24, 1934; s. John and Sarfina (Hoffman) M.; B.S. in Acctg., U. N.D., 1957, J.D. with distinction, 1959; m. Hilda Deichert, Jan. 7, 1961; children—Mary, Mark, Scott. Admitted to N.D. bar, 1959; spl. asst. atty. gen. State of N.D., 1959-71; atty. Mont.-Dakota Utilities Co., N.D., 1971-76, gen. counsel, sec., 1976-79; gen. counsel Knife River Coal Mining Co., Bismarck, 1979—; pres. Grassland, Inc., Bismarck, 1978—; tchr. bus. law, 1968-79. Mem. Am. Bar Assn., Am. Soc. Corp. Secs., North Central Electric Assn., Midwest Gas Assn., N.D. Bar Assn., Burleigh County Bar Assn. Contbr. articles to legal jours. Home: 1914 N 2d St Bismarck ND 58501 Office: 400 N 4th St Bismarck ND 58501

MAICKEL, ROGER PHILIP, pharmacologist, educator; b. Floral Park, N.Y., Sept. 8, 1933; s. Philip Vincent and Margaret Mary (Rose) M.; B.S., Manhattan (N.Y.) Coll., 1954; postgrad. Poly. Inst. Bklyn., 1954-55; M.S., Georgetown U., 1957, Ph.D., 1960; m. Lois Louise Pivonka, Sept. 8, 1956; children—Nancy Ellen, Carolyn Sue. Biochemist, Nat. Heart Inst., Bethesda, Md., 1955-65; asso. prof. pharmacology Ind. U., 1965-69, prof., 1969—, head sect. pharmacology med. scis. program, 1971-77; prof. pharmacology and toxicology, head dept. Sch. Pharmacy and Pharmacal Scis. Purdue U., W. Lafayette, Ind., 1977—; cons. Pennwalt Corp. Recipient Alumni award in medicine Manhattan Coll., 1972. Fellow AAAS, Am. Coll. Neuropsychopharmacology, Am. Inst. Chemists, Collegium Internat. de Neuro-Psychopharmacologicum; mem. Am. Chem. Soc., Am. Soc. Pharmacology and Exptl. Therapeutics, Am. Soc. Clin. Pharmacology and Therapeutics, ASTM, Soc. Forensic Toxicologists, Internat. Assn. Chiefs Police, Internat. Soc. Psyconeuroendocrinology, N.Y. Acad. Scis., Soc. Neurosci., Soc. Toxicology, Chem. Soc. (London), Sigma Xi, Rho Chi. Adv. editor Pergamon Press, 1970—; adv. editorial bd. Neuropharmacology, 1974—. Home: 3567 Canterbury Dr Lafayette IN 47905 Office: 202 Pharmacy Bldg Purdue U West Lafayette IN 47907

MAIDEN, CONDE GEORGE, former appliance co. exec.; b. Sydney, Australia, Oct. 7, 1911; s. Gordon and Dolores (MacFarlane) M.; ed. St. Joseph Coll., Sydney; m. Patricia Slatter, Apr. 30, 1949; children—Carol Anne (Mrs. Anthony Thorne), Susan, Peter Conde. Came to U.S., 1963. Vice pres., gen. mgr. appliance div. Malleys, Ltd., Sydney, 1953-58; v.p. Whirlpool Internat. Bahamas S.A., Nassau, 1958-62, pres., 1965—; v.p. Whirlpool Internat. Switzerland, Lucerne, 1963—; pres. Whirlpool Enterprises Can., Ltd., Whirlpool Internat. Switzerland, 1965—; v.p. Whirlpool Corp., Benton Harbor, Mich., 1966—; chmn. bd., chief exec. officer John Inglis Co., Ltd., Toronto, Ont., Can., 1969-76; ret., 1976. Chmn. adv. council Better Bus. Bur. Can. Mem. Canadian Elec. Mfrs. Assn. (bd. dirs., pres. 1975), Can. Appliance Mfrs. Assn. (dir.). Clubs: Toronto Hunt; Jupiter Hills Country, Tequesta Country (Tequesta, Fla.). Home: 21 Bay Harbor Tequesta FL 33458

MAIER, CORNELL C., aluminum and chem. co. exec.; b. Herreid, S.D., Jan. 12, 1925; s. Phillip and Ann Riedlinger M.; B.S. in Engring., U. Calif. at Berkeley, 1949. With Kaiser Aluminum & Chem. Corp., Oakland, Calif., 1949—, v.p., mgr. European region Kaiser Aluminum Internat., 1963-68, v.p., gen. mgr. Mill Products div. parent co., 1969, v.p., gen. mgr. N.Am. aluminum ops., 1969-70, exec. v.p., 1970-72, gen. mgr. in charge day-to-day ops., 1971-72, pres., chief exec. officer, 1972—, chmn. bd., 1978—, also dir.; dir. Kaiser Industries Corp., Anglesey Aluminum (London) Metal Ltd., Comalco Industries (Australia) Pty. Ltd., Volta Aluminum Co. Ltd.; dir., dep. chmn. Fed. Res. Bank San Francisco; mem. industry advisory council U.S. Dept. Def. Trustee Nat. Urban League. Served with USAAF, 1943-45. Mem. U.S. Council Internat. Chambers Commerce, Internat. Primary Aluminum Inst., Aluminum Assn. Clubs: Round Hill Country, Alamo. Home: 565 Bellevue Ave Oakland CA 94610 Office: Kaiser Aluminum & Chem Corp Kaiser Center 300 Lakeside Dr Oakland CA 94643

MAIER, FRANK MAGNER, journalist; b. Oak Park, Ill., June 1, 1933; s. Walter Louis and Merrie Boyd (Mitchell) M.; A.B., U. Notre Dame, 1955; m. Virginia Anne Ryan, Nov. 12, 1955; children—Michael, Katie, Daniel, Heidi. Sports editor Elgin (Ill.) Daily Courier News, 1958-60; polit. editor Rockford (Ill.) Morning Star, 1960-66; reporter Chgo. Daily News, 1966-70; corr. Newsweek mag., 1970—, bur. chief Midwest, Chgo.; instr. Medill Sch. Journalism, Northwestern U. Served with USNR, 1955-58. Roman Catholic. Club: Chgo. Press (past dir.). Office: 200 E Randolph Chicago IL 60601

MAIER, HENRY W., mayor; b. Dayton, Ohio, Feb. 7, 1918; s. Charles, Jr. and Marie L. (Knisley) M.; B.A., U. Wis., 1940; M.S. in Polit. Sci., U. Wis.-Milw., 1964. Mem. Wis. Legislature, 1950-60, floor leader for Senate, 1953, 55, 57, 59; mayor of Milw., 1960—. First pres. Nat. Conf. Democratic Mayors, 1976—. Mem. U.S. Conf. Mayors (pres. 1971-72, adv. council), Am. Municipal Assn. (exec. com.), Nat. League Cities (pres. 1964-65, adv. council 1966-67, mem. exec. com. 1968—). Served to lt. USNR, World War II; PTO. Democrat. Name one of 60 most influential men in Am., U.S. News and World Report, 1975, 76. Author: Challenge to the Cities, 1966. Home: 1129 N Jackson St Milwaukee WI 53202 Office: City Hall Milwaukee WI 53202

MAIER, IRWIN, newspaper exec.; b. Mellen, Wis., July 25, 1899; s. Louis A. and Mary E. (Ryan) M.; A.B., U. Wis., 1921, LL.D., 1964; L.H.D., Marquette U., 1965; D.Pub. Service, Northland Coll., 1973; m. Loraine Greve, Apr. 9, 1926; children—Sallyann (Mrs. Thomas L. Tolan, Jr.), Mary Clare (Mrs. Conrad P. Bittner), Victor Irwin, John Peter. Chmn. bd., dir. Jour. Co., pubs. Milw. Jour., Milw. Sentinel and operators radio stas. WTMJ, WTMJ-TV. Recipient award for distinguished service in journalism U. Minn., 1962; Vocat. Service award Rotary Club, 1964; Printers' Ink Mag. Silver Medal award Advt. Fedn. Am., 1965; Milw.-Found. Com. Frye Community Service award, 1965; Distinguished Service award Wis. Alumni Assn., 1966, Distinguished Service award Wis. Newspaper Assn., 1976; award Nat. Assn. Secondary Sch. Prins., 1973, award Pub. Expenditure Survey Wis., 1977, Knight of Golden Quill award Milw. Press Club, 1977. Mem. Milw. Assn. Commerce, Greater Milw. Com. (founder), Newspaper Advt. Execs. Assn. (dir. Bur. Advt. 1943-57, chmn. Bur. Advt. 1951, 52), Am. Newspaper Pubs. Assn. (vice chmn. 1960-61, chmn. 1962-63), Chi Phi, Phi Kappa Phi, Sigma Delta Chi. Rotarian (vocational service award 1964). Clubs: Milw. Athletic, Univ., Milw. Country, Milw. Home: 2620 E Newberry Blvd Milwaukee WI 53211 Office: 333 W State St Milwaukee WI 53201

MAIER, PETER KLAUS, lawyer; b. Wurzburg, Germany, Nov. 20, 1928; s. Bernard and Joan (Sonder) M.; came to U.S., 1939, naturalized, 1945; B.A. cum laude, Claremont Men's Coll., 1949; J.D. cum laude, U. Calif. at Berkeley, 1952; LL.M. in Taxation, N.Y. U., 1953; m. Melanie L. Stoff, Dec. 15, 1963; children—Michele Margaret, Diana Lynn. Admitted to Calif. bar, 1953, U.S. Supreme Ct. bar, 1957; atty. tax div. U.S. Dept Justice, Washington, 1956-59; mem. firm Bacigalupi, Elkus, Salinger & Rosenberg, San Francisco, 1959-69, Brookes & Maier, San Francisco, 1970-73, Winokur, Schoenberg, Maier & Zang, San Francisco, 1974—; prof. law Hastings Coll. Law, U. Calif., San Francisco, 1967—; pres. Calif. Property Devel. Corp., San Francisco, 1969—; chmn. Property Resources Inc., San Jose, Calif., 1968-77. Served to capt. USAF, 1953-56. Cert. specialist in taxation law, Calif. Mem. San Francisco Bar Assn. (chmn. sect. taxation 1970-71). Author books on taxation. Home: PO Box 391 Belvedere CA 94920 Office: Winokur Schoenberg & Maier 1 California St San Francisco CA 94111. *Having been born in Europe, I appreciate my personal liberties as well as the enormous opportunities afforded all of us fortunate enough to live in America. There is little one cannot accomplish in this country-given only the motivation and abilities. I do not take for granted our freedoms. I enjoy my life here.*

MAIER, WILLIAM MORRIS, lawyer; b. Phila., June 11, 1909; s. Paul D.I. and Anna (Shinn) M.; A.B., Haverford Coll., 1931, LL.D., 1972; LL.B., U. Pa., 1935; m. Margaret Clarke Waterman, Aug. 14, 1943; children—James Hollingsworth, Anthony Morris. With Internat. Grenfell Assn., Labrador, 1931-32; admitted to Pa. bar, 1936; partner firm Cahall & Maier, Phila., 1936-42, 45-48; with Am. Friends Service Com., Hawaii, 1942-45; asso. William Nelson West 3d, Phila., 1948-54, MacCoy, Evans and Lewis, 1954—. Dir. Friends Fiduciary Corp. Trustee Phila. Friends Yearly Meeting, Westtown Sch.; bd. mgrs. Haverford Coll., 1938—, treas., 1949-75; trustee Cheyney State Coll., 1941-68, chmn. 1947-68; treas. Ludwick Inst., 1956, Univ. Settlements, 1945—, Friends Freedmens Assn., 1954—; bd. mgrs. Am. Friends Service Com., 1953-69, Am. Sunday Sch. Union, 1937-69; trustee Internat. Grenfell Assn., 1948—, vice chmn., 1963-67, chmn., 1967-75; pres. Friends Edn. Fund. Mem. Am., Pa., Phila. bar assns. Mem. Soc. of Friends. Clubs: Philadelphia Skating, Rittenhouse (Phila.); Merion (Pa.) Cricket. Home: Harriton Bryn Mawr PA 19010 Office: 2 Penn Center Plaza Philadelphia PA 19102

MAILER, NORMAN, author; b. Long Branch, N.J., Jan. 31, 1923; s. Issac B. and Fanny (Schneider) M.; S.B., Harvard, 1943; postgrad. Sorbonne, Paris, France; m. Beatrice Silverman, 1944 (div. 1952); 1 dau., Susan; m. 2d, Adele Morales, 1954 (div.); children—Danielle, Elizabeth; m. 3d, Jean Campbell (div.); 1 dau., Kate; m. 4th, Beverly Bentley, 1963; children—Michael, Steven; m. 5th, Carol Stevens; 1 dau., Maggie. Served with AUS, 1944-46. Recipient 14th ann. award for outstanding service to arts McDowell Colony, 1973. Author: (war novel) The Naked and the Dead, 1948; Barbary Shore, 1951; The Deer Park (dramatized 1967), 1955; Advertisements for Myself, 1959; (poetry) Deaths for the Ladies and Other Disasters, 1962; The Presidential Papers, 1963; An American Dream, 1965; Cannibals and Christians, 1966; Why are We in Viet Nam?, 1967; The Armies of the Night (Nat. Book award, co-winner Pulitzer prize), 1968; Miami and the Siege of Chicago (Nat. Book award), 1968; Of A Fire On The Moon, 1971; The Prisoner of Sex, 1971; Existential Errands, 1972; St. George and the Godfather, 1972; Marilyn, 1973; The Faith of Graffiti, 1974; The Fight, 1975; Some Honorable Men, 1975; Genius and Lust, 1976; A Transit to Narcissus, 1978; The Executioner's Song, 1979. Dir. (feature films) Wild 90, 1967; Beyond the Law, 1967; Maidstone, 1968. Editor: Dissent, 1953-69. Co-founder Village Voice, 1955. Contbr. to numerous publs. Office: care Molly Malone Cook PO Box 338 Provincetown MA 02657

MAILLIARD, JOHN WARD, III, food broker; b. Belvedere, Calif., July 4, 1914; s. John Ward, Jr. and Kate (Peterson) M.; B.A., Yale U., 1935; m. Peggy Field, 1937; children—Carolyn Whitaker, Kathy Rende, Margot Mailliard; m. 2d, Charlotte Smith, 1966. With Mailliard & Schmeidell Co., 1937-74, chmn., 1964-74; chmn. bd. Bromar Inc., Sausalito, Calif., since 1974; dir. Wells Fargo Bank, Pacific Mut. Life Ins. Co. Pres. San Francisco Police Commn., 1966-68; with Am. Cancer Soc., 1962-64. Served to maj. AUS, 1942-45. Mem. Nat. Food Brokers Assn. (chmn. 1964, treas. 1968-77), San Francisco C. of C. (pres. 1953). Republican. Clubs: Pacific Union, Rancheros Visitadiros. Home: 2740 Green St San Francisco CA 94123 Office: 2658 Bridgeway St Sausalito CA 94965

MAILLOUX, NOEL, psychologist; b. Napierville, Que., Can., Dec. 25, 1909; s. Edmond and Ida (Gregoire) M.; B.A., U. Montreal (Que.), 1930; Ph.D., St. Thomas U., Rome, 1934, S.Th.L., 1938; D.Sc.Edn. (hon.), U. Sherbrooke (Que.), 1971. Joined Dominican Order, 1930, ordained priest Roman Catholic Ch., 1937; prof. psychology U. Montreal, 1942-75, prof. emeritus, 1975—, chmn. dept. psychology, 1942-57, 69-73; dir. Center of Research in Human Relations, Montreal, 1952—; cons. to govt. orgns. Decorated officer Order of Can. Can. Mental Health Assn. research fellow, 1957-58. Mem. Canadian Psychol. Assn. (pres. 1954-55), Internat. Soc. Criminology (v.p. 1962-74), Internat. Union Psychol. Sci. (exec. bd. 1954-77), Royal Soc. Can. Author books, the latest being: Jeunes sans Dialogue, 1973; editor Contributions a l'Etude des Sciences de l'homme, 1954. Home and Office: 2715 Chemin Cote Ste Catherine Montreal PQ H3T 1B6 Canada

MAIMAN, THEODORE HAROLD, physicist; b. Los Angeles, July 11, 1927; B.S. in Engring. Physics, U. Colo., 1949; M.S. in Elec. Engring., Stanford U., 1951, Ph.D. in Physics, 1955. Sect. head Hughes Research Labs., 1955-61; pres., founder Korad Corp., Santa Monica, Calif., 1961-68, Maiman Assos., Los Angeles, 1968-76; v.p., founder Laser Video Corp., Los Angeles, 1972-75; v.p. advanced tech. TRW Electronics Co., Los Angeles, 1975—. Served with USNR, 1945-46. Recipient award Fannie and John Hertz Found., 1966; Ballantine award Franklin Inst., 1962; award for devel. laser Aerospace Elec. Soc.-Am. Astron. Soc., 1965; named Alumni of Century, U. Colo., 1976. Fellow Am. Phys. Soc. (Oliver E. Buckley prize 1966), Optical Soc. Am. (R.W. Wood prize 1976); mem. Nat. Acad. Engrs., IEEE, Soc. Info. Display, Soc. Motion Picture and TV Engrs., Sigma Xi, Sigma Pi Sigma, Sigma Tau, Pi Mu Epsilon. Author papers in field. Adv. bd. Indsl. Research mag. Responsible devel. 1st laser. Office: 10880 Wilshire Blvd Los Angeles CA 90024

MAIN, JACKSON TURNER, educator; b. Chgo., Aug. 6, 1917; s. John Smith and Dorothy Kinsey (Turner) M.; B.A., U. Wis., 1939, M.A., 1940, Ph.D., 1949; m. Gloria Jean Lund, June 16, 1956; children—Jackson Turner, Eifiona Llewelyn, Judson Kempton. Asst. prof. Washington and Jefferson Coll., Washington, Pa., 1948-50; prof. San Jose (Cal.) State U., 1953-65, U. Md., College Park, 1965-66; prof. history State U. N.Y. at Stony Brook, 1966—. Served to sgt. USAF, 1941-45. Am. Council Learned Socs. fellow, 1962-63. Mem. Am., Wis. hist. assns., Orgn. Am. Historians, others. Author: The Antifederalists 1781-1788, 1961; The Social Structure of Revolutionary America, 1965; The Upper House in Revolutionary America, 1967; Political Parties Before the Constitution, 1973; The Sovereign States, 1775-1783, 1973. Home: 3 Coraway Rd Setauket NY 11733 Office: Dept History State U NY Stony Brook NY 11794

MAINES, CLIFFORD BRUCE, ins. co. exec.; b. Tacoma, Wash., Aug. 14, 1926; s. Clifford McLean and Ida Vera (Wardall) M.; student Central Coll., Fayette, Mo., 1944-45, U. Mich., 1945-46; B.S., U. Wash., 1948, LL.B., 1949, J.D., 1949; m. Mary Jean Marshall, Sept. 4, 1948; children—Molly, Janet Lynn. Admitted to Wash. bar, 1950; mem. legal staff Safeco Corp., Seattle, 1950-62, asso. gen. counsel, 1962-66, gen. counsel, 1966-68, v.p., gen. counsel, 1968-74, sr. v.p., 1974—, dir., 1977—; exec. v.p., chief operating officer, dir. Gen. Ins. Co. Am., 1974-77, pres., dir., 1977—; exec. v.p. 1st Nat. Ins. Co. Am., 1974-77, pres., dir. 1977—; exec. v.p. Safeco Ins. Co., 1974-77, pres., dir., 1977—; sr. v.p. Safeco Life Ins. Co., also dir.; exec. v.p. GSL; Served with USNR, 1944-46. Mem. Mcpl. League, Am., Wash., Seattle-King County (past trustee) bar assns., Wash. Ins. Council (past pres.), Pacific Coast Casualty and Surety Execs. (exec. com.), Beta Theta Pi. Methodist (past chmn. bd.). Clubs: Washington Athletic, Broadmoor Golf, Seattle Golf, Lions (Seattle). Office: Safeco Plaza Seattle WA 98185

MAINOUS, BRUCE HALE, educator; b. Appalachia, Va., Aug. 2, 1914; s. William Lazarus and Sibyl (Hale) M.; A.B., Coll. William and Mary, 1935; M.A., U. Ill., 1939, Ph.D., 1948; certificates, Sorbonne, Paris, France, 1958, U. Besançon (France), 1975; m. Ruth Marie Daugherty, June 7, 1941; children—Mary Michele, Martha Hale. Asst. d'anglais Lycée de Nîmes (France), 1935-36; prin. Derby (Va.) Grade Sch., 1936-37; mem. faculty U. Ill. at Urbana, 1937—, prof. French, 1964—, head dept., 1965-73, dir. Unit for Fgn. Lang. Study and Research, 1972-76, dir. Lang. Learning Lab., 1976—. Served to lt. USNR, 1942-46; comdr. Res. ret. Decorated officier Ordre des Palmes Académiques. Mem. Modern Lang. Assn., Am. Assn. Tchrs. French, Ill. Fgn. Lang. Tchrs. Assn. (pres 1966-68), Am. Council Teaching Fgn. Langs., Inst. d'Etudes Occitanes, Corda Fratres Assn. Cosmopolitan Clubs, Phi Kappa Phi, Sigma Delta Pi, Pi Delta Phi. Methodist. Author: (with H.C. Woodbridge) A Sainte-Beuve Bibliography, 1954; Basic French, 2d edit., 1968; (with Donald J. Nolan) Basic French, Workbook and laboratory Manual, 1968. Home: 502 W Washington St Urbana IL 61801

MAINS, GILBERT JOSEPH, educator, chemist; b. Clairton, Pa., Apr. 20, 1929; s. Gilbert Henry and Lois (Smith) M.; B.S. magna cum laude, Duquesne U., 1951; Ph.D., U. Calif. at Berkeley, 1954; m. Jacqueline Taschler, Aug. 25, 1951; children—Kathleen, Barbara Ann. Asst. prof. Carnegie Inst. Tech., 1955-61, asso. prof., 1961-65; with Lawrence Radiation Lab., U. Calif. at Berkeley, 1959-60; prof. chemistry, chmn. dept. U. Detroit, 1965-68, Poetker prof. physics and chemistry, 1969-71; prof. chemistry Okla. State U., 1971—, chmn. dept., 1971-76; cons. to govt. Fulbright fellow R.G.W. Norrish Lab., Cambridge, Eng., 1955. Mem. Am. Chem. Soc. (sect. officer Pitts. 1960-65, chmn. Detroit sect. 1970), Am. Phys. Soc., Internat. Solar Energy Soc., Inter-Am. Photochem. Soc., Sigma Xi. Author research publs. in photochemistry, theoretical chemistry, fuel chemistry, radiation chemistry. Home: 301 E Redbud Dr Stillwater OK 74074

MAINWARING, THOMAS LLOYD, motor freight co. exec.; b. Cleve., Aug. 25, 1928; s. Hugh Trevor and Mary Beatrice (Ottman) M.; B.A., Albion Coll., 1950; M.B.A., Western Res. U., 1958; m. Mary Farrell, Aug. 14, 1954; children—Kevin, James, Eileen, Scott, Bruce. Controller, Cleve. Cartage Co., 1959-61, v.p., treas., 1961-64; controller Asso. Truck Lines, Inc., Vandenberg Center, Grand Rapids, Mich., 1964-69; v.p. finance Asso. Transport, Inc., N.Y.C., 1969-70, exec. v.p., finance and adminstrn., 1970-72; pres. Ryder Truck Lines Inc., Jacksonville, Fla., 1972—, chief operating officer, 1978—. Vice pres. Mich. Accounting and Finance Council, 1968; trustee Albion Coll., 1977. Served with AUS, 1950-53. C.P.A., Ohio. Mem. Am. (nat. accounting and finance council 1964, pres. 1971), Fla. (dir. 1973, pres. 1979) trucking assns., Am. Mgmt. Assn. (lectr. seminars), Sigma Nu. Contbr. articles profl. jours. Home: 2211 Cheryl Dr Jacksonville FL 32217 Office: 2050 Kings Rd Jacksonville FL 32209

MAINWARING, WILLIAM LEWIS, author, publishing co. exec.; b. Portland, Oreg., Jan. 17, 1935; s. Bernard and Jennie (Lewis) M.; B.S., U. Oreg., 1957; postgrad. Stanford, 1957-58; m. Mary E. Bell, Aug. 18, 1962; children—Anne Marie, Julia Kathleen, Douglas Bernard. With Salem (Oreg.) Capital Jour., 1958-76, editor, pub., 1962-76; pub. Oreg. Statesman, 1974-76; pres. Statesman-Jour. Co., Inc., Salem, 1974-76; pres. Westridge Press, Ltd., 1976—. Pres., Salem Beautification Council, 1968, Marion-Polk County United Good Neighbors, 1970, Salem Social Services Commn., 1978-79, Salem Hosp. Found., 1978-79. Served as 2d lt. AUS, 1958; capt. Res. Mem. Oreg. Newspaper Pubs. Assn. (pres. 1969-70), Salem Area C. of C. (pres. 1972-73), Oreg. Symphony Soc. Salem (pres. 1973-75), Pacific Northwest Newspaper Assn. (v.p. 1971), Sigma Chi. Republican. Presbyn. (ruling elder). Club: Salem City (pres. 1977-78). Author: Exploring the Oregon Coast, 1977; Exploring Oregon's Central and Southern Cascades, 1979. Home: 1090 Southridge Pl S Salem OR 97302

MAISANO, FRANKLIN, life ins. co. exec.; b. Newark, Sept. 30, 1933; s. Phillip and Esther (Miloscia) M.; B.A., Mich. State U., 1955; m. Dorothy F., Nov. 11, 1978. With Manhatten Life Corp., and subs. Manhattan Life Ins. Co., N.Y.C., 1963—, exec. v.p., 1973-78, pres., 1978—, dir. parent co., 1974—. Mem. N.Y. State's Task Force on Hypertension; bd. dirs. Found. for Research on Heart Disease, N.Y. Heart Assn., Madison Sq. Boys Club, N.Y.C., Casa Italian—Columbia U., Family Service Assn. Am. Mem. Am. Soc. C.L.U.'s, Alpha Kappa Psi. Roman Catholic. Clubs: N.Y. Athletic, Mich. State Alumni of N.Y. (pres.). Home: 1979 William St Union NJ 07083 Office: 111 W 57th St New York NY 10019

MAISCH, LOUIS WILLIAM, hotel exec.; b. N.Y.C., Dec. 18, 1930; s. William Michael and Frances Felice (Frango) M.; B.S., Fla. So. Coll., 1952; m. Rebecca H. O'Brien, Sept. 13, 1969; 1 dau., Morgan Ashley. With Sheraton Corp., 1956—, resident mgr. Sheraton Russell, N.Y.C., 1970-71, gen. mgr. Sheraton Fort Wayne (Ind.), 1971-72, gen. mgr. Sheraton Motor Inc., N.Y.C., 1972-76, gen. mgr. Sheraton Ritz, Mpls., 1976-77, gen. mgr. Sheraton Atlanta, 1977—. Served with USMC. Mem. Ga. Hospitality and Travel Assn. Democrat. Roman Catholic. Office: Sheraton Atlanta Hotel 590 W Peachtree St NW Atlanta GA 30308

MAISEL, SHERMAN JOSEPH, educator, economist; b. Buffalo, July 8, 1918; s. Louis and Sophia (Beck) M.; A.B., Harvard, 1939, M.P.A., 1947, Ph.D., 1949; m. Lucy Cowdin, Sept. 26, 1942; children—Lawrence C., Margaret L. (Mrs. Keith P. Rasey). Economist, Bd. Govs. FRS, Washington, 1939-41, bd. govs., 1965-72; economist, fgn. service res. officer Dept. State, 1945-46; teaching fellow Harvard, 1947-48; asst. prof., asso. prof., prof. bus. adminstrn. U. Calif. at Berkeley, 1948-65, 72—; sr. economist Nat. Bur. Econ. Research-West, 1973-78; fellow Fund For Advancement Edn., 1952-53, Inst. Basic Math. with Application to Bus., 1959-60, fellow Center for Advanced Study in Behavioral Scis., 1972; mem. adv. coms. to Bur. Census, FHA, State of Calif., Ford Found., Social Sci. Research Council; mem. bldg. research adv. bd. NRC. Bd. dirs. Berkeley Unified Sch. Dist., 1962-65; trustee Population Ref. Bur. Served to capt. AUS, 1941-45. Mem. Am. Fin. Assn. (pres. 1973), Am. Econ. Assn., Am. Statis. Assn., Econometric Soc., Regional Sci. Assn. Author: Housebuilding in Transition, 1953; Fluctuations, Growth, and Forecasting, 1957; Managing the Dollar, 1973; Real Estate Investment and Finance, 1976. Home: 2164 Hyde St San Francisco CA 94109 Office: 350 Barrows Hall U Calif Berkeley CA 94720

MAISLIN, ISIDORE, hosp. adminstr.; b. N.Y.C., Aug. 4, 1919; s. Solomon and Rose (Baruch) M.; B.S., Columbia, 1950, M.S., 1951; m. Frances Mussman, Jan. 18, 1948; children—Wendy Sue (Mrs. Neil Robbins), Steven William. Asso. dir. Albert Einstein Med. Center, Phila., 1950-59; asso. dir. Mt. Sinai Hosp. Greater Miami, Mimai Beach, Fla., 1959-63; adminstr. Scranton (Pa.) Gen. Hosp., 1963-64; exec. dir. Jewish Home of Eastern Pa., Scranton, 1964-67; adminstr. South Mountain (Pa.) Restoration Center, 1967—. Served with AUS, 1943-46. Fellow Am. Coll. Hosp. Adminstrs., Am. Pub. Health Assn., Royal Soc. Health. Home: 535 Colfax Ave Scranton PA 18510 Office: South Mountain Restoration Center South Mountain PA 17261

MAISON, GEORGE L., physician, educator, business exec.; b. Frankfort, Ky., Oct. 13, 1911; s. Louis G. and Louise (Bear) M.; A.B., Northwestern U., 1930, M.S., 1934, M.D., 1935; m. Elizabeth Platt, July 25, 1935; children—Susan Maison Johnson, Sally. Instr. physiology U. Wis., 1935-37, St. Louis U., 1937-40; asst. prof. Wayne U. Med. Sch., 1941-42; asso. prof. physiology Boston U., 1945-46, prof., head dept. pharmacology, 1946-52; dir. research and devel. Riker Labs., Los Angeles, 1952-53, pres., 1953-61, chmn. bd., 1962-66; v.p. Dart Industries, Inc., 1962-66, staff officer, 1966-76; staff psychiatrist Gateways Hosp., Los Angeles, 1970—. Served to maj. USAAF, 1942-45. Mem. Calif. Med. Assn., Am. Soc. Pharmacology and Exptl. Therapeutics, Am. Physiol. Soc., Soc. Exptl. Biology and Medicine, AMA, AAAS, Am. Assn. Marriage and Family Counselors, Sigma Xi, Alpha Omega Alpha. Home: 555 N Wilcox Ave Los Angeles CA 90004

MAISONROUGE, JACQUES GASTON, business machine co. exec.; b. Cachan Seine, France, Sept. 20, 1924; s. Paul and Suzanne (Cazas) M.; Diplomed Engr., Ecole Centrale de Paris, 1948; m. Francoise Andree Feron, Mar. 27, 1948; children—Christine, Florence, Sylvie, Francois, Anne-Sophie. With IBM Corp., 1948—, asst. to sales mgr. France, 1954-56, mgr. market planning and research IBM Europe, 1956-58, regional mgr. Europe, 1958-59, asst. gen. mgr., 1959-62, v.p. World Trade Corp., 1962-64, pres. IBM/Europe, 1964-67, pres., 1967-73, pres., chief exec. office IBM World Trade Corp., 1973-74, chmn. bd., chief exec. officer IBM World Trade Europe/Middle East/Africa Corp., 1974—, chmn. bd., 1976—; dir. Philip Morris, Inc., L'Air Liquide. Bd. dirs. European Inst. Bus. Adminstrn.; chmn. bd. trustees Ecole Centrale des Arts et Manufacturers. Mem. Inst. Internat. Edn. (hon.). Club: Automobile of France. Office: 360 Hamilton Ave White Plains NY 10601

MAITIN, SAMUEL CALMAN, artist; b. Phila., Oct. 26, 1928; s. Isaac Boris and Ruth (Pollack) M.; grad. Phila. Coll. Art, 1949; B.A., U. Pa., 1951; m. Lilyan Miller, Aug. 29, 1964; children—Izak Joshua, Ana Raquel. One-man shows include: Phila. Mus. Art, 1972, Associated Am. Artists Gallery, Phila., 1979; group shows include: Phila. Mus. Art Bicentennial Exhbns., 1976, Tate Gallery, 1977, Tel Aviv, 1978; represented in permanent collections: Library of Congress, Mus. Modern Art, N.Y.C., Nat. Gallery Art, Oakland Mus. (Calif.), Phila. Mus. Art, Tate Gallery, London, Pa. Acad Fine Arts, Smithsonian Instn., USIA, U. Pa.; instr. art Phila. Coll. Art, 1949-59, Moore Coll. Art, 1950-52, Phila. Mus. Art, 1961-73, Annenberg Sch. Communications U. Pa., 1964-70; graphics dir., creator 50 posters. YM/YWHA Arts Council. Guggenheim fellow, 1968. Home and Studio: 704 Pine St Philadelphia PA 19106

MAITLAND, LESTER JAMES, army officer, clergyman; b. Milw., Feb. 8, 1899; s. James William and Bertha M.; student Army Service schs.; grad. Air Force Tactical Sch., 1935; m. Ruth Thurston, May 25, 1922 (div. 1930); 1 dau, Patricia Ruth; m. 2d, Kathleen McManus, Sept. 30, 1931; 1 dau, Eileen McDermott. Enlisted Wis. Aviation sect., Signal Corps, U.S. Army, 1917; commd. 2d lt., res. mil. aviator, 1918, advanced through grades to brig. gen., 1951; aide to Gen. William Mitchell and Gen. Patrick, chief staff A.C., 1921-25; flew world's 1st 200 mile-per-hour airplane, winning 2d place Pulitzer Air Race, Detroit, 1922; broke existing world speed race, Dayton, Ohio, 1923; piloted 1st airplane to cross Pacific, Oakland, Calif. to Hawaii, 1927; comdg. officer 4th Composite Group and Clark Field, Manila, P.I., 1940; served on Munitions Bd., 1941; A.S. comdr. Far Eastern Air Force, 1941-42; after fall of Manila moved all A.C. troops to Bataan, then ordered to Australia, organized, trained 386th Bomb Group (B26), 1942, combat E.T.O., 1943; dir. Wis. Aeros.; 1948-49; apptd. dir. Mich. Dept. Aeros., 1949; chmn. Mich. Civil Def. Planning Com. 1950-56; dir. Civil Def., State Mich., 1951-56; ordained to diaconate, 1956; minister Episcopal St. John's Ch., Iron River, Mich., 1956-57; priested, 1957; rector St. Stephen's Ch., Escanaba, Mich., 1958- 60, St. Peter's Ch., Red Bluff, Calif., 1960-62; canon pastor Cathedral St. Andrew, Honolulu, 1962; rector Ch. Good Shepherd of Hills, Cave Creek, Ariz., 1963-72, rector emeritus, 1972—. Decorated Silver Star, D.F.C. with oak leaf cluster, Air medal with oak leaf cluster, Presdl. Unit Citation (2). Recipient McKay Trophy. Mem. Am. Legion. Episcopalian. Mason. Author: Knight of the Air, 1928. Address: PO Box 1101 Red Bluff CA 96080

MAJER, GERALD HENRY, interior furnishings co. fin. exec.; b. Chgo., Apr. 29, 1940; s. Henry Edward and Alice Dolores (Behnke) M.; A.B. in Polit. Sci., Stanford U., 1962; M.B.A. in Fin., Wharton Sch., U. Pa., 1964; m. Diane Cunningham Lewis, May 20, 1967; 1 dau., Emily Marshall. With Brown Bros. Harriman & Co., pvt. bankers, N.Y.C., 1964-77, asst. mgr., 1969-73, dep. mgr., 1973-77; treas. Mohasco Corp., Amsterdam, N.Y., 1977—. Trustee, treas. Schenectady Museum, 1979. Home: RD 2 Charlton Rd Ballston Spa NY 12020 Office: 57 Lyon St Amsterdam NY 12010

MAJEWSKI, LAWRENCE JAMES, conservator; b. Mason City, Iowa, Feb. 10, 1919; s. Frank and Elizabeth (Krumrey) M.; B.F.A., Yale U., 1951, M.F.A., 1954; student Iowa State Coll., 1938-39; A.A. in Chemistry and Biology, Mason City Jr. Coll., 1938. Conservator of paintings Met. Mus. Art, N.Y.C., 1953-56; dep. dir. Byzantine Inst. Am., Istanbul, Turkey, 1956-60; conservator, lectr. Conservation Center, Inst. Fine Arts, N.Y. U., 1960-66, prof. conservation, chmn. Conservation Center, 1966—; consultative chmn. of objects conservation and Research Lab., Met. Mus. Art, 1976—; chief conservator Archaeol. Expdn. to Sardis, Turkey, 1964—; mem. sci. advisory council Winterthur Mus. Served with USN, 1942-45; ETO. Met. Mus. Art fellow, 1952. Fellow Internat. Inst. for Conservation of Hist. and Artistic Works (council), Am. Inst. Conservation; mem. Am. Assn. Museums, ASTM, Am. Inst. Archaeologists. Editor: Art and Archaeology. Home: 123 Sheate Rd Wappinger Falls NY 12590 Office: Conservation Center 1 E 78 St New York NY 10021

MAJNO, GUIDO, physician; b. Milan, Italy, Feb. 9, 1922; s. Edoardo and Elda (Bernstein) M.; came to U.S., 1952, naturalized, 1959; M.D., U. Milan, 1947; M.A. (hon.), Harvard U., 1961; children—Corinne, Lorenzo, Luca. Resident and chief resident in pathology Hôpital Cantonal, Geneva, Switzerland, 1947-52; mem. faculty Med. Sch., Harvard U., Cambridge, Mass., 1953-68; guest investigator Rockefeller Inst., 1958-59; dir. Inst. Pathology, U. Geneva, Switzerland, 1968-73; chmn. dept. pathology U. Mass., Worcester, Mass., 1973—. Recipient Award for Sci., Phi Beta Kappa, 1975. Fellow Am. Acad. Arts and Scis.; mem. Am. Soc. Pathology, Soc. for Cell Biology, Internat. Acad. Pathology, Soc. for Health and Human Values, Am. Antiquarian Soc. Author: The Healing Hand, 1975. Home: 16J Brandywine Dr Worcester MA 01605 Office: 55 Lake Ave N Worcester MA 01605

MAJOR, ANDRÉ WILFRID, radio producer, writer, educator; b. Montréal, Que., Can., Apr. 22, 1942; s. Arthur and Anna (Sharp) M.; student Coll. de Montréal, 1955-60; m. Ginette Lepage, June 30, 1970; children—Eric, Julie. Lit. critic La Presse, Montreal, 1965-79, Le Devoir, Montreal, 1967-70, lecteur Editions du Jour, Montreal, 1964-67, Lemeac, Montreal, 1972-75; radio producer CBC, Radio Canada, Montreal, 1973—; prof. lit. and creative writing Ottawa U., 1977-78, U. Que., 1977; works include La Chair de poule, 1965, L'Epouvantail, 1974, L'Epidémie, 1975, Les Rescapés (award of Gov. Gen. Can.), 1976; poetry collections include Poèmes pour durer, 1969; dramas include Une soirée en octobre, 1975. Mem. Union des Ecrivains québécois (sec. 1976-79). Roman Catholic. Home: 10595 Tanguay Montréal PQ H3L 3G9 Canada Office: 1400 E Boulevard Dorchester Montréal PQ Canada

MAJOR, COLEMAN JOSEPH, univ. dean; b. Detroit, Sept. 7, 1915; s. Coleman I. and Anna (Galik) M.; B.S., U. Ill., 1937; Ph.D., Cornell U., 1941; m. Marjorie Lois Shenk, Nov. 21, 1941; children—Roy Coleman, Marilyn Anne (Mrs. Parker E. Phillips). Chief prodn. engr., supt. services Sharples Chems., Inc., Wyandotte, Mich., 1941-50; asso. prof. chem. engring. U. Iowa, 1950-56; head high energy chems. Am. Potash & Chem. Corp., Whittier, Calif. and Henderson, Nev., 1956-59; prof. chem. engring. U. Iowa, 1959-64; prof., head dept. chem. engring. U. Akron, 1964-70, dean Coll. Engring., also dir. Inst. Technol. Assistance, 1970—, dir. Inst. Biomed. Engring. Research, 1979—; cons. materials and environ. engring. Chmn., Akron Regional Air Pollution Control Bd. Registered profl. engr., Ohio, Calif. Fellow Am. Inst. Chem. Engrs.; mem. Am. Chem. Soc., Am. Soc. Engring. Edn., Ohio Acad. Sci., Sigma Xi, Tau Beta Pi. Rotarian. Contbr. articles to tech. jours. Patentee in field. Home: 55 Fir Hill Akron OH 44304 Office: 302 E Buchtel Ave Akron OH 44325. *A few guidelines that I have used: 1. Work very hard but find time to relax. 2. Push yourself ahead, but don't hold anyone else back. 3. When gathering facts, be rigorous and unrelenting but when making decisions involving people, use the art of compromise.*

MAJOR, JAMES RUSSELL, educator, historian; b. Riverton, Va., Jan. 7, 1921; s. Julian Neville and Jean (Richards) M.; A.B., Va. Mil. Inst., 1942; M.A., Princeton, 1948, Ph.D., 1949; m. Blair Louise Rogers, June 9, 1945; children—Blair Louise, Randon Leigh, Clara Jean, James Russell. Mem. faculty Emory U., 1949—, prof. history, 1961—, chmn. dept., 1966-70, 76-79; vis. prof. Harvard, 1965-66; mem. Inst. Advanced Study Princeton, 1967-68, 79-80. Vice pres. H.W. Dick Co., 1975—. Served to capt. AUS, 1942-46. Decorated Silver Star, Bronze Star, Purple Heart with 2 clusters; Fulbright fellow, France, 1952-53; Guggenheim fellow, 1953-54, 67-68; Faculty Research fellow Soc. Sci. Research Council, 1955-58, fellow, 1961-62; sr. fellow Nat. Endowment for Humanities, 1973-74. Mem. Am. Hist. Assn. (mem. research div. 1979—), Internat. Commn. History Representative and Parliamentary Instn. (pres. N.Am. sect. 1975—), Renaissance Soc. Am. (mem. Council 1971-73), Am. Soc. Reformation Research, Soc. French Hist. Studies, Am. Assn. U. Profs. (pres. S.E. regional conf. 1965-67, mem. nat. council 1966-69), So. Hist. Assn. (chmn. European Sect. 1970-71), Société d'histoire de France, Phi Beta Kappa (senator United chapts. 1970-76). Author: The Estates General of 1560, 1951; Representative Instns. in Renaissance France, 1421-1559, 1960; The Deputies to the Estates General of Renaissance France, 1960; The Western World: Renaissance to the Present, 2d edit., 1971; The Age of the Renaissance and Reformation, 1970; Bellièvre, Sully and the Assembly of Notables of 1596, 1974; Representative Government in Early Modern France, 1980; also articles. Bd. editors Jour. Modern History, 1966-69. Home: 752 Houston Mill Rd Atlanta GA 30329

MAJOR, JEAN ARMOUR, librarian; b. Dixon, Ill., Aug. 28, 1939; d. Robert Henry and Martha Elizabeth (Henderson) Armour; student No. Ill. U., 1957-59; B.A., Lake Forest Coll., 1961; M.A.L.S., Rosary Coll., 1964; postgrad. Ind. U., 1977—; m. Robert Lear Major, Feb. 19, 1972. Cataloger, S.D. State U., 1964-65, U. Ill., Chgo. Circle, 1965-68; reference librarian U. Ill., Urbana, 1968-74; head undergrad. libraries Ohio State U., 1974-76; grad. teaching asst. Ind. U., 1977-78; dir. libraries No. Ill. U., 1978—. Mem. ALA, Ill. Library Assn., Assn. Coll. and Research Libraries, ACLU, Beta Phi Mu. Contbr. articles to profl. jours. Home: 102 Augusta Apt 203 DeKalb IL 60115 Office: No Ill U DeKalb IL 60115

MAJOR, JEAN-LOUIS, author, educator; b. Cornwall, Ont., Can., July 16, 1937; s. Joseph and Noella (Daoust) M.; B.A. with honors, U. Ottawa (Ont.), 1959, B.Philosophy, 1959, Licenciate of Philosophy, 1960, M.A., 1961, Ph.D., 1965; research asso. Ecole Pratique des Hautes Etudes, Paris, 1968-69; m. Bibiane Landry, June 4, 1960; 1 dau., Marie-France. Lectr. philosophy College Bruyere, Ottawa, 1960-61; lectr. dept. philosophy U. Ottawa, 1961-65, asst. prof. departement lettres Francaise, 1965-67, asso. prof., 1967-71, prof., 1971—; author books, including: Saint-Exupery, l'ecriture et la penseé, 1968; Leoné de Jean Cocteau, 1975; Anne Hébert et le miracle de la parole, 1976; Radiquet, Cocteau "Les joues enfeu", 1977; Le jeu en étoile, 1978; Paul-Marie Lapointe: la nuit incendice, 1978; contbr. numerous articles to profl. jours., 1962—; lit. critic, dir. lit. sect. Le Droit, newspaper, 1963-65; vis. prof. U. Toronto (Ont.), 1970-71. Can. Council fellow, 1968, 69, 71; Humanities Research Council Can. grantee, 1970. Fellow Royal Soc. Can.; mem. Association des Litteratures Canadiennes et Quebecoises, Academie des Lettres et des Sciences humaines. Home: 1676 Boyer St Orleans ON K1C 1R1 Canada Office: Faculty Arts U Ottawa Ottawa ON K1N 6N5 Canada

MAJOR, JOHN KEENE, radio broadcasting exec.; b. Kansas City, Mo., Aug. 3, 1924; s. Ralph Hermon and Margaret Norman (Jackson) M.; student U. Kansas City, 1940-41; B.S., Yale, 1943; M.S., 1947, D.Sc. (Fulbright fellow), U. Paris, 1951; m. Gracemary Somers Westing, Apr. 9, 1950 (div.); children—John Westing, Ann Somers, Richard Jackson; m. 2d, Lee Adair Jordan, June 25, 1970. Lab. asst. physics Yale, 1943-44; instr., research asst. physics, 1952-55; sci. staff spl. studies group, div. war research Columbia, 1944; instr. physics and chemistry Am. Community Sch., Paris, France, 1948-49; research fellow Centre National de la Recherche Scientifique, Laboratoire de Chimie Nucleaire, Coll. de France, Paris, 1951; Carnegie Found. fellow Laboratoire Curie, Institut du Radium, Paris, 1951; asso. prof. physics Western Res. U., 1955-57, chmn. dept., 1955-60, 61-64, Perkins prof. physics, 1957-66; staff asso. univ. sci. devel. sect. div. instl. programs NSF, 1964-68; prof. physics, dean Grad. Sch. Arts and Scis., U. Cin., 1968-71; prof. physics N.Y. U., 1971-74, dean Grad. Sch. Arts and Scis., 1971-73; vis. scholar Alfred P. Sloan Sch. Mgmt., Mass. Inst. Tech., 1973-74; prof. physics Northeastern Ill. U., Chgo., 1974-77, v.p. acad. affairs, 1974-75; cons. NSF, 1968-69; sci. cons. Sonar Analysis Group, 1946-47; gen. mgr. WONO (radio sta.), Syracuse, N.Y., 1977, dir. research and mktg. WFMT (radio sta.), Chgo., 1978—. Dir. T. Rowe Price Growth Stock Fund, Rowe Price New Horizons Fund. Served to lt. (j.g.) USNR, 1944-46. Fellow at Laboratorium fur Technische Physik, Technische Hochschule München, W. Germany, 1960-61. Fellow AAAS; mem. Am. Phys. Soc., Concert Music Broadcasters Assn. (exec. v.p., mem. exec. com. 1979-80), Sigma Xi. Clubs: Cosmos; Chgo. Press, Arts (Chgo.). Contbr. articles profl. jours. Home: 740 W Webster Ave Chicago IL 60614 Office: 500 N Michigan Ave Chicago IL 60611

MAJOR, WINFIELD WATSON, accountant; b. Slaughters, Ky., May 14, 1925; s. Carl King and Frances (Smith) M.; B.S., Bowling Green Coll. Commerce, 1949; C.P.A.; m. Margaret Wells, May 18, 1946; 1 son, Winfield W. Partner in charge Ernst & Ernst, Rochester, N.Y., 1963-78, joined Shelbyville (Tenn.) office through merger with Albert B. Maloney & Co., transferred to Murfreesboro, Tenn., 1952, Shelbyville, 1953, Rochester, 1959, Charlotte, N.C., 1978—, partner, 1963—; mem. N.Y. State Bd. Pub. Accountancy, 1966-76, chmn., 1975-76. Trustee Colgate Rochester Div. Sch., chmn., 1978. Served with USNR, 1944-46. Named Ky. col. Mem. Am. Inst. C.P.A.'s, Rochester C. of C. (trustee 1968-74), N.Y. Soc. C.P.A.'s (dir. 1973-75, pres. Rochester chpt. 1966-67). Clubs: Oak Hill Country (bd. govs. 1968-72, treas. 1970-72), Genesee Valley, Country of Rochester, Charlotte City. Home: 1911 Carmel Rd Charlotte NC 28211 Office: 2800 Wachovia Center Charlotte NC 28285

MAJORS, LEE, actor; b. Wyandotte, Mich., Apr. 23, 1940; student U. Ind.; grad. Eastern Ky. State Coll.; student acting with Estelle Harmon, MGM Studio Acting Sch.; m. Farrah Fawcett, July 28, 1973. Film appearances include: Will Penny, 1967, The Liberation of L.B. Jones, 1970, Killer Fish, 1979; TV films: The Six Million Dollar Man, 1973, Just a Little Convenience, 1977, The Ballad of Andy Crocker, 1969, Weekend of Terror, 1970, Francis Gary Powers: The U-2 Incident, 1977; TV series: The Big Valley, 1965-68, The Men from Shiloh, 1970-71, Owen Marshall, Counselor at Law, 1971-73, The Six Million Dollar Man, 1973-78; other TV appearances include: The Bionic Woman, Alias Smith and Jones, Bracken's World, Gunsmoke. Mem. AFTRA, Acad. Motion Picture Arts and Scis. Office: care William Morris Agy 151 El Camino Blvd Beverly Hills CA 90212*

MAJTHENYI, LADISLAUS D., mgmt. cons.; b. Kiscell, Hungary, Jan. 13, 1903; s. Alexander de and Maria (de Skublics) M.; student Acad. Commerce, Budapest, Hungary and Graz, Austria, 1920-24; m. Gabriella de Roboz, July 9, 1934; children—Klara, Alexander. Came to U.S., 1949, naturalized, 1954. With Nat. Bank Hungary, 1924-44, sect. chief Presdl. Dept., 1938-44; rep. of Austro-Impex, Linz, Austria, 1946-49; with affiliated companies Hambros Bank Ltd. (London, Eng.) in U.S., 1950-53; sr. partner Hambar Co., White Plains, N.Y., 1953-58, 69—; v.p. Pergamon Press Inc., 1954-63, pres., 1963-67, dep. chmn. bd., chmn. exec. com., 1967-69. Mem. com. to establish free port in Linz, 1948. Pres. Szechenyi Istvan Soc., Inc., N.Y.C., 1968—. Bd. dirs. Am. Found. for Hungarian Lit. and Edn., Ltd., N.Y.C., 1970—. Mem. AAAS, Am. Forestry Assn., Nat. Soc. Lit. and Art, several Am.-Hungarian socs. Club: K.C. Office: 84 Sterling Ave White Plains NY 10606

MAJUMDAR, MUKUL KUMAR, economist; b. Krishnagar, India, Dec. 6, 1944; s. Nirmal Kanti and Sita (Mitra) M.; came to U.S., 1965, naturalized, 1971; B.A. in Econs. with honors 1st class, Calcutta (India) U., 1966; Ph.D. in Econs., U. Calif., Berkeley, 1970; m. Malabika Dutta, Aug. 8, 1969. Asst. prof. econs. Stanford U., 1969-72; lectr. London Sch. Econs., 1972-73; asso. prof. Cornell U., 1973-77, prof., chmn. dept. econs., 1977—; Ford rotating research prof. U. Calif., Berkeley, 1976-77. Guggenheim fellow, 1976-77. Fellow Econometric Soc. Coordinating editor The Rev. Econ. Studies, 1976—; asso. editor Jour. Math. Econs., 1974—, Jour. Econ. Theory, 1977—. Office: Dept Econs Uris Hall Cornell U Ithaca NY 14850

MAK, DAYTON SEYMOUR, econ. cons.; b. Sioux Falls, S.D., July 10, 1917; s. Leo Leroy and Helen Martha (Dayton) M.; B.S., U. Ariz., 1939; student U. Pa., 1950-51; M.A., George Washington U., 1964; m. Julia Nelson Easley, Mar. 26, 1951; 1 dau., Helen Dayton. With Ill. Central R.R. Co., 1939-40; joined U.S. Fgn. Service, 1946; assigned Hamburg, Germany, 1946-48, Dhahran and Jidda, Saudi Arabia, 1949-50, Tripoli, Libya, 1951-53, London, Eng., 1954-56, State Dept., 1956-60 69-71; charge d'affaires embassy, Kuwait, 1961-63; assigned Naval War Coll., 1963-64, Am. embassy, Beirut, 1964-68, Nat. War Coll., 1969-70; dep. chief mission to Lebanon, 1968-69; ret. Dept. State, 1970; investment broker Leo L. Mak, Inc., Waterloo, Iowa, 1971-72, Ferris & Co., Washington, 1972-73; cons. Middle East Inst., Washington, 1974—. Served to 2d lt. AUS, 1941-45. Decorated Bronze Star, Purple Heart. Mem. Diplomatic and Consular Officers Ret., Sigma Alpha Epsilon. Clubs: City Tavern, Army and Navy; Am. (London). Home: 3247 P St NW Washington DC 20007

MAKAROVA, NATALIA, ballerina; b. Leningrad, Russia, Nov. 21, 1940; grad. Kaganova Ballet Sch., Leningrad Choreographic Sch., 1959; m. Edward Karkar, 1976; 1 son, Andre Michel. Formerly ballerina Leningrad Kirov Ballet; performed at Royal Opera House, Covent-Garden, London, 1961; toured U.S., 1961, 64; defected from Russia, 1970; danced with Rudolf Nureyev; roles include Giselle, Swan Lake, Chopiniana (Les Sylphides), Sleeping Beauty, Cinderella, Raymonda, others; joined Am. Ballet Theatre, 1970-72; guest appearances U.S. and London, 1972—. Recipient Gold medal 2d Internat. Ballet Competition, Varna, Bulgaria, 1965. Home: London England Office: care American Ballet Theatre 888 7th Ave New York NY 10019*

MAKDISI, GEORGE, educator, Arabist-Islamist; b. Detroit, May 15, 1920; s. Abraham George and Sophie (Chater) M.; B.A., U. Mich., 1947; M.A., Georgetown U., 1950; Docteur ès-Lettres, Sorbonne,

Paris, France, 1964; M.A. (hon.), Harvard, 1961, U. Pa., 1973; m. Margaret Anderson Gray, June 7, 1948 (dec.); children—John, Catherine, Thomas, Theresa, Anne, Jeanne; m. 2d, Nicole Renée Guillemette, Jan. 5, 1979. Asst. prof. Near Eastern studies U. Mich., then asso. prof., 1953-59; mem. faculty Harvard, 1959-73; prof. Arabic, 1964-73; prof. Arabic and Islamic studies U. Pa., 1973—, chmn. dept. Oriental studies, 1975—; dir. Center for Study of Byzantium, Islam and the Latin West, 1979—; chaire d'Etat, College de France, U. Paris, 1969; vis. prof. U. Paris, Sorbonne, 1978-79. Mem. Inter-univ. lang. com. Social Sci. Research Council, 1955-68; founding mem., then chmn. Am. Assn. Tchrs. Arabic, 1963-66; mem. adv. council Nat. Undergrad. Program Overseas Study Arabic, 1965; chmn. bd. dirs. Am. Inst. Islamic Studies, 1967-68; mem. nat. screening com. Inst. Internat. Edn., 1967; dir. Summer Inst. in Basic Disciplines in Medieval Studies, 1976. Served with AUS, 1942-45. Guggenheim fellow, 1957-58, 67-68; Fulbright-Hays fellow, 1967. Mem. Am. Oriental Soc., Mediaeval Acad. Am., Am. Hist. Soc., Middle East Inst., Middle East Studies Assn. (pres. 1976-77) Royal Asiatic Soc., AAUP, Am. Soc. Legal History, Asociacion Espanola de Orientalistas (Madrid), Middle E. Studies Assn. N.Am. Author: Kitab at-Tauwabin: Le Livre des Pénitents d'Ibn Qudáma 1961; Ibn Qudama's Censure of Speculative Theology, 1962; Ibn Aqil et la Resurgence de l'Islam Traditionaliste au XIe Siecle, 1963; Arabic and Islamic Studies in Honor of Hamilton A.R. Gibb, 1965; Le Livre de la Dialectique d'Ibn Aqil, 1967; Notebooks of Ibn Aqil, 1969-71; The Scholastic Method in Medieval Education, 1974; L'Islam Hanbalisant, 1977; Medieval Education in Islam and the West, 1977; also articles and monographs. Home: 751 Farnum Rd Media PA 19063 Office: 841 Williams Hall U Pennsylvania Philadelphia PA 19174

MAKECHNIE, GEORGE KINSLEY, coll. dean emeritus; b. Everett, Mass., Jan. 6, 1907; s. Charles A. and Mabel (Downing) M.; B.S., Boston U., 1929, Ed.M., 1931, L.H.D., 1979; m. Anne Schonland, June 12, 1933; children—Norman H., Arthur K., Joan D. Diver. Asst. to dean Boston U. Sch. Edn., 1930-35, registrar and asso. prof. edn., 1935-43. curriculum dir., civil affairs tng. sch. U.S. Army, 1943-45, prof., dir. undergrad. studies, 1943-45; dean Boston U. Sargent Coll. of Allied Health Professions, 1945-72, dean emeritus, 1972—, acting dean Sch. Fine and Applied Arts, 1959-61. Dir. Perceptual Edn. Center, 1966-68; former pres. Mass. Assn. Health, Phys. Edn. and Recreation. Author monographs in Bellman Series on Vocational Guidance; Optimal Health: The Quest, 1979; also contbr. to jours. Home: 50 Winthrop Rd Lexington MA 02173

MAKELA, BENJAMIN R., editor, research dir.; b. Hancock, Mich., Mar. 23, 1922; s. Charles Robert and Engel (Kruka) M.; B.A., George Washington U., 1943; M.A., Stanford, 1954; m. Betty Virginia Shade, June 26, 1954; 1 son, Gregory Strickler. Statistician, Dept. Commerce, 1946, Nat. Fertilizer Assn., 1947-48; research economist U.S. C. of C., 1948-53; asso. dir. Financial Execs. Inst., N.Y.C., 1953-63; editor Financial Exec., 1963-72; research dir. Financial Execs. Research Found., 1966—. Served with AUS, 1943-46, 51-53. Mem. Am. Finance Assn., Am. Accounting Assn., Am. Mgmt. Assn., Phi Beta Kappa, Pi Gamma Mu, Omicron Delta Gamma, Sigma Nu. Republican. Baptist. Clubs: Stanford Alumni (N.Y.C.); Squadron A. Editor: How to Use and Invest in Letter Stock, 1970; (with William Chatlos) Strategy of Corporate Tender Offers, 1971; (with D.R. Carmichael) Corporate Financial Reporting: The Benefits and Problems of Disclosure, 1976. Editorial adv. bd. Financial Exec.'s Handbook, also author chpt. Home: 88-A Heritage Hills Somers NY 10589 Office: 633 3d Ave New York City NY 10017

MAKHOLM, MARK HENRY, ins. co. exec.; b. Maple Valley, Wis., Jan. 10, 1915; s. Henry and Emma Dorothy Agnet (Johnson) M.; B.A. magna cum laude, Northland Coll., Ashland, Wis., 1937; LL.B., U. Wis., 1950; m. Phylis Shoger, Nov. 11, 1950; children—Linda Marie, Mark Henry, Martha Marie. Asst. prof. Northland Coll., 1937-38; high sch. tchr., Washburn, Wis., 1939-41; operational supr. E.I. duPont de Neumours & Co. Inc., also U.S. Rubber Co., Kankakee, Ill., 1941-45; high sch. tchr., West Bend, Wis., 1945-47; engaged in retail clothing bus., West Bend, 1947-48; admitted to Wis. bar, 1950, U.S. Supreme Ct., 1950; practice in Ashland, 1950-52; with Sentry Ins. a Mut. Co.-Sentry Life Ins. Co., Stevens Point, Wis., 1952—, v.p., gen. counsel, 1962-78, exec. v.p., 1978—, also dir.; dir. Middlesex Ins. Co., Gt. S.W. Fire Ins. Co., The Sentry Corp., Dairyland Ins. Co., Sentry Indemnity Co. Mem. Am., Wis. bar assns., Internat. Assn. Ins. Counsel, Order of Coif, Phi Delta Phi. Kiwanian. Club: Madison (Wis.). Home: 616 Greenbriar Ave Park Ridge Stevens Point WI 54481 Office: 1800 North Point Dr Stevens Point WI 54481

MAKI, KAZUMI, physicist; b. Takamatsu, Japan, Jan. 27, 1936; s. Toshio and Hideko M.; B.S., Kyoto U., 1959, Ph.D., 1964; m. Masako Tanaka, Sept. 21, 1969. Research asso. Inst. for Math. Scis., Kyoto U., 1964; research asso. Fermi Inst., U. Chgo., 1964-65; asst. prof. physics U. Calif., San Diego, 1965-67; prof. Tohoku U., Sendai, Japan, 1967-74; vis. prof. Universite Paris-Sud, Orsay, France, 1969-70; prof. physics U. So. Calif., Los Angeles, 1974—. Fulbright scholar, 1964-65; Guggenheim fellow, 1979-80. Recipient Nishina prize, 1972. Mem. Am. Phys. Soc., Phys. Soc. Japan, AAAS. Contbr. articles to profl. jours. Home: 2615 33d Santa Monica CA 90405 Office: Physics Dept U So Calif Los Angeles CA 90007

MAKLEY, TORRENCE ALOYSIUS, JR., ophthalmologist, educator; b. Dayton, Ohio, Jan. 11, 1918; s. Torrence Aloysius and Katherine (Fitzpatrick) M.; B.S., U. Dayton, 1940; M.D., Washington U., St. Louis, 1943; m. Anne Gorham, Mar. 24, 1945; children—Torrence Aloysius III, Mary Jane, Heleanor, William, Katherine, John, Michael. Intern Barnes Hosp., St. Louis, 1944; fellow ophthalmic pathology Armed Forces Inst. Pathology, Washington, 1947; resident ophthalmology Ohio State U. Hosp., 1948-50; practice medicine specializing in ophthalmology, Columbus, 1950—; mem. faculty Ohio State U., 1950—, prof. ophthalmology, 1963—, chmn. dept., 1963-73. Served as capt., M.C., AUS, 1945-46. Clubs: Scioto Country, Serra (Columbus). Contbr. articles to profl. jours. Home: 1760 Roxbury Rd Columbus OH 43212

MAKY, WALTER, lawyer; b. Cleve., June 4, 1916; s. Viktor and Saimi (Pahkala) M.; B.S., Cleve. State U., 1940, J.D., 1947; m. Helen Marian Rancken, Dec. 3, 1938; children—Pamela (Mrs. Ronald Boyarsky), Bonita (Mrs. Stephen Swift). Spot welder Gray Wire Splty. Co., 1934-37; trouble shooter Ohio Bell Telephone Co., 1937-38; patent agt. Parker-Hannifin Corp., 1938-45; admitted to Ohio bar, 1947, since practiced in Cleve.; mem. firm Maky, Renner, Otto & Boiselle, Cleve., 1945—. Consul of Finland, State of Ohio, 1951—. Mem. Am., D.C., Greater Cleve. bar assns., Nat. Council Patent Law Assns. (councilman 1972-73), Am., Cleve. (pres. 1971-72) patent law assns. Club: Ashtabula (Ohio) Country. Home: 33320 Cromwell Dr Solon OH 44139 Office: 1200 One Public Square Bldg Cleveland OH 44113

MALACH, MONTE, physician; b. Jersey City, Aug. 15, 1926; s. Charles and Yetta (Pascher) M.; B.A., U. Mich., 1949, M.D., 1949; m. Ann Elaine Glazer, June 15, 1952; children—Barbara Sandra, Cathie Tara, Matthew David. Intern, Beth Israel Hosp., Boston, 1949-50, resident, 1950-52; chief resident Kings County Hosp., Bklyn., 1954-55; practice medicine specializing in internal medicine and cardiology, Bklyn., 1955—; dir. coronary care unit Bklyn. Hosp., 1965—; pres. profl. staff Bklyn.-Cumberland Med. Center, 1966-69, chmn. med. bd., 1971-72; attending staff Caledonian Hosp.; cons. cardiology Baptist Hosp., Kings County Hosp.; teaching fellow Tufts Med. Sch., 1951-52; instr. medicine Downstate Med. Center, Bklyn., 1955-59, clin. asst. prof. medicine, 1959-68, clin. asso. prof., 1969-76, clin. prof., 1976—. Kings County committeeman Democratic Party, 1964, 65. Served to ensign USNR, 1944-46; 1st lt. M.C., U.S. Army, 1952-54. Diplomate Am. Bd. Internal Medicine, Nat. Bd. Med. Examiners. Fellow Am. Coll. Chest Physicians, A.C.P., Am. Coll. Cardiology; mem. N.Y. Heart Assn., AMA (vice chmn. sect. council for internal medicine), Am. Soc. Internal Medicine (trustee 1975-79, sec.-treas. 1979—), N.Y. State Soc. Internal Medicine (pres. 1973-74, dir. 1966—, chmn. Bklyn. chpt., v.p. 1971, award of merit 1978), Bklyn. Soc. Internal Medicine (mem. council 1965, pres. 1969-72), Med. Soc. State of N.Y. (chmn. sect. internal medicine 1976), Fed. Council for Internal Medicine (vice chmn.). Address: 55 Rugby Rd Brooklyn NY 11226. *There is a place for hard work, scrupulous ethics and pride of accomplishment. A great marriage and a fine close family are buffers against adversity.*

MALAFRONTE, DONALD, health exec.; b. Bklyn., Dec. 16, 1931; s. Pasquale and Amalia (Castaldo) M.; B.S., N.Y.U., 1954; m. Diane Freedenberg, Jan. 7, 1960 (dec. Nov. 1970); children—Philip, Victor. Reporter, L.I. Daily Press, 1956-58; reporter, editor Newark Star-Ledger, 1958-65, art columnist, 1963-70; adminstrv. asst. to mayor of Newark, 1965-70; dir. Newark Model Cities Program, 1967-70; dir. Newark Community Devel. Adminstrn., 1968-70; chief urban field operations N.J. Regional Med. Program, 1970-73; dir. Urban Health Inst., East Orange, N.J., 1973—; cons. to local, state govts., 1970—. Served with AUS, 1954-56. Recipient Joyce Kilmer fiction prize N.Y.U., 1953. Author articles in field. Home: 78 Crestview Rd Mountain Lakes NJ 07046 Office: Urban Health Inst 7 Glenwood Ave East Orange NJ 07017

MALAMED, SEYMOUR H., motion picture co. exec.; b. N.Y.C., June 17, 1921; s. Abraham and Bess (Kaisin) M.; B.B.A., City Coll. N.Y., 1942; m. Doris Raphael, May 19, 1946; children—Margery, Susan, Nancy. Engaged in entertainment field, 1954—; asst. to v.p., treas. Screen Gems Co., 1956-62; treas. parent co. Columbia Pictures Corp., 1962—, v.p., 1963-73, exec. v.p., 1973—. Served with AUS, World War II. Mem. Motion Picture Acad. Arts and Scis. Clubs: Friars (N.Y.C.); Glen Head Country. Home: 425 E 58th St New York City NY 10022 Office: 711 Fifth Ave New York City NY 10022

MALAMUD, BERNARD, writer; b. Bklyn., Apr. 26, 1914; s. Max and Bertha (Fidelman) M.; B.A., Coll. City N.Y., 1936; M.A., Columbia, 1942; m. Ann de Chiara, Nov. 6, 1945; children—Paul, Janna. Tchr. English eve. high schs., N.Y.C., 1940-49; instr. to asso. prof. English, Oreg. State U., 1949-61; mem. lang. and lit. div. Bennington (Vt.) Coll., 1961—; vis. lectr. Harvard, 1966-68; pres. P.E.N. Am. Center, 1979. Partisan Review fellow fiction, 1956-57; recipient Rosenthal award Nat. Inst. Arts and Letters, 1958; Daroff Meml. award, 1958; Nat. Book award for fiction, 1959, 67; Ford fellow humanities and arts program, 1959-61; Jewish Heritage award B'nai B'rith, 1976; Gov.'s award Vt. Council on the Arts, 1979. Mem. Am. Acad. and Inst. Arts and Letters, Am. Acad. Arts and Scis. Author: The Natural, 1952; The Assistant, 1957; The Magic Barrel (Fiction prize Nat. Book award 1959), 1958; A New Life, 1961; Idiots First, 1963; The Fixer, 1967 (fiction prize Nat. Book award 1967, Pulitzer prize 1967); Pictures of Fidelman, 1969; The Tenants, 1971; Rembrandts Hat, 1973; Dubin's Lives, 1979. Contbr. short stories, periodicals, collections. Address: care Russell and Volkening 551 Fifth Ave New York NY 10017

MALAMUD, PHYLLIS CAROLE, journalist; b. Bklyn., Sept. 15; d. Louis and Hannah (Unterman) M.; B.A., CCNY, 1960; postgrad. (Russell Sage Found. fellow), Washington U., St. Louis, 1968-69. Publicity asst. Newsweek mag., N.Y.C., 1960-62, researcher, 1962-64, feature reporter, 1964-74, N.Y. polit. reporter, N.Y.C., 1975-77, chief New Eng. bur., Boston, 1977—. Recipient Gavel award Am. Bar Assn., 1968; award for article Am. Psychol. Assn., 1975, N.Y. Newspaper Guild, 1977. Office: Prudential Tower Suite 1918 Boston MA 02199

MALAN, JOSEPH VERNON, credit union exec.; b. Linn, Mo., Apr. 5, 1934; s. Joseph W. and Beulah (Mantle) M.; B.S. in Bus. Adminstrn., U. Mo., 1956; m. Barbara Sue Medley, Mar. 14, 1964; children—Lawrence Edward, Lori Dawn. Accountant, U.S. Army Audit Agy., 1956-57; sr. accountant Peat, Marwick, Mitchell & Co., 1959-65; with City Nat. Bank, Detroit, 1965-77, v.p., cashier, 1969-74, exec. v.p., 1974-77; mgr. Central Credit Union of Mich., Southfield, 1978—. C.P.A., Mo. Mem. Am. Inst., C.P.A.'s Mich. Soc. C.P.A.'s, Credit Union Execs. Soc., Delta Sigma Pi, Beta Gamma Sigma. Home: 25043 St Christopher St Mount Clemens MI 48045 Office: 15600 Providence Dr Southfield MI

MALANGA, GERARD JOSEPH, poet, photographer; b. N.Y.C., Mar. 20, 1943; s. Gerardo and Emma (Rocco) M.; student Coll. Applied Arts U. Cin., 1960-61, (Sch. scholar) New Sch. for Social Research, 1961; B.A. (anonymous fund fellow), Wagner Coll., 1964; studied Dharma under Geshey Ngawang Dargay, Tibetan lama tchr., at Library of Tibetan Works and Archives, Dharmsala, India, 1972; designated to collect manuscripts of Beat poets for Harris Poetry Collection, beginning 1961; idea man, silk screen technician for paintings, actor, asst. dir. for films with Andy Warhol, 1963-70; portrait photographer, 1969—; one-man shows: Rice U., Internat. Mus. Photography at George Eastman House, Rochester, N.Y., Spl. Collections Library at U. Tex., U. Wis.-Parkside Library, Nat. Gallery of Australia, Sydney; with UU World newspaper Unitarian Universalist Assn., Boston, 1973; numerous poetry readings at univs.; condr. poetry writing workshops; participant writers' confs.; choreographer, dancer Velt Underground's Exploding Plastic Inevitable multimedia show, 1966. Nat. Inst. Arts and Letters grantee; Am. Film Inst. grantee; recipient Avant-Garde Poetry prize Gotham Book Mart, Dylan Thomas Meml. Poetry prize New Sch. for Social Research. Mem. Film-maker's Coop., Poetry Soc. Am. Author numerous books, the most recent being: 10 Poems For 10 Poets, 1970; the blue book, 1970; beatle calendar, 1970; chic death, 1971; poetry on film, 1972; Wheels of Light, 1972; The Poetry of Night, Dawn and Dream/Nine Poems for Cesar Vellejo, 1972; Licht/Light, 1973; (with A. T. Mann) A Portfolio of Four Duographs, 1973; 7 Poems For Pilar Crespi, 1973; Incarnations (Poems 1965-1971), 1974; Rosebud, 1975; Leaping Over Gravestones, 1976; Ten Years After: 1965-71, 1977; 100 Years Have Passed, 1978; contbg. author anthologies: The Young American Poets; The East Side Scene; The World Anthology; Another World; The New Yorker Book of Poems. Editor: Intransit: The Andy Warhol-Gerard Malanga Monster Issue, 1968; The Personal Cinema of Gerard Malanga, 1968; Film Culture No. 45-The Superstar Issue, 1968; Underground Cinema Eroticism & Visual Poetry Supplement of Other Scenes, 1969; co-founder (with Andy Warhol), editor inter/VIEW, Vol. 1, Nos. 1, 2, 3, 1969; editor The Ant's Forefoot #7/8, 1971; The Transatlantic Rev. #52; Little Caesar #9, 1979; Coldspring Jour. #12, 1979. English translator poems and prose poems of Cesar Vallejo. Holographs, papers and archive part of permanent poetry collections at libraries U. Tex., Syracuse U., U. Calif. at Los Angeles. Home: 203 E 14th St New York NY 10003

MALARKEY, MARTIN FRANCIS, JR., cable television and radio exec.; b. Pottsville, Pa., May 1, 1918; s. Martin Francis and Gertrude (Cress) M.; B.S. in Law and Accounting, LaSalle Coll., Phila.; m. Catherine Clare McCarthy, May 30, 1935; 1 dau., Clare Ann (Mrs. John E. Hampford); m. 2d, Elizabeth Koehn Onesto, May 29, 1961. Vice pres. Malarkey's, Inc., Pottsville, 1939-42, pres., 1946-50; pres., dir. Trans Video Corps., Washington, 1950-59, radio sta. WRTA, Altoona, Pa., 1956—; owner Eastern Shore Microwave Relay Co., Washington, 1961-75; pres. Malarkey, Taylor and Assos. Inc., Washington, 1959—; pres. radio sta. WMBT, Shenandoah, Pa., 1970—; pioneer in devel. cable television. Pres. Washington Internat. Horse Show Assn., 1976-77; trustee Nat. Symphony Orch. Assn., Washington Hosp., Center. Served with USNR, World War II. Mem. Nat. Cable TV Assn. (founder, 1st pres.). Clubs: Nat. Broadcasters (pres. 1966-68), Georgetown, City Tavern Assn. (Washington). Home: 1817 Kalorama Sq NW Washington DC 20008

MALARKEY, THOMAS B., JR., lumber co. exec.; b. Portland, Oreg., Nov. 2, 1928; B.A., Yale U., 1952; m. Catharine Brent Hord, Oct. 1, 1960; children—Thomas, Tucker, Sarah. With United Press Asso., 1952-55; with Pacific Lumber Co., San Francisco, 1955—, exec. v.p. mktg. and adminstrn., 1976—. Office: 1111 Columbus Ave San Francisco CA 94133

MALAS, SPIRO, basso; b. Balt., Jan. 28, 1936; s. Sam and Lillian (Lambros) M.; B.S., Towson State Coll., 1960; m. Marlena Kleinman, Sept. 30, 1963; children—Alexis, Nicol. Debuts include: Covent Garden, 1967, Vienna State Opera, 1967; appearances in U.S. and Europe, including: N.Y.C. Opera, San Francisco Opera, Lyric Opera Chgo.; Command Performance for Queen, Covent Garden, 1968; performed in operas for NBC-TV, Pub. Broadcasting System-TV. Served with Mil. Police, U.S. Army, 1953-55. Winner Met. Opera Auditions and Am. Opera Auditions, 1961; recipient citation and Key to City, Mayor of Balt., 1970. Democrat. Greek Orthodox. Home: 245 W 104th St New York City NY 10025 Office: care New York City Opera Lincoln Center Plaza New York City NY 10023

MALCOLM, GEORGE (JOHN), musician; b. London, Feb. 28, 1917; s. George Hope and Johanna (Brosnahan) M.; ed. Royal Coll. Music, London; M.A. (hon. fellow), Balliol Coll. Oxford (Eng.) U., 1942; D.Mus. (hon.), Sheffield U., 1978. Master of cathedral music Westminster Cathedral, 1947-59; concert harpsichordist, pianist, condr., 1959—, including continuous European tours and U.S. appearances; rec. artist. Served with Royal Air Force Vol. Res., 1940-46. Decorated comdr. Order Brit. Empire, papal knight Order St. Gregory. Fellow Royal Coll. Music. Roman Catholic. Contbr. numerous articles to musical jours.; composer: Missa ad Praesepe, 1956. Home: 38 Cheyne Walk London SW 3 5HJ England Office: care Kazuko Hillyer Internat 250 W 57th St New York NY 10019

MALDEN, KARL (MALDEN SEKULOVICH), actor; b. Chgo., Mar. 22, 1913; s. Peter and Minnie (Sebera) Sekulovich; student Art Inst., Chgo., 1935-36, Goodman Theatre, Chgo., 1937-38; m. Mona Graham, Dec. 18, 1938; children—Mila, Carla. Actor, 1935—; stage plays include: Golden Boy, 1938, Gentle People, 1939, Key Largo, 1940, Flight to the West, 1942, Uncle Harry, 1940, All My Sons, 1949, A Streetcar Named Desire, 1950, Desire Under the Elms, 1952; in motion pictures, 1940—, including: Boomerang, Gunfighter, 1945, Halls of Montezuma, 1950, A Streetcar Named Desire, 1950, Ruby Gentry, 1952, I Confess, 1953, On the Waterfront, 1954, Baby Doll, 1956, Desperate Hours, 1957, Fear Strikes Out, 1957, The Hanging Tree, 1959, Pollyanna, 1960, One Eyed Jacks, 1961, Parrish, The Adventures of Bullwhip Griffin, 1967, Patton, 1970, Beyond the Poseidon Affair, 1978, Meteor, 1979; dir. Time Limit, 1957, Billion Dollar Brain, 1967, Hot Millions, 1968, Blue Hotel, Cat O'Nine Tails, 1971, Wild Rovers, 1971, Summertime Killer, 1973; star TV series Streets of San Francisco, 1972-77, Skag, 1980—. Recipient Donaldson award, 1950, Oscar award, 1951. Home: care William Morris Agy 151 El Camino Dr Beverly Hills CA 90212

MALE, ROY RAYMOND, educator; b. Bklyn., Mar. 15, 1919; s. Roy Raymond and Mary Edwards (Brooks) M.; B.S., Hamilton Coll., 1939; M.A., Columbia, 1940; Ph.D., U. Tex., 1950; m. Carolyn Kate Conlisk, Aug. 19, 1944; children—Marilyn, Frank. Instr. English, U. Tex., 1946-50; asst. prof. Tex. Tech. Coll., 1950-55; mem. faculty U. Okla., 1955—, now Boyd prof. English; vis. prof. Bowling Green U., 1962, U. Wash., 1968, U. Tex. at Arlington, 1971. Served with AUS, 1940-45. Ford Found. fellow, 1954-55. Recipient Regents award excellence teaching U. Okla., 1968. Mem. A.A.U.P., Assn. U. Profs., Modern Lang. Assn., A.C.L.U., Lambda Chi Alpha. Author: Hawthorne's Tragic Vision, 1957; Enter, Mysterious Stranger, 1979; editor: Types of Short Fiction, 2d edit., 1970. Home: 709 Chautauqua St Norman OK 73069

MALEC, WILLIAM FRANK, utilities co. exec.; b. Broadalbin, N.Y., June 22, 1940; s. Henry and Anna Frances M.; B.S. cum laude, Niagara U., 1962; M.B.A., Ind. U., 1967; m. Sarah Powell, Sept. 11, 1965; children—Charles, Mariah. Mgmt. trainee Marine Midland Bank, Buffalo, 1962-63; project budget analyst Cleve. Electric Illuminating Co., 1967-68; asst. treas. Mid Continent Telephone Co., Hudson, Ohio, 1968-75; v.p., treas. Gulf States Utilities, Beaumont, Tex., 1975-78; v.p., treas. Central and South West Services, Inc., Dallas, 1978—; treas. Central and South West Corp., Dallas, Central and South West Fuels, Denver. Chmn. large industry United Appeal, 1977-78; precinct chmn. Republican Party, Jefferson County, Tex., 1977. Served with U.S. Army, 1963-65. Mem. Edison Electric Inst., Fin. Execs. Inst., Beaumont C. of C. (chmn. govt. affairs com. 1977-78). Roman Catholic. Clubs: Spring Valley Country, Northpark Racquet Ball. Office: 2700 One Main Pl Dallas TX 75250

MALECKI, HENRY RAYMOND, coll. adminstr.; b. Chgo., Mar. 10, 1922; s. Andrew and Maryanne (Baginski) M.: B.S., No. Ill. U., 1947; M.S., Purdue U., 1949, Ph.D., 1952. Dir. student tchrs. Loyola U., Chgo., 1957-62, dir. tchr. certification and placement, 1962-67, dir. tchr. edn., 1962-67, dir. summer sessions, 1970-77, dean Univ. Coll., 1967—. Served with AUS, 1943-46. Fellow AAAS; mem. Am. Personnel and Guidance Assn., Nat. Vocational Guidance Assn., Am. Ednl. Research Assn., Am. Psychol. Assn., Phi Delta Kappa, Kappa Delta Pi. Home: 155 N Harbor Dr Chicago IL 60601

MALEK, FREDERIC VINCENT, food and hotel co. exec.; b. Oak Park, Ill., Dec. 22, 1937; s. Fred W. and Martha (Smicklas) M.; B.S., U.S. Mil. Acad., 1959; M.B.A., Harvard, 1964; m. Marlene A. McArthur, Aug. 5, 1961; children—Fred W., Michelle A. Asso., McKinsey & Co., Inc., Los Angeles, 1964-67; chmn. Triangle Corp., Columbia, S.C., 1967-69; dep. under sec. HEW, 1969-70; spl. asst. to Pres. U.S., 1970-73; dep. dir. Office Mgmt. and Budget, 1973-75; exec. v.p. Marriott Corp., Washington, 1975—; dir. Sun Line Greece, Inc., Oceanic Spl. Shipping Co., Inc., Sargent Welch Sci. Co., Automatic Data Processing Corp.; adj. prof. U. S.C., 1968-69; lectr. Kennedy Sch. Govt. Harvard U., 1976. Mem. President's Commn. on White House Fellows, 1971-75, White House Domestic Council, 1974-75, President's Commn. on Personnel Interchange, 1974-76. Mem. Calif. Republican Central Com., 1967-68; dep. dir. com. for Re-election of

Pres., 1972. Mem. adv. bd. Teach Found. Served to 1st lt. AUS, 1959-62. Clubs: Harvard So. Calif. (bd. dirs., 1st v.p. 1965-67), University (com. chmn. 1966-68) (Los Angeles). Author: Washington's Hidden Tragedy: The Failure to Make Government Work, 1978. Contbr. articles to mgmt. jours. Home: 6709 Lupine Ln McLean VA 22101 Office: Marriott Dr Washington DC 20058

MALENBAUM, WILFRED, economist; b. Boston, Jan. 26, 1913; s. Harry and Bertha (Brandwyn) M.; A.B., Harvard, 1934, A.M., 1935, Ph.D., 1941; postgrad. London Sch. Econs., 1937, Inst. Econs., Oslo, Norway, 1938; m. Josephine J. Orenstein, Feb. 26, 1950 (dec. 1965); children—Bruce, Roxanne, Ronald; m. 2d, Gloria B. Balaban, Oct. 31, 1976. Instr. econs. Harvard, 1938-41; chief food and agr. sect. OSS, 1941-45; chief div. internat. and functional intelligence Dept. State, 1946-48, chief div. investment and econ. devel., 1948-53; tech. specialist 1st UNRRA conf., Atlantic City, 1943; U.S. mem. combined Working Party, London, Algiers, Rome, 1944-45; U.S. del. London Conf. on Food and Agrl. Statistics, 1945; tech. cons. FAO, WHO; specialist Meeting on Urgent Food Problems, 1946; adviser U.S. Delegation to Interim Commn. of Internat. Trade Orgn., Geneva, 1948; dir. India project Center for Internat. Studies, also vis. prof. econs. Mass. Inst. Tech., 1953—; in India directing Mass. Inst. Tech. research project, 1955-56; prof. econs. Wharton Sch., U. Pa., 1959—; vis. prof. U. Hawaii, 1961, Harvard, 1964; chair internat. econs. Heidelberg U., spring 1966. Cons., Govt. of India, 1963; U.S. del. Colombo Plan Conf., Karachi, Pakistan, 1952; U.S. del. SEATO, Baguio, P.I., 1960; cons. tech. assistance-internat. health AID; mem. U.S. Council for Internat. Health, 1971—; prin. investigator Nat. Commn. on Materials Policy, 1972-73, NSF research project on fgn. demand for raw materials, 1975—; mem. com. on resources and the environment Nat. Acad. Scis., 1973-75. Exchange scientist Council Sci. and Indsl. Research (India), NSF, 1971, 72; Ford Found. grantee, 1973; Smithsonian Instn. sr. fellow, India, 1977-78. Recipient Detur Award, 1931; Rogers Traveling fellow, 1937-38; David A. Wells prize, 1943. Mem. Am. Econ. Assn., Am. Farm Econ. Assn., Assn. Asian Studies, Asia Soc., Soc. for Internat. Devel., Phi Beta Kappa, Sigma Alpha Mu. Author: The World Wheat Economy, 1885-39, 1953; India and China; Development Contrasts, 1956; East and West in Indian Development, 1959; Prospects for Indian Development, 1962; Modern India's Economy: Two Decades of Planned Growth, 1971; Materials Requirements in the United States and Abroad in the Year 2000, 1973; World Demand for Raw Materials in 1985 and 2000, 1978. Home: 527 S 41st St Philadelphia PA 19104

MALENKA, BERTRAM JULIAN, educator, physicist; b. N.Y.C., June 8, 1923; s. Morris and Mollie (Wichtel) M.; A.B., Columbia, 1947; M.A., Harvard, 1949, Ph.D., 1951; m. Ruth D. Stolper, Mar. 28, 1948; children—David Jonathan, Robert Charles. Research fellow Harvard, 1951-54; asst. prof. physics Washington U., St. Louis, 1954-56; asso. prof. Tufts U., Medford, Mass., 1956-60; faculty Northeastern U., Boston, 1960—, prof. physics, 1962—. Mem. sci. adv. group Harvard-Mass. Inst. Tech. Cambridge Electron Accelerator, 1956—. Mem. Am., Italian phys. socs., N.Y. Acad. Scis., Phi Beta Kappa, Sigma Xi. Research and publs. on theory of nuclear forces and structure of nucleus, explanation polarization phenomena in high-energy scattering, gamma radiation, electric polarization deuteron, accelerator design. Home: 16 Rutledge Rd Belmont MA 02178 Office: Dept Physics Northeastern U Boston MA 02115

MALETZ, HERBERT NAAMAN, U.S. judge; b. Boston, Oct. 30, 1913; s. Reuben and Frances (Sawyer) M.; A.B., Harvard, 1935, LL.B., 1939; m. Catherine B. Loebach, May 8, 1947; 1 son, David M. Admitted to Mass. bar, 1939, D.C. bar, 1952; mem. staff Truman com. U.S. Senate, 1941-42; atty. anti-trust div. Dept. Justice, 1946-50; with OPS, 1950-53, chief counsel, 1952-53; chief counsel anti-trust subcom. U.S. Ho. of Reps., 1955-61; commr. U.S. Ct. Claims, 1961-67; judge U.S. Customs Ct., N.Y.C., 1967—. Served with AUS, 1942-46; lt. col. Res. Home: 17 S Morris Ln Scarsdale NY 10583 Office: 1 Federal Plaza New York City NY 10007*

MALEY, DONALD, educator; b. Buena Vista, Pa., Jan. 6, 1918; s. William and Christina (Hartmann) M.; B.S., State Tchrs. Coll. (California, Pa.), 1944; M.A., U. Md., 1947, Ph.D., 1950. Foundryman, Fort Pitt Steel Casting Co., McKeesport, Pa., 1936-40; faculty dept. indsl. edn. U. Md., College Park, 1949—, instr., 1949-51, asst. prof., 1951-53, asso. prof., 1953-56, prof., 1956—, head dept., 1957—; guest lectr. Arabian Am. Oil Co., Saudi Arabia, 1954. Cons. to industry and Md. schs. Mem. state bd. mgrs. Md. Congress Parents and Tchrs., 1966-73, audio-visual chmn., 1966-69, vocational-tech. chmn., 1969-73. Bd. dirs. Md. Ednl. TV Council; chmn. Westminster Found., U. Md., Harold R.W. Benjamin Nat. Meml. Fund. Served to lt. USNR, 1943-46. Mem. Am. Indsl. Arts Assn., Am. Vocational Assn., Md. Vocational Assn. (pres. 1963), Am. Council Indsl. Arts Tchr. Edn. (Man of Year 1970, pres. 1960-61). Author: (textbook) The Maryland Plan: A Program in the Industrial Arts, 1973; Cluster Concept as an Approach to Teaching in the Vocational Fields, 1974. Producer-writer ednl. films: Tomorrow Begins Yesterday, 1971, The Group Project, 1967, Research and Experimentation in Industrial Arts, 1961, The Seminar, 1965. Author: The Industrial Arts Teacher's Handbook: Techniques, Principles, and Methods, 1978; contbr. yearbooks. Home: 3310 Powder Mill Rd Hyattsville MD 20783. *The mental and physical gifts with which each of us is endowed brings with such endowment the moral obligation to use them to their fullest for the betterment of all mankind. To do less would be the highest form of self indulgence as well as an abandonment of our reason for being.*

MALEY, SAMUEL WAYNE, educator; b. Sidney, Neb., Mar. 1, 1928; s. Samuel Raymond and Inez (Moore) M.; B.S., U. Colo., 1952, M.S., 1957, Ph.D., 1959; student U. N.M., 1957-58; m. Elizabeth Anne Green, June 11, 1963; children—Karen Margaret, Laura Elaine. Geophysicist, Stanolind Oil Co., Lubbock, Tex., 1952; design engr. Beach Aircraft Corp., Wichita, Kan., 1952-53; design engr. Dynalectron Corp., Cheyenne, Wyo., 1953-56; research scientist U. Colo., 1959-60, vis. lectr., 1960-61, asst. prof., 1961-62, asso. prof. elec. engring., 1962-67, prof., 1967—; cons. Nat. Center Atmospheric Research, 1964, Automation Industries Research Div., Boulder, Colo. 1960-71, Midwec Corp., Ogallala, Neb., 1969-70, IBM, Boulder, 1969—. Served with AUS, 1946-47, USAF, 1947-48. Mem. I.E.E.E., Am. Assn. U. Profs., A.A.A.S., Soc. Indsl. and Applied Math. Methodist. Author: Combinational Logic Circuits, 1969. Research electromagnetic theory; communication theory; computer design. Home: 3760 N 57th St Boulder CO 80301

MALEY, WILLIS EVERETT, former chem. co. exec.; b. Vancouver, Wash., Dec. 27, 1912; s. Joseph Edwin and Esther Whipple (Converse) M.; A.B., U. Redlands, 1933; m. Fay McFarland, June 1, 1934 (dec.); 1 dau., Carolyn; m. 2d, Marion Pratt, Oct. 27, 1974; stepchildren—Jean (Mrs. Leland Larsen), Susan. With U.S. Borax & Chem. Co., 1940-79, dir. traffic, 1959-79, dir. distbn., 1965-79; pres. Nat. Freight Traffic Assn., 1965; chmn. exec. com. Nat. Indsl. Traffic League, 1962—, v.p., 1965-66, pres., 1967-68; gov. bd. Calif. chpt. Am. Soc. Traffic and Transp., 1962—; pres. Traffic Mgrs. Conf. Calif., 1949. Served with AUS, 1942-45. Clubs: Los Angeles Transp.; Long Beach Yacht. Home: 2107 Del Hollow St Lakewood CA 90712

MALFITANO, CATHERINE, opera singer; b. N.Y.C., Apr. 18, 1948; d. Joseph and Maria (Flynn) M.; B.A., Manhattan Sch. Music, 1971; m. Stephen Jon Holowid, Oct. 28, 1977. Debuts include: role in Falstaff, Central City, Colo., 1972, in Le Nozze di Figaro, Holland Festival, 1973, in La Boheme, N.Y.C. Opera, Los Angeles, 1973; appeared with Met. Opera, 1979. Mem. Am. Guild Musical Artists. Office: care Columbia Artists Mgmt Inc 165 W 57th St New York NY 10019

MALHOTRA, JAGADISH CHANDRA, psychiatrist; b. Dera Ghazi Khan, Pakistan-India, Mar. 21, 1916; s. Hardasram Malik and Moolobai (Kakar) M.; came to U.S., 1957, naturalized, 1971; student Med. Sch. Hyderabad, Sind, India, 1935-40; license Coll. Physicians and Surgeons Bombay, 1940; diploma in Psychol. Medicine, Grant Med. Coll., Bombay, 1954; licensing exam. Kans. Bd. Healing Arts, 1967; m. Sumitra Devi, Nov. 26, 1941; children—Raj Kumar, Ashok Kumar. Second asst. N.M. Mental Hosp., Thana, Bombay, India, 1948-50; resident psychiatrist Topeka State Hosp., 1957-58; clin. dir. Huntington (W.Va.) State Hosp., 1967-69; supt. Spencer (W.Va.) State Hosp., 1969-73; chief mental hygiene clinic VA Hosp., Huntington, W.Va., 1973; asst. supt. Moccasin Bend Mental Health Inst., Chattanooga, 1973—; speaker 5th World Congress Psychiatry, Mexico City, 1971, 6th, Honolulu, 1977. Fellow Indian Psychiat. Soc.; mem. Am. Psychiat. Assn. Author articles on yoga and mental hygiene. Address: Moccasin Bend Mental Health Inst Chattanooga TN 37405

MALICK, TERRENCE, film producer, dir., writer; b. Waco, Tex., 1943; grad. Harvard U.; postgrad. (Rhodes scholar) Oxford U. Reporter for Time, Newsweek, New Yorker; lectr. in philosophy M.I.T.; studied and produced short films at Am. Film Inst., Calif.; writer The Gravy Train, 1974; producer, writer, dir. Badlands, 1973; writer, dir. Days of Heaven, 1978. Office: care Evarts Ziegler Assos Inc 9255 W Sunset Blvd Los Angeles CA 90069*

MALIK, CHARLES HABIB, philosopher; b. Bterram, Al-Koura, Lebanon, 1906; s. Habib Khalil and Zareefi (Karam) M.; B.A., Am. U., Beirut, 1927; M.A., Ph.D., Harvard, 1937; student U. Freiburg (Germany), 1935-36; hon. doctoral degrees 50 univs. and colls. in U.S., Can. and Europe including Princeton U., Harvard U., Yale U., Columbia U., U. Calif. at Los Angeles, Notre Dame U., Brown U., Georgetown U., Williams Coll., Dartmouth Coll., U. Freiburg, St. Mary's U., others; m. Eva Badr, 1941; 1 son, Michael Habib Charles. Teaching and adminstrv. positions Am. U. Beirut, 1927-76, dean grad. studies, 1955-60, distinguished prof. philosophy, 1962-76; vis. prof. Dartmouth and Harvard, 1960; Univ. prof. Am. U., Washington, 1961-62; E.E. and M.P. to U.S., 1945-53, to Cuba, 1946-55; ambassador E. and P. to U.S., 1953-55; mem., sometime chmn. Lebanese del. UN, 1945-54, Signatory Charter UN, San Francisco, 1945, chmn. delegations Lebanon to UN, 1956-58; chmn. 3d Com. UN Gen. Assembly, 1948-49; pres. 13th Session, UN Gen. Assembly, 1958-59; mem. UN Security Council, 1953-54, pres., Feb. 1953, Jan., Dec. 1954; mem. UN ECOSOC Council, 1946-49, pres., 1948; mem. UN Human Rights Commn., 1947-54, chmn. commn., 1951, 52; rep. Lebanon Internat. Bank Fund and UNESCO, various times, 1947-52; Signatory for Lebanon, Japanese Peace Treaty, 1951; del. Bandung Conf., 1955; minister fgn. affairs Lebanon, 1956-58, minister nat. edn. and fine arts, 1956-57, mem. Parliament, 1957-60. Grand 1st magistrate Holy Orthodox Ch.; pres. World Council Christian Edn., 1967-71; v.p. United Bible Socs., 1966-72; former pres. bd. trustees Orthodox Coll. Annunciation, Beirut; dir. Woodrow Wilson Found., 1961-63; sometime vis. com. philosophy dept. Harvard and physics dept. Tufts U. Fellow AAAS, Am. Geog. Soc., Spring Arbor Coll.; mem. Am. Bible Soc. (hon. life), Am. Philos. Assn., Am. Philos. Soc., Assn. Realistic Philosophy, Assn. Symbolic Logic, Metaphys. Soc. Am., Am. Acad. Arts and Scis., Am. Polit. Sci. Assn., Am. Acad. Polit. and Social Sci., Am. Soc. Internat. Law, Internat. Law Assn., Union Internat. Assns., Internat. Polit. Sci. Assn., Nat. Geog. Soc., Acad. Human Rights, Internat. Movement for Atlantic Union, Internat. Platform Assn., Lebanese Acad. (a founder), Société européenne de Culture, Assn. mondiale de la Culture. Decorated by the governments of Lebanon, Italy, Jordan, Syria, Iraq, Cuba, Iran, Brazil, Dominican Republic, Austria, Greece, Nationalist China; holder highest order Lebanon for distinguished service. Clubs: Cosmos (Washington); Century, Harvard (N.Y.C.). Author: (essays) War and Peace, 1950, Problem of Asia, 1951; Christ and Crisis, 1962; Man in the Struggle for Peace, 1963; God and Man in Contemporary Christian Thought, 1971; God and Man in Contemporary Islamic Thought, 1972; The Wonder of Being, 1973; author numerous books in Arabic, most recent Almuqaddimah, 1977; contbr. parts to 20 books; author over 200 articles, Am., European, Near Eastern mags. Address: Harvard Club 27 W 44 St New York NY 10036 also Am Univ Beirut Lebanon

MALIN, IRVING, educator, lit. critic; b. N.Y.C., Mar. 18, 1934; s. Morris and Bertha (Silverman) M.; B.A., Queens Coll., 1955; Ph.D., Stanford, 1958; m. Ruth Lief, Dec. 18, 1955; 1 son, Mark. Acting instr. English, Stanford, 1955-58; instr. English, Ind. U., 1958-60, Coll. City N.Y., 1960-63, asst. prof., 1964-68, asso. prof. English, 1969-72, prof., 1972—; cons. Jewish Publ. Soc., 1964, Am. Quar., 1964, Nat. Endowment for Humanities, 1972, B'nai B'rith, 1974-75, Yaddo, 1975-77, Jewish Book Council, 1976, also PEN, Princeton U. Press, Fairleigh Dickinson Press; fellow Yaddo, 1963, Nat. Found. for Jewish Culture, 1963-64, Huntington Library, 1978. Mem. MLA, Am Studies Assn., Am. Jewish Hist. Soc., Melville Soc., PEN (cons. 1978-79), Authors League Am., Soc. for Study So. Lit., AAUP, Poe Studies Assn., English Inst., Popular Culture Assn., Nat. Book Critics Circle, Sherwood Anderson Soc., Am. Jewish Congress, Phi Beta Kappa. Jewish. Author: William Faulkner: An Interpretation, 1957; New American Gothic, 1962; Jews and Americans, 1965; Saul Bellow's Fiction, 1969; Nathanael West's Novels, 1972; Isaac Bashevis Singer, 1972. Co-editor: Breakthrough: A Treasury of Contemporary American Jewish Literature, 1964; William Styron's The Confessions of Nat Turner: A Critical Handbook, 1970; The Achievement of William Styron, 1975. Editor: Psychoanalysis and American Fiction, 1965; Saul Bellow and the Critics, 1967; Truman Capote's In Cold Blood: A Critical Handbook, 1968; Critical Views of Isaac Bashevis Singer, 1969; Contemporary American-Jewish Literature: Critical Essays, 1973; Carson McCullers: Essays in Criticism, 1981. Adv. editor Studies in American Jewish Literature. Reviewer New Republic, Va. Quar. Rev., Congress Monthly, Commonweal. Home: 96-13 68th Ave Forest Hills NY 11375 Office: Coll City NY New York NY 10031

MALIN, ROBERT ABERNETHY, investment banker; b. Mt. Vernon, N.Y., Dec. 13, 1931; s. Patrick Murphy and Caroline Cooper (Biddle) M.; A.B., Dartmouth, 1953, M.B.A., 1954; m. Gail Lassiter, Nov. 5, 1960; children—Alison Campbell, Robert Lassiter. Asst. to comptroller Biddle Purchasing Co., N.Y.C., 1958-59; with Blyth & Co., Inc., N.Y.C., 1960-71, v.p., 1965-71, dir., 1968-71, sr. v.p., mem. exec. com., 1971-72; sr. v.p. corporate fin. Reynolds Securities Inc., N.Y.C., 1972-74, dir., 1973-74; mng. dir. First Boston Corp., N.Y.C., 1974—. Mem. adv. council Fin. Acctg. Standards Bd., 1973-78. Served as lt. (j.g.) USNR, 1954-57. Mem. Investment Bankers Assn. Am. (v.p., exec. com. 1970-71), Securities Industry Assn. (accounting com.), N.Y. Soc. Security Analysts. Republican. Clubs: Links, Bond, Wall Street (gov. 1971—) (N.Y.C.); Calif. (Los Angeles); Beacon Hill (Summit, N.J.). Home: 2 Ox Bow Ln Summit NJ 07901 Office: 20 Exchange Pl New York NY 10005

MALINA, JOSEPH FRANCIS, JR., educator, civil engr.; b. Bklyn., Aug. 24, 1935; s. Joseph Francis and Mary (Wesolowski) M.; B.S. in C.E., Manhattan Coll., Riverdale, N.Y., 1957; M.S., U. Wis., 1959, Ph.D., 1961; m. Ida Marie Klein, Jan. 9, 1965; children—Kristyn Rosemarie, Joseph Alexander, Mary Amelia, Alexandra Frances. Instr., Manhattan Coll., 1957; instr. U. Wis., 1957-58; asst. prof. U. Tex., Austin, 1961-64, asso. prof., 1964-70, prof. civil engring., 1970—, chmn. dept., 1976—, dir. Environmental Health Engring. Labs., 1970-76. Diplomate Am. Acad. Environ. Engrs. Mem. ASCE, Assn. Environ. Engring. Profs., Internat. Assn. Water Pollution Research, Nat., Tex. socs. profl. engrs., Water Pollution Control Fedn., Tex. Water Pollution Control Assn., Sigma Xi, Epsilon Sigma Pi, Chi Epsilon, Tau Beta Pi, Omicron Delta Kappa, Phi Kappa Phi. Editor: (with R.E. Speece) Applications of Commercial Oxygen to Water and Wastewater Systems, 1973; (with B.P. Sagik) Virus Survival in Water and Wastewater Systems, 1974; (with E.F. Gloyna and E.M. Davis) Stabilization Ponds as a Wastewater Treatment Alternative, 1976. Home: 4508 Crestway Dr Austin TX 78731

MALINA, JUDITH, theatrical collective exec., actress, dir., writer; b. Kiel, Germany, June 4, 1926; d. Max and Rosel (Zamora) M.; student Dramatic Workshop, New Sch. Social Research, 1945-47; m. Julian Beck, Oct. 31, 1948; children—Garrick Maxwell, Isha Manna. Founder, The Living Theatre, 1947; producer, dir., actress Childish Jokes, Ladies Voices, He Who Says Yes and He Who Says No, The Dialogue of the Mannequin and The Young Man, The Thirteenth God, 1951; producer numerous stage plays, 1951—, including Mysteries and Smaller Pieces, 1964, The Maids, 1965, Frankenstein, 1965, Paradise Now, 1968, play cycle The Legacy of Cain, 1970—, Seven Meditations on Political Sadomasochism, 1973, Strike Support Oratorium, 1974, Six Public Acts, 1975, The Money Tower, 1975; actress films including Amore, Amore, 1966, Wheel of Ashes, 1967, Le Compromis, 1968, Etre Libre, 1968, Paradise Now, 1969, Dog Day Afternoon, 1974. Vice chmn. U.S. Com. for Justice to Latin Am. Polit. Prisoners, 1973-74; sponsor Am. Friends of Brazil, 1973. Recipient Lola D'Annunzio award, 1959, Page One award Newspaper Guild, 1960, Obie, 1960, Brandeis U. Creative Arts citation, 1961, Grand Prix de Théatre des Nations, 1961, medallion Paris Critics Circle, 1961, Prix de l'Université Paris, 1961, New Eng. Theatre Conf. award, 1962, Olympio prize, Italy, 1967, Village Voice awards, 1969. Author: Paradise Now, 1971; The Enormous Despair, 1972; The Legacy of Cain (3 pilot projects), 1973, also numerous collections of The Living Theatre. Address: care ML Beck 800 West End Ave New York City NY 10025

MALINA, MARSHALL ALBERT, chem. co. exec., chemist; b. Chgo., July 11, 1928; s. Maximillian and Laura (Kaufman) M.; B.S. in Chemistry, Ill. Inst. Tech., 1949; postgrad. Mass. Inst. Tech., 1956; M.B.A. (Distinguished scholar), Northwestern U., 1969; m. Corinne Miles, Aug. 14, 1955; children—Jill Ann, Karen Maurene. Chemist, Capitol Chem. Co., Chgo., 1949-50, prodn. mgr., Hamilton, Ind., 1950-52; mgr. analytical sect. Velsicol Chem. Corp., Chgo., 1952-68, mgr. quality control, 1968-69, dir. quality control, 1969-70, dir. research, 1970-74, dir. corporate devel., 1974—. Mem. Collaborative Internat. Pesticides Council. Mem. Chgo. Council on Fgn. Relations, 1969—. Ill. Inst. Tech. fellow, 1948-49; Assn. Ofcl. Analytical Chemists fellow, 1973. Mem. Comml. Devel. Assn., Am. Chem. Soc., Am. Soc. Testing Materials, Assn. Official Analytical Chemists, Am. Soc. Quality Control, Soc. Plastics Engrs., Weed Sci. Soc. Am., Council on Fabric Flammability, Plant Growth Regulant Soc., Beta Gamma Sigma. Contbr. articles on chemistry of pesticides, plastics and foods to profl. jours. Patentee in field. Home: 6007 N Sheridan Rd Chicago IL 60660 Office: 341 E Ohio Chicago IL 60611

MALIS, LEONARD IRVING, neurosurgeon; b. Phila., Nov. 23, 1919; s. Morris Melvin and Dorothy (Brodsky) M.; M.D., U. Va., 1943; m. Ruth Gornstein, June 24, 1942; children—Larry Alan, Lynne Paula. Intern, Phila. Gen. Hosp., 1943-44; resident in neurology Mt. Sinai Hosp., N.Y.C., 1947, neurosurgery, 1948-50; fellow in neurophysiology Yale U. Med. Sch., 1951; practice medicine specializing in neurosurgery, N.Y.C., 1951—; neurosurgeon in chief, dir. dept. neurol. surgery Mount Sinai Hosp., N.Y.C., 1970—; prof., chmn. dept. neurosurgery Mt. Sinai Sch. Medicine City U. N.Y., 1970—; cons. in field. Served as capt. MC, U.S. Army, World War II. Mem. Am. Assn. Neurol. Surgery, Congress Neurol. Surgeons, Am. Physiol. Soc., Soc. Neurosci., Am. Acad. Neurol. Surgery, A.C.S., Soc. Neurol. Surgeons, Alpha Omega Alpha. Contbr. numerous articles in field to med. jours.; developer various surg. and electronic instruments. Office: 1176 Fifth Ave New York City NY 10029

MALIS, LOUISE (MRS. LOUIS A. MALIS), civic worker; b. Atlanta, Apr. 6, 1921; d. Benjamin and Helen (Aarons) Clein; grad. Wright Jr. Coll., Chgo., 1939; student Northwestern U., 1939-40; m. Louis Albert Malis, Feb. 20, 1943; children—Susan Linda, Amy Beth Malis Berland. Dir. pub. affairs and pub. relations Rehab. Inst. Chgo., 1973-77. Mem. PTA, 1949—, various local and council positions, 1949-54, sch. edn. chmn. Chgo. region Ill. Congress Parents and Tchrs., 1954-58, v.p. Chgo. region, 1958-60, pres., 1960-62; pub. relations, financial devel. exec. Inst. Internat. Edn., Chgo., 1962-71. Mem. curriculum council Chgo. Bd. Edn., 1954-58, 60-62; sec. Mayor's Commn. on Sch. Bd. Nominations, 1960-61; apptd. to Chgo. Bd. Edn., 1964, 70, 75; sec.-treas. Council Great City Schs., 1969-70, 1969-71, v.p., 1977-78, pres., 1978-79, bd. dirs., 1964—; mem. steering com. Midwest Program on Airborne RV Instrn., Chgo., 1960-62; Chgo. del. to Conf. on Out-of-Sch. Unemployed Youth, Washington, 1961; first aid instr. Chgo. chpt. A.R.C., 1941-43. Bd. dirs. Jewish Children's Bur., 1971-73; mem. adv. council Nat. Humanities Inst., 1976—; bd. govs. Aspira, Inc. of Ill. Recipient Woman of Yr. award Gregorian Soc., 1976, Guildford-Waters Club, 1977. Mem. Ill. (life), Nat. (life) congresses parents and tchrs., Ill. Assn. Sch. Bds. (exec. com. large dist. council 1974), Nat. Edn. Com., B'nai B'rith Anti-Defamation League. Democrat. Jewish. Contbr. articles ednl. publs. Home: 5757 N Sheridan Rd Chicago IL 60660

MALITZ, SIDNEY, physician; b. N.Y.C., Apr. 20, 1923; s. Benjamin and Etta (Cohen) M.; student N.Y. U., 1940-42, Tulane U., 1942-43; B.M., Chgo. Med. Ch., 1946, M.D., 1947. Intern, St. Mary's Hosp., Huntington, W.Va., 1946-47; sr. intern Bethesda, Hosp., Cin., 1947-48; resident N.Y. State Psychiat. Inst., N.Y.C., 1948-51, sr. research psychiatrist, 1954-56, acting prin. research psychiatrist, 1956-58, acting chief psychiat. research, chief dept. exptl. psychiatry, 1958-64, chief psychiat. research dept. exptl. psychiatry, 1964-72, dep. dir., 1972-75, acting dir., 1975-76, dep. dir., 1976-78; in charge psychiat. drug clinic Vanderbilt Clinic, Presbyn. Hosp., N.Y.C., 1955-75, asst. attending psychiatrist, 1960-66, asso. attending psychiatrist, 1966-71, attending psychiatrist, 1971—, acting dir. psychiatry service, 1975-76; asst. dept. psychiatry Coll. Physicians and Surgeons, Columbia U., N.Y.C., 1955-57, asso., 1957-59, asst. clin. prof., 1959-65, asso. prof., 1965-69, prof., 1969—, vice chmn. dept. psychiatry, 1972-75, acting chmn., 1975-76, vice chmn., 1976-78; mem. panel impartial psychiat. experts N.Y. State Supreme Ct., 1960—; mem. adv. com. subcom.; cons. U.S. Pharmacopeia; mem. adv. com. subcom. health N.Y. State Constl. Conv.; cons. div. med. scis. NRC, Washington, 1967-70; cons. Rush Found., Los Angeles,

1968—; mem. ad hoc rev. com. to select Nat. Drug Abuse Research Centers, Center Studies Narcotic and Drug Abuse, NIMH, 1972—. Diplomate Am. Bd. Psychiatry and Neurology. Fellow Am. Psychiat. Assn. (chmn. com. biol. psychiatry 1961-62, program com., 1961-62, sec-treas. chpt. 1962-63, mem. com. research 1966-68, pres. chpt. 1969-70, chmn. Council Research and Devel. 1971-73), N.Y. Acad. Medicine, AAAS (council 1969—), Am. Coll. Neuropsychopharmacology, Collegium Internationale Neuropsychopharmacologicum, Am. Coll. Psychiatrists (archivist-historian 1978—), Royal Coll. Psychiatrists, Am. Coll. Psychoanalysts, N.Y. Soc. Clin. Psychiatry, Assn. Research Newvous and Mental Disease, N.Y. State, N.Y. County med. socs., AMA (cons. council drugs 1960—), N.Y. Acad. Scis, N.Y. Psychiat. Soc., Am. Psychopath. Assn., Soc. Biol. Psychiatry, Schilder Soc. Contbr. numerous articles to profl. jours. Address: Coll Physicians and Surgeons Columbia U Dept Psychiatry 161 Fort Washington Ave New York NY 10032

MALKIEL, BURTON GORDON, educator; b. Boston, Aug. 28, 1932; s. Sol and Celia (Gordon) M.; B.A., Harvard, 1953, M.B.A., 1955; Ph.D., Princeton, 1964; m. Judith Ann Atherton, July 16, 1954. Asst. prof. dept. econs. Princeton, 1964-66, asso. prof., 1966-68, prof., 1968—, Rentschler prof. econs., 1969—, chmn. dept. econs., 1974-75, 77—; mem. Pres.'s Council Econ. Advisors, 1975-77; dir. Vanguard Group, Prudential Life Ins. Co. Am.; bd. govs. Am. Stock Exchange. Served to 1st lt. AUS, 1955-58. Mem. Am. Fin. Assn. (pres. 1978). Author: The Term Structure of Interest Rates, 1966; (with others) Strategies and Rational Decisions in the Securities Options Market, 1969; A Random Walk Down Wall Street, 1973, 75. Home: 74 Wilson Rd Princeton NJ 08540

MALKIEL, YAKOV, educator; b. Kiev, Russia, July 22, 1914; s. Léon and Claire (Saitzew) M.; Matura, Werner-Siemens Realgymnasium, Berlin-Schöneberg, 1933; Ph.D. magna cum laude, Friedrich-Wilhelms Universität, Berlin, 1938; L.H.D., U. Chgo., 1969; LL.D., U. Ill., 1976; m. María Rosa Lida, Mar. 2, 1948 (dec. Sept. 1962). Came to U.S., 1940, naturalized, 1946. Instr. U. Wyo., 1942; lectr. U. Calif. at Berkeley, 1942-45, instr., 1945-46, asst. prof., 1946-48, asso. prof., 1948-52, prof. Romance philology, 1952-66, mem. grad council, 1953-57, asso. dean grad. div., 1963-66, prof. linguistics and Romance philology, 1966—, research fellow in the humanities, 1968-69; research asso. Mills Coll., summers 1942-43; vis. asso. prof. U. So. Calif., summer 1949; vis. lectr. Ind. U., summer 1953; vis. prof. U. Colo., summer 1958, U. Tex. Linguistic Inst., summer 1960, Linguistic Inst., Ind. U., summer 1964, Linguistic Inst., UCLA, 1966; Collitz prof. Linguistic Inst., U. N.Mex., 1980. Recipient Guggenheim Meml. Found. 3d award, 1967; Guggenheim fellow, 1948-49, 59; NSF sr. postdoctoral fellow, 1966; Princeton U. fellow, 1977. Mem. Am. Acad. Arts and Scis., Linguistic Soc. Am. (pres. 1965), Modern Lang. Assn. (founder Romance linguistics group 1946), Am. Oriental Soc., Philol. Assn. Pacific Coast (v.p. 1963, pres. 1965), Société de Linguistique Romane (exec. com. 1977, 79). Editor-in-chief Romance Philology Quar., 1947—; author: Essays on Linguistic Themes, 1968; Etymological Dictionaries: A Typological Survey, 1976; also monographs, articles U.S. and fgn. countries; contbr. Ency. Brit., Internat. Ency. Social Scis., Current Trends in Linguistics (vols. III, IV, IX), Dictionary of the Middle Ages. Home: 1 Arlington Ln Berkeley CA 94707

MALKIN, MYRON SAMUEL, ofcl. NASA; b. Youngstown, Ohio, Aug. 6, 1924; s. Morris and Sarah (Magidson) M.; B.S. in Physics, Yale U., 1948, M.S., 1949, Ph.D., 1951; m. Jocelyn Schoen, June 27, 1948; children—Martha, Peter. Nuclear physicist Schlumberg Well Surveying Corp., Ridgefield, Conn., 1951-52; asso. dir. Heavy Ion Accelerator Lab., Yale U., 1953-60; program mgr. Minuteman III and Titan II reentry vehicles Gen. Electric Co., Phila., 1961-66, program mgr. Manned Orbiting Lab., 1966-68, gen. mgr. Manned Orbiting Lab. program, 1968-69; pres. NUS Corp., Rockville, Md., 1969-71; dep. asst. sec. Dept. Def., Washington, 1972-73; dir. space shuttle program NASA, 1973—. Served with USMCR, 1943-45. Mem. AIAA, Phi Beta Kappa, Sigma Xi. Club: Cosmos. Home: 7004 Orkney Pkwy Bethesda MD 20034 Office: NASA 600 Independence Ave Washington DC 20546

MALKIN, PETER LAURENCE, lawyer; b. N.Y.C., Jan. 14, 1934; s. Samuel and Gertrude (Greenberger) M.; grad. cum laude Poly. Prep. Country Day Sch., 1951; A.B. summa cum laude, Harvard, 1955, LL.B. magna cum laude, 1958; m. Isabel L. Wien, July 10, 1955; children—Scott David, Cynthia Allison, Anthony Edward. Admitted to N.Y. bar, 1958, Conn. bar, 1976, Fla. bar, 1977; asso. Wien, Lane & Klein, N.Y.C., 1958-60; partner Wien, Lane & Malkin, N.Y.C. and Palm Beach, Fla., 1960—; mem. Empire State Bldg. Assos., 1961—; dir. Rapidata, Inc., Southwide Inc., Prevue Products, Inc., WM Capital & Mgmt. Corp.; trustee Harlem Savs. Bank; mem. Eastside adv. bd. Chem. Bank N.Y. Overseer Wien Internat. Scholarship Program. Brandeis U., 1958—, fellow, 1970—; trustee at large Fedn. Jewish Philanthropies N.Y., 1971—, v.p., 1972-74, 77-79, chmn. com. on deferred giving, 1973-79; nat. vice chmn. Harvard Law Sch. Fund, 1967-71, chmn. nat. scholarship com., 1972-75, chmn. maj. gifts com., 1975-76; bd. dirs. Urban League Southwestern Fairfield County, 1969-73, treas., 1969-71; bd. dirs. Lincoln Center for Performing Arts, Inc., 1979—; mem. devel. com. N.Y. Public Library, 1979—; v.p., mem. exec. com. Greenwich (Conn.) chpt. NAACP, 1967-69; trustee Citizens Budget Commn., N.Y.C., 1971—, Jewish Communal Fund N.Y., 1976—; hon. trustee Asso. YM and YWHA Greater N.Y.; overseers com. univ. resources Harvard, 1972-75; overseers com. to visit Kennedy Sch. Govt. Harvard, 1976—, to visit Harvard Law Sch., 1977—; exec. com. Program for Center for Jewish Studies, Harvard, 1974—; nat. vice chmn. Harvard Capital Fund Campaign, 1979—; chmn. schs. and scholarship com. Harvard, Greenwich, 1973-79; bd. dirs. Assn. Better N.Y., 1972—; dir. Coalition for N.Y.C., 1976—. Mem. Harvard Law Sch. Assn. N.Y.C. (trustee, 1968-70, v.p. 1973-74), Assn. Bar City N.Y. (mem. com. admissions 1965-68, com. assn. bldgs. 1968-72, chmn. com. ins. assn. bldgs. 1967-78), Am., N.Y. State, Conn., Fla. bar assns., Am. Arbitration Assn. (nat. panel arbitrators), Harvard Law Sch. Assn. (mem. council). Clubs: Hasty Pudding Institute 1770, Harvard Varsity (Cambridge, Mass.); Harvard (bd. mgrs. 1979—) (N.Y.C.); Harvard (v.p. 1974-75, dir. 1976—) (Fairfield County, Conn.); City-Midday (N.Y.C.); Golf of Aspetuck (Easton, Conn.); Bailiwick (founding pres.) (Greenwich, Conn.). Home: Bobolink Ln Greenwich CT 06830 Office: 60 E 42d St New York NY 10017 also 249 Royal Palm Way Palm Beach FL 33480

MALLARDI, MICHAEL PATRICK, broadcasting co. exec.; b. N.Y.C., Mar. 17, 1934; s. Michael Cosmo and Gaetana Mallardi; B.Phil. magna cum laude, U. Notre Dame; m. Sylvia J. Mandalios, Aug. 19, 1961; children—Karen, Stephanie. With ABC, Inc., 1956-61, 71—, v.p. corp. planning, N.Y.C., 1971-74, pres. ABC Record and Sales Corp., Seattle, also Fairfield, N.J., 1974-75, v.p., chief fin. officer ABC, 1975—, also dir.; location auditor Metro-Goldwyn-Mayer, Inc., Los Angeles, 1961; bus. mgr. Radio-Press Internat., Inc., N.Y.C., 1961-65; treas. Straus Broadcasting Group, Inc., N.Y.C., 1965-69, v.p., gen. mgr., 1969-71; mem. adv. bd. Chem. Bank. Served with U.S. Army, 1956. Mem. Internat. Radio and TV Soc. Roman Catholic. Office: 1330 Ave of the Americas New York NY 10019

MALLARY, RAYMOND DEWITT, lawyer; b. Lenox, Mass., Oct. 5, 1898; s. R. DeWitt and Lucy (Walker) M.; A.B., Dartmouth, 1921; J.D., Harvard, 1924; m. Gertrude Slater Robinson, Sept. 15, 1923; children—R. DeWitt, Richard Walker. Admitted to Mass. bar, 1924, Vt. bar, 1953; partner Wooden, Small & Mallary, 1924-31, Mallary & Gilbert, 1931-51; pvt. practice, counsel to Richardson, Dibble & Atkinson, Springfield, Mass., 1951-56, Bulkley, Richardson. Godfrey & Burbank, 1956-64, Wilson, Keyser and Otterman, Chelsea and Bradford, Vt., 1961-63, Otterman & Allen, Bradford, Vt., 1965-70. Dir., mem. exec. com. Mass. Mut. Life Ins. Co., 1944-73; partner Mallary Farm; dir. P.M.G. Co., West Springfield, Mass.; dir., mem. exec. com. Central Vt. Pub. Service Corp.; dir. Vt. Electric Power Co. Chmn. bd. selectmen, Fairlee, Vt., 1953-57, moderator, 1972-76; chmn. Orange County Tax Appeal Bd., 1964-65; Vt. mem. New Eng. Govs. Com. Pub. Transp., 1955—; mem. Conn. River Watershed Council, Inc. Trustee emeritus Am. Internat. Coll.; trustee, mem. livestock com. Eastern States Exposition, 1942—, chmn. exec. com., 1943-53, pres., 1953-58, chmn. bd., 1958-68, hon. chmn. bd., 1968—, dir., chmn. Vt. trustees, 1975-76; trustee Hitchcock Found., 1970-78, emeritus, 1978—. Served with U.S. Army, 1918; capt. Res. ret. Recipient citations for outstanding service North Atlantic region Future Farmers Am., 1963, 4-H U. Conn. Coll. Agrl. Extension Service, 1965; achievement award Internat. Assn. Fairs and Expns. Mem. New Eng. Fellowship Agrl. Adventurers, Holstein-Friesian Assn. Am. (dir., mem. exec. com. 1957-64, v.p. 1965- 67, pres., mem. exec. com. 1967-69), Am., Mass., Vt., Hampden County, Orange County bar assns., N.E. States Holstein Friesian Assn. (past pres., dir.), Purebred Dairy Cattle Assn. Am. (past pres.), Psi Upsilon. Club: Dartmouth of Hanover Area. Home: Mallary Farm Bradford VT 05033 Office: Bradford VT 05033

MALLARY, RICHARD WALKER, state ofcl., former congressman; b. Springfield, Mass., Feb. 21, 1929; s. Raymond DeWitt and Gertrude Slater (Robinson) M.; A.B., Dartmouth, 1949; LL.D., Am. Internat. Coll., 1973; children—Richard Walker, Anne C., Elizabeth H., Sarah R. Dairy farmer, Bradford, Vt., 1950-70; partner, mgr. Mallary Farm, 1956-71; commr. adminstrn. State of Vt., 1971; mem. 92d-93d congresses from Vt.; v.p. Farm Credit Banks, Springfield, 1975-77; sec. of adminstrn. State of Vt., 1977—. Chmn., Bd. Selectmen, Fairlee, Vt., 1951-52; mem. Vt. Ho. of Reps., 1961-68, speaker, 1966-68; del. Republican Nat. Conv., 1968; mem. Vt. Senate, 1969-70; Republican candidate for U.S. senate from Vt., 1974. Trustee Eastern States Expn. Mem. Phi Beta Kappa. Home: Mallary Farm Bradford VT 05033

MALLARY, ROBERT, sculptor; b. Toledo, Dec. 2, 1917; s. Benjamin E. and Laura (Grossman) M.; certificate La Escuela de las Artes del Libro, Mexico D.F., 1939; m. Margot Handrahan, Oct. 29, 1942; children—Michelle, Michael, Martine, Dion. Exhbt. one-man shows San Francisco Mus. Art., 1944, Crocker Art Gallery, Sacramento, 1944, Cal. Exhibitors Gallery, Los Angeles, 1951, Santa Barbara Mus. Art, 1952, Gumps, San Francisco, 1953, Fine Arts Gallery San Diego, 1953, Urban Gallery, N.Y.C., 1954, Coll. Fine Arts, U. N.M., 1956, Jonson Gallery, Albuquerque, 1957-59, Santa Fe, 1958, Allan Stone Gallery, N.Y.C., 1961, 62, 66; exhbt. group shows Los Angeles Mus. Art, 1951, 53, 54, Colorado Springs Fine Art Center, 1953, Denver Art Mus., 1955, Sao Paulo, Brazil, 1955, 63, Mus. Modern Art, 1959, 61, 65, Gt. Jones Gallery, N.Y.C., 1959, Guggenheim Mus., 1960, Whitney Mus. Am. Art, 1960, 62, 64, 66, 68, Pace Gallery, Boston, 1960, Stable Gallery, N.Y.C., 1960, Martha Jackson Gallery, N.Y.C., 1961, Inst. Contemporary Art, Houston, 1961, 62; traveling exhbns. Am. Fedn. Art, Riverside Mus., N.Y.C., 1961, Paris, France, 1962, Seattle Worlds Fair, 1962, Carnegie Inst., 1962, Denver Mus. Fine Arts, 1962, Art Inst. Chgo., 1962, Allan Stone Gallery, 1961, 62, 66, N.Y. State Coll., Potsdam, 1969; rep. permanent collections Mus. Modern Art, Whitney Mus. Am. Art, Maremont Found., Smith Coll., Brandeis U., Womens Coll. of U. N.C., U. Tex., Kalamazoo Art Center, U. Cal. at Berkeley, Roswell (N.M.) Mus., Los Angeles Mus. Art, U. N.M., Santa Fe, Drew Coll., N.J.; commd. by N.Y. Worlds Fair, 1963-64; collaborator (with Dale Owne) mural Beverly Hilton Hotel, Beverly Hills, Cal., 1955; mem. faculty U. N.M., 1955-59, Pratt Inst., 1959-67; prof. art U. Mass., Amherst, 1967—. Dir. Arstecnica: Interdisciplinary Center for Art and Tech. Guggenheim grantee, 1964-65; fellow Tamarind Workshop, 1962. Mem. Computer Arts Soc., Coll. Art Assn. Research in computer art and computer-supported studies in aesthetics; projects in art and tech.; aesthetics of surface mine reclamation; application of computer-aided design techniques to large-scale environ. sculpture and landscape design. Home: PO Box 48 Conway MA 01341

MALLENDER, FRED, II, lawyer; b. Bloomfield Twp., Mich., Jan. 3, 1931; s. Milton Fred and Eleanor Mary (Rainey) M.; A.B., Yale, 1952; J.D. with honors, U. Mich., 1955; m. Ellen Farwell Lewis, Feb. 15, 1958; children—John Stanton, Mary Eleanor, William David. Admitted to Mich. bar, 1955, since practiced in Detroit; asso. firm Lewis & Watkins, Detroit, 1955-60, partner, 1960-67; partner firm Dahlberg, Mallender & Gawne, Detroit, 1967—; dir. R.M. Wright Co., Henderson Glass, Inc., Saf-Ti Glass Inc., Knight Constrn. Co., Inc. Chmn., Planned Parenthood League, 1971-73; bd. dirs. Planned Parenthood Fedn. Am., 1974—. Mem. Yale Alumni Assn. Mich. (sec. 1957-60), Am., Mich., Detroit bar assns., Order of Coif, Phi Beta Kappa, Phi Delta Phi. Republican. Club: Detroit. Home: 3710 Burning Tree Dr Bloomfield Hills MI 48013 Office: 1022 Ford Bldg Detroit MI 48226

MALLENDER, MILTON FRED, lawyer; b. Birmingham, Mich., Nov. 6, 1905; s. Fred and Sarah Ann (Riley) M.; student Albion (Mich.) Coll., 1923-24; A.B., U. Mich., 1927; J.D., Wayne State U., 1929; m. Eleanor M. Rainey, Aug. 3, 1929 (dec. Apr. 21, 1973); children—Fred II, William Harry. Admitted to Mich. bar, 1929, since practiced in Detroit; partner firm Lewis & Watkins, 1936-67, Dahlberg, Mallender & Gawne, 1967—. Commr., Birmingham, 1943-52, mayor, 1946-49. Bd. dirs. Childrens Aid Soc. Detroit, 1950-74, Birmingham Community House Assn., 1952-60. Mem. Am., Detroit bar assns., State Bar Mich., Sigma Nu, Sigma Delta Kappa. Republican. Presbyn. Home: 6015 E Surrey Lane Birmingham MI 48010 Office: Ford Bldg Detroit MI 48226

MALLENDER, WILLIAM HARRY, diversified co. exec.; b. Birmingham, Mich., May 21, 1935; s. Milton Fred and Eleanor Mary (Rainey) M.; B.A., Yale, 1957; LL.B., U. Mich., 1960; m. Carole Mae Miller, Aug. 8, 1964; children—W. Drew, Gregory Blair. Admitted to Mich. bar, 1960, N.Y. State bar, 1962, Fla. bar, 1970; asso. Donovan Leisure Newton & Irvine, N.Y.C., 1961-69; fed. and state compliance officer Riter & Co., Fort Lauderdale, Fla., 1969-70; v.p. Gibraltar Investment Co., Inc., Fort Lauderdale, 1970; v.p. GAC Investments, Fort Lauderdale, 1970-71; exec. v.p., sec., gen. counsel Talley Industries, Inc., Mesa, Ariz., 1971—, sec., 1973—, also dir. Home: 6340 E Sage Dr Scottsdale AZ 85253 Office: PO Box 849 Mesa AZ 85201

MALLER, ROBERT RUSSELL, mgmt. cons. and banker; b. N.Y.C., July 4, 1928; s. Louis and Lucille (Haberman) M.; B.S., U. Coll., N.Y. U., 1950, M.B.A., 1957; m. Lois Fischel, June 17, 1951; children—Caryn J., Jay S. With U.S. Trust Co. of N.Y., 1956-72, municipal analyst, asst. sec., 1958-61, asst. v.p., 1961-65, v.p., 1965-69, sr. municipal officer, 1959-69, sr. v.p. adminstrn., 1969-72; sr. v.p. consumer banking services and ops. Central Savs. Bank, N.Y.C., 1972-74, exec. v.p., 1974-77; pres. CenBan Mgmt. Services, 1976-77; prin. Mgmt. by Design, Consultants, 1977—; sr. v.p. Washington Fed. Savs. & Loan Assn., 1979—; mem. com. consumer credit, com. bank ops. Savs. Bank Assn. N.Y. State, 1972-77; lectr. banking and finance Hofstra U., 1957-59. Bd. govs. Municipal Forum of N.Y., 1964-70, v.p., 1967-68, pres., 1968-69; alt. instl. investor adv. com. SEC, 1969-70. Pres. Huntington (N.Y.) Union Free Sch. Dist. No. 3 Bd. Edn., 1966-69, trustee, 1965-70; mem. exec. com. Nassau-Suffolk Sch. Bds. Assn., 1967-69. Served with AUS, 1950-52. Mem. Soc. Municipal Analysts, Municipal Analysts Group, Nat. Assn. Mut. Savs. Banks (internal ops. com. 1972-77), Soc. Profl. Mgmt. Cons.'s (accredited asso.), Phi Sigma Delta. Club: University (N.Y.C.). Author: Financing Public Education, 1959; A System for a Certificateless Society, 1971. Home: 12 Skyline Dr Huntington NY 11743

MALLERY, RICHARD, lawyer; b. Akron, Ohio, June 7, 1937; s. William Harrison and Elizabeth Mae (Whitmer) M.; B.A., DePauw U., 1959; M.A. (Woodrow Wilson fellow 1959), Cornell U., 1960; J.D., Stanford U., 1963; m. Frances Ann Kohfeldt, June 7, 1964; children—Kathleen Ann, Craig Taylor, David Whitmer, Patricia Lynn. Admitted to Ariz. bar, 1964; law clk. to chief justice Ariz. Supreme Ct., 1963-64; practiced law as partner firm Snell & Wilmer, Phoenix, 1964—; spl. counsel to appropriations com. Ariz. Ho. of Reps., 1967-68; lectr. law U. Ariz., 1969-71; gen. counsel, dir., mem. exec. com. Southwest Savs. & Loan Assn., 1972-76; lectr. real estate trans. Ariz. State U., 1976-79. Bd. visitors Law Sch., Stanford U., 1967-72; v.p., bd. dirs. Combined Met. Phoenix Arts Assn., 1967-76, chmn. adv. bd., 1976-79; pres., bd. dirs. men's arts council Phoenix Art Mus., 1968-70; chmn. charter govt. com. City of Phoenix, 1973, chmn. environ. quality commn., 1971-73; mem. Ariz. Council on Humanities and Pub. Policy, 1977-78; bd. dirs., chmn. exec. com. Ariz. Tomorrow, Inc., 1977—; mem. San Francisco regional panel Pres.'s Commn. on White House Fellows, 1975—; trustee Heard Mus. Indian Art and Anthropology, 1971-78, Phoenix Country Day Sch., 1972-76, DePauw U., 1978—, Hudson Inst., 1979—. Am. Field Service Internat. scholar, Germany, 1954; Fulbright scholar, Eng., 1960. Mem. Am., Ariz., Maricopa County bar assns., Ariz. Acad., Council Fgn. Relations, Sigma Chi. Democrat. Catholic. Clubs: Paradise Valley Country, Univ., Ariz., Pinnacle Peak Country. Home: 2201 E Georgia Ave Phoenix AZ 85016 Office: 3100 Valley Center Phoenix AZ 85073

MALLETT, JANE DAWSON, actress, script writer; b. London, Ont., Can., Apr. 18, 1899; d. Clifford Benjamin and Emily Isabel (Daly) Keenleyside; B.A., Victoria Coll., U. Toronto, 1921; m. Frederick John Mallett, Apr. 14, 1925; 1 son, John Christopher Aldworth. Regular mem. Empire Stock Co., Toronto, 1927-28; appeared in first radio plays; first Trans Can. Network series, 1930; writer, producer, actress satirical rev. Town Tonics, 1934-44, troop shows, 1939-45, Spring Thaw rev. and dramas, 1944-55; began filmwork, 1951; appears on CBC-TV, 1952—; founder Jane Mallett Assos. Ltd., 1955. Active mem. South Rosedale Ratepayers Assn.; mem. Archtl. Conservancy, Canadian Peace Research Inst. Pres., Actors Fund of Can., 1957—. Decorated Order of Can.; recipient John Drainie award for disting. contbn. to broadcasting, 1976. Mem. AFTRA (life mem., past exec. councillor), Can. Actors Equity (life mem., past councillor). Clubs: Toronto Heliconian; Celebrity. Home: 26 Chestnut Park Rd Toronto ON M4W 1W6 Canada

MALLETTE, MALCOLM FRANCIS, journalist, educator; b. Syracuse, N.Y., Jan. 30, 1922; s. Ralph Joseph and Hermia Ruth (Barry) M.; B.S. magna cum laude, Syracuse U., 1947; m. Eleanor Christine Ingram, Sept. 21, 1946; children—Gary, Bruce, David. Profl. baseball pitcher, Norfolk, Va., Newark, Kansas City, Memphis, Sacramento, Bklyn., Montreal, 1946-52; sports reporter Asheville (N.C.) Times, 1951-54; sports editor Asheville Citizen, 1954-56; sports dir. Winston-Salem (N.C.) Jour. & Sentinel, 1956-59; mng. editor Winston-Salem Jour., 1959-66; asso. dir. Am. Press Inst., Reston, Va., 1966-69, mng. dir., 1969-75, sec., dir., 1975—. Guest lectr. Grad. Sch. Journalism, Columbia, 1969-71, Am. Press. Inst., Columbia, 1961-66, U. N.C. Sch. Journalism, 1964. Served to capt. Signal Corps, AC, AUS, 1944-46. Mem. AP Mng. Editors Assn. (dir. 1961-66, regent 1976—), AP News Council (pres. N.C. 1964), Assn. Profl. Baseball Players (life). Baptist. Rotarian. Contbr. articles to various mags. Home: 2419 Silver Fox Ln Reston VA 22091 Office: 11690 Sunrise Valley Dr Reston VA 22091

MALLEY, FRANCIS JOHN, advt. and pub. relations co. exec.; b. Youngstown, O., Aug. 23, 1923; s. John P. and Mary (Hunt) M.; B.A., Manhattan Coll., 1947; postgrad. Fordham U., 1949-53; m. Gloria T. Kane, Oct. 23, 1948; children—Francis, Joseph, Regina, Ethel, Stephen, Mary Theresa, Thomas J.V. Mng. editor The Spectator, N.Y.C., 1947-53; with Doremus & Co., N.Y.C., 1953—, dir. pub. relations dept., 1965—, sr. v.p., 1966-73, exec. v.p., 1973—, also dir., mem. exec. com.; joint chmn. Doremus Internat. Pub. Relations Ltd., London, 1973. Mem. alumni adv. council Manhattan Coll., 1967-72; scoutmaster, committeeman Nassau County council Boy Scouts Am., 1957-72. Served to cpl. USAAF, 1943-45; ETO. Mem. Public Relations Soc. Am. (chmn. counselors sect.), Fin. Communications Soc. (past pres.). Club: City Midday. Home: 55 Murray Ave Port Washington NY 11050 Office: 120 Broadway New York NY 10005

MALLEY, JOHN WALLACE, lawyer; b. Parkersburg, W.Va., Feb. 17, 1906; s. Robert J. and Adelia (Carney) M.; B.S.; U.S. Naval Acad., 1927; LL.B., George Washington U., 1934; grad. Indsl. Coll. Armed Forces, 1941; m. Kathleen Pendleton, June 20, 1936; children—Kathleen Montague, John Wallace. Admitted to D.C. bar, 1934, since practiced in Washington; sr. partner firm Cushman, Darby & Cushman, specializing patent, trademark and anti-trust law, 1934—; professorial lectr. patent law George Washington U., 1964-65. Area chmn. Patent, Trademark and Copyright Research Inst., 1954. Served from ensign to lt. (j.g.), U.S. Navy, 1927-31; from lt. to comdr., USNR, 1941-45. Mem. Phi Delta Phi. Democrat. Clubs: Chevy Chase (Md.); Army and Navy (Washington). Home: 24 Quincy St Chevy Chase Village Chevy Chase MD 20015 Office: 1801 K St NW Washington DC 20006

MALLEY, ROBERT JOSEPH, mfg. co. exec.; b. Nashwauk, Minn., July 17, 1923; s. Joseph Cyril and Eva May (Troumbly) M.; B.S. in Mil. Engring., U.S. Mil. Acad., 1946; M.S. in Civil Engring., U. Minn., 1953; m. Betty Josephine Gregg, Aug. 10, 1957; children—Robert, Gregg Philip, Elizabeth Lee, Kelly Lynn, Kenneth John. Commd., U.S. Army, 1946, advanced through grades to maj. gen., 1975; assignments in airborne and engring. units, 1946-56; instr. physics U.S. Mil. Acad., West Point, N.Y., 1956-59; with programs div. SHAPE, Paris, 1960-63; bn. comdr. engring. bn. 1st cav. div., Ft. Benning, Ga. and Vietnam, 1963-66; dist. engr., Los Angeles, 1969-71; with Americal div., 1971-72; project mgr. production base modernization, Picatinny Arsenal, N.J., 1973-76; dir. combat support systems Dept. Army, Washington, 1976-78; ret., 1978; v.p. internat. ops. Chamberlain Mfg. Corp., Arlington, Va., 1978—. Decorated D.S.M., Legion of Merit with 3 oak leaf clusters, Bronze Star, Air Medal with 5 oak leaf clusters; licensed civil engr., Vt. Fellow Soc. Am. Mil. Engrs. (Wheeler award 1965); mem. Am. Def. Preparedness Assn. Roman Catholic. Clubs: Army-Navy Country, K.C. Home:

1122 Ormond Ct McLean VA 22101 Office: Suite 600 Hayes Bldg 2361 S Jefferson Davis Hwy Arlington VA 22202

MALLICK, EARL WILLIAM, steel co. exec.; b. Pitts., Jan. 18, 1926; s. Frederick and Nora Margaret (Kroll) M.; student Stevens Inst. Tech., 1943-44; B.S. in Elec. Engring., Northwestern U., 1946; LL.B., Harvard, 1949; m. Evelyn Mae Hill, June 6, 1950; children—Craig David, Keith William, Joy Evelyn. Admitted to Pa. bar, 1949; with U.S. Steel Corp., 1949—, asst. dir. personnel services Tenn. Coal and Iron div., 1962-64, v.p. South, 1964-71, v.p. environmental control, Pitts., 1971-75, v.p. environ. affairs, 1975-77, v.p. pub. affairs, 1977—. Trustee So. Research Inst., Birmingham, Ala. Served with USNR, 1943-46. Mem. Am. Iron and Steel Inst., U.S. Indsl. Council (dir.), Hwy. Users Fedn. (exec. com.), Internat. C. of C. (trustee U.S. council). Presbyterian. Home: 4368 Westover Pl NW Washington DC 20016 Office: 818 Connecticut Ave NW Washington DC 20006

MALLINSON, GEORGE GREISEN, educator; b. Troy, N.Y., July 4, 1918; s. Cyrus James and Mathilda (Greisen) M.; B.A., N.Y. State Coll. Tchrs., Albany, 1937, M.A., 1941; Ph.D., U. Mich., 1947, Burke Aaron Hinsdale scholar, 1947-48; m. Jacqueline V. Buck, Aug. 21, 1954; children—Carol Lynn, Cyrus James, Virginia Alice, Charles Evans, Carolyn Louise. Tchr. sci., Whitesboro, N.Y., 1937-40, Eden, N.Y., 1940-42; dir. sci. edn. Iowa State Tchrs. Coll., 1947-48; prof. psychology, sci. edn. Western Mich. U., 1948-54, dean Grad. Coll., 1954-77, disting. prof. sci. edn., 1977—. Mem. Gov. Mich. Sci. Adv. Bd., 1958-62; mem. regional adv. bd. Social and Rehab. Service, 1971-73. Served to sgt., AUS, 1942-45. Recipient Distinguished Alumnus award State U. N.Y. at Albany, 1970. Mem. Nat. Assn. Research Sci. Teaching (pres. 1953), Mich. Sci. Tchrs. Assn. (pres. 1954), AAAS (council), Am. Soc. Engring. Edn., Nat. Sci. Tchrs. Assn., Nat. Assn. Biology Tchrs., Sch. Sci. and Math. Assn., Am. Edn. Research Assn., Mich. Council Coll. Pres. (chmn. sci. study com. 1957-61), Mich. Acad. Sci., Arts and Letters (v.p. 1968- 70, pres. 1970-71), Council of Central States Univs. (chmn. council 1965-67, pres. bd. dirs. and corp. 1970, 71-73, 77—), Am. Assn. Workers for Blind (dir. 1968-73, chmn. publs. advisory bd. 1974—, pres. Mich. chpt. 1974, pres. Midwest region 1975—). Author: Science in Daily Life, 1953; General Physical Science, 1960; Science in Modern Life, 1969; Science, 1-6, 1975; Science: Understanding Your Environment, 1-6, 1978; also articles. Editor: Newsletter Mich. Sci. Tchrs. Assn., 1954-63, School Science and Math., 1957—. Home: 535 Kendall St Kalamazoo MI 49007

MALLON, FRANCIS BERNARD, ret. army officer; b. Middletown, N.Y., Sept. 17, 1886; s. Bernard James and Ella Marie (Koch) M.; cadet U.S. Mil. Acad., 1908-09; grad. Command and Gen. Staff Sch., 1923, Army War Coll., 1927; m. Eunice Marion Casey, Oct. 21, 1916 (dec.); 1 son, Richard. Pvt. and cpl., 5th Inf., 1909-12; commd. 2d lt. U.S. Army, 1912, advanced through grades to maj. gen., 1944; comdr. Replacement Tng. Center, Camp Jos. T. Robinson, Ark. and Army Ground Forces Replacement Depot No. 1, Fort George G. Meade, Md., World War II; mem. War Dept Gen. Staff, 1927-30, 39-41; gen. staff with troops, 1933-37; acting comdr. VII Corps, i945-46; ret., 1946. Clubs: Army and Navy (Washington); Bohemian (San Francisco). Home: 509 W Hillsdale Blvd San Mateo CA 94403

MALLORY, ARTHUR LEE, state ofcl.; b. Springfield, Mo., Dec. 26, 1932; s. Dillard A. and Ferrell (Claxton) M.; B.S., S.W. Mo. State Coll., 1954; M.Ed., U. Mo., 1957, Ed.D., 1959; H.H.D., S.W. Bapt. Coll., Mo., 1972; m. Joann Peters, June 6, 1954; children—Dennis Arthur (dec.), Christopher Lee, Stephanie Ann, Jennifer Lyn. History supr. U. Mo. Lab. Sch., Columbia, 1956-57; asst. to supt. schs., Columbia, 1957-59; asst. supt. schs. Parkway Sch. Dist., St. Louis County, Mo., 1959-64; dean eve. div. U. Mo., St. Louis, 1964; pres. S.W. Mo. State Coll., Springfield, 1964-70; commr. edn. Mo. Dept. Edn., Jefferson City, 1971—; dir. Internat. House, U. Mo., Columbia, 1956-59; mem. vis. team Nat. Council for Accreditation Tchr. Edn., 1968—. Vice pres. Ozarks council Boy Scouts Am., 1967, pres. Gt. Rivers council, 1972-73; mem. adv. com. Mo. 4-H Found.; mem. juvenile delinquency task force Mo. Law Enforcement Assistance Council. Bd. dirs. Meml. Community Hosp., Mid-Continent Regional Ednl. Lab., St. Louis Ednl. TV Commn.; pres. Mo. Council on Econ. Edn.; bd. regents Mo. State Colls.; trustee Pub. Sch. Retirement, William Jewell Coll., 1972-74; chmn. com. bds. So. Bapt. Conv., 1972-73; mem. exec. bd. Mo. Bapt. Conv., 1972-75, 77—; mem. Hache task force Edn. Commn. States. Served with U.S. Army, 1954-56. Recipient Distinguished Service award Mo. Jr. C. of C., 1966; Distinguished Service award U. Mo., 1976, Faculty/Alumni award, 1976; hon. life mem. Mo. Congress Parents and Tchrs.; named Springfield's Outstanding Young Man of Yr., 1965; Champion of Excellence, PUSH, 1978. Mem. Am. Assn. State Colls. and Univs., N. Central Assn. Colls. and Secondary Schs., Council Chief State Sch. Officers, Mo. Assn. Sch. Adminstrs., NEA, Mo. Tchrs. Assn. So. Baptist (deacon). Mason (33 deg.), Rotarian. Home: 3261 S Ten Mile Dr Jefferson City MO Office: State Commr Edn Dept Elementary and Secondary Edn Jefferson City MO 65101

MALLORY, FRANK BRYANT, educator; b. Omaha, Mar. 17, 1933; s. Deane Havercroft and Helen (Bryant) M.; B.S., Yale, 1954; Ph.D., Calif. Inst. Tech., 1958; m. Patricia Ann Livingston, June 30, 1951; children—Mary Susan, Paul Deane, Philip Howard (dec.), Michele; m. 2d, Clelia Sara Wood, Nov. 26, 1965. Asst. prof. Bryn Mawr (Pa.) Coll., 1957-63, asso. prof., 1963-69, prof. chemistry, 1969—, acad. dep. to pres., 1978—; vis. asso. Calif. Inst. Tech., 1963-64; vis. prof. Yale, 1968, 78-79, lectr., 1977-78; vis. prof. State U. N.Y., Albany, summer 1967; vis. fellow Cornell U., 1970-71. John Simon Guggenheim fellow, 1963-64, Alfred P. Sloan research fellow, 1964-68, NSF sr. postdoctoral fellow, 1970-71. Recipient Bond award Am. Oil Chemists Soc., 1970. Mem. Am. Chem. Soc., Phila. Organic Chemists Club (past sec., chmn.). Contbr. articles to profl. jours. Home: 217 N Roberts Rd Bryn Mawr PA 19010

MALLORY, G. BARRON, lawyer; b. Port Chester, N.Y., Apr. 25, 1919; s. Philip Rogers and Dorothea (Barron) Lillie; grad. magna cum laude Kent Sch., 1937; B.A. with honors, Yale, 1941, LL.B., 1947; m. Eleanor Moore Davis, July 14, 1941 (div.); children—Peter D., George B., Mary R., Elizabeth P.; m. 2d, Margaret Pierson Leary, Feb. 22, 1972. Admitted to Conn. bar, 1947, N.Y. bar, 1948, Ind. bar, 1959; asso. firm Brown, Wood, Fuller, Caldwell & Ivey, N.Y.C., 1947-51, partner, 1951-58; dir. P.R. Mallory & Co. Inc., Indpls., 1956—, adminstrv. v.p., 1958-60, pres., 1960-68, chmn., 1968-71, dir., to 1978; counsel firm Jacobs Persinger & Parker, N.Y.C., 1971—; dir. Am. Fletcher Corp., Sutton Pl. South Corp.; dir., mem. audit com. Consol. Freightways, Inc. Trustee Mystic Seaport Mus.; trustee, mem. membership, edn., research and policy coms. Com. for Econ. Devel. Served to lt. comdr. USNR, 1941-45. Mem. Assn. Bar City N.Y., Electronics Industries Assn. (life), Zeta Psi, Phi Delta Phi. Democrat. Episcopalian. Clubs: Yale, Downtown Assn., Union (N.Y.C.); Apawamis (Rye, N.Y.); Chicago; Mill Reef (Antiqua, W.I.). Author: Profit Sharing Plans. Home: 1 Sutton Pl S New York NY 10022 Office: 70 Pine St New York NY 10005

MALLORY, GEORGE KENNETH, physician, educator; b. Boston, Feb. 14, 1900; s. Frank Burr and Persis McClain (Tracy) M.; A.B., Harvard, 1922, M.D., 1926; m. Carol Fisher, Sept. 30, 1931; children—Margaret Persis, George Kenneth. Resident pathology Boston City Hosp., 1928, 4th asst., 1928, 2d asst., 1929, 1st asst., 1930, asst. pathologist, 1933-51, pathologist-in-chief, 1951-56, physician-in-chief for pathology, 1956-66, dir. Mallory Inst., 1951-66; prof., chmn. dept. pathology Med. Sch. Boston U., 1948-66, prof. emeritus, 1966—; chief anatomic pathology Boston VA Hosp., 1966-76, sr. pathologist, 1976—. Served as lt. comdr. USNR, 1934-50. Fellow Coll. Am. Pathologists; mem. New Eng. Path. Soc. (v.p. 1945, pres. 1946), Am. Soc. Exptl. Pathology, Am. Assn. Pathologists and Bacteriologists, AMA. Author articles in med. jours. Home: 88 Laurel Rd Chestnut Hill MA 02167 Office: 150 S Huntington Ave Boston MA 02130

MALLORY, JAMES RUSSELL, educator; b. St. Andrews, N.B., Can., Feb. 5, 1916; s. Charles Wesley and Eva (Outhouse) M.; B.A., U. N.B., 1937, LL.D. (hon.), 1968; LL.B., U. Edinburgh (Scotland), 1940; M.A., Dalhousie U., 1941; LL.D. (hon.), Queen's U., 1978; m. Frances Daniel Keller, June 24, 1940; children—James Russell, Charles Daniel. Instr. polit. sci. U. Sask., 1941-43; lectr. polit. economy U. Toronto, 1943-44; asst. prof. polit. economy Brandon (Man., Can.) Coll., 1944-46; mem. faculty McGill U., 1946—, prof. polit. sci., 1958—, R.B. Angus prof. polit. sci., 1977—, chmn. dept. econs. and polit. sci., 1959-69. Chmn. Social Sci. Research Council Can., 1964-67; mem. acad. panel Can. Council, 1965-68; mem. nat. selection com. Woodrow Wilson Fellowship Found., 1965-68. Bd. govs. Labour Coll. Can. Nuffield Found. travelling fellow,, 1953-54; leave fellowship Can. Council, 1969-70, 77-78; recipient Centennial of Can. medal, 1967; Queen's Silver Jubilee medal for Can., 1977; hon. fellow Faculty Law, U. Edinburgh, 1969-70; vis., fellow Australian Nat. U., 1977-78. Fellow Royal Soc. Can. (pres. sect. II 1973-74); mem. Can. Assn. U. Tchrs. (sec. 1952-54), Can. Polit. Sci. Assn. (v.p. 1964-66). Author: Social Credit and the Federal Power in Canada, 1955; The Structure of Canadian Government, 1971. Home: 632 Grosvenor Ave Montreal PQ H3Y 2S8 Canada

MALLORY, V(IRGIL) STANDISH, geologist, educator; b. Englewood, N.J., July 14, 1919; s. Virgil Sampson and Sarah Lauris (Baum) M.; A.B., Oberlin Coll., 1943; M.A., U. Calif. at Berkeley, 1948, Ph.D. (Standard Oil of Calif. fellow in paleontology), 1952; m. Miriam Elizabeth Rowan, Feb. 3, 1946; children—Charles Standish, Stefan Douglas, Peter Sommers, Ingrid Lauris. Preparator U. Calif. Museum Paleontology, Berkeley, 1946-48, curator foraminifera, 1948-50, cons., 1951; lectr. paleontology U. Calif. at Berkeley, 1951; asst. prof. geology U. Wash., 1952-59, asso. prof., 1959-62, prof., chmn. div. geology and paleontology, curator of paleontology Burke Meml. Wash. State Mus., 1962—. Cons. in petroleum geology; mem. Gov. Wash. Commn. on Petroleum Regulations, 1956-57; mem. NSF Paris Basin Field Inst., Paris, Belgium and Luxembourg, 1964; co-dir. NSF Inst. Secondary Sch. Tchrs., Western Wash. State Coll., summers 1963, 65. Served with AUS, 1944-46; PTO. Am. Assn. Petroleum Geologists Revolving Fund grantee, 1957; U. Wash. Agnes Anderson Fund grantee, 1963. Fellow AAAS (council 1964—), Geologic Soc. Am.; mem. Am. Assn. Petroleum Geologists (sect. council 1964—), Paleontologic Soc. (chmn. sect. 1956-58), Geol. Soc. Am., Soc. Econ. Paleontology and Mineralogy, Paleontol. Research Soc., Paleontogogische Gesellschaft, Geologische Gesellschaft, Internat. Paleontological Union, N.W. Sci. Soc., Am. Assn. Museums, Mineral Mus. (adv. council 1974—), Sigma Xi, Theta Tau. Author: Lower Tertiary Biostratigraphy of California Coast Ranges, 1959; Lower Tertiary Foraminifera From Media Agua Creek Drainage Area, Kern County, California, 1970; Biostratigraphy—A Major Basis of Paleontologic Correlation, 1970; contbg. author: Lincoln Library Essential Knowledge, 1965; Ency. Brit., 15th edit., 1974. Editor paleontology Quaternary Research Jour., 1970-77. Contbr. articles to profl. jours. Home: 5209 Pullman Ave NE Seattle WA 98105 Office: Burke Meml Wash State Mus DB10 U Wash Seattle WA 98195

MALLOY, DANIEL VICTOR, ins. brokerage co. exec.; b. S.I., N.Y., May 27, 1935; s. Daniel Victor and Adele M. M.; B.A., Wagner Coll., 1957; m. Eleanor L. Hartnett, May 3, 1958; children—Daniel Victor, III, Neil M., Susan L. Group sales rep. N.Y. Life, 1958-60; sales rep. Reid-Collins & Co., N.Y.C., 1960-63; v.p. R. C. Rathbone/Fred S. James, N.Y.C., 1963-75; sr. v.p. Fred S. James & Co. of N.Y., N.Y.C., 1975-77, chmn. bd., 1977-78; exec. v.p. Fred S. James & Co., Chgo., 1978—, also dir. Bd. dirs. Mid Am. chpt. ARC, Chgo. Served with U.S. Army, 1957-58. Clubs: Chgo., Met. (Chgo.); Navesink Country (Red Bank, N.J.). Home: 513 Walnut St Winnetka IL 60093 Office: 230 W Monroe St Chicago IL 60606

MALLOY, JOHN CYRIL, lawyer; b. Jackson, Tenn., June 7, 1930; s. John Cyril and Jennie May (Mathis) M.; B.S., Roosevelt U., Chgo., 1953; postgrad. Ill. Inst. Tech., 1953; J.D., Northwestern U., 1958; postgrad. in patent law George Washington U., 1959; m. Marlene Oradei, June 8, 1957; children—Angela May, Jennie Sue, John Cyril. Admitted to Fla., Ill., D.C., U.S. Patent and Trademark Office, U.S. Supreme Ct. bars; legal asst. to U.S. atty. D.C., 1958-59; individual practice patent and trademark law, Miami, Fla., 1959—; pres. Energy Div., Inc., FLA Corp.; prof. law U. Miami Sch. Law, 1978—; mem. Fla. Ho. of Reps., 1972-74, 1976—, mem. appropriations com., vice chmn. commerce com., 1978—; mem. Pres.'s Nat. Hwy. Safety Adv. Com., Washington, 1975-78. Past dir. Leukemia Fund dr., 1970-71. Served to 1st lt. U.S. Army, 1953-55. Mem. Fed. (pres. So. Fla. chpt. 1971-72), Am. (chmn. com. 503 1963-65, com. 601 1965-66), Fla. bar assns., Am. Patent Law Assn. Office: Alfred I duPont Bldg 169 E Flagler St Miami FL 33131

MALLOY, JOHN MICHAEL, mgmt. cons.; b. Burlington, Vt., Oct. 5, 1918; s. Patrick J. and Sarah (Gibbons) M.; A.B., Boston Coll., 1940; M.B.A., Harvard, 1947; m. Grace Fielding, Aug. 7, 1945; children—Virginia, Patricia. Commd. ensign U.S. Navy, 1941, advanced through grades to capt., 1960; with Navy Purchasing Office, Washington, 1947-51, Los Angeles, 1951-53; with Naval Supply Depot, Yokosuka, Japan, 1953-55, Office Naval Material, 1955-57, Office Sec. Def., 1958-61; retired, 1963; asst. corp. dir. contracts and proposals N.Am. Aviation, Inc., 1963-65; dep. asst. sec. def. for procurement, 1965-74; asst. to pres. Teledyne Ryan Aero., San Diego, 1974-76, v.p. adminstrn., 1977-78; mgmt. cons. in govt. contracting, 1978—; chmn. Armed Services Procurement Regulations Com., 1958-61; mem. Pres.'s Commn. Patent System, 1966. Decorated Legion of Merit. Mem. Nat. Contract Mgmt. Assn. (v.p. 1964-65, nat. bd. advisers 1966—). Home and Office: 1450 Calle Altura LaJolla CA 92037

MALM, JAMES ROYAL, surgeon; b. Cleve., Sept. 7, 1925; s. Royal Dinsmore and Theodora (Drumont) M.; A.B., Princeton, 1947; M.D., Columbia, 1949; m. Constance Brooks, July 8, 1950; children—Martha, Melissa, Karen, Sarah. Intern, Pa. Hosp., Phila., 1949-51; surg. resident Presbyn. Hosp., N.Y.C., 1953-57, thoracic surg. resident, 1957-59, attending surgeon, 1967—, instr. surgery Columbia, 1959-60, asst. prof., 1960-63, asso. prof., 1963-67, prof. clin. surgery, 1967—. Served to lt., M.C., USNR, 1951-53. Diplomate Am. Bd. Thoracic Surgery, Am. Bd. Surgery. Mem. A.C.S., N.Y. Heart Assn. (dir.), AMA, Internat. Cardiovascular Soc., Am. Assn. Thoracic Surgery, N.Y. Soc. Cardiovascular Surgery, N.Y. Soc. Thoracic Surgery (past pres.), Asian Thoracic and Cardiovascular Soc. (hon.), Soc. Thoracic Surgeons, Soc. U. Surgeons, Soc. Vascular Surgeons, Am. Surg. Assn. Pioneer in use of tissue valves for heart valve replacement and surgery for congenital heart disease; leader in improving the quality of thoracic training in the U.S. Home: 25 Sleepy Hollow Rd Scarborough NY 10510 Office: 161 Fort Washington Ave New York NY 10032

MALOFF, SAUL, educator, author; b. N.Y.C., Sept. 6, 1922; s. David and Yetta (Friedman) M.; B.A., Coll. City N.Y., 1939-42; M.A., U. Iowa, 1947, Ph.D., 1952; married; 1 dau., Jadis Karla Lorca Norman. Mem. faculty English and Am. lit. U. Iowa, 1946-49, U. Mich., 1949-51, U. Ind., 1951-55, Coll. City N.Y., 1955-56, Pratt Inst., 1956-59, U. P.R., 1959-60, N.Y.U., 1960-62, New Sch. Social Research, 1960-62, Bennington Coll., 1962-64; books editor Newsweek mag., 1964-68; prof. English, Hunter Coll., 1968—; frequent guest lectr. at colls. and univs.; cons. Guggenheim Found. Exec. bd. Am. Center P.E.N. Served with AUS, 1943-46. Guggenheim fellow; recipient George Polk Meml. award lit. criticism. Author: (novel) Happy Families, 1968; (novel) Heartland, 1973; also editor poetry and prose anthologies, author short stories, revs., articles, essays in lit. criticism. Home: Second Hill Rd Bridgewater CT 06752 Office: Dept English Hunter Coll City Univ NY New York City NY 10003

MALONE, DAVID HENRY, educator; b. Washington, Aug. 9, 1919; s. Maurice Drummond and Clara (Hanna) M.; A.B. with honors, U. N.C., 1940, Ph.D. in Comparative Lit., 1948; student La. State U., 1940-41; m. Alice Bond Wells, Aug. 15, 1942; children—Stephen David, Bruce Hanna, Kirk Wells. Asst. prof., then prof. English, Auburn U., 1948-62; mem. faculty U. So. Calif., 1962, prof. comparative lit. and English, 1962—, chmn. English dept., 1964-68, chmn. comparative lit. program, 1962-72, dean humanities, 1972—. Vis. Fulbright prof. U. Vienna (Austria), 1958-60. Pres. Auburn City Bd. Edn., 1961-62. Served to lt. USNR, 1942-46; comdr. Res. (ret.). Fellow Fund Advancement Edn., 1954-55. Mem. Modern Lang. Assn., AAUP (chpt. pres. 1950-52, 64, state conf. pres. 1956-57, mem. nat. council 1970-73), Nat. Council Tchrs. English, Am. Comparative Lit. Assn. (v.p. 1974-77), Assn. Internat. de Litterature Comparee, Phi Beta Kappa, Omicron Delta Kappa. Author: (with W.P. Friederich) Outline of Comparative Literature, 1954. Editor: The Frontiers of Literary Criticism, 1974. Chmn. editorial bd. U. So. Calif. Studies in Comparative Lit., 1968—. Home: 4764-C La Villa Marina Venice CA 90291 Office: Bovard Hall 200 Univ So Calif Los Angeles CA 90007

MALONE, DENNIS PHILIP, educator; b. Buffalo, Sept. 3, 1932; s. Robert G. and Mildred (Mitchell) M.; B.A., U. Buffalo, 1954; M.Sc., Yale, 1955, Ph.D., 1960; m. Ann Irene Navelle, June 21, 1954; children—Christopher D., Elisabeth Ann. Research asso. Yale, 1955-60; head modern physics br. Cornell Aero. Labs., Buffalo, 1960-65; asso. prof. engring. and applied sci. State U. N.Y. at Buffalo, 1965-70, prof., chmn. dept. elec. engring., 1970—. Dir. N.Y. Astronautical Corp., Albany. Mem. Am. Phys. Soc., Sigma Xi, Phi Beta Kappa, Pi Mu Epsilon. Patentee in ion cyclotron resonance in ionized gases. Research in lasers. Home: 101 Cummings Ave Silver Springs NY 14550 Office: Dept Elec Engring State U NY Buffalo NY 14214

MALONE, DUMAS, historian; b. Coldwater, Miss., Jan. 10, 1892; s. John W. and Lillian (Kemp) M.; A.B., Emory U., 1910, Litt.D., 1936; B.D., Yale, 1916, A.M., 1921, Ph.D., 1923; LL.D., Northwestern U., 1935; Litt.D., U. Rochester, 1936, Dartmouth Coll., 1937, Coll. William and Mary, 1977, Hampden-Sydney Coll., 1979; L.H.D., U. Chattanooga, 1962; m. Elisabeth Gifford, Oct. 17, 1925; children—Gifford Dumas, Pamela. Instr. history Yale, 1919-23, vis. prof. Am. history, 1926-27, sr. Sterling traveling fellow, 1927; asso. prof. history U. Va., 1923-26, prof., 1926-29, Thomas Jefferson Found. prof. history, 1959-62, biographer-in-residence, 1962—; an editor Dictionary Am. Biography, 1929-31, editor in chief, 1931-36; dir. Harvard U. Press, 1936-43; prof. history Columbia, 1945-59. Bd. dirs. Thomas Jefferson Meml. Found.; mem. adv. coms. on publ. Papers of Jefferson and Madison. Served from pvt. to 2d lt., USMC, 1917-18. Recipient John Addison Porter prize Yale, 1923, Wilbur L. Cross medal, 1972; Thomas Jefferson award U. Va., 1964; chmn.'s citation Nat. Endowment for Humanities, 1979; Guggenheim fellow, 1951-52, 58-59. Mem. Am. Hist. Assn., Am. Antiquarian Soc., Am. Acad. Arts and Scis., Mass. Hist. Soc. (Kennedy medal 1972), So. Hist. Assn. (pres. 1967-68), Soc. Am. Historians, Va. Hist. Soc., Phi Beta Kappa (vis. scholar 1964-65, 66-67), Omicron Delta Kappa, Raven Soc. Clubs: Century, Virginians (N.Y.C.); Cosmos (Washington). Democrat. Author: The Public Life of Thomas Cooper, 1926; Saints in Action, 1939; Edwin A. Alderman; A Biography, 1940; Jefferson the Virginian (vol. I of projected 6 vol. work entitled Jefferson and His Time), 1948, Vol. II: Jefferson and the Rights of Man, 1951, Vol. III: Jefferson and the Ordeal of Liberty, 1962, Vol IV: Jefferson the President: First Term, 1970, Vol. V: Jefferson the President: Second Term, 1974 (5 vols. awarded Pulitzer prize in history 1975); The Story of the Declaration of Independence, 1954; Thomas Jefferson as Political Leader, 1963; (with Basil Rauch) Empire for Liberty, 2 vols., 1960. Joint author The Interpretation of History, 1943. Editor: Correspondence between Thomas Jefferson and P.S. du Pont de Nemours, 1930. Contbr. mags. Editor: (with Allen Johnson) Dictionary Am. Biography, vols. IV to VII, 1930-31, as editor in chief vols. VIII to XX, 1932-36; editor Hist. Book club 1948—. Cons. Nat. Assn. Ednl. Broadcasters on The Jeffersonian Heritage, 1952. Mng. editor Polit. Sci. Quar., 1953-58. Home: 2000 Lewis Mountain Rd Charlottesville VA 22903 also West Falmouth MA 02574 Office: Alderman Library U Va Charlottesville VA 22901

MALONE, EDWARD H., elec. co. financial exec.; b. Forest Hills, N.Y., Nov. 11, 1924; s. Edward H. and Gertrude (Gibson) M.; B.S., Columbia, 1949; M.B.A., N.Y. U., 1950; m. Margaret A. Rakers, Sept. 8, 1951; children—Mary (Mrs. David W. Tilney), Edward, Patricia J., Jo-Ann. Bank examiner Fed. Res. Bank of N.Y., N.Y.C., 1949-52; trust officer Lincoln Rochester (N.Y.) Trust Co., 1952-55; with Gen. Electric Co., 1955—, mgr. private placement investments, N.Y.C., 1959-61, mgr. trust portfolios, N.Y.C., 1961-67, mgr. trust investment ops., N.Y.C., 1967-70, v.p., Stamford, Conn., 1970—; trustee Prudential Savs. Bank, 1966-77; dir. Gen. Electric Credit Corp.; mem. N.Y. State Comptroller's Investment Adv. Com.; mem. Pres.'s Commn. for Fin. Structure and Regulation, 1970-71; chmn. Elfun Trusts, Stamford, 1975—. Served with USAAF, 1943-45. Mem. N.Y. Soc. Fin. Analysts. Clubs: Landmark (Stamford); Woodway Country (Darien, Conn.). Home: 9 Old Parish Rd Darien CT 06820 Office: 112 Prospect St Stamford CT 06904

MALONE, EDWIN SCOTT, III, public relations cons.; b. Vernon, Tex., Mar. 25, 1938; s. Edwin Scott and Pauline (King) M.; B.A., So. Meth. U., 1960; m. Sandra Sue Ballard, Aug. 19, 1960; children—Melissa, Michael Scott, Paula Sue. TV performer Gourmet TV Series, Dallas and Ft. Worth, 1955-60; pres. Ed Malone Enterprises, pub. relations and investments, Arlington, Tex., 1960—; account exec. David Wade & Assos., Dallas, 1963-66; v.p. radio services So. Baptist Radio-TV Commn., Ft. Worth, 1965—; partner COMAL Pub. Relations Cons., Arlington, 1970—; producer series Accent on Youth, Assignment Travel; cons. Tyndale House Pubs., Inc., Wheaton, Ill.; dir. Cherrywood Farms, Inc., Ft. Worth. Tex. del. White House Conf. Children and Youth, 1960, 70; exec. com. Longhorn Council Boy Scouts Am. Mem. Am. Soc. Travel Writers, Am. Acad. TV Arts and Scis., Ft. Worth Religious Pub. Relations

Council (past pres.), Ft. Worth C. of C., Religious Heritage Am., S.A.R., Soc. War of 1812, Ky. Hist. Soc., Friends of LBJ Library, Dallas Press Club, Sertoma (past pres.), Acacia, Order of Pythagorus (hon.), Order St. Dennis of Zante (grand cross, charge d'affair Tex.), Order Crown of Thorns (chevalier). Clubs: Masons (33 deg.), Shriners (past presiding officer York Rite), DeMolay Legion of Honor. Author: Douglas Genealogy, 1959; Malone Genealogy, 1960; Religious Landmarks of America, 1973. Home: 1902 Mossy Oak St Arlington TX 76012

MALONE, JAMES (RICHARD), mfg. co. exec.; b. Cleve., Dec. 2, 1942; s. William R. and Marian (Bentley) M.; B.Sc., Ind. U., 1965; married; children—Deanna Lynn, Lisa Suzanne. Ops. mgr. Bendix Corp., South Bend, Ind., 1969-70; plant mgr. Western Acadia, Chgo., 1970-74; v.p. mfg. Haskell of Pitts., 1971-74; pres., chief exec. officer Mgmt. Concepts Co., Pitts., 1974-79; pres. chief operating officer Facet Enterprises Inc., Tulsa, 1979—, also dir.; dir. Malibu Corp., Pennhurst Burial. Bd. dirs. Jefferson County Indsl. Devel. Authority, Tulsa Ballet Theatre, Jr. Achievement of Tulsa. Mem. Young President's Orgn., Newmark Assos. (dir.). Republican. Presbyterian. Clubs: Pitts. Field, Pitts. Athletic; Tulsa, Cedar Ridge Country. Home: 3548 E 110 Tulsa OK 74136

MALONE, JAMES WILLIAM, bishop; b. Youngstown, Ohio, Mar. 8, 1920; s. James Patrick and Katherine V. (McGuire) M.; A.B., St. Mary Sem., Cleve., 1945; M.A., Cath. U. Am., 1952, Ph.D., 1957. Ordained priest Roman Catholic Ch., 1945; asst. pastor, Youngstown, 1945-50; supt. schs. Diocese of Youngstown, 1950-65; instr. ednl. adminstrn. St. John's Coll., Cleve., 1953; aux. bishop of Youngstown, 1960-68, bishop, 1968—; apostolic adminstr. Diocese Youngstown, 1966-68; adv. Bishops' Com. Ecumenical and Interreligious Affairs Nat. Conf. Cath. Bishops, co-chmn. Cath./United Meth. Nat. Dialogue, Internat. Commn. English in The Liturgy, rep., 1st vice chmn. bd. dirs., mem. Episcopal Bd., consultor bishops' com. liturgy. Office: 144 W Wood St Youngstown OH 44503

MALONE, JOSEPH LAWRENCE, linguist; b. N.Y.C., July 2, 1937; s. Joseph Timothy and Katherine Veronica (O'Connor) M.; B.A., U. Calif., Berkeley, 1963, Ph.D., 1967; m. Pamela Joan Altfeld, Jan. 31, 1964; children—Joseph Timothy, II, Otis Taig. Mem. faculty Barnard Coll., N.Y.C., 1967—, prof. linguistics, 1975—, chmn. dept., 1967—; part-time vis. lectr. U. Pa., spring and fall 1970; linguistics adviser Arete Publishing Co., also editor, contbr. co. Acad. Am. Ency. Served with U.S. Army, 1957-60. Grad. fellow U. Calif., Berkeley, 1965-66, Am. Council Learned Socs., 1966-67; recipient Faculty research grant Barnard Coll., 1969, 76. Mem. Linguistics Soc. Am., Am. Oriental Soc., AAUP, N. Am. Conf. Afro-Asiatic Linguistics, Phi Beta Kappa. Democrat. Author articles in field. Address: 169 Prospect St Leonia NJ 07605. *A surprisingly large variety of admirable things can be accomplished by simply walking out to the sun of day and doing them.*

MALONE, LEE HARRISON BROWN, museum exec., artist; b. Las Cruces, N.M., May 28, 1913; s. Lee Quayle and Doris Jennison (Brown) M.; grad. U. Sch., 1931; student Yale Art Sch., 1933-34, A.B., 1939; m. Joan Gilroy Reilly, Sept. 29, 1945; children—Michael, Caroline, John S., Monica, Thomas, Mary Christina. Art historian, lectr.; curator Clearwater Art Mus., 1936-37; instr. history art Notre Dame Coll. of S.I., 1939-40; aide to co-ordinator inter-Am. affairs, Dept. of State, 1940-41; dir. Columbus (Ohio) Gallery Fine Arts, 1946-53; dir. Mus. Fine Arts Houston, 1953-59; exec. dir. nat. devel. com. Pierpont Morgan Library, N.Y.C.; dir. Mus. Fine Arts, St. Petersburg, Fla., 1968—. Served as lt. comdr. USNR, 1943-46. Recipient W.L. Ehrich Meml. prize, Yale, 1939. Mem. Assn. Art Museum Dirs. (sec. 1973-74), Am. Assn. Museums, Fla. Art Mus. Dirs. Assn. Roman Catholic. Author: Sacred Art, 1953; also exhibit catalogs and mag. articles. Home: 701 15th Ave NE St Petersburg FL 33704 Office: 255 Beach Dr N St Petersburg FL 33701

MALONE, MOSES, profl. basketball player; b. Petersburg, Va., Mar. 23, 1954. Mem. Utah Stars (Am. Basketball Assn.), 1974-75, St. Louis Spirits (Am. Basketball Assn.), 1975-76, Buffalo Braves (Nat. Basketball Assn.), 1976, Houston Rockets (Nat. Basketball Assn.), 1976—. Office: care Houston Rockets The Summit Ten Greenway Plaza E Houston TX 77046*

MALONE, RICHARD HENRY, hosp. adminstr.; b. Logansport, La., June 15, 1925; s. James Drew and Mary Amanda (Bryant) M.; B.S. in Chemistry, La. State U.; M.B.A., U. Chgo., 1958; m. Betty Jane Tucker, Feb. 12, 1950; children—Richard, Tucker, Jay, Drew. Asst. adminstr. Baton Rouge Gen. Hosp., 1952-58; adminstr. Jefferson Davis Meml. Hosp., Natchez, Miss., 1958-64; pres., chief exec. officer Hinds Gen. Hosp., Jackson, Miss., 1964-74; asso. exec. dir. Baylor U. Med. Center, 1974-77; exec. dir. Baptist Med. Center, Jacksonville, Fla., 1977—; bd. dirs. Estes Park Inst., Englewood, Calif., Commn. on Profl. and Hosp. Activities, Ann Arbor, Mich. Served with USAAF, 1943-45; ETO. Fellow Am. Coll. Hosp. Adminstrs.; mem. Am. Hosp. Assn., Fla. Hosp. Assn., Am. Protestant Hosp. Assn. Baptist. Club: Rotary. Contbr. articles to trade jours. Home: 5217 Santa Rosa Way Jacksonville FL 32207 Office: 800 Prudential Dr Jacksonville FL 32207*

MALONE, RICHARD SANKEY, newspaper pub.; b. Owen Sound, Ont., Can., Sept. 18, 1909; s. Willard Park and Mildred Villiers (Sankey) M.; student Bishop Ridley Coll., St. Catherines, Can., 1928; m. Helen Mary Cook, Sept. 9, 1936; children—Robert Nesbit, Richard Cook, Deirdre Louise. With Toronto Star, 1928-30, Regina Leader-Post, 1930-36, Saskatoon Star-Phoenix, 1933; pub. Winnipeg Free Press, 1960-74; publisher Globe & Mail, Toronto, 1974-78; chmn. F.P. Publs. Ltd., 1959—; dir. Monarch Life Assurance Co.; founder, Canadian Army newspaper, Maple Leaf, 1941; hon. mgr. Imperial Press Conf., 1950. Bd. dirs. Dafoe Found. Served to brig. Canadian Army, 1939-45. Decorated Order Brit. Empire. Mem. Canadian Daily Newspaper Pub. Assn., Internat. Inst. Strategic Studies, Winnipeg C. of C. (pres. 1956-57). Mem. Ch. of Eng. Clubs: Rideau (Ottawa); Manitoba, St. Charles Country (Winnipeg); Toronto, York (Toronto). Author: Missing From the Record, 1947. Compiler: Book Shelf Free Press, 1955-56. Home: 63 St Clair Ave W Toronto ON Canada Office: FP Publications Box 139 Royal Trust Tower Toronto Dominion Centre Toronto ON Canada

MALONE, ROBERT ROY, artist; b. McColl, S.C., Aug. 8, 1933; s. Robert Roy and Anne (Matthews) M.; A.B., U. N.C., 1955; M.F.A., U. Chgo., 1958; postgrad. U. Iowa, 1959; m. Cynthia Enid Taylor, Feb. 26, 1956; 1 son, Brendan Trevor. Instr. art Union U., Jackson, Tenn., 1959-60, Lambuth Coll., 1959-61; asst. prof. art Wesleyan Coll., Macon, Ga., 1961-67, asso. prof., 1967-68; asso. prof. W.Va. U., 1968-70; asso. prof. So. Ill. U., Edwardsville, 1970-75, prof., 1975—; one-man shows at Gallery Illien, Atlanta, 1969, De Cingue Gallery, Miami, 1968, 71, Ill. State Mus., Springfield, 1974, U. Del., Newark, 1978, others; group shows include Bklyn. Mus., 1966, Asso. Am. Artists Gallery, N.Y.C., 1968, Musée d'Art Modern, Paris, 1970, DeCordova Mus., 1973, 74, Dason-Zaks Gallery, Chgo., 1971; represented in numerous permanent collections, including Smithsonian Instn., Washington, USIA, Washington, Library of Congress, Calif. Palace of Legion of Honor, San Francisco, N.Y. Pub. Library, N.Y.C., Victoria and Albert Mus., London, Chgo. Art Inst., Indpls. Mus. Art. Recipient numerous regional, nat. awards in competitive exhbns.; Ford fellow, 1977; So. Ill. U. at Edwardsville sr. research scholar, 1976. Democrat. Home: 600 Chapman St Edwardsville IL 62025 Office: Dept Art and Design So Ill U Edwardsville IL 62025

MALONE, ROWENA JAMES, editor; b. Hastings, Iowa, Aug. 6, 1915; d. Mearl Arthur and Ethelyn Leota (McKie) Gable; A.B., U. Iowa, 1937; M.S., Iowa State U., 1959; m. Gerald E. Malone, Aug. 14, 1975; 1 dau. by previous marriage, Margaret Elizabeth. Research asst. and writer, sec. to editor editorial page Des Moines Register & Tribune, 1949-52; writer, asst. producer sta. WOI-TV, Ames, Iowa, 1954-55; instr. journalism Iowa State U., Ames, 1953-55, promotion mgr., asso. editor univ. press, 1958-63, mng. editor, 1963—. Mem. Women in Communications, P.E.O., Zeta Phi Eta, Delta Delta Delta. Democrat. Episcopalian (vestry). Club: Altrusa. Contbr. articles to profl. jours. Home: 1116 Kennedy Rd Ames IA 50010

MALONE, THOMAS FRANCIS, univ. adminstr., meteorologist; b. Sioux City, Iowa, May 3, 1917; s. John and Mary (Hourigan) M.; B.S., S.D. Sch. Mines, 1940, D.Eng., 1962; Sc.D., Mass. Inst. Tech., 1946; L.H.D., St. Joseph Coll., West Hartford, Conn., 1965; m. Rosalie Doran, Dec. 30, 1942; children—John H., Thomas Francis, Mary E., James K., Richard K., Dennis P. Instr. Mass. Inst. Tech., 1942-43, asst. prof., 1943-51, asso. prof., 1951-56; dir. Travelers Research Center, Travelers Ins. Co., Hartford, Conn., 1955-56, dir. research, 1956-69, sr. v.p., 1968-70; chmn. bd. Travelers Research Center, Inc., 1961-70; dean Grad. Sch., U. Conn., Storrs, 1970-73; dir. Holcomb Research Inst., Butler U., Indpls., 1973—; chmn. bd. Center for Environment and Men, 1970-71; chmn. bd. Univ. Corp. for Atmospheric Research. Mem. Conn. Weather Control Bd., 1959-73; mem. panel on sci. and tech., com. on sci. and astronautics U.S. Ho. of Reps., 1960; nat. adv. com. community air pollution HEW, 1962-66; mem. sci. info. council NSF, 1962-66; rep. Am. Geophys. Union to U.S. Nat. Commn. for UNESCO, 1963—, chmn. U.S. Nat. Commn., 1965-67; mem. nat. adv. com. on oceans and atmosphere, 1972-75; mem. Conn. Research Commn., 1965-71; mem. com. application sci. and tech. New Eng. Council; chmn. Nat. Motor Vehicle Safety Adv. Council, 1967-70. Bd. dirs. Engrs. Joint Council, 1968-70; bd. govs. Ins. Inst. Hwy. Safety, 1966-70. Recipient Robert M. Losey award Inst. Aero. Sci., 1960, Charter Oak Leadership medal Greater Hartford C. of C., 1962, Charles Franklin Brooks award, 1964, Cleveland Abbe award Am. Meteorol. Soc., 1968, Conn. Conservationist of Yr. award, 1966; Guy E. March Silver medal S.D. Sch. Mines, 1976. Fellow N.Y. Acad. Scis., AAAS, Am. Meteorol. Soc. (pres. 1960-62), Am. Geophys. Union (past pres., sec. internat. participation 1964); mem. Nat. Acad. Scis. (chmn. geophysics research bd. 1969-76, chmn. bd. on internat. orgns. and programs, dep. fgn. sec. 1969-73, fgn. sec. 1978—), Am. Acad. Arts and Scis., Internat. Council Sci. Unions (v.p., sec.-gen. sci. com. problems environ. 1970-76, treas. 1978—), Nat. Acad. Engring. (space applications bd. 1973—), Am. Geog. Soc. (council 1971—). Editor: Compendium of Meteorology, 1951. Home: 6421 Sunset Ln Indianapolis IN 46260

MALONE, WEX SMATHERS, educator, lawyer; b. Asheville, N.C., Nov. 17, 1906; s. Charles Neilson and Joanna (Smathers) M.; student U. Chgo., 1925-27; B.A., U. N.C., 1928, J.D. with honors, 1931; LL.M., Harvard, 1933; m. Helen Lawrence Jeffress, June 14, 1933; children—Helen Lawrence, Charles Neilson II. Admitted to N.C. bar, 1934; prof. law U. Miss., 1931-32, 35-39; asso. firm Reed, Hoyt & Washburn, N.Y.C., also mem. legal dept. Irving Trust Co., N.Y.C., 1933-35; prof. law La. State U., 1939-42, 45-66, Boyd prof., 1966-75, Boyd prof. emeritus, 1975—; sr. atty. Fed. Pub. Housing, 1942-45; Legion Lex disting. vis. prof. law U. So. Calif., 1962; disting. vis. prof. U. Wash., 1977; vis. prof. law Northwestern U., U. Tex., U. N.C., Rutgers U., Stanford, Chgo., Hastings Coll. Law, U. Mich., U. Denver; adviser for restatement of torts and mem. Am. Law Inst. Recipient Disting. Service award Am. Trial Lawyers Assn., 1964, William L. Prosser award Torts sect. Assn. Am. Law Schs., 1976; La. State U. Found. Distinguished Faculty fellow, 1965. Mem. Assn. Am. Law Schs. (exec. com. 1962, pres. 1967), Order of Coif (nat. pres. 1961-64), Chi Psi, Phi Alpha Delta, Omicron Delta Kappa. Author: Louisiana Workmen's Compensation Law and Practice, 1951, 2d edit. (with H.A. Johnston). Editor: (with Green, Pedrick, Rahl) Cases on Torts, 1956; Cases on Injuries to Relations, 1958; (with M.L. Plant) Cases on Workmen's Compensation, 1962, Cases on the Employment Relation, 1974; (with Guerry) Studies in Louisiana Torts Law, 1970, supplement, 1975; Torts in a Nutshell: Injuries to Relations, 1979; also articles. Home: 1895 E Lakeshore Dr Baton Rouge LA 70808

MALONE, WILLIAM JAMES, cons. engr.; b. Toronto, Ont., Can., Sept. 23, 1924; s. Charles Stewart and Charlotte Lamont (Davidson) M.; B.S., U. Toronto, 1949; m. Heidemarie Wilmshen, July 4, 1968; children—Jennifer, Charles; children by previous marriage—Linda, John. Research engr. Hydro-Electric Power Commn. of Ont., Toronto, 1949-52; resident engr. Catskill sect. N.Y. Thruway, 1952-54; transp. cons. DeLeuw Cather Co. of Can., Ltd., Don Mills, Ont., 1954—, chmn. bd., 1960-69; chmn. MASCON Internat. Ltd., 1968. Served with RCAF, 1942-45. Recipient Canadian Centennial medal, 1967; Distinguished Service award Rds. and Transp. Assn. Can. Mem. Assn. Profl. Engrs. Ont. Inst. Traffic Engrs., ASCE, Am. Concrete Inst., Engring. Inst. Can., Cons. Engrs. Council. Club: York Downs Golf and Country (Toronto). Home: Jevington House Knotty Green Beaconsfield Bucks England Office: 135 Shannon Industrial Estate Shannon Ireland

MALONEY, CHARLES GARRETT, clergyman; b. Louisville, Sept. 9, 1912; s. David J. and Imelda Mary (Shea) M.; student St. Joseph Coll., Rensselaer, Ind., 1926-32; Ph.B., S.T.L., Gregorian U., Rome, 1938; J.C.L., Catholic U. Am., 1942. Ordained priest, Roman Cath. Ch., 1937; chaplain St. Thomas Orphanage, Louisville, 1938; asst. pastor St. Frances of Rome, Louisville, 1939; chaplain St. Joseph Infirmary, Louisville, 1942-46; sec., asst., chancellor Archdiocese of Louisville, 1946-55, vicar gen., 1954—, aux. bishop, 1955—. Mem. Vatican Council II. Office: 212 E College St Louisville KY 40203

MALONEY, DAVID MONAS, bishop; b. Littleton, Colo., Mar. 15, 1912; s. James Edward and Margaret (Flynn) M.; student U. Colo., 1929-30; A.B., St. Thomas Sem., Denver, 1933; S.T.L., Gregorian U., Rome, 1937; J.C.D., Apollinaire U., Rome, 1940. Ordained priest Roman Catholic Ch., 1936, consecrated bishop, 1961; curate St. Philomena Ch., Denver, 1940-43; asst. chancellor Archdiocese of Denver, 1943-54, chancellor, 1954-60; domestic prelate, 1949; titular bishop Ruspae, aux. bishop Diocese of Denver, 1960-67; bishop Diocese of Wichita (Kans.), 1967—. Home: 424 N Broadway Wichita KS 67202*

MALONEY, DOUGLAS WILLIAM, banker; b. Salmon Arm, B.C., Can., July 8, 1920; s. James William and Maude Elizabeth (Holliday) M.; B.Commerce, U. B.C., 1942; m. Alix McPhail, Dec. 23, 1942; children—Dianne Maloney Hand, Sharon Maloney McBurney. With IAC Ltd., 1948—, sr. v.p. bus. devel., Montreal, Que., Can., 1968-70, sr. v.p., gen. mgr., Toronto, Ont., Can., 1970-72, sr. v.p., sr. gen. mgr., 1973-74, exec. v.p. and sr. gen. mgr., 1974-76, pres., 1976—, vice-chmn., 1979—; vice-chmn., chief exec. dir., dir. Continental Bank Can., IAC Ltd.; dir. Niagara Fin. Co. Ltd., Niagara Realty of Can. Ltd., Premier Property Ltd. Served with Canadian Army, 1942-46. Mem. Phi Gamma Delta, Sigma Tau Chi. Clubs: Granite, Lambton Golf, Rosedale Golf, Badminton and Racquet, Toronto, Univ. (Toronto); M.A.A.A., Kaniwaki (Montreal). Home: 619 Avenue Rd Toronto ON M4V 2K6 Canada Office: 130 Adelaide St W Toronto ON M5H 3R2 Canada

MALONEY, SISTER ELIZABETH ANN, coll. pres.; b. Baldwin, N.Y., Dec. 12, 1925; d. Francis Xavier and Julia (Mueller) M.; A.B., Coll. of St. Elizabeth, 1947; M.A., Fordham U., 1951; postgrad. U. Notre Dame, summers 1957-61, full time, 1960-66, Yeshiva U., 1962-63. Joined Sisters of Charity, 1947; tchr. math. St. John's High Sch., Paterson, N.J., 1949-55, St. Cecilia High Sch., Englewood, N.J., 1958-60; faculty Coll. St. Elizabeth, Convent Station, N.J., 1961—, chmn. math. dept., 1963-69, asst. to pres., 1967-70, dean of studies, 1970-71, pres., 1971—; bd. mgrs. Morris County Savs. Bank. Mem. council So. province Sisters of Charity of St. Elizabeth; trustee N.J. Coll. Fund Assn., St. Elizabeth Hosp., Elizabeth, N.J. Mem. Am. Math. Assn., Assn. Ind. Colls. and Univs. N.J. Address: College of Saint Elizabeth Convent Station NJ 07963

MALONEY, FRANK EDWARD, educator; b. Niagara Falls, N.Y., Mar. 27, 1918; s. Frank E. and Florence (Bielman) M.; B.A., U. Toronto (Can.), 1938, grad. student philosophy, 1938-39; LL.B., U. Fla., 1942; m. Lucille Tinker, Feb. 20, 1943; children—Frank Edward, Jo Ann, Elizabeth. Admitted to Fla. bar, 1942, also Supreme Ct. U.S.; with firm Jordan, Lazonby & Dell, Gainesville, Fla., 1942; asso. prof. law U. Fla., 1946- 50, prof. law, 1950-58, acting dean Law Sch., 1958-59, dean Law Sch., 1959-70, dean emeritus, 1970—, prof. law, 1959—, dir. Eastern Water Law Center, 1965—; grad. fellow Sch. Law, Columbia, 1950-51; vis. prof. N.Y. U. Law Sch., 1957-58, Vanderbilt Law Sch., 1970-71, George Washington Law Center, summers 1968, 69, Tex. Tech. U., summer 1971; cons. internat. water law problems U.S. Dept. State. Served to maj. USAAF, 1942-46; CBI; col. USAF Res. ret. Fellow Am. Bar Found.; mem. Am. Law Inst., Am. Bar Assn., Fla. Bar, Assn. Am. Law Schs. (chmn. com. fed. legislation 1964-70), Internat. Assn. Water Law, U. Fla. Law Center Assn. (vice chmn. 1961-70), Bar Assn. 8th Jud. Circuit Fla., Nat. Conf. Bar Examiners (chmn. torts com. multistate bar exam.), Fla. Soc. Profl. Land Surveyors (hon. life), Phi Beta Kappa, Order of Coif, Fla. Blue Key, Phi Kappa Phi, Phi Alpha Delta, Pi Kappa Phi. Rotarian. Co-author: Water Law and Adminstration, 1968; A Model Water Code, 1972; drafted Fla. Water Resources Acts, 1957, 72, Tenn. Water Quality Act, 1971. Contbr. numerous articles to profl. jours. Home: 1823 NW 10th Ave Gainesville FL 32605

MALONEY, GERALD P., utilities co. exec.; b. Lawrence, Mass., Mar. 9, 1933; s. Thomas P. and Concetta M.; S.B. in Elec. Engring., M.I.T., 1955, S.B. in Bus. Adminstrn., 1955; M.B.A., Rutgers U., 1962; m. Dorothea Ames. With Am. Electric Power Co., Inc., N.Y.C., 1955—, controller, 1965-70, v.p. fin., 1970-75, sr. v.p. fin., 1975—; dir., v.p. fin. Appalachian Power Co., Ind. and Mich. Electric Co., Ohio Power Co., Ky. Power Co., Mich. Power Co., Wheeling Electric Co., Kingsport Power Co. Mem. Edison Electric Inst. (fin. com.), Beta Gamma Sigma. Club: Morris County Golf. Office: Am Electric Power Co 2 Broadway New York NY 10004

MALONEY, JAMES A., state judge; b. Las Vegas, N.Mex., Sept. 1, 1925; s. James and Gwynne (Heydt) M.; A.B., U. N.Mex.; J.D., Cath. U. of Am., 1950; m. Janet D. Wilson, Oct. 1, 1955; children—Ann, Sharon. Admitted to N.Mex. bar, 1950; pvt. practice law, Albuquerque, 1950-59; judge Municipal Ct., Albuquerque, 1959-68; probate judge Bernalillo County, 1953-56, 58-59; atty. gen. N.Mex., Santa Fe, 1969-71; dist. judge 2d N.Mex. Jud. Dist., 1971—. Served with AUS, 1943-46. Mem. Am. Automobile Assn. (nat. dir. 1966—). Home: 1324 Morningside NE Albuquerque NM 87110 Office: PO Box 488 Albuquerque NM 87103

MALONEY, JOHN ALEXANDER, hosp. adminstr.; b. Knoxville, Tenn., Mar. 1, 1927; s. Harry Lotspeich and Gertrude (Blaetz) M.; student U. Tenn., 1947-50; certificate in hosp. adminstrn., Ga. State Coll., 1958; m. Doris Ann Akes, Oct. 21, 1964; children—John Patrick, Christopher Michael; stepchildren—Thomas Kent Gaskins, Shelley Arlene Gaskins, William Glenn Gaskins. Adminstr., Lawrence County Gen. Hosp., Lawrenceburg, Tenn., 1958-60, Morristown-Hamblen (Tenn.) Hosp., 1960-64, Central State Psychiat. Hosp., Nashville, 1964-67, Eastern State Psychiat. Hosp., Knoxville, 1967-72; cons. Project Devel. Corp., Knoxville, 1971-72; adminstr. R.J. Taylor Meml. Hosp., Hawkinsville, Ga., 1972-73; health services cons., 1973-77; asso. adminstr. Walter Reed Army Med. Center, Washington, 1977—. Served with USNR, 1944-46; to 2d lt. AUS, 1952-53. Mem. Am. Coll. Hosp. Adminstrs., Tenn. Hosp. Assn., Knoxville Hosp. Council (pres. 1969-70), Am. Pub. Health Assn., Pi Epsilon Rho. Episcopalian. Clubs: Kiwanis, Rotary. Address: 5678 Stevens Forest Rd Columbia MD 21045

MALONEY, JOHN FREDERICK, research cons.; b. Watertown, N.Y., Apr. 28, 1913; s. John Francis and Grace (Gott) M.; grad. Mt. Hermon Sch., 1931; A.B., Princeton, 1935; m. Lucia Howard McKellar, Apr. 27, 1940; children—John Frederick, Robert McKellar, Bonnie Patton, Lucia Howard. With Gallup Poll, 1935-38; v.p. Peoples Research Corp., 1939-40; research analyst Young & Rubicam, 1940; Eastern mgr. Nat. Opinion Research Center, 1941; devel. analyst Curtis Pub. Co., 1946; research dir. internat. and U.S., Reader's Digest, 1946-66, corp. research dir., 1966-70; exec. v.p. Reader's Digest Found., 1970-71; cons. Advt. Research Found., N.Y.C., 1972—; exec. dir. Council of Am. Survey Research Orgns., 1976—. Pres. World Assn. Pub. Opinion Research, 1952-53, Market Research Council, 1958-59; chmn. research com. Mag. Pubs. Assn., 1961-65; vice chmn. tech. com. Advt. Research Found., 1956-70. Chmn. Westchester County Social Agys., 1953-57; v.p. Nat. Social Welfare Assembly, 1964-68; nat. chmn. Princeton Ann. Giving, 1968-69; vice chmn. Princeton U. Fund, 1968-69; pres. United Fund Westchester, 1968-71, Princeton Class of 1935, 1970-75; chmn. Westchester County adv. com. N.Y. State Urban Devel. Corp., 1970—. Served with USNR, 1941-45; comdg. officer destroyer escort. Decorated Commendation medal. Mem. Am. Mktg. Assn. (pres. N.Y. chpt. 1960, v.p. internat. div. 1972-73). Conglist. (chmn. bd. deacons 1962-63). Clubs: Princeton, Knickerbocker, Coffee House (N.Y.C.). Home: 48 Hamilton Rd Chappaqua NY 10514 Office: 3 E 54th St New York NY 10022

MALONEY, JOSEPH PATRICK, ret. distbn. co. exec.; b. Boston, Jan. 25, 1909; s. Patrick Henry and Ellen (Mathews) M.; A.B. cum laude, Harvard, 1930, M.B.A., 1932; m. Virginia Lee Stevens, Feb. 10, 1939; children—Joellen (Mrs. Joseph P. Toussaint), Virginia Lee, Stephen W. With Eastern Co., Westwood, Mass., 1938-73, pres. 1963-69, chmn. bd., chief exec. officer, 1969-73, now dir.; ltd. partner Westco Realty Co., Westwood, Mass. Mem. future sch. needs com. Town of Bedford, 1955, chmn. finance com., 1956. Vice pres., mem. corp. Emerson Hosp., Concord. Mem. Electric Inst. Boston (past pres.). Clubs: Harvard (Boston); Harvard Varsity (Cambridge, Mass.); Weston Golf; Nashua (N.H.) Country; Port Royal, Hole-in-The-Wall Golf, Naples Yacht (Naples, Fla.). Home: Thatcher Dr The Meadows Amherst NH 03031 also Spyglass Lane Naples FL 33940. *Freedom of choice in education, occupational pursuits, religious beliefs, political convictions, and life-style are to me the most important foundation of American life. This is why my parents came to this* *country at the turn of the century and why, within one generation, my name can appear in Who's Who.*

MALONEY, KENNETH MORGAN, chemist; b. New Orleans, Oct. 11, 1941; s. Henry Wadsworth and Alma (Johnson) M.; B.S. (T.H. Harris scholar), So. U., 1963; Ph.D., U. Wash., 1968; m. Yolanda Alfaro, Oct. 14, 1964; children—Sean, Shana. With Battelle Meml. Research Inst., Richland, Wash., 1968-70; engr. lighting research lab. Gen. Electric Co., Nela Park, Cleve., 1970-74, mgr., 1974-76; with Joseph C. Wilson Center Tech., Xerox Corp., Webster, N.Y., 1976—. Fellow Am. Inst. Chemists; mem. Am. Chem. Soc., NRC, Pi Mu Epsilon. Contbr. articles to profl. jours. Patentee in field. Home: 11 Courtenay Circle Pittsford NY 14534 Office: Xerox Corp 800 Phillips Rd Bldg 103 Webster NY 14580

MALONEY, THOMAS JAMES, publisher, editor, advt. exec.; b. Milw., Oct. 23, 1906; s. Edward Martin and Anna (Mangner) M.; m. Ruth Birdsall, 1924; children—Patricia, Terry, Judy, Jill; m. 2d, Sally Lee Woodall, Jan. 10, 1946; children—Patrick, Sally Lee; m. 3d, Mary Crosby, Sept. 1960; children—Mary L., Patrick James, Daniel Egerton. Engr., Am. Locomotive Co., 1926-28; pub., editor U.S. Camera Ann. and mag., 1935-70; pres. T. J. Maloney, Inc., advt. and pub. relations, 1935-42; partner Nevell Emmett Advt. Agy., 1942-50; exec. v.p., pres. Cecil Presley Advt. Agy., 1950-56; chmn. exec. com. Hicks & Greist, Inc., advt., 1960; chmn. bd. Telepro Industries, 1974—; author children's books, poetry, 1940—. Contbr. articles to nat. mags. Home: Crestview Lawrenceville NJ 08648

MALONEY, THOMAS JOSEPH, chem. co. exec.; b. Phila., Mar. 11, 1927; s. Thomas L. and Grace (McCarry) M.; B.S. in Accounting, St. Joseph's Coll., Phila., 1951; M.B.A., U. Del., 1958; m. Ina L. McCloskey, Sept. 9, 1950; children—Maureen, Sheila, Kevin. Adminstrv. asst. to div. gen. mgr. E.I. duPont de Nemours & Co., Inc., 1958-59; sr. systems cons. to corp. controller CBS, 1959-60; with ICI Ams. Inc., 1960—, controller, 1967-72, v.p., controller, 1972—, exec. v.p., 1979—; v.p., dir. ICI U.S. Inc., 1974—; dir. Bank of Del. vis. dir. plastics div. ICI Ltd. Bd. dirs. Wilmington Med. Center, Del. Cancer Soc. Mem. Fin. Execs. Inst., Am. Mgmt. Assn., Bus. Internat., Pharm. Mfrs. Assn. Club: Wilmington Country (dir.). Home: 402 Foulkstone Rd Woodbrook Wilmington DE 19803 Office: ICI Americas Inc Wilmington DE 19897

MALONEY, WALTER E., lawyer; b. Phillipsburg, N.J., May 5, 1911; s. Michael E. and Mary Huston (Cooper) M.; A.B., Lafayette Coll., 1933; J.D., Columbia, 1936; m. Mary C. Reynolds, June 26, 1937 (dec. 1955); children—James, Thomas; m. 2d, Hilda R. Donohoe, Jan. 26, 1957; children—Walter E. Maloney, Peter B. Maloney; stepchildren (adopted)—John F., Mary Claire, Edgar H., Katheryn A., Thomas M., William R., Anne Marie, Michael J. Admitted to N.Y. bar, 1936, since practiced in N.Y.C.; gen. law practice, 1936-39; asst. corp. counsel, City N.Y., 1939-41; specialized in maritime law, 1941-52; mem. firm Burns, Currie & Rich, 1946-52, Burns, Currie, Maloney & Rice, 1955-61, Bigham, Englar, Jones & Houston, N.Y.C., 1961—; atty. Am. Mcht. Marine Inst., Inc., 1942-52, pres., 1952, gen. counsel, 1957, chmn. mcht. marine com. of whole, com. of cos. and agts. Atlantic and Gulf coasts. Served as lt. U.S. Coast Guard Res., 1943-45. Mem. Am. Bar Assn., Maritime Law Assn. U.S., Kappa Sigma. Republican. Roman Catholic. Clubs: India House (N.Y.C.); Baltusrol Golf (N.J.). Home: 186 Hartshorn Short Hills NJ 07078 Office: 14 Wall St New York City NY 10005

MALONEY, WILLIAM GERARD, investment co. exec.; b. Dansville, N.Y., Apr. 8, 1917; s. William J. and Fannie K. (Kirschner) M.; B.S., U. Pa., 1939; m. Katherine R. Kenney, Oct. 21, 1940; children—William J., Elizabeth Ann, Stephen G. Trainee, Hemphill, Noyes & Co., N.Y.C., 1939, mem. research dept., 1940-42, 44-45, mgr. corporate fin. dept., 1949, partner, 1951-63, co-mng. partner, 1963-64; coordinating partner Hornblower & Weeks-Hemphill, Noyes, N.Y.C., 1965-71, mgr. br. office adminstrn., 1969-71, vice chmn. exec. com., dir., 1972—; sr. mng. dir. Loeb Rhoades, Hornblower & Co., 1978—, Loeb Rhoades Shearson, 1979—; dir. Servomation Corp., Continental Investment Corp., N.Am. Royalties Inc.; dir., vice chmn. Hanover Petroleum Corp., 1969-76. Served with U.S. Army, 1942-43. Mem. N.Y. Soc. Security Analysts. Republican. Roman Catholic. Clubs: Met., India House, Assn. Knights and Ladies of Equestrian Order of Holy Sepulchre of Jerusalem, Knights of Malta. Home: 39 Louise's Ln New Canaan CT 06840 Office: 14 Wall St New York NY 10005

MALONEY, WILLIAM RUSSELL, marine corps officer; b. Pitts., Oct. 13, 1929; s. James Lawrence and Elisabeth Sarah (Daugherty) M.; B.A., Brown U., 1951; M.A., Stanford U., 1963; M.S., George Washington U., 1970; m. Virginia Ann Fellows, Apr. 11, 1953; 1 dau., Lisa Louise. Commd. 2d lt. U.S. Marine Corps, 1951, advanced through grades to maj. gen., 1978; leadership instr., exec. asst. to acad. dean U.S. Naval Acad., 1963-66; comdg. officer Marine Observation Squadron 6 1st MAW, Vietnam, 1966-67; mem. staff of comdr. 6th Fleet, Mediterranean, 1970-72; comdg. officer Marine Aircraft Group 36, Okinawa, 1972-73; head joint strategic br. plans div. Hdqrs. Marine Corps, Washington, 1973-74, dir. info., 1975-77. Decorated Silver Star, Legion of Merit, Air medal, Bronze Star. Mem. Marine Corps Assn., Marine Corps Aviation Assn., Marine Corps Combat Corrs. Assn. U.S. Naval Inst. Episcopalian. Address: CG 3d MAW El Toro CA 92709

MALOON, JAMES HAROLD, airline exec.; b. Union City, Ohio, June 22, 1926; s. Charles E. and Bertha (Creviston) M.; A.B., Miami U., Oxford, Ohio, 1949; M.A., Ind. U., 1951, Ph.D., 1960; children—Sharon Maloon Wilt, Craig J., Elizabeth M. Maloon Ter Haar, Douglas C.T. Dir. finance State of Ohio, 1959-63; exec. v.p. Reston, Va., Inc., 1963-64; sr. v.p., chief fin. officer, dir. Columbia Gas System Service Corp., 1965-72; exec. v.p. Pan-Am. World Airways, Inc., 1972—, also dir.; dir. Intercontinental Hotels Corp., Falcon Jet Corp., Grand Central Bldg. Corp., Fred F. French Investing Co. Pres., Ohio Bd. Pub. Welfare, 1959-63; mem. Ohio Commn. Higher Edn., 1960-63; bd. dirs. Ohio Community Colls., 1960-63. Served with USNR, 1944-45. Mem. Am. Econ. Assn., Nat. Tax Assn. Clubs: Sky, Univ., Wings; Fairfield County (Conn.) Hunt. Research in pub. and bus. adminstrn., econ. devel. underdeveloped nations, higher edn., corporate fin. and mgmt. Home: 6000 Olentangy River Rd Delaware OH 43015 also 200 E 66th St New York NY 10021 Office: 200 Park Ave New York NY 10017

MALOTT, JAMES RAYMOND, JR., lawyer; b. Globe, Ariz., Feb. 23, 1917; s. James Raymond and Edith (Spencer) M.; student U. Ariz., 1934-36; A.B., Stanford, 1938, LL.B., 1941; m. Carol Hover, Sept. 9, 1939 (div. Sept. 1948); children—James Spencer, Lucinda; m. 2d, Barbara Farr, Feb. 20, 1949 (div. Jan. 1974); m. 3d, Ruth Austin, Jan. 10, 1975. Admitted to Ariz. bar, 1940; dep. county atty. Gila County, 1943; practice in Globe, 1945—; mem. firm Morris & Malott, 1948—. Served to 2d lt. USAAF, 1944-45. Mem. State Bar Ariz. (bd. govs. 1955-60, v.p. 1959-60). Home: 1220 Skyline St Globe AZ 85501 Office: 1450 South St Globe AZ 85501

MALOTT, ROBERT HARVEY, mfg. co. exec.; b. Boston, Oct. 6, 1926; s. Deane W. and Eleanor (Thrum) M.; A.B., Kans. U., 1948; M.B.A., Harvard U., 1950; postgrad. N.Y. U. Law Sch., 1953-55; m. Elizabeth Harwood Hubert, June 4, 1960; children—Elizabeth Hubert, Barbara Holden, Robert Deane. Asst. to dean Harvard Grad. Sch. Bus. Adminstrn., 1950-52; with FMC Corp., 1952—, asst. to exec. v.p. chems. div., N.Y.C., 1952-55, controller Niagara Chem. div., Middleport, N.Y., 1955-59, controller organic chems. div., N.Y.C., 1959-62, asst. div. mgr., 1962-63, div. mgr., 1963-65, v.p., mgr. film ops. div. Am. Viscose div., 1966-67, exec. v.p., mem. president's office, 1967-70, mgr. machinery divs., Chgo., 1970-72, pres., chief exec. officer, 1972—, chmn., 1973—; dir. FMC Corp., Standard Oil Ind., Bell & Howell, Continental Ill. Corp., Continental Ill. Bank. Trustee U. Kans. Endowment Assn., U. Chgo., Orchestral Assn., Chgo. Served with USNR, 1944-46. Mem. Chem. Mfrs. Assn., Machinery and Allied Products Inst. (exec. com.), Bus. Council, Bus. Roundtable, Phi Beta Kappa, Beta Theta Pi, Alpha Chi Sigma. Clubs: Econ., Chgo., Mid-Am. (Chgo.); Links, Explorers (N.Y.C.); Indian Hill (Kenilworth, Ill.); Bohemian (San Francisco). Office: 200 E Randolph Dr Chicago IL 60601

MALOY, RICHARD JOSEPH, newspaperman; b. New Castle, Pa., June 7, 1924; s. Frank Joseph and Helen (Flynn) M.; A.B., U. Mich., 1949; m. Berneice A. Kinahan, Apr. 7, 1951; children—Michael, Timothy. Reporter, Balt. Sun, 1949-50, Detroit Free-Press, 1950-51; telegraph editor Lorain (Ohio) Jour., 1951-52; mem. staff Washington Post, 1952-67, city editor, 1964-65, London editor, 1965-67; asso. editor Nat. Jour., 1970; Washington bur. chief Thomson Newspapers, Inc., 1971—. Served with inf. AUS, World War II; ETO. Home: 8313 Meadowlark Ln Bethesda MD 20034 Office: Nat Press Bldg Washington DC 20004

MALOY, ROBERT MICHAEL, librarian; b. Cleve., July 12, 1935; s. Harry J. and E.M. (Barnes) M.; B.A., U. Dayton, 1956; A.M., U. Chgo., 1961; S.T.D. summa cum laude, Universitat Freiburg (Switzerland), 1966; postgrad. St. Benet Hall, Oxford U., 1966, Ludwig-Maximilians Universitat, Munich, 1966-67, Harvard U., 1972. Asst. prof. ch. history, dir. spl. collections U. Dayton, 1967-71; vis. lectr., cons. Grad. Liturgical Program, U. Notre Dame, summers 1971-72; asst. prof. Rosary Coll. Grad. Library Sch., Chgo., 1971-72; library dir., asso. prof. ch. history Sch. Theology at Claremont and Claremont Grad. Sch., 1972-75; library dir., asso. prof. Union Theol. Sem., N.Y.C., 1975-79; dir. libraries Smithsonian Instn., Washington, 1979—; bd. dirs. Marianists of Ohio, 1968-70, Missionary Research Library, N.Y.C., 1975-79; ednl. cons. Faculty research fellow U. Dayton, 1970; Mediaeval Acad. Am. fellow, 1972. mem. ALA, Bibliog. Soc. Am., Cath. Theol. Soc. Am., Mediaeval Acad. Am., Phi Beta Mu. Mem. editorial bd. Marian Library Studies, 1969—, Catholic Periodical and Literature Index, 1973—. Office: Smithsonian Instn Washington DC 20560

MALOZEMOFF, PLATO, mining exec.; b. Russia, 1909; student U. Calif., 1931, Mont. Sch. Mines, 1932. Chmn., chief exec. officer Newmont Mining Corp., N.Y.C.; pres., dir. Resurrection Mining Co., Newmont Exploration Ltd., Carlin Gold Mining Co.; chmn. Newmont Mines Ltd., Newmont Proprietary Ltd.; chmn., dir. Idarado Mining Co.; v.p., dir. Newmont Exploration of Can., Ltd.; vice chmn., dir. Magma Copper Co.; dir. O'Okiep Copper Co., Cassiar Asbestos Corp., Ltd., So. Peru Copper Corp., Sherritt Gordon Mines, Ltd., Atlantic Cement Co. Inc., Peabody Coal Co., Bankers Trust Co., Palabora Mining Co., Ltd., Tsumeb Corp., Ltd., Foote Mineral Co., Bethlehem Copper Corp., Browning-Ferris Industries, Highveld Steel & Vanadium Corp. Bd. dirs. Boys' Clubs Am.; trustee Am. Mus. Natural History. Office: 300 Park Ave New York NY 10022

MALPASS, LESLIE FREDERICK, univ. pres.; b. Hartford, Conn., May 16, 1922; s. Fred J. and Lilly (Elmslie) M.; B.A., Syracuse U., 1947, M.A., 1949, Ph.D., 1952; m. Winona Helen Cassin, May 17, 1946; children—Susan Heather (Mrs. Poulton), Peter Gordon, Jennifer Joy, Michael Andrew. Psychologist, Onondaga County (N.Y.) Child Guidance Center Syracuse, 1948-52; lectr. Syracuse U., also U. Buffalo, 1949-52; asst. prof., then asso. prof. So. Ill. U., 1952-60; vis. prof. U. Fla., 1959-60; prof. psychology, chmn. div. behavioral scis. U. So. Fla., 1960-65; dean Coll. Arts and Scis., Va. Poly Inst., Blacksburg, 1965-68, v.p., 1968-74; pres. Western Ill. U., Macomb, 1974—. cons. in field. Dir. First Nat. Exchange Bank Va., 1965-74. Served with M.C., AUS, 1945-46. Diplomate Am. Bd. Examiners Profl. Psychology. Fellow Am. Psychol. Assn.; mem. AAAS, AAUP, Assn. Higher Edn., Sigma Xi, Psi Chi, Theta Chi Beta, Omicron Delta Kappa, Beta Gamma Sigma. Author books and articles in field. Home: 2001 Wigwam Hollow Rd Macomb IL 61455

MALSACK, JAMES THOMAS, mfg. and distbg. co. exec.; b. Milw., Apr. 4, 1921; s. Leonard Henry and Florence Alice (Webb) M.; B.S.B.A., Marquette U., 1946; m. Joyce Irene Niemi, Aug. 1, 1963; children—Thomas James, Claudia Irene, Robert Richard, Thomas John, Pamela Joyce. Acct., Price Waterhouse & Co., Milw., 1946-51; with Lake Shore, Inc., Iron Mountain, Mich., 1951—, exec. v.p., 1959-72, pres., chief exec. officer, 1972—; dir. First Nat. Bank, Iron Mountain. Trustee, Dickinson County (Mich.) Hosp., 1972—, No. Mich. U., 1977—. Served with USN, 1943-46. Mem. Dickinson County (Mich.) Area C. of C., Mich. State C. of C. (dir. 1972-75), Soc. Naval Architects and Marine Engrs., Soc. Mining Engrs., Am. Mining Congress, Mich. Mfrs. Assn. (dir. 1975-77). Republican. Episcopalian. Clubs: Chippewa, Rotary (dir. 1960-63) (Iron Mountain); Univ., Milw. Athletic (Milw.); Marquette (Mich.); Union (Cleve.); Masons, Shriners. Home: PO Box 427 Iron Mountain MI 49801 Office: PO Box 809 Iron Mountain MI 49801

MALSH, WILLIAM RONALD, lawyer, educator; b. July 23, 1913; s. Paul and Amalie (Samuel) M.; B.S., U. San Francisco, 1951; M.A., U. Ariz., 1954, J.D., 1955; m. Rebecca Jaffe, June 8, 1951. Admitted to Ariz. bar, 1955, also U.S. Supreme Ct.; practice in Tucson, 1955-76; judge, 1976-78; prof. polit. sci. U. Ariz., 1955. Bd. dirs. Handmaker Home for Aged, 1964-70. Served to capt. AUS, 1942-49. Decorated Bronze Star; Medaille de Metz, Medaille de Verdun (France). Fellow Internat. Acad. Law and Sci.; mem. Internat., Am., Ariz., Pima County bar assns., AAUP, Am. Judicature Soc., Am. Trial Lawyers Assn., Council Fgn. Relations, World Assn. Judges, Phi Alpha Delta. Clubs: Press (dir.), Old Pueblo, Tuscon Nat. Golf (Tucson). Author numerous legal essays. Home: 7120 N Via Venezia Tucson AZ 85704

MALSIN, ARTHUR, dept. store exec.; b. 1913; B.A., Yale U., 1935; M.F.A., Harvard U., 1939; m. Louise M. Howe, Aug. 18, 1939; children—Arthur, Louise M. (Mrs. Tom Rothschild), Lane (Mrs. William Dunn), Mary (Mrs. Robert L. Merrow). Partner, Malsin Reiman, 1946-64, also lectr. Columbia and Vassar Coll.; with Lane Bryant Inc., 1964—, sec., 1964-67, v.p., sec., 1967-69, exec. v.p., 1969-70, pres., 1970-72, pres., chief exec. officer, 1972-77, chmn. bd., chief exec. officer, 1977—, also dir.; adv. bd. Mfrs. Hanover Trust Co. Bd. dirs. Fifth Ave. Assn., Phelps Meml. Hosp., Tarrytown, N.Y. Served with USNR, 1942-46. Mem. Nat. Retail Mchts. Assn. (dir.). Office: Lane Bryant 11 W 42 St New York NY 10036

MALSKY, STANLEY JOSEPH, physicist; b. N.Y.C., July 15, 1925; s. Joseph and Nellie (Karpinski) M.; B.S., N.Y. U., 1949, M.A., 1950, M.S., 1953, Ph.D., 1963; m. Gloria E. Gagliardi, Oct. 15, 1965; children—Randolph H., Roy W., Mark A. Nuclear physicist Dept. Def., 1959-64; chief physicist VA, 1954-63; adj. asso. prof., then prof. radiol. sci. Manhattan Coll., Bronx, N.Y., 1960-74; non-resident research collaborator med. div. Brookhaven Nat. Labs., Upton, N.Y., 1964-69; research prof. radiology N.Y. U. Sch. Medicine, N.Y.C., 1975—; pres. Radiol. Physics Assn., White Plains, N.Y., 1965—. Served with U.S. Army, 1945-46. Recipient James Picker Found. award, 1963-67; Founder's Day award N.Y. U., 1964; Leadership award Manhattan Coll., 1969. Fellow Am. Public Health Assn., AAAS, Royal Soc. Health; charter mem. Am. Assn. Physicists in Medicine, Health Physics Soc. Roman Catholic. Contbr. chpts. to books. Address: 809 Hartsdale Rd White Plains NY 10607

MALTBY, GEORGE LANGFORD, neurosurgeon; b. Jamestown, N.Y., Nov. 3, 1909; s. George L. and Gladys Y. (Broadhead) M.; A.B., Yale, 1932; M.D., Harvard, 1936; m. Isabella Beyer Murphy, May 23, 1936; children—Mary, MacDougall, Ellen Askari, Susan, Michael. Intern, Boston City Hosp., 1937-39; resident in neurosurgery Boston City Hosp. and Lahey Clinic, 1939-40; practice medicine specializing in neurosurgery, Cin., 1940-42, Portland, Maine, 1945-79; pres. staff Maine Med. Center, 1958-63; asst. prof. neurology Tufts Med. Sch., 1974-79, U. Cin. Med. Sch., 1940-42. Served with M.C., AUS, 1942-45. Mem. Am. Acad. Neurosurgery (pres. 1966), Fedn. State Med. Bds. U.S. (pres. 1975), Am. Acad. Neurology, Am. EEG Soc. Home: Garrison Ln Prouts Neck Scarborough ME 04074

MALTESE, GEORGE JOHN, educator; b. Middletown, Conn., June 24, 1931; s. Giorgio and Sebastiana (Morello) M.; B.A., Wesleyan U., 1953; postgrad. U. Frankfurt (Germany), 1953-54; Ph.D., Yale, 1960; m. Marlene Erika Kunz, Apr. 14, 1956; children—Christopher, Michelle. Postdoctoral fellow U. Göttingen, 1960-61; instr. M.I.T., 1961-63; faculty U. Md., College Park, 1963-73, prof., 1969-73; prof. U. Münster, 1973—; vis. prof. U. Frankfurt, 1966-67, 70-71, U. Palermo (Italy), 1967, 71. Served with AUS, 1954-56. Fulbright fellow, 1953-54; NATO postdoctoral fellow, 1960-61. Mem. Am., Austrian, German, Italian math. socs. Contbr. articles to profl. jours. Address: Mathematisches Institut Roxeler Strasse 64 44 Münster Federal Republic of Germany

MALTESE, SERPHIN RALPH, lawyer; b. N.Y.C., Dec. 7, 1932; s. Paul and Frances (Scafidi) M.; B.A., Manhattan Coll., 1958; LL.B., J.D. (War Service scholar 1958-62), Fordham U., 1962; m. Constance Mary Del Vecchio, Aug. 27, 1955; children—Andrea Constance, Leslie Serphine, Serphin Ralph (dec.). Admitted to N.Y. bar, 1963; trial atty. for ins. cos., 1963-66; asst. dist. atty., dep. chief homicide bur. Queens County (N.Y.), 1966-69; asso. counsel N.Y. State Com. Campus Disorders, 1969-70; counsel N.Y. State Com. Deaf and Multiple Impaired, 1970; chmn. law com. Buckley for U.S. Senator, 1970; counsel N.Y. State Assembly, 1972-76, N.Y. State Senate, 1976—; exec. dir. N.Y. State Conservative Party, 1971—, exec. vice chmn., 1978—, chmn. Queens County com., 1972—. Chmn. trustees Christ the King Regional High Sch., 1976—; pres. We Care Civic Assn., 1968-76, chmn. exec. bd., 1978—; past community chmn. local Boy Scouts Am. Served with AUS, 1952-54; Korea. Recipient Charles Edison Meml. award N.Y. State Conservative Party, 1977. Mem. N.Y. State Bar Assn., Nat. Dist. Attys. Assn., Queens Asst. Dist. Attys. Assn., Christopher Columbus Assn. (chmn. 1970—), Young Americans for Freedom (nat. sr. adv. bd.), Am. Conservative Union, Citizens for Responsible Taxation (dir.), Internat. Assn. Space Philatelists, Am. Mgmt. Assn., Queens C. of C., Alexander Hamilton Conservative Club (chmn. exec. com. 1971—), Harold Gray Collectors Soc. (pres.), Met. Post Card Collectors Club, Am. Legion, VFW, Alpha Phi Delta. Roman Catholic. Club: Elks. Home: 60-16 74th St Middle Village NY 11373 Office: 468 Park Ave S New York NY 10016

MALTZ, ALBERT, author; b. Bklyn., Oct. 28, 1908; s. Bernard and Lena (Sherry) M.; A.B., Columbia U., 1930; student Yale U. Sch. Drama, 1930-32; m. Margaret Larkin, 1937 (div. 1963); children—Peter, Katherine; m. 2d, Rosemary Wylde, 1964 (dec. 1968); m. 3d, Esther Engelberg, 1969. Instr. Playwrighting Center, Sch. Adult Edn., N.Y.U., 1937-41; instr. playwriting Writers Conf. Rocky Mountains, 1939, 40; mem. exec. bd. Theatre Union, 1933-37; former arbitrator Am. Arbitration Soc.; editor Equality, 1939, 1940. Mem. Authors League Am. (mem. council 1936-41), Phi Beta Kappa. Author: (plays) Merry Go Round (with George Sklar), 1932; Peace on Earth (with George Sklar), 1933; Black Pit, 1935; (short stories) The Way Things Are, 1938; Afternoon in the Jungle, 1971; (novels) The Underground Stream, 1940; The Cross and The Arrow, 1944; The Journey of Simon McKeever, 1949; A Long Day in a Short Life, 1957; A Tale of One January, 1966; (essays) The Citizen Writer, 1950; (films) This Gun for Hire, 1942; Destination Tokyo, 1943; Pride of the Marines, 1945; The House I Live In (spl. award Acad. Motion Picture Arts and Scis.); The Naked City, 1948; Two Mules for Sister Sara, 1970. Contbr. to New Yorker mag., Scribner's, Harper's, New Masses, Time and Tide, So. Review, Scholastic, others. Short stories have appeared in Best Short Stories, 1936, 39, 41; O'Henry Memorial Award Prize Stories (1st award), 1938, 41; Best American Short Stories, 1914-39; and other anthologies. Address: Author's League of Am 234 W 44th St New York NY 10036

MALTZ, J. HERBERT, physician, hosp. dir.; b. Passaic, N.J., Jan. 8, 1920; s. Michael and Esther (Rinzler) M.; student U. Wis., 1938-41; B.A., U. Miami, 1942; M.D., Chgo. Med. Sch., 1947; m. Sybil Zun, Sept. 27, 1947; 1 son, Roger A. Intern Wilmington (Del.) Gen. Hosp., 1947-48; psychiat. resident Ill. Dept. Pub. Welfare, 1948-51; clin. instr. psychiatry Chgo. Med. Sch., 1951-55; practice medicine specializing in psychiatry, Chgo., 1951-58; asst. to supt. Chgo. State Hosp., 1956-58, supt., 1958-66; med. dir. Ridgeway Hosp., 1966-69; med. dir. Chgo. Lake Shore Hosp., 1970—; mem. faculty Northwestern U. Med. Sch., Chgo. Med. Sch.; mem. staff Ill. Masonic Hosp. Diplomate Am. Bd. Psychiatry and Neurology. Fellow Am. Psychiat. Assn. Jewish. Home: 3260 North Lake Shore Dr Chicago IL 60657 Office: 8 S Michigan Ave Chicago IL 60603

MALTZ, MAXWELL, plastic surgeon; b. N.Y.C., Mar. 10, 1899; s. Joseph and Tobey (Ellsweig) M.; B.S., Columbia, 1919; M.D., Coll. Phys. and Surg., Columbia, 1923; postgrad. in plastic surgery, Europe, 1924-25; hon. Sc.D., U. Guatamala; m. Anne Harabin, Feb. 10, 1966. Plastic surgeon Beth Israel Hosp., 1925-35, Met. Hosp., 1930-36; plastic reconstructive surgeon Beth David Hosp., 1930-39; dir. dept. plastic reconstructive surgery West Side hosp.; distinguished hon. lectr. in plastic surgery to mil. hosps., and univs., Cuba, Panama, Costa Rica. Hon. prof. surgery Univs. of Santo Domingo, Nicaragua, Honduras, El Salvador, Guatemala, Athens; prof. psychocybernetics, dir. Inst. Psychocybernetics, Ft. Lauderdale (Fla.) U., 1972. Fellow Internat. Coll. Surgeons, Latin-Am. Soc. Plastic Surgeons, N.Y. Acad. Scis., Am. Physicians Lit. Guild, AAAS; hon. fellow Brazilian Coll. Surgeons, Mexican Coll. Mil. Surgeons, Acad. Medicine, U. of Santo Domingo. Pres. Tobey Maltz Found. for Research in Tissue Growth, Degeneration and Repair. Fellow Mexican Assn. Plastic Surgeons; mem. AMA, N.Y. County Med. Soc., N.Y. State Med. Soc. Author: New Faces- New Futures; Rebuilding Character With Plastic Surgery, 1936; They Challenged Fate, 1940; The Open Window, 1963; The Long and Short of It, 1943; Cyrano's Dream; The Evolution of Plastic Surgery; Text Book on Rhino-plastic Surg.; (novels) Goddess with the Golden Eye, 1956; The Miracle of Dr. Fleming, 1957; The Unseen Scar (play) 1945; Doctor Pygmalion, 1953; Adventures in Staying Young, 1954; Galatea (play), 1957; Doctor Pygmalion's Mirror (play), 1958, The Private Life of Doctor Pygmalion, 1958; The Face of Love,

1959; The Other Door (play), 1959; Psycho-Cybernetics: A New Way To Get More Living Out of Life, 1960; Fifty Two Prescriptions, 1960; The Sound of the Ram's Horn (play), 1960; Juliets Daughter (play), 1961; The Four of Us (play), 1961; The Fountain of Youth (play), 1961; Somewhere to Go (play), 1963, Emma (play); Dorothy (play), 1964; The Quest for Success and Happiness, 1964; The Magic Power of Self Image Psychology, 1964; Cracks in the Wall (play), 1965; Creative Living for Today, 1967; The Conquest of Frustration, 1969; Psycho-Cybernetics and Self-Fulfillment, 1970; Secrets-Cassettes for Children 6-12, 1970; Power Psycho-Cybernetics for Youth, 1971; The Maltz Cassette System of Self Fulfillment, 1971; The Search for Self Respect, 1973; (novel) The Time is Now, 1973; Psycho-Cybernetic Principles for Creative Living, 1974; Thoughts to Live By, 1974. Contbr. to profl. jours. Address: 300 E 56th St New York NY 10022

MALTZ, MILTON SELWYN, broadcasting co. exec.; b. South Bend, Ind., July 26, 1929; s. Louis and Anna (Lerman) M.; B.S. in Journalism, U. Ill., 1951; m. Thelma Silverman, Feb. 4, 1950; children—Julie, Daniel, David. Radio actor, writer stas. in Chgo. and Urbana, Ill., 1943-50; founder Sta. WTTF, Tiffin, Ohio, 1959, Sta. WBRB, Mt. Clemens, Mich., 1960; pres. Malrite Broadcasting Co., Cleve., 1956—; prin. stockholder stas. WHK-WMMS, Cleve., WZUU-AM-FM, Milw., KEEY-AM-FM, Mpls., WNYR, WEZO, Rochester, N.Y., WCTI-TV, New Bern, N.C., WUHF-TV, Rochester. Vice chmn. Better Bus. Bur. Cleve.; trustee Coll. Jewish Studies, Cleve. Served with USNR, 1951-53; Korea. Mem. Nat. Assn. Broadcasters, Advt. Club Cleve. Office: Malrite Broadcasting Co 12th and Euclid Sts The Plaza Cleveland OH 44115

MALTZMAN, IRVING MYRON, educator; b. Bklyn., May 9, 1924; s. Israel and Lillian (Mass) M.; B.A., N.Y. U., 1946; Ph.D., State U. Iowa, 1949; m. Diane Seiden, Aug. 21, 1949; children—Sara, Kenneth, Ilaine. Mem. faculty U. Calif. at Los Angeles, 1949—, asso. prof., 1957-60, prof. psychology, 1961—, chmn. dept., 1970-77. Mem. Am. Psychol. Assn., AAAS, Phi Beta Kappa, Sigma Xi. Co-author: Handbook of Contemporary Soviet Psychology, 1969. Home: 11260-22B Overland Ave Culver City CA 90230 Office: U Cal Dept Psychology 405 Hilgard Ave Los Angeles CA 90024

MALVERN, DONALD, aircraft mfg. co. exec.; b. Sterling, Okla., Apr. 22, 1921; s. George Michael and Anna Francesca (Elsass) M.; B.S., U. Okla., 1946; m. Ruth Marie Vogler, June 4, 1949; 1 son, Michael John. Engr., Victory Architects and Engrs., Clinton, Ohio, 1943, Douglas Aircraft Co., Santa Monica, Calif., 1943; with McDonnell Aircraft Co., St. Louis, 1946—, exec. v.p., 1973—; v.p. McDonnell Douglas Corp., 1973—; pres. McDonnell Douglas F-15 Tech. Services Co., Inc., 1978—, McDonnell Douglas Saudi Arabia, Inc., 1978—. Served to 1st lt. USAAF, 1943-46. Asso. fellow AIAA (Tech. Mgmt. award 1968); mem. Am. Def. Preparedness Assn. (pres. 1979-80), Navy League U.S. (life), Nat. Aeros. Assn., Air Force Assn., Armed Forces Mgmt. Assn., Pi Tau Sigma, Tau Beta Pi, Tau Omega. Club: Bellerive Country. Home: 37 Baron Ct Rural Route 2 Florissant MO 63034 Office: PO Box 516 Saint Louis MO 63166

MALVILLE, JOHN MCKIM, astronomer; b. San Francisco, Apr. 24, 1934; s. Neptune John and Laura Rebecca (Carpenter) M.; B.S., Calif. Inst. Tech., 1956; Ph.D., U. Colo., 1961; m. Nancy Jean Koontz, Mar. 26, 1960; children—Katherine Lowry, Leslie Ellen. Expdn. scientist Ellsworth Sta., Antarctica, 1956-58; asst. prof. astronomy U. Mich., 1962-65; staff scientist High Altitude Obs., Boulder, Colo., 1965-70; asso. prof. astrogeophysics U. Colo., 1970-73, prof., 1973—, chmn. dept. astrogeophysics, 1977-80. Asst. dir. Colo. Outward Bound Sch., Denver, 1969. Alfred P. Sloan research fellow, 1964-66. Mem. Am. Astron. Soc., Internat. Astron. Union, Sierra Club, Am. Alpine Club, Colo. Mountain Club. Author: A Feather for Daedalus, 1973; research in solar physics, aurora, radio astronoma. Home: 220 Manhattan Boulder CO 80303 Office: U Colo Boulder CO 80309

MALVIN, RICHARD LESTER, physiologist; b. Bklyn., Aug. 19, 1927; s. Isodore and Anna C. (Weschler) M.; B.S., McGill U., 1950; M.S., N.Y. U., 1954; Ph.D., U. Cin., 1956; m. June 9, 1949; children—Gary M., Lori F. Teaching fellow N.Y. U., 1951-54; research fellow U. Cin., 1954-56; research asso. U. Mich., Ann Arbor, 1956-57, instr., 1957-59, asst. prof., 1959-64, asso. prof., 1964-67, prof. physiology, dir. Mich. Scholars Program, 1967—; mem. sci. adv. bd. Nat. Kidney Found.; mem. adv. panel metabolic biology NSF, 1969-71. Served with USN, 1945-46. Recipient Lederle Med. Faculty award, 1959, USPHS Research Career Devel. award, 1962. Porter fellow Am. Physiol. Soc.; mem. Am. Soc. Nephrology, Brit. Med. Assn. (Gold award Film Competition). Mem. editorial bd. Am. Jour. Physiology, 1966-72, Jour. Applied Physiology, 1966-72. Home: 2707 Englave St Ann Arbor MI 48103 Office: Dept Physiology U Mich 7730 Med Sci Bldg II Ann Arbor MI 48109

MALZAHN, RAY ANDREW, univ. adminstr.; b. Fort Madison, Iowa, July 8, 1929; s. Arnold Frederick and Inez (Russel) M.; B.A., Gustavus Adolphus Coll., 1951; M.S., U. N.D., 1953; Ph.D., U. Md., 1962; m. Elizabeth Mae Barrett, Aug. 23, 1953; children—Karen Louise, Janet Elizabeth. Research asso. U. Ariz., Tucson, 1961-63; asst. prof. chemistry W. Tex. State U., Canyon, 1963-65, asso. prof., 1965-67, prof. chemistry, 1967—, dean Coll Arts and Scis., 1967-71, v.p. acad. affairs, 1971-77. Served with AUS, 1954-56. Mem. Am. Chem. Soc., Tex. Assn. Coll. Tchrs., Sigma Xi. Home: 1700 Hillcrest Dr Canyon TX 79015

MAMATEY, VICTOR SAMUEL, educator; b. North Braddock, Pa., Feb. 19, 1917; s. Albert Paul and Olga (Darmek) M.; diploma Comenius U., Czechoslovakia, 1938; student Wittenberg Coll., 1938-39, U. Chgo., 1939-40; A.M., Harvard, 1941; Ph.D., U. Paris (France), 1949; m. Denise M. Perronne, Nov. 20, 1945; children—Albert R., Peter V. Asst. prof. history Fla. State U., 1949-55, asso. prof., 1955-58, prof., 1958-67, chmn. dept. history, 1964-67; research prof. history U. Ga., 1967—, acting dean Coll. Arts and Scis., 1972-73; vis. prof. Columbia, 1961, Tulane U., 1963. Served with AUS, 1942-46. Guggenheim fellow, 1959. Mem. Am. Hist. Assn. (George Louis Beer prize for best book in internat. history 1958), Am. Assn. Advancement Slavic Studies. Author: The United States and East Central Europe, 1914-1918, 1957; Soviet Russian Imperialism, 1964; (with Geoffrey Brunn) The World in the Twentieth Century, 1967; The Rise of the Habsburg Empire, 1526-1815, 1971; (with Radomir Luza) History of the Czechoslovak Republic, 1918-1948, 1973. Home: 142 Spruce Valley Rd Athens GA 30605

MAMER, STUART MIES, lawyer; b. East Hardin, Ill., Feb. 23, 1921; s. Louis H. and Anna (Mies) M.; A.B., U. Ill., 1942, J.D., 1947; m. Donna E. Jordan, Sept. 10, 1944; children—Richard A., John S., Bruce J. Admitted to Ill. bar, 1947; asso. firm Thomas & Mulliken, Champaign, 1947-55; partner firm Thomas, Mamer, Haughey & Miller, Champaign, 1955—; lectr. U. Ill. Coll. Law, Urbana, 1965—. Mem. Atty. Registration and Disciplinary Commn. Ill., 1976—. Chmn. fund drive Champaign County Community Chest, 1955; 1st pres. Champaign County United Fund, 1957. Pres., dir. U. Ill. McKinley Found., Champaign, 1957-69; trustee Ill. Children's Home and Aid Soc., v.p., 1977—. Served as pilot USAAF, 1943-45. Mem. Am. Coll. Probate Counsel, Phi Beta Kappa, Phi Gamma Delta. Republican. Presbyterian. Home: 6 Montclair Rd Urbana IL 61801 Office: First Nat Bank Bldg Champaign IL 61820

MAMET, DAVID ALAN, author, dir.; b. Chgo., Nov. 30, 1947; s. Bernard Morris and Lenore June (Silver) M.; B.A., Goddard Coll., Plainfield, Vt., 1969; m. Lindsay Crouse, Dec., 1977. Artist-in-residence Goddard Coll., 1971-73; artistic dir. St. Nicholas Theatre Co., Chgo., 1973-75; guest lectr. U. Chgo., 1975, 79; asso. artistic dir. Goodman Theater, Chgo., 1978; author: (plays) The Duck Variations, 1971, Sexual Perversity in Chicago (Village Voice Obie award 1976), 1973, Reunion, 1973, Squirrels, 1974, American Buffalo (Village Voice Obie award 1976, N.Y. Drama Critics Circle award 1977), 1976, A Life in The Theatre, 1976, The Water Engine, 1976, The Woods, 1977, Lone Canoe, 1978, Prairie du Chien, 1978, (screen play) The Postman Always Rings Twice, 1979. Recipient Outer Critics Circle award for contbn. to Am. theater, 1978. CBS Creative Writing fellow Yale U. Drama Sch., 1976-77; Rockefeller grantee, 1977. Mem. Randolph Hollister Assn.

MAN, EUGENE HERBERT, chemist, educator; b. Scranton, Pa., Dec. 14, 1923; s. E. Lester and Celia (Cohen) M.; A.B., Oberlin Coll., 1948; Ph.D. (Office Naval Research fellow, E.I. duPont fellow), Duke, 1952; m. Priscilla R. Perry, Sept. 15, 1976; children by previous marriage—Elizabeth Sue (Mrs. Carl Eichenberger), Barbara Ruth, Linda Jeanne, Bruce Jonathan. Research chemist E.I. duPont de Nemours & Co., Inc., Wilmington, Del., 1952-60, supr. tech. sect., Chattanooga, 1960-61, sr. supr., 1961-62; coordinator research U. Miami, Coral Gables, Fla., 1962-66, dean research coordination, 1966-77, prof. chemistry, 1967—, prof. marine and atmospheric chemistry, 1971—, dean research and sponsored programs, 1977-79; vis. investigator Scripps Instn. Oceanography, 1971-72. Bd. dirs. Health Planning Council, Dade County, Fla., 1970-71; dir. Gulf Univs. Research Consortium, Galveston, Tex., chmn., 1969-71; trustee, v.p. Community Mental Health Service, Dade County, 1967-71; trustee United Fund Dade County, 1967-69; mem., chmn. exec. com. Mental Health Consortium Dade County, 1969-71; mem. exec. com. Nat. Council U. Research Adminstrs., 1967-72; mem. council Oak Ridge Asso. Univs., 1973-79. Served to 1st lt. AUS, 1943-46. Recipient Harry N. Holmes award in chemistry Oberlin Coll., 1948. Fellow Am. Inst. Chemists; mem. Am. Chem. Soc., AAAS, Nat. Council Univ. Research Adminstrs., Phi Beta Kappa, Sigma Xi, Phi Lambda Upsilon. Contbr. articles profl. jours. Patentee in field. Home: 5740 SW 64 Pl Miami FL 33143

MANASCO, CARTER, lawyer, pub. relations exec.; b. Townley, Ala., Jan. 3, 1902; s. John Claude and Dora Letitia (Beaty) M.; student Howard Coll., Birmingham, Ala., 1920-22; LL.B., J.D., U. Ala., 1927; m. Mae Emma Guyton, Aug. 1, 1942 (dec. June 1963); two sons. Admitted to Ala. bar, 1927; legislative counsel Nat. Coal Assn., 1949—; mem. Ho. of Reps. of Ala., 1930-34; mem. 77th-80th Congresses, 7th Ala. Dist., 1941-49. Mem. Commn. on Orgn. of Exec. Br. of Govt. (Hoover Comm.). Democrat. Mem. Ala. Bar Assn. Clubs: Masons, Lions. Home: 5932 Chesterbrook Rd McLean VA 22101

MANASSERO, HENRI J.P., hotel exec.; b. Carcassonne, France, July 2, 1932; s. Jean and Paule (Guiraud) M.; Degree Hotel Adminstrn., French Hotel Sch., 1950; m. Moya Corrigan, June 7, 1962. Mgr. Carlton Hotel, Cannes, France, Park Hotel, Bremen, Germany, Midland Hotel, Manchester, Eng.; gen. mgr. Royal Hibernian Hotel, Dublin, Ireland, 1963-69; dir. food and beverage Trust Houses Forte Internat., 1970-72, asst. mng. dir., London, 1973-74, v.p., gen. mgr. Pierre Hotel, N.Y.C., 1974—, also v.p. ops. DeLuxe Hotels div. Trust Houses Forte Hotels Inc.; guest lectr. confs., India and Ireland. Mem. Irish Hotels and Restaurants Mgrs. Assn. (pres. 1969), Hotel and Catering Inst. Brit., Wine and Food Soc. (dir.), N.Y. Hotel Assn. (dir.). Clubs: Rotary, Westchester Country (Rye, N.Y.); Paris-Am. Contbr. articles on food and beverage to European trade mags. Address: Pierre Hotel Fifth Ave at 61st St New York NY 10021

MANATOS, ANDREW EMANUEL, govt. ofcl.; b. Washington, July 7, 1944; s. Mike N. and Dorothy V. (Varanakis) M.; B.A., Am. U., 1968, M.A., 1969; m. Tina G. Weber, June 25, 1967; children—Mike A., Nick A., Tom A. Staff post office and civil service com. U.S. Senate, Washington, 1969-73, asso. staff dir. D.C. com., also legis. asst. Senator Thomas Eagleton, 1973-77; asst. sec. congressional affairs Dept. Commerce, Washington, 1977—. Pres., Brookmont Civic Assn., Bethesda, Md., 1974-76; pres. Tulip Hill Civic Assn., Bethesda, 1978-80; Democratic precinct chairperson, 1974-80; chairperson Montgomery County Dollars for Democrats, 1975. Democrat. Greek Orthodox. Home: 6713 Tulip Hill Terr Bethesda MD 20016 Office: Room 5835 Dept Commerce Washington DC 20230

MANATOS, MIKE, ret. corp. exec.; b. Gunn, Wyo., Aug. 30, 1914; s. Nick and Anna (Anezakis) M.; B.S., Strayer's Coll., 1941; student George Washington U.; m. Dorothy Varanakis, July 3, 1938; children—Ann (Mrs. George Hatsis), Andrew, Kathleen (Mrs. Bruce Shand). Adminstrv. aide U.S. Senator Schwartz Wyo., 1937-43, U.S. Senator O'Mahoney Wyo., 1943-52; adminstrv. asst. to U.S. Senators Hunt, O'Mahoney and Hickey, all Wyo., 1953-61; adminstrv. asst. to Pres. Kennedy, 1961-63, Pres. Johnson, 1963-69; dir. for nat. govt. relations Procter & Gamble, Washington, 1969-79; ret. 1979. Democrat. Home: 5926 Overlea Rd Sumner MD 20016 Office: 1801 K St NW Washington DC 20006. *I read many years ago of an ancient Cretan saying from the land of my forefathers which impressed me very much; translated from the Greek it said, "Reach that which you can not."*

MANATT, CHARLES TAYLOR, lawyer; b. Chgo., June 9, 1936; s. William Price and Lucille (Taylor) M.; B.S., Iowa State U., 1958; J.D., George Washington U., 1962; m. Margaret K. Klinkefus, Dec. 29, 1957; children—Michele, Timothy, Daniel. Legislative asst. to Congressman, Washington, 1959-60; admitted to Calif. bar, 1962; practiced in Los Angeles, 1962-63, Beverly Hills, Calif., 1963-64, Van Nuys, Calif. and Los Angeles, 1964—; now mem. firm Manatt, Phelps, Rothenberg & Tunney, Los Angeles; chmn. bd. dirs. 1st Los Angeles Bank. Exec. sec. Young Democratic Clubs Am., 1961-62; chmn. Young Citizens for Johnson So. Calif., 1964; chmn. Calif. Dem. Com., 1971-73, 75-77; dep. dir. J.V. Tunney for Senator campaign, 1970; mem. Dem. Nat. Com., 1976—, chmn. nat. fin. council, 1978; mem. Dem. Exec. Com., 1976—; chmn. Western States Conf., 1972-76; bd. dirs. Tiger Internat.; chmn. bd. dirs. Frat. Friends of Music Center. Served with AUS. Mem. Am., San Fernando Valley (pres.), Fed. bar assns., State Bar of Calif., Delta Sigma Rho, Phi Kappa Phi, Delta Chi. Methodist. Mason. Office: 1888 Century Park E Los Angeles CA 90067

MANCHESKI, FREDERICK JOHN, automotive co. exec.; b. Stevens Point, Wis., July 21, 1926; s. John Stanley and Luella (Zwaska) M.; B.S. in Mech. Engring., U. Wis., 1948; m. Judith; children—Mary Lou, Laura, Marcia, Bruce, Amy Fredericka. With Timken Roller Bearing Co., Canton, Ohio, 1948-57, McKinsey & Co., mgmt. cons., N.Y.C., 1957-63; with Echlin Mfg. Co., Branford, Conn., 1963—, chmn. bd., chief exec. officer, 1969—; dir. Armstrong Rubber Co., Marlin Firearms, First New Haven Nat. Bank, Simmonds Precision Products, Inc., Russel, Burdsall & Ward, United Illuminating Inc. Mem. New Haven Devel. Commn., U.S. Indsl. Council Commn.; bd. dirs. Quinnipiac council Boy Scouts Am., New Haven Symphony, Hosp. St. Raphael's Found., Jr. Achievement, United Way of New Haven; trustee Conn. Pub. Expenditure Council. Named Automotive Man of Yr., Automotive Warehouse Distbrs. Assn., 1973. Mem. Young Pres.'s Orgn., Nat. Soc. Profl. Engrs., NAM (dir.), Conn. Bus. Industry Assn. (dir.), Greater New Haven Co. of C. (dir.), Sigma Alpha Epsilon. Clubs: Pine Orchard Country, Quinnipiack, New Haven Country (New Haven). Contbg. author: Turnaround Management, 1974. Home: 90 Ogden St New Haven CT 06511 Office: PO Box 451 Branford CT 06405

MANCHESTER, HUGH WALLACE, lawyer; b. Youngstown, Ohio, Mar. 25, 1905; s. Curtis A. and Leona (Eckis) M.; A.B., Cornell U., 1926; LL.B., Harvard, 1929; m. Helen L. Tinney, May 31, 1930; children—Jane (Mrs. David L. Wheeler), Hugh Wallace, Virginia (Mrs. Watson), Elizabeth (Mrs. John F. Gilpatric), Gilbert Mott. Admitted to Ohio bar, 1930, since practiced in Youngstown; partner, dir. firm Manchester, Bennett, Powers & Ullman Co., L.P.A., 1944—. Commr., Boardman Twp. Park Dist., 1947-69; trustee, sec., Youngstown U., 1930-67; sec. to trustees Youngstown State U., 1968—; trustee Youngstown YMCA, 1930—; pres. Belmont Park Cemetery Assn., 1940-78. Mem. Am., Ohio, Mahoning County bar assns., Beta Theta Pi. Republican. Presbyn. (elder 1945-65). Clubs: Youngstown, Youngstown Country. Home: 4257 Oak Knoll Dr Youngstown OH 44512 Office: Union Nat Bank Bldg Youngstown OH 44503

MANCHESTER, MELISSA TONI, singer, song writer; b. Bronx, N.Y., Feb. 15, 1951; d. David and Ruth Manchester; grad. High Sch. Performing Arts, N.Y.C., 1969; m. Larry Brezner, Feb. 13, 1971. Singer with Bette Midler, 1971-72; rec. artist Bell and Arista records; recordings include Home to Myself, Bright Eyes, Melissa (Gold Album award), Better Days and Happy Endings, 1975, Help Is On The Way, 1976; pres., owner Rumanian Pickleworks Music. Recipient Best New Female Vocalist of Year award Cashbox mag., 1974; New Female Vocalist of Year award Billboard mag., 1975; Wright award for Midnight Blue, Broadcast Music Inc., 1975. Mem. Broadcast Music Inc., AFTRA, Screen Actors Guild, Am. Fedn. Musicians. Address: care Wm Morris Agy Inc 1350 Ave of the Americas New York NY 10019

MANCHESTER, ROBERT ASA, II, lawyer; b. Canfield, Ohio, Dec. 14, 1901; s. Josiah Isaac and Gertrude (Stitle) M.; A.B., U. Mich., 1925, LL.B., J.D., 1927; m. Mary Barber, Feb. 6, 1931; children—Robert Asa III, James Russell. Admitted to Ohio bar, 1927, since practiced in Youngstown; partner Harrington, Huxley & Smith, 1927—; solicitor, Canfield, Ohio, 1938-41. Sec., dir. Research Cons.; formerly treas., dir. Manchester Co. Mem. Mahoning County Bd. Health, 1932-39, Mahoning County Charter Commn., 1934-35; mem. exec. bd. Mahoning Valley council Boy Scouts Am., 1934-71, pres., 1948-54, mem. exec. bd. region IV Nat. council, 1948-73, vice chmn., 1949-54; mem. Mahoning County Bd. Edn., 1950-55, pres., 1950, 55; mem. Mahoning County chpt. Nat. Found., 1932-74, pres., 1952-65; mem. Ohio Bd. Edn., 1956-67, pres., 1956-57; mem. exec. bd. Nat. Assn. State Bds. Edn., 1957-65, pres. 1961-63, chmn., 1963-65; pres. Youngstown Area Council Chs., 1964-66, Mahoning County Soc. for Crippled Children and Adults, 1972-74; bd. dirs. Ohio Soc. Crippled Children and Adults, 1973—. Mayor, Canfield, 1928-37. Recipient Silver Beaver award Boy Scouts Am., 1941, Silver Antelope award, 1949, disting. Eagle Scout award, 1976; named Man of Yr., Orgn. Protestant Men, 1964. Mem. Am., Ohio, Mahoning and Columbiana County bar assns., Youngstown C. of C. (chmn. youth com. 1957-65), Orgn. Protestant Men (pres. 1949), Pi Kappa Alpha, Delta Theta Phi. Presbyn. Mason (33 deg.), Rotarian (pres. 1976-77). Home: 405 Montridge Dr Canfield OH 44406 Office: 1200 Mahoning Bank Bldg Youngstown OH 44503

MANCHESTER, WILLIAM, writer; b. Attleboro, Mass., Apr. 1, 1922; s. William Raymond and Sallie E. R. (Thompson) M.; B.A., U. Mass., 1946, L.H.D., 1965; A.M., U. Mo., 1947; L.H.D., U. New Haven, 1979; m. Julia Brown Marshall, Mar. 27, 1948; children—John Kennerly, Julie Thompson, Laurie. Reporter, Daily Oklahoman, 1945-46; reporter, fgn. corr., war corr. Balt. Sun, 1947-55; mng. editor Wesleyan U. Publs., 1955-65, fellow Wesleyan U. Center for Advanced Studies, 1959-60, Wesleyan U. East Coll., 1968—; mem. faculty Wesleyan U., 1968-69, writer-in-residence, 1975—, adj. prof. history, 1979—. Pres. bd. trustees Friends of U. Mass. Library, 1970-71, trustee, 1970-74. Served with USMC, 1942-45. Decorated Purple Heart. Recipient Dag Hammarskjöld prize, 1966; citation for best book on fgn. affairs Overseas Press Club, 1968; U. Mo. honor award for distinguished service in journalism, 1969; Conn. Book award, 1975. Guggenheim fellow, 1959-60. Mem. Soc. Am. Historians, Am. Hist. Assn., Authors Guild. Club: Williams. Author: Disturber of the Peace, 1951; The City of Anger, 1953; Shadow of the Monsoon, 1956; Beard the Lion, 1958; A Rockefeller Family Portrait, 1959; The Long Gainer, 1961; Portrait of a President, 1962; The Death of a President (Book-of-the-Month Club selection), 1967; The Arms of Krupp (Lit. Guild selection), 1968; The Glory and the Dream (Lit. Guild Selection), 1974; Controversy and Other Essays in Journalism, 1976; American Caesar—Douglas Macarthur, 1880-1964 (Book-of-Month Club selection), 1978. Contbr. to various periodicals, Ency. Britannica. Address: PO Box 329 Wesleyan Station Middletown CT 06457

MANCHIN, A. JAMES, state govt. ofcl.; b. Farmington, W.Va., Apr. 7, 1927; s. Joseph and Kathleen (Roscoe) M.; B.A. in Polit. Sci. and Sociology, W.Va. U., 1951, M.A., 1962; tchrs. certificate Fairmont (W.Va.) State Coll., 1953; m. Stephanie Machel, June 9, 1951; children—Patricia Lee, Mark Anthony, Rosanna Stache. Tchr. citizenship, athletic coach pub. schs., W.Va.; dir. for W.Va., Farmers Home Adminstrn., spl. asst. to nat. adminstr., dir. for W.Va., REAP, 1973; mem. W.Va. Ho. of Dels. from Marion County, 1949; sec. of state State of W.Va., 1977—. Recipient Outstanding Service award Dept. Agr., 1968; Freedom Found. at Valley Forge award, 1969; Law and Order award Fairmont Police Dept., 1973; named Mr. W.Va., Salem Coll., 1974. Home: Farmington WV 26571 Office: State Capitol Charleston WV 25305

MANCILL, FRANK H., former lawyer; b. Port Kennedy, Pa., Aug. 26, 1891; s. Francis Shunk and May (Hoy) M.; ed. Wharton Sch., U. Pa.; LL.B., U. Pa., 1914; m. M. Louise Gibney, Sept. 22, 1915. Admitted to Pa. bar, 1914, bar of U.S. Supreme Ct., 1932; now ret.; instr., Wharton Sch., U. Pa., 1915-22, Drexel Inst. Tech., 1919-22; pres. Delaware-Montgomery Mortgage Co. Pres. bd. commrs. Lower Merion Twp., 1932-35. Vice pres. bd. trustees Am. Flag House and Betsy Ross Meml.; trustee Atwater Kent Mus. Mem. Pa. State, Philadelphia County, Am., Fed. bar assns., Franklin Inst., Baronial Order of Magna Charta, Sigma Phi Epsilon. Republican. Roman Catholic. Clubs: Lawyers, Union League, Philadelphia County (Phila.); Hare Law. Home: Apt 102 The Tedwyn Bryn Mawr PA 19010

MANCINI, HENRY, composer; b. Cleve., Apr. 16, 1924; s. Quinto and Anna (Pece) M.; student Juilliard Inst. Music, 1942; D.Mus. (hon.), Duquesne U., 1977; m. Virginia O'Connor, Sept. 13, 1947; children—Christopher, Monica and Felice (twins). Pianist, arranger Tex Beneke Orch., 1945-47; staff composer Universal Pictures, 1952-58; scores include Glenn Miller Story (nominated for Oscar award), Benny Goodman Story, Touch of Evil, The Hawaiians, The Great Waldo Pepper, 1974, Return of the Pink Panther, 1975; scored

TV series Peter Gunn, 1958, Mr. Lucky, 1959; with RCA Victor Records, 1959—; recordings include The Blues and the Beat, Mrs. Lucky Goes Latin, Breakfast at Tiffany's, Combo, Experiment in Terror, Hatari, Our Man in Hollywood, Uniquely Mancini, Days of Wine and Roses. Active in Share, Inc., for mentally retarded children. Hon. mayor, Northridge, Calif.; recipient 3 Acad. Awards for Breakfast at Tiffany's, song Moon River (with Johnny Mercer), Days of Wine and Roses (lyrics by Mercer); recipient 20 Grammy awards; named hon. alumni U. Calif. at Los Angeles, 1974; endowed yearly film music scholarship U. Calif. at Los Angeles, yearly composition scholarship Juilliard Sch. Music, N.Y.C. Mem. Composers and Lyricists Guild Am. (exec. bd.), A.S.C.A.P. Author: Sounds and Scores, 1962. Home: Regency Artists Ltd 9200 Sunset Blvd Suite 823 Los Angeles CA 90069

MANCY, KHALIL HOSNY, chemist, educator; b. Alexandria, Egypt, Nov. 4, 1928; s. Khalil and Nehmet M. (Ahmed) M.; B.S., Cairo U., 1952; M.S., U. N.C., 1959, Ph.D., 1962; postgrad. Harvard, 1964; m. Patricia Worley, Dec. 20, 1958; children—Mona Kay, Joseph Wayne, David Glenn. Chief chemist Cairo Water Co., 1952-57; research asst. U. N.C., 1957-62; asst. prof. U. Cin., 1962-64; research fellow Harvard, 1964; asso. prof., prof. chemistry U. Mich., Ann Arbor, 1965—. Research scientist Monaco Oceanographic Inst.; cons. WHO, UN Devel. Programs for Water Pollution Control in Europe, Africa and S.Am. Recipient grants from EPA, Smithsonian Instn., Ford Found., Internat. Atomic Energy Agy., USIA, other pvt. agys. Author: books. Contbr. articles to profl. jours. Patentee in field. Home: 719 Scio Church Rd Ann Arbor MI 48103

MANDAC, EVELYN LORENZANA, singer; b. Malaybalay, Philippines, Aug. 16; d. Manuel D. and Noemi (Lorenzana) Mandac; came to U.S., 1964; B.A., U. Philippines, 1963; M.A., Juillard Sch. Music, 1967; m. Sanjoy Bhattacharya, Dec. 30, 1967. World premieres include: Berio's Passagio, 1968, Pasatieri's Black Widow, 1972, Pasatieri's Inez de Castro, 1976; Am. Premiere: Bennett's Mines of Sulphur, 1967; appearances with the following opera cos.: Met., San Francisco, Houston, Seattle, Santa Fe, Pitts., Miami (Fla.), Balt., Hawaii, San Antonio, Netherlands Opera Co., Geneva, Switzerland, Toulouse (France), Glyndebourne (U.K.), Turino (Italy), Rome, Salzburg (Austria); opera roles include: Mimi in La Boheme, Manon, Despina in Cosi Fan Tutte, Zerlina in Don Giovanni, Suzannah in Figaro, Adina in L'Elixir, Norina in Don Pasquale, Melisande in Pelleas, Juliet in Romeo and Juliet, Gilda in Rigoletto, Pamina in Magic Flute, Liu in Turandot, Micaela in Carmen, Marzelline in Fidelio, Gretel in Hansel and Gretel, Leila in the Pearl Fishers; soloist with the following orchs.: Boston, Phila., Chgo., Los Angeles, Pitts., Dallas, Houston, San Antonio, Cleve., Mpls., Milw., Seattle; recordings include Orff's Carmina Buranawwith Boston Symphony (condr.: Ozawa), Mahler's Symphony #2 with Phila. Orch. (condr.: Ormandy). Winner Queen Elizabeth Voice Competition, Brussels, 1966, Met. Opera Auditions, 1966; Fulbright scholar, 1964; Rockefeller fellow, 1964-67. Office: Columbia Artists 165 W 57th St New York NY 10019

MANDAN, ROBERT, actor; b. Clever, Mo., Feb. 2; ed. Pomona Coll., N.Y. U.; studied with Lee Strasberg, Herbert Berghof, Alan Miller, Stella Adler, Lee Sweetland, Dan Marek; m. Sherry. Appeared TV series Caribe, 1975, Search for Tomorrow, Soap, 1977—; other TV roles include: The Defenders, Kraft Television Theatre, U.S. Steel Hour, Armstrong Circle Theatre, Maude, All in the Family, Redd Foxx Show, Cannon, Mannix, Kojak, Most Wanted, Police Story, Phyllis, Streets of San Francisco, One Day at a Time, Tony Randall Show; Broadway debut in There's a Girl in My Soup; appeared in play Applause, N.Y.C. and London; off-Broadway appearances include: No Exit, Julius Caesar, King Lear, The Trojan Woman, Much Ado About Nothing.

MANDANICI, JOHN C., mayor, Bridgeport (Conn.); b. Bridgeport, Jan 1, 1918; s. Virgil and Mary (Guardina) M.; grad. high sch.; m. Mary Grace Mullins, Aug. 31, 1940; children—Mary Louise, John C., Francis V., Cecelia E. With A.&P. Tea Co., Bridgeport, 1938—, store mgr., Bridgeport; mem. Bridgeport Zoning Commn., 1965-68, city clk., after 1969, now mayor. Democrat. Roman Catholic (trustee counsel, pres. adv. bd. treas. Bridgeport diocese). Club: Unico. Office: City Hall Bridgeport CT 06604*

MANDEL, H(AROLD) GEORGE, pharmacologist; b. Berlin, June 6, 1924; s. Ernest A. and Else (Crail) M.; came to U.S., 1937, naturalized, 1944; B.S., Yale U., 1944, Ph.D., 1949; m. Marianne Klein, July 25, 1953; children—Marcia Vivian, Audrey Lynn. Lab. instr. in chemistry Yale U., 1942-44, 47-49; research asso. dept. pharmacology George Washington U., 1949-50, asst. research prof., 1950-52, asso. prof. pharmacology, 1952-58, prof., 1958—, chmn. dept. pharmacology, 1960—; Advanced Commonwealth Fund fellow Molteno Inst. Cambridge (Eng.) U. 1956; Commonwealth Fund fellow U. Aukland (N.Z.) and U. Med. Scis., Bangkok, Thailand, 1964; Am. Cancer Soc. Eleanor Roosevelt Internat. fellow Chester Beatty Research Inst. London, 1970-71; Am. Cancer Soc. scholar U. Calif., San Francisco, 1978-79; mem. cancer chemotherapy com. Internat. Union Against Cancer, 1966-73; mem. external rev. com. Howard U. Cancer Research Center, 1972—; cons. Bur. Drugs, 1975—; mem. toxicology adv. com. FDA, 1975-78; mem. med. research service merit rev. bd. in alcoholism and drug dependence VA, 1975-78; mem. cancer spl. program adv. com. Nat. Cancer Inst., 1974-78, chmn., 1976-78; mem. com. on toxicology NRC-Nat. Acad. Sci., 1978—. Served with AUS, 1944-46. Recipient John J. Abel award in pharmacology Eli Lilly and Co., 1958, Distinguished Achievement award Washington Acad. Scis., 1958, Golden Apple Teaching award Student AMA, 1969. Mem. Am. Chem. Soc., Am. Soc. Biol. Chemists, Am. Soc. Pharmacology and Exptl. Therapeutics (pres. 1973-74), Am. Assn. Cancer Research, AAAS, Assn. Med. Sch. Pharmacology (pres. 1976-78), Internat. Soc. Biochem. Pharmacology, Alpha Omega Alpha, Sigma Xi. Democrat. Club: Cosmos (Washington). Research, numerous publs. on cancer chemotherapy, mechanism of growth inhibition, antimetabolites, drug disposition; contbr. numerous articles, revs. to profl. publs.; editorial bd. Jour. Pharmacology and Exptl. Therapeutics, 1960-65, field editor, 1978—; editorial bd. Molecular Pharmacology, 1965-69, Research Communications in Chem. Pathology, Pharmacology, 1972—; editorial bd. Cancer Research, 1974-76, asso. editor, 1977—. Home: 5500 Christy Dr Washington DC 20016 Office: 2300 Eye St NW Washington DC 20037

MANDEL, IRWIN DANIEL, dentist; b. Bklyn., Apr. 9, 1922; s. Samuel A. and Shirley (Blankstein) M.; B.S., City Coll. N.Y., 1942; D.D.S., Columbia U., 1945; m. Charlotte Lifschutz, Apr. 1, 1944; children—Carol, Nora, Richard. Research asst. Columbia U. Dental Sch., 1946-48, mem. faculty, 1946—, prof. dentistry, dir. div. preventive dentistry, 1969—, dir. lab. clin. research, 1960—; part-time dental practice, 1946-68; vis. prof. various dental schs.; chmn. oral biology and medicine study sect. Nat. Inst. Dental Research, 1974-76. Active local ACLU, Am. Vets. Com., SANE. Served to lt. Dental Corps, USNR, 1945-46, 52-54. Recipient Career Scientist award N.Y.C. Health Research Council, 1969-72; Leadership award in periodontology Tufts U. Dental Sch., 1971, Internat. award U. Conn. Sch. Dental Medicine, 1979. Fellow AAAS, Am. Coll. Dentists; mem. Am. Dental Assn. (chmn. council on dental research 1979), First Dist. Dental Soc. (Henry Spenadel award 1973), Am. Assn. Dental Research (pres.-elect 1979), Internat. Assn. Dental Research, N.Y. Acad. Scis., Sigma Xi, Omicron Kappa Upsilon. Mem. Am. Ethical Union. Author articles, chpts. in books; co-author: The Plaque Diseases, 1972. Home: 60 Pine Dr Cedar Grove NJ 07009 Office: 630 W 168th St New York NY 10032

MANDEL, JOSEPH C., bus. exec.; married; children—Michele, Penni. Partner, Mandel Bros., 1936-39; co-founder Premier Indsl. Corp., Cleve., 1940, now chmn. exec. com., dir. Office: 4415 Euclid Ave Cleveland OH 44103

MANDEL, LEONARD, physicist; B.Sc., U. London (Eng.), 1947, B.Sc., 1948, Ph.D., 1951; m. Jeanne Elizabeth Kear, Aug. 20, 1953; children—Karen Rose, Barry Paul. Tech. officer Imperial Chem. Industries, 1951-54; lectr., sr. lectr. Imperial Coll., U. London, 1954-64; prof. physics U. Rochester, N.Y., 1964—, prof. optics, 1977—. Fellow Am. Phys. Soc., Optical Soc. Am. Contbr. numerous sci. articles to profl. jours. Office: Dept Physics and Astronomy U Rochester Rochester NY

MANDEL, MORTON LEON, corp. exec.; b. Cleve., Sept. 19, 1921; s. Simon and Rose (Nusbaum) M.; student Case Western Res. U., 1940-42, Pomona Coll., 1943; m. Barbara Abrams, Feb. 27, 1949; children—Amy, Thomas, Stacy. With Premier Indsl. Corp., Cleve., 1946—, sec.-treas., dir., 1946-58, pres., dir., 1958-70, chmn., 1970—. Pres., Jewish Community Centers of Cleve., 1952-58, life trustee, 1958—; trustee Jewish Community Fedn., v.p., 1971-74, pres., 1974-76, life trustee; trustee Nat. Jewish Welfare Bd., v.p., 1964-70, pres., 1970-74, hon. pres., 1974—; trustee Jr. Achievement of Cleve., Community Chest Cleve.; chmn. Found. Adv. Council, 1967-75; chmn. unit plan div. United Appeal of Cleve., 1959-61, group chmn. Div. A, 1962-67, chmn. div. A, 1968-69, asso. chmn., 1970; v.p. United Way Cleve., 1971-77, pres., 1977-79, chmn., 1979—; v.p. Council Jewish Fedns., 1971-74, pres., 1978—, trustee, 1967—; pres. Bur. Careers in Jewish Service, 1967-70; mem. Commn. on Health and Social Services, Cleve., 1970-71; mem. vis. com. Sch. Applied Social Sci., Case Western Res. U., 1958-74; bd. overseers Case Western Res. U., 1970-74, trustee, 1977—; trustee Mt. Sinai Hosp., Cleve., 1970-79, Cleve. Zool. Soc., 1970-73; mem. Businessmen's Inter-racial Com., 1969-74; pres. World Confedn. Jewish Community Centers, 1977—; bd. govs. Jewish Agy., 1979—; trustee United Israel Appeal, 1977—. Recipient Outstanding Young Man of Year award Cleve. Jr. C. of C., 1956; Businessman of Year award Urban League of Cleve., 1973; Frank L. Weil award Nat. Jewish Welfare Bd., 1974; Charles Eisenman award Cleve. Jewish Community Center, 1977; Citizen of Year award Cleve. Area Bd. Realtors, 1973. Home: 17250 Parkland Dr Shaker Heights OH 44120 Office: 4415 Euclid Ave Cleveland OH 44103

MANDEL, ROBERT D., retail trade exec.; b. N.Y.C., Oct. 4, 1923; s. Max and Dora (Katz) M.; B.A., Yale, 1945; children—Alison Jane, Hilary Joan. Sr. v.p., treas., sec. Petrie Stores Corp., Secaucus, N.J., 1950—, dir., 1971—. Served to capt. AUS, 1942-45. Decorated Silver Star. Clubs: Yale (N.Y.C.); Fairview Country; Lake Placid N.Y.); Morris Yacht; Stuyvesant Yacht. Home: 1203 River Rd Edgewater NJ 07020 Office: 70 Enterprise Ave Secaucus NJ 07094

MANDEL, SIEGFRIED, educator; b. Berlin, Germany, Dec. 20, 1922; s. Nathan and Pauline (Scheinman) M.; came to U.S., 1933, naturalized, 1938; B.A., Bklyn. Coll., 1946; M.A., Columbia, 1947; Ph.D., U. Denver, 1967; m. Dorothy Isaacs, Feb. 3, 1946; children—Elise Judith, Theodore Scott. Part-time instr. Poly. Inst. Bklyn., 1948-55; sr. editor Inst. Econ. Affairs, N.Y.C., 1952-53; writer, editor Asso. Transp., Inc., 1954-55; book rev. columnist Newsday, 1954-55; lectr. N.Y.U., 1955; from instr. to asso. prof. Poly. Inst. Bklyn., 1955-62; mem. faculty U. Colo., 1962—; prof. English, 1965—, chmn. dept. English in engring., 1969-70, dir. grad. studies, dept. English, 1977—; indsl. lectr. writing workshops Internat. Tel. & Tel Corp., 1959-60. Served with AUS, 1943-46. Faculty fellow lit. research U. Colo., 1968-69, 75-76. Mem. Modern, Rocky Mt. Modern lang. assns., Coll. English Assn., Am. Comparative Lit. Assn. Editor, contbr., author: Writing in Industry, 1959; (with D.L. Caldwell) Proposal and Inquiry Writing, 1962; Modern Journalism, 1962; (Rainer Maria Rilke) The Poetic Instinct, 1965; (with Aaron Kramer) Rainer Maria Rilke: Visions of Christ, 1967; Contemporary European Novelists, 1968; Dictionary of Science, 1969; Writing for Science and Technology, 1970; Group 47: The Reflected Intellect, 1973. Home: 355 Balsam Ln Pine Brook Hills Boulder CO 80302

MANDELBAUM, BERNARD, rabbi, educator; b. N.Y.C., Jan. 12, 1922; s. Jacob and Ida (Cohen) M.; B.A., Columbia, 1942; M.H.L., Jewish Theol. Sem. Am., 1946, D.H.L., 1951; m. Judith Werber, May 27, 1945; children—Joel, Dasi, David, Debra, Naomi. Ordained rabbi, 1946; with Jewish Theol. Sem. Am., 1946—, prof. homiletics, prof. Midrash rabbinical dept., 1963—, dir. Religious Psychiat. Center, 1960—, pres., 1966-71; program editor Eternal Light, 1955-61. Mem. exec. com. Histadruth Invt., 1955—; pres. Am.-Israel Cultural Found., 1973-77; exec. v.p. Synagogue Council Am., 1979. Recipient Sylvania TV award, 1959. Fellow Internat. Conf. Jewish Scholarship; mem. Am. Acad. Jewish Research, Phi Beta Kappa. Author: Pesikta de Rab Kahana, 1962; The Wisdom of Solomon Schecter, 1963: The Maturing of the Conservative Movement, 1967; Choose Life, 1968; Add Life to Your Years, 1973. Editor: From the Sermons of Milton Steinberg, 1954; Assignment in Israel, 1960; Only Human: The Eternal Alibi, 1963. Home: 920 Park Ave New York NY 10028 Office: 432 Park Ave S New York NY 10022

MANDELBAUM, DAVID GOODMAN, anthropologist, educator; b. Chgo., Aug. 22, 1911; s. Samuel and Lena (Goodman) M.; B.A., Northwestern U., 1932; Ph.D., Yale, 1936; m. Ruth Weiss, May 23, 1943; children—Michael E., Susan F., Jonathan E. (dec.). Instr., asst. prof. U. Minn., 1938-46; research analyst U.S. Govt. agys., 1942-43; chief Indian-Cylon sect. Office Research and Intelligence, Dept. of State, 1946; asso. prof. anthropology U. Calif. at Berkeley, 1946-48, prof., 1948—, chmn. dept., 1955-57, chmn. Center South Asia Studies, 1965-68; vis. Fulbright prof. U. Cambridge (Eng.), 1953; dir. Ednl. Resources in Anthropology Project, 1959-61. Mem. U.S. Nat. Commn. for UNESCO, 1957-62, 75. Served from 1st lt. to maj., AUS, 1943-46. Fellow NRC, 1937-38, Carnegie Corp., 1941-42; Guggenheim fellow, 1949-50; fellow Center Advanced Studies Behavioral Scis., 1957-58; sr. fellow Am. Inst. Indian Studies, 1963-64, 75; recipient citation of merit U. Calif., 1979. Mem. Am. Anthrop. Assn., Am. Oriental Soc., Soc. Applied Anthropology, Am. Ethnol. Soc., Assn. Asian Studies, AAAS (chmn. anthropology sect. 1976), Sigma Xi. Author: The Plains Cree, 1940, 2d edit., 1978; Soldier Groups and Negro Soldiers, 1952; Society in India, 1970; Human Fertility in India, 1974. Editor: Selected Writings of Edward Sapir, 1949; co-editor The Teaching of Anthropology, 1963. Home: 911 Mendocino Ave Berkeley CA 94707

MANDELBAUM, MAURICE H., educator: b. Chgo., Dec. 9, 1908; s. Maurice H. and Ida (Mandel) M.; A.B., Dartmouth Coll., 1929, M.A., 1932, D.H.L., 1979; Ph.D., Yale U., 1936; m. Gwendolyn Norton, Oct. 1, 1932; children—Ann, John D.; m. 2d, Alice L. Moran, Mar. 21, 1949. Asst. instr. biography and comparative lit. Dartmouth, 1931-32; from instr. to asso. prof. philosophy Swarthmore Coll., 1934-47; prof. philosophy Dartmouth Coll., 1947-57; prof. philosophy Johns Hopkins U., 1957-67, Andrew W. Mellon prof. philosophy, 1967-78, prof. Humanities Center, 1974-78; adj. prof. philosophy Dartmouth Coll., 1979—; vis. prof. Harvard, Haverford Coll., U. Mich.; mem. Council Philos. Studies, 1969-72. Mem. Nat. Bd. Grad. Edn., 1971-75; mem. Md. Commn. Humanities and Pub. Policy, 1974-77. Guggenheim fellow, 1946; Fellow Center Advanced Study Behavioral Scis., 1967-68. Mem. Am. Philos. Assn. (pres. 1962, chmn. bd. officers 1968-74), Am. Acad. Arts and Scis., Am. Assn. U. Profs., Phi Beta Kappa. Author: The Problem of Historical Knowledge, 1938; The Phenomenology of Moral Experience, 1955; Philosophy, Science, and Sense Perception, 1964; History, Man, and Reason, 1971; The Anatomy of Historical Knowledge, 1977. Am. collaborator: Bibliographie de la Philosophie, 1937-40. Editor: Art, Perception, and Reality, 1972. Co-editor: Philosophic Problems, rev., 1967; Phenomenology and Existentialism, 1967; Spinoza: Essays in Interpretation, 1975. Address: Philosophy Dept Dartmouth Coll Hanover NH 03755

MANDELKER, DANIEL ROBERT, educator; b. Milw., July 18, 1926; s. Adolph Irwin and Marie (Manner) M.; B.A., U. Wis., 1947, LL.B., 1949; J.S.D., Yale, 1956; div.; children—Amy Jo, John David; m. 2d, Jana Marija Kovac, Mar. 7, 1968. Admitted to Wis. bar, 1949; asst. prof. law Drake U., 1949-51; atty. HHFA, Washington, 1952-53; asst. prof., then asso. prof. law Ind. U., 1953-62; mem. faculty Washington U., St. Louis, 1962—, prof. law, 1963-74, Howard A. Stamper prof. law, 1974—; Walter E. Meyer research prof. law Columbia, 1971-72; Ford Found. Law Faculty fellow, London, Eng., 1959-60. Cons. Hawaii Dept. Planning and Econ. Devel., 1972-78; mem. adv. commn. on housing and urban growth Am. Bar Assn., 1976. Mem. adv. com. legal research Transp. Research Bd., 1964—; cons. housing subcom., banking and currency com. U.S. Ho. Reps., 1970-71, Nat. Commn. Urban Problems, 1967-68, UN Centre Housing, Bldg. and Planning, 1972-73. Mem. Nat. Acad. Scis. (com. social and behavioral urban research 1967-68), Phi Beta Kappa, Order of Coif, Phi Kappa Phi. Author: Green Belts and Urban Growth: English Town and Country Planning in Action, 1962; Controlling Planned Residential Developments, 1966; Managing Our Urban Environment-Cases, Text and Problems, 2d edit., 1971; Case Studies in Land Planning and Development, 1968; The Zoning Dilemma, 1971; (with W.R. Ewald) Street Graphics, 1971; (with R. Montgomery) Housing in America: Problems and Perspectives, 1973, 2d edit., 1979; Housing Subsidies in the United States and England, 1973; New Developments in Land and Environmental Controls, 1974; Environmental and Land Controls Legislation, 1976, supplement, 1978; (with D. Netsch) State and Local Government in a Federal System, 1977; (with R. Cunningham) Planning and Control of Land Development, 1979. Office: Washington Univ Sch Law St Louis MO 63130

MANDELKERN, LEO, educator; b. N.Y.C., Feb. 23, 1922; s. Israel and Gussie (Krostich) M.; B.A., Cornell U., 1942, Ph.D., 1949; m. Berdie Medvedoff, May 19, 1946; children—Irwin, Marshal, David. Postdoctoral research asso. Cornell U., 1949-52; phys. chemist Nat. Bur. Standards, Washington, 1952-62; prof. chemistry and biophysics Fla. State U., Tallahassee, 1962—. Vis. prof. U. Miami Med. Sch., 1963, U. Calif. Med. Sch. at San Francisco, 1964, Cornell U., 1967; cons. in field. Mem. NIH biophysics fellowship com. 1967-70; NRC study panel crystal growth and morphology. Served with USAAF, 1942-46. Recipient Arthur S. Flemming award Washington Jr. C. of C., 1958; Commerce Dept. Meritorious Service award, 1957; named an Outstanding Educator Am., 1973, 75; NIH grantee, 1962-67, 72—; NSF grantee, 1972—. Fellow Am. Phys. Soc., N.Y. Acad. Sci., AAAS, Biophys. Soc.; mem. Am. Chem. Soc. (award in polymer chemistry 1975), Sigma Xi, Alpha Epsilon Pi. Club: Cosmos (Washington). Author: Crystallization of Polymers, 1964; Introduction to Macromolecules, 1972. Contbr. articles to profl. jours. Home: 1503 Old Fort Dr Tallahassee FL 32301

MANDELL, ABE, TV and movie prodn. co. exec.; student U. Cin. Actor on Cin. radio sta.; gen. mgr., then Far East supr. Frieder Films, 1946-56; network-regional sales exec. Ziv TV, 1956-58; with ITC Entertainment Inc., 1958—, dir. fgn. ops., 1958-60, v.p. fgn. ops., 1960-61, v.p. sales and adminstrn., 1961-62, exec. v.p., 1962-65, pres., 1965—. Served in U.S. Army, 1942-45; PTO. Office: ITC Entertainment Inc 115 E 57th St New York NY 10022

MANDELL, ARNOLD JOSEPH, psychiatrist; b. Chgo., July 21, 1934; s. Allen and Rose (Sugarman) M.; B.A., Stanford U., 1954; M.D., Tulane U., 1958; children—Donnan Avery, Ross Benjamin. Intern, Ochsner Found. Hosp., New Orleans, 1958-59; resident psychiatry U. Calif., Los Angeles, 1959-62, chief resident, 1962-63, asst. prof. psychiatry, 1963-66, asso. prof., 1966-68; asso. prof. psychiatry U. Calif. at Irvine, 1968-69; chmn. dept. psychiatry U. Calif. at San Diego, La Jolla, 1969-74, co-chmn. dept. psychiatry, 1975-77, prof., 1969—; cons. U. Calif. Med. Center, Los Angeles, 1961-67, Peace Corps Tng. Program, 1961-63, Rancho Los Amigos Geriatric Research Hosp., 1961-63, NASA Space Biology Lab., 1967-70, Ill. Dept. Mental Health Research Program, 1968-69, VA Hosp., Long Beach, Calif., 1969-70, Calif. Dept. Mental Hygiene Research Programs, 1968-70, NIMH Lab. Clin. Sci., 1968, 70—, Naval Neuropsychiat. Research Inst., 1969-70, Nat. Com. for Effective Drug Abuse Legis., 1970-72, San Diego Chargers Football Team, 1971-73, Sen. John Tunney, 1971-72, VA Hosp., San Diego, 1971—, VA Nat. Narcotic Abuse Program, 1972; cons. sci. adviser Pres.'s Spl. Action Office for Drug Abuse Prevention, 1970-73, Nat. Commn. on Marijuana and Drug Abuse, 1970-73; mem. sci. adv. com. Nat. Soc. for Autism, 1966-71; bd. dirs. Nat. Tng. Labs., 1969-72; mem. internat. adv. bd. Israeli Center for Psychobiology, 1973—; sci. adviser Stanford U. Addiction Research Lab., 1973—; mem. profl. adv. bd. Jerusalem Mental Health Center, 1973—; mem. NRC Commn. on Human Resources, 1974—; mem. research adv. bd. Nat. Inst. Neurol. Diseases and Blindness, 1977—; cons. San Francisco Fine Arts Mus., 1977-78. Recipient Borden research prize Tulane U., 1958, A.E. Bennett award for research in biol. psychiatry, 1962, NIMH Career Tchr. award, 1963-65; Johananoff Internat. fellow Mario Negri Inst. Pharmacol. Research, Milan, Italy, 1977—. Mem. Am. Acad. Psychoanalysis, AAAS, Am. Coll. Neuropsychopharmacology, Am. Coll. Psychiatrists, Am. Inst. Chemists, Am. Psychiat. Assn. (Found.'s Fund prize for research in psychiatry 1979), Am. Psychopath. Assn., Am. Psychosomatic Soc., Assn. Academic Psychiatry, Assn. Am. Profs. Psychiatry, Psychiat. Research Soc., Soc. Biol. Psychiatry (pres. 1976-77), Soc. for Neuroscis., Psychophysiol. Study Sleep, So. Calif. Psychiat. Soc., Phi Beta Kappa, Sigma Xi, Alpha Omega Alpha. Author: The Nightmare Season, 1976; Coming of (Middle) Age: A Journey; editor: (with Mary P. Mandell) Psycho-chemical Research in Man., 1969; New Concepts in Neurotransmitter Regulation, 1973; Neurobiological Mechanisms of Adaptation and Behavior, 1975; (with E. Usdin) The Biochemistry of Mental Disorders, 1977; contbr. articles to med jours. Office: Dept Psychiatry U Calif at San Diego La Jolla CA 92093

MANDELL, LEON, educator; b. Bronx, N.Y., Nov. 19, 1927; s. Harry and Yetta (Burnstein) M.; B.S., Poly. Inst. Bklyn., 1948; M.A., Harvard, 1949, Ph.D., 1951; m. Jane Barker, Oct. 2, 1959 (div. 1969); children—P. Bradford, David L.; m. 2d, Sara Ross Sindel, Apr. 23, 1971. Sr. chemist Merck & Co., Rahway, N.J., 1951-53; mem. faculty

Emory U., Atlanta, 1955—, asso. prof. chemistry, 1958-65, prof., 1965—, also chmn. dept. chemistry. Cons. Houndry Labs. div. Air Products Schering Corp., 1958—. Served with chem. corps AUS, 1953-55. Mem. Am., Brit. chem. socs., Phi Beta Kappa, Sigma Xi, Phi Lambda Upsilon, Omicron Delta Kappa. Contbr. articles profl. jours. Home: 2788 Galahad Dr NE Atlanta GA 30345

MANDELSTAM, ROBERT STANLEY, corp. exec.; b. Sioux City, Iowa, Apr. 30, 1919; s. Benjamin and Mary (Pickus) M.; A.B., Johns Hopkins, 1940; student Navy Oriental Lang. Sch., U. Colo., 1942-43; grad. Nat. War Coll., 1960; m. Rosemary Rogers, Feb. 8, 1944. With Marlboro Co., Balt., 1940-41; with Dept. Navy, 1946-49, Dept. Def., 1949-56; assigned Germany, 1951-53; fgn. service officer Dept. State, 1956-69, assigned Greece, 1956-58; dir. spl. projects Internat. Security Affairs, Dept. Def., 1961-69; v.p. Resources Devel. and Analysis Corp., N.Y.C. and Washington, 1965—; asso. Kermit Roosevelt and Assos., 1969-77; pres. EMS Inc., 1977—. Served with USNR, 1941-46. Decorated Presdl. Unit citation. Mem. Phi Beta Kappa. Clubs: Tudor and Stuart (Balt.); Timber Ridge Bassets (Md.); McNair Officers, Fed. City, Internat. (Washington). Home: 4620 Reservoir Rd Washington DC 20007 Office: 6817 Tennyson Dr McLean VA 22101

MANDEVILLE, ROBERT CLARK, JR., naval officer; b. Princeton, W.Va., July 18, 1927; s. Robert Clark and Grace (Oney) M.; B.S., U.S. Naval Acad., 1950; M.S., Naval Postgrad. Sch., 1959; m. Elizabeth Anne Perry, Oct. 10, 1953; children—Cathy, Karen, Christy, Scott. Commd. ensign U.S. Navy, 1950, advanced through grades to rear adm., 1976; assigned carrier-based fighter and attack squadrons; project mgr. A-6/EA-6 Weapons Systems, Washington, 1970-73; comdg. officer Naval Air Sta. Oceana, Virginia Beach, Va., 1973-74; dir. aviation plans and requirements Navy Dept., Washington, 1974-78, comdr. Light Attack Wing, Pacific, Lemoore, Calif., 1978—. Decorated D.F.C. (6), Air medal (13), Bronze Star, Meritorious Service medal, Legion of Merit. Mem. Soc. Old Crows, Sigma Xi. Home: 2466 Nimitz Circle NAS Lemoore CA 93245 Office: Comdr Light Attack Wing US Pacific Fleet NAS LeMoore CA 93245

MANDIL, I. HARRY, nuclear engr.; b. Istanbul, Turkey, Dec. 11, 1919 (parents U.S. citizens); s. Harry Robert and Bertha (Presente) M.; B.S., U. London (Eng.), 1939; M.S., Mass. Inst. Tech., 1941; grad. Oak Ridge Sch. Reactor Tech., 1950; D.Sc. (hon.), Thiel Coll., Greenville, Pa., 1960; m. Beverly Ericson, June 22, 1946; children—Jean Dale, Eric Robert. Devel., design process controls for textile mills and chem. plants Norcross Corp., 1941-42, asst. to pres. charge field engring., 1946-49; asst. to tech. dir. naval reactors br. reactor devel. div. AEC, 1950-54, dir. reactor engring. div. Bur. Ships, also chief reactor engring. br. naval reactors reactor devel. div., 1954-64; prin. officer, dir. MPR Assos., Inc., engrs., Washington, 1964—; devel. nuclear power propulsion naval vessels, also for Shippingport Atomic Power Central Sta. Served with USNR, 1942-46. Recipient Meritorius Civilian Service award Navy Dept., 1952, Distinguished Civilian Service award, 1959. Author numerous papers in field. Home: 6900 Forest Hill Dr University Park MD 20782 Office: 1140 Connecticut Ave NW Washington DC 20036

MANDINO, OG, author; b. Boston, Dec. 12, 1923; s. Silvio and Margaret T. (Lee) M.; student Bucknell Jr. Coll., 1941; m. Bette L. Lang, Dec. 9, 1957; children—Dana, Matthew. Sales mgr. Combined Ins. Co., Chgo., 1960-65; sales rep. Met. Life Ins. Co., Boston, 1948-60; exec. editor Success Unlimited mag., Chgo., 1965-72; pres. Success Unltd., Inc., Chgo., 1972-76, Matt-Dana Ltd., 1974—, also dir. Served to 1st lt. USAAF, 1942-45. Decorated D.F.C., Air medal with 5 oak leaf clusters. Mem. Authors Guild, Authors League, Nat. Speakers Assn. Author: A Treasury of Success Unlimited, 1967; The Greatest Salesman in the World, 1968; (with Edward R. Dewey) Cycles, The Mysterious Forces That Trigger Events, 1970; U.S. in a Nutshell, 1971; The Greatest Secret in the World, 1972; The Greatest Miracle in the World, 1975; (with Buddy Kaye) The Gift of Acabar, 1978; The Christ Commission, 1980. Home: 6130 E Via Estrella Ave Scottsdale AZ 85253

MANDL, INES, biochemist; b. Vienna, Austria, Apr. 19, 1917; d. Ernst and Ida (Bassan) Hochmuth; came to U.S., 1945, naturalized, 1950; Dip. Chem., Nat. U. Ireland, Cork, 1944; M.S., Poly. Inst. Bklyn., 1947, Ph.D., 1949; m. Hans Alexander Mandl, May 31, 1936. Asst. to Carl Neuberg at Interchem. Corp. and N.Y. U., 1945-49; research asso. Columbia U. Coll. Physicians and Surgeons, 1949-55, asst. prof. biochemistry, 1956-73, asso. prof. reproductive biochemistry, 1973-76, prof., 1976—. Recipient Disting. Alumnus award Poly. Inst. Bkly., 1972, Carl Neuberg medal Virchow-Pirquet Med. Soc., 1977. Mem. Am. Chem. Soc., AAAS, Am. Soc. Biol. Chemists, Soc. Exptl. Biology and Medicine, Biochem. Soc. (Eng.), Am. Assn. Cancer Research, Gerontol. Soc., Soc. Complex Carbohydrates, Am. Thoracic Soc., Am. Heart Assn., Basic Sci. Council, Cardiopulmonary Council, N.Y. Acad. Sci., Virchow-Pirquet Med. Soc., Sigma Xi, Iota Sigma Pi. Contbr. numerous articles, revs. to profl. jours.; editor-in-chief Connective Tissue Research, 1972—. Home: 166 W 72d St New York NY 10023 Office: 630 W 168th St New York NY 10032

MANDREKAR, VIDYADHAR SHANTARAM, statistician; b. India, Mar. 26, 1939; s. Shantaram Narayan and Kamalabai (Sabnis) M.; came to U.S., 1960, naturalized, 1968; B.A., Elphinstone Coll., Bombay, 1959; Ph.D., Mich. State U., 1964; m. Veena Dixit, June 15, 1968; children—Paraj V., Tushar V. Asst. prof. U. Minn., 1965-67; asso. prof. Mich. State U., East Lansing, 1968-72, prof., 1972—, chmn. dept. stats. and probability, 1975—; vis. mem. MRC, U. Wis., 1967-68; vis. prof. EPF, Lausanne, Switzerland, 1974-75, Ecole Polytechnique Palaiseau, France, 1977. Mem. Ad Hoc Com. on Traffic Safety, City of East Lansing, 1976. Merit scholar Elphinstone Coll., 1958-59; fellow Ind. U., 1960-61; NSF grantee, 1978-80. Mem. Am. Math. Soc. Author: Benchmark Papers in Electrical Engineering and Computer Science, 1973. Contbr. chpt. to Book on Probabilistic Analysis and Related Topics, 1978. Contbr. articles to profl. jours. Office: Dept Statistics and Probability Mich State U East Lansing MI 48824

MANDRELL, BARBARA ANN, entertainer; b. Houston, Dec. 25, 1948; d. Irby Matthew and Mary Ellen (McGill) M.; grad. high sch.; m. Kenneth Lee Dudney, May 28, 1967; children—Kenneth Matthew, Jaime Nicole. Country music singer and entertainer, 1959—; performed throughout U.S. and in various fgn. countries; mem. Grand Ole Opry, Nashville, 1972—. Named Miss Oceanside (Calif.), 1965; Most Promising Female Singer, Acad. Country and Western Music, 1971, Female Vocalist of Year, 1978; Female Vocalist of Year, Music City News Cover Awards, 1979, Country Music Assn., 1979. Mem. Musicians Union, Screen Actors Guild, AFTRA, Country Music Assn. (v.p.), Assn. Country Entertainers. Mem. Order Eastern Star. Home: PO Box 332 Hendersonville TN 37075

MANDRY, WILFRED JOHN, chem. co. exec.; b. London, Apr. 3, 1922; came to Can., 1955; B.Sc. in Engring., U. London; m. Kathleen Rains, 1944; children—Michael, David, Rosemary, Angela. Works engr. G.A. Harvey & Co. Ltd., London, 1946-55; with Canadian Industries Ltd., 1955—, pres., chief operating officer, dir., 1975-76, pres., chief exec. officer, dir., 1976—; v.p., dir. ICI Americas, Wilmington, Del., 1973-75. Served with RAF, 1940-46. Chartered engr., U.K. Mem. Soc. Chem. Industry, Inst. Mech. and Civil Engrs. (U.K.). Clubs: St. James's, Mt. Royal, Forest and Stream. Address: Can Industries Ltd PO Box 10 Montreal PQ H3C 2R3 Canada

MANEGOLD, ROBERT LOUIS, mfr., industrialist; b. Milw., Apr. 4, 1916; s. Robert A. and Lili A. (Muench) M.; B.A., Dartmouth, 1938; m. Sally S. Schley, May 9, 1942; children—Joan, Kathe, Marilyn, Robert H. Gen. mgr. Dings Magnetic Separator Co., 1940-45, pres., 1945-65: pres. Chisholm Boyd & Co., 1955-65, Carnes Corp., 1957-65. Wehr Steel Co., 1958-65; chmn. Wehr Corp., 1965—; dir. First Wis. Nat. Bank, First Wis. Trust Co., Congoleum Industries, Inc., Mattel Corp., Twin Disc Corp., First Wis. Corp., Employers Mut. Wausau, Western Pub. Co. Home: Route 1 Hartland WI 53029 Office: Wehr Corp Milwaukee WI 53227

MANEKER, DEANNA MARIE, publisher; b. Albany, N.Y., Dec. 13, 1938; d. Marion K.G. and Florence Ruth (Krell) Colle; A.B., Barnard Coll., 1960; m. Morton M. Maneker, Sept. 15, 1957; children—Meryl, Amy, M. Kenneth. Circulation dir. Westchester mag., Mamaroneck, N.Y., 1970-73; publisher Change mag., Ednl. Change, Inc., New Rochelle, N.Y., 1973-78; dir. Change Mag. Press, 1973-78; gen. mgr. Center for Direct Mktg., seminar mktg., Westport, Conn., 1978—. Trustee Jewish Home and Hosp. for Aged, N.Y.C., 1972—. Home: 4 Coolidge St Larchmont NY 10538 Office: 3 Sylvan Rd S Westport CT 06880

MANELL, ABRAM E., govt. ofcl.; b. Ostrog, Russia, Mar. 25, 1912; s. Harry and Edith Manell; brought to U.S., 1921, naturalized, 1928; B.S., Middlebury Coll., 1934: M.A., U. Calif. at Berkeley, 1936, Ph.D., 1948; m. Rosemary Grimes, Sept. 14, 1947. Staff, Internat. House, Berkeley, Calif., 1938-42; with Dept. Justice, 1942-43; staff Dept. of State, 1948—, fgn. service officer, 1955—; attache, Marseilles, 1948-50; dep. pub. affairs officer for France and Algeria, Paris, 1950-53; pub. affairs officer, Lisbon, Portugal, 1953-55; 1st sec., Brussels, Belgium, 1955-58; adviser U.S. del. 10th Gen. Conf. UNESCO, Paris, 1958; dir. secretariat U.S. Nat. Commn. for UNESCO, Washington, 1959-60; adviser pub. affairs Bur. Far Eastern Affairs, State Dept., 1960-64; assigned to Far Eastern and Russian Inst., U. Wash., Seattle, 1964-65; bd. examiners Dept. State, Washington, 1965-67; spl. asst. to sec. state for liaison with govs., 1967-73; cons. Dept. of State, 1973—. Served to lt. (s.g.) USNR, 1943-46. Home: 824 New Hampshire Ave NW Washington DC 20037 Office: Dept State Washington DC 20525

MANELLA, ARTHUR, lawyer; b. Toronto, Ont., Can., Aug. 7, 1917; B.S., U. So. Calif., 1939, LL.B., 1941; LL.M., Harvard, 1942; m. Nancy Holme, Oct. 30, 1942; children—David, Nora. Admitted to Calif. bar, 1941, since practiced in Los Angeles; mem. firm Irell & Manella; spl. asst. to atty. gen. U.S., tax div. Dept. Justice, 1942-43; lectr. fed. income taxes U. So. Calif. Grad. Sch. Law, 1951-57. Mem. planning com. U. So. Calif. Tax Inst., 1948-73. Bd. govs. Otis Art Inst., 1968-71. Mem. Am., Los Angeles, Beverly Hills bar assns., State Bar Calif. (taxation adv. commn.), Am. Law Inst. (tax adv. group), Order of Coif. Author: Current Developments in Taxation of Alimony, 1948; Non-Business versus Business Bad Debts, 1950; Capital Gains and Losses Under the Internal Revenue Code of 1954. Editor-in-chief So. Calif. Law Rev., 1940-41. Home: 12017 Iredell Studio City CA 91604 Office: 900 Gateway East Century City Los Angeles CA 90067

MANELLA, DANIEL JOHN, corp. exec.; b. Chgo., June 23, 1925; s. Joseph J. and Mary (Usillo) M.; B.S. in Indsl. Engring., Northwestern U., 1946, M.B.A., 1949; m. Gladys (Pat) Luchs, Jan. 13, 1945; children—Daniel J., Susan M., Diane D. Indsl. engr. Bell & Howell Co., Chgo., 1943-46; mgmt. cons., Chgo., 1946-48; v.p. Am. Colortype Co., Chgo., 1948-56, Rapid Am. Co., N.Y.C., 1957-60; exec. v.p. Am. Paper Splty. Co., N.Y.C., 1961-62, pres., chmn. bd. Am. Paper Splty. Paper Corp., Chgo., 1962-64; pres. SCM/Allied Paper Converting Co., Chgo., 1964-69; mgmt. cons., Chgo. and N.Y.C., 1969-71; v.p. Feldco Corp., Waukegan, Ill., 1971-73; pres., chief exec. officer KGA Industries, N.Y.C., 1973-74, also dir. B.V.D. Co., Inc., N.Y.C., 1974-76; pres. Anvil Brand, Inc., N.Y.C., 1977, Botany Shirt Co., Inc., N.Y.C., 1977—; chmn. bd., chief exec. officer Kenton Corp., N.Y.C., 1979—; chmn. exec. com., dir. AITS, Boston. Clubs: North Shore Country, Lake Shore. Home: 255 Old Farm Rd Northfield IL 60093 Office: 711 Fifth Ave New York NY 10019

MANES, MILTON, educator; b. Bklyn., Oct. 14, 1918; s. Philip and Rose (Buxbaum) M.; B.S., Coll. City N.Y., 1937; postgrad. George Washington U., 1938-41; Ph.D., Duke, 1947; m. Carol Freeman, Aug. 15, 1945; children—Stephen, Eleanor (Mrs. Jack P. Mann, Jr.). Lab. asst., jr. chemist FDA, Washington, 1937-42; phys. chemist U.S. Bur. Mines, Pitts., 1947-52; sr. chemist, mgr. statis. design group Koppers Research Lab., Verona, Pa., 1952-58; supr. phys. chemistry research Pitts. Chem. Co., 1958-64; sr. fellow, head adsorption fellowship Mellon Inst., Pitts., 1964-67; prof. chemistry Kent State U., 1967—; vis. prof. Cornell U., 1964. Mem. Am. Chem. Soc. (chmn. phys. chemistry group Pitts. 1953, chmn. coal tech. group 1958), AAAS, Phi Beta Kappa, Sigma Xi. Research, publs. and patents in phys. adsorption, nonequilibrium thermodynamics, thermodynamics and kinetics, catalysis, activated carbon. Home: 1613 Chadwick Dr Kent OH 44240

MANES, NELLA CELLINI, advt. agy. exec.; b. Steubenville, Ohio, July 25, 1920; d. Benvenuto Marcello and Liberata (DeMarco) C.; student Steubenville Bus. Coll., 1939-41; m. Robert V. Manes, Jan. 8, 1946 (div. June 1947); 1 dau., Michele (Mrs. James W. Broadfoot III). Procurement specialist Q.M.C., U.S. Army, Washington, 1942-46; time buyer, media dir., v.p. media Kal, Ehrlich & Merrick, Advt., Washington, 1949-68; v.p. media, exec. v.p. Ehrlich-Linkins & Assos., Washington, 1968-70; exec. v.p. Ehrlich-Manes & Assos., Washington, 1970-79, pres., 1979—; organizer, dir. First Women's Bank of Md., Inc., 1978. Bd. dirs., exec. com. Friends of Nat. Zoo; mem. pub. relations com. Montgomery County (Md.) chpt. Am. Heart Assn. Recipient Silver medal Am. Advt. Fedn., 1978. Mem. Nat. Acad. TV Arts and Scis., Advt. Club Met. Washington (Advt. Woman of year 1963), Media Research Council, Am. Women in Radio and TV, Fashion Group. Republican. Roman Catholic. Home: 4620 N Park Ave Chevy Chase MD 20015 Office: Ehrlich-Manes & Assos 4901 Fairmont Av Bethesda MD 20014

MANES, STEPHEN GABRIEL, concert pianist, educator; b. Bennington, Vt., Apr. 11, 1940; s. Julius H. and Edna E. (Silberstein) M.; B.S., Juilliard Sch. Music, 1961, M.S., 1963; postgrad. (Fulbright fellow), Acad. Music, Vienna, 1963-64; m. Frieda Green, July 7, 1963; children—Sonya Ruth, Daniel Ira. Concert piano soloist major orchs. U.S. and abroad; debuts in Washington, 1962, N.Y.C., 1963, Vienna, Austria, 1964, Berlin, 1975, Amsterdam, 1975, London, 1975; chamber music concerts, radio, TV appearances; four-hand piano recitals with Frieda Manes; vis. instr. music Oberlin (Ohio) Coll. Conservatory, 1966-67; asst. prof. Ball State U., Muncie, Ind., 1967-68; prof. music SUNY, Buffalo, 1968—. Recipient Kosciuszko Chopin prize, 1960; Town Hall award Concert Artists Guild, 1962, finalist Leventritt Internat. Competition, 1962; Harriet Cohen Internat. Beethoven prize, 1964. Mem. Music Tchrs. Nat. Assn., Coll. Music Soc., Am. Fedn. Musicians. Rec. artist Orion Master Recordings, 1974—. Home: 384 Voorhees Ave Buffalo NY 14216 Office: Music Dept State U NY at Buffalo Pritchard Hall Buffalo NY 14214

MANEY, MICHAEL MASON, lawyer; b. Taihoku, Japan, Aug. 13, 1936; s. Edward Strait and Helen M. M.; B.A., Yale U., 1956; M.A., Fletcher Sch. Law and Diplomacy, Tufts U., 1957; LL.B., U. Pa., 1964; m. Suzanne Cochran, Oct. 22, 1960; 1 dau., Michele. Case officer CIA, 1957-61; admitted to N.Y. bar, 1966, D.C. bar, 1977; law clk. Justice John Harlan, Supreme Ct. U.S., Washington, 1964-65; asso. firm Sullivan & Cromwell, N.Y.C., 1965-70, partner, 1971-77, partner, Washington, 1977—; law fellow Salzburg Seminar in Am. Studies, 1967. Served to lt. USAF, 1958-60. Mem. Am. Law Inst., Am. Bar Assn., N.Y. State Bar Assn., Assn. Bar. City N.Y., D.C. Bar Assn. Clubs: Internat. (Washington); Yale (N.Y.C.); Recess, Madison Beach, Met. Opera. Home: 2900 Woodland Dr NW Washington DC 20008 also 48 Neptune Ave Madison CT 06443 Office: Sullivan & Cromwell 1775 Pennsylvania Ave NW Washington DC 20006

MANFRED, CARL LAWRENCE, clergyman; b. St. Peter, Minn., May 10, 1918; s. Conrad A. and Eda (Anderson) Peterson; B.A., Gustavus Adolphus Coll., 1939; grad. Augustana Theol. Sem., Rock Island, Ill., 1943; D.D., Northwestern Luth. Sem., 1975; m. Miriam Hildegard Peterson, Dec. 27, 1942; children—Peter Timothy, Mark Thomas, Carol Miriam, David John. Ordained to ministry Lutheran Ch., 1943; pastor in Cedar Rapids, Iowa, 1943-46, Duluth, Minn., 1946-52; asso. youth dir. Augustana Luth Ch., 1952-62; youth dir. Luth. Ch. Am., Phila., 1963-64; asst. to pres. Minn. Synod, Luth. Ch. Am., 1965-76; sr. pastor Normandale Luth. Ch., Edina, Minn., 1976—. Author: Living Our Faith, 1970. Co-author: Adventuring with Christ in the Church Staff Vocations, 1955. Editor: Youth's Favorite Songs, 1955; The Uniting Word, annual devotional guides, 1954-62, Jr. High Programs, vol. 2, 1963. Home: 5227 Oaklawn Ave Edina MN 55424 Office: 6100 Normandale Rd Edina MN 55436

MANFRED, FREDERICK FEIKEMA, writer (pseudonym Feike Feikema from 1944-51); b. Doon, Iowa, Jan. 6, 1912; s. Feike Feikes, VI and Aaltje (Van Engen) Feikema (Old Frisic Feike means Frederick, ma means man); A.B., Calvin Coll., Grand Rapids, Mich., 1934; student Nettleton Comml. Coll., Sioux Falls, S.D., 1937, (corr.) U. Minn., 1941-42; m. Maryanna Shorba, Oct. 31, 1942 (div. Oct. 1978); children—Freya, Marya, Frederick Feikema. Engaged in various work traveling in U.S., 1934-37; reporter Mpls. Jour., 1937-39; editor Modern Medicine, 1942-43; writer-in-residence Macalester Coll., 1949-52; writer-in-residence U. S.D., 1968—. Recipient 1000 fiction grant-in-aid Am. Acad. Arts and Letters, 1945; U. Minn. Rockefeller Found. Regional Writing fellowship, 1944-46; Field Found. fellowship, 1948-49; Andreas Found. fellowships, 1949, 52; McKnight Found. fellow, 1958-59; Huntington Hartford Found. fellow, 1963-64; Avon Found. fellow, 1958-59. Mem. P.E.N., Author's League Am., Soc. Midland Writers (v.p.). Club: Players (N.Y.C.). Author: The Golden Bowl, 1944; Boy Almighty, 1945; This Is The Year, 1947; The Chokecherry Tree, 1948; Lord Grizzly, 1954; Morning Red, 1956; Riders of Judgment, 1957; Conquering Horse, 1959; (stories) Arrow of Love, 1961; Wanderlust (trilogy including The Primitive, The Brother, The Giant), 1962; Scarlet Plume, 1964; The Man Who Looked Like The Prince of Wales (in paperback The Secret Place), 1965; (poems) Winter Count, 1966; King of Spades, 1966; (stories) Apples of Paradise, 1968; Eden Prairie, 1968; Conversations, 1974; Milk of Wolves, 1976; The Manly-Hearted Woman, 1976; Green Earth, 1977; (reminiscence) The Wind Blows Free, 1979. Contbr. articles and stories mags. Home: Roundwind Rural Route 3 Luverne MN 56156. *The biggest fact of the human being is that he is still mostly primitive, a primate, no matter how many theories of relativity he may invent. If one doesn't think as a primitive first and an intellectual after, one is more apt to fall into error, and live miserably.*

MANFULL, MELVIN LAWRENCE, fgn. service officer; b. Utah, Feb. 24, 1919; A.A., Weber Coll., 1939; B.A., U. Utah, 1941; postgrad. Nat. Inst. Pub. Affairs, Am. U., Washington, 1941-42; m. Suzanne Dunning, Oct. 23, 1942; children—Lisa (Mrs. David Harper), Gregory L., William Townsend. Adminstrv. officer OPA, 1946; with Office Sec., Dept. State, 1946-52; exec. sec. U.S. mission to NATO, other regional organs., Paris, 1952-57; with Office Internat. Confs., 1958-59; officer in charge peaceful uses atomic energy, 1959-61; dep. exec. sec., 1961-62; counselor polit. affairs Am. embassy, Saigon, Vietnam, 1962-65; assigned to Imperial Def. Coll., London, Eng., 1966; dep. chief mission, minister-counselor Am. embassy, Brussels, Belgium, 1967-70; ambassador to Central African Republic, 1971-72, to Republic of Liberia, 1972-75; sr. insp. Dept. State, 1976—. Served to lt. USNR, 1942-45. Address: 4610 Rodman St NW Washington DC 20016

MANGAN, ROBERT MARTIN, lawyer, ret. govt. ofcl.; b. Binghamton, N.Y., Aug. 23, 1916; s. Martin John and Olive (Perrault) M.; A.B., U. Wis., 1939; student U. Minn., 1940-41, U. N.C., 1941; LL.B., Georgetown U., 1949; m. Dorothy Dobson, Aug. 16, 1941; children—Kathleen (Mrs. Robert F. Poi), R. Lawrence, Peter, Norma (Mrs. Bob Weakley), Michele (Mrs. David W. Dunlap). Research asst. Minn. Municipal Reference Bur., 1940-41; teaching fellow U. N.C., 1941; various civilian adminstrv., personnel and legal positions War Dept. and Dept. Army, 1942-61; spl. asst. to asst. sec. for public land mgmt. Dept. Interior, 1961-63, dep. asst. sec. for public land mgmt., 1963-65, dep. under sec., 1965-69; asst. to commr. FPC, 1969-72; practice law, Washington, 1972—; sec. Virgin Islands Corp., 1962-64. Mem. Fairfax County Council on Human Relations. Mem. D.C. Bar, Fed. Bar Assn., Smithsonian Assos., Nat. Lawyers Club. Unitarian (trustee 1958-60). Author articles. Asso. editor Personnel Adminstrn., 1942-45. Home: 2449 Fardale St Vienna VA 22180 Office: 1625 I St NW Washington DC 20006

MANGANARO, FRANCIS FERDINAND, naval officer; b. Providence, Feb. 27, 1925; s. Ralph and Ada Susanna (Hobden) M.; student U. R.I., 1943-44; B.S. in Elec. Engring., U.S. Naval Acad., 1944-47; Naval Engr., M.I.T., 1956; cert. Advanced Mgmt. Program, Harvard U. Sch. Bus., 1971; m. Carol Anne Slater, Sept. 8, 1948; children—Carol Sue, William Francis, John Thomas, Linda Anne, Mary Kathryn. Commd. ensign U.S. Navy, 1947, advanced through grades to rear adm., 1975; served in destroyers, Atlantic Fleet, 1947-49; served in submarines Pacific Fleet, 1949-53; repair officer, submarines Pearl Harbor Naval Shipyard, 1956-59; design project officer, submarines Bur. Ships, 1959-63; inspection and planning officer Office Supr. of Shipbldg., Groton, Conn., 1963-68; prodn. officer Portsmouth Naval Shipyard, 1968-72; comdg. officer Puget Sound Naval Shipyard, 1972-76; chmn. navy claims settlement bd. Naval Material Command, 1976-78; vice comdr. Naval Sea Systems Command, Arlington, Va., 1978—. Decorated Legion of Merit; registered profl. engr., Conn. Mem. Soc. Naval Architects and Marine Engrs., Am. Soc. Naval Engrs., Sigma Xi, Tau Beta Pi, Beta Psi Alpha. Office: Naval Sea Systems Command Dept Navy 2521 Jefferson-Davis Hwy Arlington VA 22202

MANGAROO, JEWELLEAN SMITH (MRS. ARTHUR S. MANGAROO), nurse, coll. dean; b. Jackson, Miss., July 25, 1937; d. Aaron and Ollie Mae Smith; B.S., Meharry Med. Coll., 1958; M.S., Washington U., St. Louis, 1961; Ph.D. (HEW fellow), Ohio State U., 1968; m. Arthur S. Mangaroo, Aug. 31, 1966; children—William A., Tereese Yvette. Dir. health services Providence Sch. Nursing, Chgo., 1958-60; adminstrv. supr. Homer G. Phillips Hosp. Sch. Nursing, St.

Louis, 1960-61; asst. prof. Sch. Nursing, N.C. A. and T. State U., 1961-62; teaching asso. Ohio State U., 1963-64, nursing fellow, 1967-68; grad. asst. U. B.C. Nursing fellow, 1965-66; dean, prof. Sch. Nursing A. and T. U., 1968-69; dean Sch. Nursing, Prairie View A. and M. Coll., 1969—. Mem. Houston Model Cities Planning Com.; mem. exec. adv. council Houston chpt. A.R.C. Mem. Am. Nurses Assn., Nat. League Nursing, Delta Sigma Theta. Democrat. Home: 10819 Cypresswood Dr Houston TX 77070 Office: 2600 SW Freeway Houston TX 77098

MANGEL, MARGARET WILSON, emeritus univ. dean; b. Tell City, Ind., May 13, 1912; d. Emil H. and Lena (Wilson) Mangel; A.B., Ind. U., 1932, dietetic certificate Sch. Medicine, 1934; M.S., U. Chgo., 1940, Ph.D., 1951. Tchr. schs., Union City, Ind., 1934-39; mem. faculty U. Mo., Columbia, 1940—, prof. home econs., 1950—, chmn. home econs. dept., 1955-60, dir. Sch. Home Econs., 1960-73, dean Coll. Home Econs., 1973-77, dean emeritus, 1977—. Past pres. Altrusa Club, Columbia, Mo. Fellow AAAS, Am. Inst. Chemistry; mem. C. of C. (chmn. total health task force 1971-73), Am. Home Econs. Assn. (chmn.-elect council for profl. devel. 1974-75, chmn. 1975-76), Am., Mo. dietetics assns., Internat. Fedn. Home Econs., USPHS Assn., Am. Chem. Soc., N.Y. Acad. Sci., AAUP, Assn. Adminstrs. Home Econs. U.S. (pres. 1972-73), Phi Beta Kappa, Sigma Xi, Omicron Nu, Sigma Delta Epsilon, Gamma Sigma Delta, Pi Lambda Theta, Phi Upsilon Omicron, Delta Kappa Gamma. Contbr. articles to profl. jours. Home: 705 Morningside Dr Columbia MO 65201

MANGELS, JOHN DONALD, banker; b. Victoria, B.C., Can., Apr. 14, 1926; s. August and Marguerite E. M. (parents Am. citizens); B.A. in Bus. and Econs., U. Wash., 1950; Grad. Sch. Credit and Fin. Mgmt., Stanford U., 1961; m. Mary Ann Hahn, Nov. 25, 1954; children—Susan, Meg, John Donald. With Rainier Nat. Bank and affiliates, Seattle, 1950—, vice chmn. Rainier Bancorp., 1975—, pres. Rainier Nat. Bank, 1976—. Trustee, Downtown Seattle Devel. Assn., 1976, United Arts Council, 1979; bd. dirs. United Way of King County, 1978. Served with USAAF, 1944-46. Mem. Am. Inst. C.P.A.'s, Assn. Res. City Bankers, Robert Morris Assos. Presbyterian. Clubs: Rotary, Wash. Athletic, Rainier, Glendale Golf and Country. Office: One Rainier Sq PO Box 3966 Seattle WA 98124

MANGER, JULIUS, JR., former hotel exec.; b. N.Y.C., Oct. 2, 1915; s. Julius and Lilian (Weissinger) M.; grad. Hackley Prep. Sch., Tarrytown, N.Y., 1935; L.H.D., Lafayette Coll., 1968; m. Marion G. Martin, June 15, 1940; children—Lilian Muir, William Carter, Jules Neville, Marion Bell, Philip Martin, Margery Bullitt, John Joseph. With Manger Corp., 1935-73, operating head, 1937-42, 45—, chmn. bd., 1948-73; pres. J & P Mgmt. Corp., 1976. Emeritus trustee Lafayette Coll., Easton, Pa.; hon. trustee Wilbraham (Mass.) and Monson Acad., 1967—; former trustee Wilson Coll., Chambersburg, Pa; bd. govs. Am. Bible Soc. Served as lt., aircraft carrier, USNR, 1942-45. Mem. SAR, Nat. Inst. Social Scis. Presbyterian (elder). Clubs: Field, Round Hill (Greenwich). Home: 33 Lismore Ln Greenwich CT 06830 Office: 25 3d St PO Box 3226 Stamford CT 06905

MANGES, HORACE S., lawyer; b. N.Y.C., July 20, 1898; s. Samuel F. and Alice (Bamberger) M.; A.B., Columbia, 1917, A.M., LL.B., 1919; m. Natalie Bloch, June 24, 1924; children—James H., Gerard H. Admitted to N.Y. bar, 1920, D.C. bar, 1953; partner firm Gleason, McLanahan, Merritt & Ingraham, 1924-26, Weil, Coursen & Manges, 1926-31; partner Weil, Gotshal & Manges, N.Y.C., 1931-76, counsel, 1976—; spl. asst. to atty. gen U.S., 1953-55; cons. to Librarian of Congress on Gen. Revision of U.S. Copyright Law; counsel Am. Book Pubs. Council, Inc.; former trustee, v.p., Copyright Soc. U.S.A. Govt. appeal agt. SSS, 1940-47. Trustee Mt. Sinai Hosp., N.Y.C., 1942-63. Fellow Am. Coll. Trial Lawyers; mem. Assn. Bar City N.Y. (exec. com. 1949-53, com. on grievances 1954-57, vice chmn. 1956-57, com. on judiciary 1943-48, 61-64), N.Y. County Lawyers Assn., Am. Bar Assn., Am. Arbitration Assn. (arbitrator, past dir.), Delta Sigma Rho, Pi Lambda Phi. Clubs: Century Assn., Univ. (N.Y.C.); Century Country (Purchase, N.Y.). Home: 936 Fifth Ave New York NY 10021 Office: 767 Fifth Ave New York NY 10022

MANGIONE, CHARLES FRANK, jazz musician, composer; b. Rochester, N.Y., Nov. 29, 1940; Mus.B. in Music Edn., Eastman Sch. Music, 1963; children—Nancy, Diana. Formed quintet with brother Gap, called Jazz Bros., 1958-64; played flugelhorn and trumpet with Mangione Bros., 1960-63; tchr. elem. sch. music, Rochester, 1 year; with bands led by Woody Herman, Kai Winding, Maynard Ferguson, 1964-65; with Art Blakey's Jazz Messengers, 1965-67; dir. Eastman Jazz Ensemble, mem. faculty Eastman Sch. Music, 1968-72; with Chuck Mangione Quartet, 1969—; composer sound track for movie The Children of Sanchez, 1978; compositions include: Hill Where the Lord Hides, Friends and Love, Lagacy, Feel of a Vision, El Gato Triste, Give It All You Got, You're The Best There Is, Pina Colada, I Never Missed Someone Before, But Slowly, Fun and Games; recs. include: Friends and Love, Land of Make Believe, Chase the Clouds Away, Feels So Good (past double platinum), An Evening of Magic, Fun and Games, Bellavia (Grammy award for best instrumentalist composition 1976), Children of Sanchez (Grammy award for best pop instrumental performance 1978); guest condr. Rochester Philharm. Orch., 1970; appeared with Oakland (Calif.), Edmonton (Alta., Can.), and Hamilton (Ont.) philharmonic orchs.; appeared at numerous festivals, including: Montreux, Newport, Concord, Monterey, Pescara (Italy), Pori (Finland), Kansas City, Niagara Falls; numerous TV appearances, including own TV spl., Live from Wolftrap, Public Broadcasting System, and Las Vegas Entertainer of the Yr. telecast. Named Most Promising Male Jazz Artist, Record World, 1975; named Jazz Artist of Yr., Instrumentalist of Yr., Most Promising Instrumentalist, Top Fusion Artist, Top Producer, Top Instrumentalist, Outstanding Jazz Artist; recipient Internat. Jazz award; Georgie award for instrumental act of yr. AGVA. Office: Gates Music 1 Marine Midland Plaza Suite 1635 Rochester NY 14604

MANGIONE, JERRE GERLANDO, author, educator; b. Rochester, N.Y., Mar. 20, 1909; s. Gaspare and Giuseppina (Polizzi) M.; B.A., Syracuse U., 1931; M.A. (hon.), U. Pa., 1971; m. Patricia Anthony, Feb. 18, 1957. Writer, Time mag., 1931; book editor Robert M. McBride & Co., N.Y.C., 1934-37; nat. coordinating editor Fed. Writers' Project, 1937-39; spl. asst. to U.S. commr. immigration and naturalization, 1942-48; advt. writer, pub. relations dir., 1948-61; mem. faculty U. Pa., 1961—, dir. writing program, 1965—, prof. English, 1968-77, emeritus, 1977—, acting dir. Italian Studies Center, 1978—; vis. lectr. Bryn Mawr Coll., 1966-67; vis. prof. Trinity Coll., Rome, summer 1973, Queens Coll., 1980; editor WFLN Phila. Guide, 1960-61; book reviewer, 1932—; adv. editor The Humanist, 1979—; judge Nat. Book award in fiction, 1968; adv. editor Italian Americana, 1974—. Chmn. lit. arts com. Phila. Art Alliance, 1958-61; mem. exec. bd. Am.-Italy Soc., 1959—, Inst. Contemporary Art, U. Pa., 1964—, Am. Inst. Italian Studies, 1975—. Pres. Friends Danilo Dolci, Inc., 1969-71; acting dir. Yaddo, 1977-78. Guggenheim fellow, 1945; Fulbright research fellow, 1965; MacDowell Colony fellow, Yaddo fellow; Rockefeller grantee, 1968; Am. Philos. Soc. grantee, 1971; Earhart Found. grantee, 1975; recipient Key to City Rochester, 1963, 10th ann. Lit. award Friends Rochester Pub. Library, 1966, Justinian Soc. award, 1966, Phila. Athenaeum Lit. award, 1973; named Person of Yr., Italian Ams. of Delaware County; decorated knight comdr. Order Star Solidarity (Italy), 1971. Fellow Soc. Am. Historians; mem. P.E.N., Authors Guild, AAUP, Phila. Art Alliance. Author: Mount Allegro, 1943; Ship and the Flame, 1948; Reunion in Sicily, 1950; Night Search, 1965; Life Sentences for Everybody, 1966; A Passion for Sicilians: The World Around Danilo Dolci, 1968; America is Also Italian, 1969; The Dream and the Deal: Federal Writers Project (1935-43), 1972; Mussolini's March on Rome, 1975; An Ethnic At Large: A Memoir of America in the Thirties and Forties, 1978. Contbr. to newspapers and mags. Home: 1901 Kennedy Blvd Apt 2404 Philadelphia PA 19103 Office: Dept English Univ Pa Philadelphia PA 19104

MANGO, WILFRED GILBERT, JR., fin. exec.; b. Weehawkin, N.J., July 11, 1940; s. Wilfred Gilbert and Mildred B. M.; B.S., Lehigh U., 1963; M.B.A., N.Y. U., 1969; m. Phyllis J. Dickson, Feb. 12, 1967; children—Christian P., Peter H. Auditor, Hurdman & Cranstown, N.Y.C., 1963-69; dir. fin. Thomas Crimmins Contracting Co., N.Y.C., 1969-77; v.p. fin. ITT Teleplant, Inc. and mgr. fin. controls ITT, N.Y.C., 1977-78; v.p. fin. George A. Fuller Co. div. Northrop Corp., N.Y.C., 1978—. Mem. Am. Soc. C.P.A's, N.Y. State Soc. C.P.A.'s. Clubs: Lehigh U. of Fairfield County; Tokeneke. Home: 15 Rocaton Rd Darien CT 06820 Office: 595 Madison Ave New York NY 10022

MANGONE, GERARD J., educator; b. N.Y.C., Oct. 10, 1918; s. Gerard Francis and Viola (Schumm) M.; A.B., Coll. City N.Y., 1938; M.A., Harvard, 1947, Ph.D. (Charles Summer prize), 1949; m. Emma Haddad, Apr. 13, 1958; children—Cleopatra, Regina, Flaminia. Asst. prof. polit. sci. Wesleyan U., Middletown, Conn., 1948-51; asso. prof. Swarthmore Coll., 1951-56; prof. polit. sci. and internat. relations Syracuse U., 1956-67, dir. grad. overseas tng. program, exec. officer Maxwell Center Study Overseas Operations, 1958-60, exec. asst. to dean Maxwell Grad. Sch., 1961-64, asso. dean dir. internat. relations program, 1961-67; dean Coll. Liberal Arts, v.p., provost Temple U., Phila., 1967-69; sr. fellow Woodrow Wilson Internat. Center, 1970-72; prof. internat. law U. Del., 1972—, dir. Center for Study Marine Policy, 1973—, H. Rodney Sharp prof. internat. law and orgn., 1975—, univ. coordinator grad. studies, 1976-79; vis. prof. Trinity Coll., Mt. Holyoke Coll., Yale, Princeton, Johns Hopkins; Tagore law prof. U. Calcutta, 1979. Mem. Presdl. Commn. Trust Territory Pacific, 1963; cons. AID, 1965-67, Nat. Commn. Marine Resources and Engrng. and State Dept., 1967—, UN, 1965; vice chmn. exec. com. Commn. Study Orgn. Peace; exec. dir. Pres.' Commn. on UN, 1970-71. Candidate for City Council, Middletown, 1950, for county comptroller Delaware County, Pa., 1952, for Congress, 1954. Served to capt. AUS, 1942-46. Mem. Am. Soc. Internat. Law, Internat. Law Assn., Internat. Studies Assn., AAAS. Club: Cosmos (Washington). Author several books including The Idea and Practice of World Government, 1951; A Short History of International Organization, 1954; The Elements of International Law, 2d edit., 1967; Marine Policy for America, 1977; co-author, editor several books including The Art of Overseasmanship, 1958; The Overseas Americans, 1960; European Political Systems, 1960; UN Administration of Economic and Social Programs, 1966; Energy Policies of the World, 3 vols., 1976-79; Internat. Straits of the World, 3 vols., 1978-79. Home: 201 Unami Trail Newark DE 19711 Office: Coll Marine Studies U Del Newark DE 19711

MANGOUNI, NORMAN, publisher; b. Detroit, Oct. 19, 1932; s. Nazareth Lazarus and Isabelle (Garabedian) M.; A.B., U. Mich., 1954; M.S., Columbia U., 1955; m. Anahid Apelian, May 10, 1964; 1 dau., Marie-Isabelle. Reporter, Ann Arbor (Mich.) News, 1957-59; editor Mich. Alumnus, U. Mich., Ann Arbor, 1959-62; sr. editor Coll. Entrance Exam. Bd., N.Y.C., 1962-64; dir. fin. aid U. Miami, Coral Gables, Fla., 1965-66; dir. State U. N.Y. Press, Albany, 1966-78; pres., gen. editor Scholars' Facsimiles & Reprints, Delmar, N.Y., 1972—; pres. Caravan Books, Delmar, 1972—; corr. DuPont-Columbia Survey and Awards, 1976-78; rep. to com. on standards in field of library work, documentation and related pub. practices Am. Nat. Standards Inst. 1974-78. Exec. asst. to majority caucus Mich. State Senate, 1964. Served to lt. USAF, 1955-57. Mem. Modern Lang. Assn., Middle East Studies Assn. N. Am., Nat. Assn. Armenian Studies and Research, Soc. Armenian Studies. Club: Univ. of Ann Arbor. Mem. Armenian Apostolic Ch. Co-translator: The Gaucho Martin Fierro, 1974; contbr. articles to profl. jours.; mem. editorial bd. Ararat mag., 1962-66, 77-78. Home: 33 Devon Rd Delmar NY 12054 Office: PO Box 344 Delmar NY 12054

MANGUAL, ARTHUR MYRON, hotel exec.; b. Lawrence, Kans., Nov. 5, 1932; s. Charles William and Helen (McGrath) M.; A.S., N.Y.C. Community Coll., 1955; m. Gloria Edith Romano, Aug. 28, 1955; children—Valerie, Douglas, Bruce, Brian. Mgr., Union News Co., Boston and N.Y.C., 1955-60; mgr., dir. ops. Win Schuler, Grand Haven, St. Joseph and Marshall, Mich., 1960-72; v.p., gen. mgr. Milw. Marriott, 1972-73; gen. mgr. Doubletree Inc., Seattle, 1973-74; v.p., gen. mgr. AIRCOA/Stouffer's, Denver Inn, Denver, 1975—. Bd. dirs. Metro State Coll. Served with USMC, 1951-52. Mem. Nat. Restaurant Assn., Am. Hotel and Motel Assn., Colo.-Wyo. Hotel Assn. (dir.). Roman Catholic. Clubs: Rotary, Elks. Home: 8824 E Fremont Circle Englewood CO 80112 Office: 3203 Quebec St Denver CO 80207

MANGUM, GARTH LEROY, economist; b. Delta, Utah, July 23, 1926; s. James L. and Golda (Elder) M.; B.S. Brigham Young U., 1956; M.P.A., Harvard, 1958, Ph.D., 1960; m. Marion Poll, Nov. 20, 1953; children—Stephen, David, Mary, Elizabeth. Instr. econs. Harvard, 1960; asso. prof. econs. Brigham Young U., 1960-63; sr. staff analyst Presdl. R.R. Commn., 1961; research dir., subcom. employment and manpower U.S. Senate, 1963-64; exec. dir. President's Com. Manpower, 1964-65; exec. sec. Nat. Com. Tech., Automation and Econ. Progress, 1965-66; research prof. econs. George Washington U., 1967-71, co-dir. Center Manpower Policy Studies, 1967-69; McGraw prof. econs., dir. Human Resources Inst., U. Utah, Salt Lake City, 1968—; lectr. U. Tel Aviv (Israel), 1969, Am. Seminar at Salzburg, 1975, U. South Africa, 1977; chmn. bd. Olympus Publishing Co. Spl. mediator Fed. Mediation and Conciliation Service, 1962-63; mem. Adv. Council Vocational Edn., 1966-67; vice chmn. Nat. Manpower Policy Task Force, 1966-69, chmn., 1969-71, mem., 1966-76; mem. Nat. Council on Employment Policy, 1976—, chmn., 1979—; chmn. Nat. Inst. Career Edn., 1976—; cons. fed., state and local govts., bus. firms, govts. of Saudi Arabia, Kuwait, Jordan, Yemen, Bahrain, United Arab Emirates, Indonesia, Yugoslavia and Romania; arbitrator Am. Arbitration Assn., Fed. Mediation and Conciliation Service. Ford Found. fellow, 1962-63, grantee, 1966-71. Mem. Am. Econ. Assn., Indsl. Relations Research Assn. (exec. bd. 1967-70), Phi Kappa Phi. Mem. Ch. of Jesus Christ of Latter-day Saints (missionary 1950-53, bishop 1971-78). Author: The Operating Engineers: Economic History of a Trade Union, 1964; MDTA, Foundation of Federal Manpower Policy, 1968; The Emergence of Manpower Policy, 1969: Federal Work and Training Program in the 1960's, 1969; Economic Opportunity in the Ghetto, 1970; Human Resources and Labor Markets, 1971; Career Education: What It Is and How To Do It, 1972; A Decade of Manpower Development and Training, 1973; Career Education and the Elementary School Teacher, 1973; Career Education in the Middle/Junior High School, 1973; Manpower Planning for Local Labor Markets, 1974; Career Education for the Academic Classroom, 1975; Employability, Employment and Income, 1976; Career Education in the High School, 1976; Your Child's Career, 1977; The Lingering Crisis of Youth Unemployment, 1978; Coming of Age in the Ghetto, 1978; Job Market Futurity, 1979; also articles, monographs. Editor: The Manpower Revolution: Its Policy Consequences, 1965; Automation and Economic Progress, 1966; Metropolitan Impact of Manpower Programs, 1973. Home: 4316 Adonis Dr Salt Lake City UT 84117

MANGUM, HARVEY KARL, lawyer; b. Pima, Ariz., Dec. 8, 1908; s. James Harve and Charlotte (Kempe) M.; A.B., Gila Coll., 1928; J.D., U. Ariz., 1931; m. Jessie Lee, June 23, 1934; children—Richard Karl, Linda Lee (Mrs. Thomas Bubaker). Admitted to Ariz. bar, 1931, since practiced in Flagstaff; county atty., Coconino County, 1932-38, 50-55; judge Superior Ct. Ariz. 1939-44; sr. partner firm Mangum, Wall, Stoops & Warden, 1946—. Dir. Ariz. Bank, Ariz. Title Guarantee & Trust Co. Served to lt. USNR, 1944-46. Fellow Am. Coll. Trial Lawyers; mem. Internat. Soc. Barristers, Ariz. Bar Assn. (bd. govs., pres. 1967-68). Mason (32 deg.), Elk (past exalted ruler). Home: 613 W Navajo Rd Flagstaff AZ 86001 Office: 222 E Birch Ave Flagstaff AZ 86001

MANHARD, PHILIP WALLACE, fgn. service officer; b. Cambridge, Mass., Nov. 13, 1921; B.A., U. So. Cal., 1943; m. Margaret Booth, 1953; children—Philip L., Virginia R., Richard K. Joined Fgn. Service, 1948; served Peking and Tienstsin, China, 1948-51, Pusan and Seoul, Korea, 1951-53, Tokyo, 1954-58, East Asia Bur., State Dept., Washington, 1959-62, 64-67; dep. polit. adviser Comdr. in Chief of Pacific, Honolulu, 1962-64; province sr. adviser, Hue, South Vietnam, 1967-68; prisoner of war, North Vietnam, 1968-73; mem. Sr. Seminar in Fgn. Policy, State Dept., 1973-74; ambassador to Mauritius, 1974-76; U.S. dep. rep. Micronesian Status Negotiations, 1976-77; sr. fellow Research Directorate, Nat. Def. U., 1977-78; vice chmn. bd. dirs. Presdl. Classroom for Young Ams., Washington, 1979—. Served with USNR, 1943-44, USMCR, 1944-46, 53. Recipient award for valor State Dept., 1973. Mem. Phi Beta Kappa. Address: care Dept State Washington DC 20520

MANHART, ROBERT AUDLEY, elec. engr.; b. Charleston, Ill., Oct. 5, 1925; s. Carl Robert and Christa Matyl (Beavers) M.; B.E.E., Rose Poly. Inst., 1945; M.S., U. Ill., 1947; Ph.D., Stanford U., 1961; m. Betty Jo Ange, July 2, 1949; children—Pamela Ann Manhart Hultberg, Craig Robert. Design engr. RCA, 1945-46; devel. engr. N. Am. Aviation Inc., 1947-48; head electronic dept., research and devel. div. N.Mex. Sch. Mines, 1948-50; servo engr. Bell Aircraft Corp., 1950-51; supr. Calif. Research & Devel. Co., 1951-54; research engr. Calif. Research Corp., 1954-55; asst. prof., then asso. prof. elec. engring. U. Ariz., 1955-58; asso. prof. Ariz. State U., 1959-61; prof. elec. engring., chmn. dept. U. Nev., Reno, 1961—; cons. Los Alamos Sci. Lab. Served with USNR, 1944. NSF sci. faculty fellow, 1958-59; registered profl. engr., Ariz., Nev. Sr. mem. IEEE; mem. Am. Soc. Engring. Edn., Nat. Soc. Profl. Engrs., Sigma Xi, Tau Beta Pi, Sigma Pi Sigma, Sigma Tau, Phi Kappa Phi. Patentee in field. Home: 2310 Mueller Dr Reno NV 89509

MANHEIM, EDWARD, advt. co. exec.; b. Cleve., Jan. 12, 1926; s. Harry Sol and Belle (Speiser) M.; B.A., Northwestern U., 1948; m. Suzanne Ellen Uberstine, Mar. 20, 1949; 1 son, Kenneth L. Vice pres. sales L. Manheim Fish Co., Cleve., 1948-59; v.p. Howard Marks Advt., Cleve., 1959-65, Marcus Advt., Cleve., 1965-72, exec. v.p., 1972-79; pres. Manheim Advt., Inc., 1979—; mem. pub. relations bd. Fedn. for Community Planning; keynote speaker Am. Drycleaners Conv., 1967. Bd. dirs. Bellefaire Foster Parents Program. Recipient Gold medal for Best of Show TV Spot, 1966; Drycleaning Advt. awards (9), internat. broadcasting award, 1970, 71, outstanding achievement award Nat. Acad. TV Arts and Scis., 1971; CLIO Radio award, 1976; Emmy award, 1976; N.Y. Film Festival award, 1979. Mem. Am. Advt. Fedn. (recipient 48 5th dist. awards), Cleve. Advt. Club. Jewish. Columnist Am. Dry Cleaner, 1966-67. Home: 28000 S Woodland Rd Cleveland OH 44124 Office: 23200 Chagrin Blvd Cleveland OH 44122

MANHEIM, ERNEST, educator; b. Budapest, Hungary, Jan. 27, 1900; s. Joseph and Hermin (Wengraf) M.; Ph.D., U. Leipzig (Germany), 1928, U. London (Eng.), 1937; m. Ann Sophy Vitters, Aug. 10, 1930; 1 son, Frank T. Came to U.S., 1937, naturalized, 1943. Lectr., U. Leipzig, 1929-33; asst. prof. sociology U. Chgo., 1937-38; mem. faculty U. Kansas City, 1938—, prof. sociology, 1948—, Henry Haskell prof., 1958—; Fulbright prof. Univs. Graz and Vienna, 1955-56, U. Tehran, 1960-61. Recipient Thomas Jefferson award U. Mo., 1973. Mem. Am. Sociol. Assn., Midwest Sociol. Soc. (pres. 1945-46), AAUP. Author: Die Trager der Offtlichen Meinung, 1933; Die Logik des Konkreten Begriffs, 1930; La Opinion Publica, 1936; Kansas City and its Neighborhoods, 1943; Youth in Trouble, 1945; Aufklärung und Offentliche Meinung, 1979; editor, translator: Karl Mannheim, Essays in the Sociology of Culture, 1956. Composer of a symphony, a quartet, a concerto. Home: 408 W 59th Terr Kansas City MO 64113

MANHEIM, MARVIN LEE, educator; b. Elizabeth, N.J., May 14, 1937; s. Isadore and Jean (Litin) M.; B.S., M.I.T., 1959, Ph.D. in Transp. and Urban Planning, 1964; m. Margaret Donovan, June 20, 1974; 1 dau., Susannah Leigh. Research asst. Joint Center for Urban Studies, M.I.T.-Harvard U., 1959-64; asst. prof. dept. civil engring. M.I.T., Cambridge, 1964-69, asso. prof., 1969-73, prof., 1973—, head transp. systems div., dept. civil engring., 1966-69, 78—), dir. tech. and community values project Center for Transp. Studies, 1968—; founding prin. Cambridge Systematics, Inc., 1972—; cons. to U.S. and fgn. govt. agys.; steering com. 4th World Conf. on Transp. Research. Served to capt. U.S. Army, 1964-66. Decorated Army Commendation medal; Samuel A. Stouffer fellow, 1962-64. Mem. Transp. Research Bd. (exec. com.), Transp. Research Forum, Internat. Wine and Food Soc. Jewish. Author: Fundamentals of Transportation Systems Analysis, vol. 1, 1979. Home: 1 Highland St Cambridge MA 02138 Office: MIT Cambridge MA 02139

MANHEIM, MICHAEL, educator; b. N.Y.C., Mar. 4, 1928; s. Leonard F. and Eleanor (Blackman) M.; B.A., Columbia, 1949, M.A., 1951, Ph.D., 1961; m. Martha Bradshaw, Mar. 6, 1955; children—James, Daniel. Instr. English, U. Del., Newark, 1953-61; asst. prof. English, U. Toledo (Ohio), 1961-63, asso. prof., 1963-67, prof. English, 1967—, asso. dean div. humanities, 1962-66, chmn. dept. English, 1966-72; vis. prof. Dartmouth, summer 1972; project dir. Nat. Endowment for Humanities; cons. WGTE-TV-FM, Toledo, 1976. Author: The Weak King Dilemma in the Shakespearean History Play, 1973. Mem. Midwest Modern Lang. Assn. (exec. com. 1976—). Contbr. articles and reviews to Renaissance Drama, Studies in English Lit., Shakespeare Studies, Studies in Philology. Home: 3426 Kirkwall Rd Toledo OH 43606

MANHEIM, PAUL ERNEST, investment banker; b. N.Y.C., June 16, 1905; s. Armin and Thersa (Quittner) M.; B.S., U. Va., 1925; m. Simone Gardner; children—Martha Green, Anthony, Emily Goldman. With A. Manheim & Co., N.Y.C., 1925, Dunbar Molasses Co., 1926; Am. consul, Brit. Guiana, 1927; ltd. partner Lehman Bros., N.Y.C.; dir. 1 William St. Fund, Gen. Sugar Estates, Cuban Sugar Plantations, Inc., Brascan, Ltd., Media Gen., Inc.; chmn. Vertientes Camaguey Sugar Co. Mem. art adv. com. Met. Mus., Boston Mus. Dartmouth, Notre Dame U. Trustee Bklyn. Mus.; bd. sponsors U. Va. Grad. Sch. Bus. Home: 2 E 67th St New York City NY 10021 Office: 1 William St New York City NY 10004

MANIER, MILLER, lawyer; b. Nashville, Jan. 15, 1897; s. Will Rucker and Mary (Owsley) M.; B.S., Vanderbilt U., 1917, LL.B., 1920; grad. U.S. Army Sch. Mil. Aeros., U. Tex., 1918; m. Ada Childers, Mar. 8, 1956. Admitted to Tenn. bar, 1919; asso., later partner Manier & Crouch, Nashville, 1919-48; partner firm Manier, White, Herod, Hollabaugh & Smith, and predecessors, 1948—; instr. Nashville YMCA Night Law Sch., 1924-53. Mem. Davidson County bd. Tenn. War Price and Rationing Bd., 1941-42. Mem. Uniform Law Commn. Tenn., 1940-60. Served as pfc. (flying cadet) A.S. Aeronautics, U.S. Army, 1917-18; from lt. to lt. comdr. USNR, 1942-52; active duty PTO, 1944-45. Recipient Presdl. certificate, Tenn. certificate for services Registration Day, 1940; H. Laird Smith Alumni award Nashville chpt. Phi Delta Theta Alumni Club, 1972. Fellow Internat. Acad. Trial Lawyers; mem. Am., Tenn. (life mem., chmn. ins. sec. 1957-58), Nashville (50-Yr. award 1970), Inter-Am. bar assns., Internat. Ins. Counsel Assn., Am. Judicature Soc., Vets. World War I of U.S.A., Assn. Ins. Attys. (gov. Tenn., exec. com 1953-58, pres. 1956-57), Probate Attys. Assn. (pres. 1956-57, exec. com., 1955-58, chmn. bd., 1958), Comml. Law League Am. (life), Law Sci. Acad. (diplomate), Am. Coll. Trial Lawyers, C. of C., Nat. Conf. Uniform Law Commrs. (life), SAR, VFW, Retreads, Inc., Am. Coll. Probate Counsel (pres. 1957-59, bd. regents 1960-67), Am. Legion (adj. Davidson County post 1919-22, Golden certificate 1973), 40 and 8, Scribes, Phi Delta Phi (internat. pres. 1927-29, mem. ct. appeals, 1929-39), Phi Delta Theta (past pres. Gamma province, mem. survey commn.). Methodist (chmn. bd. stewards 1946-48, mem. ofcl. bd. 1924—, now trustee). Clubs: Rotary (50 yr. button), Elks, Cumberland (Nashville). Asso. editor Ins. Counsel Jour., 1947-57. Home: 1868 Laurel Ridge Dr Nashville TN 37215 Office: 7th Floor Home Fed Tower 230 4th Ave N Nashville TN 37219

MANIGAULT, PETER, newspaper publisher; b. Charleston, S.C., Jan. 13, 1927; s. Edward and Mary (Hamilton) M.; A.B., Princeton, 1950; m. Landine Sanford Legendre, Aug. 8, 1959 (div.); children—Gabrielle, Pierre. With Eve. Post Pub. Co. and subsidiaries, Charleston, 1950—, pres., pub. 1960—. Trustee Nat. Trust Historic Preservation, 1963, vice chmn., 1965-74. Served with USNR, 1945-46, 52-53; capt. Res. Decorated Legion of Merit with combat V; Order Mil. Merit (Republic Korea). Mem. Nat. Audubon Soc. (dir. 1968-74). Office: 134 Columbus St Charleston SC 29403

MANILOW, LEWIS, lawyer; b. Chgo., Aug. 11, 1927; s. Nathan and Minnie (Vihon) M.; Ph.B., U. Chgo., 1948; LL.B., Harvard U., 1951; m. Mar. 22, 1973; children—Karen, David, John. Admitted to Ill. bar, 1951; asst. states atty. Cook County (Ill.) Criminal Br., 1952-56; sr. partner firm Epstein, Manilow & Sachnoff and predecessor, Chgo., 1956-69; pres. Park Forest South Devel. Co. (Ill.), 1969-75; partner firm Devoe, Shadur & Krupp, Chgo., 1976—; chmn. bd. Heritage Bank of Park Forest South; chmn. League New Community Developers, 1972-74. Pres., Mus. Contemporary Art, Chgo.; mem. Northeastern Ill. Planning Commn., 1974-78; mem. adv. commn. U.S. Internat. Communication Agy.; bd. dirs. Better Govt. Assn., Chgo., Trust, Inc., Chgo., Beaubourg Found., Inc., N.Y.C. Mem. Chgo. Bar Assn., Am. Bar Assn., Art Inst. Chgo. (governing life), Lambda Alpha. Office: 208 S LaSalle St Room 1200 Chicago IL 60604

MANINGS, ALLAN S., writer; b. Newark, Mar. 28, 1924; s. Irving and Dora (Silver) M.; B.A., Sarah Lawrence Coll., 1948; grad. Neighborhood Playhouse, Am. Theatre Wing, 1950; m. Whitney Blake, Aug. 23, 1968. Writer for TV, stage and films in U.S., Can. and Eng., 1952—; Broadway prodns. include New Faces, 1956, Littlest Revue, 1956, Evelyn, 1964; head writer Laugh-In, 1968-71, Lily Tomlin Show, 1973, Helen Reddy Show, 1973; head writer, producer David Frost Revue, 1971-72; exec. producer TV series Good Times, 1973-76; co-creator, producer TV series One Day At A Time, 1976—; writer Freestyle, 1978, Not a Penny More . . . Not a Penny Less, 1978; producer Suitcase Full of Dreams, 1978-79, I Won't Take No For An Answer, 1978-79; writer, producer Open House. Tchr. summer session creative writing Okanagan Sch. Arts, 1967. Served with USAAF, World War II. Recipient Silver Rose award Montreaux TV Film Festival, 1963; Emmy award Acad. TV Arts and Scis., 1968; award NAACP, 1974, Am. Heart Assn., 1975. Mem. Writers Guild Am. (dir. West. sect. 1974-75, v.p. West sect. 1975-77, dir. 1977-79, dir. found. 1978). Home: 510 Arkell Dr Beverly Hills CA 90210 Office: Paramount Pictures 5451 Marathon St Hollywood CA 90038

MANION, CLARENCE E., lawyer; b. Henderson, Ky., July 7, 1896; s. Edward and Elizabeth (Carroll) M.; A.B., St. Mary's (Ky.) Coll., 1915; A.M., Ph.M., Cath. U. Am., 1917; J.D., Notre Dame U., 1922; J.U.D., Boston U., 1942; m. Virginia O'Brien, Aug. 3, 1936; children—Marilyn, Carolyn, Daniel, Diana, Christopher. Tchr. history and govt. U. Notre Dame, 1919; admitted to Ind. bar, 1922; practice in Evansville, until 1925; prof. constl. law U. Notre Dame, 1925-52, dean Coll. Law, 1941-52; mem. firm Doran, Manion, Boynton & Kamm, South Bend; dir. Manion Forum radio network, St. Joseph Bank & Trust Co., South Bend. Pres. Commn. on Intergovtl. Relations. Mem. Ind. Bd. Edn., 1956-60. Recipient 3d ann. Notre Dame Faculty award, 1950; Nat. Gold Medal award D.A.R., 1974; Nat. Man of Year award Am. Religious Town Hall Meeting, Inc., 1979. Mem. Am., Ind., St. Joseph County bar assns., Am. Legion. K.C. Club: Indianapolis Athletic. Author: American History, 1926; What Price Prohibition, 1927; Liberty and the Police Power, 1928; Catholics in Our Country's Story, 1929; Lessons in Liberty, 1939; Cases and Materials on the Law of the Air, 1950; The Key to Peace; Let's Face It, 1956; The Conservative American, 1964; Cancer in the Constitution, 1972. Home: Laurel Rd South Bend IN 46637 Office: St Joseph Bank Bldg South Bend IN 46601 Died July 28, 1979.

MANION, JOHN JOSEPH, JR., pub. co. exec.; b. Phila., July 24, 1929; s. John Joseph and Catherine (Horan) M.; B.S., St. Joseph's Coll., Phila., 1953; m. Patricia Ann Igoe, Feb. 3, 1951; children—Dennis, Maureen, Francis, John Joseph III, Michael, Christine. Sr. auditor firm Stauffer, Bunn & Chambers, C.P.A.'s, Phila., 1953-60; controller computer div. Philco, Willow Grove, Pa., 1960-63; mem. central finance staff Ford Motor Co., Dearborn, Mich., 1964-66; asst. corp. controller C.B.S. Inc., N.Y.C., 1966-70, v.p. tech. group planning, 1971-72, v.p., treas., 1973-75, v.p., controller, 1975, v.p. devel., 1976—. Mem. Pa. Inst. C.P.A.'s. Roman Catholic. Home: 920 Fernwood Rd Moorestown NJ 08057 Office: WB Saunders Co W Washington Sq Philadelphia PA 19105

MANIRE, GEORGE PHILIP, educator, bacteriologist; b. Roanoke, Tex., Mar. 25, 1919; s. Ernest L. and Zera (Ballew) M.; B.S., N. Tex. State Coll., 1940, M.S., 1941; Ph.D., U. Calif. at Berkeley, 1949; m. Ruth Jacobs, Apr. 10, 1943; children—Sarah, Philip. Instr., Southwestern Med. Sch., U. Tex., Dallas, 1949-50; mem. faculty U. N.C. Med. Sch., Chapel Hill, 1950—, prof. bacteriology and immunology, 1959—, asst. vice chancellor health affairs, 1965-66, chmn. dept., 1966-76, Kenan prof., 1971—, vice chancellor, dean grad. sch., 1979—; vis. scientist Lister Inst., London, Eng., 1971-72. Fulbright Research scholar Statens Seruminstut, Copenhagen, Denmark, 1956; Alan Gregg Travel Fellow in med. edn. China Med. Bd., 1963-64; vis. prof. Inst. for Virus Research, Kyoto (Japan) U., 1963-64. Club: Cosmos (Washington). Research, publs. on chem. biol. and structural characteristics of chlamydial, microbial pathogenesis. Home: PO Box 41 Bynum NC 27228

MANIRE, JAMES MCDONNELL, lawyer; b. Memphis, Feb. 22, 1918; s. Clarence Herbert and Elizabeth (McDonnell) M.; LL.B., U. Va., 1948; m. Nathalie Davant Latham, Nov. 21, 1951 (div. Jan. 1979); children—James McDonnell, Michael Latham, Nathalie Latham. Admitted to Tenn. bar, 1948, since practiced in Memphis; partner firm Manire & Pemberton, 1956—; city atty. Memphis, 1968-71. Served to lt. comdr. USNR, 1941-46. Fellow Am. Coll. Trial Lawyers, Am. Bar Found.; mem. Am., Tenn. (pres. 1966-67), Memphis and Shelby County (pres. 1963-64) bar assns. Clubs: Memphis Country, Hunt and Polo (Memphis). Editor-in-chief Va. Law Rev., 1947-48. Home: 443 Perkins Rd S Memphis TN 38117 Office: 1195 Poplar Ave Memphis TN 38105

MANISCHEWITZ, BERNARD, corp. exec.; b. Cin., Dec. 24, 1913; s. Jacob U. and Pearl (Quitman) M.; certificate in factory mgmt., U. Cin., 1940; B.C.S., N.Y.U., 1944; m. Esther Manischewitz, July 19, 1932 (div.); children—Elaine (Mrs. Yehiel Sorki), Ruby (Mrs. Yitzchok Gass), Edith E. (Mrs. Howard Best); m. 2d, Beatrice Hoffman, Apr. 11, 1976. Asst. supt. B. Manischewitz Co., 1934-42, dir., sec., 1942-49, pres., 1949-76, chmn. bd., 1976-78, chmn. exec. com. and chief exec. officer, 1978—. Ofcl. del. 7th-11th Internat. Mgmt. Congresses. Chmn. Manhattan div. State of Israel Bonds, 1960-61. Mem. Chief Execs. Forum, Inc. Home: 2 Greenwood Ave West Orange NJ 07052 Office: 340 Henderson St Jersey City NJ 07302

MANKIEWICZ, DON M(ARTIN), writer; b. Berlin, Germany, Jan. 20, 1922 (parents U.S. citizens); s. Herman J. and Sara (Aaronson) M.; B.A., Columbia, 1942, student Law Sch., 1942; m. Ilene Korsen, 1946 (div.); children—Jane, John; m. 2d, Carol Bell Guidi, July 1, 1972; children—Jan, Sandy. Reporter, New Yorker mag., 1946-48; free-lance writer, 1948—; instr. N.Y.U. Inst. Film and TV, 1969. Democratic-Liberal candidate for N.Y. State Assembly, 1952; vice chmn. Nassau County (N.Y.) Dem. Com., 1953-72; Dem. town leader, Oyster Bay, N.Y., 1960-61; charter mem. E. Norwich (N.Y.) Dem. Club; del. N.Y. State Constl. Conv., 1967. Served with AUS, 1942-46; ETO. Mem. Writers Guild Am. East, TV Acad. Arts and Scis. (bd. govs. N.Y. chpt. 1968-72), Producers Guild Am. Author: (novels) See How They Run, 1950; Trial (Harper prize), 1955; It Only Hurts A Minute, 1966; also numerous articles, short stories; TV plays include Playhouse 90, Studio One; TV pilot scripts: Ironside, Marcus Welby, M.D.; motion picture scripts include Trial, 1955; I Want to Live, 1959. Home and office: Box 122 Sea Cliff NY 11579

MANKIEWICZ, FRANK FABIAN, pub. broadcasting exec., journalist; b. N.Y.C., May 16, 1924; s. Herman J. and Sara (Aaronson) M.; A.B., U. Calif. at Los Angeles, 1947; M.S., Columbia, 1948; LL.B., U. Calif. at Berkeley, 1955; m. Holly Jolley, Apr. 23, 1952; children—Joshua, Benjamin. Engaged in journalism in Washington and Los Angeles, 1948-52; admitted to Calif. bar, 1955; practice in Beverly Hills, 1955-61; dir. Peace Corps in Lima, Peru, 1962-64; Latin Am. regional dir. for Peace Corps, Washington, 1964-66; press sec. Senator Robert F. Kennnedy, 1966-68; syndicated columnist and TV news commentator, 1968-71; nat. polit. dir. Presdl. campaign of Senator George McGovern, 1971-72; columnist Washington Post, 1976-77; pres. Nat. Pub. Radio, 1977—. Democratic candidate for Calif. Legislature, 1950. Served with inf., AUS, 1943-46. Mem. State Bar Calif. Author: Perfectly Clear: Nixon from Whittier to Watergate, 1973; U.S. v. Richard M. Nixon: The Final Crisis, 1974; With Fidel: A Portrait of Castro and Cuba, 1975; Remote Control, Television and the Manipulation of American Life, 1977. Contbr. articles to newspapers and mags. Office: Nat Public Radio 2025 M St NW Washington DC 20036

MANKIEWICZ, JOSEPH LEO, writer, dir.; b. Wilkes-Barre, Pa., Feb. 11, 1909; s. Frank and Johanna (Blumenau) M.; A.B., Columbia, 1928; m. Rosa Stradner, July 28, 1939; (dec. 1958); children—Eric (by previous marriage), Christopher, Thomas; m. 3d, Rosemary Matthews, 1962; 1 dau., Alexandra. Writer, dir., producer motion pictures, 1929—, including: Skippy, 1930, If I Had a Million, 1931, Million Dollar Legs, 1932, Manhattan Melodrama, 1934, Fury, 1936, Three Comrades, 1937, Philadelphia Story, 1939, Woman of the Year, 1940, Keys of the Kingdom, 1944, A Letter to Three Wives, 1948, No Way Out, 1950, All About Eve, 1950, 5 Fingers, 1951, Julius Caesar, 1952, Guys and Dolls, 1954; dir. La Boheme, Met. Opera, 1952; formed Figaro, Inc., 1952; author screen play, dir. The Barefoot Contessa, also The Quiet American produced by Figaro, Inc.; dir. Suddenly Last Summer, 1959, There Was A Crooked Man, 1969, Sleuth, 1972; writer, dir. The Honey Pot, 1965. Recipient Screen Dirs. Guild Ann. award for directorial achievement, 1949, 50; Screen Writers Guild Ann. award for best Am. comedy, 1949, 50; Acad. Motion Picture Arts and Scis. first award for direction and first award for screen play, 1950, 51; comdr. Order Merit Italian Republic for contbn. to arts, 1965; asso. fellow Yale U., 1979—. Mem. Screen Dirs. Guild Am. (pres. 1950). Author: All About Eve, a screenplay, 1951; More About All About Eve, a colloquy, 1972. Club: Bedford Golf & Tennis. Address: RFD 1 Box 121 Bedford NY 10506

MANKIN, CHARLES JOHN, educator; b. Dallas, Jan. 15, 1932; s. Green and Myla Carolyn (Bohmert) M.; student U. N.Mex., 1949-50; B.S., U. Tex. at Austin, 1954, M.A., 1955, Ph.D., 1958; m. Mildred Helen Hahn, Sept. 6, 1953; children—Sally Carol, Helen Francis, Laura Kay. Asst. prof. geology Calif. Inst. Tech., 1958-59; asst. prof. geology U. Okla., 1959-63, asso. prof., 1963-66, prof., 1966—, dir. Sch. Geology and Geophysics, 1964-77, also dir. Energy Resources Center; mem. U.S. Nat. Commn. on Geology, 1977—. Dir. Okla. Geol. Survey, 1967—; Vice chmn. bd. mineral and energy resources, mem. commn. on natural resources Nat. Acad. Scis. Fellow Geol. Soc. Am., Mineral. Soc. Am.; mem. Am. Assn. Petroleum Geologists, Assn. Profl. Geol. Scientists, Clay Minerals Soc., Geochem. Soc., AAAS, Assn. Am. State Geologists (past pres.), Am. Geol. Inst. (past pres.), Soc. Econ. Paleontologists and Mineralogists, Sigma Gamma Epsilon (nat. sec.-treas.). Contbr. articles profl. jours. Home: 2220 Forister Ct Norman OK 73069

MANKIN, HART TILLER, lawyer; b. Cleve., Dec. 26, 1933; s. Howard Edmonn and Fantine (Tiller) M.; student Northwestern U., 1950-52; B.A., U. South, 1954; J.D., U. Houston, 1960; m. Ruth A. Larson, Aug. 14, 1954; children—Margaret, Theodore, Susan. Admitted to Tex. bar, 1960, U.S. Supreme Ct. bar, 1968, D.C. bar, 1971; individual practice law, Houston, 1960-67; counsel, asst. to pres. Triumph Industries, Houston, 1967-69; gen. counsel GSA, Washington, 1969-71, Dept. Navy, Washington, 1971-73; v.p., gen. counsel Columbia Gas System, Wilmington, Del., 1973—; dir. Del. Trust Co. Bd. dirs. Com. of 100, Del. Law Sch., Del. Humanities Council, Grand Opera House, Inc. Served with USAF, 1954-57. Recipient spl. achievement award GSA, 1970, Disting. Pub. Service award Dept. Navy, 1973. Mem. State Bar Tex., D.C. Bar Assn., Del. Bar Assn., Am. Bar Assn., Fed. Bar Assn., Fed. Energy Bar Assn., Maritime Law Assn., U.S., Del. C. of C. (dir.). Episcopalian. Clubs: Greenville Country, Univ., Whist. Home: 1101 Westover Rd Wilmington DE 19807 Office: 20 Montchanin Rd Wilmington DE 19807

MANKIN, HENRY JAY, physician; b. Pitts., Oct. 9, 1928; s. Hyman Isaac and Mary (Simons) M.; B.S. magna cum laude, U. Pitts., 1952, M.D., 1953; M.A. (hon.), Harvard, 1973; m. Carole Jane Pinkney, Aug. 20, 1952; children—Allison Joan, David Philip, Keith Pinkney. Intern U. Chgo. Clinics, 1953-54; resident orthopaedics Hosp. for Joint Diseases, N.Y.C., 1957-60; instr. orthopaedics U. Pitts. Sch. Medicine, 1960-62, asst. prof., 1962-64, asso. prof., 1964-66; dir., prof. orthopaedics Hosp. for Joint Diseases and Mt. Sinai Sch. Medicine, 1966-72; chief orthopaedics Mass. Gen. Hosp., Boston, 1972—; Edith M. Ashley prof. orthopaedics Harvard Med. Sch., 1972—; Mem. surgery B study sect. NIH, 1969-73; mem. adv. com. on surg. treatment FDA, 1973-75; bd. dirs., awards com. John Polachek Found., N.Y.C. Served to lt. comdr. USNR, 1955-57. Diplomate Am. Bd. Orthopaedic Surgery (mem. bd. 1976—). Fellow A.C.S.; mem. Am. Acad. Orthopaedic Surgeons, Am. Orthopaedic Assn., Orthopaedic Research Soc. (pres. 1969-70), N.Y. Acad. Medicine (chmn. orthopaedic sect. 1971-72), Am. Rheumatism Assn., SICOT, Hip Soc., Interurban, Forum orthopaedic clubs. Asso. editor Arthritis and Rheumatism, 1967-77, Jour. Bone and Joint Surgery, 1967—. Contbr. numerous articles to profl., med. jours. Home: 185 Dean Rd Brookline MA 02146 Office: Dept Orthopaedic Surgery Mass Gen Hosp Boston MA 02114

MANKOFF, RONALD MORTON, lawyer; b. Gettysburg, S.D., Oct. 13, 1931; s. Harry B. and Sarah (Frank) M.; B.S.L., U. Minn., 1952, J.D., 1954; LL.M. in Taxation, N.Y. U., 1959; m. Joy Faith Shechtman, Nov. 3, 1959; children—Jeffrey Walker, Douglas Frank. Admitted to Minn. bar, 1954, Tex. bar, 1959; with firm Leonard, Street & Deinard, Mpls., 1957-58, Lyne, Blanchette, Smith & Shelton, Dallas, 1959-60; partner firm Durant, Mankoff, Davis, Wolens & Francis, Dallas, 1960—; lectr. law So. Methodist U. Sch. Law, 1974-77; columnist Dallas-Fort Worth Bus.; dir. Allen Publs. of Tex., Inc. Chmn. bd. Dallas chpt. Am. Cancer Soc., 1976-77, chmn. Dallas crusade, 1974-75, bd. dirs., mem. exec. com., 1963—; mem. bd. Dallas Municipal Library, 1973-75; exec. com. Dallas Citizens Charter Assn., 1971-75; pres. Dallas Arts Found., Inc., 1973-75; mem. exec. com. Nat. Pooled Income Fund, Council Jewish Welfare Fedns. and Funds, 1975-77; adv. dir. Dallas Community Chest Trust Fund; chmn. found. Dallas Jewish Fedn., 1976-77; pres. Temple Emanuel, Dallas, 1977-79; bd. dirs. Jewish Fedn. Greater Dallas, 1977—, Union Am. Hebrew Congregations, 1978—. Served to lt. (j.g.) USNR, 1954-57. Mem. Am., Tex., Dallas bar assns., State Bar Tex., Zeta Beta Tau, Delta Sigma Rho. Democrat. Clubs: Columbia Country (bd. govs.), City, Chandlers Landing Yacht (Dallas). Contbr. legal jours. Home: 5839 Colhurst St Dallas TX 75230 Office: 3900 First Nat Bank Bldg Dallas TX 75202

MANKOWSKI, BRUNO, sculptor; b. Germany, Oct. 30, 1902; s. Tadeusz and Emily (Kaselow) M.; student Municipal and State Art Schs., Berlin, Beaux Arts Inst., N.Y.C.; came to U.S., 1928, naturalized, 1933. Works exhibited Corcoran Gallery, 1935, 39, N.A.D., 1940, 42, 46-49, Met. Mus., 1942, Pa. Acad. Fine Arts, 1947-49, Montclair Art Mus., Internat. Exhbn. Sculpture, Phila., 1949, Nat. Sculpture Soc., Syracuse Mus. Fine Arts, Pa. Mus., Am. Acad. Arts and Letters; one-man shows: Philbrook Art Center, Tulsa, Archtl. League, 1948, Garden Club of Am., 1948-49; sculpture in U.S. Post Office and Agrl. Bldg., Chesterfield, S.C., S.S. Independence, S.S. Constitution, Met. Museum, N.Y. World's Fair, Macomb Jr. High Sch., N.Y. carvings Mich. State Coll., U.S. Capitol, War Monument, Poly. Inst., Blacksburg, Va., Loyola Sem., Shrub Oak, N.Y., Mus. Sztuki Medalierskie, Wroclaw, Poland, Brookgreen Gardens Permanent Sculpture Collection; Pres. James F. Oates Junior portrait medal for Equitable Life Assurance Soc., Am. Folklore Medal 79th issue Soc. Medalists, 1969, Franklin D. Roosevelt commemorative medal Nat. Commemorative Soc., 1967, Asa Gray Medal for Hall of Fame for Gt. Americans, N.Y. U., 1972, Leonard Stone portrait bust; carved reconstructed marble pediment main entrance of the Capitol, Washington. Served with AUS, 1942-45. Recipient award for superior craftsmanship N.Y. Bldg. Congress, 1937; best work of art N.J. State Exhbn., Montclair Mus., 1945; citation N.Y. City Golden Anniversary Medals competition, 1948; sculpture prize 14th Nat. Ceramics Exhbn., Syracuse Mus. Fine Arts, 1949; 1st prize Medallic Art Co., 50th Anniversary medal competition, 1949; grant in recognition creative works in art Nat. Inst. and Acad. Arts and Letters, 1950; Louis Bennet prize Nat. Sculpture Soc., 1953; 2d prize Am. Artists Profl. League, 1955, 1st prize, 1956; 1st prize Arts and Crafts Assn., Meridan, Conn., 1956; Lindsay Morris Meml. prize, Allied Artists Am., 1960; J. Sanford Saltus Silver Medal award for medallic excellence, Am. Numismatic Soc.; Daniel Chester French award Allied Artists Am., 1964, Herbert Adams meml. medal Nat. Sculpture Soc., 1972, Bas Relief prize Allied Artist Am., 1970. Fellow Nat. Sculpture Soc. (mem. council 1970—, Silver medal Bicentennial Exhbn. 1976, Gold medal 1978, Lindsey Morris Meml. award for excellence in medallic art 1978), Allied Artists (Gold medal 1978), Am. Numis. Soc. (life), Am. Artists Profl. League. Works reproduced Sculpture in Modern America, 1948. Address: 16 Windsor Ave Scarborough ON M1N 1A7 Canada

MANLEY, ALBERT EDWARD, ret. coll. pres.; b. San Pedro Sula, Spanish Honduras, Jan. 3, 1908; s. Wilfred and Anita (Derwin) M.; came to U.S., 1919, naturalized, 1939; B.S., Johnson C. Smith U., 1930; M.A., Columbia Tchrs. Coll., 1938; student U. Chgo., 1942; Ed.D., Stanford, 1946; LL.D., Johnson C. Smith U., 1966; m. Dorothy Shepard, Mar. 8, 1943 (dec.); m. 2d, Audrey Elaine Forbes, Apr. 3, 1970. Tchr. Stephens-Lee High Sch., Asheville, N.C., 1931-34, prin., 1935-41; supr. Negro high schs., N.C., 1941-45; dean Coll. Arts and Scis., prof. edn. N.C. Coll., Durham, 1946-53; pres. Spelman Coll., Atlanta, 1953-76, pres. emeritus, 1976—. Mem. N.C. Commn. Interracial Cooperation; 1941-49, also mem. Ga. Commn. Interracial Cooperation; pres. N.C. Coll. Conf., 1950; chmn. council of presidents Atlanta Univ. Center, also Univ. Center in Ga. Bd. dirs. United Negro Coll. Fund, Altanta High Mus. Art; trustee Atlanta U., chmn. Gallaway Recipient Alumni citation Johnson C. Smith U., 1950. Mem. N.E.A., Am. Tchrs. Assn., Internat. Speakers platform, Phi

Delta Kappa Omega Psi Phi. Contbr. articles to ednl. jours. Home: 2807 18th St NW Washington DC 20009

MANLEY, FRANK, educator; b. Scranton, Pa., Nov. 13, 1930; s. Aloysius F. and Kathryn L. (Needham) M.; B.A., Emory U., 1952, M.A., 1953; Ph.D., Johns Hopkins U., 1959; m. Carolyn Mary Holliday, Mar. 14, 1952; children—Evelyn, Mary. Instr., then asst. prof. Yale U., New Haven, 1959-64; asso. prof., then prof. dept. English, Emory U., Atlanta, 1964—, chmn. dept., 1968-70. Served with U.S. Army, 1952-55. Guggenheim Found. fellow, 1966-67, 78-79; Am. Inst. Pakistan Studies fellow, 1979-80. Mem. MLA, AAUP. Roman Catholic. Editor: The Anniversaries (John Donne), 1963; A Dialogue of Comfort (St. Thomas More), vol. 12 Yale edit. More's complete works, 1977. Home: Route 5 Box 228 Ellijay GA 30540 Office: Dept English Emory U Atlanta GA 30322

MANLEY, HAROLD WHEATLEY, oil and gas co. exec.; b. Chanute, Kans., Aug. 26, 1905; s. Bert John and Viola (Wheatley) M.; B.M.E., Okla. State U., 1929; m. Barbara Louise Schooler, Sept. 18, 1929; children—Jeanne Manley Hines, Beverly Manley Bowman. With Barnsdall Oil Co., Tulsa, 1929-50; v.p. Sunray Oil Corp., Tulsa, 1950-53; ind. oil producer, drilling contractor, Tulsa, 1953-56; v.p. oil and gas div. Jefferson Lake Sulphur Co., 1956-64; v.p., mng. dir. Jefferson Lake Petrochems. of Can., Ltd., 1958-60, pres., mng. dir., 1962-68; pres. Petrogas Processing, Ltd., 1960-68; chmn. bd. dirs. Cansulex Ltd., Calgary, Alta., Can., 1965-68; pres. Manbar Corp., 1968—. Registered profl. engr., Okla., Province Alta. Mem. Nat., Okla., Alta. socs. profl. engrs., Am. Inst. Mining and Metallurgy, Inst. Mining and Metallurgy. Presbyterian. Club: Masons. Home: 5534 E 61st Pl Tulsa OK 74136

MANLEY, HARRY STOCKWELL, coll. adminstr.; b. Oil City, Pa., Apr. 10, 1920; s. Frank Eugene and Frances (Peterson) M.; B.A., Westminster Coll., 1942, LL.D. (hon.), 1966; LL.B., U. Pitts., 1945; Ph.D., Duke, 1955; m. Carolyn B. Hamilton, June 12, 1948; children—Melinda Ann, Martha Carol, Judith Lynn. Asst. prof. polit. sci. Westminster Coll., 1945-52; prof. polit. sci., head dept. Millsaps Coll., Jackson, Miss., 1955-60; dep. staff dir. Ill. Commn. Higher Edn., 1960-61; acad. dean Monmouth (Ill.) Coll., 1961-65; pres. Muskingum Coll., New Concord, Ohio, 1965-70; asst. to chancellor U. N.C. at Greensboro, 1970-71; provost, v.p. acad. affairs Willamette U., 1971-74, v.p. devel., 1974—. Mem. N. Central Assn. Colls. and Secondary Schs., Am. Polit. Sci. Assn., Am. Inst. Banking, Alpha Sigma Phi. Home: 3485 Balsam Dr S Salem OR 97302

MANLEY, JOAN A. DANIELS, publisher; b. San Luis Obispo, Calif., Sept. 23, 1932; d. Carl and Della (Weinmann) Daniels; B.A., U. Calif. at Berkeley, 1954; D.B.A. (hon.), U. New Haven, 1974; LL.D. (hon.), Babson Coll., 1978; m. Jeremy C. Lanning, Mar. 17, 1956 (div. Sept. 1963); m. 2d, Donald H. Manley, Sept. 12, 1964. Sec., Doubleday & Co., Inc., N.Y.C., 1954-60; sales exec. Time Inc., 1960-66, v.p., 1971-75, group v.p., 1975—, also dir.; circulation dir. Time-Life Books, 1966-68, dir. sales, 1968-70, pub., 1970-76; chmn. bd. Time-Life Books Inc., 1976—, Alva Mus. Replicas, Inc., Pacifica Ltd. (Tokyo); alt. dir. Orgn. Editorial Novaro S.A. (Mexico City); chmn. bd. Book-of-the-Month Club, Inc., N.Y.C.; supervising dir. Time-Life Internat. (Nederland) B.V., Amsterdam; chmn. bd., dir. N.Y. Graphic Soc.; dir. Little Brown & Co., Boston, Edits. Robert Laffont, Paris; adv. bd. Center for the Book. Trustee Bennington Coll., Babson Coll.; adv. council Stanford U. Bus. Sch. Mem. Assn. Am. Pubs. (past chmn.), Direct Mail Mktg. Assn. (past dir.). Clubs: Publishers Lunch, Hemisphere; Belle Haven Country (Alexandria, Va.). Office: Time and Life Bldg Rockefeller Center New York NY 10020

MANLEY, JOHN FREDERICK, polit. scientist; b. Utica, N.Y., Feb. 20, 1939; s. John A. and Gertrude M.; B.S., Le Moyne Coll., 1961; Ph.D., Syracuse U., 1966; children by previous marriage—John, Laura. Asst. prof. polit. sci. U. Wis., 1966, asso. prof., to 1971; prof., chmn. dept. polit. sci. Stanford U., 1971—; fellow Center for Advanced Study in Behavioral Scis., 1976-77. Congressional fellow, 1963-64; Brookings Instn. fellow, 1965-66; Guggenheim fellow, 1974-75. Author: The Politics of Finance, 1970; American Government and Public Policy, 1976. Home: 598 Vista Ave Palo Alto CA 94306 Office: Dept Polit Sci Stanford U Stanford CA 94305

MANLEY, JOHN H., physicist; b. Harvard, Ill., July 21, 1907; s. Benjamin F. and Effie (Justice) M.; B.S., U. Ill., 1929; Ph.D., U. Mich., 1934; m. Kathleen Porter Baird, Sept, 4, 1935; children—Kathleen Elizabeth, Harriet Jeanne. Lectr. Columbia, 1934-37; asso. U. Ill., 1937-42; research asso. metall. lab., U. Chgo., 1942; sci. Los Alamos Sci. Lab., 1942-46, asso. dir., 1946-51; asso. prof. Washington U., 1946; dep. dir. div. research AEC, 1947, sec. gen. adv. com., 1947-51; prof., exec. officer dept. physics U. Wash., 1951-57; research advisor, Los Alamos Sci. Lab., 1957-72, cons., 1972—; cons. AEC, 1972-74; vis. prof. U. Wash., 1973. Sr. scientist U.S. mission to Internat. Atomic Energy Assn., Vienna, 1957. Guggenheim fellow, 1954. Fellow Am. Phys. Soc., AAAS; mem. Sigma Xi, Tau Beta Pi. Home: 1469 46th St Los Alamos NM 87544

MANLEY, ROBERT EDWARD, lawyer, economist; b. Cin., Nov. 24, 1935; s. John M. and Helen Catherine (McCarthy) M.; Sc.Bd. in Econs., Xavier U., 1956; A.M. in Econ. Theory, U. Cin., 1957; J.D., Harvard U., 1960; postgrad. London Sch. Econs. and Polit. Sci., 1960, M.I.T., 1972; m. Roberta L. Anzinger, Oct. 21, 1971; 1 son, Robert Edward. Admitted to Ohio bar, 1960, U.S. Supreme Ct. bar; practice law, Cin., 1960—; now partner firm Manley, Jordan & Fischer; Taft teaching fellow econs. U. Cin., 1956-57, vis. lectr. community planning law Coll. Design, Architecture and Art, 1967-73, adj. asso. prof. urban planning, 1972—, lectr. law Coll. Law, 1977—, adj. prof. edn., 1978—. Mem. Hamilton County Public Defender Commn., 1976—; trustee HOPE, Cin., Albert J. Ryan Found.; counsel, co-founder Action Housing for Greater Cin.; mem. Spl. Commn. on Formation U. Cin. Health Maintenance Orgn.; mem. Mayor Cin. Spl. Com. on Housing; chmn. Cin. Environ. Adv. Council, 1975-76. Mem. Cin. Bar Assn., Am. Bar Assn. (council sect. local govt. law 1976—), Ohio State Bar Assn., Am. Judicature Soc., Law and Soc. Assn., Nat. Council Crime and Delinquency, Harvard Law Sch. Assn. Cin. (pres. 1970-71), Am. Econ. Assn., Am. Acad. Polit. and Social Sci., Ohio Planning Conf. Republican. Roman Catholic. Club: Queen City. Author: Metropolitan School Desegregation, 1978; (with Robert N. Cook) Managing Land and the Environment, 1979, others. Home: Dexter and Wold Aves Cincinnati OH 45206 Office: 4500 Carew Tower Cincinnati OH 45202

MANLEY, WILLIAM TANNER, govt. ofcl.; b. Bath County, Ky., Aug. 18, 1929; s. Nathan and Flora (Whaley) M.; B.S., U. Ky., 1951, M.S., 1955; Ph.D., U. Fla., 1958; m. Vertna Jane Alexander, Oct. 30, 1951; 1 son, William Conway. Asst. prof. U. Fla., 1958-60, asso. prof., 1960-66; economist Dept. Agr., Washington, 1960-66, dep. dir. mktg. econs. div., 1966-68, dir., 1968-73, dir. nat. econ. analysis div., 1973-76, dep. adminstr. Agr. Mktg. Service, 1976—. Bd. dirs. Bureaucrat, Inc. Served with USAF, 1951-53. Recipient cert. of merit Dept. Agr., 1963, 69, Superior Service award, 1979. Mem. Internat., So. assns. agrl. economists, Am. Agrl. Econs. Assn., Fed. Exec. Inst. Alumni Assn. (dir. 1976-78), Res. Officers Assn. Methodist. Contbr. articles on econs. of mktg. to profl. jours. Home: 6928 Girard St McLean VA 22101 Office: 14th and Independence Sts SW Washington DC 20250

MANLY, WILLIAM DONALD, metallurgist; b. Malta, Ohio, Jan. 13, 1923; s. Edward James and Thelma (Campbell) M.; student Antioch Coll., 1941-42; B.S., U. Notre Dame, 1947, M.S., 1949; postgrad. U. Tenn., 1950-55; m. Jane Wilden, Feb. 9, 1949; children—Hugh, Ann, Marc, David. Metallurgist, Oak Ridge Nat. Lab., 1949-64; mgr. materials research Union Carbide Corp., N.Y.C., 1964-65, gen. mgr., Stellite div., N.Y.C., 1967-69, v.p., Kokomo, Ind., 1969-70; sr. v.p. Cabot Corp., Boston, 1970—, also dir.; dir. Union Bank & Trust Co., Kokomo. Served with USMC, 1943-46. Recipient Honor award U. Notre Dame, 1974. Fellow Am. Soc. Metals, AIME, Am. Nuclear Soc. (Merit award 1966); mem. Nat. Acad. Engring., Nat. Assn. Corrosion Engrs., Metall. Soc. Presbyterian. Clubs: Cosmos, Masons. Home: 36 Valley Rd Wellesley Hills MA 02181 Office: Cabot Corp 125 High St Boston MA 02110

MANN, ABBY, motion picture script writer; b. Phila.; s. Ben Goodman; ed. pub. schs., Pa.; student Temple U., also N.Y. U.; m. Harriet Karr (div.). Served with AUS, World War II. Author: (campus musicals) Freud Has a Word for It, The Happiest Days; (drama) (with Herbert Cobey) Exodus; Sweet Lorraine; (musical) Just Around the Corner; author TV scripts for Studio One, Alcoa Goodyear Theatre, Robert Montgomery Theatre Playhouse 90; film scripts include: Judgement at Nuremberg (based on own TV script) (Oscar award), 1961, A Child is Waiting (based on own TV script), 1963, The Condemned of Altona (adaptation from Sartre), 1963, Ship of Fools (Katharine Porter), 1965, The Detectives, 1968, Report to the Commissioner, 1975; TV scripts The Marcus-Nelson Murders, 1973, King, 1978; creator TV series Kojak, 1973-78; exec. producer TV series Medical Story, 1975-76.*

MANN, ALAN MACDONALD, psychiatrist; b. Halifax, Can., Sept. 6, 1924; s. Alan James and Lillian Grace (Cole) M.; M.D., McGill U., 1949, diploma in psychiatry, 1954; m. Mary Evelyn Coffey, Feb. 18, 1950; children—Alan John, Debra Sue, Mary Ann, Robert Bright. Intern Royal Victoria Hosp., Montreal, 1949-50; resident in psychiatry Montreal Gen. Hosp., 1951-53; practice psychiatry, Montreal, 1954—; prof. McGill U., Montreal, 1972—; dir. Campeau Corp., Ottawa. Served with Royal Can. Navy, 1943-45. Mem. Royal Coll. Psychiatrists Eng., Can. Med. Assn. Mem. Progressive Conservative Party. Presbyterian. Club: Montreal Indoor Tennis. Contbr. articles to profl. jours. Home: 170 Simcoe Ave Montreal PQ H3P 1W5 Canada Office: 1650 Cedar Ave Montreal PQ H3G 1A4 Canada

MANN, ALFRED EUGENE, med. equipment co. exec.; b. Portland, Oreg., Nov. 6, 1925; s. Charles Emanual and Anna (Schnitzer) M.; student Reed Coll., 1941-42, Oreg. State Coll., 1942-43; B.A., U. Calif., Los Angeles, 1949, M.S., 1951; married; children—Brian, Howard, Richard, Carla, Alfred, Kevin. Research group supr., mgr. physical optics and instrumentation research and devel. Technicolor Corp., Los Angeles, 1951-56; pres. Spectrolab, Sylmar, Calif., 1956-60, pres. Spectrolab and Heliotek div. Textron, 1960-72; chmn. Pacesetter Systems, Inc., Sylmar, 1972—. Vice pres., chmn. S.W. Devel. Co., Los Angeles, 1969—. Founder Alfred E. Mann Found., Johns Hopkins, 1972, bd. dirs., 1972—. Served to lt., USAAF, 1943-46. Mem. Optical Soc. Am., Nat. Space Inst., Am. Rocket Soc., Spectroscopy Soc., Am. Chem. Soc., Photovoltaic Specialist's Panel IEEE, Inst. Environ. Scis., Soc. Motion Picture and TV Engrs., Am. Heart Assn., Phi Beta Kappa, Pi Mu Epsilon. Patentee in field. Address: 12740 San Fernando Rd Sylmar CA 91342

MANN, ARTHUR, educator, author; b. Bklyn., Jan. 3, 1922; s. Karl and Mary (Koch) Finkelman; B.A. summa cum laude, Bklyn. Coll., 1944; M.A., Harvard, 1947, Ph.D., 1952; m. Sylvia Blut, Nov. 6, 1943; children—Carol Ruth, Emily Betsy. Tutor, Bklyn. Coll., 1946; from instr. to asst. prof. Mass. Inst. Tech., 1948-55; from asst. prof. to prof. Smith Coll., 1955-66; prof. Am. history U. Chgo., 1966—, Preston and Sterling Morton prof. Am. history, 1971; vis. prof. Columbia, U. Mass., Williams Coll., U. Mich., U. Wyo., Harvard, Salzburg (Austria) Seminar Am. Studies. Served with AUS, 1943-46. Recipient Alumni award of merit Bklyn. Coll., 1968. Fellow Am. Council Learned Socs., 1962-63; Fulbright-Hays sr. scholar, Australia, 1974; U.S. Dept. State lectr., Venezuela, 1970; USIA lectr., Fiji, Indonesia, New Zealand, Singapore, 1974, Portugal, Germany, Yugoslavia, Rumania, 1976, Hong Kong, Japan, 1979. Mem. Am. Hist. Assn., Orgn. Am. Historians, Soc. Am. Historians, Am. Studies Assn. Author: Yankee Reformers in the Urban Age, 1954; Growth and Achievement, Temple Israel, 1854-1954, 1954; La Guardia, A Fighter Against His Times, 1882-1933, 1959; The Progressive Era, 1963, rev. edit., 1975; La Guardia Comes to Power, 1933, 1965; Immigrants in American Life, 1968, rev. edit., 1974; (with Harris and Warner) History and the Role of the City in American Life, 1972; The One and the Many: Reflections on the American Identity, 1979. Editor: (series) The University of Chicago Press Documents in American History. Adv. editor Am. History, U. Chgo. Press; mem. editorial bd. Ethnicity; editorial cons. Social Service Rev. Home: 4919 S Woodlawn Ave Chicago IL 60615

MANN, BARRY STUART, hotel exec.; b. Boston, Sept. 15, 1940; s. Melvin Albert and Ethel Anita (Yaffe) M.; student public schs., Boston; m. Susan Lynn Entner, Dec. 30, 1967; 1 son, Jason Harris. Credit mgr. Warwick Hotel, N.Y.C., 1965-67; asst. mgr., resident mgr. Belmont Plaza Hotel, 1967-74; rooms div. mgr. St. Regis Sheraton Hotel, 1974-76; sr. v.p., mng. dir. Barbizon Hotel for Women, N.Y.C., 1976—. Mem. Am. Hotel/Motel Assn., N.Y. State Hotel/Motel Assn., Hotel Assn. N.Y.C., Hotel Execs. Club N.Y.C. (dir.). Office: The Barbizon 140 E 63d St New York NY 10021

MANN, BRUCE ALAN, lawyer; b. Chgo., Nov. 28, 1934; s. David I. and Lillian (Segal) M.; B.B.A., U. Wis., 1955, S.J.D., 1957; children—Sally Mann Poeschl, Jonathan Hugh, Andrew Ross. Admitted to Wis. bar, 1957, N.Y. bar, 1958, Calif. bar, 1961; asso. firm Davis, Polk & Wardwell, N.Y.C., 1957-60; asso. firm Pillsbury, Madison & Sutro, San Francisco, 1960-66, partner, 1967—; cons. SEC, 1978; vis. prof. law Georgetown U., 1978; dir. Victoria Sta. Inc.; lectr. in field. Mem. adv. bd. U. Calif. Securities Regulation Inst., 1973—; mem. nat. law com. Anti-Defamation League, 1977—; chmn. lawyers com. San Francisco Jewish Welfare Fedn. Served with USAR, 1957. Mem. Am. Law Inst., Am. Bar Assn., State Bar Calif., Bar Assn. San Francisco (dir. 1974-75). Clubs: The Family, San Francisco Barristers (pres. 1966). Contbr. articles to profl. jours. Office: 225 Bush St San Francisco CA 94104

MANN, CHARLES AUGUST, govt. ofcl.; b. Mannheim, Germany, Mar. 22, 1916; s. Ludwig and Anna (Lindmann) M.; student U. N.Mex., 1940; m. Sara Louise Lockwood, July 22, 1953; 1 dau., Sara Susan. Came to U.S., 1938, naturalized, 1943. Asst. mechanic Champagne Paper Factory, N.Y.C., 1938-39; gasoline sta. attendant, Trenton, N.J., 1939; ins. salesman, N.Y.C., 1939; salesman Montgomery Ward & Co., Albuquerque, 1939, Bernalillo Merc. Corp. (N.Y.), 1939; with Albuquerque Gas & Electric Co., 1939-42; mem. staff UNRRA (now UNWRRA), Italy, 1945-47, Dept. of Army, 1948; with AID and predecessors, Korea, 1949-51, Vietnam, 1951-57; asst. dir. USOM/Cambodia, 1957-58, dep. dir., 1958-60, acting dir., 1959-60, dir., 1960-62; dir. USAID/Laos, counselor econ. affairs, 1962-65; dir. USAID/Vietnam, minister, 1965-66; sr. seminar fgn. policy, 1966-67; dir. USAID/Kinshasa, counselor econ. affairs, 1967-68; dir. USAID/Laos, counselor econ. affairs, 1969-75; asst. adminstr. AID, Dept. State, 1975-77, ret., 1977; program devel. officer IHAP, N.Y.C., 1977-78; econ. devel. adviser Conseil de l'Entente, Abidjan, Ivory Coast, 1978—. Served with AUS, 1942-45. Recipient Meritorious Service award ICA, 1958. Mem. Am. Fgn. Service Assn. Home: 2475 Virginia Ave NW Washington DC 20037 Office: Abidjan/REDSO Dept State Washington DC 20520

MANN, CHARLES KENNETH, educator; b. Fairmont, W.Va., Jan. 2, 1928; s. Lytle Earl and Lena Gay (Wamsley) M.; B.S.E., George Washington U., 1950, M.S., 1952; Ph.D., U. Va., 1955; m. Dorothy Anita McClellan, Aug. 31, 1957; children—Richard, Amy. Analytical chemist Nat. Bur. Standards, Washington, 1950-52; instr. chemistry U. Tex., 1955-58; faculty chemistry Fla. State U., Tallahassee, 1958—, prof., 1968—. Mem. Am. Chem. Soc., Soc. Applied Spectroscopy, Sigma Xi, Sigma Tau, Phi Lambda Upsilon, Alpha Chi Sigma. Unitarian. Author: Electrochemical Reactions in Nonaqueous Systems, 1970; Basic Concepts in Electronic Instrumentation, 1974; Instrumental Analysis, 1974. Contbr. articles to profl. jours. Home: 1446 Marion Ave Tallahassee FL 32303 Office: Dept Chemistry Fla State U Tallahassee FL 32306

MANN, DAVID EMERSON, asst. sec. Navy; b. N.Y.C., Nov. 4, 1924; m. Vera Deane; 1 son, James H. F.B. Jewett postdoctoral fellow Harvard U., 1950-51; physicist Heat div. Nat. Bur. Standards, Washington, 1951-60, chief molecular spectroscopy sect., 1960-66; chief applied research br. Ballistic Missile Def. Office, ARPA, Dept. Def., 1966-67, dep. dir., 1967-68, dir. Strategic Tech. Office, 1968-73; spl. asst. to CNO for Navy Adv. Systems Projects, Dept. Navy, Washington, 1973-77, asst. sec. Navy for research, engring. and systems, 1977—. Recipient Meritorious Civilian Service medal Sec. Def., 1974, Navy Distinguished Civilian Service medal, 1977; Guggenheim Found. research fellow/Fulbright sr. research fellow, 1957. Mem. IEEE. Club: Cosmos. Home: 4827 Broad Brook Dr Bethesda MD 20014 Office: Dept Navy The Pentagon Washington DC 20350

MANN, DELBERT, film, theater, TV dir. and producer; b. Lawrence, Kan., Jan. 30, 1920; s. Delbert Martin and Ora (Patton) M.; B.A., Vanderbilt U., 1941; M.F.A., Yale, 1973; LL.D. (hon.), Northland Coll.; m. Ann Caroline Gillespie, Jan. 13, 1942; children—David Martin, Frederick G., Steven P. With Gen. Shoe Corp., Nashville, 1941-42; dir. Town Theatre, Columbia, S.C., 1947-49; stage mgr. Wellesley Summer Theater, 1947-48; dir. Philco-Goodyear TV Playhouse, 1949-55, also Omnibus, Ford Star Jubilee, Playwrights 56, Producers Showcase, DuPont Show of the Month, Playhouse 90; dir. films: Marty, 1954, The Bachelor Party, 1956, Desire Under The Elms, 1957, Separate Tables, 1958, Middle of the Night, 1959, The Dark at the Top of the Stairs, 1960, The Outsider, 1960, Lover Come Back, 1961, That Touch of Mink, 1962, A Gathering of Eagles, 1962, Dear Heart, 1963, Mister Buddwing, 1965, Fitzwilly, 1967, Kidnapped, 1972, Birch Interval, 1976; dir. TV spl. Heidi, 1968, David Copperfield, 1970, Jane Eyre, 1971, The Man Without A Country, 1973, A Girl Named Sooner, 1975, Tell Me My Name, 1977, Breaking Up, 1978, Home To Stay, 1978, All Quiet on the Western Front, 1979; dir. plays A Quiet Place, 1956, Speaking of Murder, 1957, Zelda, 1969; opera Wuthering Heights, N.Y.C. Center, 1959. Bd. trust Vanderbilt U. Served as 1st lt. USAAF, World War II; B-24 pilot and squadron intelligence officer, 1944-45. Recipient Acad. Award for dir. Marty, 1955. Mem. Dirs. Guild Am. (past pres.), Producers Guild, Kappa Alpha. Office: Caroline Prodns Inc 401 S Burnside Ave Los Angeles CA 90036

MANN, DONALD NATHANIEL, radio exec.; b. Chgo., Dec. 15, 1920; s. Henry J. and Rose (Bonner) M.; B.S., Northwestern U., 1943; M.A., Columbia U., 1946; J.D., John Marshall Law Sch., 1948; m. Rhoda Fiener, Nov. 8, 1952; children—Gary Kevin, Eric Scott, Holly Jada. Program dir., asst. communications mgr. KWWL, Waterloo, Iowa, 1948-49; gen. mgr. communications mgr. WKNK, Muskegon, Mich., 1949-51; account exec. WBBM Radio & TV CBS, Chgo., 1951-54; gen. mgr. WOKY-TV, Milw., 1954; mgr. spl. projects, account exec. WBBM Radio, 1954—; prof. communications Columbia Coll., Chgo., 1967; dir. Cosmopolitan Nat. Bank Chgo.; pres. Am. Coll. Radio Arts, Crafts and Scis., Chgo., 1961—. Asst. chmn. communications div. Combined Jewish Appeal, Chgo., 1959-69; mem. Chgo. Crime Commn., 1974; dir. Niles Twp. (Ill.) Community Concerts, 1961—; co-chmn. Red Feather drive, Chgo., 1960; pres. Timber Ridge Home Owners, Skokie, Ill., 1957-60; mem. Chgo. Council Fgn. Relations, 1965—; pres. Bus. and Profl. Men City of Hope, Chgo., 1961; chmn. Bike-A-Thon, Am. Diabetes Assn.; pres. Skokie Caucus Party, 1957-64; master Chancery Village Ct. of Skokie, 1962; bd. dirs. Edward T. Lee Found., 1978, Easter Seal Soc., 1978; chmn. Sportsman of Yr. award, 1978; police and fire commr., Skokie, 1965; pres. Deere Park, 1970—; trustee, chmn. 50th Ann. com. Mt. Sinai Hosp.; trustee Columbia Coll., John Marshall Law Sch., Chgo. chpt. Am. Diabetes Assn. Served with AUS, 1942-46. Recipient Distinguished Alumni award John Marshall Law Sch., 1968; named Radio Man of Year, Am. Coll. Radio, 1964, Most Successful Media Person, 1972. Mem. Am., Ill., 7th Fed. Dist., Chgo. bar assns., Am. Fedn. Musicians, Am. Judicature Soc., Sales Exec. Club, Alpha Sigma Iota, Grocery Sales Mfg. Execs., John Marshall Alumni Assn. (pres. 1971-73), Decalogue Soc., Am. Legion, Jewish War Vets., Sales Exec. Club, Merchandising Exec. Club. Democrat. Jewish (trustee temple). Clubs: B'nai B'rith, Elk; Standard, Variety (Chgo.). Co-author: Pvt. Droop Has Lost the War, 1944; author: History of Sault St. Marie, 1942; How to Become Your Company's Top Salesman thru Showmanship. Home: 111 S Deere Park Dr E Highland Park IL 60035 Office: WBBM Radio CBS 630 N McClurg Ct Chicago IL 60611. *I have always believed that success in one's chosen field is not enough. A successful man must give of himself to civic, social, political, affairs in his community, city, state, and country-and not just lip service or money but rather time, energy, and actual participation. Only through this participation (total) will one be considered "a successful man."*

MANN, EDWARD BEVERLY, author; b. Hollis, Kans., Jan. 31, 1902; s. Grant and Mattie (Hill) M.; A.B., U. Fla., 1927; m. Helen Frazier Cubberly, Oct. 18, 1928 (div. 1939); m. 2d, Elizabeth Goodell Parkhurst, July 2, 1942. With Willard Price & Co., advt., N.Y.C., 1927-29; free-lance writer fiction and articles, 1928—; dir. U. N.Mex. Press, 1949-56; editor Guns mag., Guns Ann., The Shooting Industry, Pubs. Devel. Corp., 1956-68, contbg. editor, 1968—. Mem. Nat. Rifle Assn. (life). Republican. Club: Bird Key Yacht (Sarasota, Fla.). Author: The Man from Texas, 1931; The Blue-Eyed Kid, 1932; The Valley of Wanted Men, 1932; Killers Range, 1933; Stampede, 1934; Gamblin' Man, 1934; Rustlers' Round-up, 1935; Thirsty Range, 1935; El Sombra, 1936; Boss of the Lazy Nine, 1936; Comanche Kid, 1936; With Spurs, 1937; Shootin' Melody, 1938; Gun Feud, 1940; The Mesa Gang, 1940; Troubled Range, 1940; Gunsmoke Trail, 1941; The Whistler, 1953; New Mexico: Land of Enchantment (with others), 1955; mng. editor American Rifleman, 1943-45; asso. editor Mil. Service Pub. Co., 1945-48; guns and gunning editor Sun Trails, 1946-56; guns editor Field and Stream, 1975—. Address: Regency House Apt 901 435 S Gulfstream Ave Sarasota FL 33577

MANN, FLETCHER CULLEN, lawyer; b. Pittsboro, N.C., Sept. 21, 1921; s. F.C. and Bertie (Outlaw) M.; A.B., U. N.C., 1942; LL.B., 1948; m. Blanche Poole, Mar. 11, 1944; children—Sharon (Mrs. J. A. Piper), Fletcher C., William P. Admitted to S.C. bar, 1948; partner Leatherwood, Walker, Todd & Mann, Greenville, S.C., 1948—. Chmn. Greenville chpt. A.R.C., 1960-62, dir., 1962-65; vice-chmn. resolutions com. A.R.C., 1964, S.E. adv. com., 1965-68. Atty. S.C. Republican Party, 1967—. Bd. dirs. United Fund Greenville, 1962-65, Greenville Symphony, 1959-61, Am. Field Service, 1962-63. Served to lt. USNR, 1943-45; ETO. Recipient Humanitarian award A.R.C., 1970. Mem. Greenville (bd. dirs. 1960-63, pres. 1956, outstanding contbn. award 1957), U.S. (govt. operations com. 1964-69) chambers commerce, Greenville Lawyers Club (pres. 1965—), Greenville County, S.C. (chmn. procedural and law reform com. 1975—), Am. (vice-chmn. labor com. adminstrv. law sect. 1969—), N.C. bar assns., Greenville County Pub. Defender Corp. (chmn. 1972—), Internat. Assn. Ins. Counsel, Am. Judicature Soc., Assn. Ins. Attys., Phi Alpha Delta. Republican. Episcopalian (chmn. stewardship program 1970—, pres. Christ Ch. Endowment Corp.). Clubs: Rotary; Greenville Country (bd. dirs. 1963-66); Green Valley Country; Biltmore Forest Country; Poinsett. Home: 110 Rock Creek Dr Greenville SC 29605 Office: 217 E Coffee St Greenville SC 29602

MANN, FORBES, bus. exec.; b. Rochester, N.Y., Sept. 25, 1918; s. Abram Joseph and Helen (Forbes) M.; student Phillips Acad., Andover, Mass., 1933-34, Peekskill Mil. Acad., 1934-36; ed. Brown U.; m. Elizabeth Reese Jones, June 27, 1942; children—Robin Mann Gyovai, Richard Forbes. Design engr. Brewster Aeros. Corp., L.I. City, N.Y., 1940-41; with LTV Corp., Bridgeport, Conn., Dallas, 1941-47, chief preliminary design, 1947-52, chief mil. sales, 1952-55, program control mgr., 1955-57, dir. long range planning, 1957-59, v.p. govt. and fgn. relations, Washington, 1959-69; pres. Vought Aero. div. LTV Aerospace Corp., Dallas 1969-70; pres. LTV Aero. Space Corp., 1970-72; sr. v.p. LTV Corp., 1972—. Cubmaster, scoutmaster D.C. council Boy Scouts Am., 1959-63. Bd. dirs. Jr. Achievement Dallas. Mem. Air Force Assn., Navy League, Assn. U.S. Army, Aero. Club Washington, Am. Iron and Steel Inst., Phi Gamma Delta. Clubs: Chevy Chase, Burning Tree, Congressional Country (Washington). Home: 10700 Stanmore Dr Potomac MD 20854 Office: 1155 15th St NW Washington DC 20005

MANN, FRANK EUGENE, city ofcl., mgmt. cons.; b. Atlanta, May 1, 1920; s. Frank J. and Louise M.; A.B., George Washington U., 1941; m. Anita, Oct. 23, 1975; children—Patricia, Erik, Amy. Vice pres. Sunshine Biscuit Co., N.Y.C., 1965-69; pres. Mann Potato Chip Co., Washington, 1955-65; asso. Homer Pettit Assos., Washington, 1975-76; partner Port of Alexandria, 1970—; v.p. Kidstuff, Inc., Alexandria, 1976—; mgmt. cons. Alexandria, 1970—; mayor City of Alexandria, 1961-67, 76—; dir. PepCom Industries, 1st Commonwealth Savs. and Loan. Mem. Alexandria City Council, 1952-58, Va. Ho. of Dels., 1970-76; mem. exec. com. Va. Bicentennial Commn.; bd. dirs. No. Va. Transp. Commn., No. Va. 4-H Club Ednl. Center; mem. Va. Ins. Bd.; trustee Southeastern U. Served with USN, 1943-46. Decorated Bronze Star; recipient Distinguished Service award Alexandria Jaycees, 1955. Mem. Am. Legion, VFW. Clubs: Grandstand Mgrs., Old Dominion Boat. Home: 200 N Quaker Ln Alexandria VA 22304 Office: City Hall Room 302 Alexandria VA 22314

MANN, GERALD C., corp. exec., lawyer; b. Sulphur Springs, Tex., Jan. 13, 1907; s. Grover Cleveland and Edna Lenora (McClimons) M.; B.A., So. Meth. U., 1928; LL.B., Harvard Law Sch., 1933; m. Anna Mary Mars, June 23, 1929; children—Gerald C., Lola Ann, Robert Mars. Admitted to Tex. bar, 1933; pvt. practice, Dallas, 1933-35; sec. state, Tex., 1935; Washington rep. Tex. Planning Bd., 1935-36; pvt. practice, 1936-39, 72—; atty. gen Tex., 1939-44. Clubs: Salesmanship (Dallas). Home: 3631 Northwest Pkwy Dallas TX 75225 Office: Braniff Tower Dallas TX 75235

MANN, HERBERT FREDERICK, univ. press exec.; b. N.Y.C., Aug. 27, 1927; s. Herbert Frederick and Florence (Fleming) M.; A.B., U. Mich., 1951; m. Zofia Cowley, Oct. 26, 1958. Salesman, Overbeck Book Store, Ann Arbor, Mich., 1951-52; salesman, book buyer Oxford Univ. Press, N.Y.C., 1952-63, 67-72; salesman, editor, exec. editor, sr. editor U. Calif. Press, Berkeley, 1963-67; dir. Rutgers Univ. Press, New Brunswick, N.J., 1976—. Served with USN, 1944-46. Mem. Princeton Ballet Soc. Democrat. Episcopalian. Clubs: Trazom Soc., Road Runners N.Y. Home: 19B Phelps Ave New Brunswick NJ 08901 Office: Rutgers Univ Press 30 College Ave New Brunswick NJ 08903*

MANN, HERBIE, flutist; b. N.Y.C., Apr. 16, 1930; s. Harry C. and Ruth (Brecher) Solomon; student Manhattan Sch. Music, 1952-54; m. Ruth Shore, Sept. 8, 1956 (div. 1971); children—Paul J., Claudia; m. 2d, Jan Clonts, July 11, 1971; 1 dau., Laura. Founder, pres. Herbie Mann Music Corp., N.Y.C., 1959—; toured Africa for Dept. State, 1960, Brazil, 1961-62, Japan, 1964, Scandanavia, Cyprus and Turkey, 1971; recorded over 30 albums under own name, 1954—; pres. Herbie Mann Orch., Inc., 5 Face of Music Prodns., Inc., Rupadia Music, Inc. Served with AUS, 1948-52. Recipient Downbeat award for flute, 1958-70. Mem. ASCAP, Nat. Acad. Rec. Arts and Scis. Address: Atlantic Records 75 Rockefeller Plaza New York NY 10019*

MANN, JAMES HAROLD, lawyer; b. Edmonton, Ky., Nov. 23, 1913; s. James Harbert and Margaret Bell (Walker) M.; A.B with honors, Centre Coll., 1935; LL.B. with distinction, Cornell U., 1938; m. Margaret Ellis Blackwell, Aug. 31, 1940; children—Margaret B., Judith W. Admitted to Ky. bar, 1938, D.C. bar, 1948, U.S. Supreme Ct. bar, 1962; atty. U.S. Treasury Dept., Washington, 1938-40, 41-42; asst. prof. law U. Ark., 1940-41; spl. asst. to ambassador Am. embassy, Buenos Aires, Argentina, 1942-44, London, 1944-45; Am. mem. Joint Commn. U.S., U.K., France, Switzerland; financial attache Treasury Dept. rep. U.S. Legation, Berne, Switzerland, 1945-47; partner firm Lucas, Friedman & Mann and predecessor firms, Washington, 1948—. Exec. vice chmn. Democratic Central Com., Montgomery County, Md., 1954-58; mem. resolutions com. Md. Dem. Conv., 1956; Dem. candidate for nomination U.S. Congress, 1958; del. Dem. Nat. Conv., 1960. Mem. D.C. Bar Assn., Cornell Law Assn. (exec. com. 1957-60), Am. Judicature Soc., Delta Theta Phi, Delta Kappa Epsilon. Episcopalian. Clubs: Metropolitan, Cornell, Dacor House (Washington). Home: Rocklands 14525 Montevideo Rd Poolesville MD 20837 Office: 810 18th St NW Washington DC 20006

MANN, JAMES ROBERT, congressman; b. Greenville, S.C., Apr. 27, 1920; s. Alfred Cleo and Nina (Griffin) M.; B.A., The Citadel, 1941, LL.D. (hon.), 1978; LL.B., U.S.C., 1947; m. Virginia Thomason Brunson, Jan. 15, 1945; children—James Robert, David Brunson, William Walker, Virginia Brunson. Admitted to S.C. bar, 1947; practice in Greenville, 1947-69; del. S.C. Ho. of Reps. from Greenville County, 1949-52; solicitor 13th Jud. Circuit, 1953-63; mem. 91st-95th Congresses 4th Dist. S.C. Sec. Greenville County Planning Commn., 1963-67. Trustee Greenville Hosp. System, 1965-68; bd. visitors Presbyn. Coll., 1972-75; bd. devel. New Orleans Baptist Theol. Sem.; mem.-at-large Nat. council Boy Scouts Am. Served to lt. col. AUS, 1941-46; col. USAR ret. Mem. Am., S.C., Greenville County bar assns., Am. Judicature Soc., Greater Greenville C. of C. (pres. 1965), V.F.W. (dep. comdr. 1951-52), Am. Legion. Democrat. Baptist. Mason (Shriner), Kiwanian, Elk; mem. Woodmen of World. Home: 118 W Mountain View Ave Greenville SC 29609 Office: 812 E North St Greenville SC 29601

MANN, JEWELL RUSSELL (MRS. JOHN HENRY CLAY MANN), lawyer; b. Aurora, Ark., June 13, 1903; d. Stephen Yell and Flora (Smithson) Russell; grad. Okla. Sch. Accountancy, Tulsa, 1945; LL.B., U. Tulsa, 1928; m. John Henry Clay Mann, Sept. 1, 1928. Admitted to Okla. bar, 1928, since practiced in Tulsa; atty. Midstates Oil Corp., 1928-33; atty., sec.-treas., dir. Toklan Oil Corp., 1933-56; atty. Imperial Royalties Co., 1933-42; atty., sec.-treas., dir. Bryan Petroleum Corp., 1933-46, Toklan Prodn. Co., 1946-54, Fidelity Royalty Co., 1947-54, Lucey Products Corp., 1957-65; sec., dir. Fraber Oil Co., 1957-64; pvt. practice, 1959-68; partner firm Harrington & Mann, 1968—; dir. Admiral State Bank, Tulsa, 1977—. Mem. Tulsa Com. for UN, 1958-65, local and state coms. for aging, 1960-61, Gov.'s Commn. on Status of Women, 1963—; mem. Selective Service Bd. 76, Tulsa County, 1968-72, adviser to registrants, 1972—; mem. Okla. council Nat. Womans Party, 1970—; sec., past pres., bd. dirs. Tulsa County Legal Aid Soc.; bd. dirs. YWCA, 1965-68, Econ. Opportunity Task Force Tulsa, 1965-69; mem. exec. com. Tulsa Council Chs., 1958-69; mem. Internat. Women's Year Commn. in Okla., 1976-77. Recipient Guardsman award N.G. Bur. for outstanding leadership as pres. Okla. Fedn. Bus. and Profl. Women, 1961. Mem. Am., Okla., Tulsa County (past sec., mem. exec. com.) bar assns., Internat., Okla. (past pres.) assns. women lawyers, Tulsa League Women Voters, Nat. Fedn., Okla. (past pres., com. chmn.), Tulsa (treas., dir., past pres.) bus. and profl. women, Phi Alpha Delta (past pres. Phi Delta Delta). Mem. Christian Ch. Club: Order Eastern Star. Home: 2417 S Owasso St Tulsa OK 74114 Office: 1108 Thompson Bldg Tulsa OK 74103

MANN, JOHN H., educator; b. N.Y.C., July 15, 1928; s. Harvey T. and Edna (Brand) M.; B.A., Harvard, 1949; M.A., Coll. City N.Y., 1954; Ph.D., Columbia, 1956; m. Carola Honroth, Aug. 18, 1955 (div. Jan. 1970); children—Susan Elizabeth, Karen Patricia, Robert Christopher, Lisa Christina. Asso. research scientist USAF Project, N.Y. U., 1957-59; coordinator research Jewish Bd. Guardians, N.Y.C., 1964-65; asst. prof. sociology Grad. Sch. Arts and Sci., N.Y.U., 1957-60, asso. prof., 1960-68; chmn. dept. sociology State U. Coll. at Geneseo, N.Y., 1968-72, prof., 1968—; cons. Ednl. Policy Research Center, Stanford Research Inst., 1967-68, Bristol Labs., 1970-71, NIMH, 1964-66, U.S. Children's Bur., 1962-64, U.S. Office Vocational Rehab., 1961-63. Bd. dirs. Center for Exploration of Human Potential, San Diego, 1967-70; trustee Aureon Inst., N.Y.C. Mem. Am. Psychol. Assn., Am. Sociol. Assn., Am. Acad. Psychotherapists, N.Y. Soc. Clin. Psychologists. Author: Frontiers of Psychology, 1963; Sigmund Freud, 1964; Louis Pasteur, 1964; Changing Human Behavior, 1965; (with H. Otto) Ways of Growth, 1968, Encounter, 1970; Students of the Light, 1972; Learning to Be, 1972; (with M. Richard) Exploring Social Space, 1973. Home: 26 Linden St Livonia NY 14487 Office: Dept Sociology State U Coll Geneseo NY 14454

MANN, KENNETH WALKER, clergyman; b. Nyack, N.Y., Aug. 22, 1914; s. Arthur Hungerford and Ethel Livingston (Walker) M.; A.B., Princeton U., 1937; S.T.B., Gen. Theol. Sem., N.Y.C., 1942; M.S., U. Mich., 1950, Ph.D., 1956. Ordained priest Episcopal Ch., 1941; vicar in Valley Cottage, Pearl River, N.Y., 1941-43; priest in charge, Yonkers, N.Y., 1943-45; dir. youth work and Christian edn. Diocese Los Angeles, 1945-47; curate in Beverly Hills, Calif., 1947-49; counselor Bur. Psychol. Services, U. Mich., 1951-52; chaplain, clin. psychologist dept. psychiatry St. Luke's Hosp., N.Y.C., also priest-psychotherapist Cathedral St. John Divine, N.Y.C., psychol. examiner ministerial candidates Diocese N.Y., 1952-58; asso. chaplain Hosp. Good Samaritan, Los Angeles, 1958-65; exec. pastoral services, exec. council Episc. Ch. N.Y.C., 1965-70; program officer Acad. Religion and Mental Health, N.Y.C., 1970-72; sr. adviser profl. affairs Insts. Religion and Health, 1972—; sr. psychol. staff Silver Hill Found., New Canaan, Conn., 1974—; pres. Rockland County (N.Y.) Ministers Assn., 1942-43; exec. sec. social service commn. Diocese N.Y., 1943-45; chmn. div. pastoral services Diocese Los Angeles, 1958-65; field dir. Western region Acad. Religion and Mental Health, 1958-61; asso. nat. chaplain U.S. Power Squadrons, 1956-57. Pres. Adoption Inst. Los Angeles, 1964; mem. edn. com. Calif. Heart Assn., 1962-64; trustee, treas. Acad. Religion and Mental Health, 1954-59, mem. profl. bd., 1960-70; trustee Vis. Nurse Assn. Los Angeles, 1963-65, Children's Home Soc. Calif. in Los Angeles, 1964-65, N. Conway Inst., 1966—. USPHS grantee, 1950-51. Diplomate Am. Assn. Pastoral Counselors; licensed clin. psychologist, Calif., Conn.; lic. marriage, family and child counselor, Calif. Fellow AAAS; mem. Am. Psychol. Assn. (chmn. com. relations between psychology and religion 1956-58), Western, Calif., Los Angeles County psychol. assns., Assembly Episc. Hosps. and Chaplains. Republican. Clubs: Upper Nyack (N.Y.) Tennis; The Club (Diocese N.Y.). Author: On Pills and Needles, 1969; Deadline for Survival — A Survey of Moral Issues in Science and Medicine, 1970; contbr. articles to profl. jours. Home: 32 Tallman Ave Nyack NY 10960 Office: Silver Hill Foundation New Canaan CT 06840. *I have strongly held to the principle that the total "health" of man cannot be considered apart from the values and aspirations by which men live, and by which they may even be prepared to die. Amidst the confusions that exist today over loyalties, traditions, and ideals, many are asking: What is the right way to behave? How should I think? What kind of person am I supposed to be? To help such people in quandary to live responsibly, and still be true to their individuality, is a large task, but it is one that is central to a religious ministry. It has always been my chief concern.*

MANN, LEONARD ANDREW, coll. dean; b. Cleve., June 30, 1915; s. Andrew E. and Emma (Bartelme) M.; B.S., U. Dayton, 1937; M.S., Ohio State U., 1945; Ph.D., Carnegie Inst. Tech., 1954. Joined Soc. of Mary, 1933; high sch. tchr., 1937-48; mem. faculty U. Dayton, 1954—, chmn. physics, prof., 1955—, dean Coll. Arts and Scis., 1961—. Mem. Assn. Higher Edn., Am. Assn. Physics Tchrs., N. Central Assn. Deans, Nat. Assn. Standard Med. Vocabulary. Address: U Dayton Dayton OH 45469

MANN, LOWELL KIMSEY, mfg. exec.; b. LaGrange, Ga., June 28, 1917; s. Otis A. and Georgia B. (Mundy) M.; grad. Advanced Mgmt. Program, Harvard, 1962; m. Helen Margaret Dukes, Feb. 11, 1944; children—Margaret Ellen, Lowell Kimsey. Foreman, Callaway Mills, LaGrange, 1935-39, indsl. engr., 1939-42; indsl. engr. Blue Bell, Inc., Greenboro, N.C., 1946-52, chief engr., 1952-61, v.p. engring., 1961-62, v.p. mfg., 1962-68, dir., 1963—, exec. v.p., 1968-73, pres., 1973—, chief exec. officer, 1974—; dir. Shadowline Inc., Morganton, N.C., Wachovia Bank & Trust Co., Greensboro; So. adv. bd. Arkwright-Boston Ins. Co., 1975—. Bd. dirs. Learning Inst. N.C., 1969-76; trustee Southeastern Legal Found., 1977—. Served to capt. AUS, 1942-46. Mem. Piedmont Assn. Industries (dir.; pres. 1966-68), Am. Apparel Mfrs. Assn. (dir. 1972-78), Nat. MS Soc., N.A.M. (dir. 1977—). Democrat. Baptist. Home: 5503 Currituck Pl Sedgefield Greensboro NC 27407 Office: 335 Church Ct Greensboro NC 27401

MANN, LYLE EUGENE, ret. air force officer; b. Robinson, Ill., Nov. 19, 1923; s. Clarence Alvin and Carolyn Amanda (Ping) M.; B.A., U. Ala., 1956; M.S. in Internat. Affairs, George Washington U., 1966; grad. Air Command and Staff Coll., 1959, Air War Coll., 1966; m. Maurine McClelland Hawley, May 31, 1942; children—Robert Wayne, Lynda Sue, David Alan, Mark Stephen. Enlisted USAAF, 1942, commd. 2d lt., 1944, advanced through grades to brigadier gen. USAF, 1972; served with 49th Fighter Bomber Group, Taequ Air Base, Korea, 1950-51; instr. Squadron Officer Sch., Maxwell AFB, Ala., 1951-53; aide-de-camp to comdr. Air U., Maxwell AFB, 1953-55; comdr. 357th Fighter Interceptor Squadron, Nouasseur Air Base, Morocco, 1956-58; air staff officer internat. liaison div. hdqrs. USAF, Washington, 1959-62; project officer William Tell '63, Air Def. Command, Tyndall AFB, Fla., 1962-63; dir. tng. and operations 4756th Air Def. Wing, Air Def. Command, Tyndall AFB, 1963-64; chief air operations center Hdqrs. 314th Air Div. Air Forces Korea, Osan Air Base, 1964-65; staff officer, br. head Joint War Games Agy., Politico-Mil. Div. Joint Chiefs Staff, Washington, 1966-69; asst. dir. operations 363d Tactical Reconnaissance Wing, Shaw AFB, S.C., 1969, dir. operations, 1970; vice comdr. 432d Tactical Fighter/Reconnaisance Wing, Udorn Air Base, Thailand, 1970-71, wing comdr., 1971; dep. chief staff intelligence Hdqrs. Pacific Air Forces, Hickam AFB, Hawaii, 1972-75, chief of staff PACAF, 1975-76; ret., 1976. Decorated D.S.M., Legion of Merit, D.F.C., Meritorious Service medal with 1 oak leaf cluster, Air Medal with 18 oak leaf clusters, Air Force Commendation medal. Mem. Air Force Assn., Air Force Acad. Athletic Assn., Am. Legion, Daedalians, Quiet Birdmen, Phi Alpha Theta. Mason (32 deg., Shriner). Home: 1608 Courtland Rd Alexandria VA 22306

MANN, MARION, physician, educator; b. Atlanta, Mar. 29, 1920; s. Levi James and Cora Ellen (Casey) M.; B.S. in Edn., Tuskegee Inst., Ala., 1940; M.D., Howard U., 1954; Ph.D., Georgetown U., 1961, D.Sc. (hon.), 1979; grad. U.S. Army Command and Gen. Staff Coll., 1965, U.S. Army War Coll., 1970; m. Ruth Maurine Reagin, Jan. 16, 1943; children—Marion, Judith (Mrs. Kenneth Walk). Intern USPHS Hosp., Staten Island, N.Y., 1954-55; resident Georgetown U. Hosp., 1956-60; practice medicine, specializing in pathology, Washington, 1961—; instr. pathology Georgetown U., 1960-61, professorial lectr. Sch. Medicine, 1970-73; asst. prof. pathology Howard U. Coll. Medicine, 1961-67, asso. prof., 1967-70, prof., 1970, dean, 1970-79. Bd. dirs. Nat. Med. Fellowships, Inc. Served to capt. AUS, 1942-50; brig. gen. Res. Diplomate Nat. Bd. Med. Examiners, Am. Bd. Pathology. Mem. Internat. Acad. Pathology, AMA, Nat. Med. Assn., Assn. Mil. Surgeons U.S., Inst. Medicine, Nat. Acad. Scis., Alpha Omega Alpha. Mem. Ch. of Christ. Home: 408 N St SW Washington DC 20024 Office: 520 W St NW Washington DC 20059

MANN, MARTY, founder Nat. Council Alcoholism; b. Chgo., Oct. 15, 1904; d. William Henry and Lillian (Christy) Mann; student Chgo. Latin Sch., Santa Barbara (Calif.) Girl's Sch., 1921-22, Montemare, Adirondacks and Fla., 1922-24, Miss Nixon's Sch., Florence, Italy, 1924-25; D.Hum., Adelphi U., 1975; divorced. Asst. editor Internat. Studio, 1928-30; contbr. Town and Country mag., 1929-34; partner photography bus., London, Eng., 1930-36; publicity for jubilee season Covent Garden Opera, 1935; fashion publicity dir. R.H. Macy & Co., N.Y.C., 1940-42; research dir., radio script writer ASCAP, 1942-44; exec. dir. Nat. Council on Alcoholism, 1944-68, now founder-cons.; lectr. alcoholism, profl. and lay orgns.; cons. on alcoholism, social agys., ednl., indsl., med., ch. groups; ofcl. del. Internat. Congress on Alcoholism, Luzerne, Switzerland, 1948; guest of Govt. Union S. Africa to advise on govt. action on alcoholism, and to address 1st Nat. Conf. on Alcoholism, 1951; guest lectr., adviser alcoholism groups, New Zealand, Australia, 1961, London, Eng., Belfast and Dublin, Ireland, 1964; addressed joint sessions state legislatures, S.C., 1946, Mich., 1952, Utah, 1957, Tenn., 1965; lectr. Sch. Alcohol Studies, Yale, U. Wash., U. Utah, U. Tex., U. Colo., U. Ga., U. La., Menninger Found.; research asso. Columbia Tchrs. Coll.; lectr. pharm. scis. U. Ariz.; del. Third Conf Internat. Union for Health Edn. of Pub., Rome, Italy, 1956; spl. cons. to dir. Nat. Inst. on Alcohol Abuse and Alcoholism; cons. on alcoholism Silver Hill Found. Recipient Elizabeth Blackwell award Hobart and William Smith Colls., 1963. Hon. fellow Am. Psychiat. Assn.; fellow Am. Pub. Health Assn., Soc. Pub. Health Educators, Royal Soc. Health, London. Author: Primer on Alcoholism, 1950 (pub. Eng. 1952, Afrikaans trans. pub. S. Africa), 1954; Marty Mann's New Primer on Alcoholism, 1958 (Finnish transl. 1962, Spanish transl. 1969, Japanese transl. 1973); Marty Mann Answers Your Questions About Drinking And Alcoholism, 1970. Contbr. articles popular, profl. jours. Office: 733 3d Ave New York NY 10017

MANN, MAURICE, investment banker; b. Peabody, Mass., Feb. 22, 1929; s. Abram S. and Jennie (Goldberg) M.; B.A., Northeastern U., 1951, LL.D. (hon.), 1977; M.A., Boston U., 1952; Ph.D., Syracuse U., 1955; m. Betty M. Melnick, Sept. 6, 1953; children—Deborah Ellen, Pamela Sue. Asst. prof. econs. Ohio Wesleyan U., 1955-58; fin. economist Bur. Old Age and Survivors Ins., U.S. Govt., Balt., 1958-60; sr. economist Fed. Res. Bank Cleve., 1960-62, sr. monetary economist, 1962-63, v.p., gen. economist, 1963-69; asst. dir. office of mgmt. and budget Exec. Office U.S. Pres., Washington, 1969-70; exec. v.p. Western Pa. Nat. Bank (now Equibank), Pitts., 1970-73; pres. Fed. Home Loan Bank San Francisco, 1973-78; vice chmn. Warburg Paribas Becker, Inc., 1978—, A.G. Becker, Inc., 1978—; dir. Bekins Co. Mem. nat. alumni council Northeastern U., Boston, 1969—; trustee City of Hope; mem. policy adv. bd. Joint Center for Urban Studies Mass. Inst. Tech.-Harvard. Recipient Alumni citation for disting. achievement in banking Northeastern U., 1973; Chancellor's medal for disting. achievement Syracuse U., 1977; Ford Found. faculty research fellow, 1956. Mem. Nat. Assn. Bus. Economists, Am. Econ. Assn., Am. Fin. Assn., Lambda Alpha. Clubs: Nat. Economists, Bankers, Concordia-Argonaut; Commonwealth (San Francisco). Contbr. articles to profl. jours. Home: 3255 Jackson St San Francisco CA 94118 Office: 555 California St Suite 2760 San Francisco CA 94104

MANN, ROBERT HENRY, lawyer; b. Plainfield, N.J., July 10, 1935; s. Oscar and Alice (Keizer) M.; A.B., Miami U., 1957; J.D., N. Y. U., 1961; M.A., Columbia, 1960; m. Joan Barbara Papkin, Sept. 3, 1962; 1 dau., Jennifer Karen. Admitted to Ohio bar, 1961, N.Y. bar, 1963; atty. Hahn, Loeser, Freedheim, Dean & Wellman, Cleve., 1961-63, Fried, Frank, Harris, Shriver & Jacobson, N.Y.C., 1963-65; corporate counsel Pepsi Co, Inc., N.Y.C., 1965-69, v.p. Pepsi Co Internat., 1969-70; gen. counsel Chesebrough-Pond's Inc., Greenwich, Conn., 1970-72, v.p., sec., gen. counsel, 1972—, dir., mem. exec. com., 1974—. U.S. Steel Found. fellow, 1958; Ford Found. fellow, 1959; Root-Tilden fellow, 1957-61. Mem. Am. Bar Assn., Assn. Bar City N.Y., Miami U. Alumni Club N.Y. (pres. 1966-69), Phi Beta Kappa, Omicron Delta Kappa, Phi Eta Sigma, Zeta Beta Tau. Home: 50 Londonderry Dr Greenwich CT 06830 Office: 33 Benedict Pl Greenwich CT

MANN, ROBERT NATHANIEL, violinist; b. Portland, Oreg., July 19, 1920; s. Charles Emanuel and Anna (Schnitzer) M.; grad. Inst. Musical Art; diploma Juilliard Sch. Music; m. Lucille Rowan Zeitlin, July 27, 1952; children—Lisa, Nicholas. First violinist Juilliard Quartet, 1946—; mem. faculty Juilliard Sch., 1946—; mem. faculty, artist in residence Mich. State U., 1977—; resident mem. quartet Library of Congress, 1963—; panelist Nat. Endowment for Arts. Pres., Walter Naumburg Found. Served with AUS, 1943-46. Mem. Am. Composers Alliance, Juilliard Sch. Music Alumni Assn. Clubs:

Century, Bohemian. Composer numerous works for violin, piano, orch., chamber music. Office: Juilliard Sch Lincoln Center New York NY 10023

MANN, ROBERT TRASK, lawyer, state govt. exec.; b. Tarpon Springs, Fla., June 5, 1924; s. William Edgar and Lenora Eunice (Trask) M.; B.S.B.A., U. Fla., 1946, J.D., 1951; M.A. in Govt., George Washington U., 1948; LL.M., Harvard U., 1953, Yale U., 1968; LL.D. (hon.), Stetson U., 1979; m. Elizabeth Brown, Dec. 27, 1947; children—Robert Trask, Margaret Elizabeth. Admitted to Fla. bar, 1951, Mass. bar, 1952; asst. prof. law Northeastern U., 1951-53; practice law, Tampa, Fla., 1953-68; judge Ct. of Appeal, 2d Dist. Fla., 1968-74, chief judge, 1973-74; prof. law U. Fla., 1974—; mem. Fla. Public Service Commn., Tallahassee, 1978—, chmn., 1979—; mem. Fla. Ho. of Reps., 1956-68. Served with AUS, 1943-45. Recipient award as most outstanding rep St. Petersburg (Fla.) Times, 1967. Fellow Am. Bar Found.; mem. Am. Bar Assn., Am. Law Inst., Am. Judicature Soc. Democrat. Methodist. Club: Kiwanis. Contbr. articles to law jours. Home: 2520 Harriman Circle Tallahassee FL 32304 Office: 101 E Gaines St Tallahassee FL 32304

MANN, ROBERT WELLESLEY, educator, engr.; b. Bklyn., Oct. 6, 1924; s. Arthur Wellesley and Helen (Rieger) M.; S.B., Mass. Inst. Tech., 1950, S.M., 1951, Sc.D., 1957; m. Margaret Ida Florencourt, Sept. 4, 1950; children—Robert Wellesley, Catherine Louise. With Bell Telephone Labs., N.Y.C., 1942-43, 46-47; research engr. Mass. Inst. Tech., 1951-52, research supr., 1952-57, mem. faculty, 1953—, prof. mech. engring., 1963-70, Germeshausen prof., 1970-72, prof. engring., 1972-74, Whitaker prof. biomed. engring., 1974—, head systems and design div., mech. engring. dept., 1957-68, founder, engring. projects lab., 1959-62; founder, chmn. steering com. Center Sensory Aids Evaluation and Devel., 1964—, chmn. div. health scis., tech., planning and mgmt., 1972-74; lectr. engring. in faculty of medicine Harvard, 1973—; exec. com. program in health scis. and tech. Harvard-Mass. Inst. Tech., 1972—; research asso. in orthopedic surgery Children's Hosp. Med. Center, 1973—; cons. in engring. sci. Mass. Gen. Hosp.; cons. in field, 1953—; mem. Commn. Engring. Edn., 1962-69; com. prosthetics research and devel. Nat. Acad. Scis., 1963-69, chmn. sensory aids subcom., 1965-68, com. skeletal system, 1969; mem. com. interplay engring. with biology and medicine Nat. Acad. Engring., 1969-73, chmn. sensory aids subcom., 1968-73; mem. com. sci. policy for medicine and health Inst. Medicine, 1973-74; mem. com. on nat. needs for rehab. physically handicapped Nat. Acad. Scis., 1975-76; mem.-at-large confs. com. Engring. Found., 1975—. Pres., trustee Amanda Caroline Payson Scholarship Fund, 1965—; bd. dirs. Carroll Rehab. Center, 1967-74, pres., 1968-74; mem. corp. Perkins Sch. for Blind, 1970—, Mt. Auburn Hosp., 1972—. Served with AUS, 1943-46. Recipient Sloan award for outstanding performance, 1957; Talbert Abrams photogrammetry award, 1962; award Assn. Blind of Mass., 1969; IR-100 award for Braillemboss, 1972; Bronze Beaver award Mass. Inst. Tech., 1975; UCP Goldenson Research for Handicapped award, 1976, H.R. Lissner award, 1977. Fellow Am. Acad. Arts and Scis., Nat. Acad. Engring.; mem. Inst. Medicine of Nat. Acad. Scis., ASME (gold medal 1977), Am. Soc. Engring. Edn., AAAS, Biomed. Engring. Soc., IEEE (fellow; chmn. group on engring. in biology and medicine 1974-78), Sigma Xi (nat. lectr. 1979-81), Tau Beta Pi, Pi Tau Sigma. Roman Catholic. Author numerous articles in field. Cons. editor Ency. Sci. and Tech., also Design Research; editorial bd. Advances in Biomed. and Med. Physics, Jour. Visual Impairment and Blindness, 1976—; asso. editor IEEE Trans. in Biomed. Engring., 1969-78, ASME Jour. Biomed. Engring., 1976—. Patentee in field. Home: 5 Pelham Rd Lexington MA 02173 Office: 77 Massachusetts Ave Cambridge MA 02139

MANN, SEYMOUR ZALMON, educator, union ofcl.; b. Chgo., Mar. 29, 1921; s. Morris and Sarah (Julius) M.; student Wright Coll., 1938-40; B.E., No. Ill. U., 1942; M.A., U. Chgo., 1947, Ph.D., 1951; m. Irene Eincig, Aug. 30, 1942; children—Martin R., Sheldon H., Jeanette P. Instr. polit. sci. Triple Cities Coll., Syracuse U., 1948-51; asst. prof. Harpur Coll., State U. N.Y., 1951-55, asso. prof. polit. sci., 1955-60, chmn. dept., 1953-58; dir. pub. adminstrn. and met. affairs program, prof. govt. So. Ill. U., Edwardsville, 1960-67; chmn., prof. urban affairs dept. urban affairs Hunter Coll., 1967-77, dir. Urban Research Center, 1967-68, chmn. dept. urban affairs, 1968-73; dep. to execs. dist. council 37, Am. Fedn. State, County and Mcpl. Employees, AFL-CIO, 1977-79; prof. govt. and public adminstrn., asso. dir. Center Public Mgmt., John Jay Coll., City U. N.Y., 1980—; vis. expert research staff Office Pub. Affairs, High Commr.'s Office, Germany, 1954; cons. Southwestern Ill. Govtl. Study Commn., 1961-62; vis. prof. U. So. Calif. Sch. Pub. Adminstrn., 1967. Co-chmn. Ill. U.-State Agy. Council, 1965-67; co-chmn. nat. commn. on urban affairs Am. Jewish Congress, 1977—; cons. dist. council 37 Am. Fedn. State, County and Municipal Employees, N.Y.C., 1972—, coordinator spl. projects, 1977—. Fellow Social Sci. Research Council, 1949-50; Fulbright prof., W. Germany, 1953-54, Tel Aviv (Israel) U., 1974-75. Served with AUS, 1943-45; ETO. Mem. Am. Polit. Sci. Assn., Am. Soc. for Pub. Adminstrn. (pres. St. Louis met. chpt. 1964-65), AAUP. Author: (with Charlotte B. Smart) Land Use and Planning in the Cleveland Metropolitan Area, 1959; (with R.R. Boyce) Urbanism in Illinois: Its Nature Importance and Problems, 1965; Chicago's War on poverty, 1966; also articles. Home: 120 E 81st St New York NY 10028 Office: 445 W 59 St New York NY 10019

MANN, STANLEY JAY, lawyer; b. Chattanooga, July 15, 1929; s. Lester and Lee (Baras) M.; B.A., Hobart Coll., 1949; J.D., Harvard, 1953. Admitted to N.J. bar, 1953, N.Y. bar, 1966, Fla. bar, 1972, Calif. bar, 1973, also U.S. Supreme Ct., U.S. Ct. Mil. Appeals; mem. firm Frederick M. Adams, Woodbridge, N.J., 1957-60, Stanley J. Mann, Woodbridge, 1960-65; staff atty. Levitt & Sons., Inc., Lake Success, N.Y., 1965-68, sec., asst. gen. counsel, 1968; sec., v.p., gen. counsel, dir. ITT Community Devel. Corp., Miami, Fla., 1968-72; asso. counsel Larwin Group, Inc., Beverly Hills, Calif., 1972-74; partner firm Mann & Dady, Miami, 1974—. Fla. chmn. HUD Equal Opportunity Com., 1974—; mem. Miami Human Resources Commn., 1976—; bd. dirs. Nat. Land Council, Miami, 1970—. Senator, Jr. Chamber Internat.; trustee Players State Theatre, 1979—. Served to lt. USNR, 1953-57. Mem. Am., N.J., Fla., Los Angeles, Dade County bar assns. Jewish. Mason. Home: Apt 4-D 550 Ocean Dr Key Biscayne FL 33149 Office: 1438 Brickell Ave Miami FL 33131

MANN, THEODORE, theatrical producer; b. N.Y.C., May 13, 1924; s. Martin M. and Gwen (Artson) Goldman; Asso. B.A., Salinas (Calif.) Jr. Coll., 1945; LL.B., Bklyn. Law Sch., 1949; m. Patricia A. Brooks, Oct. 5, 1953; children—Andrew, Jonathan. Co-founder, co-producer Circle in the Square Theatre, N.Y.C., 1951—; co-founder Circle in the Sq. Theatre Sch., 1961; co-producer Long Day's Journey into Night (Antoinette Perry award as best prodn. of year 1956-57, Pulitzer prize, N.Y. Drama Critics award), 1956; producer Carnegie Hall Concert Series, 1955-69; co-producer Washington Sq. Park Concert Series, 1955; producer-dir. Ford's Theatre, Washington, 1968—; host radio show Conversations with Circle in the Square Sta. WNYC, 1978. Served with USAAF, 1943-45. Recipient Vernon Rice award, 1956, Page One award Newspaper Guild, 1960, Tony spl. award, 1976. Author: Producers on Producing, 1975. Home: 853 7th Ave New York NY 10019 Office: Circle in the Square Theatre 1633 Broadway New York NY 10019

MANN, THEODORE RALPH, lawyer; b. Kosica, Czechoslovakia, Jan. 31, 1928; s. Aaron and Bertha (Schreiber) M.; came to U.S., 1929, naturalized, 1930; B.A., Pa. State U., 1949; LL.B., Temple U., 1952; m. Rowena Joan Weiss, 1954; children—Julie Ellen, Rachel Beth, Marc Elliott. Admitted to Pa. bar, 1952; practice in Phila., 1953—; partner firm Mann & Ungar; advocate in civil liberties, anti-trust and securities fraud cases. Chmn. Conf. of Pres.'s of Maj. Am. Jewish Orgns., 1978—, Nat. Jewish Community Relations Adv. Council, 1976—, Nat. Israel Task Force, 1973-76, commn. law and social action Am. Jewish Congress, 1972-76; bd. dirs. Phila. chpt. ACLU, 1960-73. Home: 303 Barwynne Ln Wynnewood PA 19096 Office: 1711 Rittenhouse Sq Philadelphia PA 19103

MANN, THURSTON JEFFERSON, educator; b. Lake Landing, N.C., June 22, 1920; s. Thomas J. and Blanche (Bonner) M.; B.S., N.C. State U., 1941, M.S., 1947; Ph.D., Cornell, 1950; m. Lela B. Davenport, June 13, 1945; children—Thurston Jeffrey, Raymond Thomas, Richard Harvey. Mem. faculty N.C. State U., Raleigh, 1949—, prof. crop sci., 1955-64, prof. genetics and crop sci., 1964—, asst. dir. research Sch. Agr. and Life Scis., 1976—. Served to lt. USNR, 1942-45. Fellow Am. Soc. Agronomy; mem. Am. Genetics Assn., Genetics Soc. Am., Sigma Xi, Phi Kappa Phi, Kappa Phi Kappa, Gamma Sigma Delta. Home: 710 Runnymede Rd Raleigh NC 27607

MANN, WALTER, industrialist; b. Eastman, Ga., July 31, 1898; s. William W. and Lola Vinton (Brassels) M., student U. Fla., 1917-18, H.H.D. (hon.); m. Gertrude Orcutt Guasti, Jan. 1946; 1 son, Walter. With Irving Trust Co., N.Y.C, 1928-31, Am. Chicle Co., L.I., 1931-37; pres. Wilbur-Suchard Chocolate Co., Inc., Lititz, Pa., 1935-55, chmn. 1955—; dir. Rock City Packaging Co. Pres. Lola Mann Meml. Fund; trustee Berry Schs., Stetson U.; bd. dirs. Charles A. Dana Found.; overseer, treas. Stetson Law Coll. Baptist. Clubs: Racquet and Tennis (N.Y.C.); Mountain Lake (Fla); Naples (Fla.) Yacht. Home: 2500 Gulf Shore Blvd N Naples FL 33940 Office: 4375 East Lake Dexter Winter Haven FL 33880. *I want persons to feel better in my company. Principle-It is wrong to impose one's will on another.*

MANN, WILLIAM RICHARD, univ. dean; b. Battle Creek, Mich., Apr. 29, 1916; s. Alexander Richard and Mary Amelia (Williams) M.; D.D.S., U. Mich., 1940, M.S., 1942; Sc.D. (hon.), Mich. State U., 1973; m. Margaret Alice Limberg, Sept. 16, 1940; 1 son, Alexander William. Mem. faculty U. Mich. Sch. Dentistry, 1940—, prof., 1955—, dean Sch. Dentistry, dir. W. K. Kellogg Found. Inst. Grad. and Postgrad. Dentistry, 1962—. Instr. dental seminars, cons. in field, 1956—; dir. sect. dental edn., survey dentistry in U.S., Am. Council Edn., 1958-60; mem. expert com. dental edn. WHO, 1962, expert adv. panel dental health, 1962—; mem. dental research adv. com. Med. Research and Devel. Bd., Office Surgeon Gen., Dept. Army, 1954-62; mem. dental tng. com. Nat. Inst. Dental Research, USPHS, 1961-63; dental adv. com. W. K. Kellogg Found., 1963-67, Latin Am. study com., 1964-65, Latin Am. adv. com., 1966-67; adv. com. dental tng. USPHS, 1963-66; med. adv. bd. FDA, 1965-70; hon. prof. dental sci. Yonsei U., Seoul, S. Korea, 1970—. Bd. dirs. Am. Fund Dental Edn., 1956-73; bd. dirs. Mich. Health Council, 1973—, pres., 1977. Mem. Am., Mich. dental assns., Washtenaw Dist. Dental Soc. (past pres.), Internat., Am. colls. dentists, Am. Assn. Dental Schs. (pres. 1970-71), Fedn. Dentaire Internat., Internat. Assn. Dental Research, Mich. Assn. Professions, Pierre Fauchard Acad., Sigma Xi. Omicron Kappa Upsilon (nat. pres. 1958-59), Phi Eta Sigma, Phi Kappa Phi, Phi Kappa Sigma, Delta Sigma Delta; hon. mem. Am. Acad. Periodontology, Assn. Latinoamericana de Facultades de Odontologia, Detroit Dental Clinic Club, Korean Dental Assn., Soc. Odontologica Antioquena. Author articles, chpts. in books. Editor: (with K. A. Easlick) Practice Administration for the Dentist, 1955. Home: 1329 Glendaloch Circle Ann Arbor MI 48104

MANNE, ALAN SUSSMANN, educator, economist; b. N.Y.C., May 1, 1925; s. Isidor and Ruth (Liberman) M.; A.B., Harvard, 1943, M.A., 1948, Ph.D., 1950; m. Jacqueline Copp, July 2, 1954; children—Edward, Henry, Elizabeth. Instr., Harvard, 1950-52; economist RAND Corp., 1952-56; asso. prof. Yale, 1956-61; prof. econs. and ops. research Stanford, 1961-74, 76—; prof. polit. economy Harvard, 1974-76 econ. adviser U.S. AID mission to India, 1966-67. Served to lt. (j.g.) USNR, 1944-46. Recipient Lanchester prize ORSA. Fellow Center for Advanced Study in Behavioral Scis., 1970-71. Fellow Econometric Soc.; mem. Phi Beta Kappa. Author: Scheduling of Petroleum Refinery Operations, 1956; Economic Analysis for Business Decisions, 1961; Studies in Process Analysis, 1963; Investments for Capacity Expansion, 1967; Multi-Level Planning: Case Studies in Mexico, 1973. Home: 834 Esplanada Way Stanford CA 94305

MANNE, HENRY GIRARD, educator, lawyer; b. New Orleans, May 10, 1928; s. Geoffrey and Eva (Shainberg) M.; B.A., Vanderbilt U., 1950, J.D., U. Chgo., 1952; LL.M., Yale, 1953, J.S.D., 1966; m. Bobbette Lee Taxer, Aug. 19, 1968; children—Emily Kay, Geoffrey Adam. Admitted to Ill. bar, 1952, N.Y. bar, 1969; practice in Chgo., 1953-54; asso. prof. Law Sch., St. Louis U., 1956-57, 59-62; asst. prof. Law Sch., U. Wis., Madison, 1957-59; prof. Law Sch., George Washington U., 1962-68; Kenan prof. law and polit. sci. U. Rochester, 1968-74; Distinguished prof. law, dir. Law and Econs. Center, U. Miami Law Sch., 1974—; vis. prof. Stanford Law Sch., 1971-72; law cons. Bd. dirs. Econs. Insts. Fed. Judges, 1976—. Served to 1st lt. USAF, 1954-56. Mem. Am. Bar Assn., Am. Econs. Assn., Phila. Soc., Phi Beta Kappa, Order of Coif, Mont Pelerin Soc. Author: Insider Trading and the Stock Market, 1966; (with H. Wallich) The Modern Corporation and Social Responsibility, 1973; (with E. Solomon) Wall Street in Transition, 1974. Editor: (with Roger LeRoy Miller) Gold, Money and the Law, 1975, Auto Safety Regulation: The Cure or the Problem, 1976; Economic Policy and the Regulation of Corporate Securities, 1968; The Economics of Legal Relationships, 1975. Home: 3102 Granada Blvd Coral Gables FL 33134

MANNE, SHELLY, musician, band leader, composer, jazz club owner; b. N.Y.C., June 11, 1920; s. Max Harold and Anna (Cozlin) M.; student pub. schs., N.Y.C.; m. Florence Butterfield, Aug. 26, 1943. Alto saxophonist, 1938, drummer, 1939—; played on boats to Europe, 1939; with Bobby Byrne Band, 1939, Bob Astor Band, 1940, Jo Marsala Band, 1940, Raymond Scott Band, 1941, Will Bradley Band, 1941-42, Les Brown Band, 1942; musician NBC, CBS Studios, 1945, 52d Street Jazz Clubs, 1945-46, Stan Kenton Band, 1946-47, 47-48, 49-52, Charlie Ventura, 1947, Jazz at Philharmonic and Woody Hermann Orch., 1948-49; free lance musician, Los Angeles, 1952-55; organized own band, 1955; recordings for Capitol Records, 1954—; owner The Manne-Hole, Hollywood, Calif., 1960—; tech. adviser motion picture Man with the Golden Arm; actor motion pictures I Want to Live, The Five Pennies, The Gene Krupa Story; music scored movie The Proper Time; guest star numerous TV shows; composer score for TV series Daktari, motion pictures Trial of Catonsville Nine, 1972, Trader Horn, 1973. Served with USCGR, 1942-45. Recipient pollwinner plaque Down Beat mag., 1947-51, 54, 56-60; poll winner Metronome mag., 1949-50, 52- 53, 55-59; silver medal Playboy mag., 1957-62, spl. award All Stars All Star, 1959, 60; award internat. poll Melody Maker mag., Eng., 1957-59. . *Belief in yourself. Confidence in yourself. Honesty in your art and to your art. Truth.*

MANNER, HAROLD WALLACE, biologist, educator; b. Bklyn., July 31, 1925; s. Arthur James and Erna (Muller) M.; B.S., John Carroll U., 1949; M.S., Northwestern U., 1950, Ph.D., 1952; m. Marguerite Jean Lauria, Dec. 29, 1945; children—Cynthia Lee (Mrs. John Frederick Tolpa), Faith Anne. Vis. asst. prof. biology Kenyon Coll., Gambier, Ohio, 1952-53; mem. faculty Utica (N.Y.) Coll. of Syracuse U., 1952-69, prof. biology, chmn. div. sci. and math., 1963-69; prof. biology, chmn. dept. biology St. Louis U., St. Louis, 1969-72; prof., chmn. dept. biology Loyola U., Chgo., 1972—. Democratic candidate for N.Y. senator, 1962. Served with USNR, 1942-46. Mem. AAAS, Am. Inst. Biol. Scientists, Am. Soc. Zoologists, Sigma Xi. Author: Elements of Anatomy and Physiology, 1962; Elements of Comparative Vertebrate Embryology, 1963; (with J. Mavor) General Biology, 6th edit., 1966; (with J. Mavor) Laboratory Manual in General Biology, 6th edit., 1967; Vertebrate Anatomy, 1975; The Death of Cancer, 1978. Home: 1136 Brandywyn Ct Buffalo Grove IL 60090

MANNERING, GILBERT JAMES, educator, pharmacologist, biochemist; b. Racine, Wis., Mar. 9, 1917; s. John Knight and Louise (Holm) M.; B.S., U. Wis., 1940, M.S., 1943, Ph.D., 1944; m. Virginia Agnes Krahn, Feb. 1, 1939 (dec.); children—Michael John, Gail Phyllis, Barbara Lynn; m. 2d, Dagny Blanchard H. Flynn, Oct. 27, 1969. Sr. research biochemist Parke, Davis & Co., Detroit, 1944-50; cons. in chemistry 406th Med. Gen. Lab., Tokyo, Japan, 1950-54; with U. Wis., 1954-62; prof. pharmacology U. Minn., Mpls., 1962—. Cons. toxicology Wis. Crime Lab., 1954-62, Wis. Dept. Agr., 1954-57; spl. cons. interdepartmental com. on nutrition for nat. def. NIH, Ethiopia, 1958; mem. toxicology study sect. USPHS, 1962-65, mem. pharmacology-toxicology rev. com., 1965-67, pharmacology study sect. 1968-69; mem. com. problems drug safety NRC, 1967-71. Mem. Am. Soc. Pharmacology and Exptl. Therapeutics, Am. Soc. Biol. Chemistry, Sigma Xi. Studies, publs. drug metabolism; metabolism of narcotics, alcohols, kinetics of drug metabolizing enzymes, inhibition of drug metabolism; devel. chem. analytical procedures used in drug metabolism studies and in toxicology. Home: 1865 N Fairview St St Paul MN 55113 Office: Dept Pharmacology U Minn Minneapolis MN 55455

MANNERS, DOROTHY, columnist; b. Ft. Worth; d. Mason and Gertrude (Green) Harwell; student pub. schs.; m. John E. Haskell, Aug. 19, 1947. Actress, Old Fox Co.; former asst. to Louella Parsons; columnist Hearst King Features Syndicate. Mem. Greater Los Angeles Press Club, Womens Press Club Calif., A.F.T.R.A. Home: 744 N Doheny Dr Los Angeles CA 90069 Office: 205 S Beverly Dr Beverly Hills CA 90212*

MANNERS, GEORGE EMANUEL, coll. ofcl.; b. N.Y.C., Nov. 26, 1910; s. John Emanuel and Demetra (Kremida) M.; B.S. in Commerce, Ga. State U., 1935; M.B.A. in Econs., U. Ga., 1946; Ph.D. in History, Emory U., 1959; m. Claire Gibson, Oct. 14, 1939; children—George Emanuel, Susan Demetra. Bookkeeper and accountant in Ga., 1927-37; engaged in practice pub. accounting, 1937; high sch. tchr., Atlanta, 1937-39, 41-42, 46-47; test technician merit system Ga. Labor Dept., 1939-41; mem. faculty Ga. State U., and predecessor, 1947—, dean Sch. Bus. Adminstrn., 1950-69, asst. v.p., 1969-70, asso. v.p., 1970—, Regents' prof., 1971—, dean emeritus, 1977—; dean Sch. Mgmt., Rensselaer Poly. Inst., Troy, N.Y., 1979-80. Mem. Met. Planning Commn., Atlanta, 1949-59, Atlanta Regional Export Expansion Council. Served to maj. AUS, 1942-46. Mem. So. Econ. Assn., So. Hist. Assn., Atlanta C. of C., Hellenic Study Group, Delta Sigma Pi, Beta Gamma Sigma. Methodist (Sunday sch. tchr.). Kiwanian. Author: History of Life Insurance Company in Georgia, 1891-1955, 1959; also articles. Home: 338 Nelson Ferry Rd Decatur GA 30030 Office: 33 Gilmer St SE Atlanta GA 30303. *I have noted that a life devoted to a sound ideal, pursued steadily with character and tolerance, brings the keenest and most lasting happiness. Others feel the fire and assist on the way; impediments become adventures. Challenge and zest accompany one each day; horizons widen. This spirit can be applied by all, in every walk of life, in every field of endeavor, in every land, at all times in history.*

MANNERS, ROBERT ALAN, anthropologist; b. N.Y.C., Aug. 21, 1913; s. Abraham Rosen and Dora (Kniaz) M.; B.S., Columbia U., 1935, M.A., 1939, Ph.D., 1950; m. Margaret D. Hall, July 6, 1943 (div. July 1955); children—Karen Elizabeth, John Hall; m. 2d, Jean I. Hall, Sept. 12, 1955; children—Stephen David, Katherine Dora. Instr., U. Rochester, 1950-52; lectr., asst. prof., asso. prof., prof. Brandeis U., Waltham, Mass., 1952—, Ralph Levitz prof. anthropology, 1973—, chmn. dept. anthropology, 1963-68, 78—; mem. social sci. subcom. NIH, 1965-69. Bd. dirs. Research Inst. For Study Man. Served to capt. AUS, 1942-46. Fellow Am. Anthrop. Assn.; mem. N.E. Anthrop. Assn. (pres. 1978-79), Am. Ethnol. Soc. Author: (with others) People of Puerto Rico, 1956; editor: (with James Duffy) Africa Speaks, 1961; Process and Pattern in Culture, 1964; The Kipsigis of Kenya, 1967; (with David Kaplan) Theory in Anthropology: A Sourcebook, 1968, Culture Theory, 1972; Southern Paiute and Chemehuevi: An Ethnohistorical Report, 1974; An Ethnological Report on the Hualapai Indians of Arizona, 1975; Havasupai Indians: An Ethnohistorical Report, 1975; editor Am. Anthropologist, 1974-76; contbr. articles to profl. jours. Home: 134 Sumner St Newton Centre MA 02159

MANNING, ALFRED PAUL, coast guard officer; b. Cambridge, Mass., Sept. 28, 1928; s. Alfred Paul and Katherine Frances (Kinney) M.; B.S., U.S. Coast Guard Acad., 1951; M.S.E.E., U. Conn., 1958; M.M.A., U. R.I., 1971; m. Claire Florine Cote, June 9, 1951; children—Carol Irene, Maureen Claire, David Brian. Commd. ensign U.S. Coast Guard, 1951, advanced through grades to rear adm., 1978; chief electronics devel. br. U.S. Coast Guard Hdqrs., Washington, 1967-70; comdg. officer U.S. Coast Guard Base, Honolulu, 1971-74; dep. chief Office of Engring., U.S. Coast Guard Hdqrs., Washington, 1974-77; chief of ops., Seattle, 1977-78; chief research and devel. U.S. Coast Guard Hdqrs., Washington, 1978—. Mem. IEEE, Inst. Nav., U.S. Naval Inst. (bd. control), Marine Tech. Soc., Soc. Naval Architects, U.S. Coast Guard Acad. Alumni Assn. Roman Catholic. Home: 3621 Camelot Dr Annandale VA 22003 Office: USCG Hdqrs Washington DC 20590. *The only unforgivable failure is the failure to act when the situation demands it.*

MANNING, ARTHUR BREWSTER, newspaper editor; b. Atlanta, Mar. 31, 1913; s. James Arthur and Rose (Word) M.; m. Mildred J. Dalton, July 11, 1945; children—March Word, James Brewster, William Dalton. Editorial positions Atlanta Constn., 1932-55; press-radio dir. Ga. War Finance Com., 1944-46; copy chief Robert Scott Advt. Agy., Atlanta, 1943-50; with Jacksonville (Fla.) Times-Union, 1955—, mng. editor, 1959-76. Home: 414 Oglethorpe Rd Jacksonville FL 32216 Office: PO Box 1949 Jacksonville FL 32201

MANNING, BAYLESS ANDREW, lawyer; b. Bristow, Okla., Mar. 29, 1923; s. Raphael Andrew and Helen Mahala (Guffy) M.; A.B., Yale, 1943, LL.B., 1949, M.A. (hon.), 1960; LL.D., Grinnell Coll., Northeastern U.; m. Marjorie Jolivette, July 10, 1945 (div. 1972); children—Bayless Andrew, Elizabeth Jane Beecher, Lucia Harrison, Matthew Dexter; m. 2d, Donna Dillon, Mar. 7, 1972. Admitted to

D.C. bar, 1950, Ohio bar, 1951, Conn. bar, 1957, N.Y. State bar, 1977; law clk. to U.S. Supreme Ct. justice Stanley F. Reed, 1949-50; with firm Jones, Day, Cockley, & Reavis, Cleve., 1950-56; prof. law Yale U., 1956-64, chmn. Latin Am. studies program, 1958-60; spl. asst. to undersec. state, 1962-63; dean, prof. law Stanford Law Sch., Palo Alto, Calif., 1964-71; pres. Council Fgn. Relations, 1971-77; partner firm Paul, Weiss, Rifkind, Wharton & Garrison, N.Y.C., 1977—; dir. Aetna Life & Casualty, Scovill Mfg. Co., J. Henry Schroder Bank & Trust Co., Amcon Group. Chmn., Conn. Commn. Revision Corp. Laws, 1959-61; mem. Pres.'s Ethics Commn., 1961, Pres.'s Emergency Mediation Panel, 1967, Pres.'s Commn. on Campus Unrest, 1970; cons. U.S. Dept. Commerce, 1961-62, Peace Corps, 1961, Senate Com. Govt. Ops., 1960, Conn., Calif. legislatures. Trustee, chmn., pres. Sun Valley Forum on Nat. Health; trustee China Med. Bd.; trustee Yale U. Served to 1st lt. AUS, 1943-46. Mem. Am. Bar Assn., Am. Soc. Internat. Law, Am. Acad. Arts and Scis., Council Fgn. Relations, Order of Coif, Phi Beta Kappa. Author: Conflict of Interest and Federal Service, 1960; Federal Conflict of Interest Law, 1964; U.S. Foreign Policy in Nation's Third Century, 1976; Legal Capital, 1977; contbr. articles on law and fgn. affairs to profl. jours. Editor-in-chief Yale Law Jour., 1948. Address: 345 Park Ave New York NY 10022

MANNING, BURT, advt. exec. Asso. creative dir. Leo Burnett Co., Chgo., 1964-66; vice chmn. bd. J. Walter Thompson Co., N.Y.C., 1977—. Address: 420 Lexington Ave New York NY 10017

MANNING, DONALD WADDINGTON, mfg. co. exec.; b. Phila., Feb. 9, 1927; s. William Perry and Ida Mae (Waddington) M.; B.S. in Commerce and Finance, Bucknell U., 1952; m. Mary Tompkins, Apr. 22, 1955; children—Peter Bruce, Douglas Tompkins, Gary Waddington. With Budd Co., 1952—, gen. mgr. electronic controls sect., 1961, with instruments div., 1961-64, sec., 1964—. Home: 1309 Sandringham Way Birmingham MI 48010 Office: 3155 W Big Beaver Rd Troy MI 48084

MANNING, EDWARD PETER, lawyer, state legislator; b. Providence, Nov. 16, 1924; s. John J. and Margaret M. (Cahir) M.; A.B., Iowa Wesleyan Coll., Mt. Pleasant, 1949; J.D., Cath. U., Washington, 1952; m. Regina A. Fitzpatrick, May 11, 1957; children—John, Mary, Stephanie, Edward Peter, Amy, Melanie. Admitted to R.I. bar, 1953; partner firm Manning, West, Santaniello & Pari, Providence, 1953—; mem. R.I. Ho. of Reps., 1967—, dep. majority leader, 1968-76, speaker, 1977—; past legal counsel R.I. Dept. Pub. Works, R.I. Dept. Health. Active, Sherman LeClerc Monteiro Civic Center; moderator Cumberland Town Meeting, 1964-76; bd. dirs. Cumberland Housing Authority, Cumberland Heart Fund; bd. dirs. R.I. Lung Assn. Served with USAAF, 1943-45. Decorated Air medal; recipient Ann. Alumni Achievement award in field govt. and politics Cath. U. Am. Alumni Assn., 1977. Mem. R.I. Bar Assn. (past dir., bd. dels.), VFW, Am. Legion, Friendly Sons St. Patrick, Sons of Irish Kings. Clubs: Elks; St. Joseph Vets.; Turks Head; Serra. Office: 711 Indsl Bank Bldg Providence RI 02903

MANNING, HON. ERNEST C., former premier of Alta.; b. Carnduff, Sask., Can., Sept. 20, 1908; s. George Henry and Elizabeth Mara (Dickson) M.; LL.D., U. Alta., 1948, McGill U., 1967, U. Lethbridge, 1972; D.U.C., U. Calgary, 1967; m. Muriel Aileen Preston, Apr. 14, 1936; children—William Keith, Ernest Preston. Provincial sec., 1935; minister trade and industry Province of Alta., 1935-43; premier Province Alta., 1943-68, provincial treas., 1944-56, minister mines and minerals, 1952-62, atty. gen., 1955-68; mem. Canadian Privy Council, 1967; mem. Canadian Senate, 1970; chmn. Manning Cons.'s Ltd.; dir. Steel Co. Can., Ltd., Fluor Can. Ltd., Mfrs. Life Ins. Co., Melcor Devels. Ltd., McIntyre Mines, Ltd., Burns Food Ltd., OPI Ltd. Decorated Companion Order Can. Address: 54 Westbrook Dr Edmonton AB T6J 2C9 Canada

MANNING, FARLEY, pub. relations counsel; b. Shelburne Falls, Mass., Oct. 30, 1909; s. John Farley and Bessie (Learmont) M.; student Northeastern U., 1927-29, Boston U., 1929-31; m. Ruth Fulton Koegel, Jan. 23, 1932; 1 dau., Toni Ruth. With various New Eng. papers, 1932-43; with firm Dudley-Anderson-Yutzy, 1946-54; pres. Farley Manning Assos., N.Y.C., 1954-72; pres. Manning, Selvage & Lee, N.Y.C., 1972-73, chmn. bd., 1973—; chmn. bd. G & M Creative Services, Inc., 1958—; dir. Bankers Fed. Savs. & Loan Assn. Served to maj. USAAF, 1943-46. Mem. Pub. Relations Soc. Am. Clubs: N.Y. Yacht, Sleepy Hollow Country, Overseas Press. Contbr. articles on dog care and tng. to nat. mags. Home: 137 E 36 St New York NY 10016 also Roscoe NY 12776 Office: 99 Park Ave New York NY 10016

MANNING, FRANCIS SCOTT, educator; b. Barbados, W.I., Sept. 16, 1933; s. Francis Fyles and Eileen (Robinson) M.; B.Eng., McGill U., 1955; M.S., Princeton, 1957, A.M., 1957, Ph.D., 1959; m. Nancy Elizabeth Free, Apr. 16, 1960 (div. May 1977); children—Francis Charles, Helen Eileen. Came to U.S., 1955, naturalized, 1964. Instr., Carnegie Inst. Tech., 1959, asst. prof., 1959-64, asso. prof. chem. engring., 1964-68; prof., chmn. chem. engring. dept. U. Tulsa, 1968-76; dir. Petroleum and Energy Research Inst., 1977—. Cons. St. Joseph Lead Co., 1964-68, Westinghouse Electric Corp., 1968-69, U.S. Bur. Mines, 1966-68, Maloney-Crawford Tank Corp., 1968—. Prin. investigator, grantee NSF, 1960-64, Petroleum Research Found., 1965-68, Am. Iron and Steel Inst., 1963-68, EPA, 1968—, ERDA, 1968—. Mem. Am. Inst. Chem. Engrs., Am. Inst. Mining, Metall. Engrs., Am. Soc. Engring. Edn. (chmn. Allegheny sect. 1965), Sigma Xi, Tau Beta Pi. Club: Princeton (Tulsa). Author: (with L.N. Canjar) Thermo Properties and Reduced Correlations for Gases, 1967. Contbr. articles to profl. jours. Home: 4987-A S 72d East Ave Tulsa OK 74145

MANNING, GEORGE WILLIAM, physician; b. Toronto, Ont., Can., Aug. 4, 1911; s. George Arthur and May (Wright) M.; ed. Malvern Collegiate, 1927-31, Trinity Coll., Toronto, 1931-35; B.A., U. Toronto, 1935, M.D., 1940; m. Marie Lillian Collins, Dec. 14, 1940; children—Cheryl, Helen, Christopher. Jr. intern St. Michael's Hosp., Toronto, 1940; intern Toronto Gen. Hosp., 1945; aviation med. research RCAF, 1940-45; Nuffield fellow cardiac unit London (Eng.) Hosp., 1946-47; mem. faculty U. Western Ont., London, 1947-77, prof. medicine dept. cardiology, 1960-77; chief cardiology, prof. medicine U. Hosps., 1972-77, ret., 1977; dir. heart unit Victoria Hosp., London, 1947-77, now cons.; cardiac cons. Can. Armed Forces, 1948-77, dept. vets. affairs Westminster Hosp., London, 1949-77. Chmn. med. com. Ont. and Can. Heart Found., 1952—, Can. Heart Found., Can. Cardiovascular Soc. Fellow A.C.P.; mem. Can., Am. phys. socs., Am. Coll. Cardiology (v.p.), Can. Soc. Clin. Investigation, others. Research and publs. on exptl. and clin. cardiovascular diseases and electro and vectorcardiography; developed vector rec. apparatus. Home: 9 Harrison Crescent London ON N5Y 2V3 Canada Office: Univ Hosp London ON Canada

MANNING, GORDON, journalist; b. New Haven, May 28, 1917; s. John G. and Katherine L. (Godber) M.; grad. Boston U., 1941; m. Edna May Currier, Oct. 1, 1942; children—Jack, David, Glenn, Douglas. Reporter, United Press, 1940-48; staff writer Collier's, 1948-49, acting mng. editor, 1949-50, mng. editor, 1950-56; sr. editor (features) Newsweek mag., 1956-61, exec. editor, 1961-64; v.p., dir. news CBS News, 1964-72, sr. v.p., 1972-74, documentary producer, 1974-75; exec. producer NBC News, 1975-78, v.p. politics and spl. programs, 1978—. Served as lt., deck officer, USNR, 1942-46. Home: 169 Newton Turnpike Westport CT 06880 Office: NBC News 30 Rockefeller Plaza New York NY 10020

MANNING, JOHN THOMAS, lawyer; b. Clearwater, Fla., May 29, 1921; s. Jacob Thomas and Carrie (Owen) M.; B.S., U. Fla., 1943; LL.B., U. Va., 1947; m. Anne Louise Zeigler, May 28, 1943; children—John Thomas, Robert Henry, Elizabeth Anne, Rebecca Leigh. Admitted to Va. bar, 1947, N.C. bar, 1959; pvt. practice law, Charlottesville, Va., 1947-48, Greensboro, N.C., 1971—; with antitrust div. U.S. Dept. Justice, 1948-50; mem. bd. appeals War Claims Commn., 1952-53; pvt. practice law, Richmond, Va., 1953-58; gen. counsel Pilot Life Ins. Co., Greensboro, N.C., 1958-71, exec. com., 1958-71, v.p., 1964-71; past dir. So. Fire & Casualty Co., Pilot Fire & Casualty Co., Pilot Title Ins. Co. Past vice chmn. laws and legislative com. Life Insurers Conf.; permanent mem. 4th Fed. Circuit Jud. Conf. Bd. dirs. Gen. Greene council Boy Scouts Am., 1968-70. Served with AUS, 1943-45; PTO. Mem. Assn. Life Ins. Counsel (permanent mem.), Am. (anti-trust and ins. sects.), Va., Va. State, N.C., Greensboro, 18th N.C. Judicial Dist. bar assns. Methodist. Clubs: Masons, Shriners, Rotary (pres. Jamestown club 1972-73). Home: 5313 Wayne Rd Greensboro NC 27407 Office: 232 W Market St PO Box 1845 Greensboro NC 27402

MANNING, MARGARET RAYMOND, editor; b. Omaha, Sept. 1, 1921; d. Anan and Florence (Hostetler) Raymond; A.B. cum laude, Vassar Coll., 1943; m. Robert J. Manning, Dec. 28, 1944; children—Richard, Brian, Robert. Book editor Boston Globe; v.p. Hostetler Land and Investment Co. Office: Boston Globe 135 Morrissey Blvd Boston MA 02107*

MANNING, NOEL THOMAS (TOMMY), publishing co. exec.; b. Ayden, N.C., Oct. 10, 1939; s. James Samuel and Tinie (McGlohon) M.; B.S. in Intermediate Edn., East Carolina U., 1978; student Free Will Baptist Bible Coll., 1960; m. Edith Joyce Reagan, Jan. 1, 1964 (div. Jan. 1973); 1 son, Noel Thomas. Bookkeeper, teller First Nat. Bank Ayden, 1963; staff illustrator Free Will Bapt. Press, Ayden, 1963-68; editor Free Will Bapt. Press Found., 1968—; tchr. creative writing Pitt Tech. Inst., Greenville, N.C., 1972—, instr. piano, 1974—; tchr. composition and creative writing Greenville Recreational Dept., 1974—. Youth dir. Cragmont Assembly Religious Camp, Black Mountain, N.C., 1968—. Columbus (Ohio) Sch. Art scholar, 1959. Mem. Free Will Bapt. Hist. Soc. (charter), Ayden Jr. C. of C., Kappa Delta Pi. Democrat. Baptist (organist). Composer ch. music. Home: 406 NE College St Ayden NC 28513 Office: 811 N Lee St Ayden NC 28513. *How be it so? I have the choice to live or die — And in my hands I hold the tools to make life good — or to make it bad . . . One abbreviates his life when he dissociates himself from others and their concerns. In order to relate meaningfully, one must share both the sorrows and the joys of his fellowman. Identifying thusly has certainly made life for me more beneficial. Accordingly, each day I live, I try to make life more livable for at least one person—be it a needed pat on the back or an extended word of greeting. I am convinced that the manner in which one approaches all situations will determine the outcome. I further believe that a smile communicates all messages best and receives in like measure.*

MANNING, REGINALD, (Reg) West, cartoonist, copper wheel crystal designer and engraver; b. Kansas City, Mo., Apr. 8, 1905; s. Charles Augustus and Mildred Ann (Joslin) M.; student pub. schs., Kansas City, Phoenix; m. Ruth Elizabeth Littlefield, Oct. 1, 1926; 1 son, David Clark. Free lance cartoonist, 1924-26; cartoonist Ariz. Republic Phoenix, 1926—; editorial cartoonist McNaught Syndicate, Inc., N.Y.C., 1948-71; owner Reganson Cartoon Books; lectr. illus. polit. satire; exhibited one-man show crystal engravings at Phoenix Art Mus., 1973-74. Bd. dirs. Pioneer Ariz. Found. Recipient Pulitzer prize for cartooning, 1951, Freedoms Found. Cartoon Awards, 1950, 51, 52, 55, 59, 61, 63, 67, 68, 69, 73, 74, 75, Nat. Safety Council award, 1957, Abraham Lincoln award Freedom's Found., 1971, 72. Mem. Assn. Am. Editorial Cartoonists, Nat. Cartoonists Soc., S.A.R., Ariz. Srs. Golf Assn. (pres. 1966), S.W. Parks and Monuments Assn. (chmn. bd. 1967-68), Ariz. Hist. Soc., Syracuse U. Library Assos. (life), Ariz. State U. Library Assos. (chmn. bd. 1974-75). Clubs: Prescott Country, Ariz. Press (life), Phoenix Press. Author: Cartoon Guide of Arizona, 1938; What Kinda Cactus izzat?, 1941; From Tee to Cup, 1954; What Is Arizona Really Like?, 1968; Desert in Crystal, 1973. Home: 5724 E Cambridge Ave Scottsdale AZ 85257 Office: care Ariz Republic PO Box 1950 Phoenix AZ 85001. *It is unimportant whether my editorial cartoon opinions are right or wrong if the reader is encouraged to THINK.*

MANNING, ROBERT JOSEPH, journalist; b. Binghamton, N.Y., Dec. 25, 1919; s. Joseph James and Agnes Pauline (Brown) M.; Nieman fellow Harvard, 1945-46; Litt.D. (hon.), Tufts U., 1966; L.H.D., St. Lawrence U., 1971; m. Margaret Marinda Raymond, Dec. 28, 1944; children—Richard Raymond, Brian Gould, Robert Brown. Reporter, Binghamton (N.Y.) Press, 1936-41, Asso. Press, 1941; State Dept. and White House corr. United Press, 1944-46, chief UN corr., 1946-49; writer Time mag., 1949-55, sr. editor, 1955-58; chief London bur. Time, Life, Fortune, Sports Illus. mags., 1958-61; Sunday editor N.Y. Herald Tribune, 1961-62; asst. sec. state for pub. affairs, Washington, 1962-64; exec. editor Atlantic Monthly, 1964-66, editor-in-chief, 1966—; v.p. Atlantic Monthly Co., 1966—. Served with AUS, 1942-43. Clubs: Century Assn. (N.Y.C.); Garrick (London); Tavern (Boston). Home: 191 Commonwealth Ave Boston MA 02116 Office: 8 Arlington St Boston MA 02116

MANNING, ROBERT THOMAS, physician, educator; b. Wichita, Kans., Oct. 16, 1927; s. Thomas Earl and Mary Francis (Ray) M.; A.B., Wichita U., 1950; M.D., Kans. U., 1954; m. Elizabeth Jane Bell, July 29, 1949; children—Mary Kay, Phillip Trenton, Susan Ann. Intern, Kansas City (Mo.) Gen. Hosp., 1954-55; resident Kans. U. Med. Center, 1955-58; trainee Nat. Inst. Arthritis and Metabolic Disease, 1956-58; instr. to prof. internal medicine, asso. prof. biochemistry Kans. U. Med. Center, 1958-69, asso. dean, 1969-71; dean Eastern Va. Med. Sch., Norfolk, 1971-75, prof., chmn. dept. internal medicine, 1975-77, asso. prof. biochemistry, 1973-77; prof. medicine U. Kans. Sch. Medicine, Wichita, 1977—. Served with USAAF, 1945-47. Diplomate Am. Bd. Internal Medicine. Fellow A.C.P.; mem. Am. Fedn. Clin. Research, Central Soc. Clin. Research, Am. Assn. Study Liver Disease, Sigma Xi, Alpha Omega Alpha. Editor: Major's Physical Diagnosis, 1975. Contbr. articles to profl. jours. Home: 31-156 N Maize Rd Wichita KS 67212 Office: 1001 N Minneapolis Wichita KS 67214

MANNING, TIMOTHY, Cardinal, clergyman; b. Cork, Ireland, Oct. 15, 1909; s. Cornelius and Margaret (Cronin) M.; came to U.S., 1928, naturalized, 1945; student St. Patrick's Sem., Menlo Park, Calif., 1928-34; D.C.L., Gregorian U., Rome, 1938. Ordained priest Roman Catholic Ch., 1934; asst. pastor Immaculate Conception Ch., Los Angeles, 1934-35; consecrated bishop, 1946; aux. bishop and chancellor Roman Catholic Archdiocese of Los Angeles, 1946—; created cardinal, 1973. Home: 114 E 2d St Los Angeles CA 90012 Office: 1531 W 9th St Los Angeles CA 90015*

MANNING, TRAVIS WARREN, educator; b. Jester, Okla., June 17, 1921; s. John William and Ida (Young) M.; student Paris Jr. Coll., 1946, U. Okla., 1947; B.S., Okla. State U., 1949, M.S., 1950; Ph.D., U. Minn., 1954; m. Bobbie Jean Fulton, Jan. 26, 1943; children—Barbara, Mary, Patricia, Nancy, John, Linda. Research fellow agrl. econs. U. Minn., 1950-52, instr., 1952-53; asst. prof. econs. S.D. State U., 1953-55, asso. prof., 1955-56, asso prof., 1957-58, prof., 1958-59; asso. prof. agrl. econs. U. Ark., 1956; agrl. economist Fed. Res. Bank Kansas City, Mo., 1959-62; prof. agrl. econs. U. Alta., 1962—, chmn. dept., 1962-74; vis. prof. agrl. econs. U. Calif. at Berkeley, 1967-68. Served with AUS, 1941-45. Mem. Agrl. Inst. Can., Can. Agrl. Econs. Soc., AAAS, Am. Econ. Assn., Am., Western agrl. econs. assns., Internat. Assn. Agr. Economists, Phi Kappa Phi, Pi Gamma Mu. Author bulls., articles. Home: 10430-31A Ave Edmonton AB T6J 3B4 Canada

MANNING, WILLIAM FREDERICK, wire service photographer; b. Gardner, Mass., Aug. 18, 1920; s. Seth Newton and Jennie May (Bennett) M.; A.A., Boston U., 1950, B.S. in Communications, 1952; m. Yvonne J.C. Winslow, Feb. 29, 1964; children—Pamela Ann, Jeffrey Newton. With A.P., Boston, 1951-53; photographer U.P.I., Boston, 1953—. Served with USN, 1940-46; PTO. Recipient Look 1st Prize All Sports award, 1958; Pictures of the Yr. award U. Mo., 1964, 74; Nat. Headliners Club award for outstanding syndicate photography, 1974. Mem. Boston Press Photographers Assn., Delta Kappa Alpha. Congregationalist. Club: Nat. Headliners. Contbr. photos to books, mags., newspapers throughout the world. Home: 23 Sunset Dr Beverly MA 01915 Office: 20 Ashburton Pl Boston MA 02108

MANNING, WILLIAM JOSEPH, lawyer; b. N.Y.C., Aug. 11, 1926; s. Joseph Michael and Eileen Johanna (Walsh) M.; B.B.A. magna cum laude, St. John's U., N.Y.C., 1949, LL.B. magna cum laude, 1952; m. Maryanne Cullen, June 23, 1956; children—William Joseph, Michael P., Maura G., Marian T., John A., Mary E. Admitted to N.Y. bar, 1952; asso. firm Simpson Thacher & Bartlett, N.Y.C., 1952-62, partner, 1962—, sr. partner, 1968—; dir. Brascan Ltd., Toronto, Ont., Can.; bd. dirs. N.Y. Lawyers for Public Interest, 1977—. Trustee Inst. for Muscle Disease, N.Y.C., 1963-70; bd. dirs. Mercy Hosp., Rockville Centre, N.Y., 1975—. Served with inf. U.S. Army, 1944-46. Fellow Am. Coll. Trial Lawyers, Am. Law Inst., Am. Bar Found.; mem. Am. Bar Assn. (chmn. sect. litigation 1977-78, founding mem. council 1973), Assn. Bar City N.Y., N.Y. State Bar Assn., N.Y. County Lawyers Assn., Am. Judicature Soc. Roman Catholic. Clubs: Recess, Garden City Golf, Westhampton Country. Notes editor St. John's Law Rev., 1951-52. Home: 18 Lefferts Rd Garden City NY 11530 also 156 Dune Rd Westhampton Beach NY 11978 Office: One Battery Park Plaza New York NY 10004

MANNING, WILLIAM RAYMOND, town ofcl.; b. Vancouver, B.C., Can., May 17, 1920; s. William and Mary (Gysels) M.; came to U.S., 1922, derivative citizen; B.A., San Jose (Calif.) State Coll., 1941; M.A., U. Pacific, 1949; Ed.D., Stanford, 1956. Tchr., Galt, Calif., 1946-49; prin., Lodi, Calif., 1949-50; supt. schs., Orangevale, Calif., 1950-58, Petaluma, Calif., 1958-64, Lansing, Mich., 1964-67, Washington, 1967-70; chmn. ednl. bd. Xerox Edn. Publs., 1969-73; pres. BFE Ednl. Consultants, 1973—; town adminstr., Bel Air, Md., 1973—; vis. prof. U. Hawaii, Sacramento State Coll., San Francisco State Coll., No. Mich. U., Mich. State U. Served with USAAF, 1942-46. Recipient community and profl. awards. Contbr. to books and profl. jours. Home: 344 Harlan Sq Bel Air MD 21014 Office: 39 Hickory Ave Bel Air MD 21014

MANNING, WILLIAM SINKLER, mfg. co. exec.; b. 1925; B.S., N.C. State U., 1948; married. Plant gen. mgr. Deering Milliken, 1949-56; div. mgr. Burlington Draper div. Burlington Industries Co., 1956-58, div. mgr., mfg. v.p. Burlington House div., 1958-69; pres., chief exec. officer Bibb Co., Macon, Ga., 1970—. Served to lt. (j.g.) USNR, 1943-45. Office: 237 Coliseum Dr Macon GA 31208

MANNONI, RAYMOND, univ. adminstr.; b. Pittsburg, Kans., July 11, 1921; s. Espartero and Mary Katherine (Scalet) M.; B.S., Kans. State U., 1944; M.Ed., U. Mich., 1946; postgrad. Northwestern U., 1947-48; D.Mus. Edn., Chgo. Mus. Coll., 1956; m. Karen Whittet, June 2, 1956; 1 dau., Barbara Gwen. Dir. bands U. Tulsa, 1946-48; 1st horn Tulsa Symphony Orch., 1946-48; dir. bands, instr. music Kans. State Tchrs. Coll., Emporia, 1949-50; prof. music, dean Coll. Fine Arts, U. So. Miss., Hattiesburg, 1960—. Cons. music edn. dept. Lyon & Healy, Chgo., 1949-50; nat. adv. bd. LeBlanc Music Educators, 1958-68. Served with USN, World War II. Recipient Alumni certificate U. So. Miss., 1954-55; award of merit Nat. Fedn. Music Clubs, 1962. Mem. Music Educators Nat. Conf. (life), Phi Kappa Phi, Phi Delta Kappa, Kappa Kappa Psi, Alpha Psi Omega, Phi Mu Alpha Sinfonia, Phi Kappa Lambda. Mason (Shriner), Elk. Club: Exchange (Hattiesburg). Co-author: Music Theory for Beginners, 1956. Home: 45 Fairlake Dr Country Club Estates Hattiesburg MS 39401. *In the ultimate sense, success is not inherent; it depends upon traits that can be developed. Self-improvement is important. Accomplishment is a totality—a totality which is a result of everything a person does in every aspect of his job and in his daily living.*

MANNY, CARTER HUGH, JR., architect, found. adminstr.; b. Michigan City, Ind., Nov. 16, 1918; s. Carter Hugh and Ada Gage (Barnes) M.; A.B. magna cum laude, Harvard, 1941, Indsl. Adminstr., 1942; Taliesin fellow, Scottsdale, Ariz., 1946; B.S. in Architecture, Ill. Inst. Tech., 1948; m. Mary Alice Kellett, Dec. 6, 1942; children—Elizabeth, Carter Hugh III. With C. F. Murphy Assos., Chgo., 1948—, partner, 1957—, sr. v.p., 1978—; projects include Chgo.-O'Hare Internat. Airport, FBI Hdqrs., Washington, First Nat. Bank Chgo., Chgo. Civic Center; dir. Citizens Bank of Michigan City; exec. dir. Graham Found. Advanced Studies Fine Arts, 1971—. Fellow AIA (pres. Chgo. chpt. 1973, dir. Ill. council 1972-73); mem. Phi Beta Kappa. Clubs: Tavern, Mid-Day, Arts (Chgo.); Pottawattomie, Michigan City Yacht (Michigan City). Home: 200 Lake Ave Michigan City IN 46360 also 1448 Lake Shore Dr Chicago IL 60610 Office: 224 S Michigan Ave Chicago IL 60604

MANO, D. KEITH, novelist; b. N.Y.C., Feb. 12, 1942; s. William F. and Marion Elizabeth (Minor) M.; B.A. summa cum laude, Columbia, 1963; postgrad. Clare Coll., Cambridge (Eng.) U., 1964-65; children—Roderick Keith, Christopher Carey. Vice pres. X-Pando Corp., bldg. maintenance materials firm, Long Island City, 1964—; contbg. editor, columnist Nat. Rev. mag., 1972—; contbg. editor Oui mag., 1972—. Recipient Best Religious Book award Publs. of Modern Lang. Assn., 1969, Best Non-Fiction award Playboy Mag., 1977. Author: Bishop's Progress, 1968; Horn, 1969; War is Heaven!, 1970; The Death and Life of Harry Goth, 1971; The Proselytizer, 1972; The Bridge, 1973. Contbr. articles to profl. jours. Office: X-Pando Corp 43-15 36th St Long Island City NY 11101

MANOFF, MARCUS, lawyer; b. Phila., Dec. 25, 1916; A.B., U. Pa., 1937; LL.B. cum laude, Harvard U., 1940, LL.M., 1941; m. Lilliah, Nov. 10, 1946; children—Kenneth L., Susan B. Admitted to Mass. bar, 1940, Pa. bar, 1941, U.S. Dist. Ct. bar, 1947; atty. SEC, 1942, 46; asso. firm Roewer & Reel, Boston, 1941-42; partner firm Dilworth, Paxson, Kalish, Levy and Kauffman, Phila., 19—. Mem. Zoning Hearing Bd. of Marple Twp. (Pa.), 1966-70; solicitor for Marple Twp.,

1978—. Served with AUS, 1942-46. Mem. Am. Bar Assn., Pa. Bar Assn., Phila. Bar Assn., Fed. Bar Assn., Am. Law Inst., Am. Arbitration Assn. (mem. nat. panel labor arbitrators). Mem. editorial bd. Practical Lawyer. Contbr. articles to profl. jours. Home: 229 Foxcroft Rd Broomall PA 19008 Office: 2600 Fidelity Bldg Philadelphia PA 19109

MANOFF, RICHARD KALMAN, advt. exec.; b. Bklyn., June 24, 1916; s. Kalman and Sarah (Glatman) M.; B.S., Coll. City N.Y., 1937, M.S., 1940; m. Lucy B. Deutscher, Nov. 27, 1942; children—Robert K., Gregory P. Asst. regional dir. War Manpower Commn., 1942-45; marketing dir. Welch Grape Juice Co., 1949-53; v.p. Kenyon & Eckhardt Advt., N.Y.C., 1953-56; pres., chmn. bd. Manoff Geers Gross Inc., N.Y.C., 1956—; adj. prof. dept. health Scis. Sargent Coll. Allied Health Professions, Boston U., 1978—. Mem. U.S. delegation FAO World Conf., Rome, Italy, 1966; bd. advisers Manhattan Tribune, 1968—; mem. steering com. Nat. Library Week, 1968; mem. nat. bd. Nat. Book Com., 1971—; cons. spl. mission to Food and Agr. Ministry, Govt. India, AID, 1969, Ford Found. offices Pub. Edn. Pub. Broadcasting for children's TV; participant 1st World Conf. on Social Communication for Devel. Mass Communications, Mexico, 1970, 7th Asian Advt. Congress, Delhi, 1970, 3d Western Hemisphere Nutrition Congress, Fla., 1971, Internat. Conf. Nutrition, Nat. Devel. and Planning, Mass. Inst. Tech., 1971, Symposium Eating Patters and Their Influece on Purchasing Behavior and Nutrition, Nev., 1971, Nutrition Workshop, AID, 1971, 9th Annual Summer Workshop Family Planning, 1971, 4th & 5th Seminar Workshop on Mgmt. and Planning of Population Family Planning Programs, 1971, New Products Symposium, 1971, Communication Seminar series Cornell U., 1971, Exploration The Frontiers of Nutritional Edn. Seminar, 1972, 9th Internat. Congress of Nutrition, Mexico, 1972, East-West Center Comml. Resources Conf. on Family Planning, Hawaii, 1972, Protein adv. group UN Systems Annual Mtg., 1973; mem. panel White House Conf. Food, Nutrition and Health, 1969; mem. Sec.'s Adv. Com. on Population Affairs, Dept. HEW, 1971—. Mem. Nelson A. Rockefeller's Commn. on Critical Choices for Ams. Bd. dirs. Planned Parenthood World Population, The Acting Co., Pathfinder Fund, Boston, 1977—, United Nutrition Edn. Found., Alexandria, Va., 1978—; mem. com. on internat. nutrition programs Nat. Acad. Scis.-NRC, 1973; founder, mem. Com. for Shakespeare Festival, N.Y.C.; bd. visitors Grad. Sch. and Univ. Center, City U. N.Y. Mem. Am. Assn. Advt. Agys. (gov. 1967—, sec.-treas. 1975—), Nat. Planning Council, Mystery Writers Am. Clubs: City, City College, Advertising, Friars, Harmonie (N.Y.C.). Home: 322 E 57th St New York NY 10022 Office: 845 3d Ave New York NY 10022

MANOLIS, PAUL GEORGE, newspaper exec.; b. Sacramento, Feb. 4, 1928; s. George G. and Vasileki (Kalanjopoulos) M.; B.A., U. Calif., Berkeley, 1952; M.A., Harvard, 1954; m. Elene Angelica Zahas, Mar. 7, 1964; children—Alexandra, George, Dimitri, Damian. Exec. sec. U.S. Sen. William F. Knowland, Washington, 1954-59; with Oakland (Calif.) Tribune, 1959-77, exec. editor, 1965-74, asst. gen. mgr., 1968-72; sec. Tribune Pub. Co., Oakland, 1965-77; dir. Franklin Investment Co., Tribune Bldg. Co. Vice chmn. Calif. Arts Commn., 1967-71; mem. jury Pulitzer Prizes, 1972, 73. Bd. dirs. Oakland Mus., Oakland Symphony, Western Opera Theatre, Holy Cross Coll., Brookline, Mass., Archdiocesan Council Greek Orthodox Ch.; trustee Grad. Theol. Union, Berkeley, Calif., Anna Head Sch., Oakland, Calif. Served with U.S. Army, 1945-48. Decorated Gold Cross, Crusader of Holy Sephulcre, Patriarch of Jerusalem; Gold Cross of Mounth Athos (Ecumenical Patriarch of Constantinople); Archon of Ecumenical Patriarchate. Mem. Am. Soc. Newspaper Editors, Calif. Newspaper Pubs. (dir.), Sigma Delta Chi, Sigma Alpha Epsilon. Republican. Chmn. publishing bd. Orthodox Observer. Home: 100 Guilford Rd Piedmont CA 94611 Office: Oakland Tribune Oakland CA 94610

MANOOGIAN, RICHARD ALEXANDER, mfg. co. exec.; b. Long Branch, N.J., July 30, 1936; s. Alex and Marie (Tatian) M.; B.A. in Econs., Yale U., 1958; children—James, Richard, Bridget. Asst. to pres. Masco Corp., Taylor, Mich., 1958-62, exec. v.p., 1962-68, pres., 1968—, also dir.; dir. Emco Ltd., London, Ont., Can., Nat. Bank of Detroit, Flint & Walling, Kendallville, Ind. Trustee Archives Am. Art, U. Liggett Sch., Assos. of Am. Wing Detroit Inst. Arts, Center for Creative Studies. Mem. Young Presidents Orgn. Clubs: Grosse Pointe Yacht, Grosse Pointe Hunt; Country of Detroit, Detroit Yacht, Detroit Athletic. Home: 204 Provencal Rd Grosse Pointe Farms MI 48236 Office: 21001 Van Born Rd Taylor MI 48180

MANOUKIAN, NOEL EDWIN, justice Nev. Supreme Ct.; b. Livingston, Calif., Jan. 1, 1938; B.A., U. Pacific, 1961; J.D., U. Santa Clara, 1964. Admitted to Nev. bar, 1964, U.S. Supreme Ct. bar, 1971; law clk., bailiff to judges Washoe County (Nev.) Dist. Ct., 1964-65; dep. dist. atty. Douglas County (Nev.), 1965-66; asso. firm Manoukian & Manoukian, Carson City, Nev., 1965-70; individual practice law, Carson City, Lake Tahoe and Carson Valley, 1971-74; judge 1st Jud. Dist. Ct., Carson, Churchill, Douglas, Lyon and Storey counties, Minden, Nev., 1973-76; judge multiple ct. dist. 9th Jud. Dist. Ct., Carson City, 1976-77; justice Nev. Supreme Ct., 1977—; lectr. numerous schs., profl. orgns. Mem. Nev. div. Am. Cancer Soc., 1966—, bd. dirs., 1969—, vice chmn. bd. dirs., 1970, chmn. bd. chmn. exec. com., 1973-74, 74-75, now hon. life mem.; vice chmn. Nev. Small County Allocation Com., 1974-77; mem. Nev. State Personnel Adv. Commn.; mem. Nev. Commn. Crime, Delinquency and Corrections, 1979—, Nev. State Planning and Allocations Com., 1979—. Recipient Lawyer of Yr. award Santa Clara Law Sch., 1978. Mem. Am. Bar Assn., Nev. Bar Assn., Am. Judicature Soc., Nev. Dist. Judges Assn. (chmn. bd., pres. 1975-76, 76-77). Contbr. articles to profl. jours. Office: Supreme Ct Capitol Complex Carson City NV 89501

MANRING, EDWARD RAYMOND, physicist; b. Springfield, Ohio, Mar. 21, 1921; s. George and Emma (Buehl) M.; student Wittenberg Coll., 1939-40, U. Chile, 1940-41; B.S., Ohio State U., 1944, M.S., 1948, Ph.D., 1953; m. Berta Jimenez, June 1940; children—Jorge, Andrew, Viqui. Research physicist Monsanto Chem. Co., 1948-50; research asso. Ohio State U., 1950-53; physicist on night airglow Sacramento Peak Obs., 1953-56; chief spectroscopic studies sect. Geophysics Research Directorate, 1956-59; head observational physics dept. Geophysics Corp. Am., 1959-64; prof. physics U. N.C. at Raleigh, 1964—. Aurora and airglow com., equitorial com. IGY; mem. Rocket and Satellite Research Panel, Mem. Am. Phys. Soc., Am. Geophys. Union, Sigma Xi, Tau Beta Pi, Sigma Pi Sigma. Home: 1601 Dixie Trail Raleigh NC 27607

MANSAGER, FELIX NORMAN, appliance mfg. co. exec.; b. Dell Rapids, S.D., Jan. 30, 1911; s. Hoff and Alice (Qualseth) M.; grad. high sch.; LL.D. (hon.), Capitol U., Columbus, Ohio, 1967, Strathclyde U. (Scotland), 1970; D.H.L., Malone Coll., Canton, Ohio, 1972; Pd.D. (hon.), Walsh Coll., 1974; H.H.D., Wartburg Coll., 1976; m. Geraldine Larson, July 5, 1931; children—Donna Mansager Hogsven, Eva Kay Mansager Sieverts, Douglas Norman. With Hoover Co., Canton, 1929—, exec. v.p., dir., 1961-63, exec. v.p. Hoover Group, 1976—; pres., chmn. bd. Hoover Co., Hoover Worldwide, 1966-75, dir., mem. exec. com., 1976—; Goodyear exec. prof. bus. adminstrn. Akron (Ohio) U., 1978-79; dir. Hoover, Ltd., Harter Bank & Trust Co., Canton. Trustee, Ohio Found. Ind. Colls., Gustavus Adolphus Coll., Grad. Theol. Union, Augustana Coll.; trustee at large, chmn. Ind. Coll. Funds Am.; bd. govs. Ditchley Found. Decorated grand officer Dukes Burgundy, chevalier Order Leopold (Belgium); knight 1st class Order St. Olav (Norway); chevalier Legion of Honor (France); knight Brit. Empire; grand ufficiale Order Al Merito (Italy); recipient medal of honor Vaasa U. (Finland), 1972, Mktg. award Brit. Inst. Mktg., 1971; Univ. Coll. fellow, Cardiff, Wales, 1973. Fellow Brit. Inst. Mgmt.; mem. Council Fgn. Relations, Newcomen Soc. N.Am., Pilgrims U.S., Assn. Ohio Commodores, World League Norsemen (hon.), Beta Gamma Sigma. Clubs: Rotary, Masons (32 deg.), Shriners; Met. (N.Y.C.); Capitol Hill, Met. (Washington); Congress Lake Country, Canton, Torske Klubben (hon.). Home: 3421 Lindel Ct NW Canton OH 44718

MANSELL, FRANK LUTHER, investment banker; b. Omaha, Feb. 3, 1922; s. George E. and Jessie T. (McDonald) M.; B.S. with distinction, U. Nebr. at Omaha, 1943; M.B.A. with distinction, Harvard U., 1948; m. Edmona Elmore Lyman, June 19, 1957; children—Devon Bothin, Jessica Lyman; stepchildren—Robert Lyman Miller, Charles Bothin Miller, Christian Folger Miller, Gordon Edmunds Miller. With Lee Higginson Corp., N.Y.C., 1948-52; with Blyth & Co., Inc., 1952-72, pres., N.Y.C., 1971-72; vice chmn. bd., chmn. exec. com. Blyth, Eastman, Dillon & Co., Inc., N.Y.C., 1972—; dir. The Stanley Works, New Britain, Conn. Trustee, Boys' Club N.Y. Served to lt. USNR, 1943-46. Mem. Investment Bankers Assn. Am. (past gov.). Clubs: N.Y.C. Bond (past gov.), Links, Pacific-Union (San Francisco); Apawamis (Rye, N.Y.); Maidstone (E. Hampton, L.I.); Burlingame (Calif.) Country; Lyford Cay (Nassau, Bahamas). Office: Blyth Eastman Dillon & Co Inc 1221 Ave of Americas New York NY 10020

MANSELL, IRVING LAWSON, ret. newspaper editor; b. McKeesport, Pa., June 4, 1908; s. Irving Van Voorhis and Cordelia Wheeler (Smith) M.; B.A., Westminster (Pa.) Coll., 1929, D.Litt. (hon.), 1954; m. Agnes Lucille McConaghy, June 30, 1931; children—John Lawson, Jane Lucille. Reporter, Youngstown Vindicator, 1929-38, copy reader, make-up editor, financial editor, telegraph editor, 1938-44, asst. city editor, 1946-49, mng. editor, 1949-76; editor New Wilmington (Pa.) Globe, 1935-36. Trustee Westminster Coll.; pres. bd. dirs. Shenango United Presbyn. Home. Served as lt. armed guard USNR, 1944-46. Mem. Westminster Coll. Alumni Assn. (nat. pres. 1950-52), Pi Delta Epsilon, Alpha Sigma Phi. Home: Brookhill New Wilmington PA 16142

MANSELL, THOMAS NORMAN, architect; b. Morrisville, Pa., May 16, 1904; s. Benjamin T. and Pauline (Skeath) M.; B.A. summa cum laude, U. Pa., 1926; F.A.D. (hon.), Wittenberg U., 1957; m. Dorothy E. Hershey, June 22, 1929; children—Barry Norman, Anthony Alan. Designer, partner Richard Erskine, Architect, 1925-38; pvt. archtl. practice, 1938-55; partner Mansell Lewis & Fugate, Wynnewood, Pa., 1955-77; lectr. archtl. design, master planning and color; works include bldgs. Wittenberg U., Leeds & Northrup Research Lab. and Engring. Center, North Wales, Pa., 2 Phila. pub. schs., office bldg. United Luth. Ch., St. Peters Ch., Miami. Asst. to dir. Old Phila. Planning Commn.; mem. adv. com. dept. church architecture United Luth. Ch., 1960-63; chmn. Springfield Twp. Delaware County Zoning Hearing Bd., 1945-75; chmn. Delaware County Edn. and Recreation Div., 1939-41; organizer Upper Darby Boys Club, Delaware County Day Camp; v.p., dir. Delaware Valley Citizens Council for Clean Air, 1968-75, pres., 1976-77; pres. Delaware County Tb and Health Assn., Delchester Lung Assn., 1969-73. Recipient award for excellence in design and arts Guild Religious Architecture, 1957. Fellow AIA (pres. Phila. chpt. 1965-66); mem. Pa. Soc. Architects (dir. 1968-70), U. Pa. Archtl. Alumni Soc. (sec. 1947-49), Guild for Religious Architecture (pres. 1951-52), Tuscarora Lapidary Soc. (pres. 1972). Clubs: Union League, Phila. Sketch (pres. 1963-64) (Phila.); Upper Darby (Pa.) Lions (past pres.), Masons. Contbr. articles profl. jours. Home: 143 Powell Rd Springfield PA 19064

MANSFIELD, EDGAR OWEN, hosp. adminstr.; b. LaPorte, Ind., Nov. 14, 1918; s. Owen R. and Alzora P. (Pratt) M.; B.S., Northwestern U., 1950, M.S. in Hosp. Adminstrn., 1952; Dr. P.H. (hon.), Ohio No. U., 1956; m. Corinne D. Mansfield, June 25, 1975; children by previous marriage—Thomas R., Mary Ann, Barbara S., John D. Supr., dept. head Montgomery Ward & Co., Balt., 1945-47; adminstrv. asst. Mound Park Hosp., St. Petersburg, Fla., 1952-53; asso. for instl. services Nat. Bd. Hosps. and Homes Meth. Ch., Chgo., 1953; pres. Riverside Meth. Hosp., Columbus, Ohio, 1953—; dir. Suburban Motor Freight Corp.; adj. instr. in hosp. and health services adminstrn. Ohio State U., Columbus; cons. in field. Trustee The Columbus Acad. Served to lt., M.C., U.S. Army, 1942-45. Fellow Am. Coll. Hosp. Adminstrs.; mem. Am. (trustee), Ohio (pres. 1964) hosp. assns., Am. Protestant Hosp. Assn. (pres. 1974), Protestant Health and Welfare Assembly (chmn. 1974), Nat. Assn. Health and Welfare Ministries of United Meth. Ch. (pres. 1973), Mid-Ohio Health Planning Fedn., Ohio State Med. Assn., Ohio Med. Indemnity, Blue Cross of Central Ohio, Beta Gamma Sigma, Delta Mu Delta, Alpha Delta Mu. Clubs: Columbus Rotary, Columbus Maennerchor, Univ. (Columbus), Scioto Country. Contbr. articles on hosp. mgmt. to profl. jours. Home: 4460 Haverford Ct Columbus OH 43220 Office: 3535 Olentangy River Rd Columbus OH 43214

MANSFIELD, HARVEY CLAFLIN, SR., educator; b. Cambridge, Mass., Mar. 3, 1905; s. George Rogers and Adelaide (Claflin) M.; student Deep Springs (Calif.) Coll., 1921-25; A.B., Cornell U., 1927, A.M., 1928; Ph.D., Columbia U., 1932; m. Grace Winans Yarrow, Sept. 6, 1930; children—Harvey C., Charles Y., John T., Margaret Ann (Mrs. Kimball M. Barnes). Instr. govt. Yale, 1929-33, asst. prof., 1933-42; acting asst. prof. Stanford, 1939-40, vis. prof. Oreg. State System, Portland, summer 1940; adminstrv. officer Consumer Goods div. OPA, Washington, 1942, asso. price exec., 1942-44, price exec., 1944-45, asst. div. dir., 1945, OPA historian, 1946-47; prof. polit. sci. Ohio State U. 1947-65, chmn. dept., 1947-59; prof. dept. pub. law and govt. Columbia, 1965-72, Ruggles prof. pub. law, 1972-73, emeritus, 1973—, spl. lectr., 1973-75; vis. prof. Columbia U., summer 1956, Yale, 1957-58, LBJ Sch. Pub. Affairs, U. Tex., 1972, 76, U. B.C., summer 1972, Harvard, summers 1973-74, Deep Springs Coll., 1976, 77, 79; Social Sci. Research Council sr. research award Brookings Instn., Washington, 1961-62; vis. prof. U. Tenn., winter 1979. Served as sr. cons., pres. com. on adminstrv. mgmt., 1936; vis. expert OMGUS Germany, 1949; project dir., writer Conn. Commn. on State Govt. Orgn., 1949-50; cons. Com. Pub. Adminstrn. Cases, 1950, Econ. Stablzn. Agy., 1951, municipal finance study, Mayor's Com. on Mgmt. Survey, N.Y.C., 1951, Governmental Affairs Inst., 1952-53; cons. Commn. on Intergovtl. Relations, 1954-55; mem. staff Commn. on Money and Credit, 1960-61; cons. House Banking and Currency Com., 1963. Pres. Telluride Assn. (endowed ednl. found.), Ithaca, N.Y., 1931-33, 1943, custodian, 1929-37, 1941-45. Chmn. bd. trustees Inter-Univ. Case Program, 1956—. Mem. Am. Polit. Sci. Assn. (sec. 1953-55, v.p. 1967-68), Nat. Acad. Pub. Adminstrn. (trustee 1973-76), Phi Beta Kappa, Delta Sigma Rho. Democrat. Club: Cosmos (Washington). Author: The Lake Cargo Coal Rate Controversy, 1932; The General Accounting Office (in Pres. Comm. Admin. Mgt. Report with Spl. Studies), 1937; The Comptroller General, 1939; A Short History of OPA, 1949; Arms and the State (with Millis and Stein), 1958. Editor, contbr.: Congress Against the President, 1975. Editor, contbr. OPA series Historical Reports on War Administration, 1947-49. Mng. editor: Am. Polit. Sci. Rev., 1956-65. Contbr. chpts. in books, articles to profl. jours. Home: 430 W 116th St New York NY 10027

MANSFIELD, JOHN HOWARD, educator; b. Morristown, N.J., Oct. 12, 1928; s. Lewis Pierce and Elinor Clifford (Perkins) M.; A.B., Harvard, 1952, LL.B., 1956. Admitted to Calif. bar, 1956, Mass. bar, 1962; law clk. to Justice Roger J. Traynor, Supreme Ct. Calif., 1956-57, to Justice Felix Frankfurter, Supreme Ct. U.S., 1957-58; asst. prof. law Harvard Law Sch., 1958-61, prof., 1961—; vis. prof. Yale Law Sch., 1971, N.Y. U. Law Sch., 1976, U. Calif., Berkeley, 1978-79. Co-editor: Cases and Materials on Evidence, 1973. Address: Langdell Hall Cambridge MA 02138

MANSFIELD, MICHAEL JOSEPH, ambassador, former U.S. senator; b. N.Y.C., Mar. 16, 1903; s. Patrick and Josephine (O'Brien) M.; student Mont. Sch. Mines, 1927-28; A.B., U. Mont., 1933, A.M., 1934; student U. Calif., 1936, 1937; m. Maureen Hayes, Sept. 13, 1932; 1 dau., Anne (Mrs. Robin Marris). Seaman U.S. Navy, 1918-19; with U.S. Army, 1919-20; with U.S. Marines, 1920-22; miner and mining engr., 1922-1931; prof. history and polit. sci., U. Mont., 1933-42; mem. 78th-82d Congresses, 1st Dist. Mont.; U.S. Senator from Mont., 1952-76, asst. majority leader, 1957-61, majority leader, 1961-77, mem. Com. on Fgn. Relations, Appropriations Com.; chmn. Dem. Conf., Policy Com., Steering Com.; ambassador to Japan, Tokyo, 1977—. Presdl. rep. in China, 1944; U.S. delegate, IX Inter-Am. Conf., Colombia, 1948, 6th UN Assembly, Paris, 1951-52; U.S. del. Southeast Asia Conf., Manila, 1954, 13th UN Gen. Assembly, 1958; Presdl. assignment, West Berlin, Southeast Asia, Vietnam, 1962, Europe, Southeast Asia, 1965, 69; visited People's Republic of China on invitation of Premier Chou-En-lai, 1972, on invitation of Govt. of People's Republic of China, 1974, 76. Home: Missoula MT 59801 Office: Am Embassy (Tokyo) 13-go No 14 Akasaka 1-chome Minato-Ku APO San Francisco CA 96503

MANSFIELD, WALTER ROE, judge; b. Boston, July 1, 1911; s. Frederick W. and Helena E. (Roe) M.; A.B., Harvard U., 1932, LL.B., 1935; m. Elizabeth P. Bergfeld, July 20, 1979; 1 stepson, Peter F. Rient; children—Matthew F., Trina P. Admitted to Mass. bar, 1935, N.Y. bar, 1936, also U.S. Supreme Ct. bar; asso. firm Donovan, Leisure, Newton & Irvine, N.Y.C., 1935-37, 41-42, 46-66, partner, 1950-66; asst. U.S. atty. So. Dist. N.Y., 1938-41; judge U.S. Dist. Ct., So. Dist. N.Y., N.Y.C., 1966-71; U.S. judge 2d Circuit Ct. Appeals, N.Y.C., 1971—. Pres. bd. New Canaan (Conn.) Country Sch., 1953-56. Served from 2d lt. to maj. USMCR, 1943-46. Fellow Am. Coll. Trial Lawyers; mem. Am. Bar Assn., Fed. Bar Council (exec. v.p. 1965-66), Bar Assn. City N.Y., Vets. OSS (pres. 1946-49). Clubs: Century Assn. (N.Y.C.); New Canaan Country. Home: 2410 Long Ridge Rd Stamford CT 06903 Office: US Court House Bridgeport CT 06604

MANSHARDT, CLIFFORD, sociologist; b. Albany, Oreg., Mar. 6, 1897; s. George A. and Ina (Green) M.; student Bradley Poly. Inst., Peoria, Ill., 1914-15; Ph.B., U. Chgo., 1918, A.M., 1921, Ph.D., 1924; B.D., Chgo. Theol. Sem., 1922, D.D., 1932; student Union Theol. Sem., 1922-23; m. Agnes Helene Lloyd, May 16, 1925 (dec.); children—Thomas Brewster, Michael Clifford. Asst. gen. sec. Religious Edn. Assn., 1924-25; dir. Nagpada Neighborhood House, Bombay, India, 1925-41; dir. Sir Dorabji Tata Trust, Bombay, 1932-41; founder, dir. Tata Inst. Social Scis., Bombay, 1936-41; vis. prof., Alden Tuthill lectr. Chgo. Theol. Sem., 1932, lectr., 1942-43; vis. prof., spl. Earl lectr. Pacific Sch. Religion, 1941; dir. Bethlehem Community Center, Chgo., 1942-51; U.S. fgn. service officer, 1951-63; cultural affairs officer, attaché Am. embassy, New Delhi, India, 1951-55, dep. pub. affairs officer, attaché, 1955-58; pub. affairs officer, sec., information counselor Am. embassy, Karachi, Pakistan, 1958-63. Served in U.S. Army, 1918-19. Mem. United Ch. of Christ. Author: The Social Settlement as an Educational Factor in India, 1931; Christianity in a Changing India, 1933; The Hindu-Muslim Problem in India, 1936; The Delinquent Child, 1939; Freedom Without Violence, 1946; The Terrible Meek-An Appreciation of Mohandas K. Gandhi, 1948; The Mahatma and the Missionary, 1949; Pioneering on Social Frontiers in India, 1967. Editor Religious Edn., 1924-25; founder, editor Indian Jour. Social Work, 1936-41. Contbr. articles periodicals and profl. jours. Address: 1745 N Gramercy Pl Hollywood CA 90028

MANSHEL, WARREN DEMIAN, U.S. ambassador; b. Jan. 6, 1924; B.A., M.A., Harvard U., 1949, Ph.D., 1952; m. Anita Coleman, 1954; children—Liane Catherine, Michael Demian. Teaching fellow Harvard U.; investment banker Coleman & Co.; pub. Public Interest mag.; pub., editor Fgn. Policy mag.; ambassador to Denmark. Office: American Embassy Dag Hammarskojold Alle 24 Copenhagen Denmark

MANSHIP, CHARLES PHELPS, JR., publisher; b. Baton Rouge, Aug. 13, 1908; s. Charles Phelps and Leora (Douthit) M.; M.B.A., Harvard, 1932; B.J., U. Mo., 1930; m. Paula Garvey, Aug. 27, 1938. Reporter State-Times and Morning Advocate, 1926-27, gen. mgr., 1938-42, pub., 1946-70; advt. salesman Times-Picayune, 1932-34; treas. Baton Rouge Broadcasting Co., La. TV Corp., Mobile Video Tapes Co.; pres. Capital City Press; dir. La. Nat. Bank. Mem. Kappa Alpha. Pres. So. Newspaper Pubs. Assn., 1959. Clubs: Internat. House, Boston (New Orleans); Rotary, Country, City (Baton Rouge). Home: 1464 Steele Blvd Baton Rouge LA 70808 Office: 525 Lafayette St Baton Rouge LA 70802

MANSHIP, DOUGLAS, radio, television and newspaper exec.; b. Baton Rouge, Nov. 3, 1918; s. Charles P. and Leora (Douthit) M.; student La. State U., 1936-41, U. Heidelberg, 1937, U. Colo., 1938-39; m. Jane French, Jan. 31, 1942; children—Douglas Lewis, Richard French, David Charles, Dina. Reporter State Times and Morning Advocate, 1945-47, pub., 1970—; with Baton Rouge Broadcasting Co., 1947—, pres. 1948—; pres. La IV Broadcasting Corp. 1953—; vice chmn. bd. Radio Free Europe/Radio Liberty, 1978—; pres. Mobile Video Tapes, Inc., 1960; sec., pub. Capital City Press, 1970; dir. City Nat. Bank, La. Fire Ins. Co., TV Stas. Inc. Dir. civil def., La., 1951-52; campaign chmn. Community Chest, 1950, bd. dirs., 1950-52, pres. 1951. Served with USAAF, World War II. Mem. Baton Rouge (pres. 1963), La. (v.p.) chambers commerce, Assn. for Profl. Broadcasting Edn., Council for A Better La., Assn. La. Chambers Commerce, So. Newspaper Pubs. Assn. (pres. 1977-78), Kappa Alpha, Sigma Delta Chi. Episcopalian. Home: 5470 Claycut Rd Baton Rouge LA 70806 Office: 525 Lafayette St Baton Rouge LA 70802

MANSKI, WLADYSLAW JULIAN, med. scientist; b. Lwow, Poland, May 15, 1915; s. Julian and Helena (Lewicka) M.; came to U.S., 1958, naturalized, 1964; M.Phil., U. Warsaw, Poland, 1939, D.Sc., 1951; m. Anna Z. Artymowicz, June 20, 1941; children—Chris, Louis. Instr., U. Warsaw, 1936-39; research asst. Inst. Lwow, 1940-41, Inst. Agr., Pulawy, Poland, 1942-44; instr. U. Lublin (Poland), 1944-45; instr. dept. microbiology Med. Sch., Wroclaw, Poland, 1945-49; Rockefeller fellow Columbia U., N.Y.C., 1949-50; head immunochemistry Inst. Immunology and Exptl. Therapy, Polish Acad. Sci., Wroclaw, 1951-55, head Macromolecular Biochemistry

Lab., Warsaw, 1955-57; head dept. virology Biochemistry Lab., State Inst. Hygiene, Warsaw, 1955-57; research worker Coll. Physicians and Surgeons, Columbia U., 1958-62, research asso., 1962-64, asst. prof., 1964-67, asso. prof. microbiology, 1967-74, prof. microbiology, 1974—. NIH grantee, 1960—. Mem. AAAS, Am. Assn. Immunologists, AAUP, Research in Vision and Ophthalmology Assn., Am. Chem. Soc., Brit. Biochemical Soc., N.Y. Acad. Scis., Soc. Exptl. Biology and Medicine, Soc. Study of Evolution, Internat. Soc. Eye Research, Harvey Soc., Transplantation Soc. Contbr. articles to profl. jours. Home: 10 Downing St New York NY 10014 Office: 630 W 168th St New York NY 10032

MANSMANN, HERBERT CHARLES, JR., pediatric allergist, immunologist; b. Pitts., Apr. 11, 1924; s. Herbert Charles and Alethe Mulcahey (Taylor) M.; B.S. in Chemistry, U. Pitts., 1947; M.D., Jefferson Med. Coll., 1951; m. Margaret Marshall Miller, 1947; children—Herbert Charles, III, Margaret Karen, Kevin Alexander, Paris Taylor, Ian Michael. Rotating intern St. Francis Hosp., Pitts., 1951-52; resident in pediatrics Children's Hosp. of Pitts., 1952-54; allergy research fellow Mass. Gen. Hosp., Boston, 1954-55, immunology research fellow, 1955-56; pathology research fellow U. Pitts., 1956-59; pvt. practice medicine specializing in allergy, Pitts., 1959-68; prof. pediatrics, dir. div. allergy/clin. immunology Jefferson Med. Coll., 1968—; mem. pulmonary/allergy com. FDA, 1975—. Served with U.S. Army, 1943-45. Decorated Purple Heart. Diplomate Am. Bd. Pediatrics, Am. Allergy and Immunology (exec. sec.). Mem. Am. Acad. Allergy, Am. Acad. Pediatrics, Am. Coll. Allergists, Am. Pediatric Soc., N.Y. Acad. Sci., Pa. Allergy Assn., Phila. Pediatric Soc., Pulmonary Research Group. Contbr. numerous articles to profl. publs. Editor: (with M.E. Rosenthale) Immunopharmacology, Procs. of Conf. Immunopharmacology, 1976; (with others) spl. issue Pediatric Allergy, 1974. Home: 1004 Garrett Mill Rd Newtown Square PA 19073 Office: 1025 Walnut St Philadelphia PA 19107*

MANSON, EDDY LAWRENCE, composer, condr., arranger; b. N.Y.C.; s. David Manuel and Evelyn (Lasky) Salmanson; student CCNY; grad. Juilliard Sch. Music, 1942; grad. N.Y. U. Sch. Radio-TV, 1953; postgrad. UCLA, 1973-75; pvt. student Vittorio Giannini, Jan Williams, Adolf Schmid, Borrah Minnevitch Rudy Schramm, Philip Springer; s. Paul Meriam Douse, Nov. 29, 1959; 1 son, David Joseph. Performer, condr. USO Camp Shows, 1943-45; leading harmonica virtuoso, performing internationally all media, 1945—; began career as film composer Little Fugitive, 1953; composer numerous features, documentaries, TV shows, also TV and radio commls.; arranger music Red Buttons, Jackson Five, Don Ho, Miracles, others; sr. extension tchr. film scoring, arranging, orchestration UCLA, 1975—; pres. Eddy Manson Prodns., N.Y.C., Los Angeles, 1960—; pres. Margery Music Inc., N.Y.C., Los Angeles, 1958—. Mem. Los Angeles Sister City Com., Eilat, Israel, 1975—; music dir. Synagogue of Performing Arts, Los Angeles, 1973-75. Recipient numerous profl. awards including Elizabeth Sprague Coolidge prize composition, 5 Venice Film Festival awards, 17 ASCAP Panel awards. Mem. Am. Fedn. Musicians, Acad. Motion Pictures Arts and Scis., Am. Fedn. TV and Radio Artists, Composers and Lyricists Guild, ASCAP, Acad. TV Arts and Scis., Am. Guild Authors and Composers, Nat. Assn. Composers and Condrs., Am. Soc. Music Arrangers (pres., founder Composer/Arrangers Workshop 1978). Democrat. Jewish. Juilliard Alumni Assn. Club: Bohemians (N.Y.C.). Contbr. articles to profl. jours. Home and Office: 7245 Hillside Ave Los Angeles CA 90046

MANSON, IRA REXON, publisher; b. Los Angeles, Dec. 15, 1936; s. Morse Packard and Kathryn (Rexon) M.; B.S., Calif. State U., Los Angeles, 1965; M.B.A., U. Calif. at Los Angeles, 1966; m. Sarah Fay Isbitz, May 2, 1969; children—Karen, Jeffrey. With Manson Western Corp., Los Angeles, 1957—, pres., 1967—, founder Human Behavior mag., 1972. Mem. Calif. Democratic Central Com., Los Angeles County Dem. Central Com.; pres. Westwood Dem. Club, 1970. Served with AUS, 1959-60. Mem. Am. Arbitration Assn., Los Angeles World Affairs Council, Los Angeles Town Hall, Direct Mail Advt. Assn. Address: 12031 Wilshire Blvd Los Angeles CA 90025

MANSON, JULIUS JOEL, educator; b. N.Y.C., June 27, 1907; s. Tobias and Mollie (Libenson) Umansky; B.A., Columbia, 1931, M.A., 1932, Ph.D., 1955; J.D., Bklyn. Law Sch., 1936; m. Elizabeth Robison Butzner, Mar. 3, 1947; children—Carol (Mrs. Lionel Bier), David, Paul. Asst. to mgr. Local 25, Internat. Ladies Garment Workers Union, N.Y.C., 1933; statistician N.Y.C. Housing Authority, 1934; sr. investigator, head law clk. div. women in industry and minimum wage N.Y. State Labor Dept., 1934-40; admitted to N.Y. bar, 1936; examiner N.Y. State Labor Relations Bd., 1940-42; with N.Y. State Mediation Bd., 1942-66, 68-69, labor mediator, arbitrator, 1942-69, exec. dir., 1957-59; adminstr.'s negotiator initial faculty union agreements City U. N.Y., 1969-70; dean Sch. Bus. and Pub. Adminstrn., Bernard M. Baruch Coll., 1970-72, prof. mgmt. and labor relations, 1973-77, prof. emeritus, 1977—; cons. Govt. of Turkey, Ankara, 1966-68; former mem. faculty Cornell U., Columbia, New Sch. for Social Research, N.Y. U., Rutgers U., U.S. Army Univ. Tng. Command; cons. to govts. Iran, Israel, U.S. depts. State, Labor, various univs., state and local govts.; radio news commentator, 1947-50. Chmn. Spl. Bd. Inquiry Civil Service Commn. Malfeasance, Putnam County, N.Y., 1962; mem. N.Y.C. Mayor's Com. on Exploitation, 1969-73; fellow Columbia Labor Seminar. Founder, Three Arrows Co-op. Soc., 1937, past pres.; pres. Columbia Socialist Club, 1933; nat. chmn. Young People's Socialist League Am., 1939. Bd. dirs. N.Y. Legislative Service, Hebrew Free Loan Soc., N.Y. Ethical Culture Soc., Coordinating Council for Edn. Disadvantaged, League for Indsl. Democracy, Nat. Com. for Rural Schs., Histadrut Cultural Exchange Inst., Hudson Shore Labor Sch., Rand Sch. Social Sci.; nat. adv. commn. Weizmann Inst. Sci., 1976. Served with Armed Forces, 1943-46. Recipient award Joint Com. Labor and Industry, 1957, Bassin award Am. Vets. Com., 1964, award Jewish Labor Com., 1965, Ann. award League for Indsl. Democracy, 1965, award New Sch. for Social Research, 1965; Wollman Distinguished lectr. Baruch Coll., 1970. Mem. Nat. Acad. Arbitrators, Am. Arbitration Assn., Am. Econ. Assn., Indsl. Relations Research Assn., Am. Acad. Polit. and Social Sci., Nat. Bur. Econ. Research, Universal Esperanto Assn., Workmen's Circle, Beta Gamma Sigma. Author: The British Health Service, 1952; (with others) Collective Bargaining, 1964; (with others) Handbook of Counseling Techniques, 1964; (with others) Roots of Open Education, 1976. Bd. editors New Leader, 1937-40; contbr. labor relations sect. N.Y. U. Law Rev., 1957, labor legislation sect. to N.Y. State Legislative Ann., 1959; chpt. to Labor-Management Relations in Turkey, 1967; Ency. of Mgmt., 1963, 73; also articles various publs. Home: 14 Stuyvesant Oval New York City NY 10009

MANSON, S. STANFORD, educator, engr.; b. Jerusalem, July 4, 1919; s. B.S. in Mech. Engring., Cooper Union Inst. Tech., 1941; M.S., U. Mich., 1942; postgrad. Case Inst. Tech., 1943-46; m. Therese Palay, Oct. 8, 1946; children—Margaret Manson Entis, Richard, Carolyn, JoAnn, Hilary. With Nat. Adv. Com. for Aeronautics, 1942-56, chief strength of materials br., 1946-55, asst. chief materials and thermodynamics div., 1955-56; chief materials and structure div. NASA, 1956-74; prof. mech. and aerospace engring. Case Western Res. U., Cleve., 1974—; cons. Die Casting Research Found., 1962-78. Recipient medal for exceptional sci. achievement NASA, 1967; Austen Lilligren award Am. Die Casting Inst., 1974; Von Karmen award TRE Corp., 1974. Registered profl. engr., Ohio. Fellow Soc. Exptl. Analysis (past nat. pres., past chmn. N.E. Ohio chpt., chmn. com. of fellows), Royal Aero. Soc.; mem. ASTM, ASME, Japan Soc. Materials Sci., Pi Tau Sigma, Tau Beta Pi. Author: Thermal Stress and Low Cycle Fatigue, 1966. Contbg. editor Aerospace Structural Metals Handbook, 1958—. Contbr. articles to profl. jours. Office: Case Western Res Univ Cleveland OH 44106

MANSON-HING, LINCOLN ROY, educator; b. Georgetown, Guyana, May 20, 1927; D.M.D. cum laude, Tufts U., 1948; M.S., U. Ala., 1961; m. Joyce Louise Chin, Aug. 21, 1949; children—Collin James, Jennifer Lynn, Jeffrey Paul. Practice dentistry, Kingston, Jamaica, also dir. Schs.' Dental Clinic, St. Mary Parish, Jamaica, 1948-56; asst. prof. dentistry, U. Ala., 1956-59, asso. prof., 1959-68, prof. dentistry, 1968, chmn. dept. dental radiology, 1962. Cons., Am. Dental Assn., Am. Standards Assn., VA Hosp., Birmingham, Ala., VA Hosp., Tuskegee, Ala., Ala. State Crippled Children Cleft Palate Clinic, 1957-69. Fulbright-Hays lectr., Egypt., 1964-65. Mem. Am. Dental Assn., Am. Acad. Dental Radiology (pres. 1967, editor 1967—), Internat. Assn. Dento-maxillofacial Radiology (dir. 1974—), Internat. Assn. Dental Research, AAAS, Sigma Xi, Omicron Kappa Upsilon. Author: (with A.H. Wuehrmann) Dental Radiology, 1965; Panoramic Dental Radiology, 1975; Fundamentals of Dental Radiology, 1979; also articles, textbook chpts.; sect. editor Jour. Oral Surgery, Oral Medicine and Pathology, 1967—. Home: 205 Mecca Ave Homewood AL 35209 Office: 1919 7th Ave S Birmingham AL 35294

MANSOOR, MENAHEM, educator, author; b. Port Said, Egypt, Aug. 4, 1911; s. Asher S. and Yonah H. (Shalom) M.; student Sch. Oriental Studies, U. London (Eng.), 1934-39; B.A. with honors, Trinity Coll., Dublin, Ireland, 1941, M.A., 1942, Ph.D., 1944; m. Claire Dora Kramer, Nov. 29, 1951; children—Yardena Miriam, Daniel Jonathan. Came to U.S., 1954, naturalized, 1963. Sr. edn. officer, Jerusalem, 1946-49; asst. press attache Brit. Fgn. Service, Tel Aviv, Israel, 1949-54; research fellow, lectr. Johns Hopkins Oriental Sem., 1954-55; mem. faculty U. Wis., 1955—, prof. Semitic langs., 1955—, chmn. dept. Semitic langs. and lits., 1955-77, Joseph L. Baron prof., 1973—. Chmn. Hebrew com. Coll. Entrance Exam. Bd., 1964-69; chmn., founder Madison Bibl. Archaeol. Soc., 1967; mem. bd. Wis. Writers' Council, 1964—. Fulbright fellow, 1954-55; grantee Am. Philos. Soc., 1958, Wis. Soc. Jewish Learning, 1965, 75; recipient Kohut award Yale, 1955; research fellow Harvard, 1962-63, 64-65; Am. Council Learned Socs. award, 1958-59; Lang. research award NDEA, 1959, 1965, 68-71, 72-73. Mem. Soc. Bibl. Lit. (Midwest pres. 1969-70), Am. Oriental Soc. (Midwest pres. 1970-71), Modern Lang. Assn., Middle East Studies Assn., Assn. Jewish Studies, Nat. Assn. Hebrew Profs. Author: Thanksgiving Hymns, 1960; English Arabic Dictionary of Political, Diplomatic and Conference Terms, 1960; The Dead Sea Scrolls, 1966; Legal and Documentary Arabic Readers, 1966; Political and Diplomatic History of the Arab World, Chronological Study, 8 vols., 1977; Advanced Modern Hebrew Literature Readers, 1971; Duties of the Heart, 1973; Biographical Dictionary of the Arab World, 1975; Political and Diplomatic History of the Arab World, Documentary Study, 8 vols., 1977; Contemporary Hebrew, 1976; Biblical Hebrew Step by Step, 1978; Modern Hebrew Conversation Course, linguaphone, 1973; (with Fuad Megally) Modern Standard Arabic Course, 1978; also textbooks, articles; editor: Hebrew Studies, Iggeret, 1978—. Home: 1225 Sweetbriar Rd Madison WI 53705

MANSOUR, TAG ELDIN, pharmacologist; b. Belkas, Egypt, Nov. 6, 1924; s. Elsayed and Rokaya (Elzayat) M.; came to U.S., 1951, naturalized, 1956; B.Sc., Cairo U., 1946; PH.D., U. Birmingham (Eng.), 1949, D.Sc., 1974; m. Joan Adela MacKinnon, Aug. 6, 1955; children—Suzanne, Jeanne, Dean. Lectr., U. Cairo, 1950-51; Fulbright instr. physiology Howard U., Washington, 1951-52; sr. instr. pharmacology Western Res. U., 1952-54; asst. prof., asso. prof. pharmacology La. State U. Med. Sch., New Orleans, 1954-61; asso. prof., prof. pharmacology Stanford U. Sch. Medicine, 1961—, Donald E. Baxter prof., chmn. dept. pharmacology, 1977—; cons. USPHS, WHO, Nat. Acad. Scis. Mem. adv. bd. Med. Sch., Kuwait U. Commonwealth Fund fellow, 1965. Fellow AAAS; mem. Am. Soc. Pharmacology and Exptl. Therapeutics, Am. Soc Biol. Chemists, Am. Heart Assn., World Affairs Council, Sierra Club, Sigma Xi. Club: Stanford Faculty. Contrbr. sci. articles to profl. jours. Home: 867 Mayfield Ave Stanford CA 94305 Office: 300 Pasteur Dr Stanford CA 94305

MANSOURI, LOTFOLLAH, opera stage dir.; b. Tehran, Iran, June 15, 1929; s. Hassan and Mehri (Jalili) M.; A.B., U. Calif. at Los Angeles, 1953; m. Marjorie Anne Thompson, Sept. 18, 1954; 1 dau., Shireen Melinda. Asst. prof. U. Calif. at Los Angeles, 1957-60; resident stage dir. Zurich (Switzerland) Opera, 1960-65; chief stage dir. Geneva (Switzerland) Opera, 1965-75; gen. dir. Canadian Opera Co., Toronto, Ont., 1976—; guest dir. opera cos., including Met. Opera, San Francisco Opera, La Scala, Vienna Staatsoper, Vienna Volksoper, Salzburg Festival, Amsterdam Opera, Holland Festival; dramatic coach Music Acad. West, Santa Barbara, Calif., 1959; dir. dramatics Zurich Internat. Opera Studio, 1961-65, Centre Lyrique, Geneva, 1967-72; artistic adviser Tehran Opera, 1973-75; opera adviser Nat. Arts Centre, Ottawa, Ont., 1977. Mem. Am. Guild Mus. Artists, Canadian Actors Equity Assn. Home: 263 Banbury Rd Don Mills ON M3B 3C7 Canada Office: Canadian Opera Co 35-39 Front St E Toronto ON M5E 1B3 Canada

MANSURE, ARTHUR LEE, clergyman; b. Phila., June 21, 1914; s. Arthur J. and Anna Grace (McWhood) M.; A.B., U. Mich., 1936; M.A., Boston U., 1938, S.T.B., 1939, Ph.D., 1950; postgrad. Harvard, 1939, 48, U. Cambridge (Eng.), 1955, U. Nairobi, 1972; m. Marie Evangeline Wachs, June 11, 1940; children—Evangeline G., Arthur J., Margaret J., Marilee J., Victor N. Supt. schs., Old Umtali, Rhodesia, 1950-55; vis. prof. Westminster Theol. Sem., Md., 1955-56; asst. prof. Scarritt Coll., 1956-57; asso. prof. U. Evansville, 1957-62; prof. Findlay Coll., 1962-66, chmn., 1963-66; prof. humanities No. Ariz. U., Flagstaff, 1966-78, chmn. dept. humanities, 1967-78; pastor Holbrook (Ariz.) United Meth. Ch., 1978—. Fraternal del. Brit. Meth. Conf., Manchester, 1955; council commr. Put-Han-Sen council Boy Scouts Am., 1964-66, mem. exec. bd. Grand Canyon council, 1968—, v.p., 1975—. Vigil mem. Order of Arrow. Mich. Alumni Undergrad. scholar, Margaret Kraus Ramsdell fellow U. Mich.; Lucinda Bidwell Beebe fellow Boston U. Mem. Am. Philos. Assn., Am. Acad. Religion, Soc. Bibl. Lit., Phi Eta Sigma, Pi Gamma Mu, Phi Delta Kappa, Phi Kappa Phi. Club: Rotary. Contbr. articles to profl. jours. Home: 614 W Buffalo St Holbrook AZ 86025

MANSURE, EDMUND F., mfg. exec., govt. ofcl.; b. Chgo., Mar. 14, 1901; s. Edmund L. and Nellie (Forsman) M.; student Princeton Prep. Sch., Bellefonte Acad.; student Dartmouth, 1924; LL.B., Kent Coll. Law; student grad. sch. Northwestern U.; m. Julia Carroll, Dec. 24, 1938. With E. L. Mansure Co. 1922—, v.p., 1925-35, pres., 1935-51, chmn. bd., 1952—, also dir.; admitted to Ill. bar, 1927, Fed. bar, 1928; adminstr. Gen. Services Adminstrn., 1953-56, Def. Materials Procurement Agy. 1953—. Dir. Value Line Mut. Funds, Value Line Fund, Inc., Income Fund, Spl. Situations Fund, Leveraged Growth Investors Money Market Fund. Mem. adv. bd. Chgo. Planning Commn., 1938-43; dir. Chgo. Crime Commn., 1933-34; pres. Crime Prevention, Inc. of Cook County; mem. Ill Revenue Laws Commn., 1947-49, Ill. State Pension Commn., 1945-51, Nat. Capital Planning Commn., 1953, Pres.'s Com. on Govt. Contracts, 1953; chmn. Ill. State Bd. Unemployment Compensation and Free Employment Advisors; mem. exec. com. Citizen's Subway Com., 1938-43, South Side Planning Bd.; chmn. Chgo. div. Red Cross War Fund drive, 1945; mem. adv. com. Civic Fedn., chmn. citizens waterway com., 1937; chmn. Community Chest campaign, govt. div., 1954; co-chmn. Washington Community Chest, 1955. Bd. dirs. Travelers Aid, 1933-35; pres. U. Ill.-Cook County Sch. Nursing, and Nursing Service Cook County Hosp., 1948-51; dir. Research Found. Elected to Wisdom Hall of Fame, 1973; recipient Winston Churchill Medal of Wisdom, 1975. Mem. Ill. Mfrs. Assn. (dir. 1939-40, treas. 1941-46, v.p. 1947-48, pres. 1949, chmn. bd. 1950), Chgo. Drapery Mfrs. Assn. (pres. 1933-47), Chgo. Assn. Commerce, South Central Assn. (pres.), Delta Kappa Epsilon. Republican. (sec. Ill. state finance com.; mem. campaign allocation com., treas. Ill. state central com. 1937-38; del. nat. conv. 1940; chmn. citizens campaign com. Cook County). Clubs: Chicago Athletic, Commercial (Chgo.). Home: Portola Park Rd La Honda CA 94020 Office: General Services Bldg Washington DC 20405. *Concentration is the secret of strength and success. There is no such thing as a person self made-everyone depends on the help of many. Picking the brains of others you listen your way to success.*

MANTEL, SAMUEL JOSEPH, JR., educator; b. Indpls., Nov. 17, 1921; s. Samuel Joseph and Beatrice Smith (Talmas) M.; A.B., Harvard U., 1948, M.P.A., 1950, Ph.D., 1952; m. Dorothy Jean Friedland, June 28, 1950; children—Michael Lee, Samuel Joseph, III, Margaret Irene, Elizabeth Baer. Asst. prof. social sci. Ga. Inst. Tech., 1953-56; asst. prof., then asso. prof. econs., dir. econs.-in-action program Case Western Res. U., 1956-69; prof. mgmt. and quantitative analysis U. Cin., 1969—, Joseph S. Stern prof. mgmt., 1973—; mgmt. cons., condr. mgmt. seminars. Vice pres. Jewish Fedn. Cin., 1978—; past pres., life mem. Cin. Hillel Found., Cleve. Hillel Found.; trustee Jewish Hosp., Cin., 1975—; historian Rockdale Temple, Cin., 1969-77; mem. mgmt. and adminstrn. com. Anti-Defamation League, B'nai B'rith, 1976—. Served to maj. USMCR, 1942-46, 51-53. Decorated D.F.C. with 3 oak leaf clusters, Air medal with 11 oak leaf clusters; Econs.-in-Action fellow, 1955; named Prof. of Year, Delta Sigma Pi, 1974. Mem. Acad. Mgmt., AAAS, Am. Econ. Assn., Am. Inst. Decision Scis., Ops. Research Soc., Soc. Advancement Mgmt., Inst. Mgmt. Scis., Sigma Xi, Gamma Alpha, Sigma Iota Epsilon, Beta Gamma Sigma. Author: Cases in Managerial Decisions, 1964; also articles, chpts. to in books. Home: 608 Flagstaff Dr Cincinnati OH 45215 Office: Univ Cin Cincinnati OH 45221

MANTELL, CHARLES L., chem. engr.; b. Bklyn., Dec. 9, 1897; s. John Henry and Emma (Smith) M.; student McGill U., Montreal, 1914-16; A.B., Coll. City of N.Y., 1918, B.S., 1918; A.M., Columbia, 1924, Chem.E., 1924, Ph.D., 1927; m. Adelaide M. Smithenner, 1926; children—Cynthia Adelaide, Keith Charles. Chem. engr. Aluminum Co. of Am., 1918-21, Celluloid Corp., 1921-22; prof. chem. engring. Pratt Inst., Bklyn., 1922-37; cons. engr., 1924; dir. research Am. Gum Importers Assn., 1934-39; tech. adviser Netherlands Indies Govt., 1934-50; tech. dir. W. B. Driver Co., Newark, 1934-39; tech. dir. United Mchts. & Mfrs. Corp., 1940-47; v.p. United Mchts. Labs., Inc., 1945; prof. chem. engring. Newark Coll. Engring., 1948-68, chmn. dept., 1948-63; engring. cons. to various govt. agys., cos. and govts. in Near East. Trustee Newark Coll. Engring. Research Found. Served as lt. Royal Flying Corps, Brit. Army, 1917-18. Recipient Cullimore medal, 1966. Fellow Am. Inst. Chem. Engrs., Legion of Honor; mem. Am. Inst. Mining and Metall. Engrs., Am. Chem. Soc., Electro-chem. Soc., Am. Soc. Metals, Phi Lambda Upsilon, Sigma Xi, Epsilon Chi (life), Tau Beta Pi. Republican. Episcopalian. Mason. Author: Industrial Carbon, 1928, 46; Tin, 1929, 49, 72; Industrial Electrochemistry, 1931, 40, 50; Sparks from Electrode, 1932; Technology of Natural Resins, 1942; Adsorption, 1945, 51; Calcium Metallurgy and Technology, 1945; Water Soluble Gums, 1947, 71; Electrochemical Engineering, 1960. Editor-in-chief Engring. Materials Handbook, 1958; Carbon and Graphite Handbook, 1968; Batteries and Energy Systems, 1970; Solid Wastes, 1973; Our Fragile Water Planet, 1975; others; also transls. Contbr. to Chem. Engr.'s Handbook. Contbr. numerous articles to tech. jours. Address: 447 Ryder Rd Munsey Park Manhasset NY 11030

MANTELL, MURRAY IRWIN, educator, civil engr.; b. N.Y.C., Sept. 6, 1917; s. John and Anna (Sidman) M.; B.M.E., U. Fla., 1940, M.E., 1948; M.S. in Civil Engring., U. So. Calif., 1945; Ph.D., U. Tex., 1952; m. Rose Plansky, Apr. 29, 1944; children—Melodie, Andrea, Tobi, John. Pres., supt. Mantell Constrn. Co., Miami, Fla., 1940-41, 46; structural design R. Belsham, cons. engr., Miami 1941; supr. sci. sect., also engring.-in-service tng. Charleston Navy Yard, 1941-43; supr. alignment sect. Terminal Island (Cal.) Naval Shipyard 1943-45; mem. faculty U. Miami, 1946—, prof. civil engring., chmn. dept., 1948-74, chmn. sch. grad. faculty, 1974-78; vis. sr. lectr. U. Sheffield (Eng.), 1965-66. Pres. Tigertail Civic Assn., Miami, Fla., 1960-62. Sec. Learning Disabilities Found., 1968—. Recipient commendation for engring. achievement British Admiralty, 1942. Registered profl. engr., Fla. Mem. ASCE (pres. S. Fla. sect. 1958), Am. Arbitration Assn. (mem. nat. panel), ASME (sr. award 1940), Nat. Soc. Profl. Engrs. (vp. Miami 1958; Engr. of Yr. award Miami chpt. 1961), Am. Soc. Engring. Edn. (pres. S.E. sect. 1969-70; Western Electric Fund award 1969), Fla. Engring. Soc. (pres. S.E. sect. 1950, award for outstanding service to engring. 1973), AAUP, Fla. Planning and Zoning Assn. (v.p. sect. 1971-74), Tau Beta Pi, Phi Kappa Phi, Sigma Tau, Omicron Delta Kappa, Iron Arrow. Author: Structural Analysis, 1962; Orientation in Engineering, 2d edit., 1963; Ethics and Professionalism in Engineering, 1964; Strength of Materials, 1968; Sliderule, 1968; contbr. Contributions to a Philosophy of Technology, 1974. Home: 8505 SW 56th St Miami FL 33155 Office: Civil Engring Dept U Miami Coral Gables FL 33124

MANTELL, SUZANNE, editor; b. West Orange, N.J., Nov. 26, 1944; d. Milton A. and Florence B. Mantell; student U. Chgo., 1962; B.F.A., Pratt Inst., 1967. Formerly asso. editor Harper's mag., N.Y.C., editor Harper's Bookletter, 1974-77, exec. editor, 1977—. Mem. PEN, Nat. Book Critics Circle. Home: 302 W 12th St New York NY 10014 Office: 2 Park Ave New York NY 10016

MANTLE, MICKEY CHARLES, athlete, marketing cons.; b. Spavinaw, Okla., Oct. 20, 1931; s. Elvin Clark and Lovell (Richardson) M.; grad. high sch.; m. Merlyn Louise Johnson, Dec. 23, 1951; children—Mickey Elvin, David Harold, Billy Giles, Danny Merle. Signed with N.Y. Yankees, 1949, played with Independence (Mo.) team, 1949, Joplin (Mo.) team, 1950, N.Y. Yankees (1st base, outfield), 1951-68, appearing in many World Series games. Vice pres. spl. markets Res. Life Ins. Co., Dallas, 1973—. Inducted into Baseball Hall of Fame, Cooperstown, N.Y., 1974. Office: care Roy J True The True Firm 1515 Dallas Fed Savs Tower Dallas TX 75225

MANTON, EDWIN ALFRED GRENVILLE, ins. co. exec.; b. Earls Colne, Essex, Eng., Jan. 22, 1909; s. John Horace and Emily Clara (Denton) M.; student London (Eng.) U., 1925-27, N.Y. Ins. Soc., 1933-35; m. Florence V. Brewer, Feb. 2, 1936; 1 dau., Diana H. (Mrs. William Hugh Madison Morton). Came to U.S., 1933. Trainee B.W. Noble Ltd., Paris, 1927-33; casualty underwriter Am. Internat. Underwriters Corp., N.Y.C., 1933-37, sec., 1937-38, v.p., 1938-42, pres., 1942-69, chmn., 1969-75, also dir.; cons. Am. Internat. Group, Inc.; dir. Am. Internat. Aviation Agy., Inc., AIG Oil Rig, Inc.; chmn., dir. Am. Internat. Marine Agy. N.Y. Inc., N.Y.C., Starr Tech. Risks Agy. Bd. dirs. Starr Found., N.Y.C., 1955. Episcopalian. Clubs: Salmagundi, Drug and Chem., Mendelssohn Glee (sec. 1969). Home: 40 Fifth Ave New York NY 10011 Office: Am Internat Group Inc 70 Pine St New York NY 10005

MANTON, RUTH MCCARTHY, fashion mktg. exec.; b. N.Y.C.; d. Irving and Irene (Klein) Constad; A.B., Pa. State U.; m. John Manton, Apr. 19, 1973; children—Keith McCarthy, Kyle McCarthy. Mktg. editor Harper's Bazaar, 1968-74; exec. mktg. dir. Vogue mag., N.Y.C., 1974—; pres. Anne Klein Design Studio, 1975—; pres. Aries Design Mgmt., 1976—. Mem. Fashion Group, Advt. Women of New York, Trends & Women's Forum, Inc. Home: 15 W 72d St New York NY 10023 Office: 1345 Ave of the Americas Suite 4402 New York NY 10019

MANTONYA, JOHN BUTCHER, lawyer; b. Columbus, Ohio, May 26, 1922; s. Elroy Letts and Blanche (Butcher) M.; A.B. cum laude, Washington and Jefferson Coll., 1943; postgrad. U. Mich. Law Sch., 1946-47; J.D., Ohio State U., 1949; m. Mary E. Reynolds, June 14, 1947; children—Elizabeth Claire, Mary Kay, Lee Ann. Admitted to Ohio bar, 1949; asso. A.S. Mitchell, Atty., Newark, Ohio, 1949-50, C.D. Lindrooth, Newark, 1950-57; partner firm Lindrooth & Mantonya, Newark, 1957—. Mem. North Fork Local Bd. Edn., 1962-69; adv. com. Salvation Army, Licking County, 1965—. Mayor of Utica, Ohio, 1953-59. Served with AUS, 1943-45. Mem. Am. Bar Assn., Ohio Bar Assn., Licking County Bar Assn. (pres. 1967), Phi Delta Phi, Beta Theta Pi. Home: 136 Mill St Utica OH 43080 Office: Trust Bldg Newark OH 43055

MANUEL, ERNEST HARRY, diversified mfg. corp. exec.; b. Cleve., May 7, 1922; s. Harry and Barbara Manuel; B.S. in Elec. Engring., Case Inst. Tech., 1943, M.S. in Indsl. Engring., 1953; m. Shirley Baker, Mar. 16, 1946; children—Bettina Ruth, Roger Baker, Ernest Harry. Plant engr. autonetics div. N. Am. Rockwell, 1955-60, v.p., gen. mgr. Minuteman div.-autonetics div., 1960-67, v.p., gen. mgr. oceans systems ops., space div., 1967-70; v.p., dir. ops. avionics div. ITT, Nutley, N.J., 1970-71, div. pres., 1971-76, group gen. mgr. def. space group, Nutley, N.J., 1976—, v.p., 1978—. Served to lt. (j.g.) USNR, 1944-46. Mem. Air Force Assn., Assn. U.S. Army, Armed Forces Communications and Electronics Assn., Soc. Logistics Engrs. (bd. advs. 1975—), Inst. Nav., Navy League U.S., Am. Def. Preparedness Assn. Presbyterian. Club: Pennington (Passaic, N.J.). Office: ITT Def Space Group 500 Washington Ave Nutley NJ 07110

MANUEL, FRANK EDWARD, historian, educator; b. Boston, Sept. 12, 1910; s. Morris and Jessica (Fredson) M.; A.B., Harvard, 1930, A.M., 1931, Ph.D., 1933; postgrad. Ecole des Hautes Etudes Politiques et Sociales, Paris, 1933; m. Fritzie Prigohzy, Oct. 6, 1936. Instr., lectr. depts. history, govt., econs. Harvard, 1935-37, vis. prof., 1960; various govtl. positions, 1938-43; with OPA, Washington, 1945-47; prof. history Brandeis U., 1949-65, Univ. prof., 1977—; prof. N.Y. U., 1965-76, Kenan prof., 1970-76; Camp Meml. lectr. Stanford, 1964; vis. prof. Hebrew U., Jerusalem, 1972; Eastman vis. prof. Oxford U., 1972-73; vis. research fellow Australian Nat. U., 1974; vis. prof. U. Chgo., 1975, U. Calif. at Los Angeles, 1976. Served with AUS, 1943-45. Rogers Traveling fellow, 1932-33; Guggenheim fellow, 1957-58; fellow Center for Advanced Study in Behavioral Scis., 1962-63; vis. mem. Inst. for Advanced Study, Princeton, 1976-77; Phi Beta Kappa vis. scholar, 1978. Fellow Am. Acad. Arts and Scis. (mem. com. on publs. 1969-71); mem. Am. Hist. Assn. (mem. exec. com. modern history sect. 1961-63), Phi Beta Kappa. Author: Politics of Modern Spain, 1938; American-Palestine Relations, 1949; Age of Reason, 1951; The New World of Henri Saint-Simon, 1956; The Eighteenth Century Confronts the Gods, 1959; The Prophets of Paris, 1962; Isaac Newton, Historian, 1963; Shapes of Philosophical History, 1965; A Portrait of Isaac Newton, 1968; Freedom From History, 1971; The Religion of Isaac Newton, 1974. Editor: The Enlightenment, 1965; Utopias and Utopian Thought, 1966; Herder's Reflections on the Philosophy of the History of Mankind, 1968; co-author: Utopian Thought in the Western World, 1979. Co-editor: French Utopias: An Anthology of Ideal Societies, 1966. Cons. editor Psychoanalysis and Contemporary Sci.; adv. editor Clio. Home: 85 E India Row Boston MA 02110

MANUEL, RALPH NIXON, coll. dean; b. Frederick, Md., Apr. 21, 1936; s. Ralph Walter and Frances Rebecca (Nixon) M.; A.B., Dartmouth Coll., 1958; M.Ed., Boston U., 1967; Ph.D., U. Ill., 1971; m. Sarah Jane Warner, July 22, 1960; children—Mark, David, Stephen, Bradley. Asst. dir. admissions Dartmouth Coll., Hanover, N.H., 1962-68, asso. dean, 1971-72, dean of freshmen, 1972-75, dean coll., 1975—. Trustee, Kimball Union Acad., Meriden, N.H., 1976—; mem. Hanover Parks and Recreation Bd., 1974—, chmn., 1975-76; bd. corporators Mary Hitchcock Meml. Hosp., Hanover, 1975—. Served to comdr. USNR, 1958-62, 62—. NDEA fellow, 1968-69. Mem. Am. Assn. Higher Edn., Nat. Assn. Student Personnel Adminstrs., Am. Coll. Personnel Assn. Home: 13 Choate Rd Hanover NH 03755 Office: Dartmouth Coll Hanover NH 03755

MANUEL, WILEY WILLIAM, asso. justice Calif. Supreme Ct.; b. Oakland, Calif., Aug. 28, 1927; s. Curtis W. and Gradella M.; A.B., U. Calif., 1959; LL.B., Hastings Coll. Law, 1953; LL.D. (hon.), U. San Diego Law Sch., 1978; m. Eleanor Williams, June 20, 1948; children—Yvonne Temple, Gary Manuel. Admitted to Calif. bar, 1954; dep. atty. gen. State of Calif., 1953-70, asst. atty. gen., 1970-71, chief asst. atty. gen., 1971-76; judge Superior Ct. of Alameda County (Calif.), 1976-77; asso. justice Calif. Supreme Ct., 1977—; mem. sentencing adv. com. Jud. Council Calif., 1976—. Served with U.S. Army, 1946-47. Mem. Charles H. Houston Bar Assn. (pres. 1962), Calif. State Employees Assn., Calif. Judges Assn., Calif. Jud. Council, U. Calif. Alumni Assn. Democrat. Roman Catholic. Club: K.C. Home: 4107 Sequoyah Rd Oakland CA 94605 Office: 350 McAllister St San Francisco CA 94102

MANULIS, MARTIN, producer; b. N.Y.C., May 30, 1915; s. Abraham and Anne (Silverstein) M.; B.A., Columbia, 1935; m. Katharine Bard, June 14, 1939; children—Laurie, Karen, John Bard. Producer, dir. (with John C. Wilson), Broadway, also on tour and Westport Country Playhouse, 1946-50; mng. dir. Bahamas Playhouse, 1951-52; producer, dir. with CBS-TV, Suspense, Studio One, Best of Broadway, Climax, also Playhouse 90, 1952-58; exec. head television prodn. Twentieth Century Fox, 1958-60, now ind. motion picture producer; producer Days of Wine and Roses, Dear Heart for Warner Bros., Luv and Duffy for Columbia pictures; dir. Am. Film Inst., West, 1974-76. Served as lt. USNR, World War II, 1942-45. Recipient spl. service award Crusade for Freedom, 1954; Look TV award for best dramatic series, 1955, 56, 57; five TV Emmy awards for Playhouse 90, 1956, 57. Office: Martin Manulis Prodns Ltd Box 818 Beverly Hills CA 90210

MANVILLE, ALFRED R., constrn. co. exec.; b. N.J., 1917; s. Keith Rollin and Kirsten (Tonning) M.; B.S. in Elec. Engring., Rutgers U., 1938; m. Michael Burdett, Jan. 28, 1968; children—Florence, Suzanne, David, Richard, Catherine, Peggy Jane, Elizabeth. Vice pres. J. Livingston & Co., N.Y.C., 1938-64; exec. v.p. L.K. Comstock Co., N.Y.C., 1964-70; pres., chief exec. officer Fischbach and Moore, Inc., N.Y.C., 1970—. Served with AUS, 1942-46. Decorated Legion of Merit. Home: 223 Chapel Hill Rd Red Bank NJ 07701 Office: 485 Lexington Ave New York NY 10017

MAPEL, WILLIAM, writer, editor; b. Osborn, Mo., July 24, 1902; s. Frank Joseph and Ada Louise (Latta) M.; student N.W. Mo. State U., Maryville, 1920-23; B.J., U. Mo., 1925; LL.D., Lincoln Coll. of James Millikin U., 1950; m. Evelyn Edith Raines, Oct. 17, 1925; children—Evelyn Louise, William M.R. Editorial work Democrat-Forum, Maryville, 1920-23; corr. Kansas City Star, 1923-25; asso. editor Sentinel, Edina, Mo., 1925; sports editor and city editor Forum, Maryville, 1926; dir. information N.W. Mo. State U., 1926-27; head dept. publs. and publicity Kent (O.) State Coll., 1927-28; asst. prof. journalism Washington and Lee U., Lexington, Va., 1928-30, dir. Sch. Journalism, 1930-34; asst. editor Am. Boy Mag., Detroit, 1931; pres. Virginian Pub. Co., 1930-34; exec. editor, dir. Wilmington (Del.) Morning News and Evening Jour., 1934-37; with Inst. Pub. Relations, 1937; pres. William Mapel Assos., 1938-40; co-founder, gen. mgr. Newsday, Nassau County, N.Y., 1940-42; exec. sec. Pubs. Assn. N.Y.C., 1942-44, vice chmn., 1944, pres., 1952-58; cons., 1958-61; adminstrv. v.p. Am. Soc. Prevention Cruelty to Animals, 1961-72, emeritus, 1972—; editor Anglers' Club Bull., 1973-75. Oberlaender traveling fellow German univs., summer 1934. Mem. adv. com. N.Y. State Conservation Dept., 1968—. Capt. specialized res. U.S. Army, 1932-37. Recipient medal for distinguished service to journalism, U. Mo. Mem. Am. Assn. Tchrs. Journalism (v.p. 1931-33, pres. 1934), S.R., Huguenot Soc. S.C., Alpha Delta Sigma, Phi Gamma Delta, Pi Delta Epsilon, Kappa Tau Alpha, Sigma Delta Chi (nat. treas. 1931-33). Clubs: Anglers (dir.) (N.Y.C.); Mill Reef (Antigua, West Indies); DeBruce Fly Fishers (Catskills). Author: When in Doubt; The Fifth Commandment, Legend of a Family. Home: 3 Stoneleigh Plaza Bronxville NY 10708

MAPEL, WILLIAM MARLEN RAINES, banker; b. Maryville, Mo., Sept. 17, 1931; s. William and Evelyn (Raines) M.; B.A., Yale U., 1953; m. Gail Manchee, June 21, 1958; children—Daniel B., Susan L., Stephen W. Indsl. relations asst. Union Carbide Corp., N.Y.C., 1953-57; with Citibank, N.A., N.Y.C., 1957—, asst. cashier, 1959-62, asst. v.p., 1962-64, v.p., 1964-69, sr. v.p., 1969—; dir. Merc. & Gen. Reins. Co. Am. Trustee Chubb Found., N.Y.C. Mem. Wolf's Head, Delta Kappa Epsilon. Clubs: Woodway Country (Darien); Links, Anglers (N.Y.C.); Pine Valley Golf (Clementon, N.J.). Home: 18 Stephanie Ln Darien CT 06820 Office: 399 Park Ave New York NY 10022

MAPELLI, ROLAND LAWRENCE, cattle co. exec.; b. Denver, June 10, 1922; s. Herman and Della (Borelli) M.; student Regis Coll., 1959-61; m. Neoma Robinson, Apr. 1942; children—Terralyn Mapelli DeMoney, Geraldine. Vice pres. Monfort of Colo., Inc., Greeley, 1969-76, sr. v.p., 1976—, co-chmn. bd., 1971—; pres. Monfort Food Distbg. Co., Greeley, 1969—; owner, operator Mapelli Farms, Eaton, Colo., 1974—; chmn. bd. Denver Union Stock Yards Co., 1969-70; dir. 1st Nat. Bank, Greeley, 1st Nat. Bancorp. Mem. Gov.'s 100-Man Local Affairs Commn., 1962-66; div. chmn. 1962 Mile High United Fund campaign; mem. Colo. Bd. Agr.'s Frozen Food Provisioners Bd., 1967-71; mem. Colo. Agrl. Adv. Com., 1966-73; chmn. Denver Off-Street Parking Commn., 1960-72; mem. Denver City Council, 1955-59; mem. Colo. Ho. of Reps. (to fill vacancy), 1961; mem. Colo. Senate, 1962-66; state fin. chmn. Democratic Party, 1963-66; mem. adv. bd. Ft. Logan Mental Health Center, 1961-64; bd. dirs. North Denver Civic Assn., 1955-65, Better Bus. Bur., 1966-69; mem. bd. ambassadors Loretto Heights Coll., 1960-65; adv. bd. St. Anthony's Hosp., 1960-65; bd. dirs., exec. com. Nat. Western Stock Show, 1966—. Served to 2d lt. USAF, 1942-45; ETO. Recipient Knute Rockne award for outstanding civic achievement, 1961. Mem. Colo. Meat Dealers Assn. (pres. 1968-69), Colo. Cattlemen's Assn., Colo. Cattlefeeders Assn., Colo.-Wyo. Restaurant Assn., Nat. Assn. Meat Purveyors. Roman Catholic. Home: Route 2 Box 206A Eaton CO 80615 Office: PO Box G Greeley CO 80631

MAPLE, CLAIR GEORGE, educator; b. Glennwood, Ind., Mar. 17, 1916; s. Clair Albert and Ora Edna (Dunn) M.; B.A., Earlham Coll., 1939; M.Ed., U. Cin., 1940; D.Sc., Carnegie Inst. Tech., 1948; m. Mary Louise Catron, Sept. 20, 1942. Instr. math. W.Va. Inst. Tech., Montgomery, 1940-41, Ohio State U., Columbus, 1941-44; research asso. Carnegie Inst. Tech., 1946-48; asso. prof. math. North Tex. State U., Denton, 1948-49; mem. faculty Iowa State U., 1949—, prof. math., 1956—, dir. computation center, 1963—, prof. computer sci., 1968—; div. chief math. and computer sci. div. Ames Lab., Dept. Energy, 1966-78; cons. Nat. Security Agy., 1953-60, Zenith Radio Corp., 1954-66, Land Air Corp., 1960-61, United Electro-Dynamics, 1961, Collins Radio Co., 1959-60. Mem. Gov. Iowa Sci. Adv. Com., 1966-69. Trees. YMCA Iowa State U., 1960-68. Served with USNR, 1944-46, 50-52. Mem. IEEE (midwest area com. 1968—), Am. Math. Soc., Math. Assn. Am., Assn. Computing Machinery, AAUP, AAAS, Iowa Acad. Sci., Sigma Xi, Phi Kappa Phi, Pi Mu Epsilon, Soc. Indsl. and Applied Math. (chmn. Iowa 1964-65; nat. council 1970). Methodist. Author: (with Holl and Vinograde) Introduction to the Laplace Transform, 1959; also articles. Home: 333 Pearson Ave Ames IA 50010

MAPOTHER, DILLON EDWARD, physicist, acad. adminstr.; b. Louisville, Aug. 22, 1921; s. Dillon Edward and Edith (Rubel) M.; B.S. in Mech. Engring., U. Louisville, 1943; D.Sc. in Physics, Carnegie-Mellon U., 1949; m. Elizabeth Beck, June 29, 1946; children—Ellen, Susan, Anne. Engr., Westinghouse Research Labs., East Pittsburgh, Pa., 1943-46; instr. Carnegie Inst. Tech., Pitts., 1946; mem. faculty U. Ill., Urbana, 1949—, prof. physics, 1959—, dir. Office Computing Services, 1971-76, asso. vice chancellor for research, 1976—, acting dean grad. coll., vice chancellor research, 1977-78; cons. in field. Alfred P. Sloan fellow, 1958-61, Guggenheim fellow, 1960-61. Fellow Am. Phys. Soc.; mem. Am. Assn. Physics Tchrs., Assn. for Computing Machinery, Sigma Xi. Research on ionic mobility in alkali halides, thermodynamic properties of superconductors, calorimetric study of critical points, adminstrn. of univ. computing resources. Home: 1013 Ross Dr Champaign IL 61820 Office: 330 Adminstrn Bldg U Ill Urbana IL 61801

MAPP, ALF JOHNSON, JR., author, historian; b. Portsmouth, Va., Feb. 17, 1925; s. Alf Johnson and Lorraine (Carney) M.; A.A., Coll. William and Mary, 1945, A.B., 1961; m. Hartley Lockhart, Mar. 28, 1953; 1 son, Alf Johnson III; m. 2d, Ramona Hartley Hamby, Aug. 1, 1971. Editorial writer Portsmouth Star, 1945-46, asso. editor, 1946-48, editorial chief, 1948-54; news editor, editorial writer Virginian-Pilot, Norfolk, 1954-58; free-lance writer, 1958—; lectr. Old Dominion U., 1961-62, instr., 1962-67, asst. prof. English and history, 1967-73, asso prof. English, journalism, creative writing, history, 1973-79, prof., 1979—; profl. lectr., 1948—; host TV series Jamestown to Yorktown, 1975-77. Mem. Portsmouth-Norfolk County Savs. Bond Com., 1948-51; mem. Va. Com. on Library Devel., 1949-50; mem. publs. com. 350th Anniversary of Rep. Govt. in the Western World, 1966-69; mem. publs. com War of Independence Commn., 1967—; mem. editorial bd. Jamestown Found., 1967—; chmn. Portsmouth, Revolutionary Bicentennial Com., 1968—; chmn. awards jury Baruch award United Daus. Confederacy-Columbia U., 1976; chmn. Southeastern Va. Anglo-Am. Friendship Day, 1976. Bd. dirs. Portsmouth Pub. Library, 1948-58, v.p., 1954-56; bd. dirs. Portsmouth Area Community Chest, 1948-52, Va. YMCA Youth and Govt. Found., 1950-52; mem. All-Am. cities com. for award-winning city Nat. League Municipalities, 1976. Named Portsmouth Young Man of Year, 1951; recipient honor medal Freedoms Found., 1951, English award Old Dominion Coll., 1961, Troubadour Great Tchr. award, 1969, Outstanding Am. Educator award, 1972, 74; Nat. Bicentennial medal Am. Revolution Bicentennial Adminstrn., 1976; medal Comité Francais du Bicentennial de l'Independence des Etas-Unis, France, 1976. Mem. Am. Hist. Assn., Va., Portsmouth (historiographer 1975—), Norfolk (dir. 1965-72), No. Neck hist. socs., Hist. Socs. Eastern Va. (dir. 1971—), S.A.R., Am. Assn. U. Profs., Authors Guild, Va. Library Assn. (legislative com. 1950-51), Poetry Soc. Va. (pres. 1974-75), Va. Writers Club, Assn. Preservation of Va. Antiquities, Order of Cape Henry (dir. 1970—, nat. pres. 1975-76), Jamestowne Soc. (chief historian 1975-77, internat. sec. state 1978-79), English Speaking Union (dir. 1976-77), Modern Lang. Assn., Phi Theta Kappa, Delta Phi Omega (chpt. pres. 1961). Author: The Virginia Experiment, 1957, 2d edit., 1974; Frock Coats and Epaulets, 1963, 71; America Creates Its Own Literature, 1965; Just One Man, 1968; The Golden Dragon: Alfred the Great and His Times, 1974, 75; co-author: Chesapeake Bay in the American Revolution, 1978; also film and TV scripts. Co-editor: Place Names of Early Portsmouth, 1973, 74. Contbr. articles to N.Y. Times, other newspapers, mags. Home: Willow Oaks 2901 Tanbark Ln Portsmouth VA 23703 Office: Old Dominion U Norfolk VA 23508. *Reared in an intellectual family with high ethical standards, enthusiasm for the arts, and firm belief in hard work, I also had impressed on me that advantages conferred obligations. In an historic environment, I became aware of my generation's responsibility to those that preceded it (to preserve the good they had created) and to those that would follow (to create things that would enrich their lives. This concept, with personal ambition, imbues my professional life.*

MAQUET, JACQUES JEROME PIERRE, educator, anthropologist; b. Brussels, Belgium, Aug. 4, 1919; s. Jerome and Jeanne (Lemoine) M.; LL.D., U. Louvain (Belgium), 1946, D.Phil., 1948; student Harvard, 1946-48; Ph.D., U. London (Eng.), 1952; Dr. ès-lettres, Sorbonne (France), 1973; m. Emma de Longree, June 17, 1946; children—Bernard, Denis; m. 2d, Gisele Cambresier, Nov. 13, 1970. Came to U.S., 1967, naturalized, 1974. Field anthropologist Inst. Sci. Research in Central Africa, 1949-51, head Social Scis. Center, 1951-57; prof. State U. of Congo, Elisabethville, 1957-60; research dir. Ecole pratique des Hautes Etudes, U. Paris, 1961-68; prof. anthropology Case Western Res. U., 1968-71; prof. U. Calif. at Los Angeles, 1971—, chmn. dept. anthropology, 1978—; vis. prof. Northwestern U., 1956, Harvard, 1964, U. Montreal, 1965, U. Pitts., 1967; extraordinary prof. U. Brussels, 1963-68. Recipient Waxweiler award Royal Acad. Belgium, 1961; First World Festival of Negro Arts award, Dakar, 1966. Mem. Am. Anthrop. Assn., Current Anthropology, Assn. Asian Studies, Internat. Assn. Buddhist Studies, Pali Text Soc., AAUP, Fedn. Am. Scientists, Assn. Internat. des Sociologues de Langue française. Author: The Sociology of Knowledge, 1951; Aide-mémoire d'ethnologie africaine, 1954; Ruanda, 1957; (with others) Elections en Société féodale, 1957; The Premise of Inequality in Ruanda, 1961; Power and Society in Africa, 1971; Civilizations of Black Africa, 1972; Africanity, The Cultural Unity of Black Africa, 1972. Co-editor: Dictionary of Black African Civilization, 1974. Home: 2081 Linda Flora Dr Los Angeles CA 90024 Office: Dept Anthropology UCLA Los Angeles CA 90024

MAR, BRIAN WAYNE, civil engr.; b. Seattle, Aug. 5, 1933; s. Frank W. and Ruth L. (Dott) M.; B.S. in Chem. Engring., U. Wash., Seattle, 1955, M.S., 1957, Ph.D., 1958, M.S.E. in Civil Engring., 1967; m. Hazel Joy Woo, Dec. 17, 1955; children—Melanie, Marnie, Murray, Monte, Mimi. Research specialist Boeing Co., Seattle, 1959-67; mem. faculty U. Wash., 1967—, prof. civil engring. Inst. for Environ. Studies, 1973-75, chmn. water and air resources div., 1975-77, asso. dean Coll. Engring., 1976—; cons. in field. Mem. ASCE, AAAS, Am. Geophys. Union, Phi Beta Kappa, Sigma Xi, Tau Beta Pi. Author: (with others) The Natural Environment, Waste and Control, 1973; Environmental Modeling and Decision Making-The U.S. Experience, 1976; also articles, reports. Home: 10615 60th Ave S Seattle WA 98178 Office: Dept Civil Engring Coll Engring Univ Wash Seattle WA 98106. *It is not what you know, but how you use what you know in working with others.*

MARA, RICHARD THOMAS, educator; b. Bklyn., Mar. 18, 1923; s. Edward Thomas and Pauline Ann (Hluboky) M.; A.B., Gettysburg (Pa.) Coll., 1948; M.S., U. Mich., 1950, Ph.D., 1953; m. Joy Anine Nelson, Sept. 7, 1946; children—Richard Nelson, Kristin Anine, Daniel Nathan. Mem. faculty Gettysburg Coll., 1953—, prof. physics, chmn. dept., 1959-73; asso. Aspen Inst. for Humanistic Studies, summer 1964, U. Wash., summer 1965, Harvard, 1966-67; cons. AEC, 1961-69, Am. Inst. Physics, 1970—. Regional councilor in physics for Pa., 1967-71; commr. Commn. on Coll. Physics, 1968-72; mem. com. examiners Ednl. Testing Service, 1968-70. Served with U.S. Army, 1942-46. Mem. Am. Assn. Physics Tchrs. (council physics in edn. 1971), Am. Phys. Soc., Phi Beta Kappa, Sigma Xi. Home: Route 6 Gettysburg PA 17325

MARA, VINCENT JOSEPH, coll. pres.; b. Worcester, Mass., Sept. 19, 1930; s. Edward Stephan and Mary Stephanie (Kavanaugh) M.; B.S. in Edn., Ed.M., Worcester State Coll.; Ph.D., U. Conn.; m. M. Clare Owens, Feb. 15, 1958; children—John, Kevin, Maryellen, Thomas, Clare. Asst., then asso. prof. Framingham (Mass.) State Coll., 1960-63, dir. admissions, 1963-69, acad. dean, 1969-76; acting pres. Salem (Mass.) State Coll., 1974-75; pres. Fitchburg State Coll., 1976—; corporator Fitchburg Savs. Bank, 1976—. Trustee, Worcester Public Library, 1967-70, pres. bd. trustees, 1970; bd. dirs. Fitchburg Civic Center, 1977, Cushing Acad., 1978. Served with U.S. Army, 1953-55. Named Outstanding Young Man of Yr., Worcester C. of C., 1960. Mem. Am. Conf. Acad. Deans, NEA, Am. Assn. State Colls. and Univs., Fitchburg C. of C. (dir. 1977—), Phi Delta Kappa, Kappa Delta Pi. Democrat. Roman Catholic. Club: Fay (Fitchburg). Contbr. articles to profl. jours. Home: Juniper Rd Fitchburg MA 01420 Office: 160 Pearl St Fitchburg MA 01420

MARAFINO, VINCENT NORMAN, aircraft co. exec.; b. Boston, June 8, 1930; s. Nicholas and Rose M.; A.B. in Acctg. and Econs., San Jose State Coll., 1951; M.B.A., Santa Clara U., 1964; m. Doris Marilyn Vernall, June 15, 1958; children—Marli Ann, Sheri Louise, Wendi Joan. Chief acct. Am. Standard Advance Tech. Lab., Mt. View, Calif., 1956-59; with Lockheed Missiles & Space Co., Sunnyvale, Calif., 1959-70, chief accountant, 1967-68, dir. fin. mgmt. and controls, research and devel. div., also asst. dir. fin. ops., 1968-70; v.p. controller Lockheed Corp., Burbank, Calif., 1971-77, sr. v.p. fin., 1977—; dir. Lockheed Fin. Corp., Murdock Machine & Engring. Co. Tex., CTL Corp. Pres. bd. trustees Holy Cross Hosp., Mission Hills, Calif., 1978—. Served with USAF, 1953-55. Mem. Fin. Execs. Inst., Nat. Assn. Accts., Am. Inst. C.P.A.'s. Office: PO Box 551 Burbank CA 91520

MARAKAS, JOHN LAMBROS, ins. co. exec.; b. Connellsville, Pa., July 16, 1926; s. Gust John and Elizabeth Hamilton (Cutler) M.; A.B., U. Mich., 1949; m. Alice Dixon, Dec. 26, 1948; children—Andy,

Nancy, Donna. Actuarian asst. Acacia Mut., Washington, 1949-50; actuary Continental Assurance, Chgo., 1950-53; v.p., actuary, exec. v.p., pres. Res. Life Ins. Co., Dallas, 1953-70; v.p., then pres. Nationwide Corp., Columbus, Ohio; dir. Gates, McDonald & Co., Gulf Atlantic Life, Mich. Life, Nat. Casualty Co., Nat. Services, Inc., Nationwide Community Urban Redevelopment Corp., Nationwide Funding, Nationwide Life, Nationwide Profl. Services Corp., Nationwide Properties, Pacific Life, West Coast Life; trustee Nationwide Real Estate Services, Real Estate Investors, Heritage Securities Inc. Bd. dirs. Mt. Carmel Med. Center, Buckeye Boys Ranch, Planned Parenthood, Capital U. Served with U.S. Army, 1946-47. Mem. Am. Acad. Actuaries. Home: 1950 Brandywine Dr Columbus OH 43220 Office: One Nationwide Plaza Columbus OH 43216

MARAMOROSCH, KARL, virologist, educator; b. Vienna, Austria, Jan. 16, 1915; s. Jacob and Stefanie Olga (Schlesinger) M.; M.S. magna cum laude in Entomology, Agrl. U., Warsaw, Poland, 1938; student Poly. U. Bucharest (Rumania), 1944-46; fellow Bklyn. Bot. Garden, 1947-48; Ph.D. (predoctoral fellow Am. Cancer Soc. 1948-49), Columbia, 1949; m. Irene Ludwinowska, Nov. 15, 1938; 1 dau., Lydia Ann. Came to U.S., 1947, naturalized, 1952. Civilian internee in Rumania, 1939-46; asst., then asso. Rockefeller Inst., N.Y.C., 1949-61; sr. entomologist Boyce Thompson Inst., Yonkers, N.Y., 1961-74, program dir. virology and insect physiology, 1962-74; prof. microbiology Waksman Inst., Rutgers U., New Brunswick, N.J., 1974—; vis. prof. agr. U. Wageningen (Netherlands), 1953, Cornell U., 1957, Rutgers U., 1967-68, Fordham U., 1973, Sapporo U. (Japan), 1980; Mendel lectr. St. Peters Coll., Jersey City, 1963; virologist FAO to Philippines, 1960; cons. World-wide survey, 1963; chmn. U.S.-Japan Coop. Seminar, 1965, 74; mem. panel food and fiber Nat. Acad. Scis., 1966; cons. rice virus diseases AID-IRRI, Hyderabad, India, 1971; cons. UNDP, Bangalore, India, 1978-79; AIBS lectr., 1970-72; Found. Microbiology Nat. lectr., 1972-73; Fulbright Distinguished prof., Yugoslavia, 1972-73, 78; mem. tropical medicine and parasitology study sect. NIH, 1972-76; chmn. 1st-3d Internat. Confs. Comparative Virology, 1969, 73, 76. Recipient Sr. Research award Lalor Found., 1957; Nat. Ciba-Geigy award in agr., 1976. Fellow N.Y. Acad. Scis. (A. Cressy Morrison prize natural sci. 1951; chmn. div. microbiology 1956-60, rec. sec. 1960-61, v.p. 1962-63), AAAS (Campbell award 1958); mem. Harvey Soc., Growth Soc., Phytopath. Soc. (councellor), Entomol. Soc. Am., Indian, Japan, Can. phytopath. socs., Internat. Com. Virus Nomenclature, Electron Microscope Soc., Am. Soc. Microbiology (Waksman award 1978), Tissue Culture Assn. (pres. N.E. br. 1978-80), Sigma Xi. Author: Comparative Symptomatology of Coconut Diseases of Unknown Etiology, 1964. Editor: Biological Transmission of Disease Agents, 1962; Insect Viruses, 1968; Viruses, Vectors and Vegetation, 1969; Comparative Virology, 1971; Mycoplasma Diseases, 1973; Viruses, Evolution and Cancer, 1974; Invertebrate Immunity, 1975; Legume Diseases in the Tropics, 1975; Invertebrate Tissue Culture: Research Applications, 1976; Invertebrate Tissue Culture: Applications in Medicine, Biology and Agriculture, 1976; Aphids as Virus Vectors, 1977; Insect and Plant Viruses: An Atlas, 1977; Viruses and Environment, 1978; Practical Tissue Culture Applications, 1979; Leafhopper Vectors and Plant Disease Agents, 1979. Editor: Methods in Virology, 1964—, Advances in Virus Research, 1972—, Archiv ges. Virusforschung, 1973—, Intervirology, 1973—, Advances in Cell Culture, 1979—. Editor-in-chief: Jour. N.Y. Entomol. Soc., 1972—. Asso. editor Virology, 1964-68, 75—. Home: 17 Black Birch Ln Scarsdale NY 10583 Office: Waksman Inst Microbiology Rutgers U New Brunswick NJ 08903

MARAN, STEPHEN PAUL, astronomer; b. Bklyn., Dec. 25, 1938; s. Alexander P. and Clara F. (Schoenfeld) M.; B.S., Bklyn. Coll., 1959; M.A., U. Mich., 1961, Ph.D., 1964; m. Sally Ann Scott, Feb. 14, 1971; children—Michael Scott, Enid Rebecca, Elissa Jean. Astronomer Kitt Peak Nat. Obs., Tucson, 1964-69; project scientist for orbiting solar observatories NASA-Goddard Space Flight Center, Greenbelt, Md., 1969-75, head advanced systems and ground observations br., 1970-77, mgr. operation Kohoutek, 1973-74, sr. staff scientist, 1977—. Cons. Westinghouse Research Labs., 1966; vis. lectr. U. Md., College Park, 1969-70; sr. lectr. U. Calif. at Los Angeles, 1976. Named Distinguished Visitor, Boston U., 1970; recipient Group Achievement awards NASA, 1969, 74, Hon. Mention AAAS-Westinghouse Sci. Writing Award, 1970. Mem. Internat. Astron. Union, AAAS, Am., Royal astron. socs., Am. Phys. Soc., Am. Geophys. Union, Am. Inst. Aeros. and Astronautics. Author: (with John C. Brandt) New Horizons in Astronomy, 1972, 2d edit., 1979, Arabic edit., 1979. Editor: Physics of Nonthermal Radio Sources, 1964; The Gum Nebula and Related Problems, 1971; Possible Relations Between Solar Activity and Meteorological Phenomena, 1975; New Astronomy and Space Science Reader, 1977; asso. editor Earth, Extraterrestrial Scis., 1969—; editor Astrophys. Letters, 1974-77, asso. editor, 1977—. Contbr. articles on astronomy, space to popular mags. Office: Code 680 NASA-Goddard Space Flight Center Greenbelt MD 20771

MARANDA, PIERRE JEAN, anthropologist; b. Quebec, Que., Can., Mar. 27, 1930; s. Lucien and Marie Alma (Rochette) M.; B.A., U. Laval, Quebec, 1949; M.A., U. Montreal (Que.), 1953; Ph.D., Harvard U., 1966; m. Elli Kongas, Mar. 12, 1963; children—Erik Pierre, Nicolas Martin. Asst. prof. anthropology U. Laval, 1955-58, research prof., 1975—; tutor Harvard U., 1964-65, research fellow, 1966-70; dir. studies École Pratique des Hautes Études, 6th Sect., Paris, 1968-69; asso. prof. U. B.C. (Can.), Vancouver, 1969-73, prof., 1973-75; prof. étranger College de France, Paris, 1975; bd. dirs. several internat. research insts. Pres., Comité des Citoyens de Belvedere, Quebec, 1976—. Recipient Medaille du College de France, 1975. Fellow Royal Soc. Can., Am. Anthrop. Assn.; mem. Internat. Semiotics Assn., Internat. Center Linguistics and Semiotics, Can. Ethnol. Soc. (pres.), Can. Anthropology and Sociology Assn. (pres.), Can. Semiotics Research Assn., Can. Folklore Studies Assn. Author books, including: (with E. Kongus Maranda) Structural Models in Folklore and Transformational Essays, 1962, 2d rev. edit., 1970; Introduction to Anthropology: A Self-Guide, 1972; French Kinship: Structure and History, 1974; Soviet Structural Folkloristics, 1974; contbr. numerous articles to profl. publs. Office: Dept Anthropology U Laval Quebec PQ G1K 7P4 Canada

MARANTIS, ZACHARY, lawyer, mfg. co. exec.; b. N.Y.C., Sept. 20, 1930; s. Constantine Z. and Eftyhia (Mpoukas) M.; B.A., Coll. City N.Y., 1952; LL.B., J.D., Fordham U., 1957; m. Cleo Veras, Feb. 19, 1954; children—Dean Z. (dec.), Denise M., Demetrios J. Admitted to N.Y. bar, 1958; law clk.-atty. firm Webster, Sheffield & Chrystie, N.Y.C., 1956-57; atty. N.Y. Central R.R., 1958-60; mem. firm Loeb, McDonald & Marantis, N.Y.C., 1958-61; atty. CIT Fin. Corp., N.Y.C., 1961-63, Kayser-Roth Corp., N.Y.C., 1963-65; gen. atty. Gen. Time Corp., Stamford, Conn., 1965-67; v.p., gen. counsel Norlin Corp., N.Y.C., 1967—; dir. Aiken Industries, Inc., Norlin Music, Inc., Norlin Music Ltd. Dist. leader Democratic Club, Yonkers, N.Y., 1965-67; trustee Holy Trinity Greek Orthodox Ch., New Rochelle, N.Y., 1970-78, pres., 1977-78; mem. Fordham U. Council, 1978—. Served with AUS, 1952-54. N.Y. U. scholar, 1948; recipient Constl. Law medal Fordham U. Sch. Law. Mem. Am., N.Y. State bar assns., Bar Assn. City N.Y. Clubs: Princeton, Masons, Lions, AHEPA (pres. 1972). Home: Genesee Trail Harrison NY 10528 Office: 44 S Broadway White Plains NY 10601

MARAVICH, PETE, basketball player; b. Aliquippa, Pa., June 22, 1948; grad. La. State U., 1970. With Atlanta Hawks, 1970-74, New Orleans Jazz, 1974-80, Boston Celtics, 1980—; played Nat. Basketball Assn. All-Star Game, 1973, 74, 77. Named Coll. Basketball Player of Yr., 1970. Office: care New Orleans Jazz La Superdome Box 53213 New Orleans LA 70153*

MARBLE, SAMUEL DAVEY, social service agy. exec.; b. Mitchell, S.D., Nov. 15, 1915; s. Samuel William and Elsie Naomi (Davey) M.; A.B., U. N.Mex., 1937; M.A., Syracuse U., 1939, Ph.D., 1941; Certificate in Internat. Adminstrn., Columbia, 1943; LL.D., Cedarville Coll., 1951; L.H.D., Wilmington Coll., 1969; m. Rebecca Sturtevant, Feb. 15, 1947; children—Mary, Anne, Rebecca; m. 2d, Gladys Kearns, Jan. 13, 1977. Resident adviser Syracuse U., 1937-39, fellow and instr. Maxwell Sch. Citizenship and Pub. Affairs, 1939-41; procedure analyst Office of Civilian Supply, 1941-42; asso. sec. Am. Friends Service Com., 1943-46; chmn. Licensed Agys. for Relief in Asia, 1946; chmn. com. on Japan and com. on Korea, Am. Council of Vol. Agys., 1946; prof. polit. sci. W.Va. Wesleyan Coll., 1946-47; pres. Wilmington Coll., 1947-58; dir. Clinton County Red Cross and Cummunity Chest, 1958-61; pres. Delta Coll., Saginaw, Mich., 1961-64; pres. Saginaw Valley Coll., 1964-74; prof. polit. sci. John Wesley Coll., Owosso, Mich., 1975-77, pres., 1977-79; exec. Family Service Agy., Port Huron, Mich., 1979—. Dir., Midstate Broadcasting Corp., Wickes Corp. Mem. commn. on internat. aspects tchr. edn. Am. Assn. Colls. for Tchr. Edn., 1948. Rep. Friend's World Com. to UN, 1956; candidate for Congress, 10th Dist. Mich., 1974, 76. Bd. dirs. Saginaw County United Appeal, Community Service, Inc., Saginaw Symphony Orch., Internat. Symphony Orch., Multiple Sclerosis Soc. Mich., Nat. Council for Prevention of War; bd. mgrs. Pendle Hill; trustee Seasongood Good Govt. Fund. Recipient citation of merit DAV. Mem. Am. Polit. Sci. Assn., Am. Acad. Social and Polit. Sci., Nat. Mental Health Found., Soc. Advancement Edn., Quaker Coll. Assn. (pres. 1951-53), Green Key, Mich. farm bur. fedns., Phi Alpha Theta, Kappa Alpha, Phi Kappa Phi, Pi Sigma Alpha and Alpha Phi Gamma. Mem. Soc. of Friends. Clubs: Saltans, Rotary. Author: Guide to Public Affairs Organizations (with C. R. Read), 1946; Glimpses of Africa, 1973; Passages to the West, 1980. Regular contbr. to various mags. and papers. Home: 4152 Quaker Hill Rd Port Huron MI 48060 Office: Family Service Agy Port Huron MI 48060

MARBURGER, RICHARD EUGENE, coll. adminstr.; b. Detroit, May 26, 1928; s. Victor Reginald and Elsie Beth M.; student Kenyon Coll., 1946-48; B.S., Wayne State U., 1950, M.S., 1952, Ph.D., 1962; m. Mary Eva Kupalian, Dec. 23, 1950; children—Dennis, Kathryn. Sr. research physicist Gen. Motors Research Labs., 1952-69; prof. physics Lawrence Inst. Tech., Southfield, Mich., 1969-70, dir. Sch. of Arts and Sci., 1970-72, v.p. for acad. affairs, 1972-77, pres., 1977—. Trustee Armenian Congregational Ch. of Greater Detroit, 1973-79; trustee Bus.-Edn. Alliance of Greater Detroit, 1975—. Served with USAF, 1953-55. Mem. Engring. Soc. Detroit (pres. elect), Sigma Xi, Tau Beta Pi. Clubs: Econs., Renaissance., (Detroit). Office: 21000 W Ten Mile Rd Southfield MI 48075

MARBURY, BENJAMIN EDWARD, anesthesiologist; b. Farmington, Mo., May 23, 1914; s. Benjamin H. and Annie (Eversole) M.; A.B., U. Mo., 1939; M.S., La. State U., 1941; M.D., Washington U., St. Louis, 1944. Intern, St. Luke's Hosp., St. Louis, 1944-46; asst. resident N.Y. Hosp.-Cornell Med. Center, N.Y.C., 1948-49, mem. staff, 1949—; practice medicine specializing in anesthesiology, N.Y.C., 1949—; prof. anesthesiology Cornell U. Med. Coll., N.Y.C., 1948—. Served to capt. M.C., U.S. Army, 1946-48. Mem. AMA, N.Y. Acad. Medicine, N.Y. State Med. Soc., N.Y. County Med. Soc., Am. Soc. Anesthesiology, N.Y. Soc. Anesthesiology. Episcopalian. Club: Univ. (N.Y.C.). Home: 76 Flat Rock Hill Rd Old Lyme CT 06371 Office: 525 E 68th St New York NY 10021

MARBURY, WILLIAM LUKE, lawyer; b. Baltimore County, Md., Sept. 12, 1901; s. William Luke and Silvine von Dorsner (Slingluff) M.; student Va. Mil. Inst., 1918-19; A.B., U. Va., 1921; LL.B., Harvard, 1924, LL.D., 1970; D.M.A., Peabody Inst., 1967; m. Natalie Jewett Wheeler, Dec. 3, 1935; children—Luke, Anne Jewett, Susan Fendall. Admitted to Md. bar, 1925, since practiced in Balt.; mem. firm Piper & Marbury and predecessor firms, 1931—. Gen. counsel Md. Port Authority, 1956-67; trustee Peabody Inst. of Balt. 1935-67, pres., 1948-57, chmn. bd. trustees, 1957-67; asst. atty. gen. State of Md., 1930-31; chief counsel procurement program War dept., 1942-45; expert cons. procurement to Sec. War, 1940-41; mem. Md. Commn. on Judicial Disabilities, 1971—. Mem. U.S. del. to 2d session Signatories of GATT, Geneva, 1948. Fellow Harvard Coll., 1948-70; chmn. Md. Commn. on Higher Edn., 1946- 47; chancellor Episcopal Diocese of Md., 1962-71; adv. bd. Center for Advanced Studies, U. Va., 1971-78. Recipient Presdl. medal for Merit, 1945. Fellow Am., Md. (chmn. 1975-76) bar founds., Am. Coll. Trial Lawyers; mem. Am. Acad. Arts and Scis., Nat. Inst. of Trial Advocacy (dir. 1971-76), Am. Law Inst. (mem. council 1946), Md. Inst. for Continuing Profl. Edn. Lawyers (pres. 1976-78, trustee 1976—), Am. Judicature Soc. (dir. 1939-41), Am. (mem. com. jud. conduct 1969), Md. (pres. 1965-66), Balt. bar assns., Phi Beta Kappa. Episcopalian. Clubs: Elkridge, 14 West Hamilton St (Balt.); Harvard, Century Assn. (N.Y.C.). Home: 43 Warrenton Rd Baltimore MD 21210 Office: 1100 Charles Center South 36 S Charles St Baltimore MD 21201

MARBUT, ROBERT GORDON, newspaper-broadcast corp. exec.; b. Athens, Ga., Apr. 11, 1935; s. Robert Smith and Laura Gordon (Powers) M.; B.Indsl. Engring., Ga. Inst. Tech., 1957; M.B.A. with distinction, Harvard U., 1963; m. Berta Dodd, Mar. 16, 1957; children—Robert Gordon, Laura Dodd, Michael Powers. Engr., Esso Standard Oil Co., Baton Rouge, 1957; mgmt. trainee Copley Newspapers, Los Angeles, 1963; engring. services coordinator, La Jolla, Calif., 1965, corp. dir. engring. and plans, 1966-70; v.p. Harte-Hanks Newspapers, San Antonio, 1970-71, pres., chief exec. officer, 1971—, mem. exec. com., 1974—, also dir.; dir. A.P.; instr. Armstrong Coll., 1951, Calif. State, Los Angeles, 1964, Woodbury Coll., 1964. Mem. adv. bd. U. Ga. Henry W. Grady Sch. Journalism, 1975—; mem. adv. Found. for Communications Sch. U. Tex., 1975—; mem. nat. adv. bd. Up With People, Ga. Inst. Tech.; bd. dirs. Tex. Research League, 1975—, Salzburg Seminar in Am. Studies. Served with USAF, 1958-61. Registered profl. engr., Calif. Mem. Newspaper Advt. Bur. (exec. com., dir. 1974—), Am. Newspaper Pubs. Assn. Research Inst. (exec. com. 1973—), Am. Newspaper Pubs. Assn. (chmn. task group on future, chmn. press communications com. 1974—, vice-chmn. internat. press communications com. 1975—, bd. dirs. 1976—, chmn. future task group), So. Newspaper Pubs. Assn. (pres. 1978-80, dir. 1975—, treas. 1977—, chmn. bus. and adminstrn. com. 1976—), Am. Newspaper Pubs. Assn. Found. (dir.), Tex. Daily Newspaper Assn. (pres. 1979), Greater San Antonio C. of C. (chmn. long range planning task force, dir.), Delta Tau Delta, Omicron Delta Kappa, Phi Eta Sigma. Methodist. Club: Oaks Hills Country. Author: (with Healy, Henderson and others) Creative Collective Bargaining, 1965; also articles in mags., jours.; frequent speaker. Office: PO Box 269 San Antonio TX 78291

MARCASE, MICHAEL PAUL, supt. schs.; b. Phila., Apr. 27, 1925; s. Harry and Elvira (Pelosi) M.; B.F.A., Temple U., Phila., 1959, M.F.A., 1961; postgrad. Stanford U., 1965-71; Ed.D., U. Sarasota (Fla.), 1973; m. Marie Barrett; 1 dau., Diane Marcase McCartney. Insp., then chief insp. U.S. Navy Dept., 1943-53; mem. staff Sch. Dist. Phila., 1954—, tchr. high sch., 1958-62, dept. head, 1962-65, dir. sch. planning, 1966-68, asso. supt. sch. facilities planning, 1968-70, dep. supt. planning, 1970-75, supt. schs., 1975—; mem. evaluation coms. Middle States Assn.; cons. Univs. City Sci. Center project, Phila., 1966-68. Mem. Dante Sch. Commn., Order Sons Italy in Am., 1971—; trustee Chapel Four Chaplains, 1972—, United Way Southeastern Pa., 1977—; bd. dirs. S. Phila. Area Rehab. Center, 1973, Olympia Flag Ship Assn., 1975, Phila. Police Athletic League, 1975, Phila. Civic Center, 1975, Phila. Flag Day Assn., 1976, World Affairs Council Phila., 1976, Phila. March of Dimes, 1976, Community Coll. Phila., 1976, Youth Service Commn. Phila., 1976, Research for Better Schs., 1976; mem. bd., exec. com. Phila. Urban Coalition; adv. bd. Dairy Council, 1976; steering com. Am. Found. Negro Affairs, 1977—. Recipient 1st prizes Phila. Art Alliance, 1961-62, Little Gallery, 1961, Phila. Mus. Art, 1962, N.J. Tercenterary Exhbn., 1963, Woodmere Art Exhbn., 1963, Atlantic City Country Club, 1973; commn. John F. Kennedy Sculpture LaSalle Coll., 1965. Mem. NEA, Indsl. Arts Assn. Pa. (life), Indsl. Arts and Vocat. Edn. Assn. Pa. (dir. 1964-67), Phila. Arts Tchrs. Assn. (dir. 1964-65), Phila. Art Alliance, Met. Sch. Facilities Planning Group, Gt. Cities Council Sch. Improvement, Fellowship Commn., Am. Assn. Sch. Adminstrs., Schoolmen's Club, Temple U., U. Sarasota alumni assns., Nat. Council Edn., Pa. Soc., Assn. Large City Supts., Sons of Italy, Phi Delta Kappa. Club: Varsity (Temple U.). Contbr. articles to profl. jours. Home: 3326 W Queen Ln Philadelphia PA 19129 Office: Office Supts Schs Phila Parkway at 21st St Philadelphia PA 19103. *I attribute any success that I have achieved to the fact that nothing came easy to me in my lifetime. In addition, I never perceived any position I held as a stepping stone for a promotion or a higher position. I enjoyed each job, and the promotions came as a consequence of my job contentment and enthusiasm.*

MARCEAU, J. EDWARD, orthodontist; b. Rutland, Vt., Apr. 20, 1912; s. Joseph E. and Irene Nancy (Seward) M.; A.B., Dartmouth, 1934; D.D.S., U. of Mich., 1938, M.S., 1946; m. Mildred Marie Leach, May 15, 1939 (div.); children—J. Edward, Suzanne; m. 2d, Jacqueline Marion LeMay, Dec. 1955; children—Michelle, Michael, Marcy. Dental practice, Rutland, 1938-41; teaching fellow orthodontics U. Mich., 1941-42; practice orthodontics, Burlington, Vt. 1946—; dir. Sch. Dental Hygiene U. Vt., 1949—, also asso. prof. dental hygiene. Mem. Vt. State Bd. Dental Examiners. Served as capt. AUS, 1942-46. Fellow Internat. Coll. Dentists; mem. Champlain Valley, Vt. (pres. 1961-62), New Eng. dental socs., Am. Dental Assn. Am. Assn. Orthodontists, Omicron Kappa Upsilon, Phi Kappa Phi. Rotarian. Home: 1545 Hinesburg Rd South Burlington VT 05401 Office: 91 N Winooski Ave Burlington VT 05401

MARCEAU, MARCEL, French actor, pantomimist; b. Strasbourg, France, Mar. 22, 1923; s. Charles and Anne (Werzberg) Mangel; student Sch. Dramatic Art, Sarah Bernhardt Theatre, Paris 1946. Performed role of Arlequin, pantomime Baptiste; performed Praxitele and the Golden Fish, Sarah Bernhardt Theatre; organized pantomime co., Paris, 1949, producer The Overcoat, Pierrot de Montmartre, Paris qui rit-Paris qui pleure; appeared on TV, worldwide and in films including Shock, 1973, Shanks, 1975, Silent Movie, 1976; created character Bip. First appeared N.Y.C., 1955; numerous world tours; TV debut NBC, 1955. Decorated chevalier Legion d'Honneur, comdr. Order Arts and Letters (France). Address: Musee des arts et traditions populaires 6 Route du Mahatma Gandhi Paris France 75116*

MARCELLO, AMEDEO ALFRED, newspaper editor; b. Providence, Apr. 19, 1904; s. Luigi and Teresa (Villani) M.; student Byrant-Stratton Coll., 1919-20, Am. Press Inst., Columbia, 1948; m. Elsie Ann Lynum, June 2, 1930. Reporter, Providence News, 1923; state editor, city editor, drama editor, news editor News-Tribune, Providence, 1925-37; pub. weekly West Warwick (R.I.) News, 1937-38; reporter Worcester (Mass.) Telegram, 1938, asst. city editor, 1938-49, city editor, 1949-66, exec. news editor, 1966-71; founder OSIA News, nat. publ. Sons of Italy, 1946, dir., 1946-63, nat. pub. relations chmn., 1957-63; mem. adv. council Freedom Fed. Savs. Mem. Pres.'s Com. Employment Handicapped, 1950—; mem. Mass. Gov.'s Com. for Refugees, 1954-58; chmn. bd. communications Worcester Catholic Diocese. Sec., bd. dirs. Worcester County Safety Council; bd. dirs. St. Vincent Hosp. Research Found., Worcester Hist. Soc.; incorporator St. Vincent Hosp.; nat. exec. sec. Sons of Italy Found., 1957-63. Recipient Pall Malls Big Story award, 1953, citation for work with Com. Employment Handicapped, 1957, Star of Solidarity Italian Republic, 1957, Order of Merit Italian Republic, 1966. Mem. Sigma Delta Chi. Author: Ready for Retirement?, 1972; Blueprint for Retirement, 1973. Home: 222 Lovell Rd Holden MA 01520 Office: 22 Pearl-Elm Sts Worcester MA 01608. *It is better to serve than to be served. And it's far more rewarding to build up than to tear down.*

MARCELLUS, JOHN LINDSLEY, JR., tableware and indsl. wire mfg. co. exec.; b. New Hartford, N.Y., Dec. 16, 1922; s. John Lindsley and Dorothy (Wattenbe) M.; B.S. cum laude in Bus., Syracuse U., 1946; m. Joan C. Burns, Aug. 23, 1947; children—Alexandra L. Marcellus Boyce, John Lindsley III. With Oneida, Ltd. (N.Y.), 1946—, dir. product ops., 1971-73, mem. exec. com., 1973, v.p., gen. mgr., 1974-75, exec. v.p., gen. mgr., 1975-78, pres., 1978—; dir. Camden Wire Co., Oneida Mexicana, S.A., Rena Ware, Inc. Mem. profl. adv. com. State U. Coll. at Utica, Rome, N.Y. Served with Ski Troops, AUS, 1943-44. Mem. Sterling Silversmiths Guild Am. (exec. com.), Alpha Kappa Psi. Office: Kenwood Ave Oneida NY 13421. *Set realistic goals, be willing to accept new ideas and respect the ability of your associates. The integrity of the individual is a necessity if one is to build a solid foundation for the future.*

MARCELLUS, JOHN ROBERT, III, trombonist, educator; b. Overton, Tex., Sept. 17, 1939; s. John Robert and Grace (Stockman) M.; B.S., U. Md., 1964; Mus.M., Catholic U. Am., 1970, D.Mus. Arts, 1972; m. Mardele Johnson, Dec. 7, 1976; children—Robert Gray, John Fredrick. Trombonist, U.S. Navy Band, Washington, 1960-64, Balt. Symphony, 1964-65; trombonist Nat. Symphony, Washington, 1965-78, prin. trombone, 1970-78; adj. prof. trombone Cath. U. Am., dir. trombone choir and brass ensembles, 1966-78; prof. N.C. Sch. Arts, 1965-68; mem. rotating faculty Inst. Advanced Mus. Studies, Montreaux, Switzerland, 1974, Am. U., 1970-78; prof. trombone Eastman Sch. Music, Rochester, N.Y., 1978—; mem. Eastman Brass Quintet; clinician, soloist Conn Corp. Ltd.; co-dir. ann. Eastern Trombone Workshop, Towson, Md. Mem. Internat. Trombone Assn. (dir.), Am. Fedn. Musicians, Nat. Assn. Wind and Percussion Instruments, Music Educators Nat. Conf., Phi Mu Alpha. Democrat. Contbr. articles to Instrumentalist Mag., Internat. Trombone Newsletter, Music Educators Jour. Office: Eastman Sch Music 26 Gibbs St Rochester NY 14625

MARCH, BERYL ELIZABETH, poultry scientist; b. Port Hammond, B.C., Can., Aug. 30, 1920; d. James Roy and Sarah Catherine (Wilson) Warrack; B.A., U. B.C., Vancouver, 1942, M.S.A., 1962; m. John Algot March, Aug. 31, 1946; 1 dau., Laurel Allison.

Mem. indsl. research staff Can. Fishing Co. Ltd., 1942-47; mem. research staff, faculty U. B.C., 1947—, prof. poultry sci., 1970—. Recipient Poultry Sci. Assn.-Am. Feed Mfrs. award, 1960, Queen's Jubilee medal, 1977. Fellow Agrl. Inst. Can., Royal Soc. Can., Poultry Sci. Assn.; mem. Profl. Agrologists, Agr. Inst. Can., Nutrition Soc. Can., AAAS, Poultry Sci. Assn., World's Poultry Sci. Assn., Am. Soc. Exptl. Biology and Medicine, Am. Inst. Nutrition, Can. Soc. Animal Sci., Am. Nutrition Research Council, Nat. Research Council Can. Research, numerous publs. on poultry nutrition and physiology. Office: Dept Poultry Sci U BC Vancouver BC V6T 1W5 Canada

MARCH, EUGENE AIREY, steel co. exec.; b. Winamac, Ind., May 26, 1919; s. George and Rhena (Airey) M.; B.S., Mass. Inst. Tech., 1941; m. Margaret Jourdain Adams, Sept. 4, 1942; children—Glenn Adams, Nancy Jane. Metallurgist, Inland Steel Co., 1941-42; metallurgist Sanderson-Halcomb Works, Crucible Steel Co. Am., 1946-53, chief metallurgist, 1953-55, asst. mgr., 1955-58, div. supt. tech. service Midland works, 1958-59, asst. mgr., 1959-60, v.p. tech., 1961-63, v.p. operating services, 1963-67, group v.p., 1967-68; group v.p. Colt Industries, Inc., 1968—. Served from 2d lt. to maj., ordnance dept., AUS, 1942-46. Decorated Bronze Star. Fellow Am. Soc. Metals; mem. Am. Inst. Mining and Metall. Engrs., Am. Iron and Steel Engrs., Am. (dir.), Brit. iron and steel insts. Presbyn. Clubs: Duquesne (Pitts.); Edgeworth (Sewickley). Home: 601 Academy Ave Sewickley PA 15143 Office: PO Box 88 Pittsburgh PA 15230

MARCH, FREDERIC CLIFTON, mfg. co. exec.; b. Cleve., June 8, 1931; s. James Herbert and Mildred (MacCorkle) M.; B.S., U. Wis., 1953; m. Mary Trebilcock, May 15, 1954; children—Madelyn, Michael, Lauren, Bruce, John, David. Sales rep. Marathon Corp., 1953-56; v.p. Caldwell Packaging Co., 1956-60; plant mgr. Mich. Carton Co., 1960-62; product mgr. Mead Corp., Atlanta, 1962-65; sales mgr. Pierce Glass Co., Port Allegany, Pa., 1965-70, v.p. sales, 1970-73, pres., 1973-78; pres. Indian Head Glass Container Group, Laurens, S.C., 1978—; pres. E.V.P. Indian Head Inc., Laurens, 1978—; chmn. bd. Madera Glass Co. Pres., Port Allegany United Way, 1976-77. Republican. Presbyterian. Home: 17 Quail Hill Dr Greenville SC 29607 Office: PO Box 966 Laurens SC 29360

MARCH, GEORGE PATRICK, naval officer; b. Corvallis, Oreg., Jan. 16, 1924; s. George Clayton and Margaret Isobel (Motley) M.; B.S., U.S. Naval Acad., 1946; M.A., Georgetown U., 1952, Ph.D., 1965; m. Betty Eileen Saum, Dec. 20, 1946; children—Maureen, Terese, Margaret. Commd. ensign U.S. Navy, 1946, advanced through grades to rear adm., 1973; staff and command assignments Atlantic and Pacific fleets, shore duty in Morocco, Cyprus, Germany, Eng. and Japan, 1946-73; asst. dep. dir. Nat. Security Agy., Washington, 1973-74; comdr. Naval Security Group Command, dir. electronic warfare and cryptology div. on staff of chief of naval ops., 1974—. Decorated Legion of Merit. Mem. U.S. Naval Inst., Assn. Old Crows, Am. Hist. Soc., Phi Gamma Delta. Address: 4356 Punihi St Honolulu HI 96818. *The key to human survival and progress is discipline—not a harsh one imposed from above, but rather one based on mutual understanding and acceptance of that very basic Christian precept—the Golden Rule. Whatever success I have achieved in command and management of people is owed to the effective application of this simple, fundamental idea.*

MARCH, JAMES GARDNER, educator, social scientist; b. Cleve., Jan. 15, 1928; s. James Herbert and Mildred (MacCorkle) M.; B.A., U. Wis., 1949; M.A., Yale, 1950, Ph.D., 1953; hon. doctorate Copenhagen Sch. Econs., 1978, Swedish Sch. Econs. (Helsinki), 1979; m. Jayne Mary Dohr, Sept. 23, 1947; children—Kathryn Sue, Gary Clifton, James Christopher, Roderic Gunn. From asst. prof. to prof. Carnegie Inst. Tech., 1953-64; prof., dean Sch. Social Scis., U. Calif. at Irvine, 1964-70; prof. mgmt., higher edn., polit. sci. and sociology Stanford U., 1970—; cons. in field, 1954—. Mem. Nat. Council Ednl. Research, 1975-78; mem. Nat. Sci. Bd., 1968-74; mem. sociol.-social psychology panel NSF, 1964-66; social sci. tng. com. NIMH, 1967-68; mem. math. social sci. com. Social Sci. Research Council, 1958-60; mem. Assembly Behavioral and Social Sci., NRC, 1973-79, chmn. com. on aging, 1977—. Fellow Center Advanced Study in Behavioral Scis., 1955-56, 73-74; recipient Wilbur Lucius Cross medal Yale, 1968. Mem. Nat. Acad. Scis., Nat. Acad. Edn., Am. Acad. Arts and Scis., Am. Econ. Assn., Am. Polit. Sci. Assn., Am. Psychol. Assn., Am. Sociol. Assn., Phi Beta Kappa, Sigma Xi. Author: (with H.A. Simon) Organizations, 1955; (with R.M. Cyert) A Behavioral Theory of the Firm, 1963; Handbook of Organizations, 1965; (with B.R. Gelbaum) Mathematics for the Social and Behavioral Sciences, 1969; (with M.D. Cohen) Leadership and Ambiguity, 1974; Academic Notes, 1974; (with C.E. Lave) An Introduction to Models in the Social Sciences, 1975; (with J.P. Olsen) Ambiguity and Choice in Organizations, 1976; Aged Wisconsin, 1977. Home: 837 Tolman Dr Stanford CA 94305

MARCH, JOHN WILLIAM, accounting standards exec.; b. Cleve., Aug. 9, 1923; s. James Herbert and Mildred (McCorkle) M.; B.B.A., U. Wis., 1945; m. Ruth Mary Jaeger, Dec. 16, 1944; children—William J., Roger J., Peter B. With Arthur Andersen & Co., C.P.A.'s, 1945-78, partner, 1956-78, vice chmn. worldwide accounting and audit practice, Chgo., 1970-75, sr. partner, 1975-78; mem. Fin. Accounting Standards Bd., 1978—; founding mem. adv. com. Northeastern U. Sch. Pub. Accounting, Boston, 1962. Mem. U. Wis. Found.; exec. com. Bascom Hill Soc.; treas. Lake Forest (Ill.) Acad., 1966-70, trustee, 1966-77; mem. corp. Bentley Coll., Waltham, Mass.; mem. nat. adv. council U. Fla. Sch. Acctg., 1979—, gov. mem. Chgo. Orchestral Soc., 1975-78; bd. dirs. Donors' Forum Chgo., 1976-78; mem. Wellesley (Mass.) Town Meeting, 1964-65, chmn. adv. and finance com., 1965. C.P.A., Wis., Mass., Ill., N.C. Mem. Am. Inst. C.P.A.'s, Ill., Mass., Wis. socs. c.p.a.'s, Am., Nat. accounting assns. Republican. Presbyn. Clubs: Landmark, Bob O'Link Golf, Pinehurst Country, Aspetuck Valley Country, Aspetuck Golf, Weston Golf. Home: 15 Godfrey Rd W Weston CT 06883 Office: High Ridge Park Stamford CT 06905. *Fairness and freedom are refined or destroyed within the crucible which holds truth and conscience to the heat of temptations of advantage and convenience. Quality in a profession, as in life, is measured by the ability of truth and conscience to survive the heat.*

MARCH, RALPH BURTON, educator; b. Oshkosh, Wis., Aug. 5, 1919; s. Albert Harold and Vanita Ida Cora (Siewert) M.; student Oshkosh State Tchrs. Coll., 1937-38; B.A., U. Ill., 1941, M.A. (Grad. scholar 1941-42), 1946, Ph.D. (Grad. fellow 1947-48), 1948; m. Robinetta Tompkin, Dec. 26, 1942; children—John S., Janice A., Susan E. Faculty, U. Calif. at Riverside, 1948—, entomologist, 1957—, prof. entomology, 1961—, dean grad. div., 1961-68, head div. toxicology and physiology dept. entomology, 1968-72, chmn. dept. entomology, 1978—. Served with USAAF, 1942-46. Mem. Entomol. Soc. Am., Am. Chem. Soc., AAAS, Phi Beta Kappa, Sigma Xi, Phi Kappa Phi, Phi Sigma. Home: 2004 Elsinore Rd Riverside CA 92506

MARCHAND, ERNEST LEROY, educator, translator, editor; b. Douglas County Wash., Nov. 6, 1898; s. Alexis and Clara Adella (Buckingham) M.; student Wash. State Coll., 1916-18; B.A., U. Wash., 1925, M.A., 1926; student Columbia, summer 1931; Ph.D., U. Wis., 1938; m. Eunice Dorothea Ottestad, Aug. 26, 1926; children—Eunice Louise, Ernest Roger. Teaching fellow English, U. Wash., 1925-26; instr. Ore. State Coll., 1926-28, U. Wis., 1928-35; George Loomis fellow Am. lit., Stanford, 1935-37, instr., 1935-40, asst. prof., 1940-46; asso. prof. San Diego State U., 1946-49, prof., 1949-68, emeritus, 1968—, chmn. dept., 1960-63, 64-66. Mem. Modern Lang. Assn. Am., Am. Studies Assn., AAUP, Philol. Assn. Pacific Coast (sec.-treas. 1944-47), Phi Kappa Phi, Phi Beta Kappa. Author: Frank Norris: A Study, 1942. Compiler: (with others) American Literary Manuscripts: A Checklist of Holdings in Academic, Historical and Public Libraries in the United States, 1961. Editor: Ormond (Charles Brockden Brown), 1937; News from Fort Craig, New Mexico, 1863, 1966; (with Stanley J. Pincetl, Jr.) War Books: A Study in Historical Criticism (Jean Norton Cru), 1976. Translator, editor (with Stanley J. Pincetl Jr.): Notes of a Lost Pilot (Jean Beraud Villars), 1975. Contbr. articles, revs. to profl. jours. Home: 4763 Constance Dr San Diego CA 92115

MARCHAND, JEAN, Canadian govt. ofcl.; b. Champlain, Que., Can., Dec. 20, 1918; s. Gustave and Laura (Cousineau) M.; ed. Sch. Social Scis., Laval U., D. Social Scis. (hon.); D. Indls. Relations (hon.), U. Montreal; m. Georgette Guertin; 1 dau., Marie-Eve. Pres. Gen. Confedn. Nat. Trade Unions, 1942-65; mem. Canadian Ho. Commons. from 1965; Minister of Citizenship and Immigration, 1965-66; Minister of Manpower and Immigration, Can., 1966-68, Minister of Forestry and Rural Devel., 1968-69, Minister of Regional Econ. Expansion, 1969-72; Minister of Transport, 1972-75; minister without portfolio, 1975-76; Minister of the Environment, 1976; senator, 1977—. Mem. Royal Commn. of Enquiry on Bilinqualism and Biculturalism, 1963-65; former mem. Econ. Council Que., Nat. Employment Com. of Unemployment Ins. Commn., Joint Canadian-Am. Com. of Nat. Planning Commn. No. Am. Internat. Bur. Christian Trade Unionists. Office: The Senate Parliament Bldgs Ottawa ON K1A 0A6 Canada*

MARCHAND, LAURENT GERMAIN, mfg. co. exec.; b. Chateauguay, Que., Can., Oct. 24, 1918; s. Zotique Elzear and Maria (Brunet) M.; B.A., Coll. Montreal, 1939; M.Commerce, U. Montreal, 1942; m. Marcelle Beausoleil, Aug. 28, 1944; children—Suzanne, Yves, Denise. Auditor, P.A. Gagnon & Cie, C.A., Montreal, Que., Can., 1942-43; cost accountant Sorel Industries Ltd. (P.Q.), 1944-46; chief cost accountant Marine Industries, Ltd., Sorel, 1946-49, chief accounts payable dept., 1949-54, chief accountant, 1954-62, treas., 1962—. Gov. Que. div. Canadian Red Cross Soc. Mem. Corp. of Chartered Adminstrs. Que. Roman Catholic. Club: Club de la Marina de Sorel. Home: 40 Matton St Sorel PQ J3P 2S5 Canada Office: Marine Industries Ltd Tracy PQ J3P 5P5 Canada

MARCHAND, LESLIE ALEXIS, educator; b. Bridgeport, Wash., Feb. 13, 1900; s. Alexis and Clara Adele (Buckingham) M.; B.A., U. Wash., 1922, M.A., 1923; Ph.D., Columbia U., 1940; postgrad. Sorbonne, Paris, 1927-28, U. Munich (Germany), summer 1932; L.H.D., U. Alaska, 1976; m. Marion Knill Hendrix, July 8, 1950. Asst. in English, U. Wash., Seattle, 1920-23, instr., summer 1924, vis. prof., 1925, 58; prof. English and French, Alaska Agrl. Coll. and Sch. Mines (now U. Alaska), 1923-27, 34-35; extension tchr. English, Columbia U., 1928-34, instr., summers 1929-31, vis. prof., summers 1945-46, 65, lectr. Coll. Pharmacy, 1936-37; instr. Rutgers U., 1937-42, asst. prof., 1942-46, asso. prof., 1946-53, prof., 1953-66, emeritus, 1966—; Fulbright prof. U. Athens (Greece), 1958-59; lectr. English, Hunter Coll., 1960-62; Berg vis. prof. N.Y. U., 1962-63; vis. prof. Ariz. State U., 1966-67; Adams chair English, Hofstra U., 1967-68; vis. prof. U. Calif. at Los Angeles, summer 1949, U. Ill., summer 1954, Harvard U., summer 1969. Guggenheim fellow, 1968-69, 79-80; Nat. Endowment for Humanities grantee, 1972-73, 74-75, 76-79. Mem. MLA (James Russell Lowell prize), Keats-Shelley Assn. Am. (dir.), Byron Soc., Phi Beta Kappa. Author: The Athenaeum: A Mirror of Victorian Culture, 1941; Byron: A Biography, 1957; Byron's Poetry: A Critical Introduction, 1965; Byron: A Portrait, 1970; editor: Letters of Thomas Hood, 1945; Selected Poetry of Lord Byron, 1951; Lord Byron: Don Juan, 1958; Byron's Letters and Jours., Vol. 1-2, 1973, Vol. 3, 1974, Vol. 4, 1975, Vols. 5-6, 1976, Vol. 7, 1977, Vol. 8, 1978, Vol. 9, 1979; editorial bd. Keats-Shelley Jour.; contbr. articles to profl. jours. Home: 97 Lakeview Ln Englewood FL 33533

MARCHAND, NANCY, actress; b. Buffalo, June 19, 1928; d. Raymond L. and Marjorie F. M.; B.F.A., Carnegie Inst. Tech., 1949; m. Paul Sparer, July 7, 1951; children—David, Kathryn, Rachel. Vol. actress Am. Theater Wing, N.Y.C.; TV appearances include: Jo in Little Women, Studio One, Mrs. Phillip in Love of Life, The Edge of Night, Another World, Lovers and Friends, Search for Tomorrow, Look Homeward Angel, After the Fall, A Touch of the Poet; series regular on Beacon Hill, Lou Grant, 1977—; theater engagements at Circle in the Sq., N.Y.C., Los Angeles Music Center, Lincoln Center, N.Y.C., Am. Shakespeare Festival, Goodman Theater, Chgo., appeared on on Broadway in Much Ado About Nothing, After the Rain, 40 Carats, And Miss Reardon Drinks a Little, in Off Broadway plays Heartbreak House, Children, 19—. Recipient Obie award, 1960, Emmy award, 1978. Office: c/o Arcara Bauman Hiller 9220 Sunset Blvd Los Angeles CA 90069

MARCHANT, MAURICE PETERSON, librarian; b. Peoa, Utah, Apr. 20, 1927; s. Stephen C. and Beatrice (Peterson) M.; B.A., U. Utah, 1949, M.S., 1953; A.M. in L.S., U. Mich., 1966, M.A., 1968, Ph.D., 1970; m. Gerda Valoy Hansen, June 3, 1949; children—Catherine, Barrie, Alan, Roxanne, Claudia, David, Theresa. High sch. tchr., Altamont, Utah, 1949-50; high sch. librarian, Salt Lake City and Preston, Idaho, 1950-53; chief tech. librarian Dugway (Utah) Proving Ground, 1953-58; librarian Carnegie Free Library, Ogden, Utah, 1958-66; mem. faculty Brigham Young U., Provo, Utah, 1969—, prof. library and info. scis., 1976—, dir. Sch. Library and Info. Scis., 1975—; exec. dir. Nat. Library Week, Utah, 1961-62. Served with USN, 1945-46. Mid-career fellow Council Library Resources, 1972. Mem. Am. (research paper award Library Research Round Table 1975), Mountain Plains, Utah (pres. 1964-65; Disting. Service award 1977) library assns., AAUP. Author: Participative Management in Academic Libraries, 1976; SPSS as a Library Research Tool, 1977; also articles. . *Man has the potential of learning to love or exploit, to become wise or remain ignorant. God intends us to become charitable and wise, preparing us to contribute to human progress. My measure of success as a librarian and educator must reflect my commitment to lifelong learning and to honest respect of others.*

MARCHELLO, JOSEPH MAURICE, ednl. adminstr.; b. East Moline, Ill., Oct. 6, 1933; s. Anton Joseph and Katherine Margaret (Scavarda) M.; B.S. in Chem. Engring., U. Ill., 1955; Ph.D., Carnegie-Mellon U., 1959; m. Mary Louise Coulson, Jan. 27, 1960; children—Sara Leigh, Katherine C. Asst. prof. chem. engring. Okla. State U., 1959-61; asst. prof. U. Md., 1961-62, asso. prof., 1962-66, prof., 1966-78, chmn. dept. chem. engring., 1967-73, provost div. math. and phys. scis. and engring., 1973-78; chancellor U. Mo., Rolla, 1978—; mem. Md. Air Quality Control Adv. Council, 1966-78, chmn., 1971-78; mem. Md. Adv. Commn. on Atomic Energy, 1973-78; chmn. Md. Power Plant Siting Com., 1978. Mem. Air Pollution Control Assn., Am. Inst. Chem. Engrs., Am. Chem. Soc., AAAS, Mo. Soc. Profl. Engrs., Nat. Soc. Profl. Engrs., N.Y. Acad. Sci., Mo. Acad. Sci. Presbyterian. Club: Rotary. Author: Control of Air Pollution Sources, 1976; editor: (with John J. Kelly) Gas Cleaning for Air Pollution Control, 1975; (with Albert Gomezplata) Gas-Solids Handling in the Process Industry, 1976; contbr. numerous articles to profl. jours. Home: 506 W Eleventh St Rolla MO 65401 Office: 210 Parker Hall U Mo Rolla MO 65401

MARCHESI, VINCENT THOMAS, educator; b. N.Y.C., Sept. 4, 1935; s. John H. and Tomasina R. (Marett) M.; B.A., Yale U., 1957; M.D., 1963; D.Phil., Oxford U., 1961; m. Sally Lockwood, July 25, 1959; children—Peter, Christopher, Sarah, Joseph, Thomas. Intern, resident in pathology Barnes Hosp., St. Louis, 1963-65; research asso. Rockefeller U., N.Y.C., 1965-66; med. officer USPHS-NIH, Bethesda, Md., 1966-72; asso. prof. pathology Yale Med. Sch., New Haven, Conn., 1972-73, prof. pathology, chmn. dept., 1973—. Mem. Am. Assn. Pathologists, Am. Soc. Cell Biology, Am. Assn. Immunologists, Biophys. Soc., N.Y. Acad. Sci. Contbr. articles to profl. jours. Office: 310 Cedar St New Haven CT 06510

MARCHESSAULT, ROBERT HENRY, chemist; b. Montreal, Que., Can., Sept. 16, 1928; s. Louis Auguste and Jessie (Brown) M.; B.Sc., Loyola Coll., Montreal, 1950; Ph.D., McGill U., Montreal, 1954; m. Mary D. Bonnette, Oct. 1, 1952; children—Robert L., Marie Nicole, Claude N., Janine, Kim, Jean-Pierre. Research chemist Am. Viscose Co., Marcus Hook, Pa., 1954-61; asso. prof. polymers Coll. Forestry, Syracuse, N.Y., 1961-66. prof., 1966-69; prof. chemistry U. Montreal, 1969—, dir. dept. chemistry, 1969-78; mgr. Xerox Research Centre of Can., Toronto, Ont., 1978—; adj. prof. U. Toronto, U. Waterloo (Ont.). Mem. Chem. Inst. Can., Am. Chem. Soc. (Anselme Payen award Cellulose Div. 1976), Am. Phys. Soc., TAPPI. Home: 291 Burgundy Dr Oakville ON L6J 4G3 Canada Office: 2480 Dunwin Dr Mississauga ON L5L 1J9 Canada

MARCHETTI, JEROME JOHN, educator, clergyman; b. Osage City, Kans., Mar. 12, 1916; s. Chester D. and Eva L. (Gamba) M.; student Washburn U., 1934-35, St. Stanislaus Sem., Florissant, Mo., 1935-39; A.B., St. Louis U., 1940, Ph.L., 1942, M.A., 1943, Licentiate in Sacred Theology, 1949; Ph.D., U. Minn., 1952. Instr. edn. St. Louis U., 1953-57, asst. prof., 1957-66, asso. prof., 1966-69, prof., 1969—, asst. dean Coll. Arts and Scis., 1953-55, dean, 1955-58, exec. v.p., 1958-72, sec.-treas., 1972—; regional dir. Jesuit Ednl. Assn., 1957-61. Exec. com. St. Louis Sci. Fair; past chmn. St. Louis U. Hosp. Trustee U. Detroit; sec., trustee St. Louis U. Mem. Assn. Higher Edn., North Central Assn. (examiner), Soc. for Study Edn., Kappa Phi Kappa. Asso. editor Modern Schoolman, 1940-42, Jesuit Ednl. Quar., 1957-60. Contbr. articles profl. jours. Address: St Louis U St Louis MO 63103

MARCHIORO, THOMAS LOUIS, surgeon; b. Spokane, Wash., Aug. 1, 1928; s. Americo A. and Gertrude (Dennehy) M.; student Colo. Coll., 1945-46, U. Calif., Berkeley, 1949; B.S. cum laude, Gonzaga U., 1951; M.D., St. Louis U., 1955; m. Karen Byus, Apr. 2, 1956; children—Thomas, John, Elizabeth, Stephen, Joan, Katherine, Robert. Intern St. Mary's Group of Hosps.-St. Louis U. Hosp., 1955-56; resident in gen. surgery Henry Ford Hosp., Dearborn, Mich., 1956-57; resident in gen. and thoracic surgery Colo. Gen. Hosp., Denver, 1957-60, chief resident in surgery, 1961-62; resident Peter Bent Brigham Hosp., Boston, 1958, resident etrangere surgery L'Hopital Leennec, Paris, 1960-61; asst. in surgery U. Colo., 1959-60, instr., 1960-63; asst. prof. surgery, 1963-66, asso. prof., 1966-67; asso. prof. U. Wash., 1967-69, prof., 1969—, chmn. div. organ transplantation dept. surgery, 1971—; mem. surg. staff U. Wash. Hosp., 1967—, co-dir. Transplant Clinic, 1967—; cons. in surgery to hosps., Seattle; project dir. profl. transplant capability Wash.-Alaska Regional Med. Program, 1972-73, mem. kidney disease adv. com., program services, 1973—; mem. various profl. coms. and bds., including med. adv. bd. N.W. Kidney Center, nat. renal transplantation adv. group Central Office VA, Chronic Uremia Coordinating Com.; chmn. network 2 End-Stage Renal Disease Network Coordinating Council. Served with USNR, 1945-46. Markle scholar, 1965-71; diplomate Am. Bd. Surgery, Am. Bd. Thoracic Surgery. Fellow A.C.S.; mem. Soc. Univ. Surgeons, Soc. Vascular Surgery, Assn. Acad. Surgery (founding; sec. 1967-72, pres. 1974), Transplantation Soc. (charter; editorial bd. Transplantation 1976-78), Internat. cardiovascular Soc., AAAS, Renal Physicians Assn., European Soc. Surg. Research, Societe Internationale de Chirurgie, N.Y. Acad. Scis., Soc. Golden Pouch, Am. Soc. Nephrology, Pacific Coast Surg. Soc., Seattle Surg. Soc., Wash. State Med. Soc. (sci. adv. council), King County Med. Soc., Nat. Kidney Found., Am. Heart Assn. (sect. council), Surg. Biology Club III, Am. Soc. Transplant Surgeons (pres. 1976), Am. Surg. Assn., Alpha Omega Alpha, Alpha Sigma Nu. Democrat. Roman Catholic. Reasearch in organ transplantation and preservation, immunobiology, portal circulation, hepatrophic factors, pancreatic function and disease, parathyroid physiology and pathology. Office: Univ Hosp Dept Surgery RF-25 Seattle WA 98195

MARCIL, WILLIAM CHRIST, publisher, broadcasting exec.; b. Rolette, N.D., Mar. 9, 1936; s. Max L. and Ida (Fuerst) M.; B.S. in Bus. Adminstrn., U. N.D., 1958; m. Jane Black, Oct. 15, 1960; children—Debra Jane, William Christ. Br. mgr. Community Credit Co., Mpls., 1959-61; with Forum Pub. Co., Fargo, N.D., 1961—, pres., pub., 1969—; pres. S.D. Broadcasting Co., KSFY-TV, Sioux Falls, S.D., KABY-TV, Aberdeen, S.D., KPRY, Pierre, S.D.; pres. WDAY Inc., operator WDAY-TV, WDAY radio, Fargo, WDAZ-TV, Devils Lake/Grand Forks, 1970—; pres. Dakota Photo Engraving Co., Fargo, 1969—, KMMJ Radio, Grand Island, Nebr.; dir. Am. Life & Casualty Co., Fargo, First Bank of N.D., Fargo, Blue Cross N.D. Pres. Norman Black Found. Bd. dirs. N. Central region Boy Scouts Am.; trustee N.D. State U. Served with AUS, 1958-59. Mem. Inland Newspaper, N.D. press assns., Am. Newspaper Pubs. Assn. (dir., sec.), Fargo and Moorhead C. of C., Sigma Delta Chi, Lambda Chi Alpha. Republican. Clubs: Masons, Shriners, Elks, Rotary. Home: 1618 S 8th St Fargo ND 58102 Office: 101 N 5th St Fargo ND 58102

MARCINKUS, PAUL C., bishop; b. Cicero, Ill., Jan. 15, 1922. Ordained priest Roman Catholic Ch., 1947; served in Vatican secretariat, Rome, from 1952; ordained titular bishop of Orta, 1969; sec. Inst. for Religious Works (Vatican Bank), 1968-71, pres., 1971—. Office: Inst for Religious Work The Vatican Vatican City Rome Italy*

MARCO, GUY ANTHONY, librarian; b. N.Y.C., Oct. 4, 1927; s. Gaetano Mongelluzzo and Evelyn Capobianco; student DePaul U., 1947-50; B.Mus., Am. Conservatory Music, Chgo., 1951; M.A. in Music, U. Chgo., 1952, M.L.S., 1955, Ph.D. in Musicology, 1956; m. Karen Csontos, July 23, 1949; 1 son, Howard William. Librarian, instr. musicology Chgo. Mus. Coll., 1953-54; asst. classics library U. Chgo., 1954; asst. librarian, instr. music Wright Jr. Coll., Chgo., 1954-56; vis. lectr. library sci. U. Wis., summer 1955; reference librarian Chgo. Tchrs. Coll., summer 1957; librarian, instr. music Amundsen Jr. Coll., Chgo., 1957-60; asso. prof. library sci., chmn. dept. Kent State U., 1960-66, prof., dean Sch. Library Sci., 1966-77; chief gen. reference and bibliography div. Library of Congress, Washington, 1977-78; dir. for N.Am., Library Devel. Cons.'s, London, 1979—; vis. prof. library sci. N.Y. State Coll. Tchrs., Albany, summer 1956, 58; guest lectr. library sci. U. Denver, summer 1959; vis. prof. U. Okla., summer 1960, Coll. Librarianship, Wales, summer 1974, 76, 77. Served with AUS, 1946-47. Mem. ALA, Assn. Am. Library Schs., Music Library Assn., Am. Musicol. Soc., AAUP, Internat. Fedn. Library Assns.,

Beta Phi Mu. Author: The Earliest Music Printers of Continental Europe, 1962; An Appraisal of Favorability in Current Book Reviewing, 1959; (with Claude Palisca) The Art of Counterpoint, 1968; Information on Music, Vol. I, 1975, Vol. II, 1977; also articles, book reviews. Composer various works. Home: 349 O St SW Washington DC 20024 Office: Library Devel Cons's Saint Peter's Sq London W6 England

MARCONI, DOMINIC ANTHONY, clergyman; b. Newark, Mar. 13, 1927; s. Sabato Joseph and Antoinette (Ricciardi) M.; B.A., Seton Hall U., 1949; postgrad. Immaculat Conception Sem., Mahwah, N.J., 1952; S.T.L., Catholic U., Washington, 1953. Ordained priest, Roman Cath. Ch., 1953; asso. pastor St. Anthony's Ch., Union City, N.J., 1953-66; asso. dir. family life apostolate Archdiocese of Newark, 1966-70, dir., 1970-75, co-dir. div. for services to elderly Associated Cath. Charities, 1975-76; aux. bishop, Episcopal vicar for Union County, 1976—. Club: K.C. Address: 131 E 4th Ave Roselle NJ 07203

MARCOSSON, THOMAS I., service co. exec.; b. N.Y.C., Jan. 31, 1936; s. Mark and Mollie (Schreiber) M.; student Union Coll., Schenectady, 1953-55; B.S., N.Y. U., 1959; m. Lorene E. Potenberg, Nov. 18, 1973; children—Mark, Susan, Samuel, Jill. Mgr., Touche Ross & Co., N.Y.C., 1959-63; v.p. fin., dir. Superior Surg. Mfg. Co., Inc., Huntington, N.Y., 1964-66; div. pres., gen. mgr. OEI div., Vernitrun Corp., Great Neck, N.Y., 1967-71; controller Allied Maintenance Corp., N.Y.C., 1972-75, v.p. fin., 1975—. Home: 2 Fifth Ave New York NY 10011 Office: 2 Penn Plaza New York NY 10011

MARCOTTE, ROBERT SERAPHIN, ins. co. exec.; b. Glen Ridge, N.J., Nov. 1, 1932; s. Robert Louis and Ruth Mabel (Bacon) M.; B.A., U. Vt., 1954; m. Betty Lou Respess, Oct. 19, 1957; children—Robert Louis II, Anne Marie, Katherine A. Successively cost analyst, comptroller, v.p. EDP, Bankers Nat. Life N.J., 1958-68; successively v.p. info. systems, sr. v.p., now exec. v.p. Equitable Life Ins. Co., McLean, Va., 1968—, also dir. Pres. bd. dirs. West Essex Public Health Nursing Assn., 1966-68; chmn. United Giver Campaign, West Essex 1966; pres. Wooton Booster Club, 1975-76. Served with U.S. Army, 1954-57, Club: Congressional Country. Home: 9308 Wooden Bridge Rd Potomac MD 20854 Office: Equitable Life Ins Co 1700 Old Meadow Rd McLean VA 22101

MARCOUX, CHARLES ROSS, JR., transp. co. exec., lawyer; b. Bristol, Conn., July 14, 1935; s. Charles Ross and Barbara (Johnston) M.; B.A. cum laude, Niagara U., 1956; LL.B., Georgetown U., 1962; m. Mary Kathryn Chartier, Oct. 10, 1959; children—Susan, Michele, Edward, Christopher. Admitted to Va. bar, 1962; atty. SEC, Washington, 1961-65; gen. counsel Leaseway Transp. Corp., Cleve., 1966-75, vice chmn., dir., 1975—; chmn. bd. Signal Delivery Service, Inc., 1968—; dir. Chagrin Valley Co. Ltd. Served to 1st lt. AUS, 1956-58. Mem. Va. Bar Assn. Home: 15702 Albersybe Rd Shaker Heights OH 44120 Office: 3700 Park East Dr Cleveland OH 44122

MARCOUX, WILLIAM JOSEPH, lawyer; b. Detroit, Jan. 20, 1927; s. Lona J. and Anna (Ransom) C.; B.A., U. Mich., 1949, LL.B., 1952; m. Kae Marie Sanborn, Aug. 23, 1952; children—Ann K., William C. Admitted to Mich. bar, 1953; practiced in Pontiac, 1953, Jackson, 1953—; pres. Marcoux, Allen, Beaman & Cheney, P.C., 1965—. Mem. exec. bd. Land O'Lakes council Boy Scouts Am., pres., 1965-66. Served with USNR, 1945-46. Fellow Am. Coll. Trial Lawyers; mem. Am., Mich., Jackson County (pres. 1979-80) bar assns. Methodist (chmn. adminstrv. bd., chmn. bd. trustees 1976-78). Rotarian (pres. 1963-74). Clubs: Town, Country, Clark Lake Yacht (hon. mem.; commodore 1959). Home: 1745 Malvern St Jackson MI 49203 Office: 145 S Jackson St Jackson MI 49201

MARCOVICCI, ANDREA LOUISA, actress, singer; b. N.Y.C.; d. Eugene Ernst and Helen (Figura) M.; student Bennett Coll. Appeared on TV commls.; appeared regularly on TV series Love Is A Many Splendered Thing; TV guest appearances include Medical Center; TV movies: Cry Rape, Smile Jenny, You're Dead, 1975, also episodes of Kojak, Baretta and Mannix; appeared in motion picture The Front (Golden Globe nomination), 1976; stage performances include Hamlet; Nefertiti, 1976. Recipient Jefferson award nomination for original musical Dance on a Country Grave. Mem. ASCAP, AFTRA, Screen Actors Guild, Actors Equity. Office: 8899 Beverly Blvd Los Angeles CA 90048*

MARCOVICH, MIROSLAV, educator; b. Belgrade, Yugoslavia, Mar. 18, 1919; s. Svetozar and Mila (Sakich) M.; came to U.S., 1969; B.A., U. Belgrade, 1942; m. Verica Tosich, May 30, 1948; 1 son, Dragoslav. Lectr. in classics, U. Belgrade, 1946-55; prof. Los Andes U., Merida, Venezuela, 1955-69; prof. classics U. Ill., Urbana, 1969—, chmn. dept., 1973-77. Recipient Premio Sesquicentenario Gold medal, Venezuela, 1962, 64, Silver Cross, Mt. Athos, Greece, 1963, Distinguished Scholarship award U. Ill., 1973. Mem. Am. Philol. Assn. (mem. adv. com. Thesaurus Linguae Graecae 1973—), Phi Kappa Phi. Author: M. Maruli Davidias, 1957; Fr. Natalis Carmina, 1958; Bhagavadgita, 1958; Heraclitus, 1967; Eraclito: Frammenti, 1978, and others. Contbr. numerous articles to profl. jours. Home: 2509 Cottage Grove St Urbana IL 61801

MARCUCCIO, PHYLLIS ROSE, editor; b. Hackensack, N.J., Aug. 25, 1933; d. Filippo and Rose (Henry) Marcuccio; A.B., Bucknell U., 1955; M.A., George Washington U., 1976. Trainee, Time, Inc., 1956-57; art prodn. for mags. of Med. Economics, Inc., 1958-60; mem. staff Nat. Sci. Tchrs. Assn., Washington, 1961—, asso. editor Sci. and Children, 1963-65, editor, 1965—, dir. div. elementary edn., 1974-78, dir. div. program devel. and continuing edn., 1978—; lectr., cons. in field. Recipient Citizenship medal D.A.R., 1951; hon. life mem. Ohio Council Elementary Sch. Sci., 1974. Life mem. Nat. Sci. Tchrs. Assn.; mem. Council Elementary Sci. Internat. (Internat. award outstanding contbns. sci. edn. 1971, 72), Am. Nature Study Soc., Soil Conservation Soc. Am., Nat. Free Lance Photographers Assn., Photog. Soc. Am., Nat. Wildlife Fedn., Nat. Audubon Soc., Nat. Geog. Soc., Wilderness Soc., AAAS, Nat. Assn. Industry-Edn. Coop., Washington Edn. Press Assn. (treas. 1966-67, pres. 1975-76), Ednl. Press Assn. Am. (regional dir. 1969-71, sec. 1979—; Distinguished Achievement award 1969, 71-74, Eleanor Fishburn award 1978), Theta Alpha Phi, Phi Delta Gamma, Phi Delta Kappa. Author, photographer, illustrator numerous articles; co-author: Investigation in Ecology, 1972; editor: Science Fun, 1977; illustrator: Selected Readings for Students of English as a Second Language, 1966; compiler: Opportunities for Summer Studies in Elementary Science, 1968, 2d edit., 1969. Home: 406 S Horners Ln Rockville MD 20850 Office: Nat Sci Tchrs Assn 1742 Connecticut Ave NW Washington DC 20009

MARCUM, JOSEPH LARUE, ins. co. exec.; b. Hamilton, Ohio, July 2, 1923; s. Glen F. and Helen A. (Stout) M.; B.A., Antioch Coll., 1947; M.B.A. in Fin., Miami U., 1965; m. Sarah Jane Sloneker, Mar. 7, 1944; children—Catharine Ann, Joseph Timothy, Mary Christina, Sarah Jennifer, Stephen Sloneker. With Ohio Casualty Ins. Co. and affiliates, 1947—, now pres.; also dir. Mem. library and human relations bds. Butler County (Ohio). Served to capt., inf. U.S. Army. Mem. Soc. C.P.C.U. (nat. dir.), Am. Inst. Property and Liability Underwriters (trustee), Ohio C. of C. (v.p.). Presbyterian. Clubs: Queen City, Bankers (Cin.); Canadian, Met. (N.Y.C.); El Dorado Country (Indian Wells, Calif.); Little Harbor (Mich.); Walloon Lake Country (Mich.). Home: 475 Oakwood Dr Hamilton OH 45013 Office: 136 N Third St Hamilton OH 45025

MARCUS, DONALD HOWARD, advt. agy. exec.; b. Cleve., May 16, 1916; s. Joseph and Sarah (Schmitman) M.; student Fenn Coll., 1934-35; m. Helen Olen Weiss, Feb. 12, 1959; children—Laurel Kathy Marcus Heifetz, Carol Susan, James Randall (dec.), Jonathan Anthony. Mem. publicity dept. Warner Bros. Pictures, Cleve., 1935-37; mem. advt. dept. RKO Pictures, Cleve., 1937-40; mem. sales dept. Monogram Pictures, Cleve., 1940-42; pres. Marcus Advt. Inc., Cleve., 1946—; v.p. Marcus Advt. Art Inc., Cleve., 1950—; partner Cleve. Baseball Co., 1974—, Budget Inns Am., Cleve., 1973—; dir. Women's Fed. Savs., Cleve., 1978—. Guarantor, N.E. Ohio Opera Assn., 1965—; mem. Ohio Democratic exec. com., 1969-70, del. nat. conv., 1968; vice-chmn. communication div. Jewish Welfare Fund Appeal Cleve., 1964-70, chmn., 1971-72; trustee Jewish Community Fedn., 1973-74, Better Housing Inc., 1968-72, Cleve. Israel Bond Com., 1964-73, Cleve. Jewish News, 1974—; bd. dirs. Cuyahoga County unit Am. Cancer Soc. Served to 1st lt. USAAF, 1942-46. Mem. Ohio Commodores, Cleve. Brandeis U. Club (trustee 1964—), Mid-Day Club, Commerce Club Cleve., Cleve. Advt. Club, Cleve. Growth Assn., Mensa. Jewish (trustee temple). Club: Beechmont Country (pres. 1973-74). Home: 22449 Shelburne Rd Shaker Heights OH 44122 Office: Marcus Advt Inc 29001 Cedar Ave Lyndhurst OH 44124

MARCUS, EDWARD, educator, economist; b. Bklyn., Apr. 29, 1918; s. Herman and Rose (Marayna) M.; B.S., Harvard, 1939, M.B.A., 1941; student King's Coll., Cambridge (Eng.) U., 1946-47; Ph.D., Princeton, 1950; m. Mildred Rendl, Aug. 10, 1956. Economist, Fed. Res. Bd., 1950-52; prof. econs. Bklyn. Coll., 1952—, chmn. dept., 1966-79; cons. Nat. Acad. Scis., 1959, UN Conf. Trade and Devel., 1966; dir. Syracuse U. Maxwell Sch. Nigerian Project, 1961; participant Internat. Econometrics Assn., Amsterdam, Holland, 1968. Served with AUS, 1941-42, USCGR, 1942-46. Grantee Merrill Found., 1953. Mem. Am., Canadian, N.Y. Met. (pres. 1966-67) econ. assns., Am. Finance Assn., Royal Econ. Soc., Econ. Soc. S. Africa, Am. Assn. U. Profs., Phi Beta Kappa. Author: Canada and the International Business Cycle, 1927-1938, 1954; (with Mildred Rendl Marcus) Investment and Development Possibilities in Tropical Africa, 1960, International Trade and Finance, 1965, Monetary and Banking Theory, 1965, Economic Progress and the Developing World, 1971; Economics, 1978. Home: PO Box 814 New Canaan CT 06840 Office: Econs Dept Brooklyn Coll Brooklyn NY 11210

MARCUS, FRANK ISADORE, educator, physician; b. Haverstraw, N.Y., Mar. 23, 1928; s. Samuel and Edith (Sattler) M.; B.A., Columbia, 1948; M.S., Tufts U., 1951; M.D. cum laude, Boston U., 1953; m. Janet Geller, June 30, 1957; children—Ann, Steve, Lynn. Intern, Peter Bent Brigham Hosp., Boston, 1953-54, asst. resident, 1956-57, research fellow in cardiology, 1957-58; clin. fellow in cardiology Georgetown U. Hosp., 1958-59, chief med. resident, 1959-60; chief of cardiology Georgetown U. Med. Service, D.C. Gen. Hosp., Washington, 1960-68; instr. medicine Georgetown U. Sch. Medicine, 1960-63, asst. prof., 1963-68, asso. prof., 1968; prof. medicine, chief cardiology sect. U. Ariz. Coll. Medicine, Tucson, 1969—; cons. cardiology VA Hosp., Tucson, 1969, USAF Regional Hosp., Davis-Monthan AFB, Tucson, 1969; mem. courtesy staffs Tucson Med. Center, St. Mary's Hosp., Tucson. Mem. panel drug efficacy study, panel on cardiovascular drugs Nat. Acad. Scis.-NRC, 1967-68; chmn. undergrad. cardiovascular tng. grant com. HEW-NIH, 1970. Chmn., Washington Heart Assn. High Sch. Heart Program, 1966-68. Served to capt., USAF, 1954-56. Recipient Career Devel. award NIH, 1965, Student AMA Golden Apple award Georgetown U. Sch. Medicine, 1968; Mass. Heart Assn. fellow, 1957-58; John and Mary Markle scholar, 1960-65. Diplomate Am. Bd. Internal Medicine, subspecialty cardiovascular diseases. Fellow Council on Clin. Cardiology Am. Heart Assn., A.C.P., Am. Coll. Cardiology; mem. Am. Fedn. Clin. Research, Am. Soc. Pharm. and Exptl. Therapeutics, Assn. Univ. Cardiologists, Inc., Am., Ariz. (dir. 1970, v.p. 1972-73, chmn. research com. 1970-72), So. Ariz. (dir. 1969) heart assns., Alpha Omega Alpha. Mem. editorial bd. Circulation, Current Problems in Cardiology. Contbr. numerous articles to med. jours. Home: 4949 E Glenn Tucson AZ 85712 Office: U Ariz Ariz Med Center Tucson AZ 85724

MARCUS, HYMAN, corp. ofcl.; b. Roumania, May 3, 1914; s. Morris and Fannie Marcus, A.B., Columbia, 1932; m. Sydelle Allen, June 29, 1935; children—Beverly Faith, Carole Ann. Instr. math., 1932-39; pres. Empire Designing Corp., 1939-46, Manhattan Capital Co., 1946-54; pres., chmn. U.S. Hoffman Machinery Corp., 1954-58; partner van Alstyne Noel & Co., 1956-59; chmn. bd. Hoffmann Internat., 1957-59; chmn. bd. Artloom Industries, 1958—, pres., 1959—; pres., chmn. bd. Trans-United Industries, 1958; chmn. First Nat. Capital Corp., 1968—, Maralco Enterprises Inc., 1969—. Chmn., Village of Atlantic Beach Planning Commn.; trustee Riverside Sch., Jewish Meml. Hosp. Home: 159 W 53d St New York City NY 10019 Office: 200 W 51st St New York City NY 10019

MARCUS, JACOB RADER, educator; b. Connellsville, Pa., Mar. 5, 1896; s. Aaron and Jennie (Rader) M.; A.B., U. Cin., 1917, LL.D., 1950; rabbi, Hebrew Union Coll., 1920, Ph.D., U. Berlin, 1925; attended Lane Theol. Sem., 1914, U. Chgo., 1915, U. Kiel, 1923; spl. study in Paris and Jerusalem, 1925-26; LL.D., Dropsie Coll., 1955; D.H.L., Spertus Coll. Judaica, Chgo., 1977, Brandeis U., 1978, Gratz Coll., Phila., 1978; m. Antoinette Brody, Dec. 30, 1925 (dec.); 1 dau., Merle Judith (dec.). Instr. Bible, rabbinics Hebrew Union Coll., 1920, asst. prof. Jewish history, 1926-29, asso. prof., 1929-34, prof. Jewish history, 1934-59; apptd. Adolph S. Ochs prof. Jewish history, 1946, Adolph S. Ochs prof. Am. Jewish history, 1959-65, Milton and Hattie Kutz Distinguished Service prof. Am. Jewish history, 1965—; dir. Am. Jewish Archives, 1947—, Am. Jewish Periodical Center, 1956—; v.p. Central Conf. Am. Rabbis, 1947, pres., 1949, hon. pres., 1978. Served as 2d lt., 145th Inf., U.S. Army, 1917-19. Recipient Frank L. Weil award Nat. Jewish Welfare Bd., 1955; Lee M. Friedman medal for distinguished service to history, 1961; honored with publ. Essays in American Jewish History, on 10th anniversary of founding Am. Jewish Archives, 1958, A Bicentennial Festschrift for Jacob Rader Marcus, 1976. Mem. Jewish Publ. Soc. Am. (trustee), Jewish Acad. Arts and Scis., Am. Jewish Hist. Soc. (hon. pres.), Am. Acad. Jewish Research, Phi Beta Kappa. Club: B'nai B'rith. Author: The Rise and Destiny of the German Jew, 1934; An Index to Jewish Festschriften, 1937; The Jew in the Medieval World-a Source Book, 1938; Communal Sick-Care in the German Ghetto, 1947; Early American Jewry, 2 vols., 1951-53; Memoirs of American Jews 1775-1865, 3 vols., 1955-56; American Jewry Documents Eighteenth Century, 1959; On Love, Marriage, Children . . . and Death, Too, 1966; Studies in American Jewish History, 1969; The Colonial American Jew, 3 vols., 1970; Israel Jacobson: The Founder of the Reform Movement in Judaism, 1972; editor: The American Jewish Archives. Home: 401 McAlpin Ave Cincinnati OH 45220. *The most important thing in life is integrity.*

MARCUS, JOSEPH, child psychiatrist; b. Cleve., Feb. 27, 1928; s. William and Sarah (Marcus) Schwartz; B.S.c., Western Res. U., 1963; M.D., Hebrew U., 1958; m. Cila Furmanovitz, Nov. 2, 1951; children—Oren, Alon. Intern, Tel Hashomer Govt. Hosp., Israel, 1956-57; resident in psychiatry and child psychiatry Ministry of Health, Govt. of Israel, 1958-61; acting head dept. child psychiatry Ness Ziona Rehab. Center, 1961-62; sr. psychiatrist Lasker dept. child psychiatry Hadassah U. Hosp., 1962-64; research asso. Israel Inst. Applied Social Research, 1966-69; practice medicine specializing in psychiatry, Jerusalem, 1966-72; asso. dir. devel. neuropsychiatry Jerusalem Infant and Child Devel. Center, 1969-70; dept. head Eytanim Hosp., 1970-72; cons. child psychiatrist for Jerusalem Ministry of Health, 1970-72; dir. dept. child psychiatry and devel. Jerusalem Mental Health Center, 1972-75; prof. child psychiatry, dir. unit for research in child psychiatry and devel. U. Chgo., 1975—. Mem. Am. Acad. Child Psychiatry (com. on research, com. on psychiat. aspects of infancy), Soc. Research in Child Devel., Internat. Assn. Child Psychiatry and Allied Professions (asst. gen. sec. 1966-74), European Union Paedopsychiatry (hon.), World, Israel psychiat. assns., Internat. Coll. Psychosomatic Medicine, Israel Center Psychobiology. Chief editor Early Child Devel. and Care, 1972—; mem. editorial bd. Israel Annals of Psychiatry and Related Disciplines, 1965-70, Internat. Yearbook of Child Psychiatry and Allied Professions, 1968-74; contbr. articles to med. jours. Home: 5816 S Blackstone Chicago IL 60637 Office: 950 E 59th St Chicago IL 60637

MARCUS, JULES ALEXANDER, physicist, educator; b. Coytesville, N.J., May 10, 1919; s. Alexander and Julia (Parks) M.; B.S., Yale, 1940, Ph.D., 1947; m. Ruth C. Barcan, Aug. 28, 1942 (div. 1975); children—James S., Peter W., Katherine H., Elizabeth P. Instr., Yale, 1943-44, research asst., 1946-47; physicist Johns Hopkins, 1944-46; postdoctoral fellow U. Chgo., 1947-49; faculty physics Northwestern U., 1949—, prof., 1961, acting chmn. dept., 1966-67. Fellow Am. Phys. Soc.; mem. Am. Assn. Physics Tchrs., Sigma Xi. Contbr. articles profl. jours. Basic research low temperature solid state physics; 1st observation of quantum oscillations of magnetic properties of normal metals. Home: 2801 Girard Ave Evanston IL 60201

MARCUS, LEONARD MARSHALL, editor, writer, musician; b. N.Y.C., Aug. 2, 1930; s. Murray Jack and Hannah Muriel (Simon) M.; student U. Wis., 1947-49; A.B. cum laude, Harvard, 1951, M.A., 1953; student U. Minn., 1955-56; m. Beverle Ruth Slaney Reimann, Nov. 6, 1959; children—Jason Dean, Peter Jonathan, Theodore Henry. Instr. music, condr. univ. symphony U. Minn., 1955-56; asst. to condr. Mpls. Symphony, 1955-56; author movie scores; tchr. Henry St. Music Sch., Met. Music Sch., N.Y.C., 1957-59; asst. mgr. classical dept. London Records, 1959-61; mgr. information services Columbia Records, 1961-62; editor Carnegie Hall Program, 1963-65; program annotator Am. Symphony Orch., 1964-67; spl. project editor, later mng. editor High Fidelity mag., 1965-68, editor in chief High Fidelity mag., also editorial dir. Musical Am. mag., 1968—; pres. jury Montreux Internat. Record Awards, 1969; condr. Stockbridge (Mass.) Chamber Orch., 1975—; host syndicated radio program Concert Stage, 1977-79; founder, pres. Internat. Record Critics Awards, 1977—; chmn. Koussetvitzky Internat. Record Awards, 1977—; mem. 1st cultural del. to People's Republic of China, 1979. Served with AUS, 1953-55. Contbr. to Ency. Brit., 1971. Home: Undermountain Rd Lenox MA 01240 Office: 825 7th Ave New York NY 10019 also The Publishing House Great Barrington MA 01230

MARCUS, MARVIN, mathematician, educator; b. Albuquerque, July 31, 1927; s. David Clarence and Esther (Rosenthal) M.; B.A., U. Calif. at Berkeley, 1950, Ph.D., 1954; m. Arlen Ingrid Sahlman, Sept. 14, 1951; children—Jeffrey Thomas, Karen Melissa; m. 2d, Rebecca Elizabeth Michael, Oct. 12, 1965. Instr., then asst. prof. U. B.C., 1954-56, asso. prof., 1957-62; postdoctoral research fellow Nat. Bur. Standards, Washington, 1956-57; prof. U. Calif. at Santa Barbara, 1962—, dir. Inst. for Interdisciplinary Applications of Algebra and Combinatorics, 1973-79, chmn. dept. math., 1963-68, dean research devel., 1978, asso. vice-chancellor research and acad. devel., 1979—; vis. distinguished prof. U. Islamabad, West Pakistan, 1970. Cons. Bur. Naval Ordance, Pasadena, Calif. Served with USNR, 1945-46. Mem. Am. Math. Soc., Math. Assn. Am., Soc. Indsl. and Applied Math., Sigma Xi, Pi Mu Epsilon. Author books and articles in field. Editor Linear and Multilinear Algebra. Home: 2937 Kenmore Pl Santa Barbara CA 93105

MARCUS, PHILIP IRVING, microbiologist; b. Springfield, Mass., June 3, 1927; s. Julius and Marley Amelia (Speir) M.; B.S., U. So. Calif., 1950; M.S., U. Chgo., 1953; Ph.D., U. Colo., 1957; m. Angela Joan Francis, Dec. 4, 1953; children—Craig F., Wendy L., Valerie L. Asst. prof. biophysics U. Colo. Sch. Medicine, Denver, 1957-60; asso. prof. microbiology Albert Einstein Coll. Medicine, Bronx, N.Y., 1961-66, prof., 1967-69; prof. microbiology U. Conn., Storrs, 1969-75, head dept., 1969-75, prof. virology, 1976—; dir. Nat. Cancer Inst. Program Project, 1973—; cons. NIH, NSF; mem. sci. adv. council Damon Runyon-Walter Winchell Cancer Fund, 1970-74. Served with USAAC, 1945-47. Recipient USPHS research career devel. award, 1960-70; NIH grantee; NSF grantee. Mem. AAAS, Am. Soc. Microbiology, Am. Soc. Cell Biology, Conn. Acad. Sci. and Engring. Editor Jour. Cellular Physiology, 1969—; contbr. articles to profl. jours. Home: 24 Thompson Rd Storrs CT 06268 Office: Microbiology Sect U-44 U Conn Storrs CT 06268

MARCUS, RICHARD CANTRELL, retail co. exec.; b. Dallas, Oct. 2, 1938; s. Stanley and Mary (Cantrell) M.; B.A., Harvard U., 1960, Advanced Mgmt. Program, 1973; m. Heather Jo Johnson, Mar. 23, 1968; children—Catherine, Charles Allen. Mem. exec. tng. program Bloomingdales Inc., 1960-63; with Neiman-Marcus, Dallas, 1963—, exec. v.p., store mgr., 1971-72, pres., 1972-77, vice chmn., 1977-79, chmn., chief exec. officer, 1979—; dir. Republic Nat. Bank Dallas. Chmn. exec. com. Dallas Theater Center, also bd. dirs.; bd. dirs. Dallas Civic Opera, Dallas Symphony Orch., Dallas C. of C. Mem. Dallas Retail Mchts. Assn. (past pres.), Young Pres.'s Orgn., Dallas Assembly. Home: 7031 Turtle Creek Blvd Dallas TX 75205 Office: Main and Ervay Sts Dallas TX 75201

MARCUS, ROBERT, aluminum co. exec.; b. Arlington, Mass., Feb. 24, 1925; s. Hymen David and Etta (Arbetter) M.; A.B., Harvard U., 1947; M.B.A., U. Mich., 1949; M.Ed., Tufts U., 1950; m. Naomi Kaitz, Nov. 23, 1949; children—Lawrence Brian, Janie Sue, Clifford Scott, Emily. Market analyst Govt. Commodity Exchange, N.Y.C., 1952-54; mkt. research analyst Gen. Electric Co., 1954-55; corp. mkt. analyst Amax Inc., N.Y.C., 1955-62, staff mkt. mgr. aluminum group, 1962-65, pres. internat. aluminum div., 1965-70, v.p., 1970-71; exec. v.p. Amax Pacific Corp., San Mateo, Calif., 1971-72; exec. v.p. Alumax Inc., San Mateo, 1972—; dir. Advanced Memory Systems, 1973-76, Alumax Inc., Intalco, Eastalco, Alumex S.A.; trustee World Affairs Council, 1974—. Served with USN, 1943-46. Mem. Bankers Club San Francisco, Harvard Club N.Y. Home: 44 Reed St San Francisco CA 94109 Office: 400 El Camino San Mateo CA 94402

MARCUS, RUDOLPH ARTHUR, chemist; b. Montreal, P.Q., Can., July 21, 1923; s. Myer Mark and Esther (Cohen) M.; B.Sc., McGill U., Montreal, 1943, Ph.D., 1946; m. Laura Hearne, Aug. 27, 1949;

children—Alan Rudolph, Kenneth Hearne, Raymond Arthur. With Nat. Research Council Can., Ottawa, 1946-49; research asso. U. N.C., 1949-51; from asst. prof. to prof. chemistry Poly. Inst. Bklyn., 1951-64; prof. U. Ill., 1964-78; vis. prof. theoretical chemistry, fellow Univ. Coll., Oxford U., 1975-76; temp. mem. Coursnt Inst. Math. Scis., N.Y. U., 1960-61; Arthur Amos Noyes prof. chemistry Calif. Inst. Tech., Pasadena, 1978—; chmn. trustee Gordon Research Confs., 1968-69. Recipient Anne Molson prize chemistry McGill U., 1943, Alexander von Humboldt sr. U.S. scientist award, 1976; sr. postdoctoral fellow NSF, 1960-61; Sloan fellow, 1960-63; Fulbright-Hays sr. scholar, 1971-72. Fellow Am. Acad. Arts and Scis.; mem. Nat. Acad. Scis., Am. Chem. Soc. (Irving Langmuir award chem. physics 1978), Am. Phys. Soc., Am. Electrochem. Soc., Alpha Chi Sigma. Author articles in field; co-editor: Tunneling in Biological Systems, 1979. Home: 331 S Hill Ave Pasadena CA 91106 Office: 110 Noyes Lab Pasadena CA 91125

MARCUS, RUDOLPH ARTHUR, chemist; b. Montreal, Que., Can., July 21, 1923; s. Myer and Esther (Cohen) M.; B.S., McGill U., 1943, Ph.D., 1946; m. Laura Hearne, Aug. 27, 1949; children—Alan Rudolph, Kenneth Hearne, Raymond Arthur. Came to U.S., 1949, naturalized, 1958. Postdoctoral research asso. NRC of Can., Ottawa, 1946-49, U. N.C., 1949-51; asst. prof. Poly. Inst. Bklyn., 1951-54, asso. prof., 1954-58, prof., 1958-64; prof. U. Ill., Urbana, 1964-78; Arthur Amos Noyes prof. chemistry Calif. Inst. Tech., Pasadena, 1978—; temp. mem. Courant Inst. Math. Scis., N.Y. U., 1960-61; trustee Gordon Research Confs., 1966-69, chmn. bd., 1968-69, mem. council, 1965-68; mem. rev. panel Argonne Nat. Lab., 1966-72, chmn., 1967-68; mem. rev. panel Brookhaven Nat. Lab., 1971-74; mem. adv. council in chemistry Princeton U., 1972-78; mem. rev. com. Radiation Lab., U. Notre Dame, 1975—; mem. panel on atmospheric chemistry climatic impact com. Nat. Acad. Scis.-NRC, 1975-78, mem. com. kinetics of chem. reactions, 1973-77, chmn., 1975-77, mem. com. chem. scis., 1977-79; vis. com. div. chemistry and chem. engring. Calif. Inst. Tech., 1977-78; adv. council chemistry Poly. Inst. N.Y., 1977—; adv. com. for chemistry NSF, 1977—; vis. prof. theoretical chemistry U. Oxford (Eng.), 1975-76, also professorial fellow Univ. Coll. Recipient Anne Molson prize in chemistry McGill U., 1943, Alexander von Humboldt Found. Sr. U.S. Scientist award, 1976; Alfred P. Sloan fellow, 1960-63; NSF sr. postdoctoral fellow, 1960-61; sr. Fulbright-Hays scholar, 1972. Fellow Am. Acad. Arts and Scis. (exec. com. Western sect.); mem. Nat. Acad. Scis., Am. Chem. Soc. (past div. chmn., mem. exec. com., mem. adv. bd. petroleum research fund; Irving Langmuir award Chem. Physics 1978), Am. Phys. Soc. (exec. com. div. chem. physics), Electrochem. Soc., AAUP, Sigma Xi, Alpha Chi Sigma. Mem. editorial bd. Jour. Chem. Physics, 1964-66, Ann. Rev. Phys. Chemistry, 1964-69, Jour. Phys. Chemistry, 1968-72, Accounts of Chem. Research, 1968-73, Internat. Jour. Chem. Kinetics, 1976—, Molecular Physics, 1977—; contbr. articles to profl. jours. Home: 331 S Hill Ave Pasadena CA 91106

MARCUS, RUTH BARCAN, philosopher, educator; b. N.Y.C.; d. Samuel and Rose (Post) Barcan; B.A., N.Y. U., 1941; M.A., Yale U., 1942, Ph.D., 1946; children—James Spencer, Peter Webb, Katherine Hollister, Elizabeth Post. AAUW fellow, 1947-48; vis. prof. Northwestern U., 1950-57, Guggenheim fellow, 1953-54; asst. prof., asso. prof. Roosevelt U., Chgo., 1957-60; NSF fellow, 1963-64; prof. philosophy U. Ill., Chgo. Circle, 1964-70, head philosophy dept., 1964-68, Center for Advanced Study, 1968-69; prof. philosophy Northwestern U., 1970-73; Reuben Post Halleck prof. philosophy Yale, 1973—; fellow Center Advanced Study in Behavioral Sci., 1979. Mem. Council on Philos. Studies, Assn. for Symbolic Logic (past exec. council, exec. com. 1973-76, v.p. 1980—), Am. Philos. Assn. (past sec.-treas., nat. dir. 1967—, pres. 1975-76, chmn. nat. bd. officer 1977—), Aristotelian Soc., Mind Assn., Institut International de Philosophie, Am. Acad. Arts and Scis., Phi Beta Kappa. Editor: (with Anderson and Martin) The Logical Enterprise. Editorial bd. The Monist, Jour. Philos. Logic, Philosophy of Sci., Philos. Studies, Metaphilosophy. Contbr. to books and profl. jours. Home: 311 St Ronan St New Haven CT 06520 Office: Dept Philosophy Yale U New Haven CT 06520

MARCUS, SAMUEL HERMAN, meat packing co. exec.; b. Romania, Nov. 1, 1906; s. Herman and Anna (Weiss) M.; came to U.S., 1909; student U. Chgo., 1924-28; m. Mildred J. Gross, May 7, 1932; children—Howard, Jerome. Salesman, Swift and Co., 1928-35; founder, pres. Excel Packing Co. (name changed to Kans. Beef Industries, Inc. 1970), 1936-70, chmn. bd., 1971-74; vice chmn. bd., dir. MBPXL Corp., Wichita, 1974—; co-founder, dir. Enmar Co., Wichita, 1940—. Trustee Wichita State U.; pres. Kans. Coliseum Corp.; bd. dirs. Wichita Central YMCA, Temple Emanu-El, Wichita, Legal Aid Soc., Sedgwick County Health Facilities Planning Council, United Fund, Wichita Environ. Task Force; exec. bd. Urban League; governing bd. Wichita Met. Council. Recipient Super Salesman award Swift and Co., 1935; Salesman of Year award Sales and Mktg. Execs., 1969; Service to Youth award YMCA, Wichita, 1969; Outstanding Citizen's Brotherhood award NCCJ, 1970; citation Kans. Found. Pvt. Colls., 1975; Outstanding Contbn. award Urban League, 1977; Recognition award Wichita U., 1977. Mem. Am. Meat Inst. (dir. 1969-74). Republican. Clubs: Rotary, Rolling Hills Country, Wichita. Home: 2 Douglas St Wichita KS 67207 Office: PO Box 2519 Wichita KS 67201

MARCUS, SHELDON, ednl. adminstr.; b. N.Y.C., Aug. 4, 1937; s. Manny and Sarah (Lande) M.; B.A., City Coll. N.Y., 1959; M.S., 1960; Ed.D., Yeshiva U., 1970; children—Beth, Jonathan. Tchr. social studies, assoc. prin. guidance counselor N.Y.C. Pub. Schs., 1959-68; lectr. social sci. City U. N.Y., Queensborough Community Coll., 1965-68; mem. faculty Fordham U., N.Y.C., 1968-70, chmn. div. urban edn., 1970-76, asst. dean grad. edn. Tarrytown campus, 1976—. Bd. dirs. Encampment for Citizenship, Inc., 1975—; exec. bd. Tchr. Corps. Program, U.S. Office of Edn., 1974—; trustee Doctoral Assn., N.Y. Edn., 1973—. Served with U.S. Army. Recipient citation N.Y.C. Bd. Edn., 1975. Mem. N.Y. State United Tchrs. Assn. Author: Conflicts in Urban Education, 1970; Urban Education: Crisis or Opportunity?, 1972; Father Coughlin: The Tumultuous Life of the Priest of the Little Flower (nominated for Pulitzer Prize), 1973; The Urban In-Service Education Experience, 1977; contbr. articles to profl. jours. Home: 410 Benedict Ave Tarrytown NY 10591 Office: Fordham U Sch Edn Lincoln Center Campus New York NY 10023 also Fordham U Marymount Coll Campus Tarrytown NY 10591

MARCUS, STANLEY, retail mcht., lectr., mktg. cons., miniature book pub.; b. Dallas, Apr. 20, 1905; s. Herbert and Minnie (Lichtenstein) M.; student Amherst Coll., 1921; B.A., Harvard, 1925, postgrad. Bus. Sch., 1926; D.Humanities, So. Meth. U., 1965; m. Mary Cantrell, Nov. 7, 1932 (dec.); children—Jerrie (Mrs. Frederick M. Smith, II), Richard and Wendy (Mrs. Henry Raymont) (twins). With Neiman-Marcus, Dallas, Houston, Fort Worth, Bal Harbour, Atlanta, Newport Beach, Beverly Hills, Calif., St. Louis, Washington and Chgo., 1926—, sec. treas., dir., 1928, mdse. mgr. sportswear shop, 1928, mdse. mgr. all apparel divs., 1929, exec. v.p., 1935-50, pres., 1950-72, chmn. bd., 1972-75, chmn. exec. com., 1975-77, chmn. emeritus, 1977—; with Stanley Marcus Consultancy Services; owner, operator Somesuch Press, Inc.; past corp. exec. v.p., hon. dir. Carter Hawley Hale Stores, Inc., Los Angeles; dir. Republic Tex. Corp., N.Y. Life Ins. Co., Jack Lenor Larsen Inc. Mem. exec. com. Center for the Book, Library of Congress; past mem. adv. com. Nat. Assn. for U.S. Art in UN, Hemisfair; form advisory dir. Ft. Worth Art Assn.; former co-chmn. Interracial Council for Bus. Opportunity, Dallas br.; founding mem. Bus. Com. for Arts; mem. exec. com. Nat. Council Arts and Edn.; past regional v.p. Nat. Jewish Hosp., Denver; bd. govs. Common Cause, 1976-79; past bd. dirs. Dallas Council World Affairs, Grad. Research Center of Southwest; former bd. govs. USO; bd. dirs., past pres. Dallas Symphony Soc.; past pres., past dir. Dallas Citizens Council; bd. dirs., chmn. internat. mktg. com. North Tex. Commn.; former dir. Tex. Law Enforcement Found.; dir. Am. Council to Improve Our Neighborhoods, Center Study Democratic Instns.; trustee Tex. Research Found., Com. Econ. Devel., Pub. TV Found. North Tex., Eisenhower Exchange Fellowships; bd. dirs. Urban Inst.; mem. bd. publs., trustee So. Meth. Univ., also past chmn. library advancement program; past mem. Tex. Fine Arts Commn.; past pres. Dallas Art Assn.; former overseer Harvard U., mem. vis. com. univ. of resources, 1978-79; chmn. Tex. Com. Selection Rhodes scholarship; past trustee, chmn. exec. com. Hockaday Sch. Girls, Dallas. Mem. wage and hour millinery com. War Prodn. Bd., 1940. Decorated chevalier Legion of Honor, officier Legion of Honor, comdr. Nat. Order Merit (France); Star of Solidarity, Commandetore of Merito della Republica Italiana (Italy); Hon. Order of Brit. Empire; chevalier Order of Leopold II (Belgium); Royal Order of Dannebrog (Danish Govt.); Great Cross of Austria; recipient Tobe award for distinguished service to Am. retailing, 1945; N.Y. Fashion Designers award, 1958; Ambassador award for achievement, London, 1963; 1st Milw. Medallion, 1968; Gold medal Nat. Retail Merchants Assn., 1961; named Headliner of Year Dallas Press Club, 1958; B.A.M.B.I. Flying Colors award, 1978; Library of Fashion So. Meth. U. established in his honor, 1976. Research fellow Southwestern Legal Found.; fellow AIA (hon.); mem. Am. Retail Fedn. (chmn. 1948-50, exec. com.), Nat. Urban League (trustee), Council on Fgn. Relations (dir.), Am. Arbitration Assn. (past dir.), Chgo. Art Inst., Dallas (chmn. aviation com.), Internat. (trustee U.S. council), Eta Mu Pi (hon.). Clubs: Harvard (N.Y.C. and Dallas); City Athletic, Grolier (N.Y.C.); Columbian, City, Chaparral, Dallas (Dallas). Author: Minding the Store, 1974; My Fashion Business, 1976; Quest for the Best, 1979; contbr. numerous articles to mags. Home: 1 Nonesuch Rd Dallas TX 75214 Office: 4800 Republic Bank Tower Dallas TX 75201

MARCUS, STEVEN, lit. critic, educator; b. N.Y.C., Dec. 13, 1928; s. Nathan and Adeline Muriel (Gordon) M.; Ph.D., Columbia, 1961; m. Gertrud Lenzer, Jan. 20, 1966; 1 son, John Nathaniel. Prof. English Columbia, George Delacorte prof. humanities, 1976—, chmn. dept. English and comparative lit., 1977—, dir. planning Nat. Humanities Center, 1974-76, chmn. exec. com. bd. dirs., 1976—, chmn. Lional Trilling Seminars, 1976—. Served with AUS, 1954-56. Fellow Am. Acad. Arts and Scis., Acad. Lit. Studies, mem. Columbia Soc. Fellows in Humanities (co-chmn.). Author: Dickens: From Pickwick to Dombey, 1965; The Other Victorians, 1966; Engels, Manchester and the Working Class, 1974; Representations, 1976; Doing Good, 1978. Asso. editor Partisan Rev. Home: 39 Claremont Ave New York NY 10027

MARCUS, WALTER F., JR., state justice; b. 1927; B.A., Yale U.; J.D., Tulane U. Admitted to La. bar, 1955; now asso. justice Supreme Ct. La. Mem. Am. Bar Assn. Office: Supreme Ct La 301 Loyola Ave New Orleans LA 70112*

MARCUSE, JAMES EDGAR, chem. co. exec.; b. Far Rockaway, N.Y., July 4, 1906; s. Moses M. and Marion (Shrier) M.; B.A., Princeton, 1926; M.B.A., Harvard, 1928; m. Doris B. Korn, Nov. 30, 1933; children—Donald J., Edgar K. With West Chem. Products, Inc. (formerly West Disinfecting Co.), Long Island City, 1927—, pres., 1942-74, chmn. bd., 1960-74, now dir. Bd. dirs. Marcuse Fund, Jewish Guild for Blind. Home: 875 Fifth Ave New York City NY 10021 Office: 42-16 West St Long Island City NY 11101

MARCUSE, JUDITH ROSE, dancer, choreographer; b. Montreal, Que., Can., Mar. 13, 1947; d. Frank Howard and Phyllis Sheila (Salomons) Margolick; G.C.E., Cambridge (Eng.) U., and Oxford U. Bd., 1965; m. Richard Marcuse, Aug. 28, 1972. Dancer, Les Grands Ballets Canadiens, Montreal, 1965-68, Ballets de Geneve (Switzerland), 1969, Bat-Dor Dance Co., Tel-Aviv, Israel, 1970-72, Festival Ballet of Can., 1973, Ballet Rambert, London, 1974-76; choreographed works include: Fusion, 1974, Baby, 1975, Four Working Songs, 1976, Session, 1977, Apart, 1977, Puttin' on the Ritz, 1977, Re-Entry, 1978, Speakeasy, 1978, Twelfth Night, 1978, Celebration, 1979, Sadaana Dhoti, 1979; instr. dance Simon Fraser U., 1977, 79, York U., 1977, 78, 79; guest tchr. Oakland (Calif.) Ballet, 1972-74, Ballet Rambert, Eng., 1974-76, Alvin Ailey Dance Am. Theater, N.Y.C., 1977, Dance in Can. Conf., 1978, 79; TV appearances include: Israel TV, CBC, BBC; guest dancer Classical Ballet of Israel, Tel Aviv, 1972. Recipient Chalmers award in choreography Chalmers Found., 1976; Clifford E. Lee award for choreography; Que. Govt. scholar, 1961-62; Koerner Found. grantee, 1960; Can. Council short term grantee, 1968; Brit. Arts Council grantee, 1975-76; Can. Council arts grantee, 1977, 78. Mem. Dance in Can. Assn. (dir.), Canadian Actors' Equity Assn., Brit. Actors Equity Assn. Home and Office: 7290 Arbutus Pl West Vancouver BC V7W 2L6 Canada

MARCUSS, STANLEY JOSEPH, govt. ofcl.; b. Hartford, Conn., Jan. 24, 1942; s. Stanley Joseph and Anne Sutton (Leone) M.; B.A., Trinity Coll., 1963; B.A., Cambridge U., 1965, M.A., 1969; J.D., Harvard U., 1968; m. Rosemary Daly, July 6, 1968; children—Elena Daly, Aidan Stanley. Admitted to D.C., Conn., U.S. Supreme Ct. bars; staff atty. office of gen. counsel HUD, Washington, 1968; atty. firm Hogan and Hartson, Washington, 1968-73; counsel to internat. fin. subcom. U.S. Senate Com. on Banking, Housing and Urban Affairs, 1973-77; dep. asst. sec. for trade regulation Dept. Commerce, Washington, 1977-78, sr. dep. asst. sec. for industry and trade, 1978—. Bd. fellow Trinity Coll., Hartford. Mem. Am. Bar Assn., D.C. Bar Assn., Phi Beta Kappa. Contbr. articles to profl. jours. Office: Dept Commerce 14th and Constitution Ave NW Washington DC 20230

MARCUVITZ, NATHAN, educator; b. Bklyn., Dec. 29, 1913; s. Samuel and Rebecca (Feiner) M.; B.E.E., Poly. Inst. Bklyn., 1935, M.E.E., 1941, D.E.E., 1947; m. Muriel Spanier, June 30, 1946; children—Andrew, Karen. Engr., RCA Labs., 1936-40; research asso. Radiation Lab., Mass. Inst. Tech., 1941-46; asst. prof. elec. engring. Poly. Inst. Bklyn., 1946-49, asso. prof., 1949-51, prof., 1951-65, dir. Microwave Research Inst., 1957-61, v.p. research, acting dean Grad. Center, 1961-63, prof. electrophysics, 1961-66, dean research, dean Grad. Center, 1964-65; asst. dir. def. research and engring. Dept. Def., Washington, 1963-64; prof. applied physics N.Y.U., 1966-73; prof. electrophysics Poly. Inst. N.Y., 1973—, inst. prof., 1978—; vis. prof. Harvard U., spring 1971. Fellow IEEE; mem. Nat. Acad. Engring., Am. Phys. Soc., Sigma Xi, Tau Beta Pi, Eta Kappa Nu. Author: Waveguide Handbook, Vol. 10, 1951; (with L. Felsen) Radiation and Scattering of Waves, 1973; also numerous articles. Home: 7 Ridge Dr E Great Neck NY 11021 Office: Poly Inst NY Grad Center Rt 110 Farmingdale NY 11735

MARCY, CARL MILTON, govt. ofcl.; b. Falls City, Oreg., June 11, 1913; s. Milton A. and Nellie (Rickson) M.; B.A., Willamette U., 1934; M.A., Columbia, 1936, LL.B., 1939, Ph.D., 1942; m. Mildred Kester, Dec. 21, 1934; children—Karen Christine, Eric Bruce. Admitted to N.Y. bar, 1941, D.C. bar, 1975; instr. Columbia, 1935-39, Coll. City N.Y., 1939-42; officer Dept. State, Washington, 1942-49, legis. counsel, 1949-50; cons. Senate Com. on Fgn. Relations, 1950-55, chief staff, 1955-74; dir. Am. Com. on East-West Accord, 1977—. Recipient Rockefeller Pub. Service award, 1963. Mem. Am. Soc. Internat. Law. Club: Nat. Lawyers (Washington). Author: Presidential Commissions, 1945; Proposals for Changes in UN Charter, 1955. Home: 3271 Harness Creek Rd Annapolis MD 21403 Office: 227 Massachusetts Ave NE Washington DC 20002

MARCZYNSKI, THADDEUS JOHN, scientist, educator; b. Poznan, Poland, Nov. 30, 1920; s. John Adam and Wanda Catherine (Sielski) M.; M.D., Jagiellonian U. and Acad. Medicine, Cracow, Poland, 1951; Sc.D., Acad. Medicine, 1959; m. Barbara Konieczny, Oct. 10, 1956; children—Gregory Thaddeus, John Thaddeus. Came to U.S., 1964, naturalized, 1973. Asst. physician dept. medicine Mil. Hosp., Cracow, 1951-52; emergency physician Ambulance of City of Cracow, 1953-54; sr. research asst. dept. pharmacology Acad. Medicine, Cracow, 1956-62, asst. prof., 1962-64; asst. prof. pharmacology U. Ill. at Chgo., 1964-69, asso. prof., 1969-73, prof., 1973—; vis. scientist Brain Research Inst., UCLA, 1961-62. Rockefeller found. fellow, 1961-62. Mem. AAAS, Am. Soc. Pharmacology and Exptl. Therapeutics, Soc. Neurosci., N.Y. Acad. Sci. Contbr. articles to sci. jours. Home: 1217 Hinman St Evanston IL 60202 Office: U Ill at Chgo 835 S Wolcott St Chicago IL 60612

MARDAGA, THOMAS JOSEPH, bishop; b. Balt., May 14, 1913; s. Thomas J. and Agnes (Ryan) M.; B.A., St. Charles Coll., Catonsville, Md., also St. Mary's Sem., Balt., 1936; S.T.L., St. Mary's Sem., 1940; LL.D., Mt. St. Mary's Coll., 1968. Ordained priest Roman Catholic Ch., 1940; asst. pastor in Balt., 1940-62; archdiocesan dir. Cath. Youth Orgn., 1946-55; dir., archdiocesan Confraternity of Christian Doctrine, also exec. sec. Cath. Charity Fund Appeal, Balt., 1955-68; mem. archdiocesan bd. consultors, Balt., 1966; rector Basilica of Assumption, Balt., 1965-67; aux. bishop of Balt., 1967-68, vicar gen., 1967-68; bishop of Wilmington (Del.), 1968—; mem. U.S. Cath. Bishops' Adv. Council, 1973; mem. nominating com. Nat. Conf. Cath. Bishops, 1972, univ. com., 1972, com. on budget and finance, 1972, adviser to com. on doctrine, 1973, mem. bishops com. on priestly life and ministry, 1974, chmn. region IV, 1974, alt. adminstrv. com. and bd.; mem. Nat. Hon. Com. for Black Catholics Concerned, 1972; chmn. Delmarva Ecumenical Agy., 1975; trustee Mount Saint Mary's Coll., Emmitsburg, Md.; bd. dirs. Cath. Diocese Found., Greater Wilmington Devel. Council; Episcopal adv. Region II, Cursillo Movement. Mem. Nat. Conf. Cath. Bishops (adminstrv. com. 1970—; mem. com. doctrine), regional rep. Am. Coll. Immaculate Conception Cath. U. Louvain (Belgium), 1970—. Office: PO Box 2030 Wilmington DE 19899

MARDELL, FRED ROBERT, distilling co. exec.; b. Chgo., Oct. 2, 1934; s. Sam and Clara (Feldman) M.; B.S., DePaul U., 1955; J.D., U. Chgo., 1958; m. Jacqueline E. Hacker, Sept. 2, 1956; children—Elizabeth, Caleb, Sarah. Admitted to Ill. bar, 1958; practice in Chgo., 1961-65; law clk. Justice U.S. Schwartz, Ill. Appellate Ct., 1958-59; research asso. U. Chgo. Law Sch., 1959; asso. Devoe, Shadur & Krupp, 1961-65; v.p., sec. Barton Brands, Ltd., Chgo., 1965—. Served with AUS, 1959-61. Mem. Pi Gamma Mu. Asso. editor: U. Chgo. Law Rev., 1957-58. Home: 1070 Cobblestone Ct Northbrook IL 60062 Office: 55 E Monroe St Chicago IL 60603

MARDEN, BRICE, painter; b. Bronxville, N.Y., Oct. 15, 1938; s. Nicholas Brice and Kathryn (Fox) M.; student Fla. So. Coll., 1957-58; B.F.A., Boston U., 1961; M.F.A., Yale U., 1963; m. Pauline Thalia Baez, 1960 (div. 1964); 1 son, Nicholas Brice; m. 2d, Helen Regina Harrington, Nov. 7, 1968; 1 dau., Maya Mirabelle Zahara. Exhibited in one man shows throughout U.S. and Europe, 1966—, including S.R. Guggenheim Mus., N.Y.C., 1975; represented in permanent collections: Albright-Knox Art Gallery, Buffalo, Ft. Worth Art Mus., Solomon R. Guggenheim Mus., Mpls. Inst. Arts, Musée de Peinture et Sculpture, Grenoble, France, Mus. Modern Art, N.Y.C., Nat. Gallery Can., Ottawa, Neue Galerie, Aachen, W.Ger., Richmond (Va.) Mus. Fine Art, Stedelijk Mus. Fine Art, Amsterdam, Holland, U. Tex. Michener Collection, Austin, U. Mich. Mus. Art, Ann Arbor, Walker Art Center, Mpls., Whitney Mus. Am. Art, N.Y.C.; pres. Plane Image, Inc. Recipient 3d prize 72d Ann. Exhbn. Art Inst. Chgo., 1976. Author: Suicide Notes, 1974. Office: 105 Bowery New York NY 10002

MARDEN, MORRIS, mathematician; b. Boston, Feb. 12, 1905; s. Abraham and Fannie B. (Lieberman) M.; A.B. (highest honors in math.), Harvard, 1925, A.M., 1927, Ph.D., 1928; postgrad. Princeton, Swiss Fed. Tech. U., U. Paris, 1928-30; m. Miriam L. Goldman, Sept. 11, 1932; children—Albert, Philip. NRC fellow U. Wis., Princeton, U. Zurich (Switzerland), U. Paris (France), 1928-30; instr. math. Harvard, 1925-27; mem. faculty U. Wis., Milw., 1930—, chmn. math. dept., 1957-61, 63-64, distinguished prof. math., 1964-75, emeritus distinguished prof., 1975—; cons. Allis-Chalmers Co., 1948-60; vis. lectr. Math. Assn. Am., 1963-66; vis. distinguished prof. math. dept. Calif. Poly. State U., San Luis Obispo, 1975-77; invited lectr. Poland, 1958, Israel, Greece, Poland, 1962, Japan, India, Madrid, London, 1964, Mexico City, S.Am., 1965, Belgrade, Budapest, Goteburg, 1967, Israel, Stuttgart, Montreal, 1968, Finland, New Zealand, Australia, Honolulu, Montreal, 1970-71, Israel, 1973. NSF grantee, 1961-73. Fellow AAAS; mem. Am. Math. Soc., Math. Assn. Am., AAUP, London Math. Soc., Acad. Ind. Scholars, Phi Beta Kappa, Sigma Xi, Phi Kappa Phi. Author: Geometry of Zeros of a Polynomial in a Complex Variable, 1949; Geometry of Polynomials, 1966. Asst. editor Bull. Am. Math. Soc., 1942-45. Reviewer staff Math. Revs., 1940—. Research, numerous publs. on harmonic functions, polynomials and other functions of a complex variable. Home: 7100 N Barnett Ln Milwaukee WI 53217 Office: Math Dept U Wis-Milw Milwaukee WI 53201

MARDEN, PHILIP AYER, physician, educator; b. Newport, N.H., Oct. 31, 1911; s. Albion Sullivan and Laura Isobel (McEchern) M.; A.B., Dartmouth, 1933, student Med. Sch., 1933-34; M.D., U. Pa., 1936; m. Magdalen Rekus, Aug. 5, 1950. Intern Presbyn. Hosp., Phila., 1936-38; chief resident Delaware County Hosp., Drexel Hill, Pa., 1938-39; fellow otolaryngology, U. Pa. Hosp., 1939-40, chief otolaryngology, 1959-72; mem. faculty U. Pa. Med. Sch., 1940—, prof. dept. otolaryngology, 1959—; chief otolaryngology, div. A, Phila. Gen. Hosp., 1960-75; cons. Presbyn. Hosp., Phila., VA Hosp., Phila., Phila. Gen. Hosp. Served to maj., M.C., AUS, 1942-46; CBI. Mem. AMA, Am. Acad. Ophthalmology and Otolaryngology, A.C.S., Coll. Physicians Phila., Phi Beta Kappa, Sigma Xi. Home: 163 Vassar Rd Bala-Cynwyd PA 19004 Office: 3400 Spruce St Philadelphia PA 19104

MARDEN, VIRGINIA MCAVOY (MRS. ORISON SWETT MARDEN), civic worker; b. N.Y.C., Mar. 1, 1906; d. John Vincent and Marian (Newcomb) McAvoy; B.A., Barnard Coll., 1927; m. Orison Swett Marden, Mar. 1, 1930; children—Orison Swett III, John Newcomb. Asst. to supt., West Side Hosp., 1927-29; sec. to bd.

Friends of Music, 1929-30; dir., pres. Family Service of Scarsdale, N.Y., 1955-57; 1st vice chmn. Westchester County Council Social Agys., 1955-65; dir. Family Service Assn. Am., 1959, sec., 1961-66; dir. Westchester Legal Aid Soc., 1963—, sec., 1964—; exec. com. Plays for Living, 1965-70, women's div. N.Y. Legal Aid Soc., 1960—; bd. Nat. Study Service, Inc., 1960. Club: Cosmopolitan (N.Y.C.). Home: 11 Stonehouse Rd Scarsdale NY 10583

MARDER, ARTHUR JACOB, educator, author; b. Boston, Mar. 8, 1910; s. Maxwell J. and Ida (Greenstein) M.; A.B., Harvard, 1931, A.M., 1934, Ph.D., 1936; M.A., Oxford U. (Eng.), 1969, D.Litt. (hon.), 1971; m. Jan. North, Sept. 13, 1955; children—Toni Anne, Tod Allen, Kevin North. Asst. prof. history U. Oreg., 1936-38; research asso. Bur. Internat. Research, Harvard and Radcliffe colls., 1939-41; research analyst OSS, 1941-42; asso. prof. history Hamilton Coll., 1943-44; asso. prof. history U. Hawaii, 1944-51, prof., 1951-58, sr. prof., 1958-64; prof. history U. Calif. at Irvine, 1964-77; vis. prof. Harvard, 1949-50; George Eastman prof. Oxford, 1969-70. Decorated hon. comdr. Order Brit. Empire; recipient George Louis Beer prize Am. Hist. Assn., 1941; Bd. Admiralty citation, 1970; Distinguished Faculty Lectureship award U. Calif., Irvine, 1977; fellow John Simon Guggenheim Found., 1939, 45-46, 58, Am. Philos. Soc., 1956, 58, 63, 66, Rockefeller Found., 1943, Japan Found., 1976; U.K. Fulbright fellow alt., 1954; Chesney Meml. gold medal Royal United Service Instn., 1968. Fellow Royal Hist. Soc., Am. Acad. Arts and Scis.; corr. fellow Brit. Acad.; mem. Am. Philos. Soc., Am. Hist. Assn. (pres. Pacific Coast br. 1971-72, council 1973-75), Phi Beta Kappa, Phi Kappa Phi. Author: The Anatomy of British Sea Power, 1940; Portrait of an Admiral, 1952; Fear God and Dread Nought, 3 vols., 1952, 56, 59; From the Dreadnought to Scapa Flow, vol. 1, 1961, vol. 2, 1965, vol. 3, 1966, vol. 4, 1969, vol. 5, 1970; From the Dardanelles to Oran, 1974; Operation Menace, 1976. Home: 730 Woodland Dr Santa Barbara CA 93108

MARDER, JOHN G., advt. and mktg. exec.; b. N.Y.C., Dec. 27, 1926; s. Joseph T. and Rhea (Greenspun) M.; student Cornell, 1944-45; B.S., Columbia U. Sch. Bus., 1950; m. Barbara Sand, June 3, 1956 (div. 1971); children—Jonathan Allen, Susan Beth, Jane Allison; m. 2d, Joan Kron. Merchandising exec. Macy's, N.Y.C., 1951-56; exec. v.p. Grey Advt., Inc., N.Y.C., 1956—. Served as radio officer U.S. Maritime Service, U.S. Army Transport Service, 1945-46; 2d lt. Q.M.C., AUS, 1951-53. Home: 205 E 63d St New York City NY 10021 also Hedges Banks Dr East Hampton NY 11937 Office: 777 3d Ave New York City NY 10017

MARDER, LOUIS, educator; b. Bklyn., Sept. 26, 1915; s. Isidor and Clara (Freund) M.; B.A., Bklyn. Coll., 1941; M.A., Columbia U., 1947, Ph.D., 1950; m. Miriam Kugler, Aug. 31, 1940; children—Daniel Spencer, Diana Lynn. Indexer, N.Y. Times, 1946; lectr.-instr. Bklyn. Coll., 1946-53; chmn. dept. English, Pembroke (N.C.) State Coll., 1953-56; asso. prof. English, Kent (Ohio) State U., 1956-65; prof. English, U. Ill. at Chgo. Circle, 1965—; vis. prof. U. Toledo, summer 1968; lectr., spl. studies on Shakespeare; lectr. Antioch Coll. Shakespeare Festival, 1953, Utah Shakespearean Festival, 1975. Mem. President's Com. to Celebrate Shakespeare's 400th Anniversary, 1964; del. to Internat. Shakespeare Conf., Stratford-on-Avon, Eng., 1964, 66, 68, 72, 74, 76, 78; mem. com. for Internat. Coop. World Shakespeare Congress, 1971; cons. mem. World Center for Shakespeare Studies, London, mem. adv. com., also rec. sec.; chmn. Shakespeare Groundlings, 1972-76. Bd. dirs. Shakespeare Soc. Am. Served with AUS, 1943-46. Recipient Sr. Distinguished Service award, Student Council award Bklyn. Coll., 1941; Shakespeare Curriculum Devel. award U. Ill., 1975; Friends of Lit. citation for Shakespearean Letters; Laureate medal Chgo. Cliff Dwellers, 1978; Research fellow Folger Shakespeare Library, 1957. Mem. Shakespeare Assn. Am. (chmn. Shakespeare's fellow dramatists sect.), Shakespeare Soc. Am. (dir. 1968—), Renaissance Assn. Am., Modern Lang. Assn. (chmn. seminar medieval and renaissance symbolism and allegory 1969; Midwest Sec. seminar on computer studies in humanities 1970-71, sect. chmn. 1972, Southeastern Renaissance Assn., Nat. Council Tchrs. English (chmn. Shakespeare sect. 1960, 61, 64). Author: His Exits and His Entrances: The Story of Shakespeare's Reputation, 1963; also numerous articles; contbr. revs. to newspapers. Founder, editor, pub.: The Shakespeare Newsletter, 1951—; editor Study Master Shakespeare Series, 1967-70, Library Shakespearean Scholarship and Criticism, 1966-70; mem. editorial bd. Shakespeare on Film News Letter, 1976—. Contbr. encys., bibliographies. U.S. corr. Shakespeare Survey, 1957-65. Home: 1217 Ashland Ave Evanston IL 60202 Office: Univ Illinois Circle Campus Chicago IL 60680. *When I was young I worried about money; now I worry about time. The longer I live the more I become aware of the truth of the last words of Cecil Rhodes: "So much to do; so little time to do it." There is the hope that what I'm doing now may give some pleasure when my time is spent.*

MARDIAN, SAMUEL, JR., constrn. co. exec.; b. Pasadena, Calif., June 24, 1919; s. Samuel Z. and Akabe (Lekerian) M.; A.A., Pasadena Jr. Coll., 1941; B.C.S., Southwestern U., 1941; m. Lucy Keshian, Dec. 1, 1942; children—Samuel, James Kenneth, Carol Ann, Douglas David, Steven Kermit. Auditor, Haskins & Sells, C.P.A.'s 1947; sec., treas. Mardian Constrn. Co., Phoenix, 1947-65, exec. v.p., treas., 1965-78, pres., 1978—; sec., treas. Glen-Mar Door Mfg. Co., Phoenix, 1947-68, exec. v.p., treas., 1968-72, pres., 1972—; dir. 1st Nat. Bank Ariz.; mayor City of Phoenix, 1960-64. Bd. dirs. Phoenix and Valley of the Sun YMCA, 1951-70, pres., 1965-67; mem. internat. com. U.S. and Can., 1954-58, mem. Pacific S.W. area bd., 1957- 66, pres. S.W. area, 1962-63, mem. nat. council, 1962-66, mem. planning com., 1964-65; steering com. Phoenix Community Council Recreation and Group Work Survey, 1957; mem. dean's adv. council Coll. Bus. Adminstrn. Ariz. State U., 1968-71; v.p. Valley Forward Assn., 1969-75, pres., 1975-77, chmn. bd., 1977—; chmn. Maricopa County Citizens Action Com., 1971-73; campaign mgr. Gov. Pyle, 1954; chmn. Senator Fannin Campaign Com. 1964, 70; chmn. Ariz. Com. to Re-elect Pres. Nixon, 1972; mem. citizen's adv. com. Madison Sch., 1953-54, trustee Madison Sch. Dist., 1957-59; bd. dirs. Phoenix Symphony Assn., 1959-70, v.p., 1962-65; treas. Citizens Conf. on Ariz. Cts.; trustee, treas. Phoenix Fine Arts Assn., v.p., 1970-76; bd. dirs. Phoenix chpt. NCCJ, Hosp. Devel. Assn. Maricopa County, 1964-65, Ariz. Kidney Found., 1964-67, State Compensation Fund Ariz., 1969-71, Comprehensive Health Planning Council of Maricopa County, 1974-75, Central Ariz. Project Assn., 1974—; bd. dirs. Combined Phoenix Met. Arts, 1966—, pres., 1972-74; mem. exec. bd. Theodore Roosevelt council Boy Scouts Am.; pres. Valley Beautiful Citizens Council, 1967-69; trustee Haigazian Coll. Beirut; bd. dirs. Ariz. State U. Found., 1976—. Served from pvt. to capt. Signal Corps, USAAF, 1941-46. Mem. Phoenix C. of C. (pres. 1973-74, dir., chmn. bus. and govt. div. 1970), League Ariz. Cities and Towns (exec. com. 1960-64), Am. Municipal Assn. (exec. com. 1962-63), Ariz. Acad. Pub. Affairs (dir., mem. exec. com. 1968-75, chmn. research com. 1968-72, 2d v.p. 1973-75), Newcomen Soc. N.Am. Republican. Methodist (exec. com., chmn. fin. commn., chmn. ofcl. bd.). Clubs: Kiwanis (dir. 1959), Ariz., Phoenix Country. Home: 7310 N 4th Dr Phoenix AZ 85021 Office: 3815 N Black Canyon Hwy Phoenix AZ 85015

MAREK, GEORGE RICHARD, mfg. exec., author; b. Vienna, Austria, July 13, 1902; s. Martin and Emily (Weissberger) M.; student Vienna U., 1918-20; m. Muriel Hepner, Aug. 19, 1926; 1 son, Richard. Came to U.S. 1920, naturalized, 1925. Vice pres. J. D. Tarcher Advt. Agy., 1930-50, Radio Corp. of Am., N.Y.C., 1950—; music editor Good Housekeeping mag., 1941-57. Mem. panel radio program Met. Opera Quiz. Clubs: Players, Dutch Treat (N.Y.C.). Author: A Front Seat at the Opera, 1948; Good Housekeeping Guide to Musical Enjoyment, 1949; Puccini, 1950; The World Treasury of Grand Opera, 1957; Opera as Theater, 1962; Richard Strauss: The Life of a Non-Hero, 1967; Beethoven: Biography of A Genius, 1969; Mendelssohn: Gentle Genius, 1971; The Eagles Die: Franz Joseph and Elizabeth of Austria, 1974; Toscanini: a biography, 1975; The Bed and the Throne: Isabella d'Este, 1976; Chopin: a biography, 1978. Home: 151 Central Park W New York NY 10023

MAREK, RICHARD WILLIAM, pub. co. exec.; b. N.Y.C., June 14, 1933; s. George R. and Muriel (Hepner) M.; B.A., Haverford Coll., 1955; M.A., Columbia, 1956; m. Margot Lynn Ravage, June 17, 1955; children—Elizabeth, Alexander. Writer, editor McCall's mag., N.Y.C., 1958-64; sr. editor Macmillan Pub. Co., N.Y.C., 1964-69; asso. dir. World Pub. Co., N.Y.C., 1969-72; editor-in-chief Dial Press subs. Dell Pub. Co., Inc., N.Y.C., 1972-76; pres., pub. Richard Marek Pubs., Inc., N.Y.C., 1977—. Served with AUS, 1956-58. Mem. Phi Beta Kappa. Home: 12 W 96th St New York City NY 10025 Office: 200 Madison Ave New York City NY 10016

MARELLA, PHILIP DANIEL, broadcasting co. exec.; b. Italy, Sept. 9, 1929; s. T. Joseph and Julia (Santolina) M.; came to U.S., 1930; B.S., Calif. State Coll., 1955; M.S., Syracuse U., 1956; m. Lucinda Minor, Dec. 30, 1955; children—Philip Daniel, Laura Ann, William Scott. Account exec. WGR-TV, Buffalo, 1956-57; account exec., sales mgr. WIIC-TV, Pitts., 1957-66; gen. mgr. WCHS-TV, Charleston, W.Va., 1966-68; v.p. radio and television Rollins, Inc., Atlanta, 1968-70; pres. WAVY-TV, Inc., Tidewater, Va., 1970—; v.p. Lin Broadcasting, Inc., N.Y.C., also dir.; pres., owner WMGC-TV, Binghamton, N.Y., 1978—. Bd. dirs. Salvation Army, 1966-68; bd. dirs., v.p. United Fund; bd. dirs. Portsmouth chpt. A.R.C., Tidewater Regional Health and Planning Commn. Served with USMC, 1948-49, 50-52. Mem. Nat. (v.p.), Va. assns. broadcasters, Variety Club Pitts., Radio and TV Club, Portsmouth (pres. elect), Norfolk, Newport News chambers commerce. Clubs: Cavalier Golf and Yacht (Virginia Beach, Va.); N.Y. Athletic. Home: 43 Pine Ridge Rd Greenwich CT 06830 Office: PO Box 813 Binghamton NY 13902

MAREN, THOMAS HARTLEY, educator, pharmacologist; b. N.Y.C., May 26, 1918; s. James Meyer and Roxane (Holstein) M.; A.B., Princeton, 1938, student Grad. Coll., 1940-42; M.D., Johns Hopkins, 1951; M.D. honoris causa, Uppsala U. (Sweden), 1977; m. Ruth Hendricks, Sept. 5, 1941; children—Peter, James, David. Research chemist Wallace Labs., 1938-43; chemotherapist Office Naval Research, 1943-46; instr. pharmacology Johns Hopkins Med. Sch., 1946-51; group leader chemotherapy div. Am. Cyanamid Co., 1951-55; prof., chmn. pharmacology and therapeutics U. Fla. Coll. Medicine, 1955-78, grad. research prof., 1978—. Recipient class award Princeton U. Mem. Am. Soc. Pharmacology and Exptl. Therapeutics (Theodore Weicker award 1979), So. Soc. Clin. Research, Assn. for Med. Sch. Pharmacology (pres. 1972-74), Johns Hopkins Soc. Scholars. Research in chemistry and physiology of carbonic anhydrase and drug devel. Home: 1228 SW 14th Ave Gainesville FL 32601

MARGACH, CLARENCE STUART, business exec.; b. Utica, N.Y., Jan. 8, 1915; s. Andrew Lewis and Jennie (Boyd) M.; m. Catharine Little, Feb. 26, 1938; children—William Charles, Vicki Louise. With Addressograph-Multigraph Corp., 1935—, v.p. research and engring. div., 1959-63, v.p. market research and product planning, 1963-66, v.p. edn. and tng., 1966-72, cons., 1972—; v.p. Patterson Corp., Tampa, Fla., 1973—; pres. Specialized Exec. Services, 1973—. Mem. Bus. Equipment Mfrs. Assn. (past chmn. bd.), Nat. Soc. Sales Tng. Execs. (chmn. tng. research com.), Am. Soc. Tng. and Devel. Club: Pembroke Lakes Country (Hollywood, Fla.). Office: 1121 W Fairway Rd Pembroke Pines FL 33026

MARGAIN, HUGO B., Mexican diplomat; b. Mexico City, Feb. 13, 1913; Law Degree, Nat. U. Mexico, 1937; m. Margarita Charles, 1941; 6 children. Prof. constl. law Nat. U. Mex., 1947-52, prof. fiscal legis., 1952—; dir.-gen. Fed. Retail Mchts. Taxes, 1951, Fed. Income Tax Bur., 1952-59; exec. officer Ministry Industry and Commerce, 1959-61; under-sec. industry and commerce Mexico, 1961-64; dir. Nat. Commn. Profit Sharing, 1963-64; Mexican ambassador to U.S., 1964-70, AEP to U.S., Washington, 1977—; minister of fin. Mexico, 1970-73; Mexican ambassador to U.K., also accredited to Ireland, 1973-76. Author: Importance of Fiscal Law in the Economic Development, 1960; An Adequate Public Administration, 1971. Address: Embassy of Mexico 2829 16th St NW Washington DC 20009. *I have always tried to model my conduct on the old aphorism: "Equate your thinking to your life."*

MARGETTS, WALTER THOMAS, JR., corp. exec., lawyer, former state treas.; b. N.Y.C., Jan. 23, 1905; s. Walter and Edith Pearl (Lawson) M.; student Am. Inst. Banking, 1923-25, N.Y. U., 1925-26; advanced agronomy Columbia U., 1936; LL.B., St. Lawrence U., 1928, LL.M., 1930; LL.D., Fairleigh Dickinson U., 1953; m. Josephine Sharon, July 18, 1935; children—Sharon McLean Margetts Doremus, Cynthia Margetts Robinson, Walter Thomas, Susan Meredith Margetts Connell. With Bklyn. Trust Co., 1923-29; asso. Beekman, Bogue & Clark, N.Y.C., 1929-35; partner law firm Bainton, McNaughton & Douglas, 1935-43; asso. McLanahan, Merritt & Ingraham, 1943-54; past chmn. bd. Laythan Foundry Inc., Paterson, N.J.; chmn. exec. com., dir. Franklin Bank, Paterson; pres. Holly Hill Corp.; past dir., chmn. pension-fin. exec. com. U.G.I. Corp., now cons.; pres., treas., dir. Hudson Rapid Tubes Corp., Hudson and Manhattan Corp., Washington Valley Farms, Inc.; dir., chmn. audit fin. com. Kayser-Roth Corp., N.Y.C.; mem. N.Y. adv. bd. Am. Mut. Ins. Co.; dir. SFM Corp., Plainfield, N.J., Tech-Torch Co., Carlstadt, N.J.; chmn. Komline Sanderson Engring. Corp., Peapack, N.J.; dir., v.p., treas. Found. Life Ins. Co. Am., Chatham, N.J.; cons. Vornado Inc., Garfield, N.J.; dir. Automatic Data Processing Corp., Clifton, N.J.; trustee N.J. Dental Service Plan, Inc. Industry mem. Nat. War Labor Bd., 1943-45; treas. State of N.J., 1949-54; chmn. N.J. Mediation Bd., 1945-49, N.J. Commn. Intergovtl. Relations; pres. N.J. Citizen's Transp. Council; mem. adv. bd. on econ. devel. U.S. Dept. Commerce, Washington, 1970—; past chmn., treas. N.J. Republican Fin. Com.; N.J. del. Rep. Conv.; presdl. elector from N.J., 1964; dir., former pres. Passaic Taxpayers Assn.; bd. dirs. Tax Found., Inc.; bd. govs. Passaic Gen. Hosp., N.J.; chmn. bd. trustees, dir. N.J. Camp Blind Children, Inc.; pres., trustee Frost Valley Assn.; trustee Margetts Found. Fellow Fairleigh Dickinson U. (vice chmn. bd.), Wroxton Coll. Mem. Patrolmen's Benevolent Assn. (hon. life), Spring Valley Hunt Assn., Am., N.Y. State, Ariz. bar assns., N.J. Foundrymen's Assn. (pres., dir.), N.J. Taxpayers Assn. (past pres.), Am. Arbitration Assn. (panel arbitrators), N.Y. Zoology Soc. (life), St. Andrews Soc. (life), Alpha Chi Epsilon, Delta Theta Phi. Clubs: Downtown Athletic (life); Met., Nat. Press, Capitol Hill (Washington); Essex (Newark); Morristown, Morris County Golf (Morristown, N.J.); Elks (life mem.), Masons. Home: Holly Hills Farms Blue Mill Rd RFD Morristown NJ 07960

MARGILETH, ANDREW MENGES, physician, ret. naval officer; b. Cin., July 17, 1920; s. Elmer C. and Bertha (Menges) M.; B.A., Washington and Jefferson Coll., 1943; B.S., Mass. Inst. Tech., 1944; M.D., U. Cin., 1947; m. Ellee Nichols, Jan. 20, 1951; children—R. Lynn, Andrew C., Ellee C. Commd. ensign USN, 1943, advanced through grades to capt., 1963; intern, resident pediatrics Nat. Naval Med. Center, 1947-49; resident pediatrics Johns Hopkins Hosp., 1949-50; chief pediatrics U.S. Naval Hosps., Corona, Calif., 1953-57, Chelsea, Mass., 1957-63, Bethesda, Md., 1963-67; council mem. Nat. Inst. Child Health and Human Devel., 1963-67; sr. attending physician Childrens Hosp., Washington; asso. clin. prof. pediatrics Med. Sch., Howard U., prof. pediatrics Med. Sch., George Washington U., Uniformed Services U. Health Scis. Fellow Am. Acad. Pediatrics, A.C.P.; mem. Assn. Mil. Surgeons, Am. Pediatric Soc., Soc. Pediatric Dermatologists, Alpha Omega Alpha. Contbr. chpt. to Current Pediatric Therapy, 1970, 72, 74, 76, 80, to textbooks Neonatology, 1975, Pediatrics, 1977, 80, Medicine, 1978, Pediatric Dermatology, 1978; also articles profl. jours. Co-editor Clin. Procs. of Children's Hosp. Nat. Med. Center. Home: 6901 Old Stage Rd Rockville MD 20852 Office: Uniformed Services U Health Scis 4301 Jones Bridge Rd Bethesda MD 20014

MARGOLIASH, EMANUEL, biochemist; b. Cairo, Feb. 10, 1920; s. Wolf and Bertha (Kotler) M.; B.A., Am. U. Beirut, 1940, M.A., 1942, M.D., 1945; m. Sima Beshkin, Aug. 22, 1945; children—Reuben, Daniel. Research fellow, lectr., acting head cancer research labs. Hebrew U., Jerusalem, 1945-58; research asso. U. Utah, Salt Lake City, 1958-60, McGill U., Montreal, Que., Can., 1960-62; research fellow Abbott Labs., N.Chicago, Ill., 1962-69, sr. research fellow, 1969-71, head protein sect., 1962-71; prof. biochemistry and molecular biology Northwestern U., Evanston, Ill., 1971—; mem. com. on cytochrome nomenclature Internat. Union Biochemistry, 1962—; mem. adv. com. Plant Research Lab., Mich. State U./AEC, 1967-72; co-chmn. Gordon Research Conf. on Proteins, 1967. Fellow Am. Acad. Arts and Scis.; mem. Nat. Acad. Scis., Biochem. Soc. (Keilin Meml. lectr. 1970), Harvey Soc. (lectr. 1970-71), Am. Soc. Biol. Chemists (publs. com. 1973-76), Am. Chem. Soc., Canadian Biochem. Soc., Soc. Developmental Biology, N.Y., Ill. acads. scis., Am. Soc. Naturalists, Sigma Xi (nat. lectr. 1972-73, 74-77). Editorial bd. Jour. Biol. Chemistry, 1966-72, Biochem. Genetics, 1966—, Jour. Molecular Evolution, 1971—; contbr. articles and revs. to sci. jours. Home: 353 Madison Ave Glencoe IL 60022 Office: Dept Biochemistry and Molecular Biology Northwestern U Evanston IL 60201

MARGOLIN, ABRAHAM EUGENE, lawyer; b. St. Joseph, Mo., Oct. 16, 1907; s. Jacob and Rebecca (Cohn) M.; LL.B., J.D., Washington U., St. Louis, 1929; m. Florence Solow, Feb. 1, 1931; children—Robert J., Judith (Mrs. Goodman), James S. Admitted to Mo. bar, 1929, since practiced in Kansas City; sr. partner firm Margolin & Kirwan, 1949—. Dir. Security Nat. Bank Kansas City, City Bond & Mortgage Co., Tension Envelope Corp., Massman Constrn. Co. Mem. nat. exec. council Am. Jewish Com., mem. nat. council Am. Jewish Joint Distbn. Com., 1970; v.p. Jewish Fedn. and Council Greater Kansas City, 1968—; mem. Pres.'s Council, also fellow, Brandeis U., Waltham, Mass., 1970—; mem. council of fellows Nelson Gallery Found. Chmn. bd. dirs., chmn. bd. trustees Menorah Med. Center, Kansas City; bd. dirs. Met. Health Planning Council Kansas City, Truman Med. Center, Kansas City, Mo.; bd. dirs., pres. central governing bd. Children's Mercy Hosp. Kansas City, Mo.; trustee B'nai B'rith Found. Recipient Brotherhood citation NCCJ, 1978. Mem. Am., Mo. bar assns., Lawyers' Assn. Kansas City, Supreme Ct. Hist. Soc., Order Coif, Delta Sigma Rho, Pi Lambda Phi. Jewish (life dir. congregation). Mem. B'nai B'rith. Clubs: Oakwood Country (Kansas City, Mo.); Nat. Lawyers (Washington); Racquet (Palm Springs, Calif.). Home: 1201 W 57th St Kansas City MO 64113 Office: 1000 United Missouri Bank Bldg 928 Grand Ave Kansas City MO 64106

MARGOLIN, EDWARD, transp. cons.; b. Atlantic City, Oct. 17, 1912; s. Max and Katie (Henzeloff) M.; B.S., Temple U., 1935; grad. study U. Pa., 1937-40, Am. U., 1943-45; m. Freda Ladin, Mar. 27, 1938; children—Meryl L., Michele L. Domestic, export traffic mgmt. pvt. industry and govt.; with Sears, Roebuck & Co., 1936-41; China Def. supplies Lend-Lease program, 1941-42; with U.S. Treasury Dept., 1942-45; transp. economist Dept. Interior, 1945-47; supervisory transp. economist, chief policy staff, asst. to under sec. of commerce for transp. Dept. Commerce, 1948-59; dir. bur. transp. econs. and statistics ICC, 1959-65, dir. bur. econs., 1965-73, ret., 1973, cons. transp. and econs.; lectr. Wharton Sch. U. Pa., 1973—; dir. transp. programs, dir. Center for Transp. Studies, Am. U., Washington, 1975-77; cons. Nat. Transp. Policy Study Commn., 1977-79, Nat. Alcohol Fuel Com., 1979. Chmn. coms. Transp. Research Bd., Nat. Acad. Scis. Recipient Certificate award Dept. Commerce, 1957, Meritorious Service award, 1950. Mem. Am. Soc. Traffic and Transp., Am. Econ. Assn., Am. Statis. Assn. (past nat. pres.), Transp. Research Forum, Nat. Def. Transp. Assn. Home: 8500 Freyman Dr Chevy Chase MD 20015

MARGOLIN, EPHRAIM, lawyer; b. Berlin, Oct. 16, 1926; s. Julius and Eva (Spector) M.; came to U.S., 1957, naturalized, 1962; B.A., Hebrew U., Jerusalem, 1949; LL.B., Yale U., 1952; postgrad. (Univ. fellow) U. Pa. Law Sch., 1953; m. Gilda Lasko. June 24, 1954; children—Alexander Zev, Evan David. Admitted to Israel bar, 1956, Calif. bar, 1962, U.S. Supreme Ct. bar, 1970; clk. Supreme Ct. Israel, Jerusalem, 1956-57; gen. counsel ACLU of No. Calif., San Francisco, 1970—; atty. State of Israel for Pacific N.W., 1969—; adj. prof. law Hastings Coll. Law, U. Calif., San Francisco, 1971-72, 80; chmn. Practicing Law Inst. Ann. Defending Criminal Cases, 1976, 77, 78, 79, 80; lectr. in field. Pres. Am. Jewish Congress of No. Calif., 1968, Calif. Criminal Defence Bar, 1973; active Jewish Welfare Fedn. N.Calif. Mem. Lawyer's Club San Francisco (dir. 1968—, sec.). Author: State, School and Family Casebook, 1973, 75, 79; Frontiers of Criminal Law and Procedure, 1976, 77, 78, 79; contbr. numerous articles to profl. jours. Home: 60 Scenic Way San Francisco CA 94121 Office: 240 Stockton St San Francisco CA 94108

MARGOLIN, HAROLD, metallurgist; b. Hartford, Conn., July 12, 1922; s. Aaron David and Sonia (Krupnikoff) M.; B.Engring., Yale U., 1943, M.Engring., 1947, D.Eng. (Internat. Nickel fellow) 1947-49), 1950; m. Elaine Marjorie Rose, July 4, 1946; children—Shelley, Deborah, Amy. Research asso., research scientist, research div. N.Y. U., N.Y.C., 1949-56; asso. prof. metall. engring., 1956-62, prof., 1962-73; prof. phys. metallurgy Poly. Inst. N.Y., Bklyn., 1973—; cons. in field. Served with USNR, 1944-46. Fellow Am. Soc. Metals (edn. award N.Y. chpt. 1967); mem. AIME, Metals Soc. (Britain), Yale Engring. Assn., AAAS, Sigma Xi. Democrat. Jewish. Contbg. author books; contbr. articles to profl. publs.; patentee in field. Home: 19 Crescent Rd Larchmont NY 10538 Office: 333 Jay St Brooklyn NY 11201. *Achievement, work, and refusal to accept defeat are intimately intertwined.*

MARGOLIN, STUART, actor, dir.; b. Davenport, Iowa, Jan. 31. Appeared in TV films Intruders, The California Kid, This Is the West That Was, Lanigan's Rabbi, Perilous Voyage; regular on TV series Nichols, The Rockford Files; other TV appearances include He and She, Bewitched, It Takes a Thief, That Girl, Partridge Family, MASH, Gunsmoke, Mary Tyler Moore Show, My World and Welcome to It, Love, American Style, Rhoda; dir. TV films Texas Wheelers, Suddenly Love; dir. episodes of The Rockford Files; scored movies and TV shows; writer film Ballad of Andy Crocker. Recipient Emmy award Nat. Acad. TV Arts and Scis., 1979. Office: care Public Relations Universal TV 100 Universal City Studios Universal City CA 91608*

MARGOLIS, DAVID I., diversified co. exec.; b. N.Y.C., Jan. 24, 1930; s. Benjamin and Celia (Kosofsky) M.; B.A., Coll. City N.Y., 1950, M.B.A., 1952; post-grad. N.Y.U., 1952-55; m. Barbara Schneider, Sept. 7, 1958; children—Brian, Robert, Peter, Nancy. Asst. treas. Raytheon Co., 1956-59; asst. to pres. and treas. IT&T, N.Y.C., 1959-63; v.p., treas. Fairbanks Whitney Corp., N.Y.C., became Colt Industries, Inc., formerly exec. v.p., treas., dir., now pres.; dir. Istel Fund; mem. N.Y. State Emergency Fin. Control Bd. for City N.Y., 1975-77. Mem. Fin. Execs. Inst. Address: Colt Industries Inc 430 Park Ave New York NY 10022

MARGOLIS, GEORGE, physician, educator; b. Montgomery, W.Va., Dec. 12, 1914; s. Simon and Sara Reba (Blumberg) M.; A.B., Johns Hopkins, 1936; M.D., Duke, 1940; M.A. (hon.), Dartmouth, 1966; m. Anne Maria McCabe, Sept. 23, 1950; children—Susan, George McCabe, Joshua David, Dan Leo. Intern pathology Duke Med. Sch., 1940-41, asst. resident pathology, then resident, 1941-44, prof. pathology Duke Med. Sch., prof. pathology, chmn. dept. Med. Coll. Va., Richmond, 1959-63; prof. pathology Dartmouth Med Sch., 1963—. Served to maj., M.C., AUS, 1944-47; ETO. Home: Rennie Rd Lyme Center NH 03769 Office: Dartmouth Med Sch Hanover NH 03755

MARGOLIS, HENRY MELVILLE, industrialist; b. N.Y.C., Nov. 2, 1909; s. Nathan and Dora (Boverman) M.; B.S. in Social Sci., City Coll. N.Y., 1929; J.D., N.Y.U. 1932; m. Nexhmie Zaimi, Feb. 1, 1940; 1 son, Eric S.; m. 2d Irene Broza, May 21, 1956. Admitted to N.Y. bar, 1933; practice in N.Y.C., 1934-44; engaged in industry, 1945—; chmn. bd. Elgin Nat. Watch Co., 1960—, Aero-Flow Dynamics, Inc., 1957—, Schmieg Industries, Inc., 1955—, Cortland Line Co., Inc., 1959—; pres., dir. C. E. Jamieson & Co. (Dom.), Ltd., 1952—; co-owner, dir. Cafe Chambord, N.Y.C., 1950—; dir. Alaska Airlines; producer plays The Reclining Figure, 1954, Tiger at the Gates, 1955, Moby Dick (London), 1955, King Lear (Orson Welles), 1956, Hidden River, 1957. Once More, With Feeling, 1958. Alternate del. NATO Conf., 1959. Bd. dirs. N.Y. Sch. for Nursery Years, Am. com. Weizman Inst. Sci., Alvin Ailey Dance Theatre Found., 1975; trustee Internat. Fund for Concerned Photography; chmn. bd. Internat. Center Photography, 1974—. Served with USMCR, 1944-45. Home: 785 Park Ave New York City NY 10021 Office: 2051 Ambassador Dr Windsor ON Canada

MARGOLIS, JOSEPH, author, educator; b. Newark, May 16, 1924; s. Harry J. and Bluma (Goldfarb) M.; B.A., Drew U., 1947; M.A., Columbia, 1950, Ph.D., 1953; m. Clorinda Goltra Hunter, Aug. 24, 1968; children—Ann, Paul, Michael, Jennifer, Ellen. Prof. philosophy, sr. research asso. psychiatry U. Cin., 1960-65; vis. prof. U. Minn., 1964; vis. prof. philosophy and psychology Case Western Res., 1965; vis. prof. philosophy Columbia, 1965; prof., head dept. philosophy U. Western Ont., 1965-67; vis. prof. philosophy U. Toronto, 1967-68, U. Calgary, U. Utah, 1968; prof. philosophy Temple U., Phila., 1968—; vis. prof. philosophy N.Y.U., 1970-71; spl. fellow NIMH, 1962-63; asso. editor Mt. Adams Rev., 1970-71. Cons. Phila. Geriatric Center, 1973—; exec. com. Conf. on Methods in Philosophy and Scis., 1978. Served with AUS, 1943-45. Decorated Purple Heart; recipient Can. Council grant, 1966, 67. Mem. Am. Philos. Assn., AAUP. Author: Philosophy Looks at the Arts, 1962, rev. edit., 1978; The Language of Art and Art Criticism, 1965; Psychotherapy and Morality, 1966; Contemporary Ethical Theory, 1966; An Introduction to Philosophical Inquiry, 1968, 2d edit., 1978; Fact and Existence, 1969; Values and conduct, 1971; Knowledge and Existence, 1973; Negativities: The Limits of Life and Death, 1975; Art and Philosophy, 1979; Persons and Minds, 1978. Editor: Philos. Monographs, 1975—; mem. adv. bd. Social Theory and Practice, 1972—; cons. editor Jour. Theory of Social Behavior, 1976—; contbg. editor Book Forum, 1972—; cons. Jour. Critical Analysis, 1973—; cons. editor Behaviorism, 1976—; editorial bd. Philosophy and Tech. Ann., 1976—, Speculative Letters, 1978—. Home: 500 Catharine St Philadelphia PA 19147

MARGOLIS, JULIUS, educator; b. N.Y.C., Sept. 26, 1920; s. Sam and Fannie (Weiner) M.; B.S.S., City Coll. N.Y., 1941; Ph.M. in Econs., U. Wis., 1943; M.P.A. in Econs., Harvard, 1947, Ph.D., 1949; m. Doris Lubetsky, Oct. 30, 1942; children—Jane S., Carl W. Instr. econs. Tufts Coll., 1947-48; asst. prof. econs. and planning U. Chgo., 1948-51; asst. prof. econs. Stanford, 1951-54; prof. bus adminstrn. U. Calif. at Berkeley, 1954-64; prof. econs. and engring. econ. systems Stanford, 1964-69; prof., dir. Fels Center of Govt., U. Pa., 1969-76; prof. econs. U. Calif. at Irvine, 1976—; cons. to govt. and industry, 1958—. Served with AUS, 1943-46. Mem. Am. Econ. Assn., Royal Econ. Soc. Author: (with others) The Public Economy of Urban Communities, 1965; (with others) The Northern California's Water Industry, 1966; (with others) Public Economics, 1969; also articles. Home: 2337-D Ave Sevilla Laguna Hills CA 92653 Office: Social Scis Univ Calif Irvine CA 92717

MARGOLIS, LEO, biologist; b. Montreal, Que., Can., Dec. 18, 1927; B.Sc., McGill U., 1948, M.Sc., 1950, Ph.D., 1952; m. Ruth Anne Lall; children—Rhonda Lee, Robert Allan, Murray Howard, Conrad Anton. Research scientist Pacific Biol. Sta., Can. Dept. Environ., Fish and Marine Service, Nanaimo, B.C., 1952-67, head various research divs., 1967-77, head fish culture research div., resource services br., fisheries and oceans Can., 1977—; co-chmn. Can. Com. on Fish Diseases, 1970-73; mem. com. on biology and research Internat. N. Pacific Fisheries Commn., 1971—; mem. adv. bd. sci. info. and publs. Fisheries and Oceans Can., 1979—; mem. research evaluation com. Sci. Council B.C., 1979—. Pres., B.C. Amateur Hockey Assn., 1963-66, hon. v.p., 1966—. Fellow Royal Soc. Can.; mem. Canadian Soc. Zoologists (chmn. parasitology sect. 1977-78), Am. Soc. Parasitologists, Am. Fisheries Soc., Wildlife Disease Assn. Asso. editor Can. Jour. Zoology, 1971—; mem. editorial bd. Jour. of Parasitology, 1977—; author 2 books; contbr. articles on parasites and diseases of fishes and other aquatic animals, and on biology of salmon to various profl. jours. Office: Pacific Biol Sta Nanaimo BC V9R 5K6 Canada

MARGOLIS, PHILIP MARCUS, psychiatrist, educator; b. Lima, Ohio, July 7, 1925; s. Harry Sterling and Clara (Brunner) M.; B.A. magna cum laude, U. Minn., 1945, M.D., 1948; m. Nancy Nupuf, July 26, 1959; children—Cynthia, Marc, David, Laurence. Intern, Milw. County Hosp., 1948-49; resident VA Hosp. and U. Minn., 1949-52, Mass. Gen. Hosp. and Harvard U., Boston, 1952-54; instr. U. Minn., Milw., 1953-55; asst. prof. dept. psychiatry Med. Sch., U. Chgo., 1955-60, asso. prof., 1960-66; prof. psychiatry Med. Sch., U. Mich., 1966—, prof. community mental health, 1968—; chief psychiat. inpatient service U. Chgo. Hosps. and Clinics, 1956-66; dir. Washtenaw County Community Mental Health Center, Ann Arbor, 1966-72; dir. adult inpatient service neuropsychiat. inst. U. Mich., Ann Arbor, 1971-72, dir. adult services, 1973-75; cons. Forensic Psychiat. Center, State of Mich., 1974—, coordinator med. student edn. program, 1975-78, dir., 1978—. Recipient Commonwealth Fund fellow award, 1964. Fellow Am. Coll. Psychiatrists, Am. Psychiat. Assn. (chmn. consultation bd. 1973-75, membership com. 1977—, chmn. membership com. 1979—); mem. Am. Orthopsychiat. Assn., Washtenaw County Med. Soc., Mich. Psychiat. Soc. (pres.-elect 1979-80, pres. 1980-81), Internat. Assn. Social Psychiatry, World Fedn. Mental Health, Am. Acad. Psychoanalysis, Nat. Acad. Psychiatry and Law. Author: Guide for Mental Health Workers, 1970; Patient Power: The Development of a Therapeutic Community in a General Hospital, 1974; also articles. Cons. editor Community Mental Health jour., 1967—. Home: 228 Riverview Dr Ann Arbor MI 48104 Office: 900 Wall St Ann Arbor MI 48105

MARGOLIUS, SIDNEY SENIER, journalist, author; b. Perth Amboy, N.J., May 3, 1911; s. Max and Helen (Senier) M.; B.A., Rutgers U., 1934; m. Esther Papert, Nov. 14, 1942; 1 son, Richard. Asso. editor Retail Exec., N.Y.C., 1937-40; consumer editor Newspaper PM, N.Y.C., 1940-42, 45-48; syndicated columnist trade union newspapers, 1949—, United Features Syndicate, N.Y.C., 1971—; author 20 books, including: Consumers Guide to Better Buying - The Innocent Consumer vs. The Exploiters, 1967, new edit., 1972, Your Guide to Successful Retirement, 1969, How to Make the Most of Your Money, 1970, Great American Food Hoax, 1971, Health Food Facts and Fakes, 1973 (Nat. Press Club award 1973); former bd. dirs. Consumers Union; mem. Pres.'s Consumer Adv. Council-Nat. Comml. Product Safety; cons. Pres.'s Commn. on Consumer Interests, FTC; mem. N.Y. State and Nassau County Consumer Adv. Com. Recipient Media award Family Service Assn. Am., 1969, award Consumer Fedn. Am., 1972, Internat. Labor Press Assn., 1962, N.Y. Central Labor Council, 1962, Nat. Council Sr. Citizens. Home and Office: 74 Davis Rd Port Washington NY 11050

MARGRAVE, JOHN LEE, coll. dean, chemist; b. Kansas City, Kans., Apr. 13, 1924; s. Orville Frank and Bernice J. (Hamilton) M.; B.S. in Engring. Physics, U. Kans., 1948, Ph.D. in Chemistry, 1950; m. Mary Lou Davis, June 11, 1950; children—David Russell, Karen Sue. AEC postdoctoral fellow U. Calif. at Berkeley, 1951-52; from instr. to prof. chemistry U. Wis., Madison, 1952-63; prof. chemistry Rice U., 1963—, chmn. dept., 1967-72, dean advanced studies and research, 1972—; Reilly lectr. Notre Dame, 1968; vis. distinguished prof. U. Wis., 1968, U. Iowa, 1969, U. Colo., 1975, Ga. Inst. Tech., 1978, U. Tex. at Austin, 1978; Seydel-Wooley lectr. Ga. Inst. Tech., 1970; Dupont lectures U. S.C., 1971; Abbott lectures U. N.D., 1972, Cyanamid lectrs. U. Conn., 1973; cons. to govt. and industry, 1954—. Pres. Mar Chem., Inc., 1970—, High Temperature Sci., Inc., 1976—. Dir. Rice Design Center; v.p. U. Kans. Research Found., Gulf Univs. Research Consortium, Energy Research and Edn. Found., 1972-78. Served with AUS, 1943-46; capt. Res. Sloan research fellow, 1957-58; Guggenheim fellow, 1960; recipient Kiekhofer Teaching award U. Wis., 1957; IR-100 award for CFX lubricant powder, 1970, Tex. Honor Scroll award, 1978. Fellow Am. Inst. Chemists, Tex. Acad. Sci., Am. Phys. Soc.; mem. Nat. Acad. Sci., Am. Chem. Soc. (Inorganic Chemistry award 1967, Southwest Regional award 1973), Am. Ceramic Soc., A.A.A.S., Electrochem. Soc., Faraday Soc., Tex. Philos. Soc., Am. Soc. Mass Spectrometry (dir.), Sigma Xi, Omicron Delta Kappa, Sigma Tau, Tau Beta Pi, Alpha Chi Sigma. Methodist. Contbr. profl. jours. Contbg. editor; Characterization of High Temperature Vapors, 1967; Mass. Spectrometry in Inorganic Chemistry, 1968. Procs. editor Jour. High Temperature Science, 1969—; editor Procs. XXIII and XXIV Confs. on Mass Spectrometry, 1975, 76. Patentee in field. Home: 5012 Tangle Ln Houston TX 77056

MARGULIES, HAROLD, govt. ofcl.; b. Sioux Falls, S.D., Feb. 13, 1918; s. Samuel Saul and Nellie (Graceman) M.; A.B., U. Minn., 1938, M.S. (Mayo Found.), 1948, D.Sc. (hon.), 1974; B.S., U. S.D., 1940, D.Sc. (hon.), 1972; M.D., U. Tenn., 1942; m. Marjory Gutfreund, Apr. 12, 1952; children—Marc, Amy. Intern Iowa Meth. Hosp., Des Moines, 1943-44; fellow in internal medicine Mayo Clinic, 1944-45, 46-49; practice medicine, specializing in internal medicine and cardiology, Des Moines, 1949-61; prof. medicine, party chief, mem. advisory group Ind. U. contract AID Postgrad. Med. Center, Karachi, Pakistan, 1961-64; asso. dir. div. internat. med. edn., dir. AID contract Assn. Am. Med. Colls., Washington, 1965-67; asso. dir. socio-econ. activities div. AMA, Washington, 1967-68, sec. council on health manpower, 1968-69; dep. asst. adminstr. program planning and evaluation Health Services and Mental Health Adminstrn., HEW, Rockville, Md., 1969-70, dir. regional med. programs, service, 1970-73, dep. adminstr. Health Resources Adminstrn., 1973-79, spl. asst. environ. health USPHS, 1979—. Cons. internal medicine VA, 1949-61; dir. electrocardiographic lab Iowa Med. Hosp., Des Moines, 1949-61, also dir. edn., 1949-59, and mem. teaching staff, 1949-61; adviser med. edn. Eastern Mediterranean regional office WHO, Alexanderia, Egypt, 1965-66; cons. for Pakistan programs evaluation White House Office Sci. and Tech., 1966-67, Nat. Advisory Commn. on Health Manpower, 1966-67. Trustee Des Moines Art Center, 1958-61. Served with USNR, 1945-46. Diplomate Am. Bd. Internal Medicine. Fellow A.C.P., Am. Public Health Assn.; mem. AAAS Mayo Alumni Assn. Contbr. articles to profl. jours. Home: 11401 S Glen Rd Potomac MD 20854 Office: 5600 Fishers Ln Rockville MD 20857

MARGULIES, JOSEPH, artist; b. Austria, July 7, 1896; s. Elias and Mary (Schachter) M.; brought to U.S. in infancy; ed. Cooper Union, Arts High Sch., Ethical Culture Sch., Nat. Acad. Design, Art Students League (all N.Y.C.), also in Paris, Vienna and Rome; m. Mary Polisuk, Nov. 22, 1921; 1 son, Herbert Felix. Formerly instr., Coll. City N.Y. Prin. works, portraits of many famous Americans. Represented collections numerous large galleries and museums throughout U.S., including Nat. Portrait Gallery Smithsonian Instn., also graphics in Library Congress. Recipient Chandler 1st prize in black and white at Salmangundi, in oil, North Shore Art Assn., for best portrait, Rockport Art Assn.; Louis E. Seley purchase prize Salmagundi Club, 1959; Gold medal for the black and white Am. Artists Profl. League, 1965; Gorton's of Gloucester Seas of the World award for oil Rockport Art Assn., 1970; Acad. Artists award for lithograph Springfield Mus., 1970; Stow Wengeroth award, 1974, 79; Eric Hudson Meml. award for Drypoint, 1974; Gold medal for graphics Acad. Artists Assn., 1976; Gold medal Acad. Artists Assn. for Graphics, 1977; Hugh Botts Meml. award Salmagundi Club, 1977. Mem. North Shore (award 1977), Rockport art assns., Soc. Am. Graphic Artists and Etchers, Art Students League, Louis C. Tiffany Guild, Audubon Artists, Provincetown Art Assn., Am. Water Color Soc., Allied Artists Am., Soc. Western Artists. Contbr. articles to profl. publs. Club: Salmagundi. Home: 27 W 67th St New York NY 10023 also 15 Grapevine Rd East Glouster MA 01930

MARGULIS, LYNN ALEXANDER, biologist; b. Chgo., Mar. 5, 1938; d. Morris and Leone (Wise) Alexander; A.B., U. Chgo., 1957; A.M., U. Wis., 1960; Ph.D., U. Calif., Berkeley, 1965; m. Thomas N. Margulis, Jan. 18, 1967; children—Dorion Sagan, Jeremy Sagan, Zachary Margulis, Jenny Margulis. Mem. faculty Boston U., 1963—, asst. prof. biology, 1967-71, asso. prof., 1971-77, prof., 1977—; coordinator biology Colombia program Peace Corps, summer 1965, 66; Sherman Fairchild Disting. scholar Calif. Inst. Tech., 1976-77. Guggenheim fellow, 1979. Fellow AAAS; mem. Nat. Acad. Sci. (chmn. com. planetary biology and chem. evolution). Author: Origin of Eukaryotic Cells, 1970; contbr. articles to profl. jours. Office: 2 Cummington St Boston MA 02215. *We must, as E. M. Forster admonished, "only connect" and lower our growth rate. The sciences, the quest for knowledge about the universe, life and man, are intrinsically united. Only small minds arbitrarily chop them into disciplines. Like all other species ever to have lived on Earth, ours too will be replaced. The quality of that demise depends directly on our attitudes toward birth and death and their control.*

MARGUTTI, VICTOR MARIO, physician; b. Oakland, Calif., May 22, 1906; s. Louis Henry and Estelle (Rodust) M.; A.B., U. Calif. at Berkeley, 1931; D.O., Coll. Osteo. Physicians and Surgeons, Los Angeles, 1945; M.D., Calif. Coll. Medicine, 1962; Ph.D. Fremont Coll., Okla., 1977; m. Mary Belle Dibble, Nov. 25, 1933; children—Marilyn (Mrs. William Gary Pickens), Laura (Mrs. Michael Kramer), Elizabeth. Practice osteopathy, Elsinore, Calif., 1946-48, Pasadena, Calif., 1948-55, San Diego, 1955—; practice medicine, specializing in internal medicine, especially homeotherapeutics and psychosomatic medicine, San Diego, 1962—. Diplomate Am. Bd. Homeotherapeutics. Fellow Royal Soc. Health (London), Am. Inst. Homeopathy (pres. 1972-73), Calif. Homeopathic Soc. (pres. 1973-74, 76-77); mem. Am. Med. Writers Assn., Am. Pub. Health Assn., Internat. Platform Assn. Club: Commonwealth (San Francisco). Contbr. articles to profl. jours. Office: 1508 W Lewis St San Diego CA 92103. *Mind is the key to man, and man consists of what he thinks, does and loves. Man, as mind, can be brilliant, dramatic, and intense, and so filled with self-adulation that "truth," which is only relative at best, becomes over-laden with ideas and incrustations of organization, with little relation to reality. Knowledge is the result of study. Wisdom is the fructification of study and time resulting in the consciousness of being. Thus, consciousness is the ultimate of ultimates. Consciousness itself expresses through belief, faith, hope, and love; and the greatest of these is love, for without this all is in vain, for we indeed become as the crashing of brass and the tinkle of cymbals.*

MARICHAL, JUAN, educator; b. Tenerife, Spain, Feb. 2, 1922; s. Jose Lopez Marizatt and Concepcion M.; student U. Mex., 1942-45; M.A. Princeton U., 1948 Ph.D., 1949; M.A. (hon.), Harvard U., 1958; m. Solita Salinas, June 8, 1947; children—Carlos, Miguel (dec.). Mem. faculty Harvard U., 1949-53, 58—, prof. Romance langs. and lit., 1961—, chmn. dept. Romance langs., 1966-70; asso. prof. Bryn Mawr Coll., 1953-58. Mem. ednl. adv. bd. Guggenheim Found. Guggenheim fellow, 1959, 72; fellow OAS, 1960. Fellow Am. Acad. Arts and Scis.; corr. mem. Hispanic Soc. Am. Author: La voluntad de estilo, 1957; El nuevo pensamiento politico espanol, 1966; La vocacion de Manuel Azana, 1968; Tres voces de Pedro Salinas, 1975. Editor: (Pedro Salinas) Poesias completas, 1955, Teatro completo, 1957, Ensayos de literatura hispanica, 1958; (Manuel Azana) Obras Completas, 4 vols., 1966; Luminous reality (collective volume homage to Jorge Guillen), 1969; Cuatro fases de la historia intelectual latinoamericana, 1978. Home: 29 Lancaster St Cambridge MA 02140

MARIELLA, RAYMOND P., chemist, assn. exec.; b. Phila., Sept. 5, 1919; s. Angelo Raphael and Sophia (Peel) M.; B.S., U. Pa., 1941; M.S., Carnegie Inst. Tech., 1942, D.Sc., 1945; postdoctoral fellow, U. Wis., 1946; m. Miriam Margaret McMahon, Nov. 26, 1943; children—Miriam Margaret, Raymond P., Anne Marie, Patricia Sue. Instr., then asst. prof. chemistry Northwestern U., 1946-51; mem. faculty Loyola U., Chgo., 1951-77, prof. chem., 1955-77, chmn. dept., 1951-70, asso. dean Grad. Sch., dir. grad. sci. programs, 1968-69, dean Grad. Sch., 1969-77, sci. cons. indsl. orgns., 1951-77; asso. exec. dir. Am. Chem. Soc., 1977, exec. dir., 1978—; producer, performer sci. TV shows Chgo. networks, 1956-65. Sec.-treas. Midwestern Assn. Grad. Schs., 1972-77; exec. com. Council of Grad. Schs., 1972-74. Scientific adviser to gov. Ill. Recipient McCormack Freud Hon. lectr. award chemistry and chem. engring. Omicron chpt. Phi Lambda Upsilon, 1961; Merit award Chgo. Tech. Socs. Council, 1962. Mem. Am. Chem. Soc. (chmn. Chgo. 1960-61, nat. councilor 1956—; chmn. bd. com. on profl. relations 1974-75), AAAS, N.Y. Acad. Scis., Sigma Xi (pres. Loyola chpt. 1956-57), Phi Kappa Phi, Alpha Chi Sigma, Phi Lambda Upsilon, Lambda Chi Sigma, Sigma Delta. Author: Laboratory Manual of Organic Chemistry and Biochemistry, 1953; Inorganic Qualitative Analysis (with J. L. Huston), 1958; Chemistry of Life Processes (with Rose Blau), 1968; Selected Laboratory Experiments for Chemistry of Life Processes, 1968; also articles. Home: 1800 Old Meadow Rd McLean VA 22102 Office: 1155 16th St NW Washington DC 20036

MARIEN, ALBERT EMMETT, ret. internal auditor, univ. adminstr.; b. St. Louis, Sept. 7, 1911; s. Charles Anthony and Adelaide Dorothy (Kennel) M.; B.S., U. Ill., 1933, M.S., 1953; M.S., U. Denver, 1942; m. Camille Davis, June 7, 1949; children—Kent Karraker, Kay (Mrs. James R. Cook). Prin., Francis-Howell High Sch., St. Charles, Mo., 1942-43; prof., head bus. adminstrn. dept. Berry Coll., 1943-47; instr. St. Louis U., 1947-48; instr. U. Ill., Urbana, 1948-51, chimesmaster, 1958—; sectional editor Internal Auditor, 1965-67, internat. editor, 1967-68. Pres., The Mabel A. Greeley Players of Champaign, 1974—; bus. affairs chmn. U. Ill. div. United Fund, 1970-72; sec.-treas. Tau of Delta Phi Found., 1971—. Recipient Dean Turner award U. Ill. Interfrat. Council, 1969. Certified internal auditor. Mem. Inst. Internal Auditors (Outstanding Service award Central Ill. chpt. 1963), Delta Phi (treas. Tau alumni chpt. 1957-71, pres. 1975-78). Methodist (audit com., policy bd. 1962—). Author: College Sales Course, 1947; Safeguarding the Hospital's Assets, 1971; Hospital Internal Control and Auditing, 1973. Contbr. numerous articles on internal control to profl. publs. Home: 70 Greencroft Dr Champaign IL 61820 Office: 273 Altgeld Hall Urbana IL 61801

MARIENTHAL, GEORGE, govt. ofcl.; b. Kansas City, Mo., Nov. 15, 1938; s. George and Sadie (James) M.; B.S., U.S. Naval Acad., 1962; M.S., Stanford U., 1963; M.B.A., Am. U., 1974; m. Mary Biswell, June 19, 1963; children—Shawn Ann, Patrick James, Shannon Lee. Sr. research asso. Logistics Mgmt. Inst., Washington, 1967-71; dir. regional liaison EPA, 1971-75; dep. asst. sec. def. Dept. Def., Washington, 1975—. Served with USAF, 1962-67. Mem. Am. Inst. Indsl. Engrs. Episcopalian. Club: Masons. Home: 6904 Breezewood Terr Rockville MD 20852 Office: Office of Manpower Res Affairs and Logistics US Dept Def Pentagon Washington DC 20301

MARIL, HERMAN, artist; b. Balt., Oct. 13, 1908; s. Isaac H. and Celia (Maril) Becker; student Balt. Poly. Inst.; grad. Md. Inst. Fine Arts, 1928; m. Esta C. Maril, June 8, 1948; 2 children. Exhibited one-man shows in galleries and mus. in U.S., 1935—; represented in pub. and pvt. collections including Santa Barbara (Calif.) Mus., N.Y. U. Gallery, Walter's Art Gallery, Balt., Whitney Mus. Am. Art; commd. by fed. govt. to paint murals for Alta Vista (Va.) P.O. and West Scranton (Pa.) P.O.; instr. painting Cummington Art Sch. in Mass., 1935-40, King-Smith Sch., Washington, 1945-46; asst. prof. Fine Arts, U. Md., 1947-64, prof., 1964-79, prof. emeritus, 1979—. Hon. trustee Balt. Mus. Art. Served with spl. service AUS, 1942-45.

Awarded Municipal Art Soc. Prize for best work in All-Md. Exhbn., 1935; Municipal Art Soc. Purchase Prize, Balt., 1939; Balt. Mus. Art Purchase Prize, 1940; first prize for best painting, Peale Museum, Balt., 1947, and several other prizes including Berney Mem. Prize, Balt. Mus. Art, 1952. Stefan Hirsch Meml. award Audubon Soc. Artists, Nat. Acad., N.Y.C., 1972, award Hoschild-Kohn Dept. Store, Balt., 1972, Pres.'s award, ann. exhbn. Soc. Audubon Artists, NAD, 1975, award for painting Am. Acad./Inst. Arts and Letters, 1978. Mem. Coll. Art Assn., Artists Equity Assn., Provincetown Art Assn., AAUP. Address: 5602 Roxbury Pl Baltimore MD 21209

MARIMOW, WILLIAM KALMON, journalist; b. Phila., Aug. 4, 1947; s. Jay and Helen Alma (Gitnig) M.; B.A., Trinity Coll. (Conn.), 1969; m. Diane K. Macomb, Oct. 18, 1969; children—Ann Esther, Scott Macomb. Asst. editor Comml. Car Jour., Chilton Co., Bala Cynwyd, Pa., 1969-70; asst. to econ. columnist Phila. Bull., 1970-72; staff writer Phila. Inquirer, 1972—; instr. urban studies U. Pa., 1979—. Recipient 1st place award for team reporting Phila. Press Assn., 1977, 1st place award for deadline reporting AP Mng. Editors of Pa., 1977, 1st place award for best news story Sigma Delta Chi of Phila., 1977, Pulitzer prize for disting. pub. service, 1978, Silver Gavel award Am. Bar Assn., 1978, Roy W. Howard Pub. Service award Scripps-Howard Found., 1978, Robert F. Kennedy Journalism award, 1978, Nat. Pub. Service award Sigma Delta Chi, 1978, Pub. Service awards AP Mng. Editors of Pa., 1978, Sigma Delta Chi of N.J., 1978, Sigma Delta Chi of Phila., 1978, 2d place award for investigative reporting Keystone Press Assn., 1978. Mem. Pen and Pencil Club. Office: care Phila Inquirer 400 N Broad St Philadelphia PA 19101

MARIN, RICHARD ANTHONY ("CHEECH"), writer, actor; b. Los Angeles, July 13, 1946; s. Oscar and Elsa Meza M.; B.S., Calif. State U., Northridge; m. Rikki Mae Morley, Nov. 1, 1975. Co-founder improvisational group City Works, Vancouver; formed comedy duo with Tommy Chong called Cheech and Chong; appeared in clubs throughout U.S. including Carnegie Hall; recordings include: Cheech and Chong, Big Bambu, Los Cochinos, The Wedding Album, Sleeping Beauty; co-writer, co-star film: Up in Smoke, 1978; Cheech & Chong's Next Movie, 1980; co-writer title song Up in Smoke. Recipient Grammy award for Los Cochinos, Best Comedy recording, 1973. Office: C&C Brown Productions 100 Universal Plaza Universal City CA 91608

MARINACCIO, ANTHONY, educator, cons.; b. Bridgeport, Conn., Aug. 26, 1912; s. Paul and Louisa (DeLibero) M.; B.E., Conn. State Coll., 1937; M.A., Ohio State U., 1939; Ph.D., Yale U., 1949; LL.D., Parsons Coll., 1961; m. Elsie Kleps, Sept. 5, 1936 (dec. Sept. 1964); children—Warren, Karen Marinaccio Beacon, Dianna Judd Carlisi, Nancy Judd Wilber, Linda, Lee; m. 2d, M. Maxine Reynolds, Oct. 15, 1965. Tchr. jr. high sch., Hartford, Conn., 1935-41; elem. sch. prin., 1941-46; prof. edn., prin. campus sch. Tchrs. Coll. State U. N.Y., Oswego, 1946-49; asst. supt. charge instrn. and supervision Peoria (Ill.) pub. schs., 1949-53; supt. schs., Mexico, Mo., 1953-55, Kankakee, Ill., 1955-59, Davenport, Iowa, 1959-64; dean Parsons Coll., 1964-65; founding pres. The Hiram Scott Coll., Scottsbluff, Nebr., 1964-69; prof. higher edn. adminstrn. George Washington U., Washington, 1969—; professorial lectr. edn. George Washington U., summers 1952-69; prof. edn. Bradley U., part-time, 1949-53, supr. instrn. research extension courses, 1956-58; vis. prof. secondary edn. Ohio State U., summers 1953-54; dir. staff devel. program DODD Schs. Consortium, 1978—. Speaker various civic, bus., indsl. and ednl. groups; world-wide cons. colls. and sch. systems on orgn., adminstrn., accreditation. Active various local civic, religious and ednl. groups; organized South End Council, Hartford, 1944-46, Peoria Citizens Council for Pub. Schs., 1951-52, in-service tchr. edn. program, Peoria, 1949-53; pres. Kankakee Community Chest, 1957-58. Mem. Davenport (Iowa) Planning Commn., 1960-63; bd. dirs. Peoria council Boy Scouts Am., 1951-53, ARC, Peoria, 1951-53; trustee Hiram Scott Coll., 1964-69, Palmer Found., 1974-78; adviser to Palmer Coll. Bd. Dirs. Mem. Sheldon Forum, Phi Delta Kappa, Epsilon Pi Tau, Phi Sigma Phi, Psi Phi. Clubs: Masons, Shriners. Author: Exploring the Graphic Arts, 1959; Human Relations: The New Dimension in American Education, 1974; Human Relations and Cooperative Planning in Education and Management, 1977-78; contbr. articles to profl. pubs. Home: 13919 Turnmore Rd Silver Spring MD 20906 Office: George Washington U Washington DC 20052. *To teach—not the subject, but the human—has been my joy and pleasure for these two score and five years. To help establish a world of values that considers man to live in a society in which he is free to think and to believe as his conscious guides him has not been the labor of fatigue, but a labor of love. Although at times long continuous hours of such labor may have seemed a killing course, success has always generated new energy in my soul to spur me on in this joyful, never ending goal.*

MARINAKOS, PLATO ANTHONY, hospital adminstr.; b. Pitts., Dec. 26, 1935; B.S. in Zoology, U. Pitts., 1957, M.S. with honors in Hosp. Adminstrn., 1961; postgrad. Duquesne U. Sch. Law, 1964; m. Vaselia Pecunes; children—Plato Anthony, Constantine, Theodore, Alexia. Adminstrv. asst. Homestead (Pa.) Gen. Hosp., 1960-61; asst. exec. dir. Allegheny Gen. Hosp., Pitts., 1961-65, asso. exec. dir., 1965-68, exec. dir., 1968-73; pres. Conemaugh Valley Meml. Hosp., Johnstown, Pa., 1973-77; exec. v.p. Mercy Catholic Med. Center, Darby, Pa., 1977—; lectr. U. Pitts., Pa. State U.; preceptor U. Pitts., George Washington U., Duke U.; chmn. ad hoc com. on statewide coordination of Nat. Energy Conservation Act; cons HEW; mem. Sec.'s Commn. on Med. Malpractice; bd. dirs. Hosp. Purchasing Service Pa., Delchester Health Edn. Consortium, Camillus-Mercy Sch. Practical Nursing, Greater Delaware Valley Health Care, Inc. Mem. Adv. council Pitts. Allegheny C. of C.; bd. dirs. Better Bus. Bur. Southeastern Pa., Better Bus. Bur. Eastern Pa. Mem. Hosp. Assn. Pa. (chmn. com. public relations), Hosp. Council Western Pa. (chmn. com. ambulatory care), Council Teaching Hosps., Am. Assn. Med. Colls., Allegheny County Council on Mental Health/Mental Retardation (dir.), Regional Health Services Council, Am. Mgmt. Assn., Am. Public Health Assn., Nat. League Nursing, Delaware Valley Hosp. Council, United Mental Health Services Allegheny County, Alumni Assn. U. Pitts. (vp.). Greek Orthodox. Home: 112 Ringwood Rd Rosemont PA 19010 Office: Lansdown Ave and Baily Rd Darby PA 19023

MARINATOS, ANTHONY, communications co. exec.; b. Antiparos, Greece, Feb. 15, 1946; s. Tom and Flora (Kalargirou) M.; came to U.S., 1960, naturalized, 1965; B.S. in Accounting, St. John's U., Jamaica, N.Y., 1968, M.B.A. in Finance, 1971; m. Anna X. Fuentes, Aug. 16, 1969; children—John Alexis, Derek Thomas. With Downe Communications, Inc., N.Y.C., 1970—, v.p., treas., 1975—; controller Bartell Media Corp., N.Y.C., 1974-75. Intercollegiate Debate scholar, 1965-68. Mem. Paros Soc. N.Y. (dir.). Democrat. Greek Orthodox. Home: 22 Fernwood Terr Stewart Manor NY 11530 Office: 641 Lexington Ave New York City NY 10022

MARINE, GENE, author; b. San Francisco, Dec. 31, 1926; s. Fred and Gloria (Rodrigues) M.; student San Francisco State Coll., 1948-49; children—April, Craig, Sheila, Kevin. News analyst radio sta. KPFA, Berkeley, Calif., 1951-57; West coast corr. The Nation, 1954-64; asso. editor Frontier mag., 1957-59; pub. affairs and program dir. radio sta. KPFK, Los Angeles, 1959-60; news dir. radio sta. KPFA, 1960-62; polit. campaign mgr., 1962-63; contbg. editor Pacific Scene, 1964-65; with CBS News, 1964; sr. editor Ramparts mag., 1966-69. Served with USMCR, 1943-46. Recipient Radio-TV Newswriting award Sigma Delta Chi, 1960; award Calif. Asso. Press Radio & TV Assn., 1961. Mem. Author's Guild Am., San Francisco Zool. Soc. Author: America the Raped, 1969; The Black Panthers, 1969; A Male Guide to Women's Liberation, 1972. Co-author: Food Pollution, 1972; also numerous articles. Address: 1740 Rose St Berkeley CA 94703

MARINI, FRANK, ednl. adminstr.; b. Melrose Park, Ill., June 18, 1935; s. Joseph and Lillian Lee (Stuart) M.; B.A., Ariz. State U., 1960, M.A., 1961; Ph.D., U. Calif., Berkeley, 1966; children by previous marriage—Lisa M., Katherine D. Instr., U. Mo., Columbia, 1963-64; asst. prof. polit. sci. U. Ky., 1966-67; asst. prof. Syracuse U., 1967-70, asso. prof., asso. dean Maxwell Sch., dir. public adminstrn. programs, 1970-73; dean Coll. Arts and Letters, San Diego State U., 1973—. Served with USAF, 1954-58. Mem. Am. Soc. Public Adminstrn. Author pamphlets; contbr. numerous articles to profl. jours.; editor: Toward a New Public Administration, 1971; mng. editor Public Adminstrn. Rev., 1967-77. Office: Coll Arts and Letters San Diego State U San Diego CA 92182

MARINI, ROBERT CHARLES, environ. engr.; b. Quincy, Mass., Sept. 29, 1931; s. Larry and Millie Marini; B.S. in Civil Engring. cum laude, Northeastern U., Boston, 1954; S.M. in San. Engring., Harvard U., 1955; m. Myrna Lydia Pellegrini, June 26, 1955; children—Debra, Robert Charles, Larry. Pres. environ. engring. div. Camp Dresser & McKee Inc., Boston, 1977—, also partner, dir. parent co.; sr. v.p. CDM Internat. Inc. Dir. nat. council Northeastern U. Served to 1st lt. AUS, 1956-58. Named Young Engr. of Year, Mass. Soc. Profl. Engrs., 1966. Registered profl. engr., Mass., 20 other states. Diplomate Am. Acad. Environ. Engrs. Fellow ASCE; mem. Am. Pub. Works Assn., Am. Water Resources Assn., Am. Water Works Assn., Boston Soc. Civil Engrs., Inter-Am. Assn. San. Engring., Maine Water Utilities Assn., Mass., New Eng., N.Y. State water works assns., New Eng., N.H., N.Y. State water pollution control assns., Tau Beta Pi. Clubs: Neighborhood (Quincy). Home: 1 Nevin Rd South Weymouth MA 02190 Office: 1 Center Plaza Boston MA 02108

MARINO, AMERIGO ANGELO, conductor; b. Chgo., Feb. 5, 1925; s. Angelo and Julia (Ottavianni) M.; student Chgo. Mus. Coll., Sherwood Music Sch., Chgo. Conservatory; pupil of Nicolai Malko, George Szell, Fritz Zweig, Alfred Wallenstein, Max Rudolph. Violinist, Los Angeles Philharmonic, 1947-49, Hollywood Bowl Orch., 1947-49, Paramount Pictures, 1952-54; condr., composer CBS Radio and TV, 1953-56, also Liberty, Capitol and RCA records, 1959-63; music dir. Glendale (Calif.) Symphony, 1958-63, St. Louis Little Symphony, 1964-76, Birmingham (Ala.) Symphony Orch., 1964—; guest condr. N.Y. Philharmonic, Chgo., Nat., St. Louis, Houston symphonies. Served with AUS, 1941-44. Ford fellow, 1963; recipient Silver Bowl award Birmingham Festival of Arts, 1966; Obelisk award Birmingham Children's Festival, 1976. Mem. Condrs. Guild, Am. Symphony Orch. League. Composer for chorus, orch., chamber groups. Office: care Birmingham Symphony Orch PO Box 2125 2114 1st Ave N Birmingham AL 35201*

MARINO, ANTHONY WAYNE MARTIN, intestinal surgeon; b. N.Y.C., Jan. 5, 1894; s. Francis and Camille (Jarratan) M.; M.D., L.I. Coll. Medicine, 1916; m. Doris Guarin, Oct. 31, 1923; 1 son, Martin. Intern St. Mary's Hosp., 1916-17, 1919; postgrad. study surgery Mayo Clinic, 1917-18, clin. asst. medicine, 1919-21, gastroenterology, 1922-24, chief rectal clinics, 1925, asst. surgeon, 1930-31, asso. surgeon, 1932-33; attending surgeon Bklyn. Hosp., 1933-63, sr. attending surgeon, 1963—; proctologist Kingston Ave. Hosp., 1933-43, Bushwick Hosp., 1934-56; cons. proctologist Wyckoff Heights Hosp., 1940—, Kingston Av. Hosp., 1943-56, St. Mary's Hosp., Bklyn., 1951-70; instr. L.I. Coll. Med., 1930-43, asst. clin. prof. surgery, 1943-48, asso. prof. clin. surgery, 1948-54; clin. prof. surgery State U. N.Y. Coll. Medicine, 1954-66, clin. prof. emeritus surgery, 1966—. Served as 1st lt. M.C., AUS, 1918-19. Decorated Fatiga di Guerra, Zona di Guerra (Italian govt.); Order Crown of Italy. Diplomate Am. Bd. Surgery (founders group proctology), Am. Bd. Colon and Rectal Surgery (pres. 1958-59, 63-64). Fellow A.C.S., N.Y. Acad. Medicine, N.J. (hon.), New Eng. (hon.) proctologic socs., Pa. Soc. Colon and Rectal Surgery (hon.), Am. (v.p. 1939-40, pres. 1954), N.Y. (pres. 1941-45) proctologic socs.; mem. AMA (past chmn. sect. gastroenterology and proctology, Physician's award 1971-73), Med. Soc. County of Kings (pres. 1948), Med. Soc. State N.Y. (v.p. 1966), Alumni Assn. L.I. Coll. Medicine (pres. 1948), Pan Am. Med. Assn. (pres. Bklyn. and L.I. chpt.), Bklyn. Surg. Soc., Research Soc. State Med. Center in N.Y., N.Y. Soc. Ind. Research, Bklyn. Assn. Mental Health. Mem. editorial bd. Diseases of Colon and Rectum, 1957—. Contbr. articles med. jours. Home: 8301 Ridge Blvd Brooklyn NY 11209 Office: One Hanson Pl Brooklyn NY 11243

MARINO, EUGENE ANTONIO, bishop; b. Biloxi, Miss., May 29, 1934; s. Jesus M. and Lottie Irene (Bradford) M. Ordained priest Roman Catholic Ch.; instr. Epiphany Coll., Newburgh, N.Y., 1962-68; spiritual dir. St. Joseph's Sem., Washington, 1968-71; vicar gen., dep. adminstr. Soc. St. Joseph, Balt., 1971-74; aux. bishop Archdiocese of Washington, 1974—; mem. U.S. Cath. Conf.; chmn. Bishops' Com. on Permanent Diaconate. Trustee Cath. U. Am.; mem. devel. com. Nat. Shrine of Immaculate Conception. Mem. Nat. Conf. Cath. Bishops, Conf. Major Superiors of Men of U.S. Address: St Gabriel's Rectory 26 Grant Circle NW Washington DC 20011*

MARINO, SAMUEL JOSEPH, librarian; b. New Britain, Conn., Nov. 29, 1916; s. Mariano and Josephine (Pandolfo) M.; A.B., La. State U., 1940, B.S., 1948, M.A. in French, 1949; A.M. in L.S., U. Mich., 1952, Ph.D., 1962; m. Dorothy Quinney, Feb. 7, 1949; children—Mary Leila, Joseph, Michael. Acting dir. libraries U. Miss., 1952-53; dir. libraries, chmn. dept. library sci. Ind. State Tchrs. Coll., 1954-58; head librarian McNeese State Coll., Lake Charles, La., 1958-67; prof. library sci. Tex. Woman's U., 1967—, librarian, 1973—; dir., chmn. library sect. Louisiana Coll. Conf.; instr. London Bibliographic Seminar, 1978, 79. Bd. dirs. Terre Haute (Ind.) Civic Symphony. Served to capt. AUS, 1942-46. Mem. Am., Tex. (chmn. publs. com.), Southwestern, La. (chmn. coll. and univ. sect.; 2d v.p. 1965-66) library assns., Book Club Calif., Phi Mu Alpha Sinfonia, Beta Phi Mu, Phi Sigma Iota. Kiwanian. Author: French Travellers in the United States, 1765-32, 1961; Your Library: What's In It for You, 1974. Editor: La. Library Assn. Bull. Contbr. articles to profl. jours. Home: 3205 Darby Ln Denton TX 76204

MARINOS, PETER NICK, elec. engr., educator; b. Sparta, Greece, July 9, 1935; s. Nicholaos P. and Voula N. Marinakos; student Athens U., 1953-55; B.S.E.E., Clemson U., 1959; M.S.E.E., N.C. State U., 1961, Ph.D., 1964; m. Joan C. Marinos, Sept. 1, 1968; 1 dau., Maria S. Electronics engr. Lockheed Aircraft, Marietta, Ga., 1959-61; instr. N.C. State U., 1961-64; asst. prof. Clemson U., 1959-61, 65-66; asso. prof. U. Ala., Huntsville, 1966-68; asso. prof. elec. engring. Duke U., Durham, N.C., 1968-72, prof., 1972—; cons. in field. Pres., Hellenic Community of Durham, 1977—. NASA fellow; NSF fellow. Mem. IEEE, Sigma Xi, Tau Beta Pi, Phi Kappa Phi. Greek Orthodox. Contbr. articles to profl. jours. Office: Elec Engring Dept Duke Univ Durham NC 27706

MARION, ANDREW BURNET, lawyer; b. York, S.C., Apr. 22, 1919; s. John Alexander and Mary (Burnet) M.; A.B. magna cum laude, U. S.C., 1939, LL.B., 1941; m. Evelyn R. Cantey, Sept. 20, 1946; children—Evelyn C., Andrew Burnet, Margaret B. Admitted to S.C. bar, 1941; partner firm Savage & Marion, Camden, 1945-53, Haynsworth, Perry, Bryant, Marion & Johnstone, Greenville, 1953—; dir. First Bankshares Corp. of S.C., First Nat. Bank of S.C., So. Weaving Co., Carolina Fed. Savs. & Loan Assn. Pres. bd. St. Francis Community Hosp., Greenville County Hist. Soc., Greenville Arts Festival Assn., Community Council; bd. dirs. U. S.C. Ednl. Found. Served to capt. USAAF, 1941-45. Mem. Am. Law Inst., Jud. Conf. U.S. 4th Circuit, Am. Judicature Soc., Am. Bar Assn., S.C. Bar Assn., Wig and Robe, Phi Beta Kappa, Omicron Delta Kappa, Alpha Tau Omega. Clubs: Cotillion; Poinsett; St. Andrews Soc. (Greenville). Office: Haynsworth Perry Bryant Marion & Johnstone 409 E North St PO Box 2048 Greenville SC 29602

MARION, CECIL PRICE, JR., educator; b. Amory, Miss., Sept. 26, 1919; s. Cecil Price and Lola (Jarvis) M.; B.S., U. Okla., 1941; M.S., Miss. State U., 1951; m. Eleanor Hand Freeman, June 24, 1945; children—Diane Elizabeth, Ellen Hand, Cecil Price III. Instr. engring. graphics Miss. State U., 1941-42, 47-51, asst. prof., 1951-53, asso. prof., 1953-57; geophysicist Petty Geophys. Engring. Co., Ambato, Ecuador, 1945-46; asso. prof., asst. to dean engring. U. Miami, Coral Gables, Fla., 1957-62, prof., chmn. engring. graphics dept., 1962—; instr., dir. marine sedimentation Gulf Coast Research Lab., Ocean Springs, Miss., summers 1948-50; cons. Agrl. Expt. Sta. Miss., 1954-56; dir. sch. Decatur Iron & Steel Co. (Ala.), summer 1956. Served with AUS, 1942-45. Recipient AAAS, grant-in-aid Miss. Acad. Sci., 1950. Mem. Am. Soc. Engring. Edn. (past div. chmn. Southeastern sect., sec.-treas. Southeastern sect. 1970-76, pres. sect. 1976-77), Miss. Acad. Sci., Civil Air Patrol (officer Internat. Air Cadet Exchange, France, 1962), Sigma Gamma Epsilon. Home: 9551 SW 25th Dr Miami FL 33165 Office: U Miami Coral Gables FL 33124

MARION, JERRY BASKERVILLE, educator, author, physicist; b. Mobile, Ala., Dec. 10, 1929; s. Lester L. and Virginia (Hensel) M.; B.A., Reed Coll., 1952; M.A., Rice U., 1953, Ph.D., 1955; m. Adelia I. Macnab, May 31, 1952; children—Forrest Lee, Kathryn Ann. Research asso. Rice U., 1955; NSF fellow Calif. Inst. Tech., 1955-56, vis. asso. in physics, Guggenheim fellow, 1965-66; faculty U. Rochester, 1956-57; physicist Los Alamos Sci. Lab., 1957; mem. faculty U. Md., College Park, 1957—, prof. physics, 1962—; sr. staff scientist Convair/San Diego, 1960-61. Com. mem. Nat. Acad. Sci.-NRC; cons. govt. agys., indsl. firms. Recipient Sci. Teaching award Washington Acad. Scis., 1973. Fellow Am. Phys. Soc., AAAS. Author: Nuclear Reaction Graphs, 1960; Classical Dynamics of Particles and Systems, 1965; Classical Electromagnetic Radiation, 1965; Principles of Vector Analysis, 1965; Nuclear Reaction Analysis, 1968; Physics and the Physical Universe, 1971; Mathematical Preparation for General Physics, 1972; Mathematical Preparation for General Physics with Calculus, 1973; Physics—The Foundation of Modern Science, 1973; Mathematical Review for the Physical Sciences, 1974; Energy in Perspective, 1974; Physical Science in the Modern World, 1974; Physics in the Modern World, 1976; Essential Physics in the World Around Us, 1977; Our Physical World, 1978; General Physics with Bioscience Essays, 1979. Editor: (with J.L. Fowler) Fast Neutron Physics, 1960; (with G.C. Phillips, J.R. Risser) Progress in Fast Neutron Physics, 1963; (with D.M. Van Patten) Research with Low Energy Accelerators, 1967; A Universe of Physics, 1970. Mem. internat. editorial bd. Nuclear Data, 1965—. Research, numerous publs. on structure of light nuclei, especially effects relative to isobaric spin, single particle states, configuration mixing. Home: 103 Peninsula Dr Indian Lake Boro Rural Delivery 1 Central City PA 15926 Office: Dept Physics and Astronomy U Md College Park MD 20742

MARION, JOHN FRANCIS, writer; b. Norfolk, Va., Feb. 23, 1922; s. Everett Edward and Aileen (McCarthy) M.; B.A., Pa. State U., 1948. Editor, Commercial America mag., Phila., 1948-49, Philadelphia mag., 1949-50; dir. publicity J.B. Lippincott Co., Phila., 1952-53; editor Graphic Arts Rev., Phila., 1953-55; dir. publicity Phila. Conv. and Visitors Bur., 1957; head John F. Marion Lit. Agy., Phila., 1958-62; editor-in-chief Chilton Book Co., Phila., 1962-72. Served with AUS, 1943-46. Democrat. Roman Catholic. Club: Franklin Inn. Author: Lucrezia Bori of the Metropolitan Opera, 1962; Bicentennial City, 1974; Philadelphia Medica, 1976; Famous and Curious Cemeteries, 1977; The Charleston Story, 1978. Home: 1836 Delancey Pl Philadelphia PA 19103. *As a writer I feel I have been extremely fortunate in being able to pursue such a career for over 30 years. The rewards have been immeasurable, the satisfactions great, the road often a rough, unpaved one, the way fraught with danger. I would have it no other way. It has been a rich, full life.*

MARION, JOHN LOUIS, fine arts auctioneering and appraising co. exec.; b. N.Y.C., Nov. 27, 1933; s. Louis John and Florence Adelaide (Winters) M.; B.S.-S.S., Fordham U., 1956; postgrad. Columbia, 1960-61; m. Mary Anne Crowley, Aug. 27, 1960; children—John L., Deborah Mary, Therese Marie, Michelle Marie. With Sotheby Parke Bernet Inc., N.Y.C., 1960—, dir., 1965—, v.p., 1966-70, exec. v.p., 1970-72, pres., 1972—, chmn. bd., 1975—; dir. Sotheby Park Bernet Group Ltd., London, Eng., 1968—. Chmn. antique dealers div. appeal Arthritis Found., Inc., 1966-75; vice chmn. bldg. steering com. Dobbs Ferry Hosp., 1975; bd. dirs. Internat. Found. Art Research; co-chmn. Channel 13 Auction, 1978—. Served as lt. (j.g.) USN, 1956-60. Mem. Appraisers Assn. Am., Inc. Clubs: Dutch Treat, Wee Burn Country; Lotos. Home: 175 Brookside Ave Darien CT 06820 Office: 980 Madison Ave New York City NY 10021

MARION, LORETTA HUNT, pub. exec.; b. Glen Rock, Pa., Mar. 1, 1939; d. Nevin Elias and Ruth (Adams) Hunt; B.A., Wilson Coll., 1961; M.Ed., Rutgers U., 1965; postgrad. N.Y. U., 1961-62; m. John Addison Marion, June 29, 1968; 1 dau., Cynthia Anne. Elementary tchr., New Providence, N.J., 1961-63; writer Scholastic News Trails, 1963-64; asst. editor Scholastic Newstime, 1964-65; asst. editor Scholastic Tchr. of Scholastic Mags., Inc., N.Y.C., 1965-66, asso. editor, 1966-67, mng. editor, 1967-68, editor, 1968-75, editorial coordinator Sch. div., 1975-77, bus. mgr. Text div., 1977—. Mem. N.Y. Choral Soc., 1964-65, Com. on Sexism and Social Justice, 1976-78. Named Outstanding Young Woman of Am., Ednl. Press Assn. Am., 1966, recipient award for feature articles, 1971, 75. Mem. Women's Nat. Book Assn., Ednl. Press Assn. Am. (treas. 1975-79), Assn. Supervision and Curriculum Devel., Edn. Writers Assn. Lutheran. Club: Wilson College (N.Y.C.). Author: Map Skills Project Book III, 1965. Office: 50 W 44th St New York NY 10036

MARION, WILLIAM FRANCIS, lawyer; b. York, S.C., Oct. 8, 1923; s. John Alexander and Mary (Burnet) M.; A.B., U. S.C., 1943, LL.B., 1945; m. Elizabeth A. Marshall, May 5, 1945; children—Helen Bruton, Mary Burnet, William Francis, Alexander Douglas. Admitted to S.C. bar, 1945, since practiced in Greenville; sr. partner firm Haynsworth, Perry, Bryant, Marion & Johnstone, and predecessors, 1958—. Dir. Greenville div. S.C. Nat. Bank. Permanent mem. 4th Circuit Jud. Conf. Served with USMCR, 1943. Fellow Am. Coll. Trial Lawyers; mem. Internat. Assn. Ins. Counsel, Am. Judicature Soc., Am., S.C. (chmn. com. unauthorized practice 1964), Greenville bar assns., Alpha Tau Omega. Episcopalian. Clubs: Torch, Greenville

Country, Poinsett (govs. 1955-57, pres. 1957) (Greenville); Palmetto (Columbia, S.C.). Home: 144 Fernwood Ln Greenville SC 29607 Office: 409 E North St Greenville SC 29602

MARIS, ALBERT BRANSON, judge; b. Phila., Dec. 19, 1893; s. Robert Wood and Elma (Branson) M.; grad. Westtown (Pa.) Sch., 1911, Drexel U., 1926, LL.D, 1946; LL.B., Temple U., 1918, LL.D., 1940; LL.D., Haverford Coll., 1957, Swarthmore Coll., 1968; D.C.L., Villanova U., 1974; m. Edith M. Robinson, July 3, 1917 (dec. Oct. 1967); children—William Robinson, Robert Wood; m. 2d, Mildred C. Butler, Oct. 24, 1968. Admitted to Pa. bar, 1918; practiced in Chester, Pa., 1918, Phila., 1919-36; mem. firm White, Maris and Clapp; appointed judge U.S. Dist. Ct., Eastern dist. Pa., 1936; apptd. judge U.S. Court of Appeals. 3d Circuit, 1938; designated judge U.S. Emergency Ct. of Appeals, 1942, designated chief judge, 1943; sr. circuit judge, 3d Circuit (ret.), 1959—; spl. master Supreme Ct. Lake Mich. water diversion cases, 1959-67, Atlantic continental shelf case, 1970-74; adj. prof. law Temple U. Law Sch., 1941-55. Chmn. com. revision laws Jud. Conf. U.S., 1944-67, chmn. com. rules practice and procedure, 1959-73; mem. adv. com. on codification laws of V.I., 1955-57; mem. U.S. adv. com. internat. rules jud. procedure, 1959-63; adv. com. pvt. internat. law State Dept., 1964-69. Democratic county chmn., Delaware County, Pa., 1924-30; mem. Pa. Dem. State Com., 1930-34; auditor Borough of Lansdowne, Pa., 1928-34; pres. People's Assn. of Delaware County, 1935-36; mem. council Borough of Yeadon, Pa., 1935-36. Served as 2d lt. coast arty., U.S. Army, 1918. Recipient V.I. Medal of Honor, 1956. Fellow Am. Bar Found. (hon.); mem. Am., Fed., Pa., Phila., Delaware County, Montgomery County, City of N.Y. bar assns., Am. Law Inst., Inst. Jud. Adminstrn., Am. Judicature Soc., Order of Coif. Mem. Religious Soc. of Friends (presiding clk. Phila. yearly meeting 1966-67). Club: Lawyers. Editor: The Legal Intelligencer, Phila., 1933-36. Home: Apt K13 Foulkeways Gwynedd PA 19436 Office: 18613 US Courthouse Philadelphia PA 19106

MARISOL (MARISOL ESCOBAR), sculptress; b. Paris, May 22, 1930; ed. Ecole des Beaux-Arts, Paris, 1949, Art Students League, N.Y.C., 1950, New Sch. for Social Research, 1951-54, Hans Hofmann Sch., N.Y.C., 1951-54. Exhibited in one-man shows at Sidney Janis Gallery, N.Y.C., 1966, 67, 75, Hanover Gallery, London, 1967, Boymans-van Beuningen Mus., Rotterdam, Netherlands, 1968, Moore Coll. Art, Phila., 1970, Worcester (Mass.) Art Mus., 1971, N.Y. Cultural Center, 1973, Columbus (Ohio) Gallery of Fine Arts, 1974, numerous others; exhibited in group shows, including Painting of a Decade, Tate Gallery, London, 1964; New Realism, Municipal Mus., The Hague, 1964; Carnegie Internat., Pitts., 1964; Art of the U.S.A. 1670-1966, Whitney Mus. Am. Art, N.Y.C., 1966; American Sculpture of the Sixties, Mus. of Art, Los Angeles, 1967; Biennale, Venice, 1968; Art Inst. Chgo., 1968; Image of Man Today, Inst. Contemporary Arts, London, 1968; represented in permanent collections at Mus. Modern Art, N.Y.C., Whitney Mus. Am. Art, Albright-Knox Gallery, Buffalo, Hakone Open Air Mus., Tokyo, Nat. Portrait Gallery, Washington, Harry N. Abrams Collection, N.Y.C., Yale U. Art Gallery, numerous others. Mem. Am. Acad., Inst. Arts and Letters. Address: care Sidney Janis Gallery 6 W 57th St New York City NY 10019*

MARK, DAVID EVERETT, fgn. service officer; b. N.Y.C., Nov. 15, 1923; s. Leslie and Lena (Tyor) M.; B.A., Columbia, 1943, LL.B., 1946; m. Elisabeth Anne Lewis, Dec. 24, 1959; children—Leslie, Andrea, Clayton. Admitted to N.Y. bar, 1946; staff Office Polit. Adviser, U.S. Army Forces in Korea, 1946-48; 3d sec. Am. embassy, Seoul, Korea, 1948-49; mem. U.S. Mission, Berlin, Germany, 1949-51; 2d sec., dep. chief mission U.S. Legation, Bucharest, Rumania, 1952-54; Yugoslav desk officer Dept. State, Washington, 1954-57; 1st sec. embassy, Moscow, USSR, 1957-59; co-ordinator U.S. delegations to confs. on nuclear test ban, also 18 nation Com. on Disarmament, Geneva, Switzerland, 1959-63; fellow Center Internat. Affairs, Harvard, 1963-64; dir. Office West European Research and Analysis, Dept. State, Washington, 1964-69, dep. dir. Bur. Intelligence and Research, 1969-74; U.S. ambassador to Republic of Burundi, 1974-77; diplomat in residence U. Wis. at Milw., 1977-78; sr. dep. dir. Bur. Intelligence and Research, Dept. State, 1978—. Served with AUS, 1943-46. Mem. Council on Fgn. Relations. Author: Cessation of Nuclear Weapon Tests-Problems and Results of Negotiations to Date (pub. in German), 1965. Home: 8314 Loring Dr Bethesda MD 20034 Office: INR Dept State Washington DC 20520

MARK, HANS MICHAEL, govt. ofcl., physicist, engr.; b. Mannheim, Germany, June 17, 1929; s. Herman Francis and Maria (Schramek) M.; came to U.S., 1940, naturalized, 1945; A.B. in Physics, U. Calif. at Berkeley, 1951; Ph.D., Mass. Inst. Tech., 1954; Sc.D. (hon.), Fla. Inst. Tech., 1978; m. Marion G. Thorpe, Jan. 28, 1951; children—Jane H., James P. Research asso. Mass. Inst. Tech., 1954-55, asst. prof., 1958-60; research physicist Lawrence Radiation Lab., U. Calif. at Livermore, 1955-58, 60-69, exptl. physics div. leader, 1960-64; asso. prof. nuclear engring. U. Calif. at Berkeley, 1960-66, prof., 1966-69, chmn. dept. nuclear engring., 1964-69; lectr. dept. applied sci. U. Calif. at Davis, 1969-73; cons. prof. engring. Stanford, 1973—; dir. NASA-Ames Research Center, 1969-77; undersec. Air Force, Washington, 1977-77, sec. Air Force, 1979—. Mem. Pres.'s Adv. Group Sci. and Tech., 1975-76. Recipient Distinguished Service medal NASA, 1972, 77. Fellow Am. Phys. Soc., AIAA; mem. Nat. Acad. Engring., Am. Nuclear Soc., Am. Geophys. Union. Author: (with N.T. Olson) Experiments in Modern Physics, 1966; also numerous articles. Editor: (with S. Fernbach) Properties of Matter Under Unusual Conditions, 1969. Research on nuclear energy levels, nuclear reactions, applications nuclear energy for practical purposes, atomic fluorescence yields, measurement X-rays above atmosphere. Home: 2704 George Mason Pl Alexandria VA 22305 Office: Dept Air Force Pentagon Washington DC 20330

MARK, HERMAN F(RANCIS), educator; b. Vienna, Austria, May 3, 1895; s. Herman Carl and Lili (Mueller) M.; Ph.D., U. Vienna, 1921; E.D. (hon.), U. Liége (Belgium); Ph.D. (hon.), U. Berlin, U. Upsala (Sweden), Karl Franzens U., Graz; D.Sci. (hon.), Johannes Gutenberg U., Mainz, Lowell Inst.; Eng.D., Tech. U., Munich; m. Mary Schramek, Aug. 19, 1922; children—Hans Michael, Peter Herman. Came to U.S., 1940, naturalized, 1945. Research asso. Kaiser Wilhelm Inst., Berlin, 1922-26, I.G. Farben at Ludwigshafen, 1927-32; prof. chemistry U. Vienna, 1932-38; research mgr. Can. Internat. Paper Co., Hawkesbury, Can., 1938-40; prof. organic chemistry Poly. Inst., Bklyn., 1940-44, dir. Inst. Polymer Research, 1944-64, dean faculty, 1961-74; mem. faculty dept. textile chemistry NC State U., Raleigh, 1974—. Recipient numerous awards. Fellow N.Y. Acad. Scis., Am. Phys. Soc., Textile Inst. Gt. Britain; mem. Am. Chem. Soc. (chmn. N.Y. and Met. L.I. sects.), AAAS, Nat., N.Y. acads. scis., Am. Acad. Arts and Scis., Dutch, Hungarian, Roumanian, Austrian, Spanish acads. sci., Max Planck Soc.; hon. mem. Indian Acad. Sci., Weizmann Inst. Sci., Istituto Politecnico Milan. Author numerous books on fibers, rubbers and plastics. Contbr. articles to profl. jours. Synthesized several organic free radicals remaining uncombined in solid crystalline state; determined structure various compounds including urea and pentaerythritol; 1st quantitative measurement of anamalous dispersion and polarization of X-rays; determined structure of cellulose, silk, rubber, chitin and starc; developed new plymers including polyvinyls and polyacrylics. Home and office: 333 Jay St Brooklyn NY 11201

MARK, JAMES LELAND, sugar co. exec.; b. El Reno, Okla., Dec. 23, 1933; s. Robert Ellsworth and Marguerite A. (Murray) M.; student U. Colo., 1958-60; B.A.B.A., U. Denver, 1962; m. Geneva Arlene Craig, Mar. 12, 1960; 1 son, Robert R. With Gt. Western Sugar Co., Denver, 1951-78, group v.p. mktg. and sr. v.p. sales and mktg., 1975-76, exec. v.p., 1976-78; pres., chief exec. officer Bodchaux-Henderson Sugar Co., Inc., Denver, 1978—. Mem. Colo. Public Expenditures Council. Served with U.S. Army, 1945-46. Mem. Sugar Club, Sugar Assn. (Judge-Dyer Meml. award 1979), Colo. Assn. Commerce and Industry. Republican. Presbyterian. Office: 1530 16th St Denver CO 80202

MARK, LESTER CHARLES, anesthesiologist; b. Boston, July 16, 1918; s. Harry and Jean (Akabas) M.; M.D., U. Toronto, 1941; postgrad. anesthesiology N.Y. U.; m. Muriel Harriet Widman, Nov. 17, 1946; children—Dana F., Laurence Peter. Practice medicine specializing in anesthesiology, N.Y.C.; staff Presbyn. Hosp., N.Y.C.; research fellow N.Y.U. Research Service, Goldwater Meml. Hosp., 1948-51; Am. Heart Assn. research fellow, 1949-51; clin. instr. State U. N.Y., Bklyn., 1952-53; with Columbia Coll. Phys. and Surg., 1953—, prof. anesthesiology, 1965—; attending anesthesiologist Presbyn. Hosp., N.Y.C., 1965—; Fulbright prof., Denmark, 1960-61; China Med. Bd. prof. Sapporo Med. Coll., Japan, 1967; vis. scientist Sandoz Labs., Basel, Switzerland, 1974. Cons. Anaesthesiology Centre, Copenhagen, Denmark, 1960-61, A.M.A. Council on Drugs, 1963—; guest scientist med. dept. and vis. attending physician med. research center Brookhaven Nat. Lab., 1968-71; counselor Cancer Internat. Research Co-op., N.Y.C., 1968—; mem. adv. com. respiratory and anesthetic drugs FDA, 1966-70; mem. pharmacology-toxicology rev. com. Nat. Inst. Gen. Med. Scis., 1968-70, mem. pharmacology-toxicology program com., 1970-72, chmn., 1971-72, cons., 1972-74. Mem. profl. adv. bd. Found. of Thanatology, 1968—, mem. exec. com., 1973—; mem. over-the-counter sedatives, tranquilizers, sleep aids and stimulants rev. panel FDA, 1972-78; mem. reference panel Am. Hosp. Formulary Service, Am. Soc. Hosp. Pharmacists, 1974—. Guggenheim Meml. fellow, 1960-61; Macy Faculty scholar, 1974; recipient Distinguished Service award N.Y. State Jour. Medicine, 1967, Hiroshima (Japan) U. medal, 1967. Diplomate Am. Bd. Anesthesiology. Fellow Am. Coll. Anesthesiologists, N.Y. Acad. Medicine, AAAS; mem. Am., N.Y. socs. anesthesiologists, Pan Am. Med. Assn. (Med. Ambassador of Good Will bronze plaque, 1962; past pres.), Am. Soc. Pharmacology and Exptl. Therapeutics (exec. com. clin. pharmacology div. 1967-72), N.Y. Soc. Acupuncture for Physicians and Dentists (founding mem., pres. 1978-80), Am. Acad. Acupuncture, Am. Coll. Acupuncture (founding mem., pres. 1975—), Am. Fedn. Clin. Research, Assn. U. Anesthetists (sr. mem.), Union Scientifique Mondiale des Medecins Acupuncteurs et des Societes d'Acupuncture (hon.), Sigma Xi. Co-author: Anesthesiology—Progress Since 1940, 1973. Editor: Clin. Anesthesia Conf., 1967; co-editor; Advances in Anesthesiology; Muscle Relaxants, 1967; Highlights of Clin. Anesthesiology, 1971; Anestesiologia Clinica, 1974; collaborator Medicina et Pharmacologia Experimentalis, 1959-67; editorial bd. Jour. Oral Therapeutics and Pharmacology, 1964-68, Pharmacology and Therapeutics in Dentistry, 1968—, Am. Jour. Therapeutics and Clinical Reports, 1968—, Acupuncture and Electrotherapeutics Research, 1975—; editorial cons. Jour. Pharmacology and Exptl. Therapeutics, 1959—. Research, numerous publs. in field. Home: 100 Haven Ave New York NY 10032 Office: 622 W 168th St New York NY 10032

MARK, MELVIN, educator; b. St. Paul, Nov. 15, 1922; s. Isadore William and Fannye (Abrahamson) M.; B.M.E., U. Minn., 1943, M.S., 1946; Sc.D. (Teaching, Research fellow), Harvard, 1950; m. Elizabeth J. Wyner, Sept. 9, 1951; children—Jonathan S., David W., Peter B. Instr., N.D. State U., 1943-44, U. Minn., 1945-47; project mgr. Gen. Electric Co., Lynn., Mass., 1950-52; mgr. Raytheon Co., Wayland, Mass., 1952-56; cons. engr., 1956—; prof. Lowell Technol. Inst., 1957-59, dean faculty, 1959-62; prof. mech. engring. Northeastern U., Boston, 1963—, dean engring., 1968-79, provost, sr. v.p. for acad. affairs, 1979—; vis. lectr. Mass. Inst. Tech., 1955. Brandeis U., 1958. Served with USAAF, 1944-45. Recipient prize Lincoln Arc Welding Found., 1947. Registered profl. engr., Mass., Minn. Hon. fellow ASME (fellow 1948-50); mem. Am. Soc. Engring. Edn., Sigma Xi, Tau Beta Pi, Pi Tau Sigma, Phi Kappa Phi, Phi Epsilon Pi. Author: Thermodynamics: An Auto-Instructional Text, 1967; Concepts of Thermodynamics, 1975; Thermodynamics: Principles and Applications, 1979. Contbr. articles to profl. jours. Patentee in field. Home: 17 Larch Rd Newton MA 02168 Office: 111 Hayden Hall Northeastern U Boston MA 02115

MARK, PETER ALAN, director, conductor; b. N.Y.C., Oct. 31, 1940; s. Irving and Edna M.; B.A.(Woodrow Wilson fellow), Columbia U., 1961; M.S., Juilliard Sch. Music, 1963; m. Thea Musgrave, Oct. 2, 1971. Concert violist, U.S., S. Am., Europe, 1961-67; asso. prof. music and dramatic art U. Calif., Santa Barbara, 1965—; artistic dir., condr. Va. Opera Assn., Norfolk, 1975—, gen. dir., 1978—, condr. Am. première of Mary, Queen of Scots (Musgrave), 1978, world première of A Christmas Carol (Musgrave), 1979; fellow Creative Arts Inst., U. Calif., 1968-69, 71-72. Recipient Elias Lifchey viola award Juilliard Sch. Music, 1963, named hon. citizen of Norfolk, Va. Opera Assn., Musicians Union, Phi Beta Kappa. Office: 261 W Bute St Norfolk VA 23510

MARK, REUBEN, consumer products co. exec.; b. Jersey City, N.J., Jan. 21, 1939; s. Edward and Libbie (Berman) M.; A.B., Middlebury Coll., 1960; M.B.A., Harvard U., 1963; m. Arlene Slobzian, Jan. 10, 1964; children—Lisa, Peter, Stephen. With Colgate-Palmolive Co., N.Y.C., 1963—, pres., gen. mgr. Colgate-Palmolive Venezuela, 1972-73, pres., gen. mgr. Colgate-Palmolive Can., 1973-74, v.p., gen. mgr. Far East div., 1974-75, v.p., gen. mgr. household products div., 1975-79, group v.p. domestic ops., 1979—. Lectr., Sch. Bus. Adminstrn., U. Conn., 1977. Served with U.S. Army, 1961. Mem. Soap and Detergent Assn. (bd. dirs.). Office: Colgate-Palmolive Co 300 Park Ave New York NY 10022

MARK, SHELLEY M., economist, govt. ofcl.; b. China, Sept. 9, 1922; s. Hing D. and S. (Wong) M.; came to U.S., 1923, naturalized, 1944; B.A., U. Wash., 1943, Ph.D., 1956; M.S., Columbia, 1944; postgrad. (Ford Found. fellow) Harvard, 1959-60; m. Janet Chong, Sept. 14, 1946 (dec. Mar. 1977); children—Philip, Diane, Paul, Peter, Steven; m. 2d, Tung Chow, July 8, 1978. Fgn. news reporter CBS, N.Y., 1945-46; instr. U. Wash., 1946-48; asst. prof. Ariz. State Coll., 1948-51; territorial economist OPS, Honolulu, 1951-53; prof. econs. U. Hawaii, 1953-62, dir. econ. research center, 1959-62; dir. planning and econ. devel. State of Hawaii, 1962-74, state energy coordinator, 1973-74; dir. Office Land Use Coordination EPA, Washington, 1975-77; prof. econs. U. Hawaii, 1978—; also econ. cons. various orgns. Mem. Hawaii Land Use Commn., 1962-74, Gov.'s Adv. Com. Sci. and Tech., 1963-74, Oahu Transp. Policy Com., 1964-74, Regional Export Expansion Council, 1964-74, Gov.'s Agrl. Coordinating Com., 1969-74, Gov.'s Commn. on Year 2000, 1969-74, Hawaii Found. History and Humanities, 1969-74, Hawaii Bicentennial Commn., 1971-74, Hawaii Transp. Control Commn., 1972-74, Gov.'s Ad Hoc Commn. Ops., Revenues and Expenditures, 1973-74, Hawaii Manpower Council, 1974; state liaison officers U.S. Bur. Outdoor Recreation and HUD; econ. adviser Hawaii Legislature, 1954-62; mem. platform com. Democratic Party, 1954-70. Bd. dirs. U. Hawaii Research Corp.; bd. dirs. Council State Planning Agys., pres., 1973-74, hon. mem., 1975—; governing bd. Council State Govts., 1972-74. Recipient Sackett Meml. award Columbia, 1944. Mem. Hawaii Govt. Employees Assn. (pres. univ. chpt., dir. 1958-59), Am. Econ. Assn., Royal Econ. Soc., Western Regional Sci. Assn. (pres. 1974-75, dir.), Phi Beta Kappa, Sigma Delta Chi. Baptist. Author: Economics in Action, 4th edit., 1969; also other books and articles. Home: 2036 Keeaumoku St Honolulu HI 96822 Office: U Hawaii Honolulu HI 96822

MARK, STEWART WINSTON, lawyer; b. Swayzee, Ind., Feb. 18, 1915; s. Raymond Winston and Gertrude (Stewart) M.; A.B., U. Okla., 1937, LL.B., 1939; m. Ruth Eleanor Grimes, Sept. 3, 1938; children—Mary Anne (Mrs. Hal L. Malone II), Stephen S. Admitted to Okla. bar, 1939; practiced in Oklahoma City, 1939-50, 58—, Tulsa, 1950-58; asso. Hayes, Richardson, Shartel & Gilliland, 1939-42; partner Tomerlin, High & Mark, 1946-50; with law dept. Gulf Oil Corp., 1950-59; partner McAfee, Taft, Mark, Bond, Rucks & Woodruff, 1959—. Chmn. legal div. United Appeal, 1969; trustee Okla. Bar Found. Served to lt. col. AUS, 1942-46. Fellow Am. Bar Found.; mem. Am., Okla., Oklahoma County (pres. 1973) bar assns., Order of Coif, Phi Beta Kappa. Editor: Oil and Gas Reporter, 1960-64. Home: 1716 Coventry Ln Oklahoma City OK 73120 Office: 100 Park Ave Bldg Oklahoma City OK 73102

MARK, VERNON HERSCHEL, physician, educator; b. Mpls., July 6, 1925; s. Daniel Benjamin and Diana (Dworsky) M.; B.S., U. Minn., 1944, M.B., 1946, M.D., 1947, M.S., 1949; m. Alexandra Joyce Globe, Mar. 17, 1952; children—Daniel Benjamin, David Bryan, Valerie Ann, Jeffrey Paul. Intern surgery U. Minn. Hosp., 1947-48, fellow Nat. Found. Infantile Paralysis, 1948-49; asst. resident neurosurgery Mass. Gen. Hosp., 1949-50; resident neurosurgery New Eng. Med. Center and Tufts Med. Coll., 1950-51; mem. staff Mass. Gen. Hosp., 1951—, chief resident neurosurgery, 1953-54, from asst. in neurosurgery to asst. neurosurgeon, 1957-63; clin. asso. neurosurgery, 1964—; research fellow Harvard Med. Sch., 1951-53, teaching fellow surgery, 1953-54, asst. clin. prof. surgery, 1965-68, asso. clin. prof. surgery, then asso. prof. surgery, 1968—, tutor med. sci., 1964-65; dir. neurosurg. service, vis. surgeon Boston City Hosp., 1964—; cons. neurosurgeon Faulkner Hosp., Cambridge Hosp., Parker Hill Med. Center, Brookline Hosp., Lowell Gen. Hosp. Asst. treas., bd. dirs., trustee Neuro-Research Found. Served to capt., M.C., USAF, 1955-57. Sr. fellow NIH, 1951-52; Damon Runyon Cancer Found. fellow, 1952-53. Diplomate Am. Bd. Neurol. Surgery, Nat. Bd. Med. Examiners. Fellow A.C.S., Boston Med. Library; mem. Am., Mass. (chmn. public relations com.), Suffolk med. assns., Boston Soc. Psychiatry and Neurology (pres. 1969-70), Boston Surg. Soc., New Eng. Neurosurg. Soc., Soc. Neurol. Surgeons Am. Assn. Neurol. Surgeons, Pavlovian Soc. N.Am., Soc. Neurosci., World, Am. socs. for stereotactic, functional neurosurgery (council), Internat. Assn. Study Pain, Alpha Omega Alpha. Club: Harvard (Boston). Editor: Neurosurgical vol. of Lewis' Monographs in Surgery, 1971-76. Spl. research nonspecific pain pathways in thalamus human brain, the limbic system, correlation of function and structure within human brain, computerized tomography of the brain. Author: Violence and the Brain. Contbr. articles in field. Office: Neurosurg Service Boston City Hosp 818 Harrison Ave Boston MA 02118

MARKE, JULIUS JAY, educator, law librarian; b. N.Y.C., Jan. 12, 1913; s. Isidore and Anna (Taylor) M.; B.S., Coll. City N.Y., 1934; LL.B., N.Y. U., 1937; B.S. in L.S., Columbia, 1942; m. Sylvia Bolotin, Dec. 15, 1946; 1 dau., Elisa Hope. Reference asst. N.Y. Pub. Library, 1937-42; admitted to N.Y. bar, 1938; pvt. practice, N.Y.C., 1939-41; prof. law., law librarian N.Y. U., 1949—, interim dean of libraries, 1975—; lectr. Columbia Sch. Library Service, 1962—, adj. prof., 1978—. Cons. Orientation Program Am. Law, 1965—, Found. Overseas Law Libraries Am. Law, 1968—; cons. copyright Ford Found.; cons. to law libraries, others. Mem. publs. council N.Y.U., 1964—. Served to sgt. AUS, 1943-45. Decorated Bronze Star. Mem. Am. Assn. Law Libraries (pres. 1962-63), Am. Bar Assn., Assn. Am. Law Schs., Council of Nat. Library Assns. (exec. bd., v.p. 1959, 60), Law Library Assn. Greater N.Y. (pres. 1949, 50, chmn. joint com. on library edn. 1950-52, 60-61), Columbia Sch. Library Service Alumni Assn. (pres. 1973-75), Order of Coif (pres. N.Y. U. Law Sch. br.). Club: N.Y. University Faculty (pres. 1965-66). Author: Vignettes of Legal History, 1965, 2d Series, 1977; Copyright and Intellectual Property, 1967. Editor: Modern Legal Forms, 1953; The Holmes Reader, 1955; The Docket Series, 1955—; Bender's Legal Business Forms, 4 vols., 1962. Compiler, editor: A Catalogue of the Law Collection at N.Y. U. with Selected Annotations, 1953; Dean's List of Recommended Reading for Pre-Law and Law Students, 1958; co-editor, contbr. Internat. Seminar on Constl. Rev., 1963; Coordinated Law Research, 1977; editor: Holmes Reader, rev. edit., 1964; co-editor Commerical Law Information Sources, 1971. Contbr. articles to profl. jours. Home: 4 Peter Cooper Rd New York NY 10010

MARKELL, ROBERT JOSEPH, TV producer; b. Boston, Apr. 12, 1924; s. Abraham and Frances (Poley) M.; B.S. in Civil Engring., Northeastern U., 1944; student Art Students League, N.Y.C., 1948-49; D.F.A., Northeastern U., 1965; m. Joan Gloria Harris, Nov. 4, 1949; children—Mariana Sari, Gordon Denis. With Grumman Aircraft Co., 1944-46; engaged in civil engring. and architecture, Boston, 1946-48; scenic designer summer stock prodns., also Off Broadway prodns., 1948-49; scenic designer for CBS-TV, 1949-59; asso. producer Playhouse 90, 1959-60; asso. producer The Defenders, 1960-61, producer, 1961-65; producer N.Y. P.D., 1967-69, Ceremony of Innocence for NET, 1970, Dr. Cooks Garden for ABC-Paramount Pictures, 1971; producer Metromedia Producers, 1971-72; exec. producer Tomorrow Entertainment, 1973-74; exec. producer dramatic programs CBS-TV, 1974—, v.p. creative services, 1978—. Recipient Emmy award, 1954, 62, 63, 64, 76, Screen Producers Guild award, 1962, 63. Mem. Acad. TV Arts and Scis., Screen Producers Guild, United Scenic Artists, Tau Beta Pi. Address: Brooklyn Heights NY also Shelter Island NY 11965 also 28 Sidney Pl Brooklyn NY 11201

MARKER, ROBERT SYDNEY, advt. exec.; b. Nashville, July 27, 1922; s. Forest M. and Lassie (Weatherford) M.; B.A., Emory U., 1946; M.A., Vanderbilt U., 1947; m. Elizabeth Davis, Oct. 27, 1943; children—Christopher, Andrew. Account exec. Griswold-Eshleman, 1949-51; advt. mgr. B.F. Goodrich Co., 1947-49; copy group head Maxon, Inc., 1951-56; sr. v.p., dir. creative services McManus, John & Adams, 1956-63; v.p. McCann-Erickson, Inc., 1963-64, sr. v.p., 1964-67, mgr. Detroit office, 1964-68, exec. v.p., N.Y.C., 1967-68, pres., 1968-71, chmn. bd., chief exec. officer, 1971-74, also dir., mem. exec. com.; pres. Times Herald Printing Co., Dallas, 1974—; chmn. exec. com. Needham, Harper & Steers, Inc., 1975—. Bd. dirs. Am. Assn. Advt. Agys., Detroit Adcraft Club, 1965, Detroit Advt. Assn., 1965, N.Y. Bd. Trade. Mem. Mayor's Council on Environment. Served with USAAC, 1943-46. Recipient Creative Advt. awards N.Y. Art Dirs. Club, Detroit Advt. Club, Chgo. Copy Club, Alpha Delta Sigma. Mem. Am. Assn. Advt. Agys. (dir., chmn. Eastern region), Alpha Delta Sigma, Sigma Delta Chi. Clubs: Bloomfield Hills (Mich.)

Country; Greenwich (Conn.) Country; Winged Foot (Mamaroneck, N.Y.). Home: 7 Stepping Stone Ln Greenwich CT 06830 Office: 909 3d Ave New York City NY 10022

MARKERT, CLEMENT LAWRENCE, educator; b. Las Animas, Colo., Apr. 11, 1917; s. Edwin John and Sarah (Norman) M., B.A. summa cum laude, U. Colo., 1940; M.A., U. Calif. at Los Angeles, 1942; Ph.D., Johns Hopkins, 1948; m. Margaret Rempfer, July 29, 1940; children—Alan Ray, Robert Edwin, Betsy Jean. Merck-NRC fellow Calif. Inst. Tech., 1948-50; asst. prof. zoology U. Mich., 1950-56, asso. prof., 1956-57; prof. biology Johns Hopkins, 1957-65; chmn. dept. biology Yale, 1965-71, prof. biology, 1965—, dir. Center for Reproductive Biology, 1974—. Panelist NSF, 1959-63; panelist subcom. on marine biology President's Sci. Adv. Com., 1965-66; mem. council Am. Cancer Soc., 1975-78; co-chmn. developmental biology interdisciplinary cluster President's Biomed. Research Panel, 1975; mem. com. on animal models and genetic stocks NRC, 1979—; trustee Bermuda Biol. Sta. for Research, 1959—; trustee BioScis. Info. Service, 1976—, v.p., 1980; bd. sci. advisers La Jolla Cancer Research Found.; mem. bd. sci. advs. Jane Coffin Childs Meml. Fund for Med. Research, 1979—. Served with Internat. Brigades, Spain, 1938; with Mcht. Marine, 1944-45. Mem. Am. Inst. Biol. Scis. (pres. 1965), Nat. Acad. Scis. (governing council 1977-80), Inst. Medicine, Am. Soc. Biol. Chemists, Internat. Soc. Developmental Biologists, Am. Soc. Developmental Biology (pres. 1963-64), Soc. for Study of Reprodn., Am. Acad. Arts and Scis., Am. Genetic Assn. (v.p. 1979), Am. Soc. Naturalists (v.p. 1967), Am. Soc. Zoologists (pres. 1967), Genetics Soc. Am., Am. Soc. for Cell Biology, Phi Beta Kappa, Sigma Xi. Editor: Prentice-Hall Series in Developmental Biology, Procs. 3d Internat. Conf. Isozymes, 1974. Mng. editor Jour. Exptl. Zoology, 1963—; editorial bd. Archives of Biochemistry and Biophysics, 1963—, Sci. mag., 1979—, Differentiation, 1973—; Developmental Genetics, 1979—. Home: 64 Hartford Turnpike Hamden CT 06517

MARKERT, WALLACE, JR., mfg. co. exec.; b. Long Branch, N.J., Aug. 13, 1924; s. Wallace and Margaret (Phelan) M.; M.E., Stevens Inst. Tech., Hoboken, N.J., 1944; m. Kathryn H. McConnell, Apr. 29, 1945; children—Thomas H., Daniel H. With Babcock & Wilcox Co., 1947—, v.p. research and devel., 1977. Served with USNR, 1943-45. Mem. ASME, Am. Nuclear Soc., Am. Soc. Metals, Am. Chem. Soc., IEEE. Club: Alliance Country. Home: 959 Glenwood Dr Alliance OH 44601 Office: PO Box 835 Alliance OH 44601

MARKEY, EDWARD JOHN, Congressman; b. Malden, Mass., July 11, 1946; s. John E. and Christine M. (Courtney) M.; B.A., Boston Coll., 1968, J.D., 1972. Admitted to Mass. bar; mem. Mass. Ho. of Reps., 1973-76; mem. 94th-96th Congresses from 7th Mass. Dist., mem. Commerce Com., Interior Com.; mem. New Eng. Congressional Caucus, N.E.-Midwest Econ. Advancement Coalition, Democratic Study Group, Environ. Study Conf., Freshman Caucus 95th Congress. Mem. Mass. Bar Assn. (Mass. Legislator of Year 1975). Club: K.C. Mem. editorial staff Boston Coll. Law Rev. Home: 7 Townsend St Malden MA 02148 Office: 213 Cannon House Office Bldg Washington DC 20515

MARKEY, GENE, writer; b. Jackson, Mich., Dec. 11, 1895; s. Eugene Lawrence and Alice (White) M.; B.S., Dartmouth, 1918; student Art Inst. Chgo., 1919-20; L.H.D., Rollins Coll., 1957; m. Joan Bennett, 1932 (div. 1937); 1 dau., Melinda; m. 2d, Hedy Lamarr, 1939 (div. 1940); m. 3d, Myrna Loy (div. 1950); m. 4th, Lucille Parker Wright, 1952. Served as 1st lt., 19th Inf., AUS, 1917-19; with USNR 1930-55; on active duty, 1941-46; promoted commodore, 1945; ret. rear adm., 1955. Spl. asst. Sec. of Navy, 1944, 46. Decorated Legion of Merit, Bronze Star, Navy Commendation Medal (U.S.); Star of Solidarity (Italy); Legion of Honor (France). Mem. Delta Kappa Epsilon. Mem. Roman Catholic Ch. Clubs: White's (London); Army and Navy (Washington); Knickerbocker, Brook, Jockey (N.Y.C.). Author: Literary Lights, 1923; Men About Town, 1924; The Dark Island (with Charles Collins), 1928; Anabel, 1928; Stepping High, 1929; The Road to Roman, 1930; His Majesty's Pyjamas, 1934; The Great Companions, 1949; Kingdom of the Spur, 1953; Kentucky Pride, 1956; That Far Paradise, 1960; Women, Women, Everywhere, 1964; The Little Emerald, 1978; (plays) Right You Are, 1925, (with Samuel Hoffenstein) The Eskimo, 1926. Contbr. short stories to mags. Home: 18 La Gorce Circle La Gorce Island Miami Beach FL 33139

MARKEY, HOWARD THOMAS, chief judge U.S. ct.; b. Chgo., Nov. 10, 1920; s. Thomas Joseph and Vera Marie (Dryden) M.; J.D. cum laude, Loyola U., Chgo., 1949; M. in Patent Law, John Marshall Law Sch., 1950; m. Elizabeth Catherine Pelletier, Mar. 17, 1942; children—Jeffrey, Christopher, Thomas (dec.), Mary Frances. Admitted to Ill. bar, 1950, practiced in Chgo., 1950-72; partner firm Parker & Carter; Parker, Markey & Plyer, 1956-72; chief judge U.S. Ct. of Customs and Patent Appeals, Washington, 1972—. Lectr. on jets, rockets, missiles and space, 1946-50, on U.S. Constitution, 1950—; instr. patent law Loyola U., 1970-71. Served to lt. col. USAAF, 1941-46, USAF, 1950-52; pioneer jet test pilot, 1944-46; maj. gen. Res. Decorated Legion of Merit, D.F.C., Soldier's medal, Air medal, Bronze Star (U.S.); Mil. Merit Ulchi medal (Korea). Recipient George Washington Honor medal Freedoms Found., 1964. Mem. Am. Bar Assn., Am. Judicature Assn., Am. Legion (post comdr.), Air Force Assn. (pres. 1960-61, chmn. 1961-62). Republican. Club: Rotary. Office: US Ct Customs and Patent Appeals 717 Madison Pl NW Washington DC 20439*

MARKEY, LUCILLE PARKER, thoroughbred breeder and owner; b. Maysville, Ky., Dec. 14, 1896; d. John W. and Sarah B. (Owens) Parker; ed. Weston Sch.; m. Warren Wright, Mar. 26, 1919 (dec. Dec. 1950); 1 son, Warren; m. 2d, Gene Markey, Sept. 27, 1952. Owner, propr. Calumet Farm, breeding establishment and racing stable, Lexington, Ky., 1950—; 8 winners Ky. Derby. Address: 18 La Gorce Circle La Gorce Island Miami Beach FL 33141

MARKEY, WILLIAM ALAN, health care adminstr.; b. Cleve., Dec. 29, 1927; s. Oscar Bennett and Claire (Feldman) M.; student Case Inst. Tech., 1945-48; B.A., U. Mich., 1950; M.S., Yale, 1954; m. Irene Nelson, Oct. 31, 1954; children—Janet Ellen, Suzanne Katherine. Resident hosp. adminstrn. Beth Israel Hosp., Boston, 1953-54; asst. dir. Montefiore Hosp., Pitts., 1954-56; asst. adminstr. City of Hope Med. Center, Duarte, Calif., 1956-57, adminstrv. dir., 1957-66; asso. dir. cancer hosp. project, instr. pub. health U. So. Calif. Sch. Medicine, 1966-67, asst. clin. prof. pub. health and community medicine, 1968-70, asst. prof., 1970—, dep. dir. regional med. programs, 1967-71; adminstr. Health Care Agy., County of San Diego, 1971-74, health services cons., 1974-75; dir. Maricopa County Dept. Health Services, Phoenix, 1975—; lectr. pub. health Sch. Pub. Health, U. Calif. at Los Angeles, 1969-74; lectr. community medicine Sch. Medicine, U. Calif. at San Diego, 1973-75; cons. Los Angeles County Dept. of Hosps., 1966-71. Mem. bd. edn. Duarte Unified Sch. Dist., 1967-72, pres., 1970-72; bd. dirs. Hosp. Council So. Calif., 1963-67, sec. 1966-67; bd. dirs. Duarte Pub. Library Assn., 1965-72, Duarte-Bradbury chpt. Am. Field Service, 1965-72, Duarte-Bradbury Community Chest, 1961-68, Central Ariz. Health Planning Assn., 1975—. Served with USAF, 1950-52. Fellow Am. Coll. Hosp. Adminstrs.; mem. Am. Hosp. Assn., Am. Pub. Health Assn., Royal Soc. Health, Calif. Hosp. Assn. (trustee 1966-69). Clubs: Kiwanis, Rotary (past pres. Duarte). Home: 3532 E Orange Dr Phoenix AZ 85018 Office: 2601 E Roosevelt St Phoenix AZ 85008

MARKEY, WINSTON ROSCOE, educator; b. Buffalo, Sept. 20, 1929; s. Roscoe Irvin and Catherine L. (Higgins) M.; B.S., Mass. Inst. Tech., 1951, Sc.D., 1956; m. Phoebe Anne Sproule, Sept. 10, 1955; children—Karl Richard, Katherine Ilse, Kristina Anne. Engr., Mass. Inst. Tech., 1951-57, asst prof., 1957-62, asso. prof. 1962-66, prof., 1966—, dir. Measurement Systems Lab., 1961—; chief scientist USAF, 1964-65, mem. scientific adv. bd., 1966-69. Recipient Exceptional Civilian Service award USAF, 1965. Asso. fellow Am. Inst. Aeros. and Astronautics; mem. Sigma Xi, Tau Beta Pi, Gamma Alpha Rho. Author: (with J. Hovorka) The Mechanics of Inertial Position and Heading Indication, 1961. Asso. editor: Am. Inst. Aeros. and Astronautics Jour., 1963-66. Home: 11 Edgewood Rd Lexington MA 02173 Office: MIT Measurement Systems Lab Cambridge MA 02139

MARKHAM, JESSE WILLIAM, economist; b. Richmond, Va., Apr. 21, 1916; s. John James and Edith (Luttrell) M.; A.B., U. Richmond, 1941; postgrad. Johns Hopkins U., 1941-42; M.A., Harvard U., 1947, Ph.D., 1949; m. Penelope Jane Anton, Oct. 15, 1944; children—Elizabeth Anton Markham McLean, John James, Jesse William. Accountant, E.I. duPont de Nemours Co., Richmond, 1935-38; teaching fellow Harvard U., 1946-48; asst. prof. Vanderbilt U., 1948-52, asso. prof., 1952-53; chief economist FTC, Washington, 1953-55; asso. prof. Princeton U., 1955-57, prof. econs., 1957-68; prof. Harvard Grad. Sch. Bus. Adminstrn., 1968-72, Charles Edward Wilson prof., 1972—; vis. prof. Columbia U., 1958; Ford Found. vis. prof. Harvard Grad. Sch. Bus. Adminstrn., 1965-66; research staff, mem. bd. editors Patent Trademark Copyright Research Inst., George Washington U., 1955—; econs. editor Houghton Mifflin Co., 1961—; U.S. del. commn. experts on bus. practices European Productivity Agy., OEEC, 1956, 57, 58, 59, 61; vis. prof. Harvard U., 1961-62; dir. Ford Found. Seminar Region II, 1961; adv. com. mktg. to sec. commerce, 1967-71; mem. Am. Bar Assn. Commn. to study FTC, 1969. Active Boy Scouts Am.; chmn. Harvard Parents Com. Served as lt. USNR, World War II. Ford Found. research prof., 1958-59. Mem. Am., So. econ. assns., U.S. C. of C. (econ. policy com.), Phi Beta Kappa. Episcopalian. Club: Harvard (N.Y.C.). Author: Competition in the Rayon Industry, 1952; The Fertilizer Industry: Study of an Imperfect Market, 1958; The American Economy, 1963; (with Charles Fiero and Howard Piquet) The European Common Market: Friend or Competitor, 1964; (with Gustav Papanek) Industrial Organization and Economic Development, 1970; Conglomerate Enterprise and Public Policy, 1973; sect. on oligopoly Internat. Ency. Social Scis.; contbr. articles to econ. jours. Home: Leverett Towers F-112 28 De Wolfe Cambridge MA 02138 Office: 14 Anderson Harvard Grad Sch Bus Adminstrn Boston MA 02163

MARKHAM, JORDAN J., physicist; b. Samokov, Bulgaria, Dec. 25, 1916 (parents U.S. citizens); s. Reuben Henry and Mary (Gall) M.; B.S., Beloit (Wis.) Coll., 1938; M.S., Syracuse U., 1940; Ph.D., Brown U., 1946; m. Lillian Cagnon, Feb. 6, 1943; children—Linda C., Roger H. With div. war research Columbia U., 1942-45; trainee Clinton Lab., Oak Ridge, 1946-47; instr. physics U. Pa., 1947-48; asst. prof. Brown U., 1948-50; physicist Applied Physics Lab., Johns Hopkins U., 1950-53, research lab. Zenith Radio Corp., 1953-60; sci. adv. Armour Research Found., 1960-62; prof. physics Ill. Inst. Tech., 1962—; vis. prof. Phys. Inst., U. Frankfurt (Germany), summer 1965; sabbatical leave U. Reading (Eng.), 1977. Fellow Am. Phys. Soc. Author: F-centers in Alkali Halides, 1966; also articles. Home: 1528 Tyrell Ave Park Ridge IL 60068 Office: 3301 S Dearborn St Chicago IL 60616

MARKHAM, RONALD VICTOR, mining co. exec.; b. Toronto, Ont., Can., Mar. 12, 1928; s. Albert V. and Laura (Barrett) M.; grad. Vaughan Road Coll., 1942; LL.D., Pepperdine U., 1973. Pres., Canadian South African Diamond Corp. Ltd., 1968—, United Copper Corp. Ltd., 1966—, Paramount Mining Ltd., 1967—, Mut. Pacific Investments Ltd., 1966—, Haldane Silver Mines Ltd., 1966—, Pacific Projects Ltd., 1967—; dir. Dynasty Explorations Ltd., Atlas Explorations Ltd., Atlas Oil & Gas Ltd., Cima Mines Ltd., Pelly River Mines Ltd., Allied Minerals Ltd. Has provided financing in excess of 50,000,000 for Canadian mining and petroleum corps. Recipient Horatio Alger award, 1975.

MARKIN, DAVID ROBERT, motor co. exec.; b. N.Y.C., Feb. 16, 1931; s. Morris and Bessie (Markham) M.; B.S., Bradley U., 1953; m. Barbara C. Flaherty, July 3, 1967; children—Sara, Tom, John, Chris, Meredith. Foreman, Checker Motors Corp., Kalamazoo, 1955-57, factory mgr., 1957-62, v.p. sales, 1962-70, pres., 1970—, also dir.; dir. Continental Air Transport Co. Trustee Kalamazoo Coll. Served to 1st lt. USAF, 1953-55. Mem. Alpha Epsilon Pi. Clubs: Standard (Chgo.); Park (Kalamazoo). Home: 1400 Whites Rd Kalamazoo MI 49001 Office: 2016 N Pitcher St Kalamazoo MI 49007

MARKLE, GEORGE BUSHAR, IV, surgeon; b. Hazleton, Pa., Oct. 29, 1921; s. Alvan and Gladys (Jones) M.; B.S., Yale U., 1943; M.D., U. Pa., 1946; m. Mildred Donna Umstead, July 3, 1944; children—Donna Markle Partee, Melanie Jones Markle, George Bushar, Christian. Intern, Geisinger Med. Center, Danville, Pa., 1946-47, resident, 1947-49; surg. fellow Mayo Clinic, Rochester, Minn., 1949-52; chief surgery U.S. Army Hosp., Ft. Monroe, Va., 1952-54; practice gen. surgery, Carlsbad, N.Mex., 1954—; surg. staff Carlsbad Regional Med. Center, 1954-77, Guadalupe Med. Center, 1977—. Panelist, Voice of Am. Served with M.C., U.S. Army, 1952-54. Recipient Distinguished Service award Jr. C. of C., 1956. Diplomate Am. Bd. Surgery. Fellow Internat. Coll. Surgeons, Southwestern Surg. Congress, Priestley Surg. Soc.; mem. Eddy County Med. Soc., Am. Med. Assn. Republican. Presbyn. Club: Kiwanis. Author: Ill Health and Other Foolishness, 1966; How to Stay Healthy All Your Life, 1968. Contbr. articles to profl. jours. Home: 1003 N Shore Dr Carlsbad NM 88220 Office: 911 N Canal St Carlsbad NM 88220. *Those blest in family and fortune, things not of their own making, ought, I believe, to strive, as they are able, to deserve those blessings through service to God and Man. Even the least of us has some power to influence others through our examples and attitudes, and through each we influence, for good or bad, we may affect sequentially many others, like ever widening ripples on the water.*

MARKLE, ROGER A(LLAN), mining co. exec.; b. Sidney, Mont., Dec. 12, 1933; s. Forrest William and Mary Elizabeth (Hartley) M.; B.S. in Mining Engring., U. Alaska, 1959; M.S. in Mine Mgmt., Stanford U., 1965; M.B.A., U. Chgo., 1972; m. Mary Elizabeth Thompson, Jan. 13, 1967. Mgr. mine devel. Amoco Minerals, Inc., Chgo., 1973-74; pres. western div. Valley Camp Coal Co., Salt Lake City, 1974-78, pres., chief exec. officer Valley Camp Coal Co., Cleve., 1979—; dir. U.S. Bur. Mines, Washington, 1978-79; dir. Quaker State Oil Refining Corp. Vice chmn. Energy Conservation and Devel. Council of Utah, 1977-78; chmn. Interagy. Task Force for Power Plant Siting, Salt Lake City, 1978-79. Served with USN, 1951-54. Mem. AIME, Nat. Coal Assn. (dir.). Clubs: Alta, Ft. Douglas-Hidden Valley Country (Salt Lake City); Univ. Office: 700 Westgate Tower Cleveland OH 44116

MARKLE, SUSAN MEYER, educator; b. Buffalo, Nov. 11, 1928; d. Alden and Ruth (Alden) Rogers; student Smith Coll., 1946-49; B.A., U. Buffalo, 1951, M.A., 1954, Ph.D., 1960; 1 son, Alden Merrill Meyer. Research fellow Harvard U., 1956-60; dir. programming Center for Programed Instruction, N.Y.C., 1960-62; asst. prof. U. Calif., Los Angeles, 1962-65; head instructional design U. Ill., Chgo., 1965—, Media Prodn. Center, 1977—, asso. prof. psychology, 1965-69, prof., 1969—; cons. AID, India, 1966, 70, Air Tng. Command, 1963-73, Pres.'s Commn. on Instructional Tech., 1969-70, Nat. Inst. Edn., 1973—, Ednl. Products Info. Exchange, 1974—, others. Recipient Publ. of Year award Nat. Soc. Programmed Instruction, 1965; (with P.W. Tiemann) Outstanding Instructional Product award, 1968. Fellow AAAS, Am. Psychol. Assn. (edn. and tng. bd. 1970-73, 78-81, div. rep. council 1975-78); mem. Nat. Soc. Programmed Instruction (life, pres. 1966, chmn. editorial bd. 1965-66, 68-72), Am. Ednl. Research Assn., Sigma Xi. Author: Good Frames and Bad, 1964; film (with P.W. Tiemann) Programming is a Process, 1967, Really Understanding Concepts, 1969; Designs for Instructional Designers, 1978; also articles; editorial bd. Brit. Jour. Ednl. Tech., 1970—, Improving Human Performance, 1973—, Audiovisual Communication Rev., 1974—. Home: 19 E Cedar St Chicago IL 60611

MARKLEY, HERBERT EMERSON, bearing co. exec.; b. Elmore, Ohio, Oct. 5, 1914; s. Henry J. and Amelia (Wilde) M.; B.S. in Bus. Adminstrn., Miami U. Oxford, Ohio, 1938; LL.B., William McKinley Sch. Law, Canton, Ohio, 1943; m. Nancy Mulligan, June 22, 1946; children—Sheila, Herbert James, Maura, Noreen. Admitted to Ohio bar, 1943; with Timken Co., Canton, 1938—, exec. v.p., 1959-68, pres., 1968-79, chmn. exec. com., 1979—; dir. Firestone Tire & Rubber Co., Am. Electric Power Co. Trustee, Case Western Res. U. Served with AUS, 1943-46. Mem. NAM (dir. 1967—, chmn.), Conf. Bd. (sr.) Republican. Methodist. Clubs: International (Washington); Congress Lake (Hartville, Ohio); Union (Cleve.); Downtown Athletic (N.Y.C.); Canton Brookside Country (Canton); Ocean Reef (Fla.). Home: 256 Tanglewood Dr North Canton OH 44720 Office: 1835 Dueber Ave SW Canton OH 44706

MARKLEY, RODNEY WEIR, automobile mfg. co. exec.; b. Denver, Nov. 18, 1912; s. Rodney Weir and Hazel M. (Hayes) M.; student Occidental Coll., 1931-35; m. 2d, Annabel Pugh, Dec. 21, 1968; children—Judith Cornick, Mary Helen. Indsl. paint sales rep. Andrew Brown Co., Sherwin Williams Co., Los Angeles, 1935-42; contract termination mgr. Douglas Aircraft, Santa Monica, Calif., 1942-49; account exec. Aircraft Industries Assn., Washington, 1949-51; asso. Ford Motor Co., Washington, 1951-54, mgr., 1954-64, mng. dir., 1964-66, v.p. Washington staff, 1966-76, v.p. govtl. relations staff, 1976—. Trustee, Sidwell Friends Sch., Washington, 1962-67; mem. Fed. City Council, Washington. Mem. Bus.-Govt. Relations Council, Inc., Kappa Sigma. Clubs: Carlton, Burning Tree, 1925 F St., Internat. (gov.). Home: 3909 Watson Pl NW Washington DC 20016 also 52 Ave de la Reale Port la Galere 06590 Theoule France Office: 815 Connecticut Ave NW Washington DC 20006 also Ford Motor Co The American Rd Dearborn MI 48121

MARKMAN, RAYMOND JEROME, publishing co. exec.; b. Bklyn., Dec. 26, 1927; s. Julius and Celia Markman; B.J., U. Mo., 1949; m. June 4, 1949; 3 children. Vice pres., mgmt. supr. McCann-Erickson, advt. agy., 1963-71; v.p. mktg. GRI Corp., 1971-73; v.p. United Equitable Corp., 1974; exec. v.p. Ency. Brit. U.S.A., Chgo., 1974—; dir. Seago Group, real estate; founder FACT-Found. for a Constructive Tomorrow, econ. edn. Mem. Direct Mail Mktg. Assn., Broadcast Advt. Club, Chgo. Direct Mktg. Assn., Execs. Club Chgo. Home: 424 Lakeside Manor Highland Park IL 60035 Office: 425 N Michigan Ave Chicago IL 60611

MARKMAN, SIDNEY DAVID, art historian; b. Bklyn., Oct. 10, 1911; s. Samuel and Eva (Bodie) M.; A.B., Union Coll., Schenectady, 1934; M.A., Columbia U., 1936, Ph.D., 1943; m. Malvina Man, Mar. 10, 1945; children—Sarah Dinah, Alexander Jacob, Charles William. Prof., Universidad Nacional de Panama, 1941-45; chmn. Junta de Conservación y Restauración de Monumentos Históricos de Panamá, 1942-45; asst. prof. Duke U., 1947-52, asso. prof., 1952-64, prof. art history and archaeology, 1964—, acting chmn. dept. art, 1963, 75-78, dir. grad. studies in art history, 1970-78; adj. prof. Sch. Design, N.C. State U., 1964; Fulbright fellow, Spain, 1961-62; Inst. Internat. Edn. grantee, 1939; Am. Council Learned Socs. grantee, 1943, 66, 68; Am. Philos. Soc. grantee, 1959, 68; Instituto de Cultura Hispánica grantee, 1964; Fulbright fellow, Ecuador, 1979. Mem. Soc. Archtl. Historians, Latin Am. Studies Assn., Internat. Congress Americanists, Soc. Am. Archaeology, Sociedad de Geografía e Historia de Guatemala, Real Academia de Bellas Artes de Santa Isabel de Hungría de Sevilla (Spain). Democrat. Jewish. Author: The Horse in Greek Art, 1943; San Cristóbal de las Casas, 1963; Colonial Architecture of Antigua Guatemala, 1966; Colonial Central America: A Bibliography, 1977; contbr. articles to profl. jours. Home: 919 Urban Ave Durham NC 27701 Office: Art Dept 234 Social Sci Bldg Duke U Durham NC 27706

MARKO, HAROLD MEYRON, diversified industry exec.; b. Detroit, Oct. 29, 1925; s. Louis Meyron and Mae (Goldberg) M.; B.A., U. Mich., 1948; m. Barbara Soss, July 2, 1951; children—Clifford S., Neil L., Matthew P. Salesman, Core Industries, Inc. (formerly SOS Consol. Inc.), Birmingham, Mich., 1951-57, v.p. sales, 1957-60, pres., 1960—, also dir. Mem. founders soc. Detroit Inst. Arts; trustee Nat. Jewish Hosp., Denver, North Detroit Gen. Hosp. Served with AUS, 1943-45. Mem. World Bus. Council. Clubs: Renaissance, Standard (Detroit); Bloomfield Open Hunt. Contbr. chpt. to book. Home: 530 E Long Lake Rd Bloomfield Hills MI 48013 Office: 1411 N Woodward Birmingham MI 48011

MARKOE, FRANK, JR., pharm. co. exec.; b. Balt., Sept. 5, 1923; s. Frank and Margaret (Smith) M.; A.B., Washington and Lee U., 1947; LL.B., U. Md., 1950; m. Margaret McCormack (now div.); children—Andree Sutherland, Ritchie Harrison. Admitted to Md., N.J. bars; practiced law with Karl F. Steinmann, Balt., 1948-50, 50-53; partner Cable & McDaniel, Balt., 1954-55; gen. counsel, dir. Emerson Drug Co., Balt., 1955-56, adminstrv. v.p., 1957-58; v.p., sec., dir., gen. counsel Warner-Lambert Pharm. Co., 1958-67, exec. com., sr. v.p., dir., gen. counsel, sec., 1967-69, exec. asst. chmn. bd., 1970-71, sr. v.p., 1971-73; exec. v.p. Warner-Lambert Co., Morris Plains, N.J., 1973-77, vice chmn. bd., 1977—; hon. holder Alfred E. Driscoll chair Fairleigh Dickinson U. Trustee Morristown Meml. Hosp., Morris County Soc. for Crippled Children and Adults; bd. dirs. N.J. Coll. Medicine and Dentistry, Bd. Internat. Broadcasting, Radio Free Europe/Radio Liberty, Kips Bay Boys; bd. dirs., exec. com., pres. N.J. Ballet. Served with USAAF, 1942-45; PTO. Mem. U.S. C. of C., Proprietary Assn. (chmn., dir., exec. com.), Pharm. Mfrs. Assn. (dir., exec. com.), N.J. State C. of C. (dir.), Phi Beta Kappa. Home: Holland Rd Far Hills NJ 07931 Office: 201 Tabor Rd Morris Plains NJ 07950

MARKOVITZ, HERSHEL, educator; b. McKeesport, Pa., Oct. 11, 1921; s. Morris and Regina (Spiegel) M.; B.S. in Chemistry, U. Pitts., 1942; A.M., Columbia, 1943, Ph.D., 1949; m. Marion Florence Lamson, Aug. 7, 1949; children—Naomi, Joshua, Sarah. Mathematician, Kellex Corp., N.Y.C., 1943-49; fellow Mellon Inst., Pitts., 1949-51, sr. fellow, 1951—; lectr. U. Pitts., 1956-58; vis. lectr.

Johns Hopkins, 1958-59; prof. mechanics and polymer sci. dept. chemistry Carnegie-Mellon U., Pitts., 1967—; adj. prof. U. Pitts., 1972—; mem. U.S. Nat. Com. Theoretical and Applied Mechs., 1976—. Bd. dirs. United Jewish Fedn. Pitts., 1972-75. Fulbright-Hays fellow Weizmann Inst., Rehovoth, Israel, 1964-65. Fellow Am. Phys. Soc.; mem. Soc. Rheology (pres. 1969-71, Bingham medal 1967), Am. Inst. Physics (governing bd. 1970-72), Soc. for Natural Philosophy (treas. 1965-66), Am. Chem. Soc., Com. Concerned Scientists (nat. dir.). Author: (with B.D. Coleman and W. Noll) Viscometric Flows of Non-Newtonian Fluids, 1966. Editor: Polymers in the Engineering Curriculum, 1971; (with E.F. Casassa) Polymer Science, Achievements and Prospects, 1976; asst. editor Jour. Polymer Sci., 1965-68, asso. editor, 1969—. Research and publs. in rheology, polymer physics, continuum mechanics. Home: 5734 Solway St Pittsburgh PA 15217

MARKS, ARNOLD, journalist; b. Phila., Aug. 4, 1912; s. Morris M. and Esther (Joel) M.; B.A., U. Wash., 1935; M.S., Columbia, 1939; m. Isabelle Ruppert, Oct. 3, 1942; 1 son, Rupert William Joel (dec.). Editor, Pasco (Wash.) Herald, 1946; with Oreg. Jour., Portland, 1946—, drama, TV, entertainment editor, 1948-58, entertainment editor, 1958-78, ret., 1978, now spl. columnist and free-lance writer. Served with AUS, 1942-46. Mem. Sigma Delta Chi, Sigma Alpha Mu. Home: 15 Greenridge Ct Lake Oswego OR 97034

MARKS, BERNARD BAILIN, lawyer; b. Sioux City, Iowa, Sept. 6, 1917; s. Meyer A. and Beulah (Bailin) M.; B.S., Harvard, 1939, J.D., 1942; 1 dau., Susan E. Admitted to Iowa bar, 1942; with firm Shull, Marshall & Marks, Sioux City, 1946—, partner, 1949—. Sec., asst. treas., dir. Flavorland Industries, Inc. (formerly Needham Parking Co., Inc.), Sioux City, 1962—; sec., dir., KTIV TV Co., Sioux City, 1965-74; dir. Home Fed. Savs. & Loan Assn.; dir. First Nat. Bank Sioux City; v.p., dir. Valley State Bank, Sioux City, 1965-74. Bd. dirs. Iowa Heart Assn., 1960, Woodbury County chpt., 1958—, pres., 1962-64; bd. dirs. Sioux City Art Center, 1952-54, Sioux City United Fund, 1965-71, Sioux City Community Appeals Bd., 1965-68; trustee Briar Cliff Coll., Sioux City, 1968-74. Served with USAAF, 1942-46. Mem. Am., Iowa, Woodbury County (pres. 1958) bar assns., Am. Coll. Probate Counsel, Sioux City C. of C. (bd. dirs. 1964-67, treas. 1965-66). Mason (Shriner). Clubs: Sioux City Lawyers (pres. 1951), Sioux City Country (bd. dirs. 1963-64). Home: 2619 Jackson St Sioux City IA 51104 Office: 1109 Badgerow Bldg Sioux City IA 51102

MARKS, BERNARD HERMAN, physician, educator; b. Cleve., Apr. 21, 1921; s. Morris and Rose M.; B.S., Ohio State U., 1942, M.D., 1945, M.S., 1950; m. Mary Sears, Sept. 4, 1943; children—Martha, Ellen. Intern, Del. Hosp., Wilmington, 1945-46; practice medicine, specializing in pharmacology, Columbus, Ohio, 1950-74, Detroit, 1974—; instr., asst. prof., asso. prof., prof. Ohio State U., 1950-64, chmn. dept. pharmacology, 1964-74; prof., chmn. dept. pharmacology Wayne State U., 1974—. Served from lt. to capt., M.C., 1946-48. Research grantee NIH, 1954-79, Mem. Am. Soc. Pharmacology and Exptl. Therapeutics, Endocrine Soc., Soc. Exptl. Biology and Medicine, N.Y. Acad. Sci. Office: 540 E Canfield St Detroit MI 48201

MARKS, BRUCE, artistic dir., choreographer; b. N.Y.C., Jan. 23, 1937; s. Albert and Helen (Kosersky) M.; student Brandeis U., 1954-55, Julliard Sch., 1955-56; m. Toni Pihl Petersen, Jan. 27, 1966; children—Erik Anthony, Adam Christopher, Kenneth Rikard. Prin. dancer Met. Opera, 1956-61, Am. Ballet Theatre, 1961-72, Royal Swedish Ballet, 1963, Festival Ballet, London, 1965, Royal Danish Ballet, 1971-76; artistic dir. Ballet West, Salt Lake City, 1976—; choreographer Eliot Field Ballet Co., 1970, Royal Danish Ballet, 1972-73, Netherlands Dance Theatre, 1974, Ballet West, 1976—. Mem. dance adv. panel Nat. Endowment for Arts, 1979, chmn. internat. selection com., 1979. Artistic fellow Aspen Inst. for Humanistic Studies, 1979. Home: 4739 Fairfield Rd Salt Lake City UT 84117 Office: Box 11336 Salt Lake City UT 84147

MARKS, CHARLES, surgeon, educator; b. Nr. Kiev, Ukraine, USSR, Jan. 28, 1922; s. Abe and Sonia (Beck) M.; came to U.S., 1963, naturalized, 1968; M.D., U. Cape Town, 1945; M.S., Marquette U., Milw., 1966; Ph.D., Tulane U., 1973; m. Joyce Wernick, Dec. 11, 1949; children—Malcolm, Peter, Ian, Anthony. Intern, Groote Schuur Hosp., Cape Town, S. Africa, 1946, resident, 1947-49; resident Royal Coll. Surgeons affiliated hosps., Guys Hosp., London, 1950-53; cons. surgeon Salibury, Rhodesia, 1953-63; asso. prof. surgery Marquette U. Med. Sch., 1963-67; dir. surgery Mt. Sinai Hosp., Cleve., 1967-71, asso. clin. prof. surgery Case Western Res. U. Med. Sch., Cleve., 1967-71; prof. surgery La. State U. Med. Sch., New Orleans, 1971—; surgeon Charity, VA, Touro, Hotel Dieu hosps., (all New Orleans). Named Hunterian Prof., Royal Coll. Surgeons Eng., 1956, Clin. Tchr. of Year, Aesculapian Honor Soc., 1973, 74, 77. Fellow A.C.S., Am. Coll. Cardiology, Royal Coll. Surgeons Eng., Royal Coll. Physicians Edinburgh (hon.), Am. Coll. Chest Physicians, Royal Soc. Medicine; mem. Phi Delta Epsilon. Clubs: New Orleans Lawn Tennis, Cleve. Racquet. Author: Applied Surgical Anatomy, 1972; The Portal Venous System, 1973; A Surgeons World, 1972; Carcinoid Tumors, 1979. Home: 1680 State St New Orleans LA 70118. *I am grateful for the opportunities to have served others while enjoying a sense of fulfillment. The pursuit of professional goals has required persistence and perseverance balanced by a target of high ideals and commitment to excellence.*

MARKS, CHARLES CALDWELL, indsl. distbn. co. exec., b. Birmingham, Ala., June 1, 1921; s. Charles Pollard and Isabel (Caldwell) M.; student Birmingham U., 1930-38; B.S. in Physics, U. of South, 1942; grad. mgmt. seminar Harvard U., 1957; m. Jeanne Vigeant, Jan. 12, 1945; children—Randolph C., Margaret Marks Porter, Charles P. With Owen-Richards Co. (name changed to Motion Industries, Inc. 1970), Birmingham, 1946—, chmn. bd., 1952-73, pres., 1973—; dir. Home Fed. Savs. & Loan Assn.; bd. dirs. So. Research Inst. Pres., Workshop for Blind, Birmingham, 1958-61, Children's Aid Soc. Birmingham, 1962; chmn. Com. of 100, Birmingham, 1963; co-chmn. United Appeal of Jefferson County, 1963; trustee, regent U. of South. Served to lt. USNR, World War II; ATO, MTO. Mem. Bearing Specialist Assn. (adv. bd.), Navy League, Blue Key, Phi Beta Kappa, Sigma Alpha Epsilon. Episcopalian. Clubs: The Club, Redstone, Sewanee of Birmingham, Mountain Brook. Home: 2828 Charokee Rd Birmingham AL 35223 Office: PO Box 1477 Birmingham AL 35201

MARKS, CLAUDE, artist; b. London, Eng., Nov. 13, 1915; s. Joseph Morris and Hylda Rose (Davis) M.; M.A. in Modern Langs., Trinity Coll., Cambridge U., 1936; M.F.A., State U. Iowa, 1948; m. Sue Blagden, Sept. 8, 1942; 1 son, David. Came to U.S., 1938, naturalized, 1942. Asst. prof. art State U. Ia., 1948-50; painter, scenic designer in Gt. Britain and N.Y.C., 1951-61; guest lectr. art Met. Mus. Art, N.Y.C., 1959—; tchr. courses art history and appreciation Parsons Sch. Design, New Sch. for Social Research, Juilliard Sch. Music, Sch. Visual Arts, N.Y.C.; exhibited in one man shows FAR Gallery, N.Y.C., 1961, Am. embassy, London, 1965, The Room, Greenwich, Eng., 1970, Lincoln Center, N.Y.C., 1971, Mus. City N.Y., 1966, Dimitria Gallery, Princeton, N.J., 1972, Margo Feiden Galleries, N.Y.C., 1979. Served with USAAF, 1942-45. Mem. United Scenic Artists Union. Democrat. Author: From the Sketchbooks of the Great Artists, 1972; Pilgrims, Heretics and Lovers: A Medieval Journey, 1975. Scriptwriter The Lute and the Sword, CBS-TV, 1977. Home: 315 Central Park W New York NY 10025

MARKS, DOROTHY LOUISE AMES (MRS. LEONARD H. MARKS), journalist; b. Washington, Sept. 18, 1919; d. Frank Diman and Mary (Gannett) Ames; A.B., George Washington U., 1940; postgrad. U. N.C., 1941; m. Leonard H. Marks, June 3, 1948; children—Stephen Ames, Robert Evan. Asst. dir. pub. info. FCC, Washington, 1941-45; Washington corr. Variety, San Diego Jour., Sioux Falls (S.D.) Argus Leader, 1945-50; contbg. editor Democratic Nat. Com., Washington, 1952-60; corr. N.Am. Newspaper Alliance and Women's News Service, Washington, 1969—. Mem. exec. com. Fgn. Student Service Council, 1968-69. Pres., Woman's Nat. Democratic Club, 1965-67. Bd. governance George Washington U., 1970-71; bd. dirs. Meridian House; trustee Corcoran Gallery Art, 1976—. Clubs: Washington Press, Am. Newspaper Women's, 1925 F Street. Home: 2833 McGill Terr NW Washington DC 20008

MARKS, EDWARD, ambassador; b. Chgo., Apr. 22, 1934; B.A., U. Mich., 1956; M.A., U. Okla., 1975. Exchange program officer, 1959-60; econ. officer, Nairobi, Kenya, 1960-63; consular officer, Nuevo Laredo, Mex., 1963-65, consular adminstrv. officer, 1965-66; econ. officer, Lusaka, Zambia, 1966-69, internat. relations officer, 1970, econ.-comml. officer, 1970-71; econ.-comml. officer, Brussels, 1971-74; prin. officer, Lubumbashi, 1974-76; alt. dir. Office Central African Affairs, 1976-77; ambassador to Republic of Guinea-Bissau and Republic of Cape Verde, 1977—. Served with U.S. Army, 1956-58.

MARKS, EDWIN S., securities dealer; b. N.Y.C., June 3, 1926; s. Carl and Edith R. (Smith) M.; student Princeton, 1944-45; B.S., U.S. Mil. Acad., 1949; m. Nancy Lucille Abeles, June 21, 1949; children—Carolyn Gail, Linda Beth, Constance Ann. Commd. 2d lt. U.S. Army, 1949, 1st lt., 1951, ret., 1953; v.p. Carl Marks & Co., N.Y.C., 1958-61, pres., 1961—, also dir.; exec. v.p., dir. CMNY Capital Co., Inc., 1962—. Trustee Lincoln Center Fund, 1967-77, Hofstra U., 1974-79, Sarah Lawrence Coll., 1979—; bd. dirs. Chief Execs. Forum; trustee North Shore Child Guidance, Inc. Mem. Nat. Assn. Securities Dealers (mem. fgn. com.), West Point Soc., N.Y. Bd. Trade, Mexican C. of C. Club: Harmonie (N.Y.C.). Author: What I Know About Foreign Securities, 1958. Home: 15 Eagle Point Dr Kings Point NY 11024 Office: 77 Water St New York City NY 10005

MARKS, FREDERICK HOWE, journalist; b. Boston, Mar. 22, 1942; s. George Aaron and Emily (Howe) M.; B.A., Hamilton Coll., Clinton, N.Y., 1964; m. Marcia Regnier, Oct. 5, 1968. Reporter, Worcester (Mass.) Telegram & Gazette, 1968; with UPI, 1968—, bur. chief, Bangkok, 1973-75, mgr. N. Asia, Tokyo, 1975—; mem. Fulbright Selection Com. for Journalists from Japan, 1976. Served to lt. USNR, 1964-68. Decorated Bronze Star with combat V, Purple Heart. Mem. fgn. corr. clubs Japan (pres. 1977-78), Hong Kong. Home: 7-19-7 chome Koyama Shinagawa-ku Tokyo Japan Office: care UPI CPO Box 665 Tokyo Japan. *The profession of journalism is synonomous with the truth. If that value is absent, journalism becomes not a profession, but an expedient—and thereby spurious.*

MARKS, J(OSEPH) DAVID, automotive co. exec.; b. Balt., July 28, 1913; s. Abraham and Mollie (Orentreich) M.; student Cooper Union, 1929-34, Newark U., 1935-36; div.; children—Barbara Joan, Marjorie Jayne. Exec. v.p. Bolton Mfg. Co., West Haven, Conn., 1941-45; cons. engr. Conn., N.Y., N.J., 1945-56; mgr. engrng. G-V Controls, Livingston, N.J., 1956-59; v.p. Lehigh Valley Industries, N.Y.C., 1959-66; v.p. Echlin Mfg. Co., Branford, Conn., 1966—, dir., 1969-73, pres. Sensor Engrng. Co. div., 1978—; dir. Megatech Corp., Billerica, Mass., Echlin-Charger Pty. Ltd., Johannesburg, S. Africa. Pres. West Orange Citizens Charter Assn., 1955-60; mem. West Orange Bd. Edn., 1957-58; chmn. West Orange Redevl. Commn., 1962-64. Mem. Soc. Automotive Engrs., Am. Inst. Aeros. and Astronautics, Am. Def. Preparedness Assn. (life), Nat. Rifle Assn. (life). Patentee electromechanics, optics. Home: Pilgrim's Harbor 21-B Wallingford CT 06492 Office: Echlin Mfg Co 175 N Branford Rd Branford CT 06405

MARKS, JOHNNY (JOHN D.), songwriter; b. Mt. Vernon, N.Y., Nov. 10, 1909; s. Louis B. and Sadie (Van Praag) M.; B.S., Colgate U., 1931; m. Margaret Hope May, Oct. 25, 1947 (dec.); children—Michael, Laura, David. Pres., St. Nicholas Music, Inc.; tour with U.S.O.-ASCAP, Far East, 1968. Trustee, chmn. pres.'s club Colgate U. Served as capt. AUS, 1942-46. Decorated Bronze Star with 4 battle stars; named Songwriter of Year by Songhits mag., 1949; Gold award for comml. Internat. Film and Television Festival of N.Y., 1967, Internat. Soc. Santa Claus award. Mem. ASCAP (dir. 1957—, bd. rev., adv. com.), Marshall Chess Club (dir.), Phi Beta Kappa, Kappa Phi Kappa, Mu Pi Delta. Composer popular songs including: Rudolph The Red-Nosed Reindeer (named to Songwriters Hall of Fame), Address Unknown, She'll Always Remember, Night Before Christmas Song, I Heard the Bells on Christmas Day, Rockin Around the Christmas Tree, A Holly Jolly Christmas, Anyone Can Move a Mountain, Silver and Gold, When Santa Claus Gets Your Letter, A Caroling We Go, Joyous Christmas, Don't Cross Your Fingers, Cross Your Heart, Who Calls, Everything I've Always Wanted (ASCAP award). Editor and arranger two carol books. Originator of melody and harmony method of easy piano arrangements. Composer 1 hr. ann. Christmas TV color spectacular Rudolph the Red-Nosed Reindeer with 8 songs for NBC and CBS, longest running spl. in TV history, 1963—. TV spectacular Ballad of Smokey the Bear, with 8 songs for NBC, 1965, 67, 68, TV spl. The Tiny Tree with eight songs NBC, 1975, 76, 77, 78, TV spl. Rudolph's Shiny New Year ABC, 8 songs, 1976, 77, 78, 79; also comml. Gen. Electric Corp.; also appearances maj. network talk shows; also composer motion picture score, cabaret act, 1977. Home: 117 W 11th St New York NY 10011 Office: 1619 Broadway New York NY 10019

MARKS, JOSEPH, pub. cons.; b. Hull, Eng., Sept. 11, 1907; s. Gabriel and Jane (Brown) M.; grad. Hull Tech. Coll., 1921-24; m. Lillian Shapiro, Feb. 21, 1932; children—Daniel, Sheila, Jonathan. Came to U.S., 1927, naturalized, 1935. Vice pres. Doubleday & Co., Inc., N.Y.C., 1951-63; pub. cons., N.Y.C., 1963—; chmn. bd. Am.-Israel Pub. Co., 1967-69; v.p., dir. BCMA Assos., Inc., 1971—. Lectr. pub. procs. N.Y. U., Columbia, Radcliffe Coll., New Sch.; cons. pub. and printing govt. P.R., 1958; chmn. fgn. trade com. Am. Book Pubs. Council, 1953-56; treas. Am. Com. for Anne Frank Found. Chmn. pres.' council Borough Manhattan Community Coll. Mem. Internat. Assn. Book Pub. Consultants (v.p.), Inst. Ret. Profls., Am. Arbitration Assn. (panel of arbitrators). Clubs: Overseas Press (N.Y.C.); English Speaking Union (London, Eng.). Home: 117-16 Park Ln S Kew Gardens NY 11418 Office: 485 Fifth Ave New York NY 10017

MARKS, LAWRENCE, pharm. co. exec.; b. Jersey City, Oct. 26, 1926; s. David Maxwell and Bess (Harris) M.; B.Sc., Rutgers U., 1948; J.D., N.Y. U., 1952, M.D., 1959; m. Elinor Kleiner, July 29, 1951; children—Anthony and David (twins). Admitted to N.J. bar, 1953, practiced in Paterson, N.J., 1953-55; mem. firm Kleiner & Marks, Paterson, 1953-55; intern USPHS Hosp., S.I., N.Y., 1959-60; resident VA Hosp., East Orange, N.J., 1960-61; practice medicine, specializing in legal medicine, New Brunswick, N.J., from 1961; with E.R. Squibb and Sons, Inc., New Brunswick, 1961—, pres. Mfg. Enterprises, Inc., Humacao, P.R., from 1969, pres. Squibb Chem. Co., Humacao, from 1969, also dir, v.p. Squibb Corp., from 1974, also dir, chmn. Squibb Inst. Med. Research, from 1974, now exec. v.p.; mem. drug research bd. Nat. Acad. Scis.-NRC, 1971-73. Served with U.S. Army, 1945-46. Fellow Am. Coll. Legal Medicine. Home: 12 Sunset Dr Summit NJ 07901 Office: PO Box 4000 Princeton NJ 08540

MARKS, LEONARD HAROLD, lawyer; b. Pitts., Mar. 5, 1916; s. Samuel and Ida (Levine) M.; B.A., U. Pitts., 1935, LL.B., 1938; m. Dorothy Ames, June 3, 1948; children—Stephen Ames, Robert Evan. Admitted to Pa. bar, 1938, D.C. bar, 1946; asst. prof. law U. Pitts. Law Sch., 1938-42; prof. law Nat. U., 1943-55; asst. to gen. counsel FCC, 1942-46; partner firm Cohn & Marks, Washington, 1946-65, 69—; head USIA, 1965-68; chmn. exec. com. Nat. Savs. and Trust Co., 1977—. Chmn., Internat. Conf. on Communications Satellites, 1968-69; Am. del. Internat. Broadcasting Confs., 1948-69; pres. Internat. Rescue Com., 1973-79, Honor Am. Com., 1977—; chmn. U.S. Adv. Commn. on Internat. Ednl. and Cultural Affairs, 1973-78; vice chmn. Fgn. Policy Assn. 1979—. Mem. Am. (mem. ho. of dels. 1962-64), Fed. Communications (pres. 1959-60), bar assns., Bar Assn. D.C., Phi Beta Kappa, Order of Coif, Omicron Delta Kappa, Sigma Delta Chi. Clubs: Cosmos, Metropolitan, Fed. City, 1925 F Street, Broadcasters (pres. 1957-59) (Washington). Home: 2833 McGill Terr NW Washington DC 20008 Office: 1333 New Hampshire Ave NW Washington DC 20036

MARKS, MARC LINCOLN, Congressman; b. Farrell, Pa., Feb. 12, 1927; s. Benjamin H. and Myrtle S. M.; LL.B., U. Va., 1954; m. Jane London, June 22, 1952; children—Leslie, Patricia Mari. Admitted to Pa. bar; sr. partner firm Rodgers, Marks & Perfilio, Sharon, Pa.; mem. 95th-96th Congresses from 24th Pa. Dist.; solicitor Mercer County (Pa.), 1960-66. Served with USAAF, 1945-46. Mem. Am., Pa., Mercer County bar assns., Am., Pa. trial lawyers assns. Republican. Jewish. Clubs: B'nai B'rith, Kiwanis. Office: 1127 Longworth House Office Bldg Washington DC 20515*

MARKS, MEYER BENJAMIN, pediatric allergist; b. Chgo., Feb. 16, 1907; s. Simon and Rose (Block) M.; B.S., U. Ill., 1929, M.D., 1933, M.S., 1934; m. Golda A. Nathan, Sept. 27, 1932; children—Linda, Stephen. Intern Cook County Hosp., Chgo., 1934-35, resident, 1935-36; practice medicine, specializing in pediatrics, Miami Beach, Fla., 1937-57, specializing in pediatric allergy and gen. allergy, 1957—; mem. staffs Mt. Sinai Hosp., Jackson Meml. Hosp.; chief med. officer, v.p. Kraver Inst Ashthmatic Children, North Miami Beach, Fla., 1970—; clin. prof. pediatrics, chief div. pediatric allergy U. Miami, 1970—; v.p. Asthmatic Children's Found. Fla., 1964—; bd. dirs. Asthma Care Assn. Am., 1976—. Hon. pres. med. div. Southeastern div. Am. Friends Hebrew U., 1958-68; pres. Assn. Convalescent Homes and Hosp. for Asthmatic Children, 1971. Recipient Bela Schick Meml. Lecture award in pediatric allergy, Paris, 1974, Bronze award Am. Acad. Pediatrics, 1977; numerous others. Diplomate Am. Bd. Pediatrics, Am. Bd. Allergy and Immunology. Fellow Am. Acad. Pediatrics (Silver award 1975), Am. Coll. Allergists (Fellow Disting. award 1979), Am. Acad. Allergy; mem. Am., Fla., Dade County (Fla.) med. assns., Fla., Miami (pres. 1954-55) pediatric socs., Am. Assn. Certified Allergists, Internat. Assn. Asthmology, Internat. Assn. Allergology, Am. Med Writers Assn., Fla. Acad. Scis., Fla. Allergy Soc. (pres. 1970), Sigma Xi. Jewish. Author: Physical Signs of Allergy in the Respiratory Tract in Children, 1967; Stigmata of Respiratory Tract Allergies, 1972, rev. edit., 1978 (Italian transl. 1976, Spanish transl. 1978). Contbg. author: The Allergic Child, 1963; Allergy and Immunology in Childhood, 1973. Contbg. editor Ear, Nose and Throat Jour., 1976-78. Contbr. articles to profl. jours. Established Golda and Meyer Marks Cobra Art Collection, Ft. Lauderdale Mus. Arts, 1979. Home: 105 E San Marino Dr Miami Beach FL 33139 Office: 333 Arthur Godfrey Rd Miami Beach FL 33140

MARKS, PAUL ALAN, physician, biochemist; b. N.Y.C., Aug. 16, 1926; s. Robert R. and Sarah (Bohorad) M.; A.B. with gen. honors, Columbia, 1945, M.D., 1949; m. Joan Harriet Rosen, Nov. 28, 1953; children—Andrew Robert, Elizabeth Susan, Matthew Stuart. Fellow, Columbia Coll. Phys. and Surgeons, 1952-53, asso., 1955-56, mem. faculty, 1956—, dir. hematology tng., 1961-74, prof. medicine, 1967—, dean faculty of medicine, v.p. med. affairs, 1970-73, dir. Cancer Research Center, 1972—, v.p. health scis., 1973—, prof. human genetics and devel., 1969—, Frode Jensen prof. medicine, 1974—; attending physician Presbyn. Hosp., N.Y.C., 1967—; instr. Sch. Medicine, George Washington U., 1954-55; cons. VA Hosp., N.Y.C., 1962-66. Asso. investigator Nat. Inst. Arthritis and Metabolic Diseases, NIH, Bethesda, Md., 1953-55; mem. adv. panel hematology tng. grants program NIH, 1969-73, chmn. hematology tng. grants program, 1971-73; vis. scientist Lab. Cellular Biochemistry, Pasteur Inst., 1961-62; vis. prof. 1st di Chemica Biologica, U. Genoa (Italy), 1963; mem. adv. panel on developmental biology NSF, 1964-67; mem. Delos Conf., Athens, Greece, 1971, 72; mem. founding com. Radiation Effects Research Found., Japan, 1975; mem. Pres.'s Biomed. Research Panel, 1975-76, Pres.'s Cancer Panel, 1976—; mem. Pres.'s Commn. on Accident at Three Mile Island, 1979; chmn. exec. com. div. med. scis. Nat. Acad. Scis.-NRC, 1973-76; dir. Pfizer, Inc., 1978—, Dreyfus Leverage Fund. Trustee, St. Luke's Hosp., 1970—, Roosevelt Hosp., 1970—, Presbyn. Hosp., 1972—; mem. jury Albert Lasker Awards, 1974—; bd. dirs. Pub. Health Research Inst., N.Y.C., 1971-74; bd. govs. Weizmann Inst., 1976—; mem. council div. biol. scis. and Pritzker Sch. Medicine, U. Chgo. mem. tech. bd. Milbank Meml. Fund, 1978—; trustee Metpath Inst. Med. Edn., 1977—. Recipient Charles Janeway prize Columbia, 1949, Joseph Mather Smith prize, 1959, Stevens Triennial prize, 1960, Swiss-Am. Found. award in med. research, 1965. Commonwealth Fund fellow, 1961-62. Fellow Am. Acad. Arts and Scis.; mem. Inst. Medicine (mem. council 1973-76), Nat. Acad. Scis., Red Cell Club (past chmn.), Am. Fedn. Clin. Research (past councillor Eastern dist.), Am. Soc. Clin. Investigation (pres. 1972-73), Am. Soc. Biol. Chemists, Am. Soc. Human Genetics (past mem. program com.), Am. Assn. Cancer Research, A.C.P., Am. Soc. Cell Biology, Am. Soc. Hematology, Assn. Am. Physicians, Enzyme Club, Harvey Soc., Internat. Soc. Developmental Biologists, Interurban Clin. Club, Soc. for Study Devel. and Growth, World Soc. Ekistics. Editor: Monographs in Human Biology, 1963. Contbr. articles to profl. jours. Mem. editorial bd. Blood, 1964-71, asso. editor, 1976-77, editor-in-chief, 1978—; editor-in-chief Jour. Clin. Investigation, 1967-72. Research on biochemistry erythrocyte aging, predisposing factors to anemia, messenger RNA for hemoglobin, polyribosomes, molecular defect in thalassemia, erythroid cell differentiation and leukemia. Home: Beach Hill Rd Bridgewater CT 06752 Office: 630 W 168th St New York City NY 10032

MARKS, RAYMOND H., chem. co. exec.; b. N.Y.C., July 4, 1922; s. Harry S. and Rebecca (Pollak) M.; B.S., N.C. State Coll., 1943; m. Anne Cohen, Nov. 30, 1952; children—Victoria, Michael, Andrea. Sales exec. Monsanto Chem. Co., Springfield, Mass., 1946-51, Chgo., 1951-52, N.Y.C., 1952-55; sales exec. Knickerbocker Toy & Plastic, N.Y.C., 1955-57; with Cary Chems., Inc., East Brunswick, N.J., 1957-65, exec. v.p., 1960-65, pres., 1965-68; v.p. Tenneco Chems., Inc. (absorbed Cary Chems.), N.Y.C., 1968-70, pres., 1970—, also dir.; dir. Tenneco Chems. Internat. Sales Corp., Tenneco Chems.

Europe Ltd., Bristol, Eng., Albright & Wilson Ltd., London, Eng., Gentech Industries Inc., AMA Internat. Served to 1st lt. Signal Corps, AUS, 1943-46. Mem. Am. Chem. Soc., Soc. Plastics Engrs., Soc. Plastics Industry (dir.), Mfg. Chemists Assn., N.Y. Rubber Group. Office: Park 80 Plaza West-1 Saddlebrook NJ 07662

MARKS, ROBERTA GRACE, med. writer, mag. editor; b. N.Y.C., Mar. 9, 1934; s. Harold Murray and Henrietta (Good) Fillmore; student Hunter Coll., 1951, New Sch. Social Research, 1960. Sec., Rockefeller Inst. Med. Research, N.Y.C., 1951-53; editorial asst. Popular Sci. Monthly, N.Y.C., 1955-60; mng. editor of Modern Drug Ency., also Vet. Drug Ency., Reuben H. Donnelley Corp., N.Y.C., 1961-63; tech. editor Drug Trade News, Topics Pub. Co., N.Y.C., 1963-67, 68-72; exec. editor of Product Mgmt., Med. Econs. Co., Oradell, N.J., 1972-74, Current Prescribing mag., 1974-79. Recipient Jesse H. Neal award Am. Bus. Press, 1976. Democrat. Home: 401 E 81st St New York NY 10028

MARKS, SIDNEY, lawyer, pub. relations counsel; b. N.Y.C.; s. Julius and Anne M.; ed. Coll. City N.Y., N.Y. Law Sch., Bklyn. Law Sch., New Sch. for Social Research, Columbia, U. Chgo.; m. Fahimie Maria Goldenberg, July 15, 1951; 1 son, Joel Abraham. Admitted to N.Y. bar, pvt. practice of law in N.Y.C.; prof. N.Y. Law Sch.; former sec., exec. dir. Zionist Orgn. Am.; former exec. dir. United Cerebral Palsy Assn. Nassau County, Inc., L.I. Lectr. Coll. Law and Econs., Municipal U., Tel Aviv, Israel. Del. World Zionist Congress, Jerusalem; observer non-govtl. orgns., rep. U.S. Mission to UN. Bd. dirs. Keren Hayesod (Palestine Found. Fund), Keren Kayemeth L'Israel (Jewish Nat. Fund), Am. Friends of Municipal U., Tel Aviv. Mem. N.Y. County Lawyers Assn., B'nai Zion (v.p.), Pub. Relations Am. (mem. counselors sect.), Internat. Pub. Relations Assn., Fgn. Policy Assn., Grand Street Boys Assn., Mus. Modern Art, Acad. Polit. Sci., N.Y. Young Men's Hebrew Assn., N.Y. State Bar Assn., Kappa Phi Sigma, Iota Theta. Clubs: Rotary, B'nai B'rith. Office: 300 West End Ave New York City NY 10023. *I ascribe to the precepts laid down by Blackstone, the English law-giver; the belief in the creator and that the Creator has divided all things into good and evil, to which He himself must conform. That these principles for the conduct of human actions include, among others, that we should live honestly, should hurt nobody, and should render to everyone his due.*

MARKUN, PATRICIA MALONEY (MRS. DAVID JOSEPH MARKUN), editor, author; b. Chisholm, Minn., Aug. 24, 1924; d. Andrew Michael and Helen Edith (Ryan) Maloney; B.A. magna cum laude in Journalism, U. Minn., 1945; m. David Joseph Markun, June 14, 1948; children—Sybil, Meredith, David Joseph, Paul. News writer, advt. writer, announcer radio stas. WMFG, Hibbing, Minn., KSTP, St. Paul and WCCO, Mpls., 1942-45; editor employees mag. Electric Machinery Mfg. Co., 1945-46; pub. relations Mpls. Inst. Arts, 1946-48; advt. and publicity dir. Hotel Nicollet, Mpls., 1948; free-lance writer, 1948—; exec. editor Funk & Wagnalls Young Students Ency., 1971-72; editorial asso. Assn. for Childhood Internat., 1973-75; exec. editor Petroleum Today mag. Am. Petroleum Inst., 1975-78; fin. writer Fed. Home Loan Mortgage Corp., 1979—; conducted TV interview show, Bienvenido on Caribbean Forces Network and So. Command Network, C.Z., 1962-64, Pat Markun Show, 1964. Mem. credentials and platform coms. Dem. Nat. Conv., 1964; mem. Dem. Nat. Com. for C.Z., 1964-68; mem. Beauvoir-Sidwell Friends Schs. Lang. Arts Seminar, 1968-70. Active Girl Scouts U.S.A. Named Woman of Distinction, Soroptomist Club of Colon, 1962. Mem. Wash. Childrens Book Guild (pres. 1976-77), Women in Communications, Zeta Phi Eta. Author: (with J. Bailey and E. Lamb) The Pelican Tree and Other Panama Adventures, 1953; The First Book of the Panama Canal, 1957, rev. edit., 1979; The Secret of El Baru, 1958; The First Book of Mining, 1960; The First Book of Central America and Panama, 1963, 72; The First Book of Politics, 1969. Editor: The Future of American Oil, 1976; Witnesses for Oil, 1976. Roman Catholic. Home: 4405 W St NW Washington DC 20007. *I am fortunate to be among the tiny number of American women included in this book for the past 15 years. To women of the post-liberation wave, I say, welcome! In 20 years this reference work may list as many women as men. Where women my age met stifling obstacles to career progress, the world is now wide open to you on the basis of your talents. As a mother of part of this new generation, I wish you Godspeed! Make it a better world than a few women ever could!*

MARKUS, LAWRENCE, mathematician; b. Hibbing, Minn., Oct. 13, 1922; s. Benjamin and Ruby (Friedman) M.; B.S., U. Chgo., 1942, M.S., 1946; Ph.D., Harvard U., 1951; m. Lois Shoemaker, Dec. 9, 1950; children—Sylvia, Andrew. Instr. meteorology U. Chgo., 1942-44; research meteorologist Atomic Project, Hanford, 1944; instr. math. Harvard U., 1951-52; instr. Yale U., 1952-55; lectr. Princeton U., 1955-57; asst. prof. U. Minn., 1957-58, asso. prof., 1958-60, prof. math., 1960—, asso. chmn. dept. math., 1961-63, dir. control scis., 1964—, Leverhulme prof. control theory, dir. control theory centre U. Warwick (Eng.), 1970-73, Nuffield prof. math., 1970—; regional conf. lectr. NSF, 1969; vis. prof. Yale U., Columbia U., U. Calif.; dir. conf. Internat. Centre Math., Trieste, 1974; lectr. Internat. Math. Congress, 1974, Iranian Math. Soc., 1975, Brit. Math. Soc., 1976; lectr. Japan Soc. for Promotion Sci., 1976; vis. prof. U. Tokyo, 1976; mem. panel Internat. Congress Mathematicians, Helsinki, 1978; sr. vis. fellow Sci. Research Council, Imperial Coll., London, 1978; vis. prof. Tech. U. Denmark, 1979. Mem. adv. bd. Office Naval Research, Air Force Office Sci. Research. Served to lt. (j.g.), USNR, 1944-46. Recipient Research prize, Kiev, 1969; Fulbright fellow, Paris, 1950; Guggenheim fellow, Lausanne, Switzerland, 1963. Mem. Am. Math. Soc. (past mem. nat. council), Am. Geophys. Soc., Soc. Indsl. and Applied Math. (past nat. lectr.), Phi Beta Kappa, Sigma Xi. Author: Flat Lorentz Manifolds, 1959; Flows on Homogeneous Spaces, 1963; Foundations of Optimal Control Theory, 1967; Lectures on Differentiable Dynamics, 1971; Generic Hamiltonian Dynamical Systems, 1974; editor Internat. Jour. Nonlinear Mechanics, 1965-73, Jour. Control, 1963-67; contbr. articles to profl. jours. Office: Dept Math U Minn Minneapolis MN 55455

MARKUS, RICHARD M., judge; b. Evanston, Ill., Apr. 16, 1930; s. Benjamin and Ruby Markus; B.S. magna cum laude, Northwestern U., 1951; J.D. cum laude, Harvard U., 1954; m. Carol Joanne Slater, July 26, 1952; children—Linda, Scott, Kent. Admitted to D.C. bar, 1954, Ohio bar, 1965; appellate atty., civil div. Dept. Justice, Washington, 1954-56; partner various civil litigation law firms, Cleve., 1956-76; judge Cuyahoga County (Ohio) Common Pleas Ct., 1976—; instr. M.I.T., 1952-54, Case Western Res. U. Law Sch., 1972-78; adj. prof. Cleve. State U. Law Sch., 1960—; mem. Nat. Commn. on Med. Malpractice, 1971-73; chmn. bd. trustees Nat. Inst. Trial Advocacy, 1978—; Republican nominee Justice of Ohio Supreme Ct., 1978; co-founder Nat. Advocacy Coll., 1970. Bd. dirs. Lutheran Council Greater Cleve., 1979—; trustee Roscoe Pound Found., Cambridge, Mass. Recipient various awards for outstanding jud. service Ohio Supreme Ct., 1976-79. Mem. Assn. Trial Lawyers Am. (nat. pres. 1970-71), Ohio Acad. Trial Lawyers (pres. 1965-66), Am. Bar Assn., Ohio State Bar Assn. (council of dels. 1969—), Cuyahoga County Bar Assn., Greater Cleve. Bar Assn. (trustee 1967-70), Phi Beta Kappa, Pi Mu Epsilon, Delta Sigma Rho, Phi Alpha Delta. Author: Trial Handbook for Ohio Lawyers, 1973, and ann. supplements, 1974—; contbr. articles to profl. jours.; editor Harvard U. Law Rev., 1952-54. Home: 4769 Edenwood Rd South Euclid OH 44121 Office: Justice Center Cleveland OH 44113

MARKWARD, JOHN OLIVER, paper co. exec.; b. Ft. Worth, June 30, 1921; s. Martin Forrest and Ada (Moore) M.; B.S.M.E., U. Tex., 1947; m. Joyce Reid Ingalls, Feb. 3, 1951; children—John Oliver, Anne. With S.D. Warren Co. (became div. Scott Paper Co.), Westbrook, Maine, 1949—, salesman, 1954-67, v.p., 1967-69, v.p. research, 1972—; exec. dir. Scott Graphics Internat., Bornem, Belgium, 1969-72. Alderman, City of Westbrook, 1951-53; mem. exec. bd. Pine Tree council Boy Scouts Am. Served with C.E. U.S. Army, 1943-46; Guam, Okinawa. Mem. Sales Assn. Paper Industry (pres. 1967), TAPPI. Club: Rotary.

MARKWARDT, KENNETH MARVIN, chem. co. exec.; b. St. Paul, Mar. 6, 1928; s. Rudy A. and Kathryn M. (Thell) M.; B.B.A., Coll. St. Thomas, 1950; m. Bernice M. Kimmel, Aug. 1, 1950; children—Ronald, Mary Ellen, Gary, Thomas, Jean. with Econs. Lab., Inc., St. Paul, 1951—, controller, 1961-69, v.p., controller, 1968—, v.p., treas., 1969-73, sr. v.p. finance, 1973—, also dir.; dir. 1st Trust Co., St. Paul, Econ. Lab. Mfg. Co., P.R.; treas., dir. Econs. Lab. Internat. Ltd., St. Paul. Treas., St. Patrick's Guild, bd. dirs., 1951—; trustee St. Joseph Hosp., St. Paul. Served with AUS, 1946-47. Mem. Catholic Athletic Assn. (pres. 1956-57, dir. 1953), Internat. Assn. Assessing Officers, Tax Execs. (pres. Minn. chpt. 1962-63). K.C. Clubs: Minn., St. Paul Athletic (sec. dir. 1971). Home: 1202 Niles St St Paul MN 55116 Office: Osborn Bldg St Paul MN 55102

MARKWARDT, L(ORRAINE) J(OSEPH), cons. engr.; b. Lansing, Iowa, Nov. 26, 1889; s. Joseph F. and Louisa (Besch) M.; B.S., U. Wis., 1912, C.E., 1922; m. Lula May Starks, June 21, 1917. Asst. city engr., Madison, Wis., 1912; instr. drawing, descriptive geometry, engring. coll. U. Wis., 1915-17; research engr. U.S. Forest Products Lab., Madison, 1912-14, asst. chief div. timber mechanics, 1917-39, chief, 1939-43, asst. dir., 1943-59, cons. engr., 1959—. Del. timber research conf. Internat. Union Forest Research Orgns., Princes Risborough, Eng., 1937, 39; U.S. del. internat. confs. mech. wood tech. FAO, UN, Geneva, Switzerland, 1948, 49, Igls, Austria, 1951, Paris, France, 1954, Madrid, Spain, 1958; chmn. program com. Forest Products sect. 5th World Forestry Congress, 1958-59; mem. subcom. wood and plastics for aircraft NACA, 1944-47, aircraft structural materials, 1947-49. Dep. mem. materials com. Resources and Devel. Bd., Dept. Def., 1952-53; mem. materials adv. bd. and bldg. research adv. bd. Nat. Acad. Scis., NRC, 1954-59. Recipient hon. citation for engring. achievement U. Wis., 1950, Superior Service award USDA 1957; Hitchcock award for outstanding research accomplishments in wood industry Hitchcock Pub. Co. and Forest Products Research Soc., 1963; Ann. L.J. Markwardt Wood Engring. Research award established by ASTM and Forest Products Research Soc. Fellow ASTM (Edgar Marburg lectr. award 1943; bd. dir. 1944-54, v.p. 1948-50, pres. 1950-51, chmn. com. methods testing bldg. constrns. 1946-48, chmn. com. wood 1948-64 hon. mem.; recipient Walter C. Voss award in bldg. tech. 1965); mem. Am. Standards Assn. (chmn. sect. com. methods testing wood, 1922—, sect. com. safety code constrn., care, use of ladders 1950—, mem. constrn. standards bd., 1943—, sect. com. specifications wood poles, 1946—), Am. Wood Preservers Assn., Am. Ry. Engring. Assn. (com. wood bridges and trestles 1944-48), ASCE (hon. life), Nat. Soc. Profl. Engrs. (life), Soc. Am. Foresters, AAAS, Forest Products Research Soc., Internat. Wood Research Soc. (v.p.), Am. Inst. Timber Constrn. (chmn. tech. rev. bd. 1960-75, profl. life mem.), Sigma Xi, Tau Beta Pi, Chi Epsilon. Presbyterian. Clubs: Masons, Rotary (pres. Madison 1950-51), Black Hawk Country (hon. pres. 1973, Madison). Author: Descriptive Geometry (with Millar and Maclin), 1919, also subsequent revisions; Autobiography of the Spirit Oak, 1975; Blackhawk Indian Mounds on National Register of Historic Places, 1979; The Blackhawk Country Club and its Historic Indian Heritage, 1976; also sects. on timber several engring. handbooks; govt. bulls., tech., sci. papers. Address: 12 Lathrop St Madison WI 53705. *Early in life I was challenged by the admonition of Dr. Henry Van Dyke, which has proven to provide excellent guidelines for a rewarding life. "Four things a man must learn to do, If he would make his record true; To think without confusion clearly; To love his fellow man sincerely; To act from honest motives purely; To trust in God and Heaven securely." Hobbies are an essential part of a well rounded life. Of some six or more hobbies, I have found "The Music of Words to Remember," Poetry, as a most gratifying and rewarding resource.*

MARLAS, JAMES CONSTANTINE, mfg. co. exec.; b. Chgo., Aug. 22, 1937; s. Constantine J. and Helen (Cotsirilos) M.; A.B. cum laude, Harvard, 1959; M.A. in Jurisprudence, Oxford (Eng.) U., 1961; J.D., U. Chgo., 1963; m. Kendra S. Graham, Aug. 24, 1968 (div. Sept. 1971). Admitted to Ill. bar, 1963, N.Y. bar, 1966; asso. firm Baker & McKenzie, London and N.Y.C., 1963-66; exec. v.p. South East Commodity Corp., N.Y.C., 1967-68; chmn. bd. Union Capital Corp., N.Y.C., 1968—; vice chmn. bd. Mickelberry's Food Products Co., N.Y.C., 1970-71; pres., dir. Mickelberry Corp., N.Y.C., 1972—, chief exec. officer, 1973—; chmn. bd., chief exec. officer Newcourt Industries, Inc., 1976—; chmn. bd. Bowmar Instrument Corp., 1976—; dir. mem. Blue Cross and Blue Shield Greater N.Y. Bd. dirs. Assn. Mentally Ill Children in Manhattan. Mem. Am. Fgn. Law Assn., Young Pres.'s Orgn. Clubs: Boodle's (London); Racquet and Tennis (N.Y.C.). Co-editor Univ. Chgo. Law Rev., 1962-63. Contbr. articles to profl. jours. Office: 405 Park Ave New York NY 10022

MARLATT, ABBY LINDSEY, food scientist, educator; b. Manhattan, Kans., Dec. 5, 1916; d. Frederick Albert and Annie Elsie (Lindsey) M.; B.S. in Home Econs., Kans. State U., 1938; certificate in Hosp. Dietetics, U. Calif. at Berkeley, 1940, Ph.D. in Animal Nutrition, 1947. Asso. prof. foods and nutrition Kans. State U., Manhattan, 1945-52, prof., 1952-56; dir. Sch. Home Econs. U. Ky., Lexington, 1956-63, prof., 1963-68, prof. nutrition and food sci., 1968—. Vis. prof. Beirut (Lebanon) Coll. for Women, 1953-54; vis. research prof. Ky. State Coll., Frankfort, 1968-71. Chmn. Lexington Youth Devel. Center, 1973; bd. dirs. Emerson Center, 1972—. Mem. bd. Community Action Lexington Fayette County, 1967-71, 72—, sec., 1970-71, treas., 1974-78, mem. bd. Micro-City Govt., 1972—; bd. dirs. Bluegrass Community Services, Inc., 1976—, chmn., 1977—. Fellow AAAS; mem. Am. Dietetic Assn., Am. Home Econs. Assn., Soc. Nutrition Edn., Am. Sch. Health Assn., Nutrition Today Soc., Gerontol. Soc., Ky. Nutrition Council, AAUP, AAUW, ACLU, Sigma Xi, Phi Kappa Phi, Omicron Nu, Phi Upsilon Omicron, Iota Sigma Pi. Unitarian-Universalist (Ohio Valley council pres. 1972-74). Contbr. articles on research in nutrition to profl. jours. Home: 256 Tahoma Rd Lexington KY 40503

MARLENEE, RONALD CHARLES, Congressman; b. Scobey, Mont., Aug. 8, 1935; student Mont. State U., U. Mont., Reisch Sch. Auctioneering; m. Cynthia Tiemann; children—Sheila, Casey, Allison. Farmer, rancher; mem. 96th Congress from 2d Mont. Dist. Mem. Mont. Stockgrowers Assn., Daniels County Fair Bur., Daniels Fair Assn., Mont. Beef Performance Assn., Mont. Grain Growers Assn. Republican. Lutheran. Clubs: Masons, Lions. Office: 126 Cannon House Office Bldg Washington DC 20515*

MARLER, PETER ROBERT, research biologist; b. London, Eng., Feb. 24, 1928; s. Robert A. and Gertrude (Hunt) M.; B.Sc., U. London, 1948, Ph.D. in Botany, 1952; Ph.D. in Animal Behavior, U. Cambridge (Eng.), 1954; m. Judith Golda Gallen, Sept. 1, 1954; children—Christopher, Catherine, Marianne. Came to U.S., 1957, naturalized, 1963. Research fellow Jesus Coll., Cambridge (Eng.) U., 1954-56; from asst. prof. to prof. U. Cal. at Berkeley, 1957-66; prof. Rockefeller U., N.Y.C., 1966—, dir. Center for field Research in Ecology and Ethology, 1972—; sr. research zoologist N.Y. Zool. Soc., 1966-69, dir. Inst. Research Animal Behavior, 1969-72. Guggenheim fellow, 1964-65. Fellow N.Y. Zool. Soc., Am. Acad. Arts and Scis., Nat. Acad. Scis., Am. Psychol. Assn.; mem. Animal Behavior Soc. (pres. 1968-69), Am., Brit. ornithologists unions, Cooper Ornithol. Soc., Am. Soc. Zoologists, Internat. Primatological Soc. Author: (with W.J. Hamilton III) Mechanisms of Animal Behavior, 1966. Home: Reservoir Rd Staatsburg NY 12580 Office: Rockefeller U New York NY 10021

MARLETT, DE OTIS LORING, real estate exec.; b. Indpls., Apr. 19, 1911; s. Peter Loring and Edna Grace (Lombard) M.; B.A., M.A., U. Wis., 1934; postgrad. Northwestern U. (part time), 1934-39; postgrad. Harvard U. (Littauer fellow in econs. and govt.), 1946-47; m. Ruth Irene Pillar, Apr. 10, 1932 (dec. Feb. 1969); children—De Otis Neal, Marilynn Ruth; m. 2d, Marie Manning Ostrander, May 1, 1970. Staff mem. Ill. Commerce Commn., 1934-39; lectr. in econs. and pub. utilities Northwestern U. (part time), 1936-39; staff mem. Bonneville Power Adminstrn., U.S. Dept. Interior, 1939-45, asst. adminstr., 1945-52; acting adminstr. Def. Electric Power Adminstrn., 1950-51; asst. to v.p., also gen. mgr. Dicalite and Perlite divs. Gt. Lakes Carbon Corp., 1952-53, v.p., also gen. mgr. Mining and Mineral Products div., 1953-62, v.p. Property Investment dept., 1962—; pres., dir. Del. Amo Properties Co.; dir., v.p. Great Lakes Properties, Inc., Rancho Palos Verdes Corp., G.L.C. Bldg. Corp.; v.p. Gt. Lakes Carbon Internat. Ltd.; gen. mgr. Palos Verdes Properties. Past bd. dirs. United Cerebral Palsy Assn. Los Angeles County; bd. dirs., past co-chmn. So. Calif. region NCCJ, past mem. nat. bd. trustees; mem. Orthopaedic Hosp. Adv. Council; trustee City of Hope; past pres., dir. Los Angeles area council, past chmn. relationships com., past pres. Sunshine area, pres. Western region Boy Scouts Am.; past mem. Western Govs. Mining Adv. Council, Calif. State Mining Bd.; bd. govs. Western div. Am. Mining Congress, chmn., 1962-63. Recipient Distinguished Service medal U.S. Dept. Interior, 1952; named knight Order of Crown (Belgium); commd. Ky. Col. Mem. Fin. Execs. Inst., Los Angeles World Affairs Council, Wis. Alumni Assn., Perlite Inst. (past pres., dir.), Am. Inst. Mining and Metall. Engrs., Los Angeles C. of C. (past dir., chmn. mining com.), Mining Assn. So. Calif. (past pres., dir.), Calif. Mine Operators Assn. (past dir.), Bldg. Industry Assn. So. Calif., Town Hall, Phi Kappa Phi, Beta Gamma Sigma, Phi Beta Kappa, Beta Alpha Psi. Democrat. Clubs: Calif., Portuguese Bend (pres.), Rolling Hills Country, Rotary. Contbr. articles and reports on public utility regulation, operation and mgmt. to profl. jours. Home: 3200 W La Rotonda Dr Apt 318 Rancho Palos Verdes CA 90274 Office: Suite 220 Del Amo Exec Plaza 3838 Carson St Torrance CA 90503

MARLEY, FRANCIS MATTHIAS, lawyer; b. Muncie, Ind., June 9, 1910; s. William B. and Emma (Haney) M.; B.A. cum laude, U. Notre Dame, 1932, J.D. cum laude, 1934; m. Barbara O. Reinhard, Aug. 30, 1939; children—William Edmund, Francis Matthias, Susan Ann, Michael Joseph, Barbara Louise. Admitted to Ohio bar, 1934, since practiced in Fostoria; asst. pros. atty. Seneca County, Ohio, 1934-36. Dir. Midwest Plant Foods, Inc., Napoleon, Ohio, 1950-72. Chmn. Fostoria Planning Commn., 1954-58, Fostoria Civil Service Commn., 1959-63. Pres. Fostoria Democratic Club, 1950-58, treas., 1959-60; Democratic state central committeeman, 1958-68; Seneca County Democratic chmn., 1970-72. Mem. Am., Ohio (exec. com. 1972-75), Seneca County (pres. 1942-45) bar assns., Law-Sci. Acad. Am., Notre Dame Law Assn., Academia Internationali Lex et Scientia, Am. Judicature Soc., Am., Ohio title assns., Fostoria United Sportsmen (sec. 1935), Ohio Acad. Trial Lawyers. Roman Catholic. Clubs: Elks (presiding justice 1953-62), Eagles (pres. 1939-41), K.C. (4 deg.; grand knight 1938-40). Home: 311 W North St Fostoria OH 44830 Office: 100 N Poplar St Fostoria OH 44830. *I have tried to live my life honestly, truthfully respecting the fundamental rights of man: honesty with myself, with my clients (in the practice of law), with the Courts, and with associates; doing my best to ascertain the truth of each situation and honestly applying such truth in the interest of justice; and recognizing, defending, and promoting the fundamental rights of man as expressed in the Declaration of Independence of the United States, the Constitution of the United States and the moral law contained in the Bible.*

MARLEY, JOHN, actor, dir.; b. N.Y.C., Oct. 17; student Coll. City N.Y.; m. Sanra Ulusevich; 1 dau., Alexis; children by previous marriage—Peter, Julia, Ben. Appeared in numerous motion pictures, including Faces (Best Actor award Venice Film Festival), A Man Called Sledge, 1970, The Godfather, 1972, Love Story, Framed, 1975, W.C. Fields and Me, 1976, The Car, 1977, The Greatest, 1977, Hooper, 1978; dir. Cleve. Playhouse, Center Stage, Balt., Civic Playhouse, Calif., Pasadena (Calif.) Playhouse; producer, dir. summer stock. Served with Armed Forces, World War II. Recipient Oscar nomination for best supporting actor for Love Story, Golden Globe nomination for Love Story.

MARLOWE, DONALD E., engr., assn. exec.; b. Worcester, Mass., Mar. 27, 1916; s. Daniel J. and Helene (Gilogly) M.; B.S., U. Detroit, 1938; M.S., U. Mich. (Rackham scholar), 1939; Sc.D., Merrimack Coll., 1962; m. Corinne M. Ingersoll, Nov. 23, 1939; children—Donald E., Christopher J. Instr., U. Detroit, 1940-41; engring. research asst. U. Mich., 1940-41; research engr. Naval Ordnance Lab., 1941-45, chief tech. evaluation dept., 1945-50, asso. dir. for engring., 1950-55; dean Sch. Engring. and Architecture, Cath. U. Am., 1955-70, v.p. for adminstrn., 1970-75; exec. dir. Am. Soc. Engring. Edn., Washington, 1975—; mem. com. on ordnance Research and Devel. Bd., Dept. Def., 1950-55; nat. reporter for U.S.A. Conf. Engr. Socs. Western Europe and U.S., 1957-60; sec. D.C. Bd. Registration Profl. Engrs., 1959-62, chmn., 1962-66. Recipient Naval Ordnance Devel. award, 1945, Naval Distinguished Service award, 1946; Distinguished Alumni citation U. Mich., 1953, U. Detroit, 1969; award of merit Am. Inst. Cons. Engrs., 1970; named Engr. of Year, Washington Met. Area, 1966; registered profl. engr., D.C. Fellow ASME (hon. mem.; exec. council 1962-65, 67-68, pres. 1969, chmn. history com. 1974-78, treas. 1975, chmn. fin. com. 1976-80, disting. service award 1965, 68), AAAS (council, sec. engring. sect. 1976—); mem. Nat. Council Engring. Examiners (dir. 1964-65, pres. 1966-67), IEEE (sr. mem.), Engrs. Joint Council (dir., exec. com. 1962-65), Am. Phys. Soc., Am. Soc. Engring. Edn., Nat. Soc. Profl. Engrs. (dir.), Sigma Xi, Alpha Sigma Nu, Phi Eta Sigma, Tau Beta Pi, Blue Key. Clubs: Cosmos, Argyle. Home: 15402 Short Ridge Ct Silver Spring MD 20906 Office: 1 Dupont Circle Suite 400 Washington DC 20036

MARLOWE, SYLVIA (MRS. LEONID BERMAN), harpsichordist; b. N.Y.C.; d. Harry and Anna (Riklan) Sapira; student Ecole Normale de Musique (Paris), 1929-32; m. Leonid Berman, Jan. 6, 1948. First harpsichordist to tour Asia sponsored by U.S. govt. under ANTA; concert tours U.S., Europe, Asia; rec. artist Decca Gold

Label Records; appeared radio and TV stas. including NBC, CBS, ABC, BBC, Can. Broadcasting Co.; faculty Mannes Coll. Music, N.Y.C., 1953—. Decorated chevalier Arts et Des Lettres (France); recipient Handel medallion N.Y.C. Mem. The Harpsichord Music Soc. (mus. dir.). Recs. include Bach Goldberg Variations, RCA Gold Label. Home: 108 E 60th St New York NY 10022 also 6 Bridge St Newport RI 02840 Office: Mannes Coll Music 157 E 74th St New York NY 10021

MARMAS, JAMES GUST, coll. dean; b. Virginia, Minn., July 11, 1929; s. Gust George and Angela (Fatili) M.; B.S., St. Cloud (Minn.) State Coll., 1951; M.A., U. Minn., 1956; Ed.D., Stanford, 1961; m. Ruth Phyllis Leinonen, May 23, 1952; children—James Matthew, Lynn Marie, Brenda Kay. Tchr. bus. Littlefork (Minn.) High Sch., 1951-53, Lake City (Minn.) High Sch., 1953-55, Austin (Minn.) High Sch., 1955-59; asst. prof. bus. edn. Los Angeles State Coll., 1961-62; chmn. dept. bus. edn., dir. Center Econ. Edn., St. Cloud State Coll., 1962-66, dean Sch. Bus., 1966—. Bd. dirs. Minn. Council Econ. Edn. Mem. Nat., Minn., N. Central (2d v.p.) bus. edn. assns., Midwest Bus. Adminstrn. Assn., St. Cloud C. of C., Phi Delta Kappa, Delta Pi Epsilon (nat. research com.). Rotarian (pres. St. Cloud). Author articles in field. Home: 1747 Woodland Rd St Cloud MN 56301

MARMET, PAUL, physicist; b. Levis, Que., Can., May 20, 1932; s. Albert and Corinne (Filteau) M.; B.Sc., Laval U., Quebec, Que., 1956, D.Sc., 1960; m. Jacqueline Cote, June 6, 1959; children—Louis, Marie, Nicolas, Frederic. Research asst. Commonwealth Sci. and Inds. Research Orgn., Melbourne, Australia, 1960-61; asst. prof. physics Laval U., 1961-66, asso. prof., 1966-70, prof., 1970—; vis. prof. U. Liège (Belgium), 1967; com. mem. NRC Can. Recipient Sci. prize Province Que., 1962; Royal Soc. Can. Rutherford Meml. fellow, Melbourne, 1960. Fellow Royal Soc. Can.; mem. Can. Assn. Physicists (v.p.-elect), Herzberg medal 1971), Am. Phys. Soc., Royal Astron. Soc. Can. (Service award 1977), AAAS, Assn. canadienne-française pour l'avancement des sciences (Parizeau medal 1976), Chem. Inst. Can. Roman Catholic. Author: (with others) Case Studies in Atomic Physics I, 1969; contbr. numerous articles to internat. sci. jours.; patentee energy analyser of charged particules. Home: 1001 De Grenoble St Ste-Foy PQ G1V 2Z8 Canada Office: Physics Dept Quebec PQ G1K 7P4 Canada

MARMION, HARRY ALPHONSUS, coll. pres.; b. N.Y.C., June 14, 1931; s. Alphonsus and Catherine (Smyth) M.; B.S.S., Fairfield U., 1953; J.D., Georgetown U., 1958, LL.M., 1959; M.A., U. Conn., 1963, Ph.D., 1965; m. Particia Anne Hurley, June 28, 1954; children—Elizabeth, Sarah, Sheila. Admitted to Iowa bar, 1959; financial analyst SEC, Washington, 1957-58; corp. sec., house counsel Atomic Devel. Mgmt. Corp., Washington, 1958- 59; atty. Dept. Labor, Washington, 1959-60; asso. prof., chmn. econs. mgmt. dept. U.S. Coast Guard Acad., New London, Conn., 1960-64; dir. field services, fifth year program, financial aids Moorhead (Minn.) State Coll., 1964-66; staff asso. commn. on fed. relations Am. Council on Edn., Washington, 1966-68; mem. exec. staff, dir. Inst. for Coll. and Univ. Adminstrn., 1968-69; pres. St. Xavier Coll., Chgo., 1969-72, Southampton Coll. of L.I. U., 1972-78; dir. commn. collegiate athletics and Insts. Coll. and Univ. Adminstrs., Am. Council Edn.; lectr. U. Md., George Washington U., 1966-69; cons. ednl. matters various colls. and univs. Mem. East Lyme (Conn.) Charter Commn., 1962-63; mem. East Lyme Democratic Town Com., 1961-64, Southampton Town Dem. Com., 1974—; cons. Pres.'s Council on Youth Opportunity, Washington, 1968-69. Trustee Iona Coll., 1974-78. Served with USMCR, 1953-55; lt. col. Res. Recipient Fairfield U. Alumni Assn. award, 1966. Mem. A.A.U.P., Am. Assn. for Higher Edn., Am. Acad. Polit. and Social Sci., Phi Alpha Delta. Author: Selective Service Conflict and Compromise, 1968; The Case Against the Voluntary Army, 1971. Home: 465 Hill St Southampton NY 11968

MARMION, WILLIAM HENRY, clergyman; b. Houston, Oct. 8, 1907; s. Charles Gresham and Katherine (Rankin) M.; A.B., Rice Inst., 1929; B.D., Va. Theol. Sem., 1932, D.D. (hon.), 1954; m. Mabel Dougherty Nall, Dec. 28, 1935; children—William Henry, Roger Mills Nall. Ordained deacon Episcopal Ch., 1932, priest, 1933; priest in charge St. James, Taylor, Tex., and Grace Ch., Georgetown, Tex., 1932-35; asso. rector St. Mark's Ch., San Antonio, 1935-38; rector St. Mary's-on-the-Highland, Birmingham, Ala., 1938-50, St. Andrew's Ch., Wilmington, Del., 1950-54; bishop Episcopal Diocese of Southwestern Va., Roanoke, 1954—. Former dir. diocesan camps for young people in Tex. and Ala., headed diocesan youth work, several yrs.; dep. to Gen. Conv. Episcopal Ch., 1943, 46, alternate dep., 1949, 52; del. to Provincial Synod; mem. exec. council Episcopal Ch., 1963-69; chmn. Ala. Com. on Interracial Cooperation, 4 yrs. Trustee Va. Theol. Sem., Va. Episcopal Sch., St. Paul's Coll. and Boys' Home Inc. Home: 2730 Avenham Ave SW Roanoke VA 24014 Office: 1000 1st St SW Roanoke VA 24016

MARMOR, JUDD, psychiatrist, educator; b. London, May 1, 1910; s. Clement K. and Sarah (Levene) M.; came to U.S., 1911, naturalized, 1916; A.B., Columbia U., 1930, M.D., 1933; D.H.L., Hebrew Union Coll., Los Angeles, 1972; m. Katherine Stern, May 1, 1938; 1 son, Michael Franklin. Intern, St. Elizabeth Hosp., Washington, 1933-35; resident neurologist Montefiore Hosp., N.Y.C., 1935-37; psychiatrist Bklyn. State Hosp., 1937; psychoanalytic tng. N.Y. Psychoanalytic Inst., N.Y.C., 1937-41; pvt. practice psychiatry, psychoanalysis and neurology, N.Y.C., 1937-46, Los Angeles, 1946—; instr. asso. in neurology Columbia Coll. Physicians and Surgeons, 1938-40; adj. neurologist, neurologist-in-charge clinic Mt. Sinai Hosp., N.Y.C., 1939-46; lectr. New Sch. Social Research, N.Y.C., 1942-43; instr. Am. Inst. Psychoanalysis, N.Y.C., 1943; lectr. psychiatry N.Y. Med. Coll., 1944-46; lectr. social welfare U. Calif. at Los Angeles, 1948-49, vis. prof. social welfare, 1949-64, clin. prof. psychiatry sch. medicine, 1953—; vis. prof. psychology U. So. Calif., 1946-49; tng. analyst So. Calif. Psychoanalytic Inst., also pres., 1955-57; sr. attending psychiatrist Los Angeles County Gen. Hosp., 1954—; dir. divs. psychiatry Cedars-Sinai Med. Center, Los Angeles, 1965-72; Franz Alexander prof. psychiatry U. So. Calif. Sch. Medicine, 1972—; sr. cons. regional office social service VA, Los Angeles, 1946-50; cons. psychiatry Brentwood (Calif.) VA Hosp., 1955-65; mem. Council Mental Health of Western Interstate Commn. Higher Edn. Bd. dirs. Human Interaction Research Inst., Neumeyer Found., Behavioral Sci. Research Found.; v.p. Psychosomatic Research Found. Served as sr. attending surgeon USPHS, USNR, 1944-45. Diplomate Am. Bd. Psychiatry and Neurology, Nat. Bd. Med. Examiners. Fellow Am. Psychiat. Assn. (life, pres. 1975-76), N.Y. Acad. Medicine (life), Am. Acad. Psychoanalysis (pres. 1965-66), Am. Orthopsychiat. Assn. (dir. 1968-71), AAAS, Am. Coll. Psychiatrists; mem. AMA, Calif. Med. Assn., Group for Advancement Psychiatry (dir. 1968-70, pres. 1973-75), Am. Fund for Psychiatry (dir. 1955-57), So. Calif. Psychiat. Soc., So. Calif. Psychoanalytic Soc. (pres. 1960-61), Am. Psychoanalytic Assn., Los Angeles County Med. Soc., Phi Beta Kappa, Alpha Omega Alpha. Editor: Sexual Inversion-The Multiple Roots of Homosexuality; Modern Psychoanalysis: New Directions and Perspectives; Psychiatry in Transition: Selected Papers of Judd Marmor; Homosexual Behavior: A Modern Reappraisal; editorial bd. Am. Jour. Psychoanalysis, Contemporary Psychoanalysis, Psychiatry Digest, Archives Sexual Behavior, Am. Jour. Community Psychology, Jour. Sex and Marital Therapy; contbr. articles in field to profl. jours. Home: 655 Sarbonne Rd Los Angeles CA 90024 Office: U So Calif Sch Medicine 2025 Zonal Ave Los Angeles CA 90033

MARMORSTEIN, IRWIN, construction co. exec.; b. Transilvania, Romania, Apr. 29, 1928; came to U.S., 1948, naturalized, 1954; s. Louis and Violet (Geiszt) M.; B.A., Calif. Western U., 1976; m. Ruth Lederman, Aug. 30, 1953; children—Daniel, Debra, Amy, Michael. Partner, Willow-Shore Builders, Cleve., 1955-67, Multiplex, Inc., Cleve., 1967-69; v.p. Titan Group, Inc., Paramus, N.J., 1969-79; partner F.R.A. Assos., Pitts., 1979—; cons. Titan Group, Inc. Served with U.S. Army, 1950-52. Decorated Purple Heart. Mem. Sullivan County Bd. Realtors, Air Force Assn., DAV, Jewish War Vets. Club: B'nai B'rith. Office: 1046 Union Trust Bldg Pittsburgh PA 15219

MARMORSTON, JESSIE, physician; b. Kiev, Russia, Sept. 16, 1903; d. Aaron and Ethel (Wark) M.; B.S., M.D., U. Buffalo, 1924; m. Lawrence Weingarten, Feb. 2, 1945; children—Lailee Bakhtiar Marmorston Mommaerts, Elizabeth Marmorston Horowitz, Norma Marmorston Pisar. Intern, Montefiore Hosp., N.Y.C., 1924-25; bacteriologist, 1924-32; asso. bacteriology and exptl. pathology Cornell U., Ithaca, N.Y., 1931-38; attending staff Dr.'s Hosp., N.Y.C., 1938—; sr. attending staff Los Angeles County Hosp., 1943—; attending staff Cedars-Sinai Med. Center, Los Angeles, 1944—, research staff, 1948—; research staff Med. Research Inst., Los Angeles, 1948—; asso. prof. medicine U. So. Calif., 1943-53, prof. exptl. medicine, 1953-57, clin. prof. medicine, 1957—; supervising dir. Calif. Found. Med. Research, Los Angeles. Adv. com. emergency med. care Los Angeles County, 1972—; bd. dirs. Research Found., St. Joseph Hosp., Burbank. Recipient numerous awards. Fellow A.C.P., N.Y. Acad. Medicine, Am. Geriatrics Soc., Am. Coll. Cardiology, Royal Soc. Promotion Health; mem. N.Y. Acad. Scis., Am., Los Angeles County heart assns., Soc. Exptl. Biology and Medicine, N.Y. Pathol. Soc., Gerontol. Soc., Reticuloendothelial Soc., Assn. Immunology, AMA, Calif., Los Angeles County med. assns., other orgns. Author: (with David Perla) Spleen and Resistance, 1935; Natural Resistance and Clinical Medicine, 1941; (with E. Stainbrook) Psychoanalysis and The Human Situation, 1964; (with J. Weiner and M. Allen) Manuel of Computer Programs for Preliminary Multivariate Analysis, 1965; (with J. Weiner and P. Geller) Scientific Methods in Clinical Studies, 1970. Contbr. numerous articles to profl. publs. Home: 2821 Forrester Dr Los Angeles CA 90064 Office: 2025 Zonal Ave Los Angeles CA 90033

MARON, EDWARD B., JR., retail merchandiser; b. Hollywood, Calif., Jan. 10, 1927; s. Edward B. and Minnie V. M.; student U. So. Calif., 1947-48, UCLA, 1970; m. Jesslyn Langseth, Jan. 11, 1950; children—Barbara, Craig, Mike, Dareen. Grocery buyer Ralphs Grocery Co., 1968-72, merchandising mgr., 1972-74, v.p. grocery and liquor div., 1974-78; exec. v.p. merchandising FedMart Corp., San Diego, 1978—. Served with U.S. Army, 1943-45. Republican. Home: 14804 Satanas St San Diego CA 92129 Office: 3851 Rosecrans St San Diego CA 92110

MARON, MELVIN EARL, educator, philosopher; b. Bloomfield, N.J., Jan. 23, 1924; s. Hyman and Florence (Goldman) M.; B.S. in Mech. Engring., U. Nebr., 1945, B.A. in Physics, 1947; Ph.D. in Philosophy, U. Calif. at Los Angeles, 1951; m. Dorothy Elizabeth Mastin, Aug. 16, 1948; children—Nadia, John. Lectr. philosophy U. Calif. at Los Angeles, 1951-52; tech. engr. IBM Corp., San Jose, Calif., 1952-55; mem. tech. staff Ramo-Wooldridge Corp., 1955-59; mem. sr. staff, computer scis. dept. RAND Corp., 1959-66; prof. library sci. U. Calif. at Berkeley, asso. dir. Inst. Library Research, 1966—. Served with AUS, 1943-46. Mem. Assn. Computing Machinery, Am. Soc. Info. Sci., AAAS, Philosophy Sci. Assn. Contbr. profl. jours. Home: 63 Ardilla Rd Orinda CA 94563 Office: Sch of Library and Info Scis U Calif Berkeley CA 94720

MARONEY, DANIEL VINCENT, JR., union exec.; b. Notamine, W.Va., June 10, 1921; s. Daniel Vincent and Eula Mary (Mays) M.; student Beckley Coll., Morris Harvey Coll.; m. Mary Louise Callison, Sept. 15, 1944; children—Daniel Vincent, Deborah, Margaret, Elizabeth, Mary Emma. With Western Electric Co., 1947; with Atlantic Greyhound Co., 1948—, Charleston Transit Union, 1947; pres. local union, 1954-65; internat. v.p. Amalgamated Transit Union, 1965-73, internat. pres., Washington, 1973—; mem. exec. bd. dept. pub. employees AFL-CIO; dir. Union Labor Life Ins. Co. Served with inf. U.S. Army, 1941-45, to lt., 1950-52; Korea. Decorated Bronze Star. Democrat. Roman Catholic. Clubs: Elks, Am. Legion, VFW. Home: 505 Alder Ave N Sterling VA 22170 Office: 5025 Wisconsin Ave NW Washington DC 20016

MAROTTA, JOSEPH THOMAS, educator; b. Niagara Falls, N.Y., May 28, 1926; s. Alfred and Mary (Montemuro) M.; brought to Can., 1930; M.D., U. Toronto, 1949; m. Margaret Hughes, Aug. 31, 1953; children—Maureen, Patricia, Margaret, Fred, Thomas, Jo Anne, Michael, Martha, John, Virginia. Trainee in internal medicine U. Toronto, 1949-52; trainee in neurology, Presbyn. Hosp., N.Y.C., 1952-55, U. London (Eng.), 1955-56; mem. faculty U. Toronto, 1956—, prof. medicine, 1969—. Fellow Royal Coll. Physicians (Can.); mem. Acad. Medicine (Toronto), Alpha Omega Alpha, Phi Chi. Home: 8 Peebles Ave Don Mills ON M3C 2N8 Canada Office: Wellesley Hosp Toronto ON Canada

MAROUS, JOHN CHARLES, JR., mfg. co. exec.; b. Pitts., June 25, 1925; s. John Charles and Mary Ellen (Ley) M.; B.S. in Elec. Engring., U. Pitts., 1949, M.S., 1953; m. Lucine O'Brien, May 25, 1957; children—Julia, John, Leslie. With Westinghouse Electric Corp., 1949—, gen. mgr. div., Youngwood, Ohio, 1968-70, gen. mgr. 5 divs., 1970—72, exec. v.p. constrn. group, Pitts., 1973-79, pres. Internat. Westinghouse Electric Corp., 1979—. Bd. dirs. Allegheny County ARC, YMCA, Pitts.; mem. World Affairs Council Pitts. Served with U.S. Army, 1943-46. Mem. Pitts. Engring. Alumni Assn. (pres.). Republican. Roman Catholic. Clubs: Duquesne, Pitts. Field; Congressional Country (Washington). Office: Westinghouse Bldg Gateway Center Pittsburgh PA 15222

MAROVITZ, ABRAHAM LINCOLN, judge; b. Oshkosh, Wis., Aug. 10, 1905; s. Joseph and Rachel (Glowitz) M.; J.D., Chgo.-Kent Coll. Law, 1925; L.H.D., Lincoln (Ill.) Coll., 1956; LL.D., Winston Churchill Coll., 1968. Admitted to Ill. bar, 1927; asst. state's atty. Cook County (Ill.), 1927-33; practiced in Chgo., 1933-50; judge Superior Ct. Cook County, 1950-63; chief justice Cook County Criminal Ct., 1958-59; U.S. judge No. dist. Ill., 1963-75, sr. judge, 1975—; chmn. bd. Lincoln Nat. Bank, 1946-63. Past nat. chmn. Nat. Conf. State Ct. Trial Judges; past mem. lawyer's adv. council U. Ill. Law Forum. Mem. Ill. Senate, 1938-50. Bd. dirs. Hebrew Theol. Coll.; mem. adv. bd. YMCA Met. Chgo.; trustee Chgo.-Kent Coll. Law, Chgo. Med. Sch.; former trustee Ill. Hist. Library; past mem. Jewish Bd. Edn. Served to sgt. maj. USMCR, 1943-46. Named outstanding legislator Ind. Voters Ill., 1949; recipient Founders' Day award Loyola U. in Chgo., 1967; Annual award merit Decalogue Soc. Lawyers, 1968; awards Chgo. Press Club, Chgo. Press Photographers Assn., 1968; Man of Year awards Jewish Nat. Fund, Israel Bond Orgn. Mem. Chgo. Bar Assn. (past mgr.), Jewish War Vets. U.S. (past dept. comdr.), Am. Legion (comdr. Marine post Chgo.). Jewish religion (bd. dirs. synagogue). Home: 3260 N Lake Shore Dr Chicago IL 60613 Office: 219 S Dearborn Chicago IL 60604

MARPLE, DOROTHY JANE, church exec.; b. Abington, Pa., Nov. 24, 1926; d. John Stanley and Jennie (Stetler) Marple; A.B., Ursinus Coll., 1948; M.A., Syracuse U., 1950; Ed.D., Columbia Tchrs. Coll., 1969; L.H.D., Thiel Coll., 1965, Gettysburg Coll., 1979; D. Humanitarian Services, Newberry Coll., 1977. Counselor, asst., office dean undergrad. women Women's Coll., Duke, 1950-53; dean women, fgn. student adv. Thiel Coll., 1953-61; asst. social dir. Whittier Hall, Columbia Tchrs. Coll., 1961-62; exec. dir. Luth. Ch. Women, Luth. Ch. Am., Phila., 1962-75; asst. to pres. Luth. Ch. Am., 1975—; coordinator Luth. Ch. in Am. commn. on function and structure, 1970-72. Mem. Nat. Assn. Women Deans and Counselors, Pi Lambda Theta. Home: 8018 Anderson St Philadelphia PA 19118 Office: 231 Madison Ave New York NY 10016

MARQUARD, WILLIAM ALBERT, diversified mfg. co. exec.; b. Pitts., Mar. 6, 1920; s. William Albert and Anne (Wild) M.; B.S., U. Pa., 1940; m. Margaret Thoben, Aug. 13, 1942; children—Pamela, Suzanne, Stephen. With Westinghouse Electric Corp., Pitts. and Mexico City, 1940-52; with Mosler Safe Co., Hamilton, Ohio, 1952-67, sr. v.p., 1961-67, pres., 1967-70; with Am.-Standard, Inc., N.Y.C., 1967—, sr. exec. v.p., 1970, pres., chief exec. officer, 1971—; dir. Chem. N.Y. Corp., Chem. Bank, N.Y. Life Ins. Co., Shell Oil Co., N.L. Industries, Inc. Trustee U. Pa., bd. overseers Wharton Sch. Bus.; mem. Com. Corporate Support Pvt. Univs.; bd. dirs. Nat. Minority Purchasing Council; trustee N.Y.C. Citizens Budget Commn. Mem. Conf. Bd. Home: 1020 Fifth Ave New York NY 10028 Office: American Standard Inc 40 W 40th St New York NY 10018

MARQUARDT, FREDERIC SYLVESTER, editor; b. Manila, Philippines, Dec. 10, 1905; s. Walter William and Alice (Hollister) M.; A.B., Hamilton Coll., 1927; m. Alice Wilcox, June 17, 1932 (dec. Aug. 19, 1968); 1 son, Philip. Reporter, Utica (N.Y.) Daily Press, 1927-28; mem. staff Philippines Free Press, Manila, 1928-35, asso. editor, 1937-41; mem. editorial staff Canton (Ohio) Repository, 1936-37; Manila corr. Internat. News Service, 1929-36, 37-41, Reuters, 1933-36, Detroit News, 1928-31; asst. fgn. editor and Far Eastern expert Chgo. Sun, 1941-43, fgn. news editor, 1945-48; telegraph editor Chgo. Sun-Times, fgn. assignment in Far East, 1948-49; chief O.W.I. in S.W. Pacific area, 1943-45; lectr. on Far Eastern subjects; editorial page editor Phoenix Gazette 1950-54, Ariz. Republic, Phoenix, 1954-70, editor, 1956-79, sr. editor, 1979—, European assignment, 1958, Asian assignment, 1960, 70-76, Near East assignment, 1966, Caribbean assignment, 1979; editor-in-residence Tex. Tech. U., Lubbock, 1975, 79, No. Ariz. U., 1979. Mem. Gov.'s Com. on Aging, 1959-60; bd. dirs. Heard Mus. Anthropology, 1956—, pres., 1959-62; bd. dirs. Ariz. Acad., 1962-73, Lincoln Found., 1968—; bd. dirs. Ariz. Blue Cross, 1963-77, pres., 1968-71; bd. dirs. Blue Cross & Blue Shield of Ariz., 1977—; trustee Claremont (Calif.) Men's Coll., 1970-74; bd. dirs. Health Facilities Planning Council Maricopa County, 1967-73, Land Reform Tng. Inst. Taiwan, 1969—; bd. dirs. Lincoln Inst. Land Policy, 1974—; lay adv. bd. St. Joseph's Hosp., Phoenix, 1966-74, governing bd., 1974—. Recipient Medal of Freedom for meritorious civilian service U.S. Army, 1945; decorated comdr. Philippine Legion of Honor, 1958. Mem. Am. Soc. Newspaper Editors, Nat. Conf. Editorial Writers, Emerson Lit. Soc., Internat. Press Inst., Ariz. Acad. Pub. Affairs, Assn. Asian Studies, Pi Delta Epsilon, Sigma Delta Chi. Clubs: Rotary, Phoenix Press, Ariz. Press, Ariz. Circumnavigators. Author: Before Bataan and After, 1943; contbr. articles to jours. Home: 1130 E Bethany Home Rd Phoenix AZ 85014 Office: Republic & Gazette Phoenix AZ 85004

MARQUIS, HAROLD HOLLIDAY, JR., advt. agy. exec.; b. San Mateo, Calif., Aug. 13, 1928; s. Harold Holliday and Rose (Wester) M.; student Occidental Coll., 1946-48; B.A. in Journalism, U. Calif. at Berkeley, 1950; m. Nancy Josephine Heinz, July 20, 1957; children—Jefferson Peter, Julie Diane, Christopher Holliday, Matthew Eliot. With Hoefer, Dieterich & Brown, Inc., San Francisco, 1956-79, copywriter, 1956-57, copy chief, 1958, account exec., 1959-60, account supr., 1961-64, exec. v.p., 1965-76, pres., 1976-77, pres., chief exec. officer Regis McKenna Advt., Palo Alto, Calif., 1977-78; pres. Hoefer, Dieterich & Brown, San Francisco, 1979—; instr. grad. mktg., advt. and mgmt. San Francisco State U. Sch. Bus., 1979; dir. Advt. Prodns., Inc., 1964—, John H. Hoefer Co., 1958—. Chmn. pack com. Cub Scouts Am., 1966-67; v.p. San Francisco Spring Opera Soc.; trustee Monterey (Calif.) Inst. of Fgn. Studies, San Domenico Sch. for Girls; bd. dirs. Bay Area chpt. Planned Parenthood Assn., 1968-70. Served to 1st lt. USAF, 1951-56. Mem. Affiliated Advt. Agys. Internat. (pres. 1964-65), Am. Assn. Advt. Agys. (chmn. No. Calif. council), San Francisco Advt. Club, San Francisco C. of C. (dir., v.p. for communications), Sigma Alpha Epsilon. Clubs: Commonwealth (San Francisco); Ross Landing (Marin County). Home: 409 Crown Rd Kentfield CA 94904 Office: 414 Jackson Sq San Francisco CA 94111

MARQUIS, ROBERT B., architect; b. Stuttgart, Ger., July 9, 1927; s. Paul Charles and Marianne (Gutstein) M.; came to U.S., 1937, naturalized, 1934; student Sch. Architecture, U. So. Calif., 1946-49, Acad. di Belle Art, Florence, Italy, 1949-50; m. Ellen Godfrey, Dec. 20, 1950; children—Lisa Leeds, Tessa, David. Established Marquis Assos. Architects, San Francisco, 1953-56; pres. Marquis & Stoller Architects and Planners, San Francisco and N.Y.C., 1956-74, Marquis Assos., Architects, Planners & Interior Design, San Francisco, 1974—; vis. critic Stanford U.; prin. works include Novato (Calif.) Library (Design award); Sonoma State Coll. Cafeteria (Instn. Mags. award), housing for elderly (Design awards), St. Francis Sq. Co-op (Design awards); St. Francis Yacht Club, San Francisco; energy-conserving Calif. Dept. Justice Office Bldg., Sacramento; numerous pvt. residences. Mem. adv. com. Thomas Jefferson Found. at U. Va. Grantee Nat. Endowment Arts; recipient Albert J. Evers Environ. award No. Calif. AIA, 1975; Fellow AIA (past pres. No. Calif. chpts.), San Francisco Planning and Urban Renewal Assn., Sierra Club. Works included in publs., exhibited museums. Address: 243 Vallejo St San Francisco CA 94111

MARQUIS, ROBERT HENRY, lawyer, educator; b. Evanston, Ill., July 6, 1913; s. Henry and Elizabeth (Schram) M.; A.B., Am. U., 1933; LL.B., George Washington U., 1936; LL.M., Georgetown U., 1938; m. Ruth Longstreet Belden, June 21, 1940; children—Robert Stillwell, Richard Longstreet. Admitted to D.C. bar, 1936, Tenn. bar, 1940; spl. atty. U.S. Dept. Justice Knoxville, Tenn., 1938, Washington, 1938-39, Los Angeles, 1939; atty. TVA, Knoxville, 1939-43, 46-47, asst. gen. counsel, 1947-58, solicitor, 1958-67, gen. counsel, 1967-75; prof. law U. Ark. at Little Rock, 1975—; vis. prof. law U. Tenn., 1979. Served to capt. AUS, 1943-46. Mem. Am., Tenn., Knoxville, Fed. bar assns., Order of Coif. Rotarian. Home: 902 Ruffian Ln Knoxville TN 37919 Office: 1505 W Cumberland Ave Knoxville TN 37916

MARQUIS, ROLLIN PARK, librarian; b. Badin, N.C., Nov. 29, 1925; s. Rollin Howard and Carmen (Park) M.; B.A., Columbia, 1948; postgrad. linguistics St. Catherines Soc. U. Oxford, 1948-50, painting Art Students League N.Y., 1950-52; M.L.S., Carnegie Inst. Tech., 1958; m. Marian Horton Bonstein, Aug. 21, 1954; children—Rollin Hilary, Jeffrey Perrin, Anne-Louise. Catalog asst. Columbia Med. Library, 1952-53; adminstrv. asst. Nat. Council Chs. Christ in U.S.A., N.Y.C., 1953-56; adminstrv. asst. Friends Com. on Nat. Legislation, Washington, 1956-57; reference asst. Carnegie Library, Pitts., 1957-58; dir. Citizens Library, Washington, Pa., 1958-59; dir. River

Edge (N.J.) Free Pub. Library, 1959-63; dir. Allegany County Library, Cumberland, Md., 1963-64; city librarian Dearborn (Mich.) Dept. Libraries, 1964—. Served with AUS, 1944-46. Mem. Am., Mich. library assns., Adult Edn. Assn. Mich., Detroit-Suburban Librarians Round Table, Dearborn Choral Arts Soc., Dearborn Orchestral Soc., Fair Lane Music Guild. Democrat. Mem. Soc. Friends. Rotarian. Club: Torch (Detroit). Home: 23849 Lloyd Ct Dearborn MI 48124 Office: Henry Ford Centennial Library Dearborn MI 48126. *The things obtained through cooperation, sharing and mutual goodwill are the achievements which satisfy—as significantly for public and business life, as for private life.*

MARR, ALLEN GERALD, educator; b. Tulsa, Apr. 24, 1929; s. Elisha Allen and Hallie (Hedrick) M.; B.S., U. Okla., 1948, M.S., 1949; Ph.D., U. Wis., 1952; m. Kathryn Ann Pultz, Aug. 15, 1970; children—Catherine Marr Barzo, Gregory, Elizabeth Marr Timm, Margaret, Stephen, Allen. Instr. to prof. bacteriology U. Calif. at Davis, 1952—, dean grad. studies and research, 1969—; mem. life scis. com. NASA, 1974—; chmn. council on research policy and grad. edn. Nat. Assn. State Univs. and Land Grant Colls., 1975-76. Sec. Yolo County (Calif.) Grand Jury, 1964; chmn. Yolo County Democratic Central Com., 1960—; mem. Calif. Dem. Central Com., 1966-68. Fellow USPHS, 1950-51. Mem. Am. Soc. Microbiology. Editor: Jour. Bacteriology, 1968-73. Contbr. articles to profl. jours. Home: 722 Hawthorn Ln Davis CA 95616

MARR, CLINTON, JR., architect; b. Ontario, Calif., Sept. 28, 1925; s. Clinton Herbert and Luella Josephine (Tuell) M.; student U. Redlands, 1943, Murray Coll., 1944-45, St. Mary's Coll., 1945; B. Arch., U. So. Calif., 1953; m. Geraldine Lois McMahan, June 3, 1945; children—Cynthia Louise, Bruce Wayne. Designer, Albert C. Martin & Assos., Los Angeles, 1952-54; project architect Clare Day, Architect, Redlands, Calif., 1954, Herman O. Rhunu, Architect, Riverside, Calif., 1955; owner, architect Clinton Marr & Assos. Inc., Architects and Planners, Riverside, 1956-66, pres., 1966—. Mem. bd. zoning examiners City of Riverside, 1959; adv. council Riverside Easter Seal Soc., 1964-66; vice-chmn. Riverside Gen. Plan Citizens Com., 1965-67; citizens univ. com. U. Calif., Riverside, 1965—, sec., 1970-71, vice-chmn., 1971-72, chmn., 1973-75; chmn. founders club Riverside Community Hosp., 1975-76; bd. dirs. YMCA Riverside, 1966-69, Riverside Art Assn., 1970-72. Served with USNR, 1943-46. Recipient Award of Merit for Clinton Marr residence AIA, 1969, other awards. Fellow AIA (dir. Calif. council 1975, 77). Methodist (pres. bd. trustees 1971). Kiwanian (dir. chpt. 1962-64). Home: 6816 Hawarden Dr Riverside CA 92506 Office: 3602 University Ave Riverside CA 92501

MARR, DAVID FRANCIS, profl. golfer, television announcer; b. Houston, Dec. 27, 1933; s. David Francis and Grace Anne (Darnell) M.; student Rice U., 1950-51, U. Houston, 1951-52; m. Caroline Elizabeth Dawson, Sept. 25, 1972; children by previous marriage—Elizabeth S., David Francis III, Anthony J. Profl. golfer, 1953—; tour player, 1960-72, part time tour player, 1973—; golf announcer ABC Sports, 1970—; golf dir. Princeville, Kauai, Hawaii. Mem. Profl. Golfers Assn. (nat. champion 1965, Player of Year 1965), AFTRA. Roman Catholic. Clubs: Brae Burn Country, Champions Golf (Houston).

MARR, LUTHER REESE, film co. exec.; b. Kansas City, June 23, 1925; s. Luther Dow and Aileen (Shimfessel) M.; A.B., U. Calif. at Los Angeles, 1946; J.D., U. So. Calif., 1950; m. Christelle Lois Taylor, July 12, 1956; children—Michelle Lois, Stephen Luther, Christelle Elizabeth. Admitted to Calif. bar, 1951; with firm Hasbrouck & Melby, Glendale, 1952-54; atty. Walt Disney Prodns., Burbank, Calif., 1954—, corp. sec., 1957-78, v.p. corp. and shareholder affairs, 1978—, also officer, dir. subsidiaries. Trustee, v.p., gen. counsel Le Lycee Francais de Los Angeles. Served with USNR, 1946-47. Mem. Am. Soc. Corp. Secs., Calif., Los Angeles bar assns., Phi Beta Kappa, Phi Alpha Delta. Republican. Methodist. Home: 2323 Via Saldivar Glendale CA 91208 Office: 500 S Buena Vista St Burbank CA 91521

MARR, ROBERT BRUCE, physicist, educator; b. Quincy, Mass., Mar. 25, 1932; s. Ralph George and Ethel (Beals) M.; B.S., M.I.T., 1953; M.A., Harvard U., 1955, Ph.D., 1959; m. Nancy Rosa Parkes, June 12, 1954; children—Richard, Jonathan, Rebecca. Research asso. Brookhaven Nat. Lab., Upton, N.Y., 1959-61, asso. physicist, 1961-64, physicist, 1964-68, sr. physicist, 1968—, asso. chmn. applied math. dept., 1974-75, chmn., 1975-78; adj. asso. prof. Columbia U., 1969; lectr. SUNY at Stony Brook, 1969-70, vis. prof. dept. computer sci., 1979; guest mathematician U. Colo., 1970; vis. mathematician Lawrence Berkeley Lab., 1978; cons. NSF, NIH, 1969—. Served with U.S. Army, 1958-59. NSF grantee, 1974. Mem. Assn. Computing Machinery, AAAS, Am. Phys. Soc., Sigma Xi. Contbr. articles to profl. jours. Home: 368 Private Rd East Patchogue NY 11772 Office: Applied Math Dept Brookhaven Nat Lab Upton NY 11973

MARR, WARREN QUINCY, II, editor; b. Pitts., July 31, 1916; s. Warren Quincy and Cecelia Antoinette (McGee) M.; student Wilberforce U., 1934-37, N.Y. Sch. Interior Decoration, 1948-49, New Sch. for Social Research, 1962-63; m. Carmel Dolores Carrington, Apr. 11, 1948; children—Charles Carrington, Warren Quincy III. Linotype operator St. Louis Argus, 1938-39; with The Plaindealer, Kansas City, Kans., 1939-42, asst. editor, 1941-42; impressario Warren Marr, II, Presents, N.Y.C., 1943-48; decorator James Lassiter & Sons, Madison, N.J., 1948-52; pres. Dilworth-Leslie Sponsors, 1949-66; propr. House of Marr, Inc., Bklyn., 1952-56; plant mgr. Nisonger Corp., New Rochelle, N.Y., 1956-60; sec. Am. Missionary Assn. Coll. Centennials, N.Y.C., 1961-68; public relations asst. NAACP, N.Y.C., 1968-74, editor The Crisis mag., 1974—. Founder, dir. Amistad Awards, 1962-67; co-founder Amistad Research Center, Dillard U., New Orleans, 1966; founder, vol. exec. dir. Friends of Amistad, 1971—; pres. art com. Tougaloo Coll., Jackson, Miss., 1966-67; chmn. bd. dirs. Waltann Sch. Creative Arts, 1963-70; bd. dirs. Bklyn. Arts and Culture Assn., Community Council of Medgar Evers Coll., Internat. Art of Jazz, Access. Recipient various awards; named hon. citizen of New Orleans, 1979. Editor: (with Maybelle Ward) Minorities and the American Dream: A Bicentennial Perspective, 1976; (with Harry Ploski) The Negro Almanac, 1976; contbr. articles to various jours. Office: The Crisis Mag 1790 Broadway New York NY 10019

MARRA, EDWARD FRANCIS, physician, educator; b. Poughkeepsie, N.Y., May 25, 1916; s. Thomas Jefferson and Mary Agnes (Powers) M.; B.S., Trinity Coll., Hartford, Conn., 1945; M.D., Boston U., 1950; M.P.H. (Commonwealth Fund fellow), Harvard, 1955. Intern Harrisburg (Pa.) Polyclinic Hosp., 1950-51, resident, 1951-52; resident Mass. Meml. Hosp., Boston, 1952-54; instr. Boston U. Sch. Medicine, 1953-56, asst. prof., 1956-59, asso. prof., 1959-60; prof., chmn. dept. social and preventive medicine, also asso. prof. medicine, lectr. med. sociology State U. N.Y., Buffalo, 1960-76, emeritus prof., 1976—; chief service Mass. Meml. Hosps., Boston, 1959-60; lectr. Harvard Sch. Pub. Health, 1959-60. Served with USNR, 1945-46. W.H. Russell fellow Trinity Coll., 1946-47. Home: Arundel House PO Box 49 Orange Springs FL 32682 Office: State Univ New York at Buffalo 2211 Main St Buffalo NY 14214

MARRIN, PAUL S., lawyer; b. Hyannis, Nebr., May 18, 1894; s. T.L. and Ida T. (Watts) M.; A.B. and J.D., U. Calif.; m. Mary Fair, Aug. 29, 1932; children—Robert S., Suzanne F. Gen. law practice in San Francisco, 1919—; gen. counsel Henry J. Kaiser Co. and affiliates. Mem. Am., San Francisco bar assns., Calif. Bar, Phi Alpha Delta. Republican. Club: Bohemian. Office: 2 Embarcadero Center San Francisco CA 94111

MARRINER, NEVILLE, orchestral dir.; b. Lincoln, Eng., Apr. 15, 1924; s. Herbert Henry and Ethel May (Roberts) M.; ed. Royal Coll. Music, Paris Conservatory; m. Diana Margaret Corbutt, May 10, 1949 (div. 1957); m. 2d, Elizabeth Sims, Dec. 20, 1957; children—Susan Frances, Andrew Stephen. Prof., Eton Coll., 1947, Royal Coll. Music, 1952; violinist Martin String Quartet, 1946-53, Virtuoso String Trio, 1950, Jacobean Ensemble, 1952, London Philharmonia, 1952-56, London Symphony Orch., from 1956; condr. Los Angeles Chamber Orch., 1969-77; music dir. Minn. Orch., 1979—; guest condr. Gulbenkian Orch., Lisbon, Spain, Israel Chamber Orch., Australian Chamber Orch., N.Y. Chamber Orch., N.Y. Philharm. Orch., Orchestre de Paris, others; dir. South Bank Festival of Music, 1975-78, Meadowbrook Festival, Detroit, 1979—. Bd. dirs., founder Acad. St. Martin-in-the Fields, 1959—. Recipient Grand Prix du Disque, Edison award, Mozart Gemeinde prize, Tagore prize, others. Office: care Columbia Artists Mgmt 165 W 57th St New York NY 10019*

MARRIOTT, ALICE SHEETS (MRS. JOHN WILLARD MARRIOTT), restaurant chain exec., Republican nat. committeewoman; b. Salt Lake City, Oct. 19, 1907; d. Edwin Spencer and Alice (Taylor) Sheets; A.B., U. Utah, 1927, L.H.D., 1974; m. John Willard Marriott, June 9, 1927; children—John Willard, Richard Edwin. Partner Marriott Corp. (formerly Marriott-Hot Shoppes, Inc.), Washington, 1927—, v.p., dir., 1929—. Mem. Republican Nat. Com., 1959-76, vice chmn., 1965-76, mem. exec. com., 1965-76; mem. D.C. Republican Com., 1959-76; treas. Republican Nat. Conv., 1964, 68, 72, mem. arrangements com., 1960, 64, 68, 72; vice chmn. inaugural com., 1969, hon. chmn., 1973; mem. Women's Nat. Rep. Club, Rep. Coodinating Com., 1965-69, 73-76; chmn. adv. com. on arts John F. Kennedy Center For Performing Arts, 1970-76. Bd. dirs. Washington Ballet Guild, Washington Home Rule Com., Arthritis and Rheumatism Found. of Met. Washington; trustee John F. Kennedy Center, 1972—. Mem. League Republican Women D.C. (treas. 1955-57, v.p. 1957-59), Nat. Symphony Orch. Assn., Am. Newspaper Womens Club (asso. mem.), Capitol Speakers Club (membership chmn.), Welcome to Washington Internat. Clubs (treas., dir.), Chi Omega, Phi Kappa Phi. Mem. Ch. of Jesus Christ of Latter-Day Saints. Clubs: Washington, Capitol Hill, 1925 F Street. Home: 4500 Garfield St Washington DC 20007 Office: Marriott Dr Washington DC 20058

MARRIOTT, DAVID DANIEL, congressman; b. Bingham, Utah, Nov. 2, 1939; s. Raymond D. and Gladys (Syeuri) M.; B.A., U. Utah, 1967; C.L.U., 1968; m. Marilynn Tingey, Aug. 19, 1965; children—David, Michael, Katherine, Lindsay. Gen. agt. Guardian Life Ins. Co. Am.; pres. Marriott Assos., 1968-76; mem. 95th-96th Congresses from 2d Dist. Utah. Coach, Little League Baseball, 1969-76. Recipient Pub. Address award U. Utah, 1968. Mem. C.L.U. Assn. (past pres. Utah), Mountain States Pension Conf. (past dir.), Estate Planning Council, Nat. Fedn. Ind. Bus., Salt Lake City C. of C. Republican. Mormon. Club: Salt Lake City Exchange. Author: (booklet) Cash Value Life Insurance, 1968; also articles. Home: 2024 Princeton Dr Salt Lake City UT 84108 Office: Longworth House Office Bldg Washington DC 20515

MARRIOTT, JOHN WILLARD, restaurant and motel exec.; b. Marriott, Utah, Sept. 17, 1900; s. Hyrum Willard and Ellen (Morris) M.; grad. Weber Coll., Ogden, Utah, 1922; A.B., U. Utah, 1926; LL.D. (hon.), Brigham Young U., 1958; m. Alice Sheets, June 9, 1927; children—John Willard, Richard Edwin. Franchise holder A. & W. Root Beer Co., Washington, 1926-28; pres. Marriott Corp. (formerly Hot Shoppes, Inc.), 1928-64, now chmn., dir.; dir. Am. Motors Corp., Detroit, Riggs Nat. Bank, Chesapeake & Potomac Telephone Co., Washington Bd. Trade. Mem. commrs. adv. planning bd. Fed. City Council. Bd. govs. United Service Orgns.; chmn. Presdl. Inaugural Com., 1969, 73; chmn. Honor Am. Com. Recipient Hall of Fame award Am. Restaurant Mag., 1954; Achievement award Advt. Club, 1957; award Am. Marketing Assn., 1959; U. Utah, 1959; Chain Store Age award, 1961; Businessman of Yr. award Religious Heritage Am., 1971; Capt. of Achievement award Am. Acad. Achievement, 1971; Horatio Alger award, 1974. Mem. N.A.M. (dir.), Com. for Econ. Devel. (trustee), Nat. (pres. 1948), Washington (pres. 1939, 43) restaurant assns. Mem. Ch. of Jesus Christ of Latter-Day Saints (pres. Washington stake 1948-57). Clubs: Burning Tree (Bethesda, Md.); Indian Creek Country (Miami Beach, Fla.); Bald Peak Colony (Melvin Village, N.H.); Columbia Country (Chevy Chase, Md.); Paradise Valley Country (Ariz.); Washington Admirals, Capitol Hill (Washington). Biography: The J. Willard Marriott Story, 1977. Home: 4500 Garfield St NW Washington DC 20007 Office: Marriott Corp 1 Marriott Dr Washington DC 20058

MARRIOTT, JOHN WILLARD, JR., restaurant-hotel, cruise ship, entertainment park chain exec.; b. Washington, Mar. 25, 1932; s. John Willard and Alice (Sheets) M.; B.S. in Banking and Fin., U. Utah, 1954; m. Donna Garff, June 29, 1955; children—Deborah, Stephen Garff, John Willard, David Sheets. Vice pres. Marriott Hot Shoppes Inc., 1959-64, exec. v.p., 1964; pres., dir. Marriott Corp., 1964—, chief exec. officer, 1972—; dir. S.E. Banking Corp. Chmn. bd. Citizens Choice; bd. advs. U. Utah Coll. Bus.; nat. adv. council Brigham Young U. Coll. Bus.; nat. adv. council Ariz. Heart Inst. Served to lt. USNR, 1954-56. Mem. Fla. Council 100, Nat. Alliance Businessmen, U.S. C. of C. (dir.), Sigma Chi. Clubs: Burning Tree, Met. (Washington). Office: Marriott Corp Washington DC 20058

MARRIOTT, RICHARD EDWIN, restaurant and theme park exec.; b. Washington, Jan. 9, 1939; s. John Willard and Alice Taylor (Sheets) M.; B.S., U. Utah, 1963; M.B.A., Harvard U., 1965; m. Nancy Peery, Mar. 20, 1962; children—Julie Ann, Sandra, Karen, Mary Alice. With Marriott Corp., 1965—, group v.p. restaurant ops., Washington, 1976-78, corp. group v.p. restaurant and theme park ops., Washington, 1979—; dir. Riggs Nat. Bank of Washington; chmn. bd. dirs. Media Corp., 1973—. Bd. dirs. David Meml. Goodwill Industries, Washington, 1971—; trustee Holton Arms Sch., Bethesda, Md., 1979—; bd. dirs. Nat. Com. for Prevention Child Abuse, 1979—. Mem. Sigma Chi. Mormon. Office: Marriott Corp Marriott Dr Washington DC 20058

MARROCCO, WILLIAM THOMAS, musician, educator; b. West New York, N.J., Dec. 5, 1909; s. Julius Thomas and Elisa (Faccin) M.; Licentiate and Master's diplomas, Royal Conservatory Naples, Italy, 1930; Mus.B., Eastman Sch. Music, U. Rochester, 1934; M.A., 1934; Ph.D., U. Calif. at Los Angeles, 1952; m. Audrey Jeanette Grein, Sept. 14, 1937; children—Richard Thomas, Sandra Beth. Instr., U. Iowa, 1945-46; asso. prof. U. Kans., 1946-49; prof. U. Calif. at Los Angeles, 1949-79; violinist Roth String Quartet. Decorated Order of Merit (Italy). Fulbright fellow, 1949-50. Fellow Am. Philos. Soc., Am. Council Learned Socs.; mem. Mediaeval Acad. Am., Am. Musicol. Soc., Phi Kappa Lambda. Author: Fourteenth Century Italian Cacce, 1961; Music of Jacopo da Bologna, 1954; (with Harold Gleason) Music in America, 1964; Music of Fourteenth Century Italy, 6 vols.; (with Nicholas Sandon) Oxford Anthology of Medieval Music, 1977; contbr. articles to profl. publs. Home: 2101 Buck St Eugene OR 97405

MARRON, DONALD BAIRD, investment banker; b. Goshen, N.Y., July 21, 1934; s. Edward Joseph and Ethel (Baird) M.; student Baruch Sch. Bus., 1949-51, 55-57; m. Gloria Swope, June 19, 1961; children—Jennifer Ann, Donald Baird. Investment analyst N.Y. Trust Co., N.Y.C., 1951-56, Lionel D. Edie Co., N.Y.C., 1956-58; mgr. research dept. George O'Neill & Co., 1958-59; pres. D.B. Marron & Co., Inc., N.Y.C., 1959-65; co. combined with Mitchell, Hutchins & Co., Inc., 1965, pres., chief exec. officer, 1969-77; pres. Paine Webber Inc., N.Y.C., 1977—; pres., chief exec. officer M-H Holdings, Inc., Wilmington, Del., 1977—; chmn. bd. Data Resources, Inc., Lexington, Mass. Bd. dirs. N.Y. Stock Exchange; chmn. exec. com., trustee Mus. Modern Art; trustee World Inst. Computer Assisted Teaching, Calif. Inst. Arts, Valencia, Trust for Cultural Resources City of N.Y.; mem. Research Inst. on Internat. Change, Columbia U. Mem. Council Fgn. Relations, Securities Industry Assn. (past dir.), Young Pres.'s Orgn. Clubs: Economic, Down Town Assn., Recess, Bond, Regency Whist, Maidstone (past gov.) (East Hampton, N.Y.); Brook, River (N.Y.C.). Home: 791 Park Ave New York NY 10021 Office: 140 Broadway New York NY 10005

MARRS, DOUGLAS CHARLES, mfg. co. exec.; b. Hamilton, Ont., Can., Sept. 27, 1913; s. Charles Hawkins and Mina Grace (Longhurst) M.; student mgmt. course U. Western Ont.; m. Hilda Elaine Witherspoon, June 8, 1946; children—Robert Douglas, Pamela Anne. With Westinghouse Can. Ltd., 1936—, pres., chief exec. officer, now chmn. bd., also dir.; dir. Toronto Dominion Bank, Slater Steel Industries, Ltd. Bd. govs. McMaster U. Served with RCAF, 1942-45. Mem. Hamilton C. of C. Mem. United Ch. Clubs: Hamilton, Toronto, Hamilton Golf and Country. Home: 386 Bluebird Ct Burlington ON L7T 2P7 Canada Office: 286 Sanford Ave N Hamilton ON L8L 6A1 Canada

MARSAGLIA, GEORGE, mathematician, educator; b. Denver, Mar. 12, 1925; s. John and Mabel (Tappan) M.; B.A. in Physics, Colo. State U., 1947; M.A., Ohio State U., 1948, Ph.D. in Math., 1950; m. Lee Ann Stewart, Sept. 7, 1954 (div. Mar. 1969); 1 son, John Winston; m. 2d, Doris Adele Goodale, May 9, 1970. Instr., Ohio State U., Columbus, 1948; Fulbright scholar U. Manchester (Eng.), 1949-50; asst. prof. math. and astronomy, dir. statistics lab. U. Mont., 1950-53; vis. lectr., research asso. U. N.C., 1953-54, Okla. State U., 1954-55; Fulbright prof. U. Rangoon (Burma), 1955-56, also adviser to Burmese govt.; mem. staff Boeing Sci. Research Labs., Seattle, 1957-70; prof. computer sci., dir. Sch. Computer Sci., McGill U., Montreal, Que., Can., 1970-76; prof., chmn. dept. computer sci. Wash. State U., 1976—; vis. lectr. U. Wash., Seattle, 1958-62, vis. prof., 1962-70; vis. nat. lectr. Inst. Math. Statistics-Am. Statis. Assn., 1972-73; cons. to govt. and industry. Served with AUS, 1943-44. Mem. Am. Math Soc., Am. Statis. Assn. (asso. editor jour. 1968-72), Assn. Computing Machinery, Soc. Indsl. and Applied Math. Joint editor Numerische Mathematik Jour., 1970—. Contbr. articles to profl. jours. Home: SW 945 Alcora Dr Pullman WA 99163

MARSCHALK, HARRY ROBERT, corp. ofcl.; b. N.Y.C., Aug. 3, 1915; s. Harry C. and Katherine (Schnaufer) M.; A.B., Dartmouth, 1937; m. Anne Wynne McKay, Mar. 4, 1944; children—Karen, Peter, Andrea. Asst. sales mgr. Vick Chem. Co. (now Richardson-Merrell, Inc.), N.Y.C., 1940-41, v.p., 1952-58, exec. v.p., 1952-61, pres., dir., 1961-75, vice chmn. bd., 1976—, pres., chmn. various subsidiaries, 1948-61; dir. Philip Morris, Inc., Thyssen-Bornemisza Group NV, Piedmont Mgmt. Corp. Chmn. fin. devel. com. Nat. Urban Coalition, 1977-78; bd. overseers Dartmouth Med. Coll., 1979—. Served as lt. USNR 1941-45. Home: Ferris Hill Rd New Canaan CT 06840 Office: 10 Westport Rd Wilton CT 06897

MARSCHING, RONALD, precision instrument co. exec.; b. N.Y.C., Mar. 30, 1927; s. Robert and Christine Marsching; B.A., Princeton, 1950; J.D., Harvard, 1953; m. Marjory Fleming Duncan, Dec. 31, 1964; children—Christine, Jane. Admitted to N.Y. bar, 1954; with firm White & Case, N.Y.C.; sr. v.p., sec., gen. counsel, dir. Timex Corp., Middlebury, Conn., 1967—. Served with AUS, 1953-55. Mem. Am. Bar Assn., Assn. Bar N.Y., Westchester-Fairfield Corp. Counsel Assn. Clubs: Waterbury, Highfield. Home: Charcoal Ave Middlebury CT 06762 Office: Timex Corp Waterbury CT 06720

MARSDEN, DONALD DEARBORN, mfg. co. exec.; b. Orange, Mass., Nov. 6, 1921; s. George C. and Anna (Dearborn) M.; B.A., Yale, 1942; student Amos Tuck Sch., Dartmouth, 1946; M.B.A., Stanford, 1947; m. Constance Vose, June 17, 1949; children—Peter Vose, Jane Dearborn, Ann Haywood, Donald Dearborn. Auditor, Scovell Wellington & Co., Boston, 1947-52; with Ford Motor Co., 1952-62, regional fin. exec. Latin Am., 1961-62; with Singer Co., 1962-67, v.p., 1965-66, controller, 1964-66, v.p., gen. mgr. Far East div., 1966-67; v.p. finance, treas. Dictaphone Corp., Rye, N.Y., 1967-68, v.p. fin. and adminstrn., 1968-70, dir., group v.p., 1970-71; dir. fin. analysis Xerox Corp., Stamford, Conn., 1972-73; v.p. fin., treas. Acco Industries Inc. (formerly Am. Chain & Cable Co.), Bridgeport, Conn., 1973—. Served with USAAF, 1942-45, C.P.A., Mass. Mem. Am. Inst. C.P.A.'s, Mass. Soc. C.P.A.'s, Fin. Execs. Inst., Phi Beta Kappa, Sigma Xi. Club: Riverside Yacht. Presbyterian (elder). Home: 55 Winthrop Dr Riverside CT 06878 Office: 929 Connecticut Ave Bridgeport CT 06602

MARSDEN, RALPH WALTER, geologist, educator; b. Jefferson County, Wis., Apr. 11, 1911; s. Walter and Inger (Evenson) M.; Ph.B., U. Wis., 1932, Ph.M., 1933, Ph.D., 1939; m. Ellen E. Pletcher, Aug. 31, 1957; children—Jean Inger, Katherine Ellen. Asst. instr. U. Wis., 1936-39; geologist Wis. Geol. Survey, summers 1936, 38-39; geologist Jones & Laughlin Steel Corp., Pitts., summer 1937, 1945-46, 47-51; geologist Philippine Geol. Survey, Philippine Bur. Mines, 1939-40, chief geol. survey div., 1940-45; intern, Cebu City, Philippines, also Santo Tomas, Los Banos, 1942-45; asso. prof. geology U. Okla., 1946-47; geologist U.S. Steel Corp., Duluth, Minn., 1951-53, mgr. geol. investigations iron ore, 1953-67; dir. explorations Cartier Mining Co., Ltd., Duluth, 1954-57; dir. explorations Quebec Cartier Mining Co., 1957-59; prof. geology U. Minn., Duluth, 1967—, head dept., 1967-74; treas. Econ. Geology Pub. Co., 1976—. Mem. steering com. Earth Sci. Curriculum Project. Fellow Geol. Soc. Am.; mem. Soc. Econ. Geologists (past councilor), Am. Inst. Mining, Metall. and Petroleum Engrs. (past v.p.), AAAS, Mining and Metall. Soc. Am., Am. Inst. Profl. Geologists, Soc. Econ. Geologists (treas., treas. found.). Mem. editorial bd. Econ. Geology, 1968-73; editorial adv. bd. Mining Engring Handbook; mem. adv. com., contbr. to Ore Deposits of the United States 1933-1967. Home: 1112 Missouri Ave Duluth MN 55811

MARSEE, SUSANNE IRENE, lyric mezzo; b. San Diego, Nov. 26, 1941; s. Warren Jefferson and Irene Rose (Wills) Dowell; student Santa Monica City Coll., 1961; B.A. in History, UCLA, 1964; m. Brett Basil Hamilton, Mar. 3, 1970. Appeared with numberous U.S. opera cos., 1970—, including N.Y.C. Opera, San Francisco Opera, Boston Opera; appeared with fgn. cos., festivals: Mexico City Bellas Artes, 1973, 78, Canary Islands co., 1976, Opera Metropolitana, Caracas, Venezuela, 1977, Spoleto (Italy) Festival, 1977, Aix en Provence (France) Festival, 1977; recorded Tales of Hoffman, ABC/Dunhill Records; TV appearances. Named winner Liederkranz Club Contest, 1970; recipient 2d pl. award Met. Opera Regional Auditions, 1968, San Francisco Opera Regional Auditions, 1968; Gladys Turk Found. grantee, 1968-69; Corbett Found. grantee, 1969-73; Martha Baird Rockefeller grantee, 1969-70, 71-72. Mem. Am. Guild Musical Artists, AFTRA. Democrat. Office: care Shaw Concerts 1995 Broadway New York NY 10023

MARSH, BENJAMIN FRANKLIN, lawyer; b. Toledo, Apr. 30, 1927; s. Lester Randall and Alice (Smith) M.; B.A., Ohio Wesleyan

U., 1950; J.D., George Washington U., 1954; m. Martha Kirkpatrick, July 12, 1952; children—Samuel, Elizabeth. Admitted to Ohio bar, 1955, since practiced in Toledo; mem. firm Doyle, Lewis and Warner, 1955-71; partner Ritter, Boesel, Robinson & Marsh, 1971—; personnel officer AEC, 1950-54; asst. atty. gen. Ohio, 1969-71; solicitor City of Maumee (Ohio), 1963—, asst. solicitor, 1959-63. Adminstrv. asst. Legis. Service Commn., Columbus, Ohio, 1954-55; mem. Lucas County Charter Commn., Toledo, 1959-60; vice chmn. U.S. Nat. Commn. for UNESCO, mem. legal com., del. 17th Gen. Conf., Paris, 1972, U.S. observer meeting of nat. commns. of Africa, 1974, UNESCO, Addis Ababa, Ethiopia; U.S. rep. with rank spl. ambassador to 10th Anniversary Independence of Botswana, 1976; pres. Toledo and Lucas County Tb Soc., Citizens for Metroparks; mem. Judges Com. Notaries Pub.; formerly mem. Lucas County Bd. Elections; chmn. Lucas County Republican Exec. Com., 1973-74; precinct commiteeman, Maumee, 1959-73; legal counsel, dir. Nat. Council Rep. Workshops, 1960-65; pres. Rep. Workshops Ohio, 1960-64; alt. del. Rep. Nat. Conv., 1964; pres. Young Rep. Club, 1957; candidate 9th dist. U.S. Ho. of Reps., 1968; adminstrv. asst. to Rep. state chmn. Ray C. Bliss, 1954; bd. dirs. Ohio Tb and Respiratory Disease Assn. Served with USNR, 1945-46. Named Outstanding Young Man of Toledo, 1962. Mem. Maumee C. of C., Am., Ohio, Toledo bar assns., Nat. Inst. Municipal Law Officers, Ohio Municipal League (trustee), Toledo Council World Affairs, Am. Legion, Maumee Valley Hist. Soc., Internat. Platform Assn., World Peace through Law, Toledo Mus. Art, Alumni Assn. Ohio Wesleyan U. (pres.), Ohio Land Title Assn., Omicron Delta Kappa, Delta Sigma Rho, Theta Alpha Phi, Phi Delta Phi. Presbyterian. Clubs: Toledo Country, Press (Toledo); Capitol Hill (Washington). Home: 124 W Harrison St Maumee OH 43537 Office: United Savings Bldg Toledo OH 43604

MARSH, BURTON WALLACE, traffic and transp. engr.; b. Worcester, Mass., Jan. 9, 1898; s. Luman Wallace and Florence Duncan (Wells) M.; B.S. in Civil Engring., Worcester Poly. Inst., 1920, D.Engring. (hon.), 1961; postgrad. Yale, 1920-21; m. Mary Elizabeth Allison, Oct. 8, 1927; children—Jean Allison Marsh Adams, Mary Elizabeth Marsh McCartor, Alan Burton. Engaged in work on housing projects, city planning, zoning, traffic planning various cities, including Worcester, Norfolk, Va., Dayton, Ohio, 1921-24; city traffic engr., Pitts., 1924-30, Phila., 1930-33; dir. traffic engring. and safety dept. Am. Automobile Assn., Washington, 1933-64; exec. dir. AAA Found. for Traffic Safety, 1964-66; exec. dir. Inst. Traffic Engrs., 1967-70; cons. engr., 1970—; lectr., instr., dean in traffic courses and schs. including Traffic Engring. and Traffic Officer Tng. Schs. at Yale, Harvard, Northwestern U., Pa. State U., U. Md.; pioneer municipal traffic engr. Mem., past chmn. exec. com. Transp. Research Bd. of Nat. Acad. Scis.-Nat. Acad. Engring.; mem., past chmn. Nat. Com. Uniform Traffic Laws and Ordinances; emeritus mem., past chmn. Nat. Adv. Com. on Uniform Traffic Control Devices; mem. U.S. delegation Pan Am. Hwy. Congresses, Panama City, Panama, 1957, Bogota, Colombia, 1960, Washington, 1963, Montevideo, Uruguay, 1967, Quito, Ecuador, 1971, San Jose, Costa Rica, 1975. Trustee Worcester Poly. Inst., 1953-67, emeritus, 1967—; pres. Theodore M. Matson Meml. Fund, Inc., 1978. Recipient Roy W. Crum award Hwy. Research Bd., 1954; Paul Gray Hoffman award, 1959; Theodore M. Matson Meml. award 1960; Arthur Williams Meml. medal, 1970; Burton W. Marsh award named in his honor, Inst. Traffic Engrs., 1970, also first recipient; citation for distinguished service to safety Nat. Safety Council, 1974; named hon. life chmn. tech. com. on hwy. ops. Pan Am. Hwy. Congresses, OAS, 1974; named life hon. trustee AAA Found. for Traffic Safety, 1975; named hon. mem. Inst. Transp., Am. Pub. Works Assn., 1975. Fellow Am. Soc. C.E., Inst. Transp. Engrs. (past pres., a founder, hon. mem.); mem. Sigma Xi, Tau Beta Pi. Presbyn. Club: Cosmos (Washington). Address: 3126 Rittenhouse St NW Washington DC 20015

MARSH, DON E., supermarket exec.; b. Muncie, Ind., Feb. 2, 1938; s. Ermal W. and Garnet (Gibson) M.; B.A., Mich. State U., 1960; m. Marilyn Faust, Mar. 28, 1959; children—Don Ermal, Arthur Andrew, David Alan, Anne Elizabeth, Alexander Elliott. With Marsh Supermarkets, Inc., Yorktown, Ind., 1961—, pres., 1968—, also dir.; dir. Mchts. Nat. Bank, Muncie, Universal Tank and Iron Works, Indpls. Mem. Nat. Assn. Food Chains (dir.), Am. Mgmt. Assn., Internat. Food Congress, Internat. Assn. Food Distbn. (adv. bd.), Indpls., Muncie chambers commerce, Young Pres.'s Orgn., Newcomen Soc. N.Am., Pi Sigma Epsilon, Lambda Chi Alpha. Presbyterian. Clubs: Columbia (Indpls.); Delaware Country, Masons, Elks, Rotary. Home: 1250 Warwick Dr Muncie IN 47304 Office: Marsh Supermarkets Inc Yorktown IN 47396

MARSH, EDWARD WILLIAM, lawyer; b. Mt. Pleasant, Pa., Oct. 7, 1916; s. Rabe Ferguson and Jessie (Dalbey) M.; A.B., Lafayette Coll., 1938; LL.B., U. Pitts., 1941; m. Rebecca Weaver, Nov. 29, 1941; children—Edward William, John W., David R. Admitted to Pa. bar, 1942; individual practice law, Greensburg, 1941-42; asso. firm Reed, Smith, Shaw & McClay, Pitts., 1942-59, partner, 1959—; tchr. bank loan documentation course Mellon Bank, N.A. Served with AUS, 1942-44. Mem. Am. Law Inst., Am. Bar Assn., Pa. Bar Assn., Allegheny County Bar Assn., Westmoreland County Bar Assn., Order of Coif, Phi Beta Kappa, Chi Phi. Democrat. Presbyterian. Clubs: Elks; Greensburg Country. Home: 138 Underwood Ave Greensburg PA 15601 Office: 747 Union Trust Bldg Pittsburgh PA 15230

MARSH, FLORENCE GERTRUDE, educator; b. Rochester, N.Y., Sept. 15, 1916; d. Charles D. and Ruth (Galloway) Marsh; A.B., Mt. Holyoke Coll., 1937; M.A., U. Tenn., 1943; Ph.D., Yale, 1951. Tchr., Cayuga Lake Acad., Aurora, N.Y., 1939-41; teaching fellow U. Tenn., 1941-43; instr. English Western Coll. for Women, Oxford, 1943-45; instr. English Mt. Holyoke Coll., 1948-49; instr. English, Case Western Res. U., Cleve., 1950-51, asst. prof., 1951-60, asso. prof., now prof., chmn. dept., 1972-74. Ford Found. grantee for improvement teaching, 1954-55. Mem. AAUP, Modern Lang. Assn., Nat. Council Tchrs. English. Author: Wordsworth's Imagery: A Study in Poetic Vision, 1952. Contbr. articles to profl. jours. Home: 4883 Countryside Rd Lyndhurst OH 44124

MARSH, FRANK, state ofcl.; b. Norfolk, Nebr., Apr. 27, 1924; s. Frank and Della (Andrews) M.; B.S. in Edn., U. Nebr., 1950; m. Shirley Mac McVicker, Mar. 5, 1943; children—Sherry Anne Marsh Tupper, Dory Michael, Stephen Alan, Corwin Frank, Mitchell Edward, Melissa Lou. Builder, tchr., businessman, 1946-52; sec. state Nebr., 1953-71, lt. gov., 1971-75, state treas., 1975—. Mem. State Canvassing Bd., State Claims Bd., Unclaimed Property Adminstrn.; govt. liaison adviser Mayor's Com. Internat. Friendship; past pres. Nat. Council Internat. Visitors; past internat. trustee Am. Field Service/Intercultural Programs, U. Nebr. Fgn. Student Host Program; chmn. bd., pres. Am. Youth Hostels, Inc. Mem. Combined Orgn. Police Services, Am., Nebr. correctional assns., Central States Corrections Assn. (past pres.), Capitol City Footprinters, Nebraskaland Found., Nat. Assn. State Treasurers (pres.), Midwest Internat. Trade Assn. (dir.), V.F.W., Am. Legion, Scottish Soc. Nebr., Nebr. Hist. Soc., Nebr. Chamber Orch. (v.p.), Nebraska land Found., D.A.V., U. Nebr. Alumni Assn. (life). Republican. Methodist (bd. trustees). Clubs: Lincoln Gem and Mineral, Lincoln Stamp, Polemic, Univ. Home: 2701 S 34th St Lincoln NE 68506 Office: State Capitol Bldg Lincoln NE 63509

MARSH, HAROLD NEWMAN, JR., banker; b. Washington, Sept. 1, 1923; s. Harold N. and Dorothy (Dennis) M.; B.A., Bowdoin Coll., 1948; postgrad. in Advanced Sch. Credit and Fin. Mgmt., Amos Tuck Sch., Dartmouth Coll., 1966; grad. Advanced Mgmt. Program, Harvard U., 1975; m. Marion Carhart, Dec. 28, 1946; children—Harold, Addison, Mandana, Frederick, Meredith. Officer, Hartford Nat. Bank (Conn.), 1959-66, Franklin Nat. Bank (N.Y.C.), 1966-69; v.p. European Am. Bank, N.Y.C., 1969-72, sr. v.p., 1972-75, exec. v.p., 1976—; dir. Luxo Lamp Corp., Port Chester, N.Y. Mem. adv. council N.Y. Urban League, N.Y.C., 1967-73; mem. corp. gifts com. N.Y.C. Public Library, 1978—. Served to capt., inf., USMC, 1942-46, 51-52. Mem. Newcomen Soc. N. Am., Econ. Club N.Y., Assn. Res. City Bankers. Episcopalian. Clubs: Broad St., Chevy Chase, Union. Home: 169 E 69th St New York NY 10021 Office: 10 Hanover Sq New York NY 10015

MARSH, JEAN LYNDSEY TORREN, actress, writer; b. London, July 1, 1934; d. Henry Charles John and Emmeline Susannah Nightingale Poppy (Bexley) M.; student in dance, piano, voice and mime; m. Jon Devon Richard Pertwee, Apr. 2, 1955 (div. 1960). Worked as singer in cabarets, photographers' model, and with repertory cos.; Broadway debut in Much Ado About Nothing, 1959; other theatrical appearances include: Habeas Corpus, Broadway, 1975, Travesties, The Importance of Being Earnest, 1977, Too True to Be Good, 1977, My Fat Friend, Whose Life Is It Anyway?, 1979; movie appearances include: Where's Charley?, Tales of Hoffmann, The Horsemasters, Cleopatra, 1963, Frenzy, 1972, Dark Places, The Eagle Has Landed, 1977, The Limbo Line, 1969; co-creator, story cons. BBC series Upstairs, Downstairs, also starred; TV appearances include: The Grover Monster/Jean Marsh Cartoon Spl., 1975, A State Dinner for Queen Elizabeth II, 1976, Mad About the Boy: Noel Coward—A Celebration, 1976. Winner Emmy award, 1975; named Most Outstanding New Female Actress of 1972. *

MARSH, JOSEPH FRANKLIN, JR., coll. pres.; b. Charleston, W.Va., Feb. 24, 1925; s. Joseph Franklin and Florence (Keller) M.; student Concord Coll., 1941-42, W.Va. U., 1942-43; A.B., Dartmouth, 1947; student Nat. Inst. Pub. Affairs, Washington, 1947-48; M.P.A., Harvard, 1949; Rotary fellow Oxford (Eng.) U., 1950-52; LL.D., Davis and Elkins Coll., 1968. Cons. Hoover Commn., Washington, 1948; instr. in gt. issues Dartmouth, 1952-54, instr. econs., 1953-55, asst. prof., 1955-59; pres. Concord Coll., Athens, W.Va., 1959-73; ednl. cons., 1973-74; pres. Waynesburg (Pa.) Coll., 1974—. Dir. Bank of Athens. Mem. State Dept. Ednl. Mission to U.A.R., 1964; vice chmn. W.Va. Com. for Constnl. Amendments, 1966; mem. regional council Internat. Edn. Study Mission to Europe, 1970. Bd. dirs. Am. Assn. State Colls. and Univs., 1972-73, Regional Council for Internat. Edn., 1973; bd. dirs. Pa. Commn. for Independent Colls. and Univs., 1974—, sec.-treas., 1976-77, vice chmn., 1977—; trustee Found. Ind. Colls. Pa., 1974—, mem. exec. com., 1979—; bd. visitors Midway Coll., Ky., 1979—. Served as gunnery officer USNR, 1943-46. Named Outstanding Young Man W.Va. Jr. C. of C., 1960; Concord Coll. Alumnus of Yr., 1973. Mem. Am. Assn. U. Adminstrs., AAUP, Am. Econ. Assn., Royal Inst. Pub. Adminstrn., Greene County (Pa.) Hist. Soc., Oxford Union Debating Soc. (life), Oxford Soc. (life), Phi Beta Kappa, Phi Tau, Phi Delta Pi, Phi Sigma Kappa, Alpha Kappa Psi (hon.). Methodist. Clubs: Duquesne (Pitts.); Univ. (Bluefield), Masons, Rotary. Author articles. Home: President's House 74 E Wayne St PO Box 586 Waynesburg PA 15370

MARSH, JULIAN BUNSICK, educator; b. N.Y.C., Jan. 21, 1926; s. Arin and Natalie (Bunsick) M.; M.D., U. Pa., 1947; m. Priscilla Kent, June 18, 1948; children—Constance (dec.), Gail. Intern, Episcopal Hosp., Phila., 1947-48; USPHS postdoctoral fellow biochemistry dept. research medicine U. Pa., Phila., 1948-50, asso., asst. prof., asso. prof., prof. Grad. Sch. Medicine, 1952-65, prof., chmn. dept. biochemistry Sch. Dental Medicine, 1965-75; prof., chmn. dept. physiology and biochemistry Med. Coll. Pa., 1975—. Cons. VA Hosp., Phila. Served with AUS, 1944-46, to capt. M.C., 1950-52. Lalor fellow Marine Biol. Labs., Woods Hole, 1959; John S. Guggenheim fellow Nat. Inst. Med. Research, London, 1960-61. Mem. Am. Soc. Biol. Chemists, Am. Phys. Soc., Phila. Coll. Physicians, Biochem. Soc. (Gt. Britain), Soc. for Exptl. Biology and Medicine, Phila. Biochem. Club (pres. 1968), ACLU. Author: (with N. Haugaard) Action of Insulin, 1953. Contbr. chpts. to books, articles to profl. jours. Home: 4054 Irving St Philadelphia PA 19104

MARSH, PAMELA OLIVE, editor; b. Warwickshire, Eng.; d. James Frederick and Alice Irene (Ashmore) Marsh; ed. Sutton Coldfield High Sch., Warwickshire. Editor spl. sects. Christian Sci. Monitor, Boston. Office: 1 Norway St Boston MA 02115

MARSH, QUINTON NEELY, banker; b. Omaha, July 1, 1915; s. Arthur J. and Rose L. (Baysel) M.; B.S.C., Benjamin Franklin U., Washington, 1949, M.C.S., 1950; student Am. U., 1950-51; diploma Bank Adminstrn. Inst. Sch., U. Wis., 1959; m. Thelma May Beck, Nov. 24, 1944. With Western Electric Co., Omaha, 1935-37, Lamson Bros. & Co., Omaha, 1937-39, C.A. Swanson & Sons, Omaha, 1939-42; with Am. Security & Trust Co., Washington, 1946—, auditor, 1958—, security officer, 1968—, gen. auditor, 1969, v.p., 1972-77; sr. v.p., cashier Bank of Columbia, N.A., Washington, 1977-79; sr. v.p. United Nat. Bank, Washington, 1979—. Lectr. banking schs., security and law enforcement seminars, 1961—; vice chmn. exam. com. Chartered Bank Auditor Program, 1968. Served with USNR, 1942-45. Chartered bank auditor, 1968, certified internal auditor, 1973; cert. protection profl. Mem. Bank Adminstrn. Inst. (pres. D.C. 1966-67), Inst. Internal Auditors (pres. Washington 1962-63), Internat. Assn. Chiefs Police, Am. Soc. Indsl. Security. Contbr. articles to profl. jours. Home: 4801 Connecticut Ave NW Apt 312 Washington DC 20008 Office: Suite 290 1850 K St NW Washington DC 20006

MARSH, RABE FERGUSON, JR., judge; b. Greensburg, Pa., Apr. 26, 1905; s. Rabe Ferguson and Jessie (Dalbey) M.; A.B., Lafayette Coll., 1927; LL.B., U. Pitts., 1930; m. Marguerite Elizabeth Dayton, Sept. 14, 1935; children—Rabe Ferguson III, Deborah Elizabeth (dec.). Admitted to Pa. bar, 1930, practiced in Greensburg, 1930-50; asst. dist. atty. Westmoreland County (Pa.), 1942-50; U.S. dist. judge for Western Dist. Pa., Pitts., 1950—, chief judge, 1969-75, sr. dist. judge, 1977—. Chmn. Westmoreland County Democratic Com., 1940-48. Mem. Law Club Pitts., Phi Delta Phi, Phi Kappa Psi. Presbyn. Elk. Home: 905 Summit Dr Greensburg PA 15601 Office: US Courthouse Pittsburgh PA 15219

MARSH, ROBERT CHARLES, writer, music critic; b. Columbus, Ohio, Aug. 5, 1924; s. Charles L. and Jane A. (Beckett) M.; B.S., Northwestern U., 1945, A.M., 1946; Sage fellow Cornell U., 1946-47; postgrad. U. Chgo., 1948; Ed.D., Harvard, 1951; postgrad. U. Oxford, 1952-53, U. Cambridge, 1953-56; m. Kathleen C.. Moscrop, July 4, 1956. Instr. social sci. U. Ill., 1947-49; lectr. humanities Chgo. City Jr. Coll., 1950-51; asst. prof. edn. U. Kansas City, 1951-52; vis. prof. edn. State U. N.Y., 1953-54; humanities staff U. Chgo., 1956-58, lectr. in social thought, 1976; music critic Chgo. Sun-Times, 1956—. Co-recipient Peabody award for ednl. broadcasting, 1976. Ford Found. fellow, 1965-66. Fellow Internat. Inst. Arts and Letters; mem. Sigma Delta Chi. Episcopalian. Club: Tavern (Chicago). Author: Toscanini and the Art of Orchestral Performance, 1956, rev. edit., 1962; The Cleveland Orchestra, 1967. Editor: Logic and Knowledge, 1956. Contbg. editor High Fidelity, 1955-66, 71-77. Home: 1825 N Lincoln Plaza Chicago IL 60614 Office: Chicago Sun-Times Chicago IL 60611

MARSH, ROBERT MORTIMER, educator, sociologist; b. Everett, Mass., Jan. 22, 1931; s. Henry Warren and Ruth (Dunbar) M.; student Boston U., 1948-50; A.B., U. Chgo., 1952; M.A., Columbia, 1953, Ph.D., 1959; m. Susan S. Han, Oct. 12, 1957; children—Eleanor L., Christopher S.H., Diana E. Fellow Ford Found., Japan, Taiwan, Hong Kong, 1956-58; instr. sociology U. Mich., 1958-61; asst. prof. sociology Cornell U., 1961-65; asso. prof. Duke, 1965-67; mem. faculty Brown U., 1967—, prof. sociology, 1968—, chmn. dept., 1971-75. East Asian Inst. summer fellow Chinese, Columbia, 1955; Ford Found. and Guggenheim Found. fellow, Japan, 1969-70. Mem. Am., Eastern sociol. assns., Assn. Asian Studies, Internat. Studies Assn. (exec. com. comparative interdisciplinary studies sect. 1971-76), Japan Human Relations Assn. (councilor 1970—). Author: The Mandarins: The Circulation of Elites in China, 1961; Comparative Sociology: A Codification of Cross-Societal Analysis, 1967; (with H. Mannari) Modernization and the Japanese Factory, 1976; also articles. Asso. editor Adminstrv. Sci. Quar., 1963-67, Jour. Comparative Family Studies, 1970-74. Office: Dept Sociology Brown Univ Providence RI 02912

MARSH, THAD NORTON, hosp. exec.; b. Wichita, Kans., Aug. 25, 1926; s. Paul Norton and Ethel (Reaugh) M.; A.B. (Summerfield scholar 1943-48), U. Kans., 1948; B.A. (Rhodes scholar), U. Oxford (Eng.), 1951, M.A., 1955, B. Litt., 1957; m. Patricia Anne Cunningham, Dec. 23, 1955; children—Anne Catherine, Alice Jean, Paul Norton. Instr. English, U. Kans., 1948-49, Kans. State Coll., 1951-52; asst. prof. English, Rice U., 1954-62, asst. to pres., 1959-61; dean coll., prof. English, Muhlenberg Coll., Allentown, Pa. 1962-66; dean of coll., prof. English, Centenary Coll. of La., Shreveport, 1966-73; provost, v.p., lectr. English, U. of South, Sewanee, Tenn., 1973-77, prof. English, 1977-78; v.p. Meth. Hosp., Tex. Med. Center, 1978—; mem. Rhodes Scholarships Selection Com., Tex., 1955-61, 78—, Pa., 1962-65, La., 1966-76, Mo., 1977, sec., 1970-73; asso. adv. council The Danforth Found., 1964-67. Mem. bd. higher edn. United Luth. Ch. Am., 1960-62; mem. nat. selection bd. Harbison award for gifted teaching, 1965-68. Fellow Royal Geog. Soc.; mem. So. Conf. Acad. Deans (pres. 1969), Renaissance Soc. Am., Assn. Am. Rhodes Scholars, Nat. Soc. Fund-Raising Execs., Nat. Assn. for Hosp. Devel., Phi Beta Kappa. Democrat. Club: Doctors (Houston). Contbr. articles on 16th century English lit. to profl. jours.; editor: (with Wilfred S Dowden) The Heritage of Freedom, 1962. Home: 5438 Cheena Dr Houston TX 77096. *The longer I live, the more committed I am to the proposition that the truly liberating education is that which compels a person to measure and test himself against the thought, achievement-and style-of the past.*

MARSHAK, ROBERT EUGENE, physicist, educator; b. N.Y.C., Oct. 11, 1916; s. Harry and Rose (Shapiro) M.; A.B., Columbia U., 1936; Ph.D., Cornell U., 1939; hon. degree Utkal U., India, 1977; m. Ruth Florence Gup, Apr. 18, 1943; children—Ann, Robert Stephen. Instr. dept. physics U. Rochester (N.Y.), 1939-43, asst. prof., 1943-46, asso. prof., 1946-49, prof., 1949-70, chmn. dept. physics and astronomy, 1950-64, Disting. Univ. prof., 1964-70; pres. CCNY, 1970-79; Disting. prof. physics Va. Poly. Inst. and State U., Blacksburg, 1979—; lectr. Harvard Obs., summer 1940; professeur d'Echange (Guggenheim fellow) at Sorbonne, 1953-54; vis. prof. Columbia U., summer 1950, U. Mich., 1952, Tata Inst. Bombay, 1953, French Sch. for Theoretical Physics, 1954, Tokyo, 1965, Goteburg, 1970; guest prof. at CERN, Geneva, Switzerland; Ford Found. and Guggenheim fellow, 1960-61, Guggenheim fellow, 1967-68; Nobel Found. prof., Sweden, 1970; mem. Inst. Advanced Study, Princeton, spring 1948; physicist radiation lab. Mass. Inst. Tech., 1942-43, Montreal Atomic Energy project, 1943-44; dep. group leader in theoretical physics Los Alamos Sci. Lab., 1944-46; vice chmn. N.Y. State Adv. Com. on Atomic Energy, 1958; Avco vis. prof. Cornell U., 1959; chmn. vis. physics com. Brookhaven Nat. Lab., 1964-65; Niels Bohr vis. prof. Inst. Math. Sci., Madras, India, 1963; lectr. Yalta Internat. Sch., 1966, Hercig Novi Internat. Sch., 1967; head Nat. Acad. Sci. del. to Poland, 1964, to Yugolsavia, 1965; mem. Sloan Fellowship Com., 1967-73; mem. sci. council Internat. Center of Theoretical Physics, Trieste, 1967-75; Buhl vis. prof. Carnegie-Mellon U., 1968; distinguished visitor U. Tex., 1970; mem. Solvay Congress, 1967, Pugwash Conf., 1967; mem. U.S.-Japan Com. on Sci.-Cooperation, 1969-72; mem. nat. com. UNESCO, 1970-73; trustee Univ. Research Assn., 1968-70; chmn. div. particles and fields, 1970-71; trustee Atoms for Peace Award, 1958-70; founder Rochester Confs. on High Energy Physics, 1950—; vis. com. physics Carnegie Mellon U., 1967-70; bd. dirs. Internat. Found. for Sci., 1970-75. Recipient A. Cressy Morrison Astron. prize N.Y. Acad. Scis., 1940. Fellow Am. Phys. Soc. (exec. com. 1968-69, council 1965-69), AAAS; mem. AAUP, Fedn. Am. Scientists (chmn. 1947-48), Nat. Acad. Scis. (past chmn. adv. com. on sci. exchanges with USSR and Eastern Europe; council 1971-74), Am. Acad. Arts and Scis. (council fgn. affairs 1974—), Internat. Union Pure and Applied Physics (past sec. commn. on high energy phsyics), Phi Beta Kappa, Sigma Xi (nat. lectr. 1969), Phi Kappa Phi. Author: Meson Physics, 1952; (with L.I. Schiff and E.C. Nelson) Our Atomic World, 1946; (with E.C.G. Sudarshan) Elementary Particles, 1961; (with Riazuddin and C. Ryan) Theory of Weak Interactrons, 1969. Asso. editor Phys. Rev., 1953-55; editor interscience Tracts and Monographs in Physics and Astronomy, 1955-70; dir. Jour. History of Ideas, 1973—. Researcher in theoretical particle physics. Office: Va Poly Inst and State U Dept Physics Blacksburg VA 24061

MARSHAK, ROBERT REUBEN, univ. dean; b. N.Y.C., Feb. 23, 1923; s. David and Edith (Youselovsky) M.; student U. Wis., 1940-41; D.V.M., Cornell U., 1945; D.V.M. (hon.), U. Bern, 1968; M.A. (hon.), U. Pa., 1971; m. Ruth Emilie Lyons, Dec. 4, 1948; children—William Lyons, John Ball, Richard Best. Practice vet. medicine, Springfield, Vt., 1945-56; prof., chmn. dept. medicine Sch. Vet. Medicine, U. Pa., Phila., 1956-58, prof. medicine Grad. Sch. Medicine, 1957-64, chmn. dept. clin. studies Sch. Vet. Medicine, 1958-73, dir. Bovine Leukemia Research Center, 1965-73, dean Sch. Vet. Medicine, 1973—, co-dir. Center on Interactions Animals and Soc., also mem. grad. group com. in comparative med. scis. Bd. dirs. Humane Soc. U.S., Bide-a-wee Home Assn.; adv. council James A. Baker Inst. and N.Y. State Coll. Vet. Medicine (both Cornell U.); adv. bd. Pa. Dept. Agr.; mem. com. on vet. medicine scis. Nat. Acad. Scis. Served with AUS, 1943-44. Charter diplomate Am. Coll. Vet. Internal Medicine. Fellow N.Y. Acad. Scis., Phila. Coll. Physicians; mem. John Morgan Soc. (pres. 1967-68), AAAS, Am. Assn. Cancer Research, Am., Pa. vet. med. assns., Pa. Livestock Assn. (dir.), Conf. Research Workers in Animal Diseases, Am. Assn. Vet. Med. Colls., Sigma Xi, Phi Zeta. Mem. editorial bd. Jour. of Am. Vet. Radiology Soc., 1964—, Cornell Veterinarian, 1972—. Contbr. numerous articles to sci. jours. Home: Bartram Rd RD 1 Kennett Sq PA 19348 Office: U Pa Sch Vet Medicine 3800 Spruce St Philadelphia PA 19174

MARSHALL, ALBERT PRINCE, librarian; b. Texarkana, Tex., Sept. 5, 1914; s. Early and Mary Louise (Bland) M.; A.B., Lincoln U., 1938; B.L.S., U. Ill., 1939, M.A. in History, 1953; postgrad. U. Mo., 1956-63; m. Ruthe Helena Langley, June 12, 1941; 1 dau., Satia Marshall Orange. Asst. librarian Lincoln U., Jefferson City, Mo., 1939-41; librarian Winston-Salem State Coll., 1941-48; univ. librarian Lincoln U., Jefferson City, Mo., 1950-69; dir. library Eastern Mich. U., Ypsilanti, 1969-72, dean acad. services, 1972-76, spl. asst. to v.p., acad. affairs, 1976-77, prof., social sci. librarian, 1977—; cons. library collection bldg. and Black studies resources, 1967—; cons. bd. Nat. Endowment for Humanities. Mem. Mayor's Commn. on Human Rights, Winston-Salem, N.C., 1946-48, Jefferson City, Mo., 1952-54;

state conf. pres. Mo. Conf. Branches, NAACP, 1954-55; exec. sec. Mo. Commn. for UNESCO, 1955-56; mem. dist. com. Boy Scouts Am., 1955-73; bd. dirs. Child and Family Service of Washtenaw County, 1972-75, Washtenaw County unit Mich. Heart Assn., 1974-76, Washtenaw County Opportunities Industrialization Center, 1974-77; mem. Ypsilanti Hist. Commn., 1978—. Served with USCGR, 1943-45. Recipient Alumni Achievement award Lincoln U., 1965; cited by Mo. Library Assn., 1969, Lincoln U. Alumni Assn., 1969. Mem. Am. Hist. Assn., AAUP, Assn. for Higher Edn., ALA (2d v.p. 1971), Mich., Mo. (pres. 1961-62) library assns., Ann Arbor-Ypsilanti Bus. and Profl. League, Alpha Phi Alpha. Mem. African Methodist Episcopal Ch. (chmn. steward bd. 1961-77). Club: Rotary (dist. gov. 1977-78). Author: A Soldiers' Dream: A Centennial History of Lincoln University, 1966; compiler, pub. A Guide to Negro Periodical Literature, 1940-46; editor Mo. Library Assn. Quar., 1952-54, Lincoln U. Alumni Bull., 1956-69. Home: 1616 Gregory St Ypsilanti MI 48197. *A leader must exhibit three qualities which loom important if he is to remain successful. First, he must have the sensitivity of a lamb's skin in order to recognize the human needs around him. Second, he must have the roughness of a rhinoceros' hide in order to fend off attacks from those who would impede his progress. Third, he must be able to determine when to utilize one over the other.*

MARSHALL, ANTHONY WALLACE, television producer; b. N.Y.C., Mar. 29, 1906; s. Joseph and Anastasia (Pascucci) Masciarelli; B.C.S., N.Y. U., 1930; m. Marjorie Ward, Oct. 1, 1931; children—Garry K., Ronnelle, Penny. Advt. dept. Ruberoid Co., N.Y.C., 1930-35; sales promotion dir. Bryant Press, Inc., N.Y.C., 1935-48; pres. Marshall Orgn., Inc., N.Y.C., 1948-69; producer Paramount Studios, Hollywood, Calif., 1970—. Recipient Peoples Choice award for television comedy Happy Day. Mem. Advt. Club N.Y.C., Indsl. Advt. Club N.Y.C., Producers Guild, Inc. Hollywood, Alpha Kappa Psi. Democrat. Episcopalian. Clubs: Lakeside Golf (North Hollywood); Wilshire Country (Los Angeles).

MARSHALL, ARTHUR K., lawyer, judge, educator, writer; b. N.Y.C., Oct. 7, 1911; s. Louis and Fanny (Kurgan) M.; B.S., Coll. City N.Y., 1933; LL.B., St. John's U., N.Y.C., 1936; LL.M., U. So. Calif., 1952; m. Mary Jane Ratliff, June 26, 1948; 2 children. Admitted to N.Y. bar, 1937, Calif. bar, 1947; practice law, N.Y.C., 1937-43, Los Angeles, 1947-50; atty. VA, Los Angeles, 1947-50; tax counsel Calif. Bd. Equalization, Sacramento, 1950-51; inheritance tax atty. State Controller, Los Angeles, 1951-53; commr. Superior Ct. Los Angeles County, 1953-62; judge Municipal Ct., Los Angeles jud. dist., 1962-63; judge Superior Ct., Los Angeles, 1963—, supervising judge probate dept., 1968-69, appellate dept., Superior Ct., 1973—; presiding judge Appellate Dept., 1976—. Acting asst. prof. law U. Calif. at Los Angeles, 1954-59; mem. grad. faculty U. So. Calif., 1955-75; lectr. Continuing Edn. of Bar. Served with AUS, 1943-46. Named Judge of Yr., Lawyers Club of Los Angeles County, 1975. Fellow Am. Bar Found.; mem. Internat. Acad. Estate and Trust Law (founder, 1st pres., now chancellor), Am. Bar Assn., Calif. State Bar (adv. to exec. com. estate planning, probate and trust sect. 1970—), Santa Monica (Calif.) (pres. 1960), Westwood (pres. 1959), Los Angeles bar assns., Lawyers Club, Am. Judicature Soc., Am. Legion (comdr. 1971-72), Men of All Sts. Soc. (pres. 1968-69, 76, U. So. Calif. Law Alumni Assn. (pres. 1969-70), Phi Alpha Delta (1st justice alumni chpt. 1976-77). Episcopalian (vestryman 1966-70). Clubs: Lincoln, Jonathan. Author: Joint Tenancy Taxwise & Otherwise, 1953; Branch Courts, 1959; California State and Local Taxation, Text, 2 vols., 1962, rev. edit., 1969, supplement, 1979; California State and Local Taxation Forms, 2 vols., 1961-75, rev. edit., 1979; California Probate Procedure, 1961, rev. edits., 1968, 73, 79; Guide to Procedure Before Trial, 1975; (with others) Survey of California Law, 1953, rev. edit., 1954, Family Law, 1956, Civil Procedure Before Trial, 1957. Office: Superior Ct Los Angeles CA 90012

MARSHALL, C. PENNY, actress; b. N.Y.C., Oct. 15, 1943; d. Anthony W. and Marjorie Irene (Ward) Marshall; student U. N.Mex., 1961-64; m. Robert Reiner, Apr. 10, 1971; 1 dau., Tracy Lee. Appeared on numerous television shows, including The Odd Couple (series), 1972-74, Friends and Lovers (co-star), 1974, Let's Switch, 1974, Wives (pilot), 1975, Chico and the Man, 1975, Mary Tyler Moore, 1975, Heaven Help Us, 1975, Saturday Night Live, 1975-77, Happy Days, 1975, Battle of Network Stars (ABC special), 1976, Barry Manilow special, 1976, The Tonight Show, 1976-77, Dinah, 1976-77, Mike Douglas Show, 1975-77, Merv Griffin Show, 1976-77, Blansky's Beauties, 1977, $20,000 Pyramid, 1976-77, Network Battle of the Sexes, 1977; star Laverne and Shirley, 1976—; TV film More Than Friends, 1978; appeared in motion pictures How Sweet It Is, 1967, The Savage Seven, 1968, The Grasshopper, 1968, 1941, 1979. Office: Creative Artists Agy 1888 Century Park E Suite 1400 Los Angeles CA 90067*

MARSHALL, CARTER LEE, JR., physician, educator; b. New Haven, Mar. 31, 1936; s. Carter Lee and Grace Wilna (Lofton) M.; A.B. magna cum laude, Harvard, 1958; M.D., Yale, 1962, M.P.H., 1964; m. Carol Lynn Paul, Dec. 19, 1970; 1 son, Carter Lee III; children by previous marriage—Wendy Elizabeth, Holly Louise. Intern, Michael Reese Hosp., Chgo., 1962-63; fellow Sch. Pub. Health, Yale, 1964-65; with New Haven Health Dept., 1964-65; asst. prof. U. Kans. Med. Sch., 1967-69; asso. prof. community medicine Mt. Sinai Sch. Medicine, 1969-74, prof. community medicine, 1975-76, asso. dean for continuous edn., 1974-76; dean for health affairs City U. N.Y., 1972-73; prof., chmn. dept. community medicine Sch. Medicine, Morehouse Coll., 1976-77; prof. medicine and dir. Office of Primary Care, Coll. Medicine and Dentistry of N.J., 1977—. Mem. health tech. study sect. Nat. Center Health Services Research, 1973-77; cons. Children's TV Workshop; trustee Williston-Northampton Sch., Easthampton, Mass., 1972-73. Served as capt. AUS, 1965-67. Decorated Commendation medal. Diplomate Am. Bd. Preventive Medicine. Fellow Am. Pub. Health Assn., Am. Coll. Preventive Medicine; mem. AAAS, Assn. Tchrs. Preventive Medicine (exec. bd.). Author: Dynamics of Health and Disease, 1972; Toward An Educated Health Consumer: Mass Communication and Quality Assessment in Medical Care, 1977. Contbr. articles to profl. jours. Home: 146 Lenox Terr Maplewood NJ 07040 Office: Coll Medicine and Dentistry of NJ NJ Med Sch Newark NJ 07103

MARSHALL, CHARLES, utility co. exec.; b. Vandalia, Ill., Apr. 21, 1929; s. William F. and Ruth C. M.; B.S. in Agr., U. Ill., 1951; m. Millicent Bruner, Jan. 2, 1953; children—Ruth Ann, Marcia Kay, William Forman, Charles Tedrick. With Ill. Bell Telephone Co., 1953-59, 61-64, 65-70, 71-72, 77—, pres., chief exec. officer, Chgo., 1977—; with AT&T, 1959-61, 64-65, 70-71, v.p., treas., N.Y.C., 1972-77; v.p. Tex. ops. Southwestern Bell Telephone Co., Dallas, 1975-76; mem. bus. advisory council Chgo. Urban League; mem. Econ. Devel. Commn. of Chgo.; mem. governing bd. Ill. Council Econ. Edn.; dir. Harris Bankcorp., Inc. and subs. Harris Trust & Savs. Bank, GATX Corp., Inland Steel Corp. Bd. dirs. Chgo. Central Area Com., Protestant Found. Greater Chgo., United Way of Met. Chgo.; trustee Adler Planetarium, Chgo., Chgo. Symphony Orch., U. Chgo., Garrett-Evang. Theol. Sem., Museum Sci., Industry, Chgo., Rush-Presbyn.-St. Luke's Med. Center, Chgo.; mem. adv. council Northwestern U. Grad. Sch. Mgmt.; trustee Lakefront Garden; mem. Gov.'s Council on Jobs and the Economy; mem. MERIT Employment Steering Com. Served to 1st lt. USAF, 1951-53. Mem. Chgo. Council Fgn. Relations (dir.), Nat. Alliance Businessmen (advisory council), Econ. Club Chgo. (dir.), Northwestern U. Assos., U. Ill. Found. Clubs: Chgo., Comml., Econ., Mid-Am. (bd. govs.) (Chgo.); Barrington Hills Country. Home: 69 Brinker Rd Barrington IL 60010 Office: 225 W Randolph St Chicago IL 60606

MARSHALL, CHARLES BURTON, educator; b. Catskill, N.Y., Mar. 25, 1908; s. Caleb Carey and Alice (Beeman) M.; B.A., U. Tex., 1931, M.A., 1932; Ph.D., Harvard, 1939; m. Betty Louise O'Brien, Aug. 1, 1958; children (by previous marriage)—Charles Richard, Jean Mary (Mrs. Charles E. Vickery). With newspapers in El Paso and Austin, Tex., 1925-31, Detroit, 1934-38; instr., tutor govt. Harvard and Radcliffe Coll., 1938-42; vis. lectr. Harvard, summer 1963; cons. Intergovtl. Com. Refugees, 1946-47; staff cons. com. fgn. affairs U.S. Ho. of Reps., 1947-50; mem. policy planning staff State Dept., 1950-53; adviser to prime minister Pakistan, 1955-57; research asso. Washington Center Fgn. Policy Research, 1957-74, acting dir., 1969-70; vis. prof. Sch. Advanced Internat. Studies, Johns Hopkins, 1965-66, prof., 1966-67, Paul H. Nitze prof. internat. politics, 1967-75; Alumni prof. internat. studies U. N.C., 1960-61; Centennial vis. prof. Tex. A&M U., 1976; cons. in field, 1961—; U.S. govt. rep. XIV Conf. Internat. Red Cross, Toronto, Can., 1952. Served to lt. col. AUS, 1942-46. Fellow Carnegie Endowment Internat. Peace, 1934-35, vis. scholar, 1958-59. Mem. Council Fgn. Relations, Washington Inst. Fgn. Affairs, Com. on Present Danger (mem. exec. com.). Clubs: Cosmos, Harvard (Washington). Author: The Limits of Foreign Policy, 1954; The Exercise of Sovereignty, 1965; The Cold War: A Concise History, 1965; Crisis Over Rhodesia: A Skeptical View, 1967. Home: 4106 N Randolph St Arlington VA 22207 Office: 1500 Wilson Blvd Suite 1700 Arlington VA 22209

MARSHALL, CHARLES LOUIS, govt. ofcl.; b. N.Y.C., Sept. 28, 1912; s. Joseph Francis and Josephine (Tassi) M.; B.S., Fordham U., 1934, M.S., 1939; m. Noel Berry, June 24, 1939; children—Noel, Suzanne. Supr. sci., Eastchester, N.Y., 1936-40; instr. chemistry Fordham U., 1935-36; research chemist United Fruit Co., 1946; chemist Manhattan Engr. Project 1946; classification analyst AEC, 1947-49, dep. dir. Office of Classification, 1949-55, dir. div. classification, 1955—; cons. U.S. Dept. Energy. Pres., Homeowners Assn., Boca Raton, Fla. Served as lt. col., C.E., AUS, 1940-46; asst. harbor def. arty. engr.; comdg. officer, Ft. Taylor, Fla. Recipient Distinguished Service award AEC, 1974. Fellow Am. Inst. Chemists; mem. Am. Nuclear Soc., Am. Chem. Soc., Res. Officers Assn., Holy Name Soc., U.S. Coast Guard Aux. (officer). Clubs: Cosmos; Kenwood Golf and Country, Boca Raton Hotel and Club. Holder patent lab. apparatus. Contbr. articles to profl. publs. Home: 783 Enfield St Boca Raton FL 33431

MARSHALL, CLIFFORD WALLACE, educator; b. N.Y.C., Mar. 11, 1928; s. Clifford Wallace and Virginia (Roe) M.; B.A., Hofstra U., 1949; M.A., Syracuse U., 1950; M.S., Poly. Inst. Bklyn., 1954; Ph.D., Columbia, 1961; m. Adele Kentoffio, Nov. 21, 1955; children—Wallace F., James A. Staff mem. Inst. Def. Analyses, Washington, 1958, prin. engr., 1959-60, cons. summer staff mem., 1965-68; specialist operations analyst Republic Aviation Corp., Farmingdale, N.Y., 1963; cons. USN Strategic Systems Project Office, Washington, 1968-69; asso. prof. math. Poly. Inst. N.Y., 1963-68, prof. math., 1968—. Cons., Urban Inst., 1971—. Mem. Am. Math. Soc., Math. Assn. Am., Operations Research Soc. Am., Soc. Indsl. and Applied Math., Sigma Xi. Author: applied Graph Theory, 1971. Home: 264 N Ocean Ave Patchogue NY 11772 Office: 333 Jay St Brooklyn NY 11201

MARSHALL, COLIN MARSH, vehicle rental and leasing co. exec.; b. Edgware, Eng., Nov. 16, 1933; s. Edward Leslie and Florence Mary (Chandler) M.; student Univ. Coll. Sch., 1946-51; certificate Cambridge U., 1949; m. Janet Winifred Cracknell, May 10, 1958; 1 dau., Joanna Sarah. Cadet purser to dep. Orient S.N. Co., Ltd., 1951-58; asst. to v.p. adminstrn., mgr. Mexico, gen. mgr. U.K. and Benelux, Hertz Rent-A-Car, 1958-64; former v.p., exec. v.p., pres., chief exec. officer Avis, Inc., N.Y.C., 1964-79; exec. v.p., secter exec. food products and consumer services Norton Simon Inc., N.Y.C., 1979—. Home: Pheasant Ln Greenwich CT 06830 Office: 277 Park Ave New York NY 10017

MARSHALL, DOROTHY NEPPER, educator; b. Brighton, Mass., Aug. 26, 1913; d. Christian V. and Anna C. (Jacobsen) Nepper; A.B., Smith Coll., 1935, M.A., 1937, LL.D., 1972; Ph.D., Bryn Mawr (Pa.) Coll., 1944; LL.D., Regis Coll., 1972, Worcester Poly. Inst., 1975; m. J. Nathaniel Marshall, Sept. 3, 1948; children—Nicholas Nepper, Emily Rachel. Mem. faculty Bryn Mawr Coll., 1942-69, dean, 1948-69; dir. spl. studies Holy Cross Coll., Worcester, Mass., 1970-71; vice chancellor for acad. affairs U. Mass., Boston, 1971-74, Commonwealth prof., 1973—, dir. Latin Am. studies, 1973—. Dir. Charlestown Savs. Bank, Boston. Past pres. Internat. Inst. in Spain. Mem. nat. bd. cons. Nat. Endowment for the Humanities, 1973; trustee Smith Coll., 1959-69, 73—, chmn. bd., 1976-79; trustee, sec. Bryn Mawr Coll., 1971—; trustee Ford Found., 1970—, Coll. Holy Cross, 1971—. Dorothy Marshall Chair in Hispanic Studies established Bryn Mawr Coll., 1975. Mem. Modern Lang. Assn., Am. Acad. Polit. Sci., Alumnae Assn. Bryn Mawr Coll., Alumnae Assn. Smith Coll., Phi Beta Kappa. Home: 280 Beacon St Boston MA 02116

MARSHALL, E. G., actor; b. Owatonna, Minn., June 18, 1910; s. Charles G. and Hazel Irene (Cobb) M.; student Carlton Coll., 1930, U. Minn., 1932; m. Helen Wolf, Apr. 26, 1939 (div. 1953); children—Jill, Degen. Began profl. career on radio stas., St. Paul, Mpls., Chgo., 1932; appeared in motion pictures including: House on 92d Street, 13 Rue Madeleine, Swamp Angel, Call Northside 777, Bachelor Party, 1957, Twelve Angry Men, 1957, Compulsion, 1959, The Journey, 1959, Town Without Pity, 1961, The Chase, 1966, The Bridge at Remagen, 1969, Tora! Tora! Tora!, 1970, The Pursuit of Happiness, 1971, Interiors, 1978; featured on radio program Theatre Guild on the Air; featured in Eugene O'Neill's The Iceman Cometh, 1946-47; appeared in plays The Crucible, Red Roses for Me, Waiting for Godot, The Gang's All Here, 1959; star TV show The Defenders; now frequently on TV, appeared The Doctors segment of show The Bold Ones, 1969-73, appeared in TV film Vampire, 1979; Disaster on the Coastliner, 1979. Recipient Emmy award for best actor in Defenders series, 1963. *

MARSHALL, EVERETT LAWRENCE, univ. dean; b. DeKalb, Ill., July 10, 1908; s. William Lawrence and Amanda (Burt) M.; B.Edn., No. Ill. U., 1930; M.A., U. Iowa, 1934, Ph.D., 1936; m. Helen O. Hartman, Aug. 24, 1935. Tchr. elementary sch. LaGrange, Ill., 1931-33; asst. prof. Ill. State U., Normal, 1936-37; supr. U.S. Dept. Agr., 1937-38; instr. No. Ill. U., DeKalb, 1938; mem. faculty Eastern Mich. U., Ypsilanti, 1938—, prof. edn., 1945—, dean acad. records and tchr. certification, 1949—. Mem. Am., Mich. (pres. 1959-60) assns. coll. registrars and admissions officers, Alpha Phi Omega. Methodist. Lion (Man of Yr. award 1964). Office: Acad Records and Tchr Certification Eastern Mich U Ypsilanti MI 48197

MARSHALL, FRANCIS JOSEPH, aero. engr.; b. N.Y.C., Sept. 5, 1923; s. Francis Joseph and Mary Gertrude (Leary) M.; B.S. in Mech. Engring., CCNY, 1948; M.S., Rensselaer Poly. Inst., 1950; Dr. Eng. Sci., N.Y. U., 1955; m. Joan Eager, June 14, 1952; children—Peter, Colin, Stephen, Dana. Engr., Gen. Electric Co., Schenectady, 1948-50; engr. Wright-Aero Corp., Woodridge, N.J., 1950-52; group leader Lab. for Applied Scis., U. Chgo., 1955-60; instr. Ill. Inst. Tech., 1957-59; prof. Sch. Aeros. and Astronautics, Purdue U., West Lafayette, Ind., 1960—; engr. U.S. Naval Underseas Warfare Center, Pasadena, Calif., 1966-68; faculty fellow NASA-Langley, 1969-70. Served with AUS, 1943-46. Decorated Combat Inf. badge. NASA research grantee, 1970-76. Asso. fellow AIAA; mem. Am. Soc. Engring. Edn., AAUP. Contbr. articles to profl. jours. Home: 120 Leslie Ave West Lafayette IN 47906 Office: Sch Aeros and Astronautics Purdue U West Lafayette IN 47907

MARSHALL, GEORGE NICHOLS, clergyman, author; b. Bozeman, Mont., July 4, 1920; s. James Wallace and Grace (Nichols) M.; A.B., Tufts U., 1941, S.T.B., 1941, A.M., 1943; M.A., Columbia, 1942; Th.M., Harvard, 1946; Ph.D., Walden U.; D.D., Meadville/Lombard Theol. Sch., 1976; m. Barbara Ambrose, June 14, 1946 (div. 1966); 1 son, Charles Hopkinson. Ordained to ministry Unitarian Ch., 1941; pastor, Natick, Mass., 1941-43, Plymouth, Mass., 1946-52, Niagara Falls, N.Y., 1952-60, Ch. of Larger Fellowship, Boston, 1960—. Asso. dir. dept. extension Unitarian-Universalist Assn., 1960-70; treas. Unitarian Ministers Assn., 1954-56; chmn. Unitarian Commn. Ch. and Returning Servicemen, 1944-46; sec. Commn. Unitarian Universalist Union, 1949-53, Council Liberal Chs., 1953-55; pres. Niagara Falls Religious Fellowship, 1950-52. Bd. dirs. N.Y. chpt. Americans for Democratic Action, 1955-56; pres. Niagara County Planned Parenthood Assn., 1953-59, mem. N.Y. State bd., 1955-59; chmn. Unitarian Univeralist Commn. Scouting; mem. Nat. council Boy Scouts Am. 1960—; del. White House Conf. Against Discrimination, 1958. Served as chaplain USAAF, 1943-46. Recipient Freedom House award merit, 1949. Mem. African Study Assn. (pres. 1966-67), Albert Schweitzer World Confedn. (sec.), Am. Friends of Albert Schweitzer. Author: Church of the Pilgrim Fathers, 1950; Unitarians and Universalists Believe, 1960; When a Family Faces Death, 1961; Unitarian Universalism as a Way of Life, 1966 (revised and enlarged as Challenge of A Liberal Faith 1979); An Understanding of Albert Schweitzer, 1966; (with David Poling), Schweitzer, A Biography, 1971; Buddha, the Quest for Serenity, A Biography, 1978. Home: 174 Marlborough St Boston MA 02116 Office: 25 Beacon St Boston MA 02108

MARSHALL, GORDON BRUCE, shipbuilding and marine transp. co. exec.; b. Hamilton, Ont., Can., Sept. 26, 1943; (parent Am. citizen); s. J. Gordon and Mae J. (Tucker) M.; B.S.B.A., Northwestern U., 1965; M.B.A., U. Chgo., 1970; A.A.S., Coll. Lake County, 1975; m. Rita J. Penca, Apr. 22, 1979. Comptrollership trainee Continental Ill. Nat. Bank, Chgo., 1967-68; profit analyst Morton Salt Co., Chgo., 1968-70; sr. fin. specialist Abbott Labs., North Chicago, Ill., 1970-76; treas. Pott Industries Inc., St. Louis, 1976—; instr. Coll. Lake County, 1975-76. Fund raiser Jr. Achievement, St. Louis, 1977-79. Served with USNR, 1965-67. C.P.A., Mo. Mem. St. Louis Cash Mgmt. Assn., Am. Inst. C.P.A.'s, Mo. Soc. C.P.A.'s. Office: 611 E Marceau St Saint Louis MO 63111

MARSHALL, HENRIETTA HARRISON, civic worker; b. Phila., Apr. 17, 1924; d. Joseph and Lucretia Stevens (Heckscher) Harrison; student pvt. schs., Bryn Mawr, Pa.; m. Julian McIlvaine Marshall, Aug. 19, 1944; children—John Randolph, Stevens Heckscher, Elizabeth Rodman, Julia Harrison. Officer, Planned Parenthood Assn. Pa., 1967-74, chmn. bd., 1972-74, dir., 1974-79; dir. Planned Parenthood Fedn. Am., Inc., N.Y.C., 1973-78, 79—, chmn., 1975-78, acting pres., 1977-78; mem. exec. com. Internat. Planned Parenthood Fedn.-Western Hemisphere region, 1976—. Trustee Shipley Sch., Bryn Mawr, 1971—; bd. dirs. Marriage Council Phila., 1972-75, Alan Guttmacher Inst., 1977—, Population Crisis Com., Washington; bd. dirs., mem. exec. com. Population Inst., 1978—; exec. dir. Women's Way. Recipient Human Rights award City of Phila., 1976. Mem. Nat. Soc. Colonial Dames in Commonwealth Pa. (dir. 1970-76). Club Rome. Independent Republican. Episcopalian. Home: 626 Railroad Ave Haverford PA 19041 Office: 1501 Cherry St Philadelphia PA 19102

MARSHALL, HERBERT A., lawyer; b. Clinton, Ill., Aug. 20, 1917; s. Harry A. and Andrea (Pederson) M.; A.B., Washburn U., 1940, LL.B., J.D., 1943; m. Helen Christman, May 3, 1941; children—James A., Thomas A., Mary (Mrs. William Nichols). Admitted to Kans. bar, 1943; law clk. U.S. Ct. Appeals, 1943-44; asst. county atty., Shawnee County, Kans., 1944-50; practiced in Topeka, 1944—; mem. firm Marshall, Hawks, McKinney & Hendrix, 1946—; instr. practice ct. Washburn U. Law Sch., 1963—; mem. Kans. Supreme Ct. Nominating Commn., 1968-79. Trustee, elder Presbyn. Ch. Fellow Am. Coll. Trial Lawyers; mem. Am., Kans. (exec. council 1968—, v.p. 1977, pres. 1979), Topeka (pres. 1968) bar assns., Topeka C. of C. Clubs: Masons, Elks, Moose; Topeka Optimist. Home: 4722 Brentwood St Topeka KS 66606 Office: 810 Mchts Bank Bldg Topeka KS 66612

MARSHALL, J. HOWARD, II, lawyer; b. Phila., Jan. 24, 1905; s. S. Furman and Annabelle (Thompson) M.; A.B., Haverford Coll., 1926; LL.B. magna cum laude, Yale U., 1931; m. Eleanor Pierce, June 20, 1931; children—J. Howard III, Pierce; m. 2d, Bettye M. Bohanan, Dec. 10, 1961. Instr. and asst. cruise dir. Floating Univ., 1926-27, cruise dir., 1928-29; asst. dean, asst. prof. law Yale U., 1931-33; mem. Petroleum Adminstrv. Bd., U.S. Dept. Interior, 1933-35, spl. asst. to U.S. atty. gen., and asst. solicitor Dept. Interior, 1933-35; spl. counsel Standard Oil Co. Calif., 1935-37; partner Pillsbury, Madison & Sutro, San Francisco, 1938-44; chief counsel Petroleum Adminstrn. for War, 1941-44, asst. dep. adminstr., 1943-44; gen. counsel U.S. del. to Allied Commn. on Reparations, 1945; mem. firm Meyers, Marshall & Meyers, Attys., Washington. Mem. Mil. Petroleum Adv. Bd. to joint chiefs staff, 1944-50, 54-59; pres., dir. Ashland Oil & Refining Co., and subsidiary corps., 1944-51; v.p., dir. Signal Oil & Gas Co., 1952-59, exec. v.p., dir., 1959-60, also subsidiary and affiliated corps.; pres., dir. Union Texas Natural Gas Corp., 1961-62, also subs. and affiliated corps.; pres. Union Tex. Petroleum div., dir. Allied Chem. Corp., 1962-68; exec. v.p. Allied Chem. Corp., 1965-67; dir. Internat. Oil and Gas Corp., Northland Oils Ltd., Tex. Commerce Bank Nat. Assn., Houston; dir., mem. exec. com. M-K-T R.R.; chmn., dir. Petroleum Corp.; chmn. exec. com., dir. Coastal States Gas Corp.; cons. sec. interior petroleum def. program, 1950-52. Bd. mgrs. Haverford Coll. Mem. 25 Year Club, Am. Petroleum Inst. (v.p., dir.), Nat. Petroleum Council, Soc. Petroleum Engrs., Am., Calif., Ky. bar assns., Am. Inst. M.E., Order of Coif, Beta Rho Sigma. Mem. Soc. of Friends. Clubs: Bohemian (San Francisco); 29 (N.Y.C.); River Oaks Country (Houston). Author: (with N.L. Meyers) series monographs Yale Law Jour., 1931, 33. Home: 11100 Meadowick Houston TX 70024 Office: Esperson Bldg Houston TX 77002

MARSHALL, JAMES, lawyer; b. N.Y.C., May 12, 1896; s. Louis and Florence (Lowenstein) M.; student Columbia Sch. Journalism, 1913-16; LL.B., Columbia, 1920; m. Lenore K. Guinzburg, Aug. 20, 1919 (dec. 1971); children—Ellen F. Scholle, Jonathan; m. 2d, Eva Garson Levy, May 6, 1974. Admitted to N.Y. bar, 1921, bar U.S. Supreme Ct., 1924; asso. Guggenheimer, Untermyer & Marshall, N.Y.C., 1920-29, mem., 1929-30; pvt. practice law, 1930-34; mem. Marshall, Bratter, Greene, Allison & Tucker and predecessor firms, 1934-47, counsel, 1947—. Lectr. pub. adminstrn. N.Y. U., 1953-59, adj. prof. pub. adminstrn., 1959-65; tng. asso. Human Relations Center, Boston U., 1966-70. Bd. dirs. N.Y. State Tng. Sch. for Boys, 1933, pres., 1934-35; mem. N.Y.C. Charter Commn., 1934; mem. N.Y.C. Bd. Edn., 1935-52, pres. 1938-42; mem. U.S. Nat. Commn. for UNESCO, 1946-51; adv. U.S. delegation UNESCO Conf., Paris, 1946, Mexico City, 1947, cons., Florence, Italy, 1950; ednl. cons. on prejudice and discrimination ECOSOC Conf. Non-Govt. Orgns., Geneva, 1959; v.p. Am. Jewish Com., 1959-62, hon. v.p., 1962—; mem. exec. com. Am. Jewish Joint Distbn. Com. Gov. Hebrew U.; v.p. Natural Resources Def. Council, 1970—; v.p. Citizens' Com. Children; bd. dirs. Martha Graham Found. Contemporary Dance. Enlisted June, 1917 and served as 2d lt. San. Corps, U.S. Army, 1918-19; with A.E.F. Recipient Butler Silver medal for contbn. to polit. philosophy and edn. Columbia, 1941; Distinguished Pub. Service award Educators lodge B'nai B'rith, 1946; Gold medal for distinguished service to N.Y.C. pub. schs. Public Edn. Assn., 1952; Public Service award N.Y. region Am. Vets. Commn., 1952. Mem. Am. Bar Assn., Assn. Bar City of N.Y., Inst. Internat. Edn. (hon. trustee), Am. Friends of Hebrew U. (hon. v.p., past chmn. bd.), Jewish Publ. Soc. (hon. v.p.), Am. Assn. for Internat. Office Edn. (v.p. 1943-47), N.A.A.C.P. (past dir., counsel), Wilderness Soc. (governing council), P.E.N. (dir. Am. chpt. 1972-78). Clubs: Cosmos (Washington); Coffee House. Author: Ordeal by Glory, 1927; Swords and Symbols; The Technique of Sovereignty, 1939, rev. edit., 1969; The Freedom to Be Free, 1943; Law and Psychology in Conflict, 1966, rev. edit., 1979; Intention in Law and Society, 1968. Contbr. articles to publs. Office: 430 Park Ave New York City NY 10022

MARSHALL, JAMES ARTHUR, educator; b. Oshkosh, Wis., Aug. 7, 1935; s. Claude Wendal and Alice (Rodat) M.; B.S., U. Wis., 1957; Ph.D., U. Mich., 1960; postdoctoral research, Stanford, 1962; m. Mary Wilder, Mar. 26, 1971; 1 dau., Amy Sue. Mem. faculty Northwestern U., 1962—, prof. chemistry, 1968—; cons. to industry. Mem. com. phys. scis. NRC, 1969, mem. U.S.-Brazil grad. edn. in chemistry study group, 1971—; lectr. Am. Swiss Found., 1972; chmn. U.S.-Japan Conf. on Organic Synthesis, 1973; mem. medicinal chemistry study sect. USPHS, 1977—. Named Depth Charger of Yr., 1978; Alfred P. Sloan fellow, 1967-68. Mem. Am. Chem. Soc. (mem. exec. com. Organic div. 1978—, Ernest Guenther award 1979), Chem. Soc. (London). Author papers in field. Mem. editorial bd. Organic Reactions, 1970—, Jour. Organic Chemistry, 1972—; editor Synthetic Communications, 1972—. Home: 1617 Ridge Rd Highland Park IL 60035

MARSHALL, JAMES EDWARD, author, illustrator; b. San Antonio, Oct. 10, 1942; s. George Edward and Cecille (Harrison) M.; student New Eng. Conservatory Music, 1960-61, Trinity Coll., Hartford, Conn., 1967-68. Recipient N.Y. Times award for illus. book, 1972, 75. Author, illustrator 40 children's books, including George and Martha, 1972; What's The Matter with Carruthers?, 1972; Yummers!, 1973; George & Martha Encore, 1973; Willis, 1974; The Guest, 1975; Four Little Troubles, 1975; Speedboat, 1976. Illustrator: Plink, Plink, Plink (Byrd Baylor), 1971; All the Way Home (Lore Segal), 1973; The Stupids Step Out (Harry Allard), 1974; The Piggy in the Puddle (Charlotte Pomerantz), 1974; The Frog Prince (Edith Tarcov), 1974; Dinosaur's Housewarming Party (Norma Klein), 1974; The Tutti-Frutti Case (Harry Allard), 1975; Mary Alice, Operator No. 9 (Jeffrey Allen), 1975; A Summer in The South, 1977; The Stubids have a Ball (Allard), 1978; Mac Gooses' Grocery (Asch), 1978; Carrot Nose (Wahl), 1978; George and Martha One Fine Day, 1978; I Will Not Go to Market Today (Allard), 1979; Portly Mc Swine, 1979; James Marshall's Mother Goose, 1979. Address: 300 W 23d St New York NY 10011

MARSHALL, JAMES FREDERICK, educator; b. Indpls., Aug. 15, 1912; s. James Harrison and May (Weaver) M.; A.B., Ind. U., 1937; M.A., U. Ill., 1939, Ph.D., 1948; m. Sarah Elizabeth Shinn, June 3, 1943. Asst. prof. French, U. Ariz., Tucson, 1948-49; prof. French and Spanish, Whittier (Calif.) Coll., 1949-58; prof. French, U. Wis.-Milw., 1958-75, prof. emeritus, 1975—, chmn. dept. French and Italian, 1958-63, 68-70. Vice pres. orgn. com. to celebrate bicentennial of birth of Madame de Stael, Coppet, Switzerland, 1966. Served with AUS, 1942-46. Recipient Research grants U. Wis., 1959, 63, 64, Ford Found., 1955-56, Eleutherian Mills-Hagley Found., 1964, Am. Council Learned Socs., 1953. Mem. Modern Lang. Assn., Midwest Modern Lang. Assn., Am. Assn. Tchrs. French, Academie Delphinale (Grenoble), Societe d-Etudes staeliennes (Paris), Phi Beta Kappa. Editor: Stendhal, Henri III, 1952; Victor Jacquemont, Letters to Achille Chaper, 1960; De Stael-du Pont Letters, 1968. Contbr. to Madame de Stael et l'Europe, 1970. Contbr. articles profl. jours. Home: 4746 N Oakland Ave Milwaukee WI 53211

MARSHALL, JEAN MCELROY, physiologist; b. Chambersburg, Pa., Dec. 31, 1922; d. Frank Lester and Florence (McElroy) Marshall; A.B., Wilson Coll., 1944; M.A., Mt. Holyoke Coll., 1946; Ph.D., U. Rochester, 1951. Instr., Johns Hopkins U. Med. Sch., Balt., 1951-56, asst. prof., 1956-60; research postdoctoral fellow Oxford (Eng.) U., 1954-55; asst. prof. Harvard U. Med. Sch., Boston, 1960-66; asso. prof. physiology Brown U., Providence, 1966-69, prof., 1969—; mem. physiology study sect. NIH, 1967-71, mem. tng. com. engring. in biology and medicine, 1971-74, mem. tng. com. lab. medicine, 1976-77; physiol. test com. Nat. Bd. Med. Examiners, 1972-76, neurobiology adv. com., 1977—. Mem. Am. Physiol. Soc., Am. Pharmacol. Soc., N.Y. Acad. Scis., Soc. Reproductive Biology, Soc. Gen. Physiologists, Phi Beta Kappa, Sigma Xi. Editor: The Initiation of Labor, 1964; mem. editorial bd. Jour. Pharmacology and Exptl. Therapeutics, 1963-69, Am. Jour. Physiology, 1969-73, Circulation Research, 1973—; contbr. articles to profl. jours. Home: 14 Aberdeen Rd Weston MA 02193 Office: Div Medical Scis Brown U Providence RI 01912

MARSHALL, JOHN ALOYSIUS, bishop; b. Worcester, Mass., Apr. 26, 1928; s. John A. and Katherine T. (Redican) M.; A.B. cum laude, Holy Cross Coll., Worcester, 1949; postgrad. Sem. de Philosophie, Montreal, Can., 1949-50; S.T.L., Pontifical Gregorian U., Rome, 1954; M.A. in Guidance and Psychology, Assumption Coll., Worcester, 1964. Ordained priest Roman Catholic Ch., 1953, consecrated bishop, 1972; parish priest in Mass., 1954-57; asst. vice rector Pontifical N. Am. Coll., 1957-61; instr. Acad. Sacred Heart, Worcester, 1961-62, St. Vincent Hosp. Sch. Nursing, Worcester, 1961-62; headmaster St. Stephen Cath. High Sch., Worcester, 1962-68; spiritual dir. Pontifical N. Am. Coll., 1968-71, bus. mgr., 1969-71; bishop of Burlington, Vt., 1972—; chmn. com. priestly formation Nat. Conf. Cath. Bishops, 1975-78. Bd. dirs. Champlain Coll., Burlington, 1974—, Wadhams Hall, Ogdensburg, N.Y., 1974—. Address: 351 North Ave Burlington VT 05401

MARSHALL, JOHN ELBERT, III, found. exec.; b. Providence, July 2, 1942; s. John Elbert Marshall and Millicent Edna (Paige) M.; B.A., Brown U., 1964; m. Diana M. Healy, Aug. 26, 1968; children—Nelson John, Priscilla Anne. Advt. mgr. U.N. Alloy Steel Corp., Boston, 1968-70; asso. dir. devel. Brown U., 1970-74; exec. dir. R.I. Found., Providence, 1974-79; v.p. Kresge Found., Troy, Mich., 1979—. Served with USNR, 1964-68; Vietnam. Club: Providence Art. Office: 2401 W Big Beaver Rd Troy MI 48084

MARSHALL, JOHN RICHARD, opera dir.; b. Schenectady, July 28, 1929; s. Abraham Lincoln and Edith Marion (Lambert) M.; B.A., U. Rochester, 1951; M.M. Ind. U., 1953, D.Mus., 1963; cert. (Mass. Arts Council fellow) Harvard U. Inst. Arts Mgmt., 1971; postgrad. U. So. Calif., 1953-54, Stanford U., 1956, Goethe Inst., Bad Aibling, W. Ger., 1964; m. Jean Deresieuski, June 20, 1953. Dir. opera and choral music U. Buffalo, 1959-62; coach Internat. Opera Center—Switzerland, Zürich, 1964-65; dir. opera Boston Conservatory, 1965-68; founder, dir. New Eng. Regional Opera, Boston, 1967-76; gen. dir. Charlotte (N.C.) Opera Assn. and N.C. Opera, 1976—. Served with U.S. Army, 1954-56. Recipient award of merit Assn. Performing Arts. Mem. OPERA Am., Nat. Opera Assn., Am. Arts Alliance, So. Opera Conf. (founder), Assn. Symphony Orchs. N.C. Unitarian. Office: 110 E 7th St Charlotte NC 28202

MARSHALL, JOHN SEDBERRY, educator; b. Fullerton, Calif., May 25, 1898; s. John Lundy and Emma Elizabeth (Gawley) M.; A.B., Pomona Coll., 1921; Ph.D., Boston U., 1926; student Harvard U., 1924-25, U. Basel (Switzerland), 1923-25, U. Calif., 1928, Russ. U. Prague (Czechoslovakia), summers 1935-36; m. Elizabeth Southard, May 26, 1923; 1 son, James Edward. Instr. philosophy Syracuse (N.Y.) U., 1926-29; prof. philosophy Albion Coll., 1929-46; prof. philosophy U. of the South, Sewanee, Tenn., 1946-68, prof. emeritus, 1968—, prof. grad. sch. theology, 1950-62. Editor, Anglican Theol. Rev., 1959-65. Mem. Am. Philos. Assn., AAAS, AAUP, Brit. Inst. Philosophy, So. Soc. for Philosophy of Religion (past pres.), Guild of Scholars (past pres.), Realist Soc., Phi Beta Kappa, Lambda Chi Alpha. Democrat. Episcopalian. Author: (with N.O. Lossky), Value and Existence 1935; Hooker's Polity in Modern English, 1948; The Genius and Mission of the Episcopal Church, 1949; The Word Was Made Flesh, 1949; Hooker's Theology of Common Prayer, 1953; Hooker and the Anglican Tradition, 1963; contbr. various articles to The Anglican Theol. Review, The Sewanee Review, The Monist, The Personalist, The Review of Politics, Ency. Brit. Address: The Univ of the South Sewanee TN 37375

MARSHALL, JOHN STEWART, meteorologist; b. Welland, Ont., Can., July 18, 1911; s. John Wells and Catherine (Stewart) M.; B.A., Queen's U., Kingston, Can., 1931, M.A., 1933; Ph.D., Cambridge U., 1940; m. Helen Elizabeth Reburn Scott, Dec. 19, 1940; children—Claire Elizabeth, Heather. Research physicist NRC Labs. Can., Ottawa, 1939-42; operational research scientist Canadian Army Operational Research Group, 1943-45; mem. faculty McGill U., Montreal, 1945—, Macdonald prof. physics, 1959—, prof. meteorology, 1961—, chmn. dept. meteorology, 1961-64; chmn. Inter-Union Com. on Radio Meteorology, 1960-67. Recipient Patterson medal for Canadian meteorology, 1961, Hugh Robert Mill Brit. rainfall medal, 1962. Fellow Am. Meteorol. Soc. (councillor 1965-67); mem. Canadian Assn. Physicists (pres. 1950), Phys. Soc. London, Royal Meteorol. Soc., Am. Phys. Soc., Royal Soc. Can. (pres. sect. 1966). Author: (with E.R. Pounder) Physics, 1957, rev. (with E.R. Pounder, R.W. Stewart), 1967; Why the Weather, 1964; also articles. Developed use of radar to study rain, snow, hail. Home: 604 Lakeshore Rd Beaurepaire PQ H9W 4K4 Canada Office: McGill Radar Weather Obs Box 241 Macdonald Coll PQ H0A 1C0 Canada

MARSHALL, KEITH COOPER, performing arts dir.; b. New Orleans, Nov. 19, 1946; s. Harold Karin and Naomi Vernon (Damonte) M.; B.A., Yale, 1968; B.Phil. (Rhodes scholar), Oxford U., 1970, D.Phil., 1978; postgrad. Courtauld Inst., U. London, 1970-71. Owner, Downtown Gallery and Dixie Art Supplies, New Orleans, 1970—; freelance writer and lectr., 1968-70; founder, dir. Madewood Center for Visual and Performing Arts, New Orleans, 1974—. Lectr. dept. edn. Victoria and Albert Mus., London, 1971-74; vis. curator New Orleans Mus. Art, 1975. Mem. Thackeray Soc., Phi Beta Kappa. Club: Round Table (New Orleans). Author: John McCrady: 1911-1968, 1975. Home: Madewood Plantation House Napoleonville LA 70390 Office: 530 Chartres St New Orleans LA 70130. *In a time of disintegrating family ties, I have found my family to be the most important factor in any success that I have achieved. Not only does our family work together to reach mutual goals; each member is always ready to lend support to an individual's projects. In times of trouble, a close-knit family is always a blessing; and I find that the happiness and security of such a loving and stable "community" lends an ease and honesty to one's more casual relationships.*

MARSHALL, KNEALE THOMAS, educator; b. Filey, Eng., Feb. 13, 1936; came to U.S., 1962, naturalized, 1970; m. John Bertram and Winnifred Millicent (Taylor) M.; B.S., U. London, 1958; M.S., U. Calif., Berkeley, 1964, Ph.D., 1966; m. Dolores V. Bellig, Nov. 26, 1964. Metallurgist, Eldorado Mining & Refining, Sask., Can., 1958-62; mem. tech. staff Bell Labs., Holmdel, N.J., 1966-68; asst. prof. Naval Postgrad. Sch., Monterey, Calif., 1968-70, asso. prof., 1970-75, prof., 1975—; sci. adviser to dep. chief naval ops. Dept. Navy, Washington, 1978—; cons. USMC, U. Calif.; vis. prof. U. Calif., Berkeley, 1972, London Sch. Econs., 1978. Named an Outstanding Young Man Am., 1969. Mem. Ops. Research Soc. Am. (past chmn. western sect.), Inst. Mgmt. Scis., Am. Inst. Indsl. Engrs. (sr.). Author: (with R.C. Grinold) Manpower Planning Models, 1977; mem. editorial bd. Ops. Research, 1970-78, Jour. Applied Math., 1971-78. Office: DCNO (MPT) OP-O1T Dept Navy Washington DC 20370

MARSHALL, LANE LEE, landscape architect; b. Rochester, N.Y., Sept. 19, 1937; s. Arthur Straton and Leeta Margaret (Garlock) M.; B.Landscape Architecture, U. Fla., 1960; m. Marian Horton, Feb. 14, 1964; children—Kenneth, Shelley, Merelee. Asso. firm Bailey O. Breedlove, Ft. Lauderdale, Fla., 1960-61; prin. Lane L. Marshall and Assos., Inc., landscape architects, planners and golf course architects, Sarasota, Fla., 1961—; chmn. Nat. Forum on Growth Policy, 1976—; bd. dirs. Landscape Architecture Found.; vis. instr. dept. landscape architecture U. Ill., 1979. Vice pres. Sarasota County Hist. and Natural Sci. Center, 1976-78; pres. Family Service Assn. Sarasota County, 1971-73. Served with AUS, 1963-64. Recipient Distinguished Alumnus award U. Fla. Dept. Landscape Architecture, 1977; registered landscape architect, Fla., S.C., N.C. Fellow Am. Soc. Landscape Architects (pres. 1977-78); mem. Fla. Planning and Zoning Assn., Am. Soc. Golf Course Architects. Author: Trees and Man, 1970. Home: 2174 Hibiscus St Sarasota FL 33519 Office: 1800 Siesta Dr Sarasota FL 33579

MARSHALL, LOIS, mezzo-soprano; b. Toronto, Ont., Can., Jan. 29, 1925; d. David and Florence M.; grad. Royal Conservatory, Toronto (Eaton award). First recital at age 15, then sang with leading Canadian orchestras; debut at Town Hall, 1952; soloist with Arturo Toscanini in Missa Solemnis, also with Sir Thomas Beecham in works of Handel and Mozart; opera debut in La Boheme, Boston Opera Co., 1959; other appearances include Royal Festival Hall, London, Amsterdam Concertgebouw, Edinburgh Festival also in Hamburg, Dublin and USSR; music faculty U. Toronto. Recipient Naumburg award 1952. Address: U Toronto Faculty of Music Toronto ON M5S 1A1 Canada*

MARSHALL, MARTIN VIVAN, educator, business cons.; b. Kansas City, July 22, 1922; s. Vivan Dean and Marie (Church) M.; A.B., U. Mo., 1943; M.B.A., Harvard, 1947, D.C.S., 1953; m. Rosanne Borden, Sept. 5, 1951; children—Martin Dean, Michael Borden, Neil McNair. Instr. marketing and advt. U. Kans., 1947-48; mem. faculty Harvard, 1948—, Henry R. Byers prof. bus. adminstrn., 1960—, chmn. marketing area faculty, 1962-66. Cons. U.S. and internat. businesses, 1950—; dir. annual seminar mktg. and advt. Am. Advt. Fedn., 1958—; vis. prof. marketing IMEDE Mgmt. Inst. Lausanne, 1965-66; sr. prof., ednl. dir. Internat. Marketing Inst., 1967-71; vis. prof. Indian Inst. Mgmt., Agra, India, 1968, IPADE, Mexico City, 1969, U. Melbourne (Australia), 1977, 79. Served to lt. (s.g.) USNR, 1943-46. Mem. Am. Mktg. Assn., Nat. Assn. Broadcasters (dir. annual seminar), Am. Acad. Advt. (dean New Eng. 1962-65), Author: Automatic Merchandising, 1954; (with N.H. Borden) Advertising Management, 1960. Home: 29 Bradyll Rd Weston MA 02193 Office: Morgan Hall Harvard Univ Boston MA 02163

MARSHALL, MICHAEL ANDREW, bus. exec.; b. London, Dec. 14, 1924; s. William Brown and Dorothy Jessie (Colicott) M.; student Glasgow U., 1942-43, Royal Mil. Coll., Sandhurst, 1943-44; m. Helen Marjorie Elizabeth Humphries, Jan. 30, 1954; children—David John, Peter James, Andrew Michael. Asst. mcht. Maclaine Watson & Co., Ltd., Singapore, 1949-51; asst. mgr. Engelhard Industries of Can. Ltd., Toronto, 1951-55, sales dir., London, 1955-68, mng. dir., 1968-72, mng. dir., chief exec. officer Engelhard Industries Ltd. Europe, 1972-76, exec. v.p. Engelhard Industries div., 1976—, sr. v.p. Engelhard Minerals and Chems. Corp., N.Y.C., 1977—. Served to capt. Brit. Army, 1943-47. Clubs: Baltusrol Golf, Canadian, Short Hills, English-Speaking Union. Home: Short Hills NJ 07078 Office: 70 Wood Ave S Iselin NJ 08830

MARSHALL, NELSON, oceanographer; b. Yonkers, N.Y., Dec. 16, 1914; s. Ernest Woods and Mable (Austin) M.; B.S., Rollins Coll., 1937; student Brown U., 1935-36; M.S., Ohio State U., 1938; Ph.D., U. Fla., 1941; m. Grace Terry, Feb. 3, 1940; children—Terry Sue, John Murray, Catherine, Richard Nelson. Instr., U. Conn., Storrs, 1941-44, asst. prof. zoology, 1944-45; research fellow Woods Hole Oceanographic Instn., summers 1943, 44; asst. prof. and fishery biologist Marine Lab., U. Miami (Fla.), 1945-46; asso. prof. U. N.C., 1946-47; dir. Va. Fisheries Lab., Gloucester Point, 1947-50; prof. biology Coll. William and Mary, 1947-51, dean coll., 1949-51; asso. dir. Oceanographic Inst. Fla. State U. 1952-54; vis. investigator Bingham Oceanographic Lab., Yale U., 1954-55; dean Coll. Liberal Arts, Alfred U., 1955-59; prof. oceanography and marine affairs U. R.I., 1959—, dir. Internat. Center for Marine Resource Devel., 1972-75; exec. com. Chesapeake Bay Inst., Johns Hopkins U., 1948-51, Adv. Council of Va. Economy, 1948-51; mem. research council Richmond Area U. Center, 1949-51; adminstrv. council, 1950-51, exec. sec. (part-time) So. regional com. marine scis. So. Regional Edn. Bd., 1952-54; mem. New Eng. Interstate Water Pollution Control Commn., chmn., 1970-71; R.I. rep. to Coastal States Orgn. Pres. R.I. Peace Corps Council, 1968-69; trustee Rollins Coll., 1952-67, now hon. trustee. Fellow AAAS; mem. Am. Soc. Limnology and Oceanography, Atlantic Estuarine Research Soc. (hon.), Ecol. Soc. Am., World Federalists U.S.A. (vice chmn. R.I.), World Affairs Council R.I. (pres.), Sigma Xi, Delta Upsilon. Office: Grad Sch Oceanography U RI Kingston RI 02881

MARSHALL, PAUL MACKLIN, oil co. exec.; b. Toronto, Ont., Can., Sept. 21, 1923; s. Griffith Macklin and Josephine Angela (Hodgson) M.; B.C.L., McGill U., Montreal, Que., Can., 1949; m. Carol Ann Dickie; children—Blake, Gregory, Jonathan, Kirk. Called to bar Que., 1949; legal asst. Sun Life Assurance Co., Montreal, 1949-52; exec. asst. to Canadian minister nat. def., Ottawa, Ont., 1952-54; with Canadian Chem. & Cellulose Co. Ltd., Montreal, 1955-69, v.p., 1958-59; v.p., sec.-treas. Chemcell Ltd., 1959-67, chmn. bd., 1967-69; v.p., treas. Columbia Cellulose Co. Ltd., 1959-62, pres., chief exec. officer, 1962-66; v.p., treas. Can. Chem. Co. Ltd., Celgar Ltd., 1959-62; v.p. Hamilton Bros. Petroleum Corp., 1969-72; pres. Hamilton Bros. Exploration Co., Denver, 1972; exec. v.p. Hamilton Bros. Oil Co., 1972; pres. Canadian Hydrocarbons Ltd., Calgary, Alta., 1972-77; pres. Brascan Resources, 1978—; dir. Western Mines Ltd., West Mills Carpets Ltd. Served to lt. Royal Canadian Army, 1943-45. Clubs: Mount Royal (Montreal); Vancouver (B.C.); Ranchmens, Petroleum, Glenco (Calgary). Home: 805 Prospect Ave Calgary AB T2T 0W6 Canada Office: 1800 Bow Valley Sq III Calgary AB Canada

MARSHALL, PHILIP RICHARD, coll. adminstr.; b. Decatur, Ind., Nov. 13, 1926; s. E. Howard and Eurah Lucille (Ratliff) M.; A.B., Earlham Coll., 1949; M.S., Purdue U., 1951, Ph.D., 1954; m. Helen Rebecca Emmons, Aug. 19, 1951; children—Amy, Karen, Rebecca, Mary Ann. Asst., Purdue U., 1949-51, 52-53; research engr. Battelle Meml. Inst., 1951-52; instr. Albion Coll., 1953-55, asst. prof., 1955-58; asst. prof. Cornell Coll., 1958-61, asso. prof., 1961-65; prof., dean Lycoming Coll., 1965-69; asso. program dir. NSF, 1969; dean acad. affairs Eastern Wash. State Coll., Cheney, 1969-70, v.p. acad. affairs, 1970-76, exec. v.p., 1976-79; chancellor U. Wis., Stevens Point, 1979—; vis. prof. U. Iowa, summer 1962; resident faculty dir. Asso. Colls. of Midwest-Argonne Semester Program, Argonne Nat. Lab., 1964-65. Bd. dirs. Williamsport (Pa.) Hosp., 1965-69, Wash. State Ins. Bd., 1977—. Recipient Research Corp. grants, 1957, 60, NSF grants, 1957, 59. Mem. Sigma Xi, Phi Lambda Upsilon. Sci. editor: North American Review, 1964-65. Home: 21 Oakcrest Dr Stevens Point WI 54481

MARSHALL, PRENTICE H., fed. judge; b. 1926; B.S., J.D., U. Ill.; Admitted to Ill. bar, 1951; now judge U.S. Dist. Ct. for No. Ill. Office: US Courthouse 219 S Dearborn St Chicago IL 60604*

MARSHALL, RAY, sec. of labor; b. Oak Grove, La., Aug. 22, 1928; s. Thomas J. and Virginia (Foster) M.; B.A., Millsaps Coll., 1949; M.A., La. State U., 1950; Ph.D., U. Calif., Berkeley, 1954; m. Patricia Williams, Nov. 27, 1946; children—Jill, Susan, John, Sarah. Asst. prof. econs. U. Miss., 1953-57; asso. prof. econs. La. State U., 1957-62; prof. econs. U. Tex., 1962-67; prof. econs., dept. chmn. U. Ky., 1967-69; prof. econs., dir. Center Study of Human Resources, U. Tex., 1969—, chmn. dept., 1970-72; on leave as sec. of labor, Washington, 1977—; chmn. Fed. Commn. on Apprenticeship, 1974-76; pres. Nat. Rural Center; dir. Task Force So. Rural Devel.; mem. Nat. Manpower Policy Task Force, 1969-76. Served with USNR, 1943-46. Fulbright research scholar, 1955-56; Ford Found. faculty fellow, 1954-55; Wertheim fellow in indsl. relations, 1960. Mem. Indsl. Relations Research Assn. (pres.), Am., So. (pres. 1973-74) econ. assns., Am. Arbitration Assn., AAUP, Beta Gamma Sigma, Omicron Delta Kappa, Phi Kappa Phi. Presbyterian. Author: The Negro and Organized Labor, 1965; The Negro Worker, 1967; (with Vernon Briggs) The Negro in Apprenticeship, 1967; Labor in the South, 1967; (with Lamond Godwin) Cooperatives and Rural Poverty in the South, 1971; Rural Workers in Rural Labor Markets, 1974; (with Allan Cartter) Labor Economy: Wages, Employment and Trade Unions, 1976; (with Brian Rougeling) The Role of Unions in the American Economy, 1976. Office: 3d and Constitution Ave NW Washington DC 20210

MARSHALL, RICHARD DOUGLASS, educator; b. Washington, May 24, 1930; s. Garland Green and Ruby Elizabeth (Grymes) M.; A.B., Lincoln U., 1953; LL.B., Howard U., 1956; grad. Sch. Mortgage Banking, Northwestern U., 1973; m. Marie Bernadine Johnson, July 12, 1956. Mortgage loan appraiser Prudential Ins. Co. Am., Newark, 1962-66, sr. personnel cons., 1966-68; asso. dir. loans govt. Nat.

Mortgage Assn., HUD, 1971-72; prof. bus. adminstrn. Grad. Sch. Bus. Adminstrn., Rutgers U., Newark, 1972—; cons. Urban Inst., Washington. Pres. Econ. Devel. and Planning Com. Essex County, N.J.; chmn. bd. dirs. Newark Housing Devel. and Rehab. Corp., 1972-77. Trustee Lincoln U.; bd. dirs. Trust for Public Land, San Francisco. Mem. Mortgage Bankers Assn. Am., Am. Real Estate and Urban Econs. Assn., Nat. Assn. Rev. Appraisers, Urban League Essex County (past pres., dir.). Contbr. articles to profl. jours. Home: 555 Mt Prospect Ave Newark NJ 07104 Office: 92 New St Newark NJ 07102

MARSHALL, ROBERT CREEL, army officer; b. Washington, Nov. 10, 1921; s. James Creel and Mabel Estelle (Wolff) M.; B.S., U.S. Mil. Acad., 1943; B.C.E., Cornell U., 1948; m. Mary Elizabeth Pie, Apr. 19, 1947; children—James Creel, Elton Allen (dec.), Mary Marshall Berry, Michael Smith, Sarah Constance, Robert Creel, John O'Byrne, Priscilla Loudon. Commd. 2d lt. U.S. Army, 1943, advanced through grades to maj. gen., 1971; company comdr. 305th Engrs., 80th Inf. Div., ETO, World War II, 1944-45; adviser Greek Nat. Army, 1951-54; asst. prof. mil. history U.S. Mil. Acad., 1955-58; asst. dir. civil works Office Chief Engrs., 1961-64; dist. engr., Mobile, 1964-67; comdr. engring. combat group, Viet Nam, 1967-68; comdg. gen. Safeguard System Command, Huntsville, Ala., 1968-73; dep. chief staff HQS Forces Command, Atlanta, 1973—; program mgr. ballistic missile def. system Office Chief Staff U.S. Army, Washington, 1974-76, dep. chief engrs., 1976-77; pres. Miss. River Commn., Vicksburg, Miss., 1977—. Decorated D.S.M., Silver Star, Legion of Merit, Bronze Star, Air medal, Purple Heart; registered profl. engr., D.C. Mem. ASCE, Soc. Am. Mil. Engrs. Home: 1 Tennessee Rd Vicksburg MS 39180

MARSHALL, ROBERT GERALD, educator; b. Houston, Feb. 19, 1919; s. Luther Pierce and Nancy (May) M.; B.A., Rice U., 1941, M.A., 1946; Ph.D., Yale, 1950; diploma U. Siena (Italy), 1954; m. Kathryn Keller, Aug. 27, 1949; children—Christoph Patton, Ann Patteson, Philip Sanburn. Asst., then instr. French, Yale, 1947-49; asst. prof. fgn. langs. Tex. Women's U., 1949-51; mem. faculty Wells Coll., Aurora, N.Y., 1951—, prof. Romance langs., 1958—, chmn. dept., 1956-72, coordinator summer programs, 1963-67, dir. NDEA Inst. Advanced Study French, 1963-67; prof.-in-charge Sweet Briar Coll. Jr. Year In Paris, France, 1967-68, dir. Jr. Year in France, 1972—. Served to capt. AUS, 1942-46. Grantee Am. Council Learned Socs., 1953; Fulbright research grantee, Rome, Italy, 1959-60. Mem. Am. Assn. Tchrs. French (v.p. Central N.Y. chpt. 1965-67, pres. Va. chpt. 1979—), South Atlantic Modern Lang. Assn., Soc. Profs. Francai/#a/#1' Etranger. Episcopalian. Contbr. profl. jours. Editor-in-chief Catalogue of 16th Century Italian Books in American Libraries, 1970; editor (with F. C. St.t. Aubyn) Les Mouches (Sartre), 1963; Trois pièces Surréalistes, 1969. Home: Box 54 Sweet Briar VA 24595

MARSHALL, ROBERT HERMAN, educator; b. Decatur, Ill., June 26, 1925; s. Edwin Herman and Ethel (Pinkerton) M.; B.S., Ill. State Normal U., 1947, M.S., 1950; Ph.D., U. Ill., 1954. Research chemist Ethyl Corp., Ferndale, Mich. and Baton Rouge, La., 1954-58; asso. prof. La. Poly. Inst., Ruston, 1958-60; asso. prof. Memphis State U., 1960-67, prof. chemistry, 1967—, acting chmn. dept. chemistry, 1970-71. Served with USNR, 1943-46. Mem. Am. Chem. Soc., Alpha Chi Sigma. Patentee in field. Research on organometallic compounds. Home: 3277 Carrington Rd Memphis TN 38111 Office: Dept Chemistry Memphis State U Memphis TN 38152

MARSHALL, ROBERT HERMAN, educator; b. Harrisburg, Pa., Dec. 6, 1929; s. Mathias and Mary (Bubich) M.; A.B. magna cum laude, Franklin and Marshall Coll., 1951; M.A., Ohio State U., 1952, Ph.D., 1957; m. Billie Marie Sullivan, May 30, 1958; children—Mellisa Frances, Howard Hylton, Robert Charles. Teaching asst. Ohio State U., 1952-57; faculty U. Ariz., Tucson, 1957—, prof. econs., head dept., 1967-69, dir. Internat. Bus. Studies Project, 1969-71; research observer Sci.-Industry Program, Hughes Aircraft Co., Tucson, summer 1959. Bd. dirs. Com. for Econ. Opportunity, Tucson, 1968-69. Faculty fellow Pacific Coast Banking Sch., summer 1974. Mem. Am. Econ. Assn., Phi Beta Kappa, Beta Gamma Sigma, Pi Gamma Mu, Phi Kappa Phi, Delta Sigma Pi. Democrat. Roman Catholic. Author: Commercial Banking in Arizona: Structure and Performance Since World War II, 1966; (with others) The Monetary Process, 1974. Home: 6700 N Abington Rd Tucson AZ 85704

MARSHALL, ROBERT JAMES, ch. exec.; b. Burlington, Iowa, Aug. 26, 1918; s. Robert McCray and Margaret Emma (Gysin) M.; A.B., Wittenberg U., 1941; B.D., Chgo. Luth. Theol. Sem., 1944; postgrad. U. Chgo., 1949-52; D.D., Carthage Coll., 1961, Wittenberg U., 1963, Northwestern Luth. Sem., 1969, Waterloo U., 1970; L.H.D., Gettysburg Coll., 1965; LL.D., Augustana Coll., 1968, Wagner Coll., 1968, Muhlenberg Coll., 1969, Upsala Coll., 1969, Wittenberg U., 1969; S.T.D., Thiel Coll., 1971; J.C.D., Susquehanna U., 1969; Litt.D., Roanoke Coll., 1970; Lit.D., Newberry Coll., 1972; D. Theol., St. Olaf Coll., 1974; m. Alice Johanna Hepner, Feb. 6, 1943; children—Robert Edward, Margaret Alice Niederer. Ordained to ministry Lutheran Ch., 1944; pastor Grace Luth. Sch., Alhambra, Calif., 1944-47; instr. religion Muhlenberg (Pa.) Coll., 1947-49, head dept. religion, 1952-53; prof. O.T. interpretation Chgo. Luth. Theol. Sem., Maywood, Ill., 1953-62; pres. Ill. Synod Luth. Ch. in Am., 1962-68; pres. Luth. Ch. in Am., N.Y.C., 1968-78; dir. mission, service and devel. Luth. World Ministries, 1978—. Mem. exec. com. Luth. World Fedn., 1968-78; mem. central com., exec. com. World Council Chs.; mem. governing bd. Nat. Council Chs. of Christ in U.S.A., 1968-78; mem. exec. com. Luth. Council in U.S.A., 1968-78, mem. exec. council, 1964-68; chmn. on Evangelism Luth. Ch. Am., 1963-64; ann. prof. Am. Sch. Oriental Research, Jerusalem, 1958-59; exec. bd. Chgo. Conf. on Religion and Race, 1964-68. Bd. dirs. Grand View Coll., 1966-68, Augustana Coll., 1963-68, Luth. Sch. Theology, 1963-68, Augustana Hosp., Chgo., 1963-68, Luth. Hosp., Moline, Ill., 1963-68. Mem. Chgo. Soc. Bibl. Research (sec. 1962-68), Nat. Assn. Profs. Hebrew, Soc. Bibl. Lit. and Exegesis, Am. Bible Soc. (bd. mgrs.). Author: The Mighty Acts of God. Home: 300 E 40th St Apt 31N New York NY 10016 Office: 360 Park Ave S New York NY 10010

MARSHALL, ROBERT PEARSON, JR., constrn. co. exec.; b. Ashbourne, Pa., July 20, 1918; s. Robert Pearson and Lillian (Dobbins) M.; B.S., U. Pa., 1940; m. Frances Ives, Aug. 30, 1946 (div.); children—George B., Robert Pearson III, Geoffrey I.; m. 2d, Nancy Leahy Halsted, July 26, 1962. With Turner Constrn. Co., N.Y.C., 1940—, successively constrn. engr., constrn. supt., sales engr., 1940-61, v.p. sales, N.Y., 1961-65, v.p., gen. mgr. Phila. br. office, 1965-70, corporate sr. v.p., N.Y.C., 1971-76, vice chmn. bd., 1977—, also dir. Served with USNR, 1940-41, 43-46; comdr. Res. ret. Decorated Silver Star. Mem. ASCE, Soc. Am. Mil. Engrs. Clubs: N.Y. Yacht; Stanwich, Indian Harbor Yacht (Greenwich). Home: Dartmouth Rd Cos Cob CT 06807 Office: 150 E 42d St New York NY 10017

MARSHALL, SARAH CATHERINE WOOD (PEN NAME CATHERINE MARSHALL), author; b. Johnson City, Tenn.; d. John Ambrose and Leonora (Whitaker) Wood; B.A., Agnes Scott Coll., 1936; D. Litt., Cedar Crest Coll., 1954; L.H.D., Taylor U.; m. Rev. Peter Marshall, Nov. 4, 1936; 1 son, Peter John; m. 2d, Leonard Earl LeSourd, Nov. 14, 1959. Faculty Nat. Cathedral Sch. for Girls, Washington, 1949-50. Trustee Agnes Scott Coll. Mem. of the Authors Guild, Inc., Nat. League Am. Pen Women, Phi Beta Kappa. Presbyn. Author: A Man Called Peter, 1951 (became motion picture 1955); To Live Again, 1957; Beyond Ourselves, 1961; Christy, 1967; Something More, 1974; Adventures in Prayer, 1975; The Helper, 1978; (with Leonard LeSourd) My Personal Diary, 1979. Author, compilor: God Loves You, 1953; Friends with God, 1956 (juveniles). Editor: Mr. Jones, Meet the Master, 1949; Let's Keep Christmas, 1953; The Prayers of Peter Marshall, 1954; The Heart of Peter Marshall's Faith, 1956; The First Easter, 1959; John Doe, Disciple, 1963; Woman's editor Christian Herald mag., 1958-60; roving editor Guideposts mag., 1960—. Home: 3003 Fernwood Dr Boynton Beach FL 33435

MARSHALL, STANLEY, educator; b. Cheswick, Pa., Jan. 27, 1923; s. Walter W. and Mildred (Crawford) M.; B.S., Slippery Rock (Pa.) State Tchrs. Coll., 1947; M.S., Syracuse U., 1950, Ph.D., 1956; m. Ruth Cratty, June 10, 1944 (div. 1966); children—David, Sue, John; m. 2d, Shirley Ann Slade, Sept. 10, 1966; children—Kimberly, James Andrew. Tchr. sci. Mynderse Acad., Seneca Falls, N.Y., 1947-52; asst. prof. sci. State U. N.Y. Coll. Edn., Cortland, 1953-55, asso. prof., 1956-57, prof., 1957-58; instr. Syracuse U., 1955-56; prof., head dept. sci. edn. Fla. State U., Tallahassee, 1958, asso. dean Sch. Edn., 1965-67, dean Coll. Edn., 1967-69, pres., 1969-76, asso. dir. Center for Ednl. Tech., prof. edn., 1976—; pres. Sonitrol of Tallahassee, Inc., 1978—; pres. So. Scholarship and Research Found., 1968-69. Mem. U.S. Navy Undersec.'s adv. bd. edn. and tng., U.S. Army adv. panel ROTC, 1975—. Bd. regents Nat. Library Medicine, 1970-75. Served with AUS, 1943-46, ETO. Fellow AAAS; mem. Am. Inst. Physics, Nat. Sci. Tchrs. Assn., Fla. Acad. Scis., Fla. Assn. Sci. Tchrs., So. Assn. State Univs. and Land-Grant Colls (pres. 1971-72). Nat. Assn. Research Sci. Teaching, NEA, Fla. Edn. Assn., Phi Delta Kappa, Kappa Delta Pi. Author: (with E. Burkman) Current Trends in Science Education, 1966; (with I. Podendorf and C. Swartz) The Basic Science Program, 1965. Editor: Jour. of Research in Sci. Teaching, 1962-66. Mem. editorial bd. Science World, 1962-65. Contbr. articles profl. jours. Home: Route 13 Box 227-S Tallahassee FL 32312

MARSHALL, STANLEY CHARLES, mktg. and communications co. exec.; b. N.Y.C., Feb. 25, 1919; s. Milton and Ethel (Marshall) M.; B.E.E., Bucknell U., 1943; grad. student bus. mgmt. Ill. Inst. Tech., 1947-49; m. Alice Zindel, Sept. 12, 1943; children—Lisa Jo, Dianne Marshall-Hild, Laurie Ann. Elec. engr. Gen. Electric Co., 1943-45; editor tech. publs., sales promotion mgr. Sauerman Bros., Inc., Chgo., 1946-50; asst. to dir. Pa. Tech. Inst., 1951-52; pres., chief exec. officer, dir. Lando Inc., Pitts., 1952-77; v.p., gen. mgr. Marsteller, Inc., 1978-79, sr. v.p., 1979—. Pres., dir. Pitts. Commerce Inst., 1967—; bd. dirs. Partnership for Productivity Found., 1969—, chmn. bd., 1970—; pres. bd. dirs. Mgmt. Spectrum, Inc.; trustee Center for Mktg. Communications, 1967-73; chmn. Pitts. area mktg. adv. council U.S. Dept. Commerce, 1971-73; mem. Media Comparability Com., 1969-73; chmn. Pitts./Allegheny County Tourism Adv. Bd., 1971-76; mem. Pa. Bd. Edn., Council on Higher Edn., 1976—, Pa. Bd. Vocat. Edn., 1976—, Pa. Council Higher Edn., 1976—. Vice chmn. Pa. Week, 1954, Neighborhood Center Assn., 1954, bd. dirs., 1959-67, 69—, mem. exec. com., 1969—; bd. dirs. Negro Ednl. Emergency Drive, 1965—, exec. com., 1967—; Pa. chmn., Pitts. co-chmn. Get-Out-The-Vote drives, 1952; Pitts. chmn. UN Decennial Celebration, 1955; bd. dirs. Pitts. Ballet Theatre, 1978—. Recipient award Am. Heritage Found., 1952, George Washington award Freedom Found., 1952, President's award Pitts. Jr. C. of C., 1966, award of excellence Am. Mktg. Assn., 1970. Mem. Bus./Profl. Advertisers Assn. (pres. Pitts. chpt. 1967-68, nat. dir. 1968-70, chmn. internat. research com.), Pub. Relations Soc. Am. (counsellor 1960). Mem. Soc. of Friends. Home: 183 Gilkeson Rd Pittsburgh PA 15228 Office: 600 Grant St Pittsburgh PA 15219

MARSHALL, SYLVAN MITCHELL, lawyer, TV producer; b. N.Y.C., May 14, 1917; s. Louis H. and Kitty Markowitz; B.A., CCNY, 1938; J.D., Harvard U., 1941; m. Mara Byron, Feb. 11, 1951; children—Douglas Wayne, Bradley Ross. Admitted to N.Y. State bar, 1946, D.C. bar, 1953; mem. firm Garey & Garey, N.Y.C., 1946-51; spl. asst. to chief counsel OPS, Washington, 1951-53; partner firm Granik & Marshall, Washington, 1953-58; asst. producer Youth Wants to Know and Am. Forum, NBC-TV and radio, 1953-58; spl. dep. atty. gen. N.Y. State, 1946-50; pvt. practice law, Washington, 1958—; sr. partner law firm Marshall, Leon Weill & Mahony; counsel Leon, Weill & Mahony, N.Y.C.; Washington counsel Community Fed. Savs. & Loan Assn., St. Louis, First Fed. Savs. & Loan Assn., Chgo., First Fed. Savs. & Loan Assn., Jacksonville, Fla., Standard Fed. Savs., Cin., Franklin Soc. Fed. Savs. & Loan, N.Y.C., Diamond & Precious Stone Bourse, Idar-Oberstein, W. Ger., also fgn. embassies; Presidl. ambassador to Inaugural Pres. of Mexico. Hon. dep. police commr. N.Y.C., 1950-53; hon. consul Finland. Served from 2d lt. to lt. col. U.S. Army, 1941-46. Decorated knight comdr. Order of Falcon (Iceland); knight comdr. Order of Vasco Nunez de Balboa (Republic of Panama); comdr. Order of Lion (Finland); Order of Taj (Iran); comdr. Order Aztec Eagle (Mexico); Order So. Cross (Brazil); Order Ruben Dario (Nicaragua); comdr. Order of Lion and Sun (Iran). Mem. Acad. TV Arts and Scis. Club: Cosmos (Washington). Office: 4200 Wisconsin Ave NW Suite 419 Washington DC 20016 also 405 Lexington Ave 15th Floor New York NY 10017

MARSHALL, TERRELL, lawyer; b. Little Rock, July 14, 1908; s. J. C. and Jenice (Thomas) Marshall-Small; LL.B., Ark. Law Sch., 1931; m. Lourie Darland Jan. 2, 1927; 1 son, Terrell. Admitted to Ark. bar, 1931; U.S. Supreme Ct. bar, 1938; pvt. practice in Little Rock, 1931-60; asso. Joseph Marshall, 1960—; atty. Pulaski County Legal Aid Bur., 1938-42. Bd. dirs. Ark. Property Owners Found.; trustee Ark. Law Sch. Fellow Ark. Bar Found.; mem. Am., Ark. (past pres., mem. exec. com.), Pulaski County (past pres.) bar assns., Am. Judicature Soc. Club: Lakeside Country (past pres.) (Saline County, Ark.). Contbr. to Birds of Ark., 1951. Home: 372 Skyline Dr North Little Rock AR 72116 Office: Pyramid Bldg Little Rock AR 72201

MARSHALL, THOMAS OLIVER, JR., educator; b. Buffalo, Dec. 17, 1907; s. Thomas Oliver and Cynthia (MacNaughton) M.; A.B., Colgate U., 1929; Ed.M., U. Buffalo, 1932; Ed.D., Harvard, 1941; m. Evelyn Glade, Aug. 10, 1936 (dec. Nov. 1977); children—Anthony Glade, Robert Glade. Tchr., organizer Buffalo Adult Edn. Center, 1932; dir. adult edn. Genesee County (N.Y.), 1934; research asso. Regents' Inquiry, Albany, N.Y., 1936-37; instr., asst. prof. U. Rochester, 1938-42; dir. student personnel Colo. A. and M. Coll., 1942-45, dir. summer session, 1942-45, acting dean vocat. edn., 1942-45; dean Coll. Arts and Scis., Am. U., Washington, 1945-46, prof., chmn. dept. edn., 1946-47, dir. summer sch., 1946-47; prof., chmn. dept. edn. U. N.H., 1947-59, prof., 1959-73; prof. emeritus, 1973—, v.p. Center for Constructive Change, 1972—, chmn. div. tchr. edn., 1947-59, on leave as spl. asst. to dean Grad. Sch., Harvard U., 1955-56; chmn. N.H. Council for Tchr. Edn.; pres. N.H. Dept. Higher Edn.; dir., mem. exec. com. N.H. Council Better Schs.; coordinator N.H. regional center New Eng. Sch. Devel. Council; chmn. steering com., inter-univ. coop. com. Coop. Program in Ednl. Adminstrn., Center for Field Studies, Harvard; cons. Ednl. Systems Corp., Ednl. Projects Inc., migrant farm workers program Office Econ. Opportunity. Del. N.H. Dem. Conv., 1966, 68, 70, 72. Ford Found. grantee, London, 1965-66. Mem. N.H. Edn. Assn. (chmn. study tchrs. load 1959-61), Nat. Soc. Study Edn., AAUP, NEA, Soc. Advancement Edn., Kappa Delta Pi, Theta Chi, Gamma Delta Psi. Author: (with Ruth E. Eckert) When Youth Leaves School, 1939; Teaching Time: A Study of Teacher Load in N.H. Public Schools, 1961; editor: Resource Persons in the New Eng. Area on Various Aspects of Ednl. Adminstrn., 1952; asso. editor Jour. Constructive Change, 1979—; contbr. articles to ednl. publs. Home: 17 Madbury Rd #6 Durham NH 03824 Office: Center for Constructive Change 16 Stratford Ave Durham NH 03824

MARSHALL, THOMAS OLIVER, JR., judge; b. Americus, Ga., June 24, 1920; s. Thomas Oliver and Mattie Louise (Hunter) M.; B.S. in Engring., U.S. Naval Acad., 1941; J.D., U. Ga., 1948; m. Angie Ellen Fitts, Dec. 20, 1946; children—Ellen Irwin Marshall Beard, Anne Hunter Marshall Peagler, Mary Olivia Marshall Pryor. Admitted to Ga. bar, 1947; individual practice law, Americus, Ga., 1948-60; judge S.W. Judicial Circuit, Americus, 1960-74; judge Ga. Ct. Appeals, Atlanta, 1974-77; justice Ga. Supreme Ct., Atlanta, 1977—; chmn. bd. visitors U. Ga. Law Sch., 1970. Trustee Andrew Coll., So. Ga. Meth. Home for Aged, 1965-78; active ARC, 1948-60, United Givers Fund, 1948-54. Served with USN, World War II, Korean War. Decorated Bronze Star; named Young Man of Yr., Americus, 1953. Mem. Am., Ga. (bd. govs. 1958-60) Atlanta bar assns., State Bar Ga., Am. Judicature Soc., Jud. Coll. Ga. Democrat. Methodist. Clubs: Elks, VFW, Kiwanis, Am. Legion, Masons, Shriners. Home: 238 15th St NE Condominium 3 Atlanta GA 30309 Office: 541 State Judicial Bldg Atlanta GA 30334

MARSHALL, THURGOOD, asso. justice U.S. Supreme Ct.; b. Balt., July 2, 1908; s. William and Norma (Williams) M.; A.B., Lincoln U., 1930, LL.D., 1947; LL.B., Howard U., 1933, LL.D., 1954; LL.D., Va. State Coll., 1948, Morgan State Coll., 1952, Grinnell Coll., 1954, Syracuse U., 1956, N.Y. Sch. Social Research, 1956, U. Liberia, 1960, Brandeis U., 1960, U. Mass., 1962, Jewish Theol. Sem., 1962, Wayne U., 1963, Princeton U., 1963, U. Mich., 1964, Johns Hopkins U., 1966; hon. degree Far Eastern Univ., Manila, 1968, Victoria U. of Wellington, 1968, U. Calif., 1968, U. Otago, Dunedin, New Zealand, 1968; m. Vivian Burey, Sept. 4, 1929 (dec. Feb. 1955); m. 2d, Cecilia S. Suyat, Dec. 17, 1955; children—Thurgood, John. Admitted to Md. bar, 1933; practiced in Balt., 1933-37; asst. spl. counsel N.A.A.C.P., 1936-38, spl. counsel, 1938-50, dir., counsel legal def. and ednl. fund, 1940-61; U.S. circuit judge for 2d Jud. Circuit, 1961-65; solicitor gen. U.S., 1965-67; justice U.S. Supreme Ct., 1967—. Civil rights cases argued include Tex. Primary Case, 1944, Restrictive Covenant Cases, 1948, U. Tex. and Okla. Cases, 1950, sch. segregation cases, 1952-53; visited Japan and Korea to make investigation of ct. martial cases involving Negro soldiers, 1951. Cons. Constl. Conf. on Kenya, London, 1960; rep. White House Conf. Youth and Children. Recipient Spingarn medal, 1946; Living History award Research Inst. Mem. Nat. Bar Assn., N.Y. County Lawyers Assn., Am. Bar Assn., Bar Assn. D.C., Alpha Phi Alpha. Episcopalian. Mason (33 deg.). Home: Falls Church VA Office: Supreme Ct US Washington DC 20543

MARSHALL, VICTOR FRAY, physician, educator; b. Culpeper, Va., Sept. 1, 1913; s. Otis and Marie Josephine (Riton) M.; M.D., U. Va., 1937; D.Sc., Washington and Lee U., 1975; m. Barbara Walsh, Dec. 11, 1943; children—Fray F., Victor R., Philip S. Intern, N.Y. Hosp., 1937-38, asst. resident gen. surgery, 1938-41, asst. resident urology, 1941-42, resident urology, 1943, staff mem., 1943—, attending-in-charge urology James Buchanan Brady Found., 1949—; faculty Med. Coll., Cornell U., 1938-78, asso. prof. clin. surgery urology, 1947-57, prof. clin. surgery (urology), 1957-78, James J. Colt prof. urology in surgery, 1970-78, head service urology, 1946-78; prof. urology pro tem U. Va., Charlottesville, 1979—; asst. attending surgeon Meml. Center for Cancer and Allied Diseases, 1943-52, asso. attending, 1952—. Diplomate Am. Bd. Urology (past pres.). Fellow A.C.S., A.M.A., N.Y. Acad. Medicine (Valentine medal 1974); mem. A.A.A.S., N.Y. Urol. Soc. (past pres.), Am. Urol. Assn. (Guiteras award 1975), James Ewing Soc., N.Y. Cancer Soc. (past pres.), Soc. Pelvic Surgeons (past pres.), Mexican Acad. Surgery, Am. Surg. Assn., Am. Acad. Pediatrics, Soc. Pediatric Urology, Clin. Soc. Genito-Urinary Surgeons (pres. 1976), Surg. Soc. Venezuela, Mexican Urol. Soc., Brit. Assn. Urol. Surgeons, Venezuelan Soc. Urology, Am. Assn. Genito-Urinary Surgeons (Barringer medal 1970), Canadian Urol. Assn. (hon.), Royal Coll. Surgeons Ireland (hon.), Alpha Omega Alpha, Pi Kappa Alpha, Nu Sigma Nu. Contbr. articles to med. jours. Home: Rt 3 Box 131 Gordonsville VA 22942 Office: Univ Hosp Charlottesville VA 22903

MARSHALL, WILLIAM, JR., architect; b. Ashland, Ky., Nov. 24, 1925; s. William and Lee (Powers) M.; student Va. Mil. Inst., 1943-44; B.S., U. Va., 1949; postgrad. Columbia, 1949-50; m. Joan Goodyear Ellingston, June 16, 1951; children—William III, Jenefer, Charles, Elizabeth, Christopher. Designer, draftsman, 1950-53; architect Lublin, McGaughy & Assos., Architects and Cons. Engrs., Norfolk, Washington, 1953-55, architect, partner, 1955-60; chief architect, partner McGaughy, Marshall & McMillan, Architects and Cons. Engrs., Norfolk, Va., Washington, Houston, Frankfort, Germany, Athens, Greece, 1960—. Mem. Profl. unit United Community Fund, Norfolk, 1962-71; mem. adhoc com. to establish city planning dept., Norfolk, 1961-62; mem. citizens adv. com. to the Mayor, Norfolk, 1962-68, chmn. codes sub-com., 1962-68, mem. exec. com., 1962-68; mem. adv. com. bldg. constrn. curriculum Norfolk State Coll., 1968—. Trustee Hermitage Found., 1974—; trustee AIA Research Corp., 1975—. Served with AUS, 1944-46. Fellow AIA (pres. Tidewater sect. Va. chpt. 1964-65, pres. Va. chpt. 1969-70, v.p. nat. 1971, mem. exec. com. 1974-75, bd. dirs. 1974-75, chmn. commn. govt. affairs 1972-73, commr. spl. assessment program 1973-74, 1st v.p. 1974, chmn. planning com. 1974, pres. 1975—); mem. Am. Inst. Steel Construction (archtl. awards of excellence jury 1974), Am. Iron and Steel Inst. (honor awards jury 1975), Prestressed Concrete Inst. (chmn. honor awards jury 1975), Va. Assn. Professions (bd. dirs. 1970-71, regional v.p. 1970), Downtown Norfolk Assn. (bd. dirs. 1966-72). Prin. works include United Va. Bank, Norfolk, 1970; Kirn Meml. Library, Norfolk, 1962; Ministry of Def. Hdqrs., Riyadh, Saudi Arabia, 1976; Zahid Housing Complex, Jedda, Saudi Arabia, 1976; Kuwait Ministry of Def. in Interior Design Project, 1976. Office: 229 W Bute St Norfolk VA 23510

MARSHALL, WILLIAM EDWARD, hist. assn. exec.; b. St. Paul, Apr. 19, 1925; s. William Edward and Louise (White) M.; B.A., Mont. State U., 1950; B.F.A., Wittenberg U., 1951; postgrad. Ohio State U., 1951-52; m. Ruth Marie Winner, Sept. 3, 1947 (div.); children—Michael Scott, Terry Lee, Sharon; m. 2d, Loretta E. Slota, Nov. 6, 1976; 1 son, Marc William. Graphic and exhibits designer Ohio Hist. Soc., 1952-60; graphic and exhibits designer State Historic Soc. Colo., Denver, 1960-61, dep. exec. dir., 1961-63, exec. dir., 1963—. Bd. dirs. Rocky Mountain Center on Environment, 1967-72; chmn. Colo. Humanities Program Com., 1971, 75. Served with USMCR, 1943-45. Mem. Am. Assn. Museums, Am. Assn. State and Local History (mem. council). Lutheran. Contbr. articles to profl. jours. Home: 4747 W 31st Ave Denver CO 80206 Office: Colo Hist Soc Colo Heritage Center 1300 Broadway Denver CO 80203

MARSHALL, WILLIAM JEFFERSON, former naval officer, beverage inst. adminstr.; b. Henderson, Ky., Feb. 15, 1903; s. William Jefferson and Lelia Triplett (Yeaman) M.; student Centre Coll., Danville, Ky., 1920-21; B.S., U.S. Naval Acad., 1925; M.S., U. Calif., 1933; student Indsl. Coll. Armed Forces, 1946-47; m. Catharine Oliver, June 13, 1956. Commd. ensign USN, 1925, advanced through grades to vice adm., 1959; assigned destroyers escorting convoys North Atlantic, participating Normandy invasion, Philippine invasion, Okinawa, World War II; naval attache, Rome, 1951-53; exec. asst., sr. aide to chief Naval Operations, 1953-54; comdr. Destroyers Western Pacific, 1954-56; dir. material Navy Dept., 1956-59; pres. Bourbon Inst., Washington, 1959—. Decorated Silver Star medal, D.S.C. (U.S.); Croix de Guerre with Palm (France); Order of War (Brazil); Order of Merit (Italy). Named Industry Man of Year Ed Gibbs Newsletter, 1960. Mem. U.S. Naval Inst., Chevalier du Tastevin, Phi Delta Theta. Clubs: N.Y. Yacht, Army-Navy, Internat. (Washington); Fairfax Hunt. Home: 9738 Lawyers Rd Vienna VA 22180 Office: 1300 Pennsylvania Bldg Washington DC 20004

MARSHALL, WILLIAM ROBERT, JR., educator; b. Calgary, Alta., Can., May 19, 1916; s. William Robert and May (Barnum) M.; brought to U.S., 1925, naturalized, 1944; B.S. in Chem. Engring., Armour Inst. Tech., 1938; Ph.D., U. Wis., 1941; m. Dorothy Robbins, Jan. 9, 1943; children—Margaret O., Mary J., William Robert. Chem. engr. E. I. duPont Co. Expt. Sta., 1941-47; cons. to industry, 1948—; mem. faculty U. Wis., Madison, 1948—, prof. chem. engring., 1953—, asso. dir. engring. experiment sta., 1953-66, 66-71, exec. dir., 1971—, dean Coll. Engring. Mem. engring. scis. adv. panel Nat. Sci. Found., 1957-59, chmn. adv. com. to engring. div., 1966-67, mem. sci. applications task force, 1977; chmn. chem. engring. rev. com. Argonne Nat. Lab., 1959, 66, mem., 1958-66. Chmn. Wis. Licensing Bd. Architects, Profl. Engrs., Land Surveyors and Designers; mem. Korea-U.S. joint commn. Nat. Acad. Sci., 1977—. Pres. Wis. Ballet Co., 1963-66. Fourth Inst. lectr. Am. Inst. Chem. Engrs., 1952. Mem. adv. com. dept. applied sci. Brookhaven Nat. Lab., 1973-75. Recipient William H. Walker award 1953; Gold medal Verein Deutsches Inqineurs, W. Ger., 1975. Registered profl. engr. Trustee Argonne U. Assn., chmn. nuclear engring. edn. com., 1967-69, chmn. bd. commn. on edn.; bd. dirs. Commn. on Engring. Edn., 1965-68. Fellow Am. Acad. Arts and Scis., Am. Inst. Chem. Engrs. (chmn. com. on equipment testing procedures 1951-56, dir. 1956-58, Profl. Progress award 1959, pres. 1963, chmn. continuing edn. com. 1964-67, Founders award 1973, treas. 1976—); mem. Engrs. Joint Council (v.p. 1963-65, exec. com., dir.), Assn. Midwest U.'s (pres. 1962-63, dir. 1960—), Am. Assn. Land Grant Colls. (chmn. research sect. engring. div. 1957-58), Am. Soc. Engring. Edn., Soc. for History Tech. (exec. council 1966-68), Engring. Colls. Consortium for Minorities (pres. 1975—), Nat. Acad. Engring. (com. on interplay engring. with biology and medicine 1967—, vice chmn. 1969-70, chmn. 1970—; mem. commn. on edn. 1968-70, chmn. 1970-73; membership com. 1967-69), Phi Kappa Phi. Co-author: Application of Differential Equations to Chemical Engineering, 1949. Author articles in field, sect. in handbook. Home; 4917 Tonyawatha Trail Madison WI 53716

MARSICANO, NICHOLAS, artist; b. Shenandoah, Pa., Oct. 1, 1914; s. Nicholas and Rose M.; student Pa. Acad. Fine Arts, 1931-33, Barnes Found., 1934-38; m. Merle Marsicano, Jan., 1954. One-man exhbns. include: A.M. Sachs Gallery, N.Y.C., 1971-74, Howard Wise Gallery, N.Y.C., 1963, Bertha Schaefer Gallery, 1957-61, Des Moines Art Center, 1963, 64, Davenport Mcpl. Art Galleries, 1972, Huntington (W.Va.) Galleries, 1967; represented in permanent collections Mus. Modern Art, N.Y.C., Art Inst. Chgo., San Francisco Mus. Art, Larry Aldrich Mus., Dallas Mus. Fine Arts; mem. faculty dept. art Cooper Union, N.Y.C., SUNY, Purchase. Served with AUS, 1943-46. Guggenheim Found. fellow, 1974-75. Address: 42 W 15th St New York NY 10011

MARSON, ARNALDO (MARIO), game and toy mfg. co. exec.; b. San Mateo, Calif., Apr. 10, 1934; s. Arnaldo Mario and Isabelle (Keys) M.; B.S., U. So. Calif., 1955; grad. Exec. Mgmt. Program, UCLA, 1969; m. Cynthia Mauzey, Dec. 19, 1953; children—Bradley (dec.), Janet, Linda. With So. Calif. Gas Co., 1957-60, Gallo Winery, Modesto, Calif., 1961; with Mattel, Inc., Hawthorne, Calif., 1962-70, dir. ops., 1970-72; asst. to pres. Litton Dental Supply Co., Toledo, 1972; v.p. ops. Lakeside Games div. Leisure Dynamics, Inc., Mpls., 1973-74, div. pres., 1975-76; exec. v.p. Leisure Dynamics, 1977-78, pres., 1978—; dir. Cox Internat. Co., A.S. Barnes & Co. Served with U.S. Army, 1955-57. Mem. Toy Mfrs. Assn. Am. (dir.), Am. Mgmt. Assn., UCLA Grad. Sch. Exec. Program Mgmt. Assn. Office: 4400 W 78th St Minneapolis MN 55435

MARSTELLER, WILLIAM A., advt. exec.; b. Champaign, Ill., Feb. 23, 1914; s. P. L. and Minnie (Finder) M.; B.S., U. Ill., 1937; m. Gloria Crawford, Apr. 22, 1938; children—Elizabeth A. (Mrs. Stuart M. Gordon), Julie. Reporter Champaign News-Gazette, 1932-37; agy. counselor Mass. Mut. Life Ins. Co., Chgo., 1937-41; advt. and sales promotion mgr. Edward Valves, Inc., East Chicago, Ind., 1941-43, sec., 1943-45, v.p., dir., 1945-51; mgr. advt. and market research Rockwell Mfg. Co., Pitts., 1945-49, v.p., 1949-51; pres. Marsteller Research, Inc., Chgo., 1951—; pres. Marsteller Inc., 1951-60, chmn., 1960-76, chmn. exec. com., chief exec. officer 1976—; chmn. Burson-Marsteller, Assos., 1953-68, Marsteller Internat., S.A., Geneva, Switzerland, 1961—. Trustee Barnard Coll., Whitney Mus. Am. Art; mem. U. Ill. Pres.'s Club; mem. Barnard Council. Recipient Achievement award U. Ill., 1973, Pres.'s award, 1976. Mem. Am. Mgmt. Assn., Am. Assn. Advt. Agys., Chgo. (pres. 1945-46), Nat. (pres. 1947-49) indsl. advertisers assns., Football Writers Assn. Am., U. Ill. Found., Art Inst. Chgo. (life), AAUP, Sigma Chi. Clubs: Tavern, Arts (Chgo); Pinnacle (N.Y.C.); Duquesne (Pitts.). Author: The Wonderful World of Words, 1972. Contbr. articles to marketing and advt. publs. Home: 900 Lake Shore Dr Chicago IL 60611 also 1060 Fifth Ave New York NY Office: 1 E Wacker Dr Chicago IL 60601 also 866 3d Ave New York NY 10022

MARSTELLER, WILLIAM A., advt. exec.; b. Champaign, Ill., Feb. 23, 1914; s. P. L. and Minnie (Finder) M.; B.S., U. Ill., 1937; m. Gloria Crawford, Apr. 22, 1938; children—Elizabeth A. (Mrs. Stuart M. Gordon), Julie. Reporter Champaign News-Gazette, 1932-37; agy. counselor Mass. Mut. Life Ins. Co., Chgo., 1937-41; advt. and sales promotion mgr. Edward Valves, Inc., East Chicago, Ind., 1941-43, sec., 1943-45, v.p., dir., 1945-51; mgr. advt. and market research Rockwell Mfg. Co., Pitts., 1945-49, v.p., 1949-51; pres. Marsteller Research, Inc., Chgo., 1951—; pres. Marsteller Inc., 1951-60, chmn., 1960-76, chmn. exec. com., chief exec. officer, 1976—; chmn. Burson-Marsteller, Assos., 1953-68, Marsteller Internat., S.A., Geneva, 1961—. Trustee, Barnard Coll., Whitney Mus. Am. Art; mem. U. Ill. Pres.'s Club; mem. Barnard Council, Whitney Circle. Recipient Achievement award U. Ill., 1973, Pres.'s award, 1976; named to Advt. Hall of Fame, 1979; Barnard medal of distinction, 1979. Mem. Am. Mgmt. Assn. (trustee), Am. Assn. Advt. Agys., Chgo. (pres. 1945-46), Nat. (pres. 1947-49) indsl. advertisers assns., Football Writers Assn. Am., U. Ill. Found., Art Inst. Chgo. (life), AAUP, Sigma Chi. Clubs: Tavern, Arts (Chgo.). Author: The Wonderful World of Words, 1972; Words and People, 1979; contbr. articles to marketing and advt. publs. Office: 1 E Wacker Dr Chicago IL 60601 also 866 3d Ave New York NY 10022

MARSTERS, ANN PIERCE (MRS. STEWART S. BATTLES), author; b. Boston, Mar. 1, 1916; d. Ernest Reginald and Edith Armina (Bonnell) Marsters; student Cambridge Haskell Sch. for Girls, Mass., 1926-33, Child-Walker Sch. Art, Boston, 1933; m. Sabie La Vigna, Oct. 23, 1948 (dec. Dec. 1968); m. 2d, Stewart S. Battles, Oct. 25, 1969. Joined staff, Boston Sunday Advertiser and Boston Evening-Am., 1935, features on major sporting events; columnist (Girl About Town) for Boston Evening-American, 1937; feature writer Chgo. Herald-Am. (frequent series on Hollywood); syndicated by King Features; motion picture editor Chgo. Am., 1944-50, drama critic, 1950-54, columnist movies, drama, showbusiness, 1954-69; free-lance writer, 1969—; lectr. on show business and spiritualism-truth or trickery. Mem. ASCAP, Am. Guild Authors and Composers. Conglist. Contbr. short stories and poetry to mags. Address: 249 Fair Acres Dr Galesburg IL 61401

MARSTON, ROBERT ANDREW, public relations co. exec.; b. Astoria, N.Y., Aug. 6, 1937; s. Frank and Lena (DiDomenico) M.; B.A., Hofstra U., 1959; m. Carolyn Barris, June 30, 1973. Sr. v.p. Rowland Co., N.Y.C., 1959-68, Rogers & Cowen, Inc., N.Y.C., 1968-70; founder, pres. Robert Marston and Assos., N.Y.C., 1970—; founder, chmn. bd., chief exec. officer Marston and Rothenberg Public Affairs, Inc., N.Y.C., 1977—. Mem. Public Relations Soc. Am. Roman Catholic. Clubs: Bailiwick Tennis, Madison Sq. Garden, N.Y. Athletic, Marco Polo, Doubles. Contbr. articles, photographs to profl. jours. and popular mags. Home: 10 Deer Park Ct Greenwich CT 06830 Office: 645 Madison Ave New York NY 10022

MARSTON, ROBERT ANDREW, pub. relations co. exec.; b. Astoria, N.Y., Aug. 6, 1937; s. Frank and Lena (DiDomenico) M.; B.A., Hofstra U., 1959; m. Carolyn Barris, June 30, 1973; Sr. v.p. Rowland Co., N.Y.C., 1959-68, Rogers & Cowen, Inc., N.Y.C., 1968-70; founder, pres. Robert Marston and Assos., N.Y.C., 1970—; co-founder, chmn., chief exec. officer Marsten and Rothenberg Public Affairs, Inc., N.Y.C., 1977—. Mem. Public Relations Soc. Am. Roman Catholic. Clubs: Bailiwick Tennis, Madison Sq. Garden, N.Y. Athletic, Marco Polo, Doubles. Contbr. articles and photographs to profl. jours. and popular mags. Home: 10 Deer Park Ct Greenwich CT 06830 Office: 645 Madison Ave New York NY 10022

MARSTON, ROBERT QUARLES, univ. pres.; b. Toano, Va., Feb. 12, 1923; s. Warren and Helen (Smith) M.; B.S., Va. Mil. Inst., 1943; M.D., Med. Coll. Va., 1947; B.Sc. (Rhodes scholar 1947-49), Oxford (Eng.) U., 1949; hon. degrees Coll. William and Mary, 1969, Albany Med. Coll., Union U., 1969, Hahnemann Med. Coll., 1977, Colo. State U., 1977, Fla. Tech. U., 1977; m. Ann Carter Garnett, Dec. 21, 1946; children—Ann, Robert, Wesley. Intern Johns Hopkins Hosp., 1949-50; resident Vanderbilt U. Hosp., 1950-51, Med. Coll. Va., 1953-54, asst. prof. medicine, 1954; asst. prof. bacteriology and immunology U. Minn., 1958-59; asso. prof. medicine, asst. dean charge student affairs Med. Coll. Va., 1959-61; dean U. Miss. Sch. Medicine, 1961-66, dir. Med. Center, 1961-65, vice chancellor, 1965-66; asso. dir. div. regional med. programs NIH, 1966-68; adminstr. Fed. Health Services and Mental Health Adminstrn., 1968; dir. NIH, Bethesda, Md., 1968-73; scholar in residence U. Va., Charlottesville, 1973-74; Distinguished fellow Inst. of Medicine, Nat. Acad. Scis., 1973-74; pres. U. Fla., 1974—; dir. Johnson and Johnson. Bd. visitors Charles R. Drew Postgrad. Sch., Air U.; mem. Fla. Council of 100; exec. council Assn. Am. Med. Coll., 1964-67; mem. council Inst. Medicine. Served to 1st lt. AUS, 1951-53. Markle scholar, 1954-59; hon. fellow Lincoln Coll., Oxford U. Fellow Am. Pub. Health Assn.; mem. Am. Hosp. Assn. (hon.), Nat. Med. Assn. (hon.), Assn. Am. Rhodes Scholars, AMA, Assn. Am. Physicians, AAAS, Assn. Am. Med. Colls., Am. Clin. and Climatol. Assn., Soc. Scholars Johns Hopkins, Alpha Omega Alpha. Episcopalian. Author articles in field. Home: 2151 W University Ave Gainesville FL 32601

MARSTON, ROLAND F., ins. co. exec.; b. Rock Island, Ill., July 13, 1924; s. Frank and Mildred (Wainwright) M.; student DePauw U., 1942-44; B.A. in Bus. Adminstrn., Ill. Wesleyan U., 1947; m. Margaret Ann Fuller, Nov. 23, 1944; children—Roland Michael, William Frank, Gertrude Ann, Rebecca Kay. Salesman, sales mgr. Corn Belt Motor Co., Bloomington, Ill., 1947-50; owner Marston Buick Co., Kewanee, Ill., 1950-55; with State Farm Ins. Cos., 1956—, dep. regional v.p., Winter Haven, Fla., 1962-65, regional v.p., St. Paul, 1965-72, v.p. State Farm Mut. Automobile Ins. Co., Bloomington, 1972-77, exec. v.p., 1977—. Mem. allocations com. United Fund, St. Paul, 1968-70; trustee Ill. Wesleyan U., Bloomington, 1975. Served as ensign USNR, 1944-46. Mem. Phi Delta Theta. Clubs: Rotary, Masons. Home: Route 2 Bloomington IL 61701 Office: State Farm Mut Automobile Ins Co 1 State Farm Plaza Bloomington IL 61701

MARTEKA, VINCENT JAMES, JR., editor, author; b. Uxbridge, Mass., Jan. 29, 1936; s. Vincent James and Genevieve (Ramian) M.; B.S. in Geology, U. Mass., 1958; M.S., Rensselaer Poly. Inst., 1959; m. Janet Littler, May 26, 1962; children—Andrew, Peter, Katherine. Editor, U.S. Geol. Survey, Washington, 1959-60; sci. writer, news editor Sci. Service, Washington, 1961-63; sci. editor My Weekly Reader, children's newspaper, Middletown, Conn., 1964-65; editor Current Sci., sci. mag. jr. high sch. students, Middletown, 1966—; author: Bionics, 1965; also numerous articles. Served with AUS, 1960. Recipient writing awards Edn. Press Assn. Mem. Nat. Assn. Sci. Writers, Mycological Soc. Am., N.Am. Mycological Assn., Nat., Mattabeseck (pres. 1976) Audubon socs. Home: Jobs Pond Rd Portland CT 06480 Office: Xerox Edn Publs 245 Long Hill Rd Middletown CT 06457

MARTELL, ARTHUR EARL, chemist; b. Natick, Mass., Oct. 18, 1916; s. Ambrose and Dorina (Lamoureaux) M.; B.S., Worcester Poly. Inst., 1938, D.Sc. (hon.), 1962; Ph.D., N.Y. U., 1941; m. Norma June Saunders, Sept. 2, 1944; children—Stuart A., Edward S., Janet E., Judith S., Jon V., Elaine C.; m. 2d, Mary Austin, 1965; children—Helen E., Kathryn A. Instr., Worcester Poly. Inst., 1941-42; mem. faculty Clark U., 1942-61, prof. chemistry, 1951-61, chmn. dept., 1959-61; prof. chemistry, chmn. dept. Ill. Inst. Tech., 1960-66, Tex. A. and M. U., College Station, 1966—, Distinguished prof., 1973—. Mem. sch. bd. Northborough, Mass., 1958-61, chmn., 1959-61. Research fellow U. Calif. at Berkeley, 1949-50; Guggenheim fellow U. Zurich (Switzerland), 1954-55; NSF sr. postdoctoral fellow, also fellow Sch. Advanced Studies, Mass. Inst. Tech., 1959-60; NIH Spl. fellow U. Calif. at Berkeley, 1964-65. Fellow N.Y. Acad. Scis. (hon.); mem. Am. Chem. Soc. (chmn. central Mass. sect. 1957-58, S.W. Regional award 1976, Nat. award for Disting. Service 1980), AAAS, Am. Acad. Arts and Scis., Sigma Xi. Author: (with M. Calvin) Chemistry of the Metal Chelate Compounds, 1952; (with S. Chaberek, Jr.) Organic Sequestering Agents, 1959; (with L.G. Sillen) Stability Constants, 1964, supplement, 1971; (with M.M. Taqui Khan) Homogeneous Catalysis by Metal Complexes, 2 vols., 1973; (with R.M. Smith) Critical Stability Constants, Vol. 1, 1974, Vol. 2, 1975, Vol. 3, 1977, Vol. 4, 1976. Editor: ACS Monograph on Coordination Chemistry, Vol. 1, 1973, Vol. 2, 1978, Jour. Coordination Chemistry; editorial bd. Biorganic Chemistry, Jour. Inorganic and Nuclear Chemistry; contbr. articles to profl. jours. Research on chem equilibria, kinetics, catalysis, metal chelate compounds in solution. Home: Box 1136 Rt 5 Bryan TX 77801

MARTEN, JOHN FRANCIS, JR., investment banker; b. San Jose, Calif., July 28, 1914; s. John Francis and Mary (Twohy) M.; B.S., U. Santa Clara, 1936; m. Patricia Boyle, Nov. 9, 1946 (dec. Oct. 1977); children—Maureen, John Francis; m. 2d, Nadine Mormandin, Apr. 7, 1979. Title examiner, escrow officer Calif. Pacific Title Ins. Co., 1936-41; v.p. Inglewood Fed. Savs. and Loan Assn., 1946-50; exec. v.p. Am. Savs. and Loan Assn., 1951-55; pres. Gt. Western Savs. and Loan Assn., Los Angeles, 1955-64, Gt. Western Financial Corp., 1955-64; investment banker, securities broker, 1963—. Bd. dirs. adv. bd. Daniel Freeman Meml. Hosp., Inglewood, pres. 1962-63; bd. dirs. Calif. Mus. Sci. and Industry, pres., 1970-71; regent U. Santa Clara; trustee St. John's Hosp. and Health Center Found., 1976—. Served from pvt. to lt. col. AUS, 1941-46. Decorated Bronze Star. Mem. Calif. Savs. and Loan League (pres. 1962-63), Sovereign Mil. Order Malta. Roman Catholic. Clubs: Los Angeles Country, Calif. (Los Angeles); Beach (Santa Monica, Calif.).

MARTENS, ROBERT JOHN, fgn. service officer; b. Kansas City, Nov. 24, 1925; s. John Lewis and Esther (Flora) M.; B.Fgn. Service, U. So. Calif., 1949; student Russian Inst., Columbia, 1955-56; m. Patricia Catherine Glavin, Oct. 11, 1958; children—Anne Patricia, John, Thomas. Dep. probation officer Los Angeles County, 1949-50; joined U.S. Fgn. Service, 1951; vice consul, Naples, Italy, 1951-53; 3d sec., Vienna, Austria, 1953-54; vice consul, Salzburg, Austria, 1953-54; assigned State Dept., 1955-56; 2d sec., Moscow, 1956-58; assigned State Dept., 1958-63; 1st sec., consul, Djakarta, Indonesia, 1963-66; chief Bloc Internat. Polit. Div., Bur. Intelligence and Research, Dept. State, 1966-68; assigned Nat. War Coll., 1968-69; 1st sec., consul, Rangoon, Burma, 1969-70; dep. chief of mission, Bucharest, Rumania, 1971-74, charge d' affaires, 1973-74; dir. Office Regional Affairs, Bur. East Asian Affairs, Dept. State, Washington, 1974-78; dep. chief mission, Stockholm, Sweden, 1978—. Served with AUS, 1943-46: ETO. Home: 8629 Hempstead Ave Bethesda MD 20034 Office: Dept State Washington DC 20525

MARTH, ELMER HERMAN, bacteriologist; b. Jackson, Wis., Sept. 11, 1927; s. William F. and Irma A. (Bublitz) M.; B.S., U. Wis., 1950, M.S., 1952, Ph.D., 1954; m. Phyllis E. Menge, Aug. 10, 1957. Teaching asst. bacteriology U. Wis., Madison, 1949-51, research asst., 1951-54, project asso., 1954-55, instr. bacteriology, 1955-57, asso. prof. food sci. and bacteriology, 1966-71, prof., 1971—; with Kraft, Inc., Glenview, Ill., 1957-66, research bacteriologist, 1957-61, sr. research bacteriologist, 1961-63, group leader microbiology, 1963-66, asso. mgr. microbiology, 1966; mem. Intersoc. Council on Standard Methods for Exam. Dairy Products, 1968—, chmn., 1972-79. Sec., Luth. Acad. Scholarship, 1961-71. WHO travel fellow, 1975. Recipient Pfizer award for research, 1975, Educator award for research and teaching food hygiene, 1977; Nordica award for research, 1979. Mem. Am. Soc. Microbiology, Am. Dairy Sci. Assn., Internat. Assn. Milk, Food, and Environ. Sanitarians, Inst. Food Technologists, AAAS, Council Biology Editors, Sigma Xi, Alpha Zeta, Kappa Eta Kappa, Phi Sigma, Delta Theta Sigma, Gamma Alpha. Contbg. author books; editor Jour. Milk and Food Tech., 1967-76, Jour. Food Protection, 1977—. Contbr. articles to profl. publs. Patentee in field. Home: 3414 Viburnum Dr Madison WI 53705

MARTICELLI, JOSEPH JOHN, lawyer, editor; b. Freeland, Pa., Feb. 24, 1921; s. Frank Anthony and Carmela (DiSpirito) M.; A.B., Lafayette Coll., 1941; LL.B., U. Pa., 1947; m. Alva Mae Aubrey, Oct. 22, 1952; children—Frank Anthony, Barbara Ruth. Admitted to Pa. bar, 1948, N.Y. bar, 1954, also Supreme Ct. bar; practiced law, Freeland, 1948-53, Rochester, N.Y., 1953—; mng. editor Lawyers Coop. Pub. Co., Rochester, N.Y., 1953—, editor Case & Comment; adj. prof. bus. law Monroe Community Coll., Rochester. First dep. town atty. Henrietta, N.Y., 1962—; legis. asst. N.Y. Assembly, 1970-71; counsel to minority N.Y. Senate, 1976-78. Chmn. Republican Town and County Com., Henrietta, N.Y., 1961. Served with AUS, 1942-46. Mem. Am., N.Y. bar assns., Scribes Assn. Legal Writers (sec. 1978-79), Am. Trial Lawyers Assn., Am. Legion. Republican. Roman Catholic. Author, editor law books; contbr. articles to profl. jours. Home: 301 Butler Dr Pittsford NY 14534 Office: Aqueduct Bldg Rochester NY 14603

MARTIN, A. RICHARD, journalist; b. Salt Lake City, Apr. 30, 1939; s. Albert Rasband and Mildred Alice (Bush) M.; B.A., U. Denver, 1961; m. Karen Ann Hein, June 11, 1961; children—Wendy Karol, Cynthia Lynne. Reporter, Wall St. Jour., 1961, 63-73, asst. bur. chief, N.Y.C., 1973, bur. chief, Boston, 1973-76, Cleve., 1976-77, bur. chief, asst. mng. editor, Chgo., 1977—. Served with U.S. Army, 1962-63. Mem. Phi Beta Kappa, Phi Kappa Sigma. Office: 200 W Monroe St Chicago IL 60606

MARTIN, ABNER BROADWATER, air force officer; b. Fairforest, S.C., May 25, 1927; s. John Landrum and Blanche Ballenger (Wheeler) M.; student Elec. Engring., Clemson A. and M. Coll., S.C., 1943-44, N.C. State Coll., 1944-45; B.S., U.S. Mil. Acad., 1949; M.S., Mass. Inst. Tech., 1954, George Washington U., 1965; grad. Advanced Mgmt. Program, Harvard U., 1968; m. Agnes Madolyn Smith, June 7, 1949; children—Alan, Dan, Melanie. Commd. 2d lt. USAF, 1949, advanced through grades to lt. gen., 1977; grad. Army War Coll., 1965; engaged in research and devel.; comdr., dir. Armament Lab., 1968-70; program dir. Advanced Ballistic Re-entry Systems, SAMSO, 1970-71, dep. for Minuteman, SAMSO, Norton AFB, Calif., 1971, SPD, Wright-Patterson AFB, Ohio, now dir. Def. Mapping Agy. Decorated Legion of Merit, Bronze Star. Asso. fellow Am. Inst. Aeros. and Astronautics, Daedalians, Air Force Assn. Address: Def Mapping Agy Naval Obs Massachusetts Ave at 34th St Washington DC 20305

MARTIN, AGNES, painter; b. Macklin, Can., 1912; B.A., M.F.A., Columbia U. One-woman shows: Betty Parsons Gallery, N.Y.C., 1959, 60, 61, Robert Elkton Gallery, N.Y.C., 1962, 64, 65, 66, 67, Pace Gallery, N.Y.C., 1975, 76, 77, 79; exhibited Mus. Modern Art, 1973, Inst. Contemporary Art, 1973, Heyward Gallery, London, Eng., 1977, Stedelijk Mus., Amsterdam, Holland, 1977. Author: The Perfection Underlying Life and the Untroubled Mind, 1973. Address: Galisteo NM 87540. *Not to think but to live directly.*

MARTIN, ALASTAIR BRADLEY, radio chain exec.; b. N.Y.C., Mar. 11, 1915; s. Bradley and Helen Margaret (Phipps) M.; A.B., Princeton, 1938; m. Edith Park, June 15, 1938; children—Dorothy Bradley (Mrs. William H. Moore III), Robin Bradley. Now radio chain exec.; dir. Bessemer Securities Corp., Bessemer Trust N.A., Phipps Guest Agy., N.Y., Bessemer Trust Co., N.J. Formed Guennol Art Collection, exhibited at Met. Mus. Art, N.Y.C., 1970-71; pres. Nat. Tennis Found., 1971-77; pres. A.S.P.C.A., 1973-75; hon. trustee Met. Mus. Art; bd. govs. Bklyn. Mus., 1976—. Served to capt. AUS, 1942-46. U.S. amateur ct. tennis singles champion, 1950-56; elected to Tennis Hall of Fame, 1973. Mem. Regional Broadcasters Group (pres.), U.S. Tennis Assn. (pres. 1969-70), Sherlock Holmes Soc. (Five Orange Pips 1970). Clubs: Racquet and Tennis, Bedford Country. Home: The Belfry Holly Branch Rd Katonah NY 10536 Office: 245 Park Ave 36th Floor New York NY 10017

MARTIN, ALBERT SIDNEY, JR., petroleum co. exec.; b. Edmonson, Tex., Apr. 9, 1930; s. Albert Sidney and Mary Etta (Clift) M.; B.A., U. Tex., 1951; postgrad. Ohio State U., 1971-72; m. Winona

Perkins, June 14, 1952; children—Mary Elizabeth, John, Linda. Asst. mgr. regulatory gas accounting Sun Oil Co., St Davids, Pa., 1961-67, coordinator prodn. accounting, 1968-69, mgr. corporate projects accounting, 1970-71, controller, 1972-79, gen. auditor, chief control auditor, 1979—. C.P.A., Tex. Mem. Am., Pa. insts. C.P.A.'s, Fin. Execs. Inst., Am. Petroleum Inst., Inst. Internal Auditors. Methodist (adminstrv. bd.). Contbr. chpt. to Financial Executives Handbook, 1970. Home: 709 Camp Woods Rd Villanova PA 19085 Office: 100 Matsonford Rd Radnor PA 19087

MARTIN, ALBERTUS, bishop; b. Southbridge, Mass., Oct. 4, 1913; s. Arthur and Parmelie (Beaudoin) M.; B.A., Nicolet Coll., 1935; S.T.D., Laval U., 1941. Ordained priest Roman Cath. Ch., 1939; prof. philosophy Nicolet Coll., 1939-46, dir., 1946-49; vicar gen. Diocese Nicolet, 1949-50, coadjutor bishop, 1950, bishop, 1950—. Mem. commn. for liturgy Council Vatican II. Address: Bishop House PO Box 820 Nicolet PQ J0G 1E0 Canada*

MARTIN, ALBRO, historian, educator; b. Clarksville, Ark., Nov. 21, 1921; s. Albro and Fannie (Taylor) M.; A.B., George Washington U., 1948; A.M., Harvard, 1950; Ph.D. (Ford Found. New Careers fellow, Pres.'s fellow), Columbia, 1970. Economist, U.S. Dept. Agr., Washington, 1949-52; asst. mgr. comml. research and devel. Am. Machine & Foundry Co., N.Y.C., 1953-57; research account exec. J. Walter Thompson Co., N.Y.C., 1957-66; vis. prof. Coll. at New Paltz, N.Y., 1968-69; asso. prof. history Am. U., Washington, 1970-76, on leave, 1973-75; lectr. in bus. history, editor Bus. History Rev., Harvard U., 1976—; cons. in econs. and mktg. Served with USAAF, 1943-46. Recipient Columbia prize in Am. Econ. history in honor of Allan Nevins, 1970. Mem. Am. Hist. Assn., Orgn. Am. Historians (Binkley-Stephenson prize 1975), Econ. History Assn., Bus. History Conf., Phi Beta Kappa, Phi Kappa Phi. Club: Harvard (N.Y.C). Author: Enterprise Denied—Origins of the Decline of American Railroads 1897-1917, 1971; James J. Hill and the Opening of the Northwest, 1976. Home: 34 Nashville Rd Extension Bethel CT 06801 also 6 Soldiers Field Park Boston MA 02163. *It is never too late to take up the work that you ultimately decide is what you really want to do. The man or woman who undertakes at the beginning of his life the work he most wants to do has a lifetime to become disenchanted with it. But he who takes up at 35 or 45 or even 55 the work he really wanted to do at 21 has a self-assurance that is priceless.*

MARTIN, ALEXANDER ROBERT, bus. exec.; b. Toronto, Ont., Can., Sept. 23, 1928; s. Alexander and Janet Murray (McEwan) M.; student pub. schs., Toronto; m. Dorothy Louise Martin, June 13, 1953; children—David Jeffrey, Peter George. With Peat, Marwick, Mitchell & Co., Toronto, 1947-55, Hawker Siddley of Can., Toronto, 1955-57; with Emco, Ltd., London, Ont., 1957—, v.p. Emco Wheaton Internat. Ltd., 1978—. Past pres., bd. dirs. Madame Vanier Children's Services, London; bd. dirs. United Community Services. Chartered accountant, Ont. Mem. Fin. Execs. Inst. Clubs: Sunningdale Country; London. Home: 217 Deer Park London ON N6A 3C2 Canada Office: Suite 303 Plaza One 2000 Argentia Rd Mississauga ON L5N 1P7 Canada

MARTIN, ALFRED, educator; b. Pitts., May 1, 1919; s. Alfred Nicholas and Rachel (Church) M.; B.S., Phila. Coll. Pharmacy and Sci., 1942; M.S., Purdue U., 1948, Ph.D., 1950; m. Mary Ziegler, July 27, 1946; children—Neil, Douglas. Asst. prof. Temple U., 1950-53, asso. prof. 1953-55; asso. prof., then prof. Purdue U., 1955-66; prof. Med. Coll. Va., 1966-68; dean, prof. phys. medicinal chemistry Sch. Pharmacy, Temple U., 1968-73; prof., dir. Drug Dynamics Inst. Coll. Pharmacy U. Tex., 1973-78, C.R. Sublett prof. indsl. pharmacy, 1977—; vis. lectr. Am. Assn. Colls. Pharmacy, 1963, 64; lectr. Indsl. Pharmacy Conf., Arden House, N.Y.C., 1966, 67; Pfeiffer Research fellow Center Applied Wave Mechanics, Paris, 1962, 63; indsl. cons., 1961—. Served with USMCR, 1942-46; PTO. Decorated Navy Air medal, Navy Gold star. Sturmer lectr. Phila., 1967, Kauffman lectr. Ohio State U., 1970; 1st distinguished vis. pharm. scientist U. Manchester (Eng.), 1976. Fellow Acad. Pharm. Scis. (chmn. basic pharmaceutics sect.); mem. Am. Chem. Soc., Am. Pharm. Assn. (Ebert medal 1967, Research Achievement award 1967), Sigma Xi, Rho Chi (Nat. award 1968), Kappa Psi. Author: Physical Pharmacy, 2d edit., 1969; co-author: Burger's Medicinal Chemistry, 1970; American Pharmacy, 1965, 74. Editor pharmaceutics sect. Remington's Pharmaceutical Sciences, 1970, 74. Home: 5404 Ridge Oak Dr Austin TX 78731

MARTIN, ALFRED MANUEL (BILLY), profl. baseball mgr.; b. Berkeley, Calif., May 16, 1928; s. Jack and Joan (Salvini) Downey; grad. Berkeley High Sch., 1946; m. Lois E. Berndt, Oct. 4, 1950 (div. Oct. 1953); 1 dau., Kelly Ann; m. 2d, Gretchen Winkler, Oct. 7, 1959; 1 son, Billy Joe. With Oakland (Calif.) Oaks, 1947-50; 2d baseman N.Y. Yankees, 1950-57, Kansas City Athletics, 1957; short stop Detroit Tigers, 1957-58; infielder Cleve. Indians, 1959; 2d baseman Cin. Reds, 1960, Milw. Braves, 1961; with Minn. Twins, 1961-69, coach, scout, 1965-68, mgr., 1968-69; mgr. Denver Bears, 1969, Minn. Twins, 1969, Detroit Tigers, 1970-73, Tex. Rangers, 1974-75, N.Y. Yankees, 1975—; asst. to pres. Valjon Corp., Mpls., 1970; dir. Bank Jacomo, Blue Springs, Mo.; exec. v.p. Shiloh Devel. Co., Lee's Summit, Mo., 1973. Mem. tribal council Nat. Congress Am. Indians, 1953—. Served with AUS, 1950-51, 53-55. Clubs: Moose, Elks. Office: NY Yankees Yankee Stadium Bronx NY 10451*

MARTIN, ALILEA HAYWOOD, food processing co. exec.; b. Ft. Worth, Oct. 12, 1921; d. William Franklin and Ophelia (Ferrell) Haywood; B.A., U. Mich., 1943; m. Thomas Martin, June 15, 1973. Adminstrv. asst., civilian in charge Signal Office, Stockton (Calif.) Ordnance Depot, 1943-47; sec. to v.p., treas. Tillie Lewis Foods, Inc. (named changed to Ogden Food Products Corp. 1979), Stockton, 1947-59, sec. to pres., adminstrv. supr., 1961—, sec., 1965—. Mem. Citizens Com. to Study Area-Wide Jr. Coll., Stockton, 1961-62; mem. World Affairs Council, Stockton, 1971—. Mem. AAUW (past pres.), Assn. Women in Public Office (past chmn. Calif. chpt), Bus. Profl. Women's Club (Bus. Woman of Yr. 1965, chmn. Calif. public relations com. 1963-64), LWV, Friends Public Library. Club: Order Eastern Star. Office: Ogden Foods Products Corp PO Drawer J Stockton CA 95201

MARTIN, ALLEN, lawyer; b. Manchester, Conn., Aug. 12, 1937; s. Richard and Ruth Palmer (Smith) M.; B.A., Williams Coll., 1960; B.A., Oxford U., 1962; LL.B., Harvard, 1965; children—Elizabeth Palmer, Samuel Bates; m. Bonnie Williams Reid, Sept. 8, 1979. Admitted to Vt. bar, 1970; partner firm Downs, Rachlin and Martin, St. Johnsbury and Burlington, Vt., 1971—; dir. Union Mut. Fire Ins. Co., New Eng. Guaranty Ins. Co. Chmn., Vt. Bd. Edn., 1979—; vice chmn. Vt. Judicial Responsibility Bd., 1978—. Mem. Am. Law Inst., Am., Vt. bar assns. Republican. Office: 9 Prospect St Saint Johnsbury VT 05819

MARTIN, ALVIN CHARLES, lawyer; b. Bklyn., Oct. 25, 1933; s. George and Dora (Gitlin) M.; B.B.A., Coll. City N.Y., 1954; J.D., Harvard U., 1957; LL.M. in Taxation, N.Y. U., 1963; m. Susan Goldman, Sept. 3, 1959; children—Robert, Peter. Admitted to N.Y. bar, 1958, N.J. bar, 1977; practiced in N.Y.C., 1958-76, Newark, 1977—; formerly with Office of Regional Counsel, IRS, firm Curtis Mallet-Prevost Colt & Mosle; partner firm Zissu, Halper & Martin, 1966-76, Shanley & Fisher, 1977—; sec. Vornado, Inc., 1966-79, exec. v.p., gen. counsel, asst. to chmn. bd., 1971-76, v.p., 1977-79, also dir., 1967-79, mem. exec. com., 1971-79; adj. prof. Taxation N.Y. U., 1972—; dir. Gen. Microwave Corp., 1972-75; mem. taxation faculty Pace Coll. Grad. Sch. Bus. Adminstrn., 1964-70, Baruch Sch. Bus. and Pub. Adminstrn. Served with U.S. Army, 1957. Clubs: Montammy Golf (Alpine, N.J.); Essex (Newark); Ahdeek Tennis (Bergenfield, N.J.). Home: 192 Elm St Tenafly NJ 07670 Office: 550 Broad St Newark NJ 07102

MARTIN, ANTHONY ALPHONSE, librarian; b. Pitts., Aug. 18, 1920; s. John A. and Anna (Pocunis) M.; B. Ed., Duquesne U., 1942; B.S., Carnegie Library Sch. Carnegie Inst. Tech., 1946; postgrad. U. Pitts., 1946-49; m. Julia Claire Wallace, June 28, 1952; children—Michele, Anthony J., Anita. Chief librarian North side brs. Carnegie Library, Pitts., 1956-64, asst. dir. library, 1964-69, dir., 1969—; dir., pres. City Pitts. Northside Parking Corp., 1963—, Pitts. Regional Library Center, Inc., 1969—; dir. WQED Ednl. TV. Treas., Council for Computerized Library Networks, 1974—. Mem. Pa. Adv. Com. Service to Blind and Phys. Handicapped; bd. visitors U. Pitts., 1976; bd. dirs. OCLC, 1978—; mem. Pa. Adv. Council on Library Devel., 1978—. Served with USAAF, 1942-45. Decorated Air Medal with oak leaf cluster; recipient Distinguished Alumnus award U. Pitts., 1975. Mem. Am., Pa. library assns., Spl. Libraries Assn., World Affairs Council, Pitts. Bibliophiles. Editor: Tech. Book Rev. Index, 1956-69; mem. adv. bd. Inter Poetry Forum. Home: 3338 Sylvan Rd Bethel Park PA 15102 Office: 4400 Forbes Ave Pittsburgh PA 15213

MARTIN, ARCHER JOHN PORTER, chemist; b. London, Eng., Mar. 1, 1910; s. William Archer Porter and Lilian Kate (Brown) M.; student Peterhouse, Cambridge, Eng., 1929-32, M.A., 1936, PH.D.; D.Sc., Leeds U., 1968; LL.D. (hon.), Glasgow, 1973; m. Judith Bagenal, Jan. 9, 1943; 5 children. Chemist, Nutritional Lab., Cambridge, Eng., 1933-38, Wool Industries Research Assn., Leeds, Eng., 1938-46; research dept. Boots Pure Drug Co., Nottingham, Eng., 1946-48; staff Med. Research Council, 1948-52; head phys. chemistry div. Nat. Inst. Med. Research, Mill Hill, 1952-56; chem. cons., 1956-59; dir. Abbotsbury Labs. Ltd., 1959-73; profl. fellow U. Sussex (Eng.), 1973—; Robert A. Welch prof. chemistry U. Houston, 1974—. Cons., Wellcome Research Labs., Beckenham, Kent, Eng., 1970-73; Extraordinary prof. Tech. U., Eindhoven, The Netherlands, 1965-74. Decorated comdr. Brit. Empire; Order of Rising Sun (Japan); recipient Berzelius Gold medal Swedish Med. Soc., 1951; Nobel prize chemistry (with R. L. M. Synge) for invention of partition chromatography, 1952; John Scott award, 1958; John Price Wetherill medal, 1959; Franklin Inst. medal, 1959; Koltoff medal Acad. Pharm. Sci., 1969; Callendar medal Inst. Measurement & Control, 1971. Fellow Royal Soc.; mem. Royal Soc. (Leverhulme medal 1964). Club: Chemist's (hon.) (N.Y.C.). Home: Abbotsbury Barnet Ln Elstree Herts England Office: U Houston Houston TX 77004*

MARTIN, ARMOUR EMERSON, lawyer; b. N.Y.C., May 11, 1917; s. Emile F. and Alice (Sadowich) M.; A.B., Columbia, 1938, J.D., 1940; m. Mary Sirman, July 6, 1946; children—Mary Alison, Armour Emerson II. Exec. sec. stock trust certificate holders com. So. Ry., Mobile, Ala. and Ohio, 1940-42; admitted to N.Y. State bar, 1942, U.S. Supreme Ct. bar, 1970; practiced in N.Y.C., 1946—; mem. firm Appleton, Rice and Perrin, 1961-63, Emmet, Marvin and Martin, 1963-68, Armour Emerson Martin, 1946-61, 69—. Pres., dir. Internat. Turbocar Industries Corp., 1973—. Lectr. Columbia Law Sch., N.Y.C., 1952; mem. policy planning staff internat. security affairs Office Sec. Defense, 1961-62. Commr. Nassau County council Boy Scouts Am., 1958; campaign chmn. Community Chest, Port Washington, N.Y., 1953-54, also mem. exec. com., 1953-59, pres., 1955-56. Trustee Bie Family Found., 1966—. Served to capt. AUS, 1942-46; lt. col. Res. ret. Mem. N.Y. State Bar Assn., Mil. Order Fgn. Wars (judge adv., mem. council 1975—), Delta Phi. Clubs: Sands Point (N.Y.) Bath and Racquet (dir. 1963-70, treas. 1964-70, v.p. 1965-70); Princeton of N.Y. (N.Y.C.). Home: Bedford Rd Port Washington NY 11050 Office: 230 Park Ave New York NY 11017

MARTIN, BEN, sports cons.; b. Prospect Park, Pa., June 28, 1921; s. Benjamin S. and Elsie (Wilson) M.; student Princeton, 1940-42; B.S., U.S. Naval Acad., 1946; m. Harriet Jones, June 9, 1945; children—Lawrence A., Ben R. Commd. ensign U.S. Navy, 1945, advanced through grades to lt., 1949; asst. football coach U.S. Naval Acad., Annapolis, Md., 1946-55; resigned, 1955; head coach U. Va., 1956-57, USAF Acad. (Colo.), 1958-78; sports cons. Mem. Am. Football Coaches Assn. (past pres.). Episcopalian. Rotarian. Author: Flexible T Offense, 1961; Football End Play, 1962. Home: 6440 Nanette Way Colorado Springs CO 80907

MARTIN, BERNARD, educator; b. Seklence, Czechoslovakia, Mar. 13, 1928; s. Benjamin Adam and Helen Hersh (Kowitz) M.; came to U.S., 1934, naturalized, 1939; B.A., U. Chgo., 1947; M.H.L., Hebrew Union Coll., 1951; Ph.D., U. Ill., 1961; m. Nancy Louise Platt, June 30, 1955; children—Rachel, Joseph Louis. Ordained rabbi, 1951; rabbi in Champaign, Ill., 1951-57; asso. rabbi, Chgo., 1957-61; sr. rabbi, St. Paul, 1961-65; Abba Hillel Silver prof. Jewish studies Case Western Res. U., 1966—, chmn. dept. religion, 1967—. Chmn. com. theology Central Conf. Am. Rabbis, 1965-71. Bd. dirs. Cleve. chpt. NCCJ, 1966-71; trustee Cleve. Jewish Fedn., 1967-74. Served with AUS, 1953-55. Mem. Am. Acad. Jewish Research, Am. Philos. Assn., Am. Acad. Religion, Central Conf. Am. Rabbis, Nat. Assn. Profs. Hebrew. Author: The Existentialist Theology of Paul Tillich, 1963; Prayer in Judaism, 1968; Great Twentieth Century Jewish Philosophers, 1969; (with Daniel J. Silver) A History of Judaism, 1974; (novel) That Man from Smyrna, 1978. Translator: Athens and Jerusalem (Lev Shestov) 1966; Potestas Clavium, 1968; History of Jewish Literature, 12 vols. (Israel Zinberg), 1972-78; When All is Said and Done (David Bergelson), 1978. Editor: Contemporary Reform Jewish Thought, 1968; A Shestov Anthology, 1970; Issues and Movements in American Judaism, 1978; Jour. Central Conf. Am. Rabbis, 1975-77, Jour. Reform Judaism, 1977—. Home: 2593 Dysart Rd University Heights OH 44118 Office: Yost Hall Case Western Res Univ Cleveland OH 44106

MARTIN, BERNARD LEE, coll. dean; b. Dayton, Ohio, May 29, 1923; s. Harley L. and Clare (Murphy) M.; B.A., Athenaeum of Ohio, 1941-45; M.A. in History, Xavier U., 1950, M.B.A., 1955; Ph.D. in Econs., U. Cin., 1963; Ph.D. Humane Letters (hon.), Canisius Coll., 1978; m. Mary Patricia McDonald, Nov. 23, 1950; children—Joseph, Mary, David, Patrick, Paul, Timothy, Michael, Christopher. Mem. faculty Xavier U., Cin., 1948-65, asst. prof. bus. adminstrn., 1955-62, asso. prof. mktg., 1962-65, chmn. mktg. dept., 1961; chmn., prof. mktg. Eastern Mich. U., Ypsilanti, 1965-66; dean Sch. Bus. Adminstrn., Canisius Coll., Buffalo, 1966-71, acting acad. v.p., 1971-73, dean sch. bus. adminstrn., 1973-78; dean McLaren Coll. Bus. Adminstrn., U. San Francisco, 1978—. Ford Found. grantee Harvard, 1964. Mem. Am. Mktg. Assn., Am. Econ. Assn., Sales and Mktg. Execs., Am. Assn. Univ. Adminstrs. Author: (with others) Contemporary Economic Problems and Issues, 3d edit., 1973. Home: 3670 Trintel Ct Walnut Creek CA 94598 Office: 2130 Fulton St San Francisco CA 94117

MARTIN, BOYD ARCHER, educator; b. Cottonwood, Idaho, Mar. 3, 1911; s. Archer Olmstead and Norah Claudine (Imbler) M.; student U. Idaho, 1929-30, 35-36, B.S., 1936; student Pasadena Jr. Coll., 1931-32, U. Calif. at Los Angeles, summer 1934; A.M., Stanford, 1937, Ph.D., 1943; m. Grace Charlotte Swingler, Dec. 29, 1933; children—Michael Archer, William Archer. Research asst. Stanford U., 1936-37, teaching asst., 1937-38; instr. polit. sci. U. Idaho, 1938-39; acting instr. polit. sci. Stanford U., 1939-40; John M. Switzer fellow, summer, 1939-40; chief personnel officer Walter Butler Constrn. Co., Farragut Naval Tng. Center, summer 1942; instr. polit. sci. U. Idaho, 1940-43, asst. prof. polit. sci., 1943-44, asso. prof. polit. sci., 1944-47, prof., head dept. social sci., asst. dean Coll. Letters and Sci., 1947-55, dean, 1955-70, Borah Distinguished prof. polit. sci., 1970-73, prof., dean emeritus, 1973—. Vis. prof. Stanford U., summer 1946, spring 1952, U. Calif., 1962-63, affiliate Center for Study Higher Edn., at Berkeley, 1962-63; mem. steering com. N.W. Conf. on Higher Edn., 1960-67, pres. conf., 1966-67; mem. bd. Am. Assn. of Partners of Alliance for Progress; chmn. Ida. Adv. Council on Higher Edn.; del. Gt. Plains UNESCO Conf., Denver, 1947, chmn. bd. William E. Borah Found. on the Causes of War and the Conditions of Peace, 1947-55; mem. Commn. to Study Orgn. Peace; dir. Bur. Pub. Affair Research, 1959-73, dir. emeritus, 1973—; dir. Inst. Human Behavior, 1970—. Mem. Am. Polit. Sci. Assn., (exec. council 1952-53), Nat. Municipal League, Am. Soc. Pub. Adminstrn., Fgn. Policy Assn., UN Assn., AAUP, Western Polit. Sci. Assn. (pres. 1950), Phi Beta Kappa, Pi Gamma Mu, Kappa Delta Pi, Pi Sigma Alpha. Author: The Direct Primary in Idaho, 1947; (with others) Introduction to Political Science, 1950; (with other) Western Politics, 1968; Politics in the American West, 1969; (with Sydney Duncombe) Recent Elections in Idaho (1964-70), 1972; Idaho Voting Trends: Party Realignment and Percentage of Voters for Candidates, Parties and Elections, 1890-1974, 1975. Editor: The Responsibilities of Colleges and Universities, 1967. Contbr. to Ency. Britannica, 1974, also articles in polit. sci. to reviews. Home: 1314 Walenta Dr Moscow ID 83843. *Attempt to contribute to society to the maximum of your ability. Assume responsibility in positions commensurwith the obligations and accountability of the position. In making decisions, first gather all factual data, interpret it fairly, make the decision, and assume responsibility for the decision. In dealing with people, whether family, friends, professionals, or adversaries, try to remember the sensitivity of personal feelings and personal pride. Commend people who achieve and contribute. Be completely honest; when you don't know, admit it.*

MARTIN, BRUCE DOUGLAS, univ. dean; b. Rochester, N.Y., Apr. 8, 1934; s. Frederic and Harriet Emily (Krieger) M.; B.S. in Pharmacy, Albany Coll. Pharmacy, 1955; M.S. in Pharm. Chemistry, U. Ill., 1959, Ph.D., 1962; m. Geraldine Ann Coughlin, July 6, 1957; children—James Scott, Robert Douglas. Asst. prof. Sch. Pharmacy Duquesne U., 1961-64, asso. prof., 1964-68, prof., chmn. dept. pharm. chemistry, 1968-73, dean, 1971—, acting dean health professions, 1979-80. Mem. Council Pharmacy Pa. Fulbright lectr. U. Sci. and Tech., Kumasi, Ghana, 1968-69. Mem. Pa., Allegheny County (exec. bd. 1970—), Am. pharm. assns., Am. Chem. Soc., Chem. Soc. London, Acad. Pharm. Scis., Am. Inst. Chemists, Pa. Acad. Sci. (pres. elect 1978-80), AAUP, Sigma Xi, Kappa Psi, Rho Chi, Sigma Pi Sigma, Alpha Epsilon Delta, Phi Delta Chi, Omicron Delta Kappa. Home: 2648 Sapling St Allison Park PA 15101 Office: Duquesne U Sch Pharmacy Pittsburgh PA 15219

MARTIN, CHARLES E., artist; b. Chelsea, Mass., Jan. 12, 1910; s. Charles and Barbara (Cady) Mastrangelo; m. Florence J. Taylor, June 2, 1934; 1 son, Jared Christopher. Painting supr. teaching div. Fed. Art Project, 1933-37; under contract to New Yorker mag., 1937—; art cartoonist PM, 1939-42; one-man shows include Rockland Found., 1951, Ruth White Gallery, N.Y.C., 1955, 60, Bklyn. Mus., 1954-65, Graham Gallery, 1973; continual exhibit Nicholls Gallery, N.Y.C.; represented permanent collections Met. Mus., Mus. City N.Y., Library of Congress, Syracuse U.; tchr. painting Bklyn. Mus. Art Sch., 1965; cover designs for nat. mags., including 160 for New Yorker under initials C.E.M. Served with AUS, 1942-44; ETO. Mem. Cartoonist Guild Am. (past pres.), Soc. Mag. Cartoonists, Overseas Press Club. Home: Monhegan Island ME 04852 also 39-22 47 St Sunnyside Long Island City NY 11101

MARTIN, CHARLES WALLACE, travel exec., ret. univ. adminstr.; b. Columbia, S.C., Feb. 1, 1916; s. Earle Purkerson and Caroline Louise (Keenan) M.; B.A., U. S.C., 1936; m. Nancy Miles Chisolm, Sept. 30, 1944; children—Nancy Miles, Charles Wallace, Louise Elizabeth. Br. office employee N.Y. Life Ins. Co., Columbia, 1936-38; mgr. Palmetto Theatre Co., Columbia, 1938-42; mgr. Reamer Appliance Co., Columbia, 1946-47; local sales mgr. WIS Radio, Columbia, 1947-50; pres., gen. mgr. WMSC Radio, Columbia, 1950-60; dir. devel. U. S.C., Columbia, 1960-66, exec. dir. ednl. found., 1960-77, v.p. for devel., 1966-77, instr. English, 1948-52. Dir. Security Fed. Savs. and Loan, Columbia; adv. bd. Bankers Trust S.C., Columbia, 1960-78. Chmn. United Way Columbia, 1954; pres. Columbia Philharmonic Orch., 1967-68. Commr., Columbia Housing Authority, 1971-76, chmn. 1974-76. Bd. dirs. Bus. Partners Found., 1969-77; co-chmn. S.C. Gov.'s Mansion Found., 1979—; vestryman Trinity Cathedral, Columbia; chmn. Trinity Found. Served to lt. USNR, 1942-45. Named Young Man of Year Columbia, 1951. Mem. Columbia Stage Soc. (dir. 1947-59, 66-69), Greater Columbia C. of C. (pres. 1959), S.C. Broadcasters Assn. (pres. 1954), Am. Coll. Pub. Relations Assn. (dir., treas. Mason-Dixon dist., 1967-72), English-Speaking Union U.S. (pres. Columbia br. 1973-75, nat. dir. 1972-75), Sigma Nu, Omicron Delta Kappa, Pi Gamma Mu. Episcopalian. Kiwanian (pres. 1957), Clubs: Forest Lake, Pine Tree Hunt, Centurion Soc., Columbia Ball, Forum. Home: 1424 Heatherwood Rd Columbia SC 29205

MARTIN, CLARENCE EUGENE, JR., lawyer; b. Martinsburg, W.Va., Sept. 10, 1909; s. Clarence E. and Agnes G. (McKenna) M.; A.B., Cath. U. Am., 1931, LL.B., 1934; m. Catherine duBois Silver, June 6, 1942; 1 son, Clarence Eugene III. Admitted to W.Va. bar, 1934; since practiced in Martinsburg; chmn. bd. Mchts. & Farmers Bank. Mem. W.Va. State Senate, 1950-70. Served as lt. USNR, World War II. Fellow Am. Coll. Trial Lawyers, Am. Bar Found.; mem. Am. Bar Assn., West Va. State Bar (pres. 1954-55), W.Va. (pres. 1962-63), Berkeley County Bar assns., Am. Judicature Soc., Internat. Assn. Ins. Counsel, Am. Law Inst. Home: 107 N Rosemont Ave Martinsburg WV 25401 Office: 119 S College St Martinsburg WV 25401

MARTIN, CLAUDE RAYMOND, JR., mktg. cons., educator; b. Harrisburg, Pa., May 11, 1932; s. Claude R. and Marie Teresa (Stapf) M.; B.S., U. Scranton, 1954, M.B.A, 1963; Ph.D., Columbia U., 1969; m. Marie Frances Culkin, Nov. 16, 1957; children—Elizabeth Ann, David Jude, Nancy Marie, William Jude, Patrick Jude, Cecilia Marie. Newsman, Sta. WILK-TV, Wilkes-Barre, Pa., 1953-55; news dir. Sta. WNEP-TV, Scranton, Pa., 1955-60; dir. systems Blue Cross & Blue Shield Ins., Wilkes-Barre, 1960-63; lectr. mktg. St. Francis Coll., Bklyn., 1964; lectr. mktg. U. Mich., Ann Arbor, 1965-68, asst. prof., 1968-73, asso. prof., 1973-77, prof., 1977—; dir. Huron Valley Bank, Ann Arbor; cons. mktg., 1966—. Served with USNR, 1955-57. Mem. Acad. Mktg. Sci., Am. Mktg. Assn., S.W. Mktg. Assn., Bank Mktg. Assn., Assn. Consumer Research, Am. Collegiate Retailing Assn. Roman Catholic. Contbr. articles on mktg. analysis, consumer research to profl. publs. Home: 1116 Aberdeen Dr Ann Arbor MI 48104

MARTIN, DANIEL WILLIAM, acoustical physicist; b. Georgetown, Ky., Nov. 18, 1918; s. Dean William and Ethel (Weigle) M.; A.B., Georgetown Coll., 1937; M.S., U. Ill., 1939, Ph.D., 1941; m. Martha Elizabeth Parker, June 9, 1941; children—Mary Elizabeth, David William, Nancy Jane, Donald Warren. Asst. physics U. Ill. at Urbana, 1937-41; with RCA, 1941-49, tech. coordinator, 1946-49; acoustical research supr. Baldwin Piano Co., Cin., 1949-57; research dir. D.H. Baldwin Co., Cin., 1957-70, 74—, chief engr., 1970-74; extension instr. math. Purdue U., 1941-46; asst. prof. mus. acoustics U. Cin., 1964-73, asso. prof., 1973-75. Fellow Acoustical Soc. Am. (exec. council 1957-60), Audio Engring. Soc. (pres. 1964-65), IEEE (nat. chmn. audio group 1956-57); mem. Engring. Soc. Cin. (dir. 1964-67, pres. 1969-70), Tech. and Sci. Socs. Council Cin. (pres. 1967-68; Cin. Engr. Year 1972), Am. Soc. Engring. Edn., Cin. Patent Law Assn., Nat. Council Presbyn. Men (pres. 1977), Nat. Soc. Profl. Engrs. (Ohio Engr. Year 1972). Republican. Presbyterian. Author, patentee in field. Editor: I.R.E. Trans. on Audio, 1953-55; asso. editor Sound, 1961-63; patent reviewer Jour. Acoustical Soc. Am., 1950—, asso. editor, 1977—. Home: 7349 Clough Pike Cincinnati OH 45244 Office: 1801 Gilbert Ave Cincinnati OH 45202. *A Christian home, economic need, and early choice of profession gave me momentum. Generous personal assistance and teaching, professional opportunity and family stability sustained my efforts. The byproducts of striving for goals are just as valuable as the realization of goals. Building bridges between disciplines is difficult but intellectually stimulating. Great are the rewards of service to profession, people and the church.*

MARTIN, DAVID ALLAN, economist; b. Providence, Mar. 27, 1937; s. Raymond A. and Jane (Wood) M.; B.A., U. R.I., 1958, M.S., 1960; certificate U. Oslo, 1959; Ph.D., Syracuse U., 1964; m. Heather Ann Page, June 21, 1961; 1 dau., Kristen Ann. Instr. econs. U. R.I., 1960-61; asst. prof. Harpur Coll., State U. N.Y., 1963-66; vis. prof. Syracuse U., 1965-66; prof. econs., head Sch. Bus., State U. Coll., Geneseo, N.Y., 1966—; exec. dir. Genesee Region Council Econ. Edn., 1967—. Bd. dirs. Consumer Credit Counseling Service, Rochester, N.Y.; regional dir. Omicron Delta Epsilon. Recipient 1st prize, coll. div. Kazanjian Found., 1965. Mem. Am. Econ. Assn., Am. Fin. Assn., Econ. History Assn., Assn. Evolutionary Econs. Author: Introductory Economic Theory, 1971; also articles. Home: 22 Melody Ln Geneseo NY 14454

MARTIN, DAVID NATHAN, advt. agy. exec.; b. Tucson, Ariz., Apr. 19, 1930; s. Hawley P. and Evelyn (Stadelman) M.; B.S., Hampden-Sydney Coll., 1952; m. Charlotte Louise Williams, Aug. 9, 1952; children—Sarah, Susan, Robert, David. Advt. mgr. Eastern Shore Times, Berlin, Md., 1952-53; broadcast producer Vansant Dugdale & Co., Balt., 1953-56; v.p. Cargill Wilson & Acree Inc., Richmond, Va., 1956-65; pres. Martin Agy. Inc., Richmond, 1965—. Mem. Gov.'s Com. Consumer Edn., 1974—; chmn. Team of Progress Richmond, 1971-73; v.p. United Givers Fund, 1972-74; pres. Richmond Ballet, 1966-69; pres. Better Bus. Bur. Richmond, 1964-65. Bd. dirs. Richmond Meml. Hosp., Richmond Eye Hosp., J. Sargeant Reynolds Community Coll., 1970-76. Named Outstanding Young Man, Richmond Jaycees, 1961, Advt. Man of Year, Richmond Advt. Club, 1966. Mem. Young Pres.'s Orgn., Am. Assn. Advt. Agys., Va. C. of C. Episcopalian. Clubs: Commonwealth, Country of Va. (Richmond); Princess Anne Country (Virginia Beach, Va.). Home: 328 Clovelly Rd Richmond VA 23221 Office: Martin Bldg 500 N Allen Ave Richmond VA 23220

MARTIN, DEAN, actor; b. Steubenville, Ohio, June 17, 1917; ed. high sch.; m. Elizabeth Ann McDonald, 1940 (div. 1949); children—Craig, Claudia, Gail, Deanna; m. 2d, Jeanne Bieggers, 1949 (div.); children—Dino, Ricci, Gina; m. 3d, Cathy Hawn, 1973 (div.). Successively employed odd jobs Weirton, W.Va.; welterweight boxer; amateur dance band singer; singer with Ernie McKay's band, later in night clubs; formed comedy team with Jerry Lewis, 1946, appeared in night clubs, theatres, radio and TV programs, also motion pictures; now appearing as single; former star on weekly TV show NBC; appeared various motion pictures including You've Never Too Young, 1955, Artists and Models, 1955, Pardners, 1956, Ten Thousand Bedrooms, 1957, Young Lions, 1958, Some Came Running, Career, 1959, Who Was That Lady, Bells Are Ringing, Ocean's 11, 1960, Ada, 1961, Toys in the Attic, 1963, What A Way to Go, Silencers, Texas Across The River, Murderer's Row, Airport, 1970, Mr. Ricco, 1975; recorded albums including That's Amore, Everybody Loves Somebody, Welcome to My World, Memories Are Made of This. Home: 601 Mountain Dr Beverly Hills CA 90210 Office: care of Chasin-Park-Citron Agy 9255 Sunset Blvd Los Angeles CA 90069*

MARTIN, DEAN FREDERICK, chemist, educator; b. Woodburn, Iowa, Apr. 6, 1933; s. Herman A. and Frances M. (Rausis) M.; A.B., Grinnell Coll., 1955; Ph.D., Pa. State U., 1958; m. Barbara Bursa, Dec. 22, 1956; children—Diane, Bruce, John, Paul, Brian, Eric. NSF postdoctoral fellow Univ. Coll., London, 1958-59; instr. inorganic chemistry U. Ill., 1959-61, asst. prof., 1961-64; asso. prof. chemistry U. South Fla., Tampa, 1964-69, prof., 1969—; vis. prof. physiology and pharmacology Duke, 1970-71. Recipient Alumni award Grinnell Coll., 1971. USPHS research career award, 1969-74. Mem. Am. Chem. Soc., Chem. Soc. (London), Alpha Chi Sigma, Phi Beta Kappa, Sigma Xi. Roman Catholic. Author: (with Barbara B. Martin) Coordination Compounds, 1964; (with Therald Moeller) Laboratory Chemistry, 1965; Marine Chemistry, 2 vols., 1968, 70. Editor: (with George M. Padilla) Marine Pharmacognosy, 1973. Home: 3402 Valencia Rd Tampa FL 33618

MARTIN, DON STANLEY, JR., educator; b. Indpls., Feb. 19, 1919; s. Don Stanley and Laura (Beck) M.; B.S., Purdue U., 1939; Ph.D., Calif. Inst. Tech., 1944; m. Marion Adele Campbell, Dec. 20, 1949; children—Marion A., Don Stanley III, Laura J. Research and devel. Los Alamos Labs., 1941-44; mem. faculty Iowa State U., 1946—, prof. inorganic chemistry, sr. chemist Ames Lab. of AEC, 1946—. Mem. Am. Chem. Soc., Am. Phys. Soc., Soc. Ia. Acad. Scis., Sigma Xi. Asso. editor Inorganica Chimica Acta Reviews, 1967-73; adv. bd. Inorganica Chimica Acta, 1974—. Research and publs. on isotopic exchange reactions, chemistry of platinum group of metals, kinetics of ligand replacement reactions, crystal spectroscopy, radioactivities and radiochemistry. Home: 2033 Ashmore Dr Ames IA 50010

MARTIN, DONALD RAY, educator, chemist; b. Marion, Ohio, Oct. 21, 1915; s. Royal Frederick and Goldia Ferne (Gelbaugh) M.; A.B., Otterbein Coll., 1937; M.S., Western Res. U., 1940, Ph.D. in Inorganic Chemistry, 1941; m. Katherine Gertrude Newton, Feb. 4, 1939; children—Donald Ray II, Thomas Newton. Lectr. chemistry Western Res. U., 1940-42, lab. mgr. Naval research project, 1941-43; instr., then asst. prof. chemistry U. Ill., 1943-51; head chem. metall. br., metall. div. U.S. Naval Research Lab., 1951-52; lab. mgr. govt. research. Mathieson Chem. Corp., 1952-56; mgr. chem. research, aviation div. Olin Mathieson Chem. Corp., 1956-57, asso. dir. fuels research, energy div., 1957-60; dir. research Libbey-Owens-Ford Glass Co., 1960-61; with Harshaw Chem. Co., 1961-68, v.p. research and devel., 1967-68; prof. inorganic chemistry U. Tex. at Arlington, 1969—, chmn. dept. chemistry, 1969-76. Mem. Coll. Chemistry Consultants Service, 1971-76. Mem. com. examiners Grad. Record Exam. for Advanced Chemistry, 1962-70; mem. chem. tech. adv. com. Cuyahoga Community Coll., 1965-70. Adv. bd. Euclid (Ohio) Orch. and Chorus, 1965-68, pres., 1966; trustee Otterbein Coll., 1962-72. Recipient Distinguished Sci. Achievement award Otterbein Coll., 1970. Life fellow AAAS; fellow Chem. Soc. (London); mem. Am. Chem. Soc. (chmn. div. inorganic chemistry 1962), Electrochem. Soc., Sigma Xi (chpt. v.p. 1975-77, chpt. pres. 1978-80), Phi Lambda Upsilon, Sigma Zeta, Alpha Chi Sigma. Presbyterian (elder). Kiwanian (pres. Arlington 1970-71, distinguished lt. gov. 1973-74, dist. sec. 1976-77, Kiwanian of Yr. award Euclid Club 1966). Author: (with H.S. Booth) Boron Trifluoride and Its Derivatives, 1949. Home: 3311 Cambridge Dr Arlington TX 76013

MARTIN, DONALD WILLIAM, psychiatrist; b. Columbus, Ohio, Aug. 13, 1921; s. Olin R. and Clara (Jahraus) M.; B.A., Ohio State U., 1942, M.D., 1944; m. Clara Jane Jones, June 23, 1951; children—Jennifer Christine, David Lawrence. Intern, Met. Hosp., N.Y.C., 1944-45; resident psychiatrist Kings Park (N.Y.) State Hosp., 1945-46, sr. psychiatrist, 1948-49; supervising psychiatrist Central Islip (N.Y.) State Hosp., 1950-56; staff psychiatrist Summit County Receiving Hosp. (name now Fallsview Psy. Hosp.), Cuyahoga Falls, Ohio, 1956-59, supt., 1959-63; dir. Pontiac (Mich.) State Hosp. (name now Clinton Valley Center), 1963-79; pvt. practice cons. psychiatry, 1979—. Served from 1st lt. to capt., M.C., USAAF, 1946-48. Fellow Am. Psychiat. Assn.; mem. Mich. Med. Soc. Address: 2859 E Maple Rd Apt 10 Birmingham MI 48008

MARTIN, EDLEY WAINRIGHT, JR., educator; b. Texarkana, Tex., Apr. 29, 1927; s. Edley Wainright and Catherine (Smith) M.; B.S., Hendrix Coll., 1947; B.E.E., Ga. Inst. Tech., 1946; Ph.D., Ohio State U., 1953; m. Charlene Ruth Studor, Sept. 2, 1950; children—Robert, Linda, Nancy, Anne. Applied sci. rep. IBM, 1953-56; asso. prof. bus. adminstrn. Ind. U., Bloomington, 1956-61, prof. bus. adminstrn., 1961—; vis. prof. U. Hawaii, 1968-69. Served with USNR, 1944-46. Author: Electronic Data Processing, 1961, rev., 1965; Mathematics for Decision Making, 1969; (with others) Computers and Information Systems, 1973. Home: 3703 Brownridge Rd Bloomington IN 47401

MARTIN, EDWARD DANA, govt. ofcl.; b. Honolulu, Mar. 27, 1941; s. Edward and Kathryn (Kitchen) Redington (adopted by Geoffrey Matthew Martin); A.B., U. Kans., 1966, M.D., 1970; m. Dana Foster, Oct. 8, 1976; children—Therese, Brendan. Intern, then resident in pediatrics Montefiore Hosp., N.Y.C., 1970-71; resident in pediatrics Dr. Martin Luther King, Jr. Health Center, N.Y.C., 1971, dir. health services, 1971-73; dir. Nat. Health Service Corps, Rockville, Md., 1974-75; dir. Bur. Community Health Services, USPHS, Rockville, 1975—. Served with USN, 1959-64. Contbr. articles to profl. jours. Home: 314 New Mark Esplanade Rockville MD 20850 Office: 7-05 Parklawn Bldg 5600 Fishers Ln Rockville MD 20857

MARTIN, EDWIN (JOHN), psychologist; b. Washington, Mar. 14, 1934; s. Richard Edwin and Florence (Johnson) M.; B.S. in Math., N.Mex. State U., 1960; Ph.D. in Psychology, U. Iowa, 1963; m. Helen Onis Tilley, Aug. 22, 1959; children—Theresa, John Charles. Mem. faculty dept. psychology U. Mich., Ann Arbor, 1963-74, asso. prof., 1967-71, prof., 1971-74; prof. dept. psychology U. Kans., Lawrence, 1974—. Served with USN, 1953-57. Fellow AAAS, Am. Psychol. Assn.; mem. Psychonomic Soc., Sigma Xi. Editor Jour. Verbal Learning and Verbal Behavior, 1972-76; (with A.W. Melton) Coding Processes in Human Memory, 1972. Home: RFD 2 Lawrence KS 66044

MARTIN, EDWIN WEBB, educator, fgn. service officer; b. Madura, India, Aug. 31, 1917 (parents Am. citizens); s. Azel Anson and Emma (Webb) M.; A.B., Oberlin (Ohio) Coll., 1939; M.A., Fletcher Sch. Law and Diplomacy, Medford, Mass., 1940, postgrad., 1940-41; postgrad. Yale U., 1945-46; m. Emma-Rose Hubbard, Aug. 17, 1940; children—Marguerite L. Cairns, Sylvia M. Lindsay, Edwin H., David W. Vice consul, Hamilton, Bermuda, 1941-44, Leopoldville, Belgian Congo, 1944, Peiping, China, 1946-48, Hankow, China, 1948-49; consul, Taipei, Formosa, 1949-50; consul, also 2d sec. embassy, Rangoon, Burma, 1950-51; with Dept. State, Washington, 1976-79; chancellor U. Wis., Stevens Point, 1979—; dep. dir. Office Chinese Affairs, 1953-55, dir., 1958-61; assigned Nat. War Coll., 1955-56, 1st sec. embassy, London, 1956-58; polit. adviser with personal rank minister to comdr. in chief Pacific, Hawaii, 1961-64; counselor with personal rank of minister, consul gen. Am. embassy, Ankara, Turkey, 1964-67; consul gen. with personal rank minister, Hong 21 Oakcrest Dr Stevens Point WI 54481 ambassador to Burma 1971-73; professorial lectr Sch Advanced Internat Studies Washington 1975; distinguished prof diplomacy Hiram (Ohio) Coll 1976— Served with AUS 1945 Mem Internat Studies Assn Assn Asian Studies Asia Soc Am Fgn Service Assn Phi Beta Kappa Congregationalist Author: Southeast Asia and China: The End of Containment Office: Dept Polit Sci Hiram Coll Hiram OH 44234

MARTIN, EDWIN WILSON, JR., govt. ofcl., speech pathologist; b. Oceanside, N.Y., Sept. 3, 1931; s. Edwin W. and Jean (Carbone) M.; A.B., Muhlenberg Coll., 1953; M.A., U. Ala., 1955; Ph.D., U. Pitts., 1961; L.H.D., Emerson Coll., 1974; m. Peggy Anne Smith, Sept. 5, 1953; children—Scott Andrew, Bruce Leslie. Asst. prof. speech and speech pathology U. Ala., Tuscaloosa, 1960-63, asso. prof., 1963-66, co-dir. speech and hearing clinic, 1963-66; dir. ad hoc subcom. on handicapped U.S. Ho. Reps., Washington, 1966-67; dep. asso. commr. U.S. Office Edn., 1967-70, asso. commr., 1970—, acting dep. commr., 1974-77, dep. commr., 1977—, dir. Bur. Edn. for the Handicapped, 1969—; lectr. Harvard U., 1979; exec. in residence Ohio State U., 1977. Pres. Churchill Rd. Sch. PTA, McLean, 1972-73; mem. exec. com. Pres.' Com. Employment Handicapped, 1972—. Recipient Superior Service award Dept. Health, Edn. and Welfare, 1970, citation of honor League Sch. N.Y., 1970, Distinguished Service award Nat. Rehab. Inst., 1971; named Old Master, Purdue U., 1972; Legis. award Children With Learning Disabilities, 1977; Leadership award Nat. Assn. State Dirs. Spl. Edn., 1978. Fellow Am. Speech and Hearing Assn. (cons. editor jours. 1960—); mem. Am. Psychol. Assn., Council Exceptional Children. Contbr. articles on edn. of handicapped children to profl. publs. Editorial bd. Jour. Autism and Schizophrenia, 1971-76. Home: 7013 Churchill Rd McLean VA 22101 Office: Bureau of Education for the Handicapped US Office of Education Washington DC 20202

MARTIN, ERNEST H., theatrical and motion picture exec; b. Pitts., Aug. 28, 1919; s. Samuel and Cecilia (Sklar) Markowitz; A.B., U. Calif. at Los Angeles, 1942; m. Nancy Frank (div.); m. 2d, Nancy Guild (div.); children—Elizabeth, Cecilia, Polly; m. 3d, Twyla Elliott. Producer stage plays (with Cy Feuer): Where'e Charley?, 1948, Guys and Dolls, 1950, Can-Can, 1953, The Boy Friend, 1954, Silk Stockings, 1955, Whoop-Up, 1958, How to Succeed in Business Without Really Trying, (Pulitzer prize for drama), 1961, Little Me, 1962, Skyscraper, 1965, Walking Happy, 1966, The Goodbye People, 1968; The Act, 1977; motion picture with Cy Feuer, Cabaret (winner 8 Acad. awards), 1972; motion picture Piaf, 1975; mng. dir. Los Angeles and San Francisco Civic Light Opera Assn., 1975—. Office: 135 N Grand Ave Los Angeles CA 90012

MARTIN, ETHELBERT COWLEY, ret. research adminstr.; b. Eng., Nov. 1, 1910; s. William Patrick and Margaret (Cowley) M.; came to U.S., 1950, naturalized, 1955; B.S., U. Guelph (Can.), 1933; M.S., Cornell U., 1938, Ph.D., 1957; m. Grace Ronningen, June 6, 1941; children—Margaret (Mrs. John D. Flanagan), Erik John, Lois Jane. Lectr. apiculture U. Guelph, 1933-39; instr. entomology U. Man., 1939-42; provincial apiarist, Man., 1945-50; mem. faculty Mich. State U., East Lansing, 1950-75, prof. entomology, 1963-75, emeritus, 1975—; mem. nat. program staff Agrl. Research Service, Dept. Agr., Beltsville, Md., 1975-79; sci. adviser U. Nigeria, 1961-63; adviser entomology U. Gadja Mada and Inst. Pertanian, Bogor, Indonesia. Served to lt. comdr. Canadian Navy, 1942-45. Recipient coop. agreement grant Dept. Agr., 1967-73. Mem. Entomol. Soc. Am., Bee Research Assn., Am. Beekeeping Fedn., Sigma Xi. Author articles, chpts. in books. Home: 4445 Greenwood Dr Okemos MI 48864

MARTIN, FLETCHER, artist; b. Palisade, Colo., Apr. 29, 1904; s. Clinton Howard and Josephine (Reed) M.; grad. Clarkston (Wash.) High Sch., 1921; m. Cecile Booth, 1925 (div.); 1 son, Robin; m. 2d, Helen Donovan, 1946 (div. 1962); children—Clint, Donovan; m. 3d, Jean Mele, 1963. Began as printer, 1916; self-taught painter; first exhbn. Fine Arts Gallery, San Diego, 1934, since shown in all leading museums in U.S.; rep. exhbns. S.A., South Africa and Europe including the Venice Biennial (1950); taught drawing and painting Art Center Sch., Los Angeles, 1938-39; artist-in-residence U. Iowa, 1940-41; dir. painting and graphic arts Kansas City Art Inst., 1941-42; artists war corr. Life mag. on African and Normandy campaigns, 1943-44; tchr. painting Art Students League of N.Y., 1948-49; vis. prof. art U. Fla., 1950-52; vis. artist Mills Coll. Cal., 1951; tchr. Albany (N.Y.) Inst. History and Art, 1952-53, Claremont (Cal.) Coll., summer 1953; Duluth br. U. Minn., summers 1954-57, North Mich. Coll., San Antonio Art Inst., 1958; head dept. drawing Los Angeles County (Cal.) Art Inst., 1958-59; tchr. Rochester (Minn.) Art Center, 1963; Am. Fedn. Art-Ford Found. artist-in residence Roswell (N.M.) Mus., 1964, Art Students League N.Y., 1965, Roberson Meml. Center, Binghamton, N.Y., 1967-68; represented in many important pub. collections including Met. Mus., Mus. Modern Art, Whitney Mus. Art, N.Y.C., Witte Meml. Mus., San Antonio. Prizes include 1st mus. award Los Angeles Mus., 1935, 2d mus. prize, 1939; U.S. sect. Fine Art mural award, 1936; Lippincott prize for figure painting Pa. Acad., 1947; Altman prize N.A.D., 1949; Clark prize, 1953; numerous honorable mentions. Painted several murals in the west. Mem. N.A.D., Woodstock Artists Assn. Democrat. Work reproduced in mags. including Life, Newsweek, Time, Art News, Art Digest; book illustration The Jungle (Upton Sinclair), 1965, Of Mice and Men (John Steinbeck), 1969; books pub. on his life and works by Barbara Eversole, 1954, H. Lester Cooke, Jr., 1977. Home: Apartado 73 Guanajuato GTO Mexico also 474 Bowdoin Circle Sarasota FL 33577

MARTIN, FOWLER WARD, ret. educator, ret. naval officer; b. Seattle, Nov. 24, 1916; s. Fowler Ward and Jennie (Herren) M.; B.A., U. Wash., 1938; M.B.A., Stanford, 1950; m. Lois Maxine Riedel, Nov. 25, 1942; children—Fowler III, Wendy (Mrs. Steven Woolson). Commd. ensign U.S. Navy, 1938, advanced through grades to rear adm., 1966; participated numerous operations afloat PTO, World War II; comdr. Navy Ordnance Supply Office, 1954-55, Yards and Docks Supply Office, 1961-63, Def. Fuel Supply Center, 1966-69, Def. Electronics Supply Center, Dayton, Ohio, 1969-72; dir. energy div. State of N.C., Raleigh, 1972-75; vis. lectr. N.C. State U., 1976-79. Pres. Navy Fed. Credit Union, 1967-69; bd. dirs. Navy Mut. Aid, 1967-69. Mem. Chi Psi. Methodist. Clubs: Army-Navy Country (Arlington, Va.). Home: 6024 Dixon Dr Raleigh NC 27609

MARTIN, FRANCIS DAVID, philosopher, educator; b. Johnstown, Pa., Mar. 29, 1920; s. Francis Clarence and Agnes (Stover) M.; A.B., U. Chgo., 1942, Ph.D., 1949; m. Doris Elizabeth Georg, June 26, 1942; children—Marilyn Suzanne (Mrs. William Gale Reish), Timothy Patterson, Amy Lucinda (Mrs. Robert M. Coy, Jr.), Janice Kay. Instr. humanities U. Chgo., 1947-49; asst. prof. philosophy Bucknell U., Lewisburg, Pa., 1949-50, asso. prof., 1950-56, prof. philosophy, 1956—, chmn. dept. philosophy, 1969—. Served to 1st lt. AUS, 1942-46. Recipient Christian Lindback award for distinguished teaching, 1967. Fulbright scholar in Italy, 1957-59, Lilly Found. fellow, 1966-67. Mem. AAUP (past div. v.p.), Am. Philos. Assn., Am. Soc. for Aesthetics, Metaphys. Soc. Am., Soc. Process Philosophy, Renaissance Soc. Am., Phi Beta Kappa, Phi Gamma Delta, Phi Sigma Tau. Author: Art and the Religious Experience, 1972; The Humanities through the Arts, 1975, 2d edit., 1978. Contbr. articles to profl. jours. Home: RD 1 Box 337 Lewisburg PA 17837

MARTIN, FRED, artist; b. San Francisco, June 13, 1927; s. Ernest Thomas and Leona (Richey) M.; B.A., U. Calif. at Berkeley, 1949, M.A., 1952; postgrad. Calif. Sch. Fine Arts, 1949-50; m. Genevieve Catherine Fisette, Jan. 29, 1950; children—T. Demian, Fredricka C., Anthony J. Registar, Oakland (Calif.) Art Mus., 1955-58; dir. exhbns. San Francisco Art Inst., 1958-65, dir. coll., 1965-75; exhibited one man shows Zoe Dusanne Gallery, Seattle, 1952, M.H. deYoung Meml. Mus., San Francisco, 1954, 64, Oakland Art Mus., 1958, San Francisco Mus. Art, 1958, 73, Dilexi Gallery, San Francisco, 1961, Minami Gallery, Tokyo, 1963, Royal Marks Gallery, N.Y.C., 1965-70, Hansen Fuller Gallery, San Francisco, 1974, 75; represented in permanent collections Mus. Modern Art, N.Y.C., San Francisco Mus. Modern Art, Oakland Art Mus., Whitney Mus. Recipient prizes Oakland Art Mus., 1951, 58, San Francisco Mus. Art, 1957, 58, Richmond (Calif.) Art Center, 1962, Nat. Found. for Arts, 1970. Author. Beulah Land, 1966, Log of the Sun Ship, 1969; Liber Studiorum, 1973; A Travel Book, 1976; From an Antique Land, 1979; Bay area corr. Art Internat.; contbg. editor Art Week. Home: 232 Monte Vista St Oakland CA 94611

MARTIN, GEORGE (WHITNEY), writer; b. N.Y.C., Jan. 25, 1926; s. George Whitney and Agnes Wharton (Hutchinson) M.; grad. Groton Sch., 1944; B.A., Harvard, 1948; student Trinity Coll., Cambridge (Eng.) U., 1950; LL.B., U. Va., 1953. Admitted to N.Y. bar, 1955; with firm Emmet, Marvin & Martin, N.Y.C., 1955-59; engaged in writing, 1959—. Bd. dirs. Met. Opera Guild, 1958-70, sec., 1963-67; bd. dirs. Leake and Watts Childrens Home, N.Y.C., 1959-67. Author: The Opera Companion, A Guide for the Casual Operagoer, 1961; The Battle of the Frogs and Mice, An Homeric Fable, 1962; Verdi, His Music, Life and Times, 1963; The Red Shirt and The Cross of Savoy, The Story of Italy's Risorgimento, 1748-1871, 1969; Causes and Conflicts, The Centennial History of the Association of the Bar of the City of New York, 1870-1970, 1970; Madam Secretary: Frances Perkins, 1976; The Opera Companion to Twentieth Century Opera, 1979. Contbr. articles to profl. jours., mags. Address: 333 E 68th St New York NY 10021

MARTIN, GEORGE CLARKE, land devel. co. exec., assn. exec.; b. Lexington, Ky., Jan. 25, 1922; B.S. in Comm., U. Ky., 1949; m. Georgeann Beauvais; children—Mary Evelyn, Elizabeth Patience, Victoria. Pres. Bollinger-Martin, Inc., Louisville, 1954—. Past housing adviser U.S. Mission to European Econ. Council, Home Loan Bank Bd. Founder, chmn. bd. dirs. Home Owners Warranty Corp., Washington, 1973—. Chmn. bd. govs. Nat. Housing Center, Washington, 1978—; chmn. selection com. Housing Industry Hall of Fame, 1978. Served with AUS, 1943-45. Named Man of Year, Am. Home Mag., 1973; Builder of Year, Homebuilders of Louisville, 1973.

Mem. Nat. Assn. Homebuilders (pres. 1973—), Ky. Home Builders Assn. (past pres.). Home: Greenwillow Box 282 Anchorage KY 40223

MARTIN, GEORGE COLEMAN, aero. engr.; b. Everett, Wash., May 16, 1910; s. Walter Franklin and Minnie (Coleman) M.; B.S. cum laude, U. Wash., 1931; m. Mary Sturart Patrick, June 29, 1935; children—Marian Coleman, Edith Patrick. With Boeing Airplane Co., Seattle, 1931—, successively chief of stress, staff engr. stress and power plant, XB-47 project engr., preliminary design chief, B-47 project engr., chief project engr., 1941-53, chief engr. Seattle div., 1953-58, v.p., 1958-64, v.p. engring., 1964-72, cons., 1972—. Fellow Am. Inst. Aeros. and Astronautics; mem. Aerospace Industries Assn. (chmn. aerospace tech. council 1969), Phi Beta Kappa, Tau Beta Pi. Club: Seattle Yacht. Home: 425 SE Shoreland Dr Bellevue WA 98004 Office: 7755 E Marginal Way Seattle WA 98108

MARTIN, GEORGE RAYMOND RICHARD, author; b. Bayonne, N.J., Sept. 20, 1948; s. Raymond and Margaret (Brady) M.; B.S. summa cum laude, Northwestern U., 1970, M.S. cum laude, 1971; m. Gale Burnick, Nov. 15, 1975. Journalism intern Medill News Service, Washington, 1971; sportswriter, pub. relations officer N.J. Dept. Parks, Bayonne, 1971; coordinator communications and edn. Cook County (Ill.) Legal Assistance Found., Chgo., 1972-74; instr. journalism Clarke Coll., Dubuque, Iowa, 1976-78, writer-in-residence, 1978-79; author sci. fiction: A Song for Lya, 1976; Songs of Stars and Shadows, 1977; Dying of the Light, 1977; editor: New Voices I, 1977; New Voices II, 1979; contbr. short stories to mags.; founder, chmn. Windy City Sci. Fiction Writers' Workshop, Chgo., 1972-76. Mem. Sci. Fiction Writers Am. (dir. Central region), Nat. Council Coll. Publs. Advisers, Kappa Tau Alpha. Home: Burnick and Martin Manor 1205 Declovina Santa Fe NM 87501

MARTIN, GEORGE WILBUR, assn. exec.; b. Oklahoma City, Aug. 24, 1930; s. Jeff Frank and George Mullineaux (Bullard) M.; student Okla. A. and M. Coll., 1951; m. Maryellen Brokaw, June 20, 1953; 1 son, Michael Blake. Real estate salesman, Washington, 1955-59; jr. analyst CIA, Washington, 1953-55; advt. mgr. Guns and Ammo Mag., Petersen Pub. Co., Los Angeles, 1959-66, mktg. mgr., 1966-67, editor, 1967-73, pub. Petersen's Hunting, Guns and Ammo, and shooting splty. books, 1973-74, Hunting Mag., 1974-77, pub. outdoor div., shooting splty. books, 1977-78; exec. dir. publs. Nat. Rifle Assn., Washington, 1978—; cons. White House Com. Firearms Legis., 1971—. Served with USAF, 1951-52. Named hon. lt. gov. State of Okla. Mem. Am. Sportsman's Club, Alaska Profl. Hunters Assn., Hunting Hall of Fame Found. (charter, life), Am. Handgunner Awards Orgn. (endowment), Game Coin Assn. (dir. legis.), Outdoor Writers Assn. Am., Ducks Unltd., Nat. Skeet Shooting Assn., Nat. Sporting Goods Assn., Nat. Shooting Sports Found., Nat. Rifle Assn. (endowment mem.), Wildflower Assn. Scotland. Home: 11017 Gainsborough Rd Potomac MD 20854 Office: 1600 Rhode Island Ave NW Washington DC 20036

MARTIN, GORDON MATHER, physician, educator; b. Brookline, Mass., Mar. 2, 1915; s. Harry O. and Mary Alice (Mather) M.; student U. N.H., 1932-34; A.B., Nebr. Wesleyan U., 1936; M.D., U. Nebr., 1940; M.S., U. Minn. (fellow in phys. medicine Mayo Found. 1941-44), 1944; m. Neva M. Cocklin, June 14, 1940; children—Richard, Lawrence, Douglas. Intern U. Nebr. Hosp., Omaha, 1940-41; 1st asst. phys. medicine Mayo Clinic, 1943-44, cons. phys. medicine and rehab., 1947-65, chmn. dept. phys. medicine and rehab., 1965-73, sr. cons., 1973—; asst. prof. phys. medicine, dir. dept. U. Kans. Sch. Medicine, 1944-47, dir. sch. phys. therapy, 1944-47; asso. prof. phys. med. and rehab. Mayo Grad. Sch. Med., U. Minn. Grad. Sch., now prof. Mayo Med. Sch. Chmn. sub-com. phys. medicine and rehab. Gov.'s Adv. Council Mental Health for Minn., 1956-60; cons. chronic diseases program USPHS, 1959-62; chmn. residency rev. com. phys. medicine and rehab. Am. Bd. Med. Specialties, 1976—. Recipient Alumni Achievement award Nebr. Wesleyan U., 1957. Diplomate Am. Bd. Phys. Medicine and Rehab. (asst. sec. 1974-77, exec. sec.-treas. 1977—). Fellow A.C.P.; mem. Am. Guild of Organists, Rochester C. of C., Am. Congress Rehab. Medicine (pres. 1955-56, mem. exec. council), Nat. Rehab. Assn., AAAS, Am. Acad. Phys. Medicine and Rehab. (v.p.), Am. Rheumatism Assn., AMA (sec. phys. medicine and rehab. sect., council 1963-69, chmn. 1970-76), Minn. Rehab. Assn. (pres. 1970), Assn. Acad. Physiatrists, Sigma Xi, Alpha Omega Alpha. Author chpts. med. books. Home: 807 Sierra Ln NE Rochester MN 55901 Office: Mayo Clinic 200 1st St SW Rochester MN 55901

MARTIN, GORDON PERSHING, librarian; b. Frankfort, Mich., July 16, 1918; s. Donald and Janet (Ford) M.; student Fenn Coll., 1936-39; Ph.B., U. Chgo., 1948, M.A., 1952; m. Martha Gray Murray, Jan. 4, 1950 (div. July 1955). Librarian, Harper Res. Book Room, U. Chgo., 1948-51; head circulation desk service U. Minn., 1951-52; order librarian San Jose (Calif.) State Coll., 1952-53; reference librarian U. Calif. at Riverside, 1954-63, asst. univ. librarian, 1957-63; project dir. Library 21 Exhibit, Seattle World's Fair, 1962, Library U.S.A. Exhibit, N.Y. World's Fair, 1964-65; librarian Calif. State U., Sacramento, 1966—. Cons. library orgn., bldg. planning, 1953—. Mem. A.L.A., Calif. Library Assn. Author: (with Dorothea M. Berry) A Guide to Writing Research Papers, 1971. Contbr. numerous articles profl. jours. Home: 2249 Sierra Blvd Sacramento CA 95825 Office: 2000 Jed Smith Dr Sacramento CA 95819

MARTIN, GUY, lawyer; b. Los Angeles, Jan. 22, 1911; s. I.G. and Mary Pearl (Howe) M.; A.B., Occidental Coll., 1931; B.A. (hons.), Oxford U., 1934, M.A., 1944; LL.B., Yale, 1937; m. Edith Kingdon Gould, Oct. 12, 1946; children—Guy III, Jason Gould, Christopher Kingdon, Edith Maria Theodosia Burr. Admitted to N.Y. bar, 1938; practiced with Donovan, Leisure, Newton & Lumbard, N.Y.C., 1938-41; gen. counsel All Am. Aviation, Inc., 1942, Am. Mexican Claims Commn., U.S. Dept. State, 1945-47; partner Martin, Whitfield, Smith & Bebchick, and predecessors, Washington, 1952—; vice chmn. bd., chief exec. officer, dir. United Fin. Corp. Va.; gen. counsel, mem. exec. com., dir. Internat. Bank; dir. IB Realty & Mortgage Corp. Served with USN, sea duty, 1942-45. Mem. Am., N.Y.C., D.C. bar assns., Bar Assn. D.C, Phi Beta Kappa, Sigma Alpha Epsilon. Episcopalian. Clubs: Yale, Brook, Knickerbocker (N.Y.C.); Metropolitan, City Tavern (Washington). Home: 3300 O St NW Washington DC 20007 Office: 1701 Pennsylvania Ave NW Washington DC 20006

MARTIN, GUY RICHARD, govt. ofcl.; b. Denver, April 25, 1942; s. George and Sally (Garkie) M.; B.S., U. Colo., 1964, J.D., 1967; m. Nancy Jane Sand, Aug. 26, 1967. Asso. prof. polit. sci. Alaska Meth. U., 1967-71; individual practice law, Anchorage, 1968-71; legis. asst. to Congressman Nick Begich of Alaska, 1972-73; Washington counsel for State of Alaska, 1973-75; commr. Nat. Resources for State of Alaska, 1975-77; asst. sec. for land and water resources U.S. Dept. Interior, 1977—. Home: 707 Massachusetts Ave NE Washington DC 20002 Office: Main Interior Bldg Room 6616 Washington DC 20240

MARTIN, HAROLD CLARK, educator; b. Raymond, Pa., Jan. 12, 1917; s. Henry Floyd and Anna May (Clark) M.; A.B., Hartwick Coll., Oneonta, N.Y., 1937, LL.D., 1965; A.M., U. Mich., 1941; Ph.D., Harvard, 1954; student U. Wis., 1936, Columbia, 1941; L.H.D., Elmira Coll., 1967, Siena Coll., 1968, Concord Coll., 1968; D.H.L., Trinity Coll. (Conn.), 1970; Litt.D., Skidmore Coll., 1974; L.H.D., Coll. St. Rose, 1974, Union Coll., 1975; m. Elma Hicks, Dec. 21, 1939; children—Thomas, Joel, Ann, Rebecca. High sch. tchr. English and French, Adams, N.Y., 1937-39; high sch. tchr. English, Goshen, N.Y., 1939-44, prin. high sch., 1944-49; mem. faculty Harvard, 1951-65, dir. gen. edn., 1951-65, lectr. comparative lit., 1954-65; chancellor Union U., also pres. Union Coll., Schenectady, 1965-74; pres. Am. Acad., Rome, Italy, 1974-76; Margaret Bundy Scott prof. Williams Coll., 1977; Charles A. Dana prof. humanities Trinity Coll., Conn., 1977—. Dir. Schenectady Trust Co. Chmn. Mass. Com. Fulbright Awards, 1955-65, Coll. Bd. Com. English, 1959-64. Trustee Hartwick Coll., Siena Coll., Franklin Coll., Switzerland. Served with USNR, 1944-46. Mem. Modern Lang. Assn. Author: Logic and Rhetoric of Exposition, 1958. Editor Inquiry and Expression (with Richard Ohmann), 1958; Style in Prose Fiction, 1959. Home: 37 Harwich St Hartford CT 06114

MARTIN, HAROLD HARBER, author, mag. writer, columnist; b. Commerce, Ga., Sept. 17, 1910; s. Gabriel Pierce and Mary Edna Augusta (Harber) M.; A.B. in Journalism, U. Ga., 1933; m. Boyce Lokey, Apr. 23, 1935; children—Marian Hamilton (Mrs. E. Thorpe Mealing), Harold Harber, John P., Nancy Boyce (Mrs. David Sparks). Sports and feature writer Atlanta Georgian and Sunday Am., 1932-39; feature writer, columnist Atlanta Constn., 1939-74; contbr. to Harper's, Collier's, Liberty, Sat. Eve. Post, 1944-50; asso. editor Sat. Eve. Post, 1951-53, contbg. editor, 1958-63, editor at large, 1964-69. Lectr. journalism Ga. State U., Atlanta, 1972—. Mem. F.D. Roosevelt Warm Springs Meml. Commn.; bd. dirs. St. Judes House, Atlanta, pres., 1976; bd. dirs. Ga. Coop. Services for the Blind, Decatur. Served to 1st lt. USMCR, 1943-45. Decorated Bronze Star; recipient award for non-fiction Southeastern Writers Assn., 1979. Mem. Sigma Delta Chi (Distinguished Service award and Bronze medal 1958). Club: Nat. Press (Washington). Episcopalian. Author: (with Gen. M. B. Ridgway) Soldier, 1956; (humor) Father's Day Comes Once a Year and Then it Always Rains, 1960; Starlifter, 1972; Ralph McGill, Reporter, 1973; Three Strong Pillars, 1974; History of Georgia, 1977; Atlanta Mayor William B. Hartsfield, 1978; This Happy Isle, 1978; Harold Martin Remembers a Place in the Mountains, 1979. Address: 2895 Normandy Dr NW Atlanta GA 30305

MARTIN, HARRY VICTOR, publisher; b. San Francisco, Mar. 26, 1939; s. Lorne Philip and Irene Esworthy (Marshall) M.; ed. San Francisco State Coll., Nat. Sch. Aeros.; m. Mary Elizabeth Stubbs, Feb. 24, 1968; children—Thomas Victor, Amber Laraine. With grocery industry, 1959-62, airlines, 1963; owner Loch Lomond Food Mart (Calif.), 1966-67; columnist Lake County Record Bee, 1967; with Sydney (Australia) Telegraph, 1968; sports editor Forbes Advocate, 1968; polit. editor Dubbo Daily Liberal, 1968; feature editor Townsville (Australia) Daily Bull., 1969; copy desk The Australian, Sydney, 1969; editor/writer Contra Costa (Calif.) Time and Suns, 1969-71; asst. editor Napa Register, 1971-73; feature writer/editor Oakland Tribune, 1973-74; pres. Info. Research Services of No. Calif., Loch Lomond, 1974-76; pres. Bicentennial Tours Ltd., Harry V. Martin & Assos.; v.p. Spirit of 76 Retreat; gen. mgr. Pacific Midwest Mktg. Corp., Honolulu; pub. Hawaii Bicentennial Publs.; editor Peninsula Clarion, Kenai, Alaska, 1977-78; pub., owner Cook Inlet Chronicles, 1978—. Founding pres., exec. dir. North Bay News Assn., 1970—, recipient awards, 1973-74; chmn. Contra Costa County Environ. Health Planning, 1970, Napa Revenue Water Bond Com., 1973, Am. Revolution Bicentennial Com. of Napa, 1973—; mem. Napa County Republican Central Com., 1970, Calif. Rep. Central Com., 1974, Calif. Rep. Speakers Bur., 1974; v.p. Reps. in Action, 1974; assemblyman Kenai Peninsula Borough, Assembly, 1978—; adminstr. Bicentennial World Hawaiian Canoe Championships, 1976, Friends of Bicentennial, Honolulu, 1976; community coordinator Jr. Achievement of Kenai; chmn. Kenai Peninsula Conv. Bur., 1978-79. Recipient Edward Meeman Conservation award Scripps Howard Found., 1973, Edward McQuade award for social justice reporting Catholic Newsmens Assn., 1973. Mem. Australian Journalist Assn., DeMolay (pres. San Francisco chpt.), League Women Voters, Contra Costa Press Club (Best Headline, Best News Story awards 1971, Best Feature Series award 1972, Best New Series award 1974), C. of C. Hawaii, Napa C. of C., C. of C. Greater Kenai. Clubs: Alaska Press, Contra Costa Press, Masons, Order Eastern Star. Author: Peoples of Hawaii, 1976; HawaiiUSA 200, 1976; Kenai—A Business Prospectus, 1977; Tourism Almanac of the Kenai Peninsula, 1979. Home: Ciechanski Rd Soldotna AK 99669 Office: Cook Inlet Chronicles PO Box 1250 Soldotna AK 99669

MARTIN, HENRY H., motion picture exec.; b. Holcomb, Miss., Mar. 22, 1912. Poster clk. Universal Pictures, Oklahoma City, 1935, then booker and salesman, br. mgr., dist. mgr., 1951-56, so. div. mgr., N.Y.C., 1956-57, gen. sales mgr., 1957-59, v.p. Universal Pictures Co., Inc., 1959-73, pres., 1973—. Served in USN, 1943-46. Office: Universal Pictures 445 Park Ave New York City NY 10022 also Universal City Studios 100 Universal City Plaza Universal City CA 91608

MARTIN, HUGH JACK, JR., educator; b. San Diego, Sept. 1, 1926; s. Hugh Jack and Eva (Price) M.; B.S., Calif. Inst. Tech., 1951, Ph.D., 1956; m. Susan Swartz, Sept. 13, 1950; children—Kate, Hugh, Molly, Phillip, William, Daisy. Faculty, Ind. U., Bloomington, 1956—, prof. physics, 1965—. Served with AUS, 1944-46. Mem. Am. Phys. Soc., AAAS, Assn. Computing Machinery, Pattern Recognition Soc., Sigma Xi. Spl. research exptl. high energy physics, pattern recognition techniques. Home: 1108 E University St Bloomington IN 47401

MARTIN, HUNTER LENON, JR., oil and gas exploration co. exec.; b. Tulsa, Oct. 26, 1926; s. Hunter Lenon and Monta (Cook) M.; B.A. cum laude, Amherst Coll., 1947; LL.B., Harvard U., 1949; m. Lore Fleck, Feb. 17, 1978; children—Hunter Lenon, III, David P. Admitted to Okla. bar, 1949; individual practice, Tulsa, 1950-51; atty. Bolin Oil Co., Wichita Falls, Tex., 1951-52; public relations rep. Exxon Co., 1952-64; asst. to gov. Mont., 1965; v.p. Pennzoil Co., Houston, 1967-77; v.p., sec. Pogo Producing Co., Houston, 1977—. Served with AUS, 1944-45. Mem. Am. Bar Assn., Okla. Bar Assn. Clubs: Houston, Tulsa. Office: 707 McKinney St Houston TX 77002

MARTIN, JAMES ALFRED, JR., educator; b. Lumberton, N.C., Mar. 18, 1917; s. James Alfred and Mary (Jones) M.; A.B., Wake Forest Coll., 1937, Litt.D. (hon.), 1965; M.A., Duke, 1938; Ph.D., Columbia, 1944; student Union Theol. Sem., 1940-43; M.A. (hon.), Amherst Coll., 1950; m. Ann Bradsher, June 1, 1936. Ordained to ministry Bapt. Ch., 1944; asst. pastor Roxboro (N.C.) Ch., 1937-38; instr. philosophy and psychology Wake Forest Coll., 1938-40; asst. philosophy religion Union Theol. Sem., N.Y.C., 1941-44, Danforth prof. religion in higher edn., 1960-67, adj. prof. philosophy religion, 1967—; prof. religion Columbia, 1967—, adj. prof. religion, 1963—, chmn. dept., 1968-77; asst. prof. religion Amherst Coll., 1946-47, asso. prof., 1947-50, prof., 1950-54, Marquand and Stone prof., 1954-57, Crosby prof. religion, 1957-60. Ordained deacon P.E. Ch., 1953; vis. prof. Cornell U., summer 1948, Mt. Holyoke Coll., 1949-50, 52-53, 59-60, State U. Iowa, summer 1959, U. N.C., summer 1964; asso. mem. East-West Philosophers' Conf., U. Hawaii, 1949. Served as lt. chaplain, USNR, 1944-46: PTO. Recipient Distinguished Alumnus award Wake Forest U., 1971. Mem. Soc. Values in Higher Edn. (Kent fellow, pres.), Am. Theol. Soc., Soc. Theol. Discussion, Phi Beta Kappa, Omicron Delta Kappa, Pi Kappa Alpha. Author: Empirical Philosophies of Religion, 1944; Ways of Faith (with J. A. Hutchison), 1953, rev., 1960; Fact, Fiction, and Faith, 1960; The New Dialogue Between Philosophy and Theology 1966. Contbr. chpts. to books, articles to jours., encys. Home: 99 Claremont Ave New York NY 10027 also Box 667 Roxboro NC. *My experience of life has increasingly underscored the central importance of honesty-in understanding of oneself, and in perceptions of and relations to others. The quest for honesty entails a relentless and often painful search for truth. Acceptance of truth, and of others as they truly are, requires grace. The goal is to speak the truth in love.*

MARTIN, JAMES BLAKELY, judge; b. Muskogee, Okla., Dec. 7, 1930; s. Fred W. and Ruth (Blakely) M.; student Northeastern State Coll., Tahlequah, Okla., Okla. State U.; J.D., Cumberland U.; m. Virginia Lee Craig, Apr. 5, 1959; children—Larry Ray, Cindy Lou. Admitted to Okla. bar; county atty. Wagoner County, Okla.; dist. atty.; asso. dist. judge Pittsburg County, Okla.; individual practice law, McAlester, Okla., 1979—; city atty. City of Wagoner, Okla.; atty. Mo. Pacific R.R.; atty. E-M Devel. Co., also dir., County chmn. March of Dimes. Mem. Nat. Assn. Probate Judges (life), County Bar Assn. (pres.). Clubs: Masons (32 deg.), Elks. Office: 122 1/2 Carl Albert Pkwy McAlester OK 74501

MARTIN, JAMES GILBERT, univ. provost; b. Paris, Ill., Dec. 10, 1926; s. James and Ruth Ann (Gilbert) M.; B.A., Ind. State Coll., 1952, M.A., 1953; Ph.D., Ind. U., 1957; m. Doris E. Edmonson, Aug. 23, 1969; children—Bradley Keith, Philip Roger. Instr., Ind. State Coll., Terre Haute, 1952-53; lectr. Ind. U., Bloomington, 1953-56; instr. sociology Okla. U., Norman, 1956-57; asst. prof. sociology No. Ill. U., DeKalb, 1957-65, asso. prof., 1959-64; asst. dean Coll. Arts and Scis., Ohio State U., Columbus, 1965-68, asso. dean Coll. Social and Behavioral Scis., 1968-70, acting dean, 1970-71; v.p., provost U. No. Iowa, Cedar Falls, 1971—; intern academic adminstrn. E.L. Phillips Found., 1963-64. Served with AUS, 1945-48. Mem. Am. Sociol. Assn. Author: The Tolerant Personality, 1964; Minority Group Relations, 1973. Home: 1609 W 5th St Cedar Falls IA 50613

MARTIN, JAMES GRUBBS, congressman; b. Savannah, Ga., Dec. 11, 1935; s. Arthur Morrison and Mary Julia (Grubbs) M.; B.S., Davidson Coll., 1957; Ph.D., Princeton, 1960; m. Dorothy Ann McAulay, June 1, 1957; children—James Grubbs, Emily Wood, Arthur Benson. Asso. prof. chemistry Davidson (N.C.) Coll., 1960-72; mem. 93d to 96th congresses from N.C. Mem. Mecklenburg (N.C.) Bd. County Commrs., 1966-72, chmn., 1967-68, 70-71; founder, 1st chmn. Centralina Council Govts., Charlotte, N.C., 1968-70; v.p. Nat. Assn. Regional Councils, 1970-72; pres. N.C. Assn. County Commrs., 1970-71. Del. Republican Nat. Conv., 1968. Danforth fellow, 1957-60. Mem. Beta Theta Pi (v.p., trustee 1966-69, pres. 1975-78). Presbyterian (deacon). Clubs: Masons (32 deg.), Shriners. Home: Box 638 Davidson NC 28036 Office: 115 House Office Bldg Washington DC 20515

MARTIN, JAMES LUTHER, JR., clergyman, educator; b. Lone Wolf, Okla., July 22, 1917; s. James Luther and Nora Belle (Williams) M.; A.B., Oklahoma City U., 1938; B.D., Yale, 1941, Ph.D., 1951; fellow Fund Advancement Edn., Cambridge U., 1954-55. Ordained to ministry Meth. Ch., 1944; asst. pastor St. John's Meth. Ch., New Rochelle, N.Y., 1941-43; pastor Port Jefferson (N.Y.) Meth. Ch., 1943-46; asso. prof. dept. philosophy and religion Coll. Idaho, 1946-55, prof., 1955-57, chmn. dept., 1951-57; prof. religion Denison U., 1957—, chmn., 1957-63, 67-73, coordinator non-Western studies, 1965—, chmn. senate, 1972-73. Asso. dir. leadership tng. sch., nat. student YM and YWCA, Berkeley, Calif., 1953, nat. adv. bd. student YMCA, 1956-57; chmn. Northwest Conf. Religion in Higher Edn., 1956. Am. Inst. Indian Study fellow, Poona, Madras, India, 1963-64. Mem. Assn. for Asian Studies, Am. Acad. Religion, AAUP, ACLU, Internat. Assn. for Tamil Research. Democrat. Contbr. to scholarly publs. Home: 20 Samson Pl Granville OH 43023

MARTIN, JAMES MORDECAI, life ins. co. exec.; b. Charleston, W.Va., Mar. 2, 1923; s. Robert Cleveland and Ethel Margaret (Lowry) M.; A.B., W.Va. U., 1943; m. Anne McKown Miller, Jan. 24, 1948; children—Robert, Marianne. Mgr., underwriter Home Life Ins. Co. N.Y., Huntington, W.Va., 1952-65, dir. field adminstrn., N.Y.C., 1965-74, corporate sec., 1974-78. Served with USN, 1943-46, 52-54. C.L.U., W.Va. Democrat. Methodist. Club: Masons. Home: 107 S Red Hill Rd Martinsburg WV 25401

MARTIN, JAMES PERRY, educator; b. Vernon, B.C., Can., Feb. 12, 1923; s. James Thomas and Mary Sheppard (Morgan) M.; B.A.Sc., U. B.C., 1946; B.D., Princeton Theol. Sem., 1950, Th.M., 1951, Ph.D., 1958; m. Edith Mary Titcombe, Aug. 27, 1949; children—James Paul, John Thomas, Diane Ruth, David Luther. Ordained to ministry Presbyn. Ch., 1952; received into United Ch. of Can., 1978; instr. N.T., Princeton Theol. Sem., 1954-58, asst. prof., 1958-62, asso. prof. N.T., Union Theol. Sem., Richmond, Va., 1962-66, prof., 1967-72; prin., prof. N.T., Vancouver Sch. Theology, 1972—; summer lectr. Luther Theol. Sem., Princeton Theol. Sem., Young Life Inst. Assn. Theol. Schs. fellow, 1968. Mem. Studiorum Novi Testamenti Societas, Canadian Theol. Soc., Karl Barth Soc. N.Am. Club: U. B.C. Faculty. Author: The Last Judgement in Protestant Theology, 1962; also articles. Address: 6000 Iona Dr Vancouver BC V6T 1L4 Canada

MARTIN, JAMES ROBERT, JR., judge; b. Greenville, S.C., Nov. 30, 1909; s. James Robert and Lyda (Rankin) M.; LL.B., Washington and Lee U., 1931; m. Lydia Prichard, Dec. 19, 1929; children—Belle Mead Martin Heckel, Lydia Martin Sawyer, Bobbie Jane Martin Traylor. Admitted to S.C. bar, 1931; practiced in Greenville, 1931-44; judge 13th Jud. Circuit S.C., 1944-61; U.S. judge Eastern and Western dists. S.C., 1961-67; chief judge U.S. Dist. S.C., 1967—. Mem. S.C. Ho. of Reps. from Greenville County, 1943-44. Mem. Am., S.C., Greenville County bar assns. Home: 401 Crescent Ave Greenville SC 29605 Office: Federal Bldg and US Courthouse Greenville SC 29603*

MARTIN, JAMES RUSSELL, life ins. co. exec.; b. Peoria, Ill., Dec. 3, 1918; s. Ray and Gertrude Irene (Tilley) M.; B.S. in Bus. Adminstrn., U. Ill., 1940; m. Minnie Woodward Faucett, Mar. 6, 1942; children—Sally Lee, James Philip. With Home Life Ins. Co. N.Y., 1940-41, 46-51, mgr., Rochester, N.Y., 1950-51; with Mass. Mut. Life Ins. Co., Springfield, 1951—, 2d. v.p., 1958-62, v.p. agy. sales, 1962-67, sr. v.p., 1967-68, pres., chief exec. officer, 1968-74, chmn., chief exec., 1974—, also dir., chmn. exec. com. of bd. dirs.; dir. 1st Nat. Bank Boston, 1st Boston Corp., Mo. Pacific Corp., Stanley Home Products, Milton Bradley Co. Trustee Pioneer Valley United Fund, Springfield United Fund; bd. dirs. Jr. Achievement of Springfield, Inc.; corporator Springfield Coll.; mem. vis. com. Grad. Sch. Bus. Adminstrn., U. Mich.; mem. fin. com. Nat. Urban League; chmn. Mass. Bus. Roundtable. Served to lt. col. USAAF, 1941-46. Mem. Nat. Assn. Life Underwriters, Am. Coll. Life Underwriters, Health Ins. Assn. Am. (dir.), Am. Council Life Ins. (mem. exec. roundtable, mem. com. on coms.), Am. Mgmt. Assn. (dir.), Kappa Sigma. Republican. Home: 231 Knollwood Dr Longmeadow MA 01106 Office: 1295 State St Springfield MA 01109

MARTIN, JAY HERBERT, educator; b. Newark, Oct. 30, 1935; s. Sylvester K. and Ada M. (Smith) M.; A.B., Columbia U., 1956; M.A., Ohio State U., 1957, Ph.D., 1960; m. Helen Bernadette Saldini, June 9, 1956; children—Helen E., Laura A., Jay Herbert. Instr. English, Pa. State U., 1957-58; instr. English and Am. studies Yale U., 1960-64, asst. prof., 1964-67, asso. prof., 1967-68; prof. English and Am. studies U. Calif., Irvine, 1968-79, chmn. Am. studies, 1968-71, lectr. in psychiatry Med. Sch., 1978—; Leo S. Bing prof. lit. U. So. Calif.; lit. cons. to pub. houses; lectr. abroad: Moscow, Leningrad, Tashkent, Samarkand, Krasnodar, Wroclaw, San Jose, Costa Rica, Berlin; vis. prof. Moscow U., 1976; research psychoanalyst; research clin. asso. So. Calif. Psychoanalytic Inst. Stillman Coll. fellow, 1962—; Morse research fellow, 1963-64; Am. Philos. Soc. fellow, 1966; Guggenheim fellow, 1966-67; Rockefeller fellow, 1975-76. Mem. MLA, Authors Guild, Aurelian Honor Soc., So. Calif. Am. Studies Assn. (pres. 1970-72), Phi Beta Kappa. Author: Conrad Aiken: A Life of His Art, 1962; Harvests of Change: American Literature, 1865-1914, 1967; A Collection of Critical Essays on the Waste Land, 1968; Nathanael West: The Art of His Life (U. Calif. Friends of Library award), 1970; Robert Lowell, 1970; Twentieth Century Views of Nathanael West, 1970; A Singer in the Dawn: Reinterpretations of Paul Laurence Dunbar, 1975; The Dunbar Reader, 1975; Always Merry and Bright: The Life of Henry Miller (U. Calif. Friends of Library award), 1978; Winter Dreams: An American in Moscow, 1979; contbr. articles to profl. publs. Home: 18651 Via Palatino Irvine CA 92715. *I believe that it is the responsibility of every creative person to aid in the evolution of consciousness and to bring about the deepening and enlarging of sensibility that is the task of mankind.*

MARTIN, JERRY CHAMBERS, pub. relations exec., journalist; b. Austin, Tex., Feb. 6, 1933; s. Thomas Green and Molly Gladys (Chambers) M.; student U. Houston, 1953-55, U. Calif. at Berkeley, 1967-68; m. Helen Jean Rowland, June 11, 1967; 1 dau., Kelly Lynn. Corr., bur. mgr. U.P.I., Cheyenne, Wyo., also Albuquerque, 1955-56; news editor A.P., Dallas and Salt Lake City, 1958-62; polit. writer Oakland (Calif.) Tribune, 1963-65, chief editorial writer, editor editorial page, 1965-69; spl. asst. to Calif. Gov. Reagan for research and spl. projects, 1969-75; pub. affairs counsel Chevron U.S.A. Inc., 1975—. Exec. sec. Utah Republican Central Com., 1962-63; mem. Eastbay Rep. Alliance, 1964-67. Served with USAF, 1950-53. Recipient George Washington Honor medal Freedoms Found., 1965, 66, 67. Profl. Journalism seminar fellow Stanford, 1968. Mem. Nat. Journalism Soc., Sigma Delta Chi. Presbyn. Home: 3115 English Hills Rd Vacaville CA 95688 Office: 595 Market St San Francisco CA 94104

MARTIN, JOHN ANDREW, lawyer; b. Birmingham, Ala., Apr. 29, 1938; s. John Harlan and Bernice (Teal) M.; A.B. magna cum laude, Birmingham-So. Coll., 1959; LL.B. magna cum laude, Harvard U., 1962; m. Anne Bowles, Aug. 11, 1961; children—Charles Harlan, John Andrew. Admitted to D.C. bar, 1962, Tex. bar, 1965; atty. civil rights div. U.S. Dept. Justice, 1962-65; asso. firm Carrington, Johnson & Stephens, Dallas, 1965-70; partner firm Carrington, Coleman, Sloman & Blumenthal, Dallas, 1970—; lectr. So. Meth. U. Law Sch. Sec., mem. exec. com. Children's Med. Center, 1977; chmn. bd. DAL-Worc, Inc., 1973, pres., 1972; mem. Greater Dallas Planning Council, 1979—; pres. Dallas Symphony Orch. Guild, 1974-75; bd. dirs. Met. YMCA, 1975—. Mem. Am. Law Inst., Tex. Bar Found., Am. Bar Assn., Tex. Bar Assn., Dallas Bar Assn. Democrat. Baptist. Clubs: Idlewild, Terpsichorean. Home: 7155 Blairview Dallas TX 75230 Office: 3000 One Main Pl Dallas TX 75250

MARTIN, JOHN BARTLOW, author; b. Hamilton, Ohio, Aug. 4, 1915; s. John Williamson and Laura (Bartlow) M.; B.A., DePauw U., Greencastle, Ind., 1937; LL.D. (hon.), Ind. U., 1971; L.H.D. (hon.), Knox Coll., Galesburg, Ill., 1975; m. Frances Rose Smethurst, Aug. 17, 1940; children—Cynthia Ann Martin Coleman, Daniel Bartlow, John Frederick. Reporter, Indpls. Times, 1937-38; freelance writer, 1938—; ambassador to Dominican Republic, 1962-64; sr. fellow Center Advanced Studies Wesleyan U., Middletown, Conn., 1964-65; vis. fellow pub. affairs Princeton U., 1966-67; vis. distinguished prof. Grad. Center City U. N.Y., 1968; prof. journalism Medill Sch. Journalism Northwestern U., 1970-; author 14 books including: Why Did They Kill, 1953; Break Down the Walls, 1954; The Deep South Says Never, 1957; The Pane of Glass, 1959; Overtaken By Events, 1966; The Life of Adlai Stevenson, 1976, 77; U.S. Policy in the Caribbean, 1978; also numerous factual articles. Mem. campaign staff Adlai Stevenson, 1952, 56, John F. Kennedy, 1960, Lyndon B. Johnson, 1964, Robert F. Kennedy, 1968, Hubert Humphrey, 1968. Recipient Benjamin Franklin Mag. award, 1953, 56, 57. Mem. Author's Guild, Soc. Midland Authors, Caribbean Studies Assn., Sigma Delta Chi (Mag. award 1950, 57). Democrat. Clubs: Century (N.Y.C.); Federal City (Washington); Arts (Chgo.). Address: 185 Maple Ave Highland Park IL 60035

MARTIN, JOHN BUTLIN, lawyer, assn. exec.; b. Grand Rapids, Mich., Oct. 3, 1909; s. John B. and Althea (Winchester) M.; A.B., Dartmouth, 1931; Litt.B. (Rhodes scholar), Oxford U., 1933; J.D., U. Mich., 1936; m. Helen Hickam, Sept. 5, 1934; children—Richard, Judith, Gillian. Admitted to D.C. bar, 1936, Ohio bar, 1938, Mich. bar, 1946; legal sec. to commr. SEC, 1936, dep. chief Ohio div. securities, 1941; dep. dir. Nat. Office Civilian Def., 1944; practice law, Grand Rapids, 1946-69; U.S. commr. on aging Adminstrn. on Aging, HEW, Washington, 1969-73, spl. asst. on aging to Pres., 1969-73; cons. Am. Assn. Ret. Persons, 1973—. Chmn. Gov.'s Spl. Commn. Crime. Mem. Mich. Senate from Kent County, 1948-50; auditor gen. State of Mich., 1950-54; mem. Republican Nat. Com., 1957-68. Served as lt. comdr. USNR, 1944-46. Mem. Am., Mich., Grand Rapids bar assns. Baptist (trustee). Club: Rotary (pres. 1957-58). Home: 7607 Glendale Rd Chevy Chase MD 20015 Office: 1909 K St Washington DC 20006

MARTIN, JOHN GILBERT, beverage mfg. exec.; b. Coventry, Eng., Dec. 27, 1905 (parents U.S. citizens); s. Percy and Alice (Heublein) M.; B.A., Cambridge U., 1927; m. Jane Weeks, Oct. 17, 1948. Salesman Heublein, Inc., 1928-32, v.p. 1932-37, pres., 1937-61, chmn., chief exec. officer, 1961-66, chmn. bd., 1964-66, mem. exec. com., 1966—, chmn. exec. com., 1966-76, mem. exec. com., 1976—, also dir. Clubs: Hartford, Hartford Golf. Home: 2490 Gordon Dr Naples FL 33940 Office: Munson Rd Farmington CT 06032

MARTIN, JOHN GUSTIN, investment banker; b. Bay Port, Mich., Dec. 25, 1928; s. Rig and Phoebe (Ballard) M.; B.A., Mich. State Coll., 1952; student U. Detroit Law Sch., 1952-54; m. Patricia Jean Martell, Nov. 16, 1957; children—James Martell, John Douglas. With First of Mich. Corp., Detroit, 1952—, sr. v.p., 1966-69, exec. v.p., 1969, pres., 1970—, dir., 1966—. Trustee Bon Secours Hosp., Grosse Pointe, Mich. Mem. Bond Club Detroit (pres. 1961), Security Traders Detroit (pres. 1963), Investment Bankers Am. (nat. com. 1969—), Nat. Assn. Security Dealers (nat. com. 1973), Mich. State U. Bus. Alumni Assn. (dir., recipient Outstanding Alumni award 1974). Clubs: Detroit; Grosse Pointe Yacht; Renaissance. Home: 112 Vendome Rd Grosse Pointe Farms MI 48236 Office: First of Mich Corp Buhl Bldg Detroit MI 48226

MARTIN, JOHN HUGH, lawyer, aircraft co. exec.; b. Los Angeles, Apr. 19, 1918; s. John Hume and Carrie Suzanne (Hatcher) M.; B.S., Monmouth Coll., 1939; J.D., U. Chgo., 1942; m. Jean Morrison Park, Sept. 17, 1945; 1 dau., Suzanne L. Admitted to Ill. bar, 1943, Calif. bar, 1962; practice law, Chgo., 1943-52; sec., gen. counsel Am. Community Builders, Park Forest, Ill., 1952-54; dep. counsel Bur. Aero., Dept. Navy, Washington, 1954-57; with Lockheed Aircraft Corp., Burbank, Calif., 1957—, European counsel, 1960-61, div. counsel, 1961-71, asst. sec., chief counsel, 1971-77, corp. adv., 1977—; dir. Am. Pacific State Bank. Trustee, Kubani Found. Trust. Mem. Am., Fed., Internat., Los Angeles County bar assns., Phi Alpha Delta. Republican. Episcopalian. Clubs: Legal (Chgo.); Nat. Lawyers (Washington). Home: 1611 Arboles Dr Glendale CA 91207 Office: 200 W Glenoaks Blvd Suite 207 Glendale CA 91202

MARTIN, JOHN JOSEPH, journalist; b. N.Y.C., Dec. 3, 1938; s. John and Marie Agnes (Jacobsen) M.; student San Diego State U., 1956-62; m. Elizabeth Anne Thompson, Dec. 14, 1963; children—Sophie Suzanne, Claire Catherine. Copy editor, reporter San Diego Union, 1958-62; copy editor Augusta (Ga.) Chronicle, 1963; copy editor N.Y. Times Internat. Edit., Paris, 1964-65; editorial asst. Temple Fielding Publs., Mallorca, Spain, 1965-66; reporter, producer Sta. KCRA-TV News, Sacramento, 1966-75; corr. ABC-TV News, N.Y.C., 1975—. Served with U.S. Army, 1962-64. Mem. Assn. Radio and TV News Analysts, AFTRA, Mus. Broadcasting, Mus. Modern Art, Am. Mus. Natural History, U.S. Tennis Assn., Sigma Delta Chi. Office: 7 W 66th St New York NY 10023

MARTIN, JOHN JOSEPH, mfg. co. exec., former govt. ofcl.; b. Detroit, Oct. 19, 1922; s. Anthony L. and Helen (Jason) M.; B.S. in Mech. Engring., U. Notre Dame, 1943, M.S., 1950; Ph.D., Purdue U., 1951; m. Carol C. Kline, June 10, 1948; children—Peter, Anne, Stephen. Instr., U. Notre Dame, 1946-47, 49-50; research engr. N. Am. Aviation, Inc., Downey, Calif., 1951-53; chief engr. Bendix Corp., South Bend-Mishawaka, Ind., 1953-60; resident cons. Royal Aircraft Establishment, Farnborough, Eng., 1963-64; mem. staff Inst. Def. Analysis, Arlington, Va., 1960-63, 64-69, spl. asst. to v.p. for research, 1966-67, asst. to pres., 1967-68, dir. systems eval. div., 1968-69; profl. staff mem. Office Sci. and Tech., Exec. Office of Pres., 1969-73; asso. dep. to dir. CIA, 1973-74, spl. asst. to dir., Apr.-Sept. 1974; prin. dep. asst. sec. Air Force, 1974-76; acting asst. sec. for research and devel. Air Force, 1976—, asst. sec. research, devel. and logistics, 1976-79; v.p., gen. mgr. research labs. Bendix Corp., Southfield, Mich., 1979—. Mem. Sigma Xi, Tau Beta Pi, Pi Tau Sigma. Author: Atmospheric Reentry, 1966; also numerous articles. Research on atmospheric reentry ballistic missiles and manned space craft; description of reflection characteristics of ocean surfaces and bottoms. Home: 7818 Fulbright Ct Bethesda MD 20034*

MARTIN, JOHN JOSEPH, mfg. co. exec.; b. N.Y.C., July 11, 1931; s. John J. and Vera (Moran) M.; B.A., N.Y.U., 1958, J.D., 1962; m. Marilyn E. Hughes, Jan. 8, 1955; children—John Joseph, Kieran, Robert, Paul. Admitted to N.Y. bar, 1962, Conn. bar, 1975; with Huber, Magill, Lawrence & Farrell (and predecessor firm), N.Y.C., 1962-68; v.p., sec., asso. gen. counsel Bangor Punta Corp., 1968-79; v.p., gen. counsel, sec. Lone Star Industries, Inc., 1979—; v.p., sec., dir. Piper Aircraft Corp., 1970-79. Served with AUS, 1951-53. Mem. Am. Soc. Corp. Secs., N.Y. State Bar Assn., Conn. Bar Assn. Home: 96 Valley Rd Cos Cob CT 06807 Office: 1 Greenwich Plaza Greenwich CT 06830

MARTIN, JOHN L., state legislator; b. Eagle Lake, Maine, June 5, 1941; s. Frank and Edwidge (Raymond) M.; B.A. in History and Govt., U. Maine, 1963, postgrad., 1963-64. Tchr. Am. govt. and history Fort Kent (Maine) Community High Sch., 1966-72; instr. U. Maine at Fort Kent, 1972—; mem. Maine Ho. of Reps. from Eagle Lake and St. Francis Dist., 1964—, minority floor leader, 1970-74, speaker of ho. 1975—; mem. intergovtl. relations com. Nat. Legis. Conf., 1970—; chmn. Maine Land Use Regulation Commn., 1972-73, Maine Bur. Human Relations, 1972. Trustee Eagle Lake Water and Sewer Dist., 1966—, People's Benevolent Hosp., Fort Kent. Democrat. Home: Box 250 Eagle Lake ME 04739 Office: State Capitol Bldg Augusta ME 04330

MARTIN, JOHN LYNTON, museum dir.; b. Bridgewater, N.S., Can., Feb. 6, 1922; s. Zenas Freeland and Grace Pearl (Patterson) M.; diploma N.S. Agrl. Coll., 1942; B.S. in Agr., McGill U., 1946; M.S., Dalhousie U., 1954; m. Nora Catherine Fulton, Sept. 15, 1947; children—Elizabeth Anne, James Laurin. Pres., Woodlands Biol. Lab. Ltd., 1946-50; curator Nova Scotia Mus., Halifax, 1950-54, dir., 1965—; research scientist Can. Dept. Forestry, 1954-65. Mem. Mus. Dirs. Assn. Can. (pres.), Canadian Museums Assn., Atlantic Inst. Edn. (dir.), Canadian Inst. Forestry, N.S. Inst. Sci. Author numerous articles on human and natural history. Home: 50 Piers Ave Halifax NS B3N 1Z5 Canada Office: 1747 Summer St Halifax NS B3H 3A6 Canada

MARTIN, JOHN MCKENZIE, former chem. co. exec.; b. Opp, Ala., Jan. 7, 1913; s. Benjamin Hutchinson and Mary Ellen (McKenzie) M.; B.S. in Mech. Engring., Ga. Inst. Tech., 1934; m. Mary Malone, Sept. 7, 1942; children—John McKenzie, Mary Ellen, Janet Malone Martin Jones, Josephine Comer Martin Bayard, Alice Anne, Elizabeth Danforth, James Benjamin. With Hercules, Inc., Wilmington, Del., 1934-78, v.p., 1960-70, chmn. bd., 1970-78; dir. Lehman Corp., Chem. Fund, Greyhound Corp., Del. Trust Co., P.H. Glatfelter Co., Perini Corp. Chmn. bd. Greater Wilmington Devel. Council; bd. dirs. United Way Del., Del. Mus. Natural History. Mem. Am. Inst. Mining and Metall. Engrs., Am. Mining Congress, Nat. Security Indsl. Assn. (past chmn. trustees), Mining Club N.Y.C. Clubs: Pacific-Union (San Francisco); Augusta (Ga.) Nat. Golf; Wilmington, Wilmington Country, Bidermann Golf, Vicmead Hunt, Rehoboth Beach Country. Home: 1100 Westover Rd Westover Hills Wilmington DE 19807

MARTIN, JOHN RUPERT, educator; b. Hamilton, Ont., Can., Sept. 27, 1916; s. John Smith and Elizabeth (Hutchinson) M.; came to U.S., 1941, naturalized, 1959; B.A., McMaster U., 1938, D.Litt., 1976; M.F.A., Princeton, 1941, Ph.D., 1947; m. Barbara Janet Malcolm, Aug. 23, 1941; 1 dau., Hilary Jane. Instr. art U. Iowa, 1941-42; mem. faculty Princeton, 1947—, prof. art and archaeology, 1961—, Marquand prof. art and archaeology, 1970—, chmn. dept. art and archaeology, 1973—. Mem. Comité Internat. d'Histoire de l'Art. Served to maj. Canadian Army, 1942-46. Recipient Charles Rufus Morey book award Coll. Art Assn., 1974. Am. Council Learned Socs. fellow, 1965-66. Mem. Coll. Art Assn. Am., Renaissance Soc. Am. Author: The Illustration of the Heavenly Ladder of John Climacus, 1954; The Portrait of John Milton at Princeton and Its Place in Milton Iconography, 1961; The Farnese Gallery, 1965; The Ceiling Paintings by Rubens for the Jesuit Church in Antwerp, 1968; Rubens: the Antwerp Altarpieces, 1969; The Decorations for the Pompa Introitus Ferdinandi, 1972; Baroque, Style and Civilization, 1977; (with G. Feigenbaum) Van Dyck as Religious Artist, 1979; also articles. Editor: Rubens before 1620, 1972. Editor-in-chief Art Bull., 1971-74. Home: 3 Westfield Ct Princeton NJ 08540

MARTIN, JOSEPH, JR., lawyer, diplomat; b. San Francisco, May 20, 1915; A.B., Yale, 1936, LL.B., 1939; m. Ellen Chamberlain Martin, July 5, 1946; children—Luther Greene, Ellen Myers. Asso. firm Cadwalader, Wickersham & Taft, N.Y.C., 1939-41; partner firms Wallace, Garrison, Norton & Ray, San Francisco, 1946-55, Pettit & Martin, San Francisco, 1955-70, 73—; gen. counsel FTC, Washington 1970-71; ambassador, U.S. rep. to Disarmanent Conf., Geneva, Switzerland, 1971-77; mem. Pres.'s Adv. Com. for Arms Control and Disarmament, 1974-78. Pres. Pub. Utilities Commn., San Francisco, 1956-60; Republican nat. committeeman for Calif., 1960-64, treas. Rep. Party Calif., 1956-58; dir. Nat. Fair Campaign Practices Com., 1965—; bd. dirs. Patrons of Art and Music, 1959-63, Arms Control Assn., 1977—; bd. dirs. Calif. Palace of Legion of Honor, 1958-70, pres., 1963-68. Served to lt. comdr. USNR, 1941-46. Recipient ofcl. commendation for outstanding service as gen. counsel FTC, 1973, Distinguished Honor award U.S. ACDA, 1973. Fellow Am. Bar Found. Clubs: Burlingame Country, Pacific Union. Home: 2580 Broadway San Francisco CA 94115 Office: 600 Montgomery St San Francisco CA 94111

MARTIN, JOSEPH ALBERT, bishop; b. Southbridge, Mass., Oct. 14, 1913; s. Arthur and Parmelie (Beaudoin) M.; B.A., Nicolet Seminary; student Laval U. Ordained priest Roman Catholic Ch., 1939; prof. philosophy, history and Greek, Nicolet (Que., Can.) Sem., 1939-46, rector, 1946-49, vicar gen., diocese Nicolet, 1949-50, coadjutor bishop, 1950, bishop, 1950—. Home: Bishop House PO Box 820 Nicolet PQ J0G 1E0 Canada

MARTIN, JOSEPH J., chem. engr.; b. Anita, Iowa, Dec. 23, 1916; s. Joseph Wesley and Merle (Baker) M.; B.S. in Chem. Engring., Iowa State U., 1939; M.S., U. Rochester, 1944; D.Sc., Carnegie Mellon U., 1948, U. Nebr., 1971; m. Merrylin Louise Baxter, Aug. 30, 1941; children—Judy, Joseph, Jacque, Jon. Chem. engr. Eastman Kodak Co., Rochester, N.Y., 1939-41; from instr. to asst. prof. U. Rochester, 1940-45; instr. Carnegie Mellon U., Pitts., 1945-47; mem. faculty U. Mich., Ann Arbor, 1947—, prof. chem. engring., 1956—, asso. and acting dir. Inst. Sci. and Tech., 1965—; cons. to govt. and industry, 1942—; mem. NRC, 1966-72. Div. head Ann Arbor United Fund, 1966; pres. bd. Ann Arbor Hills Assn., 1950; mem. Ann Arbor Republican City Com., 1961, Ann Arbor Housing Commn., 1968-78. Recipient award for teaching Phi Lambda Upsilon, 1955; Distinguished Service award U. Mich., 1966; award N.Y. Acad. Sci., 1962. Fellow Am. Inst. Chem. Engrs. (dir., pres. 1971; Founders award 1973); mem. Am. Chem. Soc. (chmn. div. nuclear tech.), Am. Soc. Engring. Edn. (v.p. 1968-70, pres. 1978—) Engrs. Joint Council (dir., pres. 1973-75), Am. Nuclear Soc., Engrs. Council Profl. Devel., Assn. for Cooperation in Engring. (founder, 1st chmn. 1975-76), Sigma Xi, Alpha Chi Sigma, Tau Beta Pi. Contbr. articles in field to profl. jours. Home: 1565 Roxbury Rd Ann Arbor MI 48104

MARTIN, JUDSON PHILLIPS, educator; b. Butler, Wis., Feb. 4, 1921; s. Darwin H. and Emma (Phillips) M.; B.S., U. Wis., 1942, M.A., 1946, Ph.D., 1955; m. June Ruth Elletson, June 19, 1948 (div.); children—Christopher Alan, Karen Marie; m. 2d, Mary Belle Jepson, Sept. 23, 1971; children—Stephen, Susan, Sandra, Christopher. Registrar, coordinator student personnel services, acad. dean Bemidji (Minn.) State Coll., 1946-68; dean grad. study, prof. edn. N.E. Mo. State U., 1968-71, prof. edn., 1971—. Dist. chmn. Minn. Boy Scouts Am. Mem. Bemidji City Council, 1951. Served with AUS, 1942-45. Decorated Bronze Star, Croix de Guerre (France). Mem. Am. Legion, NEA, Minn. (past pres. higher edn. sect.), Mo. edn. assns., Am. Assn. Higher Edn., Mo. Fiber Artists Assn., Phi Delta Kappa. Methodist. Clubs: Masons, K.T., Elks, Kiwanis (dist. lt. gov. 1974-75). Home: Rt 4 Kirksville MO 63501

MARTIN, JULIAN S. (JULIAN SIENKIEWICZ), publisher, editor; b. Bklyn., June 27, 1929; s. Paul and Lucy (Glowacki) Sienkiewicz; m. Gladys Kaplan, Aug. 4, 1951; children—Kathi (Mrs. Jay Handt), Paul. Project dir. McLaughlin Research Corp., N.Y.C., 1953-56; publs. dir. Belock Instrument Corp., College Point, N.Y., 1956-58; mng. editor Ziff-Davis Pub. Co., N.Y.C., 1958-63; editor-in-chief, coordinator electronics group, asso. pub. Davis Publs., Inc., N.Y.C., 1963—. Served with USNR, 1948-51, AUS, 1951-53. Fellow Radio Club Am. Clubs: Chgo. Press, K.P. (dep. grand chancellor 1978-79). Author: 50 Vacuum Tube Circuits for the Electronics Experimenter, 1960; How to Read Schematic Diagrams, 1965; contbr. articles to profl. jours., consumer mags. Home: 2480 E 7th St Brooklyn NY 11235 Office: 380 Lexington Ave New York NY 10017

MARTIN, KEITH JUSTIN, ballet dancer and adminstr.; b. Doncaster, Yorkshire, Eng., June 15, 1943; s. Clifford and Ellen (Swan) M.; ed. Royal Ballet Sch., 1960-62; m. Barbarajean Martin, Jan. 6, 1973; 1 son, Jason Keith C. Prin. dancer Royal Ballet, London, 1962-70, Pa. Ballet, Phila., 1971-74, Md. Ballet, Balt., 1974-75; prin. dancer San Francisco Ballet, 1975—, dir., 1976—. Mem. Actors Equity, Am. Guild Musical Artists. Mem. Conservative Party of Eng. Roman Catholic. Office: 526 Market St San Diego CA 92101

MARTIN, KENNETH DOUGLAS, writing instrument co. exec.; b. Fort Thomas, Ky., Mar. 13, 1940; s. George Kenneth and Edith (Caudell) M.; B.S., Washington and Lee U., 1962; M.B.A., U. N.C., 1963; m. Ann Helm Hoffmann, Sept. 1, 1962; children—Mark Thomas, Scott Douglas, Edith Louise. With The Gillette Co., 1963-78, v.p. PaperMate div., Boston, 1975-78; pres., chief exec. officer Scripto, Inc., Atlanta, 1978—, also dir. Mem. Writing Instrument Mfrs. Assn. (bd. dirs.), Nat. Office Products Assn., Wholesale Stationers Assn., Nat. Assn. Writing Instrument Distbrs., Nat. Inst. Premium Sales Execs., Nat. Assn. Service Merchandisers, Nat. Premium Reps. and Mfrs. Club: Cherokee Town and Country (Atlanta). Office: PO Box 47800 Doraville GA 30362

MARTIN, KNOX, painter; b. Baraquilla, Colombia, Feb. 12, 1923; s. William Knox and Isabel M.; student Art Students League, N.Y.C. Exhibitions include: Gallery Modern Art, Washington, 1963, Santa Barbara Mus. Art, 1964, Concrete Expressionism, Loeb Student Center N.Y. U., 1965, Yale U. Art Gallery, 1966, Whitney Mus. Am. Art, 1972, Brit. Print Biennial, Bradford Mus., Eng., 1974, Jankovsky Gallery, N.Y.C., 1975; represented in permanent collections: Corcoran Gallery Art, Washington, Mus. Modern Art, Whitney Mus. Am. Art, Mus. Art, Austin, Tex., U. Calif., Berkeley; commd. works include: City Walls, Inc., West Side Hwy, N.Y.C., 1971, Wall Painting Mercor, Inc., Merritt Complex, Fort Lauderdale, Fla., Houston and McDouglas St. mural, N.Y.C.; asst. prof. drawing and painting Yale U., 1965-70. Nat. Endowment Arts grantee, 1972. Address: 128 Fort Washington Ave New York NY 10032

MARTIN, LEE, business exec.; b. Elkhart, Ind., Feb. 7, 1920; s. Ross and Esther Lee (Schweitzer) M.; B.M.E., Mass. Inst. Tech., 1943, M.S., 1943; m. July 20, 1945; children—Jennifer L., Casper, Rex, Elizabeth. Student engr. Gen. Electric Co., 1940-42; with Nibco, Inc., 1946—, v.p., gen. mgr., Elkhart, 1950-56, pres., 1957-76, chief exec. officer, 1976—; dir. First Nat. Bank, Elkhart. Served with USN, 1943-45. Mem. Chemists Club N.Y.C. Republican. Presbyterian. Clubs: Mid-Am. (Chgo.); Renaissance (Detroit). Office: 500 Simpson Ave Elkhart IN 46514

MARTIN, LEE GWYNNE, ins. co. exec.; b. N.Y.C., Dec. 7, 1917; s. Clarence Clark and Lillian Somers (Curtiss) M.; m. Georgina Walton Green, Aug. 11, 1950; children—Eleanor Townsend Hoagland, Howard Curtiss, Martha Kate, Mary Archer. With Gude, Winmill & Co. mem. N.Y. Stock Exchange, 1936-38, W.J. Roberts & Co., ins. underwriters, 1938-40; with Chubb & Son, Inc., ins. underwriters, N.Y.C., 1946—; sr. v.p., treas. Chubb Corp.; v.p., treas. Fed. Ins. Co.; v.p., treas., dir. Vigilant Ins. Co.; V.p. Pacific Indemnity Co. Tex. Pacific Indemnity Co., Northwestern Pacific Indemnity Co., Chubb Ins. Co. Ill.; treas., dir. Gt. No. Ins. Co. Trustee, v.p. Diocesan Investment Trust, Estate and property of Diocesan Conv. of N.Y. Served to 1st lt., inf., AUS, 1941-45. Decorated Bronze Star. Mem. Assn. Ex-Mems. Squadron A, Mil. Order Loyal Legion U.S., N.Y. Soc. Security Analysts, Am. Bur. Shipping. Episcopalian. Club: Downtown Assn. (N.Y.C.). Home: 7 Gracie Sq New York NY 10028 Office: 100 William St New York NY 10038

MARTIN, LOCKETT BROOKS, architect; b. Colorado City, Tex., Sept. 23, 1913; s. A. D. and Ury (Brooks) M.; B.Arch., Tex. A. and M. Coll., 1940; B.Arch., Harvard U., 1952, M.Arch., 1953; m. Orabel Foster, May 16, 1941. Individual practice architecture, Bryan, Tex., 1948-51, San Antonio, 1959-71; cons. Fehr & Granger, Austin, Tex., 1950; asso. Carl Koch, Boston, 1952, Hugh Stubbins, Jr., Architect, Cambridge, Mass., 1952-54, Samuel Glaser & Assos., Boston, 1955; sr. research architect S.W. Research Inst., San Antonio, 1956-58; pres. Martin & Ortega, Architects, San Antonio, 1971—; vis. critic in design Harvard U., 1953, Boston Archtl. Center, 1955; archtl. adviser Jackson-Todd Found. Cancer Research, San Antonio, 1959—; adj. prof. architecture U. Tex. at Arlington, fall 1977, 78. Served from 2d lt. to capt. U.S. Army, 1941-45. Decorated Purple Heart. Fellow AIA (2d prize Journalism award 1959); mem. Tex. Soc. Architects. Democrat. Episcopalian. Archtl. editor La Prensa, 1959-60. Home: 122 Downing Dr San Antonio TX 78209 Office: 615 Soledad St Suite 304 San Antonio TX 78205

MARTIN, LOUIS EDWARD, librarian; b. Detroit, Sept. 16, 1928; s. Emerick G. and Irene Rose (Fuhrman) M.; Ph.B., U. Detroit, 1951, M.A., 1954; A.M. in L.S., U. Mich., 1960; m. Barbara Hilda Heinrich, Apr. 7, 1951; children—Paul Emerique, Clare Ellen, Ann Maureen. Instr. English, U. Detroit, 1953-58, circulation librarian, 1958-60; asst. librarian Oakland U., Rochester, Mich., 1960-62; asst. dir. libraries U. Rochester (N.Y.), 1962-65, asso. dir. libraries, also asso. prof. bibliography, 1965-68; asso. exec. dir. Assn. Research Libraries, 1968-72; librarian Harvard Coll., Cambridge, Mass., 1972-79; univ. librarian Cornell U., Ithaca, N.Y., 1979—; cons. library bldgs. and mgmt. Served with USMCR, 1946-47. Mem. ALA. Democrat. Roman Catholic. Office: Olin Library Cornell U Ithaca NY 14853

MARTIN, LOUIS EMANUEL, govt. ofcl.; b. Shelbyville, Tenn., Nov. 18, 1912; s. Louis Emanuel and Willa (Hill) M., A.B., U. Mich., 1934; LL.D., Wilberforce U., Ohio, 1951, Harvard U., 1970, Howard U., 1979; m. Gertrude E. Scott, Jan. 2, 1937; children—Trudy, Anita, Toni, Linda, Lisa. Editor, pub. Mich. Chronicle, Detroit, 1936-47; editor Chgo. Defender, 1947-59, Amalgamated Pub. Ltd., Nigeria, 1959-60; v.p., editorial dir. Sengstacke Newspapers, Chgo., 1969-76, pres., 1976-78; spl. asst. to Pres., Washington, 1978—; dir. Chgo. City Bank & Trust Co., Amalgamated Bank Chgo., Service Fed. Savs. & Loan Assn. Mem. Wayne County Bd. Suprs., Detroit, 1942-44; dep. chmn. Democratic Nat. Com., 1961-69; chmn. bd. Joint Center for Polit. Studies, D.C., 1970—. Bd. dirs. United Way, Chgo. YMCA, Community Fund, Boys Club; trustee DePaul U.; trustee Nat. Urban League, Russwurm award, 1965, Equal Opportunity award, 1972. Mem. Nat. Newspaper Pubs. Assn. (pres. 1949-52), Am. Soc. Newspaper Editors, Nat., Chgo., Overseas press clubs, Sigma Delta Chi. Club: Fed. City (Washington). Home: 5500 Friendship Blvd Chevy Chase MD 20015 Office: West Wing - White House Washington DC

MARTIN, MALCOLM WOODS, lawyer; b. St. Louis, Feb. 21, 1912; s. William McChesney and Rebecca (Woods) M.; A.B., Yale, 1933; LL.B., City Coll. Law, St. Louis, 1941. With St. Louis Southwestern Ry., 1933-41; admitted to Mo. bar, 1941, since practiced in St. Louis; atty., partner Peper, Martin. Jensen, Maichel & Hetlage and predecessor firms, 1941—. Mem. St. Louis Bd. Edn., 1965—, pres., 1969-71; sec. Higher Edn. Coordinating Council, 1967—, chmn. 1973-77. Pres. Gateway Center Met. St. Louis; bd. dirs. Greater St. Louis Arts and Edn. Council. Served to capt., Transp. Corps, AUS, 1942-45. Decorated Bronze Star medal. Mem. Am., Mo., St. Louis bar assns., Council on Fgn. Relations. Presbyn. Clubs: Noonday, Media, Mo. Athletic. Home: 300 Mansion House Center 2210 St Louis MO 63102 Office: 720 Olive St St Louis MO 63101

MARTIN, MARIE YOUNG, educator, former govt. ofcl.; b. Peterborough, Can., Apr. 11, 1908; d. William and Loretta (Allen) Young; came to U.S., 1913, naturalized, 1919; B.A., U. Calif. at Berkeley, 1930; M.S., U. So. Calif., 1950, Ed.D., 1954; 1 son, William Young. Instr.-counselor Compton (Calif.) Coll., 1940-46; instr., dir. admissions Los Angeles State Coll., 1947-50, asst. dean instrn., 1947-50; dean ednl. services Los Angeles City Coll., 1958-62; lectr. Pepperdine Coll., 1943-44; acting pres. Los Angeles Valley Coll., 1962-63; pres. Los Angeles Met. Coll., 1963-66, Los Angeles Pierce Coll., 1971—; dir. community coll. unit Office Edn. U.S. Dept. Health, Edn., Welfare, Washington, 1971-77; nat. lectr. Nova U., Fort Lauderdale U., 1978—. Mem. com. profl. women Hollywood Bowl. Recipient Minerva award for Calif. AWARE Internat., 1967; award in edn. Calif. Fedn. Women's Club, 1968; named Newsmaker of Year, 1970; Educator of Year, Soc. Mfg. Engrs., 1969; Ednl. Achievement award for Western U.S., 1970; award Cal. Jr. Coll. Assn., 1973; distinguished service award Council N. Central State Council Community Colls., 1973-74, Assn. Community Coll. Trustees, 1975. Home: 435 S Curson Ave Los Angeles CA 90036

MARTIN, MARK, lawyer; b. Shawnee, Okla., June 26, 1914; s. Mark Mehael and Louise (Kraft) M.; B.B.A., U. Tex., 1935, LL.B., 1937; m. Marion Norton, Nov. 18, 1939; children—John Harris, Anne. Admitted to Tex. bar, 1937, since practiced in Dallas; partner firm Strasburger & Price, and predecessors, 1937—; mem. faculty So. Meth. U. Sch. Law, 1938-42; dir. Toreador Royalty Co. Chmn. bd. Def. Research Inst., 1966-70, hon. chmn., 1970—; mem. Tex. Constl. Revision Commn., 1973; commr. City of University Park (Tex.), 1972-74; trustee U. Tex. Law Sch. Found., 1968—. Served with USNR, 1942-45. Fellow Am. Coll. Trial Lawyers (regent); mem. Am. (Fed. Judiciary com.), Dallas (pres. 1967) bar assns., State Bar Tex. (chmn. bd. 1972-73), Tex. Assn. Def. Counsel (pres. 1965-65), Dallas C. of C. (dir. 1969-72). Home: 3525 Wentwood Dr Dallas TX 75225 Office: One Main Pl Dallas TX 75250

MARTIN, MARY, actress, singer; b. Weatherford, Tex., Dec. 1, 1913; d. Preston and Junita (Pressly) M.; ed. Ward-Belmont Sch., Nashville, Tenn.; m. Benjamin Hagman; 1 son, Larry; m. 2d, Richard Halliday, May 5, 1940 (dec. 1973); 1 dau., Mary Heller. Singer in mus. comedy Leave It to Me, N.Y.C., 1938; with Paramount Pictures, Inc., Hollywood, Calif., 1939-43; films include: The Great Victor Herbert, Rhythm On the River, Kiss the Boys Goodbye, Love Thy Neighbors, Birth of the Blues, Star Spangled Rhythm, Happy Go Lucky, True to Life; One Touch of Venus (stage), Night and Day (motion picture); Lute Song (stage); starred in Eng., 1946-47, Noel Coward's musical, Pacific 1860, 1947-48; star in tour of U.S. in musical Annie Get Your Gun, 1948, South Pacific (stage), N.Y. and London, 1949-52, Kind Sir, 1953-54, Peter Pan, 1954-55, The Skin of our Teeth (play), 1955, The Sound of Music, 1959-61, Jennie, 1963; on tour U.S., Japan, Vietnam, London, Hello Dolly, 1965; I Do, I Do, N.Y. stage and on tour, 1968-70; A Celebration of Richard Rogers, 1972; stage Do You Turn Somersaults, 1977; appeared in TV film Valentine, 1979. Recipient numerous awards including Tony, 1948, 55, 60, Emmy, 1955; winner N.Y. Drama Critics Poll, 1944, 49, 60. Episcopalian. Author: Needlepoint, 1969; (autobiography) My Heart Belongs, 1976. Address: care William Morris Agy 151 El Camino Beverly Hills CA 90212*

MARTIN, MAURICE JOHN, psychiatrist; b. Tuscola, Ill., July 6, 1929; s. Daniel Ambrose and Mary Alta (Payne) M.; B.S., U. Ill., 1951, M.D., 1954; M.S., U. Minn., 1960; m. Ada Himma, Aug. 15, 1953; children—Daniel, Mark, Matthew, Tina, Lisa. Intern, Presbyterian Hosp., Chgo., 1954-55; resident Mayo Grad. Sch. Medicine, Rochester, Minn., 1955-57, 59-62; cons. in adult psychiatry Mayo Clinic, Rochester, 1962—, head adult psychiatry, 1968-74, chmn. dept. psychiatry and psychology Mayo Clinic and Mayo Med. Sch., 1974—, asst. prof. psychiatry and psychology Mayo Clinic and Mayo Med. Sch., 1965-70, asso. prof., 1970-75, prof., 1975—, chmn. dept. psychiatry and psychology, 1974—. Served to col., M.C., USAR, 1955—. Recipient H. V. Jones award Mayo Found., 1960. Diplomate Am. Bd. Internal Medicine, Am. Bd. Psychiatry and Neurology. Fellow Am. Psychiat. Assn., Am. Coll. Psychiatrists, Acad. Psychosomatic Medicine (pres. 1974-75); mem. Minn. Psychiat. Soc. (pres. 1979—), Sigma Xi, Alpha Omega Alpha. Contbr. articles on psychiatry and psychosomatic medicine to profl. jours. Home: 914 Sierra Ln Rochester MN 55901 Office: 200 First St SW Rochester MN 55901. *Diligence, perseverance, and hard work — all virtues learned on the farm in Illinois, along with a strong desire for excellence in the altruistic service of sick patients have led to accomplishment. The jump from horse-drawn farm equipment to professor and chairman of a large department of psychiatry in 25 years required the above factors in addition to being in the right place at the right time.*

MARTIN, MICHAEL MCCULLOCH, educator; b. Junction City, Kans., Mar. 21, 1935; s. Thomas Lyle and Malvina (Rucks) M.; A.B., Cornell U., 1955; Ph.D., U. Ill., 1958; m. Joan Stadler, Dec. 10, 1965; children—Jeffrey Thomas, Linda. Mem. faculty U. Mich., 1959—, prof. chemistry and biology, 1970—. NSF postdoctoral fellow, 1958-59, faculty fellow in sci., 1976-77; Sloan Found. fellow, 1966-68. Mem. Am. Soc. Zoologists, Soc. Study Evolution, AAAS, Am. Inst. Biol. Sci. Home: 5530 Warren Rd Ann Arbor MI 48105

MARTIN, MONROE HARNISH, mathematician; b. Lancaster, Pa., Feb. 7, 1907; s. Amos Z. and Mary (Harnish) M.; B.S., Lebannon Valley Coll., 1928, D.Sc., 1958; Ph.D., Johns Hopkins, 1932; m. Virginia Parker, June 18, 1932; 1 dau., Mary Helen (Mrs. Timothy H. Goldsmith). Inst. math. Trinity Coll., 1933-36; asst. prof. math. U. Md., 1936-38, asso. prof., 1938-42, prof., acting head dept. math., 1942-43, prof., head dept., 1943-54; mem. Inst. for Fluid Dynamics and Applied Math., part time 1949—, chmn. Conf. on Differential Equations 1950, acting dir., 1952-54, dir., 1954-68, prof., 1968-71, research prof. emeritus, 1971—. Exec. sec. div. math. Nat. Acad. Sci.-NRC, 1955-57, 58-59, 61-64, chmn. com. on application math., 1958-59. NRC fellow Harvard, 1932-33; Guggenheim fellow, vis. lectr. St. Andrews, 1960. Mem. Am. Math. Soc. (chmn. com. applied math. 1951-54, rep. U.S. Nat. Commn. on Theory and Applied Mechs. 1953-56), Am. Math. Assn., Sigma Xi, Phi Beta Kappa, Kappa Sigma, Gamma Alpha. Contbr. articles fields of celestial mechs., dynamics, analysis and gas dynamics in profl. jours. Home: PO Box 64 Rural Route 2 Denton MD 21629

MARTIN, MORGAN GRAHAM, hosp. supt.; b. Hamilton, Can., Apr. 19, 1921; s. Charles and Gladys (Graham) M.; M.D., C.M., Queen's U., Kingston, Can., 1944; M.S., Columbia, 1961; m. Mary Folger, May 6, 1944; children—Susan, Sally, Nancy. Came to U.S., 1966. Intern, Hamilton Gen. Hosp., 1944-45; resident Sask. Hosps., Weyburn and N. Battleford, 1947-51; dir. Regina (Can.) Mental Health Clinic, 1953-57, Munroe Wing, Regina Gen. Hosp., 1957-59; chief mental health div. Nat. Health and Welfare Can., 1960-66; supt. Norwich (Conn.) Hosp., 1966-78, Eastern State Hosp. Wash., 1978—; lectr. Yale, 1966. Served with Royal Canadian Army Med. Corps., 1943-46. Author: The Mental Ward: A Personnel Guidebook, 1962; also articles. Home: Box A Medical Lake WA 99022

MARTIN, NORMAN MARSHALL, educator; b. Chgo., Jan. 16, 1924; s. Harry Eugene and Fay (Kaplan) Cohen; student Central YMCA Coll., 1941-42; M.A., U. Chgo., 1946; postgrad. U. Amsterdam (Netherlands), 1949-50; Ph.D., U. Calif. at Los Angeles, 1952; m. Emilia Regina van Deene, Aug. 16, 1950; children—Gabrielle, Gwenwyn, Michael John Edward. Instr. philosophy U. Ill. at Urbana, 1950-51, U. Calif. at Los Angeles, 1952-53; research asso. Willow Run Research Center, U. Mich., 1953-55; mem. tech. staff Space Tech. Labs., El Segundo, Calif., 1955-61, head logic techniques group, 1957-61; staff logician, dir. Logicon, Inc., Los Angeles, 1961-65, treas., 1962-65; asso. prof. philosophy U. Tex. at Austin, 1965-68, asso. prof. computer sci., 1967-68, prof. philosophy and computer sci., 1968-74, prof. computer sci., philosophy and elec. engring., 1974—, asso. chmn. computer sci., 1975-78; lectr. engring. U. Calif. at Los Angeles, 1956-65; cons. Logicon, Inc., 1965-71. Served with F.A., AUS, 1943-45. Decorated Purple Heart. Fulbright grantee, Netherlands, 1949. Mem. Am. Math Soc., Math Assn. Am., Am. Philos. Assn., Assn. Symbolic Logic, Assn. Computing Machinery, Internat. Significs Soc., Netherlands Assn. Logic and Philosophy Exact Scis., Sigma Xi. Democrat. Unitarian. Home: 4423 Crestway Dr Austin TX 78731

MARTIN, OSCAR THADDEUS, lawyer; b. Springfield, Ohio, Jan. 27, 1908; s. Harrie B. and Margaret L. (Buchwalter) M.; A.B., Princeton, 1929; J.D. cum laude, Harvard, 1932; m. Dorothy Traquair, June 15, 1937; children—Cecily M. (Mrs. Jack A. Lupovich), Nancy S. (Mrs. Roger L. Saunders), David M., Robert M.; m. 2d, Lydia Kauffman, July 15, 1966. Admitted to Ohio bar, 1932, since practiced in Springfield; asso. firm Martin & Corry, 1932-40; partner in successor firms and now sr. partner Martin, Browne, Hull & Harper, 1960—. Sec., dir. Vernay Labs., Inc.; dir. First Nat. Bank of Springfield, Morris Bean & Co. Vice pres. nat. council YMCA, 1979—, mem. nat. bd.; v.p., trustee Springfield Found.; trustee Springfield Symphony. Mem. Am., Ohio, Springfield (past pres.) bar assns., Am. Law Inst., Am. Coll. Probate Counsel, Nat. Assn. Coll. and Univs. Attys., Phi Beta Kappa. Clubs: Springfield Country (past pres.); Scioto (Columbus); Princeton of New York. Home: 601 Westchester Park Dr Springfield OH 45504 Office: First Nat Bank Bldg Springfield OH 45502

MARTIN, OTIS ORVAL, ret. financial mgmt. cons.; b. Gadsden, Ala., Aug. 10, 1906; s. Walter and Clara (Pickett) M.; student U. Calif. at Los Angeles, 1926, Tex. Tech. Coll., 1926-27; B.C.S., Benjamin Franklin U., Washington, 1936, M.C.S., 1937; postgrad. Am. U.; m. Jean Mildred Zeiders, June 25, 1930; 1 dau., Carol Lee. With Clovis Nat. Bank (N.Mex.), 1924, Los Angeles First Nat. Bank, 1925, FHA, 1934-38; bank examiner Treasury Dept., 1938-46; treas., comptroller, dir. Paul Stone, Inc., realtors, builders and developers, Washington, 1946-56; internal auditor HHFA, 1956-59; mem. staff Smithsonian Instn., 1959-66, treas., 1959-66, financial mgmt. adviser, 1966-70; financial mgmt. cons., 1970-77. Served with AUS, 1944-45. C.P.A., Md. Mem. Men's Forum (treas.), Fed. Govt. Accountants Assn., Rho Epsilon. Christian Scientist. Mason. Home: 1241 Arden St Longwood FL 32750

MARTIN, PAUL CECIL, physicist, educator; b. Bklyn., Jan. 31, 1931; s. Harry and Helen (Salzberger) M.; A.B., Harvard, 1952, Ph.D., 1954; m. Ann Wallace Bradley, Aug. 7, 1957; children—Peter, Stephanie, Daniel. Faculty Harvard, 1957—, prof. physics, 1964—, chmn. dept. physics, 1972-75, dean div. applied scis., 1977—; vis. prof. Ecole Normale Superieure, Paris, France, 1963, 66, U. Paris, 1971. Bd. dirs. Asso. Univs. for Research in Astronomy, 1979. NSF postdoctoral fellow, 1955; Sloan Found. fellow, 1959; Guggenheim fellow, 1966, 71. Fellow Am. Phys. Soc., Am. Acad. Arts and Scis., Nat. Acad. Scis.; mem. Nat. Inst. for Theoretical Physics (chmn. adv. com. 1979). Bd. editors Jour. Math Physics, 1965-68, Annals of Physics, 1968—, Jour. Statis. Physics, 1975—. Home: 27 Stone Rd Belmont MA 02178 Offices: Lyman Lab Physics Pierce Hall Harvard U Cambridge MA 02138

MARTIN, PAUL EDGAR, transp. co. exec.; b. Windsor, Ont., Can., Aug. 28, 1938; s. Paul Joseph and Eleanor (Adams) M.; B.A. in Philosophy and History with honours, U. Toronto (Ont.), 1962, B.Law, 1965; m. Sheila Ann Cowan, Sept. 11, 1965; children—Paul William James, Robert James Edward, David Patrick Anthony. Admitted to Ont. bar, 1966; exec. asst. to pres. Power Corp. Can. Ltd., 1966-69, v.p., 1969-71; v.p. spl. projects Consol.-Bathurst Ltd., 1971-73; v.p. planning and devel. Power Corp. Can., 1973-74; pres. Can. S.S. Lines Ltd., Montreal, 1974—, chief exec. officer, 1976—; chmn. bd., chief exec. officer Kingsway Transports Ltd., Voyageur Enterprises Ltd., Canadian Shipbldg. & Engring. Ltd.; dir. Domglas Ltd., Power Corp. of Can. Ltd. Bd. dirs. Canadian Econ. Policy Com., North-South Com., Lloyds Canadian Com., Council Canadian Unity, Sci. Council Com. on Transp., Conf. Bd. Can. Mem. Law Soc. Upper Can. Clubs: University, Royal Montreal Golf (Montreal); St. James. Home: 939 Moncrieff Rd Town of Mount Royal PQ Canada Office: 759 Victoria Sq Montreal PQ Canada

MARTIN, PAUL EDWARD, ret. ins. co. exec.; b. Santa Claus, Ind., Sept. 10, 1914; s. James F. and Anna (Singer) M.; B.A., Hanover Coll., 1936; m. Pauline Peva, Dec. 22, 1939; 1 son, Peter McDowell. With actuarial dept. State Life Ins. Co., Indpls., 1936-42; asst. actuary Ohio Nat. Life Ins. Co., Cin., 1946-48, asso. actuary, 1948-49, actuary, 1949-55, actuarial v.p., 1955-56, adminstrv. v.p., 1956-67, sr. v.p. ins. adminstrn., 1967-71, pres., 1971-72, chmn. bd., chief exec. officer, 1972-79, also dir.; dir. First Nat. Cin. Corp. Trustee, Hanover (Ind.) Coll., Bethesda Hosp. of Cin. Served to maj. F.A., AUS, 1942-46; PTO. Fellow Soc. Actuaries, Acad. Actuaries; mem. Gamma Sigma Pi, Beta Theta Pi. Presbyn. Mason (Shriner). Clubs: Commercial, Cincinnati Country. Home: 101 Clubhouse Ln Naples FL 33942

MARTIN, PAUL J., psychologist, educator; b. Chgo., Nov. 23, 1945; s. Frank R. and Christine M. (Colbert) M.; B.S. with honors, Chgo. State U., 1967; M.A., U. Ky., 1968, Ph.D., 1972. Area team supr. Upper Ky. Mental Health-Mental Rehab. Center, 1969-70; psychology intern Larue D. Carter Meml. Hosp., Indpls., 1970-71, staff psychologist, 1971-74, research psychologist, 1975—; asst. prof. psychology Ind. U. Med. Sch., 1975—. Asso. faculty Marion Coll., 1971-73, Ind. U., Indpls., 1971-75; pres., dir. Psychol. Assessment, Inc., Indpls., 1975—. USPHS fellow; NIMH research grantee, 1971-76. Mem. Ind., Central Ind. (pres. elect 1976-77), Ky. psychol. assns., Am. Psychology-Law Assn., Am. Acad. Polit. and Social Scis. Contbr. articles to profl. jours. Home: 2210 E 46th St Indianapolis IN 46205 Office: 1800 N Meridian St Suite 408 Indianapolis IN 46202. *I believe that every person has primary responsibility to contribute to the well-being of all forms of life. Success, measured in these terms, can be achieved through intelligent, active pursuit of clearly defined goals.*

MARTIN, PAUL SIMEON, lawyer; b. Berlin, Sept. 20, 1914; s. Simeon and Rochlya (Trifon) M.; came to U.S., 1915; B.S. in Engring., Coll. City N.Y., 1935, E.E., 1936; LL.B., J.D., George Washington U., 1942; m. Claire Bond, Apr. 7, 1940; children—Daniel, George, Lawrence. Admitted to D.C. bar, 1942, N.Y. bar, 1948, U.S. Ct. Customs and Patent Appeals, 1952; patent examiner U.S. Patent Office, Washington, 1938-44; mem. staff Columbia U./War Contracts Div., Mineola, N.Y., 1944-46; patent atty. Sylvania Elec. Products, N.Y.C., 1946-54; patent counsel Fed. Pacific Electric Co., Newark, 1954-73, gen. counsel, 1973—. Mem. Bar Assn. D.C., Am., N.Y., N.J. patent law assns. Patentee. Home: 189 54 43d Rd Flushing NY 11358 Office: 150 Ave L Newark NJ 07101

MARTIN, PRESTON, pvt. mortgage ins. co. exec.; b. Los Angeles, Dec. 5, 1923; s. Oscar and Gaynell (Horne) M.; B.S. in Finance, U. So. Calif., 1947, M.B.A., 1948; Ph.D. in Econs., U. Ind., 1952; m. Adrienne Hatch, Dec. 11, 1955; children—Jeffrey Ellsworth, Barbara Gay, Pier Preston. Research fellow U. Ind., Bloomington, 1948-49; prin. in housebldg. firm, 1952-56, mortgage finance and consumer financial firms, 1954-57; propr. econ. research group specializing in savs. and loan matters, 1956-66; dir. Lincoln Savs. and Loan Assn., Los Angeles, 1959-66; developer, adminstr. Pakistan Project for Grad. Bus. Edn., Los Angeles, 1960-63; developer, dir. Programs for Bus. and Govt. Execs., U. So. Calif., 1959-63; commr. savs. and loan State of Calif., 1967-69; chmn. Fed. Home Loan Bank Bd., Washington, 1969-72; chmn., chief exec. officer PMI Mortgage Ins. Co., 1972—; from asst. prof. to prof. bus. adminstrn. U. So. Calif., 1950-66; tchr. U. Ind., 1948-50. Mem. Town Hall, Los Angeles, 1952-66, Republican Assembly, Los Angeles, 1959-60; mem. Joint Center Urban Studies M.I.T. Served with AUS, 1943-46. Recipient House and Home award, 1969, award Engring. News Record, 1971, NAHB Turntable award, 1973. Mem. Am. Econ. Assn., Am. Fin. Assn., Lambda Chi Alpha. Presbyn. Clubs: Circus (Menlo Park, Calif.); Congl. Country (Bethesda, Md.). Author: Principles and Practices of Real Estate, 1959. Contbr. articles to profl. jours. Home: 399 Atherton Ave Atherton CA 94025 Office: 555 California St San Francisco CA 94104

MARTIN, RALPH GUY, writer; b. Chgo., Mar. 4, 1920; s. Herman and Tillie (Charno) M.; B.J., U. Mo., 1941; m. Marjorie Jean Pastel, June 17, 1944; children—Maurice Joseph, Elizabeth, Tina. Reporter, mng. editor Box Elder News Jour., Brigham, Utah, 1940-41; contbr. mags. including Sunday N.Y. Times, Look, Harpers mag., 1945-53; asso. editor New Republic mag., 1945-48; asso. editor charge spl. reports Newsweek mag., 1953-55; exec. editor House Beautiful mag., 1955-57; pub., pres. Bandwagon, Inc. Dep. dir. pub. relations Nat. Vols. for Stevenson-Kefauver, 1956; mem. Dem. Nat. Campaign Com. Combat corr. Stars and Stripes, Yank mag., 1941-45. Mem. Author's League Am., Author's Guild, English-Speaking Union, Tenn. Squires, Dramatist's Guild. Clubs: Century, Overseas Press, Princeton. Author: Boy From Nebraska, 1946; The Best is None Too Good, 1948; Ballots and Bandwagons: Five Key Conventions since 1900, 1964; Skin Deep, 1964; The Bosses, 1964; President from Missouri, 1964; Wizard of Wall Street, 1965; World War II; Pearl Harbor to V-J Day, 1966; The GI War, 1967; A Man for All People, 1968; Jennie: The Life of Lady Randolph Churchill, The Romantic Years, 1969, vol.

II, The Dramatic Years, 1971; Lincoln Center for the Performing Arts, 1971; The Woman He Loved: The Story of the Duke and Duchess of Windsor, 1974; Cissy, The Extraordinary Life of Eleanor Medill Patterson, 1979; co-author: Eleanor Roosevelt: Her Life in Pictures, 1958; The Human Side of FDR, 1960; Front Runner, Dark Horse, 1960; Money, Money, Money, 1960; Man of Destiny: Charles DeGaulle, 1961; Man of the Century: Winston Churchill, 1961; The Three Lives of Helen Keller, 1962; World War II: From D-Day to VE-Day, 1962. Contbr. to Yank The GI History of The War: Stevenson Speeches, 1952; Social Problems in America, 1955; Democracy in Action, 1962; others. Home: 135 Harbor Rd Westport CT 06880

MARTIN, RALPH HARDING, packaging co. exec.; b. Youngstown, Ohio, Dec. 22, 1923; s. Walter H. and Helen Jane (Metcalf) M.; B.S., Carnegie Inst. Tech., 1944, M.S., 1948; m. N. Suzanne Scott, July 7, 1945; children—Lois Elizabeth, Jeffrey Scott. Sales rep. Osborn Mfg. Co., Cleve., 1947-48; research engr. Pitts. Consol. Coal Co., 1948-53, project mgr., 1954-55; engrng. supr. Pitts. Coke & Chem. Co., 1953-54; gen. mgr. Pitts. Consol. Chem. Co., 1955-58; v.p. Dixon Chem. & Research Co., also Dixon Chem. Industries, Bloomfield, N.J., 1958-59; asst. to pres. Standard Packaging Corp., N.Y.C., 1959-60, v.p., 1960-64; exec. v.p., dir. C. H. Dexter & Sons., Inc., 1964-66, pres., 1966—, now chmn. bd. C.H. Dexter Ltd., Chirnside, Scotland and London, Eng., 1970—; vice chmn. Dexter Internat. S.A., pres. Dexter Far East, Inc., 1972—. Mem. Newark Indsl. Devel. Com., 1956-58, Newark Rivers and Harbors Com., 1956-58. Corporator Hartford Hosp., 1972—; regent U. Hartford, 1974—. Served to lt. (j.g.) USNR, 1945-46. Registered profl. engr., Pa. Mem. Am. Chem. Soc., Am. Inst. Chem. Engrs., T.A.P.P.I., Alpha Tau Omega. Conglist. Clubs: Hartford, Hartford Golf, Canoe Brook Country (Summit, N.J.); Card Sound Golf, Ocean Reef (Key Largo, Fla.). Home: 157 Westmont West Hartford CT 06117 Office: C H Dexter & Sons Inc Windsor Locks CT 06096

MARTIN, RICHARD, profl. hockey player; b. Montreal Que., Can., July 26, 1951. Left wing Buffalo Sabres Nat. Hockey League team, 1971—. Mem. East div. All-Star team Nat. Hockey League, 1972; NHL East Div. Rookie of Year, 1972; mem. NHL All-Star First Team, 1974, 75, 2d Team, 1976, 77. Address: care Buffalo Sabres Memorial Auditorium Buffalo NY 14202*

MARTIN, RICHARD HARRISON, art historian; b. Bryn Mawr, Pa., Dec. 4, 1946; s. Frank Harrison and Margaret Dever M.; B.A., Swarthmore Coll., 1967; M.A., Columbia U., 1969, M.Phil., 1971. Instr., William Paterson Coll. of N.J., Wayne, 1972-73; editor Arts Mag., N.Y.C., 1974—; asst. prof. Fashion Inst. Tech., State U. N.Y., N.Y.C., 1973—; adj. faculty Sch. Visual Arts, N.Y.C., 1975—; adj. asst. prof. N.Y. U., N.Y.C., 1977—. Mem. Coll. Art Assn. Am., Victorian Soc. in Am., Soc. Archtl. Historians, Am. Soc. for Aesthetics, Internat. Assn. Art Critics, Art Libraries Soc. N.Am., N.Y. Hist. Soc., Nat. Art Edn. Assn., Soc. for History of Tech. Club: Nat. Arts. Home: 235 E 22d St New York NY 10010 Office: Arts Mag 23 E 26th St New York NY 10010

MARTIN, RICHARD MILTON, philosopher, author; b. Cleve., Jan. 12, 1916; s. Frank Wade and Lena Beatrice (Bieder) M.; A.B., Harvard U., 1938; M.A., Columbia U., 1939; Ph.D., Yale U., 1941; m. Marianne von Winter, Oct. 23, 1948. Instr. math. Princeton U., 1942-44; instr. math. U. Chgo., 1944-46; asst. prof. philosophy Bryn Mawr Coll., 1946-48; asst. prof., asso. prof. philosophy U. Pa., 1948-59; prof. philosophy U. Tex., 1959-63; prof. philosophy N.Y. U., 1963-73; prof. philosophy Northwestern U., 1973—; guest prof. U. Bonn, 1960-61, U. Hamburg, 1970-71; vis. prof. Yale U., 1964-65, New Sch. for Social Research, 1972, Temple U., 1973, U. Conn., 1980; cons. Alderson & Sessions, mktg. cons., Phila., 1950-55; chmn. exec. com. Conf. on Method in Philosophy and the Scis., N.Y., 1970; mem. East-West Philosophers Conf., U. Hawaii, 1973; mem. Workshop on Kinship Relations sponsored by Maths. Social Sci. Bd., NSF at Center for Advanced Study in Behavioral Scis., Stanford U., 1974; mem. Inst. for Advanced Study, Princeton, N.J., 1975-76; mem. adv. bd. Peirce Edit. Project, NSF and Nat. Endowment for Humanities, 1976—; research asso. Boston U. Center for Philosophy and History of Sci., 1977—. John Simon Guggenheim Meml. Found. fellow, 1951-52, Fund for Advancement Edn. fellow, 1955-56, Am. Council Learned Socs. fellow, 1961, asso. fellow Clare Hall, Cambridge U., 1971—; research grantee NSF, 1958-74, Vaughn Found., 1970, 77. Mem. Assn. for Symbolic Logic (exec. com. and council 1950-53), Am. Philos. Assn. (exec. com. Eastern div. 1964-67), New York Philosophy Club (chmn. 1971-74), Charles S. Peirce Soc. (treas., pres. elect 1978), Metaphysical Soc. Am. (chmn. program com. 1978—), Internat. Soc. Metaphysics. Author: Truth and Denotation, A Study in Semantical Theory, 1958; The Notion of Analytic Truth, 1959; Towards A Systematic Pragmatics, 1959; Intension and Decision, A Philosophical Study, 1963; Belief, Existence and Meaning, 1969; Logic, Language and Metaphysics, 1971; Whitehead's Categoreal Scheme and Other Papers, 1974; Events, Reference and Logical Form, 1978; Semiotics and Linguistic Structure, 1978; Peirce's Logic of Relations and Other Studies, 1979; Pragmatics, Truth, and Language, 1979; Primordiality, Science, and Value, 1980. Editor: (with Alan Anderson and Ruth Marcus) The Logical Enterprise, 1975; Studies in the Scientific and Mathematical Philosophy of Charles S. Peirce (Essays by Carolyn Eisele), 1979; mem. editorial bd. The Monist, 1961—, Philosophy and Phenomenological Research, 1966—, The Ency. of Philosophy, 1967, Transactions of the Charles S. Peirce Soc., 1969—, Philosophia, 1969—, Kant-Studien, 1971—, Philosophical Studies, 1971-76, The Philosophy Research Archives, 1974—, Eidos, 1976—, The Southern Jour. of Philosophy, 1978—. Contbr. articles to profl. jours. Home: 582 Blue Hill Ave Milton MA 02186

MARTIN, ROBERT BRUCE, educator; b. Chgo., Apr. 29, 1929; s. Robert Frank and Helen (Woelffer) M.; B.S., Northwestern U., 1950; Ph.D., U. Rochester, 1953; m. Frances May Young, June 7, 1953. Asst. prof. chemistry Am. U., Beirut, Lebanon, 1953-56; research fellow Calif. Inst. Tech., 1956-57, Harvard, 1957-59; asst. prof. chemistry U. Va., 1959-61, asso. prof., 1961-65, prof., 1965—, chmn. dept., 1968-71; spl. fellow Oxford U., 1961-62. Program dir. Molecular Biology Sect., NSF, 1965-66. Mem. Am. Chem. Soc., Am. Soc. Biol. Chemists, AAAS. Author: Introduction to Biophysical Chemistry, 1964. Office: Dept Chemistry U Va Charlottesville VA 22901

MARTIN, ROBERT FINLAY, JR., judge; b. Akron, O., May 4, 1925; s. Robert Finlay and Olive (Dexter) M.; B.A., Kent State U., 1949; J.D., U. Akron, 1954; m. Eleanor A. Gunn, Sept. 3, 1948; children—Roberta C. (Mrs. Jesse E. Brown), Craig J., Scott D. Admitted to Ohio bar, 1955, Okla. bar, 1963, U.S. Supreme Ct. bar, 1974, Supreme Ct. Okla. bar, 1963, Supreme Ct. Ohio bar, 1955, U.S. Dist. Ct. Northeastern Dist. Okla. bar, 1971; claims atty. Ohio Farmers Ins. Cos., LeRoy, 1951-59; claims supr. Selman & Co., Tulsa, 1959-63; practiced in Tulsa, 1963-66; judge Common Pleas Ct., Tulsa, 1967-69; judge Dist. Ct., Tulsa, 1969—. City solicitor City of Seville (Ohio), 1958-59. Trustee Bd. Pub. Affairs, LeRoy, 1957-59, Ct. Fund Trustees Tulsa County, 1971-74. Served with USNR, 1943-46. Mason. Home: 2315 S Fulton Pl Tulsa OK 74114 Office: 312 W 5th St Tulsa OK 74103

MARTIN, ROBERT LAWRENCE, educator; b. Washington, Nov. 18, 1933; s. Robert Fitz-Randolph and Thalia (Alden) M.; student Farmington State Tchrs. Coll., 1952-54; B.S. in Secondary Edn., U. Maine, 1956; postgrad. (NSF fellow) U. Md., summer 1957; M.S. in Zoology, Kans. State U., 1959; postgrad. U. Ill., 1959-61, (NSF fellow) U. Wash., Friday Harbor, summer 1969; Ph.D. in Zoology (NASA fellow), U. Conn., 1971; m. Shirley Ann Grunert, Dec. 23, 1955. Tchr. biology Madison Sr. High Sch., 1956-57; instr. zoology State U. N.Y., Plattsburgh, 1961-63, asst. prof., 1963-64; asso. prof. biology U. Maine, Farmington, 1966-71, prof., 1971—; vis. scientist Whiteface Mountain Field Sta., Atmospheric Scis. Research Center, N.Y., summers 1962-65; research asso. Mt. Washington Obs., N.H., 1969-74, U. Conn. Chaco Boreal (Paraguay) Expdns., 1973, 74, 75; mem. U.S. Fish and Wildlife Service Ind. bat recovery team, 1975-78; mem. bat specialist group Survival Services Commn., Internat. Union for Conservation of Nature and Natural Resources. Recipient Disting. Scholar award U. Maine, 1975; NSF fellow, 1965. Fellow Zool. Soc. London, AAAS, Explorers Club; mem. Am. Soc. Mammalogists (life), Australian Mammal Soc., Mammal Soc. Brit. Isles, N.Y. Acad. Scis., So. Calif. Acad. Scis., Nat. Rifle Assn. (life), Biol. Soc. Washington, Wildlife Soc. (cert. wildlife biologist), SAR (life), Soc. Mayflower Descs. (life), Mensa (life), Jaguar Drivers Club (life), Sigma Xi, Alpha Chi, Beta Beta Beta, Beta Kappa Chi, Phi Sigma, Phi Sigma Pi (honor award 1975), Gamma Theta Upsilon, Kappa Delta Pi (Compatriot in Edn. award 1976). Editor-pub. Bat Research News, 1969-76; contbr. numerous articles to profl. jours. Home: Cape Cod Hill New Sharon ME 04955 Office: Sci Research Annex U Maine Farmington ME 04938. *Underexercised talent is worth little; it is the exercise of talent which advances mankind, and it is my duty to myself and others to exercise what talent I possess.*

MARTIN, ROBERT RICHARD, coll. pres.; b. McKinney, Ky., Dec. 27, 1910; s. Henry Franklin and Annie Frances (Peek) M.; A.B., Eastern Ky. U., 1934; M.A., U. Ky., 1940; Ed.D., Columbia U. Tchrs. Coll., 1951; m. Anne French Hoge, May 31, 1952. Tchr., prin. pub. schs., Mason and Lee counties, Ky., 1935-48; with Ky. Dept. Edn., 1948-59, beginning as auditor, successively dir. finance, head bur. adminstrn. and finance, 1948-55, supt. pub. instrn., 1955-59; commr. finance Commonwealth Ky., 1959-60; pres. Eastern Ky. U., Richmond, 1960—; dir. State Bank & Trust Co., Begley Drug Co.; mem. Ky. Senate. Assisted devel. found. program for financing of edn. in Ky. Bd. dirs. Pattie A. Clay Hosp., Telford Community Center. Served as tech. sgt. USAAF, 1942-46, meteorologist. Recipient Outstanding Alumnus award Eastern Ky. State Coll., 1956; named Kentuckian of Yr., Ky. Press Assn., 1964; recipient Service award Joint Alumni Council Ky., 1970; Civilian Service award Dept. Army, 1971. Danforth Found. grantee, 1971. Mem. NEA, Am. Assn. Sch. Adminstrs., English-Speaking Union, Civil War Roundtable (bd. dirs.), Ky. Hist. Soc. (pres. 1974—), Ky. Edn. Assn., Am. Assn. State Colls. and Univs. (pres. 1971-72), Phi Delta Kappa, Kappa Delta Pi. Democrat. Presbyn. (trustee, elder). Mason (Shriner), Rotarian. Club: Filson. Home: 300 Summit St Richmond KY 40475 Office: Adminstrn Bldg Eastern Ky U Richmond KY 40475

MARTIN, ROBERT ROY, securities brokerage co. exec.; b. Gary, Ind., Mar. 12, 1927; s. Thomas Stuart and Leora (Vanaman) M.; B.S., Ind. U., 1950; m. Nancy Davis, Jan. 26, 1952; children—Thomas Davis, Molly Vanaman. With Minn. Mining & Mfg. Co., 1950-65, new products mktg. retail tape div., 1963-65; v.p. Springstead, Inc., St. Paul, 1965-69; with Dain Kalman & Quail, Mpls., 1969—, sr. v.p., 1974-75, exec. v.p., 1975—, mem. exec. com., 1976—; pres. Carnegie Capital Mgmt., Dain Bosworth Mortgage Corp.; v.p. Liquid Capitol Income, Inc.; mem. Inter-Regional Fin. Group Planning Com.; dir. Glanton Constrn. Co. Bd. dirs. Minn. Planned Parenthood, 1975-76; mem. Republican State Central Com. Minn., 1978; mem. task force com. Minn. Dept. Econ. Devel., 1979—; vestryman St. John's Episcopal Ch., St. Paul. Served with USN, 1945-46. Public Fin. Inst. grantee, 1975; Ind. U. Bd. Aeons grantee, 1949-50. Mem. Citizens League, Security Industry Assn. (mcpl. securities com.), Public Securities Assn. (bd. govs., legis. com.), Alpha Kappa Psi. Clubs: Informal, Mpls. Office: 100 Dain Tower Minneapolis MN 55401

MARTIN, ROBLEE BOETTCHER, cement mfg. exec.; b. St. Louis, Apr. 21, 1922; s. Henry W. and Esther (Boettcher) M.; B.S. in Chem. Engring., Columbia, 1943, M.S. in Chem. Engring., 1947; D.Sc. (hon.) in Bus. Adminstrn., Cleary Coll., 1962; m. Lillian Seegraves, July 15, 1940; children—Mary Katherine, Bruce Daniel, Amy Lee. Prodn. supr. Monsanto Chem. Co., St. Louis, 1946-49; dir. research and devel. Miss. Lime Co., Ste. Genevieve, Mo., 1949-59; pres. Dundee Cement Co. (Mich.), 1959-69; v.p. Fruehauf Corp.; gen. mgr. Fruehauf Bldgs. div., Detroit, 1969-72; pres. Presidents Assn. div. Am. Mgmt. Assn., N.Y.C., 1972-74; pres. insulation div. Keene Corp., Princeton, N.J., 1974-76; pres., dir. Keystone Portland Cement Co., Allentown, Pa., 1976—; dir. Miller Industries Inc., Miami, Fla. Served to lt. (j.g.) USNR, 1944-46; PTO. Mem. Am. Inst. Chem. Engrs., Sigma Xi, Tau Beta Pi, Phi Lambda Upsilon. Baptist. Home: 1214 Knossos Dr Apt 3 Whitehall PA 18052 Office: PO Box 1785 Allentown PA 18105

MARTIN, ROGER BOND, landscape architect; b. Virginia, Minn., Nov. 23, 1936; s. Thomas George and Audrey (Bond) M.; B.S., U. Minn., 1958; M.Landscape Arch., Harvard U., 1961; m. Janis Ann Kloss, Aug. 11, 1962; children—Thomas, Stephen, Jonathan. Asst. prof. U. Calif., Berkeley, 1964-66; asso. prof. U. Minn., Mpls., 1966, prof., 1968—, chmn. dept. landscape architecture, 1968-77; owner Roger Martin & Assos., site planners and landscape architects, Mpls., 1966-68; prin. Interdesign, Inc., Mpls., 1968—; vis. prof. U. Melbourne, 1979-80. Mem. N.G., 1962. Mem. Am. Soc. Landscape Architects (pres. Minn. chpt. 1970-72), Nat. Council Instrs. Landscape Architecture (pres. 1973-74). Home: 2912 45th Ave Minneapolis MN 55406 Office: Arch Bldg U Minn Minneapolis MN 55455

MARTIN, SAMUEL PRESTON, III, physician; b. East Prairie, Mo., May 2, 1916; s. Samuel Preston and Lucy (Simmons) M.; M.D. cum laude, Washington U., 1941; m. Cornelia Ruth Campbell, July 2, 1939; children—Samuel Preston, William Barry, Celia Susan; m. 2d, Dorothy E. Matson, Sept. 5, 1970. Intern, resident Barnes Hosp., St. Louis, 1941-44; chief med. resident Duke Hosp., 1947; vis. investigator Rockefeller Inst. Med. Research, 1948; asso. medicine and microbiology Duke U. Sch. Medicine, 1949-50, asst. prof. medicine and microbiology, 1950-53, asso. prof., 1953-56; prof., head dept. medicine U. Fla., 1956-62, provost Health Center, 1962-70; vis. prof. Harvard Med. Sch., 1970; prof. medicine, exec. dir. Leonard Davis Inst. for Health Econs., U. Pa., Phila., 1971-78, dir. Robert Wood Johnson Clin. Scholars Program, 1975—; cons. USPHS; dir. Smith Kline Corp. Served to capt. AUS, 1944-47. Decorated Order of Leopold. Diplomate Am. Bd. Internal Medicine. Mem. Am. Assn. Physicians, A.C.P., Am. Soc. Clin. Investigation, Am. Assn. Immunologists, Soc. Exptl. Biology and Medicine. Home: 3641 Locust Walk Philadelphia PA 19104

MARTIN, STANLEY WILLIAM, health adminstr.; b. Toronto, Ont., Can., Jan. 2, 1914; s. William and Ada Elizabeth (Mayo) M.; grad. Malvern Collegiate Inst., 1931; m. Dorothy Lillian Jones, June 17, 1939; children—Judith Anne, Robert Stanley. Exec. sec. dept. pub. welfare City Toronto, 1931-41; asst. adminstr. Toronto East Gen. Hosp., 1941-51; mem. staff Ont. Hosp. Assn., 1951-66, exec. dir., 1963-66; chmn., gen. mgr. Ont. Hosp. Services Commn., 1966-70; chmn. Ont. Health Ins. Commn., 1970-72; dep. minister of health Province of Ont., 1972-76; chmn. Ont. Council Health, 1976—. Vice pres. Canadian Council Blue Cross Plans, 1957-59; mem. spl. com. hosp. care ins. Province Ont., 1956-59; chmn. Ont. Adv. Council Nursing, 1960-61. Recipient George Findlay Stephens award 1964. Fellow Am. Coll. Hosp. Adminstrs. (chmn. bd. research and devel. 1965-67; Silver medal 1975), Chartered Inst. Secretaries (council Toronto 1961-64); mem. Canadian (dir. 1957-63, pres. 1959-61), Am. (trustee 1961-64; Disting. Service award 1968) hosp. assns., Internat. Hosp. Fedn. (bd. mgmt. 1965-71), Can. Council Hosp. Accreditation (bd. 1965-67). Home: 165 Kingswood Rd Toronto ON M4E 3N5 Canada Office: 14th Floor 700 Bay St Toronto ON M5S 1Z6 Canada

MARTIN, STEVE, comedian; b. Calif.; s. Glenn Martin; ed. Long Beach State Coll., U. Calif. at Los Angeles. TV writer for Smothers Bros., Sonny and Cher, Pat Paulsen, Ray Stevens, Dick Van Dyke, John Denver, Glen Campbell; nightclub comedian; appeared, sometimes hosted Tonight Show, NBC's Saturday Night Live; recorded comedy albums Let's Get Small, 1977, A Wild and Crazy Guy, 1978, Comedy is Not Pretty, 1979; appeared short feature film The Absent Minded Waiter; writer screenplay The Jerk; appeared in films Sgt. Pepper's Lonely Hearts Club Band, 1978, The Muppet Movie, 1979, The Jerk, 1979. Recipient Emmy award Nat. Acad. Television Arts and Scis., 1969; Georgie award Am. Guild Variety Artists, 1977; Grammy award, 1978.

MARTIN, STEVEN CULVER, advt. exec.; b. Mpls., July 30, 1928; s. Royce Carlyle and Sylvia Gray (Hawe) M.; B.S., U. Minn., 1950; m. Betty Jeanne Bergquist, June 27, 1951; children—Cynthia Anne, Steven Carl, Peter Royce, Todd Culver, Jeffrey James, Molly Kay. With Martin-Williams Advt., Mpls., 1953—, pres., 1963-76, chmn. bd., 1976—, also dir.; co-founder, 1971, since v.p., treas., dir. Collateral Inc.; co-founder, 1971, since v.p., treas., dir. Earful, Inc.; co-founder, 1973, since v.p., treas., dir. Neighborhood Ministries Inc.; guest speaker Sch. Journalism Advt., U. Minn.; past bd. dirs. N.W. Council Advt. Agencies, Minn. Advt. Fedn. Served to 1st lt. AUS, 1951-53. Mem. Sales Execs. Club. Clubs: Lafayette, U. Minn. Alumni. Home: 115 Loring Dr Mound MN 55364 Office: 89 S 9th St Minneapolis MN 55402

MARTIN, STROTHER, actor; b. Kokomo, Ind.; student U. Mich. Films include The Asphalt Jungle, Storm Over Tibet, The Big Knife, The Shaggy Dog, Invitation to a Gunfighter, The Sons of Katie Elder, Harper, Nevada Smith, Cool Hand Luke, True Grit, Butch Cassidy and the Sundance Kid, The Ballad of Cable Hogue, Fool's Parade, Pocket Money, Rooster Cogburn, Hard Times, The Great Scout and Cathouse Thursday, Slap Shot, The End, Cheech and Chong's Up in Smoke, The Champ, Love and Bullets, Nightwing, The Villan.*

MARTIN, THEODORE KRINN, univ. ofcl.; b. Blue Mountain, Miss., Jan. 2, 1915; s. Thomas Theodore and Ivy (Manning) M.; A.B., Georgetown (Ky.) Coll., 1935; M.A., La. State U., 1941; Ph.D., George Peabody Coll., 1949; m. Lorene Garrison, Sept. 6, 1947; children—Glenn Krinn, Mary Ann, Janet Kay. Tchr. Consol. Sch., Dumas, Miss., 1935-36; prin. Mississippi Heights Acad., 1936-39; tchr. Murphy High Sch., Mobile, Ala., 1940-41; registrar Miss. State U., 1949-53, registrar, adminstrv. asst. to pres., 1953-56, dean Sch. Edn., 1956-61, exec. asst. to pres., 1961-66, v.p., 1966—, dir. Summer Sch., 1956-70. Served as capt. AUS, 1941-46. Mem. Kappa Alpha, Phi Kappa Phi, Omicron Delta Kappa, Kappa Delta Pi, Phi Delta Kappa. Presbyn. Mason. Home: Sheely Hills Mississippi State MS 39762

MARTIN, THOMAS JOSEPH, electronics co. exec.; b. Boston, July 5, 1939; s. Thomas J. and Anna E. (Norton) Considine; B.S. in Bus. Adminstrn., Boston Coll., 1961; m. E. June Tortorella, June 23, 1962; children—Thomas, Timothy, Christopher, Shawn, Gregory, Julie. Acct., Arthur Andersen Co., 1962-67; successively controller, regional sales mgr., exec. v.p. sales Cramer Electronics, Inc., Newton, Mass., 1967—. Mem. Boston Coll. Alumni Assn. (past dir.). Club: Woodland Golf. Mem. 1964 Olympic Hockey Team. Office: 85 Wells Ave Newton MA 02159

MARTIN, THOMAS LYLE, JR., univ. pres.; b. Memphis, Sept. 26, 1921; s. Thomas Lyle and Malvina (Rucks) M.; B.E.E., Rensselaer Poly. Inst., 1942, M.E.E., 1948, D.Eng., 1967; Ph.D., Stanford U., 1951; m. Helene Hartley, June 12, 1943; children—Michele Marie, Thomas Lyle. Prof. elec. engring. U. N.Mex., 1948-53; prof. engring. U. Ariz., 1953-63, dean engring., 1958-63; dean engring. U. Fla., Gainesville, 1963-66, So. Meth. U., Dallas, 1966-74; pres. Ill. Inst. Tech., IIT Research Inst., Chgo., 1974—; dir. Stewart-Warner Co., Inland Steel Co., Amsted Industries, Cherry Elec. Products Corp., Hyatt Internat. Mem. Dallas-Fort Worth Regional Airport Bd., 1970-74; bd. dirs. Museum Sci. and Industry, 1975—. Served to capt. Signal Corps, AUS, 1943-46. Decorated Bronze Star. Fellow IEEE; mem. Nat. Acad. Engring., Inst. Gas Tech. (dir.), Sigma Xi, Tau Beta Pi, Eta Kappa Nu, Sigma Tau. Author: UHF Engineering, 1950; Electronic Circuits, 1955; Physical Basis for Electrical Engineering, 1957; Strategy for Survival, 1963; Electrons And Crystals, 1970; Malice in Blunderland, 1973. Home: 990 Lake Shore Dr Apt 19C Chicago IL 60611

MARTIN, THOMAS ROBERT, univ. dean; b. Emmetsburg, Iowa, Sept. 21, 1920; s. Thomas Raphael and Mary (Laughlin) M.; B.S., Marquette U., 1942; M.B.A., Harvard, 1947; Ph.D., Stanford, 1957, m. Mary Louise Hellrung, Nov. 24, 1947; children—Paul J., Kathleen T., Thomas Raphael II, Gerald K., Mont L. Sales promotion mgr. McCormack & Co., San Francisco, 1948-50; prof. U. San Francisco, 1950-59; prof. U. Nev., 1959-62; dean Coll. Bus. Adminstrn., Marquette U., Milw., 1962—, prof., 1978—; dir. Gt. Midwest Savs. & Loan Assn., Scott, Foresman & Co. Served to capt. USMCR, 1942-46. Mem. Beta Gamma Sigma (nat. pres. 1974-76). Home: 12555 Green Meadow Pl Elm Grove WI 53122 Office: 615 N 11th St Milwaukee WI 53233

MARTIN, THOMAS STEPHEN, govt. ofcl.; b. N.Y.C., Aug. 31, 1946; s. Stephen Paul and Kathleen Mary (Redmond) M.; B.A. maxima cum laude, King's Coll., 1968; J.D., U. Chgo., 1972; m. Lynne Kathryn Mallory, Oct. 2, 1968; 1 dau., Laura Kathryn. Admitted to D.C. bar, 1973; asso. firm. Steptoe & Johnson, Washington, 1972-75; spl. asst. to asst. atty. gen., civil div. Dept. Justice, Washington, 1975-76, asst. to solicitor gen., 1976-78, dep. asst. atty. gen. civil div., 1978—. Mem. D.C. Bar Assn. Comment editor U. Chgo. Law Rev., 1971-72. Office: Dept Justice Washington DC 20530

MARTIN, TONY, entertainer; b. San Francisco, Dec. 25, 1913; s. Edward Morris and Hattie (Smith) M.; grad. St. Mary's Coll., 1934; m. Tula Finklea (Cyd Charisse), May 15, 1948; children—Tony, Nicky. Began career as saxophonist in orch.; now singer; was under contract R.K.O., now with Metro Goldwyn-Mayer; motion pictures include: Sing Baby Sing, Follow the Fleet, You Can't Have Everything, Ali Baba Goes to Town, Music in My Heart, Ziegfeld Girl, Till the Clouds Roll By, Casbah, Two Tickets to Broadway, Here Come the Girls, Easy to Love, Deep in My Heart, Hit the Deck, Quincannon Frontier Scout, Let's Be Happy; rec. artist various rec. cos.; appeared London Paladium Theatre, 1948, 50, 51. Served as sgt.

USAAF, 1942-45. Decorated Bronze Star. Mem. Am. Fedn. Musicians, Escalapias. Clubs: Masons (32 deg.), Moose, Hillcrest Country, Grand Street Boys, Friars. Address: care ICM 8899 Beverly Blvd Los Angeles CA 90048*

MARTIN, TOWNSEND BRADLEY, sports exec.; b. N.Y.C., Dec. 27, 1907; s. Bradley and Helen Margaret (Phipps) M.; student pvt. schs., N.Y. and R.I.; m. Irene Redmond, May 7, 1948; children by previous marriage—Michael, Alan. Officer, Bessemer Securities Corp., N.Y.C., 1948-70; owner, dir. N.Y. Jets Football Team, 1963—; dir. Monmouth Park Jocky Club. Republican. Episcopalian. Clubs: Rumson, Ocean, Stratton, Jockey Office: 245 Park Ave New York NY 10017

MARTIN, VINCENT GEORGE, mgmt. cons.; b. N.Y.C., Feb. 9, 1922; s. Joseph R. and Mae B. (Mulligan) M.; student Pace Coll., 1948-49, Am. Internat. Coll., 1950; m. Alice Ann McGovern, June 8, 1946; children—Kathleen (Mrs. Michael Greiner), Joseph F. Salesman Lavigna Jewels, N.Y.C., 1945-47; indsl. engr. Barton Watchase Mfg., N.Y.C., 1948-49; office procedures Local Loan Co., N.Y.C., 1950-51; sr. time study engr. Perkins Machine & Gear Co., West Springfield, Mass., 1951-52; with Milton Bradley Co., East Longmeadow, Mass., 1952-79, mgr. mfg., 1962-64, v.p. mfg., 1964-69, exec. v.p., 1969—, dir., 1971—, gen. mgr., 1972-79; with Vincent G. Martin Assos., Mgmt. Consultants, 1979—; trustee Springfield Inst. for Savs.; dir. Armoury Corp., Stockbridge Corp. Past pres. Springfield Speech and Hearing Center; mem. East Longmeadow Indsl. Park Steering Com.; gen. campaign chmn. United Fund Pioneer Valley, 1976; bd. dirs. Springfield Symphony Orch.; corporate Springfield Coll., Wesson Meml. Hosp. Served with AUS, 1942-45. Decorated Bronze Star. Mem. Soc. Advancement Mgmt. (pres. Western Mass. chpt. 1954-56), Am. Mgmt. Assn., Toy Mfrs. Am. (dir. 1973-75), Springfield C. of C. (dir. 1974—), Newcomen Soc. N.Am., East Longmeadow C. of C. (pres., dir. 1965-68). Rotarian (dir. 1970-72). Home and office: 8 Flume Ave PO Box 505 Marstons Mills MA 02648

MARTIN, WALTER EDWIN, educator; b. DeKalb, Ill., Jan. 14, 1908; s. Walter Sylvester and Tillie Lula (Secora) M.; B.E., No. Ill. State Tchrs. Coll., 1930; M.S., Purdue U., 1932, Ph.D., 1937; m. Ruth Virginia Butler, June 16, 1934; children—Carol Ann, John Walter, Judith Kathryn, David Butler. Asst. Purdue U., 1930-34, instr., 1934-37; instr. No. Ill. State Tchrs. Coll., summers 1930-31; mem. sci. expdn. Honduras, summer 1934; mem. staff Marine Biol. Lab., summers 1935-42; asst. prof. DePauw U., 1937-41, asso. prof., 1941-46, prof., 1946-47, staff Invertebrate Zoology, 1939-42; asso. prof. U. So. Calif., 1947-48; prof., 1948—, head zoology dept., 1948-54, head biology dept., 1954-58; naval technician to Egypt, summer 1953, 55, Japan, Taiwan and Philippines, 1957; sabbatical leave Marine Lab., U. Hawaii, 1956-57; sabbatical year, Neuchatel, Switzerland, 1963-64, U. Queensland, Brisbane, Australia, 1970-71. Fellow Ind. Acad. Sci., AAAS, So. Calif. Acad. Sci.; mem. Am. Soc. Zoologists, Am. Soc. Parasitologists, Am. Micros. Soc., Western Soc. Naturalists, Phi Sigma, Alpha Epsilon Delta. Home: 2185 Warmouth St San Pedro CA 90732 Office: U of Southern California Los Angeles CA 90007

MARTIN, WALTER PATRICK, physician; b. Los Angeles, Nov. 3, 1912; s. George M. and Viola (Rimill) M.; B.S., UCLA, 1933; M.D., St. Louis U., 1937; children by previous marriage—Judith (Mrs. Lewis Joseph Fisher), Kathlyn (Mrs. John Gausephol), Timothy Martin, James Martin; m. 2d, Margaret Ann Byrnes, Sept. 1, 1966; children—Mark DiPiazza, Greg DiPiazza, Walter Patrick II; adopted children—Paul Wegner, Mary Wegner (Mrs. Bryan McGee). Intern, Los Angeles County Hosp., 1937-38, resident internal medicine, 1938-40; chmn. attending staff Harbour Gen. Hosp., Torrance, Calif., 1950—; chief staff St. Mary's Hosp., Long Beach, Calif., 1970—; clin. prof. U. Calif. at Los Angeles Sch. Medicine, 1960—, pres. Harbour Collegium, 1977-78. Chmn. bd. dirs. Harriman Jones Clinic, Long Beach, 1976-79. Served to maj., M.C., AUS, 1941-45. Recipient Distinguished Service and Leadership award Harbor Gen. Hosp., 1969; named hon. clin. prof. internal medicine for meritorious services U. Calif. at Los Angeles, 1977. Rockefeller fellow, 1940-41; Fellow A.C.P. (regional gov. 1973-77), Am. Coll. Cardiology, Los Angeles Acad. Medicine (gov., pres. 1975-76), Calif. Med. Assn. (chmn. continuing med. edn. 1975, chmn. sci. bd. 1975, chmn. adv. panel internal medicine 81, mem. sci. bd. 1976-81); mem. Alpha Omega Alpha. Trustee Audio Digest, 1974-78. Home: 3039 E 1st St Long Beach CA 90803

MARTIN, WALTER TILFORD, educator; b. Sherwood, Oreg., Aug. 26, 1917; s. J. Tilford and Clara (Brown) M.; B.A., U. Wash., 1943, M.A., 1947, Ph.D., 1949; m. Elizabeth Buckley, Jan. 7, 1939; children—Susan Elizabeth, Kathleen Ann, Lawrence Arthur, David Tilford. Mem. faculty U. Oreg., Eugene, 1947—, chmn. dept. sociology, 1957-68, prof., 1959—. Vis. asst. prof. U. Kans., summer 1951; vis. asso. prof. Whittier Coll., summer 1955, U. Calif. at Berkeley, 1956-57, U. Wis., 1958; vis. lectr. U. New England, Armidale, Australia, 1973-74; field rep. Population Council. Research fellow Inst. Devel. Studies, U. Coll. Nairobi, Kenya; 1968-69; Postdoctoral fellow Social Sci. Research Council, 1952-53. Served with AUS, 1944-45. Mem. Population Assn. Am., Am., Pacific sociol. assns., AAUP. Author: The Rural Urban Fringe, 1953; (with J.P. Gibbs) Status Integration and Sucide, 1963. Editor (with O'Brien and Schrag) Readings in General Sociology, 1969; (with David L. Dodge) Social Stress and Chronic Illness, 1970. Contbr. articles in field. Home: 2730 Emerald St Eugene OR 97403

MARTIN, WILBUR FORREST, journalist; b. Austin, Tex., July 23, 1924; s. Tom G. and Molly Gladys (Chambers) M.; student Nixon-Clay Bus. Coll., 1941; m. Margaret Presnall, Dec. 15, 1951; children—Gail, Michael Dana. Sports writer, editor Austin (Tex.) Dispatch, 1939; sports writer Austin Am.-Statesman, 1939-42; reporter, sports writer San Antonio Express-News, 1942-44; writer, editor AP, Dallas, 1946-50, corr., Houston, 1950-51, news editor, Dallas, 1952-55, chief Okla. bur., 1955-64, Washington corr., 1964-66; asso. editor Nation's Bus. mag., Washington, 1966-69, mng. editor, 1969-78, editor, 1978—; adj. prof. journalism Am. U., 1970. Served with AUS, 1945-46. Mem. White House Corrs. Assn., State Dept. Corrs., Sigma Delta Chi. Home: 5905 Ryland Dr Bethesda MD 20034 Office: 1615 H St NW Washington DC 20006

MARTIN, WILLIAM ELLSWORTH, psychologist, educator; b. Idaho Falls, Idaho, May 17, 1918; s. Leroy and Margaret (Van Houtin) M.; B.S., Neb. State Coll. at Chadron, 1939; M.A., U. Minn., 1941, Ph.D., 1948; m. Phyllis Kathryn Hoffman. From instr. to asst. prof. U. Minn., 1947-49; from asst. prof. to prof. U. Ill., 1949-56; prof. child devel. Purdue U., West Lafayette, Ind., 1956-74, head dept. child devel. and family life, 1961-72, prof. psychology, 1973—. Bd. dirs. Ind. Civil Liberties Union, 1961-64. Served to capt. USAAF, 1942-46. Recipient Research award Am. Personnel and Guidance Assn., 1953. Fellow Am. Psychol. Assn. (pres. div. devel. psychology 1966-67), AAAS; mem. Am. Sociol. Assn., Soc. Research Child Devel., ACLU, Sigma Xi. Author: Child Development, 1953; Readings in Child Development, 1954; Child Behavior and Development, 1959. Editor Child Development, 1954-64; Child Development Abstracts and Bibliography, 1954-64; Monographs of the Society Research in Child Development, 1954-64. Home: 2315 N 600 St W West Lafayette IN 47906 Office: Dept Psychological Sciences Purdue Univ West Lafayette IN 47907

MARTIN, WILLIAM FREDERICK, oil co. exec.; b. Blackwell, Okla., Mar. 31, 1917; s. Fred and Emma (Buchholz) M.; B.S., U. Okla., 1938; m. Betty Jean Randall, Mar. 24, 1941; children—Sharol Ann, William Scott. With Phillips Petroleum Co., Bartlesville, Okla., 1939—, various positions treasury dept., 1939-59, treas., 1960-62, sec.-treas., 1962-65, sr. v.p., 1965-68, exec. v.p., 1968-71, pres., 1971-73, pres., chief exec. officer, 1973-74, chmn., chief exec. officer, 1974—, also dir., mem. exec. com.; dir. 1st Nat. Bank Bartlesville, Bank of Okla., Tulsa. Served to 1st lt. USAAF, 1942-44. Mem. Am. Petroleum Inst. (dir.), Nat. Assn. Mfrs. (dir.), Nat. Petroleum Council, Am. Legion, Phi Delta Theta, Beta Gamma Sigma. Mason (Shriner, Jester). Home: 615 E 16th Pl Bartlesville OK 74003 Office: 18 Phillips Bldg Bartlesville OK 74004

MARTIN, WILLIAM HENRY, III, heater mfg. co. exec.; b. Sheffield, Ala., Feb. 17, 1931; s. William Henry, Jr. and Mary (Lynes) M.; B.A. in Bus. Adminstrn., Vanderbilt U., 1952; N.S.E., Rutgers U., 1956; m. Cornelia Blanche Lipscomb, Oct. 27, 1952; children—Martha Jane, Cornelia Elizabeth. With Martin Industries Inc., Florence, Ala., 1955—, pres. King Stove div., 1966-74, corp. exec. v.p., 1974-77, pres., chief exec. officer, 1977—; chmn. bd. govs. Birmingham br. Fed. Res. Bank Atlanta; dir. Aluma-Form, Inc., Martin Supply Co., CNO&TP R.R. Co.; bd. dirs. Asso. Industries Ala., Florence-Lauderdale Indsl. Expansion Com., Jr. Achievement Quad Cities; bd. advisers Grad. Sch. Bus., U. N.Ala. Served as officer USNR, 1952-55. Named Muscle Shoals Citizen of Year, 1978, Boss of Year, 1978. Mem. Young Pres. Orgn., Gas Appliance Mfrs. Assn. (dir.). Episcopalian. Home: 413 Darby Ave Sheffield AL 35660 Office: 301 E Tennessee St Florence AL 35630

MARTIN, WILLIAM MCCHESNEY, JR., former govt. ofcl., broker; b. St. Louis, Dec. 17, 1906; s. William McChesney and Rebecca (Woods) M.; B.A., Yale, 1928; student Benton Coll. of Law, St. Louis, 1931; postgrad. Columbia, part time 1931-37; LL.D., Temple U., Amherst Coll., Tulane U., Marietta Coll., Washington U., Trinity Coll., U. Pa., Yale, Bowdoin Coll., Washington and Lee U., Hamilton Coll., Harvard U., Tufts U., Princeton, Columbia, N.Y. U., Rutgers U., Middlebury Coll., Bishop's U., Williams Coll., New Sch. Social Research, U. Del., U. Mich.; m. Cynthia Davis, Apr. 3, 1942; children—Cynthia, Diana, William III. In bank examination dept. Fed. Res. Bank, St. Louis, 1928-29; head statis. dept. A.G. Edwards & Sons, St. Louis, 1929-31, partner, 1931-38; mem. N.Y. Stock Exchange, 1931-38, gov., 1935-38, chmn. com. on constn., 1937-48, sec. Conway com. to reorganize the Exchange, 1937-38, chmn. bd., pres. protem May-June 1938, pres., 1938-41; pub., editor Econ. Forum, 1932-34; bd. dirs. Export-Import Bank, 1945, chmn. bd., 1946-48; asst. sec. U.S. Treasury, 1949; U.S. exec. dir. IBRD, 1949-52; chmn. Fed. Res. Bd., 1951-70, ret, 1970; apptd. chmn. com. to reorganize N.Y. Stock Exchange, 1971—; dir. Freeport Minerals Co., Scandinavian Securities Corp.; adv. Riggs Nat. Bank, Washington, 1970—; mem. adv. bd. IBM. Trustee emeritus Barry Schs.; fellow Johns Hopkins U. Drafted as pvt. under Selective Service Act, U.S. Army, 1941; sgt. G.H.Q., Army War Coll., 1941; commd. 1st lt., Inf., 1942, advanced through ranks to col., 1945; asst. to exec. Munitions Assignments Bd., Washington, and asst. exec. President's Soviet Protocol Com. Presbyterian. Clubs: West Side Tennis, Yale, Metropolitan, Alibi, Chevy Chase (Washington). Home: 2861 Woodland Dr NW Washington DC 20008 Office: 800 17th St NW Washington DC 20006. *If you don't take yourself seriously by 50 years out, you never will, but it is also important not to take yourself too seriously. In my freshman year at college, I came across a poem by Arthur Hugh Clough — "Say not the struggle nought availeth" — which I learned by heart and can still recite. It has been an inspiration to me and in spite of the headaches and heartaches of this life I am more confident than ever the struggle is worthwhile. Faith in God and positive thinking are the keys to contentment.*

MARTIN, WILLIAM PAXMAN, educator, soil scientist; b. American Fork, Utah, July 15, 1912; s. Thomas Lysons and Hattie (Paxman) M.; A.B., Brigham Young U., 1934; M.S. (fellow), Iowa State Coll., 1936, Ph.D., 1937; m. Harriet Hammond, June 15, 1933; children—Phillip H., Stephen H., Franklin H. Instr. soil microbiology Agrl. Expt. Sta., U. Ariz., 1937-40, asst. prof., 1940-45; soil chemist Soil Conservation Expt. Sta., U.S. Dept. Agr., 1940-45, microbiologist U.S. Regional Salinity Lab., 1945, chief divs. forest influences Southwestern Forest and Range Expt. Sta., U.S. Forest Service, 1945-48; prof. agronomy and bacteriology Ohio State U. and Agr. Expt. Sta., 1948-54; prof., head dept. soil sci. U. Minn., St. Paul, 1954—. Fellow Am. Soc. Agronomy (exec. com. 1965-67, 74-76, pres. 1975—), Soil Conservation Soc. Am., AAAS, Soil Sci. Soc. Am. (pres. 1966); mem. Internat. Soc. Soil Sci., Council Agrl. Sci. and Tech., Blue Key, Sigma Xi (Minn. pres. 1969), Phi Kappa Phi, Phi Lambda Upsilon, Gamma Sigma Delta. Home: 2285 W Hoyt Ave Saint Paul MN 55108

MARTIN, WILLIAM ROBERT, physician; b. Aberdeen, S.D., Jan. 30, 1921; s. William E. and Anna Louise (Hawkins) M.; B.S., U. Chgo., 1948; M.D., M.S., U. Ill., 1953; m. Catherine J. Reynolds, July 2, 1949; children—Catherine Anne, Charles David, Richard Douglas. Intern, Cook County Hosp., Chgo., 1953-54; instr., then asst. prof. pharmacology U. Ill. Coll. Medicine, Chgo., 1954-57; neuropharmacologist Nat. Inst. Drug Abuse Addiction Research Center, Lexington, Ky., 1957-63, dir. center, 1963-77; adj. prof. pharmacology U. Ky. Coll. Medicine, Lexington, 1962-77, prof., chmn., 1977—; prof. pharmacology U. Ill., 1968—. Mem. A.A.A.S., A.M.A., Am. Soc. Pharmacology and Exptl. Medicine, Am. Soc. Clin. Pharmacology and Therapeutics, Internat. Brain Research Orgn., Am. Coll. Neuropsycho-pharmacology, Soc. Neurosci., Internat. Assn. Study of Pain, Sigma Xi. Editorial bd. Jour. Pharmacology and Exptl. Therapeutics, 1961-68; adv. bd. Psychopharmacologia, 1962—. Home: Route 1 Versailles KY 40383 Office: U Ky Coll Medicine Lexington KY 40506

MARTIN, WILLIAM ROYALL, JR., assn. exec.; b. Raleigh, N.C., Sept. 3, 1926; s. William Royall and Edith Ruth (Crocker) M.; A.B., U. N.C., 1948, M.B.A., 1964; B.S., N.C. State U., 1952; m. Betty Anne Rader, June 14, 1952; children—Sallie Rader Martin Busby, Amy Kemp Martin Bass. Chemist, Stamford (Conn.) research labs. Am. Cyanamid Co., 1952-54, Dan River Mills, Danville, Va., 1954-56, Union Carbide Corp., South Charleston, W.Va., 1956-59; research asso. Sch. Textiles, N.C. State U., 1959-63; tech. dir. Am. Assn. Textile Chemists and Colorists, Research Triangle Park, N.C., 1963-73, exec. dir., 1974—; adj. asst. prof. Sch. Textiles, N.C. State U., 1966—, spl. lectr. dept. econs. and bus., 1966—; del. Internat. Orgn. Standardization, Pan Am. Standards Commn. Served with USNR, 1944-46. Fellow Am. Inst. Chemists, Soc. Dyers and Colourists; mem. Am. Chem. Soc., Textile Inst., Fiber Soc., Am. Assn. Textile Chemists and Colorists, Phi Kappa Phi, Phi Gamma Delta. Methodist. Clubs: Masons, Rotary. Home: 224 Briarcliff Ln Cary NC 27511 Office: PO Box 12215 1 Davis Dr Research Triangle Park NC 27709

MARTIN, WILLIAM TED, educator, mathematician; b. Springdale, Ark., June 4, 1911; s. James Ellsworth and Dora Frances (Smyer) M.; A.B., U. Ark., 1930; A.M., U. Ill., 1931, Ph.D., 1934; m. Lucy Dodge Gray, July 26, 1938; children—Seelye, James, William, Thomas. Instr. math. Mass. Inst. Tech., 1936-38, asst. prof., 1938-43, prof. math., 1946-73, prof. edn. and math., 1973-76, prof. emeritus, 1976—, sr. lectr. edn. and math., 1976-79, spl. Green lectr., 1980, dir. div. study and research in edn., 1973-75, exec. officer dept. math., 1946-47, head dept. math., 1947-68, chmn. faculty, 1969-71; prof. math., chmn. dept. Syracuse U., 1943-46. NRC fellow Princeton and Inst. for Advanced Study, 1934-36. Fellow AAAS (chmn. sect. A., v.p. 1951), Am. Acad. Arts and Scis.; mem. Am. Math. Soc. (v.p. 1949-50, trustee 1953, 54, 56-73, editor bull. 1951-56, treas. 1965-73), Math. Assn. Am., Phi Beta Kappa, Sigma Xi, Pi Mu Epsilon, Lambda Chi Alpha, Phi Eta. Editor: Math. Surveys, 1950-52, Internat. Jour. Math. Edn. in Sci. and Tech., 1970-75. Contbr. articles on functions of one or more complex variables, integration in function space, difference equations and related topics to math. jours. Home: Box 327 Block Island RI 02807 Office: DSRE Room 20C-109 MIT Cambridge MA 02139

MARTIN, YVES, univ. adminstr.; b. Lachine, P.Q., Can., Nov. 22, 1929; s. Hector and Jose (DeCary) M.; B.A., U. Montreal, 1949; M.A. in Sociology, Laval U., Quebec, 1954; m. Louise-Marie Chouinard, May 22, 1954; children—Claire, Catherine, Anne-Marie, Pierre, Laurent, Paul. Prof. dept. sociology Laval U., Quebec, 1956-64; dir. gen. planning Que. Dept. Edn., 1964-66, asst. dept. minister edn., 1966-69, dep. minister edn., 1969-73; pres., dir. gen. Que. Health Ins. Bd., 1973-75; recteur U. Sherbrooke (P.Q.), 1975. Editor: (with M. Rioux) French-Canadian Society, 1962; Recherches Sociographiques, 1960-64. Home: 975 Dominion St Sherbrooke PQ J14 1C4 Canada Office: U Sherbrooke Office of the Pres 2500 Blvd de l'Universite Sherbrooke PQ J1K 2R1 Canada

MARTINDALE, DON ALBERT, educator; b. Marinette, Wis., Feb. 9, 1915; s. Don Lucien and Elsie Caroline (Tetzloff) M.; B.A., U. Wis., 1939, M.A., 1940, Ph.D., 1948; D.Litt. (hon.), Meml. U. Nfld., 1971; m. Edith Plotkin, Feb. 2, 1943. Instr. sociology U. Wis., Madison, 1945-48; from asst. prof. to prof. sociology U. Minn., Mpls., 1948—. Served to capt. AUS, 1942-46. Mem. Am. Sociol. Assn., Am. Assn. U. Profs., Am. Acad. Polit. and Social Sci., Phi Beta Kappa. Author: Nature and Types of Sociological Theory, 1960; American Society, 1960; American Social Structure, 1960; Community Character and Civilization, 1963; Social Life and Cultural Change, 1963; Institutions, Organizations and Mass Society, 1967; Small Town and the Nation, 1969; Sociological Theory and the Problem of Values, 1974; Prominent Sociologists Since World War II, 1975; The Romance of a Profession, 1976; editor: Sociology Monograph Series; Ideals and Realities: Some Problems of Professional Social Science, 1979. Home: 2900 W Owasso Blvd Saint Paul MN 55112

MARTINDALE, JAMES VAUGHAN, publisher; b. Chgo., Oct. 16, 1894; s. George Boyd and Martha (Vaughan) M.; student Bklyn. Poly. Prep. Sch., 1911; m. Ruth Helen McDermott, Sept. 1, 1960. Vice pres., sec. Martindale-Hubbell, Inc., Summit, N.J., 1930-46, pres., treas., 1947-57, dir., 1930—, chmn. bd. dirs., 1943-46, 57—; pres. Bar Register Co., Inc., Summit, 1947-57, dir., 1935—; cons. to Survey Legal Profession, 1949-52. Served as yeoman, USNRF, 1917-18. Club: Sports Car of Am. Home: 189 Rugby Rd Brooklyn NY 11226 Office: 1 Prospect St Summit NJ 07901

MARTINDELL, ANNE CLARK, diplomat; b. N.Y.C., July 18, 1914; d. William and Marjory Bruce (Blair) Clark; student Smith Coll., 1931-32, Sir George Williams Coll., Montreal, Que., Can., 1945-46; m. Jackson Martindell, Aug. 12, 1948; children—Marjory S. Luthes, George C. Scott, David C. Scott, Roger Martindell. Tchr., reading supr. Miss Mason's Sch., 1963-67; mem. N.J. Public Broadcasting Authority, 1970-73; mem. N.J. Senate, 1973-77, vice chmn., acting chmn. edn. com., chmn. joint state library com.; dir. Office Fgn. Disaster Assistance Aid, 1977-79; ambassador to N.Z., Dept. State, 1979—. Trustee North Country Sch., 1967-79, chmn. bd., 1969-72; trustee Mercer County Coll., 1972-76; chmn. N.J. delegation Democratic Conv., 1972, del., 1976. Office: US Embassy NZ FPO San Francisco CA 96690

MARTINEK, OTTO CHARLES, savs. and loan assn. exec.; b. Chgo., Jan. 14, 1922; s. Vincent and Anna (Vachuda) M.; student Northwestern U., 1942, U. Ind., 1959; m. Grace Jane Andreasen, Jan. 26, 1952; 1 son, Robert Charles. Exec. v.p. Olympic Savs. & Loan Assn., Berwyn, Ill., 1946-72; pres., chief exec. officer Republic Fed. Savs. & Loan Assn., Chgo., 1972-75; pres., dir. Republic Fed. div. 1st. Fed. Savs., Chgo., 1975-78, corporate sr. v.p. parent co., 1975—; pres. Chgo. area Council Insured Savs. Assns., 1977—. Founding pres. Savs. Assn. Council, 1970-71; bd. dirs. Boys' Club, Cicero, Ill., Greater SW Service Corp., 1976-77; pres., chmn. bd. SW Devel. Corp., 1977. Served with USAAF, 1942-46. Mem. Pub. Relations Soc. Am. (pres. 1965-66), Chicago Lawn (Ill.) C. of C. (v.p. 1973—), Ill. Savs. and Loan League (dir. 1975-78), Savs. Inst. Mktg. Soc. Am. (charter), Soc. Savs. and Loan Controllers, Methodist. Clubs: Amvets (comdr. post 1950), Am. Legion, Masons, Shriners, Elks. Home: 4125 Howard Ave Western Springs IL 60558 Office: 1st Fed Savs 1 S Dearborn Ave Chicago IL 60603

MARTINELLI, EZIO, sculptor; b. West Hoboken, N.J., Nov. 27, 1913; s. Joseph and Josephine (Besso) M.; student Acad. Fine Arts, Bologna, Italy, 1931, NAD, 1932-36, Tiffany Found., 1936, Barnes Found., Merion, Pa., 1940; studied with Leon Kroll, Gifford Beal, Ivan Olinsky, Robert Aitken; m. Marian Reid Wilson, Sept. 22, 1945 (dec. June 1975); children—Ezio Gaetano, Josephine Valentina, Shelley J. Tchr. graphic arts Phila. Coll. Art, Phila. Mus. Art, 1946; prof. sculpture Sarah Lawrence Coll., 1947-74, prof. emeritus, 1974—; faculty Parsons Sch. Design, 1953-69; tchr. Skowhegan (Maine) Sch. Painting and Sculpture, summer 1969; exhibited one man shows, including Philip Ragan Gallery, Phila., 1943, Willard Gallery, 1946, 47, 52, 55, 56, 57, 59, 64, 66, Art Alliance, Phila., 1953, Seattle Art Mus., 1956, U. Minn., 1956, Art Inst. Chgo., 1962, Benson Gallery, 1968, 69; group shows include Whitney Mus., 1948, 60, 61, 62, 66, Chgo. Art Inst., 1941, 47, 52, 60, Am. Fedn. Art, 1957, Pa. Acad. Fine Arts, 1958, 64, 67, 68, Nat. Inst. Arts and Letters, 1959, 66, Gallery Claude Bernard, Paris, 1960, Newark Mus., 1962, Gallery Modern Art, N.Y.C., 1965, DeCordova Mus., Lincoln Mass., 1965, St. Thomas U., Houston, 1966, Bklyn. Mus., 1968, Ark. Arts Center, 1970, Lindenwood Coll., St. Charles, Mo., 1970-71, Storm King Art Center, 1971, Bucknell U., 1975, U. Wis., 1977, numerous others; works represented in permanent collections Seattle Mus., Whitney Mus., Brooks Meml., Memphis, Guggenheim Mus., Newark Mus., Phila. Mus. Art, U. Wis., Chgo. Art Inst., Bucknell U., Colby Coll., Waterville, Maine; commd. for 30 foot aluminum sculpture Gen. Assembly Bldg. UN, 1960; artist-in-residence museum project Am. Fedn. Arts, John and Mabel Ringling Mus., Sarasota, Fla.; artist-in-residence Ford Found., 1964; sculptor in residence Am. Acad. in Rome, 1964-65, trustee, 1966-68; mem. jury of selection John Simon Guggenheim Meml. Found., 1963-68. Recipient Ford Found. purchase award, 1963; Guggenheim fellow, 1958, 62; Tiffany Found. grantee, 1964; Nat. Inst. Arts and Letters grantee, 1966. Home: 11 Jane St Saugerties NY 12477

MARTINES, LAURO RENÉ, historian, educator; b. Chgo., Nov. 22, 1927; A.B., Drake U., 1950; Ph.D., Harvard, 1960; m. Julia O'Faolain, Nov. 20, 1957; 1 son, Lucien. Asst. prof. history Reed Coll., 1958-62; fellow Villa I Tatti, Harvard Center for Italian Renaissance Studies, Florence, Italy, 1962-65; prof. history U. Calif., Los Angeles, 1966—. Served with AUS, 1945-47. Fellow Am. Council Learned Socs., 1962-63; fellow Guggenheim Meml. Found., 1964-65; Sr. fellow Nat. Endowment for Humanities, 1971, 78-79. Fellow Mediaeval Acad. Am., Italian Deputation for History Tuscany (fgn.); mem. Am. Hist. Assn., Renaissance Soc. Am. Author: The Social World of the Florentine Humanists, 1963; Lawyers and Statecraft in Renaissance Florence, 1968; Power and Imagination: City-States in Renaissance Italy, 1979. Co-author: Not in God's Image: Women in Western Civilization, 1973. Editor: Violence and Civil Disorder in Italian Cities 1200-1500, 1972. Home: 15 Glenloch Rd London NW3 4DJ England Office: Dept History U Calif Los Angeles CA 90024

MARTINEZ, ARABELLA, ofcl. HEW. Former welfare case worker; exec. dir. Spanish-Speaking Unity Council of Oakland (Calif.); pvt. practice cons., to 1977; asst. sec. for human devel. services HEW, Washington, 1977-79. Office: HEW 200 Independence Ave SW Washington DC 20201

MARTINEZ, LUIS APONTE, archbishop; b. Lajas, P.R., Aug. 4, 1922; s. Santiago E. Aponte and Rosa (Martinez) M.; student San Idlefonso Sem., San Juan, P.R., 1944, St. John's Sem., Boston, 1950; LL.D. (hon.), Fordham U., 1965. Ordained priest Roman Catholic Ch., 1950; asst. pastor in Patillas, P.R., 1950-51; pastor in Maricao, P.R., 1951-53, Santa Isabel, P.R., 1953-55, Aibonito, P.R., 1957-60; sec. to bishop of Ponce, P.R., 1955-57; aux. bishop of Ponce, 1960-63, bishop, 1963-64; archibishop of San Juan, 1964-73; created cardinal, 1973; chancellor Cath. U. P.R. at Ponce, 1964—. Served as chaplain P.R. N.G., 1957-60. Club: Lions. Address: 50 Cristo St Box 1967 San Juan PR 00903*

MARTINEZ-LOPEZ, JORGE IGNACIO, physician; b. Santurce, P.R., Oct. 5, 1926; s. Jorge and Dolores (Lopez) Martinez; student U. P.R., 1943-44; M.D., La. State U., 1950; m. Mona Hagan, June 12, 1950; children—Jorge Alan, Anthony James, Ricardo, Matthew Joseph. Intern, Arecibo (P.R.) Dist. Hosp., 1950-51; gen. practice medicine, Elizabeth, La., 1953-54; resident Charity Hosp., New Orleans, 1954-57; cardiovascular trainee Med. Center, La. State U., New Orleans, 1957-59, mem. faculty, 1957—, asso. prof. medicine, 1963-70, prof., 1970—; practice medicine specializing in cardiology, New Orleans, 1957—; mem. staff, dir. heart sta. Charity Hosp., mem. staff Hotel Dieu, Delgado Rehab. Center (all New Orleans). Pres. Club de P.R., New Orleans, 1972-73; mem. council Boy Scouts Am. Served with M.C., AUS, 1951-53; Germany. Diplomate Am. Bd. Internal Medicine. Fellow Am. Coll. Cardiology, Am. Coll. Chest Physicians, A.C.P., Am. Heart Assn. Council Clin. Cardiology; mem. La. Heart Assn. (pres. 1974-75), New Orleans Acad. Internal Medicine (pres. 1970), La. Orleans Parish med. socs., Assn. Army Cardiology, Res. Officers Assn., Southeastern Clin. Club (pres. 1972-73), Alpha Omega Alpha. Contbr. to profl. jours. Office: 1542 Tulane Ave New Orleans LA 70112

MARTINEZ-TEJEDA, JUAN J., mfg. co. exec.; b. Hda. Hornos, Coah., Mexico, June 7, 1908; s. Claudio J. and Luz Maria (Tejeda) M.; M.E., Cornell U., 1927; m. Maria Teresa Orvananos, May 12, 1936; children—Claudio, Maria Teresa. With Mexican Light & Power Co., Ltd., 1927-60, v.p., 1960, also dir.; pres., gen. mgr. Autoelectrica, S.A. de C.V., Toluca and Mexico City, 1961-68, Automagneto, S.A. de C.V., 1966-68; pres., chmn. bd. trustees Centro Educacional Ingeniero Juan Martinez Teieda. A.C., Mexico City and Toluca, 1967—; pres. Durit. S.A. de C.V., Toluca and Mexico City, 1967—, Simpson S.A. de C.V., 1964—; pres. Pactol S.A. de C.V., 1970-75; dir. Mexico City, Inmobiliaria Geógrafos, S.A., Immobiliaria Circunvalación, S.A., Immobiliaria Edison S.A., Mexico City. Bd. dirs. Nat. Chamber Electricity, 1946-47; mem. bd. exec. com. Confedn. Chambers of Industry, 1959-60. Trustee Cornell U., 1961-66. Mem. Phi Kappa Theta. Clubs: University (Mexico); Cornell (N.Y.C.). Home: Paseo de la Reforma 2125 Mexico 10 DF Mexico Office: Taine 134-A Mexico 5 DF Mexico also PO Box 260 Toluca Mexico

MARTINO, DONALD, composer, educator; b. Plainfield, N.J., May 16, 1931; s. James Edward and Alma Ida (Renz) M.; B.Mus., Syracuse U., 1952; M.F.A., Princeton, 1954; m. Mari Rice, Sept. 5, 1953 (div. June 1968); 1 dau., Anna Maria; m. 2d, Lora Harvey, June 5, 1969; 1 son, Christopher James. Instr. music Princeton, 1957-59; asst. prof. theory music Yale, 1959-66, asso. prof., 1966-69; chmn. dept. composition New Eng. Conservatory Music, Boston, 1969—; tchr. composition Berkshire Music Center, summers 1965-67, 69, 73; vis. lectr. Harvard, 1971. Recipient BMI Student Composer awards, 1952, 53; Bonsall fellow, 1953-54; Kosciuszko scholar, 1953-54; Nat. Fedn. Music Clubs award, 1953; Kate Neal Kinley fellow U. Ill., 1954-55; Fulbright grantee, Florence, Italy, 1954-56; Pacifica Found. award, 1961; Creative Arts citation Brandeis U., 1963; Morse Acad. fellow, 1965; Nat. Inst. Arts and Letters grantee, 1967; Guggenheim fellow, 1967-68, 73-74; Nat. Endowment on Arts grantee, 1973, 76; Mass. Council on Arts grantee, 1973, 79; Pulitzer prize in music, 1974. Mem. Coll. Music Soc., Am. Composers Alliance, Broadcast Music Inc., Am. Music Center, Internat. Soc. Contemporary Music (a founder New Haven chpt. 1964; dir. U.S. sect. 1961-64), Am. Soc. U. Composers (founding mem., exec. com. 1965-66, trustee 1965—). Composer: Separate Songs, 1951, for high voice and piano; Sonata for Clarinet and Piano, 1951; The Bad Child's Book of Beasts, 1952, for high voice and piano; Suite of Variations on Medieval Melodies, 1952, cello solo; A Set for Clarinet, 1954; Quodlibets for Flute, 1954; Three Songs, 1955; Portraits, a secular cantata for chorus, soloists and orch., 1955; Sette Canoni Enigmatici, 1956; Contemplations for Orchestra (commd. by Paderewski Fund), 1956; Quartet for Clarinet and Strings, 1957; Piano Fantasy, 1958; Trio for violin, clarinet and piano, 1959; Cinque Frammenti, 1961; Two Rilke Songs, 1961; Fantasy-Variations for violin, 1962; Concerto for Wind Quintet (commd. by Fromm Found. and Berkshire Music Center), 1964; Parisonatina Al'Dodecafonia, for cello solo, 1964; Concerto for Piano and Orchestra (commd. by New Haven Symphony), 1965; B, a, b, b, it, t, for clarinet, 1966; Strata, for bass clarinet, 1966; Mosaic for grand orch. (commd. by U. Chgo.), 1967; Pianississimo (sonata for piano), 1970; Seven Pious Pieces, 1971; Concerto for Violoncello and Orchestra, 1972; Augenmusik, 1972; Notturno (Naumburg Chamber Music award commn., Pulitzer prize in music 1974), 1973; Paradiso Choruses for Chorus, Soloists, Orch. and Tape (Paderewski Fund commn., Classical Critics citation Record World mag. 1976), 1974; Ritorno for Orch. (Plainfield Symphony commn.), 1975; Triple Concerto for Clarinet, Bass Clarinet and Contrabass Clarinet with Chamber Ensemble (N.Y. State Council on Arts and Andrew W. Mellon Found. commn.), 1977. Author articles. Home: 11 Pembroke St Newton MA 02158 Office: New Eng Conservatory of Music Boston MA 02111

MARTINO, FRANK DOMINIC, union exec.; b. Albany, N.Y., Apr. 9, 1919; s. Benedetto and Rosina (Esposita) M.; student Rutgers U., Cornell U., Oxford U.; m. Phyllis E. Higgins, June 15, 1963; children—Michael M., Lisa R. Timekeeper, N.Y.C. R.R., 1937-41; chem. operator Sterling Drug Co., 1946-56; internat. rep. Internat. Chem. Workers Union, Akron, Ohio, 1956-70, internat. v.p., 1970-72, sec.-treas., 1972-75, internat. pres., 1975—, Washington rep., dir., 1962-70. Served with USAF, 1941-45. Democrat. Roman Catholic. Office: 1655 W Market St Akron OH 44313*

MARTINOVSKY, EUGENE SIMEON, physician, chessplayer; b. Skopje, Yugoslavia, Oct. 3, 1931; s. Simeon Yevgenievich and Penelopa (Shahovich) M.; M.D., U. Skopje, 1957; m. Mary Ann Piemonte, Jan. 9, 1965 (div. Mar. 1979); children—Anna, Charles, Dario. Came to U.S., 1962, naturalized, 1967. Intern, tng. and practice of psychiatry and neurology, Yugoslavia and Eng., 1957-62; resident Ill. State Psychiat. Inst., Chgo., 1963-66; staff psychiatrist Northville (Mich.) State Hosp., 1968-69, dir. edn., 1969-72; practice medicine, specializing in psychiatry, Oakbrook and Aurora, Ill., 1972—; dir. alcoholism treatment program Mercyville Hosp., Aurora, 1972-75. Winner numerous chess tournaments in Yugoslavia and Midwestern U.S.; correspondence chess champion of U.S. Mem. AMA, Am. Psychiat. Assn., Chgo. Chess Club (pres. 1967). Home: 11 Ivy Ln Oakbrook IL 60521 Office: 120 Oakbrook Center Mall Oakbrook IL 60521. *I have always admired men who were dedicated searchers of the truth, no matter how pleasant or unpleasant the truth was. I particularly strive to know myself as I really am with all good and bad points. I don't necessarily want to admit my weaknesses to others, but I must admit them to myself and give them always a realistic consideration.*

MARTINS, HEITOR MIRANDA, educator; b. Belo Horizonte, Brazil, July 22, 1933; s. Joaquim Pedro and Emilia (Miranda) M.; came to U.S., 1960; A.B., U. Federal de Minas Gerais, 1959, Ph.D., 1962; m. Teresomja Alves Pereira, Nov. 1, 1958 (div. 1977); children—Luzia Pereira, Emilia Pereira. Instr., U. N.M., Albuquerque, 1960-62; asst. prof. Tulane U., New Orleans, 1962-66, asso. prof., 1966-68; prof. dept. Spanish and Portuguese, Ind. U., Bloomington, 1968—, chmn. dept., 1972-76. Vis. prof. U. Tex., Austin, 1963, Stanford, 1968. Social Sci. Research Council grantee, 1965; Fulbright-Hays Commn. grantee, 1966; Ford Found. grantee, 1970, 71. Mem. Modern Lang. Assn., Renaissance Soc. Am., Am. Comparative Lit. Assn., Am. Assn. for 18th Century Studies. Author: (poetry) Sirgo nos Cabelos, 1961; (essay) Manuel de Galhegos, 1964; (essays) Oswald de Andrade e Outros, 1973. Editor: Luso-Brazilian Literary Studies. Home: 1919 Kinser Pike Bloomington IN 47401 Office: Dept Spanish and Portuguese Indiana U Bloomington IN 47401

MARTINS, PETER, ballet dancer; b. Copenhagen, Denmark, Oct. 27, 1946; came to U.S., 1967, naturalized, 1970; pupil of Vera Volkova and Stanley Williams with Royal Danish Ballet; m. Lise La Cour (div. 1973); 1 son, Nilas. Mem. Royal Danish Ballet, 1965-67, prin. dancer (including Bournonville repertory), 1967; guest artist N.Y.C. Ballet, 1967-70, prin. dancer, 1970—; guest artist regional ballet companies U.S., also Nat. Ballet Can., Royal Ballet, London, Grand Theatre Geneva, Paris Opera, Vienna State Opera, Munich State Opera, London Festoval Ballet, Ballet Internat., Royal Danish Ballet; TV appearance in series of Balanchine works, 1974; film The Turning Point; tchr. Sch. Am. Ballet, 1975, N.Y.C. Ballet, 1975; dir.-choreographer Calcium Light Night, 1977. Recipient Dance mag. award, 1977, Cue's Golden Apple award, 1977. Address: Lincoln Center Plaza New York NY 10023*

MARTINUZZI, LEO SERGIO, JR., banker; b. Newton, Mass., Aug. 1, 1928; s. Leo Sergio and Jessica (Stewart) M.; B.A., Harvard, 1950; B.Litt., Oxford U., 1952; m. Helen Renfrew Gibson, Oct. 26, 1957; children—John James, Georgiana Gibson, Samuel Stewart. With Chase Manhattan Bank, N.Y.C., 1956—, asst. treas., 1960, asst. v.p. Japanese brs., 1961-64, v.p., 1964-68, marketing exec. internat. staff, 1968-72, sr. v.p., 1971—; corporate devel. officer Chase Manhattan Corp., 1972-75, group exec. info. services, 1975—; chmn. Chase Econometric Assos. Inc., Interactive Data Corp., Chase World Info. Inc.; dir. Managistics Inc. Mem. Council Fgn. Relations. Club: Nassau Racquet. Home: 93 Elm Rd Princeton NJ 08450 Office: 1 Chase Manhattan Plaza New York City NY 10015

MARTLAND, RONALD, judge; b. Liverpool, Eng., Feb. 10, 1907; s. John and Ada (Wild) M.; came to Can., 1911; B.A., U. Alta., 1926, LL.B., 1928, LL.D. (hon.), 1964; B.A., Oxford (Eng.) U., 1930, B.C.L., 1931, M.A., 1935; m., Mar. 30, 1935; children—Patricia Martland Roscoe, John, Brigid Martland Stewart. Admitted to Alta. bar, 1932; asso. firm Milner & Steer, Edmonton, Alta., Can., 1932-58; judge Supreme Ct. Can., Ottawa, Ont., 1958—; past dir. Northwestern Utilities Ltd., Montreal Trust Co.; lectr. in law U. Alta., 1936-45. Named Hon. Prof. law U. Alta., U. Calgary. Mem. Can. Bar Assn. Mem. Anglican Ch. Can. Clubs: Edmonton, Rideau, Royal Ottawa Golf, Masons. Home: 55 Placel Rd Rockcliffe Park Ottawa ON K1L 5B9 Canada Office: Supreme Ct Can Ottawa ON K1A 0J1 Canada

MARTON, EMERY, chem. co. exec.; b. Nasna, Rumania, Aug. 11, 1922; s. Julius and Esther (Fritsch) M.; B.S., U. Mich., 1947; M.S., Harvard, 1948; LL.B., N.Y. U., 1953, J.D., 1968; m. Marian C. Pruden, Dec. 25, 1948; children—Peter D., Elise J., Eric M., Susan A. Instr. civil engring. Newark Coll. Engring., 1948-51; project engr. Belco Indsl. Equipment, Paterson, N.J., 1951-53; admitted to N.Y. bar, 1954; asst. gen. counsel Dorr-Oliver, Inc., Stamford, Conn., 1953-63; sec., house counsel Foster Grant Co., Inc. subs. Am. Hoechst Corp., Somerville, N.J., 1963-77, v.p., 1973-77; v.p., gen. counsel Am. Hoechst Corp., 1978—. Served with AUS, 1940-42. Kellogg Found. fellow pub. health, 1947. Mem. Am. Bar Assn., N.Y. Acad. Scis., Harvard Engring. Soc. Home: 40 Montadale Dr Princeton NJ 08540 Office: Route 202-206 N Somerville NJ 08876

MARTON, GEORGE EMIL, office equipment mfg. co. exec.; b. Paris, Dec. 4, 1940; came to U.S., 1957, naturalized, 1962; s. Matthew and Renata M.; B.S.E.E., Syracuse U., 1962; M.B.A., Harvard U., 1967; m. Jacqueline Vick, Sept. 2, 1962; children—Matthew Vick, Adam, Seth. Design engr. Univac div. Sperry Rand and Raytheon Corp., Sudbury, Mass., 1962-65; market devel. mgr., tech. product div. Brunswick Corp., Chgo., 1967-69; cons. Booz Allen & Hamilton, Inc., Chgo., 1969-72; mgr. mktg. info. products div. A.B. Dick Co., Chgo., 1972-76, mgr. mktg. and fin., 1976-77; pres. microfilm products div. Bell & Howell Co., Chgo., 1977-78, pres. microfilm systems group, 1978-79, corp. v.p. and pres. microimagery group, 1979—. Bd. dirs. North Evanston (Ill.) West Neighborhood Orgn. 1970-73; chmn. 6th Ward Democratic Com., Evanston, 1971-74. George F. Baker, William C. Decker, Joseph Kolodny fellow, 1967-69. Office: 6800 N McCormick Rd Chicago IL 60645

MARTON, KATI ILONA, journalist; b. Budapest, Hungary, Apr. 3, 1947; d. Endre and Ilona (Nyilas) M.; came to U.S., 1957, naturalized, 1963; student Wells Coll., Aurora, N.Y., 1965-67, Sorbonne, Paris, 1967-68; B.A., George Washington U., 1969, M.A. in Internat. Relations, 1971. Tchr. French, George Washington U., 1960-70; reporter, producer Nat. Pub. Radio, Washington, 1971-73; reporter WCAU-TV, Phila., 1973-77; fgn. corr. ABC News, Bonn. W. Germany, 1977—. Recipient Pub. Broadcasting award for best local television feature story, 1973, George Foster Peabody award for journalism, 1974, Spl. award for bravery Pa. Gov. Milton Shapp, 1977. Office: ABC News Heussallee (Allianzplatz) Presshaus II Bonn 53 Fed Republic of Germany

MARTORANA, SEBASTIAN VINCENT, educator; b. Farnham, N.Y., Jan. 7, 1919; s. Francis and Jennie (Mancuso) M.; B.S., N.Y. State Coll. at Buffalo, 1939; postgrad. U. Buffalo, 1940; M.A., U. Chgo., 1946, Ph.D., 1948; m. Carrie Mae Stephenson, Sept. 20, 1947; children—Vincenne (Mrs. Alfred Kirmss), Francis Stephen, John Charles. Prof. Wash. State Coll., 1948-53; dean Ferris State Inst., 1953-55; specialist community colls. U.S. Office Edn., Washington, 1955-57, chief state and regional orgns., 1957-63; asst. commr. for higher edn. planning N.Y. State Bd. Regents, 1963-65; vice-chancellor for community colls., provost tech. edn. State U. N.Y., 1965-72; research asso. Center Study Higher Edn., prof. higher edn. Pa. State U., 1972—; mem. nat. bd. inservice edn. project Edn. Commn. States, 1976—; pres., chmn. bd. Assos. Cons. in Edn., 1976—; lectr. in field. Pres. Wakefield Forest Civil Assn., Annandale, Va., 1958-59, Pearse Rd. Civic Assn., Schenectady, 1966-67. Trustee Coll. Entrance Exam. Bd., 1966-70, Washington Internat. Coll., 1974—; lay adv. bd. Notre Dame High Sch., Schenectady, 1968-72. Served with USAAF, 1942-45. Decorated Legion of Merit; recipient Distinguished Alumnus award State U. N.Y. Coll. at Buffalo, 1959, Distinguished Service award HEW, 1960. Danforth Found. grantee. Mem. Am. Assn. Higher Edn., Am. Ednl. Research Assn., Assn. Instl. Research, Am. Assn. Community and Jr. Colls. (dir. 1977—), Nat. Soc. Study Edn., Am. Acad. Polit. and Social Sci., NEA, Pa. Higher Edn. Assn., Internat. Platform Assn., Res. Officers Assn., Phi Delta Kappa. Author: (with E. Hollis) State Boards Responsible for Higher Education, 1960; College Board of Trustees, 1963; (with C. Blocker, L. Bender) The Political Terrain of American Postsecondary Education, 1975; (with E. Kuhns) Managing Academic Change, 1975; (with Gary McGuire) State Legislation Relating to Community and Junior Colleges, 1975; (with L. Nespoli) State Legislating to Community and Junior Colleges, 1976; (with L. Nespoli) Regionalism in American Postsecondary Education: Concepts and Practices, 1978; (with L. Nespoli) Study, Talk, and Action, 1978. Editor: (with W. Toombs, D. Breneman) Graduate Education and Community Colleges, 1975. Editorial bd. Community Coll. Rev.; editorial adv. bd. Jour. Edn. Finance. Home: Box 84 Rural Delivery Centre Hall PA 16828 Office: 322 Pond Lab Bldg University Park PA 16802

MARTY, MARTIN EMIL, educator, editor; b. West Point, Nebr., Feb. 5, 1928; s. Emil A. and Anne Louise (Wuerdemann) M.; M.Div., Concordia Sem., 1952; S.T.M., Luth. Sch. Theology, Chgo., 1954; Ph.D. in Am. Religious and Intellectual History, U. Chgo., 1956; Litt.D., Thiel Coll., Thomas More Coll.; L.H.D., Marian Coll., W.Va. Wesleyan Coll., Providence Coll., Willamette U., St. Olaf Coll., DePaul U., D.D., Bethany Sem., Muhlenberg Coll., U. So. Calif., Valparaiso U., Christ Sem.-Seminex; LL.D., Keuka Coll.; m. Elsa Schumacher, June 21, 1952; children—Joel, John, Peter, James, Micah. Ordained to ministry Luth. Ch., 1952; pastor, Washington, 1950-51, Elk Grove Village, Ill., 1956-63; asst. pastor, River Forest, Ill., 1952-56; prof. history of modern Christianity, Div. Sch. U. Chgo., 1963—, Fairfax A. Cone disting. service prof., 1978—; asso. editor Christian Century, Chgo., 1956—; co-editor Ch. History, 1963—. Fellow Am. Acad. Arts and Scis., Soc. Am. Historians; mem. Am. Soc. Ch. History (pres. 1971), Am. Antiquarian Soc. Author: A Short History of Christianity, 1959; The New Shape of American Religion, 1959; The Improper Opinion, 1961; The Infidel, 1961; Baptism, 1962; The Hidden Discipline, 1963; Second Chance for America Protestants, 1963; Church Unity and Church Mission, 1964; Varieties of Unbelief, 1964; The Search for a Usable Future, 1969; The Modern Schism, 1969; Righteous Empire, 1970 (Nat. Book award 1971); Protestantism, 1972; You Are Promise, 1973; The Fire We Can Light, 1973; The Pro and Con Book of Religious America, 1975; A Nation of Behavers, 1976; Religion, Awakening and Revolution, 1978; contbr. articles to religious publs.; editor Context, 1969—; Home: 239 Scottswood Rd Riverside IL 60546 Office: Swift Hall Univ Chicago Chicago IL 60637

MARTYL (MRS. ALEXANDER LANGSDORF, JR.), artist; b. St. Louis, Mar. 16, 1918; d. Martin and Aimee (Goldstone) Schweig; A.B., Washington U., St. Louis, 1938; m. Alexander Langsdorf, Jr., Dec. 31, 1941; children—Suzanne, Alexandra. One-man shows include Cal. Palace of Legion of Honor, 1956, Chgo. Art Inst., 1949, 76, Feingarten Galleries, N.Y.C., Beverly Hills and Chgo., 1961, 62, 63, St. Louis, 1962, Feingarten Gallery, N.Y.C., 1963, Los Angeles, 1964, Kovler Gallery, Chgo., 1967, Washington U., St. Louis, 1967, U. Chgo. Oriental Inst. Mus., 1970; Deson-Zaks Gallery, 1973, Fairweather-Hardin Gallery, 1977, Ill. State Mus., 1978; represented in permanent collections Met. Mus. Art, Chgo. Art Inst., Pa. Acad. Fine Arts, Ill. State Mus., Los Angeles County Mus., Whitney Mus. Am. Art, Davenport (Iowa) Municipal Mus., City Art Mus., St. Louis, Washington U., U. Ariz., Arnot Gallery, Elmira, N.Y., Greenville (S.C.) Mus., Nat. Coll. Fine Arts, Hirshhorn Mus. and Sculpture Gallery; Instr. art dept. U. Chgo.; artist in residence Tamarind Inst., U. N.M., Albuquerque, 1974. Recipient 1st prize City Art Mus., St. Louis, 1943, 44; Armstrong prize Chgo. Art Inst., 1947, William H. Bartels award, 1953; Frank Logan medal and prize, 1950; Walt Disney purchase award Los Angeles Museum; purchase prize Portrait of America competition, Colo. Springs Fine Arts Center, 1961; honor award for mural AIA, 1962; named Artist of Year Am. Fedn. Arts, 1958. Mem. Artists Equity, Renaissance Soc. Unitarian. Address: Rural Route 1 Box 228 Meacham Rd Schaumburg IL 60172

MARTYN, JAMES LOUIS, educator; b. Dallas, Oct. 11, 1925; s. William Pitt and Ruby (Bettis) M.; B.S. in Elec. Engring., Tex A. and M. Coll., 1946; B.D., Andover Newton Theol. Sch., 1953; M.A., Yale, 1956, Ph.D., 1957; m. Dorothy Lee Watkins, June 10, 1950, children—Timothy, Peter C., David P. Instr., Wellesley Coll., 1958-59; mem. faculty Union Theol. Sem., N.Y.C., 1959—, Edward Robinson prof. Bibl. theology, 1967—, adj. prof. religion, 1973—. Chmn. N.T. seminar Columbia U., 1965-67, 75—; seminar dir. Ecumenical Inst. for Advanced Theol. Studies, Jerusalem, 1974-75. Fulbright scholar, Germany, 1957; Guggenheim fellow, 1963. Mem. Soc. Bibl. Lit. (past pres. Mid-Atlantic sect.), Studiorum Novi Testamenti Societas. Author: History and Theology in the Fourth Gospel, 1968, rev. and enlarged edit., 1979; (with Charles Rice) Proclamation of Easter, 1975; The Gospel of John in Christian History: Essays for Interpreters, 1979; also articles. Editor: (with L.E. Keck) Studies in Luke-Acts, 1966, 2d edit., 1980. Home: 606 W 122d St New York NY 10027

MARTZ, BILL L., med. educator; b. Anderson, Ind., Jan. 17, 1922; s. Carl and Roxie Dell (Clark) M.; A.B., DePauw U., 1944; M.D., Ind. U., 1945; m. Mary Elizabeth Holder, July 31, 1948; children—Michael, David, Sharon. Intern Indpls. Gen. Hosp., 1945-46, resident, 1948-51; research physician Lilly Lab. for Clin. Research, Indpls., 1951-56, head clin. research lab., 1956-60, dir. 1960-72; vis. staff Marion County Gen. Hosp., 1956; prof. medicine Ind. U. Med. Sch., 1967—; prof. medicine U. Mo. at Kansas City Sch. Medicine, 1972-74; dir. medicine and clin. investigation Dow Chem. Co., 1974—. Precinct committeeman, twp. chmn. Republican Party, 1966-72. Bd. dirs. Indpls. Urban League. Served with AUS, World War II. Diplomate Am. Bd. Internal Medicine. Fellow Am. Coll. Cardiology (pres. 1969). A.C.P., Am. Soc. Clin. Pharmacy and Therapeutics (dir. 1970), AAAS, Am. Fedn. Clin. Research, Am. Assn. Advancement Med. Instrumentation; mem. Ind. Heart Assn. (pres. 1946-48), Sigma Xi, Alpha Omega Alpha. Mason (33 deg.). Contbr. articles to profl. jours. Home: 216 W Tilden Rd Brownsburg

IN 46112 Office: Dow Chem Co PO Box 68511 Indianapolis IN 46268. *Alertness and sensitivity to what goes on about us are the fuels for self-renewal - to power us to the goal of full realization of our potential.*

MARTZ, GEORGE E., lawyer; b. Indpls., Apr. 26, 1926; s. Joseph Arthur and Addie May (Hoss) M.; B.S., Ind. U., 1949, J.D., 1957; m. Patricia Lee Terry, Dec. 29, 1973; children by previous marriage—George E., Linda, Steven, Dennis, Christopher, Kimberly. Admitted to Ind. bar, 1958, U.S. Supreme Ct. bar, 1969, Ct. of Mil. Appeals bar, 1969, U.S. Dist. Ct. bar, 1958, Circuit Ct. of Appeals bar, 1969; practice law, Indpls., 1957—; partner firm Martz and Threlkeld, 1973—; chief pub. defender Marion County Criminal Ct., 1959-62; spl. trial dep. Marion County prosecutor's officer, 1975-79; sec., dir. Dunkin Mobile Homes Ind., Inc., Instant Living Fla., Inc. Elder, Presbyn. Ch. Served with USAAF, 1943-44, USAF, 1949-53. Mem. Am., Ind., Indpls. bar assns., Am., Ind. trial lawyers assns., Am. Judicature Soc., Smithsonian Inst., Frat. Order Police (asso.), Phi Alpha Delta. Democrat. Clubs: Masons, Shriners. Home: 9060 Stonegate Rd Indianapolis IN 46227 Office: 915 First Fed Bldg Indianapolis IN 46204

MARTZ, JOHN DANHOUSE, III, educator; b. Latrobe, Pa., July 8, 1934; s. John Danhouse and Margaret Elizabeth (Sipe) M.; A.B. magna cum laude, Harvard, 1955; A.M., George Washington U., 1960; Ph.D., U. N.C., Chapel Hill, 1963. Asst. prof. polit. sci. U. N.C., 1963-66, asso. prof., 1966-70, asso. dir. Latin Am. Inst., 1966-78, prof., 1970-78, chmn. dept. polit. sci., 1970-75; prof., head dept. polit. sci. Pa. State U., 1978—; cons., lectr. in field. Served to lt., AUS, 1957-59. Ford Found. fellow, 1962-63; Social Sci. Research Council fellow, 1963-64; Guggenheim fellow, 1966-67; NSF fellow, 1973-77. Mem. Am., So. polit. sci. assns., Latin Am. Studies Assn., Southeastern Latin Am. Studies Assn. (pres. 1973-74). Democrat. Presbyn. Author: Central America, 1959; Colombia, 1962; Evolution of a Modern Political Party in Venezuela, 1966; Ecuador: Conflicting Political Cultures, 1972; (with Miguel Jorrin) Latin American Political Thought and Ideology, 1970; (with Enrique Baloyra) Political Mobilization in Venezuela, 1976. Editor: Dynamics of Political Change in Latin America, 1st edit., 1965, 2d edit., 1971; (with David J. Myers) Venezuela: The Democratic Experiment, 1977; (with E. Baloyra) Political Attitudes in Venezuela, 1979; Latin Am. Research Rev., 1974-79. Contbr. numerous articles, revs. to profl. jours. Home: 2619 Acacia Dr State College PA 16801

MARTZ, LOUIS LOHR, educator; b. Berwick, Pa., Sept. 27, 1913; s. Isaiah Louis Bower and Ruth Alverna (Lohr) M.; A.B., Lafayette Coll., 1935, Litt.D., 1960; Ph.D., Yale, 1939; m. Edwine Montague, June 30, 1941; children—Frederick, Louis, Ruth Anne. Instr. English, Yale, 1938-44, asst. prof., 1944-48, asso. prof., 1948-54, prof., 1954-57, Douglas Tracy Smith prof. English and Am. lit., 1957-71, Sterling prof. English, 1971—, dir. Beinecke Rare Book and Manuscript Library, 1972-77, chmn. dept., 1956-62, 64-65, dir. div. humanities, 1959-62, chmn. coll. seminar program, 1968-71. Fellow Saybrook Coll. Guggenheim fellow, 1948-49; Rockefeller fellow, 1966-67; NEH fellow, 1977-78; recipient Christian Gauss prize, 1955. Mem. Modern Lang. Assn., Am. Acad. Arts and Sci., Am. Antiquarian Soc., Amici Thomae Mori, Renaissance Soc. Am., Phi Beta Kappa, Kappa Delta Rho. Club: Elizabethan (New Haven); Grolier, Yale (N.Y.C.); Athenaeum (London). Author: The Later Career of Tobias Smollett, 1942; The Poetry of Meditation, 1954; The Paradise Within, 1964; The Poem of the Mind, 1966; The Wit of Love, 1969. Editor: Pilgrim's Progress, 1949; The Meditative Poem, 1963; Milton: Critical Essays, 1966; Anchor Anthology of 17th Century Verse, vol. I, 1969; (with R. Sylvester) Thomas More's Prayer Book, 1969; Marlowe's Hero and Leander, 1972; (with F. Manley) Thomas More's Dialogue of Comfort, 1976. Editorial bd. Yale Edit. Prose Works of John Milton; chmn. Yale Edit. Works of Thomas More. Contbr. articles, revs. Brit. and Am. periodicals. Home: 46 Swarthmore St Hamden CT 06517 Office: 994 Yale Station New Haven CT 06520

MARTZ, WALTER ATLEE, dairy coop. exec.; b. Frederick, Md., Dec. 18, 1923; s. Walter Clayton and Alta Irene (Ramsburg) M.; student Frederick pub. schs.; m. Barbara Jean Winebrener, Dec. 1, 1950; children—Walter Clayton II, Byron W., Barbara S., Elizabeth S., Stephen C., Julia A. Pres., Penmarva Dairymen's Fedn., Inc., Balt., 1973, Md. and Va. Milk Producers, Arlington, Va., 1973—; asst. treas. Nat. Milk Producers Fedn., 1975—; pres. Atlantic Dairy Assn., 1977; pres. Dairy Council of Greater Met. Washington, 1978—; chmn. Order 4 Advt. Agency, 1978. Pres. Republican Club of Frederick County, 1964-65; mem. Rep. State Central Com. from Frederick County, 1966-74; mem. Economic Commn. Frederick County, 1979. Lutheran. Club: Frederick Cotillion. Home: 8619 Yellow Springs Rd Frederick MD 21701 Office: 1530 Wilson Blvd Arlington VA 22209

MARTZ, WILLIAM EDWARD, lawyer, chess master; b. Detroit, Mar. 21, 1945; s. Edward V. and Ellen (Legerat) M.; B.A., U. Wis., 1965; J.D., Marquette U., 1970. Admitted to Wis. bar, 1970, since practiced in Hartland. Chess tchr., exhibitor, lectr., 1965—; rep. of U.S. in internat. chess competition, 1967-76; Wis. chess champion, 1964, 65, 66, 69, 70, 74, 75; Wis. del. U.S. Chess Fedn., 1968-79; internat. chess master, 1975; twice participant U.S.A. team World Chess Olympics. Mem. U.S. Chess Fedn. (life master), Waukesha Chess Club, Wis., Milw. Municipal (pres. 1972-74) chess assns. Contbr. to ofcl. state chess publs., Wis., Minn., N.D., Ill., Mich. Home: N56 W30650 Hwy K Hartland WI 53029

MARUMOTO, MASAJI, lawyer, former state justice; b. Honolulu, Jan. 27, 1906; s. Tamajiro and Matsu (Nakayama) M.; Ph.B., U. Chgo., 1927; J.D., Harvard, 1930; m. Shigeko Ozu, Sept. 23, 1933; children—Wendell Hiroshi, Claire Mitsu. Admitted to Hawaii bar, 1930; practice in Honolulu, 1931-43, 46-56, 60-67, 74—; asso. justice Supreme Ct. Territory of Hawaii, 1956-59; asso. justice Supreme Ct. Hawaii, Honolulu, 1959-60, 67-73. Chmn. compilation commn. Revised Laws of Hawaii, 1955; chmn. adv. com. Hawaii Revised Statutes, 1966-69. Pres. Kuakini Hosp. and Home, 1948-50; chmn. Hawaii chpt. ARC, 1966-67. Served with AUS, 1943-46. Fellow Am. Bar Found.; mem. Bar Assn. Hawaii (pres. 1954), Am. Bar Assn. Japan Am. Soc. Honolulu (pres.). Club: Waialae Country (Honolulu). Home: 4999 Kahala Ave Apt 343 Honolulu HI 96816

MARUSI, AUGUSTINE RAYMOND, former food processing exec.; b. N.Y.C., Nov. 30, 1913; s. Dante R. and Victoria (Sacchi) M.; B.S. in Chem. Engring., Renssalaer Poly. Inst., 1936; m. Ruth Sinclair Travis, Aug. 31, 1940; children—Frederic, Raymond, Margo. Chemist, Catalin Corp. Am., N.Y.C., 1938-39; mem. sales staff Chem. div. Borden Co., N.Y.C., 1939-42, chem. div. So. regional mgr., 1945-47, v.p. parent co., Borden, Inc., 1955-63, exec. v.p., 1964-67, pres., 1967-73, chmn. bd., chief exec. officer, 1968-79, also dir., 1959—; dir., gen. mgr. Alba S.A., Sao Paulo, Brazil, 1947-52, v.p. Chem. div., 1952-54, pres. Chem. div. 1954-64. Served as lt. USN, 1942-46. Clubs: Econ., Univ. (N.Y.C.). Office: Borden Inc 277 Park Ave New York NY 10017

MARUSKA, EDWARD JOSEPH, zoo ofcl.; b. Chgo., Feb. 19, 1934; s. Edward M.; student Wright Coll., Chgo., 1959-61; m. Nancy; children—Donna, Linda. Keeper hoofed animals Lincoln Park Zoo, Chgo., 1956-62, head keeper Children's Zoo, 1959-62; gen. curator Cin. Zoo, 1962-68, dir., 1968—; lectr. biol. sci. U. Can.; numerous TV appearances. Recipient Cin. Conservation Man of Year award, 1973, Ambassador award Cin. Conv. and Visitors Bur., 1974. Fellow Am. Assn. Zool. Parks and Aquariums (pres. 1978-79); mem. Am. Soc. Ichthyologists and Herpetologists, Whooping Crane Conservation Assn., Langdon Club, Cin. Naturalists Soc. Club: Rotary of Cin. Office: Cin Zoo 3400 Vine St Cincinnati OH 45220

MARUYAMA, YOSH, physician, educator; b. Pasadena, Calif. Apr. 30, 1930; s. Edward Yasaki and Chiyo (Sakai) M.; A.B., U. Calif., Berkeley, 1951; M.D., U. Calif. at San Francisco, 1955; m. Fudeko Tsuji, July 18, 1954; children—Warren H., Nancy C., Marian M., Karen A. Intern San Francisco Hosp., 1955-56; resident Mass. Gen. Hosp., Boston, 1958-61; James Picker advanced acad. fellow Stanford U., 1962-64; asst. prof. radiology Coll. Med. Scis., U. Minn., Mpls., 1964-67, asso. prof., 1967-70, dir. div. radiotherapy, 1968-70; prof., chmn. dept. radiation medicine Coll. Medicine, U. Ky., Lexington, 1970—, dir. Radiation Cancer Center, 1975—; cons. VA Hosp., Lexington. Served with M.C., AUS, 1956-58. Am. Cancer Soc. fellow, 1960-61. Diplomate Am. Bd. Radiology. Mem. Am. Coll. Radiology (commn. on radiation therapy and patterns of care study), AAAS, Am. Radium Soc., Cell Kinetics Soc., Ky. Cancer Commn., Radiation Research Soc., Soc. Exptl. Biol. Medicine, Am. Assn. Cancer Research, Radiol Soc. N.Am., Am. Soc. Therapeutic Radiology, Soc. Chmn. Acad. Radiology Oncology Programs, Am. Assn. Immunologists, Southeastern Cancer Research Assn. (dir.), Ky. Med. Assn., Order Ky. Cols. Minn., N.Y. Acad. Scis., Japan Soc. Ky., Shodan Judoka, Kodokan Inst. (Tokyo), Phi Beta Kappa, Sigma Xi, Alpha Omega Alpha. Club: Spindletop Hall (Lexington). Asso. editor Applied Radiology; editor: New Methods in Tumor Localization, 1977. Contbr. articles to profl. jours. Home: 1739 Lakewood Dr Lexington KY 40502

MARVEL, JOHN A., educator; b. Forgan, Okla., Mar. 13, 1922; s. Floyd Hoyt and Fronia Mae (Bixler) M.; B.S., Northwestern Okla. State U., 1946; M.Ed., U. Okla., 1952, Ed.D., 1955; m. Frances Joanna Smith, Aug. 15, 1945; children—Merrill Ann Martin, John Alan, Marvin Kim. Tchr. bus., coach, prin. Hazelton (Kans.) Pub. Schs., 1946-52; prin. Eugene Field Sch., Manhattan, Kans., 1952-53; prin. U. Wyo. Lab. Sch., 1955-58; dir. adult edn. and community service U. Wyo., 1958-62, dean Coll. Edn., 1962-66; pres. Adams State Coll., Alamosa, Colo., 1966-77; pres. Colo. State Colls. and Univs. Consortium, Denver, 1977—; mem. higher edn. evaluation team People's Republic of China; leader higher edn. evaluation team, Taiwan; dir. Survey of Internat. Needs of Mexico as Part of Internat. Linkages, Washington; Bd. fellows Gallaudet Coll., Washington; bd. dirs., past pres. Am. Assn. State Colls. and Univs.; bd. dirs., past sec. Am. Council Edn. Served with AUS, 1943-46. Presdl. fellow Danforth Found. Mem. Internat. Edn. Com., Assn. State Colls. and Univs. (cons.), Internat. Assn. Educators World Peace, Phi Delta Kappa, Sigma Tau Gamma. Methodist. Clubs: Rotary, Denver, Petroleum. Author: (with F. Harlan Bryant) Public Schools in Nevada-A Further Look; Basic Education Program for Wyoming Schools; Appraisal of Overseas American Schools; Identity Crisis and Intercultural Education; contbg. author: Role of Impressions of Modern China; Can Man Transcend His Culture; Extra-Institutional Governance in Colorado Higher Education; Fresh Approaches to Common Sense; also articles. Address: 203 State Services Bldg 1525 Sherman St Denver CO 80203

MARVEL, WILLIAM, state ofcl.; b. Wilmington, Del., Sept. 29, 1909; s. Josiah and Mary Belle (Jackson) M.; student Groton, 1923-28; B.A., Yale, 1932, Cambridge, 1934, M.A., 1944; postgrad. U. Va., 1934-36; m. Peggy Potter, Dec. 22, 1934; m. 2d, Laura Blair, Aug. 1, 1964. Admitted to Del. bar, 1936; with firm Marvel & Morford, Wilmington, 1936-42, partner, 1946-54; asst. U.S. atty., 1941-42; U.S. atty. dist. Del., 1948-53; vice chancellor State of Del., 1954-76, chancellor, 1976—. Served from 2d lt. to capt. AUS, 1942-45; N. Africa, ETO. Mem. Am., Del. bar assns., Hist. Soc. Del. (dir.), Soc. Colonial Wars. Democrat. Episcopalian. Clubs: Wilmington, Country. Home: Barley Mill Rd Greenville DE 19807 Office: Court House 11th and King Sts Wilmington DE 19801

MARVELL, ELLIOT NELSON, educator; b. New Bedford, Mass., Sept. 10, 1922; s. Sumner Edward and Irene (Nelson) M.; B.S., Brown U., 1943; Ph.D., U. Ill., 1948; m. Jean Carpenter, July 2, 1944; children—Linnaea (Mrs. Wayne Mell), Kristan Peter. Mem. faculty dept. chemistry Oreg. State U., Corvallis, 1948—, asso. prof., 1957-62, prof., 1962—. Vice chmn. Benton County Democratic party, 1955. NSF postdoctoral fellow, Zürich, Switzerland, 1956-57; recipient Petroleum Research Fund internat. award, 1965-66. Mem. Am., Brit., Swiss chem. socs., AAUP, Sigma Xi. Author: two textbooks, 1945, 65. Contbr. articles profl. jours. Home: 1740 Alta Vista Dr Corvallis OR 97330

MARVIN, BURTON WRIGHT, educator; b. Somerville, Mass., Dec. 23, 1913; s. Henry Howard and Alma Ethel (Wright) M.; A.B., U. Nebr., 1935; M.Sc., Columbia U., 1937; Dr. Journalism, Southwestern Coll., 1964; m. Margaret Fiske Medlar, Jan. 15, 1938; children—Mary (dec.), Charles, Robert, Anne. Reporter, Lincoln (Nebr.) Star, 1935-36; reporter, copyreader, asst. city editor, cable editor, telegraph editor Chgo. Daily News, 1937-46; lectr. Medill Sch. Journalism, Northwestern U., 1945-46, asst. prof., 1946-47; asso. prof. Columbia U. Grad. Sch. Journalism, 1947-48; dean William Allen White Sch. Journalism and Pub. Info., dir. William Allen White Found., U. Kans., 1948-65; asso. gen. sec. for communication Nat. Council Chs., N.Y.C., 1966-68; prof. journalism Syracuse (N.Y.) U., 1968-79, dir. mental health info. program, 1968-71, head religious journalism program, 1969-79, asst. dean Sch. Pub. Communications, 1970-79; vis. prof. Tel Aviv U., 1965-66; Fulbright lectr. U. Tehran (Iran), 1960-61; lectr. journalism African-Am. Inst., summer 1963; mem. Nat. Commn. on Pub. Relations and Meth. Info., 1956-68. Bd. dirs. Laubach Literacy Internat., Inc., 1970-79; mem. interpretation and support conf. U.S. Conf. World Council Chs., Inc., 1969-75. Hitchcock scholar Columbia U. Grad. Sch. Journalism, 1936, recipient Alumni Achievement medallion, 1963. Mem. Am. Assn. Schs. and Depts. Journalism (pres. 1953), Assn. Edn. Journalism, Am. Council Edn. Journalism (chmn. accrediting com. 1956-60), Kappa Tau Alpha, Sigma Delta Chi, Theta Chi Beta. Universalist. Home: 318 DeForest Rd Syracuse NY 13214 Died Mar. 8, 1979.

MARVIN, DANIEL E., JR., univ. pres.; b. East Stroudsburg, Pa., Apr. 25, 1938; s. Daniel E. and Hazel E. M.; student Susquehanna U., 1956-58; B.S., East Stroudsburg State Coll., 1960; M.S., Ohio U., 1962; Ph.D., Va. Poly. Inst., 1966; m. Maxine James, June 15, 1958; children—Brian, Laurie, Amy. Grad. asst. Ohio U., 1960-61, instr. biology, 1961-62; asst. prof. biology Radford Coll., 1962-67, prof. biology, dean div. natural scis., 1967-68, v.p. acad. affairs, 1968-70, acting pres., 1968-69; asso. dir. State Council of Higher Edn. for Va., 1970-72, dir., 1972-77; pres. Eastern Ill. U., Charleston, 1977—. Mem. Nat. Center Higher Edn. Mgmt. Systems (dir.), Am. Assn. State Colls. and Univs., Am. Council Edn. (Commn. Acad. Affairs), AAAS. Methodist. Contbr. articles to profl. jours. Office: Eastern Ill Univ Charleston IL 61920. *I often advise young administrators that their success will be measured not by how many good decisions they make, but by how many bad ones.*

MARVIN, DAVID KEITH, educator; b. Lincoln, Nebr., Apr. 8, 1921; s. Henry Howard and Alma (Wright) M.; B.A., U. Nebr., 1943; M.A., Northwestern U., 1955, Ph.D., 1957; m. Frances Parks Cash, Dec. 14, 1946; children—Margaret Elaine, Keith Wright, Martha Jean. Mem. UNRRA, Austrian Mission, 1946; vice consul Am. Fgn. Service, Peiping, 1947-50; 2d sec., London, 1950-53; consul, Dar-es-Salaam, 1953; Ford Found. fellow Tanganyika, 1956-58; vis. asst. prof. Northwestern U., 1958; asst. prof. San Francisco State U., 1958-62, asso. prof., 1962-67, prof., 1967—, asst. chmn. social sci. div., 1960-64, chmn. dept. internat. relations, 1964-70, 77-78; vis. prof. U. Calif. at Berkeley, 1967. Chmn. North Coastside Community Council, 1962-64. Bd. dirs. Diablo Valley Edn. Project. Served with inf., AUS, 1943-46. Fellow African Studies Assn.; mem. Phi Beta Kappa. Author: Emerging Africa in World Affairs, 1965. Office: Program Internat Relations San Francisco State U San Francisco CA 94132

MARVIN, JAMES CONWAY, librarian; b. Warroad, Minn., Aug. 3, 1927; s. William C. and Isabel (Carlquist) M.; B.A., U. Minn., 1950, M.A., 1966; m. Patricia Katharine Moe, Sept. 8, 1947; children—Heidi C., James Conway, Jill C., Jack C. City librarian, Kaukauna, Wis., 1952-54; chief librarian, Eau Claire, Wis., 1954-56; dir. Cedar Rapids (Iowa) Pub. Library, 1956-67, Topeka Pub. Library, 1967—; Am. Library Assn.-Rockefeller Found. vis. prof. Inst. Library Sci. U. Philippines, 1964-65; vis. lectr. dept. librarianship Emporia (Kans.) State Coll., 1970—; chmn. Kans. del. to White House Conf. on Libraries and Info. Services. Served with USNR, 1945-46. Mem. Am., Iowa (past pres.), Kans., Philippine (life) library assns. Rotarian. Home: 40 Pepper Tree Ln Topeka KS 66611 Office: 1515 W 10th St Topeka KS 66604

MARVIN, JAMES LAMAR, mfg. co. exec.; b. Kirkwood, Mo., Mar. 4, 1927; s. Charles Ohmer and Emma Louise (Hayhurst) M.; B.S., Yale U., 1949; m. Annette Barbatelli, Sept. 14, 1949; children—Andrew, Victoria, James LaMar. With Anaconda Co., 1950—, group v.p., N.Y.C., 1974-77, sr. v.p. ARCO, subs., Los Angeles, 1977-80, pres. Anaconda Industries, subs., Denver, 1979—. Bd. dirs. Central City Opera Assn., Denver; mem. fin. com. Mt. Airy Psychiat. Hosp., Denver. Served with USN, 1945-47. Mem. Aluminum Assn. (chmn.'s adv. bd.), Internat. Copper Research Assn. (dir.), Tau Beta Pi. Episcopalian. Clubs: Denver, Denver Petroleum. Office: 555 17th St Suite 3609 Anaconda Tower Denver CO 80217

MARVIN, LEE, actor; b. N.Y.C., Feb. 19, 1924; s. Lamont W. and Courtenay D. M.; m. Pamela Feeley, Oct. 18, 1970. Appeared with summer stock cos.; Broadway debut in Billy Budd; film debut You're in the Navy Now, other films include: Diplomatic Courier, We're Not Married, Down Among the Sheltering Palms, Eight Iron Men, Stranger Wore a Gun, Big Heat, Gun Fury, Wild One, Caine Mutiny, Gorilla at Large, The Raid, Bad Day at Black Rock, Life in the Balance, Violent Saturday, Not as a Stranger, Pete Kelly's Blues, I Died a Thousand Times, The Rack, Shack Out on 101, Attack, Cat Ballou, The Professionals, The Dirty Dozen, Paint Your Wagon, Point Blank, Sergeant Ryer, Hell in the Pacific, Prime Cut, Pocket Money, Emperor of the North Pole, Iceman Cometh, The Spikes Gang, The Klansman, The Great Scout and Cathouse Thursday, Shoot at the Devil, Avalanche Express. Served with USMC, World War II. Recipient Best Actor award Berlin Film Festival; Acad. award for Cat Ballou, 1965; Brit. Acad. award for best fgn. actor, 1965; Spanish Silver Film award, 1970. Address: care Mishkin Agy Inc 9255 Sunset Blvd Los Angeles CA 90069*

MARVIN, MURRAY JOSEPH, life ins. co. exec.; b. Green County, Ohio, June 15, 1918; s. Murray Joseph and Iona (Gee) M.; B.S., W.Va. State Coll., 1936; M.B.A., U. Chgo., 1960; m. Delores Kathleen Jackson, Dec. 31, 1946. Partner with wife Marvin & Marvin, Chgo., 1947-52; exec. dir. Nat. Ins. Assn., Chgo., 1950-61; dir. planning N.C. Mut. Life Ins. Co., Durham, 1961-71, v.p. planning and communication, 1971-76, sr. v.p., 1976—; instr. Grad. Sch. Bus. N.C. Central U., Durham, part time, 1962-66. Mem. 3 man cons. team reviewing activities local anti-poverty agy. Operation Breakthrough, 1965-66; mem. Pres. Nixon's Urban Renewal Task Force, 1969; mem. budget com. United Fund, 1966-71, v.p. 1973-74. Bd. dirs. N.C. Mus. Life and Sci. Community Planning Services, 1970—; mem. gov.'s adv. council Dept. Cultural Resources, 1977—. Served with USNR, 1944-46. Recipient Crosthwait award Chgo. Ins. Assn., 1961, 40th Anniversary award Nat. Ins. Assn., 1961. Mem. Am. Mgmt. Assn., Am. Inst. Mgmt., Pub. Relations Soc. Am., Life Advertisers Assn., Kappa Alpha Psi, Sigma Pi Phi. Republican. Episcopalian. Club: Rotary. Home: 909 Dupree St Durham NC 27701 Office: Mutual Plaza Durham NC 27701

MARVIN, OSCAR MCDOWELL, hosp. adminstr.; b. Statesville, N.C., Apr. 12, 1924; s. Oscar McDowell and Gladys (Early) M.; A.B., U. N.C., 1948; M.B.A., U. Chgo., 1953; M.S., U. Louisville, 1971; m. Jane Everitt Krauss, June 16, 1951 (div. 1975); children—Frederick McDowell, Elizabeth Anne, Robert Doyle; m. 2d, Marcia Ann Benefiel Jackson, Dec. 2, 1977; children—Jonathan Paul, Katherine Susanne. Foreman, Hanes Dye & Finishing Co., Winston-Salem, N.C., 1948-51; adminstrv. resident N.C. Bapt. Hosp., Winston-Salem, 1952-53; asst. adminstr. City Meml. Hosp., Winston-Salem, 1953-55, N.C. Med. Care Commn., Raleigh, 1955-57; hosp. adminstr., missionary Bd. World Missions, Presbyn. Ch. U.S., Yodogawa Christian Hosp., Osaka, Japan, 1957-60; asst. adminstr. City Memphis Hosp., 1960-62, adminstr., 1962-68; exec. dir. Louisville Med. Center, Inc., 1968—; lectr. dept. preventive medicine U. Tenn., 1963-68, asso. prof. Coll. Pharmacy, 1965-68; organizer N.C. chpt. Hosp. Accountants, 1954, pres., 1955-56; treas. Memphis Hosp. Council, 1963, v.p., 1964, pres., 1965; sec. Memphis Inst. Medicine and Religion, 1966-68. Mem. Memphis Mayor's Com. to Employ Handicapped, 1963; chmn. hosp. div. Shelby United Neighbors, Memphis, 1965; sec.-treas. Assn. Coop Hosp. Laundries, 1970-71; trustee Med. Benevolence Found., 1971; pres. Jefferson County Assn. Children with Learning Disabilities, 1973-74, Ky. Assn. Children with Learning Disabilities, 1974-78. Served with AUS, 1942-45. Mem. Am. Coll. Hosp. Adminstrs., Sigma Nu. Presbyterian (deacon, elder). Club: Rotary. Contbr. articles to profl. jours. Home: 225 Bramton Rd Louisville KY 40207 Office: 334 E Broadway Suite 323 Louisville KY 40202

MARVIN, PHILIP, educator; b. Troy, N.Y., May 1, 1916; s. George G. and Marjorie (Moston) M.; B.S., Rensselaer Poly. Inst., 1937; M.B.A., Ind. U., 1951, D.B.A., 1951; LL.B., LaSalle U., 1954; m. Grace E. Meerbach, Aug. 22, 1942. Research scientist Gen. Electric Co., 1937-42; dir. chem. and metall. engring. Bendix Aviation Corp. marine div., N.Y.C., 1943-44; dir. research and devel. Penn Controls, Inc., Milw., 1945-51; v.p., dir. Commonwealth Engring. Co., Dayton, Ohio, 1952-54; cons. to chmn. bd., pres. Am. Viscose Corp., 1955-56; mgr. research and devel. div. Am. Mgmt. Assn., 1956-64; pres., dir. Clark, Cooper, Field and Wohl, Inc., N.Y.C., 1964-65; dean profl. devel. U. Cin., 1965-73, prof. profl. devel. and bus. adminstrn., 1965—; lectr., cons. in field, 1965—; dir. Basic Research, Inc., Dunlap Assos., Inc. Fellow Fin. Analysts Fedn.; mem. Inst. Chartered Fin. Analysts, IEEE, Nat. Acad. TV Arts and Scis., Newcomen Soc. N.Am., N.Y. Soc. Security Analysts, Sigma Xi, Tau Beta Pi, Beta Gamma Sigma. Club: Cin. Author: Top Management and Research, 2d edit., 1953; Administrative Management, 2d edit., 1954; Planning

New Products, vol. 1, 1958, vol. 11, 1964; Management Goals, 1968; Multiplying Management Effectiveness, 1971; Developing Decisions for Actions, 1971; Man in Motion, 1972; Product Planning Simplified, 1972; The Right Man for the Right Job at the Right Time, 1973; Fundamentals of Effective Research and Development Management, 1973; Managing Your Career, 1974; Managing Your Successful Career, 1978; also articles, TV programs. Patentee in field. Home: 2750 Weston Ridge Dr Cincinnati OH 45239 Office: U Cin Mail Code 20 Cincinnati OH 45221

MARVIN, WILLIAM GLENN, JR., fgn. service officer; b. Dobbs Ferry, N.Y., Oct. 30, 1920; s. William Glenn and Charlotte (Linden) M.; student U. Calif., Berkeley, 1938-40; B.S., Harvard U., 1942; M.A., Stanford U., 1948; m. Sheila Wells, June 6, 1945 (dec.); children—Sally Marvin Lockhart, William Glenn III, Wells. European rep. Hoover Instn., 1948-49; polit. scientist Stanford Research Inst., 1949-52; commd. fgn. service officer Dept. State, 1952; consul gen., Bordeaux, France, 1977—. Served to capt. U.S. Army, 1942-46. Mem. U.S. Fgn. Service Assn. Clubs: Connetablie de Guyenne, Ordre de Tursan. Office: 4 Rue Esprit des Lois Bordeaux France

MARX, ANNE (MRS. FREDERICK E. MARX), poet; b. Germany; d. Jacob and Susan (Weinberg) Loewenstein; grad. U. Heidelberg, U. Berlin; m. Frederick E. Marx, Feb. 12, 1937; children—Thomas J., Stephen L. Came to U.S., 1936, naturalized, 1938. Poet, more than 1000 poems published in nat. mags., anthologies, lit. jours. and newspapers; mem. staffs N.Y.C. Writers Conf., 1965, Iona Coll., 1964, 65, 70, Wagner Coll., 1965, Poetry Workshop, Fairleigh Dickinson U., 1962, 63, 64, Poetry Soc. Am. Workshop, 1970-71, 78-79; Bronxville Adult Sch. Lecture Series, 1972; poetry recs. Lamont Library at Harvard, stas. WFAS, WRNW, WEVD, WRVR, Voice of Am., others; dir. poetry series Donell Library Center (N.Y. Pub. Library) 1970-74; poetry day chmn. Westchester County, 1959—; Poetry Day Workshop, Ark., 1966, 70, Ark. Writers Conf., 1971, South and West Conf. (Okla.) 1972; tchr., poetry readings, Jakarta, Indonesia, summer 1979; judge various nat. poetry contests. Recipient Am. Weave Chapbook award, 1960, Nat. Sonnet prize, 1959, 67, prizes Nat. Fedn. Women's Clubs, 1959, 60, Nat. Fedn. State Poetry Socs., 1962, 65, 66, 73, South and West Publn. award, 1965, Greenwood prize Eng., 1966, 2d Ann. Viola Hayes Parsons award, 1977, award Delbrook Center Advanced Studies, 1978. Mem. Poetry Soc. Am. (mem. exec. bd. 1965-70, v.p. 1971-72, two fellowships, life mem, Cecil Hemley Meml. award 1974), Poetry Soc. Gt. Britain, Nat. League Am. Pen Women (pres. Westchester County br. 1962-64, North Atlantic regional chmn. 1964-66), nat. letters bd. 1972-74, nat. poetry editor 1974-78, N.Y. State lit. chmn. 1979-80, Biennial book award 1976), Acad. Am. Poets, Poet Soc. Pa., Composers, Authors and Artists Am., Inc. (poetry editor mag. 1973-78), Poets and Writers, Inc. Author: Ein Buechlein, 1935; Into the Wind of Waking, 1960; The Second Voice, 1963; By Grace of Pain, 1966; By Way of People, 1970; A Time to Mend (selected poems) 1973. Nat. poetry editor The Pen Woman, 1974-78. Co-editor Pegasus in the Seventies, 1973. A Conversation with Anne Marx (2 hour talking book for blind), 1974, Hear of Israel and Other Poems, 1975; 40 Love Poems for 40 Years, 1977. Home: 315 The Colony Hartsdale NY 10530. *To be undeterred is the key to any achievement that is important to our lives. Undeterred by detractors asserting that one's goal is impossible to reach. Undeterred by blame or praise. Undeterred by demands of custom and fashion. Undeterred by all but the most essential bonds of family and friends. Undeterred even by the knowledge that there will be no greatness at the end of the long climb - only the satisfaction that we have tried to bring out the best that is in us, that we have added to our years that special ingredient we needed most to add zest to existence.*

MARX, ARTHUR (JULIUS), author, playwright; b. N.Y.C., July 21, 1921; s. Groucho and Ruth (Johnson) M.; student U. So. Calif., 1939-40; m. Feb. 1943; children—Steve, Andy; m. 2d, Lois Goldberg, June 27, 1961. Copywriter, Hal Horne Agy., 1941; radio comedy writer Milton Berle Show, 1942, Sealtest Show, 1942, Edgar Bergen Show, 1948; writer films: Blondie in the Dough, 1947, A Global Affair, 1963, I'll Take Sweden, 1965, Eight on the Lam, 1967, Cancel My Reservation, 1972; free-lance mag. writer for Cosmopolitan, Redbook, Collier's, Good Housekeeping, Sport, others; writer for TV series: All in the Family, Maude, My Three Sons, The Jeffersons, McHale's Navy, others; Broadway playwright: The Impossible Years, 1965, Minnie's Boys, 1970; author books: The Ordeal of Willie Brown, 1951, Life With Groucho, 1954, Not as a Crocodile, 1958, Son of Groucho, 1972, Everybody Loves Somebody Sometime—Especially Himself, 1974, Goldwyn, 1976, Red Skelton, 1979; exec. script cons. TV series Alice, 1976-80. Served with USCG, 1942-45; PTO. U.S. Intercollegiate Freshman Tennis Champion, 1940. Mem. Dramatists Guild, Authors Guild, Writers Guild Am., West, Acad. Motion Picture Arts and Scis. Jewish. Office: care John Schallert Agy 9350 Wilshire Blvd Suite 214 Beverly Hills CA 90212. *Use whatever talent you happen to have been blessed with wisely. Don't waste time; aside from his talent, it's the most important thing a writer has to work with. Don't deliberately step on anybody in order to achieve your goals. And above all, be lucky. But luck is a funny commodity—I've always found that the harder I work, the luckier I get.*

MARX, GEORGE L., educator; b. Sioux City, Iowa, Jan. 5, 1932; s. Leo and Teresa (Merry) M.; B.A., Yankton Coll., 1953; M.A., Iowa U., 1958, Ph.D., 1959; m. Carolyn Evans, Sept. 4, 1958. Mem. faculty counseling and personnel services U. Md., College Park, 1959—, now prof., head dept. Trustee Am. Coll. Testing Program, 1964-66, 71-74. Mem. Am. Personnel Guidance Assn., Am. Psychol. Assn. Home: 7520 Wellesley Dr College Park MD 20740

MARX, GERTIE FLORENTINE, anesthesiologist; b. Frankfurt am Main, Germany, Feb. 13, 1912; d. Joseph and Elsa (Scheuer) Marx; came to U.S., 1937, naturalized, 1943; student U. Frankfurt (Germany), 1931-36; M.D., U. Bern (Switzerland), 1937; m. Eric P. Reiss, Sept. 26, 1940 (dec. 1968). Intern, resident in anesthesiology Beth Israel Hosp., N.Y.C., 1939-43, adj. anesthesiologist, 1943-50, asso. anesthesiologist, 1950-55; attending anesthesiologist Bronx Municipal Hosp. Center, 1955—; attending anesthesiologist Bronx VA Hosp., 1966-72, cons., 1972—; asst. prof. anesthesiology Albert Einstein Coll. Medicine, 1955-60, asso. prof., 1960-70, prof., 1970—. Diplomate Nat. Bd. Med. Examiners, Am. Bd. Anesthesiology. Fellow Am. Coll. Anesthesiology, N.Y. Acad. Medicine, Am. Coll. Obstetricians and Gynecologists; mem. Am., N.Y. State socs. anesthesiologists, AMA, Bronx County Med. Soc., N.Y. Acad. Scis. Author: (with Orkin) Physiology of Obstetric Anesthesia, 1969; asso. editor Survey Anesthesiology, 1957—; editor Parturition and Perinatology, 1973; Clinical Management of Mother and Newborn, 1979; contbr. articles to profl. jours. Home: 155 Crary Ave Mount Vernon NY 10550

MARX, HENRY MOSLER, lawyer; b. Birmingham, Ala., Mar. 18, 1908; s. Otto and Agnes (Mosler) M.; A.B. cum laude, Princeton, 1930; LL.B. cum laude, Harvard, 1933; m. Peggy Esberg, Mar. 19, 1937 (dec.); children—Henry E., Otto III; m. 2d, Anna Duval, Dec. 24, 1969 (dec.). Admitted to N.Y. bar, 1933, Conn. bar, 1954; asso. lawyer White & Case, N.Y.C., 1933-41, 45; partner Kramer, Marx, Greenlee and Backus, and predecessor firms, 1946-74, Windels & Marx, 1974-77, Windels, Marx, Davies & Ives, 1978—; dir. Thyssen Inc., Gafulco Co., Inc., Chromasco Ltd., Chromium Mining & Smelting Corp., Birmingham Corp. Town rep. Greenwich (Conn.), 1949-51; coordinator atomic devel. activities, State of Conn., 1955-68; formerly mem. Conn. Research Commn.; mem. AEC Adv. Commn. of State Ofcls. Patron, mem. Met. Opera Nat. Council, dir. Am. Friends of Covent Garden and Royal Ballet, Inc. Served from 1st lt. to maj. AUS, 1942-45. Decorated Bronze Star medal. Mem. Am., N.Y. bar assns., Assn. Bar City N.Y., N.Y. County Lawyers Assn., Conn. Bar Assn., Am. Arbitration Assn. (mem. nat. panel), Newcomen Soc. N.A. Clubs: Hemisphere, Princeton, Wings, New York Yacht. (N.Y.C.); Byram Yacht (Conn.); Royal Norwegian Yacht; Royal Scandinavian Yacht, Nylandska Jaktklubben; Princeton Yacht, Wharf Rat; Storm Trysail; Mount Royal (Montreal). Home: 303 E 57th St New York NY 10022 also Casana Tortola BWI Office: 51 W 51st St New York NY 10019

MARX, LEO, educator; b. N.Y.C., Nov. 15, 1919; s. Leo and Theresa (Rubinstein) M.; S.B. magna cum laude, Harvard U., 1941, Ph.D. in History Am. Civilization, 1950; M.A. (hon.) Amherst Coll., 1959; m. Jane T. Pike, Aug. 14, 1943; children—Stephen P., Andrew R., Lucy T. Teaching fellow, tutor Harvard U., 1946-49; asst. prof. English, U. Minn., Mpls., 1949-53, asso. prof., 1953-58; prof. English and Am. studies Amherst (Mass.) Coll., 1958-76; William R. Kenan, Jr. prof. Am. cultural history Mass. Inst. Tech. Cambridge, 1976—. Fulbright lectr. U. Nottingham (Eng.), 1956-57, U. Rennes (France), 1965-66. Guggenheim fellow, 1962-63, 65-66. Served with USNR, 1941-45. Fellow Am. Acad. Arts and Scis.; mem. Am. Studies Assn. (pres. 1975-77), Modern Lang. Assn., Signet Soc., Phi Beta Kappa (Bicentennial fellow). Author: The Machine in the Garden: Technology and the Pastoral Ideal in America, 1964. Editor: The Americanness of Walt Whitman, 1960; Henry Thoreau, Excursions, 1962; Adventures of Huckleberry Finn (Mark Twain), 1966; Anthology of American Literature, 1974. Home: 19 Joy St Boston MA 02114 Office: 20D-201 Mass Inst Tech Cambridge MA 02139

MARX, OTTO, JR., investment banker; b. Birmingham, Ala., Nov. 26, 1909; s. Otto and Agnes (Mosler) M.; B.S., U. Va., 1932; m. Harriott P. Maxfield, Nov. 8, 1937; stepchildren—John V. Summerlin, Harriott Summerlin (Mrs. Page Summerlin). Partner, Ladenburg Thalmann & Co., N.Y.C., 1954-61; pres. Marx & Co., N.Y.C., 1961-65, now dir., mem. exec. com.; pres., then chmn. Paribas Corp., N.Y.C., 1965-69, also dir., mem. exec. com.; pres. Marx & Co., Inc., N.Y.C., 1969—; pres., dir. Ohio Hotel Corp., Otmar Real Estate Corp., 2 E. 88th St. Corp., Birmingham Corp., Lehman Capital Fund, Video Internat., Inc., Video Variations, Inc. Trustee N.Y. Zool. Soc. Served to lt. comdr. USNR, 1941-45. Clubs: N.Y. Yacht; Royal Bermuda Yacht, Coral Beach (Bermuda); Rockefeller Center Lunch. Home: 2 E 88th St New York NY 10028 Office: 600 Fifth Ave New York NY 10020

MARX, WESLEY, author; b. Los Angeles, Nov. 2, 1934; s. Edward Howard and Kathleen W.; B.A., Stanford U., 1956; m. Judith Marx, 1962; children—Christopher, Heather, Tyler. Reporter, Pasadena (Calif.) Star-News, 1960-61; contbg. editor Los Angeles mag., 1962-63; Los Angeles corr. Nat. Observer, 1964-65; lectr. communications dept. Calif. State U. at Fullerton, fall 1969; environ. lectr. extension and social ecology program U. Calif., Irvine, 1970—; cons. marine plan Calif. Coastal Zone Conservation Commn., 1974. Participant EASTROPAC Oceanographic Expdn., 1968. Bd. govs. Marine Studies Inst.; bd. dirs. Friends Newport Bay. Recipient Phelan award for non-fiction, 1968; Orange County Authors award for non-fiction, 1967, 78. Mem. Calif. Atty. Gen.'s Environment Task Force, 1970-76; adv. bd. Fund for the Environment, 1970—; mem. Irvine Planning Commn., 1972-73; mem. Orange County Fair Housing Council, Planning and Conservation League; trustee Center for Law in the Public Interest. Author: The Frail Ocean, 1967 (softcover 1969, German edit. Bis das Meer Zum Himmel Stinkt); (with others) The California Revolution, 1968, The Enviromental Handbook, 1969; Man and His Environment: Waste, 1971; Oil Spill, 1971; The Protected Ocean (juvenile) 1972; (with others) What We Save Now, 1973; The Pacific Shore, 1974; Acts of God, Acts of Man, 1977; (with others) Land and Water, 1978; also articles. Address: 18051 Butler St Irvine CA 92715

MARYLANDER, STUART JEROME, hosp. adminstr.; b. Oakland, Calif., Nov. 13, 1931; s. Philip and Lilyan (Wolf) M.; M.P.H. in Hosp. Adminstrn., U. Calif. at Berkeley, 1956; m. Judith Rosenblatt, June 3, 1956; children—Steven Mark, Grant. Research asst. med. care adminstrn. Sch. Pub. Health, U. Calif. at Berkeley, 1955-56; adminstrv. resident Mt. Zion Hosp., San Francisco, 1956-57; asst. adminstr. Cedars of Lebanon Hosp., Los Angeles, 1957-62; adminstr. Mt. Sinai Hosp. div. Cedars-Sinai Med. Center, Los Angeles, 1963-64, adminstrv. dir. center, 1964-66, asso. exec. dir. and adminstrv. dir., 1967-71, exec. dir. 1971-74, exec. v.p., 1974-78, pres., 1979—; instr. U. So. Calif. Sch. Pub. Adminstrn., 1965-70; dir. Blue Cross of So. Calif., 1976—. Bd. dirs. Commn. Adminstrv. Services to Hosps., 1967-76; bd. dirs. Hosp. Council So. Calif., 1968-76, pres., 1975-76; adminstrv. bd. Council Teaching Hosps. Served with AUS, 1953-55. Fellow Am. Pub. Health Assn., Royal Soc. of Health (Eng.), Am. Coll. Hosp. Adminstrs.; mem. Am., Calif. (dir. 1974—, chmn. 1979) hosp. assns., Assn. Am. Med. Colls. (mem. assembly, mem. exec. council), Internat. Hosp. Fedn., Sigma Alpha Mu. Home: 3644 Ballina Cyn Rd Encino CA 91436 Office: 8700 Beverly Blvd Los Angeles CA 90048

MASAMUNE, SATORU, chemist, educator; b. Fukuoka, Japan, July 24, 1928; s. Hajime and Chikako (Kondo) M.; A.B., Tohoku U., Sendai, Japan, 1952; Ph.D. in Chemistry, U. Calif., Berkeley, 1957; m. Takako Nozoe, July 25, 1956; childre—Hiroko, Tohoru. Fellow, Mellon Inst., Pitts., 1961-64; asso. prof. chemistry U. Alta., Can., 1964-67, prof., 1967-79; prof. chemistry M.I.T., Cambridge, 1978—. Recipient Am. Chem. Soc. award for creative work in synthetic organic chemistry, 1978. Fellow Royal Soc. Can.; mem. Am. Chem. Soc., Chem. Soc. (London), Can. Inst. Chemistry, Japan Chem. Soc. Contbr. numerous articles in field of organic chemistry. Office: Mass Inst Tech Cambridge MA 02139

MASANI, PESI RUSTOM, educator; b. Bombay, India, Aug. 1, 1919; s. Rustom Pestonji and Monijeh (Wadia) M.; student Elphinstone Coll., 1936-38, Royal Inst. Sci., 1938-40; B.Sc., Bombay U., 1940; M.A., Harvard, 1942, Ph.D., 1946. Came to U.S., 1941, naturalized, 1969. Fellow Royal Inst. Sci., Bombay, 1940-41; teaching fellow math. Harvard, 1943-45; mem. Inst. Advanced Studies, Princeton, N.J., 1946-48; sr. research fellow Tata Inst. Fundamental Research, Bombay, 1948-49; prof., head math dept. Inst. Sci., Bombay, 1949-59; vis. lectr., Harvard U., MIT, 1957-58, Brown U., 1959-60; prof. math Ind. U., 1960-72; prof. math. U. Pitts., 1972, univ. prof., 1973—; vis. prof. Math. Research Center, Madison, Wis., 1965-66, Statis. Lab. Cath. U., 1966-67, L'Ecole Polytechnique Federale Lausanne, summer 1975; vis. researcher Battelle Seattle Research Center, 1969-70; Fulbright-Hays sr. scholar State U. Tbilisi, Georgian SSR, USSR, Summer 1977; cons. in field. Mem. Am. Math. Soc., Math. Assn. Am., Author: (with R.C. Patel and D.J. Patil) Elementary Calculus, 1965. Editor: Collected Works of Norbert Wiener, Vol. I, 1976, Vol. II, 1979. Address: U Pittsburgh Dept Math Pittsburgh PA 15260

MASER, EDWARD ANDREW, educator; b. Detroit, Dec. 23, 1923; s. Andrew J. and Bozena (Slezak) M.; student U. Mich., 1941-43; M.A., U. Chgo., 1948, Ph.D., 1957; postgrad. U. Frankfurt-am-Main (Germany), 1949-50, U. Florence (Italy), 1950-52; m. Inge Besas, Mar. 31, 1956. Instr. Northwestern U., 1952-53; dir. U. Kans. Mus. Art, 1953-61, asso. prof. history art, 1957-61; prof. art U. Chgo., 1961—, chmn. art dept., 1961-64; dir. D. and A. Smart Gallery, U. Chgo. 1972—. Cons. S.H. Kress Found. Fulbright Research scholar, 1965-66; Guggenheim fellow, 1969-70. Served with USAAF, 1943-45. Decorated Austrian Cross of Honor for Letters and Art 1st class, 1974. Mem. Coll. Art Assn., Am. Assn. U. Profs., Phi Beta Kappa. Author: Catalog of Museo del Opificio delle Pietre Dure, 1952; Giovanni Domenico Ferretti, 1968; Iconologia of Cesare Ripa, 1971; Drawings of J.M. Rottmayr, 1971. Home: 5318 Hyde Park Blvd Chicago IL 60615

MASEY, JACK, designer; b. N.Y.C., June 10, 1924; s. Max and Anna (Ziskin) M.; student Cooper Union, 1941-43; B.F.A., Yale, 1950; m. Mary Lou Leach, Dec. 27, 1959. Cartoonist, Esquire mag., 1946; exhibits officer USIS, New Delhi, India, 1951-55; designer U.S. Pavilion, Kabul Internat. Fair, 1956; dir. design Am. Nat. Exhbn., Moscow, 1959; chief East-West exhibits br. USIA, Washington, 1960-67, chief design U.S. Pavilion, Montreal (Que., Can.) Worlds Fair, 1967, dep. commr. gen. for planning and design U.S. Pavilion Osaka (Japan) World Exposition, 1970; dir. design Am. Revolution Bicentennial Commn., Washington, 1971-73; mgr. bicentennial parks program, 1973-77; dir. design and exhbns. Am. Revolution Bicentennial Adminstrn., 1974-77; dir. design Internat. Communication Agy., Washington, 1977—. Lectr., Sch. Art and Architecture, Yale, 1968-69; designer Medicine-U.S.A. exhbn. for USSR exchange program, 1962, Tech.-Books exhbns., 1963. Served with AUS, 1943-45; ETO. Recipient Meritorious Service award USIA, 1959, Superior Service award, 1964, Superior Honor award, 1967, 75; award of excellence Fed. Design Council, 1975, Outstanding Achievement award, 1979; award of excellence Soc. Fed. Artists and Designers, 1971; Gold medal Art Dirs. Club, 1965; certificated of excellence Am. Inst. Graphic Arts, 1964. Mem. Pi Alpha. Home: 2716 N St NW Washington DC 20007 Office: Internat Communication Agy Washington DC 20547

MASHAW, WILLIAM GORDON, trade assn. exec.; b. Lewisville, Ark., Sept. 1, 1921; s. Andrew Louis and Martha Aurelia (Thatcher) M.; student Ark. A. and M. Coll., 1940-42; J.D., Columbia U., 1948; m. Dorothy Dix Maggard, Apr. 2, 1944; children—Terry Lynn Mashaw Gibbons, Dorothy Catherine Mashaw Senecal, Laura Beth Mashaw Dolezal, Mary Angela. With FBI, 1948-54, agt. supr., Washington, 1953-54; with Nat. Retail Hardware Assn., Indpls., 1954—, exec. v.p., then pub. Hardware Retailing mag., 1956-67, mng. dir., sec.-treas. assns., 1967—; bd. dirs. Am. Retail Fedn., 1967-73, 78-79. Pres., Washington Twp. (Ind.) Sch. Bd., 1963-67; bd. dirs. Pub. Action in Corrections Effort, 1963-77, pres., 1967-69; nat. bd. dirs. Big Bros./Big Sisters Am., 1975-77, v.p., 1978-79. Served to lt., aviator, USNR, 1942-46. Mem. Am. Soc. Assn. Execs. (dir. 1972-75). Republican. Baptist. Club: Highland Golf and Country (Indpls.). Home: 4903 Seville Ct Indianapolis IN 46208 Office: 770 N High Sch Rd Indianapolis IN 46224

MASHECK, JOSEPH DANIEL, art critic, educator; b. N.Y.C., Jan. 19, 1942; s. Joseph Anthony and Dorothy Anna (Cahill) M.; A.B., Columbia U., 1963, M.A., 1965, Ph.D., 1973. Editorial researcher Bollingen Found., Princeton U. Press, 1967-69; lectr. liberal studies Maidstone Coll. Art, Kent, Eng., 1968-69; preceptor in art history Columbia U., 1969-71, instr. art history Barnard Coll., 1971-73, asst. prof., 1973—; editor Artforum mag., N.Y.C., 1977-80. Nat. Endowment Arts fellow, 1972-73, 75-76; Guggenheim fellow, 1977-78. Mem. AAUP, Internat. Assn. Art Critics. Roman Catholic. Editor: Marcel Duchamp in Perspective, 1975; contbr. articles to publs. Office: Dept Art History Barnard Coll New York NY 10027

MASI, ALFONSE THOMAS, medical educator; b. N.Y.C., Oct. 29, 1930; s. Antonio and Mary (Genese) M.; B.S., City U. N.Y., 1951; M.D., Columbia, 1955; Dr.P.H., Johns Hopkins, 1963; m. Nancy Ann Bouton, Aug. 27, 1960; children—Anthony Mark, Christopher Maurice, Maria Lisa, Amy Elizabeth. Intern Johns Hopkins Hosp., 1955-56; resident Johns Hopkins Hosp. and U. Calif. at Los Angeles Med. Center, 1958-60; practice medicine specializing in rheumatology; asst. prof. epidemiology Johns Hopkins Sch. Hygiene, 1963-65, asso. prof., 1965-67; prof. medicine, dir. div. connective tissue diseases Coll. Medicine, U. Tenn., Memphis, 1967-78, prof. dept. health care scis., 1967-78; prof., head dept. medicine Peoria Sch. Medicine, U. Ill. Coll. Medicine, 1978—; prof. epidemiology U. Ill. Sch. Pub. Health, Chgo., 1978—; cons. various divs. NIH, 1971—; com. mem. various projects NRC, 1972—. Served with USPHS, 1956-58. Sr. Investigator The Arthritis Found. 1966-71, also, recipient Russell L. Cecil fellow award. Fellow A.C.P., Am. Pub. Health Assn.; mem. Am. Rheumatism Assn. Home: 6710 N Skyline Dr Peoria IL 61614

MASIKO, PETER, JR., coll. pres.; b. Vera Cruz, Pa., Mar. 18, 1914; s. Peter and Sophia (Baker) M.; B.A. with highest honors, Lehigh U., 1936; M.A. (fellow), U. Ill., 1937, Ph.D., 1939; m. Anna E. Fetterolf, July 9, 1932; children—Elaine Irene (Mrs. James Salapatas), Peter III. Instr. U. Ill., 1936-39; with Wright Jr. Coll., Chgo., 1939-56, successively instr., chmn. social sci. dept., asst. dean, dean, 1939-56; exec. dean Chgo. City Jr. Coll., 1956-62; pres. Miami (Fla.)-Dade Community Coll., 1962—. Economist Bd. Investigation and Research, Washington, summer 1942; mem. adv. com. on edn. U.S. Dept. Def., 1963-66; mem. steering com., mental health tng. and research So. Regional Edn. Bd.; mem. Fla. Post-Secondary Planning Com.; trustee Ednl. Testing Service; bd. dirs. South Fla. Comprehensive Health Planning Council, Am. Council Edn., Pub. TV Sta., Miami; mem. adv. com. Dade County Oceanographic Sci. Park, Internat. Oceanographic Found.; mem. adv. com. marine scis. Oceanographic Activities and Devel. Virginia Key; bd. dirs. United Way, Greater Miami. Mem. Am. Econ. Assn. (adv. com. on structure of profession), Am. Council on Edn. (commn. fed. relations, dir. 1972—, sec. 1973-74), Am. Assn. Sch. Adminstrs. (commn. on founds.), Am. Assn. Community and Jr. Colls. (dir. 1969—, chmn. 1973—), Am. Council Edn., Commn. on Women in Higher Edn., Ill. Assn. Jr. Colls. (sec.-treas. 1951-52), North Central Assn. (commr. commn. on colls. and univs. 1956-60), Phi Beta Kappa, Phi Kappa Phi. Lutheran. Author: Introduction to Social Science (with Atteberry, Auble and Hunt), rev. ed. 1951. Editorial bd. Edn. Digest. Home: 10270 S W 102d Terrace Miami FL 33176

MASKO, GEORGE, food co. exec.; b. Columbia Heights, Minn., July 29, 1924; s. Andrew and Mary (Hallahan) M.; B.S., U. Minn., 1950; postgrad. Stanford U., 1968; m. Lucille Eleanor Hollopeter, Sept. 22, 1951; children—Marshall Thomas, Melissa Grahame. With Pillsbury Co., Mpls., 1951-79, v.p., gen. mgr., 1968-77, pres. Am. Beauty Macaroni div., 1977-78, group v.p., 1978-79; pres. Jeno's, Inc., Duluth, Minn., 1979—. Served with U.S. Army, 1943-46. Office: Jeno's Inc 525 Lake Ave S Duluth MN 55802

MASLACH, GEORGE, lawyer, ins. co. exec.; b. Los Angeles, Mar. 15, 1915; s. George Michael and Anne (Scalla) M.; student U. Calif. at Los Angeles, 1932-34; J.D., Loyola U., Los Angeles, 1938; m.

Daisy Lu Condon, Feb. 15, 1942; children—Michael James, Anne. Admitted to Calif. bar, 1938; mem. firm Early, Maslach, Leavey & Nutt, Los Angeles, 1950—; chmn. bd., dir. Farmers Group, Inc.; v.p., dir. Investors Guaranty Life Ins. Co.; pres. New World Fund, Inc.; dir. Mid-Century Ins. Co., Ohio State Life Ins. Co. Bd. councillors U. So. Calif. Law Center. Mem. Assn. So. Calif. Def. Counsel (past pres., dir.), Calif. Ins. Fedn. (v.p., dir.), Phi Alpha Delta. Home: 10924 Savona Rd Los Angeles CA 90024 Office: 4680 Wilshire Blvd Los Angeles CA 90005 Died July 2, 1979.

MASLACH, GEORGE JAMES, educator; b. San Francisco, May 4, 1920; s. Michael J. and Anna (Pszczolkowska) M.; A.A., San Francisco Jr. Coll., 1939; B.S., U. Calif., 1942; m. Doris Anne Cuneo, Mar. 12, 1943; children—Christina, James, Steven. Staff mem. radiation lab. Mass. Inst. Tech., 1942-45, Gen. Precision Labs., 1945-49; research engr. Inst. Engring. Research, 1949-52, asst. dir., 1956-58; asso. prof. U. Calif. at Berkeley, 1952-58, prof., 1959-72, dean Coll. Engring., 1963-72, provost profl. schools and colls., 1972—. Adv. aeros. research and devel. NATO, 1960—, U.S. Naval Acad. Rev. Bd., 1966—, Dept. Commerce Tech. Adv. Bd., 1964-69, Ford Found. and Am. Soc. Engring. Edn., 1966—. Mem. ASME, AAAS, Sigma Xi. Home: 265 Panoramic Way Berkeley CA 94704

MASLAND, FRANK ELMER, III, carpet co. exec.; b. Carlisle, Pa., Aug. 23, 1921; s. Frank Elmer, Jr. and Mary Virginia (Sharp) M.; A.B., Princeton U., 1944; M.B.A., Harvard U., 1948; LL.D. (hon.) Grove City (Pa.) Coll., 1970; m. Marie Perry, May 22, 1943; children—Ellen C. Masland Anderson, Frank Elmer, IV, Jonathan L. With C.H. Masland & Sons, Carlisle, 1956—, exec. v.p., 1959-61, pres., gen. mgr., 1961-71, pres., chmn. bd., 1971, chmn. bd., 1971—, also dir.; dir. Dauphin Deposit Trust Co., Harsco Corp.; pres. Carpet and Rug Inst. Pres. trustees Carlisle Hosp.; bd. dirs. Pennsylvanians for Effective Govt., Americans for Competitive Enterprise System. Served with U.S. Army, World War II. Decorated Bronze Star. Mem. NAM (dir.). Republican. Methodist. Clubs: Princeton (N.Y.C.); Tavern (Chgo.); Racquet (Phila.). Home: RD 6 Box 417 Carlisle PA 17013 Office: Masland & Sons Spring Rd Carlisle PA 17013

MASLON, SAMUEL HENRY, lawyer; b. Kapulia, Russia, Apr. 15, 1901; s. Hyman and Ida (Craneberg) M.; brought to U.S., 1903, naturalized, 1910; A.B., U. Minn., 1920; LL.B. cum laude (Jonathan Fay diploma), Harvard, 1923; m. Luella Rykoff, Feb. 7, 1929; children—James I., Enid (Mrs. Sherman H. Starr), Patricia. Admitted to Minn. bar, 1923; law clk. Mr. Justice Brandeis, 1923-24; instr. law U. Minn. at Mpls., 1927-32; partner firm Brill & Maslon, Mpls., 1924-48; practice in Mpls., 1948-56; partner firm Maslon, Kaplan, Edelman, Borman, Brand & McNulty, Mpls., 1956—. Dir. North Central Airlines, Inc., Dr. S.E. Rykoff & Co. Bd. dirs. Mpls. Soc. Fine Arts, Twin City Ednl. TV Assn., Phillips Found.; trustee, pres. The Maslon Found.; bd. govs. Mt. Sinai Hosp. Assn. Mem. Am., Minn., Hennepin County bar assns., Phi Beta Kappa, Delta Sigma Rho, Sigma Alpha Mu. Home: 2800 Northview Rd Minnetonka Beach MN 55361 Office: Midwest Plaza Minneapolis MN 55402

MASLOW, WILL, lawyer, assn. exec.; b. Kiev, Russia, Sept. 27, 1907; s. Saul and Raeesa (Moonves) M.; brought to U.S., 1911, naturalized, 1924; A.B., Cornell U., 1929; J.D., Columbia, 1931; m. Beatrice Greenfield, Dec. 21, 1933; children—Laura, Catha. Admitted to N.Y. bar, 1932, also U.S. Supreme Ct. bar; reporter N.Y. Times, 1929-31; asso. Arthur Garfield Hays, 1931-34; asso. counsel Dept. Investigation, N.Y.C., 1934-36; trial atty., examiner NLRB, 1937-43; dir. field operations Pres.'s Com. Fair Employment Practice, 1943-45; gen. counsel Am. Jewish Congress, 1945—, exec. dir., 1960-72. Faculty N.Y. Sch. Social Research, 1948-60; adj. prof. Coll. City N.Y., 1965—. Trustee Meml. Found. for Jewish Culture; bd. dirs. Interracial Council for Bus. Opportunity, A. Philip Randolph Inst. Mem. World Jewish Congress (exec. com.), ACLU (dir. 1963-72), Am. Jewish Congress (Stephen Wise laureate 1972), Phi Beta Kappa. Home: 401 E 86th St New York City NY 10028 Office: 15 E 84th St New York City NY 10028

MASNICK, GEORGE STEPHAN, educator; b. Elizabeth, N.J., Sept. 10, 1942; s. George and Genevieve (Komoroski) M.; B.A., Cornell, 1965, M.A., 1966; Ph.D., Brown U., 1970; 1 son, Joshua. Asst. prof. sociology U. Pa., 1970-74, asst. dir. Population Studies Center, 1971-73, acting dir., 1973-74; asso. prof. population scis. and sociology Harvard, 1974—, head population scis., 1975-77. Fellow AAAS; mem. Population Assn. Am., Social Sci. History Assn., Internat. Union for Sci. Study Population. Home: 15 Davis Ave Brookline MA 02146

MASON, AARON S., psychiatrist; b. Russia, Mar. 5, 1912; s. Zussman and Libby (Plotkin) M.; came to U.S., 1915, naturalized, 1927; student Crane Jr. Coll., Chgo., 1928-30, Loyola U., Chgo., 1930-31; B.S., U. Ill., 1933, M.D., 1935; m. Jessie Warshawsky, June 7, 1942; children—Howard Gary, Steven Jay, Kenneth Glen. Intern psychiatry Chgo. State Hosp., 1935; gen. rotating intern Los Angeles County Gen. Hosp., 1935-36; staff physician Lincoln (Ill.) State Sch. and Colony, 1937-38; staff psychiatrist VA Hosp., Little Rock, Knoxville, Iowa, 1938-40; staff psychiatrist, chief reconstrn. service, chief admitting and outpatient service, chief acute and intensive treatment service, asst. chief profl. service VA Hosp., Downey, Ill., 1940-53, hosp. dir., 1972-74; chief mental health br. div. remedial services Ky. Dept. Human Resources, 1974—; chief staff VA Hosp., Brockton, Mass., 1953-62; hosp. dir. VA Hosp., Tomah, Wis., 1962-63; dir. VA Hosp., Lexington, Ky., 1963-72, now cons.; asso. prof. clin. psychiatry U. Ky., 1962-71, prof., 1971-72; asso. prof. psychiatry Northwestern U., 1972-74; prof. clin. psychiatry U. Ky. Med. Center, 1974—; pres. bd. trustees Central Ky. Regional Mental Health-Mental Retardation Bd.; adv. bd. Mental Health Assn. Central Ky.; adviser Lexington Commn. Human Rights; commr. Human Resources Coordinating Council, Commonwealth of Ky.; chmn. bd. Bluegrass Youth Services, Inc.; mem. health planning council Lake County, Ill. Served to col., M.C., AUS, 1944-46. Named hon. Ky. col. Diplomate Am. Bd. Psychiatry. Fellow Am. Psychiat. Assn. (life), Am. Geriatric Soc.; mem. AMA, Assn. Mil. Surgeons U.S., Assn. Med. Supts. Mental Hosps., Fayette County Med. Soc., Fed. Hosp. Inst. Alumni Assn., Ky. Psychiat. Assn. (chmn. rehab. com.), Res. Officers Assn. U.S., Ret. Officers Assn. Club: B'nai B'rith (v.p.). Address: 500 Lake Tower Dr #48 Lexington KY 40502

MASON, ALPHEUS THOMAS, educator, author, lectr.; b. Snow Hill, Md., Sept. 18, 1899; s. Herbert William and Emma Leslie (Hancock) M.; A.B., Dickinson Coll., 1920, Litt.D., 1947, LL.D., 1963; A.M., Princeton U., 1921, Ph.D., 1923, LL.D., 1974; D.Litt., U. Louisville, 1957, Centre Coll. Ky., 1977; L.H.D., Washington Coll., 1969, Brandeis U., 1973; Sc.D., Utah State U., 1976; m. Christine Este Gibbons, June 12, 1934; 1 dau., Louise Este Mason Bachelder. Proctor fellow Princeton U., 1922-23; asst. prof. polit. sci. Trinity Coll. (now Duke U.), 1923-25; asst. prof. politics Princeton U., 1925-30, asso. prof., 1930-36, prof., 1936-47, McCormick prof. jurisprudence, 1947-68, McCormick prof. jurisprudence emeritus, 1968—; Doherty prof. govt. and law U. Va., 1968-70; lectr. constl. law Mercer Beasley Sch. Law, Newark, 1928-32; lectr. Liberal Summer Sch., Cambridge, Eng., 1935; mem. Inst. Advanced Study, Princeton, N.J., 1938; acting prof. polit. sci. Stanford U., summer 1947; lectr. Conn. Coll., 1947, Syracuse U., 1948; Messenger lectr. Cornell U., Ithaca, N.Y., 1955; Edward Douglass White lectr. La. State U., 1957; Ford research prof., 1960; William W. Cook lectr. U. Mich., 1962; lectr. Hebrew U., Jerusalem, 1967; Henry L. and Grace Dougherty Found. prof. U. Va., 1968-70; vis. prof. govt. Harvard U., 1970-71, U. Calif. at Santa Barbara, 1971, Dartmouth Coll., 1971; Hill Found. vis. prof. U. Minn., 1971, U. Mich., 1972; Robb vis. prof. Barnard Coll., 1972, Johns Hopkins U., 1973; William A. Johnson Meml. distinguished vis. prof. Pomona Coll., 1974; Milton R. Merrill vis. prof. Utah State U., 1975; vis. prof. Claremont Men's Coll., 1976, Centre Coll. Ky., 1977, Humboldt State U., 1978, Yale U., 1979; Walter E. Edge lectr. Princeton U., 1979; bd. editors Am. Polit. Sci. Rev., 1936-40; mem. com. of experts to make survey of adminstrn. and expenditures of N.J. state govt., 1932, dir. Nat. Endowment for Humanities Summer Seminar, 1979; Recipient grants-in-aid Social Sci. Research Council for study of Mr. Justice Brandeis, 1933, for study of trade unions and the state in London, 1935; Guggenheim fellow for biography of Harlan Fiske Stone, 1950; Northwestern U. Centennial lectr., 1951; Guggenheim fellow, 1952; Gasper G. Bacon lectr. Boston U., 1953; mem. Am. Studies Seminars, Tokyo U., 1953; $5,000 prize in history and biography ALA, 1957; Rockefeller Found. study award, 1960-63; McCosh Faculty fellow, 1963-64. Fellow Am. Acad. Arts and Scis.; mem. Am. Polit. Sci. Assn. (v.p.), Phi Beta Kappa, Sigma Alpha Epsilon. Presbyterian. Clubs: Nassau (Princeton); Princeton (N.Y.C.); Authors (London). Author or co-author numerous books, 1925—, latest being American Constitutional Law, 1954, 6th edit., 1978; Security Through Freedom, 1955; Harlan Fiske Stone: Pillar of the Law, 1956; The Supreme Court from Taft to Burger, rev. edit., 1979; In Quest of Freedom, 1959, 2d edit., 1973; The Supreme Court: Palladium of Freedom, 1962; The States Rights Debate: Antifederalism and the Constitution, 1964, 2d edit., 1972; Free Government in the Making, 1965; William Howard Taft: Chief Justice, 1965; The Supreme Court in a Free Society, 1969; contbr. articles to profl. jours. Home: 8 Edgehill St Princeton NJ 08540

MASON, ARTHUR WINFRED, JR., educator; b. Fremont, Nebr., June 10, 1921; s. Arthur Winfred and Mary (Brown) M.; B.S. in Bus. Adminstrn., U. Nebr., 1942, M.A., 1946; Ph.D., U. Pa., 1958; m. Pollyann Petty, June 12, 1944; children—Judith Ann, Pamela, Sally Jean. Asst. actuary Great Eastern Mut. Life Ins. Co., Denver, 1946; asst. prof., then asso. prof. ins. U. Denver, 1947-52; dir. coll. relations Am. Coll. Life Underwriters, Phila., 1952-56; prof., asso. dean Washington U., St. Louis, 1956-66; dean Coll. Bus. Adminstrn., U. Denver, 1966-74, dir. ins. research program, 1963-69, prof., 1966—; mgmt. cons., 1956—. Mem. ins. adv. com. St. Louis County, 1964-66. Adviser Kirkwood Sch. Dist., Ladue Sch. Dist., 1964-66, Regional Export Expansion Council, 1969-72, Gov.'s Revenue Estimating Com., 1969-74. Served to lt. USNR, 1942-45. Heubner Found. fellow; recipient Top Hat award Colo. Fedn. Bus. and Profl. Women, 1968. C.L.U. Mem. Am. Soc. C.L.U.'s (editorial bd. jour. 1966-68), Am. Risk and Ins. Assn., Western Econ. Assn., Sigma Chi, Pi Mu Epsilon, Beta Gamma Sigma, Omicron Delta Kappa, Delta Sigma Pi, Beta Alpha Psi. Rotarian. Home: 3649 S Narcissus Way Denver CO 80237

MASON, AUSTIN BLAKE, mfg. co. exec.; b. Weston, Mass., Oct. 28, 1921; s. Austin Blake and Margaret (Bliss) M.; student Harvard, 1944; m. Joan Jackson, Apr. 19, 1943 (div. July 1969); children—Austin Blake III, Stephen D., Joanne; m. 2d, Connie Bell, May 28, 1970. Dir., asst. mgr., buyer Mass. Mohair Plush Co., Lowell, Mass., 1951-53; mgr. No. div. Pacific Mills, Boston, 1954-55; asst. to pres. Ludlow Corp., Needham Heights, Mass., 1956, exec. v.p., 1956-57, pres., dir., 1957—; pres., dir. Ludlow Can. Ltd.; dir. Sociedade de Industrias Texteis do Norte, Liberty Mut. Ins. Co., Boston, Ludlow Jute Co., Ltd., First Nat. Bank of Boston, First Nat. Boston Corp., Liberty Mut. Fire Ins. Co. Trustee Children's Hosp., Nashoba Community Hosp.; mem. industry adv. council U. Lowell. Served as 1st lt., F.A., AUS, World War II. Decorated Bronze Star medal, Purple Heart. Home: Prescott St Pepperell MA 01463 Office: 145 Rosemary St Needham Heights MA 02194

MASON, BARRY JEAN, banker; b. Big Spring, Tex., June 3, 1930; s. Vernon E. and Irene E. (Owen) M.; B.S., U. Tex., 1957; B.F.T., Am. Inst. Fgn. Trade, 1958; postgrad. Advanced Mgmt. Program Harvard, Auspices U. Hawaii, 1968; m. Alexana Petroff, Aug. 31, 1958; children—Scott Alexander, Lydia Claire. Trainee First Nat. City Bank, N.Y., Hong Kong, 1959-60, asst. accountant, Toyko, Japan, 1960-63, asst. mgr., 1963-66, mgr., Hong Kong, 1966-67, resident v.p., 1967-68, resident v.p., Tokyo, 1968-69, v.p., Japan, Korea, Okinawa, 1969; v.p. Republic Nat. Bank Dallas, 1969-70, sr. v.p., 1970-72, exec. v.p. 1972—. Mem. adv. bd. PEFCO. Trustee Am. Sch. Japan; bd. advisers Internat. Sch. Hong Kong. Served with AUS, 1948-49, USNR, 1952-53, USMCR, 1953-55. Mem. Bankers Assn. for Fgn. Trade (past dir.), Am. Bankers Assn. Clubs: Hong Kong; T Bar M Racquet. Home: 7730 Yamini Dr Dallas TX 75230 Office: PO Box 5961 Dallas TX 75222

MASON, BIRNY, JR., chem. co. exec.; b. Brownsville, Pa., Feb. 27, 1909; s. Birny and Mary (Carmack) M.; B.S., Cornell U., Ithaca, N.Y., 1932; m. Elizabeth Brownson Smith, Mar. 22, 1935; 1 son, Jerome Acheson. With Union Carbide Corp., 1932—, beginning with research and devel. dept. Union Carbide Chems. Co. div., South Charleston, W.Va., successively asst. plant supt., Louisville, asst. dir. indsl. relations, South Charleston, exec. asst. to v.p. indsl. relations, N.Y.C., mgr. indsl. relations, asst. sec., asst. treas., 1932, 1958-60, pres., 1960-66, chief exec. officer, 1963-71, chmn. bd., 1966-71, chmn. exec. com., 1971-74, also dir.; pres. div. Union Carbide Devel. Co., 1956-57, v.p., mem. appropriations com. corp., 1957-65. Trustee, Nat. Safety Council. Mem. Am. Inst. Chem. Engrs., Alpha Delta Phi. Clubs: Larchmont (N.Y.) Yacht; Blind Brook (Port Chester, N.Y.). Home: 6 Island Dr Rye NY 10580 Office: 270 Park Ave New York NY 10017

MASON, BRIAN HAROLD, geologist; b. N.Z., Apr. 18, 1917; s. George Harold and Catherine (Fairweather) M.; M.Sc., U. New Zealand, 1938; Ph.D., U. Stockholm, 1943. Came to U.S., 1947, naturalized, 1953. Lectr. geology Canterbury Coll., N.Z., 1944-47; prof. mineralogy Ind. U., 1947-53; chmn. dept. mineralogy Am. Mus. Natural History, N.Y.C., 1953-65; research curator U.S. Nat. Mus., Washington, after 1965; now with dept. mineral scis. Smithsonian Instn., Washington. Fellow Mineral. Soc. Am., Geol. Soc. Am.; mem. Geochem. Soc., Royal Soc. N.Z., Swedish Geol. Soc. Author: Principles of Geochemistry, 3d edit., 1967; Meteorites, 1962; The Literature of Geology, 1958; (with L. G. Berry) Mineralogy, 1959; (with W.G. Melson) The Lunar Rocks, 1970. Office: Dept Mineral Scis Smithsonian Instn Washington DC 20560

MASON, CHARLES ELLIS, III, editor; b. Boston, Oct. 31, 1938; s. Charles Ellis, Jr. and Ada Brooks (Trafford) M.; B.A., Yale U., 1960. Loan officer State St. Bank, Boston, 1963-68; asso. editor Sail mag., Boston, 1968-74, exec. editor, 1974—. Bd. dirs. Save Our Shores, 1972—. Served with USNR, 1960-62. Home: 16 Joy St Boston MA 02114 Office: 38 Commercial Wharf Boston MA 02110

MASON, DAVID DICKENSON, educator; b. Abingdon, Va., Jan. 22, 1917; s. William Thomas and Eva (Dorton) M.; B.A., King Coll., 1936; M.S. (Acad. Merit fellow), Va. Poly. Inst., 1938; postgrad. Ohio State U., 1939-40; Ph.D., N.C. State U., 1948; m. Virginia Louise Pendleton, Oct. 28, 1944; children—Margie F., David P. Asst. soil scientist Va. Poly. Inst., 1938-39; asst. prof. soils Ohio State U., 1947-49; prin. biometrician Dept. Agr., Beltsville, Md., 1949-53; prof. statistics N.C. State U., 1953-62, prof., head dept. statistics, 1962—, head Inst. Statistics, 1962—. Sr. cons. United Fruit Co., Boston, 1957—. Instl. rep. So. Regional Edn. Bd. com. statistics, 1963—, chmn., 1973-75. Bd. dirs. Triangle Univs. Computation Center Corp., chmn., 1968-70. Served with AUS, 1941-45. Fellow Am. Statis. Assn., Am. Soc. Agronomy, Soil Sci. Soc. Am.; mem. Biometric Soc., Sigma Xi, Phi Kappa Phi, Gamma Sigma Delta. Presbyn. (elder, deacon). Rotarian. Contbr. articles to profl. jours. Home: 4212 Arbutus Dr Raleigh NC 27612 Office: Inst Statistics Box 5457 Raleigh NC 27650

MASON, DAVID ERNEST, mgmt. cons., author, clergyman; b. Natchitoches, La., Jan. 3, 1928; s. Charles Culberson and Marjorie (O'Bannon) M.; B.A., La. State U., 1949; B.D., So. Bapt. Theol. Sem., 1952; Th.M., So. Bapt. Theol. Sem., 1952; D.D., U. Corpus Christi, 1958; M.A. in Journalism, Syracuse U., 1964; m. Betty D. Oxford, Aug. 11, 1950 (div.); m. 2d, Alberta Martin, July 2, 1964; children—David Ernest, Paul Alexander; stepchildren—Hobart, Jeffrey, William, Suzanne. Ordained to ministry Bapt. Ch., 1950; student dir. Bapt. Student Union La. Poly. Inst., 1950; asst. to pastor 2d Ponce de Leon Ch., Atlanta, 1952-53; pastor 1st Ch., Jefferson, Ga., 1953-55, Jonesboro, La., 1955-60, Alice, Tex., 1960-62; asso. dir. Laubach Literacy, Inc., 1963-66, exec. dir., 1967-68; dir. Manpower Ednl. Corp., N.Y.C., 1968-69; chmn. bd. Supportive Services, Inc., N.Y.C., 1969-74; also chmn. bd. Westchester Learning Center, 1971-74, N.Y. Jobs Consortium, Inc., 1971-74. Cons. to Internat. Paper Co., Am. Cyanamid, U.S. Industries, Hertz, Inc., Indian Head Corp., Prudential Life Ins. Co., Nat. Bank N.Am., others. Mem. L.I. Econ. Devel. Corp., 1969-72; mem. Mayor's Com. on Jobs for Vets., 1972—; mem. New Orleans Civic Council, 1972—, New Orleans Human Relations Commn., Orleans Parish Prison Bd., 1972—, Legal Aid Bur. Chmn. home missions com. La. Bapt. Conv., 1957; pres. exec. bd. Dist. IV Bapt. Conv., 1958-59; chmn. New Orleans White Collar Crime Com., 1979; mem. Sch. Bd. Sch. Fin. Com., 1979; Am. rep. com. on evangelism of Jamaica (B.W.I.) Bapt. Union, 1960, 61; exec. dir. Greater New Orleans Fedn. Chs., 1972—. La. chmn. James P. Boyce Library Fund, 1957-59; trustee So. Bapt. Theol. Sem., 1959-60; bd. dirs. Am. Council of Vol. Agys. for Fgn. Service, 1967-68, Koinoia Found., Balt., 1967-68; chmn. adv. bd. Afrlo-Lit., Africa. Bd. overseers Dag Hammariskold Coll., 1970-72; mem. bd. Greater New Orleans Housing Corp., 1972—, Inst. Human Understanding, 1972-78, New Orleans Tragedy Fund, 1973-78; mem. steering com. Goals Found., 1972-77; chmn. New Orleans Nat. Alliance Businessmen JOBS program; chmn. La. Renaissance, Religion and Arts, 1976-77; bd. dirs. Luth. Home New Orleans, 1976-78; mem. Westchester County (N.Y.) Council on Arts. Served as 2d lt., F.A., AUS, 1950. Mem. So. Bapt. Theol. Sem. Alumni Assn. La. (past pres.), Assn. Internat. Vol. Orgns. (chmn. 1966-69), Adult Edn. Assn., Bapt. Writers Assn. (past chmn.), Fellowship of Religious Journalists (pres.), Soc. Internat. Devel., Religious Pub. Relations Assn., Assn. Edn. Journalism. Rotarian. Author: Now Then, 1957; The Charley Matthews Story, 1958; Eight Steps Toward Maturity, 1962; The Vacant Hearted, 1963; Apostle to the Illiterates, 1965; Frank C. Laubach, Teacher of Millions, 1967; Reaching The Silent Billion, 1967; The Compulsive Christian, 1968. Author numerous articles. Home: 527 St Philip St New Orleans LA 70116 Office: 332 Carondelet St New Orleans LA 70130 also 200 Park Ave New York City NY 10017

MASON, DAVID MALCOLM, educator; b. Los Angeles, Jan. 7, 1921; s. David Malcolm and Anna Pride (McKelvy) M.; B.S. in Applied Chemistry, Calif. Inst. Tech., 1943, M.S. in Chem. Engring., 1947, Ph.D., 1949; m. Honora Elizabeth MacPherson, Sept. 12, 1953. Chem. engr. Standard Oil of Calif., 1943; instr. chem. engring. Calif. Inst. Tech., 1949-52; research group supr. Jet Propulsion Lab., 1952-55; asso. prof. chem. engring. and chemistry Stanford, 1955-58, prof., 1958—, chmn. dept. chem. engring., 1960-72, asso. dean undergrad. studies, 1974-76; liaison scientist Office of Naval Research, London, 1972-73; Nat. Sci. fellow Imperial Coll., London, 1964-65. Served from ensign to lt. (s.g.), USNR, 1943-46. Recipient Alumni Distinguished Service award Calif. Inst. Tech., 1966; registered profl. engr., Calif. Fellow Am. Inst. Chem. Engrs.; mem. Am. Chem. Soc., Am. Soc. Engring. Edn., AAAS, Am. Electrochem. Soc., Sigma Xi, Tau Beta Pi. Home: 148 Doud Dr Los Altos CA 94022

MASON, DEAN TOWLE, cardiologist; b. Berkeley, Calif., Sept. 20, 1932; s. Ira Jencks and Florence Mabel (Towle) M.; B.A. in Chemistry, Duke U., 1954, M.D., 1958; m. Maureen O'Brien, June 22, 1957; children—Kathleen, Alison. Intern, then resident in medicine Johns Hopkins Hosp., 1958-61; clin. asso. cardiology br., sr. asst. surgeon USPHS, Nat. Heart Inst., NIH, 1961-63, asst. sect. dir. cardiovascular diagnosis, attending physician, sr. investigator cardiology br., 1963-68; prof. medicine, prof. physiology, chief cardiovascular medicine U. Calif. Med. Sch., Davis-Sacramento Med. Center, 1968—; co-chmn. cardiovascular-renal drugs U.S. Pharmacopeia Com. Revision, 1970-75; mem. life scis. com. NASA; med. research rev. bd. VA, NIH; vis. prof. numerous univs., cons. in field. mem. Am. Cardiovascular Splty. Certification Bd., 1972—. Recipient Research award Am. Therapeutic Soc., 1965; Theodore and Susan B. Cummings Humanitarian award State Dept.-Am. Coll. Cardiology, 1972, 73, 75, 78; Skylab Achievement award NASA, 1974; U. Calif. Faculty Research award, 1978; named Outstanding Prof., U. Calif. Med. Sch., Davis, 1972. Diplomate Nat. Bd. Med. Examiners, Am. Bd. Internal Medicine (cardiovascular diseases). Fellow Am. Coll. Cardiology (pres. 1977-78), A.C.P., Am. Heart Assn., Am. Coll. Chest Physicians, Royal Soc. Medicine; mem. Am. Soc. Clin. Investigation, Am. Physiol. Soc., Am. Soc. Pharmacology and Exptl. Therapeutics (Exptl. Therapeutics award 1973), Am. Fedn. Clin. Research, N.Y. Acad. Scis., Am. Assn. U. Cardiologists, Am. Soc. Clin. Pharmacology and Therapeutics, Western Assn. Physicians, AAUP, Western Soc. Clin. Research (past pres.), Phi Beta Kappa, Alpha Omega Alpha. Republican. Methodist. Club: El Macero Country. Author: Cardiovascular Management, 1974; Congestive Heart Failure, 1976; Advances in Heart Disease, Vol. 1, 1977, Vol. 2, 1978; Cardiovascular Emergencies, 1978; also numerous articles. Editor: Clin. Cardiol. Jour.; mem. editorial bds. sci. jours. Home: 3015 Country Club Dr El Macero CA 95618 Office: Cardiovascular Medicine Univ Calif Medical Sch Davis CA 95616. *Many of us are more capable than some of us, but none of us is as capable as all of us. If you think you are outclassed, you are. Think small and you'll fall behind; think big and your achievements will rise. Success in life belongs to the person who knows he can. To accomplish your goals, you must maintain an end-zone orientation without sideline distractions.*

MASON, EARL HENRY, banker; b. Webster, Mass., Nov. 6, 1924; s. Edward C. and Catherine L. M.; grad. Bentley Coll., Boston, 1949. Auditor, asst. cashier, asst. v.p. and cashier First Nat. Bank of Webster, 1950-65; sr. v.p., treas. Guaranty Bank & Trust Co., Worcester, Mass., 1965-75, exec. v.p., treas., 1975—, also dir.; v.p., treas., dir. The Conifer Group Inc., bank holding co., 1973—. Served with Signal Corps, AUS. Mem. Nat. Assn. Accountants, Assn. Bank Auditors and Comptrollers. K.C. Home: Oscar St Webster MA 01570 Office: 370 Main St Worcester MA 01608

MASON, EDWARD ALLEN, scientist, educator; b. Atlantic City, Sept. 2, 1926; s. Edward Paul and Olive Margaret (Lorah) M.; B.S., Va. Poly. Inst., 1947; Ph.D., Mass. Inst. Tech., 1951; A.M., Brown U., 1968; m. Ann Courtenay Laufman, July 6, 1952; children—Catherine Hubbard, Stephen Edward, Elizabeth Margaret, Sarah Lois. Research asso. Mass. Inst. Tech., 1950-52; NRC fellow U. Wis., 1952-53; mem. faculty Pa. State U., 1953-55, U. Md., 1955-67; prof. chemistry and engring. Brown U., Providence, 1967—. Fellow Am. Phys. Soc., Washington Acad. Scis. (Phys. Scis. award 1962), Random Soc.; mem. AAAS, Am. Assn. Physics Tchrs., Sigma Xi, Phi Kappa Phi, Phi Lambda Upsilon. Author: (with J. T. Vanderslice and H. W. Schamp) Thermodynamics, 1966; (with T. H. Spurling) Virial Equation of State, 1969; (with E.W. McDaniel) Mobility and Diffusion of Ions in Gases, 1973. Asso. editor Physics of Fluids, 1963-65, Jour. Chem. Physics, 1964-66 adv. editor Case Studies in Atomic Physics, 1971-75. Research publs. on interaction and collisions among atoms, molecules and ions, their effects on properties and behavior of gases; membrane transport theory. Home: 26 Nayatt Rd Barrington RI 02806 Office: Dept Chemistry Brown U Providence RI 02912

MASON, EDWARD ARCHIBALD, chem. and nuclear engr.; b. Rochester, N.Y., Aug. 9, 1924; s. Henry Archibald and Monica (Brayer) M.; B.S., U. Rochester, 1945; M.S., Mass. Inst. Tech., 1948, Sc.D., 1950; m. Barbara Jean Earley, Apr. 15, 1950; children—Thomas E., Kathleen M., Paul D., Mark J., Anne M., Mary Beth. Asst. prof. chem. engring. Mass. Inst. Tech., Cambridge, 1950-53, asso. prof. nuclear engring., 1957-63, prof., 1963-77, dept. head, 1971-75; commr. Nuclear Regulatory Commn., Washington, 1975-77; v.p. research Standard Oil Co. (Ind.), Chgo., 1977—; dir. research Ionics, Inc., Cambridge, Mass., 1953-57; sr. design engr. Oak Ridge Nat. Lab., 1957; mem. adv. com. reactor safeguards AEC, 1972-75; cons. other govt. agys., industry. Mem. adv. com. M.I.T., U. Chgo., U. Tex. Served with USNR, 1943-46. NSF Sr. Postdoctoral fellow, 1965-66. Fellow Am. Acad. Arts and Scis., Am. Nuclear Soc., Am. Inst. Chemists; mem. Nat. Acad. Engring. (councilor 1978—), N.Y. Acad. Scis., Am. Inst. Chem. Engrs. (R.E. Wilson award in nuclear chem. engring. 1978), Western Soc. Engrs., Am. Chem. Soc., AAAS, Phi Beta Kappa, Sigma Xi, Tau Beta Pi. Clubs: Execs. (Chgo.); Hinsdale (Ill.) Golf. Contbr. articles to profl. jours. Patentee in field. Home: 145 Hillcrest Ave Hinsdale IL 60521 Office: 200 E Randolph Dr Chicago IL 60601

MASON, EDWARD SAGENDORPH, economist, educator; b. Clinton, Iowa, Feb. 22, 1899; s. Edward Luther and Kate (Sagendorph) M.; A.B., U. Kans., 1919; A.M., Harvard, 1920, Ph.D., 1925, LL.D., 1956; B.Litt., Oxford (Eng.) U., 1923; Litt.D. (hon.), Williams Coll., 1948; LL.D., Yale, 1964, Concord Coll., 1971; m. Marguerite Sisson La Monte, Apr. 4, 1930; children—Robert La Monte (step son), Jane Carroll (Mrs. Roger Manasse), Edward H.L. Instr., Harvard, 1923-27, asst. prof. econs., 1927-32, asso. prof., 1932-37, prof. econs., 1937—, George F. Baker prof. econs., 1958-61, Thomas W. Lamont Univ. prof., 1961-69, Lamont prof. emeritus, dean Grad. Sch. Pub. Adminstrn., 1947-58. Econ. cons. Dept. Labor, 1938-39, Def. Commn., 1940-41, OSS, Washington, 1941-45; dep. to asst. sec. state charge econ. affairs, 1945; econ. cons. Dept. State, 1946-47; chief econ. adviser Moscow Conf., 1947; mem. Adv. Com. on Mgmt. Improvement to Assist in Improving Govt. Orgn.; mem. Materials Policy Commn., 1951-52; chmn. adv. com. econ. devel. AID; cons. World Bank; chmn. Sloan Found. commn. on cable communications. Bd. dirs. Internat. Council for Ednl. Devel., Resources for the Future, Asian Devel. Corp. Recipient Medal of Freedom, 1946; Star of Pakistan, 1967; Distinguished Alumni award U. Kans.; hon. fellow Lincoln Coll., Oxford. Mem. Am. Philos. Soc., Am. Econ. Assn. (past pres.), Royal Econ. Soc. London, Am. Acad. Arts and Scis., Phi Beta Kappa, Delta Sigma Rho. Unitarian. Club: The Saturday. Home: 1010 Memorial Dr Cambridge MA 02138

MASON, ELLSWORTH GOODWIN, librarian; b. Waterbury, Conn., Aug. 25, 1917; s. Frederick William and Kathryn Loretta (Watkins) M.; B.A., Yale, 1938, M.A., 1942, Ph.D., 1948; L.H.D., Hofstra U., 1973; m. Rose Ellen Maloy, May 13, 1951 (div. Oct. 1961); children—Kay Iris, Joyce Iris; m. 2d, Joan Lou Shinew, Aug. 16, 1964; 1 son, Sean David. Reference asst. Yale Library, 1938-42; with office exports Bd. Econ. Warfare, 1942-43; instr. English, Williams Coll., 1948-50; mem. humanities div. Marlboro (Vt.) Coll., 1951-52; serials librarian U. Wyo. Library, 1952-54; reference librarian Colo. Coll. Library, 1954-58, librarian, lectr. English, 1958-63; prof., dir. library services Hofstra U., Hempstead, N.Y., 1963-72; prof., dir., U. Colo. Libraries, 1972-76; pres. Mason Assos., Ltd., 1977—. Research asso. U. Calif. at Berkeley, 1965; vis. lectr. Colo. Coll., 1965, Syracuse U., 1965-68, Elmira Coll., 1966, Columbia, 1966-68, U. Ill., summer 1968, 72, Lincoln U., 1969, U. B.C. (Can.), 1969, U. Toronto, 1970, U. Tulsa, 1971, 76, Rutgers U., 1971, Colgate U., 1972, Simmons Coll., 1972, U. Oreg., 1973, U. Ky., 1973, U. N.C., 1976, U. Ala., 1976, Ball State U., 1977, U. Lethbridge (Can.), 1977; v.p., pres.-elect Bibliog. Center Research, Rocky Mountain Region, 1961-63; exec. bd. Hist. Soc. Pikes Peak Region, 1960; chmn. Colo. Council Library Devel., 1962-63; chmn. Conf. on U. Library Standards, Boston, 1967; planning com. L.I. Library Resources Council, 1967-68, trustee, 1970-72, chmn. personnel com., 1970-72; dir. Workshop on surveys Canadian Assn. Coll. and Univ. Libraries, 1968; lectr. Conf. on Acad. Library Bldgs., Drexel Inst. Tech., 1966; library bldg. cons. 121 ednl. instnl. libraries. Served with USNR, 1943-46. Recipient hon-mention in design N.Y. State Assn. Architects-A.I.A., 1974; Progressive Architecture award, 1974; Harry Bailly award Assn. Colls. of Midwest, 1975. Council on Library Resources fellow, 1969-70. Mem. Am. (councillor-at-large), Colo. (pres. So. dist. 1960-61) library assns., Bibliog. Soc. Am., Library Assn. (London), Modern Lang. Assn., Pvt. Libraries Assn., Alcuin Soc., Conf. Editors Learned Jours., Colo. Book Collectors (founder, pres. 1975—), James Joyce Found. (chmn., sect. on translation from Joyce, 2d Internat. James Joyce Symposium, Dublin, 1969), Alpha Sigma Lamda, Sigma Kappa Alpha (pres. 1969-70). Clubs: Caxton, Archons of Colophon; Ghost Town (Colorado Springs). Editor: (with Stanislaus Joyce) The Early Joyce, 1955, Xerox U.M. edit., 1964; (with Richard Ellmann) The Critical Writings of James Joyce, 1959; Critical Commentary on A Portrait of the Artist as a Young Man, 1966. Translator, (S. Joyce) Recollections of James Joyce, 1951; Essais de J. Joyce, 1966; Escritos Criticos de James Joyce, 1973; James Joyce's Ulysses and Vico's Cycle, 1973; Kritische Schriften v. James Joyce, 1975; editor: Colorado College Studies, 1959-62. Editor and compiler, Focus on Robert Graves, 1972—, editor The Booklover's Bounty, 1977—; editorial bd. The Serials Librarian, 1977—. Home: 756 6th St Boulder CO 80302

MASON, FRANK HERBERT, artist, educator; b. Cleve., Feb. 20, 1921; s. Walter Harrison and Mildred Mary (Corbin) M.; student Nat. Acad. Design, 1937-38, Art Students League, N.Y.C., 1938-51; m. Anne Cary Crosby, Mar. 12, 1966; 1 son, Arden Harriman. Represented in permanent collections at Ch. of San Giovanni di Malta, Venice, Italy (Cross of Merit for eight canvas murals on life of St. Anthony of Padua Sovereign Mil. Order of Malta), Am. embassy, London, Eng., AEC, Washington, Duke, Butler Inst. Am. Art, Indpls., Eureka Coll.; instr. fine arts Art Students League, 1951—. Served with AUS, 1945-46. Recipient North Am. Continent award Expn. Intercontinentale, Monaco, 1968. Mem. NAD (past treas.), Nat. Mural Soc. Home: 385 Broome St New York NY 10013

MASON, FRANKLIN ROGERS, fin. exec.; b. Washington, June 16, 1936; s. Franklin Allison and Jeannette Morgan (Rogers) M.; B.S. in Engring., Princeton U., 1958; M.B.A., Northwestern U., 1959; m. Aileen Joan Larson, July 29, 1961; children—William Rogers, Elisa Ellen. With Ford Motor Co., 1960-75, finance mgr., Portugal, 1969-72; fin. analysis mgr. Ford subs. Richier S.A., France, 1972-75; sr. v.p. finance Raymond Internat. Inc., Houston, 1975—; dir. First City Nat. Bank-Inwood Forest, Houston. Served with arty. U.S. Army, 1960. Mem. Fin. Execs. Inst., Assn. Corp. Growth, Am. Mgmt. Assn., Princeton U. Alumni Assn., Alliance Francaise, Houston-Nice Sister City Assn. Republican. Episcopalian. Clubs: University, Racquet (Houston); Princeton (N.Y.C.). Home: 420 Chapelwood Ct Houston TX 77024 Office: PO Box 27456 Houston TX 77027. *Business is people, and success is dependent on good communication with people. Effective communication must be accompanied by fairness, consistency, patience, and a willingness to compromise.*

MASON, GEORGE ROBERT, surgeon, educator; b. Rochester, N.Y., June 10, 1932; s. George Mitchell and Marjorie Louise (Hooper) M.; B.A., Oberlin Coll., 1955; M.D. with honors, U. Chgo., 1957; Ph.D. in Physiology (Giannini fellow 1966-67), Stanford U., 1968; m. Grace Louise Bransfield, Feb. 4, 1956; children—Douglas Richard, Marcia Jean, David William. Tchg. asst. pathology U. Chgo., 1954-56; rotating intern U. Chgo. Clinics, 1957-58; tchg. asst. surgery, NIH postdoctoral fellow, USPHS fellow surgery Stanford U., 1960-62; from asst. resident in surgery to sr. and chief resident in surgery, Stanford U. Hosps., 1962-66; mem. faculty Stanford Med. Sch., 1965-71, asso. prof., 1970-71; prof., chmn. dept. surgery U. Md. Med. Sch., Balt., 1971—, also prof. physiology. Served to capt. M.C., USAF, 1958-60. Recipient Markle scholarship in acad. medicine, 1968-74. Diplomate Am. Bd. Surgery, Am. Bd. Thoracic Surgery. Mem. Am. Assn. Thoracic Surgery, AAUP, Am. Coll. Chest Physicians, A.C.S., AMA, Am. Physiol. Soc., Pacific Coast Surg. Assn., Assn. Acad. Surgery, Balt. Acad. Surgery, Balt. Med. Soc., Halsted Soc., Med. and Chirurg. Faculty Md., Soc. Internat. de Chirurgie, Soc. Clin. Surgery, Soc. Surgery Alimentary Tract, Soc. U. Surgeons, SE Surg. Congress, Sigma Xi, Alpha Omega Alpha. Contbr. to profl. jours., med. textbooks. Home: 112 Tunbridge Rd Baltimore MD 21212 Office: U of Md Sch Medicine Dept Surgery 22 S Greene St Baltimore MD 21201

MASON, GORDON FARMER, radio sta. exec.; b. Pitts., Mar. 26, 1929; s. Thomas Gordon and Dorothy (Farmer) M.; B.A., U. Calif., Los Angeles, 1951; m. Linda Booth, May 3, 1974; children—Catherine Dorothy, Craig Campbell. Various positions Sta. KNX, Los Angeles, 1952-58, gen. sales mgr., 1958-62; field mgr. affiliate relations CBS Radio Network, 1962; nat. sales mgr. Golden West Broadcasters Radio, 1962-63; gen. sales mgr. Sta. KTLA-TV, Los Angeles, 1964-66; v.p., asso. pub. Western Advt. Co., Los Angeles, 1966-67; v.p. sales MAC Pubs., Inc., Los Angeles, 1967-69; v.p., sta. mgr. Sta. KBIG, Los Angeles, 1969-74; v.p., gen. mgr. CCLA Communications Co., Los Angeles, 1974—, Sta. KJOI-FM, Los Angeles, 1974—; instr. broadcast mgmt. U. Calif. extension, Los Angeles. Advisor to bd. dirs. Los Angeles County Epilepsy Soc., 1977—. Served with USNR, 1944-46. Mem. Advt. Club Los Angeles (past pres.), So. Calif. Broadcasters Assn. (dir. 1977—, past chmn.), Advt. Industry Emergency Fund. (pres. 1979—), Milline Club So. Calif. (dir. 1977—, past pres.). Home: 1445 N Bundy Dr Los Angeles CA 90049 Office: 2555 Briarcrest Rd Beverly Hills CA 90210

MASON, HAROLD JESSE, communications exec.; b. Bklyn., Dec. 13, 1926; s. Irving and Belle (Solomon) M.; B.A., Emory U., 1952, M.A., 1954; Ph.D., Columbia, 1966; m. Selma Ruth Werner, May 22, 1947; children—Lori Karen, Dione Ellen. Serials Librarian Ga. Inst. Tech., 1953-54; asst. mgr. Kraus Reprint Corp., N.Y.C., 1954-66; pres. Greenwood Press Inc., Westport, Conn., 1967-72; pres. Harold J. Mason, Inc., Weston, Conn., 1973—. Mem. Phi Beta Kappa. Republican. Jewish. Contbr. articles to profl. publs. Home: 32 Farrell Rd Weston CT 06883 Office: PO Box 1267 Weston CT 06883

MASON, HENRY LLOYD, educator; b. Berlin, Germany, Nov. 4, 1921; s. Hugo L. and Maria (Werner) M.; came to U.S., 1940, naturalized, 1943; B.A., Johns Hopkins, 1942; Ph.D., Columbia, 1951; m. Mathilde Jessé, Jan. 23, 1946; children—Monica (Mrs. Robert Mimeles), Paul. Mem. faculty Tulane U., New Orleans, 1952—, prof., chmn. dept. polit. sci., 1966-75; vis. asso. prof. Columbia, 1958; Fulbright prof. U. Innsbruck, 1958-59; Fulbright prof. Free U. Berlin, 1965; vis. prof. U. Amsterdam, 1973-74. Bd. dirs. Urban League Greater New Orleans, 1961-69. Served to 1st lt., M.I., AUS, 1942-46; ETO. Mem. AAUP (mem. nat. council 1966-69), Internat. Studies Assn. (pres. so. region, 1972-73), So. Polit. Sci. Assn. (mem. exec. council, 1973-76). Author: The Purge of Dutch Quislings, 1952; The European Coal and Steel Community, 1955; Toynbee's Approach to World Politics, 1959; Mass Demonstrations Against Foreign Regimes, 1966; University Government, 1972. Home: 1821 Upperline St New Orleans LA 70115

MASON, HERBERT WARREN, JR., author, educator, translator; b. Wilmington, Del., Apr. 20, 1932; s. Herbert Warren and Mildred Jane (Noyes) M.; A.B., Harvard U., 1955, A.M., 1965, Ph.D., 1969; m. Mary Stauffer Grimley, Sept. 11, 1954; children—Cathleen, Paul, Sarah. With summer theatre, 1950-52; schooner crewman, 1950; pvt. detective, 1954-55; writer, tchr., Maine, 1960-62; tchr. Simmons Coll., Boston, 1962-63, Tufts U., 1966-67, Harvard U., 1964-68; Univ. prof., prof. religion and Islamic history Boston U., 1972—. Sec., Inter-racial Riverside Assn., Cambridge, Mass., 1965-67; trustee Bd. Charity of Edward Hopkins, Boston Athenaeum. Mem. Medieval Acad. Am., Am. Oriental Soc., Am. Acad. Religion, Mark Twain Soc., P.E.N. Author: Reflections on the Middle East Crisis, 1970; Two Statesmen of Medieval Islam, 1971; Gilgamesh (Nat. book award nomination), 1971; The Death of al-Hallaj, 1979; Moments in Passage, 1979; (novel) Summer Light, 1980; translator: La Passion d'al-Hallaj, 4 vols., Bollingen Series, by Louis Massignon; co-editor Humaniora Islamica; contbr. articles, essays, fiction, poetry to fiction mags. Address: 227 Payson Rd Belmont MA 02178

MASON, JAMES, actor; b. Huddersfield, Eng., May 15, 1909; s. John and Mabel Hattersley (Gaunt) M.; student Marlborough Coll., 1923-28; B.A., Peterhouse, Cambridge U., 1931, M.A., 1943; m. Pamela Kellino, Feb. 1941 (div.); children—Portland Allen, Alexander Morgan; m. 2d, Clarissa Kaye, 1971. Resident U.S., 1946-62, Switzerland, 1962—. Began career in theatre, 1931; screen debut in Late Extra, 1935; films include The Mill on the Floss, Secret of Stamboul, High Command, Man in Grey, Fanny by Gaslight, Pandora and the Flying Dutchman, Lady's Possessed, Desert Fox, 5 Fingers, Botany Bay, Story of Three Loves, Face to Face, Desert Rats, Man Between, Prince Valiant, The Decks Ran Red, Prisoner of Zenda, Julius Caesar, A Star is Born, 20,000 Leagues Under the Sea, Forever Darling, Journey to the Center of the Earth, Marriage Go Round, Lolita, 1961, Island in the Sun, Cry Terror, North by Northwest, Georgy Girl, 1966, The Deadly Affair, 1966, Age of Consent, 1968, Spring and Port Wine, 1969, Childs Play, 1971, The Last of Sheila, 1972, Dr. Frankenstein, 1973, The Marseilles Contract, 1974, Great Expectations, 1974, Mandingo, 1974, The Devil and the Schoolteacher, 1975, Autobiography of a Princess, 1975, The Voyage, 1975, Water Babies, 1976, Cross of Iron, Fear in the City, 1976, The Passage, Murder by Decree, Bloodline, 1978, Heaven Can Wait, Boys From Brazil, 1977; actor, producer film Bigger than Life; producer 20th Century-Fox Studio; actor television programs Your Readers' Series, 1955, documentary Search for the Nile, also Plot to Kill Hitler, Love and Hate, The Roots of the Mafia, 1975, Jesus of Nazareth, 1976; Broadway play Faith Healer, 1979. Office: care Maggie Parker 55 Park Ln London W1 England

MASON, JAMES TATE, surgeon; b. Seattle, June 17, 1913; s. James Tate and Laura (Whittlesey) M.; student U. Wash., 1936; M.D., U. Va., 1940; m. Margaret Elisabeth Thomas, Jan. 10, 1942; children—Laura Mason Foster, Anne Mason Curti, James Tate, Mary Mason Paul. Intern, Bellevue Hosp., N.Y.C., 1940-41; resident Lahey Clinic, Boston, 1942-43, U. Mich., 1946-49; practice medicine, specializing in urologic surgery, Seattle, 1949—; staff Mason Clinic, Virginia Mason, Univ., Harborview hosps. (all Seattle); clin. prof. urology U. Wash., Seattle, 1974—. Bd. dirs. Virginia Mason Hosp., 1956-79, pres., 1975-78; trustee Virginia Mason Research Found., Seattle, 1960-79; trustee King County (Wash.) chpt. Boys' Clubs Am., 1965-76. Served to comdr., M.C., USNR, 1941-46. Diplomate Am. Bd. Urology (trustee 1974—, pres. 1979-80). Mem. Am. Urol. Assn. (pres. Western sect. 1968-69, exec. com. assn. 1973-76), SAR (pres. chpt. 1957-58). Clubs: Rotary, Univ., Seattle Tennis. Contbr. articles to profl. jours. Home: 1121 39th Ave E Seattle WA 98112 Office: U Wash Med Sch Seattle WA 98195

MASON, JERRY, publisher; b. Balt., Apr. 6, 1913; s. Daniel A. and Esther (Schapira) Myerberg; A.B., Johns Hopkins U., 1933; M.S. in Journalism, Columbia U., 1934; m. Clarise Finger, Nov. 26, 1936; children—Michael Maury, Judy Ann Mason Underhill. Writer for magazines, also engaged in pub. relations, 1934-41; mem. staff This Week mag., N.Y.C., 1941-49, asso. editor, 1945-49; editor-in-chief Argosy mag., 1949-53, also editorial dir. Popular Publs. Co.; pres., founder Maco Mag. Corp., N.Y.C., 1953-57; founder, 1957, since pres. Ridge Press, N.Y.C.; author: I Find Treason, 1939; editor, pub.: Family of Man, 1955, Private World of Pablo Picasso, 1958, Family of Women, 1979. Advisory council Internat. Center Photography; pres. Hiram Halle Meml. Library, Pound Ridge, N.Y. Mem. Phi Beta Kappa. Clubs: Golf at Aspetuck (Easton, Conn.); Book Table. Home: Upper Shad Rd Pound Ridge NY 10576 Office: 25 W 43d St New York NY 10036

MASON, JIMILU, sculptor; b. Las Cruces, N.Mex., Oct. 19, 1930; d. Lowell Blake and Rose (d'Amore) Mason; A.A., Am. U., 1951; A.B., George Washington U., 1953. One woman show Potters House Gallery, 1962, Atheneum, Alexandria, Va., 1974; exhibited group shows Smithsonian Instn., Washington, 1953, 56, Corcoran Gallery, Washington, 1952, 53, 57, 62, Pa. Acad. Fine Arts, Phila., 1956, Detroit Mus. Fine Art, 1957, Arts Club Washington, 1957, Potter's House Gallery, Washington, 1957; represented in permanent collections Colo. State Capitol, Denver, U.S. Supreme Ct., Bklyn. Inst. Tech., Consumer's Coop. Assn. Bldg., Kansas City, Mo., S.C. Johnson & Son, Inc., Racine, Wis., S.C. Johnson & Son, Ltd., London, YMCA, Racine, Nat. Portrait Gallery, U.S. Capitol, also numerous pvt. collections; executed stained glass trilon meml. to Alma White, Denver, 1962; works include bronze busts of numerous prominent U.S. govt. figures; executed bust of Pres. Lyndon B. Johnson, 1964, 8-foot bronze figure of Pres. Johnson for Johnson City, Tex., bronze bust of Pres. Harry S. Truman, 1975; busts of Dag Hammarskjold, 1969, Constantino Brumidi, U.S. Capitol, Fred Vinson, Chief Justice U.S. Supreme Ct., bronze figure of Audie L. Murphy for Audie L. Murphy Meml. Hosp., San Antonio, 1975; executed stainless steel circle fountain Columbia (Md.) Shopping Mall (HUD award 1972), 1971, stained glass window St. Albans Sch., Washington, 1971, Bronze Dove Fountain, Internat. Women's Yr. Conf., Houston, 1976, steel circle fountain VA Hosp., Los Angeles; Bronze bust of James Norris, Nat. Shrine of Immaculate Conception, Washington, 1978, 7-foot Madonna and Child marble figure, 1979; mgr., dir. Heritage Art and Framing, Inc., Alexandria, Va., 1963-73; dir. Potters House Gallery, 1960-67. Mem. Nat. Council Art, 1967-72; mem. bd. overseers Dag Hammarskjold Coll. (Washington). Recipient hon. mention for bronze of Peter Vaghi, Corcoran Art Gallery, 1962, Alumna award George Washington U., 1971, 1st Gov.'s award for Arts in Va. Mem. Artists Equity. Mem. Ch. of Saviour. Office: 415 Jefferson St Alexandria VA 22314

MASON, JOHN CLARKE, lawyer; b. Charlotte, N.C., May 2, 1912; s. Edwin Lowell and Mamie R. (Badgett) M.; student Furman U., 1931; A.A., George Washington U., 1936, J.D., 1940; m. Germaine J. Bernard, Aug. 27, 1939; children—John Clarke, G. Jeanne, Kathleen M., Janice M., Claire (dec.), Michael. Admitted to D.C. bar, 1940, U.S. Supreme Ct., 1953, also other U.S. cts.; clk. FPC, 1934-41, atty. gen. 1941-53, asst. gen. counsel, 1953-56, dep. gen. counsel, 1956-60, 61-67, gen. counsel, 1960-61; counsel Morgan Lewis and Bockius, Washington, 1967—; FPC rep. Adminstrv. Conf. U.S., 1961-62, Adv. Council Pub. Land Law Rev. Commn., 1966. Mem. Pub. Utilities Commn. Fairfax County, Va., 1951-52; active local Boy Scouts Am., Poplar Heights Recreation Assn. Served to lt. (s.g.) USNR, 1944-46; PTO. Mem. Am., Fed. bar assns. Home: 3177 Lindenwood Ln Fairfax VA 22031 Office: 1800 M St NW Washington DC 20036

MASON, JOHN LEMEAR, publishing co. exec.; b. Cin., Dec. 9, 1921; s. Walter R. and Ella N. (Snodgrass) M.; B.B.A., U. Cin., 1946, J.D., 1948; m. Betty Jean Bauman, Sept. 21, 1946; children—David J., Susan Lee. Admitted to Ohio bar, 1948; with Anderson Pub. Co., Cin., 1948—, editor-in-chief, 1965-73, pres., 1973—; sec. Court Index Press Inc., Cin., 1956-72, chmn. bd., 1972—. Served with U.S. Army, 1943-46. Mem. Ohio, Cin. bar assns. Editor: Ohio Legal Digest, 1961; Ohio Form Book, 1965. Office: 646 Main St Cincinnati OH 45202*

MASON, JOHN LEONARD, savs. and loan exec.; b. Upper Sandusky, Ohio, Feb. 26, 1931; s. Harold L. and Helen (Cox) M.; A.B., Ohio Wesleyan U., 1953; M.B.A., Ind. U., 1957, D.B.A., 1960; m. Anne Lepley, Apr. 3, 1954; children—John R., Jennifer L. With Gen. Elec. Co., 1957; asst. prof. to prof. marketing U. Toledo, 1960-74, dean Coll. Bus. Adminstrn., 1966-74; exec. v.p., dir. People's Savs. Assn., Toledo, 1974—. Trustee Toledo Area Regional Transit Authority, 1970-73; chmn. Crestview of Ohio, 1975—; trustee Flower Hosp., 1978—, Community Planning Council Northwestern Ohio, 1978—. Served to 1st lt. USAF, 1954-55. Named one of the 10 outstanding young men Toledo Jr. C. of C., 1966, Northwestern Ohio mktg. Man of Year, Am. Mktg. Assn., 1966; recipient Civic award Alpha Kappa Psi, 1974. Mem. Am. Econ. Assn., Am. Mktg. Assn., Toledo Area C. of C. (trustee 1978—), Beta Gamma Sigma, Phi Kappa Phi. Mason. Home: 5315 Brooklawn Dr Toledo OH 43623

MASON, JOHN RUSSELL, ret. librarian, curator; b. Phila., Jan. 1, 1900; s. Charles Lincoln and Martha Ann (Taylor) M.; A.B., George Washington U., 1923, A.M., 1925; Summer Library Sch., U. Birmingham (Eng.), 1930; B.S. in L.S., Columbia, 1933; unmarried. Asst. in library George Washington U., 1920- 23, asst. librarian, 1923-29, asso. librarian, 1929-33, librarian, 1933-65, curator of art, 1944-65; organist, commencements and convocations, 1930-65. Reorganized geo-phys. lab. library Carnegie Inst., Washington, 1928-29; profl. organist for churches, Washington, 1920—, Central Presbyn. Ch., 1926-44. Trustee Powder River Found., Inc. Recipient Alumni Achievement award George Washington U., 1951. Mem.

A.L.A., Library Assn. Great Britain, D.C. Library Assn. (pres. 1940-42), Am. Guild Organists, Theta Delta Chi. Clubs: Washington Arts, Cosmos, Home: Arts Club 2017 Eye St NW Washington DC 20006

MASON, JOSEPH BARRY, educator; b. Memphis, Mar. 24, 1941; s. Rufus Crawford and Joyce (Fontenot) M.; B.S. in Bus. Adminstrn., La. Poly. U., 1963; M.A. in Mktg., U. Ala., 1964, Ph.D. in Bus. Adminstrn. (Loveman's Scholar), 1967; m. Linda Sue Fairchild, Dec. 20, 1961; children—Michael Barry, Michele Rene. Mem. faculty dept. mktg. and urban studies U. Ala., University, 1967—, asso. prof., 1969-71, prof., 1971—, dir. research, spl. program Grad. Sch. Bus., 1971—, chmn. mgmt. and mktg., 1974—; research asso. Ala. Hwy. Research Project, 1964-67, project dir., co-principal researcher, 1967-72; partner Market Research Assos., Tuscaloosa, 1970—; mem. hwy. research bd. Nat. Acad. Scis., 1967—; dir. Peoples Bank. Mem. community advisory com. Family Services Task Force, Tuscaloosa (Ala.) Community Council, 1972; bd. dirs. Ala. Credit Union, 1978—. Mem. Assn. Consumer Research, Am. Mktg. Assn., So. Mktg. Assn., Ala. Acad. Sci., Regional Sci. Assn., Delta Sigma Pi, Beta Gamma Sigma. Home: 44 Sherwood Dr Tuscaloosa AL 35401 Office: PO Box 2312 University AL 35486

MASON, LOWELL BLAKE, lawyer, former chmn. FTC; b. Chgo., July 25, 1893; s. William E. and Edith J. (White) M.; LL.B., Northwestern U., 1916, LL.D., 1954; m. Grace F. Gilbert, 1916; children—William E., III, Barbara Grace, Nancy Gilbert, Lowell B., Jr.; m. 2d, Rose d'Amore, 1938; children—Jimilu, Bianca. Admitted to Ill. bar, 1916, D.C. bar, 1936, practiced in Chgo. and Washington; asst. corp. counsel, City of Chgo., 1916; mem. Ill. Senate, 1922-30; gen. counsel Nat. Industry Recovery Bd. (Darrow Bd.), 1934; counsel U.S. Senate Judiciary subcom. investigating NRA, 1935; counsel U.S. Senate Interstate Commerce subcom., 1936; mem., later chmn. FTC, 1945-56. Mem. 1st Ill. State Aviation Commn., 1927. Bruno Leoni fellow Inst. Humane Studies, Menlo Park, Calif. Mem. Bar Assn. D.C. Republican. Unitarian. Mason (32 deg., Shriner). Author: The Language of Dissent; The Bull on the Bench; Changing Forms of Government. Address: 5117 Chevy Chase Pkwy Washington DC 20008

MASON, LUCIUS RANDOLPH, lawyer; b. Frederick, Md., Jan. 23, 1886; s. William Pinckney and Elizabeth R. (McGill) M.; student lit. dept. George Washington U., 1903-04, law dept., 1905-08, LL.B., 1908; m. Sophy Stanton Johnston, Dec. 3, 1918; 1 dau., Sophy (Mrs. Caperton Burnam). Began practice Washington, 1910; asst. U.S. atty. for D.C., 1919-21; asst. gen. counsel Fed. Res. Bank of N.Y.C., 1921, gen. counsel, 1922-28; practice law, N.Y.C., 1928-37; counsel Turk, Marsh, Kelley and Hoare, and predecessor firms, 1937—. Mem. local bd. 15 SSS, 1942-43. Served as capt. inf. O.R.C., U.S. Army. 1916-18. Mem. Am. Bar Assn., N.Y. County Lawyers Assn., SAR, Downtown Assn. Democrat. Episcopalian. Clubs: Port Royal (Naples, Fla.); Chevy Chase (Md.). Home: 200 E 66th St New York City NY 10021. *There is light to be found, and a chain of moral principles applicable.*

MASON, MADELINE, poet, author, critic; b. N.Y.C., Jan. 24, 1913; d. Jacob and Maud Frederica (Mason) Manheim; student pvt. tutors U.S. and abroad: pupil piano and composition with Siloti, Ganz and Bloch; m. Malcolm Forbes McKesson, May 6, 1942. Poet in residence Shenandoah Coll., Winchester, Va., Dellbrook Centre for Advanced Studies, Riverton, Va., 1969-76. Recipient Edna St. Vincent Millay award, also diploma for internat. distinction Centro Studi E. Scambi Internazionali, 1968; Internat. award of honor, diploma of distinction, life mem. Internat. Council Leaders and Scholars, 1969. Mem. Composers, Authors and Artists Am. (nat. 1st v.p., pres. N.Y. state 1966-68), N.Y. Jr. League, Poetry Soc. Am. (v.p., exec. bd.), Authors League Women's Aux., N.Y. Philharmonic Soc., Pen and Brush, N.Y. Women's Bible Soc., Nat. League Am. Pen Women (recipient Diamond Jubilee award 1957), Woman's Press, P.E.N. Author: Hill Fragments, 1925; Riding for Texas, 1936; (with Colonel E. M. House) The Cage of Years, 1949; At the Ninth Hour, A Sonnet Sequence in a New Form, 1958; Le Prophete (trans. into French of the Prophet by Kahlil Gibran); Our Home on the Range (radio script); Sonnets in a New Form, 1971, Journey in a Room-Poems; As I Knew Them (memoirs); The Challengers (poems), 1975. also syndicated column Polit. Undercurrent. Contbr. nat. mags. Exhbn. Poetry and Prose of Madeline Mason, Harvard; works also in collection of 20th Century Am. Poets, Lockwood Meml. Library, Buffalo U. Lectures; Edinburgh Festival, 1953, Library of Congress reading of own work, 1956; lectr., reader City Lit. Inst. of London, 1961-62, Anthroposophical Soc., N.Y.C., 1962—, Chautauqua, 1963, Bd. Edn. City N.Y. U. Coll., London. 1965—. Inventor Mason sonnet 1st presented at Library of Congress, 1956. Address: 22 E 29th St New York City NY 10016. *My aim as poet is to hear the inner voice, to express as fully as possible the inward vision. I would bar the self-defeating search for "success" for "originality." My human goal is to return the kindnesses that helped to shape my own career and to leave in no one's memory a cruel word or act.*

MASON, MARSHA, actress; b. St. Louis, Apr. 3, 1942; d. James and Jacqueline Mason; grad. Webster (Mo.) Coll.; m. Gary Campbell, 1964 (div.); m. 2d, Neil Simon, Oct. 25, 1973. Mem. cast Broadway and nat. tour Cactus Flower, 1968; other stage appearances include: The Deer Park, 1967, The Indian Wants the Bronx, 1968, Happy Birthday, Wanda June, 1970, Private Lives, 1971, You Can't Take It With You, 1972, Cyrano de Bergerac, 1972, A Doll's House, 1972, The Crucible, 1972, The Good Doctor, 1973, King Richard III, 1974; film appearances include: Blume in Love, 1973, Cinderella Liberty, 1973, Audrey Rose, 1977, The Goodbye Girl, 1977, Promises in the Dark, 1979, Chapter Two, 1979; TV appearances include: daytime series Love of Life, Cyrano de Bergerac, 1974, The Good Doctor, 1978, The Cheap Detective, 1978. Recipient Golden Globe award for Cinderella Liberty, 1974, The Goodbye Girl, 1978. Address: care Warner Bros 4000 Warner Blvd Burbank CA 91522

MASON, MEARLE D., lawyer; b. Nowata, Okla., Mar. 1, 1921; s. Mearle D. and Lois (Kellogg) M.; A.B., Kans. State Coll., 1943; LL.B., J.D., U. Mich., 1949; m. Dorothy Ann Altepeter, Mar. 7, 1946; children—Steven F., L. Lorrain, Dana K., Diann. Admitted to Kans. bar, 1949; asso. firm Ratner & Allen, Wichita, 1949-50; partner firm Hill & Mason, Wichita, after 1950, Hill, Mason & Gilchrist, Wichita, 1972—; municipal ct. judge, Wichita and Haysville; pres. Prepaid Legal Services of Kans., Inc.; dir., sec., treas. Clear Lakes, Inc., Wichita, 1968—. Served to lt. USNR, 1943-46; PTO. Mem. Sedgwick County-Wichita Bar Assn. (pres.), Am. Judges Assn. (bd. govs.), Kappa Delta Kappa. Republican. Methodist. Club: Lions. Home: 3109 N St Clair St Wichita KS 67204 Office: Suite C Southwest Citizens Fed Bldg 810 W Douglas St Wichita KS 67203

MASON, PAMELA HELEN, actress, producer, writer; b. London, Mar. 10, 1922; d. Isadore and Helen Spear (Morgan) Ostrer; ed. pvt. schs., Eng.; m. Roy Kellinu (div. 1941); m. 2d, James Mason (div. 1964); children—Portland, Morgan. State appearances include Broadway prodn. Bathsheba, 1969, others; over 20 film appearances; commentator Pamela Mason TV show, 1960-68, The Weaker Sex, 1969, also appearances on all nat. TV talk shows; propr. vitamin co. Author: (novels) This Little Hand, 1942; Del Palma, 1944; The Blinds Are Down, 1946; Ignoramus Ignormus, 1950; Marriage is the First Step Toward Divorce; The Female Pleasure Hunt; (with James Mason) An Anthology of Cat Stories; also articles. Office: 1018 Pamela Dr Beverly Hills CA 90210

MASON, PAUL JOSEPH, lawyer; b. N.Y.C., Sept. 16, 1932; s. Harry and Esther M.; B.A. summa cum laude, Bklyn. Coll., 1953; M.A. in Am. History with distinction, Harvard U., 1954; J.D., George Washington U., 1958; m. Zena Sapperstein, Dec. 22, 1957; children—Miles, Stacy, Robert. Admitted to Md. bar, 1957, D.C. bar, 1958; practiced law, Washington, 1958-63; spl. counsel div. corp. regulation, spl. counsel div. trading and markets and asst. dir. div. trading and markets SEC, Washington, 1963-68; chief counsel Securities of Am. Council Life Ins., Washington, 1968—. Vice pres. Washington Hebrew Congregation; mem. Md. Value Edn. Commn., 1979. Served with U.S. Army, 1954-56. Mem. Am. Bar Assn., Fed. Bar Assn. (Disting. Service award 1977,78), Am. Law Inst. Home: 7916 Robison Rd Bethesda MD 20034 Office: 1850 K St NW Washington DC 20006

MASON, PAUL WARREN, banker; b. Wichita, Kans., Sept. 27, 1920; s. Harvey Ritchie and Cora (Jones) M.; A.B., U. Kans., 1947; LL.B., U. Tex., 1949; student U. Wichita, 1937-39; m. Lily Olivia Gouger, June 2, 1944; children—Carol Olivia, Nancy Hall, Olivia Cora. Admitted to Tex. bar 1949; practice in Corpus Christi, 1949-50; cashier, dir. Robstown Nat. Bank (Tex.), 1950-58, pres., 1958-61; sec., treas., dir. Robstown Savs. & Loan Assn., 1953-61; v.p. 1st Nat. Bank, Fort Worth, 1961-62, exec. v.p., dir., 1963, pres., 1963, chief exec. officer, pres., 1970, chmn. bd. chief exec. officer, 1971—; pres., dir. First United Bancorp., Inc., Ft. Worth, 1972—; dir. Southland Royalty Co., Ft. Worth, Allied Bank Internat., N.Y.C. Mem., vice chmn. Dallas-Fort Worth Regional Airport Bd. Past chmn. bd. trustees Robstown Independent Sch. Dist.; bd. dirs. ARO, Tarrant County, United Fund, Tex. Christian U.; numerous others. Served to lt. (j.g.) USNR, 1942-46. Mem. Ft. Worth C. of C. (pres., dir. 1971, mem. and ex officio exec. com.), W. Tex. C. of C. (dir.), N. Tex. Commn. (dir., mem. advt. Com.), Am. (legal-legislative task force com., bank mgmt. com.), Tex. (vice chmn. nat. bank div. 1972-73) bankers assns., Assn. Res. City Bankers (bank credit policies com.), Am., Tarrant County bar assns., State Tex. Bar, Assn. Bank Holding Cos. (chmn.-elect). Episcopalian. Rotarian (past pres.). Clubs: Exchange (pres.), Ft. Worth; Rivercrest Country (dir.); Shady Oaks Country. Home: 325 Rivercrest Dr Fort Worth TX 76107 Office: PO Box 2260 Fort Worth TX 76113

MASON, RALPH EDWARD, educator; b. Armington, Ill., Aug. 7, 1919; s. Ralph and Agnes Lorraine (Cross) M.; B.S., Ill. State U., 1940; M.S., Northwestern U., 1949; Ph.D., U. Ill., 1961; m. Ann Scott Maher, June 9, 1947. Tchr. bus. Shelbyville (Ill.) Community Pub. Schs., 1940-42, 46-47; coordinator distributive edn., dir. vocat. edn. Springfield (Ill.) Pub. Schs., 1947-55; asst. prof. to asso. prof. bus. edn. U. Ill., 1955-64; prof. bus., chmn. dept. bus. distributive edn. and office adminstrn. Ind. State U., Terre Haute, 1964—. Served to sgt. Signal Corps, AUS, 1942-45. Decorated Bronze Star medal. Mem. Ill. (pres. 1960-61), Ind. (pres. 1968-69) bus. edn. assns., Am., Ind. vocat. assns., Nat. Bus. Edn. Assn. (Distinguished Service award 1976), Council Distributive Tchr. Edn. (Outstanding Educator award 1975), Am. Mktg. Assn. (sec. Central Ill. chpt. 1962-63). Author: (with Peter Haines) Cooperative Occupational Education and Work Experience in the Curriculum, 1965, 2d edit., 1972, rev. edit., 1976; (with Patricia M. Rath) Marketing and Distribution, 1968, 2d edit. (with Patricia M. Rath and Herbert L. Ross), 1973, 3d edit. (with Rath and Ross) Marketing Practices and Principles, 1980; contbr. articles to profl. jours. Home: 206 Terre Vista Dr Terre Haute IN 47803

MASON, RALPH SCHWEIZER, lawyer, YMCA exec.; b. Trenton, N.J., May 18, 1913; s. Ralph Silas and Emilia (Schweizer) C.; A.B., Princeton U., 1936; LL.B., U. Pa., 1939; D.H.L. (hon.), George Williams Coll., 1976; m. Jean Louise Harris, Sept. 23, 1950; children—Ralph Schweizer III, Karen A., Thomas S. Admitted to N.J. bar, 1939; asst. counsel Commn. Statutes of State of N.J., 1940, 42, 46; individual practice law, Trenton, N.J., 1940-46, Princeton, N.J., 1951-55; partner firm Montgomery & Mason, 1946-51, Mason, Griffin & Pierson and precessors, Princeton, 1955—; sec.-treas., dir. Nassau Broadcasting Co.; mem. exec. com. of bd. Princeton Savs. & Loan Assn. Pres. Nat. Council YMCA's of U.S.A., 1975-77; cons. to exec. com., mem. council World Alliance YMCA's; chmn. bd. trustees Med. Center, Princeton, 1967-76; trustee, former pres. Princeton United Community Fund; sec.-treas., trustee Hun Sch., Princeton; elder, former chmn. bd. trustees Nassau Presbyterian Ch.; former trustee New Brunswick (N.J.) Presbytery; incorporator Nat. USO, 1967-73; mayor Princeton Twp., 1956-57; chmn. Princeton Twp. Planning Bd., 1959-60. Served with U.S. Army, 1942-46. Decorated Bronze Star Medal; recipient Gerard B. Lambert award Princeton United Community Fund, 1961. Fellow Am. Coll. Probate Counsel; mem. Greater Princeton C. of C. (bd. dirs., man of year 1972), Am., N.J., Mercer County (past pres.), Princeton (past pres.) bar assns. Republican. Clubs: Nassau, Rotary (past trustee). Home: 265 Brookstone Dr Princeton NJ 08540 Office: 201 Nassau St Princeton NJ 08540

MASON, RAUSEY WOOD, banker; b. Atlanta, July 22, 1937; s. Rausey Wood and Grace Virginia (Robbins) M.; B.S., Ga. Inst. Tech., 1959; postgrad. S.E. Sem., 1959-60, Emory U., 1960-62; m. Diane Danner, Feb. 7, 1970. Asst. v.p. First Nat. Bank of Atlanta, 1962-69; v.p. La Salle Nat. Bank, Chgo., 1969-72; exec. v.p. Pioneer Bank and Trust Co., Chgo., 1972-75, pres., 1975—; pres. W. N. Lane Interfinancial, 1979—. Mem. Chgo. Crime Commn. Mem. Robert Morris Assos., Am. Bankers Assn. (exec. planning com.), Nat. Assn. Creditmen, Bankers Club, Young Presidents Orgn. (dir.). Republican. Unitarian. Clubs: Economic, La Grange Country. Office: 4000 W North Ave Chicago IL 60639

MASON, RAYMOND ADAMS, brokerage firm exec.; b. Lynchburg, Va., Sept. 28, 1936; s. Raymond Watsi and Marion (Adams) M.; B.A., Coll. William and Mary, 1959; m. Suzanne M. Arble, Aug. 10, 1959; children—Paige Adams, Pamela Ann, Carter Meade. Registered rep. Mason & Lee Inc., Richmond, Va., 1960-62; pres. Mason & Co. Inc., Newport News, Va., 1962-70; pres. Legg, Mason & Co., Inc., Washington, 1970—, also chmn. bd.; pres., chmn. bd. Legg, Mason Wood Walker, Inc., Balt., 1975—; dir. Am. Motor Inns; chmn. regional firms com. N.Y. Stock Exchange. Chmn. bd. trustees Coll. William and Mary Endowment Fund, 1969, dir. Grad. Sch. Bus., 1970; trustee, mem. exec. com. Balt. Mus. Art. Served with AUS, 1959-60. Mem. Nat. Assn. Securities Dealers (chmn. bd. govs. 1974-75). Home: 1911 Ruxton Rd Baltimore MD 21204 Office: 7 E Redwood St Baltimore MD 21203

MASON, RICHARD DEAN, lawyer; b. Sickles, Okla., Aug. 2, 1906; s. Hall Adelphia and Grace (McWhinney) M.; B.S., U. Okla. 1929, A.B., 1931, E.E., 1931; M.S., Mass. Inst. Tech., 1931; LL.B., George Washington U., 1935; m. Alice Mary Eckman, Feb. 20, 1937; children—Patricia Anne, Marilyn Whiley. Admitted to Ill. bar, 1938, D.C. bar, 1935, also U.S. Supreme Ct. bar; engr. Gen. Electric Co., Lynn, Mass., 1929-31, patent dept., Washington, 1931-35, patent atty., Schenectady, 1935; patent atty. Hazeltine Corp., N.Y.C., 1936; mem. Davis, Lindsey, Smith & Shonts, 1937-43. Mueller, Dodds & Mason, 1944-48; founding partner Mason, Kolehmainen, Rathburn & Wyss, Chgo., 1948—; lectr. patent law U. Okla., 1949-50. Mem. Ill., Am., Chgo. bar assns., Chgo. Patent Law Assn., Ill. C. of C., Phi Kappa Psi, Sigma Tau, Phi Delta Phi. Presbyn. Clubs: American (London); Legal, University, Tower, Curling, Executives (Chgo.); Indian Hill (Winnetka, Ill.); Tucson Country; Pres.'s (U. Ariz.). Home: 970 Green Bay Rd Winnetka IL 60093 Office: 20 N Wacker Dr Chicago IL 60606

MASON, ROBERT JOSEPH, automotive parts co. exec.; b. Muskegon, Mich., Nov. 17, 1918; s. Robert J. and Delora (Houle) M.; M.B.A., U. Chgo., 1941; m. M. Kathleen Carr, June 24, 1944 (dec. Nov. 1965); children—Marcia (Mrs. Richard Dwyer), Eileen A. (Mrs. Thomas Wilhelm); m. 2d, Carol F. Fales, Jan. 31, 1967. Accounting analyst Carnegie-Ill. Steel Corp., Gary, Ind., 1941-45; with Sealed Power Corp., Muskegon, 1945—, sec.-treas., 1959-70, v.p. finance, 1970—, dir., 1972—; dir. Hackley Union Nat. Bank & Trust Co. Bd. dirs. Muskegon County United Appeal, Muskegon Area Devel. Council; adv. bd. Mercy Hosp. Mem. C. of C., Fin. Execs. Inst., Am. Soc. Corporate Secs. Clubs: Century (pres., dir.); Muskegon Country (past bd. dirs.). Home: 320 W Circle Dr North Muskegon MI 49445 Office: 100 Terrace Plaza Muskegon MI 49443

MASON, RONALD LAWRENCE, banker; b. Cleve., Mar. 12, 1928; s. Lawrence Edward and Agnes Cecelia (Fitzgibbon) M.; student Loyola Coll., Balt., 1947; Eastern Coll. Commerce, Balt., 1948; grad. Am. Inst. Banking, 1958, Brown U. Grad. Sch. Savs. Banking, 1967; mgmt. devel. program, U. Mass., 1972; m. Mary Jane Kroupa, May 10, 1952; children—Ronald L., Nancy M., Ruth M., Thomas E., Michele M. With Provident Savs. Bank, Balt., 1948—, br. mgr., 1951-60, asst. treas., 1960-66, asst. v.p., 1966-68, treas., 1968-70, v.p., treas., 1969, sr. v.p., 1970, exec. v.p., 1971-76, pres., 1976—, dir., 1975—. Served with USNR, 1945-46. Mem. Am. Inst. Banking (past pres. Balt. chpt., life), Chesapeake Toastmasters (past pres.). Clubs: Center, Exchange (pres. 1975-76) (Balt.); Towson Golf and Country. Home: 55 Belfast Rd Timonium MD 21093 Office: 240 N Howard St Baltimore MD 21201

MASON, STANLEY GEORGE, phys. chemist; b. Montreal, Mar. 20, 1914; s. David MacCallum and Margaret (Fraser) M.; B.Eng. in Chem. Engring., McGill U., 1936, Ph.D. in Phys. Chemistry, 1939; m. Renata Vincenzi, June 14, 1969; children—Cheryl, Andrea. Lectr., Trinity Coll., Hartford, Conn., 1939-41; sr. scientist, dept. head Suffield Exptl. Sta., Ralston, Alta., Can. Dept. Nat. Def., 1941-45; asso. research chemist atomic energy div. NRC, Montreal, 1945-46; dir. applied chem. div., head phys. chemistry Pulp and Paper Research Inst. Can., Montreal, 1946-79, prin. scientist, 1979—; research asso. chemistry McGill U., Montreal, 1946-66, prof., 1966-79, Otto Maass prof., 1979—. Recipient Kendall award in colloid and surface chemistry, 1967; Anselme Payne award in cellulose chemistry Am. Chem. Soc., 1969; Bingham medal Soc. Rheology, 1969; Chem. Inst. Can. medal, 1973; Dunlop award, 1975. Fellow Royal Soc. Can., Chem. Inst. Can., TAPPI. Office: Dept Chemistry McGill Univ 3420 University St Montreal PQ H3A 2A7 Canada

MASON, THOMAS BOYD, lawyer; b. Lynchburg, Va., Jan. 12, 1919; s. Leonard Tyree and Beulah Elizabeth (Coffey) M.; student Hampden-Sydney Coll., 1936-38; LL.B., U. Va., 1941; m. Emily Ann Wilkins, Jan. 22, 1949; children—Martha Wyatt (Mrs. Malloy), Ann Corinne Courtney. Admitted to Va. bar, 1940; practice in Arlington, 1941-42, Lynchburg, 1946-56; mem. trust dept. Peoples Nat. Bank & Trust Co., Lynchburg, 1956-61; U.S. atty. Western dist. Va., 1961-69; gen. solicitor Norfolk & Western Ry. Co., Roanoke, Va., 1969—. Served with USNR, 1942-46. Mem. Am., Va., Roanoke bar assns., Pi Kappa Alpha, Phi Alpha Delta. Home: 2608 Richelieu Ave SW Roanoke VA 24014 Office: 8 N Jefferson St Roanoke VA 24011

MASON, TONY JAMES, football coach; b. Sharon, Pa., Mar. 2, 1930; s. Tony James and Julia Verna (Monaco) M.; B.S., Clarion (Pa.) State Coll., 1950; B.Ed., U. Westminster, 1963, M.A.; m. Carolyn Pelyak, Aug. 14, 1966; 1 dau., Carey Julia. Football coach high schs. in Ohio, 1955-65, U. Mich., 1965-70, Purdue U., 1971-76, U. Cin., 1976, U. Ariz., Tucson, 1976—. Served with AUS, 1950-52; Korea. Decorated Bronze Star. Republican. Roman Catholic. Address: Athletic Dept Univ Ariz SUPO Box 21106 Tucson AZ 85720

MASONER, PAUL HENRY, educator; b. Middletown, Ohio, Mar. 25, 1908; s. Paul and Emma Martha (Hayes) M.; student Capital U., 1926-28; B.A. in English, Ohio State U., 1930, M.A. in Sociology, 1931; postgrad. Wilmington Coll., summer 1931; Ph.D. in Counseling, U. Pitts., 1949; postgrad. U. London (Eng.), summers 1964, 66; D.Litt. (hon.), Hanyang U., Seoul, Korea, 1978; m. Liliana Mühlman, 1976; children—Paul, David, Linda. Tchr. English, Central High Sch., Uhrichsville, Ohio, 1930-32; tchr. social scis. Bellevue High Sch., Pitts., 1932-34, counselor, vice prin., 1934-43, acting prin., 1943-44; adminstrv. head Engring. and Sci. Mgmt. War Tng. Center, Bellevue, Pa., 1942-44; sr. analyst Nat. Def. Research Com., U. Pa., 1944-45; counselor, lectr. psychology Vets. Counseling Center, U. Pitts., 1945-46, instr. Sch. Edn., 1946-48, asst. prof., 1948-50, asso. prof., 1950-51, prof., 1953—, asst. dean Sch. Edn., 1952-54, acting dean, 1954, dean, 1955-73, dean emeritus, 1973—, Univ. prof., 1973—. Mem. adv. com. Learning Research and Devel. Center, Pitts., 1965-73; cons. scholarship aid programs; ednl. cons. to sch. systems, colls., univs., ednl. orgns., govt. agys., others; mem. accreditation teams Middle States Assn. and Nat. Council for Accreditation of Tchr. Edn., 1954-75; mem. adv. com. Pa. Grad. Tchr. Edn., 1964-70; mem. Pa. Curriculum Commn., 1964-70; mem. Com. of One Hundred Citizens for Better Edn., 1963-67; mem. council Nat. Council Accreditation Tchr. Edn., 1968-70; mem. Nat. Adv. Council Edn. Professions Devel., 1970-73; mem. exec. bd. Nat. Reading Center, Washington, 1970-73. Bd. dirs. Falk Elementary Sch., Pitts., 1955-73, Westminster Found., Pitts., 1964-66, Pitts. Council of Chs., 1964-66; pres. bd. trustees Robert Morris Coll. Recipient Outstanding Service to Edn. award Commonwealth of Pa., 1962, Effective Leadership to Tchr. Edn. award, 1964. Fellow Coll. Preceptors (hon.) (Eng.); mem. Western Pa. Scholarship Assn. (exec. sec. 1950-70), Nat., Pa. State (exec. council 1966-68) edn. assns., Western Pa. Edn. Conf. (chmn. 1955-70), Pa. Schoolman's Club (pres. 1963), (Pa. Assn. Liberal Arts Colls. for Advancement of Teaching (pres. 1959), AAUP, Am. Personnel and Guidance Assn., Nat. Vocat. Guidance Assn. (profl.), Am. Assn. Sch. Adminstrs. (profl.), Internat. Council Edn. for Teaching (trustee 1972-76, pres. 1976—), Am. Assn. Colls. Tchr. Edn. (pres. 1970-71), AAAS, Civic Club Allegheny County (Pa.), Allegheny Roundtable (pres. 1964-70), Omicron Delta Kappa, Delta Pi Epsilon (hon.), Iota Lambda Sigma, (hon.), Phi Delta Kappa, Kappa Phi Kappa. Conglist. Clubs: Cosmos (Washington); University (Pitts.). Contbg. author: Standards for the 60's, 1962; Counseling: Selected Readings, 1962; Changes in Teacher Education: An Appraisal, 1964. Author: Design for Teacher Education, 1964; An Imperative: A National Policy for Teacher Education, 1972. Extensive fgn. travel and study. Address: Univ Pitts Forbes Quadrangle Pittsburgh PA 15260

MASORO, EDWARD JOSEPH, JR., educator, physiologist; b. Oakland, Calif., Dec. 28, 1924; s. Edward Joseph and Louise Elizabeth (DePaoli) M.; A.B., U. Calif. at Berkeley, 1947, Ph.D., 1950; m. Barbara Weikel, June 25, 1947. Asst. prof. physiology Queen's U., Kingston, Ont., Can., 1950-52; asst. prof., then asso. prof.

Tufts U. Sch. Medicine, 1952-62; research asso. prof., then research prof. physiology and biophysics U. Wash., 1962-64; prof. physiology and biophysics, chmn. dept. Med. Coll. Pa., 1964-73; prof. physiology, chmn. dept. U. Tex. Health Sci. Center, San Antonio, 1973—; cons. council basic sci. Am. Heart Assn., 1965-67. Mem. Med. Adv. Bd. Ednl. Film Prodn., 1967—; chmn. metabolic discussion group Fed. Am. Soc. Exptl. Biology, 1969-73. Served with USNR, 1943-46. Recipient Christian R. and Mary F. Lindback Distinguished Teaching award Med. Coll. Pa., 1967; Golden Apple award Student Am. Med. Assn., 1966, 71. Fellow AAAS (council 1970—), Gerontol. Soc. (chmn. elect biol. scis. sect. 1977-78); mem. AAUP, Canadian, Am. physiol. socs., Soc. Exptl. Biology and Medicine, Canadian Biochem. Soc., Am. Chem. Soc., N.Y. Acad. Scis., Am. Soc. Biol. Chemists, Phila. Physiol. Soc. (pres. 1966-67). Author: Physiological Chemistry of Lipids in Mammals, 1967; co-author Acid-Base Regulation: Its Physiology and Pathophysiology, 1971, 2d edit., 1977. Contbr. articles to profl. jours. Editor sect. 24 Internat. Ency. Pharmacology and Therapeutics, 1974; editorial bd. Jour. Lipid Research, 1964—. Address: Dept Physiology Univ Tex Health Sci Center San Antonio TX 78229

MASOTTA, ROBERT EDWARD, diversified co. exec.; b. Boston, Dec. 12, 1939; s. John J. and Susan M. (Ferullo) M.; A.B., Boston Coll., 1961; J.D., Suffolk U., 1970; m. Cynthia J. Deimantas, June 3, 1967; children—Victoria, Michael. With Liberty Mut. Ins. Co., Boston, 1964-67; asst. ins. mgr. United Fruit Co., Boston, 1967-69; sec., corporate counsel Standex Internat. Corp., Salem, N.H., 1969—, v.p., 1979—. Served to 1st lt. U.S. Army, 1962-64. Decorated D.S.M. Mem. Am., Mass., Boston bar assns. Home: 131 Sandra Ln North Andover MA 01845 Office: Manor Pkwy Salem NH 03079

MASOTTI, LEWIS RICHARD, waterworks co. exec.; b. Stamford, Conn., Dec. 15, 1933; s. Peter V. and Lee (Bohiem) M.; B.S. in Acctg., U. R.I., 1955; m. Florence L. Masson, Aug. 18, 1956; children—Patricia L., Carol L., Peter L., Richard L. Accountant, Masotti & Masotti, Stamford, 1955; treas. Bertie, Inc., Stamford, 1955-57; controller Citizens Utilites Co., Stamford, 1957-65; dir. accounting services Gilbert Assos., N.Y.C., 1965-66; v.p. finance Gen. Waterworks Corp., Phila., 1966-72, sr. v.p., 1975—; v.p. devel. group IU Internat., Phila., 1973-75; dir. Gen. Waterworks Corp., Round Valley, Inc., New Rochelle Water Co.; guest lectr. Grad. Sch. Bus. Adminstrn., Drexel U., 1967. Treas. Stamford Pioneers, 1960-65. Named Ark. traveler, 1968. Mem. AIM, Nat. Assn. Water Cos. (dir. 1974—), Scabbard and Blade, Lambda Chi Alpha (alumni trustee 1962-64). Clubs: Toastmasters (treas. Phila. 1970), Blue Line Firebird Hockey (dir. 1974-79). Home: 1315 Prospect Hill Rd Villanova PA 19085 Office: 1500 Walnut St Philadelphia PA 19102

MASOTTI, LOUIS HENRY, educator; b. N.Y.C., May 16, 1934; s. Henry and Angela Catherine (Turi) M.; A.B., Princeton U., 1956; M.A., Northwestern U., 1961, Ph.D., 1964; m. Iris Patricia Leonard, Aug. 28, 1958; children—Laura Lynn, Andrea Anne. Fellow, Nat. Center for Edn. in Politics, 1962; asst. prof. polit. sci. Case Western Res. U., Cleve., 1963-67, asso. prof., 1967-69, dir. Civil Violence Research Center, 1968-69; sr. Fulbright lectr. Johns Hopkins U. Center for Advanced Internat. Studies, Bologna, Italy, 1969-70; asso. prof. polit. sci. Northwestern U., Evanston, Ill., 1970-72, prof., 1972—, prof. public mgmt., 1979—, dir. Center for Urban Affairs, 1971—, dir. program public mgmt., 1979—; cons. in field; vis. asso. prof. U. Wash., summer 1969. Research dir. Carl Stokes for Mayor City of Cleve., 1967; exec. dir. Mayor Byrne transition com., Chgo.; mem. Cleveland Heights (Ohio) Bd. Edn., 1967-69. Served to lt. USNR, 1956-59. Recipient Disting. Service award Cleve C. of C., 1967; numerous fed. and found. research grants, 1963—. Mem. Am., Midwest (v.p. 1976-77) polit. sci. assns., Council of Univ. Insts. for Urban Affairs, Policy Studies Assn. Author: Education and Politics in Suburbia, 1967; Shootout in Cleveland, 1969; A Time to Burn?, 1969; Surburbia in Transition, 1973; The New Urban Politics, 1976; The City in Comparative Perspective, 1976. Editor (with others): Metropolis in Crisis, 1968, rev. 1971; Riots and Rebellion, 1968; The Urbanization of the Suburbs, 1973. Editor Edn. and Urban Soc., 1968-71, Urban Affairs Quar., 1973—. Home: 200 E Delaware Pl Chicago IL 60611

MASQUELETTE, PHILIP ABBOTT, lawyer; b. Port Arthur, Tex., Jan. 16, 1926; s. Philip Reddington and Nelia Elizabeth (Wilkins) M.; student Tex. A. and M. Coll., 1942-43, Harvard Bus. Sch., 1944-45; B.B.A., Tulane U., 1945; M.B.A., U. Tex., 1947; LL.B., U. Houston, 1952; postgrad. Southwestern Grad. Sch. Banking, So. Meth. U., 1960; m. Elizabeth Daggett Simmons, Mar. 17, 1948; children—Laura Masquelette Selig, Philip E., Pamela A. Masquelette Howard, David S. Acct., Masquelette Bruhl & Co., accts., Houston, 1947-53; admitted to Tex. bar, 1952; asso. firm Butler, Binion, Rice & Cook, Houston, 1953-57; v.p., dir. Bank Tex., Houston, 1957-61, sr. v.p., 1961-62; pres., dir. Perpetual Corp., Houston, 1962-65; practice law, Houston, 1965-71; partner firm Masquelette, Bailey, Donisi & Haynes, Houston, 1971-72, Dillingham, Schleider & Masquelette, 1973-76, Dillingham & Masquelette, 1976-77, Dillingham, Masquelette & Boerstler, 1977-79, Masquelette & Mas dir. Ch. Life Ins. Corp., N.Y.C., Ch. Ins. Co., N.Y.C. Trustee Episcopal Ch. Pension Fund, N.Y.C. Served with USNR, 1943-46. C.P.A., Tex. Mem. Am., Houston bar assns., State Bar Tex., Am. Coll. Probate Counsel, Am. Inst. C.P.A.'s, Tex. Soc. C.P.A.'s, Sigma Alpha Epsilon, Beta Gamma Sigma, Beta Alpha Psi, Phi Delta Phi. Republican. Episcopalian. Home: 2201 Welch St Houston TX 77019 Office: 2121 San Felipe Houston TX 77019

MASSALSKI, THADDEUS BRONISLAW, educator, scientist; b. Warsaw, Poland, June 29, 1926; s. Piotr and Stanislawa (Andrukaniec) M.; B.Sc., Birmingham (Eng.) U., 1952, Ph.D., 1954, D.Sc., 1964; fellow Inst. Study Metals, U. Chgo., 1954-56; D.Sc. (h.c.), Warsaw (Poland) U., 1973; m. Sheila Joan Harris, Sept. 19, 1953; children—Irena, Peter, Christopher. Came to U.S., 1959. Lectr. Birmingham U., 1956-59; head. metal physics group Mellon Inst., Pitts., 1959-75, staff fellow, 1961—, prof. metal physics and materials sci. Carnegie-Mellon U., 1968—; vis. prof. U. Buenos Aires, 1962, Calif. Inst. Tech., 1962, Stanford, 1963, U. Calif., 1964, 66, Inst. Physics, Bariloche Argentina, 1966, 70, Harvard, 1969; exchange prof., Krakow (Poland) U., 1968. Guggenheim fellow Oxford U., 1965-66. Fellow Am. Soc. Metals, Brit. Inst. Metals, Brit. Inst. Physics; mem. Polish Inst. Arts and Scis. in Am. (council), AIME, Phys. Soc. Co-author: Structure of Metals, 3d edit., 1966; Advanced Physical Metallurgy, 1965. Co-editor: Progress in Materials Science, 1969—. Papers and articles on alloy theory, crystallography, metal physics, meteorites. Home: 900 Field Club Rd Pittsburgh PA 15238 Office: 4311 Science Hall Carnegie-Mellon U Pittsburgh PA 15213

MASSAQUOI, HANS JURGEN, mag. editor; b. Hamburg, Germany, Jan. 19, 1926; s. Al-Haj and Bertha (Baetz) M.; came to U.S., 1950, naturalized, 1960; student Elgin (Ill.) Community Coll., 1953-55; B.S. in Journalism, U. Ill., 1957; grad. Medill Sch. Journalism, Northwestern U., 1957; m. Joan Elizabeth DeBerry, Oct. 20, 1956 (div. 1971); children—Steve Gordon, Hans Jurgen. Interpreter, Brit. Mil. Govt., Hamburg, 1945-48; travel in Africa, 1948-50; editor Nat. Assn. Ednl. Broadcasters, Urbana, Ill., 1956-57; asso. editor Jet. mag., Chgo., 1958-59; asso. editor Ebony mag., Chgo., 1959-65, asst. mng. editor, 1965-67, mng. editor, 1967—; lectr. European tour Dept. State, 1976. Served as parachutist 82d Airborne Div., AUS, 1951-53. Recipient Outstanding Achievement award Immigrants' Service League of Travelers Aid Soc., 1970; citation for outstanding reporting from abroad Overseas Press Club Am., 1975. Office: 820 S Michigan Ave Chicago IL 60605

MASSEL, MARK S., lawyer, economist; b. N.Y.C., Aug. 6, 1910; s. Jacob and Sophie (Massel) M.; B.S., N.Y. U., 1930, M.A., J.D., 1933; postgrad. Columbia U., 1936-37; m. Jean Eleanor Magnus, Sept. 2, 1935 (dec. June 1965); children—Lynn Massel Sedway, Joan Massel Morrall; m. 2d, Katharine Douglas Pringle, Jan. 1, 1966. Admitted to N.Y. bar, 1933, Ill. bar, 1945; gen. mgr. Massel Press, Inc., 1929-30; asst. chief auditor Brownsville Savs. Bank, 1930-31; lectr. econ. law, accounting N.Y. U., 1932-33, U.S. Dept. Agr. Grad. Sch., 1937-42, Am. U., 1941-42; dir. study postwar bus. reserves, capital adjustments Nat. Planning Assn., 1942-43; chief pricing policy br., purchases div. ASF, 1943-44; partner firm Bell, Boyd, Marshal & Lloyd, Chgo., 1944-58; pres. Lyon & Healy, Inc., 1952-53; sr. staff mem. Brookings Instn., 1958-67; part-time cons. to Common Market Commn., 1965-67, UN Conf. on Trade and Devel., 1969-73; cons. N.R.A., 1933-35, W.P.A., 1935-39, Temporary Nat. Econ. Com., 1939-40, Dept. Interior, 1940, WPB, 1940-43; chmn. exec. com., dir., Sanford Corp.; dir. Tri-Rental Co., Sanford de Mexico; professorial lectr. U. Chgo., 1956, U. Calif., 1956, Cath. U., 1972; vis. prof. U. Mich. Grad. Sch. Bus. Adminstrn. and Law Sch., 1964, U. Wis. Grad. Sch. and Law Sch., 1968; Fulbright lectr. Poly. Inst., Quito, Ecuador, 1974; mem. panel invention and innovation Sec. of Commerce, 1965-66; chmn. panel fgn. maritime policy NRC, 1969-70. Trustee Monterrey Inst. Internat. Studies. Mem. Law and Soc. Assn., Fed., Am. (chmn. com. on info. and edn. antitrust law sect.), N.Y., Ill., Chgo. bar assns., Am. Mgmt. Assn., Am. Econ. Assn., Am. Accounting Assn., Nat. Assn. Cost Accountants, Nat. Planning Assn., Am. Soc. Internat. Law, U.S. C. of C., Evolutionary Econ. Assn. Clubs: Cliff Dwellers (Chgo.); Columbia Univ.; Club de la Fondation Universitaire (Brussels); Cosmos (Washington). Author: Business Reserves for Post-War Survival; Competition and Monopoly: Legal and Economic Issues, 1962; contbr. articles to profl. publs. Home: 2540 Massachusetts Ave NW Washington DC 20008

MASSELINK, BRUCE HERSCHEL, clergyman; b. Kalamazoo, July 26, 1905; s. Benjamin H. and Senie (Welandt) M.; B.A., Kalamazoo Coll., 1931; grad. student U. Mich., 1931-32; B.D., Chgo. Theol. Sem., 1936; D.D., Piedmont Coll., Demorest, Ga., 1959; m. Donna Dee Parrish, Nov. 24, 1934; children—Mara Gay (Mrs. John Comer), Gerrit Parrish. Ordained to ministry Congl. Ch., 1936; asst. minister Park Congl. Ch., Grand Rapids, Mich., 1936-39; minister First Congl. Ch., Burlington, Iowa, 1939-58, Mayflower Congl. Ch., Grand Rapids, 1958-72, minister emeritus, 1973—; minister Little Stone Ch., MacKinac Island, Mich., 1977—. Bd. dirs. Iowa Congl. Conf., 1940-48; moderator Nat. Assn. Congl. Christian Chs., 1964-65, bd. dirs., 1956-59, mem. missionary soc., 1949-56. Pres. sch. bd., Burlington, 1944-50; mem. Des Moines County Health Bd., 1945-50; mem. Sr. Citizens Co-ordinating Com., Grand Rapids, 1965-68. Trustee Grinnell (Iowa) Coll., 1946-49, Piedmont Coll., Demorest, 1973—; adv. bd. Chgo. Theol. Sem., 1956-61. Republican. Home: 3413 Burton Ridge Rd SE Apt C Grand Rapids MI 49506 also Box 513 MacKinac Island MI 49757

MASSELL, SAM, business exec.; b. Atlanta, Aug. 26, 1927; s. Sam and Florence (Rubin) M.; student Emory U., 1944-45, U. Ga., 1947-48; LL.B., Atlanta Law Sch., 1949; B.C.S., Ga. State U., 1951, postgrad. certificate in selling, 1952, postgrad. diploma in real estate, 1953; m. Doris M. Middlebrooks, Oct. 25, 1952; children—Cynthia Diane, Steven Alan, Melanie Denise. Chief publs. Nat. Assn. Women's and Children's Apparel Salesmen, Inc., 1949-51; with Allan-Grayson Realty Co., 1951-69, 74-75, v.p., 1955-69, pres. devel. div. 1974-75; propr. Your Travel Agt., Sam Massell, 1975—; instr. real estate Smith-Hughes Atlanta Vocational Sch., 1956; v.p. Mallin Developers, Inc., 1956-65; dir. Security Fed. Savs. and Loan Assn. Atlanta, 1961-67, United Trust Life Ins. Co., 1964-68. Councilman City Mountain Park, Ga., 1950-52; sec. Atlanta City Exec. Com., 1953-61; pres. bd. aldermen, vice mayor Atlanta, 1962-69; mayor of Atlanta, 1970-74. Dir., U.S. Conf. of Mayors, 1971-74; v.p., Inter-Am. Municipal Orgn., 1972-74; pres. Nat. League of Cities, 1972, chmn. adv. council, 1973. Served with USAAF, 1946-47. Democrat. Jewish. Club: Standard. Home: 2750 Wyngate NW Atlanta GA 30305 Office: Suite 100 3330 Peachtree Rd NE Atlanta GA 30326

MASSENGALE, JOHN EDWARD, 3D, lawyer; b. Kansas City, Mo., Nov. 18, 1921; s. John Edward, Jr. and Frances (Haig) M.; A.B., Harvard, 1942, LL.B., 1948; m. Jean Mitchell Montague, Dec. 8, 1942; children—Sarah Choate (Mrs. George D. Billock, Jr.), John Edward IV, Thomas Haig. Admitted to N.Y. bar, 1949, D.C. bar, 1971; practice in N.Y.C., 1948—; partner firm Paul, Weiss, Rifkind, Wharton & Garrison, 1958—. Dir. Babcock Internat. Inc., Colonial Penn Group, Inc., Cullman Ventures Inc., Roland Internat. Corp., Wellington Tech. Industries, Inc. Rep., town meeting, Darien, Conn., 1955-61, 63-70. Served to lt. USNR, 1942-45. Mem. Assn. Bar City N.Y., N.Y. State Bar Assn., Am. Bar Assn. Club: Noroton Yacht. Home: Goodwives River Rd Noroton CT 06820 Office: 345 Park Ave New York NY 10022

MASSENGALE, MARTIN ANDREW, agronomist, educator; b. Monticello, Ky., Oct. 25, 1933; s. Elbert G. and Orpha (Conn) M.; B.S., Western Ky. U., 1952; M.S., U. Wis., 1954, Ph.D., 1956; m. Ruth Audrey Klingelhofer, July 11, 1959; children—Alan Ross, Jennifer Lynn. Research asst. agronomy U. Wis., 1952-56; asst. prof., asst. agronomist U. Ariz., 1958-62, asso. prof., asso. agronomist, 1962-65, prof., agronomist, 1965—, head dept., 1966-74, asso. dean Coll. Agr., asso. dir. Ariz. Agr. Expt. Sta., 1974-76; vice chancellor for agr. and natural resources U. Nebr., 1976—; chmn. pure seed adv. com. Ariz. Agrl. Expt. Sta.; chmn. bd., pres. Midam. Internat. Agrl. Consortium; mem. EPA-Dept. Agr. Land Grant Univ. Coordinating Com. Environ. Quality. Served with AUS, 1956-58. Named One of Outstanding Educators Am., 1970; Faculty Recognition award Tucson Trade Bur., 1971. Cert. profl. agronomist, profl. crop scientist. Fellow Am. Soc. Agronomy (dir.), AAAS; mem. Am. Grassland Council, Ariz. Crop Improvement Assn. (dir.), Crop Sci. Soc. Am. (past dir., pres. 1972-73), Am. Soc. Plant Physiology, Nat. Assn. Colls. and Tchrs. of Agr., Ariz. Acad. Sci., Agrl. Council Am. (dir., mem. issues com.), Sigma Xi, Phi Kappa Phi, Gamma Sigma Delta, Alpha Zeta, Phi Sigma, Gamma Alpha, Alpha Gamma Rho. Pioneer in floral initiation and photoperiodism in alfalfa and water-use efficiency in forage crops. Home: 6701 Everett St Lincoln NE 68506

MASSERMAN, JULES HOMAN, psychoanalyst; b. Chudnov, Poland, Mar. 10, 1905; s. Abraham and Czerna (Baker) M.; M.D., Wayne U., 1931; came to U.S., 1908, naturalized, 1917; m. Christine McGuire, 1943. Instr., then asst. prof. U. Chgo., 1937-46; asst. prof. neurology and psychiatry Northwestern U. Med. Sch., 1946-48, asso. prof., 1948-52, prof. neurology and psychiatry, 1952—, co-chmn. dept. psychiatry, 1960-69; dir. edn. Ill. Psychiat. Inst., 1958-62; Roche vis. prof. Australia and N.Z., 1968; fellow Center Advanced Study of Behavioral Scis., 1968-69; chmn. Chgo. Psychiat. Council, 1967-69, Ill. Research and Tng. Authority, 1965-68; chmn. council Stone-Brandell Found., 1966-69. Recipient nat. award in pathology Phi Lambda Kappa, 1929; Presdl. award for selective service duty, 1946; Lasker award for research mental hygiene, 1946; Taylor Manor award as psychiatrist of year, 1972; Sigmund Freud award, 1974. Diplomate Am. Bd. Psychiatry and Neurology. Mem. AMA, Am. Psychiat. Assn. (council 1965-68, v.p. 1974-75, sec. 1975-77, pres. 1978—), Am. Acad. Psychoanalysis (past pres.), Am. Soc. Biol. Psychiatry (past pres.), Internat. Assn. Social Psychiatry (hon. life pres. 1969—), Am. Soc. Group Therapy (past pres.), Am. Assn. Social Psychiatry (pres. elect 1972), Am. Acad. Stress Disorders (exec. v.p. 1971—). Author: A Psychiatric Odyssey, 14 text books, 380 articles, 16 motion pictures; editor 42 books, jours.; composer, violinist. Home: 2231 E 67th St Chicago IL 60649 Office: 8 S Michigan Ave Chicago IL 60603

MASSEY, CHARLES KNOX, JR., advt. exec.; b. Durham, N.C., Jan. 16, 1936; s. Charles Knox and Louise (Southerland) M.; B.S. in Bus. Adminstrn., U. N.C., 1959; m. Mary Ann Keith, Aug. 27, 1960; children—Elizabeth, Knox, Louise. Vice pres. C. Knox Massey & Assoc., Inc., advt. agy., Durham, N.C., 1959-64; account exec. Tucker Wayne & Co., At (advt. agy.), Atlanta, 1964-69, v.p., 1969-71, sr. v.p., 1971-74, exec. v.p., gen. mgr., 1975-78, pres., 1978—, also dir. Dir. Quadrant Corp., Atlanta, K.M. Corp., Durham. Trustee The Lovett Sch., Atlanta; chmn. bd. trustees Literary Action, Inc. Mem. Ga. Conservancy (trustee), Am. Mktg. Assn. Episcopalian. Club: Piedmont Driving (Atlanta). Home: 67 Brighton Rd NE Atlanta GA 30309 Office: 230 Peachtree St NW Atlanta GA 30303

MASSEY, CHARLES L., health orgn. exec.; b. Waco, Tex., Aug. 19, 1922; s. Charles L. and Corinne Laney (Flood) M.; B.S., U. Ark., 1948; m. Edris Haynes, Dec. 16, 1944; children—Charles W., Priscilla. Field rep. Nat. Found.-March of Dimes, 1948-56, asst. dir. field staff, 1956-60, dir. field staff, 1960-65, exec. v.p., 1965-78, pres., chief exec. officer, White Plains, N.Y., 1978—; trustee Ga. Warm Springs Found.; dir. Nat. Health Council; trustee Salk Inst. Biol. Studies. Served to 1st lt. AUS, 1943-46. Decorated Purple Heart. Home: 16 Hobe St West Nyack NY 10994 Office: 1275 Mamaroneck Ave White Plains NY 10605

MASSEY, GERALD J(AY), educator; b. Wauseon, Ohio, Feb. 11, 1934; s. Charles Arnold and Ethel P. (Pry) M.; B.A. maxima cum laude, U. Notre Dame, 1956, M.A., 1960; postgrad. (Fulbright fellow) U. Louvain (Belgium), 1956-57; Ph.D., Princeton U., 1964; m. Ann Schultheis, Aug. 17, 1957; children—Charles Daniel, Mary Cecelia, Stephane Ethel, Roberta Ann. Asst. prof. philosophy Mich. State U., 1963-66, asso. prof., 1966-68, prof., 1968-70; prof. U. Pitts., 1970—, chmn. dept. philosophy, 1970-77; vis. asso. prof. U. Mich., fall 1967. Served as lt. USMC, 1958-61. Hon. Woodrow Wilson fellow, 1956-57; Danforth fellow, 1956-63; Mellon postdoctoral fellow, 1969-70. Mem. Assn. Symbolic Logic, Am. Philos. Assn. Author: Understanding Symbolic Logic, 1970; contbr. numerous articles to profl. jours. Home: 6035 Bunker Hill St Pittsburgh PA 15206 Office: 724 Schenley Hall U Pitts Pittsburgh PA 15260

MASSEY, HAROLD WALLACE, coll. adminstr.; b. Salem, Mo., June 10, 1914; s. William Edward and Carrie (Wallace) M.; student Mo. Central Coll., 1933-35; B.S., S.W. Mo. State U., 1940; postgrad. U. Florence (Italy), 1945; M.Ed., U. Mo. 1948, Ed.D., 1951; m. Alzada Keeney, May 29, 1946; children—Bill, Marilyn. Tchr., adminstr. pub. schs., Licking, Mo., 1940-43, 46-47, 48-49, Phoenix, Oreg., 1947-48; Mo. rep. Nat. Found. Infantile Paralysis, 1951-53, dir. tchr. edn. Okla. Panhandle State U., Goodwell, 1953-61, dean instrn., 1961-63; grad. dean Southwestern Okla. State U., Weatherford, Okla., 1963—. Chmn. Okla. Profl. Standards Bd., 1969-70; mem. higher edn. com. on grad. and profl. edn. Okla. State Regents. Served with AUS, 1943-46. Mem. Okla. Council Tchr. Edn. (past chmn.), Okla. Assn. Higher Edn. (past chmn.), Okla. Edn. Assn., N.E.A., C. of C. (dir.), Assn. Higher Edn., Phi Delta Kappa, Pi Gamma Mu. Mem. Federated Ch. Lion. Author: (with E.E. Vineyard) The Profession of Teaching, 1961; also articles. Home: 416 Texas St Weatherford OK 73096

MASSEY, JAMES LEE, educator; b. Wauseon, Ohio, Feb. 11, 1934; s. Charles Arnold and Ethel (Pry) M.; B.S.E.E., U. Notre Dame, 1956; S.M., M.I.T., 1960, Ph.D., 1962; children—Thomas, Robert, Peter, John. Asst. prof. elec. engring. U. Notre Dame, 1962-65, asso. prof., 1965-66, prof., 1966-72, Freimann prof. elec. engring., 1972-77; prof. system sci. UCLA, 1977—; guest prof. Tech. U. Denmark, Lyngby, 1971-72; vis. asso. prof. Mass. Inst. Tech., 1966-67; vis. prof., Vinton Hayes fellow Mass. Inst. Tech., 1977-78; cons. Codex Corp., Newton, Mass., 1962—; cons. Calif. Inst. Tech. Jet Propulsion Lab., 1978—. Served with USMC, 1956-59. Fellow IEEE; mem. Am. Soc. Engring. Edn., AAUP, Sigma Xi, Tau Beta Pi, Eta Kappa Nu. Democrat. Roman Catholic. Author: Threshold Decoding, 1963. Editor IEEE Trans. on Info. Theory, 1974-77. Office: Dept System Sci UCLA CA 90024

MASSEY, JOHN, art dir.; b. Chgo., 1931; B.F.A., U. Ill., 1954. Former instr. design Inst. Design, Ill. Inst. Tech.; now dir. communication Container Corp. Am., Chgo.; designer civic posters for Field Mus. Natural History, Chgo. Lakefront, Adler Planetarium, Lincoln Park; designer banners on Civic Center Plaza; represented in permanent collection at Mus. Modern Art, N.Y.C., and Library of Congress. Recipient over 200 awards from design instr.; named Art Dir. of Year Nat. Soc. Art Dirs., 1967; Gold Metal award Art Dirs. Club N.Y., 1979; Bronze medal Brno, 1979. Mem. Am. Inst. Graphic Arts, Soc. Typographic Arts (hon. 1977), Alliance Graphique Internat. Address: Container Corp Am One First Nat Plaza Chicago IL 60603

MASSEY, LEON R., assn. exec.; b. Grand Island, Nebr., Jan. 16, 1930; s. James Moore and Iva Pearl (Richardson) M.; student U. Colo., 1948-49; B.A., U. Nebr., 1955; postgrad. N.Y. Inst. Fin., 1963; m. Jean M. Nielsen, June 17, 1951; children—Dean R., Maureen L. Salesman consumer products Union Carbide Corp., Memphis, 1956-57, Greenville, Miss., 1957-58, Albuquerque, 1958-61, Dallas, 1962-63; with GC Electric div., Textron Corp., Dayton, Ohio, 1963-64, regional sales mgr., 1963-64; account exec. Merrill Turben Co., Dayton, 1964-66; with Nat. Electric Contractors Assn., Dayton, 1967-72, Denver, 1972—, exec. sec., 1967—, also dir. Rocky Mountain chpt.; instr. adult edn. Wayne State U., Dayton, 1964-66. Active Democratic party, 1960; bd. dirs. Cherry Creek Civic Assn., 1973-74. Served with USAF, 1950-54; Korea. Cert. assn. exec. Mem. Am., Colo. (pres. 1979) socs. assn. execs., Cherry Creek Civic Assn. (pres. 1979-80), Phi Kappa Psi. Methodist. Clubs: Masons, Civitan. Office: Nat Electric Contractors Assn 450 Decatur St Denver CO 80204

MASSEY, PEYTON HOWARD, JR., coll. dean; b. Zebulon, N.C., Oct. 4, 1922; s. Peyton Howard and Roselle (Sears) M.; B.S., N.C. State Coll., 1947, M.S., 1951; Ph.D., Cornell U., 1952; m. Elizabeth Lorelei Shumaker, Oct. 3, 1942; children—Elizabeth Howard Massey Alls, Carol Anne, Suzanne Frances Massey Hughes. Teaching asst. N.C. State Coll., 1947-49; research asst. Cornell U., 1949-52; asso. prof., then prof. horticulture Va. Poly. Inst. and State U., Blacksburg, 1952—, asso. dean Grad. Sch., 1964-65, asso. dean, dir. agronomic and plant scis. div. Coll. Agr., 1966-78, asso. dean, dir. internat. agr. Coll. Agr., 1979—; cons. to govt. and industry. Past pres. Blacksburg PTA. Served with U.S. Army, World War II; ETO. Decorated Purple Heart; recipient certificate and medal City of Paris (France), 1968.

Mem. AAAS, Am. Legion (past post comdr), Sigma Xi, Phi Kappa Phi, Alpha Zeta, Omicron Delta Kappa, Gamma Sigma Delta, Epsilon Sigma Phi. Baptist (past chmn. bd. deacons). Club: Rotary (dir., pres.) Author articles. Address: 807 Gracelyn Ct Blacksburg VA 24060

MASSEY, RAYMOND, actor, dir., producer; b. Toronto, Ont., Can., Aug. 30, 1896; s. Chester D. and Anna (Vincent) M.; ed. Appleby Sch. (Oakville, Ont.), Toronto U., Balliol Coll., Oxford U. (Eng.); D.Litt. (hon.), Lafayette U., 1939, Hobart and Smith Colls., 1952; LL.D., Queens U., 1949; A.F.D., Northwestern U., Ripon Coll.; Dr. Humanics, Am. Internat. Coll., 1960; L.H.D., Coll. of Wooster, 1966; m. Margery Hilda Fremantle, 1921 (dissolved); 1 son, Geoffrey; m. 2d, Adrianne Allen, 1929 (dissolved); children—Daniel, Anna; m. 3d, Dorothy Ludington, 1939. Naturalized Am. citizen, 1944. Acted in many plays on London stage, including St. Joan, Spread Eagle, The Shining Hour, Idiot's Delight, The Man in Possession, Five Star Final, I Never Sang for My Father, 1970; dir. some 35 plays including The Rats of Norway, Grand Hotel, Five Star Final, Idiot's Delight, The Silver Tassie; N.Y. stage debut as Hamlet, 1931; starred in 11 Broadway prodns. including Ethan Frome, Candida, The Doctor's Dilemma, Pygmalion, Abe Lincoln in Illinois, J.B.; starred in Night of the Iguana, Los Angeles; appeared in over 60 motion pictures including The Scarlet Pimpernel, Things to Come, Hurricane, The Prisoner of Zenda, East of Eden, Abe Lincoln in Illiois; appeared in TV series Dr. Kildare as Dr. Gillespie. Served as lt., Canadian F.A., 1915-19; in France (wounded), 1916, in U.S. as instr. in field arty., Yale and Princeton, 1917, in Siberia, 1918; maj. on staff adj. gen. Canadian Army, 1942; officer in Res., 1943. Clubs: Garrick (London); Century (N.Y.C.); Pilgrims of U.S. Author: (play) The Hanging Judge, produced in London, 1952; (autobiography) When I Was Young, 1976, A Hundred Different Lives, 1979.

MASSEY, RICHARD WALTER, investment counselor; b. Birmingham, Ala., May 19, 1917; s. Richard Walter and Elizabeth (Spencer) M.; B.S., U. Va., 1939; M.A., Birmingham-So. Coll., 1959; Ph.D., Vanderbilt U., 1960; m. Ann Hinkle, Sept. 4, 1959; children—Richard Walter, Dale Elizabeth. Owner, mgr. Massey Bus. Coll., Birmingham, Ala., 1946-56; asst. to chancellor Vanderbilt U., 1959-60; chmn. dept. econs. Birmingham-So. Coll., 1960-66; investment trust officer 1st Nat. Bank of Birmingham, 1966-67; prof. econs. U. Ala., Tuscaloosa, 1967-68; v.p., dir. investment research Sterne, Agee & Leach, Inc., Birmingham, 1968-75; pres. Richard W. Massey & Co., Inc., Investment Counsel, Birmingham, 1975—. Served to maj. U.S. Army, 1941-46. Club: Country of Birmingham. Home: 3000 Cherokee Rd Birmingham AL 35223 Office: Suite 116 10 Office Park Circle Birmingham AL 35223

MASSEY, ROBERT UNRUH, physician, univ. dean; b. Detroit, Feb. 23, 1922; s. Emil Laverne and Esther Elisabeth (Unruh) M.; student Oberlin Coll., 1939-42, U. Mich. Med. Sch., 1942-43; M.D., Wayne State U., 1946; m. June Charlene Collins, May 28, 1943; children—Robert Scott, Janet Charlene. Intern, resident internal medicine Henry Ford Hosp., Detroit, 1946-50; asso. Lovelace Clinic, Albuquerque, 1950-68, chmn. dept. medicine, 1958-68, bd. govs., 1957-68; dir. med. edn. Lovelace Found. for Med. Edn. and Research, 1960-68; clin. asso. U. N.M. Sch. Medicine, 1961-68; prof. medicine U. Conn. Sch. Medicine, Farmington, 1968—, asso. dean for grad. edn., 1968-71, dean Sch. Medicine, 1971—, acting univ. v.p. for health affairs, 1975-76; chief staff Newington (Conn.) VA Hosp., 1968-71. Trustee Am. Assn. Med. Clinics, 1966-68; exec. com., regional adv. group Conn. Regional Med. Program, 1971-76; trustee, v.p. Capitol Area Health Consortium, 1974-78; bd. dirs. Health Planning Council, Inc., 1974-76, Hartford Inst. for Criminal and Social Justice, 1976—, Conn. Easter Seal Soc., 1977—, Hospice Inst. for Edn., Tng. and Research, 1979—. Served with AUS, 1955-57; maj. Res. Named Distinguished Alumnus, Wayne State U. Fellow A.C.P.; mem. Am. Group Practice Assn. (accreditation commn. 1968—), Am. Diabetes Assn., Assn. Am. Med. Colls., Hartford County Med. Assn., Conn., Hartford med. socs., Soc. Med. Adminstrs., Sigma Xi, Alpha Omega Alpha. Episcopalian. Club: Twilight (Hartford). Home: 10 Lord Davis Ln Avon CT 06001 Office: U Conn Sch Medicine Farmington CT 06032

MASSEY, VINCENT, biochemist, educator; b. Berkeley, New South Wales, Australia, Nov. 28, 1926; s. Walter and Mary Ann (Mark) M.; B.Sc. with honors, U. Sydney (Australia), 1947; Ph.D., U. Cambridge (Eng.), 1953; m. Margot Grunewald, Mar. 4, 1950; children—Charlotte, Andrew, Rachel. Mem. research staff Henry Ford Hosp., Detroit, 1955-57; from lectr. to sr. lectr. U. Sheffield, 1957-63; prof. Med. Sch., U. Mich., 1963—. Mem. fellowship rev. panel NIH, 1965-69, sect. biochemistry study, 1972—. Recipient Alexander Von Humboldt U.S. Sr. Scientist award, 1973-74. Imperial Chem. Industries Research fellow, 1953-55. Fellow Royal Soc. London; mem. Biochem. Soc., Am. Soc. Biol. Chemists, Am. Chem. Soc. (exec. bd. div. biol. chemistry 1975—). Contbg. author numerous books. Contbr. numerous articles, chiefly on oxidative enzymology, to profl. jours. Home: 2536 Bedford Rd Ann Arbor MI 48104

MASSEY, WALTER EUGENE, physicist; b. Hattiesburg, Miss., Apr. 5, 1938; s. Almar Cleveland and Essie (Nelson) M.; B.S., Morehouse Coll., 1958; M.A., Washington U., St. Louis, 1966, Ph.D., 1966; m. Shirley Streeter, Oct. 25, 1969; children—Keith Anthony, Eric Eugene. Physicist, Argonne (Ill.) Nat. Lab., 1966-68; asst. prof. physics U. Ill., Urbana, 1968-70; asso. prof. Brown U., Providence, 1970-75, prof., dean Coll., 1975-79; cons. Argonne Nat. Lab., dir., 1979—; NSF, cons. Nat. Acad. Scis., NRC. Mem. Human Relations Commn., Urbana, 1967-68; bd. dirs. Urban League R.I., 1972-74. NSF fellow, 1962; NDEA fellow, 1959-60. Mem. Am. Phys. Soc., Am. Assn. Physics Tchrs. (Distinguished Service award 1975), AAAS, Sigma Xi. Contbr. articles on sci. edn. in secondary schs. and in theory of quantum fluids to profl. jours. Home: 5811 S Dorchester Ave Chicago IL 60637 Office: Argonne Nat Lab Argonne IL 60439

MASSEY, WILLIAM S., educator, mathematician; b. Granville, Ill., Aug. 23, 1920; s. Robert R. and Alma (Schumacher) M.; student Bradley U., 1937-39; B.S., U. Chgo., 1941, M.S., 1942; Ph.D., Princeton, 1948; m. Ethel Heap, Mar. 14, 1953; children—Eleanor, Alexander, Joan. Mem. research dept. Princeton, 1948-50; from asst. prof. to prof. Brown U., 1950-60; prof. math. Yale, 1960—, Erastus L. Deforest prof. math, 1964—, chmn. dept. math., 1968-71. Served as officer USNR, 1942-46. Fellow Am. Acad. Arts and Scis.; mem. Am. Math. Soc. Author: Algebraic Topology: An Introduction, 1967; Homology and Cohomology Theory, 1978. Mem. editorial staff math. jours. Home: 101 Haverford St Hamden CT 06517 Office: Math Dept Yale Univ New Haven CT 06520

MASSI, FRANK, communications exec.; b. N.Y.C., Nov. 25, 1909; s. Frank and Mary Grace (Lobue) M.; ed. Coll. City N.Y., N.Y. U.; m. Madeline D'Angelo, Sept. 15, 1935; children—Lucille Massi Cazzetto, Martha Massi Polemeni. With McGraw-Hill Pub. Co., 1927-32, Pictorial Rev., 1932-34; with Hearst Corp., 1934—, asst. treas., 1953-61, treas., 1961-68, exec. v.p., 1968-73, pres., chief exec. officer, 1973-75, vice-chmn. bd., 1975—, also dir.; dir. S.W. Forest Industries, Inc., Charter Indemnity Co.; mem. regional adv. bd. Mfrs. Hanover Trust Co. Bd. dirs. Bur. Advt., Alcoholism Recovery Inst., Inc. Mem. Fifth Ave. Assn., N.Y. C. of C. Club: Knights of Malta. Office: 959 8th Ave New York NY 10019*

MASSIE, ROBERT KINLOCH, author; b. Lexington, Ky., Jan. 5, 1929; s. Robert K. and Mary (Kimball) M.; B.A., Yale, 1950; (Rhodes scholar), Oxford U., 1952; m. Suzanne L. Rohrbach, Dec. 18, 1954; children—Robert Kinloch, Susanna, Elizabeth. Reporter, Collier's mag., 1955-56; writer, corr. Newsweek mag., 1956-62; writer USA-1 mag., 1962, Sat. Eve. Post, 1962-65; free-lance writer, 1965—; Ferris prof. journalism Princeton U., 1977. Served to lt. (j.g.) USNR, 1952-55. Mem. Author League Am. Author: Nicholas and Alexandra, 1967; (with Suzanne Massie) Journey, 1975. Address: Irvington NY 10533

MASSING, BERTRAM KERMIT, lawyer; b. Cleve., July 13, 1933; s. George and Minnie (Fuss) M.; B.S., UCLA, 1955; J.D., U. So. Calif., 1960; m. Phyllis Liebman, Mar. 4, 1956; children—Gregory Irwin, Robert Andrew, Lisa Ann. Acct., Price Waterhouse & Co., Los Angeles, 1955, 57-60; admitted to Calif. bar, 1961, also U.S. Dist. Ct., Tax Ct. U.S.; practice in Beverly Hills, 1961—; atty. Ervin, Cohen & Jessup, 1961-64, partner, 1964—; lectr. UCLA extension div., 1962-63, U. So. Calif. Law Sch., 1965-66, 76-77; dir. Intermark Investing, Inc., 1968-70. Mem. exec. bd. Los Angeles chpt. Am. Jewish Com. Served with AUS, 1955-57. C.P.A., Calif. Mem. Am., Beverly Hills bar assns., State Bar Calif., UCLA Bus. Adminstrn. Alumni Assn. (mem. dean's roundtable grad. sch. of mgmt., chancellor's assos.), Order Coif, Nu Beta Epsilon, Tau Epsilon Phi, Beta Gamma Sigma. Mem. bd. editors: U. So. Calif. Law Rev., 1959-60. Home: 17101 Strawberry Dr Encino CA 91436 Office: 9401 Wilshire Blvd Beverly Hills CA 90212

MASSON, ROBERT HENRY, consumer products co. exec.; b. Boston, June 27, 1935; s. Robert Louis and Henrietta Hill (Worrell) M.; B.A., (Travis and Woods award), Amherst Coll., 1957; M.B.A., Harvard U., 1964; m. Virginia Lee Morton, Dec. 28, 1957; children—Linda Anne, Kenneth Morton, Robert Louis. Fin. staff Ford Motor Co., Dearborn, Mich., 1964-68, mktg. services div. controller, 1968-70; pres. Knutson Constrn. Co., Mpls., 1970-72; v.p. fin., treas. Ellerbe, Inc., Bloomington, Minn., 1972-77; fin. dir. CirTech, Inc., Mpls., 1973-77; v.p. fin. transp. div. PepsiCo., Inc., Tulsa, 1977, corp. v.p., treas., Purchase, N.Y., 1978—; Westchester adv. bd. Mfrs. Hanover Trust Co., 1979—. Pres., North Georgtown Homeowner's Assn., Birmingham, Mich., 1968-70; U.S. Presdl. Advance Man, 1972—. Served to lt. USN, 1957-62; lt. comdr. Res. Mem. Theta Delta Chi. Presbyterian (fin. trustee 1968-70). Clubs: Wayzata Yacht (dir.-treas. 1973-77), Riverside Yacht. Author: (with others) The Management of Racial Integration in Business, 1964. Home: 20 West Way Lucas Point Old Greenwich CT 06870 Office: PepsiCo 700 Anderson Hill Rd Purchase NY 10577

MASSOW, ROSALIND (MRS. NORTON LUGER), journalist; b. N.Y.C.; d. Morris and Ida (Kahn) Massow; B.A., Hunter Coll.; m. Dr. Norton Luger, Jan. 31, 1959. Reporter, city desk, feature writer, ski, travel columns N.Y. Jour. Am., 1951-61; feature writer, women's editor Parade Publs., N.Y.C., 1961-71; free lance writer, 1971—; travel editor Medical/Mrs. Mem. Gov.'s Com. on Minorities in Media, 1968; mem. Women's Aux. Booth Meml. Hosp.; mem. Pres.'s Commn. on Status of Women, 1964. Mem. Overseas Press Club (gov. 1965-66, 71-73, 74—), Newspaper Women's Club N.Y. (Front Page awards 1956, 60, 66, pres. 1965-66, Pegasus award 1966), Soc. of Silurians, Travel Writers N.Y., Am. Soc. Travel Writers, Am. Soc. Journalists and Authors, Sigma Delta Chi. Club: Deadline. Author: Now It's Your Turn to Travel, 1976. Office: 530 E 72d St New York NY 10021

MAST, JAMES WILLIAM, govt. ofcl., lawyer; b. Laredo, Tex., Jan. 19, 1928; s. Clifford Arp and Eileen Warren (Quick) M.; B.A. in Econs., Tex. A&M Coll., 1950; LL.B., Tex. U., 1953; m. Mary Evelyn Holt, Nov. 1, 1956; stepchildren—Jean Abney Mast Hynes, William T. Abney, Gerald W. Abney. Admitted to Tex. bar, 1953, U.S. Supreme Ct., 1958; asst. dist. atty. El Paso (Tex.), 1955-58; atty. NLRB, El Paso, 1958-61, Albuquerque, 1961-68, regional atty., Albuquerque, 1968-73, Fort Worth, 1973-75; chief adminstrv. law judge HUD, Washington, 1975—. Served with U.S. Army, 1945-46, 53-55. Mem. Am. Bar Assn., Tex. Bar Assn. Democrat. Roman Catholic. Home: 1200 N Courthouse Arlington VA 22201 also 9206 Chimney Corner Dallas TX 75243 Office: HUD 451 7th St SW Washington DC 20410

MASTEN, JOHN TALBOT, educator; b. Newark, Mar. 13, 1914; s. Glen Arnold and Janet Elizabeth (Turner) M.; B.S., U. Ill., 1936, M.S. (fellow), 1937; Ph.D., U. N.C., 1942; m. Elizabeth Bluemke, Aug. 17, 1938; children—Patricia Sue Masten Barnes, John Talbot. Asst. prof. econs. DePauw U., Greencastle, Ind., 1941-45; regional price economist Bur. Labor Statistics, Chgo., 1945-47; chmn. dept. econs. Kalamazoo Coll., 1947-48; prof. money and banking, dir. grad. studies econs., chmn. dept. econs. U. Ky., Lexington, 1948-67; Ga. Bankers Assn. prof. banking U. Ga., Athens, 1967-79, prof. emeritus, 1979—; vis. prof. fin. U. So. Calif., 1964; vis. prof. econs. U. Ky., 1975-76, 79-80; program dir. Ky. Banking Sch., 1969; ednl. dir. Ga. Banking Sch., 1967; mem. faculty advanced banking sch. Kans., Nebr., Mo., 1969; cons. in field. Mem. Ky. State Plan for Emergency Mgmt. Resources, 1965-68. Mem. Am. Econs. Assn., Am. Fin. Assn., Beta Gamma Sigma. Author: A Programmed Text in Money and Banking, 1969; The Structure of Commercial Banking in the U.S., 1969; contbr. articles to profl. jours. Home: 130 Devereux Dr Athens GA 30606 Office: Dept Econs U Ky Lexington KY 40506. *A successful life requires a personal philosophy that will stand the test of time and enough luck in life that one's philosophy is not tested too sternly or frequently.*

MASTERMAN, JACK VERNER, ins. co. exec.; b. Calgary, Alta., Can., Aug. 8, 1930; s. Lawrence Arthur and Mary F. G. (Robinson) M.; B.Com. with honors, U. Man. (Can.), 1953. m. Isabel Christine Kaitting, June 25, 1953; children—Christine, Lawrence, Sheila, Keith. With Mut. Life Assurance Co. of Can., Waterloo, Ont., v.p. ops., 1971-75, v.p. individual ins. and annuities, 1975-78, exec. v.p., 1978—. Fellow Soc. Actuaries, Can. Inst. Actuaries. Mem. United Ch. of Can. Home: 163 Tennyson Pl Waterloo ON N2L 2T2 Canada Office: 227 King S Waterloo ON N2J 4C5 Canada*

MASTEROFF, JOE, playwright; b. Phila., Dec. 11, 1919; s. Louis P. and Rose (Pogost) M.; B.S., Temple U., 1940. Author: The Warm Peninsula, 1959; She Loves Me, 1963; Cabaret (Tony award, N.Y. Drama Critics Circle award 1967), 1966; 70, Girls, 70 (adaptation of own book), 1971; pres. New Dramatists Com., 1952—. Served with USAAF, 1942-46. Address: 2 Horatio St New York City NY 10014*

MASTERS, CHARLES DAY, geologist; b. Pawhuska, Okla., Aug. 4, 1929; s. Alan Dunning and Maxine Lueretta (Day) M.; B.S., Yale U., 1951, Ph.D., 1965; M.S., Colo. U., 1957; m. Anna Ruth Sandin, June 6, 1953; children—Cynthia Ruth, Eric Alan, Carolyn Frances. Exploration geologist Pan Am. Petroleum Corp., Denver, 1957-62, 65-68, research geologist, Tulsa, 1968-70; chmn. div. sci. and math., asso. prof. geology W. Ga. Coll., Carrollton, 1970-73; chief Office Energy Resources, also acting chief Office Marine Geology, Geol. Div., U.S. Geol. Survey, Reston, Va., 1973—. Activities chmn. Tulsa YMCA, 1968-70; founder pres. W. Ga. chpt. Ga. Conservancy, 1971-73. Served with USNR, 1951-55. Fellow Geol. Soc. Am.; mem. Am. Assn. Petroleum Geologists, AAAS, Sigma Xi. Democrat. Unitarian. Home: 1028 Walker Rd Great Falls VA 22066 Office: US Geol Survey National Center MS 915 Reston VA 22092

MASTERS, DEXTER WRIGHT, author, editor; b. Springfield, Ill., June 15, 1908; s. Thomas Davis and Gertrude (Mettler) M.; grad. Choate Sch., 1926; Ph.B., U. Chgo., 1930; m. Christina Malman, Mar. 8, 1941 (dec. Jan. 1959); m. 2d, Joan Brady, Sept. 23, 1963; one son, Alexander Wright. Editor, Tide mag., 1930-36, Consumer Reports, 1937-42; editor Radar, also mem. staff Radiation Lab., Mass. Inst. Tech., 1943-45; editorial cons. McGraw-Hill Pub. Co., 1945-46; publs. dir. Consumers Union, 1947-51, dir., 1957-63, editorial cons., 1963-67. Author: (radio series) One World Or None (Peabody award 1947), 1947; (novel) The Accident, 1955; (essays) The Intelligent Buyer and the Telltale Seller, 1966; (novel) The Cloud Chamber, 1971. Editor: (with K. Way) One World or None: A Report on the Full Meaning of the Atomic Bomb, 1946. Contbr. nat. mags. Home: The Hermitage South St Totnes Devon England Office: care Consumers Union Mount Vernon NY 10550

MASTERS, EDWARD E., ambassador; b. Columbus, Ohio, June 21, 1924; s. George Henry and Ethel Verena (Shaw) M.; student Denison U., 1942-43; B.A. with distinction, George Washington U., 1948; M.A., Fletcher Sch. Law and Diplomacy, 1949; m. Allene Mary Roche, Apr. 2, 1956; children—Julie Allene, Edward Ralston. Joined U.S. Fgn. Service, 1950; intelligence research analyst Near East, Dept. State, 1949-50; resident officer, Heidelberg, Germany, 1950-52; polit. officer embassy, Karachi, Pakistan, 1952-54; Hindustani lang. and area tng. U. Pa., 1954-55; consul, polit. officer, Madras, India, 1955-58; intelligence research specialist South Asia, Dept. State, 1958-60, chief Indonesia-Malaya br. Office Research Asia, 1960-61, officer-in-charge Thailand affairs, 1961-63; grad. Nat. War Coll., 1964; counselor embassy for polit. affairs Am. embassy, Djakarta, 1964-68; country dir. for Indonesia, Dept. State, 1968-70; dir. Office East Asian Regional Affairs, 1970-71; minister Am. embassy, Bangkok, Thailand, 1971-75; ambassador to Bangladesh, 1976-77, to Indonesia, 1977—. Mem. Am. Fgn. Service Assn., Phi Beta Kappa, Omicron Delta Kappa, Pi Gamma Mu, Delta Phi Epsilon. Home: PO Box 214 Savannah OH 44874 Office: American Embassy Djakarta Indonesia

MASTERS, FRANK WYNNE, surgeon, educator; b. Pitts., Nov. 1, 1920; s. Frank Wynne and Estabrook (Taylor) M.; A.B., Hamilton Coll., Clinton, N.Y., 1943; M.D., U. Rochester, 1945; m. Eleanor Jean Cooper, Oct. 13, 1945; children—Francis, Patricia Ann, Robert Randall. Intern Strong Meml. Hosp., Rochester, N.Y., 1945-46, resident, 1948-51; resident plastic surgery Duke Hosp., 1951-54; practice plastic surgery, Charleston, W.Va., 1954-58; asso. plastic surgery Duke Med. Sch., 1953-54; mem. faculty Med. Center U. Kans., Kansas City, 1958—, prof. plastic surgery, 1967—; asso. dean, 1973-76; mem. staff Kansas City VA Hosp. chief, plastic surgery sect, vice chmn. dept. surgery, 1972-77, chmn. dept. surgery, 1977—. Diplomate Am. Bd. Surgery, Am. Bd. Plastic Surgery. Fellow A.C.S.; mem. Am. Soc. Plastic and Reconstructive Surgeons, Am. Assn. Plastic Surgeons, Am. Surg. Assn., Soc. Head and Neck Surgeons, Soc. Univ. Surgeons, Am., Western surg. assns., Am. Assn. Surgery Trauma, Am. Assn. Cleft Palate Rehab., Plastic Surgery Research Council, Kansas City Surg. Soc., AMA, Kans. Med. Soc., Clin. Soc. Univ. Plastic Surgeons, Central Surg. Assn., Rocky Mountain Traumatological Soc. Contbr. articles to profl. jours. Home: 6738 Rainbow St Shawnee Mission KS 66208 Office: Univ Kans Med Center Kansas City KS 66103

MASTERS, JOHN, author; b. Oct. 26, 1914; s. John and Ada (Coulthard) M.; student Royal Mil. Coll., Sandhurst, Eng.; m. Barbara Allcard, 2 children. Served with Indian Army, 1934-48, active service in N.W. Frontier, 1936-37, Iraq, Syria, Persia, 1941, Burma, 1944-45; author: Nightrunners of Bengal, 1951, The Deceivers, 1952, The Lotus and the Wind, 1953, Bhowani Junction, 1954, Coromandel, 1955, Bugles and a Tiger, 1956, Far, Far The Mountain Peak, 1957, Fandango Rock, 1959, The Venus of Konpara, 1960, The Road Past Mandalay, 1961, To The Coral Strand, 1962, Trial at Monomoy, 1964, Fourteen Eighteen, 1965, The Breaking Strain, 1967, The Rock, 1969, Pilgrim Son, 1971, The Ravi Lancers, 1972, Thunder at Sunset, 1974, The Field Marshall's Memoirs, 1975, The Himalayan Concerto, 1976, Now, God Be Thanked, 1979. Decorated companion Disting. Service Order, officer Order Brit. Empire. Office: care Brandt 101 Park Ave New York NY 10017*

MASTERS, JON JOSEPH, lawyer; b. N.Y.C., June 20, 1937; s. Arthur Edward and Esther (Shady) M.; B.A., Princeton U., 1958; J.D., Harvard U., 1964; m. Rosemary Dunaway Cox, June 16, 1962; children—Brooke Alison, Blake Edward. Admitted to N.Y. bar, 1965; cons. asst. to under sec. army, 1961; mem. policy planning staff asst. sec. def. internat. security affairs, Washington, 1962; mem. President Johnson's Spl. Polit. Research Staff, Washington, 1964; asso. firm Shearman & Sterling, N.Y.C., 1965-68, 69; mem. staff Bedford-Stuyvesant D & S Corp., Bklyn., 1968-69; v.p., sec., gen counsel Baker, Weeks & Co., Inc., N.Y.C., 1969-76, also dir.; mem. firm Christy & Viener, N.Y.C., 1976—; mem. SEC adv. com. broker-dealer compliance, 1972-74. Mem. Implementation Com. of Economic Devel. Task Force of N.Y. Urban Coalition, 1968; mem. bd. Internat. Social Service, Am. Br., Inc., 1978—, pres., 1979—; bd. dirs. The Arts Connection, 1979—. Served with USN, 1958-61. Mem. Assn. Bar of City N.Y. (com. on municipal affairs 1977—), N.Y. State Bar Assn., Am. Soc. Internat. Law. Home: 530 E 86th St New York NY 10028 Office: 620 Fifth Ave New York NY 10020

MASTERS, RICHARD E., mech. engr.; b. Bklyn., Mar. 15, 1928; s. William and Mollie (Beckerman) M.; B.M.E., Poly. Inst. N.Y., 1949; m. Joan Marilyn Hecker, Apr. 3, 1954; children—Cary, Amy, William. Engr., Nonpareil Concrete Constrn. Co., N.Y.C., 1949-50; cons. engr., partner Jaros, Baum & Bolles, N.Y.C., 1953—. Mem. adv. com. to Center of Bldg. Tech., Nat. Bur. Standards. Served to 1st lt. C.E., U.S. Army, 1950-53. Decorated Bronze Star; registered profl. engr., Calif., Conn., D.C., Fla., Ill., Ky., Mass., Md., Mich., Mo., N.C., N.Y., N.J., Ohio, Pa., R.I., Tex., Va., W.Va. Fellow Am. Cons. Engrs. Council; mem. ASME, Am. Soc. Heating, Refrigeration and Air Conditioning Engrs., Nat. Soc. Profl. Engrs., N.Y. Assn. Cons. Engrs. (chmn. mech. code com. 1973, gov. 1974), Soc. Fire Protection Engrs., Tau Beta Pi. Republican. Club: Metropolis Country (White Plains, N.Y.). Home: 3 Well House Ln Mamaroneck NY 10543 Office: 345 Park Ave New York NY 10022

MASTERS, ROGER DAVIS, educator; b. Boston, June 8, 1933; s. Maurice and S. Grace (Davis) M.; B.A., Harvard, 1955; M.A., U. Chgo., 1958, Ph.D., 1961; M.A. (hon.), Dartmouth Coll., 1974; m. Judith Ann Rubin, June 6, 1956; children—Seth J., William A., Katherine R. Instr. dept. polit. sci. Yale U., 1961-62, asst. prof., 1962-67; asso. prof. dept. govt. Dartmouth Coll., Hanover, N.H., 1967-73, prof., 1973—; cultural attache Am. embassy, Paris, France, 1969-71. Chmn., France-Am. Commn. for Ednl. and Cultural Exchange, 1969-71. Served with AUS, 1955-57. Fulbright fellow Institut d'Etudes Politiques, Paris, 1958-59; joint Yale U.-Social Sci. Research Council fellow, 1964-65; Guggenheim fellow, 1967-68; fellow Inst. Soc., Ethics and Life Scis., 1973-78. Mem. Am. Polit. Sci. Assn., Am. Soc. for Legal and Polit. Philosophy, AAAS. Author: The Nation is Burdened, 1967; The Political Philosophy of Rousseau, 1968. Editor: Rousseau's Discourses, 1964, Rousseau's Social

Contract, 1978; sect. editor Social Sci. Info., 1971—. Home: Dogford Rd Etna NH 03750 Office: Dept Govt Dartmouth Coll Hanover NH 03755

MASTERS, WILLIAM HOWELL, physician, educator; b. Cleve., Dec. 27, 1915; s. Francis Wynne and Estabrooks (Taylor) M.; B.S., Hamilton Coll., 1938, Sc.D. (hon.), 1973; M.D., U. Rochester, 1943; m. Virginia E. Johnson, Jan. 7, 1971; children by previous marriage—Sarah Worthington, William Howell III. Intern obstetrics and gynecology St. Louis Maternity and Barnes Hosp., 1943, asst. resident, 1944; intern pathology Washington U. Sch. Medicine, St. Louis, 1944; asst. resident gynecology Barnes Hosp. 1944, intern internal medicine, 1945, resident gynecology, 1946-47; resident obstetrics St. Louis Maternity Hosp., 1945-46; mem. faculty Washington U. Sch. Medicine, 1947—, asso. prof. clin. obstetrics and gynecology, 1964-69, prof., 1969—, dir. Reproductive Biology Research Found., 1964-73; co-dir. Masters & Johnson Inst. (formerly Reproductive Biology Research Found.), 1973—; asso. physician St. Louis Maternity Barnes and St. Louis Children's hosps., Washington U. Clinics; asst. attending physician Jewish Hosp., St. Louis. Meml. Hosp. Bd. dirs. St. Louis Family and Childrens Service, Planned Parenthood Assn., St. Louis Health and Welfare Council. Served to lt. (j.g.) USNR, 1942-43. Recipient Paul H. Hoch award Am. Psychopathol. Assn., 1971; award STECUS, 1972; Distinguished Service award Am. Assn. Marriage and Family Counselors, 1976; award for distinguished achievement Modern Medicine, 1977; award Am. Assn. Sex Educators, Counselors and Therapists, 1978; Paul Harris fellow, 1976. Diplomate Am. Bd. Obstetricians and Gynecologists; cert. Am. Assn. Sex Educators, Counselors and Therapists. Mem. Gerontol. Soc., Am. Fertility Soc., Internat. Fertility Assn., Endocrine Soc., Am. Coll. Obstetricians and Gynecologists, N.Y. Acad. Sci., Soc. Sci. Study Sex, AAAS, Comprehensive Med. Soc., Pan Am. Med. Assn., Internat. Soc. for Research in Biology Reprodn., Am. Geriatric Soc., Am. Soc. Cytology, Soc. for Study Reprodn., AMA, Eastern Mo. Psychiat. Soc. (hon.), Authors Guild, Alpha Omega Alpha, Alpha Delta Phi. Club: Racquet (St. Louis). Episcopalian. Author: (with Virginia E. Johnson) Human Sexual Response, 1966, Human Sexual Inadequacy, 1970, The Pleasure Bond, 1975, Homosexuality in Perspective, 1979; (with Kolodny et al) Textbook of Human Sexuality for Nurses, Textbook of Sexual Medicine; editor: (with V.E. Johnson and R.C. Kolodny) Ethical Issues in Sex Therapy and Research, 1977. Home: 2221 S Warson Rd Saint Louis MO 63124

MASTERSON, CHARLES FRANCIS, social scientist; b. N.Y.C., Nov. 3, 1917; s. Frank Joseph and Harriett Geneva (Whittaker) M.; A.B., L.I. U., 1938; M.A., Columbia U., 1939, Ph.D., 1952; m. 2d, Vivian Ethel Reppke, May 8, 1954; children by previous marriage—Michael Charles, Susan Jane. Dir. pub. relations Poly. Prep., Bklyn., 1946-49, Bklyn. C. of C., 1949-50, N.Y.C. Mission Soc., 1950-53; spl. asst. White House, Washington, 1953-56, Rumbough Co., N.Y., 1957-60; spl. asst. Nat. Safety Council, 1960-62, exec. dir. Office of Trustees, 1962-77; sr. asso. Clark, Phipps, Clark & Harris, 1978—. Bd. dirs. N.Y.C. Mission Soc. Mem. Pub. Relations Soc. Am., Nat. Inst. Social Scis., Phi Delta Kappa. Presbyterian (elder). Author: World History, 1949; History of Asia, 1950. Home: 9801 Shore Rd Brooklyn NY 11209 Office: 60 E 86th St New York NY 10028

MASTERSON, HARRIS, estate mgmt. exec.; b. Houston, July 9, 1914; s. Neill Turner and Libbie (Johnston) M.; student N.Mex. Mil. Inst., 1928-31; B.A., Rice U., 1955; m. Carroll Sterling, Jan. 17, 1951. Producer, God and Kate Murphy, N.Y.C., 1959, The Villa of Madame Vidac, off Broadway, 1959, From A to Z, N.Y.C., 1960, New Faces of 1962, N.Y.C.; asso. producer Masterpiece, London, Eng., 1961; co-producer A Second String, N.Y.C., 1960, Beg, Borrow, or Steal, N.Y.C., 1960, Lady of the Camellias, N.Y.C., 1963, Traveller Without Luggage, N.Y.C., 1964, Bajour, 1965. Pres., C & HM Corp. Chmn. Bayou Bend Founders Fund; chmn. bd. Houston Mus. Fine Arts, Houston Lyric Theatre Found., Inc.; chmn. Houston Ballet Found. Bd. dirs. Houston Symphony, Nat. Symphony, Friends of Rice U.; chmn. Bayou Bend Adv. Council; v.p. Theater Under the Stars; dir. Tex. Fine Arts Soc; arts adv. council Rice U. Served to capt. AUS, 1941-45; ETO, 1951-52. Decorated Sovereign Order of Hospitaliers of St. John of Jerusalem, Knights of Malta, Grand Cross of Malta, Knight of Mil. and Hospitaller Order St. Lazarus of Jerusalem; named hon. Ky. Col. Mem. Sons of Confederacy, Ams. of Royal Descent, Magna Charta Barons, Colonial Order of Crown, SAR, Sons Confederate Vets., Plantagenet Soc., Sons Republic Tex., Order Washington, Order Stars and Bars. Episcopalian. Clubs: American (London); Houston-River Oaks Country, Bayou, Allegro (Houston); Tex. Corinthian Yacht. Home: 1406 Kirby Dr Houston TX 77019 also Diamond C Ranch Rosenberg TX also 2319 Park Baycliffe TX 77518 Office: 2001 Kirby Dr Suite 900 Houston TX 77019

MASTERSON, JOHN PATRICK, educator; b. Chgo., Mar. 15, 1925; s. Michael Joseph and Delia Frances (Dolan) M.; B.A., St. Mary of the Lake, 1947; M.A., De Paul U., 1952; Ph.D., U. Ill., 1961; m. Jean Frances Wegrzyn, Aug. 18, 1956; children—Mary Beth, Michael, Maureen, Laura. Chmn. English dept. De Paul U., Chgo., 1964-67, head humanities div., 1967-70, prof. English, 1970, dean Coll. Liberal Arts and Scis., 1970-76, prof. mgmt., 1976—; cons. in field. Recipient award Shell Oil Co., 1968; fellow adminstrn. program Am. Council Edn. Mem. Am. Assn. Higher Edn., North Central Assn. Accreditation Com., AAUP. Roman Catholic. Home: 1922 S Belleview Westchester IL 60153 Office: 23 E Jackson Blvd Chicago IL 60604

MASTERSON, KLEBER SANDLIN, former orgn. exec., ret. naval officer; b. San Jon, N.Mex., July 12, 1908; s. John Patrick and Leila (Johnson) M.; student U. N.Mex., 1925-26; B.S., U.S. Naval Acad., 1930; grad. U.S. Naval Postgrad. Sch., 1939, Naval War Coll., 1953; m. Charlotte Elizabeth Parker, Oct. 3, 1931; 1 son, Kleber Sandlin, Jr. Commd. ensign U.S. Navy, 1930, advanced through grades to vice adm., 1964; assigned various ships, 1930-41; main battery asst. U.S.S. Arizona, Pearl Harbor; gunnery officer U.S.S. Pennsylvania, to 1944; staff research and devel. div., bur. ordnance Navy Dept., Wash., 1944-46; mem. staff CINCLANT FLT, 1946-47; comdr. Destroyer Div. 102, 1947-48; head ammunition br. Bur. Naval Ordnance, 1950-52; comdr. officer U.S.S. Lenawee, 1953-54; comdr. Naval Adminstrv. Unit, also asst. comdr. operations, field command, Armed Forces Spl. Weapons Project, 1954-56; comdg. officer U.S.S. Boston, 1956-57; dir. guided missile div. Office Chief Naval Operations, exec. mem. navy ballistic missile com., 1958-60; comdr. Cruiser Div. 1, 1960-61; asst. chief naval operations devel. Office Chief Naval Operations, 1961; dep. chief Bur. Naval Weapons, 1961-62; chief Bur. Naval Weapons, 1962-64; comdr. 2d Fleet and comdr. Striking Fleet Atlantic, 1964-66; dir. Weapons Systems Evaluation Group. Office of Sec. of Def., Washington, 1966-69, ret., 1969; pres. Navy Relief Soc., 1969-73. Decorated D.S.M., Legion of Merit, Navy Commendation; commandeur del'Ordre National du Mérite (France). Club: Army Navy Country (Arlington, Va.). Home: 1600 S Eads St Arlington VA 22202

MASTERSON, PETER, writer, director, producer, actor; b. Houston, June 1, 1934; s. Carlos Bee and Josephine Yeager (Smith) M.; B.A. in History, Rice U., 1957; m. Carlin Glynn, Dec. 29, 1960; children—Carlin Alexandra, Mary Stuart, Peter Carlos. Appeared on Broadway: Marathon '33, 1963, Blues For Mr. Charlie, 1964, title role in Trial of Lee Harvey Oswald, 1967, The Great White Hope, 1968, That Championship Season, 1974, The Poison Tree, 1975; appeared in films: The Exorcist, 1972, Man On A Swing, 1973, The Stepford Wives, 1974; Author play: The Best Little Whorehouse in Texas, 1978, Broadway dir., 1978 (Drama Desk award for best dir. of musical 1978); screenwriter and dir. film: The Best Little Whorehouse in Texas, 1980; producer TV film: City in Fear, 1980. Mem. Actors Equity Assn., Screen Actors Guild, Soc. Stage Dirs. and Choreographers, AFTRA, Writers Guild Am., Actors Studio, Dirs. Guild Am. Episcopalian. Clubs: Seawanhaka Corinthian Yacht, Tex. Corinthian Yacht.

MASTERSON, THOMAS ROBERT, educator; b. Crystal Lake, Ill., Sept. 17, 1915; s. Peter Aloysius and Isobel Cherry (Woods) M.; Ph.B., U. Chgo., 1946, M.B.A., 1948, Ph.D., 1955; m. Dorothy Jean Mandabach, Aug. 17, 1940; children—Katherine Irene, Judith Amanda, Miriam Alicia. Underwriter, supr. Hartford Accident and Indemnity Co., Chgo., 1935-41; asst. prof. DePaul U., Chgo., 1948-56, asso. prof., 1957-60; asso. prof. mgmt. Grad. Sch. Bus., Emory U., Atlanta, 1960-66, prof., 1967—, exec. officer Center for Corp. Policy Direction, 1975—; bd. dirs. various trusts. Served with USAAF, 1941-45. Mem. Acad. of Mgmt., Am. Mgmt. Assn., Am. Soc. for Personnel Adminstrn. (accredited personnel diplomate), AAUP (pres. DePaul U. chpt. 1955, pres. Emory U. chpt. 1967), So. Mgmt. Assn., Beta Gamma Sigma. Club: Druid Hills Golf. Author books and jour. articles. Office: Grad Sch Bus Emory U Atlanta GA 30322. *A social system which indiscriminately rewards mediocrity and merit alike is in trouble.*

MASTERTON, WILLIAM LEWIS, educator; b. Conway, N.H., July 24, 1927; s. Fred Richard and Elsie Marion (Wickens) M.; B.S., U. N.H., 1949, M.S., 1950; Ph.D., U. Ill., 1953; m. Loris Ruth Matthys, June 20, 1953; children—Frederick, Reynold. Instr. chemistry U. Ill., 1953-55; prof. chemistry U. Conn., Storrs, 1955—. Served with AUS, 1946-47. Mem. Am. Chem. Soc., AAUP, Sigma Xi, Phi Lambda Upsilon. Author: Chemical Principles, 1965, 69, 73, 75, 77. Contbr. articles to profl. jours. Home: 1 Ridge Rd Storrs CT 06268

MASTIN, THOMAS WILLIAM, chem. co. exec.; b. New Castle, Ind., Dec. 19, 1913; s. Thomas William and Minnie Lee (Garner) M.; B.A. in Chemistry, Wabash Coll., 1938, D.Sc. (hon.), 1973, 78; M.S. in Chemistry, U. Ill., 1939, Ph.D., 1942; m. Lillian Elizabeth Hungate, June 20, 1937; children—Thomas W., Dennis A. Research chemist Lubrizol Corp., Wickliffe, Ohio, 1942-43, dir. chem. research labs., 1943-53, asst. dir. research and devel., 1953-56, v.p. research and devel., 1956-67, exec. v.p., v.p. research and devel., 1967-69, exec. v.p., 1969-72, pres., 1972-76, chief exec. officer, 1972—, chmn., 1976—, also dir.; dir. Keithley Instruments, Inc., Roadway Express, Inc., Splty. Composites, Inc. Trustee Cleve. Mus. of Natural History, Euclid Gen. Hosp., Grand River Acad., Lake Erie Coll., Wabash Coll., N.E. Ohio council Boy Scouts Am. Recipient Comml. Devel. Assn. award, 1977. Mem. Am. Chem. Soc. Republican. Presbyterian. Clubs: Union, Kirtland Country, Pepper Pike. Contbr. articles to chem. and petroleum jours. Patentee in field of lubricant additives. Home: 7265 Markell Rd Willoughby OH 44094 Office: 29400 Lakeland Blvd Wickliffe OH 44092

MASTOR, GEORGE CONSTANDINE, lawyer, utility exec.; b. Bemidji, Minn., Dec. 2, 1925; s. Philip M. and Agnes (Sekula) M.; B.S. in Law, U. Minn., 1949, LL.B., 1952; m. Margaret McDaniel, Sept. 16, 1950; children—Andrea, Barbara, Connie, Michael, John. Admitted to Minn. bar, 1952, since practiced in Mpls.; partner firm Mastor and Bale, 1953-79; gen. counsel Minn. Gas Co., 1979—. Served to 1st lt. AUS, 1944-47, 50-51. Mem. Minn. (sec. 1970-74, pres. 1975-76), Hennepin County (pres. 1968-69) bar assns., Am. Right of Way Assn. (pres. Tri-State chpt. 1962). Club: Edina Country (treas. 1969-70, sec. 1970-71). Home: 5720 Tucker Ln Edina MN 55436 Office: Peavey Bldg Minneapolis MN 55402

MASTROIANNI, LUIGI, JR., physician; b. New Haven, Nov. 8, 1925; s. Luigi and Marion (Dallas) M.; A.B., Yale U., 1946; M.D., Boston U., 1950, D.Sc. (hon.), 1973; M.A. (hon.), U. Pa., 1970; m. Elaine Catherine Pierson, Nov. 4, 1957; children—John James, Anna Catherine, Robert Luigi. Intern, Met. Hosp., N.Y.C., 1950-51, resident obstetrics and gynecology, 1951-54; practice medicine specializing in obstetrics and gynecology, New Haven, 1955-61, Los Angeles, 1961-65, Phila., 1965—; fellow in fertility and endocrinology Med. Sch., Harvard and Free Hosp., 1954-55; instr. obstetrics and gynecology Yale Sch. Medicine, 1955-56, asst. prof., 1956-61; prof. obstetrics and gynecology U. Calif. at Los Angeles, 1961-65; chief obstetrics and gynecology Harbor Gen. Hosp., Torrance, Calif., 1961-65; prof., chmn. obstetrics and gynecology U. Pa., 1965—, Goodell prof. gynecology, 1967—; chief obstetrics and gynecology Woman's Hosp. of Hosp. U. Pa., 1965—; chmn. primate research centers adv. com. NIH, 1965-68; sci. adv. bd. Internat. Planned Parenthood Fedn., 1966—. Bd. dirs. Sex Info. Ednl. Council U.S., 1968-71. Recipient Squibb prize Am. Fertility Soc., 1965; Ortho medal for contbns. to reprodn., 1966; Lindback Found. award for disting. teaching, 1969; Barren Found. medal, 1977. Diplomate Am. Bd. Obstetrics and Gynecology (subsplty. gynecol. endocrinology). Fellow A.C.S., Am. Coll. Obstetricians and Gynecologists, Coll. Physicians Phila., Am. Gynecol. Soc.; mem. Am. Physiol. Soc., Soc. Exptl. Biology and Medicine, Soc. Gynecologic Investigation, Am., Pacific Coast (hon.) fertility socs., Obstet. Soc. Phila., Endocrine Soc., Soc. Study of Reprodn. (dir. 1972—), Soc. Study of Fertility, Central Assn. Obstetricians and Gynecologists (hon.), Peruvian Obstet. and Gynecol. Soc. (hon.), Brazilian Fertility Soc. (hon.), Sigma Xi, Alpha Omega Alpha. Roman Catholic. Editor Jour. Fertility and Sterility, 1969-76; contbr. articles to profl. jours. Home: 351 Laurel Ln Haverford PA 19041 Office: 3400 Spruce St Philadelphia PA 19104

MASUBUCHI, KOICHI, naval architect; b. Otaru, Hokkaido, Japan, Jan. 11, 1924; s. Yosaku and Tomi (Ota) M.; B.S., U. Tokyo, 1946, M.S., 1948, Ph.D., 1959; m. Fumiko Kaneno, Oct. 24, 1950. Research engr. Transp. Tech. Research Inst., 1948-58; vis. fellow, cons. Battelle Menl. Inst., Columbus, Ohio, 1958-62, research asso., fellow, tech. adviser, 1963-68, chief welding mechanics sect., welding div. Ship Research Inst., 1962-63; asso. prof. naval architecture Mass. Inst. Tech., Cambridge, 1968-71, prof. ocean engring. and Materials sci., 1971—. Recipient Disting. Service award Transp. Tech. Research Inst., Ministry Transp., Japan, 1959. Mem. Am. Welding Soc. (R.D. Thomas Meml. award 1977), Japan Welding Soc., Am. Soc. Metals, Soc. Naval Architects and Marine Engrs., Soc. Naval Architects Japan, Internat. Inst. Welding (commn. vice chmn.), Sigma Xi. Author: Materials for Ocean Engineering, 1970; Analysis of Welded Structures, 1980; co-author 3 books on residual stresses in weldments, materials for ocean engring.; contbr. tech. papers to profl. lit. Home: 34 Hamilton Rd Arlington MA 02174 Office: Mass Inst Tech Cambridge MA 02139

MASUDA, GEORGE THEODORE, bishop; b. Mpls., Mar. 3, 1913; s. Roy T. and Minnie (Gilbertson) M.; B.A., Carleton Coll., Northfield, Minn., 1934; B.D., Seabury Western Sem., Evanston, Ill., 1942, D.D., 1965; m. Jeanne Bennett, Oct. 20, 1951; children—David, Michael. Ordained to ministry Episcopal Ch., 1942; vicar in Whitefish, Mont., 1942-48; rector in Billings, Mont., 1948-65; bishop of N.D., 1965—. Home: 707 S 8th St Fargo ND 58102 Office: 809 S 8th Ave Fargo ND 58102*

MASUR, ERNEST FRANK, educator; b. Berlin, July 15, 1919; came to U.S., 1939, naturalized, 1944; s. Martin M. and Else (Brukstein) M.; B.S., U. Pitts., 1941; M.S., Ill. Inst. Tech., 1948, Ph.D., 1952; m. Eva Henriette Magnus, Dec. 16, 1944; children—Robert Edward, Howard Alan, Sandra. From instr. to asso. prof. civil engring. Ill. Inst. Tech., 1948-55; from asso. prof. to prof. engring. mechanics U. Mich., 1955-64; head dept. materials engring. U. Ill., Chgo. 1964—; cons. in field; Nat. Acad. Scis. exchange scientist with Bulgaria, 1972, with Poland, 1977; dir. div. civil and mech. engring. NSF, 1979-80. Served with AUS, 1943-46. Recipient Laurie award ASCE, 1960. Fellow ASCE (past chmn. div. engring. mechanics), Am. Acad. Mechanics; mem. ASME, AAUP, Sigma Xi, Chi Epsilon, Sigma Tau. Editor: Jour. Structural Mechanics; contbr. articles to profl. jours. Home: 510 Elmwood Ave Evanston IL 60202 Office: U Ill at Chgo Circle Box 4348 Chicago IL 60680

MASUR, ERNEST FRANK, educator; b. Berlin, Germany, July 15, 1919; s. Martin M. and Else (Brukstein) M.; came to U.S., 1939, naturalized, 1944; B.S., U. Pitts., 1941; M.S., Ill. Inst. Tech., 1948, Ph.D., 1952; m. Eva Henriette Magnus, Dec. 16, 1944; children—Robert Edward, Howard Alan, Sandra. Instr., asst. prof., then asso. prof. civil engring. Ill. Inst. Tech., 1948-55; asso prof., prof. engring. mechanics U. Mich., 1955-64; head dept. materials engring. U. Ill., Chgo., 1964—. Structural, aerospace engring. cons., 1948—; cons. NSF, 1962—, dir. div. civil and mech. engring., 1979-80; Nat. Acad. Scis. exchange scientist with Bulgaria, 1972, with Poland, 1977. Served with AUS, 1943-46. Recipient Laurie award Am. Soc. C.E., 1960. Fellow Am. Soc. C.E. (past chmn. engring. mechanics div.), Am. Acad. Mechanics; mem. Am. Soc. M.E., Am. Assn. U. Profs., Sigma Xi, Chi Epsilon, Sigma Tau. Editor: Jour. Structural Mechanics. Contbr. articles to profl. jours. Home: 510 Elmwood Ave Evanston IL 60202 Office: U Ill at Chgo Circle Box 4348 Chicago IL 60680

MASUROVSKY, GREGORY, artist; b. Bronx, N.Y., Nov. 26, 1929; s. Benjamin Israel and Lillian Mary (Hugel) M.; student Black Mountain Coll., 1947-48, Sorbonne, Paris, 1954-62; m. Shirley Goldfarb, Feb. 20, 1953; 1 son, Marc Jean. Exhbns. include: Palais des Beaux Arts, Brussels, 1964, Documenta, Kassel, 1964, Mpls. Inst. Arts, 1967, Gallery Betty Parsons, N.Y.C., 1969, 71, 73, Galerie Albert Loeb, Paris, 1971, 73, Librairie/Galerie Obliques, Paris, 1978; represented in permanent collections: Mus. Modern Art, N.Y.C., Fogg Mus., Cambridge, Mass., Carnegie Inst., Pitts., Art Inst. Chgo., Mpls. Inst. Arts, Library of Congress, Bibliothèque Nationale, Paris; vis. prof. drawing Mpls. Coll. Art and Design, 1966-67. Served with U.S. Army, 1948-49, 50-51. Recipient award William and Noma Copley Found., 1963. Mem. Artists Equity N.Y. Address: 43 rue Liancourt Paris France 75014

MASURSKY, HAROLD, geologist; b. Ft. Wayne, Ind., Dec. 23, 1923; s. Louis and Celia (Ochstein) M.; B.S. in Geology, Yale U., 1943, M.S., 1951; m. Jean Anne Stormont, 1969; 4 children. With U.S. Geol. Survey, 1951—, chief astrogeologic studies br., 1967-71, chief scientist Center Astrogeology, Flagstaff, Ariz., 1971-75, sr. scientist, 1975—, lunar orbiter Surveyor Project, 1965-67; team leader, prin. investigator TV experiment Mariner Mars, 1971; co-investigator Apollo field geol. team Apollo 16 and 17, also mem. Apollo orbital sci. photog. team, Apollo site selection group; leader Viking landing site staff, dep. team leader orbiter visual imaging systems Viking Mars, 1975; mem. teams Voyager (Jupiter, Saturn), 1977, chmn. mission ops. group Venus Pioneer, 1978, co-chmn. mission operational group Galileo, 1981; mem. Space Sci. Adv. Com., 1978-79; sec. Coordinating Com. of Moon and Planets. Served with AUS, 1943-46. Fellow Geol. Soc. Am., AAAS, Am. Geophys. Union, Internat. Astron. Union, Am. Astron. Assn., Com. Space Research, Asso. editor Geophys. Research Letters. Address: US Geol Survey 2255 N Gemini St Flagstaff AZ 86001. *The vigorously ongoing exploration of outer space continues the exploration tradition of man. It has been exhilarating to be involved with the manned and unmanned exploration programs. Each of the nine programs so far has required new thinking and approaches to solving the problems.*

MATA, EDUARDO, conductor; b. Mexico City, Mexico, 1942; student Nat. Conservatory of Music, 1954-63; pupil Carlos Chaves, 1960-65; advanced conducting work Tanglewood, 1964; m. Carmen Cirici-Ventalló, Nov. 5, 1968. Resident condr. Tanglewood, 1964; guest condr. with U.S. orchs. including Boston Symphony, Chgo. Symphony, Cleve. Orch., Pitts. Orch., Detroit Symphony Orch., also orchs. in South and Central Am., Poland, Yugoslavia, Luxembourg, France, W. Ger., Sweden, Gt. Britain, Italy, Israel, Japan; music dir., condr. Orch. Philharmonic Mexico, 1966-75; prin. condr., musical adviser Phoenix Symphony, 1969-74, dir., 1975-78; also music dir. Dallas Symphony, 1977-79; artistic dir. Puebla Music Festival, 1975—. Mem. Mexico Soc. Composers. Composer symphonies, chamber and vocal music. Address: Dallas Symphony PO Box 26207 Dallas TX 75226

MATARAZZO, JOSEPH DOMINIC, psychologist; b. Caiazzo, Italy, Nov. 12, 1925 (parents Am. citizens); s. Nicholas and Adeline (Mastroianni) M.; student Columbia U., 1944; B.A., Brown U., 1946; M.S., Northwestern U., 1950, Ph.D., 1952; m. Ruth Wood Gadbois, Mar. 26, 1949; children—Harris, Elizabeth, Sara. Fellow in med. psychology Washington U., 1950-51, instr., 1951-53, asst. prof., 1953-55; research asso. Harvard Med. Sch., asso. psychologist Mass. Gen. Hosp., 1955-57; prof., head med. psychol. dept. U. Oreg. Med. Sch., Portland, 1957—; mem. nursing research and patient care study sect. NIH; spl. research com. Am. Cancer Soc. Bd. regents Uniformed Service U. Health Scis., 1974—. Served to ensign USNR, 1943-47; capt. Res. Recipient Hofheimer prize Am. Psychiat. Assn., 1962. Fellow Am. Psychol. Assn. (pres. div. health psychology 1978-79), AAAS; mem. Western, Oreg. psychol. assns., Am. Assn. State Psychology Bds. (pres. 1963-64), Nat. Assn. Mental Health (dir.), Oreg. Mental Health Assn. (dir., pres. 1962-63), Internat. Council Psychologists (dir. 1972-74, pres. 1976-77), Sigma Xi. Author: Wechsler's Measurement and Appraisal of Adult Intelligence, 5th edit., 1972; (with A.N. Wiens) The Interview: Research on its Anatomy and Structure, 1972; (with Harper and Wiens) Nonverbal Communication, 1978; asso. editor Human Orgn., 1954-66; mem. editorial bd. Jour. Clin. Psychology, 1962—, Psychotherapy: Theory, Research and Practice, 1964-68, Mental Hygiene, 1969—, Jour. Continuing Edn. in Psychiatry, 1975—; cons. editor Contemporary Psychology, 1962-70, Jour. Community Psychology, 1974—, Behavior Modification, 1976—, Intelligence: An Interdisciplinary Jour., 1976; editor Psychology series Aldine Pub. Co., 1964-74; psychology editor Williams & Wilkins Co., 1974-77; contbr. articles to psychol. jours. Home: 1934 SW Vista Ave Portland OR 97201

MATARAZZO, RUTH GADBOIS, psychologist; b. New London, Conn., Nov. 9, 1926; d. John Stuart and Elizabeth (Wood) Gadbois; A.B., Brown U., 1948; M.A., Washington U., St. Louis, 1952, Ph.D., 1955; m. Joseph D. Matarazzo, Mar. 26, 1949; children—Harris Starr, Elizabeth Wood, Sara Holt. Research fellow pediatrics Washington U. Med. Sch., 1954-55; research fellow psychology Harvard U. Med. Sch., 1955-57; asst. prof. med. psychology U. Oreg. Med. Sch.,

Portland, 1957-63, asso. prof., 1963-68, prof., 1968—, also woman liaison officer to Assn. Am. Med. Colls.; bd. dirs. Community Child Guidance Clinic, Mental Health Assn. Oreg., Portland Met. Mental Health Assn., N.W. Center for Devel. Human Potential; Western regional bd. Am. Bd. Profl. Psychologists; cons. Portland Center Hearing and Speech, N. Clackamas Pub. Sch. Dist., Tillamook Job Corps. Bd. dirs., past sec. Portland Opera Assn. Diplomate Am. Bd. Examiners in Profl. Psychology. Fellow Am. Psychol. Assn. (del. to council reps.); mem. Western (dir.), Oreg. (past sec.-treas.), Portland (past pres.) psychol. assns., AAUP, AAAS, Oreg. Soc. Mayflower Descs. past treas., dep. gov., gov., dep. gov.-gen.), Asso. Alumni/ae Brown U. (bd. dirs., regional dir.), Sigma Xi. Editorial bd. Women, An Annual; contbr. articles to profl. jours., chpts. to books. Home: 1934 SW Vista Ave Portland OR 97201

MATAXIS, THEODORE CHRISTOPHER, ednl. adminstr., ret. army officer; b. Seattle, Aug. 17, 1917; s. Chris P. and Edla (Osterdahl) M.; B.A., U. Wash., 1940; student Def. Services Staff Coll., India, 1950-51, Army War Coll., 1957-58; M.A. in Internat. Relations, George Washington U., 1965; m. Helma Mary Jensen, Aug. 27, 1940; children—Shirley Jeanne (Mrs. John M. Howell), Theodore Christopher, Kaye Louise (Mrs. Vernon P. Isaacs, Jr.). Commd. 2d lt. U.S. Army, 1940, advanced through grades to brig. gen., 1967; inf. bn. comdr., Europe, World War II; regt. comdr., Korea, 1952-53; mem. Gov. Harriman's Presdl. Mission to Establish Mil. Aid Program, India, 1962; mil. asst., speech writer for chmn. Joint Chiefs of Staff, 1962-64; sr. adviser II Vietnamese Army Corps, Pleiku, 1964-65; dep. comdr. 1st Brigade, 101st Airborne Div., 1966; asst. div. comdr. 82d Airborne Div., 1967; chief army sect. Army Mission/MAAG, Iran, 1968-70; asst., acting div. comdr. Americal Div., Vietnam, 1970; chief mil. equipment delivery team, Cambodia, 1971-72; ret., 1972; ednl. and systems mgmt. cons. Republic of Singapore, 1972-74; asst. supt., comdt. cadets Valley Forge Mil. Acad., Wayne Pa., 1975—. Decorated D.S.M., Silver Star, D.F.C., Bronze Star with 3 oak leaf clusters with V, Commendation medal with 3 oak leaf clusters and V, Joint Services Commendation medal, Purple Heart with oak leaf cluster, Legion of Merit with 2 oak leaf clusters, Air medal with V and 30 oak leaf clusters, Combat Inf. Badge with 2 stars (U.S.); Nat. Order 5th class, Distinguished Service Order, 4 Gallantry crosses, Honor medal 1st class, Air medal (Vietnam); Def. medal Order of Republic (Cambodia). Mem. Am. Assn. Univ. Adminstrs., Oral History Assn., Am. Mil. History Inst., U.S. Commn. on Mil. History, Mil. Order World Wars (life), Am. Legion, VFW, Airborne Assn., 70th Div. Assn., Assn. U.S. Army, Nat. Rifle Assn. (life), 101st Airborne Div. Assn., (life), Ends of the Earth, Scabbard and Blade (adv. council nat. soc.). Elk. Clubs: Army Navy (Washington); Tanglin (Singapore). Author: (with Seymour Goldberg) Nuclear Tactics, 1958; also numerous mil. and hist. articles. Address: Valley Forge Mil Acad and Jr Coll Wayne PA 19087

MATCHAM, CHARLES ORMROD, architect; b. Allentown, Pa., Apr. 24, 1903; s. Charles A. and Margaret (Ormrod) M.; grad. Hotchkiss Sch. 1921; Ph.B., Yale, 1925, B.F.A., 1928; student Fountainbleau Sch., 1927; m. Harriet Quinlan, Nov. 21, 1929; children—Charles Ormrod, Michael Quinlan. Individual practice architecture, Palm Springs, Calif., 1932-39, Los Angeles, 1936—; prin. works include instl., ednl., comml., recreational bldgs., pub. works and residential projects throughout So. Calif. Bd. govs. Los Angeles County Mus. Natural History; past trustee Los Angeles County Mus. Art. Fellow AIA (past regional dir.). Clubs: California, Turf (Los Angeles); Balboa de Mazatlan (Mexico); Valley Hunt (Pasadena, Calif.). Address: 740 S Orange Grove Blvd Pasadena CA 91105

MATE, HUBERT EMERY, coll. dean; b. Lima, N.Y., Sept. 2, 1917; s. Joseph Simeon and Inez Louise (Butler) M.; A.B. cum laude, Samford U., 1937; M.A., U. Ala., 1938; Ph.D., Northwestern U., 1949; m. Agnes Eileen Eddleman, June 3, 1937; children—Janet (Mrs. David W. Parr), Carolyn (Mrs. D. Randall Williams). Research asso. Rockefeller Found., Brazil, 1941-42; instr. Spanish, Ind. U., 1946-49; mem. faculty U. Ala., University, 1949—, prof. Romance langs., 1958—, dean admissions and records, 1961-74, dir. curriculum studies, 1974—; cons. So. Assn. Colls. and Schs., 1964—. Chmn. So. Humanities Conf., 1969-70. Mem. Devel. Program Bur., Tuscaloosa, 1966—, Police Adv. Com., 1964—. Trustee Wesley Found., 1962—. Served to capt. USNR, 1942-46. Decorated Ordem do Cruzeiro do Sul (Brazil); Pi Kappa Phi scholar, 1937; recipient Distinguished Service award Theta Chi, 1970. Mem. Omicron Delta Kappa, Sigma Delta Pi, Phi Sigma Iota, Pi Tau Chi, Delta Kappa. Author: Handbook of Brazilian Studies, 1954; Conferencias Sobre O Ventura, 1943; Dicionario de Termos Tecnicos De Aviacao, 1944; Manual de Fornecimento de Aviacao, 1947; Guide to Equivalence and Transfer of Junior College Credits, 1976. Home: 2713 Claymont Circle Tuscaloosa AL 35404 Office: Box 6255 University AL 35486. *I have faith in others, finding that an investment of faith and trust seldom fails to pay good dividends. And I do not worry about the friends of the mighty. My concern is for the obscure one who knows no one.*

MATEER, ROBERT NELSON, comml. banker; b. Elizabeth, N.J., Dec. 12, 1933; s. George L. and Millicent (Watkins) M.; B.A. in Chemistry, Middlebury Coll., 1955; postgrad Stanford, 1955-56; M.B.A., Tulane U., 1960; m. Gladys Sulm, Mar. 19, 1960; children—George Dirk, Marianne Elizabeth. Asst. treas. Chase Manhattan Bank, N.Y.C., 1960-65; sr. v.p. Nat. Bank of Commerce, New Orleans, 1965-70; exec. v.p. Bank of New Orleans and Trust Co., 1970-71; pres., chief exec. officer Elpac, Inc., Houston, 1971-73; exec. v.p. Bankers Comml. Corp., San Diego, 1973-76; sr. v.p. Calif. 1st Bank, 1976; investment banker, fin. cons., La Jolla, Calif., 1976-78; sr. v.p., regional mgr. City Nat. Bank, La Jolla, 1979—. Mem. adv. bd. Tulane Bus. Sch. Served with AUS, 1956-58. Club: Rancho Santa Fe Country. Home: PO Box 1044 Rancho Santa Fe CA 92067 Office: City National Bank La Jolla Village Dr La Jolla CA 92037

MATEJKA, LADISLAV, educator; b. Czechoslovakia, May 30, 1919; s. Joseph and Anna (Kocka) M.; came to U.S., 1954, naturalized, 1959; Ph.D., Charles U., Prague, 1948; Ph.D., Harvard, 1961; m. Gudrun I. Ebenfelt, Sept. 14, 1957; children— Jan P., Anne Elizabeth. Mem. faculty U. Lund (Sweden), 1949-54; with Radio Free Europe, Munich, Germany and N.Y.C., 1954-56; research asst. Harvard, 1956-59; asso. prof. U. Mich., Ann Arbor, 1959-65, prof. dept. Slavic langs. and lit., 1965—, gen. editor Slavic publs., 1962—. Fulbright fellow, 1965; Ford Found. fellow, 1972; Guggenheim fellow, 1979. Mem. Linguistic Soc. Am. Author: (with others) Word Accent in Serbocroatian, 1971; Crossroads of Sound and Meaning, 1975. Editor: Readings in Russian Poetics, 1971; Am. contbns. to 7th Internat. Congress Slavists, 1973; Semiotics of Art: Prague School Contributions, 1976; Sound, Sign and Meaning: Quinquagenary of the Prague Linguistic Circle, 1976; Readings in Soviet Semiotics, 1976; The Sign: Semiotics Around the World, 1978. Home: 2003 Day St Ann Arbor MI 48104 Office: U Mich Modern Lang Bldg Ann Arbor MI 48104

MATEJU, JOSEPH FRANK, hosp. adminstr.; b. Cedar Rapids, Iowa, Oct. 18, 1927; s. Joseph Frank and Adeline (Smid) M.; B.A., U. N.Mex., 1951; M.A., N.Mex. State U., 1957. Sr. juvenile probation officer San Diego County, 1958-64; adminstr. Villa Solano State Sch., Hagerman, N.Mex., 1965-67; state coordinator on mental retardation planning N.Mex. Dept. Hosps. and Instns., Santa Fe, 1969-70; adminstr. Los Lunas (N.Mex.) Hosp. and Tng. Sch., 1968-69, 70—. Served with USAAF, 1946-47. Fellow Am. Assn. Mental Deficiency; mem. Nat. Assn. Supts. Residential Facilities for Mentally Retarded (dir.), Assn. Mental Health Adminstrs., Nat. Assn. Retarded Children, N.Mex. Hosp. Assn., Am. Coll. Nursing Home Adminstrs., Pi Gamma Mu. Home: 405 Fontana Pl NE Albuquerque NM 87108 Office: PO Box 1269 Los Lunas NM 87031

MATER, GENE P., broadcasting co. exec.; b. N.Y.C., Nov. 27, 1926; s. Albert and Anne (Lande) M.; student Bklyn. Poly. Inst., 1943-44; m. Jeanne M. Blanc, Mar. 7, 1947; children—Richard L., Gene A., Philip E. Editor news agy., various newspapers, Germany, 1946-48; reporter, county editor, city editor San Bernardino (Calif.) Sun-Telegram, 1949-53; copy editor, makeup editor, asst. night editor, news editor N.Y. World-Telegram & Sun, N.Y.C., 1953-59; news dir. Radio Free Europe, Munich, Germany, 1959-65; exec. v.p., sec. Radio Free Europe Fund, Inc., N.Y.C., 1965-70; spl. asst. to pres. CBS/Broadcast Group, CBS, Inc., N.Y.C., 1970-72, v.p., asst. to pres., 1972—. Served with AUS, 1944-46. Mem. Internat. Radio and TV Soc., Nat. Acad. TV Arts and Scis. Office: 51 W 52d St New York NY 10019

MATHEKE, OTTO GEORGE, JR., surgeon; b. Newark, Sept. 28, 1912; s. Otto George and Anna E. (Schaub) M.; B.S., U. Md., 1934, M.D., 1937; m. Elsa Calkins, July 1, 1939; children—Marian E. (Mrs. John S. Melish), Grant E., Steven Jon, Cynthia Ann, Otto George III. Intern Newark City Hosp., 1937-39; postgrad. surgery N.Y.U. Sch. Medicine, 1939-42; practice medicine specializing in surgery, Newark, 1946—; mem. staff Presbyn., St. Barnabas, St. Michael and City hosps.; dir. surgery Presbyn. Hosp., 1963-66, chief staff, 1966—. Trustee United Hosps. Newark. Served to maj., M.C., AUS, 1942-46; CBI. Fellow A.C.S.; mem. A.M.A., Acad. Medicine N.J., N.J. Med. Soc. Home: 151 Eagle Rock Way Montclair NJ 07042 Office: 109 S Munn Ave East Orange NJ 07018

MATHENY, EDWARD TAYLOR, JR., lawyer; b. Chgo., July 15, 1923; s. Edward Taylor and Lina (Pinnell) M.; B.A., U. Mo., 1944; J.D., Harvard, 1949; m. Marion Elizabeth Shields, Sept. 10, 1947; children—Nancy Elizabeth, Edward Taylor III. Admitted to Mo. bar, 1949, since practiced in Kansas City; partner firm Blackwell, Sanders, Matheny, Weary & Lombardi, 1954—; atty. Kansas City (Mo.) Sch. Dist., St. Luke's Hosp., Kansas City; sec., dir. C.J. Patterson Co. Pres. Community Service Broadcasting of Mid-Am., Inc., 1971-72. Chmn. Citizens Assn. Kansas City, 1958; bd. dirs. Kansas City area council Boy Scouts Am.; trustee of city trusts City of Kansas City (Mo.); bd. dirs. St. Luke's Found. for Med. Edn., Kansas City; bd. dirs. U. Mo. Devel. Fund; trustee U. Kansas City. Served to lt. (j.g.) USNR, 1944-46. Mem. Am., Kansas City bar assns., Mo. Bar, Lawyers Assn. Kansas City, Newcomen Soc. N. Am., Phi Beta Kappa, Sigma Chi (Balfour Nat. award 1944). Episcopalian (chancellor Diocese West Mo.). Clubs: River, Mission Hills Country. Home: 5400 Cherry St Kansas City MO 64110 Office: 5 Crown Center Kansas City MO 64108

MATHENY, RUTH ANN, editor; b. Fargo, N.D., Jan. 17, 1918; d. Jasper Gordon and Mary Elizabeth (Carey) Wheelock; B.E., Mankato State Coll., 1938; M.A., U. Minn., 1955; postgrad. Universidad Autonoma de Guadalajara (Mex.), summer 1956, Georgetown U., summer, 1960; m. Charles Edward Matheny, Oct. 24, 1960. Tchr. in U.S. and S.Am., 1939-61; asso. editor Charles E. Merrill Pub. Co., Columbus, Ohio, 1963-66; tchr. Confraternity Christian Doctrine, Washington Court House, Ohio, 1969-70; asso. editor Jr. Cath. Messenger, Dayton, Ohio, 1966-68; editor Witness Intermediate, Dayton, 1968-70, Today's Cath. Tchr., Dayton, 1970—; editor-in-chief Catechist, Dayton, 1976—, Ednl. Dealer, Dayton, 1976—. Mem. EDPRESS, Cath. Press Assn., Nat. Cath. Ednl. Assn., 3d Order St. Francis. Editorial collaborator Dimensions of Personality series, 1969—; co-author: At Ease in the Classroom; author: Why Religious Education?, and Why a Catholic School?. Home: 3840 Briar Pl Dayton OH 45405 Office: 2451 E River Rd Dayton OH 45439

MATHER, ALLEN FREDERICK, lawyer; b. Kansas City, Mo., Apr. 28, 1922; s. William Frederick and Alberta (Stephenson) M.; A.B., Colgate U., 1943; LL.B., Harvard, 1949; m. Patricia T. Mitchell, June 23, 1972; children—Allen Frederick, Nathaniel J., J. Miles Mitchell. With Agrl. Council of Calif., Sacramento, 1950-57, exec. sec., 1954-57; admitted to Calif. bar, 1953; gen. counsel Sunkist Growers, Los Angeles, 1958-66; pres. Sun-Maid Raisin Growers of Calif., Kingsburg, 1966-72; pres. Sunland Marketing, Inc., Menlo Park, Calif., 1971-72; pres. First Nat. Bank Fresno (Calif.), 1973-77; mem. firm Wild, Carter, Tipton & Quaschnick, 1977—; mng. partner Agribus. Group, 1977—. Mem. Calif. Industry and World Trade Commn., 1969—; pres. Sequoia council Boy Scouts Am., 1969—. Served with USNR, 1943-46. Mem. Dried Fruit Assn. (dir.), Fresno C. of C. (dir.). Club: Sunnyside Country (Fresno). Home: 1228 W San Madele St Fresno CA 93711 Office: 2300 Civic Center Sq Fresno CA 93721

MATHER, AUSTIN WHEELER, architect; b. Norwalk, Conn., Dec. 13, 1904; s. Harry Wakefield and Maude (Wheeler) M.; grad. Pratt Inst., 1927, Beaux Arts Inst. Design, 1930; m. Marjorie Kellogg, Sept. 5, 1938; 1 dau., Melinda K. Partner, Lyons & Mather, Bridgeport, Conn., 1939—; instr. Pratt Inst., 1927-28, 38-40, U. Bridgeport, 1946-48; guest lectr. Mass. Inst. Tech., 1937-38. Mem. UN Site Com., 1945; cons. Fairfield County Planning Assn., 1934-58; pres. Conn. Fedn. Planning and Zoning Agy. 1955. Pres., Bd. Assos., U. Bridgeport. Fellow AIA (regional dir. 1955-58, pres. New Eng. regional council 1955-58, exec. com. 1955-58; pres. Conn. 1953-54); mem. Conn. Soc. Architects (pres. 1947-48), Conn. Fedn. Planning and Zoning Agys. (pres. 1955). Author publs. Fairfield County Planning Assn.; contbr. articles periodicals. Home: Creeping Hemlock Dr Norwalk CT 06851 Office: 855 Main St Bridgeport CT 06603

MATHER, BETTY BANG, musician, educator; b. Emporia, Kans., Aug. 7, 1927; d. Read Robinson and Shirley (Smith) Bang; B.Mus., Oberlin Conservatory, 1949; M.A., Columbia U., 1951; m. Roger Mather, Aug. 3, 1973. Faculty, U. Iowa, Iowa City, 1952—, prof. flute, 1973—; rec. artist. Author: Interpretation of French Music from 1675-1775, 1973; (with David Lasocki) Free Ornamentation for Woodwind Instruments from 1700-1775, 1976; (with David Lasocki) The Classical Woodwind Cadenza, 1978. Editor: 30 Virtuosic Selections in the Gallant Style for Unaccompanied Flute, 1975; Opera Duets Arranged for Two Flutes by Berbiguier, 1976; 60 Favorite Airs in the Gallant Style for Unaccompanied Flute, 1978. Contbr. articles to profl. publs. Home: 308 4th Ave Iowa City IA 52240

MATHER, BRYANT, research adminstr.; b. Balt., Dec. 27, 1916; s. Leon Bryant and Julia (Ferguson) M.; grad. Balt. City Coll., 1934; A.B. in Geology, Johns Hopkins, 1936, postgrad., 1936-38, 40-41, Am. U., 1938-39; D.Sc. (hon.), Clarkson Coll., 1978; m. Katharine Selden Kniskern, Mar. 27, 1940. Curator mineralogy Chgo. Mus. Natural History, 1939-41; with U.S. Army Corps Engrs., 1941—, geologist Central Concrete Lab., U.S. Mil. Acad., 1941-42, Mt. Vernon, N.Y., 1942-43; supervisory research civil engr., chief engring. scis. br., concrete lab. Waterways Expt. Sta., Vicksburg, Miss., 1946-65, asst. chief concrete lab., 1965-66, chief, 1966-76, acting chief structures lab., 1978—; research asso. Fla. Dept. Agr. and Consumer Services, 1968—; charter mem. U.S. Sr. Exec. Service, 1979—; research asso. Miss. Mus. Natural Scis., 1979—; chmn. concrete div., dept. materials and constrn. Transp. Research Bd., Nat. Acad. Scis.-NRC, 1963-69; mem. U.S. Com. of Internat. Commn. Large Dams, 1959—; lectr. Purdue U., 1961, U. Notre Dame, 1964, Mass. Inst. Tech., 1966, Clemson U., 1967; Henry M. Shaw lectr. N.C. State U., 1967, U. Wis., 1978, 79; Stanton Walker lectr. U. Md., 1969, Edgar Marburg lectr. ASTM, 1970; mem. 4th, 5th and 6th internat. symposia chemistry cement Internat. Symposium Movement Water in Porous Bodies, Paris, 1964. Meritorious Civilian Service award Dept. Army, 1965, Exceptional Civilian Service award, 1968; Roy C. Crum Distinguished Service award Transp. Research Bd., 1966. Fellow AAAS, ASTM (sec. com. C-9 1952-60, chmn. 1960-66; chmn. com. C-1 1968-74, chmn. com. E-39 1973-75; dir. 1970-73, v.p. 1973-75, pres. 1975-76; Award of Merit 1959, Sanford E. Thompson award 1961, Frank E. Richart award 1972); mem. Am. Concrete Inst. (pres. 1964, Henry C. Turner medal 1973, Charles S. Whitney medal 1974), Natural Hist. Soc. Md., Orleans County (Vt.) Hist. Soc., Soc. Petroleum Engrs., Lepidopterists Soc., Miss. Acad. Sci., Am. Inst. Biol. Scis., Miss. Gem and Mineral Soc., Am. Mus. Natural History (hon. mem. 1968, hon. patron 1974, research asso. 1979—), Am. Inst. Mining, Metall. and Petroleum Engrs., Phi Beta Kappa, Sigma Xi. Co-author: Butterflies of Mississippi, 1958. Editor: Handbook for Concrete and Cement, 1942, 49; also quar. supplements, 1949—. Address: 213 Mt Salus Dr Clinton MS 39056

MATHER, CHARLES HAROLD, ins. exec.; b. Wabash County, Ind., Mar. 5, 1927; s. Harold S. and Lois E. (Bates) M.; student Manchester Coll., 1948-49; B.S., U. Oreg., 1951; m. Betty J. Settergren, June 19, 1948; children—Jonathan C., Sarah E., Kathleen A., Susan J. With Cole, Clark & Cunningham, Inc., 1951— (merged with Rollins Burdick Hunter Co. 1971), pres., chief operating officer, Chgo., 1975-78, pres., chief exec. officer, 1978—. Served with USNR, 1945-46. Clubs: Chgo., GlenView, Metropolitan, Arlington, Portland Golf, Pinnacle. Office: 10 S Riverside Plaza Chicago IL 60606

MATHER, JEAN PAUL, educator; b. Del Norte, Colo., Dec. 15, 1914; s. John Bruce and Leona Hawie (Coe) M.; student U. Colo., 1932-35; B.S.C. U. Denver, 1937, M.B.A., 1948; student U. Chgo., 1939; M.A., Princeton, 1951; LL.D., Am. Internat. Coll., 1955, Amherst Coll., 1956, Northeastern U., 1958, U. R.I., 1960, U. Hokkaido, 1963, U. Mass., 1974; D.Sc., Lowell Technol. Inst. 1955; Litt.D., Lesley Coll., 1958; m. Marie Lorraine Wick, Mar. 1, 1936; children—Shirley Jeanne, Barbara Lorraine. Instr. economics Colo. Sch. Mines, 1938-39, asst. prof., 1939-43; instr. econs. U. Denver, 1946-47, asst. prof. econs. and statistics, dir. curriculum and instrn., 1947-48; lectr. Woodrow Wilson Sch. Pub. and Internat. Affairs, Princeton, 1948-51, research asso. Princeton Surveys State and Local Govt., 1948-51; staff asso., asst. treas. Am. Council Edn., Washington, 1951-53; provost U. Mass., Amherst, 1953-54, pres., 1954-60; pres. Coll. Testing Program, 1960-62; cons. N.J. State Tax Commn., 1948-51, Mass. State Tax Commn., 1949-50, Nat. Found. Consumer Credit, Washington, 1951-52, VA, 1958-61; asst. gen. mgr. Purdue Research Found., Lafayette, Ind., 1962-63, v.p., gen. mgr., 1963-64; exec. v.p. Univ. City Sci. Center, Phila., 1964-67, pres., 1967-69; head dept. mineral economics Colo. Sch. of Mines, Golden, 1969—; dir. Fidelity Mut. Growth Fund; cons. Maine Commn. Higher Edn., 1966. Served as lt. USNR, 1943-46. Fellow Am. Acad Arts and Sci.; mem. Beta Gamma Sigma, Phi Eta Sigma, Alpha Kappa Psi, Blue Key. Democrat. Conglist. Home: 23715 Waynes Way Golden CO 80401

MATHER, JOHN RUSSELL, climatologist, educator; b. Boston, Oct. 9, 1923; s. John and Mabelle (Russell) M.; B.A., Williams Coll., 1945; B.S. in Meteorology, Mass. Inst. Tech., 1947, M.S., 1948; Ph.D. in Geography-Climatology, Johns Hopkins, 1951; m. Amy L. Nelson; 1946; children—Susan, Thomas, Ellen. Research asso., climatologist Lab. Climatology, Seabrook, N.J., 1948-54, prin. research scientist, Centerton, N.J., 1954-63; pres. Lab. Climatology, C.W. Thornthwaite Assos., Centerton, 1963-72; asst. prof. Johns Hopkins, 1951-53; asso. prof. climatology Drexel Inst. Tech., Phila., 1957-60; prof. geography U. Del., Newark, 1961—, chmn. dept. geography, 1966—. Vis. lectr. geography U. Chgo., 1957-61. Mem. Am. Meteorol. Soc., Assn. Am. Geographers, Am. Geog. Soc., Am. Geophys. Union, Tau Beta Pi, Phi Kappa Phi. Author 2 books on applied climatology. Contbr. numerous articles to tech. jours. Contributed to concept of potential evapotranspiration, its measurement, use in climatic water balance; application of climatic water balance to studies in agr., hydrology, applied climatology. Home: RD 3 Elmer NJ 08318 Office: Dept Geography U Del Newark DE 19711

MATHER, KATHARINE, geologist; b. Ithaca, N.Y., Oct. 21, 1916; d. Walter Hamlin and Katharine Emily (Selden) Kniskern; A.B. in Geology, Bryn Mawr Coll., 1937; student Sch. Higher Studies, Johns Hopkins, 1937-40; D.Sc. (hon.), Clarkson Coll., 1978; m. Bryant Mather, Mar. 27, 1940. Research asst. Johns Hopkins, 1939; research asso. Field Mus. Natural History, Chgo., 1940-41; geologist Corps Engrs., U.S. Army, 1942—, assigned Waterways Expt. Sta., Vicksburg, Miss., 1946—, chief petrography and X-ray br., engring. scis. div., concrete lab., 1947-76, chief engring. scis. div., 1976—. Mem. Internat. Symposia Chemistry Cement, 1960, 68, 4th Internat. Congress Non-Destructive Testing, 1963; mem., chmn. tech. coms. Transp. Research Bd. of Nat. Acad. Scis.-NRC; mem. U.S. panel Tech. Coop. Program. Recipient Exceptional Service award Sec. Army, 1962; Fed. Woman's award, 1963; Disting. Civilian Service award Sec. Def., 1964. Fellow Mineral. Soc. Am., Am. Concrete Inst. (co-recipient Wason Research medal 1955; dir. 1968—); life mem. Mineral. Soc. London; mem. Soc. Mining Engrs. (hon.), ASTM (Sanford E. Thompson award 1952), Am. Ceramic Soc., Am. Crystallographic Assn., Geochem. Soc., Am. Geophys. Union, Soc. Econ. Paleontologists and Mineralogists, Clay Minerals Soc. (sec. 1964-67, pres. 1973), Clay Sci. Soc. Japan, Alumnae Assn. Bryn Mawr Coll. (past dist. councillor), Sigma Xi. Co-author: Butterflies of Mississippi, 1958. Bd. dirs., editor Jour. Miss. Acad. Scis., 1960-66. Address: 213 Mt Salus Dr Clinton MS 39056

MATHER, NORMAN WELLS, educator; b. Upland, Calif., Apr. 29, 1914; s. Wiley Wells and Glenn (Shaw) M.; student Chaffey Jr. Coll., 1932-33; B.S. in Elec. Engring., U. Calif. at Berkeley, 1936; M.S. in Engring., Princeton, 1947; m. Mary Adele Clark, June 10, 1939; children—John Norman, Margaret Ann. Engr. Otis Elevator Co., San Francisco, Los Angeles, also Yonkers, N.Y., 1936-42; mem. faculty Princeton, 1946—, asso. prof. elec. engring., 1947-58, prof., 1958—, asso. Project Matterhorn, 1952-61; asso. Plasma Physics Lab., 1961-71. Served from ensign to lt. USNR, 1942-46. Mem. I.E.E.E., Assn. Princeton Grad. Alumni (sec.-treas., 1963-71), Sigma Xi, Eta Kappa Nu. Address: 522 Prospect Ave Princeton NJ 08540

MATHER, WILLIAM GREEN, JR., clergyman, former educator; b. Chgo., July 15, 1901; s. William Green and Julia (King) M.; B.S., Denison U., 1924; B.D., Rochester Theol. Sem., 1927; M.S., Cornell U., 1934; Ph.D., 1936; m. Bertha Gladys Williams, Dec. 24, 1934; children—William Green II, Eleanor Julia (Mrs. Frank P. Saul). Ordained to ministry Baptist Ch., 1927; was pastor, Cuba, N.Y., 1928-31; head dept. sociology and econs. Franklin Coll., 1934-42; prof. sociology DePauw U., 1942-45; prof. rural sociology Pa. State U., 1945-54, head dept. sociology and anthropology, 1954-62, research prof. sociology, 1962-69, prof. emeritus, 1969—. Past pres. Pa. Baptist Conv., chmn. council on Christian social progress. Am. Bapt. Conv.; chmn. Pa. Action Com. for Clean Air. Bd. dirs. Pa. Tb and Respiratory Disease Soc. Recipient gold medal Pa. Sabbath Sch. Assn., citation Pa. Rural Safety Council, Benjamin Rush med. award Centre County, McKay Donkin award Pa. State U., Alumni citation Denison U., 1974. Mem. Am. Sociol. Assn., Am. Pub. Health Assn., Am. Rural Sociology Assn., Pa. Health Council (sec., past pres.), Pa. Pub. Health Assn. (past pres.), Royal Soc. Health (Eng.), AAUP (faculty welfare chmn. Pa. div.), Phi Beta Kappa, Sigma Xi, Pi Gamma Mu, Alpha Kappa Delta. Home: 2304 S Colonial Dr Melbourne FL 32901. *I have tried to proceed on the conviction that the true goal of research is the betterment of the lot of humankind.*

MATHERS, WILLIAM HARRIS, lawyer; b. Newport, R.I., Aug. 27, 1914; s. Howard and Margaret I. (Harris) M.; A.B., Dartmouth, 1935; J.D., Yale, 1938; m. Myra T. Martin, Jan. 17, 1942; children—William Martin, Michael Harris, John Grinnell, Myra, Ursula. Admitted to N.Y. bar, 1940; with Milbank, Tweed & Hope, 1938-48; mem. Milbank, Tweed, Hope & Hadley, 1948-57; v.p., sec., dir. Yale & Towne Mfg. Co., Stamford, Conn., 1957-60; partner firm Chadbourne, Parke, Whiteside & Wolff, 1960-75; sr. v.p., gen. counsel United Brands Co., 1975—. Mayor Village of Cove Neck, N.Y. Trustee Barnard Coll., 1958-69. Served as pvt. to maj. U.S. Army, 1942-46. Mem. Am., N.Y. State, Nassau County bar assns., Assn. Bar City of N.Y., New Eng. Soc. in City of N.Y., Casque and Gauntlet, Corbey Court, Phi Beta Kappa, Psi Upsilon. Clubs: Down Town Assn., Piping Rock, Seminole Golf, N.Y. Yacht, Yale (N.Y.C.); Somerset (Boston); Cold Spring Harbor Beach. Home: Cove Neck Rd Cove Neck Oyster Bay NY 11771 Office: 1271 Ave of Americas New York NY 10020

MATHES, RACHEL CLARKE, soprano, educator; b. Atlanta, Mar. 14, 1941; d. Frank Alfred and Jacqueline Eugenia (Woolfolk) M.; B.A. (Fulbright scholar), Birmingham-So. Coll., 1962; postgrad. Akademie F Musik U Darst Kunst, Vienna, Austria, 1962-63. Leading soprano Stadttheater, Basel, Switzerland, 1965-66, Deutsche Oper Am Rhein, Dusseldorf, W. Ger., 1966-71, Stadttheater, Bonn, W. Ger., 1971-72; appeared opera houses throughout Europe and Am., 1972-74; debut Met. Opera, N.Y.C., 1974, N.Y. State Theater, N.Y.C., 1975; prof. music Birmingham-So. Coll., 1977—; regional judge Met. Opera Auditions. Bd. dirs. Birmingham Civic Opera. Birmingham Music Club Auditions winner, 1960; Met. Regional Auditions winner, 1962; Friday Morning Music Club Auditions winner, 1962; Balt. Opera Auditions winner, 1965; Alpha Chi Omega Achievement award, 1978. Mem. Am. Guild Mus. Artists, Am. Music Teachers Assn., Nat. Assn. Tchrs. Singing, AAUW, Coll. Music Soc., Inc., Ala. Music Tchrs. Assn., Music Tchrs. Nat. Assn., Inc. Presbyterian. Office: Box A-33 Birmingham Southern College 800 8th Ave W Birmingham AL 35204. *Faith in God, belief in one's own ability, and total commitment to develop that ability to the fullest, as well as loving and supportive parents, family, and friends are needed for success in one's chosen career. Even more important are a sense of humor and an enormous amount of work.*

MATHESON, KENNETH WILLIAM, lawyer; b. Cabano, Que., Can., May 23, 1909; s. William and Mame (Wallace) M.; B.A., Dalhousie U., 1930, LL.B., 1933; m. Anita Marie Gagnon, Nov. 8, 1941; 1 son, James Neal. With Fraser Cos. Ltd., Edmundston, N.B., Can., 1933-68, with asso. cos., 1933-37, secretarial dept., 1937-41, organizer, dir. legal dept., 1941-49, asst. to gen. mgr., 1949-60, v.p., dir., 1960-64, sr. v.p., dir., 1965-68; dep. chmn. Appeals Tribunal, 1968-72. Trustee Student Aid Fund Inc. Mem. N.B. Barristers Soc. Home: 16 Lawson St Edmundston NB E3V 1Z4 Canada

MATHESON, MAX SMITH, research chemist; b. McGill, Nev., May 24, 1913; s. Henry Thompson and Ethel (Smith) M.; A.B., U. Utah, 1936; M.S., Brown U., 1938; Ph.D. in Chemistry, U. Rochester, 1940; m. Gladys H. Mulchahey, Sept. 30, 1939; m. 2d, Georgine M. Sims, April 29, 1967; children—Linda Jean, Marc Edward. Research chemist gen. labs. U.S. Rubber Co., Passaic, N.J., 1940-50; asso. chemist Argonne (Ill.) Nat. Lab., 1950-52, sr. chemist, 1952-78, cons., 1978—; dir. chemistry div., 1965-71; chmn. Gordon Conf. Radiation Chemistry, 1960; Guggenheim fellow Inst. du Radium and Lab. de Chimie Physique, Paris, 1960-61; vis. prof. Hebrew U., Jerusalem, 1972. Mem. AAAS, Am. Chem. Soc., Am. Phys. Soc., Chem. Soc. Britain, Radiation Research Soc. (council 1975-78), Sci. Research Soc. Am., Phi Beta Kappa, Sigma Xi, Phi Kappa Phi. Contbr. articles on photo and radiation chemistry and kinetics to profl. jours. Home: 611 E Taylor Ln Unit H Murray UT 84107

MATHESON, MURRAY, actor; b. Casterton, Victoria, Australia, July 1, 1912; s. Kenneth Murray and Ethel Sunderland (Barrett) M.; student Sandord State Sch., 1918-26; Came to U.S., 1956. First appeared on stage in Dangerous Corner, Melbourne, Australia, 1933, later appeared in numerous plays in London, Eng. and throughout Europe; Broadway debut in The Relapse, 1950, also appeared in Escapade, 1953, Electra, 1959, Harlequinade, 1959, Oh, Kay, 1960; appeared in numerous films, 1940—, including Way to the Stars, 1940, Journey Together, 1945, The Fool and the Princess, 1946, Hurricane Smith, 1952, Plymouth Adventure, 1952, Botany Bay, 1953, Flight to Tangier, 1953, King of the Khyber Rifles, 1953, The Bamboo Prison, 1954, Love Is a Many-Splendored Thing, 1955, Wall of Noise, 1963, Signpost to Murder, 1964, How to Succeed in Business, 1967, Star, 1968, Rabbit Test, 1978; appeared in numerous TV films, including The Cocktail Party, 1949, Archers Ring, 1959, The Yellow Sedan, 1959, Patience, 1960, Perils of Penrose, 1960, The Poisoner, 1960, Letter to a Lover, 1961, A Husband for Oona, 1961, The Fugitive, 1962, The Apple Cart, 1962, The Case of the Accosted Accountant, 1963, Ticket to Alaska, 1963, Knights Gambit, 1964, Murder Case, 1964, Laburnum Grove, 1964, also on Twilight Zone, Sam Benedict, Naked City, Route 66, The Islanders, Laramie, Tall Man, Banacek, McMillan and Wife, Marcus Welby, Lucy Show, Hec Ramsay, Circle of Fear, Mannix, Vegas, Galactica, Charlie's Angels, others. Served with RAF, 1940-45. Mem. A.F.T.R.A., Actors Equity Assn., Screen Actors Guild. Home: Otter Lake Parry Sound ON Canada Office: PO Box 5758 Santa Monica CA 90405

MATHESON, SCOTT MILNE, gov. Utah; b. Chgo., Jan. 9, 1929; s. Scott Milne and Adele (Adams) M.; B.S. in Polit. Sci., U. Utah, 1950; J.D., Stanford U., 1952; m. Norma Warenski, Aug. 25, 1951; children—Scott Milne, Mary Lee, James David, Thomas Douglas. Admitted to Utah bar, 1953; practice in Iron County, Utah, 1953-54; atty. Parowan City (Utah), 1953-54; dep. atty. Iron County, 1953-54; law clk. to U.S. dist. judge, 1954-56; pvt. practice, Salt Lake City, 1956-58; dep. atty. Salt Lake County, 1956-57; asst. gen. atty., then gen. atty. Union Pacific R.R., 1958-69, gen. solicitor, 1972-76; asst. gen. counsel Anaconda Co., 1970-72; gov. Utah, 1977—; lectr. Coll. So. Utah, 1953-54; chmn. Utah R.R. Assn., 1972-76. Pres. Utah Young Democrats, U. Utah, 1948; mem. Utah Water Pollution Com., 1970-76. Mem. Am. Bar Assn., (chmn. spl. com. youth edn. for citizenship), Am. Judicature Soc. (dir.), Utah State Bar (pres. 1968-69; del. 1973-76), Utah Tennis Assn. Mormon. Clubs: Rotary, Alta, Ft. Douglas Hidden Valley, Salt Lake Swimming and Tennis. Home: 2253 Hubbard Ave Salt Lake City UT 84104 Office: 210 Capitol Bldg Salt Lake City UT 84114

MATHESON, WALLACE ALEXANDER, publisher; b. Montreal, Que., Can., July 29, 1931; s. Alexander G. and Grace deF. (Wallace) M.; B.A., Acadia U., 1953; m. Martha Ann Driscoll, May 25, 1957; children—Heather Ann, Alexander James, Martha Jean. Canadian field rep. coll. div. Prentice-Hall, Inc., Englewood Cliffs, N.J., 1953-58, dir., 1976—, Can. dist. mgr., 1958-61, v.p. Prentice-Hall of Can., Ltd., 1961-65, pres., 1965—, also dir. Bd. govs. Canadian Copyright Inst., 1973—; bd. dirs. Montreal Internat. Book Fair, 1973—. Mem. Canadian Book Pubs. Council (past v.p., pres. 1972-73), Canadian Library Exhibitors Assn. (pres. 1966-68, dir. 1968-70). Mason. Home: 8 Palomino Crescent Willowdale ON M2K 1W1 Canada Office: 1870 Birchmount Rd Scarborough ON M1P 2J7 Canada

MATHESON, WILLIAM ANGUS, mfr., business cons., dir. pub. relations; b. Oregon City, Ore., Aug. 30, 1895; s. Angus and Elizabeth (Williams) M.; student pub. schs.; m. Maude Moore, Dec. 13, 1917; 1 son, William Angus. Served in World War I May 1917-19. Sales mgr. Mt. Hood Ice Cream Co., Portland, Oreg., 1921-23, Power Plant Engrng. Co., 1923-26; sales mgr. Hart Oil Burner Corp., Phila., 1926-30; br. mgr. Williams Oil-O-Matic Heating Corp., Chgo., 1930-36, N.Y.C. br. mgr. GMSC Delco Appliance Div., 1936-40, v.p., asst. to pres. Williams Oil-O-Matic Heating Corp., 1940; dir. 1940-44, pres. 1944-45; became mgr. Williams Oil-O-Matic div. (Bloomington, Ill.), Eureka Williams Corp. (merger 1945), 1945; gen. sales mgr. Lustron Corp., 1949-50; bus. cons., dir. dealer relations Am. Bildrok Co., Chgo.; pres. Portable Elevator Mfg. Co., Bloomington, 1952-75; pres. Amco div. Dynamics Corp. Am., 1970-75, asst. to pres. parent corp., 1975—; v.p., dir. Implement Splty. Co., Inc., St. Louis; dir. Am. Foundry & Furnance, Nat. Bank of Bloomington, Lindsay Bros. Co., Mpls., Capital Equipment Co. Treas., Brokaw Hosp., chmn. bd., 1974-75; mem. exec. com. Oil Heat Inst. Am., Inc. (past pres.). Chmn., McLean County Savs. Bond Com.; nat. asso. Boys Clubs Am. Chmn., McLean County United Republican Fund; v.p. United Republican Fund. Ill. Mem. Farm Equipment Mfrs. Assn. (pres. 1956-57, dir.), Bloomington Assn. Commerce (pres. 1965), Ill. Mfrs. Assn. (dir.). Republican. Presbyn. Mason, Rotarian. Clubs: Union League, Chicago Athletic (Chgo.); Bloomington Country, Bloomington (Ill.); Ill. Farm Equipment (pres. 1964). Author: The Selling Man. Home: 15 Country Club Pl Bloomington IL 61701 Office: Portable Elevator Mfg Co Bloomington IL 61701

MATHESON, WILLIAM LYON, lawyer, utility co. exec.; b. Coeburn, Va., Dec. 5, 1924; s. Julius Daniel and Ruth Steele Lyon M.; student Emory U., 1946-47; A.B., Mercer U., 1944; LL.B., U. Va., 1950; m. Katrina B. Hickox; children—Katherine, William Lyon, Alline, Thornton; m. 2d, Marjorie H. Anderson, Nov. 26, 1977. Admitted to N.Y. State bar, 1951; asso. firm Patterson, Belknap & Webb, N.Y.C., 1950-57; asso. Wertheim & Co., investments, N.Y.C., 1957-58; partner Webster & Sheffield, N.Y.C., 1959-65; individual practice law, N.Y.C., 1965—; chmn. bd., treas. Mich. Gas Utilities Co., Monroe, 1959—. Bd. dirs. Madison Sq. Boys' Club, N.Y.C., 1958-76, asso. mem. bd. dirs., 1977—; trustee Police Athletic League, N.Y.C., 1962—. Served to lt. (j.g.) USN, 1942-46. Mem. Assn. Bar City N.Y., Am. Gas Assn. Democrat. Clubs: Links (N.Y.C.); Piping Rock (Locust Valley, N.Y.); Meadow Brook (Jericho, N.Y.); Nat. Golf Links (Southampton, N.Y.); Farmington Country (Charlottesville, Va.); Seminole Golf (North Palm Beach, Fla.). Home: 870 UN Plaza New York NY 10017 also 11188 Turtle Beach Rd North Palm Beach FL 33408 Office: 277 Park Ave Suite 4701 New York NY 10017

MATHEWS, ARTHUR FRANCIS, lawyer; b. Herkimer, N.Y., Feb. 27, 1938; s. Glen and Tessa (Kraszewski) Wright; B.A., Union Coll., 1959; LL.B., Albany Law Sch., 1962, J.D., 1965; LL.M., Georgetown Law Center, 1964; children by previous marriage—Scott, Susan, Clarissa; m. Nancy C. Crisman, Jan. 4, 1980. Admitted to D.C. bar, 1962, N.Y. State bar, 1962, U.S. Supreme Ct. bar, 1966; with SEC, Washington, 1962-69, asst. dir. criminal reference, 1967-69, dep. asso. dir. enforcement, 1969—; partner firm Wilmer & Pickering and predecessor, Washington, 1969—; adj. prof. law George Washington Law Center, 1969—, Cornell U. Law Sch., 1976-77, Georgetown U. Law Center, 1977—, Am. U. Law Sch., 1978; mem. Georgetown Law Center Continuing Legal Edn. Adv. Bd. Served with USAR, 1955-62. Mem. Am. Bar Assn., Fed. Bar Assn. (Outstanding Younger Fed. Lawyer award 1969). Author books, the most recent being: (with others) The Foreign Corrupt Practices Act of 1977—Do You Know This Act Covers Domestic Business Activities?, 1978; (with A. Levenson) Negotiating SEC Consent Decrees—Targets and Tactics for Settling Civil Injunctive Actions, 1979; SEC Enforcement and White Collar Crimes, 1979; contbr. articles to profl. publs. Home: 4508 17th St NW Washington DC 20011 Office: Wilmer & Pickering 1666 K St NW Washington DC 20006

MATHEWS, CARMEN SYLVA, actress; b. Phila., May 8, 1918; d. Albert Barnes and Matilde (Keller) Mathews; student Bennet Jr. Coll., 1936-38, Royal Acad. Dramatic Art (Eng.), 1938, 39. Appeared numerous stage plays, roles include Ophelia in Hamlet, Queen in Richard II, Lady Mortimer in Henry IV, Varya in Cherry Orchard, 1943, Violet in Man and Superman, 1945, Mrs. Sullen in Beaux Strategem, 1945, Miss Ronberry in Corn is Green, 1946, Miss Neville in She Stooped to Conquer, 1946, Madame Ducotel in My Three Angels, 1952, Mary in Holiday for Lovers, 1957, Candida in Shaw's Candida, 1958, Eileen in Man in Dogsuit, 1958, Lady Utterword in Heartbreak House, 1959-60, appeared as Contessa in Candide, musical adapted from Voltaire, 1956, Ceil in Night Life, 1962, Maria in Lorenzo, 1963, Louise in Zenda, 1963, Queen, in Hamlet, 1964, Grandma Hutto in musical adaptation The Yearling, 1965, Edna in A Delicate Balance, 1966, Bathsheeba in I'm Solomon, 1967-68, Constance in Dear World, 1968; Fraulein Schneider in Cabaret, 1970, Wife in All Over, 70, Grandma in Ring around the Bathtub, 1971, Mrs. Boatwright in movie Sounder, 1971, Gloriani in Ambassador, 1972, Mrs. Aigreville in In Fashion, 1973, Mamita in Gigi, 1974, Arietta in Morning's at Seven, 1974, Mrs. Higgins in Pygmalion, 1975, A Rage to Live (movie), Rabbit Run, 1969, Mother in Children, 1976, Mrs. Ellis in The Autumn Garden, 1976, Madame Arcati in Blithe Spirit, 1977, Mrs. Tilford in The Children's Hour, Catherine in Arms and the Man, 1979; also various dramatic TV shows. Records books Am. Found. for Blind. Home: West Redding CT 06896 also 400 E 52d St New York NY 10022

MATHEWS, CHARLES DRAYTON, lawyer, judge; b. Trickham, Tex., Sept. 16, 1912; s. Luke G. and Ethyl R. (Featherston) M.; LL.B. with highest honors, U. Tex., 1937; m. Billy N. Eubanks, May 29, 1943; 1 dau., Betty. Admitted to Tex. bar, 1937; practiced in Lubbock, Tex., 1937-41; legal examiner, chief law enforcement officer Tex. R.R. Commn., 1941-42; asst. atty. gen. Tex., Austin, 1947-50, 1st asst. atty. gen., 1950-52; sr. partner firm Looney, Clark, Moorhead and Mathews, Austin, 1952-61, v.p., gen. counsel, sec. Red Ball Motor Freights, Inc., Dallas, 1961-67, pres., 1967—, also dir.; now judge 200th Dist. Ct., Austin. Mem. Tex. Bd. Ins., 1969—. Bd. dirs. Tex. Technol. Coll., 1962-65. Served to capt. AUS, 1942-46. Mem. Am. Bar Assn., State Bar Tex., also numerous transp. assns., Order of Coif, Chancellors. Author: History of the Anti-Trust Laws of Texas, 1950. Mem. editorial staff Tex. Law Rev., 1936-37. Home: 7611 Rustling Rd Austin TX 78731

MATHEWS, CHRISTOPHER KING, biochemist; b. N.Y.C., May 5, 1937; s. Frank Pelletreau and Alison Barstow (Murphy) M.; B.A. in Chemistry, Reed Coll., 1958; Ph.D. in Biochemistry (USPHS fellow), U. Wash., 1962; m. Catherine Anne Zitcer, June 19, 1960; children—Lawrence Stuart, Anne Catherine. USPHS postdoctoral fellow in biochemistry U. Pa., 1962-63; asst. prof. biology Yale U., 1964-67; asso. prof. biochemistry U. Ariz. Coll. Medicine, 1967-73, prof. biochemistry, 1973-77; prof., chmn. dept. biochemistry and biophysics Oreg. State U., 1978—; mem. microbial chemistry study sect. NIH. Mem. Democratic Precinct Com., Tucson, 1970-77; scoutmaster, com. chmn. Catalina council Boy Scouts Am., 1971-75. Am. Cancer soc. scholar grantee, 1973-74; USPHS research grantee, 1964—; Am. Heart Assn. grantee, 1968-78. Mem. Am. Soc. Biol. Chemists, Am. Soc. Microbiology, Am. Chem. Soc., Am. Soc. Cell Biology, AAAS, AAUP (v.p. chpt. 1971-72, pres. chpt. 1972-73), Sierra Club, Nat. Wilderness Soc., Defenders Wildlife, Nat. Audubon Soc., Nat. Wildlife Fedn., Zero Population Growth. Author: Bacteriophage Biochemistry, 1971; contbr. numerous articles on nucleotide and nucleic acid metabolism, biochemistry of virus replication, and regulation of cellular metabolism to profl. jours.; editorial bd. Jour. Virology, 1970—, Archives Biochemistry and Biophysics, 1973—. Home: 3336 SW Willamette Ave Corvallis OR 97330 Office: Dept Biochemistry and Biophysics Oreg State U Corvallis OR 97331

MATHEWS, ELMER CLARENCE, univ. dean; b. Potsdam, N.Y., Jan. 6, 1917; s. George B. and Daisy (O'Neal) M.; diploma Potsdam Normal Sch., 1940; B.S., N.Y. State Coll. Tchrs., Albany, 1941; M.A., Columbia Tchrs. Coll., 1947, Ed.D., 1956; m. Janet Busacker, Sept. 20, 1942; children—Ann Christine, Catherine Dale, Susan Janet. Tchr. jr. high social studies Jefferson Sch., South Schenectady, N.Y., 1941-42; tchr. secondary social studies Martin Van Buren High Sch., Kinderhook, 1946-47; mem. faculty N.Y. State Coll. Tchrs., Albany, 1947-60, asso. dean, 1959-60; dean personnel adminstrn. SUNY at Albany, 1960—. Served to capt. C.E., AUS, 1942-46; col. Res. ret. Mem. Schenectady Pipe Band, St. Andrews Soc. Home: 54 E Knightsbridge Guilderland NY 12084 Office: 1400 Washington Ave Albany NY 12222

MATHEWS, FERRIN YOUNG, lawyer; b. Florala, Ala., July 10, 1924; s. Murray Hilliard and Oliva Mae (Womble) M.; student U. Ala., 1942-43; B.S. in Textile Engring., Ga. Tech. U., 1948; J.D., Emory U., 1951; m. Carol Ann Barge, Mar. 20, 1949; children—Holly Ferralynn, Ferrin Young. Textile engr. Reeves Bros. Inc., 1948; instr. So. Tech. Inst., 1949-50; admitted to Ga. bar; practiced in Atlanta, 1951-56; asso. city atty. Atlanta, 1956-59, 63-65, first asst. city atty., 1965-76, city atty., 1976—; arbitrator Fed. Mediation and Conciliation Service, Am. Arbitration Assn., 1961—; spl. master Fla. Pub. Employees Relations Commn., 1974—. Served with USN, 1943-46. Mem. Am., Atlanta bar assns., Lawyers Club Atlanta, Am. Judicature Soc., Old War Horse Lawyers Club, Phi Alpha Delta. Democrat. Methodist. Club: Roswell Country. Home: 345 7th St Unit 3 Atlanta GA 30309 Office: 2000 Fulton Nat Bank Bldg Atlanta GA 30303

MATHEWS, GEORGE DONALD, oil co. exec.; b. Evanston, Ill., Sept. 5, 1927; s. George Clifford and Mista Viglenna (McNaughton) M.; student U. Wis.-Madison, 1945, Ind. State U., 1945—, Stevens Inst. Tech., 1945-46; B.S. in Geology, U. Wyo., 1949; m. Dawn Keller Dally, Apr. 8, 1950; children—Michael Reed, Mista Maureen. With Superior Oil Co., 1949-51, 52—, dist. geologist, Albuquerque and Farmington, N.Mex., 1960-62, Midland, Tex., 1962-69, regional geologist fgn. exploration, Houston, 1969-72, sr. v.p. exploration, Houston, 1972-76, also dir.; oil and gas cons., Houston, 1976-79; exec. v.p. H.H.G. Oil Co., Midland, Tex., 1979—. Served with USNR, 1945-46, 51-52; Korea. Mem. Am. Assn. Petroleum Geologists, Houston, West Tex. geol. socs., Petroleum Club Houston. Club: Inwood Forest Country. Home: 3209 Stanolind Midland TX 79701 Office: HHG Oil Co Box 2267 Midland TX 79701

MATHEWS, HARLAN, state ofcl.; b. Sumiton, Ala., Jan. 17, 1927; s. John William and Lillia Mae (Young) M.; B.A., Jacksonville (Ala.) State U., 1949; M.A. in Public Adminstrn., Vanderbilt U., 1950; LL.B., YMCA Law Sch., Nashville, 1962; m. Patsy Jones, May 15, 1973; children—Stanley, Lester K. With State of Tenn., 1950—, commr. dept. fin. and adminstrn., 1961-71; with Amcon, Internat., Memphis, 1971-73; treas. State of Tenn., 1974—; admitted to Tenn. bar, 1962; dir. Murray Guard, Inc. Served with USNR, 1944-46. Mem. Nat. Mcpl. Fin. Officers Assn., Nat. Assn. State Auditors, Comptrollers and Treasurers, Nat. Assn. State Treasurers (past pres.), Tenn. Mcpl. Fin. Officers Assn. Democrat. Baptist. Club: Nashville City, Capitol, Capitol Hill (Nashville). Home: 184 Boxwood Dr Franklin TN 37064 Office: Treasurer's Office State Capitol Nashville TN 37219

MATHEWS, JAMES KENNETH, bishop; b. Breezewood, Pa., Feb. 10, 1913; s. James Davenport and Laura Mae (Wilson) M.; A.B., Lincoln Meml. U., 1934, D.D. (hon.), 1954; S.T.B., N.Y. Theol. Sem., 1937; grad. student Boston U. Sch. Theology, 1937-38; spl. student Cambridge (Eng.) U., 1955; Ph.D., Columbia, 1957; D.D., Wesleyan U., 1965, Colby Coll., 1971; L.H.D., Lycoming Coll., 1966, Ohio Wesleyan U., 1969, Norwich U., 1970; m. Eunice Jones, June 1, 1940; children—Anne, Janice (Mrs. William R. Stromsem), James Stanley. Ordained to ministry Methodist Ch., 1938; missionary to India, 1938-42; asso. sec. div. world missions Meth. Bd. Missions, 1946-52, asso. gen. sec., 1952-60; bishop United Meth. Ch., resident in Boston Area, 1960-72, Washington area, 1972—; Fondren lectr. So. Meth. U., 1962; Lowell lectr. Boston U., 1964, Jones lectr., 1976; Gray lectr. Duke, 1967; Showers lectr. Lebanon Valley Coll., 1977; sec. Council of Bishops; mem. Bd. Higher Edn. and Ministry, Gen. Council on Ministries, Gen. Commn. Archives and History; mem. governing bd. Nat. Council Chs.; mem. exec. com. World Meth. Council; mem. central com. World Council Chs.; chmn. United Christian Ashrams. Trustee, Boston U., also bd. visitors Sch. Theology; trustee Western Md. Coll., Wesley Coll., United Meth. Union, Morristown Coll., Samoan Heritage, Inc., Sibley Meml. Hosp., Asbury Meth. Home, Morgan Christian Center United Meth. Home, Providence, Nur Manzil Psychiat. Center, Lucknow, India; chmn. bd., trustee Am. U.; chmn. bd. dirs. Chs. Center for theology and Pub. Policy; chmn. trustees Santiago (Chile) Coll.; bd. govs., mem. exec. com. Wesley Theol. Sem.; pres. Nat. Coalition for Public Edn. and Religious Liberty; trustee, mem. exec. com. Internat. Councils Religion, Inc.; bd. dirs. Friends of WCC Inc., Wesley Found., U. Del. Served to maj. AUS, 1942-46. Club: Cosmos. Author: South of the Himalayas, 1955; To the End of the Earth, 1959; Eternal Values in a World of Change, 1960; A Church Truly Catholic, 1969; (with Eunice J. Mathews) Selections from E. Stanley Jones, 1972; also numerous articles. Home: 4120 48th St NW Washington DC 20016 Office: 100 Maryland Ave NE Room 400 Washington DC 20002

MATHEWS, JON, physicist; b. Los Angeles, Feb. 10, 1932; s. John H. and Grace (Logie) M.; B.A., Pomona Coll., 1952; Ph.D., Calif. Inst. Tech., 1957; m. Charlotte Dallett, June 10, 1952 (div. 1976); children—Valerie, Jancis, Richard Hays, William Salisbury; m. 2d, Jean Vontobel, Oct. 15, 1977. Mem. faculty Calif. Inst. Tech., Pasadena, 1957—, prof. physics, 1966—. Mem. Am. Phys. Soc., AAAS. Author: (with R.L. Walker) Mathematical Methods of

Physics, 1964; contbr. articles to profl. jours. Home: 130 S Wilson Ave Pasadena CA 91106 Office: 405-47 Physics Dept Calif Inst Tech 1201 E California Blvd Pasadena CA 91125

MATHEWS, KENNETH PINE, physician; b. Schenectady, Apr. 1, 1921; s. Raymond and Marguerite Elizabeth (Pine) M.; A.B., U. Mich., 1941, M.D., 1943; m. Alice Jean Elliott, Jan. 26, 1952 (dec.); children—Susan Kay, Ronald Elliott, Robert Pine; m. 2d, Winona Beatrice Rosenburg, Nov. 8, 1975. Intern, asst. resident, resident in medicine Univ. Hosp., Ann Arbor, Mich., 1943-45, 48-50; mem. faculty dept. medicine U. Mich. Med. Sch., 1950—, asso. prof. internal medicine, 1956-61, prof., 1961—, head div. allergy, 1967—; cons. Ann Arbor VA Hosp., Wayne County Gen. Hosp. Served to capt. M.C., AUS, 1946-48. Diplomate Am. Bd. Internal Medicine. Recipient Disting. Service award Am. Acad. Allergy, 1976. Mem. Am. Acad. Allergy (past pres.), A.C.P., Am. Assn. Immunologists, Central Soc. Clin. Research, Am. Fedn. Clin. Research, Am. Bd. Allergy and Immunology (sec.), Am. Thoracic Soc., Mich. Allergy Soc. (past pres.), Washtenaw County Med. Soc., Mich. State Med. Soc., Alpha Omega Alpha, Phi Beta Kappa. Co-author: A Manual of Clinical Allergy, 2d edit., 1967; editor Jour. Allergy and Clin. Immunology, 1968-72; contbr. numerous articles in field to profl. jours. Home: 1145 Aberdeen Dr Ann Arbor MI 48104 Office: Box 27 Univ of Mich Med Center Ann Arbor MI 48109

MATHEWS, RICHARD ALBERT, communications co. exec.; b. Trenton, N.J., Apr. 15, 1924; s. Albert Hart and Hazel Eva (Richards) M.; B.E.E., Rutgers U., 1948; m. G. Elizabeth Morss, July 19, 1946; children—JoAnn Mathews Higgins, Linda Jane Mathews Mitchell, Richard Hart, Theodore Morss. With N.J. Bell Telephone Co., 1948-50; with N.Y. Telephone Co., 1950-59, 59-61, 62-66, 72—, gen. mgr., Utica, 1959-61, v.p. mktg., 1962-64, v.p. planning, 1964-66, v.p. ops. and engring., 1972—; planning engr. AT&T, 1959, asst. v.p. mktg., 1961-62; gen. dir. Bell Telephone Labs., Piscataway, N.J., 1966-72. Registered profl. engr., N.Y. Mem. Phi Beta Kappa, Tau Beta Pi. Home: Ravine Lake Rd Bernardsville NJ 07924 Office: NY Telephone Co 1095 Ave of Americas New York City NY 10036

MATHEWS, ROBERT EDWARD, banker; b. Columbus, Ohio, Dec. 30, 1909; s. John Sherman and Mary (Stump) M.; student Ohio State U., 1931; m. Alice Nelleny, Sept. 10, 1934; children—Marianne, Robert Edward. With Ohio Nat. Bank, Columbus, 1929—, v.p., 1951-66, v.p., cashier, 1966-67, sr. v.p., dir., 1967—. Pres., Franklin County chpt. Am. Cancer Soc., also chmn. bd. trustees Ohio div.; bd. dirs. Ohio Regional Med. Program, Health Careers Ohio; mem. community adv. bd. Ohio State U. Cancer Research Center; bd. dirs., exec. dir. Vision Center of Central Ohio; Mem. Columbus C. of C., Res. City Bankers Assn., Am. Inst. Banking, Nat. Assn. Accountants, Bank Adminstrv. Inst. (past pres. Central Ohio chpt.), Aquinas, Ohio State U. alumni assns., Am. Mgmt. Assn. Roman Catholic. Clubs: Brookside Country (past pres.) (Worthington, Ohio); Columbus Atheltic, Columbus Maennerchor, Ambassadors National (Columbus); Scioto Country (Upper Arlington, Ohio). Home: 2299 Abington Rd Columbus OH 43221 Office: 51 N High St Columbus OH 43215

MATHEWS, WARREN EDWARD, aerospace co. exec.; b. Osborne, Kans., Nov. 10, 1921; s. Chester Ora and Selma Martha (Rader) M.; B.A. with high honors, Ohio Wesleyan U., 1942; B.S. in Elec. Engring., M.S. (Inst. scholar), Mass. Inst. Tech., 1944; Ph.D. in Physics cum laude (Howard Hughes fellow), Calif. Inst. Tech., 1953; m. Elizabeth Mills Uptegrove, Apr. 2, 1949; children—Carole Ellen, Margaret Mills, Gael Ann; m. 2d, Joyce Whitehead Larson, Apr. 23, 1971. Mem. tech. staff Bell Telephone Labs., Murray Hill, N.J., 1946-49, developed coupled transmission line theory of traveling wave amplifiers; mem. tech. staff Hughes Aircraft Co., Culver City, Calif., 1950-54, head advanced planning staff, 1954-57, corp. dir. planning, 1957-60, dir. infrared labs., 1960-67, asso. dir. research and devel. div., 1962-66, mgr. missile systems div., 1966-70, asso. mgr. systems divs., 1970-71, mgr. equipment engring. divs., 1971-74, asst. group exec. electro-optical and data systems group, 1974-75, corp. dir. product effectiveness, 1975—. Bd. dirs. Santa Barbara Research Center, 1960-66; nat. exec. com. Infrared Information Symposia, 1960-65; gen. chmn. WINCON, 1971; bd. govs. Electronic Industries Assn., 1976—. Composer, arranger, dir., performer choral music. Mem. Handel and Haydn Soc., Boston, 1943-44; mem. Collegiate Chorale, N.Y.C., 1947-49; choral dir. Community Ch., Summit N.J., 1947-49; dir. Murray Hill Male Quartet, 1947-49; mem. Masterworks Chorale, Los Angeles, 1950-52; pres. Los Angeles Met. Chorus, 1952-54; mem. Gregg Smith Singers, Los Angeles, 1959-60; mem. Pacifica Singers, Los Angeles, 1967-70. Served to 1st lt., Signal Corps, AUS, 1944-46. Fellow IEEE, Am. Inst. Aeros. and Astronautics (asso.); mem. N.Y. Acad. Scis., Phi Beta Kappa, Sigma Xi, Tau Beta Pi, Omicron Delta Kappa, Beta Gamma Sigma (hon.), Sigma Alpha Epsilon, Phi Mu Alpha, Pi Mu Epsilon, Sigma Pi Sigma, Theta Alpha Phi. Unitarian (dir. ch. 1970-73, 79—, treas. 1976-78), Editor: Were We Guinea Pigs?, 1938. Contbr. sci. articles to profl. jours. Patentee in field. Home: 1010 Centinela Ave Santa Monica CA 90403 Office: Hughes Aircraft Co Centinela Ave at Teale St Culver City CA 90230

MATHEWSON, HUGH SPALDING, physician, educator; b. Washington, Sept. 20, 1921; s. Walter Eldridge and Jennie Lind (Jones) M.; student Washburn U., 1938-39; A.B., U. Kans., 1942, M.D., 1944; m. Judith Ann Mahoney, Aug. 6, 1979; children—Jane Mathewson Holcombe, Geoffrey K., Brian E., Catherine E., Jennifer A. Intern, Wesley Hosp., Wichita, Kans., 1944-45; resident anesthesiology U. Kans. Med. Center, Kansas City, 1946-48; practice medicine, specializing in anesthesiology, Kansas City, Mo., 1948-69; chief anesthesiologist St. Luke's Hosp., Kansas City, 1948-69; med. dir., sect. respiratory therapy U. Kans. Med. Center, 1969—, asso. prof., 1969-75, prof., 1975—; examiner schs. respiratory therapy, 1975—; oral examiner Nat. Bd. Respiratory Therapy; mem. Council Nurse Anesthesia Practice, 1974—; dir. Empire State Bank. Trustee, Kansas City Mus. Served to lt. comdr., USNR, 1956. Recipient Bird Lit. prize Am. Assn. Respiratory Therapists, 1976. Mem. Mo. (pres. 1963), Kans. (pres. 1974-77) socs. anesthesiologists, Kans. Med. Soc. (council), Sigma Xi, Phi Beta Kappa. Club: Carriage (Kansas City, Mo.). Author: Structural Forms of Anesthetic Compounds, 1961; Respiratory Therapy in Critical Care, 1976; Pharmacology for Respiratory Therapists, 1977; contbr. articles to profl. publs.; editorial bd. Anesthesia Staff News, 1975—. Home: 6523 Overbrook Rd Shawnee Mission KS 66208 Office: 39th and Rainbow Sts Kansas City KS 66103

MATHEWSON, KENT, urbanologist; b. N.Y.C., Aug. 6, 1917; s. Park and Alice (Clarke) M.; B.S., U. N.C., 1939; M.A. in Public Adminstrn., Syracuse U., 1942; m. Mariana Worth Moore, Sept. 7, 1940; children—Worth, Kent, William Carroll. Asst. city mgr., San Diego, 1939-40, Durham, N.C., 1942; spl. rep. Office of Sec. of War, Washington, 1943; city mgr. Asheboro, N.C., 1946-48, Martinsville, Va., 1948-56, Salem, Oreg., 1956-63; pres. Met. Fund, Inc., Detroit, 1963-80, sr. cons., 1980—; adj. prof. U. Tex., Austin, 1980—; vis. prof. San Diego State U. Bd. govs. Grad. Program in Public Adminstrn., Nova U.; mem. Mich. State Library Bd., 1964-67; mem. Nat. Hwy. Research Bd., 1964-66; mem. Mich. Gov.'s Commn. on Local Govt., 1971-73. Served to capt. USAAF, 1943-46. Recipient Distinguished Service award Internat. City Mgmt. Assn., 1978; Distinguished Citizen award Nat. Mcpl. League, 1979; inductee Intergovernmental Hall of Fame, Nat. Assn. Regional Councils, 1979. Mem. Internat. City Mgmt. Assn. (v.p.), Am. Soc. Public Adminstrn. (past dir.), Nat. Inst. Public Affairs (past dir.), Nat. Acad. Public Adminstrn., Nat. Assn. Regional Councils, Pi Alpha Alpha. Episcopalian. Club: Detroit. Editor, author works in field. Home: 4080 Chablis Dr West Bloomfield MI 48033 also 1801 Lavaca Blvd Austin TX 78701 Office: 200 Renaissance Center Suite 2233 Detroit MI 48243 also LBJ Sch Public Affairs Univ Tex Austin TX 78712

MATHIA, DOYLE V., hotel/casino exec.; b. Lawrence, Kans., Apr. 14, 1933; s. David H. and Victoria Mathia; B.A. in History, Washburn U., Topeka, Kans., 1956; m. Alice Jean Herzog, May 17, 1974; children—Clay David, Tracy Lyn. Mem. staff Harrah's Inc., Reno, 1956-77; v.p., gen. mgr. Del Webb's Sahara Reno Hotel & Casino, 1977-78; pres. Del Webb Hotels, Las Vegas, Nev., 1978—. Served with USAF, 1957-59. Office: 300 S 4th St Suite 1200 Las Vegas NV 89101

MATHIAS, CHARLES MCCURDY, JR., U.S. senator; b. Frederick, Md., July 24, 1922; s. Charles McCurdy and Theresa McElfresh (Trail) M.; B.A., Haverford Coll., 1944; student Yale, 1943-44; LL.B., U. Md., 1949; m. Ann Hickling Bradford, Nov. 8, 1958; children—Charles Bradford, Robert Fiske. Admitted to Md. bar, 1949, U.S. Supreme Ct. bar, 1954; asst. atty. gen. of Md., 1953-54; city atty. City of Frederick, 1954-59; mem. Md. Ho. of Dels., 1958; mem. 87th-90th Congresses from 6th Dist. Md.; mem. U.S. Senate from Md., 1968—. Served from seaman to capt. USNR. Republican. Episcopalian. Home: RFD #2 Frederick MD 21701 also 3808 Leland St Chevy Chase MD 20015 Office: Fed Office Bldg Baltimore MD

MATHIAS, JAMES HERMAN, lawyer; b. N.Y.C., Nov. 12, 1913; s. J. Herman and Alma Rosenstein M.; B.A., Columbia, 1934, J.D., 1936; m. Shirl Seeman, Aug. 2, 1975. Admitted to N.Y. State bar, 1937, since practiced in N.Y.C.; mem. firm Cahn & Mathias, N.Y.C., 1950—. Served to capt., Judge Adv. Gen. Dept., AUS, 1942-46. Mem. Soc. for Strings Inc. (sec. 1955-75), Assn. Bar City N.Y., N.Y. County Lawyers Assn., Confrerie des Chevaliers du Tastevin, Harmonie Club, Phi Beta Kappa. Home: 848 Fenimore Rd Larchmont NY 10538 Office: Cahn & Mathias 22 E 40th St New York City NY 10016

MATHIAS, JOSEPH SIMON, metall. engr.; b. Bombay, India, Oct. 28, 1925; s. Pascal Lawrence and Dulcine Applina (De Souza) M.; came to U.S., 1948, naturalized, 1954; B.S., U. Bombay, 1944, B.A., 1946; Ph.D., Lehigh U., Bethlehem, Pa., 1954; M.Engr., U. Calif., Berkeley, 1951; m. Anna Katrina Elliott, Nov. 10, 1956. Research asso. Lehigh U., 1951-54; chief metallurgist Superior Metals, Inc., Bethlehem, Pa., 1954-56; mgr. process metall. research Foote Mineral Co., Easton, Pa., 1956-59; mgr. materials research, then group mgr. physics and materials Sperry Univac Co., Blue Bell, Pa., 1959-67, dir. research, 1967—; mem. program com. Internat. Magnetic Conf., 1969, 70; cons. in field. Fellow Am. Inst. Chemists, N.Y. Acad. Sci.; sr. mem. IEEE; mem. Am. Soc. Electrochemistry, Am. Inst. Mining and Metall. Engrs., Sigma Xi, Tau Beta Pi. Clubs: Rotary (past chmn. membership com.), Riverton Country. Author, patentee in field. Home: 105 Thomas Ave Riverton NJ 08077 Office: Sperry Univac Co PO Box 500 Blue Bell PA 19422

MATHIES, ALLEN WRAY, JR., physician, univ. adminstr.; b. Colorado Springs, Colo., Sept. 23, 1930; s. Allen W. and Esther S. (Norton) M.; B.A., Colo. Coll., 1952; M.S., Columbia, 1953, Ph.D., 1958; M.D., U. Vt., 1961; m. Lewise Austin, Aug. 23, 1956; children—William A., John N. Research asso. U. Vt., 1957-61; intern, Los Angeles County Hosp., 1961-62; resident in pediatrics Los Angeles Gen Hosp., 1962-64; asst. prof. pediatrics U. So. Calif., 1964-68, asso. prof., 1968-71, prof., 1971—, asso. dean Sch. Medicine, 1969-74, interim dean, 1974-75, dean, 1975—; head physician Communicable Disease Service, 1964-75; bd. dirs. Orthopedic Hosp., Ear Research Inst., Hollywood Presbyn. Hosp., Huntington Meml. Hosp. Served with U.S. Army, 1953-55. Mem. Am. Acad. Pediatrics, Infectious Disease Soc. Am., Am. Pediatric Soc., Soc. Pediatric Research. Republican. Episcopalian. Contbr. articles to med. jours. Home: 314 Arroyo Dr South Pasadena CA 91030 Office: 2025 Zonal Ave Los Angeles CA 90033

MATHIESON, ANDREW WRAY, investment mgmt. exec.; b. Pitts., June 11, 1928; s. Andrew Russell and Margaret (Wray) M.; B.S. in Mech. Engring., Bucknell U., 1950; M.S. in Indsl. Adminstrn., Carnegie-Mellon U., 1952; m. Helen Fricke, Dec. 5, 1953; children—Margaret Adele, Andrew Fricke, Peter Ferris. With elevator div. Westinghouse Electric Corp., 1955-63, dist. mgr., Cleve., 1960-62, asst. group v.p. constrn. group, Pitts., 1962-63; with T. Mellon and Sons., Pitts., 1963-71, v.p., gov., 1967-71; v.p. Richard K. Mellon and Sons, Pitts., 1971-78, exec. v.p., 1978—; dir. Koppers Co., Inc., Gen. Reins. Corp., Gen. Reassurance Corp., Gen. Reins. Life Corp., N. Star Reins. Corp., Gen. Reins. (Europe), Hana Ranch, Inc. Trustee, treas. Richard King Mellon Found., Richard King Mellon Charitable Trusts; trustee R.K. Mellon Family Found., Koppers Found., Bucknell U.; bd. dirs. St. Margaret Meml. Hosp., Pitts., 1966—, pres., 1976; exec. com. Allegheny Conf. Community Devel., 1976. Served with USNR, 1952-55. Episcopalian. Clubs: Duquesne, Fox Chapel Golf (dir. 1974) (Pitts.); Laurel Valley Golf, Rolling Rock (Ligonier, Pa.); Unversity, Links (N.Y.C.). Home: 10 Fairview Manor Pittsburgh PA 15238 Office: Richard K Mellon and Sons PO Box 1138 Pittsburgh PA 15230

MATHIEU, ALAIN ETIENNE, retail chain exec.; b. Paris, June 24, 1937; s. Robert Etienne and Genevieve M.; came to U.S., 1979; student Ecole Polytechnique, Paris, 1957-59; Ph.D. in Econs., U. Paris, 1967; m. Anne Brizay, Jan. 13, 1963; children—Jean-Fabrice, Alexandre, Constance. Chargé de mission French Ministry of Fin., Paris, 1963-66; mng. dir. Procredit, Paris, 1967-72; chief fin. officer Au Bon Marche, dept. store chain, Paris, 1972-76, pres., 1973-76; pres. Conforama, discout furniture store chain, Paris, 1976-79; chmn., chief exec. officer Korvettes, N.Y.C., 1979—. Served with French Air Force, 1959-60. Home: 1088 Park Ave New York NY 10028 Office: 430 W 33d St New York NY 10001

MATHIEU, JEAN, physician, educator; b. Montreal, P.Q., Can., Aug. 7, 1926; s. Emile and Marie-Berthe (Larviere) M.; B.A., Coll. Stanislas, Montreal, 1944; M.D., U. Montreal, 1950; m. Anne-Marie Mouren, Aug. 16, 1956; children—Bernard, Yves, Nicolas. Intern, Hotel-Dieu de Montréal, 1949-50; resident Hosp. St.-Luc, Montreal, 1950-51, Toronto Gen. Hosp., 1951-54, Hosp. Boucicaut, Paris, 1955; physician Hosp. Maisonneuve-Rosemont, Montreal, 1956—; prof. medicine U. Montreal, 1972—, asso. dean post grad studies Faculty of Medicine, 1968-77, head dept. medicine, 1977—; bd. govs. Coll. Physicians and Surgeons, P.Q., 1966-74. Fellow Royal Coll. Physicians and Surgeons Can. Roman Catholic. Office: 1150 Saint Joseph Blvd Montreal PQ H2J 1L5 Canada

MATHIEU, ROBERT P., hosp. adminstr.; b. Providence, June 6, 1926; s. Peter N. and Ida (Racine) M.; A.B., Providence Coll., 1950; postgrad. Providence Coll., 1950-51, Boston U., 1951, Northwestern U., 1953; m. Jane Frances Corley, Aug. 25, 1951; children—Jane Frances, Robert Phillip, Patricia Anne, Peter Frances, Susan Marie. Adminstrv. asst. R.I. Hosp., Providence, 1950-51, Michael Reese Hosp., Chgo., 1951-52; adminstrv. resident Worcester (Mass.) City Hosp., 1952-53; asst. adminstr. Meml. Hosp., Pawtucket, 1953-58; asso. adminstr., coordinator med., nursing and profl. relations and edn., 1958-61; adminstr. Dr. U.E. Zambarano Meml. Hosp., Wallum Lake, R.I., 1961—, Charles V. Chapin Hosp., Providence, 1966-69; asst. dir. div. hosps. Dept. Mental Health, Retardation and Hosps., 1970—; prof. hosp. and nursing home adminstrn. U. R.I. Cons. Nat. Commn. Nursing Services, 1955—, to dir. health, Pawtucket, 1955—; mem. Gov.'s Adv. Commn. Vocational Rehab., 1967—, tech. adv. com. Health Facilities Planning Council, 1968—; chmn. extended care facilities study commn. USPHS, 1968—. Bd. dirs. Foster Grandparent Program Office Equal Opportunity, 1967-69. Served with USNR, 1944-46. Fellow Am. Coll. Hosp. Adminstrs., Am. Pub. Health Assn.; mem. Am. Hosp. Assn., Hosp. Assn. R.I. (trustee, 1970—), New Eng. Hosp. Assembly, New Eng. Pub. Health Assn. Author: Hospital and Nursing Home Management, 1971. Home: 62 Greenfield St Pawtucket RI 02861 Office: Office of Governor Room 13 State House Providence RI 02903

MATHIS, BYRON CLAUDE, psychologist, educator; b. Longview, Tex., Mar. 10, 1927; s. Byron Claude and Pearl (Livsey) M.; B.A., Tex. Christian U., 1949, M.A., 1950; Ph.D., U. Tex., 1956; m. Patricia Ann Purtell, June 7, 1958; children—Byron Claude III, Deborah Ann. Asst. prof. ednl. psychology U. Tex., 1955-56; asst. prof. edn. Northwestern U., 1956-60, asso. prof., 1960-64, asso. prof. edn. and psychology, 1964-65, prof., 1965—, asst. dean grad. Sch., 1964-65, asso. dean, 1966-69, asso. dean Sch. Edn., 1969-78, dir. Center for the Teaching Professions, 1969—. Bd. dirs. Family Counseling Service Evanston and Skokie Valley, 1971-77, pres., 1974-77; trustee Roycemore Sch., 1978—. Served with USNR, 1944-46. Fellow Am. Psychol. Assn.; mem. Am. Ednl. Research Assn., AAUP, AAAS. Author: (with John Cotton and Lee Sechrest) Psychological Foundations of Education-Learning and Teaching, 1970. Asso. editor Psychology In The Schools, 1964-70; editor, 1970-71; editor (with William McGaghie) Profiles in College Teaching, 1972; (with Stephen Holbrook) Teaching: A Force for Change in Higher Education. Contbr. articles to profl. jours. Home: 9350 Nashville Ave Morton Grove IL 60053 Office: 2003 Sheridan Rd Evanston IL 60201. *Marcus Aurelius once wrote that "people exist for the sake of one another. Teach them, then, or bear with them." Creative teaching is an essential part of existence. Study the teacher as well as what is taught, and learn the difference between understanding and simply knowing.*

MATHIS, HAROLD FLETCHER, educator; b. Wichita Falls, Tex., July 19, 1916; s. Henry Fletcher and Annie Martha (Petty) M.; B.S., U. Okla., 1939, E.E., 1954; M.S., Tex. A. and M. U., 1941, E.E., 1952; Ph.D., Northwestern U., 1953, Case Western Res. U., 1961; m. Lois Reno, June 6, 1942; children—Robert, Betty. Research asso. Northwestern U., 1946-49; asso. prof. elec. engring. U. Okla., 1949-54; research specialist Goodyear, Akron, O., 1954-60; prof. elec. engring. Ohio State U., Columbus, 1960—. Cons. N.Am. Rockwell Corp., 1962-70. Served with USNR, 1942-46, 51-53. Mem. IEEE, Am. Soc. Engring. Edn., Am. Bell Assn., Sigma Xi, Phi Eta Sigma, Sigma Tau, Eta Kappa Nu, Kappa Delta Pi. Contbr. articles to profl. jours. Home: 2905 Halstead Rd Columbus OH 43221

MATHIS, JERRY NASH, packaging co. exec.; b. Knoxville, Tenn., July 25, 1934; s. Harry Rhubart and Doris Bradford (Dietz) M.; B.A., Lake Forest Coll., 1957; postgrad. U. Pitts. Exec. Program, 1969, Dartmouth Inst., 1977; m. Joyce Marion Stocer, Feb. 9, 1957; children—Jay, Jennifer. With Am. Can Co., Greenwich, Conn., v.p., gen. mgr. spl. products, 1974-75, v.p., gen. mgr. beverage packaging, 1975-77, sr. v.p., 1977—, sector exec.-internat., 1979—. Trustee, Daytop Village, N.Y.C. Served with AUS, 1957. Mem. U.S. Brewers Assn. (asso. dir.), Can Mfrs. Inst. (dir.). Office: Am Can Co American Ln Greenwich CT 06830

MATHIS, JOHN SAMUEL, educator; b. Dallas, Feb. 7, 1931; s. Forrest and Mattie Mae (Godbold) M.; B.S., M.I.T., 1953; Ph.D., Calif. Inst. Tech., 1956; m. Carol Simpelaar, Sept. 11, 1954; children—Matthew, Alice, Jeffrey, Emily, Sarah. NSF Postdoctoral fellow Yerkes Obs., U. Chgo., 1956-57; asst. prof. Mich. State U., 1957-59; mem. faculty U. Wis.-Madison, 1959—, prof. astronomy, 1969—. U.S. Sr. Scientist awardee Alexander-von-Humboldt Found., 1975-76. Mem. Am. Astron. Soc. Asso. editor Astrophys. Jours. Letters, 1971-73. Home: 29 N Yellowstone Dr Madison WI 53705

MATHIS, JOHNNY, singer; b. San Francisco, Sept. 30, 1935; student San Francisco State Coll. Numerous recordings, film, concerts and TV appearances; tours of Europe, Africa, Australia, S.Am., Orient, Can.; rec. artist Columbia Records. Address: care Rojon Prodns 6290 Sunset Blvd Hollywood CA 90028

MATHIS, LUSTER DOYLE, coll. adminstr., polit. scientist; b. Gainesville, Ga., May 5, 1936; s. Luster and Fay Selena (Wingo) M.; A.B., Berry Coll., 1958; M.A., U. Ga., 1958, Ph.D. (Univ. Alumni Found. fellow), 1966; m. Rheba Burch, June 5, 1958; children—Douglas James, Deborah Jane. Asst. prof. polit. sci. Brenau Coll., Gainesville, 1960-61; asso. prof. Calif. Baptist Coll., 1961-62; asso. prof. Belmont Coll., Nashville, 1962-64; asso. prof., head dept. polit. sci. W.Ga. Coll., Carrollton, 1965-68, prof., 1969-75, head dept., 1969-71, chmn. div. grad. studies, 1970-73; research asso., asst. editor Papers of Thomas Jefferson, Princeton U., 1968-69; v.p., dean of coll. Berry Coll., Mt. Berry, Ga., 1975—; cons. Citizens Com. on Ga. Gen. Assembly. Mem. Ga. Democratic Charter Commn., 1974-75; mem. consumer adv. com. Floyd Med. Center, 1978—. Nat. Hist. Publs. Commn. fellow, 1968-69. Mem. Am. Assn. Higher Edn., Am. Conf. Acad. Deans, So. Conf. Deans of Faculties and Acad. Vice Pres's., Ga. Polit. Sci. Assn. (pres. 1968-69). Democrat. Baptist. Club: Kiwanis. Co-author: Courts as Political Instruments, 1970. Office: Berry Coll Mount Berry GA 30149

MATHIS, M. DAWSON, Congressman; b. Nashville, Ga., Nov. 30, 1940; s. Marvin W. and Nell Dawson (Abel) M.; student So. Ga. Coll., 1958-60; m. Sharon R. Beavers; children by previous marriage—Anthony Dawson, Dawson, Craig Steven, Jason Everett, Russell Dean. News dir. Sta. WALB-TV, Albany, Ga., 1964-70; mem. 92d-96th congresses from 2d Dist. Ga., mem. House Com. Agr. Active Chehaw Boy Scouts Am., 1967-70. Mem. Ga. Assn. Newscasters, Fraternal Order Police. Clubs: Elks, Masons, Shriners. Office: Rayburn House Office Bldg Washington DC 20515

MATHIS, PATRICIA ANN, govt. ofcl.; b. Hearne, Tex., Aug. 23, 1939; s. Julius E. and Johnoween Smyth M.; B.A., U. Tex., 1961; postgrad. Cath. U., 1968-69, U. Vt., 1970-72, Boston U., 1974-76. Legis. aide Sen. Ralph Yarborough, 1959-62; dir. speakers bur. Peace Corps, Washington, 1962-63; dir. Canterbury Sch., Accokeek, Md., 1963-67; v.p. for adminstrn. Urban Inst., Washington, 1968-70; v.p. for personnel mgmt. Boston U., 1972-76; dep. asst. sec. Dept. Treasury, Washington, 1977-79; dir. Merit Systems Rev., Washington, 1979—; chairperson Interagy. Com. on Women Bus. Enterprise. Mem. Coll. and Univ. Personnel Adminstrs. Democrat. Episcopalian. Club: Women's Nat. Democratic.*

MATHIS, PAUL CARL, educator; b. Dubuque, Iowa, May 26, 1917; s. Paul Carl and Alma (Petersen) M.; B.A. cum laude, U. Dubuque; student U. Mich., 1938-39; M.A., U. Iowa, 1940, Ph.D., 1946; m. L. Edna Viken, June 4, 1941; children—Karen, Paul, William, John. Instr., McCook (Neb.) Jr. Coll., 1941-42; asst. prof. Carleton Coll., Northfield, Minn., 1946-47; prof. U. S.D., 1947-62; prof. Central Mich. U., Mt. Pleasant, 1962—, chmn. dept. econs., 1962-72; cons. in field. Served with AUS, 1942-46. Gen. Electric Found. fellow; Found. Econ. Edn. fellow. Mem. Am., Midwest econ. assns., AAAS, Econs. Soc. Mich., Omicron Delta Gamma. Mason (32 deg.). Author articles and monographs. Home: 900 E Maple St Mount Pleasant MI 48858

MATHIS, ROBERT COUTH, air force officer; b. Eagle Pass, Tex., July 3, 1927; s. Harry Poynter and Marjorie Roberta (Couth) M.; B.S., U.S. Mil. Acad., 1948; M.S., U. Ill., 1953; Ph.D., U. Tex., 1963; postgrad. Indsl. Coll. Armed Forces, 1966-67; m. Greta Gay, Apr. 13, 1952; children—Harry Poynter III, Carol Gay Mc Bane, Robert Couth, Donald H., Kristi Anne. Commd. 2d lt. USAF, 1948, advanced through grades to lt. gen., 1977; jet fighter pilot, Korea, 1950-51; instr. electronics U.S. Naval Acad., 1953-56; adviser to Vietnamese Air Force, 1967-68; with Office Dir. Def. Research and Engring., 1968-69; comdr. Rome (N.Y.) Air Devel. Center, 1968-71; dir. F-111 aircraft program Wright-Patterson AFB, Ohio, 1971-73, dir. F-15 aircraft program, 1974-76; vice comdr. Air Force Systems Command, Washington, 1977-79; vice comdr. Tactical Air Command, Langley AFB, Va., 1979—. Decorated D.S.M., Silver Star medal, D.F.C., Air medal, Purple Heart, Legion of Merit, also fgn. decorations. Home: 437 Ridgemont Ave San Antonio TX 78209 Office: HQ Tactical Air Command Langley AFB VA 23665

MATHIS, SHARON BELL, educator, author; b. Atlantic City, Feb. 26, 1937; d. John Willie and Alice Mary (Frazier) Bell; B.A., Morgan State Coll., 1958; M.Sc., Catholic U. Am., 1975; m. Leroy F. Mathis, July 11, 1957 (div. Jan. 1979); children—Sherie, Stacy, Stephanie. Interviewer, Children's Hosp. of D.C., 1958-59; tchr. Holy Redeemer Elementary Sch., Washington, 1960-65, Charles Hart Jr. High Sch., Washington, 1965-72, Stuart Jr. High Sch., Washington, 1972-74; librarian Benning Elementary Sch., Washington, 1975-76, Friendship Ednl. Center, 1976—; writer-in-charge children's lit. div. D.C. Black Writers Workshop; writer-in-residence Howard U., 1972-73; bd. advisers lawyers com. D.C. Commn. on Arts, 1972. Nominated by Nat. Conf. Christians and Jews for Books for Brotherhood list, 1970 award of Council on Interracial Books for Children for Sidewalk Story, Child Study Assn. award, 1971, 72, Outstanding Book of Year award N.Y. Times, 1972, Coretta Scott King award, 1974; Arts and Humanities award Secretariat for Black Caths., 1978; award D.C. Assn. Sch. Librarians, 1976, others. Weekly Reader Book Club fellow Bread Loaf Writers Conf., 1970. Author: Brooklyn Story, 1970; Sidewalk Story, 1971; Teacup Full of Roses, 1972; Ray Charles, 1973; Listen for the Fig Tree, 1974; The Hundred Penny Box, 1975 (Boston Globe-Horn Book Honor book 1975, Newberry Honor Book, 1976); Cartwheels, 1977. Address: care Curtis Brown Ltd 575 Madison Ave New York NY 10022. *My success is due to the glorious African blood which flows throughout my body—and to the dignity, intelligence, strength, pride, efforts, and faith of my very creative parents—and all other Black people who have helped me.*

MATHIS, WILLIAM LOWREY, lawyer; b. Jackson, Tenn., Dec. 19, 1926; s. Harry Fletcher and Syrene (Lowrey) M.; B.M.E., Duke U., 1947; J.D., George Washington U., 1951; m. Marilyn Jayne Cason, Sept. 10, 1949; children—Amanda Jayne, Amy Susan, Peter Andrew, Perry Alexander, Anne Lowrey. Examiner, U.S. Patent Office, 1947-52; admitted to D.C. bar, 1951, Fla. bar, 1972, Va. bar, 1977; mem. firm Swecker & Mathis, Washington, 1952-61, Burns, Doane, Swecker & Mathis, Washington and Alexandria, Va., 1961—; adj. prof. law Georgetown U. Law Center, 1974—. Mem. Am., D.C. bar assns., Am. Patent Law Assn., Order of Coif. Roman Catholic. Co-author: Trademark Litigation in the Trademark Office and Federal Courts, 1977. Home: 3709 Chanel Rd Annandale VA 22003 Office: George Mason Bldg Washington and Prince Sts Alexandria VA 22313

MATHOG, ROBERT HENRY, otolaryngologist, educator; b. New Haven, Apr. 13, 1939; s. William and Tiby (Gans) M.; A.B., Dartmouth Coll., 1960; M.D., N.Y. U., 1964; m. Deena Jane Rabinowitz, June 14, 1964; children—Tibye, Heather, Lauren, Jason. Intern, Duke Hosp., Durham, N.C., 1964-65, resident surgery, 1965-66, resident otolaryngology, 1966-69; practice medicine, specializing in otolaryngology, Mpls., 1971-77, Detroit, 1977—; chief of otolaryngology Hennepin County Med. Center, Mpls., 1972-77; asst. prof. U. Minn., 1971-74, asso. prof., 1974-77; prof., chmn. dept. otolaryngology Wayne State U. Sch. Medicine, 1977—; editor-in-chief Vido Med. Edn. Systems, 1972-77; book rev. editor Am. Jour. Otolaryngology, 1978—. Bd. Dirs. Bexer County Hearing Soc., 1969-71. Served to maj. USAF, 1969-71. Recipient Valentine Mott medal for proficiency in anatomy, 1961; Deafness Research Found. grantee, 1979. Mem. A.C.S., AMA, Mich. Med. Soc., Am. Acad. Otolaryngology (cert. of award 1976, cert. of appreciation 1978), Triological Soc., Am. Acad. Facial Plastic and Reconstructive Surgery, Am. Neurotology Soc., Am. Head and Neck Soc., Soc. Univ. Otolaryngologists, Assn. Acad. Depts. Otolaryngology. Author: Otolaryngology Clinics of North America, 1976; Contbr. articles to med. jours. Home: 27115 Wellington St Franklin MI 48025 Office: 540 E Canfield St Detroit MI 48201

MATHUES, THOMAS OLIVER, auto mfg. co. exec.; b. Dayton, Ohio, Jan. 26, 1923; s. John Leslie and Florence (Killen) M.; student Grove City Coll., 1944-45, U. Ill., 1945-46; B.M.E., Gen. Motors Inst., 1947; m. Patricia McFarland, May 20, 1944; children—Thomas P., Rebecca, John, Jennifer. With Inland div. Gen. Motors Corp., Dayton, 1940-78, gen. mgr., 1966-78; v.p. mfg. staff Gen. Motors, Warren, Mich., 1978—. Bd. dirs. U. Dayton; bd. regents Gen. Motors Inst., Flint, Mich. Served with USNR, 1944-46. Mem. Soc. Automotive Engrs., Phi Gamma Delta. Mem. Christian Ch. Club: Sycamore Creek Country. Patentee in field. Home: 910 Sunningdale Rd Bloomfield Hills MI 48013 Office: Gen Motors Tech Center 12 Mile and Mound Rds Warren MI 48090

MATHUR, VISHNU SAHAI, physicist, educator; b. Asansol, India, Apr. 28, 1934; s. Jagdish Sahai and Rup (Rani) M.; came to U.S., 1965, naturalized, 1968; B.Sc. with honors (All India Merit scholar), Delhi (India) U., 1953, M.Sc. (All India Merit scholar), 1955, Ph.D., 1958; m. Kusum Mathur, Feb. 5, 1961; children—Sharmila, Dipika, Madhulika. Postdoctoral fellow Fermi Inst. Nuclear Studies, U. Chgo., 1958-60; pool officer Delhi U., 1960-63, reader Centre for Advanced Studies in Physics, 1963-65; vis. sr. research asso. U. Rochester (N.Y.), 1965-68, sr. research asso., 1968—, prof., 1970—. Mem. Am. Phys. Soc. Contbr. articles to profl. jours. Home: 45 Hampshire Dr Rochester NY 14618

MATIUK, ALEXANDER, engr.; b. N.Y.C., May 28, 1917; s. Daniel and Mary (Zwarico) M.; B.M.E., Cooper Union Inst. Tech., 1938; M.M.E., Poly. Inst. Bklyn., 1944; m. Ann Meleshko, May 25, 1940; children—Alexander, Gregory, Conrad. Project engr. Ebasco Services, N.Y.C., 1938-47; head steam and power div. Douglas M. McBean, Rochester, N.Y., 1947; group supervising engr. United Engrs. and Constructors, Phila., 1947-51; v.p., dir. engring. div. Burns & Roe, Inc., N.Y.C., 1955-62; pres. Gibbs & Hill, Inc., N.Y.C., 1962—. Recipient award for outstanding leadership ASME, 1969. Fellow ASME. Office: 393 7th Ave New York NY 10001*

MATKIN, GEORGE GARRETT, banker; b. Ennis, Tex., Jan. 21, 1898; s. George Garrett and Clemens (Loggins) M.; student pub. schs., El Paso, Tex.; m. Lucile Ross, June 22, 1929 (dec. Feb. 1976); children—Margaret (Mrs. George H. Jackson), Nancy Clemens (Mrs. Raymond Marshall). With State Nat. Bank of El Paso, 1917—, pres. 1949-67, chmn. bd., 1967—; chmn. bd., dir. Pannational Bank Group, El Paso; dir. El Paso Electric Co.; hon. dir. Mountain States Tel. & Tel. Co. Mem. El Paso C. of C. Mason (32). Clubs: El Paso Country; Internat.; Coronado. Home: 810 E Blanchard Ave El Paso TX 79902 Office: State Nat Bank El Paso TX 79901

MATLICK, DAYTON HARRIS, mag. editor; b. Haviland, Kans., Nov. 14, 1934; s. John Orville and Helen (Dayton) M.; B.A., U. Ky., 1957; M.A., Mich. State U., 1977—; m. Mary Patricia Castle, Dec. 8, 1968; children—Scott Dayton, Gregory Trent, Leslie Ann, Peter Scott, Joseph Paul, Heather Lynn. Field editor Ky. Farmer, Tenn. Farmer, Ind. Farmer mags., Louisville, 1959-60; asso. editor Ky. Farmer, Tenn. Farmer mags., 1960-61; editor Tenn. Farmer, Nasville, 1961-62; mng. editor Mich. Farmer, Lansing, 1962-66, editor, 1966-76; v.p., editorial dir. Harvest Pub. Co., Cleve., 1976-78, sr. v.p. editorial prodn. and circulation, 1978—; lectr. journalism Mich. State U., 1970-73. Mem. Mich. Health Council, 1966-77, Mich. Rural Safety Council, 1966-77, Pork Council, 1968-75; mem. poultry adv. com. Mich. State U., 1967-69, dairy adv. council, 1969-75. Asso. chmn. Nat. Amateur Athletic Union Taekwon Do Jr. Olympics subcom., 1977—. Served with AUS, 1957-59. Hon. State Future Farmers Am. degree, 1968; Animal Agr. award Am. Feed Mfrs. Assn., 1965; Soil Mgmt. award for editors Nat. Plant Food Inst., 1969; Oscar in Agr., Dekalb Agresearch, Inc., 1969; Soil Conservation Certificate Merit, Mich. chpt. Soil Conservation Soc. Am., 1969, Profl. Invprovement award for editors Chgo. Bd. Trade, 1971, Mich. 4-H citation, 1973; 4th deg. Black Belt Taekwon Do, 1975. Mem. Am. Agrl. Editors Assn., Agrl. Criculation Mgrs. Assn., Am. Mgmt. Assn., Mich. Agrl. Conf. (dir.), Am. Soc. Bus. Press Editors, Mich. Kang Duk Won Assn. (pres. 1970-73, adviser 1973—), Am. Midwest Taekwon Do-Karate Fedn. (pres. 1973-75, adviser 1975—), Sigma Delta Chi. Home: 2035 Mattingly Rd Hinckley OH 44233 Office: 9800 Detroit Ave Cleveland OH 44102

MATLOCK, CLIFFORD CHARLES, ret. foreign service officer; b. Whittier, Cal., Nov. 6, 1909; s. William Holland and Clara Louisa (Wallace) M.; A.B., Stanford, 1932; A.M., Harvard, 1940, certificate pub. adminstrn. (Littauer fellow), 1940; m. Nina Stolypin, Nov. 6, 1934 (dec. Dec. 1969); m. 2d, Elisabeth Thompson Scobey, May 3, 1971. Economist, USDA, 1938-41, U.S. Treasury, 1941-42; economist, adminstr. Bd. Econ. Warfare, Fgn. Econ. Adminstrn., 1942-45; econ., polit. officer Dept. State, 1946-62, polit. adviser European coordinating com., London, 1949-50, polit. officer U.S. delegation North Atlantic Council, London, 1950-52, polit. officer, then dir. plans and policy staff Office U.S. spl. rep. in Europe, Paris, 1952-53, spl. asst. Am. ambassador, Tehran, 1955-57, spl. asst. econ. affairs asst. sec. state for Far Eastern affairs, also alternate to Dep. Asst. Sec., 1959-62, ret.; acting dep. asst. Sec. of State, 1959; spl. asst. for polit. and econ. affairs to asst. adminstr. East Asia, AID, Dept. of State, 1962-68, dir. East Asia tech. adv. staff, 1966-68, cons. Bur. for East Asia, 1968-71; coordinator interdisciplinary devel. Cycles Research Project, 1971-76, prin., 1977—. U.S. del. Econ. Commn. for Asia and Far East (UN), Tokyo, Japan, 1962; U.S. del. to devel. assistance com. Orgn. for Economic Cooperation and Devel., Paris, France, 1962. Member U.S. delegation Colombo Plan Consultative Com., Seattle, 1958, London, 1964, Development Assistance Group, Orgn. Econ. Coop. and Development, Washington, 1960; U.S. alternate rep. UN Econ. Commn. for Asia and Far East, Bangkok, 1960; adviser, mem. U.S. del. bds. govs. Internat. Monetary Fund, Internat. Bank for Reconstrn. and Devel., Tokyo, Japan, 1964; exec. com. SE Asia Devel. Adv. Group, 1965-70. Recipient Superior Honor award AID, 1968. Mem. Fgn. Service Assn., Diplomatic and Consular Officers Ret., Phi Beta Kappa. Clubs: Metropolitan, Harvard (Washington); Harvard of Western N.C. Author: Man and Cosmos: A Theory of Endeavor Rhythms, 1977. Home: Route 1 Box 388 Lowry Rd Balsam Heights Waynesville NC 28786

MATLOCK, JACK FOUST, JR., fgn. service officer; b. Greensboro, N.C., Oct. 1, 1929; s. Jack Foust and Nellie (McSwain) M.; A.B. summa cum laude, Duke, 1950; M.A., Columbia, 1952; certificate Russian Inst., 1952; m. Rebecca Burrum, Sept. 2, 1949; children—James, Hugh, Nell, David, Joseph. Instr. Dartmouth, 1953-56; fgn. service officer Dept. State, 1956—; assigned Washington, 1956-58, Am. embassy, Vienna, Austria, 1958-60; Am. consulate gen., Munich, Germany, 1960-61; assigned Am. embassy, Moscow, 1961-63, Am. embassy, Accra, Ghana, 1963-66, Am. consulate, Zanzibar, 1967-69, Am. embassy, Dar es Salaam, Tanzania, 1969-70, Sr. Seminar in Fgn. Policy, Dept. State, 1970-71; country dir. for USSR, State Dept., 1971-74; minister-counselor, dep. chief mission Am. embassy, Moscow, 1974-78; diplomat-in-residence Vanderbilt U., Nashville, 1978-79; dep. dir. Fgn. Service Inst., Washington, 1979—. Compiler, editor Index to J.V. Stalin's Works, 2d edit., 1971. Home: 2913 P St NW Washington DC 20007 Office: Fgn Service Inst US Dept State Washington DC 20520

MATLOCK, KENNETH JEROME, bldg. materials co. exec.; b. Oak Park, Ill., May 30, 1928; s. Harvey and Lillian (Sivertsen) Samuelson; student James Millikin U., 1946-48, B.S. in Accountancy, U. Ill., 1950; postgrad. Northwestern U. Inst. Mgmt., summer 1963; m. Dorothy Belowski, Nov. 3, 1956; children—Geoffrey, Barbara, Gail, Paul. Sr. audit mgr. Price Waterhouse & Co., Chgo., 1950-64; with Celotex Corp., Chgo., 1964-65, v.p. fin. ops., Tampa, Fla., 1965-74; asst. to v.p. Jim Walter Corp., Tampa, 1966-79, controller, 1970-72, v.p., 1972-74, v.p., chief fin. officer, 1974—; v.p. Jim Walter Research Corp., St. Petersburg, Fla., 1967—. Adviser, Jr. Achievement, Chgo., 1958-60; active Heart Fund, United Fund, Chgo., 1956-58. Served with USNR, 1945-46. C.P.A., Ill., Fla. Mem. Am. Inst. C.P.A.'s, Ill., Fla. socs. C.P.A.'s, Fin. Execs. Inst. Home: 1401 87th Ave N Saint Petersburg FL 33702 Office: 1500 N Dale Mabry St Tampa FL 33607

MATLOFF, MAURICE, govt. ofcl., author, historian; b. Bklyn., June 18, 1915; s. Joseph and Ida (Glickhouse) M.; B.A. (N.Y. State scholar 1932-36), Columbia Coll., 1936; M.A. (Harvard-Henry Ware Wales scholar), Harvard, 1937, Ph.D. (Edward Austin fellow, Francis Parkman fellow), 1956; postgrad. Yale, 1943-44; m. Gertrude Glickler, Oct. 21, 1942; children—Howard Bruce, Jeffrey Lewis, Jody Matloff Dove. Instr. dept. history Bklyn. Coll., 1939-42, asso. prof., 1946; sr. historian ops. div. War Dept. Gen. Staff, Washington, 1946-47, sr. historian, Hist. div., Dept. Army, Washington, 1947-49, chief strategic plans sect., Office Chief of Mil. History, 1949-60, sr. hist. adviser, Post World War II br., 1960-62, chief Current History br., 1962-66, chief Gen. History br., 1966-68, dep. chief historian, 1969-70, chief historian, 1970-73, chief historian U.S. Army Center Mil. History, 1973—; lectr. U. Md., 1957-71; adj. prof. Am. U., 1965-68; vis. prof. San Francisco State Coll., summer 1966; vis. prof. U. Calif. at Davis, 1968-69; distinguished vis. prof. U. Ga., spring 1974; vis. prof. Dartmouth Coll., spring 1977; Regents prof. U. Calif., Berkeley, spring 1980; cons. govt. coms.; lectr. Nat. War Coll., Army and Navy War Colls., Service Acads., various univs. Mem. exec. bd. Am. Com. History Second World War; adv. council George C. Marshall Research Found., 1975—. Served with AUS, USAAF, 1942-46. Sec. Army Study and Research fellow 1959-60; Meritorious Civilian Service medal, 1965; Dept. Army Outstanding Performance awards, 1972, 74, 75, 76, 78. Mem. U.S. Commn. Mil. History, Am. Hist. Assn. (historian, fed. govt. com. 1958-61), Internat. Inst. Strategic Studies, Am. Mil. Inst. (mem. nominating com. 1970-72, trustee 1976—), Orgn. Am. Historians, Soc. Historians Am. Fgn. Relations, Phi Beta Kappa. Club: Cosmos. Author: Strategic Planning for Coalition Warfare, 1941-42, 1953; Strategic Planning for Coalition Warfare 1943-44, 1959. Gen. editor Am. Military History, 1969, rev., 1973. Contbr. numerous articles to profl. jours. Home: 4109 Dewmar Ct Kensington MD 20795 Office: Pulaski Bldg 20 Massachusetts Ave NW Washington DC 20314. *I have tried to carry forward in my professional and personal life the principles, ideals and standards instilled in me by my immigrant parents—a sense of commitment, hard work, the satisfaction of a job well done, perfecting one's capacities, the pursuit of truth, respect for one's own faith and that of others, the golden rule, and dedication to the ideals upon which the United States was founded.*

MATRE, RICHARD ANTHONY, univ. adminstr.; b. Chgo., Feb. 27, 1922; s. Richard Joseph and Gertrude (O'Rourke) M.; Litt.B., Xavier U., Cin., 1945; A.M., Loyola U., Chgo., 1949; Ph.D., Northwestern U., 1961; m. Marilu Flanagan, Aug. 9, 1947; children—Patrick, Michael, Margaret Hartley, Elizabeth, Jeanne, Teresa Baldwin, Richard, Loretta, John. Instr. history and polit. sci. Loyola U. Chgo., 1947-53, asst. prof. history, 1953, asst. dean Coll. Arts and Scis., 1951, dean Univ. Coll., 1952-65, dir. summer session, 1954-64, asso. prof., 1965-69, prof., 1969—, dean Grad. Sch., 1965-69, v.p., dean faculties, 1969-79, provost med. center, 1979—. Adv. council Chgo. Building Commr., 1954-56. Mem. Holy Name Soc. Union (officer Archdiocese of Chgo. 1955-56), Am. Hist., Soc., Nat. Cath. Edn. Assn. (sec. coll. and univ. dept., 1962-68, v.p. coll. and univ. dept. 1968- 70, pres. 1970—), Assn. for Continuing Higher Edn. (chmn. research and study com. 1955-58, pres. 1960-61), North Central Assn. (cons.-examiner 1969—), Am. Assn. Univ. Adminstrs. (dir.), Pi Gamma Mu, Blue Key. Home: 4030 Fairway Dr Wilmette IL 60091 Office: 2160 S First Ave Maywood IL 60153

MATRICCIANI, JOSEPH STEPHEN, lawyer; b. Balt., Sept. 18, 1943; s. Stephen Thomas and Margaret (Modo) M.; A.A., Eastern Coll., 1965; LL.B., Mt. Vernon Coll., 1968; J.D., U. Balt., 1974; m. Roberta Jean Moxley, June 10, 1967; 1 dau., Melinda Anne. Admitted to Md. bar, 1968; pvt. practice law, Balt., 1968-72; asst. city solicitor Balt., 1972—; partner McManus & Matricciani, Balt., 1972—. Dir., Ro-Jo Enterprises Ltd. Pres., Concept 70's, 1973—; mem. Baltimore County Charter Revision Commn., 1977; bd. dirs. People for Community Action, 1972-73. Contbr. articles polit. jours. Home: 20705 Keeney Mill Rd Freeland MD 21053 Office: 321 Fallsway Baltimore MD 21202 Racquet and Tennis

MATSCHULLAT, WAYNE EMIL, retail exec.; b. Page, Nebr., Jan. 18, 1917; s. Otto F. and Elizabeth M.; B.S., U. Nebr., 1940, J.D., 1942; m. Harriet J. Bowman, Apr. 1942; children—Dale, Robert, Bettiann Matschullat Cassidy, Kay. Mgmt. trainee to met. mgr. Los Angeles met. retail stores Sears Roebuck & Co., 1947-68; v.p. N. Central states, dir. Montgomery Ward & Co., Chgo., 1968-72; pres., dir. Gamble-Skogmo, Inc., Mpls., 1972—; instr. mktg. Drury Coll. Active Jr. Achievement, Boy Scouts Am., various fund drives. Served with AUS, 1942-46. Club: Rotary (v.p.). Home: 6620 Iroquois Trail Edina MN 55435 Office: 5100 Gamble Dr Minneapolis MN 55416*

MATSEN, FREDERICK ALBERT, educator; b. Racine, Wis., July 26, 1913; s. Frederick Albert and Karen (Iversen) M.; B.S., U. Wis., 1937; Ph.D., Princeton, 1941; m. Cecilia Kirkegaard, Aug. 7, 1938; children—Frederick Albert III, Megan Cecilia (Mrs. Albert E. Meisenbach). Instr. Bucknell U., 1940-42; prof. chemistry and physics U. Tex. at Austin, 1942—. Cons. Humble Oil & Refining Co., Exxon Research & Engring. Co., NSF, NIH, 1965—. Guggenheim fellow, 1951-52; NSF sr. postdoctoral fellow, 1961. Fellow Am. Phys. Soc.; mem. Am. Chem. Soc., Faraday Soc. Home: 1800 San Gabriel St Austin TX 78705

MATSLER, FRANKLIN GILES, educator, orgn. exec.; b. Glendive, Mont., Dec. 27, 1922; s. Edmund Russell and Florence Edna (Giles) M.; B.S., Mont. State U., Bozeman, 1948; M.A., U. Mont., Missoula, 1952; Ph.D., U. Calif. at Berkeley, 1959; m. Lois Josephine Hoyt, June 12, 1949; children—Linda, Jeanne, David, Winfield. Tchr., Missoula County (Mont.) High Sch., 1949-51, Tracy (Calif.) Sr. Elem. Schs., 1952-53, San Benito County (Calif.) High Sch. and Jr. Coll., 1953-55; grad. asst. U. Calif. at Berkeley, 1955-58; asst. prof. Humboldt State Coll., Arcata, Calif., 1958-62, asso. prof., 1962-63, asst. exec. dean, 1958-63; chief specialist higher edn. Calif. Coordinating Council for Higher Edn., Sacramento, 1963-68; exec. dir. Ill. Bd. Regents, Springfield, 1968—; prof. higher edn. Ill. State U., Normal, 1968—. Bd. dirs. Ill. Edn. Consortium, 1972-76; bd. dirs. Central Ill. Health Planning Agy., 1970-76, Springfield Symphony Orch. Assn. Served to 1st lt. AUS, 1943-46. Mem. Am. Assn. State Colls. and Univs., Assn. for Instl. Research, Phi Delta Kappa, Lambda Chi Alpha. Clubs: Sangamo (Springfield). Home: 1100 Woodland Ave Springfield IL 62704 Office: 616 Myers Bldg Springfield IL 62701

MATSON, GEORGE DONALD, bank exec.; b. White Deer, S.D., Aug. 26, 1919; s. S. R. and Ellen M. (Peterson) M.; Ph.B., U. Wis., 1940; m. Margaret J. Hawkes, June 1942; children—Thomas H., James G. Pub. accountant Arthur Andersen & Co., 1940-52; with NBC, N.Y.C., 1952-61, beginning as financial analyst, successively asst. treas., controller, v.p. and treas., 1952-59, v.p., gen. mgr. TV Network, 1959-61, asst. to pres., 1960-61; financial v.p., treas. Essex Chem. Corp., Paulsboro Chem. Industries, 1961-73; sr. v.p. Nat. Bank N.Am., N.Y.C., 1973-79, exec. v.p., dir., 1979—. Mem. Financial Execs. Inst., Am. Inst C.P.A's, Am. Mgmt. Assn. Home: Pleasantville Rd New Vernon NJ 07976 Office: 44 Wall St New York NY 10005

MATSON, GRETA, artist; b. Claremont, Va., June 7, 1915; d. Mathew Augustus and Elina (Lansilehto) Matson; student Grand Central Sch. Art, 1935-36, Jerry Farnsworth Sch., 1938-41; B.A. magna cum laude, City U. N.Y., 1978; m. Alfred Alexander Khouri, July 13, 1946 (dec. July 1962); children—Lance Christopher, Janine Alexandra. Works exhibited Carnegie Inst., Chgo. Art Inst., John Herron Art Inst., Albany Art Inst., Pa. Acad., N.A.D., Bklyn. Mus.; represented permanent collections New Britian (Conn.) Art Inst., Va. Mus. Fine Arts, Norfolk Mus. Arts and Scis., William and Mary Coll., Tex. Technol. Art Inst., Tex. Coll. Arts and Industry, Fla. So. Coll., Museum of Fine Arts, Little Rock, Ark., others. Tchr. art Norfolk Mus., summer 1959, 66-67. Recipient 1st Hallgarten prize N.A.D., 1943, Altman prize, 1945; purchase prize Norfolk Mus. Arts and Scis., 1943, 48, 54, 56; portrait prizes So. States Art League, 1945-46; Stroud prize Am. Water Color Soc., 1949, Am. Artist Mag. citation, 1955; popular prize Isaac Delgado Mus., 1951, 2d graphics prize, 1952; Dunham prize Conn. Acad., 1952, Penrose prize, 1953; George B. Zaloom prize watercolor, Nat. Assn. Women Artists, 1960; prizes Nat. Assn. Women Artists Annuals, U.S., 1956; Lillian Cotton Meml. prize Knickerbocker Artists, 1963. Mem. Am. Water Color Soc., Audubon Artists (corr. sec. 1961, dir., 1962-64), Allied Artists (pub. relations chmn. 1962-63), Nat. Assn. Women Artists (pres. 1961-65, mem. exec. bd. 1966-68), Bklyn. Soc. Artists (1st v.p. 1961), Painters and Sculptors Soc. N.J. (dir. 1958-60); Michael L. Tagliaremi prize 1962), Tidewater Artists. Home: 8750 Old Ocean View Rd Norfolk VA 23503

MATSON, SIGFRED CHRISTIAN, music educator; b. Chgo., Feb. 17, 1917; s. Sigfred William and Wilhelmine (Janke) M.; B.Mus., Am. Conservatory Music, Chgo., 1937, M.Mus. (piano), 1938, M.Mus., (composition), 1939; A.B., Ohio Wesleyan U., 1942; Ph.D., Eastman Sch. Music, Rochester, N.Y., 1947; m. Mildred Zimmer, Aug. 8, 1940; children—Marie Judith, Sigfred, Lois Carolyn, Paul, Carol, Sharon. Instr. music Sioux Falls (S.D.) Coll., 1939-41, Ohio Wesleyan U., 1941-44; prof. music Monmouth (Ill.) Coll., 1947-48, head music dept., 1948-49; head music dept. Miss. U. for Women, Columbus, 1949-78, prof. music, 1978—; composition grantee, summers 1964-75. Adv. council Miss. Dept. Edn., 1956-60; mem. com. on liturgics and hymnology So. Dist. of Luth. Ch.-Missouri Synod, 1960-66. Mem. Music Educators Nat. Conf. (chmn. editors of state periodicals So. div. 1965-66), Music Tchrs. Nat. Assn. (exec. bd. So. div. 1971—, nat. exec. bd. 1971-74, 76—, v.p. program So. div. 1974-76, pres. div. 1976-78, rec. sec. 1979—), Miss. Music Educators Assn. (v.p. 1958-59, sec.-treas. 1959-60, sec. 1960-61, pres. 1961-62, editor publ. 1960-66), Nat. Assn. Schs. Music (v.p. region VIII 1962-64), Miss. Music Tchrs. Assn. (pres. 1966-70, certification chmn. 1964-76), Phi Mu Alpha-Sinfonia. Lutheran. Home: Star Route Box 220-2 Columbus MS 39701

MATSON, WALLACE I., educator; b. Portland, Oreg., June 18, 1921; s. Henry I. and Nelle (Newton) M.; A.B., U. Calif. at Berkeley, 1942, Ph.D., 1949; m. Olga Luiba Matveyenko, Jan. 30, 1953; children—Alexander Paul, Philip Newton. Vis. asst. prof. philosophy Pomona Coll., 1949-50; asst. prof. U. Wash., 1950-55; mem. faculty U. Calif. at Berkeley, 1955—, prof. philosophy, 1965—, chmn. dept., 1968-71. Vis. prof. U. Alta., 1955, U. Rochester, 1964, U. Hawaii, 1965. Served with AUS, 1942-46. Guggenheim fellow, Cambridge (Eng.) U., 1961-62; Nat. Endowment for Humanities sr. fellow, 1971-72; vis. fellow Wolfson Coll., Cambridge U., 1978. Mem. Am. Philos. Assn., Mind Assn. Great Britain, Aristotelian Soc. (London), Phi Beta Kappa. Author: The Existence of God, 1965; A History of Philosophy, 1968; Sentience, 1976; (with Thomas B. Warren) The Warren-Matson Debates, 1978; also articles. Home: 2511 Hill Ct Berkeley CA 94708

MATSUDA, FUJIO, univ. pres.; b. Honolulu, Oct. 18, 1924; s. Yoshio and Shimo (Iwasski) M.; B.S. in Civil Engring., Rose Poly. Inst., 1949; D.Sc., Mass. Inst. Tech., 1952; m. Amy M. Saiki, June 11, 1949; children—Bailey Koki, Thomas Junji, Sherry Noriko, Joan Yuuko, Ann Mitsuyo, Richard Hideo. Research engr. Mass. Inst. Tech., 1952-54; asst. prof. U. Ill., Urbana, 1954-55; asst. prof. engring. U. Hawaii, Honolulu, 1955-57, asso. prof., 1957-62, chmn. dept. civil engring., 1960-63, prof., 1962-63, dir. engring. research center, 1962-63, v.p. bus. affairs, 1973-74, pres., 1974—; dir. Hawaii Dept. Transp., Honolulu, 1963-74; v.p. Park & Yee, Ltd., Honolulu, 1957-58; pres. SMS & Assos., Inc., 1959-63; pvt. practice as structural engr., 1958-60; dir. C. Brewer & Co., Ltd., Hawaiian Electric Co., UAL, Inc., United Air Lines. Mem. Bd. Water Supply, Honolulu, 1963-73; mem. adv. bd. Trans-Pacific Soc., 1963-74; pres. Pacific Coast Assn. Port Authorities, 1969; mem. Gov.'s adv. task force on energy policy, 1974; bd. dirs. Aloha United Way, 1973, Honolulu Symphony Soc., 1974—; trustee U. Hawaii Found., 1968-74, Oceanic Found., 1973-74. Served with AUS, 1943-45. Mem. ASCE, Nat. Acad. Engring., Nat. Soc. Profl. Engrs., Am. Soc. Engring. Edn., Am. Concrete Inst., Sigma Xi, Tau Beta Pi. Home: 2234 Kamehameha Ave Honolulu HI 96822 Office: U Hawaii Honolulu HI 96822

MATSUI, ROBERT TAKEO, congressman; b. Sacramento, Sept. 17, 1941; s. Yasuji and Alice (Nagata) M.; A.B. in Polit. Sci., U. Calif., Berkeley, 1963; J.D., Hastings Coll. Law, U. Calif., San Francisco, 1966; m. Doris Kazue Okada, Sept. 17, 1966; 1 son, Brian Robert. Legal intern Calif. Dept. Water Resources, Sacramento, 1966; admitted to Calif. bar, 1967; practiced law, Sacramento, 1967-78; mem. Sacramento City Council, 1971-78, vice mayor, 1977; mem. 96th Congress from 3d Dist. Calif. City rep. Sacramento Area CD and Disaster Council, from 1972; chmn. Employee Relations Com., 1972; chmn. Budget and Fin. Com., 1975. Campaign chmn. Congressman John E. Moss re-election campaign, 1972, 74, 76. Named Young Man of Yr., Jr. C. of C., 1973; recipient Disting. Service award, 1973. Mem. Sacramento Japanese Am. Citizens League (pres. 1969), Sacramento Met. C. of C. (dir. 1976). Democrat. Clubs: 20-30 (pres. 1972), Rotary (Sacramento). Home: 1340 Gable Way Sacramento CA 95831 Office: 502 Cannon House Office Bldg Washington DC 20515

MATSUMOTO, GEORGE, architect; b. San Francisco, July 16, 1922; s. Manroku F. and Ise (Nakagawa) M.; student U. Calif. at Berkeley, 1938-42; B.Arch., Washington U., 1944; M.Arch., Cranbrook Acad. Art, 1945; m. Kimi Nao, Dec. 15, 1951; children—Mari-Jane, Kiyo-Ann, Kei-Ellen, Kenneth Manroku, Miye-Eileen. Designer, Heathers Garden Devel. Co., Calif., 1941-42; designer with George F. Keck, Chgo., 1943-44; sr. designer, planner Saarinen & Swanson, Birmingham, Mich., 1945-46; sr. designer Skidmore, Owings & Merrill, Chgo., 1948; partner Runnells, Clark, Waugh, Matsumoto, Kansas City, Mo., 1946-47; practice architecture Okla., N.C., 1948-61, San Francisco, 1962—; instr. U. Okla., 1947-48; prof. N.C. State Coll., 1948-61, U. Calif. at Berkeley, 1961-67. Bd. dirs. Young Audiences, Oakland Mus. Assn., Oakland Art Council. Recipient over 50 archtl. awards and prizes. Fellow AIA, Internat. Inst. Arts and Letters; mem. Mich. Soc. Architects, Assn. Coll. Sch. Architecture, Raleigh Council Architects, San Francisco Planning and Urban Renewal Assn., Nat. Council Archtl. Registration Bds., Calif. Assn. Architects, Bldg. Research Inst. Important works include office bldgs., schs., chs., govt. bldgs. and pvt. residences. Home: 1170 Glencourt Dr Oakland CA 94611 Office: 215 Leidesdorff St San Francisco CA 94111

MATSUMOTO, TERUO, educator, surgeon; b. Fukuoka City, Japan, Jan. 2, 1929; s. Yoshinari and Fumie (Hayashi) M.; M.D., Kyushu U., 1953, Ph.D., 1956; m. Mary L. Cousino, July 29, 1961; children—Louisa Michi, Maria Chieko, Monica Mieko, Nelson Tateru. Came to U.S., 1956, naturalized, 1964. Intern Cook County Hosp., Chgo., 1956-57; surg. resident Med. Coll. Ohio, Toledo, 1957-61; commd. capt. U.S. Army, 1961, advanced through grades to lt. col., 1967; gen. surgeon U.S. Army Camp Zama Hosp., Japan, 1961-63, chief gen. surgery sect., 1963-64, chief surg. service, 1964-65; chief dept. exptl. surgery Walter Reed Army Inst. Research, 1966-68, acting dir. div. surgery, 1968; prof. surgery Hahnemann Med. Coll. and Hosp., Phila., 1969—, chmn. dept. surgery, 1975—. Recipient Sir Henry Wellcome medal and prize, 1967; gold medal Southeastern Sug. Congress, 1968; Outstanding Achievement award U.S. Army Sci. Conf., 1970; Golden Apple award Student AMA, 1972. Diplomate Am. Bd. Surgery. Fellow Southeastern Surg. Congress, A.C.S., Am. Coll. Angiology, Am. Assn. for Surgery of Trauma, Pan Am. Med. Assn., Assn. Surgery for Alimentary Tract, AMA, Japanese Coll. Surgeons, Internat. Cardiovascular Surgery, Soc. Vascular Surgery, AOA, Phila. Acad. Surgery, Pan Pacific Surg. Congress, Soc. Surg. Chairmen (council cardiovascular surgery and society, surg. oncology). Contbr. to profl. jours. and books. Home: 515 Fishers Rd Bryn Mawr PA 19010 Office: Hahnemann Med Coll and Hosp Philadelphia PA 19102

MATSUNAGA, RONALD SHIGETO, facial plastic surgeon; b. Fresno, Calif., Feb. 17, 1927; s. Gunta and Sueno (Motoshima) M.; D.D.S., U. So. Calif., 1953; M.D., UCLA, 1958; m. Helen Morita, Aug. 19, 1951; children—Marsha Judd, Mark, Laura. Intern, Los Angeles County Gen. Hosp., 1958-59; resident head and neck surgery Wadsworth VA Hosp. and UCLA Med. Center, 1959-62; practice medicine, specializing in plastic surgery, otolaryngology, Los Angeles, 1962—; chief dept. head and neck surgery, cons. staff plastic surgery Daniel Freeman Hosp., Inglewood, Calif., 1972-77; chief staff Viewpark Hosp., Los Angeles, 1971-72, bd. govs.; clin. prof. facial plastic and maxillofacial surgery U. So. Calif. Med. Sch., Los Angeles, 1971—. Served with AUS, 1945-47. Fellow Am. Acad. Facial Plastic and Reconstructive Surgery, A.C.S. Clubs: Optimist, Bel Air Country. Office: 6200 Wilshire Blvd Los Angeles CA 90048

MATSUNAGA, SPARK MASAYUKI, U.S. senator; b. Kauai, Hawaii, Oct. 8, 1916; s. Kingoro and Chiyono (Fukushima) M.; Ed.B. with honors, U. Hawaii, 1941; J.D., Harvard U., 1951; LL.D. (hon.), Soochow U., 1973, St. John's U., 1977, Eastern Ill. U., 1978, U. Md., 1979; H.L.D., Lincoln U., 1979; m. Helene Hatsumi Tokunaga, Aug. 6, 1948; children—Karen (Mrs. Hardman), Keene, Diane, Merle, Matthew. Vets. counsellor U.S. Dept. Interior, 1945-47; chief priority claimants div. War Assets Adminstrn., 1947-48; admitted to Hawaii bar, 1952; asst. pub. pros. City and County of Honolulu, 1952-54; practice of law, Honolulu, 1954-62; mem. Hawaii Ho. of Reps., 1954-59, majority leader, 1959; mem. 88th-94th congresses, mem. Rules, Aging, Steering and Policy coms., dep. majority whip; U.S. senator from Hawaii, 1976—, mem. Fin., Energy and Natural Resources, Vets.' Affairs coms., chief dep. whip. Mem. Hawaii statehood delegations to Congress, 1950, 54, Pacific War Meml. Commn., 1959-62; adv. com. Honolulu Redevel. Agy., 1953-54. Chmn. bd. Kaimuki YMCA; pres. Naturalization Encouragement Assn. Honolulu. Bd. dirs. World Brotherhood. Soc. Crippled Children and Adults, Honolulu Council Social Agys. Served from 2d lt. to capt., inf., AUS, 1941-45; ret. lt. col. JAGC, 1969. Decorated Bronze Star with valor clasp, Purple Heart with oak leaf cluster. Mem. Am., Hawaii bar assns., D.A.V., V.F.W., Japan-Am. Soc., U. Hawaii Alumni Assn. Democrat. Episcopalian. Clubs: Lions, Club 100 (Honolulu). Author: Rulemakers of The House, 1976. Home: 4020 Glenrose St Kensington MD 20795 Office: Russell Senate Office Bldg Washington DC 20510

MATSUSHIMA, SATOSHI, astronomer, educator; b. Fukui, Japan, May 6, 1923; s. Kyoyu and Hatsuye (Isaka) M.; B.S., U. Kyoto, 1946; Ph.D., U. Utah, 1954; postgrad. Harvard, 1952-54; Sc.D., U. Tokyo, 1966; m. Reiko Hori, Oct. 25, 1955; children—Peter Koichi, Anne Yuko. Came to U.S., 1950, naturalized, 1963. Asst. U. Kyoto, 1946-50; research asso. U. Pa., 1954-55; sr. research fellow Paris (France) Obs., 1956-57; research asso. U. Kiel (Germany), 1957-58; asst. prof. physics Fla. State U., 1958-60; asso. prof. astronomy U. Iowa, 1960-67; prof. astronomy Pa. State U., University Park, 1967—, head dept., 1976—; vis. astronomer Utrecht Obs., Netherlands, 1956; sr. research fellow Calif. Inst. Tech., 1958-60; vis. prof. U. Tokyo, 1965-66, 74, Tohoku U., 1974; cons. U.S. Naval Research Lab., 1963; panel mem. Nat. Acad. Scis.-NRC, 1970-73. UNESCO-IAU grantee, 1956-58; German Humboldt Found. fellow, 1957-58; German Astron. Soc. grantee, 1957-58; Research Corp. grantee, 1958; U.S.-Japan Coop. Sci. program fellow, 1965-66; NSF research grantee, 1963—. Fellow Royal Astron. Soc. Eng.; mem. Am. Astron. Soc., Am. Geophys. Union, Astron. Soc. Pacific, Internat. Astron. Union, Sigma Xi. Contbr. articles to profl. jours. Home: 274 Osmond St State College PA 16801 Office: 525 Davey Lab University Park PA 16802

MATTE, PIERRE VICTOR, librarian; b. Shawinigan, Que., Can., July 31, 1918; s. Auguste and Josephine (Gaillardetz) M.; B.A., Trois-Rivieres Coll., 1942; B.Phil., Laval U., 1944; B.L.S., U. Montreal, 1948; m. Clothilde Lessard, Oct. 20, 1951; children—Johanne, Louise and Michelle (twins). Prof., St. Mary Coll., Shawinigan, 1944-45; speaker CHLN Radio, Trois-Rivieres, Que., 1949; librarian Ballarmin House, Montreal, P.Q., 1950; editor plant organ Shawinigan Chems. Ltd., 1951-55; librarian City of Shawinigan, 1956-59; asst. dir. Quebec Pub. Library Service, Govt. of Quebec, 1960-75, dir., 1975—; mem. Pub. Library Commn. Govt. of Quebec, 1960—. Mem. Association des bibliothecaires de langue francaise (pres. 1960), Association pour l'avancement des sciences et des techniques de la documentation, Canadian Library Assn. (councillor 1963-65, 2d v.p. 1966-67), ALA (mem. council 1967-72), Corp. Profl. Librarians. Roman Catholic. Home: 1228 De Repentigny Quebec PQ G1S 1Y3 Canada Office: 1700 St Cyrille Blvd 17th Floor Quebec PQ G1R 5A9 Canada

MATTERN, DONALD EUGENE, banker; b. Mapleton Depot, Pa., Feb. 11, 1930; s. John Franklin and Lizzie May (Fiss) M.; B.A., Pa. State U., 1951; M.B.A., U. Pa., 1955; m. Anna Mae Bard, Nov. 24, 1951, children—Debra Jeanne, Cynthia Ann, James Franklin. Exec. trainee Fed. Res. Bank of Phila., 1953-55; asst. cashier to cashier Cumberland County Nat. Bank, New Cumberland, Pa., 1955-63; v.p. 1st Nat. Bank of State College (Pa.), 1963-64; asst. v.p., v.p., sr. v.p., sec. Reading Trust Co. (Pa.), 1964-70; sr. v.p., cashier Nat. Central Bank, Lancaster, Pa., 1970—; sec., v.p. Nat. Central Financial Corp., 1972—. Treas., bd. dirs. Reading-Berks Human Relations Council, 1967-70; v.p. bd. dirs. local chpt. Ams. Competitive Enterprise System; bd. dirs., past pres. United Way of Berks County; bd. dirs. Nat. Council Alcoholism, 1967-68; treas., bd. dirs. Housing Opportunities in the Met. Environment, 1968-73; bd. dirs., v.p. Community Gen. Hosp. of Reading; mem. adv. bd. Hawk Mountain council Boy Scouts Am.; bd. dirs. Reading Center City Devel. Fund. Served to 1st lt. USAF, 1951-53. Mem. Greater Reading Bd. Realtors (treas., dir.), Berks County Bankers Assn. (pres.). Republican. Lutheran. Clubs: Masons, Shriners, Berkshire Country. Home: 20 Birchwood Rd Wyomissing PA 19610 Office: 100 N Queen St Lancaster PA 17604 also 515 Penn St Reading PA 19603

MATTERN, DONALD HECKMAN, civil engr.; b. Johnstown, Pa., July 19, 1905; s. Hays Waite and Helen (Heckman) M.; B.S., Pa. State U., 1926; M.S., Iowa State U., 1928, C.E., 1933; m. May Foster, July 21, 1930; children—Mary Jane (Mrs. Owens), James Waite. Grad. asst. civil engring. Iowa State Coll., 1926-28; with prodn. and transmission dept. Consumers Power Co., Jackson, Mich., 1928-31; staff J. Paul Blundon, cons. engr., Keyser, W.Va., 1933; design orgn. TVA, Knoxville, 1934-38, project planning orgn., 1938-70, chief project planning br., 1954-70; water resources cons., 1970—. Registered engr., Tenn. Hon. mem. Am. Soc. C.E. (nat. dir. 1957-60, nat. v.p. 1960-62; profl. recognition award 1962); mem. Tech. Soc. Knoxville, Tau Beta Pi, Chi Upsilon. Mason. Address: 2524 Craghead Ln Knoxville TN 37920

MATTERN, WALTER GRAY, JR., assn. exec.; b. Tarrytown, N.Y., Dec. 31, 1926; s. Walter Gray and Helen (Furman) M.; A.B., Yale, 1946, grad. student, 1948-49; M.A. (hon.), Wesleyan U., 1961; Litt.D., Western New Eng. U., 1971; m. Virginia Kingswood Vogel, Jan. 3, 1959; children—Heather K., Candice B., Jennifer Vogel, Walter Gray III. Instr. Taft Sch., Watertown, Conn., 1946-48; headmaster Irving Sch., Tarrytown, N.Y., 1949-55; headmaster Wilbraham (Mass.) Acad., 1955-71, trustee, 1956-74; exec. sec. European Council Internat. Schs., 1974—. Republican. Address: Heather Hill Hydon Heath Godalming Surrey GU8 4BB England

MATTERS, CLYDE BURNS, coll. pres.; b. Fargo, N.D., Nov. 10, 1924; s. Lester H. and Pearl Lila (Burns) M.; B.S., Whitworth Coll., Spokane, Wash., 1950, M.Ed., 1951; Ph.D., U. Wash., 1960; m. Anna R. Skeels, Mar. 24, 1948; children—Cynthia (Mrs. Charles V. Carroll), Richard B. Tchr. Spokane Pub. Schs., 1950-51; prof. Whitworth Coll., 1950-57, 70-72; research asso. U. Wash., 1957-60; asst. supt. schs., King County, Wash., 1960-63; program adviser Ford Found., West Africa, 1963-70; pres. Hastings (Nebr.) Coll., 1972—. Pres. Nebr. Ind. Coll. Found.; mem. nexus com. Presbyn. Coll. Union; v.p. Assn. Ind. Colls. and Univs. Nebr. Resident camp dir. Spokane YMCA, 1952-57, bd. dirs., 1970-72. Bd. dirs. United Good Neighbors, Spokane County, 1969-70. Served with AUS, 1943-46. Decorated Bronze Star, Combat Inf. badge. Mem. Assn. Ind. Colls. and Univs. (pres. Nebr. 1979-80), Phi Delta Kappa. Presbyterian (elder). Club: Kiwanis. Home: 1340 Pershing Rd Hastings NE 68901

MATTESON, ROBERT ELIOT, coll. adminstr.; b. St. Paul, Sept. 13, 1914; s. Charles Dickerman and Adelaide Gridley (Hickcox) M.; B.A., Carleton Coll., Northfield, Minn., 1937; intern Nat. Inst. Pub. Affairs, 1937-38; M.A., Harvard, 1940; student Nat. War Coll., 1964-65; m. Jane Elizabeth Paetzold, June 21, 1940; children—Adelaide (Mrs. David Elliott Donnelley), Robert Eliot, Fredric L., Sumner W., Elizabeth C. Instr. polit. sci. Carleton Coll., 1940-42; dir. Stassen staff, Republican presdl. nomination, 1946-48; asst. to pres. U. Pa., 1948-52; asst. dir. Fgn. Operation Adminstrn., Washington, 1953-55; dir. White House Disarmament Staff, 1955-58; asst. to Sherman Adams, White House, 1958; mem. bd. nat. estimates CIA, 1959-62; dir. policy planning staff U.S. Disarmament Adminstrn., 1961; dir. research council, dir. program planning staff, sr. adviser U.S. Arms Control and Disarmament Agy., 1962-67; dep. CORDS, II Corps, Vietnam, 1967-68; dir. Office Internat. Tng., AID, Washington, 1968-71; dir. Sigurd Olson Inst. Environmental Studies, Northland Coll., Ashland, Wis., 1972-74. Mem. planning bd. Nat. Security Council, 1955-58; dep. dir. U.S. Disarmament delegation, London, 1956-57; adviser to U.S. delegation Fgn. Ministers Conf., Geneva, 1957, Summit Meeting and Geneva 10 Nation Disarmament Talks, Paris, 1960, 18 Nation Disarmament Talks, 1962, Geneva; mem. adv. bd. Wis. Environ. Edn. Council, 1972-76; mem. Wis. Wild Resources Adv. Council, 1974—, Wis. Snowmobile Council, 1974-76; chmn. Pres.'s Adv. Com. on Quetico-Superior Area, 1976-78; bd. dirs. Duluth-Superior Area Ednl. TV, 1977—, Environ. Learning Center Minn., 1977—, Minn. Sci. Mus., St. Paul, 1972—; trustee Northland Coll., 1974-75. Served with 80th Inf. Div., 3d Army, AUS, 1943-46; ETO. Decorated Combat Infantry badge, Silver Star for capture of Nazi Gestapo chief SS Gen. Kaltenbrunner; Littauer fellow, 1938-40. Mem. Assn. Governing Bds. Am. Colls. and Univs. (bd. mentor 1976—), Minn. Environ. Balance Assn. (dir. 1977-78). Lion. Clubs: Somerset (St. Paul); Harvard of Wis.; Explorers (N.Y.C.); Mill Reef (Antigua). Home: Cable WI 54821

MATTESON, ROBERT JOHNSON MONTGOMERY, public affairs cons.; b. Bennington, Vt., June 25, 1916; s. Peleg Austin and Amelia (Armbruster) M.; B.A., Middlebury Coll., 1938; student Nat. Inst. Pub. Affairs, 1938-39; M.P.A., Harvard, 1941, Ph.D., 1953; m. Janet Lucille Meditch, June 22, 1940 (div. 1962); 1 dau., Brenda Kathleen; m. 2d, Mary Makiko Okimoto, 1963; children—Mollie, Ruth, Carol. Adminstrv. asst. REA, 1938-39; adminstrv. officer Dept. Agr., 1941-43; dir. tng., research staff, project dir. Inst. Pub. Adminstrn., 1946-56; staff dir. Govtl. Research Assn., 1954-55; spl. asst. to city adminstr. City of N.Y., 1955; exec. dir. Am. Soc. Pub. Adminstrn., 1956-61; prin. cons. Matteson Assos., pub. affairs counseling, 1962—; research dir. Temporary Commn. on City Finances, N.Y.C., 1964-66; program cons. Center for Environ. Studies, Williams Coll., 1968-69. Served to lt. (j.g.) USNR, 1944-45. Mem. Am. Soc. Pub. Adminstrn. (pres. N.Y. chpt. 1954-55, Chgo. chpt. 1964-65), Am. Polit. Sci. Assn., Govtl. Research Assn., Vt. Antique Dealers Assn. (pres. 1974-76), Middlebury Coll. Alumni Assn., Sigma Phi Epsilon. Unitarian. Club: Rotary (pres. Bennington 1975-76). Survey reports on intergovtl. relations, regional planning, pub. welfare, pub. service edn., govtl. manpower, assn. mgmt., state constns., legislative orgn., resources devel., adminstrv. seminars, govtl. finance. Address: South St at Grandview Bennington VT 05201

MATTESON, WILLIAM BLEECKER, lawyer; b. N.Y.C., Oct. 20, 1928; s. Leonard Jerome and Mary Jo (Harwell) M.; B.A., Yale U., 1950; J.D., Harvard U., 1953; m. Marilee Brill, Aug. 26, 1950; children—Lynn, Sandra, Holly. Clk. to judge U.S. Ct. Appeals, 1953-54; admitted to N.Y. bar, 1954; clk. to U.S. Supreme Ct. Justice Harold H. Burton, 1954-55; asso. firm Debevoise, Plimpton, Lyons & Gates, and predecessors, N.Y.C., 1955-61, partner, 1961—, partner European office, Paris, 1973-78; lectr. Columbia U. Law Sch., 1972-73, 78—. Trustee Peddie Sch., Highstown, N.J., 1968-73, Kalamazoo Coll., 1972-77, Miss Porter's Sch., Farmington, Conn., 1977—, Nat. Council of Salk Inst., La Jolla, Calif., 1977—. Mem. Internat., Am., Fed., N.Y. State bar assns., Assn. Bar City N.Y. (chmn. securities regulation com. 1968-71), Harvard U. Law Sch. Assn. N.Y.C. (trustee 1968-73). Clubs: Union, Yale (N.Y.C.); Sankaty Head (Nantucket, Mass.); Circle Interallie (Paris). Home: 201 E 62d St New York NY 10021 Office: 299 Park Ave New York NY 10017

MATTEUCIG, GIACINTO, educator; b. Udine, Italy, June 11, 1915; s. Giuseppe and Rosa (Sibau) M.; came to U.S., 1931; A.B., U. Calif., Berkeley, 1936, M.A., 1938, postgrad., 1939-40; postgrad. U. Florence, Italy, 1938-39; Ph.D., Harvard, 1942; m. Iole Louise Cagnoni, June 26, 1948; children—Catherine Rose, Michael Joseph, Laurence Anthony. Research asso. U. Calif., Berkeley, 1942-43, lectr. in Italian, 1944; instr. ASTP, Stanford, 1943-44; instr. St. Marys Coll., Calif., 1945-46; asst. prof. U. San Francisco, 1946-51, asso. prof., 1951-60, prof., 1960—; vis. prof. lang. lab. techniques Nat. Def. Edn. Act Inst., U. Calif., Berkeley, summer 1961. Recipient Richardson Latin Composition prize U. Calif., 1934, 35, 36. Inst. Internat. Edn. traveling fellow, 1938, P.B. Wall Meml. scholar U. Calif., 1939, Amy Bowles Johnson Meml. Traveling fellow, 1940, Am. Council Learned Socs. fellow, 1941, Fulbright research fellow Am. Acad. Rome, 1964-65. Mem. Am. Philol. Assn., Archeol. Inst. Am., Pi Sigma, Pi Mu Iota. Author: Poggio Buco, the Necropolis of Statonia, 1951. Contbr. articles to profl. jours. Home: 55 Aerial Way San Francisco CA 94116

MATTFELD, JACQUELYN PHILLIPS ANDERSON, coll. pres.; b. Balt., Oct. 5, 1925; d. David Lindsay and Dorothy (Wheless) Anderson; diploma Peabody Conservatory Music, 1943-47; B.A. magna cum laude, Goucher Coll., 1948; Ph.D., Yale U., 1959; D.H.L., Kalamazoo Coll., 1979, Wagner Coll., 1976, Columbia U., 1976; M.A., Brown U., 1972; LL.D., U. Mass., 1972, Goucher Coll., 1972; m. Victor Henry Mattfeld, Aug. 28, 1949 (div. Aug. 1970); children—Stefanie, Felicity. Dir. fin. aid Radcliffe Coll., 1958-60, asso. dean instrn., also dean of East House, 1960-63; asso. dean student affairs Mass. Inst. Tech., 1963-65; dean Sarah Lawrence Coll., Bronxville, N.Y., 1965-69, prof. music history, 1965-71, provost, dean of faculty, 1969-71; asso. provost, dean faculty, dean acad. affairs, prof. music Brown U., Providence, 1971-76; pres. Barnard Coll., 1976—; lectr. dept. music Harvard U., 1960-63; ednl. cons. Kenyon

Coll., 1965; cons., asso. Kirkland Coll., 1965-72; cons. on coedn. Princeton U., 1967-68; mem. project selection com. Nat. Endowment for Humanities, 1970-73, project panel, 1970-74, devel. grant panel, 1974-75, nat. bd. cons., 1976—; mem. New Eng. adv. com. Higher Edn. Resource Service to Women, 1972-76, Mid-Atlantic adv. com., 1976—; mem. Nat. Com. Cultural Resources, 1974-75, Coop. Assessment Exptl. Learning, 1973-76, Conf. Faculty Adminstrv. Mgmt. U. Mich., 1974—. Adv. bd. Assn. Mentally Ill Children of Westchester, 1967-71; ednl. bd. dirs. Coop. Coll. Center, State U. N.Y., 1967-68, 70-71; mem. corp. Cambridge Sch. of Weston, 1970-72; trustee Goucher Coll., 1972—; bd. dirs. Japan Internat. Christian Found., 1966-68, N.Y. Philharmonic, 1976-77; bd. dirs., pres. bd. trustees Exptl. Center for Visual Edn. Recipient Wilbur Lucius Cross medal Yale U., 1979; Rockefeller fellow Aspen Inst., 1978—. Mem. Am. Council Edn. (commn. leadership devel. 1974-75, commn. acad. affairs 1976—), Am. Conf. Acad. Deans, Eastern Assn. Coll. Deans and Advisers Students (exec. com. 1969-71), Am. Musicol. Soc., Am. Mgmt. Assn. (trustee 1977—), Renaissance Soc., AAUW, Yale U. Council (chmn. com. edn. women 1973—, mem. com. on music 1972—), Phi Beta Kappa. Address: 606 W 120th St New York NY 10027

MATTHAEI, CHARLES WILLIAM HENRY, corp. exec.; b. Tacoma, May 6, 1920; s. William Peter and Hazel Margaret (Pfeffer) M.; B.S., U. Wash., 1943; grad. Exec. Program, Stanford U. Bus. Sch.; m. Helen Barbara Leon, June 28, 1946; children—William L., C. Frederick, Richard H. Test engr. Seattle-Tacoma Shipbuilding, 1943; with Roman Meal Co., Tacoma, 1947—, pres., 1964—, chmn. bd., chief exec. officer; trustee United Mutual Savs. Bank. Mem. adv. com. Tacoma Gen. Hosp. Served to lt. USNR, 1943-46. Mem. Assn. Wash. Bus. (trustee), Am. Inst. Baking (trustee), Am. Bakers Assn. (gov.), Indsl. Conf. Bd. (dir.), Am. Assn. Cereal Chemists, Bakery Engrs. Republican. Clubs: Rotary, Tacoma Yacht, Masons, Elks. Office: 2101 S Tacoma Way Tacoma WA 98409*

MATTHAU, WALTER, actor; b. N.Y.C., Oct. 1, 1920; s. Milton and Rose (Berolsky) M.; ed. pub. schs., N.Y.C.; m. Carol Grace Marcus, Aug. 21, 1959; children—David, Jenny, Charles. Broadway appearances include Anne of a Thousand Days, 1948, The Liar, 1949, Season in the Sun, 1950, Fancy Meeting You Again, 1951, Twilight Walk (N.Y. Drama Critics award), 1951, One Bright Day, 1951, In Any Language, 1952, The Grey-Eyed People, 1952, The Ladies of the Corridor, 1953, Will Success Spoil Rock Hunter, 1955, Once More with Feeling (N.Y. Drama Critics award), 1958, Once There Was a Russian, 1960, A Shot in the Dark (Antoinette Perry award), 1961, My Mother, My Father and Me, 1963, The Odd Couple (Antoinette Perry award), 1964; motion pictures include The Fortune Cookie (Academy award), A Guide for the Married Man, Lonely Are the Brave (Film Daily award), Secret Life of An American Wife, Cactus Flower, Mirage, Charade, The Kentuckian, The Indian Fighter, Voice in the Mirror, Slaughter on Tenth Avenue, Ride A Crooked Trail, Hello Dolly, A Face in the Crowd, Bigger Than Life, Island of Love, Where's The Action, Fail-Safe, Odd Couple, A New Leaf, Plaza Suite, Kotch, Pete 'n Tillie, Charley Varrick, Laughing Policeman, The Sunshine Boys, The Bad News Bears, Pelham, One Two Three, Casey's Shadow, 1978, House Calls, 1978. Served with USAAF, 1941-45; ETO. Home: 10100 Santa Monica Blvd Suite 2200 Los Angeles CA 90067

MATTHEIS, DUANE JOHN, ednl. ofcl.; b. Ellendale, N.D., Oct. 20, 1927; s. John and Katherine (Ammon) M.; B.S. in Sci., State Normal and Indsl. Coll., Ellendale, 1950; M.S. in Sch. Adminstrn., Colo. State Coll. Edn., 1954; M.Ednl. Adminstrn., Stanford, 1971; m. Beverly Tjosvold, June 26, 1955; children—Peter, Erik. Tchr. science and math. Granite Falls (Minn.) High Sch., 1950-53; prin., also tchr. sci., math., coach basketball LeRoy (Minn.) High Sch., 1953-54; prin. Granite Falls High Sch., 1954-56; asst. prin. Owatonna (Minn.) High Sch., 1956-58, supt. schs., 1958-64; commr. edn. Minn., 1964-69; dep. commr. for sch. systems U.S. Office of Edn., Washington, 1971-74, exec. dep. commr. edn., 1974-76; asso. dir. Ednl. Research Council Am., Cleve., 1976—. Served 1946-48. Mem. NEA (life), Am. Assn. Sch. Adminstrs., Phi Delta Kappa. Home: 20756 Parkcliff Dr Fairview Park OH 44126

MATTHES, M. C. (CHARLES), former fed. judge; b. DeSoto, Mo., Jan. 29, 1906; legal edn. Benton Coll. Law, St. Louis; m. Mildred M. Smelser, Dec. 23, 1931; 1 dau., Joanna May Matthes Smith. Admitted to Mo. bar, 1928; city atty. City of DeSoto, 2 yrs.; apptd. spl. dep. fin. commr. State Mo., 1929, 31; practiced law in DeSoto and Hillsboro, Mo., until 1955; then apptd. mem. St. Louis Ct. Appeals, 3 yrs.; judge U.S. Ct. Appeals, 8th Circuit, 1958-70, chief judge, 1970-76; mem. Mo. Senate, from 1942, pres. pro tem; former lectr. Washington U. Sch. Law, St. Louis. Mem. Mo. Hwy. Commn., 1954-55. Recipient citation of merit U. Mo. Sch. Law Alumni Assn., 1971. Mem. Am. Judicature Soc., Lawyers Assn. St. Louis, Alumni Assn. U. Mo. (hon.; public service award 1968), Order of Coif, Phi Delta Phi. Presbyterian. Club: Mo. Athletic (St. Louis). Office: US Ct Appeals 510 US Ct and Customs House 1114 Market St Saint Louis MO 63101

MATTHEWS, A(LAN) BRUCE, corporate exec.; b. Clarksburg, W.Va., Dec. 11, 1923; s. Ezra Wilson and Hilma (Nelson) M.; B.S., Ohio U., 1945; m. Marjorie Phillips, 1944 (div. 1962); m. 2d, Marjorie Nelson, Dec. 31, 1963; children—Bruce, Thomas, Jennifer, David, Michelle, Bradford, Christopher. Partner Arthur Andersen & Co., Detroit, 1945-56, mng. partner, Denver, 1956-65; v.p. finance and adminstrn. Communications Satellite Corp., Washington, 1965-70; pres., dir. Bliss & Laughlin Industries, Inc., Oak Brook, Ill., 1970-71; sr. v.p. CNA Financial Corp., Chgo., 1972-75; chmn., pres. Larwin Group, Inc., Beverly Hills, Calif., 1974-75; chmn. bd., dir. Healthco, Inc., 1972-75, 1st Healthcare Corp., 1972-75, Coaxial Communications, Inc., 1973-75, CNA Mgmt. Corp., 1973-75; pres. The Matthews Group, Washington, Cairo and London, 1975—; chmn. bd. Egyptian Service & Supply Co., Cairo, 1975-77, Washington Communications Group, 1977—. Pres., Jr. Achievement Met. Denver, 1960-62, chmn. bd., 1962-64, chmn. bd. Western Region, 1964-66, mem. nat. exec. com., 1962—; pres. bd. trustees Graland Country Day Sch., Denver, 1960-61, trustee, 1959-65; treas. Denver Symphony, 1964-65, trustee, 1958-65; chmn. Red Rocks Music Festival, 1960-61; treas., dir. Chgo. Crime Commn., 1970-72; trustee Nat. Symphony Orch., Washington, 1966-70; trustee Avery Coonley Sch., 1971-74, pres., 1973-74; bd. govs. Chgo. Symphony Orch. Assn., 1972—. Served with AUS, 1942-43. Mem. Financial Execs. Inst., Am. Inst. C.P.A.'s, President's Assn., Am. Mgmt. Assn., Nat. Assn. Bus. Economists, Newcomen Soc. Clubs: Chicago, Mid-America, Economic (Chgo.); Mile High (Denver); Hinsdale Golf; Met., Congressional Country, Internat. (Washington); Sky (N.Y.C.). Home: 4970 Rockwood Pkwy NW Washington DC 20016 Office: 2626 Pennsylvania Ave NW Washington DC 20037

MATTHEWS, ALBERT BRUCE, corp. exec.; b. Ottawa, Ont., Can., Aug. 12, 1909; s. Albert E. and Maud (Whiteside) M.; student Upper Can. Coll., Toronto; m. Victoria Thorne, Sept. 25, 1937; children—Bryn Corse, Victor Bruce, Harriet Matthews Harris. Engaged in investment bus., N.Y.C., 1928-30; gen. partner Matthews & Co., Toronto, 1932-39; with Excelsior Life Ins. Co., Toronto, 1946—, pres., 1949-63, chmn. bd., 1963-74, now dir.; dep. chmn., dir. Argus Corp. Ltd., 1964-79; pres. Matthews & Co., Inc., Toronto, hon. v.p. Toronto-Dominion Bank; chmn. Dome Mines Ltd.; dir. Can. Permanent Trust Co., Can. Permanent Mortgage Corp., Massey-Ferguson Ltd., 3d Canadian Gen. Investment Trust, Canadian Gen. Investments Ltd., Standard Broadcasting Corp., Dome Petroleum Ltd. Served to maj. gen. Royal Canadian Arty., 1939-45. Decorated comdr. Brit. Empire, Distinguished Service Order, Efficiency Decoration, Canadian Forces Decoration; Legion of Honour, Croix de Guerre with palm (France); grand officer Order Orange Nassau (Netherlands). Mem. Royal Canadian Mil. Inst. Clubs: Toronto, York, Toronto Golf, Nat. (Toronto); Mount Royal (Montreal); Rideau (Ottawa); Brook (N.Y.C.). Home: 19 Riverview Dr Toronto ON Canada Office: 320 Bay St Suite 700 Toronto ON M5H 2P6 Canada

MATTHEWS, ALFRED ST. JOHN, JR., hotel exec.; b. Macon, Ga., Dec. 19, 1939; s. Alfred St. John and Willa (Perry) M.; B.A., Randolph-Macon Coll., 1961; m. Pamela Ruth DeYoung, Aug. 19, 1972; children—Alfred St. John, III, Joseph Douglas, Kristen Elizabeth. With Marriott Hotels, Inc., 1962—, exec. asst. mgr. Saddlebrook (N.J.) Marriott Hotel, 1971-74, resident mgr. Denver Marriott Hotel, 1974-76, Chgo. Marriott O'Hare, 1976-77, gen. mgr. Atlanta Marriott Hotel at Perimeter Center, 1977—. Mem. Ga. Hospitality and Travel Assn., Atlanta C. of C., DeKalb County C. of C. Episcopalian. Club: Atlanta Country. Office: Atlanta Marriott Hotel at Perimeter Center 236 Perimeter Center Pkwy Atlanta GA 30346

MATTHEWS, BENJAMIN ALFONZO, lawyer; b. Culloden, Ga., Apr. 18, 1890; s. Alfonzo Horton and Augusta Louise (Vaughan) M.; LL.B., Georgetown U., 1913; m. Emilie May Johnston, June 2, 1917 (dec. Oct. 1962); children—Benjamin A. (dec.), David L., Anne (Mrs. Kenneth S. Rawson). Admitted to Ga. bar, 1912; also cts. of N.Y., D.C., Supreme Ct. U.S. and lower Fed. cts.; clk. Ordnance Office, later Judge Adv. Gen.'s Office, War Dept., Washington, 1909-12; sec. to William H. Hunt, Circuit Judge on U.S. Commerce Ct., 1913-14; asst. U.S. atty. So. Dist N.Y., 1914-21; partner firm Rothwell, Harper & Matthews, 1921-28, Harper & Matthews, 1928-29, Clarke, Allen, Harper & Matthews, 1929-32, Harper & Matthews, 1932-77. Asst. chief counsel N.Y. State Crime Commn., 1951, chief counsel, 1952-54. Served with Ga. N.G., 1906-09; with N.Y. Naval Militia, 1914-17. Govt. appeal agt. local bd. No. 1, SSS, N.Y.C., 1940-45. Recipient first honor awards Class of 1913, Georgetown U. Law Sch., 1911, 12, 13. Mem. Am., N.Y. State (50 Year Lawyer award 1970), Fed. bar assns., N.Y. County Lawyers Assn. (pres. 1956-58), Assn. Bar City of N.Y., Georgetown Alumni Assn., N.Y. So. Soc. Methodist (alternate mem. jud. council 1940-48, pres. N.Y.C. soc. 1926-66; ch. trustee). Clubs: Quill, Lawyers (past pres.), University (N.Y.C.); Nat. Lawyers (Washington). Home: 993 Park Av New York City NY 10028 also (summer) Secret Acres Route 224 Ely VT 05044 Office: 82 Wall St New York NY 10005. *Do the next thing next. Aim high, but don't shoot straight up. If it is worth doing at all, it's worth doing well.*

MATTHEWS, BURNITA SHELTON, judge; b. Burnell, Miss., Dec. 28, 1894; d. Burnell and Lora Drew (Barlow) Shelton; LL.B., George Washington U., (formerly Nat. U.), 1919, LL.M., 1920, LL.D., 1950; LL.D., Am. U., 1966; m. Percy Ashley Matthews, Apr. 28, 1917. Admitted to D.C., Miss., U.S. Supreme Ct. bars; practice in Washington, 1920; active in securing equal rights for women; formerly mem. faculty Washington Coll. Law; judge U.S. Dist. Ct., D.C., 1949-68, sr. judge, 1968—. Past mem. Com. Experts Women's Work ILO; formerly mem. research com. Inter-Am. Commn. Women; former mem. Nat. Woman's Party. Mem., past v.p. nat. bd. Med. Coll. Pa. (formerly Woman's Med. Coll. Pa.); nat. devel. com. Am. Recipient Alumni Achievement award George Washington U., 1968; Distinguished Service award Bar Assn. D.C., 1968. Mem. Am. Bar Assn., Nat. Assn. Women Lawyers (past pres.). Drafted many laws sponsored by Nat. Woman's Party. Home: 5420 Connecticut Ave NW Washington DC 20015 Office: US Courthouse 3d and Constitution Ave NW Washington DC 20001

MATTHEWS, BURTON CLARE, univ. pres.; b. Kerwood, Ont., Can., Dec. 16, 1926; s. Clarence DeLloyd and Dora Meryl (Freer) M.; B.S., U. Toronto, 1947; A.M., U. Mo., 1948; Ph.D., Cornell U., 1952; m. Lois Verna Lewis, June 23, 1951; children—David Lewis, Thomas Dale. Prof. soil sci. Ont. Agrl. Coll., 1950-64; prof. soil sci. U. Guelph, 1964-70, v.p. acad., 1966-70; pres., vice-chancellor U. Waterloo, Ont., 1970—; dir. Ont. Ednl. Communications Authority, Campbell Soup Co. Ltd. Nuffield Found. fellow Oxford U., 1960-61. Mem. Agrl. Inst. Can., Am. Soc. Agronomy, Canadian Soc. Higher Edn., Assn. Univs. and Colls. Can. (dir. 1977-78), Sigma Xi, Gamma Alpha. Anglican. Clubs: Masons; Kitchener Rotary. Sci. editor Canadian Jour. Soil Sci., 1962-64; contbr. articles to various jours. Home: 12 Westgate Walk Kitchener ON N2M 2T8 Canada Office: 75 University Ave Waterloo ON Canada

MATTHEWS, CHARLES ARNOLD, educator; b. Brunswick County, Va., May 6, 1916; s. James Edward and Patty Sue (Epperson) M.; B.C.S., Washington and Lee U., 1937; M.A. in Econs., U. Va., 1939, Ph.D., 1941; m. Mary Dawson Lippitt, Sept. 9, 1950 (dec. 1957); children—Mary Katherine, Charles Arnold; m. 2d, Reta Garris, Jan. 27, 1962. Instr. econs. W.Va. U., 1939-40; econ. analyst U.S. Dept. Treasury, 1945-48; prof. fin. U. Fla., Gainesville, 1948—, chmn. dept. fin. and ins., 1957—, chmn. dept. finance, ins., real estate and urban land studies, 1971-76, asso. dean Coll. Bus. Administrn., 1976—. Served from ensign to lt. comdr., Supply Corps, USNR, 1941-45, from lt. comdr. to comdr., 1951-53. Mem. Am., So. econ. assns., Am., So. fin. assns. Democrat. Methodist. Kiwanian. Contbr. articles to profl. jours. Home: 2000 NW 23d Terr Gainesville FL 32601

MATTHEWS, CHARLES WILLIAM, cons. engr., city planner; b. Milw., Sept. 29, 1904; s. Alfred Cookman and Mayme Helen (Disch) M.; B.S. in Civil Engring., U. Wis.-Madison, 1928, certificate in civil affairs, 1943; M. City Planning, Mass. Inst. Tech., 1937; postgrad. Am. Sch. Center, Shrivenham, Eng., 1944; m. Janet Ruth Beckwith, Nov. 12, 1930; children—Susan Matthews Byrnes, Sara (Mrs. Robert C. Stocker), Elizabeth Matthews Wallace. Engr., Milw. County Regional Planning Dept., 1928-35; town planner U.S. Resettlement Adminstrn., Washington, 1935-36; engr. New Eng. Regional Planning Commn., planning cons., Boston, 1936-37; engr. N.Y. Div. State Planning, Albany, 1937-38; resident engr. Ladislas Segoe and Assos., Cin., Charleston, W.Va. and Tucson, 1938-42, prin. assos., Cin., collaborative projects with Balke Engrs., Cin., Howard, Needles, Tammen & Bergendoff, Kansas City, Tippetts-Abbett-McCarthy-Stratton, N.Y.C., Vogt, Ivers & Assos., Cin., and others, 1946-65; cons. engr., city planner in individual practice, Cin., also cons. asso. Community Cons., Inc., Charleston, W.Va., and John R. Snell Engrs., Inc., Lansing, Mich., 1965—; planning cons. over 100 cities, towns and counties in 15 states and Can.; vis. lectr. U. Ariz., 1941, U. Cin., 1959-61. Mem. Pleasant Ridge Community Council, Cin., 1972—. Served from capt. to lt. col., AUS, 1942-46; ETO. Decorated L'Ordre Grand Ducal de la Couronne de Chene (Luxembourg). Registered profl. engr., Ohio, W.Va., Wis.; registered community planner, Mich.; certified Nat. Council Engring. Examiners. Fellow ASCE; mem. Am. Assn. Engring. Socs., Am. Inst. Certified Planners (awards jury), Am. Planning Assn., Soc. Am. Mil. Engrs., Engrs. and Scientists Cin. (ASCE sect.), Engrs. and Scientists Milw., Ret. Officers Assn., Pi Kappa Alpha. Republican. Presbyn. Mason. Clubs: Officers (Wright-Patterson AFB, Dayton, Ohio); Statesman's, Mass. Inst. Tech. Alumni, University of Wisconsin Alumni (Cin.). Contbr. articles to various publs. Address: 3212 Beredith Pl Cincinnati OH 45213

MATTHEWS, CLARK J(IO), II, retail co. exec.; b. Arkansas City, Kans., Oct. 1, 1936; s. Clark J. and Betty Elizabeth (Stewart) M.; B.A., So. Meth. U., 1959, J.D., 1961; m. Janice Eleanor Hill, June 28, 1959; children—Patricia Eleanor, Pamela Elaine, Katherine Joy. Admitted to Tex. bar, 1961; trial atty. Ft. Worth Regional Office, SEC, 1961-63; law clk. to chief U.S. dist. judge No. Dist. Tex., Dallas, 1963-65; atty. Southland Corp., Dallas, 1965-73, v.p., gen. counsel, 1973-79, exec. v.p., chief fin. officer, 1979—. Mem. Tex., Dallas, Am. bar assns., Am. Judicaturé Soc., Alpha Tau Omega, Pi Alpha Delta. Methodist. Club: DeMolay. Home: 7005 Stefani St Dallas TX 75225 Office: 2828 N Haskell Ave Dallas TX 75204

MATTHEWS, CLIFFORD NORMAN, educator; b. Hong Kong, Dec. 20, 1921; s. Thomas and Anna (Braun) M.; student U. Hong Kong, 1938-41; B.Sc., U. London, 1950; Ph.D., Yale, 1955; m. Magdalen I. Javor, July 5, 1947; children—Sandra Anna, Christopher Thomas. Chem. research Conn. Hard Rubber Co., New Haven, 1950-51, Diamond Alkali Co., Painesville, O., 1955-59, Monsanto Research Corp., Everett, Mass., 1959-64, central research dept. Monsanto Co., St. Louis, 1964-69; prof. chemistry U. Ill. at Chicago Circle, 1969—. Served with Brit. Army, 1941-45. Mem. Am. Chem. Soc., Chem. Soc. London, AAAS. Research on organic chemistry, chem. evolution, origin of proteins. Office: University of Ill at Chgo Circle Chicago IL 60680

MATTHEWS, DAVID, clergyman; b. Indianola, Miss., Jan. 29, 1920; s. Albert and Bertha (Young) M.; A.B., Morehouse Coll., Atlanta, 1950; student Atlanta U., 1950, Memphis Theol. Sem., 1965, Delta State U., Cleveland, Miss., 1969, 71, 72; D.D. (hon.), Natchez (Miss.) Jr. Coll., 1973; m. Lillian Pearl Banks, Aug. 28, 1951; 1 dau., Denise. Ordained minister Nat. Baptist Conv. U.S.A., 1946; pastor chs. in Miss., 1951—, Bell Grove Baptist Ch., Indianola, 1951—, Strangers Home, Greenwood, 1958—; instr., chmn. dept. social sci. Gentry High Sch., Indianola, 1958—; vice moderator Sunflower Baptist Assn., 1957—; v.p. Gen. Baptist Conv. Miss., 1958—, lectr., conv. congress religious edn., 1958—; v.p. Nat. Baptist Conv. U.S.A., 1971—, del. to Nat. Council Chs., 1960, supr. oratorial contest, 1976; pres. Gen. Missionary Bapt. State Conv. Miss., 1974—. Mem. Sunflower County Anti-Poverty Bd., 1965-71, Indianola Bi-Racial Com., 1965—; mem. Gov.'s Advisory Com.; col. on staff Gov. Finch, 1976-80; mem. budget com. Indianola United Fund, 1971—; chmn. bd. Indianola FHA, 1971—; trustee Natchez Jr. Coll. Served with U.S. Army, 1942-45; PTO. Recipient citation Morehouse Coll., 1950, Miss. Valley State Coll., 1956; J.H. Jackson Preaching award Midwestern Baptist Laymen Fellowship, 1974; Gov.'s Merit award, 1975. Mem. NEA, Miss., Indianola tchrs. assns. Democrat. Home: PO Box 627 Indianola MS 38751. *I have learned not to seek honors and success but to become so involved in worthwhile works that I lose myself and by such actions success and honors have come.*

MATTHEWS, DONALD RAY BILLY, public relations cons.; b. Micanopy, Fla., Oct. 3, 1907; s. David Horace and Flora (Turney) M.; A.B., U. Fla., 1929, M.A., 1947; m. Sara Lewis, Apr. 5, 1941; children—Mary Carolyn, Sara Ann Dailey, Donald Ray. Pub. sch. tchr., Leesburg and Orlando, Fla., 1929-35; prin. Newberry (Fla.) schs., 1935-36; dir. Student Activity Center, U. Fla., 1936-47, dir. alumni affairs, 1947-52; mem. 83d-89th congresses, 8th Dist. Fla., mem. house com. on appropriations; tchr. Am. instns. Santa Fe Jr. Coll., Gainesville, Fla., until 1978; public relations cons., 1978—. Past chmn. Alachua County chpt. Nat. Found. Infantile Paralysis; past pres. Alachua County chpt. Health and Welfare; 1st chmn. Fla. Council for Blind. Mem. Fla. Legislature, 1935. Served as capt., inf., AUS, 1942-46. Mem. Nat. Assn. Coll. Student Activity Centers (pres. 1946-47), Am. Alumni Council (panel leader), C. of C. Gainesville (past dir.), Am. Legion, Fla. Blue Key, Scabbard and Blade, Sigma Phi Epsilon, Alpha Phi Omega, Tau Kappa Alpha, Pi Gamma Mu, Phi Kappa Phi. Presbyn. (elder). K.P., Kiwanian (past pres.), Lion (past dist. gov.). Home: 2611 SW 8th Dr Gainesville FL 32601

MATTHEWS, DONALD ROWE, polit. scientist, educator; b. Cin., Sept. 14, 1925; s. William Proctor and Janet Birch (Williams) M.; student Kenyon Coll., 1943, Purdue U., 1944-45; A.B. with high honors, Princeton, 1948, M.A., 1951, Ph.D., 1953; m. Margie C. Richmond, June 28, 1947 (div.); children—Mary, Jonathan; m. 2d, Carmen J. Onstad, July 7, 1970; children—Christopher, Amy. Instr., Smith Coll., Northampton, Mass., 1951-53, asst. prof. govt., 1953-57; lectr. polit. sci. U. N.C., Chapel Hill, 1957-58, asso. prof., 1958-63, prof., 1963-70, research prof. Inst. for Research in Social Sci., 1963-70; sr. fellow in govtl. studies Brookings Instn., Washington, 1970-73; prof. polit. sci. and research asso. Inst. for Research in Social Sci., U. Mich., Ann Arbor, 1973-76; prof. polit. sci., chmn. dept. polit. sci. U. Wash., Seattle, 1976—; fellow Center for Advanced Study in the Behavioral Scis. 1964-65; cons. to U.S. Commn. on Civil Rights, 1958-60, NBC News, 1966-68, Ford Found., 1967-68, U.S. Ho. of Reps., 1970-72, others. Served with USNR, 1943-46. Recipient Sr. Award for Research in Govtl. Affairs, Social Sci. Research Council, 1962; Ford Found. fellow, 1969-70; Fellow Am. Acad. Arts and Scis.; mem. Am. (treas. 1970-72), Pacific N.W. (pres. 1977-78), Western (pres. 1979-80), So., Midwestern polit. sci. assns., Inter-Univ. Consortium for Polit. Research (exec. com. 1970-72). Democrat. Author: The Social Background of Political Decision-Makers, 1954; U.S. Senators and Their World, 1960; (with James Prothro) Negroes and the New Southern Politics, 1966; Perspectives on Presidential Selection, 1973; (with William Keech) The Party's Choice, 1976; (with James Stimson) Yeas and Nays: A Theory of Decision-Making in the U.S. House of Representatives, 1975. Contbr. articles to profl. jours. Home: 1429 E Valley St Seattle WA 98112 Office: Dept of Polit Sci DO-30 U Wash Seattle WA 98195

MATTHEWS, DOYLE JENSEN, univ. adminstr.; b. Liberty, Idaho, Apr. 13, 1926; s. William and Idell (Jensen) M.; B.S., Utah State U., 1950, M.S., 1951; Ph.D., Kans. State U., 1959; m. Edith Passey, Feb. 11, 1946; children—Shirlene, Mardyne, Neal, Karen, Larry. Mem. faculty dept. animal husbandry Utah State U., Logan, 1952-63, extension livestock specialist, 1963-65, asst. dean Coll. Agr., 1965-71, dean Coll. of Agr., dir. Agr. Experiment Sta., 1971—; vice chmn. Agrl. Devel. Council, State of Utah. Served with USNR, 1945-46. Mem. Phi Kappa Phi, Sigma Xi, Alpha Gamma Rho. Mormon. Home: 485 S 400 E Logan UT 84321 Office: Coll of Agr Utah State Univ Logan UT 84322

MATTHEWS, EDWARD JOSEPH, JR., food co. exec.; b. N.Y.C., Oct. 20, 1935; s. Edward Joseph and Regina Theresa (Taylor) M.; B.A. in Econs., Dartmouth Coll., 1957; M.B.A. in Finance and Accounting, Amos Tuck Sch., 1959; m. Michelle McQueeny; children—Edward Joseph, IV, Peter M., Paul T., Margot Lynn. Sr. accountant Haskins & Sells, C.P.A.'s, N.Y.C., 1959-64; v.p. finance Strawberry Hill Press Inc., N.Y.C., and Asheville, N.C., 1964-69; asst. controller Inmont Corp., N.Y.C., 1969-70, v.p., gen. mgr. Inmont Confections Co., N.Y.C., 1970-71; asst. treas., Inmont Corp., N.Y.C.,

1971-73; asst. treas. Nabisco, Inc., N.Y.C., 1973-75, treas., 1975-78, v.p. corporate devel., 1978—; dir. Morris County Savs. Bank. Served with USMCR, 1959-60. C.P.A. Mem. Am. Inst. C.P.A.'s, N.Y. State Soc. C.P.A.'s, Financial Execs. Inst., Morris County C. of C., Beta Theta Pi. Republican. Clubs: Roxiticus Golf, Mantoloking Yacht; Yale (N.Y.C.). Address: Nabisco Inc East Hanover NY 07936

MATTHEWS, EUGENE EDWARD, artist; b. Davenport, Iowa, Mar. 22, 1931; s. Nickolas Arthur and Velma (Schroeder) M.; student Bradley U., 1948-51; B.F.A., U. Iowa, 1953, M.F.A., 1957; postgrad. (fellow in painting) Am. Acad. Rome, 1957-60; m. Wanda Lee Miller, Sept. 14, 1952; children—Anthony Lee, Daniel Nickolas. Exhibited in 1-man shows U. Wis., Milw., 1960, Wustum Art Mus., Racine, Wis., 1961, Brena Gallery, Denver, 1963, 65, 67, 70, 74, Boulder (Colo.) Pub. Library Gallery, 1963, U. Colo. Fine Arts Gallery, 1964, Davenport Municipal Art Gallery, 1965, Colorado Springs Fine Arts Center, 1967, Sheldon Art Gallery, U. Nebr., 1968, Denver Art Mus., 1972, James Yu Gallery, N.Y.C., 1973; exhibited numerous group shows U.S., fgn. countries; represented in permanent collections Nat. Collection Fine Arts, Washington, others; prof. fine arts Grad. Faculty, U. Colo., Boulder, 1961—. Creative Research fellow, 1966-67. Recipient Gold Medal of Honor, 1st. oil award Milw. Art Center, 1960, Penello d'Argento award Acitrezza Internazionale, 1958, Bicentennial award Rocky Mountain Nat. Watercolor Exhbn., 1976. Home: 2865 Jay Rd Boulder CO 80301

MATTHEWS, FRANCIS RICHARD, lawyer; b. Calgary, Alta., Can., Aug. 19, 1920; s. Charles Curtice and Grace (Cathro) M.; Com., U. Alta., 1941, LL.B., 1948; m. Joyce Winter Jarvis, Nov. 10, 1944; children—James Richard, Frances Elizabeth, Michael John. Called to Alta. bar, 1949; created Queen's Counsel. 1963; asso. firm Mackimmie, Matthews, Calgary, 1949-54, partner, 1954—; dir. Murphy Oil Co. Ltd., Ranger Oil (Can.) Ltd., Westburne Internat. Industries Ltd. Served to lt., Royal Canadian Naval Vol. Res., 1941-45. Mem. Calgary Philharmonic Orchestra Soc. (bd. govs., pres. 1955-56, 61-62), Calgary C. of C., Can., Alberta bar assns., Soaring Assn. Can., Delta Kappa Epsilon. Mem. Anglican Ch. Clubs: Glencoe; Calgary Petroleum. Home: 4612 5th St SW Calgary AB Canada Office: 240 4th Ave SW Calgary AB Canada

MATTHEWS, G(EORGE) HUBERT, educator; b. Kingston, N.Y., Apr. 12, 1930; s. George B. and Barbara Helene (Davis) M.; B.A., U. Pa., 1952, M.A., 1954, Ph.D., 1958; m. Clara Moos, Nov. 21, 1973. Research asso. Mass. Inst. Tech., 1961-65, asso. prof., 1965-67, prof., 1967-74; dir. Crow bilingual edn. program Crow Agy. Pub. Sch., Crow Agency, Mont., 1972-76; linguist Pretty Eagle Sch., St. Xavier, Mont., 1976-78; asso. prof. Mont. State U., Bozeman, 1976—. Mem. Linguistic Soc. Am. Author: Hidatsa Syntax, 1965. Home: 8117 Alamosa Circle Bozeman MT 59715 Office: Mont State U Bozeman MT 59717

MATTHEWS, GARETH BLANC, educator; b. Buenos Aires, Argentina, July 8, 1929; s. Louis Brown and Reka (Blanc) M.; A.B., Franklin Coll., 1951; Rotary Found. fellow, Free U. Berlin, 1952-53; A.M., Harvard, 1952, Ph.D. (Kent fellow), 1961; m. Mary Howorth, Aug. 16, 1958; children—Sarah Ruth, Rebecca Mary, John Peter. Asst. prof. U. Va., 1960-61; asst. prof. U. Minn., 1961-64, asso. prof., 1964-69; prof. philosophy U. Mass., Amherst, 1969—; vis. lectr. Smith Coll., 1972, 74, Amherst Coll., 1973, Cambridge U., 1975-76, Mt. Holyoke Coll., 1977; Mead-Swing lectr. Oberlin Coll., 1976. Served to lt. USNR, 1954-57. George Santayana fellow, 1967-68. Home: 1170 N Pleasant St Amherst MA 01002

MATTHEWS, GARY NATHANIEL, baseball player; b. San Fernando, Calif., July 5, 1950. With San Francisco Giants, 1972-76, Atlanta Braves, 1976—. Named Nat. League Rookie of Year, 1973.*

MATTHEWS, JACK, psychologist, speech pathologist, educator; b. Winnipeg, Man., Can., June 17, 1917; s. Samuel and Ellen (Walker) M.; A.B., Heidelberg Coll., 1938, D.Sc., 1976; M.A., Ohio U., 1940; Ph.D., Ohio State U., 1946; student Vanderbilt U., 1942-43; m. Hannah Miriam Polster, Aug. 16, 1942; children—Rachel Sophia, Rebecca. Asst. dir. speech clinic Purdue U., 1946-48; dir. speech clinic, asst. prof. psychology and speech U. Pitts., 1948-55, dir. speech clinic, dir. div. psychol. services, asso. prof. psychology, 1950-55, prof., chmn. speech dept., 1955—, dean humanities, 1967-68, pres. univ. senate, 1969—. Bd. dirs. Community Hearing Council, Pitts. Hearing Soc.; pres. Am. Bd. Examiners Speech Pathology and Audiology, 1966-67; sec. Speech and Hearing Found., 1964-68; mem. Edn. Commn. States, Nat. Adv. Com. on Handicapped Children; trustee Western Pa. Sch. for Deaf. Served as sgt. AC Psychol. Research Unit, USAAF, 1942-45. Mem. Am. Speech and Hearing Assn. (pres. 1963-64, asso. editor jours. 1959—), Am. Assn. Cleft Palate Rehab. (pres. 1957-59), Am. Psychol. Assn., Speech Assn. (mem. adminstrv. council; mem. research bd. 1966—, chmn. 1967—), Am. Assn. Mental Deficiency, AAAS, Soc. Psychol. Study Social Issues, Pa. Speech Assn. (pres. 1959-60), Assn. for Communication Adminstrn. (exec. com. 1978—), AAUP, Sigma Xi, Pi Kappa Delta, Alpha Psi Omega, Tau Kappa Alpha, Sigma Alpha Eta. Asst. editor Jour. Speech and Hearing Disorders, 1952-54, editorial bd., 1965—; editorial bd. Speech Monographs, 1951-53, 56-65; editorial bd. Jour. Communications, 1961—. Deafness, Speech and Hearing pubs.; cons. editor Today's Speech, 1968- 70, ERIC, 1975—. Contbr. articles to profl. jours. Home: 825 Old Mill Rd Pittsburgh PA 15238

MATTHEWS, JAMES BENNING, educator; b. Ft. Benning, Ga., May 15, 1933; s. Max Audrey and Frieda Aurora (Sexton) M.; B.S., Rose-Hulman Inst. Tech., 1954; M.S., Mass. Inst. Tech., 1959; Ph.D., U. Ariz., 1966; m. Doris Louise Miller, Aug. 16, 1953; children—James Michael, Lynn Michelle, Melissa Ann. Instr., Rose-Hulman Inst. Tech., Terre Haute, Ind., 1956-58, asst. prof., 1959-63, asso. prof., 1966-68, prof., 1968-75, chmn. dept. mech. and aerospace engring., 1966-70, dean of faculty, 1970-73, v.p. acad. affairs, 1973-75; prof., chmn. dept. mech. engring. Western Mich. U., Kalamazoo, 1978—. Served with C.E., AUS, 1954-56. NSF Sci. faculty fellow, 1963-65. Registered profl. engr., Ind., Mich. Mem. ASME, Am. Soc. for Engring. Edn., Soc. Automotive Engrs. (Ralph Teetor Ednl. award 1968), Nat. Soc. Profl. Engrs., Tau Beta Pi, Pi Tau Sigma. Clubs: Elks, Rotary. Home: 414 Pinewood Circle Portage MI 49081

MATTHEWS, JOHN BOWERS, JR., educator; b. Norway, Maine, Aug. 25, 1922; s. John Bowers and Marion (Smith) M.; A.B., Bowdoin Coll., 1943; M.B.A., Harvard, 1949, D.C.S., 1957; m. Margaret Elizabeth William, Mar. 15, 1952; children—Martha Anne, Laurel Marion. With State Dept., then War Manpower Commn., 1943-47; mem. faculty Harvard Grad. Sch. Bus. Adminstrn., 1949—, prof., 1962—, Joseph C. Wilson prof., 1978—. Ednl. adviser Nat. Assn. Ind. Schs., 1960—; cons. to industry, 1952—. Dir. Rust Craft Greeting Cards, Inc., Passaic Herald News, Handleman Co. Trustee Dana Hall Sch., 1966—. James Bowdoin scholar, 1943, Baker scholar, 1949. Mem. Phi Beta Kappa. Conglist. (trustee). Author books in marketing and social responsibility of business. Home: 35 Longmeadow Rd Belmont MA 02178 Office: Harvard Business Sch Boston MA 02163

MATTHEWS, JOHN FLOYD, writer, educator; b. Cin., Apr. 8, 1919; s. Floyd L. and Helen (Orth) M.; student Wooster Coll., 1935-37, Northwestern U., 1937; B.A., U. Cin., 1940, postgrad., 1940-41; postgrad. Columbia U., 1943-44, New Sch. for Social Research, 1944-45; m. Maurine Zollman, Mar. 4, 1945 (dec. 1959); children—Lauralee Alice, Caroline Elaine (dec.); m. 2d, Brenda Martin, Aug. 27, 1966. Network radio actor, writer, producer, 1939-45; screenwriter Warner Bros., 1945; lectr. New Sch. for Social Research, 1948-50; lectr., chmn. faculty Dramatic Workshop and Tech. Inst., N.Y.C., 1950-52; lectr. in playwriting CCNY, 1947-63; asst. prof. dramatic lit. and history Brandeis U., 1952-59, asso. prof., 1959-67, Schulman prof., 1967-71, chmn. dept. theatre, 1955-58, prof. Am. studies, 1971—, chmn. dept. Am. studies, 1973-74, Richter prof. Am. civilization and instns., 1972—; author plays, including: The Scapegoat, 1950; Michael and Lavinia, 1956, Barnum, 1962; author books: (with Edward Choate) The Old Vic In America, 1946; El Greco, 1952, Shaw's Dramatic Criticism, 1959, George Bernard Shaw, 1969, Reflections on Abortion, 1976; contbr. fiction to lit. mags.; cons., play doctor for script and prodn. problems of numerous Broadway and off-Broadway plays and musicals; TV scriptwriter for maj. networks, 1955-64; screenwriter MGM, United Artists, Asso. Screen Prodns., Toronto, Ont., Can., 1958-64; vis. critic Yale Sch. Drama, 1965; mem. Seminar in Am. Studies, Circle Cultural de Royaumont, France; founding mem. Brandeis Creative Arts Awards Commn. Mem. Wesport (Conn.) Democratic Town Com., 1959-64; mem. Newton (Mass.) Republican City Com., 1977-79; mem. Mass. Rep. Platform Com., 1978; bd. dirs. Newton Taxpayers Assn., 1979—. Recipient Arts of the Theatre Found. award, 1950. Mem. Brit. Drama League, English Speaking Union, Trustees of Reservations. Episcopalian. Contbg. editor: Library of Living Painters, 1949-51; Dictionary of the Arts, 1946; Ency. World Biography, 1970. Home: 162 Pine Ridge Rd Waban MA 02168 also 80 Upper North St Brighton Sussex England Office: Brandeis U Waltham MA 02154

MATTHEWS, JOHN ROUPEE, savs. and loan exec.; b. Bklyn., Aug. 1, 1928; s. Jay Butlin and Mildred (Roupee) M.; B.S., Hofstra U., 1952; C.P.A., N.Y., 1957; m. Carolyn Bedell, Sept. 6, 1952; children—Dale Carol Hart, Lynn Patricia, J. David, Paul, Mark. Engaged in pub. accounting, 1952-57; investment analyst Allstate Ins. Co., Skokie, Ill., 1957-62; controller Allstate Savs. & Loan Assn., North Hollywood, Calif., 1962-63; financial v.p. State Mut. Savs. & Loan Assn., Los Angeles, 1963-70; treas. parent co. Far West Financial Corp., Los Angeles, 1963-70; sr. v.p. Coast Fed. Savs. & Loan Assn., Los Angeles, 1970-76, treas., 1973-76; sr. v.p. Republic Fed. Savs. and Loan Assn., Altadena, Calif., 1976—. Served with USN, 1946-48. Mem. Cal. Soc. C.P.A.'s. Mem. Ch. of Jesus Christ of Latter-day Saints. Home: 5400 Wilbur Ave Tarzana CA 91356 Office: 2246 N Lake Ave Altadena CA 91001

MATTHEWS, LEMUEL HATCH, lawyer; b. Chgo., June 5, 1909; s. Avery Putnam and Fannie (Hatch) M.; A.B., U. Calif. at Berkeley, 1931, LL.B., 1934; m. Gwen Turner Matthews, Feb. 14, 1947; 1 son, George Putnam. Advt. mgr. Salinas Index Jour., 1931; admitted to Calif. bar, 1935, also U.S. Supreme Ct. bar; asso. firm Sterling Carr, San Francisco, 1935-51, with CIA, Washington, 1951-52; partner firm Jonas and Matthews, San Francisco, 1952—. Lectr., Calif. Continuing Edn. of Bar, 1955—; dir. Overseas Central, Inc., Tropicraft Corp., Chan Nat., Inc. Pres. San Francisco Legal Aid Soc., 1968. Bd. dirs. Calif. Roadside Council, 1954-58, San Francisco Planning and Housing Assn., 1956-59; trustee Calif. Rural Legal Assistance Program, 1968, San Francisco Ladies Protection and Relief Soc., 1970—; trustee San Francisco Bar Found., 1972-73, pres., 1974—. Served to lt. col. AUS, 1941-47; ETO. Fellow Am. Bar Found., Am. Coll. Probate Counsel; mem. Am., San Francisco (pres. 1965, dir., 1962-66) bar assns., State Bar Calif. (del. 1958-69, exec. com. 1970-72), UN Assn. Calif. (pres. 1960), UN Assn. (hon.). Clubs: Bohemian, World Trade, Commonwealth (San Francisco). Home: 405 Davis Ct San Francisco CA 94111 Office: 300 Montgomery St Room 930 San Francisco CA 94104

MATTHEWS, LEONARD SARVER, advt. exec.; b. Glendean, Ky., Jan. 6, 1922; s. Clell and Zetta Price (Sarver) M.; B.S. summa cum laude, Northwestern U., 1948; m. Dorothy Lucille Fessler, June 27, 1942; children—Nancy, James, Douglas. With Leo Burnett Co., Inc., Chgo., 1948-76, v.p., dir., 1958-59, v.p. charge mktg. services, 1959-61, exec. v.p., 1961-70, pres., 1970-75; asst. sec. commerce for domestic and internat. bus., 1976; pres., mem. exec. com., dir. Young and Rubicam, 1977-78; pres. Am. Assn. Advt. Agys., 1979—. Trustee Better Govt. Assn., Chgo. Ednl. TV Assn. Served as ensign USCGR, 1942-46. Mem. Advt. Council (dir., exec. com., sec.), Council Better Bus. Burs. (dir., exec. com.), Delta Sigma Pi, Beta Gamma Sigma. Republican. Lutheran. Clubs: Mid-America, University, Executive, Economic (Chgo.); Skokie Country, Glencoe; Sky (N.Y.C.); Pine Valley Golf (N.J.). Home: Kenilworth IL 60043 Office: AAAA Pan Am Bldg Suite 1400 New York NY 10017. *Reach for the stars in everthing you do!*

MATTHEWS, LUTHER WHITE, III, railroad exec.; b. Ashland, Ky., Oct. 5, 1945; s. Luther White and Virginia Carolyn (Chandler) M.; B.S. in Econs., Hampden-Sydney Coll., 1967; M.B.A., in Fin. and Gen. Mgmt., U. Va., 1970; m. Mary Jane Hanser, Dec. 30, 1972; 1 dau., Courtney Chandler. Fin. cons. Chem. Bank, N.Y.C., 1970-72, asst. sec., 1972-74, asst. v.p., 1974-75, v.p., 1976-77; treas. Mo. Pacific Corp., St. Louis, 1977—; v.p. fin. Mo. Pacific R.R. Co., subs. Mo. Pacific Corp., St. Louis, 1979—; dir. Trailer Train Co. Treas., Samuel Cupples House Found., St. Louis, 1977—; trustee Hampden-Sydney Coll., 1978—. Served with USCGR, 1967-68.

MATTHEWS, MARK STANLEY, lawyer; b. Chgo., June 16, 1906; s. Rev. Dr. William H. and Eva (Chandler) M.; A.B., Columbia, 1928, LL.B., J.D., 1930, postgrad. polit. sci., 2 years; m. Betty Middleton, June 10, 1940; children—George Gregory, Mark Stanley (dec.), Judith Foster. Admitted to N.Y. bar, 1930, practiced law with Barber, Fackenthal & Giddings, N.Y.C.; apptd. asst. corp. counsel of City of N.Y. in charge of legislation; attended in behalf of N.Y.C., N.Y. State Constl. Conv., 1938; resumed law practice, 1940; asst. head Fed.-State Relations Sect., Dept. Justice, 1942-43. Mem. Gen. Assembly of Conn. Served on staff Supreme Comdr., AEF, 1943-45. Pres. U.S. Jaycees, 1940-41; past v.p. Nat. Municipal League; former pres. Greenwich C. of C. Recipient Distinguished Service award one of ten outstanding young men in U.S., U.S. Jaycees, 1940. Mem. Am. Bar Assn., Alpha Delta Phi. Republican. Presbyn. Clubs: Greenwich Country; Country of Florida; Ocean. Author: Guide to Community Action; Special Acts and Ordinances Concerning the Town of Greenwich, other acts enacted by N.Y. and Conn. legislatures. Home: 418 N Ocean Blvd Delray Beach FL 33444 also 83 Oneida Dr Indian Harbor Greenwich CT 06830 Office: 55 Lewis St Greenwich CT 06830

MATTHEWS, MARY JEAN O'LEARY, pathologist; b. Holyoke, Mass., Apr. 11, 1923; d. Martin Joseph and Agnes (Burke) O'Leary; A.A., Immaculata Jr. Coll., 1942; A.B., George Washington U., 1946, M.D., 1949; m. John Lee Matthews, June 19, 1948; children—Mary Ann, Susan Jean, John Edward, Margaret Louise, Robert Joseph. Intern, D.C. Gen. Hosp., 1949-50, asso. dir. Main Lab., 1954-62; resident in pathology Georgetown U., 1950-54, asst. clin. prof. pathology, 1961-72; Nat. Cancer Inst. fellow, 1950-53; practice medicine specializing in pathology, Washington, 1954—; asst. chief VA Hosp. Lab. Service, Washington, 1962-64, chief, 1964-70; asso. clin. prof. pathology Howard U., 1965-68, prof., 1968-72; professorial lectr. George Washington U., 1968-72, prof. pathology, 1972—; sr. pathologist, med. oncology service Nat. Cancer Inst.-VA, 1971—, chmn. working party for lung cancer therapy Nat. Cancer Inst., 1972-73, co-chmn., 1973-76. Recipient Achievement citation Washington Womens Advt. Club, 1967; diplomate Am. Bd. Pathology. Fellow Am. Coll. Chest Physicians; mem. Washington Soc. Pathologists, Internat. Acad. Pathology, D.C. Med. Soc., Am. Women's Med. Assn., Am. Soc. Clin. Oncology, Am. Soc. Cytology, Met. Washington Cytology Assn. Roman Catholic. Home: 6604 Virginia View Ct Washington DC 20016 Office: Veterans Administration Hospital 50 Irving St Washington DC 20422. *In grammar school I formulated my H1 P3 prayer that has helped me most of my life: "Dear God, I am proud and vain; give me the gift of humility. You have given me beauty and decency; keep me pure. You know my anger and resentments; give me patience. You know my doubts about my religion; give me piety."*

MATTHEWS, ROBERT EMIL, utility co. exec.; b. Elizabeth, N.J., May 1, 1925; s. Emil Charles and Mae Margaret (McLaughlin) M.; B.M.E., Catholic U. Am., 1950; M.B.A., Morehead State U., 1978; m. Jeanne Frances Corbett, Jan. 20, 1951; children—Robert Edward, Patricia, Thomas, John, Anne. Mech. engr. Am. Gas & Electric Service Corp. (now Am. Electric Power Service Corp.), N.Y.C., 1950-58, head engring. sect. 1958-64, dir. sales engring., 1964-67, dir., 19—; comml. mgr. Ky. Power Co., Ashland, 1967-74, div. mgr., Ashland, 1974-78, exec. v.p., Ashland, 1978—, also dir.; dir. Second Nat. Bank, Ashland. Bd. dirs. Hack Estep Home for Boys, Boyd County. Served with AC, U.S. Army, 1943-46. Mem. ASHRAE, Ashland Area C. of C. (dir. 1975-78, pres. 1977). Roman Catholic. Clubs: Rotary (dir. club), Elks (Ashland). Office: 1701 Central Ave Ashland KY 41101

MATTHEWS, ROBERT LLOYD, banker; b. Omaha, Sept. 23, 1937; s. Lloyd Dale and Henrietta Ann (Voss) M.; B.A., U. Omaha, 1959; grad. Am. Inst. Banking, 1968, Pacific Coast Banking Sch., 1970; m. Elizabeth Ann Martell, Feb. 17, 1962; children—Charles Robert, John Lloyd. With Ariz. Bank, Phoenix, 1959—, beginning as mgmt. trainee, successively loan officer, br. mgr., loan supr., asst. to pres., exec. v.p. charge loan div., 1959-75, exec. v.p. charge earning assets div., 1975-77, pres., 1978—. Bd. dirs., mem. exec. com., former pres. Valley Big Bros.; mem. Phoenix Thunderbirds; mem. Fiesta Bowl Adv. Bd., Heard Mus.; bd. dirs. United Way, Sun Angel Found.; trustee St. Luke's Med. Center. Served with Air N.G., 1959-65. Mem. Robert Morris Assos. (past pres.), Ariz. Bankers Assn. (pres.), Am. Bankers Assn., Phoenix Met. C. of C. (dir.). Republican. Roman Catholic. Home: 309 W Flynn Ln Phoenix AZ 85013 Office: Ariz Bank PO Box 2511 Phoenix AZ 85002

MATTHEWS, TIMOTHY JOHN, bishop; b. London, July 8, 1907; s. John Colmworth and Ethel May (Burns) M.; came to Can., 1913, naturalized, 1974; B.A., Bishop's U., Lennoxville, Que., Can., 1932, L.S.T., 1932, D.C.L., 1975, S.Th., Gen. Synod, Cupar, Sask., Can., 1932; S.Th., Tatterford (Eng.) Sch., 1942; m. Mary Eileen Montgomery, June 27, 1933; children—Peter, John, Thomas, Philip, Margaret Matthews Larass. Ordained priest Anglican Ch. of Can., 1933; vicar of Viking, Alta., 1932-36; rector of Edson, Alta., 1936-40, Coaticook, Que., Can., 1940-44, Lake St. John, 1944-52; rural dean Que., 1944-52; archdeacon Gaspe, Que., 1952-57, St. Francis, Que., 1957-71; lord bishop of Que., Quebec, 1971-77; counsellor Nat. Ch., 1977—; mem. corp. Kings Hall, Bishop's U. Address: 23 High St Lennoxville PQ J1M 1E6 Canada

MATTHEWS, WANDA (LEE) MILLER, artist; b. Barry, Ill., Sept. 15, 1930; d. Harry Leonard and Gladys (Smith) Miller; B.F.A., Bradley U., Peoria, Ill., 1952; M.F.A., U. Iowa, 1957; m. Eugene Edward Matthews, Sept. 14, 1952; children—Anthony Lee, Daniel Nicholas. Spl. services artist U.S. Army, Ft. Riley, Kans., 1954-55; research asst. printmaking U. Ia., 1956-57; travel in Italy and Europe, 1957-60; producing, exhibiting printmaker, Boulder, Colo., 1961—; one-woman exhbns. include Lehigh U., Bethlehem, Pa., 1973, Gettysburg (Pa.) Coll., 1973, U. Colo., 1976, U. N.D., 1976; group exhbns. include USIS Gallery, Naples, Italy, 1960, Nat. Invitational Print Exhbn., Otis Art Inst., Los Angeles, 1962, 63, Brit. Internat. Print Biennale, Bradford, Eng., 1970, 79, Invitational Graphics, Minot (N.D.) State Coll., 1972, Printmaking Now, W. Tex. Mus., Lubbock, 1973, Colorprint USA, Tex. Tech U., Lubbock, 1974, 78, Nat. Invitational Print Show, Central Wash. State Coll., Ellensburg, 1975, 11th Internat. Exhbn. Graphic Art, Ljubljana, Yugoslavia, 1975, 6th, 7th Internat. Print Biennales, Cracow, Poland, 1976, 78, Internat. Book Fair, Leipzig, E. Ger., 1977, others; rep. permanent collections Nelson Gallery Art/Atkins Mus., Kansas City, Mo., Boston Pub. Library, Los Angeles County Mus., Nat. Collection Fine Arts, Washington, Phila. Mus. Art, Library of Congress, others. Tiffany grantee, 1957-58, 58-59; recipient numerous awards, 1956—, including Purchase prize Prints 1962 Nat. Exhbn., State U. Coll., Potsdam, N.Y., 1962, Prints 10th ann. print exhbn., 1970; purchase prize 4th Dulin Nat. Print and Drawing competition Dulin Gallery Art, Knoxville, Tenn., 1968, 22d ann. nat. exhbn. Boston Printmakers, 1970; purchase award Graphics '71, Nat. Print and Drawing Exhbn., Western N.Mex. U., Silver City, 1971, Soc. Am. Graphic Artists; Benton Spruance prize Print Club Phila., 1971. Mem. Calif. Soc. Printmakers, Print Club Phila. Address: 2865 Jay Rd Boulder CO 80301

MATTHEWS, WARREN WAYNE, JR., state supreme ct. justice; b. Santa Cruz, Calif., Apr. 5, 1939; s. Warren Wayne and Ruth Ann (Maginnis) M.; A.B., Stanford U., 1961; LL.B., Harvard U., 1964; m. Donna Stearns, Aug. 17, 1963; children—Holly Maginnis, Meredith Sample. Admitted to Alaska bar, 1965; asso. firm Burr, Boney & Pease, Anchorage, 1964-69; asso. firm Matthews & Dunn, Matthews, Dunn and Baily Anchorage, 1969-77; justice Alaska Supreme Ct., Anchorage, 1977—. Bd. dirs. Alaska Legal Services Corp., 1969-70. Mem. Alaska Bar Assn. (bd. govs. 1974-77), Am. Bar Assn. Office: 303 K St Anchorage AK 99502

MATTHEWS, WILBUR LEE, lawyer; b. Big Spring, Tex., Jan. 20, 1903; s. Robert D. and Sallie (Bourland) M.; LL.B. with highest honors, U. Tex., 1926; m. Mary LeNoir Kenney, June 22, 1932 (dec. Oct. 1972); children—Wilbur Lee, John Kenney; m. 2d, Helen P. Davis, May 28, 1976. Admitted to Tex. bar, 1926, since practiced in San Antonio; with Matthews, Nowlin, Macfarlane & Barrett, and predecessor firms, 1926—, partner, 1930—. Mayor, City of Terrell Hills, 1939-41; mem. Tex. Finance Adv. Commn., 1960; trustee, chmn. San Antonio Med. Found. Fellow Am. Coll. Trial Lawyers; mem. Am. Law Inst., Am. Judicature Soc., Am. Bar Assn. Clubs: San Antonio Country, Argyle, San Antonio. Contbr. articles to legal pubs. Home: 711 Alta Ave San Antonio TX 78209 Office: Alamo Nat Bldg San Antonio TX 78205

MATTHEWS, WILLIAM D(OTY), lawyer, consumer products mfg. co. exec.; b. Oneida, N.Y., Aug. 25, 1934; s. William L. and Marjorie L. (Doty) M.; A.B., Union Coll., 1956; LL.B., Cornell U., 1960; m. Ann M. Morse, Aug. 4, 1956; children—Judith Anne, Thomas John. Admitted to N.Y. bar, 1960, D.C. bar, 1962; atty. div. corp. fin. SEC,

Washington, 1960-62; asso. firm Whitlock, Markey & Tait, Washington, 1962-69; with Oneida Ltd. (N.Y.), 1969—, gen. counsel, 1973-, v.p., 1977-78, sr. v.p., 1978—, also dir.; dir. Leavens Mfg. Co., Inc., Oneida Valley Nat. Bank, Camden Wire Co., Inc. Alderman City of Oneida, 1972-79. Mem. Am. Bar Assn., Madison County Bar Assn. Presbyterian. Home: 621 Patio Circle Dr Oneida NY 13421 Office: Oneida Ltd Oneida NY 13421

MATTHEWS, WILLIAM LEWIS, JR., educator; b. Livermore, Ky., Jan. 13, 1918; s. William Lewis and Grace (Vass) M.; A.B., Western Ky. State Coll., 1941; LL.B., U. Ky., 1941; LL.M., U. Mich., 1946, S.J.D., 1950; m. Carol Torrence, Nov. 27, 1946; 1 dau., Camille Torrence Schwert. Admitted to Ky. bar, 1941; practice in Bowling Green, Ky., 1946; asso. prof. law U. Ky., 1947-49, prof., 1949-74, Alumni prof., 1974—, acting dean Coll. Law, 1951-52, 56-57, dean, 1957-71; vis. prof. U. N.C., summer 1958, N.Y. U., summer 1959, 66-67, U. Mich., summer 1962. Mem. state, nat. legal adv. coms., commns.; mem. Ky. Pub. Service Commn., 1975-76. Served from pvt. to maj., USAAF, 1941-45; ETO. Decorated Bronze Star, Presdl. Unit citation, 6 campaign stars; Cook fellow grad. study law U. Mich., 1941- 42. Mem. Am., Ky. bar assns. Omicron Delta Kappa, Phi Alpha Delta, Order of Coif. Presbyn. Contbr. articles to legal periodicals. Home: 1752 Mooreland Dr Lexington KY 40502

MATTHEY, LOUIS WOODWARD, diversified industry exec.; b. St. Louis County, Mo., Jan. 2, 1920; s. Leon Henri and Elizabeth (Heibel) M.; B.S., Washington U., St. Louis, 1941; m. Jacqueline Tankersley, Mar. 1, 1947; children—Andrew, Harriet. Sales engr. Gen. Electric Co., St. Louis, 1941-48; v.p. Key Co., East St. Louis, Ill., 1948-54; pres. Matthey Engring. Co., St. Louis, 1954-58; prin. Worden & Risberg, mgmt. cons.'s, Phila., 1958—, pres., 1971-73, chmn., 1973-79; pres. KDI Corp. Cin., 1970—. Served to lt. (j.g.) USNR, 1944-46. Mem. Phi Delta Theta. Republican. Clubs: Hyde Park Country, Bankers (Cin.); Union League (N.Y.C.). Home: 1253 Rookwood Dr Cincinnati OH 45208 Office: 5721 Dragon Way Cincinnati OH 45227

MATTHIAS, BERND TEO, physicist; b. Frankfurt on Main, Germany, June 8, 1918; s. Ludwig and Marta (Lippman) M.; Ph.D. in Physics, Fed. Inst. Tech., Zürich, Switzerland, 1943; Sc.D. (hon.), U. Lausanne, 1978; m. Joan Trapp, Aug. 5, 1950. Came to U.S., 1947, naturalized, 1951. Sci. collaborator Fed. Inst. Tech., 1942-47; mem. staff., div. indsl. coop. Mass. Inst. Tech., 1947-48; mem. tech. staff Bell Labs., Inc., Murray Hill, N.J., 1948—; asst. prof. physics U. Chgo., 1949-51; prof. physics U. Calif. at San Diego, 1961—, also dir. Inst. for Pure and Applied Phys. Scis., 1971—. Recipient Research Corp. Found. award, 1962; John Price Wetherill medal Franklin Inst., 1963; Indsl. Research Man of Year award, 1968; Oliver E. Buckley solid state physics prize, 1970; Internat. prize for new materials Am. Phys. Soc., 1979. Fellow AAAS, Am. Phys. Soc.; mem. Nat. Acad. Scis., N.Y. Acad. Scis., Am. Acad. Arts and Scis., Swiss Phys. Soc., Sigma Xi. Home: PO Box 1354 La Jolla CA 92038

MATTHIAS, RUSSELL HOWARD, lawyer; b. Milw., Aug. 7, 1906; s. Charles G. and Lena (Martin) M.; A.B., Northwestern U., 1930, J.D., 1932; m. Helene Seibold, Dec. 28, 1932; children—Russell Howard, William Warrens, Robert Charles. Admitted to Ill. bar, 1933, D.C. bar, 1947, Okla. bar, 1947, Fla. bar, 1979; spl. asst. to atty. gen. U.S. R.R. Retirement Act, 1934-35; sec. Ill. Fraternal Congress, 1935-40, 45-60; partner firm Meyers & Matthias, Chgo., 1951-78; pres., treas. Meyers & Matthias, P.C., 1978—; chmn. bd., dir. Old Orchard Bank & Trust Co.; dir. Kemper Municipal Bond Fund, Inc., Kemper Option Income Funds, Inc., Kemper Total Return Fund, Inc., Kemper Growth Fund, Inc., Kemper Summit Fund, Inc., Kemper Income & Capital Preservation Fund, Inc., Kemper Money Market Fund, Inc., Kemper High Yield Fund, Inc., Republic Nat. Life Ins. Co., Dallas; exec. v.p., dir., gen. counsel Bankers Mut. Life Ins. Co.; dir., gen. counsel United Founders Life Ins. Co. of Ill., United Founders Life Ins. Co. of Okla.; dir., gen. counsel Wesco Inc. Drafting com. Ill. Ins. Code, 1938, annotating com., 1940; mem. drafting com. La. Ins. Code, 1948. Trustee Valparaiso U. Law Sch., Luth. Gen. Hosp., Deaconess Hosp.; sec., treas., dir. Technology Fund, Inc. Served capt. to lt. col., AUS, 1942-46. Recipient Alumni award Northwestern U., 1973. Mem. Luth. Brotherhood (dir., gen. counsel), Internat. Assn. Life Ins. Counsel, Phi Delta Theta. Republican. Lutheran. Clubs: Indian Hill Country; Mid-Day, University (Chgo.); Kenilworth; Army and Navy (Washington); Minneapolis; Citrus, Country (Orlando, Fla.). Home: 1500 Sheridan Rd Wilmette IL 60091 Office: 230 W Monroe St Room 2200 Chicago IL 60606

MATTHIAS, WILLARD C., govt. ofcl.; b. Fennimore, Wis., Mar. 6, 1914; s. Nathaniel and Ernestine Caroline (Braun) M.; B.A. magna cum laude, U. Iowa, 1936; M.A., U. Minn., 1938; M.A. (Littauer fellow 1938-39), Harvard, 1944; m. Sally L. Seashore, June 26, 1937; children—Jane Iris, Theodore Willard. Staff mem. Brookings Instn., Washington, 1939-40; instr., then asst. prof. govt. Miami U., Oxford, Ohio, 1940-43; intelligence officer CIA, 1947-58, 59-64, 66-73, mem. bd. nat. intelligence estimates, 1961-64, 66-73; research dir. Am. Com. on East-West Accord, 1978—; U.S. rep. Brit. Joint Intelligence Com., London, 1953-55; fellow Center Internat. Affairs, Harvard, 1958-59; 1st sec. embassy, Rome, 1964-66; research dir. Am. Com. East-West Accord, Washington, 1978—. Served with AUS, 1943-46. Mem. Phi Beta Kappa. Episcopalian. Home: 408 Clover Way Alexandria VA 22314

MATTHIESSEN, PETER, author; b. N.Y.C., May 22, 1927; s. Erard A. and Elizabeth (Carey) M.; student The Sorbonne, Paris, France, 1948-49; B.A., Yale, 1950; m. Patricia Southgate, Feb. 8, 1951 (div.); m. 2d, Deborah Love, May 8, 1963 (dec. Jan. 1972); children—Lucas C., Sara C., Rue, Alexander F.L. Trustee N.Y. Zool. Soc., 1965-78. AAAL grantee, 1963. Mem. Nat. Inst. Arts and Letters. Author: Race Rock, 1954; Partisans, 1955; Raditzer, 1960; Wildlife in America, 1959; The Cloud Forest, 1961; Under the Mountain Wall, 1963; At Play in the Fields of the Lord, 1965; Sal si Puedes, 1969; Blue Meridian, 1971; The Tree Where Man Was Born, 1972; The Wind Birds, 1973; Far Tortuga, 1975; The Snow Leopard (Nat. Book award), 1978. Home: Bridge Ln Sagaponack NY 11962

MATTICK, THOMAS CHARLES, mfg. co. exec.; b. Milw., Aug. 7, 1939; s. Raymond William and Audrey Lillian (Reeves) M.; B.B.A., U. Wis., 1962; m. Nancy Kay, Aug. 24, 1963; children—Kathryn Lynn, Bradley Thomas. Audit mgr. Arthur Andersen & Co., Chgo., 1962-71; controller Mark Controls Corp., Evanston, Ill., 1972-74, v.p., 1975, v.p. fin., sec., 1975—, also dir.; dir. United Centrifugal Pumps. Pres., Kenilworth (Ill.) United Fund, 1979-80. Served with USAR, 1960-61. C.P.A., Ill. Mem. Am. Inst. C.P.A.'s, Fin. Execs. Inst. Clubs: Mich. Shores, Kenilworth (dir.). Home: 138 Winnetka Ave Kenilworth IL 60043 Office: 1900 Dempster St Evanston IL 60204

MATTIL, EDWARD LA MARR, educator; b. Williamsport, Pa., Nov. 25, 1918; s. Jacob and Louise B. (Feigles) M.; B.S., Pa. State U., 1940; M.A., 1946, D.Ed., 1953; m. Pauline G. Davis, Oct. 4, 1941; son, Michael Davis. Art tchr. pub. schs., Cumberland, Md., 1940-41, art supr., Wallingford, Pa., 1941-42, 45-46; art supr., State College (Pa.) pub. schs., 1945-53; asst. prof., asso. prof. Pa. State U., 1948-60, prof., head art edn. dept., 1960-70; dean Sch. Fine Arts, St. Cloud (Minn.) State Coll., 1970-71; chmn. dept. art N. Tex. State U., Denton, 1971—. Prod. TV series for children, Key to the Cupboard; prof. film Meaning in Child Art. Recipient Nat. Gallery Art 25th medal for Distinguished Service, 1966. Mem. Nat. Art Education Assn. (pres. 1963-65), Pa. Art Edn. Assn. (past pres.), Eastern Arts Assn. (past mem. council), Am. Craftsmens Council, N.E.A., Nat. Council Arts Edn., Phi Delta Kappa, Pi Gamma Alpha. Author: Meaning in Crafts, 1959, 3d edit., 1971; (with others) Providing for Individual Differences in the Elementary Schools, 1960, The Arts in Higher Education, 1969; El Valor Educativo de las Manualidades, 1973. Editor: Everyday Art, 1957—. Home: 600 Roberts Ave Denton TX 76201

MATTINGLY, RICHARD FRANCIS, physician, educator; b. Zanesville, Ohio, Oct. 25, 1925; s. James Joseph and Frances Katherine (Shaw) M.; B.A., Ohio State U., 1949; M.D., Cornell U., 1953; m. Mary Elizabeth Kohlmann, Sept. 19, 1948; children—Kevin, Kerry, Kent, Kathleen, Keith, Kelly, Kristen. Intern, then resident obstetrics and gynecology Johns Hopkins Hosp., 1953-58, instr., then asst. prof. obstetrics and gynecology, 1958-61; prof., chmn. dept. gynecology and obstetrics Med. Coll. Wis., Milw., 1961—; dir. dept. gynecology and obstetrics Milw. County Gen. Hosp., 1961—; mem. cons. staff Milw., St. Joseph's, St. Luke's, St. Mary's, Mt. Sinai, Columbia hosps. Served with M.C. AUS, 1944-46. Diplomate Am. Bd. of Obstetrics and Gynecology (mem. exam. bd.). Fellow AMA, Am. Coll. Obstetrics and Gynecology; mem. Am. Assn. Obstetrics and Gynecology, Med. Soc. Milw. County, AAUP, Assn. Profs. Gynecology and Obstetrics, Central Assn. Obstetricians and Gynecologists, Wis. Med. Soc., Wis. Soc. Obstetrics and Gynecology, Am. Fertility Soc., Soc. Pelvic Surgeons, Am. Soc. Cytology, N.Y. Acad. Sci., Am. Gynecol. Soc., Am. Radium Soc. Editor-in-chief Obstetrics and Gynecology. Home: 4762 N Lake Dr Milwaukee WI 53211

MATTINGLY, THOMAS K., astronaut; b. Chgo., Mar. 17, 1936; s. Thomas K. Mattingly; B. Aero. Engring., Auburn U., 1958. Commd. officer U.S. Navy, 1958, now comdr. assigned to space shuttle ops. NASA; astronaut NASA Manned Spacecraft Center, Houston; crew mem. Apollo 16, 1972. Address: NASA Manned Spacecraft Center Houston TX 77058*

MATTISON, GEORGE AUGUSTUS, JR., slag and aggregate co. exec., Shrine ofcl.; b. Talladega, Ala., Nov. 5, 1898; s. George Augustus and Mary (Ferguson) M.; B.S. in Elec. Engring., Auburn U., 1919, D.Sc. (hon.); m. Ernestine Carriger, Dec. 20, 1923 (dec.); children—George Augustus III (dec.), William Ernest, Mary. Co-founder Woodstock Slag Corp., Anniston, Ala., 1919, pres., 1937-56; partner Houston Slag Materials Co., 1944—; pres. Hurock, Inc., Houston, 1952—; mem. So. adv. bd. Am. Mut. Liability Ins. Co.; dir. Ala. Gt. So. R.R. Co. Mem. Anniston lodge Masons, 1922—, Scottish Rite, Birmingham, 1949—, Anniston Commandery K.T., 1922—, Red Cross of Constantine (past sovereign St. Dunstan Conclave), 1956—, Royal Order Jesters (past dir. Court 127), 1944—; mem. Ancient Arabis Order Nobles of Mystic Shrine For N.A., 1922, potentate Zamora Temple, 1947, imperial potentate Imperial Council, 1960-61; trustee, chmn. bldg. and equipment com. Shriners' Hosps. for Crippled Children. Chmn. Ala. Community Chest appeal, 1943, Ala. March of Dimes, 1943, USO Appeal, Birmingham, 1942, Birmingham Committee of 100, 1958-59. Former mem. bd. dirs. Auburn Research Found.; bd. dirs. Birmingham Boys Club, Boys Club Am.; trustee, past pres. Crippled Childrens Clinic, Birmingham. Served to 2d lt., inf., U.S. Army, World War I. Recipient Algermon Sydney Sullivan medallion award for humanitarian traits Auburn U., 1958, Disting. Engr. award Auburn U., 1978; named to Ala. Acad. Honor, 1976. Mem. Am. Concrete Inst., Am. Soc. Testing Materials, So. Research Inst., So. Assn. Sci. and Industry, Nat. Slag Assn. (past pres.), Auburn Alumni Assn. (past pres.), Newcomen Soc., Am. Legion (past post comdr.), 40 and 8 (past chef passe), Birmingham C. of C. (past pres.), Ala. Acad. Honor, Omicron Delta Kappa. Episcopalian (past sr. warden, vestryman). Clubs: A Club (Auburn U.); Mt. Brook, The Club (past pres.), Engineers, Kiwanis (past pres.), Traffic and Transportation (past pres.), Monday Morning Quarterback (past capt.) (Birmingham). Home: 3016 Weatherton Circle Birmingham AL 35223 Office: Transportation Bldg Birmingham AL 35203

MATTOON, HENRY AMASA, JR., advt. and mktg. cons., writer; b. Waterbury, Conn., Jan. 14, 1914; s. Henry A. and Sarah Currie (Hallock) M.; B.S., Yale, 1935; m. Dorothy Ann Teeter, June 20, 1936; children—Ann Brooks Mattoon Wofford, David Scott, Sara Halsey, Judith Scott. Mail boy, then copywriter, copy supr. Compton Advt. Inc., N.Y.C., 1935-44, v.p., creative dir., 1944-50; v.p., chmn. plans bd. Ruthrauff & Ryan, Inc., 1950-52; v.p., creative dir. Dancer-Fitzgerald-Sample, Inc., 1952-54; pres., dir. Reach, Yates & Mattoon, Inc., 1954-56; chmn. marketing plans bd. McCann-Erickson, Inc., 1956-57, v.p., asso. creative dir., 1957-62, v.p., gen. mgr., Los Angeles office, 1962-65, sr. v.p. and mgr., Houston office, 1965-68; v.p., dir. advt., pub. relations and sales promotion Yardley of London, Inc., 1968-69; partner Walter Weintz & Co., Inc., Stamford, Conn., 1969-70; prin. Otto Man Assos., 1967—; pres. Hamandot Co., 1976—. Mem. Chi Phi. Clubs: Yale, Sky (N.Y.C.); Aspetuck Valley Country (Weston, Conn.). Home: 11 October Dr Weston CT 06883 Office: 60 Wilton Rd Westport CT 06880

MATTOX, CLYDE EUGENE, lawyer; b. Bethel, Ohio, Apr. 30, 1915; s. Clarence Ceil and Flora Duckwall (Butler) M.; B.S.Ed., Wilmington Coll, 1938; grad. USAAF Tech. Sch., 1942; cert. accomplishment Republic Aviation Corp. Tng. Sch., 1943; LL.B., U. Cin., 1948; m. Shirley Alice Ritchie, Sept. 16, 1946; children—Karen Sue Mattox McClanahan, Kayla Jean Mattox Collier. Admitted to Ohio bar, 1949; tchr. public schs., Clermont County, Ohio, 1936-41, Hamilton County, Ohio, 1941-42; individual practice law, Bethel, 1949-50; asso. firm Ely, White & Davidson, Batavia, Ohio, 1951-52; asso. firm Cors. Hair & Hartsock, Cin., 1953-56, partner, 1957—, sr. partner, 1966—; solicitor Village of Amelia, 1951, Village of Bethel, 1950-73. Mem. numerous sch. supporting orgns. and coms. Served with USAAF, 1942-46; CBI. Cert. permanent tchr., Ohio. Mem. Am. Bar Assn., Ohio State Bar Assn., Cin. Bar Assn., Clermont County Bar Assn. (pres. 1960-61), Am. Trial Lawyers Assn., Ohio Trial Lawyers Assn. Democrat. Methodist. Clubs: Oasis, Ridge, Masons, Shriners, Am. Legion, China, Burma, India Vets. Editorial bd. U. Cin. Law Rev., 1948; instrumental in the financing of banking facilities by Indsl. Revenue Bonds, 1970. Home: 2655 Williamsburg-Bantam Rd Bethel OH 45106 Office: 1700 Carew Tower Cincinnati OH 45202

MATTOX, JAMES ALBON, Congressman; b. Dallas, Aug. 29, 1943; s. Norman and Mary Kathryn (Harrison) M.; B.B.A. magna cum laude, Baylor U., 1965; J.D., So. Meth. U., 1968. Admitted to Tex. bar, 1968; asst. dist. atty. Dallas County, 1968-70; partner firm Crowder & Mattox, Dallas, 1970—; mem. Tex. Ho. of Reps. from 33d Dallas Dist., 1972-76; mem. 95th-96th Congresses from 5th Tex. Dist.; chmn. nat. def. and internat. affairs task force Ho. budget com., mem. banking, fin. and urban affairs com. Del. Tex. Democratic Conv., 1972. Named Outstanding Freshman Rep., Tex. Intercollegiate Students Assn., 1973; Legislator of Yr., Dallas County Women's Polit. Caucus. Baptist. Home: 1110 Valencia St Dallas TX 75223 Office: 1127 Longworth House Office Bldg Washington DC 20515

MATTOX, KARL RUSSELL, phycologist; b. Cin., Aug. 22, 1936; s. Karl Russell and Virginia Lee (Slye) M.; B.S., Miami U., Oxford, Ohio, 1958, M.A., 1960; Ph.D., U. Tex., 1962; m. Beverly Ann Clark, Aug. 31, 1957; children—Jennifer, Benjamin, Katherine. Asst. prof. botany U. Toronto, Ont., Can., 1962-66; asst. prof. Miami U., Oxford, Ohio, 1966-70, asso. prof., 1970-75, prof., 1975—, chmn. dept., 1977—. Mem. Oxford Bd. Edn., 1972-75. Mem. Bot. Soc. Am. (co-recipient Darbaker prize in phycology 1976), Phycological Soc. Am., Brit. Phycological Soc., Sigma Xi. Methodist. Contbr. articles in field to books and profl. jours. Home: 729 Melissa Dr Oxford OH 45056 Office: Dept Botany Miami Univ Oxford OH 45056

MATTOX, RICHARD BENJAMIN, educator; b. Middletown, Ohio, May 15, 1921; s. Arthur Bennett and Nellie (Kriick) M.; B.A., Miami U., Oxford, Ohio, 1948, B.S., 1949; Ph.D., U. Iowa, 1954; m. Helen Jeanne Wagner, Aug. 28, 1948; children—Richard Lee, Jane Wade. Instr. Miami U., Oxford, 1948-49; geologist Magnolia Petroleum Co., San Antonio, 1950; asst. instr. U. Ia., 1951-52; asso. prof. geology Miss. State U., State College, 1952-54; prof. geology Tex. Tech. Coll., Lubbock, 1954—, chmn. dept. geoscis., 1964-70, prof. geology, 1970—; cons. geologist on groundwater, petroleum, 1954—; mem. steering com. Internat. Conf. on Saline Deposits, 1962-63. Served to lt. USAAF, 1942-45. Fellow Geol Soc. Am.; mem. AAAS, Am. Assn. Petroleum Geologists, Nat. Assn. Geology Tchrs. Home: 3413 53d St Lubbock TX 79413

MATTSON, JOE OLIVER PHILIP, safety cons.; b. Los Angeles, Nov. 17, 1903; s. Harry Colburn and Bertha T. (Jackson) M.; student Oreg. State Coll., 1923-27; m. Helen Louise Goodwin, May 20, 1937; children—James Eric, Judith Lynn. Pres. Mattson-Jacot Co., importers, exporters, Long Beach, Calif., 1931-34; mgr. dept. motor vehicles State of Calif., Pasadena, 1934-37, asst. chief clk., Sacramento, 1937-39, dir., 1940; with Automotive Safety Found., 1941-69, asst. to pres., 1948-53, pres., 1953-69; cons. hwy. adminstrn., planning and safety Wilbur Smith & Asso., Washington, 1969-73; mem. Pres.'s Highway Safety Conf. Mem. adv. com. Inst. Transp. and Traffic Engring., U. Calif., 1948—; adv. com. Yale Bur. Hwy. Traffic; mem. nat. adv. com. edn. and safety research Columbia; state legislature cons. engring. studies hwy. needs, Calif., 1946, Wash., Oreg., 1948; cons. traffic law study, Colo.; dir. motor vehicle study, Mich.; mem. traffic and transp. com., Los Angeles; mem. traffic safety com. PanAm Hwy. Congress, U.S. del., 1957-68; mem. 1st World Traffic Engrs. Conf., 3d Triennial Congress of Internat. Assn. for Accident and Traffic Medicine; mem. accident prevention adv. com. USPHS; chmn. exec. com. Pres.'s Com. Traffic Safety. Mem. Am. Assn. Motor Vehicle Adminstrs., Inst. Traffic Engrs. (asso.), Internat. Assn. Chiefs of Police (hon.), Calif. State C. of C., Beta Theta Pi. Clubs: Columbia Country, University. Home: 8108 Kerry Ln Chevy Chase MD 20015

MATTSON, MARCUS, lawyer; b. Ogden, Utah, July 3, 1904; s.David and Blanche (Allison) M.; A.B., U. Calif. at Berkeley, 1927, J.D., 1930; m. Eleanor L. Hynding, Dec. 30, 1933; 1 son, Peter H. Admitted to Calif. bar, 1930, since practiced in Los Angeles; sr. partner firm Lawler, Felix & Hall, 1942—; lectr. antitrust law. Mem. Jud. Council Calif., 1969-73; adv. council FTC, 1970-74. Trustee Pacific Legal Found., 1973—. Fellow Am. Bar Found., Am. Coll. Trial Lawyers (bd. regents 1973-77, pres. 1978-79); mem. Am. (chmn. antitrust law sect. 1965-66, mem. com. on multi-dist. litigation 1968-74), Los Angeles bar assns., State Bar Calif. (v.p., gov. 1959-60; chmn. com. bar examiners 1962-63, chmn. com. law sch. edn. 1960-67), U. Calif. Law Sch. Alumni Assn. (pres. 1958). Mem. Ch. of Jesus Christ of Latter-day Saints. Clubs: California, Los Angeles Country (Los Angeles); Pacific-Union (San Francisco); Pauma Valley (Calif.) Country. Office: 700 S Flower St 31st Floor Los Angeles CA 90069

MATTSON, ROY HENRY, engring. educator; b. Chisholm, Minn., Dec. 26, 1927; s. Gust and Hilma (Appel) M.; B.Elec. Engring., U. Minn., 1951, M.S. in Elec. Engring., 1952; Ph.D., Iowa State U., 1959; m. June Eileen Lindstrom, June 14, 1948; children—Kristi Lynn, Lisa Kay, Greta Lee, Linnea Jean, Marla Jo, Brent Anders, Brian Alan. Mem. tech. staff Bell Telephone Labs., Inc., 1952-56; asst. prof., then asso. prof. Iowa State U., 1956-61; asso. prof. U. Minn., 1961-66; prof. elec. engring., head dept. U. Ariz., 1966—. Del. to A.S. Popov Congress, Moscow USSR, 1972; non-govt. observer to UN Conf. on Human Environment, Stockholm, 1972. Mem. Amphitheater Bd. Sch. Trustees, 1971-76, pres., 1976. Served with USNR, 1946-47. Registered profl. engr. Fellow IEEE (editor Transactions on Edn. 1970-73, chmn. validation of ednl. achievement program 1976—), AAAS; mem. Am. Soc. Engring. Edn., Sigma Xi, Theta Tau, Eta Kappa Nu, Tau Beta Pi. Author: Basic Junction Devices and Circuits, 1963; Electronics, 1966; also articles. Patentee in field. Home: 9060 N Riviera Dr Tucson AZ 85704

MATTSON, VERNON LINNAEUS, oil co. cons.; b. Chgo., July 12, 1902; s. Axel Linnaeus and Stella (Buck) M.; student Carnegie Inst.Tech., 1920-22; E.M., Colo. Sch. Mines, 1926; m. Carribelle Pitcher, Aug. 9, 1928 (div. 1975); 1 son, Joseph T.; m. 2d, Thelma Makeig (dec. 1977); m. 3d, Aliece Makeig, 1978. Mine examiner Mazapil Copper Co., also Norrie & Tower Co., 1926-30; v.p., gen. mgr. Celo Mines, Inc., Burnsville, N.C., 1930-44; chief engr. Consol. Feldspar Corp., 1944-49; dir. Colo. Sch. Mines Research Found., 1949-55; formerly mgr. mines and mills, v.p. and tech. adviser to the pres. Kerr-McGee Corp., v.p. research, 1968-69, v.p. spl. projects, 1969-71; now cons. in mineral and petroleum bus. Mem. Governor's Adv. Com. Sci. and Industry. Recipient Distinguished Achievement award Colo. Sch. Mines, 1960. Registered profl. engr., Colo., N.M. Mem. Am. Inst. Mining, Metall. and Petroleum Engrs. (named to Legion of Merit 1973), Okla., Colo. sci. socs., Okla., N.Y. acads. sci., Colo. Soc. Engrs., Colo. Mining Assn., Am. Nuclear Soc., Geol. Soc. Am., Navy League. Clubs: Teknik, Mt. Vernon Country (Denver); Mining (N.Y.C.); Sierra. Address: PO Box 2690 Estes Park CO 80517

MATTSON, WALTER EDWARD, communications co. exec.; b. Erie, Pa., June 6, 1932; s. Walter Edward and Florence Evelyn (Anderson) M.; B.S., U. Maine, 1955; A.S., Northeastern U., 1959; postgrad. Harvard U. Advanced Mgmt. Program, 1973; m. Geraldine Anne Horsman, Oct. 10, 1953; children—Stephen, William, Carol. Printer various cos., 1948-53; advt. mgr. Anderson Newspapers Co., Oakmont, Pa., 1954; asst. prodn. mgr. Boston Heral Traveler, 1955-58; cons. Chas. T. Main Co., Boston, 1959; with N.Y. Times Co., N.Y.C., 1960—, sr. v.p., 1972-74, exec. v.p., 1974—. Bd. dirs. nat. council Northeastern U. Served with USMC, 1951. Named Distinguished Alumni Northeastern U., 1974. Mem. ANPA (vice chmn. prodn. mgmt. com.). Home: 34 Heather Dr Stamford CT 06903 Office: 229 W 43d St New York NY 10036

MATTSSON, CARVEL, lawyer; b. Salina, Utah, Aug. 30, 1907; s. Carl Albert and Elnora Christena (Beal) M.; B.S. magna cum laude, U. Utah, 1928; LL.B. summa cum laude, George Washington U., 1932; m. Wanda F. Ashley, Sept. 2, 1931; children—Marilyn, Jon Michael, Mary Melinda, Marc Carvel. High sch. tchr., Jerome, Idaho, 1928-29; admitted to Utah bar, 1932; practiced in Richfield, 1933-49,

Richfield and Salt Lake City, 1949—; mem. firm Gustin, Richards & Mattsson, 1949-65, Mattsson & Jackson, 1966-68, Mattsson, Jackson and McIff, 1968-78; atty. for Salina City, 1935-58, 66-71, Sevier County, 1935-40, 6th Jud. Dist., 1940; legal counsel Ideal Nat. Ins. Co., Salt Lake City, 1970-75. Appeal agt. Selective Service Bd., 1941-44, 48-71. Bd. dirs. Utah Mental Health Assn., 1963-67; vice chmn. bd. regents U. Utah, 1963-65; mem. Utah Coordinating Council Higher Edn., 1960-61. Recipient Scholarship key Delta Sigma Pi, 1928. Fellow Am. Bar Found.; mem. Utah Bar Assn. (commr. 1946-49; pres. 1948-49), Order of Coif, Delta Theta Phi (key 1932), Phi Kappa Phi. Republican. Mem. Ch. of Jesus Christ of Latter-day Saints (ch. organist 1933-43). Home: 952 Eastgate Rd Salt Lake City UT 84117 Office: 151 N Main St Richfield UT 84701

MATULA, RICHARD ALLEN, univ. dean; b. Chgo., Aug. 22, 1939; s. Ludvig A. and Leone O. (Dufeck) M.; B.S., Purdue U., 1961, M.S., 1962, Ph.D., 1964; m. Brenda C. Mather, Sept. 5, 1959; children—Scott, Kristropher, Daniel, Tiffiny. Instr., Purdue U., 1963-64; asst. prof. mech. engring. U. Calif., Santa Barbara, 1964-66; asst. prof. mech. engring. U. Mich., 1966-68; asso. prof. mech. engring. Drexel U., Phila., 1968-70, prof., 1970-76, chmn. thermal and fluid sci. advanced study group, 1969-72, chmn. Environ. Studies Inst., 1972-73, chmn. dept. mech. engring. and mechanics, 1973-76; dean Coll. Engring., prof. mech. engring. La. State U., Baton Rouge, 1976—. Treas., bd. dirs. Wexford Leas Swim and Racquet Club, Inc., 1968-73; v.p. Wexford Leas Civic Assn., 1969-71. Mem. Air Pollution Control Assn., Am. Soc. Engring. Edn., ASME, AAAS, Combustion Inst., Soc. Automotive Engrs., Sigma Xi, Pi Kappa Phi, Pi Tau Sigma, Sigma Pi Sigma, Tau Beta Pi. Roman Catholic. Contbr. articles to profl. jours. Home: 5536 Valley Forge Ave Baton Rouge LA 70808 Office: Coll Engring 3304-U CEBA La State U Baton Rouge LA 70803

MATUSIAK, LOUIS WAYNE, accountant; b. Streator, Ill., June 25, 1924; s. Walter Anthony and Anne Catherine (Kozak) M.; student Northwestern U., 1942-43; B.S., U. Ill., 1949, M.S., 1950; postgrad. in Bus. Adminstrn., U. Mich., 1950-57; m. Alberta (Pat) Porter, July 3, 1949; children—Louis Wayne, Richard A., James E., Nancy A. Asso. prof. accounting, chmn. dept. U. Detroit, 1950-57; nat. dir. tng. and edn. Touche Niven Bailey & Smart, Detroit, 1957-58; dir. profl. devel. Am. Inst. C.P.A.'s, N.Y.C., 1958-64; with Alexander Grant & Co., Chgo., 1964-78, asst. nat. mng. partner, 1976-78; exec. dir. Public Oversight Bd. of SEC practice sect. Am. Inst. C.P.A.'s, N.Y.C., 1978—. Mem. Ill. State Bd. Accountancy, 1970-74, chmn., 1971-72. Bd. dirs., mem. exec. com. Chgo. Conv. and Tourism Bur., 1973-78. Served with U.S. Army, 1943-46. Mem. Am. Inst. C.P.A.'s, Ill. Soc. C.P.A.'s, Nat. Assn. State Bds. Accountancy (dir. 1971-74, 75-78, pres. elect 1978-79), Beta Gamma Sigma, Beta Alpha Psi. Republican. Roman Catholic. Clubs: Country of Darien (Conn.); Rotary. Home: 6 Canaan Close New Canaan CT 06840 Office: Public Oversight Board 1270 Ave of Americas New York NY 10020

MATUSZAK, STEPHEN ANTHONY, banker; b. Erie, Pa., Jan. 18, 1931; s. Stephen Joseph and Elizabeth Catherine (Konopka) M.; B.S., U.S. Mil. Acad., 1955; M.B.A., N.Y. U., 1964; postgrad. Rutgers, 1963-65; m. Violet Marques, June 11, 1955; children—Nanciann, Stephen M., Donna M., David. Editor-analyst, Value Line Investment Survey, N.Y.C., 1959-62; pres. Nat. Bank of Westchester, White Plains, N.Y., 1962—; PM Life Ins. Co.; instr. bank investments Am. Inst. Banking, 1963-64. Treas., bd. dirs. Westchester Urban Coalition, 1970-71. Served with AUS, 1950, 55-59. Mem. Financial Execs. Inst., Financial Analysts Fedn., N.Y. Soc. Security Analysts, Westchester County Assn., N.Y. State Bankers' Assn. Club: Westchester Country. Author: Modern Investment Guide, 1959.

MATZ, JOHN EDWIN, life ins. co. exec.; b. Hamburg, Pa., Sept. 2, 1916; s. Harry L. and Florence (Smith) M.; M.A., Pa. State U., 1939; m. Phoebe Land, July 4, 1941; children—Susan Eugenia, John Edwin. With John Hancock Mut. Life Ins. Co., Boston, 1949—, v.p., 1961-65, sr. v.p., 1965-67, exec. v.p., 1967-72, sr. exec. v.p., 1972-73, pres., chief ops. officer, vice chmn. bd., 1974-78, chmn., chief exec. officer, 1979—, also dir.; dir. Shawmut Bank Boston N.A., Shawmut Corp. Trustee Am. Coll. Life Underwriters; mem. corp., trustee Northeastern U., Tax Found., Inc.; bd. dirs. Council Fin. Aid to Edn.; trustee, bd. govs. New Eng. Med. Center Hosp., New Eng. Colls. Fund; vis. com. Harvard Grad. Sch. Bus. Adminstrn.; mem. nat. bd. Jr. Achievement, Inc. Fellow Soc. Actuaries; mem. Phi Beta Kappa. Clubs: Comml. (Boston), St. Botolph, Algonquin, Weston Golf; Univ.; Bald Peak Colony (N.H.). Home: 60 Robin Rd Weston MA 02193 Office: John Hancock Pl Box 111 Boston MA 02117

MATZKE, FRANK J., architect, cons.; b. Akron, Ohio, Jan. 28, 1922; s. Frank G. and Erna (Weibel) M.; student State Tchrs. Coll. at Buffalo, 1940-41; B.Arch., Rensselaer Poly. Inst., 1951; m. Shirley Elizabeth Hall, Nov. 27, 1952 (div. Dec. 1966); children—Kim Elizabeth, Karla Jo. Field rep., project architect W. Parker Dodge Assos., Rensselaer, N.Y., 1951-54; sr. architect div. architecture N.Y. State Dept. Pub. Works, Albany, 1954-58; asso. architect State U. N.Y., Albany, 1958-62; dep. mgr. planning State U. Constrn. Fund, Albany, 1962-68, dep. gen. mgr., 1968-72; asso. commr. for project mgmt. Pub. Bldgs. Service, GSA, Washington, 1972-75, acting asst. commr. for constrn. mgmt., 1974-75; exec. dir. Ill. Capital Devel. Bd., 1975-76; v.p. for tech. and programs Nat. Inst. Bldg. Scis., Washington, 1978—; mem. Bldg. Research Adv. Bd., Washington, 1976-79; chmn. Mgmt. Resource Council, 1974-75; cons. to pub. agys., colls. and univs. on methods to expedite design and constrn. of phys. facilities. Chmn. planning bd. Town of Johnsburg, 1962-65; nat. ski patrolman, past patrol leader O.C. Ski Club Ski Patrol. Bd. dirs. Bldg. Research Inst., 1973-75. Served to 1st lt., inf., AUS, 1942-46; PTO. Decorated Bronze Star, Combat Infantryman's badge. Recipient Ricketts prize for best archtl. thesis, 1951, N.Y. Soc. Architects medal, 1951. Registered architect, N.Y. Fellow A.I.A. (pres. E. N.Y. chpt. 1959-60, dir. 1960-63, mem. nat. com. on architecture for edn. 1966-72, chmn. nat. com. on architects in govt. 1975, medal for excellence in architecture 1951), N.Y. State Assn. Architects (dir. 1966-69); mem. Soc. for Coll. and U. Planning, Council Ednl. Facility Planners, Assn. Gen. Contractors (research adv. council 1974-75), Sigma Xi, Tau Beta Pi, Sigma Phi Epsilon. Contbr. articles to profl. jours. Home: 1100 6th St SW Washington DC 20024

MATZKE, HOWARD ARTHUR, educator; b. Winona, Minn., Mar. 22, 1920; s. William Louis and Daisy (Harders) M.; B.S., St. Mary's Coll., Winona, 1941; M.S., St. Louis U., 1943; Ph.D., U. Minn., 1949; m. Grace Lucille Mahlke, June 6, 1942; children—Lourdes S. (Mrs. Jeffrey Oliver), Judith (Mrs. Jerry Jan Foster), Charles S. Teaching fellow in biology St. Louis U., 1941-43; instr. anatomy Creighton U., 1943-47; research asso. neuropathology U. Minn., 1947-50; asst. prof. anatomy State U. N.Y., Downstate Med. Center, 1950-53; asso. prof. anatomy U. Kans., Kansas City, 1953-59, prof., 1959—, chmn. dept. anatomy, 1962—; vis. lectr. anatomy Makerere Med. Coll., Kampala, Uganda, E.Africa, 1960; researcher Inst. for Sci. Research in Central Africa, Lwiro, Belgian Congo, 1960-61; founding mem., Western Hemisphere secretariat Commn. on Comparative Neuroanatomy, World Fedn. Neurology, 1959—; exchange prof. U. Philippines Coll. Medicine, 1961, 1st Ann. Emilio Bulatoo Meml. lectr., 1961; 84th Luis Guerrero lectr. U. Santo Tomas Coll. Medicine, Philippines, 1961; cons. in neurosciences U. Calif., San Diego, summer 1967; vis. prof. Autonomous Universitad de Guadalajara, Mexico, 1968. Recipient Jayhawker award, 1960. Mem. Am. Assn. Anatomists, Am. Acad. Neurology (chmn. neuroanatomy sect.), AMA (affiliate), Kansas City Neurol. Soc., Soc. for Neuroscience, Assn. Anatomy Chairmen, Cajal Club (sec.-treas.), Phi Beta Pi. Adv. editor Jour. Neurol. Scis., 1965—; editorial bd. Jour. fur Hurnforschung, 1965—. Contbr. articles profl. jours. Home: 11002 W 72 Terr Shawnee KS 66203 Office: Dept Anatomy U Kans Kansas City KS 66103

MATZKIN, ROSE ELLIS (MRS. MAX N. MATZKIN), clubwoman; b. N.Y.C.; d. Louis and Jennie (Susman) Cohen; student New Haven State Tchrs. Coll., 1929-31; m. Max N. Matzkin, Dec. 23, 1934; children—Michael, Hannah (Mrs. Barry Lavine). Tchr. grammar sch. and spl. courses in remedial reading and dramatics, 1932-36; v.p., nat. chmn. Youth Aliyah, Zionist affairs, Am. affairs, tourism, wills and bequests Hadassah, 1962-72, nat. pres., 1972-76; chmn. Hadassah Med. Orgn., 1976—; Hadassah del. 23d, 25th, 26th, 27th, 28th sessions World Zionist Congress, Jerusalem; mem. exec. bd. World Confedn. Gen. Zionists, Am. Israel Pub. Affairs Com., Am. Zionist Fedn., Nat. Conf. on Soviet Jewry; trustee United Israel Appeal Bd., Am. Friends of Hebrew U.; mem. bd. Inst. Jewish Affairs, London; mem. bd., v.p. Am. Zionist Youth Fedn.; bd. govs. Hebrew U., Jerusalem; rep. from Am.-Israel Public Affairs Com. to Conf. Presidents Maj. Am. Jewish Orgns.; mem. women's aux. Am., Waterbury dental assns., Waterbury Hosp., St. Marys Hosp., Temple Israel. Home: Waterbury CT 06708 Office: 50 W 58th St New York NY 10019

MAU, CHUCK, lawyer; b. Honolulu, Jan. 10, 1907; s. Tin Kee and Jane (Ching) M.; B.A., U. Colo., 1932, LL.B., 1932; m. Karen Chun-Hoon, Dec. 19, 1942; children—Gordon James, Susan. Admitted to Hawaii bar, 1935; law sec. to justices Supreme Ct. Hawaii, 1933-35; dep. atty. gen. Hawaii, 1936-40; pvt. practice, Honolulu, 1940-50, 51—; now sr. partner firm Mau, White & Yee, Honolulu; judge Hawaii Tax Appeal Ct., 1948, First Circuit Ct. Hawaii, 1950-51; dir. sec., gen. counsel Hawaii Nat. Bank, Wadco, Inc., Town Properties, Ltd., Town Investments, Ltd., Industrial Investors, Inc., Chun-Hoon Pharmacy, Ltd., World-Wide Factors, Inc.; chmn. exec. com. Hawaii Nat. Bank. Mem. bd. suprs. City and County Honolulu, 1940-46, 48-50; bd. examiners Hawaii Bar, 1949. Del. Democratic Nat. Conv., 1948, Hawaii Constl. Conv., 1950; chmn. Central Com. Dem. Party Hawaii, 1950. Pres. Oahu chpt. Assn. Crippled Children and Adults, 1957-60, pres. Hawaii, 1961-62, nat. trustee, 1961-62, hon. life dir., 1973—; vice chmn. governing bd. Hawaii chpt. Arthritis Found.; bd. dirs. U. Colo. Found., Kokokahi Trust, Kapiolani Maternity and Gynecol. Hosp., Leahi Hosp., Honolulu Community Theatre, Hawaii Child and Family Service; chmn. Honolulu Symphony Fund Drive, 1962; adv. com. Hawaii chpt. Am. Freedom Found. Recipient Alumni award U. Colo., 1954; founder Mau Law Scholarship Fund, U. Colo. Sch. Law, Chuck Mau Scholarship Fund, Mid-Pacific Inst., Honolulu; named Law Father of Year, Honolulu C. of C., 1957; named to Hall Fame "C" Club U. Colo., 1969. Fellow Am. Coll. Mortgage Attys.; mem. Am. Bar Assn. (adv. bd. Standing Com. on Communism and its contrast to Liberty under law), Delta Sigma Rho. Conglist. Clubs: Waialae Country; Lotos (N.Y.C.). Home: 3077 LaPietra Circle Honolulu HI 96815 Office: 1000 Bishop St Honolulu HI 96813

MAU, WILLIAM KOON-HEE, financier; b. Honolulu, Apr. 25, 1913; s. Wah Hop and Mau (Ho Shee) M.; ed. pub. schs., Hawaii; LL.D., Pacific U., 1969; m. Jean Lau, Oct. 17, 1936; children—Milton, Cynthia, Lynette, Leighton, Letitia. Chmn. bd., chief exec. officer Am. Security Bank, Honolulu, 1958-69; pres. Tropical Enterprises, Ltd. and Ambassador Hotel of Waikiki, Honolulu, Top of Waikiki Revolving Restaurant, Honolulu, 1955—; owner, developer Waikiki Bus. Plaza; owner, developer Waikiki Shopping Plaza, Aloha Motors Properties; pres. Empress Ltd., Hong Kong, 1962-70, Aloha Motors, Inc. Vice chmn. Hawaii Bd. Land Natural Resources, 1959-63. Bd. dirs. Chinese Cultural Found., Hawaii, 1960—, Aloha United Fund, 1966—, Am. Nat. Red Cross, 1965—; past mem. exec. bd. Boy Scouts Am.; trustee Kauikeolani Children's Hosp., 1959-61. Recipient Golden Plate award Am. Acad. Achievement Bd. Govs., 1969; Wisdom Hall of Fame award of honor, 1969; named Bus. Man of Year, Hawaii Bus. and Industry mag., 1966. Mem. Am., Hawaii bank assns., Newcomen Soc. N.Am., Am. Bd. Arbitration, Downtown Improvement Assn., United Chinese Soc., Tsung Tsin Assn., Hawaii Visitors Bur., Hawaii Islanders, Hawaii Pub. Links Golf Assn., Chinese C. of C. (dir., auditor 1959-62). Home: 3938 Monterey Pl Honolulu HI 96816 Office: Waikiki Bus Plaza 2270 Kalakaua Ave Honolulu HI 96815

MAUCH, GENE W., profl. baseball mgr.; b. Salina, Kans., Nov. 18, 1925; s. George W. and Mamie (Peterson) M.; grad. high sch.; m. Nina Lee Taylor, Dec. 15, 1945; 1 dau., Leanne. Player with Bklyn. Dodgers, Pitts. Pirates, Chgo. Cubs, Boston Braves, St. Louis Cardinals, Chgo. White Sox; mgr. Atlanta Baseball Club, then Mpls. Club, 1958-60, Phila. Phillies, 1960-68, Montreal Expos team, Can., 1969-75, Minn. Twins, 1976—. Named Mgr. of Year, 1973; AP Mgr. of Year, 1964. Home: 3210 Las Marias St Hacienda Heights CA 91745 Office: Minn Twins Met Stadium 8001 Cedar Ave Bloomington MN 55428*

MAUCK, ELWYN ARTHUR, educator, adminstr.; b. Toledo, Iowa, May 5, 1910; s. Garfield Arthur and Elsie Caroline (Buck) M.; A.B., Cornell Coll., Iowa, 1932, LL.D., 1973; A.M. (Roberts fellow 1932-36), Columbia U., 1933, Ph.D., 1937; m. Mary Frank Helms, June 4, 1948. Staff mem. Inst. Pub. Adminstrn., N.Y.C., 1935, N.Y. Commn. for Rev. of Tax Laws, 1935-37; asst. prof. polit. sci. U. N.C., 1937-45, asso. prof., 1945-47 (on leave 1942-47); chief reports and awards div. Office Civilian Def., Washington, 1942-45; teaching staff Dept. Agr. Grad. Sch., Washington; vis. prof. pub. adminstrn. U. P.R., Rio Piedras, 1945-46; chief orgn. and methods div. War Assets Adminstrn., Nashville region, 1946-47; prof. govt. and politics U. Md., 1947-49; dir. Md. Fiscal Research Bur., Balt., 1948-53; lectr. McCoy Coll., Johns Hopkins U., 1949-53; vis. lectr. Goucher Coll., 1951, 52; pub. adminstrn. adviser Inst. Inter-Am. affairs, 1953-57; chief pub. and bus. adminstrn. div. USOM, Brazil, 1954-57; prof. pub. adminstrn. N.Y. U. in Ankara, Turkey, 1958-59; prof. U. Minn. Project in Seoul, Korea, 1959-62; prof. pub. adminstrn. U. Pitts., 1962-75, prof. emeritus, 1975—; chief party U. Mich. Project in Taipei, Taiwan, 1963-64; chief party U. Pitts. Project in Zaria, Nigeria, 1965-67; dean Faculty of Adminstrn., Ahmadu Bello U., Nigeria, 1967; coordinator of GSPIA Doctoral Study, 1968-73; dir. GSPIA Nigeria program, 1968-73; mem. Md. Commn. on Pub. Welfare, 1948; exec. sec. Md. Joint Legis. Com. to Study State Mental Hosps., 1949, 51; cons. Md. Tax Survey Commn., 1949-51; staff dir. Md. Commn. on Adminstrv. Orgn. of State, 1951-53. Mem. Am. Polit. Sci. Assn. (sec. D.C. home rule com. Washington chpt. 1947-48, exec. council 1948-50), Am. Soc. Pub. Adminstrn. (pres. Md. chpt. 1949-50), Phi Beta Kappa, Pi Sigma Alpha (nat. sec., treas. 1949-52, nat. pres. 1952-54), Tau Kappa Alpha. Author: Financial Control in the Suburban Areas of N.Y. State, 1937; contbg. author: Public Administration in Puerto Rico, 1948; Outside Readings in American Government, 1949; County Government Across the Nation, 1951; editor County and Twp. Sect., Nat. Municipal Rev., 1940-53; contbr. numerous articles to profl. mags., other publs. Address: Route 1 Box 155-U Indian Head MD 20640

MAUCK, HENRY PAGE, JR., educator; b. Richmond, Va., Feb. 3, 1926; s. Henry Page and Harriet Hutcheson (Morrison) M.; B.A., U. Va., 1950, M.D., 1952; m. Janet Garrett Horsley, May 14, 1955; children—Henry Page III, John Waller. Intern, Henry Ford Hosp., Detroit, 1952-53; resident Med. Coll. Va., Richmond, 1953-56, asst. prof. medicine and pediatrics, 1961-66, asso. prof., 1966-72, prof., 1972—; fellow in cardiology Am. Heart Assn., 1956-57; cons. cardiology Langley Field Air Force Hosp., Hampton, Va., McGuire's VA Hosp., Richmond. Served with U.S. Army, 1944-46. Diplomate Am. Bd. Internal Medicine. Fellow A.C.P., Am. Coll. Cardiology; mem. Am. Physiol. Soc., So. Soc. Clin. Investigation, Am. Fedn. Clin. Research, So. Soc. Clin. Research. Presbyterian. Contbr. chpt. to Pathophysiology, Autonomic Control of Cardiovascular System, 1972. Home: 113 Oxford Circle W Richmond VA 23221 Office: Box 281 Med Coll Va Richmond VA 23298

MAUDE, EDWARD JOSEPH, banker; b. Orange, N.J., Aug. 6, 1924; s. William L. and Katharine (Vickers) M.; grad. Kent Sch., 1942; student Va. Mil. Institute, 1942; A.B. in Econs., Princeton, 1948; m. Suzanne Norman Fleet, May 21, 1949 (div. 1971); children—Cynthia Vickers, William Lupton III; m. 2d, Ann Lang Balmos, 1972. Asst. v.p. Chem. Bank N.Y. Trust Co., 1948-60; exec. v.p., trustee Community Savs. Bank, Rochester, N.Y., 1960-61; treas. Greenwich Savs. Bank, N.Y.C., 1962-64; pres. trustee Union Sq. Savs. Bank, (merger, formed United Mut. Savs. Bank 1969), N.Y.C., 1965-74, chmn., chief exec., 1974—; dir. Instl. Investors Mut. Fund, 1977—. Trustee Bloomfield (N.J.) Coll., 1975—. Served with inf. AUS, 1943-45; ETO. Mem. Savs. Bank Assn. of N.Y. State (dir. 1977—). Episcopalian. Clubs: Montclair (N.J.) Golf; Princeton (N.Y.C.); N.Y. Yacht; Boothbay Harbor (Maine) Yacht. Home: 215 N Mountain Ave Montclair NJ 07042 Office: 1370 Ave of Americas New York City NY 10019

MAUER, ALVIN MARX, physician, hosp. adminstr.; b. LeMars, Iowa, Jan. 10, 1928; s. Alvin Milton and Bertha Elizabeth (Marx) M.; B.A., State U. Iowa, 1950, M.D., 1953; m. Theresa Ann McGivern, Dec. 2, 1950; children—Stephen James, Timothy John, Daria Maureen, Elizabeth Claire. Intern, Cin. Gen. Hosp., 1953-54; resident in pediatrics Children's Hosp. Cin., 1954-56; fellow in hematology dept. medicine U. Utah, Salt Lake City, 1956-59; dir. div. hematology Children's Hosp. Cin., prof. dept. hematology, 1959-73; prof. dept. pediatrics U. Cin. Coll. Medicine, 1959-73; prof. pediatrics U. Tenn. Coll. Medicine, Memphis, 1973—; dir. St. Jude Children's Research Hosp., Memphis, 1973—; mem. hematology study sect. NIH; mem. clin. cancer investigation rev. com. Nat. Cancer Inst.; mem. com. on maternal and infant nutrition NRC. Served with U.S. Army, 1946-Home: 4583 Laurelwood Dr Memphis TN 38117

MAUGHAN, RICHARD JOHNSON, judge; b. Logan, Utah, Nov. 13, 1917; s. Heber Chase and Ragna (Johnson) M.; B.S., Utah State U., 1948; J.D., U. Utah, 1951; grad. Appellate Judges Seminar Sch. Law, N.Y. U., 1975; m. Laura Dell Torgeson, July 12, 1946; children—Margith, Joyce, Eloise, Richard, Mary. Admitted to Utah bar, 1951, Fed. Dist. Ct. bar, 1951, Circuit Ct. Appeals bar, 1962, U.S. Supreme Ct. bar, 1967; asst. to Atty. Gen. for Utah, 1951-52; practice law, Salt Lake City, 1951-74; justice Supreme Ct. Utah, 1975—. Mem. Utah State Bd. Regents, 1969-75; exec. com. Western Interstate Commn. for Higher Edn., 1969-75; Democratic candidate for Congress, Utah, 1968; chmn. Dem. Central Com., Davis County, 1967-71; pres. Peter Maughan Family Orgn., 1964-74; trustee Utah State U., 1965-69, chmn. bd., 1968-69. Served with U.S. Army, 1942-45. Mem. Utah State (chmn. continuing legal edn. com. 1966-69, mem. profl. competence com. 1974, mem. judiciary com. 1975—), Davis County (pres. 1961-62) bar assns., Utah Jud. Council, Newcomen Soc. N.Am., Pi Sigma Alpha, Phi Alpha Delta. Mormon. Contbr. articles to jours. Office: Utah Supreme Court State Capitol Salt Lake City UT 84114

MAUKE, OTTO RUSSELL, coll. pres.; b. Webster, Mass., Jan. 26, 1924; s. Otto G. and Florence (Giroux) M.; A.B., Clark U., 1947, A.M., 1948; Ph.D. (Kellogg fellow), U. Tex., 1965; m. Leah Louison, June 18, 1950. Tchr. history, acad. dean Endicott Jr. Coll., Beverly, Mass., 1948-65; acad. dean Cumberland County Coll., Vineland, N.J., 1966-67; pres. Camden County Coll., Blackwood, N.J., 1967—. Served with U.S. Army, 1943-46; PTO. Home: PO Box 126 Blackwood NJ 08012

MAULDEN, WESLEY M., aerospace co. exec.; b. Spokane, June 23, 1925; s. Robert W. and Willena (Morrison) M.; B.A., U. Puget Sound, 1951; S.M., M.I.T., 1961; children—Penny, Gregory, Dean, David. With Boeing Co., Seattle, 1951—, successively asst. mgr. SST div., asst. mgr. group programs comml. airplane group, v.p., asst. gen. mgr., exec. v.p., now sr. v.p.; lectr. econs. U. Puget Sound, Tacoma, 1950-51. Served with AUS, 1943-46. Mem. Mu Sigma Delta. Home: 3223 SW 319th Federal Way WA 98003 Office: 7755 E Marginal Way Seattle WA 98124

MAULDIN, ROBERT RAY, banker; b. China Grove, N.C., Jan. 15, 1935; s. Raymond Ray and Hazel Inez (Luther) M.; student N.C. State U., 1953-54; B.S., U. N.C., 1959; m. Patricia Crain Jarman, Aug. 29, 1959; children—John Clayton, Patricia Crain, Elizabeth Jarman, Anne Luther, Katherine Purnell. Trainee, asst. trust officer N.C. Nat. Bank, Charlotte, 1959-62; cashier Bank of York (S.C.), 1962-65; v.p. Colonial Am. Nat. Bank, Roanoke, Va., 1965-69; exec. v.p., dir. Peoples Bank & Trust Co., Rocky Mount, N.C., 1969—; dir. Stoney Creek Knitting Mills, N.C. Payments System Inc. Campaign chmn., dir. Western York County United Fund, 1963-65; dir. Palmetto Area council Boy Scouts Am., 1964-65; treas., dir. Family Service-Travelers Aid of Roanoke Valley, 1967-69; pres. Rocky Mount United Community Services, 1974-75; dir. Downtown, Inc., 1970—. Bd. dirs. York County Mental Health Clinic, 1964-65, Rocky Mount area N.C. Wesleyan Coll. Found., 1970—, Carolinas United Community Services, 1972-73, Rocky Mount Family YMCA, 1971-74; treas. Central City Revitalization Corp., 1976—; mem. Rocky Mount City Schs. Bd., 1979—. Served with AUS, 1954-56. Mem. N.C. Young Bankers (pres. 1974-75), Am. Inst. Banking, Robert Morris Assos., N.C. Bankers Assn. (dir. 1975-76), Bank Adminstrn. Inst., Rocky Mount C. of C. (dir. 1975—, v.p. 1977, pres. 1978-79), Chi Phi. Presbyn. Club: Kiwanis (pres. Rocky Mount 1976-77). Home: 109 Essex Ct Rocky Mount NC 27801 Office: PO Drawer 872 Rocky Mount NC 27801

MAULDIN, WILLIAM H., cartoonist; b. Mountain Park, N.Mex., Oct. 29, 1921; s. Sidney Albert and Edith Katrina (Bemis) M.; ed. pub. schs. and high schs., N.Mex. and Ariz.; studied art, Chicago Acad. of Fine Arts; M.A. (hon.), Conn. Wesleyan U., 1946; Litt.D., Albion Coll., 1970, N.Mex. State U., Las Cruces, 1972; L.H.D., Lincoln Coll., 1970; m. Norma Jean Humphries, Feb. 28, 1942 (div. 1946); children—Bruce Patrick, Timothy; m. 2d, Natalie Sarah Evans, June 27, 1947 (dec. Aug. 1971); children—Andrew, David, John, Nathaniel; m. 3d, Christine Ruth Lund, July 29, 1972; 1 dau., Kaja Lisa. Cartoonist St. Louis Post-Dispatch, until 1962, Chgo. Sun-Times, 1962—. Tech. adviser, actor film Teresa, 1950; actor The Red Badge of Courage, 1950. Served with U.S. Army, 1940-45, with 45th Inf. Div. and Stars and Stripes; campaigns Sicily, Italy, France, Germany. Decorated Purple Heart, Legion of Merit; recipient Pulitzer prize for cartoons, 1944, 59, Sigma Delta Chi Award for cartoons, 1963, 69, 72, Distinguished Service award, 1969; Prix Charles Huard de dessin de presse Fondation pour l'Art et la Recherche, Paris, France, 1974. Fellow Sigma Delta Chi. Author or cartoonist: Star Spangled Banter, 1941; Sicily Sketch Book, 1943; Mud, Mules and Mountains, 1943; This Damn Tree Leaks, 1945; Up Front (Book of the Month selection), 1945; Back Home (Book of the Month selection), 1947; A Sort of a Saga, 1949; Bill Mauldin's Army, 1951; Bill Mauldin in Korea, 1952; What's Got Your Back Up?, 1961; I've Decided I Want My Seat Back, 1965; The Brass Ring, 1971 (Book of Month Club selection). Author, illustrator numerous articles Collier's, Life, Sat. Eve. Post, Sports Illus. Address: care Chicago Sun-Times 401 N Wabash Ave Chicago IL 60611

MAULDON, JAMES GRENFELL, educator; b. London, Feb. 9, 1920; s. Philip George and Eileen Grenfell (Hicks) M.; student Jesus Coll., Oxford, Eng., 1938-39, 46-47, M.A. First Class, 1947; M.A. (hon.), Amherst Coll., 1970; m. Margaret Capron, July 11, 1953; children—Jane, Matthew, Maria, Lucy. Mem. faculty Oxford U., 1947-68, C.U.F. lectr., 1951-68, chmn. math. faculty, 1966-68, fellow Corpus Christi Coll., 1950-68, dean, 1951-57, emeritus fellow, 1977—; mem. faculty U. Calif. at Berkeley, 1960-61; prof. Amherst (Mass.) Coll., 1968—. Cons. on APL math. notation, Paris, 1974-75. Served to maj. Brit. Army, 1939-46. Decorated Mil. Cross; mentioned in despatches. Mem. Royal Statis. Soc., Inst. Math. Statistics, Am. Math. Soc., Math. Assn. Am., AAUP, Elizabethane Soc., Sigma Xi. Mem. Ch. of Eng. Clubs: Royal Tank Regiment Officers' (London); Oxford Alpine. Contbr. articles on probability, statistics, combinatorics, geometry, real analysis, abstract algebra, games and chess problems to tech. jours. Home: 97 Lincoln Ave Amherst MA 01002

MAULE, HAMILTON BEE, author; b. Ojus, Fla., Mar. 19, 1915; s. Claude Wendell and Zelita (Bee) M.; student St. Mary's U., 1934-37; B.J., U. Tex. at Austin, 1947; m. Ann Moore (div. Feb. 1958); children—Hamilton Bee, Halsey Coykendall, Robin Hamilton, Frederica (Mrs. James Rosenfield); m. 2d, Dorothy Levins, Apr. 25, 1959. Sports writer Austin (Tex.) Am.-Statesman, 1946, Dallas Morning News, 1947-48; pub. dir. Los Angeles Rams Football Club, 1949-52, Dallas Football Club, 1952; sports writer Dallas News, 1953-56; sr. editor Sports Illus., N.Y.C., 1957-75; sr. writer Classic Mag., 1975—; author: Jeremy Todd, 1958; The Pros (with Robert Riger), 1959; Footsteps, 1960; The Rookie, 1961; The Quarterback, 1962; The Shortstop, 1962; The Game, 1963, 65, 68, Championship Quarterback, 1963; Beatty of the Yankees, 1963; Rub-a-Dub-Dub, 1964; The Running Back, 1964; The Last Out, 1965; The Linebacker, 1965; The Corner Back, 1966; The Receiver, 1967; The Players, 1968; The Pro Season, 1970; Running Scarred, 1972; Bart Starr, Quarterback, 1973. Served with U.S. Merchant Marine, 1939-45. Mem. Authors Guild, Writers Guild Am. Home: 25 Sutton Pl S New York NY 10022 Office: Classic Mag 551 Fifth Ave New York NY 10020

MAULL, FLORA DAVIS (MRS. BALDWIN MAULL), sculptor, civic worker; b. March 1, 1904; d. A.S. Johnston and Ella (Thomas) Davis; A.B., Vassar Coll., 1925; ed. Art Students League, N.Y.C., 1925-26; study sculpture, N.Y.C., Paris, France, 1927-33; m. Baldwin Maull, Dec. 7, 1929; children—Baldwin, Diana. One man show Milch Gallery, N.Y.C.; exhibited jury shows Archtl. League; represented in pvt. collections. Benefit chmn. United Neighborhood Houses, Inc., N.Y.C., 1942-43; founder, chmn. women's com. Payne Whitney Clinic, N.Y. Hosp., 1943-46; dir., del. 5th Internat. Inst. Child Psychiatry, Toronto, Can., 1954; dir., sec., treas. bd. Grosvenor Neighborhood House, Inc., N.Y.C., 1936-54, mem. bd. assos., 1954—; dir., sec., treas. bd. Psychiat. Clinic Buffalo and Erie County, 1953-62; mem. Children's Aid Soc. Com. Foster Home Care, Buffalo, 1960-68; mem. White House Conf. Com., 8th Jud. Dist. Mental Health, 1959-60; bd. dirs. N.Y. State Assn. for Mental Health, 1964-66; mem. Nat. Council on Crime and Delinquency, 1967-69; life fellow Albright-Knox Art Gallery, Buffalo; mem. McCall Corp. Conf. on Woman Power, 1968—; del. N.Y. Gov.'s Conf. on Natural Beauty, 1966; mem. N.Y. Bot. Garden Symposium Challenge for Survival, 1968. Docent Princeton U. Art Mus., 1972—, also life mem. Mem. Mental Health Assn. N.J. (dir. 1950-52), Nat. Soc. Colonial Dames in State N.Y. (mem. Gunston Hall com., hist. activities com.), Marquis Biog. Soc. Library (pres. 1965, trustee 1966-69). Clubs: Colony, Badminton (N.Y.C.); Vassar (founder, pres. Central N.J. 1947-52, 70—, Western N.Y. 1952-69); Present Day (Princeton). Author: Custom Houses of New York State in Three Centuries of Custom Houses, 1972. Address: 25 Alexander St Princeton NJ 08540

MAUMENEE, ALFRED EDWARD, physician, educator; b. Mobile, Ala., Sept. 19, 1913; s. Alfred Edward and Lulie Martha (Radcliff) M.; A.B., U. Ala., 1934, student Med. Sch., 1935; M.D., Cornell U., 1938; Sc.D. (hon.), U. Ill., 1974; m. Anne Elizabeth Gunnis, July 1949; children—Anne Elizabeth, Alfred Edward; m. 2d, Irene Hussels, 1972; children—Niels Kim, Nicholas Radcliff. Intern, resident Wilmer Inst. Johns Hopkins Hosp., 1938-44, chief resident, 1942-43, asso. prof. ophthalmology 1944-48, now ophthalmologist-in-chief; prof. chief div. surgery in ophthalmology Stanford U. Sch. Medicine and Hosp., 1948-55; prof. ophthalmology Johns Hopkins U. Sch. Medicine, 1955, also dir. Wilmer Ophthalmol. Inst. civilian cons. Walter Reed Army Hosp. Clin. Center NIH, U.S. Naval Hosp., Bethesda, Md.; civilian cons. postgrad. med. tng. to Surgeon Gen. USN; cons. Balt. City Hosp., 1959—; USPHS Hosp., Wyman Park, 1965—, Nat. Acad. Scis., 1974—; mem. numerous adv. coms.; vis. prof., lectr. numerous univs. Vice pres. Ophthalmic Pub. Co., 1973. Chmn. adv. com. Variety Club Blind Babies Found, 1949-55; adv. com. Nat. Soc. for Prevention of Blindness; sci. adv. council Nat. Council to Combat Blindness, Inc.; bd. dirs. Pan-Am. Ophthalmol. Found., 1967—. Diplomate Am. Bd. Ophthalmology (mem. bd. 1959-67, chmn. 1967). Recipient numerous awards including award Soc. Mil. Ophthalmologists, 1959, Beverly Myers Achievement award Ednl. Found. Ophthalmic Optics, 1967, Howe medal Am. Ophthalmol. Soc., 1969, Lucian Howe Gold medal AMA sect. ophthalmology, 1970, Howe medal Buffalo Ophthalmol. Soc., 1970, Francis I. Proctor Research medal, 1972, Jorge Malbran Gold medal, 1974, John M. McLean Gold medal Internat. Eye Found., 1976, Trustees award Research to Prevent Blindness, 1976, award Cornell U. Med. Coll., 1977, Distinguished Service award Dept. Navy, 1977. Hon. fellow Puget Sound Acad. Ophthalmology and Otolaryngology, Royal Coll. Surgeons Edinburgh; mem. Internat. Agy. for Prevention of Blindness (pres. 1968-70), Med. and Chirurg. Faculty Md., Nat. Acad. Scis. (adv. com. ophthalmology 1955-58), AMA (chmn. sect. 1965), Am. Ophthalmol. Soc., Am. Acad. Ophthalmology and Otolaryngology (pres. 1971), Assn. of Univ. Profs. of Ophthalmology (chmn.), Assn. for Research Ophthalmology (chmn. trustees 1968), Pan-American Assn. Ophthalmology (pres. 1972-75, sec.), Ophthalmic Pathology Club; hon. mem. Pacific Coast Oto-Ophthalmol. Soc., La.-Miss. Ophthalmol. and Otol. Soc., Argentine Ophthalmol. Soc., Hellenic Ophthalmol. Soc., South African Ophthalmol. Soc., Ariz. Ophthalmol. Soc., Alpha Omega Alpha. Wilmer Residents Assn. Co-author: Atlas of Ophthalmic Pathology. Co-editor: Progress in Ophthalmology and Otology, 1952. Author 190 articles on corneal transplantation, other subjects. Corr. editor of Bull. of Tissue Transplantation: co-editor Am. Jour. Ophthalmology, pres. bd. dirs. 1975; asso. editor: Investigative Ophthalmology, 1963-74; editorial adv. bd. Audio-Digest Ophthalmology, 1963—. Home: 1700 Hillside Rd Stevenson MD 21153 Office: 601 N Broadway Baltimore MD 21205

MAUN, JOSEPH ANGUS, lawyer; b. Laurel, Nebr., June 24, 1909; s. Angus E. and Rosa (Gallagher) M.; B.A. cum laude, U. Minn., 1932, LL.B., 1935; m. Lucille McDermott, July 31, 1937; children—Lawrence, Sheila, Janis, Jeanne, James, Thomas. Admitted to Minn. bar, 1935, since practiced in St. Paul; partner firm Maun, Green, Hayes, Simon, Aretz & Murray, St. Paul, and predecessor firms, St. Paul, 1943—; dir. Northland Co., Northland Mortgage Co., Northland Fin. Corp., Aslesen Co., Bayard Realty Co., Uptown Mgmt. Co., Anchor Paper Co., C.,M.,St.P.&P. R.R., Chgo. Milw. Corp., Vulcan-Hart Corp., Universal Title Co., St. Paul. Former mem. Met. Planning Commn., 1965-67, Met. Airports Council St. Paul-Mpls.; mem. Met. Improvement Commn. St. Paul-Mpls. Bd. dirs. United Fund St. Paul. Served as pvt. AUS, 1944-45. Mem. Am., Minn. bar assns., St. Paul Area C. of C. (past pres.), St. Paul Winter Carnival Assn. (past. pres.), Am. Legion, St. Paul Jr. Assn. Commerce (past. pres.), Am. Mgmt. Assn., Phi Beta Kappa. Kiwanian (dir. St. Paul). Clubs: Town and Country (pres., dir.), Minn. Home: 1077 Sibley Memorial Hwy Saint Paul MN 55105 Office: Hamm Bldg Saint Paul MN 55102

MAUPIN, ARMISTEAD JONES, lawyer; b. Raleigh, N.C., Nov. 10, 1914; s. Alfred McGhee and Mary Armistead (Jones) M.; A.B., U. N.C., 1936; J.D., George Washington U., 1940; m. Diana Jane Barton, May 16, 1942; children—Armistead Jones, Anthony Westwood, Jane Stuart. Admitted to N.C. bar, 1939; since practiced in Raleigh, partner firm Maupin, Taylor & Ellis. Pres., Occoneechee council Boy Scouts Am., 1962-64; pres. Carolina Charter Corp., 1976—. Served from ensign to lt. (s.g.), USNR, 1941-45; comdr. Res. Decorated chevalier French Legion of Honor. Fellow Am. Bar Found.; mem. N.C. State Bar (pres. 1959-60, council 1955-60), Am. Bar Assn. (ho. dels. 1960-72), Soc. of Cincinnati (v.p. gen. 1968-70, pres. gen. 1971-74, pres. N.C. soc. 1964-67). Episcopalian (former vice chancellor N.C. Diocese, former sr. warden Christ Ch. Parish). Clubs: Carolina Country, Circle, Triangle Hounds. Home: 2005 Banbury Rd Raleigh NC 27608 Office: Insurance Bldg Raleigh NC 27602

MAURER, ARMAND AUGUSTINE, clergyman, educator; b. Rochester, N.Y., Jan. 21, 1915; s. Armand Augustine and Louise (Ribson) M.; came to Can., 1933; B.A., U. Toronto (Ont., Can.), 1938, M.A., 1943, PH.D., 1947; M.S.L., Pontifical Inst. Mediaeval Studies, Toronto, 1945. Joined Congregation Priests of St. Basil, Roman Catholic Ch., 1940. ordained priest, 1945; lectr. in philosophy St. Michael's Coll., U. Toronto, 1946-55, asst. prof. philosophy, 1955-58, asso. prof., 1948-62, prof., 1962—; asst. prof. philosophy Pontifical Inst. Maediaeval Studies, 1949-53, prof., 1953—. Guggenheim fellow, 1954-55. Mem. Royal Soc. Can., Am. Cath. Philos. Assn., Metaphys. Soc., Can. Philos. Assn. Author: Medieval Philosophy, 1962; (with others) Recent Philosophy: Hegel to the Present, 1966; contbr. numerous articles to philos. Jours. Home and Office: 59 Queens Park Crescent Toronto ON M5S 2C4 Canada

MAURER, EVAN MACLYN, curator; b. Newark, Aug. 19, 1944; s. Myron P. and Belle (Cloth) M.; B.A., Amherst Coll., 1966; M.A., U. Minn., 1968; Ph.D., U. Pa., 1974; m. Naomi E. Margolis, Mar. 17, 1968; 1 son, Noah Anthony Samuel. Asst. to dir., curator Mpls. Inst. Arts, 1970-73; curator primitive art Art Inst. of Chgo., 1973—. Author: The Native American Heritage, 1977. Office: Art Inst Chicago Michigan Ave Chicago IL 60603

MAURER, FRED DRY, coll. dean; b. Moscow, Idaho, May 4, 1909; s. Oran J. and Lavina (Stone) M.; B.S., U. Idaho, 1934; D.V.M., Wash. State Coll., 1937; Ph.D., Cornell U., 1948; m. Irene L. Haworth, Aug. 25, 1935; children—Allen D., Linda J. Commd. lt. Vet. Corps, U.S. Army, 1941, advanced through grades to col., 1959; research on equine diseases, Front Royal, Va., 1941-43; virus research War Disease Control Sta., Grosse Isle, Can., Africa, 1943-46, Walter Reed Army Inst. Research, Washington, 1946-47, 48-51; research on fgn. animal diseases Africa, 1951-54; research in virology and pathology Armed Forces Inst. Pathology, Washington, 1954-61; dir. pathology div. Army Med. Research Lab., Ft. Knox, Ky., 1961-64; ret., 1964; asso. dean, distinguished prof. pathology Coll. Vet. Medicine, Tex. A. and M. U., College Station, 1964-74, coordinator Inst. Tropical Vet. Medicine, 1974-76, emeritus, 1976—; cons., 1976—; cons. USDA, 1951—, Morris Animal Found., 1963—, Ill. Zoonoses Center, 1963-66, Animal Health Com., NRC, 1965-71, Army Surgeon Gen., 1973—; mem. com. on research priorities for Africa, NSF, 1971-73; mem. horse industry adv. com. USDA, 1972—; sci. adv. bd. Armed Forces Inst. Pathology, 1972-77; chmn. sci. adv. bd. Yerkes Primate Center, Emory U., 1974—. Decorated Legion of Merit; mem. U.S. Animal Health Livestock Assn. (chmn. fgn. animal disease com. 1965-66), Am. Vet. Med. Assn. (research council 1965-75), Am. Coll. Vet. Pathologists (pres. 1964). Contbg. author: Diseases of Cattle, 1956; Diseases of Swine, 2d edit., 1970; Virus Diseases, 1964. Research in diagnosis and control of infectious diseases in animals with emphasis on virology and pathology of fgn. diseases of food producing animals; devel. tng. aids. Home: 2408 Morris Ln Bryan TX 77801 Office: Coll Vet Medicine Tex A and M U College Station TX 77843

MAURER, GILBERT CHARLES, pub. co. exec.; b. Bklyn., May 24, 1928; s. Charles and Mildred (Petite) M.; A.B., St. Lawrence U., 1950; M.B.A., Harvard, 1952; m. Ann D'Espinosa, May 17, 1951; children—Christopher, David, Peter, Jonathan, Meredith. With Cowles Communications, Inc., N.Y.C., 1952-71, Look Mag., 1952-62; pub. Venture mag., 1963-67; pres. Family Circle mag., 1967-69, v.p., dir. corporate planning, exec. com., 1969-71, also dir.; sr. v.p. F.A.S. Internat., Inc., 1971-73; v.p. mag. div. Hearst Corp., 1973-74, exec. v.p., 1974-76, pres., 1976—. Mem. N.Y. adv. bd. Salvation Army, 1979—. Mem. Mag. Pubs. Assn. (chmn. 1979—). Clubs: Harvard, Metropolitan (N.Y.C.). Home: 15 Burritts Landing Westport CT 06880 Office: 959 8th Ave New York NY 10019

MAURER, HAROLD MAURICE, pediatrician; b. N.Y.C., Sept. 10, 1936; s. Isador and Sarah (Rothkowitz) M.; A.B., N.Y. U., 1957; M.D., SUNY, Bklyn., 1961; m. Beverly Bennett, June 12, 1960; children—Ann Louise, Wendy Sue. Intern pediatrics Kings County Hosp., N.Y.C., 1961-62; resident in pediatrics Babies Hosp., Columbia-Presbyn. Med. Center, N.Y.C., 1962-64; fellow in pediatric hematology/oncology Columbia-Presbyn. Med. Center, 1966-68; asst. prof. pediatrics Med. Coll. Va., Richmond, 1968-71, asso. prof., 1971-75, prof., 1975—, chmn. dept. pediatrics, 1976—; chmn. Intergroup Rhabdomyosarcoma Study; mem. Cancer and Leukemia Group B. Mem. Gov.'s Adv. Com. on Handicapped. Served to lt. comdr. USPHS, 1964-66. Diplomate Am. Bd. Pediatrics (written exam. task force). NIH grantee, 1974—. Mem. Am. Acad. Pediatrics (com. oncology-hematology), Am. Soc. Hematology, Soc. Pediatric Research, Am. Pediatric Soc., Va. Pediatric Soc. (exec. com.), Assn. Med. Sch. Pediatric Dept. Chairmen, Va. Hematology Soc., Am. Cancer Soc., Sigma Xi, Alpha Omega Alpha. Republican. Jewish. Editorial bd. Am. Jour. Hematology; contbr. articles to profl. jours. Home: 405 Berwickshire Dr Richmond VA 23229 Office: Med Coll Va Richmond VA 23298

MAURER, J. PIERRE, life ins. co. exec.; b. Montreal, Que., Can., June 10, 1924; s. Alexis Antoine and Jeanne (Marcotte) M.; B.A., St. Ignatius Coll., Montreal, 1946; hon. degree Ottawa U., 1978; m. Armande Crete, Feb. 15, 1947; 1 son, Michel. With Met. Life Ins. Co., 1950—, pres. Can. ops., 1974-78, exec. v.p., mem. exec. com., N.Y.C., 1978—; dir. Royal Bank Can., TIW Industries, Ltd., Warnock Hersey Internat., Ltd. Mem. Life Ins. Mktg. Research Assn. (sr. mktg. officer research group). Clubs: Rideau (Ottawa); Mt. Royal (Montreal); Ontario (Toronto); Metropolitan (N.Y.C.). Home: 8 Peter Cooper Rd New York NY 10010 Office: 1 Madison Ave New York NY 10010*

MAURER, JAMES RICHARDSON, mfg. co., exec.; b. Tulsa, June 9, 1930; s. James Miller and Haseltine Antoinette (Richardson) M.; B.A., Stanford, 1951, LL.B., 1953; m. Susan Ellen Gustine, Aug. 15, 1953; children—Stephen, Elizabeth, Joseph, Caroline (dec.), Margaret, Mary Rose, Thomas, Sarah, Katharine, John, Benjamin. Contract adminstr. Boeing Airplane Co., Seattle, 1953-55; admitted to Wash. bar, 1954, Calif. bar, 1955; tax and legal counsel Ryan Aero. Co., San Diego, 1955-68; partner Madruga & Maurer, Indio, Calif., 1968-69; asst. gen counsel Xerox Corp. div., Pasadena, 1969-70; asst. gen counsel Brown Co., Pasadena, 1970-71, v.p., sec., gen. counsel, 1971, also dir.; dir. Symons Corp. Instr. bus. law Calif. State Coll., San Diego, 1959-60. Newhouse scholar, 1949-51; Ira S. Lillick scholar, 1951-53. Mem. Los Angeles County, Am. bar. assns., Am. Soc. Corp. Secs., Town Hall. Editorial bd. Stanford Law Rev., 1952-53. Home: 286 Alegria Ave Sierra Madre CA 91024 Office: 251 S Lake Ave Pasadena CA 91101

MAURER, JOSEPH ABELE, educator; b. Bethlehem, Pa., Sept. 29, 1911; s. Andrew and lydia (Abele) M.; A.B., Moravian Coll. Theol. Sem., 1932; M.A., Lehigh U., 1936; Ph.D., U. Pa., 1948; m. Kathleen E. Danneberger, Jan. 19, 1957. Instr. Latin and English, Moravian Coll., 1932-36, asst. prof., 1936-43; Latin master Princeton (N.J.) Country Day Sch., 1943-47; instr. Greek and Latin, Lehigh U., 1947-49, asst. prof., 1949-53, asso. prof. classical langs., 1953-55, head dept. classical langs., 1956-75, prof., 1964-77, prof. emeritus, 1977—, asso. dean langs., chmn. pro tem modern fgn. langs., 1975-77; lectr. N.T. Greek at Acad. New Church, Bryn Athyn, Pa., 1948-49. Recipient Lindback Found. award for distinguished teaching, 1973, Hillman award Lehigh U., 1977. Mem. Am. Philol. Assn., Moravian Hist. Soc., Classical Assn. Atlantic States (pres. 1964-65), Phi Beta Kappa (hon.; sec.-treas. Middle Atlantic dist. United chpts. 1970-76), Pi Gamma Mu, Phi Alpha Theta, Eta Sigma Phi, Alpha Chi Rho. Democrat. Episcopalian. Mason (K.T.). Author: A Commentary on C. Suetonii Tranquilli Vita C. Caligulae Caesaris, 1949. Editor-in-chief The Classical World, vols. 62-64, 1968-71. Home: Bridle Path Woods Apt D-12 400 Bridle Path Rd Bethlehem PA 18017

MAURER, PAUL HERBERT, biochemist, educator; b. N.Y.C., June 29, 1923; s. Joseph and Clara (Vogel) M.; B.S., City Coll. N.Y., 1944; Ph.D., Columbia, 1950; m. Miriam Esther Merdinger, June 27, 1948; children—Susan Gail, David Mark, Philip Mitchell. Research biochemist Gen. Foods Corp., Hoboken, N.J., 1944-46; instr. City Coll. N.Y., 1946-51; research asso. Coll. Phys. and Surg., Columbia, 1950-51; asst. research prof. Sch. Medicine, U. Pitts., 1951-54, asso. prof. immunochemistry, 1954-60; asso. prof. microbiology Seton Hall Coll. Medicine, 1960-62; prof. microbiology N.J. Coll. Medicine, 1962-66; prof., chmn. dept. biochemistry Jefferson Med. Coll., Phila., 1966—; mem. allergy and infectious diseases tng. grant com. NIH, 1961-66; mem. commn. on albumin Protein Fedn.; mem. NRC com. on plasma. Served with USNR, 1946-48. Recipient Research Career award Nat. Inst. Allergy and Infectious Diseases, 1962-66, Chemistry medal City Coll. N.Y., 1944. Mem. Am. Chem. Soc., N.Y. Acad. Scis., Biochem. Soc. (London), Harvey Soc., Am. Assn. Immunologists, Am. Soc. Biol. Chemistry, AAAS, Societe de Chimie Biologique (France), Soc. Exptl. Biology and Medicine, Sigma Xi. Asso. editor: Immunochemistry, 1964; Science, 1966. Contbr. profl. jours. Home: 1001 Dell Ln Wyncote PA 19095 Office: Dept Biochemistry Jefferson Med Coll 1020 Locust St Philadelphia PA 19107

MAURER, RICHARD SCOTT, airline exec.; b. Cleve., July 16, 1917; s. Horace C. and Nelle (Dunn) M.; A.B., Ohio Wesleyan U., 1938; J.D., Yale, 1941; m. Mary Fleming, Aug. 7, 1942 (dec.); children—Mary, Nancye; m. 2d, Lella Levine, July 28, 1962; children-Ske, Lyle. Admitted to Ohio bar, 1941, Tenn. bar, 1944, Ga. bar, 1954, U.S. Dist. Ct., No. Dist. of Ga., 1955, U.S. Circuit Ct. Appeals of 5th Circuit, 1956; mem. gen. counsel's staff Civil Aero. Bd., 1941-43; asst. gen. counsel Chgo. & So. Airlines, Memphis, 1943-45, sec., gen. counsel, 1946-50, v.p., sec., gen. counsel, 1950-53; legal v.p. Delta Air Lines, Atlanta, 1953-59, dir., 1954—, v.p. legal, sec., 1960-64, v.p. gen. counsel sec., 1965-66, sr. v.p., gen. counsel, sec., 1967-77, vice chmn., sec., 1978—. Mem., past chmn. adv. bd. Salvation Army, Atlanta. Pres. bd. dirs. Memphis Better Bus. Bur., 1952-53. Mem. Atlanta C. of C., Am. Arbitration Soc. (nat. panel arbitrators), Am. (past chmn., ins., negligence and compensation law sect.; past chmn. corporate law depts. com., bus., banking and corp. law sect.), Ga., Atlanta bar assns., Corporate Counsel Assn. Greater Atlanta (1st pres.), Am. Soc. Corporate Secs. (past chmn. bd., chief exec. officer, 1st pres. Southeastern Regional Group), Phi Beta Kappa, Omicron Delta Kappa, Delta Sigma Rho, Phi Gamma Delta, Phi Alpha Delta (hon.). Episcopalian. Clubs: Lawyers, Capital City (Atlanta); Nat. Aviation (Washington). Home: 2601 Arden Rd NW Atlanta GA 30327 Office: Delta Air Lines Atlanta Airport Atlanta GA 30320

MAURER, ROBERT DISTLER, indsl. physicist; b. St. Louis, July 20, 1924; s. John and Elizabeth J. (Distler) M.; B.S., U. Ark., 1948; Ph.D., M.I.T., 1951; m. Barbara A. Mansfield, June 9, 1951; children—Robert M., James B., Janet L. Mem. staff M.I.T., 1951-52; with Corning Glass Works (N.Y.), 1952—, mgr. physics research, 1963-78, research fellow, 1978—. Served with U.S. Army, 1943-46. Recipient Indsl. Physics prize Am. Inst. Physics, 1978; L.M. Ericsson Internat. prize in telecommunications, 1979. Fellow Am. Ceramic Soc. George W. Morey award 1976); mem. IEEE (Morris N. Liebmann award 1978), Am. Phys. Soc., Nat. Acad. Engring. (bd. telecommunications-computer applications). Patentee in field; contbr. articles to profl. jours., chpts. to books. Home: 6 Roche Dr Painted Post NY 14870 Office: Sullivan Park Corning Glass Works Corning NY 14830

MAURER, STEWART ANDERSON, JR., hotel exec.; b. Rochester, N.Y., Nov. 3, 1935; s. Stewart Anderson and Ruth Marie (Rohr) M.; B.S., Cornell U., 1957; m. Priscilla Bronson Smith, July 20, 1957; 1 son, Stewart Anderson III. Mgr., Sheraton Corp., Rochester and Buffalo, Omaha, Mpls., N.Y.C., 1957-75; v.p., gen. mgr. Sheraton Russell Hotel, N.Y.C., 1971-72, Sheraton Cadillac, Detroit, 1972-74, Sheraton Palace, San Francisco, 1975-76; gen. mgr. Adams Hotel, Phoenix, 1976-78; v.p., gen. mgr. Indpls. Hilton Hotel, 1978—. Mem. Phoenix Fire Safety Adv. Bd., 1977-78; mem. Mayor's Central Phoenix Redevel. Com., 1977-78; v.p. Phoenix Bus. and Profl. Assn., 1977-78; bd. dirs. Commn. for Downtown Indpls., Conv. and Visitors Bur., Indpls., Indpls. Christmas Com., Inc. Served to capt. U.S. Army Res., 1957-69. Recipient Very Outstanding Phoenician award, 1978, Gold award United Way of Indpls., 1979. Mem. Am. Hotel and Motel Assn., Ind. Hotel and Motel Assn., Indpls. Hotel and Motel Assn. (v.p.), Cornell Soc. Hotelmen, Ind. C. of C., Indpls. C. of C., Hotel

Sales Mgmt. Assn., Sigma Alpha Epsilon. Republican. Presbyterian. Clubs: Rotary (Indpls.); Columbia. Home and office: Indpls Hilton Hotel PO Box 1966 Indianapolis IN 46206

MAURER, WALTER HARDING, educator; b. N.Y.C., July 13, 1921; s. Carl and Frieda (Geib) M.; B.A., U. Vt., 1943; postgrad. Princeton, 1947-48; Ph.D., U. Pa., 1962; m. Geraldine Kaufman, Feb. 18, 1961. Tchr. classical Greek and German, U. Vt., 1946-47; reference librarian South Asia sect. Orientalia div. Library of Congress, Washington, 1950-62; curator South Asia collection East-West Center U. Hawaii, Honolulu, 1962-63, prof. Sanskrit, 1962—, prof. history, 1964—, lang. cons. Philosophy East and West, 1967—, chmn. dept. Indo-Pacific langs., 1971—; vis. research fellow Inst. Advanced Studies in Humanities, U. Edinburgh (Scotland), summer 1978. Served with AUS, 1943-46. Am. Numis. Soc. grantee, 1948; Fulbright fellow Deccan Coll., Poona, India, 1953-55; Am. Council Learned Socs. Area study grantee U. Tübingen (Germany) and London, 1968-69. Mem. Am. Oriental Soc., Tibet Soc., Royal Asiatic Soc., Sigma Alpha Epsilon, Phi Beta Kappa. Author: Sugamanvaya Vrtti, 1965; also articles revs. Home: 2333 Kapiolani Blvd Apt 813 Honolulu HI 96826

MAURER, WESLEY HENRY, educator, publisher; b. Bunker Hill, Ill., Jan. 18, 1897; s. Henry P. and Emilia Anna (Boechkler) M.; A.B., U. Mo., 1921, B.S., 1922, B.J., 1923; m. Flossie Wilson, Aug. 31, 1921, (div. May 1943); m. 2d, Margaret Elizabeth Weber, Feb. 26, 1944; children—Margaret E., Wesley H. Jr., Marilyn. News editor Evening Ledger, Mexico, Mo., 1922-24; corr. St. Louis Post Dispatch, Kansas City Star, other newspapers, 1922-24; city editor, editorial writer, editor Athens (Ohio) Messenger, 1925-28; editorial cons. various publs., 1938—, editorial writer, since 1935; instr. Journalism U. Mich., 1924-25; asst. prof. journalism, dir. journalism lab. Ohio 1925-28; instr. U. Mich., 1928-32, asst. prof., 1932-42; acting chmn., 1937-38, asso. prof. journalism, 1941-48, exec. sec. dept. journalism, 1947, prof., 1948—, chmn. dept., 1949-66, mem. exec. com. Coll. Lit., Sci. and Arts, 1949-57, com. on deanship, 1951, chmn. senate adv. com. on univ. affairs, 1960-61; pub. Town Crier, Mackinac Island, Mich., 1959—, Harbor Light, Harbor Springs, Mich., 1964-70; editor, pub. St. Ignace (Mich) News and St. Ignace Enterprise, 1975—; pres. Assn. Accredited Sch. and Depts. Journalism, 1953-54; pub. relations cons. Essex Co. Med.-Econ. Research, Windsor, Ont., Can., 1938; cons. Mainichi Newspapers, Tokyo and Osaka, Japan, 1963; U.S. State Dept. specialist Center for Advanced Studies in Journalism for Latin Am., Quito, Ecuador, 1964. Organizer, chmn., mem. exec. bd. Ann Arbor Citizens' Council; bd. dirs. Council Am. Affairs and World Events, Detroit, 1930-74; lectr. Mott Found., Flint, 1942; asso. organizer Mich. Fedn. Tchrs. (pres. 1936-37); pres. Wesleyan Found., 1948. Recipient U. Mich. Distinguished Faculty Achievement award, 1961; Mem. Am. Soc. Newspaper Editors (distinguished achievement in journalism, life mem.), AAAS, Am. Assn. Tchrs. Journalism, AAUP, Am. Fedn. Tchrs. (past pres., sec.), ACLU (mem. nat. com.), Jackson Fund for Civil Liberties. Democrat. Unitarian. Author series of 12 articles on report of com. on survey of med. service and health agys. for Detroit News, Detroit Free Press, other Mich. newspapers; series of 3 articles for Canadian Press; sound film on Federal Aid to the States for Edn. for Am. Fedn. Tchrs., 1938; sound films Human Priorities, Our Town is a Neighborhood, for Community Fund; Children and Youth of Mich., for Mich. Youth Commn. and Mid-Century White House Conf. Home: 60 Keightley St Saint Ignace MI 49781 Office: 539 Reagon St Saint Ignace MI 49781

MAURICE, ALFRED PAUL, educator, artist; b. Nashua, N.H., Mar. 11, 1921; s. Paul and Gertrude (Martel) M.; student U. N.H., 1940-42; B.A., Mich. State U., 1947, M.A., 1950; m. J. Dolores Robson, Feb. 23, 1946. Muralist, Nat. Youth Adminstrn., 1939-40; instr. Macalester Coll., 1947-49; teaching asst. Mich. State U., 1949-50; asst., then asso. prof. State U. N.Y. at New Paltz, 1950-57; exec. dir. Md. Inst., 1957-59; dir. Kalamazoo Inst. Arts, 1959-65; prof. art, U. Ill. Chgo. Circle Campus, 1965—, chmn. dept., 1965-67, asso. dean faculties, 1969-72, acting dean Coll. of Architecture and Art, 1975-77; typographer-calligrapher, painter-printmaker, 1947—, art and museum cons., lectr., 1957—. Dir. Stuart Town Homes Corp., 1970. Mem. Gov. Mich. Council Arts, 1964-65. Served with AUS, 1942-46. Mem. Coll. Art Assn. Home: 2725 A S Michigan Ave Chicago IL 60616

MAURIN, MARIO LEON, educator; b. Neuilly s/Seine, France, Dec. 22, 1928; s. Joaquin and Jeanne (Lifchitz) M.; came to U.S., 1941, naturalized, 1953; B.A., Yale, 1948, M.A., 1949, Ph.D., 1951; m. Margaret Simpson, Aug. 31, 1960; 1 dau., Elana Celia. Mem. faculty Bryn Mawr Coll., 1953—, prof. French, 1965-79, Eunice M. Schenck 1907 prof. French, 1979—, chmn. dept., 1958-67; vis. lectr. Haverford Coll., 1955, U. Pa., 1956, Johns Hopkins, 1968, Inst. d'Etudes Francaises, Avignon, 1962, 64, 67, 69, 72, 75, 78. Served with USMCR, 1951-53. Recipient Prix de la Langue Française, French Acad., 1973; Palmes académiques French Govt., 1976. Guggenheim fellow, 1960. Mem. Modern Lang. Assn., Am. Assn. Tchrs. French, Soc. des Profs. Francais en Amerique. Author: Leopardi, 1961; Henri de Régnier, 1972; also articles; syndicated columnist Agencia latino americana. Home: 14 Westview Rd Bryn Mawr PA 19010

MAURO, ALEXANDER, biophysicist; b. New Haven, Conn., Aug. 14, 1921; s. John and Maria Grazia (Rapuano) M.; B.Elec. Engring., Yale U., 1942, Ph.D. in Biophysics, 1950; m. Jean Gilpatrick, Nov. 27, 1955. Electronics engr. Gen. Electric Co., 1942-45; asst. prof. dept. physiology Yale U. Med. Sch., 1951-59; asst. prof. biophysics Rockefeller U., N.Y.C., 1959-62, asso. prof., 1963-71, prof., 1971—; vis. prof. U. Geneva, 1972-73; Rockefeller Found. fellow U. Copenhagen, Denmark, 1950-51. Mem. fellowship com. Muscle Dystrophy Assn., 1974—. Mem. Am. Physiol. Soc., Biophysics Soc., IEEE, Sigma Xi. Designer original heart pacemaker. Editor: Regeneration of Striated Muscle and Myogenesis, 1970; Muscle Regeneration, 1979. Home: 392 Central Park W New York NY 10025 Office: 1230 York Ave New York NY 10021

MAURO, ANDREW EMIL, glass co. exec.; b. N.Y.C., July 25, 1916; s. Thomas Andrew and Concetta (Maurelli) M.; B.S., Alfred U., 1937; M.S., St. Bonaventure U., 1941; m. Warda Alice Vincent, July 3, 1938; children—Thomas, Andrew, Alice, Elizabeth. Plant supt. Olean Glass Co. (N.Y.), 1938-42; plant mgr. Thatcher Glass Mfg. Co., N.Y.C., 1942-44, Elmira, N.Y., 1944-54, Lawrenceburg, Ind., 1955-60, Saugus, Calif., 1960-63; factories mgr. Glass Container Corp., Fullerton, Calif., 1963-65, v.p. mfg., 1965-68, v.p. operations, 1968-69, sr. v.p., 1969—; instr. glass tech. St. Bonaventure U., 1940-41. Fund-raising chmn. Elmire Community Chest, 1952; chmn. Dearborn County (Ind.) Red Cross, 1958; chmn. Dearborn County Community Chest, 1959. Trustee Holy Cross Hosp., San Fernando, Cal., 1963. Mem. Am. Ceramic Soc. Roman Catholic. K.C. Home: 13381 Kootenay Dr Santa Ana CA 92705 Office: 535 N Gilbert Ave Fullerton CA 92634

MAURY, REUBEN, editorial cons.; b. Butte, Mont., Sept. 2, 1899; s. Henry Lowndes and Anne Henderson (Perkins) M.; LL.B., U. Va., 1924, J.D., 1970; m. Thomasine Lafayette Rose, July 21, 1928. Admitted to Mont. bar, 1923; mem. firm Maury & Maury, Butte, 1923-26; reporter N.Y. Daily News, 1926, movie critic, 1926, chief editorial writer, 1926-72, editorial cons., 1973—. Mem. S.A.T.C., U. Va., 1918. Decorated Order Brilliant Star, Taiwan (Republic of China), 1972. Recipient Pulitzer Prize for editorials printed in 1940, also Christopher editorial award, 1954; award Assembly Captive European Nations, 1965; George Sokolsky award Am. League Against Communism, 1965; Freedoms Found. at Valley Forge editorial honor certificate, 1973. Mem. Beta Theta Pi, Sigma Delta Chi, Silurian Soc. Club: Dutch Treat (N.Y.). Roman Catholic. Author: The Wars of the Godly: The Story of Religious Conflict in America, 1928; Americans to Remember, 1958; (with Karl G. Pfeiffer) Effective Editorial Writing, 1960; What Made the U.S. Great, 1968. Contbr. articles, short stories, editorials, etc., to Collier's Weekly, Woman's Home Companion, Red Book, Blue Book, Old Scribners, Old American Mercury, Liberty, Adventure, Sea Stories, Chicago Tribune-N.Y. News Blue Ribbon Fiction Features. Address: PO Box 305 Saugatuck CT 06880

MAUTNER, HENRY GEORGE, chemist; b. Prague, Czechoslovakia, Mar. 30, 1925; s. Frank Thomas and Maria (Neumann) M.; came to U.S., 1941, naturalized, 1946; B.S., U. Calif. at Los Angeles, 1946, Ph.D., at Berkeley, 1955; M.S., U. So. Calif., 1950; M.A. (hon.), Yale U., 1967; m. Dorothea Johanna Barkemeyer, Nov. 21, 1967; children—Monica Ann, Matthew Erich, Andrea Christina. Teaching asst. U. Calif., 1951-55; research chemist Productol Co., Santa Fe Springs, Calif., 1950; faculty Yale U., New Haven, 1955-70, prof. dept. pharmacology, 1967-70, head sect. medicinal chemistry, 1962-70; prof. biochemistry and pharmacology, chmn. depts. Tufts U. Sch. Medicine, 1970—; mem. med. chemistry study sect. NIH, 1968-72, chmn., 1971-72; mem. neurobiology panel NSF, 1977—. Mem. Am. Chem. Soc., Chem. Soc. (London), Am. Assn. Pharmacology, Am. Assn. Cancer Research, Biophys. Soc., Am. Soc. Biol. Chemists, AAAS. Editorial bd. Jour. Med. Chemistry, 1967-70, 76—; contbr. articles to profl. jours., chpts. to books. Home: 183 Ward St Newton Centre MA 02159

MAUTZ, BERNHARD, paint and varnish co. exec.; b. Madison, Wis., Feb. 8, 1899; s. Bernhard and Amalia (Meyer) M.; B.S., U. Wis., 1922; m. Jane Allison Fuller, Nov. 22, 1926; children—Betsy (Mrs. James Klode), Bernhard F. With Mautz Paint Co., Madison, 1922—, pres., 1930—, chmn. bd., 1964—. Sec., treas. Wis. Alumni Research Found. Served U.S. Army, World War I. Mem. Chi Psi. Mason (Shriner). Clubs: Madison, Maple Bluff Country (Madison). Home: 57 Cambridge Rd Madison WI 53704 Office: 939 E Washington Ave Madison WI 53701

MAUTZ, ROBERT BARBEAU, educator; b. Marion, Ohio, Jan. 22, 1915; s. Albert Edward and Bessie (Barbeau) M.; B.A., Miami U., Oxford, Ohio, 1937; J.D., Yale, 1940, postgrad., 1949-50; hon. degrees U. Miami, U. Fla., Miami U., Oxford, Jacksonville U., Fla. Inst. Tech.; m. Esther Guthery, Feb. 22, 1947. Admitted to N.Y. bar, 1941; asso. Root, Clark, Buckner & Ballantine, N.Y.C., 1940-41; atty. Pan Am. Airways, Brit. W. Africa, 1941-42; exec. officer legal div. Office Mil. Govt., Berlin, Germany, 1945-48, dep. legal dir., Hesse, 1948-49; prof. law, asst. dean Coll. Law, U. Fla., 1950-58, dean acad. affairs U. Fla., Gainesville, 1958-63, v.p. acad. affairs, 1963; chancellor State Univ. System of Fla., 1968-75, Regent's prof., dir. Inst. Learned Scholars, Gainesville, 1975—; dir. Nat. City Bank of Marion (Ohio). Trustee, past pres. Fla. Beta Students Aid Fund, Inc. Past pres. Fla. Assn. Colls. and U.; past pres. sect. acad. v.p. and deans So. Assn. Colls. and Univs.; commr. Edn. Commn. of States; mem. exec. bd. So. Regional Edn. Bd. Bd. dirs. Am. Coll. Testing Program, Nat. Center for Higher Edn. Mgmt. Systems; adv. council Nat. Center for Edn. Statistics; mem. Fla. Commn. on Post-Secondary Edn.; adv. council Def. Systems Mgmt. Coll.; exec. com. Yale Law Sch. Served to col. USAAF, 1942-45; maj. gen. U.S. Air Force Ret. Decorated chevalier Swedish Royal Order North Star; Star of Yugoslavia with gold wreaths; D.S.M. (U.S.); named Man of Yr. by several orgns. Mem. Phi Beta Kappa, Beta Theta Pi, Omicron Delta Kappa, Phi Alpha Delta, Order of Coif. Club: Army-Navy. Author legal and other articles. Contbr. to Ency. Internat. Home: 611 SW 27th Ct Gainesville FL 32601 Office: 182 Grinter Hall U Fla Gainesville FL 32611

MAUTZ, ROBERT KUHN, acct., univ. ofcl.; b. Ft. William, Ont., Can., Apr. 12, 1915 (parents Am. citizens); s. William Frederick and Caroline Barbara (Kuhn) M.; B.S., U.N.D. 1937, M.S., U. Ill., 1938, Ph.D., 1942; m. Ruth S. Sundby, Sept. 9, 1939; children—Robert Kuhn II, Carl David, Kristin Barbara. Instr., U. Ill., 1937-42; with Haskins & Sells, C.P.A.'s, 1942-43, 45-46, Alexander Grant & Co., C.P.A.'s, 1946-48; faculty U. Ill. at Urbana, 1948-72, prof. accountancy, 1954-72, Weldon Powell meml. prof. accountancy, 1969-72; Am. Inst. C.P.A.'s Distinguished vis. prof. U. Minn., 1969; partner Ernst & Ernst, Cleve., 1972-78; dir. Paton Acctg. Center, U. Mich., Ann Arbor, 1978—. Mem. Cost Acctg. Standards Bd., 1971-77. Served to lt. (j.g.) USNR, 1943-45; ETO. Recipient Notable Contbn. to Accounting Lit. award Am. Inst. C.P.A.'s, 1970, gold medal award, 1979; Public Service award GAO, 1976; named to Acctg. Hall of Fame, 1978. Mem. Am. Acctg. Assn. (pres. 1965, mem. exec. com.), Am. Inst. C.P.A.'s (mem. council 1965-68, dir. 1970-71), Beta Gamma Sigma, Beta Alpha Psi, Phi Kappa Phi. Mem. Ch. of Jesus Christ of Latter-day Saints. Author: Fundamentals of Auditing, 2d edit., 1964; (with Donald E. Kieso and C.A. Moyer) Intermediate Principles of Accounting, 1969; (with Hussein A. Sharaf) Philosophy of Auditing, 1961; Financial Reporting by Diversified Companies, 1968; (with F.L. Neumann) Corporate Audit Committees, 1970; Corporate Audit Committees-Practices and Procedures, 1977; Effect of Circumstances on the Application of Accounting Principles, 1972; (with W.G. May) Financial Disclosure in a Competitive Economy, 1978; also articles. Editor The Accounting Review, 1958-61. Home: 2989 Hickory Ln Ann Arbor MI 48104 Office: Paton Accounting Center U of Mich Ann Arbor MI 48109

MAUZY, OSCAR HOLCOMBE, lawyer; b. Houston, Nov. 9, 1926; s. Harry Lincoln and Mildred Eva (Kincaid) M.; B.B.A., U. Tex., 1950, J.D., 1952; m. Anne Rogers; children—Catherine Anne, Charles Fred, James Stephen. Admitted to Tex. bar, 1952, since practiced in Dallas; pres. Mullinax, Wells, Mauzy & Baab, Inc., P.C., 1970-78; mem. Tex. Senate from 23d Dist., 1967—, chmn. edn. com., 1971—, pres. pro tempore, 1973. Mem. Tex. Adv. Commn. Intergovtl. Relations, Nat. Conf. State Legislators, Edn. Commn. of the States, Am. Edn. Finance Assn. Vice chmn. judiciary com. Tex. Constl. Conv., 1974; nat. committeeman Young Democrats, 1954. Served with USNR, 1944-46. Kiwanian. Home: 904 Evergreen Hill Rd Dallas TX 75208 Office: 1025 Elm St 9th Floor Dallas TX 75202

MAVES, PAUL BENJAMIN, clergyman, educator; b. Burwell, Nebr., Apr. 21, 1913; s. Benjamin C. and Ellen Alverda (Craun) M.; A.B., Nebr. Wesleyan U., 1936; B.D., Drew U., 1939, Ph.D., 1949; student N.Y. U., 1945-46, Harvard, 1957-58; student (vis. scholar) Columbia U., 1964-65; m. Mary Carolyn Hollman, Sept. 10, 1939; children—Margaret Alverda, David Hollman. Ordained to ministry Methodist Ch., 1940; pastor in Albany, N.Y., 1940-42, Middlebury, Vt., 1942-45; instr. edn. N.Y. U., 1945-46; research asso. dept. pastoral services Fed. Council Chs., 1946-48, acting exec. sec. dept., 1948-49; faculty Drew U., 1949-67, George T. Cobb prof. religious edn., 1956-67; asso. exec. dir., dept. of ednl. devel. Nat. Council of Churches of Christ, 1967-70; dir. field edn., prof. ch. adminstrn. St. Paul Sch. Theology, 1970-75; adminstr. Kingsley Manor, Los Angeles, 1975-78; staff asso. Mid-Am. Resource and Tng. Center on Aging, Kansas City, Mo., 1978—. Mem. Nebr. Ann. Conf. Meth. Ch. Del. White House Conf. Aging, 1961. Author: The Best is Yet to Be, 1951; Understanding Ourselves as Adults, 1959; On Becoming Yourself, 1962; (with J. Lennart Cedarleaf) Older People and the Church, 1949; (with Mary Carolyn Maves) Finding Your Way Through The Bible, 1970, Learning More About The Bible, Exploring How The Bible Came To Be, 1973, Discovering How The Bible Message Spread, 1974. Editor: The Church and Mental Health, 1953. Home: 10200 Edelweiss Circle Merriam KS 66203 Office: 5218 Oak St Kansas City MO 64112. *I have tried to be, to let be, and to cooperate with others in a mutual becoming.*

MAVIS, FREDERIC THEODORE, cons. civil engr.; b. Crocketts Bluff, Ark., Feb. 7, 1901; s. Martin John and Hinda (Cassens) Mewes; B.S. in C.E., U. of Ill., 1922, M.S., 1926, C.E., 1932, Ph.D., 1935; student Technische Hochschule Karlsruhe, Baden, Germany, 1927-28; m. Edith Frances Foley, June 7, 1930. Jr. engr. to asst. engr. Kelker, DeLeuw & Co., Chgo., 1922-25; research asst. ASCE (com. on concrete, reinforced concrete arches), U. Ill., 1925-26; office engr. in charge design Kelker, DeLeuw & Co., 1926-27; Freeman traveling fellow ASCE, 1927-28; successively asst. prof. mechs. and hydraulics, prof., head dept. State U. Iowa, asso. dir. in charge lab. to cons. engr. Iowa Inst. Hydraulic Research, 1928-39; prof., head dept. civil engring. Pa. State Coll., 1939-44; prof., head dept. civil engring. Carnegie Inst. Tech., Pitts., 1944-57; dean Coll. Engring., prof. civil engring., U. Md., 1957-65, prof. mech. engring., 1965-67; cons. engr., 1967—. Chmn. panel Research and Devel. Bd., 1947-48; mem. and mem. at large Div. Engring. and Indsl. Research NRC, 1955-64. Recipient Wason medal for research Am. Concrete Inst., 1959. Mem. ASCE, ASME, Am. Soc. for Engring. Edn., Soc. Am. Mil. Engrs., Am. Water Works Assn., Internat. Assn. Hydraulic Research, Pi Kappa Phi, Theta Tau, Chi Epsilon, Gamma Alpha, Tau Beta Pi, Phi Kappa Phi, Sigma Xi, Pi Tau Sigma, Pi Mu Epsilon, Kappa Alpha Mu. Club: Rotary (Paul Harris fellow). Author papers on response of structures and materials to dynamic loading. Author and editor monographs on hydraulic and structural engring., engring. edn., applied math.; (with Edith F. Mavis) photographs and feature stories of Western Ill. Home: 215 W Piper St Macomb IL 61455

MAVRINAC, ALBERT ANTHONY, educator; b. Pitts., Nov. 24, 1922; s. Anthony and Mary Theresa (Kvaternik) M.; A.B., U. Pitts., 1943; M.A., 1950; student Columbia, summer 1948; Ph.D., Harvard, 1955; A.M., Colby Coll., 1960; Fulbright scholar, Inst. Superieur de Philosophie, U. Louvain (Belgium), 1950-51; Carnegie fellow law and polit. sci., Harvard Law Sch., 1961-62; m. Marilyn Parks Sweeney, July 3, 1954; children—Georgia Ireland, Susan Edwards, Sarah Clay, Emily Gregor, Anthony Edwards. Labor relations specialist Office Mil. Govt., Hesse, Germany, 1946-48; lectr. polit. sci. U. Pitts., 1948-50; instr. Wellesley Coll., 1953; teaching fellow Harvard, 1953-55, instr., 1955-57, lectr., 1958, Allston Burr sr. tutor, 1956-58; Fulbright prof. univs Rennes and Montpellier (France), 1958-59; prof. govt. Colby Coll., Waterville, Maine, 1958-78, Charles A. Dana prof. govt., 1978—, chmn. dept. govt., 1979—, acting dean students 1970-71; fellow Duke, summer 1960; asso. dir. Insts. Communism and Am. Constitutionalism Am. U., summer 1963; project specialist Ford Found. and Inst. Pub. Adminstrn. for Egyptian Adminstrn., also adviser Govt. UAR, 1965-67; spl. asst. for legislation to gov. Maine, 1968-69; faculty fellow NASA, 1969; chief party Inst. Pub. Adminstrn. Adv. Group to Nat. Inst. Adminstrn., Vietnam, 1971-72; chmn. Nat. Fulbright-Hays Scholarship Screening Com. for France, 1976; Nat. Endowment for Humanities fellow Princeton U., summer 1977; lectr., cons. in field. Com. chmn. Gov. Maine Task Force Govt. Reorgn., 1967-68; founding mem. No. Kennebec Valley Community Action Com., 1965; mem. Maine Council Humanities and Pub. Policy, 1975—; active numerous Democratic campaigns in Maine; chmn. Maine for Muskie, 1970. Served to 1st lt. AUS, 1943-46; ETO. Decorated Bronze Star, Combat Inf. badge; recipient Toppan prize Harvard, 1955. Mem. Am., New Eng. (past pres.) polit. sci. assns., Am. Soc. Polit. and Legal Philosophy, Am. Soc. Pub. Adminstrn. Roman Catholic. Author monographs, articles. Home: 47 Winter St Waterville ME 04901

MAVROULES, NICHOLAS, congressman; b. Peabody, Mass., Nov. 1, 1929; student M.I.T.; m. Mary Silva, 1950; children—Debbie, Gail, Brenda. Supr. personnel Sylvania Electronics Corp., 1949-67; ward councillor, Peabody, Mass., 1958-61, councillor-at-large, Peabody, 1964-65, mayor city of Peabody, 1967-79; mem. 96th Congress from 6th Mass. Dist. Recipient David Ben Gurion award State of Israel. Mem. Mass. Mayor's Assn. Democrat. Greek Orthodox. Clubs: Rotary, Kiwanis. Office: 1204 Longworth House Office Bldg Washington DC 20515

MAW, CARLYLE ELWOOD, lawyer; b. Provo, Utah, Oct. 13, 1903; s. Charles E. and Margaret (Peterson) M.; B.S., Brigham Young U., 1925; LL.B. cum laude, Harvard, 1928; m. Margot Bell, Sept. 8, 1934; children—Carlyle Elwood, Michael Bailey, Susan Margot Maw Hykin. Admitted to N.Y. bar, 1928, D.C. bar, 1976; asso. firm Cravath, Swaine & Moore, N.Y.C., 1928-39, partner, 1939-73, counsel, 1976—; legal adviser State Dept., Washington, 1973-74, undersec. state for security assistance, 1974-76, cons., 1976—; chief counsel Pub. Works Adminstrn., 1933-34; chmn. exec. com. Com. for Def. of Constn. by Preserving Treaty Power, 1953-57. Chmn., Harvard Law Sch. Fund, 1961-63, vis. com. Law Sch., 1966-71; advisory bd. Internat. and Comparative Law Center, Southwestern Legal Found., 1964—. Fellow Am., N.Y. bar founds.; mem. Inter-Am., Am. (chmn. internat. trade com. antitrust law sect. 1971-73), N.Y. State (chmn. com. internat. law 1970-71), Internat. bar assns., Assn. Bar City N.Y. (v.p. 1954-55, mem., chmn. numerous coms.), Council Fgn. Relations, Am. Soc. Internat. Law (exec. council 1968-72), Internat. Law Assn. (exec. com. Am. br. 1971—), Harvard Law Sch. Assn. (pres. N.Y.C. 1965-66, pres. assn. 1969-71), Union Internationale des Avocats. Clubs: University (N.Y.C.); Metropolitan, Chevy Chase (Washington). Editor: Harvard Law Rev., 1926-28. Contbr. articles to profl. jours. Home: 870 UN Plaza New York City NY 10017 Office: One Chase Manhattan Plaza New York City NY 10005

MAWARDI, OSMAN KAMEL, plasma physicist; b. Cairo, Egypt, Dec. 12, 1917; s. Kamel Ibrahim and Marie (Wiennig) M.; B.S., Cairo U., 1940, M.S., 1945; A.M., Harvard U., 1947, Ph.D., 1948; m. Betty Louise Hosmer, Nov. 23, 1950. Came to U.S., 1946, naturalized, 1952. Lectr. physics Cairo U., 1940-45; asst. prof. Mass Inst. Tech., 1951-56, asso. prof., 1956-60; prof. engring., dir. plasma research program Case Inst. Tech., Cleve., 1960—; dir. Energy Research Office, Case Western Res. U., 1977—; pres. Collaborative Planners, Inc.; mem. Inst. Advanced Study, 1969-70; also cons.; dir. Rhikon Corp. Bd. dirs. Cleve. Soc. Contemporary Arts; trustee Print Club Cleve., Cleve. Inst. Art, Cleve. Art Assn. Recipient Biennial award Acoustical Soc. Am., 1952; CECON medal of achievement, 1979. Fellow Acoustical Soc. Am., AAAS, Am. Phys. Soc., IEEE (Edison lectr. 1968-69); mem. N.Y. Acad. Scis., Soc. Indsl. and Applied Math., Groupement des Acousticiens de Langue Française, Sigma Xi, Eta Kappa Nu. Contbr. articles to profl. jours. Home: 15 Mornington Ln Cleveland Heights OH 44106 Office: 10900 Euclid Ave Cleveland OH 44106

MAWBY, RUSSELL GEORGE, found. exec.; b. Grand Rapids, Mich., Feb. 23, 1928; s. Wesley G. and Ruby (Finch) M.; B.S. in Horticulture, Mich. State U., 1949, Ph.D. in Agrl. Econs., 1959, LL.D., 1972; M.S. in Agrl. Econs., Purdue U., 1951, D.Agr. (hon.), 1973; L.H.D., Luther Coll., Decorah, Iowa, 1972; LL.D., N.C. A. and T. State U., Greensboro, 1974; L.H.D., Alma (Mich.) Coll., 1975, Nazareth Coll., 1976; D.P.A., Albion Coll., 1976; D.C.L., U. Newcastle (Eng.), 1977; LL.D. (hon.), Tuskegee Inst., 1978; m. Ruth E. Edison, Dec. 16, 1950; children—Douglas, David, Karen. Extension specialist Mich. State U., East Lansing, 1952-56, asst. dir. coop. extension service, 1956-65; dir. div. agr. W.K. Kellogg Found., Battle Creek, Mich., 1965-66, mem., trustee, 1967—, v.p. programs, 1966-70, pres., 1970; dir. Kellogg Co. Trustee, Youth for Understanding, Ann Arbor, Mich., 1973-79, Arabian Horse Trust, 1978; bd. dirs. Gateway Tech. Inst. Found., Kenosha, Wis., 1977, Council on Founds., 1978—. Served with AUS, 1953-55. Decorated knight 1st class Royal Order St. Olaf (Norway); knight's cross Order of Dannebrog 1st class (Denmark); recipient Distinguished Service award U.S. Dept. Agr., 1963, Distinguished Alumni award Mich. State U., 1971, Nat. Alumni award 4-H Clubs, 1972, Distinguished Eagle Scout award Boy Scouts Am., 1973, Meritorious Achievement award Fla. A. and M. U., 1973, Nat. Partner in 4-H award Dept. Agr. Extension Service, 1976; named hon. fellow Spring Arbor (Mich.) Coll., 1972. Mem. Am. Agrl. Econ. Assn., Alpha Gamma Rho (dir. 1976—, Man of Year Chgo. Alumni chpt. 1976), Alpha Zeta, Phi Kappa Phi (Disting. Mem. award Mich. State U. 1978), Epsilon Sigma Phi (certificate of recognition 1974). Home: 8400 N 39th St Augusta MI 49012 Office: 400 North Ave Battle Creek MI 49016

MAWHINNEY, EUGENE ALBERTO, educator; b. Jonesboro, Maine, Oct. 14, 1921; s. Bert and Estella (Whitney) M.; B.S., U. Maine, 1947, M.A., 1949; Ph.D. in Polit. Sci., U. Ill., 1955; m. Anne Dowling, Aug. 24, 1946; children—Meredith, Mark Allen. Asso. prof. polit. sci. NE Mo. State Coll., 1951-55; mem. faculty Elmira (N.Y.) Coll., 1955-59, prof. polit. sci., 1958-59, head dept. social sci., 1956-59; mem. faculty U. Maine, 1959—, prof. polit. sci., 1963—, head dept., 1966-75. Mem. Maine Task Force Govtl. Reorgn., 1967-68, 76-77, Maine Jud. Council, 1965-77, Maine Commn. Senate Apportionment, 1966-67, 71, Maine Commn. House Apportionment, 1971-72, Maine Task Force Regional and Dist. Govt., 1977-78; cons. N.Y. State Commn. Constl. Revision, 1957-58; exec. dir. Maine Mgrs. Inst., 1960-65; trustee Washington Acad., 1969—. Served with AUS, 1942-46. Mem. Am., New Eng. (pres. 1974-75) polit. sci. assns., Kappa Delta Pi, Kappa Delta Phi, Phi Kappa Phi, Pi Sigma Alpha. Conglist. Mason (32 deg., Shriner). Author: Profile of Metropolitan Elmira, 1958; Maine Legislative Apportionment, 1967; (with others) Downeast Politics: The Government of Maine, 1975. Home: Spearin Dr Orono ME 04473

MAX, PETER, artist; b. Germany, Oct. 19, 1937; s. Jacob and Salla (Zeisel) Finkelstein; came to U.S., 1953; student Art Students League, Pratt Graphic Arts Center, Sch. Visual Arts; m. Elizabeth Ann Nance, May 1, 1963; children—Adam Cosmo, Libra Astro. Artist; pres. Peter Max Enterprises, N.Y.C.; published 29 books, 160 posters, 310 ltd. edit. graphics, TV specials, designs for 52 corps.; commd. to design U.S. postage stamp; commd. by U.S. govt. to create 200 murals at border sta. points between U.S./Can. and U.S./Mex.; exhbns. of paintings in numerous galleries and museums, U.S. and abroad. Recipient numerous art awards. Office: New York City NY

MAXA, RUDOLPH JOSEPH, JR., journalist; b. Cleve., Sept. 25, 1949; s. Rudolph Joseph and Christine Marie (Kimpel) M.; B.S. in Journalism cum laude, Ohio U., 1971; m. Kathleen Ann Zolciak, June 19, 1971; 1 dau., Sarah Lynn. Staff writer Washington Post, 1971—. Lectr. on journalism. Recipient John Hancock award for excellence in bus. and financial writing, 1972. Mem. Soc. Profl. Journalists, Sigma Delta Chi. Author: Dare to be Great, 1977; Public Trust, Private Lust, 1977. Home: 2841 29th St NW Washington DC 20008 Office: 1150 15th St NW Washington DC 20071

MAXEINER, CLARENCE WILLIAM, lawyer, constrn. co. exec.; b. Sioux City, Iowa, Mar. 24, 1914; s. Frank A. and Dora A. (Olson) M.; student Columbia Coll., 1933-34, Columbia U. Law Sch., 1938-39; A.B., Grinnell Coll., 1936; J.D., U. Calif. at Berkeley, 1941; m. Julie Frazer, Sept. 8, 1937; children—Martha Ann, Jay Frank, Mary Katherine, Nancy Carol; m. 2d, Rosalie F. Steele, May 29, 1974. Admitted to Calif. bar, 1941; partner firm Thelen, Marrin, Johnson & Bridges, San Francisco and Los Angeles, 1941-60; sr. v.p., gen. counsel, dir. J.H. Pomeroy & Co., Inc. and affiliated cos., San Francisco, 1959-65; v.p., gen. counsel Dillingham Corp. and affiliated cos., Honolulu, 1966—, sr. v.p., gen. counsel, sec., dir., mem. exec. com., 1968-71, spl. counsel, 1971—. Chmn. equipment fund com. Somona State Hosp., 1956-65. Bd. overseers Grinnell Coll., 1964; adv. council David W. Cogswell & Assos. Mem. Am., San Francisco bar assns., State Bar Calif., Am. Judicature Soc., Hawaii State Bar (asso.), Columbia, U. Calif. law schs. assns., Phi Beta Kappa, Phi Delta Phi. Conglist. Clubs: Commonwealth of Cal., The Family (San Francisco). Home: 4071 Sunset Ln Pebble Beach CA 93953

MAXEY, DAVID ROY, editor, communications cons.; b. Boise, Idaho, Oct. 22, 1936; s. Roy Gess and Dott Elizabeth (Brown) M.; B.S., U. Idaho, 1958; M.B.A., Harvard, 1961; m. Francisca Juliana Guenther, Apr. 15, 1966; 1 son, Brian Guenther. Researcher, asst. editor Look mag., N.Y.C., 1961-63, sr. editor, 1964-66, adminstrv. editor, asst. mng. editor, 1967-69; mng. editor Careers Today mag., Del Mar, Calif., 1969; Washington editor Look, 1969-70, mng. editor, N.Y.C., 1970-71; staff writer Life mag., N.Y.C., 1971-72; editor Psychology Today mag., Del Mar, 1972-75, N.Y.C., 1975-77; editor Sports Afield mag., N.Y.C., 1977-78; now communications cons., editor, writer. Served to 2d lt. Arty., AUS, 1958-59. Home: 225 W 86th St New York NY 10024

MAXFIELD, JAMES ROBERT, JR., radiologist; b. Grand Saline, Tex., Nov. 11, 1910; s. James Robert and Marie (Streeter) M.; A.B., M.D., Baylor U., 1935; Dr. Aerospaceology, Air Force Systems Command, 1966; m. Kathryn Morgan Jester, Aug. 21, 1936; children—James Robert III, Morgan Jester, Jordan Henley Work Streeter (dec.), Jordan II. Intern United Hosp., Port Chester, N.Y., 1935-36; resident radiology Baylor U., 1937-39; resident roentgenology U. Calif. at San Francisco, 1939-40; dir. dept.radiology, also Mattie Fair Meml. Tumor Clinic, Parkland Hosp., Dallas, 1941-43; dir. dept. radiology, chmn. tumor clinic St. Paul's Hosp., Dallas, 1941-45; clin. asst. prof. radiology Southwestern Med. Sch., U. Tex., 1945—; sect. chief radiology br. VA. Hosp., 1945-49; cons. radioisotope unit Lisbon VA Hosp., 1949-50, Los Alamos Sci. Labs., 1949-57, Lawrence Radiation Lab., Livermore, Calif.; dir. Tex. Radiation and Tumor Inst., Dallas, 1946—; lectr. Blackford Meml. Cancer Lectures, Grayson County Med. Soc., 1957; Equen Meml. lectr. Ga. Med. Soc., 1958. Mem. regional adv. council nuclear energy So. Gov.'s Conf.; mem. Tex. Gov.'s Radiation Study Commn., AEC, past mem. adv. com. div. isotope devel.; chmn. Tex. Radiation Adv. Bd.; mem. permanent adv. com. So. Interstate Nuclear Bd.; mem. energy com. So. States Energy Bd.; mem. Tex. Hosp. Adv. Com.; dir. Tex. Law Enforcement and Youth Devel. Found.; mem. nat. adv. bd. Am. Security Council, Washington; mem. power plant Siting Com. State Tex. Bd. trustees, past pres. Dallas Health and Sci. Museum; trustee Fla. Inst. Tech., Melbourne; past trustee Episcopal Radio-TV Found.; past nat. commr. for Tex., Freedoms Found. of Valley Forge; mem. Fla. Council of 100. Recipient Antarctic Service medal. Fellow Internat. Coll. Surgeons, Am. Coll. Nuclear Medicine (sec.-treas, past pres., gold medal for outstanding service to nuclear medicine 1979); asso. fellow AIAA; mem. Am., So. med. assns., Tex., Dallas County med. socs., Am. Coll. Radiology, Radiol. Soc. N.A., Inter-Am. Congress Radiology, Am. Radium Soc., Brit. Inst. Radiology, Tex., Dallas-Fort Worth, Rocky Mountain radiol. socs., Soc. Nuclear Medicine (sec., treas., past pres.), Flying Physicians Assn., Airplane Owners and Pilots Assn., Soc. of South Pole, Dallas Execs. Assn., Dallas C. of C. Rotarian (past pres. Dallas-Park cities; named Rotarian of Year, 1956). Contbr. papers to tech. lit. Home: 5920 Lomo Alto Dallas TX 75205 Office: 2711 Oak Lawn Ave Dallas TX 75219

MAXFIELD, JOHN EDWARD, educator; b. Los Angeles, Mar. 17, 1927; s. Chauncey George and Rena Lucile (Cain) M.; B.S., Mass. Inst. Tech., 1947; M.S., U. Wis., 1949; Ph.D., U. Oreg., 1951; m. Margaret Alice Waugh, Nov. 24, 1948; children—Frederick George (dec.), David Glen, Elaine Rebecca, Nancy Catherine, Daniel John. Instr. U. Oreg., 1950-51; mathmatician U.S. Naval Ordnance Test Sta., China Lake, Calif., 1949-56, head computing br., 1956-57, head math. div., 1957-60; lectr. U. Calif. at Los Angeles, 1951-60; head prof. dept. math. U. Fla., 1960-67; prof., chmn. dept. math. Kans. State U., 1967—. Mem. Am. Math. Soc., Math. Assn. Am., Soc. Indsl. and Applied Math., Sigma Xi. Home: 417 N 17th St Manhattan KS 66502

MAXFIELD, JOHN FRANK, lawyer; b. Pitts., Mar. 31, 1922; s. Frank B. and Rebecca Mellon (Lyle) M.; B.B.A., So. Meth. U., J.D., 1949; m. Vera Smith, Dec. 18, 1948; 1 son, Robert F. Admitted to bar; asst. dist. atty. Dallas County (Tex.), 1951-53; partner firm Stigall, Maxfield & Collier, Dallas, 1953—; dir. Am. Exchange Life Ins. Co., Erban Realty Co. Mem. charter study commn., Richardson, Tex., 1961, chmn. zoning bd. adjustment, 1961-65; mem. nat. exploring com. Boy Scouts Am., 1975—. Mem. Dallas County Democratic Exec. Com., 1974—. Served with USAAF. Decorated Air medal with four oak leaf clusters. Recipient Vigil Honor Boy Scouts Am., 1968, award of Merit, 1974. Mem. Am., Dallas, Richardson (pres. 1962) bar assns., State Bar Tex. Club: Dallas Athletic. Home: 904 Newberry St Richardson TX 75080 Office: 740 1 Main Pl Dallas TX 75250

MAXFIELD, KENNETH WAYNE, transp. co. exec.; b. Leo, Inc., Oct. 26, 1924; student Loyola U., Chgo., 1946-48; LL.B., De Paul U., 1950; m. Jean; 2 children. Admitted to Ind., Ill. bars, 1950; with N.Am. Van Lines Inc., 1950—, exec. v.p. corp. world hdqrs., Fort Wayne, Ind., 1966-77, pres., chief operating officer, chmn. bd., 1977—. Pres. bd. Jr. Achievement, Ft. Wayne, 1976-77. Served with U.S. Army, 1943-46; Aleutians. Mem. Ft. Wayne C. of C. (pres. 1974). Clubs: Summit (dir.); Rotary (Ft. Wayne). Office: North Am Van Lines Inc 5001 US Hwy 30 W Fort Wayne IN 46818

MAXHEIM, JOHN HOWARD, utility co. exec.; b. Clinton, Iowa, Oct. 4, 1934; s. Vincent J. and Dorothy F. Maxheim; B.S. in Indsl. Engring., Iowa State U., 1958. Indsl. sales engr. Mobil Oil Co., Chgo., 1958-59; indsl. sales engr. and mgr. Milw. Gas Light Co., 1959-62; asst. to pres. United Cities Gas Co., Nashville, 1962-65, v.p., 1965-66, exec. v.p., 1966-70, pres., dir., 1970-78, chief exec. officer, 1970-78; pres., chief operating officer Piedmont Natural Gas Co., Inc., Charlotte, N.C., 1978—, dir., 1979—. Mem. Am. Gas Assn., So. Gas Assn. (past dir.), Southeastern Gas Assn., Nat. Assn. of Mfrs. (mem. adv. council S.E. region), Greater Charlotte C. of C. (mem. energy task force com.), Alpha Tau Omega. Episcopalian. Clubs: Nashville City; Carolina Ambassadors, Charlotte Athletic; Capital City; Carmel Country. Home: 4100 Beresford Rd Charlotte NC 28211 Office: PO Box 33068 Charlotte NC 28233

MAXON, ROBERT GEORGE, ins. co. exec.; b. Floresville, Tex., June 14, 1939; s. Robert George and Louise (Maxon) Wighaman; B.A. in Math., U. Tex., 1962; postgrad. Profl. Mgmt. Inst., Purdue U., Dartmouth Inst., 1976; m. Judith A. Bergan, Apr. 7, 1959; children—Pamela F., Robert E. Actuarial intern Am. Nat. Ins. Co., 1962-64; with Life Ins. Co. N. Am., 1965-74, life actuary, 1969-71, v.p., actuary in charge life reins. and equity products, 1972-74; v.p. life products Aetna Life & Casualty Ins. Co., Hartford, Conn., 1974-78, v.p., corp. comptroller, 1978—. Fellow Trustee, Mark Twain Meml., Miss Porter's Sch., Conn. Public Expenditure Council. C.P.C.U. Soc. Actuaries; mem. Am. Acad. Actuaries. Club: Hartford. Home: 237 Farmington Ave Hartford CT 06105 Office: 151 Farmington Ave Hartford CT 06156

MAXSON, A. L., airline exec.; b. Erie, Pa., Dec. 27, 1935; B.S. in Bus. Adminstrn., Pa. State U., 1957; M.B.A., Ga. State U., 1973; grad. Advanced Mgmt. Program, Harvard U., 1976; m. Linda K. Kiger, Apr. 18, 1964; children—Barbara L., Janet E., Patricia A. Sr. accountant Price Waterhouse & Co., Pitts., 1957-66; controller, then v.p. fin., treas. So. Airways, Inc., Atlanta, 1966-79; v.p., treas. Republic Airlines, Inc., Mpls., 1979—. C.P.A., Ga. Mem. Fin. Execs. Inst., Am. Inst. C.P.A.'s. Methodist. Home: 2663 Canna Ridge Circle NE Atlanta GA 30345 Office: 7500 Airline Dr Minneapolis MN 55450

MAXSON, WILLIAM BURDETTE, air force officer; b. Akron, Ohio, Sept. 4, 1930; s. Herbert William and Lorah Shively M.; B.S. in Engring., U.S. Naval Acad., 1952; M.S. in Aero. Engring., USAF Inst. Tech., 1962; m. Nancy Jean Hewett, July 12, 1952; children—Suzanne Burdette, Robert William. Commd. 2d lt. U.S. Air Force, 1952, advanced through grades to maj. gen., 1978; pilot with concurrent research and devel. positions through world, including Philippines and Europe, 1954-71; asst. sec. for atomic energy Office Sec. Def., Washington, 1974-77; dir. devel. and programming Hdqrs. USAF, Washington, 1977—; lectr. on maj. weapon system devel. and acquisition. Decorated Silver Star, Legion of Merit with oak leaf cluster, D.F.C., Air medal with 14 oak leaf clusters, Air Force Commendation medal with oak leaf cluster. Mem. Air Force Assn., AIAA, Quiet Birdmen, Daedalions, U.S. Naval Acad. Athletic Assn., U.S. Naval Acad. Alumni Assn. Republican. Episcopalian. Contbr. articles to sci. and tech. jours. Home: Quarters 251 Lowry AFB CO 80230 Office: Comdr Lowry Tech Tng Centre Lowry AFB CO 80230

MAXSON, WILLIAM LESLIE, JR., electronics co. exec.; b. Honolulu, Dec. 3, 1925; s. William Leslie and Mary Irene (Steely) M.; student Williams Coll., Franklin and Marshall Coll., N.Y. U.; m. Mary Alice Brown, Nov. 1, 1947; children—Caryl Ann, Mary Leslie, Holly Brown, William Leslie. With Maxson Electronics Corp., N.Y.C., 1942—, v.p., 1959-62, pres., 1962-69, chmn., 1969-70, also dir.; chmn. bd. Unimax Group Inc., 1969-72, dir., 1972—; chmn. bd. Sealord Inc., 1970-71; dir. Ofcl. Industries Corp., Victoria Investment Co. Bd. dirs. Oceanographic Fund; trustee Southside Hosp., Dowling Coll. Served with USNR, 1943-45. Mem. Army Ordnance Assn., Nat. Security Indsl. Assn., Nat. Rifle Assn., Nat. Skeet Shooting Assn. Home: 7300 NE 8th Ave Boca Raton FL 33431

MAXWELL, ALBERT LELAND, utility exec.; b. Fresno, Calif., May 22, 1921; s. Ernest E. and Vida (Rice) M.; B.S. in Bus. Adminstrn., UCLA, 1948; postgrad. in mgmt., econs. and finance, U. So. Calif., also Stanford U.; m. Phyllis Hope Thurner, July 3, 1962. With So. Calif. Edison Co., 1949—, mgr. taxes, 1959-65, asst. treas., asst. controller, 1965-68, controller, 1968-75, v.p., controller, 1975—; dir., v.p., comptroller Asso. So. Investment Co.; comptroller, dir. So. Surplus Realty Co. Served with AUS, 1942-45. Mem. UCLA Alumni Assn., Tax Execs. Inst. (dir. 1962-65), Pacific Coast Elec. Assn., Edison Electric Inst. (mem. accounting exec. com. 1968—). Home: 7257 1/2 Hollywood Blvd Hollywood CA 90046 Office: PO Box 800 Rosemead CA 91770

MAXWELL, ART VERNON, cons. engr.; b. Kanab, Utah, Jan. 24, 1916; s. Charles Bennet and Josephine (Anderson) M.; student Coll. So. Utah, 1933-36; B.S., Utah State U., 1942; m. JenaVee Williams, Sept. 3, 1940; children—Anita Maxwell Major, Vernon Lee, Paula Maxwell Jamison, Shirleen Maxwell Hayes. Hydraulic engr., office engr. Water Resources Div., U.S. Geol. Survey, Salt Lake City, 1942-55; v.p. Nielsen & Maxwell, Salt Lake City, 1955-72; v.p Nielsen, Maxwell & Wangsgard, Salt Lake City, 1972-77, pres., gen. mgr., 1977—; treas. ARENCO, architects and engrs. Recipient Utah Engr. of Yr. award Utah Engring. Council, 1968. Registered profl. engr., Utah, Idaho, Colo. Fellow ASCE, Am. Cons. Engrs. Council (nat. pres. 1969-70); mem. Am. Water Works Assn., Phi Kappa Phi. Mormon. Home: 850 E 1050 N Bountiful UT 84010 Office: 624 N 300 W Salt Lake City UT 84103

MAXWELL, ARTHUR EUGENE, educator; b. Maywood, Calif., Apr. 11, 1925; s. John H. and Nelle I. (Arnold) M.; B.S. in Physics with honors, N.Mex. State U., 1949; M.S. in Oceanography, Scripps Instn. Oceanography, U. Calif., 1952, Ph.D. in Oceanography, 1959; m. Rita Louise Johnson, Nov. 24, 1964; children—Delle Rae, Eric, Lynn, Brett, Gregory James. Research geophysicist Scripps Instn. Oceanography, 1949-55; head oceanographer Office Naval Research, Washington, 1955-59, head geophysics br., 1959-65; asso. dir. Woods Hole (Mass.) Oceanographic Instn., 1965-69, dir. research, 1969-71, provost, 1971—; sec.-treas. Joint Oceanographic Instns., Inc., 1977—; mem. Nat. Adv. Com. on Oceans and Atmosphere, 1973-76. Served with USNR, 1942-45. Recipient Distinguished Civilian Service award USN. Mem. Am. Geophys. Union (pres. 1976-78, pres. oceanography sect. 1970—), Marine Tech. Soc. (pres.-elect 1979-80). Club: Cosmos (Washington). Editor: The Sea, vol. IV. Home: 4 Quissett Cove Ln Woods Hole MA 02543 Office: Water St Woods Hole MA 02543

MAXWELL, ARTHUR GRAHAM, educator; b. Watford, Eng., July 18, 1921; s. Arthur Stanley and Rachel (Joyce) M.; came to U.S., 1936; B.A., Pacific Union Coll., 1943, M.A., 1944; Ph.D., U. Chgo. Div. Sch., 1959; m. Rosalyn Gildersleeve, Sept. 9, 1943; children—Lorna (Mrs. George Andersson), Audrey (Mrs. David Zinke), Alice (Mrs. Don Lucas). Asst. prof. bibl. langs. Pacific Union Coll., Angwin, Calif., 1944-52, asso. prof., head dept. bibl. langs., 1952-59, prof., chmn. div. religion, 1959-61; dir. div. religion, prof. N.T., Loma Linda (Calif.) U., 1961-76, prof. N.T., 1976—. Mem. Soc. Bibl. Lit., Am. Acad. Religion, Soc. for Sci. Study Religion, Cath. Bibl. Assn. Am. Author: You Can Trust the Bible, 1967; I Want to be Free, 1970; Can God Be Trusted?, 1977. Contbr. Seventh-Day Adventist Bible Commentary, 1957. Home: 11588 Lawton Ct Loma Linda CA 92354

MAXWELL, BARRY R., engr., univ. adminstr.; b. New Brunswick, N.J., Jan. 20, 1937; s. Sherman O. ano Edna M. (Robbins) M.; B.S., Bucknell U., 1959, M.S., 1961; Ph.D. in Mech. Engring., U. N.Mex., 1971; m. Marjorie A. Savoye, June 15, 1957; children—Kimberley, Bradley, Ryan. Mem. faculty dept. mech. engring. Bucknell U., Lewisburg, Pa., 1963—, asso. prof., 1974-79, prof., dean engring., 1979—. Served with U.S. Army, 1961-63. Recipient Lindback award for teaching, 1975, Western Electric Fund award, 1978. Mem. ASME, Soc. Automotive Engrs., Am. Soc. Engring. Edn., Tau Beta Pi. Republican. Office: Coll Engring Bucknell Univ Lewisburg PA 17837

MAXWELL, BRYCE, educator, engr.; b. Glen Cove, N.Y., July 26, 1919; s. Howard W. and Helen (Young) M.; B.S. in Engring., Princeton, 1943, M.S. in Engring., 1948; m. Margurite Kulsar, June 5, 1953 (dec. 1974); children—Bryce, Margaret H., Stephen H. Research asso. Princeton, 1948-53, asst. prof., 1953-57, asso. prof., 1957-66, asst. dean Sch. Engring., 1962-66, prof. chem. engring., 1966-68, prof. chem. engring. for polymer studies, chmn. polymer materials program, 1968—. Dir. U.S. Rubber Reclaiming Co., Inc., Vicksburg, Miss., 1962—; cons. several chem. cos. Trustee Plastics Inst. Am. Served with USNR, 1943-46. Mem. ASME, ASTM, Soc. Rheology, Soc. Plastics Engrs. (gold medal and internat. award in plastics sci. and engring. 1976), Sigma Xi. Research and publn. in polymer viscoelastic behavior, polymer melt rheology. Inventor elastic melt extruder, orthogonal rheometer, melt elasticity tester. Home: 19 McCosh Circle Princeton NJ 08540

MAXWELL, CARLA LENA, dancer, choreographer, educator; b. Glendale, Calif., Oct. 25, 1945; d. Robert and Victoria (Carbone) M.; student Bennington Coll., 1963-64; B.S., Juilliard Sch. Music, 1967. Mem. Jose Limon Dance Co., N.Y.C., 1965, prin. dancer, 1969—, acting artistic dir., 1977-78, artistic dir., 1978—; soloist Louis Falco Dance Co., 1967-71, Harkness Festival at N.Y.C. Delacorte Theater, 1964—; artist-in-residence Gettysburg Coll., 1970, Luther Coll., Decorah, Iowa, 1971, U. Idaho, 1973; guest tchr., performer Centre Internat. de la Danse, Vichy, France, 1976; choreography works includes: A Suite of Psalms, 1973; lectr., tchr. in field; toured East and West Africa, 1969. N.Y. State Cultural Council grantee, 1971. Home: 7 Great Jones St New York NY 10012 Office: Jose Limon Dance Co PO Box 5373 Grand Central Sta New York NY 10017

MAXWELL, CHESTER ARTHUR, broadcasting exec.; b. San Antonio, Mar. 29, 1930; s. Chester A. and Clara A. (Olle) M.; student Trinity U., San Antonio, 1948-51; M.B.A. candidate, U. Dallas; m. Carolyn King, Aug. 7, 1969; children by previous marriage—Sheryl Ann, Karen Kay Maxwell Cervantes. With advt. dept. Joskes of Tex., dept. store, San Antonio, 1952-56; account exec., sales mgr. Sta. KBAT, San Antonio, 1956-63; account exec. Sta. KILT, Houston, 1964-68; asst. gen. mgr. Sta. KBOX/KME2, Dallas, 1969-71, v.p., gen. mgr., 1972—; instr. Tex. Assn. Broadcasters Student Clinic, Howard Payne U., Abilene, Tex., 1962. Pres., Greater Dallas chpt. Muscular Dystrophy Assn., 1971-73; vice chmn., trustee Dallas Multiple Sclerosis Soc. Served with USMC, 1946-48. Named one of Dallas Men of Year, Women's Equity Action League, 1975, 76; Hope Chest award Nat. Multiple Sclerosis Soc., 1979. Mem. Dallas Advt. League, Assn. Broadcast Execs. Tex. (sec. 1971, pres. 1974), N. Tex. Real Estate Investors Assn. Club: Las Colinas Country (Dallas). Office: 9900 McCree Rd Dallas TX 75238

MAXWELL, DAVID F., lawyer; b. Phila., Nov. 7, 1900; s. Alexander and Rachel Sellers (Farrow) M.; B.S., U. Pa., 1921, LL.B., 1924; hon. degrees. Nat. U. Ireland, Dickinson Law Sch.; m. Emily Ogden Nelson, Nov. 16, 1925; children—Fairlie (Mrs. William H. Pasfield), David O. Admitted to Pa. bar, 1924; asso. firm. Edmonds, Obermayer & Rebmann (name now Obermayer, Rebmann, Maxwell & Hippel), Phila., 1924-29, partner, 1929-75, of counsel, 1975—. Hon. bd. dirs. Crime Commn. of Phila., pres., 1965-67; trustee Woods Schs.; trustee emeritus Dickinson Law Sch. Recipient Citizenship award SAR; award merit U. Pa. Mem. Am. Bar Assn. (pres. 1956-57; mem. ho. of dels. 1944—, chmn. ho. of dels. 1952-54), Pa. Bar Assn. (chmn. ho. dels. 1966-68), Phila. bar assns., Am. Bar Found. (pres. 1956-57), St. Andrew's Soc. Phila. (pres. 1958-59), Fellows of Am. Bar Found.

(chmn. 1958-59), Am. Coll. Trial Lawyers (regent 1966-69), Internat. Acad. Astronautics (dir. 1959-60), Beta Gamma Sigma, Pi Kappa Alpha (Distinguished Achievement award), Phi Alpha Delta, (hon.). Episcopalian. Mason (past master). Clubs: Kiwanis (pres. 1951), Penn; University (Sarasota, Fla.). Author articles in field. Home: Apt F107 2100 Benjamin Franklin Dr Sarasota FL 33577 Office: Packard Bldg Philadelphia PA 19102

MAXWELL, DAVID OGDEN, ins. co. exec., former govt. ofcl.; b. Phila., May 16, 1930; s. David Farrow and Emily Ogden (Nelson) M.; B.A., Yale, 1952; LL.B., Harvard, 1955; m. Joan Clark Paddock, Dec. 14, 1968. Admitted to Pa. and D.C. bar, 1955; with firm Obermayer, Rebmann, Maxwell & Hippel, Phila., 1959-67, partner, 1963-67; ins. commr. State of Pa., 1967-69, sec. adminstrn. and budget sec., 1969-70; gen. counsel HUD, Washington, 1970-73; pres., chief exec. officer Ticor Mortgage Ins. Co., 1973—; mem. med. assistance adv. council HEW, 1969-70; mem. adv. com. Fed. Nat. Mortgage Assn., 1979—; mem. adv. bd. Nat. Savs. and Loan League, 1979—. Treas., Los Angeles Philharm. Assn., 1977—. Served with USNR, 1955-59. Mem. Am. Bar Assn., Am. Bar Found. Home: 2511 Benedict Canyon Beverly Hills CA 90210 Office: 6300 Wilshire Blvd Los Angeles CA 90048

MAXWELL, DAVID SAMUEL, educator; b. Bremerton, Wash., Feb. 13, 1931; s. Samuel Wallace and Merry Cecil (Musgrave) M.; B.A., Westminster Coll., 1954; B.A., (Rhodes scholar) Oxford U., 1957, M.A., 1968; Ph.D., U. Calif. at Los Angeles, 1960; m. Evelyn Mae Hourigan, Aug. 26, 1957; children—Mary Lisa, Anne Patricia, Stephen Daniel. Faculty U. Calif. Sch. Medicine, Los Angeles, 1959—, prof. anatomy, 1968—; prof. surgery anatomy Charles Drew Postgrad. Med. Sch., Los Angeles, 1973—; cons. in field. John and Mary R. Markle scholar, 1960-65. USPHS research grantee, 1960—. Mem. Am. Assn. Anatomists, ElectronMicroscopy Soc. Am., Am. Soc. Cell Biology, Soc. Neurosci. Home: 4143 Hayvenhurst Dr Encino CA 91436 Office: Dept Anatomy U Calif Los Angeles CA 90024

MAXWELL, DIANA LOUISE, magazine editor; b. Evanston, Ill., Dec. 5, 1942; d. Alexander and Ester (Sexton) Maxwell; B.A. in Anthropology and Psychology, Northwestern U., 1968; m. Leonard I. Tafel, 1961 (div. 1971); 1 son, Brian L. Advt. copywriter Spiegel's, Chgo., 1968-71; mng. editor Concrete Products mag., Chgo., 1971-74; pub. relations dir. Center Photog. Arts, Chgo., 1974; exec. editor Success Unlimited mag., Chgo., 1974-79. Mem. Am. Assn. Handwriting Analysts, Publicity Club Chgo., Social Service Communications. Home: 7210 N Paulina St Chicago IL 60626

MAXWELL, FOWDEN GENE, educator; b. Brownwood, Tex., Sept. 29, 1931; B.S., Tex. Technol. U., 1957; M.S., Kans. State U., 1958, Ph.D. in Entomology, 1961; m. Katherine Gant, July 14, 1955; children—Steve, Rebecca Ann, David Randal. Grad. research asst. Kans. State U., 1957-60, instr. entomology, 1960-61; entomologist Dept. Agr. Boll Weevil Research, State College, Md., 1961-68; prof., head dept. entomology Miss. State U., 1968-75; coordinator environ. activities USDA, 1975-76; chmn. dept. entomology U. Fla., Gainesville, 1976-78; head dept. entomology Tex. A & M U., College Station, 1978—; mem. panel experts on integrated pest control FAO, UN. Served with USNR, 1951-55. Charter mem. Soc. Univ. Fellows Miss. State U.; mem. Am. Inst. Biol. Scis., Miss., Kans. acad. scis., Agronomy Soc. Am., Nat. Soc. Solar Energy, Miss. Entomol. Soc. (past v.p., pres., Distinguished Service award 1975), Entomol. Soc. Am. (program chmn. sec. C 1971; Bussard award 1972, Meml. Founders award 1976), Sigma Xi, Gamma Sigma Delta Distinguished Research award 1975), Alpha Zeta, Phi Kappa Phi. Lion (past pres. Starkville). Contbr. to books, numerous articles profl. jours. Home: PO Box 9507 College Station TX 77840 Office: Dept Entomology Tex A & M U College Station TX 77840

MAXWELL, IAN ROBERT, publisher, film producer; b. Selo Slatina, Czechoslovakia, June 10, 1923; s. Michael and Ann (Hoch) M.; self- educated; m. Elisabeth Meynard, Mar. 15, 1945; children—Anne, Philip, Christine, Isabel, Ian, Kevin, Ghislaine. Became British citizen, 1945. Head press and publs. div. German sect. British Fgn. Office, 1945-47; founder, chmn., pub. Pergamon Press Ltd., Oxford, Eng., 1949—, also dir.; chmn. Harmony Films Ltd., 1950—; chmn. bd., pres. Pergamon Press Inc., N.Y.C., 1950—; film producer Mozart's Don Giovanni at Salzburg Festival, also Bolshoi Ballet, London; film producer Swan Lake, 1968. Labour mem. Parliament for Buckingham, 1964-70. Chmn. Labour Fund Raising Found., 1960-68. Kennedy fellow Harvard, 1971. Mem. Am. Nuclear Soc., Am. Vacuum Soc., Human Factors Soc., Fabian Soc. Great Britain, Internat. Acad. Astronautics (hon.). Author: Public Sector Purchasing, 1968. Editor: Progress in Nuclear Energy: The Economics of Nuclear Power, 1963; gen. editor: Info.: U.S.S.R., 1962. Home: Headington Hill Hall Oxford England Office: Maxwell House Fairview Park Elmsford NY 10523

MAXWELL, JACK ERWIN, automobile co. exec.; b. Cleve., July 17, 1926; s. Fred A. and Gertrude F. (Haug) M.; B.S., Case Inst. Tech., 1949; M.B.A., Harvard U., 1952; m. Martha Jane Miller, Dec. 28, 1966; children by previous marriage—Laura Jane, Frederic, Elizabeth Grant, Carla Moore, Linda Hanson. Indsl. engr. Lincoln Electric Co., Cleve., 1952-53; mgr. purchase analysis Ford Motor Co., Dearborn, Mich., 1953-57; v.p. Booz, Allen & Hamilton, Inc., Detroit, 1957-69; v.p. corp. devel. Am. Motors Corp., Detroit, 1969-71, v.p. adminstrn., 1971-76, v.p. non-automotive subsidiaries, 1976—; dir. GTI Corp., San Diego. Served with USNR, 1944-46. Mem. Case Inst. Tech. Alumni Assn., Harvard Bus. Sch. Alumni Assn., Tau Beta Pi, Theta Tau. Clubs: Detroit Athletic, Detroit Yacht, Old Club. Home: 3541 Bradway Blvd Birmingham MI 48010 Office: 27777 Franklin Rd Southfield MI 48034

MAXWELL, JAMES LIVINGSTON, cons.; b. Tulsa, May 12, 1926; s. William Raymond and Mary Pauline (O'Donnell) M.; B.A., Okla. State U., 1950. Mayor, Tulsa, 1958-66; bd. dirs. Airport Authority, 1958-66, Park and Recreation Commn., 1958-66, Tulsa Metropolitan Area Planning Commn., 1958-66; mem. City Commn., 1958-66; mem. bd. dirs. Utility Bd., 1958-66; cons., Tulsa and Washington, 1966—; v.p. First Exploration, Inc., 1973-75; v.p., gen. mgr. Trans Port Terminal, 1973—; pres. Tulsa Real Estate Investment Trust; cons. to Washington for Okla. with Econ. Devel. Adminstrn. Hon. senator Jr. Chamber Internat. Served with AUS, 1944-46. Mem. Tulsa Hist. Soc. (pres. 1968, chmn. bd. 1970), Sigma Chi. Home: 4805 S Knoxville Tulsa OK 74135 Office: 218 Court Arcade Bldg 6th and Boulder Sts Tulsa OK 74103

MAXWELL, JEWELL CLINTON, former aerospace co. exec.; b. Cockrum, Miss., June 18, 1917; s. John Clinton and Annie (Greer) M.; B.S. in Mech. Engring., U. Tenn., 1947; M.S. in Aero. Engring., Princeton, 1949; m. Harriett Parrish Caldwell, Aug. 24, 1946; children—Jewell Clinton, George Caldwell (dec.). Flying cadet USAAF, 1941-42, commd. 2d lt., 1942, advanced through grades to maj. gen. USAF, 1965; squadron comdr. ETO, 1943-45; wing instr. Dobbins AFB, Ga., 1947; assigned bomber aircraft sect., research and devel. Hdqrs. USAF, 1949-52; engaged in systems mgmt. Wright-Patterson AFB, Ohio, 1952-58; chief staff Hdqrs. Air Force Systems Command, 1958-63; comdr. Air Force Western Test Range, Vandenberg AFB, Calif., 1963-65; dir. supersonic transp. program Hdqrs. USAF, 1965-69; comdr. Air Force Armament Test Center, Eglin AFB, Fla., 1969-73; ret. 1973; v.p., gen. mgr. mil. airplane devel. Boeing Aerospace Co., Seattle, 1973-79. Decorated D.S.M., Legion of Merit, Bronze Star, D.F.C., Air medal; Croix de Guerre with palm (France). Mem. Alpha Tau Omega, Tau Beta Pi, Phi Kappa Phi. Home: 17100 151st Ave SE Renton WA 98055

MAXWELL, JOHN BRYAN, supt. schs.; b. Atwater, Ohio, Sept. 29, 1911; s. Jesse Lloyd and Nellie (Bryan) M.; B.S., Ohio State U., 1936, M.S., 1940; postgrad. Miami U., Oxford, Ohio, 1960-64; m. Jeannette Reese, July 28, 1938 (dec. June 1979); children—John Bryan, Johnnetta Lee Maxwell Mumma. High sch. coach, Plymouth, Ohio, 1936-38; tchr. elementary sch., Dayton, Ohio, 1938-40, tchr. high sch., 1940-50; prin. Highview Elementary Sch., Dayton, 1951-60, Meadowdale High Sch., Dayton, 1970-72; supt. schs. Dayton Public Schs., 1973—. Trustee, Dayton Art Inst., Dayton Mus. Natural History, Jr. Achievement Dayton. Mem. NEA (life), Nat. Congress Parents and Tchrs. (life), Ohio, Western Ohio edn. assns., Am., Buckeye (mem. standing com. 1974) assns. sch. adminstrs., Ohio Assn. Secondary Sch. Prins. (mem. activities com. 1972-73), Nat. Assn. Secondary Sch. Prins., North Central Assn. Colls. and Secondary Schs., Dayton Sch. Mgmt. Assn., Phi Delta Kappa, Epsilon Pi Tau, Lambda Chi Alpha. Conglist. Home: 5829 Algoma St Dayton OH 45415 Office: 348 W 1st St Dayton OH 45402

MAXWELL, JOHN CRAWFORD, educator; b. Xenia, Ohio, Dec. 28, 1914; s. William and Addie (Crawford) M.; B.A., DePauw U., 1936; M.A. (Thomas F. Andrews fellow), U. Minn., 1937; Ph.D., Princeton, 1946; m. Marian Ruth Buchanan, Nov. 4, 1939; children—Judith Margaret, Marilyn Jane. Geologist, geophysicist Sun Oil Co., 1938-40; instr. Princeton, 1946-47, asst. prof., 1947-52, asso. prof., 1952-55, prof. geology, 1955—, chmn. dept. geol. engring., 1955-66, chmn. dept. geology, 1966-67, chmn. dept. geol. and geophys. scis., 1967-70; Farish prof. geol. scis. U. Tex., Austin, 1970—; cons. geologist oil and non-metallic minerals. Chmn. earth sci. div. NRC, 1970-72; chmn. U.S. Nat. Com. for Geodynamics, 1979—. Served as lt. USNR, 1942-45. Recipient Distinguished Grad. award U. Minn., 1972; NSF sr. post-doctoral fellow, Italy, 1961-62. Fellow Geol. Soc. Am. (pres. 1973), Am. Geophys. Union; mem. Am. Geol. Inst. (pres. 1971), Am. Assn. Petroleum Geologists, Yellowstone-Bighorn Research Assn., Societa Geologica Italiana, Sigma Xi (Distinguished lectr. 1967), Phi Beta Kappa. Home: 5322 Western Hills Dr Austin TX 78731

MAXWELL, MICHAEL, symphony orch. adminstr.; b. Westport, N.Z., Jan. 6, 1936; s. Eric and Phyllis (Christian) M.; ed. King's Coll., Auckland, N.Z., 1949-53. Asst. program officer N.Z. Broadcasting Service, 1955-59; orch. mgr. Philharmonia Orch., London, 1960-63; tour mgr. Royal Philharmonic Orch., London, 1963; mgr. Princeton Chamber Orch., 1964-65; promotion dir. N.Y. Philharmonic, 1965-66; asst. mgr. Cleve. Orch., 1966-70, gen. mgr., 1970-76; mng. dir. Opera Co. of Boston, 1976-77; cons., 1978; gen. mgr. San Diego Symphony Orch., 1978—; former profl. adv. trustee Cleve. Music Sch.; mem. recommendation com. Avery Fisher Artist Award Program; adv. bd. Kirk Artists Series, Ft. Lauderdale, Fla.; bd. dirs. Cleve. Ballet Guild; spl. adviser Boston Chamber Orch. Mem. Cleve. Super Sesqui Commn.; trustee Univ. Circle, Inc., Cleve. Mem. Am. Symphony Orch. League (patron, past dir.), Assn. Calif. Symphony Orchs. (dir.), Nat. Soc. Lit. and Arts, Am. Film Inst., Ohio Arts Council (former mem. music advisory panel). Home: 7956 Paseo del Ocaso La Jolla CA 92037 Office: PO Box 3175 San Diego CA 92103. *The sensitivity to the needs of others and a human response to them are essential attitudes in life.*

MAXWELL, OTIS ALLEN, editor, publisher; b. Waco, Tex., Nov. 24, 1915; s. Otis Allen and Myra (Vesey) M.; B.A., So. Methodist U., 1937, B.S. in Commerce, 1937, M.A., 1940; m. Emma Vee Dunlap, Aug. 31, 1940; children—Otis Allen III, Mary Susanna, Rebecca Agnes. Asst. book editor Dallas Morning News, 1937-42, 48-58, book editor, 1958—; asst. dir. So. Meth. U. Press, 1939-42, dir., 1946—; mng. editor Southwest Rev., 1939-42, editor, 1946-63; adj. prof. English, So. Meth. U., 1973—; vice pres. Assn. Am. U. Presses, 1955. Mem. adv. fine arts com. Dallas C. of C., chmn., 1948-50; mem. exec. com. Jno. E. Owens Meml. Found., 1954—, chmn. 1955-57. Served from ensign to lt. comdr. Supply Corps, USNR, 1942-46. Mem. Tex. Inst. Letters (past v.p., councilor), Tex. Folklore Soc. (past asso. editor, past treas.), Phi Beta Kappa, Kappa Sigma. Democrat. Methodist. Editor: The Present Danger: Four Essays on American Freedom, 1953; (with Mody C. Boatright and Wilson M. Hudson) Folk Travelers: Ballads, Tales and Talk, 1953; Texas Folk and Folklore, 1954; Mesquite and Willow, 1957; Madstones and Twisters, 1958; And Horns on the Toads, 1959; Singers and Storytellers, 1961; The Golden Log, 1962; (with Lon Tinkle) The Cowboy Reader, 1959; (with Boatright and Hudson) A Good Tale and a Bonnie Tune, 1964; (with Hudson) The Sunny Slopes of Long Ago, 1966. Home: 6610 Northwood Rd Dallas TX 75225 Office: So Meth U Dallas TX 75275 also Dallas Morning News Dallas TX 75265

MAXWELL, RICHARD CALLENDER, educator; b. Mpls., Oct. 7, 1919; s. Bertram Wayburn and Blossom (Callender) M.; B.S.L., U. Minn., 1941, LL.B., 1947; m. Frances Lida McKay, Jan 27, 1942; children—Richard Callender, John McKay. Asso. prof. U. N.D., 1947-49; asso. prof. U. Tex., 1949-51, prof., 1951-53; counsel Amerada Petroleum Corp., 1952-53; prof. U. Calif. at Los Angeles, 1953—, dean Sch. Law, 1959-69, Connell prof., 1979—; vis. prof. Columbia, 1955; vis. Alumni prof. U. Minn., 1970-71; Fulbright lectr. Queen's U., No. Ireland, 1970, vis. Ford Found. prof. U. Singapore, 1971; vis. prof. Hastings Coll. Law, 1976, Duke U., 1979-80; pres. Minn. Law Rev., 1946; chmn. Council Legal Edn. Opportunity, 1971-72; pres. Assn. Am. Law Schs., 1972; chmn. adv. com. law Fulbright Program, 1971-74, chmn. adv. com. U.K., 1974-77; mem. com. on gas prodn. opportunities NRC, 1977-78. Mem. Los Angeles Employee Relations Bd., 1971-74; bd. dirs. Constl. Rights Found.; bd. visitors Duke U. Sch. Law, 1973-79. Recipient Disting. Teaching award UCLA, 1977. Mem. Am. Bar Assn. (com. on youth edn. for citizenship 1975-79, spl. com. on public understanding about the law 1979—), Order of Coif. Author: (with S. A. Riesenfeld) Cases and Materials on Modern Social Legislation, 1950; (with H.R. Williams, C.J. Meyers) Cases on Oil and Gas Law, 1956, 4th edit., 1979; (with S. A. Riesenfeld) California Cases on Security Transactions, 1957, 2d edit. (with S.A. Riesenfeld, J.R. Hetland, W.D. Warren), 1975. West Coast editor Oil and Gas Reporter, 1953—. Home: 18083 Sandycape Dr Pacific Palisades CA 90272

MAXWELL, (IAN) ROBERT, publisher; b. Selo Slatina, Czechoslovakia, June 10, 1923; s. Michael and Ann Hoch; Kennedy fellow Harvard U., 1971; m. Elisabeth Meynard, Mar. 14, 1945; 7 children. Founder, pub. chmn. bd. Pergamon Press, Oxford, Eng., London and N.Y.C., 1949—; mem. Parliament for Buckingham, 1964-70; dir. Computer Tech. Ltd., 1966-77, Gauthier-Villars, pubs., Paris, 1961-70; chmn., chief exec. Internat. Learning Systems Corp., 1968-69; treas. Round House Trust Ltd., 1965—. Chmn. Labour Party Nat. Fund Raising Found., 1960-69; chmn. Labour Working Party on Sci., Govt. and Industry, 1963-64; mem. Council of Europe, 1965-67. Served with Brit. Army, 1940-45. Decorated Mil. Cross. Mem. Acad. Astronautics (hon.). Author: Public Sector Purchasing, 1968; (with Keith Hindle) Man Alive, 1968; editor: Information USSR, 1963; The Economics of Nuclear Power, 1965; co-producer films: Mozart's Don Giovanni, 1954; Bolshoi Ballet, 1957; Swan Lake, 1968. Office: Maxwell House Fairview Park Elmsford NY 10523

MAXWELL, ROBERT EARL, judge; b. Elkins, W.Va., Mar. 15, 1924; s. Earl L. and Nellie E. (Rexstrew) M.; student Davis and Elkins Coll.; LL.B., W.Va. U., 1949; m. Ann Marie Grabowski, Mar. 29, 1948; children—Mary Ann, Carol Lynn, Ellen Lindsay, Earl Wilson. Admitted to W.Va. bar, 1949; practiced in Randolph County, 1949; pros. atty. Randolph County, 1952-61; U.S. atty. for No. Dist. W.Va., 1961-64; judge U.S. Dist. Ct. for No. Dist. W.Va., Elkins, 1965—; chmn. budget com. Jud. Conf. U.S. Recipient Alumni Disting. Service award Davis and Elkins Coll., 1969; award Religious Heritage Am., 1979. Mem. Dist. Judges Assn. 4th Circuit (past pres.). Home: Elkins WV 26241 Office: US Courthouse Elkins WV 26241

MAXWELL, ROBERT LEROY, hosp. ofcl.; b. Dundy County, Nebr., Jan. 15, 1930; s. George Lee and Hannah J. (Russell) M.; grad. high sch.; m. Iris Elaine Pursley, Aug. 9, 1952; children—Lisa Ann, Gregg Alan. Patrolman, San Diego Police Dept., 1954-56; with Bank of Am., San Diego, 1956-58; with U.S. Nat. Bank, San Diego, 1958-73, sr. v.p., 1971-73; v.p. retail mktg. Crocker Nat. Bank, San Francisco, 1973-74; adminstrv. mgr. Otay Mcpl. Water Dist., Spring Valley, Calif., 1974-77; personnel officer San Miguel Hosp. Assn., San Diego, 1977—. Pres. region X1V Nat. Cystic Fibrosis Found., 1971—; event coordinator Chicano Community Center. Bd. dirs. Project Jove; treas. Leukemia Soc., 1973. Served with USN, 1950-54. Mem. Am. Inst. Banking (past pres., dir. Calif.), Bank Adminstrn. Inst., San Diego County Taxpayers Assn. Presbyterian. Home: 1974 Harbison Canyon Rd El Cajon CA 92021 Office: 1940 El Cajon Blvd San Diego CA 92104

MAXWELL, ROBERTA, actor; b. Toronto, Ont., Can., June 17, 1945; d. Robert Gilbert and Patricia Maher (MacGregor) M.; student pvt. schs., Toronto. Appeared in plays: The Prime of Miss Jean Brodie, 1967, Equus, Broadway, 1974, Ashes, N.Y.C., 1977, The Merchant, 1977; appeared at: Stratford (Ont., Can.) Festival, 1966-67, Tyrone Guthrie Theatre, Mpls., Long Wharf Theatre, New Haven, 1968-76, Stratford, Conn., 1969-74. Recipient Drama Desk award for Whistle in the Dark, 1969; Obie award for Slag, 1970; Obie award for Ashes, 1977. Mem. AFTRA, Actors Equity. Christian Scientist. Office: 236 W 45 St New York NY 10036

MAXWELL, RONALD F., filmmaker; b. Jan. 5, 1947; s. John F. and Eliane S. Maxwell; ed. N.Y. U., 1968, Inst. Film and TV, 1970; children—Olivia Anne, Jonathan Frederick. With Folio Films, London, 1970-71; staff producer Am. Bible Soc., N.Y.C., 1971-73; producer, dir. Bi-Centennial Prodns., Inc., N.Y.C., 1973-74; Sta.-WNET-13, Ednl. Broadcasting Corp., N.Y.C., 1974-78; free-lance producer, dir. and writer, 1978; U.S. rep. Deauville Film Festival, 1975. Recipient Spl. award of Merit, USO, 1978. Mem. Acad. TV Arts and Scis., Dirs. Guild Am. Lutheran. Producer, dir. films: The Guest, 1970; Sea Marks, 1976; Verna: USO Girl, 1978 (Atlanta Film Festival Grand prize 1978); Little Darlings, 1980. Home: 112 W 81st St New York NY 10024 Office: 4541 Marathon St Hollywood CA 90038

MAXWELL, STEVEN CHARLES, wholesale grocery co. exec.; b. Sioux City, Iowa, Sept. 23, 1940; s. Lyle Charles and Corinne Zenobia (Knudson) M.; B.S., Drake U., Des Moines, 1962, postgrad., 1963-64; m. Jerrilyn Lee Mammen, Dec. 30, 1961; 1 son, Timothy Allen. Engring. planner Douglas Aircraft Co., 1962-63; staff acct. Hunzelman, Putzier & Co., C.P.A.'s, Storm Lake, Iowa, 1964-67; mem. chancellor's staff U. Ill., Chgo. Circle, 1967-69; bus. mgr. Shive-Hattery & Assos., Cedar Rapids, Iowa, 1969-74; controller Am. Coll. Testing Program, Iowa City, 1974-75; treas. Thompson Industries Ltd., Storm Lake, 1975-77, dir., 1976; treas. May Co., Mpls., 1977—. C.P.A., Iowa, Minn. Mem. Am. Inst. C.P.A.'s, Minn. Soc. C.P.A.'s, Iowa Soc. C.P.A.'s. Methodist. Home: 16905 27th Ave N Plymouth MN 55447 Office: 3501 Marshall St NE Minneapolis MN 55418

MAXWELL, VERA HUPPE, fashion designer; b. N.Y., Apr. 22, 1904; d. Bernard Alexander and Iram Torges (Honthumb) Huppe; student pub., pvt. schs., Bronx, N.Y., Leonia, N.J.; m. Raymond John Maxwell, Oct. 21, 1923; 1 son, R. John. Mem. co. Met. Opera Ballet, N.Y.C., 1919-22; model, designer Linken & Klien, 1929-35, Linken Hehpert, 1935-39, Adler & Adler, 1939-46, Jacobson Linde, 1947—; pvt. practice fashion designing, N.Y.C., 1947—; mem. faculty Parsons Sch. Design; lectr., judge Fashion Inst. Tech.; lectr. Tobe-Coburn; exhibited retrospective fashion show Smithsonian Instn., 1966, retrospective show Vera Maxwell clothes, 1935-78, Mus. City N.Y., 1978; tchr., cons. in field. Recipient Coty Spl. award, 1951, award Mraaivi Sch., Florence, Italy, 1951, award Nieman Marcus, 1955, award Jewish Fedn., 1960, award Lord & Taylor, 1960, award N.Y. Fashion Designers award, 1962, Fresh Air Fund award, 1970, N.J. Cultural Council award, 1976. Mem. Inner Circle Fashion, Met. Opera Guild, Am. Arbitration Assn. Office: 530 7th Ave New York NY 10018

MAXWELL, W. RICHARD, assn. pres.; b. Troy, Ohio, June 20, 1920; s. Wilbur D. and Gertrude (McDowell) M.; student Ohio Wesleyan U., 1938-41; B.S., Richmond (Va.) Profl. Inst. of Coll. William and Mary, 1955; m. Roberta Mae Kennedy, June 29, 1942; children—Douglas R., Jean Ann. Sec., Troy C. of C., 1948-50, Va. C. of C., 1950-55; asst. to pres., later chmn. bd. Reynolds Metals Co., 1955-64; v.p. Reynolds Fgn. Sales Inc., 1964-68; pres. Nat. Better Bus. Bur., 1968-70, Jr. Achievement, Inc., Stamford, Conn., 1970—; instr. Richmond Profl. Inst., part-time 1955-57; sponsor-trustee U. Va. Grad Bus. Sch., 1956-68. Civilian employee USAAF and USN, 1942-45. Clubs: Old Greenwich Yacht; University (N.Y.C.). Home: 12 Pleasant View Pl Old Greenwich CT 06870 Office: 550 Summer St Stamford CT 06904

MAXWELL, WILLIAM, writer; b. Lincoln, Ill., Aug. 16, 1908; s. William Keepers and Eva Blossom (Blinn) M.; student U. Ill., 1926-30, 31-33, D.Litt., 1973; student Harvard, 1930-31; m. Emily Gilman Noyes, May 17, 1945; children—Katharine Farrington, Emily Brooke. Mem. English faculty U. Ill., 1931-33; editorial staff New Yorker mag., 1936-76. Mem. Nat. Inst. Arts and Letters (pres.). Clubs: Coffee House, Century Assn. (N.Y.C.). Author: Bright Center of Heaven, 1934; They Came Like Swallows, 1937; The Folded Leaf, 1945; The Heavenly Tenants, 1946; Time Will Darken It, 1948; (with Jean Stafford, John Cheever, Daniel Fuchs) Stories, 1956; The Chateau, 1961; The Old Man at the Railroad Crossing, 1966; Ancestors, 1971; Over by the River, 1977; So Long, See You Tomorrow, 1979; also stories, book reviews. Office: care Alfred A Knopf Press Relations 201 E 50th St New York NY 10022

MAXWELL, WILLIAM DAVID, coll. dean; b. Fayetteville, N.C., Oct. 13, 1926; s. Thomas Marion and Lois (Purdue) M.; student N.C. State U., 1943-44; A.B. in econs., U. N.C., 1949, M.A., 1954; Ph.D. in Polit. Economy, Johns Hopkins U., 1958; children—Susan, Marian. Asst. prof. econ. U. S.C., 1956-57; asst., then asso. prof. econ. Tulane U., New Orleans, 1959-65, chmn. dept., 1961-65; vis. scholar Thammasat U., Bangkok, Thailand, 1965-66; prof. bus. econ. Ind. U.,

Bloomington, 1966-70; dean Coll. Liberal Arts, prof. econs. Tex. A. and M. U., College Station, 1970—. Cons. various univs.; mem. regional selection com. Woodrow Wilson fellowships, 1964-65; cons. Rockefeller Found., 1966-68. Served with USNR, 1944-47, 50-52. Earhart sr. fellow, Southern fellow. Mem. Am. Econ. Assn. (mem. nominating com. 1964-65), So. Econ. Assn. (v.p. 1964-65), Phi Beta Kappa, Sigma Pi Alpha, Beta Gamma Sigma, Delta Sigma Pi. Author: Price Theory and Application in Business Administration, 1970. Mem. bd. editors The Southern Economic Journal, 1962-64, Applied Economics jour., 1969-71. Contbr. articles to profl. jours. Office: Office Dean College Liberal Arts Tex A and M Univ College Station TX 77843

MAY, ADOLF DARLINGTON, educator; b. Little Rock, Mar. 25, 1927; s.Adolf Darlington and Inez (Shelton) M.; B.Sc. in Civil Engring., So. Meth. U., 1949; M.Sc., Iowa State U., 1950; Ph.D., Purdue U., 1955; m. Margaret Folsom, Dec. 23, 1948; children—Dolf, Barbara, David, Larry. Asst. prof., then asso. prof. Clarkson Coll. Tech. 1952-56; asso. prof. Mich. State U., 1956-59; research engr. Thompson-Ramo Wooldridge, 1959-62; project dir. Ill. Div. Hwys., 1962-65; mem. faculty U. Calif. at Berkeley, 1965—, prof. civil engring., 1965—; guest prof. numerous univs., 1965—; cons. to industry, 1965—. Served with USNR, 1944-47. Fulbright scholar to Netherlands, 1977. Mem. Transp. Research Bd., Am. Soc. Engring. Edn., Inst. Traffic Engrs., Sigma Xi, Tau Beta Pi. Contbr. to profl. jours., books. Home: 1645 Julian Dr El Cerrito CA 94530 Office: McLaughlin Hall Univ Calif Berkeley CA 94720

MAY, DANIEL, ret. hosiery mfr.; b. Nashville, Dec. 25, 1898; s. Jacob and Rebecca (Weingarten) M.; A.B., Vanderbilt U., 1919; m. Dorothy Fishel, June 14, 1927; children—Joseph Leserman, Elizabeth (Mrs. Walter P. Stern). Partner, Bloch Clothing Co., 1924-27; with May Hosiery Mills, 1927—, treas., 1933-46, chmn. bd., 1946-59, 64-65, pres., 1959-63, chmn. exec. com., 1965-75, ret., 1975; dir. Wayne Gossard Corp., 1966-75. Cons., WPB Office Civilian Requirements, 1945; former mem. bd. edn., Nashville, pres., 1950-53; v.p. Tenn. Council Econ. Edn.; pres. Nashville Jewish Community Council, 1953-56; magistrate Davidson County, Tenn., 1954-66; chmn. sch. com. County Ct., 1955-62; councilman-at-large Met. Govt. of Nashville and Davidson County, 1962-66; chmn. met. action com. Office Econ. Opportunity, 1967-69; pres. Mid-Cumberland Comprehensive Health Council, 1969-74. Trustee Vanderbilt U.; mem. bd. Fisk U., 1950-59 vice chmn., 1959-61; mem. bd. Joint Univ. Library. Recipient Distinguished Citizenship award City of Nashville, 1970. Mem. Zeta Beta Tau. Republican. Jewish religion. Clubs: Rotary, Shamus, University. Home: 4200 Harding Rd Nashville TN 37205 Office: 425 Chestnut St Box 1207 Nashville TN 37202

MAY, DONALD, actor; b. Chgo., Feb. 22; student Western Res. Coll., U. Okla.; m. Ellen Cameron; children—Christopher, Douglas. Regular on TV series Colt .45, The Roaring Twenties, 1960-62, The Edge of Night, 1967—. Served as lt. USN; Korea. Mem. AFTRA. Office: care Pub Relations Dept ABC 1330 Ave of Americas New York City NY 10019*

MAY, EDGAR, journalist, state legislator; b. Zurich, Switzerland, June 27, 1929; s. Ferdinand and Renee (Bloch) M.; brought to U.S., 1940, naturalized, 1954; B.J. with highest distinction, Northwestern U., 1957; m. Judith A. Hill, June 30, 1973. Reporter, acting editor Bellows Falls (Vt.) Times, 1951-53; reporter Fitchburg (Mass.) Sentinel, 1953; part time reporter Chgo. Tribune, 1955-57; reporter Buffalo Evening News, 1958-61; dir. pub. welfare projects State Charities Aid Assn., 1962-64; mem. President's Task Force on War Against Poverty, 1964, spl. asst. to dir., asst. dir. Office Econ. Opportunity, 1964; spl. adviser to Ambassador Sargent Shriver, 1968-70; cons. Ford Found., 1970-75; mem. Vt. Legislature, 1975—. Served with AUS, 1953-55. Recipient Page One award Buffalo Newspaper Guild, 1959, Walter O. Bingham award, 1959; Pulitzer prize for local reporting, 1961; Merit award Northwestern U. Alumni Assn., 1962. Author: The Wasted Americans, 1964. Home: Muckross Springfield VT 05156

MAY, ELAINE, entertainer; b. Phila., 1932; d. Jack Berlin; ed. high sch.; studied Stanislavsky method of acting with Marie Ouspenskaya; m. Marvin May (div.); 1 dau., Jeannie Berlin; m. 2d, Sheldon Harnick (div.). Stage and radio appearances as child actor; performed Playwright's Theatre, Chgo.; appeared in student performance Miss Julie, U. Chgo.; with Mike Nichols, others, appeared with improvisational theatre group in night club The Compass, Chgo., to 1957, with Mike Nichols appeared N.Y. supper clubs Village Vanguard, Blue Angel, also night clubs other cities; TV debut on Jack Paar Show, also appeared Steve Allen Show, Omnibus, 1958, Dinah Shore Show, Perry Como Show, TV specials; mem. panel Laugh Line, NBC, 1959; recording spoken comedy Improvisations to Music, Mercury Records; weekly appearance NBC radio show Nightline; appeared with Mike Nichols, N.Y. Town Hall, 1959, An Evening with Mike Nichols and Elaine May, Golden Theatre, N.Y.C., 1960-61; dir. films A New Leaf (also acted), 1972, The Heartbreak Kid, 1973, Mikey and Nicky, 1976; appeared in film Luv, 1967, California Suite, 1978; co-author screenplay Heaven Can Wait, 1978; author: (play) Better Part of Valor. Office: care Dirs Guild Am 110 W 57 St New York NY 10019*

MAY, ELIZABETH STOFFREGEN (MRS. GEOFFREY MAY), govt. ofcl., educator; b. St. Louis, Apr. 25, 1907; d. Carl H. and Caroline (Stumpf) Stoffregen; A.B., Smith Coll., 1928; postgrad. Radcliffe Coll., 1930-31; Ph.D., London U., 1931; LL.D., Wheaton Coll., 1962, Goucher Coll., 1975; m. Geoffrey May, Sept. 22, 1931 (dec. 1964). Instr., asst. prof., asso. prof. Goucher Coll., 1931-39; asso. in social studies AAUW, 1936-37; econ. analyst Treasury Dept., 1939-41; prin. fiscal analyst U.S. Bur. Budget, 1941-47; cons. Am. Mission Aid to Greece, 1947-48, Com. Econ. Devel., 1949; prof. econs., dean Wheaton Coll., Norton, Mass., 1949-64, acting pres., 1961-62; dir. Export-Import Bank U.S., 1964-69. Bd. dirs. Wolf Trap Found. for Performing Arts, Consortium of Univs., Washington. Mem. Internat. Fedn. Univ. Women (pres. 1974-77), AAUW, Am. Econ. Assn., Soc. for Internat. Devel. Clubs: Cosmopolitan (N.Y.C.); Univ. Women's (London). Author: Government, Business and the Individual, 1936; (with others) International Control in the Nonferrous Metals, 1937. Home: Harvard MA 01451

MAY, ERNEST MAX, charitable orgn. ofcl.; b. Newark, July 24, 1913; s. Otto Bernard and Eugenie (Morgenstern) M.; B.A., Princeton, 1934, M.A., 1935; Ph.D. in Organic Chemistry, U. Chgo., 1938; m. Harriet Elizabeth Dewey, Oct. 12, 1940; children—Ernest Dewey, James Northrup, Susan Elizabeth. With Otto B. May, Inc., Newark, 1938-73, successively chemist, gen. mgr., 1938-52, pres., 1952-73; trustee Youth Consultation Service Diocese Newark, 1952-59, 61-66, 68—, pres., 1971-75; dir. Cone Mills Corp., 1960-73, mem. exec. com., 1968-71. Tech. adviser to spl. rep. trade negotiations, 1964-67. Councilman, Summit, N.J., 1963—70. Mem. Summit Environ. Com., 1971—, chmn., 1974; pres. Family Service Assn. Summit, 1959-61, Mental Health Assn. Summit, 1954, Summit Council Chs. Christ, 1962-63; mem. exec. com. Christ Hosp., Jersey City, 1971—, v.p., chmn., 1974—. Trustee, organizer Summer Organic Chemistry Inst., Choate Sch., Wallingford, Conn.; mem. Union County Mental Health Bd., 1973-76; bd. dirs. N.J. Mental Health Assn., 1974—; trustee Montclair (N.J.) State Coll., 1975—, vice-chmn., 1976—; adviser applied prof. psychology Rutgers U., 1976—. Fellow Am. Inst. Chemists; mem. Am., Swiss, German chem. socs., Synthetic Organic Chem. Mfrs. Assn. (bd. govs. 1952-54, 63-70, v.p., 1966-68, chmn. internat. comml. relations com. 1968-73, hon. mem.), Sigma Xi. Republican. Episcopalian (vestry 1950-60). Clubs: Metropolitan Opera, Chemists (N.Y.); Beacon Hill (Summit, N.J.); Essex (Newark); Nassau (Princeton). Home: 57 Colt Rd Summit NJ 07901 also State Rd Chilmark MA 02535. *To live right and help others live right too, each in his own way.*

MAY, ERNEST RICHARD, historian. educator; b. Ft. Worth, Nov. 19, 1928; s. Ernest and Rachel (Garza) M.; A.B., U. Calif. at Los Angeles, 1948, M.A. (Native Sons of Golden West fellow in history), 1949, Ph.D. (Univ. fellow), 1951; M.A. (hon.), Harvard U., 1959; m. Nancy Caughey, Dec. 15, 1950; children—John Ernest, Susan Rachel, Donna LaRee. Lectr. history Los Angeles State Coll., 1950; mem. hist. sect. Joint Chiefs of Staff, 1952-54; instr. history Harvard U., 1954-56, asst. prof., 1956-59, asso. prof., 1959-63, prof., 1963—, Allston Burr sr. tutor Kirkland House, 1960-66, mem. Inst. Politics, 1967—, dir. inst., 1971-74, dean of coll., 1969-71; mem. Council on Fgn. Relations. Chmn. bd. control John Anson Kittredge Trust. Served as lt. (j.g.) USNR, 1951-54. Guggenheim fellow, 1958-59; faculty research fellow Social Sci. Research Council, 1959-61; fellow Center for Advanced Study Behavioral Scis., 1963-64. Mem. Mass. Hist. Soc., Am. Hist. Assn., AAUP, Am. Acad. Arts and Scis. Episcopalian. Club: Belmont Hill. Author: The World War and American Isolation, 1914-17, 1959; The Ultimate Decision; The President as Commander in Chief, 1960; Imperial Democracy; The Emergence of America as a Great Power, 1961; The American Image, 4 vols., 1963; (with John W. Caughey) A History of the United States, 1964; (with editors of Life) The Progressive Era, 1964, War, Boom and Bust, 1964; From Isolation to Imperialism, 1898-1919, 1964; (with John W. Caughey and John Hope Franklin) Land of the Free, 1966; American Imperialism; A Speculative Essay, 1968; Lessons of the Past: The Use and Misuse of History in American Foreign Policy, 1973; The Making of The Monroe Doctrine, 1975; also numerous articles. Office: History Dept Harvard U Cambridge MA 02138

MAY, FRANCIS BARNS, educator; b. Cascilla, Miss., Dec. 24, 1915; s. James Marshall and Hallye (Rice) M.; B.B.A. with highest honors, U. Tex., 1941, M.B.A., 1943, Ph.D., 1957; m. Janice Evelyn Christensen, June 9, 1956. Mem. faculty U. Tex., 1941—, prof. statistics, 1961—, chmn. dept. gen. bus., 1964-68; cons. in field, 1946—; vis. prof. bus. statistics U. Minn., 1960. Dir. San Antonio br. Fed. Res. Bank Dallas, 1966-68, 68-71, chmn., 1968-70. Mem. Gov. Tex. Com. Industrialization State, 1969-70. Served to capt. USAAF, 1943-46. Mem. Am. Statis. Assn. (council 1969-70), Phi Eta Sigma, Beta Gamma Sigma, Beta Alpha Psi, Sigma Iota Epsilon, Phi Kappa Phi. Author: (with others) Executive Management Decision Simulation Computerized Model, 3 vols., 1962; Introduction to Games of Strategy, 1970. Home: 6504 Auburn Hill Austin TX 78723

MAY, FRANCIS HART, JR., bldg. materials and indsl. products mfg. exec.; b. Dunkirk, Ind., Apr. 2, 1917; s. Francis Hart and Agnes (Elabarger) M.; A.B., U. Notre Dame, 1938; M.B.A., Harvard, 1940; m. June Breen, Aug. 31, 1940; children—Francis Hart, John Joseph, Marcia Ann. Mgr. war contracts div. Owens-Ill. Glass Co., Toledo, 1940-44; v.p., sec. Glass Fibers, Inc., Toledo, 1946-54; v.p., sec., treas. L-O-F Glass Fibers Co., Toledo, 1955-58; v.p., gen. mgr. Johns-Manville Fiber Glass, Inc., 1959-60; asst. v.p. finance Johns-Manville Corp., N.Y.C., 1960-61, v.p. fin., dir., 1962-70, exec. v.p. fin. and adminstrn., 1971-79, vice-chmn. bd., 1979—; dir. Allegheny Power System, also subsidiaries. Bd. dirs. Denver Symphony, Boys' Clubs of Denver, Easter Seal Soc.; mem. council fin. execs. Conf. Bd. Served with inf. AUS, 1944-46. Mem. Fin. Execs. Inst. Clubs: Harvard Notre Dame (N.Y.C.); Denver and Cherry Hills (Colo.) Country. Home: 13 Lynn Rd Englewood CO 80110 Office: Ken-Caryl Ranch PO Box 5108 Denver CO 80217

MAY, GEORGES CLAUDE, educator, univ. ofcl.; b. Paris, France, Oct. 7, 1920; s. Lucien Léopold and Germaine (Samuel) M.; B.A., U. Paris, 1937; Licence es Lettres, U. Montpellier (France), 1941, Diplôme d'Etudes Supérieures, 1941; Ph.D., U. Ill., 1947; m. Martha Corkery, Feb. 19, 1949; children—Anne Charlotte, Catherine Ellen. Came to U.S., 1942; naturalized, 1943. Asst., U. Ill., 1942-43, 46-47; faculty Yale, 1947—, successively instr., asst. prof., asso. prof., 1947-56, prof. French, 1956-71, dean Yale Coll., 1963-71, Sterling prof. French, 1971—, chmn. dept. French, 1978—, provost, 1979—; prof. summers U. Ill., 1946, Middlebury Coll., 1951, 54, U. Minn., 1948, U. Mich., 1952, U. Calif. at Berkeley, 1959; sec. Fourth Internat. Congress Enlightenment, 1975. Trustee Hopkins Grammar Day Prospect Hill Sch., 1970-78. Served with French Army, 1939-40, AUS, 1943-45. Decorated chevalier French Legion of Honor; Guggenheim Found. fellow, 1950-51. Mem. Am. Acad. Arts and Scis., Am. Soc. 18th Century Studies (pres. 1974-75), Am. Assn. Tchrs. French, Modern Lang. Assn., Assn. des Etudes Francaises, Société d'Etude du XVIIIe Siècle, Phi Beta Kappa. Author: Tragédie cornélienne, tragédie racinienne, 1948; D'Ovide à Racine, 1949; Quatre Visages de Denis Diderot, 1951; Diderot et La Religieuse, 1954; Rousseau par lui-même, 1961; Le Dilemme du roman au XVIIIe siècle, 1963; L'Autobiographie, 1979. Editor: Corneille's Polyeucte and Le Menteur, 1964; Diderot's Commentary on Hemsterhuis' Lettre sur l'homme, 1964; Diderot's La Religieuse, 1975. Contbr. articles French lit., profl. publs. Home: 35 Hillhouse Ave New Haven CT 06511

MAY, GITA, educator; b. Brussels, Sept. 16, 1929; d. Albert and Blima (Sieradska) Jochimek; came to U.S., 1947, naturalized, 1950; B.A. magna cum laude, Hunter Coll., 1953; M.A., Columbia U., 1954, Ph.D., 1957; m. Irving May, Dec. 21, 1947. Lectr. in French, Hunter Coll., N.Y.C., 1953-56; instr. French, Columbia U., 1956-58, asst. prof., 1958-61, asso. prof., 1961-69, prof., 1968—, deptl. rep., 1968—, mem. senate, 1979—; lecture tour English univs., 1965. Decorated Chevalier Ordre des Palmes Academiques, 1968; recipient award Columbia U. Council for Research in Humanities, 1960, 67, 69, Am. Council Learned Socs., 1961, award for outstanding achievement Hunter Coll., 1963; Fulbright research grantee, 1964-65; Guggenheim fellow, 1964-65; Nat. Endowment for Humanities sr. fellow, 1971-72. Mem. AAUP, Am. Assn. Tchrs. of French, Modern Lang. Assn. Am. (del. assembly 1973-75, mem. com. research activities 1975-78), Am. Soc. 18th Century Studies (exec. bd. N.E. 1976-79), Société Française d'Etude du Dix-Huitieme Siècle, Am. Soc. French Acad. Palms, Phi Beta Kappa. Author: Diderot et Baudelaire, critiques d'art, 1957; De Jean-Jacques Rousseau à Madame Roland: essai sur la sensibilité préromantique et revolutionnaire, 1964; Madame Roland and the Age of Revolution, 1970 (Van Amringe Distinguished Book award); Stendhal and the Age of Napoleon, 1977; co-editor: Diderot Studies III, 1961; mem. editorial bd. 18th Century Studies, 1975-78, French Rev., 1975—, Romanic Rev. 1959—; contbg. editor: Oeuvres complètes de Diderot, 1975—; contbr. articles and revs. to profl. jours. Home: 404 W 116th St New York NY 10027

MAY, HENRY FARNHAM, educator; b. Denver, Mar. 27, 1915; s. Henry F. and May (Rickard) M.; A.B., U. Calif. at Berkeley, 1937; M.A., Harvard, 1938, Ph.D., 1947; m. Jean Louise Terrace, June 18, 1941; children—Hildegarde Clark Lomas, Ann Rickard. Instr. history Lawrence Coll., 1941-42; asst. prof., then asso. prof. Scripps Coll., 1947-49; vis. asso. prof. Bowdoin Coll., 1950-51; mem. faculty U. Calif. at Berkeley, 1952—, prof. history, 1956—, Margaret Bryne prof. Am. history, 1963—, chmn. dept., 1964-66; summer tchr. Salzburg (Austria) Seminar Am. Studies, also U. Minn.; Fulbright lectr. Belgian Univs., 1959-60; Pitt prof. Am. history and instns. Cambridge U., 1971-72. Served to lt. (j.g.) USNR, 1942-45. Fellow Social Sci. Research Council, 1946-47, 63-64, Am. Council Learned Socs., 1963-64; Nat. Endowment for Humanities Sr. fellow, 1974-75. Mem. Am. Hist. Assn. (Beveridge prize 1977), Orgn. Am. Historians (Merle Curti prize 1976), Am. Soc. Ch. History, Am Acad. Arts and Scis., Am. Antiquarian Assn. Democrat. Episcopalian. Author: Protestant Churches and Industrial America, 1949; The End of American Innocence, 1959; (with C.G. Sellers) A Synopsis of American History, 1963; The Enlightenment in America, 1976; also articles. Home: 612 Coventry Rd Berkeley CA 94707

MAY, J. PETER, educator; b. N.Y.C., Sept. 16, 1939; s. Siegmund H. and Jane (Polachek) M.; B.A., Swarthmore Coll., 1960; Ph.D., Princeton, 1964; m. Maija Bajars, June 8, 1963; children—Anthony David, Andrew Daniel. Instr. Yale, 1964-65, asst. prof., 1965-67; asso. prof. math. U. Chgo., 1967-70, prof., 1970—; mem. Inst. Advanced Study, 1966. Fulbright fellow, 1971-72; hon. Woodrow Wilson fellow, 1960. Mem. Am. Math. Soc., AAUP, Phi Beta Kappa. Author: Simplicial Objects in Algebraic Topology, 1967; The Geometry of Iterated Loop Spaces, 1972; (with V.K.A.M. Gugenheim) On the Theory and Applications of Differential Torsion Products, 1974; Classifying Spaces and Fibrations, 1975; (with F.R. Cohen and T.J. Lada) The Homology of Interated Loop Spaces, 1976; E-infinity Ring Spaces and E-infinity Ring Spectra, 1977; also articles. Office: Dept Math U Chicago 5736 University Ave Chicago IL 60637

MAY, J. T., psychiatrist; b. Roland, Ark., Nov. 17, 1922; s. John Rye and Nona (Porter) M.; student Hendrix Coll., Conway, Ark., 1939-41; M.D., U. Ark. 1944; m. Helen Louise Hearn, Feb. 19, 1943; children—Susan (Mrs. Joe Milder), Steven. Michael, Marilyn (Mrs. Neil Montz), Robin. Intern, Ark. Bapt. Hosp., Little Rock, 1944-45, resident in medicine, 1945-46; resident psychiatry VA Hosp., Little Rock, 1952-55, staff mem., 1955-58; clin. instr. dept. psychiatry U. Ark. Sch. Medicine, 1952-56, asst. clin. prof., 1956-58; chief of service Mental Health Inst., Cherokee, Iowa, 1958-61, clin. dir. inpatient services, 1962-67, supt., 1969-73; cons., 1973-76; staff VA Hosp., North Little Rock, 1976-78; supt. Mental Health Inst., Independence, Iowa, 1978—; dir. profl. services for research and edn. VA Hosp., Gulfport, Miss., 1961-62; asst. prof. Sch. Medicine, N.Y. U., Buffalo, also chief psychiatry and neurology VA Hosp., Buffalo, 1967-69; acting dir. Bur. Mental Health, Iowa Dept. Social Services, 1972-73. Served to capt., M.C., Aus, 1946-48. Fellow Am. Psychiat. Assn.; mem. Iowa Psychiat. Assn. (past pres.). Address: Mental Health Inst Independence IA 50644

MAY, JAMES BRENDAN, lawyer; b. Bklyn., Nov. 21, 1929; s. Morford S. and Mary L. (Ryan) M.; B.A., Williams Coll., 1951; LL.B., Harvard U., 1957; m. Ann M. Powers, Apr. 17, 1955; children—Patricia, Peter, Timothy, Susan. Admitted to N.Y. bar, 1958; asso. firm Brown, Wood, Ivey, Mitchell & Petty and predecessor, N.Y.C., 1957-67, partner, 1967—; lectr. on litigation under fed. securities laws Am. Law Inst-Am. Bar Assn.; arbitrator Nat. Assn. Securities Dealers, Inc. Served with U.S. Army, 1951-54. Decorated Bronze Star. Mem. Am. Bar Assn., N.Y. State Bar Assn., Am. Judicature Soc., Am. Law Inst., Phi Beta Kappa. Clubs: City Midday; Rockville Country Club. Home: 12 Arsdley Pl Rockville Centre NY 11570 Office: One Liberty Plaza New York NY 10006

MAY, JAMES C., constrn. co. exec.; b. Richmond, Ill., Dec. 15, 1929; s. Charles N. and Jucia A. (Freund) M.; B.S. in Archtl. Engring., U. Ill.; m. Mary E. Bruce, Jan. 10, 1952; children—Bruce, Robert, Linda, Barbara, Patricia, Thomas. Structural engr. dept. plant engring. Fairbank-Morse Co., Beloit, Wis., 1953-55; structural design engr. Henry Wolfe, Logansport, Ind., 1955-56; with Huber, Hung & Nichols Inc., Indpls., 1956—, exec. v.p., now pres., also dir.; pres. AGC of Ind., 1976. Served to 1st lt. USAF, 1951-53. Mem. Bldg. Contractors Assn. Indpls. (pres. 1972). Club: Elks (Plainfield, Ind.). Home: 1537 Hardin Ct Plainfield IN 46148 Office: 2450 S Tibbs St Indianapolis IN 46206

MAY, JOHN LAWRENCE, bishop; b. Evanston, Ill., Mar. 31, 1922; s. Peter Michael and Catherine (Allare) M.; M.A., St. Mary of Lake Sem., Mundelein, Ill., 1945, S.T.L., 1947. Ordained priest Roman Catholic Ch., 1947; asst. pastor St. Gregory Ch., Chgo., 1947-56; chaplain Mercy Hosp., Chgo., 1956-59; v.p., gen. sec. Cath. Ch. Extension Soc. U.S., 1959-67, pres., 1967—; tchr. St. Gregory High Sch., Chgo., 1949-56, Loyola U., Chgo., 1948-49; lectr. Cana Conf. Chgo., 1949-65; defender of bond. met. tribunal Archdiocese Chgo., 1949-58, prosynodal judge, 1958-69; part-time mem. personnel bd. Archdiocese Chgo., 1967-69; aux. bishop Chgo., 1967-69; vicar gen. Archdiocese Chgo., 1967-69; pastor Christ The King Parish, Chgo., 1968-69; bishop of Mobile, Ala., 1969—. Home: PO Box 1966 400 Government St Mobile AL 36601

MAY, MELVIN ARTHUR, sugar co. exec.; b. Cortez, Colo., Oct. 22, 1940; s. Everett James and Viola Christina (Lair) M.; A.A., Pueblo Coll., 1959; B.S., U. Colo., 1961; m. Dale Charlene Kelly, Oct. 3, 1963; children—Diana, Michael. Accountant, Haskins & Sells, C.P.A.'s, San Diego, Denver, and Colorado Springs, Colo., 1961-68; asst. to v.p., treas. Holly Sugar Corp., Colorado Springs, 1968-69, asst. treas., 1970-71, treas., 1972—, v.p., 1977—; v.p., treas., dir. Holly World Foods, Inc., San Francisco, Ashley's Inc., El Paso. Served with USMCR, 1963-64. Mem. Am. Inst. C.P.A.'s, Colo. Soc. C.P.A.'s, Fin. Execs. Inst., Nat. Rifle Assn., Izaak Walton League Am. Home: 637 Dexter St Colorado Springs CO 80911 Office: PO Box 1052 Colorado Springs CO 80901

MAY, ORVILLE EDWARD, chemist, research adminstr.; b. New Albin, Iowa, Aug. 22, 1901; s. George Burton and Frances Margaret (Dailey) M.; student Loras Coll., 1918-20, U. Minn., 1920-23; A.B., George Washington U., 1924, M.S., 1926, Ph.D., 1929; m. Katherine Marie Barrett, Oct. 27, 1926; children—Elaine Marie, George Barrett. Research chemist on fermentation U.S. Dept. Agr., Washington, 1923-36, dir. U.S. Regional Soybean Lab., developing wider uses for soybeans at U. Ill., Urbana, 1936-39, dir. U.S. No. Regional Research Lab., Peoria, Ill., 1939-42, coordinator for chem. research U.S. Dept. Agr., Washington, 1942-44, chief Bur. Agrl. and Indsl. Chemistry, U.S. Dept. Agr., 1944-46; tech. exec. Coca-Cola Co., Atlanta, 1946-48, v.p., tech. dir., 1948-66. Bd. regents Loras Coll., 1965-67, hon. life mem., 1972—. Recipient Alumni Achievement award George Washington U., 1962; gold medal award Am. Inst. Chemists, 1968. Hon. life mem. Am. Inst. Chemists, AAAS; mem. Am. Chem. Soc. (emeritus), Inst. Food Technologists (emeritus), Sigma Xi, Alpha Chi Sigma, Phi Lambda Upsilon. Clubs: Cosmos (Washington); Captial City (Atlanta). Home: Big Rock 6130 Lower Roswell Rd Marietta GA 30067

MAY, PAUL WHITE, state legislator; b. Hot Springs, Va., Jan. 2, 1928; s. Paul White and Sue Ellen (Haskins) M.; m. Lucille Helen Doran, July 8, 1956; children—Paul White, Sandra K., April Ann. Real estate salesman, Las Vegas, Nev., 1972—, broker, 1972—; mem.

Nev. Ho. of Reps., 1966—, chmn. assembly taxation com., 1971-77, speaker of house, 1979-80; chmn. North Las Vegas Legis. Del., 1970-77; mem. Western States Multi-State Tax Compact Adv. Commn., 1973-77; mem. urban com. Fed. State Assembly, 1977-78. Bd. dirs. Clark County unit March of Dimes, FitzSimmons House, Regia Hall. Served with U.S. Army, 1948-51. Democrat. Clubs: Elks, Am. Legion. Home: 3309 Wright St North Las Vegas NV 84030 Office: 846 E Sahara St A Las Vegas NV 89102

MAY, PETER WILLIAM, mfg. co. exec.; b. N.Y.C., Dec. 11, 1942; s. Samuel D. and Isabel (Meyer) M.; A.B., U. Chgo., 1964, M.B.A., 1965; m. Leni Finkelstein, Aug. 16, 1964; children—Jonathan, Leslie. Mgr. audit dept. Peat Marwick Mitchell & Co., N.Y.C., 1965-72; v.p. fin. FSF Industries Inc., N.Y.C., 1972-74, exec. v.p., treas., 1974—; exec. v.p., sec., dir. Coffee-Mat Corp., N.Y.C., 1975-76. Chmn. bd. dirs. Ethical-Fieldston Fund. of N.Y. Ethical Culture Schs.; active Little League, Cub Scouts. C.P.A., N.Y. Mem. Fin. Execs. Inst., Am. Inst. C.P.A.'s, N.Y. Soc. Pub. Accountants, U. Chgo. Alumni Assn. Clubs: City Athletic (N.Y.C.); New Milford (Conn.) Racquet. Home: 176 E 71st St New York NY 10021 Office: 600 Madison Ave New York NY 10022

MAY, ROBERT A., lawyer; b. Grand Rapids, Mich., May 8, 1911; s. Adam F. and Myra Ethel (Shedden) M.; A.B., U. Mich., 1933, J.D., 1936; m. Margrethe Holm, Aug. 30, 1934 (dec. Dec. 1970); children—Marcia, Margrethe; m. 2d, Virginia L. Salisbury, Mar. 20, 1973. Admitted to Mich. bar, 1936; practiced in Grand Rapids, 1936-41; admitted to Ariz. bar, 1941, U.S. Supreme Ct. bar, 1960; practice law, Tucson, 1941—; partner May, Dees & Barassi and predecessors. Mem. State Bar Ariz., vice chmn., 1952-55, chmn. group ins. com., 1955-72, co-founder, chmn. bd. trustees Client's Security Fund, 1961—, mem. Am. Bar Assn. standing com. Clients Security Fund, 1968-73; mem. com. on revision probate code Ariz. State Bar, 1970—; Ariz. chmn. Joint Editorial Bd. for Uniform Probate Code, 1972—; mem. com. on revision Ariz. probate code Ariz. Legis. Council, 1970-72; mem. com. jud. selection, tenure, and discipline, 1957-72. Co-founder Def. Info. Office: charter mem. Def. Research Inst.; dir., gen. counsel St. Luke's in the Desert, charitable san. clinic, 1944—, pres., 1964-77, pres. emeritus, 1977—; bd. dirs. Pima County Legal Aid Soc., 1952-77, emeritus, 1977—, pres., 1958-60; advisory bd. Tucson Med. Center, 1946-49; co-founder Tucson Conv. Bur., 1945-74, exec. bd., 1957-67; regional chmn. U. Mich. Law Sch. Fund, 1963-66, mem. nat. com., 1967-72, now emeritus; vice chmn. coms. Ariz. hosp. com. ARC, 1942-45; mem. Citizens Adv. Com. for Public Schs., 1944-46; vis. com. U. Mich. Law Sch., 1964-67. Recipient Outstanding Service award Ariz. State Bar Assn., 1977. Fellow Am. Coll. Probate Counsel (bd. regents 1966-69, 73-77); mem. Nat. Coll. Probate Judges (life), Internat. Acad. Law and Sci., Tucson C. of C., Ariz. Pioneers Hist. Soc., Am. (vice chmn. health ins. com. 1958-70, chmn. 1970-72), Internat., Mich., Pima County (pres. 1955-56), Fed. bar assns., Am. Bar Found., Found for Temple Bar, So. Ariz. Estate Planning Council (co-founder, pres. 1956), Mich. Alumni Assn. (dist. dir. 1943-46), Internat. Assn. Ins. Counsel, Tucson (mem. exec. bd., chmn. fin. com. 1948-64, pres. 1956-58), Ariz. (v.p. 1956-58) councils chs., Internat. Acad. Law and Sci., Am. Judicature Soc. (nat. dir. 1963-67), Assn. Ins. Attys., Internat. Platform Assn., Phi Sigma Kappa Found., Phi Sigma Kappa (pres. Tucson Alumni Club 1960-74), Alpha Epsilon Mu (hon.). Episcopalian (parish chancellor 1943-78, chancellor emeritus 1978—, vestryman 1943-73, 74-77, rector's warden 1977-78, vice chancellor Ariz. diocese 1959—). Clubs: Round Table Internat. (pres. 1944-46), Old Pueblo; University of Mich. Alumni (pres. Grand Rapids 1938-40, Tucson 1945-50, 76-77); Inst. for Dirs., Wig and Pen (London). Home: 1915 E 3d St Tucson AZ 85719 Office: United Bank Bldg 3d Floor 120 W Broadway Tucson AZ 85701

MAY, ROLLO, psychoanalyst; b. Ada, Ohio, Apr. 21, 1909; s. Earl Tittle and Matie (Boughton) M.; A.B., Oberlin Coll., 1930; B.D. cum laude, Union Theol. Sem., N.Y.C., 1938; Ph.D. summa cum laude, Columbia U., 1949; D.H.L., U. Okla., 1970; LL.D., Regis Coll., 1971; L.H.D. (hon.), St. Vincent Coll., 1972, Mich. State U., 1976, Rockford Coll., 1977, Ohio No. U., 1978; m. Florence DeFrees, June 5, 1938 (div. 1968); children—Robert Rollo, Allegra Anne, Carolyn Jane; m. 2d, Ingrid Schöll, 1971. Tchr., Am. Coll., Saloniki, Greece, 1930-33; student adviser Mich. State Coll., 1934-36; student counselor Coll. City N.Y., 1943-44; mem. faculty William Alanson White Inst. Psychiatry, Psychology and Psychoanalysis, 1958-70; lectr. New Sch. Social Research, N.Y.C., 1955-76; tng. fellow supervisory analyst Williams Alanson White Inst. Psychiatry, 1958—; co-chmn. Conf. on Psychotherapy and Counseling, N.Y. Acad. Scis., 1953-54; vis. prof. Harvard U., summer 1964, Princeton U., 1967, Yale U., 1972; Dean's scholar N.Y. U., 1971; Regents' prof. U. Calif. at Santa Cruz, 1973; disting. vis. prof. Bklyn. Coll., 1974-75. Trustee Am. Found. Mental Health; bd. dirs. Soc. Arts, Religion and Culture. Recipient award distinguished contbn. profession and sci. of psychology N.Y. Soc. Clin. Psychology, 1955; Ralph Waldo Emerson award for Love and Will, Phi Beta Kappa, 1970; Distinguished Contbns. award N.Y. U., 1971; Centennial Medallion, St. Peter's Coll., 1972; ann. citation Merrill-Palmer Inst., Detroit, 1973; spl. Dr. Martin Luther King, Jr. award N.Y. Soc. Clin. Psychologists, 1974; Disting. Grad. award Columbia U. Tchrs. Coll., 1975; fellow Branford Coll., Yale U., 1960—. Fellow Am. Psychol. Assn. (award for disting. contbn. to sci. and profession of clin. psychology 1971), Nat. Council Religion Higher Edn., William Alanson White Psychoanalytic Soc. (past pres.); mem. N.Y. State Psychol. Assn. (past pres.). Author: Art of Counseling, 1939, Meaning of Anxiety, 1950, rev. edit., 1977; Man's Search for Himself, 1953; Psychology and the Human Dilemma, 1966; Existence: A New Dimension in Psychiatry and Psychology, 1958, Love and Will, 1969; Power and Innocence, 1972; Paulus-Reminiscences of a Friendship, 1973; The Courage to Create, 1975. Editor: Existence: A New Dimension in Psychiatry and Psychology, 1958; Existential Psychology, 2d edit., 1961; Symbolism in Religion and Literature, 1960;

MAY, RONALD ALAN, lawyer; b. Waterloo, Iowa, Sept. 8, 1928; s. John W. and Elsie (Finlayson) M.; B.A., State U. Iowa, 1950; LL.B., Vanderbilt U., 1953; m. Naomi Gray, Aug. 18, 1950 (div. Feb. 1974); children-Sarah, Jonathan, Andrew, Rachel; m. 2d, Susan East Gray, May 9, 1975. Admitted to Ark. bar, 1953; practiced in Marianna, 1953-57, Little Rock, 1957—; partner Wright, Lindsey & Jennings, 1960—. Pres., Spl. Com. on Pub. Edn., Ark. Assn. for Mental Health, Friends of Library, Central Ark. Radiation Therapy Inst.; bd. dirs. Nat. Assn. for Mental Health, Ark. State Hosp., Gaines House; trustee Mus. Sci. and Natural History, Little Rock, chmn., 1973. Served with AUS, 1946-47. Mem. Am. (chmn. sci. and tech. sect. 1975-76), Ark., Pulaski County bar assns., Order of Coif, Phi Beta Kappa. Republican. Episcopalian. Clubs: Capital, Little Rock, Little Rock Country. Editor: Automated Law Research, 1972; Sense and Systems in Automated Law Research, 1975. Home: 420 Midland St Little Rock AR 72205 Office: Worthen Bank Bldg Little Rock AR 72201

MAY, STEPHEN, state govt. ofcl., lawyer; b. Rochester, N.Y., July 30, 1931; s. Arthur J. and Hilda (Jones) M.; grad. Wesleyan U., 1953; LL.B., Georgetown U., 1961. Exec. asst. to Rep. Kenneth B. Keating, 1955-64; admitted to N.Y. bar, 1963; asso., mem., then of counsel firm Branch, Turner & Wise, Rochester, 1965—; city councilman-at-large Rochester, 1966-73, mayor, 1970-73; commr. N.Y. State Bd. Elections, Albany, 1975—. Vice chmn. Temporary State Commn. on Powers of Local Govt., 1970-73; mem. 20th Century Fund Task Force on Future of N.Y.C., 1979; mem. Nat. Adv. Commn. Higher Edn. for Police Officers, 1977-79; mem. Joint Com. Assn. Bar City N.Y. and Drug Abuse Council on N.Y. Drug Law Evaluation, 1977-78; chmn. Rochester Interfaith Com. on Israel, 1973—; del.-at-large Republican Nat. Conv., 1972; mem. N.Y. State Crime Control Planning Bd., 1970-73; bd. dirs. Police Found., 1970—, Nat. Com. for Labor Israel, 1977-, Empire State Report, 1974—, Inst. Mediation and Conflict Resolution, 1973—. Served with U.S. Army, 1953-55. Mem. Phi Beta Kappa. Contbr. numerous articles to newspapers and profl. periodicals. Home: 9-A Prince St Rochester NY 14607 Office: NY State Bd Elections Agency Bldg 2 Empire State Plaza Albany NY 12223

MAY, TIMOTHY JAMES, lawyer; b. Denver, Aug. 3, 1932; s. Thomas Henry and Helen Frances (O'Connor) M.; B.A., Cath. U. Am., 1954; LL.B., Georgetown U., 1957, LL.M., 1960; m. Monica Anita Gross, Aug. 24, 1957; children—Stephanie Jean, Maureen, Cynthia Marie, Timothy James, Anthony C. Admitted to D.C. bar, 1957; with firm Covington & Burling, Washington, 1958-61; cons. Exec. Office President Kennedy, 1961-62; acting chief counsel subcom. stock piling U.S. Senate, 1962-63; mng. dir. Fed. Maritime Commn., 1963-66; gen. counsel Post Office Dept., Washington, 1966-69; partner firm Patton, Boggs, Blow, Verrill, Brand & May, and predecessor, Washington, 1969—; gen. counsel New Process Co., Parcel Post Assn., Mail Order Assn. Am., Nat. Assn. Postal Suprs. Lectr. English lit. Catholic U. Am., 1955-57. Mem. Nat. Finance Council Dem. Nat. Com. Recipient Presdl. award for economy achievement, 1964; Jump Meml. Found. Meritorious award, 1965, 66, 67; Arthur Flemming award, 1965; Postmaster Gen.'s Benjamin Franklin award, 1969; named Young Lawyer of the Year, Fed. Bar Assn., 1967. Mem. Blue Key. Clubs: Metropolitan, Congressional Country (Washington). Home: 3828 52d St NW Washington DC 20016 Office: 2550 M St NW Washington DC 20037

MAY, WALTER GRANT, chem. engr.; b. Saskatoon, Sask., Can., Nov. 28, 1918; s. George Alfred and Abigail Almira (Robson) M.; came to U.S., 1946, naturalized, 1954; B.Sc., U. Sask., Saskatoon, 1939, M.Sc., 1942; Sc.D., M.I.T., 1948; m. Mary Louise Stockan, Sept. 26, 1945; children—John R., Douglas W., Caroline O. Chemist British Am. Oil Co., Moose Jaw, Sask., 1939-40; asst. prof. U. Sask., 1943-46; with Exxon Research & Engring. Co., Linden, N.J., 1948—. sci. adv., 1969-76, sr. sci. adv., 1976—; with Advanced Research Projects Agy., Dept. Def., 1959-60; industry based prof. Stevens Inst. Tech., 1968-74, Rensselaer Poly. Inst., 1975-77. Recipient Process Indsl. Div. award ASME, 1972. Mem. Am. Inst. Chem. Engrs., ASME, Combustion Inst., Nat. Acad. Engring. Home: 73 Stoneridge Rd Summit NJ 07901 Office: PO Box 45 Linden NJ 07036

MAY, WILLIAM FREDERIC, container mfg. exec.; b. Chgo., Oct. 25, 1915; s. Arthur W. and Florence (Hartwick) M.; B.S., U. Rochester, 1937; grad. Advanced Mgmt. Program, Harvard, 1950; D. Engring., Clarkson U.; LL.D., Okla. Christian Coll.; L.H.D., Livingstone U.; LL.D., Lafayette U.; m. Kathleen Thompson, June 14, 1947; children—Katherine Hartwick (Mrs. Edward W. Bickford), Elizabeth Shaw (Mrs. Ralph P. Jessen). Research worker E.I. Du Pont de Nemours Co., 1937-38; with Am. Can Co., 1940—, mgr., Chgo., 1957-58, v.p., 1958-64, exec. v.p., 1964-65, vice chmn. bd., 1965, chmn., chief exec. officer, 1965—, mem. exec. com., dir., 1960—, dir., mem. exec. com. Johns-Manville Co.; dir. N.Y. Times, Bankers Trust Co., B.T. Corp., Bus. Internat. Corp., Engelhard Minerals & Chems. Corp. Nat. chmn. NCCJ; bd. dirs. Lincoln Center, Nat. Council on Crime and Delinquency; trustee Am. Ditchley Found., Am. Mus. Natural History, Taft Inst. Govt., Columbia-Presbyn. Hosp., U. Rochester; mem. corp. Poly. Inst. N.Y.; bd. overseers Dartmouth. Mem. Can Mfrs. Inst. (dir.), Phi Beta Kappa, Alpha Delta Phi. Episcopalian. Clubs: Union League, River, Links, Economic (N.Y.C.); Round Hill; Nat. Golf Links; Blind Brook; Coral Beach. Home: 16 Fort Hills Ln Greenwich CT 06830 Office: American Ln Greenwich CT 06830

MAYALL, JOHN BRUMWELL, blues singer, musician; b. Macclesfield, Eng., Nov. 29, 1933; s. Frederick Murray Hyde and Beryl (Leeson) M.; nat. diploma design, also diploma associateship, Regional Coll. Art, Manchester Eng., 1959; m. Pamela Barlow Heap, May 5, 1957 (div. May 1972); children—Gary vincent, Jason Walter, Tracey Ann, Benedict. Display work Kendals Dept. Store, Manchester, 1949-52; graphic designer, typographer, studio mgr. various advt. agys., Manchester and London, 1959-63; profl. musician, band leader The Bluesbreakers, 1963-68; solo artist, 1968—; rec. artist for Decca, Eng./London U.S.A. Records, 1964-69, Polydor Europe/U.S.A., 1969-74, ABC Records, U.S.A., 1974—; formed own co. Crusade, 1969; pres. Hibiscus Prodns., Inc., U.S.A., 1974—; dir. John Mayall Ltd. Served with Brit. Army, 1952-55; Korea. Composer over 200 compositions. Address: care Artists/Heller Agy 6430 Sunset Blvd Los Angeles CA 90028

MAYBERRY, WILLIAM EUGENE, physician; b. Cookeville, Tenn., Aug. 22, 1929; s. Henry Eugene and Beatrice Lucille (Maynard) M.; student Tenn. Technol. U., 1947-49; M.D., U. Tenn., 1953; M.S. in Medicine, U. Minn., 1959; m. Jane G. Foster, Dec. 29, 1953; children—Ann Graves, Paul Foster. Intern, U.S. Naval Hosp., Phila., 1953-54; resident Mayo Grad. Sch. Medicine, Rochester, Minn., 1956-59; mem. staff New Eng. Med. Center, Boston, 1959-60, Nat. Inst. Arthritis and Metabolic Diseases, 1962-64; staff Mayo Clinic, Rochester, 1960-62, 64—, cons. internal medicine, endocrine research and lab. medicine, chmn. dept. lab. medicine, 1971-75, bd. govs., 1971—, vice chmn., 1974-75, chmn., chief exec. officer, 1976—; asst. in medicine Tufts U. Med. Sch., 1959-60; faculty Mayo Grad. Sch. Medicine and Mayo Med. Sch., 1960—, now prof. lab. medicine. Trustee, Mayo Found., 1971—, vice chmn., 1974—. Diplomate Am. Bd. Internal Medicine. Fellow A.C.P.; mem. Am. Thyroid Assn., Am. Clin. and Climatological Soc., Am. Fedn. for Clin. Research, Endocrine Soc., Central Research Club, Central Soc. for Clin. Research, Sigma Xi. Clubs: Rochester Golf and Country, Mpls. Recipient Distinguished Alumni award Tenn. Technol. U., 1976; NIH research fellow, 1959-60, Am. Cancer Soc. research fellow, 1962-64; NIH research grantee, 1965-71; mem. editorial bd. Jour. of Clin. Endocrinology and Metabolism, 1971-73; contbr. articles to profl. jours. Home: 705 SW 8th Ave Rochester MN 55901 Office: 200 SW 1st St Rochester MN 55901

MAYBURY-LEWIS, DAVID HENRY PETER, educator, anthropologist; b. Hyderabad, Pakistan, May 5, 1929; s. Sydney Alan and Constance Louise (Hambleton) Maybury-L.; came to U.S., 1960; B.A., Trinity Hall, Cambridge (Eng.) U., 1952, M.A., 1956; M.A., Oxford U., 1956, D.Phil., 1960; A.M. (hon.), Harvard, 1966; m. Elsebet Helga Henningsen, Apr. 6, 1953; children—Alan Biorn, Niels Anthony. Mem. faculty Harvard, 1960—, prof. social anthropology, 1969—, chmn. dept. anthropology, 1973—; Ford Found. cons., Brazil, 1968—. Pres. Cultural Survival, Inc., 1972—. Served to 2d lt. Brit. Army, 1948-49. Fellow Center Advanced Study Behavioral Scis., 1964-65; vis. fellow Clare Hall, Cambridge, Eng., 1977-78; grantee NIH, 1963-68. Fellow Am. Acad. Arts and Scis., Royal Danish Acad. Scis., Société Suisse des Américanistes, Am. Anthrop. Assn., Royal Anthrop. Inst.; mem. Assn. Social Anthropologists, Latin Am. Studies Assn. Author: The Savage and The Innocent, 1965; Akwe-Shavante Society, 1967; editor: Dialectical Societies, 1979. Home: 30 Bowdoin St Cambridge MA 02138

MAYDA, JARO, educator; b. Brno, Czechoslovakia, 1918; s. Francis and Maria (Hornova) M.; came to U.S., 1949, naturalized, 1955; Dr. Juris Utriusque, Masaryk U., Brno, 1945; J.D., (Rockefeller fellow 1955-56), U. Chgo., 1957; m. A. Raquel Chamberlain, 1951; children—Jaro II, Maria Raquel, Pavel; m. 2d, Maruja del Castillo, 1967. Legal counsel export div. Skodaworks, Pilsen-Prague, 1946-48; vis. prof. polit. sci. Denison U., Granville, Ohio, 1949-50, Ohio State U., Columbus, 1950-51; asst. prof. law and polit. sci. U. Wis., Madison, 1951-56; mem. faculty U. P.R., Rio Piedras, 1957—, prof. law and public policy, 1958—, dir. Inst. Policy Studies and Law, 1972-75, spl. asst. to pres., 1972; Fulbright research prof. Inst. Comparative Law, U. Paris, 1967-68; fellow Woodrow Wilson Internat. Center for Scholars, Smithsonian Instn., 1971; Bailey lectr. La. State U., 1 969; lectr. Am. specialist program Dept. State, 1960; dep. sec. gen. 42d Conf. Internat. Law Assn., 1947; cons. Internat. Assn. Legal Sci., UNESCO, 1972—, FAO, 1974—, UN Environ. Program, 1977—; mem., policy adv. Gov.'s Study Group P.R. and Sea, 1972; research asso. Center Energy and Environ. Research, U. P.R.-U.S. Dept. Energy, 1977—; mem. com. environ. policy and law Internat. Union Conservation Nature, 1972—; adv. panel on Ecosystem Data Handbook, NSF, 1976-77. Author: Introduction to Law, 1959, 74; Environment and Resources: From Conservation to Ecomanagement, 1967; Francois Geny and Modern Jurisprudence, 1976; also articles; translator: Geny Method of Interpretation, 1963; also law treatises; editorial bd. Am. Jour. Comparative Law, 1958—; dir. U. P.R. Law Rev., 1958-62. Office: Sch Law Univ PR Rio Piedras PR 00931

MAYEDA, WATARA, educator; b. Shizuoka, Japan, June 21, 1928; s. Toshita and Taki (Mayeda) M.; came to U.S., 1950; B.S., Utah State U., 1954; M.S., U. Utah, 1955; Ph.D., U. Ill., 1958; Ph.D. in Engring., Tokyo Inst. Tech., 1965; m. Yoko Ando, June 27, 1957; children—Arthur H., James N. Asst. prof. elec. engring. U. Ill., at Urbana, 1958-59, asso. prof., 1960-65, prof., 1965—; staff engr. IBM Research Center, 1959-60; vis. prof. Tokyo Inst. Tech., 1966, U. Tex., 1967-69. Mem. IEEE, Inst. Electronics and Communications Engrs. Japan, Sigma Xi, Phi Kappa Phi, Pi Mu Epsilon, Eta Kappa Nu. Patentee ednl. apparatus. Research in theory of linear graphs and its application to communication systems, traffic control and computers. Home: 1106 S Western St Champaign IL 61820 Office: CSL Univ Illinois Urbana IL 61801

MAYER, ARNO JOSEPH, educator; b. Luxembourg, June 19, 1926; s. Frank J. and Ida (Lieben) M.; brought to U.S., 1941, naturalized, 1944; B.B.A., CCNY, 1949; M.A., Yale U., 1950, Ph.D., 1953; m. Nancy Grant, June 19, 1955 (div. Dec. 1965); children—Carl, Daniel. Asst. prof. politics Brandeis U., 1954-58; asst. prof. history Harvard, 1958-61; prof. history Princeton, 1961—; vis. prof. Columbia, 1966-71, N.Y. U., 1971-72; research asso. Ecole Pratiques des Hautes Etudes, Paris, 1973. Served with intelligence service AUS, 1944-46. Recipient Herbert Baxter Adams prize Am. Hist. Assn., 1968; Am. Council Learned Socs. fellow 1960-61, Soc. Sci. Research Council fellow, 1961-62, Rockefeller Found. fellow, 1963-64; Guggenheim fellow, 1967-68; Research fellow Inst. War and Peace, Columbia, 1971-72, Lehrman Inst., 1976-77. Fellow Am. Acad. Arts and Scis.; mem. Am. Hist. Assn. Author: Political Origins of the New Diplomacy, 1959; Politics and Diplomacy of Peacemaking, 1967; Dynamics of Counterrevolution, 1971. Home: 58 Battle Rd Princeton NJ 08540

MAYER, DENNIS THOMAS, biochemist, educator; b. Lexington, Mo., Jan. 3, 1901; s. August John and Agatha (Gavin) M.; student U. Ill., 1923-25; A.B., U. Mo., 1931, M.A., 1933, Ph.D., 1938; m. Virginia Louise Miller, May 8, 1937; children—Dennis T., David R., Michael J. Agt., U.S. Dept. Agr., 1937-42; mem. faculty U. Mo. at Columbia, 1937—, prof. agrl. biochemistry, 1952—, dir. research in physiology and biochemistry reprodn., 1942—, dir. interdisciplinary reproductive biology tng. program, 1966, chmn. dept. agrl. chemistry, dir. grad. studies, 1968-71, prof. emeritus, 1971—. Mem. Am. Soc. Biol. Chemists, Soc. for Exptl. Biology and Medicine, Am. Soc. Animal Sci., N.Y. Acad. Scis., Mo. Acad. Sci., Phi Beta Kappa, Sigma Xi, Gamma Sigma Delta. Contbr. articles to profl. jours. Home: Apt 305 606 Shamrock Ave Lee's Summit MO 64063

MAYER, EDGAR NATHAN, educator; b. N.Y.C., Sept. 24, 1924; s. Edgar August and Frances Beatrice (Silberstein) M.; B.A., Cornell U., 1944; M.A., Harvard, 1948, Ph.D., 1952; postgrad. Sorbonne, U. Paris, 1953-54, Middlebury Coll., 1946-48, 50-51; m. Yvonne Marie Boulard, Aug. 21, 1950; 1 son, Andrew Paul. Instr. French and Russian, Williams Coll., 1948-50, Princeton, 1950-51, Washington U., St. Louis, 1951-52, Lafayette Coll., Easton, Pa., 1953-55; asst. prof., dir. English for Foreigners, Wayne State U., 1956-59; asso. prof. French and Russian, U. Buffalo and State U. N.Y. at Buffalo, 1959-70; prof. French, U. Colo., Boulder, 1970—, chmn. dept., 1970-72; prof. linguistics at seven NDEA Insts., including Tours, France, summers 1963-68. Served with USNR, 1944-46. Am. Council Learned Socs. grantee for summer study linguistics, 1953; Fulbright lectr. Tokyo U. Edn., Japan, 1964-65. Mem. Linguistics Soc. Am., Am. Assn. Tchrs. French, Am. Assn. Tchrs. Slavic and East European Langs., AAUP. Author: Handbook of French Structure, 1968; Structure of French, 1969; others. Contbr. articles to profl. jours. Home: 2003 Bluebell Ave Boulder CO 80302

MAYER, FRED CHRISTIAN, univ. dean; b. Detroit, June 23, 1911; s. Frederick C. and Elizabeth (Patzer) M.; B.S.M., Capital U. Conservatory Music, 1933, D.Mus., 1974; M.A., Ohio State U., 1936; postgrad. Mich. State U., 1954; m. Ruth Ackerman, June 5, 1937; children—Fred Charles, Robert. Head dept. music Wilmington (Ohio) Coll., 1937-47; dir. Sch. Music, Friends U., Wichita, Kans., 1947-59; dir. music First Meth. Ch., Dallas, 1959-62; dean Sch. Music, Oklahoma City U., 1962—; prod. Piano Playtime, TV series, 1956-57. Organizer-dir. ann. Baroque Music Festival, Wichita, 1951-59; toured Asia with choral group, 1963, Europe, 1965; pres. Oklahoma City Chamber Music Series, 1968-70; chmn. music panel Okla. Arts and Humanities Council, 1964-73. Vice pres. Civic Music Assn., Wichita, 1951-59. Recipient Community Arts Council award, Wichita, 1955. Mem. Music Tchrs. Nat. Assn. (pres. S.W. div. 1968-70, nat. exec. bd. 1968-72), Kans. Music Tchrs. Assn. (pres. 1956), Music Educators Nat. Conf., Am. Choral Dirs. Assn., Okla. Coll. and Univ. Music Adminstrs. Assn. (chmn. 1971-74), Pi Kappa Lambda, Phi Mu Alpha Sinfonia. Methodist. Rotarian. Home: 2608 NW 42d Circle Oklahoma City OK 73112

MAYER, FREDERICK MILLER, ret. business exec.; b. Youngstown, Ohio, Oct. 8, 1898; s. Rev. Frederick and Carrie Ann (Miller) Mayer; B.A., Heidelberg Coll., Tiffin, Ohio, 1920, LL.D., 1948; J.D., Harvard, 1924; m. Mildred Katherine Rickard, Nov. 25, 1926; children—Frederick Rickard, Elizabeth Ann (Mrs. Boeckman). Admitted to Ohio bar, 1924; practice in Akron, 1924-26, Youngstown, 1926-32; treas. Continental Supply Co., Dallas, 1932-33, v.p., 1933-45, dir., 1933-55, pres., 1945-56; pres. Continental-Emsco Co. div. Youngstown Sheet and Tube Co., 1957-64; v.p. Youngstown Sheet and Tube Co., 1956-64, mem. exec. com., 1964-69, dir., 1958-69; pres., dir. Continental-Emsco Co., Ltd.,

Continental-Emsco Co. Compania Anonima (Venezuela), 1956-64, Continental-Emsco Co. de Mexico S.A. de C.V., 1962-64; pres. Fibercast Co. div. Youngstown Sheet and Tube Co., 1960-64; chmn. Continental-Emsco Co. (Gt. Britain), Ltd. (Eng.), 1957-64; dir. Gen. Am. Oil Co. of Tex. Trustee Dallas Art Assn. (pres. 1959-61, chmn. bd. 1966-68), Heidelberg Coll. Mem. Am. Petroleum Inst., Mid-Continent Oil and Gas Assn., Petroleum Equipment Suppliers Assn. (hon. dir., past pres.), Ind. Petroleum Assn., Acacia, Huguenot Soc. Ohio, S.A.R., Pi Kappa Delta. Republican. Conglist. Clubs: Idlewild, Brook Hollow, Dallas Petroleum, Dallas Hunting and Fishing, Dallas (Dallas); Ponte Vedra (Fla.). Home: 3131 Maple Ave Dallas TX 75201 Office: Mercantile-Continental Bldg Dallas TX 75221

MAYER, FREDERICK RICKARD, oil and gas exploration and drilling, uranium exploration co. exec.; b. Youngstown, Ohio, Jan. 25, 1928; s. Frederick Miller and Mildred Kathryn (Rickard) M.; B.A., Yale U., 1950; m. Jan MacCasler Perry, Nov. 1, 1958; children—Frederick MacCasler, Anthony Rickard, Perry Ellen. Pres., Exeter Drilling Co. (name changed to Exeter Drilling and Exploration Co. 1970-75, to Exeter Co. 1975—), Dallas and Denver, 1953-70, chmn. bd., chief exec. officer, 1970—. Chmn. Wallace Vill. for Children, 1971-74; trustee Garland Country Day Sch., 1973-79; mem. arts adv. com. Phillips Exeter Acad., 1974—; chmn. bd. trustees Denver Art Museum, 1975-79; trustee Am. Fedn. Arts, 1977—. Served with U.S. Army, 1950-52. Mem. Ind. Petroleum Assn. Am. (exec. com.), Chief Execs. Forum, Metro Denver Exec. Club, Am. Petroleum Inst., Ind. Petroleum Assn. Mountain States, Ind. Assn. Drilling Contractors, Nat. Petroleum Council. Clubs: Cherry Hills Country, Univ. of Denver, Garden of the Gods, Denver and Dallas Petroleum. Home: 37 Sunset Dr Englewood CO 80110 Office: PO Box 17349 Denver CO 80217

MAYER, HAROLD MAX, meat packing co. exec.; b. Chgo., Mar. 18, 1917; s. Oscar G. and Elsa (Stieglitz) M.; B.S., Cornell U., 1939; m. June Sirotek, Nov. 16, 1963; children—Harold F., Richard A., Robert O. With Oscar Mayer & Co., 1939—, trainee Madison (Wis.) plant, 1939-41, plant mgr., Chgo., 1953-61, v.p., 1948-66, sec., 1962—, dir., 1951—, exec. v.p., 1966—, vice chmn. bd., 1973-77, chmn. exec. com., 1977—; pres. Kartridg Pak Co., 1953-73, chmn. bd., 1973-77; past v.p., dir. Chgo. Profl. Basketball Team; past dir. Gen. Life Ins. Co., Milw., Williams Bros. Paper Box Co., St. Joseph, Mich. Mem. Chgo. Com. Alcoholism, 1957—, v.p., 1959, exec. v.p., 1960, vice chmn., 1972. Bd. dirs. Skokie Valley Community Hosp.; past trustee U. Chgo. Cancer Found., Ill. Children's Home Aid Soc., Elmhurst (Ill.) Coll. Served to maj. AUS, 1942-46. Mem. Chgo. Assn. Commerce and Industry (dir.), Young Pres.'s Orgn. (past chpt. chmn.), Ill. C. of C., Chgo. Pres.'s Orgn. (pres. 1967-68), Cornell Alumni Assn., Cornell Soc. Hotelmen. Mason (Shriner). Clubs: Executives, Economic, Mid-Am., Metropolitan, Chgo. Yacht, Chgo. Athletic Assn. (Chgo.); Meadow (Rolling Meadows, Ill.); Imperial Golf (Naples, Fla.); North Shore Country (Glenview, Ill.). Home: 1420 Sheridan Rd #4-E Wilmette IL 60091 Office: 5725 E River Rd Chicago IL 60631

MAYER, HENRY MICHAEL, transit system exec.; b. Wauwatosa, Wis., Oct. 20, 1922; s. Henry and Rose (Daas) M.; B.S. in Bus. Adminstrn., Marquette U., 1947; m. Colleen C. Reisner, July 25, 1944; children—Michael, Michele, David, Jennifer. With Milw. Transit System, 1947-75, exec. asst., 1959-67, v.p., gen. mgr., 1965-75; pres., mng. dir. Milw. Transport Services, Inc., 1975—; lectr., cons. mass transit. Mem. adv. com. Southeastern Wis. Regional Planning Commn; bd. dirs. Wis. Kidney Found.; bd. overseers St. Francis Sem., Milw. Served to lt. USNR, 1943-46. Mem. Am. Public Transit Assn. (dir., v.p. bus. ops.), Inst. Transp. Engrs. Originator bus service using pvt. shopping centers as park-ride lots for freeway express service to downtown. Home: 1620 N 124th St Wauwatosa WI 53226 Office: 4212 W Highland Blvd Milwaukee WI 53208

MAYER, J. GERALD, lawyer, business exec.; b. N.Y.C., May 2, 1908; s. Charles A. and Lillian P. (Morgan) M.; B.S., George Washington U., 1928; LL.B., St. Lawrence U., Canton, N.Y., 1931; LL.D. (hon.), Hartwick Coll., Oneonta, N.Y., 1962; m. Marian Louese Swayze, July 25, 1931; 1 son, Timothy Swayze. Engr., Western Electric Co., 1928-33; admitted to N.Y. bar, 1933, D.C. bar, 1950; pvt. practice, Schenectady, 1933-41; spl. corp. counsel City of Schenectady, 1937-40; sr. partner firm Mayer, Kline, Rigby, Washington, 1945; v.p., dir., then exec. v.p. Gen. Instrument Corp., Newark, 1954-63; pres. Colonial (Radio) Network, Inc., Cortland, N.Y., 1947-50; pres., dir. Radio Receptor Corp., 1958-59, Harris Transducer Corp., 1959-63; chmn. Radio Norwich, Inc. (N.Y.), 1956—, Gladding Corp., Boston, 1962—. Served with AUS, 1942-45. Mem. Am., D.C., Fed., N.Y. State bar assns., Cornell Soc. Engrs., Administrv. Law Assn. Clubs: Kenwood Country; Nat. Press (Washington). Home: 17 Arnold Gifford Rd Falmouth MA 02540 Office: 441 Stuart St Boston MA 02116

MAYER, JACK FARLEY, consumer products mfg. co. exec.; b. Birmingham, Ala., Jan. 4, 1927; s. Louis A. and Mayme M. Mayer; B.S., Samford U., 1950; m. Betty Brock, June 7, 1947; children—Dana Marie, Jack Douglas. Shipping/billing clk. Graham Brokerage Co., Birmingham, 1946-50; salesman Borden Co., Birmingham, 1950-51; with Texize Chems. Co., Greenville, S.C., 1951—, v.p. sales/mktg., 1969-75, pres., 1975—. Served with USCG, 1944-45. Presbyterian. Home: 4 Hunting Hollow Rd Greenville SC 29615 Office: PO Box 368 Greenville SC 29602*

MAYER, JAMES B., banker; b. Los Angeles, Jan. 13, 1914; s. James B. and Mary Belle (Preston) M.; A.B., Fresno State U., 1937; m. Wilda L. Lightsey, June 6, 1945; children—Bradley W., Wanda L., Donald L., Barbara A.; m. 2d, Betty Jane Izenour, Oct. 22, 1966; children—Janet McLaughlin, Nancy McLaughlin. Dep. commr. pub. safety and welfare City of Fresno (Calif.), 1937-41; asst. to pres. Sunland Industries, 1941-42; engaged in promotional and pub. relations activities, 1945-46; with Producers Cotton Oil Co., Fresno, 1946-72, v.p. charge ops. Ariz., Imperial Valley and Mex., 1955-58, exec. v.p., 1958-67, pres., 1967-72; chmn. bd. Valley Nat. Bank of Ariz., 1972-76, chmn. exec. com., dir., 1976—; dir. Producers Cotton Oil Co.; mem. adv. council Fed. Res. Bd. Bd. dirs. Theodore Roosevelt council Boy Scouts Am., Central Ariz. Project, Valley Forward; mem. bus. adv. bd. Ariz. State U. Served to maj. USAAF, 1942-45. Mem. Nat. Cotton Council Am., Nat. Cottonseed Products Assn. (pres. 1964), Cotton Council Internat., Assn. Res. City Bankers, Fresno County and City C. of C. (pres. 1962), Calif. C. of C., Sigma Chi, Alpha Kappa Psi. Clubs: Ariz.; Univ.; Phoenix Country; Sunnyside Country. Home: 125 E Palm Ln Phoenix AZ 85004 Office: Valley Nat Bank Ariz PO Box 71 Phoenix AZ 85001*

MAYER, JEAN, univ. pres., scientist; b. Paris, France, Feb. 19, 1920; s. Andre and Jeanne Eugénie (Veille) M.; B.Litt. summa cum laude, U. Paris, 1937, B.Sc. magna cum laude, 1938, M.Sc., 1939; Ph.D. in Physiol. Chemistry (Rockefeller Found. fellow), Yale U., 1948; Dr.-ès-Sc. in Physiology summa cum laude, Sorbonne, 1960; hon. degrees; A.M., Harvard U., 1965; M.D., J.E. Purkyne Coll. Medicine, Prague, Czechoslovakia, 1968; D.Sc., Wittenberg U., 1975, Mass. State Coll. at Framingham, 1976; D.B.A., Johnson and Wales Coll., 1976; L.H.D., Northeastern U., 1976, Worcester Poly. Inst., 1977, Western New Eng. Coll., 1977, Starr King Sch. for Ministry, 1977; LL.D., Curry Coll., 1978; m. Elizabeth Van Huysen, Mar. 16, 1942; children—Andre, Laura, John-Paul, Theodore, Pierre. Fellow, Ecole Normale Superieure, Paris, 1939-40; nutrition officer FAO, UN, 1948-49; from asst. prof. to prof. nutrition Harvard U., 1950-76, lectr. history pub. health, 1961-76, mem. Center for Population Studies, 1968-72, 75-77, co-dir., 1975-76, master Dudley House, 1973-76, hon. asso., former master, 1976—; pres. Tufts U., Medford, Mass., 1976—. Spl. cons. to Pres. U.S., 1969-70; chmn. White House Conf. on Food, Nutrition and Health, 1969; chmn. nutrition div. White House Conf. on Aging, 1971—; mem. Pres.'s Consumer Adv. Council, 1970-77; mem., vice chmn. President's Commn. on World Food Problems, 1978—; gen. coordinator U.S. Senate Nat. Nutrition Policy Study, 1974; mem. FAO-WHO Adv. Mission to Ghana, 1959, to Ivory Coast and West Africa, 1960, UNICEF mission to Nigeria-Biafra, 1969; mem. FAO-WHO Joint Expert Com. on Nutrition, 1961—; mem. protein adv. group UN, 1973-75; dir. Priorities on Child Nutrition UNICEF, 1973-75; dir. Monsanto Co. Adv. bd. Sargent Coll. Boston U., 1955-72; mem. subcom. on med. services U.S. Olympic Com., 1966-70; mem. child health adv. com. Hood Found., 1964-69, chmn., 1968-69; mem. bd. inquiry on hunger in U.S., Citizens' Crusade against Poverty, 1967; chmn. Nat. Council on Hunger and Malnutrition in U.S., 1968-69; mem. food and nutrition bd. Nat. Acad. Scis., 1973-76. bd. dirs. Action for Boston Community Devel., 1964-70, Am. Kor-Asian Found., 1976—, French-Am. Found., 1976—, World Affairs Council, 1976—; bd. overseers Shady Hill Sch., Cambridge, Mass., 1965-68; mem. New Eng. Bd. Higher Edn., 1978—. Served to capt. French Army, 1940-45. Decorated Croix de Guerre with two palms, Gold Star and Bronze Star, knight Legion of Honor, Resistance medal, numerous others; recipient Gold medal City of Paris, 1936, Calvert Smith prize Harvard Alumni Assn., 1961, Alvarenga prize Coll. Physicians Phila., 1968, Atwater prize Agrl. Research Adminstrn., 1971; Presdl. citation AAHPER, 1972; Bradford Washburn prize Boston Mus. Sci., 1975; Golden Door award Internat. Inst., 1975; Poiley Gold medal N.Y. Acad. Sci., 1975; Pub. Edn. award Greater Boston chpt. Am. Heart Assn., 1976; gold medal Franklin Inst., 1978; numerous lectureships. Fellow Am. Acad. Arts and Scis. (mem. council 1970-73), AAAS, fgn. mem. French Academie des Sciences; mem. Am. Inst. Nutrition (mem. council 1972-75), Am. Physiol. Soc. (editorial bd. 1960-66), Soc. for Nutrition Edn. (pres. 1974-75), Am. Soc. for Clin. Nutrition, Am. Pub. Health Assn. (chmn. food and nutrition sect. 1972-73), Phi Beta Kappa, Delta Omega, Sigma Xi, Beta Beta Beta. Unitarian (chmn. bd. trustees 1st parish, Sudbury, Mass., moderator 1959-66, vestryman 1970-74, sr. warden King's Chapel, Boston 1974—). Clubs: Harvard, Bay (Boston); Annisquam Yacht (Gloucester, Mass.); University (N.Y.C.). Author: Overweight: Causes, Cost, Control, 1969; Human Nutrition, 1971; A Diet for Living, 1975; Food and Nutrition in Health and Disease, 1977. Editor: U.S. Nutrition Policies in the Seventies 1973; (with W. Aykroyd) Nutrition Terminology, 1973; Health, 1974; also numerous sci. articles. Asso. editor: Nutrition Revs., 1951-54; nutrition editor: Postgrad. Medicine, 1959-71; editorial bd. Am. Jour. Physiology, Jour. Applied Physiology, 1960-65, Family Health, 1969—; Postgrad. Medicine, 1976—; cons. editor: Environ. Research, 1967—, Jour. Nutrition Edn., 1968-70, Geriatrics Digest, 1968—. Syndicated columnist. Home: 161 Packard Ave Pres's House Medford MA 02155 Office: Tufts U Medford MA 02155

MAYER, JOHN ANTON, banker; b. Terre Haute, Ind., July 30, 1909; s. Herman and Antoinette (Brinkman) M.; B.S., U. Pa., 1932, M.B.A., 1933; LL.D, Ind. State U., 1971; m. Effie F. Disston, Oct. 1, 1937; children—John Anton, Christopher, Mark Disston. Asst. sec. Penn Mut. Life Ins. Co., 1936-39, asst. to pres., 1939-47, sec., 1947-49; pres., dir. Reliance Life Ins. Co. of Pitts., 1949-51; v.p. Mellon Nat. Bank & Trust Co. (now Mellon Bank, N.A.), 1951-57, exec. v.p., 1957-59, pres., 1959-67, chief exec. officer, 1963-74, chmn. bd., 1967-74; chmn. bd., chief exec. officer Mellon Nat. Corp., 1972-74; dir. H.J. Heinz Co., Aluminum Co. of Am., Pitts., Gen. Motors Corp., PPG Industries, Inc., Norfolk & Western Ry. Co. Trustee U. Pa.; bd. dirs. Western Pa. Hosp. Served as comdr. USNR, World War II. Decorated Legion of Merit. Mem. Assn. Res. City Bankers (pres. 1963-64, now hon. mem.), Sigma Chi. Episcopalian. Clubs: Links (N.Y.C.); Duquesne, Fox Chapel Golf, Laurel Valley Golf, Pittsburgh Golf (Pitts.); Rolling Rock (Ligonier, Pa.); Gulf Stream Golf (Fla.). Home: RD 4 Ligonier PA 15658 Office: care Mellon Bank NA Mellon Sq Pittsburgh PA 15230

MAYER, JOSEPH E., chem. physicist; b. N.Y.C., Feb. 5, 1904; s. Joseph and Catherine (Proescher) M.; B.S., Calif. Inst. Tech., 1924; Ph.D., U. Calif., 1927; Dr.h.c., U. Libre de Bruselles, 1963; m. Maria Goeppert, Jan. 18, 1930 (dec. 1972); children—Marianne, Peter Conrad; m. 2d, Margaret Griffin, June 20, 1972. Asst. dept. chemistry U. Calif., 1927-28; Internat. Edn. Bd. Research fellow U. Goëttingen Germany, 1929-30; asso. dept. chemistry Johns Hopkins, 1930-35, asso. prof., 1935-39; asso. prof. dept. chemistry Columbia, 1939-45; prof. Inst. of Nuclear Studies and chem. dept. U. Chgo., 1945-55, Carl Eisendraht prof. chemistry, 1955-60; prof. chemistry U. Calif. at La Jolla, 1960—. Cons., Ballistic Research Lab., Aberdeen Proving Ground, Ordinance Dept., U.S. Army, 1942-77; cons. Los Alamos Sci. Lab., Rand Corp. Recipient Gilbert N. Lewis medal Calif. sect. Am. Chem. Soc., 1958, Debye medal, 1967; Charles F. Chandler medal Columbia, 1966; J.G. Kirkwood medal Yale, 1968; James Flack Norris award Am. Chem. Soc., 1969; Distinguished Alumni award Cal. Inst. Tech., 1971. Fellow Am. Phys. Soc. (v.p. 1972, pres. 1973); mem. Am. Acad. Arts and Scis., Am. Chem. Soc., Nat. Acad. Sci. (chmn. class I 1967-68), Internat. Union Pure and Applied Physics (pres. com. thermodynamics 1951-56, v.p. com. on constants), NRC (chmn. div. phys. inorganic chemistry 1954-58), Heidelberg Acad. Sci. (corr. mem.), Am. Philos. Soc., Sigma Xi, Tau Beta Pi, Alpha Chi Sigma, Phi Lambda Upsilon, Gamma Alpha. Author: Statistical Mechanics (with Maria Goeppert Mayer), 1940; Equilibrium Statistical Mechanics, 2d edit., 1977. Editor: (with Smoluchowski and Weyl) Phase Transformation in Solids, 1951. Co-editor-in-chief: Internat. Ency. Phys. Chemistry and Chem. Physics, to 1970; editor Jour. Chem. Physics, 1940-52. Home: 2345 Via Siena La Jolla CA 92037

MAYER, KLAUS, physician; b. Mayence, Germany, May 21, 1924; s. Stephan Karl and Caecilie Matilda (Mueller) M.; came to U.S., 1934; B.S., Queens Coll., 1945; M.D., U. Groningen (Holland), 1950; m. Vera Strasser, May 6, 1950; children—Rulon Richard, Carla Christina. Intern Hosp. St. Raphael, New Haven, 1950-51; resident Meml. Hosp. Cancer and Allied Diseases, N.Y.C., 1952-55; scientist Brookhaven Nat. Lab., 1951-52; mem. staff Meml. Hosp. Cancer and Allied Diseases, 1952—; practice medicine specializing in internal medicine and hematology, N.Y.C., 1956—; attending hematologist, dir. blood bank Hosp. Spl. Surgery, 1957—; dir. blood banks Meml. Hosp. for Cancer and Allied Diseases, 1966—, dir. hematology labs., 1971—, attending physician, 1972—; attending physician N.Y. Hosp., 1979—; prof. clin. medicine Cornell U. Med. Coll., N.Y.C., 1979—; cons. Rockefeller U. Hosp. and Manhattan Eye and Ear Hosp., 1978—; mem. Mayor's Com. Radiation, 1968—; mem. Bd. Examiners Blood Banks N.Y.C., 1971-74; mem., prin. ad hoc com. to create Am. Blood Commn., 1974-75, sec.-treas., 1975-76, chmn. utilization com., 1976—; mem. N.Y. State Council on Human Blood and Transfusion Services, 1976—. Served with AUS, 1943-46. Damon Runyon Cancer Research fellow, 1955-58. Fellow A.C.P., Am. Coll. Nuclear Medicine, Am. Soc. Clin. Pathology; mem. Am. Assn. Blood Banks (pres. 1973-74; Disting. Service award 1976). Research use radioactive isotopes in hematology. Home: 45 Sutton Pl S New York NY 10022 Office: 1275 York Ave New York NY 10021

MAYER, MANFRED MARTIN, biochemist; b. Frankfurt on Main, Germany, June 15, 1916; s. Gustav and Julie (Sommer) M.; B.S., Coll. City N.Y., 1938; Ph.D., Columbia, 1946; Dr. Med. Sci. (hon.), Johannes Gutenberg U., Mainz, Germany, 1969; m. Elinor S. Indenbaum, Dec. 6, 1942; children—Jonathan Marnin, David Michael, Dan Ellis, Matthew Jared. Sci. staff OSRD, Columbia, 1942-45, instr. biochemistry, 1946; asst. prof. bacteriology Sch. Hygiene and Pub. Health, Johns Hopkins, 1946-48, asso. prof. microbiology, 1948-61, prof. microbiology Sch. Medicine, 1961—; cons. USPHS, NSF, U.S. Dept. Agr., Office Naval Research. Recipient Kimble award methodology, 1953; Karl Landsteiner award Am. Assn. Blood Banks, 1974; Albion O. Bernstein award Med. Soc. State N.Y., 1976. Fellow AAAS; mem. Am. Chem. Soc., Am. Assn. Immunologists (councillor 1971, pres. 1976), Soc. Exptl. Biology and Medicine, Internat. Coll. Allergists, Nat. Acad. Sci., Am. Soc. Biol. Chemists, Biochem. Soc., Phi Beta Kappa, Sigma Xi. Author: Experimental Immunochemistry (with Elvin A. Kabat), 1948, rev. edit., 1960; editorial bd. Jour. Immunology. Home: 562 Sudbrook Ln Baltimore MD 21208

MAYER, MARTIN PRAGER, writer; b. N.Y.C., Jan. 14, 1928; s. Henry and Ruby (Prager) M.; A.B., Harvard, 1947; D.Litt. (hon.), Wake Forest U., 1977; m. Ellen Moers, June 23, 1949 (dec. Aug. 1979); children—Thomas, James. Reporter, N.Y. Jour. Commerce, 1947-48; asst. editor Labor and Nation, 1948-49; editor Hillman Periodicals, 1949-51; asso. editor Esquire mag., 1951-54, record critic, 1952-75; freelance writer, 1954—; research dir. study of internat. secondary edn. Twentieth Century Fund, 1965-66. Cons. Am. Council Learned Socs., 1961-63; mem. President's Panel on Ednl. Research and Devel., 1961-66; mem. edn. com. Music Critics Assn., 1978—. Chmn., N.Y.C. Local Sch. Bd., 1962-67; commr. Nat. Commn. on Reform Secondary Edn., 1972-73; bd. visitors Wake Forest U., 1972—; mem. bd. Exodus House, narcotics treatment center, 1965—. Democrat. Jewish. Clubs: Century (N.Y.C.); Gardiner's Bay (Shelter Island, N.Y.). Author: (novel) The Experts, 1955; Wall Street, Men and Money, 2d edit., 1960; Madison Avenue, USA, 1958; (novel) A Voice That Fills the House, 1959; The Schools, 1961; Where, When & Why, Social Studies in American Schools, 1963; The Lawyers, 1967; Emory Buckner, 1968; Diploma, 1968; (with Cornell Capa) New Breed on Wall Street, 1969; Bricks, Mortar and the Performing Arts, 1970; All You Know Is Facts, 1970; The Teachers Strike, 1970; About Television, 1972; The Bankers, 1975; Conflicts of Interest: Broker-Dealer Firms, 1975; Today and Tomorrow in America, 1976; The Builders, 1978; (novel) Trigger Points, 1979; The Fate of the Dollar, 1980; others. Office: care Curtis Brown Ltd 575 Madison Ave New York NY 10022

MAYER, MILTON, newspaperman; b. Chgo., Aug. 24, 1908; s. Morris Samuel and Louise (Gerson) M.; student U. Chgo., 1925-28; Litt.D., Windham Coll., 1973; eminence credential Community Colls. Calif., 1976; m. Bertha Hagedorn Tepper, Sept. 13, 1929 (div. 1945); children—Julie (Mrs. Robert Vognar), Amanda (Mrs. Theodore B. Stinchecum); m. 2d, Jane Stoddard Scully, Aug. 6, 1947; stepchildren—Rock Robert Scully, Richard Spencer Scully. Newspaperman for A.P., Chgo. Evening Post, Chgo. Am., 1928-37; tutor, asst. prof. com. on social thought U. Chgo., 1937-48; acad. dir. Great Books Found., 1948-51, cons., 1951-76; vis. prof. William Penn Coll., 1948-51, Frankfurt (Germany) U., 1951-52, Comenius Theol. Faculty, Prague, Czechoslovakia, 1961-62, U. Paris, 1974, Max Planck Inst., Ger., 1978; prof. English, U. Mass., 1964-73; prof. humanities Windham Coll., 1969—; Regents lectr. U. Calif., 1969; adj. prof. journalism Hampshire Coll., 1976—; Bingham prof. humanities U. Louisville, 1977; vis. tutor Ecole d'Humanité, Switzerland, 1955—; cons. Center for Study Democratic Instns., 1964—; dean faculty Internat. Coll., 1972—; John Woolman resident at Woolman Hill, 1966-72; roving reporter Broadcasting Found. Am., 1979—; lectr., guest preacher U.S. and Europe, 1939—. Recipient George Polk Meml. award, 1955; Benjamin Franklin citation journalism, 1955; Communicator of Year award U. Chgo., 1967; Ralph Atkinson award ACLU, 1979. Jewish; mem. Soc. of Friends. Author: They Thought They Were Free: The Germans, 1933-45, 1955; (with M.J. Adler) The Revolution in Education, 1958; (with others) Humanistic Education and Western Civilization, 1964; What Can A Man Do?, 1964; (with others) The Anatomy of Anti-Communism, 1969; The Art of the Impossible: A Study of the Czech Resistance, 1969; Man v. the State, 1970; If Men Were Angels, 1972; The Nature of the Beast, 1975; also numerous articles. Editor: The Tradition of Freedom, 1958; contbg. editor Ency. Brit., 1960-67; roving editor The Progressive, 1942—. Home: 25995 Junipero Carmel CA 93923

MAYER, MORRIS LEHMAN, educator; b. Demopolis, Ala., Dec. 14, 1925; s. Lehman Morris and Anne (Rochotsh) M.; B.S. in Bus. Adminstrn., U. Ala., 1949; M.S. in Retailing, N.Y. U., 1950; Ph.D. in Bus. Orgn., Ohio State U., 1960; m. Judith Marion Morton, Dec. 22, 1957; children—Susan Morton, Elizabeth Anne. Buyer, Goldblatts Dept. Store, Chgo., 1951-55; mem. faculty U. Ala., 1955—, prof., 1960—, chmn. dept. mktg., 1969-74; instr. Ohio State U., Columbus, 1956-60; cons. Mgmt. Horizons Co., Columbus, 1966—, N.C.R. Co., Dayton, Ohio, 1967—. Served with AUS, 1944-46, 50-51, Ford Found. fellow, 1962-63. Mem. Am., So. (pres.) mktg. assns., Ala. Retail Assn. (mem. bd.), Am. Coll. Retail Assn. (pres.), Beta Gamma Sigma, Eta Mu Pi, Pi Sigma Epsilon, Zeta Beta Tau, Omicron Delta Kappa. Jewish (temple trustee). Co-author: Modern Retailing, 1978. Home: 1321 Montclair Circle Tuscaloosa AL 35404 Office: PO Box 5444 University AL 35486

MAYER, OSCAR G., former meat packing co. exec.; b. Chgo., Mar. 16, 1914; s. Oscar G. and Elsa (Stieglitz) M.; A.B., Cornell, 1934; LL.D. (hon.), U. Wis., 1977; m. Rosalie Harrison, Nov. 21, 1942; children—Oscar Harrison, Donald Lawrence, William Edward. With Oscar Mayer & Co., 1936-77, dir., 1939—, v.p. ops., 1950-53, exec. v.p., 1953-55, pres., 1955-66, chmn. bd., 1966-73, chmn. exec. com., 1973-77; trustee Northwestern Mut. Life Ins. Co.; dir. Wis. Telephone Co. Mem. U. Chgo. Bus. Sch. Council; hon. trustee Com. for Econ. Devel.; bd. dirs. U. Wis. Found., Lyric Opera Chgo. Clubs: Chicago (Chgo.); Madison, Maple Bluff Country (Madison). Home: 722 Wilder Dr Madison WI 53704 Office: One S Pinckney St Suite 713 Madison WI 53703

MAYER, PAUL GUSTAV WILHELM, civil engr.; b. Frankfurt/Main, Ger., Nov. 3, 1923; s. Frederick and Alice Lucia (Waldin) M.; came to U.S., 1947, naturalized, 1952; B.S. in Civil Engring., U. Cin., 1953; M.S., Cornell U., 1955, Ph.D., 1957; m. Virginia Calvert Wagner, July 2, 1955; children—Frederick, Marianne, Laura, Donald. Asst. prof. Cornell U., 1957-59; mem. faculty Ga. Inst. Tech., Atlanta, 1959—, prof. civil engring., 1965—, Regents prof., 1974—. Recipient Outstanding Tchr. award Ga. Inst. Tech., 1970, Outstanding Faculty award, 1973; registered profl. engr., Ga. Mem. ASCE (pres. Ga. sect. 1978), Am. Soc. Engring. Edn., Internat. Assn. Hydraulic Research, Sigma Xi (chpt. pres. 1977).

Author papers, reports in field. Home: 1126 Lullwater Rd NE Atlanta GA 30307 Office: Sch Civil Engring Ga Inst Tech Atlanta GA 30332

MAYER, RAYMOND RICHARD, educator; b. Chgo., Aug. 31, 1924; s. Adam and Mary (Bogdala) M.; B.S., Ill. Inst. Tech., 1948, M.S., 1954, Ph.D., 1957; m. Helen Lakowski, Jan. 30, 1954; children—Mark, John, Mary, Jane. Indsl. engr. Standard Oil Co., Whiting, Ind., 1948-51; orgn. analyst Ford Motor Co., Chgo., 1951-53; instr. Ill. Inst. Tech., Chgo., 1953-56, asso. prof., 1958-60; asst. prof. U. Chgo., 1956-58; Walter F. Mullady prof. bus. adminstrn. Loyola U., Chgo., 1960—. Served with USNR, 1944-46. Ingersoll Found. fellow, 1955-56, Machinery and Allied Products Inst. fellow, 1954-55, Ford Found. fellow, 1962. Mem. Acad. Mgmt., Am. Econ. Assn., Am. Statis. Assn., Am. Inst. for Decision Scis., Nat. Assn. Purchasing Mgmt., Polish Inst. Arts and Scis. in Am., Alpha Iota Delta, Alpha Kappa Psi, Beta Gamma Sigma. Author: Financial Analysis of Investment Alternatives, 1966; Production Management, 1962, rev. edit., 1968; Production and Operations Management, 1975; Capital Expenditure Analysis, 1978. Home: 1705 Ridge Ave Evanston IL 60201 Office: 820 N Michigan Ave Chicago IL 60611

MAYER, RICHARD DEAN, educator; b. Ft. Wayne, Ind., May 26, 1930; s. Lester Blyle and Velma Lucille (Maulsby) M.; B.S., Purdue U., 1952, M.S., 1954; Ph.D., U. Wash., 1959; m. Patsy Jean Hartwell, Aug. 31, 1952; children—Susan, Joann, John. Teaching asst. Purdue U., 1952-54, U. Wash., 1954-59; research engr. Boeing Airplane Co., Seattle, summer 1959; asst. prof. math. Idaho State U., 1959-61, asso. prof. math., chmn. dept., 1961-67; research engr. Carter Oil Co., Billings, Mont., summer 1960; chmn. dept., prof. math. State U. N.Y. at Oswego, 1967—. Mem. Am. Assn. U. Profs., Math. Assn. Am., Am. Math. Soc., Sigma Xi, Sigma Pi Sigma, Delta Rho Kappa, Pi Mu Epsilon, Kappa Mu Epsilon. Home: RD 3 Edwards Circle Oswego NY 13126

MAYER, RICHARD HENRY, publisher; b. Johnstown, Pa., Jan. 27, 1930; s. W. Stephens and Hilda (Ellis) M.; B.S. in Fin., Lehigh U., 1956; m. Constance Imhoff, Dec. 13, 1975; children—Pamela J., Debra A.; step-children—David J. Hantke, Michael K. Hantke. With Johnstown Tribune Pub. Co., 1956—, pub., 1963—, pres., 1974—; dir. U.S. Nat. Bank, WJAC Inc., Winston Corp. (all Johnstown). Chmn., Community Chest Johnstown, 1975; sec. Conemaugh Valley Meml. Hosp., Johnstown; chmn. Floor Recovery Coordinating Com., Johnstown, 1977. Served with U.S. Army, 1952-54. Named Outstanding Young Man, Jaycees, 1963 and recipient other honors in connection with Johnstown flood. Mem. Pa. Newspaper Pubs. Assn. (pres. 1976), Am. Newspaper Pubs. Assn., Johnstown C. of C. (pres. 1968), Sigma Delta Chi. Office: 425 Locust St Johnstown PA 15901

MAYER, ROBERT ANTHONY, mgmt. cons.; b. N.Y.C., Oct. 30, 1933; s. Ernest John and Theresa Margaret (Mazura) M.; B.A. magna cum laude, Fairleigh Dickinson U., 1955; M.A., N.Y. U., 1967; m. Laura Wiley Christ, Apr. 30, 1960. With N.J. Bank and Trust Co., Paterson, 1955-61, mgr. advt. dept., 1959-61; program supr. advt. dept. Mobil Oil Co., N.Y.C., 1961-62; asst. to dir. Latin Am. program Ford Found., N.Y.C., 1962-65, asst. rep. for Brazil, 1965-67, asst. to v.p. adminstrn., 1967-73, officer in charge logistical services, 1968-73; asst. dir. programs N.Y. Community Trust, N.Y.C., 1973-76; exec. dir. N.Y. State Council on the Arts, N.Y.C., 1976-79; mgmt. cons., N.Y.C., 1979—. Mem. state programs adv. panel Nat. Endowment Arts, 1977—; mem. Mayor's Com. on Cultural Policy, N.Y.C., 1974-75; mem. pres.'s adv. com. Bklyn. campus L.I. U., 1978-79; bd. dirs. Fedn. Protestant Welfare Agys., N.Y.C., 1977-79; mem. dean's adv. com. Grad. Sch. Social Welfare, Fordham U., 1976. Served with U.S. Army, 1956-58. Recipient Nat. award on advocacy for girls Girls Clubs Am., 1976. Mem. Nat. Assembly of State Arts Agys. (bd. dirs. 1977-79, 1st vice chmn. 1978-79). Mem. editorial adv. bd. Grants mag., 1978—. Author: (plays) La Borgia, 1971; Alijandru, 1971; They'll Grow No Roses, 1975. Address: 50 W 69th St New York NY 10023

MAYER, ROBERT GEORGE, banker; b. N.Y.C., Dec. 17, 1917; s. Albert B. and Katherine (Monak) M.; B.S., Rutgers U., 1957; certificate Stanford, 1968; m. Shirley S. Smith, June 25, 1942 (dec.); children—Robert Grosvenor, Jane Ridgeley; m. 2d, June Driscoll, Mar. 30, 1973. With bond dept. Bankers Trust Co., 1936-37, trust dept. Guaranty Trust Co., 1938-41; with internat. banking dept. Chase Nat. Bank, N.Y.C., 1945-46; sr. v.p. exec. adminstrn. Bank of Am., N.Y.C., 1947-74; exec. v.p. Bank of Calif. Internat., N.Y.C., 1975—; v.p., gen. mgr. M and T Bank, N.Y.C., 1976-78; sr. v.p. Internat. L.I. Trust Co., N.Y.C. Served to maj. Ordnance Dept., AUS, 1941-45. Decorated Army Commendation medal, Star of Solidarity (Italy). Mem. Am. Mgmt. Assn., Bankers Assn. for Fgn. Trade, Com. on Internat. Banking, Rutgers U., Stanford alumni assns. Home: 7 Ferndale Rd Chatham Township NJ 07928 Office: 665 Fifth Ave New York NY 10022

MAYER, ROBERT WALLACE, educator; b. Mt. Pulaski, Ill., Apr. 17, 1909; s. Edward Otto and Minnie Laura (Clark) M.; B.S., U. Ill., 1930, M.S., 1931, Ph.D., 1933; m. Nella Coryell DeAtley, Aug. 2, 1933; children—Nancy (Mrs. Donald G. Wyatt), Anne (Mrs. Robert M. Shannon), Caroline (Mrs. Chester R. Keller), Melinda. Statistician, Libby McNeill & Libby, Chgo., 1929, Commonwealth Edison Co., Chgo., 1930; from instr. to asst. prof. Lehigh U., 1933-42; sr. economist WPB, Washington, 1942-45; asso. prof. econs. U. Ill., Urbana, 1945-52, prof., 1952-57, prof. finance, 1957-77, prof. emeritus, 1977—, vice chmn. dept. econs., 1953-57; vis. prof. fin. Ill. State U., Normal, 1978-79. Exec. sec. Combined (Brit.-Am.) Steel Com., 1943-45; cons. Rand Corp., 1951-53. Cert. ofcl. U.S. Track and Field Fedn. Mem. Am., Midwest (pres. 1967-68) finance assns., Am. Econ. Assn., Chgo. Fin. Writers Assn., SAR, U. Ill. Varsity Assn. (hon.), Beta Gamma Sigma, Phi Kappa Phi, Alpha Kappa Psi, Tau Kappa Epsilon. Republican. Presbyn. Kiwanian (pres. 1969-70). Contbr. articles to profl. jours. Home: 17 Greencroft Dr Champaign IL 61820 Office: U Ill Urbana IL 61801

MAYER, STEVEN EDWARD MAX, pharmacologist; b. Frankfurt, Germany, Feb. 11, 1929; s. Ernest Bernhard and Irmgard (Kaufman) M.; came to U.S., 1938, naturalized, 1942; B.A., U. Chgo., 1947, B.S., 1950, postgrad., 1950-52; M.S., U. Ill., 1953, Ph.D., 1954; m. Jean Needelman, June 17, 1951; children—Stephanie Susan, Alex Simon. Asst. scientist NIH, USPHS, Bethesda, Md., 1954-56; postdoctoral fellow dept. pharmacology Washington U., St. Louis, 1956-57; asst. prof. pharmacology Emory U., Atlanta, 1957-62, asso. prof., 1962-66, prof., 1966-69; prof. medicine U. Calif., San Diego, 1969—. Recipient Career Devel. award USPHS-NIH, 1957-67; Josiah Macy Found. faculty scholar, 1976; Nat. Heart Inst. grantee, 1959—. Fellow AAAS; mem. Am. Physiol. Soc., Am. Soc. Biol. Chemists, Am. Soc. Pharmacology and Exptl. Therapeutics (John J. Abel award 1963, pres. 1977-78), Fedn. Am. Scientists, Sigma Xi. Democrat. Jewish. Contbr. numerous articles to profl. jours.; asso. editor Jour. Pharmacology and Exptl. Therapeutics, 1961-64; asso. editor: Pharmacol. Basis Therapeutics (Goodman and Gilman), 1978—; editor Molecular Pharmacology, 1971-74. Office: Dept Medicine M-013 U Calif At San Diego La Jolla CA 92093

MAYER, WILLIAM DIXON, physician, educator; b. Beaver Falls, Pa., Oct. 5, 1928; s. Emil Leroy and Elizabeth (Townsend) M.; A.B., Colgate U., 1951; M.D. with honor, U. Rochester, 1957; m. Ann Woolsey Trainer, June 10, 1953; children—Elizabeth Ann, David Dixon, William Dixon. Intern, then resident pathology Strong Meml. Hosp., Rochester, N.Y., 1957-61; instr., mem. faculty U. Mo. Sch. Medicine, 1961-76, dir. Univ. Med. Center, 1967-74, dean Sch. Medicine, 1967-74, prof. pathology, 1967-76; asst. chief med. dir. for acad. affairs VA, Washington, 1976-79; pres. Eastern Va. Med. Authority, Norfolk, Va., 1979—; asso. dir. div. regional med. programs NIH, 1966-67. Served with USMC, 1946-48. Markle scholar acad. medicine, 1962-67. Fellow Coll. Am. Pathologists; mem. AMA, Assn. Am. Med. Colls. (Disting. Service mem.), Sigma Xi, Alpha Omega Alpha. Episcopalian. Home: 945 Winwood Dr Virginia Beach VA 23451

MAYERS, DAVID, metal mfg. co. exec.; b. N.Y.C., May 2, 1913; s. David and Elizabeth (Kupferer) M.; B.S., Newark Coll. Engring., 1936; m. Katherine Teed, Oct. 12, 1934; children—David, William, Judith, Thomas. Pres., Intalco Aluminum Corp., 1964-67; pres. Hunter Engring. Co., 1966-68; group v.p. Amax Aluminum Co., Riverside, Calif., 1967-68; v.p. Am. Metal Climax, Inc., N.Y.C., 1968-71; pres. AMAX Pacific Aluminum Co., San Mateo, Calif., 1971-72, AMAX Aluminum Co., Inc., San Mateo, 1972-74; pres., chief exec. officer Alumax, Inc., San Mateo, 1974—, also dir. Mem. Am. Inst. Mining Engrs., Aluminum Assn. (dir.). Clubs: Peninsula Country, Coyote Point Yacht, San Mateo, Club de Cazadores La Grulla. Office: 400 S El Camino Real San Mateo CA 94402*

MAYERS, EUGENE DAVID, educator, philosopher; b. N.Y.C., July 30, 1915; s. Sylvester and Estelle (Weinstein) M.; A.B., Yale, 1936, LL.B., 1940; Ph.D., Columbia, 1956; m. Odette Marguerite Julia Gilchriest, Dec. 30, 1950; children—David Allan, Marilyn Anne, Judith Odette, Peter Michael. Admitted to N.Y. State bar, 1941; with Nat. Bur. Econ. Research, N.Y.C., 1941, Office Gen. Counsel, Navy Dept., 1946; mem. faculty Carleton Coll., Northfield, Minn., 1950-61, Columbia, 1959-60, Mills Coll., Oakland, Calif., 1961-63; mem. faculty Calif. State U., Hayward, 1963—, prof. philosophy, 1963—. Served to capt. AUS, 1941-46, 51-52. Fellow Soc. Values in Higher Edn.; mem. Am. Philos. Assn. (chmn. conf. dept. chmn. Pacific div. 1973-75, chmn. exec. com. Pacific div. 1978—), Am. Soc. Polit. and Legal Philosophy, Pacific Coast Theol. Soc., Internat. Assn. Philosophy Law and Social Philosophy, A.A.U.P., Am. Acad. Religion. Democrat. Author: Some Modern Theories of Natural Law, 1957. Contbr. articles to profl. jours. Home: 3191 Frye St Oakland CA 94602 Office: Calif State Univ 25800 Hillary St Hayward CA 94542

MAYERS, JEAN, educator; b. N.Y.C., June 8, 1920; s. Lou and Ida (Edrich) M.; B.Aero. Engring., Poly. Inst. Bklyn., 1942, M.Aero. Engring., 1948; m. Reva Lee Bookbinder, May 20, 1945; children—Eileen, Laurence. Research asst. aero. engring. Poly. Inst. Bklyn., 1946-48; aero. research scientist, structures research div. NACA, Langley Field, Va., 1948-56; successively prin. engr., engring. sec. head, engring. dept. head Sperry Utah Co. div. Sperry Rand Corp., 1956-61; vis. asso. prof. Stanford, 1961-63, mem. faculty, 1963—, prof. aero. engring., 1967—, vice chmn. dept. aero. and astronautics, 1966-71; vis. prof. Technion-Israel Inst. Tech., Haifa, 1970; Naval Air Systems Command Research prof. U.S. Naval Acad., 1978-79. Sci. adviser U.S. Army, 1962-74; cons. to govt. and industry, 1962—; mem. ad hoc vis. com. on aero. engring. curricula Engrs. Council for Profl. Devel., 1969-70. Served to lt. comdr. USNR, 1942-46. Recipient U.S. Army Outstanding Civilian Service medal, 1972. Asso. fellow Am. Inst. Aero. and Astronautics (asso. editor jour. 1967-70); mem. Aircraft Owners and Pilots Assn., Naval Res. Assn., Am. Soc. Engring. Edn., Sigma XI. Author articles, reports in field. Home: 830 Tolman Dr Stanford CA 94305 Office: Dept Aero and Astronautics Stanford U Stanford CA 94305

MAYERS, ROY ELLIOT, publishing co. exec.; b. N.Y.C., Oct. 26, 1943; s. Bernard Herman and Doris (Roey) M.; B.B.A., City Coll. N.Y., 1966, M.B.A., 1970; m. Nancy Jane Keusch, June 28, 1969; children—Beth Michele, Aaron Eli. With Globe Book Co., N.Y.C., 1962-75, exec. v.p., 1972-75; pres. Modern Curriculum Press, Inc., Cleve., 1975—; guest lectr. U. Nev., C.W. Post Coll. of L.I. U. Mem. Internat. Reading Assn., Nat., Nat. Cath. edn. assns., Strongsville (Ohio) C. of C. Office: 13900 Prospect Rd Cleveland OH 44136

MAYERSON, PHILIP, educator; b. N.Y.C., May 20, 1918; s. Theodore and Clara (Fader) M.; A.B., N.Y. U., 1947; Ph.D., N.Y. U., 1956; m. Joy Gottesman Ungerleider, Nov. 25, 1976; children—Miriam Mayerson, Clare Mayerson, Peter Ungerleider, Steven Ungerleider, Jeanne Ungerleider, Andrew Ungerleider. With Puritan Fed. Clothing Stores, N.Y.C., 1935-42; instr. N.Y. U., N.Y.C., 1948-56, asst. prof., 1956-60, asso. prof., 1960-66, prof. classics, 1966—, vice dean, 1969-71, acting dean, 1971-73, dean Washington Sq. and U. Coll. of Arts and Sci., 1973-78. Served with USN, 1942-45. Rockefeller Found. grantee, 1956-57; Am. Council of Learned Socs. fellow, 1961-62. Mem. Am. Philological Assn., Am. Research Center of Egypt, Am. Schs. of Oriental Research. Author: The Ancient Agricultural Regime of Nessana and the Central Negeb, 1961; Classical Mythology in Literature, Art and Music, 1971; contbr. articles in field to profl. jours. Home: 4 Oak Ln Larchmont NY 10538 Office: 100 Washington Sq E New York NY 10003

MAYES, CHARLES RAY, educator; b. Warrensburg, Mo., Feb. 8, 1922; s. William Ray and Chloe Racine (Miller) M.; B.S. in Edn., Central Mo. State U., 1942; M.A., U. Md., 1948; postgrad. U. Paris, 1948-49; Fulbright scholar, U. London, 1951-52; Ph.D., U. Minn., 1955. Instr. social studies Wentworth Mil. Acad., Lexington, Mo., 1945-47; instr. history U. Ky., 1952-53; from instr. to asso. prof. history Ohio U., Athens, 1953-64; prof. history Monmouth Coll., West Long Branch, N.J., 1964—, chmn. dept. history and govt., 1964-76. Internat. councillor Phi Alpha Theta, 1969-72; mem. adv. bd. Phi Alpha Theta, 1972-74. Served to 2d lt. USAAF, 1942-45. Decorated Air medal, Purple Heart. Mem. Am. Assn. U. Profs. (pres. Monmouth Coll. chpt. 1965-66), Am. Hist. Assn., Conf. Brit. Studies, Can. Studies Conf. of N.J., Phi Kappa Tau, Phi Alpha Theta, Kappa Delta Pi. Democrat. Mem. Ch. of the Brethren. Bd. editors Ohio U. Rev., 1959-64. Contbr. articles to profl. jours. Home: 16 Clarence Ave Long Branch NJ 07740 Office: Dept History Monmouth Coll West Long Branch NJ 07764

MAYES, HERBERT RAYMOND, editor, publisher; b. N.Y.C., Aug. 11, 1900; s. Herman and Matilda (Hutter) M.; m. Grace Taub, Dec. 6, 1930; children—Victoria, Alexandra. Editor, The Inland Merchant, mag., 1920-24; editor bus. paper div. Western Newspaper Union, 1924-26; editor Am. Druggist, mag., 1926-34; editor Pictorial Rev., 1934-37; mng. editor Good Housekeeping, 1937-38, editor, 1938-58; editor McCall's, 1959-62; pres. McCall Corp., 1961-65; cons. Norton Simon, Inc., 1966—. Recipient Editor of Year award Mag. Editors Council, 1960, Distinguished Achievement award, field of periodicals U. So. Calif., 1960, N.Y. Art Dirs. Club medal, 1960, and others. Clubs: Book Table, Illustrators Soc., Dutch Treat. Author: Alger, A Biography Without a Hero, 1928; Editor's Choice, 1956; An Editor's Treasury, 1968. Home: 910 Fifth Ave New York NY 10021

MAYES, PAUL EUGENE, elec. engr.; b. Frederick, Okla., Dec. 21, 1928; s. Robert Franklin and Bertha Ellen (Walter) M.; B.S.E.E., U. Okla., 1950; M.S.E.E., Northwestern U., 1952, Ph.D., 1955; m. Lola Mae Davis, June 4, 1950; children—Gwynne Ellen, Linda Kay, Stuart Franklin, Patricia Gail, Steven Lee, David Thomas. Grad. Asst. Northwestern U., 1950-52, research asso., 1952-54; asst. prof. elec. engring. U. Ill., Urbana, 1954-58, asso. prof., 1958-63, prof., 1963—; cons. in field. Pres., Champaign-Urbana Youth Hockey Assn., 1967-68. Recipient certificate achievement Group on Antennas and Propagation, 1968, 69. Fellow IEEE; mem. Internat. Union Radio Scientists, Sigma Xi, Tau Beta Pi, Eta Kappa Nu. Methodist. Patentee various antennas. Home: 1508 Waverly Dr Champaign IL 61820 Office: 155 Elec Engring Bldg U Ill Urbana IL 61801

MAYES, WENDELL WISE, JR., broadcasting co. exec.; b. San Antonio, Mar. 2, 1924; s. Wendell Wise and Dorothy Lydia (Evans) M.; student Schreiner Inst., 1941-42, U. Tex. at Austin, 1942, Daniel Baker Coll., 1946; B.S., Tex. Tech. Coll., 1949; m. Mary Jane King, May 11, 1946; children—Cathey Mayes Rollins, Sarah Mayes Yost, Wendell Wise, III. Program dir., sta. mgr. Sta. KBWD, Brownwood, Tex., 1949-57; mgr. Sta. KCRS, Midland, Tex., 1957-63, pres., 1965—; pres. Sta. KNOW, Austin, Tex., 1970—, Stas. KVIC and KCWM, Victoria, Tex., 1970—, Sta. KWMJ, Midland, Tex., 1976—, Sta. KCSW, San Marcos, Tex., 1976—; dir. Capital Nat. Bank, Austin; lectr. Coll. Communications, U. Tex., Austin, 1978—. Chmn. bd. Am. Diabetes Assn., 1974-77, now mem. Nat. Diabetes Adv. Bd.; pres. Tex. Broadcast Edn. Found., 1973-76. Served with USNR, 1943-46. Recipient Addison B. Scoville award Am. Diabetes Assn., 1977; named to Tex. Tech. Mass Communications Hall Fame, 1978. Mem. Tex. Assn. Broadcasters (pres. 1964 named Pioneer Broadcaster of Year 1978), Nat. Assn. Broadcasters (dir. 1969-72), Am. Council on Edn. in Journalism (dir. 1977—), Broadcast Edn. Assn. (dir. 1973-77). Episcopalian. Home: 1510 W 24th St Austin TX 78703 Office: PO Box 2197 Austin TX 78768

MAYFIELD, CHARLES HERBERT, banker; b. Oilton, Okla., Jan. 14, 1924; s. Harmon Dodson and Bertha Odell (Smith) M.; student U. Southwestern La., 1944-45; B.B.A., Tulane U., 1947; certificate La. State U. Sch. Banking of South, 1952; m. Mary Ellin Voizin, Sept. 20, 1947; children—Charles David, Martha Ann. Sr. v.p. First Nat. Bank of Commerce, New Orleans. Chief Naval Ops. Res. Affairs Adv. Bd.; vice chmn. mil. affairs com. City of New Orleans. Served with USN, World War II; rear adm. USNR. Fellow Nat. Inst. Credit; mem. La. Bankers' Assn., Am. Inst. Banking, Tulane Assn. Bus. Alumni, New Orleans C. of C., Naval Res. Assn., Res. Officers' Assn., Navy League Council New Orleans, Supply Corps Assn. Greater New Orleans, U.S. Naval Inst., Navy Supply Corps Assn. and Found., Info. Council Ams., Internat. House, Kappa Alpha. Home: 4767 Franklin Ave New Orleans LA 70122 Office: 210 Baronne St New Orleans LA 70130

MAYFIELD, CURTIS LEE, musician; b. Chgo., June 3, 1942; s. Kenneth and Marion (Washington) M.; children—Tracy, Curtis, Todd, Sharon, Tymphani, Kirk. Performer with group Impressions, 1958-70; solo albums include Curtis, 1970, Curtis Live, Roots, 1971, Back to the World, 1973, Sweet Exorcist, 1974, America Today, 1975; Never Say You Can't Survive, 1977, Do It; composer, arranger, performer soundtrack, also actor film Super Fly, 1972; now rec. artist, producer, songwriter; co-pres. Curtom Records Inc.

MAYFIELD, DEMMIE GAMMON, psychiatrist; b. Kerrville, Tex., June 27, 1932; s. Greydon Strickland and Julie Charlotte (Wilzin) M.; B.A., U. Tex., Austin, 1954; M.D., U. Tex., Galveston, 1958; M.A. ad eundem, Brown U., 1976. Intern, So. Pacific Gen. Hosp., San Francisco, 1958-59; resident in psychiatry U. Tex. Med. Br., Galveston, 1959-62; sr. psychiatrist Clin. Neuropharmacology Research Center, NIMH, St. Elizabeth's Hosp., Washington, 1962-64; asso. prof. psychiatry Duke U. Med. Sch., Durham, N.C., 1964-73; asso. chief of staff for research Providence VA Med. Center, 1974-76, chief mental health services, 1973—; prof. psychiatry Brown U. Program in Medicine, Providence, 1973—; cons. staff Butler Hosp., Roger Williams Hosp., Providence. Bd. dirs. Durham Council on Alcoholism, 1965-73, Hope Council on Alcoholism, 1973-75. Served with USPHS, 1962-64. Diplomate Am. Bd. Psychiatry and Neurology. Fellow Am. Psychiat. Assn., Am. Coll. Clin. Pharmacology; mem. Soc. Biol. Psychiatry, Am. Soc. Clin. Pharmacology and Therapeutics, Am. Coll. Psychiatrists, Sigma Xi. Presbyterian. Contbr. articles in field to profl. jours. Office: VA Medical Center 4801 Linwood Blvd Kansas City MO 64128

MAYFIELD, GENE, food co. exec., lawyer; b. Billings, Mo., May 1, 1915; s. Waldo Clarence and Nellie (Nagle) M.; LL.B., U. Mo., 1938; m. Winifred Neill Horner, July 1, 1941; children—Douglas Eugene, Allan Horner. Admitted to Mo. bar, 1938; with firm Bartley & Mayfield, St. Louis 1938-42; with Pet Milk Co., St. Louis, 1946—, asst. sec., 1952—, gen. counsel, 1956—, v.p., 1966—. Active local Boy Scouts Am., Community Chest. Served to lt. USNR, 1942-45. Mem. Am., Mo., St. Louis bar assns., N.A.M., U.S. C. of C., Beta Theta Pi. Presbyterian. Home: 2 Maryhill Dr St Louis MO 63124 Office: PO Box 392 St Louis MO 63166

MAYFIELD, RICHARD HEVERIN, lawyer; b. Washington, Sept. 29, 1921; s. Robert Edwin and Helen May (Benton) M.; A.B., Swarthmore Coll., 1943; LL.B., Harvard U., 1948; m. Caroline C. Mayfield; children—Elinor D., Nancy L., Anne W. Admitted to D.C. bar, Md. bar; asso. firm McKenney, Flannery & Craighill (name later changed to Craighill, Mayfield & McCally), Washington, 1948-54, partner, 1954—. Bd. govs. Beauvoir Sch., 1961-67, chmn., 1967. Served with AUS, 1943-46. Fellow Am. Coll. Probate Counsel; mem. Washington Estate Planning Council, D.C. Bar Assn. (chmn. sect. young lawyers 1955-56), Barrister Club (sec. 1959), Lawyers Club. Rotarian, Mason (Shriner). Clubs: Columbia Country, Farmington Country. Editor: Will Forms and Clauses, 1969; Trust Forms and Clauses, 1975. Home: 5 E Kirke St Chevy Chase MD 20015 Office: 725 15th St NW Washington DC 20005

MAYFIELD, THOMAS BRIENT, III, dairy co. exec.; b. Athens, Tenn., Nov. 11, 1919; s. Thomas Brient and Goldie (Denton) M.; student U. Tenn. Coll. Agr., 1937-40; m. Alma Bolton, Dec. 4, 1945 (dec. Aug. 1969); children—Thomas Brient IV, Robert Bolton, Evelyn Anne, David Earl; m. 2d, Regenia Lawson Davis, May 31, 1970; 1 stepson, William M. Davis. Partner, Mayfield's Creamery, 1950-57; sec.-treas. Mayfield Realty Co., Inc., 1955—; pres., gen. mgr. Mayfield Dairy Farms, Inc., Athens, 1957—; pres. Dixie Dairy Products Assn., Inc., Tuscaloosa, Ala., 1959-60; dir. First Nat. Bank, Athens. Bd. dirs. Milk Industry Found., 1973—. Served to lt. USNR, 1942-45. Mem. Tenn. Dairy Products Assn. (past pres.), So. Assn. Ice Cream Mfrs. (pres., 1952, 76), Internat. Assn. Ice Cream Mfrs. (v.p. 1960-62, dir.; pres. 1962-64), U. Tenn. Alumni Assn. (bd. govs. 1968-69), Coll. Agr. Alumni (past pres.), Athens C. of C. (past pres.), Def. Orientation Conf. Assn., Phi Gamma Delta. Kiwanian. Home: Mayfield Farms Madisonville Rd Athens TN 37303 Office: Mayfield Dairy Farms Inc 813 Madison Ave PO Box 310 Athens TN 37303

MAYHER, LAURENCE THOMPSON, mgmt. cons.; b. Easthampton, Mass., Feb. 17, 1910; s. Philip and Katharine (Thompson) M.; A.B., Amherst Coll., 1930; m. Matilda Lawrence Dunham, Jan. 25, 1947; children—Madeleine C. Mayher, Eleanor J.

(Mrs. Thomas P. Hackett), Margaret E. (Mrs. Robert W. Ramsdell, Jr.), Philip L., Katharine D. (Mrs. Thomas P. Kane), Gretchen. Salesman, sales supr. Socony-Vacum Oil Co., Inc. 1930-38; asso. Robert Heller & Assos., Inc., 1939-50, v.p., 1950-58, sr. v.p., 1958-63, dir., 1954-63; pres. Robert Heller Assos., Inc., 1963-68, dir., 1963-69; mgmt. cons., 1968—; exec. dir. Commn. on Pub. Sch. Personnel Policies in Ohio, 1970-73. Exec. dir. Citizens' Council for Ohio Schs., 1974-78. Mem. Shaker Heights Bd. Edn., 1954-61, pres., 1957-60. Trustee Cleve. Inst. Music, Cleve. Inter-Faith Housing Corp.; former trustee Greater Cleve. Neighborhood Centers Assn. Mem. Newcomen Soc., Alpha Delta Phi, Delta Sigma Rho. Episcopalian. Clubs: City, Union (Cleve.). Home: 2655 Haddam Rd Cleveland OH 44120

MAYHEW, DAVID RAYMOND, educator; b. Putnam, Conn., May 18, 1937; s. Raymond William and Jeanie (Nicholson) M.; B.A., Amherst Coll., 1958; Ph.D. (Delancey K. Jay dissertation prize 1964), Harvard U., 1964. Teaching fellow Harvard U., 1961-63; instr., then asst. prof. polit. sci. U. Mass., Amherst, 1963-67; vis. asst. prof. Amherst Coll., 1965-66; mem. faculty Yale U., 1968—, prof. polit. sci., 1977—, chmn. dept., 1979—. Woodrow Wilson fellow, 1958-59; vis. fellow Nuffield Coll., Oxford, 1978; Guggenheim fellow, 1978-79; Hoover nat. fellow, 1978-79. Mem. Am. (nat. council 1976-78, Congl. fellow 1967-68), So., New Eng. polit. sci. assns. Author: Party Loyalty Among Congressmen, 1966; Congress: The Electoral Connection (Washington Monthly ann. polit. book award 1974), 1974. Editorial bd. Polity. Home: 3238 Yale Station New Haven CT 06520 Office: Polit Sci Dept Yale Univ New Haven CT 06520

MAYHEW, KENNETH EDWIN, JR., transp. co. exec.; b. Shelby, N.C., Sept. 27, 1934; s. Kenneth Edwin and Evelyn Lee (Dellinger) M.; A.B., Duke, 1956; m. Frances Elaine Craft, Apr. 7, 1957; 1 dau., Catherine Lynn. Sr. auditor Arthur Andersen & Co., Atlanta, 1956-58, 60-63; controller Trendline, Inc., Hickory, N.C., 1963-66; with Carolina Freight Carriers Corp., Cherryville, 1966—, treas., 1969—, v.p., 1971-72, exec. v.p., 1972—, also dir.; pres., dir. Robo Auto Wash, Shelby, Inc., 1967-73, Robo Auto Wash Cherryville, Inc., 1968-73; dir. Cherryville Nat. Bank. Served with AUS, 1958-60. C.P.A., N.C., Ga. Mem. Am. Inst. C.P.A.'s, Nat. Assn. Accountants, Nat. Accounting and Finance Council, Am. Trucking Assn., Phi Beta Kappa, Omicron Delta Kappa, Phi Eta Sigma. Methodist. Lion (pres. Cherryville 1972-73). Home: 507 Spring St Cherryville NC 28021 Office: Highway 150 E Cherryville NC 28021

MAYHEW, LAWRENCE LEE, electronics co. exec.; b. Santa Paula, Calif., Mar. 17, 1933; s. Paul Donald and Lucille Francis M.; B.S.E.L., Calif. State Poly. U., 1961; m. Kathleen Joan McCown, Feb. 6, 1955; children—Taryn Lee, Jeffrey Park, Kimberly Anne. With Tektronix Inc., Beaverton, Oreg., 1961—, ops. mgr. Tektronix Holland, 1965-69, internat. mfg. mgr., Holland, 1969-70, div. mgr., 1970-73, v.p., 1973-76, group v.p., 1976—. Bd. dirs. Oreg. Museum Sci. and Industry, Portland. Served to lt. USNR, 1953-58. Mem. IEEE (sr.), Am. Electronics Assn. (dir.), Computer and Bus. Equipment Mfrs. Assn. (dir.). Republican. Office: Tektronix PO Box 500 Beaverton OR 97077

MAYHEW, LEON HINCKLEY, educator; b. Ogden, Utah, May 15, 1935; s. Wayne Elijah and Vera Lenore (Hinckley) M.; B.A., U. Calif. at Berkeley, 1956; M.A., Harvard, 1960, Ph.D., 1964; m. Janet Ellsworth, June 15, 1956; children—Deborah Lee, Jonathan Ellsworth, Stewart James. Instr., then asso. prof. U. Mich., 1962-68; prof., chmn. dept. sociology U. Calif. at Davis, 1969-75, vice chancellor acad. affairs U. Calif. at Davis, 1975—; vis. prof. U. Calif.; Berkeley, 1969. Served to lt. (j.g.) USNR, 1956-58. Recipient Distinguished Service award U. Mich., 1967. Mem. Am. Sociol. Assn. Author: Law and Equal Opportunity, 1968; Society, 1971. Co-editor: Social Problems; Am. Sociol. Rev., 1967-70; editor: Am. Sociologist, 1973-75. Office: Office Acad Affairs Univ California Davis CA 95616

MAYHEW, LEWIS BALTZELL, educator; b. Pontiac, Ill., Dec. 18, 1917; s. Herman and Edna (Baltzell) M.; B.S., U. Ill., 1938, M.S., 1947; Ph.D., Mich. State U., LL.D. Loyola U., Chgo., 1970; m. Dorothy Cord, June 6, 1939; children—Lewis Baltzell, Madeline, Robert Milton. From instr. to prof. evaluation and social sci. Mich. State U., 1947-59; prof. social sci., dir. Office Research and Planning, U. S.Fla., 1960-62; prof. higher edn. Stanford, 1962—; dir. research Stephen's Coll., 1957-71. Cons., Coll. Entrance Exam. Bd. 1962-70; dir. study future higher edn. Acad. Ednl. Devel.; mem. U.S. Office Edn. Commn. Grad. Studies. Bd. visitors Def. Intelligence Sch.; trustee Golden Gate U., to 1979, New Coll. Calif., to 1976; mem. bd. scholars Higher Edn. Research Inst., 1974—. Served to maj. AUS, 1940-46; ETO. Decorated Medal of Merit. Mem. Am. Assn. Higher Edn. (pres. 1967), AAUP, Nat. Soc. Study Edn. Author: The Smaller Liberal Arts College, 1962; American Higher Education: Contemporary College Students and the Curriculum, 1969; Colleges Today and Tomorrow, 1969; Graduate and Professional Education 1980, 1970; Arrogance on Campus, 1970; The Literature of Higher Education, 1971; Changing Education for the Professions, 1971; Reform in Graduate Education, 1972; The Time is Now, 1972; The Literature of Higher Education-1972, 1972; The Carnegie Commission on Higher Education, 1973; Occupations in Higher Education, 1974; Educational Leaderships—Declining Enrollments, 1974; (with Patrick J. Ford) Reform in Graduate and Professional Education, 1974; (with Paul L. Dressel) Higher Education as a Field of Study; How Colleges Change, 1976; Legacy of the Seventies, 1977; Surviving the Eighties, 1979; editor: General Education: An Account and Appraisal, 1960—; Higher Education in the Revolutionary Decades; editorial bd. Jour. Higher Edn., 1969-72. Home: 945 Valdez Pl Stanford CA 94305

MAYHEW, RICHARD, artist; b. Amityville, L.I., N.Y., Apr. 3, 1924; s. Alvin and Lillian (Goldman) M.; student Bklyn. Mus. Art Sch., 1948; m. Dorothy Zuccarini, Nov. 3. 1951; children— Ina, Scott. Numerous one man shows N.Y.C., Hamilton Coll., Clinton, N.Y., 1974, Montclair (N.J.) State Coll., 1975; group exhbns. Bklyn. Mus., Whitney Mus. Biennial, N.A.D., Carnegie Inst., Chgo. Art Inst., San Francisco Mus. Art, N.Y. Cultural Center, N.Y.C., Gallery Modern Art, N.Y.C., Butler Inst. Ohio, Chgo. Art Inst., Am. Acad. Arts and Letters, New Sch. Social Research, Smith Coll., San Francisco Mus. Art, Pa. Acad. Fine Arts; represented in permanent collections Bklyn. Mus., Whitney Mus., Albion (Mich.) Coll., Mus. African Art, Miles Coll., Mendel Art Gallery, Can., Evansville (Ind.) Mus., Tougaloo (Miss.) Coll., Olson Found. Conn., N.Y. U., R.I. Sch. Design, N.Y. U., Transam., San Francisco, Newark Mus., Minn. Mus. Art, R.I. Sch. Design, and others; represented by Midtown Galleries, N.Y.C. Tchr. Smith Coll., Pratt Inst., Art Students League; asst. prof. Hunter Coll., San Jose State U., 1975-76. Bd. dirs. Rockland Center for Arts, Rockland County, N.Y., Macdowell Colony Assn., N.Y. State Council on Arts, 1973-74; mem. advisory bd. Calif. Council Arts. John Hay Whitney fellow, 1958; recipient Macdowell Colony award, 1958, Ingram Merrill Found. grant, 1960, Childe Hassam Purchase award, 1963-64, Ford Found. Purchase award, 1962, Tiffany Found. grant, 1963; Henry Ward Ranger Purchase award, 1964, Nat. Inst. Arts and Letters award, 1965, Benjamin Altman award, N.A.D., 1970; Butler Inst. award, 1974. N.A. Address: 541 S Mountain Rd Rockland County New City NY 10956

MAYMAN, MARTIN, educator; b. N.Y.C., Apr. 2, 1924; s. Abraham and Anna (Mann) M.; B.S., Coll. City N.Y., 1943; M.S., N.Y. U., 1947; Ph.D., U. Kans., 1953; m. Rosemary Walker, Oct. 12, 1960 (div.); children—Sara, Stephen, Daniel. Clin. psychologist Menninger Found., Topeka, 1944-46; clin. instr. U. Kans. and Winter VA Hosp., Topeka, 1946-51; dir. psychol. tng. Menninger Found., 1951-65; prof. psychology U. Mich., Ann Arbor, 1966—, also co-dir. Psychol. Clinic; vis. prof. U. Colo., Boulder, 1965-66, U. Calif. at Berkeley, 1966; faculty Topeka Psychoanalytic Inst., 1960—, Mich. Psychoanalytic Inst., Detroit, 1967—; participant Nat. Conf. on Profl. Tng. in Clin. Psychology, 1960. Fellow Am. Psychol. Assn., Am. Bd. Examiners Profl. Psychology; mem. Mich. Psychoanalytic Assn., Topeka Psychoanalytic Assn., Soc. for Personality Assessment (pres. 1967-68). Editor: Psychoanalytic Inquiries, 1979—; adv. editor Jour. Consulting Psychology, 1965-70, Psychotherapy, 1975—. Author: Psychoanalytic Research; Three Approaches to the Experimental Study of Subliminal Processes, 1973; (with K.A. Menninger and P. Pruyser) The Vital Balance, 1963; (with K.A. Menninger and P. Pruyser) A Manual for Psychiatric Case Study, 2d edit., 1963. Home: 230 Wildwood Ann Arbor MI 48104

MAYNARD, ARTHUR HOMER, educator; b. Centerville, Mich., Aug. 28, 1915; s. Floyd Ray and Harriet (Crumb) M.; B.A., Cornell Coll., 1936; M.A., Boston U., 1938, S.T.B., 1939; postgrad. Pacific Sch. Religion, 1946-47; Ph.D., U. So. Calif., 1950; m. Pauline E. Schroeder, Aug. 29, 1941; children—Paulette Ann, Kent Arthur. Ordained to ministry Methodist Ch., 1938; minister Meth. Chs., Wis. and Calif., 1939-50; vis. prof. religion Willamette U., 1950-52; asso. prof. U. Miami, Fla., 1952-55, prof., 1955-58, chmn. dept. religion, 1952-58; prof. Bible, U. of Pacific, Stockton, Calif., 1958—, chmn. dept. religious studies, 1962-75; teaching, research Leonard Theol. Sem., Jabalpur, India, 1965; study tours Israel and Jordan, 1960, Eastern Europe, 1969. Pres., Stockton chpt. UN Assn., 1964-66; v.p. No. Calif. Council, 1967-68; chmn. com. on accreditation Calif.-Nev. Conf. Bd. Edn., 1962-72. Mem. Soc. Bibl. Lit. (v.p. Pacific Coast sect. 1972, pres. 1973-74), Am. Acad. Religion, Phi Beta Kappa, Phi Kappa Phi, Phi Chi Phi. Author: The Enduring Word: A Study of Old Testament Literature in Historical Perspective, 1964. Contbr. articles to profl. jours. Home: 2009 Meadow Ave Stockton CA 95207 Office: U of Pacific Stockton CA 95211

MAYNARD, AUBRE DE LAMBERT, physician; b. Georgetown, Brit. Guinna, Nov. 17, 1901; s. Percival Conrad and Gertrude (Johnson) M.; B.S., Coll. City N.Y., 1922; M.D., N.Y. U., 1926; Professor Extraordinario, Catholic U. of La Plata (Argentina), 1972; m. Janine Delcroix July 7, 1960. Mem. staff dept. surgery Harlem Hosp. Center, N.Y.C., 1928-52, dir. surgery, 1952-67, now emeritus cons. surgery; emeritus cons. surgery St. Clare's Hosp.; cons. Misericordia Hosp., Harlem Hosp., Columbus Hosp., St. Joseph's Hosp., Barbados, W.I.; spl. lectr. in surgery Coll. Phys. and Surg., Columbia, clin. prof. surgery, 1962-67; hon. prof. surgery Pahlavi U. Med. Sch., Shiraz, Iran, 1976-77. Trustee N.Y. Acad. Medicine, Godfrey Nurse Fund. Aubre de L. Maynard Cardiac Operating Suite, Harlem Hosp. Center, N.Y.C., named in his honor, 1972. Diplomate Am. Bd. Surgery. Fellow A.C.S.; mem. N.Y. Acad. Medicine, N.Y. Soc. Thoracic Surgery, N.Y. Surg. Soc., Westchester Acad. Medicine, N.Y. Cancer Soc., Soc. Internat. de Chirurgie, Acad. of Surgery (Paris). Author: Surgeons to the Poor; Surgery of the Traumatic Heart, others. Contbr. numerous articles to profl. jours. Home: 270 Convent Ave New York NY 10027

MAYNARD, DON ROGERS, football player; b. Crosbyton, Tex., Jan. 25, 1937; s. Ernest Thomas and Marian Arletta (Sharpe) M.; student Rice Inst., 1953; B.A. in Phys. Edn., Tex. Western Coll., M.A. in Indsl. Arts; m. Marilyn Frances Weaver, Dec. 13, 1956; children—Terry Lynn, Tim Scott. Sales Don Maynard Co.; plumber Brown & Olds; tchr. Ysleta pub. schs., El Paso pub. schs.; sales and pub. relations Prices Creameries; former account exec. Bowen Co., El Paso and Houston; football player N.Y. Jets, N.Y.C.; now broker Cancer & Intensive Care Ins.; formerly in pub. relations and mktg. Farah slacks, El Paso; athletic cons. high schs., colls. and profl. teams. Active Boy Scouts Am. Mem. Fellowship Christian Athletics. Lion. Address: 6545 Butterfield Dr El Paso TX 79932

MAYNARD, DONALD NELSON, plant scientist; b. Hartford, Conn., June 22, 1932; s. Harry Ashley and Elsie Frances (Magnuson) M.; B.S., U. Conn., 1954; M.S., N.C. State U., 1956; Ph.D., U. Mass., 1963; m. Charlotte Louise Grybko, Mar. 23, 1974; 1 son, David Nelson. Instr. plant sci. U. Mass., Amherst, 1956-62, asst. prof., 1962-67, asso. prof., 1967-72, prof., 1972-79, asst. dean, 1974-75; prof., chmn. vegetable crops U. Fla., Gainesville, 1979—; cons. Greenleaf, Inc., Hackensack, N.J. Recipient Aid to Edn. award Gulf Oil Corp., 1965. Fellow Am. Soc. for Hort. Sci. (Environ. Quality Research award 1975, Marion W. Meadows award 1977); mem. Am. Soc. Agronomy, Sigma Xi, Phi Kappa Phi, Alpha Zeta, Phi Tau Sigma. Republican. Episcopalian. Asso. editor Jour. Am. Soc. Hort. Sci., 1976-80, Hortsci., 1975-80. Home: 2531 NW 63d Terr Gainesville FL 32601 Office: Dept Vegetable Crops U Fla Gainesville FL 32611

MAYNARD, FREDERICK CHARLES, JR., ins. co. exec.; b. Rexburg, Idaho, Jan. 21, 1922; s. Frederick Charles and Ruth (Edgerton) M.; B.A., Wesleyan U., Middletown, Conn., 1946; J.D., Duke, 1949; m. Carol Caldwell Houston, July 5, 1952; children—Carol E., Livingston H., Frederick Charles III, James C. Admitted to Conn bar, 1949; with Travelers Ins. Cos., 1949—, sr. v.p., 1968-74, exec. v.p., 1974-77, asst. to chmn., 1977—; dir. Travelers Investment Mgmt. Co. Inc., United Bank and Trust Co., TravCan Ltd. Regent, U. Hartford; bd. dirs. Greater Hartford Process, Inc., Greater Hartford Arts Council, Coordinating Council for Founds., Inc., Jr. Achievement of Hartford, Hartford Stage Co.; trustee Wadsworth Atheneum, Hartford Grad. Center, Hartford Sem. Found. Served with USNR, 1943-46. Recipient Medal of Merit, Treasury Dept., 1970. Mem. Psi Upsilon. Clubs: Hartford, Hartford Golf; 20th Century (Hartford); Weekapaug (R.I.) Yacht; Misquamicut (Watch Hill, R.I.). Home: 40 Mohawk Dr West Hartford CT 06117 Office: 1 Tower Sq Hartford CT 06115

MAYNARD, HARRY LEE, banker; b. DeWitt, Iowa, Nov. 5, 1927; s. Hosea J. and Mildred (Bourne) M.; student Colgate U., 1945-46; St. Ambrose Coll., 1946-47; B.A., U. No. Iowa, 1950; m. Carolyn Messersmith, June 22, 1952; children—Linda Lea, Harry Lee (dec.). Tchr.-coach, Stuart (Iowa) High Sch., 1950-52; tchr. El Rio Elementary Sch., Oxnard, Calif., 1952-53; mgr. Beneficial Finance Co., Los Angeles, 1952-59; asst. mgr. Security First Nat. Bank, Ventura, Calif., 1959-63; exec. v.p. Channel Islands State Bank, Ventura, 1963-69; v.p., mgr. Wells Fargo Bank (merger with Channel Islands State Bank), Ventura, 1969-76; pres. Am. Comml. Bank, 1976—, also dir. Founding father Ventura Boys Club, 1962; city chmn. Heart Fund, 1963-64; publicity chmn. Community Meml. Hosp. drive, 1963; mem. 4-H Fair Auction Com., 1964—, chmn., 1967—, treas. 31st Agrl. Dist., 1976; mem. BBQ com. Bob Pyles Boys Camp, 1963—; gen. chmn. Citizens' Com. Water and Sewer Bond Issue, 1970; chmn. Comprehensive Plan Adv. Com., Ventura; pres. adv. bd. Salvation Army, Ventura County; bd. dirs. Redevel. Agy. Ventura, Ventura County Fair, 1977—; treas., trustee Community Meml. Hosp., 1978—. Recipient Distinguished Service award Ventura Jr. C. of C., 1963; named Outstanding Citizen of Year, Ventura C. of C., 1969. Mem. Am. Inst. Banking, Calif. (group bd. dirs. 1968-71, pres. region 7, 1973), Ind. bankers assns., State Coll. Iowa Alumni Assn., Air Force Assn. (treas. 1962-63), Am. Legion, Ventura C. of C. (pres. 1965), Am. Bankers Assn. (mem. nat. adv. council savs. and marketing div. 1967-69). Mason (33 deg. Scottish Rite, Shriner), Lion (pres. Ventura Downtown 1971-72). Club: Campus View (Ventura). Home: 5448 Bryn Mawr St Ventura CA 93003 Office: 494 E Main St Ventura CA 93001

MAYNARD, JOSEPH ALFRED, advt. agy. exec.; b. Lawrence, Mass., Dec. 30, 1923; s. Joseph Waldemar and Alice Ethyl (La Bonte) M.; student U. N.H., 1945-48; grad. New Eng. Sch. Art, 1948; m. Patricia A. Parker, Jan. 30, 1949; children—Michael, Joseph, Carol. Pres. Mayhoff Co., Lynn, Mass., 1948; art dir. Ingalls Assos. Inc., Boston, 1948-56, v.p. creative, 1956-60, pres., 1961-79, chmn. bd., 1979—. Chmn. Community Relations and Communications, United Way Mass. Bay, 1975; active Buten (Pa.) Museum. Bd. dirs. Dare Inc. Served with USAAF, 1943-45. Mem. New Eng. Broadcasters Assn. (1st v.p. 1975), Ad Club Greater Boston, Copley Soc. (Boston). Club: Annisquam Yacht. Home: Annisquam MA Office: Ingalls Assos Inc 857 Boylston St Boston MA 02116

MAYNARD, ROBERT CLYVE, journalist; b. Bklyn., June 17, 1937; s. Samuel Christopher and Robertine Isola (Greaves) M.; student (Nieman fellow) Harvard U., 1966; m. Nancy Hicks, Jan. 1, 1975; children—Dori J., David H., Alex Caldwell. Reporter, Afro-Am. News, Balt., 1956; reporter York (Pa.) Gazette and Daily, 1961-67; reporter Washington Post, 1967-72, asso. editor/ombudsman, 1972-74, editorial writer, 1974-77; editor Oakland (Calif.) Tribune, 1977—; chmn. Inst. for Journalism Edn., U. Calif. Mem. panel on behavioral scis. Nat. Acad. Sci., 1978—; mem. Mexican-Am. Legal Def. and Ednl. Fund, 1978—; mem. commn. on public understanding about law Am. Bar Assn. 1979—. Mem. Am. Soc. Newspaper Editors. Office: 409 13th St Oakland CA 94612*

MAYNARD, ROBERT WYNFIELD, computer and controls mfg. co. exec.; b. North Haledon, N.J., July 20, 1922; s. Wynfield Johnson and Nathalie (Benz) M.; A.B., Princeton U., 1946; LL.B., Harvard U., 1949. Admitted to N.J. bar, 1950, Mass. bar, 1954, Minn. bar, 1977; asso. firm Evans, Hand & Evans, Paterson, N.J., 1949-53; asst. fgn. counsel USM Corp., Boston, 1953-59, fgn. counsel, 1959-60, asst. gen. counsel, 1960-68, v.p., gen. counsel, 1968-77; v.p., gen. counsel, sec. Honeywell Inc., Mpls., 1977—. Served to 1st lt. OSS, AUS, 1943-45, CIC, AUS, 1950-53. Mem. Am. Bar Assn. Clubs: The Country, Longwood Cricket (Brookline, Mass.); Union (Boston); Mpls., Minikahda (Mpls.). Home: 3200 W Calhoun Pkwy Minneapolis MN 55416 Office: Honeywell Plaza Minneapolis MN 55408

MAYNE, WILEY EDWARD, lawyer; b. Sanborn, Iowa, Jan. 19, 1917; s. Earl W. and Gladys (Wiley) M.; S.B. cum laude, Harvard, 1938, student Law Sch., 1938-39; J.D., State U. Iowa, 1939-41; m. Elizabeth Dodson, Jan. 5, 1942; children—Martha (Mrs. F.K. Smith), Wiley Edward, John. Admitted to Iowa bar, 1941; practiced in Sioux City, 1946-66, 75—; mem. firm Shull, Marshall, Mayne, Marks & Vizintos, 1946-66, Mayne, Probasco, Berenstein, 1975—; spl. agt. FBI, 1941-43. Mem. 90th-93d Congresses, 6th Dist. Iowa; mem. judiciary com., agr. com. Commr. from Iowa, Nat. Conf. Commrs. Uniform State Laws, 1956-60; chmn. grievance commn. Iowa Supreme Ct., 1964-66; del. FAO, 1973; chmn. Woodbury County Compensation Bd., 1975—. Chmn. Midwest Rhodes Scholar Selection Com., 1964-66; pres. Sioux City Symphony Orch. Assn., 1947-54. Vice chmn. Young Republican Nat. Fedn., 1948-50. Bd. dirs. Iowa Bar Found., 1962-68. Served to lt. (j.g.) USNR, 1943-46. Fellow Am. Coll. Trial Lawyers; mem. Am. (ho. of dels. 1966-68), Iowa (pres. 1963-64), Sioux City bar assns., Internat. Assn. Ins. Counsel (exec. com. 1961-64). Mason (33 deg.). Clubs: Harvard (N.Y.C.); Capitol Hill; Sioux City Country. Home: 2728 Jackson St Sioux City IA 51104 Office: 300 Commerce Bldg Sioux City IA 51101

MAYNE, WILLIAM, writer; b. Kingston-upon-Hull, Eng., Mar. 16, 1928; s. William and Dorothy (Fea) M.; grad. Cathedral Choir Sch., Canterbury, Eng., 1942. Mem. Aysgarth Rural Dist. Council, 1961-74; chmn. Parish Meeting Thornton Rust, 1966-75; lectr. creative writing Deakin U., Geelong, Victoria, 1976-77. Recipient Carnegie medal for best children's book of year, 1957. Author: Follow The Footprints, 1953; The World Upside Down, 1954; A Swarm in May, 1955; Choristers' Cake, 1956; The Member for the Marsh, 1956; The Blue Boat, 1957; A Grass Rope, 1957; Underground Alley, 1958; The Thumbstick, 1958; The Rolling Season, 1959; Cathedral Wednesday, 1959; Summer Visitors, 1960; The Changeling, 1961; A Parcel of Trees, 1961; The Twelve Dancers, 1962; Words and Music, 1962; Plot Night, 1962; Pig in the Middle, 1963; Whistling Rufus, 1963; The Fishing Party, 1963; A Day Without Wind, 1963; Sand, 1964; No More School, 1964; On The Stepping Stones, 1963; Earthfasts, 1965; Rooftops, 1965; The Man From the North Pole, 1965; The Glass Ball, 1965; The Last Bus, 1966; The Old Zion, 1967; The Yellow Aeroplane, 1968; The Toffee Join, 1968; (with Fritz Wegner) The House on Fairmount, 1968; The Hill Road, 1969; Ravensgill, 1969. Editor: A Book of Giants, 1968; A Game of Dark, 1971; Royal Harry, 1971; The Incline, 1972; Skiffy, 1972; Robin's Real Engine, 1972; The Jersey Shore, 1973; A Year and a Day, 1976; Max's Dream, 1977; It, 1977; Party Pants, 1977; While the Bells Ring, 1979; An Egg for Tea, 1979; Salt River Times, 1979; editor: A Book of Heroes, 1967. Address: care Harold Ober Assos 40 E 49th St New York NY 10017

MAYNES, CHARLES WILLIAM, ofcl. Dept. State; b. Huron, S.D., Dec. 8, 1938; s. Charles William and Almira Rose (Summers) M.; B.A., Harvard U., 1960; M.A., Oxford (Eng.) U., 1962; m. Gretchen Schiele, July 17, 1965; children—Stacy Kathryn, Charles William. UN polit. affairs ofcl. Dept. State, Washington, 1962-65, chief monetary economist AID, Laos, 1965-67, econ. officer Am. Embassy, Moscow, 1968-70, asst. sec. for internat. orgn. affairs Dept. State, 1977—; Congressional fellow, 1971; sr. legis. asst. to Sen. Fred R. Harris, 1972; sec. Carnegie Endowment for Internat. Peace, 1972-76. Mem. issues staff Sargent Shriver's Vice Presdl. Campaign, 1972. Recipient Meritorious Service award Dept. State. Mem. Council Fgn. Relations, Ams. Dem. Action, UN Assn., Phi Beta Kappa. Democrat. Club: Century Assn. Office: Dept State Room 6323 2201 C St NW Washington DC 20520

MAYNES, E. SCOTT, economist; b. Meriden, Conn., Oct. 6, 1922; s. Edwin and E. Janet (Scott) M.; B.S., Springfield Coll., 1947; M.A., Wesleyan U., Middletown, Conn., 1949; Ph.D., U. Mich., 1956; m. Blanche Rivero, Nov. 11, 1953; children—Lisa, Philip, Christina. Asst. study dir. Survey Research Center, U. Mich., 1949-53, study dir., 1953-56; faculty U. Minn., Mpls., 1956-74, prof. econs., 1968-74, dir. research, 1972-74; prof. dept. consumer econs. Cornell U., Ithaca, N.Y., 1974—, chmn. dept., 1976—. Econ. cons. Nat. Council Applied Econ. Research, New Delhi, India, 1958-59; statistician Bur. Census, 1962-63; econ. cons. Instituto DiTella, Buenos Aires, Argentina, 1965-66; vis. prof. econs. U. Calif., San Diego, 1971-72; vis. scholar Survey Research Center, U. Mich., 1974-75; cons. CAB, 1976, UN Centre for Transnat. Corps., 1978. Organizer, Nat. Conf. on Automobile Ins. Reform, 1970; mem. adv. com. Econ. Behavior Program, Survey Research Center, 1966—, Nat. Bur. Econ. Research, 1967-70; bd. dirs. Consumers Union U.S., 1968-77, treas., 1972-75.

Bd. dirs. State Capitol Credit Union, 1968-74; bd. govs. Credit Research Center, Purdue U., 1979—. Served with USAAF, 1943-45. Mem. Am. Econ. Assn., Am. Statis. Assn., Am. Council on Consumer Interests, Assn. Consumer Research (adv. council 1979—). Democrat. Unitarian. Author: Decision-Making for Consumers, 1976. Mem. editorial bd. Jour. Consumer Affairs, 1974—, Jour. Consumer Research, 1977—, Jour. Consumer Policy, 1977—. Contbr. articles on consumer econs., consumption, survey methods to profl. jours. Home: 112 N Sunset Dr Ithaca NY 14850

MAYNOR, DOROTHY, soprano; b. Norfolk, Va., Sept. 3, 1910; ed. Rev. J. Mainor; early musical edn. in choir of father's Meth. church; student home econs., then music Hampton (Va.) Inst., pupil music J. Nathaniel Dett, and became mem. of choir which toured Europe; student voice with Westminster Choir, Princeton, N.J., later with Klamroth, N.Y.C.; D.Mus., Bennett Coll., 1945, Howard U., 1960, Duquesne U., 1970; L.H.D., Oberlin Coll., 1971; m. Rev. Shelby Rooks, June 27, 1942. Auditioned by Koussevitzky at Berkshire Musical Festival, 1939; awarded Town Hall Endowment Series award for outstanding performance at Town Hall, N.Y.C., 1939; has appeared with N.Y. Philharmonic and Boston, Phila., Chgo., Cleve., San Francisco, Los Angeles symphony orchs.; founder, exec. dir. Harlem Sch. of the Arts, N.Y.C., 1965—. Bd. dirs. Westminster Choir Coll., Princeton, Met. Opera Assn., N.Y.C. Address: Harlem Sch Arts 409 W 141st St New York NY 10031

MAYNOR, HAL WHARTON, JR., educator; b. Nashville, Oct. 5, 1917; s. Hal Wharton and Ophelia Abbigail (Hill) M.; B.S., U. Ky., 1944, M.S., 1947, D.Eng., 1954; m. Marjorie Mae Baker, Mar. 16, 1946; children—Sandra Maynor Averhart, Susan Maynor Bromberg, Hal Wharton III. X-ray technician, lab asst. Henry Vogt Machine Co., Louisville, 1936; lab. asst. Jones Dabney Co., Louisville, 1936-39; asst. prof. mech. engring., asso. engr. atomic research inst. Iowa State Coll., 1947-51; research engr. major appliance div. Gen. Electric Co., Louisville, 1954-57; prin. investigator scaling of titanium and titanium base alloys USAF contract, U. Ky., 1951-54, asso. prof., 1957-59; prof. mech. engring. Auburn (Ala.) U., 1959-78, prof. emeritus, 1978—; project leader fracture of high strength materials Army Missile Command, 1959-70. Chmn., Auburn High Sch. Kiwanis Career Day, 1961; bd. dirs. Friends Auburn Library. Served with USNR, 1943-46. Decorated Bronze Star (6), Silver Star. ASTM grantee, 1967-68; registered profl. engr., Ala., Ky. Fellow Am. Inst. Chemists; mem. Ala. Acad. Sci., Ky. Acad. Sci., AIME, Am. Soc. Engring. Edn., Nat. Soc. Profl. Engrs., Ala. Soc. Profl. Engrs. (pres. Auburn chpt. 1964-65), ASME, Sci. Research Soc. Am., Sigma Xi, Alpha Chi Sigma, Tau Beta Pi, Pi Tau Sigma. Mem. Christian Ch. (elder, bd. dirs., past chmn. ofcl. bd.). Reviewer papers and books Applied Mechanics Revs.; contbr. articles to profl. jours. Home: 518 Cary Dr Auburn AL 36830. *Living and all it entails seems to be increasingly competitive. If it is one's ambition to make even a modest contribution to society, it is probable that he must submit to self-discipline, i.e., condition himself to the idea that while life has its pleasant aspects, it also requires a significant proportion of dedication to less pleasant, if not downright unpleasant, aspects.*

MAYO, BYRON W., advt. agy. exec.; b. Portland, Oreg., 1922; ed. U. Oreg., U. Wash.; m. Mary Bovee, 1950; children—Byron Robert, Cathye Marie. Pres., Sea & Ski Corp., 1966-71; sr. v.p., dir. Foote, Cone & Belding, Inc., San Francisco and Los Angeles, 1972-75; pres. Jennings & Thompson/FCB, Phoenix, 1975—. Bd. dirs. Maricopa County Jr. Achievement, Valley Forward; mem. exec. com. Combined Phoenix Arts Assn. Mem. Am. Assn. Advt. Agys. (chmn. Sun Country council, bd. govs. Western region), Assn. Corp. Growth (chpt. dir.), Ariz. Acad., Alpha Delta Sigma, Alpha Tau Omega. Office: 3003 N Central Ave Phoenix AZ 85012

MAYO, CHARLES GEORGE, coll. pres.; b. Long Beach, Calif., Aug. 1, 1931; s. Maurice Melvin and Irene Marie (Jost) M.; A.B., Reed Coll., 1953; A.M., U. So. Calif., 1960, Ph.D., 1963; m. Iris Jean Cook, July 12, 1953; 1 dau., Carolyn Ann. Insp., Equitable Life Assurance Soc. U.S., 1956-57; teaching asst. U. So. Calif., 1958-62; asst. prof. San Francisco State Coll., 1963-66; asso. dean Grad. Sch., asst. prof. polit. sci. U. So. Cal., 1966-68, asso. prof. polit. sci., 1968-74, chmn. dept., 1968, dean Grad. Sch., 1968-74, interim dean coll. Letters, Arts and Scis., 1968-69; pres., prof. polit. sci. West Chester (Pa.) State Coll., 1974—. Pres., Western Assn. Grad. Schs., 1972-73; mem. exec. com. Pa. Assn. Colls. and Univs., 1978—. Trustee Chadwick Sch., 1971-74. Served with AUS, 1954-56. Malcolm fellow, 1958-59. Mem. Am. Polit. Sci. Assn., AAUP, Blue Key, Phi Kappa Phi, Pi Sigma Alpha. Co-editor, contbr. Dimensions of Political Analysis; An Introduction to Contemporary Study of Politics, 1966; American Political Parties; A Systemic Perspective, 1967. Contbr. to profl. jours. Home: Tanglewood E Rosedale Ave West Chester PA 19380

MAYO, DANA WALKER, educator; b. Bethlehem, Pa., July 20, 1928; s. Dana H. N. and Ethel (Chapman) M.; B.Sc., Mass. Inst. Tech, 1952; Ph.D., Ind. U., 1959; m. Odile Jeanne D'Arc Mailhiot, Jan 12, 1962; children—Dana Lawrence, Chapman Scott, Sara Walker. Research asso. Mass. Inst. Tech., 1959-60, fellow Sch. Advanced Study, 1960-62; asst. prof. Bowdoin Coll., 1962-65, asso. prof, 1965-68, prof., 1968—, chmn. dept. chemistry, 1969—, 75, 77-78, Charles Weston Pickard prof. chemistry, 1970—; lectr. chemistry Mass. Inst. Tech., 1962-71; adj. prof. chemistry U. N.H., 1975—; adj. marine organic chemistry Bigelow Lab. Ocean Scis., West Boothbay Harbor, Maine, 1975—; vis. scientist Explosives Research and Devel. Establishment, Walthan Abbey, Essex, Eng., 1975. lectr. Raman Inst., U. Md., 1967, 70-73; cons. USAF, U.S. Army, Scott Paper, Keyes Fibre Co., Sadtler Research Lab., Perkin-Elmer Corp. Mem. Citizens' Adv. Com., Brunswick, Maine, 1966-67; coll. chmn. United Fund Campaign, 1968. Served with USAF, 1957-59. Spl. fellow NIH, 1967, 69-70, Mem. Chem. Soc. Gt. Britain, Soc. Applied Spectroscopy, Coblentz Soc. (bd. mgmt. 1978—, chmn. archives com.), Am. Chem. Soc. (chmn. Me. sect. 1973), Soc. Chem. Industry (London), AAAS, Sigma Xi, Phi Lambda Upsilon, Alpha Chi Sigma. Home: RFD 5 Princes Point Rd Brunswick ME 04011

MAYO, FRANK REA, chemist; b. Chgo., June 23, 1908; s. Frank and Clara (Rea) M.; B.S., U. Chgo., 1929, Ph.D., 1931; m. Eleanor Louise Pope, Dec. 25, 1933; children—Carolyn (Mrs. Roger Mansell), Jean Louise (Mrs. John L. Howell). Research chemist DuPont Co., Deepwater Point, N.J., 1933-35; instr. U. Chgo., 1936-42; research chemist U.S. Rubber Co., Passaic, N.J., 1942-50; research asso. Gen. Electric Research Lab., Schenectady, 1950-56; sci. fellow SRI Internat. (formerly Stanford Research Inst.), Menlo Park, Calif., 1956—; lectr. Stanford U., 1957-65. Eli Lilly fellow U. Chgo., 1931-32. Recipient Am. Chem. Soc. award in polymer chemistry, 1967. Mem. Am. Chem. Soc. (div. and sect. chmn.). AAAS, Chem. Soc. (London), Phi Beta Kappa. Mem. editorial bd. Jour. Am. Chem. Soc., 1951-60, Jour. Organic Chemistry, 1964-68, Jour. Polymer Sci., 1967—. Home: 89 Larch Dr Atherton CA 94025 Office: SRI Internat Menlo Park CA 94025

MAYO, JAMES WELLINGTON, physicist, sci. cons.; b. Atlanta, Mar. 2, 1930; s. James Otis and Thelma Grace (Session) M.; B.S. with honors in Math., Morehouse Coll., 1951; M.S. in Math. Physics, Howard U., 1953; M.S., M.I.T., 1961, Ph.D. in Physics, 1964; m. Sandra Joanna Bratton, July 20, 1963; children—Joanna Marie, Janell Grace, Jamila Safiya. Physicist, Nat. Bur. of Standards, Washington, 1952-53; instr. dept. physics Howard U., Washington, 1955-57; research asst. A.R. Von Hippel Lab. for Insulation Research, M.I.T., Cambridge, 1958-61, research asst. Research Lab. of Electronics, 1961-63; physicist IBM Thomas Watson Lab., Yorktown, N.Y., summer 1964; asso. prof., chmn. dept. physics Morehouse Coll., Atlanta, 1964-67, prof., 1967-72; cons. Inst. for Services to Edn., 1967-69; program dir. coll. sci. improvement program NSF, Washington, 1971-73, head instructional improvement implementation sect. div. higher edn. in sci., 1973-75, dep. dir. sci. edn. resources improvement div., 1975-77, spl. asst. to asst. dir. sci. edn., 1977-78; sci. adv. asst. sec. for energy tech. Dept. Energy, Washington, 1978—; vis. lectr. U. Calif., Santa Barbara, 1971, Berkeley, 1971, Los Angeles, 1971; vis. scientist Am. Inst. Physics, 1969-71; cons. Atlanta public schs., 1969-71; field reader physics HEW, 1969-70. Pres., Brown Sta. Sch. PTA, 1971; mem. bd. govs. Center for Research in Coll. Sci. and Math., 1969-71; mem. com. of visitors U.S. Army Intelligence Sch., 1978—; trustee Morehouse Coll., 1969-71. Served with M.S.C., U.S. Army, 1953-55. Recipient Spl. Achievement award Dept. Energy, 1979. Mem. Am. Phys. Soc., Nat. Inst. Sci., Am. Assn. Physics Tchrs., AAAS, Ga. Acad. Sci., Sigma Xi, Beta Kappa Chi, Phi Beta Kappa, Sigma Pi Sigma. Contbr. articles on physics to sci. jours.; inventor optical microwave cavity, 1962. Office: 1000 Independence Ave SW Washington DC 20545

MAYO, JOHN SULLIVAN, research and devel. co. exec.; b. Greenville, N.C., Feb. 26, 1930; s. William Louis and Mattie (Harris) M.; B.S., N.C. State U., 1952, M.S., 1953, Ph.D., 1955; m. Lucille Dodgson, Apr. 1957; children—Mark Dodgson, David Thomas, Nancy Ann, Lynn Marie. With Bell Telephone Labs., Inc., Murray Hill, N.J., 1955—, exec. dir. toll electronic switching div., 1973-75, v.p. electronics tech., 1975-79, exec. v.p. network systems, 1979—; chmn., program chmn. Internat. Solid State Circuits Conf.; bd. dirs. Nat. Engring. Consortium, Inc. Recipient Alexander Graham Bell award; named Outstanding Engring. Alumnus, N.C. State U., 1977. Fellow IEEE; mem. Nat. Security Indsl. Assn. (chmn. study of global communications, mem. COMCAC adv. com.), Nat. Acad. Engring. Contbr. articles to profl. jours. Patentee in field.

MAYO, LOUIS HARKEY, univ. ofcl.; b. Prestonburg, Ky., May 20, 1918; s. Walker Porter and Reba (Harkey) M.; student East Ky. State Coll., 1935-36; B.S., U.S. Naval Acad., 1940; LL.B., U. Va., 1949; J.S.D., Yale, 1953; m. Mary Leah Mayo, Sept. 17, 1943; children—Richard, Harkey, David. Prof., George Washington U. Law Sch., 1950—, acting dean, 1958-59, dean Grad. Sch. Pub. Law, 1960-66, v.p. for policy studies and spl. projects, 1966—, dir. program policy studies sci. and tech., 1966—; cons. White House Spl. Projects. Disarmament, 1956; exec. sec. FCC Network Study, 1956-57. Mem. panel tech. assessment com. sci. and pub. policy Nat. Acad. Scis., 1968-69, mem. com. hearing, bioacoustics and biomechanics, 1972—; adv. bd. Center Adminstrv. Justice, 1979—. Served from ensign to lt. comdr. USN, 1940-47. Decorated Bronze Star. Mem. Am., Va., Fed., D.C. bar assns. Research in law, sci. and tech. Editorial adv. bd. Solar Law Reporter, 1979—. Home: 3018 Wallace Dr Falls Church VA 22042 Office: George Washington U Washington DC 20052

MAYO, MAURICE GEORGE, mfg. co. exec.; b. Manchester, N.H., May 22, 1929; s. Earl G. and Yvonne B. (Hemond) M.; B.S., Bentley Coll., Waltham, Mass., 1970; m. Theresa Vander-Heyden, May 27, 1950; children—David, Daniel, Diane, Peter, Gregory. Exec. v.p. Improved Machinery, Inc., Nashua, N.H., 1970-72; comptroller Ingersoll-Rand Co., Woodcliff Lake, N.J., 1972-74, v.p., comptroller, 1974—; dir. No. Research & Engring. Corp., Cambridge, Mass. Committeeman, Boy Scouts Am., 1956-60; mem. Pres.'s adv. com. Bentley Coll.; trustee Bentley Coll., 1976. Bd. advisers Castle Secretarial Sch., 1971-72. Mem. Financial Execs. Inst., Nat. Assn. Accountants, Machinery and Applied Products Inst. (financial council), T.A.P.P.I., Nashua C. of C. (dir. 1972-73). Home: 101 Tam O'Shanter Dr Mahwah NJ 07430 Office: 200 Chestnut Ridge Rd Woodcliff Lake NJ 07675

MAYO, ROBERT PORTER, banker; b. Seattle, Mar. 15, 1916; s. Carl Asa and Edna Alberta (Nelson) M.; A.B. magna cum laude, U. Wash., 1937, M.B.A., 1938; m. Marian Aldridge Nicholson, Aug. 28, 1942; children—Margaret Alice, Richard Carl, Carolyn Ruth (Mrs. Gregory Brown), Robert Nelson. Research asst., auditor Wash. State Tax Commn., 1938-41; economist U.S. Treasury, 1941-47, asst. dir. office of tech. staff, 1948-53, chief debt div. analysis staff, 1953-59; asst. to sec. Treasury Dept., 1959-60; v.p. Continental Ill. Nat. Bank & Trust Co. of Chgo., 1960-69; chmn. Boye Needle Co., 1963-67; staff dir. Pres. Commn. on Budget Concepts, 1967; dir. U.S. Bur. of Budget, 1969-70; counsellor to Pres. U.S., 1970; pres. Fed. Res. Bank of Chgo., 1970—. Chmn. mng. bd. YMCA, Chgo.; mem. bus. advisory council Grad. Sch. Bus. U. Wis. Mem. Chartered Financial Analysts, Chgo. Assn. Commerce and Industry (sr. council), Am. Econ. Assn., Am. Fin. Assn., Phi Beta Kappa. Presbyterian. Clubs: Cosmos (Washington); Bankers, Comml., Execs., Econ. (Chgo.); Galena (Ill.) Ter. Home: 302 Woodley Rd Winnetka IL 60093 Office: 230 S LaSalle St Chicago IL 60604

MAYO, ROBERT WILLIAM, editor; b. Gardner, Ill., July 25, 1919; s. George A. and Nelle E. (Worthington) M.; B.S., Ill. Wesleyan U., 1943; postgrad. Medill Sch. Journalism, Northwestern U., 1943-44; m. Betty Jane Tibbetts, Mar. 13, 1943; children—Bruce R., Bradford W. Financial writer Chgo. Jour. Commerce, 1944; mng. editor Haywood Pub. Co., Chgo., 1945-47; editor Today's Bus. Mag., Martin Publs., Chgo., 1947-60; exec. editor sci. publs. AMA, Jour. of AMA and 9 med. splty. jours., 1960-72, 74-76, div. dir. sci. publs. AMA, 1977—; pres. Mayo Publs., Inc., 1972-74; cons. Canadian Med. Assn., 1967, Conf. Execs. of Am. Schs. for Deaf, Am. Med. Illustrators. Pres. United Fund, Downers Grove, Ill., 1963, campaign chmn., 1961, dir., 1958-67. Mem. alumni council Ill. Wesleyan U., 1968—. Mem. Soc. Profl. Journalists, Am. Soc. Mag. Editors, Am. Med. Writers Assn., Am. Assn. Med. Soc. Execs., Am. Numis. Assn., Sigma Delta Chi, Tau Kappa Epsilon. Clubs: Chgo. Headline, Chgo. Press. Editor, publisher Dir. of Programs and Services directory Am. Annals of the Deaf, 1970-71. Home: 1200 Brookside Ln Downers Grove IL 60515 Office: 535 N Dearborn St Chicago IL 60610

MAYO, SELZ CABOT, sociologist, educator; b. Mesic, N.C., Sept. 20, 1915; s. Sebastian Cabot and Cora Ethel (Gaskins) M.; A.B., Atlantic Christian Coll., Wilson, N.C., 1935; M.S., N.C. State Coll., 1938; Ph.D., U. N.C., 1942; m. Anna Fay Hall, Sept. 11, 1940; 1 dau., Ann Tremayne. Mem. faculty N.C. State Coll., 1939—, prof. sociology, 1955—, head dept. rural sociology, 1960—, head dept. of sociology and anthropology, 1963—. Mem. Am. Sociol. Assn., So. (pres. 1963-64), Rural sociol. socs. Author articles, bulls. in field. Home: 1317 Kimberley Dr Raleigh NC 27609

MAYO, THOMAS TABB, IV, educator, physicist; b. Radford, Va., June 15, 1932; s. Thomas Tabb and Martha (Lavinder) M.; B.S. in Physics, Va. Mil. Inst., 1954; M.S. in Physics, U. Va., 1957; Ph.D. in Physics, 1960; m. Elna Ann Wilson, June 22, 1957; children—Thomas Tabb, Ann Burgess, Chester Wilson. Sr. scientist Research Lab. for Engring. Scis., Charlottesville, Va., 1960-61; asst. prof. physics Hampden-Sydney (Va.) Coll., 1962-64, asso. prof., 1964-67, prof., 1967—, asst. acad. dean, 1971-73, asso. acad. dean, 1973-75, 76-77, acting acad. dean, 1975-76; research asso. Quantum Theory Project, U. Fla. at Gainesville, 1969-70. Served to 1st lt. Chem. Corps, AUS, 1961-62. Mem. Am. Phys. Soc., Am. Assn. Physics Tchrs., Sigma Xi, Lambda Chi Alpha. Democrat. Presbyn. (deacon 1967—). Home: Venable Ln Hampden-Sydney VA 23943 Office: Hampden-Sydney Coll Hampden-Sydney VA 23943

MAYOCK, ROBERT LEE, internist; b. Wilkes-Barre, Pa., Jan. 19, 1917; s. John F. and Mathilde M.; B.S., Bucknell U., 1938; M.D., U. Pa., 1942; m. Constance M. Peruzzi, July 2, 1949; children—Robert Lee, Stephen Philip, Holly Peruzzi. Intern, Hosp. U. Pa., Phila., 1943-44, resident, 1944-45, chief med. resident, 1945-46, attending physician, 1946—, chief pulmonary disease sect. Phila. Gen. Hosp., 1959-72; asst. prof. clin. medicine U. Pa., 1959-70, prof. medicine, 1970—. Served to capt. U.S. Army, 1952-54. Diplomate Am. Bd. Internal Medicine. Fellow A.C.P., Am. Coll. Chest Physicians (regent 1972—); mem. Pa. Med. Soc., Phila. County Med. Soc., Physiology Soc. Phila., Laennec Soc. Phila. (pres. 1963-64), Am. Thoracic Soc., N.Y. Acad. Scis., AMA, Am. Fedn. Clin. Research, Am. Lung Assn., (dir. Phila. and Montgomery County 1961—, pres. 1966-69), Am. Heart Assn., Pa. Lung Assn. (dir. 1976—), Sigma Xi, Alpha Omega Alpha. Clubs: Merion Cricket, Swiftwater Reserve. Contbr. articles in field to med. jours. Home: 244 Gypsy Ln Wynnewood PA 19096 Office: Hosp U Pa 214 Maloney Bldg Philadelphia PA 19104

MAYOR, JOHN ROBERTS, educator; b. LaHarpe, Ill., July 9, 1906; s. James Cary and Edna May (Roberts) M.; B.S., Knox Coll., 1928, LL.D., 1959; M.A., U. Ill., 1929; Ph.D., U. Wis., 1933; m. Darlene Louise Miller, Jan. 25, 1934; children—Berta Edna, James Otto. Instr. math. U. Wis., 1929-35, asso. prof. math. and edn., 1947-51, prof. math. and edn., 1951-57, chmn. dept. edn., 1951-54, acting dean Sch. Edn., 1954-55; dir. sci. teaching improvement program A.A.A.S., 1955-57, dir. edn., 1957-74; part-time prof. math. and edn. U. Md., 1957-67, asst. provost for research div. human and community resources, 1974—; prof. math., chmn. dept. So. Ill. U., 1935-47; faculty cons. math. Knox Coll., 1954-66. Dir. Study of Influence Higher Edn. Accreditation Tchr. Edn., Nat. Commn. Accrediting, 1963-65; chmn. Central Atlantic Regional Ednl. Lab., 1965-66. Recipient Alumni Achievement award Knox Coll., 1957. Fellow A.A.A.S.; mem. Soc. Indsl. and Applied Math., Math. Assn. Am. (gov. 1957-60), Am. Ednl. Research Assn., Assn. Supervision and Curriculum Devel., Nat. Sci. Tchrs. Assn., Central Assn. Sci. and Math. Tchrs. (dir. 1951-53), Am. Math. Soc., NEA, Nat. Assn. Secondary Sch. Prins., Nat. Assn. Research in Sci. Teaching, Nat. Council Tchrs. Math. (dir. 1949-52, pres. 1952-54). Conf. Bd. Math. Scis. (council, sec. 1960-71, treas. 1961-72), Phi Beta Kappa, Sigma Xi, Pi Mu Epsilon, Gamma Alpha. Author publs. in field. Asso. editor Am. Math. Monthly, 1960-68. Home: 411 Windsor St Silver Spring MD 20910 Office: Div Human and Community Resources U Md College Park MD 20742

MAYOR, RICHARD BLAIR, lawyer; b. San Antonio, Mar. 27, 1934; s. E. Allan and Elizabeth Ann (Hastings) M.; B.A., Yale U., 1955; postgrad. (Fulbright scholar), Melbourne (Australia) U., 1955-56; J.D., Harvard U., 1959; m. Heather Donald, July 28, 1956; children—Diana Boyd, Philip Hastings. Admitted to Tex. bar, 1960; asso. firm Butler, Binion, Rice, Book & Knapp, Houston, 1959-67, partner, 1967—. Trustee, mem. exec. com. Contemporary Arts Mus., Houston, 1972-78. Mem. Am. Bar Assn., Am. Law Inst., Tex. Bar Assn., Phi Beta Kappa. Home: 226 Pine Hollow St Houston TX 77056 Office: 11 Esperson Bldg Houston TX 77002

MAYO-SMITH, RICHMOND, educator; b. Boston, July 3, 1922; s. Richmond and Elizabeth (Farrington) Mayo-S.; grad. Noble and Greenough Sch., 1940; B.A., Amherst Coll., 1944, M.A. (hon.), 1959; M.A.T, Harvard, 1950; m. Nancy Umstad Fox, Dec. 17, 1949; children—Richmond III, Michael Fox, Katrina. Instr. sci. Philips Exeter Acad., 1946-62; rep. World Edn. Inc., then acting dir. Literacy House, Lucknow, India, 1962-64; headmaster Roxbury Latin Sch., West Roxbury Mass., 1965-73; field dir. for Mass., Common Cause, Boston, 1974-75. Fulbright exchange tchr., Eng., 1950-51; con. Gen. Sci. Project, Delhi, India, 1961-62. Chmn. bd. trustees World Edn. Inc.; chmn. fin. com. Bridge Fund Inc.; treas. Mass. chpt. Common Cause. Served with F.A., AUS, 1943-45; ETO. Mem. Phi Beta Kappa, Phi Delta Kappa. Co-author series gen. sci. textbooks pub. in India. Home: 156 Mt Vernon St Boston MA 02108

MAYR, ERNST (WALTER), scientist; b. Kempten, Germany, July 5, 1904; s. Otto and Helene (Pusinelli) M.; student U. Greifswald, Berlin, 1923-26; Ph.D., U. Berlin, 1926; Ph.D. (hon.), Uppsala U. (Sweden), 1957; D.Sc. (hon.), Yale, 1959, U. Melbourne, 1959, Oxford U., 1966, U. Mûnchen, 1968, U. Paris, 1974; m. Margarete Simon, May 4, 1935; children—Christa E., Susanne. Came to U.S., 1931, naturalized. Asst. curator zool. mus. U. Berlin, 1926-32; mem. Rothschild expdn. to Dutch New Guinea, 1928, expdn. to Mandated Ty. of New Guinea 1928-29, Whitney Expdn., 1929-30; research asso. Am. Mus. Natural History, N.Y.C., 1931-32, asso. curator, 1932-44, curator, 1944-53; Jesup lectr. Columbia, 1941; Alexander Agassiz prof. zoology Harvard, 1953-75, emeritus, 1975—, dir. Mus. Comparative Zoology, 1961-70. Pres. XIII Internat. Ornith. Congress, 1962. Recipient Leidy medal, 1946; Wallace Darwin medal, 1958; Brewster medal Am. Ornithologists Union, 1965, Daniel Giraud Elliot medal, 1967; Nat. Medal of Sci., 1970; Molina prize Accademia delle Scienze, Bologna, Italy, 1972; Linnean medal, 1977. Fellow Linnean Soc. N.Y. (past sec. editor), Am. Ornithol. Union (pres. 1956-59), New York Zool. Soc.; mem. Am. Philos. Soc., Nat. Acad. Sci., Am. Acad. Arts and Scis., Am. Soc. Zoologists, Soc. Systematic Zoology (pres. 1966), Soc. Study Evolution (sec. 1946, pres. 1950); hon. or corr. mem. Royal Australian, Brit. ornithol. unions, Zool. Soc. London, Soc. Ornithol. France, Royal Soc. New Zealand, Bot. Gardens Indonesia, S. Africa Ornithol. Soc., Linnean Soc. London, Deutsche Akademie der Naturforsch Leopoldina. Author: List of New Guinea Birds, 1941; Systematics and the Origin of Species, 1942; Birds of the Southwest Pacific, 1945; Birds of the Philippines (with Jean Delacour), 1946; Methods and Principles of Systematic Zoology (with E. G. Linsley and R. L. Usinger), 1953; Animal Species and Evolution, 1963; Principles of Systematic Zoology, 1969; Populations, Species and Evolution, 1970; Evolution and the Diversity of Life, 1976. Editor: Evolution, 1947-49. Office: Mus Comparative Zoology Harvard U Cambridge MA 02138

MAYS, BENJAMIN ELIJAH, educator; b. Epworth, S.C., Aug. 1, 1895; s. S. Hezekiah and Louvenia (Carter) M.; A.B. with honors, S.C. State Coll., 1916, Bates Coll., Lewiston, Maine, 1920, D.D., 1947; M.A., U. Chgo., 1925, Ph.D., 1935; LL.D., Denison U., Granville, Ohio, 1945, Virginia Union U., 1945, Centre Coll. Ky., 1970; D.D. (hon.), Howard U., 1945, Bucknell U., 1954, Berea Coll., 1955, Kalamazoo Coll., 1959, Morris Coll., Sumter, S.C., 1966, Ricker Coll., 1966, Interdenominational Theol. Center, Atlanta, 1974; LL.D., U. Liberia, Monrovia, 1960, Lincoln U., 1965, Alderson-Broaddus Coll., 1972; Litt.D., S.C. State Coll., 1946; L.H.D., Shaw U., Raleigh, N.C., 1966, Keuka Coll., 1962, Morehouse Coll., 1967, N.Y. U., 1968, Emory U., 1970, Brandeis U., 1970, Yeshiva U., 1971, Coe Coll., 1972, Pratt Inst., 1971, Edward Waters Coll., Jacksonville, 1974, Duke, 1975, Dillard U., New Orleans, 1975, Kean Coll., Union, N.J., 1975, Bethune Cookman Coll., Daytona Beach, Fla., 1976; LL.D., St. Augustine's Coll., Raleigh, 1963, Harvard, 1967, Morgan Coll., Balt.,

1967, Mich. State U., 1968, Dartmouth Coll., 1975, Bishop Coll., Dallas, 1977; Ed.D., St. Vincent Coll., Latrobe, Pa., 1964; Litt.D., Grinnell Coll., 1967, U. Ife (Nigeria), 1971; H.H.D., Boston U., 1950, Benedict Coll., 1970, Lander Coll., 1974, Talladega (Ala.) Coll., 1978, U. S.C., 1978; D.C.L., Middlebury (Vt.) Coll., 1969, Atlanta U., 1979; D.S.T., Olivet (Mich.) Coll., 1974; m. Sadie Gray, Aug. 9, 1926. Tchr. higher math. Morehouse Coll., 1921-24; pastor Shiloh Bapt. Ch., Atlanta, 1921-24; instr. English, State Coll. S.C., Orangeburg, 1925-26; exec. sec. Tampa (Fla.) Urban League, 1926-28; nat. student sec. YMCA, 1928-30; dir. study of Negro chs. in U.S. for Inst. of Social and Religious Research, N.Y., 1930-32; dean Sch. of Religion, Howard U., Washington, 1934-40; pres. Morehouse Coll., Atlanta, 1940-67, pres. emeritus, 1967—; vis. prof., adviser to pres. Mich. State U., 1968-69. Cons., Office Edn., HEW, Washington, 1969, Ford Found., 1970, United Bd. Coll. Devel. Pres. United Negro College Fund, 1958-61, now bd. dirs.; v.p. Fed. Council Chs. Christ in Am., 1944-46; rep. U.S. at Oxford Conf. on Church, Community and State, Oxford (Eng.) U., 1937, YMCA of U.S. at Plenary Session of World Com., Stockholm, 1938; leader Youth Conf., Amsterdam, 1939; mem. U.S. del. World Conf. of YMCA, Mysore, India, 1937; del. to 1st assembly World Council Chs., 1948, mem. central com., 1949-54; del. Commn. on Ch. Amidst Racial and Ethnic Tensions, Geneva, 1953; del., leader Baptist World Alliance Assembly, Cleve., 1950; mem. U.S. Adv. Com. for UN, 1959, U.S. nat. commn. UNESCO, 1962; mem. nat. adv. council to Peace Corps, 1961; mem. Atlanta Bd. Edn., 1969-81, pres., 1970-81; v.p. World Student Service Fund; co-chmn. Citizens Crusade Against Poverty; Peace Corps rep. All-African Conf. on Edn., Addis Abada, 1961. Chmn. bd. trustees Benedict Coll.; past trustee Danforth Found., Nat. Fund for Med. Edn.; chmn. bd. dirs. Nat. Sharecropper Fund; bd. dirs. Inst. Internat. Edn. N.E. Region, Butler St. YMCA, Atlanta, Paine Coll., Religious Heritage Am., Martin Luther King, Jr. Center for Social Change; past bd. dirs. Nat. YMCA. Recipient Alumnus of Year award U. Chgo. Div. Sch., 1949; 2d Ann. Tex. State Fair Negro Achievement award, 1950; Christian Culture award Assumption U., Windsor, Ont., Can., 1961; Religious Leaders award NCCJ, 1970; Amistad award Am. Missionary Assn., 1968; Merrick-Moore-Spaulding award N.C. Mut. Life Ins. Co., 1968; Man of Year award Soc. Advancement of Mgmt., Greenville, S.C., 1968; Myrtle Wreath award Atlanta chpt. Hadassah, 1969; Achievement award Black Ednl. Services, Chgo., 1970; Russwurm award Nat. Newspapers Pubs., Chgo., 1970; citation Am. Bapt. Chs. of South, 1971; 1st recipient Dorie Miller award Dorie Miller Found., Chgo., 1971; Nat. Freedom Day award, Phila., 1972; James Bryant Conant award Edn. Commn. of the States, 1977; Top Hat award The Chgo. Defender, 1978; Disting. Am. Educator award U.S. Office of Edn., 1978; Roy Wilkins award NAACP, 1977; Hale Woodruff award United Negro Coll. Fund, 1978; award Nat. Black Child Devel. Inst., 1978; Nat. Leadership award Nat. Assn. Equal Opportunity in Higher Edn., 1978; Alumni medal U. Chgo., 1978; Humanitarian award Internat. New Thought Alliance, 1978; numerous others; Kent fellow Nat. Council Religion in Higher Edn. Mem. U. Chgo. Alumni Assn. (dir., mem. cabinet), Phi Beta Kappa, Delta Sigma Rho (Distinguished Service award), Delta Theta Chi, Omega Psi Phi. Democrat. Baptist. Author: The Negro's Church, 1933; The Negro's God, 1938, 2d edit., 1968; Seeking to be Christian in Race Relations, 1957; Disturbed About Man, 1969; Born to Rebel, 1971. Contbr. numerous works in field to encys., books and several mags. and newspapers. Weekly columnist for Pittsburgh Courier. Compiler: A Gospel for the Social Awakening, 1950. Home: 3316 Pamlico Dr SW Atlanta GA 30311. *I have attempted to do well whatever I set out to do. I have aimed to deal fairly with all men. Honesty is an obsession with me, including intellectual honesty. I have no prejudice against anyone because he belongs to a different ethnic or racial group than my own.*

MAYS, CARL W., JR., banking exec.; b. 1925; B.S., UCLA; married. With U.S. Nat. Bank of Oreg., until 1973, asst. v.p., 1961-66, v.p., personnel dir., 1966-68, v.p., corp. planning dir., 1968-70, sr. v.p.-staff services group, 1970-73, exec. v.p. staff services, 1973; with U.S. Bancorp, Portland, Oreg., 1973—, now pres. Served to lt. USNR, 1944-46. Office: 309 SW 6th Ave PO Box 8837 Portland OR 97208*

MAYS, GERALD AVERY (JERRY), constrn. co. exec.; b. Dallas, Nov. 24, 1939; s. Avery and Blanche (Ponder) M.; B.S. in Civil Engring., So. Methodist U., 1962, postgrad., 1962-63; m. Shirley Ann Pike; children—Gerald Avery, Sandra Jo, Sherrie Lynn, Sarah Elisabeth; stepchildren—Donald K. Turner, Bruce R. Turner, Barry K. Turner. Laborer, engr. Avery Mays Constrn. Co., Dallas, 1950-63, v.p., 1967-71, pres., 1971—; football player Kansas City Chiefs, 1961-70; engr. Howard, Needles, Tammen & Bergendoff, cons. engrs., 1964-67; partner Mays, Flowers, Grady & Burruss Ins.; pres. GAMCO Constructors, Inc., 1972—. Campaign chmn. Greater Dallas March Dimes, 1973; mem. Dallas Community Relations Bd. Adv. bd. Dallas Opportunities Industrialization Com., 1972; bd. dirs. Kansas City chpt. ARC, 1969-70, pres. Heart of Am. chpt., 1973; bd. dirs. Baker U., 1970-73; exec. com. Met. Dallas YMCA; chmn. Met. Y Sustaining Fund Campaign, 1976; exec. com. Goodwill Industries Dallas, Goals for Dallas. Recipient football awards All Am. Football League, 1962, 64-68; All Am. Football Conf., 1970; named Am. Football League Sportsman of Year, 1965; Young Engr. of Month, Kansas City, 1970; Alpha Tau Omega Man of Year, 1970; capt. Kansas City Chiefs, 1963-70. Registered profl. engr., Tex., Kans., Mo. Mem. Nat. Soc. Profl. Engrs., ASCE, Salesmanship Club Dallas, Young Pres.'s Orgn., Dallas C. of C. (chmn's council), Sigma Tau, Chi Epsilon, Alpha Tau Omega. Home: 75 Mays Pl Denton TX 76201 Office: 2030 Empire Central Dallas TX 75235

MAYS, L. LOWRY, broadcasting co. exec.; b. Houston, July 24, 1935; s. Lester T. and Virginia (Maddox) M.; B.S., Tex. A. and M. U., 1957; M.B.A., Harvard U., 1962; m. Peggy Pitman, July 29, 1959; children—Kathryn, Linda, Mark, Randall. Sr. v.p. Russ & Co., N.Y.C., 1962-70; pres. Mays and Co., fin. cons., 1970—; pres. San Antonio Broadcasting, Inc., 1973—; pres. Clear Channel Communications, Inc., 1974—, Prime Time, Inc., San Antonio, 1976—; mem. CBS Radio Affiliates Bd.; dir. UniCapital Corp., Atlanta, Gulf Energy and Devel. Corp., San Antonio, Herald Pub. Co., San Antonio Press, Prodn. Operators, Inc., Houston. Bd. dirs. YMCA, San Antonio, Baptist Meml. Hosp. System. Served to 1st lt. USAF, 1958-60. Mem. Greater San Antonio C. of C. (vice chmn.). Episcopalian. Clubs: Harvard, San Antonio, Country, Argyle, Order of Alamo. Home: 400 Geneseo Rd San Antonio TX 78209 Office: 540 Travis Park W San Antonio TX 78205

MAYS, MARSHALL TRAMMELL, lawyer; b. Greenwood, S.C., July 21, 1924; s. Calhoun Allen and Mae Marshall (Trammell) M.; B.S., U.S. Naval Acad., 1945; LL.B., U. S.C., 1950. Admitted to S.C. bar, 1950; partner firm Mays & Mays, Greenwood, 1954-69; dep. dir. ins. div. AID, Washington, 1969-71; gen. counsel Overseas Pvt. Investment Corp., Washington, 1971-73, pres., 1973-77; pvt. practice law, Washington, 1977—. Mem. S.C. State Legislature, 1959-60. Served to lt. comdr. USNR, 1945-47, 51-54. Home: 616 S Lee St Alexandria VA Office: 1101 Connecticut Ave NW Washington DC 20036

MAYS, MORLEY JOSIAH, coll. pres.; b. Johnstown, Pa., Dec. 13, 1911; s. William Oscar and Essie (Oaks) M.; A.B. cum laude, Juniata Coll., 1932; A.M., U. Pitts., 1936; Ph.D., U. Va., 1949; D.D. (hon.), Bethany Theol. Sem., 1968; LL.D. (hon.), Elizabethtown (Pa.) Coll., 1977; L.H.D. (hon.), Albright Coll., 1978; m. Lucinda Miller; m. 2d, Lettie B. Perry; children—Elisabeth Louise, Randall Morley. Instr. English, Juniata Coll., Huntingdon, Pa., 1932-38, prof. philosophy, coll. dean, 1948-66, v.p. acad. affairs, 1963-66; pres. Elizabethtown Coll., 1966-77, Albright Coll., Reading, Pa., 1977-78; asso. prof. English, Bridgewater (Va.) Coll., 1941-46; chmn. bd. dirs. Univ. Center at Harrisburg, 1967-77; cons. higher edn. Md. Dept. Edn. Report analyst commn. on higher edn., Middle States Assn. Colls. and Secondary Schs., 1964-69. Chmn., Huntingdon County Planning Commn., 1962-66. Sec. Gen. Conf. Ch. of Brethren, 1964-67, moderator, 1968-69; chmn. bd. dirs. Bethany Theol. Sem., Oak Brook, Ill., 1958-67; trustee Huntingdon County Pub. Library, 1956-66, Lancaster Theol. Sem., 1972-77. Mem. Phi Beta Kappa. Lutheran. Home: 76 Highland Dr Lancaster PA 17602

MAYS, ROY MARK, petroleum and mgmt. cons.; b. Denton, Tex., July 25, 1915; s. Roy and Grace (Hovenkamp) M.; LL.B., N. Tex. Sch. Law, Ft. Worth, 1937; grad. Advanced Mgmt. Program, Harvard, 1957; m. Thelma Powers, Jan. 21, 1940; children—Marilyn (Mrs. M.C. Mays), Roy Mark. With Continental Oil Co., 1951—, So. regional mgr., 1963—, v.p., 1964-68, v.p., gen. mgr. Ponca City (Okla.) activities, 1968-72, v.p., gen. mgr., Denver, 1972-74; petroleum and mgmt. cons., 1974—; agt. FBI, 1942-45; dir. Frontier Fed. Savs. & Loan Assn. Trustee Austin Coll.; hon. mem. Internat. Petroleum Expn. Mem. Soc. Former Agts. FBI, Mid-Continent Oil and Gas Assn. (past pres. Okla.-Kans. div.). Clubs: Petroleum (pres. 1966), Ft. Worth, Rivercrest (Ft. Worth); Ponca City Country. Home: 5 Stoneridge Rd Ponca City OK 74601

MAYS, WILLIE HOWARD, JR., ret. profl. baseball player; b. Westfield, Ala., May 6, 1931; s. William Howard and Ann Mays; ed. Fairfield (Ala.) High Sch.; m. Mae Louise Allen, Nov. 27, 1971; 1 adopted son, Michael. Mem. Birmingham Black Barons Baseball Team, 1948-50; joined N.Y. (now San Francisco) Giants system, 1950; mem. Trenton (N.J.) team, 1950-51, Mpls. Millers, 1951; mem. Giants 1951-72, capt.; coach N.Y. Mets, 1972-73, ret., 1973. Named Nat. League's most valuable player, 1954, 65; named Player of Year, Sporting News, 1954, Baseball Player of Decade, 1970; named Male Athlete of Year, A.P., 1954; recipient Hickok belt, 1954; 1st Commr.'s award, 1970; Golden Plate award, 1975; named to Baseball Hall of Fame, 1979, City of Hope Hall of Fame, 1978. Served with AUS, 1952-54. Author: Willie Mays: My Life In and Out of Baseball, 1966. Address: care Park Pl Hotel Park Pl and Boardwalk Atlantic City NJ 08401

MAYSENT, HAROLD WAYNE, hosp. adminstr.; b. Tacoma, Wash., June 26, 1923; s. Wayne L. Shivley and Esther Pierce M.; B.A., U. Wash., 1950; M.S. in Hosp. Adminstrn. with distinction, Northwestern U., 1954; m. Marjorie Ellen Hodges, June 13, 1953; children—Jeffrey, Nancy, Brian, Gregory. Adminstrv. resident Passavant Meml. Hosp., 1953-54, adminstrv. asst., 1954-55; research asso. hosp. adminstrn. Northwestern U., Evanston, Ill., 1954-55; with Lankenau Hosp., Phila., 1955-72, dir., 1963-67, exec. dir., 1967-72; exec. v.p. Rockford (Ill.) Meml. Hosp., 1972-75, pres., 1975—; clin. asso. Rockford Sch. Medicine, U. Ill., 1974—. Coach, adminstr. Broomal (Pa.) Little League, 1962-72. Bd. dirs. Community Health Assn., 1964-70, Rockford Med. Edn. Found., 1972—, Tri State Hosp. Assembly, 1978. Served with AUS, 1942-46. Recipient Malcom T. MacEachern award Northwestern U., 1954. Fellow Am. Coll. Hosp. Adminstrs. (Ill. regent 1979—); mem. Am. Hosp Assn. (com. on vols. 1976—, ho. of dels. 1977), Pa. Hosp. Assn. (dir. 1965-68), Ill. Hosp. Assn. (trustee 1973-79, sec. 1974-76, chmn. elect 1977, chmn. bd. trustees 1978, named an outstanding leader in hosp. industry 1978). Contbr. articles to profl. jours. Office: Rockford Meml 2400 N Rocton Ave Rockford IL 61101

MAYSON, JOSEPH DOUGLAS, former indsl. exec.; b. Atlanta, Mar. 14, 1915; s. Thomas Clifford and Margie (Spearing) M.; student Va. Mil. Inst., 1931-32, Vanderbilt U., 1932-34; B.S., U. Ga., 1936, LL.B., 1937; m. Lucile Gaston Jordan, Aug. 18, 1934; children—Joseph Douglas, James Spearing. Admitted to Ga. bar, 1937; with Md. Casualty Co., 1938-40; tax atty. U.S. Steel Corp., 1940-44; tax Supr. Dresser Industries, Inc., 1944-49, dir. law dept. 1949-56, asst. sec., dir. law dept., 1956-57, sec., dir. law dept., 1957-60, v.p., sec., gen. counsel, 1960-75, sr. v.p., sec., gen. counsel, 1975; formerly officer and/or dir. various affiliated cos. and subsidiaries Dresser Industries, Inc. Mem. Am., Dallas bar assns., Am. Soc. Corporate Secs., Phi Delta Theta, Phi Delta Phi. Clubs: Brook Hollow Golf (Dallas); Riomar Country, Riomar Bay Yacht (Vero Beach, Fla.). Home: 515 Bay Dr Vero Beach FL 32960

MAYTAG, LEWIS B., airline exec.; b. Rochester, Minn., 1926; ed. Colo. Coll. Chmn. bd., chief exec. officer Nat. Airlines, Inc.; dir. Maytag Co. Office: PO Box 592055 AMF Miami FL 33159

MAYTUM, DONALD NEIL, oil co. exec.; b. Alexandria, S.D., Feb. 11, 1924; s. Cecil Syferd and Vivian (Field) M.; B.Chem. Engring., U. Minn., 1948; m. Winifred E. Workman, Sept. 18, 1948; children—Marilyn, Marsha. Pres. Iran Calif. Oil Co., London, 1967-69; mgr. fgn. staff Standard Oil Co. of Calif., San Francisco, 1969-71, asst. sec., 1971-75, sec., 1975—. Served with USNR, 1943-45. Mem. Am. Soc. Corporate Secs., Western Pension Conf., World Affairs Council No. Calif. Club: World Trade (San Francisco). Office: 225 Bush St San Francisco CA 94104

MAZAN, WALTER LAWRENCE, govt. ofcl.; b. Center Rutland, Vt., June 5, 1921; s. Lawrence Walter and Henrietta (Mazur) M.; student Norwich U., 1941; B.S. in Commerce, U. Vt., 1949; LL.D., So. Colo. State Coll., 1971; m. Lee Duffy, July 14, 1956; children—Walter Lawrence II, Lorilee, Michelle, Michael. With investigations dept. Gen. Adjustment Bur., N.Y.C., 1949-52; dir. civil def. for Vt., also asst. to gov., 1951- 57; with Office Emergency Preparedness, Exec. Office Pres., 1957-69, dir. Office Liaison, 1969; asst. sec. of transp. for pub. affairs, 1969-70; dir. intergovtl. affairs White House Conf. on Children and Youth, 1970-71, exec. dir., 1971-72; spl. programs adviser to Sec. Transp., 1972-73; mng. dir. WLM Assos., Washington, 1973-74; staff asst. Com. Pub. Works, U.S. Ho. of Reps., 1974—; lectr. in field, 1963—. Vice pres. Nat. Conf. State Socs., 1967; pres. Office Emergency Preparedness Credit Union, 1965-66. Served with USAAF, 1942-46. Recipient Outstanding Performance award Office Emergency Preparedness, Sustained Superior Performance award, 1967; Merit certificate Nat. Jr. Achievers, 1970; Recognition award U. Tenn., 1969; Appreciation certificate U. Fla., 1970. Mem. Nat. Geog. Soc., Arlington County Civic Assn., Vt. State Soc., Nat. Platform Assn. Roman Catholic. Author reports. Home: 8360 Greensboro Dr McLean VA 22102. *This society, this nation-yes, this world, stands in awesome need of what I shall call "energetic excellence". And I hope you will not do me the disservice of confusing "excellence" with "perfection". Because while the latter is unattainable, the former is readily achievable. For "excellence" is by definition, the fact or condition of excelling; to raise oneself; to surpass. And that certainly we all can do. And it is only in that way, that we may truly improve ourselves, our nation and our society.*

MAZANEC, GEORGE LAD, utility exec.; b. Chgo., May 30, 1936; s. Charles and Catherine Ceclia (Traczyk) M.; A.B. in Econs., DePauw U., 1958; M.B.A., Harvard, 1960; m. Elsa Barbara Weiffenbach, Oct. 1, 1960; children—Robert, John. Asst. v.p. Leighly & Prince, Inc., Chgo., 1960- 64; with No. Natural Gas Co., Omaha, 1964—, supr. investment analysis, 1964-65, adminstrv. mgr. People's Natural Gas div., 1965-67, v.p. People's Natural Gas div., 1968, treas. co. and subsidiaries, 1969-71, v.p., treas. co. and subsidiaries, 1971-78; pres. No. Liquid Fuels Cos., 1978—; dir. First Nat. Bank Council Bluffs (Iowa). Sec.-treas. Harvard Bus. Sch. Assn. Neb. Bd. dirs., pres. Omaha Zool. Soc.; chmn. bus. adminstrn. adv. council U. Nebr. at Omaha. Mem. Soc. Financial Analysts, Ind. Natural Gas Assn., Am. Gas Assn., Alpha Tau Omega. Clubs: Omaha, Happy Hollow. Home: 2512 S 95th St Omaha NE 68124 Office: 2223 Dodge St Omaha NE 68102

MAZANKOWSKI, DONALD FRANK, Canadian govt. ofcl.; b. Viking, Alta., Can., July 27, 1935; s. Frank and Dora (Lonowski) M.; student Viking schs.; m. Lorraine Poleschuk, Sept. 6, 1958; children—Gregory, Roger, Donald. Mem. House of Commons, 1968—, chmn. Progressive Conservative com. transp., 1972-74, com. govt. ops., 1976-77, com. trans. and communication, 1977-79; minister of transp., also minister responsible Can. Wheat Bd., 1979—. Trustee Vegreville Sch. Bd., 1963-68; mem. Vegreville and Dist. Credit Union; regional dir. Alta. Progressive Conservative Assn., 1962, No. v.p., 1963, No. chmn. orgn., 1964; pres. Vegreville Progressive Conservative Assn., 1963-68. Mem. Commonwealth Parliamentary Assn., Interparliamentary Union, Can. NATO Parliamentary Assn., Can. World Federalist Parliamentary Assn., Vegreville C. of C., Royal Can. Legion, Alta. Fish and Game Assn. Roman Catholic. Club: Vegreville Rotary (past dir.). Office: Tower C Pl de Ville Ottawa ON K1A 0N5 Canada

MAZE, CLARENCE, JR., ednl. adminstr.; b. Industry, W.Va., Nov. 24, 1931; s. Clarence Harvey and Nona May (Rose) M.; A.B., Glenville State Coll., 1953; M.A., W.Va. U., 1956; Ed.D., Ind. U., 1962; m. Marlene Dotson, Dec. 22, 1956; children—John Marshall, Thomas Charles. Chmn. USAID project Ohio U., Ibadan, Nigeria, 1962-64; prof. bus. edn. and office adminstrn. U. Tenn., Knoxville, 1965-72; dean of academic affairs Glenville (W.Va.) State Coll., 1972-75; pres. Richard Bland Coll., Coll. William & Mary, Petersburg, Va., 1975—. Mem. advisory bd. Sch. Nursing, Petersburg Gen. Hosp., 1975—; bd. dirs. United Way Southside Va., 1975-78; treas., bd. dirs. Southside Va. Community Concert Assn., 1976-79; bd. dirs. Petersburg chpt. Am. Cancer Soc., 1979—, Ft. Henry br. Assn. Preservation of Va. Antiquities, 1978—; sr. warden, vestryman, lay reader Christ and Grace Episcopal Ch. Served with U.S. Army, 1953-55. Mem. Am. Assn. Univ. Adminstrs., Am. Higher Edn. Assn., Council of Pres.'s in Va., Petersburg C. of C. (dir.), Phi Delta Kappa, Delta Pi Epsilon. Club: Rotary. Author: Business Education in the Junior High School, 1965. Editor Tenn. Bus. Edn. Quarterly, 1967-71. Contbr. articles to profl. jours. Home and Office: Richard Bland College College of William and Mary Route 1 Box 77-A Petersburg VA 23803

MAZER, HENRY, conductor; b. Pitts., July 21, 1921; s. Samuel and Irene M.; student Duquesne U., 1935-39, Carnegie Inst. Tech., 1939-40, U. Pitts., 1945-46; m. Kathryn Foulk, Oct. 3, 1949; children—Kathryn E., Thomas Samuel. Condr., Wheeling (W.Va.) Symphony Orch., 1947-59, Fla. Symphony Orch., Orlando, 1959-66; asso. condr. Pitts. Symphony Orch., 1966-70, Chgo. Symphony Orch., 1970—; music dir., condr. DePaul U. Symphony Orch., 1978—. Served with C.E., AUS, 1942-45. Address: care Chgo Symphony Orch 220 S Michigan Ave Chicago IL 60604*

MAZER, MORRIS BILL, sports announcer; b. Soslov, Russia, Nov. 2, 1920; s. Ben and Betha (Lerner) M.; came to U.S., 1923, naturalized, 1928; B.A., U. Mich., 1941; m. Dora Sudarsky, Apr. 7, 1946; children—Francine, Beverly, Arnold. Sports div Sta. WKBW, Buffalo, 1948-52, Sta. WGR-TV, Buffalo, 1952-64; Sports announcer NBC Radio and TV, N.Y.C., 1964-68; host, interview program Sta. WOR, N.Y.C., 1968-70; sports dir. Sta. WHN, N.Y.C., 1970-77; sports announcer CBS-TV, N.Y.C., 1970-72,78-79; sports announcer Sta. WNEW-TV, N.Y.C., 1973—; appeared in film Raging Bull; free lance comml. announcer. Served to 1st lt. USAF, 1942-46. Named N.Y.C. Sportcaster of Year, 1964, 65, 66. Mem. AFTRA, screen Actors Guild. Jewish. Club: Metropolis Country. Author: Sports Answers Book, 1967; Answer Book of Sports, 1970. Office: 205 67th St New York NY

MAZER, WILLIAM, paper mfr.; b. N.Y.C., July 30, 1905; s. Abraham and Rose (Kamensky) M.; B.S., N.Y.U., 1926; student Columbia, 1927; m. Helen Cohen, July 16, 1932; children—Linda, Frank, Robert. With Hudson Pulp & Paper Corp., 1927—, purchasing agt., 1932, v.p., 1937, exec. v.p. 1947-55, pres., 1955-73, chmn. bd., 1973—. Chmn. pulp and paper div. Fedn. Jewish Philanthropies; pres. Muscular Dystrophy Assn., 1953—; pres. Am.-Israel Cultural Found., 1968, chmn. bd., 1973—; pres. Inst. for Muscle Disease, 1959-64. Bd. dirs., pres. The Family Inst.; fellow Brandeis U., 1953, trustee, 1954; trustee Lebanon Hosp., Jewish Sanitarium and Hosp. for Chronic Diseases. Mem. Pi Lambda Phi. Club: Metropolis Country. Office: Hudson Pulp & Paper Co 477 Madison Ave New York NY 10022

MAZIA, DANIEL, biologist; b. Scranton, Pa., Dec. 18, 1912; s. Aaron and Bertha (Kurtz) M.; A.B. U. Pa., 1933, Ph.D., 1937; Ph.D.h.c., U. Stockholm, 1976; m. Gertrude Greenblatt, June 19, 1938; children—Judith Ann, Rebecca Ruth. National Research Council fellow in biology sci., Princeton, 1937-38; asst. prof. zoology, U. Mo., 1938-41, asso. prof., 1942-47, prof. since 1947; asso. prof. zoology U. Calif., Berkeley, 1951-53, now prof. Mem. corp. Marine Biol. Lab., Woods Hole. mem. bd. trustees and physiology teaching staff, 1950—. Served as 1st lt. AAF, 1942-44, capt. aviation medicine, 1944-45. Fellow Am. Acad. Arts and Scis.; mem. Am. Soc. Cell Biology, Soc. Gen. Physiologists, Nat. Acad. Scis. Mem. editorial bd. Exptl. Cell Research. Home: 900 Shattuck Berkeley CA 94707

MAZIARZ, EDWARD ANTHONY, educator; b. Milw., Mar. 6, 1915; s. John and Mary (Matusiak) M.; B.S., St. Joseph's Coll., Rensselaer, Ind., 1944; M.A., Cath. U. Am., 1941; M.S., U. Mich., 1945; Ph.D, U. Ottawa (Can.), 1949; summer student, U. Va., 1944, U. Laval, 1947. Ordained priest Roman Catholic Ch., 1940; instr. philosophy Marian Coll., Fond du Lac, Wis., 1941-42; faculty St. Joseph's Coll., 1943-66, prof. philosophy and math., 1958-66, acad. dean, 1955-63; prof. philosophy Loyola U., Chgo., 1966—. Mem. AAAS, Am. Math. Soc., Am. Cath. Philos. Assn., Am. Philos. Assn., Assn. Symbolic Logic, History of Sci. Soc., Philos. Sci. Assn., Delta Epsilon Sigma (nat. pres. 1951—). Author: The Philosophy of Mathematics, 1950. Translator: A Short History of Philosophy, 1955; Redemption Through the Blood of Jesus, 1960; A Short History of Philosophy, 2d edit., 1960; co-author: Greek Mathematical Philosophy, 1967; Human Being and Being Human, 1969; editor: Value and Values in Evolution: A Symposium, 1979. Address: Dept Philosophy Loyola U 6525 N Sheridan Rd Chicago IL 60626

MAZLISH, BRUCE, educator, historian; b. N.Y.C., Sept. 15, 1923; s. Louis and Lena (Reuben) M.; B.A., Columbia, 1944, M.A., 1947, Ph.D., 1955; m. Anne A. Austin, Nov. 12, 1960; children—Anthony, Jared; children by previous marriage—Cordelia, Peter. Instr. history U. Maine, 1946-48, Columbia, 1949- 50, Mass. Inst. Tech., 1950-53; dir. Am. Sch. in Madrid (Spain), 1953-55; mem. faculty Mass. Inst.

Tech., 1955—, prof. history, 1965—, chmn. history sect., 1965-70, head dept. humanities, 1974-79; mem. NSF evaluating panel Worcester Poly. Inst., 1972-75; hist. cons. com. space Am. Acad. Arts and Scis., 1963-65. Served with inf. and OSS, AUS, 1943-45. Social Sci. Research Council fellow, 1967-68; vis. mem. Inst. for Advanced Study, 1972-73. Fellow Am. Acad. Arts and Scis. Clubs: Badminton and Tennis; Cambridge Tennis; Harbor (Seal Harbor, Me.). Author: (With J. Bronowski) The Western Intellectual Tradition, 1960; The Riddle of History, 1966; In Search of Nixon, 1972; James and John Stuart Mill: Father and Son in the 19th Century, 1975; The Revolutionary Ascetic, 1976; Kissinger, The European Mind in American Policy, 1976; (with Edwin Diamond) Jimmy Carter, An Interpretive Biography, 1980. Editor: Psychoanalysis and History, 1963, rev. edit., 1971; The Railroad and the Space Program: An Exploration in Historical Analogy, 1965; asso. editor Interdisciplinary History. Home: 3 Channing Circle Cambridge MA 02138

MAZO, EARL, writer; b. Warsaw, Poland, July 7, 1919; s. Samuel George and Sonia (Portugal) M.; grad. Clemson Coll., 1940; m. Rita Vane, 1941; children—Judith Frances, Mark Elliot. Staff Charleston News and Courier (S.C.), also Greenville News, 1939-41; editor, editorial page Camden Courier Post (N.J.), 1945-50; staff N.Y. Herald Tribune, 1950-64, nat. polit. corr.; with New York Times, N.Y.C., 1964-65; with Reader's Digest, 1965—. Served to lt. AUS, World War II; combat corr. European Stars and Stripes. Fellow Woodrow Wilson Internat. Center for Scholars, Smithsonian Instn., 1972. Decorated Air medals, Bronze Star medal, Presidential citations. Mem. Acad. Polit. Sci., Sigma Delta Chi. Clubs: Overseas Press (New York); National Press (Washington). Author: Richard Nixon, A Political and Personal Portrait, 1959; The Great Debates, 1961; (with Stephen Hess), Nixon, A Political Portrait, 1968. Address: 5915 Nebraska Ave NW Washington DC 20015

MAZO, ROBERT MARC, educator; b. Bklyn., Oct. 3, 1930; s. Nathan and Rose Marion (Mazo) M.; B.A., Harvard, 1952; M.S., Yale, 1953, Ph.D., 1955; m. Joan Ruth Spector, Sept. 5, 1954; children—Ruth, Jeffrey, Daniel. Research asso. U. Chgo., 1956-58; asst. prof. Calif. Inst. Tech., 1958-62; asso. prof. U. Oreg., Eugene, 1962-65, prof. chemistry, 1965—, head chemistry dept., 1978—, dir. Inst. Theoretical Sci., 1964-67, asso. dean Grad. Sch., 1967-71; program dir NSF, 1977-78. Alfred P. Sloan fellow, NSF Sr. Postdoctoral fellow, vis. prof. U. Libre de Bruxelles Belgium, 1968-69. NSF Postdoctoral fellow U. Amsterdam (Netherlands), 1955-56. Mem. Am. Phys. Soc., AAAS, AAUP. Author: Statistical Mechanical Theories of Transport Processes, 1967; also research articles. Home: 2460 Charnelton St Eugene OR 97405

MAZUR, ABRAHAM, educator; b. N.Y.C., Oct. 8, 1911; s. David and Anna (Rubin) M.; B.S., City Coll. N.Y., 1932; M.A., Columbia U., 1934, Ph.D., 1938; m. Miriam Becker, July 7, 1940; children—Ellen (Mrs. James T. Thomson), Stephen. Fellow to prof. City Coll. City U., N.Y., 1932—; chmn. dept. chemistry, 1969-72; chief biochemistry sect. med. research div. CWS, 1943-46; research asso. to asso. prof. Cornell U. Med. Coll., N.Y.C., 1941-75; v.p. for research N.Y. Blood Center, 1975—. Chmn. bd. trustees New Lincoln Sch., N.Y.C., 1964-65. Served to capt. San. Corps, AUS, 1943-44. Decorated Army Commendation medal; recipient research grants NIH, 1956-75; Am. Cancer Soc., 1968-71; AEC, 1968-75; Townsend Harris medal City Coll. N.Y. Alumni Assn., 1976. Carnegie Corp. fellow, 1938; Guggenheim fellow, 1949. Fellow AAAS; mem. Am. Chem. Soc., Am. Soc. Biol. Chemists, Brit. Biochemical Soc., Harvey Soc. Author: (with B. Harrow) Textbook of Biochemistry, 1971; Biochemistry: A Brief Course, 1968; also articles. Home: 254 E 68th St New York NY 10021

MAZUR, ALLAN CARL, sociologist; b. Chgo., Mar. 20, 1939; s. Joseph and Esther (Markowitz) M.; B.S., Ill. Inst. Tech., 1961; M.S., U. Calif., Los Angeles, 1964; Ph.D., Johns Hopkins U., 1969; m. Minnette Albrecht, Jan. 21, 1968; children—Julie Elizabeth, Rachel Lee. Research engr. North Am. Aviation Co., Los Angeles, 1961-64; instr. polit. sci. Mass. Inst. Tech., 1966-67; ops. research analyst Lockheed Missile & Space Corp., Sunnyvale, Calif., 1967-68; asst. prof. sociology Stanford U., 1968-71; mem. faculty Syracuse (N.Y.) U., 1971—, prof. sociology, 1976—. Mem. Am. Sociol. Assn., AAAS. Jewish. Co-author: Biology and Social Behavior, 1972. Contbr. profl. jours. Home: 246 Scottholm Terr Syracuse NY 13224 Office: 500 E University Pl Syracuse NY 13210

MAZUR, MICHAEL, artist; b. N.Y.C., Nov. 2, 1935; s. Burton Boris and Helen (Isaacs) M.; B.A., Amherst Coll., 1958; M.F.A., Yale, 1961; m. Gail Lewis Beckwith, Dec. 28, 1958; children—Daniel Isaac, Kathe Elizabeth. Exhibited in one man shows Kornblee Gallery, N.Y.C., 1960,63, 66, Boris Mirski, Boston, 1963, 65, Phila. Print Club, 1964, Silvermine Guild, 1964, Fla. State U., 1966, Shoemaker Gallery Juniata Coll., 1966, Alpha Gallery, Boston, 1967, 68, 74, OGL Gallery, Los Angeles, Calif., 1968, Rose Art Mus., Brandeis U., 1969, A.A.A. Gallery, 1969, Inst. Contemporary Art, Boston, 1970, Terry Dintenfass, N.Y.C., 1974, 76, Alpha Gallery, Boston, 1974, Picker Gallery, Colgate U., 1973, Trinity Coll., 1976, Ohio State U., 1975, Robert Miller Gallery, N.Y.C., 1977, 80, Harkus-Krakow, Boston, 1977, 79; exhibited group shows at Mus. Modern Art, 1964, 75, Bklyn. Mus., 1960, 62, 64, 66, 76, Fogg Art Mus., 1966, 76, Art. Inst. Chgo., 1964, Pa. Acad., 1966, Phila. Mus., 1966, Boston Mus. Fine Arts. 1967, 68, 76, 77, DeCordova Mus., Lincoln, Mass., 1965-67, 75, Whitney Mus. Am. Art, 1965, Nat. Inst. Arts and Letters, 1965, 74, Sivermine Guild, 1965, Print Biennial of Americas, Santiago, Chile, 1965, Paris Biennale, 1969, Venice Biennale, 1970, Finch Coll. Mus., 1971-72, 2d and 3d Biennial Graphic Art, Cali, Colombia, N.A.D. Ann., 1974, Butler Inst., Youngstown, Ohio, 1974, Ball State U., 1974, America-1976, Sense of Place, Met. Mus., N.Y.C., 1979, 80, Montreal Mus. Fine Arts, 1977, Palais Royale, Brussels, 1979; traveling exhbns. include Bicentennial Exhbn., 1976, State Arts Councils, Iowa, Kans., Mo., Nebr., 1973, Am. Monotypes, Smithsonian Instn., 1977; represented in permanent collections Met. Mus., N.Y.C., Mus. Modern Art, Smith Coll. Art Mus., Library Congress, Fogg Art Mus., Art Inst. Chgo., Whitney Mus., Los Angeles County Art Mus., Mus. R.I. Sch. Design, Oreg. Art Mus., U. Maine, Mpls. Inst., Pa. State U., Toledo Art Mus., Phila. Art Mus., U. Ohio Westminster Found., Boston Mus. Fine Arts, Boston Pub. Library, Bklyn. Mus., Addison Gallery, Andover Acad., Yale Art Gallery, Montreal Mus. Fine Arts; instr. R.I. Sch. Design, 1962-65; asst. prof. fine arts Brandeis U., Waltham, Mass., 1965-76; vis. prof. Yale U. Sch. Art and Architecture, 1972, Queens Coll., 1973, U. Calif. at Santa Barbara, 1974-75; lectr. Mus. Fine Arts, Boston, Brown U.; vis. lectr. Carpenter Center, Harvard U., 1976, 78. Cons. dept. prints and drawings Mus. Fine Arts, Boston, 1974. Bd. dirs. Mass. Arts and Humanities Found.; mem. Mass. Council on Arts and Humanities, 1978—. Recipient 2d prize Soc. Am. Graphic Artists, 1963; Nat. Inst. Arts and Letters award, 1965; Tiffany Found. grant, 1964; Tamarind Lithography Workshop grant, 1968; also numerous purchase awards. Guggenheim Found. fellow, 1964-65. Mem. Boston Visual Artists Union. Home: 5 Walnut Ave Cambridge MA 02140

MAZUR, PAUL MYER, investment banking; b. Boston, Dec. 9, 1892; s. Louis and Eva (Siskin) Mazur; A.B., Harvard, 1914; D.C.S., N.Y. U., 1960; L.H.D., Rutgers U., 1961; m. Adolphia Kaske, June 21, 1922; children—Peter, Ann. Partner of Lehman Bros., investment bankers, N.Y.C., 1927-69, ltd. partner, 1969-79; vis. prof. investment banking Wharton Sch., 1965-67. With AUS, 1917-19. Recipient Tobe award for contbn. to nation's system of distbn. Clubs: Harvard, Lotos, Wall Street (New York). Author: Principles of Organization Applied to Modern Retailing, 1927; American Prosperity, 1928; America Looks Abroad, 1930; New Roads to Prosperity, 1931; The Standards We Raise, 1953; The Dynamics of Economic Growth, 1965; Unfinished Business: A Banker Looks at the Economy, 1973. Home: 1 Gracie Square New York NY 10028 Office: 1 William St New York NY 10004 Died July 30, 1979. *My lifework has consisted of a career as an investment banker, a worker, and a teacher of young people both in business, and educational institutions in the subject of economics, banking, and distribution. This guidance of younger people, exposition of economic factors, and the planning of organizational procedures have brought me a relative sense of fulfillment.*

MAZURSKY, PAUL, motion picture writer-dir.; b. Bklyn., Apr. 25, 1930; s. David and Jean (Gerson) M.; B.A., Bklyn. Coll., 1951; m. Betsy Purdy, Mar. 12, 1953; children—Meg, Jill. Actor, stage, TV and films, 1951—, including (film) Blackboard Jungle, (film and play) Deathwatch; night club comedian, 1954-60; writer Danny Kaye Show, 1963-67; co-writer film I Love You, Alice B. Toklas, 1968; writer-dir. films Bob & Carol & Ted & Alice, 1969, Alex in Wonderland, 1970, Blume in Love, 1972, Harry & Tonto, 1973, Next Stop, Greenwich Village, 1976, An Unmarried Woman, 1977-78, Willie & Phil, 1979-80. Office: care Creative Mgmt 8899 Beverly Blvd Los Angeles CA 90048

MAZZEO, JOSEPH ANTHONY, educator; N.Y.C., June 25, 1923; s. Joseph and Lia (Soraci) M.; A.B., Columbia, 1946, A.M., 1947, Ph.D., 1950; student U. Florence (Italy), 1948-49; m. Lucy Bates Welch, May 8, 1948. From instr. to asst. prof. English, Columbia, 1948-55; from asso. prof. to prof. English, Cornell U., 1955-60; prof. comparative lit. Columbia, 1960-73, Parr prof. English and comparative lit., 1973-77, Avalon Found. prof. humanities, 1977—. Served with AUS, 1943-46. Decorated Bronze Star. Recipient Gold medal Dante Soc., 1959. Guggenheim fellow, 1959. Mem. Comparative Lit. Assn. Author: Structure and Thought in the Paradiso, 1958; Medieval Cultural Tradition in Dante's Comedy, 1960; Renaissance and 17th Century studies, 1964; Renaissance and Revolution, 1965; The Design of Life: Major Themes in Biological Thought, 1967; Varieties of Interpretation, 1978. Home: 470 W 24th St New York NY 10011

MAZZIA, VALENTINO DON BOSCO, educator, physician, lawyer; b. N.Y.C., Feb. 17, 1922; s. Alexander Lloret and Francesca (D'Alessandro) M.; B.S. cum laude, City Coll. N.Y., 1943; M.D., N.Y. U., 1950; postgrad. U. So. Calif. Sch. Law, 1973-74; J.D., U. Denver, 1978; children—Lisa Mitchell, Donald Mitchell, Christopher Mitchell; m. 2d, Rosana Sgarlata, Sept. 2, 1974. Intern, Kings County Hosp., Bklyn., 1950-52; resident N.Y. Hosp., N.Y.C., 1952-54; from asst. to asst. prof. Cornell U. Med. Coll., 1952-61; prof. anesthesiology, chmn. dept. N.Y. U. Coll. Medicine, 1961-72, N.Y.U. Postgrad. Med. Sch., 1961-72; prof. anesthesiology N.Y.U. Coll. Dentistry, 1962-72; dir., attending anesthesiology Univ. Hosp., N.Y.C., 1961-72; vis.-in-charge, dir. anesthesia service Bellevue Hosp. Center, N.Y.C., 1961-72; cons. N.Y. VA Hosp., Manhattan State Hosp., 1961-72; dir. anesthesiology Los Angeles County/Martin Luther King Jr. Gen. Hosp., 1971-73; chief anesthesiology Kern County Gen. Hosp., Bakersfield, Calif., 1973; then practice, Bakersfield, Los Angeles and Las Vegas; staff 35 hosps., 1973-75; prof. anesthesiology U. Colo. Health Scis. Center and Dental Sch., Denver, 1976—; clin. dir. operating room for anesthesiology Colo. Gen. Hosp., 1976—. Vis. prof., chmn. anesthesiology Charles R. Drew Post Grad. Med. Sch., Los Angeles, 1971-73; vis. prof. anesthesiology U. Calif. at Los Angeles, 1972; asst. med. examiner, cons. forensic anesthesiology Office of Chief Med. Examiner, City of N.Y., 1962-73; dep. coroner, asst. med. examiner County of Los Angeles, 1973—; admitted to Colo. bar, 1978. Served with USAAF, 1943-45; surgeon USPHS Res. Diplomate Am. Bd. Anesthesiology. Fellow Am. Coll. Anesthesiology, N.Y. Acad. Medicine, Am. Coll. Chest Physicians, Am. Osteo. Coll. Anesthesiologists, Am. Coll. Legal Medicine; mem. Am., Colo., Denver socs. anesthesiologists, Am. Soc. Pharmacology and Exptl. Therapeutics, Harvey Soc., Soc. Exptl. Biology and Medicine, Assn. Advancement Med. Instrumentation, Am., Colo., Denver bar assns., Assn. Trial Lawyers Am., Colo. Trial Lawyers Assn., Bellevue Hosp. Alumni (asso.), Phi Beta Kappa, Sigma Xi, Beta Lambda Sigma, Alpha Omega Alpha. Club: New York Athletic (life). Co-author: Practical Anethesiology, 1962—; also articles. Address: B 113 Dept Anesthesia Univ Colo Med Center 4200 E 9th Ave Denver CO 80262 . *When one's progress appears to be blocked by circumstances or people, change location or vocation.*

MAZZO, KAY, ballet dancer; b. Evanston, Ill., Jan. 17, 1946; d. Frank Alfred and Catherine M. (Hengel) Mazzo; student Sch. Am. Ballet, 1959-61. Joined Ballet's U.S.A., touring Europe with co., performing for Pres. Kennedy at White House, 1961; joined N.Y.C. Ballet, 1962—, soloist, 1965-69, prin. ballerina, 1969—; leading roles include Jewels, Movements for Piano and Orch., Afternoon of A Faun, Midsummer Night's Dream, La Valse, Nutcracker, La Sonnambula, Agon, Stravinsky Violin Concerto and Duo Concertant; appeared as guest artist with Boston Ballet, Washington Ballet, Berlin Ballet, Geneva Ballet; appeared on television in U.S., Can., Germany. Recipient Mademoiselle Merit award, 1970. Office: NYC Ballet Lincoln Center Plaza New York NY 10023

MAZZOLA, ANTHONY THOMAS, editor, art cons., designer; b. Passaic, N.J., June 13, 1923; s. Thomas and Jennie (Failla) M.; grad. Cooper Union Art Sch., N.Y.C., 1948; m. Michele Morgan, Nov. 18, 1967; children—Anthony Thomas II, Marc Eden, Alisa Morgan. Art dir. Street & Smith Publs., N.Y.C., 1948, Town and Country mag., pub. by Hearst Corp., N.Y.C., 1948-65, editor-in-chief, 1975-72; editor-in-chief Harpers Bazaar, 1972—. Pres. Anthony Mazzola Design Corp., N.Y.C., 1963—; cons. designer United Nations Childrens' Fund, Assn. Jr. Leagues Am., Columbia Pictures Corp., Sells Spltys., Gen. Foods, Paramount Pictures, Princess Marcella Borghese, Inc., Huntington Hartford, Ltd., N.Y. World's Fair, 1965; exhibited Art Dirs. Club. N.Y. ann. exhbns., 1948—. Decorated Knight Officer of Order of Merit (Italy); recipient Certificate of Merit awards N.Y. Art Dirs. Club; medal Art Dirs. Club N.Y.C., 1955. Served with AUS, 1943-46. Home: 15 W 55th St New York NY 10022 Office: 717 Fifth Ave New York NY 10022

MAZZOLA, JOHN WILLIAM, performing arts center exec.; b. Bayonne, N.J., Jan. 20, 1928; s. Roy Stephen and Eleanor Burnett (Davis) M.; A.B., Tufts U., 1949; LL.D., Fordham U., 1952; m. Sylvia Drulie, Mar. 7, 1959; children—Alison, Amy. Admitted to N.Y. bar, 1956; mem. firm Milbank, Tweed, Hadley & McCloy, N.Y.C., 1952-64; sec., exec. v.p. Lincoln Center for Performing Arts, N.Y.C., 1964-68, gen. mgr., 1969-70, mng. dir., 1970-77, pres., 1977—; cons. performing arts centers in U.S. and abroad. Bd. dirs. Maurice Ravel Acad., France, Broadway Assn., N.Y.C.; adv. bd. Chopin Found. U.S., Van Cliburn Internat. Piano Competition, Avery Fisher Artist Awards. Served with CIC, U.S. Army, 1953-55. Decorated cavaliere ufficiale Ordine al Merito della Repubblica Italiana. Benjamin Franklin fellow Royal Sch. Arts. Episcopalian. Clubs: Watch Hill (R.I.) Yacht; Misquamicut (R.I.). Home: 12 Beekman Pl New York NY 10022 Office: 140 W 65th St New York NY 10023

MAZZOLA, VINCENT PONTORNO, physician; b. Italy, May 2, 1898; s. Paul and Antoinetta (Pontorno) M.; came to U.S., 1905, naturalized, 1912; B.S., Fordham U., 1919, M.S., 1926; M.D., L.I. Coll. Hosp., 1923; hon. D.Sc., Alfred U., 1938. Intern, resident medicine and obstetrics and gynecology L.I. Coll. Hosp. and New York Lying-In Hosp., 1927-28; attending obstetrician and gynecologist L.I. Coll. Hosp. and St. Peters Hosp., 1928—; med. dir. St. Peters Hosp., 1963—; asst. clin. prof., dir. obstetrics and gynecology L.I. Coll. Medicine; cons. Ob-Gyn, L.I. Coll. Hosp.; ltd. partner Coleman & Co.; v.p., dir. Green Acre Wood Lands, Inc., East Paterson, N.J.; ltd. partner Coleman & Co.; dir. Loon Mountain Recreation Corp., Lincoln, Lodi Trust Co. (N.J.). Mem. med. grievance com. N.Y. State Bd. Regents, 1938-43; mem. appeal bd. SSS, 1940—; mem. N.Y. State Hosp. Rev. and Planning Council, 1972—; mem. Mayor's Screening Panel for selection of mems. Bd. Higher Edn., 1964—, also Citizens Adv. Com. for Constl. Conv.; mem. Gov.'s Med. Adv. Com. for Health and Social Welfare; spl. asst. to Gov. Rockefeller for profl. activities, 1968—; mem. Bishops Lay Com. for Charities, 1953—; adviser to undersec. for adminstrn., 1968. Bd. dirs. Assn. for Children with Retarded Mental Devel.; pres., life trustee Bklyn. Benevolent Soc.; trustee U.S.O.; bd. visitors Elmira Reformatory, 5 terms. Served with U.S. Army, World War I; brig. surgeon N.Y. Guard, 1940. Recipient By-Line award New York Newspaper Reporters Assn., 1950, Distinguished Service award N.Y. Dept. State, 1972, Meritorious Service award Selective Service System, 1972, citation of merit Am. Correctional Chaplains Assn., 1959; named hon. citizen N.H., 1968. Fellow Mediterranean Acad., 1950. Diplomate Am. Bd. Obstetrics and Gynecology. Fellow N.Y. Acad. Medicine, N.Y. Obstet. Soc., Bklyn. Gynecol. Soc., A.C.S., Internat. Coll. Surgeons, Am. Coll. Obstetrics and Gynecology; mem. New York Reporters Assn. (hon.), Soc. of Silurians, Circus Saints and Sinners; hon. mem. Bordeaux, Madrid, Rome, Brazil surg. socs. Clubs: Downtown Athletic; Turf and Field. Mem. bd. contbg. editors Medical Times, 1940—. Contbr. articles profl. jours. Address: 133 Clinton St Brooklyn NY 11201. *Health, hard work, honesty are the pillars of peace, happiness and prosperity. There is no compromise with the Truth; expediency, pragmatism and complacency, are false truths. Respect consultation and experience.*

MAZZOLI, ROMANO L., congressman; b. Louisville, Ky., Nov. 2, 1932; B.S. in Bus. Adminstrn. magna cum laude, U. Notre Dame, 1954; J.D., U. Louisville, 1960; m. Helen Dillon, 1959; children—Michael, Andrea. Admitted to Ky. bar, 1960; mem. law dept. Louisville and Nashville R.R. Co., 1960-62; pvt. practice, 1960-70; mem. Ky. Senate, 1967-70; mem. 92d-96th congresses from 3d Ky. Dist.; pres. House Freshman Democrats, 1972. Lectr. bus. law Bellarmine Coll., Louisville, 1963-67. Served with AUS, 1954-56. Named Outstanding Freshman Ky. State Senator, 1968, Best Ky. State Senator from Public Standpoint, 1970. Mem. Louisville, Ky., Am. bar assns., Notre Dame Clubs of Ky. and D.C. Home: Louisville KY Office: House Office Bldg Washington DC 20515

MAZZONE, A. DAVID, judge; b. Everett, Mass., June 3, 1928; s. A. Marino and Philomena M.; B.A., Harvard U., 1950; J.D., DePaul U., 1957; m. Eleanor G. Stewart, May 10, 1951; children—Margaret Clark, Andrew David, John Stewart, Jan Eleanor, Martha Ann, Robert Joseph, Carolyn Cook. Admitted to Ill. bar, 1957, Mass. bar, 1959, U.S. Supreme Ct. bar, 1964; asst. dist. atty., Middlesex County, Mass., 1961-65; asst. U.S. atty., Mass., 1965; partner firm Moulton, Looney & Mazzone, Boston, 1965-75; asso. justice Superior Ct., Boston, 1975-78; U.S. dist. judge, Boston, 1978—. Served with U.S. Army, 1951-52. Mem. Mass. Trial Lawyers Assn., Am. Law Inst., Mass. Bar Assn., Boston Bar Assn., Middlesex Bar Assn., Fed. Bar Assn. Democrat. Roman Catholic. Home: 7 Shumway Circle Wakefield MA 01880 Office: McCormack Post Office and Courthouse Bldg Boston MA 02109

MCADAM, CHARLES VINCENT, newspaper syndicate exec.; b. N.Y.C., May 28, 1892; s. John and Mary (Barrett) M.; student pub. schs., N.Y.C.; m. Marguerite Wimbey, Sept. 28, 1920 (dec. Jan. 1965); children—Patricia Thom, Charles Vincent, Marguerite Lois Cook; m. 2d, Joanne Farris, Nov. 27, 1965; m. 3d, Sybil S. Speiller, June 15, 1979; stepchildren—Paul B., Joyce M. With McClure Newspaper Syndicate, 1914-17, Internat. and King Features Syndicate, 1917-19; v.p. McNaught Syndicate Inc., 1922, chmn., 1930—; dir. emeritus Storer Broadcasting Co., Miami; v.p. Calder Race Course, Miami. Named Ky. Col. Mem. Soc. Magicians. Roman Catholic. Clubs: Westchester Country (Rye, N.Y.); Artists and Writers; Blind Brook, Indian Creek; Bal Harbour Beach; LaGorce Country (Miami Beach, Fla.). Home: 107 Bal Cross Dr Bal Harbour Miami Beach FL 33154 Office: 60 E 42d St New York NY 10017

MC ADAM, DALE WILLIAM, psychologist; b. Lansing, Mich., Oct. 23, 1934; s. Ray Malvern and Henrietta Marie (Behnke) McA.; B.A., U. Iowa, 1957, M.A., 1961, Ph.D., 1961. From research asso. to asso. prof. U. Iowa, 1961-67; mem. faculty U. Rochester (N.Y.), 1967—, prof. psychology, 1972—. Author papers on biol. substrates of complex behavior. Home: 1025 Goler House Rochester NY 14620 Office: Psychology Dept Univ Rochester Rochester NY 14627

MC ADAMS, ANDREW JACK, physician; b. Pitts., Nov. 25, 1911; s. Robert Joseph and Miriam (Snow) McA.; B.S., M.D., U. Pitts., 1935; m. Elizabeth von Senden, Sept. 11, 1937; children—Marilyn (Mrs. Robert J. White), Andrew Jack. Intern Western Pa. Hosp., Pitts., 1935-36, asst. to chief div. surgery, 1936-39, asso. div. surgery, 1939-48, sr. div. surgery, 1948—, interim chief div. surgery, 1971; cons. div. surgery Braddock Gen. Hosp., 1946—; clin. instr. surgery U. Pitts. Bd. dirs. Western Pa. Hosp., 1973-74. Served to maj., M.C., AUS, 1943-45. Diplomate Am. Bd. Surgery, Am. Bd. Colon and Rectal Surgery (pres. 1969-71, adv. council 1972—). Fellow A.C.S., Am. Soc. Colon and Rectal Surgeons (pres. 1971-72, chmn. self-assessment program 1971-76); mem. AMA (sect. chmn. 1970). Methodist (trustee). Clubs: Univ. (Pitts.), Longue Vue (Verona, Pa.). Research, publs. on colonic anastomoses. Home: 5804 Wayne Rd Pittsburgh PA 15206 Office: 4815 Liberty Ave Pittsburgh PA 15224

MC ADAMS, HERBERT HALL, banker; b. Jonesboro, Ark., June 6, 1915; s. H.H. and Stella (Patrick) McA.; B.S., Northwestern U., 1937; postgrad. Harvard, 1937-38, Loyola U., Chgo., 1938-39; J.D., U. Ark., 1940; m. Shelia Wallace, Nov. 27, 1970; children (by previous marriage)—Judith (Mrs. Walter A. DeRoeck), Sandra (Mrs. Robert C. Connor), Hall, Penny (Mrs. Tim Hodges); 1 dau., Nicole Patrick McAdams. Admitted to Ark. bar, 1940; chmn. bd., chief exec. officer Citizens Bank, Jonesboro, 1959—; chmn. bd., chief exec. officer Union Nat. Bank, Little Rock, 1970—; dir. Little Rock br. Fed. Res. Bank, 1974-76, Ark. La. Gas Co., 1964-73, 76—. Pres., Jonesboro Sch. Dist., 1947, mem., 1948-50; mem. Ark. Indsl. Devel. Commn., 1965-73, chmn., 1967-72; trustee Ark. Children's Hosp., 1972-75, Baptist Med. Center, 1975-77, Bapt. Found., 1975; bd. govs. Ark. State Fair and Livestock Show Assn.; pres. Bapt. Med. Center System Real Estate Corp., 1977—; mem. Bapt. Med. Center System Corp.; exec. com. Democratic Nat. Fin. Com., 1977—; state chmn. Citizens Com. on Edn., 1950; chmn. bd. govs. Ark. State U. Found.; bd. visitors U. Ark. at Little Rock, 1978—. Served with USNR, World War II. Recipient

Purple Heart. Mem. Am., Ark. bar assns., Am., Ark. bankers assns., Ark. Council Econ. Edn., Met. C. of C. (dir.), Sales and Marketing Execs. (Top Mgmt. Honoree 1972), Sigma Nu. Bapt. Clubs: Rotary, Country of Little Rock, Little Rock, Pleasant Valley Country (Little Rock); Summit (Memphis). Home: 47 Egdehill Little Rock AR 72207 Office: Union National Bank Little Rock AR also Citizens Bank Bldg Jonesboro AR 72401

MC ADAMS, JOE B., JR., newspaper exec.; b. Hot Springs, Ark., Oct. 13, 1943; s. Joe B. and Dorothy D. (Rushing) McA.; B.A., So. Ill. U., 1969; M.B.A., Loyola U., 1972; postgrad. John Marshall Law Sch., 1974; m. Marcia Cates, Jan. 25, 1964 (div.); children—Joe, Kevin. Composing room supr. St. Louis Post Dispatch, 1965-69; cost and efficiency analyst Meredith Pub. Co., 1969-70; mgr., v.p., gen. mgr. Met. Printing, 1970-73; v.p. prodn. Chgo. Sun-Times, 1973-78, exec. v.p., gen. mgr., 1978—; dir. Met. Printing, F.S.C. Paper Corp. Served with U.S. Army, 1966-68. Mem. Am. Newspaper Pubs. Assn. (mem. telecommunications com.), Research and Engring. Council Graphic Arts, So. Prodn. Planning Inst., Chgo. Club Printing Craftsmen. Office: 401 N Wabash Ave Chicago IL 60611

MC ADAMS, JOHN V., advt. exec.; b. N.Y.C., Nov. 1, 1917; s. John and Helen McAdams; ed. Ohio State U., Columbia U. With Albert Frank-Guenther Law, Inc., advt., N.Y.C., pres., 1947-70, chmn. bd., 1970—. Address: Albert Frank-Guenther Law Inc 61 Broadway New York NY 10006*

MCADAMS, RONALD EARL, cons. geologist; b. Tulia, Tex., Aug. 6, 1910; s. Earl A. and Laura Ann (Hutchinson) McA.; B.A., Tex. A. and M. Coll., 1932, M.S., 1935; m. Lucy Grace Harris, Aug. 24, 1927; children—Elizabeth Ann, John Harris. Field geologist Shell Oil Co., 1936-42, dist. geologist, 1946-47, exploration mgr., Tulsa, 1947-53, Denver, 1954, mgr. exploration and land, head office N.Y.C., 1955-57, v.p. exploration, 1957-70; cons. petroleum geologist, 1970-76; chmn., chief exec. officer McAdams, Roux, O'Connor Assos., Inc., oil and gas exploration, 1977—. Served from 1st lt. to lt. col., AUS, 1942-45. Fellow Geol. Soc. Am; mem. Am. Assn. Petroleum Geologists, Am. Inst. Profl. Geologists, Tau Beta Pi. Clubs: Cherry Hills Country (Englewood, Colo.); Champions Golf (Houston); Denver Petroleum. Home: 3401 S Race St Englewood CO 80110

MC ADAMS, WILLIAM ALFRED, mfg. co. exec.; b. Hagerstown, Md., Feb. 24, 1918; s. Marvin L. and Vida (Huffer) McA.; B.S. in Math. and Physics, Washington Coll., 1940; m. Anna M. McKay, Feb. 10, 1945; children—Susan Hansbury, Robert W. Ballistics engr. E.I. duPont Co., N.J. and Ind., 1940-43; research physicist Manhattan project at U. Chgo., E.I. duPont Co., 1943-44; radiation protection engr., supr. Hanford atomic project E. I. duPont Co. and Gen. Electric Co., 1944-55; cons. radiation protection, corporate engring. Gen. Electric Co., Schenectady, 1955-59, mgr. industry, corporate engring. and tech. staffs, Schenectady, 1960-66, N.Y.C., 1966-79, Fairfield, Conn., 1974-78; chmn. Nat. Acad. Sci. evaluation panel for a div. of Nat. Bur. Standards, 1975—; dir. Am. Nat. Metric Council, 1975-76; del. internat. orgns. Recipient Alumni citation Washington Coll., 1960; Gold Standards medal Am. Standards Assn., 1965; Spl. award Am. Nat. Standards Inst., 1974; Leo B. Moor award Standards Engrs. Soc. Fellow IEEE, Standards Engrs. Soc.; mem. Nat. Elec. Mfrs. Assn. (com. officer), Nat. Fire Protection Assn. (chmn. bd. 1976—), ASTM (dir., pres. 1977—). Patentee in field; pioneer standards work. Home: 220 Ingleside Rd Fairfield CT 06430 Office: Gen Electric Co Fairfield CT 06431

MCADOO, BOB, basketball player; b. Greensboro, N.C., Sept. 25, 1951; grad. U. N.C., 1973. With Buffalo Braves, 1972-76, N.Y. Knickerbockers, 1976-79, Boston Celtics, 1979—. Named Rookie of Year, NBA, 1973. Office: Boston Celtics Boston Garden North Sta Boston MA 02114*

MC ADOO, DONALD ELDRIDGE, artist; b. Chgo., Feb. 8, 1929; s. Frank Joseph and Marion Louise (Weigler) Kovarik; student public schs.; m. Carolyn Westbrook, Oct. 20, 1970. Exhibited 25 one-man shows; retrospective exhibit toured La. Art Commn. Gallery, Columbus (Ga.) Mus., Columbia (S.C.) Mus., Mint Mus., Charlotte, N.C., Birmingham (Ala.) Mus., Rogers (Miss.) Mus., Telfair Mus., Savannah, Mobile (Ala.) Mus., Macon (Ga.) Mus., 1972-74; exhibited in 49 group shows including: Springfield (Mass.) Mus. 1966, Va. Mus., 1967, Norfolk (Va.) Mus., 1967, S.E. Center Contemporary Art, 1969-72, Nat. Acad. Galleries, N.Y.C., 1970, High Mus., Atlanta, 1971, El Paso (Tex.) Mus., 1972, Greenwich (Conn.) Workshop, 1979; represented in permanent collections: Va. Mus., Richmond, Ga. Mus. Art, Athens, Springfield (Mo.) Mus., Birmingham Mus., Columbia Mus., Columbus (Ohio) Mus., Mint Mus., Mus. of South at Mobile, Macon (Ga.) Mus. Art and Sci.; tutor, lectr., instr. to art groups, 1972—; judge art exhibits, 1968—. Recipient numerous awards for paintings and graphics. Mem. La. Watercolor Soc., Ala. Watercolor Soc., Southeastern Center for Contemporary Arts, Nat. Audubon Soc. Roman Catholic. Author: (with Carol McAdoo) Reflections of the Outer Banks, 1975. Home: 5070 Sunset Trail NE Marietta GA 30067. *I have one primary goal—to paint the bark without the dog. With this seemingly unattainable aim always before me, complacency and stagnation cannot exist and growth becomes a constant factor.*

MC ADOO, RICHARD BUDD, publishing co. exec.; b. Ft. Washington, Pa., Mar. 25, 1920; s. Henry M. and Margaret (Nice) McA.; A.B., Harvard U., 1942; m. Mary Wigglesworth, June 26, 1948; children—Mary Parkman, Pamela Dwight, Julia Minot. With Harper and Row, and predecessor, N.Y.C., 1946-68, editor nature and outdoor books, 1956-61, editor social and econ. books, 1962-65, v.p., gen. mgr., 1965-68; sr. editor Houghton Mifflin Co., Boston, 1968-69, trade div. editor-in-chief, 1969-73, sr. v.p., dir. trade div., 1973—, also dir., mem. exec. com.; chmn. bd. Ticknor & Fields, 1979—. Trustee, Center House Found., Boston Philharm. Orch. Served to capt. AUS, 1942-45. Woodrow Wilson Found. sr. fellow. Episcopalian. Clubs: Harvard (N.Y.C.); Tavern, Somerset (Boston). Contbr. articles Harper's mag. Home: 7 Lincoln Ln Cambridge MA 02138 Office: 2 Park St Boston MA 02107

MC AFEE, JERRY, oil co. exec., chem. engr.; b. Port Arthur, Tex., Nov. 3, 1916; s. Almer McD. and Marguerite (Calfee) McA.; B.S. in Chem Engring., U. Tex. at Austin, 1937; Sc.D. in Chem. Engring., Mass. Inst. Tech., 1940; student Mgmt. Problems for Execs., U. Pitts., 1952; m. Geraldine Smith, June 21, 1940; children—Joe R., William M., Loretta M., Thomas R. Research chem. engr. Universal Oil Products Co., Chgo., 1940-43, operating engr., 1944-45; tech. specialist Gulf Oil Corp., Port Arthur, Tex., 1945-50, successively dir. chemistry, asst. dir. research, v.p., asso. dir. subs. Gulf Research & Devel. Co., Hamarville, Pa., 1950-55, v.p. engring. mfg. dept. of corp., 1955-60; v.p., exec. tech. advisor of corp., 1960-64, also dir. planning and econs., 1962-64; sr. v.p. Gulf Oil Corp., 1964-67, now chmn. bd., chief exec. officer; sr. v.p. Gulf Eastern Co., London, 1964-67; exec. v.p. Brit. Am. Oil Co., Ltd., Toronto, Ont., 1967-69; pres., chief exec. officer, dir. Gulf Oil Can. Ltd., 1969-75; dir. Mellon Bank. Bd. dirs. Am. Petroleum Inst., Aspen Inst. Humanistic Studies, M.I.T. Corp., Pitts. Symphony Soc. Mem. Am. Inst. Chem. Engring. (v.p. 1959, pres. 1960), Nat. Acad. Engring., Am. Petroleum Inst., Am. Chem. Soc. Presbyterian. Clubs: Duquesne (Pitts.); York (Toronto); Fox Chapel Golf; Links (N.Y.). Patentee in field. Home: 4 Indian Hill Rd Pittsburgh PA 15238 Office: Gulf Oil Corp Gulf Bldg Pittsburgh PA 15219

MCAFEE, JOHN G., physician, educator; b. Toronto, Ont., Can., June ll, 1926; s. Robert Duncan and Susan Jane (Damery) McA.; M.D., U. Toronto, 1948; m. Joan Margaret Weber, Feb. 9, 1952; children—Paul Clifton, Carol Joan, David Robert. Came to U.S., 1951, naturalized, 1960. Intern Victoria Hosp., London, Ont., 1948, resident, 1950; resident Westminster Hosp., London, 1949-50, Johns Hopkins Hosp., 1951-53; practice medicine specializing in radiology, Balt., 1951-65, Syracuse, N.Y., 1966—; mem. faculty Johns Hopkins Med. Sch., 1953-65; prof., chmn. dept. radiology State U. N.Y. Upstate Med. Center, Syracuse, 1965-73, prof. radiology, chief nuclear medicine service, 1973-78, chief div. radiol. sci., 1978—. Mem. Soc. Nuclear Medicine, Assn. U. Radiologists, Radiol. Soc. N.Am. Contbr. numerous articles to profl. jours. Developed radioactive agts. for detection bone, inflammatory and kidney lesions in man. Home: 5 Lynacres Blvd Fayetteville NY 13066 Office: 750 E Adams St Syracuse NY 13210

MCAFEE, KENNETH EMBERRY, lawyer; b. Spadra, Ark., Aug. 27, 1903; s. Thomas W. and Corah M.B. (Dowell) McA.; B.S., LL.B., U. Okla., 1934; m. Maxine Maples, Apr. 21, 1930; 1 dau., Jacquelyn (Mrs. Gary Wayne Williams). Admitted to Okla. bar, 1934, since practiced in Oklahoma City; mem. firm McAfee, Taft, Mark, Bond, Rucks & Woodruff, 1934—. Bd. dirs. U. Okla. Found. Served to lt. comdr. USNR, 1942-45. Mem. Am. Bar Assn., Am. Inst. C.P.A.'s, Order of Coif, Beta Gamma Sigma. Lion. Clubs: Sirloin, Economics, Mens Dinner (Oklahoma City). Home: 1120 Glenwood Oklahoma City OK 73116 Office: 100 Park Ave Oklahoma City OK 73102

MC AFEE, RALPH LAVERNE, lawyer; b. Barry, Tex., Oct. 20, 1914; s. Jesse Urban and Annie (Reeves) McA.; student Southwestern U., 1931-33; B.S., Columbia, 1936, J.D., 1939; m. Carolyn Jane McDonell, June 25, 1946; children—Carolyn Jane, Horace Michael, Marc Charles. Admitted to N.Y. bar, 1940, since practiced in N.Y.C.; law asst. N.Y. County Dist. Attys. Office, 1939-40; asso. firm Cravath, Swaine & Moore and predecessor, 1940-52, mem. firm, 1952—. Served to maj. AUS, 1940-45; CBI. Fellow Am. Bar Found., Am. Coll. Trial Lawyers, N.Y. Bar Found.; mem. Am., N.Y. State, N.Y.C. bar assns., Fed. Bar Council, N.Y. County Lawyers Assn., Am. Judicature Soc., N.Y. Law Inst., Phi Delta Phi. Clubs: Wall Street (N.Y.C.); Sleepy Hollow Country (Scarborough, N.Y.); Metropolitan, National Lawyers (Washington); Shinnecock Hills Golf (Southampton, N.Y.). Home: 22 Lakeview Ave North Tarrytown NY 10591 Office: 1 Chase Manhattan Plaza New York NY 10005

MCAFEE, WILLIAM, govt. ofcl.; b. Port Royal, Jan. 25, 1910; s. French and Willietta (Anderson) McA.; B.A. Coll. of Wooster, 1932; M.A. in Am. History, Pa. State U., 1941; student Oxford (Eng.), summer 1937, Wooster in India rep. on faculty Ewing Christian Coll., Allahabad, India, 1932- 35; tchr. pub. high schs. and prep. sch., Pa., 1935-42; joined State Dept., 1946; country specialist Office Chinese Affairs, 1946-50; coordinator current intelligence Bur. Intelligence and Research, 1950-56, spl. asst. to dir., 1956-60, dir. ops. staff, 1966, asst. dep. dir. coordination, 1960-72, dep. dir. coordination, 1972—. Adviser Griffin Econ. Aid Mission to S.E. Asia, 1950. Served to lt. col. AUS, 1942-46; CBI. Decorated Legion of Merit; Order Brit. Empire, Precious Tripod (Chinese Nationalist Govt.); recipient Superior Honor award State Dept., 1964. Mem. Am. Fgn. Service Assn., Assn. U.S. Army, Delta Sigma Rho. Home: 4433 Brandywine St NW Washington DC 20016 Office: Dept of State Washington DC 20520

MC ALESTER, ARCIE LEE, JR., educator; b. Dallas, Feb. 3, 1933; s. Arcie Lee and Alverta (Funderburk) McA.; B.A., B.B.A., So. Methodist U., 1954; M.S., Yale, 1957, Ph.D., 1960; m. Virginia Wallace Savage; children—Kirstie Martine, Archibald Keven. Mem. faculty Yale, 1959-74, prof. geology, 1966-74, curator invertebrate paleontology Peabody Mus., 1966-74; prof. geol. scis., So. Meth. U., Dallas, 1974—, dean Sch. Humanities and Scis., 1974-77. Served to 1st lt. USAF, 1954-56. Guggenheim Found. fellow Glasgow (Scotland) U., 1965. Mem. Geol. Soc. Am., Paleontol. Soc., AAAS. Club: Yale (N.Y.C.). Author: The History of Life, 1977; The Earth, 1973; Physical Geology, 1975; History of the Earth, 1979; also articles. Asso. editor Am. Scientist, 1970-74. Address: Dept Geological Sciences Southern Methodist University Dallas TX 75275

MC ALISTER, ERNEST ELMO, JR., gas co. exec.; b. Stephenville, Tex., May 12, 1939; s. Ernest Elmo and Velma Lois (Moore) McA.; B.B.A., Hardin Simmons U., 1962; M.B.A., So. Methodist U., 1974; m. Verna Jane Jordan, Feb. 1958; children—Kimberly I., Dana R. With Lone Star Gas Co. div. ENSERCH Corp., Dallas, 1963—, asst. treas. payroll and credit, fin. div., 1974-75, asst. treas. credit and disbursements, 1975, co. treas., 1975—. Bd. dirs. Dallas Jr. C. of C., 1971-72, Dallas County United Way, 1974-76, Jr. Achievement Dallas, 1979—. Mem. Nat. Soc. Rate Return Analysts, Adminstrv. Mgmt. Soc., Assn. System Mgmt., Tex. Assn. Assessing Officers, Nat., Dallas assns. credit mgmt., Am. Gas Assn., So. Gas Assn. Democrat. Baptist. Clubs: Lions (treas., 3d v.p., dir. Dallas Founders club), Lancers. Home: 2321 Camp David Dr Mesquite TX 75149 Office: 301 S Harwood St Dallas TX 75201

MC ALISTER, LUTHER DURWOOD, editor; b. Bolivar, Tenn., June 16, 1927; s. Turner Dolphis and Mary Jo (Brown) McA.; B.A., Howard Coll., 1949; m. Dorris Fay Curenton, June 15, 1950; children—David Bruce, Jane Kimberly, Donald Kent. Reporter, Birmingham (Ala.) Age-Herald, 1949-50; reporter, news editor Anniston (Ala.) Star, 1950-54; with Atlanta Jour., 1954—, mng. editor, 1968-78, editor, 1978—. Served with USNR, 1945-46. Mem. A.P. Mng. Editors Assn. (dir.), Am. Soc. Newspaper Editors, Sigma Delta Chi. Baptist. Club: Atlanta Press. Home: 1643 Timberland Rd NE Atlanta GA 30345 Office: 72 Marietta St Atlanta GA 30302

MC ALISTER, ROBERT CARTER, army officer; b. Mayfield, Ky., Sept. 15, 1923; s. Samuel Edward and Orene (Cashon) McA.; student U.S. Mil. Acad., 1942-45; B.S., U.S. Army Command and Gen. Staff Coll., 1955; grad. Army War Coll., 1963; M.A., George Washington U., 1963; m. Martha Sebree, Aug. 17, 1950; children—Pauline, Mary, Robert Carter, Edmund Sebree, Samuel Edward. Commd. 2d lt. U.S. Army, 1945, advanced through grades to lt. gen., 1975; instr. tactics U.S. Mil. Acad., 1959-62; bn. comdr., 4th U.S. inf. div., 1963-64; plans officer U.S. So. Command, Panama, 1964-67; div. arty. comdr., asst. div. comdr. 4th U.S. inf. div., Vietnam, 1967-69; dir. inter-Am. regional Office Sec. Def. Internat. Security Affairs, Washington, 1969-71; comdg. gen. U.S. Army So. European Task Force, Vicenza, Italy, 1971-73; dep. chief staff U.S. Army Tng. and Doctrine Command, Ft. Monroe, Va., 1973-75; chief staff Allied Forces So. Europe, Naples, Italy, 1975-78; chief staff U.S. European Command, 1978—. Decorated D.S.M., Legion of Merit with oak leaf cluster, Bronze Star medal for valor with oak leaf cluster, Air medal with 8 oak leaf clusters, Purple Heart. Address: 403 N 6th St Mayfield KY 42066

MC ALLISTER, DECKER GORDON, mfg. exec.; b. San Francisco, Aug. 19, 1900; s. Elliott and Alice (Decker) McA.; student Stanford, 1917-18; B.S. in Elec. Engring., Mass. Inst. Tech., 1921; m. Martha Ransome, Apr. 20, 1929; children—Decker Gordon, Bruce. With Pacific Sci. Co., San Francisco, 1925—, pres., 1961-65, chmn. bd., 1965-73, hon. chmn. bd., 1973—; with Pacific Sci. Aero Products, 1928—, pres., 1954—; vice chmn. bd. Oxford Labs.; dir. Varian Assos., Chemetal Corp. Chmn. trustees, fellow Calif. Acad. Scis.; trustee Internat. Sci. Found. Clubs: Pacific Union (San Francisco); Burlingame Country (Hillborough, Calif.). Home: 700 Eucalyptus Rd Hillsborough CA 94010 also Hana Maui HI 96713 Office: 541 Taylor Way Belmont CA 94002

MC ALLISTER, DONALD, publisher; b. Ithaca, N.Y., July 12, 1902; s. Peter Francis and Margaret (O'Shea) McA.; A.B., Cornell U., 1922; m. Betty L. Myers, June 30, 1947; children—Donald, Liane Elisabeth. With Geyer-McAllister Publs., Inc., pubs. bus. mags., N.Y.C., 1922—, gen. mgr., 1946-59, pres., 1959-63, chmn. bd., 1963—; chmn. bd., chief exec. officer Geyer-McAllister Internat., Inc.; adv. com. Am. Bus. Press. Served with USAAF, 1942-45. Mem. Adminstrv. Mgmt. Soc., Am. Mgmt. Soc., AIM, Assn. 2d Class Mail Publs. (dir.), Asso. Bus. Publs. (chmn. bd. 1956-57); hon. mem., dir. Gift and Decorative Accessories Assn. Am.; hon. mem. Nat. Office Products Assn. Clubs: University (N.Y.C.); Creek (Locust Valley, N.Y.); Seawanhaka Corinthian Yacht (Oyster Bay, N.Y.). Home: 870 Fifth Ave New York NY 10021 Office: 51 Madison Ave New York NY 10010

MC ALLISTER, GERALD NICHOLAS, clergyman; b. San Antonio, Feb. 23, 1923; s. Walter Williams and Leonora Elizabeth (Alexander) McA.; student U. Tex., 1942; student Va. Theol. Sem., 1951, D.D. (hon.), 1977; m. Helen Earle Black, Oct. 2, 1953; children—Michael Lee, David Alexander, Stephen Williams, Elizabeth. Rancher, 1946-48; ordained deacon Episcopal Ch., 1953, priest, 1954; deacon, priest Ch. of Epiphany, Raymondville, Ch. of Incarnation, Corpus Christi, St. Francis Ch., Victoria (all Tex.), 1951-63; 1st canon Diocese of W. Tex., 1963-70; rector St. David's Ch., San Antonio, 1970-76; Episcopal bishop of Okla., Oklahoma City, 1977—; trustee Episcopal Theol. Sem. of S.W., 1961-72, adv. bd., 1974—; pres. Tex. Council Chs., 1966-68; bd. dirs. Presiding Bishop's Fund for World Relief, 1972-77, Ch. Hist. Soc., 1976—; chmn. Nat. and World Mission Program Group, 1973-76; mem. Structure of Ch. Standing Commn., 1979; founder Chaplaincy Program, Bexar County Jail, 1968. Bd. dirs. Econ. Opportunity Devel. Corp., San Antonio, 1968-69; mem. exec. com. United Way, 1968-70, vice-chmn., 1970. Served with U.S. Mcht. Marines, 1942, to 1st lt. USAAF, 1942-45. Recipient Agudas Achim Brotherhood award, 1968. Author: What We Learned from What You Said, 1973. Office: 1100 Classen Dr Oklahoma City OK 73101

MC ALLISTER, JAMES M., publishing co. exec.; b. Niles, Ohio, Sept. 21, 1915; s. James Robert and Osa (Hall) McA.; B.A., Western Res. U., 1937; m. Mildred Waser Morris, June 15, 1940; children—James M., Michael G. Sales promotion copy writer Union Paper Co., 1937-43; sales rep. Capper Publs., 1946-48; sales rep. Parade Publs., 1948-58, Chgo. mgr., 1958-62, Midwest mgr., 1962-72, nat. advt. dir., 1972-73, exec. v.p., 1974, pres., 1975—, chmn. bd., 1977—; also chief exec. officer Diversified Printing Corp., Atglen, Pa. Served with USMCR, 1944-46. Mem. Internat. Press Inst., Am. Newspaper Pubs. Assn., Delta Kappa Epsilon. Clubs: Sales Execs., Tavern (Chgo.); Pinnacle (N.Y.C.); Larchmont Yacht. Home: 16 Beaver Ln Highland Estates Sedona AZ 86338 Office: 733 3d Ave New York NY 10017

MC ALLISTER, KENNETH, tobacco exec.; b. Coraopolis, Pa., May 25, 1916; s. Arthur Walker and Ethalinda May (Correll) McA.; B.S. in Mech. Engring., Rutgers U., 1939; m. Betty Proudfoot, Sept. 21, 1940; children—Keith, Craig. Sales promotion mgr. radio sta. WGY, Schenectady, 1940-41; advt. exec. Columbia Records, 1941-43, 46-50; v.p., sec. plans bd. Sullivan, Stauffer, Colwell & Bayles, Inc., 1953-55; sr. v.p., dir. Benton & Bowles Inc., N.Y.C., 1950-53, 55-61; v.p. advt. Thomas J. Lipton, Inc., 1961-63, exec. v.p., 1963-67, dir., 1961-67; pres., dir. Good Humor Corp., 1965-67; pres. M & M/Mars candy div. Mars, Inc., 1967-68; pres. cigarette and tobacco div. Liggett & Myers, Inc., 1969-73; exec. v.p., dir. parent co.; dir., mem. exec. com. Coca Cola Bottling Co. N.Y. Served with USNR, 1943-46. Mem. Phi Beta Kappa, Tau Beta Pi. Clubs: Harbour Town, Plantation (Hilton Head). Home: Catbird Ln Hilton Head Island SC 29928

MC ALLISTER, LESTER BELDEN, educator; b. Chgo., Feb. 21, 1921; s. Lester Belden and Bertha (Wulpi) McA.; B.A., Coe Coll., 1942; M.A., Northwestern U., 1947; Ph.D. (Carnegie fellow 1950-52), U. Oreg., 1953; m. Elaine Schneider, Feb. 17, 1945; 1 dau., Margaret. Instr. econs. Coe Coll., 1947-50, Oreg. State Coll., 1952-53; mem. faculty Beloit Coll., 1953—, prof. econs., 1959—, chmn. dept. econs. and bus., 1960-74; prof. fgn. affairs Nat. War Coll., 1961-62; vis. prof. econs. U. Wis., 1968; cons.-examiner North Central Assn., 1974—. Mem. Wis. Banking Rev. Bd., 1974-79. Mem. Beloit Bd. Edn., 1955-58. Served to maj. USAAF, 1942-46. Ford Found. fellow U. Wis., 1957. Mem. Am., Midwest econ. assns., Phi Beta Kappa. Author articles, essays. Home: 1209 Chapin St Beloit WI 53511

MCALLISTER, ROBERT JOHN, physician; b. Geyser, Mont., Aug. 13, 1919; s. John Joseph and Laura (Lee) McA.; B.A., Loras Coll., 1941; M.A., Catholic U. Am., 1949, Ph.D., 1952; M.D., Georgetown U., 1956; m. Jane Fox; children—Frances, Robert, John, Paul, Patricia, Laura. Intern Providence Hosp., Washington, 1956- 57; resident Seton Psychiat. Inst., Balt., 1957-60; practice medicine, specializing in psychiatry, Takoma Park, Md., 1960-66, Reno, 1966-71, Grants Pass, Oreg., 1971-76, Spokane, Wash., 1976—; psychiat. cons. Dept. Def., 1963-66; supt., med. dir. Nev. State Hosp., 1966-71; adminstr. Mental Health Div. Nev., 1966-71; faculty Inst. for Mental Health, St. John's U., Collegeville, Minn., 1964-74; adj. clin. prof. U. Nev., 1967-72. Served with AUS, 1943-46. Recipient Research award Nat. Assn. Pvt. Psychiat. Hosps., 1960. Mem. AMA, Am. Psychiat. Assn., Am. Psychol. Assn., Acad. Religion and Mental Health. Address: S 2129 Rockwood Blvd Spokane WA 99203

MC ALLISTER, WALTER WILLIAMS, savs. and loan exec.; b. San Antonio, Mar. 26, 1889; s. Frank Williams and Lena (Stumberg) McA.; E.E., U. Tex., 1910; m. Lenora Alexander, Mar. 26, 1913 (dec. May 1969); children—Elizabeth McAllister Solcher, Walter Williams Jr., Gerald N. Founder, San Antonio Savs. Assn., 1921, chmn. bd., 1953-76, chmn. exec. com., 1976—; chmn. bd. South States Oil Co., San Antonio, chmn. Fed. Home Loan Bank Bd., Washington, 1953-56; chmn. nat. advisory bond com. savs. and loan U.S. Treasury, 1958-63. Pres., Planning Bd. San Antonio and Bexar County, 1948-50; chmn. San Antonio City Mgr. Charter Revision Commn., 1951—; mem. Tex. Finance Commn., 1952-53; mayor San Antonio, 1961-71, councilman, 1960. Bd. dirs. emeritus Ednl. TV Sta. KLRN, Austin, Tex.; pres. bd. trustees San Antonio Union Jr. Coll., 1946-60; chmn. bd. dirs. Witte Mus., 1952-53; trustee Internat. Union Bldg. Socs. and Savs. and Loan Assns. Recipient Golden Deeds award San Antonio Exchange Club, 1956, Outstanding Citizens award San Antonio Council Presidents, 1964. Mem. U.S. (legis. com., past pres.), Southwestern (past pres.), Tex. (past pres.) savs. and loan leagues, San Antonio C. of C. (past pres.), Phi Gamma Delta. Republican. Mason (33 deg., Shriner), Kiwanian. Clubs: San Antonio Country, Argyle.

Home: 103 Bushnell St San Antonio TX 78212 Office: 111 Soledad St San Antonio TX 78205

MCALLISTER, WALTER WILLIAMS, JR., savs. and loan assn. exec.; b. San Antonio, July 7, 1918; s. Walter Williams and Leonora Elizabeth (Alexander) McA.; student Tex. U., Austin, St. Mary's U., San Antonio, Ind. U.; m. Edith Scott, July 25, 1940; children—Walter Williams, III, Jo Ellen McAllister Taddy, Reagin, Eloise. With San Antonio Bldg. & Loan Assn. (named changed to San Antonio Savs. & Loan Assn. 1953, to San Antonio Savs. Assn. 1960), 1940-43, 45—, corp. sec., 1947-54, v.p., 1953-54, pres., 1954-76, chmn. bd., 1976—. Chmn. bd. trustees San Antonio Community Coll.; bd. dirs. Downtown, Inc., San Antonio, San Antonio Research and Planning Council. Served with USAAF, 1943-45. Mem. U.S. League Savs. and Loan Assn., Savs. and Loan Found., Inc. (vice chmn., trustee-at-large), Tex. Savs. and Loan League, San Antonio Home Builders Assn. (dir.), Tex. Mfrs. Assn., San Antonio Bd. Realtors (dir.), Alamo City Bldg. Owners and Mgrs. Assn., San Antonio C. of C. (dir.), South Tex. C. of C. Presbyterian. Clubs: San Antonio Country, Order of Alamo, Kiwanis, Argyle, German. Home: 203 Terrell Rd San Antonio TX 78209 Office: PO Box 1810 111 Soledad St San Antonio TX 78296

MC ALLISTER, WALTER WILLIAMS, III, savings and loan exec.; b. San Antonio, Apr. 9, 1942; s. Walter Williams and Edith (Scott) McA.; B.B.A. in Fin. with honors, U. Tex., Austin, 1969; m. Lida Picton Suttles, Nov. 2, 1963; children—Lida Picton, Walter Williams. With San Antonio Savs. Assn., 1965—, exec. v.p., 1971—, pres., 1976—; chmn. bd. Prestonwood Land Co., Wysong & McAllister Ins., SASA Mortgage Corp., SASA Devel. Corp.; sec. Sawtelle, McAllister & Frederich Ins. Co. Chmn. bd. Metro San Antonio YMCA, 1976-77; chmn. bd. San Antonio River Authority, 1979—, Asso. Employers San Antonio, 1977-78, Consumer Credit Counseling Service, 1976-77; bd. dirs. St. Lukes Lutheran Hosp., San Antonio, 1977-79, San Antonio United Way, 1976—, San Antonio Research and Planning Council, 1976—. Served with U.S. Army, 1963-65. Named Outstanding Young Man of San Antonio, Jaycees, 1976. Mem. Inst. Fin. Edn., U.S. League Savs. Assns. (chmn. br. ops. com. 1978-79), San Antonio C. of C. (chmn. govt. affairs council 1979). Presbyterian. Clubs: Cavaliers, Order of Alamo, German. Home: 641 Garraty Rd San Antonio TX 78209 Office: PO Box 1810 111 Soledad St San Antonio TX 78296

MC ALLISTER-JOHNSON, WILLIAM, educator; b. Columbia, Mo., Oct. 24, 1939; came to Can., 1965, naturalized, 1974; B.A., U. Mo., 1960, M.A., 1962; M.F.A., Princeton U., 1964, Ph.D., 1965. Mem. faculty U. Toronto, 1965—, prof. dept. fine art, grad. dept. history of art, 1977—. Fulbright fellow, 1960-61; Guggenheim fellow, 1978-79. Mem. Am. Numismatic Soc., Renaissance Soc. Am., Societe de l' Histoire de l'Art Francais, Phi Beta Kappa. Author: Estienne Jodelle, Le Recueil des Inscriptions, 1558, 1972; The Paris Entries of Charles IX & Elisabeth of Austria, 1571, 1974; French Lithography: The Restoration Salons, 1817-1824, 1977; The Royal Tour of France of Charles IX & Catherine de'Medici 1564-1566, 1979. Office: Dept Fine Art/Graduate Dept History Art U Toronto Toronto ON M5S 1A1 Canada

MC ALPIN, KIRK MARTIN, lawyer; b. Newark, Sept. 14, 1923; s. Aaron Champion and Margaret (Martin) McA.; LL.B., U. Ga., 1949; postgrad. Columbia, 1950; m. Sarah Frances Morgan, Dec. 14, 1951; children—Kirk Martin, Philip Morgan, Margaret. Admitted to Ga. bar, 1949; asst. solicitor gen. Eastern Jud. Circuit of Ga., 1951; asso. Bouhan, Lawrence, Williams, Levy & McAlpin, Savannah, Ga., 1952-53, partner, 1954-63; partner firm King & Spalding, Atlanta, 1963—. Pres., Atlanta Legal Aid Soc., 1971; chmn.-elect Ga. Heart Assn., 1978-79. Fellow Am. Bar Found., Am. Coll. Trial Lawyers, Internat. Acad. Trial Lawyers, Internat. Soc. Barristers; mem. Am. Bar Assn. (Jr. Bar Conf., chmn. 1958-59, ho. of dels. 1961—, state del. 1970—, gov. 1973-76), State Bar Ga. (chmn. young lawyers 1953-54, bd. govs. 1953-63, pres. 1979-80), Atlanta, Savannah (v.p. 1960-61) bar assns., Ga. Def. Lawyers Assn., Am. Judicature Soc., Assn. R.R. Trial Counsel, Internat. Assn. Ins. Counsel, Soc. of Cin., Sons of Colonial Wars, Phi Delta Phi, Sigma Alpha Epsilon, St. Andrews Soc. Episcopalian. Clubs: Oglethorpe, Chatham, Savannah Yacht and Country (Savannah); Capital City, Commerce, Atlanta City, River Bend Gun, Piedmont Driving (Atlanta); Nat. Lawyers (Washington). Home: 3085 E Pine Valley Rd NW Atlanta GA 30305 Office: 2500 Trust Co Atlanta GA 30303

MCANDREW, GORDON LESLIE, supt. schs.; b. Oakland, Calif., Aug. 29, 1926; s. James and Margaret (Watts) McA.; A.B., U. Calif. at Berkeley, 1948, M.A., 1952, Ph.D., 1962; m. Doris McGarry, Sept. 12, 1948; children—Kevin, Regan. Tchr., adminstr. pub. schs., Oakland, 1949-64; dir. N.C. Advancement Sch. and Learning Inst., Durham, 1964-68; supt. Gary (Ind.) Pub. Schs., 1968—; cons. OEO, 1965—, U.S. Office Edn., 1965—; lectr. Sch. Mgmt., Nova U.; mem. core faculty Union Grad. Sch. Served with USAAF, 1944-45. Home: 6225 Forest St Gary IN 46403 Office: 620 E 10th St Gary IN 46402

MCANDREWS, JOHN PATRICK, sporting arms and ammunition co. exec.; b. Owensboro, Ky., June 12, 1925; s. Patrick William and Ruth Louise (Pelligrin) McA.; B.S.ChE., U. Notre Dame, 1944, M.S., 1947; m. Margaret Ellen Stier, Aug. 23, 1952; children—Mary Ellen, Lawrence John, Kevin Francis, Brian Patrick, Christopher Lee. With E.I. duPont de Nemours & Co., 1947-66, asst. dir. mktg. automotive indsl. products div., 1963-64, gen. sales mgr. consumer product div. fabrics and finishes dept., 1964-66; with Remington Arms Co., Inc., Bridgeport, Conn., 1966—, asst. gen. mgr., 1974-76, pres., 1978—, also dir.; dir. Conn. Nat. Bank, Bridgeport. Bd. dirs. Bridgeport Hosp., United Way Eastern Fairfield County; trustee Fairfield U., St. Joseph's Manor; mem. adv. council Coll. Sci. U. Notre Dame. Served to lt. USNR. Mem. Sporting Arms and Ammunition Mfrs. Inst. (exec. com.), Wildlife Mgmt. Inst. (dir.), Nat. Security Indsl. Assn. (dir.). Clubs: Brooklawn Country (Fairfield, Conn.). Home: 14 Moss Ledge Rd Westport CT 06880 Office: 939 Barnum Ave Bridgeport CT 06602

MCANINCH, HAROLD D., coll. adminstr.; b. Leota, Mo., May 29, 1933; s. James Loyd and Essie L. McA.; B.S., S.W. Mo. State U., 1957; M.A., U. Ark., 1958; Ed.D., U. Mo., 1967; postgrad. Loyola U., Chgo., 1972-74; D.Hum. (hon.), Lewis U., 1974; m. Karyl Kay Woodbridge, May 25, 1956; children—Michele Kay, Michael Sean. Tchr., Smith Cotton High Sch., Sedalia, Mo., 1958-61; instr. U. Mo., Columbia, 1961-64; dean Jefferson Coll., Hillsboro, Mo., 1964-68; pres. Jackson (Mich.) Community Coll., 1968-71; pres. Joliet (Ill.) Jr. Coll., 1971-79; pres. Coll. of DuPage, Glen Ellyn, Ill., 1979—. Chmn. Will County Cancer Crusade; bd. dirs. United Crusade of Will County, YMCA, Boy Scouts Am.; mem. lay adv. bd. St. Joseph Hosp., Joliet. Served with U.S. Army, 1950-53. Mem. Council North Central Community and Jrs. Colls. (pres. 1975), Ill. Council Public Community Coll. Presidents (vice chmn. 1976, pres. 1977, past chmn. fin. com.), North Central Assn. Colls. and Secondary Schs. (evaluator), Nat. Assn. Negotiators and Adminstrs. (mem. adv. bd.), Am. Assn. Community and Jr. Colls. (chmn. President's Acad. 1979), Phi Delta Kappa. Club: Rotary. Contbr. articles to profl. jours. Home: 73 Bluebird Ln Naperville IL 60540 Office: Coll of DuPage 22d and Lambert Rds Glen Ellyn IL 60137

MC ANULTY, HENRY JOSEPH, univ. pres.; b. Pitts., Apr. 25, 1915; s. William J. and Catherine (Calpin) McA.; B.A., Duquesne U., 1936; B.Th., St. Mary's Sem., Ferndale, Norwalk, Conn., 1941; LL.D., Loyola U., Los Angeles, 1958; D.Ed., St. Vincent Coll., Latrobe, Pa., 1961; L.H.D., U. Pitts. Joined Congregation of Holy Ghost, 1936; ordained priest Roman Catholic Ch., 1940; nat. sec., Pitts. Diocesan dir. Pontifical Assn. Holy Childhood, 1941-44; commd. 1st lt. chaplain, USAAF, 1944, advanced through grades to lt. col. USAF, resigned, 1958; brig. gen. Res.; asst. to pres. Duquesne U., 1958-59, pres., 1959—. Bd. dirs. Pitts. Symphony Soc., Pitts. Regional Indsl. Devel. Corp., Pitts. Conv. and Visitors Bur., Allegheny Conf. for Community Devel., Pitts. Urban Transit Council. Mem. Am. Legion. Address: Duquesne U Pittsburgh PA 15219

MCANULTY, WILLIAM NOEL, educator; b. Howe, Okla., Nov. 26, 1913; s. Henry Clay and Jessie Anne (Armstrong) McA.; B.S., U. Okla., 1938, M.S., 1948; Ph.D. in Geology, U. Tex., 1953; m. Waldene Slagle, Jan. 25, 1939; children—Julia, William Noel, Catherine. Head dept. geology Sul Ross Coll., Alpine, Tex., 1947-51; chief geologist Dow Chem. Co., Freeport, Tex., 1953-64; head dept. geol. sci. U. Tex., El Paso, 1964-71, prof. geology, 1971-79, prof. emeritus, 1979—; dir. Rangaire Corp., Cleburne, Tex.; partner McAnulty & McAnulty, geol. cons., El Paso. Fellow Geol. Soc. Am.; mem. Soc. Econ. Geologists, Am. Assn. Petroleum Geologists, Am. Inst. Profl. Geologists, El Paso Geol. Soc. (pres. 1969). Contbr. articles to profl. lit. Home: 220 Stratus El Paso TX 79912

MCARDLE, PAUL FRANCIS, judge; b. Albany, N.Y., Nov. 26, 1918; s. Charles P. and Mary (Murray) McA.; B.S., Georgetown U., 1941, LL.B., 1948; m. Catherine Angela Manley, Nov. 8, 1952; children—Paul Francis, Peter M., Susan M., Mary M. Admitted to D.C. bar, 1948; asso. firm Cleary, Gottlieb, Friendly & Cox, Washington, 1948-51, Covington & Burling, Washington, 1951—; now judge Superior Ct. D.C. Active United Givers Fund, Chevy Chase, Md. Served to capt. USMCR, 1941-46. Mem. Am. Bar Assn., Bar Assn. D.C., Am. Bar Found. Home: 3505 Windsor Pl Chevy Chase MD 20015 Office: Superior Ct DC Washington DC 20001

MC ARDLE, RICHARD EDWIN, cons.; b. Lexington, Ky., Feb. 25, 1899; s. Maurice Herbert and Mildred Yarbrough (Johnson) McA.; B.S., U. Mich., 1923, M.S., 1924, Ph.D., 1930, D.Sc., 1952; LL.D., Syracuse U., 1961; D.Sc. (hon.), U. Maine, 1962; m. Dorothy Coppage, Dec. 29, 1927; children—Richard Coppedge, John Parker, Michael Robert. Silviculturist, Pacific N.W. Forest Expt. Sta., Portland, Oreg., 1924-34; dean. Sch. Forestry, U. Idaho, 1934-35; dir. Rocky Mountain Forest and Range Expt. Sta., Ft. Collins, Colo., 1935-38, Appalachian Forest Expt. Sta., Asheville, N.C., 1938-44; asst. chief U.S. Forest Service, 1944-52, chief, 1952-62; exec. dir. Nat. Inst. Pub. Affairs, Washington, 1962-64, adviser, 1964-65; forestry cons., 1964—; cons. Nat. Wildlife Fedn., 1967-78; dir. Olinkraft, Inc.; mem. Royal Commn. Forestry, Nfld., 1967-71; pres. 5th World Forestry Congress, 1960; hon. pres. 6th World Forestry Congress, Madrid, 1966, 7th World Congress, Buenos Aires, 1972. Recipient distinguished service award Dept. Agr., 1957; Pres. U.S. distinguished fed. civilian service award, 1961; Rockefeller public service award, 1960; Sir William Schlich Meml. medal Soc. Am. Foresters, 1962; knight comdr. Order Merit (Germany), 1962; Order Merit Miguel Angel de Quevado (Mexico), 1961; John Aston Warder Forestry award Am. Forestry Assn., 1978; named one of top ten career men in govt. Nat. Civil Service League, 1958. Fellow Soc. Am. Foresters (mem. council 3 terms), Soil Conservation Soc. Am.; mem. Royal Swedish Acad. Agr. and Forestry, Am. Forestry Assn. (dir. 1963—), Sigma Xi, Phi Sigma, Xi Sigma Pi. Home: 5110 River Hill Rd Washington DC 20016

MCARDLE, RICHARD JOSEPH, univ. dean; b. Omaha, Mar. 10, 1934; s. William James and Abby Marie (Menzies) McA.; B.A., Creighton U., 1955, M.A., 1961; Ph.D., U. Nebr., 1969; m. Katherine Ann McAndrew, Dec. 27, 1958; children—Bernard, Constance, Nancy, Susan, Richard. Tchr. pub. high schs., Nebr., 1955-65; grad. asst. romance langs. U. Nebr., 1965-66, instr. fgn. lang. methods, 1966-69; chmn. dept. edn. Cleve. State U., 1969-70, dean Coll. Edn., 1975—, chmn. dept. elementary and secondary edn. U. North Fla., 1971-75; cons. in field. Active Pop Warner Football Program. Mem. Am. Council on Teaching Fgn. Langs., Am. Assn. Colls. Tchr. Edn., Phi Delta Kappa. Author: (with others) Little League Football: Problems and Prospects, 1975; Interaction Analysis for the Foreign Language Teacher-A Programmed Approach. Home: 28276 Gardenia Dr North Olmsted OH 44070 Office: Coll of Edn Cleve State U Cleveland OH 44115

MC ARTHUR, DUNCAN ROBERT BALY, former cement co. exec.; b. Yonkers, N.Y., July 23, 1918 (Canadian citizen); s. Alexander Stanley and Dorothy Tertia (Rainbow) McA.; B.A. in Sci., U. Toronto, 1940; M.B.A., Harvard, 1947; m. Nancy Mary Smith, Mar. 12, 1943; children—Peter David, John Alexander (dec.), Robert Cameron, Christie Ann. With Stevenson and Kellogg Ltd., mgmt. cons., 1947-53; with Western Minerals Ltd., 1954-60; with Inland Cement Industries, Ltd., Edmonton, Alta., Can., 1960—, exec. v.p., 1961-68, pres., 1968—, chmn., 1973-78; dir. Canadian Utilities Ltd. Past pres., dir. Alta. Edn. Council; mem. senate U. Alta.; chmn. Metric Commn. Can. Served to lt. col. Canadian Army, 1940-46. Decorated Mem. Order Brit. Empire. Registered profl. engr., Alta. Fellow Chartered Inst. Secs.; mem. Edmonton C. of C. (past pres.), Edmonton Klondike Days Assn. (past pres.). Mem. Anglican Ch. (exec. com.). Clubs: Mayfair Golf and Country, Edmonton, Petroleum (Edmonton). Office: Inland Cement Industries 8215 112th St Edmonton AB T5J 2T Canada

MCARTHUR, GEORGE, fgn. corr.; b. Valdosta, Ga., July 15, 1924; s. George and Ann (Johnson) McA.; B.A. in Journalism, U. Ga., 1948; m. Eva Kim, Sept. 17, 1979. With AP, 1948-69, corr. in Korea, 1950-54, in Paris, 1954-60, bur. chief, Cairo, 1960-63, bur. chief, Manila, 1963-65, corr., Saigon, 1966-68, bur. chief, 1968-69; with Los Angeles Times, 1969—, bur. chief, Saigon, 1970-75, corr. for Southeast Asia, Bangkok, 1975-79. Served with USNR, 1943-45. Recipient citation for fgn. reporting Overseas Press Club, 1973. Mem. Sigma Delta Chi. Clubs: Fgn. Corrs. (Hongkong); Glen Arven Country Country (Thomasville, Ga.); River Bend Country (Gt. Falls, Va.). Address: 4633 Rockwood Pkwy NW Washington DC 20016

MC ARTHUR, JANET WARD, endocrinologist; b. Bellingham, Wash., June 25, 1914; d. Hyland Donald and Alice Maria (Frost) McA.; A.B., U. Wash., 1935, M.S., 1937; M.B., Northwestern U., 1941, M.D., 1942; Sc.D., Mt. Holyoke Coll., 1962. Intern, Cin. Gen. Hosp., 1941-42, asst. resident in medicine, 1942-43; asst. resident, research fellow in medicine H.P. Walcott fellow clin. medicine Mass. Gen. Hosp., Boston, 1943-44, asso. physician, 1959—, asso. children's service, 1968—; instr. Harvard U., 1955-57, asst. prof., 1960-64, asso. prof., 1964-73, prof., 1973—, mem. Center for Population Studies, 1970—; mem. sci. advisory com. Med. Research Inst., Worcester, Mass., 1963—; mem. reproductive biology study sect. NIH, 1974-78; co-dir. Vincent Meml. Research Lab., 1977—; mem. adv. com. Harvard Center for Population Studies, 1971—; cons. Mass. Eye and Ear Infirmary, Boston, 1952—. Diplomate Am. Bd. Internal Medicine. Fellow A.C.P.; mem. AMA, Endocrine Soc., Am. Fertility Soc., AAAS, Boston Obstet. Soc., Phi Beta Kappa, Sigma Xi, Alpha Omega Alpha. Author: (with others) Functional Endocrinology from Birth Through Adolescence, 1952; editor: (with Theodore Colton) Statistics in Endocrinology, 1970; contbr. articles to profl. jours. Home: 19 Brimmer St Boston MA 02108 Office: 32 Fruit St Boston MA 02114

MCARTHUR, JOHN HECTOR, educator; b. Vancouver, B.C., Can., Mar. 31, 1934; s. Hector and Elizabeth Lee (Whyte) McA.; B.Commerce, U. B.C., 1957; M.B.A., Harvard U., 1959, D.B.A., 1962; m. Netilia Ewasiuk, Sept. 15, 1956; children—Jocelyn Natasha, Susan Patricia; came to U.S., 1957. Dean, prof. Sch. Bus. Adminstrn., Harvard U., Boston; dir. Multibank Fin. Corp., Rohm and Haas Co.; cons. numerous cos. and govt. agys. in Can., Europe and U.S. Home: 140 Old Connecticut Path Wayland MA 01778 Office: Harvard Business Sch Boston MA 02163

MCATEE, OTT BENTON, neuropsychiatrist, hosp. adminstr.; b. Candiz, Ky., July 23, 1902; s. George Thomas and Martha Clysta (Hillman) McA.; A.B., U. Ky., 1930; M.D., Vanderbilt U., 1937; postgrad. N.Y. Psychiat. Inst., 1950, U. Chgo., 1961-62; m. Lucile Newland Kelly, June 26, 1934; children—Lloyd Thomas, George Kelly, Richard Dudley. Intern Rochester (N.Y.) Gen. Hosp., 1937-38; resident psychiatry Overbrook Hosp., Cedar Grove, N.J., 1949-52; gen. practice medicine, Stanford, Ky., 1938-41; staff psychiatrist TVA, Chattanooga, 1946-49; supt., chief med. dir. Madison State Hosp., 1952—; instr., then asst. prof. psychiatry Med. Sch. Ind. U., 1958—. Dir. Madison-Jefferson Country United Fund, 1959-62; pres. Madison Consol. High Sch. P.T.A., 1960-61; dir. Youth Commn., Madison, 1963—; pres. Greater Madison Council Chs., 1963-65; dir. at large Ind. Council Chs., Indpls., 1964-66. Served to maj. M.C., AUS, 1941-46. Recipient citation for meritorious service in advance psychiatry at Madison State Hosp. Gov. Ind., 1953-57, citation for exemplary service to people So. Ind. in achieving accreditation Madison State Hosp. Gov. Ind., 1962. Diplomate Am. Bd. Psychiatry and Neurology. Fellow Am. Psychiat. Assn.; mem. A.M.A., Am. Assn. Mental Hosps., Jefferson and Switzerland County Med. Soc. (sec.-treas., past pres.), Phi Beta Pi. Rotarian. Contbr. numerous articles profl. jours. Address: Madison State Hosp Madison IN 47250

MC ATEE, PATRICIA ANNE ROONEY, educator; b. Denver, Apr. 20, 1931; d. Jerry F. and Edna E. (Hansen) Rooney; B.S., Loretto Heights Coll., 1953; M.S., U. Colo., 1961; Ph.D., Union of Universities, 1976; m. Darrell Mc Atee, Sept. 4, 1954; 1 son, Kevin Paul. Supr., St. Anthony Hosp., Denver, 1952-55; pub. health nurse, edn. dir. Tri-County Health Dept., Colo., 1956-58; adminstr. sch. health program Littleton (Colo.) Pub. Schs., 1958-60; asst. prof. community health, academic adminstr. continuing edn. U. Colo., 1968-70; project dir. Western Interstate Commn. for Higher Edn., 1972-74; asst. prof. pediatrics, project co-dir. Sch. Medicine U. Colo., 1975—; chmn. bd. dirs. Found. for Urban and Neighborhood Devel.; cons. Colo. Safety Council; treas. Vista Neuva Assos.; mem. Arapahoe Health Planning Council. Mem. Nat. Acad. Scis., Nat. Bd. Pediatric Nurse Practitioners and Assos. (pres.), Nat. Assn. Pediatric Nurse Assos. and Practitioners (v.p.), Am. Acad. Polit. and Social Scientists, Nat. League Nursing, Western Soc. Research, Am. Pub. Health Assn., Am. Sch. Health Assn., Sigma Theta Tau. Editor Pediatric Nursing, 1975-77. Home: 877 E Panama Dr Littleton CO 80121 Office: 4200 E 9th Ave Box C-219 Denver CO 80262

MCAULAY, ARCHIBALD HENDRIE, ins. mgmt. cons.; b. Alexandria, Scotland, Mar. 21, 1904; s. Archibald Hendrie and Mary (Robertson) McA.; student Dumbarton Acad., 1919-21; M.A., Glasgow U., Scotland, 1925, B.Sc., 1927. Came to U.S., 1939, naturalized, 1946. With Sun Life Assurance Co. of Can., 1928-39; asst. actuary Northwestern Nat. Life Ins. Co., Mpls., 1939-44; asst. actuary Nat. Life Ins. Co., Montpelier, Vt., 1944-47, v.p., dir. selection, 1947-54; pres., dir. N.Am. Reassurance Co., N.Y.C., 1954-59; ins. mgmt. cons.; dir. Montgomery Ward Life Ins. Co., Chgo., Royal Globe Life Ins. Co., N.Y.C., Polypastex United, Inc., N.Y.C. Fellow Soc. Actuaries. Clubs: Pinnacle (N.Y.C.). Home: Hudson House Ardsley-on-Hudson NY 10503 Office: PO Box 113 Ardsley-on-Hudson NY 10503

MCAULAY, JAMES BOYD, hosp. adminstr.; b. North Cobalt, Ont., Can., June 29, 1927; s. Angus and Margaret (McKee) McA.; grad Runnymede Collegiate Inst., 1946; m. Jeanne Woolfrey, Apr. 10, 1953; children—Kim, Kathryn, Carol, Sharon, James. With G.H. Wood & Co., Ltd., Toronto, 1946-49; accountant Toronto Western Hosp., 1950-56; treas., 1956-63; asst. adminstr., 1963-67; asso. exec. dir., 1967-69; exec. dir., 1969—; dir. Booth Ave. Hosp. Laundry. Mem. Bd. Trade Met. Toronto. Mem. Am. Coll. Hosp. Adminstrs., Canadian Coll. Health Service Execs., Royal Canadian Inst. Club: York Downs Golf and Country (Unionville). Home: 18 Aquila Ct Rexdale ON Canada Office: 399 Bathurst St Toronto ON Canada

MCAULEY, RAYMOND REDDEN, state ofcl.; b. St. Louis, Sept. 16, 1917; s. Terry Francis and Ethel (Redden) McA.; A.B., St. Louis U., 1941, Ph.L., 1942, M.A., 1945, S.T.L., 1949. Tchr. Campion High Sch., 1942-45; tchr. St. Louis U., 1949; tchr. Marquette U., Milw., 1950-52, dean men, 1952-54, v.p. student affairs, 1954-56, v.p. bus. and finance, 1956-65, exec. v.p., 1965-70, trustee, 1956-70, trustee Sch. Medicine, 1956-67. Endowment officer San Diego County, 1971—. Mem. Nat. Assn. Student Personnel Adminstrs., Fin. Execs. Inst., Am. Assn. for Higher Edn., Nat. Assn. Coll. and Univ. Bus. Officers, Beta Alpha Psi. Home: 3583 Syracuse Ave San Diego CA 92122 Office: 1600 Pacific Hwy San Diego CA 92101

MC AULIFFE, DENNIS PHILIP, ret. army officer, govt. ofcl.; b. N.Y.C., Apr. 8, 1922; s. Michael and Mary (Ryan) McA.; B.S., U.S. Mil. Acad., 1944; M.S. in Elec. Engring., U. Pa., 1950; m. Kathleen Bolton, June 2, 1946; children—Carolyn (Mrs. Bert T. Shoemaker), Dennis Philip, Kathleen Ann. Commd. 2d lt. U.S. Army, 1944, advanced through grades to lt. gen., 1975; asst. comdr. I Corps Arty., Korea, 1964-65; with Army Gen. Staff, Washington, 1959-63, 65-66; mem., exec. to chmn. Joint Chiefs Staff, Washington 1966-69; asst. div. comdr. 1st Inf. Div., Vietnam, 1969; sr. adviser, III Corps and Mil Region 3, Vietnam, 1970; chief policy Supreme Hdqrs. Allied Powers Europe, Belgium, 1971-73; dep. comdg. gen. U.S. Army Combined Arms Center, 1973-74; dir. European region Office Sec. Def., 1974-75; comdr. in chief So. Command, 1975-79; adminstr. Panama Canal Commn., 1979—. Chmn. bd. mgmt. YMCA, Balboa, Panama; trustee Civilian-Mil. Inst., Colorado Springs, Colo. Decorated D.S.M., Legion Merit with 2 oak leaf clusters, D.F.C. with oak leaf cluster, Bronze Star with oak leaf cluster; Republic of Vietnam Gallantry Cross with palm and gold star, Republic of Vietnam Armed Forces Honor medal, Dominican Republic Honor medal. Mem. Assn. Grads. U.S. Mil. Acad., Assn. U.S. Army, Nat. War Coll. Alumni Assn., Sons of Xavier, SHAPE Officers Assn., Soc. 1st Div., Soc. 89th Div. World War II. Office: Panama Canal Commn PSC Box 44 APO Miami FL 34002

MC AULIFFE, FRANK MALACHI, author; b. N.Y.C., Dec. 3, 1926; s. Cornelius Jeremiah and Margaret (Harte) McA.; grad. high sch.; m. Rita Mary Gibbons, Mar. 17, 1951; children—Meg (Mrs. Rich Reed), Liz, Mark Conn, Mary, Kathleen, Barbara, Luke. Served with USAAF, 1945. Recipient Edgar award Mystery Writers Am.,

1971. Author: Hot Town, 1956; (series with Augustus Mandrell as protagonist) Of All the Bloody Cheek, 1965, Rather a Vicious Gentleman, 1968, For Murder I Charge More, 1971; The Maltese Falcon Commission, 1974; Bagman, 1979. Address: 1828 Swift Blvd Ventura CA 93003

MC AULIFFE, JOHN, pub.; b. Boston, Oct. 24, 1943; s. Joseph E. and Burnadette Joan (McWeeny) McA.; B.S., Columbia U., 1964; M.B.A., Am. U., 1966; postgrad. Harvard Bus. Sch., 1966-67; m. Hawley Anne Hilton, June 20, 1978. Sales mgr. Mademoiselle mag., 1966-69, dir. sales, 1970; founder, pub. Beauty Handbook Corp., N.Y.C., 1971—; pres., pub. Consumer & Trade Pub. Co., 1974—. Mem. N.Y.C. Democratic Devel. Com. Served with USAF, 1964. Mem. Am. Mktg. Assn., Nat. Assn. Chain Drug Stores. Roman Catholic. Clubs: N.Y. Athletic, Nat. Press, N.Y. Advt. Home: 220 E 67th St New York NY 10021 Office: 420 Lexington Ave New York NY 10017

MCAULIFFE, MICHAEL F., bishop; b. Kansas City, Mo., Nov. 22, 1920; student St. Louis Preparatory Seminary and Cath. U. Ordained priest Roman Cath. Ch., 1945; consecrated bishop, 1969; bishop diocese of Jefferson City (Mo.), 1969—. Address: Bishops House PO Drawer 417 Jefferson City MO 65101*

MCAVOY, WILLIAM CHARLES, educator; b. Cleve., Jan. 28, 1921; s. Charles William and Olive Charlotte (Connors) McA.; A.B., John Carroll U., 1946; M.A., U. Ill., 1948, Ph.D., 1952; m. Jerry Ferguson, Jan. 8, 1945; children—Carolyn (Mrs. Paul A. Kolodziej), Kathleen (Mrs. Alfred Messano), Michael, Thomas, William, Elizabeth (Mrs. Ronald Messano), John, Anne, David. Mem. faculty St. Louis U., 1952—, prof. English, 1964—, chmn. dept., 1971-74. Served with USAAF, 1942-45. Mem. Modern Lang. Assn. Am., AAUP, Midwest Renaissance Soc. Am. Author: (with William E. Buckler) American College Handbook of English Fundamentals, 1965; Dramatic Tragedy, 1971. Editor: Twelfth Night: The Variorum Shakespeare, 1966. Contbr. articles to profl. jours. Home: 4466 W Pine Blvd Saint Louis MO 63108

MC BAIN, LEROY DOWARD, clergyman, sem. pres.; b. Bottineau, N.D., July 18, 1917; s. Isaiah Daniel and Ada (Wassen) McB.; A.B., Eastern Baptist Theol. Sem., Phila., 1943, Th.B., 1943, D.D., 1959; spl. student Columbia, also Union Theol. Sem., N.Y.C., 1946-49, Mansfield Coll., Oxford, Eng., 1971, Harvard Div. Sch., 1973; m. Olive Ann Fountain, May 30, 1940; children—Ada Marianne (Mrs. Gary Barrett), Loren Doward, Robert Mark, Margaret Melissa (Mrs. David Mong), Joy. Ordained to ministry Bapt. Ch., 1943; minister in Allentown, N.J., 1941-43, Clifton, N.J., 1943-52, Bklyn., 1952-54, Covina, Calif., 1954-62, First Bapt. Ch., Phoenix, 1962-77; pres. Am. Bapt. Sem. of the West, Berkeley, Calif., 1977—; vis. prof. Calif. Bapt. Theol. Sem., Covina, 1956—. Pres. Am. Bapt. Conv., 1967-68, Valley of Sun Council Chs., Phoenix, 1965-66; mem. gen. bd., also dept. internat. affairs Nat. Council Chs., 1959—; del. World Council Chs., New Delhi, India, 1961; chmn. bd. Am. Bapt. Sem. West, 1970-71; nat. pres. evangelistic life style com. Am. Bapt. Conv. Merrill fellow Harvard Divinity Sch., 1972. Author: Through the Valley, 1967; also Discipleship text for Judson Press, articles. Home: 19695 San Ramon Valley Blvd San Ramon CA 94583 Office: 2515 Hillegass Ave Berkeley CA 94704

MC BAINE, TURNER HUDSON, lawyer; b. Columbia, Mo., May 5, 1911; s. James Patterson and Ethel (Hudson) McB.; A.B., U. Calif. at Berkeley, 1932; LL.B., 1936; B.A. in Jurisprudence (Rhodes scholar), Oxford (Eng.) U., 1934; m. Jane Neylan, Aug. 2, 1939 (div. 1957); children—John Neylan, James Patterson; m. 2d, Edith Zsofia Bokor, Aug. 30, 1957. Admitted to Calif. bar, 1936, N.Y. bar, 1947; asso. firm Orrick, Palmer & Dahlquist, San Francisco, 1936-39, Cahill, Gordon, Zachery & Reindel, N.Y.C., 1946-47; with firm Pillsbury, Madison & Sutro, San Francisco, 1948—, partner, 1950—, sr. partner, 1971-77; gen. counsel Standard Oil Co. of Calif., 1970-77; mem. Adminstrv. Conf. U.S., 1976-79. Bd. visitors Stanford Law Sch., 1966-69; trustee World Affairs Council No. Calif., 1948-54; trustee Asia Found., 1954—; bd. dirs. Bay Area Council, 1977-79. Served to comdr. USNR, 1941-45. Decorated Legion of Merit; Order Brit. Empire. Fellow Am. Bar Found.; mem. Am., Calif., San Francisco bar assns., Am. Judicature Soc., Calif. State Club Assn. (pres. 1976—), Phi Beta Kappa, Order of Coif, Beta Theta Pi. Republican. Episcopalian. Clubs: Commonwealth, Pacific-Union (San Francisco); Burlingame Country (Hillsborough). Home: 1765 Crockett Ln Hillsborough CA 94010 Office: 225 Bush St San Francisco CA 94104

MC BATH, JAMES HARVEY, educator; b. Watertown, S.D., Oct. 24, 1922; s. Earl A. and Edna (Harvey) McB.; B.S., Northwestern U., 1947, M.A., 1948, Ph.D., 1950; fellow Inst. Hist. Research, U. London, 1952-53; m. Jean Bloomquist, July 6, 1963 (dec. Oct. 1979); children—Margot, Douglas, Janet. Asst. prof. speech U. N.Mex., 1950-52, U. Iowa, 1953-54, U. Md. European Program, 1954-56; mem. faculty U. So. Calif., 1956—, prof. speech, 1963—, chmn. dept., 1965—, pres. faculty senate, 1977-78, vice chmn. pres.'s adv. council, 1978—; cons. Am. Student Found., 1961-64, Calif. Office Econ. Opportunity, 1972, City of Hope, 1973, RAND Corp., 1973-78, Nat. Endowment for Humanities, 1973-75, Tokyo Inst. English Lang., 1977—, Nat. Center Ednl. Stats., 1975—; mem. U.S. Dist. Ct. Com. Sch. Integration, 1978-79. Served with Psychol. Research Unit, USAAF, 1943-46. Mem. Speech Communication Assn. (exec. council 1966-70, chmn. bicentennial coordinating com. 1971-76, legis. council 1977—), Am. Forensic Assn. (pres. 1960-62), Western (pres. 1968-69), Calif. speech assns., Assn. Communication Adminstrn. (pres. 1975-76), Internat. Communication Assn., Internat. Platform Assn., Am. Assn. for Pub. Opinion Research, Brit. Hist. Assn., AAUP, Am. Assn. Higher Edn., Assn. Coll. Honor Socs. (nat. council 1975—), Communication Assn. Pacific (adv. bd. 1972—), Phi Kappa Phi, Delta Sigma Rho-Tau Kappa Alpha (pres. 1969-72). Methodist. Co-author: Guidebook for Speech Practice, 1961; British Public Addresses, 1828-1960, 1971; Guidebook for Speech Communication, 1973; Communication Education For Careers, 1975. Editor: Essays in Forensics, 1970; Forensics as Communication: The Argumentative Perspective, 1975; Argumentation and Debate, 1963. Editor Jour. Am. Forensic Assn., 1966-68; asso. editor Quar. Jour. Speech, 1967-69; contbr. Ency. of Edn., 1971. Home: 395 S San Marino Ave Pasadena CA 91107 Office: Dept Speech Communication Univ So Calif Los Angeles CA 90007

MC BAY, HENRY CECIL, chemist, educator; b. Mexia, Tex., May 29, 1914; s. William Cecil and Roberta (Ransom) McB.; B.S., Wiley Coll., 1934; M.S., Atlanta U., 1936; Ph.D. in Chemistry, U. Chgo., 1945; children—Michael H.C., Ronald P.W. Mem. faculty dept. chemistry Morehouse Coll., Atlanta, 1945—, prof., 1948—, chmn. dept., 1957—. Mem. Am. Chem. Soc. (Herty award 1976, Northeastern sect. 1978), Am. Inst. Chemists, Ga. Acad. Sci., Phi Beta Kappa, Sigma Xi. Contbr. articles to profl. jours. Home: 1719 Detroit Ct NW Atlanta GA 30314 Office: Dept Chemistry Morehouse Coll Atlanta GA 30314

MC BEAN, ALAN JOHNSTON, telephone co. exec.; b. Duluth, Minn., May 14, 1921; s. Alan Johnston and Jean Seaton (Cochran) McB.; A.B., Dartmouth, 1943; m. Jennie Dixon Bradfield, Sept. 12, 1943; children—Peter Johnston, James Shannon, Elizabeth Ann (Mrs. William H. Donald III). With So. New Eng. Telephone Co., New Haven, 1946—, asst. v.p., 1962-70, sec., treas., 1970—; dir. Colonial Bank, New Haven. Commr. bd. finance City of New Haven, 1975. Bd. dirs., pres. New Haven YMCA, 1970-74; bd. dirs. New Haven Symphony Orch. Served with AUS, 1943-46, 50-52. Mem. Am. Soc. Corporate Secs., New Haven C. of C. (dir.). Democrat. Conglist. Clubs: New Haven Lawn, Quinnipiack; Wall Street (N.Y.C.). Home: 426 Prospect St New Haven CT 06511 Office: 227 Church St New Haven CT 06506

MCBEAN, ALEXANDER MARSHALL, physician, state ofcl.; b. Summit, N.J., Mar. 10, 1942; s. Alexander and Maude Elmira (Metzger) McB.; A.B. magna cum laude, Yale U., 1964; M.D., Harvard U., 1968; M.Sc., U. London, 1976; m. Jean Catherine Ulrich, Apr. 6, 1968; children—Alexander Duncan, James Ian. Intern, Harvard service Boston City Hosp., 1968-69, resident in internal medicine, 1969-70; med. epidemiologist smallpox eradication program Center for Disease Control, Atlanta, 1970-71, Organisation de Coordination pour la Lutte Contre les Endemies en Afrique Centreale, Yaoundé, Cameroun, 1971-74; commr. Vt. Dept. Health, Burlington, 1976-78; asso. prof. health services adminstrn. Johns Hopkins U. Sch. Hygiene, Balt., 1978—; instr. pub. health Centre Universite de Science et Santé, Yaoundé, Cameroun. Mem. Am. Pub. Health Assn. Congregationalist. Home: 16507 Garfield Rd Monkton MD 21111

MC BEE, JAMES LEONARD, JR., univ. ofcl.; b. Philippi, W.Va., May 4, 1931; s. James Leonard and Nora Annabelle (Haddix) McB.; B.S., W.Va., U., 1952, M.S., 1956; Ph.D., U. Mo., 1959; m. Jean Bush, Mar. 28, 1953; children—Debra Jean, Keith Lewis. Prof., W.Va. U., Morgantown, 1959-69, chmn. dept. animal sci., 1964; chmn. dept. agrl. Ill. State U., Normal, 1970-74, asst. to pres., 1974-75, exec. officer, 1975-77; vice chancellor adminstrn. and fin. U. Mass., Amherst, 1977-78; exec. dean Potomac State Coll., 1978—. Mem. Ill. Bd. Agrl. Advisers. Active Cub Scouts, 1965-70, PTA, 1965-70. Served with USNR, 1952-55; capt. Res. Decorated Nat. Def. medal. Mem. Am. Meat Sci. Assn., Am. Soc. Animal Sci., Block and Bridle, Sigma Xi, Gamma Sigma Delta (pres. 1965-66), Phi Delta Kappa, Alpha Zeta. Kiwanian (dir. 1969). Home: 150 Mineral St Keyser WV 26726

MC BRATNEY, WILLIAM H., lawyer; b. St. Louis, July 19, 1913; s. Emmet William and Marie (Baur) McB.; A.B., Ill. Coll., 1933; J.D., Washington U., St. Louis, 1936, M.A., 1937; m. Carol Musgrove, June 17, 1944; children—Elizabeth A., Margaret L. Admitted to Mo. bar, 1936, Ariz. bar, 1951; practice in St. Louis, 1936-41, Tucson, 1951-78; lectr. U. Ariz. Coll. Bus. Adminstrn., 1960-66, 72-74. Bd. dirs. Ariz. Sch. Deaf and Blind, 1961-63, 71—, pres., 1963, 73; bd. dirs. Community Service, Inc., 1952-64, pres., 1955-56. Served with AUS, 1943-46. Mem. Am., Mo., Ariz. bar assns., Phi Beta Kappa, Kappa Alpha. Republican. Mason (32 deg.). Clubs: Old Pueblo, Tucson Country (Tucson). Home: 9402 E Lorain Pl Tucson AZ 85710

MCBRIDE, EARLE FRANCIS, geologist; b. Moline, Ill., May 25, 1932; s. Earle Curtis and Elsa Mae (Burch) McB.; B.A., Augustana Coll., 1954; M.A., U. Mo., Columbia, 1956; Ph.D., Johns Hopkins U., 1959; m. Donna JoAnn Hixson, Aug. 1, 1956; children—Deborah, Suzanne. Jr. geologist Shell Oil Co., Corpus Christi and Kilgore, Tex., summers 1955-56; instr. U. Tex., Austin, 1959-60, asst. prof. geology, 1960-65, asso. prof., 1965-70, prof., 1970—; Merrill W. Haas vis. prof. U. Kans., 1972; NATO vis. prof. U. Perugia (Italy), 1977; lectr., cons. to oil cos. Mem. Soc. Econ. Paleontologists and Mineralogists (sec.-treas. and councilor 1967, pres. 1979-80), Am. Assn. Petroleum Geologists, Geol. Soc. Am., Internat. Assn. Sedimentologists. Contbr. numerous articles on sedimentary rocks to tech. jours. Office: U Tex at Austin Dept Geology Austin TX 78712

MCBRIDE, EDWARD JOHN, educator; b. Chester, Pa., May 9, 1913; s. Peter Joseph and Ann Marie (Maguire) McB.; B.S., Villanova Coll., 1934; M.S., Harvard U., 1939, D.Sc., 1949; m. Helen Madeleine Corrigan, Aug. 22, 1942; children—Edward John, Mary Anne, Margaret Mary, Ann Marie. Design, devel., research turbo-machinery Westinghouse Corp., Lester, Pa., 1936-40, Elliott Co., Jeannette, Pa., 1941-44, Worthington Corp., Wellsville, N.Y., 1944-51; prof. U. Kans., 1952—, chmn. dept. mech. engring., 1952-62. Fellow ASME; mem. Am. Soc. Engring. Edn., Sigma Xi, Pi Tau Sigma. Patentee blade element for rotary fluid machines. Home: 2244 New Hampshire St Lawrence KS 66044 Office: U Kans Lawrence KS 66045

MC BRIDE, GUY THORNTON, JR., coll. pres.; b. Austin, Tex., Dec. 12, 1919; s. Guy Thornton and Imogene (Thrasher) McB.; B.S. in Chem. Engring. with distinction, U. Tex., 1940; Sc.D., M.I.T., 1948; D.P.S. (hon.), Regis Coll., 1979; m. Rebekah Jane Bush, Sept. 2, 1942; children—Rebekah Ann, William Howard, Ellen McBride McCarty. Instr. chem. engring. Mass. Inst. Tech., 1942-44, research asso., 1946-48; job. engr. Standard Oil Co. Calif., 1944-46; asst. prof. chem. engring Rice Inst., 1948-55, asso. dean students, 1950-57, dean, 1957-58, asso. prof., 1955-58; cons. Tex. Gulf Sulphur Co., 1950-58, asst. mgr. research dept., 1958-59, mgr., 1959-60, v.p., mgr. research, 1960-63, v.p. Phosphate div., 1963-70, gen. mgr., 1966-70; pres. Colo. Sch. Mines, Golden, 1970—. Dir. Halliburton Co., Texasgulf Inc. Registered profl. engr., Tex. La., N.Y., Colo. Mem. Am. Chem. Soc., Am. Inst. Chem. Engrs., Nat. Soc. Profl. Engrs., Soc. Chem. Industry, Sigma Xi, Phi Lambda Upsilon, Tau Beta Pi. Club: Mile High (Denver). Home: 1722 Illinois St Golden CO 80401

MC BRIDE, H. T., cement co. exec.; b. Union City, N.J., Sept. 29, 1916; s. Henry and Hazel (Topping) McB.; B.S. in Accounting, N.Y. U., 1941; m. Dorothy Burke; 1 son, H. Colin. Adminstrv. mgr., asst. sec. Bechtel Corp., San Francisco, 1942-61; v.p., treas. Atlantic Cement Co., Inc., Stamford, Conn., 1961—; dir., v.p. Atlantic Cement Co. Fla., Inc., Jacksonville, Fla., 1964—. C.P.A., N.Y. Mem. Fin. Execs. Inst. N.Y., Lambda Chi Alpha. Clubs: Coveleigh (Rye); Canadian, Metropolitan (N.Y.C.); Midtown (Stamford). Home: 80 Florence Ave Rye NY 10580 Office: PO Box 30 Stamford CT 06904

MC BRIDE, JOHN ALEXANDER, cons.; b. Altoona, Pa., Mar. 29, 1918; s. Raymond E. and Carolyn (Tinker) McB.; A.B., Miami U., Oxford, Ohio, 1940; M.Sc., Ohio State U., 1941; Ph.D., U. Ill., 1944; m. Elizabeth Ann Vogel, Aug. 28, 1942; children—Katherine M. Woodbury, Susan McBride Malick, Carolyn McBride Nafziger. Various positions in research and devel. dept. Phillips Petroleum Co., 1944-58, 59-65, dir. chem. tech., Atomic energy div., 1963-65; chief applications engring. Astrodyne, Inc., 1958-59; dir. div. materials licensing AEC, 1965-70; v.p. E.R. Johnson Assos., Inc., Washington, 1970—; asst. gen. mgr. Nuclear Chems. & Metals Corp., 1970-71. Adviser U.S. delegation 3d Internat. Conf. Peaceful Uses Atomic Energy, 1964. Mem. Am. Chem. Soc., Am. Inst. Chem. Engrs. (chmn. nuclear engring. div. 1966), Am. Nuclear Soc., AAAS, Alpha Chi Sigma, Phi Kappa Tau. Author articles, patentee petrochem. products and processes, solid propellant rockets, irradiated fuel reprocessing, radioactive waste fixation and disposal. Mailing Address: PO Box 192 Merrifield VA 22116 Home: 2027 Carr Hill Rd Vienna VA 22180 Office: 8206 Leesburg Pike Vienna VA 22180

MC BRIDE, LLOYD, union ofcl.; b. Farmington, Mo., Mar. 9, 1916; student Farmington pub. schs.; m. Dolores Neihaus, 1937; children—Larry, Sharon McBride Reynolds. Mem. Steelworkers Organizing Com., 1936; organizer Local 1295, Mo., 1936, pres., 1938-40; pres. St. Louis Indsl. Union Council, CIO, 1940, Mo. CIO Indsl. Union Council, 1942-44; staff union rep. United Steelworkers Am., AFL-CIO, Pitts., 1946-58, sub-dist. dir., 1958-65, dist. dir., 1965-77, pres., 1977—; v.p. AFL-CIO, 1977—, mem. exec. bd. indsl. union dept.; del. Internat. Metalworkers Fedn. meetings, Geneva. Bd. dirs. Nat. Center Resource Recovery, Nat. Soc. Prevention Blindness; mem. presdl. commn. to investigate accident at Three Mile Island; mem. Pay Adv. Bd.; trustee Human Resources Devel. Inst.; mem. bd. Salvation Army; mem. Com. Nat. Health Ins., Harry S. Truman Inst. Served with USNR, 1944-46. Office: 5 Gateway Center Pittsburgh PA 15222

MC BRIDE, LLOYD MERRILL, lawyer; b. Corydon, Iowa, July 20, 1908; s. Ernest Eugene and Jeannie (Randolph) McB.; A.B. cum laude, Carleton Coll., Northfield, Minn., 1930, LL.D. (hon.), 1979; student Harvard, 1931-32; J.D., Northwestern U., 1934; m. Alice Rowland, June 8, 1935; children—Patricia Ann, Barbara Jean. Admitted to bar, 1934, and since in practice of law, Chgo.; with law firm Stearns & Jones, 1934-41, partner successor firms, Stearns & McBride, 1941-43, McBride & Baker, 1943-58, McBride, Baker, Wienke & Schlosser, 1958—; sec., dir. SMI Investments Co., FRC Corp., Rydertypes, Inc., Vermilion Corp., Bayou Corp.; dir. Bornquist, Inc., Stenning Industries, Inc., Wallace Bus. Forms, Inc. Sec., trustee Morton Arboretum, Lisle, Ill.; pres. 1550 State Pkwy. Condominium Assn.; trustee emeritus Carleton Coll., Northfield, Minn. Mem. Phi Beta Kappa. Republican. Clubs: Racquet, Tower, Mid-America (Chgo.). Home: 1550 N State Pkwy Chicago IL 60610 Office: 110 N Wacker Dr Chicago IL 60606

MCBRIDE, PATRICIA, ballerina; b. Teaneck, N.J., Aug. 23, 1942; m. Jean-Pierre Bonnefous. Made profl. debut as mem. Andre Eglevsky's Petit Ballet Co., 1957; apprentice N.Y. City Ballet, 1958, mem. corps de ballet, 1959—, now prin. dancer; danced leads in ballets, including Concerto Barocco, Ivesiana, Liebeslieder Walzer, Divertimento No. 15,; roles in many ballets, including Figure in the Carpet, 1960, Swan Lake, Fantasy, The Cage, Dim Lustre, Harlequinade, A Midsummer Night's Dream, Raymonda Variations, Nutcracker, Brahms-Schoenberg Quartet, 1966, Jewels, 1967, Who Cares?, 1970, Goldberg Variations, 1971, Divertimento from Le Baiser de la Fée, 1972, Coppelia, 1974, Dybbuk Variations, 1974, The Steadfast Tin Soldier, 1975, Pavane pour une Infante défunte, 1975; many concert and TV appearances, including Coppelia, 1978. Office: care NYC Ballet Lincoln Center for Performing Arts New York City NY 10023*

MC BRIDE, RAYMOND ANDREW, physician, educator; b. Houston, Dec. 27, 1927; s. Raymond Andrew and Rita (Mullane) McB.; B.S., Tulane U., 1952, M.D., 1956; m. Isabelle Shepherd Davis, May 10, 1958 (div. 1978); children—James Bradley, Elizabeth Conway, Christopher Ramsey, Andrew Gore. Surg. intern Jefferson Davis Hosp., Baylor U. Coll. Medicine, Houston, 1956-57; asst. in pathology Peter Bent Brigham Hosp., Boston, 1957-60, sr. resident pathologist, 1960-61; resident pathologist Free Hosp. for Women, Brookline, Mass., 1959; asst. resident pathologist Children's Hosp. Med. Center, Boston, 1960; teaching fellow pathology Harvard Med. Sch., Boston, 1958-61, research trainee Nat. Heart Inst., NIH, HEW, 1958-61; spl. postdoctoral fellow Nat. Cancer Inst., HEW, McIndoe Meml. Research unit Blond Labs., East Grimstead, Sussex, Eng., 1961-63; asst. attending pathologist Presbyn. Hosp., N.Y.C., 1963-65; asst. prof. pathology Coll. Physicians and Surgeons, Columbia U., 1963-65; research asso. Mt. Sinai Hosp., N.Y.C., 1965-68, asso. prof. surgery and immunogenetics, Mt. Sinai Sch. Medicine, N.Y.C., 1965-68; career scientist Health Research Council City N.Y., 1967-73; attending pathologist Flower and Fifth Ave. hosps., N.Y.C., 1968-78, Met. Hosp. Center, N.Y.C., 1968-78; prof. pathology N.Y. Med. Coll., 1968-78, Baylor Coll. Medicine, Houston, 1978—; attending pathologist Harris County Hosp. Dist., Ben Taub Gen. Hosp., Houston, 1978—; asso. staff Meth. Hosp., Houston, 1978—; exec. dean N.Y. Med. Coll., Valhalla, 1973-75; exec. dir., chief operating officer, bd. dirs. Westchester Med. Center Devel. Bd., Valhalla, 1974-76. Bd. dirs. Westchester Artificial Kidney Found., Inc., 1974-78, Westchester Med. Center Library, 1974-78, Westchester div. Am. Cancer Soc., 1973-78; trustee Tuxedo Park (N.Y.) Sch., 1975-78, Tuxedo Library, 1976-78. Grantee Health Research Council, N.Y.C., 1963-73, Am. Cancer Soc., 1971-72, NIH, USPHS, 1964—, NSF, 1965-68. Diplomate Am. Bd. Pathology. Fellow Royal Soc. Medicine; mem. Transplantation Soc., Am. Soc. Exptl. Pathology, Reticuloendothelial Soc., AAAS, Am. Assn. Pathologists and Bacteriologists, Am. Assn. Immunologists, AAUP, AMA, Tex. Med. Assn., Harris County Med. Soc., Tex. Soc. Pathologists, Am. Assn. Clin. Pathologists, Houston Acad. Medicine, Houston Soc. Clin. Pathologists, Assn. Am. Med. Colls., Fedn. Am. Scientists, Am., N.Y. cancer socs., Alpha Omega Alpha. Democrat. Roman Catholic. Club: Tuxedo (Tuxedo Park, N.Y.). Contbr. articles to profl. jours.; editorial bd. Jour. Immunogenetics. Home: 12431 Woodthorpe Ln Houston TX 77024 Office: Dept Pathology Baylor Coll Medicine 1200 Moursund Ave Tex Med Center Houston TX 77030

MCBRIDE, ROBERT DANA, steel co. exec.; b. Decatur, Ill., Nov. 5, 1927; s. Glen Clovis and Winifred Audrey (Spates) McB.; B.S., U.S. Mil. Acad., 1950; grad. Advanced Mgmt. Program, Harvard U., 1974; m. Gloria Jean Haefner, July 8, 1950; children—Scott, Dana, Kelly, Kitty. Vice-pres. ops. Granite City Steel Co. (Ill.), from 1966; v.p., gen. mgr. Granite City Steel div. Nat. Steel Corp., pres., 1976-77, pres. Great Lakes Steel div., Detroit, 1977—; dir. Security Bank and Trust Co., Southgate, Mich. Served with U.S. Army, 1950-56. Decorated Purple Heart, Silver Star, Bronze Star. Mem. Am. Iron and Steel Inst., Assn. Iron and Steel Engrs. (dir.). Roman Catholic. Home: 181 Ridge Rd Grosse Pointe Farms MI 48236 Office: 101 Tecumseh Rd Detroit MI 48229

MC BRIDE, ROBERT GUYN, composer, teacher, instrumentalist; b. Tucson, Feb. 20, 1911; s. John Marion and Hulda (Woertz) McB.; Mus.B., U. Ariz., 1933, Mus.M., 1935; m. Carol Haines, June 21, 1941; children—Marion, Lawrence. Played clarinet in high sch. and coll. band and orch., clarinet and saxophone in dance bands; former oboist Tucson Symphony Orch.; tchr. theory and wind instruments Bennington Coll. 1935-46; tchr. Concord (Mass.) Summer Sch., 1937, Bennington Coll. Summer Sch., 1940-41; mem. Yaddo Group, 1936, 37, 40; soloist with Bennington Coll., Pioneer Valley (Greenfield, Mass.), Vt. Symphony and Boston Pops orchs., Gordon String Quartet; played clarinet, oboe and English horn in program of own works Composers Forum, N.Y.C., 1937; played wind instruments with Gregory Tucker, pianist, at schs. and colls., 1942 and 1943, under auspices Am. Assn. Colls.; clarinetist League of Composers Wind Quintet touring Central and S. Am., fall 1941; soloist Ford Hour under Reiner, May 1946; asso. prof. music U. Ariz., 1957-60, prof., 1960—, oboist woodwind quintet, 1960—. Compositions: Mexican Rhapsody, 1935; Fugato on a Well Known Theme, 1935; Prelude to a Tragedy, 1935; Workout for Chamber Orchestra, 1936; Show Piece, ballet for Erick Hawkins of Ballet Caravan (played by Radio City Orch. under Rapee, and by Phila. Orch. and Nat. Youth Orch. under Stokowski);

Swing Stuff, 1936; Wise Apple Five, clarinet and strings, performed by Jacques Gordon group, 1940; music for Martha Graham's prodn. Punch and the Judy, 1941; Strawberrry Jam (Home-Made) (performed by Nat. Orchestral Assn. under Leon Barzin, Mar. 1942), Stuff in G. conducted by composer, WNYC Music Festival, Feb. 1943; composed music for Turandot, Bennington Coll. drama, 1941; Sunday in Mexico, 1961; Hill-Country Symphony, 1963; Country Music Fantasy, 1964; Overture on Whimsical Themes, 1962; also numerous works for solo instrument and piano accompaniment, bands and instrumental groups; composed music for RKO-Pathé short subjects, 1944-45, for mus. dir. March of Time, for Movietone News, also Triumph Films, N.Y.C.; film scores Farewell to Yesterday; The Man With My Face; commns.: Symphonic Melody, 1968, Folksong Fantasy, 1970, 1776 Overture, 1975, Improvisation, 1976; (ballet) Brooms of Mexico, 1970, Light Fantastic, 1977, Sportmusic, 1977. Guggenheim fellow in composition, 1937; award Am. Acad. Arts and Letters, 1942; Composers' Press award, 1943; U. Ariz. award of merit, 1960. Mem. Am. Composers Alliance, Phi Kappa Phi. Episcopalian. Home: 3236 E Waverly St Tucson AZ 85716

MC BRIDE, ROBIN, record co. exec.; b. Pitts., June 2, 1937; s. J. Vincent and Alison Hyde (Jacobs) M.; B.A. in Music, Amherst Coll., 1959; grad. Hartt Coll. Music, 1958, St. John's U. Sch. Law, 1967; m. Mariele Moser, Jan. 29, 1966; 1 dau., Sabina Alison. With N.Y. Jazz Festival, N.Y.C., 1956-58; adminstr. artists and repertoire Columbia Records, N.Y.C., 1961-65; mgr. Folkways Records, N.Y.C., 1965-68; dir. midwest and internat. artists and repertoire Mercury (now Phonogram, Inc.), Chgo., 1968-78; ind. record producer with Bird Prodns., Chgo., 1969—. Served with USAF, 1960-66. Mem. Nat. Acad. Recording Arts and Scis. (pres. Chgo. chpt. 1973, 78, nat. trustee 1969-72, 77—), Record Industry Assn. Am. (internat. com. 1970—). Office: 1946 N Hudson Ave Chicago IL 60614

MC BRIDE, THOMAS FREDERICK, govt. ofcl.; b. Elgin, Ill., Feb. 8, 1929; s. Thomas Wallace and Sarah Rosalie (Pierce) McB.; B.A., N.Y. U., 1952; LL.B., Columbia, 1956; m. Catherine Higgs Milton, Aug. 23, 1975; children—Matthew, Elizabeth, John, Raphael, Luke. Admitted to N.Y. State bar, 1956, D.C. bar, 1966, U.S. Supreme Ct. bar, 1963; asst. dist. atty. N.Y. County, 1956-59; trial atty. organized crime sect. Dept. Justice, 1961-65; adviser to Home Ministry, Govt. India, 1964; ofcl. Peace Corps, 1965-68; dep. chief counsel select com. on crime Ho. of Reps., 1969-70; asso. dir., staff dir. Police Found., 1970-73; asso. spl. prosecutor Watergate, 1973-75; dir. bur. enforcement CAB, 1975-77; insp. gen. U.S. Dept. Agr., Washington, 1977—. Served with AUS, 1946-47. Mem. D.C. Bar Assn. Co-author: Team Policing, 1973. Home: 2922 45th St NW Washington DC 20016 Office: Dept Agr Washington DC

MCBRIDE, WILLIAM BERNARD, corp. exec.; b. N.Y.C., May 22, 1931; s. William and Nora (Hughes) McB.; B.S., Fordham U., 1952; M.B.A., Baruch Sch., 1963; m. Lorraine Barry, May 27, 1956; children—Mary, William, Stephen, Anne. Staff auditor Touche, Ross, Bailey & Smart, C.P.A.'s, N.Y.C., 1952-58; asst. v.p. Bankers Trust Co., N.Y.C., 1959-67; treas. Walter Kidde & Co., Inc., Clifton, N.J., 1967—, v.p., 1974—. C.P.A., N.Y. Mem. Am. Inst. C.P.A.'s, N.Y. State Soc. C.P.A.'s. Home: 243 Sunset Ave Ridgewood NJ 07450 Office: 9 Brighton Rd Clifton NJ 07012

MC BRIDE, WILLIAM LEON, philosopher, educator; b. N.Y.C., Jan. 19, 1938; s. William Joseph and Irene May (Choffin) McB.; A.B., Georgetown U., 1959; postgrad. (Fulbright fellow) U. Lille, 1959-60; M.A. (Woodrow Wilson fellow), Yale U., 1962, Ph.D. (Social Sci. Research Council fellow), 1964; m. Mary Angela Barron, July 12, 1965; children—Catherine, Kara. Instr. philosophy Yale U., New Haven, 1964-66, asst. prof., 1966-70, asso. prof., 1970-73; lectr. Northwestern U., Evanston, Ill., summer 1972; asso. prof. Purdue U., West Lafayette, Ind., 1973-76, prof., 1976—; lectr. Korcula Summer Sch., Yugoslavia, 1971, 73. Pres., Highland Sch. PTA, Lafayette, 1977-78. Mem. Am. Philos. Assn., Am. Soc. for Polit. and Legal Philosophy, Soc. for Philosophy and Pub. Affairs, Soc. for Phenomenology and Existential Philosophy (exec. co-sec. 1977—), AAUP. Author: Fundamental Change in Law and Society, 1970; The Philosophy of Marx, 1977. Home: 744 Cherokee Ave Lafayette IN 47905 Office: Dept Philosophy Recitation Bldg Purdue U West Lafayette IN 47907

MC BURNEY, ANDREW MARVELL, paper mfg. exec.; b. Phila., July 25, 1913; s. Andrew M. and Dorothy Irwin (Buck) McB.; student Germantown Acad., 1930; grad. Hill Sch., Pottstown, Pa., 1932; B.A., Yale, 1936; m. Lidie Lane Sloan, Feb. 26, 1938; children—A. Sloan, F. Lane. With Oxford Paper Co., N.Y.C. (became div. Ethyl Corp. 1967), 1936—, various positions West Carrollton and Rumford mills, successively mem. sales orgn, N.Y.C., asst. to exec. v.p., eastern sales mgr., sales mgr. gen. sales mgr., 1936-58, v.p., 1953-66, exec. v.p., 1966-76; sr. adviser Boise Cascade, 1976—; dir. Ethyl Corp., Lake Placid Co., Thomas Jefferson Life Ins. Co., Iroquois Brands Ltd., Mohasco Corp. Mem. Exec. Office of Pres. Office Emergency Preparedness, 1968—. Chief pulp, paper and paperboard br., forest products div. OPS, Wash., 1951-52. Trustee, mem. exec. com. Lake Placid Edn. Found.; trustee Hill Sch., Pottstown, Pa., 1965—. Served to capt. USMCR, 1943-46; comdg. officer aircraft detachment. Mem. Salesmen's Assn. Paper Industry, Boston Paper Trade Assn., Printing Paper Mfrs. Assn. (chmn. 1962-63). Republican. Presbyn. Clubs: University, The Links, Twenty-Nine, Yale, Sales Executives, Paper (N.Y.C.); Lake Placid (pres.) (Lake Placid, N.Y.). Home: Tower East 190 E 72d St New York NY 10021 Office: 330 Madison Ave New York NY 10017

MC CABE, BRIAN FRANCIS, physician; b. Detroit, June 16, 1926; s. Charles J. and Rosalie T. (Dropiewski) McC.; B.S., U. Detroit, 1950; M.D., U. Mich., 1954; m. Yvonne T. Fecteau, Sept. 8, 1951; children—Brian F., Bevin E. Intern, Univ. Hosp., Ann Arbor, Mich., 1954-55; resident U. Mich. Med. Sch., 1955-59; practice medicine specializing in otolaryngology and maxillofacial surgery, Iowa City; mem. staff Iowa City VA Hosp.; prof., head dept. otolaryngology and maxillofacial surgery U. Iowa; also chmn. residency rev. com. for otolaryngology. Dir. Bd. Examiners Otolaryngology. Mem. Am. Acad. Ophthalmology and Otolaryngology (sec. for otolaryngology), Am. Laryngol., Rhinol. and Otolaryngol. Soc., Am. Otol. Soc. (editor-librarian), Am. Laryngol. Soc., Otosclerosis Study Group, Galens Hon., Linn County, Am., Iowa med. socs., Collegium Oto-Rhino-Laryngologicum Amicitae sacrum, New Zealand Soc. Otolaryngology, Snipe Class Internat. Racing Assn., Nat. Amateur Yacht Racing Assn., DN Ice Yacht Racing Assn., Alpha Omega Alpha. Clubs: Centurion, Barton Boat, Hawkeye Sailing. Co-editor Annals of Otology, Rhinology and Laryngology. Home: 237 Ferson St Iowa City IA 52240 Office: Univ Hosps and Clinics Iowa City IA 52240. *It seems to me the greatest single attribute leading to success is the ability to transmit a thought or concept clearly and simply. It is said also that any degree of success is attended by a proportionate amount of luck. This is undoubtedly so. I am reminded at the same time, of the anonymous aphorism, "The harder I work, the luckier I get."*

MCCABE, CHARLES RAYMOND, journalist; b. N.Y.C., Jan. 24, 1915; s. Peter Joseph and Mary Catherine (Kyne) McC.; B.A., Manhattan Coll., 1937; m. Margaret Ellen Scripps, 1948 (div. 1955); children—Mary (Mrs. Peter Barmonde), Peter, Nini, Charles. Reporter, New York American, 1937-38; publicity rep. Steve Hannagen Assos., N.Y.C., 1939-42; corr. U.P.I., Washington, 1950-52; syndicated columnist San Francisco Chronicle and other papers, 1959—; cons. Howard Gossage Assos., 1962-64. Mem. San Francisco Crime Commn., 1968-69. Served with USNR, 1942-45. Decorated Navy Commendation medal; recipient Munoz-Marin Journalism award, San Juan, P.R., 1940. Mem. Newspaper Guild. Democrat. Roman Catholic. Club: Great Bedwyn Cricket (pres. 1962-66) (Witshire, Eng.). Author: Damned Old Crank, 1952; The Fearless Spectator, 1970; Tall Girls Are Grateful, 1973; The Good Man's Weakness, 1974. Office: 901 Mission St San Francisco CA 94119

MC CABE, CYNTHIA JAFFEE, mus. curator; b. N.Y.C., Feb. 8, 1943; d. Harry and Pauline (Techefsky) Jaffee; B.A., Cornell U., 1963; M.A., Columbia U., 1967. Organizer fine arts sect., catalogue, bibliography Lower East Side: Portal to American Life (1870-1924), Jewish Mus., N.Y.C. and Smithsonian Instn., Washington, 1966-67; research Nakian Retrospective, Mus. Modern Art, N.Y.C., 1966; organizer fine arts sect. Erie Canal Sesquicentennial, N.Y. State Council Arts, 1967; research Venice 34, Nat. Collection of Fine Arts, Smithsonian Instn., 1968; curator painting and sculpture Hirshhorn Mus. and Sculpture Garden, Smithsonian Instn., 1967-76, curator exhbns., 1976—; organizer The Golden Door: Artist-Immigrants of Am., 1876-1976, 1976; asst. professorial lectr. George Washington U., 1975-76; lectr. Smithsonian Resident Assos., 1976—, Spoleto (S.C.) Festival, 1978; co-chmn. Smithsonian Einstein Centennial Colloquium-The Muses Flee Hitler, 1980; organizer Twentieth Century Sculptors and Their Drawings: Selections from Hirshhorn Mus. and Sculpture Garden, Smithsonian Instn. Traveling Exhbn. Service, 1979-80, Fernando Botero Hirshhorn Mus. and Sculpture Garden, and tour, 1979-80, others. Mem. Internat. Council Museums, Am. Assn. Museums (chmn. curators com. 1977-79, credentials com. 1978—), Coll. Art Assn., Soc. Archtl. Historians, Internat. Assn. Art Critics, Women's Caucus for Art. Author: Sculptors and Their Drawings: Selections from the Hirshhorn Museum Collection, 1974; Henry Moore at the Hirshhorn Museum and Sculpture Garden, 1974; The Golden Door: Artist-Immigrants of America, 1876-1976, 1976; Fernando Botero, 1979; others. Art historian. Office: Hirshhorn Museum and Sculpture Garden Smithsonian Institution Washington DC 20560

MC CABE, EDWARD AENEAS, lawyer; b. County Monaghan, Ireland, Mar. 4, 1917; s. Patrick and Alice (McDonnel) McC.; LL.B., Columbus U., Washington, 1946; m. Janet Isabel Stevens, Nov. 17, 1951; children—Thomas, Michael, Patrick, Barbara. Admitted to D.C. bar, 1946, U.S. Supreme Ct. bar, 1950; exec. asst. Joint Congl. Com. Labor Mgmt. Relations, 1947-48; atty. for labor relations and trade assn. matters, Washington, 1949-52; gen. counsel com. on labor and edn. Ho. of Reps., 1953-55; asso., counsel to Pres. of U.S., 1956-58, adminstrv. asst., 1958-61; partner firm Hamel, Park, McCabe & Saunders, 1961—; White House cons. Presdl. transition, 1974-75. Mem. D.C. Criminal Justice Coordinating Bd. Trustee, Public Defender Service D.C., vice chmn., 1969; bd. govs. U.S.O.; trustee Immaculata Coll., Washington, Allentown Coll., Center Valley, Pa.; mem. bd. advisers DeSales Sch. of Theology, Washington; trustee United Student Aid Funds, Inc., N.Y.; chmn. bd. Student Loan Mktg. Assn. Served with U.S. Army, 1941-45. Mem. Am., Fed., D.C. bar assns., Jud. Conf. D.C. Circuit. Republican. Roman Catholic (mem. cardinal's com. laity Archdiocese of Washington, com. for deferred gifts for Archdiocese). Clubs: Capitol Hill, Metropolitan, Kenwood Golf and Country, Burning Tree (Washington). Home: 5605 Kirkwood Dr Washington DC 20016 Office: 1776 F St NW Washington DC 20006

MC CABE, EDWARD JAMES, JR., publisher; b. Worcester, N.Y., May 9, 1913; s. Edward J. and Mary (Murphy) McC.; B.S. in Elec. Engring., Cornell U., 1934; m. Ethel Corrigan, Jan. 27, 1940; children—Kathleen, Edward Owen. With Grolier, Inc. (formerly Grolier Soc., Inc.), N.Y.C., 1934—, treas., dir., 1937-47, pres., dir., 1947-67, chmn. bd., 1967-75; chmn. adv. bd. Grolier Inc., 1975—; pres. Internat. Copy Corp., 1978—; dir. Impresora y Editora Mexicana, S.A. de C.V., Grolier Found., Inc. Chmn. reference book sect. Am. Textbook Pubs. Inst., 1952-53, 66-68, dir., 1953-58, 69-70, 2d v.p., 1954-55, treas., 1955-57, v.p., 1958; dir., treas. Assn. Am. Publishers, Inc., 1970-72; assisted formation industry wide Subscription Book Pubs.-Nat. Better Bus. Bur. Coop. Program, 1950, mem. adv. and exec. com., 1950-70, chmn. adv. com., 1958-62, 65-66; dir. Nat. Better Bus. Bur., 1955-70, 2d vice chmn., 1965, 1st vice chmn., 1966-67, chmn. bd., 1968-70; dir. Council Better Bus. Burs., Inc., 1970-71; mem. State Dept. Overseas Schs. Adv. Council, 1969—; mem. Am. Pubs. Trade Delegation to USSR for studying copyrights and publishing, 1970. Mem. Korean War Industry Adv. Com., NPA; mem. joint ALA com. on relations with pubs. and Am. Book Pubs. Council com. on reading devel.; mem. joint ALA com. on relations with subscription book pubs. Bd. dirs. Grolier Found., Inc.; mem. fund bd. Cornell U., 1967-73; trustee Cath. U., 1968-73, Washington, Hutchinson River council Boy Scouts Am. Decorated knight comdr. grand cross Holy Sepulchre, Knight Malta. Mem. Eta Kappa Nu. Clubs: Siwanoy Country, Westchester Country, Cornell. Home: 3 Pine Terr Bronxville NY 10708 Office: 575 Lexington Ave New York NY 10022

MCCABE, EUGENE JOSEPH, bank and holding co. exec.; b. N.Y.C., Feb. 14, 1918; s. Eugene Joseph and Katherine Elizabeth (Owens) McC.; B.B.A., Manhattan Coll., 1939; J.D., Fordham U., 1948; m. Eleanor Genevieve Kadis, Nov. 7, 1953; children—Mary Ellen, Eugene, Suzanne, Michael, Nicholas. Adminstrv. asst. Guaranty Trust Co., N.Y.C., 1939-43; asst. sec. Colonial Trust Co., N.Y.C., 1946-56; v.p. Irving Trust Co., N.Y.C., 1956-72, v.p., sec., 1976—; sec. Charter N.Y. Corp. (name now Irving Bank Corp.), N.Y.C., 1972—. Served to lt. USN, 1943-46. Home: Rohallion Dr Rumson NJ 07760 Office: One Wall St New York NY 10005

MC CABE, FRANK JOHN, telecommunications co. exec.; b. N.Y.C., Oct. 27, 1923; s. John Charles and Anne (O'Toole) McC.; A.B. in Psychology, Fordham U., 1950, M.A., 1951, Ph.D., 1954; m. Lucille Peterson, Sept. 15, 1956 (dec.); children—Carole, Peter, David; m. 2d, Linda Holiday, Nov. 5, 1977. Mem. faculty psychology Fordham U., 1950-53; staff psychologist Sci. Research Assos., 1953-54, Met. Life Ins. Co., 1954-56; cons. psychologist Psychol. Corp., 1956-58; dir. personnel devel. Raytheon Co., 1958-59; with ITT, 1959—, v.p., dir. personnel, 1965-73, sr. v.p., 1973—. Mem. Am. Psychol. Assn., Sigma Xi. Home: 14 Park Rd Scarsdale NY 10583 Office: 320 Park Ave New York NY 10022

MCCABE, FRANK WELLS, banker; b. Brewster, N.Y., 1903; grad. Taft Sch., 1920; B.A., Yale, 1925; postgrad. Oxford U., 1925-26; m. Mary Lee Borden, 1930; children—Pauline, Mary Lee, Martha. With Nat. Comml. Bank & Trust Co., Albany, 1926-77, pres., 1955-64, chmn. bd., 1964-73, dir., 1952-74, hon. dir., 1974-77; pres., dir. Wytex Corp., Albany, N.Y.; dir. CMP Industries, Inc., Albany, Matthew Bender & Co., N.Y.C., Conroy, Inc., San Antonio. Trustee Albany Med. Coll.; hon. gov. Albany Med. Center Hosp. Clubs: Ft. Orange (Albany); Yale (N.Y.C.). Home: Brinsmade Ln Box 367 Salisbury CT 06068 Office: Wytex C Box 1867 66 State St Albany NY 12201

MC CABE, GERARD BENEDICT, univ. library adminstr.; b. N.Y.C., Jan. 22, 1930; s. Patrick Joseph and Margaret Irene (McDonald) McC.; B.A. in English, Manhattan Coll., 1952; A.M. in Library Sci. (Scholar), U. Mich., 1954; M.A. in English, Mich. State U., 1959; m. Jacqueline L. Maloney, Aug. 3, 1963; children—Theresa Marie, Rebecca Mary. Asst. acquisitions dept. U. Nebr. Library, Lincoln, 1954-56; chief bibliog. acquisitions dept. Mich. State U. Library, East Lansing, 1956-58, librarian Inst. Community Devel. and Service, Mich. State U., 1958-59; acquisitions librarian U. S. Fla., Tampa, 1959-66, asst. dir. planning and devel., 1967-70; asso. dir. U. Ark. Library, Fayetteville, 1966-67; dir. univ. libraries Va. Commonwealth U., Richmond, 1970—. Mem. ALA, Va., Southeastern library assns., Bibliog. Soc. Am. Home: 1519 Village Grove Rd Richmond VA 23233 Office: Va Commonwealth U Univ Libraries 901 Park Ave Richmond VA 23284

MC CABE, JOHN CHARLES, III, writer; b. Detroit, Nov. 14, 1920; s. Charles John and Rosalie (Dropiewski) McC.; Ph.B., U. Detroit, 1947; M.F.A. in Theatre, Fordham U., 1948; Ph.D. in English Lit., Shakespeare Inst., U. Birmingham (Eng.), 1954; m. Vija Valda Zarina, Oct. 19, 1958; children—Linard Peter, Sean Cahal and Deirdre Rose (twins). Profl. actor, 1938—; producer-dir. Milford (Pa.) Playhouse, summers 1948-53; producer N.Y. U. Summer Theatre, Sterling Forest, N.Y., 1963-65; instr. theatre Wayne State U., 1948-51, CCNY, 1955; mem. faculty N.Y. U., 1956-68, prof. dramatic art, chmn. dept., 1962-68; chmn. dept. drama and theatre arts Mackinac Coll., Mackinac Island, Mich., 1968-70; author-in-residence Lake Superior State Coll., Sault Ste. Marie, Mich., 1970—; founder, The Sons of the Desert, group devoted to works Laurel and Hardy, 1963. Served with USAAF, 1943-45; ETO. Mem. Shakespeare Assn. Am., Actors Equity Assn., Catholic Actors Guild Am., Baker St. Irregulars. Clubs: The Players, The Lambs (N.Y.C.). Author: Mr. Laurel and Mr. Hardy, 1961, rev. edit., 1967; George M. Cohan: The Man Who Owned Broadway, 1973; The Comedy World of Stan Laurel, 1974; Laurel & Hardy, 1975; (with G.B. Harrison) Proclaiming the Word, 1976; Charlie Chaplin, 1978; cons. to James Cagney for autobiography Cagney by Cagney, 1976. Home: 498 Sheridan Dr Sault Ste Marie MI 49783

MCCABE, JOSEPH CHARLES, pub. co. exec., editor; b. Plainfield, N.J., Jan. 16, 1914; s. Frank John and Margaret Mary (Ryan) McC.; B.S. in Elec. Engring., Lehigh U., 1936; postgrad. Stevens Inst. Tech., 1941-42; m. Lucy Gloria Urello, Sept. 19, 1936; children—Frank J., Judith McCabe Koru, William Joseph. Cadet engr. Jersey Central Power & Light Co., 1936-37, tech. engr. Power Plants, 1937-43; field engr. Western Electric Co., 1943-45; asso. editor Power Mag., McGraw-Hill Pub. Co., N.Y.C., 1945-53; editor Combustion Mag., Combustion Pub. Co., N.Y.C., 1953—, v.p., 1958—. Mem. Mountain Lakes (N.J.) Bd. Edn., 1953-55, pres., 1953-55; councilman City of Mountain Lakes, 1958-63. Served with USAAF, 1944-45; PTO. Registered profl. engr., N.J., Fellow ASME (chmn. div. fuels 1958-59). Home: 73 Woodland Ave Mountain Lakes NJ 07046 Office: 277 Park Ave New York NY 10017

MCCABE, JUDITH VAN BARON, mus. adminstr.; b. Mankato, Minn., Dec. 2, 1942; d. William Henry and Grace Eloise (Gerth) Appel; A.A., Waldorf Coll., 1962; B.A. magna cum laude, Luther Coll., 1963; M.A in Art History, U. Iowa, 1969, Ph.D., 1973; m. Thomas W. McCabe, Nov. 10, 1978; 1 dau., Erika Briana Gorder. Tchr., Rock Island (Ill.) High Sch., 1963-65; mng. editor Arts Mag., 1973-74; exec. dir. Bronx Mus. of the Arts, 1974-76; dir. Gallery One, Master's Gallery, San Jose State U., 1976-77; exec. dir. Monmouth (N.J.) Mus., 1977—; asst. prof. art San Jose State U., 1976-77; adj. asst. prof. William Paterson Coll. N.J., 1978; asst. prof. N.Y. U., summer 1974. Mem. vis. com. Met. Mus. Art, N.Y.C., 1974-76; mem. exec. com. Bicentennial Adv. Com.; chmn. bd. dirs. West Bronx Art League, 1975-76. Kress Found. fellow, 1971, grantee, 1972-73. Editor art news Soho Weekly News, 1976-77; author works in field. Office: Newman Springs Rd Lincroft NJ 07739

MCCABE, LEO ORVINE, lawyer; b. Canton, Minn., Aug. 8, 1899; s. Frank and Anastasia (Gossman) McC.; B.A. cum laude, Columbia Coll., Dubuque, Iowa, 1920; post-grad. U. Minn., 1920-21; J.D., Yale, 1923; spl. studies summers, State U. Iowa, Iowa State Coll.; m. Anne Hogan, Aug. 23, 1927; children—Karen Anne, John Leo. Admitted to Iowa bar, 1923; practiced with Jordan, Jordan, Wismer and McCabe, Des Moines; instr. law U. Notre Dame, 1927-29; prof. law De Paul U., Chgo., 1929-43, 46-48; practice of pub. utility corp. law, 1948-76; partner of firm Stevenson, Dendtler, & McCabe, 1950-64, Isham, Lincoln & Beale, Chgo., 1964—. Atty. pub. utilities div. SEC, Phila., 1943-46. Mem. Ill., Chgo. bar assns., Phi Alpha Delta, Pi Gamma Mu, Book & Gavel Soc., Blue Key. Roman Catholic. Clubs: Yale (Chgo.); Mich. Shores, Executives. Author: (case book) Cases on Persons and Domestic Relations; also articles law revs. Home: 2333 Central St Evanston IL 60201 Office: One First Nat Plaza Chicago IL 60603

MC CABE, ST. CLAIR LANDERKIN, publishing exec.; b. Toronto, Ont., Can., July 13, 1915; s. Herbert St. Clair and Myrtle (Landerkin) M.; m. Elsie Dorothy Stricker, Nov. 10, 1933; children—Katherine Dorothy Anne McCabe Beatson, John Timothy St. Clair. Pres., dir. Thomson Newspapers Ltd., Thomson. Newspapers Inc., Can. Newspapers Co. Ltd., Humboldt Newspapers Inc., Opelika-Auburn Pub. Co., Inc., Douglas Dispatch, Inc., Greenville Newspapers Inc., Oxnard Pub. Co., St. John's Pub. Co. Ltd., Phenix Citizen Inc., The Independent Inc., Key West Newspaper Corp., San Gabriel Valley Tribune, Inc., Lock Haven Express Printing Co., Punta Gorda Herald Inc., Replacement Sales Co. Ltd., Rocky Mt. Pub. Co., Thomson B.C. Newspapers Ltd., Thomson Newspapers (N.H.) Inc., Thomson Newspapers (Minn.) Inc., Thomson Newspapers (Pa.) Inc., Thomson Newspapers (Ala.) Inc., Thomson Newspapers (Wis.) Inc., Thomson Newspapers (Mo.) Inc., Thomson Newspapers (Fla.) Inc., Thomson Newspapers (Ill.) Inc., Thomson Publs. N.Y. Inc., Thomson Newspaper Pub. Co., Inc., Thomson-Brush-Moore Newspapers, Inc., Western Pubs. Ltd.; exec. v.p., dir. Chew Newspapers Ohio Inc.; dir. The Advocate Co. Ltd., Central Can. Ins. Service Ltd., The Guarantee Ins. Co., Scottish & York Holdings Ltd., Scottish & York Ins. Co. Ltd., Victoria Ins. Co. Can. Mem. Can. Daily Newspaper Pubs. Assn., Canadian Press (dir.), Commonwealth Press Union, Inland Daily Press Assn., Internat. Press Inst. Clubs: Masons; Ontario; National (Toronto); Mississauga (Ont.) Golf and Country. Home: 1195 Greenoaks Dr Mississauga ON Canada Office: 65 Queen St W Toronto ON M5H 2M8 Canada also 3150 Des Plaines Ave Des Plaines IL 60018

MC CABE, THOMAS BAYARD, paper co. exec., banker; b. Whaleyville, Md., July 11, 1893; s. William Robbins and Beulah (Whaley) McC.; student Wilmington Conf. Acad., Dover, Del., 1907-10; A.B., Swarthmore Coll., 1915, LL.D.; LL.D., Hahneman Med., Drexel Inst., Trinity Coll., 1949, Pa. Mil. Coll., U. Del., 1955, U. Maine, 1961, St. Joseph's Coll., 1962, U. Md., 1962; L.H.D., Temple U., 1959, Salisbury State Coll., 1979; hon. degrees U. Pa., Colo. Coll., Jefferson Med. Coll., Colby Coll.; m. Jeannette Laws, Feb. 28, 1924; children—Thomas (dec.), Richard Whaley, James. With Scott Paper Co., Chester, Pa., 1916—, salesman, 1916-17, asst. sales mgr., 1919-20, sales mgr., 1920-22, dir., 1921—, sec., sales mgr., 1922-27, v.p., 1927, pres., 1927-62, chmn., 1962-68, chmn. finance com., 1969-72, chief exec., 1927-67; dir. Fed. Res. Bank of Phila., 1938-48, chmn. bd., 1939-48; chmn. bd. govs. Fed. Res. System, 1948-51. Mem. bus. adv. council Dept. Commerce, 1940—, chmn., 1944-45; hon. chmn. Mktg. Sci. Inst.; with Council Nat. Def., 1940; dep. dir. div. of priorities Office Prodn. Mgt., 1941; dep. Lend-Lease Adminstrn., 1941-42. Public gov. N.Y. Stock Exchange, 1960-63. Trustee Com. for Econ. Devel., Army-Navy Liquidation Commn., Feb.-Sept. 1945; spl. asst. to sec. State and Fgn. Liquidation Commr., 1945-46. Trustee Eisenhower Exchange Fellowships, Inc.; bd. mgrs. Swarthmore Coll. Served from pvt. to capt. U.S. Army, 1917-19. Awarded Medal for Merit. Mem. Delta Upsilon. Presbyterian. Clubs: Rittenhouse, Union League, Pen and Pencil (hon. life) (Phila.); Corinthian Yacht. Home: 607 N Chester Rd Swarthmore PA 19081 Office: Scott Paper Co Philadelphia PA 19113

MCCABE, WILLIAM GORDON, JR., textile co. exec.; b. Petersburg, Va., July 11, 1911; s. William Gordon and Frances C. (Spicer) McC.; grad. Woodberry Forest Sch., 1930; B.S., U. Va., 1933; m. Lydia Phillips, Apr. 14, 1936; children—Katharine Gordon, Mary Scott. Asso., Am. Cotton Coop. Assn., New Orleans, 1933-36, mgr. Greenville (S.C.) office, 1936-39; partner Donkle & McCabe, Inc., Greenville, 1939-48; dir. raw cotton purchases J.P. Stevens & Co., Greenville, 1948-51, dir. raw cotton and wool policies and procurement, 1951-52, v.p., 1952-76, group v.p., dir.; pres. W. Gordon McCabe & Co., Inc., 1976—; dir. S.C. Nat. Bank, Columbia, Piedmont & Laurens Ry.; pres. bd. mgrs. N.Y. Cotton Exchange, 1977—; adviser Nat. Cotton Council, Am. Cotton Shippers. Bd. dirs. Greenville County Found., 1959—; chmn. bd. Greenville Gen. Hosp., 1950-56; chmn. Greenville Community Corp.; trustee Clemson U. Served to lt. (s.g.) USNR, 1943-46. Mem. Greenville C. of C. Episcopalian. Clubs: Boston (New Orleans); Biltmore Forest Country (Biltmore, N.C.); Poinsett (past pres.), So. Cross, Carolina Yacht (S.C.); Ponte Vedra (Fla.); Cotillion (past pres.), Green Valley Country (dir.) (Greenville); Algonquin, Metropolitan (N.Y.C.); Ocean Reef (Fla.). Home: 89 Woodvale Ave Greenville SC 29605 Office: PO Box 8188 Greenville SC 29604*

MCCAFFERTY, MICHAEL GILBERT, fin. exec.; b. Poteau, Okla., June 26, 1938; s. Rennie Earl and Anna Louise (Pope) McC.; B.S., U. Okla., 1960; M.B.A., Stanford, 1964. Asst. v.p. First Nat. City Bank, N.Y.C., 1964-68; asso. firm Thatcher Partners, N.Y.C., 1968-71; with Great Western United Corp., Denver, 1971-73, treas., 1972-73; v.p., treas. Kaiser Aetna, Oakland, Calif., 1973-76; asst. treas. Crown Zellerbach Corp., San Francisco, 1976—. Served with USNR, 1960-62. Clubs: University (N.Y.C.); Commercial (San Francisco). Home: 140 Saint James Dr Piedmont CA 94611 Office: One Bush St San Francisco CA 94119

MCCAFFERY, WILLIAM ARTHUR, graphic designer; b. Phila., Sept. 16, 1935; s. William and Mae (Panchick) McC.; B.F.A., Phila. Mus. Coll. Art, 1957; m. Sheila Schaeffer, Dec. 20, 1970; children—Kent Travis, Paisley. Art dir. Grey Advt., N.Y.C., 1959-60; sr. art dir. Marschalk Co., N.Y.C., 1960-63; creative dir., exec. v.p. Degarmo, Inc., N.Y.C., 1963-67; partner, dir. Degarmo, McCaffery, Inc., N.Y.C., 1967-70; film dir. Rima Prodns., N.Y.C.; pres. William McCaffery, Inc., 1971—; v.p., creative dir. Norton Simon Communications, 1972-75; v.p. Revlon, Inc., 1975-79; pres. McCaffery Inc., 1979—; instr. graphic design Parsons Sch. Design, N.Y.C. Trustee Phila. Coll. Art. Recipient numerous awards N.Y. Art Dirs. Club, Am. Inst. Graphic Arts, Advt. Club, 1959—. Mem. Am. Inst. Graphic Arts (past dir.), N.Y. Art Dirs. Club (v.p., dir.). Author, illustrator: How to Watch a Parade, 1958; Noses Are For Rosses, 1959. Exhibited N.Y. Cultural Center, 1972. Address: 20 Pheasant Ln Greenwich CT 06830

MCCAFFREY, ANNE INEZ, author; b. Cambridge, Mass., Apr. 1, 1926; d. George H. and Anne (McElroy) McCaffrey; B.A. cum laude Radcliffe Coll., 1947; student U. City of Dublin, 1970-71; m. Wright Johnson, Jan. 14, 1950 (div. Aug. 1970); children—Alec Anthony, Todd, Georgeanne. Advt. copywriter Liberty Music Shops, N.Y.C., 1947-50; copywriter Helena Rubinstein, N.Y.C., 1950-52. Author: Restoree, 1967; Dragonflight, 1968; Decision at Doona, 1969; Ship Who Sang, 1970; Mark of Merlin, 1971; Dragonquest, 1971; Ring of Fear, 1971; To Ride Pegasus, 1973; Out-Of-This-World Cookbook, 1973; A Time When, ltd. edit., 1975; Dragonsong; Kilternan Legacy; Dragonsinger; Dinosaur Planet; Get Off the Unicorn; White Dragon; numerous short stories, 1954—. Editor: Alchemy and Academe, 1970. Dir. musicals Brecks Mill Cronies, Wilmington Music Sch., 1962-65. Recipient Hugo award, 1967; Nebula award, 1968. Mem. Sci. Fiction Writers Am. (sec.-treas. 1968-70), Authors' Guild. Address: Dragonhold Kilquade Greystones County Wicklow Ireland

MCCAFFREY, JOSEPH FRANCIS, broadcasting corr.; b. Poughkeepsie, N.Y., May 9, 1920; s. Philip Francis and Kathryn (Shally) McC.; student State U. N.Y. at New Platz, 1939; m. Mildred M. Barrington, Oct. 27, 1945; children—Sally Ann Shumaker, Michael. With Poughkeepsie Courier, 1939-41; Washington corr. CBS, 1945-48; Washington editor Mut. Newsreel of Air, MBS, 1948-54; chief corr. WMAL-Radio, Washington, 1955—; pres. Culpeper Communications, Inc.; pub. Culpeper (Va.) News. Chmn. No. Va. fund dr. Easter Seal Soc., 1964, Christmas Seal Soc., 1970; trustee Fairfax (Va.) Hosp. Assn. Served to 1st lt. inf. AUS, 1941-44. Recipient 4 Emmy awards Washington Acad. TV Arts and Scis.; Ted Yates award outstanding TV journalist, 1971; Grad. of Year award State U. N.Y. at New Platz, 1961; mem. Washington Reporters Hall of Fame, 1976. Mem. Radio-TV Corrs. Assn. (past pres.), A.F.T.R.A. (past v.p.), Congl. Radio-TV Galleries (chmn. standing com., 1956, 71), Acad. Polit. Sci., Orgn. Am. Historians. Author: Election Guide, 1954. Home: 9201 Maria Ave Great Falls VA 22066 Office: 4400 Jenifer St NW Washington DC 20015

MC CAFFREY, NEIL, publishing co. exec.; b. Rye, N.Y., Aug. 29, 1925; s. Cornelius Thomas and Anastasia Frances (Waterman) McC.; B.A., Fordham U., 1950; m. Joan Elizabeth Melervey, Apr. 10, 1950; children—Maureen, Neil III, Eugene V., Roger A., Eileen, Susan. Employed various positions, 1948-55; editor Doubleday Co., N.Y.C., 1955-61, copywriter, 1955-61, product mgr., 1960-61; mail order mgr. Macmillan Co., N.Y.C., 1961-64, dir. advt., 1963-64; founder, pres. Arlington House Pubs., New Rochelle, N.Y., 1964-78, Conservative Book Club, New Rochelle, 1964-78, Nostalgia Book Club, New Rochelle, 1968-78, Arlray Advt., New Rochelle, 1972-78; pres. Movie/Entertainment Book Club, Harrison, N.Y., 1978—; circulation mgr. Human Events, 1978—. Direct mail cons. Nat. Republican Congl. Com., 1963-71. Bd. dirs. Am. Conservative Union, 1970-72. Served with USCGR, 1943-46. Republican. Roman Catholic. Contbr. to Nat. Rev. Office: 15 Oakland Ave Harrison NY 10528

MC CAFFREY, ROBERT HENRY, JR., corp. exec.; b. Syracuse, N.Y., Jan. 20, 1927; s. Robert Henry and May Ann (McGuire) McC.; B.S.. Syracuse U., 1949; m. Dorothy Anne Evers, Sept. 22, 1956; children—Michael Robert, Kathleen Mary. Sales asst. Sealright Corp., Fulton, N.Y., 1949-50; with TEK Hughes div. Johnson & Johnson, Metuchen, N.J., 1950-67, gen. sales mgr., 1958-59, v.p. sales, 1959-62, pres., 1962-67; gen. mgr. med. div. Howmet Corp., N.Y.C., 1967-70; group v.p. Howmedica, Inc., 1970-73, sr. v.p., 1973-74, exec. v.p., 1974-76, also dir.; pres., chief exec. officer C.R. Bard, Inc., 1976-78, chmn. bd., chief exec. officer, 1978—, also dir.; dir. Summit & Elizabeth Trust, Summit Bancorp.; v.p. Austenal Europa, Inc., 1967-70. Chmn. corp. adv. council Syracuse U., 1974-75, trustee, 1979—. Served with AUS, 1945-46. Mem. Orthopedic Surg. Mfrs. Assn., Health Industry Mfrs. Assn. (dir.), N.Y. Sales Execs. Club, Sigma Chi. Clubs: Pinnacle (N.Y.C.); Baltusrol Golf (Springfield, N.J.). Home: 483 Mark Rd Allendale NJ 07401 Office: C R Bard Inc Central Ave Murray Hill NJ

MCCAFFREY, STANLEY EUGENE, univ. pres.; b. Taft, Calif., Feb. 26, 1917; s. Joseph Cormack and Dorothy (Bunyard) McC.; A.B., U. Calif., 1938; LL.D., Golden Gate U., 1972, Pepperdine U., 1978; m. Beth Conolley, July 6, 1941; children—Stephen Conolley, Nancy. Personnel work Standard Oil Co. (Calif.), 1939-40; coordinator vets. affairs U. Calif. at Berkeley, 1946, v.p., exec. asst., 1957-60, exec. mgr. Alumni Assn., 1948-56; advt. mgr. Kaiser Aluminum, Oakland, Calif., 1946-48; exec. asst. to Vice Pres. U.S., 1960; pres., exec. officer San Francisco Bay Area Council, 1960-71; pres. U. Pacific, Stockton, Calif., 1971—. Mem. Vets. Bd. Calif., chmn., 1956; del. Gov's Conf. on Children and Youth, 1956; mem. Berkeley Recreation Commn., v.p., 1957; mem. Oakland Manpower Commn., 1965-67, State Commn. on Government Orgn. and Economy, 1966-68. Dir. Berkeley Community Chest, 1952-55, Berkeley YMCA, 1953-54, Internat. House; pres. Berkeley Service Club Council, 1954-55. Trustee Peralta Jr. Coll. Dist., 1962-68, pres., 1964-66; trustee U. Calif. Alumni Found., Pacific Med. Center, San Francisco, Golden Gate U., San Francisco; governing mem. San Francisco YMCA, 1960-66; bd. advisers Nat. Indsl. Coll. of U.S. Armed Forces, 1964-66. Served from ensign to lt. comdr., USNR, 1940-45; capt. Res. Decorated Silver Star, Legion of Merit. Mem. Am. Alumni Council (treas. 1952-54), Am. Legion, Big C Soc. of U. Calif. (dir. 1948-57), Internat. House-Assn. (nat. exec. com. 1955-60), Assn. Ind. Cal. Colls. and Univs. (v.p. 1975-76, pres. 1976-78), Western Coll. Assn. (exec. com., pres. 1979—), Ind. Colls. No. Calif. (bd. dirs.), Navy League (v.p. San Francisco council 1966), Order of Golden Bear, Phi Beta Kappa, Pi Sigma Alpha. Conglist. Clubs: Rotary (pres. Berkeley 1954-55, dist. gov., 1964-65, chmn. internat. youth com. 1966-67, internat. dir. 1969-71, 1st v.p. 1970-71); Tennis (dir. 1952-55) (Berkeley); Berkeley Fellows, Family, Commonwealth of Calif. (quar. chmn. 1955, gov.), Bohemian, St. Francis Yacht (San Francisco); West Lane Tennis (Stockton). Address: President's Office University of the Pacific Stockton CA 95211

MCCAHAN, WALTER K., retail trade exec.; b. Port Royal, Pa., Dec. 3, 1935; s. Walter C. and Mary (Gray) McC.; B.S., Susquehanna U., 1963; m. Helga Wilhelm, Aug. 5, 1958; children—Yvonne, Heidi, Patrick. Accountant Main Lafrentz & Co., C.P.A.'s, Harrisburg, Pa., 1963-68; controller Rite Aid Corp., Shiremanstown, Pa., 1968-72, v.p., 1972—. Served with USAF, 1954-59. Mem. Am., Pa. insts. C.P.A.'s. Home: 309 Blacksmith Rd Camp Hill PA 17011 Office: PO Box 3165 Harrisburg PA 17105

MCCAIN, WARREN EARL, supermarket bus. exec.; b. Logan, Kans., 1925; A.A., Oreg. State U., 1948. Supr. sales Mountain States Wholesale Co., 1951-59; with Albertson's Inc., owner, operator supermarkets, 1959—, became mgr. non-foods, 1959, mgr. store, 1962, supr. merchandise, 1965, dir. intermountain region, 1967, v.p. ops., 1968-72, exec. v.p., 1972-74, pres., 1974-76, pres., chmn. bd., chief exec. officer, Boise, Idaho, 1976—, also dir.; dir. Tras-Joist. Office: 250 Parkcenter Blvd Boise ID 83726*

MCCAIN, WILLIAM DAVID, ret. univ. pres.; b. Bellefontaine, Miss., Mar. 29, 1907; s. Samuel Woodward and Sarah Alda (Shaw) McC.; B.S., Delta State Tchrs. Coll., Cleveland, Miss., 1930; A.M., U. Miss., 1931; Ph.D., Duke, 1935; Litt.D., Miss. Coll., 1967; m. Minnie Leicester Lenz, Oct. 3, 1931; children—William David, John (dec.), Patricia. Teaching fellow in history U. Miss., 1930-31; head math. dept. East Central Jr. Coll., Decatur, Miss., 1931-32; head social sci. dept. Copiah-Lincoln Jr. Coll., Wesson, Miss., 1932-33; fellow in history Duke, 1933-35; historian Morristown (N.J.) Nat. Hist. Park. 1935; asst. archivist Nat. Archives, Washington, 1935-37; acting asso. prof. history U. Miss., summers 1942-46; lectr. history Millsaps Coll., 1941-42, 46-47; historian Miss. dept. V.F.W., 1946-48, Miss. dept. Am. Legion, 1946-48; dir. Miss. Dept. Archives and History, 1938-55; pres. U. So. Miss., Hattiesburg, 1955-75, pres. emeritus, 1975—. Mem. Miss. Geol. Commn., 1938-55; sec. bd. trustees Miss. Dept. Archives and History, 1938-55; chmn. Miss. State Library Commn., 1941-43; chmn. Miss. Hist. Commn., 1948-55. Served as 1st lt. anti-aircraft arty., Coast Arty., AUS, 1943-46, 51-53; maj. gen. Res. Mem. Soc. Am. Archivists (founding mem., mem. council 1939-44, v.p. 1946-51, pres. 1951-53), Miss. Hist. Soc. (pres. 1966-67), Miss. Library Assn. (pres. 1941-44). Miss. N.G. Assn. (pres.). S.C.V. (adj-in-chief 1953—), Order Stars and Bars (adj. gen. 1954—), Alpha Tau Omega. Baptist. Clubs: Lions (Jackson, Miss.). Author: The United States and the Republic of Panama, 1937; History of Jackson, Mississippi, 1821, 1951, 1953. Editor: Jour. Miss. History, 1939-56. Contbr. to jours. and newspapers. Address: Southern Sta Box 5164 Hattiesburg MS 39401

MC CAIN, WILLIAM DAVID, JR., engring. educator; b. Greenville, Miss., Feb. 20, 1933; s. William D. and Minnie (Lenz) McC.; B.S. in Chem. Engring., Miss. State Coll., 1956; M.S., Ga. Inst. Tech., 1961, Ph.D., 1964; m. Barbara Ann Uhalt, June 25, 1954; children—William David III, John Woodward II, Anne Leicester. Engr., Esso Research Labs., Baton Rouge, 1956-59; mem. faculty Miss. State U., 1963-76, prof. petroleum engring., head dept., 1965-76; col. U.S. Army, Washington, 1976—; cons. in field, 1962—. Served with AUS, 1951-53. Recipient Meritorious Service award N.G. Assn. U.S., 1974. Mem. Soc. Petroleum Engrs. (chmn. edn. and accreditation com. 1970-71, chmn. Miss. 1971), Sigma Xi, Tau Beta Pi, Phi Kappa Phi. Kiwanian (pres. Starkville 1970-71). Author: Properties of Petroleum Fluids, 1973. Patentee in field. Home: 603 Sherwood Rd Starkville MS 39759 Office: NGB-ARR The Pentagon Washington DC 20310

MC CALL, ABNER VERNON, lawyer, univ. pres.; b. Perrin, Tex., June 8, 1915; s. Harry Vernon and Gertrude Elizabeth (Rhoades) McC.; A.B., J.D., Baylor U., 1938; LL.M., U. Mich., 1943; m. Frances Laura Bortle, Aug. 17, 1940 (dec. June 1969); children—Anne, Bette, Richard, Kathleen; m. 2d, Mary W. Russell, Dec. 25, 1970. Admitted to Tex. bar, 1938; mem. firm Gibson, McCall & Dawson, Longview, Tex., 1938-42; instr. law Baylor U., 1938-42, prof. law, 1946-48, dean Law Sch., 1948-59, exec. v.p., 1959-61, pres., 1961—; asso. justice Supreme Ct. Tex., 1956; spl. agt. FBI, 1943-46; mem. Tex. Civil Jud. Council, 1954—, pres., 1955-58. Pres., Baptist Gen. Conv. Tex., 1963-64; 1st v.p. So. Baptist Conv., 1979-80; Tex. rep. Edn. Commn. of States; pres. Tex. Scottish Rite Found.; mem. Tex. Adult Probation Commn.; chmn. bd. Tex. System Natural Labs. Mem. State Bar Tex., Assn. Tex. Colls. and Univs. (pres. 1968-69), Ind. Colls. and Univs. Tex. (pres. 1965-71). Office: Baylor U Waco TX 76703

MC CALL, CHARLES BARNARD, univ. dean; b. Memphis, Nov. 2, 1928; s. John W. and Lizette (Kimbrough) McC.; B.A., Vanderbilt U., 1950, M.D., 1953; m. Carolyn Jean Rosselot, June 9, 1951; children—Linda, Kim, Betsy, Cathy. Intern Vanderbilt U. Hosp., 1953-54; clin. asso., sr. asst. surgeon USPHS, Nat. Cancer Inst., NIH, 1954-56; sr. asst. resident in medicine U. Ala. Hosp., 1956-57, chief resident, 1958-59; fellow chest diseases Nat. Acad. Scis.-NRC, 1957-58; instr. U. Ala. Med. Sch., 1958-59; asst. prof., then asso. prof. medicine U. Tenn. Med. Sch., 1959-69, chief pulmonary diseases, 1964-69; mem. faculty U. Tex. System, 1969-75, prof. medicine med. br., Galveston, 1971-73, asso. prof. medicine Health Sci. Center, Southwestern Med. Sch., Dallas, 1973-75, also asso. dean clin. programs, 1973-75, dir. Office Grants Mgmt. and Devel., 1973-75; dean U. Tenn. Coll. Medicine, also prof. medicine, 1975-77; dean, prof. medicine Oral Roberts U. Sch. Medicine, Tulsa, 1977-78; interim asso. dean U. Okla. Tulsa Med. Coll., 1978-79; clin. prof. medicine U. Colo. Med. Sch., Denver, 1979—; cons. in field. Diplomate Am. Bd. Internal Medicine (pulmonary diseases). Fellow A.C.P., Am. Coll. Chest Physicians; mem. AMA, Am., So. (pres. 1968-69) thoracic socs., Am. Fedn. Clin. Research, Okla. Med. Assn., Tulsa County Med. Soc., Sigma Xi, Alpha Omega Alpha. Baptist. Contbr. articles to med. jours. Home: 2800 S University Denver CO 80210 Office: 1720 S Bellaire Denver CO 80222

MC CALL, DANIEL THOMPSON, JR., ret. state justice; b. Butler, Ala., Mar. 12, 1909; s. Daniel Thompson and Caroline Winston (Bush) McC.; A.B., U. Ala., 1931, LL.B., 1933; m. Mary Edna Montgomery, Apr. 3, 1937; children—Mary Winston (Mrs. Rogers N. Laseter), Daniel Thompson III, Nancy (Mrs. John W. Poynor). Admitted to Ala. bar, 1933, also U.S. Supreme Ct. bar; practice in Mobile, 1933-60; partner firm Johnston, McCall & Johnston, 1943-60; circuit judge, Mobile County, 1960-69; asso. justice Supreme Ct. Ala., 1969-75. Dir. Title Ins. Co., 1959-69. Pres. Jr. Bar Ala., 1937. Mem. Mobile County Bd. Sch. Commnrs., 1950-56, 58-60. Trustee Julius T. Wright Sch. Girls, 1953-63; adv. bd. U. Ala. Med. Coll., 1955-65; dir. U. Ala. Law Sch. Found., Ala. bar commrs., 1957-60; trustee U. Ala., nat. alumni pres., 1963. Served to lt. USNR, World War II. Recipient Dean's award U. Ala. Law Sch., 1974; Julius T. Wright Sch. Disting. Service award, 1979. Mem. Am., Ala. (grievance com. 1954-57), Mobile (pres. 1953) bar assns., Am. Judges Assn., Am. Judicature Soc., Farrah Law Soc., Cumberland Law Sch. Order Jurisprudence, Inst. Jud. Adminstrn., Nat. Trust Historic Preservation, Navy League U.S. (pres. Mobile 1963-65), Am. Legion, Nat. Hist. Assn., Ala. Hist. Soc., Res. Officers Assn. U.S., Mil. Order World Wars, Ala. Wildlife Fedn., 40 and 8, St. Andrew's Soc. Mid-South, Omicron Delta Kappa, Phi Delta Phi, Sigma Nu. Democrat. Episcopalian. Clubs: Athelstan (pres. 1967-69); University (Tuscaloosa). Home: 2253 Ashland Pl Ave Mobile AL 36607

MCCALL, DAVID BRUCE, advt. exec.; b. N.Y.C., Mar. 13, 1928; s. Sydney C. and Katharine (Adams) McC.; student Hotchkiss Sch., Lakeville, Conn., 1942-45, Yale, 1948-49; m. Joan C. Williams, Feb. 10, 1951; children—John Percy, Peter Cortelyou, David Bruce, William Dudley, Robert Dodd, Thomas Clement; m. 2d, Susan Alder, Jan. 18, 1975 (dec.). Copywriter, Young and Rubicam, Inc., 1949-51, Hewitt, Ogilvy, Benson and Mather, 1951-53; v.p., copy chief David J. Mahoney, Inc., 1953-56; with Ogilvy, Benson and Mather, 1956-62, copy chief, sr. v.p. dir., 1961-62; vice chmn. bd. C.J. LaRoche Co., Inc. (name changed to McCaffrey & McCall, Inc.), N.Y.C., 1962—, pres., chmn. bd., 1964—. Served with AUS, 1946-47. Club: Racquet and Tennis. (N.Y.C.). Home: 172 E 95th St New York City NY 10029 Office: 575 Lexington Ave New York City NY 10022

MCCALL, ERNEST ELLERY HALL, chem. co. exec.; b. Eugene, Oreg., Jan. 10, 1935; s. William Calder and Marian Schwarz (Hall) McC.; grad. Princeton U., 1957; m. Barclay Ball, Dec. 14, 1964; children—Ernest, Marian, Ned. With McCall Oil & Chem. Corp., Portland, Oreg., 1962—, v.p., 1965-69, pres. Gt. Western Chem. Co., div. McCall Oil & Chem. Corp., 1969—. Pres. N.W. Outward Bound Sch., Portland, 1974-76; bd. dirs. Med. Research Found. Oreg., Portland. Served to lt. (j.g.) USN, 1957-61. Clubs: Arlington (Portland); Pacific Union (San Francisco); Ranier (Seattle). Office: 808 SW 15th Ave Portland OR 97205

MC CALL, HOBBY HALBERT, lawyer; b. Dallas, May 16, 1919; s. John Dean and Reba (Randolph) McC.; student Southwestern U., Georgetown, Tex., 1936-38, U. Tex., 1938-39; LL.B., So. Methodist U., 1942; m. Jane Jennings, Dec. 27, 1944; children—Hobby Halbert, Lucy McCall Dowdy. Admitted to Tex. bar, 1943; with appeals div. IRS, Pitts., 1946-49; partner firm McCall, Parkhurst & Horton, Dallas, 1949—. Bd. dirs. Camp Grady Spruce, Dallas YMCA, 1952—, chmn., 1963-64; bd. dirs. Douglas MacArthur Acad. of Freedom, Brownwood, Tex., 1950—, vice chmn., 1974-75; trustee Dallas Community Coll. Found., 1974—. Served to maj., inf., AUS, 1942-46. Decorated Silver Star, Bronze Star with oak leaf cluster, Purple Heart with oak leaf cluster, Combat Inf. badge. Mem. Am. (chmn. local govt. law sect. 1974-75), Dallas bar assns., State Bar Tex., 90th Div. Assn. (pres. 1957-58), Phi Delta Theta. Clubs: Bankers Am. (N.Y.C.); Army and Navy (Washington); Dallas Country, Dallas City. Home: 4220 Versailles Ave Dallas TX 75205 Office: 1400 Mercantile Bank Bldg Dallas TX 75201. *If I am to be considered at a point of success, or if I have accomplished something of value, in retrospect I know of nothing I possess for which payment has not been made with concentrated efforts or with material items obtained through concentrated efforts.*

MC CALL, JERRY CHALMERS, govt. ofcl.; b. Oxford, Miss., June 30, 1927; s. E. Forrest and Mariada (Huffaker) McC.; B.A., U. Miss., 1951, M.A., 1951; M.S., U. Ill., 1956, Ph.D., 1959; m. Margaret Denton, Nov. 28, 1952; children—Betsy, Lynn, Kim. Teaching asst. dept. math. U. Miss., 1950-51, instr. math., 1952-53, prof. math., 1973-76, exec. vice chancellor, 1973-76; research asso. U. Ill., 1953-57; applied sci. rep. IBM, Springfield, Ill., 1957-58, mgr., Bethesda, Md., 1966-68, Huntsville, Ala., 1968-71, Owego, N.Y., 1971-72; exec. v.p. Midwest Computer Service, Inc., Decatur, Ill., 1958-59; mem. sci. staff computation lab. Army Ballistic Missile Agy., Huntsville, 1959-60; asst. to dir. Marshall Space Flight Center, NASA, Huntsville, 1960-63, dep. dir. research and devel. ops., 1963-66; dir. info. research Miss. Test Facility, Bay St. Louis, 1972-73; pres. 1st State Bank and Trust Co., Gulfport, Miss., 1976-77; dir. NOAA Data Buoy Office, Bay St. Louis, Miss., 1977—; head math. dept. St. Bernard Coll., Cullman, Ala., part-time 1960-65; asso. prof. math. U. Ala., Huntsville, 1960-62; pub. speaker, 1960-63; chmn. incorporators First State Bank & Trust Co., Gulfport, Miss., 1973-76; tech. cons. Gen. Electric Co., 1974-75. Mem. Miss. Criminal Justice Standards Commn., 1974-75; mem. Miss. Marine Resources Council, 1974-76; bd. dirs. U. Miss. Found.; bd. advisers Sch. Engring., U. Miss., 1965-73; mem. indsl. advisors U. New Orleans; chmn. founders U. Ala. Research Inst., Huntsville, 1960-62. Mem. Am. Judicature Soc. (lay mem.), U. Miss. Alumni Assn. (dir. 1966-73). Editor: (with Ernst Stuhlinger) Astronautical Engineering and Science, 1963; (with Ernst Stuhlinger) From Peenemunde to Outer Space, 1963. Home: 40 54th St Gulfport MS 39501 Office: NOAA NSTL Sta MS 35929. *Since happiness is a result of achievement, I have tried to complete the task at hand before a more attractive task is begun, selecting only those goals that can be accomplished with reasonable effort, then pursuing those goals diligently, being as objective and analytical as possible, including recognition and acknowledgment of error.*

MCCALL, JOHN PATRICK, univ. adminstr., educator; b. Yonkers, N.Y., July 17, 1927; s. Ambrose V. and Vera E. (Rush) McC.; A.B., Holy Cross Coll., 1949; M.A., Princeton U., 1952, Ph.D., 1955; m. Mary-Berenice Morris, June 15, 1957; children—Claire, Anne,

Ambrose, Peter. Instr., Georgetown U., 1955-57, asst. prof. English, 1957-62, asso. prof., 1962-66; prof. U. Cin., 1966—, head dept. English, 1970-76, sr. v.p., provost, 1976—. Served with Signal Corps, U.S. Army, 1952-54. Am. Council Learned Socs. fellow, 1962; John Simon Guggenheim Meml. Found. fellow, 1975; Fulbright grantee, 1962. Mem. Mediaeval Acad. Am. MLA, AAUP. Democrat. Roman Catholic. Author: Chaucer Among the Gods: the Poetics of Classical Myth, 1979; contbr. articles to profl. jours.; research in medieval lit. and Chaucer's poetry. Home: 218 Glenmary Ave Cincinnati OH 45220 Office: U Cin Cincinnati OH 45221

MC CALL, JULIEN LACHICOTTE, banker; b. Florence, S.C., Apr. 1, 1921; s. Arthur M. and Julia (Lachicotte) McC.; B.S., Davidson Coll., 1942; M.B.A., Harvard, 1947; m. Janet Jones, Sept. 30, 1950; children—Melissa, Alison Gregg, Julien Lachicotte. With First Nat. City Bank, N.Y.C., 1948-71, asst. mgr. bond dept., 1952-53, asst. cashier, 1953-55, asst. v.p., 1955-57, v.p., 1957-71; 1st v.p. Nat. City Bank, Cleve., 1971-72, pres., 1972-79, chmn. bd., chief exec. officer, 1979—, also dir.; pres., dir. Nat. City Corp.; dir. GF Bus. Equipment Corp., Jarva, Inc., Progressive Corp., Russell Burdsall & Ward, Inc. Trustee, St. Luke's Hosp., Cleve. Center Econ. Edn., Corp. 1 Percent Program for Higher Edn., United Way Services, Cleve. Mus. Natural History. Served from 2d lt. to 1st lt. Ordnance Dept., AUS, 1942-46; Africa, ETO. Episcopalian. Clubs: Wee Burn Country (Darien, Conn.); Union, Pepper Pike, Tavern, Chagrin Valley Hunt (Cleve.); Rolling Rock (Ligonier, Pa.). Home: Arrowhead County Line Rd Hunting Valley OH 44022 Office: Nat City Bank 623 Euclid Ave Cleveland OH 44114

MCCALL, RAYMOND JOSEPH, psychologist, educator; b. Bronx, N.Y., Oct. 16, 1913; s. John J. and Helen G. (Whalen) McC.; A.B., Fordham U., 1934, Ph.D., 1941; M.A., Cath. U., 1936, Columbia, 1949, Ph.D., 1951; m. Mary E. McDonald, June 19, 1937; children—Raymond J., Anthony, Timothy, Debra. Instr. St. John's U., 1936-40, asso. prof., 1940-46, prof., 1946-51; lectr. N.Y.U., 1949-50; research asst. depts. research psychiatry and psychology N.Y. Psychiat. Inst., 1949-51; cons. psychologist Grace Clinic, Bklyn., 1951; chmn. dept. psychology De Paul U., 1951-56, supr. testing and counseling services, 1951-56; chmn. dept. psychology Marquette U., 1956-61, prof., 1956—, dir. Guidance Center, 1958-61; clin. prof. psychiatry Med. Coll. Wis., 1967—; dean Wis. Sch. Profl. Psychology, 1979—. Ford Found. fellow Harvard U., 1954-55. Served as lt. (j.g.), USNR, 1944-46. Author: Basic Logic, 1947, rev. edit., 1952; A Preface to Scientific Psychology, 1959; The Varieties of Abnormality, 1975. Home: 2814 E Newberry Blvd Milwaukee WI 53211 Office: 617 N 13th St Milwaukee WI 53233

MCCALL, ROBERT R., oil co. exec.; b. Norman, Okla., June 21, 1926; s. Robert R. and Ida (Smith) McC.; B.S., U. Okla., 1951, M.S., 1952; m. Jacqueline Richards, July 24, 1948; children—Claudia, Michael, Melinda, Danny. With Texaco, Inc., 1952—, gen. mgr. producing Eastern hemisphere, 1972-78, v.p. producing, Harrison, N.Y., 1978—. Bd. dirs. Near East Found. Served with USNR, 1944-46. Mem. Am. Inst. Mech. Engrs., Okla. Profl. Engrs., Pi Epsilon Tau. Republican. Home: 65 Mill Rd New Canaan CT 06840 Office: 2000 Westchester Ave White Plains NY 06050

MC CALLA, DENNIS ROBERT, educator; b. Edmonton, Alta., Can., July 30, 1934; s. Arthur Gilbert and Enid (Rice) McC.; B.Sc., U. Alta., 1957; M.Sc., U. Sask., 1958; Ph.D., Calif. Inst. Tech., 1961; m. Kathleen Mary Rachel Gardiner, June 1, 1957; children—Arthur Harold, Kathleen Louise. Asst. prof. McMaster U., 1961-66, asso. prof., 1966-71, prof., 1971—, dean Faculty of Sci., 1967-75, acting v.p. sci. and engring., 1972-74, chmn. dept. biochemistry, 1979—; vis. scientist MRC Cell Mutation Unit, U. Sussex, Brighton, Eng., 1975-76. mem. editorial bd. Jour. Protozoology, Chem. Biol. Interactions. Fellow Chem. Inst. Can.; mem. Am. Soc. Biol. Chemists, Nat. Cancer Inst. Can. (research adv. group 1973-78, chmn. 1974-75, 76-78). Contbr. articles sci. jours. Home: 18 Forsythe Ave N Hamilton ON L8S 4E1 Canada

MCCALLA, GARY EDWARD, editor; b. Chickasha, Okla., Mar. 20, 1931; s. Joseph Bailey and Marilouise (Klaeger) McC.; B.A. in Journalism, U. Okla., 1954; m. Dominique Stassinos, Dec. 17, 1955; children—Karine, Claudia, Eric, Christopher. Advt. and pub. relations mgr. Ideco div. Dresser Industries, Dallas, 1957-61; pub. Passport mag., Dallas, 1961-62; contractor NASA, Houston, Huntsville, Ala., 1962-65; with So. Living mag., Birmingham, Ala., 1965—, editor, 1969—. Served to 1st lt. AUS, 1954-57. Mem. Sigma Delta Chi. Office: 820 Shades Creek Pkwy Box 523 Birmingham AL 35201

MCCALLICK, HUGH ERNEST, coll. dean; b. El Paso, Sept. 2, 1920; s. Hugh Henry and Henrietta (Collin) McC.; student Tex. Western Coll., 1938; B.B.A., M.B.A., U. Houston, 1949; postgrad. U. Tex., 1956; m. Betty Mathis McCallick, Apr. 6, 1974. Mem. faculty Coll. Tech., U. Houston, 1947-60, 64—, asso. dean, 1955-60, prof. indsl. mgmt., 1955—, dean, 1964—, asso. dir. Office Internat. Affairs, 1964-72, cons. on internat. affairs, 1964—, mem. relations with industry com., 1950—; exec. v.p. Capitol Radio Engring. Inst., Washington, London and Frankfort, Ger., 1960-64. Exec. v.p. ERA, Inc., Washington, 1954—; exec. v.p. Holmes Inst., Washington, 1960. Chmn. membership com., pres. Nat. Council Tech. Schs., 1958—, also trustee; mem. bus. standards com. Nat. Home Study Council, 1960—, also mem. exec. bd.; chmn. Coll; Industry Conf., 1957; mem. Community Council Houston; exec. com. ASEE Tech. Council, 1965—; dir. indsl. poly. programs in India, 1963-66; vice-chmn. Edn. Devel. Center Consortium on Algeria, 1976—; mem. com. Nat. Acad. Engring.-Nat. Acad. Scis. mem. Tex. Gov.'s Adv. Council Tech.-Vocat. Edn., 1971—; cons. to U.S. govt., Brazil, Ecuador, Japan, Peru, Colombia, Guatemala, Costa Rica, Mexico, Pakistan, India, Venezuela, Algeria, 1964—; head U.S. del. internat. conf., India, 1976. Recipient Interprofl. Coop. award Soc. Mfg. Engrs., 1976. Mem. Am. Soc. Engring. Edn. (chmn. awards policy com., James H. McGraw award 1970, Chester F. Carlson award 1977), Engrs. Council Profl. Devel. (chmn. tech. com. 1968-70, dir. 1975), Council on World Affairs, Houston Engring. and Sci. Soc., Wash. Soc. Engrs., AAAS, Delta Pi Epsilon, Omicron Delta Kappa, Phi Kappa Phi, Sigma Phi Epsilon. Clubs: Houston, Houston Engineers. Rice farmer, oil and gas developer. Home: 5305 Blythewood Dr Houston TX 77021 also 501 S Robinson Edna TX 77957 Office: 4800 Calhoun Blvd Houston TX 77004

MC CALLION, HARRY JOHN, lawyer; b. N.Y.C., July 29, 1914; s. John and Katherine (Meehan) McC.; B.S. cum laude, Coll. City N.Y., 1937; J.D., Fordham U., 1941; m. Edna Johnson, May 24, 1941; children—Douglas, Kenneth, Donald, Peter. Admitted to N.Y. State bar, 1941, also bar Supreme Ct. U.S., 1959; practice in N.Y.C., 1941—; asso. firm Debevoise, Stevenson Plimpton & Page, 1941-47; atty. N.Y. Life Ins. Co., 1947-51, counsel, 1951-54, asst. gen. counsel, 1954-57, asso. gen. counsel, 1957-65, v.p., gen. counsel, 1965-72, sr. v.p., 1972—; treas., bd. dirs. Legal Aid Soc., N.Y.C., 1977—; adj. asso. prof. law Fordham Law Sch., 1977—. Mem. Council Fordham U. Served as lt. (j.g.) USNR, 1943-46; ETO, PTO. Fellow Am. Bar Found.; mem. Am., N.Y. State (past chmn. ins. sect.), Fed. bar. assns., Assn. Life Ins. Counsel (past pres.), Assn. Bar City N.Y. (past v.p., past chmn. exec. com., past chmn. admission, ins. coms., mem. judiciary com., past mem. com. profl. responsibility), Fordham U. Alumni Fedn. (dir., past chmn. bd. govs.), Fordham Law Alumni Assn. (dir., past pres.; medal of Achievement 1978), Fordham Law Rev. Assn. (dir., past pres.), Am. Law Inst. Home: 459 Siwanoy Pl Pelham NY 10803 Office: 51 Madison Ave New York NY 10010

MC CALLUM, CHARLES ALEXANDER, coll. dean; b. North Adams, Mass., Nov. 1, 1925; s. Charles Alexander and Mabel Helen (Cassidy) McC.; student Dartmouth, 1943-44, Wesleyan U., Middletown, Conn., 1946-47; D.M.D., Tufts U., 1951; M.D., Med. Coll. Ala., 1957; D.Sc. (hon.), U. Ala., 1975; m. Alice Rebecca Lasseter, Dec. 17, 1955; children—Scott Alan, Charles Alexander III, Philip Warren, Christopher Jay. Intern oral surgery Univ. Hosp., Birmingham, Ala., 1951-52, resident oral surgery, 1952-54, intern medicine, 1957-58; mem. faculty U. Ala. Sch. Dentistry, 1956—, prof., chmn. dept. oral surgery, 1959-65, dean sch., 1962-77; v.p. for health affairs U. Ala. Med. Center, Birmingham, 1977—; prof., chief sect. oral surgery Med. Coll. Ala., 1965-69. Mem. nat. adv. dental research council NIH, 1968-72. Diplomate Am. Bd. Oral Surgery (pres. 1970). Fellow Am. Coll. Dentists, Internat. Coll. Dentists; mem. Am. Dental Assn. (mem. council on dental edn. 1970-76), Am. Assn. Dental Schs. (pres. 1969), Ala. Acad. of Honor. AMA, Am. (trustee 1972-73, pres. 1975-76), Southeastern (pres. 1970) socs. oral surgeons, Omicron Kappa Upsilon, Phi Beta Pi. Home: 2328 Garland Dr Birmingham AL 35216 Office: U Ala Med Center Birmingham AL 35294

MCCALLUM, DAVID, actor; b. Scotland, Sept. 19, 1933; m. 2d, Katherine Carpenter; 4 sons (3 by previous marriage), 1 dau. Appeared as child actor on BBC, then in repertory theatres and London stage; dir. plays for Brit. Army; motion pictures include The Secret Place, Hell Drivers, Robbery Under Arms, Violent Playground, A Night to Remember, The Long and The Short and The Tall, Billy Budd, Freud, The Great Escape, The Greatest Story Ever Told, Around the World Under the Sea, Three Bites of the Apple, Sol Madrid, Mosquito Squadron, Dogs, King Solomon's Treasure, Watcher in the Woods; appeared as Illya Kuryakin in TV series The Man From U.N.C.L.E., 1964-67; also appeared TV programs including Teacher Teacher, Hauser's Memory, Invisible Man; Colditz series for BBC, 1972, 73, 74; now appearing in TV series Sapphire and Steel, ATV, Eng.; summer stock theater including Alfie, Signpost to Murder, Crown Matrimonial, The Mousetrap, Camelot; dir. Ten Who Dared film for BBC-TV, 1974; appeared on Broadway in Neil Simon's California Suite, 1977. Address: care Lionel Larner 850 7th Ave New York NY 10019

MCCALLUM, FRANCIS A., bus. cons.; b. Carsonville, Mich., Apr. 5, 1917; s. Claud and Frances (Irwin) McC.; grad. Spring Arbor Sem., 1933; m. Doris H. Mehlberg, Sept. 23, 1939; children—Robert J., Michael W. Sales mgr. Tri- Products Co., Holly, Mich., 1948-50, Pontiac Coach Co., Drayton Plains, Mich., 1950-54; v.p. Detroiter Mobile Homes, Inc., St. Louis, Mich., 1954- 66, also dir.; exec. asst. to Mich. Senate, 1966-70; bus. cons., Alma, Mich., 1971—; v.p. Mobile Homes Finance Co., Drayton Plains. Mem. Mich. Bd. of Alcoholism, 1964-72, chmn., 1970. Served with USNR, World War II. Mem. Mobile Home Mfrs. Assn. (pres. 1961), Aircraft Owners and Pilots Assn., Sacred Order Golden Dragon. Presbyn. Mason. Club: Scotsmans (Alma Coll., Mich.). Address: 1020 Orchard St Alma MI 48801. *I believe in living one day at a time ... live every day to the best of your ability and you can live a full and useful life. Yesterday is a cancelled check; tomorrow is a promissary note. Today is cash; use it wisely.*

MC CALLUM, KENNETH JAMES, educator, chemist; b. Scott, Sask., Can., Apr. 25, 1918; s. James Alexander and Alice (Fines) McC.; B.Sc., U. Sask., Saskatoon, 1936, M.Sc., 1939; Ph.D., Columbia, 1942; m. Christine Chorneyko, Sept. 2, 1950 (dec. 1971); children—Patricia Jean, Douglas James; m. 2d, Erika Connell, Aug. 16, 1974. Jr. research officer NRC Can., 1942-43; faculty U. Sask., 1943—, prof. chemistry and chem. engring., 1953—, head dept. chemistry and chem. engring., 1959—, dean grad. studies, 1970—; dir. sci. affairs Chem. Inst. Can., 1961-64, pres., 1968-69. Fellow Royal Soc. Can., AAAS, Chem. Inst. Can. Asso. editor Jour. Chem. Physics, 1947-50. Research and publs. in cement chemistry, electron affinities, radioisotope exchange reactions, chem. effects nuclear transformations, radiation chemistry. Home: 1622 Park Ave Saskatoon SK Canada

MC CALLUM, ROBERT D., business exec.; b. June 17, 1911; s. Jesse B. and Gertrude (Wyatt) McC.; B.S., U. Tenn.; children—Mrs. John B. Syer, Mrs. Michael McDonnell, Robert D. With Geo. H. McFadden & Bro., Memphis, 1933—, partner, 1948—; chmn. bd. Valmac Industries, Inc., Memphis, 1969—, also dir.; chmn. bd. Distribuco, Inc., Union City Calif.; dir. Union Planters Nat. Bank of Memphis, Union Planters Corp., Memphis; former mem. bd. mgrs. N.Y. Cotton Exchange; former dir. Nat. Cotton Council, Cotton Council Internat. Chmn. bd. trustees Southwestern U. at Memphis; mem. men's adv. bd. Crippled Children's Hosp. Sch., Memphis. Mem. Am. Cotton Shippers Assn. (past pres.), So. Cotton Assn. (past pres.). Presbyterian. Clubs: Memphis Country, Memphis Hunt and Polo; Belvedere (Charlevoix, Mich.); St. Andrews (Delray Beach, Fla.). Home: 200 S Goodlett Memphis TN 38117 Office: Valmac Industries Inc 2 S Front St Memphis TN 38103

MCCALLY, CHARLES THOMAS, lawyer; b. Washington, Jan. 24, 1929; s. Robert E. and Marguerite L. (Baird) McC.; A.A., Am. U.; LL.B., George Washington U., 1953; divorced; children—Cheryl, Thomas. Admitted to D.C. bar, 1954; asst. U.S. atty. for D.C., 1959-61; partner firm Craigbill, Mayfield & McCally, Washington, 1961—. Mem. Delta Theta Phi. Home: 6904 Old Stage Rd Rockville MD 20852 Office: Suite 901 725 15th St NW Washington DC 20005 also 7401 Wisconsin Ave Bethesda MD 20014

MCCALPIN, FRANCIS WILLIAM, lawyer; b. St. Louis, Nov. 8, 1921; s. George Ambrose and Marguerite (Miles) McC.; A.B., St. Louis U., 1943; LL.B., Harvard, 1948; m. Margaret Wickes, Feb. 27, 1954; children—Martha Helen, William Francis, Katherine Mary, Lucy Alice, David Christopher. Admitted to Mo. bar, 1948, since practiced in St. Louis; admitted to Ill. bar, 1953; mem. firm Lewis, Rice, Tucker, Allen & Chubb, 1948—, partner, 1956—. Sec., dir. Hardy Salt Co.; dir. Color Process Co. Mem. nat. adv. com. to legal services program Office Econ. Opportunity, 1965-73; mem. Mo. Coordinating Bd. Higher Edn., 1974—, chmn., 1974; dir. Legal Services Corp. Trustee, sec. St. Louis Ednl. TV Commn. KETC-TV, 1965-72; trustee Jr. Coll. Dist. St. Louis, 1962-65, St. Louis U., 1972-74; bd. dirs. Family and Childrens Service Greater St. Louis, 1972-78; bd. dirs. Am. Bar Found., 1976—, chmn. fellows, 1976-77. Served with USMCR, 1942-46, 50-51. Mem. Am. (chmn. spl. com. on availabilty of legal services 1965-70, chmn. spl. com. on prepaid legal services 1970-73, chmn. standing com. on legal aid and indigent defendants 1973-76, sec. 1979), Ill. bar assns., Mo. Bar Integrated (gov. 1967-73), Bar Assn. St. Louis (pres. 1961-62), Nat. Conf. Bar Presidents (treas. 1970-71, pres. 1973-74). Clubs: Harvard (St. Louis); Westborough Country. Home: 215 N Berry Rd St Louis MO 63122 Office: 611 Olive St St Louis MO 63101

MCCAMANT, WILLIAM CYRUS, trade assn. exec.; b. Huntingdon, Pa., Aug. 19, 1916; s. Frank Waters and Alice Florence (Conrad) McC.; student Dickinson Coll., 1934-36, U. Pa., 1949-50; m. Mary Jean Randle, July 30, 1948; 1 son, William Cyrus. With Navy Dept., Washington, 1946-54, manpower specialist, mil. manpower analyst; asst. to sec. HEW, Washington, 1954-57; dir. govt. relations Am. Retail Fedn., Washington, 1957-62; dir. govt. relations Nat. Assn. Wholesaler-Distbrs., Washington, 1962-72, exec. v.p., 1972-79, vice chmn., 1979—. Mem. Vienna (Va.) Town Council, 1957-59. Served with USNR, 1943-46. Mem. Washington Soc. Assn. Execs. (pres. 1962-63), Am. Soc. Assn. Execs. Presbyterian. Clubs: Univ., Capitol Hill (Washington). Home: 6123 Ramshorn Dr McLean VA 22101 Office: 1725 K St Washington DC 20006

MCCAMBRIDGE, MERCEDES, actress; b. Joliet, Ill., Mar. 17, 1918; d. John Patrick and Marie (Mahaffry) McC.; A.B., Mundelein Coll., 1937; Litt.D. (hon.), St. Scholastica U., 1973; 1 son, John Markle. Appeared on stage in Hope for the Best, 1945, Place of Our Own, Twilight Bar, Woman Bites Dog, The Young and Fair; films include: Lightning Strikes Twice, All the King's Men (Acad. award Best Supporting Actress 1950), Inside Straight, The Scarf, Johnny Guitar, Giant (Acad. award nomination 1956), A Farewell to Arms, Suddenly Last Summer, Cimarron, Angel Baby, 1961, Last Generation, Jigsaw, 1965, 99 Women, 1969, Thieves, 1977; voice used in film The Exorcist; artist-in-residence Cath. U., Washington, 1973. Mem. adv. council Nat. Inst. Alcohol Abuse and Alcoholism, Washington. Recipient Drama award Mundelein Coll., 1937; AP Poll, Look award, 1950; Fgn. Corr. award for Best Newcomer and Best Supporting Actress, 1950; nominated for Tony award, 1972; recipient Gold Key award Nat. Council Alcoholism. Author: The Two of Us, 1960. Address: care Brut Prodns 9200 Sunset B[vd Los Angeles CA 90069*

MCCAMERON, FRITZ ALLEN, univ. adminstr.; b. Nacogdoches, Tex. Oct. 8, 1929; s. Leland Allen and Gladys (Turner) M.; B.B.A., Stephen F. Austin State Coll., 1950, M.A., 1951; Ph.D., U. Ala., 1954; m. Jeannine Young, June 11, 1957; 1 dau., Mary Hartley. Asso. prof. La. State U., 1959-62, prof., 1962-67, chmn. dept. accounting, 1967-71, asst. vice chancellor, 1971-73, dean continuing edn., 1973—; cons. in field. C.P.A., La. Mem. Am. Inst. C.P.A.'s, La. Soc. C.P.A.'s, Am. Accounting Assn. Author: FORTRAN Logic and Programming, 1968; Cobol Logic and Programming, rev. edit., 1970, 3d edit., 1975; FORTRAN IV, 1970, rev. edit., 1974, 3d edit., 1977. Home: 930 Rodney Dr Baton Rouge LA 70808

MCCAMMON, CURTIS PAUL, physician; b. Knoxville, Tenn., Nov. 6, 1922; s. William Howard and Trula (Reynolds) McC.; B.A., U. Tenn., 1946; M.D., Temple U., Phila., 1949; M.P.H., Harvard U., 1958; m. Doris Marie Meggs, May 22, 1954; children—Nan Marie, Stanley Paul, Janet Lee, Daniel Kevin. Intern Brooke Gen. Hosp., San Antonio, 1949-50; asst. health officer Bur. Health, Knoxville, 1950-52; practice medicine specializing in gen. practice Wartburg, Tenn., 1954-57; dir. indsl. hygiene Tenn. Dept. Pub. Health, Nashville, 1957-68; med. dir. U. Tenn. Med. Research Center and Hsp., Knoxville, 1968—, also clin. prof. Med. Sch., Memphis, 1958-67; clin. prof. Vanderbilty U., Nashville, 1960-66; mem. staff U. Tenn. Med. Research Center. Mem. AMA, Tenn. Med. Assn. Methodist. Club: Masons. Home: 320 Essex Dr Concord TN 37720 Office: 1924 Aloca Hwy Knoxville TN 37920

MC CAMMON, DAVID NOEL, automobile co. exec.; b. Topeka, Nov. 6, 1934; s. Noel F. and Freda E. McC.; B.S. in Bus. Adminstrn., U. Nebr., 1957; M.B.A. (Baker scholar), Harvard U., 1962; m. Valerie L. Palliaer, May 18, 1968; children—Jeff, Mark, Scott. With Ford Motor Co., Dearborn, Mich., 1957—, controller Ford div., 1970-71, asst. corp. controller, 1971-77, exec. dir. bus. strategy, 1977-78, v.p. corp. strategy analysis, 1979—. Served with U.S. Army, 1957-58. Club: Harvard Bus. Sch. (Detroit). Office: Ford Motor Co World Headquarters American Rd Dearborn MI 48121

MCCAMPBELL, DONALD H., service co. exec.; b. Kansas City, Mo., Aug. 22, 1914; s J.P. and Bess (Sater) McC.; LL.B. cum laude, U. Mo. at Kansas City, 1938; m. Catherine Evans, June 6, 1961; children—Brian, Jerry, Laura. Admitted to Mo. bar; practice in Kansas City, 1939-44; dir. properties and facilities Trans World Airlines, Kansas City, 1944-49; with Allied Maintenance Corp., 1949—, exec. v.p., now pres., dir. Home: 17 W 54th St New York City NY 10019 Office: 2 Penn Plaza New York City NY 10001

MC CAMY, JAMES LUCIAN, former educator; b. Knoxville, Tenn., June 10, 1906; s. James Lucian and Ida Winfield (Mullendore) McC.; B.A., U. Tex. 1929, M.A., 1932; Ph.D., U. Chgo., 1938; m. Julia Texie Boggess, July 17, 1931; children—Keith, Colin. Reporter Austin (Tex.) Am., 1925-28; editor, publicity dir. Tex. Ex-Students' Assn., Austin, 1928-32; tchr. Am. govt. U. Tex., 1932-33; fellow, research asst., dept. polit. sci. U. Chgo., 1933-34; prof. of govt. Bennington Coll., 1934-39, 1941-42; asst. to sec. of agr. U.S. Dept. Agr., 1939- 41; asst. to dir. Bd. Econ. Warfare, 1942-43; exec. dir. Bur. Areas, Fgn. Econ. Adminstrn., 1943-45; econ. adviser U.S. Forces, Austria, 1945; dir. Office of World Trade Policy, also dep. dir. for policy Office of Internat. Trade, U.S. Dept. Commerce, 1946; prof. polit. sci. U. Wis., 1947-71; ret., 1971; Knapp vis. scholar to U. Wis. Centers, 1967-68, chmn. dept., 1948-52, Brittingham prof. Inst. for Environ. Studies, 1970-71; chmn. Wis. Seminar on Quality of Environment, 1967; distinguished vis. scholar Milton Coll., 1969; mem. Wis. Bd. Ethics, 1973-74. U.S. del. to Internat. Inst. Agr., Rome, 1940; adviser to U.S. delegations at meetings of Internat. Bank and Monetary Fund, Savannah, 1946, 2d and 3d sessions of UNESCO Lake Success, 1946; staff mem. Pub. Library Inquiry, Social Sci. Research Council, 1947-48. Mem. Am. Polit. Sci. Assn. (past v.p.). Author: Government Publicity, 1939; Governmental Publications for the Citizen, 1949, The Administration of American Foreign Affairs 1950 (Freedom House-Willkie award); American Government 1957; Science and Public Administration, 1960; Conduct of the New Diplomacy, 1964; The Quality of the Environment, 1972. Asso. editor Am. Polit. Sci. Rev., 1952-55. Contbr. articles to profl. jours. Home: 1610 Adams St Madison WI 53711

MCCANCE, THOMAS, banker; b. Edgewood, Pa., Aug. 25, 1902; s. William James and Nancy (Hodge) McCance; attended Phillips-Exeter Sch., 1918-21; Ph.B., Yale, 1925; m. Elizabeth Day Ferguson, Sept. 10, 1932; children—Thomas, Jr., Ellen Margaret (Mrs. Harry S. Parker, III), Henry Ferguson. With Brown Bros. Harriman & Co., N.Y.C., 1929-45, partner, 1945—; pres. Bedgolton Corp., Bedford, N.Y.; trustee, mem. exec. com. Provident Loan Soc. N.Y.; voting trustee SKF Industries Phila.; mem. N.Y. Stock Exchange. Mem. Yale Devel. Bd. Bd. trustees Fgn. Parishes, P.E. Ch. in U.S.A. Mem. Downtown Lower Manhattan Assn. (dir., mem. exec. com.), Psi Upsilon. Wolf's Head Society. Clubs: Golf and Tennis (Bedford); Yale, Links, Down Town Assn. Home: Sarles St Mt Kisco NY 10549 Office: Brown Bros Harriman & Co 59 Wall St New York City NY 10005

MC CANDLESS, BRUCE, II, astronaut; b. Boston, June 8, 1937; s. Bruce and Sue (Bradley) McC.; B.S., U.S. Naval Acad., 1958; M.S. in Elec. Engring., Stanford, 1965; m. Alfreda Bernice Doyle, Aug. 6, 1960; children—Bruce III, Tracy. Commd. ensign USN, 1958, advanced through grades to comdr., 1966; naval aviator, 1960, with Fighter Squadron 102, 1960-64; astronaut Johnson Space Center, NASA, Houston, 1966—, mem. backup crew Skylab I. Mem. IEEE, U.S. Naval Inst., Nat., Houston (past pres.) Audubon socs., Episcopalian. Office: Code CB NASA Johnson Space Center Houston TX 77058

MC CANDLESS, ROBERT CECIL, lawyer; b. Hobart, Okla., July 23, 1937; s. Cecil Reeves and Leah Marjorie (Yeager) McC.; A.A., George Washington U., 1959, B.A. in Journalism, 1961, postgrad. law; J.D., U. Okla., 1965; children—Mark Kerr, Kevin Hennings. Asst. to U.S. Senator Robert S. Kerr, 1955-63; admitted to Okla. bar, 1965, D.C. bar, 1967, U.S. Supreme Ct. bar, 1970; labor atty., asst. dir. govt. relations Internat. Paper Co., N.Y.C., 1965-67; practiced in Washington, 1968—; partner firm Burwell, Hansen & McCandless, Washington, 1968-73; partner firm Law Offices of Robert C. McCandless, 1973-76, firm McCandless & Barrett, 1977—. Gen. counsel, bd. dirs. Am. Horse Protection Assn.; trustee Ford's Theatre; mem. roster arbitrators Fed. Mediation and Conciliation Service. Spl. counsel Dem. Nat. Com., 1969; nat. del. coordinator, then nat. dir. campaign orgn. Humphrey for Pres., 1968. Mem. D.C., Okla., Am., Fed. bar assns., Bar Assn. D.C., Okla. Honor Soc., Am. Judicature Soc., Am. Acad. Polit. and Social Sci., Am. Arbitration Assn., George Washington Nat. Law Assn. (mem. exec. com. alumni 1971-76), Sigma Alpha Epsilon, Phi Delta Phi. Home: 700 New Hampshire Ave NW Washington DC 20037 Office: 1707 H St NW Suite 1005 Washington DC 20006

MCCANDLISH, FAIRFAX SHEILD, lawyer; b. Fairfax, Va., Oct. 26, 1918; s. Fairfax Sheild and Mary (Donohoe) McC.; A.B., Princeton, 1941; LL.B., Georgetown U., 1947; m. Priscilla Ann Totman, Feb. 27, 1943; children—Barbara M., Fairfax Sheild III, Margaret (Mrs. Robert Darby). Admitted to Va. bar, 1947, since practiced in Fairfax; mem. firm Boothe, Prichard & Dudley and predecessor firms, 1961-76. Dir. Gen. Personnel Investigations, Inc. Mem. Fairfax County Park Authority, 1958-63; chmn. Fairfax County Tax Equalization Bd., 1971; vice chmn. exec. com. P.E. Ch. Diocese Va., 1966-67. Trustee Diocesan Missionary Soc. Va., 1970—. Served to lt. USNR, 1942-46. Mem. Fairfax County Bar Assn. (pres. 1958-59), Va. State Bar (chmn. bd. govs. estates and property sect. 1977-78). Home: 3806 Lakeview Terr Falls Church VA 22041 Office: 4085 University Dr Fairfax VA 22030

MC CANDLISH, ROBERT JOHN, JR., lawyer; b. Hancock, Md., Mar. 8, 1909; s. Robert John and Jane Charlton (Graves) McC.; A.B., U. Md., 1930; LL.B., George Washington U., 1934; m. Josephine Meredith Sutton, May 24, 1941; children—Rebekah S., Charles S. Admitted to Va. bar, 1935, since practiced in Fairfax; sr. partner firm McCandlish, Lillard, Church & Best, 1948—; dir. Arlington-Fairfax Savs. and Loan Assn. Mem. Va. Gen. Assembly from Fairfax County, 1942-44, 48. Served as lt. USNR, 1944-46. Mem. Va. State Bar, Am., Va. (chmn. exec. com. 1958-59, pres. 1960-61) bar assns., Nat. Conf. Bar Presidents. Protestant Episcopalian (past v.p. Laymen of Diocese Va.). Clubs: Commonwealth (Richmond, Va.); Court House Country (Fairfax); Chevy Chase (Md.). Home: 3906 Chain Bridge Rd Fairfax VA 22030 Office: 4069 Chain Bridge Rd Fairfax VA 22030

MCCANLES, MICHAEL FREDERICK, educator; b. Kansas City, Mo., Mar. 8, 1936; s. Martin and Dorothy (Kaysing) McC.; B.S., Rockhurst Coll., 1957; M.A., U. Kans., 1959, Ph.D., 1964; m. Penelope A. Mitchell, May 27, 1967; children—Christopher, Stephanie, Jocelyn. Instr. dept. English, U. Cin., 1962-64; asst. prof. Marquette U., 1964-68, asso. prof., 1968-76, prof., 1976—. Guggenheim fellow, 1978-79. Mem. MLA, Renaissance Soc. Am., Malone Soc. Author: Dialectical Criticism and Renaissance Literature, 1975; contbr. articles to profl. jours. Home: 2640 N 89th St Wauwatosa WI 53226 Office: Dept English Marquette U Milwaukee WI 53233. *As educator, scholar, and citizen I try to encourage in the public domain the same qualities of open-mindedness, secular tolerance of multiple viewpoints, and critical judgement of these viewpoints that I encourage among my students and colleagues.*

MC CANN, CECILE NELKEN, art jour. editor, pub.; b. New Orleans; d. Abraham and Leona (Reiman) Nelken; student Vassar Coll., 1934-46, Tulane U., 1936-37; B.A., San Jose State Coll., 1963, M.A., 1964; postgrad. U. Calif., Berkeley, 1966-67; m. Albert Hews McCann, Jr., Mar. 6, 1937 (div. 1976); children—Dorothy Collins, Cecile Isaacs, Annette Lassen, Denise, Albert Hews III. Tool designer Convair Corp., New Orleans, 1942-45; archtl. draftsman, various companies, New Orleans and Clinton, Iowa, 1945-47, 51-53; owner, operator ceramics studio, Clinton, 1953-58; instr. San Jose State Coll., 1964-65, Calif. State U., Hayward, 1964-65, Chabot Coll., Hayward, 1966-69, Laney Coll., 1967-70, San Francisco State U., 1977-78; founder, editor, pub. Artweek mag., Oakland, Calif., 1970—; cons. Nat. Endowment Arts, 1974-78, fellow in art criticism, 1976; panelist numerous confs. and workshops; one-man shows at Davenport Mus. Art, Robert North Galleries, Chgo., Crocker Gallery, Sacramento, Calif., Calif. Coll. Arts and Crafts, Oakland, others; exhibited in group shows at DeYoung Mus., San Francisco, Everson Mus. Art, Syracuse, N.Y., Oakland Mus., Richmond Art Center, Pasadena Mus., Los Angeles County Mus. Art, others; represented in permanent collections San Jose State Coll., Mills Coll., Coll. Holy Names, City of San Francisco, State of Calif., others. Mem. Assn. San Francisco Potters, Am. Crafts Council, Women's Caucus Art, Internat. Assn. Art Critics, Coll. Art Assn. Contbr. to profl. publs. Office: Artweek 1305 Franklin St Oakland CA 94612

MC CANN, DAVID ANTHONY, publisher; b. N.Y.C., June 13, 1929; s. Patrick J. and Helen C. (McCauley) McC.; B.A., St. Johns Coll., 1950; m. Carol L. Gerard, Oct. 8, 1960; children—Peter G., Anthony D., Ellen A. With Am. Weekly div. Hearst Corp., 1950-60; advt. salesman Good Housekeeping mag., 1960-68, N.Y. mgr., 1968-69, Eastern mgr., 1969-71; pub. House Beautiful mag., v.p. Hearst Corp., N.Y.C., 1971—; pub. Town & Country Mag., 1977—. Democrat. Roman Catholic. Clubs: Huntington (N.Y.) Country; Lloyd Neck (N.Y.) Bath. Home: School Lane Lloyd Harbor NY 11743 Office: 717 Fifth Ave New York NY 10022

MC CANN, FRANCES VERONICA, physiologist; b. Manchester, Conn., Jan. 15, 1927; d. John Joseph and Grace E. (Tuttle) McCann; A.B. with distinction and honors, U. Conn., 1952, Ph.D. (Nat. Heart Inst. fellow), 1959; M.S., U. Ill., 1954; M.A. (hon.), Dartmouth Coll., 1975; m. Elden J. Murray, Sept. 20, 1962. Investigator, Marine Biol. Lab., Woods Hole, Mass., 1952-62; instr. physiology Dartmouth Med. Sch., Hanover, N.H., 1959-61, asst. prof., 1961-67, asso. prof., 1967-73, prof., 1973—, adj. prof. biol. scis. Dartmouth Coll., 1974—; cons. research Mary Hitchcock Meml. Hosp.; cons. physiology study sect. NIH, 1973—, mem. biomed. research devel. com., 1978—, chmn., 1979; cons. Hayer Inst., 1979—; established investigator Am. Heart Assn.; chmn. Internat. Symposium on Comparative Physiology of the Heart, 1968. Trustee Montshire Mus. Sci., 1977, Howe Library, 1976, Hanover Health Council, 1976, Lebanon Coll., 1978—. Grantee Nat. Heart Inst., 1960, N.H. Heart Assn., 1964-65, Vt. Heart Assn., 1966—. Mem. Am. Physiol. Soc., Soc. Gen. Physiologists, AAAS, Biophys. Soc., Am. Heart Assn. (council basic sci.), Sigma Xi, Phi Kappa Phi. Editor: Comparative Physiology of the Heart: Current Trends, 1969. Contbr. articles to numerous publs. Office: Dartmouth Med Sch Hanover NH 03755

MCCANN, GILBERT DONALD, JR., educator; b. Glendale, Calif., Jan. 12, 1912; s. Gilbert D. and Edna (Valentine) M.; student U. Calif. at Los Angeles, 1930-32; B.S., Calif. Tech. Inst., 1934, M.S., 1935, Ph.D., 1939, teaching fellow, 1934-38; m. Betty Bonebrake, Aug. 30, 1936; children—Norman D., Janice V. Central Sta. Engring. Dept., Westinghouse Electric Corp., 1938- 41; cons. transmission engr., 1941-46; prof. elec. engring. Calif. Inst. Tech., 1946-66, prof. of applied sci., 1966—, dir. Computing Center, 1961-71. Recipient Eta Kappa Nu Recognition award, 1942. Fellow IEEE; mem. Am. Soc. Elec. Engrs., Am. Soc. Engring. Edn., Biomed. Engring. Soc., Assn. Computing Machinery, AAUP. Author: Electrical Transmission and and Distribution Reference Book, 1942. Contbr. articles to profl. publs. Home: 2247 North Villa Heights Rd Pasadena CA 91107 Office: Calif Inst of Tech 286-80 Pasadena CA 91125

MC CANN, JOHN JOSEPH, lawyer; b. N.Y.C., Feb. 4, 1937; s. John and Katherine (McKeon) McC.; A.B., Fordham U., 1958; LL.B., Columbia U., 1961; married; children—Catherine Anne, John Bernard, Robert Joseph, James Patrick. Admitted to N.Y. State, N.J. bars; asso. firm Donovan, Leisure, Newton & Irvine, N.Y.C., 1962-71, partner, 1971—. Bd. govs. The Children's Village, Dobbs Ferry, N.Y., Mt. St. Mary Coll., Newburgh, N.Y. Served with U.S. Army, 1962. Mem. Am. Law Inst., Am. Bar Assn., N.Y. State Bar Assn., N.J. Bar Assn., N.Y.C. Bar Assn. Roman Catholic. Clubs: Univ., Hemisphere (N.Y.C.); Beacon Hill (Summit, N.J.). Office: 30 Rockefeller Plaza New York NY 10020

MC CANN, JOSEPH JAMES, home bldg. co. exec.; b. Pitts., Aug. 1, 1930; s. Michael Joseph and Mary (Herwood) McC.; B.S. in Bus. Adminstrn., Duquesne U., 1952, M.S., 1956; m. Emily E. Frank, Feb. 12, 1955; children—Joseph James, Garry L., Monica L., Yvonne M. Chief accountant Crown Aluminum Co., Pitts., 1960-63, asst. controller, 1963-67; controller Ryan Homes Inc., Pitts., 1967-74, treas., fin. v.p., 1974—, also dir. subs.; dir. Shearsin Daily Dividend, Inc. Served to 1st lt. U.S. Army, 1952-54. Mem. Nat. Assn. Accountants (pres. Pitts. chpt. 1977-78), Planning, Fin. execs. insts. Roman Catholic. Home: 200 Oak Park Pl Pittsburgh PA 15243 Office: 100 Ryan Ct Pittsburgh PA 15205

MCCANN, LESLIE COLEMAN, pianist, composer, photographer; b. Lexington, Ky., Sept. 23, 1935; s. James W. and Ann (Lawrence) McC.; student Westlake Coll. Music, Hollywood, Calif., Los Angeles City Coll.; m. Charlotte Watkins Lavande, Apr. 2, 1961; stepchildren—Rose-Elaine, Raphaël, Arabella. Appeared on All-Navy talent contest Ed Sullivan Show, 1956; night club appearances, 1957—; formed 1st group, N.Am., 1959, now leader quartet Les McCann Ltd.; toured Europe, Africa, Mex., Jamaica, Tahiti; rec. artist; pres. Jana Music; performed concerts in penal instns.; narrated, performed movie Soul to Soul; tchr. Sch. for Learning, Mezcales, Mex. and Los Angeles; founder Inst. Black Am. Music div. Operation Bread basket. Bd. dirs. African-Am. Cultural Exchange. Exhibited photographs in Montreux, Switzerland, 1970, Washington, Detroit, N.Y.C.; photographer book See You Tomorrow (Dr. Betty Eisner). Served with USNR, 1953-56. Democrat. Office: care Bernard & Steckler Co 9200 Sunset Blvd Suite 620 Los Angeles CA 90069*

MCCANN, ROBERT MUNSON, mining engr., steel co. exec.; b. Franklin, N.J., Oct. 7, 1930; s. Raymond L. and Fleta M. (Munson) McC.; B.S. in Mining Engring., Lehigh U., 1952; m. Ann L. Lieberman; children—William T., Susan E., Amy L. With Bethlehem Steel Corp., 1952—, gen. mgr. mining, Bethlehem, Pa., 1976-77, asst. v.p. mining, 1977-79, v.p. mining, 1979—. Mem. AIME, Am. Iron and Steel Inst., Am. Iron Ore Assn., Can. Inst. Mining. Office: Bethlehem Steel Corp 8th and Eaton Ave Bethlehem PA 18016

MC CANN, SAMUEL MCDONALD, educator, physiologist; b. Houston, Sept. 8, 1925; s. Samuel Glenn and Margaret (Brokaw) McC.; student Rice U., Houston, 1942-44; M.D., U. Pa., 1948; m. Barbara Lorraine Richardson; children—Samuel Donald, Margaret, Karen Elizabeth. Intern in internal medicine Mass. Gen. Hosp., Boston, 1948-49, resident, 1949-50; mem. faculty U. Pa. Sch. Medicine, 1952-65, prof. physiology, 1964-65, acting chmn. dept., 1963-64; prof., chmn. physiology U. Tex. Southwestern Med. Sch., Dallas, 1965—; cons., Schering Corp., Bloomfield, N.J., 1958; mem. gen. medicine B study sect. NIH, 1965-67, endocrinology study sect. 1967-69, population research com., 1974-76, reproductive biology study sect., 1978—. Recipient Spencer Morris prize U. Pa. Med. Sch., 1948; Lindback award for distinguished teaching, 1965; Oppenheimer award for research in endocrinology, 1966. Mem. Am. Physiol. Soc., Endocrine Soc. (Fred Conrad Koch award 1979), Am. Physiol. Soc. (council 1979—), Soc. for Exptl. Biology and Medicine, N.Y. Acad. Scis., Neuroendocrine Discussion Group (chmn. 1965), Internat. Neuroendocrine Soc. (council 1972—). Editorial bd. Endocrinology, 1963-68, 72-77, Neuroendocrinology, 1967-76, Ann. Rev. Physiology, 1974-79, Soc. Exptl. Biology and Medicine, 1976—; editor Endocrine Physiology, Pioneers in Neuroendocrinology. Contbr. articles to profl. jours., chpts. to books. Home: 7025 Hillgreen Dr Dallas TX 75214

MCCANN, TERRENCE JOHN, assn. exec.; b. Chgo., Mar. 23, 1934; s. John Henry and Alice Marie (Ladd) McC.; B.S., U. Iowa, 1957; M.B.A., Loyola U., Chgo., 1974; m. Lucille Creely, Dec. 11, 1953; children—Rose Ann, Deirdre, Colleen, Terrence John, Sean, Bridgid, Denise. Program mgr. U.S. Jaycees, Tulsa, 1958-65; exec. sec. Wheaties Sports Fedn., Mpls., 1965-67; mgr. communications and pub. relations SuperMarket Inst., Inc., Chgo., 1967-71; treas., asst. exec. adminstr. Lions Internat., Chgo., 1971-74; exec. dir. Toastmasters Internat., Inc., Santa Ana, Calif., 1972—; instr. mgmt. Santa Ana Coll. Elected to U.S. Wrestling Hall of Fame, 1978. Mem. Am. Mgmt. Assn., Am. Soc. Assn. Execs., Am. Soc. for Tng. and Devel., Speech Communications Assn., Am. Inst. Parliamentarians, Soc. for Advancement of Mgmt. Republican. Roman Catholic. Clubs: Lions, Toastmasters. Home: 24371 Barbados Dr Dana Point CA 92629 Office: Toastmasters Internat Inc 2200 N Grand Ave Santa Ana CA 92711

MCCANN, WILLIAM EDWARD, life ins. co. exec.; b. Lowell, Mass., Sept. 27, 1930; s. Michael Timothy and Margaret Jane (Masterson) McC.; B.A., Bradshaw Coll., Lowell, 1957; m. Virginia Ann Blouin, Sept. 5, 1969; children—E. Tiffany, W. Nevins. Life ins. salesman John Hancock Life Ins. Co., 1955-58, Hartford Life Ins. Co., 1959-62; pres., treas. Asso. Life Ins. Co., Wilmington, Del., 1962-68; pres., chief exec. officer Found. Fin. Corp., Chatham, N.J., 1968—, also Found. Life Ins. Co. Am.; dir. State Bank Chatham; mem. guest faculty La. State U., Baton Rouge. Mem. provost's bd. Fairleigh Dickinson U. Served with USNR, 1950-54; Korea. Fellow Life Mgmt. Inst.; mem. Nat., Merrimack Valley (v.p., sec., treas.) assns. life underwriters, Life Ins. Agy. Mgmt. Assn. Home: 180 Highland Ave Short Hills NJ 07078 Office: 330 Main St Chatham NJ 07928

MC CARDELL, ADRIAN LEROY, JR., banker; b. Frederick, Md., Apr. 10, 1908; s. Adrian Leroy and Eleanor (Clingan) McC.; B.S., Washington and Lee U., 1929; M.B.A., Harvard, 1931; m. Phyllis K. Green, Dec. 15, 1945; children—Katharine Claire, Adrian LeRoy III. Asst. bank examiner, Md., 1931-32; nat. bank examiner Fifth Fed. Res. Dist., 1932-42; v.p. Seaboard Citizens Nat. Bank, Norfolk, Va., 1946-56, Charleston Nat. Bank (W.Va.), 1956-58; v.p. First Nat. Bank, Balt., 1958-59, exec. v.p., 1960, pres., 1961-68, chmn. bd., 1968-73, chmn. exec. com., 1973-78, mem. trust com., 1978—; dir. First Md. Bancorp. Trustee, Keswick Home, Council Econ. Edn. in Md. Served from lt. to comdr. USNR, 1942-46. Mem. S.A.R., Md. Hist. Soc. Democrat. Episcopalian. Clubs: Princess Anne Country (Virginia Beach, Va.); Maryland (Balt.); Elkridge. Home: 1023 Winding Way Baltimore MD 21210 Office: PO Box 1596 Baltimore MD 21203

MC CARDELL, ARCHIE RICHARD, mfg. co. exec.; b. Hazel Park, Mich., Aug. 29, 1926; s. Archie and Josephine (Gauthier) McC.; B.B.A., U. Mich., 1948. M.B.A., 1949; m. Margaret Edith Martin, June 17, 1950; children—Sandra Beth, Laurie Wynne, Clay Vincent. With Ford Motor Co., 1949-60, finance exec., Dearborn, Mich., 1960; sec.-treas. Ford of Australia, 1960-63; dir. finance Ford of Germany, 1963-66; group v.p. for corporate service Xerox Corp., Rochester, N.Y., 1966-68, exec. v.p., 1968-71, pres., 1971-77, also chief operating officer, dir.; now chmn., chief exec. officer Internat. Harvester Co.; dir. Am. Express Co., Am. Express Internat. Banking Corp., Gen. Foods Corp., Harris Trust & Savs. Bank, Harris Bankcorp, Inc., Honeywell, In.; former chmn. nat. adv. com. Blue Cross Assn. Formerly mem. adv. council Stanford U. Grad. Sch. Bus.; bd. dirs. Children's Meml. Hosp.; trustee U. Chgo. Served with USAAF, 1943-45. Office: 401 N Michigan Ave Chicago IL 60611

MCCARDELL, WILLIAM MARKHAM, oil co. exec.; b. Houston, Nov. 1, 1923; s. William Kenon and Margaret Best (Bachman) McC.; B.S. in Chem. Engring., Rice U., 1948; M.S. in Chem. Engring., Calif. Inst. Tech., 1949; m. Martha McDonald, Aug. 27, 1949; children—Carol Frances, Stephen Hayward. With Humble Oil & Refining Co., Houston, 1949-70, various research assignments prodn. research div., chief research engr., 1958-60, mgr. corp. planning dept., 1961-63, various mktg. mgmt. positions, 1963-68, mktg. v.p., 1968-70; mktg. v.p. Exxon Corp., N.Y.C., 1970-75, v.p., mining and synthetic fuels dept., 1977—; exec. v.p. Esso Eastern, Inc., Houston, 1975-77. Served to capt. USAAF, 1943-46. Registered profl. engr., Tex. Mem. Soc. Petroleum Engrs., Soc. Mining Entrs., Am. Meteorol. Soc., Am. Inst. Chem. Engrs., Sigma Xi, Tau Beta Pi, Phi Lambda Upsilon. Clubs: Mining, Riverside Yacht. Home: 70 E 77th St New York NY 10021 Office: 1251 Office: Ave of Americas New York NY 10020

MC CARN, GRACE HAYDEN, librarian; b. Tompkinsville, Md., July 10, 1939; d. Robert Kermit and Annie Mae (Ryce) Hayden; B.A. in English, U. Md., 1962, M.L.S., 1971; m. Davis Barton McCarn, Aug. 4, 1973; step-children—Davis Moore, Kevin O'Brien, Michael John, Susan Ruth; dau., Stacy Kathleen. With Nat. Library Medicine, Bethesda, Md., 1963—, mem. task force new computer implementation, 1969-70, head med. lit. analysis and retrieval system mgmt., 1971-78, chief bibliog. services div., 1978—. Recipient Equal Employment Opportunity Achievement award Nat. Library Medicine, 1975, Superior Performance award, 1976, Merit award NIH, 1978. Mem. Med. Library Assn., Am. Soc. Info. Sci., Beta Phi Mu (past treas.). Democrat. Author papers in field. Home: 6455 Windermere Circle Rockville MD 20852 Office: 8600 Rockville Pike Bethesda MD 20209

MC CARRAGHER, BERNARD J., bus. exec.; b. Waukesha, Wis., Sept. 17, 1927; s. Bernard J. and Agnes A. (Brennan) McC.; B.S., Marquette U., 1951; m. Mary Horschak, June 20, 1953; four sons, seven daus. Auditor, Arthur Andersen & Co., Milw., 1951-57; accountant Elgin Watch Co., 1957-58; controller Paine Lumber Co., Oshkosh, Wis., 1958-60; accountant Bergstrom Paper Co., Neenah, Wis., 1960-62; controller, treas. Menasha Corp., Neenah, 1962—. Served with U.S. Army, 1946-48. C.P.A., Wis. Club: Rotary Internat. Home: 211 5th St Neenah WI 54956 Office: PO Box 367 Neenah WI 54956

MC CARREY, JEAN LORRAINE, ins. broker; b. Champaign County, Ill., Aug. 31, 1922; d. Alva R. and Alma M. (Kemper) McCarrey; grad. high sch. Staff asst. Ill. Welfare Dept., Tuscola, 1941-57; adminstrv. asst. Creative Bldgs. Inc., Urbana, Ill., 1957-70, also dir., sec.; sales rep. Travelers Ins. Co., Peoria, Ill., 1970—; para-legal asst. to firm Follmer, West, Erdmann & Clem; mgr. Sunnycrest Shopping Center. Mem. adv. com. SBA, 1967-71; mem. panel med. devices HEW, 1974-77; pub. mem. Fgn. Service Selection Bd., U.S. Dept. State, 1975. Speaker, lectr. on citizen responsibility and participation. Trustee Bus. and Profl. Women's Found., 1969-74, pres., 1973-74; former mem. Villa Grove Planning and Zoning Commn.; mem. Villa Grove City Council. Mem. Nat. Fedn. Bus. and Profl. Women's Clubs (pres. 1973-74). Methodist (certified lay speaker, mem. dist. council on ministries 1974-77). Address: 7 N Pine St Villa Grove IL 61956 also 1717 S Philo Rd Urbana IL 61801

MC CARRICK, THEODORE EDGAR, clergyman, educator; b. N.Y.C., July 7, 1930; s. Theodore Egan and Margaret (McLaughlin) McC.; student Fordham U., 1950-52; A.B., St. Joseph's Sem., 1954, A.M., 1958; M.A., Cath. U., 1960, Ph.D., 1963; LL.D., Mt. St. Vincent Coll., 1967; S.T.D., Inter-Am. U., i969; L.H.D., St. John's U., 1974. Ordained priest Roman Catholic Ch., 1958; asst. chaplain Cath. U., Washington 1959-61, dean students, 1961-63, asst. to rector, dir. univ. devel., 1963-65, instr. dept. sociology, 1961-65; domestic prelate 1965; pres. Cath. U. P.R., 1965-69; asso. dir. edn. Archdiocese of N.Y., 1969-71; sec. to Cardinal-Archbishop N.Y., 1971-77; titular bishop of Rusibisir, aux. bishop of N.Y., 1977—, also episcopal vicar for East Manhattan, 1977—. Asst. dir. Inst. for Inter-Cultural Communications, Cath. U. P.R., 1959-60, dir., 1960-63; mem. policy bd. Washington Consortium, Peace Corps, 1962-63; pres. Nat. Council for Spainish-Speaking People, 1961-65; chmn. Gov.'s Commn. for Higher Edn. in P.R., 1968, P.R. Adv. Council on Tech. and Vocat. Edn., 1968-69. Named knight grand cross Holy Sepulcher. Mem. Am. Sociol. Soc., Assn. Colls. and Univs. P.R. (pres. 1968), Sigma Beta Kappa, Phi Kappa Theta. Clubs: K.C., Am. Assn. Knights Malta (chaplain 1978). Address: 1011 1st Ave New York NY 10022

MC CARROLL, JAMES RENWICK, physician; b. N.Y.C., Nov. 14, 1921; s. Edward Loomis and Emma Sellers (Robertson) McC.; B.A., Colby Coll., 1942; M.D., Cornell U., 1946; m. Eleanor Hall Thomas, Feb. 9, 1962 (dec. Oct. 1966). Intern. Bellevue Hosp., N.Y.C., 1946-47, asst. resident medicine, 1947-50, psychiatry, 1950; sr. resident medicine Bklyn. VA Hosp., 1951; asso. prof., dir. epidemiology Cornell U. Med. Coll., 1954-66; prof., chmn. dept. environ. health U. Wash. Sch. Pub. Health, Seattle, 1966-73; asst. med. dir. City of Los Angeles, 1973-76; program mgr. health effects Electric Power Research Inst., Palo Alto, Calif., 1976—; clin. prof. dept. community and preventive medicine Stanford U. Med. Sch., 1977—; Mem. nat. air quality criteria com. and sci. adv. bd. EPA, coordinating research com. Am. Petroleum Inst. Bd. dirs. Tb and Respiratory Disease Assn. Served to capt. M.C. AUS, 1948-50. Recipient award for accident research Nat. Safety Council, 1964. Fellow Am. Pub. Health Assn., Am. Coll. Preventive Medicine, Am. Occupational Med. Assn., Am. Acad. Occupational Medicine; mem. Internat. Soc. Accident and Traffic Medicine (founding), Royal Soc. Medicine, AMA, Am., Internat. epidemiol. assns., Author numerous articles on health effects of air pollution. Office: 3412 Hillview Ave Palo Alto CA 94303

MC CARROLL, MICHAEL ARTHUR, publisher; b. Pitts., Apr. 1, 1938; s. Arthur Clifford and Doris Marie (Wickersham) McC.; B.A., U. Mich., 1959; M.L.S., U. So. Calif., 1969; postgrad. Sorbonne, 1963-64; m. Eleanor Gray Baird, Nov. 14, 1970. Editor, Radio Free Europe, Munich, Germany, 1964-67; librarian Dept. Interior, Washington, 1969-70; editor Info. Sci. Abstracts, Yale U., 1970-72; v.p., gen. mgr. Lexington Books div. D.C. Heath & Co., Lexington, Mass., 1972—; mem. adv. com. White House Conf. Libraries and Info. Services, 1975—. Mem. Assn. Am. Pubs. Home: 45 Whippoorwill Ln Concord MA 01742 Office: Lexington Books DC Heath and Co 125 Spring St Lexington MA 02173

MCCARTER, CHARLES VERNON, utilities exec.; b. Navarro, Tex., Aug. 1, 1925; s. Charlie Holden and Lenora Vernon (Moore) McC.; student Draughon's Bus. Coll., 1942-43. With Tex. Power & Light Co., Dallas, 1947—, sec., asst. treas., 1972—. Served with AUS, 1944-46. Decorated Purple Heart. Mem. Am. Records Mgmt. Assn. (pres. Dallas chpt. 1970). Baptist. Home: 8323 Van Pelt Dr Dallas TX 75228 Office: 1511 Bryan St Dallas TX 75201

MCCARTER, FRANCIS E.P., lawyer; b. New Brunswick, N.J., Sept. 10, 1917; s. George W.C. and Dorothy (Parker) McC.; grad. Taft Sch., 1935; A.B., Princeton, 1939; J.D., Harvard, 1947; m. Marna Kuelthau, June 19, 1948; children—George W.C., Robert Y., Lisa. Admitted to N.J. bar, 1948; asso. atty. firm McCarter & English, Newark, 1948-50, partner, 1950—. Councilman borough of Rumson (N.J.), 1963—, pres. of council, 1975—. Served to lt. col., F.A., AUS, 1940-46. Decorated Medalia Merito Di Guerra (Italy). Mem. Am., N.J. (chmn. com. on conservation and ecology 1970-73), Essex County, Monmouth County bar assns. Home: 45 Buenavista Ave Rumson NJ 07760 Office: 550 Broad St Newark NJ 07102

MC CARTER, JOHN ALEXANDER, educator; b. Wareham, Eng., Jan. 25, 1918; s. Alexander and Helen T. (McKellar) McC.; B.A., U. B.C., 1939, M.A., 1941; Ph.D., U. Toronto, 1945; m. Patricia Jocelyn St. John, Dec. 27, 1941; children—David G., Robert M., Patricia L., William A. Came to Can., 1919. Research officer NRC Can. Atomic Energy Project, Chalk River, Ont., 1945-48; asso. prof. Dalhousie U., Halifax, Can., 1948-50, prof., 1950-65; prof. biochemistry, dir. Cancer Research Lab., U. Western Ont., London, 1965—. Mem. Med. Research Council Canada, 1961-67, research adv. group Nat. Cancer Inst. Canada, 1967-72. Fellow Brit. Empire Cancer Campaign, 1959-60, Fellow Royal Soc. Can.; mem. Canadian Biochem. Soc. (pres. 1966-67), Alpha Omega, Fedn. Ont. Naturalists. Contbr. articles to profl. jours. Research tumor virology. Home: 472 Lawson Rd London ON N6G 1X8 Canada Office: Cancer Research Lab Univ Western Ontario London ON Canada

MC CARTER, JOHN WILBUR, JR., corp. exec.; b. Oak Park, Ill., Mar. 2, 1938; s. John Wilbur and Ruth Rebecca McC.; A.B., Princeton U., 1960; postgrad. London Sch. Econs., 1961; M.B.A., Harvard U., 1963; m. Judith Field West, May 1, 1965; children—James Philip, Jeffrey John, Katherine Field. Cons., asso., v.p. Booz Allen and Hamilton, Inc., Chgo., 1963-69; White House fellow, Washington, 1966-67; dir. Bur. Budget and Dept. Fin., State of Ill., Springfield, 1969-73; v.p. DeKalb AgResearch (Ill.), 1973-78, dir., 1975—, exec. v.p., 1978—. Trustee Chgo. Public Television, 1973—; vestryman St. Peter's Ch., Sycamore, Ill., 1974-77. Republican. Episcopalian. Clubs: University, Chgo., Economic. Home: 450 Somonauk Sycamore IL 60178 Office: Sycamore Rd DeKalb IL 60115*

MCCARTER, WILLIAM J., JR., broadcasting exec.; b. Phila., June 10, 1929; s. William J. and Julia R. (Miller) McC.; B.A., Lafayette Coll., 1951; postgrad. Temple U. Sch. Communication, 1957-58; m. Emma Linda Warner, Jan. 19, 1952; children—Julianne, William J. II, Amy, James Andrew. Dir., WFIL-TV, Phila., 1953-57; program dir. WHYY-TV, Phila., 1957-62; program devel. officer Nat. Ednl. Television, N.Y.C., 1962-64; pres., gen. mgr. WETA-TV/FM, Washington, 1964-71; pres., gen. mgr. WTTW-TV, Chgo., 1971—; lectr. U. Pa., Am. U., Northwestern U.; TV cons. Govt. V.I.; pres. Eastern Ednl. TV Network, 1968-71. Mem. Pres.'s Commn. on Human Rights, 1968; telecommunications adviser to mayor of Washington. Trustee, St. John's Coll., Washington; bd. mgrs. Pub. Broadcasting Service, mem. Chgo. com. bd. dirs. Served to 1st lt. AUS, 1951-53. Decorated Bronze Star medal, Purple Heart. Recipient Bd. Govs.' award Washington Acad. Television Arts and Scis., 1971. Mem. Nat. (v.p. 1967-69), Washington (pres. 1966-68) acads. television arts and scis., Public TV Mgrs. Council, Nat. Assn. Ednl. Broadcastors (dir. 1970-72, vice chmn. 1970-72), Radio and TV Corrs. Assn., Chgo. Council Fgn. Relations (dir.). Clubs: National Press, International (Washington); Mid-Am., Union League (Chgo.). Office: WTTW-TV 5400 N Saint Louis Ave Chicago IL 60625*

MC CARTHY, ALFRED LEE, ret. lawyer; b. Galveston, Tex., Dec. 23, 1901; s. John Thomas and Frances Elizabeth (Walker) McC.; student Southwestern U., 1919-20; LL.B., Washington and Lee U., 1923; m. Harriet Whyte, Oct. 9, 1926. Admitted to Fla. bar, 1923, practiced in Miami, 1923-74; partner firm McCarthy Steel Hector & Davis. Pres. Greater Miami Philharmonic Soc., Inc., 1968-70. Mem. dist. bd. trustees Miami-Dade Community Coll., 1968-75. Mem. Am. Law Inst., Am., Dade County bar assns., Fla. Bar, Omicron Delta Kappa, Phi Delta Phi. Clubs: Biscayne Bay Yacht (Miami); Riviera Country (Coral Gables, Fla.). Home: 600 Biltmore Way Apt 806 Coral Gables FL 33134

MCCARTHY, CHARLES JOSEPH, lawyer, former govt. ofcl.; b. Providence, June 19, 1907; s. John Francis and Mary Elizabeth (Quinn) McC.; A.B., Providence Coll., 1927; LL.B., Yale, 1930; m. Gladys Christina McGrail; children—Helen Jacquelyn (Mrs. James F. Hickey), Barbara Ann (Mrs. John J. McCooe), Cormac, William Bernard, Maryellen (Mrs. James A. Jaques III), Dennis Michael. Admitted to bar N.Y., 1932, R.I., 1933, Tenn., 1934, D.C., 1968, U.S. Supreme Ct., 1935; pvt. practice, N.Y.C., 1930-32, Providence, 1932-34; atty. RFC, 1934; legal staff TVA, 1934-67, gen. counsel, 1958-67; partner Swidler & Belnap, Washington, 1968-70, Belnap, McCarthy, Spencer, Sweeney & Harkaway, 1970—; spl. asst. to atty. gen. Dept. Justice, 1938-39. Mem. Am., Fed. bar assns. Co-author: A Study of the Electric Power Situation in New England, 1970-1990; also articles. Home: 6401 Lakeview Dr Falls Church VA 22041 Office: 1750 Pennsylvania Ave NW Washington DC 20006

MCCARTHY, CLARENCE FRANCIS, accountant, educator; b. Chgo., Nov. 30, 1909; s. James J. and Mary Agnes (McGann) McC.; J.D., De Paul U., 1933, A.B., 1935; student Northwestern U. Coll. Commerce, 1939-44; m. Lillian E. O'Brien, Nov. 23, 1939; children—Maribeth (Mrs. Norman Schmidt), Neil R., Carol, Gerald J. Admitted to Ill. bar, 1933; practice in Chgo., 1933-40; with Arthur Andersen & Co., C.P.A.'s 1941—, partner charge N.Y. tax dept., 1952-58, partner charge tax div. firm, Chgo. home office, 1958-67; ret., 1972; instr. Grad. Sch. Mgmt., Northwestern U., 1970-77. Bd. examiners Am. Inst. C.P.A.'s, 1966-70. C.P.A., Ill., N.Y. Author: The Federal Income Tax—Its Sources and Applications. Home: 2728 Iroquois Rd Wilmette IL 60091

MCCARTHY, CORNELIUS STEPHEN, educator; b. Worcester, Mass., Dec. 26, 1916; s. John and Mary (Shea) McC.; B.S. in Journalism, Boston U., 1940, M.Ed., 1941; m. Louise Frances Holewinski, June 10, 1950; children—Mary Louise, Stephen John, Martin Vincent, Martha Anne. Editorial and advt. work daily and weekly newspapers in Mass., 1935-39; dir. publs. Rockhurst Coll., Kansas City, Mo., 1946-48; faculty Duquesne U., 1948—, chmn. dept., 1950-77, now prof. journalism dept., founder, 1954, later dir. Duquesne Univ. Scholastic Press Assn.; founder, 1959, later editor Duquesne Journalist; founder Pittsburgh Communications Found., 1968. Mem. national alumni council Boston U., 1962—. Member Assn. Education Journalism, Am. Soc. Journalism Sch. Adminstrs. (nat. v.p. 1965-66, pres. 1966-67); asso. mem. Cath. Press Assn. Am. (supr. nat. competition annual awards newspaper div. 1959-65), Pi Delta Epsilon (hon.), Sigma Delta Chi (pres. Pitts. profl. chpt., 1969-70), Kappa Tau Alpha (nat. v.p., 1967-69, nat. pres. 1971-73). Book reviewer, author articles. Editor, bus. mgr. The Journalism Educator, 1962-66. Home: 126 Cedar Blvd Pittsburgh PA 15228

MCCARTHY, D. JUSTIN, coll. pres.; b. Brockton, Mass.; B.S., Bridgewater State Coll., 1938, Ed.M., 1939; Ed.D., Harvard U., 1955; m. Rose Mary Hoye; children—Daniel Justin, Rosemary, John Emmet, Vincent Joseph. Tchr., prin. Hanover (Mass.) Pub. Schs.; tchr., asst. prin. Belmont (Mass.) Elementary Schs.; dean instrn. U. Maine, Farmington, 1947-48, extension lectr., Orono, 1947-48; supr. student teaching U. Mass. at Amherst, 1948-55; supt. edn., asst. dir. div. state colls. Mass. State Colls., 1955-56, dir. div. state colls., 1956-61; pres. Framingham (Mass.) State Coll., 1961—. Chmn. evaluation Nat. Council Accreditation Tchr. Edn., Mass. Bd. Coll. Authority, New Eng. Assn. Colls. and Secondary Schs.; past pres. New Eng. Tchr. Prep. Assn.; mem. 1202 Commn. Higher Edn. Mass. Mem. Assn. Supervision and Curriculum Devel. (past pres.), Phi Delta Kappa, Kappa Delta Pi (hon.). Contbr. articles to profl. jours. including Harvard Educational Review. Address: Framingham State Coll Framingham MA 01701*

MCCARTHY, D. JUSTIN, coll. pres.; b. Brockton, Mass.; B.S., Bridgewater State Coll., 1938, Ed.M., 1939; Ed.D., Harvard U., 1955; m. Rose Mary Hoye; children—Daniel Justin, Rosemary, John Emmet, Vincent Joseph. Tchr., prin. Hanover (Mass.) Pub. Tic Schs.; tchr., asst. prin. Belmont (Mass.) Elementary Schs.; dean instrn. U. Maine, Farmington, 1947-48, extension lectr., Orono, 1947-48; supr. student teaching U. Mass. at Amherst, 1948-55; supt. edn., asst. dir. div. state colls. Mass. State Colls., 1955-56, dir. div. state colls., 1956-61; pres. Framingham (Mass.) State Coll., 1961—. Chmn. evaluation Nat. Council Accreditation Tchr. Edn., Mass. Bd. Coll. Authority, New Eng. Assn. Colls. and Secondary Schs.; past pres. New Eng. Tchr. Prep. Assn.; mem. 1202 Commn. Higher Edn. Mass. Mem. Assn. Supervision and Curriculum Devel. (past pres.), Phi Delta Kappa, Kappa Delta Pi (hon.). Contbr. articles to profl. jours. including Harvard Educational Review. Address: Framingham State Coll Framingham MA 01701

MCCARTHY, DANIEL CHRISTOPHER, JR., mfg. co. exec.; b. St. Paul, May 10, 1924; s. Daniel Christopher and Isobel Beatrice (Wilmot) McC.; B.Mech. Engring. with distinction, Cornell U., 1949; m. Gail Lloyd Allen, Mar. 9, 1951. Mgr. profit planning Ford div. Ford Motor Co., 1949-56; dir. mfg. staff Chrysler Corp., 1956-58; controller Chrysler Internat., Geneva, Switzerland, 1958-59; exec. v.p. Pratt & Whitney Co., 1959-61, pres., 1961-64; v.p. bus. equipment group Litton Industries, Orange, N.J., 1964-65, pres. Monroe Internat., Inc. div., 1965-67; v.p., dir. Keene Corp., 1967-74; founder, pres. Gale Corp., 1974—; founder, chmn. Sound Constrn. Corp., 1979—; dir. Hytek Corp., Luxo Corp. Mem. Cornell U. Council. Served with inf., AUS, 1942-46. Mem. Am. Soc. M.E., Tau Beta Pi, Phi Kappa Phi, Pi Tau Sigma, Psi Upsilon. Home: 78 Lloyd Rd Montclair NJ 07042 Office: 2000 Elizabeth St PO Box 183 North Brunswick NJ 08902

MC CARTHY, DANIEL DESMOND, investment banker; b. Dublin, Ireland, Mar. 25, 1927; s. Francis T. and Ellen (Hannigan) McC.; m. Alice Patricia Ean, Apr. 21, 1951; children—Regina, Patricia, Daniel, Brian, Francis. Security trader Merrill, Lynch, Pierce, Fenner and Smith, N.Y.C., 1946-50; with Blyth Eastman Dillon & Co., Inc., N.Y.C., 1956—, exec. v.p., dir., 1970—. Bd. dirs. Mercy Hosp., Rockville Centre, N.Y., Cath. Charities, Rockville Centre. Served with USNR, 1945-46. Mem. Securities Traders Assn., Corp. Bond Traders. Clubs: Bond, N.Y. Yacht. Home: 5 Glenwood Rd Rockville Centre NY 11570 Office: 1221 Ave of Americas New York NY 10020

MCCARTHY, DAVID JEROME, JR., ednl. adminstr.; b. Hartford, Conn., July 19, 1935; s. David Jerome and Flora Emily (Edmondo) McC.; A.B., cum laude, Fairfield (Conn.) U., 1957; LL.B. (now J.D.), Georgetown U., 1960; LL.M., 1962; m. Mary Elizabeth McGlynn, Aug. 13, 1960; children—Emilie Anne, Mary Theresa, Carolyn Elizabeth, Katherine Margaret. Admitted to Conn. bar, 1960, D.C. bar, 1962; law clk. U.S. Ct. Appeal for D.C. Circuit, 1960-61; law clk. to Judge John A. Danaher, 1961-62; atty. Appellate sect. civil div. U.S. Dept. Justice, Washington, 1962-63; dir. D.C. Bail Project, 1963-65; adj. prof. law Georgetown U., 1964-65, asso. prof., 1965-68, prof., 1968—, asst. dean, 1965-68, asso. dean, 1968-70, dean, 1975—, exec. v.p. Law Center Affairs, 1975—; chmn. exec. com. D.C. Pretrial Services Agy., 1966—; mem. Nat. Chamber Found. Task Force on Products Liability, 1978—; mem. Joint Com. on Clin. Legal Edn. Guidelines, Am. Bar Assn.-Am. Assn. Law Schs., 1977—; mem. Gov.'s Commn. for Modernization of Md. Exec. Br., 1966-67. Trustee Four Colls. Trust Fund, 1969-71. Named Man of Year, Fairfield U. Alumni, 1965. Mem. Am. Bar Assn., Phi Alpha Delta. Democrat. Roman Catholic. Author: Local Government Law in a Nutshell, 1975. Contbr. chpts. to books, also articles in profl. jours. Home: 12612 Orchard Brook Terr Potomac MD 20854 Office: Georgetown University Law Center 600 New Jersey Ave NW Washington DC 20001

MC CARTHY, DENIS MICHAEL, diversified mfg. co. exec.; b. Hartford, Conn., Dec. 4, 1942; s. Charles J. and Mary M. (Moynihan) McC.; B.S., U. Conn., 1964, M.A., 1965; m. Linda M. Horn, Aug. 21, 1965; children—Bryan Stephen, Kerry Ann, Kevin Michael. Asst. sec. Mfrs. Hanover Trust Co., N.Y.C., 1965-68; dir. cash mgmt. Triangle Industries, Inc., 1968-70, asst. treas., 1970, treas., asst. sec., 1970-71, v.p., treas., 1971-73, sr. v.p., treas., 1973-74, sr. v.p. finance, treas., 1974-76, sr. v.p. fin. and adminstrn., 1976-78, exec. v.p., chief fin. officer, 1978—; asso. dir. 1st Mchts. Nat. Bank. Mem. Financial Execs. Inst., NAM, Am. Mgmt. Assn. Home: Holling Rd Colts Neck NJ 07722 Office: Triangle Industries Inc Holmdel NJ 07733

MC CARTHY, DENNIS, lawyer; b. N.Y.C., Oct. 4, 1912; s. Wilson and Minerva (Woolley) McC.; student Stanford, 1932-35; J.D., Georgetown U., 1939; m. Florence Derrick, June 15, 1935 (dec. Jan. 1955); children—Maureen, Wilson, Dennis O'Shaughnessy; m. 2d, Marilyn Lindsay, June 1, 1956; children—Lindsay, Kelly. Admitted to D.C. bar, 1939, Utah bar, 1946; asst. U.S. atty., D.C., 1940-43; sr. mem. firm Van Cott, Bagley, Cornwall & McCarthy, Salt Lake City, 1946—. Served to lt. comdr. USNR, 1943-46. Fellow Am. Bar Found. (state chmn.); mem. Am., Salt Lake County (pres. 1956-57), Utah bar assns., Phi Delta Phi (hon.). Clubs: Salt Lake Country, Alta (Salt Lake City). Home: 2408 Haven Ln Salt Lake City UT 84117 Office: 141 E 1st St South Salt Lake City UT 84111

MC CARTHY, DONALD WANS, utility exec.; b. Mpls., Feb. 11, 1922; s. Donald and Carolyn (Beach) McC.; B.S., U.S. Naval Acad., 1943; m. Anne Leslie, Jan. 2, 1947; children—Donald, Peter, Thomas, Jill. Commd. ensign U.S. Navy, 1940, advanced through grades to lt., 1943; active duty, 1943-48, 52-53; resigned, 1953; with No. States Power Co., Mpls., v.p., mgr. Mpls. div., 1969-72, 1972-73, exec. v.p., 1973-76, pres., dir., 1976—, chmn. bd., 1978—; dir. Northwestern Nat. Bank, Mpls. Decorated Bronze Star. Mem. Mpls. Engrs. Club. Clubs: Mpls., Woodhill Country, Minn. Address: 414 Nicollet Mall Minneapolis MN 55401

MCCARTHY, EDWARD ANTHONY, bishop; b. Cin., Apr. 10, 1918; s. Edward E. and Catherine (Otte) McC.; M.A., Mt. St. Mary Sem. of West, Norwood, Ohio, 1944; Licentiate Canon Law, Cath. U. Am., 1946; D. Canon Law, Lateran U., Rome, Italy, 1947; S.T.D., Angelicum, Rome, 1948. Ordained priest Roman Catholic Ch., 1943; sec. to archbishop of Cin., 1944-65; aux. bishop of Cin., 1965-69; bishop of Phoenix, 1969-76; coadjutor archbishop of Miami, 1976-77; archbishop of Miami, 1977—. Office: 6301 Biscayne Blvd Miami FL 33138

MC CARTHY, EDWARD D., oil and gas exploration co. exec.; b. S.Bend, Ind., Feb. 6, 1929; s. James E. and Dorothy (Hoban) McC.; B.S., U. Notre Dame, 1950; m. Mary M. McMahon, Nov. 24, 1956; children—Michael, Maureen, Kathleen, Erin. With Mobil Oil Corp., 1953-57, Miss. River Fuel Corp., 1957-61; with La. Land and Exploration Co., New Orleans, 1961—, now sr. v.p. internat. region. Adv. bd. Hotel Dieu Hosp., New Orleans. Served with AUS, 1951-53. Mem. Nar. Assn. Indsl. and Office Parks (v.p.; spl. award), Am. Assn. Petroleum Landmen (dir.; spl. award), Petroleum Landmen's Assn. New Orleans (pres., dir.), Am. Petroleum Inst. Republican. Roman Catholic. Clubs: Metairie Country, Pickwick (New Orleans). Office: 225 Baronne St Suite 1200 New Orleans LA 70112

MC CARTHY, EDWARD JAMES (ED), publisher, writer; b. Newark, Jan. 5, 1914; s. F. Sanford and Ellen Mary (Mottley) McC.; student Essex County Jr. Coll., 1933-35; m. Virginia Patterson Drace, Sept. 19, 1943; children—Eric Drace, Sean Sanford. Reporter, feature writer N.Y. Mirror, 1937-41; mng. editor Tune In, radio mag., 1945; picture editor newspaper PM, 1946-47, Sunday editor, 1947-48; editor This Week, N.Y. Herald Tribune edit., 1949-55, asst. mng. editor nat. edit., 1955-56, mng. editor, 1956-64; founder, pub. Graphophile Assos., 1962; v.p., partner Mayo-Infurna Design, Inc., 1969-79. Served with USCGR, 1941-45; editor service mags. Author: (with Bud Finger) Little Mr. Tootle, 1937; (with Ginny McCarthy) Fruits of the Hudson Valley, 1974; contbr. to periodicals. Home and Office: 16 Hickory Hill Rd Tappan NY 10983

MC CARTHY, EUGENE JOSEPH, writer, former senator; b. Watkins, Minn., Mar. 29, 1916; s. Michael John and Anna (Baden) McC.; A.B., St. John's U., Collegeville, Minn., 1935; A.M., U. of Minn., 1939; m. Abigail Quigley, June 1945; children—Ellen, Mary, Michael, Margaret. Tchr. pub. schs., 1935-40, 45; prof. econ. edn. St. John's U., 1940-42; civilian tech. work with Mil. Intelligence Div., War Dept., 1944; instr. sociology and econs. St. Thomas Coll., St. Paul, 1946-48; mem. 81st-85th congresses from 4th Minn. dist., mem. ways and means com.; U.S. senator from Minn., 1958-70, mem. senate finance, fgn. relations and govt. ops. coms.; Adlai Stevenson prof. polit. sci. New Sch. for Social Research, 1973-74; syndicated columnist, 1977—. Roman Catholic. Author: Frontiers in American Democracy, 1960; Dictionary of American Politics, 1962; A Liberal Answer to the Conservative Challenge, 1964; The Limits of Power, 1967; The Year of the People, 1969; Other Things and The Aardvark (poetry), 1970; The Hard Years, 1975; Mr. Raccoon and His Friends, 1977; America Revisited, 1978; Ground Fog and Night (poetry), 1979; co-author: A Political Bestiary, 1978. Office: 1420 N St NW Washington DC 20005

MCCARTHY, FRANCIS JAMES, ins. co. exec.; b. N.Y.C., Aug. 8, 1918; s. Eugene T. and Louise C. (Wacker) McC.; A.B. with honors and distinction, Wesleyan U., Middletown, Conn., 1940; J.D., Yale U., 1947; grad. Nat. Jud. Coll., 1975; m. Barbara Ellen Cheney, Jan. 19, 1942; children—Morrison, Melissa. Admitted to Conn. bar, 1947; with law dept. Travelers Ins. Cos., Hartford, 1947-74; asso. firm Maxwell & Dully, Hartford, 1947-62; judge Conn. Superior Ct., 1974-76; gen. counsel Travelers Ins. Cos., 1976—; bd. dirs. Conn. Bar Found.; lectr. U. Conn. Law Sch. Chmn. Wethersfield (Conn.) Zoning Commn., 1958-59; charter mem. Capitol Region Planning Agy., 1958-60; mayor, chmn. Wethersfield Town Council, 1962-66; mem. Conn. Ho. of Reps. from 22d dist., 1967-71, chief counsel house and senate minority, 1972, majority, 1973; corporator St. Francis Hosp., Hartford. Mem. Am. Bar Assn., Assn. Life Ins. Counsel, Fedn. Ins. Counsel, Conn. Bar Assn., Hartford County Bar Assn., Sigma Chi. Republican. Club: Ocean Reef (Key Largo, Fla.). Contbr. articles to profl. jours. Home: 19 Coleman Rd Wethersfield CT 06109 Office: 1 Tower Sq Hartford CT 06115

MC CARTHY, FRANK, motion picture producer; b. Richmond, Va., June 8, 1912; s. Frank J. and Lillian (Binford) McCarthy; A.B., Va. Mil. Inst., 1933; A.M., U. Va., 1940; unmarried. Instr. and tactical officer Va. Mil. Inst., 1933-35, 36-37; reporter Richmond (Va.) News Leader, 1935-36; press agt. for theatrical prod. George Abbott, N.Y.C., 1937-39; asst. sec. state U.S. Dept. State, 1945; rep. for Motion Picture Assn. Am. in Hollywood and Europe, 1946-49; alternate del. U.N. Conf. on Freedom of Information, Geneva, 1948; exec. and producer 20th Century-Fox Studios, 1949-62, 65-72; producer Universal Studios, 1963-65, 72-77. Trustee George C. Marshall Research Found., Va. Mil. Inst. Found., Barter Theatre of Va.; mem., bd. dirs. Norton Simon Mus. Art, Los Angeles Music Center Theatre Group, Producers Guild Am., Thomas A. Dooley Found., Motion Picture and Television Fund, Motion Picture Permanent Charities Com., Served as 2d lt. field arty., res. U.S. Army, 1933, advanced through grades to brig. gen., 1957, asst. sec. War Dept. gen. staff and mil. sec. to chief staff, 1941-43, secy. of War Dept., gen. staff, 1944-45. Decorated D.S.M., Legion of Merit; officer Most Excellent Order of Brit. Empire; selected one of America's 10 outstanding young men by U.S. Jr. C. of C. for distinguished contbn. to nation's welfare during 1945; named Virginian of Yr., Va. Press Assn., 1970. Mem. Acad. Motion Picture Arts and Scis., Chevaliers du Tastevin, Council of Atlantic Union Com., U. Calif. at Los Angeles Art Council, U. So. Calif. Friends of Libraries, Va. Mil. Inst. Soc., Va. Hist. Soc. Episcopalian. Films produced include: Decision Before Dawn, Sailor of the King, A Guide for the Married Man, Patton (received Oscar for Best Picture 1970), Fireball Forward, MacArthur. Home: 1455 Seabright Pl Beverly Hills CA 90210

MC CARTHY, FRANK MARTIN, educator; b. Olean, N.Y., Aug. 27, 1924; s. Frank Michael and Joan (Quinn) McC.; B.S., U. Pitts., 1943, D.D.S., 1945, M.D., 1949; M.S. in Oral Surgery, Georgetown U., 1954; Sc.D. (hon.), St. Bonaventure U., 1956; m. Julia Richmond, Nov. 24, 1949; children—Robert Lee, Joan Lee, Med. intern Mercy Hosp., Pitts., 1949-50; practice oral surgery, Los Angeles, 1954-75; teaching fellow Georgetown U., 1952-53; research fellow NIH, 1953-54; prof. oral surgery U. So. Calif. Sch. Dentistry, 1966-75, prof., chmn. sect. anesthesia and medicine, 1975—, chmn. dept. surg. scis., 1979—, asso. dean adminstrv. affairs, 1977-79, asst. dean hosp. affairs, 1979—; dir. anesthesiology U. So. Calif. oral surgery sect. Los Angeles County Hosp., 1958—; lectr. in field; adv. panel dentistry, sect. anesthesizing agts. Nat. Fire Protection Assn., 1971-79; mem. Am. Nat. Standards Com., 1974—. Bd. councilors Sch. Dentistry, U. So. Calif., 1972-75. Served as lt., M.C., USNR, 1950-52. Fellow Internat. Assn. Oral Surgeons (founder), Am. Coll. Dentistry, Internat. Coll. Dentistry; mem. ADA, AAAS, Am. Acad. Oral Pathology, Am. Dental Soc. Anesthesiology (Heidbrink award 1977), Am. Assn. Oral-Max Surgeons (chmn. anesthesia com. 1971), So. Calif. Soc. Oral Surgeons (pres. 1974), Calif., Los Angeles County dental assns., Delta Tau Delta, Psi Omega, Phi Rho Sigma, Omicron Kappa Upsilon. Author: Emergencies in Dental Practice, 1967, rev., 1972, 79; contbr. articles to profl. publs.; cons. in field. Home: 480 S Orange Grove Blvd Apt 11 Pasadena CA 91105 Office: U So Calif Sch Dentistry 925 W 34th St Los Angeles CA 90007

MCCARTHY, HAROLD CHARLES, ins. co. exec.; b. Madelia, Minn., Dec. 5, 1926; s. Charles and Merle (Humphry) McC.; B.A., Carleton Coll., Northfield, Minn., 1950; postgrad. Butler U., Indpls.; m. Barbara Kaercher, June 24, 1949; children—David, Susan. With Federated Mut. Ins. Co., Owatonna, Minn., 1950-67; with Meridian Mut. Ins. Co., Indpls., 1967—, exec. v.p., then exec. v.p., gen. mgr., 1972-75, pres., 1975—, also dir.; dir. Meridian Life Ins. Co., Meridian Standard Ins. Co., Meridian Service Corp.; v.p., exec. com., bd. dirs. Ind. Ins. Inst.; mem. bd. All Industry Research Adv. Com.; bd. dirs. Conf. Casualty Ins. Cos.; chmn. fire and allied lines conf. Nat. Assn. Mut. Ins. Cos., 1979. Mem. Greater Indpls. Progress Com., Corp. Community Council. Served to petty officer USNR, 1944-46. Named hon. Ky. col., hon. life mem. Va. PTA. Mem. Nat. Assn. Ind. Insurers (bd. govs.), Am. Mgmt. Assn., U.S. C. of C., Ind. C. of C., Indpls. C. of C. Republican. Presbyterian. Clubs: Kiwanis, Columbia, Hillcrest Country. Office: 2955 N Meridian St Indianapolis IN 46207

MCCARTHY, JOHN EDWARD, bishop; b. Houston, June 21, 1930; s. George Gaskell and Grace Veronica (O'Brien) McC.; student St. Mary's Sem., Houston, 1949-56; M.Th., St. Thomas U., Houston, 1979. Ordained priest Roman Catholic Ch., 1956; served various Houston Cath. parishes; exec. dir. Nat. Bishops Com. for Spanish speaking, 1966-68; mem. staff Social Action Office, U.S. Cath. Conf., 1968-69; exec. dir. Tex. Cath. Conf., Houston, 1973-79; aux. bishop Diocese of Galveston-Houston, 1979—. Bd. dirs. Nat. Center for Urban Ethnic Affairs, Mexican-Am. Cultural Center, Campaign for Human Devel., St. Edwards U. Recipient First Clergyman of Year award NCCJ, 1972. Mem. Cath. Conf. for Urban Ministry. Democrat. Home and office: 1700 San Jacinto St PO Box 907 Houston TX 77001

MCCARTHY, JOHN FRANCIS, JR., aero. engr., govt. research adminstr.; b. Boston, Aug. 28, 1925; s. John Francis and Margaret Josephine (Bartwood) McC.; S.B., M.I.T., 1950, S.M. in Aero. Engring., 1951; Ph.D. in Aeros. and Physics, Calif. Inst. Tech., 1962; m. Camille Dian Martinez, May 4, 1968; children—Margaret I., Megan, Jamie M., Nicole E., John F. Supr. air/ground communications TWA, Rome, 1946-47; project mgr. aeroelastic and structures research lab. M.I.T., 1951-55, prof. aeros. and astronautics, 1971-78; ops. analyst Hdqrs. SAC, Offutt AFB, Nebr., 1955-59; dir., asst. chief engr. Apollo Space div., N.Am. Aviation, Inc., Downey, Calif., 1961-66; v.p. Los Angeles div./Space div., Rockwell Internat. Corp., 1966-71; dir. and prof. M.I.T. Center for Space Research, 1974-78; dir. NASA Lewis Research Center, Cleve., 1978—; mem. Internat. Council Aero. Scis., Koln, Germany, 1978—; mem. USAF Sci. Adv. Bd., Washington, 1970—; mem. sci. adv. group Joint Chiefs of Staff, Joint Strategic Target Planning Staff, Offutt AFB, 1976—; com. mem. Energy Engring. Bd., Assembly Engring., NRC, 1979; cons. in field. Campaign chmn. Downey Community Hosp., 1968-69; bd. govs. Nat. Space Club, Washington, 1978—; vice chmn. Fed. Exec. Bd., Cleve., 1979—. Served with USAAF, 1944-46. Recipient Apollo Achievement award NASA, 1969, Meritorious Civilian Service medal USAF, 1973, Exceptional Civilian Service medal, 1978. Fellow AIAA (dir. 1975-76); asso. fellow Royal Aero. Soc. (London); mem. Am. Soc. Engring. Edn. (exec. com. aerospace div. 1969-72), Sigma Xi, Sigma Gamma Tau. Unitarian. Clubs: Cosmos. Author numerous tech. reports; patentee impact landing system. Home: 18819 Canyon Rd Fairview Park OH 44126 Office: NASA Lewis Research Center Cleveland OH 44135. *Success is hard work and the guts to change careers when the going gets too easy.*

MCCARTHY, JOHN JOSEPH, newspaper exec.; b. N.Y.C., June 24, 1920; s. Jerry and Helen (Duffy) McC.; B.B.A., St. John's U., 1947, J.D., 1951; m. Leona Mary Hart, May 25, 1947; children—John, Mary Ellen, Robert Emmett, Eileen, Doreen, Terrence, Kathleen, Daniel, Elizabeth Ann. With Dow Jones & Co., Inc., 1946—, bus. mgr., 1963-65, treas., 1965-70, v.p. finance, 1970—, v.p. adminstrn., 1977—. Admitted to N.Y. State bar, 1952. Served with USAAF, 1941-45; ETO. Decorated Bronze Star. Mem. Delta Psi Upsilon. Home: 211 N Union Ave Cranford NJ 07016 Office: PO Box 300 Princeton NJ 08540

MC CARTHY, JOHN MICHAEL, investment co. exec.; b. Bklyn., Apr. 9, 1927; s. Michael Francis and Catherine (McCarthy) McC.; B.A., St. Francis Coll., 1951; M.B.A., N.Y. U., 1953; m. Mary Agnes Hickey, Sept. 8, 1951; children—Stephen J., Neil M., Tara Anne, Laurette E. Sr. research officer trust dept. Citibank, N.Y.C., 1951-59; sr. research analyst, then dir. research Lord Abbett & Co., N.Y.C., 1960-72, partner, 1972—; v.p., portfolio mgr., then exec. v.p. Affiliated Fund Inc., N.Y.C., 1972-77, pres., dir., 1977—; dir. Lord Abbett Bond Debenture Fund, Lord Abbett Developing Growth Fund, Lord Abbett Income Fund. Served with USAAF, 1945-47. Recipient Paper award Investment Bankers Assn., 1962, 63. Mem. N.Y. Soc. Security Analysts, Elec. and Electronic Analysts Group N.Y.C. (past pres.), Hist. Soc. Garden City. Republican. Roman Catholic. Clubs: Recess (N.Y.C.); Cherry Valley (Garden City). Home: 69 1st St Garden City NY 11530 Office: 63 Wall St New York NY 10005

MC CARTHY, JOHN ROBERT, health care adminstr., former fgn. service officer; b. N.Y.C., Mar. 27, 1923; s. James Anthony and Gertrude Madeline (Casey) McC.; A.B. with honors, Holy Cross Coll., 1943; m. Helen Ruth House, Aug. 16, 1950; children—William, Anne, Elizabeth, Christopher, Margaret, John, Michael. Free-lance writer, 1946-50; joined U.S. Fgn. Service, 1951; fgn. service information officer USIA, Paris, and Lyon, France, 1951-55, Bonn, Germany, 1956-58, Berlin, Germany, 1958-60, Washington, 1960-63, Beirut, Lebanon, 1963-64, Damascus, Syria, 1964-66, Karachi, Pakistan, 1966-71, Rabat, Morocco, 1971-73, Washington, 1973-78; adminstrv. resident N.H. Hosp. Assn., Concord, 1978—. Served with USAAF, 1943-46. Inst. Current World Affairs fellow, 1948-51. Mem. Fgn. Service Assn., Delta Epsilon Sigma, Alpha Sigma Nu. Roman Catholic. Clubs: Karachi Yacht; Skowhegan Country. Home: 22 Pine St Peterborough NH 03458 Office: 12 Loudon Rd Peterborough NH 03301. *The most precious of skills is the ability to match what is pragmatically right, i.e. that which works, with what is morally right, i.e. that which suits man's nature in God's world. To be neither ruthless nor polyannish—and these extremes have been about equally counter-productive in human history—is rare. Allende was as unhelpful as Duvalier, and the preacher often wastes our time as effectively as the militarist. What we need above all is the flair to recognize a 50-50 combination.*

MCCARTHY, JOSEPH WALTON, hotel exec.; b. Boston, Apr. 30, 1932; s. William Leo and Anna Gertrude (O'Donnell) McC.; B.S. in Econs., Boston Coll., 1958; m. Gloria Ann Klemm, June 20, 1973; 1 dau., Jennifer A. Gen. mgr. Roosevelt Hotel, N.Y.C.; sr. v.p., dir. sales Sheraton Corp., ITT, later sr. v.p., dir. ops. N.Am., now pres., chief exec. officer Quality Inns of Am., Silver Spring, Md. Served with USAF. Office: Quality Inns of Am 10750 Columbia Pike Silver Spring MD 20901

MCCARTHY, JOSEPH WESTON, editor and writer; b. Cambridge, Mass., Mar. 6, 1915; s. Dennis Francis and Elizabeth (Doyle) McC.; A.B., Boston Coll., 1939; m. Mary Dunn, Dec. 21, 1941; children—Susan (Mrs. Michael Todd, Jr.), Elizabeth Doyle (Mrs. John Huckel), Dennis, Mary Dunn (Mrs. Richard Giza). Sports writer and reporter Boston Post, 1936-39; radio and publicity writer, Boston, 1940-41; in mil. service, 1941-45; pvt., 97th F.A. Bn. (pack), U.S. Army, 1941-42, promoted staff sgt., tech. sgt., master sgt.; sports editor, Yank, Army weekly, 1942, mng. editor, 1942-45; on editorial staff Cosmopolitan mag., 1946-48; now free lance writer. Decorated Legion of Merit. Roman Catholic. Democrat. Author: The Remarkable Kennedys, 1960; In One Ear, 1962; Ireland, 1964; New England, 1967; Hurricane, 1969; (with Kenneth P. O'Donnell, David F. Powers) "Johnny, We Hardly Knew Ye", Memories of John Fitzgerald Kennedy, 1972. Editor: Fred Allen's Letters, 1965. Contbr. to nat. mags. Address: Blue Point NY 11715

MC CARTHY, KATHRYN AGNES, univ. adminstr., physicist; b. Lawrence, Mass., Aug. 7, 1924; d. Joseph Augustine and Catherine (Barrett) McCarthy; A.B., Tufts U., 1945, M.S., 1946; Ph.D., Radcliffe Coll., 1957. Instr. physics Tufts U., 1946-53, asst. prof., 1953-59, asso. prof., 1959-62, prof., 1962—, dean Grad. Sch., 1969-74, provost, sr. v.p., 1973-79. research fellow in metallurgy Harvard, 1957-59, vis. scholar, 1979-80; research asso. Baird Assos., 1947-49, 51, Boston U. Optical Research Lab., summer 1952; asso. research engr. U. Mich., summer 1957-58; dir. Mass. Electric Co., State Mut. Assurance Co. Trustee Southeastern Mass. U., 1972-74, Merrimack Coll., 1974—; corporator Lawrence Meml. Hosp., 1975—, dir., 1978—. Fellow Optical Soc. Am., Am. Phys. Soc.; mem. Soc. Women Engrs. (sr.), Phi Beta Kappa, Sigma Xi. Home: Box 905 East Orleans MA 02643 Office: Dept Physics Tufts U Medford MA 02155

MC CARTHY, MARY, author; b. Seattle, June 21, 1912; d. Roy Winfield and Therese (Preston) McC.; A.B., Vassar Coll., 1933; 1 son, Reuel K. Wilson; m. James Raymond West, Apr. 15, 1961. Editor Covici Friede, 1936-37; editor Partisan Rev., 1937-38, drama critic, 1937-48; instr. lit. Bard Coll., 1945-46; instr. English, Sarah Lawrence Coll., 1948. Guggenheim fellow, 1949-50; recipient Horizon prize, 1949; Nat. Inst. grantee, 1957; Guggenheim fellow, 1959-60. Mem. Nat. Inst. Arts and Letters, Phi Beta Kappa. Author: The Company She Keeps, 1942; The Oasis, 1949; Cast a Cold Eye, 1950; The Groves of Academe, 1952; A Charmed Life, 1955; Sights and Spectacles, 1956; Venice Observed, 1956; Memories of a Catholic Girlhood, 1957; The Stones of Florence, 1959; On the Contrary, 1961; The Group, 1963; Mary McCarthy's Theatre Chronicles, 1963; Vietnam, 1967; Hanoi, 1968; The Writing on the Wall, 1970; Birds of America, 1971; Medina, 1972; The Seventeenth Degree, 1974; The Mask of State, 1974; Cannibals and Missionaries, 1979. Contbr. articles to nat. mags. Address: Castine ME 04421

MCCARTHY, MARY FRANCES, nun, coll. pres.; b. Springfield, Mass., July 25, 1916; d. Charles James and Elizabeth Agnes (Weeks) McCarthy; B.A., Trinity Coll., Washington, 1937; M.A., Catholic U. Am., 1938; Ph.D., Johns Hopkins, 1961. Joined Sisters of Notre Dame de Namur, 1938; tchr. high schs. Archdiocese Phila., 1941-56; instr. English, Trinity Coll., Washington, 1957-59, asst. prof. German and Russian, 1960-62, asso. prof., 1962-65, prof., 1965-75; pres. Emmanuel Coll., Boston, 1975—. Mem. nat. screening com. Fulbright-Hays awards to Germany, 1971, 72, 73, chmn. com., 1972, 73. Bd. trustees Trinity Coll., Washington, 1965-68. NDEA fellow, 1959, Fulbright Travel fellow Deutscher Akademischer Austauschdienst, 1959-60, Nat. Endowment for Humanities sr. fellow 1972-73. Mem. Modern Lang. Assn., Mediaeval Acad. Am., AAUW, Am. Council Edn., Assn. Am. Colls., Assn. Independent Colls. and Univs. in Mass. Translator: On Modern German Literature, 4 vols., 1970-77. Contbr. articles to profl. jours. Address: Emmanuel College 400 The Fenway Boston MA 02115*

MC CARTHY, PATRICK EDWARD, univ. chancellor; b. Rumford, Maine, July 23, 1930; s. John W. and Margaret C. (Whalen) McC.; student Dartmouth Coll., 1951-53, U. Maine, 1954-57, Boston U., 1957; M.City and Regional Planning, Harvard U., 1960; H.H.D. (hon.), Stonehill Coll., North Easton, Mass., 1972; m. Norma Joan Leary, Dec. 2, 1956; children—Sean W., Megan E., Cait S., Hannah R., Patrick E. Planner, San Diego, 1960, City of San Leandro, Calif., 1960-61; urban renewal project dir. Boston Redevel. Authority, 1961-63; exec. dir., sec. Worcester (Mass.) Redevel. Authority, 1963-64; UN chief adviser to Govt. Ireland, 1964-67; dir. adminstrn. Mass. Bd. Higher Edn., 1967-69, dep. chancellor, then chancellor, 1969-75; chancellor U. Maine, 1975—; mem. Maine Postsecondary Edn. Commn., 1975—, Mass. Exec. Com. Ednl. TV, 1973-77; trustee Stonehill Coll., 1972—; guest lectr., cons. in field. Trustee Washingtonian Center Addictions, 1972-76, mem. corp., 1976—. Served with USMCR, 1947-50. Mem. Am. Assn. Higher Edn., Assn. Am. State Colls. and Univs., Edn. Commn. States, Am. Inst. Planners, Acad. Polit. Sci., State Higher Edn. Exec. Officers Assn., New Eng. Bd. Higher Edn., Christmas Cove Improvement Assn. (v.p. 1972-76, commodore 1973-76). Club: Harvard (Boston). Contbr. profl. publs. Home: 43 Highland Ave Bangor ME 04401 Office: 107 Maine Ave Bangor ME 04401

MCCARTHY, ROBERT VINCENT, coll. adminstr.; b. Worcester, Mass., Apr. 5, 1921; s. Thomas H. and Margaret (McDonnell) McC.; B.A., Coll. Holy Cross, 1943; M.A., Clark U., 1948; Ph.D., U. Ottawa (Can.), 1955; m. Mary C. Carroll, Jan. 12, 1946. Instr. English, Assumption Prep Sch., Worcester, 1946-48; tchr., coach Chester (Conn.) High Sch., 1948-50; asso. dir. guidance, instr. King's Coll., Wilkes-Barre, Pa., 1950-51; guidance counselor Worcester pub. schs., 1951-54; mem. faculty Seton Hill Coll., Grennsburg, Pa., 1955-65, prof. edn., 1960-65, chmn. dept. edn., 1955-65; prof. secondary edn. Boston State Coll., 1965—, dean undergrad. studies, 1969—, acting pres., 1970-71, dean of coll., 1971—, exec. v.p., 1973—. Mem. Gov.'s Com. on Edn., Pa., 1958-60, Adv. Com. to Office Program Devel., Boston pub. schs., 1968-69; mem. Mass. State Transfer Rev. Council, 1971-73; mem. program adv. com. Mass. State Bd. Higher Edn., 1972-74, chmn., 1973-74; mem. Commn. Instns. Higher Edn., New Eng. Assn. Schs. and Colls., 1976-79. Served with AUS, 1943-45. Mem. Mass. Schoolmasters' (Boston), Am. Legion, Phi Eta Sigma. Home: 44 Hazelton Av Needham MA 02192 Office: 625 Huntington Av Boston MA 02115

MC CARTHY, STEPHEN ANTHONY, cons., librarian; b. Eden Valley, Minn., Oct. 7, 1908; s. Stephen Joseph and Mary Agnes (Graham) McC.; B.A., Gonzaga U., 1929. M.A., 1930; B.L.S., McGill U., 1932; Ph.D., U. Chgo., 1941; Litt.D., McGill U., 1969; m. Mary Louise Wedemeyer, Aug. 27, 1936 (dec. June 1971); children—Stephen Graham, Louise Bert (Mrs. Xerxes J. Mehta), Kathleen Marie, David John (dec. Apr. 1970); m. 2d, Dorothy E. Ryan, July 8, 1972 (dec. July 1979). Tchr., Gonzaga High Sch., Spokane, Wash., 1929-31; asst. librarian and cataloger St. John's U., Collegeville, Minn., 1933-34; reference asst. Chicago Am., 1934-35; librarian Univ. Coll., Northwestern U., Chgo., 1935-37; asst. dir. libraries U. Nebr., 1937-41, asso. dir., 1941-42; dir., 1942-44; asst. dir. Libraries Columbia U., 1944-46; dir. Cornell U. Library, 1946-67, dir. libraries, 1960-67; exec. sec. Assn. Research Libraries, Washington, 1960-62, exec. dir., 1967-74; Fulbright lectr. in Egypt, 1953-54, Inst. U.S. Studies, U. London, 1967; vis. prof. U. Ill. Library Sch., summer 1943. Condr. surveys univ. libraries; library bldg. cons. Recipient Cornell medal, 1967. Mem. A.L.A., Assn. Coll. and Reference Libraries (chmn. univ. libraries 1948-49), Neb. Library Assn. (pres. 1940), N.Y. Library Assn. (pres. 1951-52), Phi Beta Kappa (hon.). Democrat. Roman Catholic. Clubs: Cornell (N.Y.); Cosmos (Washington). Home: 1514 Knollwood Rd Annapolis MD 21401

MCCARTHY, THOMAS K., mfg. co. exec.; b. 1909; A.B., U. Calif., 1931, LL.B., 1934; married. Admitted to bar; with firm Thelen, Marrin, Johnson & Bridges, 1941-57; v.p., dir. Kaiser Aluminum & Chem. Corp., 1957-74, sec., 1970-73, dir., to 1979; dir. Sempervirens Fund. Address: Santa Cruz CA 95062

MC CARTHY, THOMAS PATRICK, magazine publisher; b. Elizabeth, N.J., Mar. 17, 1928; s. Thomas Joseph and Genevieve Elizabeth (Duffy) McC.; B.A., Seton Hall U., East Orange, N.J., 1955; m. Joan Ellen Bodet, Jan. 16, 1954; children—Kathleen E., Patricia E., Thomas Patrick. Salesman, Joseph Davis Plastics Co., Kearney, N.J., 1955-57; nat. accounts mgr. ESB Corp., N.Y.C., 1957-65, Bekins Van & Storage Co., N.Y.C., 1965-67; nat. sales mgr. Traffic Mgmt. mag., N.Y.C., 1967-74, pub., Boston, 1974—. Served with AUS, 1950-53. Mem. Bus. Publ. Advt. Assn., Assn. R.R. Advt. Mgrs., Assn. Am. Port Authorities, Materials Handling Inst., Pvt. Truck Council. Roman Catholic. Clubs: Lions, K.C. Home: 57 Salt Meadow Way Marshfield MA 02050 Office: 221 Columbus Ave Boston MA 02116

MC CARTIN, THOMAS RONALD, newspaper pub. co. exec.; b. Jersey City, June 15, 1934; s. James A. and Margaret V. (Kelly) McC.; student Glendale Jr. Coll., 1955-56, UCLA, 1959-60; m. Ann Daley, Feb. 8, 1958; children—Margaret, Maureen, Michele, Michael, Matthew. Asst. dir. advt. Los Angeles Times, 1959-74; v.p. sales Washington Post, 1974-76; exec. v.p. Dallas Times Herald, 1975—. Trustee, Marymount Coll.; mem. exec. com. Center Mktg. and Design, North Tex. State U.; mem. adv. council Coll. Communication, U. Tex.; bd. dirs. McCartin Scholarship; vice chmn. Dallas Cultural Com.; mem. internat. bd. dirs. Up with People; mem. allocation com. United Way, Dallas; bd. dirs. North Tex. Commn., Internat. Irish Cultural Inst., St. Thomas Coll., St. Paul, St. Paul Hosp. Found., Dallas; mem. adv. bd. dirs. Salvation Army, Dallas, Goodwill Industries, Dallas; mem. cultural com. Goals for Dallas; trustee Dallas Museum Fine Arts; bd. dirs., mem. exec. com., v.p. TACA; bd. dirs., chmn. mktg. Dallas Symphony Orch.; bd. dirs. exec. com. Dallas Civic Opera; mem. Tex. Bus. Com. for Arts; bd. dirs. Shakespearean, Dallas; pres. Palos Verdes Peninsula (Calif.) Adv. Council, 1971-73. Served with USN, 1951-55. Recipient cert. and key of appreciation City of Los Angeles, 1973, The First Proclamation, City of Rancho Palos Verdes, 1974. Mem. Met. Sunday Newspapers (dir.), Newspaper Advt. Bur., Am. Assn. Newspaper Reps. (v.p. 1964-65), Navy League (dir. Dallas/Ft. Worth chpt.). Roman Catholic. Clubs: Congressional Country, Capitol Yacht, Nat. Press (Washington); Chaparral, City, Bent Tree Country, Dallas Press (Dallas). Home: 5114 Yolanda Dallas TX 75229 Office: 1101 Pacific Dallas TX 75202

MCCARTNEY, CHARLES PRICE, obstetrician and gynecologist; b. Barnesville, Ohio, Aug. 14, 1912; s. Jesse Thomas and Carrie (Price) McC.; B.S., U. Chgo., 1942, M.D., 1943; m. Phyllis Helen Graybill, Sept. 27, 1940; children—Marilyn B., Anne E. Intern U. Chgo. Clinics, 1943-44, resident, 1947-50; mem. faculty U. Chgo. Med. Sch., 1950-71, prof. obstetrics and gynecology, 1960-71, Mary Campeau Ryerson prof., 1967-71; clin. prof. obstetrics and gynecology U. Ill., 1971—; attending gynecologist and obstetrician Chgo. Lying-In Hosp., 1950—. Mem. Cook County Com. Maternal Welfare, 1965—. Served to maj., M.C., AUS, 1944-46. Diplomate Am. Bd. Obstetricians and Gynecologists. Fellow Am. Gynecol. Soc.; mem. Chgo. Gynecol. Soc. (pres. 1967), Chgo. Med. Soc. (councillor 1960—, pres. 1973, chmn. bd. trustees 1973), Am. Coll. Obstetricians and Gynecologists (chmn. Ill. sect. 1965—), Central Assn. Obstetricians and Gynecologists. Home: 12412 S 74th Ave Palos Heights IL 60463 Office: 5841 S Maryland Ave Chicago IL 60637

MCCARTNEY, JAMES PAUL, musician; b. Liverpool, Eng., June 18, 1942; s. James and Mary Patricia (Mohin) McC.; m. Linda Eastman, Mar. 12, 1969; 4 children. With John Lennon and George Harrison in groups Quarrymen, Moondogs, Silver Beatles, 1956-62, also with Ringo Starr in group The Beatles, 1962-70; solo performer and with group Wings, 1970—; film appearances include: A Hard Day's Night, 1964, Help!, 1965, How I Won the War, 1967, Let It Be, 1970; TV appearances include: Magical Mystery Tour, 1967, James Paul McCartney, 1973, Wings Over the World, 1979; producer animated film The Oriental Nightfish, 1978; composer numerous songs, including Yesterday, Michelle, Hey Jude, And I Love Her, Eleanor Rigby, Live and Let Die; albums include: McCartney, 1970, Ram, 1971, Red Rose Speedway, 1973, Band on the Run, 1973, Venus and Mars, 1975, Wings Over America, 1975, Wings at the Speed of Sound, 1976, London Town, 1978; Decorated Order of Brit. Empire, 1965; Acad. award (with Beatles) for Best Original Song Score, Let It Be, 1970; 5 Grammy awards with Beatles, 2 solo, 1 with Wings. Office: care MPL Communications 1 Soho Sq London W1V 6BQ England

MC CARTNEY, KENNETH HALL, coll. dean, economist; b. Winnipeg, Man., Can., Aug. 28, 1924; s. Robert and Mabel (Hall) McC.; B.A., U. Man., 1945; M.A., U. Minn., 1949, Ph.D., 1959; M.S.W. (hon.), Smith Coll., 1973; m. June Lois Palmer, Mar. 20, 1951; children—Kevin Hall, Brian Palmer. Came to U.S., 1947, naturalized, 1965. Instr., United Coll., Winnipeg, 1945-47; instr. U. Minn., 1947-51, 1952-54; spl. lectr. McMaster U., Hamilton, Ont., Can., 1951-52; asst. prof. Smith Coll., Northampton, Mass., 1954-60, asso. prof., 1960-64, prof., 1964—, dean of faculty, 1978—, acting dean Sch. Social Work, 1971-72, dean, 1972-76; vis. prof. Atlanta U. Center, 1968-69. Home: 15 Woodlawn Rd Hadley MA 01035 Office: Wright Hall Smith Coll Northampton MA 01063

MC CARTNEY, ROBERT CHARLES, lawyer; b. Pitts., May 3, 1934; s. Nathaniel Hugh and Esther Mary (Smith) McC.; A.B., Princeton U., 1956; J.D. (Princeton fellow), Harvard U., 1959; m. Janet Carolyn Moore, June 16, 1956; children—Ronald K., Sharon S., Carole J. Admitted to D.C. bar, 1959, Pa. bar, 1960; asso. firm Eckert, Seamans, Cherin & Mellott, Pitts., 1959-64, partner, 1965—; sec., gen. counsel Ryan Homes, Inc.; dir., sec., gen. counsel Washington Trotting Assn., Inc., Mountain Laurel Racing, Inc.; sec., gen. counsel Edn. Mgmt., Inc.; dir., v.p., sec., gen. counsel Holleran Services, Inc. Dir., United Methodist Found. of W. Pa., 1972-78; solicitor N.Pitts. Community Devel. Corp., 1968-76, alt. dir., 1968—; mem. McCandless Twp. Govt. Study Commn., 1973-74; solicitor

McCandless Indsl. Devel. Authority, 1972—; mem. exec. com. Princeton U. Alumni Council, 1966-70, 76—; trustee, mem. exec. com. Etterbein Coll., 1975—; corp. bd. North Hills Passavant Hosp., 1976—; bd. mgmt. North Hills YMCA, 1979—. Mem. Am., Pa., Allegheny County bar assns., Princeton U. Alumni Assn. of W.Pa. (pres. 1976-78), Golden Triangle YMCA. Republican. Clubs: Harvard-Yale-Princeton, Downtown (Pitts.); Allegheny. Home: 9843 Woodland Rd N Pittsburgh PA 15237 Office: 42d Floor US Steel Bldg 600 Grant St Pittsburgh PA 15219

MCCARTY, A. CLEVE, chem. co. exec.; b. Ark., May 1, 1925; s. Jesse L. and Alice Maye (Martindale) McC.; student Ark. Inst. Tech.; B.S., U. Ark.; m. Freddie Joan Campbell, Jan. 25, 1947; children—Peggy Joan, Michiel Cleve. County agt. U. Mo., 1954-55; mgr. fertilizers dept. Consumers Coop. Assn., 1955-60; v.p. Nat. Phosphate Corp., 1960-65, Woodward & Dickerson, 1966-71; exec. v.p., vice chmn. bd. Beker Industries Corp., Greenwich, Conn., 1971—. Bd. dirs. Fertilizer Inst., Washington. Served with U.S. Army, 1943-46, Res., 1946-51. Home: Meads Point Greenwich CT 06830 Office: 124 W Putnam Ave Greenwich CT 06830

MCCARTY, BRUCE, architect; b. South Bend, Ind., Dec. 28, 1920; s. Earl Hauser and Hazel (Beagle) McC.; B.A., Princeton, 1944; B.Arch., U. Mich., 1949; m. Julia Elizabeth Hayes, Apr. 5, 1945; children—Bruce Hayes, Douglas Hayes, Sarah Elizabeth. Partner Painter, Weeks & McCarty, 1955-65, Bruce McCarty & Assos., 1965-70; pres. McCarty Bullock Holsaple, Architects, Planners, Engrs., Inc., Knoxville, Tenn., 1970—; works include residential, pub. and instnl. architecture. Mem. Knox County Met. Planning Commn., 1967-72; exec. architect planner Energy Expo 82, 1976. Trustee Dulin Gallery of Art, 1969-74; dir. East Tenn. Community Design Center; mem. Knoxville Beautification Bd., 1978—. Served to 2d lt. USAAF, 1942-45. Recipient AIA EFL 1st honor for Humanities Bldg. U. Tenn.; Prestressed Concrete Inst. award for Mountain View Parking Garages; AIA regional awards for Humanities Bldg. Clarence Brown Theatre, Townview Terrace Housing, and U. Tenn. Pedestrian Bridge; AIA Competition winner for U. Tenn. Art and Architecture Bldg., 1975. Fellow AIA; mem. Tenn. Soc. Architects (pres. 1972), Knoxville C. of C. (dir. 1965-69). Presbyn. (elder). Home: Lyons Bend Rd Knoxville TN 37919 Office: 2 Northshore Center 1111 Northshore Dr Knoxville TN 37919

MCCARTY, CHESTER EARL, lawyer, ret. air force officer; b. Pendleton, Oreg., Dec. 31, 1905; s. Albert Guy and Nancy Elizabeth (Odom) McC.; J.D., Northwestern Coll. of Law (Portland, Oreg.), 1929; student at George Washington University, 1952; m. Julia Caroline Gromoff, July 17, 1926. Admitted to Oreg. bar, 1928, since practiced in Portland, sr. mem. firm McCarty, Swindells & Nelson and predecessor firms, 1929-77; of counsel firm Pattullo, Gleason, Scarborough, Trammell & Hannon, 1977—; legal adviser to Gov. of Oreg., 1931-33; spl. asst. atty. gen., Oreg., 1931-36, chmn. Republican Central Com., Multnomah County, Oreg., 1934-36; elected state senator, 1943, declined to serve due to mil. service. Served as col. A.C., U.S. Army, 1942-46; commr. Port of Portland (Oreg.), 1950-54; brig. gen. USAF, 1951-52, maj. gen., 1953; comdr. 403d Troop Carrier Wing, 1951-52, 315th Air Div. (combat cargo), also Korean Airlift, 1952-54; comdr. 18th Air Force, 1954-57, 12th Air Force, 1957-59, 14th Air Force, 1959-60; pilot first USAF aircraft flown over South Pole, 1956; asst. chief staff Reserve Forces, USAF, 1960-63; chief staff U.S. Air Forces in Europe, 1963-66, ret. as maj. gen. Trustee Lewis and Clark Coll., Northwestern Sch. Law, Air Force Hist. Soc. Decorated D.S.M., Legion of Merit with oak leaf cluster, D.F.C., Distinguished Marksman's Medal, Bronze Star, Air Medal with 4 oak leaf clusters; hon. pilot French, Thailand and Chinese Air Forces; French Fgn. Legion (hon.); Order of Cloud and Banner (China); comdr. Quissam Alouite Cherifien (Morocco); comdr. Nicham-Iftikhar (Tunis); Order of Crown (Thailand); Order of Taiguk, Presdl. Citation (Korea); Citation and medal for distinguished acts (Kingdom of Greece); hon. comdr. of mil. div. Most Execllent Order Brit. Empire. Permanent mem. Jud. Conf. 4th U.S. Circuit. Mem. Air Res. Assn. (nat. pres. 1947-48), Am., Fed. (Oreg. pres. 1977-78), Oreg. bar assns., Res. Officers Assn. (life), Nat. Rifle Assn. (life), Air Force Assn. (life), Izaak Walton League Am. (life), Lang Syne Soc. (pres. 1971), Explorers Club, Am. Rod and Gun Clubs of Europe (hon. v.p.), Mil. Order World Wars (life), Am. Legion, Order Daedalians (life), Delta Theta Phi (life). Clubs: Mason (32 deg.), Shriners, Jesters, Rotary, Arlington, Waverley Country, University (hon. life mem.), Multnomah Athletic (Portland); Ends of Earth; OX5 Aviation Pioneers; Prince Albert (Brussels, Belgium). Home: 2323 SW Park Pl Portland OR 97205 Office: 710 SW 3d Ave Portland OR 97204

MC CARTY, DANIEL JOHN, physician, educator; b. Phila., Oct. 31, 1928; s. Daniel John and Margaret M. (Gallagher) McC.; B.S., Villanova U., 1950; M.D., U. Pa., 1954; m. Constance Helen Paakh, Aug. 28, 1954; children—Constance E., Claire L., Margaret H., Daniel John IV, Brian A. Intern Fitzgerald-Mercy Hosp., Darby, Pa., 1954-55; resident U. Pa. Hosp., 1957-58, fellow in rheumatology, 1959-60; resident VA Hosp., Phila., 1958-59; asst. prof., head sect. rheumatology, dir. arthritis tng. program Hahnemann Med. Coll. Hosp., 1960, cons., 1960-67, asso. prof. medicine, 1963-67; practice medicine, specializing in rheumatology, Phila., 1960-67, Chgo., 1967-74, Milw., 1974—; past sr. attending Phila. Gen. Hosp.; now chief medicine Milwaukee County Gen. Hosp.; prof. medicine, head sect. arthritis and metabolism, dir. arthritis tng. program U. Chgo., 1967-74; prof., chmn. dept. medicine Med. Coll. Wis., Milw., 1974—; cons. Parke Davis Labs., 1967; cons. arthritis tng. program Surgeon Gen. USPHS, 1967-71; chmn. rheumatology program adv. com. VA Central Office. Mem. med. adv. com. Eastern Pa. chpt. Arthritis Found., 1960-67, mem. fellowship com., 1968-74, exec. com., bd. dirs. Wis. chpt., 1974—, nat. bd. dirs., 1974—, mem. ho. of dels., 1974, chmn. research com., 1976-78; bd. dirs. Wis. Lupus Erythematosus Found., 1974-76. Served with AUS, 1955-57. Recipient Gairdner Found. Internat. award, 1965; Hektoen Silver medal AMA, 1964; Russell Cecil award Nat. Arthritis Found., 1965; Sigmundus Albicus Gold medal Czech Rheumatism Assn., 1969. Diplomate Am. Bd. Internal Medicine (mem. rheumatology splty. bd. subcom. 1970-76). Fellow A.C.P.; mem. Am. Rheumatism Assn. (pres. 1979-80), Am. Soc. Clin. Investigation, Central Soc. for Clin. Research, Midwest Joint Club, Central Research Club (v.p. 1972-73), Coll. Physicians Phila., Am. Soc. Pharmacology and Exptl. Therapeutics, N.Y. Acad. Scis., Am. Fedn. Clin. Research, AAAS, Assn. Am. Med. Colls., Assn. Am. Physicians, Chgo. (med. and sci. com.), Central, Czechoslovakian (hon.), Italian, Brazilian (hon.) rheumatism socs. Editor in chief Arthritis and Rheumatism, 1965-70; asso. editor Arthritis and Allied Conditions, 1971, editor-in-chief 9th edit., 1977. Home: 29919 Woodfield Ct Hartland WI 53029 Office: Dept Medicine Med Coll Wis Milwaukee County Gen Hosp 8700 W Wisconsin Ave Milwaukee WI 53226

MCCARTY, DONALD JAMES, educator; b. Ulster, Pa., July 17, 1921; s. James Leonard and Louise (Golden) McC.; B.S. cum laude, Columbia, 1949, M.A., Tchrs. Coll., 1950; Ph.D., U. Chgo., 1959; m. Mary Elizabeth Donahue, Aug. 23, 1951; children—Mary Louise, Donald James, Kevin, Maureen. Jr. high sch. tchr., Brookings, S.D., 1950-51; sr. high sch. tchr., Toms River, N.J., 1951- 52, Brookings, 1952-53; supt. schs., Colman, S.D., 1953-56; staff asso. U. Chgo., 1956-59; prof. ednl. adminstrn. Cornell U., Ithaca, N.Y., 1959-66; dean U. Wis. Sch. Edn., Madison, 1966-75, prof. ednl. adminstrn., 1975—. Served to maj. USAAF, 1939-46. Mem. Am. Ednl. Research Assn., Assn. Higher Edn. Author: (with Charles E. Ramsey) The School Managers: Power and Conflict in American Public Education, 1971; The Dilemma of the Deanship, 1978; also articles. Editor: New Perspectives on Teacher Education. Home: 2926 Harvard Dr Madison WI 53705

MCCARTY, KENNETH SCOTT, biochemist; b. Dallas, June 20, 1922; s. Justin Scott and Louisa L. (Kremp) McC.; B.S. in Chemistry, Georgetown U., 1944; Ph.D. in Biochemistry, Columbia Coll. Physicians and Surgeons, 1958; m. Marketa Regan, Nov. 27, 1944; children—Kristine McCarty Hammatt, Kenneth Scott. Research biochemist FDA, 1944-45; 1st asst. to dir. cancer research Lillia Babbit Hyde Found., N.Y., 1945-52; cons. electron microscopist VA Hosp., N.Y.C., 1949-54; sr. staff mem. tissue culture, Cooperstown, N.Y., 1954; instr. biochemistry Columbia Coll. Physicians and Surgeons, 1957-59; asso. prof. biochemistry Duke U., 1959-68, prof. biochemistry, 1968—, dir. grad. studies, 1967—; cons. cancer research; adv. panel NASA Skylab. Mem. Soc. Exptl. Biology and Medicine, N.Y. Soc. Electron Microscopists, Am. Soc. Biol. Chemists, Electron Microscope Soc. Am., N.Y. Acad. Sci., Am. Assn. Cancer Research, AAAS, Tissue Culture Assn., Biol. Photography Assn., Am. Soc. Cell Biology, Enzyme Club Duke, Société de Chimie Industrielle, Harvey Soc., Sigma Xi, Phi Lambda Upsilon. Contbr. articles to profl. jours. Home: 2713 Dogwood Rd Durham NC 27706

MCCARTY, MACLYN, med. scientist; b. South Bend, Ind., June 9, 1911; s. Earl Hauser and Hazel Dell (Beagle) McC.; A.B., Stanford, 1933; M.D., Johns Hopkins, 1937; Sc.D., Columbia, 1976, U. Fla., 1977; m. Anita Alleyne Davies, June 20, 1934 (div. 1966); children—Maclyn, Richard E., Dale, Colin; m. 2d, Marjorie Steiner, Sept. 3, 1966. House officer, asst. resident physician Johns Hopkins Hosp., 1937-40; asso. Rockefeller Inst., 1946-48, asso. mem., 1948-50, mem., 1950—, prof., 1957—, v.p., 1965-78, phys. in chief to hosp., 1961-74; research in streptococcal disease and rheumatic fever. Cons. USPHS, NIH. Mem. distbn. com. N.Y. Community Trust, 1966-74; chmn. Health Research Council City N.Y., 1972-75. Mem. bd. trustees Helen Hay Whitney Found. Served with Naval Med. Research Unit, Rockefeller Hosp., USNR, 1942-46. Fellow medicine N.Y. U. Coll. Medicine, 1940-41; NRC fellow med. scis. Rockefeller Inst., 1941-42. Recipient Eli Lilly award in bacteriology and immunology, 1946, 1st Waterford Biomed. Research award, 1977. Mem. Am. Soc. for Clin. Investigation, Am. Assn. Immunologists, Soc. Am. Bacteriologists, Soc. for Exptl. Biology and Medicine (pres. 1973-75), Harvey Soc. (sec. 1947-50, pres. 1971-72), N.Y. Acad. Medicine, Assn. Am. Physicians, Nat. Acad. Scis., Am. Acad. Arts and Scis., N.Y. Heart Assn. (1st v.p. 1967, pres. 1969-71). Home: 500 E 63d St New York City NY 10021 Office: Rockefeller U 66th St and York Ave New York City NY 10021

MC CARTY, PERRY LEE, environ. engr., educator; b. Grosse Pointe, Mich., Oct. 29, 1931; s. James C. and Alice C. (Marsom) McC.; B.S. in Civil Engring., Wayne State U., 1953; M.S. in San. Engring., Mass. Inst. Tech., 1957, S.D., 1959; m. Martha Davis Collins, Sept. 5, 1953; children—Perry Lee, Cara L., Susan A., Kathleen R. Field engr. Edwin Orr Co., Dearborn, Mich., 1951-52; engr. Pate & Hirn, Detroit, 1952-53; field engr. Hubbell, Roth & Clark, Detroit, 1953; instr. civil engring. Wayne State U., 1953-54; field engr. George Jerome & Co., Detroit, 1954; engr. Civil Engrs., Inc., Detroit, 1956; asso. Rolf Eliassen Assos., Winchester, Mass., 1958-61; asst. prof. san. engring. Mass. Inst. Tech., 1958-62; mem. faculty Stanford U., 1962—, prof. civil engring., 1967-75, Silas H. Palmer prof., 1975—; chmn. Gordon Research Conf. Environ. Scis., 1972; mem. engring. adv. bd. John Wiley & Co., Inc., 1974—; vice chmn. environ. studies bd. NRC-Nat. Acad. Scis., 1976—. Served with AUS, 1954-56. NSF faculty fellow, 1968-69. Mem. Nat. Acad. Engring., Am. Water Works Assn. (chmn. water quality div. 1972-73, chmn. research com. 1976—), Water Pollution Control Fedn. (Thomas Camp award 1975, Harrison P. Eddy award 1962, 77), ASCE (Walter L. Huber research prize 1964, Simon W. Freese Environ. Engring. award 1979), Assn. Environ. Engring. Profs. (Distinguished Faculty award 1966), Am. Soc. Engring. Edn., Internat. Assn. Water Pollution Research, Sigma Xi, Tau Beta Pi (fellow 1957-58), Omicron Delta Kappa. Co-author: Chemistry for Environmental Engineering, 3d edit., 1970. Home: 823 Sonoma Terr Stanford CA 94305 Office: Civil Engring Dept Stanford Univ Stanford CA 94305

MCCARTY, PERRY ROSWELL, instrument co. exec.; b. Los Angeles, June 13, 1919; s. Robert Webster and Cora (Roberts) McC.; A.A., Santa Monica (Calif.) Jr. Coll., 1940; B.S., U. Calif., Los Angeles, 1947; m. Kathryn Elizabeth Tryon, Feb. 17, 1951. Sr. accountant Haskins & Sells, C.P.A.'s, Los Angeles, 1947-55; controller Arnold O. Beckman, Inc., South Pasadena, Calif., 1955-58; with Beckman Instruments, Inc., Fullerton, Calif., 1958—, treas., 1963-71, sec.-treas., 1971—; instr. accounting East Los Angeles Jr. Coll., 1956-61. Served with AUS, 1942-45. C.P.A., Calif. Mem. Am. Inst. C.P.A.'s, Calif. Soc. C.P.A.'s, Fin. Execs. Inst., Nat. Assn. Accountants, Am. Soc. Corporate Secs., Beta Gamma Sigma. Clubs: Rotary (Fullerton); Toastmasters (past pres. La Habra). Home: 15573 LaMoine St Hacienda Heights CA 91745 Office: 2500 Harbor Blvd Fullerton CA 92634

MCCARTY, ROBERT LEE, lawyer; b. New London, Conn., Mar. 1, 1920; s. Robert Patrick and Lyda (Griser) McC.; B.S., Bowdoin Coll., 1941; LL.B., Yale, 1948; LL.M., Georgetown U., 1953; m. Eileen Joan Noone, Sept. 1, 1945; children—Michael N., Patrick J., Charles Barry. Admitted to D.C. bar, 1948, also U.S. Supreme Ct.; asso. firm Northcutt Ely, 1948-54; mem. firm Ely, McCarty, & Duncan, 1955-60; partner firm McCarty and Wheatley, 1961-67, McCarty & Noone, 1968—. Mem. Adminstrv. Conf. U.S., 1972-74. Pres. bd. dirs. Belle Haven Citizens Assn., 1959-60. Served with USAAF, 1942-46, USAF, 1951-53; col. Res. Decorated D.F.C. (2), Air medal with 3 oak leaf clusters, Army Commendation medal. Fellow Am. Bar Found.; mem. Am. (chmn. sect. adminstrv. law 1966-67, sect. del. to ho. dels. 1968-70), Fed., D.C. bar assns. Roman Catholic. Clubs: University, Nat. Lawyers (Washington); Belle Haven Country (Va.). Contbr. chpts. to books. Home: 2108 Woodmont Rd Alexandria VA 22307 Office 490 L'Enfant Plaza E Washington DC 20024. *If you are to be satisfied with your product, there is no substitute for work.*

MCCARTY, STUART, banker; b. Kenosha, Wis., Jan. 20, 1923; s. Earl Hauser and Hazel (Beagle) McC.; A.B., Harvard, 1944; M.B.A., N.Y. U., 1951; m. Mary Dunhill Soons, Feb. 8, 1944; children—Stuart II, Martha Ann, Jane Dunhill, Mary Croft. With Mfrs. Hanover Trust Co., N.Y.C., 1946-63, v.p., 1960-63; with First City Nat. Bank, Binghamton, N.Y., 1963—, pres., 1967-77; pres., dir. Lincoln First Bank, N.A., Rochester, N.Y., 1978—; dir. Security Mut. Life Ins. Co. N.Y. Trustee Link Found.; pres. Broome County United Fund, 1970-71; campaign chmn. Broome County United Way, 1973; pres. Susquenango council Boy Scouts Am., 1965-67; chmn. finance com., treas. Nat. Assn. Mental Health, 1963-64. Served to capt., F.A., AUS, 1943-46. Clubs: Country of Rochester, Genesee Valley. Home: 4300 East Ave Rochester NY 14618 Office: Lincoln First Sq Rochester NY 14643

MC CARTY, THEODORE MILSON, mfg. co. exec.; b. Somerset, Ky., Oct. 10, 1909; s. Raymond Andrew and Jennie (Milson) McC.; Comml. Engr., U. Cin., 1933, postgrad., 1934-35; m. Elinor H. Bauer, June 14, 1935; children—Theodore F., Susan McCarty Davis. Asst. store mgr. Wurlitzer Co., Rochester, N.Y., 1936-38, mgr. real estate div. Cin. and Chgo., 1939-41, dir. procurement, DeKalb, Ill., 1942-44, mdse. mgr. retail div., Chgo., 1945-48; pres., gen. mgr., dir. Gibson Inc., 1948-66; pres., treas., dir. Bigsby Accessories, Inc., Kalamazoo, 1966—; owner, pres., dir. Flex-Lite, Inc.; v.p., dir. Command Electronics, Kalamazoo. Bd. dirs. Glowing Embers council Girl Scouts U.S., 1968-74. Mem. Am. Music Conf. (pres., adminstr. 1961-63, 70-77, dir., 1956—, hon. life dir.), Guitar and Accessory Mfrs. Assn. (past pres., hon. life dir.), Kalamazoo Symphony Soc. (past pres.), S.A.R. (charter mem.), Alpha Kappa Psi, Alpha Tau Omega, Omicron Delta Kappa. Presbyterian. Clubs: Masons, Rotary (past pres.), Kalamazoo Country (past pres.), Park. Patentee in music field. Home: 2412 Bronson Blvd Kalamazoo MI 49008 Office: Bigsby Accessories Inc 3521 E Kilgore Rd Kalamazoo MI 49001

MC CARTY, VIRGINIA DILL, lawyer; b. Plainfield, Ind., Dec. 15, 1924; d. E. Millard and Martha Gertrude (Paddack) Dill; A.B., Ind. U., 1946; LL.B., 1950; m. Mendel O. McCarty, Apr. 26, 1946 (dec. 1973); children—Michael Brent, Janet Martha. Admitted to Ind. bar, 1950; with Wasson's Dept. Store, Indpls., 1950; legal staff OPS, Indpls., 1950-52; final title examiner Union Title Co., Indpls., 1952-53; dep. atty. gen. State of Ind., 1965-66, asst. atty. gen., 1966-69; partner firm Dillon, Kelley, McCarty, Hardamon & Cohen, Indpls., 1969-77; pres. Dill-Fields Implement Co., Inc., Greenfield, Ind., 1967-77; U.S. atty. for So. Ind., Indpls., 1977—; mem. Atty. Gen.'s Adv. Com. of U.S. Attys., 1977—; mem. Fed. Corrections Adv. Com., 1978—; mem., sec. treas., v.p. Ind. Bd. Law Examiners, 1971-76. Mem. Indpls. Mayor's Task Force Women, 1972-76, chmn. legal status com., 1974-75; pres. Greater Indpls. Women's Polit. Caucus, 1971-73, Ind. Women's Polit. Caucus, 1972-73, precinct vice committeeman, 1966-69, chairperson orgn. com. Nat. Women's Polit. Caucus, 1973-75, advisory com., 1975-78; v.p. Hoosiers for Equal Rights Amendment, 1973-74, mem. steering com., 1976-77; mem. Ind. Gov.'s Commn. Privacy, 1976-77; Ind. Internat. Women's Year Com., 1977; Dem. candidate for Ind. Atty. Gen., 1976; bd. dirs. Concord Center, Info., Inc., Marin County Girls' Club. Mem. Am., Ind., Indpls. (legis. chmn. 1972) bar assns., Order of Coif, Phi Beta Kappa. Clubs: Stansfield Circle, Economic (dir.). (Indpls.). Home: 5809 Washington Blvd Indianapolis IN 46220 Office: 120 E Market St Indianapolis IN 46204. *Every individual has a responsibility to him or herself and others to achieve his or her full potential. The corollary is that each person must recognize and respect the strivings and potential of every other person.*

MCCARUS, ERNEST NASSEPH, educator; b. Charleston, W.Va., Sept. 10, 1922; s. Nasseph Mitchell and Della (Saad) McC.; student Morris Harvey Coll., 1939-40; A.B., U. Mich., 1945, M.A., 1949, Ph.D., 1956; m. Adele Najib Haddad, Sept. 10, 1955; children—Peter Kevin, Carol Ann. Translation team capt. Allied Translators and Interpreters' Service, Allied Hqrs., Tokyo, Japan, 1946-47; mem. English Lang. Inst. staff U. Mich., 1948-52, mem. univ. expdn. to Near East, 1951, instr. univ., 1952-56, asst. prof. Arabic, 1956-61; dir. Fgn. Service Inst., Field Sch. Arabic Lang. and Area Study, U.S. Dept. State, Beirut, Lebanon, 1958-60; asso. prof. dept. Near Eastern studies U. Mich., 1961-67, prof., 1967—, chmn. dept., 1969-77; cons. Ford Found., 1973; dir. Center for Arabic Study Abroad, 1974—. Served with AUS, 1942-46. Rockefeller fellow, 1951. Mem. Mich. Linguistic Soc. (pres. 1962-63), Am. Assn. Tchrs. Arabic (pres. 1973), Middle East Studies Assn. (dir. 1973-75), Linguistic Soc. Am., Am. Oriental Soc., Linguistic Circle N.Y. Author: Grammar of Kurdish of Sulaimania, Iraq, 1958; (with H. Hoenigswald, R. Noss, J. Yamagiwa) A Survey of Intensive Programs in the Uncommon Languages, 1962; (with A. Yacoub) Elements of Contemporary Arabic, 1962, 3d edn., 1966; (with Raji Rammuny) First Level Arabic: Elementary Literary Arabic for Secondary Schools, 1964; (with Raji Rammuny) Teacher's Manual to Accompany First Level Arabic, 1964; (with Jamal J. Abdullah) Kurdish Basic Course - Dialect of Sulaimania, Iraq, 1967; (with Jamal J. Abdullah): Kurdish Readers, Vol. I Newspaper Kurdish, Vol. II. Kurdish Essays, Vol. III Kurdish Short Stories, 1967; A Kurdish-English Dictionary, 1967; (with Raji Rammuny) Phonology and Script of Modern Literary Arabic, 1967; (with P. Abboud, N. Bezirgan, W. Erwin, M. Khouri, R. Rammuny) Elementary Modern Standard Arabic, 1968; (with R. Rammuny) Word Count of Elementary Modern Literary Arabic Textbooks, 1969; (with P. Abboud, E.T. Abdel-Massih, S. Altoma, W. Erwin, R. Rammuny) Modern Standard Arabic Intermediate Level, 1971; (with R. Rammuny) A Programmed Course in Modern Literary Arabic Phonology and Script, 1970. Editor Language Learning, Vol. VII, 1956-57; Language Learning, Vol. XIII, 1963; An-Nashra, 1967-74; Contemporary Arabic Readers, Vols. I-V, 1962-66. Contbr. articles to scholastic jours. Home: 1400 Beechwood Dr Ann Arbor MI 48103

MCCASHLAND, BENJAMIN WILLIAM, univ. dean; b. Geneva, Nebr., May 7, 1921; s. Ivan Leslie and Lucia (Kretke) McC.; B.S., U. Nebr., 1947, M.S., 1948, Ph.D., 1955; m. Glenrose B. Wassung, Dec. 25, 1943; children—William, David, Jean McCashland Tetz, Roberta. Mem. faculty U. Nebr., Lincoln, 1947-70, prof. physiology, 1962-70, asst. dean grad. coll., 1965-70; prof. biology, dean grad. studies Moorhead (Minn.) State U., 1970—. Served with inf. AUS, 1943-47. Decorated Purple Heart. Fellow AAAS; mem. Sigma Xi, Rho Chi. Author 1 text, co-author 3 others (all in physiology). Contbr. articles to profl. jours. Research in protozoan physiology. Office: Moorhead State U Moorhead MN 56560

MC CASKEY, AMBROSE EVERETT, JR., engring. ofcl.; b. New Martinsville, W. Va., Oct. 2, 1909; s. Ambrose Everett and Bessie (DeBolt) McC.; B.S. in Civil Engring., W.Va. U., 1932, M.S., 1936; postgrad. U. Mich.; Ph.D., U. Wis., 1955; m. Bessie Thomas, Oct. 2, 1932; 1 dau., Ann Elizabeth. San. engr. W.Va. Water Service Co., Charleston, 1932-36; head dept. engring. Marshall U., 1936-42, 51-60, dean applied scis., 1960-71; chief utilities operations Office Chief of Engrs., Washington, 1951; water resources coordinator Huntington dist. Corps Engrs., 1971—. Past pres. Huntington City Plan Commn.; mem. City of Huntington (W.Va.) San. Bd.; pres. W.Va. Bd. Registration Profl. Engrs.; mem. Gov.'s Adv. Com. on Tech. Services Act; pres. W.Va. region II Health Systems Agy.; cons. Gov.'s Adv. State Health Coordinating Council. Served from 1st lt. to lt. col., C.E., AUS, 1942-46. Decorated Legion of Merit, Medal for Mil. Merit; named W.V. Engr. of Year, 1974, W.Va. Centennial Coll. Registered profl. engr., W.Va.; diplomate Am. Acad. Environ. Engrs. Fellow ASCE (past pres. W.Va. sect.); mem. Nat. Council Engring. Examiners, W.Va. Soc. Profl. Engrs. (dir.), AAAS, Am. Water Works Assn., W.Va. Community Planners Assn., W.Va. Pub. Health Assn., Engrs. Club, Nat. Soc. Profl. Engrs., Water Pollution Control Fedn., Am. Soc. Engring. Edn., Smithsonian Assos., Nat. Audubon Soc., Sigma Xi, Chi Beta Phi, D-Rho D-Theta (founder), Alpha Sigma Phi. Methodist. Mason, Rotarian. Author tech. articles. Home: 61 Edgemont Terr Huntington WV 25701

MCCASLIN, JOHN MATHERS, JR., lawyer; b. Cin., Apr. 29, 1920; s. John Mathers and Sue Towles (Bagley) McC.; A.B., Princeton U., 1942; LL.B., U. Cin., 1948; m. Althea F. Richardson, June 28, 1948; children—Susan R., Robert B., Hugh F., John Mathers, III.

Admitted to Ohio bar, 1948; partner firm McCaslin, Inbus & McCaslin, Cin., 1950—, now sr. partner. Served with USAF, 1942-45. Decorated D.F.C., Air medal with 4 oak leaf clusters. Mem. Cin. Bar Assn., Ohio State Bar Assn. Episcopalian. Club: Glendale Lyceum. Home: 125 E Sharon Rd Cincinnati OH 45246 Office: 1200 Gwynne Bldg Cincinnati OH 45202

MCCAULEY, ALFRED ROBERT, lawyer; b. Bklyn., Feb. 25, 1922; s. John Francis and Mary Ann (Horan) McC.; student St. Bonaventure (N.Y.) U., 1940-42; LL.B., U. Va., 1948; m. Helen Patricia McQuide, Sept. 24, 1949; children—Ann, Stephen, James, Matthew, Marybeth. Admitted to Va. bar, 1948, D.C. bar, 1963; asst. to gen. counsel U.S. Tariff Commn., 1948-58; fgn. trade adviser com. ways and means Ho. of Reps., 1959-63; partner firm Graubard, Moskovitz & McCauley, Washington, 1963—. Served with U.S. Army, 1942-46, 51-52. Decorated Bronze Star, Commendation medal. Mem. Am. (chmn. com. customs 1964-73), Fed., Va. bar assns. Democrat. Roman Catholic. Clubs: Internat., Nat. Democratic (Washington). Address: 1629 K St NW Washington DC 20006

MCCAULEY, BRUCE GORDON, investment advisor; b. St. Louis; s. William Maurice and Evylin Adele (Halbert) McC.; student U. Mo., 1939-41, Yale, 1944; B.S. in Engring., U. Calif. at Berkeley, 1948, M.B.A., 1949, M.S. in Indsl. Engring., 1952; m. Barbara Allen Stevens, Mar. 16, 1945 (dec.); children—David S., Sharon; m. 2d, Gwen Crumpton Cummings, Nov. 25, 1967. Asst. purchasing agt. Curtis Mfg. Co., St. Louis, 1941-43; teaching asst. U. Calif. at Berkeley, 1948-49, asst. prof. mech. engring., 1950-56, chmn. indsl. engring. inst., 1954-55; design engr. Standard Oil Co. of Calif., 1949-50; sr. partner McCauley & Dunmire, San Francisco, 1952-56; v.p. Shand & Jurs Co., Berkeley, 1956-58, dir., 1957-60, exec. v.p., 1958-60; asst. to pres. Honolulu Star- Bulletin, 1960-62; gen. mgr. Christian Sci. Pub. Soc., Boston, pubs. Christian Science Monitor, Christian Sci. Jour., Christian Sci. Sentinel, other publs., 1962-69; gen. mgr. New York News, Inc., N.Y.C., 1969-74, sec., 1970-71, v.p., 1971-73, sr. v.p., 1973-75, asst. to pres., 1974-75, also dir., 1971-75; v.p. Daseke & Co., Inc., Greenwich, Conn., 1975-77, sr. v.p., 1977—, mgr. West Coast office, 1978—. Dir. Better Bus. Bur., N.Y.C., 1973-77, N.Y. C. Conv. and Visitors' Bur., 1974-77. Served as capt. USAAF, 1943-46; PTO. Registered profl. engr., N.Y., Calif., Hawaii. Mem. Nat. Assn. Security Dealers (registered prin.), Am. Inst. Indsl. Engrs., ASME, Nat. Assn. Accountants, Nat. Soc. Profl. Engrs., U. Calif. Alumni Assn., Principia Alumni Assn., Sigma Xi, Tau Beta Pi, Beta Gamma Sigma, Pi Mu Epsilon. Christian Scientist. Clubs: Bankers (San Francisco); Masons (32 deg.). Home: 194 Stewart Dr Tiburon CA 94920 Office: 4780 Bank of America Center San Francisco CA 94104

MCCAULEY, JOHN CORRAN, JR., physician; b. Rochester, Pa., Feb. 25, 1901; s. John Corran and Jennie Campbell (Parks) McC.; B.S., Hahnemann Coll. Sci., 1923; M.D., U. Colo., 1927; m. Mildred Catherine Steil, Sept. 30, 1939; children—Ann Hamilton (Mrs. Robert Renfrew Trostle), Marcia Miller. Intern Genesee Hosp., Rochester, N.Y., 1927-28, surg. resident, 1928-29; orthopedic resident Hosp. for Ruptured and Crippled, N.Y.C., 1929-30; practice medicine, specializing in orthopedic surgery, N.Y.C., 1930—; asst. vis. orthopedic surgeon Bellevue Hosp., 1930-35, asso. vis. orthopedic surgeon, 1935-41, vis. orthopedic surgeon, 1941—; attending orthopedic surgeon U. Hosp., 1941—; asst. attending orthopedic surgeon N.Y. State Rehab. Hosp., Haverstraw, 1941-42, attending orthopedic surgeon, 1942- 43, sr. orthopedic surgeon, 1943-47, surgeon-in-chief, 1947-67; mem. staff Neponsit Beach Hosp., 1936, Seaside Hosp. St. John's Guild, 1937, N.Y. Orthopedic Hosp., 1941, Vanderbilt Clinic Presbyn. Hosp., 1950; instr. orthopedic surgery Med. Sch. N.Y. U., 1930-39, asst. prof., 1939- 44, asso. prof. clin. orthopedic surgery, 1944-47, asso. prof. orthopedic surgery, 1947-56, prof., 1956—; cons. orthopedic surgeon Flushing (N.Y.) Hosp., Nyack (N.Y.) Hosp., Lawrence Hosp., Bronxville, N.Y., St. Agnes Hosp., White Plains, N.Y.; spl. cons. USPHS; impartial orthopedist N.Y. State Workmens Compensation Bd., Police Dept. N.Y.C., Fire Dept. N.Y.C. Mem. Med. Milk Commn. Mem. adv. bd. Selective Service; mem. med. adv. bd. St. Johnsland. Recipient Presidential citation Internat. Poliomyelitis Congress, 1949. Diplomate Am. Bd. Orthopedic Surgery. Mem. Am. Orthopedic Assn., A.C.S., Am. Acad. Orthopedic Surgeons, Internat. Soc. Orthopedic Surgery and Traumatology, N.Y. Acad. Medicine (past sect. chmn.), A.M.A., N.Y. State, County med. socs., Am. Assn. Med. Milk Commns. (past pres.). Presbyn. Club: Hospital Graduates. Contbr. articles med. jours. Home: 2452 Terry Ln Sarasota FL 33581

MCCAULEY, R. PAUL, criminologist, educator; b. Highspire, Pa., Jan. 13, 1943; s. Paul Herbert and Frances Vaden (Harper) McC.; A.S., Harrisburg Area Community Coll., 1968; B.S., Va. Commonwealth U., 1969; M.S., Eastern Ky. U., 1971; Ph.D. (fellow), Sam Houston U., 1973; certificate Home Office Detective Tng. Course (Eng.), 1967; m. Gail Lee Gummo, Jan. 30, 1965. Police comdr. Highspire Police, 1964-69; adminstr. Burns Internat. Security Services Inc., 1969-71; prof. police sci. and adminstrn., dir. grad. studies in adminstrn. of justice U. Louisville, 1973—. Mem. staff So. Police Inst., 1973—, Nat. Crime Prevention Inst., 1973—; researcher, partner McShan Assos., 1974—; cons. U.S. Congress Com. on Emergency Communications, 1967. Active Metro Child Abuse Program, Crime Clinic of Greater Harrisburg, 1965-74; mem. Lower Swatara Twp. Police Civil Service Commn., 1967-69. Served with USMC, 1962-66, to lt. USN, 1966-69. Recipient City award for community service Chesapeake, Va. Mem. Acad. Criminal Justice Scis., Am. Correctional Assn., Am. Soc. for Pub. Adminstrn., Am. Soc. for Indsl. Security, Criminal Justice Research Soc., Am. Judicature Soc., Navy League (award for distinguished community service). Lutheran. Mason (Shriner). Co-author: The Criminal Justice System, 1976. Contbr. chpts. to books, articles to profl. jours. Home: 1609 Trevillian Way Louisville KY 40205 Office: 201 Patterson Hall U Louisville Louisville KY 40208

MC CAULEY, ROBERT JOSEPH, hotel exec.; b. Montreal, Que., Can., Apr. 9, 1933; s. Robert J. and Janet (Donihee) McC.; student Loyola Coll., Montreal, 1948-51, St. Xavier U., Antigonish, N.S., 1952-53, McGill U., Montreal, 1954-55; m. Mary McCauley. With Palliser Hotel, 1957-62; asst. mgr. Hotel Georgia, Vancouver, B.C., Can., 1962-63, dir. sales, 1964-67, exec. asst. mgr., 1967-69, gen. mgr., 1970-72; mgr. Imperial Inn, Victoria, B.C., 1969-70; resident mgr. Bayshore Inn, Vancouver, 1972; gen. mgr. Edmonton (Alta.) Plaza, 1972-75; gen. mgr. Hotel Toronto, Ont., 1975-79, mng. dir., 1979—; v.p. Western Internat. Hotels, Western Internat. Hotels, Ltd. (Can.). Bd. dirs. Conv. and Tourist Bur. Toronto, Tourism Industry Assn. Can. Named Hotelier of Year, 1975. Mem. Am. Hotel and Motel Assn., Internat. Wine and Food Soc., Am. Soc. Travel Agts., Sales and Mktg. Execs. Internat., Hotel Assn. Met. Toronto (dir.), Toronto Restaurant and Foodservice Assn. (dir.), Can. C. of C., Bd. Trade of Met. Toronto, Chaine des Rotisseurs. Roman Catholic. Clubs: Skal (Toronto); Variety Internat.; Lambton Golf and Country. Office: 145 Richmond St W Toronto ON M5H 3M6 Canada

MCCAULEY, WILLIAM ANDREW, coll. dean; b. Geneseo, N.Y., Aug. 25, 1924; s. Thomas and Violet (Knox) McC.; B.Ed., State U. N.Y. at Geneseo, 1949; M.A., Colo. State Coll., 1950; Ph.D., Syracuse U., 1956; m. Ruth Norman, May 18, 1947; children—Janet Lynne, Barbara Lee, Thomas Norman. Instr. State U. N.Y. At Geneseo, 1950-53; asst. instr. Syracuse U., 1953-55; counseling psychologist VA, 1955-56; from asst. prof. to prof. George Washington U., 1956-67; Fulbright prof. U. del Valle, Cali, Colombia, 1964-65; dean grad. studies Clarion (Pa.) State Coll., 1967—; dir. Counseling Assos., Washington, 1961-64; sr. partner Counselor Assos., Kensington, Md., 1965-67; sr. asso. Leadership Resources, Inc., 1965—. Served with USCGR, 1942-45. Mem. Kappa Delta Pi, Phi Alpha Theta, Psi Chi, Omicron Delta Kappa, Phi Delta Kappa. Home: RD 2 Shippenville PA 16254 Office: Clarion State Coll Clarion PA 16214

MCCAUSLAND, THOMAS GEROME, lawyer, corp. legal counsel; b. Pitts., Dec. 4, 1924; s. Victor Roy and Gertrude (Parks) M.; B.A., Yale, 1949; LL.B., Harvard, 1952; m. Jean Kathryn Black, June 11, 1952; children—Montgomery, Ellen Douglas, Buchanan. Admitted to Md. bar, 1952, since practiced in Balt.; asso. Tydings, Sauerwein, Benson & Boyd, 1952-54; asso. Muecke, Mules & Ireton, 1954-56; asso. counsel Comml. Credit Co., Balt., 1956-57, asst. gen. counsel, 1967-71, sec., gen. atty., 1971—; dir. Calvert Fire Ins. Co., Cavalier Ins. Corp., Chesapeake Adjusters, Inc., Comco France, S.A., Comco Internat. Bank, S.A., Comco Internat., Inc., Comco Trading Corp., Comml. Credit Computer Leasing (Switzerland) A.G., Comml. Credit Leasing Services (Switzerland) A.G., Comml. Credit Europe, Inc., Comml. Credit Far East, Inc., Comml. Trading Internat., Inc., City Loan Bldg. Co., Control Data Technotec, Inc., Control Data Worldtech, Inc., Comml. Credit Mortgage Ins. Co., Comcres, Inc. Served with USAF, 1943-46. Mem. Am. Bar Assn., Am. Indsl. Bankers Assn., Nat. Consumer Finance Assn. (mem. law forum), Ill., Balt. chambers commerce, Cannon Castle Soc., Phi Lambda Theta. Republican. Clubs: Yale (Md.), Harvard (Md.), Mory's, Timberidge Hunt. Home: Round Top Monkton MD 21111 Office: 300 St Paul Pl Baltimore MD 21202

MC CAW, JOHN EMORY, clergyman, educator; b. Lomax, Ill., Mar. 10, 1917; s. Clayton Clair and Anna Mildred (Phillips) McC.; A.B., Drake U., 1939; B.D., U. Chgo., 1949; D.D., Butler U., 1958; m. Maxine Mae Gambs, May 15, 1942; children—Clayle Franklin, Milva Lou, Maxhn Herbert, Janine Gambs. Minister, Christian Ch., Humeston, Iowa, 1936-37; exec. sec. Iowa Christian Endeavor Union, 1937-39; ordained to ministry Disciples of Christ Ch., 1939; dir. Interchurch Council, U. Chgo., 1941-42; dir. Student Christian Found., So. Ill. U., 1943-45; nat. dir. student work Disciples of Christ., Indpls., 1945-50; dean, prof. ch. history Div. Sch., Drake U., Des Moines, 1950-65, prof., 1965—. Established Disciples of Christ Student Fellowship, 1946; chmn. exec. com. United Student Christian Council, 1949-50; sec. Am. Assn. Theol. Schs., 1958-60, Sealantic Found. A.A.T.S. faculty fellowships, 1957-58, 66-67; mem. Des Moines Sch. Bd., 1969-77, pres., 1972-73; mem. Des Moines Pastoral Counseling Center, pres., 1978. Am. Soc. Ch. History, Disciples Christ Hist. Soc., Soc. Sci. Study Religion, Am. Acad. Religion, AAUP, Nat. Council on Religion and Pub. Edn., Council on Christian Unity, Phi Beta Kappa, Eta Sigma Phi, Aleph Theta Xi. Club: University. Home: 4210 SW 26th St Des Moines IA 50321. *Three loves have filled my life: a love for God; a love for mankind; and a love for the soil. Three searches have led me on: a search for facts; a search for meaning; and a search for wisdom. Three labors have kept me busy: a labor for redemption of persons; a labor for a just society; and a labor for a peaceful world.*

MCCAY, MYRON STANLEY, educator; b. Pocataligo, Ga., Nov. 5, 1911; s. Edward Lee and Nettie (Burroughs) McC.; A.B., U. Ga., 1932; M.A., U. N.C., 1934; Ph.D., Ohio State U., 1937; m. Lessie Belle Peeler, June 11, 1935; children—Myron Stanley, Judith Ann (Mrs. Albert Enoch Munson). Instr., Va. Poly. Inst., Blacksburg, 1937-39, asst. prof., 1939-41, asso. prof., 1941-46, prof. physics, 1946-48; prof., head physics-astronomy dept. U. Tenn., Chattanooga, 1948-77, emeritus, 1977—. Sr. physicist Applied Physics Lab., OSRD, Johns Hopkins, World War II; summer research participant Oak Ridge Nat. Lab., 1957-58; lectr. Oak Ridge Asso. U. and AEC Mobile Lab., 1953-73. Mem. Chattanooga Elec. Licensing Bd., 1953-65. Recipient citation for civilian research OSRD, 1944; Evans award for teaching talent U. Chattanooga, 1963; George B. Pegram award for excellence in teaching physics Southeastern sect. Am. Phys. Soc., 1976; Outstanding Tchr. award U. Tenn. Alumni, 1977. Mem. Am. Phys. Soc. (treas. S.E. sect. 1957-73, chmn. S.E. sect. 1975), Am. Assn. Physics Tchrs. (asso. editor, membership com. 1964-69), AAAS (acad. conf. 1960-62), Am. Assn. U. Profs., Optical Soc. Am., Tenn. Acad. Sci. (pres. 1954, jr. acad. dir. 1958-63), Am. Nuclear Soc., Chattanooga Engrs. Club (pres. 1964), Blue Key, Phi Beta Kappa, Sigma Xi, Sigma Pi Sigma. Methodist. Home: 2120 Driftwood Rd Soddy-Daisy TN 37379. *Education for intelligent thinking and acting is society's top-priority need. The world's problems with energy, edibles, and environment may yet be solved by education and thoughtful action. Edgar Alan Poe reportedly observed, "The most outrageous ill fortune must in the end yield to the untiring courage of philosophy."*

MCCAY, PERCY LUZENBERG, ret. banker; b. New Orleans, Dec. 13, 1896; s. Percy Luzenberg and Eleanor (Conner) McC.; B.A., B.B.A., Tulane U., 1919; grad. Grad. Sch. Banking of Rutgers U., 1937; m. Bethia Caffery, Oct. 27, 1921; children—Bethia Liddell (Mrs. Edmund G. Brown, Jr.), Donelson Caffery. With W.R. Grace & Co., 1919-22; export mgr. H.T. Cottam, Inc., 1922-28; instr. Loyola U., 1931-32; with Whitney Nat. Bank of New Orleans, 1928—, mgr. Spanish Am. dept., asst. v.p., 1939-43, v.p., 1943-69, vice chmn. bd., 1969-74, dir. emeritus, 1974—. Mem. Delta Kappa Epsilon. Democrat. Presbyn. Clubs: Boston, Louisiana (New Orleans). Home: 1625 Arabella St New Orleans LA 70115

MCCHESNEY, ROBERT PEARSON, artist; b. Marshall, Mo., Jan. 16, 1913; s. John and Ruby (Pearson) McC.; student Sch. Fine Arts, Washington U., 1931-34, Otis Art Inst., Los Angeles, 1936-37; m. Mary Ellen Fuller, Dec. 17, 1949. One-man shows: San Francisco Mus. Modern Art, 1949, 53, San Francisco Art Inst., 1957, Todes Art Gallery, Chgo., 1958, Reed Coll., Portland, Oreg., 1959, Parsons Gallery, Los Angeles, 1960, 61, Bolles Gallery, San Francisco, 1959, 61, 70, 71, N.Y.C., 1962, 20th Century West, N.Y.C., 1965, Lincoln Art Center, Santa Rosa, Calif., 1978, U. Calif., Hayward, 1977; retrospective show San Francisco Art Commn., 1974; group shows include: Art Inst. Chgo., 1947, 54, 60, 61, Corcoran Gallery, Washington, 1957, San Francisco Mus. Art Ann., 1945-60, Nordness Gallery, N.Y.C., 1964, Legion of Honor, San Francisco, 1962, 64, Oakland Mus., 1972, 73; represented in permanent collections: Whitney Mus. Am. Art, N.Y.C., San Francisco Mus. Art, Oakland Art Mus., Art Inst. Chgo., Legion of Honor, Muskegon (Mich.) Mus. Art, instr. art Calif. Sch. Fine Arts, San Francisco, 1949-51, Santa Rosa Jr. Coll., 1957-58. Trustee San Francisco Art Inst., 1965-67. Address: 2955 Sonoma Mountain Rd Petaluma CA 94952. *The desert wilderness, which I truly love to be in as much as possible, has influenced me a great deal. Of course, the artist is no different from anyone else in that he is influenced by everything around him visually and psychologically, but he has the ability to digest this, you might say, and then regurgitate it as art.*

MC CHESNEY, RUSSELL JAMES, art materials co. exec.; b. West Orange, N.J., Dec. 8, 1916; s. Russell Dudley and Margaret Clothilda (Monohan) McC.; student Bloomfield Coll., 1935-39, Rutgers U., 1951-54, N.Y. U., 1965; m. Marjorie Jane Miller, Sept. 6, 1947; children—R. Douglas, Susan L., Deborah L. With Binney & Smith Inc., Easton, Pa., 1935—, v.p. mktg., 1967-70, exec. v.p., 1970-71, chmn. bd., 1971—, pres., 1973—, also dir., 1968—; dir. Binney & Smith (Europe) Ltd., Can. Crayon Co., Easton Nat. Bank & Trust; mem. joint com. Am. Assn. Sch. Adminstrs. and Ednl. Industries Assn. (dir., past pres.). Served with AUS, 1940-45. Decorated Croix de Guerre (France). Mem. Crayon, Water Color and Craft Inst. (dir., v.p., past pres.), Nat. Art Edn. Assn. (life). Clubs: Chgo. Athletic, Upper Mountain Country, Pomfret, Northampton Country, Manhattan. Home: 84 North Rd Kinnelon NJ 07405 Office: PO Box 431 1100 Church Ln Easton PA 18042

MCCLAFFERTY, JOHN JOSEPH, clergyman; b. N.Y.C., Apr. 9, 1906; s. John and Margaret (Moran) McC.; A.B., Cathedral Coll., 1927; grad. St. Joseph's Sem., 1930; A.M., Catholic U., 1932; diploma N.Y. Sch. Social Work, 1936; LL.D., Loyola U., Los Angeles, 1947. Ordained priest Roman Catholic Ch., 1930, apptd. papal chamberlain, 1943; apptd. Domestic Prelate, 1953, Protonotary Apostolic, 1965; asst. dir. div. social action Catholic Charities, N.Y.C., 1936-41, dir. div. social research, 1941-47. Exec. sec. Nat. Legion Decency, 1936-47; mem. bd. consultors Ch. of the Air CBS, 1940-47; bd. advisors Radio Chapel MBS, 1941-47; bd. dirs. Casita Maria Settlement, 1941-47; com. discrimination N.Y. State War Council, 1942-44; Am. del. to Pan-Am. Congress, Caracas, Venezuela, 1948; del. 3d Congress of Inter-Am. Cath. Social Action Confederation, Rio de Janeiro, Brazil, 1948. Dean, Nat. Cath. Sch. of Social Service, Catholic U. Am., 1947-55, asst. to rector for univ. devel., 1955-63; pastor St. Peter's Ch., S.I., 1963-66, St. Francis de Sales Ch., N.Y.C., 1966—. Mem. nat. exec. fact-finding coms., Mid-Century White House Conf. on Children and Youth, 1950. Del., White House Conf. Children and Youth, 1960. Served as capt. (chaplain) 5th regiment of N.Y. Guard, 1941-42, col. (chaplain) Hdqrs. N.Y. Guard, 1946-51. Mem. Point Four Mission to Colombia, S.A., 1951. Certified social worker, N.Y. State. Fellow Royal Soc. Health; mem. Nat. Assn. Social Workers, Acad. Certified Social Workers, Editor Cath. U. of Am. Bull., 1956-63. Home: 135 E 96th St New York City NY 10028

MCCLAIN, CHARLES JAMES, univ. pres.; b. Ironton, Mo., Sept. 1, 1931; s. John F. and Hazel (Pierce) McC.; B.S. in Edn., S.W. Mo. State Coll., 1954; M.Ed., U. Mo., 1957, Ed.D., 1961; hon. degree Busan Nat. U.; m. Norma Mae Gregory, Aug. 25, 1950; children—Anita, Melanie. Pres. Jefferson Coll., Hillsboro, Mo., 1963-70, Northeast Mo. State U., Kirksville, 1970—. Mem. advisory bd. Mo. Hist. Records; corporate assembly Blue Cross; mem. Mid-Mo. Health Consortium, NE Mo. Health and Welfare Council. Recipient Distinguished Alumnus award SW Mo. State U., 1977, Distinguished Service award U. Mo. Coll. Edn. Mem. Mo. Acad. Sci., Internat. Assn. Univ. Presidents, Phi Delta Kappa. Mason. Rotarian. Contbr. articles to profl. jours. Home: 706 Halliburton St Kirksville MO 63501

MC CLAIN, DAVID, football coach; b. Upper Sandusky, Ohio, Jan. 28, 1938; s. Vernon and Isabel (Bardon) McC.; B.S., Bowling Green U., 1960, M.S. in Edn., 1962; m. Judy Perry, June 30, 1962; children—Tom, Melinda, Marcy. Tchr., coach Crestline High Sch., 1960; coach Cornell U., 1961-62; football coach Miami U., Oxford, Ohio, 1963-66, U. Kans., Lawrence, 1967-68, Ohio State U., Columbus, 1969-70; head coach Ball State U., Muncie, Ind., 1971-77; head football coach U. Wis., Madison, 1978—. Mem. Am. FootbAll Coaches Assn., Ind. and Wis. High Sch. Coaches Assn. Baptist. Home: 22 Harwood Circle Madison WI 53717 Office: 1440 Monroe St Madison WI 53706

MCCLAIN, WILLIAM ANDREW, judge; b. Sanford, N.C., Jan. 11, 1913; s. Frank and Blanche (Leslie) McC.; A.B., Wittenberg Coll., 1934; J.D. (Henry N. Campbell Case Club and Student Judgeship award 1937), U. Mich., 1937; LL.D., Wilberforce U., 1963, U. Cin., 1971; L.H.D., Wittenberg U., 1972; m. Roberta White, Nov. 11, 1944. Admitted to Ohio bar, 1938, also U.S. Supreme Ct., other fed. cts.; practice in Cin., 1938—; asst. solicitor civil div. City Cin., 1942-57, dep. solicitor, 1957-63, city solicitor, 1963-72; judge Common Pleas Ct., 1975-77; judge Municipal Ct., 1977—; acting city mgr., Cin., 1968, 72. Bd. dirs. central clinic Cin. Gen. Hosp., Council Chs. Greater Cin.; bd. dirs. Cin. chpt. ARC, Cin. United Appeal; trustee So. Ohio conf. 3d Episcopal dist. A.M.E. Ch., McCall Ednl. Found. Cin. Served to 1st lt. AUS, 1943-46. Decorated Army Commendation award; recipient Citizens of Year award in law Beta Iota chpt. Omega Phi Psi, Distinguished Pub. Service award Nat. Inst. Municipal Law Officers, 1971, Nat. Med. Assn. merit award 1972. Mem. Am., Nat., Ohio, Cin. bar assns., Am. Judicature Soc., Cin. Lawyers Club, Queen City Assn., NAACP (pres. Cin. 1941, Ohio 1942; Certificate of Honor award 1942), Wittenberg U. Alumni Assn. (pres. 1964-65; Nat. Alumni citation 1966), Alpha Phi Alpha (Man of Year award Delta Gamma Lambda chpt. 1963), Alpha Delta Boule, Sigma Phi Pi. Mem. A.M.E. Ch. (trustee; Nat. Layman of Year award 1963, Distinguished Lawyer award 1968). Clubs: Univ. Mich. Alumni, Wittenberg Alumni (Cin.), Masons. Address: 3709 Bonfield Dr Cincinnati OH 45220. *The supreme art of living is to live each day well, as if it is the last day on this earth. What we cannot do for a lifetime, we can do for a day-time. Create the kind of self you will be happy to live with all your life. Man does not die to become immortal, he is immortal now; this is eternity. The gift of things is never as precious as the gift of one's humanity. Perfection consists not in doing extraordinary things, but in doing ordinary things well.*

MCCLAIN, WILLIAM ASBURY, lawyer; b. Sweetwater, Tenn., Apr. 1, 1901; s. William A. and Anne Lynn (Bachman) McC.; grad. Tenn. Mil. Inst., 1920; B.S., Davidson Coll., 1924; LL.B., U. Va., 1927; m. Catherine Flagler, Nov. 15, 1933; children—Martha Catherine (Mrs. Robert D. Hand, Jr.), Anne Lynn, William Asbury III. Admitted to Tenn. bar, 1927, Ga. bar, 1928; asso. firm Watkins, Asbill & Watkins, Atlanta, 1927-32, Hooper & Hooper; with gen. counsel's office SEC, Washington, 1935-38, Southeastern regional counsel, 1938-46; asst. atty. gen. State of Ga., 1932; spl. asst. atty. gen. U.S., 1943; partner Candler, Cox & McClain, Atlanta, 1946-70; mem. firm McClain, Mellen, Bowling & Hickman, 1970—; dir. Flagler Co., Flagler-Mellan Stuart Co., Atlanta, Hampton Mills, Inc., Ellijoy, Ga. Trustee Episcopal Radio-TV Found., Diocesan Found., Lovett Sch. Mem. Atlanta Lawyers Club, Ga. Hort. Soc., Commerce Club, Am., Ga., Atlanta bar assns., Garden Club Am., Beta Theta Pi. Clubs: Piedmont Driving, Nine O'clocks, Commerce (Atlanta). Home: 1776 W Wesley Rd NW Atlanta GA 30327 Office: 225 Peachtree St Box 56505 Atlanta GA 30343

MCCLAIN, WILLIAM HAROLD, educator; b. Cleve., July 22, 1917; s. William Harry and Helen (Newman) McC.; A.B., Western Res. U., 1939; M.A., U. Wis., 1940, Ph.D., 1943. Vice consul Office U.S. Polit. Adviser, SHAEF, State Dept., 1945-46; instr., then asst. prof. German, Harvard, 1946-53; mem. faculty Johns Hopkins, 1953—, prof. German, 1962—, chmn., 1972—. Trustee Julius Hofmann Fund, 1958—. Fulbright rep., 1965; recipient Lindback award distinguished teaching Johns Hopkins, 1962; Distinguished Alumni citation Western Res. U., 1968. Mem. Goethe Soc. Md. (pres. 1954-56), Am. Assn. Tchrs. German (pres. Md. 1956-58), A.A.U.P., Humanities Research Assn., German Soc., Kafka Soc., Soc. for History of Germans in Md., MLA, Phi Beta Kappa (pres. Alpha chpt.

1978—), Delta Phi Alpha. Author: Wie sie es sehen, 1952; Deutsch, 1957; Between Real and Ideal, 1963; Karl Gutzkows Briefe an Costenoble, 1971; Traditions and Transitions, 1972; Friedrich Gerstäckers Briefe an Costenoble, 1974; Friedrich von Bodenstedts Briefe an Hermann Costenoble, 1977. also articles. Editor Modern Lang. Notes, 1953—. Home: 3411 Oakenshaw Pl Baltimore MD 21218

MC CLANAHAN, RUE (EDDI-RUE), actress; b. Healdton, Okla., Feb. 21; d. William Edwin and Dreda Rheua-Nell (Medaris) McC.; B.A. cum laude, U. Tulsa, 1956; 1 son, Mark Thomas Bish. Actress, Erie (Pa.) Playhouse, 1957-58; theatrical, film and TV appearances, Los Angeles, 1959-64, N.Y.C., 1964-73; mem. cast TV series Maude, 1973-78, Apple Pie, 1978; appeared on Broadway in California Suite, 1977; star TV series The Son-In-Law, 1980. Spl. scholar Pasadena (Calif.) Playhouse, 1959; Phi Beta Gamma scholar, 1955; recipient Obie award for leading off-Broadway role in Who's Happy Now?, 1970. Mem. Actors Studio, Actors Equity Assn., AFTRA, Screen Actors Guild. Office: Sta KTTV 5752 Sunset Blvd Los Angeles CA 90028

MC CLARREN, ROBERT ROYCE, librarian; b. Delta, Ohio, Mar. 15, 1921; s. Dresden William Howard and Norma Leona (Whiteman) McC.; student Antioch Coll., 1938-40; A.B., Muskingum Coll., 1942; M.A. in English, Ohio State U., 1951; M.S. in L.S (Joseph Towne Wheeler award 1954), Columbia, 1954; m. Margaret Aileen Weed, May 31, 1947; children—Mark Robert, Todd Adams. Registration officer VA, Cin., 1946-47; instr. English, Gen. Motors Inst., 1949-50; head circulation dept. Oak Park (Ill.) Pub. Library, 1954-55, acting head librarian, 1955; head librarian Crawfordsville (Ind.) Pub. Library, 1955-58; head librarian Huntington (W.Va.) Pub. Library, also Western Counties (W.Va.) Regional Pub. Library, 1958-62; dir. Ind. State Library, 1962-67; system dir. North Suburban Library System, 1967—; del. White House Conf. on Libraries, 1979; instr. U. Wis., summer 1964; instr. Rosary Coll., 1968—, U. Tex., summer 1979. Pres., W.Va. Library Assn., 1960; mem. Gov. Ind. Commn. Arts, 1964-65; mem. Ill. State Library Adv. Com., 1972-79, chmn., 1975-79; bd. dirs. Ill. Regional Library Council, 1972—, pres., 1977; chmn. adv. commn. Nat. Periodical System, Nat. Commn. on Libraries and Info. Sci., 1978—. Served to 1st lt. AUS, 1942-46, 51-52; maj. Res. Named Ill. Librarian of Yr., 1978. Mem. Am. (councilor 1966-68, 74-78, treas. 1968-72, endowment trustee 1972-78, mem. pub. bd. 1972-75, pres. reference and adv. service div. 1975-76), Ill. (v.p.) library assns., Am. Library Trustee Assn. (v.p. 1976-77), Assn. Spl. and Coop. Library Agys. (pres. 1978-79), Ohio Hist. Soc., Am. Philatelic Soc., Soc. Philatelic Ams. Clubs: Literary, Portfolio (Indpls.). Contbr. articles to profl. jours. Home: 1560 Oakwood Pl Deerfield IL 60015 Office: 200 W Dundee Rd Wheeling IL 60090

MCCLARY, JAMES DALY, ret. contractor; b. Boise, Idaho, July 19, 1917; s. Neil Hammacker and Myrtle (Daly) McC.; student Boise Jr. Coll., 1934-36, A.A., 1957; A.B., Stanford, 1938; L.H.D., Gonzaga U., 1976; m. Mary Jane Munger, Feb. 2, 1939; children—Pamela, John. Laborer to supt. Morrison-Knudsen Co., Inc., Boise, 1932-42, project mgr., asst. dist. mgr., 1942- 47, gen. mgr. Mexican subsidiary, 1947-51, asst. to gen. mgr., 1951-53, asst. gen. mgr., 1953-60, dir., 1955-78, v.p., 1956-60, exec. v.p., 1960-72, chmn. bd., 1972-78; dir. Provident Fed. Savs., Boise, 1973—. Mem. vice chmn. Idaho Permanent Bldg. Fund Adv. Council, 1961-64, chmn., 1964-71. Treas., Idaho Republican Central Com., 1964-70; Presdl. elector, 1968. Trustee Boise Jr. Coll., 1960—, vice chmn., 1967-73, chmn., 1973—; pres. Boise State U. Found., Inc., 1970—; bd. dirs., pres. AGC Edn. and Research Found., 1974—; elector Hall of Fame for Great Ams., 1976—. Recipient George Washington medal of honor Freedoms Found., Valley Forge, Pa., 1977; decorated Chevalier and Legion of Honor, Order of DeMolay; named Alumnus of Year Boise State U. Alumni Assn., 1971, Ky. Col. Fellow ASCE, Am. Inst. Constructors; mem. Internat. Road Fedn. (dir. 1972-78, vice chmn. 1977-78), Soc. Am. Mil. Engrs., Asso. Gen. Contractors Am. (dir. 1958—, exec. com. 1961-78, pres. 1972), Cons. Constructors Council Am., Newcomen Soc., Conf. Bd. (sr. mem.), Idaho Assn. Commerce and Industry (dir., chmn. 1974-77), The Moles (hon., mem. award 1978). Episcopalian. Elk. Clubs: Hillcrest Country (dir. 1965-67, 69, pres. 1967), Arid (exec. com. 1966); Ariz. Country (Phoenix); University (Mexico City); Stanford (Boise); Capitol Hill, International (Washington). Home: 4903 Roberts Rd Boise ID 83705

MCCLARY, TERENCE E., bus. exec.; b. Lincoln, Nebr., Dec. 1, 1921; s. Terence A. and Mildred A. (Wilson) McC.; B.S. in Bus. Adminstrn., U. Nebr., 1949; m. Florence H. Harris, May 15, 1950; children—Karyl, Karyn. Financial mgr. Gen. Electric Co., Schenectady, Pittsfield, Mass., Lynn, Mass., until 1969; v.p. finance, controller Sanders Assos., Inc., Nashua, N.H., 1969-73, also dir.; asst. sec. def., comptroller, Washington, 1973-76; v.p. Gen. Electric Co., 1976—. Mem. Cost Accounting Standards Bd., 1975-76. Served as 1st sgt., inf., AUS, 1942-46. Office: 3135 Easton Turnpike Fairfield CT 06431

MCCLATCHEY, DEVEREAUX FORE, lawyer; b. Marietta, Ga., June 1, 1906; s. Devereaux Fore and Leone (Awtrey) McC.; B.Ph., Emory U., 1926, LL.B., 1929; m. Dorothy Methvin, July 12, 1930; children—Eve Leah, Devereaux Fore. Admitted to Ga. bar, 1927; practice in Atlanta, 1930—; asso. Hirsch & Smith, 1930-36; partner Kilpatrick & Cody, 1936—. Vice pres., dir., mem. exec. com. Coastal States Life Ins. Co.; adv. dir. Fulton Nat. Bank, Randall Bros., Inc. Mem. Bd. Edn., Atlanta, 1937-57, pres., 1953-57; pres. Atlanta Symphony Guild, 1947-49. Mem. Ga. Ho. of Reps., 1965-70. Fellow Am. Coll. Probate Counsel; mem. Am., Ga., Atlanta (past pres.) bar assns., Atlanta Lawyers Club, Am. Law Inst., Kappa Sigma, Phi Alpha Delta. Democrat. Presbyn. Clubs: Piedmont Driving, Commerce, Capital City, Civitan (past pres. Atlanta) Home: 66 Avery Dr NE Atlanta GA 30309 Office: 3100 Equitable Bldg Atlanta GA 30303

MCCLATCHY, CHARLES KENNY, editor; b. Fresno, Calif., Mar. 25, 1927; s. Carlos Kelly and Phebe (Briggs) McC.; grad. Deerfield Acad. (Mass.), 1945; B.A., Stanford, 1950; m. Grace Kennan, Mar. 1, 1958 (div. 1968); children—Charles, Adair, Kevin. Reporter, Washington Post, 1953-55, Washington news bur. ABC-TV, 1957-58, Sacramento Bee, 1958-63; asso. editor McClatchy Newspapers, Sacramento, 1963-68, exec. editor, 1968-74, editor, 1974—, corp. v.p., 1969-78, pres., 1978—. Asst. press sec. Adlai Stevenson Presdl. campaign, 1956. Served to 1st lt. AUS, 1951-53. Clubs: Sutter (Sacramento); Bohemian (San Francisco). Home: 1621 11th Ave Sacramento CA 95818 Office: 21st and Q Sts Sacramento CA 95813

MCCLEARY, CHARLES DAVID, chemist; b. Huntsville, Ohio, Nov. 19, 1914; s. Charles S. and Jessie Myrtle (Forsythe) McC.; B.A., Wittenburg Coll., Springfield, Ohio, 1936; Ph.D., Ohio State U., 1940; m. Mary Gilkeson, Aug. 29, 1942; children—Katharine Elizabeth, Anne Forsythe, Charles Albert, Robert Steele. With Uniroyal Chem. div. Uniroyal, Inc., Naugatuck, Conn., 1940—, tech. coordinator polyvinyl chloride ops., 1954-58, asst. dir. research and devel., 1958-61, dir. research and devel., 1961—; ret., 1979—. Bd. dirs. Waterbury (Conn.) Symphony Orch.; mem. Naugatuck Charter Revision Commn. Fellow AAAS; mem. Am. Chem. Soc., Indsl. Research Inst., Naugatuck C. of C., Sigma Xi. Republican. Mem. United Ch. Christ. Club: Waterbury. Patentee in field. Home: 170 Allerton Rd Naugatuck CT 06770 Office: EMIC Spencer St Naugatuck CT 06770

MC CLEERY, WILLIAM THOMAS, playwright, editor; b. Hastings, Nebr., Sept. 15, 1911; s. Carl Kilburn and Vera Gertrude (Lowman) McC.; A.B., U. Nebr., 1931; m. Martha Davenport, Oct. 3, 1936 (div. 1946); 1 son, Michael Carl; m. 2d, Ann Roan Robinson, Mar. 18, 1950; 1 son, Samuel Adams. Feature writer Omaha World Herald; Washington staff A.P., 1932-34, exec. editor A.P. Feature Service, 1935-38; editorial staff Life mag., 1938-39; Sunday editor PM, 1939-45; asso. editor Ladies' Home Jour. 1958-63; editor Univ., Princeton (N.J.) quar., 1964-77, lectr. in playwriting Princeton U., 1967-77. Mem. bd. dirs. MacDowell Colony, 1948-70. Mem. Beta Theta Pi, Sigma Delta Chi. Author: Wolf Story, 1947; (plays) Hope for the Best, Parlor Story, Good Housekeeping, Love Out of Town, Good Morning Miss Dove, Hardesty Park; co-author: The Way to Go, 1974. Home: 317 Edgerstoune Rd Princeton NJ 08540

MC CLELLAN, ALBERT ALFRED, ch. ofcl.; b. Bowie, Tex., Dec. 22, 1912; s. Renick Kinnard and Mary Callie (Nipper) McC.; B.A., Bapt. U., 1939; Th.M., Southwestern Bapt. Theol. Sem., 1941; D.D. (hon.), Okla. Bapt. U., 1953; m. Mabel Ruth Helm, Oct. 20, 1939; children—Renick Helm, Alan Brownlow. Ordained to ministry, So. Bapt. Conv., 1931; pastor various chs. in Tex., 1931-34, 36-42, Waurika, Okla., 1942-45; editor Okla. Publs., So. Bapt. Conv. Exec. Com., Nashville, 1949-59, dir. program planning, 1959-72, asso. exec. sec., 1972—; cons. organizational problems So. Bapt. state convs., 1962—; mem. Ch. Exec. Devel. Program, 1969—. Trustee, Okla. Bapt. U., 1944-45, New Orleans Sem., 1945-49, Belmont Coll., 1952-59. Recipient Disting. Alumnus award Southwestern Sem., 1965, G.Y. Mullins award, 1976; Outstanding Alumni Achievement award Okla. Bapt. U., 1966. Mem. So. Bapt. Pub. Relations Soc. Author: Rainbow South, 1952; The West is Big, 1953; The Faith We Hold, 1954; Christian Stewardship, 1955; Look, Look, The Cities, 1957; The Christian's Role in World Peace, 1963; The Mission Tasks of the Church, 1969; Creative Expectancy, 1971; Openness and Freedom, 1972; Share the Word Now, 1973; The Hard Sayings of Jesus, 1975; Meet Southern Baptists, 1978; contbr. articles and poems to profl. publs.; editor: Okla. Baptist Messenger, 1945-49; Baptist Program, 1949-59. Home: 701 Brownlee Dr Nashville TN 37205 Office: 460 James Robertson Pkwy Nashville TN 37219

MCCLELLAN, BRUCE, educator; b. York, Pa., Apr. 10, 1924; s. William Smith and Josephine (Niles) McC.; grad. Deerfield Acad., 1941; B.A., Williams Coll., 1945; M.A., New Coll., Oxford U., 1949; L.H.D., Williams Coll., 1962; Litt.D., Lafayette Coll., 1963, Rider Coll., 1972; m. Mary E. Wisotzkey, June 15, 1946; children—Ann Ivison McClellan Miller, William Smith, Robert Niles. Tchr. Deerfield Acad., 1946-47; asst. dean Williams Coll., 1949-50; tchr. Lawrenceville Sch., 1950—, head master, 1959—. Served to capt. USAAF, 1942-45. Presbyn. Home: Foundation House Lawrenceville Sch Lawrenceville NJ 08648

MCCLELLAN, CAROLE KEETON, mayor; b. Austin, Sept. 13, 1939; d. W. Page and Madge Anna (Stewart) Keeton; B.A. in Govt. with honors, U. Tex., 1961; m. Barr McClellan, Oct. 14, 1960 (div.); children—Mark Barr, Bradley Dean and Dudley Page (twins), Scott Keeton. Tchr. civics and history, coach girls tennis McCallum High Sch., 1961, 63; trustee Austin Ind. Sch. Dist., 1972-77, v.p., 1974-76, pres. 1976-77; founding mem., trustee Austin Community Coll., pres. bd. trustees, 1976-77; mayor City of Austin, 1977—; mem. adv. bd. U.S. Conf. Mayors; vice chmn. Austin Parks and Recreation Bd. Trustee United Fund, Austin; mem. Nat. Community Edn. Adv. Council, HEW; mem. adv. bd. John F. Kennedy Sch. Govt.; bd. dirs. Austin Symphony, Big Bros., Austin, Austin Mental Health Assn., United Cerebral Palsy of Capital Area, Austin. Named 1 of Austin's 6 Outstanding Women, Am.-Statesman, 1970; a Women of Yr., Austin Citizen, 1976; 1 of Austin's 6 Valiant Women, Church Women United, 1976; 1 of Austin's 5 Outstanding Women, Women in Communication, 1976; 1 of 50 Faces for Am.'s Future, Time Mag., 1979; recipient Pendant award Austin Assn. Children with Learning Disabilities, 1976. Mem. LWV, Austin Women's Polit. Caucus, Nat. League Cities (vice chair environ. quality com.), Tex. Municipal League (dir., 1st v.p.), Tex. Arts Alliance, Jr. League Austin, Austin Women's Teams Assn. (past pres.), Capital Area Tennis Assn., Chi Omega Alumnae, Delta Kappa Gamma. Methodist. Clubs: Austin Women's, Austin Mothers of Twins (past pres.). Office: City of Austin PO Box 1088 Austin TX 78767

MCCLELLAN, CATHARINE, educator, anthropologist; b. York, Pa., Mar. 1, 1921; d. William Smith and Josephine (Niles) McClellan; A.B. magna cum laude in Classical Archaeology, Bryn Mawr Coll., 1942; Ph.D. (Anthropology fellow), U. Calif. at Berkeley, 1950; m. John Thayer Hitchcock, June 6, 1974. Vis. asst. prof. U. Mo. at Columbia, 1952; asst. prof. anthropology U. Wash., Seattle, 1952-56; anthrop. cons. USPHS, Arctic Health Research Center, Alaska, 1956; asst. prof. anthropology, chmn. dept. anthropology Barnard Coll., Columbia, 1956-61; asso. prof. anthropology U. Wis. at Madison, 1961-65, prof., 1965—, John Bascom prof., 1973; vis. lectr. Bryn Mawr (Pa.) Coll., 1954. Served to lt. WAVES, 1942-46. Margaret Snell fellow AAUW, 1950-51; Am. Acad. Arts and Scis. grantee, 1963-64, Nat. Mus. Can. grantee, 1948-74. Fellow Am. Anthrop. Assn., Royal Anthrop. Inst. Gt. Britain and Ireland, AAAS, Arctic Inst. N.Am.; mem. Am. Ethnol. Soc. (sec.-treas. 1958-59, v.p. 1964, pres. 1965), Kroeber Anthrop. Soc., Am. Folklore Soc., Am. Soc. Ethnohistory (exec. com. 1968-71), Sigma Xi. Asso. editor Arctic Anthropology, 1961, editor, 1975; asso. editor The Western Canadian Jour. of Anthropology, 1970. Various archaeol. and ethnographic field investigations in Alaska and Yukon Territory in Can. Home: 4110 Veith Ave Madison WI 53704 Office: Dept Anthropology Social Sci Bldg U Wis Madison WI 53706

MC CLELLAN, EDWIN, educator; b. Kobe, Japan, Oct. 24, 1925; s. Andrew and Teru (Yokobori) McC.; M.A., U. St. Andrews, Scotland, 1952; Ph.D., U. Chgo., 1957; m. Rachel Elizabeth Pott, May 28, 1955; children—Andrew Lockwood, Sarah Rose. Came to U.S., 1952. Instr. English, U. Chgo., 1957-59, asst. prof. Japanese lang. and lit., 1959-63, asso. prof., 1963-65, prof., 1965-70, Carl Darling Buck prof., 1970-72, chmn. Com. Far Eastern Studies, 1963-67, chmn. dept. Far Eastern langs. and civilizations, 1966-72; prof. Japanese lit. Yale U., 1972-79, Sumitomo prof. Japanese studies, 1979—, chmn. dept. East Asian langs. and lits., 1973—, chmn. council humanities, 1975-77, chmn. council East Asian studies, 1979—; vis. lectr. Far Eastern langs. Harvard, spring 1965; mem. adv. council dept. Oriental studies Princeton, 1966-71. Served with R.A.F., 1944-48. Fellow Am. Acad. Arts and Scis.; mem. Am. Oriental Soc. (dir.-at-large 1970-73). Translator: Kokoro (Natsume Soseki), 1957; Grass on the Wayside (Natsume Soseki), 1969; A Dark Night's Passing (Naoya Shiga), 1976. Author: Two Japanese Novelists; Soseki and Toson, 1969. Contbr. articles profl. jours. Home: 641 Ridge Rd Hamden CT 06517

MCCLELLAN, JAMES EDWARD, JR., educator; b. Temple, Tex., Nov. 26, 1922; s. James Edward and Claire (Thomson) McC.; B.A. cum laude, U. Tex., 1949; M.A., U. Ill., 1953, Ph.D., 1955; m. Sara Frances Graham, Apr. 30, 1945; children—James Edward III, John Ross, Murray C., Bruce Graham; m. 2d, Dorothy L. Spektorov, Feb. 17, 1973. Asst. prof. Fla. State U., 1953-54; asso. prof. Columbia, 1954-62; prof., chmn. dept. founds. Temple U., 1962-73; prof. philosophy of edn. State U. N.Y. at Albany, 1973—; Served as ensign, USNR, 1942-46. Guggenheim Found. fellow, 1964-65; Univ. Exchange scholar, 1979. Mem. Philosophy of Edn. Soc., Am. Fedn. Tchrs., Am. Philos. Assn. Author: (with Solon T. Kimball) Education in the New America, 1962; Toward An Effective Critique of American Education, 1968; Philosophy of Education, 1976. Contbr. articles profl. jours. Home: 22 Clarendon Rd Albany NY 12203 Office: SOE State U NY 1400 Washington Ave Albany NY 12222

MCCLELLAN, STAN LEON, army officer; b. Wichita Falls, Tex., Aug. 2, 1924; s. Albert Henry and Vernia (Walker) McC.; B.S., U. Neb., 1964; M.S., George Washington U., 1968; grad. Inf. Officer Advance Course, 1952, Command and Gen. Staff Coll., 1956, Armed Forces Staff Coll., 1960, Indsl. Coll. of Armed Forces, 1968; m. Phyllis Irene Emmons, May 10, 1947; children—Johnny Mercer, Karen Lissa. Commd. 2d lt. inf., U.S. Army, 1947, advanced through grades to maj. gen., 1973; tng. adviser Mil. Assistance Group, Belgium-Luxembourg, 1960-63; mech. inf. bn. comdr. 4th Inf. Div., Ft. Lewis, Wash., 1964-65; personnel mgmt. officer Dept. Army, Washington, 1965-67; combat brigade comdr., field force operations officer, Vietnam, 1968-69; div. chief, exec. officer Dept. Army Gen. Staff, Washington, 1969-70; asst. div. comdr. 3d Inf. Div., Germany, 1970-71; dir. tng., spl. asst. to comdr. U.S. Forces, Vietnam, 1971-72; chief of staff U.S. Army, Vietnam, 1972-73; dir. logistics/J4, U.S. Support Activities Group, Thailand, 1973, dep. chief staff personnel TRADOC, Ft. Monroe, 1974-77; co-dir. U.S. Spanish Combined Staff, Madrid, 1977—. Decorated D.S.M., Silver Star medal with oak leaf cluster, Legion of Merit with oak leaf cluster, Bronze Star medal with oak leaf cluster, Air medal with 12 oak leaf clusters, Army Commendation medal with 2 oak leaf clusters, Purple Heart with oak leaf cluster, Combat Inf. badge with star, Bravery Gold medal (Greece), Korean Order Hwa Rang, Korean Order Chung Mu, knight Vietnam Nat. Order, Vietnam Cross of Gallantry with 6 palms, Vietnam Cross of Gallantry with gold star, Cambodian Order of Republic with 2 gold palms. Contbr. articles to profl. publs. Address: US-Spanish Combined Staff Am Embassy APO New York NY 09285

MCCLELLAN, THOMAS MARCUS, JR., paper co. exec.; b. Atlanta, Jan. 8, 1899; s. Thomas Marcus and Walton (Harper) McC.; B.S., U. Ala., 1920; m. Philippa Haardt, June 27, 1931; children—Thomas McClellan III, Philippa (Mrs. Frank Bainbridge). With Birmingham Paper Co. (Ala.), 1920-60, pres., 1957-60; pres. Nifty Mfg. Co., div. St. Regis Paper Co., 1960-63, chmn. bd., 1963-71, dir. parent company, 1960-75. Vice pres. Anti Tb Assn., 1948-64. Mem. N.A.M. (dir. 1957-63), Paper Stationery and Tablet Assn. (dir. 1954-63), Nat. School Supply and Equipment Assn. (dir. 1955-61), Sigma Alpha Epsilon. Episcopalian (vestryman). Clubs: Rotary; Redstone; Country; Mountain Brook. Home: 3200 Argyle Rd Birmingham AL 35213

MC CLELLAN, WILLIAM MONSON, music librarian; b. Groton, Mass., Jan. 7, 1934; s. James Lewis and Ruth Caldwell (Monson) McC.; B.A., Colo. Coll., 1956, M.A., 1961; A.M. in L.S., U. Mich., Ann Arbor, 1959; m. Jane Muir, Sept. 3, 1955; children—Jennifer, Anne, Margaret, Amy. Music librarian U. Colo., Boulder, 1959-65, U. Ill., Urbana, 1965—; cons. music library resources and services to colls. and univs.; co-dir. Inst. Music Librarianship, Kent State U., 1969. Council on Library Resources fellow, 1976-77. Mem. Music Library Assn. (pres. 1971-73, conf. panelist), Internat. Assn. Music Libraries, Am. Musicol. Soc. Editor Music Library Assn. Notes, 1977—. Home: 1020 W Hill St Champaign IL 61820 Office: Music Bldg University of Illinois Urbana IL 61801

MCCLELLAND, DAVID CLARENCE, educator; b. Mt. Vernon, N.Y., May 20, 1917; s. Clarence Paul and Mary (Adams) McC.; A.B., Wesleyan U., 1938, Sc.D. (hon.), 1957; M.A., U. Mo., 1939; Ph.D., Yale, 1941; M.A. (hon.), Harvard, 1956; D.Phil. (hon.), U. Mainz (Germany), 1958; LL.D., MacMurray Coll., 1963; D.Litt. (hon.), Albion Coll., 1970; m. Mary Warner Sharpless, June 25, 1938; children—Catherine, Duncan, Nicholas, Sarah, Jabez. Instr. to prof. psychology Wesleyan U., 1941-56; prof. psychology dept. social relations Harvard, 1956—, chmn. dept. of social relations, 1962-67, chmn. staff Center for Research in Personality, 1956- 62, 1964- 67; Peace Corps cons., spring 1968. Psychology panel NRC, 1951-55, Fulbright award com., 1953-56; dep. dir. behavioral scis. div. Ford Found., 1952-53; tng. grants com. NIMH, 1956-61, Dir., Yarway Corp. Mem. New Eng. Psychol. Assn. (pres. 1967-68), Am. Acad. Arts and Scis., Soc. Friends, Phi Beta Kappa, Sigma Xi. Author: Personality, 1951; (with J. W. Atkinson, R.A. Clark, E.L. Lowell) The Achievement Motive, 1953; The Achieving Society, 1961; (with D.G. Winter) Motivating Economic Achievement, 1969; The Drinking Man, 1972; Power: The Inner Experience, 1975. Home: 81 Washington Ave Cambridge MA 02140

MCCLELLAND, HAROLD FRANKLIN, educator; b. Omaha, Mar. 8, 1918; s. Frank Melanchthon and Nellie (Hawthorne) McC.; B.A., Hastings Coll., 1939; M.A. U. Nebr., 1940; M.S., Denver U., 1942; Ph.D., Harvard, 1959; m. Marion Lois Ludlow, July 3, 1941; children—Donald G., Nancy J., Jeanne L. Research asso. Govtl. Research Inst., St. Louis, 1942-43; treas. McClelland-Rose Motors, Inc., Hastings, Neb., 1946-55; from instr. to prof. econs. Claremont (Calif.) Men's Coll. and Claremont Grad. Sch., 1958-65, dean faculty, 1963-70. Mem. Calif. Constn. Revision Commn., 1969-72. Served to lt. USNR, 1943-46. Mem. Am., Western econ. assns., Nat. Tax Assn. (bd. dirs. 1978—). Republican. Presbyterian. Clubs: Commonwealth of Calif.; University. Author: State and Local Finance, Nebraska, 1962; (with others) Essays in Federalism, 1961; (with others) The American Property Tax, 1965; also articles. Home: 457 Blaisdell Dr Claremont CA 91711

MC CLELLAND, JAMES CRAIG, lawyer; b. New Alexandria, Pa., Sept. 8, 1901; s. James Craig and Cora Blanche (Barnhart) McC.; B.A., Coll. Wooster, 1923; LL.B., Western Res. U., 1926; m. Eleanor May Hamilton, June 15, 1929 (dec. July 1964); children—Louise (Mrs. Gerhard Urban), James Craig, Jr.; m. Marjorie Brown Hilkert, Mar. 29, 1969. Admitted to Ohio bar, 1926, practice law, Cleve., 1926—, mem. firm Boer, Mierke, McClelland & Caldwell, and predecessor firms, 1926—. Counsel, Berea City Sch. Dist., Southwest Gen. Hosp. Mem. Am., Ohio (past mem. council of dels.), Cleve. (past mem. exec. com.) bar assns., Order of the Coif, Delta Sigma Rho. Home: Apt 1411 12540 Edgewater Dr Lakewood OH 44107 Office: 1530 Williamson Bldg Cleveland OH 44114

MCCLELLAND, JOHN GORDON, publisher; b. Toronto, Ont., Can., July 30, 1922; s. John and Sarah Ethel McClelland; B.A., Trinity Coll., 1946; LL.D., Carleton U., Ottawa; m. Elizabeth Matchett; children—Susan, Carol, Sarah, Anne, Robert. With McClelland and Stewart Ltd., Toronto, now pres., pub. Served with Canadian Navy, World War II. Decorated officer Order Can., 1975; recipient Banff medal U. Alta. Home: 141 Dunvegan Rd Toronto ON Canada Office: 25 Hollinger Rd Toronto ON M4B 3G2 Canada

MCCLELLAND, LLOYD SHAW, retail corp. exec., lawyer; b. Bellevue, Pa., Feb. 1, 1922; s. William C. and Virginia L. (Shaw) McC.; student Carnegie Inst. Tech., 1940-42; LL.B., Northwestern U., 1945; m. Janet Croft Cook, May 27, 1944; children—Sandra (Mrs. David R.

Lenigan), Margo (Mrs. John R. Hattery), Debra. Atty. firm Sidley, Austin, Burgess & Harper, Chgo., 1945-50; law dept. Sears, Roebuck & Co., Chgo., 1950-61, asst. sec., 1961-71, sec., gen. counsel, 1971—, v.p., 1973—; dir. Western Forge Corp., Colorado Springs, Colo. Mem. Am., Chgo. bar assns., Legal Club Chgo., Law Club Chgo., Assn. Gen. Counsel, Am. Soc. Corp. Secs., Phi Delta Phi. Club: North Shore Country (Glenview, Ill.). Home: 72 Canterbury E Northfield IL 60093 Office: Sears Tower Chicago IL 60684

MCCLELLAND, THOMAS HUTCHISON, bus. exec.; b. N.Y.C., 1909; grad. U. Calif., 1932. Chmn. bd. Placer Devel. Ltd., Vancouver, B.C., Can.; chmn., dir. Placer Amex Inc., Marcopper Mining Corp.; dir. Craigmont Mines Ltd., Gibraltar Mines Ltd. Mem. Mining Assn. B.C. Office: 700 Burrard Bldg Vancouver BC V63 3A8 Canada

MCCLELLAND, WALTER MOORE, fgn. service officer; b. Oklahoma City, July 13, 1922; s. James Bruce and Eugenia Gunnell (Moore) McC.; B.A., U. Va., 1944; LL.B., Harvard U., 1949, M.A., 1950; m. Frances Louise Shaffer, June 1, 1947; children—James Lloyd, William Cabell, James Bruce, Katherine Ann, Mary Elizabeth. Commd. fgn. service officer, Dept. State; vice consul, Liverpool, Eng., 1950-52; polit. officer, London, Eng., 1953-55; internat. relations officer European regional affairs, Dept. State, 1956-59; consul, Dhahran, 1959-61; econ., comml. officer, Baghdad, Iraq, 1964-67; internat. relations officer, Dept. State, 1967-70; dep. chief mission, Kuwait, 1970-74; fgn. service insp., Dept. State, 1974-76, mem. bd. Fgn. Service, 1976-77; counsul gen., Alexandria, Egypt, 1977—. Served with USNR, 1943-46. Mem. D.C. Bar Assn. Episcopalian. Home: 3818 Harrison St NW Washington DC 20015 Office: American Embassy Box 27 FPO NY 09527

MCCLENDON, CHARLES YOUMANS, football coach; b. Lewisville, Ark., Oct. 17, 1923; s. Leigh Alexander and Susie (Robey) McC.; B.A., U. Ky., 1950, M.A., 1951; m. Dorothy Faye Smart, Dec. 24, 1947; children—Dolores Kaye, Charles Scott. Asst. football coach U. Ky., 1951, Vanderbilt U., 1952; asst. coach La. State U., Baton Rouge, 1953-62, head coach, 1962—. Named Nat. Co-Coach of Yr., 1970. Served with USNR, 1943-46. Mem. Am. Football Coaches Assn. (pres. 1979). Address: Athletic Dept La State U Baton Rouge LA 70303

MCCLENDON, ERNESTINE EPPS, theatrical agt.; b. Norfolk, Va.; d. Edward and Lillie (Warren) Epps; m. George Wiltshire, Aug. 20, 1946. Actress, Woodstock Playhouse, N.Y.C., 1958, Casino Theatre, Newport, R.I., 1959, North Jersey, Playhouse, 1959, Jan Hus House, N.Y.C., 1959, Lenox Hill Playhouse, 1959-60, 60-61; toured summer theatres as Lena in A Raisin in the Sun, 1961; appeared in numerous films including A Face in the Crowd, 1957, The Last Angry Man, 1959, The Apartment, 1960, The Rat Race, 1960, The Young Doctors, The World by Night, 1961, The Young Savages, 1961; TV appearances, 1950; artists rep., owner Ernestine McClendon Enterprises, Inc., N.Y.C., 1962—, Hollywood, Cal., 1972—. Mem. Actors Guild Assn., Screen Actors Guild, A.F.T.R.A. Composer songs, 1966. Home: 8440 Sunset Blvd Los Angeles CA 90069 Office: 8440 Sunset Blvd Hollywood CA 90069. *Preparation and dedication are the keynotes to success.*

MC CLENDON, SARAH NEWCOMB, writer, news service exec.; b. Tyler, Tex., July 8, 1910; d. Sidney Smith and Annie Rebecca (Bonner) McClendon; student Tyler Jr. Coll.; grad. Sch. Journalism U. Mo.; widow; 1 dau., Salley Newcomb Theresa O'Brien Mac Donald. Mem. staff Tyler Courier-Times and Tyler Morning Telegraph, 1931-39; reporter Beaumont (Tex.) Enterprise; Washington corr. Phila. Daily News, 1944; founder Sarah McClendon News Service, Washington, 1946—, also service for radio and TV 1969—. Appearances on radio and TV shows including Today, Tomorrow, Tonight, Good Morning, Merv Griffin. Served with WAC. Recipient numerous awards including honored woman grad. U. Mo., Women's Achievement award Tex. Press Women, 1978, 1st prize for book My Eight Presidents; 2nd prize Nat. Fed Press Women, 1979. Mem. Am. Women in Radio and TV, U. Mo. Alumni (pres. chpt.), Women in Communications (Margaret Caskey award, Nat. Headliner award), Am. Newspaper Women's Club (pres.) D.A.R., Sigma Delta Chi. Clubs: Nat. Press (past v.p.), Washington Press. Syndicated columnist Intercontinental Press Syndicate, 1979. Address: 2933 28th St NW Washington DC 20008. *After covering eight presidents, I still feel that I am my own self, honest and owned by no one. I believe that journalism is a public trust and that I must uphold that public trust.*

MC CLENDON, WILLIAM HUTCHINSON, III, lawyer; b. New Orleans, Feb. 19, 1933; s. William H. and Eleanor (Eaton) McC.; B.A., Tulane U., 1956, LL.B., 1958; m. Eugenia Mills Slaughter, Feb. 6, 1960; children—William Hutchinson, IV, Virginia Morris, Eleanor Eaton, Bryan Slaughter. Admitted to La. bar, 1958, U.S. Supreme Ct. bar, 1964; atty. Humble Oil & Refining Co., 1958-60; with firm Taylor, Porter, Brooks & Phillips, Baton Rouge, 1961—, partner, 1966—; instr. comml. law and negotiable instruments Am. Inst. Banking, 1963-74. Lectr. immovable Property La. Bar Assn. Bridging the Gap Inst., 1965; lectr. La. State U. Law Sch. and Real Estate Seminar chmn., 1972, 74, 76. Bd. dirs. Cancer Soc. Baton Rouge, 1968-71; trustee Episcopal High Sch., 1976-78. Served to capt. AUS. Mem. Am., La. (chmn. sect. trust estates, probate and immovable property law 1969-70), Baton Rouge (chmn. title standards com. 1968-69) bar assns., Am. Judicature Soc., Tulane Alumni Assn. Greater Baton Rouge (pres. 1968-69), La. Tulane Law Alumni (treas., 2d v.p. 1964-65), Kappa Alpha. Democrat. Episcopalian (vestry, sr. warden 1975). Rotarian (dir. 1972). Toastmasters (pres. 1970). Clubs: Baton Rouge Country, Camelot (Baton Rouge); Pickwick (New Orleans). Home: Oakland at Gurley Ethel LA 70730 Office: 451 Florida St Baton Rouge LA 70821

MCCLENNAN, WILLIAM HOWARD, union ofcl.; b. Boston, Sept. 11, 1907; s. Samuel T. and Mary (Donahue) McC.; student Boston U., 1938-40; m. Muriel C. Ross, July 4, 1932; children—Howard, Ronald. Mgr., United Markets, Boston, Cambridge, Mass., 1930-42; mem. Boston Fire Dept., 1942-69; pres. Internat. Assn. Fire Fighters, Washington, 1968—; pres. public employees dept. AFL-CIO; mem. exec. bd. AFL-CIO. Democrat. Roman Catholic. Clubs: Touchdown, Exec. (Washington). Office: Internat Assn Fire Fighters United Nations Bldg 1750 New York Ave NW Washington DC 20006

MCCLENNAN, WILLIAM HOWARD, JR., mfr.; b. Boston, Apr. 29, 1934; s. William Howard and Muriel (Ross) McC.; B.S., Boston Coll., 1959; postgrad. Syracuse U., 1959-61; m. Claire Marie Cincotta, June 20, 1959; children—John Howard, Mark William. Accounting supr. Link div. Gen. Precision, Inc., Binghamton, N.Y., 1959-61; mgr. accounting, asst. treas. G.P.E. Controls, Inc., Chgo., 1961-66; mgr. accounting, div. controller, corporate controller J.I. Case Co., Racine, Wis., 1966-77; dir. internal audit Tenneco Inc., Houston, 1977—. Fin. adviser Racine Environment Com., 1970-71; pres. Racine Cath. Edn. Com., 1970-71; mem. Unified Sch. Dist. No. 1 Sch. Bd. Racine County, 1972-77; v.p. Unified Sch. Bd., 1974-75, treas., 1976-77; mem. Racine Sch. Traffic and Safety Commn., 1973-77; Racine Park and Recreation Commn., 1973-77; mem., pres. St. Mary's Parish Ch. Council, 1976-77. Served with USNR, 1953-55. Recipient Service award St. Mary's Ch., 1976, 77. Mem. Nat. Assn. Accountants, Racine Mfg. Assn. Alpha Kappa Psi. Club: Kiwanis (chmn. vocat. guidance and scholarship com.). Home: 5414 Pine Arbor St Houston TX 77066 Office: PO Box 2511 Houston TX 77001

MC CLENNEN, LOUIS, lawyer; b. Cambridge, Mass., May 29, 1912; s. Edward F. and Mary (Crane) McC.; A.B. cum laude, Harvard, 1934, J.D., 1937; m. Miriam Jacobs, Apr. 25, 1969; children (by previous marriage)—Adams, James, Helen, Persis, Crane, Emery. Admitted to Mass. bar, 1937, Ind. bar, 1940, Ariz. bar, 1946; practice in Boston, 1937-39, Indpls., 1940-42, Phoenix, 1946—; now partner Allen, McClennen & Fels; adj. prof. law (fed. taxation) Ariz. State U., 1974—. Pres. Ariz. Bd. Edn., 1965-69; trustee No. Ariz. Mus.; former pres., bd. dirs. Maricopa County Legal Aid Soc., Phoenix Symphony Assn.; v.p., bd. dirs. Phoenix United Fund; sec., bd. dirs. Phoenix Country Day Sch.; bd. dirs. Ariz. Acad.; regional dir. Asso. Harvard Alumni. Served to maj. USAAF, 1942-46. Mem. Am., Ariz., Maricopa County (dir., past v.p.) bar assns., Harvard Law Sch. Assn. (v.p.), Lawyers Club Phoenix (pres.). Unitarian. Clubs: Country (Phoenix); Yacht (Chatham, Mass.). Author: (with others) Arizona Estate Tax, 1953; (with J. T. Melczer, Jr.) Arizona Income Tax Regulations, 1954. Contbr. articles to profl. mags. Home: 5311 La Plaza Circle Phoenix AZ 85012 Office: 101 N 1st Ave Suite 2323 Phoenix AZ 85003

MCCLENNEY, BYRON NELSON, community coll. pres.; b. San Antonio, Dec. 14, 1939; s. Thomas B. and Lorene Holley McC.; B.S., U. Tex., 1961, M.Ed., 1963, Ed.D., 1969; m. Mary Ann Zupan, Mar. 21, 1959; children—Mark Nelson, Don Alan. Asst. dean evening div. San Antonio Coll., 1966-68; dean instrn. McLennan Community Coll., Waco, Tex., 1968-70; dean instrn. Eastfield Coll., Dallas County, Tex., 1970-71, pres., 1971-78; pres. Parkersburg (W.Va.) Community Coll., 1978—; cons. Nat. Center for Higher Edn. Mgmt. Systems. Chmn. Library Bd., Garland, Tex., 1976-77; chmn. bd. dirs. YMCA, Garland, Tex., 1977. NDEA fellow, 1965-66. Mem. Commn. on Instns. of Higher Edn., N. Central Assn., Am. Assn. Community and Jr. Colls. (mem. exec. com. pres.' acad.). Baptist. Club: Rotary (past dist. gov.). Home: 117 Woodshire North Hills Parkersburg WV 26101 Office: Rt 5 Box 167-A Parkersburg WV 26101

MCCLESKEY, JAMES MILTON, JR., chem. co. exec.; b. Daisy, Tenn., Oct. 15, 1923; s. James Milton and Almyrt (Smith) McC.; student Rice U., 1940-43; B.B.A., U. Tex., El Paso, 1948; m. Cynthia Vaughn Crowe, Feb. 16, 1945; children—James Milton, Michael L. Accountant, Thurston & Grider Co., El Paso, Tex., 1946-50; treas. Mitchell Brewing Co., El Paso, 1952-56; with El Paso Products Co., Odessa, Tex., 1956—, v.p., 1960-74, exec. v.p., 1974—, also dir.; dir. Odessa Natural Corp., BEM Holding Co., Am. Bank, Odessa. Pres. Permian Playhouse, Odessa, 1970; sr. warden St. John's Episcopal Ch., Odessa, 1974; lifetime dir. Odessa YMCA. Served with Chem. Corps, U.S. Army, 1943-46, Finance Corps, 1950-52. C.P.A., Tex. Mem. Am. Inst. C.P.A.'s, Tex. Soc. C.P.A.'s. Clubs: Odessa Country, Plaza of Houston. Home: 2724 Palo Verde Odessa TX 79763 Office: PO Box 3986 Odessa TX 79760

MCCLESTER, JOHN RICHARD, finance co. exec.; b. Butler, Pa., Oct. 16, 1923; s. Robert Howard and Verna (Shull) McC.; B.A., Washington and Jefferson Coll., 1944; postgrad. Stanford U., 1968; m. Jean Donaldson, Nov. 29, 1946; children—John R., Jr., Martha Louise. Mem. treasury dept. Westinghouse Electric Corp., Pitts., 1953-64; v.p. Westinghouse Credit Corp., Pitts., 1965-70, pres., 1970—, dir., 1970—; dir. Westinghouse Leasing Corp., 1970—. Dir. Presbyn. Econ. Devel. Corp., 1973-75; trustee Washington and Jefferson Coll., 1979—, Mt. Lebanon Presbyn. Ch. Served with AUS, 1944-46. Clubs: Butler (Pa.) Country; Sewickley Heights Golf; Allegheny, Duquesne (Pitts.). Home: Fairway Dr RD 3 Sewickley PA 15143 Office: 3 Gateway Center Pittsburgh PA 15222

MCCLIMANS, JAMES DEAN, drug and dept. store exec.; b. Greenville, Pa., Apr. 4, 1922; s. James Homer and Kathryn (Dean) McC.; B.A., Allegheny, 1943; m. Nancy Lucille Martin, Sept. 23, 1943; children—James Lynn, Donald Paul, Nancy Ellen, Robert Martin. Asst. credit mgr. Talon, Inc., Meadville, Pa., 1946-50; with Joseph & Feiss Co., Cleve, 1950-70, v.p. adminstrn., 1965-67, sr. v.p., 1967-70; exec. v.p. adminstrn. Gray Drug Stores, Inc., Cleve., 1970-73, exec. v.p., dir., 1973—. Mem. bd. rev. and allocation Cleve. Welfare Fedn. Bd. dirs. Garden Valley Neighborhood House; trustee West Side YMCA, Greater Cleve. Jr. Achievement, 1974—. Served as lt. USNR, 1943-46; ETO, PTO. Mem. Phi Gamma Delta. Republican. Mem. United Ch. Christ. Clubs: Vermilion Yacht; Catawba Island (Port Clinton, Ohio); Cleveland Athletic. Home: 5372 Portage Dr Vermilion OH 44089 Office: 666 Euclid Ave Cleveland OH 44114

MCCLINTOCK, ARCHIE GLENN, justice; b. Sheridan, Wyo., Mar. 26, 1911; s. James Porter and Martie E. (Glenn) McC.; A.B., U. Wyo., 1933, LL.B., 1935; m. Ina Jean Robinson, May 27, 1939 (dec. 1974); children—Ellery, Jeffry, Kathleen. Admitted to Wyo. bar, 1935; pvt. practice law, Cheyenne, Wyo., 1935-73; justice Wyo. Supreme Ct., Cheyenne, 1973—. Mem. Wyo. Fair Employment Practices Commn., 1965-71. Served with USNR, 1944-46. Mem. Wyo. State Bar (pres. 1950-51), Am. Bar Assn., Am. Judicature Soc., Sigma Nu. Democrat. Club: Elks. Home: 1211 Richardson Ct Cheyenne WY 82001 Office: Supreme Ct Bldg Cheyenne WY 82001

MCCLINTOCK, DAVID WILLIAM, fgn. service officer; b. Los Angeles, Apr. 11, 1932; s. Albert Fletcher and Geraldine (Cheney) McC.; B.A. in Internat. Relations, U. Calif. at Los Angeles, 1954; M.A. in Polit. Sci., U. Mich., 1969, Ph.D. in Polit. Sci., 1973; m. Susan Melinda Clough, Dec. 29, 1968; children—Anna, Lesley, Nathan. Joined U.S. Fgn. Service, 1960; vice consul, Manila, Philippines, 1960-62; attache Am. embassy, Beirut, Lebanon, 1962-64; 2d sec. embassy, consul, Sanaa, Yemen, 1964-66; in charge analysis Arabian Peninsula affairs Dept. State, Washington, 1966-68; chief diplomatic mission, Sanaa, Yemen Arab Republic, 1970-72; 1st. sec., chief polit. sect. Am. embassy, Amman, Jordan, 1972-74; dep. dir. Office Security Assistance Dept. State, Washington, 1974-76; sr. tng. fellow Nat. Def. U., 1976-77; coordinator polit. studies Fgn. Service Inst., 1977-79; food and agr. adviser OES Bur., 1979—. Served to 1st lt. AUS, 1954-56. Recipient Meritorious Honor award Dept. State, 1968, 72. Ford Found. grantee, 1969; Woodrow Wilson vis. fellow, 1978-79. Author: U.S. Food—Making the Most of a Global Resource, 1978; contbr. chpts. to books, also articles to profl. jours. and mags. Home: 3825 Cathedral Ave NW Washington DC 20016 Office: US Dept State Washington DC 20520

MCCLINTOCK, ROSS AUGUSTUS, oil co. exec.; b. Corona, Calif., Apr. 29, 1921; s. Augustus and Iva A. (Roberds) McC.; student Fullerton Jr. Coll., 1939-40; B.A., U. N.Mex., 1940-41; m. Andrea Todd Hanna, Nov. 30, 1973; children—Julia (Mrs. Richard Yutuc), Ross Augustus Jr. Field engr. Drilling & Exploration Co., Los Angeles, 1947-50; sales engr. Shaffer Tool Works, Brea, Calif., 1950-56; with Western Offshore Drilling & Exploration Co., Los Angeles, 1956—, pres., 1963—; sr. v.p., dir. Fluor Corp., Los Angeles, 1969—; dir., pres. Hellenic Oil, S. China Sea and S. Pacific Oil, Inc. Mem. Orange County (Calif.) Republic and Central Com., 1956-59; 4-H Club and Future Farmers Am. sponsor, Orange, Calif. Served as pilot USAAF, World War II. Decorated air medals. Patentee offshore and drilling techniques. Home: 18141 Estes Way Santa Ana CA 92705 Office: Fluor Corporation 3333 Michelson Dr Irvine CA 92730

MC CLINTON, DONALD G., mfg. co. exec.; b. Pitts., June 30, 1933; s. Donald K. and Ethel M. McC.; B.S., Miami U., Oxford, Ohio, 1955; m. Jane Ann Knoebel, Apr. 12, 1958; children—Catherine, D. Scott. Audit mgr. Arthur Andersen & Co., Cleve., 1955-62; mgr. accounting E. Ohio Gas Co., Cleve., 1962-66; exec. v.p. Nat. Industries, Inc., Louisville, 1966—. Mem. Louisville-Jefferson County Bicentennial Commn., 1976-77; mem. council, treas. Old Kentucky Home council Boy Scouts Am., 1976-77; mem. Citizens at Large Jefferson County Budget Com., 1978—; bd. overseers Bellarmine Coll., 1978—; bd. dirs. Ky. Derby Festival, 1978—. Mem. Am. Mgmt. Assn., Am. Inst. C.P.A.'s, Ohio Soc. C.P.A.'s, Fin. Execs. Inst., Nat. Assn. Accountants, Louisville Area C. of C. Home: 6205 Deep Creek Dr Prospect KY 40059 Office: Bank of Louisville Bldg 510 W Broadway Louisville KY 40202

MC CLINTON, KATHARINE MORRISON, writer; b. San Francisco, Jan. 23, 1899; d. Robert and Leila (Perry) Morrison; A.B., Stanford, 1921; A.M., Columbia, 1922; Dr. Arts and Letters, Wheaton Coll., 1961; m. Richard Frederick Kahle, Sept. 11, 1923; 1 dau., Julianna Ashley (Mrs. Martin A. Mortensen); m. 2d, Harold Leander McClinton, Oct. 25, 1935. Decorator, W. & J. Sloane decoration dept., 1922-23; lectr. art and interior decoration U. Cal. Extension, 1925-31; art criticism column San Diego Sun, 1930-33; bd. dirs. San Diego Fine Arts Gallery, 1930-35, ofcl. lectr., 1935; editorial staff McCall's Mag., 1938-39; nat. adv. com., lectr. religious art Contemporary Crafts Mus., N.Y.C., 1957, Dallas Mus. Fine Arts, 1958, Gen. Theol. Sem., Chrysler Mus., Norfolk, Va., and others; lectr. antiques collecting San Diego Fine Arts Gallery, N.Y. Hist. Soc. Exhibited paintings So. Cal. Art Assn., Ann., 54th Ann. Expn., San Francisco Art Assn., Faulkner Meml. Art Gallery, Santa Barbara, Cal., Cal. State Fair, Santa Monica Art Assn., Pasadena Art Inst. Decorated Women's Bldg., San Diego Expn., 1935. Mem. Nat. Sculpture Soc., N.Y. Hist. Soc., Alpha Phi. Episcopalian. Author: An Outline of Period Furniture, 1929; Modern French Decoration, 1930; Flower Arrangement in the Church, 1944; A Handbook of Popular Antiques, 1946; American Glass, 1950; Good Housekeeping in the Church, 1951; Antique Collecting for Everyone, 1951; Antique Collecting, 1952; Loaves and Fishes, 1955; The Changing Church: Its Architecture, Art and Decoration, 1957; Christian Church Art Through the Ages, 1961; Complete Book of Small Antiques Collecting, 1965; Collecting American Victorian Antiques, 1966; Complete Book of Country Antiques, 1967; Collecting American 19th Century Silver, 1968; Antiques of American Childhood, 1970; Antiques in Miniature, 1970; Antiques: Past and Present, 1971; Art Deco, 1972; Antique Cats for Collectors, 1973; The Chromolithographs of Louis Prang, 1973; Lalique for Collectors, 1975; Royal Doulton Figurines and Character Jugs, 1978; Introduction to Lalique Glass, 1978. Contbr. to art and home decorating mags. Home: 25 East End Ave New York City NY 10028 (winter) 2280 Cahuilla Hills Dr Palm Springs CA 92262

MC CLINTON, ROBERT BROCK, naval officer; b. Bryn Mawr, Pa., July 1, 1925; s. Harold Leander and Elma (Dick) McC.; student Williams Coll., Williamstown, Mass., 1943-44; B.S. in Elec. Engring., U.S. Naval Acad., 1947; M.S. in Internat. Affairs, George Washington U., 1969; m. Gunvor Maria Nyzell, July 1, 1948; children—Joyce Elizabeth McClinton Mast, Kim McClinton Lyttle. Commd. ensign U.S. Navy, 1947, advanced through grades to rear adm., 1974; surface warfare specialist, 1947—; comdg. officer U.S.S. Conflict, 1955-57, U.S.S. Turner Joy, 1965-66, U.S.S. Detroit, 1970-71; comdr. Destroyer Squadron 1, 1971-72, Navy Recruiting Command, 1975-77, Naval Surface Group, Western Pacific, 1977-79; comdr. U.S. Naval Base and comdt. 6th Naval Dist., Charleston, S.C., 1979—; mem. adv. com. Naval Sea Cadet Corps. Decorated Legion of Merit with Gold Star, Meritorious Service Medal. Mem. U.S. Naval Inst., Naval Hist. Soc. Episcopalian. Club: Bohemian (San Francisco). Home: 1314 Elsinore Ave McLean VA 22102 Office: Commander US Naval Base Charleston SC 29408

MCCLORY, ROBERT, congressman; b. Riverside, Ill., Jan. 31, 1908; s. Frederick Stevens and Catherine (Reilly) McC.; student L'Institut Sillig, Vevey, Switzerland, 1925-26, Dartmouth, 1926-28; LL.B., Chicago-Kent College, 1932; m. Audrey Vasey (dec. Sept. 1967); children—Beatrice (Mrs. Etienne), Michael, Oliver; m. 2d, Doris S. Hibbard, Mar. 1969. Admitted to Ill. bar, 1932; pvt. practice, Chgo. and Waukegan, 1932-62; mem. Ill. Ho. of Reps., 1951-52, Ill. Senate, 1952-62; mem. 88th-96th congresses from 13th Ill. Dist., ranking Republican mem. Judiciary Com.; mem. House Select Com. on Intelligence, 1976. Mem. congl. del. to Interparliamentary Union, 1964—; participant Ditchley Conf., London, 1966; mem. congl. del. to Environ. Conf., Stockholm, 1972. Mem. Am., Ill., Lake County bar assns., Navy League, Waukegan-Lake County C. of C., Psi Upsilon, Phi Delta Phi. Republican. Christian Scientist. Clubs: Chgo. Law; Bath and Tennis (Lake Forest, Ill.); Capitol Hill (Washington). Home: 340 Prospect Ave Lake Bluff IL 60044 also 321 Constitution Ave NE Washington DC 20002 Office: Rayburn House Office Bldg Washington DC 20515 also County Bldg Waukegan IL 60085 also 150 Dexter Ct Elgin IL 60120 also 56 N Williams St Crystal Lake IL 60014

MCCLORY, SEAN JOSEPH, actor; b. Dublin, Ireland, Mar. 8, 1924; s. Hugh Patrick and Mary Margaret (Ball) McC.; ed. Jesuit Coll. (Ireland), Med. Sch. of Nat. U. Ireland; m. Suzanne Alexander White; children by previous marriage—Duane, Kevin, Cathleen. Actor, Gaelic Theatre, Galway, Ireland, from 1932; with Abbey Theatre, Dublin, 1944-46; with RKO, Hollywood, Calif., 1946, appeared in films Roughshod, 1947, Rogues March, Daughter of Rosie O'Grady, Lorna Doone, 1951, The Quiet Man, 1952, Plunder of the Sun, Island in the Sky, 1953, Ring of Fear, Moonfleet, 1954, Diane, I Cover the Underworld, The Long Grey Line, 1955, Guns of Fort Petticoat, 1957, Cheyenne Autumn, 1960, Valley of the Dragons, 1961, Follow Me Boys, 1966, The Gnomemobile, 1967, Bandolero, 1968, Day of the Wolves, 1971; appeared on Broadway in King of Friday's Men; appeared in plays including Juno and the Paycock, The Lady's Not for Burning, Anna Christie, Billy Budd, Dial M for Murder, Shadow of a Gunman; appeared on numerous television programs; co-star series The Californians, 1957-58, Kate McShane, 1975; producer-dir. The Tara Theatre, San Francisco, 1949-50. Mem. Actors Equity, Screen Actors Guild, AFTRA, Dirs. Guild Am., Soc. for Preservation of Variety Arts. Club: Magic Castle. Author: (play) Moment of Truth, 1971. Home: 6612 Whitley Terr Los Angeles CA 90068 Office: care Ralph A Rosner & Assos Suite 107 449 S Beverly Dr Beverly Hills CA 90212

MCCLOSKEY, JOHN MICHAEL, orgn. exec.; b. Eugene, Oreg., Apr. 26, 1934; s. John C. and Agnes M. (Studer) McC.; B.A., Harvard, 1956; J.D., U. Oreg., 1961; m. Maxine E. Mugg Johnson, June 17, 1965; stepchildren—Claire Johnson, Laura Johnson, James Johnson, Rosemary Johnson. Northwest conservation rep. Sierra Club, Fedn. Western Outdoor Clubs, Eugene, 1961-65; asst. to pres. Sierra Club, San Francisco, 1965, conservation dir., 1966-69, chief staff, 1969, exec. dir., 1970—; mem. Pres.'s Commn. on Agenda for 1980's. Past mem. adv. bd. Ford. Found. Energy Policy Project; mem. coordinating subcom. com. on strategic oil storage and enhanced oil recovery Nat. Petroleum Council; co-chmn. mining subcom. Nat. Coal Policy Project; past mem. Council on Population and Environment; past mem. Am. com. Internat. Wildlife Protection Bd. dirs. League Conservation Voters, Resolve; mem. adv. bd. Arbor Day Found.; chmn. environ. subcom., com. on surface mining and reclamation Nat. Acad. Sci. Served to capt. AUS, 1956-58. Recipient Profl. Service award Calif. Conservation Council, 1969; John Muir award Sierra Club, 1979. Mem. Mem. adv. bd. Energy Rev. Home: 93 Florada Ave Piedmont CA 94610 Office: 530 Bush St San Francisco CA 94108

MCCLOSKEY, PAUL N., JR., congressman; b. San Bernardino, Calif., Sept. 29, 1927; A.B., Stanford, 1950, LL.B., 1953; m. Caroline W. McCloskey (div.); children—Nancy, Peter, John, Kathleen. Admitted to Calif. bar, 1953; mem. firm McCloskey, Wilson, Mosher & Martin, Palo Alto, 1956-67; mem. 90th-94th congresses from 17th Calif. Dist., 95th congress from 12th Dist.; del. UN Law of Sea Conf. Served to col. USMC. Decorated Navy Cross, Silver Star, Purple Heart. Mem. Am., Palo Alto (pres. 1960-61), Santa Clara County (trustee 1965-67) bar assns., State Bar Calif. (pres. conf. barristers 1961-62), Phi Delta Phi. Republican. Author: Truth and Untruth, 1972. Home: 1344 29th St NW Washington DC 20007 Office: 305 Grant Ave Palo Alto CA 94306 also 205 Cannon House Office Bldg Washington DC 20515

MC CLOSKEY, PETER FRANCIS, trade assn. exec.; b. N.Y.C., Jan. 10, 1935; s. Joseph Michael and Frances Mary (McAllister) McC.; B.S. in Physics, Holy Cross Coll., 1956; postgrad. Georgetown U. Law Sch., 1959-62, Fordham U. Sch. Law, 1963-65; m. Louise C. Collins, Nov. 28, 1959; children—Mary Catherine, Margaret Ann, Elizabeth, Patricia. Contract adminstr. Melpar, Inc., Falls Church, Va., 1959-60; programmer, systems analyst, mktg. rep., advanced systems mgr., contract adminstr., domestic licensing mgr. IBM, 1960-65; v.p. Farrington Mfg. Co., Washington, 1965, pres., 1968-69, chmn. bd., 1969-70; pres. Peter F. McCloskey and Assos, Inc., 1970—; partner firm Hughes & McCloskey, 1971—; pres., chief exec. officer Computer and Bus. Equipment Assn., 1973-77; pres., chief exec. officer Electronic Industries Assn., 1977—; dir Janus Cons. Bd. dirs. Am. Nat. Standards Inst. Served with USMC. Recipient Am. jurisprudence prize Fordham U. Mem. Bar State N.Y., D.C. Bar, Va. Bar, Young Pres. Assn. Roman Catholic. K.C. Clubs: University (N.Y.C., Washington); Congressional Country; Regency (McLean, Va.). Home: 7625 Burford Dr McLean VA 22102 Office: 2001 Eye St Washington DC 20036

MCCLOSKEY, ROBERT, artist; b. Hamilton, Ohio, Sept. 15, 1914; s. Howard Hill and Mabel (Wismaier) McC.; student Vesper George Sch., Boston, N.Y.C., N.A.D.; Dr. of Letters, Miami U., Oxford, Ohio, 1962, Mt. Holyoke Coll., South Hadley, Mass., 1967; m. Margaret Durand, Nov. 23, 1940; children—Sarah, Jane. Artist, illustrator; host Am. Songfest, Weston Woods bicentennial film. Recipient numerous awards including President's award for creative work, Nat. Acad. Design, 1936; fellowship for painting, Prix de Rome, Am. Acad. in Rome, 1939; Caldecott medal for most distinguished picture book for children published in 1941 (awarded at A.L.A. conv., Milw.), 1942; second Caldecott medal for Time of Wonder, 1958; Regina medal Cath. Library Assn., 1974. Executed bas-reliefs for Hamilton (Ohio) Municipal Bldg., 1935. Fellow Am. Acad. Rome; mem. P.E.N., Author's League Am. Author: Lentil, 1940; Make Way for Ducklings, 1941; Homer Price, 1943; Blueberries for Sal, 1948; Centerburg Tales, 1951; One Morning in Maine, 1952; Time of Wonder, 1957; Bert Dow, Deep Water Man, 1963. Home: Little Deer Island ME 04650 Office: care Viking Press 625 Madison Ave New York NY 10022

MCCLOSKEY, ROBERT JAMES, diplomat; b. Phila., Nov. 25, 1922; s. Thomas and Anna (Wallace) McC.; B.S. in Journalism, Temple U., 1953; postgrad. George Washington U., 1958-59; m. Anne Taylor Phelan, July 8, 1961; children—Lisa Siobhan, André Taylor McCloskey. Engaged in hotel work, 1945-50, as newspaper reporter, 1952-55; joined U.S. Fgn. Service, 1955; assigned Hong Kong, 1955-57; publs. officer State Dept., 1957-58; press officer Office of News, 1958-60; assigned U.S. Mission to UN 15th Gen. Assembly, 1960-62; spl. asst. Bur. Pub. Affairs, State Dept., 1962-63, dep. dir. Office News, 1963-64, dir., 1964-66, dep. asst. sec. of state, 1966-69, dep. asst. sec., spl. asst. to sec. for press relations Office Press Relations, 1969-73; ambassador to Republic of Cyprus, 1973-74; ambassador-at-large, 1974-75; ambassador at large, asst. sec. state for congl. relations, 1975-76; ambassador to the Netherlands, 1976-78; ambassador to Greece, 1978—. Served with USMC, 1942-45. Office: American Embassy Athens Greece

MCCLOUD, JAMES FERDINAND, engring. co. exec.; b. Oakland, Calif., July 2, 1918; s. Albert Blaine and Maria Sylvia (Torre) McC.; B.M.E., Stanford U., 1941; Sc.D. (hon.), St. Mary's Coll., Moraga, Calif., 1963; m. Geneva K. Edgar, July 2, 1944; children—Kimball Patrick, Kelly William, Mark Torre, James Andrews. With Henry J. Kaiser Co., 1941—, group v.p., then dir. Kaiser Industries Corp., Oakland, Calif., 1971—, pres. Kaiser Engrs., Inc., Oakland, 1974—; dir., mem. exec. com. Raymond Internat. Inc., Houston. Mem. adv. bd. Sch. Bus., U. Santa Clara (Calif.); adv. council Sch. Engring., Stanford U.; trustee Am. Grad. Sch., Internat. Mgmt. Bd. regents, trustee St. Mary's Coll.; chmn. United Bay Area Crusade, Alameda County, Calif., 1974; bd. dirs. New Oakland Com., 1977—, Marcus A. Foster Ednl. Inst., Oakland, 1977—. Named Exec. of Year, Argentine Press Assn., 1964; knight St. Gregory the Great, Pope Paul VI, 1964; registered profl. engr., Calif. Mem. Am. Iron and Steel Inst. Roman Catholic. Clubs: Pacific Union (San Francisco); Silverado Country (Napa, Calif.); Jockey (Buenos Aires). Home: 45 Glen Alpine Rd Piedmont CA 94611 Office: 300 Lakeside Dr Oakland CA 94666

MC CLOY, JOHN JAY, lawyer; b. Phila., Mar. 31, 1895; s. John Jay and Anna May (Snader) McC.; A.B. cum laude, Amherst Coll., 1916; LL.B., Harvard, 1921; LL.D., Amherst Coll., Syracuse U., Colby Coll., U. Md., U. Pa., Yale U., Princeton U., U. Notre Dame, Swarthmore Coll., Wilmington Coll., Washington U., Harvard, Columbia U., Dartmouth Coll., Doshisha U., Tokyo U., N.Y. U., Trinity Coll., Brown U., Williams Coll., Middlebury Coll., Boston U., Haverford Coll., Lehigh U., Franklin and Marshall Coll.; D.C.L., Washington Coll.; Dr. Ing., Tech. U. Berlin (Charlottenberg); m. Ellen Zinsser, Apr. 25, 1930; children—John Jay, Ellen. Admitted to N.Y. bar, 1921; with Cadwalader, Wickersham & Taft, 1921-25; with Cravath, de Gersdorff, Swaine & Wood, 1925-40, mem. firm, 1929-40; became expert cons. to sec. of war, Oct. 1940; asst. sec. of war, Apr. 1941-Nov. 1945; mem. Milbank, Tweed, Hope, Hadley & McCloy, 1946-47; pres. World Bank, 1947-49; U.S. Mil. Gov. and High Commr. for Germany, 1949-52; chmn. bd. Chase Nat. Bank, N.Y.C., 1953; chmn. bd. Chase Manhattan Bank (merger Chase Nat. Bank and Bank of Manhattan Co.), 1955-60; co-ordinator U.S. disarmament activities, 1961-63; mem. Milbank, Tweed, Hadley, and McCloy, 1962—. Dir. Dreyfus Corp., Mercedes Benz N.Am.; chmn. exec. com. Squibb Corp. Chmn. Pres.'s Gen. Adv. Com. on Arms Control and Disarmament, 1961-74; chmn. Am. Council on Germany. Hon. trustee Lenox Hill Hosp.; trustee John M. Olin Found.; hon. chmn. bd., trustee emeritus Amherst Coll.; hon. chmn. bd. Council Fgn. Relations, Inc., Internat. House-N.Y.; hon. chmn. Atlantic Inst. (Paris); chmn. Ford Found., 1953-65; mem. exec. com. Salk Inst. Served as capt., field arty., AEF, World War I. Decorated D.S.M., Presdl. Medal of Freedom, Grand Officer Legion of Honor (France); Grand Ofcl. Order of Merit (Italy); Grand Cross Order of Merit (Germany). Mem. Am. Bar Assn., Assn. Bar City N.Y., Am. Inst. C.P.A.'s (chmn. public oversight bd.), Order of Coif. Republican. Presbyn. Clubs: Century, Clove Valley Rod and Gun, Bond, Links, Recess, University, Anglers (N.Y.C.); Metropolitan (Washington). Home: 404 June Rd Cos Cob CT 06807 Office: 1 Chase Manhattan Plaza New York NY 10005

MCCLOY, WILLIAM ASHBY, educator; b. Balt., Jan. 2, 1913; s. Charles Harold and Anna (Fisher) McC.; grad. Phillips Andover Acad., 1930; B.A., U. Ia., 1933, M.A., 1936, M.F.A., 1949, Ph.D., 1958; m. Patricia Caroline Hill, June 3, 1936. Asst. prof. art Drake U., 1937-39; instr. art edn. U. Wis., 1939-43, asst. prof., 1946-48; prof., dir. Sch. Art, U. Man. (Can.), 1950-54; prof. art, chmn. Conn. Coll., 1954-72, prof., 1954-78, Henry B. Plant prof. art, 1970-78. Bd. dirs. Fred and Florence Olsen Found. Mem. Nordica Meml. Assn. (trustee 1971—). Prints represented in several museums; paintings widely exhibited; sculptures owned by Conn. Coll. Home: 430 Kitemaug Rd Uncasville CT 06382

MC CLUNG, JIM HILL, mfg. co. exec.; b. Buena Vista, Ga., Nov. 8, 1936; s. Jim Hill and Marjorie (Oxford) McC.; B.A., Emory U., 1958; M.B.A., Harvard U., 1964; m. Jo Patrick, July 5, 1958; children—Jim Hill, Karen Mareese. With Lithonia Lighting div. Nat. Service Industries, Inc., Conyers, Ga., 1964—, now pres. Served with USAF, 1958-62. Mem. Young Pres.'s Orgn. Methodist. Office: Lithonia Lighting Box A Conyers GA 30207

MC CLUNG, LELAND SWINT, microbiologist, educator; b. Atlanta, Tex., Aug. 4, 1910; s. Joe Baker and Roxie Buelah (Swint) McC.; A.B., U. Tex., 1931, A.M., 1932; Ph.D., U. Wis., 1934; m. Ruth Wilhelmien Exner, Dec. 25, 1944. Research bacteriologist Am. Can Co., Maywood, Ill., 1934-36; instr. in fruit products and jr. bacteriologist Coll. Agr., U. Calif., 1936-37; instr. research medicine George Williams Hooper Found. for Med. Research, U. Calif., 1937-39; asst. prof. Ind. U., Bloomington, 1940-44, asso. prof., 1944-48, prof., chmn. dept. bacteriology, 1948-66, prof. microbiology, 1966—, asst. dir. div. biol. scis., 1965-68. Fellow John Simon Guggenheim Meml. Found., research fellow in bacteriology Harvard Med. Sch., 1939-40. Fellow AAAS, Am. Acad. Microbiology (gov. 1961-67, 76-77), Ind. Acad. Sci.; mem. Nat. Sci. Tchrs. Assn., Soc. Am. Archivists, Am. Soc. Microbiology (archivist 1960—), Am. Assn. of Immunologists, Soc. Am. Bacteriologists (council 1943-47, editorial bd. Jour. Bacteriology 1953-57, chmn. com. on edn. 1958-61, archivist 1953-60), Am. Inst. Biol. Scis. (governing bd. 1968-74), Inst. Food Tech. (mem. editorial bd. 1942-45, 47-50), Soc. Gen. Microbiology, Soc. Exptl. Biology and Medicine (council 1949-50), Nat. Assn. Biology Tchrs. (1st v.p. 1963, pres. 1965), Soc. Indsl. Microbiology (v.p. 1958, dir. 1960-63), Sigma Xi, Phi Sigma, Gamma Alpha, Alpha Epsilon Delta, Omega Beta Pi. Author: The Anaerobic Bacteria and Their Activities in Nature and Disease: A Subject Bibliography (with Elizabeth McCoy), 2 vols., 1939, supplement, 1941; contbr. articles to sci. jours. Address: Jordan Hall Dept Biology Ind U Bloomington IN 47405

MC CLUNG, NORVEL MALCOLM, educator; b. Mc Clungs, W.Va., June 9, 1916; s. Virgil Edward and Mary (Anderson) McC.; A.B., Glenville State Coll., 1936; M.S., U. Mich., 1940, Ph.D., 1949; m. Delia Rainey, Aug. 31, 1945 (div. Sept. 1966); children—Charles E., Margaret L., Ralph A., Susan E.; m. 2d, Hermine Friedson, Oct. 18, 1966. Tchr., Webster Springs (W.Va.) High Sch., 1936-41; asst. prof. biology U. Kans., Lawrence, 1948-57; asso. prof. U. Ga., Athens, 1957-66; prof. U. South Fla., Tampa, 1966—; vis. prof. Kyoto (Japan) U., 1962-63; cons. Fla. Dept. Health, 1968, Ocean Products, Plant City, Fla., 1968-69. Served to capt. USNR, 1941-46. Decorated Purple Heart, Navy and Marine Corps medal, La. State U. tropical medicine fellow, 1960; Fulbright Research award, Japan, 1961-62; recipient grants U. Kans. Found, 1950-53, NIH, 1954-57, Massengill Corp., 1956-58, NSF, 1960-61, 50-65, travel award Sigma Xi, 1961, Am. Soc. Microbiology, 1963. Mem. Southeastern Electron Microscopy Soc. (chmn. 1970-72), AAAS, AAUP, Am. Inst. Biol. Scis., Am. Soc. Microbiology, Bacteriol. Soc. Japan, Bot. Soc. Am., Internat. Soc. Humand and Animal Mycoses, Kans. Acad. Scis., Med. Mycology Soc. Am. (charter), Mycol. Soc. Am., Soc. Gen. Microbiology (Brit.), Am. Acad. Microbiology, Sigma Xi, Phi Kappa Phi, Phi Sigma. Author: (with A. J. Mix) Mycology for Students of Bacteriology and Medicine, 1955; (with R. G. Eagon and W. J. Payne) A Laboratory Manual for Introductory Bacteriology, 1960; contbr. sect. on Nocardia to Manual Determinative Bacteriology (Bergey), 8th edit.; also articles to profl. jours. Home: 2701 Varsity Pl Tampa FL 33612

MCCLUNG, RICHARD GOEHRING, lawyer; b. Butler, Pa., June 26, 1913; s. Frank A. and Mary A. (Goehring) McC.; A.B., Princeton, 1935; LL.B., Yale, 1939; certificate Harvard Bus. Sch., 1937; m. Jean Barrett Coffin, Dec. 1, 1951; children—Jean C., Mary G., Priscilla B. Admitted to N.Y. bar, 1940, since practiced in N.Y.C.; partner firm Carter, Ledyard & Milburn, 1948—. Served to comdr. USNR, 1942-46. Home: 30 Winding Ln Greenwich CT 06830 Office: 2 Wall St New York City NY 10005

MCCLUNG, ROY CORNELIUS, coll. pres.; b. Frederick, Okla., Sept. 17, 1917; s. Joseph Leonard and Ethel (Robinson) McC.; B.A., Okla. Bapt. U., 1941; Th.M., So. Bapt. Theol. Sem., 1944, Th.D., 1948; m. Genelle Bucklew, Aug. 5, 1941; children—Michael, Nancy (Mrs. RoGene Chaddick), Mark. Ordained to ministry Bapt. Ch., 1938; pastor in Hiseville, Ky., 1945-47, Louisville, 1947-54, Ada, Okla., 1954-58, Plainview, Tex., 1958-63; pres. Wayland Bapt. Coll., Plainview, 1963—. Chmn. Haynes dist. Boy Scouts Am., 1961-64. Lion. Mason. Home: 1307 W 6th St Plainview TX 79072

MCCLURE, BROOKS, mgmt. cons.; b. N.Y.C., Mar. 8, 1919; s. Walter Harsha and Angelica (Mendoza) McC.; A.B. summa cum laude, U. Md.; distinguished grad., U.S. Naval War Coll., 1967; m. Olga Beatrice Gallik, Oct. 15, 1949; 1 dau., Karen. N.Y. corr. Western Press Ltd., Australia, 1939-42; copy editor Washington Eve. Star, 1946-51; joined U.S. Fgn. Service, 1951; information officer, attache embassy, Copenhagen, 1951-53; press Attache embassy, Vienna, 1953-55; information officer, attache embassy, Cairo, 1956-57, Seoul, 1957-60, Bonn, 1960-63; policy officer Europe, USIA, 1963-66; pub. affairs officer, 1st sec. embassy, Copenhagen, 1967-72; spl. asst. policy plans and nat. security council affairs, internat. security affairs Dept. Def., 1972-76; internat. security adviser USIA, 1976-77; program coordinator Crisis Assessment Staff, Dept. Commerce, 1977-78; dir. ops. Internat. Mgmt. Analysis and Resources Corp., 1978—; various spl. assignments Europe, Asia, Africa. Served with AUS, 1942-46. Mem. Am. Fgn. Service Assn., Am. Acad. Polit. and Social Sci., Am. Polit. Sci. Assn., Acad. Polit. Sci., Royal United Services Inst. (London), Phi Kappa Phi, Alpha Sigma Lambda Club: Nat. Press (Washington). Author: Russia's Hidden Army in Modern Guerrilla Warfare, 1962; Dynamics of Terrorism, 1977; Hostage Survival in International Terrorism in Contemporary World, 1978; Terrorism Today and Tomorrow in Contemporary Terrorism, 1978; contbr. to Political Terrorism and Business: Threat and Response, 1979. Contbr. articles profl. jours.; contbr. to Senate Judiciary Com. report on internat. terrorism and hostage def. measures. Home: 6204 Rockhurst Rd Bethesda MD 20034 Office: IMAR Corp 1120 National Press Bldg Washington DC 20045

MC CLURE, DONALD STUART, educator, phys. chemist; b. Yonkers, N.Y., Aug. 27, 1920; s. Robert Hirt and Helen (Campbell) McC.; B.Chemistry, U. Minn., 1942; Ph.D., U. Calif. at Berkeley, 1948; m. Laura Lee Thompson, July 9, 1949; children—Edward, Katherine, Kevin. With war research div. Columbia U., 1942-46; mem. faculty U. Calif. at Berkeley, 1948-55; group leader, mem. profl. staff RCA Labs., 1955-62; prof. chemistry U. Chgo., 1962-67, Princeton, 1967; vis. lectr. various univs.; cons. to govt. and industry. Guggenheim fellow Oxford (Eng.) U., 1972-73; recipient Irving Langmuir prize, 1979. Mem. Am. Chem. Soc., Am. Phys. Soc. Author: Electronic Spectra of Molecules and Ions in Crystals, 1959; Some Aspects of Crystal Field Theory, 1964; also articles. Home: 23 Hemlock Circle Princeton NJ 08540

MCCLURE, GEORGE TARRENCE, philosopher, educator; b. Harriman, Tenn., Nov. 24, 1928; s. George Tarrence and Ruth (Martin) McC.; B.A., U. Tenn., 1952, M.A., 1953; Ph.D., Ohio State U., 1958; m. Clara Wallace, Mar. 25, 1950; children—Wendy, Laura. Mem. faculty dept. philosophy So. Ill. U., Carbondale, 1958—, prof., 1972—, chmn. dept., 1976—. Mem. Ill. Humanities Council, 1972-77. Served with U.S. Army, 1953-55. NSF grantee, 1968; Nat. Endowment Humanities grantee, 1976-79. Mem. AAAS, Am. Philos. Assn., AAUP, Am. Soc. Aesthetics and Art Criticism, ACLU. Democrat. Contbr. articles to profl. jours. Home: 1204 Hill St Carbondale IL 62901 Office: Dept Philosophy So Ill Univ Carbondale IL 62901

MC CLURE, HARLAN EWART, architect, planner, educator; b. Delaware, Ohio, Oct. 19, 1916; s. Alexander Ewart and Mary Jeanette (Huffman) McC.; A.B., B.Arch., George Washington U., 1937; archtl. diploma Royal Swedish Acad., 1938; M.Arch., Mass. Inst. Tech., 1941; m. Virginia Withers Varney, Mar. 13, 1942 (dec. Nov. 1973); children—Christopher Ewart, Wesley Alexander, Barbara Beth McClure Hahn; m. 2d, Susan Kay Watson, May 14, 1977; 1 stepdau., Melanie Kay. Asst. prof. architecture U. Minn., 1946-47, asso. prof., 1947-51, prof., 1952-55, prof., chmn. architecture faculty Clemson (S.C.) U., 1955-58, prof., dean Sch. Architecture, 1958-69, prof., dean Coll. Architecture, 1969—; town planner, pvt. practice architecture; cons. architect; designer Clemson U. Engring. Center, Clemson U. Master Plan; vis. prof. A.A. Sch. Architecture, London; founder Clemson U. Charles Daniel Center for Bldg. Research and Urban Studies, Genoa, Italy, 1973; pres. S.C. Bd. Archtl. Examiners, 1959—; sec. Nat. Archtl. Accrediting Bd., 1965-69, pres., 1969-70. Mem. S.C. Fine Arts Commn.; archtl. and fine arts cons. S.C. Tricentennial Commn.; advisor to mayors of Greenville and Charleston; mem. Interprofl. Task Force on Environ. Design; mem. design advisory panel GSA, 1969-72; design, planning cons. Redevel. Commn., City of Charlotte, 1966—. Served to lt. comdr. USN, 1941-45. Fulbright sr. fellow, U.K., 1952-53. Fellow AIA (dir. Mpls. chpt. 1948-50; mem. task force on social responsibilities 1969-70); mem. AAUP, Nat. Council Arts in Edn. (dir. 1960—), Assn. Coll. Schs. Architecture (nat. pres. 1959-61), Minaret Soc., Plumb Bob, Scarab, Tau Sigma Delta (nat. grand chpt. master 1970—), Phi Kappa Phi, Alpha Rho Chi. Episcopalian. Clubs: Univ., Egg and Dart, Campus, Gown-In-Town (Mpls.); Archtl. Assn. (London); Rotary. Author: Study of an Evolving Architectural Design, 1946; Beginning Architectural Design, 1948; Guide to Architecture of the Twin Cities, 1955; co-author: South Carolina Architecture, 1670-1970; editor: Architecture South Carolina, 1960-62; contbr. articles to profl. jours. Home: Boxwood House E Queen St Pendleton SC 29670 Office: Clemson U Clemson SC 29631

MCCLURE, JAMES A., senator; b. Payette, Idaho, Dec. 27, 1924; s. W. R. and Marie McClure; J.D., U. Idaho, 1950; m. Louise Miller; children—Marilyn, Kenneth, David. Mem. 90th-92d Congresses from 1st Idaho Dist., chmn. Task Force on Energy and Resources; U.S. Senator from Idaho, 1973—, mem. Energy and Natural Resources Com., Appropriations and Joint Econ., chmn. Senate Steering Com. Com. Recipient Watchdog of Treasury award Nat. Assn. Businessmen. Mem. Phi Alpha Delta. Methodist (trustee). Mason, Kiwanian. Address: 3467 N Venice St Arlington VA 22207

MC CLURE, JAMES J., JR., lawyer, pres. Village Oak Park (Ill.); b. Oak Park, Sept. 23, 1920; s. James J. and Ada Leslie (Baker) McC.; B.A., U. Chgo., 1942, J.D., 1949; m. Margaret Carolyn Phelps, Apr. 9, 1949; children—John Phelps, Julia Jean, Donald Stewart. Admitted to Ill. bar, 1950; partner firm Gardner, Carton & Douglas, Chgo., 1962—; mem. Oak Park Plan Commn., 1966-73; mem. Northeastern Ill. Planning Commn., 1973—, pres., 1975—; pres. Village Oak Park, 1973—. Pres. United Christian Community Services, 1967-69, 71-73, Erie Neighborhood House, 1953-55, Oak Park-River Forest Community Chest, 1967; moderator Presbytery Chgo., 1969; mem. Gov.'s Spl. Com. on MPO, 1978—. Served with USNR, 1942-46. Recipient Disting. Citizen award Oak Park, 1976; Silver Beaver award, Disting. Eagle Scout award Boy Scouts Am. Mem. Am. Coll. Probate Counsel, Am., Ill., Chgo. bar assns., Lambda Alpha. Clubs: Univ. (Chgo.); Oak Park. Home: 707 N Oak Park Ave Oak Park IL 60302 Office: One First Nat Plaza Suite 4600 Chicago IL 60603. *Love of God, love of family, awareness of both the uniqueness and the contribution of every other human being, a sense of the wholeness of life with my religious faith, my profession of law, my family and my community service each play an important part and compliment each other.*

MCCLURE, JOEL WILLIAM, JR., educator; b. Irvine, Ky., Aug. 8, 1927; s. Joel William and Mattie Collins (Riley) McC.; student U. Ky., 1945, Eastern Ky. State Coll., 1947; B.S., Northwestern U., 1949, M.S. in Physics, 1951; Ph.D. in Physics, U. Chgo., 1954; m. Ann Jacqueline Allen, June 18, 1953; children—Blanch Travis, Joel Andrew. Asst. prof. physics U. Oreg., 1954-56, asso. prof. physics 1961-65, prof., 1965—; research scientist Union Carbide Corp., Cleve., 1956-61. Served with AUS, 1945-46. Office: Dept Physics U Oreg Eugene OR 97403

MCCLURE, MICHAEL THOMAS, poet, playwright, educator; b. Marysville, Kans., Oct. 20, 1932; s. Thomas and Marian Dixie (Johnston) McC.; student U. Wichita, 1951-53, U. Ariz., 1953-54; B.A., San Francisco State Coll., 1955; m. Joanna Keera Kinnison, Oct. 10, 1954; 1 dau., Katherine Jane. Asso. prof. humanities and scis. Calif. Coll. Arts and Crafts, 1962-77, prof., 1977—. Playwright-in-residence A.C.T., 1975. Guggenheim fellow for poetry, 1974; recipient award for Poetry NEA, 1974, 75, Magic Theatre award, 1974, Playwright award Rockefeller Found., 1975. Mem. Sons of Anacreon, AAAS. Author poetry books: Hymns to St. Geryon, 1959; Dark Brown, 1961; The New Book, 1961; Ghost Tantras, 1964; Little Odes, 1967; Star, 1970; Rare Angel, 1974; September Blackberries, 1974; Jaguar Skies, 1975; also author: Meat Science Essays, 1963; Freewheelin Frank Secretary of the Angels-as told to Michael McClure, 1969; The Mad Cub, 1970; The Adept, 1971; Hail Thee Who Play, 1974; The Grabbing of the Fairy, 1978; playwright Gargoyle Cartoons, The Beard, (N.Y.C. prodn. received two Obies, 1967), The Mammals, Gorf, 1976, General Gorgeous, 1976. Office: care Calif Coll Arts and Crafts 5212 Broadway Oakland CA 94618*

MCCLURE, RICHARD FOWLER, furniture co. exec.; b. Shamokin, Pa., Nov. 8, 1927; s. James Focht and Florence (Fowler) M.C.; B.S. in Engring., U. Mich., 1949; M.B.A., U. Pa., 1951; m. Dorothy Ann Laity, Jan. 1, 1955; children—Richard Fowler, Thomas Murray. Mktg. mgr. RCA, 1953-58; v.p. marketing Lewisburg Chair & Furniture Co., 1958-64; pres. Lewisburg div., v.p. Gen. Interior Corp., N.Y.C., 1964-70, pres., chief exec. officer corp., 1970-72, also dir.; pres., chief exec. officer McClure Furniture Industries, Lewisburg, Pa., 1972—; dir. First Nat. Trust Bank, Sunbury, Pa. Bd. dirs. W.D. Himmelreich Meml. Library, Lewisburg, Pa., 1960—, pres., 1960-66; bd. dirs. Evang. Community Hosp., Lewisburg. Served to 1st lt. USAF, 1951-53. Mem. Nat. Assn. Furniture Mfrs. (v.p. 1970, pres. 1972-73, dir.), Aircraft Owners and Pilots Assn., Tex. Blockhouse Hunting and Fishing Lodge, Sigma Chi. Republican. Presbyterian. Club: Bucknell University Golf. Home: 236 S 3d St Lewisburg PA 17837 Office: Box 414 Milton PA 17847

MCCLURE, RUSSELL SCHEE, disaster mgmt. cons.; b. Seattle, Dec. 26, 1915; s. Worth and Pearl Agnes (Russell) McC.; A.B., Stanford, 1937; M.A., U. Wash., 1939; student Ohio State U., 1939-42; m. Mary Helen Pruitt, Aug. 12, 1939; children—Charles Russell, James Worth, Andrew Wilson. Analyst, State Dept., 1942-43; transp. attache embassy, Paris, France, 1945-47; chief transp. div. Office U.S. Spl. Rep., ECA, Paris, 1948-49; also transp. adviser U.S. resident delegation Econ. Commn. Europe, Geneva, Switzerland; dep. head, then head U.S. resident delegation Econ. Commn. Europe, Geneva, 1950-51; dir. Office Programs and Reports, UN Korean Reconstrn. Agy., Seoul, 1951-54; dep. dir. U.S. Interagy. Program Fgn. Econ. Research, 1954-61; dir. AID mission to Jordan, Amman, 1962-65, AID mission to Afghanistan, Kabul, 1965-70, AID mission to Congo, Kinshasa, 1970-71; fgn. disaster relief coordinator AID Dept. State, Washington, 1971-75; dir. relief coordination div. Office UN Disaster Relief Coordinator, Geneva, 1975-77; disaster mgmt. cons., 1977—; U.S. rep. Central Rhine Commn., 1946-51; fellow Harvard Center Internat. Affairs, 1960-61. Served with USNR, 1943-46. Mem. Am. Fgn. Service Assn., Foyer Interalliee Des Chemins De Fer (Paris). Clubs: American (Paris and Geneva); Cercle de Kinshasa. Home: 630 77th Ave NE Olympia WA 98506

MC CLURE, STARLING VIRGIL, retail trade co. exec.; b. Roanoke, Ala., May 29, 1920; s. James Butler and Lula Victoria (Glore) McC.; B.S., Miami U., Oxford, Ohio, 1946; m. Mary Jane Campbell, Jan. 11, 1947; children—Linda (Mrs. Harry J. Argue), John Campbell. With J.M. McDonald Co., Hastings, Nebr., 1937—, asst. to pres., 1957-58, v.p., 1958-60, exec. v.p., 1960-76, v.p. ops., 1976—, dir., editor monthly publ., 1958—. Bd. dirs. Hastings Community Chest, 1964-70, pres., 1969. Vice pres. J.M. McDonald Found., 1957-60. Served with USNR, 1942-45; PTO. Republican. Presbyn. (trustee). Mason. Club: Lochland Country (Hastings). Home: 1331 Pershing Rd Hastings NE 68901 Office: 2635 W 2d St Hastings NE 68901

MCCLURE, WILLIAM PENDLETON, lawyer; b. Washington, May 25, 1925; s. John Elmer and Helen Newsome (Pendleton) McC.; B.S., U. Pa., 1949; LL.B., George Washington U., 1951, LL.M., 1954; postgrad. The Hague (The Netherlands) Acad. Internat. Law, 1952; m. Linda Wooldridge Geoghegan, Dec. 18, 1977; children—Marilyn Alexander, Helen Pendleton. Admitted to D.C. bar, 1951; sr. partner McClure & Trotter, Washington, 1952—. Chmn. D.C. div. Crusade Against Cancer, Am. Cancer Soc., 1966, 67. Served from pvt. to 1st lt., inf. U.S. Army, 1943-46; PTO. Mem. Am. Bar Assn., Bar Assn. D.C., Am. Judicature Soc., Order of Coif, Phi Delta Phi, Phi Delta Theta. Clubs: Metropolitan, Columbia Country, Nat. Press (Washington). Home: 9505 Brooke Dr Bethesda MD 20034 Office: 1100 Connecticut Ave NW Washington DC 20036

MC CLUSKEY, EDWARD JOSEPH, educator; b. N.Y.C., Oct. 16, 1929; s. Edward Joseph and Rose (Slavin) McC.; A.B. in Math. and Physics, Bowdoin Coll., Brunswick, Maine, 1953, B.S., M.S. in Elec. Engring., 1953; Sc.D., Mass. Inst. Tech., 1956; children by previous marriage—Edward Robert, Rosemary, Therese, Joseph, Kevin, David. With Bell Telephone Labs., Whippany, N.J., 1955-59; asso. prof. elec. engring. Princeton, 1959-63, prof., 1963-66, dir. Computer Center, 1961-66; prof. elec. engring. and computer sci. Stanford, 1967—, dir. Digital Systems Lab., 1969-78; cons. Palyn Assos., Signetics Corp., Gen. Precision Co., IBM, Honeywell Co., Microtech. Corp. Fellow IEEE (pres. computer soc. 1970-71), AAAS, Am. Fedn. Info. Processing Socs. (dir., exec. com.). Author: A Survey of Switching Circuit Theory, 1962; Introduction to the Theory of Switching Circuits, 1965; Design of Digital Computers, 1975. Editor: Computer Design and Architecture Series, Am. Elsevier, 1973—. Asso. editor, IRE Transactions on Computers, 1959-65, ACM Jour., 1963-69; editorial bd. Digital Processes, 1975—, Design Automation and Fault-Tolerant Computing, 1975—; editorial bd. Annals of the History of Computing, 1978—. Patentee in field. Office: Computer Systems Lab Stanford CA 94305

MC CLUSKEY, ELLEN L., interior designer; b. N.Y.C.; d. Allan and Evelyn (Schiffer) Lehman; B.A., Vassar Coll., 1934; postgrad. Columbia, 1934-36, N.Y. Sch. Interior Design, 1936-37; m. Richard McCluskey, 1942 (div. 1952); children—Maureen, Sharon, Orin; m. 2d, Preston Long, June 1957 (div. 1971). Asso. interior decorator with Adele Dewey, 1937-38, Franklin Hughes, 1938-42, Ruth Warburton Kaufman, 1942-43; prin. Ellen L. McCluskey Assos., Inc., 1948—. Active Travelers Aid Soc., Just One Break, Inc., N.Y. Infirmary; mem. acquisitions com. benefit auction Cooper Hewitt Mus.; chmn. Am. Soc. Interior Designers Edn. Found. Fellow Am. Inst. Interior Designers (past pres. N.Y. chpt.); mem. Am. Soc. Interior Designers (mem. working com. of nat. com. on historic preservation). Home: 555 Park Ave New York NY 10021 Office: 654 Madison Ave New York NY 10021

MCCLUSKEY, ROBERT TIMMONS, physician; b. New Haven, Jan. 16, 1923; s. Charles Ayling and Lora (Timmons) McC.; A.B., Yale, 1944; M.D., N.Y. U., 1947; m. Jean Ann White, Dec. 28, 1957; children—Ann, James. Intern, Kings County Hosp., Bklyn., 1947-49; resident Bellevue Hosp., N.Y.C., 1950-53; asso. prof. pathology N.Y. U., 1956-62, prof., 1962-68; prof., chmn. dept. pathology State U. N.Y. at Buffalo, 1968-71; S. Burt Wolbach prof. pathology Harvard, 1971-74, Mallinckrodt prof. pathology, 1974—; pathologist in chief Children's Hosp. Med. Center, Boston, 1971-74; chief pathology Mass. Gen. Hosp., Boston, 1974—. Mem. allery and immunology study sect. NIH, 1970—. Served with AUS, 1953-55. Mem. Am. Assn. Immunologists, Am. Assn. Pathologists and Bacteriologists, AMA, Am. Soc. Exptl. Pathology. Editor: (with Zweifach, Grant) The Inflammatory Process, 1965; (with H. Fudenberg) Clinical Immunology and Immunopathology; (with Stanley Cohen) Series on Basic and Clinical Immunology. Editorial bd. Archives Pathology, 1971-75, Kidney Internat., 1971—. Home: 28 Gardner Rd Brookline MA 02146 Office: Mass Gen Hosp Fruit St Boston MA 02114

MC CLYMONT, HAMILTON, opera exec.; b. Montreal, Que., Can., Mar. 20, 1944; s. Hamilton, Jr. and Zoe Annis (Cook) McC.; B.A., Dalhousie U., 1970. Adminstrv. dir. Toronto Arts Prodns., 1971-74; adminstr. Neptune Theatre, Halifax, N.S., 1974-76; music officer, fin. Can. Council, Ottawa, Ont., 1976-78; dir., gen. mgr. Vancouver (B.C.) Opera, 1978—. Adviser, Community Music Sch. of Greater Vancouver. Mem. Can. Music Council, Can. Conf. of Arts, Community Arts Council Vancouver (major arts liaison com.), Can. Owners and Pilots Assn. Club: Pacific Flying. Office: 111 Dunsmuir St Vancouver BC V6B 1W8 Canada

MCCOBB, EDWARD CLYDE, lawyer; b. Franklin, Pa., Oct. 2, 1902; s. Thomas Clyde and Frances Maude (Whitling) McC.; A.B., U. Mich., 1923, J.D., 1925; m. Mary Josephine Patton, May 15, 1926; children—James Edward, Donald Clyde, Elizabeth Ann. Admitted to Mich. bar, 1925; practiced in Detroit, 1925, Grand Rapids, 1926—; counsel to Freihofer, Oosterhouse, DeBoer & Barnhart and predecessor firms; dir. King Milling Co., Lowell. Pres., East Grand Rapids Sch. Bd., 1946-47, Grand Rapids Community Chest, 1947-48; chmn. United Fund Drive, 1955; exec. dir. Grand Rapids Found., 1966-71. Mem. Mich. Commn. Uniform State Laws, 1960-63, Grand Rapids City Commn., 1966-68, Grand Rapids Charter Revision Commn., 1970-71; Mem. Grand Rapids C. of C. (pres. 1949-50), Am., Mich., Grand Rapids (pres. 1949-50) bar assns., Order of Coif, Phi Beta Kappa, Delta Upsilon, Phi Alpha Delta. Conglist. Clubs: Peninsular, Rotary. Home: 3600 E Fulton St Grand Rapids MI 49506 Office: 950 Union Bank Bldg Grand Rapids MI 49503

MCCOLL, HUGH LEON, JR., banker; b. Bennettsville, S.C., June 18, 1935; s. Hugh Leon and Frances Pratt (Carroll) McC.; B.S. in Bus. Adminstrn., U. N.C., 1957; m. Jane Bratton Spratt, Oct. 3, 1959; children—Hugh Leon III, John Spratt, Jane Bratton. Trainee, N.C. Nat. Bank, Charlotte, 1959-61, officer, 1961-65, v.p., 1965-68, sr. v.p., 1968, div. exec., 1969, exec. v.p., 1970-73, vice chmn. bd., 1973-74, pres., 1974—, also dir.; chmn. bd., dir. Bank of Fort Mill (S.C.), 1976—; dir. Korf Industries, Inc., Charlotte, Dickerson Inc., Monroe, N.C., Sonoco Products Inc., Hartsville, S.C., NCNB Corp., The Caroline Corp., Conway, S.C., Ruddick Corp., Charlotte. Mem. N.C. Bd. Conservation and Devel., 1973. Former trustee Sacred Heart Coll., Belmont, N.C., St. Andrews Presbyn. Coll., Laurinburg, N.C.; bd. dirs. Am. Council on Germany, N.Y.C., 1977-78; bd. mgrs. Charlotte Meml. Hosp. and Med. Center, 1975—; trustee Heineman Found., Charlotte, 1976—. Served to 1st lt. USMCR, 1957-59. Mem. Robert Morris Assos., Assn. Res. City Bankers, N.C. Bankers Assn. (pres. 1974—). Democrat. Presbyterian. Office: One NCNB Plaza Charlotte NC 28255

MCCOLL, WILLIAM FRAZER, JR., orthopedic surgeon; b. San Diego, Apr. 2, 1930; s. William Frazer and Esther A. (Devries) McC.; B.S., Stanford, 1952; M.D., U. Chgo., 1955; m. Barbara B. Bird, Dec. 27, 1953; children—Duncan, Bonnie, Carrie, John, Milton, Jennifer. Profl. football player with Chgo. Bears Profl. Football Team, 1952-59; intern Stanford Hosp., San Francisco, 1955-57; resident orthopedic surgery U. Ill. Hosps., 1958-62; med. missionary Presbyn. Hosp., Taegue, Korea, also Ae Rak Won Leprosarium, 1962-64; pvt. practice, West Covina, Calif., 1964—; mem. staff Queen of Valley, W. Covina Intercommunity, Covina Rancho Los Amigos hosps. Mem. Calif. Bd. Pub. Health, 1967-71, pres., 1970-71. Trustee Calif. State Univ. and Coll. System, 1971-72, Stanford, 1976—; bd. dirs. Am. Leprosy Missions. Named All Am. End, 1950, 51; One of Ten Outstanding Young Men, U.S. Jr. C. of C., 1965; recipient Achievement scroll Nat. Pro Football Hall Fame, 1966; Pub. Service citation U. Chgo., 1967; named to Nat. Football Found. Hall Fame, 1973. Home: 2877 Monte Verde Dr Covina CA 91724 Office: 1433 W Merced West Covina CA 91790

MC COLLISTER, JOHN CHARLES, clergyman, educator; b. Pitts., June 1, 1935; s. John Charles and Caroline Jesse (Hall) McC.; B.A., Capital U., 1957; B.D., Luth. Theol. Sem., Columbus, Ohio, 1961; Ph.D., Mich. State U., 1969; m. Beverly Ann Chase, Aug. 6, 1960; children—Beth Ann, Amy Susan, Michael John. Ordained to ministry Lutheran Ch., 1961; pastor Zion Luth. Ch., Freeland, Mich., 1961-65, Bethlehem Luth. Ch., Lansing, Mich., 1965-71; prof. religion and Greek, Olivet (Mich.) Coll., 1970-74; prof. Bethune-Cookman Coll., Daytona Beach, Fla., 1974-76; prof. Embry-Riddle Aero. U., Daytona Beach, Fla., 1976—, dir. profl. programs, 1979—; pres. Wright Advt. Co., Daytona Beach, Fla., 1975-76. Host, Open Phone Forum radio sta. WROD, Daytona Beach, 1974-76; vol. probation officer, Mich., 1961-71; hearing officer, Mich., 1970-74; nat. arbitrator Am. Arbitration Assn., 1974—; spl. master for Fla. Pub. Employees Relations Commn., 1975—; arbitrator Fed. Mediation and Conciliation Service, 1978—; mgmt. cons. Hoover Ball & Bearing, Charlotte, Mich.; commr. Mich. Dept. Commerce, 1969-72. Recipient Outstanding Am. award Daytona Beach Jaycees, 1974. Editor and compiler: A Child is Born, 1972; Portraits of the Christ, 1974; co-author: The Sunshine Book, 1979; contbr. articles to various mags. Home: 463 N Yonge St Ormond Beach FL 32074 Office: Embry-Riddle Aero U Daytona Beach FL 32015

MCCOLLOM, KENNETH ALLEN, univ. dean; b. Sentinel, Okla., June 17, 1922; s. Walter William and Irene Pearl (Allen) McC.; B.S., Okla. State U., 1948; M.S., U. Ill., 1949; Ph.D., Iowa State U., 1964; m. Katherine Tompkins, Jan. 4, 1944; children—Alan Tompkins, Neal Norman. Engr., Phillips Petroleum Co., Bartlesville, Okla., 1949-51, 54-57, sect. chief, br. mgr. Atomic Energy div., Idaho Falls, Idaho, 1951-54, 57-62; project leader Ames (Iowa) Lab. Research Reactor, 1962-64; prof. elec. engring. Okla. State U., Stillwater, 1964-68, asst. dean engring., 1968-73, asso. dean engring., 1973-77, dean engring., tech. and architecture, 1977—; cons. AEC. Asst. condr. Idaho Falls Civic Symphony Orch., 1958-60; bd. mem., Cub Pack leader, asst. scoutmaster Boy Scouts Am., 1960-72; campaign chmn. Stillwater United Fund, 1971-72. Served with AUS, 1942-46; ETO. Mem. I.E.E.E. (sr.), Am. Nuclear Soc. (chmn. Okla. sect. 1974-75), Nat. (nat. dir. 1975-78), Okla. (adminstrv. v.p. 1974-75, exec. v.p. 1975-76, pres. 1976-77) socs. profl. engrs., Am. Soc. Engring. Edn. (Chester F. Carlson award 1973). Lion. Patentee in field. Home: 1107 W Knapp St Stillwater OK 74074

MCCOLLOUGH, CLAIR R., radio-TV sta. exec.; b. York, Pa., July 1, 1903; s. Austin E. and Pearl E. (Robinson) M.; grad. Millersville State Coll., 1926; D.C.S. (hon.), Franklin and Marshall Coll., 1955; D.Litt. (hon.), Elizabethtown Coll., 1964; m. Velma A. Dilworth, July 12, 1926; 1 dau., Constance. Pres., gen. mgr. TV stas. WGAL-TV, Lancaster, Pa., WTEV-TV, Providence, KOAT-TV Albuquerque KVOA-TV, Tucson, 1931—; pres., dir. radio stas. WGAL, WGAL-FM, Lancaster, WORK, York, WKBO, Harrisburg, Pa., WEST, WEST-FM Easton-Allentown, Pa., WDEL, WDEL-FM Wilmington, Del., 1931—. Chmn. bd. dirs. Nat. Assn. Broadcasters, 1961-63, TV Bur. Advt., 1955-57, TV Information Office, N.Y.C., 1959-65; chmn. Nat. TV Code Rev. Bd., 1964-69; pres. Broadcasters Found., 1963—; chmn. new bldg. com. Nat. Assn. Broadcasters, 1963-70; mem. Future of Broadcasting and Communications in Am. Com., 1963—; trustee Ednl. Found. (AWRT), Inc., 1961—; bd. dirs. Soc. TV Pioneers, 1957—, Broadcast Pioneers, 1954—; mem. U.S. Broadcasters Com. for UN, 1965—. Mem. Pa. Council Crime and Delinquency, 1965—, Pa. State U. Adv. Com. Broadcasting, 1961—. Trustee Franklin and Marshall Coll., 1965—, Millersville State Coll., 1936-44, Lancaster Day Sch., 1947-52. Recipient Distinguished Achievement award Nat. Assn. Broadcasters, 1960; U.S. Radio Silver Mike award, 1960; George Foster Peabody TV award, 1963; award dedicated service to religious broadcasting United Presbyn. Ch. U.S., 1963; Alfred I. DuPont TV award (KVOA-TV), 1963; Pioneer Pres. award Pa. Assn. Broadcasters, 1958; Variety Ambassador of U.S. Radio award, 1950. Mem. Internat. Radio and TV Soc., Sigma Delta Chi. Clubs: Nat. Press, Broadcasters (Washington); Marco Polo (N.Y.C.); Old Pueblo (Tucson); Arizona (Phoenix); Wamsutta (New Bedford, Mass.); Megantic (Eustis, Maine). Home: 1021 Marietta Ave Lancaster PA 17603 Office: Lincoln Hwy West Lancaster PA 17604

MC COLLOUGH, NEWTON CLARK, III, orthopaedic surgeon; b. Butler, Pa., July 17, 1934; s. Newton C. and Margaret Elizabeth (Mattocks) McC.; B.A., Duke U., 1956; M.D., U. Pa., 1959; m. Mary Eva Semanski, Feb. 22, 1968; children—Peter Scott, Amy Marie. Intern, Jackson Meml. Hosp., Miami, Fla., 1959-60, resident in orthopaedic surgery, 1960-64; dir. orthopaedic resident edn. Orange Meml. Hosp., Orlando, Fla., 1965-66; asst. prof. orthopaedics and rehab. U. Miami Sch. Medicine, 1968-72, asso. prof., 1972-76, prof., vice chmn. dept., 1976-78, prof., chmn. dept., 1978—, dir. rehab., 1972—; dir. Am. Bd. for Certification in Prosthetics/Orthotics, 1974-77; mem. Health Planning Council So. Fla. Task Force on Long Term Patient Care, 1974-77; asst. med. dir. Div. of Children's Med. Services, State of Fla., 1975—; chmn. Statewide Com. for Spinal Cord Injury, 1976-78. Served to lt. comdr. M.C., USNR, 1966-68. Decorated Legion of Merit. Diplomate Am. Bd. Orthopaedic Surgery. Mem. Am. Acad. Orthopaedic Surgeons (bd. dirs. 1978-79), Fla. Orthopaedic Soc. (mem. exec. com. 1978—), Miami Orthopaedic Soc. (v.p. 1978-79), AMA, Fla. Med. Soc., Dade County Med. Assn., Am. Congress Rehab. Medicine, Nat. Rehab. Assn., A.C.S., Scoliosis Research Soc., Internat. Soc. Prosthetics and Orthotics, Am. Spinal Injury Assn., Internat. Med. Soc. Paraplegia, Phi Beta Kappa, Alpha Omega Alpha. Republican. Lutheran. Contbr. articles to med. jours. Home: 6040 SW 104th St Miami FL 33156 Office: Univ of Miami Sch Medicine Dept Orthopaedics and Rehab PO Box 016960 Miami FL 33101

MCCOLLOW, THOMAS J., newspaper exec.; b. Hartford, Wis., Mar. 29, 1925; s. Owen Conrad and Zita Ann (Gardien) McC.; A.B., Dartmouth Coll., 1946, M.B.A., 1947; m. Yvonne Parent, June 18, 1949; children—Mardi, Mark, John, Timothy. Acct., Ernst & Ernst, C.P.A.'s, Milw., 1947-51; asst. office mgr. Jour. Co., 1951-60, treas., office mgr., 1961-72, sr. v.p. fin. and corp. planning, 1973-77, pres., 1977—, vice chmn. bd. dirs. Newspapers, Inc. div. Jour. Co., 1977—. Bd. dirs. U. Wis.-Milw. Found.; trustee Milw. Boy's Club; mem. lay adv. bd. St. Mary's Hosp. Served to lt. USNR, 1943-46. Mem. Inst. Controller and Fin. Officers (past pres.), Am. Newspaper Pubs. Assn., Phi Beta Kappa. Roman Catholic. Clubs: University, Chenequa Country, Rotary. Office: 333 W State St PO Box 661 Milwaukee WI 53201

MCCOLLUM, CLIFFORD GLENN, coll. dean.; b. South Gifford, Mo., May 12, 1919; s. William Henry and Aultie V. (Westfall) McC.; student Central Coll., 1935-37; B.S., U. Mo., 1939, M.A., 1947, Ed.D., 1949; m. Alice Elizabeth Erickson, Aug. 18, 1940; children—Eric Edward, Lisa Buren Sommer. Tchr. pub. schs., Monett, Mo., 1938-39, Poplar Bluff, Mo., 1939-41, Boonville, Mo., 1941-42; asst. prof. sci. U. No. Ia., 1949-55, asso. prof., 1956-59, prof., 1959—, head dept. sci., 1957-68, dean Coll. Natural Scis., 1968—; prof. State U. N.Y. at Oneonta, 1955-56. Dir., instl. rep. Central States Univs., Inc.; cons. Coronet Instrnl. Films; cons. on sci. curricula to pub. schs. and colls.; speaker in field. Served with USAAF, 1943-46. Fellow AAAS (nat. committeeman 1964-67), Iowa Acad. Sci. (pres. 1979-80); mem. Am. Inst. Biol. Scis., Nat. Assn. Biology Tchrs. (regional dir. 1963-65), Nat. Assn. Research in Sci. Teaching, Nat. Sci. Tchrs. Assn., Phi Delta Kappa. Contbr. articles to profl. jours. Home: 1514 W 18th St Cedar Falls IA 50613

MCCOLLUM, JOHN ISAAC, JR., educator; b. Conway, Ark., Oct. 13, 1919; s. John Isaac and Hazel (Schroader) McC.; A.B., U. Miami (Fla.), 1946, M.A., 1949; Ph.D., Duke, 1956; m. Bettie Lou Johnson, Dec. 19, 1947; children—John Isaac III, Mark Stephen. Mem. faculty U. Miami, 1949—, prof. English, 1963—, asso. dean Univ. Coll., 1960-61, chmn. dept. English, 1961-73. Local rep. Fulbright program, Danforth Found.; mem. regional selection com. Woodrow Wilson Nat. Fellowship Found., 1959-62, local rep., 1955—; mem. Fla. Certification Com., 1966-70. Pastor Goulds Baptist Ch., Fla., 1944-46, Coral Bapt. Ch., Miami, 1950-52; trustee Coral Gables Congregational Ch., 1966-70, chmn. ch. council, pres., 1974—; mem. conf. bd. trustees United Ch. of Christ, 1976—, pres. conf. bd. dirs., 1978—. Mem. Modern Lang. Assn., S. Atlantic Modern Lang. Assn., Renaissance Soc. Am., Southeastern Renaissance Soc., Phi Kappa Phi, Omicron Delta Kappa, Phi Alpha Theta. Author: Essentials of Grammar and Style, 1966; also articles. Editor: The Age of Elizabeth, 1960; The Restoration Stage, 1961; Jonson's The Alchemist, 1965. Contbr. to Ency. Americana. Home: 1430 Mendavia Ave Coral Gables FL 33146

MCCOLLUM, JOHN MORRIS, tenor; b. Coalinga, Calif., Feb. 21, 1922; s. Fay James and Ingabord Telette (Mason) McC.; student Coalinga Coll., 1939-40; B.A. in Journalism, U. Calif. at Berkeley, 1947; student voice and acting, Am. Theatre Wing, 1951-53; m. Mary Margaret Wilson, Jan. 23, 1944; children—Kristi Elizabeth, Timothy James. Reporter, city editor Coalinga Record, 1947-50; editor agrl. news U. Calif. Coll. Agr., 1950-51; concert and opera singer, 1951—; soloist Fifth Ave. Presbyn. Ch., N.Y.C., 1953-56; debut Town Hall, N.Y.C., 1952; with Boston Symphony Orchestra, Tanglewood, Mass., summer 1952; engagements with N.Y.C., Chgo., Phila., San Francisco, Buffalo, Cleve., Pitts., Mpls., Washington, St. Louis, Detroit, New Orleans, Toronto, London, Mexican Nat. symphony orchestras; with opera companies of Boston, Washington, Toronto, Ft. Worth, Central City, Colo., also NBC-TV, music festivals and oratorio societies; European debut Festival of Two Worlds, Spoleto, Italy, summer 1958; prof. music and chmn. voice faculty U. Mich.; dir. U. Mich. div. Nat. Music Camp; with Santa Fe Opera Co.; faculty Aspen Music Festival and School, 1963; leading tenor N.Y.C. Opera Co.; performing mem. Music Assos. of Aspen. Recipient award Atwater Kent Auditions, 1950, Am. Theatre Wing award, 1952. Mem. Republican Central Com., Fresno County, Calif., 1950. Served as aviator USNR, World War II. Mem. U. Calif. Alumni Assn., Nat. Assn. Tchrs. Singing, Am. Acad. Tchrs. Singing, Alpha Tau Omega, Sigma Delta Chi, Pi Kappa Lambda. Episcopalian (lay reader). Clubs: Rotary (pres. 1977), Ann Arbor Golf and Outing (pres. 1979). Home: 2117 Brockman Blvd Ann Arbor MI 48104

MC COLLUM, ROBERT STUART, business exec.; b. Denver, Nov. 23, 1916; s. Stuart T. and Mary B. (Hadley) McC.; B.A., Amherst Coll., 1938; m. Lydia E. Nelson, May 2, 1947; children—Mary L., Patricia A., Robert Stuart, Bruce C. Tchr., Deerfield Acad., 1938-41; pres. Auto Equipment Co., Denver, 1946-57; pres. McCollum-Law Corp., Denver, 1953-56, chmn. bd., 1957-75; adminstr. refugee program bur. security and consular affairs Dept. State, 1957-60; vice chancellor U. Denver, 1960-69; pres. Robert McCollum Assos., 1969-74. Mem. Denver City Council, 1951-55, pres., 1955; mem. nat. bd. CARE; trustee Inst. Internat. Edn., 1954-57, Mills Coll., 1961—, Loretto Heights Coll., 1976—; pres. Colo. Council Econ. Edn., 1976—; v.p. Luth. Med. Center, 1974-77, pres., 1977—; elder Montview Presbyterian Ch., 1970—. Candidate for U.S. Congress, 1956. Served with USAAF, 1942-46. Decorated Order Orange Nassau (Netherlands); Cavallieri Ufficiale (Govt. of Italy); named One of Ten Outstanding Young Men, Jr. C.

of C., 1951; recipient Outstanding Community Service award Nat. Council Chs., 1952. Mem. Am. Assn. UN (state pres.). Rotarian (1st v.p. 1955, dir.). Home: 3477 S Race St Englewood CO 80110

MC COLOUGH, CHARLES PETER, office equipment mfg. co. exec.; b. Halifax, N.S., Can., Aug. 1, 1922; s. Reginald Walker and Barbara Theresa (Martin) McC.; student Dalhousie U., 1943, LL.B., 1947, LL.D., 1970; student Osgoode Hall Law Sch., Toronto, 1945-46; M.B.A., Harvard, 1949; m. Mary Virginia White, Apr. 25, 1953. Came to U.S., 1951, naturalized, 1956. Vice pres. sales Lehigh Coal Navigation Co., Phila., 1951-54; with Xerox Corp., 1954—, v.p. sales, 1960-63, exec. v.p. operations, 1963-66, pres., 1966-71, chief exec. officer, now chmn., chief exec. officer, also chmn. exec. com., dir.; dir. Union Carbide Corp., Rank Xerox Ltd., London, Eng., Fuji-Xerox Co. Ltd., Citicorp., N.Y., Citibank N.A. Mem. steering com. Nat. Com. Full Employment; chmn. Pres.'s Commn. Pension Policy; trustee Com. for Econ. Devel., U. Rochester; chmn. exec. com. Internat. Exec. Service Corps; bd. dirs. Council for Financial Aid to Edn., Overseas Devel. Council, Greenwich, Joint U.S.-USSR Trade and Econ. Council; mem. corp. Greenwich Hosp. Assn.; industries adv. com. Advt. Council; adv. mem. adv. bd. Yale. Mem. Internat. C. of C. (trustee U.S. council), Council on Fgn. Relations (bd. dirs.), Bus. Council, Bus. Com. for Arts, Bus. Roundtable. Roman Catholic. Clubs: Country, Genesee Valley (Rochester); Harvard, River (N.Y.C.); Belle Haven, Greenwich Country, Stanwich (Greenwich, Conn.). Office: Xerox Corp Stamford CT 06904

MCCOLPIN, ANDREW KERR, lawyer; b. Cleburne, Tex., Sept. 10, 1929; s. John J. and Leown Elizabeth (White) McC.; B.A., U. Tex., 1950, LL.B., 1952; m. Mary Louise Jackson, Feb. 21, 1958; children—John Kerr, Amanda Cartwright. Admitted to Tex. bar, 1952, N.Y. State bar, 1955; asso. firm Pennie, Edmonds, Morton, Barrows & Taylor, N.Y.C., 1954-56, Hutcheson, Taliaferro & Hutcheson, Houston, 1956-58; atty. Conoco Inc., Ft. Worth, N.Y.C., Stamford, Conn., 1958-77, sr. v.p., gen. counsel, Stamford, 1977—. Trustee, Long Ridge Sch., Stamford, 1971-73; mem. Norwalk (Conn.) City Council, 1976-79; alt. del. Republican Nat. Conv., 1976. Served with inf. U.S. Army, 1952, to 1st lt. JAGC, 1952-54. Mem. Assn. Bar City N.Y., Westchester-Fairfield County Corp. Counsel Assn., Assn. Gen. Counsel, State Bar Tex., Pi Sigma Alpha, Phi Delta Phi. Episcopalian. Clubs: Knickerbocker (N.Y.C.); Netherland (N.Y.C.); Landmark (Stamford). Office: Conoco Inc High Ridge Park Stamford CT 06904

MCCOLPIN, CARROLL WARREN, corp. exec., ret. air force gen.; b. Buffalo, Nov. 15, 1914; s. Joseph Warren and Doris (McCarthy) McC.; grad. Armed Forces Staff Coll., 1950, Air War Coll., 1955; B.A., Golden Gate U., 1969; m. Mary Joan Martin, Mar. 4, 1943; children—Mary Patricia, Carol Warren. Joined RAF, 1940, transferred to USAAF, 1942, advanced through grades to maj. gen. USAF, 1965; pilot, then squadron leader RAF, Eng., 1940-42; comdr. 336th Fighter Squadron 4th Fighter Group, Eng., 1942; assigned Hdqrs. USAAF, Washington, 1943; group ops. officer 423d Fighter Group, Deridder AFB, La., 1943; comdr. 407th Fighter Group, Lakeland, Fla., also Galveston, Tex., 1943-44, 404th Fighter Group, Eng., France and Belgium, 1944-45; dir. combat ops. 29th Tactical Air Command, Belgium, 1945; comdr., dep. comdr. 3d Fighter Command Gunnery Sch., Pinellas, Fla., 1945-46; comdr. 355th and 52d Fighter Group, Germany, 1946-47, 31st Fighter Group, Turner AFB, Ga., 1947-50; dir. operations and tng. Hdqrs. Air Def. Command, Colorado Springs, Colo., 1950-52; dep. for operations Hdqrs. Eastern Air Def. Force, Stewart AFB, Newburgh, N.Y., 1952-54; comdr. 64th Air Div., Newfoundland, Can., 1955-58; dir. operations Hdqrs. NORAD/CONAD, Ent AFB, Colo., 1958-62; comdr. San Francisco Air Def. Sector, Beale AFB, Calif., 1962-63, Portland Air Def. Sector, Adair AFB, Ore., 1963-64; comdr. 28th Air Div., Hamilton AFB, Cal., 1964, 1966; comdr. 4th Air Force, Hamilton AFB, 1966-68; now pres. Comprehensive Equity Corp., San Francisco; pres. Brit. Bancorp. Ltd. Decorated Legion of Merit with 3 oak leaf clusters, D.F.C., D.S.M., Air medal with 6 oak leaf clusters; Distinguished Flying Cross (Eng.); Croix de Guerre with palm, Fourragere (France); Croix de Guerre with palm, Fourragere (Belgium). Mem. Fighter Aces Assn. (charter), Air Force Assn., Order Daedalians, Nat. Rifle Assn., Air Force Acad. Athletic Assn. Home: 205 Country Club Dr Novato CA 94947

MCCOMAS, DONALD EARL, musician; b. Sioux City, Iowa, Dec. 3, 1932; s. Orvy Berry and Epha Helen (Stone) McC.; Mus.B. in Edn., U. Mich., 1955; Mus.M., Cath. U. Am., 1963; m. Sharlene E. Stewart, Feb. 4, 1956; children—Roger B., Neal S., Scot A. Trumpeter, Buffalo Philharmonic Orch., 1958-60, Nat. Symphony Orch., Washington, 1960-64, Phila. Orch., 1964—; mem. Phila. Brass Trio, 1965—; instr. trumpet and brass New Sch. Music, Phila., 1968—; pvt. tchr. trumpet, 1955—; numerous appearances ballet and opera orchs., chamber music ensembles, show and dance bands. Served with AUS, 1955-58. Home: 613 Knox Rd Wayne PA 19087 Office: Phila Orch 230 S 15th St Philadelphia PA 19102

MCCOMAS, HARROLD JAMES, lawyer; b. Coshocton, Ohio, Aug. 20, 1924; s. James R. and Evelyn L. (Swan) McC.; B.A., Coll. of Wooster, 1948; J.D., Yale U., 1951; m. Hazelyn Melconian, Sept. 10, 1949; children—James, Rachel, David, Paul. Admitted to Wis. bar, 1951, since practiced in Milw.; partner firm Foley & Lardner and predecessor firm, 1960—; counsel Ripon (Wis.) Coll.; dir. Linens, Ltd., Oak Creek Corp., Western Industries, Inc. Pres., United Performing Arts Fund, 1972; chmn. bd. Milw. Symphony Orch., 1976-78; dir. Vis. Nurse Assn., 1967-76, Suder-Pick Found., Inc., Ziegler Found.; trustee Melitta S. Pick Charitable Trust. Served with USAAF, 1943-46. Clubs: Milw. Country; Univ.; Sloane. Home: 5223 N Lake Dr Milwaukee WI 53217 Office: 777 E Wisconsin Ave Milwaukee WI 53202

MCCOMAS, JAMES DOUGLAS, univ. pres.; b. Princhard, W.Va., Dec. 23, 1928; s. Herbert and Nell (Billups) McC.; B.S., W.Va. U., 1951, M.S., 1960; Ph.D., Ohio State U., 1962; m. Francis Adele Stoltz, May 11, 1961; children—Cathleen, Patrick. High sch. tchr., 1951-54, 56-60; from asst. prof. to prof., head dept. elementary and secondary edn. N.M. State U., 1961-67; dean Coll. Edn. Kans. State U., 1967-69; dean U. Tenn., 1969-76, also prof. continuing and higher edn.; pres. Miss. State U., 1976—. Field reader U.S. Office Edn.; chmn. Southeastern Manpower Adv. Com.; mem. exec. com. Southeastern Conf.; mem. appeals bd. Nat. Council Accreditation of Tchr. Edn.; mem. Nat. Accreditation Council for Agencies Serving the Blind; mem. exec. com. Land Grant Deans Edn.; chmn. com. on equal opportunity Nat. Assn. Land Grant Colls. and State Univs.; asso. mem. Nat. Manpower Adv. Com., Gov.'s Manpower Adv. Com.; chmn. council of presidents State Univs. Miss.; pres. So. Land Grant Colls. and Univs.; chmn. Tenn. Council Deans Edn.; mem. Miss. Jr. Coll. Commn. Pres. Belmont West Community Assn., Miss. Econ. Council, East Miss. Council. Served with M.C., AUS, 1954-56. Mem. Am. Sociol. Assn., Am. Higher Edn. Assn., Am. Acad. Polit. and Social Sci., Kappa Delta Pi, Gamma Sigma Delta, Alpha Zeta, Omicron Delta Kappa, Phi Kappa Phi, Beta Gamma Sigma. Home: PO Box J Mississippi State MS 39762

MCCOMB, JAMES NEWELL, pump co. exec.; b. New Castle, Pa., Mar. 10, 1906; s. Thomas S. and Adelaide (Clark) McC.; C.E., Rensselaer Poly. Inst., 1929; m. Jessie Ellen Chase, July 26, 1930; children—Marcia, Malcolm, James C. With Goulds Pumps, Inc., Seneca Falls, N.Y., 1929—, pres., 1964—, chmn. bd., 1970-76. Mem. Seneca Falls Bd. Edn., 1948-58; pres. Community Center of Seneca Falls. Trustee, mem. exec. com. Eisenhower Coll. Mem. Fin. Execs. Inst., Hydraulic Inst. (past pres.). Home: R D 2 Romulus NY 14541 Office: 340 Fall St Seneca Falls NY 13148

MCCOMBS, G. B., pub. co. exec.; b. Waxahachie, Tex., Nov. 9, 1909; s. Robert Davis and Minnie (Parks) McC.; student Randolph Jr. Coll., Cisco, Tex., Trinity U., San Antonio; m. Mary Louise Matthews, Sept. 7, 1928; children—Robert M., Mary Ann (Mrs. James W. Patterson), Nancy K. (Mrs. David DeBusschere). Sales exec. Fishburn Motor Co., Dallas, 1928-29, Willys Overland Motor Co., Dallas, 1929-30; with Curtis Circulation Co., Phila., 1930—, v.p., dir. single copy sales, 1953-62, pres., 1962-73, chmn., chief exec. officer, 1965-69, also dir., now cons.; circulation dir., Curtis Pub. Co. Phila., 1962-66, v.p., 1963, sr. v.p., 1964-68, exec. v.p., 1968, pres., 1969-70; dir. Curtis Distbg. Co. Ltd., Toronto, Can., 1953-74, pres., 1957-66, chmn., 1969; v.p., dir. Nat. Mag. Service, Chatham, N.J., 1953-67; dir. Moore-Cottrell Subscription Agys., Inc., 1953-68, chmn. bd., 1964-68; dir. Keystone Readers, 1962-68, chmn. bd., 1963-68; v.p. Cadence Industries Corp., Inc., 1970-74; now dir., vice-chmn., mem. exec. com. Served to lt. USNR, 1944-45. Mem. Bur. Ind. Pubs. and Distbrs. (past chmn., hon. dir., also past pres., hon. dir. 25 Years Club). Club: Country (Naples, Fla.). Address: 341 Burning Tree Dr Naples FL 33942

MC COMIC, ROBERT BARRY, real estate devel. co. exec.; b. Selmer, Tenn., Nov. 6, 1939; s. Richard Donald and Ila Marie (Prather) McC.; B.S., Union U., 1961; LL.B. (Thomas Dewey Nelson award), Tulane U., 1964; postgrad. in law (Ford Found. grantee, Fredrich Ebert Found. fellow) U. Freiburg (W. Ger.), 1964-65, Hague (Netherlands) Internat. Acad. Law, 1965; children by previous marriage—Thomas Christopher, Robert Geoffrey. Exec. trainee Union Planters Nat. Bank, Memphis, 1961; admitted to Tenn. bar, 1964, N.Y. bar, 1966, Calif. bar, 1971; asso. firm Donovan Leisure Newton & Irvine, N.Y.C., 1965-68; asso. gen. counsel Avco Corp., Greenwich, Conn., 1968-70; v.p., sec., gen. counsel Avco Community Developers, Inc., San Diego, 1970-73, exec. v.p., 1973-75, pres., 1975—, also dir.; chmn. bd. Continental Escrow Co., San Diego, 1975—; pres. Coastline Mortgage Corp., Newport Beach, Calif., 1977—; dir., sec. Avco Savs. and Loan Assn., Los Angeles, 1969-73; del. Internat. Assn. New Towns, Tehran, Iran, 1977. Mem. nat., So. Calif. campaign coms. United Negro Coll. Fund, 1976-80; mem. chancellors assos. U. Calif., San Diego; bd. dirs. La Jolla Mus. Contemporary Art, 1979—. Mem. Am., Calif., N.Y., Tenn., San Diego County bar assns., Assn. Bar City N.Y., San Diego Bldg. Contractors Assn. (dir., treas. 1974-75), Order of Coif, Omicron Delta Kappa, Sigma Alpha Epsilon. Clubs: San Diego Yacht, City of San Diego, Laguna Niguel Country. Asst. editor Tulane Law Rev., 1963-64; editor Tulane Tax Inst., 1963-64. Home: 2676 Caminito Tom Morris La Jolla CA 92037 Office: 16770 W Bernardo Dr San Diego CA 92127

MCCONAGHA, ALAN, newspaperman; m. Barbara Melamed, June 22, 1966; children—William Arthur, Megan Mara, Adam Cameron. With Montgomery (Ala.) Advertiser, 1956-57; with Mpls. Tribune, 1957—, European corr., 1967-69, Washington corr., 1970—. Office: Mpls Tribune 940 National Press Bldg Washington DC 20045

MCCONAGHA, GLENN LOWERY, coll. cons.; b. New Concord, Ohio, June 2, 1910; s. David Hawthorne and Lida (Taylor) McC.; A.B., Muskingum Coll., 1932; A.M., Ohio State U., 1934, Ph.D., 1941; student U. Pitts., 1936-37; m. Pearl Esther Hook, Apr. 8, 1939. Instr. social studies Aliquippa (Pa.) High Sch., 1934-38; asst. prof. edn. Muskingum Coll., summers 1935-38; instr. edn. Ohio State U., Columbus, 1939-40; asst. dir. field service, 1941-42; pre-induction classification officer U.S. Army, Huntington, W. Va., 1943; exec. officer U.S. Armed Forces Inst., Madison, Wis., 1944-45 (commd. U.S. Army 1947), comdt., 1945-49, ednl. dir., 1949-50, civilian dir., 1950-53; exec. v.p. Muskingum Coll., 1953-62, pres., 1962-64; dean Blackburn Coll., Carlinville, Ill., 1964-65, pres., 1965-74, chancellor, 1974-77, spl. cons., 1977—. Former trustee Lincoln Acad. Ill.; former mem. Presbyn. Coll. Union (pres. 1972-73). Hon. maj. Brit. Royal Edn. Corp. Mem. Am. Council Assn., Higher Edn. Assn., Asso. Colls. Ill., Mil. Order World Wars, Am. Ednl. Research Assn., NEA, AAUP, Phi Gamma Mu, Alpha Phi Gamma, Phi Delta Kappa. Mason. Decorated: Army Commendation ribbon, Presdl. Unit Citation. Author articles in profl. jours.; contbr. to Nat. Parent-Teacher Mag., Bull. of Nat. Assn. Secondary Sch. Prins. Author: Train of Thought (monthly publ.), 1965-72. Home: 10 Taggart Dr Carlinville IL 62626. *Success requires, first of all, complete and total dedication. There must be an acceptance of change and an adherence to the goal that anything we can do we can do better. There must be a consistent philosophy which has as its central guidepost the worth and dignity of each individual. There must be honesty, firmness, and forthrightness in dealing with others. Also required is an abiding but critical confidence in the will of our country to meet adversity and there must be an abiding faith in education properly conceived as a learning process which goes on from the cradle to the grave. We must have an ability to face crossroads situations and to make decisions with the full knowledge that each of us in a democratic society must face the consequences of the decisions we make. There must be an ability to look down the track ahead so that our track record will receive attention and can be lived with. Salient throughout our professional and personal life, we must have anticipation, faith, and convictions concerning the present and future—which, in essence, means involvement.*

MCCONAHEY, WILLIAM MCCONNELL, JR., physician, educator; b. Pitts., May 7, 1916; s. William McConnell and Charlotte Maude (Hixson) McC.; A.B., Washington and Jefferson Coll., 1938; M.D., Harvard, 1942; M.S., U. Minn., 1948: m. Adrienne Parsons Magness, June 15, 1940; children—William McConnell III, Meredith McConahey Pollak, Peter Magness. Resident internal medicine Mayo Clinic, 1946-48; asst. to staff Mayo Clinic, 1949, mem. staff internal medicine and endocrinology, 1949—; cons. internal medicine St. Mary's, Rochester Methodist hosps., 1949—; chmn. dept. endrocrinology Mayo Clinic, 1967-74; prof. medicine Mayo Grad. Sch. Medicine U. Minn., 1966-73, Mayo Med. Sch., 1973—. Served with M.C., AUS, 1943-45; now Col. Res. Decorated Silver Star, Bronze Star; recipient Disting. Alumni Service award Washington and Jefferson Coll., 1978. Fellow A.C.P.; mem. Am. Thyroid Assn. (Distinguished Service award 1973, pres. 1976), Endocrine Soc., Am. Diabetes Assn., Am. Fedn. Clin. Investigation, A.A.A.S., Minn. Soc. Internal Medicine, So. Minn. Med. Assn., Central Soc. Clin. Research, Zumbro Valley Med. Soc., Royal Soc. Medicine, Phi Beta Kappa, Sigma Xi. Author articles in field. Home: 1122 6th St SW Rochester MN 55901

MCCONKEY, DALE DURANT, food co. exec.; b. Washington Court House, Ohio, Mar. 10, 1928; s. Edwin O. and Ora (Emrich) McC.; B.S., N.Y. U., 1951, M.B.A., 1953; m. Eleanor A. Intoccia, Sept. 4, 1948; children—Dale D., Lori L., Dean E., Todd E. Mgr. Spiedel Newspapers, Inc., Chillocothe, Ohio, 1940-45; examiner NLRB, 1949-50; personnel mgr. Am. Sugar Refining Co., 1952-55; mgr. indsl. relations Beech-Nut Life Savers, Inc. (merger Beech-Nut Packing Corp. and Life Savers Corp.), Canajoharie, N.Y., 1955-56, dir. indsl. relations, 1956-59, v.p., 1959-60; v.p. United Fruit Co., 1960-62, exec. asst. to pres. and v.p. adminstrn., 1962-66, group v.p., 1966-68; pres. Dale D. McConkey Assos., Madison, Wis., 1968—; dir. A & W Root Beer Co., J. Hungerford Smith Co., A & W Drive-Ins of Can., Baskin-Robbins 31 Ice Cream Co., House, Inc., Tropical Radio Telegraph Co., Flambeau Products Corp., Top-Grade Feedlots Inc., Western Co. N.Am.; instr. indsl. relations Eastern U., P.I., 1952; lectr. indsl. relations Bklyn. Coll., 1952; prof. mgmt. U. Wis., Madison, 1973—. Mem. Gov.'s Bus. Assistance Com., N.Y. Trustee Amsterdam (N.Y.) City Hosp.; mem. alumni adv. com. N.Y. U. Served with USAAF, World War II, to 1st lt. USAF, Korea. Mem. N.A.M., Grocery Mfrs. Assn., Am. Mgmt. Assn., Soc. Advancement Mgmt., Pan Am. Soc. New Eng. (trustee), Pan Am. Soc. (gov.), Ecuadorian-Am. Assn. (dir.), Alpha Kappa Psi (distinguished service award 1951). Clubs: New York University (N.Y.C.); University (Boston); Canajoharie Golf and Country. Author: How to Manage by Results, 1965, Planning Next Year's Profits, 1968, Updating The Management Process, 1971; Management By Objectives For The Staff Manager, 1971; No-Nonsense Delegation, 1976; Management by Objectives for Nonprofit Organizations, 1976; Management by Objectives for Financial Managers, 1976. Contbr. articles and papers to various publs. Address: PO Box 1746 Madison WI 53701

MC CONKIE, BRUCE REDD, clergyman; b. Ann Arbor, Mich., July 29, 1915; s. Oscar W. and Margaret V. (Redd) McC.; A.B., U. Utah, 1937, J.D., 1940; m. Amelia Smith, Oct. 13, 1937; children—Vivian, Joseph F., Stanford S., Mary E., Mark L., Rebecca, Stephen L., Sara J. Admitted to Utah bar, 1940; mem. firm McConkie, Boud, Summerhays & Hess, Salt Lake City, 1940-42; asst. city atty., city prosecutor Salt Lake City, 1940-42. Ordained to ministry Ch. of Jesus Christ of Latter Day Saints, 1946; ch. servicemen's coordinator, 1947-64; gen. authority of ch., 1946—, mem. First Council of 70, 1946-72; mem. council Twelve Apostles, 1972—; pres. So. Australian Mission, Melbourne, Australia, 1961-64. Mem. Bd. Edn. Ch. Jesus Christ Latter-day Saints, 1972—. Trustee Brigham Young U., Provo, Utah, 1972—, Ricks Coll., Rexburg, Idaho, 1973—, Ch. Coll. Hawaii, Laie, Oahu, 1973—. Served from 1st lt. to lt. col., M.I., AUS, 1942-46. Compiler 3 volumes of doctrines of salvation, sermons and writings of Joseph Fielding Smith, 1954, 55, 56. Author: Mormon Doctrine, 1958; Doctrinal New Testament Commentary, Vol. 1, The Gospels, 1965; vol. 2, Acts-Philippians, 1970; Vol. 3, Colossians-Revelation, 1972; The Promised Messiah—The First Coming of Christ, 1978; The Mortal Messiah—From Bethlehem to Calvary, Book I, 1979. Address: 47 E S Temple St Salt Lake City UT 84184

MC CONKIE, GEORGE WILSON, educator; b. Holden, Utah, July 15, 1937; s. G. Wilson and Mabel (Stephenson) McC.; A.A., Dixie Jr. Coll., 1957; B.S., Brigham Young U., 1960, M.S., 1961; Ph.D., Standord U., 1966; m. Orlene Carol Johnson, Sept. 6, 1962; children—Lynnette, Heather, April, Faline, George Wilson, Bryce Johnson, Camille, Elissa, Esther, Bryna. Asst. prof. edn. Cornell U., 1964-70, asso. prof., 1970-75, prof., 1975-78, chmn. dept. edn., 1977-78; prof. U. Ill., Champaign, 1978—. NIMH spl. fellow, 1971-72; NIMH grantee, 1974—; U.S. Office Edn. grantee, 1970-73; Nat. Inst. Edn. grantee, 1974-77. Fellow Am. Psychol. Assn.; mem. Am. Ednl. Research Assn., Am. Psychonomic Soc., Nat. Reading Conf. Mormon. Contbr. articles to profl. publs. Home: 2605 Berniece Dr Champaign IL 61820 Office: Center for Study Reading 51 Gerty Dr Champaign IL 61820

MCCONN, JAMES JOSEPH, mayor Houston; b. Tulsa, Mar. 15, 1928; student U. Notre Dame; m. Margie. Owner, McConn Constrn. Co., Houston; mayor Houston, 1978—, mem. City Council, 1971-74. Office: City Hall 901 Bagby St Houston TX 77001

MCCONNACHIE, BRIAN JOHN, editor, writer; b. N.Y.C., Dec. 23, 1942; s. Morton and Mae (Clark) McC.; student U. Dublin, 1961-63, N.Y. U., 1963-64; m. Ann Brennan Crilly, Nov. 25, 1967; 1 dau., Mary Crilly. Mem. network programming staff CBS, N.Y.C., 1967-68; mem. staff TV programming dept. Benton & Bowles Advt., N.Y.C., 1968-70; free-lance writer, cartoonist, 1970-72; editor Nat. Lampoon, N.Y.C., 1972-75, also creative dir. advt. and books. Served with AUS, 1965-67. Author: The Naked and the Nude, 1976; editor: Job of Sex, 1974; The Paperback Conspiracy, 1974; contbg. editor This Side of Parodies, 1974, Letters From The Editors, 1973; co-scripter: The Big Event (NBC), 1976, The TV TV Show (NBC), 1977, Saturday Night Live (NBC), 1978—. Home: 110 W 78th St New York City NY 10024

MC CONNAUGHEY, GEORGE CARLTON, JR., lawyer, utility co. exec.; b. Hillsboro, Ohio, Aug. 9, 1925; s. George Carlton and Nelle (Morse) McC.; B.A., Denison U., 1949; LL.B., Ohio State U., 1951, J.D., 1967; m. Carolyn Schlieper, June 16, 1951; children—Elizabeth, Susan, Nancy. Admitted to Ohio bar, 1951, since practiced in Columbus; partner firm McConnaughey & McConnaughey, 1954-57, McConnaughey, McConnaughey & Stradley, 1957-62, Laylin, McConnaughey & Stradley, 1962-67, George, Greek, King, McMahon & McConnaughey, 1967-79, McConnaughey, Stradley, Mone & Moul, 1979—; sec., gen. counsel Mid-Continent Telephone Corp., Hudson, Ohio, 1960—, also dir.; dir. N.Am. Broadcasting Co. (WMNI Radio), Columbus, Newark (Ohio) Telephone Co.; asst. atty. gen. State of Ohio, 1951-54. Pres., Upper Arlington (Ohio) Bd. Edn., 1967-69, Columbus Town Meeting Assn., 1974-76; chmn. Ohio Young Republicans, 1956; U.S. presdl. elector, 1956; trustee Buckeye Boys Ranch, Columbus; elder Covenant Presbyterian Ch., Columbus. Served with U.S. Army, 1943-45; ETO. Mem. Am. Bar Assn., Ohio Bar Assn., Columbus Bar Assn., Am. Judicature Soc. Clubs: Columbus, Scioto Country, Athletic, Rotary, Masons (Columbus). Home: 1969 Andover Rd Columbus OH 43212 Office: 100 E Broad St Columbus OH 43215

MC CONNAUGHY, JOHN EDWARD, JR., environ. control co. exec.; b. Pitts., May 9, 1929; s. John Edward and Laura (Remly) McC.; grad. Mercersburg Acad., 1946; A.B., Denison U., 1950; M.B.A., Harvard, 1952; m. Carolyn L. Saxton, Oct. 10, 1977; children—John Edward III, James Radcliffe, Lynne Ann. Asst. mgr. fin. planning elec. appliance div. Westinghouse Electric Corp., Mansfield, Ohio, 1956-58, mgr. adminstrv. services portable appliance div., 1958-62, dir. mgmt. services consumer group, Pitts., 1962-63; controller U.S. consumer products Singer Co., N.Y.C., 1963-66, regional dir. mktg., 1966; pres. Singer Co. Can. Ltd., 1967, v.p. European ops., 1967-69; chmn. bd., chief exec. officer Peabody Internat. Corp., Conn., 1969—; dir. First Bank, Mgmt. Assistance Inc., N.Y.C., Conn. Gram Industries, Inc., N.Y.C. Served to lt. (j.g.) USNR, 1953-56. Address: 4 Landmark Sq Stamford CT 06901

MCCONNELL, DAVID GRAHAM, biochemist, educator; b. Bronxville, N.Y., Dec. 3, 1926; s. Luther Graham and Helen (Slagle) McC.; A.B., Columbia, 1949, A.M., 1949; Ph.D., Ind. U., 1957; m. Patricia Barnes, Sept. 1, 1970; children—Ross, Paul D., Teresa Barnes, Alex, Debora Barnes, Kim. Research asso. Ohio State U., Columbus, 1956-61, asso. prof., 1962-71, prof., 1971-72; prof. biochemistry and biomechanics Mich. State U., East Lansing, 1973—. Labor ofcl. NAACP, 1966-72. Served with USNR, 1944-46, USMCR,

1950-52. Mem. Am. Soc. Biol. Chemists, Am. Soc. for Cell Biology, Biophys. Soc., Psychonomic Soc., Am. Neurochem. Soc. Author: (novel) The Destruction of Crown City, 1974. Home: East Lansing MI Office: Dept Biochemistry Mich State U East Lansing MI 48824

MCCONNELL, DAVID MOFFATT, lawyer; b. Chester, S.C., June 12, 1912; s. Harvey Elzaphon and Elizabeth (Simpson) McC; B.S. summa cum laude, Davidson Coll., 1933; student Harvard. Grad. Bus. Sch., 1933-34, Law Sch., 1934-35; J.D., Georgetown U., 1939, LL.M., 1940; m. Ona Altman, Dec. 31, 1952; children—David Moffatt, Lynn Torbit, Joseph Moore. Admitted to S.C. bar, 1936, D.C. bar, 1945, N.C. bar, 1946, also U.S. Supreme Ct.; with firm Henry & Henry, Chester, 1936; counsel com. govt. reorgn. U.S. Senate, 1937-38; spl. atty. to chief counsel Internal Revenue Service, 1938-41; practice in Charlotte, N.C., 1946—; v.p., gen. counsel Belk Stores, Charlotte, 1946-76; gen. counsel Leggett Stores, 1946-76; dir. So. Nat. Bank, Lumberton, N.C., also chmn. Charlotte bd., 1970-76; U.S. ambassador to UN, 1968-69. Spl. adviser UN Econ. and Social Council; mem. U.S. delegation Fed. Republic Germany Marshall Plan, 1967. Chmn., sec. N.C. Bd. Elections, 1952-62; chmn. exec. com. Mecklenburg County (N.C.) Democratic Party, 1952-57; mem. nat. platform com. Dem. Party, 1964-72; elector U.S. Electoral Coll., 1948, 52. Donor McConnell Collection Tibetan Art to Baton Rouge Arts Mus., 1965; bd. dirs. emeritus Billy Graham Evangelistic Assn.; bd. visitors Davidson Coll., 1972—; trustee Erskine Coll., Due West, S.C., 1954-58, bd. advisers, 1968-72; trustee Robert Lee Stowe, Jr. Found., Henderson Belk Found. Served to col. AUS, 1940-46; CBI. Decorated Legion of Merit with oak leaf cluster; Order Cloud with banner (Republic China). Fellow Mexican Acad. Internat. Law; mem. Am., N.C., 26th Jud. Dist. bar assns., St. Andrews Soc., Newcomen Soc., Phi Beta Kappa, Kappa Alpha. Presbyterian. Mason (Shriner). Clubs: Charlotte Country, City, Quail Hollow Country (Charlotte); University (Washington). Home: 920 Granville Rd Charlotte NC 28207 Office: McConnell Howard Pruett & Bragg City Nat Center 200 S Tryon St Charlotte NC 28202

MC CONNELL, EDWARD BOSWORTH, legal orgn. adminstr., lawyer; b. Greenwich, Conn., Apr. 3, 1920; s. Raymond Arnott and Anna Bell (Lee) McC.; A.B., U. Neb., 1941, LL.B., 1947; M.B.A. with distinction, Harvard U., 1943; m. Jeanne Rotton, Aug. 30, 1947; children—Annalee, Marilyn McConnell Behren, Edward, Barbara, William. Admitted to Nebr. bar, 1947, N.J. bar, 1950; mem. faculty Rutgers U. Sch. Bus. Adminstrn., Newark, 1947-53; asso. firm Toner, Speakman and Crowley, Newark, N.J., 1949-50; adminstrv. asst. and law sec. to Chief Justice of N.J., 1950-53; adminstrv. dir. Cts. of N.J., Trenton, 1953-73, also standing master Supreme Ct., 1953-73; dir. Nat. Center for State Cts., Williamsburg, 1973—; mem. group to study Role of Cts. in Am. Society, 1978—; mem. adv. com. Dispute Resolution Policy Com., Social Sci. Research Inst., U. So. Calif., 1975—; nat. adv. council Center Adminstrn. Justice, Wayne State U., 1973-77; nat. project com. State Jud. Info. Systems Project SEARCH Group, 1973-76; faculty Appellate Judges Seminar, Inst. Jud. Adminstrn., N.Y. U., 1962-75; vis. expert UN Asia and Far East Inst., Tokyo, 1971; mem. Cts. Task Force Nat. Advisory Commn. Criminal Justice Standards and Goals, 1971-73; nat. advisory com. D.C. Ct. Mgmt. Project, 1966-70. Trustee Inst. Ct. Mgmt., 1969-73; chmn. Nat. Conf. Ct. Adminstrv. Officers, 1956. Served to maj., C.E., AUS, 1943-46. Decorated Bronze Star medal. Recipient Warren E. Burger award for greatest contbn. to improvement of ct. adminstrn. Inst. for Ct. Mgmt., 1975; Herbert Lincoln Harley award for efficient adminstrn. justice Am. Judicature Soc., 1973; Glenn R. Winters award for outstanding service in jud. adminstrn. Am. Judges Assn., 1974. Mem. Am. (chmn. jud. adminstrn. div. 1976-77, ho. of dels. 1977—), N.J., Nebr. bar assns., Order of Coif (hon.), Delta Upsilon, Sigma Delta Phi, Phi Delta Phi. Home: 222 W Queens Dr Williamsburg VA 23185 Office: Nat Center for State Cts 300 Newport Ave Williamsburg VA 23185

MC CONNELL, FREEMAN ERTON, educator, audiologist; b. West Point, Ind., Apr. 20, 1914; s. Grant Wilson and Alma (Wyman) McC.; B.S., U. Ill., 1939, M.A., 1946; Ph.D., Northwestern U., 1950; m. Grace Boonie Conn, May 31, 1941; children—Conn Michael, Steven Grant. Audiologist, asst. prof. logopedics U. Wichita (Kans.) Inst. Logopedics, 1950-51; dir. Bill Wilkerson Hearing and Speech Center, Nashville, 1951-60, 63-76, dir. emeritus, 1976—; prof. audiology, chmn. dept. hearing and speech scis., 1951-60, 63-75, asso. prof. otolaryngology, 1969—; prof. audiology Vanderblit U. Sch. Medicine, Nashville, 1976—; prof., head dept. audiology and speech pathology U. Tenn., Knoxville, 1960-63; vis. prof. audiology Syracuse U., 1967; cons. audiology Arnold Engring. Devel. Center, Tullahoma, Tenn., 1953-72; cons. health div. Oak Ridge Nat. Lab., 1963-67; research cons. U.S. Office Edn., 1965-74; mem. Nat. Adv. Com. Ann. Survey Hearing Impaired Children and Youth, 1970—, numerous short-term consultantships to health and edn. depts. Bd. dirs. Am. Hearing Soc., 1954-60; trustee Edn. and Auditory Research Found., 1972—. Served with AUS, 1943-46. Nat. Inst. Neurol. Diseases and Stroke grantee, 1957-60, 63-65, 66-74, U.S. Office Edn. grantee, 1965-73. Fellow Am. Speech and Hearing Assn. (honors 1977); mem. Acad. Rehab. Audiology (past pres.), Council on Exceptional Children, AAAS, Acoustical Soc. Am., Tenn. Speech and Hearing Assn. (past pres., honors 1972). Democrat. Episcopalian. Editor: Deafness in Childhood, 1967. Contbr. articles to profl. jours. and chpts. to books. Research on hereditary deafness and lang. devel. Home: 3828 Richland Ave Nashville TN 37205

MCCONNELL, GRANT, educator, author; b. Portland, Oreg., June 27, 1915; s. Leslie Grant and Nellie (Nelson) McC.; B.A., Reed Coll., 1937; student Harvard, 1937-38; Rhodes scholar, Oxford (Eng.) U., 1938-39; Ph.D., U. Calif. at Berkeley, 1951; m. Jane Foster, Oct. 7, 1939: children—Ann Katherine, James Andrew. Instr. econs. Mt. Holyoke Coll., 1939-40; with Dept. Agr., also OPA, 1940-42; lectr. polit. sci. U. Calif. at Berkeley, 1951-53. asst. prof., 1953-57; asso. prof. polit. sci. U. Chgo., 1957-65, prof., 1965-69, chmn. dept. polit. sci., 1967-69; prof. govt. U. Calif. at Santa Cruz, 1969—, exec. vice chancellor, 1970-71; dir. U. Chgo.-Makerere (Uganda) Coll.- State Dept. Exchange Program, 1961—; U. Chgo.-Falk Program, 1962—; cons. on conservation, 1957—. Served to lt. USNR, 1943-46; PTO. Mem. Am. Polit. Sci. Assn., Nat. Parks Assn. North Cascades Conservation Council (bd. dirs.), Wilderness Soc., Sierra Club. Author: The Decline of Agrarian Democracy, 1953: The Steel Seizure of 1952, 1960; Steel and the Presidency, 1962, 1963; Private Power and American Democracy, 1965; The Modern Presidency, 2d edit., 1976. Home: Bonny Doon Rd Santa Cruz CA 95060

MCCONNELL, J(AMES) H(OGE) TYLER, lawyer, banker; b. Richmond, Va., Nov. 23, 1914; s. Frank Percy and Belle Norwood (Tyler) McC.; B.A., Va. Mil. Inst., 1936; LL.B., U. Va., 1939, J.D., 1970; m. Jean Ellen duPont, Sept. 23, 1944 (div. 1972); children—Marion, Susan, James, William (dec.); m. 2d, Margaret Mahler, Apr. 25, 1973. Admitted to Va. bar, 1938, Del. bar, 1944, Mo. bar, 1942; v.p., dir. Peoples Bank of Radford (Va.), 1937-41; partner firm Tyler, McConnell and Goldsmith, Radford, 1938-41; judge Civil Ct., Radford, 1940-41; asst. leader Inst. Pub. Affairs, U. Va., Charlottesville, 1939; counsel Hercules, Inc., Wilmington, Del., also plant mgr., asst. gen. counsel, asst. to pres., corporate sec., 1944-66, dir., 1959-66; pres., 1966-79, chmn., 1979—, chief exec. officer, chmn. exec. com., dir. Del. Trust Co., Wilmington, 1966—, mem. adminstrv. com., 1976—; dir. sta. WHYY-TV; dir. Del. Dept. Health and Social Services, 1967-69, Del. Dept. Indsl. Fin., 1973-75; pres. Wilmington Clearing House, 1968-69, 1979—, AAA Motor Club, 1965-75. Parent chmn. Bennett Coll., N.Y., 1965-66; chmn. fin. com. Sweet Briar Coll., 1959-71; chmn. Del. Hwy. Dept., 1949-53; 1st chmn. Delaware River and Bay Authority, 1963-65, treas., 1966—; founder, dir. Greater Wilmington Devel. Council, 1960—, also 1st pres.; mem. Del. Com. on Organized Crime, 1966-67; chmn. Fair Hill Races, 1966-75; pres. Cecil County Breeders Fair, Inc., 1966-75; mem. nat. adv. com. Camp Fire Girls, 1971-72; bd. dirs. Del. chpt. ARC, 1948—, campaign chmn., 1952; bd. dirs., exec. com. Nat. Safety Council, 1960—, chmn., 1969-71; bd. dirs. Del. Safety Council, 1950—, pres., 1960-63; bd. dirs. Block Blight, Inc., 1968-69, Urban Coalition, 1977-79, Del. Dept. Health and Social Services, 1967-69, Del. Dept. Indsl. Fin., 1973-75; trustee Lawrenceville (N.J.) Sch., 1968-71. Served to 1st. lt. field arty. USAR, 1939-42. Recipient Flame of Life award Nat. Safety Council, 1971. Mem. Am., Va., Del., Mo. bar assns., Am. Judicature Soc., Del. Bankers Assn. (pres. 1972-73), Nat. Steeplechase and Hunt Assn. (steward 1964-76, v.p. 1971-76), Del. Racing Assn. (dir. 1948—), Am. Bankers Assn. (gov. adminstrv. com. 1976—, v.p. 1972-74), Va. Mil. Inst. Alumni Assn., Phi Alpha Delta, Raven Soc. Democrat. Episcopalian. Clubs: Greenville Country; Wilmington, Wilmington Country (pres. 1965-69); River (N.Y.); Rehoboth Beach Country; Indian River Yacht. Office: Delaware Trust Co 900 Market St Wilmington DE 19899

MCCONNELL, JAMES VERNON, educator, psychologist; b. Okmulgee, Okla., Oct. 26, 1925; s. James V. and Helen (Stokes) McC.; B.A. in Psychology, La. State U., 1947; M.A., U. Tex., 1954, Ph.D., 1956; student U. Oslo (Norway), 1954-55. Mem. faculty U. Mich., 1956—, prof. psychology, 1963—; pres. Planarian Press, Ann Arbor, Mich., 1964—; editor, pub. Worm Runner's Digest, Internat. Jour. Comparative Psychology, 1959—; editor Jour. Biol. Psychology, 1966—. Served to ensign USNR, 1944-46. Recipient Distinguished Teaching award Am. Psychol. Found., 1976. Fulbright scholar, 1954-55. Fellow AAAS, Am. Psychol. Assn.; mem. Psychonomic Soc., Animal Behavior Soc., Midwestern Psychol. Assn. Author: (with others) Psychology, 1961; also numerous articles, chpts. in books. Editor: The Worm Re-Turns, 1965; (with Marlys Schutjer) Science, Sex and Sacred Cows, 1971; Understanding Human Behavior, 1974, 2d edit., 1977; (with Robert Trotter) Psychology: The Human Science, 1978. Spl. research in behavior modification, biochemistry of memory. Home: 4101 Thornoaks Rd Ann Arbor MI 48104

MC CONNELL, JOHN WILKINSON, educator, labor arbitrator; b. Phila, Oct. 18, 1907; s. John and Lucy (Wilkinson) McC.; B.A., Dickinson Coll., 1929, D.Sc., 1959; Ph.D., Yale, 1937; LL.D., U. R.I., 1967, Ricker Coll., 1968, U. N.H., 1971; m. Harriet Hawley Barlow, July 29, 1933; children—Janet (Mrs. John Alexander), Kathleen (Mrs. David Mervin), Grace (Mrs. Alfred Clark), Judith Ann (Mrs. Henry Sondheimer), John C. Instr., Am. U. at Cairo, Egypt, 1929- 32; instr. Yale, 1935, research asso. Inst. Human Relations, 1934-37; asst. prof. econs. and sociology Am. U., Washington, 1937-39; prof. sociology N.Y. U., 1939-46; prof. indsl. and labor relations Cornell U., 1946-63, dean grad. sch., 1955-59, dean sch. indsl. and labor relations, 1959-63; dir. research in indsl. retirement, 1959—; pres. U. N.H., 1963-71; counselor to coll. Ithaca (N.Y.) Coll., 1971-75, lectr., 1975; adj. prof. labor econs. Cornell U., 1971—; dir. research Twentieth Century Fund, 1951-54; Fulbright lectr. in India, 1953-54. Pub. mem. region II Nat. War Labor Bd., 1943-46, Nat. WSB, 1950-52; pub. mem. Fgn. Service Grievance Bd. Dept. State, 1974—; cons. pension and retirement systems, mem. human resources research adv. bd. USAF, 1948-53, Social Security Adminstrn.; mem. adv. council Nat. Inst. Child Health and Human Devel., NIH, 1965-69; mem. labor arbitration panel N.Y. State Mediation Service; mem. Fed. Mediation and Conciliation Service; pub. mem. minimum wage bd., P.R., 1956—, chmn., 1960, 1968; chmn. study group on edn. of fgn. students Land-Grant Coll. Assn., 1961. Recipient Outstanding Service medal Army Dept., 1967, with oak leaf cluster, 1971. Fellow AAAS, Am. Sociol. Soc.; mem. Am. Econ. Assn., Nat. Acad. Arbitrators, Am. Arbitration Assn., Indsl. Relations Research Assn. (dir. 1951-54), Portsmouth (N.H.) Fire Soc., Phi Beta Kappa, Phi Kappa Phi, Omicron Delta Kappa, Pi Gamma Mu. Methodist. Author: Evolution of Social Classes, 1942; Basic Teachings of Great Economists, 1943; (with Robert Risley) Economic Security, 1951; (with others) America's Needs and Resources, 1955; (with John Corson) Economic Needs of Older People, 1955; Contbr. articles to profl. jours. Club: Cornell N.Y. Home: 21 Cayuga St Trumansburg NY 14886

MCCONNELL, JOHN WILLIAM, JR., lawyer; b. Bessemer, Ala., Apr. 17, 1921; s. John W. and Elizabeth (Sheridan) McC.; A.B., U. Ala., 1942, M.A., 1946; LL.B., Yale, 1948; m. Margaret B. Snider, Jan. 7, 1944; children—Margaret E. (Mrs. John Evans), Rebecca L. (Mrs. A.D. Braden), Catherine L., John W. III. Admitted to Ala. bar, 1948, D.C. bar, 1977; atty. Inge, Twitty, Armbrecht & Jackson, Mobile, Ala., 1948-56, Armbrecht, Jackson, McConnell & DeMouy, 1956-65; dir. U.S. Peace Corps, Nigeria, 1965-68; v.p. legal Sea-Land Service, Inc., Menlo Park, N.J., 1968-76, also dir.; of counsel Haight, Gardner, Poor & Havens, Washington, 1977—. Mem. Ala. Democratic Exec. Com., 1963-65, chmn. Ala. Dem. Steering Com., 1963-65. Served to capt. AUS, 1943-46, 50-52. Mem. Am., Ala. bar assns., Maritime Law Assn. Methodist. Atty. for Reynolds v. Sims on legislative reapportionment, U.S. Supreme Ct., 1963-64. Home: 3744 12th St S Arlington VA 22204

MCCONNELL, RAYMOND ARNOTT, JR., newspaperman; b. North Ridgeville, Ohio, Dec. 31, 1915; s. Rev. Raymond Arnott and Anna Bell (Lee) McConnell; A.B., Williams Coll., 1936; LL.D., Doane Coll., 1951; m. Maren Ellen Dobson, May 31, 1940; children—Alice Maren, Raymond Arnott III, Judith Dobson, Christine. Reporter, Troy (N.Y.) Record, 1936-37; telegraph and news editor Nebr. State Jour., Lincoln, 1937-39; asso. editor Lincoln Evening Jour., 1940; mng. editor The Jour. Newspapers, Lincoln, 1941-57, editor 1943-57; news exec. Twin Coast Newspapers, Inc., 1958—; mng. editor Pasadena Star-News, The Independent, 1966-72, exec. editor, 1972-75; exec. editor Pasadena Star-News and Foothill Intercity newspapers, 1975—. Commr. Joint U.S.-Mexico Commn. Migrant Labor, 1954. Mem. natural conservation adv. commn. U.S. Dept. Agr., 1955-57. Studied Brit. agrl. war effort on invitation, 1943; instr. journalism, 1944-45. Bd. dirs. Pasadena Anti-Crime Program, 1978—, Pacificulture Found. and Asia Mus., 1972—; bd. govs. Pasadena-Foothill Urban League, 1975—. Organizer, Nebr. All Star presdl. primary for which Journal awarded Pultizer prize for dist. pub. service, 1948; named Outstanding Young Man of Nebr., Nebr. Jr. C. of C., 1950, Outstanding Young Man of Lincoln, Jr. C. of C., 1951; one of 10 outstanding young men of U.S., U.S. Jr. C. of C., 1951; recipient Distinguished Service award Nat. Watershed Congress, 1973. Mem. Gargoyle Soc., P.E.N., Sigma Delta Chi, Zeta Psi. Presbyn. Mason (32 deg.). Author: Trampled Terraces, 1950. Contbr. to nat. mags. Home: 650 Cordova St Pasadena CA 91101 Office: 525 E Colorado Blvd Pasadena CA 91109

MC CONNELL, ROBERT BROOKE NAYLOR, newspaper publisher; b. Vancouver, B.C., Can., Sept. 21, 1943; s. Norman Elmore and Shelagh (Tait) McC.; B.A., U. B.C., 1964; M.A., U. Chgo., 1965; m. Kay Lusty, June 6, 1964; children—Megan, Morgan. Reporter, then editor Vancouver Province, 1965-72; asst. to pub., then gen. mgr. Montreal Gazette, 1976-79, publisher, 1979—. Anglican. Office: 1000 St Antoine St Montreal PQ H3C 3R7 Canada*

MCCONNELL, ROBERT BRUCE, broadcasting exec.; b. Indpls., Apr. 17, 1921; s. Charles Bruce and Emma Lucile (Clemens) McC.; B.A., Ind. U., 1942; m. Frances Louise Hollingsworth, June 10, 1944; 1 dau., Sally Anne. Salesman radio sta. WISH, Indpls., 1944-47; v.p., gen. mgr. Universal Broadcasting Corp., Indpls., 1947-50; v.p., gen. mgr. Ind. Broadcasting Corp., Indpls., 1950—; treas. Met. Ind. TV Assn., 1971—. Pres., 500 Festival Assos., Indpls., 1966; mem. Greater Indpls. Progress Com., 1968—, pres., 1972; pres. Crossroads Rehab. Center, 1970—. Bd. dirs. United Way Indpls., 1965—. Served with USNR, 1941-45. Mem. Indpls. (dir. 1972-73), Ind. (dir. 1976—) chambers commerce, Nat. Assn. Broadcasters (dir. 1975-79), Ind. Broadcasters Assn. (dir. 1972-73), Sigma Nu. Mason. Clubs: Columbia (pres. 1970), Indianapolis Athletic, Meridian Hills Country (Indpls.). Home: 8423 Overlook Pkwy Indianapolis IN 46260 Office: 1950 N Meridian St Indianapolis IN 46202

MC CONNELL, ROBERT CHALMERS, former city ofcl., cons.; b. Santa Fe, Aug. 7, 1913; s. Chalmers and Mary (Foree) McC.; B.A., U. N.Mex., 1935; LL.B., George Washington U., 1939; m. Colleen Alford, Feb. 3, 1948; 1 dau., Julie. Admitted to N.Mex. bar, 1941, U.S. Supreme Ct. bar, 1947; law clk. to U.S. circuit judge, 1939-40; asst. dist. atty. N.Mex., 1940-41, 45-47; adminstrv. asst. to congressman from N.Mex., 1947-57, 57-61; spl. asst. to asst. sec. interior, 1961-62; asst. to sec. for congl. liaison Dept. Interior, Washington, 1962-67, asst. sec. for adminstrn., 1967-69; mayor City of Redington Beach (Fla.), 1971-72; partner McConnell-Wilroy Cons., St. Petersburg, Fla., 1976—. Mgr. Madeira Beach (Fla.) Little League Baseball; chmn. bd. govs. Redington Beach Assn., 1977-79; chmn. Chaves County Democratic Com., 1946-48. Served with AUS, 1941-45. Recipient Distinguished Service award U.S. Dept. Interior, 1967. Home: 15849 Redington Dr Redington Beach FL 33708

MC CONNELL, ROBERT EASTWOOD, architect, educator; b. Spokane, Wash., July 15, 1930; s. Robert Ervie and Alma (Eastwood) McC.; B.Archtl. Engring., Wash. State U., 1952; M.Arch., Mass. Inst. Tech., 1954; m. Beverly Ann Vincent, Sept. 12, 1953; children—Kathleen Ann, Karen Eileen, Terri Lynn. Project architect John W. Maloney, Architect, Seattle, 1956-62; asst. prof. architecture Ariz. State U., Tempe, 1962-66, asso. prof., 1966-67; prof. U. Kans., Lawrence, 1967-69; prof., head dept. art and architecture U. Idaho, Moscow, 1969-71; prof. U. Ariz., Tucson, 1971—, dean Coll. Architecture, 1971-77; partner McConnell & Peterson, Architects, Tempe, 1963-66; pvt. practice architecture, 1962—. Chmn. Idaho Gov.'s Awards Program in Arts and Humanities, 1970; project dir. Rio Salado Conceptual Study, Phoenix, 1966; bd. dirs. Tucson Regional Plan, 1972-79. Served with USAF, 1954-56. Fellow AIA (awards 1969, 76); mem. Ariz. Acad., Ariz. Soc. Architects (mem. council of dels., 1971-77, chmn. honor awards jury 1975), Phi Kappa Phi, Scarab, Tau Beta Pi, Sigma Tau. Author, project dir. Land Use Planning for Ariz., Ariz. Acad., 1974. Contbr. articles to profl. jours. Home: 7001 N Edgewood Pl Tucson AZ 85704 Office: College of Architecture U Ariz Tucson AZ 85721

MCCONNELL, THOMAS RAYMOND, educator; b. Mediapolis, Iowa, May 25, 1901; s. William John and Nell (Cox) McC.; A.B., Cornell Coll., Mt. Vernon, Iowa, 1924, LL.D., 1949; A.M., U. Iowa, 1928, Ph.D., 1933; D.H.L., Syracuse U., 1952; m. Ruth Kegley, June 20, 1925; children—Robert Willis, Carol Ruth. Instr. English and journalism Cornell Coll., 1925-26, instr. and asst. prof. edn. and psychology, 1927-29, dean of coll., prof. edn. and psychology, 1932-36; instr. edn. U. Iowa, 1930-31, summers 1931-36; prof. edn. psychology U. Minn., 1936-50, chmn. com. ednl. research, 1937-47, asso. dean Coll. Sci., Lit. and Arts, 1940-44, acting dean, 1942-44, dean, 1944-50; chancellor U. Buffalo, 1950-54; prof. U. Calif., Berkeley, 1954-68, prof. emeritus, 1968—, chmn. Center for Study of Higher Edn., 1957-66, research educator Center Research and Devel. in Higher Edn., 1966-76; mem. Pres. Truman's Commn. on Higher Edn. Fellow Center for Advanced Study of Behavioral Scis., 1959-60. Mem. com. on devel. youth Social Sci. Research Council, 1957-68; chief cons. Restudy of Needs of Calif. in Higher Edn., 1954-56; mem. U.S. Pres.'s Com. on Pub. Higher Edn. in D.C., 1963-64; adviser to subcom. mgmt. and financing undergrad. edn. Com. on Econ. Devel.; chmn. Ill. Commn. Study Non-Pub. Higher Edn., 1968-69; adv. com. Inst. Coll. & U. Adminstrs., 1958-70. Recipient 1966 award for distinguished contbns. to ednl. research Am. Ednl. Research Assn.-Phi Delta Kappa, 1966; Distinguished Service award U. Iowa, 1968; Centennial award U. Calif., Berkeley, 1968; 1st ann. award Colloquium in Higher Edn., 1970; award for contbns. Carnegie Commn. Higher Edn.-Assembly Univ. Goals and Governance-Center for Research and Devel. in Higher Edn., 1971; award for distinguished research on coll. students Am. Ednl. Research Assn. and Am. Coll. Testing Program, 1977. Mem. Nat. Acad. Edn., Phi Beta Kappa. Methodist. Author: (with others) Psychology in Everyday Living, 1938; (with others) Educational Psychology, 1948; (with T.C. Holy and H.H. Semans) A Restudy of the Needs of California in Higher Education, 1955; A General Pattern for Am. Public Higher Edn., 1962; (with others) Training for Educational Research, 1968, Omnibus Personality Inventory, 1968; Governments and the University: A Comparative Analysis, 1966; (with K.P. Mortimer) The Faculty in University Governance, 1971; The Redistribution of Power in Higher Education, 1971; (with B.R. Clark, P. Heist, M.A. Trow and G. Yonge) Students and Colleges: Interaction and Change, 1972; (with R.O. Berdahl and M.A. Fay) From Elite to Mass to Universal Higher Education: The British and American Transformations, 1973; (with Stewart Eddstein) Campus Government at Berkeley: A Study in Jurisdictions, 1977; (with Kenneth Mortimer) Sharing Authority Effectively: Participation, Interaction, and Discretion, 1977. Chmn. bd. editors Ency. Ednl. Research, 1964-69. Contbr. to books and various publs. on edn. and psychology. Home: Grand Lake Gardens 401 Santa Clara Ave Apt 214 Oakland CA 94610

MCCONNON, JAMES CHARLES, lawyer; b. Pitts., Mar. 30, 1926; s. Myles and Myra Viola (Steel) McC.; B.S., Cornell U., 1947; LL.B., U. Pa., 1951; m. Nancy Kern, Nov. 14, 1953; children—James Charles, Linda J., Nancy. Engr., U.S. Steel Co., Pitts., 1947, Westinghouse Air Brake Co., Pitts., 1948; admitted to Pa. bar, 1952, Ct. Customs and Patent Appeals, 1952; asso. firm Paul & Paul, Phila., 1952-58, partner, 1958—. Vice chmn. Southeastern Pa. Transp. Authority, 1964-68, chmn., 1968-78; bd. dirs., mem. exec. com. Am. Transit Assn., 1972-74; mem. mgmt. com. Internat. Union Pub. Transport, 1976—; mem. Nat. Transp. Policy Study Commn., 1976—; chmn. for hwy. transp. industry Payroll Savs. Bond drive, 1977, 78; mem. Phila. Met. Area Study Commn., 1963; regional chmn. Montgomery County (Pa.) Republican Com. Served with USN, 1943-46. Recipient Recognition of Service award Greater Phila. C. of C., 1974, Am. Pub. Transit Assn., 1976. Mem. Am., Phila. patent law assns., Am., Pa. (chmn. vehicle code revision), Phila. bar assns. Roman Catholic. Clubs: Union League (Phila.); Seaview Country (N.J.). Home: 104 Anton Rd Wynnewood PA 19096 Office: 1800 Land Title Bldg Philadelphia PA 19110

MCCONNOR, WILLIAM S., petroleum co. exec.; b. McKeesport, Pa., Jan 27, 1920; s. William F. and Shirley (Sandborn) McC.; B.S. in Indsl. Engring., Lehigh U., 1941; m. Eleanor Mills, June 5, 1943.

Became gen. supt. Toledo refinery Pure Oil Co. div. Union Oil Co. Calif., ops. mgr. refining div., Chgo., 1956-64, v.p., gen. mgr. refining, Palatine, Ill., 1964-67, v.p. refining and mktg., 1967-73, sr. v.p. parent co., Los Angeles and pres. Union 76 Div., 1973—; chmn. bd. Colonial Pipeline Co., Atlanta; dir. Wolverine Pipeline, Palatine Nat. Bank. Trustee Jobst Inst. Found. Recipient 25-Year Alumnus award Lehigh U. Alumni Assn., 1966. Mem. Nat. Petroleum Refiners Assn. (v.p., dir.), Am. Petroleum Inst. (v.p. refining). Club: Glen View. Office: Union Oil Center Los Angeles CA 90017*

MCCOOL, WOODFORD BETHEL, mgmt. cons., sch. adminstr.; b. McPherson, Kans., May 7, 1915; s. John H. and Nancy M. (Shirley) McC.; B.A., U. So. Calif., 1942; m. Mary Frances Bronson. Communications officer U.S. mission to UN, 1946-51, for sec. of state 2d and 3d sessions UN Gen. Assembly, 1947-48; asst. dir. Exec. Office Sec. Def., 1951-53; asst. sec. commn. AEC, 1953-54, sec. commn., 1954-72; now mgmt. cons.; v.p. adminstrv. affairs Rancho Bernardo Center for Continuing Edn. affiliate San Diego State U., 1978—; Served to lt. USNR, World War II. Recipient Outstanding Service award AEC, 1957. Mem. Am. Soc. Pub. Adminstrn., Western Gerontol. Soc., Soc. Advancement Mgmt. Democrat. Presbyterian. Club: Seven Oaks. Home: 12286 Casero Ct San Diego CA 92128 Office: Rancho Bernardo Center for Continuing Edn 12409 Rancho Bernardo Rd Suite 109 San Diego CA 92128

MCCORD, DAVID (THOMPSON WATSON), writer; b. N.Y.C., Nov. 15, 1897; s. Joseph Alexander and Eleanore Baynton (Reed) McC.; A.B., Harvard U., 1921, A.M., 1922, L.H.D., 1956; Litt. D., Northeastern U., 1954, U. N.B. (Can.), 1963, Williams Coll., 1971; LL.D., Washington and Jefferson Coll., 1955; L.H.D., Colby Coll., 1968, Framingham State Coll., 1975; Art. D., New Eng. Coll., 1956; Ed.D., Suffolk U., 1979. Asso. editor Harvard Alumni Bull., 1923-25, editor, 1940-46; mem. drama staff Boston Evening Transcript, 1923-28; exec. dir. Harvard Fund Council, 1925-63; lectr. Lowell Inst., 1950; staff mem. Bread Loaf Writers Conf., 1958, 60, 62, 64; instr. advanced writing courses Harvard U., summers 1963, 65, 66; vis. prof. Framingham State Coll., 1974; hon. curator Poetry and Farnsworth Rooms, Harvard Coll. Library; hon asso. Dudley House, Harvard U.; mem. Am. Council Learned Socs. com. on Dist. Am. Biography. Hon. trustee Boston Center for Adult Edn.; trustee Boston Atheneum, Historic Boston, Inc., Peter Bent Brigham Hosp., Boston, Charity of Edward Hopkins; trustee emeritus New Eng. Coll.; hon. trustee New Eng. Wildflower Soc.; overseer Old Sturbridge Village (Mass.), Perkins Inst. for Blind; bd. dirs. Asso. Harvard Alumni, 1965-68; councilor Harvard Soc. Advanced Study and Research, 1967-72; mem. overssers vis. com. dept. astronomy Harvard U. Served as 2d lt. F.A., U.S. Army, 1918. Guggenheim fellow, 1954; Kipling fellow Marlboro Coll.; Benjamin Franklin fellow Royal Soc. Arts, London. Fellow Am. Acad. Arts and Scis.; mem. Colonial Soc. Mass., Soc. of Cin. (N.H.), Internat. P.E.N., Am. Alumni Council, Mass. Hist. Soc., Phi Beta Kappa (poet Harvard 1938, Tufts 1938, 78, Coll. William and Mary 1950, M.I.T. 1973, Colby Coll., 1979). Recipient Golden Rose, New Eng. Poetry Club, 1941, William Rose Benet award, 1952, Sarah Josepha Hale medal, 1962, Nat. Inst. Arts and Letters grant, 1961, 1st nat. award for excellence in poetry for children Nat. Council Tchrs. English, 1977. Several one-man water color shows. Republican. Episcopalian. Clubs: Harvard, St. Botolph (past pres.), Tavern (past pres.), Club of Odd Volumes (Boston); Faculty; Signet, (Cambridge); Century (N.Y.C.). Author: Oddly Enough, 1926; Floodgate, 1927; Stirabout, 1928; Oxford Nearly Visited, 1929; The Crows, 1934; Bay Window Ballads (illustrated by John Lavalle), 1935; H.T.P.-Portrait of a Critic, 1935; Notes on the Harvard Tercentenary, 1936; An Acre for Education, 1938; Twelve Verses from XII Night, 1938; And What's More, 1941; On Occasion, 1943; About Boston, 1948; A Star by Day, 1950; Poet Always Next But One, 1951; The Camp at Lockjaw (illustrated by Gluyas Williams), 1952; Far and Few (poems for children, illustrated by Henry B. Kane), 1952; The Old Bateau, 1953; As Built With Second Thoughts, 1953; Odds Without Ends, 1954; The Language of Request, 1961; Take Sky, 1962; The Fabrick of Man, 1963; In Sight of Sever (Harvard essays), 1963; All Day Long, 1966; Every Time I Climb a Tree (illustrated by Marc Simont), 1967; Notes from Four Cities, 1969; Poem for the Occasion, 1970; For Me to Say, 1970; Pen, Paper and Poem, 1971; Mr. Bidery's Spidery Garden, 1972; Away and Ago, 1974; The Star in the Pail (illustrated by Marc Simont), 1975; One At A Time, 1977. Editor: Once and For All, 1929; What Cheer, 1945; Arthur Griffin's New England Revisited, 1967; Stow Wengenroth's New England, 1969. Mem. usage panel Am. Heritage Dictionary. Contbr. to mags., encys. Home: 374 Commonwealth Ave Boston MA 02215

MCCORD, HERBERT WEYMOUTH, radio exec.; b. Flushing, N.Y., Nov. 4, 1942; s. Frank Post and Alice (Weymouth) McC.; A.B., Darthouth Coll., 1964; M.B.A., Columbia U., 1966; m. Judith Stewart, June 18, 1966; children—Michael, Jennifer. Sta. mgr. WCBS-FM, 1969-72; account exec. CBS TV Network, 1972; v.p., gen. mgr. CKLW Radio, Southfield, Mich., 1973-74, pres., 1974—. Pres. Windsor dist. Canadian Cancer Soc., 1979; bd. dirs. Windsor United Way Campaign. Served with USMCR. Mem. Nat. Radio Broadcasters Assn., Detroit Radio Advt. Group (dir.). Clubs: Renaissance; Variety (Detroit). Office: CKLW Radio 26400 Lahser Rd Southfield MI 48037

MC CORD, JAMES ILEY, seminary pres.; b. Rusk, Tex., Nov. 24, 1919; s. Marshal Edward and Jimmie Oleta (Decherd) McC.; B.A., Austin Coll., 1938, D.D., 1949; student Union Theol. Sem., 1938-39; B.D., Austin Presbyn. Theol. Sem., 1942; M.A., U. Tex., 1942; student Harvard, 1942-43, U. Edinburgh, 1950-51; Th.D., U. Geneva, 1958; S.T.D., Knox Coll., Toronto, Can., 1958; D.D., Princeton, 1960, Victoria U., Toronto, 1963, Westmister Coll., New Wilmington, Pa., 1969, U. Edinburgh, 1970, Presbyn. Coll., U. Montreal, 1975; LL.D., Maryville Coll., 1959, Lafayette Coll., 1962, Tusculum Coll., 1964, Bloomfield Coll., 1966, United Protestant Theol. Inst., Cluj, Romania, 1974; Litt.D., Davidson Coll., 1959, Washington and Jefferson Coll., 1970, Rider Coll., 1977, Keimyung U., Taegu, Korea, 1979; L.H.D., Ursinus Coll., 1962; Th.D., Debrecen (Hungary) Ref. Theol. Faculty, 1967; LL.D., Park Coll., 1969; m. Hazel Thompson, Aug. 29, 1939; children—Vincent, Alison McCord Zimmerman, Marcia. Instr. U. Tex., 1940-42; adj. prof. Austin Presbyn. Theol. Sem., 1944-45, dean, prof. systematic theology, 1945-59; pres. Princeton Theol. Sem., 1959—. Vis. prof. Presbyn. Theol. Sem. of South, Campinas, Brazil, 1956; chmn. North Am. Area World Alliance Ref. Chs., 1958-60, N. Am. sec. alliance, 1959-77, also chmn. theol. dept., 1956-70; chmn. faith and order com., past chmn. nat. faith and order colloquium Nat. Council Chs.; mem. commn. faith and order World Council of Chs.; chmn. council theol. edn. U.P. Ch., 1964-67, chmn. council theol. sems., 1978—. chmn. com. consultation on ch. union U.P. Ch., 1961-63; past chmn. commn. on accrediting Assn. Theol. Schs. U.S. and Can.; pres. World Alliance Ref. Chs., 1977—; pres. Assn. Theol. Schs. in U.S. and Can., 1978—. Democrat. Home: 86 Mercer St Princeton NJ 08540

MC CORD, JOHN HARRISON, educator, lawyer; b. Oceanside, N.Y., Dec. 22, 1934; s. John Francis and Elsie (Powers) McC.; A.B., Fordham Coll., 1957; J.D. (St. Thomas More fellow), St. John's U., 1960; LL.M., U. Ill., 1965; m. Maureen Ursula Maclean, Dec. 30, 1961; children—John F.X., Paul V., David G., Maureen E. Admitted to N.Y. bar, 1960, Ill. bar, 1964; atty. U.S. Dept. Justice, Washington, 1960-61; mem. faculty U. Ill. Coll. Law, Champaign, 1964—, prof. law, 1965—; acad. cons. Ill. Inst. Continuing Legal Edn., 1968-72; vis. prof. law U. N.C., 1975, U. Hawaii, 1976. Served to capt. USAF, 1961-64. Mem. Am. (com. continuing legal edn. and chief reporter for study outline on buying, selling and merging businesses sect. fed. tax 1969-73, com. estate and gift taxes 1973—, chmn. subcom. gross estate issues 1976-78, subcom. tax reform 1978—), Ill. (exec. council fed. tax sect. 1966-73, chmn. sect. 1971-72), Chgo., Champaign County bar assns., Am. Judicature Soc., AAUP, Am. Arbitration Assn. (nat. panel arbitrators 1969—), Eastern Ill. Estate Planning Council (pres. 1970-71), Assn. Am. Law Schs. (fed. taxation roundtable council 1969-72), Order of Coif. Author: (with Keeton and O'Connell) Crisis in Car Insurance, 1967; Buying and Selling Small Businesses, 1969; (with O'Byrne) Deskbook for Illinois Estate Planners, 1969; Closely Held Corporations, 1971; (with O'Neill, Pearlman and Stroud) Buying, Selling and Merging Businesses, 1975; (with Lowndes and Kramer) Estate and Gift Taxes, 3d edit., 1974; (with McKee) Federal Income Taxation-A Summary Analysis, 1975; (with Kramer) Problems for Federal Estate and Gift Taxes, 1976; Estate and Gift Tax Reform, 1977; Estate and Gift Tax Summary, 1978; editor: Dimensions and Academic Freedom, 1969; With All Deliberate Speed: Civil Rights Theory and Reality, 1969; Ill. Law Forum, 1965-69; contbr. articles to profl. jours. Home: 15 Sherwin Dr Urbana IL 61801 Office: U Ill Coll Law Champaign IL 61820

MCCORD, KENNETH ARMSTRONG, cons. engr.; b. Balt., May 4, 1921; s. William Ellermeyer and Bertha (Turnt) McC.; B. Engring., Johns Hopkins U., 1941; m. Carol Blanton, Oct. 12, 1946; children—Thomas B., Kenneth Armstrong, William C., David M., Jean E. Sr. partner Whitman, Requardt and Assos., Balt., 1941—; gen. partner B&H Investments, Manassas, Va.; 1st v.p., dir. Warrenton Bldg. Material Co., Inc. (Va.). Served with C.E., U.S. Army, 1942-46. Decorated Silver Star, Croix de Guerre (France); registered profl. engr., Md., Va., N.J., D.C., Del.; registered profl. surveyor, Md., Del.; registered profl. planner, N.J. Fellow ASCE; mem. Am. Water Works Assn., Am. Cons. Engrs. Council, Water Pollution Control Fedn., Nat. Soc. Profl. Engrs. Democrat. Presbyterian. Clubs: Balt. Country, Md., Annapolis Yacht. Home: 1010 West Wind Ct Ruxton MD 21204 Office: 1111 N Charles St Baltimore MD 21202

MCCORD, LARRY REED, U.S. atty.; b. Ft. Smith, Ark., Apr. 25, 1940; s. Tilden Reed and Bryce Marie (Spencer) McC.; B.S. in Bus. Adminstrn., U. Ark., 1962, LL.B., 1965; m. Suzanne Beauchamp, Apr. 8, 1969; children—Jamie Leigh, Brent Christopher. Admitted to Ark. bar, 1965; asso. firm Bethel & Pearce, and successor, Ft. Smith, 1965-68; partner firm Pearce, Robinson & McCord, and predecessor, Ft. Smith, 1969-77; U.S. atty., Western Dist. Ark., 1977—; U.S. magistrate, 1974-77; bd. dirs. City of Ft. Smith, 1973-78, vice mayor, 1977-78. Pres. Ft. Smith United Way, 1976. Recipient Distinguished Service award Ft. Smith Jaycees, 1973. Mem. Am., Ark., Sebastian County bar assns. Clubs: Town (pres. 1977), Noon Exchange (Ft. Smith). Home: 2514 S 46th St Fort Smith AR 72903 Office: PO Box 1524 Fort Smith AR 72902

MCCORD, MARSHAL, civil engr.; b. Balt., July 4, 1917; s. William Ellermeyer and Bertha (Turnt) McC.; B. Engring., Johns Hopkins U., 1937; m. Ruth Helen Schultz, Apr. 20, 1946; 1 dau., Barbara Lynn. Draftsman, Modjeski & Masters, Harrisburg, Pa., 1937-40; design and project engr. J.E. Greiner Co., Balt., 1946-57; chief engr., v.p. Century Engring., Inc., Towson, Md., 1957-77; dir. engring. and constrn. State of Md., Balt., 1977—; mem. Md. State Bd. Registration for Profl. Engrs. and Land Surveyors, 1966-76, chmn., 1971-76. Moderator, Presbytery of Balt., 1977—. Served with C.E., U.S. Army, 1941-46. Fellow ASCE; mem. Nat., Md. (Meritorious Service award 1971) socs. profl. engrs. Club: Johns Hopkins. Home: 15 Northampton Rd Timonium MD 21093 Office: 301 W Preston St Baltimore MD 21201

MCCORD, WILLIAM CHARLES, diversified energy co. exec.; b. San Antonio, Apr. 1, 1928; s. Sam Byard and Helen (Schoepfer) McC.; B.S. in Mech. Engring., Tex. A. and M. U., 1949; m. Margaret Ann Lancaster, Oct. 17, 1947; children—Kathleen (Mrs. Gary Burnett), Martha (Mrs. Steven Pennington), Billy, Helen (Mrs. Steve Porter), Elizabeth (Mrs. David Paschal), Richard, Douglas, James, Quannah, Korrin Li, Minta Ann. With Enserch Corp. (formerly Lone Star Gas Co.), 1949—, dir. bldg. mgmt., 1965-67, v.p. Dallas div., 1967, sr. v.p. operations, 1968-70, pres., prin. exec. officer, 1970-77, chmn., pres., 1977—; sr. v.p. Nipak, Inc., chem. subsidiary, Dallas, 1967—; dir. Republic Nat. Bank, Dallas, Republic of Tex. Corp., Tex. Employers' Ins. Assn., Employers Casualty Co. Pres., Circle Ten council Boy Scouts Am., 1972-73; bd. dirs. Dallas County United Fund, Tex. Research League, Dallas Citizens Council, State Fair Tex., Baylor Coll. Dentistry, Children's Med. Center Dallas, Dallas Central Bus. Dist. Assn., Gas Research Inst.; trustee Southwestern Med. Found. Mem. Am. Petroleum Inst. (bd. dirs.), Am. Gas Assn. (bd. dirs.), Ind. Natural Gas Assn. Am., Tau Beta Pi. Baptist (deacon). Office: 301 S Harwood St Dallas TX 75201

MCCORD, WILLIAM MAXWELL, educator, social scientist; b. St. Louis, Oct. 24, 1930; s. Don Chylo and Elinor (Maxwell) McC.; B.A., Stanford, 1952; Ph.D., Harvard, 1955; children—Geoffrey, Robert, Maxwell, William, Mary; m. 2d, Arline Fujii, May 8, 1971. Instr. social psychology Harvard, 1955-58; from asst. to asso. prof. sociology Stanford, 1958-65, asst. dean Sch. Humanities, 1958-61; Lena Gohlman Fox prof. sociology Rice U., 1965-68; prof. sociology Syracuse U., 1968-71; prof., chmn. dept. sociology City U. N.Y., 1971—; distinguished lectr. Polish Acad. Scis., 1961; vis. prof. Am. U. in Cairo (Egypt), 1964; Fulbright prof. Trinity Coll., Dublin, 1977-78. Mem. President's Com. on Violence, 1965—. Bd. dirs. Palo Alto (Calif.) chpt. NAACP, 1960-65, Palo Alto Family Service Soc., 1960-62, San Francisco Salvation Army. 1961, Houston Child Guidance Clinic, 1966-68, Bklyn. Sch., 1974—. Woodrow Wilson fellow, 1952. Fellow Am. Sociol. Assn.; mem. Internat. Sociol. Assn., Phi Beta Kappa. Democrat. Author: Psychopathy and Delinquency, 1956; Origins of Crime, 1959; Origins of Alcoholism, 1960; The Psychopath. 1964; The Springtime of Freedom, 1965; Mississippi: The Long Hot Summer, 1965: Life Styles in the Black Ghetto, 1969; The Study of Personality, 1969; Urban Social Conflict, 1977; Social Problems, 1977; Power and Equity, 1977. Home: 1 Kingswood Dr Orangeburg NY 10962 Office: Sociology Dept City Coll of NY New York City NY

MC CORD, WILLIAM MELLEN, physician; b. Durban, Natal, Union South Africa, Jan 24, 1907 (parents Am. citizens); s. James Bennett and Margaret (Mellen) McC.; A.B., Oberlin Coll., 1928; Ph.D., Yale, 1931; M.D., La. State U., 1939; Litt.D., Coll. Charleston, 1974; m. Evangeline Andrews, June 14, 1930; children—James A., Marilyn Ann (Mrs. Harry S. Sloane). Instr. biochemistry La. State U. Med. Sch., New Orleans, 1931-35, asst. prof., 1935-39, asso. prof., 1939-42; intern Charity Hosp., New Orleans; mem. faculty Med. Univ. S.C., Charleston, 1945-78, prof., 1945-64, interim pres., 1964-65, pres., 1965-75; dean clin. studies St. George's U. Sch. Medicine, Grenada, W.I., 1978—. Trustee, Charleston County Hosp., 1964—. Served with AUS, 1942-45. Named S.C. chemist of the year Am. Chem. Soc., 1973. Mem. Charleston County Med. Soc. (past pres.), AMA, Am. Chem. Soc., Soc. Nuclear Medicine, AAAS, Am. Fedn. Clin. Research, S.C. Acad. Sci., Soc. Exptl. Biology and Medicine, Assn. Acad. Health Adminstrs., Sigma Xi, Alpha Omega Alpha. Elk. Club: Hibernian Society. Contbr. profl. jours. Home: PO Box 4 Lodge SC 29082

MCCORISON, MARCUS ALLEN, librarian; b. Lancaster, Wis., July 17, 1926; s. Joseph Lyle and Ruth (Mink) McC.; A.B., Ripon Coll., 1950; M.A., U. Vt., 1951; M.S., Columbia, 1954; m. Janet Buckbee Knop, June 10, 1950; children—Marcus Allen II, Judith G. McCorison Gove, Andrew Buckbee, Mary Lyle, James Rice, Peter Gardner. Librarian Kellogg-Hubbard Library, Montpelier, Vt., 1954-55; chief of rare books dept. Dartmouth Coll. Library, Hanover, N.H., 1955-59; head spl. collections dept. State U. Iowa Libraries, 1959-60; librarian Am. Antiquarian Soc., Worcester, Mass., 1960—, dir., 1967—, editor Procs., 1960-67. Lectr. in Am. history Clark U., 1967—. Mem. Com. for a New Eng. Bibliography, treas., 1970-77; overseer Old Sturbridge Village; adv. com. Eleutherian Mills-Hagley Found., 1971-74; 1st v.p. Bibliog. Soc. Am., 1978—; trustee Fruitlands Mus. Served with USNR, 1944-46, AUS, 1951-52. Mem. Am. Antiquarian Soc., Mass. Hist. Soc., Orgn. Am. Historians, Assn. Coll. and Research Libraries (chmn. rare books sect. 1965), Vt. Hist. Soc. (trustee 1956-66), Worcester Hist. Soc. (exec. com. 1967—), Ind. Research Libraries Assn. (chmn. 1972-73, 78-80), Assn. Internationale de Bibliophilie, N.E. Am. Soc. 18th Century Studies (pres. 1978-79). Clubs: Odd Volumes, Grolier (councillor 1979—), St. Botolph, Century. Author: Vermont Imprints 1778-1820, 1963; The 1764 Catalogue of the Redwood Library, 1965; contbr. chpt. to the Pursuit of Knowledge in the Early American Republic, 1976. Editor: History of Printing in America by Isaiah Thomas, 1970. Home: 4 Military Rd Worcester MA 01609 Office: Am Antiquarian Soc 185 Salisbury St Worcester MA 01609

MC CORKINDALE, DOUGLAS HAMILTON, publishing co. exec.; b. N.Y.C., June 14, 1939; s. William Douglas and Kathleen (Miles) McC.; B.A., Columbia Coll., 1961, LL.B. cum laude (Harlan Fiske Stone scholar), 1964; m. Susan Ann Whitworth; children—Laura Ann, Heather Jean. Admitted to N.Y. bar, 1964; asso. mem. firm Thacher Proffitt & Wood, N.Y.C., 1964-70, partner, 1970-71; gen. counsel, sec. Gannett Co., Inc., Rochester, N.Y., 1971-72, v.p., gen. counsel, sec., 1972-77, sr. v.p. fin. and law, 1977-79, sr. v.p., chief fin. officer, 1979—, also dir.; dir. Lincoln First Banks, Inc., El Paso Times, Inc., Gannett Pacific Corp., Honolulu, Guam Publ. Inc., Agana, Huntington Publ. Co. (W.Va.), News Press Publ. Co., Ft. Myers, Fla., Pallidium Pub. Co., Richmond, Ind., Citizen Co., Tucson, Westchester Rockland Newspapers, Inc., Harrison, N.Y., Binghamton (N.Y.) Press Co., Inc., Cape Publs., Inc., Cocoa, Fla., Courier-News Co., Bridgewater, N.J., Elmira (N.Y.) Star-Gazette, Inc., Empire Newspaper Supply Corp., Rochester, N.Y., Fremont (Ohio) Messenger Co., Gannett News Service, Inc., Washington, Gannett Newspaper Advt. Sales, Inc., N.Y.C., McClure Newspapers, Inc., Burlington, Vt., News Printing Co., New Kensington, Pa., Niagra Falls (N.Y.) Gazette Publ. Corp., Northwestern Publ. Co., Danville, Ill., The Saratogian, Inc., Saratoga Springs, N.Y., Springfield (Mo.) Newspapers, Inc., The Sun Co. of San Bernadino, Calif., Times Co., Marietta, Ohio, Hawaiian Newspaper Agy., Inc., Honolulu, New Mexican, Santa Fe, Time Enterprises, Inc., El Paso, Pacific Media Inc., Agana, Ithaca (N.Y.) Jour.-News, Pensacola (Fla.) News-Jour., Rockford (Ill.) Newspapers, Inc., So. N.J. Newspapers, Inc., Cherry Hill, Times-Herald Co., Port Huron, Mich., Utica Observer-Dispatch, Inc., Louis Harris & Assos., Inc., N.Y.C., Statesman-Jour. Co., Salem, Oreg., Okla. Press Pub. Co., Muskogee, Speidel Newspapers, Inc., Reno, Times Pub. Co., Ltd., Shreveport, La., Chillicothe (Ohio) Newspapers, Inc., Coffeyville (Kans.) Pub. Co., Poughkeepsie (N.Y.) Newspapers, Inc., Federated Publs., Inc., Battle Creek, Mich., The Cin. Enquirer, Inc., Combined Communications Corp., Phoenix, Daily News Pub. Co., Inc., St. Thomas, V.I., Newspaper Printing Corp., Nashville, Oakland (Calif.) Tribune, Inc., Tennessean Newspapers, Inc., Nashville; officer, various companies. Bd. dirs. Lend-a-Hand Inc., 1972—; trustee Keuka Coll., Genesee Hosp.; officer Frank E. Gannett Newspaper Found. Mem. Am. (chmn. com. Exchange Act of 1934, 1971-73), N.Y. State bar assns., Rochester C. of C., Am. Newspaper Pubs. Assn. (com. govt. relations, press-bar relations com.). Editorial adv. bd. The Bus. Lawyer. Clubs: Oak Hill Country; Genesee Valley. Home: 556 Allens Creek Rd Rochester NY 14618 Office: Lincoln Tower Rochester NY 14604

MC CORKLE, CHESTER OLIVER, JR., educator; b. Gilroy, Calif., Jan. 18, 1925; s. Chester Oliver and Avis Jacqueline (Kickham) McC.; student Calif. State Poly. Coll., 1941-43, 46, U. Redlands, 1943-44; B.S., U. Calif. at Berkeley, 1947, M.S., 1948, Ph.D., 1952; m. Nina Grace Mathews, June 11, 1945; children—Sandra Lee, Kenneth Carl, Timothy Kevin. Research asst. U. Calif. at Berkeley, 1947-48, asst. specialist, 1949-51; agrl. analyst Bank of Am., San Francisco, 1948-49; from research asst. to dean Coll. Agrl. Scis. and Environ. Scis., U. Calif. at Davis, 1952-70; v.p. of univ. Universitywide Office, Berkeley, 1970-78; research economist Center for Econ. Research, Athens, Greece, 1961-62; econ. cons. Ministry Coordination, Kingdom of Greece, 1965. Dir. Del Monte Corp. Chmn. bd. on agr. and renewable resources NRC-Nat. Acad. Scis., 1977—, mem. commn. on natural resources, 1976—. Served with USMCR, 1943-46, 51-52. Mem. AAAS, AAUP, Am., Western (past pres.) agrl. econ. assns., Am., Calif. (past sec.) socs. farm mgrs. and rural appraisers. Club: Bohemian (San Francisco). Home: 637 Eisenhower St Davis CA 95616 Office: Room 111 Voorhies Hall U Calif Davis CA 95616

MCCORKLE, HORACE JACKSON, educator, physician; b. Center Point, Tex., Feb. 5, 1905; s. Homer Thomas and Helen Hart (Cason) McC.; M.D., U. Calif., 1934; m. Marion Fisher, June 10, 1939; children—Alan, Donald, Malcolm, Douglas, Jeanette. Intern San Franciso City and County Hosp., 1933-34; surgeon U. Calif. Med. Sch., 1938—, prof. surgery, 1953—. Mem. Am., Pan Pacific, Western, Pacific Coast surg. assns., Internat. Surg. Soc., Pan Am. Med. Soc., Soc. Exptl. Biology and Medicine, Soc. Univ. Surgeons, Am. Gastroenterol. Assn., Nu Sigma Nu, Kappa Delta Rho. Home: 35 San Fernando Way San Francisco CA 94127

MCCORMAC, BILLY MURRAY, physicist, research instn. exec., army officer; b. Zanesville, Ohio, Sept. 8, 1920; B.S., Ohio State U., 1943; M.S., U. Va., 1956, Ph.D. in Nuclear Physics, 1957; married, 1948, 69; 5 children. Commd. officer U.S. Army, 1943, advanced through grades to lt. col.; physicist Office Spl. Weapons Devel., 1957-60, scientist Office of Chief of Staff, 1960-61, physicist Def. Atomic Support Agy., 1961-62, chief electromagnetic br., 1962-63; ret., 1963; sci. advisor Ill. Inst. Tech. Research Inst., 1963, dir. div. geophysics, 1963-68; sr. cons. scientist Lockheed Research Labs., Palo Alto, Calif., 1968-69, mgr. Radiation Physics Lab., 1969—. Chmn. radiation trapped in earth's magnetic field Adv. Study Inst., Norway, 1965, chmn. aurora and airglow, Eng., 1966, Norway, 1968, Can., 1970, chmn. physics and chemistry of atmospheres, France, 1972, Belgium, 1974, chmn. earth's particles and fields, Germany, 1967, Calif., 1969, Italy, 1971, Eng., 1973, Austria, 1975, Fellow Am. Inst. Aero. and Astronautics (asso.); mem. A.A.A.S., Am. Astronautical Soc. (sr.), Am. Phys. Soc., Am. Geophys. Union, Marine Tech. Soc., Am. Astron. Soc., Am. Ordnance Assn. Now editor Jour. Water, Air and Soil Pollution; editor Geophysics and Astrophysics Monographs. Home: 12861 Alta Tierra Rd Los Altos Hills CA 94022 Office: 3251 Hanover St Palo Alto CA 94304

MCCORMAC, JOHN WAVERLY, judge; b. Zanesville, Ohio, Feb. 8, 1926; s. Samuel D. and Phyllis (Murray) McC.; B.S., Muskingum Coll., 1951; J.D., Capital U., 1961; m. Martha Ann Cunningham, June 22, 1952; children—Michael Paul, John Mark, James Samuel. Fire protection engr. Ohio Insp. Bur., 1951-60; admitted to Ohio bar, 1961; pvt. practice, Columbus, 1961-65; prof. law Capital U., Columbus, 1965-66, 71-74; dean Capital U. Law Sch., 1966-71; judge 10th Dist. Ct. Appeals, 1975—. Mem., staff cons. rules adv. com. Supreme Ct. Ohio; chmn. adv. bd. Vols. in Probation, 1972-74; 2d vice chmn. Ohio Jud. Conf., 1978—. Served with USNR, 1943-46. Fellow Ohio Bar Assn. Found.; mem. League Ohio Law Schs. (pres. 1969-70), Am., Ohio (council of dels. 1973-77), Columbus (bd. govs. 1968-72, sec.-treas. 1973-74, pres. 1975-76) bar assns., Am. Judicature Soc., Phi Alpha Delta. Republican. Methodist. Mason. Author: Ohio Civil Rules Practice, 1970; Anderson's Ohio Civil Practice, Vol. 1, 1971, Vol. 2, 1976, Vol. 3, 1977. Home: 395 Longfellow Ave Worthington OH 43085

MCCORMACK, DONALD PAUL, journalist; b. Brockton, Mass., Jan. 15, 1926; s. Everett G. and Esther (Lufkin) McC.; B.A., U. Pitts., 1949; m. Petronella Ruth Seger, Apr. 28, 1951; 1 son, Christopher Paul. Corr., U.P.I., 1949-52; asst. city editor Pitts. Sun-Telegraph, 1952-56; pub. relations exec., 1956-64; copy reader N.Y. News, 1964-67, editorial writer, 1967-72, chief editorial writer, 1972—. Served with USAAF, 1944-46. Home: 45 Marion Rd Westport CT 06880 Office: 220 E 42d St New York City NY 10017

MC CORMACK, EDWARD JOSEPH, lawyer; b. Boston, Aug. 29, 1923; s. Edward J. and Mary T. (Coffey) McC.; student Colby Coll., 1941-42, B.S., U.S. Naval Acad., 1946; LL.B. cum laude, Boston U., 1952; m. Emily Rupils, Oct. 19, 1946; children—Edward Joseph III, John W. Admitted to Mass. bar, 1952; atty. gen. Commonwealth of Mass., 1958-63. Mem. city council, Boston, 1953-58, pres., 1956. Chmn., Com. for Boston; trustee New Eng. Sch. Law. Served with USN, 1946-49. Club: 100 of Mass. (dir.). Home: Jamaicaway Tower 111 Perkins St Boston MA 02130 Office: 225 Franklin St Boston MA 02110

MC CORMACK, ELIZABETH JANE, found. exec.; b. N.Y.C., Mar. 7, 1922; d. George H. and Natalie J. (Duffy) McCormack; B.A., Manhattanville Coll., 1944; M.A., Providence Coll., 1957; Ph.D., Fordham U., 1966; LL.D., Brandeis U., 1972, Princeton, 1974; m. Jerome I. Aron, 1976. Asst. to pres., acad. dean Manhattanville Coll., 1958-66, prof. philosophy, pres., 1966-74; asso. Rockefeller Family and Assos., N.Y.C., 1974—; dir. Gen. Goods Corp.; trustee Franklin Savs. Bank, N.Y.C. Mem. Faculty Fellowship program United Negro Coll. Fund; adv. com. Pvt. Philanthropy and Pub. Needs; trustee Spelman Coll., Atlanta, Hamilton Coll., Clinton, N.Y., N.Y.C. Police Found.; bd. dirs. Am. Ditchley Found.; bd. overseers Meml. Sloan-Kettering Cancer Center, N.Y.C. Mem. Council on Fgn. Relations. Home: 201 E 62d St New York NY 10021 Office: 30 Rockefeller Plaza New York NY 10020

MC CORMACK, FRANCIS XAVIER, oil co. exec.; b. Bklyn., July 9, 1929; s. Joseph and Blanche V. (Dengel) McC.; A.B. cum laude, St. Francis Coll., Bklyn., 1951; LL.B., Columbia, 1954; m. Margaret V. Hynes, Apr. 24, 1954; children—Marguerite, Francis Xavier, Sean Michael, Keith John, Cecelia Blanche, Christopher Thomas. Admitted to N.Y. bar, 1955, Mich. bar, 1963, Calif. bar, 1974, Pa. bar, 1975; asso. firm Cravath, Swaine & Moore, N.Y.C., 1956-62; sr. atty. Ford Motor Co., 1962-64, asst. gen. counsel, 1970-72; v.p., gen. counsel, sec. Philco-Ford Corp., 1964-72; v.p., gen. counsel Atlantic Richfield Co., 1972-73, sr. v.p., gen. counsel, 1973—. Decorated commendatore Ordine al Merito della Republica Italiana. Home: 975 Singing Wood Dr Arcadia CA 91006 Office: 515 S Flower St Los Angeles CA 90071

MCCORMACK, FRED ALLEN, hosp. adminstr.; b. Bklyn., June 10, 1930; s. Frank J. and Rhea (Del Castro) McC.; B.S., Seton Hall U., 1953; M.S.W., U. Conn., 1955; m. Ellen Anne Lockwood, June 19, 1954; children—Mary Lee, Lynn Anne, Rosemarie, Fred A., Julie Ellen, Rhea Michelle, Claire Eileen. Social worker Montrose (N.Y.) VA Hosp., 1955-61; adminstr., dir. Tappan Zee Mental Health Center, North Tarrytown, N.Y., 1957-62; supr. social worker Orange County Mental Health Clinic, Goshen, N.Y., 1961-62; dir. Sweetwater Counseling Service, Rock Springs, Wyo., 1962-65; asst. supt., dir. geriatric program Manteno (Ill.) State Hosp., 1965-68; dir. Tacoma Comprehensive Mental Health Center, 1968-69; cons. Dept. Instns. Wash., 1968-69, Laurel Haven Sch., Ballwin, Mo., 1977-78; supt. W. G. Murray Childrens Center, Centralia, Ill., 1969-71, Elisabeth Ludeman Center, Park Forest, Ill., 1971-76; dir. San Luis Valley Mental Health Center, Alamosa, Colo., 1976-77, Monroe Devel. Center, Rochester, N.Y., 1977—; part-time teaching Western Wyo. Jr. Coll., 1963-65, Prarie State Coll., 1965-68, Green River Community Coll., 1968-69; instr. Adams State Coll., Alamosa, 1977; cons. Snohomish Community Action Council, Everett, Wash., 1969. Past mem. citizens adv. bd. Sch. Dist. 162, Mattison, Ill.; chmn. Park Forest Sr. Citizens Commn. Past bd. dirs. Gavin Found., Park Forest, Ill.; bd. dirs. Jones Community Center, Chicago Heights. Recipient certificate of merit Nat. Assn. Physically Handicapped. Fellow Am. Assn. Mental Deficiency (pres. Ill. chpt. 1972); mem. Nat. Assn. Social Workers, Am. Assn. Mental Health Adminstrs., Acad. Certified Social Workers. Home: 3776 Stalker Rd Macedon NY 14502 Office: Monroe Devel Center Rochester NY

MCCORMACK, JOHN JOSEPH, investment co. exec.; b. Milw., Aug. 20, 1932; s. Thomas A. and Agnes C. (Van Elsberg) McC.; B.S. in Bus. Adminstrn., Marquette U., Milw., 1955; m. Barbara Alice Belter, Aug. 20, 1954; children—John, Timothy, Michael, Kevin, Robert, Daniel. Accountant, Horwath & Horvath, C.P.A.'s, Ft. Lauderdale, Fla., 1955-59; accountant, then partner Fonteine, McCurdy & Co., Milw., 1960-68; accountant, then partner Arthur Young & Co., Milw., 1968-70; fin. v.p. MGIC Investment Corp., Milw., 1971-75, sr. v.p. fin., 1975—; dir. Firstmark Corp., Buffalo. C.P.A., Wis. Mem. Fin. Execs. Inst. Republican. Roman Catholic. Club: Milw. Athletic. Home: 15205 Tucson Dr Brookfield WI 53005 Office: MGIC Plaza Milwaukee WI 53201

MCCORMACK, JOHN W., former congressman; b. Boston, Dec. 21, 1891; s. Joseph H. and Mary E. (O'Brien) McC.; ed. pub. schs.; LL.B., Boston U., Holy Cross Coll., 21 others; m. M. Harriet Joyce, 1920 (dec. 1971). Admitted to Mass. bar, 1913, began practice in Boston; mem. firm McCormack & Hardy; mem. Mass. Constl. Conv., 1917-18; mem. Mass. Ho. of Rep., 1920-22, Mass. State Senate, 1923-26 (Dem. leader); mem. 70th-87th Congresses from 12th Mass. Dist. (majority leader), 88th-91st Congresses from 9th Mass. Dist. (speaker of house). Mem. South Boston Citizens Assn., Am. Legion. Clubs: K.C., Elks, Moose, Cath. Order Foresters, Ancient Order of Hibernians. Knight of Malta first class, Knight St. Gregory. Home: 111 Perkins St Jamaica Plain MA 02130 Office: Post Office Bldg Boston MA 02109*

MCCORMACK, LARRY WARREN, lawyer; b. Butler, Pa., Oct. 1, 1937; s. Kenneth J. and Ronalda (Collingwood) McC.; A.B., Columbia, 1959; J.D. with distinction, U. Mich., 1962; m. Mary Carolyn Gough, Sept. 21, 1962; children—Ian Bruce, Katherine Eileen, Halley Lynn. Admitted to Ohio bar, 1962, since practiced in Toledo; partner Fuller, Seney, Henry & Hodge, 1962-70; counsel, mgr. indsl. relations Owens-Ill., Inc., 1970-75, dir. total compensation, 1975-78, plant mgr. Glass Container div., 1978—. Mem. Am., Ohio, Toledo bar assns. Home: 1535 Fieldgreen Overlook Stone Mountain GA 30088 Office: 3107 Sylvan Rd Atlanta GA 30354

MC CORMACK, LAWRENCE JOHN, pathologist; b. Kansas City, Mo., July 13, 1921; s. Lawrence Ralph and Mildred (Hungate) McC.; B.S., Northwestern U., 1942, M.D., 1945, M.S., 1950; M.S. in Pathology, U. Minn., 1951; m. Dorothy Rice; children—Lawrence R., Kathleen Ann, Thomas A., James R. Intern, Cook County Hosp., Chgo., 1945; head dept. surgery Sch. Aviation Medicine, Randolph Field, Tex., 1946-48; fellow in pathology, asso. staff mem. Mayo Clinic, Rochester, Minn., 1948-51; mem. staff Cleve. Clinic Found., 1952—, dir. labs.; clin. prof. biochemistry Cleve. State U. Served with AUS, 1943-47. Diplomate Am. Bd. Pathology. Fellow Am. Coll. Chest Physicians; mem. Coll. Am. Pathologists (pres. elect 1978-79, pres. 1979-81), AMA, Am. Soc. Clin. Pathologists, Am. Assn. Pathologists, Ohio Med. Assn. Club: Pasteur (Cleve.). Contbr. chpts. to books, articles to profl. jours. Home: 4983 Countryside Ln Lyndhurst OH 44124 Office: 9500 Euclid Ave Cleveland OH 44106

MCCORMACK, MIKE, congressman; b. Basil, Ohio, Dec. 14, 1921; student U. Toledo; B.S., M.S. in Chemistry, Wash. State U.; postgrad. law Gonzaga U.; D.Engring. (h.c.), Stevens Inst., Hoboken, N.J.; m. Margaret Higgins, 1947; children—Mark, Steven, Tim. Instr. U. Puget Sound, 1949-50; research scientist Hanford Project, 1950-70; mem. Wash. Ho. of Reps., 1956-60, Wash. Senate, 1960-70; mem. 92d to 96th congresses from 4th Wash. Dist.; chmn. House Task Force on Energy, chmn. subcom. on energy, mem. House Pub. Works and Transp. Com., mem. House Sci. and Tech. Com. Served to 1st lt. inf. AUS, 1943-46; ETO. Named Solar Energy Man of Year Solar Energy Industries, Assn., 1975. Mem. AAAS (nat. dir. 1975), Am. Nuclear Soc., Am. Chem. Soc., Am. Legion, V.F.W. Democrat. Mason (Shriner). Clubs: Grange, Richland Rod and Gun (Wash.). Sponsor of all nuclear energy legislation State Wash.; co-author and prime sponsor 1970 Thermal Power Plant Act, creating Wash. Thermal Power Plant Siting Council; author Solar Heating and Cooling Demonstration Act, 1974, Solar Research, Devel. and Demonstration Act, 1974, Geothermal Research, Devel. and Demonstration Act, 1974. Home: Richland WA Office: Longworth Office Bldg Washington DC

MCCORMACK, PATRICIA (BORN RUSSO, PATRICIA ELLEN), actress; b. N.Y.C., Aug. 21, 1945; d. Frank and Elizabeth (McCormack) Russo; m. Bob Catania (div.); children—Robert, Danielle. Formerly child model; stage appearances include: Touchstone, 1953, The Bad Seed, 1954, Time of the Cuckoo; film appearances include: Two Girls and a Guy, 1951, The Bad Seed, 1956, Kathy-O, 1958, Explosive Generation, 1961, The Young Animals, 1968, Maryjane, 1968, The Mini-Skirt Mob, 1968, Born Wild, 1968, The Young Runaways, 1968; early TV appearances include: several Playhouse 90 episodes, including The Miracle Worker; I Remember Mama, Kraft TV Theatre, Wagon Train, Peck's Bad Girl, U.S. Steel Hour, Route 66, Climax, Wagon Train, One Step Beyond, The Best of Everything; recent TV appearances include: Cannon, Barnaby Jones, Marcus Welby, M.D., As The World Turns, Fantasy Island, Friends, The Love Boat; regular on ABC-TV series The Ropers, 1979—. Office: care Contemporary-Korman Artists Ltd 132 Lasky Dr Beverly Hills CA 90212*

MCCORMACK, PATRICIA SEGER, journalist; b. Pitts., June 11, 1927; d. Arthur John and Anne Irene (McCaffrey) Seger; B.A., U. Pitts., 1949; certificate, A.P. Inst. Seminar, 1967; m. Donald P. McCormack, Apr. 28, 1951; 1 son, Christopher Paul. News editor weekly newspapers, Mt. Lebanon, Pa., 1950-52; med. editor Pitts. Sun Telegraph, 1952-57; med. sci. editor Internat. News Service (merged to U.P.I.), N.Y.C., 1958-59, columnist, family health and edn. editor, 1959—. Mem. Boy of Year selection com. Boys Clubs Am., 1966. Recipient Biennial Media award Family Service Assn. Am., 1965, Freedom Found. medal; 1st place Sci. Writing award Am. Dental Assn., 1976; Nat. Media award United Negro Coll. Fund, 1977. Mem. Nat. Assn. Sci. Writers, Edn. Writers Assn., AAAS, N.Y. Newspapers Woman's Club. Home: 45 Marion Rd Westport CT 06880 Office: 220 E 42d St New York City NY 10017

MCCORMACK, RICHARD, lawyer; b. Middletown, N.Y., Apr. 29, 1916; s. Roy David and Francis Elizabeth (Lemon) McC.; A.B., Ohio Wesleyan U., 1938; J.D., U. Mich., 1948; m. Margaret Helen Pivarnik, Nov. 8, 1941; 1 son, David Richard. Admitted to Mich. bar, 1948; with Clark Equipment Co., Buchanan, Mich., 1948-77, asst. sec., mgr. legal dept., 1962-77, v.p., gen. counsel, 1966-77, dir., 1967-76; v.p., dir. Clark Equipment Credit Corp., Clark Equipment Overseas Finance Corp., Clark Equipment Realty Corp.; v.p. Clark Equipment Can., Ltd. Served to 1st lt. AUS, 1942-45; ETO. Mem. Am., Berrien County (past pres.) bar assns., State Bar Mich., Am. Legion. Club: Pickwick (Niles). Home: 2215 Redbud Trail S Niles MI 49120 Office: Mollberg Bldg 7 Buchanan MI 49107

MC CORMACK, THOMAS JOSEPH, pub. co. exec.; b. Boston, Jan. 5, 1932; s. Thomas Joseph and Lena Carolyn (Allen) McC.; student U. Conn., 1950-51; A.B. summa cum laude (James Manning scholar), Brown U., 1954; postgrad. (G.H. Palmer scholar, Woodrow Wilson fellow), Harvard, 1956; m. Sandra Harriet Danenberg, Aug. 21, 1964; children—Daniel Aaron, Jed Charles (dec.), Jessie Ann. Writer radio news WSTC, Stamford, Conn., 1957-59; editor Doubleday & Co., Inc., N.Y.C., 1959-64, Harper & Row, N.Y.C., 1964-67; edn. editor New Am. Library, N.Y.C., 1967-69; dir. trade dept. St. Martin's Press, N.Y.C., 1969-70, pres., 1970—, also dir.; pres., chmn. bd. St. James Press, Ltd., London; dir. Macmillan Pub., Ltd., London; v.p., treas. Sandra D. McCormack, Inc., Interior Designer. Served with AUS, 1954-56. Mem. Assn. Am. Pubs. (dir. 1973-76), Phi Beta Kappa. Clubs: The Players, Century Assn. (N.Y.C.). Author: Afterwords, Novelists on Their Novels, 1969; play American Roulette, 1969. Home: 50 Central Park W New York NY 10023 Office: 175 Fifth Ave New York NY 10010

MC CORMACK, WILLIAM CHARLES, educator; b. Sutherland, Iowa, Mar. 31, 1929; s. Dan Bicknell and Wilna (Plager) McC.; B.A., U. Chgo., 1948, Ph.D., 1956; B.A. with distinction in Psychology, Stanford, 1949, M.A. in Anthropology, 1950; postgrad. U. Calif. at Berkeley, 1950-51; postdoctoral study linguistics U. Mich., summer 1956; m. Anna Mary Pikelis, June 9, 1962. Asso. research anthropologist Modern India Project, U. Calif., 1958-59; vis. lectr. Indian anthropology U. London, 1959-60; asst. prof. anthropology, linguistics and Indian studies U. Wis., 1960-64; asso. prof. anthropology Duke, 1964-69; prof. anthropology and linguistics U. Calgary, 1969—, chmn. dept. linguistics, 1972-73. Mem. nat. selection com. NIMH, 1967; mem. fellowship selection com. Shastri Indo-Canadian Inst., 1970, 71, 77, 78, chmn., 1979; cons. Peace Corps, 1965; ad hoc cons. univ. presses, profl. jours., research founds.; guest lectr. univs. in U.S., Can., Europe and India. Ford Found. fellow fgn. area tng., India, 1953-54; Rockefeller Found. jr. linguist fellow, India, 1956-58; prin. contractor lang. devel. sect., research grantee U.S. Office Edn., Madison, Wis., and India, 1962-64; Am. Council Learned Socs. fellow, India, 1962-63; recipient numerous research grants; recipient Fulbright Hays award, U.S. Office Edn., 1966. Fellow Am. Anthrop. Assn., Current Anthropology, Explorers Club, Royal Anthrop. Inst.; mem. Mythic Soc. India (life), Canadian Ethnology Soc., Conf. on Religion in South India, Canadian Assn. Sociology and Anthropology, Linguistic Assn. Can. and U.S., Internat. Soc. Comparative Study of Civilizations, Linguistic Soc. Am., Dravidian Linguistic Assn., Canadian Soc. Asian Studies, Assn. Asian Studies, Am. Acad. Religion, Soc. Sci. Study Religion, Soc. South Indian Studies, Canadian Assn. U. Tchrs., Sigma Xi. Author: (with M.G. Krishnamurthi) Kannada: a Cultural Introduction to the Spoken Styles of the Language, 1966. Editor: (with S.A. Wurm) Language and Man: Anthropological Issues, 1976, Language and Thought, 1977, Approaches to Language, 1978, Language and Society, 1979. Home: 340 40th Av SW Calgary AB T2S 0X4 Canada

MCCORMICK, BARNES WARNOCK, educator; b. Waycross, Ga., July 15, 1926; s. Barnes Warnock and Edwina (Brogdon) McC.; B.S. in Aero. Engring., Pa. State U., 1948, M.S., 1949, Ph.D., 1954; m. Emily Joan Hess, July 18, 1946; 1 dau., Cynthia Joan. Research asso. Pa. State U., University Park, 1949-54, asso. prof., 1954-55, prof. aero. engring., 1959—, head dept. aerospace engring., 1969—; asso. prof., chmn. aero. dept. Wichita U., 1958-59; chief aerodynamics Vertol Helicopter Co., 1955-58. Pres., Aero. Engring. Asso., Inc., State College, Pa., 1965—; cons. to industry. Served with USNR, 1944-46. Recipient joint award for achievement in aerospace edn. Am. Soc. Engring. Edn.-Am. Inst. Aeros. and Astronautics, 1976. Asso. fellow Am. Inst. Aeros. and Astronautics (asso.); mem. ASEE, Am. Helicopter Soc. (tech. council), Sigma Xi, Sigma Gamma Tau, Tau Beta Pi. Club: Masons. Author: Aerodynamics of V/Stol Flight, 1967; Aerodynamics, Aeronautics and Flight Mechanics, 1979. Contbr. articles to profl. jours. Patentee in field. Home: 611 Glenn Rd State College PA 16801 Office: Pa State U Coll Engring University Park PA 16802

MCCORMICK, BROOKS, mfg. exec.; b. Chgo., Feb. 23, 1917; s. Chauncey and Marion (Deering) McC.; grad. Groton Sch., 1936; B.A., Yale, 1940; m. Hope Baldwin, 1940. With Internat. Harvester Co., 1940—, mfg., sales positions various locations U.S. and Gt. Britain, 1940-54, dir. mfg., 1954-57, exec. v.p., 1957-68, pres., 1968-71, pres., chief exec. officer, 1971-77, chmn., 1977-79, chmn. exec. com., 1979—, also dir.; dir. Commonwealth Edison Co., Chgo., First Nat. Bank Chgo. Gen. chmn. Crusade of Mercy, 1961; dir. Nat. Safety council, 1964-67; chmn. bus. advisory council Chgo. Urban League, 1967-76; chmn. Motor Vehicle Mfrs. Assn., 1973-74, 79-80; mem. long range planning com. United Way Am., 1977—; pres. St. Luke's Hosp., 1956-75, life trustee, 1975—; trustee Ill. Inst. Tech., 1962-75, Art Inst. Chgo.; pres. United Way Met. Chgo., 1976-77; chmn. Polish-U.S. Economic Council, 1974-77; bd. dirs. U.S.-USSR Trade and Economic Council, 1975—; mem. nat. advisory com. Minorities in Engring., 1975—; bd. dirs. Ind. Coll. Funds Am., 1979. Mem. Farm and Indsl. Equipment Inst. (chmn. 1977-78). Clubs: Chicago, Commercial (pres. 1976-77) (Chgo.). Office: 401 N Michigan Ave Chicago IL 60611

MCCORMICK, C(LARENCE) JAMES, transp. co. exec.; b. Decker, Ind., Jan. 3, 1925; s. Clarence J. and Emma (Bobe) McC.; student Purdue U.; m. Bettye Jean Gramelspacher, Dec. 28, 1946; children—Michael D., Patrick Edward, Clarence James III, Jane Ann. Self-employed trucker, 1944-54; pres. I & S-McDaniel, Inc., 1954-76; founder, chmn./pres. McCormick, Inc., 1948—, Comml. Rentals, Inc., 1950—, Jamac Corp., 1960—, Indpls. White-Autocar, Inc., 1963—; co-founder, pres., dir. Jem, Inc., 1961—; sr. v.p., dir. Briggs Transp. Co., St. Paul, 1976—; mem. Fed. Home Loan Bank Bd., 1979; dir. 1st Fed. Savs. and Loan Assn. Vincennes (Ind.); vice chmn., dir. Sundance Transp. Co., 1977. Chmn. Aeros. Commn. Ind., 1961—. Chmn. Nat. Hwy Users Fedn., 1979; trustee Am. Trucking Assn. Found. Named Outstanding Young Man of Year Jr. C. of C., 1957. Mem. Am. Trucking Assns., Inc. (chmn. bd. 1971), Equipment Interchange Assn. (pres. 1961-62), Ind. Motor Truck Assn. (pres. 1958-59), Ind. Motor Rate & Tariff Bur. (pres. 1962-64, now dir.), Ind. Motor Carriers Labor Relations Assn. (pres. 1956), Young Presidents Orgn., Ind. C. of C. (bd. dirs.), Quiet Birdmen, Knights of Malta. Methodist (past Sunday sch. tchr.). Mason (32 deg., Shriner), Elk, Kiwanian (pres. 1957). Clubs: Vincennes Country (past pres.); Evansville (Ind.) Country; Indianapolis Athletic; Congressional Country (Washington); Innisbrook (Fla.) Golf and Country; Tamarron (Colo.). Home: 2500 Grandview Dr Vincennes IN 47591 Office: U S 41 South Vincennes IN 47591

MC CORMICK, DANIEL GILBERT, naval officer; b. Key West, Fla., May 8, 1930; s. Daniel Gilbert and Thelma (Sands) McC.; B.S. in Mech. Engring., Ga. Inst. Tech., 1952; postgrad. Naval Test Pilot Sch., 1957, Armed Forces Staff Coll., 1964; m. Barbara Jean Waldron, Aug. 15, 1953; children—Glenn A., Karen A., Chris C. Commd. ensign U.S. Navy, 1953, advanced through grades to rear adm., 1978; comdg. officer Fighter Squadron 41 and 101, 1970-71; comdg. officer U.S.S. Trenton, 1972-74, Aircraft Carrier U.S.S. America, 1974-76; dep. comdr. Naval Striking Forces So., NATO, 1978—. Active, State of Fla. Soc., Washington. Decorated Bronze Star, Navy Achievement medal. Mem. Soc. Exptl. Test Pilots, Assn. Naval Aviators. Republican.

MCCORMICK, DONALD BRUCE, biochemist, educator; b. Front Royal, Va., July 15, 1932; s. Jesse Allen and Elizabeth (Hord) McC.; B.A., Vanderbilt U., 1953, Ph.D., 1958; postdoctoral fellow U. Cal. at Berkeley, 1959-60; m. Norma Jean Dunn, June 6, 1955; children—Susan Lynn, Donald Bruce, Michael Allen. Asst. prof. Cornell U., 1960-63, asso. prof., 1963-69, prof. nutrition, biochemistry and molecular biology, biol. scis., 1969-79, Liberty Hyde Bailey prof. nutritional biochemistry, 1978-79; Fuller E. Callaway prof., chmn. dept. biochemistry Emory U. Med. Sch., Atlanta, 1979—. vis. lectr. U. Ill., 1963. Cons. biochemist Interdepartmental Com. on Nutrition for Nat. Def., Spain, 1958; chmn. nutrition study sect. NIH, 1977—. Recipient awards Bausch and Lomb, 1950, Mead Johnson, 1970, Osborne and Mendel, 1978; Westinghouse Sci. scholar, 1950; fellow NIH, 1958-60; Guggenheim fellow, 1966-67. Mem. Am. Soc. Biol. Chemists, Am. Inst. Nutrition, Soc. Exptl. Biology and Medicine, Am. Chem. Soc., Am. Inst. Biol. Sci., Microbiol. Soc., Photobiol. Soc., N.Y. Acad. Sci., AAAS, Sigma Xi. Author: (with others) Spain: Nutrition Survey of the Armed Forces, 1958; Riboflavin, 1974. Editor, author: (with others) Vitamins and Coenzymes, 1970-71, 79—. Editorial bd. Analytical Biochemistry, Arch. Biochem. Biophys., Nutrition Rev. Contbr. articles profl. jours. Home: 2245 Deer Ridge Dr Stone Mountain GA 30087

MCCORMICK, EDWARD ALLEN, educator; b. Fairfax County, Va., July 1, 1925; s. Jesse Allen and Elizabeth (Hord) McC.; A.B., Randolph-Macon Coll., 1948; Ph.D., U. Berne (Switzerland), 1951; M.A. (hon.), Dartmouth, 1965; m. Diana Festa, Mar. 1, 1952 (div. Aug. 1973); children—Allen Sergio, Marco Kevin, Carlo Brian; m. 2d, Marie Parrice, Apr. 2, 1974. Instr. German, Princeton, 1952, U. Mich., 1952-53, Harvard, 1953-54; asst. prof. German, Princeton, 1954-58, Brown U., 1958-59; mem. faculty Dartmouth, 1959—, prof. German, German and comparative lit., dir. comparative lt. Queens Coll., City U. N.Y., 1966-70, prof. German and comparative lit. Grad. Center, 1970—, exec. officer comparative lit., 1970-74. Served with 82d Airborne Div., AUS, 1943-46; ETO. Recipient Princeton Bicentennial Preceptorship, 1954-58; Dartmouth Faculty fellow,

1963. Mem. Modern Lang. Assn., Am. Comparative Lit. Assn., Am. Assn. Tchrs. German. Author: Whitman's Leaves of Grass in deutscher Ubertragung, 1953; (with F.G. Ryder) Lebendige Literatur, 1960, 2d edit., 1974; Theodor Storm's Novellen, 1964. Editor: Lessing's Laokoon, 1962; (J.E. Schlegel) On Imitation, 1965; also articles in jours., encys. Home: Route 71 Hillsdale NY 12529 Office: Ph D program in Comparative Lit Grad Center City U NY 33 W 42d St New York City NY 10036

MCCORMICK, EDWARD JAMES, JR., lawyer; b. Toledo, May 11, 1921; s. Edward James and Josephine (Beck) McC.; B.S., John Carroll U., Cleve., 1942; J.D., Western Res. U., 1948; m. Mary Jane Blank, Jan. 27, 1951; children—Mary Margaret, Edward James III, Patrick William, Michael J. Admitted to Ohio bar, 1948, since practiced in Toledo; partner, office mgr. Mulholland, Hickey, Lyman, McCormick, Fisher & Hickey and predecessor, 1948—; mem. teaching staff St. Vincent's Hosp. Sch. Nursing, 1951-69. Gen. chmn. Cancer Fund drive Am. Cancer Soc., Lucas County, Ohio, 1951, trustee, 1950-61, sec., 1953, v.p., 1954-56, pres., 1957-58; mem. Municipal League, Toledo, 1963—. Pres., trustee Toledo Small Bus. Assn., 1954, 56, 57, 67; trustee, mem. exec. com. Goodwill Industries Toledo; bd. dirs., gen. counsel Friendly Center. Served to 1st lt. Q.M.C., AUS, 1942-46. Named Outstanding Young Man of Year Toledo Jr. C. of C., 1951, Man of Nation, Woodmen of World, Omaha, 1952. Mem. Am., Ohio (com. chmn.), Toledo (com. chmn.), Lucas County (com. chmn.) bar assns., Nat. Assn. Trial Counsel Am., Nat. Assn. Immigration and Nationality Lawyers, Am. Judicature Soc., Toledo C. of C., Toledo Deanery Diocesan Council Catholic Men, U.S. Power Squadron (nat. law staff), Alpha Sigma Nu. K.C. (4 deg.), Elk (past exalted ruler), Lion (past pres.). Clubs: Toledo Torch, Toledo, Toledo Yacht (past commodore). Home: 3161 Haughton Dr Toledo OH 43606 Office: Nat Bank Bldg Toledo OH 43604

MCCORMICK, FLOYD GUY, JR., educator; b. Center, Colo., July 3, 1927; s. Floyd Guy and Gladys (Weir) McC.; B.S., Colo. State U., 1950, M.Ed., 1959; Ph.D., Ohio State U., 1964; m. Constance P. Slane, Sept. 18, 1965; children—Angela Lynn, Craig Alan, Kim Ann, Robert Guy. Tchr. vocat. agr. State Colo., 1956-62; asst. prof. agrl. edn. Ohio State U., 1964-67; mem. com. agr. edn. Commn. Edn. in Agr. and Natural Resources, Nat. Acad. Sci., 1967-69; prof. agrl. edn., head dept. U. Ariz., 1967—; cons. in-service edn., div. vocat. edn. Ohio Dept. Edn., 1963-64; vis. prof. Colo. State U., 1973. Trustee Nat. FFA Found. Served with USNR, 1945-46. Named hon. state farmer, Colo., 1958, Ariz., 1968; Hon. Am. Farmer, 1972; Outstanding Educator in Am., 1972; recipient Centennial award Ohio State U., 1970. Mem. Am. Vocat. Assn. (mem. policy com. agrl. edn. div. 1976-79), Nat. Vocat. Agr. Tchrs. Assn. (Outstanding Service award Region I 1974), Am. Assn. Tchr. Educators in Agr. (editor newsletter 1975-76, pres. 1976-77, Disting. Service award 1978), Alpha Zeta, Alpha Tau Alpha (hon.), Gamma Sigma Delta, Phi Delta Kappa. Mason. Author instructional units, tech. bulls., articles in profl. jours. Spl. editor Agrl. Edn. mag., 1970-74. Home: 6933 Paseo San Andres Tucson AZ 85710

MC CORMICK, HAROLD L., motion picture theatre co. exec., state senator; b. Florence, Colo., May 16, 1918; s. B. P. and Anna L. (Hoffman) McC.; B.S., U. Denver, 1940; m. Jeanne E. Rolfes, Jan. 8, 1941; children—Brian, Carole, Ellen. Owner, operator McCormick Theatres, Colo., N. Mex., 1940—; mem. Colo. Gen. Assembly, 1961-72; mem. Colo. Senate, 1973—, pres. pro tem.; candidate for Congress, 1980. Served with U.S. Army, 1942-47. Decorated Air Force Commendation medal, Presidential citation. Mem. Omicron Delta Kappa, Beta Theta Pi. Republican. Presbyterian. Club: Mason. Address: 927 Greenwood St Canon City CO 81212

MC CORMICK, HENRY J., librarian; b. Watertown, N.Y., July 2, 1919; s. Henry J. and Anna (Yager) McC.; B.A., Syracuse U., 1940, M.A., 1947, B.S. in L.S., 1947; m. Marie Elizabeth Atwater, Oct. 1, 1949 (dec. Nov. 1954); children—John A., Mary E., Henry Joseph, Martha M.; m. 2d, Mary Jane Heenan, Feb. 11, 1956; children—Anne C., Margaret J., Eileen F. Reference librarian Grosvenor Library, Buffalo, 1947-48; dir. Olean (N.Y.) Pub. Library, 1948-54; asst. dir. Syracuse Pub. Library, 1954-61, dir., 1962-75; asst. dir. Onondaga County Pub. Library, 1976-78; instr. English, history and ROTC, Fla. Mil. Acad., 1940-41; instr. history St. Bonaventure U., 1949-50, 52-54. Bd. mem. Assn. N.Y. Libraries for Tech. Services. Served to capt. AUS, 1942-45, 51-52. Mem. Am., N.Y. library assns., Beta Theta Pi, Beta Phi Mu (dir.). Club: Rotary. Home: 513 Scott Ave Syracuse NY 13224 Office: 335 Montgomery St Syracuse NY 13202

MCCORMICK, HOPE BALDWIN (MRS. BROOKS MCCORMICK), former mem. Republican Nat. Com.; b. N.Y.C., July 9, 1919; d. Alexander Taylor and Loise (Bisbee) Baldwin; student Ethel Walker Sch., Simsbury, Conn.; m. Brooks McCormick, June 26, 1940; children—Martha (Mrs. William O. Hunt, Jr.), Brooks II, Mark B., Abby D. Mem. Ill. Ho. of Reps., 1965-67. Past mem. women's bd. Children's Meml. Hosp., Lyric Opera; founder, past pres. Ill. Epilepsy League; mem. women's bd. Rush-Presbyn.-St. Luke's Hosp., Art Inst. Chgo., Field Mus. Natural History, U. Chgo. Past chmn. women's div. United Republican Fund, 1957-61, bd. govs., 1957-65; pres. Rep. Citizens Com. of 9th Congl. Dist., 1961-66; mem. Rep. Nat. Com. from Ill., 1964-72, vice chmn., 1972. Past bd. dirs. Chgo. Pub. Sch. Art Soc.; past trustee Chgo. Latin Sch.; trustee Ill. Children's Home and Aid Soc., Mus. Sci. and Industry, MacMurray Coll., Chgo. Symphony Orch. bd. govs. Rec. for Blind. Republican. Home: 1530 N State Pkwy Chicago IL 60610

MC CORMICK, JAMES ALBERT, publisher; b. Phillipsburg, N.J., Oct. 15, 1927; s. John and Elvira McC.; A.B. in Communications, Temple U., 1953; m. Sept. 2, 1953; children—John, Jacquelyn, Susan, Chris. With Bell Aircraft Co., 1953, RCA, 1954, IBM, 1955, Ingersoll-Rand Co., 1956-79; mgr. advt. services, pub. Compressed Air mag., Washington, N.J., 1975—. Served with USNR, 1946-48. Mem. Bus. Publ. Assn. Roman Catholic. Office: Compressed Air mag 253 E Washington Ave Washington NJ 07882

MC CORMICK, JAMES CHARLES, heavy equipment mfg. co. exec.; b. Cleve., Jan. 23, 1938; s. Michael Patrick and Agnes Christine (Mortensen) McC.; B.S. in Accounting, Regis Coll., Denver, 1960; m. Claire A. Maskaly, Nov. 28, 1963 (div. June 1978); children—Kelly, Shannon. Accountant, Ernst & Ernst, Allentown, Pa., 1963-73; treas. Fuller Co., Catasauqua, Pa., 1973—. Dist. chmn. Minsi Trails council Boy Scouts Am., 1976-77, treas., 1978—. Served with USNR, 1960-63. C.P.A. Mem. Am. Inst. C.P.A.'s. Club: Livingston (Allentown). Home: Spring Ridge Apts M-17 Whitehall PA 18052 Office: care Fuller Co PO Box 29 Catasauqua PA 18032

MCCORMICK, JAMES HAROLD, coll. pres.; b. Indiana, Pa., Nov. 11, 1938; s. Harold Clark and Mary Blanche (Truby) McC.; B.S., Indiana U. of Pa., 1959; M.Ed., U. Pitts., 1961, Ed.D., 1963, postdoctoral U. Pitts., Columbia U., U. Mich.; m. Maryan Kough Garner, June 7, 1963; children—David Harold, Douglas Paul. Tchr., Punxsutawney (Pa.) Area Joint Sch. Dist., 1959-61; adminstr. Baldwin-Whitehall Schs., Pitts., 1961-64; grad. asst. U. Pitts., 1962-63; asst. supt. instrn. Washington (Pa.) City Schs., 1964-65; prof. dept. edn. and psychology, asst. dean acad. affairs, acting dean tchr. edn., asst. to pres., v.p. adminstrn. Shippensburg (Pa.) State Coll., 1965-73; pres. Bloomsburg (Pa.) State Coll., 1973—. Appt. to Edn. Commn. of States; chmn. Commn. State Coll. and Univ. Presidents, 1979—; mem. exec. bd. Columbia-Montour council Boy Scouts Am. Recipient Ten Outstanding Young Men of Year award Pa. Jr. C. of C., 1974. Falk intern in politics, 1959. Mem. numerous nat. and state profl. orgns. Presbyn. (elder). Mason (32 deg.), Kiwanian. Club: Columbia-Montour Torch of Pa. Contbr. articles profl. jours. Home: Buckalew Pl Light St Rd Bloomsburg PA 17815

MCCORMICK, JOHN OWEN, educator; b. Thief River Falls, Minn., Sept. 20, 1918; s. Owen Charles and Marie Antoinette Beauchemin (Smith) McC.; B.A. magna cum laude, U. Minn., 1941; M.A., Harvard, 1947, Ph.D., 1951; m. Helen Manuel, 1942; m. 2d, Mairi Clare MacInnes, 1954; children—Jonathan, Peter, Antoinette, Fergus. Teaching fellow Harvard, 1947-51, sr. tutor, 1948-51; dean, lectr. Salzburg Seminar in Am. Studies, 1951-52; lectr., prof. Free U., Berlin, 1952-59; prof. comparative lit., chmn. dept. Rutgers U., 1959—; vis. prof. Nat. U. Mexico, 1961-62, Hachioji (Tokyo) seminar, 1979; Christian Gauss Seminar lectr. Princeton, 1969; resident fellow Sch. Letters of Ind. U., 1970. Served with USNR, 1941-46. Recipient prize for non-fiction Longview Found., 1960; Guggenheim fellow, 1964-65, 79-80; Bruern fellow Leeds (Eng.) U., 1975-76. Mem. Modern Lang. Assn., Internat. Comparative Lit. Assn. Clubs: Taurino (London, Eng.); Harvard (N.Y.C.). Author: The Middle Distance: a Comparative History of American Imaginative Literature, 1919-32, 1971; The Complete Aficionado, 1967; (with Mairi MacInnes McCormick) Versions of Censorship, 1962; Der moderne amerikanische Roman, 1960; Amerikanische Lyrik, 1957; Catastrophe and Imagination, 1957; Fiction as Knowledge, 1975. Home: 158 Terhune Rd Princeton NJ 08540 Office: Rutgers Univ New Brunswick NJ 08903

MCCORMICK, JOSEPH CARROLL, bishop; b. Phila., 1907; student St. Charles Sem., Phila., Pontifical Roman Sem., Rome. Ordained priest Roman Catholic Ch., 1932; vice chancellor, later chancellor Phila. Archdiocese, 1936-44; pastor St. Stephen's Ch., Phila., 1944-60; titular bishop of Ruspe, aux. bishop of Phila., 1947-60; bishop of Altoona-Johnstown (Pa.), 1960-67; bishop of Scranton (Pa.), 1967—. Address: 300 Wyoming Ave Scranton PA 18503*

MCCORMICK, KENNETH DALE, editor; b. Madison, N.J., Feb. 25, 1906; s. John Dale and Ida Pearl (Wenger) McC.; A.B., Willamette U., 1928; children—Dale, Kevin; m. Anne Hutchens, 1968; 1 son, John Bradley. With Doubleday and Co., Inc., 1930—, successively clk., mgr., bookshop, promotion mgr. pub. house, reader in editorial dept., chief asso. editor, 1938, editor in chief, 1942-71, v.p., 1948-71, sr. cons. editor, 1971—; editorial cons. Franklin Library, 1975; lectr. on books. Democrat. Conglist. Clubs: Players, Century Assn., Coffee House, Dutch Treat. Contbr. to Publishers' Weekly. Home: 670 W End Ave New York City NY 10025 Office: 245 Park Ave New York City NY 10017

MCCORMICK, MARK, state justice; b. Ft. Dodge, Iowa, Apr. 13, 1933; s. Elmo Eugene and Virgilla (Lawler) McC.; A.B., Villanova U., 1955; LL.B., Georgetown U., 1960; m. Marla Rae McKinney, June 11, 1966; children—Marcia, Michael, Paul. Admitted to Iowa bar, 1960; law clk. to judge U.S. Ct. Appeals, 1960-61; practice law, Ft. Dodge, 1961-68; asst. county atty. Webster County, 1963-67; judge 11th and 2d jud. dists., 1968-72; justice Iowa Supreme Ct., Des Moines, 1972—. Served with USN, 1955-58. Mem. Am., Iowa bar assns., Am. Judicature Soc. Office: Capitol Bldg Des Moines IA 50319*

MC CORMICK, PETER HAMILTON, bank exec.; b. Attleboro, Mass., Apr. 3, 1936; s. Samuel James and Virginia Bradford (Jones) McC.; B.S. cum laude, Harvard U., 1959; m. Fair Alice Bullock, July 2, 1960; children—Alexander, Nathaniel, Benjamin. With New Eng. Mchts. Nat. Bank, Boston, 1963—, sr. v.p., sr. loan officer, head comml. banking div., 1972-78, pres., 1978—; exec. v.p., dir. New Eng. Mchts. Co., Inc. Mem. corp. Museum of Sci., Boston, Northeastern U.; chmn. bd. trustees Jobs for Youth-Boston; bd. dirs., mem. exec. com., treas. United Community Planning Corp. Served to lt. (j.g.) USN, 1959-63. Mem. Nat. Trust Hist. Preservation, Comml. Club, World Affairs Council (dir.), New Eng. Council, Value Exchange Corp. (dir.), Boston Zool. Soc., Boston Com. Fgn. Relations, Assn. Res. City Bankers, Robert Morris Assos., Catboat Assn. Club: The Country. Office: 28 State St Boston MA 02106

MC CORMICK, RICHARD DAVID, telephone co. exec.; b. Fort Dodge, Iowa, July 4, 1940; s. Elmo Eugne and Virgilla (Lawler) McC.; B.S. in Elec. Engring., Iowa State U., 1961; m. Mary Patricia Smola, June 29, 1963; children—John Richard, Matthew David, Megan Ann, Katheirne Maura. With telephone co., 1961—, v.p., chief exec. officer for N.D., Northwestern Bell Telephone Co., Omaha, 1974-77, asst. v.p. human resources AT&T, Basking Ridge, N.J., 1977-78, sr. v.p. Northwestern Bell, Omaha, 1978—. Vice chmn. engr. adv. bd. Iowa State U., 1979-80; bd. dirs. United Way of Midlands, 1979-80; mem.-at-large Mid-Am. council Boy Scouts Am., 1978-80, mem. nat. personnel com., 1978-80, profl. tng. com., 1980. Named Outstanding Young Alumnus, Iowa State U., 1975. Roman Catholic. Clubs: The Omaha, Omaha Country; Fairmount Country (Chatham, N.J.). Office: Northwestern Bell Telephone Co 100 S 19th St (1230 Dodge) Omaha NE 68102

MC CORMICK, RICHARD PATRICK, educator; b. N.Y.C., Dec. 24, 1916; s. Patrick Austin and Anna (Smith) McC.; B.A., Rutgers U., 1938, M.A., 1940; Ph.D., U. Pa., 1948; m. Katheryne Crook Levis, Aug. 25, 1945; children—Richard Levis, Dorothy Irene. Historian, Phila. Q.M. Depot, 1942-44; instr. U. Del., 1944-45; mem. faculty Rutgers U., 1945—, univ. historian, 1948—, dean Rutgers Coll., 1974-77, Univ. prof. history, 1977—; research adviser Colonial Williamsburg, 1950-60; Fulbright lectr. Cambridge (Eng.) U., 1961-62; Commonwealth lectr. U. London, 1971; chmn. N.J. Hist. Commn., 1967-70. Mem. N.J. Tercentenary Commn., 1958-60, Am. Revolution Bicentennial Commn., 1970-72. Social Sci. Research Council fellow, 1956-57. Mem. Am. Hist. Assn. Orgn. Am. Historians, Am. Assn. State and Local History, N.J. Hist. Soc. (pres. 1950-57), Phi Beta Kappa. Club: Cranberry Valley Golf (Harwich, Mass.). Author: Experiment in Independence, 1950; History of Voting in N.J., 1953; N.J. From Colony to State, 1964; Second American Party System, 1966; Rutgers: a Bicentennial History, 1966. Home: 938 River Rd Piscataway NJ 08854 Office: 111 GSLS Rutgers Univ New Brunswick NJ 08903

MC CORMICK, THOMAS FRANCIS, printing co. exec.; b. Gardner, Mass., Feb. 20, 1929; s. Harold J. and Florence R. (Mailloux) McC.; B.S. cum laude, Holy Cross Coll., Worcester, Mass., 1950; m. Beverly G. Acey, Nov. 28, 1953; children—Stephen, Harold, Laura, Ann. With Gen. Electric Co., 1953-73, financial analyst, adminstrv. asst. to group v.p. indsl. group, N.Y.C., 1965-67, gen. mgr., treas. Maqua Co., Schenectady, 1967-72, mgr. power generation strategy devel., N.Y.C., 1972-73; pub. printer of U.S., Washington, 1973-77; pres. Telegraph Press Inc., Harrisburg, Pa., 1977—. Served to lt. (j.g.) USNR, 1950-53. Home: 454 Chocolate Ave Hershey PA 17033 Office: Telegraph Press Inc Cameron and Kelker Sts Harrisburg PA 17105

MCCORMICK, THOMAS JULIAN, educator; b. Syracuse, N.Y., Nov. 14, 1925; s. Thomas Julian and Doris (Rafferty) McC.; A.B., Syracuse U., 1948, A.M., 1949; M.F.A., Princeton, 1953, Ph.D., 1971; m. Margaret Emily Dorkey, Mar. 23, 1957; children—Sarah Elizabeth, Martha Dorcas. Research asst. Va. Mus. Fine Arts, Richmond, 1953-54; instr. Smith Coll., Northampton, Mass., 1954-56; dir., asst. prof. Robert Hull Fleming Mus., U. Vt., 1956-58; asso. prof., chmn. art dept. Wells Coll., Aurora, N.Y., 1958-60; asso. prof., dir. Art Gallery, Vassar Coll., Poughkeepsie, N.Y., 1960-70; Wright-Shippee prof., chmn. art dept. Wheaton Coll., Norton, Mass., 1970—; vis. asso. prof. Williams Coll., 1969; lectr. Worcester (Mass.) Art Mus., 1978. Bd. dirs. Dutchess County (N.Y.) Landmarks Assn., 1968-70, Olana State Historic Site, 1968-70. Served with AUS, 1944-46; ETO. Corning Mus. Glass fellow, 1954, Fulbright Sr. Research fellow to Gt. Britain, 1966-67, to Yugoslavia, 1976-77. Mem. Coll. Art Assn., Soc. Archtl. Historians (book rev. editor Jour. 1958-65, dir. 1960-63), Delta Kappa Epsilon. Episcopalian. Club: Princeton (N.Y.C.). Contbr. articles to profl. jours., exhbn. catalogs. Home: 8 Library Sq Norton MA 02766

MC CORMICK, WILFRED, author; b. Newland, Ind., Feb. 8, 1903; s. Ivor B. and Nellie (Jordan) McC.; student U. Ill., 1923-27; m. Eleanor Paddock, Nov. 2, 1935 (dec. Jan. 1952); children—Kathryn, Robert; m. 2d, Rebecca Fee, July 4, 1953 (dec. Oct. 1960); m. 3d, Helene Adele Huff, Aug. 1, 1962. Author numerous short stories and novels; profl. lectr. on lit. and hist. subjects; instr. creative writing, extension div. U. N.Mex., 1949-76; moderator weekly TV show, Albuquerque, 1954-55; pres. Bronc Burnett Enterprises, Albuquerque, 1953—; staff mem. Southwest Writers Conf., Corpus Christi, Tex., 1959-63; lectr. West Tex. State U. writing seminar, 1954; instr. Glorietta Writers Assembly, 1955; lectr. Nat. League Am. Pen Women, 1959—. Mem. armed forces adv. com. 4th Army Area, 1949—. Pres. N.Mex. Soc. Crippled Children, 1949-51, Friends of Library, Albuquerque, 1955-68; v.p. achievement and finance chmn. No. N.Mex. council Boy Scouts Am., 1953-55; Albuquerque chmn. Nat. Crusade for Freedom, 1951; N.Mex. co-chmn. Boys' Ranch expansion dir., 1949. Bd. dirs. Alburquerque Conf., NCCJ, 1954. Served to lt. col. AUS, 1942-46. Internat. Rotary Paul Harris fellow, 1973. Fellow Internat. Inst. Letters, Arts and Scis.; mem. Ret. Officers Assn., Assn. Former Mil. Intelligence Officers, Wisdom Hall Fame, Internat. Platform Assn., Am. Legion, Scabbard and Blade, C. of C., N.Mex. Com. Fgn. Relations (past chmn.), Delta Sigma Tau, Delta Alpha Epsilon. Mem. Christian Ch. Rotarian (pres. Albuquerque 1952-53, Am. del. internat. conv. 1952, 67, 68, dist. gov. 1967-68; mem. world consultative group 1968-69). Author: The Three-Two Pitch, 1948; Legion Tourney, 1948; Fielder's Choice, 1949; Flying Tackle, 1949; Bases Loaded, 1950; Rambling Halfback, 1950; Grand-Slam Homer, 1951; Quick Kick, 1951; Eagle Scout, 1952; First and Ten, 1952; The Man on the Bench, 1955; The Captive Coach, 1956; The Hot Corner, 1958; The Bigger Game, 1958; The Big Ninth, 1958; The Proud Champions, 1959; Five Yards to Glory, 1959; The Last Putout, 1959; The Automatic Strike, 1960; Too Many Forwards, 1960; The Double Steal, 1961; One O'Clock Hitter, 1961; The Play for One, 1961; Man in Motion, 1961; Rebel with a Glove, 1962; Home-Run Harvest, 1962; Too Late to Quit, 1962; The Five Man Break, 1962; The Starmaker, 1962; The Phantom Short-stop, 1963; Once a Slugger, 1963; Rough Stuff, 1963; The Two-One-Two Attack, 1963; The Long Pitcher, 1964; The Pro Toughback, 1964; The Right-End Option, 1964; The Throwing Catcher, 1964; Seven in Front, 1965; The Go-Ahead Runner, 1965; Tall at the Plate, 1966; No Place for Heroes, 1966; Rookie on First, 1967; The Incomplete Pitcher, 1967; One Bounce too Many, 1967; Fullback in the Rough, 1969. Home: Box 8857 Albuquerque NM 87198

MCCORMICK, WILLARD F., mgmt. cons.; b. Tonawanda, N.Y., Feb. 18, 1904; m. Phyllis Webb, Sept. 23, 1950; children—Willard F., Anne E., Cathleen D., Thomas L., Margaret H., John C. Chmn. Cresap, McCormick and Paget, Inc., mgmt. consultants; dir. Farrell Lines, Inc., N.Y.C., Midland Capital Corp., N.Y.C.; dir. Am. Bus. Group Inc. cardinal's com. for edn. Archdiocese N.Y. Trustee, exec. and fin. coms. Thomas Alva Edison Found. Mem. N.Y. Fgn. Policy Assn. (dir.). Clubs: Sky, Union League (N.Y.C.); Wee Burn Country (Darien, Conn.). Home: 480 Hollow Tree Ridge Rd Darien CT 06820 Office: 245 Park Ave New York City NY 10017

MCCORMICK, WILLIAM BLISS, mayor Topeka; b. Topeka, June 7, 1927; s. Joseph Bliss and Wilma (Bergundthal) McC.; B.B.A., Washburn U., 1952, J.D., 1959; m. Shirley Westfall, June 9, 1950; children—Timili, Mary, Lory, Jamie, Jennifer. Admitted to Kans. bar, 1958; practiced in Topeka; asst. city atty., Topeka, 1959-69; mayor of Topeka, 1971—. Served with USMC, 1945-47. Mem. Kans., Topeka bar assns., Am. Legion (comdr. post), VFW. Presbyterian. Clubs: Masons, Shriners, Moose. Office: Office of Mayor City Hall 215 E 7 St Topeka KS 66603*

MC CORMICK, WILLIAM FREDERICK, forensic pathologist, neuropathologist; b. Riverton, Va., Sept. 9, 1933; s. Jesse Allen and Elizabeth (Hord) McC.; B.S., U. Chattanooga, 1953; M.D., U. Tenn., 1955, M.S., 1957; m. Deanne Bourne Petersen, July 2, 1954; children—William Frederick, Cynthia Anne. Intern, Baptist Meml. Hosp., Memphis, 1956; resident in pathology U. Tenn., 1957-60, asst. in pathology, 1957-60, instr., 1960, asst. prof., 1960-64, mem. exec. com., basic med. scis., 1963-64; dep. chief med. examiner Tenn., 1961-63; spl. fellow, instr. neuropathology Columbia U., 1961-62; asso. prof. U. Iowa, 1964-68, prof., 1968-73, chmn. surgery dept. rev. com., 1968-69; prof. pathology, neurosurgery and neurology U. Tex. Med. Br., Galveston, 1973—; cons. in field; vis. scientist Armed Forces Inst. Pathology, Washington, 1965-66; dep. chief med. examiner Galveston County, 1976; mem. head injury study group Dept. Transp.; mem. com. NRC, 1978; vis. prof. U. Tenn., U. Pitts. Scoutmaster, Bay Area council Boy Scouts Am., 1975. Diplomate Am. Bd. Pathology. Mem. Am. Soc. Human Genetics, AAAS, Am. Soc. Exptl. Pathology, Assn. Am. Med. Colls., Am. Assn. Pathologists, Am. Assn. Neuropathologists, Nat. Assn. Med. Examiners, N.Y. Acad. Scis., AMA, Tex. Med. Assn., Sigma Xi. Author: (with W. E. Bell) Increased Intracranial Pressure in Children, 1972, 2d edit., 1978, Neurologic Infections in Children, 1975; (with S. S. Schochet, Jr.) Syllabus of Neuropathology, 1973, Atlas of Cerebrovascular Disease, 1976, Neuropathology Case Studies, 1976, 2d edit., 1979; Essentials of Neuropathology, 1979; contbr. articles to profl. jours. Home: 2828 Dominique St Galveston TX 77550

MCCORMICK, WILLIAM MARTIN, broadcasting exec.; b. Hackensack, N.J., Dec. 15, 1921; s. John and Delia Theresa (Murphy) McC.; student N.Y. U., 1939-43, B.S., 1946; student Harvard U., 1943-45; m. Joan Theresa Dowling, June 19, 1957; children—Jean Marie, Patricia, Joan, William Martin. Account exec. Sta. WOR, N.Y.C., 1946-54, asst. sales mgr., 1955, dir. sales, 1956-59, v.p., dir. sales, 1959-60; pres., gen. mgr. Sta. WNAC-AM and FM and WNAC-TV, Boston, 1960-64; v.p., gen. mgr. Sta. WNAC-TV, 1964-69; area v.p. New Eng., WNAC-TV, 1970-72; pres. McCormick Communications, 1972—; trustee Charlestown Savs. Bank. Bd. dirs. Catholic TV Center, 1970—, ARC, 1970—; pres. execs. club Greater Boston C. of C., 1965-66, bd. dirs., 1966-68; bd. dirs. Better Bus. Bur., 1966-70. Served with USN, 1941-46. Recipient award Greater Boston C. of C., 1962, citation of merit NCCJ, 1974. Mem. Nat. Assn. Broadcasters, Nat. Radio Broadcasters Assn., Advt. Club Boston,

New Eng. Broadcasters Assn. Roman Catholic. Clubs: Skating (Boston); Weston Golf. Office: 1 Beacon St Boston MA 02108

MCCORMICK, WILLIAM MORGAN, patent researcher; b. Perth Amboy, N.J., June 28, 1912; s. Edward Joseph and Mary Lloyd (Morgan) McC.; student Rutgers U., 1929-30; B.S., U.S. Naval Acad., 1934; student Fgn. Service Inst., 1959-60; m. Lalla Jane Cary, June 9, 1936; children—William Morgan, Jane Cary (Countess Tristan du Parc Locmaria), James Watt, John Thomas. Commd. ensign U.S. Navy, 1934, advanced through grades to rear adm., 1961; assigned battleships, destroyers, cruisers, 1934-42, patrol squadrons, 1942-45, aircraft carriers, 1945-49; comdr. Naval Air Sta., Miramar, Cal., 1949-50; assigned aircraft carriers, Korean War, 1951-53; comdr. U.S.S. Greenwich Bay, 1955-56, U.S.S. Valley Forge, 1958-59; mil. asst. to dep. sec. def., 1960-61; dep. dir. Def. Intelligence Agy., 1961-64; comdr. Carrier Div. 14, 1964-65; spl. asst. to Joint Chiefs of Staff, 1965-67; comdr. Fleet Air Wings, U.S. Atlantic Fleet, 1967-68, ret., 1968; v.p. Gen. Consultants Inc., 1968-69; v.p. Franklin Mint, Franklin Center, Pa., 1969-77; patent researcher Woolcott and Co., Arlington, Va., 1977—. Participated AEC weapons tests, 1950-51; naval attache, attache for air, Rome, Italy, 1956-58. Decorated Legion of Merit with 2 stars, Air medal; cavalier Order Mil. Merit (Italy); others. Clubs: New York Yacht (N.Y.C.); Army-Navy Country (Washington). Author: The Silver Ships, 1971. Home: 342 N Pitt St Alexandria VA 22314 Office: Woolcott and Co 1911 Jefferson Davis Hwy Arlington VA 22202

MCCORQUODALE, JOSEPH CHARLES, JR., state legislator; b. Mobile, Ala., Dec. 2, 1920; s. Joseph Charles and Winnie Lee (Griffin) McC.; student Marian Mil. Inst. Jr. Coll., 1938, U. Ala., 1941; m. Mary Elizabeth McCrary, Jan. 17, 1942; children—Joseph Charles III, Gaines Cowan. Automobile dealer, 1951-60; owner McCorquodale Agency, Jackson, Ala., 1961—; pres. Overstreet & McCorquodale, Inc., 1964—; mem. adv. bd. 1st Fed. Savs. & Loan Assn.; mem. Ala. Ho. of Reps. from 33d Dist., 1958—, speaker pro tem, 1972-74, speaker, 1975—; chmn. constn. and elections com., vice chmn. ways and means com.; mem. hwy. safety com. chmn. Ala. Toll Bridge Authority, 1969—, Ala. Forestry Commn., 1971—; mem. Gov.'s Com. for Indsl. Devel., 1961—; vice chmn. Ala. Legis. Council, 1971—. Bd. dirs. Ala. Mental Health Assn., Clarke Washington Industries Bd.; trustee Vanity Fair Found., Livingston U. Served to lt. USAAF; CBI; PTO. Decorated Air medal with 5 oak leaf clusters; named Man of Yr., City of Jackson, 1969, Most Outstanding Mem. Ho. of Reps., Capitol Press Corps, 1971. Mem. Jackson C. of C., Ala. Forestry Assn., Life Underwriters Assn., Am. Legion. Methodist. Club: Optimist. Home: Coffeeville Rd Jackson AL 36545 Office: PO Box 535 Jackson AL 36545*

MCCORQUODALE, JOSEPH CHARLES, JR., state legislator; b. Mobile, Ala., Dec. 2, 1920; s. Joseph Charles and Winnie Lee (Griffin) McC.; student Marian Mil. Inst. Jr. Coll., 1938, U. Ala., 1941; m. Mary Elizabeth McCrary, Jan. 17, 1942; children—Joseph Charles III, Gaines Cowan. Automobile dealer, 1951-60; owner McCorquodale Agency, Jackson, Ala., 1961—; pres. Overstreet & McCorquodale, Inc., 1964—; chmn. bd. Washington County State Bank, McIntosh, Ala., mem. adv. bd. 1st Sou. Savs. & Loan Assn.; mem. Ala. Ho. of Reps. from 33d Dist., 1958—, speaker pro tem, 1972-74, speaker, 1975—; chmn. constn. and elections com., vice chmn. ways and means com.; chmn. So. Speakers Conf.; chmn. Ala. Toll Bridge Authority, 1969—, Ala. Forestry Commn., 1971—; mem. Gov.'s Com. for Indsl. Devel., 1961—; vice chmn. Ala. Legis. Council, 1971—. Bd. dirs. Ala. Mental Health Assn., Clarke Washington Industries Bd.; trustee Vanity Fair Found., Livingston U. Served to lt. USAAF; CBI; PTO. Decorated Air medal with 5 oak leaf clusters; named Man of Yr., City of Jackson, 1969, Most Outstanding Mem. Ho. of Reps., Capitol Press Corps, 1971. Mem. Jackson C. of C., Ala. Forestry Assn., Life Underwriters Assn., Am. Legion, VFW, Ala. Acad. Honor, Omicron Delta Kappa. Methodist. Club: Optimist. Home: Coffeeville Rd Jackson AL 36545 Office: PO Box 928 Jackson AL 36545

MCCOSKER, JOHN EDWARD, ichthyologist, marine biologist; b. Los Angeles, Nov. 17, 1945; s. Joseph Samuel and Betty Eleanor (Hoyt) McC.; B.A., Occidental Coll., 1967; Ph.D., Scripps Instn. Oceanography, 1973; m. Sandra Smith, June 21, 1970. Research asso. Smithsonian Instn., C.Z., 1970-71; lectr. marine biology U. Calif. at San Diego, 1973; dir. Steinhart Aquarium, San Francisco, 1973—. Mem. Soc. Protection of Old Fishes, Am. Soc. Ichthyologists and Herpetologists, AAAS, Soc. Systematic Zoology, others. Club: Bohemian. Contbr. articles to profl. jours. Office: Steinhart Aquarium San Francisco CA 94118

MCCOUBREY, R. JAMES, advt. agy. exec.; b. Quebec, Que., Can., Sept. 1, 1944; s. James Addison and Margaret Genevieve Fernio (Scarratt) McC.; B.Comm., McGill U., Montreal, Que., 1966, M.A., 1967; m. Annette Louise Hebert, Sept. 16, 1972; 1 son, James Andrew. Brand mgmt. Procter & Gamble, Toronto, Ont., Can., 1967-69; with Young & Rubicam Ltd., Montreal, 1969-72, Toronto, 1972—, sr. v.p., mgr., 1974-77, pres., 1977—; dir. Young & Rubicam Internat. Publisher, Priority Mag., 1966-70; v.p. Fed. Progressive Conservative Party, 1966-70. Mem. Inst. Can. Advt. (dir.), Zeta Psi. Anglican. Club: Royal Can. Yacht. Home: 164 Walmer Rd Toronto ON M5R 2X9 Canada Office: 60 Bloor St W Toronto ON M4W 1J2 Canada

MCCOVEY, WILLIE LEE, profl. baseball player; b. Mobile, Ala., Jan. 10, 1938; s. Frank and Ester (Jones) McC. Mem. minor league profl. baseball teams, 1955-60; mem. San Francisco Giants Profl. Baseball Team, 1960-73, 77—, San Diego Padres, 1973-76, Oakland (Calif.) A's, 1976-77. Named Nat. League Rookie of Year, 1959, Home Run Champion 1963, 68, 69, Runs Batted In Leader, 1968, 69, Most Valuable Player, 1969; mem. All-Star Team, 1963, 66, 68, 69, 70, 71. Address: Candlestick Park San Francisco CA 94124*

MC COWAN, RICHARD JAMES, educator; b. N.Y.C., Oct. 10, 1931; s. Richard James and Veronica Mary (Quinn) McC.; B.A. cum laude, St. John's Coll., 1953; M.A., Niagara U., 1954, certificate, 1955; Ph.D., St. John's U., 1965; postgrad. State U. N.Y., Buffalo, 1964-66, State U. N.Y., Albany, 1967; m. Mary Elisabeth Coyle, Aug. 1957; children—Mary Elisabeth, Kathleen Mary, Maura Ann, Sheila Coyle. Tchr., counselor Baldwin (N.Y.) Jr. High Sch., 1957-61; counselor Farmingdale (N.Y.) High Sch., 1961-64; dir. guidance Eden (N.Y.) Central Schs., 1964-66; chief Bur. Sch. and Cultural Research, N.Y. State Edn. Dept., 1966-68; dir. campus lab. sch., dir. ednl. research and devel., prof. edn. State U. N.Y., Buffalo, 1968—; pres. McCowen Cons., Inc.; cons. numerous agys. and schs. Mem. adv. bd. GUILD Acad., 1968—, Erie Community Coll., City campus, 1971—; mem. Woodlawn Adv. Com., 1973-74; campaign mgr. Republican Mayoral Candidate, Buffalo, 1973. Served with U.S. Army, 1955-57. Mem. NEA, Am. Ednl. Research Assn., Inst. People, Nat. Soc. for Study of Edn., Am. Personnel and Guidance Assn., Nat. Vocat. Guidance Assn., Am. Sch. Counselors Assn., N.Y. State Tchrs. Assn., AAUP, Phi Delta Kappa. Clubs: K.C., Rotary. Editorial bd. Child Study Jour.; editor-in-chief Jour. Industry-Edn. Coop. Contbr. articles to profl. publs., poems. Home: 2466 W Oakfield Rd Grand Island NY 14072 Office: State U Coll at Buffalo Buffalo NY 14222

MCCOWAN, ROBERT TAYLOR, oil co. exec.; b. Carlisle, Ky., July 29, 1928; s. William Ray and Susan (Taylor) McC.; B.S., U. Ky., 1951, LL.D.; postgrad. U. Ill., 1964; m. Nyle Eleanor Yates, Dec. 6, 1953; children—David Wayne, Susan Jill. With Ashland Oil Inc., 1951—, salesman, Cin., 1951-54, div. mgr., Chgo., 1954-59, spl. rep., Ashland, Ky., 1959-64, asst. mgr. refinery sales, 1964-65, exec. asst., 1965-67, v.p., 1967-70, adminstrv. v.p., 1968-69, exec. v.p., dir., now pres. Ashland Petroleum Co., also dir.; dir. 2d Nat. Bank, Ashland. Active Ashland YMCA, 1963—. Fellow, U. Ky., bd. dirs. devel. council. Mem. Am. Petroleum Inst. (dir.), Nat. Petroleum Refiners Assn. (dir.), Ashland (dir.), Ky. chambers commerce, Asphalt Inst. (past dir.), U. Ky. Alumni Assn. (past pres. Boyd County), Ind. Petroleum Assn. Am., Omicron Delta Kappa, Beta Gamma Sigma, Delta Tau Delta. Mem. Christian Ch. Rotarian (dir. Ashland). Club: Bellefonte (dir.); 25 Year of Petroleum Industry. Home: 2311 Forest Ave Ashland KY 41101 Office: 1409 Winchester Ave Ashland KY 41101

MCCOWN, HAL DALE, army officer; b. Little Rock, Nov. 26, 1916; s. George Malcolm and Myrtle (Snell) McC.; B.A., La. State U., 1940; M.A. in Internat. Affairs, George Washington U., 1962; grad. Command and Gen. Staff Coll., 1943, Army War Coll., 1955; m. Rowena Merle Harmon, May 24, 1942; children—Hal Dale, David Harmon, Malcolm Lee, Marian Merle, Anne Leslie. Commd. 2d lt. U.S. Army, 1940, advanced through grades to maj. gen., 1967; co. and bn. duties 4th and 30th divs., 1940-43; combat duty with 30th Div., ETO, 1944-45; instr. tactics Inf. Sch., Ft. Benning, Ga., 1945-46; instr. inf. tactics Armored Sch., Ft. Knox, Ky., 1947-48; asst. and dep. sec. gen. staff Far East Command, Tokyo, 1948-51; comdg. officer 17th Inf. Regt., Korea, 1951-52; R.O.T.C. duty La. State U., 1952-54; chief army orgn. br. SHAPE, Paris, 1953-58; chief U.S. Army adv. group Air U., 1958-62; sr. adviser II Corps, Vietnam, 1962-63; dep. dir. mgmt. U.S. Army, 1963-64, dir. mgmt., 1964-65; dir Vietnam Support Expediting Task Force, 1965-66; dir., ground munitions Office Asst. Sec. Def., 1966-67; comdr. U.S. Mil. Assistance Command Thailand, also chief JUSMAG, Thailand, 1967-69; dep. comdg. gen. 11 Field Force, Vietnam, 1969-70; comdg. gen. Delta Mil. Assistance Command, Vietnam, 1970—. Decorated D.S.M. with oak leaf cluster, Silver Star with 2 oak leaf clusters, Legion of Merit with 4 oak leaf clusters, Bronze Star with oak leaf cluster, Air medal, Air Force Commendation medal, Purple Heart, Combat Inf. badge with star; Brit. Distinguished Service Order; Belgian Fourregere. Baptist. Home: 3409 Pope Ave North Little Rock AR 72116

MCCOWN, HALE, judge; b. Kansas, Ill., Jan. 19, 1914; s. Ross S. and Pauline (Collins) McC.; A.B., Hastings Coll., 1935; LL.B., Duke, 1937; m. Helen Lanier, July 15, 1938; children—Robert B., William L., Mary Lynn. Admitted to Oreg. bar, 1937, Nebr. bar, 1942; with firm Carey, Hart, Spencer & McCulloch, Portland, 1937-42; practice in Beatrice, 1942-65; mem. firm of McCown, Baumfalk & Dalke; asso. justice Supreme Court Nebr., 1965—. Served to lt. USNR, 1943-45. Fellow Am. Coll. Trial Lawyers, Am. Coll. Probate Counsel; mem. Am., Nebr. (chmn. ho. dels. 1955-56, pres. 1960-61) bar assns., Am. Law Inst. (mem. council 1969—), Am. Judicature Soc. Presbyn. Author articles legal jours. Home: 1301 J St Lincoln NE 68508 Office: State Capitol Bldg Lincoln NE 68509

MCCOY, CHARLES ALLAN, educator; b. Chgo., May 19, 1920; s. Charles Richard and Marie (Peterson) McC.; B.S., Ill. State U., 1948; M.A. with distinction, Colgate U., 1950; Ph.D., Boston U., 1958; m. Elaine Langan, Apr. 7, 1969; children—Sarah L., C. Ian, C. Graeme, C. Allan; children by previous marriage—Bruce A., Craig R. Asst. prof. Worcester Poly. Inst., 1950-53; research asst. Bur. Pub. Adminstrn., U. Va., 1953-56; prof. Temple U., 1956-68; prof. polit. sci., chmn. dept. govt. Lehigh U., 1968-76; leave of absence Lehigh U., 1976-77; prof. polit. sci., chmn. dept. polit. sci. and sociology U. North Fla., Jacksonville, 1976-77; prof. polit. sci. govt. dept. Lehigh U., 1977—; vis. lectr. polit. theory Leeds (Eng.) U., 1961-62; Fulbright prof. Monash U., Melbourne Australia, 1965; Fulbright prof. polit. theory U. Hong Kong, 1971. Founding officer, vice chmn. Caucus for a New Polit. Sci., 1967-69. Served to 1st lt. USAAF, 1941-46. Decorated Air medal with 2 oak leaf clusters. Mem. Am., Internat. polit. sci. assns., AAUP, Internat. Studies Assn. Author: Political Analysis: An Unorthodox Approach; Apolitical Politics: A Critique of Behavioralism, 3d edit., 1969; Polk and the Presidency, 1960. Home: Durham PA 18039 Office: Dept Govt Lehigh U Bethlehem PA 18015

MC COY, CHARLES WALLACE, banker; b. Marietta, Ohio, Feb. 5, 1920; s. John H. and Florence (Buchanan) McC.; B.A., Marietta Coll., 1942; M.B.A., Stanford, 1944; grad. Am. Bankers Assn. Sch. Banking, Rutgers U., 1947; m. Ruth Zimmerman, July 20, 1946; children—Melissa, Brent, Shelley. With City Nat. Bank, Columbus, O., 1944-59, v.p., 1952-59, also dir.; sr. v.p. La. Nat. Bank, Baton Rouge, 1959-61, pres., 1961-78, chmn., 1963-78, chmn., chief exec. officer, 1978—. Mem. faculty Comml. Bank Mgmt. Program Grad. Sch. Bus. Columbia, 1968—. Dir. Jefferson-Pilot Corp., Jefferson Standard Life Ins. Co., Greensboro, N.C., Fed. Res. Bank, New Orleans, 1974-77. Mem. La. Gov.'s Offshore Revenue Sharing Com.; mem. accreditation com. Am. Council Constrn. Edn., 1975—; mem. La Sea Grant Adv. Council, 1974—. Mem. La. State U. Found.; adv. council Coll. Bus. Adminstrn., La. State U.; bd. govs. La. Arts Found.; trustee Pub. Affairs Research Council; dir., trustee Gulf South Research Inst.; pres. United Givers Fund Baton Rouge, 1971; bd. dirs. Council for Better La., La. Exposition, Inc., 1976, So. Univ. Found., Baton Rouge; Mem. Am. (communications council), La. bankers assns., Conf. Bd., Res. City Bankers Assn., La. C. of C. (pres. 1972—), Delta Upsilon. Episcopalian. Mason (32 deg., Shriner). Clubs: Baton Rouge Country, Baton Rouge City, Rotary. Home: 17 Stone's Throw 8655 Jefferson Hwy Baton Rouge LA 70809 Office: 451 Florida St Baton Rouge LA 70801

MCCOY, CHARLIE, musician; b. Oak Hill, W.Va., Mar. 28, 1941; children—Charlie, Ginger. Rec. artist featured with other artist numerous albums; also known for harmonica on own records, including Today I Started Loving You Again, 1973. Named Number One Country Instrumentalist, Billboard Mag., 1973, Most Promising Country Instrumentalist, Cash Box, Record World, 1973, Instrumentalist of Year, Kraft Music Awards, 1973; recipient Most Promising Country Album of Year award Record World, Grammy award best country instrumentalist, 1973; Instrumentalist of Year, Country Music Assn., 1972, 73, Best Country Instrumental Performance, 1972. Address: care Jan Kurtis Mgmt PO Box 40662 Nashville TN 37204*

MCCOY, CLARENCE JOHN, JR., curator; b. Lubbock, Tex., July 25, 1935; s. Clarence John and Marguerite Ceona (McNew) McC.; B.S., Okla. State U., Stillwater, 1957, M.S., 1960; Ph.D., U. Colo., 1965; m. Patsy Ruth Kelly, June 7, 1957; children—John Kelly, Catherine Janet. Instr. zoology Okla. State U., summers 1959-60; research asso. U. Colo. Museum, 1962-64; mem. staff Carnegie Mus., Pitts., 1964—, curator amphibians and reptiles, 1972—; vis. asst. prof. zoology Ariz. State U., 1969-70; adj. asso. prof. biology U. Pitts., 1972—. Carnegie Mus. del. Latin Am. Congress Zoology, Montevideo, 1971, Mexico, 1974, Tucuman, 1977. NSF fellow, 1961. Mem. AAAS, Am. Soc. Ichthyologists and Herpetologists (gov. 1967-72), Am. Soc. Mammalogists, Herpetologists League (exec. council 1965-67, 70—), Soc. Systematic Zoology, Soc. Study Amphibians and Reptiles (chmn. 1972), Southwestern Assn. Naturalists, Latin Am. Assn. I chthyologists and Herpetologists, Okla. Acad. Sci., Pa. Acad. Sci., Sigma Xi. Author: Vertebrates, 1968; Animals of the Islands, 1969; Keys to Mexican Amphibians and Reptiles, 1978; also articles. Editor lizard accounts Catalogue Am. Amphibians and Reptiles, 1967—. Office: 4400 Forbes Ave Pittsburgh PA 15213

MCCOY, CRAIG WALPOLE, broadcasting co. exec.; b. White Plains, N.Y., May 25, 1945; s. Arthur Hatcher and Virginia Lefoy (Green) McC.; B.S., Lehigh U., 1967; M.B.A., Northwestern U., 1971. With Doyle Dane Bernbach, Los Angeles, 1972-73; sta. mgr. Sta. KGON, Portland, Oreg., 1974-76, gen. mgr., 1976-78; pres., gen. mgr. Sta. KYXI/KGON, Portland, 1978—. Served with U.S. Army, 1969-70. Mem. Portland Advt. Fedn., Portland C. of C. Club: Multnomah Athletic. Home: 1651 SW Ash St Lake Oswego OR 97034 Office: PO Box 22125 Portland OR 97222

MC COY, DONALD RICHARD, historian; b. Chgo., Jan. 18, 1928; s. Patrick Emmett and Rose Roma (Hewitt) O'Day; B.A., U. Denver, 1949; M.A., U. Chgo., 1949; Ph.D., Am. U., 1954; m. Vivian Alicia Rogers, Sept. 29, 1949; children—Patricia, Bernard, William. Archivist interior sect. Nat. Archives, 1951-52; faculty dept. social studies State U. Coll., Cortland, N.Y., 1952-57; faculty dept. history U. Kans., Lawrence, 1957—, Univ. distinguished prof., 1974—; Fulbright prof. history U. Bonn, Germany, 1962; Mary Ball Washington prof. history Univ. Coll., Dublin, Ireland, 1976-77; dir. spl. research project Harry S. Truman Library Inst., 1967-72; prin. investigator Central Am. Oral History Project, univs. Costa Rica and Kans., 1970-72; mem. adv. com. for protection archives and records centers U.S. GSA, 1974-76, mem. Nat. Archives Adv. Council, 1976-79; mem. Joint Com. Historians and Archivists, 1977—, chmn., 1979—. Alderman, Cortland, 1955-57. Served with Signal Corps, U.S. Army, 1945-47. Recipient Byron Caldwell Smith award for distinguished writing, 1970; Waldo Gifford Leland prize Soc. Am. Archivists; Nat. Endowment for Humanities research grantee, 1968-70, 73-74. Mem. Phi Beta Kappa. Author: Angry Voices, Left-of-Center Politics in the New Deal Era, 1958; Landon of Kansas, 1966; Calvin Coolidge, The Quiet President, 1967; (with R.T. Ruetten) Quest and Response: Minority Rights During The Truman Administration, 1973; Coming of Age: The United States During The 1920s and 1930s, 1973; The National Archives: America's Ministry of Documents, 1978. Editor: (with M.L. Fausold) Student Guide to the American Story, II, 1957; (with R.G. O'Connor) Readings in Twentieth Century American History, 1963; (with R.T. Ruetten and J.R. Fuchs) Conference of Scholars on the Truman Administration and Civil Rights, 1968; (with B.K. Zobrist) Conference of Scholars on the Administration of Occupied Areas, 1943-1955, 1970. Contbr. articles to profl. jours. Office: Dept History U Kans Lawrence KS 66045

MCCOY, JEROME DEAN, educator; b. Liberty, Mo., Feb. 28, 1931; s. Joseph Perrean and Thelma Rebecca (Jones) McC.; A.B., William Jewell Coll., 1952; M.A., U. Mo., 1957; Ph.D., U. Helsinki (Finland), 1965; children—Heather, Jerome Dean. Asst. prof. physics U. Tulsa, 1958-66, prof., 1970—; research specialist N.Am. Aviation, Tulsa, 1966-67; mgr. advanced systems Sylvania Electronics, Mountain View, Calif., 1967-70; cons. in field. Served with AUS, 1953-55. NSF Sci. Faculty fellow, 1963-64. Mem. Am. Phys. Soc., Finnish Phys. Soc., Am. Nuclear Soc., Am. Soc. Engring. Edn., Am. Assn. Physics Tchrs., Sigma Xi. Patentee in field. Home: 2439 E 7th St Tulsa OK 74104 Office: Dept Physics U Tulsa Tulsa OK 74104

MCCOY, JOHN BONNET, banker; b. Columbus, Ohio, June 11, 1943; s. John Gardner and Jeanne Newlove (Bonnet) McC.; B.A., Williams Coll., 1965; M.B.A., Stanford U., 1967; m. Jane Deborah Taylor, Apr. 21, 1968; children—Tracy Bonnet, Paige Taylor, John Taylor. With City Nat. Bank and Trust Co., Columbus, 1970—, br. head, 1973-75, v.p. asset mgmt., 1975-77, pres., 1977—, also dir.; dir. 1st Trust Co. Ohio. Active Boy Scouts Am.; trustee Kenyon Coll., Columbus Symphony Orch. Served to capt. USAF, 1967-70. Episcopalian. Clubs: Columbus, Golf, Muirfield, Columbus Country, Harbor Springs; Wequetonsing Golf (Little Harbor, Mich.); Univ. (N.Y.C.). Home: 230 Ashbourne Rd Columbus OH 43209 Office: 100 E Broad St Columbus OH 43215

MC COY, JOHN GARDNER, banker; b. Marietta, Ohio, Jan. 30, 1913; s. John Hall and Florence (Buchanan) McC.; A.B., Marietta Coll., 1935; M.B.A., Stanford, 1937; LL.D. (hon.), Kenyon Coll., 1970; m. Jeanne N. Bonnet, Jan. 4, 1941; children—John Bonnet, Virginia Buchanan. With City Nat. Bank & Trust Co., Columbus, 1937—, v.p., 1946-58, pres., 1958-68, chmn. bd., 1968-77, also dir.; chmn., dir. Buckeye Internat., Inc.; pres. First Banc Group Ohio, Inc., 1968—, Banc One Corp. Chief fin. adviser Office Prodn. Mgmt., 1941; asst. dir. machine tools div. WPB, 1942; chmn. Devel. Com. for Greater Columbus, 1962—. Bd. dirs., treas. Columbus Gallery Fine Arts; trustee Marietta Coll.; bd. dirs. Franklin County chpt. ARC. Served to lt. (s.g.) USNR, 1943-45. Mem. Assn. Res. City Bankers, Assn. Registered Bank Holding Cos. (officer, dir.). Episcopalian. Clubs: University (N.Y.C.); Columbus, Columbus Country, Muirfield Golf, University, Golf; Wequetonsing (Mich.) Golf, Little Harbor (Harbor Springs, Mich.); Royal Poinciana, Hole In-the-Wall Golf (Naples, Fla.). Home: 11 Sessions Dr Columbus OH 43209 Office: 100 E Broad St Columbus OH 43215

MCCOY, JOHN LOUIS, aircraft co. exec.; b. Garden City, Kans., Dec. 5, 1914; s. Louis and Grace (Small) McC.; B.S., U.S. Mil. Acad., 1939; m. Barbara Vaughn, May 31, 1953; children—Mary J., Barbara M., Patricia V., Laura A. Commd. 2d lt. U.S. Army, 1939, advanced through grades to maj. gen. USAF, 1966; ops. officer B-29 group, PTO, World War II; bomber command ops. officer, Korean War; dir. material 2d A.F., 1953-54; dep. for aircraft Wright-Patterson AFB, 1955-59; dir. Titan and Minuteman programs, 1961-66; comdr. ballistic systems div. Air Force Systems Command, 1966-67; dep. chief staff plans Air Force Logistics Command, 1967-69; v.p. aircraft div. Northrop Corp., 1970—. Bd. govs. Inst. Logo-pedics, Wichita, Kans., 1964-68. Decorated D.S.M., Legion of Merit with oak leaf cluster, D.F.C., Soldiers medal, Bronze Star, Air medal with oak leaf cluster. Mem. Kappa Sigma. Home: 1609 Via Lazo Palos Verdes Estates CA 90274

MCCOY, JOHN MILTON, II, banker; b. Dallas, Mar. 5, 1905; s. John Milton and Marie Alice (Ostrom) McC.; B.S., Tex. A. and M. U., 1926; postgrad. Columbia, 1926-27; m. Millicent Hume, Dec. 27, 1929; children—Carolyn, John III. Asst. dist. mgr. Firestone Tire & Rubber Co., Akron, O., 1930-42; regional exec. officer OPA, Dallas, 1942-47; sr. v.p. Tex. Bank & Trust Co., Dallas, 1947—; Pres. 1st Bus. Investment Corp., Dallas, 1968—. Treas., Campfire Girls Orgn., Dallas, 1954-55, Presbyn. Children's Home and Service Agy., Itasca, Tex., 1952—. Mem. Delta Kappa Epsilon, Alpha Kappa Psi. Presbyn. (treas., elder). Home: 5423 Park Ln Dallas TX 75220 Office: 1 Main Pl Dallas TX 75250

MC COY, PRESSLEY CRANE, ednl. cons.; b. Fresno, Calif., Feb. 24, 1926; s. Daniel Crane and Bessie George (Watt) McC.; B.A. cum laude, Muskingum Coll., 1948; M.A., Northwestern U., 1950. Ph.D., 1954; m. Mary Niemeyer, Mar. 15, 1974; children—Jeffrey, Rhonda Lee, Mark, Thomas. Instr. English and speech Muskingum Coll.,

1948-49; teaching fellow speech Northwestern U., 1949-51; dir. oral communication Denison U., 1951-55, asst. prof., 1953; dean students, asst. prof. U. Md. at Munich, Germany, 1955-56; asst. dir. Danforth Found., St. Louis, 1956-58, asso. dir., also dir. programs liberal edn., 1958-65; pres. Central States Coll. Assn., 1965-68; chancellor at Johnston Coll., U. Redlands (Calif.), 1968-71; dean summer quarter 1971-72; dir. U. Coll. and Middle Coll. U.S. Internat. U., San Diego, 1972-74; ednl. cons., 1974-76; pres. Dayton-Miami Valley Consortium, 1979—; cons. new dimensions Los Angeles Community Coll. Dist., 1977-78; chmn. Council Affiliated Colls. of Inst. European Studies. Bd. dirs. St. Louis Christmas Carols Assn., Victor Gruen Center Environ. Planning, Access Public TV. Served with AUS, 1945-46; PTO. Mem. Am. Acad. Polit. and Social Scis., Higher Edn. Colloquium. Presbyn. (elder). Author articles. chpts. in books. Home: 9515 Bridlewood Trail Spring Valley OH 45370

MCCOY, RALPH RICHARD, found. exec.; b. Richland, Ind., Oct. 14, 1909; s. L. Lyman and Louise (Link) McC.; student George Washington U., 1930-35; LL.B., Nat. U., 1938; m. Elizabeth Bacon, Apr. 23, 1936; children—Sankey, Noel. Service sta. sales Standard Oil Co., Washington, 1929-30; asst. purchasing agt. So. Dairies, Inc., Washington, 1930-32; accounting, sales, fgn. service Standard Oil Co. of N.J., 1932-56; pres. Pate Oil Co., Milw., Oklahoma Oil Co. of Chgo., 1956-60, pres. Oklahoma-Pate div. Humble Oil & Refining Co., Houston, 1960-61, regional marketing mgr., 1961-65; marketing coordinator Esso Standard Eastern, Inc., 1965-69; v.p. Teagle Found., N.Y.C., 1969—. Mem. Delta Phi Epsilon. Club: Wee Burn Country. Home: Horseshoe Rd Darien CT 06820 Office: 30 Rockefeller Plaza New York City NY 10020

MC COY, RAYMOND F., educator; b. Pawtucket, R.I., Sept. 17, 1913; s. John H. and Agnes (O'Connor) McC.; A.B., Xavier U., Cin., 1934; A.M., U. Cin., 1935, B.E., 1936, Ed.D., 1939; m. Margaret Hohmann, Nov. 20, 1941; children—Thomas R., Kathleen, Margaret Ann, John J., James P., Patricia. Tchr. Cin. schs., 1936-39, curriculum asst., 1939-40, adminstrv. asst. to supt., 1940-42; dir. grad. div. Xavier U., 1946-56, chmn. dept. edn., 1946-70, dean grad. sch., 1956-77, distinguished prof. ednl. adminstrn., 1977—. Mem. exec. bd. and mem. U.S. Nat. Commn. for UNESCO, 1950-56, 62-68; U.S. rep UNESCO, Paris, 1947, Lake Success, 1948. Mem. Adv. Com. on Voluntary Fgn. Aid, AID, 1959-78. Served as spl. agt. M.I., AUS, 1943-45. Mem. Cath. Assn. for Internat. Peace (pres. 1953-55), Cath. Commn. on Intellectual and Cultural Affairs, Am. Assn. of Sch. Adminstrs., Nat. Cath. Edn. Assn., Ohio Council for UNESCO, Ohio Coll. Assn. (pres. tchr. placement sect. 1947-49, mem. commn. on grad. studies 1950-53), Cin. Assn. for U.N. (pres. 1949-50), Cin. Council World Affairs (dir.), Phi Delta Kappa, Kappa Delta Pi. Author: American School Administration: Public and Catholic, 1961. Editor: Prose and Poetry of England, Prose and Poetry of America, Prose and Poetry for Enjoyment, Prose and Poetry for Appreciation, 1942; Working Together, 1957; Regions Near and Far, 1961; Our Country, 1961; mem. editorial bd. Cath. Messenger, 1947-60; editorial dir. Catholic Unified Social Studies series. Contbr. to various publs. Home: 944 Finney Trail Cincinnati OH 45224

MCCOY, RICHARD HUGH, educator, emeritus univ. dean; b. Wilmington, O., Nov. 26, 1908; s. Oliver Robert and Elizabeth (Barrett) McC.; A.B., Earlham Coll., 1929; M.S., U. Ill., 1931, Ph.D. (Rockefeller fellow 1934-35), 1935; m. Margaret Jean Stockdale, Apr. 5, 1952; 1 dau., Carolyn Jean. Instr. chemistry Earlham Coll., 1929-30; research fellow Wistar Inst., 1936-40; mem. faculty U. Pitts., 1940—, prof. chemistry, asso. dean div. natural scis., 1959—, asso. dean and dir. grad. programs, faculty of arts and sciences, 1968-73, dean emeritus, 1973—. Del. Friends Worlds Conf., Oxford, Eng., 1952. Fellow AAAS; mem. Am. Chem. Soc., Am. Inst. Nutrition, Am. Soc. Biol. Chemists, Am. Assn. U. Profs., Fedn. Am. Scientists, N.Y. Acad. Scis., Soc. Social Responsibility Sci., Sigma Xi, Phi Lambda Upsilon, Alpha Chi Sigma. Mem. Soc. Friends. Home: 1737 Williamsburg Pl Pittsburgh PA 15235

MCCOY, ROBERT BAKER, publisher; b. Arrowsmith, Ill., Mar. 26, 1916; s. Robert Benton and Charlotte (Miller) McC.; B.S., Northwestern U., 1950, M.S., 1951; postgrad. U. Ill. extension. Various positions with branches U.S. Govt., 1939-51; mng. editor book dept. Popular Mechanics Mag. Co., Chgo., 1951-60; mng. editor high sch. textbook div. J.B. Lippincott Co., Chgo., 1960-62; owner, pres., chmn. bd. Rio Grande Press Inc., pubs. non-fiction Western Americana books, Chgo., 1962—; chmn. bd., pres. Rio Grande Press of N.Mex., Inc. Served with AUS, 1941-45. Baptist. Lectr., author articles on Am. Indian, ornithology, travel. Address: The Rio Grande Press Inc La Casa Escuela Glorieta NM 87535

MCCOY, SETH, tenor; b. Sanford, N.C., 1928; grad. N.C. A. and T. Coll., Greensboro, 1950; student Pauline Thesmacher at Music Sch. Settlement, Cleve., Antonia Lavanne, N.Y.C.; m. Jane Gunter. Soloist with Robert Shaw Chorale, 1963-65; mem. Bach Aria Group, 1973—; frequent soloist with N.Y. Philharm., Boston Symphony, Phila. Orch., Chgo. Symphony, Cleve. Symphony, Pitts. Symphony, San Francisco Symphony, Los Angeles Philharm., Nat. Symphony of Washington, others; appearances at Carmel (Calif.) Bach Festival, Ravinia Festival, Blossom Music Festival, Cleve., Berkshire Festival., others; European debut at Aldeburgh Festival, 1978; recs. for RCA and Vanguard, including Bach's St. Matthew Passion, Brahms' Liebestieder Walzer; Met. opera debut as Tamino in The Magic Flute, 1979. Served with inf. U.S. Army; Korea. Office: care Herbert Barrett Mgmt 1860 Broadway Suite 1700 New York NY 10023

MCCOY, THOMAS LARUE, mathematician, educator; b. Seville, Ohio, Jan. 16, 1933; s. Calvin Armstrong and Irene Rosemund (LaRue) McC.; B.A., Oberlin Coll., 1954; M.S., U. Wis., 1956, Ph.D., 1961; m. Leslie Helene Reiwitch, Nov. 29, 1957; children—Bruce Duncan, Clare Ann. With Inst. for Air Weapons Research, Chgo., 1960; instr. Ill. Inst. Tech., 1961-62, asst. prof., 1962-64; asst. prof. Mich. State U., East Lansing, 1964-67, asso. prof., 1967-77, prof. math., 1977—. Mem. Am. Math. Soc., Soc. for Indsl. and Applied Math. Contbr. articles to math. jours. Office: Dept Math Mich State U East Lansing MI 48824

MCCOY, WESLEY LAWRENCE, educator; b. Memphis, Jan. 27, 1935; s. Harlan Eftin and Gladys (Coggin) Mc C.; B.Music Edn., La. State U., 1957, Ph.D., 1970; M.Music Edn., U. Louisville, 1958; M.Sacred Music, So. Bapt. Theol. Sem., 1960; m. Carolyn June Noble, Aug. 26, 1960; children—Jill Laurene, Scott Edward. Minister of music Beechmont Bapt. Ch., Louisville, 1959-62, also instr. music So. Bapt. Theol. Sem., Louisville; asst. prof. music, dir. bands Carson Newman Coll., Jefferson City, Tenn., 1962-67; grad. teaching fellow La. State U., Baton Rouge, 1968-69; asst. prof. music U. S.C., Columbia, 1969-72; asso. prof. music U. Ark., Little Rock, 1972-77, prof., 1977—, asst. dean for public service Coll. Fine Arts, 1978—, condr. Wind Ensemble, River City Community Band, 1972—. French horn player Knoxville (Ky.) Symphony Orch., 1962-67, Columbia Philharm. Orch. 1969-72, Ark. Symphony Orch., 1972—; mem. com. to rev. certificatio music tchrs. S.C. Dept. Edn., 1971-72; condr. Die Fledermaus, Ark. Arts Center, Little Rock, 1974. Co-chmn. Jefferson County (Tenn.) Com. for Goldwater for Pres., 1962; mem. Pulaski County Republican Com., 1977—. Mem. S.C. Music Educators Assn. (pres. coll. div. 1971-73), Ark. Music Edn. Assn. (chmn. research 1975—, chmn. higher edn. 1975-79), Music Educators Nat. Conf., Coll. Band Dirs. Nat. Assn. (Ark. chmn. 1976-78), Assn. Concert Bands Am. (membership chmn. 1979—), Phi Mu Alpha, Pi Kappa Lambda, Phi Delta Kappa, Kappa Kappa Psi. Republican. Baptist. Contbr. to Ch. Musician, 1974-76. Home: 3200 Imperial Valley Dr Little Rock AR 72212. *Persistence in attempting goals will result in attainment of most goals.*

MC CRACKEN, DANIEL DELBERT, author, computer cons.; b. Hughsville, Mont., July 23, 1930; s. Albert Ray and Blanche (Spear) McC.; B.A. in Math., Central Wash. U., 1950, B.A. in Chemistry, 1951; student N.Y. U., 1958-59; M.Div., Union Theol. Sem., N.Y.C., 1970. With Gen. Electric Co., 1951-58, dir. tng., computer dept., 1956-57; with AEC Computing Center, N.Y.U., 1958-59; cons. computer programming, writing and tng., 1958—. Pres. bd. edn., Ossining, N.Y., 1965-66. Mem. Assn. Computing Machinery (chmn. com. on computers and pub. policy 1972-76, mem. council 1974—, v.p. 1976-78, pres. 1978-80). Democrat. Author: Digital Computer Programming, 1957; (with H. Weiss and T.H. Lee) Programming Business Computers, 1959; A Guide to FORTRAN Programming, 1961; A Guide to IBM 1401 Programming, 1962; A Guide to ALGOL Programming, 1962; A Guide to COBOL Programming, 1963, (with U. Garbassi) 2d edit., 1970; (with F.J. Gruenberger) Introduction to Electronic Computers, 1963; (with W.S. Dorn) Numerical Methods and FORTRAN Programming, 1964; A Guide to FORTRAN IV Programming, 1965, 2d edit., 1972; FORTRAN with Engineering Applications, 1967; Public Policy and the Expert, 1971; (with W.S. Dorn) Numerical Methods with FORTRAN IV Case Studies, 1972; A Simplified Guide to FORTRAN Programming, 1974. Editor: (with M. Mead, R.L. Shinn and J.E. Carothers) To Love or To Perish: The Technological Crisis and the Churches, 1972; A Simplified Guide to Fortran Programming, 1974; A Simplified Guide to Structured Cobol Programming, 1976; A Guide to PL/M Programming for Microcomputer Applications, 1978. Address: 7 Sherwood Ave Ossining NY 10562

MCCRACKEN, GEORGE HERBERT, mag. publisher; b. Pitts., June 20, 1899; s. George and Anne Elizabeth (Vance) McC.; B.S., U. Pitts., 1921; Litt.D., Lafayette Coll., 1968; LL.D., Allegheny Coll., 1972; m. Martha M. Alford, Jan. 22, 1977; children—Judith (Mrs. William M. Clark), George Herbert. Head football coach Allegheny Coll., 1921-23, Lafayette Coll., 1924-35; with Scholastic Mags., Inc., N.Y.C., 1922—, sr. v.p., 1954-61, vice chmn. bd., 1961-70, chmn. exec. com., 1971—, also dir.; founder, 1931, Scholastic Coach mag., pub., 1931-68. Football Found. Hall of Fame; trustee U. Pitts., Lafayette Coll. Served with U.S. Navy, 1918. Mem. Delta Tau Delta (pres. 1946-48), Omicron Delta Kappa, Beta Gamma Sigma. Presbyn. Clubs: Delray Beach Yacht; Scarsdale Golf, Scarsdale Town. Home: South 9 Sabal Island Dr Boynton Beach FL 33435 Office: 50 W 44th St New York City NY 10036

MCCRACKEN, GUY F., steel co. exec.; b. Pitts., Apr. 20, 1924; s. Guy F. and Nora S. (McClellan) McC.; B.S., Pa. State U., 1949; m. Earleen Ramsey, June 19, 1946; children—Carol (Mrs. Michael Milligan), Linda (Mrs. Patrick Leary), Nancy. Metallurgist Crucible Steel Corp., Syracuse, N.Y., 1949-59, Midland, Pa., 1959-61, corp. v.p., 1966-68; group v.p. Steel Colt Industries, Pitts., 1968; pres. Universal Cyclops Corp., Pitts., 1968-73; exec. v.p., chief operating officer Sharon Steel Corp. (Pa.), 1973—, dir., 1973—; dir. McDowell Nat. Bank, Shenango Inn, Sharon. Chmn. indsl. div. United Way Mercer County, 1974. Bd. dirs. Pa. Economy League, Mercer County, 1973—, Sharon (Pa.) Gen. Hosp., 1973—. Served with AUS, 1943-45. Mem. Am. Iron and Steel Inst. (dir. 1975—), Delta Sigma Phi. Presbyn. Clubs: Sharon Country; Laurel Valley Golf (Ligonier, Pa.); Muirfield Village Golf (Dublin, Ohio); Duquesne (Pitts.). Home: 1220 Yahres Rd Sharon PA 16146 Office: Box 291 Sharon Steel Corp Sharon PA 16146

MC CRACKEN, HAROLD, author, explorer, mus. dir.; b. Colorado Springs, Colo., Aug. 31, 1894; s. James Owen and Laura Gladys (Crapsey) McC.; ed. Drake U., 1911-13, Ohio State U., 1914-15; Litt.D., Hope Coll., 1957, U. Alaska, 1966; L.H.D., Colo. State U., 1972; LL.D., U. Wyo., 1974; m. Angelyn Elizabeth Conrad, Oct. 23, 1924; children—Harold Conrad, Marjorie Angelyn. Ornithol. collector for Iowa State Mus., Des Moines, 1912; leader Ohio State U. expdn. to Alaska, 1915-17; mining in Alaska, 1919-20; leader Ohio State Mus. photo-sci. expdn., to secure picture record of Alaska brown bear and other big game, 1922, 23; leader Stoll-McCracken expdn. Am. Mus. Natural History for archeol. research in Aleutian Islands, discovering mummified bodies of Stone Age and collecting Arctic walrus group for museum's Hall of Ocean Life; lectr. on Alaskan and Arctic wild life; regarded as authority on Alaska brown bear. Dir. Buffalo Bill Hist. Center, also Whitney Mus. Western Art, Cody, Wyo., 1958-74, dir. emeritus, 1974—. Served as sgt. photog. sect. Signal Corps, and on spl. duty in intelligence div. and in aviation research div., dept. physics Columbia U., World War I. Clubs: Douglaston (L.I.); Explorers (hon. life mem.). Mem. Dutch Reformed Ch. Author 31 books including: Iglaome (fiction), 1930; God's Frozen Children (travel), 1930; Pershing-The Story of a Great Soldier, 1931; Alaska Bear Trails (travel), 1931; Frederic Remington-Artist of the Old West, 1947; Caribou Traveler, 1949; The Flaming Bear, 1951; Portrait of the Old West, 1952; Pirate of the North, 1953; The Beast That Walks Like Man, 1955; Winning of the West, 1955; Story of Alaska, 1956; Hunters of the Stormy Sea, 1957; The Charles M. Russell Book, 1957; Hoofs, Claws and Antlers, 1958; George Catlin and the Old Frontier, 1959; Frederic Remington's Own West, 1960; The Frederic Remington Book, 1966; Roughnecks and Gentlemen, 1968; The American Cowboy, 1973; The Frank Tenney Johnson Book, 1974. Address: Buffalo Bill Hist Center Box 1020 Cody WY 82414

MC CRACKEN, JAMES, tenor; b. Gary, Ind.; s. John A. and Doris (Hafey) McC.; D.Music (hon.), Ind. U.; m. Sandra Warfield; children—Ahna-Maureen, John. Appeared with maj. opera cos.: Met. Opera, Vienna Staatsoper, Covent Garden, Paris Opéra, Bayerische Staatsoper, Deutsche Oper Berlin, Saltzburg Festival, Hamburg Staatsoper, Arena di Verona, Zurich Opera, Rome Opera, Teatro Colón, San Francisco Opera, Seattle Opera, others; leading rôles in: Otello, Tannhäuser, Le Prophète, Carmen, Il Trovatore, Pagliacci, Fidelio, Aida, Faust, Ariadne auf Naxos, Turandot, La Forzadel Destino, La Bohème, Ballo in Maschera, Contes d'Hoffmann, others; soloist with maj. orchs.: Phila., Boston, Detroit, Dallas, San Francisco, Milw., others; recs. include: The Meeting of the Waters, Mc Cracken on Stage, Fidelio, Duets of Love and Passion, Otello (Grand Prix du Disques 1972), I Pagliacci, Le Prophète, Carmen (Grammy award 1974), Gurrelieder. Served with USN, World War II. Named Hoosier of Year, Ind. Soc. N.Y., 1977. Author: (with Sandra Warfield) A Star in the Family, 1971. Address: care Columbia Artists Mgmt Inc 165 W 57th St New York NY 10019

MCCRACKEN, JARRELL FRANKLIN, pub. co. exec.; b. Wartburg, Tenn., Nov. 18, 1927; s. Leonard Oren and Hazel Dean (Rowe) McC.; B.A., Baylor U., 1950, M.A., 1953; LL.D., John Brown U., 1969; m. Judith Murray, Aug. 21, 1953; children—Lisa McCracken Lacy, Timothy. Founder, Word, Inc., Waco, Tex., 1951, pres., 1951— (merged with ABC 1974); pres. Word Books, Word Music, Word Records; dir. Word Ednl. Products, Am. Bank of Waco, Eaton Internat.; owner Bentwood Farm. Chmn., Nat. Bible Week, 1971-72; chmn. civic affairs Waco Advancement Com., 1971-72; pres. Waco Symphony Assn., Baylor Stadium Com.; v.p. Youth For Christ Internat.; bd. dirs. So. Baptist Radio and TV Commn., YMCA, San Marcos Acad., Dag Hammarskjold Coll. Named Outstanding Young Man in Waco, 1961, One of Five Outstanding Young Men in Tex., 1961; Communications award Bapt. Gen. Conv. Tex., 1974. Mem. Record Industry Assn. Am. (pres. 1971-72), Waco C. of C. (dir.), Baylor U. Ex-Students Assn. (dir.). Baptist. Home: 4820 Hillcrest St Waco TX 76708 Office: 4800 W Waco Dr Waco TX 76710

MCCRACKEN, JOHN HARVEY, artist; b. Berkeley, Calif., Dec. 9, 1934; s. J.H. and Marjorie (Strain) McC.; B.F.A., Calif. Coll. Arts and Crafts, 1962, grad. student, 1963-65; m. Joan Stout, Jan. 21, 1961 (div. Apr. 1971); children—David Gordon, Patrick Daniel; m. 2d, Anne-Marie Baddour, Oct. 16, 1971 (div. 1974). Tchr., U. Calif. at Irvine and Los Angeles, 1965-68, Sch. Visual Arts, N.Y.C., 1968-69, Hunter Coll., N.Y.C., 1971-72, U. Nev., Las Vegas, 1972—; one-man shows include: Nicholas Wilder Gallery, Los Angeles, 1965, 67, 68, Robert Elkon Gallery, N.Y.C., 1966, 67, 68, Art Gallery Ont., Toronto, 1969, Ileana Sonnabend Gallery, Paris, 1969, Sonnabend Gallery, N.Y.C., 1970, Meghan Williams Gallery, Los Angeles, 1978, 80; group shows include: Primary Structures, Jewish Mus., N.Y.C., 1966, Am. Sculpture of the Sixties, Los Angeles County Mus. Art and Phila. Mus. Art, 1967, 5th Paris Biennale, 1967, 5th Guggenheim Internat. Exhbn., 1967, Art of the Real, Mus. Modern Art, also in Paris and London, 1969; represented in permanent collections: Whitney Mus., Guggenheim Mus., Los Angeles County Mus. Art, Pasadena (Calif.) Art Mus., Milw. Art Center, Mus. Modern Art, also pvt. collections. Recipient award Nat. Endowment for Arts, 1968. Served with USN, 1953-57. Address: care Meghan Williams Gallery 8225 1/2 Santa Monica Blvd Los Angeles CA 90046

MCCRACKEN, PAUL WINSTON, educator; b. Richland, Iowa, Dec. 29, 1915; s. Sumner and Mary (Coffin) McC.; student William Penn Coll., 1937; M.A., Harvard, 1942, Ph.D., 1948; m. Emily Ruth Siler, May 27, 1942; children—Linda Jo, Paula Jeanne. Faculty, Found. Sch., Berea Coll., Ky., 1937-40; economist Dept. Commerce, Washington, 1942-43; fin. economist, dir. research Fed. Res. Bank of Mpls., 1943-48; asso. prof. Sch. Bus. Adminstrn., U. Mich., 1948-50, prof., 1950-66, Edmund Ezra Day Univ. prof. bus. adminstrn., 1966—; mem. Council Econ. Advisers, Washington, 1956-59, chmn., 1969-71. Fellow Am. Statis. Assn.; mem. Am. Econ. Assn., Am. Finance Assn., Royal Econ. Soc. Presbyn. Clubs: Cosmos (Washington); Harvard (N.Y.C.). Author: (monographs) Hypothetical Projection of Commodity Expenditures; Northwest in Two Wars; Future of Northwest Bank Deposits; Rising Tide of Bank Lending; Balance of Payments and Domestic Prosperity; Economic Progress and the Utility Industry; Can Capitalism Survive?. Author articles on financial, econ. subjects. Home: 2564 Hawthorn Rd Ann Arbor MI 48104

MC CRACKEN, RALPH JOSEPH, agronomist; b. Guantanamo, Cuba, July 3, 1921; s. John Raymond and Ina (Ratliff) McC.; A.B., Earlham Coll., 1942; M.S., Cornell U., 1951; Ph.D., Iowa State U., 1956; m. Virginia Johnson, Aug. 27, 1949; children—Douglas Raymond, Jo Ellen. Soil scientist Bur. Plant Industry and Soils, Dept. Agr., 1947-54; asso. agronomist U. Tenn., Knoxville, 1954-56; asso. prof. N.C. State U., 1956-60, prof., 1960-63, head dept. soil sci., 1963-70, asst. dir. agr. research, 1970-73, asso. dir. agrl. research, 1973; asso. adminstr. Dept. Agr., Agrl. Research Service, Washington, 1973-78, asso. dir. Sci. and Edn. Adminstrn., 1978—. Fellow Am. Soc. Agronomy, Soil Sci. Soc. Am. (past pres.), Agrl. Research Inst. (past pres.). Club: Cosmos (Washington). Co-author: Soil Genesis and Classification. Office: US Dept Agr Sci and Edn Adminstrn Washington DC 20250

MCCRADY, JAMES DAVID, educator; b. Beaumont, Tex., June 26, 1930; s. James Homer and Lucyle (Ward) McC.; B.S., Tex. A. and M. Coll., 1952, D.V.M., 1958; Ph.D., Baylor U., 1965; m. Mary Elizabeth McDougald, Sept. 8, 1951; children—David, Diane, Darla. Instr., then asst. prof. Tex. A. and M. Coll., 1958- 62; dir. animal research, instr. Baylor U. Coll. Medicine, 1962-64; mem. faculty Tex. A. and M. Coll., 1964—, prof., head dept. vet. physiology and pharmacology, 1966—. Served with USAF, 1952-54. Mem. AVMA, Tex. Acad. Sci., Am. Physiol. Soc., Sigma Xi, Phi Kappa Phi, Phi Zeta. Research on comparative cardiovascular and respiratory physiology. Home: 511 Olive St Bryan TX 77801 Office: Tex A and M Univ College Station TX 77843

MCCRAKEN, ROBERT STANTON, newspaper and broadcasting exec.; b. Washington, June 1, 1924; s. Tracy Stephenson and Lillian G. (Davis) McC.; student Washington and Lee U., 1945, U. Denver, 1946; B.A., U. Wyo., 1948; m. A. Anne Wright, May 6, 1960; children—Michael, Cindy. Reporter, Rawlins (Wyo.) Daily Times, 1948-50; promotion mgr. Cheyenne (Wyo.) Newspapers, Inc., pubs. Wyo. Eagle, Wyo. State Tribune, Wyo. Tribune Eagle, 1950-54, asso. pub., 1955-58, pres., pub., 1958—; pres. Frontier Broadcasting Co., Cheyenne; chmn. bd. Laramie Newspapers, Inc., Rawlins Newspapers, Inc., Rock Springs Newspapers, Inc., Big Horn Basin Newspapers, Inc.; dir. Wyo. Broadcasting Co., Cheyenne Nat. Bank. Trustee U. Wyo., 1961-67. Served with AUS, World War II. Mem. Internat. Platform Assn., Cheyenne C. of C., Kappa Sigma. Presbyterian. Clubs: Elks, Kiwanis. Office: Wyo Eagle 110 E 17 St Cheyenne WY 82001*

MCCRAVEY, MARY ALVARETTA, business exec.; b. Blairsville, Ga., Jan. 3, 1921; d. Ernest Leroy and Elsie (Owensby) McCravey; A.B., U. Ga., 1948, J.D. summa cum laude, 1948. Admitted to Ga. bar, 1947; with Ga.-Pacific Corp., Portland, Oreg., 1948—, asst. sec., 1951-56, sec., 1956—; sec., dir. Ga.-Pacific Investment Co., Ga.-Pacific Bldg. Materials Ltd., Ga.-Pacific Internat. Corp., Ga.-Pacific Found. Mem. Am., Ga. bar assns., Am. Soc. Corp. Secs., Phi Beta Kappa, Phi Kappa Phi. Home: 1784 SW Montgomery Dr Portland OR 97201 Office: 900 SW 5th Ave Portland OR 97204

MC CRAW, JAMES EDWARD, mag. editor; b. Phila., Jan. 23, 1943; s. James Patrick and Elizabeth Caroline (Bird) McC.; B.S. in Journalism, Temple U., Phila., 1966; m. Joan Schwarz, Nov. 8, 1975. Asso. editor Product Design and Devel. mag., Chilton Co., Phila., 1966; editor Super Stock mag., Eastern Pub. Co., Alexandria, Va., 1967-73; competition editor, then editor Hot Rod mag., Petersen Pub. Co., Los Angeles, 1974-76, exec. editor, 1976-78; feature editor Motor Trend mag., 1978—. Recipient Media award Nat. Hot Rod Assn., 1971. Address: 8490 Sunset Blvd Los Angeles CA 90069

MCCRAY, BILLY QUINCY, state senator, real estate broker; b. Geary, Okla., Oct. 29, 1927; s. John Joel and Ivory Beatrice (Jessie) McC.; m. Wyvette M. Williams, Oct. 12, 1952; children—Frankie Leen Conley, Anthony, Melody McCray Miller, Kent. Mem. Kans. Ho. of Reps., Wichita, 1967-72, Kans. Senate, 1973—; real estate broker. Mem. Human Relations Comm., 1961-63; mem. Mayor's Adv. Com., 1964—. Served with USAF, 1947-51. Mem. African Methodist Episcopal Ch. Democrat. Mason. Home: 1532 N Ash St Wichita KS 67214 Office: Kans State Senate Topeka KS 66612

MCCREADY, ALBERT LEE, journalist; b. Portland, Oreg., Mar. 16, 1918; s. Edgar S. and Olive (Lembke) McC.; student pub. schs., Portland; m. Constance Averill, Dec. 31, 1945; children—Molly, Martha, Nancy. Mem. staff The Oregonian, Portland, 1939—, editorial writer, 1953—, asso. editor, 1955-71, asst. mng. editor, 1971-75, mng. editor, 1976—. Sec.- treas. Tri Club Islands, Inc., 1968—. Mem. Oreg. Fair Employment Practices Commn., 1949-50; mem. Adv. Com. on Oreg. Legislature, 1968; treas. Tri-County Met. Transp. Dist. Oreg., 1969—. Served with USNR, 1942-45. Mem. Portland C. of C. Club: Rose City Yacht (commodore 1963). Author: Railroads in the Days of Steam, 1959. Home: 2407 NE 27th Ave Portland OR 97212 Office: 1320 SW Broadway Portland OR 97201

MC CREADY, WARREN THOMAS, educator; b. N.Y.C., Feb. 8, 1915; s. Thomas Burns and Louise Harriet (Rudolph) Mc C.; M.A., U. Chgo., 1949, Ph.D., 1961. Instr., U. Ind., Gary, 1950-53; lectr. Queens U., Kingston, Ont., Can., 1954-56; lectr. U. Toronto (Ont.), 1956-60, asst. prof., 1960-64, asso. prof., 1964-69, prof., 1969—. Served with USAAF, 1940-45. Mem. Am. Assn. Tchrs. Spanish and Portuguese, Can. Assn. Hispanists, Asociacion Internacional de Hispanistas. Author: La heraldica en las obras de Lope de Vega y sus contemporaneos, 1962; Bibliografia tematica de estudios sobre el teatro antiguo espanol, 1966; Lope de Vega: El mejor mozo de Espana, 1967; editor Bull. Comediantes, 1967-72. Office: Dept Spanish and Portuguese U Toronto Toronto ON M5S 1A1 Canada

MCCREARY, JOHN FERGUSON, educator, physician; b. Eganville, Ont., Can., Jan. 22, 1910; s. James and Anne (Ferguson) McC.; M.D., U. Toronto, 1934; D.Sc., Meml. U., Nfld., 1968; LL.D., U. Toronto, 1970; D.Sc., U. B.C., 1975; m. Dorothy Dowling, Mar. 23, 1970; 1 son, by previous marriage, James Richard. Milbank research fellow Harvard Med. Sch. and Boston Children's Hosp., 1939-41; practice pediatrics, Toronto, 1945-51; attending physician Hosp. for Sick Children, 1945-51, cons. physician, 1951; cons. newborn nurseries Wellesley Hosp., Toronto, 1946-51, newborn nurseries Grace Hosp., Toronto, 1947-51; cons. nutrition Def. Research Bd., 1949—, Armed Forces Med. Council, 1956; asst. prof. U. Toronto, 1949-51; prof., head dept. pediatrics U. B.C., 1951-59, dean faculty medicine, 1959-72, coordinator health scis., 1971-75; pediatrician-in-chief health centre for children, Vancouver Gen. Hosp., 1951-59; cons. pediatrician Children's Hosp., Vancouver, 1952-75, St. Paul's Hosp., Vancouver, 1952-75. Mem. Canadian Council Nutrition, 1955-59; chmn. adv. com. Canadian Conf. Children, 1960-66; mem. med. team sponsored by Colombo plan studying med. ednl. methods in India, 1957; chmn. Queen Elizabeth II Fund for Research Diseases Children, 1960-74; med. adv. bd. Canadian Physiotherapy Assn., 1960—; chmn. med. div. Royal Commn. Govt., 1961-62; pres. Assn. Canadian Med. Colls., 1963-66; pres. St. John Council B.C., 1971-76; adv. fellow World Fedn. Occupational Therapists, 1972; chmn. edn. com. B.C. Med. Centre, 1973-75. Bd. dirs. B.C. Med. Research Found., Leon and Thea Koerner Found., Hamber Found., Inst. for Research on Pub. Policy, Mr. & Mrs. P.A. Woodward's Found. Served to wing comdr. Royal Canadian Air Force, 1942-45; capt. Res. Decorated officer Order Orange-Nassau (Netherlands); Order Can.; knight St. John Jerusalem. Diplomate Am. Bd. Pediatrics. Fellow Royal Coll. Physicians and Surgeons (certified pediatrics; Duncan Graham award 1977), Am. Coll. Hosp. Administrs. (hon.); mem. Canadian (chmn. com. nutrition 1954-59), B.C. med. assns., Am. Acad. Pediatrics, Am., Canadian (Ross award 1977), N. Pacific pediatrics socs., Western Soc. Pediatric Research, Canadian Dietetic Assn. (life), Alpha Omega Alpha. Home: PO Box 1021 1223 Shoal Lookout Gibsons BC V0N 1V0 Canada

MC CREARY, ROBERT G., JR., lawyer; b. Cleve., Apr. 30, 1918; s. Robert G. and Helen (Galvin) McC.; A.B., Amherst Coll., 1940; LL.B., Case Western Res. U., 1947; m. Eileen McNamee, Nov. 11, 1950; children—Robert G. III, Charles J., James B., Elizabeth. Admitted to Ohio bar, 1947, since practiced in Cleve.; partner firm Arter & Hadden, 1958—; instr. admiralty law Case Western Res. U., 1965-66, 76—. Served to lt. USNR, 1942-46. Mem. Am. Bar Assn. (chmn. com. maritime law 1968-73), Maritime Law Assn. (mem. exec. com. 1975-78), Ohio State Bar Assn., Bar Assn. Greater Cleve. (pres. 1974), Am. Coll. Trial Lawyers, Propeller Club U.S., Order of Coif, Psi Upsilon, Phi Delta Phi. Contbr. profl. jours. Home: 23300 Stanford Rd Shaker Heights OH 44122 Office: Union Commerce Bldg Cleveland OH 44115

MCCREE, WADE HAMPTON, JR., govt. ofcl.; b. Des Moines, July 3, 1920; s. Wade Hampton and Lulu H. (Harper) McC.; A.B., Fisk U., 1941; LL.B., Harvard, 1944; LL.D., Wayne State U., 1964, Tuskegee Inst., 1965, Detroit Coll. Law, 1967, U. Detroit, 1968, Harvard, 1969, Mich. State U., 1971, U. Mich., 1971, Oakland U., 1974, Lewis & Clark/Northwestern U., 1976, Howard U., 1977, Atlanta U., 1977, Boston U., 1977; Litt.D., Centre Coll., Danville, Ky.; m. Dores B. McCrary, July 29, 1946; children—Kathleen L. (Mrs. David B. Lewis), Karen L., Wade H. Admitted to Mich. bar, 1948; practice in Detroit, 1948-52; commr. Mich. Workmen's Compensation, 1952-54; circuit judge Wayne County, 1954-61; U.S. dist. judge Eastern Dist. Mich., 1961-66; U.S. circuit judge 6th Circuit, 1966-77; solicitor gen. U.S., 1977—. Mem. law faculty Salzburg Seminar Am. Studies, 1969; former mem. vis. com. Wayne State U. Law Sch., Harvard Law Sch. Vice pres. United Found. Detroit; exec. bd. Detroit Area council Boy Scouts Am.; mem. nat. council advisers U. Mid-Am.; vice chmn. bd. trustees Fisk U., Nashville; past bd. dirs. Met. Hosp., Henry Ford Hosp., Founders Soc., Detroit Inst. Arts. Served to capt., inf., AUS, 1942-46; ETO. Fellow Am. Bar Found.; mem. Am. (adv. bd. editors jour., mem. commn. on standards jud. adminstrn.), Nat., Detroit bar assns., State Bar Mich., Inst. Jud. Adminstrn., Am. Law Inst. (council), Seminar Soc. (Detroit), Phi Beta Kappa Assos. Unitarian-Universalist. Club: University (Cin.). Home: 340 N St SW Washington DC 20024 Office: Dept Justice Constitution Ave and 10th St NW Washington DC 20530

MCCREEDY, JOHN, metals co. exec.; b. Winnipeg, Man., Can., Mar. 23, 1917; s. William McNeilly and Mary Black (McInnes) McC.; B.Applied Sci., U. Toronto, 1949; m. Ila Elizabeth Maxwell, Apr. 29, 1942; 1 dau., Bonnie Franklyn. With Inco Ltd., 1949—, pres. Ont. div., 1970, sr. v.p., then chmn., chief exec. officer Inco Metals Co., 1977, vice chmn. Inco Ltd., Toronto, 1979—, also dir.; dir. St. Lawrence Cement Ltd., Bramalea Ltd.; bd. dirs. Centre Resource Studies, Queens U. Served with RCAF, 1942-45. Mem. Mining Assn. Can. (pres. 1979), Assn. Profl. Engrs. Ont., Can. Inst. Mining and Metallurgy, AIME. Mem. United Ch. Can. Clubs: Toronto, Toronto Golf, Copper Cliff. Office: 1 First Canadian Pl Toronto ON M5X 1C4 Canada

MCCREIGHT, ROBERT BAKER, stockyards exec.; b. Wichita, Kans., Apr. 4, 1910; s. Robert Raymond and Mae (Baker) McC.; LL.B., U. Mo. at Kansas City, 1932; m. Gevene Shirk, Dec. 29, 1934. Admitted to Mo. bar, 1932; partner firm Borders, Wimmell & McCreight, Kansas City, Mo., 1934-42, Wimmell & McCreight, 1946-47; v.p., sec., dir. Kansas City Stock Yards Co., 1947-52; v.p., dir. St. Paul Union Stockyards Co., 1953-60, pres., dir. 1961-67; v.p., dir. Union Stockyards Co., Fargo, N.D., 1960-67, United Stockyards Corp., Chgo., 1967-68; pres., dir. Union Stock Yards Co., Omaha, 1968-75, S. Omaha Terminal Ry. Co., 1968-72; pres., dir. Am. Stockyards Assn., 1975—; dir. Nat. Live Stock and Meat Bd., 1975—, Omaha Livestock Market, 1976—. Served with USAAF, 1942-46. Mem. Am. Judicature Soc. Rotarian. Home: 1545 S 79th St Omaha NE 68124 Office: Livestock Exchange Bldg Omaha NE 68107

MCCRENSKY, EDWARD, UN ofcl., educator; b. Boston, June 19, 1912; s. Benjamin and Anna (Miller) McC.; B.A., Boston Coll., 1933; M.Ed., Boston Tchrs. Coll., 1935; student Harvard Grad. Sch. Edn., 1940-41; m. Louise C. Marshall, Apr. 16, 1942; children—Myron Wilson, Richard Marshall. High sch. tchr., Boston, 1936-41; govt. ofcl. U.S. Civil Service Commn., 1941-46; dir. civilian personnel and service Office Naval Research, Washington 1946-66; chief personnel adminstrn. dept. social and econ. affairs UN, N.Y.C., 1966—, inter-regional adviser, 1968-77, team leader, Bangkok, Thailand, 1978—; prof. George Washington U., 1950-68; guest prof. Royal Coll. Sci. and Tech., Srathclyde U. Glasgow, Scotland, 1961; cons. U.S. and internat. orgns.; lectr. human relations and internat. sci. manpower. Recipient Rockefeller Pub. Service award and fellowship, 1957; Merit citation Nat. Civil Service League, 1955; Distinguished Civilian Service award Navy Dept., 1966. Mem. Soc. Personnel Adminstrn. (pres. 1955-56). Author: Wartime Practices in Recruitment, 1946; Scientific Manpower in Europe, 1959; Strategy and Tactics, Professional Recruitment, 1963. Contbr. articles U.S. fgn. jours. Home: 548 Ploenchit Rd Bangkok Thailand

MC CRIE, ROBERT DELBERT, editor, pub.; b. Sarnia, Ont., Can., Oct. 8, 1938; s. Robert Newton and Evelyn May (Johnston) McC.; B.A., Ohio Wesleyan U., 1960; M.S., U. Toledo, 1962; postgrad. U. Chgo., 1962-63; m. Fulvia Madia, Dec. 22, 1965; children—Carla Alexander, Mara Elizabeth. Researcher, Connective Tissues Research Lab., Copenhagen, Denmark, 1963; copywriter numerous advt. agys., 1965-70; pres., editor Security Letter, Inc., N.Y.C., 1970—; editor, pub. HBJ Publs., N.Y.C., 1973-76; pres. Mags. for Medicine, Inc., N.Y.C., 1972—; dir. Research Media, Inc.; cons. in field. Mem. Newsletter Publs. Am., Assn. Behavioral Scis. and Med. Edn. Presbyterian. Clubs: Union League (N.Y.C.); Point O'Woods. Editor: Behavioral Medicine, 1978—. Home: 49 E 96th St New York NY 10028 Office: 475 Fifth Ave New York NY 10017

MCCRIMMON, JAMES MCNAB, educator; b. Renton, Scotland, June 16, 1908; s. John and Margaret (Patterson) McC.; B.A., Northwestern U., 1932, M.A., 1933, Ph.D., 1937; m. Barbara Smith, June 10, 1939; children—Kevin M., John M. Came to U.S., 1929, naturalized, 1939. Asst. instr. English, Northwestern U., 1935; instr. English, U. Toledo, 1936-38, asst. prof., 1938-43, asso. prof., 1943-47; faculty U. Ill., 1947—, chmn. humanities div. Galesburg extension, 1947-49, asso. prof. humanities, Urbana, 1949-55, prof., 1955-65, prof. emeritus, 1965—, head div. gen. studies, 1954-62, dir. U. High Sch. English project, 1962—; vis. prof. English, Fla. State U., 1967-70, lectr., 1970-78. Mem. Nat. Council Tchrs. English, College Conf. Composition and Communication, Phi Kappa Phi. Author: Bibliography of the Writings of John Stuart Mill (with MacMinn and Hainds), 1945; Writing with a Purpose, 1950; Open Door to Education (with Loutitt and Habberton), 1951; From Source to Statement, 1968. Home: 1330 W Indian Head Dr Tallahassee FL 32301

MCCROHON, MAXWELL, newspaper editor; b. Sydney, Australia, June 19, 1928; s. Arthur and Lucy Arcadia (Sparkes) McC.; grad. high sch., Australia; m. Nancy Wilson, Dec. 17, 1955; children—Sean, Craig, Regan. Reporter, Sydney Morning Herald, 1950-52, N.Y. corr., 1952-55; reporter/feature writer Sun-Herald, Sydney, 1955-60; with Chgo. Am., 1960-68, mag. editor Sunday edit., until 1968; mng. editor Chgo. Today, 1969-72; mng. editor Chgo. Tribune, 1972-79, editor, 1979—. Mem. Am. Soc. Newspaper Editors, Chgo. Council Fgn. Relations, Internat. Press Inst., Chgo. Press Club, Sigma Delta Chi. Clubs: Arts, Chgo., Tavern (Chgo.). Home: Box 1053 Route 3 Crete IL 60417 Office: 435 N Michigan Ave Chicago IL 60611

MC CRON, RAYMOND CHARLES, ins. co. exec.; b. Flushing, N.Y., Feb. 26, 1921; s. James R. and Pauline (Meyer) McC.; B.S. in Econs., Wharton Sch., U. Pa., 1943; m. Corinne H. Mathews, June 30, 1946; children—Linda Catharine, James Robert II, John Howard, Trudy Jane. Asst. sec.-asst. treas. D. & R.G.W. R.R. Co., 1952-56; asst. to v.p. finance N.Y.C. R.R., 1956-61, treas., 1961-68, also treas. subsidiary cos.; treas. Penn Central, 1968-69; financial cons., 1969-70; v.p. Equitable Life Assurance Soc., 1971-73, v.p., treas., 1973-78, sr. v.p., treas., 1978—. Served with AUS, 1943-46, 50-52. Mem. SIgma Phi Epsilon (bd. dirs. 1957-70, chmn. chpt. investment fund 1959—, chmn. bd. trustees 1961—). Mason. Club: Larchmont (N.Y.) Yacht. Home: 8 Ferncliff Rd Scarsdale NY 10583 Office: 1285 Ave of Americas New York NY 10019

MCCRONE, ALISTAIR WILLIAM, univ. pres.; b. Regina, Sask., Can., Oct. 7, 1931; s. Hugh McMillan and Kathleen Maude Tallent (Forth) McC.; came to U.S., 1953, naturalized, 1963; B.A., U. Sask., 1953; M.S. (Shell fellow), U. Nebr., 1955; Ph.D., U. Kans., 1961; m. Judith Ann Saari, May 8, 1958; children—Bruce, Craig, Mary. Instr. geology N.Y. U., 1959-61, asst. prof., 1961-64, asso. prof., 1964-69, prof., 1969-70, chmn. dept. geology, 1966-69, asso. dean Grad. Sch. Arts and Scis., 1969-70; acad. v.p. U. of Pacific, Stockton, Calif., 1970-74, prof. geology, 1970-74; pres., prof. geology Humboldt State U., Arcata, Calif., 1974—. Lectr. geology CBS-TV network, 1969-70; editorial cons. sci. series Harcourt-Brace-Jovanovich pub., 1971, 73, 77; mem. com. on environment Am. Assn. State Colls. and Univs., 1974—. Trustee, Pacific Med. Center, San Francisco, 1971-74, Am. Fijian Found., 1973—; mem. Calif. Council for Humanities in Public Policy. Recipient Erasmus Haworth Honors award U. Kans., 1957; named Danforth Assos. convenor N.Y. U., 1966-68, Outstanding Educator of Am., 1975. Fellow Geol. Soc. Am., AAAS, Calif. Acad. Sci.; mem. Am. Assn. Petroleum Geologists, N.Y. Acad. Scis., Soc. Econ. Paleontologists and Mineralogists, St. Andrews Soc. of N.Y., Sigma Xi. Rotarian. Club: Commonwealth of Calif. Contbr. articles to profl. jours. Home: 15 Robert Ct W Arcata CA 95521

MCCRONE, HAROLD WARFIELD, JR., diversified co. exec., lawyer; b. Balt., Aug. 9, 1937; s. Harold Warfield and Annetta (McGowan) McC.; B.A., Cornell U., 1959; LL.B., Yale U., 1963; m. Barbara Roome, June 24, 1961; children—Charles Roy, Amanda Jane. Admitted to Pa. bar, 1964; asso. firm Drinker Biddle & Reath, Phila., 1963-69; sec., counsel Drexel Firestone Inc., Phila., 1969-73, v.p., 1969-73, also dir.; sec., corp. counsel Alco Standard Corp., Valley Forge, Pa., 1973—. Served as capt. USAR, 1959-60. Mem. Am., Pa. bar assns., Am. Soc. Corporate Secs. Baptist. Home: 1428 Bobolink Ln West Chester PA 19380 Office: PO Box 834 Valley Forge PA 19482

MC CRONE, WALTER COX, research co. exec.; b. Wilmington, Del., June 9, 1916; s. Walter Cox and Bessie Lillian (Cook) McC.; B.Chemistry, Cornell U., 1938, Ph.D., 1942; m. Lucy Morris Beman, July 13, 1957. Microscopist, sr. scientist Armour Research Found., Ill. Inst. Tech., Chgo., 1944-56; chmn. bd., sr. research adviser Walter C. McCrone Assos. Inc., Chgo., 1956-78; pres. McCrone Research Inst., Inc., 1961—; editor, pub. Microscope Publs. Ltd., London, 1962—; dir. McCrone Research Assos. Ltd., London. Chmn. bd. trustees Ada S. McKinley Community Services, Inc. Recipient Benedetti-Pichler award, 1970, Ernst Abbe award, 1977. Mem. Am. Chem. Soc., Am. Phys. Soc., Am. Acad. Forensic Sci., Am. Crystallographic Soc., ASTM, Air Pollution Control Assn., Australian, N.Y., La., Midwest, Royal, Ill. micros. socs., Sigma Xi, Phi Kappa Phi, Phi Lambda Upsilon. Club: Quekett. Author: Fusion Methods in Chemical Microscopy, 1957; The Particle Atlas, 1967; Particle Atlas Two, 6 vols., 1973-78; Polarized Light Microscopy, 1978; contbr. tech. articles, chpts. in books. Home: 501 E 32d St Chicago IL 60616 Office: 2508 S Michigan Ave Chicago IL 60616

MC CRORY, THOMAS MILTON, ophthalmologist; b. Dalhart, Tex., Oct. 9, 1919; s. Lon C. and Ethel (Carlton) McC.; M.D., Baylor U., 1943; student Southwestern Med. Sch., Dallas., 1943-44; m. Mauryne Jarrett, July 25, 1944; children—Thomas Milton 3d, Marsha Ann. Intern, Robert B. Greene Hosp., San Antonio, 1944; pvt. gen. practice, Dallas, 1946-48; postgrad. opthalmology Washington U. Sch. Medicine, St. Louis, 1949-50; resident ophthalmology Dallas VA Hosp., 1950-52; chief ophthal. service Baylor Med. Center, 1965-74; dir. service Children's Med. Center, 1963-74. Served to capt. M.C., AUS, 1945-46. Mem. AMA, Tex. Med. Assn., Dallas County Med. Soc., Am., Dallas acads. ophthalmologists, Tex. Soc. Ophthalmologists and Otolaryngologists, Pan Am. Assn. Ophthalmologists, Am. Assn. Ophthalmology. Home: 3544 Centenary Dallas TX 75225 Office: 2811 Lemmon A Dallas TX 75204

MCCRORY, WALLACE WILLARD, educator, pediatrician; b. Racine, Wis., Jan. 19, 1920; s. Willard L. and Beulah (St. Clair) McC.; B.S., U. Wis., 1941, M.D., 1944; m. Sylvia E. Hogben, Feb. 6, 1943; children—Pamela, Michael, Christine. Rotating intern Phila. Gen. Hosp., 1944-45; resident pediatrics Children's Hosp., Phila., 1945-46, chief resident physician, 1948-49, asso. pediatrician, 1953-55, sr. pediatrician, 1955-58; provisional asst. pediatrician to out-patients, Lewis Cass Ledyard, Jr. fellow pediatrics, N.Y. Hosp., 1949-50, pediatrician-in-chief, 1961—; chief pediatric service Univ. Hosp., Iowa City, 1958-61; instr. pathology U. Wis. Med. Sch., 1942-43; instr. pediatrics U. Pa. Sch. Medicine, 1948-49, instr., research fellow pediatrics, 1950-53, asst. prof., 1953-55, asso. prof., 1955-58; prof. pediatrics, chmn. dept. State U. Ia. Coll. Medicine, 1958-61, Cornell U. Med. Coll., 1961—. Pres. Nat. Kidney Found., 1964-66. Served to capt., M.C., AUS, 1946-48. Diplomate Am. Bd. Pediatrics. Fellow N.Y. Acad. Medicine, Royal Soc. Medicine; mem. Am. Pediatric Soc., Am. Acad. Pediatrics, Soc. Pediatric Research, Am. Soc. Nephrology, Am. Soc. Pediatric Nephrology, AAAS, Sigma Xi, Alpha Omega Alpha. Home: Route 4 Salem Rd Pound Ridge NY 10576 Office: NY Hospital Cornell Medical Center 525 E 68th St New York City NY 10021

MC CROSKEY, WILLIAM JAMES, aero. engr.; b. San Angelo, Tex., Mar. 9, 1937; s. J. M. and W. Elizabeth (Adams) McC.; B.S., U. Tex., 1960; M.S., Princeton U., 1962, Ph.D., 1966; m. Elizabeth W. Wear, Jan. 31, 1960; children—Nancy E., Susan C. Research asso. Princeton U., 1966; research engr. U.S. Army Aeromechanics Lab., Moffett Field, Calif., 1966—; exchange scientist l'Office Nat. d'Etudes et de Recherches Aérospatiale, Châtillon, France, 1972-73; mem. fluid dynamics panel NATO Adv. Group for Aerospace Research and Devel. Served with U.S. Army, 1966-68. Mem. AIAA (Outstanding Engr. San Francisco sect. 1975), Am. Helicopter Soc., ASME (Freeman Scholar award 1976). Office: Ames Research Center Moffett Field CA 94035

MC CROSSAN, JOHN ANTHONY, librarian; b. Duluth, Minn., Dec. 20, 1930; s. Charles Stewart and Mae Kathryn (Blakeley) McC.; B.A., U. Minn., M.A., 1960; Ph.D., U. Ill., 1966. Dir Eau Claire (Wis.) Pub. Library, 1960-63; research asso. U. Ill., 1963-66; prof. U. Mich., 1967-70; library devel. supr. Pa. State Library, 1970-73; state librarian Vt., Vt. Dept. Libraries, Montpelier, 1973-77; prof. dept. library sci. U. South Fla., Tampa, 1977—, chmn. dept., 1977—; cons. in field. Mem. Am. (pres. adult services div. and mem. council 1971-72), Vt. library assns., Vt. Hist. Soc. (dir.), Phi Beta Kappa. Contbr. articles to profl. jours. Home: 5309 Nancy St Tampa FL 33617 Office: Dept Library Sci Univ South Fla Tampa FL 33620

MCCRUMM, JOHN DOENCH, educator; b. Colorado Springs, Colo., Apr. 17, 1912; s. John T. and Della (Doench) McC.; B.S., U. Colo., 1933, M.S., 1934; grad. fellow, Princeton, 1950-51; grad. student part-time Mass. Inst. Tech., 1939, U. Pa., 1938-42; m. Kate F. Walker, June 25, 1938 (div. Oct. 1968); children—Martha K., Thomas A.; m. 2d, Erasmia Tsonides, July 22, 1969. Test engr. Gen. Electric Co., 1934-35; research engr. Douglas Aircraft Co., 1944-46; mem. faculty Swarthmore Coll., 1935-78, prof. engring., 1951-78, chmn. div. engring., 1951-59, Howard and Ada Eavenson prof., 1959-78, chmn. elec. engring. curriculum, 1967-78; ret., 1978; vis. prof. Stanford, 1973; asst. to v.p. research and engring. Burroughs Corp., Detroit, 1957-58, cons. to v.p., 1956-59; cons. research div. U. Pa., 1946-50, Franklin Inst., 1949- 56, Booz, Allen & Hamilton, 1956-58, Gen. Electric Co., 1960—, Scott Paper Co., 1960-65. NSF fellow Athens (Greece) Technol. Inst., 1965-66. Chmn., Tri-County Health and Welfare Council on Fluoridation, 1954-57; mem. sci. and arts award com. Franklin Inst. Mem. IEEE, Am. Soc. Engring. Edn., AAUP, Franklin Inst., Sigma Xi, Sigma Tau, Phi Kappa Psi. Author tech. articles. Patentee in field. Office: Swarthmore College Swarthmore PA 19081

MCCUBBIN, MELVIN A., corp. financial exec., lawyer; b. Louisville, Aug. 22, 1924; s. William Milton and Emma Lee (Shelton) McC.; B.S., U. Md., 1952; LL.B., U. Balt., 1961; m. Margaret Louise Thomas, June 24, 1950; children—Linda Marie, Melvin Albert, Patrick Allen, James Thomas, Thomas David. Admitted to Md. bar, U.S. Supreme Ct. bar; chief accountant Rheem Mfg. Co., Balt., 1951-56; practice law, Balt., 1956-58; controller nuclear div. Martin Marietta Corp., Balt., 1958-64, controller Denver div., 1964-69, treas., controller aerospace group, 1969-74, corp. v.p., controller, Bethesda, Md., 1974—. Served with USNR, 1942-46. Mem. Financial Execs. Inst., Nat. Assn. Accountants, Sigma Delta Kappa. Republican. Roman Catholic. Club: Ulmstead of Anne Arundel County (Md.). Home: 1000 Placid Dr Arnold MD 21012 Office: 6801 Rock Ledge Dr Bethesda MD 20034

MCCUE, CAROLYN MOORE, pediatric cardiologist; b. Richmond, Va., June 26, 1916; d. Thomas Justin and Caroline (Willingham) Moore; student Wellesley Coll., 1933-35; A.B., Leland Stanford U., 1937; M.D., Med. Coll. Va., 1941; m. Howard M. McCue, Jr., Apr. 5, 1941; children—Carolyn McCue Osteen, Howard McDowell. Intern, Wis. Gen. Hosp., Madison, 1941-42; resident in pediatrics Children's Hosp., Phila., 1942-43, Med. Coll. Va., 1946-47; dir. pediatric cardiology Med. Coll. Va., Richmond, 1947—, prof. pediatrics, 1963—; clin. dir. pediatric cardiology clinics State of Va., 1958—. Fellow Am. Acad. Pediatrics, Am. Coll. Cardiology, A.C.P.; mem. Richmond Acad. Medicine (pres. 1975), Richmond Area Heart Assn. (pres. 1959-60), Phi Beta Kappa, Alpha Omega Alpha. Country of Richmond. Contbr. articles to profl. jours. Home: 12 Huntly Rd Richmond VA 23226 Office: Box 272 Medical College of Virginia Richmond VA 23298

MCCUE, GERALD MALLON, architect, educator; b. Woodland, Calif., Dec. 5, 1928; s. Floyd F. and Lenore (Mallon) McC.; A.B., U. Calif. at Berkeley, 1951, M.A., 1952; M.A. (hon.), Harvard, 1977; m. Barbara Walrond, Sept. 1, 1951; children—Scott, Mark, Kent. Partner archtl. firm Milano-McCue, Berkeley, 1953-59; pres. architect firm Gerald M. McCue & Assos., Berkeley, 1963-70; pres. McCue, Boone, Tomsick, San Francisco, 1970-76; prin. MBT Assos., San Francisco, 1976—; mem. faculty U. Calif. at Berkeley, 1954-76, prof. architecture and urban design, 1966-76, chmn. dept., 1966-71; prof. architecture and urban design, chmn. dept., asso. dean. Grad. Sch. Design, Harvard U., 1976—; planning and design commns. executed for variety pub. and pvt. clients with over 30 nat., regional and local design awards. Fellow A.I.A. (active mem., chmn. nat. commns.). Co-author: Creating the Human Environment, 1970; Interaction of Building Components During Earthquakes, 1975; Architectural Design of Building Components for Earthquakes, 1978; Building Response and Component Designs: An Enclosure Wall Study, 1978; author: IBM's Santa Teresa Lab-Architectural Design for Program Development, 1978. Office: Gund Hall Harvard U Cambridge MA 02138

MC CUISTION, ROBERT WILEY, hosp. adminstr.; b. Wilson, Ark., June 15, 1927; s. Ed Talmadge and Ruth Wiley (Bassett) McC.; A.B. in History and Polit. Sci., Hendrix Coll., Conway, Ark., 1949; J.D., U. Ark., 1952; m. Martha Virginia Golden, June 11, 1949; children—Beth, Dan, Jed. Admitted to Ark. bar, 1952; practice in Dermott, 1952-57; dep. pros. atty. 10th Jud. Dist. Ark., 1953-57; bus. mgr. St. Mary's Hosp., Dermott, 1953-56, asst. adminstr., 1956-57; adminstr. Stuttgart (Ark.) Meml. Hosp., 1957-60, Forrest Meml. Hosp., Forrest City, Ark., 1960-68; asso. adminstr. St. Edward Mercy Hosp., Ft. Smith, Ark., 1968-70; pres. Meml. Med Center, Corpus Christi, Tex., 1970-79; adminstr. Methodist Hosp., Mitchell, S.D., 1979—; sec. Ark. Hosp. Adminstrs. Forum, 1958-59, pres., 1959-60; pres. Ark. Hosp. Assn., 1964-65; pres. Ark. Conf. Catholic Hosps., 1970; v.p. Ark. Assn. Mental Health, 1969-70; pres. Areawide Health Planning, 1970, Twin City Hosp. Council, 1968. Div. chmn. Forrest City United Community Services, 1971, Corpus Christi United Way Community Services, 1972; Dermott council Boy Scouts Am., Explorer adviser 1954-57. Served with USAAF, World War II. Recipient Emminent Leadership award DeSoto council Boy Scouts Am., 1956. Mem. Am. Assn. Hosp. Accountants (pres. Ark. chpt. 1957). Mid-West Hosp. Assn. (trustee 1963-65). Am. Coll. Hosp. Adminstrs. Methodist (vice chmn., sec. ofcl. bd. 1957). Club: Rotary (pres. Forrest City 1964-65). Home: Methodist Hosp 909 S Miller St Mitchell SD 57301

MC CULLEN, JOSEPH THOMAS, JR., mgmt. cons.; b. Phila., Mar. 15, 1935; s. Joseph Thomas and Sara Ellen (Berryman) McC.; B.A., Villanova U., 1957, D.Pub.Adminstrn. (hon.), 1976; postgrad. Johns Hopkins, 1960; m. Eleanor Joan Houder, July 5, 1958; children—Geoffrey, Jennifer, Justin Douglas. Mgr. coll. relations Merck & Co., 1961-62, mgr. planning and acquisitions analysis, 1962-64; sr. v.p., partner Spencer Stuart & Assos., mgmt. cons., N.Y.C., 1965-71; exec. dir. Pres.'s Commn. on Personnel Interchange, Washington, 1971-72; dep. spl. asst. to Pres., 1972-73; asst. sec. Navy for manpower and res. affairs, 1973-77; sr. v.p., sec. New Eng. Mut. Life Ins. Co., 1977-79; partner Canny, Bowen, Inc., mgmt. cons., N.Y.C. and Boston, 1979—. Bd. dirs. Boston Ballet Co., also mem. exec. com.; bd. dirs. Sea Scouts, Nat. Center for Career Life Planning, Crotched Mountain Rehab. Center for Handicapped. Served with USNR, 1953, AUS, 1958-61. Recipient Army Commendation medal, 1961; Disting. Public Service award Navy Dept., 1977; award for contbn. to edn. Ohio State U.; award NOW, 1976; Distinguished Pub. Service award Dept. Def., 1977. Named adm. Tex. Navy. Mem. N.J. Jaycees (v.p., dir.), Navy League. Clubs: Kenwood Country, Capital Hill; Algonquin. Home: 97 Essex Rd Chestnut Hill MA 02167 Office: 425 Park Ave New York NY 10022 also 60 State St Boston MA 02109

MC CULLOCH, ERNEST ARMSTRONG, physician, educator; b. Toronto, Ont., Can., Apr. 27, 1926; s. Albert E. and Letitia (Riddell) McC.; M.D. with honors, U. Toronto, 1948; m. Ona Mary Morganty, 1953; children—James A., Michael E., Robert E., Cecelia E., Paul A. Intern, Toronto Gen. Hosp., 1949-50, sr. intern, 1951-52; Nat. Research Council fellow dept. pathology U. Toronto, 1950-51; asst. resident Sunnybrook Hosp., Toronto, 1952-53; practice medicine specializing in internal medicine, Toronto, 1954-67; clin. tchr. dept. medicine U. Toronto, 1954-60, asst. prof. dept. med. biophysics, 1959-64, asso. prof., 1964-66, prof., 1966, asst. prof. dept. medicine, 1967-68, asso. prof., 1968-70, prof., 1970—, mem. grad. faculty Inst. Med. Sci., 1968—, dir. inst., 1975-79, asst. dean Sch. Grad. Studies, 1979—; physician Toronto Gen. Hosp., 1960-67; cons. Nat. Cancer Plan, 1972—; mem. standing com. on health research and devel. Ont. Council Health, 1974—. Trustee Banting Research Found., 1975—, hon. sec. treas., 1958 74, v.p., 1977 . Recipient William Goldie prize U. Toronto, 1964, Ann. Gairdner award Internat. Gairdner Found., 1969, Starr Medallist award Dept. Anatomy U. Toronto, 1957; Nat. Cancer Inst. Can. fellow, 1954-57. Fellow Royal Soc. Can., Royal Coll. Physicians and Surgeons Can.; mem. Can. Acad. Sci., Am. Soc. Exptl. Pathology, Am. Assn. Cancer Research, Canadian Soc. Cell Biology, Canadian Soc. Clin. Investigation, Am., Internat. socs. hematology, Internat. Soc. Exptl. Hematology. Clubs: Badminton, Racquet. Author numerous articles on research in hematology; editorial bd. Blood, 1969, Biomedicine, 1973, Clin. Immunology and Immunopathology, 1972-76; asso. editor Jour. Cellular Physiology, 1966-68, editor, 1968—. Home: 480 Summerhill Ave Toronto ON M4W 2EX Canada Office: U Toronto Sch Grad Studies 65 Saint George St Toronto ON Canada. *Research success depends on associating with agreeable and talented people.*

MCCULLOCH, FRANK W., lawyer, educator, arbitrator; b. Evanston, Ill., Sept. 30, 1905; s. Frank H. and Catharine (Waugh) McC.; A.B., Williams Coll., 1926; LL.B., Harvard Law Sch., 1929; LL.D., Olivet Coll., 1945, Chgo. Theol. Sem., 1961, Williams Coll., 1971; m. Edith F. Leverton, 1937; children—William Holt, Frank H. Admitted Ill. bar, practiced Chgo., 1930-35; asst. to Sen. Paul Douglas, 1949-61; chmn. NLRB, 1961-70; vis. prof. law U. N.C., 1971; prof. law U. Va., Charlottesville, 1971-76; also mem. Center Advanced Studies, 1971-74, scholar in residence, 1976—; vis. prof. N.Y. State Sch. Indsl. and Labor Relations, Cornell U., 1976; cons. Task Force on Labor Relations, Pres.'s Reorgn. Project, 1977. Indsl. relations sec. Council Social Action, Congregational-Christian Ch., 1935-46; mem. panel Regional War Labor Bd., World War II; dir. labor edn. div. Roosevelt U., Chgo., 1946-49. Mem. Adminstrv. Conf. U.S., 1968-70, adv. com. on fed. hearing examiners Civil Service Commn., 1962-70, Am. team Anglo-Am. adminstrv. Law Exchange, 1969; mem. roster arbitrators Fed. Mediation and Conciliation Service, 1970—, pub. rev. bd. UAW, 1971—, Com. on Pub. Employee Rights (Va.), 1972-76, Ill. Employee Labor Relations Council, 1973—; mem. com. experts on application of convs. and recommendations ILO, Geneva, Switzerland, 1974—; bd. dirs. Migrant Legal Action Program, Washington, 1973—. Mem. Am., Fed., Ill., Chgo. bar assns., Am. Arbitration Assn. (panel arbitrators), Phi Beta Kappa. Author: (with Tim Bornstein) The National Labor Relations Board, 1974. Contbr. articles to legal jours. Home: 104 Falcon Dr Charlottesville VA 22901

MCCULLOCH, FRANK WALTER, fgn. corr., editor; b. Fernley, Nev., Jan. 26, 1920; s. Frank Walter and Frieda (Sieke) McC.; B.A. in Journalism, U. Nev., 1941, Litt.D., 1967; m. Jakie Caldwell, Mar. 1, 1942; children—Michaele Lee McCulloch Parman, Candace Sue McCulloch Yee, David Caldwell. With UP, 1941-42, San Francisco Chronicle, 1945-46, Reno Eve. Gazette, 1946-52; with Time, Inc., 1952-60, 63-72, bur. chief Time-Life News Service, Dallas, 1954-56, Los Angeles, 1957-60, China and S.E. Asia, 1963-68, N.Y.C., 1969-72, Washington editor Life mag., 1968-69; mng. editor Los Angeles Times, 1960-63; v.p. Edn. Today Co., editor-in-chief Learning Mag., 1972-75; mng. editor Sacramento Bee, 1975—. Served with USMCR, 1942-45. Mem. Sigma Delta Chi, Phi Kappa Phi, Kappa Tau Alpha, Sigma Nu. Contbr. nat. mags. Home: 1638 Del Dayo Carmichael CA 95608 Office: Sacramento Bee PO Box 15779 Sacramento CA 95813

MCCULLOCH, JAMES ALOYSIUS, coll. dean; b. Braddock, Pa., July 11, 1922; s. Patrick A. and Elizabeth (Kearney) McC.; B.A., Duquesne U., 1947; M. Litt., U. Pitts., 1948, Ph.D., 1951; m. Elizabeth Kelly, Feb. 8, 1946; children—Patricia, Karen, Kathleen, Mary Ann, James B. Jr. constrn. engr. Jones and Laughlin Steel Corp., 1951-55; mem. faculty Duquesne U., 1955—, prof. classics, 1963—, chmn. dept., 1964-68, dean Coll. Arts and Scis., 1968—. Served as officer USNR, 1943-47. Danforth asso., Lawrence fellow, 1956. Mem. Am. Conf. Acad. Deans, Am. Assn. U. Adminstrs., Am. Assn. Higher Edn. Author: Selections From the Metamorphoses of Ovid, 1965; A Medical Greek and Latin Workbook, 1962, 70. Home: 2024 Thornberry Dr Pittsburgh PA 15237 Office: Coll Liberal Arts and Scis Duquesne Univ Pittsburgh PA 15219

MCCULLOCH, JOHN IRVIN BEGGS, assn. exec.; b. St. Louis, Nov. 8, 1908; s. Richard and Mary Grace (Beggs) McC.; B.A., Yale, 1930; postgrad. New College Oxford, 1931; M.A., Stanford, 1937; m. Elizabeth Ten Broeck Jones, Sept. 9, 1934 (div. 1946); children—Mary Elizabeth, Keith, Roderick, Scott; m. 2d, Patricia Robineau, Nov. 15, 1956; children—Jeanne, Darcy, Catherine. Free-lance writer, 1931—; editor, publisher Inter-American, Washington, 1939-45, English Around the World, 1969—; pres. English-Speaking Union of U.S., N.Y.C., 1972—. Mem. adv. bd. American-Hungarian Studies Found., N.Y.C., 1965—. Served to maj. OSS, AUS, 1943-45. Decorated comdr. Order Brit. Empire. Mem. Soc. of the Cincinnati. Clubs: Union, River, Yale (N.Y.C.); University (Washington); Maidstone (East Hampton, N.Y.). Author: Drums In the Balkan Night, 1936; Challenge to the Americas, 1938. Home: 770 Park Ave New York City NY 10021 Office: 16 E 69th St New York City NY 10021

MC CULLOCH, SAMUEL CLYDE, educator; b. Ararat, Victoria, Australia, Sept. 3, 1916; s. Samuel and Agnes Almond (Clyde) McC.; came to U.S., 1936, naturalized, 1944; A.B. with highest honors in History, U. Calif. at Los Angeles, 1940, M.A. (grad. fellow history), 1942, Ph.D., 1944; m. Sara Ellen Rand, Feb. 19, 1944; children—Ellen (Mrs. William Henry Meyer III), David Rand, Malcolm Clyde. Asst., U. Calif. at Los Angeles, 1943-44; instr. Oberlin Coll., 1944-45; asst. prof. Amherst Coll., 1945-46; vis. asst. prof. U. Mich., 1946-47; mem. faculty Rutgers U., 1947-60, prof. history, asso. dean arts and scis., 1958-60; dean coll., prof. history San Francisco State Coll., 1960-63; dean humanities, prof. history U. Calif. at Irvine, 1964-70, prof., 1970—, coordinator Edn. Abroad Program, 1975—; vis. summer prof. Oberlin Coll., 1945, 46, U. Calif. at Los Angeles, 1947, U. Del., 1949; Fulbright Research prof. Monash U., also Melbourne (Australia) U., 1970; Am. Philos. Soc. grantee, 1970. Mem. Calif. Curriculum Commn., 1961-67. Mem. bd. edn., Highland Park, N.J., 1959-60. Grantee Am. Philos. Soc., Social Sci. Research Council and Rutgers U. Research Council to Australia, 1951; Fulbright research fellow U. Sydney (Australia), 1954-55; grantee Social Sci. Research Council to Eng., summer 1955. Fellow Royal Hist. Soc.; mem. Am. Hist. Assn., Church, Royal Australian hist. socs., A.A.U.P., Conf. Brit. Studies (exec. sec. 1968-73, pres. 1975-77), English Speaking Union (pres. New Brunswick 1957-59), Phi Beta Kappa, Pi Gamma Mu. Episcopalian (vestry). Author: British Humanitarianism, 1950; George Gipps, 1966; also numerous articles, revs. Asso. editor Jour. Brit. Studies, 1960-68, bd. advisers, 1968-70; bd. corrs. Hist. Studies: Australia and New Zealand, 1949—. Home: 2121 Windward Ln Newport Beach CA 92660 Office: Dept of History Univ of California Irvine CA 92717

MC CULLOUGH, DAVID, author; b. Pitts., July 7, 1933; s. Christian Hax and Ruth (Rankin) McC.; B.A., Yale U., 1955; m. Rosalee Ingram Barnes, Dec. 18, 1954; children—Melissa (Mrs. John E. McDonald, Jr.), David, William Barnes, Geoffrey Barnes, Doreen Kane. Writer, editor Time, Inc., N.Y.C., 1956-61; writer, editor USIA, Washington, 1961-64; writer, editor Am. Heritage Pub. Co., N.Y.C., 1964-70; author, 1970—; mem. Bennington (Vt.) Coll. Writers Workshop, 1978 79; scholar-in-residence U. N.Mex., 1979. Recipient New York Diamond Jubilee award, 1973, cert. of merit Mcpl. Art Soc. of New York, 1973, Nat. Book award, 1978, Francis Parkman prize, 1978, Samuel Eliot Morison award, 1978, Cornelius Ryan award, 1978, Civil Engring. History and Heritage award, 1978. Fellow Soc. Am. Historians (v.p.). Author: The Johnstown Flood, 1978; The Great Bridge, 1972; The Path Between the Seas, 1977.

MCCULLOUGH, DONALD FREDERICK, textile mfr.; b. Montclair, N.J., May 6, 1925; s. Willis Gerald and Viola (Mock) McC.; student Taft Sch., Watertown, Conn.; B.S., Yale 1945; m. Mary Jane Whipple, Dec. 28, 1951 (dec. 1962); children—Gregory, Nina, Tracey, Sally; m. 2d, Louise C. Voorhees, July 23, 1963. With Collins & Aikman Corp., N.Y.C., 1946—, exec. trainee, sales mgr. yarn div., asst. automobile fabrics sales mgr., asst. to v.p. for sales, 1946-54, exec. v.p. sales, 1955-61, pres., 1961-70, chmn. bd., chief exec. officer, 1970—; dir. Bankers Trust Co., Bankers Trust N.Y. Corp., Mass. Mut. Life Ins. Co., Chesebrough-Pond's Co., Melville Corp. Mem. nat. execs.' com. Nat. Council on Crime and Delinquency. Trustee Taft Sch.; bd. dirs. Am. Textile Mfrs. Inst., pres., 1970-71. Served as lt. USNR, 1943-46, 51-53. Clubs: Union League, N.Y. Yacht, Storm Trysail, Riverside Yacht; Lyford Cay (Nassau, Bahamas); Round Hill. Home: Meads Point Greenwich CT 06830 Office: 210 Madison Ave New York City NY 10016

MCCULLOUGH, EDGAR JOSEPH, JR., educator; b. Charleston, W.Va., Nov. 29, 1931; s. Edgar Joseph and Elsie (Rapp) McC.; B.A., W.Va. U., 1953, M.S., 1955; Ph.D., U. Ariz., 1963; children—Edgar Joseph III, Deborah Jane. Instr., U. Ariz., 1957-63, asst. prof., 1963-65, asso. prof., 1965-70, prof., head, dept. geoscis., 1970—; acting asst. dir. geol. survey br. and acting state geologist Ariz. Bur. Geology and Mineral Tech., 1977-78. Writer AAAS elementary sch. sci. program Sci.-A Process Approach, 1963-65; dir. So. Ariz. Regional Sci. Fair, 1966-73. Dist. com. chmn. Boy Scouts Am., 1970—. Mem. Nat. Assn. Geology Tchrs. (pres. S.W. sect. 1971—, nat. sec.-treas. 1973-76), Geol. Soc. Am., AAAS. Author: Laboratory Manual for Physical Geology, 1961, Rocks, Minerals and Fossils, 1964, Historical Geology, 1966; editor Ari. Geol. Soc. Digest. Home: 336 Calle de Madrid Tucson AZ 85711 Office: Dept Geosciences U Ariz Tucson AZ 85721

MCCULLOUGH, GERALD W., real estate and investment co. exec.; b. Lynville, Ind., Apr. 1, 1904; s. Francis Clarence and Bertha (Thompson) McC.; student Tulsa U., 1921-22; B.S., A. and M. Coll., Stillwater, Okla., 1925; m. Opal Hope Mason, Jan. 16, 1925 (dec. Jan. 1962); children—Gerald William, Kenneth Waldo, Barbara, Linda, Patricia; m. 2d, Elizabeth Sneed, Mar. 29, 1963; stepchildren—George L., David G., Carol J., Sally E. With Phillips Petroleum Co., Bartlesville, Okla., 1925—, chmn. operating com., 1951-53, v.p., chmn. operating com., 1953-56, v.p., gen. mgr. Phillips Chem. Co., 1948-51; dir. Phillips Chem. Co., Phillips Terminal Co., 1948-56, mgr. natural gasoline dept., 1956-59, v.p. natural gasoline dept., 1956-64, v.p. engring. dept., 1964-68; v.p. Phillips Petroleum Co., 1959-68, cons. to engring. dept., 1969; pres. Hope Devel. Co., 1954—, G.W. McCullough Enterprises, Inc., 1969—; dir. Home Savs. & Loan Assn., Bartlesville, Arapaho Petroleum, Inc., Denver, Cimarron Transmission Co., Ardmore, Okla., Warrior drilling and Engring. Co., Inc., Tuscaloosa, Ala. Bd. govs. Okla. State U. Devel. Found. Recipient Hall of Fame award, 1955, Outstanding Alumnus award Okla. State U., 1956; Engr. of Year award, Okla. Soc. Profl. Engrs., 1966; Hanlon award Natural Gas Producers Assn., 1967. Mem. Nat. Soc. Profl. Engrs. (past dir.), Ind. Petroleum Assn. Am., Natural Gas Processors Assn. (pres. 1963-64, dir. 1964-66), Am. Gas Assn., Am. Petroleum Inst., Mid-Continent Oil and Gas Assn., Okla. Soc. Profl. Engrs. (pres. 1952), Bartlesville C. of C., Sigma Chi. Rotarian. Author numerous tech. papers. Holder patents pertaining to natural gasoline prodn., recovery, separation of both process and equipment nature. Home: 2009 Skyline Dr Bartlesville OK 74003 Office: Bartlesville OK 74003

MCCULLOUGH, HELEN CRAIG, educator; b. Hollywood, Calif., Feb. 17, 1918; d. Everett Emerson and Mabel (Bishop) Craig; A.B., U. Calif., Berkeley, 1939, M.A., 1952, Ph.D., 1955; m. William Hoyt McCullough, July 19, 1952; 1 son, Dundas Craig. Lectr. in history, Asian langs. Stanford (Calif.) U., 1964-69; lectr. Oriental langs. U. Calif., Berkeley, 1969-75, prof., 1975—; vis. prof. Harvard U., 1978-79. Served with WAVES, 1943-46. Fulbright fellow, 1955-56. Mem. Sierra Club. Democrat. Author: Yoshitsune, 1966; Tales of Ise, 1968; translator, author research articles in field of classical Japanese lit. Home: 40 Alta Rd Berkeley CA 94708 Office: Dept Oriental Langs U Calif Berkeley CA 94720

MC CULLOUGH, JOHN PRICE, oil co. exec.; b. Dallas, May 10, 1925; s. John A. and Alta (McGee) McC.; student U. Denver, 1942-43; B.S. in Chem. Engring., U. Okla., 1945; M.S., Oreg. State U., 1948, Ph.D. in Chemistry, 1949; m. Mary Ann Calvert, Aug. 5, 1946; children—Sherri, Cathryn, Patricia. With U.S. Bur. Mines, Bartlesville, Okla., 1949-63, phys. chemist, 1949-57, chief thermodynamics br., 1958-63; mgr. central research div. Mobil Oil Corp., Princeton, N.J., 1963-69, mgr. applied research and devel., 1969-71; gen. mgr. research and devel. Mobil Chem. Co., 1971-78; v.p. environ. affairs and toxicology Mobil Research & Devel. Corp., N.Y.C., 1978—; adj. prof. chemistry Okla State U., Stillwater, 1961-63; dir. Mobil-Tyco Solar Energy Corp. Mem. adv. com. Mercer County (N.J.) Community Coll., 1968-69; bd. dirs. Chem. Inst. Toxicology, 1979—, United Community Fund, Princeton, 1963-69, Middlesex-Somerset-Mercer Regional Study Council, 1968-69. DuPont fellow, 1947-48; recipient Meritorious Service award Dept. Interior, 1959, Distinguished Service award, 1962; Am. Chem. Soc. award petroleum chemistry, 1963, Leo Friend award, 1977. Mem. Gordon Research Conf. (trustee, chmn. bd. trustees, mem. council), Am. Chem. Soc. (editorial bd. Jour. Chem. and Engring. Data, Jour. Phys. Chemistry), Am. Inst. Chemists, AAAS, Sigma Xi. Home: 30 Boudinot St Princeton NJ 08540 Office: Mobil Research and Devel Corp 150 E 42d St New York NY 10017

MCCULLOUGH, LOUIS GARLAND, athletic dir.; b. Florence, Ala., May 17, 1925; s. Louis G. and Josephine (Stockard) M.; B.A., Wofford Coll., 1949; M.A., Columbia U., 1951; married; children—Elizabeth Ann, Jefferson Lee, Daniel Hudson, Patrick Louis. Football coach Wofford Coll., Spartanburg, S.C., 1949-52, U. Wyo., Laramie, 1953-56, Ind. U., Bloomington, Ind., 1957, Iowa State U., Ames, 1958-62, Ohio State U., Columbus, 1963-70; dir. athletics Iowa State U., 1971—. Served with USAAF, 1943-45. Mem. Am. Football Coaches Assn., Nat. Assn. Collegiate Dirs. Athletics. Clubs: Rotary, Ames Golf and Country. Home: 321 24th St Ames IA 50010 Office: 135 Olsen Bldg Iowa State Univ Ames IA 50011

MC CULLOUGH, NORMAN B., physician, microbiologist, educator; b. Milford, Mich., Feb. 23, 1909; s. George W. and Florence W. (Bird) McC.; B.S. with high honors, Mich. State Coll., 1932; M.S., 1933; Ph.D., U. Chgo., 1937, M.D., 1944; m. Mary Louise Young, July 22, 1939; children—Marilyn Kay, Robert Norman. Mem. staff Parke Davis & Co., Detroit, 1934-36, 38-40; research bacteriologist U. Tex., Austin, 1940-42; commd. sr. asst. surgeon USPHS, 1947, advanced through grades to med. dir., 1952; ret., 1968; chief brucellosis activities NIH, U. Chgo., 1947-51, asst. clin. prof. medicine, 1947-50; chief brucellosis unit Lab. Infectious Diseases, Nat. Inst. Allergy and Infectious Diseases, NIH, Bethesda, Md., 1952-56, chief Lab. Clin. Investigation, clin. dir. inst., 1952-58, chief Lab. Bacterial Diseases, 1958-68; mem. med. bd. Clin. Center, NIH, 1952-58; instr. Found. Advanced Edn. Scis., 1961-68; faculty chmn. microbiology and immunology, 1963-68; prof. medicine, microbiology and pub. health Mich. State U., East Lansing, 1968-79, part-time, 1979—; lectr. infectious diseases Georgetown U., 1952-66. Panelist WHO/FAO, 1952—; mem. Nat. Brucellosis Com., 1961-69, bd. dirs., 1963-69. Recipient Distinguished Faculty award Mich. State U., 1972. Diplomate Am. Bd. Microbiology. Fellow Am. Acad. Microbiology, Washington Acad. Sci.; mem. Am. Soc. for Microbiology, AAAS, N.Y. Acad. Scis., Sigma Xi, Phi Kappa Phi, Phi Sigma, Alpha Omega Alpha, Gamma Alpha, Phi Chi. Research, publs. on characteristics of agt. of brucellosis and diagnosis; treatment of disease; other infectious parasitic diseases of man. Home: 6 Apple Blossom Ln Okemos MI 48864 Office: Mich State U Dept Medicine East Lansing MI 48824

MC CULLOUGH, RALPH CLAYTON, II, lawyer; b. Daytona Beach, Fla., Mar. 28, 1941; s. Ralph C. and Doris (Johnson) McC.; B.A., Erskine Coll., 1962; J.D., Tulane U., 1965; m. Carolyn Rodgers Reid, Sept. 1, 1962; children—Melissa Wells, Clayton Baldwin. Admitted to La. bar, 1965, S.C. bar, 1974; asso. firm Baldwin, Haspel, Maloney, Rainold and Meyer, New Orleans, 1965-68; asst. prof. law U. S.C., 1968-71, asso. prof., 1971-75, prof., 1975—, asst. dean Sch. Law, 1970-76, instr. Med. Sch., 1970-79, adj. prof. law and medicine, 1979—; trustee S.C. dist. U.S. Bankruptcy Ct., 1979—; exec. dir. S.C. Continuing Legal Edn. Program. Bd. visitors Erskine Coll. Mem. La. Bar Assn., S.C. Bar (sec. 1975-76, exec. dir. 1972-76, award of service 1978), Am. Bar Assn., New Orleans Bar Assn., Am. Trial Lawyers Assn., Am. Law Inst., Southeastern Assn. Am. Law Schs. (pres.), Phi Alpha Delta. Republican. Episcopalian. Club: Forest Lake. Author: (with J. L. Underwood) The Civil Trial Manual, 1974 supplements, 1976, 77, 78; (with Myers & Felix) New Directions in Legal Education, 1970; co-reporter S.C. Criminal Code, 1977, S.C. Study Sentencing, 1977. Home: 113 Dibble Ln Columbia SC 29206 Office: U SC Sch Law Columbia SC 29208

MCCULLOUGH, RAY DANIEL, JR., ins. co. exec.; b. Daytona Beach, Fla., Feb. 28, 1938; s. Ray Daniel and Clarice (Malphurs) McC.; B.S. in Bus. Adminstrn., U. Fla., 1960; m. Barbara Jean Winchester, Aug. 16, 1963; children—Courtney Ann, Justin Ray. Accountant, Haskins & Sells, C.P.A.'s, Jacksonville, Fla., 1960-63; with Gulf Life Ins. Co., Jacksonville, 1963—, v.p., controller, 1971—. Mem. bus. adv. council U. Fla., Gainesville, 1979—. C.P.A., Fla. Mem. Am., Fla. insts. C.P.A.'s, Jacksonville Toastmasters Club (pres.

1966), Beta Alpha Psi, Beta Gamma Sigma. Home: 10312 Sylvan Ln W Jacksonville FL 32217 Office: 1301 Gulf Life Dr Jacksonville FL 32207

MCCULLOUGH, RICHARD LAWRENCE, advt. agy. exec.; b. Chgo., Dec. 1, 1937; s. Francis John and Sadie Beatrice McC.; B.S., Marquette U., 1959; m. Julia Louise Kreimer, May 6, 1961; children—Steven, Jeffery, Julia. Account exec. Edward H. Weiss & Co., Chgo., 1960-66; account supr. Doyle Dane Bernbach, N.Y.C., 1966-68; sr. v.p. J. Walter Thompson Co., Chgo., 1969—. Bd. dirs. Gateway Found., Chgo., 1976—, mem. exec. com., 1976—. Served with spl. forces U.S. Army, 1959-60. Roman Catholic. Home: 2720 Lincoln St Evanston IL 60201 Office: 975 N Michigan Ave Chicago IL 60611

MCCULLOUGH, ROBERT DALE, osteo. physician; b. Terre Haute, Ind., Mar. 13, 1913; s. Francis Clarence and Bertha (Thompson) McC.; student Kirksville Coll. Osteopathy and Surgery, 1931-33; D.O., Kansas City (Mo.) Coll. of Osteopathy and Surgery, 1935, D.Sc. (hon.), 1962; m. Roberta Maude Purdy, June 10, 1934; children—Robert Dale, Carol Joyce. Intern, Lakeside Hosp., Kansas City, Mo., 1935-36; surg. resident Conley Clinic Hosp., Kansas City, Mo., 1939-41; surgeon Eastern Okla. Hosp., Muskogee, 1941-43; gen. practice of surgery, Tulsa, 1943—; staff Okla. Osteo. Hosp., Tulsa, 1944—, chief of staff, 1950-51; pres. Okla. Bd. Osteo. Examiners, 1950-52; mem. Okla. Bd. Health, 1960—, v.p., 1968—; chmn. Okla. Osteo. Cross, Blue Shield Com., 1954—; dir. Life Ins. Co. Minn., Mpls., Life Stocks of Minn., Inc.; trustee Okla. Blue Cross-Blue Shield. Chmn. bd. Tulsa Youth for Christ, 1954-71, chmn. emeritus, 1971-79; mem. bd. Internat. Youth for Christ, 1956-65; chmn. adv. bd. Frances Willard Home, Tulsa, 1955-58, Leader Dog for the Blind, Rochester, Mich. Trustee Kansas City Coll. Osteopathy and Surgery, 1962-64; trustee Okla. Osteo. Hosp., 1944—, chmn. bldg. com., 1962-77; trustee George Washington Boyhood Home, Ark. Enterprises for Blind, Little Rock, Mich. Osteo. Coll. Found.; trustee Lions Internat. Found., 1974-78, pres., 1974-78; mem. adv. bd. Southwestern Bapt. Theol. Sem., 1975—. Recipient Distinguished Service award Am. Osteo. Assn., 1973. Mem. Am. (trustee 1948-55, pres. 1956-57; Okla. del. ho. of dels. 1958-73, vice speaker 1973—; del. Nat. Health Council 1959-63; chmn. Assn's. com. on hosps. 1960-64), Okla. (sec.-treas. 1938-39, jour. editor 1938-43, pres. 1943-44, trustee 1941-43) osteo. assns., Am. Coll. Osteo. Surgeons (life), Am. Osteo. Coll. Proctology, Internat. Acad. Preventive Medicine (pres. 1972-73, trustee 1973—), Soc. for Preservation and Encouragement Barber Shop Quartet Singing Am. (pres. Tulsa 1947-48), Assn. Internat. Champions, Tulsa C. of C., DeMolay Legion of Honor, Gideons Internat., Wycliffe Assos., Internat. Platform Assn., Psi Sigma Alpha, Alpha Phi Omega, Sigma Sigma Phi. Baptist (deacon). Mason (32 deg., K.T., Shriner), Lion (pres. Tulsa 1946-47, internat. dir. 1963-65, exec. com. 1964-65, 67-71, internat. pres. 1970-71). Home: 3429 S Lewis St Tulsa OK 74105 Office: 2221 E 3d St Tulsa OK 74104. *We keep only that which we give away. Jim Elliott, martyred missionary, wrote, "He is no fool who gives what he cannot keep to gain what he cannot lose." The joy of living comes from God's Love accepted by faith and giving ourselves in service to others.*

MC CULLOUGH, ROBERT WILLIS, textile mfr.; b. Monclair, N.J., Sept. 19, 1920; s. Willis G. and Viola (Mock) McC.; student Brown U., 1940-42, Phila. Textile Sch.; m. Margaret Elizabeth Hammons, Aug. 12, 1942; children—Constance Joan, Sandra Margaret, D. Scott, Linda Anne. With Collins & Aikman Corp., N.Y.C., 1946—, exec. v.p., 1955—, chmn. exec. com., 1961—, also dir. parent orgn. and subsidiaries. Adviser to supt. U.S. Naval Acad. Trustee, past chmn. South Street Seaport Mus.; trustee N.Y. State Maritime Mus., Am. Scottish Found.; chmn. bd. trustees Textile Research Inst. at Princeton. Served from ensign to lt. comdr. USCGR, 1942-46. Named to Brown U. Hall of Fame. Mem. Am. Arbitration Assn. Clubs: Riverside Yacht; N.Y. Yacht (past commodore; chmn. Am.'s Cup Com.), Storm Trysail, Cruising of Am. Home: Club Rd Riverside CT 06878 Office: 210 Madison Ave New York NY 10016

MCCULLOUGH, ROLAND ALEXANDER, banker; b. Spartanburg, S.C., Nov. 29, 1917; s. Ashton Alexander and Mary Belle (Cannon) McC.; A.B., Wofford Coll., 1939, A.M., 1942, LL.D., 1975; m. Birdie Brown West, Sept. 8, 1940; children—Emily Alexandra (Mrs. Robert Voorhees), Mary Cecilia (Mrs. Joseph S. Stall), Margaret Ann. Sch. tchr., adminstr., hosp. investigator, hosp. bus. mgr., Spartanburg County, S.C., 1939-44; mng. editor Spartanburg Herald and Sunday Herald-Jour., 1944-50; press and research sec. to Gov. Byrnes of S.C., 1950-54; adminstrv. asst. to U.S. Senator Strom Thurmond, 1955-57; v.p., then sr. v.p. S.C. Nat. Bank, Greenville and Columbia, 1957-69; bd. dirs. Export Import Bank U.S., Washington, 1969-77, spl. asst., 1978—, bank's rep. on Pres.'s Interagy. Com. on Export Expansion, 1973-75; mem. export credit group OECD, Paris, 1970-76. Contbr. articles to mags. Home: 7711 Bridle Path Ln McLean VA 22102 also Spartanburg SC Office: 811 Vermont Ave NW Washington DC 20571

MC CULLOUGH, SAMUEL ALEXANDER, banker; b. Pitts., Nov. 10, 1938; s. Alexander and Mary Ruth (Brady) McC.; B.B.A., U. Pitts., 1960; m. Katharine Graham, Sept. 23, 1967; children—Bonnie S., Elizabeth C., Rebecca D., Anne D., Mary D. With Mellon Bank, N.A., Pitts., 1956-75, asst. cashier, 1964-68, asst. v.p., 1968-71, v.p., 1971-75; sr. v.p. corp. banking group Am. Bank & Trust Co. of Pa., Reading, 1975, exec. v.p., 1977, pres., chief exec. officer, 1978—; dir. Am. Bus. Credit Corp., Berks Title Corp., Am. Venture Capital Corp. Bd. dirs. Easter Seal Soc. of Berks County, United Way of Berks County; bd. dirs. Wyomissing Property Corp.; trustee St. Joseph Hosp., Albright Coll. Mem. Am. Inst. Banking, Am. Bankers Assn., Pa. Bankers Assn., C. of C. of Reading and Berks County (dir.). Republican. Presbyterian. Clubs: Allegheny Country (Sewickley, Pa.); Berkshire Country (Reading); Moselem Springs Golf (Fleetwood, Pa.). Office: 35 N 6th St PO Box 1102 Reading PA 19603

MCCUNE, BARRON PATTERSON, judge; b. West Newton, Pa., Feb. 19, 1915; s. James Patterson and Lyda Barron (Hammond) McC.; A.B., Washington and Jefferson Coll., 1935; LL.B., U. Pa., 1938; m. Edna Flannery Markey, Dec. 23, 1943; children—Edward M., James H., Barron Patterson. Admitted to Pa. bar, 1939; practiced in Washington, Pa., 1939-64; judge 27th Jud. dist. Ct. Common Pleas, Washington, Pa., 1964-71, U.S. Dist. Ct., Western Dist. Pa., Pitts., 1971—. Trustee Washington and Jefferson Coll.; bd. dirs. Washington (Pa.) State Hosp. Served with USNR, 1942-45. Home: 144 Lemoyne Ave Washington PA 15301 Office: US Courthouse Pittsburgh PA 15219

MCCUNE, BERNARD EDWARD, constrn. and land. devel. co. exec.; b. Gresham, Nebr., Mar. 24, 1921; s. Irvin E. and Catherine (Harris) McC.; B.S. in Civil Engring., U. So. Calif., 1951; m. Genevieve Ruth Reeves, July 4, 1941; children—Garen Lee, Bernard Lynn, Steven Jon. Dep. city engr., Long Beach, Calif., 1945-58; self-employed in heavy constrn. contracting, 1958-61; sr. v.p. Shapell Industries, Inc., Beverly Hills, Calif., 1961-77, vice chmn. bd. dirs., 1973—; dir. Council Environment, Employment, Economy and Devel., Orange County, Calif. Past pres. Bixby Hill Community Assn.; past mem. Calif. Senate Interim Com.; chmn. adv. bd. Salvation Army, Long Beach, Calif., 1968, now hon. dir.; past bd. dirs., vice chmn. exec. com. Long Beach chpt. A.R.C.; pres. bd. dirs. Pacific Hosp., Long Beach, 1971-73, Boys Clubs Long Beach, 1971-72; bd. dirs. NCCJ; mem. 100 Club of Boy Scouts Am. Served to maj. C.E., AUS, 1940-45. Decorated Bronze Star with oak leaf cluster, Purple Heart; named Honor Citizen of Year, NCCJ, 1974; recipient Golden Man and Boy award Boys Clubs Am., 1973; also various resolutions. Registered profl. engr., Calif. Mem. Am. Assn. Engrs., Nat. Soc. Profl. Engrs., Am. Mil. Engrs. Assn., Bldg. Industry Assn. Calif. (past chpt. treas.), Long Beach (past bd. dirs., past chmn. sts. and hwys. com.), Orange County, Westminster, Garden Grove, Seal Beach, Cerritos, Huntington Beach chambers commerce, Navy League, Am. Legion, mil. orders Purple Heart, World Wars. Methodist. Clubs: Long Beach Exchange (past pres.); Masons, Elks (past exalted ruler), Old Ranch Country, Shadow Mountain Country. Home: 926 Palo Verde Ave Long Beach CA 90815 Office: 8383 Wilshire Blvd Beverly Hills CA 90211

MC CUNE, ELLIS E., univ. pres.; b. Houston, July 17, 1921; s. Ellis E. and Ruth (Mason) McC.; student Sam Houston State U., 1940-42; B.A., U. Calif. at Los Angeles, 1948, Ph.D., 1957; m. Hilda May Whiteman, Feb. 8, 1946; 1 son, James Donald. Teaching asst. U. Calif. at Los Angeles, 1949-51; instr. polit. sci. Occidental Coll., Los Angeles, 1951-56, asst. prof., 1956-59, asso. prof., 1959; asst. prof. Calif. State U., Northridge, 1959-61, asso. prof. 1961-63, prof., 1963; dean acad. planning Calif. State Univs. and Colls., 1963-67; pres. Calif. State U., Hayward, 1967—; cons. govtl. units and agys.; lectr., panelist. Commr. Calif. State Scholarship and Loan Commn., 1964-68, chmn., 1967-68; pres. Govtl. Adminstrn. Group Los Angeles, 1959; chmn. adv. com. inst. coll. and univ. adminstrs. Am. Council on Edn., 1973—; mem. accrediting commn. sr. colls. and univs. Western Assn. Schs. and Colls., 1974—, chmn., 1977—; mem. commn. on colls. N.W. Assn. Schs. and Colls., 1974—; dir. Assn. Am. Colls., 1971-75, vice chmn., 1975-76; dir. Assn. Western Univs., mem. Council on Postsecondary Edn., 1977—; mem. exec. com. Western Coll. Assn., 1970-72, v.p., 1972-74, pres., 1974-77; pres. Western Assn. Schs. and Colls., 1979—. Chmn. univs. and colls. div. United Bay Area Crusade, 1969-70. Bd. dirs. Oakland (Calif.) Museum Assn.; trustee Calif. Council Econ. Edn.; sec. bd. dirs. Eden Community Found., 1978-79. Served with USAAF, 1942-46. Mem. Am. Polit. Sci. Assn., AAUP, Western Polit. Sci. Assn. (exec. council 1958-61), Hayward C. of C. (dir. 1968-71, 73-76, 77—), Phi Beta Kappa, Pi Gamma Mu, Pi Sigma Alpha. Rotarian. Clubs: Bohemian, Commonwealth (San Francisco). Home: 17577 Parker Rd Castro Valley CA 94546 Office: Calif State University Hayward CA 94542

MCCUNE, GEORGE DAVID, publisher; b. Cedar Rapids, Iowa, Oct. 18, 1924; s. James and Mary Esther (Vanous) McC.; B.A., Butler U., 1948; M.A., U. Pa., 1950; m. Sara Joy Miller, Oct. 16, 1966; children—Cathy Jane, David Franklin, Keith Robert, Susan Marie. With Macmillan Co., N.Y.C., 1950-66, v.p., dir. div. Free Press, 1964-65, div. Glencoe Press, 1965-66; chmn. bd., pub., treas. Sage Publs., Inc., Beverly Hills, Calif., 1966—, chmn. bd. Sage Publs., Ltd., London, 1971—. Served with USAAF, 1943-46. Home: 1102 S Oakhurst St Los Angeles CA 90035 Office: 275 S Beverly Dr Beverly Hills CA 90212*

MC CUNE, JOHN FRANCIS, III, architect; b. New Castle, Pa., Oct. 23, 1921; s. John Francis and Alice (Miles) McC.; student Vanderbilt U., 1938-40; B.S. in Architecture, U. Mich, 1943; m. Jeanne Ramsay, Sept. 28, 1946; children—Morgan R., Martha (Mrs. Dennis L. Maddox), David M., William S. Draftsman firm Walter E. Bort, Architect, Clinton, Iowa, 1946-47, firm Pope & Kruse, Architects, Wilmington, Del., 1947-54, asso., 1955-60; partner firm Pope, Kruse & McCune, Architects, Wilmington, 1961-72, owner McCune Assos., Architects, Wilmington, 1972—. Mem. Historic Area Commn., New Castle, Del. Mem. AIA (pres. Del. chpt. 1970-71, mem. nat. com. historic resources 1975-77, state preservation coordinator Del. 1975—), Soc. Archtl. Historians, Assn. for Preservation Tech., Constrn. Specifications Inst. (dir. Del. chpt. 1974-77), Nat. Trust Hist. Preservation, Del. C. of C., Nat. Fire Protection Assn. (com. libraries, museums and hist. bldgs.), Bldg. Ofcls. and Code Adminstrs. Internat., Kappa Sigma. Lion (pres. Kennett Sq. club 1969-70). Projects include John Dickinson High Sch., Thomas McKean High Sch., Del. Power and Light Co. (in association with V.G. Kling), U.S. Court House, Custom House and Fed. Office Bldg., all Wilmington; historic preservation projects include Presbyn. Ch., New Castle, Old Court House, New Castle, Barrett's Chapel, Frederica, Del., Old State House, Dover, Del., Loockerman Hall, Dover. Home: RD 3 Box 366 Bayard Rd Kennett Square PA 19348 Office: 3411 Silverside Rd Wilmington DE 19810

MC CUNE, SARA MILLER (MRS. GEORGE D. MCCUNE), publisher; b. N.Y.C., Feb. 4, 1941; d. Nathan and Rose (Glass) Miller; B.A. (N.Y. Regents scholar), Queens Coll., 1961; m. George D. McCune, Oct. 16, 1966. Asst. to v.p. sales Macmillan Co., N.Y.C., 1961-63; sales mgr. Pergamon Press Ltd., Oxford, Eng., 1963-64; sales, N.Y.C., 1964; pres., pub. Sage Publs., Inc., Beverly Hills, Calif., 1965—; dir. Sage Publs. Ltd. Mem. Am. Polit. Sci. Assn., Am. Sociol. Assn., Evaluation Research Soc., Internat. Polit. Sci. Assn., Pi Sigma Alpha. Home: 1102 S Oakhurst Los Angeles CA 90035 Office: 275 S Beverly Dr Beverly Hills CA 90212

MC CUNE, SHANNON, geographer, educator; b. Sonchon, Korea, Apr. 6, 1913; s. George Shannon and Helen (McAfee) McC.; B.A., Coll. of Wooster, 1935; M.A., Syracuse U., 1937; Ph.D., Clark U., 1939, LL.D., 1960; LL.D., U. Mass., 1962, Eastern Nazarene Coll., 1966; m. Edith Blair, June 30, 1936; children—Antoinette McCune Bement, Shannon McCune Wagner, George Blair. Instr., asst. prof. Ohio State U., Columbus, 1939-47; econ. intelligence officer Bd. Econ. Warfare-Fgn. Econ. Adminstrn., 1942-45; asst. prof. to prof. Colgate U., Hamilton, N.Y., 1947-55; provost U. Mass., Amherst, 1955-61; dir. Dept. Edn., UNESCO, Paris, 1961-62; civil adminstr. Ryukyu Islands, 1962-64; staff asso. Office of Pres., U. Ill., Urbana, 1964-65; pres. U. Vt., Burlington, 1965-66, research prof., 1966-67; dir. Am. Geog. Soc., 1967-69; prof. geography U. Fla., Gainesville, 1969-79, prof. emeritus, 1979—. Recipient medal of freedom U.S. Presidential award, 1946, Pandit Madan Mahan Malaviya medal Nat. Geog. Soc. India, 1950, Founder's award Hampshire Coll., 1970, Distinguished Alumni award Coll. of Wooster, 1976. Mem. Assn. Am. Geographers (v.p.), Assn. Japanese Geographers, Phi Beta Kappa, Sigma Xi, Phi Kappa Phi. Mem. United Ch. of Christ. Mason. Author: Korea's Heritage, A Regional and Social Geography, 1955; Korea: Land of Broken Calm, 1965; The Ryukyu Islands, 1975. Home: 1617 NW 7th Pl Gainesville FL 32603

MC CUNE, WILLIAM JAMES, JR., mfg. co. exec.; b. Glens Falls, N.Y., June 2, 1915; s. William James and Brunnhilde (Decker) McC.; S.B., Mass. Inst. Tech., 1937; m. Janet Waters, Apr. 19, 1940; 1 dau., Constance (Mrs. Leslie Sheppard); m. 2d, Elisabeth Johnson, Aug. 8, 1946; children—William Joseph, Heather H.D. With Polaroid Corp., Cambridge, Mass., 1939—, v.p. engring., 1954-63, v.p., asst. gen. mgr., 1963-69, exec. v.p., after 1969, now pres., chief operating officer, dir.; dir. Haemonetics Corp.; trustee Mitre Corp. Mem. corp. Boston Mus. Sci.; mem. corp. devel. com. M.I.T.; trustee Mass. Gen. Hosp. Fellow Am. Acad. Arts and Scis.; mem. Nat. Acad. Engring. Home: Old Concord Rd Lincoln MA 01773 Office: Polaroid Corp 549 Technology Sq Cambridge MA 02139

MCCURDY, ALEXANDER, JR., organist; b. Eureka, Calif., Aug. 18, 1905; s. Alexander and Lillie May (Ervin) McC.; studied piano, organ. harmony and counterpoint with Wallace A. Sabin, Berkeley, Calif., 1919-24, piano with Edwin Hughes, and organ with Lynnwood Farnam, N.Y.C., 1924-27; grad. (scholar), Curtis Inst. of Music, Phila., 1934; Mus.D., Susquehanna U., 1936; Mus.D. (hon.), Curtis Inst., 1952; m. Flora Bruce Greenwood, June 6, 1932; children—Xandra (Mrs. Robert L. Schultz), Alexander III. Organist, Trinity Episcopal Ch., Oakland, Calif., 1919-21, First Congregational Ch., 1921-23; choirmaster, organist St. Luke's Episcopal Ch., San Francisco, 1923-24. Ch. of Redeemer, Morristown, N.J., 1924-27; dir. music Morristown Prep. Sch., 1925-27; debut as concert organist, Town Hall, N.Y.C., 1926; choirmaster and organist 1st Presbyn. Ch., Phila., 1927-71; comdr. Trenton Choral Art Soc., 1928-35; head organ dept. Curtis Inst. Music, 1935-72; headmaster St. James Choir Sch. for Boys, 1937-40; head music dept. Episcopal Acad., Overbrook, Pa., 1937-40; head organ dept. Westminster Choir Coll., Princeton, N.J., 1940-65; soloist Am. Guild of Organist's convs., 1930, 32, 35, 37; recitals at San Diego Expn., 1935; spl. recitalist Swarthmore Coll., 1933-41. Tchr. summers Occidental Coll., Los Angeles, and Northfield Sch., East Northfield, Mass.; organist for uncut performances St Matthew Passion (Bach) with N.Y. Philharmonic Orch., Carnegie Hall, 1943. Bd. dirs. Mus. Fund Soc. Phila., 1962—, chmn. music com., 1963-64. Mem. Art Alliance, Am. Organ Players Club (div.). Republican. Presbyn. (elder). Mason. Contbr. articles to Etude, The Am. Organist, others. Organ editor The Etude, 1946-57. Home: Box 3 Castine ME 04421 Studio: Water St Castine ME 04421

MCCURDY, EVERETT DARLING, lawyer; b. Port Townsend, Wash., Feb. 15, 1905; s. William Horace and Ella (Darling) McC.; A.B., Western Res. U., 1926, LL.B., 1934; m. Eugenia J. Somma, Feb. 12, 1938. Admitted to Ohio bar, 1928; since practiced in Cleve.; chmn. firm Spieth, Bell, McCurdy & Newell, and predecessor, 1952—; lectr. in law Cleve. Coll., Western Res. U., 1945-64. Pres., Western Res. Residences, Inc.; pres., trustee Spieth & Co.; sec. Yorktown Land Co.; dir. Bohme & Blinkmann, Inc., Nestle LeMur Co. Republican candidate for chmn. Cuyahoga County, 1966. Mem. Am., Ohio, Cleve. bar assns., Ct. of Nisi Prius, Phi Kappa Psi. Christian Scientist. Mason (32 deg., Shriner). Club: Mayfield Country (South Euclid, Ohio). Home: 1487 Burlington Rd Cleveland Heights OH 44118 Office: Union Commerce Bldg Cleveland OH 44115

MCCURDY, GILBERT GEIER, retailer; b. Rochester, N.Y., May 25, 1922; s. Gilbert J.C. and Virginia (Geier) McC.; B.A., Williams Coll., 1944; m. Katherine W. Babcock, Nov. 9, 1946; children—Gilbert Kennedy, Lynda Babcock (Mrs. Hotra). With McCurdy & Co., Inc., Rochester, 1946—, controller, asst. treas., 1953-55, v.p., 1956-59, exec. v.p., 1959-62, pres., gen. mgr., 1962—, chief exec. officer, 1969—; chmn. bd. Frederick Atkins, 1968-70; dir. Lincoln First Bank of Rochester. Dir. Rochester Better Bus. Bur. Bd. dirs. Men's Service Center, Rochester and Monroe County Community Chest; trustee U. Rochester Served to 1st lt. Signal Corps, AUS, 1943-46. Mem. Rochester C. of C. (pres. 1975). Baptist. Home: 1 Whitney Ln Rochester NY 14610 Office: Midtown Plaza Rochester NY 14604

MCCURDY, HAROLD GRIER, psychologist; b. Salisbury, N.C., May 30, 1909; s. McKinnon Grier and Nellie (Curd) McC.; A.B., Duke U., 1930, Ph.D., 1938; m. Mary Burton Derrickson, Sept. 15, 1937; children—John Derrickson, Ann Lewis. Asst. prof. biology High Point Coll., 1931-32; caseworker Fed. Transient Bur., Salisbury, N.C., 1934; prof. psychology Milligan Coll., 1938-41; asso. prof. to prof. psychology and philosophy Meredith Coll., 1941-48; asso. prof. to Kenan prof. psychology, U. N.C., Chapel Hill, 1948-71, Kenan prof. psychology emeritus, 1971—. Mem. AAAS, Am. Psychol. Assn., Sigma Xi. Democrat. Methodist. Author: Personality and Science, 1965, Barbara, 1966; (poetry) The Chastening of Narcissus, 1970; others. Home: 6 Gooseneck Rd Chapel Hill NC 27514

MCCURDY, PATRICK PIERRE, editor; b. Angers, France, Sept. 14, 1928 (parents Am. citizens); s. Joseph Alexander and Constance Yolande (Hillairet de Boisferon) McC.; B.S. in Chem. Engring., Carnegie Inst. Tech., 1949; m. Eiko Yamada, May 30, 1953; children—Alan J., Wendy C., Alec, Jeffrey R. Chem. engr., tech. service dept. Humble Oil & Refining Co., Baytown, Tex., 1949-50; chem. engr. Callery Chem. Co. (Pa.), 1954-56; sr. chem. engr. U.S. Army Engr. Research and Devel. Labs., Ft. Belvoir, Va., 1956-60; asst. editor Chem. & Engring. News, Washington, 1960-61, N.Y.C., 1961-62, bur. head, Frankfurt, Germany, 1962-64, Tokyo, 1964-67, mng. editor, Washington, 1967-69, editor, 1969-73; editor Chemical Week, 1973—. Served to 1st lt. C.E., AUS, 1950-54. Recipient Jesse H. Neal award, 1979. Mem. Am. Chem. Soc., Overseas Press Club, Fgn. Corrs. Club Japan, Chemists Club, Société de Chimie Industrielle, Tau Beta Pi, Phi Kappa Phi, Theta Tau, Phi Kappa. Club: Tokyo American. Home: 220A Riverside Ave Riverside CT 06878 Office: 1221 Ave of the Americas New York NY 10020

MC CURDY, RICHARD CLARK, cons.; b. Newton, Iowa, Jan. 2, 1909; s. Ralph Bruce and Florence (Clark) McC.; A.B., Stanford, 1931, E.M., 1933; m. Harriet Edith Sutton, Sept. 11, 1933; children—Gregor, Richard, Carolyn, Robert. Engring. and prodn. Shell Oil Co., 1933-47; prodn. mgmt. Shell Caribbean Petroleum Co., 1947-50; gen. mgr. Shell Group Companies, Venezuela, 1950-53; pres. Shell Chem. Co., N.Y.C., 1953-65; dir. Shell Oil Co., mem. exec. com., 1959-69, pres., chief exec. officer, 1965-69; asso. adminstr. orgn. and mgmt. NASA, Washington, 1970-73, cons., 1974—. Trustee United Seamans Service, 1954-70, Stanford U., 1965-70, Hood Coll., 1968—, Rensselaer Poly. Inst., 1974—. Recipient Distinguished Service medal NASA, 1972. Mem. Mfg. Chemists Assn. (dir. 1955-65, chmn. bd. 1961-62, chmn. exec. com. 1964-65), Am. Inst. Mining, Metall. and Petroleum Engrs., Am. Phys. Soc., Am. Petroleum Inst., Beta Theta Pi. Clubs: N.Y. Yacht; Noroton (Conn.) Yacht (commodore); Tokeneke (Darien, Conn.); St. Francis Yacht, Pacific Union (San Francisco); Links (N.Y.C.). Home: Contentment Island Darien CT 06820

MC CURLEY, ROBERT LEE, JR., lawyer, educator; b. Gadsden, Ala., Sept. 7, 1941; s. Robert Lee and Nellie Ruth McC.; B.S., U. Ala., 1963, J.D., 1966; m. Martha Dawson McCurley, June 21, 1969; 1 dau., Allison Leah. Admitted to Ala. bar, 1966, D.C. bar, 1973, U.S. Ct. Mil. Appeals, 1966, U.S. Supreme Ct. bar, 1970, U.S. Customs and Patents bar, 1966; asst. dir. Fed. Savs. & Loan Ins. Corp., Washington, 1966-67; partner firm Rains, Rains, McCurley & Wilson, Gadsden, Ala., 1967-75; city judge, Southside, Ala., 1970-75; dir. Ala. Law Inst., asst. dean U. Ala. Law Center, 1977—; mem. White House Conf. on Balanced Nat. Growth. Pres., Gadsden Boys Club, 1971, Etowah March of Dimes, 1973; nat. committeeman Ala. Young Democrats, 1974; mem. Nat. Democratic Charter Commn., 1974. Mem. Am. Bar Assn., Am. Law Inst., Farrah Law Soc. Baptist. Clubs: Indian Hills Country, Univ., Kiwanis (pres.) (Tuscaloosa). Editor books in field. Office: Box 1287 University AL 35486

MC CURRY, DONALD REID, mktg. research co. exec.; b. Nashville, July 21, 1928; s. Ray Reid and Victoria Wanda (Stranz) McC.; B.A., Cornell U., 1950; m. Flora McKenzie, July 21, 1950; children—Diane, Kathryn, Laura. With A. C. Nielsen Co., Northbrook, Ill., 1955—, client service exec., 1962-67, v.p., 1967-74, exec. v.p., 1974—, also dir.; chmn. bd. Compumark, Inc., Coordinated Mgmt. Systems, Inc. Served with USAF, 1951-53. Mem. Am. Mktg. Assn., Phi Beta Kappa. Club: Knollwood (Lake Forest, Ill.). Home: 600 W Westleigh Rd Lake Forest IL 60045 Office: AC Nielsen Co Nielsen Plaza Northbrook IL 60062

MCCURRY, PAUL D., architect; b. Chgo., Dec. 3, 1903; s. Daniel J. and Ella (Crissinger) McC.; B.S., Armour Inst. Tech., 1926; M.Ed., U. Chgo., 1937; m. Irene Tipler, Aug. 30, 1935; children—Margaret, Marian, Alan. With various archtl. firms, 1926-46; with Schmidt, Garden & Erikson, architects-engrs., Chgo., 1946—, now partner. Chmn. Mayor's Archtl. Com., Lake Forest, Ill.; chmn. archtl. licensing com. Ill. Dept. Registration and Edn., 1971-79; mem. Lake Forest Plan Commn., 1970-75. Fellow A.I.A. (pres. Chgo. chpt. 1968—); mem. Deerpath Art League, (pres.). Clubs: Lake Forest (Ill.); Arts, Cliff Dwellers (Chgo.). Prin. works include VA Research Hosp., Chgo., Schs. of Health Professions, U. Pitts., Amos Alonzo Stagg High Sch., Palos Hills, Ill., Marian Coll. of Fond du Lac (Wis.), John Hancock Elementary Sch., Chgo., Mary C. Terrell Elementary Sch., Chgo., Deerpath Elementary Sch., Lake Forest, Marillac High Sch., Northfield, Ill., Kenwood High Sch., Chgo., Copley Hosp., Aurora, Ill., Lake Forest Club, Lake Forest, Ill., U. Ill. Hosp., Chgo. Home: 250 E Cherokee Rd Lake Forest IL 60045 Office: 104 S Michigan Ave Chicago IL 60603

MC CUSKEY, GEORGE, fin. cons.; b. Cuyahoga Falls, Ohio, Dec. 25, 1914; s. Charles C. and Lottie (Wilcox) McC.; A.B., Denison U., 1936; LL.B., Cleve. Law Sch., 1941; m. Phyllis Herzberg, 1939; children—Anne Carolyn, Margery Sue. Investment analyst Boyd & Co., Cleve., 1937-43; asso. wage stblzn. dir. War Labor Bd., 1943-44; gen. counsel, sec.-treas. Perfection Stove Co., 1944-52; asst. to pres. Youngstown Sheet & Tube Co. (Ohio), 1952-54, v.p., 1954-70, pres., 1970-71; exec. v.p. Lykes-Youngstown Corp., 1969-71; chmn. bd. Arthur G. McKee Co., 1971-77, Liquid Capital Income Inc., 1977-78; chmn. exec. com. McKee Corp., 1977-78; fin. cons., Naples, Fla., 1978—. Trustee, Western Res. Acad. Home: Naples FL 33940

MC CUSKEY, JAMES R., corp. exec.; b. Canton, Ohio, Dec. 17, 1915; s. Emery Andrew and Margaret (George) McC.; B.A., Denison U., 1937; m. Janet Egbert, Aug. 19, 1939; children—James, Andrew, John, William. Vice-pres. Ohio Can & Crown Co., Massillon, 1946-54; pres. Central States Can Co., Massillon, 1955-78, chmn. bd., 1979—; dir., v.p. Van Dorn Co., Cleve.; dir. Harter Bank, Canton, Soc. Corp., Cleve. Mem. Can Mfrs. Inst. Am. (vice chmn. 1974-77), Massillon C. of C. (past pres.). Republican. Clubs: Brookside Country, Canton. Home: 2826 Midvale Rd NW Canton OH 44708 Office: 700 16th SE Massillon OH 44646

MCCUSKEY, RICHARD GEORGE, lawyer; b. Canton, Ohio, Mar. 23, 1912; s. Emery Andrew and Margaret (George) McC.; student Wooster (Ohio) Coll., 1930-31; grad. Mt. Union Coll., Alliance, Ohio, 1934, LL.D., 1979; grad. U. Mich. Law Sch., 1937; m. Eleanor E. Mumaw, Sept. 9, 1938; 1 son, Thomas G. Admitted to Ohio bar, 1937, practiced in Canton, to 1978; of counsel firm Black, McCuskey, Souers & Arbaugh, 1946—; dir. Union Metal Mfg. Treas., Canton Police Boys Club, 1952—; trustee Canton Scholarship Found., 1952—, Canton Pub. Library, 1950-63, pres., 1958-63; trustee Mt. Union Coll., 1953—, pres., 1964-72; trustee Aultman Hosp., 1971—, Canton Med. Edn. Found., 1978—. Served to maj. AUS, 1943-46. Decorated Bronze Star. Fellow Ohio Bar Found.; mem. Am., Ohio, N.Y. State bar assns., Am. Judicature Soc., Sigma Nu. Republican. Methodist. Clubs: Canton, Brookside Country (Canton). Home: 3003 12th St NW Massillon OH 44646 Office: Harter Bank Bldg Canton OH 44702

MCCUTCHEON, FREDERIC YORK, stockbroker; b. Toronto, Ont., Can., Sept. 19, 1940; s. Malcolm Wallace and Eva Trow (Borland) McC.; B.A. with honors in Math., U. Toronto, 1962; m. Margaret Lorna Smith, Oct. 20, 1961; children—Lorna Kristine, Ian Alexander York, Kathleen Mary Alice, Patricia Colleen. Group actuarial supr. N.Am. Life Assurance Co., Toronto, 1962-65; research analyst, underwriter, instl. salesman Pitfield, Mackay, Ross & Co., Ltd., Toronto and Montreal, 1965-69; propr. McCutcheon Securities Co., Toronto, 1969-70; v.p., sec. Loewen, Ondaatje, McCutcheon & Co. Ltd., Toronto, 1970-77; pres. Arachnae Mgmt. Ltd., Buttonville, Ont., 1976—; v.p. Martonmere Securities Ltd., Toronto, 1977—; dir. Patino N.V., The Hague. Netherlands, N.Canadian Oils Ltd., Calgary, Alta., Foodex Inc., Toronto, Can. Gen. Life Ins. Co., Can. Gen. Securities Ltd., Canbrusa Mining N.V., Edper Equities Ltd., Edper Holdings Ltd., Hatleigh Corp. Ltd., Kesmark Constrn. Ltd., others; chmn. Toronto Stock Exchange, 1976-77. Pres. Westmount Young Progressive Conservatives, Montreal, 1965-67; chmn. Ont. Waterfowl Research Found., Guelph, 1971-73; chmn. trustees Imperial Order Daus. of Empire Children's Hosp., Toronto, 1974—. Mem. Naval Officers Assn. Can. Mem. United Ch. Can. Clubs: Albany, Granite, Strollers (Toronto). Home: 58 Lympstone Ave Toronto ON M4N 1M7 Canada Office: Buttonville Airport Markham ON L3P 3J9 Canada

MCCUTCHEON, JOHN TINNEY, JR., journalist; b. Chgo., Nov. 8, 1917; s. John Tinney and Evelyn (Shaw) McC.; B.S., Harvard U., 1939; m. Susan Dart, Feb. 1, 1943; children—Anne (Mrs. Ronald Lewis), Mary, John Tinney III. Reporter, City News Bur., Chgo., 1939-40, Chgo. Tribune, 1940-51, editor column A Line O' Type or Two, 1951-57, editorial writer, 1957-71, editor editorial page, 1971—, columnist, 1967-70. Trustee, Lake Forest (Ill.) Library, pres. 1970-72. Served with USNR, 1941-46. Mem. Soc. Midland Authors, Am. Soc. Newspaper Editors, Nat. Conf. Editorial Writers, Geog. Soc. Chgo. (pres. 1955-57), Chgo. Zool. Soc. (trustee), Chgo. Hist. Soc. (trustee), Inter Am. Press Assn. (dir., freedom of press com.), Sigma Delta Chi. Clubs: Onwentsia (Lake Forest, Ill.); Tavern, Wayfarers, Press (Chgo.). Home: 281 W Laurel Ave Lake Forest IL 60045 Office: Tribune Tower 435 N Michigan Ave Chicago IL 60611

MCCUTCHEON, LAWRENCE, football player; b. Plainview, Tex., June 2, 1950; student Colo. State U. Running back Los Angeles Rams, 1972—; played in Pro Bowl, 1973, 74, 75, 76, 77, in NFC Championship Game, 1974, 75, 76. Office: care LA Rams 10271 W Pico Blvd Los Angeles CA 90064*

MCDADE, HERBERT HARDINGE, JR., pharm. co. exec.; b. Bklyn., Apr. 6, 1927; s. Herbert Hardinge and Mabel L. (Landefeld) McD.; B.S., U. Notre Dame, 1949; B. Philosophy, Laval U., Quebec, Can., 1950; m. Ann Lois Finucane, Oct. 6, 1951; children—Mary Elizabeth, Janice Ann, Mark Daniel, Herbert Hardinge III. With Upjohn Co., 1950-70, product promotion mgr., 1960-62, dir. sales planning and promotion, 1962-68, dir. lab. procedures div., 1968-70; pub. Family Health mag., N.Y.C., 1970-72; pres., chief operating officer USV Pharm. Corp., 1973—; dir. Nat. Vitamin Found., 1963—, chmn. exec. com., 1964—, chmn. bd., 1966; dir. Meloy Labs. Formerly co-chmn. indsl. com. Kalamazoo Community Chest; pres. Lansing Diocesan Area Sch. Bd.; mem. Lansing Diocese Bd. Edn.; former bd. dirs. Cath. Social Service Mich.; trustee Thomas Aquinas Coll. Club: Winged Foot Golf. Home: 4 Well House Ln Mamaroneck NY 10543 Office: 1 Scarsdale Rd Tuckahoe NY 10707

MC DADE, JOSEPH EDWARD, microbiologist; b. Cumberland, Md., Feb. 4, 1940; s. Joseph Edward and Mary Margaret (Litzenburg) McD.; B.A., Western Md. Coll., 1962, Sc.D. (hon.), 1977; M.A., U. Del., 1965, Ph.D., 1967; m. Judith Ann Firestone, Aug. 22, 1964; children—Michael, Karen. Dir. cell prodn. dept. Microbiol. Assos., Inc., Bethesda, Md., 1969-71; research asso. U. Md. Sch. Medicine, 1971-75; research microbiologist Center Disease Control, Atlanta, 1975—. Served to capt. Chem. Corps, AUS, 1967-69. Recipient Bates prize Western Md. Coll., 1962; award for Exceptional Achievement, HEW, 1978; Richard and Hinda Rosenthal award, 1979, NDEA fellow, 1962-65. Mem. Am. Soc. Microbiology. Author research articles. Home: 1295 Oxford Rd Atlanta GA 30306 Office: 1600 Clifton Rd Atlanta GA 30333

MC DADE, JOSEPH MICHAEL, congressman; b. Scranton, Pa., Sept. 29, 1931; s. John B. and Genevieve (Hayes) McD.; B.A. in Polit. Sci. with honors, U. Notre Dame, 1953; LL.B., U. Pa., 1956; LL.D., St. Thomas Aquinas Coll.; m. Mary Teresa O'Brien, Mar. 31, 1952; children—Joseph, Aileen, Deborah, Mark. Clk. to fed. judge, 1956-57; admitted to Pa. bar, 1957; pvt. practice law, Scranton, 1957—; city solicitor, Scranton, 1962; mem. 88th-95th Congresses, 10th Dist. Pa., mem. appropriations com. Mem. Am., Pa. Lackawanna County bar assns., Scranton C. of C. Republican. Clubs: K.C.; Lions, James Wilson Law (Phila.). Home: 4006 N 27th St Arlington VA 22370 Office: House Office Bldg Washington DC 20515

MCDANIEL, BOYCE DAWKINS, physicist, educator; b. Brevard, N.C., June 11, 1917; s. Allen Webster and Grace (Dawkins) McD.; B.S., Ohio Wesleyan U., 1938; M.S., Case Inst. Tech., 1940; Ph.D., Cornell U., 1943; m. Jane Chapman Grennell, Aug. 3, 1941; children—Gail P., James G. Staff mem. radiation lab. Mass. Inst. Tech., 1943; physicist Los Alamos Sci. Lab., 1943-46; mem. faculty Cornell U., Ithaca, N.Y., 1945—, prof., 1956—, asso. dir. lab. nuclear studies, 1960-67, dir. lab. nuclear studies, 1967—, Floyd R. Newman prof. nuclear studies, 1977—; head accelerator sect. Nat. Accelerator Lab., Batavia, Ill., 1972; mem. high energy physics adv. panel ERDA, 1975—. Trustee Asso. Univs., Inc., 1962-75. Vis. fellow Brookhaven Nat. Lab., 1966. Fulbright Research grantee Australian Nat. U., 1953; Guggenheim and Fulbright grantee U. Rome and Synchrotron Lab., Frascati, Italy, 1959-60. Fellow Am. Phys. Soc.; mem. Univs. Research Assn. (trustee 1971-77). Spl. research neutron spectroscopy, gamma ray spectroscopy, high energy photoprodn. K mesons and hyperons, instrumentation for high energy physics, accelerator design and constrn. Contbr. articles to profl. jours. Home: 26 Woodcrest Ave Ithaca NY 14850

MC DANIEL, CHARLES POPE, supt. schs.; b. Tucker, Ga., Dec. 28, 1922; s. Charles Pope and Loreno (Britt) McD.; A.B., Mercer U., 1947, M.Ed., 1949; M.A., Columbia U., 1953; D.Ed., U. Ga., 1967; m. Beatrice Schroeder Martin, Apr. 19, 1946; children—Mary Elizabeth McDaniel Edwards, Margaret Anne, Charles William. Tchr., Tucker Elem. Sch., 1946; tchr., counselor Ga. Mil. Coll., Milledgeville, 1947-53; prin. Metter (Ga.) High Sch., 1953-56; prin. Druid Hills High Sch., Atlanta, 1956-60; supt. schs. Thomasville (Ga.) City Schs., 1960-69, Clarke County Schs., Athens, Ga., 1969-77, State of Ga., Atlanta, 1977—. Mem. Ga. Tax Reform Commn., 1978—; bd. dirs. Athens-Clarke County Community Chest, Ga. Spl. Olympics; trustee Mercer U.; mem. governing bd. Student-Tchr. Achievement Recognition. Served with USMC Res., 1943-46. Decorated Purple Heart; named Thomasville-Thomas County Man of Year, 1966. Mem. NEA, Ga. Assn. Educators, Profl. Assn. Ga. Educators, Am. Assn. Sch. Adminstrs., Ga. Assn. Sch. Supts., Council of Chief State Sch. Officers, Athens Area C. of C. (past dir.). Democrat. Baptist. Club: Atlanta Rotary. Author: A Study of Factors in the Success or Failure of School Bond Issues, 1967. Home: 2042 Eldorado Dr NE Atlanta GA 30345 Office: State Supts Office 242 State Office Bldg Atlanta GA 30334

MCDANIEL, CHARLES-GENE, educator, writer; b. Luxora, Ark., Jan. 11, 1931; s. Charles Waite and Edith Estelle (Kelly) McD.; B.S., Northwestern U., 1954, M.S. in Journalism, 1955. Reporter, Gazette and Daily, York, Pa., 1955-58; sci. writer Chgo. bur. A.P., 1958-79; dir. journalism program, asso. prof. English and communicative arts Roosevelt U., Chgo., 1979—. Recipient writing awards Erikson Inst. for Early Edn., 1972, AMA, 1974, Chgo. Inst. for Psychoanalysis, 1971, 73, Ill. Med Soc., 1972, 73, ADA, 1975. Mem. Fellowship of Reconciliation, ACLU, War Resistors League, Art Inst. Chgo. (life), Mus. Contemporary Art (charter), Chgo. Symphony Soc., Handgun Control Inc. Contbr. articles to The Progressive, Christian Century, The Nation, Newman Reports, Today's Health, Family Health, Reader's Digest, others. Work represented in anthologies. Home: 5109 S Cornell Ave Chicago IL 60615 Office: 430 S Michigan Ave Chicago IL 60605

MCDANIEL, EARL WADSWORTH, physicist, educator; b. Macon, Ga., Apr. 15, 1926; s. James Bruce and Jewel (Wadsworth) McD.; B.S., Ga. Inst. Tech., 1948; M.S., U. Mich., 1950, Ph.D., 1954; m. Marjorie Frances Scarratt, July 2, 1948; children—Keith Bruce, Linda Frances. Asst. prof. Ga. Inst. Tech., 1954-56, asso. prof., 1956-61, prof., 1961-70, Regents prof., 1970—; vis. scholar U. Durham (Eng.), 1966-67; cons. Oak Ridge Nat. Lab., U.S. Army Missile Command, United Techs. Research Center; mem. NRC com. on basic research, 1954-57; mem. Internat. Conf. on Physics of Electron and Atomic Collisions, 1965-71; sec. Gaseous Electronics Conf., 1965-66. Served with USN, 1944-46. Named Ga. Scientist of Year, 1971. Guggenheim fellow, 1966-67; Fulbright-Hays Act sr. research scholar, 1966-67. Fellow Am. Phys. Soc. Author: Collision Phenomena in Ionized Gases, 1964; (with V. Cermak, A. Dalgarno and E. Ferguson) Ion-Molecule Reactions, 1970; (with E.A. Mason) The Mobility and Diffusion of Ions in Gases, 1973. Co-editor, 5 vols. Case Studies in Atomic Physics, 1969-77; mem. editorial bd. Physics Reports, 1974—, Atomic Data and Nuclear Data Tables, 1969—. Contbr. sci. articles to profl. jours. Home: 4565 Meadow Valley Dr NE Atlanta GA 30342 Office: Sch Physics Ga Inst Tech Atlanta GA 30332

MCDANIEL, GLEN, business exec., lawyer; b. Seymour, Tex., Mar. 21, 1912; s. Otho and Mary Burnet (Kerr) McD.; A.B., So. Meth. U., 1932, A.M., 1933; LL.B., Columbia, 1936; m. Marilyn Ballentine, Apr. 15, 1965; children—Laurie Esther, Scott Kerr. Atty. Sullivan & Cromwell, N.Y.C., 1936-42; v.p., gen. atty. R.C.A. Communications, Inc., N.Y.C., 1946-48; v.p. RCA, 1948-51; partner Lundgren & McDaniel, N.Y.C., 1951-65; chmn. exec. com., dir. Litton Industries, Inc.; dir. Air Products & Chems. Inc., Security Pacific Nat. Bank. Served from lt. (j.g.) to lt. comdr. USNR, 1942-45; chmn. Navy Bd. Contract Appeals, 1945-46. Mem. Electronics Industries Assn. (pres. 1951-55). Presbyterian. 780 Linda Flora Dr Los Angeles CA 90049 Office: 360 N Crescent Dr Beverly Hills CA 90210

MC DANIEL, JESSE WOOD, JR., lawyer; b. Little River, Tex., Dec. 8, 1910; s. Jesse Wood and Beulah Corine (Middlebrook) McD.; B.A., U. Tex., 1931, LL.B., 1934; m. Carrie Helen Bentley, June 26, 1937 (dec. 1965); m. Margaret Marie Smith, Sept. 10, 1966; children—Mildred Corine, Charles Bentley. Admitted to Tex. bar, 1934; asso. Will M. Martin, atty., Hillsboro, Tex., 1934-36; asso. Cole, Patterson & Cole, Houston, 1936-42; partner Patterson, McDaniel & Boyd (and predecessors), Houston, 1942-77; dir. Allied Metals, Inc., Offenshauser Co., Isabell Gerhart, Inc., Pernie Bailey Drilling Co., Eagle Insulators, Inc., FitzSimmons Dental, Inc.; past pres. Houston Jr. Bar Assn. Served with USNR, 1944-46. Methodist (adminstrv. bd.). Mason (33 deg., past grand prelate Tex.). Home: 6707 Buffalo Speedway Houston TX 77005

MCDANIEL, RAYMOND LAMAR, newspaper editor; b. Natalbany, La., Dec. 15, 1925; s. Franklin Pierce and Mattie (Stilley) McD.; student Southeastern La. U., 1942-43; B.S., La. Tech. U., 1949; m. Eugenia Hastings, Nov. 10, 1951; 1 son, Raymond Lamar. State editor Shreveport Times Pub. Co. (La.), 1950-53, legis. corr., 1953-58, city editor, 1958-68, exec. editor, 1968-74, editor, 1974—. Served with USMCR, 1943-46. Mem. Sigma Delta Chi, Pi Kappa Alpha, Gamma Psi. Baptist (deacon, dir. ch.). Rotarian. Home: 422 Ontario St Shreveport LA 71106 Office: 222 Lake St Shreveport LA 71101

MC DANIEL, RODERICK ROGERS, engring. cons.; b. High River, Alta., Can., 1926; s. Dorsey Patton and Daisy (Rogers) McD.; B.S., U. Okla., 1947; m. Marilyn Bouck, Oct. 16, 1948; children—Nancy, Leslie. Petroleum reservoir engr. Creole Petroleum Corp., 1947, Imperial Oil Ltd., 1948-52; chief reservoir engr. Imperial Oil Ltd., 1952-55; pres. McDaniel Cons., Calgary, 1955—; dir., chmn. Pacific Western Airlines Ltd., Calgary, 1975—. Bd. dirs. Calgary Exhbn. and Stampede. Mem. Assn. Profl. Engrs., Can. C. of C. (past pres.), Geologists and Geophysicists of Alta., Petroleum Soc. Mem. Progressive Conservative Party. Clubs: Calgary Petroleum (past pres.), Calgary Highlanders, Ranchmen's, Calgary Golf and Country. Home: #11 3231 Rideau Ridge Pl SW Calgary AB Canada Office: 800 6th Ave SW Calgary AB T2P 0T8 Canada*

MC DANIEL, THOMAS M., JR., utility exec.; b. Richmond, Calif., Feb. 13, 1916; s. Thomas M. and Marguerite (Pierson) McD.; A.B., Stanford, 1937, M.B.A., 1939; m. Clerimond W. Haug; children—Martha, Kathleen, Nancy, Laurie. Salesman, IBM; asst. to v.p. Bethlehem Steel Co.; prin. Arthur Andersen & Co.; past pres. So. Calif. Edison Co., now cons. and dir.; dir. Northrop Corp., Bank of Am. N.T. & S.A., Dillingham Corp., Asso. So. Investment Co., Bankamerica Corp., Pacific Indemnity Co. Trustee Huntington Library and Art Gallery. Clubs: California, Los Angeles Country. Office: 2244 Walnut Grove Ave Rosemead CA 91770

MCDANIEL, WILLIAM EARL, state ofcl.; b. Fresno, Calif., May 30, 1915; s. Jesse F. and Emma (Mischler) McD.; B.S. in Agr., U. Mo., 1942; M.S. in Agrl. Econs., U. Ill., 1943; Ph.D., U. Minn., 1951; m. Frances M. Bissett, Dec. 26, 1946; children—William Earl II, Michael Anthony. Instr., U. Minn. Coll. Commerce, 1947-48, Coll. Agr., 1948-51; mem. faculty U. Del., 1951—, prof. agrl. econs., 1958—, chmn. dept., 1957-65, dean Coll. Agrl. Scis., 1965-77, dir. Del. Agr. Expt. Sta., 1965-77; sec. Del. Dept. Agr., 1977-79; chmn. Gov. Del. Council Natural Resources and Environ. Control, 1970-77. Vice pres., dir. Brookside Community Assn., Newark, Del. Served with AUS, 1943-46. Mem. Am. Agrl. Econ. Assn., Am. Soc. Farm Mgrs. and Rural Appraisers, Gamma Sigma Delta, Alpha Zeta. Contbr. articles to profl. jours. Home: 404 Country Club Dr Newark DE 19711

MCDAVID, JOEL DUNCAN, bishop; b. Georgetown, Ala., June 10, 1916; s. Harry and Ola Elizabeth (McCaskill) McD.; B.A., Millsaps Coll., 1941; B.D., Emory U., 1944; D.D. (hon.), Birmingham So. U., 1959, Fla. So. Coll., 1973, Bethune Cookman Coll., 1973, Millsaps Coll., 1976; m. Milah Dodd Gibson, Aug. 29, 1942; children—Ben A., Joel G., Karen Anne. Ordained to ministry Methodist Ch., 1944; pastor in Grand Bay, Ala., 1944-46, Toulminville, Ala., 1946-50, Auburn, Ala., 1950-58, Montgomery, Ala., 1958-66, Dauphin Way Ch., Mobile, Ala., 1966-72; bishop United Meth. Ch., Lakeland, Fla., 1972—; instr. Auburn (Ala.) U., 1950-58. Mem. Ala. Ethics Commn., 1966-67. Bd. dirs. YMCA, 1959-72, A.R.C., 1955-58, Family Guidance, 1961-65; trustee Huntingdon Coll., 1951-72, Fla. So. Coll., 1972—, Bethune Cookman Coll., 1972—, Emory U., 1972—, Mobile Gen. Hosp. Sch. Nursing, 1968-72. Named Man of Year Montgomery, Ala., 1965. Mem. United Meth. Southeastern Jurisdiction Council (v.p. 1968-72, mem. higher edn. commn. 1956-60, structure commn. 1968-72, gen. conf. del. 1960, 64, 66, 68, 70, 72, gen. bd. discipleship 1972—). Author: Waiting, 1969. Home: 127 Lake Hollingsworth Dr Lakeland FL 33801 Office: 968 Callahan Court Lakeland FL 33802

MC DAVID, RAVEN IOOR, JR., linguist, educator; b. Greenville, S.C., Oct. 16, 1911; s. Raven Ioor and Marie Louise (Henderson) McD.; B.A., Furman U., 1931, Litt.D., 1966; M.A., Duke, 1933, Ph.D., 1935, Litt.D., 1972; summer student Va. Mil. Inst., 1929, U. Mich., 1937, 38, 40, 48, 52, 56, 57, 58, U. N.C. 1941; student U. Mich., 1951-52, Yale, 1942-43; m. Elizabeth Lee Harris, Mar. 7, 1942 (div. 1945); 1 dau., Bettie McClain Mason; m. 2d, Virginia Ann Glenn, June 7, 1950; children—Glenn Truxtun, Raven Ioor III, Thomas Inglesby, Ann Hamilton. Instr. English, The Citadel, Charleston, S.C., 1935-38, Mich. State U., East Lansing, 1938-39; asst. prof. S.W. La. Inst., 1940-42, Western Res. U., Cleve., 1952-57; asso. prof. English, U. Chgo., 1957-64, prof. of English and linguistics, 1964—; vis. summer prof. U. Colo., 1950, Mont. State Coll., 1951, U. Mich., 1952, 57, U. N.B., 1961, W.Va. State Coll., 1962, Mich. State U., 1964, Ill. Inst. Tech., 1967, 69; vis. prof. U. Ill., 1949-50, Cornell U., 1950-51, U. S.C., 1974, 76, La. State U., 1979; linguist lang. sect. U.S. Army, 1943-45, U.S. Bd. Geog. Names, 1947. Fellow Am. Council Learned Socs., 1942-44, 45, 50-51; Rosenwald fellow, 1941; Fulbright fellow, Mainz, 1965; sr. fellow Nat. Endowment for Humanities, 1975. Fellow Am. Anthrop. Assn., AAAS; mem. Nat. Council Tchrs. English (David Russell Research award 1969), Modern Lang. Assn. Am., Midwest Modern Lang. Assn., Linguistic Soc. Am., N.Y., Ill. acads. scis., Dutch Settlers Soc. Albany, Am. Dialect Soc. (pres. 1967-68), Internat. Assn. U. Profs. English, N.Y. Folklore Soc., Midwest Folklore Soc., Am. Oriental Soc., AAUP, Internat. Center Gen. Dialectology, Canadian Linguistic Assn., NAACP, SAR, Phi Beta Kappa. Democrat. Episcopalian. Club: Quadrangle (Chgo.). Author: Varieties of American English, 1979; co-author: Structure of American English, 1958; Pronunciation of English in the Atlantic States, 1961. Editor: (H.L. Mencken) The American Language, 1963; Linguistic Atlas of the North Central States, 1976; Linguistic Atlas of the Middle and South Atlantic States, 1979; co-editor: Lexicography in English, 1973. Field investigator, asso. editor Linguistic Atlas U.S. and Canada, 1941-64, editor, 1964—. Home: 5736 Blackstone Ave Chicago IL 60637

MCDAVID, VIRGINIA GLENN, educator, linguist; b. Mpls., Aug. 9, 1926; d. Lester Truxtun and Anna (Wurtz) Glenn; B.A., U. Minn., 1946, M.A., 1948, Ph.D., 1956; m. Raven I. McDavid, Jr., June 7, 1950; children—Glenn Truxton, Raven Ioor III, Thomas Inglesby, Ann Hamilton. Prof. English, Chgo. State U., 1958—; co. dir. Lang. Research Services, Chgo., 1961—. Mem. Modern Lang. Assn., Linguistic Soc. Am., Am. Dialect Soc. (editor publ.), Nat. Council Tchrs. English. Author: (with William Card) 99 Exercises for College Composition, 1962; (with Macklin Thomas) Basic Writing, 1973, Writing Today's English, 1977; The Random House English Handbook, 1973; American English, 1974; editor Ill. Schs. Jour.; asso.

editor Linguistic Atlas of N. Central States. Home: 5736 S Blackstone Chicago IL 60637

MCDERMOTT, ALBERT LEO, lawyer; b. Lowell, Mass., Jan. 21, 1923; s. John Thomas and Josephine (Rohan) McD.; A.B., Boston Coll., 1944; LL.B., Georgetown U., 1949. Admitted to Mass. and D.C. bars, 1950, U.S. Supreme Ct. bar, 1972; practice of law, Washington, 1950-54; asso. Ingoldsby & Coles, 1950-52, partner, 1952-54; spl. asst. to Sec. Labor, 1954-61; now partner law firm McDermott & Russell, and predecessor, Washington rep. Am. Hotel and Motel Assn., 1963—. Mem. bd. adv. Maritime Cargo Transp. Conf., Fed. Service Impasses Panel, 1972-78; alt. rep. Pres. Nixon's Pay Board, 1971-73. Served as lt. USNR, World War II. Mem. Nat. Acad. Sci. (mem. research council 1957-60), Am., Fed. bar assns., Bar Assn. D.C. Clubs: Nat. Lawyers, Counsellors, Capitol Hill (Washington). Home: 4813 Van Ness St NW Washington DC 20016 Office: Washington Bldg Washington DC 20005

MCDERMOTT, DENNIS, trade union exec.; b. Portsmouth, Eng., Nov. 3, 1922; s. John and Beatrice (Sutton) McD.; student public schs.; m. Mary Claire Elizabeth Caza, Oct. 22, 1976; children—Michael, Mark, Patrick, William, Maureen. Assembler and welder Massey-Ferguson, Toronto, Ont., Can., 1948-54; internat. rep. United Automobile Workers Am., 1954-68, Can. dir., 1968-78; pres. Can. Labour Congress, Ottawa, Ont., 1978—; lectr. on arbitration and labor law at univs. and Labour Coll. Can.; mem. Ont. Labour Relations Bd. Mem. Ont. provincial exec. and fed. exec. New Democratic Party. Served with Royal Navy, 1939-46. Decorated Centennial medal. Office: 2841 Riverside Dr Ottawa ON K1V 8X7 Canada

MC DERMOTT, EDWARD ALOYSIOUS, lawyer; b. Dubuque, Iowa, June 28, 1920; s. Edward L. and Sarah (Larkin) McD.; B.A., Loras Coll., Dubuque, 1939; J.D., State U. Iowa, 1942; J.D. (hon.), Xavier U., 1962, Loras Coll., 1973; m. Naola Spellman, Sept. 1, 1945; children—Maureen, Edward Aloysious, Charles Joseph, Daniel John. Admitted to Iowa, D.C., Nebr. bars, 1942; mem. legal dept. Travelers Ins. Co., Omaha, 1942-43, Montgomery Ward & Co., Chgo., 1943-46; atty. firm O'Connor, Thomas & O'Connor, Dubuque, 1946-50; chief counsel sub-com. privileges and elections U.S. Senate, 1950-51; partner firm O'Connor, Thomas, McDermott & Wright, Dubuque, 1951-61; prof. bus. law and econs. Loras Coll., also Clarke Coll., Dubuque; dep. dir. Office Civil and Def. Moblzn., 1961-62; dep. dir. Office Emergency Planning, 1961-62; dir., 1962-65; partner firm Hogan & Hartson, Washington, 1965—. Mem. Nat. Security Council, 1962-65; U.S. rep. to sr. com., other coms. NATO, 1962-65; chmn. Pres. Exec. Stockpile Com., 1962-65; bd. advisers Indsl. Coll. Armed Forces, 1962-65; commr. Nat. Conf. Uniform Commrs. State Laws, 1959-64; chmn. Nat. Civil Def. Adv. Council, 1962-65; mem. Pres.'s Com. Employment Handicapped, 1962-65, Pres.'s Com. Manpower, 1963-65, Pres.'s Com. Econ. Impact Def. and Rearmament, 1963-65, Pres.'s Sr. Adv. Com. on Govt. Reorgn., 1978-79; chmn. Com. on Assumptions for Nonmil. Planning, 1963-65; mem. Fed. Reconstrn. and Devel. Commn. Alaska, 1964-65. Del. Democratic Nat. Conv., 1952, 60, 64; mem. Iowa Dem. Central Com., 1956-60; co-chmn. Iowans for Kennedy, 1960. Trustee Colgate U., Coll. Notre Dame, Loras Coll.; regent emeritus U. Santa Clara (Calif); bd. advisers Lynchburg (Va.) Coll., Iowa Law Sch. Found. Decorated knight Holy Sepulchre; Knight of Malta; recipient Amvets Spl. Silver Helmet award, 1963. Mem. Am. Irish Found. (v.p., dir.), Am., Fed., Iowa (bd. govs. 1956-60), D.C. bar assns., Am. Judicature Soc., John Carroll Soc. (Pres. 1972), Friendly Sons St. Patrick (pres. 1978-79). Clubs: Nat. Lawyers, Nat. Capitol Democratic, Metropolitan, International (Washington). Home: 5400 Albermarle St NW Washington DC 20016 Office: 815 Connecticut Ave Washington DC 20006

MCDERMOTT, EDWARD H., lawyer; b. Cooperstown, N.D., Aug. 17, 1896 s. John H. and Anna (Arneson) McD.; A.B. U. N.D., 1919; LL.B., Harvard, 1922; m. Lucile Boso, May 29, 1924 (dec. Jan. 1965); children—Robert B., John H.; m. 2d, Mildred Wetten Kelly, Nov. 4, 1966. Admitted to Mass. bar, 1922; asst. counsel and counsel Joint Congl. Com. Internal Revenue Taxation, 1927-29; cons. U.S. Treas. Dept., 1929; sr. partner McDermott, Will and Emery, lawyers, Chgo., 1934-71, counsel, 1971—. Cons. Office War Moblzn., Washington, 1944. Trustee YMCA Met. Chgo. Mem. Chgo., Ill., Am. bar assns. Presbyn. Clubs: Chicago, Legal, Mid-Day, Glen View, (Chgo.). Home: 237 E Delaware Pl Chicago IL 60611 Office: 111 W Monroe St Chicago IL 60603

MCDERMOTT, JOHN FRANCIS, historian, educator; b. St. Louis, Apr. 18, 1902; s. John F. and Mary (Steber) McD.; A.B., Washington U., St. Louis, 1923, A.M., 1924; D.H.L., U. Mo., 1977; m. Mary S. Kendrick, Dec. 20, 1924; 1 son, John Francis IV. Instr. English, Washington U., St. Louis, 1924-36, asst. prof., 1936-49, asso. prof. English, 1949-61, asso. prof. Am. cultural history, 1961-63; research prof. humanities So. Ill. U., Edwardsville, 1963-71, research prof. emeritus, 1971—; cons. early Western Am. history and 19th century Am. painting. Bd. dirs. Friends of Lovejoy Library, So. Ill. U., treas., 1976—; mem. Gov. Bond's Bingham Sketches Com., 1975-76. Mem. Modern Humanities Research Assn., Bibliog. Soc. Am., Inst. Francais Washington (trustee 1958—), Academie de Macon, Orgn. Am. Historians, Mo. Hist. Soc. (trustee 1950-59, 79—, sec. bd. 1951-54, award of merit 1961, 78), Am. Name Soc., Am. Studies Assn., Am. Folklore Soc. (councillor 1958-60), Am. Antiquarian Soc., Nat. Folk Festival Assn. (pres. 1953-61; chmn. Wash. U. Folklore Conf., 1953, 55), N.Y., Kans., Ind., Ill., Minn., Mo. hist. socs., Am., Western (award of merit 1976) hist. assns., Am. Hist. Assn., Internat. Soc. for 18th Century Studies, Nat. Trust for Historic Preservation, William Clark Soc. St. Louis (pres. 1953-60), St. Louis Hist. Documents Found. (pres. 1948-78), St.Louis Westerners (pres. 1961), Instituto de Cultura Hispanica Madrid (hon.), Henry Shaw Meml. Assn. (pres. 1953-60). Served to capt. USAAF, 1942-45. Newberry Library Fellow in Midwestern Studies, 1947-48; Washington U. summer research appointments, 1950, 57, 60; Guggenheim Meml. Found. Fellow, 1954-55; research grants Am. Philos. Soc., 1939, 40, 54, 57, 58-59, 63, 64 (library research asso. 1959-62), Mich. State U., 1951, Am. Council Learned Socs., 1960, Pro-Helvetia Found., 1961, Henry E. Huntington Library, 1965, So. Ill. U., 1964—; decorated chevalier Palmes Academiques, 1965, comdr., 1976; chevalier Ordre National du Merite, 1970. Chmn. Conf. France in Miss. Valley, Washington U., 1956; chmn. Conf. Research Opportunities in Am. Cultural History, 1959; chmn. Conf. (St. Louis Bicentennial) French in Miss. Valley, 1964, Conf. Trans. Miss. Frontier, So. Ill. U., 1965, Conf. French in Miss. Valley, 1967, Conf. Travelers on Western Frontier, 1968, Conf. Spanish in Miss. Valley, 1970. Author: Private Libraries in Creole Saint Louis, 1938; Glossary of Miss. Valley French, 1941; The Lost Panoramas of the Mississippi, 1958; The Art of Seth Eastman, 1959; George Caleb Bingham, River Portraitist, 1959; Seth Eastman Pictorial Historian of the Indian, 1961; Seth Eastman's Mississippi: A Lost Portfolio Recovered, 1973. Co-author: The Technique of Composition, 1931, latest rev. edit., 1960; English Communication, 1943. Editor: Collected Verse of Lewis Carroll, 1929; Modern Plays, 1932; The Russian Journal and other Selections from Works of Lewis Carroll, 1935, 77; Tixier's Travels on the Osage Prairies, 1940, 69; Western Journals of Washington Irving, 1944, 66; Old Cahokia, 1949; Travels in Search of the Elephant, The Wanderings of Alfred S. Waugh, Artist, 1951; Up the Missouri with Audubon; the Journal of Edward Harris, 1951; The Early Histories of St. Louis, 1952; Thaddeus Culbertson's Jour. of an Expedition to the Mauvaises Terres and the Upper Missouri in 1850, 1952; John Treat Irving's Indian Sketches, 1954; Washington Irving's Tour on the Prairies, 1956; Milford's Memoir of Travels in the Creek Nation, 1956; Research Opportunities in American Cultural History, 1961, 77; Robb's Streaks of Squatter Life, 1961; The Western Journals of Dr. George Hunter, 1796-1805, 1963; The World of Washington Irving, 1965; Audubon in the West, 1965; The French in the Mississippi Valley, 1965; The Frontier Reexamined, 1967; An Artist on the Overland Trail: The 1849 Diary and Sketches of James F. Wilkins, 1968; Before Mark Twain: A Sampler of Old, Old Times on the Mississippi, 1968; Frenchmen and French Ways in the Mississippi Valley, 1969; Travelers on the Western Frontier, 1970; The Spanish in the Mississippi Valley, 1973; Philip Pittman's The Present State of the European Settlements on the Mississippi, 1977. Co-editor: College Readings in Contemporary Thought, 1929; Contemporary Opinion, 1933; Matt Fields Prairie and Mountain Sketches, 1957; contbr. periodicals. Asso. editor French Am. rev., 1950. Gen. editor Travels on Western Waters series, So. Ill. U. Press; adv. bd. Papers on Language and Literature, 1965—, Old Northwest Quar., 1974-79; publ. adv. com. Henry Francis duPont Winterthur Mus., 1968-71. Home: 6345 Westminster Pl Saint Louis MO 63130

MC DERMOTT, JOHN FRANCIS, JR., psychiatrist; b. Hartford, Conn., Dec. 12, 1929; s. John Francis and Camilla R. (Cavanaugh) McD.; A.B., Cornell U., 1951; M.D., New York Med. Coll., 1955; m. Sarah N. Schemm, Dec. 27, 1958; children—Elizabeth C., John Francis III. Intern, Henry Ford Hosp., Detroit, 1955-56; resident psychiatry U. Mich. Med. Center, 1956-62; practice medicine, specializing in psychiatry and child psychiatry, Honolulu, 1969—; instr., asst. prof., asso. prof. psychiatry U. Mich. Sch. Medicine, 1962-69; prof., chmn. dept. psychiatry U. Hawaii Sch. Medicine, 1969—; cons. numerous mental health clinics and orgns. Served with USN, 1958-60. Named Disting. Alumnus, New York Med. Coll., 1976. Diplomate Am. Bd. Psychiatry and Neurology (chmn. com. on certification in child psychiatry 1974-78). Fellow Am. Psychiat. Assn., Am. Acad. Child Psychiatry, Am. Coll. Psychiatrists, Am. Orthopsychiatric Assn. Clubs: Oahu Country; Outrigger Canoe. Author: Psychiatry for the Pediatrician, 1970; Childhood Psychopathology, 1972; Mental Health Education in New Medical Schools, 1973; Psychiatric Treatment of the Child, 1977; New Directions in Childhood Psychopathology, 1979; The Parents Book of Sibling Rivalry, 1980. Home: 1950 Judd Hillside Honolulu HI 96822 Office: 1356 Lusitana St Honolulu HI 96813

MCDERMOTT, JOHN JOSEPH, educator; b. N.Y.C., Jan. 5, 1932; s. John J. and Helen (Kelly) McD.; B.A. cum laude, St. Frances Coll., 1953; M.A., Fordham U., 1954, Ph.D., 1959; LL.D., U. Hartford, 1970; m. Virginia Picarelli, June 14, 1952; children—Marise, Michele, David, Brian, Tara. Tchr. Latin, Loughlin High Sch., Bklyn., 1953-54; instr. philosophy St. Francis Coll., Bklyn., 1954-57; mem. faculty Queens Coll., Flushing, N.Y., 1957-77, asso. prof. philosophy, 1965-67, prof., 1968-77; prof., head dept. philosophy and humanities Tex. A. and M. U., 1977—; vis. prof. Am. lit. State U. N.Y. at Stony Brook, 1970. Postdoctoral fellow Union Theol. Sem., 1964-65; recipient E. Harris Harbison award for gifted teaching, 1969-70. Mem. Am. Philos. Assn., Am. Studies Assn., History of Sci. Soc., Peirce Soc. (editorial bd. Trans.), Conf. Sci. Philosophy and Religion, Soc. for Advancement Am. Philosophy (exec. com. 1973, pres. 1977). Editor: Writings of William James, 1967; Basic Writing of Josiah Royce, 2 vols., 1969; The Philosophy of John Dewey, 2 vols., 1973; The Culture of Experience, 1976; adv. editor Collected Works of William James; editorial bd. Cross Currents, 1968—. Contbr. articles to profl. jours. Home: 705 Dexter College Station TX 77840

MCDERMOTT, RAYMUND GERALD, accountant; b. Seattle, May 23, 1927; s. William Arthur and Marjorie (Wheeler) McD.; B.A., U. Wash., 1949; m. Phyllis Ann Graham, June 25, 1950; children—Patrick Graham, Kerry Rae. Jr. accountant Longview Fibre Co. (Wash.), 1949-51; accountant John DeVille & Co., Longview, 1951-52; with Longview Fibre Co., 1952—, asst. treas., 1960-67, treas., 1968-75, v.p. finance, 1975—, also dir. Dir. Longview Sch. Dist. #122; chmn. Longview Bd. Edn., 1969-70. Trustee Cowlitz County United Fund. C.P.A., Washington. Mem. Tax Execs. Inst., Fin. Execs. Inst. Mason, Elk. Home: 2435 W Lynnwood Dr Longview WA 98632 Office: PO Box 639 Longview WA 98632

MCDERMOTT, ROBERT EMMET, univ. adminstr.; b. Maywood, Ill., Oct. 5, 1920; s. Aloysius Louis and Gertrude (Engels) McD.; B.S., Iowa State U., 1943, M.S., 1947; Ph.D., Duke, 1952; m. Barbara Jane Fawcett, Nov. 6, 1943; children—Paula Jane, Karen Denise. Asst. to asso. prof. forestry U. Mo., Columbia, 1952-59; prof. forestry, head dept. forest mgmt. Pa. State U., University Park, 1959-66, asso. dean adminstrn. Grad. Sch., 1966-69; dean Grad. Sch., dir. research, prof. botany U. Ark., Fayetteville, 1969-72; provost, prof. forestry Pa. State U., Middletown, 1972-79, prof. regional planning, 1979—. Served to lt. (j.g.) USNR, 1943-46. Mem. Soc. Am. Foresters, AAAS. Rotarian. Cotbr. articles to profl. jours. Home: 4305 Long Dr Harrisburg PA 17112

MC DERMOTT, THOMAS CHARLES, JR., electronic exec.; b. Pitts., June 1, 1927; s. Thomas Charles and Anne Horton (Morrow) McD.; B.S. in Indsl. Engring., Pa. State U., 1951; M.S. in Indsl. Adminstrn., Carnegie-Mellon U., 1954; m. Marianne Brozier, Dec. 29, 1951; children—Thomas Charles III, Karen Anne. Div. dir. quality assurance and logistics, Autonetics div. N.Am. Aviation, Anaheim, Calif., 1960-66; v.p. quality and reliability assurance space div. N.Am. Rockwell, Downey, Calif., 1966-70, mgr. operations, navigation and computers Autonetics div., Anaheim, 1970-71, dir. quality and logistics aerospace group, 1971-72, v.p. prodn. ops. Autonetics div., 1972-76, v.p. electronics prodn. ops., 1976-79, dir. mfg. plastic div., 1979—. Served with USAAF, 1945-47, USAF, 1951-60. Recipient NASA certificate appreciation contbns. Apollo program, 1969. Fellow Am. Soc. Quality Control (Pres. 1968-69, chmn. 1969-70); mem. Am. Soc. Nondestructive Testing, Am. Mgmt. Assn., Alpha Pi Mu, Sigma Tau, Phi Delta Theta. Republican. Presbyn. Home: 5106 Longview Dr Troy MI 48098

MC DERMOTT, THOMAS JOSEPH, educator, labor arbitrator; b. Somerville, Mass., May 15, 1915; s. James and Nora (Gallagher) McD.; B.B.A., Boston U., 1939, M.B.A., 1941, Ph.D., 1955; m. Patsy Ruth Harding, Nov. 21, 1944; children—Christopher, Susan Fay. Asst. prof. econs. N.Mex. State U., Albuquerque, 1946-48; asso. prof. econs. Holy Cross Coll., Worcester, Mass., 1948-59; prof. econs., coordinator econ. scis. Duquesne U., Pitts., 1959-79, prof. emeritus, 1979—; labor arbitrator, 1954—; permanent arbitrator Pitts. Steel Co. and U.S.W.A., 1962-67; contract arbitrator Owens-Ill. Glass Containers, others; mem. panels Fed. Mediation and Conciliation Service, Pa. Mediation Service, Am. Arbitration Assn.; chmn. Mass. Personnel Appeals Bd., 1958-59. Mem. Westboro (Mass.) Classification Bd., 1956-59. Served to capt. AUS, 1942-46; maj. Res. ret. Recipient Berlin award for promotion sound labor-mgmt. relations Holy Cross Coll., 1953. Fellow Dusquesne U. Inst. African Affairs; mem. Nat. Acad. Arbitrators (regional chmn. 1963-66, bd. govs. 1969-71, chmn. com. on devel. new arbitrators 1970-75), Am. Arbitration Assn., Am. Econ. Assn., AAUP, Indsl. Relations Assn., Assn. Social Econs. (exec. bd. 1965-66), Nat. Acad. Scis. Contbr. articles to profl. jours. Home: 444 Pacific Ave Pittsburgh PA 15221

MCDERMOTT, WALSH, physician, educator; b. New Haven, Oct. 24, 1909; s. Terence and Rosella (Walsh) McD.; B.A., Princeton, 1930, D.Sc. (hon.), 1974; M.D., Columbia, 1934; D.Sc. (hon.), Dartmouth Coll., 1976; D.M.S. (hon.), Med. Coll. Ohio; m. Marian Anne MacPhail, Nov. 11, 1942. Intern, asst. resident N.Y. Hosp. 1934-37; with Cornell U. Med. Coll., N.Y.C., 1937—, Livingston Farrand prof., chmn. dept. pub. health, 1955-72, prof. pub. affairs in medicine, 1972-75, emeritus prof., 1975—; spl. adv. Robert Wood Johnson Found., 1972—. Trustee Columbia U., 1973—. Recipient Lasker award, 1955, Trudeau Medal, 1963, James D. Bruce Meml. award A.C.P., 1968, Woodrow Wilson award Princeton, 1969. Fellow Royal Coll. Physicians (hon.), Societas Medica Polonorum (hon.); mem. Nat. Acad. Scis., Nat. Acad. Scis. Inst. Medicine, Am. Acad. Arts and Scis., Am. Soc. Clin. Investigation., Assn. Am. Physicians, Council on Fgn. Relations, Interurban Clin. Club. Clubs: Century Assn. (N.Y.C.); Cosmos (Washington). Co-editor Beeson-McDermott-Wyngaarden Textbook of Medicine. Office: Robert Wood Johnson Found PO Box 2316 Princeton NJ 08540

MCDERMOTT, WILLIAM VINCENT, JR., physician, educator; b. Salem, Mass., Mar. 7, 1917; s. William Vincent and Mary A. (Feenan) McD.; grad. Phillips Exeter Acad., 1934; A.B., Harvard, 1938, M.D., 1942; m. Blanche O'Riorden, May 15, 1943 (dec. July 1969); children—Blanche Anne, William Shaw, Jane Travers; m. Mary Boit Bingham, June 1, 1976. Intern, Mass. Gen. Hosp., Boston, 1942, asst. resident surgeon, 1946-49, chief resident surgeon, 1950, practice medicine specializing in surgery, Boston, 1951—; mem. staff Mass. Gen. Hosp., 1951—; USPHS fellow dept. biochemistry Sch. Medicine Yale, 1949-50; from instr. to prof. surgery Med. School Harvard, 1951-69, Cheever prof. surgery, 1969—; vis. prof. pro tem Kings Coll. Hosp. Med. Sch., London, Eng., 1960; dir. Harvard surg. unit, Sears surg. labs. Boston City Hosp., 1963-73; dir. Harvard Surg. Service and Cancer Research Inst., New Eng. Deaconess Hosp., 1973—. Pres., Med. Found. Boston, 1968-70. Served to major, M.C., AUS, 1943-46; ETO. Diplomate Nat. Bd. Med. Examiners (chmn. surgery test com.). Mem. A.C.S., Soc. U. Surgeons, Am. Surg. Assn., New Eng., Boston (pres. 1971), surg. socs., Harvard Med. Alumni Assn. (treas. 1965-68, pres. 1975—). Clubs: Aesculapian (pres. 1971), Harvard of Boston (bd. govs. 1971-77); Tavern; Country. Mem. editorial bd. Jour. Surg. Research, 1960-73, Jour. Surg. Oncology, 1970—. Home: 570 Bridge St Dedham MA 02026 Office: Med Sch Harvard Boston MA 02115

MCDEVITT, JOHN WILLIAM, educator, fraternal exec.; b. Malden, Mass., Dec. 28, 1906; s. James Francis and Margaret Agnes (Sullivan) McD.; B.A., Boston Coll., 1928, M.A., 1929; LL.D., St. Michaels Coll., 1956, Saint Francis Coll., 1964. St. Johns' U., 1967, St. Mary's Coll., 1970; L.H.D., Catholic U. Am., 1967, Catholic U. P.R., 1969, St. Leo Coll., 1973; m. Mary C. Kelley, July 3, 1936; children—John Kelley, William Paul. Tchr., prin. pub. schs., Malden, 1929-42; supt. pub. schs., Waltham, Mass., 1942-61; supreme dir. K.C., 1955—, supreme knight, 1964—. Hon. consultor Vatican City State. Dir. 1st New Haven Nat. Bank, New Haven Water Co., United Illuminating Co. Chmn. Mass. Bd. Edn., 1954, 57, Bd. dirs. Human Life Found.; trustee St. Raphael Hosp. Decorated knight grand cross Order St. Gregory, Order of Pius IX. Home: 155 Colony Rd New Haven CT 06511 Office: Drawer 1670 New Haven CT 06507

MCDEVITT, JOSEPH BRYAN, univ. adminstr., ret. naval officer; b. McGehee, Ark., Dec. 22, 1918; s. John and Mary Ann (Zimmer) McD.; student So. Ill. U., 1936-38; B.A., U. Ill., 1940, J.D., 1942; m. Catherine Irene Beatty, Jan. 30, 1965; children—Jeffrey Bryan, Paul Killian, Rodney Peter, Rita Elizabeth, John Stephen, David Andrew, Joseph Bryan, Richard Vincent, Eugena Rose, Edward Francis, Gerald Christopher. Admitted to Ill. bar, 1952; commd. ensign U.S. Navy, 1943, advanced through grades to rear adm., 1968; boat group comdr. U.S.S. Leon, 1944-46; with legal office 8th Naval Dist., New Orleans, 1950; legal officer to comdr. Amphibious Force, Atlantic Fleet, 1952; mem. mil. justice div. Office Judge Adv. Gen., 1954; naval liaison officer to U.S. Senate, 1956; staff legal officer Marine Corps. Schs., Quantico, Va., 1958; student Naval War Coll., 1958-59; assigned Joint Chiefs Staff, 1959-61; dir. internat. law div. Office Judge Adv. Gen., 1962-65; legal affairs officer to comdr. in chief Pacific, 1965-68; judge adv. gen. of navy, 1968-72; ret., 1972; chief exec. officer People to People Programs Inc., Washington, 1972-73; v.p. for exec. affairs, univ. counsel, sec. bd. trustees Clemson U., S.C., 1973—. Decorated Purple Heart, Legion of Merit, D.S.M. Mem. Am., Ill., Fed., Inter-Am. bar assns., Judge Advs. Assn., Am. Soc. Internat. Law. Catholic. Home: 201 Martin St Clemson SC 29631 Office: Office of Pres Clemson U Clemson SC 29631

MCDIARMID, IAN BERTRAND, physicist; b. Carleton Place, Ont., Can., Oct. 1, 1928; s. John and Lillian (Campbell) McD.; B.A., Queen's U., 1950, M.A., 1951; Ph.D., U. Manchester, 1954; m. Dorothy May Folger, Aug. 18, 1951; children—John Charles, Leslie-Anne. Research officer NRC Can., Ottawa, 1955-75, asst. dir. div. physics, 1970-75; asst. dir. Herzberg Inst. Astrophysics, NRC Can., 1975—. Mem. Royal Soc. Can., Am. Geophys. Union, Can. Assn. Physicists. Contbr. articles to profl. jours. Home: 901-60 McLeod St Ottawa ON K2P 2G1 Canada Office: National Research Council 100 Sussex Dr Ottawa ON Canada

MC DILL, EDWARD LAMAR, sociologist; b. Gadsden, Ala., Oct. 14, 1930; s. Edd N. and Grace Augusta (Little) McD.; B.A., Jacksonville State U., 1952; M.A., U. Ala., 1955; Ph.D., Vanderbilt U., 1959; children—Mark, Ellen. Asst. prof. sociology Vanderbilt U., 1959-64, asso. prof., 1964-65; asso. prof. social relations Johns Hopkins U., 1965-70, prof., chmn. dept. social relations, 1970—; cons. Nat. Inst. Edn. Served to 1st lt., U.S. Army, 1952-54. Ford Found. fellow, 1969-70. Mem. Am. Sociol. Assn., Am. Ednl. Research Assn., So. Sociol Soc. Author: Strategies for Success in Compensatory Education, 1969; Structures and Process in Secondary Schools, 1973; Violence in Schools, 1973. Office: Dept Social Relations Johns Hopkins Univ Baltimore MD 21218

MCDILL, THOMAS ALLISON, clergyman; b. Cicero, Ill., June 4, 1926; s. Samuel and Agnes (Lindsay) McD.; Th.B., No. Baptist Sem., Oakbrook, Ill., 1951; B.A., Trinity Coll., 1954; M.Div., Trinity Evang. Div. Sch., 1955; D.Ministries, Bethel Theol. Sem., 1975; m. Ruth Catherine Starr, June 4, 1949; children—Karen Joyce, Jane Alison, Steven Thomas. Ordained minister Evang. Free Ch. of Am., 1949; pastor Community Bible Ch., Berwyn, Ill., 1947-51; pastor Grace Evang. Free Ch., Chgo., 1951-58, Liberty Bible Ch., Valparaiso, Ind., 1959-67, Crystal Evang. Free Ch., Mpls., 1967-76; v.p., moderator Evang. Free Ch. of Am., 1973-74, chmn. home missions bd., 1968-72, chmn. exec. bd., 1973—, pres., 1976—. Chmn. bd. Trinity Coll., Deerfield, Ill., 1974-76. Mem. Evang. Free Ch. Ministerial Assn., Evang. Ministers Assn., Nat., Greater Mpls. (bd. dirs., sec. bd. 1969-73) assns. evangelicals. Contbr. articles to publs. Home: 4356 Florida Ave N Minneapolis MN 55428 Office: 6421 45th Ave N Minneapolis MN 55428

MC DIVITT, JAMES ALTON, transp. equipment exec., former astronaut; b. Chgo., June 10, 1929; s. James and Margaret (Maxwell) McD.; B.S. in Aero. Engring., U. Mich., 1959, Dr. Astro. Sci. (hon.),

1965; D.Sc. (hon.), Seton Hall U., 1969, Miami U., Oxford, Ohio, 1970; LL.D. (hon.), Eastern Mich. U., 1975; m. Patricia Ann Haas, June 16, 1956; children—Michael A., Ann Lynn, Patrick W., Kathleen M. Commd. 2d lt. USAF, 1951, advanced through grades to brig. gen., 1972; flew 145 combat missions in Korean War; grad. Exptl. Test Pilot Sch., Edward AFB, Calif., 1959-60, Aerospace Research Pilot Course, 1961; exptl. flight test officer Edward AFB, 1960-62; joined Project Gemini, NASA, 1962; command pilot on 4 day orbit in Gemini-Titan IV, 1965; comdr. Apollo IX, Mar. 3-13, 1969; mgr. for lunar landing operations Apollo program office, 1969—, mgr. Apollo Spacecraft program, 1969-72; ret.; exec. v.p. Consumer Power Co., Jackson, Mich., 1972-75; pres. Pullman Standard div. Pullman Inc., 1975-79; exec. v.p. Pullman, Inc., Chgo., 1975—; dir. Pullman Leasing Co., Chgo., Pullman Internat., Inc. Bd. dirs. Adler Planetarium, Loyola U. Chgo. Decorated D.S.M. with oak leaf cluster, D.F.C. with 3 oak leaf clusters, Air medal with 4 oak leaf clusters; Hon. Order Chung Mao (South Korea); recipient 2 NASA Distinguished Service medals, 1969, 71, NASA Exceptional Service medal, 1965. Mem. Soc. Exptl. Test Pilots, Am. Inst. Aeros. and Astronautics, Am. Astronauts Soc., U. Mich. Alumni Assn. (dir. 1970-75), Tau Beta Pi, Phi Kappa Phi. Roman Catholic. Home: 2349 Iroquois Rd Wilmette IL 60091 Office: 200 S Michigan Ave Chicago IL 60604

MCDONAGH, EDWARD CHARLES, sociologist; b. Edmonton, Alta., Can., Jan. 23, 1915 (came to U.S. 1922, naturalized 1936); s. Henry Fry and Aletta (Bowles) McD.; A.B., U. So. Calif., 1937, A.M., 1938, Ph.D., 1942; m. Louise Lucille Lorenzi, Aug. 14, 1940; children—Eileen, Patricia. Asst. prof. So. Ill. U., Carbondale, 1940-46, asst. to pres., 1942-44; asst. prof. U. Okla., Norman, 1946-47; asst. prof. U. So. Calif., Los Angeles, 1947-49, asso. prof., 1949-56, prof., 1956-69, head dept., 1958-62, chmn. div. social scis., 1960-69, asso. dean div. social scis. and communications, 1960-66; head dept. sociology U. Ala., University, 1969-71; chmn. dept. sociology Ohio State U., Columbus, 1971-74, acting dean Coll. Social and Behavioral Scis., 1974-75, dean, 1975-78, chmn. coordinating council deans Colls. Arts and Scis., 1977-78; Smith-Mundt prof. Sweden, 1956-57. Cons., Los Angeles and related sch. dists.; mem. Region XV Woodrow Wilson Selection Com., 1961-62. Served with AUS, 1944-46. Fellow Am. Sociol. Assn. (co-chmn. nat. conf. com. 1963, budget and exec. office com. 1975-78); mem. AAUP, AAAS, Am. Assn. Pub. Opinion Research, Alpha Kappa Delta (pres. united chtps. 1965-66), Phi Beta Kappa (chpt. pres. 1959-60), Blue Key, Skull and Daggar. Author: (with E.S. Richard) Ethnic Relations in the U.S., 1953; (with J.E. Nordskog, M.J. Vincent) Analyzing Social Problems, 1956; (with Jon Simpson) Social Problems: Persistent Challenges, 1965, rev., 1969. Asso. editor Sociology and Social Research, 1947-69; editorial cons. Sociometry, 1962-65. Contbr. articles to profl. publs. Home: 3090 S Dorchester Rd Columbus OH 43221 Office: Ohio State Univ Adminstrn Bldg Columbus OH 43210

MC DONALD, ALONZO LOWRY, govt. ofcl.; b. Atlanta, Aug. 5, 1928; s. Alonzo Lowry and Lois (Burrell) McD.; A.B., Emory U., 1948; M.B.A., Harvard, 1956; m. Suzanne Moffitt, May 9, 1959; children—Kenneth Alexander, Denise Carrie, Jennifer Wynn, Hans Peter Lowry. Asst. to sales mgr. air conditioning div. Westinghouse Electric Corp., Staunton, Va., 1956-57, Western zone mgr., St. Louis, 1957-60; asso. N.Y. Office, McKinsey & Co., Inc., 1960-64, prin. London Office, 1964-66, mng. prin. Zurich Office, 1966-68, mng. dir. Paris Office, 1968-73, mng. dir. firm, N.Y.C., 1973-76, dir. N.Y. office, 1976-77; dep. spl. trade rep., also ambassador in charge U.S. del. Tokyo round of Multilateral Trade Negotiations in Geneva, 1977-79; White House staff dir., 1979—. Mem. Council on Fgn. Relations, 1974—. Served with USMCR, 1950-52. Home: Indian Point Ln Riverside CT 06878 Office: Exec Office of Pres 1600 Pennsylvania Ave NW Washington DC 20500

MC DONALD, ANDREW J., bishop; b. Savannah, Ga., Oct. 24, 1923; s. James Bernard and Theresa (McGrael) McD.; A.B., St. Mary's Sem., Balt., 1945, S.T.L., 1948; J.C.B., Catholic U. Am., 1949; J.C.D., Lateran U., Rome, 1951. Ordained priest Roman Cath. Ch., 1948; consecrated bishop, 1972; curate, Port Wentworth, Ga., 1952-57; chancellor Diocese of Savannah, 1952-68; vicar gen., 1968—, vice oficialis, 1952-57, oficialis, 1957; pastor Blessed Sacrament Ch., 1963; named papal chamberlain, 1956, domestic prelate, 1959; bishop Diocese of Little Rock, 1972—. Home: 2415 N Tyler St Little Rock AR 72217

MC DONALD, ANDREW JEWETT, securities firm exec.; b. Cin., Sept. 7, 1929; s. Matthew Arnold and Jane (Jewett) Mc D.; grad. Hotchkiss Sch., 1947, Yale U., 1951. With Paine, Webber, Jackson & Curtis Inc., Boston, 1955—, dir. New Eng. region, 1972-73, sr. v.p., dir. Eastern div., 1973—; dir. F. W. Paine Found., 1973—; allied mem. N.Y. Stock Exchange, 1971—. Mem. Flight Safety Found., 1971—. Served with USAF, 1951-55. Clubs: Aero of New Eng., Fed., Down Town, Yale (Boston). Office: 100 Federal St Boston MA 02110

MCDONALD, ATWOOD, lawyer; b. Azle, Tex., Mar. 17, 1899; s. William Newton and Maud Hilliard (Bailey) McD.; LL.B., U. Tex., 1924; m. Ripple Ruth Sweet, Oct. 8, 1929; children—Myrna Marie (Mrs. William D. Winston), Paul Joseph, Marilyn Ruth (Mrs. Lenox Ligon). Admitted to Tex. bar, 1924; practiced in Ft. Worth, 1924-41, 51—; chief justice Ct. Civil Appeals, Ft. Worth, 1941-51; partner firm McDonald, Sanders, Ginsburg, Phillips, Maddox & Newkirk, 1951—. Vice pres. Tex. Civil Jud. Council, 1950-51, pres., 1951-53. Pres. Ft. Worth Bd. Edn., 1962-65. Bd. chancellors U. Tex. Law Sch., 1923—. Served with U.S. Army, 1917-19. Mem. Am., Tex. (chmn. jud. sect. 1948), Ft. Worth bar assns., Am. Coll. Probate Counsel, Kappa Alpha, Phi Delta Phi. Home: 4232 Kenwood Ct Fort Worth TX 76103 Office: Continental Bank Bldg Fort Worth TX 76102

MC DONALD, CHARLES JACK, dermatologist; b. Tampa, Fla., Dec. 6, 1931; s. George B. and Bertha C. (Harbin) Mc D.; B.S. magna cum laude, A&T Coll. N.C., 1951; M.S., U. Mich., 1952; M.D. with highest honors, Howard U. 1960; m. Rosalyn J. Hodgins, Nov. 1, 1952; children—Marc S., Norman D., Eric S. Rotating intern Hosp. St. Raphael, New Haven, 1960-61, asst. resident in medicine, 1961-63; asst. resident in dermatology Yale U., 1963-65, spl. USPHS research fellow, chief resident in dermatology, 1965-66, instr. in medicine and pharmacology, 1966-67, asst. prof. medicine and pharmacology, 1967-68; asst. prof. med. sci. Brown U., 1968-69, asso. prof., 1969-74, prof., 1974—, dir. dermatology program, 1970—, head subsect. dermatology, 1974—; head div. dermatology Roger Williams Gen. Hosp., 1968—; cons. in field; com. and task force mem., chmn. task force on minority affairs Am. Acad. Dermatology; mem. dermatology adv. panel FDA, until 1978, cons., 1978— chmn. com. public edn., dir., v.p. R.I. div. Am. Cancer Soc., pres.-elect div.; bd. dirs. Planned Parenthood R.I.; lectr. for assns., univs., including Samuel Bluefarb lectr. Northwestern U., 1977; chmn. R.I. Gov.'s Task Force on Health, 1970-73; trustee Citizens Bank R.I. Bd. dirs. Providence Health Care Found. Served to maj. USAF, 1952-56. Recipient Disting. Service award Hosp. Assn. R.I., 1971; diplomate Am. Bd. Dermatology. Mem. Am., New Eng., R.I., N. Worcester dermatol. assns., Soc. Investigative Dermatology, Am. Fedn. Clin. Research, Am. Acad. Dermatology, Nat. Med. Assn. (chmn. sect. dermatology 1973-75), Pan Am. Med. Assn., AAAS, Am. Soc. Clin. Oncology, Dermatology Found. (chmn. sci. com. 1972-76), Assn. Profs. Dermatology, Sigma Xi, Alpha Omega Alpha, Alpha Kappa Mu, Beta Kappa Chi. Democrat. Contbr. numerous articles to med. publs. Office: 825 Chalkstone Ave Providence RI 02908

MC DONALD, DAVID GEORGE, educator, psychologist; b. St. Louis, Aug. 16, 1933; s. George and Merle (Lovelady) McD.; A.B., U. Mo., 1955; M.A., Washington U., St. Louis, 1957, Ph.D., 1959; m. Barbara Eppard, May 25, 1968; children—Ellen Rae, David Gregory, Claire Louise. Research instr. med. psychology Washington U. Sch. Medicine, St. Louis, 1959-62; supervisory research psychologist U.S. Naval Med. Neuropsychiat. Research Unit, San Diego, 1962-63; asst. prof. clin. psychology U. Mo., Columbia, 1963-65, asso. prof. med. psychology, 1965-69, prof. psychology an psychiatry, chmn. dept. psychology, 1969-73, asso. dean arts and sci., 1973-76, acting dean arts and scis., 1976-77, acting asso. v.p. acad. affairs U. Mo. Central Adminstrn., 1978—; lectr. San Diego State Coll., 1962-63. Mem. Am., Midwestern, Mo. psychol. assns., AAAS, Soc. Psychophysiol. Research, Assn. Psychophysiol. Study Sleep, N.Y. Acad. Sci., Psi Chi, Kappa Sigma. Contbr. articles to profl. jours. Home: 3101 Crawford St Columbia MO 65201

MC DONALD, DAVID WILLIAM, chemist; b. Shreveport, La., Aug. 4, 1923; s. Maxwell Wood and Mary Estelle (Weber) McD.; B.S., U. Southwestern La., 1943; Ph.D., U. Tex., 1951; m. Nell Cullen Welch, July 31, 1948; children—Mason, Thomas, Daniel, David. Chemist Humble Oil & Refining Co., Baytown, Tex., 1943-44, 46-47; research chemist, group leader Monsanto Co., Texas City, Tex., 1951-59, research sect. leader, mgr., 1959-67, product adminstr., St. Louis, 1967-69, dir. research plastics div., St. Louis, 1969-74, dir. tech., 1974—. Served with USNR, 1944-46. Mem. Am. Chem. Soc., Soc. Plastics Engrs., Sigma Xi. Episcopalian. Patentee in field. Home: 9 Cedar Crest St Louis MO 63132 Office: 800 N Lindbergh Blvd St Louis MO 63166

MCDONALD, DONALD DEAN, ins. co. exec.; b. Granite City, Ill., Aug. 2, 1923; s. James Edward and Bertha (Mounts) McD.; B.S., U. Mo., 1950; M.B.A., Washington U., 1962; m. Evelyn Marie Kixmiller, Jan. 29, 1950; children—Donna Sue McDonald Preves, Linda Lee. With Combined Ins. Co. Am., Chgo., 1954-74, 79—, exec. v.p., treas., 1979—; v.p. Combined Am. Ins. Co., Dallas, 1974-79, also dir. Served with U.S. Army, 1942-46; PTO. Mem. Planning Execs. Inst., Fin. Execs. Inst. Republican. Lutheran. Home: 117 Surrey Ln Lincolnshire Woods Lake Forest IL 60045 Office: 5050 Broadway Chicago IL 60640

MCDONALD, DONALD FIEDLER, surgeon, educator; b. Chicago Heights, Ill., Aug. 13, 1919; s. Guy Arthur and Carrie (Fiedler) McD.; A.A., U. Chgo., 1939, M.D., 1942; children—Bruce Bradford, Stuart Vail, Nancy Carol. Intern, U. Chgo. Clinics, 1943-44, resident, 1944-46, instr. urol. surgery U. Chgo., 1946-49; asst. prof. urol. surgery U. Wash. Sch. Medicine, 1949-58; practice medicine, specializing in urology and genitourinary surgery, Rochester, N.Y., 1958—; prof. urol. surgery U. Rochester Sch. Medicine, 1958-69; prof. urology U. Tex., Med. br., Galveston, 1969—. Served to comdr. USNR, 1945-46. John and Mary R. Markle scholar med. scis., 1952-56. Fellow A.C.S.; mem. A.M.A., Am. Urol. Assn., Soc. Genito-Urinary Surgeons, Clin. Soc. Genito-Urinary Surgeons, Assn. Cancer Research, AAAS. Contbr. articles to profl. jours. Home: Port aux Princes No 8 Galveston TX 77550

MCDONALD, DONALD JOHN, mag. editor; b. Marinette, Wis., Nov. 27, 1920; s. John Archibald and Mary Sarah (Solper) McD.; Ph.B., Marquette U., 1948; M.A., 1953; m. Virginia M. Humbach, Dec. 1, 1945; children—Donald, Mark, Paul, Anne, Teresa. News editor Cath. Messenger, Davenport, Ia., 1949-57, editor, 1957-59; editor Marquette U. Mag., Milw., 1959-62, dean Coll. Journalism, 1962-65; sr. fellow Center for Study of Democratic Instns., Santa Barbara, Calif., 1965-69, mng. editor The Center Mag., 1969-74, editor, 1974—; vis. prof. U. Calif. at Berkeley, 1974; lectr. pub. affairs reporting U. Calif., Santa Barbara, 1976—. Served to capt. USAAF, 1942-45. Roman Catholic. Author: Catholics in Conversation, 1960. Home: 2126 E Valley Rd Santa Barbara CA 93108 Office: PO Box 4068 Santa Barbara CA 93103

MCDONALD, EDWIN ANDERSON, ret. naval officer and polar explorer and cons.; b. Hazel Creek, Calif., Nov. 23, 1907; s. Orion and Edith (Anderson) McD.; B.S. in Engring., U.S. Naval Acad., 1931; ordnance engring. degree, Naval Bur. Ordnance, 1956. Commd. ensign U.S. Navy, 1931, advanced through grades to capt., 1962; comdg. officer icebreaker U.S.S. Burton Island during TF 39 Antarctic Expdn., 1947-48; participated in 6 naval arctic expdns. as comdg. officer, ice expert or task unit comdr., 1948-53; leader 2 ship task group into Weddell Sea to construct Ellsworth Sta. (farthest penitration of ships), Deep Freeze II and III, 1956-58; comdr. 8 ships in supply antarctic stas., Deep Freeze IV, 1958-59; Deep Freeze 60, 1959-60; succeeded first time history in penetrating to coast of Bellingshausen Sea with two icebreaker task unit, 1959-60; dep. comdr. U.S. Naval Support Force, Antarctica, 1958-61; rescued beset Belgium ship Polarhov, 1959, Brit. ship Kista Dan, 1960; Deep Freeze, 1961-62; penetrated by icebreaker the Amundsen Sea Coast Antarctic for 1st time; ret. 1962; polar cons. Arctic Inst. N.Am., 1962-66; mgr. polar operations Alpine Geophys. Assos., Inc., Norwood, N.J., 1966-69; dir. ship and polar operations Lindblad Travel, Inc., N.Y.C., 1969-72. Decorated Silver Star, Legion Merit (2), Bronze Star with combat V and 2 clusters, Order of Leopold (Belgium); recipient Royal Geog. Gold Patron medal (Eng.), 2 Commendation medals, Royal Geog. Soc. Mem. Am. Geog. Soc., Antarcticans Polar Soc., Royal Geog. Soc., Arctic Inst. N.Am. Club: Explorers (N.Y.C.). Author: Polar Shiphandling, 1966; Polar Operations, 1969; also articles and papers on hydrographic and polar topics. Home: 134 Pochet Rd East Orleans MA 02643. *What has been accomplished is over and done with. New goals keep the challenge and interest going.*

MC DONALD, FRANK BETHUNE, physicist; b. Columbus, Ga., May 28, 1925; s. Frank B. and Lucy (Kyle) McD.; B.S., Duke U., 1948; M.S., U. Minn., 1951, Ph.D. (AEC fellow), 1955; m. Virginia Ballew, June 15, 1951; children—Kyle Louise, Robert Kyle, Douglas Frank. Research asso. State U. Iowa, Iowa City, 1953-56, asst. prof. physics, 1956-59; chief lab. for high energy astrophysics Goddard Space Flight Center, Greenbelt, Md., 1959—; prof. U. Md., College Park, part-time 1963—; mem. phys. scis. com. space program adv. council NASA, 1975—. Served with USNR, 1942-45. Recipient Exceptional Sci. Achievement award NASA, 1964; Presdl. Mgmt. Improvement cert., 1971. Fellow Am. Phys. Soc. (chmn. div. cosmic physics 1973-74); mem. Am. Geophys. Union, Washington Philos. Soc., Am. Astronom. Soc., Sigma Xi, Phi Beta Kappa. Editor: High Energy Particles and Quanta in Astrophysics, 1974. Asso. editor Jour. Geophys. Research, 1964-67; mem. editorial bd. Space Sci. Revs. Research in cosmic ray physics; flown expts. on 11 NASA sci. satellites; project scientist 8 NASA sci. satellites; study of planet Jupiter with expts. on Pioneer 10 and 11. Office: NASA/Goddard Space Flight Center Code 660 Greenbelt MD 20771

MC DONALD, HUGH JOSEPH, chemist, educator; b. Glen Nevis, Ont., Can., July 27, 1913; came to U.S., 1935, naturalized, 1943; s. Roderick J. and Annie Sarah (McDonell) McD.; student Queens U., 1930-32; B.Sc. with 1st class honors, McGill U., 1935; M.S., Carnegie-Mellon U., 1936, D.Sc., 1939; hon. grad. Universidade Catolica do Rio de Janeiro, 1962; m. Margaret Bilsland Taylor, Feb. 14, 1942 (dec. Jan. 14, 1963); children—George Gordon, Jean, Gail; m. 2d, Avis Eugenia Nieman, August 8, 1964. Teaching asst., part-time instr. Carnegie-Mellon U., Pitts., 1936-39; instr. in chemistry Ill. Inst. Tech., Chgo., 1939-41, asst. prof., 1941-42, asso. prof., 1943-46, prof., 1946-48; prof., chmn. dept. biochemistry and biophysics Stritch Sch. Medicine, Loyola U., Chgo., 1948—; cons. Argonne Nat. Lab., 1946—. War research Manhattan Project, Columbia U., 1943. Recipient Sigma Xi research award, 1944; Royal Soc. Advancement of Sci. scholar, 1933-34; research grantee Am. Acad. Arts and Scis., 1945. Registered profl. engr., Ill. Diplomate Am. Bd. Clin. Chemistry. Fellow AAAS; mem. Nat. Acad. Clin. Biochemistry (chmn. com. edn. 1977-78, dir. 1978—), Am. Chem. Soc., Am. Assn. Clin. Chemists (chmn. com. on edn. 1949-53, pres. 1953-54), Soc. Exptl. Biology and Medicine, Am. Soc. Biol. Chemists, Biophys. Soc., Sigma Xi, Phi Lambda Upsilon, Alpha Chi Sigma. Roman Catholic. Club: Chaos (Chgo.). Asso. editor Clin. Chemistry, 1955-60; editorial bd. Analytical Biochemistry, 1960-70. Contbr. articles on phys. chemistry, electrochemistry and biochemistry to profl. and tech. jours. Home: 5344 Cleveland St Skokie IL 60077 Office: Stritch Sch Medicine Loyola U of Chgo Maywood IL 60153

MCDONALD, JAMES BENJAMIN, petroleum co. exec.; b. Oakland, Kans., May 23, 1923; s. Chauncey Earl and Myrtle (Davenport) McD.; student Kans. State U., 1940-42, Washburn U., 1946-48; B.S. in Bus., U. Kans., 1949; m. Betty Louise Wray, Apr. 13, 1946; children—Linda (Mrs. John M. Patton), James G., Bruce S. Spl. agt. Nat. Surety Corp., Denver, 1949-53; treas. Empire Petroleum Co., Denver, 1953-63; treas., controller Tex. City Refining, Inc., Texas City, Tex., 1963-72, v.p. finance, 1972—; dir. Texas City Nat. Bank, 1975—. Active Bay Area council Boy Scouts Am., 1964-70, mem. exec. com., 1967-70; chmn. finance com. fund drive Dickinson (Tex.) Library, 1969; mem. exec. com. Jr. Achievement, Texas City, 1973—. Bd. dirs. United Fund, Texas City, 1971, teenage program Little League, Dickinson, 1964-72. Served with USAAF, 1942-46. Decorated D.F.C., 3 Air medals. Mem. Am. Petroleum Inst., Fin. Execs. Inst., Planning Execs. Inst. (v.p. 1967). Home: Cedar Creek Farm Hwy 517 Dickenson TX 77539 Office: PO Box 1271 Texas City TX 77590

MC DONALD, JAMES BENJAMIN, JR., assn. exec.; b. Agana, Guam, June 21, 1951; s. James Benjamin and Josefina Flores (Iturzaeta) McD.; B.A. in Econs., Fordham Coll., 1972; m. Genedine Ann Taitano, June 14, 1975; children—Genine, Elyze. Mgr., Ricky's Auto Co., Anigua, Guam, 1972-75; sales mgr. Toyota Motors Co., Tamuning, Guam, 1975-76; dir. Guam Dept. Commerce, 1976-78; pres. Guam C. of C., Agana, 1979—; mem. Guam Polit. Status Commn., 1976-78, Pvt. Investment Com., 1979. Bd. regents U. Guam, 1975-76; mem. Guam Adv. Council on Vocat. Edn., 1976-79, Manpower Services Council, 1977-78. Roman Catholic. Club: Rotary. Office: 102 Ada Plaza Center Agana GU 96910

MCDONALD, JAMES MICHAEL, JR., ednl. center ofcl.; b. Chgo., Jan. 19, 1924; s. James Michael and Gertrude Isabel (Dame) McD.; A.B. cum laude, Syracuse U., 1949; M.A., Sch. Advanced Internat. Studies, 1950; postgrad. Bologna Center, 1956-57; student Nat. War Coll., 1968-69; m. Helen Elizabeth Sharp, Feb. 3, 1948; children—Megan, Melissa, Rebecca. Joined U.S. Fgn. Service, 1950; assigned Germany, 1951-56, Italy, 1956-57, France, 1957-58, Washington, 1958-61, Nicaragua, 1961-65, Dominican Republic, 1969-71; dep. pub affairs officer, Rome, 1971-74, chief resource and ops. analysis USIA, Washington, 1974-75; dir. seminar and studies program Battelle Meml. Inst., 1975—. Mem. Council on Wash.'s Future, Seattle Com. Fgn. Relations; trustee Pacific Sci. Center; bd. dirs. Wash. Council on Internat. Trade; trustee Seattle Opera, Wash. State Internat. Trade Fair. Served with USAAF, 1943-47. Recipient Superior Honor award USIA, 1975. Club: Rainier. Address: 1278 NW Blakely Ct Seattle WA 98177

MCDONALD, JOHN CECIL, lawyer; b. Lorimor, Iowa, Feb. 19, 1924; s. Cecil F. and Mary Elsie (Fletcher) McD.; student Simpson Coll., 1942, So. Ill. U., 1943; J.D., Drake U., 1948; m. Barbara Joan Berry, May 8, 1943; children—Mary Elisabeth (Mrs. Dell Richard), Joan Frances (Mrs. Andrew Ackerman), Jean Maurine. Admitted to Iowa bar, 1948, U.S. Supreme Ct. bar, 1956, U.S. Ct. Mil. Appeals, 1956, U.S. Dist. Ct. for So. Dist. Iowa; practiced in Dallas Center, Iowa, 1948-71; sr. partner firm McDonald, Keller & Brown, 1971—; county atty. Dallas County, 1958-62, asst. county atty., 1963-69; city atty., Dallas Center, 1956—. Mem. Simpson Coll. Alumni Council, pres., 1977—; legal adviser Dallas Community Bd. Edn., 1953-69, pres., mem., 1968-76; nat. adv. com. Central Coll. Finance chmn. Dallas County Republican Central Com., 1954-63, chmn., 1963-68; chmn. Iowa 7th Congl. Dist. Rep. Central Com., 1968-69; chmn. Iowa Rep. Central Com., 1969-75; mem. Rep. Nat. Com., 1969—, mem. exec. com., 1973—, mem. Rule 29 com., com. on reform; mem. Gov. Iowa's inaugural com., 1969, 71, 73, 75, 79; del. Rep. Nat. Conv., 1964, 72, 76, chmn. com. on contests, 1976, chmn. com. on credentials, 1976, mem. com. on arrangements, 1976, mem. rules rev. com. for Rep. Nat. Conv., 1977—; chmn. Midwest Rep. State Chairmen's Assn., 1973-75, chmn. Nat. Rep. State Chairmen's Adv. Com., 1973-75. Trustee Dallas County Hosp., Perry, Iowa; bd. visitors U.S. Air Force Acad., 1975-78, chmn., 1977-78; trustee Simpson Coll., 1978—. Served with USAAF, 1942-46, USAF, 1951-52; col. Res. Recipient Alumni Achievement award Simpson Coll., 1974; Disting. Service award Drake U., 1978. Mem. Am., Iowa (past chmn. spl. com. on mil. affairs, mem. mil. affairs com.), Dallas County (past pres.) bar assns., Am. Legion, Farm Bur., Blackfriars, Drake U. Law Sch. Alumni Assn. (class officer). Alpha Tau Omega, Delta Theta Phi, Alpha Psi Omega. Presbyn. Mason (32 deg., Shriner), Rotarian (past pres. Dallas Center). Clubs: Commercial (past pres.) (Dallas Center); Hillcrest Country (past pres.) (Adel, Ia.); Des Moines, Lincoln, Embassy (Des Moines). Home: 1507 Vine St Dallas Center IA 50063 Office: 502 15th St Dallas Center IA 50063

MCDONALD, JOHN CLIFTON, surgeon; b. Baldwyn, Miss., July 25, 1930; s. Edgar Hone and Ethel (Knight) McD.; B.S., Miss. Coll., 1951; M.D., Tulane U., 1955; m. Martha Dennis, Sept. 9, 1956; children—Melissa Lee, Karen Ann, Martha Knight. Intern, Confederate Meml. Med. Center, Shreveport, La., 1955-56; asst. resident Meyer Meml. Hosp., Buffalo, N.Y., 1958-62, resident, 1962-63, asst. attending surgeon, 1963-66, asso. attending surgeon, 1966-67, attending surgeon, 1967-68, asso. dir. surg. research lab., 1965-68; practice medicine, specializing in surgery, Buffalo, 1963-69, New Orleans, 1969-77, Shreveport, 1977—; asst. attending surgeon Deaconess Hosp., Buffalo, 1965-66, asso. attending, 1966-68, attending surgeon, 1968-69, head, sect. of transplantation, 1966-68; cons. Roswell Park and Meml. Hosp., 1968-69, Masten Park Rehab. Center, 1968-69; dir. transplantation Charity Hosp. of La., New Orleans, 1969-77, vis. surgeon, 1969-77; cons. surgeon Lallie Kemp Charity Hosp., Independence, La., 1969-77, Pineville (La.) VA Hosp., 1969-77, Huey P. Long Charity Hosp., Pineville, 1969-77, Keesler AFB, Biloxi, Miss., 1969-77; clin. asst. surgeon Touro Infirmary, New Orleans, 1969-77; mem. med. staff So. Baptist Hosp., New Orleans, 1969-77; asso. mem. dept. surgery Hotel Dieu Hosp., 1969-77; dir. La. Organ Procurement Program, 1971-77; surgeon in chief La. State U.

Med. Center, Shreveport, 1977—; cons. N.W. La. Emergency Med. Services, 1977—; Buswell research fellow in immunology SUNY at Buffalo, 1963-65, instr. surgery, 1963-65, asst. prof., 1965-68, head, sect. transplantation, 1966-68; asso. prof. surgery Tulane U. Sch. Medicine, 1969-72, prof., 1972-77, asso. prof. microbiology and immunology, 1969-77, dir. surg. research labs., 1969-77, dir. transplantation labs., 1969-77, dir. Med. Center Histocompatability Testing Lab., 1969-77, vis. prof., 1978; prof., chmn. dept. surgery La. State U. Sch. Medicine, 1977—; vis. prof. Columbus (Ga.) Med. Center, 1978. Served to capt. USAF, 1956-58. Recipient Owl Club award for outstanding teaching Tulane U., 1977. Research grantee Kidney Found. Western N.Y., 1966-67, NIH, 1969—, Schlieder Found., 1970-73, Cancer Assn. Cancer Assn. Greater New Orleans, 1971-72, La. Regional Med. Program, 1971-73. Diplomate Am. Bd. Surgery. Mem. Am. Assn. Clin. Histocompatibility Testing (founding), Am. Assn. Immunologists, A.C.S., AMA, Am. Soc. for Artificial Internal Organs, Am. Soc. Transplant Surgeons (founding), Buffalo Surg. Soc. (sec. 1968), So. Surg. Assn. (Arthur H. Shipley award 1972), Surg. Assn. La. (dir. 1977—), Am. Assn. for Surgery of Trauma, Transplantation Soc., Southeastern Surg. Congress, Soc. U. Surgeons, La. Med. Soc., Caddo Parish Med. Soc. Contbr. sci. articles to med. jours. Office: 1541 Kings Hwy Shreveport LA 71130

MC DONALD, JOHN JOSEPH, electronics exec.; b. N.Y.C., Apr. 18, 1930; s. John J. and Margaret (Shanley) McD.; B.A., Bklyn. Coll., 1951; m. Tessa de R. Greenfield, Aug. 22, 1956; children—Kathryn, Elizabeth, Andrew. With Sperry Rand Corp., Blue Bell, Pa., 1954-75, v.p., 1972-75; mng. dir. Casio Electronics Ltd., London, 1975-78, pres. Casio Europe, 1975-78, Casio, Inc., Fairfield, N.J., 1978—; dir. Casio Electronics. Served with U.S. Army, 1952-54. Mem. Brit. Inst. Mktg., Am. Mgmt. Assn. Office: 15 Gardner Rd Fairfield NJ 07006

MCDONALD, JOHN PETER, librarian; b. Phila., Oct. 17, 1922; s. Edward David and Marguerite (Bartelle) McD.; A.B., U. Va., 1946; M.L.S., Drexel Inst. Tech., 1951; fellow Rutgers U. Library Sch., 1958; m. Josephine S. Herring, Feb. 23, 1952; children—John L., James R. Instr. English, Drexel Inst. Tech., 1946-47; mem. staff U. Pa. Library, 1949-54; from chief reference dept. to asso. dir. libraries Washington U., St. Louis, 1954-63; dir. libraries U. Conn., 1963—; cons. in field, 1964—; cons. Universidad Catolica de Chile, Santiago, 1970, Coll. of V.I.; adv. com. library research and tng. projects U.S. Office Edn. Served to lt. (j.g.) USNR, 1942-46. Fellow Carnegie Corp., 1958; travel grantee Ednl. Facilities Lab., 1964. Mem. Assn. Research Libraries (dir. 1969—), Am., Conn. State, New Eng. library assns., Bibliog. Soc. Am., Archons of Colophon, Phi Kappa Phi. Author articles. Office: U Conn Library Storrs CT 06268*

MCDONALD, JOHN RICHARD, lawyer; b. Connersville, Ind., Aug. 8, 1933; s. Vernon Louis and Thelma (Venham) McD.; B.A., U. Ariz., 1957, LL.B., 1960; m. Mary Alice Boyd, Aug. 17, 1957; children—Anne Elizabeth, John Richard, Colleen Lynn. Admitted to Ariz. bar, 1960, since practiced in Tucson; asso. Richard N. Roylston, 1961-62; pvt. practice, 1963-65; partner McDonald & Rykken, 1965-68, DeConcini & McDonald (now DeConcini, McDonald, Brammer, Yetwin & Lacy), 1968—. Pres., bd. dirs. Comstock Children's Hosp. Found.; v.p. Ariz. Sch. Bds. Assn., 1979; v.p., bd. dirs. Tucson Assn. for Blind; trustee Catalina Foothills Sch. Dist. Served with CIC, AUS, 1955-57. Mem. Am., Ariz., Pima County (dir. 1978—) bar assns., Am. Trial Lawyers Assn., Delta Chi. Republican. Presbyn. Home: 6151 Camino Almonte Tucson AZ 85718 Office: 240 N Stone Ave Tucson AZ 85701

MCDONALD, JOHN WARLICK, JR., diplomat; b. Coblenz, Germany, Feb. 18, 1922 (parents Am. citizens); s. John Warlick and Ethel Mae (Raynor) McD.; A.B., U. Ill., 1943, J.D., 1946; m. Barbara Jane Stewart, Oct. 23, 1943 (div.); children—Marilyn Ruth, James Stewart, Kathleen Ethel, Laura Ellen; m. 2d, Christel Meyer, Oct. 1970. Admitted to Ill. bar, 1946, U.S. Supreme Ct., 1951; with legal div. Office Mil Govt., Berlin, Germany, 1947; asst. dist. atty. U.S. Mil. Govt. Cts., Frankfort, Germany, 1947-50; with Allied High Commn., Bonn, Germany, 1950-52; U.S. mission to NATO and OEEC, Paris, France, 1952-54; fgn. affairs officer Dept. of State, Washington, 1954-55; exec. sec. to dir. ICA, Washington, 1955-59; U.S. econ. coordinator for CENTO, affairs, Ankara, Turkey, 1959-63; chief econ. and comml. sect. Am. embassy, Cairo, UAR, 1963-66; Nat. War Coll., Washington, 1966-67; dep. dir. office econ. and social affairs Bur. Internat. Orgn. Affairs, Dept. State, 1967-68, dir., 1968-71; coordinator UN Multilateral Devel. Programs, Dept. State, 1971-74, acting dep. asst. sec. econ. and social affairs, 1971, 73; dep. dir. gen. ILO, Geneva, Switzerland, 1974-78; pres. INTELSAT Conf. Privileges and Immunities, 1978, U.S. coordinator Tech. Coop. among Developing Countries, 1978, rep. UN Conf. with rank of ambassador, 1978—. U.S. del., alt. del. and adviser to numerous UN confs.; sec. gen. 27th Colombo Plan Ministerial Meeting, 1978; U.S. coordinator UN Decade on Drinking Water and Sanitation, 1979; U.S. coordinator, rep. Third World Conf. on Indsl. Devel., 1979. Recipient Superior Honor award, 1972. Mem. Am. Bar Assn., Am. Fgn. Service Assn., Delta Kappa Upsilon, Phi Delta Phi. Clubs: Internat. Lawyers, Am. Internat. (Geneva); Cosmos (Washington). Home: 3800 N Fairfax Dr Apt 1001 Arlington VA 22203 Office: US Dept State IO Room 1509 Washington DC

MC DONALD, JOSEPH VALENTINE, neurol. surgeon; b. N.Y.C., June 7, 1925; s. Benedict and Catherine Eleanor (Chadney) Mc D.; A.B., Coll. Holy Cross, 1945; M.D., U. Pitts., 1949; m. Carolyn Alice Patricia Petersen, Apr. 30, 1955; children—Judith Katherine, Elizabeth Ann, Catherine Eleanor, Joseph Bede, David Randolph. Intern, St. Vincent's Hosp., N.Y.C., 1949-50; research fellow neuroanatomy Vanderbilt U., 1950-51; gen. surgery asst. resident Cushing VA Hosp., Boston, 1951-52; neurology extern Lenox Hill Hosp., 1952; asst. resident neurosurgery Johns Hopkins Hosp., 1953-55, resident neurosurgeon, 1955-56; practice medicine specializing in neurol. surgery, Rochester, N.Y., 1956—; prof., chmn. div. neurosurgery U. Rochester Med. Sch.; neurosurgeon-in-chief Strong Meml. Hosp.; cons. neurosurgery to hosps. Mem. Soc. Neurol. Surgeons, A.C.S., Acad. Neurology, Am. Assn. Neurol. Surgeons, Congress Neurosurgeons. Home: 800 Allens Creek Rd Pittsford NY 14618 Office: Div Neurosurgery Strong Meml Hosp Rochester NY 14642

MC DONALD, LAWRENCE P., congressman; b. Atlanta, Apr. 1, 1935; grad. Davidson (N.C.) Coll.; M.D., Emory U., 1957; Litt.D. (hon.), Daniel Payne Coll., Birmingham, Ala.; children—Tryggvi Paul, Callie Grace, Mary Elizabeth. Resident in gen. surgery Grady Meml. Hosp., Atlanta; resident in urology U. Mich., Ann Arbor; mem. 94th-95th Congresses from 7th Ga. Dist. Served with M.C., USNR, 1957-61. Mem. John Birch Soc. (nat. council), Am. Conservative Union (adv. bd.), Conservative Caucus (adv. bd.), Com. for Survival of a Free Congress (adv. bd.). Methodist. Democrat. Club: Rotary. Office: 504 Cannon House Office Bldg Washington DC 20515

MCDONALD, LEE CAMERON, educator; b. Salem, Oreg., Feb. 22, 1925; s. O. Lyman and Mabel (Duncan) McD.; student U. Oreg., 1942-43; B.A., Pomona Coll., 1948; M.A., U. Calif. at Los Angeles, 1949; Ph.D., Harvard, 1952; m. Claire Elizabeth Kingman, Aug. 17, 1946; children—Mary, Alison, Julia, Devon (dec.), Thomas, Paul. Teaching asst. U. Calif. at Los Angeles, 1948-49; teaching fellow Harvard, 1950-52; mem. faculty Pomona Coll., Claremont, Calif., 1952—, prof. govt., 1962—, dean coll., 1970-75. Chmn. com. faculty interests, dept. higher edn. Nat. Council Chs., 1966-69; mem. adv. council Danforth Found. Assos. Program, 1964-67; mem. Commn. on Liberal Learning Assn. Am. Colls., 1974-76. Served with USAAF, 1943-45. Recipient Harbison Distinguished Teaching award Danforth Found., 1963. Mem. Am., Western (exec. council 1972-74), So. Calif. (pres. 1969-70) polit. scis. assns., Am. Soc. Polit. and Legal Philosophy, Am. Conf. Acad. Deans (dir. 1973-76), Phi Beta Kappa, Pi Sigma Alpha. Democrat. Presbyn. (elder 1958-60, 72-74). Author: Western Political Theory; The Modern Age, 1962; Western Political Theory; Origins to the Present, 1968; editor: Human Rights and Educational Responsibility, 1979. Editorial bd. Western Polit. Quar., 1963-66, 68-70, Claremont Quar., 1960-64. Home: 239 W 11th St Claremont CA 91711

MCDONALD, LESLIE ERNEST, educator; b. Middletown, Mo., Oct. 14, 1923; s. Leslie Earnest and Velma (Tagg) McD.; B.S., Mich State U., 1948, D.V.M., 1949; M.S., U. Wis., 1951, Ph.D., 1952; m. Evelyn Kubat, June 12, 1946; children—Patricia Jo, Dennis, Dale. Practice as veterinarian, Berlin, Wis., 1949-50; research fellow U. Wis., Madison, 1950-52; asso. prof. U. Ill., 1952-54; prof. head dept. physiology and pharmacology Okla. State U., Stillwater, 1954-69; asso. dean Coll. Vet. Medicine, U. Ga., Athens, 1969-71, Coll. Vet. Medicine, 1972—. dean Coll. Vet. Medicine, Ohio State U., Columbus, 1971-72. Mem. Okla. Bd. Examiners Basic Med. Scis., 1956-66; cons. NIH; com. mem. NRC. Mem. Am. Physiol. Soc., Soc. Exptl. Biology and Medicine, AVMA, Soc. Study Fertility, Sigma Xi. Presbyn. (elder). Club: Kiwanis. Author, editor: Veterinary Pharmacology and Therapeutics, 1977; Endocrinology and Reproduction, 1980. Home: 13 S Stratford St Athens GA 30605

MCDONALD, MARSHALL, utility exec.; b. Memphis, Mar. 30, 1918; s. Marshall and Nadine (Hardin) McD.; B.S. in Bus. Adminstrn., U. Fla., 1939, LL.B., 1941; M.B.A., Wharton Grad. Sch. U. Pa., 1947; m. Florence Harris, Jan. 10, 1952 (dec. Nov. 1963); m. 2d, Lucille Smoak Collins, May 7, 1965; children—Mary Linda (Mrs. Donald Caton), Charles M. Collins, Cynthia (Mrs. H.T. Langston, Jr.), Marshall III, Roger Collins, Davis, James D. Admitted to Fla. bar, 1941, Tex. bar, 1949; accountant, Houston, 1947-49; atty., Houston, 1950-52; treas. Gulf Canal Lines, 1953-54; pres. Investment Co. Houston, 1955-58; v.p. Sinclair Oil & Gas Co., Tulsa, 1959-61; v.p., gen. mgr. Oil Recovery Corp., Tulsa, 1962-63; asst. to pres. Pure Oil Co., Palatine, Ill., 1964-65; dir. affiliated cos. Union Oil Co., Los Angeles, 1966-68; pres. Sully-Miller Contracting Co., Los Angeles, 1968-71; pres., chief exec. officer Fla. Power & Light Co., Miami, 1971-79, chmn., chief exec. officer, 1979—. C.P.A., Tex. Served with AUS, 1941-46. Mem. Am. Bar Assn., Am. Inst. C.P.A.'s, Alpha Tau Omega. Republican. Presbyn. Mason. Office: 9250 W Flagler St Miami FL 33174 also PO Box 529100 Miami FL 33152

MC DONALD, MILES FRANCIS, lawyer; b. Bklyn., May 24, 1905; s. John R. and Lucy (Malone) McD.; grad. St. Johns Prep. Sch., Bklyn., 1922; A.B. cum laude, Holy Cross Coll., Worcester, Mass., 1926, LL.D., 1951; J.D., Fordham U., 1929; LL.D., St. John's U., 1946; m. Alice Shelare, Dec. 27, 1933; children—John R., Joanne (Mrs. William D. Roddy), Miles F., Alan Shelare. Admitted to N.Y. Bar, 1929; atty. Wingate & Cullen, Bklyn., 1929-40; asst. dist. atty. Kings County (N.Y.), 1940-45; U.S. atty. Eastern Dist. N.Y., 1945; dist. atty. Kings County, 1946-54; elected justice Supreme Ct. of N.Y. State, 1953, presiding justice appelate term 2d and 11th Jud. Dists., 1968, adminstrv. Judge 2d Jud. Dist., 1968-71; counsel Shea & Gould, N.Y.C., 1971—; dir. Butte Cooper and Zinc Co., 1934-37, dir., sec., 1937-42, v.p., treas., 1942-60; dir. Jonathan Logan. Past chmn. bd. trustees Nat. Conf. on Crime and Delinquency. Mem. Am., N.Y. State, Bklyn. bar assns., Bklyn. Manhattan Trial Counsel Assn. (past pres.), Nat. Conf. State Trial Judges (past chmn.), Assn. Supreme Ct. Justices N.Y. (past chmn.), N.Y. State Dist. Atty.'s Assn. (past pres.), Nat. Assn. Dist. Attys. (past pres.). Democrat. Clubs: N.Y. Yacht; Greenwich (Conn.) Country; Turtle Creek Country (Fla.). Home: 1 Putnam Hill Greenwich CT 06830 also 100 River Rd Tequesta FL 33458 Office: 330 Madison Ave New York NY 10017

MCDONALD, O. V., ins. co. exec.; b. Hale Center, Tex., July 18, 1922; B.B.A., N. Tex. State U., 1947; m. LaClair Pierce; children—Robert, Carol, Gary, Kathryn. With Employers Ins. of Tex., 1947—, now v.p. and sec.; bd. trustees Loman Found.; bd. govs. Internat. Ins. Seminars, Inc. C.P.C.U. Club: Ins. (Dallas). Home: 1611 Mapleton St Dallas TX 75228 Office: 423 S Akard St Dallas TX 75202

MCDONALD, PATRICK ALLEN, lawyer, educator; b. Detroit, May 11, 1936; s. Lawrence John and Estelle (Maks) M.; Ph.B. cum laude, U. Detroit, 1958, LL.B. magna cum laude, 1961; LL.M. (E. Barrett Prettyman Trial scholar, Hugh J. Fegan fellow), Georgetown U., 1962; m. Margaret Mercier, Aug. 10, 1963; children—Michael Lawrence, Colleen Marie, Patrick Joseph, Timothy, Margaret, Thomas, Maureen. Case worker Dept. Pub. Welfare, Detroit, 1958; field examiner NLRB, Detroit, 1961; admitted to D.C. bar, 1961, Mich. bar, 1961; practiced in Washington, 1961-62; trial cons. NIH, Bethesda, Md., 1962; staff judge adv. USAF, France, 1962-65; partner, Monaghan, Campbell, LoPrete, McDonald & Norris, Detroit, 1965—. Instr. polit. sci., law U. Md., 1963-65; instr. U. Detroit, 1959-61, adj. prof., 1965—. Mem. Detroit Bd. Edn., 1966-76, pres.; pres. Soccer Unltd.; mem. adv. bd. Providence Hosp., Southfield, Mich. Named one of Five Outstanding Young Men of Mich., Outstanding Young Man of Detroit. Mem. Detroit, Am. bar assns., State Bar Mich. (commr.), Am. Trial Lawyers, U. Detroit Alumni Assn. (dir.), Alpha Phi Omega (pres. Eta Pi chpt. 1955), Alpha Sigma Nu (v.p. 1960), Blue Key. Co-author: Law and Tactics in Federal Criminal Cases, 1963. Home: 5165 Lashbrook Ln E Brighton MI 48116 Office: Buhl Bldg Detroit MI 48226

MCDONALD, PATRICK HILL, JR., educator; b. Carthage, N.C., Dec. 25, 1924; s. Patrick Hill and Mary (Bruton) McD.; B.S., N.C. State U., 1947; M.S., Northwestern U., 1951, Ph.D. (Cabell fellow), 1953; m. Virginia Mabel Ackerman, June 14, 1951; children—Virginia Janet, Patrick Donald, Clyde Malcolm, Charles Thomas (dec.). Instr. mech. engring. N.C. State U. at Raleigh, 1947-48, mem. faculty, 1953—, prof., 1957—, head dept. engring. mech., 1960-76, Harrelson prof., 1965—. instr. mechanics and hydraulics Clemson (S.C.) U., 1948-50; Served with AUS, 1943-45. Recipient Research award Am. Soc. Engring. Edn., 1959. Mem. Am. Soc. Engring. Edn., ASME, Am. Acad. Mechanics, Soc. Exptl. Stress Analysis, N.C. Soc. Engrs., Sigma Xi, Tau Beta Pi, Pi Tau Sigma. Presbyn. (elder). Author: Unified Mechanics, 1964. Contbr. articles to profl. jours. Home: 3120 Tanager St Raleigh NC 27606

MC DONALD, ROBERT EMMETT, conglomerate exec.; b. Red Wing, Minn., Apr. 29, 1915; s. Mitchell W. and Olivia (Carlson) McD.; B.B.A., B.E.E., U. Minn., 1940; postgrad. U. Chgo., 1942; m. Marion L. Wigley, Sept. 14, 1946; children—Patricia L., Barbara C. Employment interviewer Commonwealth Edison Co., Chgo., 1940-43; supr. accessory maintenance Northwest Airlines, St. Paul, 1946-51; dir. maintenance No. region Braniff Airways, Mpls., 1951-53; mgr. operations, then v.p., mgr. def. div. Univac, St. Paul, 1953-64; pres. Univac div. Sperry Rand Corp., Blue Bell, Pa., 1966-71, exec. v.p. parent co., 1966-72, pres., chief operating officer Sperry Rand Corp., N.Y.C., 1972—, vice-chmn. bd., 1979—, also dir.; dir. CertainTeed Corp., Valley Forge, Pa., SKF Industries, Phila. Served to lt. USNR, 1943-46. Mem. IEEE, Tau Beta Pi, Eta Kappa Nu, Acacia. Clubs: Minn. (bd. govs. 1963) (St. Paul); Clove Valley Rod and Gun; Phila. Country, Union League (Phila.); Econ. (N.Y.C.); Mpls. Home: 1125 Robin Rd Gladwyne PA 19035 Office: 1290 Ave of Americas New York NY 10019

MC DONALD, ROY, newspaper publisher; b. Graysville, Tenn., Nov. 25, 1901; s. Frank Jones and Nannie (Ketner) McD.; m. Elizabeth Williams, Dec. 8, 1923. With Chattanooga News-Free Press Co., pub. Chattanooga News-Free Press, 1933—, now chmn. bd. Chmn. bd. Blue Cross-Blue Shield of Tenn. Home: 405 Scenic Hwy Lookout Mountain TN 37350 Office: 400 E 11th St Chattanooga TN 37402

MC DONALD, ROY JOSEPH, nursing home exec.; b. Charlo, Mont., May 17, 1921; s. William Matthew and Lucinda (Keller) McD.; B.P.H., Wash. State U., 1951; m. Carol Rossman, June 27, 1948; children—Dennis, Lorarine, Mary, Christina, Paul, Patrick. Sanitarian Bremerton-Kitrap County Health Dept., Bremerton, Wash., 1945-46; sanitarian Whitman County Health Dept., Colfax, Wash., 1951-56; pres. Palouse Nursing Home, Inc., Colfax, Wash., 1956—; pres. Rest Haven, Inc., Clarkston, Wash., 1956—, St. Ignatius Manor, Inc., Colfax; cons. HEW. Mem. Gov.'s Med. Adv. Com., State Wash., 1966-67; mem. State Wash. Nursing Home Adv. Council, 1961; del. White House Conf. on Aging, 1962, White House Conf. on Health, 1966; chmn. Cuban Refugee Childrens Program, Colfax, Wash. Served with USN, 1941-45. Decorated Purple Heart; named Nursing Home Adminstr. of Year, Am. Nursing Home Assn., 1967; recipient Better Life award, 1968. Mem. Wash. Sanitarians Assn. (pres. 1953), Am. Nursing Home Assn. (pres. 1966-67), Am. Coll. Nursing Home Adminstrs., Wash. State Nursing Home Assn. (pres. 1959-61), Am. Legion. Republican. Roman Catholic. K.C., Eagle. Home: E 202 James St Colfax WA 99111 Office: 907 S Mill St Colfax WA 99111

MC DONALD, STEPHEN LEE, educator; b. Arkadelphia, Ark., Aug. 8, 1924; s. Claud Bethel and Ruth Jane (Gresham) McD.; B.A., La. Poly. Inst., 1947; M.A., U. Tex., 1948, Ph.D., 1951; m. Elizabeth Gene Brewer, Aug. 14, 1945; children—Martha Elizabeth (Mrs. Harvey B. Worchel), Kathryn Ann (Mrs. John J. McGlothlin). Asst. prof. U. Tex., Austin, 1950-56, prof. econs., 1961—, chmn. dept., 1972-76; economist Humble Oil & Refining Co., 1956-57; asso. prof., prof. La. State U., 1957-61. Served with USNR, 1943-46. Ford Found. grantee, 1964; Resources for Future grantee, 1967. Mem. Am., So. (v.p. 1969-70), Southwestern (pres. 1964-65) econ. assns., Southwestern Social Sci. Assn., Gamma Epsilon, Phi Kappa Phi. Democrat. Methodist. Author: Federal Tax Treatment of Income from Oil and Gas, 1963; Petroleum Conservation in the United States, 1971. Contbr. articles to profl. jours. Home: 4002 Sierra Dr Austin TX 78731

MCDONALD, WALTER J., govt. ofcl.; b. Staten Island, N.Y., Dec. 21, 1926; B.B.A., N.Y. U.; M.B.A., Southeastern U. Formerly dep. comptroller, Fort Irwin, Calif., and in Europe; with Dept. Treasury, 1965—, dep. dir. Office of Mgmt. and Orgn., 1974-78, acting asst. Sec. of Treasury, 1978-79, asst. Sec. of Treasury, 1979—. Served with U.S. Army, World War II, Korean War. Office: Dept Treasury 15th and Pennsylvania Ave NW Washington DC 20220

MC DONALD, WALTER JOSEPH, economist; b. Boston, Sept. 20, 1925; s. William John and Estelle Helena (Petite) McD.; B.A., Boston U., 1951; postgrad. U. Minn., 1951-52, Am. U., Beirut, Lebanon, 1956; m. Mary Elizabeth St. John, Jan. 27, 1946; children—Kathleen, Dianne, Kevin, Susan, Sean, William. With CIA, 1952-79, dep. dir. econ. research, 1972-77; prin. dep. asst. sec. internat. affairs Dept. Energy, 1977-79, sr. intelligence officer, 1977-79; mem. Nat. Foreign Intelligence Bd., 1977-79; econ. cons., Annapolis, Md., 1979—; pres. Woods, Inc., Diet Centers of Annapolis, Inc., WJM, Inc., Walter McDonald Assos. Inc.; internat. dir. Nugan Hand Internat., Sydney, Australia. Served with USMC, 1942-45. Decorated Purple Heart; recipient Disting. Intelligence medal CIA, 1977. Fellow Am. Coll. Nursing Home Adminstrs; mem. Internat. Mgmt. and Devel. Inst., Council for Energy Studies, Internat. Assn. Energy Economists. Democrat. Roman Catholic. Club: Annapolis Yacht. Home: 3066 Rundelac Rd Annapolis MD 21403 Office: 1419 Forest Dr #205 Annapolis MD 21403

MCDONALD, WALTER SCOTT, city mgr.; b. Pilot Point, Tex., July 23, 1908; s. George Edwin and Jessie (Scott) McD.; B.S. in Civil Engring., So. Meth. U., 1931; m. Evelyn Foster Moore, June 8, 1934; children—Walter Scott, Steve George, Lynn Elizabeth (Mrs. Robert Murray). Asst. dist. engr., resident engr. Tex. Hwy. Dept., 1931-42; with City of Dallas, 1942—, city mgr., 1966—. Recipient Distinguished Engr. Alumnus award Inst. Tech., So. Meth. U., 1970, Disting. Alumnus award, 1978; Louis Brownlou award Internat. City Mgmt. Assn., 1969, Outstanding Achievements award civil engring. Nat. Engrs. Week, 1967; Citizen of Year award Dallas Kiwanis, 1971. Registered profl. engr., Tex. Mem. ASCE (Nat. Civil Govt. award 1970), Nat., Tex. (Engr. of Year award Dallas chpt. 1972) socs. profl. engrs., Chi Epsilon (hon.). Rotarian. Home: 6814 Desco Dr Dallas TX 75225 Office: City Hall Dallas TX 75201

MCDONALD, WARREN GEORGE, savs. and loan holding co. exec.; b. Oakland, Calif., Feb. 14, 1939; s. George Daniel and Barbara (Sainsot) McD.; B.A., San Francisco State Coll., 1962; m. Roberta Anne Peterson, Apr. 27, 1968; children—Edward Bruce, Deborah Lynn. Partner, Main Lafrentz & Co., C.P.A.'s, San Francisco, 1969-74; v.p., treas. Imperial Corp. Am., San Diego, 1975—. Comdg. officer Coast Guard Res., 1978—. C.P.A., Calif. Mem. Am. Inst. C.P.A.'s, Calif. Soc. C.P.A.'s, Nat. Assn. Accountants, Res. Officers Assn. Home: 6876 Cibola Rd San Diego CA 92120 Office: 8787 Complex Dr San Diego CA 92112

MCDONALD, WESLEY LEE, naval officer; b. Washington, July 26, 1924; s. Wesley Edwin and Thelma Elizabeth (Dulin) McD.; B.S., U.S. Naval Acad., 1946; M.S., George Washington U., 1969; m. Norma Mae Joy, June 5, 1946; children—Thomas O., Kathryn L. McDonald Overman, Joy Anne, Toni Marie. Commd. ensign U.S. Navy, 1943, advanced through grades to vice adm.; comdr. Light Attack Squadron 56, Vietnam, Attack Carrier Air Wing 15, U.S.S. Hermitage, landing ship dock, U.S.S. Coral Sea, aircraft carrier; comdt. 13th Naval Dist.; comdr. Carrier Air Group 3, Gulf of Tonkin; chief Naval Air Tng., 1974-75; comdr. Second Fleet, Norfolk, Va., 1975—. Mem. exec. bd. U.S. Olympic Com. Decorated Legion of Merit with gold star, D.F.C. with gold star, Bronze Star, Meritorious Service medal Joint Service Commendation medal, Air medal with 3 gold stars, Navy Commendation medal. Home: 423 Dillingham Blvd Norfolk VA 23511 Office: Comdr Second Fleet FPO NY 09501

MCDONALD, WILLIAM ANDREW, educator; b. Warkworth, Ont., Can., Apr. 26, 1913 (came to U.S. 1936, naturalized 1943); s. William Douglas and Jean (Lane) McD.; B.A., U. Toronto, 1935, M.A., 1936; Ph.D., Johns Hopkins, 1940; m. Elizabeth Jackson Anderson, June 28, 1941; children—Susan, Elizabeth. Asst. prof. classics Lehigh U., 1939-43; tech. writer Consol. Vultee Aircraft Co.,

1943-45; asso. prof. classics, U. Tex., Austin, 1945-46; prof. classics, chmn. dept. Moravian Coll., Bethlehem, Pa., 1946-48; prof. classics, U. Minn., 1948—, Regents' prof. classical studies, 1973—, dir. honors div. Coll. Liberal Arts, 1964-67, dir. Minn. Messenia expdn. in S.W. Greece, 1961—, dir. grad. center for ancient studies, 1973-78; Research prof. Am. Sch. Classical Studies, Athens, 1978-79; excavation staff Johns Hopkins at Olynthus, 1938, U. Cin. at Pylos, 1939, 53. Vogeler Meml. fellow Johns Hopkins, 1936-38, Royal Soc. Can. fellow Am. Sch. Classical Studies, Athens, 1938-39, Guggenheim fellow, 1958-59, 67-68. Mem. Archaeol. Inst. Am. (exec. com.), Am. Philol. Assn., Assn. for Field Archaeology (v.p.), Soc. Prof. Archaeologists (dir.). Author: Political Meeting Places of Greeks, 1943; Progress into the Past, 1967; (with D. J. Georgacas) Place Names of Southwest Peloponnesus, 1969; (with G. Rapp Jr.) Minnesota Messenia Expedition: Reconstructing A Bronze Age Regional Environment, 1972. Home: 1707 Lindig St Apt 5 St Paul MN 55113 Office: 312 Folwell Hall Univ Minn Minneapolis MN 55455

MCDONALD, WILLIAM G(ERALD), economist, govt. ofcl.; b. Providence, June 2, 1919; s. William Leo and Catherine Theresa (White) McD.; B.A. in Econs., U. Tulsa, 1949; postgrad. Georgetown U., 1950; postgrad. Columbia U., 1951-54, grad. exec. mgmt. program, 1957; grad. Command and Gen. Staff Coll., Armed Forces Staff Coll.; m. Agnes G. Sellman, Apr. 28, 1944; children—William G., Francis L., M. Brian, Catherine T. Served as enlisted man USAAF, from 1942, commd. officer, advanced through grades to col., USAF, 1959; asst. prof. U.S. Mil. Acad.; prof. polit. sci. U.S. Air Force Acad.; spl. asst. chief staff USAF, Office Sec. Def., ret., 1970; with Office Mgmt. and Budget, Washington, 1970-72; dir. plans and schedules AEC, NRC, Washington, 1972-77; exec. dir. Fed. Energy Regulatory Commn., Dept. Energy, Washington, 1977—. Active Assn. for Retarded Children. Decorated Legion of Merit, Air Force Commendation medal; recipient Presdl. commendation for work on Presdl. Commn. on Causes and Prevention of Violence, 1972, for work on FY 73 Presdl. Budget, 1972, Disting. Service award NRC. Roman Catholic. Home: 4311 Bradley Ln Chevy Chase MD 20015 Office: 825 N Capitol St Washington DC 20426

MC DONALD, WILLIAM JAMES, corp. ofcl., lawyer; b. N.Y.C., Apr. 17, 1927; s. William J. and Adelaide (Morrison) McD.; B.S., Holy Cross Coll., 1949; J.D., Georgetown U., 1952; m. Diane A. Saxer, Apr. 19, 1958; children—Brian A., Timothy R., Megan M., Christopher M. Admitted to N.Y. bar, 1952, U.S. Supreme Ct. bar; with firm Clark, Carr & Ellis, N.Y.C., 1952-69, partner, 1963-69; gen. counsel Union Pacific R.R. Co. and subsidiaries, 1968, v.p. law dept., 1969; v.p., gen. counsel Union Pacific Corp., Union Pacific R.R. Corp. and affiliates, 1969-73, sr. v.p. law, 1973—; dir. Los Angeles & Salt Lake R.R., Oreg.-Wash. R.R. & Nav., Oreg. Short Line R.R., Spokane Internat. R.R. Co., St. Joseph & Grand Island Ry. Co., Upland Industries, Union Pacific Land Resources Corp. Mem. Cardinal's Com. for Edn. in Archdiocese, 1970—, Cardinal's Com. of Laity, 1969—. Served with USNR, 1945-46; PTO. Mem. Assn. Bar City N.Y., Assn. Am. R.R. (legal affairs com., chmn. various subcoms.), N.Y. State, Am. (chmn.-elect) public utilities sect.) bar assns., Am. Arbitration Assn. (dir. 1979—, chmn. environ. dispute adv. com.). Contbr. articles to legal jours. Home: 11 Axtell Dr Scarsdale NY 10583 Office: 345 Park Ave New York NY 10022

MCDONALD, WILLIAM JOSEPH, aux. bishop; b. Kilkenny, Ireland, June 15, 1904; s. Patrick and Bridget (Foskin) McD.; B.A., St. Kieran's Coll., Kilkenny, 1924; M.A., Cath. U. Am., 1937, Ph.D., 1939; LL.D., Northwestern U., 1958, Mt. St. Mary's Coll., Emmitsburg, Md.; J.U.D. (hon.), Nat. U. Ireland, 1959; Sc.D., St. John's U., Bklyn.; Paed.D., LaSalle Coll., Phila.; Ed.D., Providence Coll.; Litt.D., St. Francis Coll., Bklyn. Ordained priest Roman Catholic Ch., 1928, invested domestic prelate, 1948; chaplain Newman Club, Stanford, 1928-30; asso. editor The Monitor, San Francisco, 1930-32; moderator Newman Club, San Francisco State Coll., 1934-36; curate St. Paul's Ch., San Francisco, 1934-36; prof. philosophy Cath. U. Am., 1940-67, vice rector, 1954-57, rector, 1957-67; aux. bishop of Washington, 1964-68, San Francisco, 1968—; titular bishop of Aquae Regiae; pres. Internat. Fedn. Catholic Univs., 1960-63. Mem. Cath. Culture Guild (founder 1934). Editor-in-chief New Cath. Ency.; contbr. articles to revs. Home: 1615 Broadway San Francisco CA 94109*

MCDONALD, WILLIAM LEO, life ins. co. exec.; b. Emmetsburg, Iowa, Feb. 6, 1938; s. Leo Raymond and Helen Marie (Boyd) McD.; B.S. in Math., Buena Vista Coll., Storm Lake, Iowa, 1960; postgrad. U. No. Iowa, U. Chgo.; m. Deanna Marie Brechwald, June 4, 1960; children—Catherine Sue, James William, Thomas Andrew, Kari Lynn. Vice pres. Zahorik Co., Pasadena, Calif., 1972-74; pres. Confidence Golf Co., Pasadena, 1974-75; with Life Investors Co. Inc. Am., Cedar Rapids, Iowa, 1975—, exec. v.p., 1976-78, pres., 1978—, also dir.; pres. Bankers United Life Assurance Co., Cedar Rapids, 1978—. Mem. Nat. Assn. Life Underwriters, Gen. Agts. and Mgrs. Assn. Roman Catholic. Club: Cedar Rapids Country. Home: 2904 Allegheny Dr Cedar Rapids IA 52402 Office: 4333 Edgewood Rd NE Cedar Rapids IA 54299

MC DONELL, HORACE GEORGE, JR., electronics co. exec.; b. N.Y.C., Sept. 23, 1928; s. Horace Gustave and Anabel (Armstrong) McD.; A.B., Adelphi Coll., 1952; postgrad. Harvard, 1962; m. Eileen Romar, Sept. 6, 1952; children—Victoria, Diane, Horace. Engr., Sperry Gyroscope Co., N.Y.C., 1952; with Perkin-Elmer Corp., Norwalk, Conn., 1963—, mgr. instrument group, 1967-77, v.p., 1966-69, sr. v.p., 1969-77, exec. v.p., 1977—, also dir.; dir. Hitachi-Perkin Elmer, Ltd. (Japan), Perkin-Elmer Ltd. (U.K.), Perkin Elmer Internat., Inc. Mem. adv. task force on export controls U.S. Def. Sci. Bd., 1975—, chmn. instrumentation subcom., 1975—. Mem. Bd. Edn., Ridgefield, Conn., 1969. Bd. dirs. Conn. Sci. Fair. Trustee, bd. dirs. Danbury (Conn.) Hosp. Served with AUS, 1946-48. Mem. Sci. Apparatus Maker Assn. (dir., chmn. analytical instrument sect.), Am. Inst. Physics, AAAS, Instrument Soc. Am. Home: Powder Horn Dr Ridgefield CT 06877 Office: Perkin-Elmer Corp Main Ave Norwalk CT

MCDONNELL, EDWARD FRANCIS, food co. exec.; b. Boston, July 27, 1935; s. John and Margaret (O'Neill) McD.; B.S., Suffolk U., 1959; m. Catherine McNamara, July 18, 1959; children—Edward, Paul, Elizabeth. With Raytheon Co., 1960-64, bus. mgr. radio and TV tube op., 1965-66; with Gen. Foods Corp., 1966-75, fin. ops. mgr. Gen. Foods Internat., 1966-67, asst. to pres., 1968, pres., chief exec. officer Kibin S.P., Subs., Brazil, 1969-75; with Pillsbury Co., Mpls., 1975—, corp. group v.p., pres. Pillsbury Internat., 1978—, v.p. Europe, 1977—. Home: 447 Peavey Rd Wayzata MN 55391 Office: 608 2d Ave S Minneapolis MN 55402

MCDONNELL, JAMES SMITH, aerospace co. exec.; b. Denver, Apr. 9, 1899; s. James Smith and Susan Belle (Hunter) M.; B.S., Princeton, 1921; M.S. in Aeronautical Engring., Mass. Inst. Tech., 1925; grad. Army Air Corps Flying Sch., San Antonio, 1923-24; D.Eng., Washington U., St. Louis, 1958, M.D., 1977; D.Eng., U. Mo. at Rolla, 1957; LL.D., Princeton, 1960, U. Ark., 1965; D.Sc., Clarkson Coll., 1976; m. Mary Elizabeth Finney, June 30, 1934 (dec. July 1949); children—James Smith III, John Finney; m. 2d, Priscilla Brush Forney, Apr. 1, 1956; children—George David, Susan Brush Boyd, Priscilla Young Canny. Aero. engr., pilot Huff Daland Airplane Co., 1924; stress analyst, draftsman Consol. Aircraft Co., 1925; asst. chief engr. Stout Metal Airplane Co., 1925; chief engr. Hamilton Aero Mfg. Co., 1926-27, McDonnell & Assos., 1928-29; v.p. Airtransport Engring. Corp., 1930-31; engr., test pilot Great Lakes Aircraft Corp., 1932; chief project engr. for landplanes Glenn L. Martin Co., 1933-38; pres. McDonnell Aircraft Corp., St. Louis, 1939-62, chmn., chief exec. officer, 1962-67; chmn., chief exec. officer McDonnell Douglas Corp., St. Louis, 1967-72, chmn., 1972—. Mem. adv. council Center for Strategic and Internat. Studies, Washington; mem. Civic Progress, Inc., St. Louis. Bd. dirs. Atlantic Council, Population Crisic Com., UN Assn. U.S.A.; hon. chmn. bd. St. Louis Country Day Sch. Recipient St. Louis award, 1959, Daniel Guggenheim medal, 1963, Robert J. Collier trophy, 1966, Founders medal Nat. Acad. Engring., 1967, Forrestal award, 1972; named to Nat. Aviation Hall of Fame. Fellow Am. Inst. Aeros. and Astronautics (hon.); mem. St. Louis C. of C., St. Louis Com. Fgn. Relations, Mo. Acad. Squires. Clubs: Log Cabin, Old Warson Country, Noonday, University, Racquet, St. Louis Country, Bellerive Country, Saint Louis, Washington University, Mo. Athletic (St. Louis); University (N.Y.C.); Met. (Washington). Home: PO Box 516 Saint Louis MO 63166 Office: McDonnell Douglas Corp Lambert-St Louis Municipal Airport Saint Louis MO 63166

MC DONNELL, JOHN THOMAS, oil and gas co. exec.; b. Tulsa, Jan. 5, 1926; s. John Thomas and Louise (Gallo) McD.; student Villanova U., 1943-44; B.S. in Chem. Engring., U. Okla., Norman, 1946; m. Dorothy Henry, June 19, 1948; children—Kevin Robert, Lisa Anne McDonnell Raynolds. Vice pres. Iberian Gulf Oil Co., Madrid, 1967-69, pres., 1969-70; pres. Warren Petroleum Co., Tulsa, 1970-75; v.p., exec. rep. Gulf Oil Exploration & Prodn. Co., Houston, 1976—; dir. Flame Gas Transmission Co., Grand Bay Co. Met. chmn. Nat. Alliance of Businessmen, 1976-77. Served as ensign, USNR, 1946. Mem. Interstate Natural Gas Assn. Am., Mid-Continent Oil and Gas Assn., Am. Inst. Chem. Engrs., Natural Gas Supply Com., Am. Petroleum Inst. Republican. Episcopalian. Club: Lakeside Country (Houston). Home: 511 Longwoods Ln Houston TX 77024 Office: PO Box 2100 Houston TX 77001. *Success is real when it involves the personal satisfaction that talents have been put to good use. Position, money or fame are poor substitutes for an inner feeling of achievement.*

MC DONNELL, MICHAEL EUGENE, food co. exec.; b. Davenport, Iowa, Nov. 9, 1941; s. Joseph Edward and Olive Marie (Dolan) McD.; B.B.A. cum laude, U. Notre Dame, 1963; m. Judith Ann Seidel, Apr. 19, 1969; children—Theresa, Jeffrey, Allison. Audit mgr. Arthur Young & Co., Chgo., 1963-70; asst. controller Swift & Co., Chgo., 1970-73, fin. v.p., 1973—, also dir. Mem. Ill. C.P.A. Soc., Am. Inst. C.P.A.'s, Fin. Execs. Inst., Beta Alpha Psi, Beta Gamma Sigma. Roman Catholic. Office: 115 W Jackson Blvd Chicago IL 60604

MCDONNELL, MICHAEL THOMAS, JR., lawyer; b. Phila., June 30, 1936; s. Michael Thomas and Florence C. (Mulligan) McD.; B.S., Villanova U., 1958, LL.B., 1961; LL.M. candidate, Temple U., 1968; m. Ellen Meisner, June 16, 1962; children—Michael Thomas III, Patrick, Ellen, Theresa, Andrew. Substitute tchr. Phila. Bd. Edn., 1959-61; admitted to Pa. bar, 1961; Pa. Supreme Ct., Delaware County Common Pleas Ct.; mem. firm Brown, Connery, Kulp & Wille, Camden, N.J., 1961-62, McClenachan, Blumberg & Levy, Chester, Pa., 1962-63; partner McDonnell & McDonnell Assos., Yeadon and Drexel Hill, Pa., 1963—; instr. real estate Pa. Mil. Coll., Chester, 1963-64; instr. bus. law Drexel Inst. Tech., Phila., 1963-64, Temple U., Phila., 1963-66. Chmn., Am. Cancer Soc. Ann. Drive, Borough of Yeadon, 1973; adviser to Selective Service System Local Bd. 58, 1972—. Mem. Am., Pa., Delaware County bar assns., Am., Pa. (chmn. Delaware County) trial lawyers assns., Am. Judicature Soc., Yeadon Businessmens Assn. (pres.), St. Louis Holy Name Soc. (pres.), Profl. Club of Yeadon (pres.). Home: 1206 N Longacre Blvd Yeadon PA 19050 Office: 712 Church Ln Yeadon PA 19050 also 4750 Township Line Rd Drexel Hills PA 19026

MCDONNELL, SANFORD NOYES, aircraft co. exec.; b. Litte Rock, Oct. 12, 1922; s. William Archie and Carolyn (Cherry) McD.; B.A. in Econs., Princeton, 1945; B.S. in Mech. Engring., U. Colo., 1948; M.S. in Applied Mechanics, Washington U., St. Louis, 1954; m. Priscilla Robb, Sept. 3, 1946; children—Robbin McDonnell Hallock, William Randall. With McDonnell Douglas Corp. (formerly McDonnell Aircraft Corp.), St. Louis, 1948—, v.p., 1959-66, pres. McDonnell Aircraft div., 1966-71, corp. exec. v.p., 1971; corp. pres., 1971—, chief exec. officer, 1972—, also dir. corp.; dir. First Nat. Union, Inc., St. Louis. Active St. Louis United Way; exec. bd. St. Louis council Boy Scouts. Trustee Washington U., St. Louis. Fellow Am. Inst. Aeros. and Astronautics; mem. Aerospace Industries Assn. (gov.), Navy League U.S. (life), Am. Helicopter Soc., Assn. U.S. Army, Air Force Assn., C. of C. of U.S., Armed Forces Mgmt. Assn., Nat. Def. Transp. Assn., Am. Ordnance Assn., Am. Security Council, Nat. Aeronautic Assn., Tau Beta Pi. Presbyterian (trustee, elder). Office: McDonnell Douglas Corp PO Box 516 Saint Louis MO 63166*

MCDONOUGH, GEORGE FRANCIS, JR., aero. engr.; b. Chgo., July 3, 1928; s. George Francis and Minnie L. (Bartoli) McD.; B.S., Marquette U., Milw., 1953; M.S., U. Ill., 1956, Ph.D., 1959; m. Louise Guthrie, June 4, 1955; children—Michael Neil (dec.), Kathleen Louise, Thomas Charles, Daniel George. Asst. prof. U. Ill., 1959-60; asso. prof. San Jose (Calif.) State Coll., 1960-61; sr. engr. E.H. Plesset Assos., Los Angeles, 1961-63; sr. scientist United Aircraft Corp., Los Angeles, 1963; with George C. Harshall Space Flight Center, NASA, Huntsville, Ala., 1963—, dep. dir. data systems labs., 1974-78, dep. asso. dir. engring., 1978—; lectr. U. Ala., Huntsville, 1965—. Chmn. Westbury Civic Assn., 1965-67. Served with USNR, 1945-47, 51-52. Recipient Superior Performance award NASA, 1964, Superior Achievement award, 1966, Exceptional Service medal, 1973; director's commendation George C. Marshall Space Flight Center, 1973. Mem. ASCE, Sigma Xi (pres. Huntsville 1972-74). Democrat. Roman Catholic. Co-author: Wind Effects on Launch Vehicles, 1970. Home: 1902 Fairmont Rd Huntsville AL 35801 Office: Code EF01 George C Marshall Space Flight Center Huntsville AL 35812

MC DONOUGH, JAMES NORMAN, educator, lawyer; b. Toledo, Mar. 2, 1911; s. Ellsworth Edward and Mary Louise (Caragher) McD; A.B. magna cum laude, St. John's U., 1931; J.D., Western Res. U., 1936, LL.M., 1937; m. Elizabeth Mildred Langley, Sept. 2, 1950. Editor, Entr'actes, publ. Chevron Players, Toledo, 1931-33; English instr. St. John's U., Toledo, 1932-33; research fellow Western Res. U. Law Sch., Cleve., 1936-37; lectr., 1947, asst. prof., 1947-48, asso. prof., adv. Law Review, 1948-51, prof., 1951-53; admitted to Ohio bar, 1936; teaching fellow N.Y. U. Law Sch., 1937-39; instr. Loyola U. Law Sch., Los Angeles, 1939-40; editorial staff Cath. Press Union, Inc., 1940-43, 46-47; dean St. Louis U. Sch. Law, 1953-62, prof., 1953—. Bd. mem. Legal Aid Soc., City and County of St. Louis, 1957-64; mem. University City Human Relations Commn., 1962-65, vice chmn., 1963-65; mem. Mo. adv. com. U.S. Commn. Civil Rights, 1959-61, chmn., 1960-61; mem. St. Louis County Pub. Defender Adv. Bd.; exec. bd. St. Louis Civil Liberties Com., 1959-65; mem. bd. Helpers of Holy Souls, 1958-65, Inst. Internationale d'Etudes et de Documentation en Matière de Concurrence Commerciale, Cath. League Religious and Civil Rights. Served from pvt. to capt. USAAF, 1943-46. Mem. John Henry Newman Honor Soc., Am. Law Inst., Inst. for Theol. Encounter with Sci. and Tech. (dir.), Am., Ohio bar assns., Bar Assn. St. Louis, Delta Theta Phi, Alpha Sigma Nu, Order of Coif. Roman Catholic. Editorial adv. bd. Social Order, 1953-58; editorial adv. Focus/Midwest, 1961-70. Author: (with D.B. King and J.E. Garrett) Juvenile Court Handbook, 1970. Contbr. articles to legal and other periodicals. Home: 515 Purdue Ave University City MO 63130 Office: 3642 Lindell Blvd Saint Louis MO 63108

MCDONOUGH, JOHN RICHARD, lawyer; b. St. Paul, May 16, 1919; s. John Richard and Gena (Olson) McD.; student U. Wash., 1937-40; LL.B., Columbia U., 1946; m. Margaret Poot, Sept. 10, 1944; children—Jana Margaret, John Jacobus. Admitted to Calif. bar, 1949; asst. prof. law Stanford U., 1946-49, prof., 1952-69; asso. firm Brobeck, Phleger & Harrison, San Francisco, 1949-52; asst. dep. atty. gen. U.S. Dept. Justice, Washington, 1967-68, asso. dep. atty. gen., 1968-69; of counsel and partner firm Keatinge & Sterling, Los Angeles, 1969-70; partner firm Ball, Hunt, Hart, Brown and Baerwitz, 1970—; exec. sec. Calif. Law Revision Commn., 1954-59, mem. commn., 1959-67, vice chmn., 1960-64, chmn., 1964-65; participant various continuing edn. programs. Served with U.S. Army, 1942-46. Mem. State Bar Calif., Am. Bar Assn., Los Angeles County Bar Assn., Beverly Hills Bar Assn., Am. Law Inst. Democrat. Office: 450 N Roxbury Dr 5th Floor Beverly Hills CA 90210

MCDONOUGH, MATHIAS JOHN, elec. equipment mfg. co. exec.; b. Pitts., Aug. 24, 1921; s. Michael and Ellen (Higgins) McD.; B.S. in Elec. Engring. U. Pitts., 1943; m. Athena Hellmann, Sept. 24, 1949; children—Michele, Charles, Garry, Brian, Loren, John. With Westinghouse Electric Corp., Pitts., 1946—, v.p. power systems marketing, 1967-71, exec. v.p. transmission and distribution group, 1971-76, sr. exec. v.p. corp. resources, 1976—. Served with AUS, 1943-46. Clubs: Duquesne, Oakmont Country (Pitts.). Home: 319 Dewey Ave Pittsburgh PA 15218 Office: Westinghouse Bldg Rm 2311 Pittsburgh PA 15222

MC DONOUGH, PATRICK JAMES, clergyman, editor; b. Boston, Nov. 30, 1928; s. Patrick J. and Katherine T. McD.; A.B. in Theology, St. Michael's Passionist Sem., 1946; Ph.D., Anglican U., Rome, 1959. Ordained priest, Roman Catholic Ch., 1956; asst. prof. philosophy Immaculate Conception Monastery, Jamaica, N.Y., 1959-64, asso. prof., 1964-68; asso. prof. philosophy LaSalle Coll., Phila., 1968-71; rector St. Ann's Monastery, Scranton, Pa., 1971-78; performer-host program CBS-Radio-TV, N.E. Pa., 1971-78; editor Sign Mag., Union City, N.J., 1978—. Mem. Cath. Philos. Soc., Cath. Press Assn. Home: 1901 West St Union City NJ 07087 Office: 526 Monastery Pl Union City NJ 07087

MC DONOUGH, RICHARD DOYLE, paper co. exec.; b. St. Stephen, N.B., Can., May 8, 1931 (parents Am. citizens); s. Kenneth Paul and Mary (Doyle) McD.; A.B., Dartmouth, 1952; m. Caroline Wilkins, July 7, 1956; children—Elizabeth Wilkins, Richard David, Philip Bradford. Financial exec. Gen. Electric Co., Mexico City, 1953-63; financial exec. Singer Co., U.S. and U.K., 1963-69, v.p., controller, N.Y.C., 1969-73, v.p., 1973-76, pres. European mail order div., 1976, corp. v.p. divestments activities, 1976-79; sr. v.p. fin., chief fin. officer Bowater, Inc., 1979—. Mem. Financial Execs. Inst., Nat. Assn. Accountants. Home: Barons Mead East Point Ln Old Greenwich CT 06870 Office: Bowater Inc 1500 E Putnam Ave Old Greenwich CT 06870

MCDONOUGH, ROBERT PAUL, polit. cons.; b. Parkersburg, W.Va., Mar. 13, 1915; s. Patrick J. and Virginia (Goff) McD.; A.B., U. Notre Dame, 1936; m. Martha Sinclair Smith, Dec. 26, 1941; children—Sarah Katherine, Robert Sinclair. Individual practice as polit. cons. County committeeman Democratic Party, 1954-60; campaign dir. county and congl. dist. campaigns, 1958; del. Dem. Nat. Conv., 1956; campaign dir. Senator John F. Kennedy in W.Va. Primary, 1960; chmn. W.Va. Dem. Exec., Com., 1961-64; Dem. nat. committeeman, 1964-65. Former dir. W.Va. Dept. Natural Resources. Served to capt. C.E., AUS, 1941-46. Decorated Bronze Star. Home: 420 Argyle Dr Alexandria VA 22305 Office: PO Box 912 Parkersburg WV 26101

MCDONOUGH, THOMAS JOSEPH, archbishop; b. Phila., Dec. 5, 1911; s. Michael Francis and Margaret Mary (Nolan) McD.; A.B., St. Charles Sem., Phila., 1935; J.C.D., Cath. U. Am., 1941. Ordained priest Roman Catholic Ch., 1938; asst. pastor Cathedral and St. Charles parish, Phila., 1938-40; vice-chancellor, chancellor, vicar gen., officialis Diocese of St. Augustine (Fla.), 1941-48; pastor of Cathedral, St. Augustine, 1943-45; apptd. domestic prelate, 1945; consecrated bishop, 1947; aux. bishop of St. Augustine, 1947-57; aux. bishop of Savannah (Ga.), 1957-60, bishop, 1960-67; archbishop of Louisville, 1967—. Author: Apostolic Administrators, 1941. Office: 212 E College St Louisville KY 40203*

MCDOUGAL, CHRISTOPHER BOUTON, lawyer; b. Chgo., June 17, 1907; s. Robert and Persis (Bouton) McD.; A.B., Princeton U., 1929; J.D., U. Chgo., 1932; LL.D., Trinity Coll., 1973; m. Winnifred Turner, Aug. 23, 1941; children—Ellen, Christopher Bouton, Edward Turner. Admitted to Ill. bar, 1932; asso., then partner Sidley & Austin, and predecessors, 1933-49; v.p., sec., gen. counsel, dir. R.R. Donnelley & Sons Co., Chgo., 1949-71, dir., 1973—. Past pres. Winnetka (Ill.) Bd. Edn. Vice pres., chmn. legal aid com. United Charities of Chgo., 1956-58; mem. Chgo. Crime Commn, dir., v.p., 1951-55. Bd. dirs. Young Life Campaign, 1966-70; pres. Chgo. Sunday Evening Club, 1969-78; trustee, 1969-78. Served with USNR, 1942-45. Decorated Legion of Merit. Mem. Order of Coif. Clubs: Law, Legal, Univ., Princeton, Comml. Commonwealth, Old Elm, Indian Hill (Winnetka). Home: 682 Ardsley Rd Winnetka IL 60093

MCDOUGAL, MILFORD MERLYN, judge; b. Clovis, Calif., July 4, 1922; s. Charles Arthur and Lina (Southerland) McD.; B.S., Okla. Baptist U., 1949; LL.B., U. Tulsa, 1958; m. Murrel Louese Goetz, Oct. 22, 1949; 1 dau., Bryn Lori. Admitted to Okla. bar, 1958; mem. staff Hawkins, Sumpter & Co., C.P.A.'s, Tulsa, Okla., 1952-54; self-employed pub. accountant, Tulsa, Okla., 1954-58; pvt. practice law, Tulsa, 1958-69; spl. dist. judge Dist. Ct. State of Okla., Jud. Dist. 14, Tulsa County, 1969-71; asso. dist. judge Probate div., 1971-75; dist. judge, 1975—. Served to capt. AUS, 1942-46, 50-52. Decorated Purple Heart medal with 1 oak leaf cluster; Air medal with 3 oak leaf clusters. Mem. Am., Okla., Tulsa County bar assns., Okla. Jud. Conf., Nat. Coll. Probate Judges. Baptist (deacon 1972—). Lion. Home: 6754 S 70th East Ave Tulsa OK 74133 Office: 403 Tulsa County Courthouse Tulsa OK 74103

MCDOUGALL, JOHN, automotive co. exec.; b. Belfast, Ireland, July 3, 1916; s. William and Ellen (Faulkner) McD.; came to U.S., 1929, naturalized, 1937; m. Ola B. Beaman, Nov. 7, 1940; 1 son, John William. With Ford Motor Co., 1935—, pres. subs. Ford Europe, London, 1973-75, chmn. Ford Europe, 1975-77, exec. v.p. ops. staff Ford Motor World Hdqrs., Dearborn, Mich., 1977-78, exec. v.p. ops. N. Am. automotive ops., 1978—, also dir. Trustee Taylor U.; active United Fund campaigns. Mem. Soc. Automotive Engrs., Engring. Soc. Detroit, ASME, Am. C. of C. (London) (dir.). Republican. Contbr.

articles to profl. jours. Home: 1893 Pine Ridge Ln Bloomfield Hills MI 48013 Office: Ford Motor Co Rotunda Dr PO Box 1522A Dearborn MI 48121

MC DOUGALL, PAMELA ANN, Canadian govt. ofcl.; b. Ottawa, Ont., Can., May 9, 1925; d. Samuel G. and Marjorie J. (Sumner) McDougall; B.Sc., Mt. Allison U., 1945, LL.D. (hon.), 1969. With Canadian Fgn. Service, 1949-76, ambassador to Poland, 1968-71, asst. sec. to cabinet, Ottawa, 1971-74, dir. gen. Bur. Econ. and Sci. Affairs, Dept. External Affairs, 1974-76; chmn. Canadian Tariff Bd., 1976—; dir. Uranium Can., 1974-76; alt. dir. Export Devel. Corp., 1974-76; dep. minister nat. health and welfare, 1979—. Mem. Ch. of Eng. Address: Jeanne Mance Bldg Ottawa ON K1A 0K9 Canada

MCDOW, JOHN JETT, univ. dean; b. Covington, Tenn., Jan. 6, 1925; s. Robert Simpson and Lucy Ann (Cocke) McD.; student Franklin and Marshall Coll., 1944-45; B.S., U. Tenn., 1948; M.S., Mich. State U., 1949, Ph.D., 1957; m. Dorothy Virginia Glass, Dec. 22, 1946; children—Ronald Allan, Jane Virginia. Instr., Mich. State U., 1949; instr. Okla. State U., 1949-51, asst. prof. agrl. engring., 1951; asso. prof. La. Poly. U., 1951-57, prof., 1957-62, head agrl. engring. dept., 1953-62; prof., head dept. agrl. engring. U. Tenn., Knoxville, 1962-73, dean admissions and records, 1973—; cons./collaborator Agrl. Research Service, U.S. Dept. Agr., 1970-76. Mem. La. Engring. Council, 1955-56. Served with USNR, World War II; comdr. Res. So. Fellowship grantee, 1957. Registered profl. engr., Tenn., La. Mem. Am. Soc. Agrl. Engring. (dir. 1973-75), Am. Soc. Engring. Edn. (sec. agrl. engring. div. 1971-72, vice chmn. 1972-73, chmn. 1973-74), Sigma Xi, Tau Beta Pi, Pi Mu Epsilon, Omicron Delta Kappa, Gamma Sigma Delta, Phi Kappa Phi (v.p. 1971-77, pres. elect 1977—, pres. found. 1974-78). Presbyn. Rotarian. Contbr. articles to profl. jours. Home: 2008 Walnut Hills Dr Knoxville TN 37920

MCDOWALL, RODDY, actor; b. London, Sept. 17, 1928; educated St. Joseph's Sch., London. With Twentieth Century Fox, 1940—; films include: Man Hunt, How Green was My Valley, My Friend Flicka, Lassie Come Home, Cleopatra, Lord Love a Duck, Planet of the Apes, Escape from the Planet of the Apes, Conquest of the Planet of the Apes, The Poseidon Adventure, Funny Lady, Embryo, The Cat from Outer Space, Laserblast, Rabbit Test, Circle of Iron, Scavenger Hunt; TV films: Flood, A Taste of Evil, The Elevator; Broadway appearances include: Misalliance, Escapade, Doctor's Dilemma, No Time for Sergeants, Camelot, The Astrakhan Coat, Mean Johnny Barrows; numerous TV appearances include: Hollywood Squares, Kraft Theater, Goodyear Playhouse, U.S. Steel Hour, Run for your Life, Ironside, Harry O, Love American Style, McCloud, Macmillan & Wife; appeared in TV drama Miracle on 34th Street, 1973; regular on TV series Planet of the Apes, 1974; dir. film The Devil's Widow. Address: care of William Morris Agency Inc 1350 Ave of Americas New York NY 10019*

MCDOWELL, CHARLES ALEXANDER, phys. chemist; b. Belfast, Ireland, Aug. 29, 1918; s. Charles and Mabel (McGregor) McD.; B.Sc., M.Sc., Queens U., Belfast, 1942; D.Sc., U. Liverpool (Eng.), 1955; m. Christine Joan Staddart, Aug. 10, 1945; children—Karen Mary Anne, Christina Anne, Avril Jeanne. Sr. asst. lectr. Queen's U., 1941-42; sci. officer U.K. Civil Def., 1942-45; lectr. U. Liverpool, 1945-55; prof., head dept. chemistry U. B.C., Vancouver, 1955—, Killiam sr. research fellow, 1969-70; vis. prof. Kyoto (Japan) U., 1965, 69-70; Distinguished vis. prof. U. Fla., Gainesville, 1974; NRC Sr. Research fellow Cambridge (Eng.) U., 1963-64; W.U.S. cons. U. Honduras, 1975; Distinguished vis. prof. U. Capetown, 1975; Frontiers of Chemistry lectr. Wayne State U., 1978; Distinguished vis. lectr. Faculty of Sci., U. Calgary, 1978. Recipient Letts Gold medal in theoretical chemistry Queen's U., 1941, Sci. medal Université de Liège (Belgium), 1955; Centennial medal Gov. of Can., 1967; Queen Elizabeth Silver Jubilee medal 1977. Mem. Chem. Soc. London, Chem. Inst. Can. (medal 1969, pres.-elect 1977), Royal Inst. Chemistry (U.K.), Royal Soc. Can., Am. Chem. Soc., Am. Mass Spectrometry Soc., Mass Spectrometry Soc. Japan, Am. Phys. Soc. Editor: Mass Spectrometry, 1963; Magnetic Resonance, 1972; contbr. articles to profl. jours. Home: 5612 McMaster Rd Vancouver BC V6T 1JB Canada

MCDOWELL, CHARLES EAGER, lawyer, naval officer; b. Manchester, N.H., Sept. 9, 1923; s. Joseph Curry and Mildred (Eager) McD.; A.B., Dartmouth Coll., 1947; J.D., U. Va., 1950; m. Carolyn A. Gibbons, June 21, 1947; children—Robin, Patricia. Served to 2d lt. AUS, 1943-46; admitted to Tex. bar, 1950; with land div. Shell Oil Co., Houston, 1950; commd. lt. (j.g.) U.S. Navy, 1951, advanced through grades to rear adm., 1976; staff legal officer Comdr. Service Force, U.S. Pacific Fleet; staff judge adv., head internat. law div. Naval War Coll., 1963-66; staff legal officer, comdr. 7th Fleet, 1966-68; sr. Navy mem. ad hoc com., dep. asst. judge adv. gen. Office Judge Adv. Gen. Dept. Def., Washington, 1968-72; staff judge adv. on staff comdr. in chief U.S. Naval Forces, Europe, London, Eng., 1972-75; comdg. officer Naval Justice Sch., Newport, R.I., 1975-76; dep. judge adv. gen. Navy Dept., Washington, 1976-78, judge adv. gen., 1978—. Decorated Bronze Star, Joint Service Commendation medal, Navy Commendation medal with Combat V, Purple Heart, Combat Inf. badge. Mem. Am. Bar Assn., Fed. Bar Assn., Tex. Bar Assn., Judge Advs. Assn., Order of Coif, Chi Phi. Methodist. Club: Square Dancer. Home: 1106 Croton Dr Alexandria VA 22308 Office: Office of Judge Adv Gen Navy Dept Washington DC 20370

MCDOWELL, EDWIN STEWART, newspaperman; b. Somers Point, N.J., May 13, 1935; s. Samuel Hamilton and Kathryn (Priser) McD.; B.S., Temple U., 1959; student N.Y. U., 1959; m. Carole Ann Foss, July 14, 1956 (div. Sept. 1971); children—Susan Carole, Amy Lyn; m. 2d, Sathie Akimoto, July 7, 1973; 1 son, Edwin Akimoto. Pub. affairs dir. McGraw-Edison Co., N.Y.C., 1958-60; editorial writer Ariz. Republic, Phoenix, 1960-70, editor editorial pages, 1970-72; editorial writer Wall St. Jour., N.Y.C., 1972-77; reporter N.Y. Times, 1978—; lectr. Ariz. State U., Tempe, 1968-71. Served with USMC, 1952-55. Author: Portrait of an Arizonan, 1964; Three Cheers and a Tiger, 1966. Home: 72 Marquand Ave Bronxville NY 10708 Office: NY Times 229 W 43 St New York NY 10036

MCDOWELL, ELMER HUGH, architect, engr.; b. Mobile, Ala., July 16, 1924; s. Henry Curtis and Bessie Cherry (Fonville) McD.; B.S. in Architecture and Engring., Hampton Inst., 1949; postgrad. Ill. Inst. Tech., 1950-51, U. Kans., 1952-56; m. Ava L. Atkinson, Dec. 9, 1955. Asso., Servis-Van Doren & Hazard, Topeka, 1952-58; with Allied Engring. Co., Topeka, 1958-60; practice architecture, Topeka; now prin. E. H. McDowell & Assos.—Architect/Engr., St. Thomas, V.I.; chmn. Com. to Update V.I. Bldg. Codes, 1967; chmn. Task Force on Archtl. Barriers and Transp., 1968-70. Served with USAAF. Fellow AIA (nat. dir.); mem. Nat. Soc. Profl. Engrs., Constn. Specifications Inst., ASCE, Institute de Arquitectos de P.R. Home: #37 40 Estate Pearl Saint Thomas VI 00801 Office: PO Box 3958 Saint Thomas VI 00801*

MCDOWELL, FLETCHER HUGHES, physician; b. Denver, Aug. 5, 1923; s. James Thomas and Gladys (Hughes) McD.; A.B., Dartmouth Coll., 1945; M.D., Cornell U., 1947; m. Electra Bostwick July 18, 1958; children—Electra, Laura, Linn. Intern N.Y. Hosp., 1947-48, resident, 1950-53; dir. Cornell Neurology Service Bellevue Hosp., N.Y.C., 1956-67; asst. prof. neurology Cornell U. Med. Coll., 1956-60, asso. prof., 1960-66, prof., 1966—, also asso. dean; med. dir. Burke Rehab. Hosp., 1974—. Served to capt. M.C., AUS, 1953-55. Mem. Am. Neurol. Assn. Office: 1300 York Ave New York City NY 10021

MC DOWELL, FRANK, plastic surgeon; b. Marshfield, Mo., Jan. 30, 1911; s. Hollie A. and Louise (North) McD.; A.B., Drury Coll., 1932; M.D., Washington U., St. Louis, 1936; Sc.D., Drury Coll., 1973; m. Mary Elizabeth Neal, June 10, 1934; children—Robert Lawrence, George Edward, Carole Louise. Intern, Barnes Hosp., St. Louis, 1936-37, asst. resident surgeon, 1937-39, attending surgeon, 1941-69; attending surgeon St. Louis Children's Hosp., cons. surgeon Shriners Hosp., Frisco, Mo. Pacific, St. Louis City hosps., 1941-69; pres. med. and surg. staff Barnes and Allied Hosps. Med. Center, 1958-59; mem. faculty Washington U. Sch. Medicine, 1939-69, asso. prof. clin. surgery, 1954-69, asso. prof. maxillofacial surgery Sch. Dentistry, 1940-69; surg. staff Queen's, Children's, Castle hosps., Honolulu, 1967—; surg. cons. Tripler Gen. Hosp., 1967—; exec. com. dept. surgery, prof. surgery U. Hawaii, 1967—; prof. clin. surgery Stanford, 1974—; v.p. Hawaii Med. Library, 1970-76; lectr. French Acad. Surgery, 1949, Hadassah U. Sch. Medicine, Jerusalem, 1954, U. Athens (Greece) Sch. Medicine, 1954, Nat. Inst. for Burned, Buenos Aires, Argentina, 1957, Am. Replantation Mission to China, 1973; vis. prof. surgery U. Calif. at Los Angeles, 1969, U. Utah, 1972, U. Mo., 1974. Mem. Adv. Bd. Med. Specialists, 1955-69; v.p. Am. Bd. Med. Specialists, 1970-71, chmn. surg. council, 1969-71; v.p. 3d Internat. Congress Plastic Surgery, 1963. Trustee Drury Coll., 1956-78, chmn. bd. trustees, 1964-65. Recipient Distinguished Alumni award Drury Coll., 1954; 1st Dow Corning Internat. award in plastic surgery, 1971; Honorary award Ednl. Found. ASPRS, 1978. Diplomate Am. Bd. Surgery, Am. Bd. Plastic Surgery (sec. 1955-60, vice chmn. 1960-61, chmn. 1961-62). Fellow A.C.S.; mem. Am. Assn. Plastic Surgeons (pres. 1962-63, hon. award 1978), Am. Soc. Plastic and Reconstructive Surgeons, Soc. Head and Neck Surgeons (founder), Am., Western surg. assns., Am. Assn. Surgery Trauma, Israel Assn. Plastic Surgeons (hon.), Société française de chirurgie reconstructive et plastique (hon.), Washington U. Med. Alumni Assn. (pres. 1960-61). Club: Pacific. Author: Skin Grafting, 3d edit., 1959; Plastic Surgery of the Nose, 2d edit., 1965; Surgery of Face, Mouth and Jaws, 1954; Neck Dissections, 1957; History of Plastic Surgical Societies, 1963; Surgical Rehabilitation in Leprosy, 1974; also numerous articles. Asso. editor Directory Med. Specialists, 1955-72, McDowell Indexes of Plastic Surgery Literature, 5 vols., 1977—, The Source Book of Plastic Surgery, 1977; cons. editor Lawyers Med., 1962-78, Stedman's Med. Dictionary, 1975—, Current Contents, 1973—, Internat. Dictionary Biology and Medicine, 1979—; editor-in-chief Jour. Plastic and Reconstructive Surgery, 1967—. Home: 100-F N Kalaheo Kailua HI 96734 Office: Alexander Young Bldg Honolulu HI 96813

MCDOWELL, JACK SHERMAN, publicist; b. Alameda, Calif., Feb. 23, 1914; s. John Sherman and Myra Lorraine (Frierson) McD.; student San Jose State Coll., 1931-32; m. Jeanette California Ofelth, June 18, 1938; children—Nancy Lynn (Mrs. Henry A. Swanson, Jr.), Peggy Joanne (Mrs. G.P. Cramer), Judy Carolina. With Alameda Times-Star, 1926-31, San Jose Evening News, 1932; owner, operator with brother Turlock Daily Jour., 1933-40, Eugene (Oreg.) Daily News, 1941-42; staff writer San Francisco Call-Bull. (now Examiner), 1942-50, corr. PTO, 1944, daily column, 1946-50, city editor, 1950-56, polit. editor, columnist, 1956-69; co-owner Woodward, McDowell & Larson, polit. campaign mgmt. advt. and pub. relations, 1969—. News dir. Gov. Ronald Reagan campaign, 1970, Senator S.I. Hayakawa campaign, 1976. Recipient best news photo award Calif. Newspaper Pub. Assn., 1939, Pulitzer prize for distinguished reporting of 1944. Mem. Sigma Delta Chi. Club: Press (San Francisco). Co-author: (with Chaplain Howell M. Forgy) And Pass the Ammunition, 1944. Contbr. mags. Home: 97 Normandy Ln Atherton CA 94025 Office: 223 Sansome St San Francisco CA 94104

MC DOWELL, JOHN B., bishop; b. New Castle, Pa., July 17, 1921; s. Bernard A. and Louise M. (Hannon) McD.; B.A., St. Vincent Coll., 1942, M.A., 1944; M.A., Catholic U. Am., 1950, Ph.D., 1952; Litt.D. (hon.), Duquesne U., 1962; grad. St. Vincent Sem., Latrobe, Pa. Ordained priest Roman Catholic Ch., 1945, consecrated as titular bishop of Tamazuca and aux. to bishop of Pitts., 1966; pastor St. Irenaeus Ch., Oakmont, 1945-49; asst. supt. schs. Diocese of Pitts., 1952-55, supt. schs., 1955-70, vicar for edn., 1970—, now vicar gen.; pastor Epiphany Parish, Pitts., 1969—; papal chamberlain to Pope Pius XII, 1956, to Pope John XXIII, 1958; domestic prelate to Pope Paul VI, 1964; chmn. ad hoc com. on moral values in our soc. Nat. Conf. Cath. Bishops, 1973—, Bishops Com. for Pastoral on Moral Values, 1976—; mem. Internat. Council for Catechesis, 1975—; bd. dirs. Allegheny County Community Coll., Western Pa. Safety Council, Duquesne U., Sta. WQED-TV, ednl. sta. Named Man of Yr. in Religion, Pitts., 1970, Educator of Yr., United Pvt. Acad. Schs. Assn., 1978. Mem. Nat. Cath. Ednl. Assn., Cath. Ednl. Assn. Pa., Omicron Delta Kappa Gamma Circle (hon.). Co-author elem. sch. religions series, jr. high sch. lit. series, elem. sci. series and elem. reading series; contbr. ednl. articles to various publs.; former editor Cath. Ednl. Assn. of Pa. Bull., Cath. Educator Mag. Office: Epiphany Ch 1018 Centre Ave Pittsburgh PA 15219

MCDOWELL, JOHN NELSON, public relations and advt. cons.; b. Bucks County, Pa., Jan. 15, 1910; s. William Franklin and Mary Jane (Boulden) McD.; B.A., U. Del., 1931; m. Irene M. Barbin, Sept. 16, 1933 (dec. Apr. 1938); 1 son, John Nelson; m. 2d, Mary B. Burnett, June 21, 1941; 1 dau., Nancy Lynn. Investigator, adminstrv. asst. various pub. agys., Pa., 1931-38; dir. alumni and pub. relations U. Del., 1938-43, 46; adminstrv. asst. to Del. congressman, 1947-50; exec. v.p. pub. relations firm, 1951-53; pres. McDowell Assos., Inc., Wilmington, Del., 1953—; sec. State of Del., 1953-58. Past mem. bd. control of So. Regional Edn. Bd. Trustee Del. State Coll., 1953-72, pres. bd., 1956-70. Served from ensign to lt. USNR, 1943-46. Mem. Phi Kappa Phi, Theta Chi. Clubs: University (Wilmington); Newark (Del.) Country. Home: 17 Hillside Rd Newark DE 19711 Office: 919 Washington St Wilmington DE 19801

MCDOWELL, JOSEPH HAMPTON, lawyer; b. Belleville, Kans., Oct. 15, 1907; s. Joseph Hampton and Nellie P. (Sandels) McD.; LL.B., Kans. U., 1931; m. Claudene Stone, Dec. 25, 1933; 1 son, Hampton. Admitted to Mo. bar, 1930, Kans. bar, 1931, Nebr. bar, 1935; atty. Kans. Corp. Commn., Topeka, 1931-33, Fed. Land Bank Wichita (Kans.), 1933-34, HOLC, Omaha, 1934-35; judge City Ct., Kansas City, 1936-40; county atty. Wyandotte County, Kans., 1940-42; practice in Kansas City, Kans., 1945—; mem. firm McDowell, Rice & Smith, and predecessor, 1948—; mayor, Kansas City, 1964-71; prof. labor law Rockhurst Coll., Kansas City, Mo., 1941, 45. Mem. Kans. Senate, 1948-64; pres. Channel 19, Pub. TV, Kansas City, Mo., 1974; bd. dirs. Greater Kansas City Fgn. Trade Zone, 1964—, Mid-Am. Arts Alliance, 1978—. Served to capt. USMCR, 1942-45. Mem. Bar Assn. State Kans., Kans. U. Alumni Assn. (dir. 1971—), Sigma Alpha Epsilon, Phi Alpha Delta. Club: Terrace. Contbr. articles to legal jours. Home: 2100 Washington Blvd Kansas City KS 66102 Office: Security Nat Bank Bldg Kansas City KS 66101

MCDOWELL, ROBERT CHARLES, engring. exec.; b. Simpsonville, Ky., Nov. 18, 1912; s. Robert A. and Bertha (Spicer) McD.; B.S., U. Ky., 1935, C.E., 1943, D.Sc. (hon.), 1962; m. Gloria Brown, Jan. 1, 1961; children—Bridge, Spicer. Project engr., field supt. R.C. Mahon Co., Detroit, 1935-41; supt. Hunkin-Conkey Constrn. Co., Cleve., 1941-43; gen. mgr. Cleve. Steel Erection Co., 1943-44; chmn. bd., chief exec. officer McDowell-Wellman Engring. Co., Cleve.; now chmn. bd., chief exec. bd. Lewis Molding Machinery Co., RCM Engring. Co.; pres. McDowell Africa, Ltd., McDowell Co. S.A., McDowell Constrn. Co. Can. Ltd., McDowell-Wellman Internat., Inc.; mem. Ohio adv. bd. Liberty Mut. Ins. Co. Mem. exec. com. U. Ky. Fellows. Mem. U. Ky. Research Found.; dir. Deaconess Hosp. Cleve., trustee Kraft Retirement Home of hosp.; trustee, chmn. planning com. Cleve. Zool. Soc. Mem. Am. Soc. C.E., Am. Inst. M.E., Ohio Soc. Profl. Engrs., Am. Iron and Steel Inst., Beavers, Moles, Newcomen Soc. N. Am. Western Res. Hist. Soc. (pres., trustee, dir.), U. Ky. Devel. Council, Cleve. Engring. Soc. (trustee), Tau Beta Pi, Alpha Sigma Phi, Omicron Delta Kappa. Mason (Shriner). Clubs: Union (Cleve.); Westwood Country, Fairlawn Country (Akron); Explorers (N.Y.). Home: 2748 Ira Rd Akron OH 44313 Office: 16300 S Waterloo Rd Cleveland OH 44110

MCDOWELL, WILLIAM RALSTON, lawyer, ry. exec.; b. Shreveport, La., Jan. 18, 1917; s. Milas R. and Mollie (Ayres) McD.; B.B.A., U. Tex., 1940, LL.B., 1940; m. Fern Bronstad, Sept. 15, 1939; children—Rebecca Gail (Mrs. W. Lionel Craver). Admitted to Tex. bar, 1940; spl. agt. FBI, Washington, 1940-41, adminstrv. asst. to dir., 1941-45; asso. law firm McBride & Johnson, Dallas, 1945-47; asst. dist. atty., Dallas County, 1947-48; atty., gen. atty. T. & P. Ry., Dallas, 1948-58, v.p., gen. counsel, 1959—, also dir.; gen. counsel So. Lines, M.P.R.R., Dallas, 1962-76, v.p., gen. counsel, 1976—; dir. Weatherford Mineral Wells, Northwestern Ry. Co. Bd. dirs. Tex. Research League. Mem. Am., Dallas bar assns., State Bar Tex., Am. Judicature Soc., ICC Practitioners, Soc. Former Agts. FBI. Lutheran. Home: 5353 Edmondson St Dallas TX 75209 Office: 505 N Industrial Blvd Dallas TX 75207

MCDUFF, ODIS PELHAM, educator; b. Gordo, Ala., May 16, 1931; s. Henry Lucious and Nolia (Strickland) McD.; B.S., U. Ala., 1952; M.S., Mass. Inst. Tech., 1953; Ph.D., Stanford, 1966; m. Peggy Joan Bobo, Dec. 24, 1953; children—Janice Marie, Carol Dianne, Anita Joan, Jeffrey Wayne. Test engr., Gen. Electric Co., 1952; circuit devel. engr., Owensboro, Ky., 1956-59; supervising engr., 1959; mem. tech. staff Bell Telephone Labs., Murray Hill, N.J., 1953-54; asst. prof. U. Ala., University 1959-66, asso. prof., 1966-68; prof., head dept. elec. engring., 1968—. Cons. Army Missile Command; instr. courses on lasers. Served to 1st lt. U.S. Army, 1954-56. NSF fellow, 1963-64, 65-66. Mem. IEEE, Am. Soc. Engring. Edn., Am. Optical Soc., Sigma Xi, Tau Beta Pi, Theta Tau, Eta Kappa Nu, Pi Mu Epsilon, Phi Eta Sigma, Omicron Delta Kappa. Contbr. articles profl. jours. Home: 27 Ridgeland Tuscaloosa AL 35401 Office: Box 6169 University AL 35846

MC EACHEN, EDMUND DAVID, lawyer; b. Lincoln, Nebr., June 12, 1928; s. James Allen and Edna Charlotte (Pegler) McE.; B.S. with high honors, U. Nebr., 1949; J.D. with honors, U. Mich., 1952; m. Nancy McEachen, June 23, 1950; children—Catherine Ann, Sarah Elizabeth, Marion Ellen, Edmund D., John Richard. Admitted to Nebr. bar, 1952; mem. firm Baird, Holm, McEachen, Pedersen, Hamann & Haggart, Omaha, 1952—, partner, 1957—. Mem. Am. Soc. Hosp. Attys. (dir. 1974—, pres. 1979—), Am. Bar Assn., Nebr. Bar Assn., Omaha Bar Assn., Am. Law Inst., Nat. Health Lawyers Assn., Phi Beta Kappa, Beta Gamma Sigma. Republican. Congregationalist. Club: Downtown Kiwanis (dir., v.p.). Office: 1500 Woodmen Tower Omaha NE 68102

MCEACHERN, EDWARD MERRITT, JR., banker; b. High Point, N.C., Feb. 11, 1933; s. Edward Merritt and Leora Cromwell (Hiatt) McE.; A.B., Guilford Coll., 1955; m. Patricia Ann Starnes, June 15, 1956; children—Sarah Ann, Edward Merritt III, Amy Starnes. Partner, McEachern Agy., Wilmington, N.C., 1957-59; with Wachovia Bank & Trust Co., N.A., Winston-Salem, N.C., 1959-78, asst. trust officer, 1962-65, trust officer, 1965-70, v.p., 1970-78; mgr. adminstrn. Anacomp, Inc., Winston-Salem, 1978—. Served from ensign to lt. (j.g.), USNR, 1955-57; now capt. Res. Mem. Naval Res. Assn., Navy League. Methodist. Home: 3011 St Claire Rd Winston-Salem NC 27106 Office: PO Box 3097 Winston-Salem NC 27102

MCEACHERN, WILBUR WASHINGTON, banker; b. Hazelhurst, Ga., Oct. 8, 1904; s. Andrew Oliver and Sarah (Yawn) McE.; B.A., Ga. Normal Coll., 1919; grad. Am. Inst. Banking, 1923; LL.B. (hon.), Furman U., 1969; m. Bonnie Loree Ehler, Sept. 8, 1925 (dec.); children—Mary Lou McEachern Trevillian, Jo Ann McEachern Leigner; m. 2d, Jean Gunter Arnau, Aug. 7, 1964 (dec.); m. 3d, Mildred Swittenberg Walsh, Apr. 14, 1972. With Atlantic Nat. Bank, Jacksonville, Fla., 1919-24, 1st Nat. Bank and 1st Security Bank, St. Petersburg, 1924-30; pres. Union Trust Co., St. Petersburg, 1931-44, vice chmn., 1944-46; exec. v.p. The Bank of Va., Richmond, 1946-50; pres. First Nat. Bank, Greenville, S.C., 1950-57; pres. S.C. Nat. Bank, Greenville, 1957-66, chmn., chief exec. officer, 1966-69, hon. chmn. bd., 1970—; dir., chmn. exec. com. S.C. Nat. Corp., Columbia; dir. S.C. Nat. Corp., Columbia, Dan River, Inc., Multimedia, Inc., Liberty Life Ins. Co., Fed. Res. Bank of Richmond, Charlotte br. Pres. bd. trustees Greater Greenville Community Chest; chmn. steering com. United Fund of Greenville County, 1955; bd. visitors Clemson Coll., 1963; gov. Greenville unit Shriner's Hosp. for Crippled Children; adv. council Furman U., Greenville, S.C. chmn. bd. trustees Greenville Gen. Hosp. System; mem. bd. St. Francis Community Hosp.; trustee F.W. Symmes Found.; chmn. Burgess Charities, Inc., SCN Charitable and Ednl. Found. Mem. Am. (adv. com. on fed. legislation 1961-62, mem. legis. com. 1964, pres. state bank div. 1944, mem. exec. council nat. bank div. 1960-63), Fla. (pres. 1941), S.C. (pres. 1958- 59) bankers assns., S.C. C. of C. (dir.). Presbyn. Mason (K.T. Shriner). Clubs: Greenville Country, Green Valley Country, Poinsett (Greenville); Country of Va., Commonwealth (Richmond). Home: 17 E Hillcrest Dr Greenville SC 29609 Office: 13-15 S Main St Greenville SC 29601

MCEACHRAN, JOHN NELSON, fin. co. exec.; b. Montreal, Que., Can., Oct. 30, 1926; s. Flora Deschenes McEachran; ed. St. Joseph's Tchrs. Coll.; m. Blanche Costello, Oct. 15, 1948; children—Gerald, Linda, Bruce, Joan, John, Susan. Sch. tchr., 1945-48; with Imperial Tobacco Co., 1948-66, credit mgr., 1957-66; v.p. M. Loeb Ltd., Ottawa, 1966—, corp. sec., 1969—; past pres. Canadian Credit Inst. Fellow Canadian Inst.; mem. Quebec C. of C., Assn. Canadian Franchisors, Ottawa Bd. Trade. Author articles in field. Home: 87 Hilliard Ave Ottawa 8 ON Canada Office: 400 Industrial Ave Ottawa 8 ON Canada

MCEACHRON, KARL BOYER, JR., univ. ofcl.; b. Ada, Ohio, June 27, 1915; s. Karl Boyer and Leila Emily (Honsinger) McE.; B.S. in Elec. Engring., Purdue U., 1937; m. Marjorie Blalock, Mar. 20, 1937; children—Norman Bruce, Lawrence Karl, Linda Louise, Donald Lynn. With Gen. Electric Co., 1937-55, project engr., 1952-55; faculty Case Inst. Tech., 1955-57, dean instrn., 1957-64, vice provost, 1964-67, dean Case Inst. Tech. of Case Western Res. U., 1967-72, dir.

admissions and financial aid, 1972-74, dean undergrad. affairs, 1974—. Named Distinguished Alumnus Purdue U., 1964. Fellow I.E.E.E. (chmn. edn. com. 1959-61, chmn. Cleve. chpt. 1961-62); mem. Am. Soc. Engring. Edn. (v.p. 1967-69), Engrs. Council Profl. Devel. (com. edn. and accreditation 1956-61, exec. com. 1964-65), Nat. Soc. Profl. Engrs., Cleve. Soc. Profl. Engrs. (pres. 1975-76), Sigma Xi, Tau Beta Pi, Eta Kappa Nu. Republican. Methodist. Contbr. articles to profl. jours. Home: 12900 Lake Ave Apt 522 Lakewood OH 44107 Office: 2040 Adelbert Rd Cleveland OH 44106

MCELDERRY, STANLEY, librarian; b. Fairfield, Iowa, Oct. 19, 1918; s. Chester Arthur and May Agnes (Young) McE.; A.B., U. So. Calif., 1940, B.S. in L.S., 1941; student U. Chgo. Grad. Library Sch., 1947-49, 56; m. Bernice Ingram, Dec. 20, 1948; children—David Allen, Thomas Arthur, Howard Ingram. Engring. librarian Lockheed Aircraft Corp., 1941-47; circulation librarian, asst. prof. U. Minn., 1950-52; asst. dir. libraries, asso. prof. U. Okla., 1952-55; librarian San Fernando Valley State Coll., 1957-68; dean, prof. library sci. Grad. Sch. Library Sci., U. Tex., Austin, 1968-72; dir. library, prof. U. Chgo., 1972—; vis. lectr. U. Tex., 1954, 55, 65, U. So. Calif., 1958, 62. Mem. Am. (counci), Calif. (pres. coll. univ. research libraries sect. 1964) library assns., Am. Soc. for Information Scis. Home: 5201 S Cornell Ave Chicago IL 60615

MCELHANEY, JAMES HARRY, biomedical engr.; b. Phila., Oct. 27, 1933; s. James H. and Olga M. (Lazuk) McE.; B.S., Villanova U., 1955; M.S., U. Pa., 1960; Ph.D., W.Va. U., 1964; m. Eileen M. Esbensen, Nov. 17, 1954; children—Kathy, Amy, Liza. Mech. engr. Philco Corp., Phila., 1955-59; asst. prof. mech. engring. Villanova (Pa.) U., 1959-62; prof. theoretical and applied mechanics W.Va. U., Morgantown, 1962-69; asso. prof. mech. engring., head biomechanics dept. Hwy. Safety Research Inst., U. Mich., 1969-74; prof. biomechanics Duke U., Durham, N.C., 1974—, dir. grad. studies, 1974-75; pres. Safety Electronics Corp.; cons. Ford Motor Co., Am. Motors Co., Chrysler Corp., Westinghouse Corp., NIH, others; chmn. com. on indsl. head protection Am. Nat. Standards Inst. Served with U.S. Army Res., 1955-63. NIH grantee, 1967—. Registered profl. engr., Pa. Mem. Am. Soc. Engring. Edn., ASME (chmn. bioengring. div. 1975—, asso. editor Trans. on Biomech. Engring.), Soc. for Exptl. Stress Analysis, Soc. Automotive Engrs. (chmn. anthropometric dummy study com.), Southeastern Neurol. Soc. (pres. elect), Biomedical Engring. Soc., Am. Acad. Mechanics, Sigma Xi, Pi Tau Sigma. Club: Duke Men's. Editor mech. engring. sect. Jour. of Bioengring., 1977—; mem. editorial adv. bd. Jour. of Biomechanics, 1967—. Contbr. articles on biomechanics to profl. jours. Home: 3411 Cambridge Rd Durham NC 27707 Office: Biomedical Engring Dept Duke U Durham NC 27707

MC ELHANEY, JAMES WILLSON, educator, lawyer; b. N.Y.C., Dec. 10, 1937; s. Lewis Keck and Sara Jane (Hess) McE.; A.B., Duke U., 1960; LL.B., 1962; m. Maxine Dennis Jones, Aug. 17, 1961; children—David, Benjamin. Admitted to Wis. bar, 1962; asso. firm Wickham, Borgelt, Skogstad & Powell, 1966; asst. prof. U. Md. Law Sch., 1966-69, asso. prof., 1969-72; vis. prof. So. Meth. U. Sch. of Law, Dallas, 1973-74, prof., 1974-76; Joseph C. Hostetler prof. trial practice and advocacy Case Western Res. U. Sch. of Law, Cleve., 1976—; mem. faculty Nat. Inst. Trial Advocacy, Boulder, Colo., 1975—; vis. prof. U. Tulsa Coll. Law, summer 1977, 79; cons. to U.S. Atty. Gen. on Justice Dept. Advocacy Tng. Programs, 1979—; lectr. in field. Recipient Outstanding Prof. award So. Meth. U., 1976. Mem. Am. Bar Assn., Assn. Am. Law Schs. (chmn. sect. trial advocacy 1974-76, chmn. sect. evidence 1978). Author: Effective Litigation: Trials, Problems and Materials, 1974; asso. editor Litigation mag.; author column Trial Notebook; contbr. articles to profl. jours. Home: 2842 E Overlook Cleveland Heights OH 44118 Office: 11075 E Boulevard Cleveland OH 44106. *Awkward language is not precision and obscurity is not great insight. New ideas may be expressed plainly, and the better the author understands them the more likely it is they will be understandable to others.*

MCELHANNEY, ROBERT GORDON, machinery mfr.; b. Vancouver, B.C., Can., Mar. 15, 1917; s. William Gordon and Marion Alice (McLaughlin) McE.; B.A. Sc., U. B.C., 1939; m. Evelyn H. Lawrence, Aug. 7, 1953; children—William, Susan, David. Came to U.S., 1966. Sales engr. The Dorr Co., Toronto, 1947-55; v.p. sales Dorr Oliver Long, Orillia, Ont., 1956-65; mgr. process equipment div. Dorr Oliver, Inc., Stamford, Conn., 1966-69, sr. v.p., 1969—; dir. Nat. Filter Media Corp. (New Haven), Dorr Oliver Can., Ont., Dorr Oliver, Pty., Sydney, Australia, Hindustan Dorr Oliver, Bombay, India. Served with RCAF, 1942-46. Mem. Am. Inst. Mining and Metall. Engrs., Canadian Inst. Mining and Metall. Engrs., Assn. Profl. Engrs. Ont. Home: 3 Victoria Ln Westport CT 06880 Office: 77 Havemeyer Ln Stamford CT 06904

MCELHENY, JOHN DANIEL, civil engr., lawyer; b. LaRue, Ohio, Aug. 5, 1914; s. John Fulton and Eva Elsie (Ziegler) McE.; B.S., U.S. Mil. Acad., 1936; M.S. in Civil Engring., Mass. Inst. Tech., 1939; grad. Army War Coll., 1952; J.D., U. Fla., 1972; m. Frances Inez Wolslagel, Aug. 30, 1939; children—Phyllis Ann, Bruce Daniel. Commd. 2d lt. U.S. Army, 1936, advanced through grades to col. C.E., 1944; engr.-in-charge reconstrn. war damaged port, Le Havre, France, 1944-45; charge engr. supply U.S. Army Forces, Far East, 1952-55; lt. gov. C.Z., also v.p. Panama Canal Co., 1958-61; chief materiel maintenence div. Dept. Army gen. staff, 1961-64; admitted to Fla. bar; atty. Johnson, Motsinger, Trismon & Sharp, Orlando, 1972—; cons. IBRD, 1965-66. Decorated Legion of Merit. Mem. ASCE, Am., Fla. bar assns. Home: 1220 Druid Rd Maitland FL 32751 Office: 213 W Comstock Ave Winter Park FL 32790

MCELHINNY, WILSON DUNBAR, banker; b. Detroit, July 27, 1929; s. William Dunbar and Elizabeth (Wilson) McE.; B.A., Yale, 1953; m. Barbara Cheney Watkins, June 6, 1952; children—David Ashton, Ward Cheney, Edward Wilson, William Dunbar. With Union and New Haven Trust Co., 1952-63; v.p. Reading Trust Co. (Pa.), 1963-68, pres., 1968-70; pres. Nat. Central Bank (formerly Reading Trust Co.), 1970—, chief exec. officer, 1975—, also dir.; dir. Educators Mut. Life Ins. Co., Black Diamond Coal Co., Nat. Central Fin. Corp., Hampden Color & Chem. Co., A C & S, Inc., K-D Mfg. Co. Bd. dirs. Lancaster Gen. Hosp.; trustee Franklin and Marshall Coll. Mem. Young Pres.'s Orgn. Clubs: Lancaster Country, Hamilton (Lancaster, Pa.). Home: 1430 Hunsicker Rd Lancaster PA 17601 Office: 100 N Queen St Lancaster PA 17604

MC ELIGOT, DONALD MARINUS, educator; b. Passaic, N.J., Mar. 9, 1931; s. Maurice Joseph and Shirley Irene (Gambling) McE.; B.S. in Mech. Engring., Yale, 1952; M.S. in Engring., U. Wash., 1958; postgrad. (AEC fellow), 1957-60; Ph.D. (Yuba Industries Research fellow), Stanford, 1963; m. Julimae Albright, July 20, 1957; children—Kim, Kyle, Sean. Engr., Gen. Electric Co., 1955-57; faculty U. Ariz., Tucson, 1963—, prof., 1968—. Vis. staff Imperial Coll., London, 1969-70; guest prof. U. Karlsruhe, 1975-76, 79; cons. Los Alamos Sci. Lab., 1967—. Served to lt. (j.g.) USNR, 1952-55; now comdr. Res. Recipient Gold badge for soaring Fedn. Aeronautique Internat., 1971; Calif. record, altitude gain, 15 meter class, 1978. Mem. Am. Phys. Soc., ASME, ASTM, Soaring Soc. Am., Naval Res. Assn. Clubs: Tucson Soaring (treas. 1972), Yale-Tucson (sec.-treas. 1967-69); Luftsportverein Albgau e.v. Research in fluid mechanics and thermal scis. Office: Dept Aero Mech Engring U Ariz Tucson AZ 85721

MC ELIN, THOMAS WELSH, medical educator; b. Janesville, Wis., Aug. 27, 1920; s. Bertrand James and Evelyn (Welsh) McE.; A.B. summa cum laude, Dartmouth, 1942, postgrad. Med. Sch., 1941-42; M.D., Harvard, 1944; M.S. in Obstetrics and Gynecology, U. Minn., 1948; m. Sylvia Dennison, June 30, 1945; children—Joan Dennison McElin Vogt, Thomas Welsh. Intern, Passavant Hosp., Chgo., 1944-45; resident Mayo Found., Rochester, Minn., 1945-48, 1st asst. gynecology and surgery, 1948-49, spl. 1st asst. obstetrics and gynecology, 1949-50; practice medicine, specializing in obstetrics and gynecology, Evanston, Ill., 1950—; mem. faculty Med. Sch., Northwestern U., Chgo., 1950—, asso. prof. obstetrics and gynecology, 1960-67, prof., 1967—, asst. chmn. dept. obstetrics and gynecology, 1974—; chmn. dept. obstetrics and gynecology Evanston Hosp., 1965—, pres. profl. staff, 1963-64; mem. editorial bd. Obstetrics and Gynecology Jour., 1973—. Diplomate Am. Bd. Obstetrics and Gynecology (asso. examiner 1967-78). Fellow Am. Coll. Obstetricians and Gynecologists (founding fellow), A.C.S. (gov.); mem. Am. Assn. Obstetricians and Gynecologists (exec. council 1974-76, pres. 1977-78), Am. Fertility Soc., Central Assn. Obstetricians and Gynecologists (pres. 1970-71), Chgo. Gynecol. Soc. (pres. 1969-70), AMA, Central Travel Club Obstetricians and Gynecologists (pres. 1968), N. Am. Obstetrics and Gynecology Soc., Endocrine Soc., Inst. Medicine (Chgo.), Phi Beta Kappa, Sigma Xi, Alpha Kappa Kappa. Clubs: Dartmouth, Harvard (Chgo.); Glen View (Golf, Ill.). Contbr. articles to profl. jours. Home: 560 Greenwood Ave Kenilworth IL 60043 Office: 2650 Ridge Ave Evanston IL 60201

MCELLISTREM, MARCUS THOMAS, JR., educator; b. St. Paul, Apr. 19, 1926; s. Marcus Thomas and Loretta Camille (Simard) McE.; B.A., Coll. St. Thomas, St. Paul, 1950; M.S., U. Wis., 1951, Ph.D., 1956; m. Eleanor DeMeuse, Aug. 17, 1957; children—Mary Ann, Marcus, Rebecca, Joan, Catherine, Deborah. Research asst. U. Wis., 1953-55; research asso. Ind. U., 1955-57; asst. prof. physics and astronomy U. Ky., 1957-60, asso. prof., 1960-65, prof., 1965—, Univ. research prof., 1978-79, dir. nuclear structure labs., 1964—; cons.; fgn. collaborator Centre d'Etudes de Bruyeres-le-Châtel, 1974, 75, 78; pres. Adena Corp. Mem. Nat. Conf. Christians and Jews, 1960-63, sponsor U. Ky. Newman Center, 1960-77, pres., 1978-79. Served with USNR, 1944-46. Recipient Newman Center service award, 1964. AEC Nuclear Faculty grantee, 1959, NSF Nuclear Research grantee. Mem. AAAS, Am. Phys. Soc, Sigma Xi. Roman Catholic. Contbr. articles to profl. jours. Home: 1841 Blairmore Ct Lexington KY 40502

MC ELRATH, GAYLE WILLIAM, educator, mgmt. cons.; b. Randolph, Minn., Dec. 15, 1915; s. William L. and Lillie (Foster) McE.; B.S. in Math., U. Minn., 1941, M.S. in Math., 1946; m. Kathryn Mary Slayton, Nov. 15, 1946; children—Susanne, Deborah, Paul, Holly, Douglas. Mem. faculty U. Minn., 1946-70, head indsl. engring. div., 1955-70, prof. mech. engring., 1958-70; v.p. Bayer & McElrath, Inc., mgmt. cons., Detroit, Mpls., 1960-77, dir. Mgmt. Acad. edn. div., 1973-77, chmn. bd., exec. officer Bayer & McElrath, 1974-77; pres. McElrath & Assos., Inc., mgmt. cons., 1978—; dir. Thermo Systems, Inc., St. Paul, 1967—; guest prof. and/or lectr. Purdue U., U. Wis., U. Calif. at Los Angeles, U. Ill., U. Miss., Marquette U., State U. Iowa, M.I.T., St. Thomas Coll., Internat. Edn. Inst., Manchester and London, Eng., Internat. Fedn. Pharm. Mfrs. Assns., Geneva, Switzerland; cons. in field, 1953—. Bd. dirs. Council Internat. Progress Mgmt., 1968-71. Registered profl. engr., Minn.; cert. quality engr. Fellow AAAS, Am. Soc. Quality Control (nat. bd. dirs. 1956-61, chmn. Midwest conf. bd. 1961, nat. v.p. 1961-65, rep. to Engrs. Joint Council 1968-71; E.L. Grant award 1969 for meritorious ednl. programs in field quality control); mem. Am. Mgmt. Assn., Am. Statis. Assn., Operations Research Soc. Am., Am. Soc. Engring. Edn., Sigma Xi, Pi Tau Sigma. Methodist (chmn. trustees 1962-68). Author: Introduction to Probability and Statistics, 3d edit., 1968. Home: 5026 Bruce Ave Minneapolis MN 55424

MCELRATH, RICHARD ELSWORTH, ins. co. exec.; b. Thompsontown, Pa., Oct. 11, 1932; s. Clayton Ellsworth and Jane Elizabeth (Shoop) McE.; B.S. cum laude, Elizabethtown (Pa.) Coll., 1955; M.B.A. cum laude, Harvard U., 1961; m. Donna Gail Booher, Aug. 18, 1952; children—Leslie Jo, Jennifer Jo, Josie Arlene Elizabeth, Rebekah Clare. Research asst. Harvard U., 1961-62; asst. to pres. Callaway Mills Co., LaGrange, Ga., 1963-65; with Irving Trust Co., N.Y.C., 1965-73, v.p., 1969-73; treas. Tchr. Ins. & Annuity Assn., N.Y.C., also Coll. Retirement Equities Fund, 1973—; dir. Tchrs. Realty Corp., Minn. Tchrs. Realty Corp., WRC Properties, Inc., GRC Properties, Inc., Res. Mgmt., Inc. Trustee Elizabethtown Coll.; mem. Soc. Valley Hosp., Ridgewood, N.J.; mem. Republican Com., Boston, 1961-63, Troup County, Ga., 1964-65. Served to lt. comdr. USNR, 1956-59. Mem. Assn. Gov. Bds. Univs. and Colls., Renaissance Soc. Am., Medieval Acad. Am., Acad. Polit. Sci. Methodist. Author articles, case studies. Home: 17 Cedar St Glen Rock NJ 07452 Office: 730 3d Ave New York NY 10017

MCELROY, GEORGE SPAHR, chem. co. exec.; b. Columbus, Ohio, July 8, 1915; s. Austin and Elizabeth (Spahr) McE.; grad. Phillips Acad., Andover, Mass., 1933; B.S.E., Princeton, 1937; m. Elvira Hazard Bullock, May 31, 1940; children—George Spahr, Candace (Mrs. James Bahrenburg), Austin Chandler. Engr., E.I. du Pont de Nemours & Co., Inc., Leominster, Mass., 1937-38; gen. foreman Rico Barton Corp., Worecester, Mass., 1938-45; marketing mgr. Owens Corning Fiberglas Corp., N.Y.C. 1945-65; pres. Ironsides Co., Columbus, 1965—. Pres., Columbus Gallery Fine Arts, 1967-73. Served with USNR, 1943-45. Mem. Wire Assn., Soc Aerospace Materials and Process Engring., Am. Inst. Steel Engrs. Clubs: Princeton (N.Y.C.); Rocky Fork, Golf, Castalia Trout, Little Sturgeon Trout, Columbus Country, Columbus Beach, Columbus, Oakmont. Home 15 Sessions Dr Columbus OH 43209 Office: 270 W Mound St Columbus OH 43216

MCELROY, JAMES RUSSELL, judge; b. McDowell, Ala., Oct. 1, 1901; s. George Roland and Annie Laurie (Harper) McE.; spl. course U. Ala. Sch. Law, 1923-24; LL.B., Birmingham Sch. Law, 1925; m. Edith Ferrell, Dec. 29, 1928; children—Marian McElroy Gillespie (dec.), James Russell. Admitted to Ala. bar, 1924; asst. city atty. City of Birmingham (Ala.), 1925-26; with firm London, Yancey & Brower, Birmingham, 1924; pvt. practice, Birmingham, 1924; mem. firm Wilkinson, Burton & McElroy, Birmingham, 1925-27; judge 10th Jud. Circuit Ala., Birmingham, 1927-77, presiding judge, 1941-60; ret., 1977; faculty Birmingham Sch. Law, 1924-27, U. Ala. Sch. Law, 1947-72, Samford U. Cumberland Sch. Law, 1965—; lectr. med. jurisprudence Med. Coll. Ala., 1946-65. Mem. Ala. Circuit Judges Assn. (pres. 1938-39), Ala., Birmingham (Law and Justice award 1972) bar assns., Farrah Order of Jurisprudence, Kappa Alpha, Phi Alpha Delta, Omicron Delta Kappa. Mason (Shriner), Lion. Home: 1603 Roseland Dr Birmingham AL 35209 Office: 305 Courthouse Birmingham AL 35203. *My parents always said to me: "Son, work hard and always do the right thing."*

MC ELROY, JOSEPH PRINCE, author; b. Bklyn., Aug. 21, 1930; s. Joseph Prince and Louise (Lawrence) McE.; B.A., Williams Coll., 1951; Ph.D., Columbia U., 1961; m. Joan Leftwich, Aug. 16, 1961; 1 dau., Hanna. Tchr. English, U. N.H., 1955-62; mem. faculty Queens Coll., 1964—, Johns Hopkins U., 1975, Columbia U., 1977; author: (novels) A Smuggler's Bible, 1966; Hind's Kidnap, 1969; Ancient History, 1971; Lookout Cartridge, 1974; Plus, 1977. Served with USCGR, 1952-54. Fellow Guggenheim Found., 1976-77, Rockefeller Found., 1969, Ingram-Merrill Found., 1971, Creative Artists Pub. Service, 1974, Nat. Endowment Arts, 1970; recipient Lit. award Nat. Acad. Arts and Letters, 1977; D.H. Lawrence fellow, 1979. Address: care Georges Borchardt 136 E 57th St New York NY 10022

MCELROY, WILLIAM DAVID, biochemist, univ. chancellor; b. Rogers, Tex., Jan. 22, 1917; s. William D. and Ora (Shipley) McE.; B.A., Stanford, 1939; M.A., Reed Coll., 1941; Ph.D., Princeton U., 1943; D.Sc., U. Buffalo, 1962, Mich. State U., 1970, Loyola U., Chgo., 1970, U. Notre Dame, 1975, Calif. Sch. Profl. Psychology, 1978; D.Pub. Service, Providence Coll., 1970; LL.D., U. Pitts., 1971; m. Nella Winch, Dec. 23, 1940 (div.) children—Mary Elizabeth, Ann Reed, Thomas Shipley, William David; m. 2d, Marlene A. DeLuca, Aug. 28, 1967; 1 son, Eric Gene. War research, com. med. research OSRD, Princeton, 1942-45; NRC fellow, Stanford, 1945-46; instr. biology dept. Johns Hopkins, 1946, successively asst. and asso. prof., prof. biology, 1951-69, chmn. biology dept., 1956-69, also dir. McCollum-Pratt Inst., 1949-64; dir. NSF, Washington, 1969-71; chancellor U. Calif., San Diego, 1972—. Mem. Sch. Bd. Baltimore City, 1958-68. Recipient Barnett Cohen award in bacteriology, 1958; Rumford prize Am. Acad. Arts and Scis., 1964. Mem. Am. Inst. Biol. Scis. (pres. 1968), Am. Chem. Soc., Nat. Acad. Sci., Am. Soc. Biol. Chemists (pres. 1963-64), Soc. Gen. Physiology (pres. 1960-61), Soc. Naturalists, Soc. Zoologists, Am. Acad. Arts and Scis., Am. Soc. Bacteriologists, Am. Philos. Soc., AAAS (pres. 1976, chmn. 1977), Sigma Xi, Kappa Sigma. Author textbook. Editor: Copper Metabolism (with Bentley Glass), 1950; Phosphorus Metabolism, 2 vols., 1951, 52; Mechanism of Enzyme Action, 1954; Amino Acid Metabolism, 1955; The Chemical Basis of Heredity, 1957; The Chemical Basis of Development, 1959; Light and Life, 1961; Cellular Physiology and Biochemistry, 1961; (with C.P. Swanson) Foundations of Modern Biology series, 1961-64. Office: Chancellor's Office Q-005 Univ Calif San Diego La Jolla CA 92093

MCELROY, WILLIAM THEODORE, judge; b. Newark, Jan. 20, 1925; s. William J. and Matilda (Hamilton) McE.; Rutgers U., 1946-50, J.D. cum laude, 1950; m. Emilie Hoinowski, Jan. 18, 1947; children—Karen L., William J., Ruth P. Admitted to N.J. bar, 1949; asso. Duggan, Shaw & Hughes, Newark, 1949-50; with McElroy, Connell, Foley & Geiser and predecessor firms, Newark, 1950—, partner, 1956-78; judge Superior Ct. N.J., Morristown, 1978—. Served with USNR, 1942-45. Fellow Am. Coll. Trial Lawyers; mem. Am., N.J. (chmn. civil procedure sect. 1973-74), Essex County, Morris County bar assns., N.J. Trial Lawyers Assn. Home: 56 Lowery Ln Mendham NJ 07945 Office: Morris County Ct House Morristown NJ 07960

MC ELWAIN, JOSEPH A., power co. exec.; b. Deer Lodge, Mont., Nov. 13, 1919; s. Lee Chaffee and Johanna (Petersen) McE.; B.A., U. Mont., 1943, LL.B., 1947; m. Mary Cleaver Witt, Mar. 8, 1945; children—Lee William and Lori Louise (twins). Admitted to Mont. bar, 1947; individual practice law, Deer Lodge, 1947-63; Washington legis. counsel Mont. Power Co., Butte, 1954-63, counsel, 1963-65, asst. to pres., 1965-67, v.p., 1967-70, exec. v.p., dir., 1970, now chmn., chief exec. officer; dir. First Bank System, Devel. Credit Corp. Mont.; mem. U.S. nat. com. World Energy Conf.; mem. Mont. Pub. Land Law Rev. Advisory Com. City atty. Deer Lodge, 1950-57, 60-63; mem. Mont. Ho. of Reps., 1949-55, majority floor leader, 1951; mem. Mont. State Senate, 1962-64; state chmn. Republican Central Com., Mont., 1952-54. Mem. adv. com. Edison Electric Inst., U. Mont. Found., Missoula, Rocky Mountain Coll., Billings. Served with AUS, World War II, Korea. Recipient Judstin Miller award, 1947. Mem. Mont., Am. bar assns. Episcopalian. Clubs: Masons, Shriners, Kiwanis. Home: 1500 Carolina Ave Butte MT 59701 Office: 40 E Broadway Butte MT 59701

MCELWAIN, KEITH DENNIS, apparel and accessories mfg. co. exec.; b. Bklyn., Mar. 27, 1926; s. George Rankin and Madeline Justin (Held) McE.; student Cornell U., 1944; B.S. in Econs. magna cum laude, Seton Hall Coll., 1949; m. Marie T. Blanch, Aug. 18, 1951; children—Therese Mary, Janis Ann, Keith Dennis, Bryan Micheal. Asst. to ins. mgr. ARAMCO, 1949-53, Union Carbide Co., 1953-62; corp. ins. mgr. ITT, N.Y.C., 1962-74; corp. ins. mgr. Culbro Corp., N.Y.C., 1975-76; sec., ins. mgr. Manhattan Industries Inc., N.Y.C., 1976—. Served with U.S. Army, 1944-46. Decorated Purple Heart, Bronze Star. Mem. Risk and Ins. Mgmt. Soc., Nottingham Soc., Am. Legion. Roman Catholic. Home: 1335 E 28th St Brooklyn NY 11210 Office: 1271 Ave of Americas New York NY 10020

MCELWAIN, WILLIAM E., pub. relations exec.; b. Terre Haute, Ind., Apr. 13, 1921; s. William E. and Anna May (Kenan) McE.; B.A., U. Pitts., 1941; m. Mercedes Perrino, Nov. 3, 1945; children—William Eric, Jeanine Shirley. Sportswriter Pitts. Press, 1941-42, reporter, 1946; asst. dean men U. Pitts., 1946-48; copy reader Pitts. Sun-Telegraph, 1948-50, rewrite and gen. assignment, 1951-54; editorial staff Rome (Italy) Daily Am., 1950-51; with Ketchum, MacLeod & Grove, Pitts., Houston, 1954-78, pub. relations account supr., Pitts., 1960-65, v.p., dir. pub. relations, Houston, 1965-76, v.p. collateral services, Houston, 1976-78; sr. pub. relations counsellor Dale Henderson, Inc., Houston, 1978—. City councilman, El Lago, Tex., 1978-79; bd. dirs. Zool. Soc. Houston, 1976-78. Served with AUS, 1942-45. Mem. Pub. Relations Soc. Am. (dir. 1966-71, 77—, v.p. 1977-78, pres. 1978-79), Omicron Delta Kappa. Address: 4445 NASA 1 Unit 377 Seabrook TX 77586

MCELWAINE, ROBERT MARSHALL, assn. exec.; b. N.Y.C., May 19, 1924; s. Donn and Ina (Fowler) M.; student U. So. Cal., 1941-44; m. Sandra Cowen, Oct. 19, 1957; 1 son, Andrew Scott. Sr. account supr. Interpublic, Inc., N.Y.C., 1957-62; exec. v.p. Maxon, Inc., N.Y.C., 1962-65; dir. pub. relations Mercedes-Benz of N. Am., Fort Lee, N.J., 1965-68; v.p., gen. mgr. Ketchum, MacLeod & Grove, Inc., Washington, 1968-71; pres. Am. Imported Automobile Dealers Assn., Washington, 1971—. Chmn. citizen's com. for police recruitment, 1969. Mem. Presdl. Inauguration Com., 1968. Trustee Fed. City Council, Washington; bd. dirs. John F. Kennedy Center Prodns. Served with USNR, 1942-46. Mem. Pub. Relations Soc. Am. Soc. Assn. Execs. Home: 2433 Tracy Pl NW Washington DC 20008 Office: 1220 19th St NW Washington DC 20036

MC ELWEE, JOHN GERARD, life ins. co. exec.; b. Port Bannatyne, Scotland, Dec. 19, 1921; s. James and Margaret (Fitzgerald) McE.; came to U.S., 1925, naturalized, 1935; student Boston Coll., 1939-42, LL.B., 1950; grad. advanced mgmt. program Harvard U. Sch. Bus., 1960; m. Barbara Sullivan, Mar. 31, 1951; children—Neal, Janet, Sheila, Brian. With John Hancock Mut. Life Ins. Co., Boston, 1945—, asst. sec., 1957-61, 2d v.p., 1961-65, v.p., 1965-71, sr. v.p., sec., 1972-74, exec. v.p., sec., 1974-79, pres., 1979—, dir., 1976—; dir. New Eng. Merchants Nat. Bank Boston, New Eng. Merchants Co., Cooper Industries, Inc.; dir., past chmn. Ins. Inst., Northeastern U. Trustee Univ. Hosp., Citizenship Tng. Group, Inc., Boston Coll., Radcliffe U.; mem. trustee council Boston U. Med. Center; past dir., past pres. Big Brother Assn. Boston. Served with USN, 1941-45. Roman Catholic. Clubs: Algonquin, Winchester Country; Univ.,

Comml. (Boston). Home: 3 Longfellow Rd Winchester MA 01890 Office: John Hancock Pl PO Box 111 Boston MA 02117

MC ELWEE, WILLIAM HENRY, lawyer; b. Statesville, N.C., Oct. 13, 1907; s. William Henry and Elizabeth (Cranor) McE.; B.A., Davidson Coll.; J.D., Wake Forest Coll.; m. Douglas Plonk, Mar. 9, 1943; children—W.H., Elizabeth McElwee Cannon, Dorothy M. McElwee Shartzer, John. Sr. partner firm McElwee, Hall, McElwee & Cannon, Wilkesboro, N.C.; dir. Lewe's Co., 1961—, gen. counsel; gen. counsel Holly Farms; mem. N.C. Bd. Law Examiners. Served with AUS, 1942-46. Decorated Bronze Star. Democrat. Presbyterian. Club: Masons. Home: 109 McElwee St North Wilkesboro NC 28659 Office: 906 R B St North Wilkesboro NC 28659*

MCENANY, MICHAEL VINCENT, univ. dean; b. Covington, La., Jan. 24, 1908; s. Michael Vincent and Edna (Ernst) McE.; B.S. in Elec. Engring., Colo. Coll., 1929; M.A., Dartmouth, 1931; student U. Okla., 1934-35; m. Helen Louise Rosenberger, Dec. 31, 1932; 1 son, Michael Vernon. With Pub. Service Co., Colo., 1929-31, New Eng. Power Constrn. Co., 1931; mem. faculty Adams State Coll., Alamosa, Colo., 1931-33; tchr. Okla. pub. schs., 1935-39; head div. sci. and math. Adams State Coll., 1940-42; asso. prof. elec. engring. S.D. State Coll., Brookings, 1942-43; mem. faculty Rice U., 1943—, prof. elec. engring., 1964—, registrar, 1954-64, dean undergrad. affairs, 1964-73; ret., 1974, prelaw adviser 1974—; cons. to industry, 1943—. Chmn. com. ednl. inquiry Carnegie Found., 1950-54. Mem. Houston Philos. Soc. (past pres., sec.), Sigma Xi, Sigma Tau. Home: 5416 Holly St Bellaire TX 77401 Office: P O Box 1892 Houston TX 77001

MC ENERY, JOHN WINN, army officer; b. San Francisco, Dec. 30, 1925; s. Douglas Wiltz and Katherine (Winn) McE.; B.S. in Mil. Sci., U.S. Mil. Acad., 1948; M.S. in Internat. Affairs, George Washington U., 1968; grad. Spanish Army Staff Coll., 1967, Air War Coll., 1968; m. Constance Aileen Markley, June 22, 1949; children—Douglas, John Winn. Commd. 2d lt. U.S. Army, 1948, advanced through grades to maj. gen., 1974; comdr. 3d Squadron, 11th Armored Cavalry Regiment, Vietnam, 1968-69, Air Cavalry Combat Brigade, 1st Cavalry Div., Ft. Hood, Tex., 1970-72; asst. div. comdr. 1st Cavalry Div., Ft. Hood, 1972-73; comdr. 101st Airborne Div., Ft. Campbell, Ky., 1974-76, U.S. Army Armor Center, Ft. Knox, Ky., 1976-78; comdr. Readiness Region VIII, FAMC, Denver, 1978-79; dep. chief of staff for ops. Hdqrs. U.S. Army Forces Command, Ft. McPherson, Ga., 1979—. Decorated Distinguished Service Cross, Silver Star with oak leaf cluster, Bronze Star, Air medal with 25 oak leaf clusters, Purple Heart. Home: 17 E Wheeler Dr Fort McPherson GA 30330

MCENROE, JOHN PATRICK, JR., profl. tennis player; b. Wiesbaden, Germany, Feb. 16, 1959; s. John Patrick and Katy McEnroe; grad. Trinity Sch., N.Y.C., 1977; student Stanford U. Winner numerous U.S. jr. singles and doubles titles; winner jr. titles for French Mixed Doubles, 1977, French Jr. Singles, 1977, Italian Indoor Doubles, 1978; winner Nat. Coll. Athletic Assn. Intercollegiate U.S. Men's Singles title, 1978; turned prof., 1978; played on victorious U.S. Davis Cup Team, 1978; winner Stockholm Open, 1978, Benson and Hedges Tournament, 1978, Grand Prix Masters singles and doubles, Wembley, 1978, Grand Prix Masters Tournament, N.Y.C., 1979, New Orleans Grand Prix, 1979, WCT Milan Internat., Italy, 1979, Stella Artois Tournament, London, 1979, U.S. Open Men's Singles Championship, 1979, World Championship Tennis Championship, 1979.*

MC ENTEE, EDWARD MATTHEW, U.S. judge; b. Providence, Oct. 21, 1906; s. Owen E. and Catherine (Hackett) McE.; A.B., Holy Cross Coll., 1928; LL.B., Boston U., 1933; Ed.D. (hon.), Cath. Tchrs. Coll. Providence, 1948; m. Gertrude M. Hauke, June 5, 1941; children—Carolyn, Edward, Owen, Mary, Matthew, Michael, Brian. Admitted R.I. bar, 1933, Supreme Ct. bar, 1938; practice in Providence; lectr. on sch. law R.I. Coll. Edn., 1936-65, Cath. Tchrs. Coll. of Providence, 1946-50; judge U.S. Ct. Appeals, Providence, now sr. judge. Mem. R.I. Ho. of Reps., 1935-39, R.I. Pub. Works Commn., 1935-39; asst. U.S. atty. Dist. R.I., 1940-52, U.S. atty., 1952, 53. Mem. White House Conf. on Children and Youth, 1948, State Released Time Commn., 1949, State Family Ct. Commn., 1956-57. Mem. Am., R.I. bar assns., R.I. Hist. Soc., Friendly Sons of St. Patrick. Club: Clover (Boston). Office: 311 Fed Bldg Providence RI 02903*

MCENTEE, KENNETH, educator; b. Oakfield, N.Y., Mar. 30, 1921; s. Michael Thomas and Florence (Bobsene) McE.; D.V.M., N.Y. State Vet. Coll., 1944; Ph.D. (hon.), Royal Vet. Coll., Sweden, 1975; m. Janet Louise Fraser, Aug. 6, 1952; children—Michael Fraser, Margaret Colleen. Vet. practice, Newport, Vt., 1944-45; mem. faculty N.Y. State Vet. Coll., 1947—, prof., 1955—, chmn. dept. large animal medicine, obstetrics and surgery, 1965-69, asso. dean clin. studies, 1969-73; vis. scientist Armed Forces Inst. Pathology, 1958-59; sr. research fellow Animal Health Research Lab., Commonwealth Sci. and Indsl. Research Orgn., Parkville, Victoria, Australia, 1965-66; vis. tchr. and lectr. Royal Vet. Coll., Stockholm, Sweden, 1973, 75, 77; vis. prof. Vet. Coll., Belo Horizonte, Brazil, 1973. Served to capt. AUS, 1945-47. Hon. diplomate Am. Coll. Theriogenologists. Recipient Borden award for cattle disease research, 1971. Mem. Am. Coll. Vet. Pathologists (pres. 1966-67), AVMA, Am. Assn. Pathologists and Bacteriologists, Internat. Fertility Assn., Sigma Xi, Phi Zeta, Phi Kappa Phi. Author numerous papers in field. Home: 128 Pine Tree Rd Ithaca NY 14850

MCENTEER, BEN, banker; b. DuBois, Pa., Dec. 30, 1913; s. Ben and Helen (Pentz) McE.; student U. Wis.; m. Mary L. Griffith, May 15, 1943; children—James B., David G. With DuBois Nat. Bank, 1931-36; examiner Pa. Dept. Banking, 1936-40, Fed. Res. Bank Cleve., 1940-47; asst. v.p., then br. mgr. Nat. City Bank Cleve., 1948-59; chmn. bd., pres., dir. Pa. Bank and Trust Co., Titusville, 1959—. Mem. Pa. Banking Bd., 1966—. Mem. Titusville (Pa.) Housing Authority; pres. Col. Drake council Boy Scouts Am., 1969-72, v.p., exec. bd. French Creek council, 1972—, Silver Beaver award, 1972; vice chmn. Redevel. Authority Titusville; v.p. Titusville Indsl. Fund, Inc. Chmn. adv. bd. U. Pitts. at Titusville; bd. dirs., pres. Titusville Hosp. Served to capt. USAAF, 1942-46. Mem. Pa. Bankers Assn. (1st v.p. 1973-74, pres. 1974-75), Pa. Soc., Newcomen Soc. N.Am. Elk, Rotarian, Mason (Shriner). Clubs: Bankers, Duquesne (Pitts.); Cleveland Athletic, Westwood Country (Cleve.); Conewango Country (Warren, Pa.); Wanango Country (Reno, Pa.); Titusville Country. Home: 814 N Monroe St Titusville PA 16354 Office: 127 W Spring St Titusville PA 16354

MC ENTYRE, PETER MICHAEL, trust co. exec.; b. Westmount, Que., Can., Aug. 15, 1917; s. John and May (Gear) McE.; student Bishop's Coll. Sch., 1928-35; B.Com., McGill U., 1939, C.A., 1941, C.F.A., 1963; m. Katharine Creelman, Mar. 15, 1941; children—David, Nancy. Partner, Creak Cushing & Hodgson, Montreal, 1939-48; sec.-treas. St. Lawrence Sugar Refineries Ltd., Montreal, 1948-63; pres., dir. Comml. Trust Co. Ltd., Montreal, Que., 1963-79, Comtrust Holdings Inc., Montreal, 1979—; chmn. bd. Canada Cement LaFarge Ltd.; dir. La Farge, S.A., Citadel Cement Corp., Starlaw Investments Ltd., Belding Corticelli Ltd. Alderman, City of Westmount, 1962-69, commr. finance City Westmount, 1962-69; mayor, 1969-71. Bd. govs. Concordia U.; chmn. Boys' Clubs of Can. Endowment Fund. Served with Royal Canadian Navy, 1941-46. Clubs: University, Mount Royal, St. James's, Royal Montreal Golf, Montreal Badminton and Squash, Royal Montreal Curling. Home: 444 Clarke Ave Westmount PQ H3Y 2C6 Canada Office: 1130 Sherbrooke St W Montreal PQ H3A 2T1 Canada

MC EVERS, ROBERT DARWIN, banker; b. Washington, May 18, 1930; s. John Henry and Beatrice (Holton) McE.; B.S. with distinction, U.S. Naval Acad., 1952; M.B.A. with distinction, Harvard U., 1958; m. Joan Manning, Mar. 29, 1954; children—Robert Darwin, Allison Holton. With First Nat. Bank of Chgo., 1958-61; spl. asst., exec. offices Trans Union Corp. (formerly Union Tank Car Co.), Chgo., 1961-64, gen. mgr. Canadian subs., Toronto, Ont., 1964, asst. to pres., Chgo., 1964-65, v.p., gen. mgr. Tank Car div., 1965-70, pres., 1970-73; v.p., dir. Trans Union Corp., 1966-73; sr. v.p. First Nat. Bank of Chgo., 1973-76, head trust dept., 1974-77, exec. v.p., 1976—, head exec. dept., 1977—; dir. Marquette Co., Cooper Industries, Inc., Reading Industries Inc. Bd. dirs. Central YMCA Community Coll., AM Fund. Served to 1st lt. USAF, 1952-56. Mem. Am. Mgmt. Assn., Chgo. Council Fgn. Relations, Newcomen Soc. N.Am., Beta Theta Pi. Clubs: Econ., Mid-Am., Univ., Mid-Day (Chgo.); Army-Navy Country (Arlington, Va.); Kenilworth (Ill.); Indian Hill (Winnetka, Ill.). Home: 48 Kenilworth Ave Kenilworth IL 60043 Office: 1 First National Plaza Chicago IL 60670

MCEVILLA, JOSEPH DAVID, univ. dean; b. Aspinwall, Pa., Sept. 11, 1919; s. Joseph Edward and Christiana (Steffler) McE.; B.A., U. Fla., 1944; B.S. in Pharmacy, U. Pitts., 1949, M.S. (Geo. A. Kelly Sr. fellow), 1952, Ph.D., 1955; m. Avis Walter, Feb. 5, 1943; children—Arlene Avis, Joseph David. Asst. prof. U. Pitts., 1955-58, asso. prof., 1959-61, prof., 1962-74; prof. pharm. econs., dean Sch. Pharmacy, Temple U., Phila., 1974—; cons. St. Clair, Armstrong County hosps.; cons. Task Force on Prescription Drugs, HEW; cons. Colombian Govt., Inst. Social Security, Nat. Assn. Bds. Pharmacy Manpower Study, Nat. Pharmacy Ins. Council, drug studies br. Social Security Adminstrn.; Pitts. area cons. Hosp. Audit, Inc., Merck, Sharp and Dohme; mem. Allegheny adv. council Western Pa. Comprehensive Health Planning Assn.; co-chmn. Pharmacy Panel on Inter-relation of Secondary Schs., Colls. and Profl. Schs.; study dir. Am. Pharm. Assn. Found. Served with USMCR, 1943-45. Fellow Acad. Pharm. Scis.; mem. Am., Pa., Chester County pharm. assns., AMA, Am. Econ. Assn., Am. Pub. Health Assn., Soc. Pa. Economists, Am. Assn. Colls. of Pharmacy Conf. Tchrs. (chmn. 1964-65), Am. Acad. Pharm. Scis. (sect. chmn.), Rho Chi, Kappa Psi. Author: Remington's Practice of Pharmacy, 1961; Pharmacy Administration, 1965; Perspectives on Medicine in Society. Home: 28 Bodine Rd Berwyn PA 19312 Office: 3307 N Broad St Philadelphia PA 19140

MCEVILLY, THOMAS VINCENT, seismologist; b. East Saint Louis, Ill., Sept. 2, 1934; s. Robert John and Frances Nathalie (Earnshaw) McE.; B.S., St. Louis U., 1956, Ph.D., 1964; m. Dorothy K. Hopfinger, Oct. 23, 1970; children—Mary, Susan, Ann, Steven, Joseph, Adrian. Geophysicst, California Co., New Orleans, 1957-60; engring. v.p. Sprengnether Instrument Co., St. Louis, 1962-67; asst. prof. seismology U. Calif., Berkeley, 1964-68, asso. prof., 1968-74, prof., 1974—, chmn. dept. geology and geophysics, 1976—, asst. dir. seismographic sta., 1968—; cons. numerous govt. agys., geotech. cos. Mem. Am. Geophys. Union, Royal Astron. Soc., Earthquake Engring. Research Inst., Seismol. Soc. Am. (editor bull. 1976—), Soc. Exploration Geophysicists, AAAS. Contbr. numerous articles to profl. jours. Office: Dept Geology and Geophysics U Calif Berkeley CA 94720

MCEVOY, CHARLES LUCIEN, printing exec.; b. Bradford, Pa., Sept. 2, 1917; s. L. Carle and Mary Ellen (McMahon) McE.; A.B., Xavier U., 1938; postgrad. Georgetown U., 1938-41; J.D., Chgo. Kent Coll. Law, 1950; m. Rosemary C. Rocca, Sept. 2, 1947. With Neo Gravure Co. of Chgo., 1947-54, asst. gen. mgr., 1950-52, gen. mgr., 1952-54; v.p. sales The Cuneo Press, Inc., Chgo., 1954-67, exec. v.p., 1967-73, pres., 1973—, dir., 1956—. Served with AUS, 1942-46; PTO. Clubs: Chicago Golf, Chicago Athletic. Home: 3000 Sheridan Rd Chicago IL 60657 Office: 2 N Riverside Plaza Chicago IL 60606

MC EWAN, JOHN M., bank exec.; b. Pitts., Aug. 17, 1934; s. James and Martha (Millin) McE.; B.A., U. Va.; postgrad. Wharton Sch., U. Pa.; m. Betsy Drew Butterworth, May 19, 1959; children—J. Stoddard, Timothy D., Ailsa E., Elizabeth D., Samantha M. With Central Pa. Nat. Bank, 1955-73, Everett Trust & Savs. Bank, 1973-75; with Central Nat. Bank of Cleve., 1975—, now exec. v.p., banking group exec. Mem. vis. com. Case Western Res. U. Sch. Mgmt., 1975—; trustee Cleve. chpt. ARC, 1978—, New Cleve. Campaign, 1978—, Hillcrest Hosp., Cleve., 1979—; sect. chmn. United Way of Cleve., 1978—. Served to 1st lt. USMC, 1957-59. Mem. Am. Mktg. Assn., Am. Bankers Assn., Bank Mktg. Assn. Clubs: Union of Cleve., Tavern, Kirtland Country, Chagrin Valley Hunt. Home: 12 Pepper Ridge Rd Pepper Pike OH 44124 Office: 800 Superior Ave Cleveland OH 44114*

MCEWAN, LEONARD, judge; b. Great Falls, Mont., Feb. 17, 1925; s. Leonard Wellington and Olga (Trinastich) McE.; B.S., U. Wyo., 1955, J.D., 1957; m. Cameon Wolfe, Sept. 2, 1953 (dec. 1977). Admitted to Wyo. bar, 1957; practice in Sheridan, 1957-58; municipal judge City Sheridan, 1958-69; justice Wyo. Supreme Ct., Cheyenne, 1969-75, chief justice, 1975; dist. judge, Sheridan, Wyo., 1975—. Trustee Sheridan Coll., 1963-69, Sheridan County YMCA, 1963 68, All-American Indian Days, 1959-63, N. Am. Indian Found., 1960-67. Served with USAAF, 1943-46. Recipient Distinguished Service award Jr. C. of C., 1960. Mem. Wyo. State Bar, Am. Bar Assn., Am. Legion, U. Wyo. Alumni Assn. (bd. dirs. 1962-66), Sigma Alpha Epsilon. Episcopalian. Elk, Eagle, Mason, Rotarian. Club: Quarterback. Address: PO Box 6066 Sheridan WY 82801

MCEWAN, OSWALD BEVERLY, lawyer; b. Orlando, Fla., 1913; s. John Singer and Roberta (Dunn) McE.; B.A., U. Fla., 1936; J.D., Washington and Lee U., 1940; m. Mary Ann Walker, 1941 (dec. Feb. 8, 1975); children—Christopher, Nancy, James; m. 2d, Betty Wilson Farrar, June 14, 1975. Admitted Fla. bar, 1940, since practiced in Orlando; partner Sanders, McEwan, Mims & McDonald, and predecessor, 1947—; U.S. referee bankruptcy, 1946; asst. county solicitor, Orange County, Fla., 1947-49; city atty., Orlando, 1949-52; counsel Fla. Real Estate Commn., 1952-53; dir. Gulf Life Ins. Co. Chmn. trustees Lawyers Title Guaranty Fund, 1968-69. Chmn. Municipal Planning Bd., City of Orlando, 1975—. Served to lt. col. Judge Adv. Gen. Corps, AUS, World War II. Decorated Legion of Merit. Fellow Am. Coll. Probate Counsel, Am. Bar Found.; mem. Am. (chmn. com. on prof. grievances, mem. ho. of dels. 1959-67), Fla. (bd. govs. 1951-59, pres. 1958-59), Orange County (pres. 1952) bar assns., Internat. Assn. Ins. Counsel, Fedn. Ins. Counsel (v.p. 1960-63), Nat. Conf. Lawyers, Ins. Cos. and Abstracters, Order of the Coif, V.F.W., Am. Law Inst., Am. Judicature Soc., Am. Legion, Phi Delta Phi, Kappa Alpha. Clubs: University, Country, Rotary (Orlando). Home: 1129 S Osceola St Orlando FL 32806 Office: 108 E Central Blvd Orlando FL 32802

MC EWEN, JAMES LEONARD, ret. educator; b. Greene, Iowa, June 1, 1909; s. Walter and Alice (Lucas) McE.; B.S., Iowa State U., 1933; M.S., N.Y. U., 1934, Ph.D., 1950; m. Edna M. Hanlon, Dec. 13, 1936 (dec. June 1973); m. Mary M. Collins, Aug. 20, 1976. Engaged in operations and personnel L. Bamberger & Co., Newark, 1934-47; asso. prof. N.Y. U., 1947-51; personnel dir. Halle Bros. Co., Cleve., 1951-56; v.p. personnel and labor relations Lit Bros. Co., Phila., 1956-64; prof. marketing, chmn. dept. L.I. U., 1964-65, Drexel U., 1965-74, now ret.; vis. prof. bus. adminstrn. Villanova U., 1975—; cons. in field. Served with AUS, 1943-45. Decorated Purple Heart with cluster; recipient Alumni Achievement award N.Y. U. Alumni Assn., 1962. Mem. Am. Mktg. Assn., Fed. Mediation and Conciliation Service, Indsl. Relations Assn., Am. Arbitration Assn., Indsl. Relations Reasearch Assn., Nat. Retail Mchts. Assn. (chmn. personnel group 1963-64), Beta Gamma Sigma, Eta Mu Phi. Presbyterian. Author: Appraising Retail Executive and Employee Performance, 1968. Home: 200 N Wynnewood Ave Wynnewood PA 19096. *As said by some philosopher: "A man's value in the world is estimated and paid for according to the ability he uses, not what he may possess." Without the help of many others, what ability I may possess would not even have been used.*

MCEWEN, JEAN, painter; b. Montreal, Que., Can., Dec. 14, 1923; s. William and Elaine (Renaud) McE.; grad. U. Montreal, 1947; m. 2d, Indra Kagis, Sept. 18, 1976; children—Jean Sabin, Marianne; children by previous marriage—Isabelle, Domenique. One-man exhbns. include Gallery Godart-Lefort, Montreal, 1962-69, Gallery Montreal, 1963, Gallery Moore, Toronto, 1963-69, Mayer Gallery, Paris, 1964; group exhbns. include Dunn Internat. Exhbn., Tate Gallery, London, 1963; rep. permanent collections Mus. Modern Art, N.Y.C., Walker Art Center, Mpls., Albright-Knox Art Gallery, Buffalo, Ottawa Mus., Toronto Mus.; commd. for stained glass window Sir George Williams U., 1966, murals for Toronto Airport, Plase Arts, Montreal. Winner Quebec Art competition, 1962; recipient Jessie Dow award Montreal Spring Exhbn., 1964; grantee Can. Council, 1977-78. Academician Royal Can. Acad. Arts. Roman Catholic. Address: 3908 Parc Lafontaine Rue Montreal PQ H2L 3M6 Canada

MCEWEN, ROBERT CAMERON, congressman; b. Ogdensburg, N.Y., Jan. 5, 1920; s. Robert H. and Mary (MacIntyre) McE.; student U. Vt., 1938-39, Wharton Sch. Finance, 1939-41, Albany Law Sch., 1941-47; m. Anita M. Sharples, July 26, 1952; children—Nancy, Mary. Admitted to N.Y. bar, 1947, since practiced in Ogdensburg; partner O'Connell, McEwen & DuPre; mem. N.Y. State Senate, 1954-64; mem. 89th-96th congresses from 30th N.Y. Dist. Mem. N.Y. State, St. Lawrence County bar assns., Am. Legion, V.F.W., Phi Delta Theta. Republican. Clubs: Masons. Elks. Office: 2210 Rayburn House Office Bldg Washington DC 20515*

MCEWEN, WILLIAM EDWIN, chemist; b. Oaxaca, Mexico, Jan. 13, 1922; s. William E. and Annabel (Miller) M.; A.B., Columbia, 1943, M.A. 1945, Ph.D., 1947; m. Miriam K. Sherman, Sept. 1, 1945 (div. Oct. 1978); children—Robert W., Joan E., Alfred S. Tech. engr. Union Carbide Corp., Oak Ridge, 1945-46; lectr. Columbia, 1947; asst. prof. U. Kans., 1947-52, asso. prof., 1952-57, prof. chemistry, 1957-62; Commonwealth head, prof. U. Mass., 1962-77, Commonwealth prof., 1977—; research collaborator Brookhaven Nat. Lab., 1962—, mem. vis. com. for chemistry, 1964-67; cons. NSF, 1966-70, mem. chemistry panel, 1966-69; cons. State Edn. Dept., Albany, N.Y., 1973-75. Mem. medicinal chemistry B study sect. NIH, 1973-77. Served with C.E., AUS, 1945-46. Fellow, N.Y. Acad. Scis.; mem. Am. Chem. Soc. (com. on nominations and elections 1968-74, com. on coms. 1974-75, com. on publs. 1977—), Chem. Soc. London, AAAS (chmn. sect. C 1978). Author textbooks of organic chemistry, research papers. Home: 252 West St Apt 6 Amherst MA 01002

MCEWEN, WILLIAM ROBERT, educator; b. Duluth, Aug. 21, 1911; s. Alexander Murdoch and Alice Maude (Metcalfe) McE.; B.E., Duluth State Tchrs. Coll., 1935; M.A., U. Minn., 1939, Ph.D., 1946; m. Dorothy Larson, June 15, 1940; children—William Robert, Claudia, Audrey, Alice, Alexander, John. With U. Minn., 1937—, with Duluth br., 1947—, successively instr., asst. prof., asso. prof., prof., 1949—. Math. cons. Office Research Analysis, USAF. Mem. Am. Math. Assn., Math. Soc. Am. Home: 2153 Sussex St Duluth MN 55803

MCFADDEN, FRANK HAMPTON, judge; b. Oxford, Miss., Nov. 20, 1925; s. John Angus and Ruby (Roy) McF.; B.A., U. Miss., 1950; LL.B., Yale, 1955; m. Jane Porter Nabers, Sept. 30, 1960; children—Frank Hampton, Angus Nabers, Jane Porter. Admitted to N.Y. State bar, 1956, Ala. bar, 1959; asso. firm Lord, Day & Lord, N.Y.C., 1955-58; asso. firm Bradley, Arant, Rose & White, Birmingham, Ala., 1958-63, partner, 1963-69; judge U.S. Dist. Ct. No. Dist. Ala., 1969-73, chief judge, 1973—. Served from ensign to lt. USNR, 1944-49, 51-53. Home: 3015 Briarcliff Rd Birmingham AL 35223 Office: Federal Courthouse Birmingham AL 35203

MC FADDEN, FRANK WILLIAM, public relations co. exec.; b. San Diego, June 3, 1914; s. Clarence Ray and Mabel Mary (Hyde) McF.; student Southwestern U. Bus., 1933-34; m. Marion Pauline Story, Aug. 31, 1935; children—Michael Frank, Judith Ann. Asst. publicity dir. Universal Pictures, Los Angeles, 1937-52; nat. publicity dir. Panoramic Prodns., Culver City, Calif., 1953; pres. Frank McFadden & Assos., Los Angeles, 1954; partner McFadden & Eddy, Asso., Los Angeles, 1955-66, McFadden, Strauss & Irwin, Los Angeles, 1966-76, ICPR Public Relations, Los Angeles, 1976—. Recipient Les Mason award Publicists Guild Am., 1977. Home: 20494 Roca Chica Dr Malibu CA 90265 Office: ICPR 9255 Sunset Blvd Los Angeles CA 90069

MCFADDEN, G. BRUCE, hosp. adminstr.; b. Winchester, Va., Feb. 19, 1934; s. S. Donald and Ruth D. McF.; B.S., Va. Poly. Inst., 1953; M.H.A., Med. Coll. Va. (Va. Commonwealth U.), 1961; m. Lois F. Richardson, Aug. 22, 1964; children—Christopher, Amy. Asst. adminstr. Meml. Hosp. at Easton, Md., Inc., 1963-70; v.p. Pa. Hosp., Phila., 1970-75; dir. U. Md. Hosp., Balt., 1975—; cons. Hosp. Joint Practice Demonstration Project, Nat. Joint Practice Commn. of AMA and ANA; preceptor for programs in health care adminstrn. Med. Coll. Va., Columbia U., N.Y. U., U. Pa., Temple U.; chmn. com. on curriculum for program in health care adminstrn. Med. Coll. Va.; mem. Task Force on Regionalization Blood Service Units, Am. Blood Commn.; bd. dirs., mem. exec. com. Central Md. Health Systems Agy. Bd. dirs. Vis. Nurse Soc., Phila.; bd. dirs., vice chmn. Community Nursing Services of Phila. Fellow Am. Coll. Hosp. Adminstrs.; mem. Am. Hosp. Assn. (council on human resources, chmn. spl. coms. on mandatory continuing edn.), Md. Hosp. Assn. Home: 259 Bowline Rd Severna Park MD 21146 Office: 22 S Greene St Baltimore MD 21201*

MC FADDEN, GEORGE LINUS, army officer; b. Sharon, Pa., Oct. 16, 1927; s. George Linus and Frances Jane (Byrne) McF.; B.E., U. Omaha, 1961; M.S., George Washington U., 1967; grad. Advanced Mgmt. Program, Harvard U., 1971; m. Floretta Theresa McFadden, Nov. 20, 1948; children—Kenneth William, Mark Edward, Mary Kathleen, Robert Bernard, George Linus, William. Pvt., U.S. Army, 1946, advanced through grades to maj. gen., 1976; comdg. officer 7th infantry div., arty., Korea, 1969-70; dep. comdg. gen. U.S. Army Security Agy., Arlington, Va., 1972-74; dep. dir. for field mgmt. and evaluation, dep. chief central security service, Fort George G. Meade, Md., 1975-78, dep. dir. ops. Nat. Security Agy., 1978-79; comdg. gen.

U.S. Army So. European Task Force, Vincenza, Italy, 1979—. Decorated D.F.C., Silver Star, Bronze Star, Purple Heart, others. Mem. Assn. U.S. Army, Field Arty. Hist. Assn. Roman Catholic. Club: Rotary. Office: CG SETAF APO New York NY 09168

MCFADDEN, HARRY WEBBER, JR., med. microbiologist, pathologist; b. Greenwood, Nebr., Dec. 9, 1919; s. Harry W. and Alma E. (Wiedeman) McF.; A.B., U. Nebr., 1941, M.D., 1943; m. Josephine Patricia Kerns, Oct. 11, 1945; children—Harry Edward, Mary Jean. Rotating intern U. Nebr. Hosp., Omaha, 1943-44; resident in pathology U. Nebr. Coll. Medicine, 1943-44, resident in clin. pathology and bacteriology, 1947-49, instr. and fellow in pathology and bacteriology, 1949-52, asst. prof. pathology and microbiology, 1952-55, asst. prof. med. microbiology, 1955, asso. prof. med. microbiology, 1955-56, prof. med. microbiology, 1956—, chmn. dept. med. microbiology, 1955—, prof. pathology, 1968—, interim asso. dean for grad. studies, 1972-79, interim chancellor U. Nebr. Med. Center, 1972, 76-77. Served with M.C., U.S. Army, 1945-47; Berlin. Recipient teaching award Sr. Class of U. Nebr. Coll. Medicine, 1953, award as outstanding educator and friend, 1955, Basic Sci. award, 1958, 59, 61, 62, 67; diplomate Am. Bd. Pathology (trustee 1970). Fellow Coll. Am. Pathologists; mem. Omaha Med. Soc., Nebr. Med. Assn. (speaker ho. of dels.), AMA, Nebr. Assn. Pathologists (pres. 1960-61), Am. Soc. Clin. Pathology (council on microbiology 1965-71, chmn. council 1969-71), Am. Soc. Microbiology, Omaha M.W. Clin. Soc. (dir. clinics 1962-64), AAAS, Am. Fedn. Clin. Research, N.Y. Acad. Scis., Am. Museum Natural History, Electron Microscopy Soc. Am., Phi Beta Kappa, Sigma Xi, Alpha Omega Alpha, Phi Chi. Author: (with others) The Bacteriology of Commercial Poultry Processing, 1954; (with others) A Laboratory Manual for Medical Mycology and Clinical Parasitology, 1954; contbr. articles to profl. publs. Home: 10710 Poppleton Omaha NE 68144 Office: U Nebr Med Center 42d and Dewey Aves Omaha NE 68105

MCFADDEN, JAMES PATRICK, publisher; b. Youngstown, Ohio, Sept. 25, 1930; s. Francis Jerome and Recelba Katherine (Onorato) McF.; B.A., Youngstown Coll., 1953; m. Faith Abbott, Apr. 18, 1959; children— Robert Arthur, Maria James, Patrick Abbott, Regina Laudis, Christina Luke. Reporter, Youngstown Vindicator, 1952-54; with Nat. Rev. mag., N.Y.C., 1956—, asso. pub., 1971—; pres. Communications Distbn., Inc., N.Y.C., 1968—; v.p. Ultra Arts, Inc., N.Y.C., 1960—. Pres., Human Life Found., 1974—; chmn. Nat. Com. Cath. Laymen, 1977—. Served with CIC, AUS, 1954-56. Roman Catholic. Editor, Human Life Rev., 1975—. Home: 1050 Park Ave New York City NY 10028 Office: 150 E 35th St New York City NY 10016

MC FADDEN, JOHN VOLNEY, tool and die mfg. co. exec.; b. N.Y.C., Oct. 3, 1931; s. Volney and Mary Lucale (McConkie) McF.; B.S. in Commerce and Fin., Bucknell U., 1953; J.D., Detroit Coll. Law, 1960; m. Marie Linstead, June 27, 1953; children—Deborah, John Scott, David. Buyer, Ford Motor Co., Dearborn, Mich., 1956-60; gen. mgr. MTD Products Inc., Cleve., 1960, now exec. v.p. and dir.; dir. Valley City Steel Co., Agri-Fab Inc., Overly Hautz Inc. Pres., Cleve. World Trade Assn. Served to lt. Supply Corps, USN. Mem. Greater Cleve. Growth Assn. Club: Cleve. Yachting. Office: PO Box 36900 Cleveland OH 44136

MCFADDEN, JOSEPH JAMES, state justice; b. Boise, Idaho, May 3, 1916; s. James J. and Augusta R. (Murphy) McF.; B.S. in Bus., U. Idaho, 1937; m. Irene D. Barrett, Mar. 15, 1948; children—Teresa, Denyse, John, Joseph. Ct. reporter, Gooding, Idaho, 1938-42; admitted to Idaho bar, 1940; practice in Hailey, 1946-59; justice Supreme Ct. Idaho, 1959—, chief justice, 1966, 69-70, 76-77. Pres., Idaho Gem Boys State, Inc., 1961-62. Served with inf. AUS, 1942-46. Mem. Am., Idaho bar assns., Am. Judicature Soc. (dir. 1968-71). Home: 2110 N Curtis Rd Boise ID 83704 Office: Supreme Court Bldg Boise ID 83720

MCFADDEN, JOSEPH MICHAEL, coll. pres.; b. Joliet, Ill., Feb. 12, 1932; s. Francis Joseph and Lucille (Adler) McF.; B.A., Lewis Coll., 1954; M.A., U. Chgo., 1961; Ph.D., No. Ill. U., 1968; m. Norma Cardwell, Oct. 10, 1958; children—Timothy Joseph, Mary Colleen, Jonathon Andrew. Tchr. history Joliet Catholic High Sch., 1957-60; mem. faculty history dept. Lewis Coll., Lockport, Ill., 1960-70, asso. prof., 1967-70, v.p. acad. affairs, 1968-70; prof. history, dean sch. Nat. and Social Sci., Kearney (Neb.) State Coll., 1970-74; prof. history, dean Sch. Social and Behavioral Scis., Slippery Rock (Pa.) State Coll., 1974-77; pres. No. State Coll., Aberdeen, S.D., 1977—. Served with USNR, 1954-56. Mem. So. Hist. Assn. Roman Catholic. Home: 504 20th Ave NE Aberdeen SD 57401

MC FADDEN, MARY JOSEPHINE, fashion industry exec.; b. N.Y.C., Oct. 1, 1938; d. Alexander Bloomfield and Mary Josephine (Cutting) McF.; ed. Sorbonne, Paris, France, Traphagen Sch. Design, 1957, Columbia, 1959-62; 1 dau., Justine. Pub. relations dir. Christian Dior, N.Y.C., 1962-64; merchandising editor Vogue South Africa, 1964-65; polit. and travel columnist Rand (South Africa) Daily Mail, 1965-68; founder sculptural workshop Vukutu, Rhodesia, 1968-70; spl. projects editor Vogue U.S.A., 1970; fashion and jewelry designer, 1973—; pres. Mary McFadden, Inc., N.Y.C., 1976—. Recipient Am. Fashion Critics award-Coty award, 1976, 78, Audemars Piguet Fashion award, 1976, Rex award, 1977, More Coll. Art award, 1977, Pa. Gov.'s award, 1977, Roscoe award, 1978, Pres.'s Fellows award R.I. Sch. Design, 1979, Neiman Marcus award of excellence, 1979; named to Fashion Hall of Fame, 1979. Mem. Fashion Group. Home: 760 Park Ave New York NY 10021 Office: 264 W 35th St New York NY 10001

MCFADDEN, PETER WILLIAM, educator; b. Stamford, Conn., Aug. 2, 1932; s. Kenneth E. and Marie (Gleason) McF.; B.S. in Mech. Engring., U. Conn., 1954, M.S., 1956; Ph.D., Purdue U., 1959; m. Kathleen Mary Garvey, Aug. 11, 1956; children—Peter, Kathleen, Mary. Asst. instr. U. Conn., 1954-56, dean Sch. Engring., prof. mech. engring., 1971—; mem. faculty Purdue U., 1956-71, prof. mech. engring., head Sch. Mech. Engring., 1965-71; postdoctoral research Swiss Fed. Inst., Zurich, 1960-61; cons. to industry, 1959—. Mem. ASME, Am. Soc. Engring. Edn. Registered profl. engr., Ind., Conn. Research in cryogenics, heat transfer, mass. transfer. Home: 85 Willowbrook Rd Storrs CT 06268

MCFADDEN, THOMAS BERNARD, assn. exec., ret. airline exec.; b. N.Y.C., Feb. 11, 1917; s. John Joseph and Agnes B. (McCabe) McF.; ed. N.Y. U. Sch. Commerce, 1934-38, Harvard Bus. Sch., 1967; m. Marjorie Hutchison, Oct. 7, 1950; children—Thomas Hutchison, Matthew John. Page boy NBC, 1934-37, news editor, 1937-39, sports editor, 1939-41, dir. NBC Spot Sales, 1952-54, v.p. NBC, 1954-62, also in charge NBC owned properties; gen. mgr. WRCA, N.Y.C., 1947, 1st gen. mgr. WRCA-TV, 1948-50, gen. mgr. KRCA, Los Angeles, 1950; pres. New Britain Broadcasting Co., 1956-59, v.p., nat. sales mgr. NBC TV Network, 1959-62; v.p. marketing Trans World Airlines, Inc., 1962-68, sr. v.p. Eastern Airlines, Inc., 1968-77; dir. Am. Dist. Telegraph Co.; now exec. dir. Am. Cancer Soc. Past chmn. tourist div. Fla. C. of C.; vice chmn. S. Fla. Council Boy Scouts Am.; mem. Gov.'s Tourist Adv. Council; bd. dirs. Miami (Fla.) Heart Inst. Served to capt. USAAF, 1941-45. Mem. Inst. Certified Travel Agts. (founding trustee), Newcomen Soc. N.Am., Broadcast Pioneers. Clubs: Miami (gov.), Palm Bay, LaGorce Country (gov.) (Miami, Fla.); Bath (Miami Beach). Home: 4401 North Bay Rd Miami Beach FL 33140

MCFADDEN, THOMAS JOSEPH, lawyer; b. S.I., N.Y., May 1, 1900; s. Frank J. and Annie G. (McMenamin) McF.; A.B., Cornell, 1922, J.D., 1925; postgrad. Yale Law Sch., 1927- 28. Admitted to N.Y. bar, 1928, D.C. bar, 1934, bar U.S. Supreme Ct., 1935; spl. asst. to atty. gen. Dept. Justice, 1928-29; counsel, mgr. Nat. Paint, Varnish and Lacquer Assn., Washington, 1929-33; partner Donovan, Leisure, Newton & Irvine, N.Y.C., 1934—. Served with U.S Army, 1918; lt. comdr., naval air liaison officer, Sicily Invasion with 45th Inf. Div., USNR, 1942-45; chief Pacific Far East Morale Operations, O.S.S., Washington, 1943-44. Mem. Am. Soc. Internat. Law, Federal, Am., N.Y. State bar assns. Clubs: Nat. Lawyers; Cornell, Yale (N.Y.C.). Home: 183d and Pinehurst Ave New York NY 10033 Office: Donovan Leisure Newton & Irvine 30 Rockefeller Plaza New York NY 10020

MC FADIN, ROBERT LEE, mfg. co. exec.; b. Milw., Dec. 16, 1921; s. Charles Lee and Madeline (Hansen) McF.; B.S. in Mech. Engring., Mich. Tech. U., 1945; m. JoAnn Metzger, Sept. 6, 1947; children—Lindsey McFadin Spake, Barbara. Engr., Carrier Corp., N.Y.C., 1945-48; with Marley Co., Mission, Kans., 1948—, exec. v.p. all domestic operating divs., 1968-75, pres., chief operating officer, dir., 1975—, also dir. subsidiaries; dir. Blue Shield Kansas City (Mo.), Charterbank Ward Pkwy., Kansas City, Mo. Bd. dirs. Rehab. Inst., Kansas City, Mo., Heart of Am. United Way; gen. campaign chmn. Kansas City United Way, 1977; pres. Kansas City United Way, 1979; trustee Mich. Tech. Fund, Houghton, Midwest Research Inst. Served with USAAF, 1943. Mem. Newcomen Soc., Atomic Indsl. Forum, Kansas City (Mo.) C. of C. (dir.), Engrs. Club Kansas City, Mo. Clubs: Mission Hills (Kans.) Country; Morris County Golf (Convent Station, N.J.); Shriners. Home: 5728 Oakwood Rd Shawnee Mission KS 66208 Office: 5800 Foxridge Dr Mission KS 66202

MC FALL, JOHN, dancer, choreographer; b. Kansas City, Mo., Nov. 12, 1946; s. John Frances and Nina (Timoschenko) McF.; student pub. schs., Raytown; m. Marolyn Victoria Gyorfi, Aug. 29, 1966. Ford Found. scholar San Francisco Ballet Sch., 1964; dancer San Francisco Ballet, 1965-69, 71—, tchr. ballet, 1972-74; dancer Bayerischen Staats Oper Ballet, Munich, Germany, 1970; choreographer Beethoven Quartets for San Francisco Ballet; choreographer Seattle Opera, San Francisco Opera Assn.; choreographer dance film Tealia (award Moscow Film Festival, Golden Eagle award USIS), 1977, We the Clown, Oakland Ballet, 1978, Quanta, San Francisco Ballet, 1978; numerous guest appearances on West Coast. Mem. Am. Guild Mus. Artists (union rep. 1967-69, exec. com. San Francisco Area), Actors Equity. Home: 316 17th Ave San Francisco CA 94121 Office: 378 18th Ave San Francisco CA 94121

MCFALL, KENNETH HELICER, coll. ofcl.; b. Cleve., Oct. 21, 1906; s. Frank H. and Mary Ella (Porter) McF.; B.S., Mt. Union Coll., 1929, LL.D., 1969; M.A., Western Res. U., 1941, Ph.D., 1947; m. Dorothy E. Vernon, Sept. 2, 1930; 1 dau., Mary Jane. Prin. Hanoverton (Ohio) High Sch., 1929-30, Franklin Sch., Kent, Ohio, 1930-32; exec. head Randolph (Ohio) Schs., 1932-34; dir. admissions Mt. Union Coll., Alliance, Ohio, 1934-43; dean freshman Bowling Green (Ohio) State U., 1943-45, dir. guidance services, 1945-47, asst. dean liberal arts, 1947-48, dean Coll. Liberal Arts, 1948-55, prof. psychology, 1948—, provost, 1955-60, v.p., 1960-72, sec. bd. trustees, 1972—; fellow higher edn. Western Res. U., 1943-45. Dir. Indsl. Devel. Corp. Mem. commn. on higher edn. Midwest Program Airborne TV. Trustee Mt. Union Coll.; bd. dirs. Wood County chpt. Am. Cancer Soc. Fellow AAAS; mem. Coll. Pub. Relations Assns. (pres. 1942-43), Ohio Assn. Coll. Admission Officers (pres. 1943-44), Ohio Coll. Assn. (treas. 1963-72, chmn. com. on inspection and membership 1957-63), C. of C., Mid Am. Athletic Conf. (pres. 1962), Am., North Central (v.p. 1951-52, pres. 1952-53), Ohio assns. acad. deans, Ohio Assn. Coll. Presidents and Deans (pres. 1953-54), Am. Ednl. Research Assn., NEA, Arnold Air Soc., Alpha Phi Omega, Omicron Delta Kappa, Alpha Tau Omega (nat. vocat. adv. bd. 1947-57), Pi Gamma Mu, Tau Kappa Alpha, Book and Mortar, Alpha Epsilon Delta. Presbyn. (elder). Mason, Kiwanian. Contbr. articles to edn. publs. Co-editor Looking Toward College, 1942-48, To College in Ohio, 1944. Home: 611 Knollwood Dr Bowling Green OH 43402

MCFARLAN, RONALD LYMAN, electronic engr.; b. Cin., Mar. 8, 1905; s. Frank Grossinger and Mary Ella (Henninger) McF.; A.B., U. Cin., 1926; Ph.D., U. Chgo., 1930; NRC fellow physics, Harvard, 1930-32; m. Ethel Warren White, Sept. 6, 1933; children—Franklin Warren, Ethel Louise Bowen. Instr. physics Harvard, 1932-35; chief physicist United Drug Co., 1935-40, B.B. Chem. Co., 1940-43; dir. research Bulova Watch Co., 1943-46; exec. asst., dir. engring. Raytheon Co., 1946-56; pres. Internat. Med. Tech., 1975—; cons. datamatic div. Mpls.-Honeywell Regulator Co., also Raytheon Co., Boston Safe Deposit and Trust Co. (Mass.), Arthur D. Little, Inc., Searle Medidata, Inc., research and advanced devel. div. AVCO Mfg. Co.; cons. Pickard & Burns div. Gorham Corp.; cons., bd. dirs. Slater Electric, Inc. Mem. engring adv. com. U. Rochester; cons. to pres. Polytech. Inst. Bklyn. Fellow IEEE; mem. IRE (dir. 1957-62, pres. 1960; chmn. profl. group on edn. 1958-59), Inst. Aero. Scis., Am. Phys. Soc., Am. Chem. Soc., Am. Soc. Naval Engrs., Sigma Xi. Home: 68 Pond St Belmont MA 02178

MC FARLAND, FRANK EUGENE, univ. adminstr.; b. Ft. Towson, Okla., Sept. 8, 1918; s. Thomas Edward and Sadie Margaret (Gayer) McF.; B.A. cum laude, Baylor U., 1950; M.A., Columbia U., 1953, Ed.D., 1959; postgrad. U. Tex., 1956, Tex. A. and M. U., 1956; m. Trudy Hudson Lively, Dec. 20, 1947; children—Marsha Lane, Martha Lynne McFarland Cox. Counselor, Tex. A. and M. U., Coll. Sta., 1950-51, acting dir. counseling, 1951, personal and vocat. counselor, 1951-55, instr., 1951-53, asst. prof. psychology, 1953-55, acting dir. testing and research basic div., asst. prof. psychology, 1955-56, dir. testing and research, basic div., asso. prof., 1956-69; dir. student personnel Coll. Arts and Scis., asso. prof. Okla. State U., Stillwater, 1959-61, dean student affairs, prof. psychology, 1961-68, prof. edn. Coll. Edn., 1968-73, dir. student services, prof. applied behavioral studies, 1973—. First v.p. United Fund Stillwater, Inc., 1963-64, pres., 1964-65; cabinet adviser Will Rogers council Boy Scouts Am., 1961-63; mem. Mayor's Com. on Hosp. Adv. Bd., 1963-66. Served with AUS, 1941-45. Decorated Purple Heart with oak leaf cluster, Bronze Star; recipient Okla. State U. Student Senate award of recognition, 1968; Columbia U. faculty fellow, 1952-53; lic. psychologist, Okla. Mem. Am. Psychol. Assn., Am. Personnel and Guidance Assn., Southwestern Assn. Student Personnel Adminstrs., Okla. Personnel, Guidance and Counseling Assn., Okla. Deans and Counselors Assn., Okla. Edn. Assn. (pres. 1972-73), Omicron Delta Kappa (achievement award for outstanding contbn. to Okla. State U. 1968), Phi Delta Kappa, Kappa Delta Pi, Alpha Chi, Psi Chi, Sigma Epsilon Sigma, Phi Kappa Phi. Rotarian. Author: Compilation of Research Studies from 1953-59, 1959; Student Attitudes Toward the Basic Division, 1958; contbr. articles to profl. jours. Home: 1224 N Lincoln St Stillwater OK 74074

MCFARLAND, GERALD WARD, historian; b. Oakland, Calif., Nov. 7, 1938; s. Frank Edimer and Florilla Marguerite (Ward) McF.; B.A., U. Calif., Berkeley, 1960; M.A., Columbia U., 1962, Ph.D., 1965; m. Dorothy June Tuck, Aug. 15, 1964. Mem. faculty dept. history U. Mass., Amherst, 1964—, asso. prof., 1970-75, prof., 1975—, chmn. dept., 1975-78, asst. dean Coll. Arts and Scis., 1966-70. Guggenheim fellow, 1978-79. Mem. Soc. Religion in Higher Edn. (chmn. central com. 1971-72), Am. Hist. Assn., Orgn. Am. Historians, Soc. Values in Higher Edn., Phi Beta Kappa. Author: Mugwumps, Morals and Politics, 1884-1920, 1975; editor: Moralists or Pragmatists? The Mugwumps, 1884-1900, 1975; contbr. numerous articles to profl. jours. Home: 62 Shutesbury Rd Leverett MA 01054 Office: Dept History Univ of Mass Amherst MA 01003

MC FARLAND, HAROLD RICHARD, food co. exec.; b. Hoopeston, Ill., Aug. 19, 1930; s. Arthur Bryan and Jennie (Wilkey) McF.; B.S., U. Ill., 1952; m. Sarah Forney, Dec. 30, 1967. With Campbell Soup Co., Camden, N.J., 1957-67, mgr. purchasing, 1961-67; dir. procurement Keebler Co., Elmhurst, Ill., 1967-69; v.p. purchasing and distbn. Ky. Fried Chicken Corp., Louisville, 1969-74, v.p. food services, sales and distbn., 1974-75; pres., dir. Mid-Continent Carton Co., Louisville, 1974-75, KFC Mfg. Corp., Nashville, 1974-75; pres., dir. McFarland Foods Corp., Indpls., 1975—; dir. Fountain Trust Co., Covington Service Corp. (Ind.), 1975—, Spring Valley Foods, Inc., Empire, Ala., 1972-75; pres., dir. K.F.C. Advt. Inc. (Ind.), 1975—. Chmn. process foods com. World's Poultry Congress, 1974. Life pres. U. Ill. Sr. Class of '52. Served to 1st lt. USAF, 1952-54. Recipient President's award Ky. Fried Chicken Corp., 1970; hon. chief police, Louisville, 1970. Mem. Ky. Restaurant Assn. (dir. 1970-75), Nat. Broiler Council (bd. dirs. 1971-74), Ind. Restaurant Assn., Am. Shorthorn Breeders Assn., Great Lakes K.F.C. Franchise Assn. (dir. 1975—, 1st v.p. 1978-79, pres. 1979-80), Delta Upsilon. Presbyn. Clubs: Main Line Ski (pres. 1964) (Phila.); Wildwood Country. Home: 6361 Avalon Ln East Indianapolis IN 46220 Office: 1815 N Meridian St Indianapolis IN 46202

MCFARLAND, KAY ELEANOR, state justice; b. Coffeyville, Kans., July 20, 1935; d. Kenneth W. and Margaret E. (Thrall) McF.; B.A. magna cum laude, Washburn U., Topeka, 1957, J.D., 1964. Admitted to Kans. bar, 1964; pvt. practice, Topeka, 1964-71; probate and juvenile judge Shawnee County, Topeka, 1971-73; dist. judge, Topeka, 1973-77; justice Kans. Supreme Ct., 1977—; owner, operator Quilts by Kay McFarland, Topeka, 1961-64. Mem. Am., Kans., Topeka bar assns., Dist. Judges Assn., Nat. Assn. Juvenile Judges, Nat. Assn. Probate Judges. Home: 4401 W 10th St Topeka KS 66604 Office: Supreme Ct Kansas State House Topeka KS 66612*

MCFARLAND, KEITH NIELSON, univ. dean; b. Mentor, Minn., Apr. 5, 1921; s. Elmer Leon and Hazel Mae (Nielson) McF.; B.S., U. Minn., 1942, M.A., 1952, Ph.D., 1955; m. Mary Ellen Hanson, June 14, 1946; children—Michael Allen, Susan Ellen. With George A. Hormel & Co., 1937-38, 39-40; faculty Inst. Agr., U. Minn., 1946—, prof., asst. dean, dir. resident instrn., 1960-70, chmn. faculty Coll. Agr., Forestry and Home Econs., 1960-70, acting dean Coll. Home Econs., 1970-73, dean, 1973—. Chmn. resident instrn. sect., div. agr. Assn. State Univs. and Land Grant Colls., 1966-67; AID cons. East Africa, 1965, 69. Bd. dirs. Nat. Council Adminstrs. of Home Econs., 1978—. Served to capt. AUS, 1942-46; lt. col. Res. Recipient Nat. Alumni award 4-H Found., 1960. Mem. Am. Home Econs. Assn., Minn. Personnel and Guidance Assn., Minn. Coll. Personnel Assn., Assn. Minn. Colls. (pres. 1968-69), Minn. Home Econs. Assn., Assn. Adminstrs. Home Econs. (pres. 1979-80), Alpha Zeta, Gamma Sigma Delta, Phi Delta Kappa, FarmHouse, Delta Theta Sigma (hon.), Phi Zeta (hon.). Home: 3254 Sandeen Rd Saint Paul MN 55112

MCFARLAND, MARVIN WILKS, hist. editor, librarian; b. Phila., Nov. 15, 1919; s. Marvin W. and Elizabeth (Foster) McF.; student Girard Coll., 1928-36; A.B., Franklin and Marshall Coll., 1940; student McGill U., 1940, Georgetown U., 1950-51; m. Monica Susan Weber, Nov. 15, 1947; children—Pamela Anne, Ian Ross, James Bruce, Elizabeth Mary, Robert Lewis. Asst. to librarian Girard Coll., 1940-41; asst. manuscripts dept. Hist. Soc. Pa., 1942; spl. cons. to chief aero. div. Library Congress, 1948-53, head aero. sect. sci. and tech. div., 1953-63, asst. chief, 1963-66, chief, 1966—; cons. on Stephen Girard papers and effects to pres. Girard Coll., 1973—; Guggenheim chair aeros., 1954-64; tech. adv. TV film The Winds of Kitty Hawk, 1978. Trustee Air Force Hist. Found., 1958—, v.p., 1963. Served from pvt. to capt. USAF, 1942-48, C.W.S., 1942-43, hist. sect. 8th Air Force, 1943, U.S. Strategic Air Forces in Europe, 1944-45, hist. asst. comdg. gen. USAAF, chief staff USAF, 1946-48. Awarded L'Alliance Francaise medal, 1935, Bronze Star Medal, 1944. Mem. Am. Aviation Hist. Soc., Am. Inst. Aeros. and Astronautics, U.S. Naval Inst., Spl. Library Assn., Phi Beta Kappa. Editor: The Papers of Wilbur and Orville Wright, 2 vols., 1953. Contbr. articles jours. Mem. editorial bd. Air Force Hist. Found., 1956; contbg. editor U.S. Air Services mag., 1956. Contbr. chpts., cons. American Heritage History of Flight, 1962. Home: 2217 Shorefield Rd Wheaton MD 20902 Office: Library of Congress Washington DC 20540

MCFARLAND, NORMAN FRANCIS, bishop; b. Martinez, Calif., Feb. 21, 1922; s. Francis Walter and Agnes (Kotchevar) McF.; A.B., St. Patrick's Coll., Menlo Park, Calif., 1943; postgrad. St. Patrick's Theologate, Menlo Park, 1943-46; J.C.D., Cath. U. Am., 1951. Ordained priest Roman Cath. Ch., 1946; asst. pastor in San Francisco, 1946-48; chief judge of tribunal, vicar gen. Archdiocese of San Francisco, 1951-74, aux. bishop, 1970-74; pastor Mission Dolores, San Francisco, 1970-74; apostolic adminstr. Diocese of Reno-Las Vegas, 1974-76, 4th bishop, 1976—. Mem. Canon Law Soc. Am., Nat. Conf. Cath. Bishops. Home: 843 Marsh Ave Reno NV 89509 Office: 515 Court St Reno NV 89501

MC FARLAND, ROBERT HAROLD, univ. adminstr.; b. Severy, Kans., Jan. 10, 1918; s. Robert Eugene and Georgia (Simpson) McF.; B.S. and B.A., Kans. State Tchrs. Coll., 1940; Ph.M. (Mendenhall fellow), U. Wis., 1943, Ph.D., 1947; m. Twilah Mae Seefeld, Aug. 28, 1940; children—Robert Alan, Rodney Jon. Sci. instr., coach high sch., Chase, Kans., 1940-41; instr. navy radio sch. U. Wis., Madison, 1943-44; sr. engr. Sylvania Elec. Corp., 1944-46; faculty Kans. State U., 1947-60, prof. physics, 1954-60, dir. nuclear lab., 1958-60; physicist U. Calif. Lawrence Radiation Lab., 1960-69; dean Grad. Sch., U. Mo., Rolla, 1969-79, dir. instnl. analysis and planning, 1979—, acting v.p. acad. affairs U. Mo. System, 1974-75. Mem. Grad. Record Exams. Bd., 1971-75. Cons. Well Surveys, Inc., Tulsa, 1953-54, Argonne Nat. Lab., Chgo., 1955-59, Kans. Dept. Pub. Health, 1956-57. Active Boy Scouts Am., 1952—, mem. exec. bd. San Francisco Bay Area council, 1964-68; chmn. Livermore (Calif.) Library Bond drive, 1964. Mem. Kans. N.G., 1936-40. Recipient Silver Beaver award Boy Scouts Am., 1968; Community Service award C. of C., 1965; Distinguished Alumnus award Kans. State Tchrs. Coll., 1969. Fellow Am. Phys. Soc.; mem. AAAS, Am. Assn. Physics Tchrs., Mo. Acad. Sci., AAUP (chpt. pres. 1956-57), Mo. Assn. Phys. Sci. Tchrs., Am. Soc. Engring. Edn., Sigma Xi, Lambda Delta Lambda, Xi Phi, Kappa Mu Epsilon, Kappa Delta Pi, Pi Mu Epsilon, Gamma Sigma Delta, Phi Kappa Phi. Patentee in field lighting, vacuum prodn., controlled thermonuclear reactions. Contbr. articles to profl. jours. Home: 309 Christy Dr Rolla MO 65401. *Continuation of the last hundred years of major progress in the quality* *of life for the human race will not only require the best of our education systems and technological talents but a sincere interest in all of us to contribute positively toward our collective well being.*

MC FARREN, GEORGE ALLEN, educator; b. Akron, Ohio, Nov. 2, 1930; s. Glenn Gilbert and Dorothy Constance (Courtney) Mc F.; B.A., Muskingum Coll., 1952; M.Ed., Kent State U., 1956; Ph.D., Ohio State U., 1962; m. Jean Ruth Finney, Aug. 10, 1957; 1 son, James Andrew. Tchr., Westfield High Sch., Le Roy, Ohio, 1954-55, Byron Jr. High Sch., Shaker Heights, Ohio, 1956-59; instr. Ohio State U., Columbus, 1960-62; asst. prof. Baldwin-Wallace Coll., Berea, Ohio, 1962-65; faculty SUNY Coll., Buffalo, 1965—, prof. social studies edn., 1967—; bd. dirs. Wesley Found., Buffalo. Served with AUS, 1952-54. Mem. Nat. Council Social Studies, Nat. Soc. Study Edn., AAUP, Kappa Delta Pi, Phi Delta Kappa, Delta Tau Kappa. Methodist. Home: 11 Willow Ln Ct Tonawanda NY 14150 Office: 1300 Elmwood Ave Buffalo NY 14222. *Respecting yourself as an individual human being is the key to personal happiness and success. Honesty, integrity, and reliability are the primary characteristics that contribute to enduring success. Individuals must fulfill their responsibilities to the best of their ability with the perspective of contributing to the general welfare of mankind.*

MCFEATTERS, DALE STITT, artist, ret. electric corp. exec.; b. Avella, Pa., Aug. 20, 1911; s. James Dale and Alice Mabel (Stitt) McF.; student Art Inst. Pitts., U. Pitts.; m. Tirzah McHenry Bigham, Sept. 29, 1938; children—Dale Bigham, Ann Carol McFeatters Koepke, Susan Love. Reporter, feature writer, news commentator, fin. editor Pitts. Press., 1931-45; with Westinghouse Electric Corp., Pitts., 1945—, dir. employee info., dir. info. services, v.p., 1954-73; now artist and cartoonist. Republican. Episcopalian. Mason. Clubs: Duquesne, Chartiers Country (Pitts.); Rolling Rock (Ligonier, Pa.); Nat. Press (Washington). Creator nationally syndicated cartoon Strictly Business. Home: 1461 Navahoe Dr Pittsburgh PA 15228 Studio: 701 Washington Rd Mt Lebanon PA 15228

MC FEE, ARTHUR STORER, physician; b. Portland, Maine, May 1, 1932; s. Arthur Stewart and Helen Knight (Dresser) McF.; B.A. cum laude, Harvard U., 1953, M.D., 1957; M.S., U. Minn., 1966, Ph.D., 1967; m. Iris Goeschel, May 13, 1967. Intern, U. Minn. Hosp., 1957-58, resident in surgery, 1958-65; asst. prof. surgery U. Tex. Med. Sch., San Antonio, 1967-70, asso. prof., 1970-74, prof., 1974—; co dir. surg. intensive care unit Bexar County Hosp., San Antonio, 1968—; spl. cons. on emergency med. care text to AAOS. Served with USNR, 1965-67. Diplomate Am. Bd. Surgery. Fellow A.C.S.; mem. Am. Assn. History of Medicine, Assn. Acad. Surgery, AMA, Tex. Med. Assn., Bexar County Med Soc., Tex. Surg. Soc., Western Surg. Soc., San Antonio Surg. Soc., Soc. Surgery Alimentary Tract, So. Med. Assn., N.Y. Acad. Scis., Royal Soc. Medicine. Contbr. articles to profl. jours. Home: 131 Brittany Dr San Antonio TX 78212 Office: 7703 Floyd Curl Dr San Antonio TX 78212

MC FEE, THOMAS STUART, govt. ofcl.; b. Delafield, Wis., Nov. 19, 1930; s. Leon Worrick and Margurette Ella (Morris) McF.; B.S., U. Md., 1953, postgrad., 1956-60; m. Mary Virginia Butler, June 7, 1952; children—Richard Stuart, John Worrick, Charles Paxton. Mathematician math. computation div. David Taylor Model Basin, Navy Dept., Washington, 1956-58, head systems analysis br. ops. research div., 1958-62; project leader weapons systems eval. group Def. Dept., 1962-65; tech. asst. to dir. Sci. and Tech. Office, White House, 1965-66; dir. systems devel. HEW, 1967-69, dep. asst. sec. planning and evaluation, 1969-71, dep. asst. sec. for mgmt. planning and tech., 1971-77, dep. asst. sec. for mgmt., 1977-78, asst. sec. for personnel adminstrn., 1978—. Served with USAF, 1954-56. Mem. Assn. for Computing Machinery, Am. Math. Assn. Office: Office of Personnel Adminstrn HEW 200 Independence Ave SW Washington DC 20201

MCFEELY, WILLIAM SHIELD, historian, educator; b. N.Y.C., Sept. 25, 1930; s. William C. and Marguerite (Shield) M.; B.A., Amherst Coll., 1952; M.A., Yale, 1962, Ph.D., 1966; m. Mary Drake, Sept. 13, 1952; children—William Drake, Eliza, Jennifer. Asst. prof. history and Am. studies Yale, 1966-69, asso. prof., 1969-70; dean faculty Mount Holyoke Coll., 1970-73, prof. history, 1970—; tchr. Yale-Harvard-Columbia intensive summer studies program, 1967-69; vis. prof. history Univ. Coll. London, 1978-79; cons. to com. on judiciary U.S. Ho. of Reps., 1974. Morse fellow, 1968-69; fellow Am. Council Learned Socs., 1974-75, Huntington Library, 1976. Mem. Am., So. hist. assns., Assn. Study Afro-Am. Life and History, Orgn. Am. Historians. Author: Yankee Stepfather: Gen. O.O. Howard and the Freedmen, 1968; (with Thomas J. Ladenburg) The Black Man in the Land of Equality, 1969; co-author: Responses of the Presidents to Charges of Misconduct, 1974. Home: 23 Ashfield Ln South Hadley MA 01075

MC FERON, DEAN EARL, mech. engr.; b. Portland, Oreg., Dec. 24, 1923; s. Wallace Suitor and Ruth Carolyn (Fessler) McF.; student Oreg. State Coll., 1942-43; B.S. in Mech. Engring. with spl. honors, U. Colo., 1945, M.S. in Mech. Engring., 1948; Ph.D., U. Ill., 1956; m. Phyllis Grace Ehlers, Nov. 10, 1945; children—David Alan, Phyllis Ann, Douglas Dean, Donald Brooks. Instr., U. Colo., Boulder, 1946-48; asso. prof. U. Ill., 1948-58; research asso. Argonne (Ill.) Nat. Lab., 1957-58; prof. mech. engring., asso. dean U. Wash., Seattle, 1958—; cons. to industry, 1959-70. Served with USNR, 1942-46. Co-recipient Outstanding Tech. Applications Paper award Am. Soc. Heating, Refrigeration and Air Conditioning Engrs., 1974; Ednl. Achievement award Soc. Mfg. Engrs., 1970; NSF faculty fellow, 1967-68. Mem. ASME, Am. Soc. Engring. Edn., Sigma Xi (nat. dir. 1972—, pres. 1978), Tau Beta Pi, Sigma Tau, Pi Tau Sigma. Home: 3634 42d Ave NE Seattle WA 98105 Office: Dept Mech Engring U Wash Seattle WA 98195

MCGAFFEY, JERE D., lawyer; b. Lincoln, Nebr., Oct. 6, 1935; s. Don Larsen and Doris (Lanning) McG.; B.A., B.Sc. with high distinction, U. Nebr., 1957; LL.B. magna cum laude, Harvard U., 1961; m. Ruth S. Michelsen, Aug. 19, 1956; children—Beth, Karen. Admitted to Wis. bar, 1961; mem. firm Foley & Lardner, Milw., 1961—, partner, 1968—; dir. Wis. Gas Co., Smith Investment Co. Dir., St. Luke's Hosp., Lakeside Children's Center. Served with U.S. Army, 1957-58. Mem. Am. Bar Assn., Wis. Bar Assn., Milw. Bar Assn., Am. Inst. C.P.A.'s, Wis. Inst. C.P.A.'s, Phi Beta Kappa, Beta Gamma Sigma, Delta Sigma Rho. Clubs: University, Milw. Country (Milw.); Harvard (N.Y.C.). Author works in field. Home: 12852 NW Shoreland Dr Mequon WI 53092 Office: 777 E Wisconsin Ave Milwaukee WI 53202

MCGAGH, WILLIAM GILBERT, automobile co. exec.; b. Boston, May 29, 1929; s. Thomas A. and Mary M. (McDonough) McG.; B.S., Boston Coll., 1950; M.B.A., Harvard, 1952; M.S. (Sloan fellow), Mass. Inst. Tech., 1965; m. Sarah Ann McQuigg, Sept. 23, 1961; children—Margaret Ellen, Sarah Elizabeth. Financial analyst Ford Motor Co., Dearborn, Mich., 1953-55; mem. staff treas. office Chrysler Corp., Detroit, 1955-64, comptroller, treas. Chrysler Can. Ltd., Windsor, 1965-67, staff exec.-finance Latin Am. ops., Detroit, 1967-68, asst. treas. Chrysler Corp., 1968-75, treas., 1975-76, v.p., treas., 1976—. Served as 2d lt. USAF, 1952-53. Mem. Fin. Analysts Soc., Fin. Execs. Inst. (pres. Detroit chpt. 1979-80). Clubs: Detroit Athletic, Orchard Lake Country; Renaissance (Detroit); Harvard (N.Y.C.). Home: 1289 Indian Mound West Birmingham MI 48010 Office: Chrysler Corp PO Box 1919 Detroit MI 48288

MCGAHAN, MERRITT WILSON, univ. dean; b. Los Angeles, Mar. 8, 1920; s. Joseph Wilson and Myrtle (Hall) McG.; A.B., U. Calif. at Berkeley, 1948; Ph.D. in Botany, U. Calif. at Davis, 1952; M.Divinity, Union Theol. Sem., N.Y.C., 1966; m. Muriel Johnson, Dec. 24, 1946; children—Susan Elizabeth, Thomas Wilson. Research asso. N.Y. State Coll. Forestry, Syracuse, 1951-52; asst. prof. botany, asst. research prof. forestry U. R.I., 1952-59; plant anatomist United Fruit Co., 1959-63; vis. asso. prof. biology Brandeis U., 1961; dir. campus ministry Riverside Ch., N.Y.C., also Protestant counselor Columbia, 1964-66; dean Grad. Sch., prof. botany, dir. Inst. Sci. Research, N.Mex. Highlands U., Las Vegas, 1966-71, prof. botany, dean acad. affairs, 1971-74, chmn. biology dept., 1974-77, prof. botany, 1977—. Mem. R.I. Sci. Workshop Com., 1956-59, chmn., 1958-59; mem. N.Mex. Certification and Approval Com., 1967-77, chmn., 1975-76; chmn. N.Mex. Adv. Com. Edn., 1968-73. Served with AUS, 1941-45; ETO. Decorated certificate meritorious achievement USAAF, 1944, certificate of merit U.S. Inf., 1945. Mem. Bot. Soc. Am., AAAS, Nat. Assn. Higher Edn., N.Mex. Acad. Sci., Sigma Xi, Phi Sigma Kappa. Presbyn. Author tech. publs. Research in embryology monocotyledons, gen. plant anatomy. Home: Old National Rd Las Vegas NM 87701

MCGANITY, WILLIAM JAMES, physician, educator; b. Kitchener, Ont., Can., Sept. 21, 1923; s. Arthur James and Ethel May (Dryden) McG.; M.D., U. Toronto, 1946; m. Mary Kathryn Hambrock, Dec. 11, 1948; children—Peter Louis James, Martha Lee Jane, Brian David. Came to U.S., 1952, naturalized, 1957. Intern, Toronto Gen. Hosp., 1946-47, fellow in nutrition, 1947-49, resident, 1949-52; practice medicine specializing in obstetrics and gynecology, Galveston, Tex., 1960—; faculty Vanderbilt U. Sch. Medicine, 1952-59, Lowell M. Palmer scholar for med. sci., 1954-56, asso. prof. obstetrics and gynecology, 1956-59; prof., chmn. dept. obstetrics and gynecology U. Tex. Med. Br., Galveston, 1960—, dean of medicine, 1964-67; cons. nutrition program HEW/USPHS, 1956-73, Air Force, 1960—. Mem. com. on internat. nutrition NRC, 1959-63, com. on dietary allowances food and nutrition bd., 1959-63, maternal nutrition food and nutrition bd., 1966-69; mem. nutrition study sect. NIH, 1963-67, mem. research panel childrens bur., 1964-66; panel mem. White House Conf. on Nutrition and Health, 1969; co-chmn. panel nutrition and health, select com. on nutrition and human needs U.S. Senate, 1974; nat. adv. council on maternal, infant and fetal nutrition U.S. Dept. Agr., 1975-78. Served with Canadian Army, 1944-46. Diplomate Am. Bd. Nutrition. Fellow Royal Coll. Physicians and Surgeons Can., Royal Coll. Surgeons Can.; mem. Am., Tex. (past pres.) assns. obstetricians and gynecologists, Am. Coll. Obstetricians and Gynecologists (chmn. task force on nutrition), Am. Inst. Nutrition, AMA (past mem. council on foods and nutrition), Am. Soc. Clin. Nutrition (past pres.) Assn. Profs. Gynecology and Obstetrics, Tex. Med. Assn. (chmn. com. on nutrition and food resources), Galveston County Med. Soc., Soc. Gynecologic Investigation, Southwest Oncology Group, Sigma Xi. Contbr. articles profl. jours. Home: 1402 Harbor View Dr Galveston TX 77550

MCGANN, JOHN RAYMOND, bishop; b. Bklyn., Dec. 2, 1924; s. Thomas Joseph and Mary (Ryan) McG.; student Cathedral Coll. Immaculate Conception, 1944, Sem. Immaculate Conception, Huntington, 1950; LL.D., St. Johns U., 1971; L.H.D., Molloy Coll., 1977; Ordained priest Roman Catholic Ch., 1950, Episcopal ordination, 1971; asst. priest St. Anne's, Brentwood, 1950-57; asst. chaplain St. Joseph Convent, Brentwood, 1950-54; tchr. religion St. Joseph Acad., 1950-54; asso. Cath. chaplain Pilgrim State Hosp., 1950-57; asst. chancellor Diocese of Rockville Centre, 1957-67, vice chancellor, 1967-71; asst. sec. to Bishop Kellenberg, 1957-59; elevated to papal chamberlain, 1959; sec. to Bishop Kellenberg, 1959-70; apptd. titular bishop of Morosbisdus and aux. bishop of Rockville Centre, 1970-76, bishop Rockville Center, 1976—. Del. Sacred Congregation for Religious to Marianists, 1973-76; del. Nat. Conf. Cath. Bishops, Rome, 1974, mem. adminstrv. com., 1977—, mem. Anglican/Roman Cath. task force on pastoral ministry of bishops, 1978—; mem. nat. adv. council U.S. Cath. Conf., 1969-70, mem. health affairs com., 1972-75, mem. adminstrv. bd., 1977—; mem. sem. admissions bd. Diocese Rockville Centre, 1971-76, diocesan boundary commn., 1971-76. Bd. Diocesan Services, Inc., 1971-76, com. that established Consultation Services for Religious, 1972-74; vicar gen. Diocese Rockville Centre, 1971-76, episcopal vicar Suffolk County, 1971-76; mem. N.Y. State Cath. Conf. Com. on Prison Apostolate, 1971-74; mem. U.S. Bishops' Com. for Apostolate of Unity, 1972-76; mem. Rockville Centre Diocesan Bd. Consultors, 1969-76; episcopal mem. N.Y. State Cath. Com., 1974-78; chmn. N.Y. State Bishops' Com. on Elective Process, 1974—, Com. Religious Studies in Pub. Edn., 1975—. Bd. dirs. Good Samaritan Hosp., West Islip, N.Y., 1972-76, chmn., 1976—; trustee Cath. Charities Diocese of Rockville Centre, 1971-76; trustee St. Charles Hosp., Port Jefferson, N.Y., 1972-76, chmn., 1976—; pres. Mercy Hosp., St. Francis Hosp., Diocesan Commodities, Inc., 1976—; chmn. Consolation Residence, 1976—; bd. advisers Sem. Immaculate Conception, 1975—. Home: 29 Quealy Pl Rockville Centre NY 11570 Office: 50 N Park Ave Rockville Centre NY 11570

MC GANNON, DONALD EDWARD, JR., geologist; b. Mpls., Oct. 12, 1929; s. Donald Edward and Bertha Marie (Hein) McG.; student Carleton Coll., 1947-51; B.A., U. Syracuse, 1952; M.S., U. Minn., 1957, Ph.D., 1960; m. Joyce Ingaborg Hafslund, Oct. 29, 1955 (dec. Apr. 1977); children—Gregory Mark, Mark Jefery, Linda Marie; m. 2d, Mary Margrot Hardin, Mar. 8, 1979. Instr., U. Minn., 1957-59; asst. prof. Trinity U., San Antonio, 1959-64, asso. prof., 1964-69, prof. geology, 1969—, chmn. dept., 1959-78, chmn. academic council, 1970, chmn. univ senate, 1973; cons. Mobil Oil Co., 1955, U.S. Geol. Survey, 1958, Shell Oil Co., 1959; Am. Geochem. Soc. translator Russian articles, 1960-68, books, 1965-69; cons. Tex. Hwy. Dept., 1963-68, Witte Mus., others. Pres., dir. Almo Div. Sci. Fair, 1963-68; state dir. sci. fairs, 1967; program dir., pres. PTA, 1970-71; sponsor campus Young Republicans, 1968—. Served with USAF, 1951-54. Trinity U. grantee, 1968-75, NSF grantee, 1965-68, 71, 77, 78; recipient Outstanding Prof. award Trinity U., 1968; Distinguished Achievement award Am. Fedn. Mineral. Socs., 1973. Mem. Geol. Soc. Am. (chmn. field trips Gulf Coast chpt.), Nat. Assn. Geology Tchrs., AAAS, Sigma Xi. Republican. Originator concept of mobil field geology lab.; research on fresh water limestones, environ. geology. Home: 10415 Burr Oak San Antonio TX 78230

MCGANNON, DONALD HENRY, broadcasting exec.; b. N.Y.C., Sept. 9, 1920; s. Robert E. and Margaret (Schmidt) McG.; B.A., Fordham U., 1940, LL.B., 1947, L.H.D., 1964; L.H.D., U. Scranton, 1963, Creighton U., 1965, Emerson Coll., 1966, Fordham U., 1964, Fairfield U., 1967; D.Sc. (hon.), St. Bonaventure U., 1965; m. Patricia H. Burke, Aug. 22, 1942. Admitted N.Y., Conn. bars, 1947; practiced in N.Y.C., 1947-50, Norwalk, Conn., 1947-51; asst. to dir. broadcasting DuMont TV Network, 1951-52, gen. mgr., asst. dir. broadcasting, 1952-55; pres., chmn. bd. Westinghouse Broadcasting Co., Inc. Ind., Md., Del., 1955; chmn. bd. TV Advt. Reps., Inc., Radio Advt. Reps., Inc., WBC Prodns., Inc., Broadcast Rating Council, Inc. Adviser to Pontifical Commn. for Communications Media; chmn. Conn. Commn. for Higher Edn.; mem. broadcasting adv. council Emerson Coll.; chmn. advt. council Coll. Liberal Arts U. Notre Dame, Coll. Arts and Scis. Georgetown U.; mem. communications com. N.Y. Urban Coalition. Trustee, pres. Nat. Urban League; trustee Ithaca Coll., N.Y. Law Sch., N.Y. U.; hon. Fordham U.; founder, dir. trustee Sacred Heart U.; mem. exec. com. council regents St. Francis Coll.; bd. dirs. Radio Free Europe, Acad. TV Arts and Scis. Found., Radio Advt. Bur.; chmn. Advt. Council, Inc. Served as maj. CAC, AUS, 1941-46. Recipient Distinguished Service award Nat. Assn. Broadcasters, 1964; Spl. Emmy award, 1968; Trustees award Nat. Acad. TV Arts and Scis., 1967-68. Clubs: Duquesne (Pitts.); Union League (N.Y.C.). Office: 90 Park Ave New York City NY 10016

MCGANNON, ROBERT EUGENE, lawyer; b. Humboldt, Kans., Jan. 24, 1928; s. Patrick J. and Jane Clare (Barry) McG.; A.B., Rockhurst Coll., 1948; J.D., Georgetown U., 1951; m. Mary Elizabeth Cavanaugh, Sept. 12, 1953; children—Mary E., Maureen C., Robert Eugene, John B., Patrick J. Admitted to Mo. bar, 1951, since practiced in Kansas City; asso. Morelock, Hoskins & King, 1951-56; partner Hoskins, King, McGannon, Hahn & Hurwitz, 1956—, also Strop Watkins Hoskins & King, St. Joseph, Mo., 1974-76. Dir. Wire Rope Corp. of Am., Inc., St. Joseph, Mo., Fidelity Security Life Ins. Co., Ry. Communications, Inc., Kansas City; founding dir. Kansas City (Mo.) Human Rescue; mem. liaison com. Mid-West region Internal Revenue Service. Bd. dirs. St. Martin Tours League, Kansas City (Kans.), Rockhurst Coll. Alumni; former chmn. adv. bd. St. Teresa's Acad., Kansas City; trustee St. Joseph Hosp., Kansas City, Mo. Served with USNR, 1946. Mem. Am., Mo., Kansas City bar assns., Lawyers Assn. Kansas City, Delta Epsilon Sigma, Phi Delta Phi. Clubs: Sertoma (dir.); Indian Hills Country (dir., past pres.) (Mission Hills, Kans.). Home: 2308 W 70th St Shawnee Mission KS 66208 Office: Commerce Bank Bldg Kansas City MO 64106

MCGARA, HOMER JOSEPH, business exec.; b. Trafford, Pa., May 13, 1913; s. Austin J. and Minerva (Young) McG.; M.E., Wayne U., 1942; m. Esther L. Skelding, Dec. 25, 1945; children—Jane A., John S. Engr., Motor Products Corp., Detroit, 1936-49, plant supt., 1949-54; mgr. Macon Arms, Inc., Decatur, Ill., 1954-58; pres. Sheridan Mfg. Co. div. Sheller Globe Corp., Wauseon, Ohio, 1958-71, group v.p., 1969-71; exec. v.p. Globe Wernicke Co., Cin., 1961-63; sr. group v.p. Sheller-Globe Corp., Toledo, 1971-74, sr. v.p., 1974-76, exec. v.p., 1976—. Pres. Wauseon Community Chest, 1971—. Served as capt. C.E., AUS, 1942-46. Mem. C. of C. Republican. Presbyn. Mason (Shriner), Elk, Rotarian (pres. 1971—). Home: 2838 Hasty Rd Toledo OH 43615 Office: 1501 Jefferson Ave Toledo OH 43697

MC GARITY, EDMUND CODY, JR., holding co. exec.; b. Birmingham, Ala., Nov. 8, 1928; s. Edmund Cody and Caroline (Covington) McG.; B.S. in Bus. Adminstrn., Auburn U., 1951; LL.B., Jones Law Sch., Montgomery, Ala., 1964; m. Ann Conway Long, Sept. 26, 1974; children by previous marriage—Marshall Edmund, Charles Alan, William Cody, Michael Laird, Nancy Marie. Admitted to Ala. bar, 1964; with U.S. Pipe and Foundry Co., Birmingham, 1953-75, controller, 1965-68, treas., 1968-75, v.p., treas. adminstrn., 1970-75; adminstrv. v.p. U.S. Home Corp., Clearwater, Fla., 1975-76; v.p. Harrison Industries, Inc., Birmingham, 1976—. Pres. Shades Mountain Community Park, Inc., 1966. Served to 1st lt. AUS, 1946-48, 51-53. Mem. Nat. Assn. Accountants, Birmingham Tax Club (pres. 1967), Financial Execs. Inst., Lambda Chi Alpha, Delta Sigma Pi, Phi Kappa Phi. Episcopalian (trustee 1966-68, sr. warden 1968). Home: 1732 Cedarwood Rd Birmingham AL 35216 Office: Suite 50 2700 Hwy 280 S Birmingham AL 35223

MC GARR, FRANK J., fed. judge; b. 1921; A.B., J.D., Loyola U., Chgo. Admitted to Ill. bar, 1950; now judge U.S. Dist. Ct. for No. Ill. Office: US Dist Ct US Courthouse 219 S Dearborn St Chicago IL 60604*

MC GARR, PAUL ROWLAND, textile co. exec.; b. Webster County, Miss., Nov. 11, 1933; s. Willie B. and Nina Mae (Rowland) McG.; B.S., Miss. State U., 1955; m. Elizabeth Ann Smith, May 1, 1955; children—Paul Rushton, Lee-anne. Indsl. engr., cost accountant ITT, Corinth, Miss. and Raleigh, N.C., 1958-62; treas., exec. v.p. So. Gen. Factors, Inc., High Point, N.C., 1962-66; v.p. fin., sec., treas., dir. Guilford Mills, Inc., Greensboro, N.C., 1966—; dir. Arcadian Shores, Inc., Jacques, Inc. Served with USN, 1955-57. C.P.A., Miss. Mem. Am. Inst. C.P.A.'s. Republican. Lutheran. Club: Masons. Home: 905 Westminster Dr Greensboro NC 27410 Office: PO Drawer U-4 Greensboro NC 27402

MCGARRAH, ROBERT EYNON, educator; b. Scranton, Pa., July 16, 1921; s. Henry Stanley and Jane May (Eynon) McG.; B.S., Lafayette Coll., 1943; M.A., Princeton U., 1948; Ph.D., Cornell U., 1951; m. Barbara Anne Moore, Oct. 20, 1943; children—Robert Eynon, Anne Louise, Douglas Moore. Instr., Princeton, 1946-48; from instr. to asso. prof. indsl. engring., Cornell U., 1948-58; asso. prof. bus. adminstrn. Harvard Grad. Sch. Bus. Adminstrs., 1958-63; prof. Imede Mgmt. Devel. Inst., U. Lausanne (Switzerland), 1963-65; asst. dir. def. research and engring., internat. programs Dept. Def., 1966-68; v.p. Logistics Mgmt. Inst., 1965-66; dir. Center Bus. and Econ. Research, 1968-72, prof. mgmt. Sch. Bus. Adminstrn., U. Mass., Amherst, 1968—, cons. in field, 1948—. Faculty fellow U.S. Gen. Accounting Office, Washington, 1974-75; expert in mgmt. edn. UN-Internat. Labor Orgn. Project on Mgmt. Devel., Nigera, West Africa, 1978. Trustee Moses Brown Preparatory Sch. Served with USNR, 1943-46, 51-53. Mem. Inst. Mgmt. Scis., Am. Assn. U. Profs., Am. Inst. Indsl. Engrs., Phi Kappa Phi. Author: Production and Logistics Management, 1963; Four Volume Production Casebook Series, 1964; also papers. Home: 17 Elm St Amherst MA 01002

MC GARRAH, WILLIAM ERWIN, JR., naval officer; b. Dallas, Feb. 24, 1927; s. William Erwin and Jewel Irene (Bain) McG.; B.S., U.S. Naval Acad., 1950; M.S. in Mech. Engring., U.S. Naval Postgrad. Sch., 1961; postgrad. George Washington U., 1965-69; m. Betty Louise Jacob, June 3, 1950; children—James Mitchell, Donald Richard, Robert Erwin. Commd. ensign U.S. Navy, 1950, advanced through grades to rear adm., 1978; instr. marine engring. U.S. Naval Acad., Annapolis, Md., 1954-56; main propulsion asst. U.S.S. Philippine Sea; engring. duty officer Charleston Naval Shipyard, 1961-64; assignment officer for engring duty officers Bur. Ships, 1964-66; asst. project mgr. Large Helicopter Amphibious Assault Ship Program, Naval Ship Systems Command, 1966-69; Large Helicopter Amphibious Assault Ship field tech. rep., Pascagoula, Miss., 1969-70, dep. supr. shipbldg., 1970-71, supr. shipbldg., 1975-79; asst. chief of staff for engring., staff of comdr. amphibious forces U.S. Atlantic Fleet, 1971-73; dir. ship programs, office of asst. sec. navy (installations and logistics), 1973-75; dep. comdr. ship systems engr. Naval Sea Systems Command, Navy Dept., Washington, 1979—. Bd. dirs. Jackson County (Miss.) United Fund, 1975-79. Registered profl. engr., Miss. Mem. ASME, Am. Soc. Naval Engrs. Methodist. Clubs: Masons, Shriners. Office: Dep Comdr Naval Sea Systems Command for Ship Systems Engring Navy Dept Washington DC 20360

MCGARRELL, JAMES, artist; b. Indpls., Feb. 22, 1930; s. James and Gretchen (Heermann) McG.; B.A., Ind. U., 1953; M.A., U. Calif., Los Angeles, 1955; m. Anna Harris, June 24, 1955; children—Andrew Rider, Flora Raven. Artist-in-residence Reed Coll., Portland, Oreg.,

1956-59; prof. fine arts, dir. grad. painting Ind. U., Bloomington, 1959—; one-man exhbns. include Allan Frumkin Gallery, N.Y.C., 1961, 64, 66, 68, 71, 73, 77, Galerie Claude Bernard, Paris, 1967, 70, 74, Galleria Il Fante de Spade, Rome and Milan, 1967, 71, 72, 74, 76, Utah Mus. Art, Salt Lake City, 1972; represented in permanent collections at Mus. of Modern Art, Whitney Mus. Am. Art, Joseph Hirshman Mus., Washington, Hamburg (Ger.) Mus. Art. Nat. adv. bd. Tamarind Inst., Albuquerque. Fulbright fellow, 1955-56; Guggenheim Found. fellow, 1965; Nat. Endowment for Arts grantee, 1967. Mem. Coll. Art Assn. (bd. dirs. 1969-73), Academie des Beaux Arts de L'Institut de France. Home: 5699 E Lampkins Ridge Bloomington IN 47401 Office: Fine Arts Dept Ind U Bloomington IN 47405

MCGARRY, EUGENE L., univ. ofcl.; b. West Chicago, Ill., June 9, 1930; s. Joseph C. and Rose (Gorgal) McG.; B.A., Cornell Coll., 1952; M.A., Northwestern U., 1956; Ph.D., U. Iowa, 1961; m. Jetta F. Grubbs, June 11, 1955; 1 son, Michael. Asst. prof. social scis. U. Minn., Mpls., 1960-62; asst. prof., advisement coordinator, asso. prof. and asso. dean edn., prof. and dean edn. Calif. State U., Fullerton, 1962-71, asso. v.p. acad. adminstrn., 1971-77, dir. Univ. Learning Center, 1977—. Served with AUS, 1952-54. Home: 403 S Paseo Serena Anaheim CA 92807 Office: 800 N State College Blvd Fullerton CA 92631

MCGARRY, FREDERICK JEROME, educator; b. Rutland, Vt., Aug. 22, 1927; s. William John and Ellen (Dunn) McG.; A.B., Middlebury (Vt.) Coll., 1950; S.B., Mass. Inst. Tech., 1950, S.M., 1953; m. Alice M. Reilly, Oct. 7, 1950 (dec. Jan. 1971); children—Martha Ellen, Alice Catherine, Joan Louise, Carol Elizabeth, Susan Elizabeth, Janet Marian; m. 2d, Ann Freeman Austin, Sept. 17, 1977; stepchildren—Gregory Jacoby, Douglas Jacoby, Alison Jacoby. Faculty, Mass. Inst. Tech., 1950—, prof. civil engring., 1965—, prof. materials sci. and engring., 1974—, head materials div., 1964—, dir. materials research lab., 1964—, asso. dir. inter-Am. program civil engring., 1961—. Recipient Best Paper award Soc. Plastics Industry, 1968. Mem. Soc. Rheology, Soc. Plastics Engrs., Am. Soc. Metals, A.A.A.S., ASTM, Am. Concrete Inst., Sigma Xi. Contbr. numerous articles to profl. jours. Home: 11 Indian Hill Rd Weston MA 02193 Office: Mass Inst Tech Cambridge MA 02139

MCGARRY, JOHN PATRICK, JR., advt. agy. exec.; b. Elizabeth, N.J., Nov. 22, 1939; s. John Patrick and Elizabeth (Weber) McG.; B.S in Mktg. Econs., Villanova U., 1961; m. Gilda R. Spurio, Oct. 24, 1964; children—Victoria Elizabeth, John Patrick, III. Salesman, Exxon Corp., Elizabeth, 1961-64; advt. exec. Young and Rubicam Inc., N.Y.C., 1965-69, sr. v.p., mgmt. supr., 1969—. Bd. dirs. New Youth Performing Theatre, Bedford, N.Y., Regional Rev. League, Westchester, N.Y. Served with U.S. N.G., 1963-69. Democrat. Roman Catholic. Club: Bedord (N.Y.) Golf and Tennis. Home: Cantitoe Rd Bedford Village NY 10506 Office: 285 Madison Ave New York NY 10017

MCGARRY, PATRICK STEPHEN, coll. adminstr.; b. N.Y.C., Sept. 10, 1929; s. Joseph J. and Catherine V. (Woods) McG.; B.A., Manhattan Coll., Bronx, N.Y., 1951; M.A., Columbia U., 1953, Ph.D., 1963. Instr., Manhattan Coll., 1955-60, De LaSalle Coll., Washington, 1961-65; asst. editor Renaissance ch. history New Catholic Ency., Washington, 1963-65; mem. faculty Manhattan Coll., 1965—, prof. history, 1975—, exec. v.p., provost, 1975—; mem. Bros. Christian Schs., Roman Catholic Ch., 1960—; cons. Office Film and Broadcasting, U.S. Cath. Conf. Acad. intern, fellow Am. Council on Edn., 1969-70. Mem. Am., Cath. hist. assns., Nat. Cath. Edn. Assn., Middle Atlantic Radical Historians Orgn., Phi Alpha Theta, Theta Alpha Kappa. Democrat. Contbr. articles to profl. publs. Home: 4415 Post Rd Riverdale Bronx NY 10471 Office: Manhattan Coll Parkway Bronx NY 10471. *I believe that God has given men and women the opportunity to create a better world. Much that is good, great, and enduring has been done by persons who have been instruments of change and goodness. Obscure, unknown, and unremembered, many of these persons may be, but the world is a better place because they touched it.*

MC GARVEY, BRUCE RITCHIE, educator; b. Springfield, Mo., Mar. 10, 1928; s. Phillip Carter and Helen Cornell (Ritchie) McG.; B.A., Carleton Coll., 1950; M.A., U. Ill., 1951, Ph.D., 1953; m. Mathilde Endrody, July 9, 1954; children—Peter, Kathleen, Paul. Instr. U. Calif., 1953-55, asst. prof., 1955-57; asst. prof. chemistry Kalamazoo Coll., 1957-59, asso. prof., 1959-62, co-chmn. dept., 1958-62; asso. prof. inorganic and phys. chemistry Poly. Inst. Bklyn., 1962-66, prof., 1966-72, acting dept. head, 1971-72; prof. chemistry U. Windsor (Ont., Can.), 1972—. Active Boy Scouts Am., Boy Scouts Can. Served with AUS, 1946. Guggenheim fellow, 1967-68; AEC predoctoral fellow, 1951-53; recipient research grants Research Fund, 1959, Petroleum Research Fund, 1960, NSF, 1964-70, Nat. Research Council Can., 1972—, NATO, 1978—. Fellow Chem. Inst. Can.; mem. Am. Chem. Soc., Am. Phys. Soc., Can. Inst. Chemists, Can. Assn. U. Tchrs., Phi Beta Kappa, Sigma Xi, Phi Lambda Upsilon. Mem. United Ch. Can. Asso. editor of Jour. Chem. Physics, 1966-69; editorial bd. Jour. Magnetic Resonance, 1976—. Contbr. articles to profl. jours. Home: 4019 Roseland Dr E Windsor ON N9G 1Y5 Canada

MC GAUGH, JAMES LAFAYETTE, psychobiologist; b. Long Beach, Calif., Dec. 17, 1931; s. William Rufus and Daphne (Hermes) McG.; B.A., San Jose State U., 1953; Ph.D. (Abraham Rosenberg fellow), U. Calif. at Berkeley, 1959; sr. post-doctoral fellow Nat. Acad. Scis.-NRC, Istituto Superiore di Sanita, Rome, Italy, 1961-62; m. Carol J. Becker, Mar. 15, 1952; children—Douglas, Janice, Linda. Asst. prof., asso. prof. psychology San Jose State U., 1957-61; asso. prof. psychology U. Oreg., 1961-64; asso. prof., founding chmn. dept. psychobiology U. Calif. at Irvine, 1964-67, 71-74, prof., 1966—, dean Sch. Biol. Sci., 1967-70, vice chancellor acad. affairs, 1975-77, exec. vice chancellor, 1978—. Mem. adv. coms. NIMH, 1962-78. Fellow Am. Psychol. Assn., AAAS; mem. Internat. Brain Research Orgn., Soc. for Neurosci., Am. Coll. Neuropsychopharmacology, Psychonomic Soc., Phi Beta Kappa, Sigma Xi. Author: (with J.B. Cooper) Integrating Principles of Social Psychology, 1963; (with H.F. Harlow, R.F. Thompson) Psychology, 1971; (with M.J. Herz) Memory Consolidation, 1972; Learning and Memory: An Introduction, 1974; (with R.F. Thompson and T. Nelson) Psychology I, 1977; (with C. Cotman) Behavioral Neuroscience, 1979. Editor: (with N.M. Weinberger, R.E. Whalen) Psychobiology, 1966; Psychobiology-Behavior from a Biological Perspective, 1971; The Chemistry of Mood, Motivation and Memory, 1972; (with M. Fink, S.S. Kety, T.A. Williams) Psychobiology of Convulsive Therapy, 1974; (with L.F. Petrinovich) Knowing, Thinking, and Believing, 1976; (with R.R. Drucker-Colin) Neurobiology of Sleep and Memory, 1977; Behavioral Biology, 1972-78, Behavioral and Neural Biology, 1979—; editorial bd. Brain Research, Psychopharmacology Communications, Behavior Research Methods and Instrumentation, Jour. Exptl. Psychology: Animal Behavior Processes. Home: 2327 Aralia St Newport Beach CA 92660 Office: Dept Psychobiology U Calif Irvine CA 92717

MC GAUGHAN, ALEXANDER STANLEY, architect; b. Phila., May 18, 1912; s. Henry T. and Mable (Colgan) McG.; B.Arch., U. Mich., 1934; m. M. Virginia Storm, July 11, 1936; 1 son, Alexander Stanley. Draftsman, designer, Pontiac, Mich., 1934-36; architect Resettlement Adminstrn. and Farm Security Adminstrn., 1936-44; labor economist, planner WPB, Washington, 1944-45; housing economist, prodn. engr. Nat. Housing Agy., Washington, 1945-47; indsl. designer Cairns Corp., N.Y.C., also Hugh Johnson Assos., Washington, 1947-50; partner McGaughan & Johnson, Washington, 1950—; spl. cons. Nat. Security Resources Bd., Def. Prodn. Adminstrn., HHFA, HUD, Dept. of Def. Mem. D.C. Bd. Examiners and Registrars of Architects, 1966-73, pres., 1969-72; dir. Middle Atlantic region Nat. Council Archtl. Registration Bds., 1966-73, chmn., 1970-71, chmn. com. on design and site planning, 1972-73; bd. govs. Washington Bldg. Congress, 1968-71, bd. dirs., 1973-76; mem. Pres.'s Com. on Employment Handicapped, 1974—; bd. dirs. Nat. Center for Barrier Free Environment, 1974-79. Works include Charred Oak Estates (Md.), doctors residence D.C. Gen. Hosp., housing Carlisle Barracks (Pa.), Washington pub. schs., Andrew Radar Clinic (Ft. Meyer, Va.), D.C. Police Acad., 2d, 4th and 5th dist. police stas., D.C. Recipient 1st award for contemporary architecture and land planning Md. Homebuilders, 1962, distinguished urban landscape award U.S. Army C.E., 1968, distinguished archtl. award U.S. Army C.E., 1969, nat. archtl. award of excellence Am. Inst. Steel Constrn., 1973. Fellow AIA (pres. Washington met. chpt. 1963, chmn. nat. com. archtl. competitions 1966-67, mem. barrier free task force 1974-77, rep. to Am. Nat. Standards Inst. A 117.1 Com. 1977—); mem. Soc. Archtl. Historians, Nat. Trust for Historic Preservation, Constrn. Specifications Inst., Am. Arbitration Assn. (nat. panel arbitrators). Club: Cosmos (Washington). Patentee aluminum bldg. systems. Home: 11509 Hornfair Ct Potomac MD 20854 Office: 1325 Massachusetts Ave NW Washington DC 20005

MC GAUGHY, JOHN BELL, civil engr.; b. Norfolk, Va., Nov. 5, 1914; s. John Bell and Frances Vivian (Coleman) McG.; student U. Va., 1933-35; B.S. in Civil Engring., Duke U., 1938; m. Charlotte Edna Schwartz, Jan. 20, 1940 (dec. Dec. 1978); 1 son, John Bell. Asst. to project engr. U.S. Dept. Agr., Farmville, Va., 1936-37; tech. asst. civil engring. sect. U.S. Coast Guard, Norfolk, Va., 1938-39; civil engr. constrn. q.m. U.S. Army, Albrook Field, C.Z., 1939-41; chief mil. design sect. U.S. Engrs. Office, Norfolk, 1941-43; sr. partner Lublin, McGaughy & Assos., architects and cons. engrs., Norfolk, 1945-65; pres. McGaughy, Marshall & McMillan, Norfolk, Washington, Grand Island, Nebr., Frankfurt, W.Ger., and Athens, Greece, 1965—; spl. cons. Office Coal Research U.S. Dept. Interior; mem. Va. Gov.'s Met. Areas Study Commn.; chmn. faculty Norfolk extension U. Va., 1943-46. Named Va. Engr. of Yr., 1970. Fellow ASCE, ASTM, Am. Cons. Engrs. Council; mem. Am. Concrete Inst., Am. Road Bldg. Assn. (dir. engring. div. 1966-68), Prestressed Concrete Inst., Nat. Soc. Profl. Engrs. (v.p. 1957-59), Va., Norfolk (dir. 1960-63) chambers of commerce, Va. Soc. Profl. Engrs. (past pres.), Engrs. Club Hampton Roads (past pres.), Soc. Am. Mil. Engrs., Va. Engring. Found. (dir. 1970-72), Phi Delta Theta, Thelta Tau. Clubs: Cedar Point Golf (Suffolk); Harbor, Norfolk Yacht and Country (Norfolk). Home: 5905 Studeley Ave Norfolk VA 23508 Office: 229 W Bute St PO Box 269 Norfolk VA 23501

MCGAVERN, JOHN HOWARD, librarian; b. Cambridge, Mass., Dec. 23, 1926; s. Howard Allen and Gertrude (Ober) McG.; B.A., Harvard, 1949; M.A., Simmons Sch. Library Sch., 1954. Circulation asst. Widener Library, Harvard, 1952-54, reference librarian Lamont Library, 1954, acquisitions librarian Baker Library, 1955-59; reference librarian Hillyer Coll., 1959-60; univ. librarian U. Hartford (Conn.), 1960—. Mem. New Eng. (treas. 1962), Conn. library assns., Capital Region Library Council (dir. 1976—), Buddhist Soc. (London). Home: 967 Asylum Ave Apt 2G Hartford CT 06105

MCGAVIN, DARREN, actor, dir., producer; b. Spokane, Wash.; s. Reid Delano Richardson and Grace (Bogart) McG.; student U. of Pacific, 1 year, Neighborhood Playhouse, 6 months; student Actors Studio; m. Kathie Browne, Dec. 31, 1969; children—York, Megan, Bridget, Bogart. Films include: Fear, 1946, Summer Madness, 1955, The Court Martial of Billy Mitchell, 1955, The Man with the Golden Arm, 1956, The Delicate Delinquent, 1957, Beau James, 1957, The Case Against Brooklyn, 1958, Bullet for a Madman, 1964, The Great Sioux Massacre, 1963, Mrs. Pollifax, Spy, 1970, The Petty Story, 1972, B Must Die, 1973, No Deposit, No Return, 1975, Mission Mars, Airport '77, 1977, Hot Lead and Cold Feet, 1978; plays include: Death of a Salesman, My Three Angels, The Rainmaker, Tunnel of Love, The Lovers, The King and I, Blood, Sweat and Stanley Poole, Dinner at Eight, Captain Brassbound's Conversion; TV series: Mike Hammer, 1958, Riverboat, 1960, The Outsider, 1968, The Night Stalker, 1974-75; TV films: The Challenge, 1970, Tribes, 1970, Something Evil, 1972, Law and Order, 1976, Brink's, 1976; directorial debut with film: Happy Mother's Day . . . Love, George, 1973; pres., chief exec. Taurean Films, S.A., Tympanum Corp. Mem. Screen Actors Guild, Actors Equity Assn., Dirs. Guild Am., Writers Guild Am., A.F.T.R.A. .

MC GAVOCK, WILLIAM GILLESPIE, educator; b. Franklin, Tenn., Dec. 31, 1909; s. John and Mary (Gillespie) McG.; B.S., Davidson Coll., 1930; M.A., Duke, 1933, Ph.D., 1939; student Princeton, 1936-37, U. Wis., 1954-55, Cornell U., 1967; m. Sarah Herbert Nolen, June 11, 1931; children—David Nolen, Martha Randal. Tchr., Branham and Hughes Mil. Acad., Spring Hill, Tenn., 1930-32, Morgan Sch., Petersburg, Tenn., 1933-34; mem. faculty Davidson (N.C.) Coll., 1934-70, prof. math., 1946-70, Dana Distinguished prof. math., chmn. dept., 1949-67; vis. prof. Duke, 1943-44, Emory U., 1944-45. Mem. So. Regional Selection Com. Ford Faculty Fellowships, 1951-54. Chmn. Mecklenburg County Civil Service Bd.; mem. Mayor Davidson Community Com.; moderator Concord Presbytery, Presbyn. Ch.; active local Boy Scouts Am. Dir. Charlotte Fresh Air Camp. Recipient Thomas Jefferson Distinguished Prof. award, 1964; Gen. Edn. Bd. fellow, 1936-38; Ford faculty fellow, 1954-55; Grantee NSF, 1956, 62, 64. Mem. Math. Assn. Am., N.C. Acad. Sci. (chmn. math. sect. 1940, 53), AAUP, Phi Beta Kappa, Omicron Delta Kappa, Sigma Pi Sigma, Kappa Alpha. Democrat. Presbyn. (elder). Author articles. Home: 225 Roundway Down Davidson NC 28036

MC GAW, ALEX JAMES, civil engr.; b. Belfast, Ireland, Mar. 2, 1909; s. Robert and Mina (McClue) McG.; came to U.S., 1912, naturalized, 1938; A.B., U. Wyo., 1933, B.S. with honors, 1934, C.E., 1937; m. Margaret Hopkins, Dec. 20, 1931 (dec. Apr. 22, 1973); children—Jo Ann, Michael Robert, Nancy Kathleen; m. 2d, Louise Olson, Nov. 21, 1973. Asst. combustion engr. Standard Oil Co., Ind., Aruba, N.W.I., 1929-31; structural engr. Standard Oil Co., N.J., Aruba, 1934; spl. engr. Wyo. State Engrs. Office, 1935; faculty U. Wyo., 1935-74, prof. civil engring., 1943-74, prof. emeritus, 1974—; head dept. civil and archtl. engring., 1948-64, acting dean Grad. Sch., 1949, Coll. Engring., 1952, dean engring., 1964-71, asst. to pres. for devel., 1971-74; city engr. City of Laramie, Wyo., 1940, 41; head structural design Toltz, King & Day, engrs., architects, air base, Casper, Wyo., 1942; cons. engr., 1940—. Chmn., Laramie Zoning Commn., 1941-46; chmn. Bldg. Com.; trustee Ivinson Meml. Hosp., 1960-66, pres., 1962-64. Named Engr. of Yr., Wyo., 1967. Fellow AAAS, ASCE (pres. Wyo. sect. 1940; life mem., hon. mem.); mem. Wyo. Engring. Soc. (pres. 1955), Wyo. Reclamation Soc., Am. Soc. Testing Materials (Rocky Mountain council 1958-60), Am. Soc. Engring. Edn. (chmn. archtl. engring. div. 1957, mem. gen. council 1958-60), Nat. Soc. Profl. Engrs. (dir. 1957-63), Laramie Planning Bd. (sec. 1943-45), Laramie C. of C., Sigma Xi, Sigma Tau, Sigma Alpha Epsilon. Republican. Episcopalian. Club: Laramie Country (pres. 1948). Home: 1221 Garfield Laramie WY 82070

MC GAW, FOSTER GLENDALE, hosp. supply exec.; b. Hot Springs, N.C., Mar. 7, 1897; s. Francis Alexander and Alice S. (Millar) McG.; grad. Keokuk (Iowa) High Sch., 1916; extension courses Northwestern U.; L.H.D., Ill. Wesleyan U., 1953, Loyola U., Chgo., 1972, Northwestern U., 1973, Nat. Coll. Edn., Evanston, Ill., 1974; D.M.S., Sch. of Ozarks, Point Lookout, Mo., 1978; m. Mary Wallace Harrison, Dec. 14, 1921 (dec.); m. 2d, Mary Wettling Vail, June 15, 1949. Founder Am. Hosp. Supply Corp., Chgo., 1922, now hon. chmn. bd., dir.; hon. dir. 1st Nat. Bank & Trust, Evanston. Life trustee Northwestern U., Nat. Coll. Edn., Evanston, Ill., Coll. of Wooster (Ohio); hon. dir. McGaw Med. Center of Northwestern U., Chgo., Presbyn. Home, Evanston. Served sgt. maj. USMC, 1918-19. Recipient Greater Chgo. Churchman award, 1968; Decision-Maker of Year award Chgo. chpt. Am. Statis. Assn., 1969; Distinguished Citizen award Ill. St. Anthony Soc., 1970; Distinguished Citizen citation Protestant Found. Greater Chgo., 1971; Trustee award Am. Protestant Hosp. Assn., 1972; Sword of Loyola, Loyola U., Chgo., 1973; Merit award Rotary Club Chgo., 1974; Maker of Chgo. award Chgo. Assn. Commerce and Industry, 1976; Outstanding Philanthropist, Nat. Soc. Fund Raising Execs., 1979; Citizen fellow Inst. Medicine Chgo. Fellow Am. Coll. Hosp. Adminstrs. (hon.); mem. Evanston C. of C., Art Inst. Chgo. (life), Chgo. Symphony Soc. (life). Presbyn. Clubs: Chicago, Rotary, Economic, Commercial, Execs., Northwestern U.; Glen View (Golf, Ill.); Indian Hill (Winnetka, Ill.); Onwentsia (Lake Forest, Ill.); Mid America. Office: PO Box 1038 Evanston IL 60204

MC GAW, ROBERT WALTER, mayor Rockford (Ill.); b. Rockford, Apr. 9, 1923; s. James Lincoln and Loren (Lynch) McG.; B.S., No. Ill. U., 1950, M.S., 1966; m. Margaret Arlene Schindler, June 21, 1946; children—Marlis Jean McGaw Young, Roberta Sue, Raymond William. With Shabhona (Ill.) Pub. Sch., 1950-52; tchr. Harlem Consol. Schs., Loves Park, Ill., 1952-72, tchr., 1952-68, adminstr. Rock Cut Sch., Rockford, 1968-72; alderman City of Rockford, 1955-63; del. Nat. Dem. Conv., 1968, 72, county chmn., 1962-64; mayor, Rockford, 1972—. Served with U.S. Army, 1942-46. Mem. NEA, Ill. Edn. Assn., Ill. Mcpl. League (pres. 1979-80). VFW. Clubs: Masons, Moose. Office: Office of Mayor City Hall 425 E State St Rockford IL 61104

MCGEACHY, JOHN ALEXANDER, JR., educator; b. Wilmington, N.C., Mar. 28, 1911; s. John Alexander and Helen (Mabry) McG.; A.B., Davidson Coll., 1934; M.A., U.N.C., 1936; Ph.D., U. Chgo., 1942; m. Margaret Cathey, Oct. 18, 1945; 1 son, John Alexander III. Asso. prof. history Davidson Coll., 1938-50, prof., 1950-77, Mary Reynolds Babcock prof. history, 1961-77, prof. emeritus, 1977—. Served to sgt., Signal Corps, AUS, 1942-45. Mem. Am. Hist. Assn. Mediaeval Acad. Am., Am. Archaeol. Inst., Phi Beta Kappa. Presbyn. (elder). Author: Q. Aurelius Symmachus and the Senatorial Aristocracy of the West, 1942. Home: Davidson NC 28036

MCGEADY, LEON JOSEPH, educator; b. Freemansburg, Pa., July 5, 1921; s. Gerald and Elda (Smock) McG.; B.S. in Metall. Engring., Lehigh U., 1943, M.S., 1946, Ph.D., 1950; m. Anne Peters, Sept. 5, 1949. Research asso. Lehigh U., 1943-49; faculty Lafayette Coll., 1949—, prof. metall. engring., chmn. dept., 1957—. Researchers, Welding Research Council, 1955—; ind. metall. cons., 1953—. Mem. Am. Soc. Metals (chmn. Lehigh Valley 1957); Am. Welding Soc., Am. Soc. Engring. Edn., Am. Inst. Mining, Metall. and Petroleum Engrs. Contbr. articles to profl. jours. Home: 404 Center St Bethlehem PA 18018

MCGEARY, ROBERT WILLIAM, corp. exec.; b. Atlantic City, June 3, 1931; s. Expedit William and Esther (Feeney) McG.; A.B., U. Ala., 1953; M.A. (Rockefeller scholar), U. Pa., 1954; m. Patricia Ann Langan, Sept. 2, 1950; children—Kathleen A., Robert W., Maureen P., Kevin J., William S., John P. Mgmt. analyst Navy Dept., Washington, 1954-56; asst. to pres. Leahy & Co., N.Y.C., 1956-58; mgr. systems planning Am. Standard Corp., N.Y.C., 1958-60; v.p. Leahy & Co., N.Y.C., 1960-62; project dir. Logistics Mgmt. Inst., Washington, 1962-63; dir. mgmt. information services Lever Bros., N.Y.C., 1963-65, asst. comptroller, 1965-67, comptroller, 1967-68; pres. Lever Data Processing Services, Inc., 1968-72; dir. data processing marketing div. Reuben H. Donelley Corp., 1972-76; v.p. Donnelley Mktg., 1976—. Vice pres. Elmsford (N.Y.) Ednl. Assn., 1964-65. Served with USMCR, 1951. Contbr. articles to profl. jours. Home: 90 Windom St White Plains NY 10607 Office: 1515 Summer St Stamford CT 06905

MC GEE, DEAN ANDERSON, petroleum co. exec.; b. Humbolt, Kans., Mar. 20, 1904; s. George Gentry and Gertrude Hattie (Sayre) McG.; B.S. in Mining Engring., Kans. U., 1926; LL.D., Oklahoma City U., 1957; D.Sc. (hon.), Bethany Nazarene Coll., 1967; D.Eng. (hon.), Colo. Sch. Mines, 1968; L.H.D., Okla. Christian Coll., 1975; m. Dorothea Antoinette Swain, June 28, 1938; children—Marcia Ann, Patricia Dean. Geology instr. Kans. U., 1926-27; petroleum geologist Phillips Petroleum Co., Bartlesville, Okla., 1927, chief geologist, 1935-37; v.p. charge prodn., exploration Kerr-McGee Oil Industries, Inc. (now Kerr-McGee Corp.), Oklahoma City, 1937-42, exec. v.p., 1942-54, pres., 1954-67, chmn., 1963-67, chmn. bd., chief exec. officer, 1967—; pres., dir. Kerr-McGee Bldg. Corp., dir. Kerr-McGee Chem. Corp.; v.p. Downtown Airpark, Inc.; v.p. Am. Potash and Chem. Corp.; trustee Okla. Authority; owner McGee-Keesee Angus Ranch; dir. Kerr-McGee Coal Corp., Kerr-McGee Iranian Oil CO., Mine Contractors, Inc., Kerr-McGee Nuclear Corp., Sunningdale Oils Ltd., Kerr-McGee Oil (U.K.) Ltd., Kerr-McGee Resources Corp., Kerr-McGee Tunisia Ltd., Southwestern Oil & Refining Co., Inc., Southwestern Refining Co., Inc., Transworld North Sea Drilling Services Ltd., Triangle Refineries, Inc., Kerr-McGee Australia, Ltd., Internat. Creosoting & Constrn. Co., Fidelity Bank N.A., Transworld Drilling Co.; dir. emeritus Gen. Electric Co. Trustee Okla. Zool. Soc., Presbyn. Hosp., Calif. Inst. Tech., Oklahoma City Indsl. and Cultural Facilities Trust, Southwest Research Inst., San Antonio, Midwest Research Inst., Kansas City, Mo., Oklahoma City U., Kans. U. Endowment Assn., Okla. Eye Found.; pres., dir. Kerr-McGee Found., Inc., McGee Found., Inc.; mem. Okla.'s Future, Inc.; dir., trustee, vice-chmn. bd. Okla. Safety Council; mem. Oklahoma City Arts Council; bd. dirs. Oklahoma City U. Found., Okla. Med. Research Found., Oklahoma City Symphony Soc., Ark. Basin Devel. Assn., NCCJ, Oklahoma City; dir. Okla. State Fair and Expn.; chmn. exec. com. Okla. Health Scis. Found.; trustee, mem. exec. com., hon. life mem. bd. dirs. Nat. Cowboy Hall Fame; trustee Scis. and Natural Resources Found. Okla.; advisory bd. Coll. Bus. Adminstrn. U. Okla., 1975; mem. governing bd. Okla. Center Sci. and Arts, Inc., 1976, Rhodes Scholarship Trust, 1968-74; mem. Rockefeller U. Council. Recipient numerous honors and awards, including Erasmus Haworth Distinguished Alumni award in geology U. Kans., 1951; Kans. U. Alumni Citation for Distinguished Service, 1951; Outstanding Civilian Service award Dept. Army, 1965; Nat.

Brotherhood citation NCCJ, 1961; Headliner of Year award, 1968; Golden Plate award Am. Acad. Achievement, 1969; Outstanding Oil Man award Okla. Petroleum Council, 1970; Oklahoma City Beautiful award, 1973; citation Midwest Research Inst., 1973; Henry G. Bennett Distinguished Service award Okla. State U., 1974; Distinguished Service citation U. Okla. Regents and Alumni Assn., 1966, Oklahoma City Advt. Club, 1976; Distinguished Friend award Okla. City U., 1978; elected to Okla. Hall of Fame, 1958, U. Okla. Med. Scis. Hall Fame, 1958, U. Okla. Acad. Fellows, 1970, Nat. Petroleum Hall of Fame Disting. Service award, 1977, 25 Year Club Petroleum Industry, 1978, others. Fellow AAAS, Okla. Acad. Sci.; mem. Oklahoma City Geol. Soc., Nat. Petroleum Council, Am. Assn. Petroleum Geologists (hon. life mem.; recipient Pub. Service award 1974 Sidney Powers award 1975), Am. Petroleum Inst. (dir., exec. com.), Am. Inst. Profl. Geologists, Ind. Petroleum Assn. Am. (dir.), Nat., Okla. socs. profl. engrs., Am. Mining Congress, Tex. Mid-Continent (dir., Distinguished Service award 1975), Mid-Continent (exec. com.) oil and gas assns., AIA (hon. life), Soc. Econ. Paleontologists and Mineralogists, U. Okla. Assos. (founding chmn. 1979), Oklahoma City C. of C. (dir.), Navy League U.S., Okla. Hist. Soc. (life), AIME (hon.), Atomic Indsl. Forum, Okla. Bus. Edn. Assn. (adv. bd. to exec. bd.), Newcomen Soc. N. Am. (award 1970), Sigma Xi, Pi Epsilon Tau, Acacia, Tau Beta Pi, Delta Sigma Pi, Theta Tau, Beta Gamma Sigma (hon.), Sachem. Democrat. Presbyn. Mason (Shriner, Jester). Clubs: Oklahoma City Golf and Country, Men's Dinner, Sirloin (dir.), Whitehall, Oklahoma City Press, Oklahoma City Petroleum, Beacon, Touchdown. Contbr. articles to profl. jours. Office: Kerr-McGee Center PO Box 25861 Oklahoma City OK 73125

MCGEE, GALE, ambassador; b. Lincoln, Nebr., Mar. 17, 1915; s. Garton W. and Frances (McCoy) McG.; A.B., Nebr. State Tchrs. Coll., 1936; M.A., U. Colo., 1939; Ph.D., U. Chgo., 1947; LL.D., U. Wyo., 1965, Eastern Ky. U., 1967, Am. U., 1967, Allegheny Coll., 1969; L.H.D., Seton Hall U., 1969; m. Loraine Baker, June 11, 1939; children—David, Robert, Mary Gale, Lori Ann. Tchr. high sch., 1936-40; instr. history Nebr. Wesleyan U., Iowa State Coll., U. Notre Dame, U. Chgo., 1940-46; prof. history U. Wyo., 1946-58, also dir. Inst. Internat. Affairs; legis. asst. Sen. Joseph O'Mahoney, 1955-56; mem. U.S. Senate from Wyo., 1958-77, chmn. Western Hemisphere affairs of senate fgn. relations com., chmn. subcom. on agr., environ. and consumer protection of senate appropriations com., chmn. post office and civil service com.; U.S. permanent rep. U.S. Mission to OAS, 1977—; mem. U.S. del. 27th Gen. Assembly UN, 1972; profl. lectr. fgn. policy; Internat. Knife and Fork lectr., 1947—. Wyo dir. Crusade for Freedom; N.W. dir. Theodore Roosevelt Centennial Observance; dir. tour to Russia, 1956; study of Soviet intentions Council Fgn. Relations, N.Y.C., 1952-53. Mem. AAUP, Am., Miss. Valley hist. assns., Theodore Roosevelt Assn., Izaak Walton League, Wyo. Edn. Assn. Club: Eagles. Author: The Responsibilities of World Power, 1968. Home: Dubois WY 82513 Office: Dept State Room 6494 Washington DC 20520

MCGEE, JAMES HOWELL, lawyer; b. Berryburg, W.Va., Nov. 8, 1918; s. Spanish and Perrie (Dalton) McG.; B.S., Wilberforce U., 1941; LL.B., Ohio State U., 1948; m. Elizabeth McCracken, Jan. 23, 1948; children—Annette, Frances. Admitted to Ohio bar, 1949, since practiced in Dayton. Past pres., bd. dirs. Dayton br. N.A.A.C.P.; pres., bd. dirs. Dayton Urban League. Commr. City of Dayton, 1967-70, mayor, 1970—. Served with AUS, 1942-45; ETO. Mem. Alpha Phi Alpha. Home: 1518 Benson Dr Dayton OH 45406 Office: 1526 W 3d St Dayton OH 45407

MC GEE, JOHN FRAMPTON, communications co. exec.; b. Charleston, S.C., Jan. 9, 1923; s. Hall Thomas and Gertrude (Frampton) McG.; B.S. in Bus. and Polit. Sci., Davidson Coll., 1943; m. Ruth Bouknight Smedley, June 19, 1971; children—Beverly C. McGee Kinder, Catharine F. McGee Mebane, Charles V. Smedley. With Charleston (S.C.) Post-News and Courier, 1946-62; asst. gen. mgr. State-Record Newspapers, Columbia, S.C., 1962-64, gen. mgr., pres., co-pub., 1964-69; gen. exec. Knight Newspaper, Inc., Miami, Fla., 1969-70; pres., associated pub. Charleston (W.Va.) Daily Mail, 1970—; pres. Clay Communications, Inc., parent co. Charleston Daily Mail, Raleigh Register, Beckley Post Herald, TV Stas.-WWAY, N.C., KFDX, Tex., KJAC, Tex., WAPI, Miss., dir. AP, N.Y.C.; Kanawha Banking & Trust Co., Charleston, W.Va.; mem. adv. bd. Sch. Journalism, W.Va. U. Bd. dirs. Charleston Area Med. Center Found.; mem. gen. exec. bd. Presbyterian Ch., U.S.A., 1974-76; mem. S.C. Commn. for Higher Edn., 1966-69. Served to capt. inf. U.S. Army, 1943-45. Decorated Purple Heart (2), Bronze Star with 3 oak leaf clusters (U.S.); Croix de Guerre with palm (France and Belgium). Mem. So. Newspaper Pubs. Assn. (chmn. labor com. 1967-68, chmn. new processes com. 1966-67, dir. 1967-69), Internat. Press Inst., W.Va. Press Assn. (pres. 1977-78), New Eng. Soc. S.C. Clubs: Cosmos (Charleston, W.Va.); Edgewood Country of W.Va. Home: 801 Louden Heights Rd Charleston WV 25314 Office: 1001 Virginia St E Charleston WV 25301

MCGEE, JOSEPH JOHN, JR., ins. co. exec.; b. Kansas City, Mo., Dec. 2, 1919; s. Joseph J. and Margaret (Cronin) McG.; student Rockhurst Coll., Kansas City, Georgetown U.; m. Anne Cunningham, Apr. 30, 1949; children—Sally, Peter, Mary, John, David, Julie, Simon. Asst. sec. Old Am. Ins. Co., Kansas City, Mo., 1939-45, v.p., 1946-51, exec. v.p., 1952-55, pres., 1956—; dir. Kansas City Title div. Chgo. Title Ins. Co., Gas Service Co., Commerce Bancshares, Safety Fed. Savs. & Loan Assn. Chmn., Kansas City Postal Customers' Council. Bd. dirs. Truman Med. Center, Truman Library Inst. for Nat. and Internat. Affairs, Am. Royal Assn.; pres. bd. trustees Notre Dame de Sion; trustee Rockhurst Coll.; trustee Kansas City Employees Retirement System; chmn. McGee Found. Home: 1045 W 54th St Kansas City MO 64112 Office: 4900 Oak St Kansas City MO 64141

MCGEE, THOMAS W., state legislator; b. Lynn, Mass., May 24, 1924; s. Thomas and Mary (O'Shea) McG.; A.A., LL.B., Boston U.; m. Ann Sorrenti; children—Thomas, Shawn, Colleen, Michael. Mem. City Council, Lynn, 1956-62, pres. council, 1958-62; mem. Mass. Ho. of Reps., 1962—, Democratic whip, 1968, majority leader, 1969-75, speaker, 1975—. Served with USMC, 1942; PTO. Recipient Distinguished Pub. Service award Boston U. Alumni, 1974. Mem. VFW (Silver medal Mass.), Am. Legion, DAV, AMVETS (Nat. Comdr.'s Spl. Achievement certificate, certificate of service/community benefactor). Roman Catholic. Club: Massassoit (West Lynn). Home: 9 Pine St Lynn MA 01901 Office: Speakers Office Room 356 State House Boston MA 02133*

MCGEE, WILLIAM SEARS, state justice; b. Houston, Sept. 29, 1917; s. James Butler and Alice (Sears) McG.; student Rice Inst., 1934-36; LL.B., U. Tex., 1940; m. Mary Beth Peterson, Mar. 8, 1941; children—James Sears, Mary Gray McGee Neilson, Claire Logan McGee Holmes, Alice Gray (Mrs. Bob Ruckman), George Sears, Erwin Smith. Admitted to Tex. bar, 1940; judge County Ct. Law, Harris County, 1948-54, 151st Dist. Ct., Harris County, 1954-55; practice, Houston, 1955-58; judge 55th Dist. Ct., Harris County, 1958-69; justice Tex. Supreme Ct., 1969—; instr. civil law procedure U. Houston Coll. Law, 1950-52. Sec.-treas. Houston Jr. Bar, 1947. Bd. dirs. central br. YMCA, Houston; mem. Houston Community Council; pres. Houston Council Deaf Children. Served to lt. USNR, 1943-46. Mem. Tex. State Bar. (dir., mem. legislative com. jud. sect.), Tex. Bar Found., Am. Bar Assn., Am. Judicature Soc., Sons of Herman, Phi Delta Theta. Home: 2300 Quarry Rd Austin TX 78703 Office: Supreme Ct Bldg Austin TX 78711

MCGEE, WINSTON EUGENE, artist, educator; b. Salem, Ill., Sept. 4, 1924; s. Elmer C. and Ida Evelyn (Chezchin) McG.; B.J., U. Mo., 1948, M.A., 1949; student (Delta Phi Delta scholar) Alliance Francaise, Paris, 1949, Ecole Superieure des Beaux Arts, Paris-Aetelier M. Jean Souverbie, 1949-50, Ecole de la Grande Chaumier, Paris, 1950, French Nat. Acad., Paris, 1951, Ecole du Louvre, Sorbonne, Paris, 1951, Atelier Andre L'Hote, Paris, 1951; m. Susan Cutler Kelley, Aug. 5, 1953; children—Chaunda, Lindsay. Mem. art staff Nat. Cathedral, Washington, 1951; prof. art, chmn. dept. art Lake Erie Coll., 1952-69; prof. painting Cleve. State U., 1970-76, chmn. dept. painting, 1970-72; prof. art, chmn. art dept. Calif. State Coll., Stanislaus; one-man shows: Barone Gallery, N.Y.C., 1960, Widdifield Gallery, N.Y.C., 1961, Trabia Gallery, N.Y.C., 1962, Lake Erie Coll., 1967, Bowman Gallery, Allegheny Coll., 1974, Mitchell Mus., Mt. Vernon, Ill., 1974, Union Gallery, Columbus, Ohio, 1974, Loyola U., Chgo., 1975, Springfield (Ohio) Fine Arts Center, 1976; group shows include: Am. Embassy, Paris, 1962, Am. Artists in Europe, Paris, 1962, Galeria XXII Marzo, Venice, Italy, 1963, Galeria Tunminelli, Milan, Italy, 1964, Galeria Minima, Milan, 1965, Musee de Chatalet, Paris, 1968, Denise Renee Gallery, Paris, 1969, Cyrus Gallerie, Maison d'Iran, Paris, 1976, Atelier II, La Defense, Paris, 1978; represented in permanent collections, including Whitney Mus. Am. Art, Brit. Mus., London, Phila. Mus. Art, Nat. Collection Fine Arts, Washington; works include: David Leach Estate mural, Madison, Ohio, 1975, Trinity Cathedral mural, Cleve., 1976, Sara Beck Meml. mural, Painesville, Ohio, 1978, Mo. State Hist. Soc., 1973; lectr., panelist in field; art dir. Internat. Expt. in Living, France and Italy, 1958-59; exchange adv. Ecole des Beaux Arts, Nice, France, winter 1962; trustee Art Guild, Calif. State Coll., Stanislaus; v.p. Turlock (Calif.) Regional Arts Council; treas. Turlock City Arts Commn., 1979-81. Served with U.S. Army, 1943-47. Recipient Annie McEngree Norton award U. Mo., 1949; Spl. award Cleve. Mus. Art, 1968; Fulbright scholar, 1950-51. Fellow Internat. Arts and Letters; mem. Calif. Art Assn., Kappa Alpha Mu. Methodist. Club: Turlock Country. Home: 1710 Smith Dr Turlock CA 95380 Office: 800 Monte Vista Turlock CA 95380

MCGEHEE, BENJAMIN HARRIS, wholesale co. exec.; b. Wilmington, Va., July 7, 1918; s. Thomas Harris and Kate (Winston) McG.; B.S. in Bus. Adminstrn., U. Richmond, 1941; m. Sarah Glen Callan, July 7, 1951; children—Susan (Mrs. Donald A. Tucker). Gen. credit mgr., treas., dir. Stephen Putney Shoe Co., Richmond, Va., 1948-50; with Noland Co., Newport News, Va., 1950—, treas., 1958-64, v.p. finance, treas., 1964—, also dir.; dir. United Va. Bank/Citizens & Marine, Newport News, Va. Indsl. Devel. Corp., Richmond. Bd. dirs. Riverside Hosp., Newport News. Mem. Financial Execs. Inst. Episcopalian. Kiwanian. Clubs: James River Country (Newport News); Williamsburg (Va.) Country. Home: 403 Woodroof Rd Newport News VA 23606 Office: 2700 Warwick Blvd Newport News VA 23607

MCGEHEE, CARDEN COLEMAN, banker; b. Franklin, Va., Aug. 11, 1924; s. Clopton Vivian and Laura (Coleman) McG.; student Va. Poly. Inst., 1941-43; B.S., U. Va., 1947; grad. Rutgers U. Grad. Sch. Banking, 1955-58, Harvard Advanced Mgmt. Program, 1970; m. Caroline Yarnall Casey, Apr. 21, 1951; children—Carden Coleman, Stephen Yarnall, Margaret Fox Verner. With First & Mchts. Nat. Bank, Richmond, Va., 1948—, asst. trust officer, 1954-56, trust officer, 1956-59, v.p., 1959-62, sr. v.p., 1962, pres., chief adminstrv. officer, 1972-73, chmn. bd., chief exec. officer, 1973—, also dir.; chmn. bd., chief exec. officer First & Mchts. Corp., 1974—; dir. Chesapeake and Potomac Telephone Co. Va., Dan River, Inc., Commonwealth Natural Resources; trustee Tr. South Mortgage Investors. Instr. evening div. U. Richmond, 1956-62, Va. Commonwealth U., 1958-64. Pres., United Givers Fund, 1971; bd. visitors Va. Commonwealth U., 1968-78; bd. govs. St. Christophers Sch., 1968-74; bd. sponsors Sch. Bus. Adminstrn., Coll. William and Mary; trea. Retreat Hosp. Served with AUS, 1943-46; maj. Va. N.G. Mem. C. of C., St. Andrews Soc., Beta Theta Pi, Delta Sigma Rho, Phi Alpha Delta, Beta Gamma Sigma, Omicron Delta Upsilon. Rotarian (pres. Richmond 1971-72). Clubs: Commonwealth; Country of Va.; Harvard, Board Room (N.Y.C.). Home: 6128 St Andrews Lane Richmond VA 23226 Office: F & M Center 12th and Main Sts PO Box 2705 Richmond VA 23261

MCGEHEE, H. COLEMAN, JR., bishop; b. Richmond, Va., July 7, 1923; s. Harry Coleman and Ann Lee (Cheatwood) McG.; B.S., Va. Poly. Inst., 1944; J.D., U. Richmond, 1949; M.Div., Va. Theol. Sem., 1957, D.D., 1973; m. June Stewart, Feb. 1, 1946; children—Lesley, Alexander, Coleman III, Donald, Cary. Admitted to Va. bar, 1949, also U.S. Supreme Ct. bar; spl. counsel Va. Dept. Hwys., 1949-51; gen. counsel Va. Employment Service, 1951; asst. atty. gen. Va., 1951-54; ordained priest Episcopal Ch., 1958; rector Immanuel Ch.-on-the-Hill, Alexandria, Va., 1960-71; bishop Diocese of Mich., Detroit, 1973—. Mem. Gov.'s Commn. on Status of Women, 1965-66, Mayor's Civic Com., Alexandria, 1967-68. Pres., Alexandria Legal Aid Soc., 1969-71, trustee, 1966-71; bd. dirs. No. Va. Fairhousing Corp., 1963-67; bd. dirs. Episc. Ch. Pub. Co., 1978—. Served to 1st lt., C.E., AUS, 1943-46. Named Feminist of Yr., Detroit NOW, 1978. Club: Detroit Economic (dir.). Home: 749 Henley Dr Birmingham MI 48008 Office: 4800 Woodward Ave Detroit MI 48201

MCGEHEE, LARRY THOMAS, univ. adminstr.; b. Paris, Tenn., May 18, 1936; s. George Eugene and Margaret Elizabeth (Thomas) McG.; B.A., Transylvania Coll., 1958; B.D., Yale, 1963, M.A., 1964, Ph.D. (Danforth fellow), 1969; m. Elizabeth Hathhorn Boden, Aug. 26, 1961; children—Elizabeth Hathhorn, Margaret Thomas. Dir., asst. v.p. for univ. relations U. Ala., 1966-68, exec. asst. to pres., 1968-69, exec. v.p., 1969-71, lectr., asso. prof. dept. Am. studies, 1969-71, acad. v.p., 1971; chancellor U. Tenn. at Martin, 1971-79; spl. asst. to pres., Knoxville, 1979—. Home: 4146 Forest Glen Dr Knoxville TN 37919 Office: U Tenn 711 E Andy Holt Tower Knoxville TN 37916

MCGEHEE, NAN ELIZABETH, univ. adminstr.; b. Chgo., Mar. 9, 1928; d. Winston Tennyson and Ethel Sue (Davis) McGehee; A.B., U. Chgo., 1947; B.S., Northwestern U., 1958, M.S. (NIMH fellow), 1959, Ph.D. (univ. research fellow), 1962; IEM Certificate, Harvard, 1972; m. William L. Dawson, Jr., Oct. 6, 1974. Instr., Northwestern U., Evening Div., 1960-61; instr. U. Ill., Chgo., 1961-62, asst. prof. Circle Campus, 1962-66, asso. prof., 1966—, dir. Univ. Honors Programs, 1967-70, asso. dean faculties, 1970-72, asso. chancellor, 1972—. Cons., U.S. Civil Service Commn., 1970-72. Bd. dirs. Ill. Regional Library Council, 1973—; policy bd. mem. Nat. Center for Study Ednl. Policy Alternatives, 1972—. Mem. Am., Ill., Midwest psychol. assns., A.A.U.P., Sigma Xi, Delta Kappa Gamma, Alpha Kappa Alpha, Alpha Lambda Delta, Phi Eta Sigma. Contbr. articles to profl. jours. Office: PO Box 4348 Chicago IL 60680

MC GHAN, WILLIAM FREDERICK, pharmacist, educator; b. Sacramento, July 6, 1946; s. Roy William and Nelleen (Zischang) McG.; Jackson Community scholar, U. Calif., Davis, 1964-66; Pharm.D., U. Calif., San Francisco, 1970; Ph.D., U. Minn., 1979; m. Kristine Ann Gunther, Aug. 24, 1968. Pharmacy intern U. Calif. Med. Center, San Francisco, 1969-70, pharmacy resident, 1970-71; pharmacy coordinator Appalachian Student Health Project, summer 1970; exec. sec. Student Am. Pharm. Assn., Washington, 1971-74, chmn. community health, 1969-70, staff dir. Project SPEED, nat. drug edn. program, 1971-73; asst. dir., 1973-74; exec. sec. Am. Pharm. Assn. Acad. Pharm. Scis., Washington, 1974-76, mem. pub. policy com., 1974—, chmn. publs. com., 1975-76; grad. fellow, instr. Coll. Pharmacy, U. Minn., 1976—; asst. prof. Sch. Pharmacy, U. So. Calif., 1978—; mem. membership com. Nat. Coordinating Council for Drug Edn., 1974-75; mem. steering com. Am. Pharm. Assn. Drug Interactions Program, 1973-76; Acad. Pharm. Scis. liaison to Nat. Acad. Scis.-NRC Assembly of Math. and Phys. Scis., 1975-76. Named One of Outstanding Young Men of Am., 1973, 76. Fellow Am. Found. for Pharm. Edn., 1976-78; mem. Am., Calif. pharm. assns., Am. Pub. Health Assn., AAAS, Delta Sigma Phi, Rho Chi, Phi Kappa Phi, Sigma Xi. Democrat. Methodist. Editor Student Am. Pharm. Assn. News, 1971-73, mng. editor, 1973-74; editor Acad. Reporter, 1974-76. Home: 12350 Reva Pl Cerritos CA 90701 Office: Sch Pharmacy U So Calif 1985 Zonal Ave Los Angeles CA 90033. *Through creativity, integrity, dedication, and compassion, we must all be the instruments for improving the welfare of all mankind and the environment.*

MCGHEE, GEORGE CREWS, petroleum producer, former govt. ofcl.; b. Waco, Tex., Mar. 10, 1912; s. George Summers and Magnolia (Spruce) McG.; student So. Meth. U., 1928, D.C.L., 1953; B.Sc., U. Okla., 1933; D.Phil. (Oxon), (Rhodes scholar), Oxford U., 1937; postgrad. U. London, 1937; LL.D., Tulane U., 1957, U. Md., 1965; D.Sc., U. Tampa, 1969; m. Cecilia Jeanne De Golyer, Nov. 24, 1938; children—Marcia Spruce, George DeGolyer, Dorothy Hart, Michael Anthony, Cecilia Goodrich, Valerie Foster. Geologist Atlantic Refining Co., 1930-31; geophysicist Continental Oil Co., 1933-34, Compagnie Generale de Geophysique, Morocco, 1935; v.p. Nat. Geophys. Co., 1937-40; partner DeGolyer, MacNaughton & McGhee, Dallas, 1940-41; ind. explorer, producer oil, 1940—, sole owner McGhee Prodn. Co.; chmn. bd. Saturday Rev., 1973-77; dir. Mobil Oil Corp., Procter & Gamble Co., Am. Security & Trust Co., Washington, TransWorld Airlines, 1976—. Coordinator for aid to Greece and Turkey, Dept. State, 1947-49, spl. asst. to sec. state, 1949, asst. sec. for Near Eastern, South Asian, African affairs, 1949-51; mem. various adv. groups to pvt., govtl. orgns. 1940—; U.S. ambassador, chief Am. Mission for Aid to Turkey, 1951-53; sr. adviser N. Atlantic Treaty Council, Ottawa, Can., 1951; mem. bd. Middle East Inst., 1953-58; cons. Nat. Security Council, 1958-59; mem. Pres.'s Com. to study U.S. Mil. Assistance program, 1958-59; chmn. policy planning council, counselor Dept. State, 1961; under-sec. state for polit. affairs, 1961-63; ambassador Fed. Republic of Germany, 1963-68; ambassador-at-large, 1968-69; spl. rep. to chmn. Urban Coalition, 1969-70; chmn. bd. Bus. Council for Internat. Understanding, 1969-73; mem. bd. Fed. City Council, Washington, 1958-61, 70—, pres., 1970-74; vice chmn. Japan-U.S. Internat. Adv. Council, 1970-74; chmn. adv. com. on housing and urban devel. Nat. Acad. Scis., 1970-74; mem. Am. Council on Germany, 1969—, Fed. City Housing Corp., 1972—; chmn. nat. adv. com. Center for Book, Library of Congress, 1978—; hon. fellow Queen's Coll., Oxford, 1968—; guest lectr. Nat., Air, Naval war colls., Salzburg Seminar, Austria, 1960. Trustee Thessalonica (Greece) Agrl. and Indsl. Inst. (Am. Farm Sch.), 1949-61; mem. bd. devel. So. Meth. U., 1949-61; mem. bd. Nr. East Found., 1956-61, Aspen Inst. Humanistic Studies, 1958—, Atlantic Inst. for Internat. Affairs, Resources for Future; trustee or dir. Com. for Econ. Devel., 1957—, Fgn. Service Edn. Found. and Sch. Advanced Internat. Studies, Johns Hopkins, 1947—, Nat. Civil Service League, 1969—, Population Crisis com., 1969—, Population Crisis Found. Tex., 1969—, Nat. Trust for Historic Preservation, 1971—, Duke U., 1962—, Asia Found., 1973—; adv. council Renewable Natural Resources Found., 1973—, Andrew Wellington Cordier fellow Columbia U.; bd. dirs., treas. Piedmont Environmental Council; internat. com. YMCA, 1949-61; adv. council dept. Oriental langs. and lits. Princeton, 1949-61; vis. com. Middle Eastern Studies and Summer Sch., Harvard, 1954-61; sponsor Atlantic Inst., 1954-60. Served with USNR, 1943-45; lt. col. USAF Res., 1945-72. Decorated Legion of Merit with 3 battle stars; Order of Cherifien Empire (Morocco); recipient Distinguished Service award U.S. Jr. C. of C., 1949, Distinguished Service citation U. Okla., 1952, So. Meth. U. Distinguished Alumnus award, 1955; named Hon. citizen, Ankara, Turkey, 1954. Registered profl. engr., Tex. Mem. several profl. and sci. assns. including Am. Assn. Petroleum Geologists, Soc. Exploration Geophysicists, Am. Inst. Mining, Metall. and Petroleum Engrs., English Speaking Union (chmn. bd. 1970-74), Smithsonian Nat. Assos. (chmn. 1975-78), Sigma Xi, Phi Beta Kappa. Episcopalian. Clubs: Metropolitan, City Tavern Assn. (Washington); Brook, Century Assn. (N.Y.C.); Colonnade (U. Va.); Mill Reef (Antigua, W.I.). Contbr. to profl. publs. Patentee in field. Home: Farmer's Delight Middleburg VA 22117 also 2808 N St NW Washington DC 20007 also Turkish Delight Alanya Turkey

MCGHEE, NANCY BULLOCK (MRS. SAMUEL C. MCGHEE), educator; b. High Point, N.C.; d. Oscar S. and Mehala C. (Morris) Bullock; A.B., Shaw U.; M.A., Columbia; Ph.D., U. Chgo.; H.H.D., Shaw U., 1973; m. Samuel C. McGhee, Nov. 9, 1955. Tchr., Louisville Municipal Coll., then Lincoln U., Jefferson City, Mo.; faculty Hampton (Va.) Inst., 1945—, dir. Pre-Coll. Inst. in Humanities, 1964-69, Avalon Found. prof. humanities, 1966-78, prof. emeritus, 1978—, dir. faculty seminar in humanities, 1969, chmn. dept. English, 1968-72; vis. prof. lit. Coll. William and Mary, Williamsburg, Va., 1971. Mem. Nat. Advanced Placement Conf., 1965-71; mem. Va. Humanities Conf., 1960—, pres., 1972-73; cons. numerous profl. groups, 1952—. Bd. dirs., pres. Am. Council on Human Rights, 1954-58; sec., bd. dirs. Va. Found. for Humanities and Pub. Policy. Recipient Distinguished Alumni award Shaw U., 1960, Distinguished Teaching award Hampton Inst., 1965. Mem. Coll. Lang. Assn., Nat. Council Tchrs. English, Nat. Council Negro Women (v.p. 1953-57), AAUW (dir.; mem. nat. com. standards in higher edn. 1972-75), Modern Lang. Assn. (exec. com. of assn. depts. English 1972-75), Va. Edn. Assn. (vice chmn. Hampton chpt.), Zeta Phi Beta (grand basileus 1948-54, chmn. exec. bd. 1955-57). Home: 20 Gayle St Hampton VA 23669

MCGHEE, ROBERT BARCLAY, scientist, educator; b. Cleveland, Tenn., Feb. 22, 1918; s. Charles McClung and Marion (Snavely) McG.; A.B. in Biology, Berea Coll., 1940; M.S. in Zoology, U. Ga., 1940-42; Ph.D. in Bacteriology and Parasitology, U. Chgo., 1948; m. Ann Lewis Hinkle, Mar. 30, 1946; children—Nancy Stuart, Terence Barclay, Michael Bruce. Asst. Rockefeller Inst. Med. Research, 1948-51, asso., 1951-54; mem. faculty U. Ga., 1954—, head dept. zoology, 1955-64, prof., 1958—, Alumni Found. Distinguished prof. zoology, 1964—. Mem. study sect. tropical medicine and parasitology USPHS, 1965-71, chmn., 1970-71; mem. adv. sci. bd. Gorgas Meml. Inst., 1972—. Served to capt. AUS, World War II. Decorated Bronze Star; recipient Michael award for research U. Ga., 1957. Fellow Am. Acad. Microbiology, Royal Soc. Tropical Medicine and Hygiene; mem. Am. Soc. Parasitologists (council 1960-64), Soc. Protozoologists (nominating com. 1961, sec. 1973-79, pres.-elect 1979-80), Am. Soc. Tropical Medicine and Hygiene, Am. Inst. Biol. Sci., AAAS, Am. Soc. Naturalists. Club: Town and Gown (pres. 1963-64) (Athens). Author articles parastic protozoa. Home: 3605

Barnett Shoals Rd Athens GA 30605 Office: Dept Zoology U Ga Athens GA 30602

MCGHEE, ROBERT EARL, mfg. co. exec.; b. Detroit, July 23, 1927; s. Earl Heistand and Vera (Fessenden) McG.; B.B.A., U. Mich., 1949; m. Ann Pilson, Aug. 15, 1953; children—Kathy Ann, Robert Neel. Brand mgr. Procter & Gamble Co., 1951-57; account supr. Lennen & Newell, Inc., 1957-59; with Lever Bros. Co., 1959—, merchandising mgr., 1961-62, marketing v.p. personal products div., 1963-69, marketing v.p. household products div., 1969-71, v.p., dir., 1971—. Served with AUS, 1945-46; CBI. Home: 35 Stag Ln Greenwich CT 06830 Office: 390 Park Ave New York NY 10022

MCGHEE, WALTER BROWNIE, blues singer, guitarist; b. Knoxville, Tenn., Nov. 30, 1915; s. George Duffield and Zella (Henely) McG.; ed. pub. schs., Tenn.; m. Ruth Dantzler, Nov. 8, 1950; children—Vedia Zella E., Vilhelmina, George Walter, Valerie R. Performed with Sonny Terry, 1939—, with Leadbelly, Woody Guthrie, 1942; recording artist for Okeh Records, 1939-42, Savoy Records, 1944-55; now recording artist for Alert, Atlantic, Prestigem Folkways and Decca records; tours throughout Europe, India, Australia; motion picture appearances include Cat on a Hot Tin Roof, 1955, Face in the Crowd, 1955; Roots of American Music, 1971, Sincerely the Blues, 1975; recorded Soundtrack for films The Roosevelt Story, 1947, Book and the Preacher, 1972, Leadbelly, 1976; concert with Paul Robson, 1942, with Harry Belafonte, 1964-67; tours for State Dept. to india and Napal; owner, operator Home of the Blues Music Sch., N.Y.C., 1942-50. Mem. Broadcast Music Inc., Am. Fedn. Musicians. Composer: Baseball Boogie, 1947; My Fault, 1948; Living with the Blues, 1958; Walk On, 1959. Address: care Agy Performing Arts 120 W 57th St New York NY 10019

MCGIBBON, PAULINE MILLS, lt. gov. Ont. (Can.); b. Sarnia, Ont., Can., Oct. 20, 1910; d. Alfred William and Ethel (French) Mills; B.A., U. Toronto, 1933, LL.D. (hon.), 1975, D.L.S., 1979; LL.D. (hon.), U. Alta., 1967, Queen's U., 1974, U. Western Ont., 1974; D.U., U. Ottawa, 1972, Laval U., 1976; B.A.A. (hon.), Ryerson Poly. Inst., 1974; D.Hum.L., St. Lawrence U., 1977; m. Donald Walker McGibbon, Jan. 26, 1935. Dir., IBM Can. Ltd., 1972-74, Imasco, 1973-74; chancellor U. Toronto, 1971-74; lt. gov. Province of Ont., Toronto, 1974—; chancellor U. Guelph, 1977—. Pres. Dominion Drama Festival, 1957-59, Can. Conf. Arts, 1972-73; mem. Can. Council, 1968-71; mem. U. Toronto Senate, 1952-61; bd. dirs. duMaurier Council for Performing Arts, 1973—; chmn. bd. govs. Nat. Theatre Sch. Can., 1966-69; bd. govs. Womens Coll. Hosp., 1960—, chmn. bd. govs., 1970-74; bd. govs. Upper Can. Coll., 1971-74; U. Toronto rep. Ont. Cancer Inst. Decorated officer Order of Can., 1967; dame comdr. Order St. Lazarus Jerusalem; dame of grace Order St. John Jerusalem; recipient Can. drama award, 1957; Centennial medal, 1967; civic award of merit City of Toronto, 1966; Centennial medal, 1967; award of merit Canadian Pub. Relations Soc., 1972; named hon. col. Toronto Service Bn., 1975, Cadet Corps St. Thomas, 1976. Fellow Royal Coll. Physicians and Surgeons Can. (hon.); mem. Imperial Order Daus. of Empire (pres. nat. chpt. 1963-65, hon. v.p. nat. chpt., hon. pres. provincial chpt., hon. vice regent Municipal chpt. Toronto), Royal Canadian Mil. Inst., Royal Canadian Legion (1st woman mem. Ft. York br.), Heraldry Soc. Can. Clubs: Heliconian; Canadian; Empire; Ladies'. Home: 20 Avoca Ave Apt 2004 Toronto ON M4T 2B8 Canada Office: Queen's Park Toronto ON Canada

MCGIFF, JOHN C(HARLES), pharmacologist; b. N.Y.C., Aug. 6, 1927; s. John Francis and Rose Rita (Rieger) McG.; B.S., Georgetown U., 1947; M.D., Columbia U., 1951; m. Sara Leighton Babb, Feb. 8, 1958; children—John, Katharine, Sara, Jeremiah, Elizabeth. Intern U. Cin., 1951-52; resident in medicine U. Va. Med. Center, 1952-53; tng. in physiology and pharmacology Columbia Presbyn. Hosp., N.Y.C., 1957-58; mem. faculty U. Pa. Med. Sch., 1961-66; dir. cardiovascular sect. St. Louis U. Med. Sch., 1966-71; dir. clin. pharmacology Med. Coll. Wis., Milw., 1971-75; prof., chmn. dept. pharmacology U. Tenn. Center Health Scis., 1975-79, N.Y. Med. Coll., Valhalla, 1979—; vis. scientist Wellcome Research Labs., Beckenham, Eng., 1974-75; adv. bd. Am. Heart Assn., Kidney Found.; cons. in field. Pres. sch. bd. St. Louis Cathedral Sch., 1970. Served as flight surgeon M.C., USMCR, 1955-57; Korea. Burroughs Wellcome Fund scholar, 1971-74; diplomate Am. Bd. Internal Medicine. Mem. Am. Physiol. Soc., Am. Soc. Pharmacology and Exptl. Therapeutics, Council High Blood Pressure Research (med. adv. bd. 1968), Am. Soc. Clin. Investigation, Brit. Pharmacology Soc. Roman Catholic. Author articles in books; contbr. articles to profl. jours. Home: 939 Long Hill Rd Briarcliff Manor NY 10510 Office: Dept Pharmacology NY Med Coll Valhalla NY 10595

MCGIFFERT, DAVID ELIOT, govt. ofcl., lawyer; b. Boston, June 27, 1926; s. Arthur Cushman and Elizabeth (Eliot) McG.; student U. Calif. at Berkeley, 1944; B.A., Harvard U., 1949, LL.B., 1953; postgrad. Cambridge (Eng.) U., 1950; m. Enud De Kibedi-Varga, Jan. 21, 1966; children—Laura, Carola. Admitted to D.C. bar, 1954; with firm Covington & Burling, Washington, 1953-55, 57-61, partner, 1969-77; lectr. law U. Wis., 1956; asst. to sec. def. for legis. affairs Dept. Def., 1962-65, under sec. army, 1965-69, asst. sec. for internat. security affairs, 1977—. Served with USNR, 1944-46. Mem. Am. Bar Assn., Am. Soc. Internat. Law, Council Fgn. Relations, Alpha Delta Phi. Club: Met. (Washington). Home: 3461 Macomb St NW Washington DC 20007 Office: Dept Def Washington DC

MC GIFFERT, JOHN RUTHERFORD, army officer; b. Jefferson Barracks, Mo., Aug. 5, 1926; s. Stephen Yates and Louise Brokenbrough (Jones) McG.; student Va. Mil. Inst., 1944; B.S., U. Md., 1967; M.S., George Washington U., 1968; m. Patricia Ann Clipp, May 2, 1946; children—William Christian, Katherine Louise, Elizabeth Ann, Mary Margaret. Joined U.S. Army as pvt., 1945, advanced through grades to lt. gen., 1977; assignments in U.S., Germany, Iceland, Vietnam; dir. of Army Staff, Office Chief of Staff Hdqrs. Dept. of Army, Washington, 1977—. Decorated D.S.M., Silver Star, D.F.C., Legion of Merit, Bronze Star, Air medal, others. Mem. Assn. U.S. Army, Field Arty. Assn., Inf. Assn., Am. Soc. Mil. Comptrollers. Episcopalian. Home: 17 Lee Ave Ft Myer VA 22211 Office: Dir of Army Staff OCSA Washington DC 20310

MC GILL, ARCHIE JOSEPH, JR., communications co. exec.; b. Winona, Minn., May 29, 1931; s. Archibald Joseph and Anne (Lettner) McG.; B.A. in Econs., St. Mary's Coll., Winona, 1956; m. Jeanne Sullivan, Mar. 17, 1974; children—Archibald Joseph, III, Mark E., Gregory P., Debora, Karen, Susan, Brian. With IBM Corp., 1956-69, v.p. market ops., White Plains, N.Y., 1956-69; founder, pres. McGill Assos., White Plains, 1970-73; dir. market mgmt. AT&T Co., 1973-78, v.p. bus. mktg., 1978—. Served with USAF, 1951-54. Named Mktg. Statesman of Year, Sales Execs. Club, 1978. Office: AT&T Co 295 N Maple Ave R 4342I1 Basking Ridge NJ 07920

MC GILL, DAN MAYS, educator; b. Greenback, Tenn., Sept. 27, 1919; s. John Burton and Jane (Mays) McG.; B.A., Maryville Coll., 1940; M.A., Vanderbilt U., 1941; Ph.D., U. Pa., 1947; m. Elaine Lucille Kem, June 22, 1952; children—Douglas Russell, Melanie Mays. Asso. prof. finance U. Tenn., 1947-48; Julian Price asso. prof. life ins. U. N.C., 1948-51; asso. prof. ins. U. Pa., 1952-56, prof., 1956-59, Frederick H. Ecker prof. life ins., 1959—. Vis. asso. prof. Stanford, summer 1950; exec. dir. S.S. Huebner Found., 1954-65, 67-74, 78—, chmn. adminstrv. bd., 1965—, research dir. Pension Research Council, 1954—, chmn., 1965—; co-dir. First Internat. Ins. Conf., 1957; mem. adv. council on employee welfare and pension benefit plans to sec. labor, 1966-74; mem. adv. panel on integration of pension plans. asst. sec. treasury, 1967; chmn. governing bd. Leonard Davis Inst. Health Econs., 1967—; trustee Northwestern Mut. Life Ins. Co., 1978—; dir. INA Cash Fund, INA Investment Securities, Inc.; mem. adv. com. Pension Benefit Guaranty Corp., 1975—, chmn., 1975-78. Chmn. bd. dirs. Maryville (Tenn.) Coll., 1974-79; chmn. bd. pensions United Presbyterian Ch., 1977—. Served to maj. USAAF, 1942-46, USAF, 1951-52. Recipient Elizur Wright award for outstanding publ. in field of ins., 1955; Distinguished Alunmi award Maryville Coll., 1962. Mem. Am. Coll. Life Underwriters (trustee 1976—), Am. Risk and Ins. Assn. (past pres., com. chmn.). Author: An Analysis of Government Life Insurance, 1949; Fundamentals of Private Pensions, 4th edit., 1979; Life Insurance, rev. edit., 1967; Fulfilling Pension Expectations, 1962; Guaranty Fund for Private Pension Obligations, 1970; Preservation of Pension Benefit Rights, 1972; Employer Guarantee of Pension Benefits, 1974; Public Pension Plans, 1979. Author, editor: Pensions, Problems and Trends, 1955; Financing the Civil Service Retirement System, 1979. Editor: (with D.W. Gregg) World Insurance Trends, 1959. Mem. editorial bd. C.L.U. Jour., 1954-59. Contbr. articles to profl. jours. Home: Sutton Terrace 50 Belmont Ave Bala-Cynwyd PA 19004 Office: 3641 Locust Walk Philadelphia PA 19104

MC GILL, ESBY CLIFTON, former coll. adminstr.; b. Omaha, Ark., Jan. 12, 1914; s. James Preston and Celia (Stafford) McG.; B.S., S.W. Mo. State U., 1940; M.S., Okla. State U., 1941; Ed.D., N.Y. U., 1955; m. Ruth Evelyn Jones, Oct. 22, 1932 (dec.); children—Barbara (Mrs. Forrest E. Nelson), Marilyn; m. 2d, Mary Elizabeth Beardsley, July 5, 1978. Tchr. public schs., Mo., 1932-33, 35-39; head bus. dept. High Sch. Stillwater, Okla., 1941-42; asso. prof. in charge of U.S. Naval Radio Sch., Tex. A. and M. U., College Station, 1942-44; chmn. div. bus. Emporia (Kans.) State U., 1945-59; chmn. bus. edn. dept. Utah State U., Logan, 1959-60; dean faculties, dir. acad. planning, dir. summer sessions So. Oreg. State Coll., Ashland, 1960-77, dir. summer sessions, 1976-79, dir. off-campus continuing edn., 1976-78, dir. non-traditional programs, 1978-79; cons. curriculum schs. in central states, 1950-69. Chmn. Downtown Redevel. Com., Ashland, 1967-71. Bd. dirs. Peter Britt Music and Arts Festival Assn., Jacksonville, Oreg., 1966-69, Ashland Rotary Found., Jackson-Josephine Oreg. Comprehensive Health Planning Unit. Recipient Founder's Day award N.Y. U., 1956, Man of Year award Ashland C. of C. 1965. Mem. NEA, Oreg. Edn. Assn., Nat. Assn. Bus. Tchr. Edn. Instns. (past pres., bd. dirs.) United, Mountain Plains (past pres., bd. dirs.) bus. edn. assns., N. Central Assn. Conf. Summer Schs. and Future Bus. Leaders Am. (past bd. dirs. both), Nat. Office Mgmt. Assn. (hon.), Ashland C. of C. (pres., bd. dirs.), Am. Assn. Colls. Tchr. Edn. (liaison officer for Oreg. 1970-73), Phi Delta Kappa, Kappa Delta Pi, Delta Pi Epsilon, Pi Omega Pi, Pi Gamma Mu, Sigma Tau Gamma. Mason, Rotarian (past sec., pres. bd. Ashland). Author: Communications Typing, 1944; Production Typing, 1955; Business Principles, Organization and Management, 1958, rev., 1963; Briefhand, 1957; manuals in field; also numerous articles. Spl. editor Nat. Bus. Edn. Quar., 1951-55; editorial bd. Bus. Edn. Forum, 1956-59, Nat. Assn. Bus. Tchr. Tng. Instns. Bull., 1951-55. Home: 1785 Zemke Rd Talent OR 97540

MCGILL, FRANK, editor, publisher; b. Phila., Nov. 23, 1943; s. Francis D. and Catherine I. (Lythgoe) McG.; B.A., Villanova (Pa.) U., 1966; m. Joyce Capozzoli, Apr. 15, 1967; children—Christopher, Brendan. Mng. editor Ames Pub. Co., Phila., 1967-72; pres. Direct Response Media Co., Willow Grove, Pa., 1972-73; exec. v.p. Walker-Davis Publications, Inc., Willow Grove, 1973—, editor, exec. pub. Plant Energy Mgmt., Engrs. Digest. Bd. dirs. Bucks County Services for Deaf. Mem. Am. Soc. Bus. Press Editors, Am. Inst. Plant Engrs. Home: 201 Penn St Newtown PA 18940 Office: 2500 Office Center Willow Grove PA 19090

MCGILL, MAURICE LEON, accountant; b. Malden, Mo., Aug. 22, 1936; s. William Howard and Iris (Phillips) McG.; student Central Coll., Fayette, Mo., 1954-55; B.S., U. Mo., 1958, M.A., 1959; m. Wanda Coral Wirt, Feb. 2, 1957; children—Melany, Melinda, William Shannon. Mgr., Touche, Ross, Bailey & Smart, Kansas City, Mo., 1959-64; financial v.p., treas. Iowa Beef Packers, Inc., Dakota City, Nebr., 1964-69; exec. v.p., treas., dir. Spencer Foods, Inc. (Iowa), 1969-71; sr. v.p. Diamond Red Trucks, Inc., Lansing, Mich., 1971-72; financial v.p. Ariz. Colo. Land & Cattle Co., Phoenix, 1972-75; partner Touche Ross & Co., Phoenix, 1975—. C.P.A., Mo., Iowa, Ariz., La., N.C. Mem. Am. Inst. C.P.A.'s, Ariz. Soc. C.P.A.'s, Assn. for Corporate Growth. Home: 8229 N 53d St Scottsdale AZ 85253 Office: 2700 Valley Center Phoenix AZ 85079

MCGILL, RAYMOND BRUCE, ednl. records bur. exec.; b. Andover, N.Y., Mar. 21, 1920; s. Clarence Raymond and Katherine Louise (Stickler) McG.; A.B., Alfred U., 1941; M.A., N.Y. U., 1947; m. Mamie Elizabeth Vincent, Nov. 20, 1941; children—Michael, David. Prin., The Middle Sch., Chappaqua, N.Y., 1953-59, Edgemont High Sch., Scarsdale, N.Y., 1959-62; supt. schs. Wayland, Mass., 1962-68, Byram Hills Sch. Dist., Armonk, N.Y., 1968-73; pres. Ednl. Records Bur., Boston, 1973—; mem. Am. Arts Awards Program, 1979—; lectr. in field. Trustee Alfred U., 1970-72; mem. dean's com. N.Y. U., 1971-72. Mem. Am. Assn. Sch. Adminstrs., New Eng. Assn. Sch. Supts., Am. Ednl. Research Assn., Nat. Corsortium on Testing, Phi Delta Kappa. Author: Experiments in High School Biology, 1950, Experiments in General Science, 1948. Home: 22 Goulding St Sherborn MA 01770 Office: 100 Worcester Rd Wellesley MA 02181

MC GILL, ROBERT ERNEST, III, mfg. co. exec.; b. San Francisco, Apr. 30, 1931; s. Robert Ernest and Madeleine Melanie (Ignace) McG.; B.A., Williams Coll., 1954; M.B.A., Harvard U., 1956; m. Daphne Urquhart Driver, Apr. 26, 1958; children—Robert Ernest, Meredith Louise, Christina Elizabeth, James Alexander. With Morgan Stanley & Co., investment bankers, N.Y.C., 1956-63; mem. fin. staff Air Products & Chems., Inc., Allentown, Pa., 1963-64, dir. corp. planning and devel., 1964-68; v.p. Gen. Interiors Corp., N.Y.C., 1968-70, exec. v.p., 1970-73; v.p. fin. Ethan Allen, Inc., Danbury, Conn., 1973-75; v.p. fin., sec. Dexter Corp., Windsor Locks, Conn., 1975—; dir. Pratt-Read Corp., Ivoryton, Conn., Travelers Equities Fund, Inc.; bd. mgrs. Travelers Funds for Variable Annuities. Mem. N.Y. Soc. Security Analysts. Office: Dexter Corp 1 Elm St Windsor Locks CT 06096

MCGILL, WILLIAM JAMES, univ. pres.; b. N.Y.C., Feb. 27, 1922; s. William E. and Edna (Rankin) McG.; A.B., Fordham Coll., 1943, A.M., 1947; Ph.D., Harvard U., 1953; m. Ann Rowe, June 14, 1948; children—Rowena, William. Teaching fellow Harvard U., 1948-49; staff mem. Lincoln Lab., M.I.T., 1951-54, asst. prof. psychology, 1954-56; asst. prof. psychology Columbia U., 1956-58, asso. prof., 1958-60, prof., 1960-65, chmn. dept., 1961-63, mem. grad. faculty pure sci., 1959-65, pres. univ., 1970—; prof. psychology U. Calif. at San Diego, 1965-68, chancellor, 1968-70, chmn. San Diego div. acad. senate, 1967-68; dir. AT&T, McGraw-Hill, Texaco, Inc. Chmn., Carnegie Commn. on Future of Pub. Broadcasting, 1977-79; trustee Trinity Sch.; bd. dirs. Am. Council Edn. Fellowship panel CDRB, NIH, 1964—. Mem. Am., Eastern psychol. assns., Am. Statis. Assn., Biometric Soc., Psychometric Soc., Psychonomic Soc. (governing bd.), AAAS, N.Y. Acad. Scis., Am. Acad. Arts and Scis., Knights of Malta, Soc. Exptl. Psychologists, Phi Beta Kappa, Sigma Xi. Home: 60 Morningside Dr New York NY 10027

MCGILLEM, CLARE DUANE, educator; b. Clinton, Mich., Oct. 9, 1923; s. Vergil and Starlie (Weaver) McG.; B.S. in Elec. Engring., U. Mich., 1947; M.S., Purdue U., 1949, Ph.D. in Elec. Engring., 1955; m. Frances Ann Wilson, Nov. 29, 1947; 1 dau., Mary Ann. Div. head U.S. Naval Avionics Facility, Indpls., 1951-56; engring. supr. Gen. Motors Corp., 1956-62; prof. elec. engring. Purdue U., 1963—, asso. dean, dir. engring. expt. sta., 1968-72; co-dir. Ind. Tech. Service Program, 1969-73; cons. to Industry; pres. Tech. Assos. Inc., West Lafayette, Ind., 1976—. Served to lt. (j.g.) USNR, 1943-46. Recipient Meritorious Civilian Services award U.S. Navy, 1955. Fellow I.E.E.E.; mem. Am. Soc. Engring. Edn., A.A.A.S., Sigma Xi, Tau Beta Pi, Eta Kappa Nu. Co-author: Methods of Signal and System Analysis, 1967; Probabilistic Methods of Signal and Systems Analysis, 1970; Continuous and Discrete Signal and System Analysis, 1974; Hermes Bound, 1978. Home: 208 Pawnee Dr West Lafayette IN 47906. *A person's behavior patterns, including successful achievement, are controlled in large measure by the subconscious mind. Proper orientation of the subconscious can be aided greatly be periodically re-examining and carefully articulating one's personal goals. The conscious mind contributes greatly by insuring that one's dealings with others are honest, fair, and sympathetic.*

MCGILLEY, SISTER MARY JANET, coll. pres.; b. Kansas City, Mo., Dec. 4, 1924; d. James P. and Peg (Ryan) McG.; B.A., St. Mary Coll., 1945; M.A., Boston Coll., 1951; Ph.D., Fordham U., 1956; postgrad. U. Notre Dame, 1960, Columbia U., 1964. Social worker, Kansas City, 1945-46; joined Sisters of Charity of Leavenworth, 1946; tchr. English, Hayden High Sch., Topeka, 1948-50, Billings (Mont.) Central High Sch., 1951-53; faculty dept. English St. Mary Coll., Leavenworth, Kans., 1956-64, pres., 1964—; bd. dirs. Asso. Ind. Colls. of Kans.; bd. dirs., exec. com. Kansas City Regional Council for Higher Edn.; bd. dirs. Kans. Found. for Pvt. Colls., pres. 1972-74, 77-78. Recipient Alumnae award St. Mary Coll., 1969. Mem. Nat. Council Tchrs. English, Am. Council Edn., Cath. Poetry Soc. Am., Am. Assn. Higher Edn., Ind. Coll. Funds Am. (exec. com. 1974-77, trustee at large 1975-76), Leavenworth C. of C. (hon. bd. dirs.), Assn. Am. Colls. (commn. higher learning 1970-73, com. on curriculum and faculty devel. 1979—), Delta Epsilon Sigma. Democrat. Contbr. articles, fiction and poetry to various jours. Address: Saint Mary College Leavenworth KS 66048

MC GILLICUDDY, JOHN FRANCIS, banker; b. Harrison, N.Y., Dec. 30, 1930; s. Michael J. and Anna (Munro) McG.; A.B., Princeton, 1952; LL.B., Harvard, 1955; m. Constance Burtis, Sept. 9, 1954; children—Michael Sean, Faith Burtis, Constance Erin, Brian Munro, John Walsh. With Mfrs. Hanover Trust Co. subsidiary Mfrs. Hanover Corp., N.Y.C., 1958—, v.p., 1962-66, sr. v.p., 1966-69, exec. v.p., asst. to chmn., 1969-70, vice chmn., dir., 1970, pres., 1971—, chmn., chief exec. officer, 1979—; dir. Cities Service Co., Kraftco Corp., Sperry & Hutchinson Co., Westinghouse Electric Co., Continental Corp., AMF Inc. Bd. dirs. Nat. Multiple Sclerosis Soc., 1969—, pres., 1977—; bd. dirs. Roosevelt Hosp., 1973. Served to lt. (j.g.) USNR, 1955-58. Mem. Assn. Res. City Bankers. Roman Catholic. Clubs: Westchester Country (Rye, N.Y.); Blind Brook (Port Chester, N.Y.); Princeton (N.Y.C.). Home: Hilltop Pl Rye NY 10580 Office: 350 Park Ave New York NY 10022

MCGIMPSEY, RONALD ALAN, oil co. exec.; b. Cleve., June 7, 1944; s. John E. and Muriel N. McGimpsey; B.S., Case Inst. Tech., 1966; M.S., Case Western Res U., 1974; m. Linda V. Tiffany, Apr. 20, 1974. With Standard Oil Co. (Ohio), 1966—, treas., 1977—. Address: 265 Midland Bldg Cleveland OH 44115

MCGIMSEY, CHARLES ROBERT, III, anthropologist; b. Dallas, June 18, 1925; s. Charles Robert, Jr. and Ellen Randolph (Parks) McG.; student Vanderbilt U., 1942-43; U. of South, 1943-44; B.A., U. N.M., 1949; M.A., Harvard, 1954, Ph.D., 1958; m. Mary Elizabeth Conger, Dec. 20, 1949; children—Charles Robert, Brian Keith, Mark Douglass. Instr., U. Ark., Fayetteville, 1957, asst. prof., 1958-62, asso. prof., 1962-67, prof. anthropology, 1967—, chmn. dept., 1969-72, asst. curator U. Ark. Mus., 1957-59, dir., 1959—, dir. Ark. Archeol. Survey, 1967—. Mem. Ark. Rev. Com., Historic Preservation Program, 1968-76; collaborator Nat. Park Service, 1971-74, adviser, 1974—; mem. Com. on Recovery Archeol. Remains, 1971—; mem. adv. bd. dirs. Red River Mus., 1975-76. Served with USNR, 1943-47. Research grantee Am. Philos. Soc., Am. Acad. Arts and Scis., Andean Research Inst., Nat. Park Service, NSF, Smithsonian Instn., Wenner-Gren Found. Fellow Am. Anthrop. Assn.; mem. Soc. for Am. Archeology (pres. 1974-75, cited for outstanding service to profession 1974), Ark. Archeol. Soc. (editor 1960—), Southeastern Museums Conf. (council 1962-71, editor 1964-71), Soc. Profl. Archeologists (founder 1976, dir. 1976—), Am. Assn. Museums. Author: (with G.R. Willey) Monagrillo Culture of Panama, 1954; Mariana Mesa, 1958; Indians of Arkansas, 1969; Public Archeology, 1972; Archeology and Archeological Resources, 1973. Contbr. articles to profl. jours. Home: 435 Hawthorn St Fayetteville AR 72701 Office: U Ark Mus Fayetteville AR 72701

MCGINLEY, EDWARD FRANCIS, banker; b. Chester, Pa., Aug. 9, 1903; s. Edward F. and Elizabeth (McFadden) McG.; B.S., U. Pa., 1925; m. Georgiamay White, Feb. 9, 1968; children—Edward Francis III, Gerald Hayes, Richard Donald. With Nat. Bank of Commerce, N.Y.C., 1925-29, Guaranty Trust Co., 1929-30; with Chem. Bank & Trust Co., N.Y.C., 1930-51; pres., dir. Liberty Bank of Buffalo, 1952-56; v.p. Fidelity-Phila. Trust Co., Phila., 1957-61; pres., dir. Beneficial Mut. Savs. Bank, 1961—, Del. & Bound Brook R.R. Co.; dir., mem. exec. com. Pittson Co. Investors Diversified Services, Inc.; dir. Phila. Life Ins. Co. Active Cath. Charities Appeal. Asso. trustee U. Pa. Decorated knight Malta, knight St. Gregory. Mem. Pa. Soc. N.Y. (v.p., treas.), Wharton Sch. Alumni Soc. (past pres., dir.), Delta Tau Delta. Republican. Roman Catholic. Clubs: University of Pa., Economic, University (N.Y.C.); Union League, Racquet (Phila.); Spring Lake (N.J.) Bath and Tennis. Home: 301 Crescent Pkwy Sea Girt NJ 08750 Office: Box 346 Sea Girt NJ 08750

MCGINN, ROBERT FRANCIS, mfg. research exec.; b. Milw., Oct. 20, 1917; s. John James and Ellen (Mooney) McG.; B.S. in Mech. Engring., Marquette U., 1940; grad. USAAF Meteorol. Coll., U.S. Signal Corps Electronics Sch., 1943; m. Elizabeth Rohr, June 26, 1948; children—James, Mark, John, Terry, Paul, William, Mary, Sally, Joseph. With A.O. Smith Corp., Milw., 1946—, staff research and devel. div., 1951-52, asst. to pres., 1953-55, asst. sec., 1955-58, dir. research, v.p., 1958—; dir. Taylor Dynamometer Corp. Served to capt. USAAF, 1942-46. Mem. Marquette U. Alumni Assn. (past pres., dir.). Home: 1550 Greenway Terr Elm Grove WI 53122 Office: AO Smith Corp Milwaukee WI 53216

MCGINN, WILLIAM DONALD, ins. co. exec.; b. Milford, Mass., Feb. 17, 1934; s. Charles T. and Eunice R. (Granger) McG.; B.A., Trinity Coll., Hartford, Conn., 1957; m. Nancy Ann Fuller, Dec. 2, 1961; children—Maureen, Melanie, William, Scott. Asst. v.p.

Northwestern Nat. Ins. Co., Milw., 1969-72, v.p., 1972-74, pres., chief operating officer, 1977—; pres. Universal Reins. Corp., Milw., 1974-77, also dir.; dir. Ore Auto Ins. Co., Pacific Nat. Ins. Co., Universal Reins. Corp., N. Pacific Ins. Co. Bd. dirs. Wis. Soc. Prevention Blindness. Served with U.S. Army, 1957-59. Mem. Chartered Property and Casualty Underwriters (pres. Wis. chpt. 1974-75). Roman Catholic. Club: Milw. Athletic. Office: Northwestern Nat Ins Co 731 N Jackson St Milwaukee WI 53201*

MCGINNES, EDGAR ALLEN, JR., educator; b. Chestown, Md., Feb. 15, 1926; s. Edgar Allen and Emily Frances (Howard) McG.; B.S., Pa. State U., 1950, M.F., 1951; Ph.D., N.Y. State Coll. Forestry, 1955; m. Jean Marie Heidemann, June 23, 1951; children—Jeffrey, Christine, Karen. Research chemist Am. Viscose Corp., 1951-52, research scientist, 1955-60; prof. forestry U. Mo. at Columbia, 1960—; cons. abnormal wood formation. Served with AUS, 1944-46. Fellow Am. Inst. Chemists; mem. Am. Chem. Soc., TAPPI, Forest Products Research Soc., AAAS (council 1970-74), Internat. Assn. Wood Anatomists, Mo. Acad. Sci., Kappa Sigma. Club: Cosmopolitan Internat. (pres. 1971-72) (Columbia). Contbr. articles to profl. jours. Home: 900 Bourn Ave Columbia MO 65201

MCGINNIS, ARTHUR JOSEPH, publisher; b. Paterson, N.J., Apr. 5, 1911; s. Arthur L. and Rose (Seyer) McG.; B.A., Fordham U., 1932; M.B.A., Harvard, 1934; m. Roselind P. Diskon, May 17, 1939; children—Roselind P. (Mrs. Joseph W. Mullen, Jr.), Carolyn M., Kathleen M. (Mrs. A.A. Stein III), Patricia A., Arthur J. Traveling auditor, 1934-35; staff statistician Western Union Telegraph Co., 1935-40; asso. editor Ry. Age, 1940-44, financial editor, 1944-46; asst. treas. Simmons-Boardman Pub. Corp., 1946-50, treas., dir., 1950-54, exec. v.p., treas., 1954-58, pres., treas., 1958-72, chmn. exec. com., treas., chief exec. officer, 1972—; pub. Am. Builder mag., 1955-61. Trustee Monmouth Med. Center, Long Branch, N.J., 1956—, chmn. devel. com. Roman Catholic. Clubs: Nat. Press (Washington); N.Y. Athletic, Harvard Business (N.Y.C.); Deal (N.J.) Golf and Country (pres.); Allenhurst (N.J.) Bathing. Home: 15 Corlies Ave Allenhurst NJ 07711 Office: 350 Broadway New York NY 10013

MCGINNIS, CHARLES IRVING, civil engr.; b. Kansas City, Mo., Jan. 31, 1928; s. Paul Sherman and Sidney (Bacon) McG.; B.S., Tex. A. and M. Coll., 1949, M. Engring., 1950; grad. Army Engring. Sch., 1955, Command and Gen. Staff Coll., 1959, Armed Forces Staff Coll., 1962, Army War Coll., 1969; m. Shirley Ann Meyer, Nov. 5, 1955; children—Gail B., Ann K., James P. Enlisted as pvt. U.S. Army, 1945, advanced through grades to maj. gen., 1976; exec. officer C.E. Beach Erosion Bd., 1955-56; comptroller, Korea, 1957-58; area engr. Ethiopia and Somali Republic, 1962-65; dist. engr., St. Paul, 1969-71; dir. engring. and constrn. bur. Panama Canal Co., 1971-72, v.p., 1972-74; lt. gov. C.Z., 1972-74; div. engr. southwestern div. C.E., Dallas, 1974-77; dir. civil works Office Civil Engring U.S. Army, Washington, 1977-79; civil engr., 1979—; mem. Mississippi River Commn., Bd. Engrs. for Rivers and Harbors. Chmn. Combined Fedn. Campaign Coordinating Com., C.Z., 1972-74; pres. C.Z. council Boy Scouts Am., 1973-74; mem. com. mgmt. Balboa YMCA, 1973-79; trustee C.Z. United Way. Decorated Legion of Merit with oak leaf cluster, D.S.M., Joint Services Commendation medal, Army Commendation medal with oak leaf cluster (U.S.); Chuong My medal 1st class (Vietnam); registered profl. engr., Tex. Mem. ASCE, Nat. Soc. Profl. Engrs., Soc. Am. Mil. Engrs. (past pres. Twin Cities post and Panama post), Assn. U.S. Army, Tau Beta Pi, Chi Epsilon. Episcopalian. Address: 4168 Elizabeth Ln Annandale VA 22003. *The simple four-part philosophy which has well served three generations of my family requires an uncompromising commitment to honesty in all things, industry, concentration on the job and on personal objectives, and economy of all resources, both natural and man-made.*

MCGINNIS, FREDERICK PATRICK, state ofcl.; b. Atlanta, Jan. 9, 1921; s. John Nicholas and Hannora (Underwood) McG.; A.B., Asbury Coll.; B.D., Asbury Theol. Sem., 1948; D.D., U. Puget Sound., 1960; L.H.D., U. Alaska; postgrad. Emory U., 1945; m. Harriet Riggs, June 19, 1948; children—Bryan Timothy, Mary Ann. Ordained to ministry Methodist Ch., 1948; pastor in Quincy, Ohio, 1947-50, Juneau, Alaska, 1950-54; adminstrv. supt. Meth. work in Alaska, 1954-60; pastor Anchorage Meth. Ch., 1957; trustee Alaska Meth. U. 1957-60, pres., 1959-71; commr. Alaska Dept. Health and Social Services, 1971-74, dep. commr., 1975—; mem. Gov.'s Commn. on Adminstrn. Justice, 1971-75; chmn. Alaska Comprehensive Health Planning Council, 1971-75; mem. Alaska Manpower Commn., 1971-75. Chaplain Alaska Senate, 1953; pres. Alaska Council Chs., 1957-60; mem. gen. assembly Nat. Council Chs.; gen. assembly del., mem. World Meth. Council. Mem. Alaska scholarship com. U.S. Naval Scholarship Program, 1960-68; mem. scholarship com. Rhodes Scholarship Trust, 1960-68; commr. Alaska Higher Edn. Facilities Act. Commn., Internat. North Pacific Fisheries Commn., 1962-68; mem. Alaska Mil. Command Adv. Bd. Named to Alaska Hall of Fame, 1968. Mem. Am. Acad. Social and Polit. Sci., Alaska Assn. Univs. and Colls., A.I.M. (pres.'s council), League Women Voters (sponsors com. Alaska 1969). Home: SRA 814 Jarvi Dr Anchorage AK 99502

MCGINNIS, GEORGE S., profl. basketball player; b. Birmingham, Ala., Aug. 10, 1950; s. Bernie and Willie (Keith) McG.; student Ind. U., 1969-71. Forward, Ind. Pacers Profl. Basketball Team, Indpls., 1971-75, Phila. 76ers, 1975-78, Denver Nuggets, 1978 . Named to High Sch. All Am. Team, 1968, 69, Coll. All Am. Basketball Team, 1971, All Rookie Profl. Team, 1971-72, All Star Profl. Team, 1972, 73, NBA All-Star Team, 1976, 77. Mem. Am. Basketball Assn. Players Assn. Address: Denver Nuggets PO Box 4286 Denver CO 80204*

MCGINNIS, JAMES DOUGLAS, lt. gov. Del.; b. Chgo., Jan. 11, 1932; s. Philip A. and Evelyn Catherine (Mousel) McG.; student Balt. City Coll.; m. Mary Jane Richards, Aug. 25, 1951; children—Philip J., James E., Donna M. Mem. Del. Ho. of Reps., 1963-65, 73-77, majority leader, 1976-77; mem. Del. Senate, 1965-67; lt. gov. Del., 1977—. Pres., Kent County (Del.) Heart Assn., 1975. Served with N.G. Named Del.'s Outstanding Young Man of Year, 1965. Democrat. Roman Catholic. Clubs: Lions, Moose. Office: Legislative Hall Dover DE 19901*

MC GINNIS, JAMES MICHAEL, physician; b. Columbia, Mo., July 12, 1944; s. Leland Glen and Lillian Ruth (Mackler) McG.; A.B., U. Calif., Berkeley, 1966; M.A., M.D., UCLA, 1971; M.P.P., Harvard U., 1977; m. Patricia Anne Gwaltney, Aug. 4, 1978; 1 son, Brian. House officer in internal medicine Boston City Hosp., 1971-72; internat. med. officer HEW, 1972-74, dir. Office for Asia and Western Pacific, 1974-75; state coordinator smallpox eradication program WHO, India, 1974-75; fellow Harvard Center for Community Health and Med. Care, Boston, 1976-77; cons. to sec. HEW, Washington, 1977, dep. asst. sec. for health, disease prevention and health promotion, 1977—; instr. medicine George Washington U. Med. Sch., 1973-75; adj. prof. public policy Duke U., 1979—. Served with USPHS, 1972-75, 77—. Mem. editorial bd. Jour. Med. Edn., 1975-78. Office: 200 Independence Ave SW Washington DC 20201

MCGINNIS, ROBERT CAMERON, univ. dean; b. Edmonton, Alta., Can., Aug. 18, 1925; s. Reginald James and Louie Mildred (Hyde) McG.; B.Sc., U. Alta., 1949, M.Sc., 1951; Ph.D., U. Man., 1954; m. Alyce Lenore Wright, July 21, 1951; children—Kathryn Mae, Robert Kelly, Shauna-Marie Claretta. Cytogeneticist, Agr. Can., Winnipeg, Man., 1951-60; asso. prof. plant sci. U. Man., 1960-65, head dept., 1965-75, dean Faculty Agr., 1979—; dir. Plant Breeding Sta., Njoro, Kenya, 1973-75; asso. dir. Internat. Crops Research Inst. for Semi-Arid Tropics, Hyderabad, India, 1975-79; cons. in field. Chmn. bd. Ft. Garry Public Library, 1968-73; mem. bd. govs. Grace Hosp., Winnipeg, 1971-73. Recipient Centennial medal, 1967. Mem. Agrl. Inst. Can., Man. Inst. Agrologists, Genetics Soc. Can., Am. Genetics Soc., N.Y. Acad. Scis. Mem. United Ch. Can. Club: Rotary. Author papers in field. Home: 800 Cloutier Dr Winnipeg R3V 1L2 Canada Office: Faculty Agr Univ Man Winnipeg MB R3T 2N2 Canada

MCGINNIS, ROBERT CAMPBELL, lawyer; b. Dallas, Jan. 1, 1918; s. Edward Karl and Helen (Campbell) McG.; B.A., U. Tex., 1938; LL.B., Yale, 1941; m. Ethel Clift, May 14, 1945; children—Mary, Campbell, John, Robert, Michael. Admitted to Ohio bar, 1941, Tex. bar, 1941; practice in Cleve., 1941-42, Dallas, 1946-49, Austin, 1949—; atty. Squire, Sanders & Dempsey, 1941-42, Carrington, Gowan, Johnson & Walker, 1946-49, McGinnis, Lochridge & Kilgore, 1949—; dir. Tex. State Bank, Austin. Instr., So. Meth. U. Law Sch., 1946-47; vis. prof. U. Tex. Law Sch., 1963-64; mem. Tex. Jud. Qualifications Commn., 1971-72, chmn., 1976. Bd. dirs. Austin YMCA, Travis County Cancer Soc. Served to lt. USNR, 1942-46. Mem. Am., Travis County (past pres.) bar assns., State Bar Tex. (past com. chmn.), Phi Beta Kappa, Phi Delta Theta. Presbyn. Home: 2708 Scenic Dr Austin TX 78703 Office: 900 Congress St Austin TX 78701

MCGINNIS, ROGER B., pub. relations cons.; b. Chgo., Sept. 24, 1916; s. Charles and Amelia (Schoenau) McG.; m. Betty Jo Reno; children—Michelle J., Linda (Mrs. Dean Cerva), Jim Ray (dec.), Ann (Mrs. Chris Ives), Kirk. With Boise (Idaho) Indsl. Found. Inc., corp. sec., 1958-72, now adminstrv. asst. to pres.; pres. McGinnis Pub. Co., Inc., 1973—; treas. Boise Devel. Corp., Inc., 1971—. Mem. Econ. Research adv. bd. Boise State Coll., food services adv. bd., Vocat. Sch. adv. bd.; mem. membership com. Am. Indsl. Devel. Council; mem. city planning commn., Fairfield, Calif., 1950; treas. Boise Municipal Golf Course Com., 1971-72; mem. adv. bd. Ebroni Learning Center, Boise, 1972-73. Treas. Bishop Rhea Sr. Center; mem. exec. bd. dirs. Oreg.-Idaho council Boy Scouts Am.; pres., bd. dirs. PAL. Recipient Distinguished Citizen award, Huntington Park, Calif. Jaycees, 1957, Boise Jaycees, 1970; Outstanding Profl. award Mountain States Assn., 1961; Distinguished Citizen award Idaho Statesman Newspapers, 1963. Mem. Treasure Valley C. of C. (sec.-treas. 1963—, Civic Leader award 1978), Idacate (pres. 4 terms), Mountain States Assn. (pres. 1959-60, dir.), Idaho Chamber Execs. (pres. 1969), Am. C. of C. Execs. (dir. 1962-64), Calif. Assn. C. of C. Execs. (dir. 1949-57, v.p. 1954-55), Central and No. Calif. C. of C. Execs. (pres. 1954), Western Inst. for Comml. Orgn. Execs. (pres. 1952, bd. govs. 1949-57), Boise-Stanley Hwy. Assn. (sec.-treas. 1960—), Idaho Trailer Coach Assn. (publicity dir. 1972-73), Greater Boise C. of C. (exec. v.p. 1957-72), Sales and Mktg. Execs. Internat., Idaho Press Assn., Idaho State Broadcasters Assn. Episcopalian (lay reader 1958-69, treas., vestryman 1960-62, pres. Brotherhood of St. Andrew 1960, pres. Brotherhood of St. Andrew State Assembly, 1961-62, mem. Bishops Council, mem. exec. com.). Mason (Shriner). Moose, Elk. Club: Hillcrest Country. Home: 1519 Harrison Blvd Boise ID 83702 Office: Box 2181 Boise ID 83701

MCGINNIS, THOMAS CHARLES, phychotherapist, marriage counselor, author, educator; b. Monroe, N.C., June 2, 1925; s. Robert Ashe and Mamie (Warlick) McG.; B.A., Catawba Coll., 1946, Litt.D., 1979; M.S. in Psychiat. Social Work, U. N.C., 1949; certificate William A. White Inst. Psychiatry, Psychoanalysis and Psychology, 1957, Inst. for Research in Hypnosis, 1977; Ed.D., Columbia U. Tchrs. Coll., 1963; m. Mary Yorke Kluttz, Feb. 15, 1947; children—Thomas Charles, Karen Yorke, John Richard. Supt. Carteret County (N.C.) Dept. Pub. Welfare, 1949-51; adj. and psychotherapist Mental Hygiene Cons. Service, Ft. Dix, N.J., 1951-53; dir. Clinic for Mental Health Service, Passaic County, N.J., 1953-59; pvt. practice, Fair Lawn, N.J., 1952—; dir., sponsor, pres. Counseling and Psychotherapy Center, P.A., Fair Lawn, 1959—; dir. Human Services Center for Edn. and Research, Fair Lawn, 1973—; pres. Internat. Union Family Orgns. in U.S.A., 1978—; non-govt. officer to UN, 1978—; instr. Fairleigh Dickinson U., 1963-65; asso. prof. N.Y.U. Grad. Sch. Edn., 1965-73, co-dir. grad. program human sexuality, marriage and family, 1969-73. Bd. dirs. N.J. League Emotionally Disturbed Children, 1955-56; sec. com. legislation for community mental health service N.J. Welfare Council, 1956-57; exec. com. Passaic County Health and Welfare Assn., 1957-58; sec. coordinating com. legislation for emotionally disturbed child N.J. Welfare Council, 1957-59; chmn. N.J. Community Mental Health Adv. Council, 1958-59; cons. Music Corp. Am., 1962-68, Major League baseball teams, 1965, Wake Forest U. Sch. Medicine, 1974—; sec. U.S. nat. com. Internat. Union Family Orgn., N.Y., 1968—, exec. bd., Paris, France, 1969—; mem. N.J. Bd. Marriage Counselor Examiners, 1969—, vice chmn., 1974-76; mem. grant rev. bd. NIMH, 1969-70; pres. Yorktom, Inc., 1970-73; cons. in USSR on invitation Soviet Women's Bur., 1966, Nat. Marriage Guidance Council Gt. Britain, 1970-73. Served with U.S. Mcht. Marine Cadet Corps, 1945-46, to lt. (j.g.) USNR, 1946-47, to 1st lt. AUS, 1948-51. Recipient Whitner medal Catawba Coll., 1946, citation for Service Clinic Men-Health Service Passaic County, 1959; O.B. Michael Outstanding Alumni award Catawba Coll., 1971, Distinguished Service award State of N.J., 1975. Fellow Am. Assn. Marriage Counselors; mem. N.J. Assn. Mental Hygiene Clinics (pres. elect 1959), N.J. Assn. Marriage Counselors (pres. 1966-69), Am. Assn. Sex Educators and Counselors (v.p. 1968-69), Am. Assn. Marriage and Family Counselors (pres. 1970-71), Am. Psychol. Assn., Sci. Soc. Study Sex, N.J. Psychol. Assn., Am. Acad. Psychotherapists, Nat. Assn. Social Workers (charter), Nat. Council Family Relations, N.J. Welfare Council, Author's Guild. Rotarian. Author: Your First Year of Marriage, 1967; A Girl's Guide to Dating and Going Steady, 1968; Sensitivity Training, 1970; co-author: Preparation for Marriage, 1971; Open Family and Marriage, A Guide to Personal Growth, 1976; Open Family Living, 1976; Extramarital Affairs, More than a friend, 1978. Mem. editorial bd. Sexual Behavior mag., 1971-73, Jour. of Divorce, 1976—. Contbr. numerous articles and papers in fields marriage counseling, psychotherapy, sensitivity tng. Pioneer in clin. and ednl. services in mental health field; designer Interactional Therapeutic System; coined and popularized concept of Open Family Living. Home: 346 Owen Ave Fair Lawn NJ 07410 Office: 0-100 27th St Fair Lawn NJ 07410

MC GINNISS, NEIL, hosp. ins. cons.; b. Cin., Apr. 30, 1927; s. Albert Neil and Winn (McDowell) McG.; B.A. in Chemistry with honors, U. Cin., 1948; M.S., Columbia U., 1956; m. Biddie Renfro, Jan. 3, 1948; children—Caroline, Kathleen, William. Asst. credit mgr., then purchasing agt., adminstrv. asst. Bethesda Hosp., Cin., 1948-53; mem. adminstrv. staff Oakwood Hosp., Dearborn, Mich., 1955—, dir., 1957-77, exec. v.p., 1977; cons. Blue Cross - Blue Shield of Mich. Recipient Tri-State Key award Merit, 1967. Fellow Am. Coll. Hosp. Administr.; mem. Am., Mich. hosp. assns., Phi Beta Kappa. Congregationalist. Club: Fairlane (Dearborn). Home: 906 S Claremont St Dearborn MI 48124

MCGINTY, JAMES SHIVER, lawyer; b. Dadeville, Ala., June 22, 1926; s. Ottie Orestes and Gladys (Shiver) McG.; student Ala. Poly. Inst., 1944; B.S., U. Ala., 1950, LL.B., 1952, J.D., 1969; grad. FBI Acad., Quantico, Va., 1952; m. Joy Faye Boman, July 7, 1951; children—Pamela Faye, Jami Lynn, Joy Dawn. Admitted to Ala. bar, 1952; practice in Scottsboro, 1954—; spl. agt. FBI, 1952-53; law clk. Judge Goodwyn, Ala. Supreme Ct., 1953-54; asso. Scott, Dawson & Scott, 1954-55; partner Scott, Dawson & McGinty, 1955-56, Dawson & McGinty, 1956-66, Dawson, McGinty & Livingston, 1966-74, Dawson & McGinty, 1974—; pres., dir. Scottsboro Convalescent & Medicare Center, Inc.; trustee Roseberry Investment Trust, Galax Investment Trust, Mamland Investment Trust, Capital Investment Trust, Fox Ridge Farms Investment Trust; partner Dawson & McGinty, rentals, McGinty & Miller, real estate investments, Derrick & McGinty, real estate investments, River Ridge Estates, real estate investment. Govt. appeal agt. Local Bd. No. 361, 1955-70; mem. Ala. Com. on Legislation for Mental Health, 1960-61. Chmn. bd. dirs. Indsl. Devel. bd. City of Scottsboro; bd. dirs. Scottsboro Community Devel. Found.; v.p., bd. dirs. Jackson County United Givers Fund. Served with inf., AUS, 1944-45; PTO. Mem. Am., Ala. (past mem. exec. council jr. bar sect.), Jackson County (pres. 1977-79) bar assns., Am. Judicature Soc., Comml. Law League Am., U. Ala. Alumni Assn. (past pres. Jackson County, nat. v.p.), Soc. Former Spl. Agts. FBI, Scottsboro C. of C. (past dir.). Baptist (deacon). Lion (past pres.). Home: 1907 Roseberry Dr PO Box 100 Scottsboro AL 35768 Office: 206 S Broad St Scottsboro AL 35768. *My faith in God, the lessons taught by my parents in words and examples, the influence of our learning institutions, my patriotic feelings, my desire to be governed by laws rather than men, the love, encouragement, and cooperation of my wife and children and the foresight, optimism and guidance of my firm and business partners have combined to make my life beautiful, meaningful, happy and successful.*

MCGINTY, JOHN, marketing cons.; b. Neosho, Mo., Dec. 5, 1911; s. Abner Crawford and Blanche (Hale) McG.; B.C.S., Drake U., 1932; LL.B., City Coll. Law, St. Louis, 1936; m. Glenella Florence Davison, July 15, 1934; children—Marilyn McGinty Stewart, Marjorie McGinty Nunn, Maureen, John Edward, Melanie McGinty Tate, Melinda. Mgr. closing div. Fed. Land Bank of St. Louis, 1933-44; admitted to Mo. bar, 1936; with Ralston Purina Co., St. Louis, 1944-73, editor sales publs., mgr. publs., sales promotion mgr., 1944-59, v.p. and dir. sales promotion, 1959-63, v.p., dir. advt. and sales promotion, 1963-69, v.p., dir. mktg. services, 1969-73; meeting cons. for firms including Ralston Purina, DeLaval Separator Co., Monsanto Co., Babcock Industries Inc., Mktg. Intercontinental, 1973—. Chmn. bd. Christian Bd. Publs., St. Louis, 1955—; chmn. bd. trustees Drury Coll., 1970-73, now trustee; trustee Disciples Div. House, U. Chgo., Drake U. Author: How to Raise the Level of Giving in Your Church, 1978. Home: 34 Flower Hill Ct Glendale MO 63122

MC GINTY, JOHN MILTON, architect; b. Houston, Apr. 24, 1935; s. Milton Bowles and Ruth Louise (Dreaper) McG.; B.S., Rice U., 1957; M.F.A., Princeton, 1961; m. Juanita Jones, May 4, 1957; children—Christopher Harold, Jacqueline Ruth. With archtl. firm Barnes, Landes & Goodman, Austin, Tex., 1957-58, Ingram & Harris, Beaumont, Tex., 1958-59; partner McGinty & Assos., Houston, 1961—; instr. archtl. design U. Houston, 1965-67; White House fellow, asst. to Sec. of Interior, 1967-68; vis. prof. architecture Rice U., 1969-70. Mem. AIA (mem. U.S. delegation to USSR 1972, pres. Houston chpt. 1973, nat. pres. 1977). Home: 5403 John Dreyer Dr Houston TX 77056 Office: 3501 W Alabama St Houston TX 77027

MC GIVERIN, ARTHUR A., state justice; b. Iowa City, Iowa, Nov. 10, 1928; s. Joseph J. and Mary B. McG.; B.S.C. with high honors, U. Iowa, 1951, J.D., 1956; m. Mary Joan McGiverin, Apr. 20, 1951; children—Teresa, Thomas, Bruce, Nancy. Admitted to Iowa bar, 1956; practice law, Ottumwa, Iowa, 1956; alt. mcpl. judge, Ottumwa, 1960-65; judge Iowa Dist. Ct. 8th Jud. Dist., 1965-78; asso. justice Iowa Supreme Ct., Des Moines, 1979—. Mem. Iowa Supreme Ct. Commn. on Continuing Legal Edn., 1975. Served to 1st lt. U.S. Army, 1946-48, 51-53. Mem. Iowa State Bar Assn. Roman Catholic. Office: Supreme Ct of Iowa Capitol Bldg 10th and Grand Des Moines IA 50319*

MCGIVERIN, DONALD SCOTT, retail co. exec.; b. Calgary, Alta., Can., Apr. 4, 1924; s. Alfred Chester and Ella (Scott) McG.; B.Comm., U. Man., 1945; M.B.A., Ohio State U., 1946; m. Margaret-Ann Weld, Sept. 9, 1950 (dec. Nov. 1968); children—Mary Edith, Richard Weld (dec.). Mng. dir. retail stores Hudson's Bay Co., Winnipeg, Man., Can., 1969-72, pres., 1972—; dep. chmn., dir. Simpson's Ltd.; chmn., dir. Markborough Properties Ltd.; dir. Mfrs. Life Ins. Co., DuPont Can. Ltd., Zeller's Ltd.; Canadian mem. Reynolds Industries Internat. Adv. Bd. Bd. govs. Olympic Trust Can. Mem. Phi Kappa Pi, Beta Gamma Sigma. Clubs: Lambton Golf and Country, Rosedale Golf, Granite, York, Toronto; LyFord Cay (Nassau, Bahamas); St. Charles Country (Winnipeg). Home: 44 Charles St W Toronto ON M4Y 1R7 Canada Office: 2 Bloor E Toronto ON M4W 1A8 Canada

MCGIVERN, WILLIAM PETER, novelist; b. Chgo., Dec. 6, 1922; s. Peter Frank and Julia Frances (Costello) McG.; student Birmingham (Eng.) U., 1946; m. Maureen Daly, Dec. 28, 1946; children—Megan, Patrick. Reporter, Phila. Bull., 1947-49; novelist, 1948—, also writer screenplays, TV scripts and articles and short stories; co-owner sta. KOWN, Escondido, Calif.; guest lectr. U. N.C., 1961; author: The Big Heat, 1952, Rogue Cop, 1953, Odds Against Tomorrow, 1955, The Caper of the Golden Bulls, 1964, Choice of Assassins, 1965, Night of the Juggler, 1974, Soldiers of '44, 1979. Served with AUS, 1942-45; ETO. Decorated Soldiers medal. Mem. Writers Guild Am., Mystery Writers Am. (pres. 1980), Crime Writer Gt. Britain, TV Acad. Arts and Scis., Author League Am. Democrat. Clubs: Players (N.Y.C.); Indian Wells Country (Palm Desert).

MC GLADE, KEITH LYNN, publishing co. exec.; b. Zanesville, Ohio, Dec. 8, 1937; s. Kenneth Edward and Dorothy Louise McG.; student Ohio U., 1955-57; B.S. in Econs., U. Pa., 1959; M.B.A., U. Mich., 1967; m. Linn Gale, Aug. 22, 1964; 1 dau., Kimberly Ann. With Chevrolet div. Gen. Motors Corp., Detroit, 1959-67; with Ernst & Ernst, C.P.A.'s, Detroit, 1967-71; controller Detroit Free Press, 1971-73, treas., controller, 1973-77, bus. mgr., treas., 1977; v.p., gen. mgr. Beacon Jour. Pub. Co., Akron, Ohio, 1977—. Vice chmn. Akron Action Com., 1979; hon. chmn. Am. Diabetes Assn., 1979; asst. treas., bd. dirs. Akron Art Inst.; bd. dirs. Akron Gen. Med. Center, United Way of Summit County; bd. dirs., mem. exec. com. Akron Regional Devel. Bd., Downtown Akron Assn.; trustee Beacon Jour. Fund, Inc. Served with U.S. Army Res., 1961. Mem. Financial Execs. Inst., Nat. Assn. Accountants, Am. Inst. C.P.A.'s, Mich. Assn. C.P.A.'s, Am. Mgmt. Assn., Inst. Newspaper Controllers and Financial Officers, Ohio Newspaper Assn. (trustee). Presbyterian. Club: Cascade; Portage Country. Home: 2390 Stockbridge Rd Akron OH 44313 Office: 44 E Exchange St Akron OH 44328

MCGLASSON, MAURICE ARGYLE, educator; b. Evansville, Ind., Aug. 31, 1917; s. Thomas D. and Nellie (Corn) McG.; A.B., DePauw U., 1937; A.M., Ind. U., 1941, Ed.D., 1953; m. Ruth Hurt, Aug. 25, 1940 (dec.); 1 son, Thomas M.; m. 2d, June Newkirk Lowe, Aug. 7, 1971. Tchr., Ind. pub. schs., 1937-46; dir. guidance, head social studies dept., Martinsville (Ind.) Sch., 1947-49; prin. New Albany (Ind.) Jr. High Sch., 1949-53; asso. prof., dir. student teaching Central Wash. State U., Ellensburg, 1953-56; mem. faculty Ind. U., 1956—, prof. edn., 1963—, chmn. dept. secondary edn., 1964-69, 74-76; tech. asst. secondary edn. Coll. Edn. and Chulalongkorn U., Bangkok, Thailand, 1957-58. Mem. Jr. High-Middle Sch. liaison Com. North Central Assn. Colls. and Schs., 1965-71, chmn., 1968-71, bd. dirs., 1972-73, 75—; mem. adminstrv. com. Commn. on Schs., 1968—, chmn., 1972-73, chmn. task force for formulation accreditation standards for elementary schs., 1972-74, hon. mem., 1975, v.p., pres.-elect, 1979-80. Served with AUS, 1943-45. Mem. NEA, Nat. Assn. Secondary Sch. Prins., Nat. Soc. Study Edn., Assn. Supervision and Curriculum Devel., Phi Delta Kappa. Methodist. Author: (with Howard T. Batchelder) Student Teaching in Secondary Schools, 1964; (with Temsiri Punyasingh) A Changing Secondary Education in Thai Culture, 1958; The Middle School: Whence? What? Whither?, 1973; also articles in profl. jours. Address: 2602A E 2d St Bloomington IN 47401

MC GLINN, FRANK CRESSON POTTS, banker; b. Phila., Nov. 19, 1914; s. John A. and Emma F., (Potts) McG.; grad. William Penn Charter Sch., 1933; A.B., U. N.C., 1937; LL.B., U. Pa., 1940; LL.D., Villanova U., 1970; m. Louise Cabeen Lea, Sept. 9, 1942; children—Marion McGlinn Lockwood, Louise McGlinn Preston, Alice McGlinn Connell, Ann Croasdale. Admitted to Pa. bar, 1941; marine counsel Reliance Ins. Co., 1942-43; asso. Pepper, Bodine, Stokes & Hamilton, 1940-42, 46-53; asst. to pres. Al Paul Lefton Co., Inc., advt., Phila., 1953-57, v.p., 1957-58; exec. v.p. Fidelity Bank, 1957-78; v.p. Western Savs. Bank, Phila., 1978—; vice consul Costa Rica, 1954-60; dir. PIPR, Inc. Chmn. bd., exec. com. Walnut St. Theatre Corp.; bd. dirs. Independence Hall Assn., 1977—; chmn. fund campaigns Red Cross, YMCA, Holland Flood Relief, Cancer Crusade, others; mem. U.S. Nat. Commn. to UNESCO, 1969-77, Commn. Orgn. Govt. for Conduct Fgn. Policy, 1972-75; Phila. chmn. Eisenhower Presdl. Library; treas. Cath. Charities Appeal, 1958-60, vice chmn., 1965, gen. chmn., 1966, exec. com., 1960-75; chmn. exec. com., pres. World Affairs Council, Phila., 1966-68, now mem. adv. com.; mem. nat. bd. Nat. Conf. Christians and Jews, 1951-53, 62-66, Phila. co-chmn., hon. Phila. chmn.; vice chmn. Found. Full Service Banks, 1969-71, trustee, 1970-73; chmn. finance com. Mayor's Com. Youth Opportunity, 1968, 69; co-chmn. Citizen's Com. for Phila. Improvement Program, 1969-72; mem. Delaware Valley Regional Planning Commn., 1967-69, Pa. Council on Arts, 1965-71, 79—; treas. Friends of Theatre, Mus. City N.Y., 1969—; bd. dirs., trustee Citizens Research Found. Exec. sec. Pa. finance com. Republican party, 1946-53, chmn., 1963-66, mem. nat. finance com., 1964—, vice chmn. nat. finance com., 1965-69, 71-73, del. at large nat. conv., 1964, 68, 72, 76, mem. state exec. com., 1948-50, 63-69; asst. sgt.-at-arms nat. conv., 1948, nat. v.p. Young Reps., 1951-53, pres. Young Reps. Pa., 1949-50; life trustee Free Library of Phila.; bd. dirs., mem. exec. com. United Way; bd. dirs. William Penn Found., 1972-78, cons., 1978—; bd. dirs. Edwin Forrest Home; past trustee, treas. Nat. Repertory Theatre; hon. trustee Temple U.; bd. govs. 41st Internat. Eucharistic Congress, 1974-76. Served as lt. USNR, 1942-46. Decorated Knight of Malta, Stella Della Solidarieta Italiana, 1948; knight comdr. Equestrian Order St. Gregory the Gt.; named Young Man of Year, Phila., 1948, Pa., 1950. Mem. U.S. (nat. dir. 1949), Phila. (pres. 1947-48) jr. chambers commerce, Navy League (regional pres. 1952-56), Pa., Phila. bar assns., Bank Mktg. Assn. (dir. 1971-74), Pub. Relations Soc. Am., Assn. Res. City Bankers, Fgn. Policy Assn. (dir. 1976—), Pa. Hist. Soc. (dir.), Phi Beta Kappa, Delta Kappa Epsilon. Roman Catholic. Clubs: Sharswood Law, Union League (Phila.); Merion Cricket. Home: Haverford PA 19041 Office: Western Savs Bank Broad and Chestnut Sts Philadelphia PA 19107. *Peace—understanding—tolerance in the world can only be achieved through complete freedom of expression and the opportunity to freely question all such expressions. To work toward such a goal is the first step toward one's own success.*

MCGLOCKLIN, JON PAUL, profl. basketball exec.; b. Franklin, Ind., June 10, 1943; s. Lesley Zion and Helen Frances (Weaver) McG.; B.S., Ind. U., 1965; m. Pamela Ruth Young, June 26, 1965; children—Shannon Jay, Meghan Lara. Player, Cin. Royals, 1965-67, San Diego Rockets, 1967, Milw. Bucks, 1968-76, adminstrv. asst., color commentator for radio and TV, 1976—. Chmn. sports sect. Easter Seal campaign, Wis., 1971; bd. dirs. Wis. Soc. Prevention of Blindness, Athletes for Youth; founder Milw. Athletes Against Child Cancer, 1976. Served with USAR, 1966-72. Home: 6290 Parkview Rd Greendale WI 53129 Office: 700 W Wisconsin Ave Milwaukee WI 53233

MC GLOTHLIN, JAMES HARRISON, lawyer, railroad ofcl.; b. Louisville, May 31, 1910; s. William Joseph and May Belle (Williams) McG.; B.A. summa cum laude, Furman U., 1929; M.A., U. Va., 1930; J.D. magna cum laude, Harvard, 1936; m. Patricia Charlotte Dowd, Dec. 31, 1944; children—Susan Louise Detchon, Patricia Anne, Kathryn Holly. Tchr., Tech. High Sch., Atlanta, 1930-33; law clk. Judge H.M. Stephens, 1936-37; admitted to D.C. bar, 1937, N.Y. bar, 1939; practice in Washington, 1940—; asso. Cravath, Swaine & Moore, N.Y.C., 1937-40; asso. Covington & Burling, 1940-50, partner, 1950-78, sr. partner, 1979—; prof. Cath. U. Law Sch., 1947-49; v.p. law So. Ry. Co., 1967-70, exec. v.p. law and fin., 1970-75, cons. to chief exec. officer, 1975—; dir. Ala. Gulf So. R.R., Central of Ga. R.R., Norfolk So. R.R.; mem. financial adv. panel Nat. Rail Passenger Transp. Corp., 1971-76. Bd. dirs. Columbia Hosp. Women, Maderia Sch.; mem. adv. council Furman U. Served with AUS, 1941-42; to lt. comdr. USNR, 1942-46. Mem. Am. (chmn. anti-trust com., P.U. sect.), D.C. bar assns., Am. Arbitration Assn., Phi Gamma Delta. Democrat. Baptist. Clubs: Metropolitan (Washington); Burning Tree, Chevy Chase (Md.). Contbr. articles to legal jours. Home: 4400 Tournay Rd Overlook MD 20016 also Cottage 247 Sea Island GA 31561 Office: 888 16th St NW Washington DC 20006 also 920 15th St NW Washington DC 20005

MCGLYNN, JOSEPH LEO, JR., judge; b. Phila., Feb. 13, 1925; s. Joseph Leo and Margaret Loretta (Ryan) McG.; B.S., Mt. St. Mary's Coll., 1948; LL.B., U. Pa., 1951; m. Jocelyn M. Gates, Aug. 26, 1950; children—Jocelyn, Leo, Timothy, Suzanne, Alisa, Deirdre, Caroline, Elizabeth, Meghan, Brendan. Admitted to Pa. bar, 1952; asst. U.S. atty., Phila., 1953-60; asso., partner firm Blank Rudenko Klaus & Rome, Phila., 1960-65; judge County Ct. of Phila., 1965-68, Ct. of Common Pleas, 1st Jud. Dist. of Pa., 1968-74, U.S. Dist. Ct. for Eastern Dist. Pa., Phila., 1974—. Served with USN, 1943-46; PTO. Home: 1029 Southampton Rd Philadelphia PA 19116 Office: 8614 US Courthouse Independence Hall W Philadelphia PA 19106

MCGLYNN, SEAN PATRICK, educator, chem. physicist; b. Dungloe, Ireland, Mar. 8, 1931; s. Daniel and Catherine (Brennan) McG.; B.S., Nat. U. Ireland, 1951, M.S., 1952; Ph.D., Fla. State U., 1956; m. Helen Magdalena Salacz-von Dohnanyi, Apr. 11, 1955; children—Sean Ernst, Daniel Julian, Brian Charles, Sheila Ann, Alan Patrick. Came to U.S., 1952, naturalized, 1957. Fellow Fla. State U., 1956, U. Wash., 1956-57; mem. faculty La. State U., 1957—, prof. chemistry, 1964—, Boyd prof. chemistry, 1967—; asso. prof. biophysics Yale, 1961; Humboldt prof. physics U. Bonn (W. Ger.), 1979-80; cons. to pvt. companies. Fellow Research Corp., 1960-63; Sloan fellow, 1964-68; recipient award Baton Rouge Council Engring. and Sci. Socs., 1962-63; Sr. Scientist award Alexander von Humboldt Found., 1979; Disting. Research medal U. Bologna (Italy), 1979. Mem. Am. Chem. Soc. (S.W. regional award 1967, Fla. sect. award 1970, Coates award 1977), AAAS, Am. Phys. Soc. Author: (with others) Molecular Spectroscopy of the Triplet State, 1969; (with others) Introduction to Applied Quantum Chemistry, 1971; also articles. Research molecular electronic spectroscopy, electronic structure, energy transfer, molecular genealogy, bioenergetics, mathematical biology. Home: 851 Delgado Dr Baton Rouge LA 70808

MC GOLDRICK, JOHN GARDINER, lawyer; b. Grand View-on-Hudson, N.Y., July 25, 1932; s. Francis Michael and Elizabeth Theresa (Leitner) McG.; student Coll. of Holy Cross, Worcester, Mass., 1950-51; seminarian Soc. of Jesus, 1951-58; A.B., Fordham U., 1957; J.D., Georgetown U., 1961; m. Cathleen Elinor Cloney, June 5, 1965; children—John Francis, Ann Cathleen. Admitted to N.Y. bar, 1962; asso. Lowenstein, Pitcher, Hotchkiss, Amann & Parr, N.Y.C., 1961-66; asso. Kaye, Scholer, Fierman, Hays & Handler, N.Y.C., 1966-69; partner Schulte & McGoldrick, N.Y.C., 1969—. Bd. dirs., mem. exec. com. Georgetown U., 1973-79, vice chmn. bd., 1975-79; bd. consultors Nat. Catholic Office Motion Pictures, 1963-67. Mem. Am., N.Y. State bar assns., Assn. Bar City N.Y. (com. on grievances 1976-79), Cath. Poetry Soc. Am. (dir., treas. 1965-67). Republican. Clubs: Board Room, University (N.Y.C.). Home: 111 E 80th St New York NY 10021 Office: 460 Park Ave New York NY 10022

MC GONIGLE, PAUL JOHN, broadcasting exec.; b. New Castle, Pa., Sept. 29, 1942; s. John Paul and Verna Alfreda (Bailer) McG.; student Ohio Wesleyan U., 1960-63, U. Va., 1968, N.C. State U., 1972. News editor Sta. WCOL, Columbus, Ohio, 1963-65; asst. mgr. Sta. WPRW, Manassas, Va., 1965-67; news/program dir. Sta. WEAM, Arlington, Va., 1967-69; news editor Sta. WJBK, Detroit, 1969-70; news dir. Sta. WKNR, Dearborn, Mich., 1970-71, Sta. WKIX, Raleigh, N.C., 1971-73, Sta. KOY, Phoenix, 1973—; instr. broadcast journalism Phoenix Coll., Ariz. State U. Co-founder, bd. dirs. Didlake Sch. for Retarded Children, 1966; rep. Phoenix Jewish Fedn. Interfaith Mission to Israel, 1978; civic speaker. Recipient Va. Public Service award Nat. Found. for March of Dimes, 1966, Nat. Disting. Service award, 1967; Best Regularly Scheduled Local Newscast award Mich. AP Broadcasters Assn., 1971, Radio-TV News Dirs. Assn. of Carolinas, 1973, Nat. certificate merit Am. Bar Assn., 1975, 78, Nat. award for outstanding public service in broadcast journalism Scripps-Howard Found., 1978. Mem. AP Broadcasters Assn. (nat. dir.), Ariz. AP Broadcasters Assn. (pres. 1978-79), Radio-TV News Dirs. Assn. (Western Regional Edward R. Murrow Documentary award 1978, Western Regional Spot News Reporting award 1978), Sigma Delta Chi (Nat. Distinguished Service award for radio reporting 1978). Republican. Baptist. Clubs: Phoenix Press (v.p., dir.), Ariz. Press (sec. 1977-78, Spot News Reporting award 1977, 78, 79, Gen. News Reporting award 1977, 78, 79). Office: KOY Radio 840 N Central Ave Phoenix AZ 85004. *A good broadcast journalist understands, accepts and considers foremost the great responsibility he or she has to the public. I've tried to do my job that way.*

MCGOOHAN, PATRICK, actor; b. Astoria, L.I., N.Y., Mar. 19, 1928; m. Joan; children—Ann, Frances, Catherine. Worked with Sheffield (Eng.) Repertory Co., Bristol (Eng.) Old Vic Co.; stage debut in London in Serious Charge, 1954; appeared stage prodn. Moby Dick, London, 1955; acted in films including: Passage Home, 1955, High Tide at Noon, 1956, Hell Drivers, 1957, The Quare Fellow, 1962, Life for Ruth, 1962, Ice Station Zebra, 1968, Mary, Queen of Scots, 1972, The Genius, 1975, Silver Streak, 1976, Brass Target, 1978; appeared TV series: Danger Man, 1961, Secret Agent, 1965-66, The Prisoner, 1968, Rafferty, 1977; TV movies: The Man in the Iron Mask, 1978, Koroshi, 1978; wrote, directed and appeared various episodes in Columbo series. Recipient Brit. award for best TV actor of year, 1962, Brit. award for best stage actor of year in play Brand; Emmy award Nat. Acad. Television Arts and Scis., 1975.*

MCGOUGH, BOBBY CORNELIUS, educator; b. Lake City, Ark., Nov. 10, 1921; B.S., Ark. State U., Jonesboro, 1948; M.B.A., Syracuse (N.Y.) U., 1951; Ph.D., U. Fla., 1962; married; 2 children. Store mgr. Goodyear Tire & Rubber Co., Cleveland, Miss., 1948-50; grad. asst. Coll. Bus. Adminstrn., U. Fla., 1951-52, real estate instr., 1953-56, 57-62; salesman Central Fla. Realty Co., Ocala, 1952-53; real estate appraiser State of Fla., U. Fla., 1953, So. and Central Fla. Flood Control Dist., 1956-57; asst. prof., asso. prof. Coll. Bus. and Pub. Adminstrn., U. Ariz., 1962-65; prof., dean Coll. Bus., Ark. State U., Jonesboro, 1965-76, Ray Worthington prof. real estate, 1975—. Served to 1st lt. USAAF, 1942-46; lt. col. Res., 1946-70. Equitable Life Assurance Soc. fellow, 1959, Am. Assn. Collegiate Schs. of Bus. fellow Ind. U., 1967, Ariz. State U., 1971, IBM fellow San Jose, Calif., 1967, Mortgage Bankers Assn. fellow Northwestern U., 1969; Brookings Inst. fellow Ark. State U., 1970-71; Mortgage Bankers Assn. fellow So. Meth. U., 1977; cert. rev. appraiser, ind. fee appraiser. Mem. Am. Fin. Assn., Am., So., Ozark econ. assns., Nat. Assn. Realtors (edn., econ. and research coms.), Ark. Realtors Assn. (edn. com.), Jonesboro Realtors, So., Am. Real Estate and Urban Econ. Assn., Southwestern Social Sci. Assn., Res. Officers Assn., Financial Mgmt. Assn., Am. Inst. for Decision Scis., Am. Soc. Real Estate Appraisers, Alpha Kappa Psi, Pi Sigma Epsilon, Omicron Delta Epsilon, Beta Gamma Sigma. Contbr. articles to profl. jours. Home: Route 1 Box 24 Jonesboro AR 72401 Office: Coll Bus Box NNN State University AR 72467. *"Work brings profit: talk brings proverty." Proverbs 14:23 (Living Bible).*

MCGOUGH, WALTER THOMAS, lawyer; b. Steubenville, Ohio, June 4, 1919; s. Frank C. and Nellie C. (Curran) McG.; student Duquesne U., 1936-41; LL.B., U. Pitts., 1948; m. Jane Fitzpatrick, Nov. 24, 1949; children—Jane Ellen, Walter T., Hugh F., Marita. Admitted to Pa. bar, U.S. Dist. Ct. bar, 1948; asso. firm Reed Smith Shaw & McClay, Pitts., 1948-58, partner firm, 1958—, head litigation dept., 1965—. Served to capt. USAAF, 1941-46. Mem. Am. Bar Assn., Am. Law Inst., Pa. Bar Assn., Allegheny County Bar Assn., Am. Judicature Soc., Acad. Trial Lawyers Allegheny County, 3d Circuit Jud. Conf., Order of Coif. Republican. Roman Catholic. Clubs: Duquesne, Press, Ross Mountain, Pitts. Athletic, Case editor U. Pitts. Law Rev. Home: 825-D Morewood Ave Pittsburgh PA 15213 Office: 647 Union Trust Bldg Pittsburgh PA 15219

MC GOUGH, WILLIAM EDWARD, psychiatrist; b. Union City, N.J., Nov. 12, 1928; s. Irving Victor and Minnie Mae (McAtee) Mc G.; B.S., St. Peter's Coll., N.J., 1950; M.D., Duke U., 1956. Intern, Duke U. Med. Center, Seton Hall Jersey City Med. Center, 1956-57; resident in psychiatry Yale-New Haven Hosp., 1957-60; instr., asst. prof. psychiatry Duke U., 1961-64; faculty Coll. Medicine and Dentistry of N.J., Rutgers Med. Sch., Piscataway, N.J., 1965—, prof. psychiatry, 1972—, asso. dean Med. Sch., 1972-76; chief psychiatry Raritan Valley Hosp., 1977—. Mem. Am. Psychiat. Assn., N.J. Psychiat. Assn. (pres. 1975-76). Roman Catholic. Clubs: Monmouth County Kennel (pres. 1967—), Camden County Kennel, Rock River Valley Kennel. Contbr. articles on psychophysiology, cultural aspects of psychiatry, stuttering therapy, edn. fgn. med. grads. to profl. jours. Home: Laird Rd Colts Neck NJ 07722 Office: Coll Medicine and Dentistry NJ Rutgers Med Sch Piscataway NJ 08854

MCGOVERN, GEORGE STANLEY, senator; b. Avon, S.D., July 19, 1922; s. Joseph C. and Frances (McLean) McG.; B.A., Dakota Wesleyan U., 1945; M.A., Northwestern U., 1949, Ph.D., 1953; m. Eleanor Stegeberg, Oct. 31, 1943; children—Ann, Susan, Teresa, Steven, Mary. Prof. history and polit. sci. Dakota Wesleyan U., 1949-53; exec. sec. S.D. Democratic Party, 1953-55; mem. 85th-86th Congresses, 1st Dist. S.D.; spl. asst. to Pres., dir. Food for Peace, 1961-62; U.S. senator from S.D., 1963—, chmn. senate select com. on nutrition and human needs. Democratic candidate for Pres. U.S., 1972. Served as pilot USAAF, World War II Decorated D.F.C. Mem. Am. Hist. Assn. Methodist. Mason (33 deg., Shriner), Elk, Kiwanian. Author: The Colorado Coal Strike, 1913-14, 1953; War Against Want, 1964; Agricultural Thought in the Twentieth Century, 1967; A Time of War, A Time of Peace, 1968; (with Leonard Guttridge) The Great Coalfield War, 1972; An American Journey, 1974; Grassroots, 1978. Office: 4236 Dirksen Senate Office Bldg Washington DC 20510*

MCGOVERN, JOHN JOSEPH, assn. exec.; b. Pitts., June 21, 1920; s. John J. and Philomene (Henigin) McG.; B.S., Carnegie Inst. Tech., 1942, M.S., 1944, Sc.D., 1946; m. Doris I. Judy, Sept. 25, 1947; children—John Joseph, Joseph Edgar, Daniel Paul, Michael James, William Patrick, Edward Vernon. Fellow, then sr. fellow Mellon Inst., Pitts., 1945-50, head research services, 1958-71, dir. ednl. and research services Carnegie-Mellon U., 1971-73, asst. dir. div. sponsored research, 1973, asst. dir. Carnegie-Mellon Inst. Research, 1974-76; info. scientist U. Pitts., 1976—; edn. services mgr. Air Pollution Control Assn., 1979—; asst. chief chemist, then chief chemist Koppers Co., Inc., 1950-58. Mem. Spectroscopy Soc. Pitts. (chmn. 1951), Am. Chem. Soc. (sec. Pitts. 1960, chmn. sect. 1964, dir.). Clubs: Chemists (pres. Pitts. 1968-69). Editor: The Crucible, 1970-76. Home: 925 Wood Bourne Ave Pittsburgh PA 15226 Office: PO Box 2861 Pittsburgh PA 15230

MCGOVERN, JOHN PHILLIP, physician; b. Washington, June 2, 1921; s. Francis and Lottie (Brown) McG.; B.S., M.D., Duke U., 1945; postgrad., London and Paris, 1949-50; Sc.D. (hon.), Ricker Coll., 1971, U. Nebr., 1973, Ball State U., 1977, Huston-Tillotson Coll., 1977, John F. Kennedy U., 1978; LL.D., Union Coll., 1972; L.H.D., Kent State U., 1973, Emerson Coll., 1976; Litt.D., Lincoln Coll., 1976; D.P.M. (hon.), Ill. Coll. Podiatric Medicine, 1975; m. Kathrine Dunbar Galbreath, 1961. Intern pediatrics New Haven Gen. Hosp., 1945-46; resident pediatrics Duke Hosp., 1948-49; chief resident Children's Hosp., 1950, chief out-patient dept., 1951-53; John and Mary R. Markle scholar med. sci., asst. prof. pediatrics George Washington U. Sch. Medicine, 1950-55; chief George Washington U. pediatric div. D.C. Gen. Hosp., 1951-54; asso. prof. pediatrics Tulane U., 1954-56; vis. physician Charity Hosp., New Orleans; practice medicine specializing in allergy, Houston, 1956—; chief of allergy service Tex. Children's Hosp., Houston; clin. prof. pediatrics (allergy), clin. prof. microbiology Baylor Coll. Medicine; prof., chmn. dept. history of medicine U. Tex. Grad. Sch., 1969-78, clin. prof. allergy Grad. Sch. Biomed. Scis., 1963—, prof. dept. biomed. communication Sch. Allied Health Scis., 1977—, adj. prof. dept. environ. scis. Sch. Pub. Health, 1978—; clin. prof. immunology and allergy U. Tex. System Cancer Center, 1976—, cons. research library, 1976—; clin. prof. medicine U. Tex., Houston, 1978—; disting. adj. prof. allied health scis. Kent State U., 1972—; adj. prof. physiology and health sci. Ball State U., 1976—; cons. USPHS, New Orleans, 1954-56, Jewish Nat. Hosp. for Asthmatics, Denver; regional cons. Lackland AFB, San Antonio; regional cons. nat. med. adv. council Asthmatic Children's Found., 1963—, bd. dirs., 1967—. Chmn. bd. dirs. Tex. Allergy Research Found., 1961—; bd. dirs. Allergy Found. Am., 1962-75; bd. regents Nat. Library Medicine, 1970-75, chmn., 1975. Served to capt., M.C., AUS, 1946-48. Diplomate Nat. Bd. Med. Examiners, Am. Bd. Pediatrics, subsplty. pediatric allergy, Am. Bd. Allergy and Immunology. Fellow Am. Coll. Allergists (pres. 1968-69), Am. Acad. Allergy, Am. Acad. Pediatrics, A.C.P., Internat. Assn. Allergology, Am. Coll. Chest Physicians (Tex. chpt. pres. 1966-67), Internat. Soc. Tropical Dermatology, Am. Assn. Study Headache (pres. 1963-64), Acad. Psychosomatic Medicine; mem. So. Soc. Pediatric Research, Am. Assn. Immunologists, Soc. Exptl. Biology and Medicine, Am. Med. Writers Assn., Am. Soc. Research Nervous and Mental Diseases, Am. Assn. Hist. Medicine, AMA, So. Med. Assn. (life mem.), Tex. Pediatric Soc., N.Y. Acad. Scis., Assn. Am. Med. Colls., AAUP, Houston Allergy Soc. (pres. 1973-76), Assn. Convalescent Homes and Hosps. for Asthmatic Children (pres. 1969-70), Duke U. Med. Alumni Assn. (pres. 1969-70), Am. Assn. Certified Allergists (pres. 1972-73), Am. Osler Soc. (pres. 1973-74), Osler Club London, Am. Sch. Health Assn. (Disting. Service award), Tex. Sch. Health Assn., Sociedad de Alergia y Ciencias Afines (Mexico, hon.), La Sociedad Mexicana de Alergia e Inmunologia (hon.), La Sociedad Venezuela de Alergologia (hon.), Westchester (hon.), Canadian (hon.) allergy socs., Asociacion Argentina de Alergia e Immunologia (hon.), Phi Beta Kappa, Alpha Omega Alpha, Sigma Xi (editor newsletter 1970-71, dir. 1972-73), Sigma Pi Sigma, Pi Kappa Alpha. Clubs: Cosmos, Army-Navy Country (Washington); Doctors (Houston), Osler (London). Author: (with Mandel) Bibliography of Sarcoidosis (1878-1961), 1963; (with James Knight) Allergy and Human Emotions, 1966; (with Charles Roland) William Osler: The Continuing Education, 1969; (with Gordon Stewart) Penicillin Allergy: Clinical and Immunological Aspects, 1970; asso. editor Annals of Allergy, ALERGIA, 1972—; asso. editor Jour. Asthma Research; editor Am. Lectures in Allergy; editorial adv. bd. Chronic Disease Mgmt., 1967—; editorial bd. Psychosomatics, Headache, Letter of Internat. Corr. Soc. of Allergists, 1961—, Geriatrics, 1974-78, Acad. Achievement, 1968—, Jour. Sch. Health, 1973—; editorial adv. bd. Consultant, 1970—, Emergency Medicine, 1971—. Office: 6969 Brompton St Houston TX 77025

MCGOVERN, JOSEPH JAMES, newspaper editor; b. N.Y.C., July 16, 1925; s. James and Mar (Ryan) McG.; m. Marion Grace Jacobs, Feb. 8, 1948. Asst. city editor N.Y. Jour. Am., 1946-58; news editor The Record, Hackensack, N.J., 1959-69; asst. mng. editor Paterson (N.J.) Morning Call 1964-66; mng. editor Morning Sentinel and Evening Star, Orlando, Fla., 1969-72, exec. editor Sentinel Star Co., 1972—. Served with USMC, 1943-46. Recipient pub. service awards N.Y. Silurians Soc., Nat. Headliners Club, 1967. Mem. Fla., Am. socs. newspaper editors, Sigma Delta Chi. Home: 138 Countryside Dr Sweetwater Oaks Longwood FL 32750 Office: 633 N Orange Ave Orlando FL 32802

MCGOVERN, JOSEPH W., lawyer; b. N.Y.C., Feb. 22, 1909; s. Philip and Jane (Fahey) McG.; B.A. magna cum laude, Fordham U., 1930, LL.B., cum laude, 1933, LL.D., 1961; L.H.D., Siena Coll., 1961, Coll. New Rochelle, 1968, LL.D., Manhattan Coll., 1968, Colgate U., Iona Coll., Keuka Coll., 1969, Marymount Manhattan Coll., 1974, Yeshiva U., 1975; D.Comml. Law, Pace Coll., 1968; Litt.D., Coll. Mt. St. Vincent, 1972; m. Marie V. Gough, Feb. 23, 1935; children—Marie T. (Mrs. Matthew M. Melillo), Raymond L., Joseph J., Philip C., Lawrence F. Admitted to N.Y. bar, 1933, since practiced in N.Y.C.; asso. firm Phillips, Mahoney, Leibell & Fielding, 1933-36; asso. Sullivan, Donovan, Hanrahan, McGovern & Lane, 1943-74, partner, 1945-74; partner McGovern & Dawson, 1974—. Faculty, Fordham U. Law Sch., 1936-43, part time prof. law, 1943-66, on leave, 1966-72. Bd. dirs. James Gordon Bennett Meml. Corp., Cath. Guardian Soc.; chmn. bd. dirs. Calvary Hosp.; pres., bd. dirs. Kennedy Child Study Center; bd. regents U. State N.Y., 1961-75, chancellor,

1968-75, chancellor emeritus, 1975—; trustee Regis High Sch., N.Y.C., 1975—. Mem. Am., N.Y. State bar assns., N.Y. County Lawyers Assn., Assn. Bar City N.Y., Guild Cath. Lawyers. Home: 262 S Buckhout St Irvington NY 10533 Office: 70 Pine St New York NY 10005

MCGOVERN, MAUREEN THERESE, entertainer; b. Youngstown, Ohio, July 27, 1949; d. James Terrence and Mary Rita (Welsh) McG.; student pub. schs., Youngstown. Exec. sec. Youngstown Cartage Co., 1968-69; sec. Assos. in Anesthesiology, Youngstown, 1970-71; entertainer, 1972—; cameo appearance in movie The Towering Inferno, 1975; appeared in film Ky. Fried Theater's Airplane, 1979; record albums for 20th Century Records include The Morning After (Gold Record award), 1973, Nice To Be Around, 1974, Academy Award Performance, 1975; record album for Warner Bros. Records, Maureen McGovern, 1979. Recipient Gold Record for single The Morning After, Record Industry Assn. Am., 1973, Can. RPM Gold Leaf award, 1973, Australian gold award, 1975; resolution for bringing fame and recognition to Ohio, Ohio Senate, 1974; Grand prize Tokyo Music Festival, 1975. Mem. ASCAP, Am. Fedn. Musicians, AFTRA, Screen Actors Guild. Composer: Midnight Storm, 1973; If I Wrote You a Song, 1973; All I Want, 1974; Memory, 1974; Little Boys and Men, 1974; Love Knots, 1974; You Love Me Too Late, 1979; Thief in the Night, 1979; Don't Stop Now, 1979; Hello Again, 1979, others. Office: care Day 5 Prodns 216 Chatsworth St San Fernando CA 91340

MCGOVERN, R. GORDON, bakery products co. exec.; b. Norristown, Pa., Oct. 22, 1926; s. James Joseph and Marion (Stritzinger) McG.; student Williams Coll., 1944-45, Coll. Holy Cross, 1945-46; A.B., Brown U., 1948; M.B.A., Harvard, 1950; m. Julia Merrow, June 4, 1955; children—Lucinda, Jennifer, Martha, Douglas. With Pepperidge Farm, Inc., 1956—, pres., 1968—, also dir.; v.p. Campbell Soup Co., 1976—; dir. N.Am. Life Assurance Co., Toronto, Ont., Can. Trustee Wheaton Coll., Norton, Mass., 1976—. Served to lt. USNR, 1944-46, 52-54. Mem. Am. Mktg. Assn., Am. Soc. Bakery Engrs., Phi Beta Kappa, Sigma Xi, Delta Upsilon. Home: 182 Lounsbury Rd Ridgefield CT 06877 Office: Westport Ave Norwalk CT 06856

MC GOVERN, RAYMOND EDWARD, advt. agy. exec.; b. N.Y.C., Apr. 6, 1928; s. Charles Patrick and Edna Frances (Bowman) McG.; B.A. cum laude, St. Francis Coll., 1951; LL.D. magna cum laude, St. John's U., Bklyn., 1953; m. Anne Burke, Nov. 19, 1955; children—Raymond, Keith, Laura, Jeffrey, Pamela, Kyle. Admitted to N.Y. bar, 1954; asso. firm Boal, McQuade & Fitzpatrick, N.Y.C., 1953-50, partner, 1961-66; sr. v.p., sec., gen. counsel Batten, Barton, Durstine & Osborn, Inc., N.Y.C., 1967—. Trustee, Village of Tarrytown (N.Y.), 1968-77, 79—. Served with USN, 1945-47. Mem. Am. Bar Assn., Assn. Bar City N.Y. Home: 24 Heritage Hill Rd Tarrytown NY 10591 Office: 383 Madison Ave New York NY 10017

MCGOVERN, WALTER T., judge; b. Seattle, May 24, 1922; s. C. Arthur and Anne Marie (Thies) McG.; B.A., U. Wash., 1949, LL.B., 1950; m. Rita Marie Olsen, June 29, 1946; children—Katrina M., Shawn E., A. Renee. Admitted to Wash. bar, 1950; practiced law in Seattle, 1950-59; mem. firm Kerr, McCord, Greenleaf & Moen; judge Municipal Ct., Seattle, 1959-65; judge Superior Ct., Wash., 1965-68; judge Wash. Supreme Ct., 1968-71; judge U.S. Dist. Ct., Western Dist. Wash., 1971—, chief judge, 1976—. Mem. Am. Judicature Soc., Wash. State Superior Ct. Judges Assn., Seattle King County Bar Assn. (treas.), Phi Delta Phi. Club: Seattle Tennis (pres. 1968). Office: 705 US Courthouse Seattle WA 98104*

MCGOVERN, WILLIAM MONTGOMERY, JR., educator; b. Evanston, Ill., July 9, 1934; s. William Montgomery and Margaret (Montgomery) McG.; A.B., Princeton, 1955; LL.B., Harvard, 1958; m Katharine Watts, Sept. 20, 1958; children—William Montgomery III, Elizabeth Lee, Katharine Margaret. Admitted to Ill. bar, 1959; asso. Sidley, Austin, Burgess & Smith, Chgo., 1959-63; asst. prof. law Northwestern U. Sch. of Law, Chgo., 1963-66, asso. prof., 1966-68, prof., 1968-72; prof. law Sch. Law, U. Calif. at Los Angeles, 1972 ; vis. prof. U. Minn. Law Sch., 1979-80. Served with U.S. Army, 1958-59. Bd. editors Harvard Law Rev., 1956-58. Contbr. articles profl. jours. Home: 17319 Magnolia Blvd Encino CA 91316 Office: 405 Hilgard Los Angeles CA 90024

MCGOWAN, CARL, judge; b. Hymera, Ind., May 7, 1911; A.B., Dartmouth, 1932; LL.B., Columbia, 1936; LL.D. (hon.), Northwestern U., 1976; m. Josephine V. Perry, Jan. 20, 1945; children—Mary, Rebecca, John, Hope. Admitted to N.Y. bar, 1936, Ill., 1940, D.C. bar, 1948; sr. mem. firm Ross, McGowan, Hardies & O'Keefe, Chgo., 1953-63; gen. counsel C. & N.-W. Ry., 1957-63; judge U.S. Ct. Appeals for D.C. Circuit, 1963—. Mem. Am., Chgo., Ill., D.C. bar assns., Am. Law Inst., Phi Beta Kappa. Home: 4717 Quebec St NW Washington DC 20016 Office: US Ct Appeals Washington DC 20001

MCGOWAN, HAROLD, real estate developer, investor, scientist, author; b. Weehawken, N.J., June 23, 1909; s. Sylvester and Grace (Kalbfleish) McG.; ed. Bklyn. Poly. Inst., Pratt Inst., N.Y. U., Hubbard (Eng.) U., Rose Croix U.; D.Sc., Coll. Fla.; m. Anne Cecelia McTiernan, Jan. 15, 1938; children—Linda Anne, Harold Charles, Janice Marie. Pres., chmn. bd. Atomic Research, Inc.; pres. Harold McGowan Builders; owner, developer Central Islip Shopping Center, Central Islip Indsl. Center; developer, builder Brinsley Gardens, Rolling Green, Slater Park, Clover Green, Maple Acres, Wheeler Acres; owner Little League Baseball Parks. Hwy. commr. Suffolk County. Recipient Wisdom award Honor, 1975. Mem. AAAS, IEEE, Explorers Club, Mensa Internat. Author: Green Flight; The Spirit of Christmas in Words and Sculpture, The Making of a Universalist; The Thoughtron Theory of Life and Matter; Born Again; The Incorigibles; Christmas Stories; Short Stories; also sculptures include Bless Them, Victory, Eternity, Love and Hate, Triumph; artist, philanthropist. Patentee in field. Address: 28 2d Ave Central Islip NY 11722. *To become a really whole and successful person, one should recognize the efforts and good will of those living and dead who developed the culture, the fruits of which he enjoys, and repay his benefactors by contributing more to that society than he takes and also by doing good deeds to make the society better than he found it. He must also strive to understand the world and his relationship to it and know that the universe is neither capricious nor mysterious, that miracles do not happen. Everything and every action can only occur within the bounds of universal laws. He must further realize that he is eternal and the basic purpose of human life is to become aware of and to live by universal laws. The acme of a person's accomplishments would be his comprehension of the structure of the physical universe, the processes of life, and the nature of his mind. When he comprehends the universe, life, and mind, he will understand his own immortality.*

MCGOWAN, JAMES ATKINSON, aluminum co. exec.; b. De Soto, Mo., Nov. 10, 1914; s. James Electra and Dora Mercer (Atkinson) McG.; A.A., Little Rock Jr. Coll., 1934; B.S. in Chem.Engring., Iowa State U., 1936; m. Barbara Louise Bevan, Apr. 5, 1941; m. 2d Margaret Mercier Johns, Dec. 21, 1974; children—James Michael, John Barrie, Susan Alexandra, Jean Christine. With Aluminum Co. Am., 1936—, dist. sales mgr., Cleve., 1959-60, gen. mgr. indsl. sales, Pitts., 1962-67, v.p., Pitts., 1967-75, exec. v.p., 1975—. Mem. Am. Inst. Chem. Engrs., Chem. Mfg. Assn. (dir.), Aluminum Assn., Nat. Assn. Corrosion Engrs., Sigma Chi. Republican. Episcopalian. Clubs: Duquesne, Laurel Valley Golf, Longue Vue. Office: 425 6th Ave Pittsburgh PA 15215

MC GOWAN, JOHN P., librarian; b. N.Y.C., May 11, 1926; s. Patrick and Nora (Naughton) McG.; B.Indsl. Engring., N.Y. U., 1966; A.M. in L.S., Columbia U., 1951; A.B. in English, Hunter Coll., N.Y.C., 1950; m. Eileen Durkin, Nov. 4, 1950; children—Carol, Joanne, John, Deirdre, Malcolm. Librarian, N.Y. U., 1951-56, Tech. Inst., Northwestern U., 1956-59; dir. library Franklin Inst., Phila., 1959-66; asso. univ. librarian Northwestern U., 1966-71, univ. librarian, 1971—; pres. MIDLNET, network consoria Mid-Western univs.; trustee EDUCOM. Served with AUS, 1944-46. Fellow Council Library Resources. Mem. ALA (pres. reference services div.). Office: Northwestern Univ Library Evanston IL 60022

MCGOWIN, NICHOLAS STALLWORTH, lawyer; b. Chapman, Ala., May 17, 1912; s. James Greeley and Essie (Stallworth) McG.; A.B., U. Ala., 1933; postgrad. Pembroke Coll., Oxford U., Eng., 1933-34; LL.B., Harvard, 1937; m. Elizabeth Brittain Smith, Apr. 21, 1945; children—Nicholas Stallworth (dec.), Peter H., Elizabeth. Admitted to Ala. bar, 1937, Pa. bar, 1939; practice in Greenville, Ala., 1937-39, Phila., 1939-41, Washington, 1941-42, Mobile, Ala., 1946—; asso. Drinker, Biddle & Reath, 1939-41; mem. legal staff Brit. Purchasing Commn., 1941-42; mem. firm Thornton & McGowin, 1956—. Chmn. Ala. Fulbright Scholarship Com., 1951-72. Pres. Mobile Symphony, 1956-58; chmn. bd. trustees Lyman Ward Mil. Acad.; chmn. bd. trustees Mobile Pub. Library, 1969-70. Served to lt. comdr. USNR, 1942-45; PTO. Decorated Order of Vasa (Sweden). Mem. Am., Ala. (chmn. real property, probate and trust sect. 1970-71), Mobile (pres. 1974) bar assns., Maritime Law Assn., Phi Beta Kappa, Delta Kappa Epsilon. Clubs: Country, Lakewood, Athelstan (Mobile); Boston (New Orleans). Home: 3604 Spring Hill Ave Mobile AL 36608 Office: Mchts Bank Bldg Mobile AL 36602

MC GOWIN, WILLIAM EDWARD, artist; b. Hattiesburg, Miss., June 2, 1938; s. William Edward and Emily (Ratliff) McG.; B.S., U. So. Miss., 1961; M.A., U. Ala., 1964; m. Claudia DeMonte, May 28, 1977; children—Leah, Jill. One-man shows include: Corcoran Gallery Art, Washington, 1962, 71, 75, Martha Jackson Gallery, N.Y.C., 1968, Am. Cultural Center, Paris, 1974, Museum Modern Art, Paris, 1978; group shows include: Contemporary Mus., Houston, Miss. Mus. Art, Whitney Mus., N.Y.C., Detroit Inst. Art, Speed Mus., Ky.; represented in permanent collections: Addison Mus. Art, Andover, Mass., Corcoran Gallery Art, Nat. Collection Fine Arts, Washington, New Orleans Mus. Art, Whitney Mus. Am. Art, N.Y.C.; asst. prof. art SUNY, Old Westbury, 1978—, Coll. Old Westbury; mem. faculty Corcoran Gallery Art, 1966-77, head sculpture dept., 1967-74; lectr. in field. Recipient Oscar for painting, 1977, Painting prize 9th Internat. Painting Festival, prize Internat. Festival, 1977, prize Cagnes-sur-Mer, France, 1977; Nat. Endowment for Arts grantee, 1967-68; GSA grantee, 1978-79; Cassandra Found. grantee, 1972—. Work reviewed in numerous newspapers, jours. and books. Home and Office: 96 Grand St New York NY 10013

MCGRAIL, JOHN SIMON, physician; b. Eng., May 28, 1931; s. William Anthony and Dorothy (John) McG.; M.D., U. Manchester (Eng.), 1955; D.L.O., U. London, 1957; M.S., U. Mich., 1964; m. Theresa Mary Jenkins, Apr. 4, 1959; children—Susan, Mark, Christopher, Justin. Practice medicine specializing in otolaryngology, Toronto, Ont., Can., 1966—; otolaryngologist-in-chief Wellesley Hosp., 1966—; cons. Ont. Cancer Inst., 1966—; prof. otolaryngology U. Toronto, 1966—, asst. prof. anatomy, 1968—. Pres., Adult Fitness Centres, Toronto; bd. dirs. Integra Found., Toronto Art Prodn. Served with M.C., Royal Army, 1956-58. Fellow Royal Coll. Surgeons (Can.); mem. Can. Med. Assn., Ont. Med. Assn., Acad. Facial and Reconstructive Surgery, Sports Medcine of Can. Roman Catholic. Author: Fitness for Fun; contbr. articles on head and neck cancer to med. jours. Office: 160 Wellesley St E Toronto ON 284 Canada

MCGRAIL, RICHARD P., health orgn. exec.; b. New Haven, Sept. 29, 1920; s. Hugh and Mary (Shannon) McG.; B.S., Syracuse U., 1943; LL.B., J.D., N.Y.U., 1957; m. Louise H. Jewell, Sept. 22, 1943; children—Patricia (Mrs. Fred Clements), Richard, Louise (Mrs. John Rathbun), Robert. With Am. Cancer Soc., 1946—, v.p. field services, 1958-60, dep. exec. v.p., 1960—; admitted to N.Y. bar, 1959, since practiced in Merrick, to 1972. Mem. Pres.'s Com. on Health Edn., 1972. Mem. bd., past pres. Nat. Health Council. Served to lt. USNR, 1943-46. Mem. N.Y. County Lawyers Assn. Home: 109 Lucinda Dr Babylon NY 11702 Office: 777 3d Ave New York City NY 10017

MCGRATH, BRENDAN, clergyman, educator; b. Chgo., Feb. 19, 1914; s. John Joseph and Irene (Quinn) McG.; A.B., Loyola U., Chgo., 1936, M.A. with honors, 1939; S.T.L., U. Ottawa (Can.), 1945, S.T.D., 1949. Teaching fellow Loyola U., Chgo., 1936-39; entered St. Procopius Abbey, Lisle, Ill., 1939, professed, 1940, ordained priest Roman Cath. Ch., 1944; faculty St. Procopius Coll., 1940—; tchr. St. Procopius Sem., 1946-67, rector, 1962-67; rector St. Maur's Sem., Indpls., 1967-70; prof. theology Loyola U., Chgo., 1970—; part-time parochial ministerial work, 1944—. Mem. priests senate Diocese of Joliet, Ill., 1966, 74—; mem. DuPage County Council Religion and Race, 1964—; pres. Am. Benedictine Acad., 1968-71. Mem. Cath. Bibl. Assn. Am. (pres. 1958-59). Contbr. articles to revs. encys. Translator (J. Chaine) God's Heralds, 1954. Address: St Procopius Abbey Lisle IL 60532

MCGRATH, EARL JAMES, educator; b. Buffalo, Nov. 16, 1902; s. John and Martha Carolyn (Schottin) McG.; B.A., U. Buffalo, 1928, M.A., 1930; Ph.D., U. Chgo., 1936; hon. degrees 51 colls. and univs., 1949—; m. Dorothy Ann Leemon, May 12, 1944. Mem. faculty U. Buffalo, 1928-45; dean Coll. Liberal Arts, State U. Iowa, 1945-48; prof. U. Chgo., 1948-49; U.S. commr. edn. Office of Edn., FSA, 1949-53; pres., chancellor U. Kansas City, 1953-56; exec. officer Inst. Higher Edn., also prof. higher edn. Tchrs. Coll., Columbia, 1956-68; chancellor Eisenhower Coll., Seneca Falls, 1966-68; dir. Higher Edn. Center, Temple U., 1968-73; sr. cons. Lilly Endowment, Indpls., 1973-76; prof. U. Ariz., 1974—. Mem. Fulbright Bd. Fgn. Scholarships, 1949-52. Mem. and former mem. many profl. coms. and commns., local state, nat. and internat. in field of edn. Frequent mem. U.S. govtl. agys. and commns. on study ednl. systems. Trustee Antioch Coll., 1958-61, Muskingum Coll., 1961-64, 68-77, St. Michael's Coll., 1966-75, Buckingham (Eng.) Coll., 1973-76, Warner Pacific Coll., 1972—; mem. adv. bd. Truman Library. Served to lt. comdr. USNR, 1942-44. Decorated Knight Order St. John of Jerusalem. Mem. many profl. orgns. and assns. related to field of edn., Phi Beta Kappa, Delta Chi, Beta Sigma Pi, Phi Delta Kappa, Delta Phi Alpha, Sigma Xi, Iota Lambda Sigma, Omicron Delta Kappa. Clubs: Cosmos (Washington); Century Assn., N.Y. Athletic; Old Pueblo, Tucson Nat. Golf (Tucson). Author and co-author several books, numerous articles. Home: 632 W Roller Coaster Rd Tucson AZ 85704

MCGRATH, FRANCIS JOSEPH, city ofcl.; b. Worcester, Mass., May 11, 1908; s. Francis G. and Elizabeth (Tivnan) McG.; A.B. cum laude, Holy Cross Coll., 1930, D.C.L., 1959; M.A., Boston Coll. 1931; D.Pub. Adminstrn., Assumption Coll., Worcester, 1978; m. Mary Estelle Wickham, July 29, 1939. Tchr., dept. head Bartlett High Sch., Webster, Mass., 1931-41; prin. Worcester Sch. System, 1941-43, 46-50; asst. city mgr., Worcester, 1950, city mgr., 1951—; trustee Worcester County Instn. for Savs. Served as lt. comdr. USNR, 1943-46. Recipient Eagle award Boy Scouts Am., 1978; award of merit Armed Forces Com. Worcester County, 1979; Irving A. Glavin award Worcester Area Assn. for Retarded Children, 1979; Francis J. McGrath Elem. Sch. named in his honor, 1979. Mem. Internat., Mass. city mgrs. assns., V.F.W., Am. Legion. Rotarian. Home: 76 Forest St Worcester MA 01609 Office: City Hall Worcester MA 01601

MCGRATH, JOHN JOSEPH, mgmt. cons.; b. Hartford, Sept. 26, 1910; s. John William and Mary Ellen (Sayers) McG.; A.B., U. Conn., 1933; postgrad. N.Y. U., 1936-37; Carnegie fellow Yale, 1937-38; m. Virginia L. Bonenfant, May 23, 1938; children—John P., Teresa L. (Mrs. John B. Winfield), Marygay C., Timothy S., Richard P. Dir. Bur. Adult Edn., Hartford, 1938-41; lectr. N.Y. U. Sch. Retailing, 1947-55; mgr. tng. dept. Macy's, N.Y.C., 1946-55; mgr. edn. dept. J.C. Penney Co., 1955-59; v.p. orgn. Allied Stores Corp., 1959-75. Past dir. Allied Stores Found. Past mem. Cardinal's Com. of Laity N.Y.C.; mem. univ. council St. John's U.; past adv. bd. Molloy Coll.; past bd. dirs., sec., treas. B. Earl Puckett Fund for Retail Edn.; former chmn. bd. Orgn. Devel. Council. Served to lt. col. AUS, 1941-45; col. Res. ret. Mem. Nat. Retail Mchts. Assn. (past v.p.), Distributive Edn. Clubs Am. (past v.p.), N.Y. Marine Corps Fathers Assn. (past v.p.). Roman Catholic. Home: 23 Lincoln Ct Rockville Centre NY 11570

MCGRATH, JOSEPH EDWARD, educator; b. DuBois, Pa., July 17, 1927; s. John Bernard and Winifred Amelia (Senard) McG.; B.S., U. Md., 1950, M.A., 1951; Ph.D., U. Mich., 1955; m. Marion Freitag, Sept. 5, 1952; children—Robert E., William D., James G., Janet W. Research scientist Psychol. Research Assos., Arlington, Va., 1955-57; v.p., sr. research scientist, dir. research office Human Scis. Research, Inc., Clarendon, Va., 1957-60; research asst. prof., asso. dir. Group Effectiveness Lab., U. Ill., Champaign, 1960-62, asst. prof. psychology dept., 1962-64, asso. prof., 1964-66, prof., 1966—, head psychology dept., 1972-76. Served with AUS, 1945-46. Fellow Am. Psychol. Assn.; mem. Midwestern Psychol. Assn., Soc. Psychol. Study Social Issues, Psychonomic Soc., Soc. Exptl. Social Psychologists, A.A.U.P., Sigma Xi, Phi Eta Sigma, Psi Chi. Author: Social Psychology: A Brief Introduction, 1965; (with Irwin Altman) Small Group Research: A Synthesis and Critique of the Field, 1966. Editor, co-author: Social and Psychological Factors in Stress, 1970; (with Philip J. Runkel) Studying Human Behavior, 1972. Home: 502 W Michigan St Urbana IL 61801 Office: Psychology Bldg U Ill Champaign IL 61820

MCGRATH, KYRAN MURRAY, lawyer; b. Chgo., Aug. 24, 1934; s. George E. and Annabelle (Colten) McG.; B.S.S. cum laude, Georgetown U., 1956, LL.B., 1959; m. Rosemary McVeigh, June 16, 1956; children—Kyran Murray, Eileen, Thomas, Roseann. Admitted to D.C. bar, 1959; practiced law, Washington, 1959-61, 75—; legis. counsel Senator Paul H. Douglas, Washington, 1961-65; chief Ill. Dept. Bus. and Econ. Devel., Washington, 1965-67; spl. asst. to chmn. Nat. Adv. Commn. on Civil Disorders, Washington, 1967-68; dir. Am. Assn. Museums, Washington, 1968-75; lectr., cons U.S. Dept. Labor, 1967; lectr., cons. dept. grad. art history George Washington U., grad. lectr. in mus. adminstrn., 1975-76; mem. U.S. Nat. Commn. to UNESCO, 1970-75; owner/mgr. Inn at Long Trail, Killington, Vt., 1977—. Pres. PTA, Washington, 1967; bd. dirs. Festival of Arts, Killington, 1979—. Roman Catholic. Club: Happy Hour Investment (pres. 1965-67) (Washington). Author salary surveys, articles and plays. Home: Plymouth VT 05056

MC GRATH, LEE PARR, author, pub. relations exec.; b. Robstown, Tex.; d. James Carl and Margaret Marden (Russ) Parr; B.A., So. Methodist U., 1955; m. Richard J. McGrath, Nov. 5, 1955; children—John Parr, Margaret Lee, Maureen Alison. Book reviewer Dallas Morning News, 1953, New Orleans Times-Picayune, 1956; guest editor Mademoiselle mag., 1952; chmn. bd. McGrath/Power Assos., N.Y.C., 1973—. Recipient Prix de Paris, Vogue, 1954. Mem. Fashion Group, Pub. Relations Soc. Am., Am. Soc. Journalists and Authors, Cousteau Soc. (dir.), Phi Beta Kappa. Author: Creative Careers For Women, 1968; Do-It-All-Yourself Needlepoint, 1971; What is a Father?, 1969; What Is a Mother?, 1969; What Is a Grandmother?, 1970; What Is a Grandfather?, 1970; What is a Brother?, 1971; What Is a Sister?, 1971; What Is a Friend?, 1971; What Is a Pet?, 1971; Celebrity Needlepoint, 1972; Housekeeping With Antiques, 1971. Home: 717 The Parkway Mamaroneck NY 10543 Office: 500 Fifth Ave New York NY 10036

MCGRATH, THOMAS, author; b. Nov. 20, 1916; student U. N.D., La. State U., New Coll. Oxford U.; m. Eugenia Johnson; 1 son, Tomasito. Instr., Colby Coll., Waterville, Maine, 1940-41; asst. prof. Los Angeles State Coll., 1950-54; author, also writer documentaries and other films. Amy Lowell Travelling Poetry scholar, 1965-66; Guggenheim fellow, 1967-68; Bush Found. fellow, 1975-76. Mem. Assn. Rhodes Scholars, Phi Beta Kappa. Author: First Manifesto; Dialectics of Love; To Walk a Crooked Mile; Longshot O'Leary's Garland of Practical Poesy; Witness to the Times; Figures From a Double World; Selected and New Poems; Letter to an Imaginary Friend, Parts I and II; The Movie at the End of the World: Collected Poems; Voyages to the Inland Sea; Voices from Behind the Walls; (children's books) About Clouds, The Beautiful Things; (novel) The Gates of Ivory, the Gates of Horn; (poems) A Sound of One Hand, 1975, Letters to Tomasito, 1976, Open Songs, 1976, Trinc: Praises II, 1979; Waiting for the Angel, 1979. Contbr. to profl. publs. Address: 615 S 11th St Moorhead MN 56560

MCGRATH, WILLIAM LOUGHNEY, inventor, ret. co. exec., research engr.; b. Duluth, Minn., Feb. 17, 1911; s. Augustus Henry and Anna (Barrington) McG.; B.S. in Archtl. Engring., U. Minn., 1932; m. Elizabeth Grobe, Sept. 17, 1934; children—Patricia (Mrs. Charles V. O'Connor), Nancy (Mrs. John M. Freyer), Kathleen (Mrs. James F. Kelly), William Loughney. Asst. mgr. air conditioning control div. Honeywell, Inc., Mpls., 1934-39, air conditioning controls mgr., Phila., 1934-43; with Carrier Corp., Syracuse, N.Y., 1943—, exec. v.p. Carrier Air Conditioning Co. subsidiary, 1962-70, exec. asst. to chmn. Carrier Corp., 1970-72, 75—; pres. Caricor Ltd., London, Eng., 1972-74; vice chmn. bldg. research adv. bd. Nat. Acad. Scis.-Acad. Engring.-NRC, 1968-71; chmn. Fed. Constrn. Agy., NRC, 1969-71; v.p. Am. Nat. Standards Inst., 1967-68. Chmn. planning com. Collier County (Fla.); other civic posts. Named Modern Pioneer, N.A.M., 1965. Registered profl. engr., N.Y. Fellow Am. Soc. Heating, Refrigeration and Air Conditioning Engrs. (nat. pres. 1966-67), Inst. Heating and Ventilating Engrs. (U.K.), Chartered Inst. Bldg. Services (U.K.); mem. ASME, ASTM, Tau Beta Pi, Alpha Delta Phi. Roman Catholic. Clubs: Junior Carlton, Pall Mall (London); Naples (Fla.) Country. Contbr. numerous articles to tech. jours. U.S., fgn. patentee in field. Home: 4005 Gulf Shore Blvd N Naples FL 33940 Office: William L McGrath Laboratory Naples FL 33940

MCGRATH, WILLIAM RESTORE, transp. planner; b. Stratford, Conn., Oct. 4, 1922; s. Thomas Christopher and Alpha Retta (Perry) McG.; B.C.E., Rensselaer Poly. Inst., 1950; diploma Yale Bur. Hwy. Traffic, 1951; m. Lillian Joyce DeAngelis, Mar. 9, 1945; children—Brian, David, Raymond, Harold, Vincent, Mary, Kevin, Rita, Beverly, Nora, Margaret. Mem. faculty Bur. Hwy. Traffic Yale,

New Haven, 1951-55; dir. traffic and parking City of New Haven, 1955-63; transp. coordinator Boston Redevel. Authority, 1963-68; commr. dept. traffic and parking City of Boston, 1968-70; v.p. Raymond Parish Pine & Weiner, Tarrytown, N.Y., 1970—. Cons., AID, Madras, India, 1963, Dublin, Ireland, 1965, World Trade Center, Moscow, USSR, 1974. Mem. exec. com. Met. Area Planning Council, Boston, 1965-70, Gov.'s Council on Transp., 1968-70; mem. urban ecology adv. council Inst. Ecology, 1973—. Served with USNR, 1943-45. Registered profl. engr. Calif., Conn., Mass., N.J., N.Y. Fellow Inst. Transp. Engrs. (nat. pres. 1973, chmn. equal opportunity com., chmn. U.S. legis. com.); mem. Nat. Soc. Profl. Engrs., Am. Road and Transp. Builders Assn., Transp. Research Bd., Sigma Xi, Tau Beta Pi, Chi Epsilon. Roman Catholic. Home: 2773 Old Yorktown Rd Yorktown Heights NY 10598 Office: 555 White Plains Rd Tarrytown NY 10591

MCGRAW, ARTHUR GARFIELD, JR., coll. dean; b. Chgo., Dec. 9, 1918; s. Arthur Garfield and Justine (Caswell) McG.; B.Ed., Whitewater State Tchrs. Coll., 1940; M.S. in Ednl. Adminstrn., U. Wis., 1948, Ph.D., 1958; m. Doris Helen Knudson, Nov. 28, 1952; children—Bruce Arthur, David Paul, Erik Steven. Tchr. pub. high sch., Ft. Atkinson, 1940-42, Whitewater, Wis., 1946-48; prin. campus elem. sch., chmn. dept. elem. edn. U. Wis.-Whitewater, 1948-68, asso. dean Grad. Sch., 1968-71, dean, 1971—; treas., mem. exec. bd. Whitewater Found., 1964-66. Mem. adv. com. Park and Recreation Bd., Whitewater, 1973. Pres. bd. edn. Whitewater Unified Sch. Dist., 1973-75. Served with M.C., AUS, 1942-46. Mem. Wis. Elementary Sch. Prins. Assn. (life; exec. bd. 1961-69), Phi Kappa Phi, Kappa Delta Pi, Phi Delta Kappa. Episcopalian (sr. warden 1965-74, 77-79, jr. warden 1975-77). Author: Ready for the Teaching Team!?, 1961. Home: 517 S Prince St Whitewater WI 53190

MC GRAW, CHARLES FRANCIS, actor; b. N.Y.C., May 10, 1914; s. Francis Park and Beatrice (Crisp) McG.; grad. high sch.; m. Freda A. Choy, Oct. 12, 1938; 1 dau., Jill McGraw Gregson. Appeared in Broadway plays Jazz Age, 1935, Dead End, 1936, Boy Meets Girl, 1936, The Night of January 16, 1936, Golden Boy, 1937-38, Native Son, 1941; motion pictures include: The Killers, 1946, The Gangster, 1947, Roses are Red, 1947, Blood On the Moon, 1948, Border Incident, 1949, His Kind of Woman, 1950, Loophole, 1953, The Bridges of Toko-Ri, 1954, Toward the Unknown, 1956, Joe Dakota, 1956, Slaughter on Tenth Avenue, 1957, Spartacus, 1960, Cimmaron, 1960, Pendulum, 1968, In Cold Blood, 1967, Johnny Got His Gun, 1971, River Blood, 1973, Twilight's Last Gleaming, 1977, others; appeared on radio for 30 years, now on TV. Served with AUS, 1943-45. Mem. Screen Actors Guild, Actors Equity Assn., AFTRA. Home: PO Box 4796 Valley Village North Hollywood CA 91607 Office: 9000 Sunset Blvd Los Angeles CA 90069

MC GRAW, DARRELL VIVIAN, JR., judge; b. Wyoming County, W.Va., Nov. 8, 1936; s. Darrell Vivian and Julia Rosella (ZeKany) McG.; A.B., W.Va. U., 1961, LL.B., J.D., 1964, M.A., 1977. Admitted to W.Va. bar, 1964; gen. atty. Fgn. Claims Settlement Commn., Dept. State, 1964; counsel to Gov., State of W.Va., 1965-68; practice law, Shepherdstown and Charleston, 1968-76; judge W.Va. Supreme Ct. Appeals, Charleston, 1977—. Served with U.S. Army, 1954-57. Democrat. Office: Supreme Ct State Capitol Bldg Charleston WV 25311

MCGRAW, HAROLD WHITTLESEY, JR., publisher; b. Bklyn., Jan. 10, 1918; s. Harold Whittlesey and Louise (Higgins) McG.; grad. Lawrenceville (N.J.) Sch., 1936; A.B., Princeton, 1940; m. Anne PerLee, Nov. 30, 1940; children—Suzanne, Harold Whittlesey III, Thomas Per-Lee, Robert Pearse. With G.M. Basford, advt. agy., N.Y.C., 1940-41, Brentano's Bookstores, Inc., 1946; with McGraw-Hill Book Co., Inc., N.Y.C., 1947—, successively promotion mgr., dir. co. advt. and trade sales, 1947-55, dir., v.p. charge trade book, indsl. and bus. book depts., co. advt., 1955-61, sr. v.p., 1961-68, pres., chief exec. officer, 1968—; dir. McGraw Hill, Inc., 1954—, pres., 1974—, chief exec. officer, 1975—, chmn. bd., 1976—. Pres., Princeton U. Press. Served as capt. USAAF, 1941-45. Clubs: University (N.Y.C.); Blind Brook (Purchase, N.Y.). Home: Watch Tower Rd Darien CT 06820 Office: 1221 Ave of Americas New York City NY 10020

MC GRAW, JAMES DUANE, hotel exec.; b. Ringling, Okla., Oct. 10, 1931; s. Sterling Porter and Ruth Ella (Fletcher) McG.; B.A., Tex. Technol. U., 1953; M.A., Columbia, 1955; m. Nelda Jo Vaughter, Sept. 22, 1956; children—Jenna Ruth, Nina Karen, Melinda Leigh. Capital project officer U.S. Devel. Loan Fund, Washington, 1959-61; loan officer, program officer AID, Washington, Nicosia, Cyprus, Ankara, Turkey, Dacca, East Pakistan, Islamabad, Pakistan, 1961-66; mgr. treas.'s ops. ITT, N.Y.C., 1966-69; v.p., treas. Sheraton Corp., Boston, 1969-72, exec. v.p., 1972—. Chmn. bd. trustees Mt. Scenario Coll., Ladysmith, Wis.; bd. advisers Brighter Day, Boston. Mem. Am. Hotel and Motel Assn. (industry real estate fin. adv. com.). Home: 8 Traill St Cambridge MA 02138 Office: 60 State St Boston MA 02210

MC GRAW, JAMES E., pharm. co. exec.; b. Mpls., Dec. 15, 1931; s. John J. and Amy McG.; grad. U. Minn., 1953; postgrad. Harvard Bus. Sch., 1963; m. Ann Padden, Mar. 27, 1951; children—Timothy, Colleen, Mark. Vice pres. sales-mktg. Dorsey Labs., Lincoln, Nebr., 1967-71; pres. gen. diagnostic div. Warner Lambert, Morris Plains, N.J., 1971-74; pres. pharm. group Marion Labs., Inc., Kansas City, Mo., 1974-79, exec. v.p., 1979—. Mem. Nat. Wholesale Druggists Assn., Pharm. Mfrs. Assn., Nat. Assn. Chain Drugs, Proprietary Assn. Club: Kansas City. Home: 6527 Overhill Shawnee Mission KS 66208 Office: 10236 Bunker Ridge Rd Kansas City MO 64137*

MC GRAW, WALTER JOHN, lawyer; b. Richmond Hill, N.Y., May 4, 1928; s. Walter Jeffries and Veronica Lillian (Kilcline) McG.; B.A., U. Richmond (Va.), 1950; LL.B., Washington and Lee U., Lexington, Va., 1955; m. Maryglyn Cooper, Aug. 15, 1953; children—Martha Glenn, Walter John. Admitted to Va. bar, 1955; asso. partner firm Christian, Marks, Scott & Spicer, Richmond, 1955-56; asso. partner firm Hunton & Williams, Richmond, 1956-63; counsel Life Ins. Co. of Va., Richmond, 1963-66, asst. gen. counsel, 1966-68, asso. gen. counsel, 1968-70; gen. counsel Richmond Corp., 1970-73, v.p., gen. counsel, 1973-77; v.p., gen. counsel Richmond Co., 1977-78; v.p., gen. counsel Continental Fin. Sers. Co., 1979—, also dir.; dir. Ins. Mgmt. Corp., Ins. Mgmt. Corp. Fla., Home Shop, Inc., Capital Printing Co., Mut. Insurers Inc., Va. Printing Co., Bank of Va., Hewitt, Coleman & Assos. Inc. Mem. exec. bd. Robert E. Lee council Boy Scouts Am.; vice rector, chmn. exec. com., bd. visitors James Madison U.; mem. agency agreements com. United Way Greater Richmond, div. chmn., 1972. Served with USN, 1951-53, USNR, 1973—. Mem. Am., Va. (chmn. young lawyers sect., bus. law sect.), Richmond (exec. com., chmn. corp. counsel sect.) bar assns., Omicron Delta Kappa, Phi Delta Phi, Theta Chi. Roman Catholic. K.C. Clubs: Country of Va., Downtown, Focus, Optimist, Richmond Cotillion (Richmond). Home: 4 Lower Tuckahoe Rd W Richmond VA 23233 Office: 6600 W Broad St Richmond VA 23230

MC GREEVY, MILTON, business exec.; b. Chgo., Jan. 27, 1903; s. Milton C. and Dora (Achenbach) McG.; A.B., Harvard, 1924, M.B.A., 1926; m. Barbara James, Apr. 17, 1929; children—Jean, Thomas James, Barbara Ann, Gail. Partner, McGreevy & Co. (mem. N.Y. Stock Exchange), 1929-30, Harris, Upham & Co. (inc. 1965), Kansas City, Mo., 1930-65, vice chmn., 1965-76; v.p. sales Smith Barney, Harris Upham & Co., Inc., Kansas City, 1976-79; chmn. bd. Jackson County Nat. Bank & Trust Co., Prairie Village, Kans., 1979—. Trustee Linda Hall Library, William Rockhill Nelson Gallery of Art. Mem. N.Y. Stock Exchange. Clubs: University, Kansas City, Kansas City Country, Mission Hills, River (Kansas City). Home: 5707 Oakwood Rd Shawnee Mission KS 66208 Office: 6940 Mission Rd Prairie Village KS 66208

MC GREGOR, DONALD THORNTON, journalist; b. McLennan County, Tex., Mar. 20, 1924; s. Marshall Thornton and Flora Elvira (Welch) McG.; B.A., Baylor U., Waco, Tex., 1947; postgrad. Southwestern Baptist Theol. Sem., Ft. Worth, 1951-52; m. Alice Carlene Barnhill, Dec. 21, 1946; children—Alice Diane McGregor Tyrone, Robert Thornton, Donald Wayne. Agr. reporter Midland (Tex.) Reporter-Telegram, 1948-49; continuity dir. Sta. KCRS, Midland, 1949-50; editorial asso. Bapt. Standard, Dallas, 1952-55; real estate editor Dallas Time Herald, 1959; pub. relations exec. Union Bankers Ins. Co., Dallas, 1955-58; asso. editor Bapt. Standard, 1959-71; editor Calif. So. Bapt., Fresno, 1971-73; publisher Kemp (Tex.) News, Ferris (Tex.) Wheel, also Dawson (Tex.) Herald, 1973-74; asso. editor Bapt. Record, Jackson, Miss., 1974-76, editor, 1976—. Chmn. public relations adv. com. So. Bapt. Conv., 1979-80. Served with AUS, 1943-45. Recipient Distinguished Service award So. Bapt. Conv., 1973. Mem. So. Bapt. Press Assn. (sec.-treas. 1964-68), Miss. Broadcasters Assn. Democrat. Home: 202 Turtle Creek Dr Brandon MS 39042 Office: PO Box 530 Jackson MS 39205

MCGREGOR, DUNCAN J(UNIOR), geologist, educator; b. St. Joseph, Mo., Jan. 3, 1923; s. Duncan Edward and Elma B. (Lawrence) McG.; B.S., U. Kans. 1943, M.S., 1948; Ph.D., U. Mich., 1953; m. Thelma A. Dewsbury, June 30, 1946; children—Lynn, Scott D., Brett D. Asst. geologist Kans. Geol. Survey, 1946-47; asst. dist. geologist Sinclair Oil & Gas Co., 1950-52; asst. prof. geology, head indsl. minerals sect. Ind. Geol. Survey, 1953-63; state geologist S.D. Geol. Survey; prof. geology U. S.D., Vermillion, 1963—, chmn. dept. earth sci./physics, 1979—. Served with USNR, 1943-46. Mem. Geol. Soc. Am., AAAS, Am. Assn. Petroleum Geology, Soc. Econ. Geology, Soc. Econ. Paleontology and Minerology, Am. Assn. State Geologists, Sigma Xi, Sigma Gamma Epsilon. Mem. United Ch. of Christ. Rotarian. Home: 945 Ridgecrest Dr Vermillion SD 57069

MC GREGOR, MALCOLM FRANCIS, educator; b. London, Eng., May 19, 1910; s. Walter Malcolm and Alice Mary (Francklin) McG.; B.A., U. B.C., 1930, M.A., 1931; postgrad. U. Mich., 1931-33; Ph.D., U. Cin., 1937; D.C.L., Bishop's U., 1970; D.Litt., Acadia U., 1971; m. Marguerite Blanche Guinn, June 8, 1938; children—Heather Mary, Malcolm Rob Roy. From teaching fellow to prof. classics and ancient history U. Cin., 1933-54, acting dean Grad. Sch. Arts and Scis., 1941-42; mem. Inst. Advanced Study, Princeton U., 1937-38, 48; vis. prof. classics U. B.C., 1952, prof. classics, 1954-77, prof. emeritus, 1977—, head dept., 1954-75, asst. to dean faculty arts and sci., 1957-64, mem. univ. senate, 1963-66, 69-77, dir. residences, 1966-68, dir. ceremonies, 1968-77, master tchr., 1974; vis. prof. ancient history U. Wash., 1953, 76, 77; vis. prof. Oxford and Cambridge univs., Am. Sch. Classical Studies, Athens, 1961, 67-68; sr. fellow Can. Council, 1967-68; mgmt. com. Am. Sch. Classical Studies, Athens; instr. Vancouver Community Coll., 1977—; hon. prof. humanities U. Calgary (Alta.). Dir. centennial com. B.C., 1955-60. John Simon Guggenheim Meml. fellow, 1948; decorated comdr. Order of Phoenix (Greece); Queen's Jubilee medal, 1977. Fellow Royal Soc. Can.; mem. Am. Philol. Assn. (Merit award 1954 v.p., 1968-69, pres. 1969-70.), Archaeol. Inst. Am., Hellenic Soc. Gt. Britain, Classical Assn. Can. (pres. 1968-70), Classical Assn. Pacific N.W. (pres. 1972-73), Ohio Classical Conf. (sec.-treas. 1949-54), B.C. Mainland Cricket League (sec. 1954-61, v.p. 1968—), B.C. Cricket Assn. (sec. 1961-67, v.p. 1969-75), Canadian Field Hockey Assn. (pres. 1969-71). Club: Literary (Cin.). Author: (with B.D. Meritt, H.T. Wade-Gery) The Athenian Tribute Lists, 4 vols., 1953; (with D.W. Bradeen) Studies in Fifth Century Attic Epigraphy, 1973. Editor: (with D.W. Bradeen) Phoros: Tribute to Benjamin Dean Meritt, 1974. Contbr. articles to profl. publs. Home: 4495 W 7th Ave Vancouver BC V6R 1X1 Canada

MC GREGOR, MAURICE, cardiologist; b. South Africa, Mar. 24, 1920; s. Frank and Eleanor (Roechling) McG.; M.B., B.Ch., U. Witwatersrand, Johannesburg, South Africa, 1942, M.D., 1947; m. Margaret Rigsby Becklake, Mar. 20, 1948; children—James Andrew, Margaret Jane. Lectr., U. Witwatersrand, 1950-57; asso. prof. medicine McGill U., Montreal, Que., Can., 1958—, prof. medicine, 1966—, dean medicine, 1967-72, vice prin. health care, 1972-74, physician-in-chief, 1974-79. Fellow Royal Coll. Physicians (London, Eng.), Royal Coll. Physicians and Surgeons Can. Contbr. numerous articles to tech. jours. Research in physiology, physiopathology of coronary circulation in health and disease. Home: 532 Pine Ave W Montreal PQ H2W 1S6 Canada Office: Royal Victoria Hospital 687 Pine Ave W Montreal PQ Canada

MCGREW, ELIZABETH ANNE, physician; b. Faribault, Minn., Aug. 30, 1916; d. Charles Dana and Edna (Rosebrook) McGrew; student Rockford Coll., 1933-36; B.A., Carleton Coll., 1938; M.D., U. Minn., 1944. Intern, Milw. County Hosp., Wauwatosa, Wis., 1944-45; asst. in pathology U. Ill. Coll. Medicine, Chgo., 1945-46, instr., 1946-50, asst. prof., 1950-55, asso. prof., 1955-62, prof. pathology, 1962—; resident in pathology Research and Ednl. Hosps., Chgo., 1945-49, asst. pathologist, 1949-55, asso. pathologist, 1955—. Diplomate Am. Bd. Pathology. Fellow Am. Soc. Clin. Pathologists, Coll. Am. Pathologists; mem. AMA, Am. Med. Women's Assn. (pres.), Internat. Acad. Pathologists, AAAS, Am. Soc. Cytology, Internat. Acad. Cytology, Sigma Xi. Home: 548 Judson Ave Evanston IL 60202 Office: 1853 W Polk St Chicago IL 60612

MCGRORY, MARY, newspaperwoman; b. Boston, 1918; d. Edward Patrick and Mary (Jacobs) McGrory; A.B., Emmanuel Coll. Reporter, Boston Herald Traveler, 1942-47; book reviewer Washington Star, 1947-54, feature writer for nat. staff, 1954—, now also syndicated columnist. Recipient George Polk Meml. award; Pulitzer prize for commentary, 1975. Office: Washington Star 225 Virginia Ave SE Washington DC 20061*

MC GRUDER, STEPHEN JONES, securities analyst; b. Louisville, Nov. 14, 1943; s. Clement W. and Elizabeth Boyer (Short) McG.; B.S. in Chemistry, Stanford U., 1966; B.A. in Econs., Claremont Men's Coll., 1966. Vice pres. Eberstadt Asset Mgmt., N.Y.C., 1978—. Chartered fin. analyst. Mem. Fin. Analysts Fedn., IEEE. Republican. Episcopalian. Club: University (N.Y.C.). Office: 1 W 54th St New York NY 10019

MCGUANE, THOMAS FRANCIS, III, author, screenwriter; b. Wyandotte, Mich., Dec. 11, 1939; s. Thomas Francis and Alice Rita (Torphy) McG.; student Mich. State U., 1958-62, Yale Sch. Drama, 1962-65; Wallace Stegner fellow Stanford U., 1966; m. Portia Crockett, Sept. 8, 1962; 1 son, Thomas Francis. Author: The Sporting Club, 1969; The Bushwhacked Piano, 1971; Ninety-Two in the Shade, 1973; screenplays include: The Bushwhacked Piano, 1970, Rancho Deluxe, 1973, Ninety-Two in the Shade, 1974, Missouri Breaks, 1974; contbr. Sports Illustrated, 1969-73. Recipient Richard and Hinda Rosenthal Found. award fiction Nat. Inst. Arts and Letters, 1972. Club: Mandible (Key West). Office: care Farrar Straus & Giroux 630 Fifth Ave New York NY 10020*

MCGUCKIN, JAMES FREDERICK, engring. and mfg. co. exec.; b. Phila., June 5, 1930; s. James B. and Catherine Marie (Faber) McG.; B.S. in Engring., Lehigh U., Bethlehem, Pa., 1952; M.B.A., Drexel U., Phila., 1966; m. Margaret Marie Sculley, Apr. 18, 1958; children—Karen, James Frederick, Richard, Brian, Margaret. With space div. Gen. Electric Co., Valley Forge, Pa., 1957-69; v.p., div. gen. mgr. Budd Co., Phila., 1969-70; gen. mgr. power circuit breaker div. I.T.E. Imperial Corp., Los Angeles, 1970-74; gen. mgr. power circuit breaker dept. Gen. Electric Co., Phila., 1974-75, gen. mgr. switchgear equipment mktg. dept., Phila., 1975-76; pres. equipment systems div. Dominion Bridge Co., Wilmington, Del., 1976-77; pres. Litton Med. Systems, Des Plaines, Ill., 1977—. Chmn. maj. gift com. Los Angeles YMCA, 1974; pres. bd. Maple Glen (Pa.) Sch., 1965-68, Maple Glen Civic Assn., 1967. Served to lt. (j.g.) USNR, 1953-57. Mem. Nat. Elec. Mfrs. Assn., Pi Tau Sigma, Alpha Pi Mu. Republican. Roman Catholic. Clubs: Jonathan, Whitemarch Valley Country, Atlantic City Country, Friendly Hills Country. Home: 2 Martins Rd Newtown Square PA 19073

MCGUIGAN, FRANK JOSEPH, psychologist, educator; b. Oklahoma City, Dec. 7, 1924; B.A., UCLA, 1945, M.A., 1949; Ph.D., U. So. Calif., 1950. Instr., Pepperdine Coll., 1949-50; asst. prof. U. Nev., 1950-51; research asso. Psychol. Corp., 1950-51; research scientist, sr. research scientist, acting dir. research Human Resources Research Office, George Washington U., 1951-55; prof. psychology Hollins Coll., Roanoke, Va., 1955-76, chmn. dept., 1955-76; research prof. Grad. Sch., prof. dept. psychology, dep. psychiatry and behavioral scis., Sch. Medicine, dir. Performance Research Lab., Inst. Advanced Study, U. Louisville, 1976—; adj. research prof. N.C. State U., 1970-72; vis. prof. U. Calif., Santa Barbara, 1966, U. Hawaii, summer 1965; Nat. Acad. Scis. vis. scientist, Hungary, 1975. Served with USNR, 1942-46. Recipient award for outstanding contributions to edn. in psychology Am. Psychol. Found., 1973. Fellow Am. Psychol. Assn., Internat. Soc. Research on Aggression; mem. Am. Assn. Advancement of Tension Control (exec. dir. 1973—), Pavlovian Soc. (mem. exec. bd. 1973—, pres. 1975-76, editor, chmn. publ. bd. Pavlovian Jour. Biol. Sci.), Am. Physiol. Soc., Biofeedback Soc. Am., Interam. Soc. Psychology, Internat. Congress of Applied Psychology, Ky. Psychol. Assn., Psychonomic Soc., Soc. Psychophysiol. Research, Sigma Xi. Author numerous books in field including: The Biological Basis of Behavior, 1963; (with P.J. Wood) Contemporary Studies in Psychology, 1972; Cognitive Psychophysiology - Principles of Covert Behavior, 1978; Experimental Psychology: A Methodological Approach, 3d edit., 1978. Editor numerous works in field. Contbr. articles to profl. jours. Mem. editorial bd. Archiv fur Arzneitherapie, Biofeedback and Self-regulation. Office: Performance Research Lab Univ of Louisville Louisville KY 40208

MC GUIGAN, FRANK JOSEPH, psychologist, educator; b. Oklahoma City, Dec. 7, 1924; s. Francis Leo and Edith Louise (Whiting) McG.; B.A., UCLA, 1945, M.A., 1949; Ph.D., U. So. Calif., 1950; m. Lillian Vidovich, July 29, 1950; children—Joan (Mrs. Broaddus C. Fitzpatrick), Constance, Richard. Instr., Pepperdine Coll., Los Angeles, 1949-50; asst. prof. U. Nev., Reno, 1950-51; sr. research scientist, dir. research Human Resources Research Office, George Washington U., Washington, 1951-55; prof., chmn. dept. psychology Hollins Coll., Roanoke, Va., 1955-76; research prof. Grad. Sch., U. Louisville, also prof. psychology Coll. Arts and Scis., prof. psychiatry Sch. Medicine, also dir. Performance Research Lab., Inst. Advanced Study, 1977—. Vis. prof. U. Hawaii, summer 1965, U. Calif. at Santa Barbara, 1966; dir. evaluation project Ency. Brit., 1961-67; adj. research prof. Adult Learning Center, N.C. State U., 1970-72; exec. dir. Am. Assn. for Advancement of Tension Control, 1973—. Pres., Roanoke Mental Health Assn., 1968. Served with USNR, 1942-46; PTO. Recipient award for outstanding contbn. to edn. in psychology Am. Psychol. Found., 1973. Fellow Am. Psychol. Assn.; mem. Am. Physiol. Soc., Psychonomic Soc., Pavlovian Soc. (pres. 1975-76), Interam. Soc. Psychology, Biofeedback Research Soc., Soc. for Psychophysiol. Research, Sigma Xi, others. Author: Experimental Psychology, 3d edit., 1978; The Psychophysiology of Thinking, 1973; Cognitive Psychophysiology, 1978; Psychophysiological Measurement of Covert Behavior, 1979; others. Contbr. articles to profl. jours. Office: Performance Research Lab U Louisville Louisville KY 40208

MCGUIGAN, JAMES EDWARD, educator, physician, scientist; b. Paterson, N.J., Aug. 20, 1931; s. Harold Taylor and Marie (Lloyd) McG.; student Coll. Holy Cross, 1949-50; B.S., Seattle U., 1952; M.D., St. Louis U., 1956; m. Mary DeLa Montanya, June 9, 1956; children—Sheila, Maura, John. Intern, Pa. Hosp., 1956-57; asst. resident in medicine U. Wash. Sch. Medicine, Seattle, 1960-62, fellow in gastroenterology, 1962-64; spl. fellow in immunology Washington U. Sch. Medicine, St. Louis, 1964-66, asst. prof. medicine, 1966-69; prof. medicine, chief div. gastroenterology U. Fla. Coll. Medicine, Gainesville, 1969—, chmn. dept. medicine, 1976—. Mem. program projects com. Nat. Inst. Arthritis, Metabolic and Digestive Diseases, NIH, 1971-73, mem. gen. medicine A study sect., 1974-76, chmn., 1976-78. Served to capt. USAF, 1957-60. Research fellow in gastroenterology; Spl. fellow in immunology, Career Devel. award, research grantee NIH; research grantee Am. Heart Assn., Am. Cancer Soc. Mem. Am. Assn. Immunologists, Am. Gastroent. Assn. (Distinguished Achievement award 1974), Am. Soc. Clin. Investigation, Assn. Am. Physicians, Assn. Profs. Medicine, Alpha Omega Alpha, Sigma Xi. Research and publs. in gastroenterology and immunology. Home: 2500 NW 21 Ave Gainesville FL 32605

MC GUINNESS, AIMS CHAMBERLAIN, physician; b. Chester, N.Y., Mar. 10, 1905; s. J. Holmes and Amy Aims (Chamberlain) McG.; A.B., Princeton, 1927; M.D., Columbia, 1931; m. Margaret A. Hatfield, Sept. 2, 1933 (dec. July 14, 1975); children—Louise Hatfield (Mrs. G.C. Ludlow, Jr.), Margaret (Mrs. John Hinman Denny), Aims C. Intern, U. Pa. Hosp., Phila., 1931-33; resident Children's Hosp., Phila., 1933-34; pvt. practice pediatrics, Phila., 1934-48; faculty U. Pa. Sch. Medicine, 1934, asst. prof. pediatrics, 1946-50, asso. prof., 1951-57, adj. prof., 1968—, dean Grad. Sch. Medicine, 1951-54; clin. dir. Miners Meml. Hosp. Assn., United Mine Workers Am. Welfare and Retirement Fund, 1954-56, cons., 1956-57. Spl. asst. for health and med. affairs to sec. HEW, 1957-59; exec. sec. Com. on Med. Edn., N.Y. Acad. Medicine, 1959-66; asso. dir. Ednl. Council Fgn. Med. Grads., 1967-74, trustee, 1957-66, pres. bd. trustees, 1963-66; asst. vis. physician Children's Hosp., Phila., 1940-46, sr. vis. physician, 1947-54, dir. hosps., 1948-51, cons. staff, 1954-57, 68-79, emeritus staff, 1979—; dir. emeritus Phila. Serum Exchange, 1934-54; mem. subcom. on blood Health Resources Adv. Bd. ODM, 1953-57; asso. mem. commn. immunization Armed Forces Epidemiological Bd., 1954-58; examiner Am. Bd. Pediatrics, 1949-65; mem. Fed. Council Sci. and Tech., 1959. Mem. U.S. del. WHO, 1957-59, City N.Y. Community Mental Health Bd., 1962-64, Health Research Council City N.Y., 1962-64. Bd. dirs. Am. Council Emigrés in Professions; trustee Keene Valley (N.Y.) Hosp. (v.p. 1955-62), Am. Nat. Council Health Edn. of Pub., 1962-68 (v.p. 1959-63). Served as lt. col. M.C., AUS, World War II. Decorated Legion of Merit. Fellow N.Y. Acad. Medicine; mem. AMA, Assn. Am. Med. Coll., Am. Acad. Pediatrics,

Am. Pediatric Soc. (past sec.), Council on Med. Adminstrn., Assn. Med. Consultants World War II, John Morgan Soc. (pres. 1942-46), Phila. Pediatric Soc. (pres. 1949), Philadelphia County Med. Soc., Soc. Pediatric Research. Episcopalian. Contbr. articles to med. jours. Home: 721 Prospect Ave Princeton NJ 08540

MCGUINNESS, WILLIAM JAMES, educator, mech. engr.; b. N.Y.C., Mar. 26, 1902; s. James W. and Angelina (Tierney) McG.; M.E., Stevens Inst. Tch., 1924; m. Mary P. Quinlan, May 12, 1934; children—William J., James, John, Jane; m. 2d, Mrs. Edward Reimann, July 27, 1973. Engr., Turner Constrn. Co. 1924-30, Vermilya Brown, builders, 1930-35; v.p. Wininger & Selby, builders, 1936-39; faculty Pratt Inst., 1940-66, prof. architecture, 1954-66, chmn. dept. structural design, 1954-66, now prof. emeritus; adj. prof. architecture Columbia, 1945-61, vis. lectr. Grad. Sch. Architecture and Planning, 1976; chief engr. N.Y.C. Dept. Investigation, 1966-68; partner McGuinness & Duncan, engrs., 1952—; adj. prof. architecture N.Y. Inst. Tech., 1971-74. Cons. to exam. com. Nat. Council Archtl. Registration Bds., 1962-72. Recipient award for excellence in design N.Y. State Assn. Architects, 1972, Honor award for excellence in architecture L.I. chpt. AIA, 1975. Fellow ASCE; mem. Am. Soc. Heating, Refrigerating and Air Conditioning Engrs., Gt. South Bay Yacht Racing Assn. Author: (with B. Stein) Mechanical and Electrical Equipment for Buildings, 1971, Building Technology: Mechanical and Electrical Systems, 1977. Contbg. editor Progressive Architecture, 1954-68. Address: 1435 Briarcliff Dr Merrick NY 11566

MC GUIRE, ALFRED JAMES, basketball coach, sports equipment co. exec.; b. N.Y.C., Sept. 7, 1931; s. John and Winifred (Sullivan) McG.; B.A., St. John's Coll., Bklyn., 1952; m. Patricia Sharkey, Aug. 22, 1953; children—Alfred J., Noreen, Robert. Coach, Dartmouth Coll., Hanover, N.H., 1955-57, Belmont Abbey Coll., Belmont, N.C., 1957-64; athletic dir., head basketball coach Marquette U., Milw., 1964-77; v.p., dir. sports edn. publs. Medalist Industries, Milw., 1970-78, also dir.; basketball commentator NBC, 1978—; profl. basketball player, N.Y., 1951-52, Balt., 1954; pres. Hall of Fame Basketball Camps, 1967—. Trustee Milw. County Stadium Recreation Commn., 1972—. Named Sports Figure of Year, Wis. C. of C., 1974; Coach of Year, AP, UPI, Sporting News, U.S. Basketball Writers Assn., 1971, 74. Mem. Nat. Assn. Basketball Coaches. Club: Westmoor Country. Office: care NBC Sports 30 Rockefeller Plaza New York NY 10020*

MCGUIRE, DELBERT, educator; b. Altus, Okla., Aug. 24, 1917; s. Clinton F. and Ella (Stevens) McG.; B.J., U. Tex., 1947, M.J., 1948; Ph.D., U. Ia., 1966; m. Virginia Wright, Feb. 6, 1942; 1 son, Delbert Allen. Reporter, sub-editor Austin Am.-Statesman, 1945-47; editor So. Florist and Nurseryman, Ft. Worth, 1948-50, Automatic World, Ft. Worth, 1948-52; asso. prof. journalism N. Tex. State U., 1950-61; prof., head journalism dept. Tex. A. and M. U., 1961-67; vis. prof. journalism U. N.C., 1967-68; prof., chmn. tech. journalism Colo. State U., Ft. Collins, 1968—. Served with USAAF, 1942-45. Mem. Am. Council for Edn. in Journalism, Am. Soc. Journalism Sch. Adminstrs. (chmn. newspaper div. 1970-71, pres.-elect 1971-72), A.P. Mng. Editors, Sigma Delta, Chi. Author: Technical and Industrial Journalism, 1957. Editorial cons., 1974—. Contbr. articles to profl. jours. Home: 160 Yale Ave Fort Collins CO 80525

MC GUIRE, DOROTHY HACKETT, actress; b. Omaha, June 14, 1918; d. Thomas Johnson and Isabel (Flaherty) McG.; student Pine Manor Jr. Coll., 1935-37; m. John Swope, July 18, 1943; 2 children. Stage debut in A Kiss for Cinderella, Omaha, 1930; played stock in Deertrees, Maine; N.Y.C. debut as understudy in Stop-Over, 1938, also understudied Our Town, 1938; tour My Dear Children, 1939; appeared in Swingin' the Dream, 1939, Kind Lady, 1940, Medicine Show, 1940, Claudia, 1941; gen. understudy The Time of Your Life, 1940; toured in USO prodn. Dear Ruth, 1945, also toured in Tonight at 8:30, 1947, Summer and Smoke, 1950; appeared in Legend of Lovers, 1951, Winesburg, Ohio, 1958, The Night of the Iguana, 1976, Cause Celebre, 1979; film appearances include: Claudia, 1943, A Tree Grows in Brooklyn, 1945, Claudia and David, 1946, The Spiral Staircase, 1946, Gentlemen's Agreement, 1947, Make Haste to Live, 1954, Three Coins in the Fountain, 1954, Trial, 1955, Friendly Persuasion, 1956, Old Yeller, 1957, This Earth is Mine, 1959, A Summer Place, 1959, The Swiss Family Robinson, 1960, The Dark at the Top of the Stairs, 1960, Summer Magic, 1962, The Greatest Story Ever Told, 1965, Flight of the Doves, 1971, Jonathan Livingston Seagull (voice only), 1973; TV movie She Waits, 1971; featured in radio serial Big Sister, 1937, in play Hamlet, 1951; TV appearances include: U.S. Steel Hour, 1954, Lux Video Theatre, 1954, Climax, 1954, 56, Another Part of the Forest, 1972, The Runaways, 1975, The Philadelphia Story, 1954, Little Women, 1978. Recipient N.Y. Drama Critics Circle award, 1941; named Best Actress by Nat. Bd. Rev., 1955. Mem. Screen Actors Guild, Actors Equity Assn., AFTRA. Office: Box 25940 Los Angeles CA 90025

MCGUIRE, EDWARD PERKINS, former govt. ofcl.; b. Boston, Oct. 22, 1904; grad. Worcester Acad.; B.Textile Engring., Lowell Textile Inst., 1928; D.Sc., Lowell Technol. Inst., 1958; m. Katherine Ward, Oct. 5, 1929. With Harris Forbes & Co., N.Y.C., 1928-29, Asso. Dry Goods Corp., 1929-31; with James McCreery & Co., N.Y.C., 1931-36, gen. mgr., 1937-39; divisional mgr. Montgomery Ward & Co., 1939-42; dir., pres. R.H. White Corp., Boston, and R.H. White Realty Corp., 1945-48; pres., mng. dir. Sterling-Lindner-Davis, Cleve., 1950-54; v.p., dir. Allied Stores of Ohio, 1952-54; dep. asst. sec. of def. for internat. security affairs, 1954-56, asst. sec. def. for supply and logistics, Washington, 1956-61; dir. Log-Etronics, Inc. Chmn. Commn. on Govt. Procurement, 1970-73. Served to comdr. U.S. Navy, 1942-45; organizer, supr. forward pricing and price revision activities, Navy Dept.; organizer negotiation group handling contracts of Bur. of Ordnance; dep. chief procurement br. of sec.'s office, chief of procurement br., 1945. Decorated Legion of Merit; recipient Pub. service medal Def. Dept., 1961. Mem. Phi Psi. Roman Catholic. Knight of Malta, Knight Comdr. Holy Sepulchre. Clubs: Metropolitan, Chevy Chase (Washington). Home: 2420 Tracy Pl Washington DC 20008

MCGUIRE, FRANCIS THOMAS, ret. mfg. co. exec.; b. N.Y.C., Oct. 2, 1912; s. Thomas Edward and Josephine Veronica (Ryan) McG.; B.S. in Mech. Engring., U. Notre Dame, 1937, M.S. in Metallurgy, 1938, Ph.D., 1941; m. Bernease Anne VanTuyl, Aug. 6, 1936; children—Patricia Anne (Mrs. Robert Kasten), Michael Francis. Hennen Jennings scholar Harvard U. Sch. Engring., 1938-39; teaching fellow U. Notre Dame, 1939-41; asso. prof. engring. U. Ky., 1941-43; lab. dir. Republic Steel Corp., 1943-46; foundry mgr. Sibley Machine & Foundry Co., South Bend, Ind., 1946-49; with Deere & Co., Moline, Ill., 1949-66, 66—, v.p. research, 1962-65, v.p., mng. dir. Europe, Africa and Middle East, 1967-70, sr. v.p. overseas div., 1970-73; v.p. research U. Notre Dame, South Bend, 1965-66. Mgr. adv. com. armor piercing projectiles of chief ordnance Nat. Acad. Sci., 1952, def. research com., 1952—; cons. Army Weapons Command, Indian Investment Centre. Past chmn., past pres. bd. Jr. Achievement Rock Island County. Mem. Am. Def. Preparedness Assn., Am. Soc. Agrl. Engrs., ASME, Brit. Iron and Steel Inst., Soc. Automotive Engrs., Sigma Xi. Clubs: Sailing, Moorings Golf (Naples, Fla.). Co-author: Ferritic Steels at Low Temperatures. 1945. Home: Executive Club Apt 312 3300 Gulf Shore Blvd Naples FL 33940

MCGUIRE, HAROLD FREDERICK, lawyer; b. N.Y.C., June 27, 1906; s. Frederick Francis and Lillian (Shaw) McG.; A.B., Columbia U., 1927, LL.B., 1929; m. Lillian Virginia Jones, Dec. 28, 1933; children—Harold Frederick, Bartlett Hoyle. Admitted to N.Y. bar, 1929; asst. Columbia U. Law Sch., 1929-30; mem. legal staff firm Cravath, de Gersdorff, Swaine & Wood, N.Y.C., 1930-39; partner firm Gardner, Morrison, Rogers & McGuire, Washington, 1939-41; partner firm Wickes, Riddell, Bloomer, Jacobi & McGuire, N.Y.C., 1942-76, 76-79; of counsel firm Morgan Lewis & Backius, 1979—; dir. Seaboard Surety Co. Chmn. gymnasium bldg. fund Columbia U., 1958—, trustee, 1960—, vice chmn. bd. trustees, 1968-77. Mem. Assn. Bar City N.Y., N.Y. County Lawyers Assn., Alumni Fedn. Columbia U. (pres. 1958-60), Phi Beta Kappa, Psi Upsilon. Clubs: Downtown Assn. (N.Y.C.); Point O'Woods (Fire Island, N.Y.). Home: 88 Morningside Dr New York NY 10027 Office: 9 W 57th St New York NY 10019

MCGUIRE, JAMES T., corp. exec.; b. Boston; grad. Boston Coll.; m. Audrey McGuire; children—Carol Ann, James T. Exec. v.p. Canteen Corp.; dir. Nat. Automatic Merchandising Assn., 1962—, mem. exec. com., 1963—, sr. v.p., 1966, pres., 1967. Clubs: Execs., Chgo. Athletic, Mchts. and Mfrs. (Chgo.); Evanston (Ill.) Golf (pres.). Home: Skokie IL 60203 Office: Canteen Corp Merchandise Mart Plaza Chicago IL 60654

MCGUIRE, JOSEPH WILLIAM, educator; b. Milw., Mar. 14, 1925; s. William B. and Marion (Dunn) McG.; Ph.B., Marquette U., 1948; M.B.A., Columbia 1950, Ph.D., 1956; m. Margaret Drewek, Aug. 20, 1946; children—Laurence, Karen, Eileen, Kevin. Asst. prof. U. Wash. Coll. Bus. Adminstrn., Seattle, 1954-56, asso. prof., 1956-61, prof., 1961-63; prof., dean U. Kan. Sch. Bus., 1963-68; dean Coll. Commerce and Bus. Adminstrn., prof. U. Ill., Urbana, 1968-71; v.p. planning U. Cal., Berkeley, 1971-74; prof. adminstrn. U. Cal., Irvine, 1973—. Vis. prof. Netherlands Coll. Econs., Rotterdam, 1957-58; vis. prof. dept. econs. U. Hawaii, 1962-63; Ford vis. research prof. Carnegie-Mellon U. Grad. Sch. Indsl. Adminstrn., 1967-68; cons. editor Goodyear Pub. Co., Wadsworth Pub. Co., 1964-70. Served with USAAF, 1943-45. Recipient McKenzie awards, 1963, 65. Fellow Am. Acad. Mgmt. (bd. govs. 1967-70); mem. Am. Assn. Collegiate Schs. Bus. (dir. 1970-71), Am. Econ. Assn., AAUP, Am. Inst. Decision Scis., Western Econs. Assn., Western Tax Assn. (dir. 1977—), Assn. for Social Econs. (exec. council 1970—, pres. 1973-74), Phi Beta Kappa, Beta Gamma Sigma. Author: Business and Society, 1963; Theories of Business Behavior, 1964; Factors Affecting the Growth of Manufacturing Firms, 1963; Inequality; The Poor and the Rich in America, 1968. Editor, contbr. Interdisciplinary Studies in Business Behavior, 1962; Contemporary Management: Issues and Viewpoints, 1973. Home: 3840 Ocean Birch Dr Corona del Mar CA 92625

MCGUIRE, LESLIE SARAH, editor; b. N.Y.C., Jan. 18, 1945; s. Timothy Strong and Hastings Virginia (Wenderoth) McG.; A.B., Barnard Coll., 1966; State Teaching certificate, N.Y. U., 1968. Pub. relations asst. Guild for Blind, N.Y.C., 1966-67; spl. reading tchr. Pub. Sch. 165, Manhattan, N.Y., 1967-69; editor Platt & Munk Pubs., Bronx, N.Y., 1969—. Mem. Barnard Coll. Alumni Assn. Democrat. Episcopalian. Author: Mosaics, 1974, also 37 children's books, 1970—. Home: 420 Riverside Dr New York City NY 10025 Office: 1055 Bronx River Ave Bronx NY 10472

MC GUIRE, MARIE C., govt. ofcl.; b. Washington; ed. George Washington, Tex., Houston univs.; hon. degree, Villanova U., 1975. Exec. dir. San Antonio Housing Authority until 1961; commr. U.S. Pub. Housing Adminstrn., 1961-66; acting dept. asst. sec. housing assistance adminstrn. HUD, 1966-68, asst. for problems elderly and handicapped, 1968; now housing specialist Internat. Center for Social Gerontology. Named Outstanding Businesswoman of Year, Houston, 1949, San Antonio, 1956; recipient Headliner award Theta Sigma Phi, 1959; award for pub. housing design AIA, 1964; Nat. Council on Aging award, 1965. Author: Housing for the Elderly, 1957; Housing for the Handicapped, 1977; Housing and the Disabled, 1976; also pamphlets, research studies in field. Home: 4501 Connecticut Ave NW Washington DC 20008 Office: Suite 840 425 13th St NW Washington DC 20004

MC GUIRE, ROBERT JOSEPH, city police ofcl., lawyer; b. N.Y.C., Dec. 8, 1936; s. James J. McG.; B.A., Iona Coll., 1958; LL.B., St. John's U., 1961; LL.M., N.Y. U., 1962. Admitted to N.Y. State bar, 1961, U.S. Supreme Ct. bar, 1966; asst. U.S. atty. So. Dist. N.Y., Dept. Justice, 1962-66; dir. Community Law Offices, East Harlem, N.Y.C., 1963-69; mem. firm McGuire & Lawler, N.Y.C., 1969—; commr. police City N.Y., 1978—. Office: NYC Police Dept 1 Police Plaza New York NY 10038*

MCGUIRE, WILLIAM, book editor; b. St. Augustine, Fla., Nov. 8, 1917; s. William Joseph and Edna Laurie (Musgrave) McG.; A.B., U. Fla., 1938, M.A., 1939; postgrad. Johns Hopkins U., 1939-41; m. Anne Georgia Collins, Nov. 13, 1947; children—John, Edward; m. 2d, Paula Van Doren, May 28, 1965; 1 dau., Mary. Reporter, Balt. Sun, 1941, The New Yorker, N.Y.C., 1943-46; information officer U.N. Secretariat, 1946-49; spl. editor Bollingen Series, Bollingen Found., N.Y.C., 1949-56, mng. editor, 1956-67; asso. editor Bollingen Series, Princeton U. Press, 1967—; editorial cons. pubs., libraries, founds. Bd. dirs., sec. Frances G. Wickes Found., 1967-73; trustee Vladimir Nabokov Lit. Trust, 1970-75; mem.-at-large bd. govs. C.G. Jung Inst., San Francisco, 1975-78; trustee C.G. Jung Found., N.Y.C., 1978—. Served with USNR, 1941-43. Exec. editor: Collected Works of C.G. Jung, 1953-79; editor: The Freud/Jung Letters, 1974; C.G. Jung Speaking, 1977; contbr. to Alchemy and the Occult (catalogue of Paul and Mary Mellon collection Yale U.), 1968, 78. Home: 219 Washington Rd Princeton NJ 08540 Office: Princeton U Press Princeton NJ 08540

MC GUIRE, WILLIAM, civil engr., educator; b. S.I., N.Y., Dec. 17, 1920; s. Edward Joseph and Phoebe (Sellman) McG.; B.S. in Civil Engring., Bucknell U., 1942; M.Civil Engring., Cornell U., 1947; m. Barbara Weld, Feb. 5, 1944; children—Robert Weld, Thomas Rhodes. Structural designer Jackson & Moreland, engrs., Boston, 1947-49; faculty Cornell U., Ithaca, 1949—, prof. civil engring., 1960—, dir. Sch. Civil Engring., 1966-68; vis. prof. civil engring. Asian Inst. Tech., Bangkok, Thailand, 1968-70; vis. research engr. Nat. Bur. Standards, 1972; Gledden vis. sr. fellow U. Western Australia, 1973; cons. structural engr., 1951—; vis. prof. U. Tokyo, 1979. Served to lt. USNR, 1942-45. Decorated Naval Letter of Commendation. Fellow ASCE (pres. Ithaca 1964, Norman medal 1962); mem. Am. Concrete Inst., Internat. Assn. Bridge and Structural Engring., Sigma Xi, Chi Epsilon, Kappa Delta Rho. Presbyn. Club: Country of Ithaca. Author: Steel Structures, 1967; (with R.H. Gallagher) Matrix Structural Analysis, 1979. Home: 216 Kelvin Pl Ithaca NY 14850

MCGUIRE, WILLIAM JAMES, educator; b. N.Y.C., Feb. 17, 1925; s. James William and Anne M. (Mitchell) McG.; B.A., Fordham U., 1949, M.A., 1950; Fulbright fellow, Louvain (Belgium) U., 1950-51; Ph.D., Yale, 1954; m. Claire Vernick, Dec. 29, 1954; children—James William, Anne Maureen, Steven Thomas. Postdoctoral fellow U. Minn., 1954-55; asst. prof. Yale, 1955-58; asso. prof. U. Ill., 1958-61; prof. Columbia, 1961-67; prof. U. Calif. at San Diego, 1967-70; fellow London Sch. Econs., 1970-71; prof. Yale, 1971—, chmn. dept. psychology, 1971-73. Mem. adv. panel for sociology and social psychology NSF, 1963-65; mem. review panel for social scis. NIMH, 1968-72; cons. NIH, 1974—; fellow Center for Advanced Study in Behavorial Scis., 1965-66. Served with AUS, 1943-46. Recipient Ann. Social Psychology award AAAS, 1964; Gen. Electric Found. awards, 1963, 64, 66. Guggenheim fellow, 1970-71. Mem. Am. Psychol. Assn. (pres. div. personality and social psychology 1973-74), Am. Sociol. Assn., Am. Assn. Pub. Opinion Research, Sigma Xi. Author: (with Carl I. Hovland and Milton Rosenberg) Attitude Organization and Change, 1960. Editor: (with Robert P. Abelson) Theories of Cognitive Consistency. Editor, Jour. Personality and Social Psychology, 1967-70; cons. editor Jour. Exptl. Social Psychology, Brit. Jour. Social and Clin. Psychology, European Jour. Social Psychology. Home: 225 St Ronan St New Haven CT 06511 Office: Dept Psychology Yale U New Haven CT 06520

MC GUIRE, WILLIAM LAWRENCE, sporting goods exec., lawyer; b. Bklyn., May 24, 1926; s. William Lawrence and Catherine Elizabeth (Ellis) McG.; A.B., Fordham U., 1950; J.D. cum laude, St. John's U., 1954; m. Gloria E. Corse, Sept. 10, 1949; children—William Lawrence, Brian James, Sharon, Mark, Susan. Admitted to N.Y. bar, 1954, also U.S. Supreme Ct.; terminal renting agt. Port of N.Y. Authority, 1950-54; partner firm Rogers, Hoge & Hills, 1954-65, Graham, McGuire & Campaign, 1965-73; v.p., exec. counsel, sec. The Garcia Corp., Teaneck, N.J., 1973-78, pres., chief exec. officer, 1978—; lectr. trade regulation Seton Hall U., 1972—. Trustee Village of Asharoken (N.Y.), 1964, village justice, 1964-68; chmn. Huntington (N.Y.) Zoning Bd. Appeals, 1968-71. Served with USCGR, 1943-46; PTO. Mem. N.Y. State Bar Assn., Assn. Bar City N.Y., N.Y. State Magistrates Assn. Democrat. Roman Catholic. Home: 101 Asharoken Ave Northport NY 11768 Office: 329 Alfred Ave Teaneck NJ 07666

MC GUIRK, WILLIAM EDWARD, JR., bank holding co. exec.; b. N.Y.C., Dec. 31, 1917; s. William Edward and Loretta Beatrice (Lanigan) McG.; B.S., U.S. Naval Acad., 1939; postgrad. Harvard U., 1940; m. Mary Tolfree Paige, Aug. 2, 1941; 15 children. Syndicate mgr. Kuhn, Loeb & Co., N.Y.C., 1945-54; with AEC, 1950-52; exec. v.p. Davison Chem. Co., Balt., 1954-56, pres., 1956-65; successively chmn. exec. com., vice chmn. bd., chmn. Merc.-Safe Deposit & Trust Co., Balt., 1967-72, now dir.; chmn. bd. Merc. Bankshares Corp., 1970—, also dir.; chmn. bd. Borlin Corp., 1961-72; dir. A.S. Abell Co., Dun & Bradstreet Corp., Kirk Corp., L&N R.R. Co., Seaboard Coast Line Industries, Inc., Seaboard Coast Line R.R. Co. Trustee, Johns Hopkins Hosp., chmn., 1972-77. Served to lt. comdr. USNR, 1941-45. Decorated Silver Star. Roman Catholic. Clubs: Md., Elkridge, Links. Office: PO Box 2257 Baltimore MD 21203

MC GURN, BARRETT, govt. ofcl.; b. N.Y.C., Aug. 6, 1914; s. William Barrett and Alice (Schneider) McG.; A.B., Fordham U., 1935, Litt.D., 1958; m. Mary Elizabeth Johnson, May 30, 1942 (dec. Feb. 1960); children—William Barrett III, Elizabeth (Mrs. John J. Hehn), Andrew; m. 2d, Janice Ann McLaughlin, June 19, 1962; children—Summers, Martin Barrett, Mark Barrett. Editor, Fordham Ram, 1934-35; with N.Y. Herald Tribune, 1935-66, asst. corr., Rome, 1939, bur. chief, Rome, 1946-52, 55-62, reporting staff, N.Y.C., 1935-42, 62-66, bur. chief, Paris, 1952-55, acting chief bur., Moscow, 1958, assignments in Morocco, Algeria, Tunisia, Hungary (1956 revolution), Egypt, Greece, Yugoslavia, Poland, Austria, Switzerland, French Equatorial Africa; press attache Am. embassy, Rome, 1966-68; dep. dir. U.S. Govt. Press Center, Vietnam, 1968, dir., 1968-69; counselor for press affairs Am. embassy, Vietnam, 1968-69; White House and Pentagon liaison for State Dept. spokesman, Washington, 1969-72; World Affairs commentator USIA, 1972-73; dir. pub. info. U.S. Supreme Ct., Washington, 1973—. Mem. Italian-Am. com. to select Italian fellowship winners for study in U.S., 1950-52; mem. U.S. Nat. Cath. Com. on Communications Policy, 1970-74; mem. White House Com. on Drug Control Information, 1970-72; mem. interdept. com. on U.S. govt. press info. policy, 1970, inter-dept. U.S. govt. task force to rescue 100 Ams. kidnapped in Jordan, 1970; one-man U.S. presdl. mission to Cambodia on media news problems, 1970. Trustee Corrs. Fund, 1965-68, Overseas Press Club Found., 1963-66; mem. bd. Anglo-Am. Charity Fund in Italy, 1967-68; adv. council Fordham U., 1970—, journalism adv. council Iona Coll. Served to sgt. AUS, 1942-45; corr. Yank, covered assignments Peliliu Invasion in Marianas, Solomon Islands, New Hebrides, New Zealand, MacArthur's return to Philippines, Hawaiian Islands. Decorated Purple Heart; grand knight Italian Order of Merit; Vietnam Psychol. Warfare medal 1st class; recipient Polk award for outstanding fgn. reporting L.I. U., 1956; named best press corr. abroad Overseas Press Club, 1957; recipient Christopher award for one of ten most inspiring books of year, 1960; named Man of Year, Cath. Inst. Press, 1962; Fordham U. Alumnus of Year in communications, 1963; co-winner ann. Golden Typewriter award N.Y. Newspaper Reporters Assn., 1965, outstanding pub. service award N.Y. chpt. Sigma Delta Chi, 1965; Page One award N.Y. Newspaper Guild, 1966; Silurians award, 1966; award N.Y. Newspaper Reporters Assn., 1966; Citation for pub. service N.Y.C. Citizens Budget Commn., 1966; Meritorious Honor award Dept. State, 1972. Mem. Fgn. Press Assn. Italy (v.p. 1951-52, pres. 1961-62), SHAPE Corrs. Assn. Paris (treas. 1955), Authors Guild, Am. Fgn. Service Assn. Roman Catholic. Clubs: Overseas Press (pres. 1963-65; life gov.) (N.Y.C.); Anglo-Am. Press (bd. govs.) (Paris); Circolo del Ministero degli Affari Esteri (Rome); Fordham, Kenwood (Washington). Author: Decade in Europe, 1959; A Reporter Looks at the Vatican, 1962; A Reporter Looks at American Catholicism, 1969; contbg. author: The Best from Yank, 1945; Yank, the GI Story of the War, 1946; Combat, 1950; Highlights from Yank, 1953; Overseas Press Club Cook Book, 1962; I Can Tell it Now, 1964; U.S. Book of Facts, Statistics and Information, 1966; New Catholic Treasury of Wit and Humor, 1967; How I Got that Story, 1967; Heroes for Our Times, 1968; Newsbreak, 1975; Saints for all Seasons, 1978; also Am. Peoples Ency. Yearbook, numerous mags. Author initial study N.Y., Herald Tribune series, New York City in Crisis. Early life papers included in Wis. Hist. Soc. U.S. journalism collection. Home: 5229 Duvall Dr Westmoreland Hills MD 20016 Office: US Supreme Court 1 1st St NE Washington DC 20543. *Providing information to our democratic public has been the work of my life both as a foreign correspondent and as a government spokesman. The newsman and the person who speaks for government share the same objective of explaining government policy. The spokesman has an added responsibility—to help government policy succeed. The reporter and the spokesman sometimes are at war with one another, but it is a war in behalf of the same beneficiary: the people.*

MCGURN, JOHN MARTIN, utility exec.; b. El Paso, Tex., Oct. 25, 1931; s. Martin James and Margaret (McGovern) McG.; B.E.E., N.Mex. State U., 1934; m. Catherine Elizabeth Pinner, Nov. 12, 1946; children—John M., Katrina C., Arthur S., Teresa C., Christopher P., Monica N. Engr., El Paso Electric Co., 1934-41; with Va. Electric and Power Co., Richmond, 1941—, sr. v.p., 1966-67, pres., chief exec. officer, 1967-70, vice chmn. bd., 1970-71, chmn. bd., chief exec. officer, 1971—, also dir.; dir. Bank of Va. Co., Va. Trust Co., Robertshaw Controls Co. Bd. dirs. Edison Electric Inst., Electric Power Research Inst., Southeastern Electric Exchange; chmn. Gov. Va. Adv. Bd. Indsl. Devel., 1970—; chmn. Met. Richmond C. of C., 1973-74; trustee Benedictine High Sch., Richmond. Recipient Nat.

Brotherhood award Richmond chpt. NCCJ, 1973. Roman Catholic. Office: PO Box 26666 Richmond VA 23261*

MCHAFFIE, ROBERT E., household goods moving co. exec.; b. Putnam County, Ind., Jan. 8, 1917; s. Robert M. and Amy N. (Ruark) McH.; LL.B., Ind. Law Sch., 1939; m. Mary Florence Miller, Aug. 1, 1945; children—Joan McHaffie Jackson, Thomas Robert, Amy Lee. Chief clk. Ind. Boys Sch., 1935-38; mem. firm Chadd and McHaffie, Danville, Ind., 1939-40; with Mayflower Corp., 1940—, exec. v.p., sec., gen. counsel, 1977-79, sr. exec. v.p., sec., gen. counsel, 1979—, also dir. Served with U.S. Army, 1942-45. Decorated Bronze star. Mem. Ind. State Bar Assn., Indpls. Bar Assn., Am. Bar Assn., Am. Judicature Soc., Assn. ICC Practitioners, Sigma Delta Kappa. Clubs: Kiwanis, Athletic (Indpls.); Masons (Danville). Home: 1240 Ridge Rd Carmel IN 46032 Office: 9998 N Michigan Rd Carmel IN 46032

MCHALE, DANIEL VINCENT, hotel exec.; b. Mpls., Apr. 30, 1946; s. Merle Clement and Dorothy Signora (Running) McH.; student Fullerton Jr. Coll., 1964-66, Woodbury Coll., 1966-68; m. Lucy Chee, Dec. 18, 1972; 1 dau., Melisa Chee. With Beverly Hilton, 1968-69; Hilton Hotel Corp., 1969; exec. asst. mgr. Washington Hilton, 1969-74; resident mgr. Omaha Hilton, 1974-76; gen. mgr. San Francisco Airport Hilton, 1976—. Second v.p. San Mateo (Calif.) Conv. and Visitors Bur., 1978-80. Mem. San Mateo Restaurant and Hotel Assn. (pres.). Republican. Roman Catholic. Address: San Francisco Airport Hilton San Francisco CA 94128

MC HALE, INEZ PECORE, interior designer; b. Houston, Feb. 6, 1908; d. Alexander Pecore and Gertrude (Yarrington) P.; ed. pvt. tutors; m. Thomas George McHale, Nov. 21, 1933 (dec.); children—Marjorie, Ann (dec.). Designer, DonCave Co., Houston, 1930-35, Harris & West Co., Houston, 1935-44; owner, designer Inez McHale Interiors, Houston, 1945—. Trustee Courtland Assn. Fellow Am. Inst. Designers (now Am. Soc. Interior Designers) (pres. Tex. chpt. 1951-52, mem. nat. bd., by-laws com., charter mem. aux.); aux. mem. AIA. Republican. Roman Catholic. Home and Office: 2 Courtland Pl Houston TX 77006

MCHALE, JOHN JOSEPH, baseball club exec.; b. Detroit, Sept. 21, 1921; s. John Michael and Catherine M. (Kelly) McH.; A.B. cum laude, U. Notre Dame, 1947; m. Patricia Ann Cameron, Feb. 15, 1947; children—Patricia Cameron II, John Joseph, Kevin F., Anne F., Brian F., Mary M. Profl. baseball player, 1941-42, 45-47; asst. dir. minor league clubs Detroit Tigers Baseball Club, 1948, asst. farm dir., 1948-53, dir. minor league clubs, 1954-55, dir. player personnel, 1956-57, gen. mgr., 1957-58; v.p., gen. mgr. Milw. Braves Baseball Club (became Atlanta Braves Baseball Club 1961), 1957-61, pres., gen. mgr., 1961-67; adminstrv. asst. to commr. baseball, N.Y.C., 1967-68; pres. Montreal Expos Baseball Club, 1968—; dir. Perini Corp. Club: Nat. Monogram (U. Notre Dame). Office: PO Box 500 Sta M Montreal PQ H1V 3P2 Canada

MCHARDY, LOUIS WILLIAM, orgn. exec.; b. Baton Rouge, Oct. 31, 1930; s. Colin Andrew and Julia Clara (Zoeller) McH.; B.A., La. State U., 1951, M.S.W., 1956; m. Ann Evelyn Carter, May 30, 1951; children—Colin Andrew, Louis William, Hugh Carter, Julie Ann. Probation officer, then chief probation officer Family Ct., Baton Rouge, 1955-64; dir. ct. services Juvenile Ct., St. Louis, 1965-72; exec. dir. Nat. Council Juvenile Ct. Judges, Reno, 1972—, also dean Nat. Coll. Juvenile Justice; adj. prof. jud. adminstrn. U. Nev., 1972—. Mem. Mo. Law Enforcement Assistance Council, 1969-72; exec. dir. Nat. Juvenile Ct. Found., 1972—. Mem. exec. bd. Nev. area council Boy Scouts Am.; bd. dirs. Nev. Catholic Welfare Bur. Served with AUS, 1951-53; lt. col. Res. Mem. Am. Soc. Assn. Execs., Internat. Assn. Youth Ct. Magistrates (hon. v.p. 1974—). Elk, K.C. Editor, pub. jours. in field. Home: 4265 Ross Dr Reno NV 89509 Office: 118 Judicial Coll Bldg Univ Nev Reno NV 89509

MCHARG, IAN LENNOX, landscape architect, regional planner, educator; b. Clydebank, Scotland, Nov. 20, 1920; s. John Lennox and Harriet (Bain) McH.; came to U.S., 1946, naturalized, 1960; B.Landscape Architecture, Harvard, 1949, M.Landscape Architecture, 1950, M.City Planning, 1951; L.H.D., Amherst Coll., 1970, Bates Coll., 1978; H.H.D., Lewis and Clark Coll., 1970; m. Pauline Crena de Iongh, Aug. 30, 1947 (dec. 1974); children—Alistair Craig, Malcolm Lennox; m. 2d, Carol Ann Smyser, May 28, 1977. Planner, Dept. Health for Scotland, 1950-54; chmn., prof. dept. landscape architecture and regional planning U. Pa., Phila., 1954—; partner Wallace, McHarg, Roberts & Todd, architects, landscape architects, city and regional planners, 1956—. Mem. White House Conf. on Children and Youth, 1970. Served to maj., comdg. parachute troops Brit. Army, 1939-46. Recipient Bradford Williams medal Am. Soc. Landscape Architects, 1968, 76; B.Y. Morrison medal N.Am. Wildlife Mgmt. Assn., 1971; Creative Arts award Brandeis U., 1972; Allied Professions medal AIA, 1972; Phila. Art Alliance award, 1975; Distinguished Sci. lectr. Brookhaven Nat. Lab., 1968; Horace Albright Meml. lectr. U. Calif., Berkeley, 1969; Danz lectr. U. Wash., Seattle, 1971; Brown and Haley lectr. U. Puget Sound, 1972. Fellow Am. Soc. Landscape Architects, Inst. Landscape Architects, Royal Inst. Brit. Architects; mem. AIA, Town Planning Inst. (Eng.), Task Force on Potomac. Author: Design With Nature, 1969. Prin. works include: Ecol. Study for Mpls.-St. Paul Met. Area, plan for New Town, Ponchartrain, New Orleans, plan for New Town, Woodlands, Tex., Environ. Park for Teheran, Iran. Home: 685 Broad Run Rd West Chester PA 19380 Office: 1737 Chestnut St Philadelphia PA 19103

MCHENDRIE, DOUGLAS, lawyer; b. Trinidad, Colo., Mar. 9, 1906; s. Andrew Watson and Frances East (Hamilton) McH.; A.B., Colo. Coll., 1927; postgrad. Harvard Law Sch., 1927-28; B.A. (Rhodes scholar Colo.), Oxford U., 1930, B.C.L., 1931; m. Frances Reed Scott, Aug. 31, 1940; children—Margret Hamilton (Mrs. Morris B. Hecox, Jr.), Andrew Graig. Admitted to Colo. bar, 1932; with McHendrie & Shattuck, Trinidad, 1932-35; with firms Grant, Ellis, Shafroth & Toll, and successor firms, Denver, 1935—, now Grant, McHendrie, Haines & Crouse; gen. atty. Colo., A.T.&S.F. Ry. Mem. Colo. Bd. Bar Examiners, 1948-57, chmn., 1957-68; pres. Denver Library Commn., 1961-64. Trustee Colo. Hist. Soc. Found., Colo. Coll., 1964-70, 72—; trustee Colo. Acad., 1964-69, also past pres. Served from 2d lt. to capt. USAAF, 1942-44; capt. OSS, AUS, 1944-46. Fellow Am. Bar Found.; mem. Am., Colo. (pres. 1958-59) bar assns., Am. Judicature Soc., Phi Beta Kappa, Phi Gamma Delta. Clubs: University, Mile High, City (Denver). Home: 101 Marion St Denver CO 80218 Office: Western Fed Bldg Denver CO 80202

MCHENRY, DEAN EUGENE, educator; b. nr. Lompoc, Calif., Oct. 18, 1910; s. William Thomas and Virgie (Hilton) McH., A.B., U. Calif. at Los Angeles, 1932; M.A., Stanford U., 1933; Ph.D., U. Calif. at Berkeley, 1936; Litt.D., U. Western Australia, 1963; LL.D., U. Nev., 1966, Grinnell Coll., 1967; m. Jane Snyder, Feb. 23, 1935; children—Sally (Mrs. Kenneth Mackenzie), Dean Eugene, Nancy (Mrs. L.S. Fletcher), Henry. Instr. govt. Williams Coll., 1936-37; asst. prof. polit. sci. Pa. State Coll., 1937-39; asst. prof. polit. sci. U. Calif. at Los Angeles, 1939-45, asso. prof., 1945-50, prof. polit. sci., 1950-63, coordinator Navy tng. program, 1943-46, dean div. social scis., 1947-50, chmn. dept. polit. sci., 1950-52; Fulbright vis. prof. U. Western Australia, 1954; acad. asst. to pres. U. Calif. (statewide), 1958-60, dean of acad. planning, 1960-61, prof. comparative govt., chancellor, Santa Cruz, 1961-74, chancellor emeritus, 1974—; cons. S. Am. univs. Ford Found., 1961; mem. Coll. Entrance Exam. Bd., 1964-67; dir. State Nev. U. Survey, 1955-57, Survey of Higher Edn. in Kansas City Area, 1957, Master Plan Survey of Higher Edn. in Cal., 1959- 60; mem. adv. bd. U.S. Naval Postgrad. Sch., 1970-74. Candidate for mayor, City Los Angeles, 1950, for rep. in Congress, 22d Dist., 1952. Carnegie fellow in New Zealand, 1946-47. Author: The Labor Party in Transition, 1931-38, 1938; California Government: Politics and Administration (with W.W. Crouch), 1945; The American Federal Government (with J.H. Ferguson), 1947, 13th edit., 1977; The American System of Government (with J.H. Ferguson), 1947, 13th edit., 1977; The Third Force in Canada, 1950; Elements of American Government (with J.H. Ferguson), 1950, 9th edit., 1970; American Government Today (with E.B. Fincher and J.H. Ferguson), 1951; State and Local Government in California (with W.W. Crouch and others), 1952, California Government and Politics, 1956, 4th edit., 1967; Academic Departments: Problems, Variations and Alternatives, 1977. Office: McHenry Library Univ of Calif Santa Cruz CA 95064

MC HENRY, DONALD F., diplomat; b. St. Louis, Oct. 13, 1936; s. Limas and Dora Lee (Brooks) McH.; B.S., Ill. State U., 1957; M.S., So. Ill. U., 1959; m. Mary Elizabeth Williamson; children—Michael Stephen, Christina Ann, Elizabeth Ann. Instr., Howard U., 1959-62; with Dept. State, 1963-73, internat. affairs officer, 1963-66, officer-in-charge dependent area affairs, 1966-68, asst. to sec., 1968-69, spl. asst. to counselor, 1969-71; internat. affairs fellow Council Fgn. Relations, guest scholar Brookings Instn., 1971-73; project dir. Carnegie Endowment Internat. Peace, 1973-77; U.S. dep. rep. UN Security Council, 1977-79; ambassador to UN, 1979—; lectr. Georgetown U., 1973-74, Am. U., 1975. Recipient Superior Service award Dept. State, 1966. Mem. Council Fgn. Relations, Am. Polit. Sci. Assn. Author: Micronesia: Trust Betrayed, 1975. Contbr. articles to profl. jours. Office: US Delegation UN 799 UN Plaza New York NY 10017*

MC HENRY, POWELL, lawyer; b. Cin., May 14, 1926; s. L. Lee and Marguerite L. (Powell) McH.; A.B., U. Cin., 1949; LL.B., Harvard, 1951, J.D., 1969; m. Venna Mae Guerrea, Aug. 27, 1948; children—Scott, Marshall, Jody Lee, Gale Lynn. Admitted to Ohio bar, 1951; asso. firm Dinsmore, Shohl, Sawyer & Dinsmore, Cin., 1951-58; partner firm Dinsmore, Shohl, Coates & Deupree and predecessors, Cin., 1958-75; gen. counsel Federated Dept. Stores, Inc., 1971-75; asso. gen. counsel Procter & Gamble Co., 1975-76, v.p., gen. counsel, 1976—. Dir., Republican Club of Hamilton County, Ohio, 1957-58. Served with USNR, 1944-46. Recipient award of merit Ohio Legal Center Inst., 1969. Mem. Am. Judicature Soc., Internat., Am., Ohio, Cin. (pres. 1979) bar assns., Harvard Law Sch. Assn. Cin. (pres. 1960-61), Def. Research Inst., Cin. Council on World Affairs, Assn. of Gen. Counsel, Hamilton County Defender Commn. Methodist. Clubs: Harvard; Western Hill Country (dir. 1964-70, sec. 1966-69, treas. 1969-70); Queen City; Commonwealth; Diogenese. Home: 1960 Beech Grove Dr Cincinnati OH 45238 Office: PO Box 599 Cincinnati OH 45201

MCHENRY, WILLIAM BARNABAS, publishing co. exec.; b. Harrisburg, Pa., Oct. 30, 1929; s. William Cecil and Louise (Perkins) McH.; A.B., Princeton, 1952; LL.B., Columbia, 1957; m. Marie Bannon Jones, Dec. 13, 1952; children—Thomas J.P., W.H. Davis, John W.H. Admitted to N.Y. bar, 1957; asso. firm Lord, Day, & Lord, N.Y.C., 1957-62; gen. counsel The Reader's Digest Assn., Inc., N.Y.C., 1962—, also dir.; dir. Palaceside Bldg. Corp., Tokyo. Mem. vis. com. on Egyptian art, vis. com. on 20th century art Met. Mus. Art; bd. dirs. Presbyn. Hosp., Boscobel Restoration, Inc., Garrison, N.Y., High Winds Fund, Inc., L.A.W. Fund, Inc., DeWitt Wallace Fund, Inc., Lakeview Fund, Inc., Franklin Coll., Center for Hudson River Valley, Joffrey Ballet Co., Nat. Corp. Fund for Dance, Inc., Children's Art Carnival, Reader's Digest Fund for Blind, Reader's Digest Assn., Inc.; chmn. Commn. for Cultural Affairs of City of N.Y.; mem. Temporary State Commn. on Restoration of the Capitol. Served with AUS, 1952-54. Mem. Am., N.Y. State bar assns., Assn. Bar City N.Y., ANTA (dir.), Am. Conservation Assn. (dir.). Clubs: Century, Sky. Racquet and Tennis (N.Y.C.); Fairfield (Conn.) Country. Home: 164 E 72d St New York City NY 10021 also 203 Greens Farms Rd Greens Farms CT 06436 Office: 32d Floor 200 Park Ave New York NY 10017

MCHOSE, ALLEN IRVINE, educator, musician; b. Lancaster, Pa., May 14, 1902; s. Clarence N. and A. Margaretta (Vollmer) McH.; B.S., Franklin and Marshall Coll., 1923, D.F.A., 1948; B.Mus., U. Rochester, 1927, Mus.M., 1929; Mus.D., Okla. City U., 1945; m. Helen Elizabeth Kelley, Apr. 8, 1928 (dec. Dec. 1964); children—David I., Allen J.; m. 2d, Dorothy Hutcheon, June 11, 1966. Instr. sci., math. Moravian Prep. Sch., Bethlehem, Pa., 1923-25; faculty Eastman Sch. Music, U. Rochester (N.Y.), 1930-67, chmn. theory dept., 1931-62, dir. summer session, 1954-67, asso. dir. sch., 1962-67; now music cons., lectr., author; Rose Morgan vis. prof. U. Kans., 1969-70. Organist, dir. music Brick Presbyn. Ch., Rochester, 1932-67. Trustee Hochstein Meml. Music Settlement Sch., Rochester, N.Y., 1970—; trustee, v.p. Music Tchrs. Nat. Assn. Scholarship Found., 1971—. Mem. Music Library Assn., Music Tchrs. Nat. Assn. (treas. 1959—), Nat., Nat. Cath. music educators confs., Am. Mus. Soc., Phi Mu Alpha, Chi Phi. Clubs: University (Rochester); Cliff Dwellers (Chgo.). Author: (with Ruth N. Tibbs) Sight Singing Manual, 1944; (with Donald F. White) Keyboard and Dictation Manual, 1949; Contrapuntal Harmonic Technique of the 18th Century, 1947; Teachers Dictation Manual, 1948; Basic Principles of the Technique of 18th and 19th Century Composition, 1951; Musical Styles 1850-1920. Composer: Sonata for Violin and Piano, 1929; Concerto for Oboe and Orchestra, 1932; others. Home: PO Box 247 Naples NY 14512

MC HOSE, JAMES H., psychologist; b. Fargo, N.D., Jan. 13, 1937; s. James Williston and Neva E. (Hayden) McH.; B.A., Carleton Coll., 1958; M.A., U. Iowa, 1960, Ph.D., 1961; m. Judith Ellen Hugg, Aug. 26, 1961; children—James Williston, Jennifer Ellen. Mem. faculty dept. psychology So. Ill. U., Carbondale, 1961—, prof., 1970—, chmn. dept., 1978—. Mem. Midwestern Psychol. Assn., Psychonomics Soc., Phi Beta Kappa, Sigma Xi. Democrat. Contbr. articles to profl. jours. Home: Rural Route 6 Carbondale IL 62901 Office: Dept Psychology So Ill Univ Carbondale IL 62901

MCHUGH, DONALD PETER, ins. co. exec.; b. Wilkes-Barre, Pa., July 26, 1917; s. Peter Francis and Agnes (Kennedy) McH.; A.B., Bucknell U., 1939; J.D., Georgetown U., 1943; m. Frances Cavanaugh, Sept. 7, 1957; children—Christine, Michael, Anne, Jean. Admitted to D.C. bar, 1943; with Treasury Dept., 1943-44, spl. asst. to atty. gen., asst. chief trial sect. anti trust div. Dept. Justice, 1944-53; mem. firm Carolan and McHugh, Washington, 1953-55; chief counsel, staff dir. antitrust and monopoly subcom. U.S. Senate Jud. Com., 1955-61; v.p., gen. counsel State Farm Ins. Cos., Bloomington, Ill., 1961—; bd. dirs. Ill. Ins. Info. Service, Ins. Inst. Hwy Safety, State Farm Internat. Services, Inc.; mem. Med. Injury Ins. Reparations Commn. Mem. Am., Fed. bar assns., Internat. Assn. Ins. Law. Democrat. Roman Catholic. Clubs: Nat. Capitol Democratic, Nat. Lawyers (Washington). Author articles in field. Home: 918 Hastings Dr Bloomington IL 61701 Office: One State Farm Plaza Bloomington IL 61701

MC HUGH, JAMES FRANCIS, III, lawyer; b. Sioux Falls, S.D., Feb. 11, 1944; s. James Francis and Katherine McH.; A.B., Brown U., 1965; J.D. magna cum laude, Boston U., 1970; m. Katherine W. Seay, Feb. 28, 1976; 1 dau., Abigail Seay. Admitted to Mass. bar, 1971, U.S. Dist. Ct. for Dist. Mass. bar 1972, U.S. Ct. Appeals for 1st Circuit bar, 1972, U.S. Supreme Ct. bar, 1974; law clk. to Hon. George E. MacKinnon, U.S. Ct. Appeals, D.C. Circuit, 1970-71; asso. firm Bingham, Dana & Gould, Boston, 1971-77, partner, 1977—; lectr. Boston Coll. Law Sch., 1978—; mem. steering com. Boston Lawyers Com. for Civil Rights Under Law, 1979—. Chmn., Bd. Zoning Appeals, Lincoln, Mass., 1979—. Served with USN, 1965-67. Mem. Boston Bar Assn., Maritime Law Assn. U.S., Am. Law Inst. Author: Desegregation: The Boston Orders and Their Origin, 1977; editor Boston U. Law Rev., 1970. Office: Bingham Dana & Gould 100 Federal St 35th Floor Boston MA 02110

MCHUGH, JOHN LAURENCE, marine biologist, educator; b. Vancouver, B.C., Can., Nov. 24, 1911; s. John and Annie Margaret (Woodward) McH.; B.A., U. B.C., 1936, M.A., 1938; Ph.D., U. Calif. at Los Angeles, 1950; m. Sophie Kleban, Mar. 30, 1979; children by previous marriage—Peter Chadwick, Heather, Jan Margaret. Came to U.S., 1946, naturalized, 1958. Summer sci. asst. Fisheries Research Bd. Can., 1929-37, fishery biologist, 1938-41; research asso. Scripps Instn. Oceanography, 1948-51; dir. Va. Fisheries Lab., Gloucester Point, 1951-59; prof. marine biology Coll. William and Mary, 1951-59; chmn. sci. com. Atlantic States Marine Fisheries Commn., 1956-58; chief div. biol. research Bur. Comml. Fisheries, Dept. Interior, 1959-63, asst. dir. for biol. research, 1963-66, dep. dir. bur., 1966-70, acting dir. Office Marine Resources, 1968-70; head NSF Office for Internat. Decade Ocean Exploration, 1970; prof. marine resources State U. N.Y., Stony Brook, 1970—. U.S. commr. Inter-Am. Tropical Tuna Commn., 1960-70, sec. commn., 1960-61, 67-68, sec. U.S. sect., 1961-67, head U.S. del., 1967-70; dep. U.S. commr. Internat. Whaling Commn., 1961-67, commr., 1967-73, vice chmn., 1968-71, chmn., 1971-72; mem. U.S. nat. com. Internat. Biol. Program, 1968-70; adv. com. marine resources research to dir.-gen. FAO, 1967-71; mem. U.S. dels. to internat. sci., fishery meetings, 1959—; mem. NRC, 1963-69; mem. com. on internat. marine sci. affairs policy, ocean affairs bd. Nat. Acad. Scis.-Nat. Acad. Engring., 1971-74, com. on aquatic food resources, food and nutrition bd., 1973-74, vice chmn., 1973; mem. blue ribbon panel to rev. fed. programs on continental shelf. Office Sci. and Tech., Exec. Office Pres., 1971; chmn. select com. to rev. Eastern Pacific Oceanic Conf., Scripps Instn. Oceanography, 1972; mem. steering com., chmn. panel on fisheries, chmn. working group on information needs for effective mgmt. Coastal Zone workshop Woods Hole Oceanographic Instn., 1971-72; hon. mem. Whaling Mus. Soc., Cold Spring Harbor, N.Y., 1972—; sec. Internat. Marine Archives, Nantucket, Mass., 1973—; cons. to Nat. Council Marine Resources and Engring. Devel., 1970-71, Smithsonian Instn., 1970-72, Nat. Oceanic and Atmospheric Adminstrn., 1971-73, Riverside Research Inst., N.Y.C., 1971-72, Town of Islip (N.Y.), 1974-78; mem. Mid-Atlantic Regional Fishery Mgmt. Council, 1976—; mem. steering com. Nat. Acad. Sci.-NRC Panel to Review Fishery Research, 1975-76. Served to capt. Canadian Army, 1941-45. Recipient Distinguished Teaching award Marine Scis. Research Center Assos., 1977. Fellow Internat. Oceanographic Found., 1955-74, trustee emeritus, 1974—; fellow Woodrow Wilson Internat. Center for Scholars Smithsonian Instn., summer 1971. Mem. AAAS (selection com., Rosenstiel award 1976), Am. Fisheries Soc., Nat. Shellfisheries Assn., Va. Acad. Scis. (past chmn. biology sect.), Atlantic Estuarine Research Soc. (hon., past pres.), Am. Inst. Fishery Research Biologists, Sigma Xi, Beta Theta Pi. Club: Cosmos (Washington). Contbr. numerous sci. papers, book chpts., articles to profl. lit. Home: 150 Strathmore Gate Dr Stony Brook NY 11790

MC HUGH, MATTHEW, congressman; b. Phila., Dec. 6, 1938; s. Peter F. and Margaret M. (Whalen) McH.; B.S., Mt. St. Mary's Coll., 1960; J.D., Villanova U., 1963; m. Eileen Alanna Higgins, 1963; children—Alanna, Kelli, Meg. Admitted to N.Y. State bar, 1964; practiced in N.Y.C.; pros. atty. City of Ithaca (N.Y.), 1968; dist. atty. Tompkins County (N.Y.), 1969-72; mem. 94th-96th Congresses from 27th N.Y. Dist. Active numerous civic orgns. Mem. Am., N.Y. State, Tompkins County bar assns. Democrat. Home: 102 Willard Way Ithaca NY 14850 Office: 1204 Longworth House Office Bldg Washington DC 20515

MC HUGH, PAUL (RODNEY), psychiatrist, neurologist, educator; b. Lawrence, Mass., May 21, 1931; s. Francis Paul and Mary Dorothea (Herlihy) McH.; A.B., Harvard, 1952; M.D., 1956; m. Jean Barlow, Dec. 27, 1959; children—Clare Mary, Patrick Daniel, Denis Timothy. Intern, Peter Bent Brigham Hosp., Boston, 1956-57; resident in neurology Mass. Gen. Hosp., 1957-60, fellow in neuropathology, 1958-59; teaching fellow in neurology and neuropathology Harvard, 1957-60; clin. asst. psychiatry Maudsley Hosp., London, Eng., 1960-61; mem. neuropsychiatry div. Walter Reed Army Inst. Research, Washington, 1961-64; asst. prof. psychiatry and neurology Cornell U., N.Y.C., 1964-68, asso. prof., 1968-71, prof., 1971; dir. electroencephalography N.Y. Hosp., 1964-68, founder, dir. Bourne Behavioral Research Lab., Westchester div. dept. psychiatry, 1967-68, clin. dir. and supr. psychiat. edn., 1968-73; prof., chmn. dept. psychiatry U. Oreg. Health Sci. Center, Portland, 1973-75; Henry Phipps prof. psychiatry Johns Hopkins, Balt., 1975—, chmn. dept. psychiatry, 1975—, prof. dept. mental hygiene, 1976—, psychiatrist-in-chief Johns Hopkins Hosp., 1975—; vis. prof. Guys Hosp., London, Eng., 1976. Mem. Md. Gov.'s Adv. Com., 1977—. Grantee NIH, 1964-68, 67-70, 70-74, 75—. Diplomate Am. Bd. Psychiatry and Neurology. Fellow Royal Coll. Psychiatry, Am. Psychiat. Assn.; mem. Am. Neurol. Assn., Am. Physiol. Soc., Harvey Soc., Am. Psychopath. Assn., Pavlovian Soc. Club: W Hamilton St. Contbg. author Cecil-Loeb Textbook of Medicine, 1974. Mem. editorial bd. Am. Jour. Physiology and Psychol. Medicine, 1976—. Contbr. articles to med. jours. Home: 3707 St Paul St Baltimore MD 21218 Office: Johns Hopkins U School of Medicine Phipps 210 Baltimore MD 21205

MCHUGH, ROBERT CLAYTON, lawyer; b. Kansas City, Mo., June 2, 1928; s. Earl Clifton and Margaret Mary (Higgins) McH.; student Northwestern U., 1946-49; J.D., U. Colo., 1951; B.A., Colo. Coll., 1959; postgrad. Stanford U. Grad. Sch. Bus., 1968, Oxford (Eng.) U., 1977; m. Ruth Mary Irish, Dec. 22, 1949; children—Stephen Robert, Jennifer. Admitted to Colo. bar, 1951; mem. firm LaGrange & McHugh, Colorado Springs, 1951-52, 54-56; with Colo. Interstate Corp., Colorado Springs, 1956-74, v.p., 1965-71, sr. v.p., 1971; pres. Colo. Interstate Gas Co. div., Colorado Springs, 1971-74; pres., dir. Trans-Colo. Pipeline Co., Trans-Wyo. Pipeline, 1971-74, CIG Exploration, Inc., 1972-74; v.p. CIC Industries, Inc., 1965-74; pvt. practice law, 1974-77; counsel Colo. Interstate Gas Co., 1977—; instr. Coll. Bus. Adminstrn., U. Colo., 1974—; mem. exec. reserve Office Oil and Gas, Interior Dept., 1972-74; mem. Colo. Gov.'s Energy Com., 1972-74, Nat. Petroleum Council, 1973-74; instr. pre-parole release center Colo. Penitentiary, Canon City, 1959-70. Mem. Colo. Commn. Higher Edn., 1968-79; mem. Community Leaders Council, U. Colo., 1979—; mem. Colo. Solar Adv. Com., 1978—. Served with AUS, 1952-54. Recipient Free Enterprise award SWAP Club, 1972. Mem.

Am., Colo., El Paso County bar assns., Am. Judicature Soc., Order of Coif, Pi Gamma Mu, Phi Alpha Delta, Alpha Epsilon Delta, Chi Psi. Home: 2114 Monteagle St Colorado Springs CO 80909

MC HUGH, ROBERT PAUL, newspaper editor; b. Cedar Rapids, Iowa, Feb. 14, 1917; s. Roy Patrick and Minnie Elizabeth (Nesper) McH.; student Loras Coll., 1936; Journalism Asso., U. Iowa, 1946; m. Frances Jordan, Sept. 9, 1948; children—Timothy, Michael Kevin, Amanda Dillard. Reporter, Waterloo (Iowa) Courier, 1947-49; reporter Balt., A.P., 1950-57, corr. charge S.C. operations, 1957-63; govt. affairs editor for the State, Columbia, S.C., 1963-66; mng. editor Columbia Record, 1966-69; editor Daily Herald, Biloxi-Gulfport, Miss., 1969-74; editor South Miss. Sun, Biloxi, 1974, exec. editor Daily Herald and South Miss. Sun, 1974—. Pres. S.C. A.P. News Council, 1967. Pres. Gulf Coast Opera Theatre, 1972—. Bd. dirs. Harrison County chpt. A.R.C., Harrison County Boys Club. Served with USAAF, 1940-44. Decorated Air medal with 3 clusters. Mem. Am. Soc. Newspaper Editors, Sigma Delta Chi. Author libretto for Elegy in Gray, mus. drama; (3-act opera) Parnell; editor, annotator, author introduction The Bathtub Hoax, collection H.L. Mencken essays, 1958. Contbr. to Am. Mercury mag., Southeast Quar. Rev., An Am. Spectator. Home: 530 2d St Gulfport MS 39501 Office: PO Box 4567 Biloxi MS 39533

MCHUGH, SIMON FRANCIS, JR., state ofcl.; b. Washington, Feb. 28, 1938; s. Simon F. and Grace (Winter) McH.; B.S., Georgetown U., 1961, postgrad. Law sch., 1963-65; M.B.A., Am. U., 1971—; m. Victoria Kay McCammon, Aug. 13, 1966; children—Gregory Lyndon, Jason Francis. Staff accountant Henry S. Owens Co., 1961-63; govt. contracts accountant IBM Corp., 1963-65; real estate investor, 1965-67; spl. asst. to adminstr. Small Bus. Adminstrn., 1967; mem. Subversive Activities Control Bd., 1967-73; asst. to Gov. Md., Annapolis, 1973—. Served with USCGR, 1956-57. Mem. Friendly Sons St. Patrick. Democrat. Clubs: Nat. Aviation, Touchdown (Washington). Home: 106 Primrose St Chevy Chase MD 20015 Office: State House Annapolis MD 21404

MCILHANY, STERLING FISHER, publishing co. exec.; b. San Gabriel, Cal., Apr. 12, 1930; s. William Wallace and Julia (Fisher) M.; B.F.A., U. Tex., 1953; student U. Cal. at Los Angeles, 1953-54, 55-57 Universita per Stranieri, Perugia, Italy, 1957; Rotary fellow Accademia Belle Arti, Rome, 1957-58. Teaching asst. art history U. Cal. at Los Angeles, 1953-54, 55-57; art supr. Kamehameha Prep. Sch., Honolulu, 1954-55; instr. Honolulu Acad. Arts, 1955; asso. editor Am. Artist mag., N.Y.C., 1958-61, editor, 1969-70; condr. network series Books and the Artist, WRVR, N.Y.C., 1961-62; sr. editor Reinhold Book Corp., N.Y.C., 1962-69; pres. Art Horizons, Inc., N.Y.C., 1962—; instr. Sch. Visual Arts, N.Y.C., 1961-69. Recipient First award tour European art centers Students Internat. Travel Assn., 1952. Author: Banners and Hangings, 1966; Art as Design-Design as Art, 1970; Wood Inlay, 1973. also articles. Address: 52 Morton St New York City NY 10014. *I am concerned with awakening an awareness of the visual world in all people. Empathic and rational encounter with the visual arts, good or bad, is a key to understanding our time.*

MCILHENNY, HENRY PLUMER, museum exec.; b. Phila., Oct. 7, 1910; s. John Dexter and Frances Galbraith (Plumer) McI.; student Episcopal Acad., 1922-28, Milton Acad., 1928-29; A.B. magna cum laude, Harvard, 1933, postgrad., 1933-34. Curator decorative arts Phila. Mus. Art, 1935-64, trustee, 1964—, v.p., 1968-76, chmn. bd. trustees, 1976—; resident art historian Am. Acad. in Rome, Italy, 1947-48. Mem. Smithsonian Art Commn., 1957-77. Washington, Harvard Vis. Com., Royal Oak Found.; dir. Phila. Orch. Assn., Met. Opera Assn., N.Y.C., 1949-62. Served to lt. comdr. USNR, 1942-46. Mem. Phila. Soc. for Preservation Landmarks (dir.) Am.-Italy Soc. Phila. (dir.), Phi Beta Kappa. Clubs: Philadelphia, Rittenhouse (Phila.); Century Assn., Grolier (N.Y.C.). Home: 1914 Rittenhouse Sq Philadelphia PA 19103

MCILHENNY, JAMES HARRISON, pub. co. exec.; b. Cleve., Nov. 9, 1927; s. Edward Lott and Noreen Isobel (Spence) McI.; student USCG Acad., 1945-47; B.A. in Econs., U. Mich., 1950; m. Dorothy Dean Johnson, Aug. 11, 1951; 1 dau., Claire Brookes. Pres., I. Miller & Sons, Inc., 1962-65; v.p. Hickok Mfg. Co., Rochester, N.Y., 1965-68; sr. v.p. Macmillan, Inc. (formerly Crowell, Collier & Macmillan, Inc.), N.Y.C., 1968-72, exec. v.p., 1972—, also dir. Trustee Hackley Sch., Tarrytown, N.Y., 1975—. Served with USCG, 1945-47. Mem. Gravure Tech. Assn. (dir.), Sigma Nu. Home: 5 River Terr Tarrytown NY 10591 Office: 866 3d Ave New York City NY 10022

MC ILRATH, WAYNE JACKSON, educator; b. Laurel, Iowa, Oct. 18, 1921; s. Robert Kenneth and May Lee (Custard) McI.; B.A., U. No. Iowa, 1943; M.S., State U. Iowa, 1947, Ph.D., 1949; student Oak Ridge Inst. Nuclear Studies, 1948; m. Mary Celia Wilson, Dec. 24, 1942; children—Janet Elaine, Peggy Jane, Nancy Jean. Asst. biology Iowa State Tchrs. Coll., 1939-42; grad. asst. botany State U. Iowa, 1946-47, instr., 1947-49; asst. prof. plant physiology A. and M. Coll. Tex., also Tex. Agrl. Expt. Sta., 1949-51, from asst. prof. to prof. botany U. Chgo., 1951-64; dean Grad. Sch., prof. biol. scis. No. Ill U., DeKalb, 1964-73, now prof.; chmn. bd. No. Ill. U. Press, 1966-73; resident research asso. Argonne Nat. Lab., 1956, 58, 60, cons., 1956—; research asso. U. Chgo., 1964-66; sr. vis. fellow in sci. OEEC, France, 1961. Chmn. Central States Univs., Inc., 1967-68, bd. dirs., 1969—, treas., 1971—; mem. council mem. instns., mem. governing bd. Quad-Cities Grad. Study Center, Rock Island, Ill., 1970-73; commn. scholars state Ill. Bd. Higher Edn., 1968-71. Served with AUS, 1943-46; col. Res. ret. Mem. Inst. Biol. Scis. (vis. biologist colls. program 1960-71), Iowa Acad. Sci., Am., Scandanavian, Japan socs. plant physiologists, Bot. Soc. Am., AAAS, Ill. Acad. Sci., Indian Soc. Plant Physiology, Res. Officers Assn. U.S., Sigma Xi, Beta Beta Beta, Lambda Delta Lambda, Kappa Delta Pi, Blue Key. Asso. editor Bot. Gazette, 1959-66; editorial bd. Trans. Ill. Acad. Sci., 1961-64. Home: 1513 E Fairview Rd DeKalb IL 60115

MCILROY, ROBERT STEWART, accountant; b. Toronto, Ont., Can., Oct. 15, 1935; s. Cecil Stewart and Inez (Branch) McI.; came to U.S., 1955, naturalized, 1966; B.Sc. in Accounting, U. Calif. at Berkeley, 1958, M.B.A., 1963; m. Maureen Patricia Luther, May 28, 1966; children—Robert Stewart, William, James, John, Maureen Michelle, Michael. Auditor, Arthur Andersen & Co., C.P.A.'s. San Francisco, 1958-60; loan officer Pacific Finance Corp., Los Angeles, 1963-64; mgr. fin. analysis Ford Motor Credit Co., 1964-69; comptroller Cleve. Trust Co., 1969-74; v.p. Premier Indsl. Corp., Cleve., 1974-78; owner, act. exec. Whitehill Bus. and Fin. Services, Chagrin Falls, Ohio, 1978—. C.P.A., Ohio, Calif. Home and office: 5242 Maple Springs Dr Chagrin Falls OH 44022

MCILVAINE, JOHN HARMON, JR., banker; b. Chgo., Feb. 23, 1936; s. John Harmon and Mildred (Petrina) McI.; student Cornell U., 1954-55; B.A., Rollins Coll., 1964; postgrad. Wharton Grad. Sch. U. Pa., 1964-66; m. Barbara Blackburn Mohler, July 9, 1960; children—Joan Harmon, William Mohler, Andrew W. Accountant, Germantown Savs. Bank, Bala Cynwyd, Pa., 1966-69, asst. treas., 1970-71, comptroller, 1971—, v.p., 1975—; treas. GSB Service Co., 1971—. Served with USAF, 1956-60. Mem. Nat. Assn. Accountants, Fin. Execs. Inst. Republican. Presbyn. Home: 267 Hathaway Ln Wynnewood PA 19096 Office: City Line and Belmont Aves Bala Cynwyd PA 19004

MCILVAINE, ROBINSON, found. exec.; b. Downingtown, Pa., July 17, 1913; s. Gilbert and Elizabeth Malbone (Breese) McI.; A.B., Harvard, 1935; m. Jane W. Stevenson, June 3, 1939 (div. 1956); children—Stevenson, Mia Carol (dec. 1971); m. 2d, Alice W. Nicolson, Sept. 1961; children—Ian, Katherine. Publisher Downingtown Archive, 1946-58; chmn. U.S. sect. Caribbean Commn., 1953-56; dep. asst. sec. of State, 1954-56 counselor Am. Embassy, Lisbon, Portugal, 1956-59; consul gen. Leopoldville, Congo, 1960-61; 1st resident ambassador Republic of Dahomey, 1961-64; dir. Nat. Interdept. Seminar, Washington, 1964-66; ambassador to Republic of Guinea, 1966-69; ambassador to Kenya, 1969-73; dir. African Wildlife Leadership Found., 1973—. Served with USNR, 1941-46. Home: 2266 48th St NW Washington DC 20007 Office: African Wildlife Leadership Found 1717 Massachusetts Ave NW Washington DC 20036

MCILWAIN, CARL EDWIN, physicist; b. Houston, Mar. 26, 1931; s. Glenn William and Alma Ora (Miller) McI.; B.A., N. Tex. State Coll., Denton, 1953; M.S., State U. Iowa, 1956, Ph.D., 1960; m. Mary Louise Hocker, Dec. 30, 1952; children—Janet Louise, Craig Ian. Asst. prof. State U. Iowa, 1960-62; asso. prof. physics U. Calif., San Diego, 1962-66, prof., 1966—; mem. space scis. steering com., fields and particles subcom. NASA, 1962-66; mem. anti-submarine warfare panel President's Sci. Adv. Com., 1964-67; mem. com. potential contamination and interference from space expts. Space Sci. Bd., Nat. Acad. Scis.-NRC, 1964-71; mem. advisory com. for radiation hazards in supersonic transports FAA, 1967-71; mem. Fachbeirat Inst. Extraterrestrial Physics, Max Planck Inst., Garching, Ger., 1977. Guggenheim fellow, 1968, 72; recipient Space Sci. award Am. Inst. Aeros. and Astronautics, 1970; Computer Art award U.S. Users Automatic Info. Display Equipment, 1971; Sr. U.S. Scientist award Alexander von Humboldt Found., Ger., 1976. Fellow Am. Geophys. Union (John A. Fleming award 1975); mem. Am. Phys. Soc., Am. Astron. Soc. Author, patentee in field. Home: 6662 Avenida Manana LaJolla CA 92037 Office: Physics Dept B-019 Univ Calif San Diego LaJolla CA 92093

MC ILWAIN, WILLIAM FRANKLIN, writer, editor; b. Lancaster, S.C., Dec. 15, 1925; s. William Franklin and Docia (Higgins) McI.; B.A., Wake Forest Coll., 1949; postgrad. Harvard, 1957-58; m. Anne Dalton, Nov. 28, 1952 (div. 1973); children—Dalton, Nancy, William Franklin III. Various positions with Wilmington (N.C.) Star, 1943, Charlotte (N.C.) Observer, 1945, Jacksonville (Fla.) Jour., 1945, Winston-Salem (N.C.) Jour.-Sentinel, 1949-52, Richmond (Va.) Times-Dispatch, 1952-54; chief copy editor Newsday, Garden City, N.Y., 1954-57, day news editor, 1957-60, city editor, 1960-64, mng. editor, 1964-66, editor, 1967-70; writer-in-residence Wake Forest U., 1970-71; dorm leader Alcoholic Rehab. Center, Butner, N.C., 1971; dep. mng. editor Toronto Star, 1971-73; mng. editor The Record, Hackensack, N.J., 1973-77; editor Boston Herald Am., 1977-79; dep. editor Washington Star, 1979—; Stone Ridge lectr., 1978. Mem. Pres. Johnson's Commn. on Civil Rights. Served with USMCR, 1944. Mem. Am. Soc. Newspaper Editors, Soc. Nieman Fellows. Author: The Glass Rooster, 1960; (with Walter Friedenberg) Legends of Baptist Hollow, 1949; (collaborator) Naked Came The Stranger, 1969; A Farewell to Alcohol, 1973. Contbr. to Harper's, Atlantic Monthly, Esquire, Reader's Digest. Office: Washington Star 225 Virginia Ave SE Washington DC 22061

MCILWAINE, ELLEN, singer, guitarist, rec. artist; b. Nashville, Oct. 1, 1945; d. William Andrew and Frances Aurine (Wilkins) McI.; student King Coll., Bristol, Tenn., 1964-65, Dekalb Coll., Clarkston, Ga., 1965. Soloist various clubs in Atlanta, N.Y.C., Can., 1966—; toured with Lily Tomlin, 1973—; records include Fear Itself for Dot Records, 1969, Honkey Tonk Angel, 1972, We The People, 1973 both for Polydor Records, The Real Ellen McIlwaine for Kot'ai Records, 1975, Ellen McIlwaine for United Artists Records, 1978. Recipient Ellen McIlwaine Day proclamation Atlanta mayor, 1978; apptd. lt. col., aide de camp gov. Ga. staff, 1978. Mem. Am. Fedn. Musicians, ASCAP, AFTRA. Office: PO Box 8811 Atlanta GA 30306. *Get in the way and stay there.*

MCINALLY, LEROY BURDETTE, lawyer; b. North Branch, Mich., Dec. 19, 1906; s. Melvin Clark and Jessie Louise (Beacom) McI.; LL.B., Detroit Coll. Law, 1931; m. Reta M. Ingram, June 26, 1931; 1 dau., Janet Lee McInally Campbell. Admitted to Mich. bar, 1931, since practiced in Detroit; partner firm McInally, Rockwell, Brucker, Newcombe & Wilke, 1931—. Republican. Methodist. Clubs: Detroit Athletic, Lochmoor, Masons (33 deg.). Home: 832 Lakeland St Grosse Pointe MI 48230 Office: 3800 City Nat Bank Bldg Detroit MI 48226

MCINDOE, DARRELL WINFRED, air force officer, physician; b. Wilkinsburg, Pa., Sept. 28, 1930; s. Clarence Wilbert and Dorothy Josephine (Morrow) McI.; B.S., Allegheny Coll., 1952; M.D., Temple U., 1956, M.S., 1960; m. Carole Jean McClain, Aug. 23, 1952; children—Sherri L., Wendy L., Darrell B., Ronald S., Holly B. Commd. 2d lt. M.C., U.S. Air Force, 1956, advanced through grades to col., 1971; intern Brooke Army Med. Center, San Antonio, 1956-57; resident in medicine Temple U. Med. Center, Phila., 1957-60; chief internal medicine and hosp. services Norton AFB, 1960-64, 7520 U.S. Air Force Hosp., U.K., 1964-68; vis. research fellow Royal Post Grad. Med. Sch., London, 1968-69; chief endocrinology services, chmn. dept. nuclear medicine USAF Med. Center, Keesler AFB, Miss., 1969-75; dep. dir. Armed Forces Radiobiology Research Inst., Def. Nuclear Agy., Bethesda, Md., 1975-77, dir., 1977—; sr. lectr. mil. medicine Uniformed U. of Health Scis., Bethesda; cons. in field. Fellow Royal Soc. Medicine; mem. Am. Coll. Nuclear Physicians, Air Force Soc. Physicians (bd. govs. 1973-77), Uniformed Services Nuclear Medicine Assn. (pres. 1975), Soc. Nuclear Medicine, Assn. Mil. Surgeons U.S., Alexander Graham Bell Soc. Home: 12405 Borges Ave Silver Spring MD 20904 Office: Armed Forces Radiobiology Research Inst Defense Nuclear Agency Bethesda MD 20014

MCINERNEY, JAMES EUGENE, JR., air force officer; b. Springfield, Mass., Aug. 3, 1930; s. James Eugene and Rose Elizabeth (Adikes) McI.; B.S., U.S. Mil. Acad., 1952; M.S. in Engring., Princeton U., 1960; postgrad. Royal Air Force Staff Coll., 1964; M.S., George Washington U., 1970; m. Mary Catherine Hill, July 17, 1963; children—Anne Elizabeth, James Eugene, III. Commd. 2d lt. USAF, 1952, advanced through grades to maj. gen. USAF, 1976; fighter pilot, Korea, Japan and Ger.; comdr. tactical fighter squadron, Thailand, 1967, tactical fighter wing, Ger., 1971; sr. U.S. adviser Turkish Air Force, 1973; dir. mil. assistance and sales Hdqrs. USAF, 1975-78; comdt. Indsl. Coll. Armed Forces, 1978-79; dir. programs Hdqrs. USAF, 1979—; Decorated Air Force Cross, D.S.M., Silver Star (3), D.F.C. (7), D.S.M., Bronze Star, Meritorious Service medal (2), Air medal (18), Air Force Commendation medal; Vietnamese Crosses of Gallantry with palm and star; Republic of Korea Cheongsu medal Mem. Air Force Assn. (citation of honor 1968). Roman Catholic. Home: 1031 Delf Dr McLean VA 22101 Office: Dir Programs Hdqrs USAF Washington DC

MCINERNEY, JAMES MARTIN, springs mfg. co. exec.; b. Chgo., Jan. 8, 1920; s. James Lawrence and Kathryn (Keller) McI.; M.E., U. Notre Dame, 1940; m. Marjorie Lane Dumas, June 29, 1944; children—James Lawrence II, Gary John, Kirk Martin, Michael. With McInerney Spring & Wire Co., Grand Rapids, Mich., 1939—, charge plant layout and installation new plant, Grand Rapids, 1939-40, asst. to gen. mgr., 1945-47, v.p. charge mfg., 1947-53, pres., 1953—, also dir.; dir. Mich. Nat. Bank. Prodn. analyst shipbuilding br. WPB, 1940-41. Served as pilot USMCR, 1941-45. Mem. Soc. Automotive Engrs., Wire Assn., Grand Rapids C. of C. K.C. Clubs: Económic (Detroit); Peninsular, Kent Country (Grand Rapids); Lost Tree (Fla.). Office: 655 Godfrey Ave SW Grand Rapids MI 49502

MCINERNEY, WILLIAM KELLER, corp. exec.; b. Chgo., Sept. 26, 1921; s. James Lawrence and Kathryn (Keller) McI.; student Campion Prep. Sch., 1935-39, Purdue U., 1939-42; m. Ruth Katherine Weber, June 1, 1943; children—Katherine, William K., Laurie Ann, Sara Louise. With McInerney Spring & Wire Co., Grand Rapids, Mich., 1945—, successively prodn. engr., v.p. ops., now exec. v.p. and dir. Past pres. Grand Rapids and Kent County Cath. Service Bur.; dir. Grand Rapids Youth Commonwealth, Community Chest; trustee Grand Rapids Art Gallery, St. Mary's Hosp.; v.p., dir. Mich. United Fund; mem. budget com. United Community Funds of Am. Served as capt. USAF, 1942-45; ETO. Mem. Soc. Automotive Engrs., Am. Ordnance Assn., Wire Assn., Grand Rapids C. of C., Phi Kappa Sigma. Clubs: Rotary, Kent Country, Peninsular, Univ., Macatawa Yacht, Little Harbor, Detroit Athletic, Recess (Detroit). Home: 3142 E Gatehouse Dr Grand Rapids MI 49508 Office: 655 Godfrey Ave SW Grand Rapids MI 49502

MCINERNY, RALPH MATTHEW, educator, author; b. Mpls., Feb. 24, 1929; s. Austin Clifford and Vivian Gertrude (Rush) McI.; B.A., St. Paul Sem., 1951; M.A., U. Minn., 1952; Ph.D. summa cum laude, Laval U., 1954; m. Constance Terrill Kunert, Jan. 3, 1953; children—Cathleen, Mary, Anne, David, Elizabeth, Daniel. Instr., Creighton U., 1954-55; prof. U. Notre Dame, Ind., 1955—, Michael P. Grace prof. Medieval Studies, dir. Medieval Inst., 1978—, dir. Jacques Maritan Center, 1979—. Served with USMCR, 1946-47. Fulbright research fellow, Belgium, 1959-60; Nat. Endowment for Humanities fellow, 1977-78. Mem. Am., Am. Cath. (pres.) philos. assns., Am. Metaphysical Soc., Societe Internationale pour l'Etude de la Philosophie Medievale, Mediaeval Acad., Authors Guild. Author: The Logic of Analogy, 1961; History of Western Philosophy, Vol. 1, 1963; Thomism in an Age of Revewal, 1966; Studies in Analogy, 1967; New Themes in Christian Philosophy, 1967; Jolly Rogerson, 1967; History of Western Philosophy, Vol. 2, 1968; A Narrow Time, 1969; The Priest, 1973; Gate of Heaven, 1975; Rogerson at Bay, 1976; St. Thomas Aquinas, 1976; Her Death of Cold, 1977; The Seventh Station, 1977; Romanesque, 1977; spinnaker, 1977; Quick As a Dodo, 1978; Bishop as Pawn, 1978; La Cavalcade Romaine, 1979; Lying Three, 1979; Abecedary, 1979. Editor: The New Scholasticism, 1967—. Home 2158 Portage Ave South Bend IN 46616 Office: Box 495 Notre Dame IN 46556

MCINERNY, RALPH MATTHEW, educator; b. Mpls., Feb. 24, 1929; s. Austin Clifford and Vivian Gertrude (Rush) McI.; B.A., St. Paul Sem., 1951; M.A., U. Minn., 1952; Ph.D. summa cum laude, Laval U., 1954; m. Constance Terrill Kunert, Jan. 3, 1953; children—Cathleen, Mary, Anne, David, Elizabeth, Daniel. Instr., Creighton U., 1954-55; prof. medieval studies U. Notre Dame, Ind., 1955—, also dir. Medieval Inst. Served with USMCR, 1946-47. Fulbright research fellow, Belgium, 1959-60; Nat. Endowment for Humanities fellow, 1977-78. Mem. Am., Am. Cath. (pres.) philos. assns., Am. Metaphysical Soc., Societe Internationale pour l'Etude de la Philosophie Medievale, Authors Guild, Medieval Acad. Am., Mystery Writers Am. Author: The Logic of Analogy, 1961; History of Western Philosophy, Vol 1, 1963; Thomism in an Age of Revewal, 1966; Studies in Analogy, 1967; New Themes in Christian Philosophy, 1967; Jolly Rogerson, 1967; History of Western Philosophy, Vol. 2, 1968; A Narrow Time, 1969; The Priest, 1973; Gate of Heaven, 1975; Rogerson at Bay, 1976; St. Thomas Aquinas, 1976; Her Death of Cold, 1977; Romanesque, 1977, Bishop as Pawn, 1978. Editor: The New Scholasticism, 1967—. Home: 2158 Portage Ave South Bend IN 46616 Office: Box 495 Notre Dame IN 46556

MCININCH, RALPH AUBREY, banker; b. Manchester, N.H., June 15, 1912; s. John A. And Gula (Ruiter) McI.; B.S., Harvard, 1934; grad. Rutgers U. Sch. Banking, 1938; m. Elizabeth B. Farmer, Sept. 16, 1938; children—Richard D., Douglas A. Asst. trust officer Mchts. Nat. Bank, Manchester, 1936-42, pres, 1948-78, chmn. bd., 1978—; chmn. bd. Londonderry Bank & Trust Co., 1979—; examiner Fed. Res. Bank, Phila., 1942-45; v.p., trust officer Union Trust Co., Providence, 1945-48; v.p., treas., trustee Mchts. Savs. Bank, Manchester, 1948-73; treas., dir. 1st Bancorp. of N.H., Inc.; dir. First Bank Mortgage, N.H. Ins. Co., Amoskeag Industries, Inc., N.H. Ins. Co., Laconia Peoples Nat. Bank & Trust Co., (N.H.); dir. Fed. Res. Bank Boston, 1971-73. Mem. exec. bd. Daniel Webster council Boy Scouts Am.; treas. Manchester Inst. Arts and Scis. Trustee Gale Home, City of Manchester Cemetery Trust Funds, Manchester City Library, Colby-Sawyer Coll., New London, N.H.; co-trustee Samuel P. Hunt Found.; bd. dirs. Federated Arts of Manchester. Mem. Manchester C. of C., Am. Automobile Assn. (dir.), New Eng. Council, Newcomen Soc. Rotarian. Clubs: Harvard of N.H., Manchester Country, Hundred of N.H. Home: 847 Maple St Manchester NH 03104 Office: Mchts Nat Bank Manchester NH 03105

MC INNES, ROBERT MALCOLM, mining co. exec.; b. Pictou, N.S., Can., July 17, 1930; naturalized U.S. citizen, 1964; s. John Logan and Jenny MacKay (Malcolm) McI.; B.S., Dalhousie U., Halifax, N.S., 1952, LL.B., 1953; postgrad. Harvard U. Bus. Sch., 1968; m. June Hughena O'Brien, Apr. 19, 1952; children—Donald, Elizabeth, Susan. Asso. firm Duquet, MacKay, Weldon & Tetreault, Montreal, Que., Can., 1953-57; with Pickands Mather & Co., Cleve., 1957-69, 71—, v.p., 1971-73, exec. v.p., 1973—; gen. counsel, treas. Diamond Shamrock Corp., 1969-71; dir. Moore McCormack Resources, Inc., Brush Wellman Inc. Mem. Am. Iron and Steel Inst., Lake Carriers' Assn., Cleve. Bar Assn. Republican. Methodist. Clubs: Mayfield Country, Cleve. Skating, Mid-Day, Union. Home: 32300

Meadowlark Way Pepper Pike OH 44124 Office: 1100 Superior Ave Cleveland OH 44114

MCINNES, WILLIAM CHARLES, ednl. assn. exec.; b. Boston, Jan. 20, 1923; s. William Charles and Mary (Byrne) McI.; B.S., Boston Coll., 1946, A.B., 1950, M.A., 1951; S.T.L., Weston Coll., 1958; Ph.D., N.Y. U., 1955. Joined Soc. of Jesus, 1946, ordained priest Roman Cath. Ch., 1957; prof. mktg. and bus. ethics Boston Coll. Sch. Bus. Adminstrn., 1959-63, asso. dean, 1961-63, dir. honors program, 1963-64, mem. citizens seminar planning com., 1959-63; pres. Fairfield (Conn.) U., 1964-73, prof. urban problems, 1969-72; pres. U. San Francisco, 1972-77; pres. Assn. Jesuit Colls. and Univs., 1977—. Past chmn. bd. ABCD (community action agys.); pres. Conn. Assn. for Community Action Programs; founder Fairfield County Community Forum; life mem. United Cerebral Palsy Assn. Fairfield County; vice chmn. San Francisco Consortium; pres. Stewardship Services, Inc.; bd. dirs. Nat. Better Bus. Bur.; trustee Loyola U., Chgo., U. Detroit, Wheeling, Scranton U. Served to capt. USAAF, 1942-46; CBI. Mem. Beta Gamma Sigma, Alpha Sigma Nu, Delta Sigma Pi, Phi Kappa Theta, Alpha Epsilon Delta. Home: 1726 N Hampshire Ave NW Washington DC Office: 1717 Massachusetts Ave Washington DC 20036

MCINNIS, EDWIN, lawyer; b. Oakland, Calif., May 19, 1902; s. Michael A. and Margaret Anne (Mulgrew) McI.; A.B., St. Marys Coll., Oakland, 1924; LL.B., Oakland Coll. Law, 1934; m. Mary Frances Costello, Sept. 9, 1927; children—Mary F. McInnis Glass, Margaret A. McInnis Verge, Jeanne McInnis Flynn, George E., E. Catherine McInnis Yonke, Therese McInnis Pedemont. Instr. St. Marys Coll., 1924-25; v.p. Bank of Am. N.T. and S.A., 1925-67; admitted to Calif. bar, 1936; practicing atty. O'Gara & McGuire, 1967—; sr. trust officer Calif. 1st Bank (formerly The Bank of Tokyo of Calif.), San Francisco, 1967-76. Counsel, Hanna Boys Center; past pres. bd. regents St. Marys Coll., past pres. internat. alumni. Decorated Knights of Malta. Mem. San Francisco Estate Planning Council (founding mem.), Calif., San Francisco bar assns. K.C. Author legal and trust lit. including Am. Inst. Banking textbook, Trust Functions and Services, 1971. Home: 515 Haddon Rd Oakland CA 94606 Office: Alcoa Bldg San Francisco CA 94111

MCINTIRE, JUNIUS M., biochemist; b. Price, Utah, Jan. 27, 1918; s. Brigham F. and Effie (Cottam) McI.; A.B. in Chemistry, Brigham Young U., Provo, Utah, 1940; M.S. in Biochemistry, U. Wis., 1942, Ph.D., 1944; m. Vivian Richardson, Apr. 10, 1947; children—John R., Paul C. Head food products devel. Western Condensing Co., Appleton, Wis., 1944-49; head dairy, oil and fat products div. Q.M. Food and Container Inst., Chgo., 1950-54; asst. dir. research Carnation Co., Van Nuys, Calif., 1954-66, gen. mgr. research, 1967—; mem. food industry liaison com. AMA; council industry liaison panel Food and Nutrition Bd., Nat. Acad. Scis.; indsl. panel sci. and tech. NSF. Fellow Inst. Food Tech., Am. Chem. Soc., Indsl. Research Inst., Am. Dairy Assn., AAAS, Nutrition Found., N.Y. Acad. Scis., Soc. Nutrition Edn., Sigma Xi, Gamma Alpha. Mormon. Author numerous papers in field. Home: 6939 Columbus St Van Nuys CA 91405 Office: 8015 Van Nuys Blvd Van Nuys CA 91412

MCINTIRE, RICHARD LEE, investment banking exec.; b. Rochester, Ind., Nov. 12, 1934; s. Lewis Herman and Hazel Ruth (Gohn) McI.; B.S., Ind. U., 1957, LL.B. with distinction, 1959; m. Carol Anne Mitchell, Dec. 26, 1954 (dec. July 1977); children—Steven, Stacy; m. 2d, Joan L. Wolfe, May 12, 1979; children—Jennifer Wolfe, Bradford Wolfe. Admitted to Ind. bar, 1959, D.C. bar, 1960, Ill. bar, 1961; atty. Covington & Burling, Washington, 1959-61; atty. Rothschild, Hart, Stevens & Barry, Chgo., 1961-65; atty. Baxter Labs., Inc., Morton Grove, Ill., 1965-69, dir. corporate devel., 1969-70, pres. Am. Instrument Co. div., Silver Spring, Md., 1970-72, v.p. corporate devel. parent co., 1972-74, pres. Hyland div., Costa Mesa, Calif., 1974-75, chmn. Hyland Diagnostics div. and Am. Instrument div., Deerfield, Ill., 1975-77; with R.L. McIntire and Assos., Winnetka, Ill., 1977-78; v.p. Warburg, Paribas Becker, Chgo., 1978—; village atty., Clarendon Hills, Ill., 1965-69. Mem. Order of Coif, Sigma Pi, Phi Delta Phi, Beta Gamma Sigma. Note editor: Ind. Law Jour., 1958-59. Home: 90 Locust Rd Winnetka IL 60093 Office: Two First Nat Plaza Chicago IL 70603

MC INTOSH, ALEXANDER MCCOMBIE, oil co. exec.; b. Blackburn, Scotland, Mar. 11, 1926; s. George William and Clementine (Pender) McI.; B.Sc. in Petroleum Engring., U. Alta., 1951; m. Irene Isobelle Leckie, Sept. 17, 1947; children—Sandra Ann McIntosh Burdylo, Laurie Gene and Leslie Gail (twins). Pres., chief operating officer Home Oil Co. Ltd., Calgary, Alta., Can., 1979—. Served with RCAF, 1944, Royal Canadian Armored Corps, 1944-46. Mem. Assn. Profl. Engrs. Alta., Canadian Petroleum Assn. (chmn. bd. govs. 1977), Clubs: Earl Grey Golf and Country; Calgary Golf and Country, Ranchmen's, Calgary Petroleum. Home: 2629 Linden Dr SW Calgary AB T3E 6C8 Canada Office: 2300 Home Oil Tower 324 8th Ave SW Calgary AB T2P 2Z5 Canada

MCINTOSH, CAMERON IRWIN, lt. gov. Sask., Can.; b. North Battleford, Sask., July 1, 1926; s. Cameron Ross and Pearl Susan (Irwin) McI.; student U. Sask., 1945-49; m. Barbara Lee Aylesworth, Oct. 9, 1954; children—William, Rebecca, Jean Ann. Editor, North Battleford News, 1951-53; editor North Battleford News-Optimist, 1953-71, pub., 1971-77; pub. Western Can. Outdoors, 1977-78; lt. gov. of Sask., Regina, 1978—. Mem. North Battleford Public Sch. Bd., 1962-78, chmn., 1968-70; mem. North Battleford Planning Commn., 1960-78; chmn., 1976-78; chmn. Table Mountain Regional Park, 1974-78. Mem. Outdoor Writers Am., Outdoor Writers Can., Can. Community Newspapers Assn. (past pres.). Presbyterian. Clubs: Kinsmen, Masons, Elks. Editor, Sask. Ski Jour., 1976-78. Office: 511A Hotel Saskatchewan Regina SK S4P 0S3 Canada

MCINTOSH, DONALD LESTER, accountant; b. Seattle, Jan. 12, 1924; s. Herbert W. and Mildred (Anderson) McI.; B.S., U. Oreg., 1947; m. Margaret K. Broten, Feb. 15, 1947; children—Scott Lester, Pamela Ann. With Price Waterhouse & Co., C.P.A.'s, 1948—, partner-in-charge, Columbus, Ohio, 1964—; sr. v.p. fin. and adminstrn. NCR Corp., Dayton, Ohio, 1972—. Bd. dirs. Aviation Hall of Fame. Served to ensign AC, USNR, 1943-45. C.P.A., Ohio. Mem. Fin. Execs. Inst., Nat. Fgn. Trade Council (dir.), Sigma Phi Epsilon. Lutheran. Home: 1495 Westwicke Pl N Dayton OH 45459 Office: 1700 S Patterson Blvd Dayton OH 45479

MC INTOSH, HARRIS, corporate dir.; b. Cayuga, N.Y., July 25, 1904; s. John Esterley and Mary Luella (Witbeck) McI.; Ph.B., Yale, 1927; m. Elizabeth Ross Knight, June 24, 1939; children—Harris, John W., Daniel K., Elizabeth Ross. Prodn. mgr. Allen & Hills, Inc., Auburn, N.Y., 1928-30; securities analyst 5th Ave. Bank, N.Y.C., 1931-33; sales promotion Garrett & Co., Bklyn., 1933-34; asst. to pres., gen. mgr. Dura Co., Toledo, 1935-37; v.p., gen. mgr. Conklin Pen Co., 1937-38; prodn. mgr. Owen Dyneto div. Electric AutoLite Co., Syracuse, N.Y., 1938-40; pres. Fostoria Screw Co. (Ohio), 1940-41; mgr. prodn. control Vega Aircraft Corp., Burbank, Calif., 1942-43; asst. to pres. Lockheed Aircraft Corp., 1943-45; v.p. charge mfg. Toledo Scale Corp., 1945-46, pres., 1946-68; dir., pres. Nicholas Corp., Toledo, 1977—; v.p., treas. Ottawa Bay Devel. Co.; hon. dir. Toledo Trust Co. Mem. Toledo Labor-Mgmt. Citizens Com., 1946-76; trustee Toledo Hosp.; past trustee Wells Coll., Aurora, N.Y. Club: Belmont Country (Perrysburg, Ohio). Home: 29727 East River Rd Perrysburg OH 43551 Office: 1630 Nat Bank Bldg Toledo OH 43604

MC INTOSH, J(OHN) RICHARD, biologist; b. N.Y.C., Sept. 25, 1939; s. Rustin and Millicent Margaret (Carey) McI.; B.A. in Physics, Harvard U., 1961, Ph.D. in Biophysics, 1968; m. Marjorie Rogers Keniston, Aug. 30, 1961; children—Robert K., Elspeth R., Craig T. Instr. in math. and physics Cambridge Sch., Weston, Mass., 1961-63; asst. prof. biology Harvard U., 1968-70; asst. prof. U. Colo., Boulder, 1970-72, asso. prof., 1972-76, prof., 1977—, chmn. dept. molecular, cellular and devel. biology, 1977-78. Recipient Teaching Recognition award U. Colo., 1974; Scholar award Am. Cancer Soc., 1976; Am. Cancer Soc. grantee, 1971-79; NSF grantee, 1970-79; NIH grantee, 1973-78. Mem. AAAS, Am. Soc. Cell Biology (council). Contbr. numerous articles to profl. jours.; editorial bd. Jour. Cell Biology, 1978—. Home: 870 Willowbrook Rd Boulder CO 80302 Office: Dept Molecular Cellular and Devel Biology U Colo Boulder CO 80309

MCINTOSH, JAMES ALEXANDER, banker; b. Danbury, Conn., July 30, 1934; s. James Alexander and Margaret Helen (Brew) McI.; B.S., Mt. St. Mary's Coll., Emmitsburg, Md., 1956; m. Elizabeth Ann McCarron, June 28, 1957; children—James Alexander, Mary E., Gregory W., Patricia A. With Fed. Res. Bd., Washington, 1957-73, 1st v.p. Fed. Res. Bank, Boston, 1973—. Fellow Nat. Inst. Pub. Affairs; mem. Am. Inst. Banking (adv. bd. Boston chpt.). Home: 108 Cornwell Hill Marshfield Hills MA 02051 Office: 600 Atlantic Ave Boston MA 02106

MCINTOSH, JAMES BOYD, life ins. co. exec.; b. Milton, Mass., Feb. 18, 1920; s. James A. and Margaret (Wilkie) McI.; B.B.A., Boston U., 1950; m. Frances Glading, Feb. 20, 1943; children—Judith Boyd (Mrs. William C. Carr, Jr.), Gaye Glading, Linda Jane, James Boyd. With New Eng. Mut. Life Ins. Co., Boston, 1945-67, asst. sec., asst. to pres., 1954-56, 2d v.p., asst. to pres., 1956-57, v.p., asst. to pres., 1957-59, adminstrv. v.p., 1959-64, exec. v.p., 1964-67; pres., dir. Midland Mut. Life Ins. Co., 1967—; dir. Lifetime Communities, Inc., Columbus Trust Co., Orange-Co, Inc. Trustee Center Sci. and Industry, Columbus Symphony, Ohio Dominican Coll., Griffith Found., Boston U., Children's Hosp. Served as capt. USAAF, World War II. Mem. Life Office Mgmt. Assn. (dir.), Ohio C. of C. (dir.). Clubs: Columbus Country, University, Columbus, Columbus Athletic; Dedham (Mass.) Country and Polo. Home: 80 Bishop Sq Bexley OH 43209 Office: 250 E Broad St Columbus OH 43215

MC INTOSH, JAMES COLIN, fgn. service officer; b. Boston, Aug. 18, 1923; s. James William and Helen Theresa (Lally) McI.; student Boston U., 1941-42; B.S. in Fgn. Service, Georgetown U., 1948; M.S., Columbia, 1950; m. Marie Lalague, July 4, 1964; 1 dau., Isabel. Reference librarian Enoch Pratt Free Library, Balt., 1950-52, 53-55; with USIA, 1952-53, 55—; fgn. service info. officer, France, 1952-53, 63-65, Germany, 1955-61, Gabon, 1961, Can., 1961-62, Ivory Coast, 1962, Tunisia, 1967-70; counselor for pub. affairs, also dir. USIS, Am. embassy, Kinshasa, Zaire, 1970-72; dep. asst. dir. for Europe, USIA, 1972-75; counselor for pub. affairs Am. embassy, Brussels, Belgium, 1975-78; cultural attaché Am. embassy, Rome, 1978—. Served with AUS, 1943-46. Recipient superior merit award USIA, 1965. Roman Catholic. Editor Am. series translated to French, 1963-65. Contbr. articles to mags. Address: Am Embassy Via Veneto 119a Rome 00187 Italy

MCINTOSH, JAMES EUGENE, JR., interior designer; b. Dadeville, Ala., Nov. 13, 1938; s. James Eugene and Jessie (Latimer) McI.; B.Interior Design, Auburn (Ala.) U., 1961. Designer contract div. Rich's Dept. Store, Atlanta, 1961-64; asso. William Trapnell & Assos., Atlanta, 1964-70; dir. Interior Concepts, Inc., Atlanta, 1970-72; dir. design comml. design div. Rich's Dept. Store, 1972—. Adv. bd. interior design dept. Ga. State U. Fellow Am. Soc. Interior Designers (Presdl. citation 1974); mem. Nat. Trust Hist. Preservation, Ala. Hist. Soc., High Mus. Art. Home: 1824 Colland Dr NW Atlanta GA 30318 Office: PO Box 4576 Atlanta GA 30302

MC INTOSH, ROBERT LLOYD, univ. dean; b. Montreal, Can., Feb. 16, 1915; s. Alexander Douglas and Bella (Marcuse) McI.; B.A., Dalhousie U., 1935, M.Sc., 1936; Ph.D., McGill U., 1939, D.Sc. (hon.), 1972; m. Margaret Jean Callaghan, Mar. 31, 1966; children—Sharon McIntosh Lamb, Janet McIntosh Truant, Alexander David. Research chemist Shawinigan Chems. Co., 1939-40; asst. dir. extramural research NRC Can., 1941-45; officer charge extramural research Directorate Chem Warfare and Smoke, Dept. Nat. Def., 1943-45; sr. research chemist NRC Can., 1947-48; asso. prof. chemistry, then prof. U. Toronto, 1948-61; prof. chemistry, head dept. Queen's U., Kingston, Ont., 1961-69, asso. dean scis., 1969-70, dean Sch. Grad. Studies and Research, 1969-79, prof. chemistry, 1979—; mem. sci. adv. council Can. Soc. for Weizman Inst. Sci., 1968—. Royal Exhbn. of 1851 scholar, 1939; decorated Order Brit. Empire, 1942. Fellow Royal Soc. Can., Chem. Inst. Can. Clubs: Royal Canadian Yacht (Toronto); Kingston Yacht. Author: Dielectric Constant of Physically Adsorbed Gases, 1966; also articles. Research in surface chemistry specializing in properties of physically adsorbed gases on solids. Home: 35 Kensington Ave Kingston ON Canada

MCINTYRE, BRUCE HERBERT, publishing co. exec.; b. Takoma Park, Md., Jan. 24, 1930; s. Orrin Raymond and Leila Hazel (Olmsted) McI.; student Gannon Coll., 1954-57, U. Akron, 1958-61; m. Natalie Ann Wolff, Oct. 10, 1953; children—Douglas A., Elizabeth W., Emily O., Catherine N., Jane A. Reporter, city editor Erie (Pa.) Times and News, 1949-57; reporter, city editor, asst. to exec. editor Akron (Ohio) Beacon Jour., 1958-67; with Battle Creek (Mich.) Enquirer & News, 1967-71, asst. mng. editor, 1967-68, mng. editor, 1968-71; exec. v.p., editor Oakland Press, Pontiac, Mich., 1971-77, pub., 1977—; lectr. Am. Press Inst., 1968—; journalism juror Pulitzer Prizes, 1972—. Served with AUS, 1951-53; lt. col. Res. Mem. Sigma Delta Chi. Episcopalian. Club: Pine Lake Country (Bloomfield, Mich.). Office: Oakland Press PO Box 9 Pontiac MI 48056*

MCINTYRE, CHARLES JOHN, educator; b. Camden, N.J., Mar. 15, 1921; s. Charles John and Margaret (Dunion) McI.; B.A., Lafayette Coll., 1949; M.S., Pa. State U., 1950, Ph.D., 1952; m. Joanne Elizabeth Johnson, Sept. 2, 1950; children—Elizabeth, Jennifer. Research asso. Pa. State U., 1952-55; chief instructional procs. br. Office Armed Forces Information and Edn. edn. div., Washington, 1955-59; prof. ednl. psychology U. Ill., Urbana, 1959—, also dir. Office Instructional Resources, 1959—. Bd. dirs., mem. exec. com. Nat. Assn. Ednl. Broadcasters, 1962-67; bd. dirs., exec. com. Midwest Program Airborne TV Instrn., 1960-70. Served with AUS, 1943-46, ETO. Leverhulme fellow, 1969-70. Mem. Am. Edn. Research Assn., NEA, Am. Psychol. Assn., AAAS, ACLU, Phi Beta Kappa, Sigma Xi, Phi Kappa Phi. Author: Planning For Instructional Resources At A Rapidly Growing Urban University, 1967. Home: 2016 Zuppke Dr Urbana IL 61801

MCINTYRE, DONALD B., geologist, educator; b. Edinburgh, Scotland, Aug. 15, 1923; s. Robert E. and Mary (Darling) McI.; B.Sc., U. Edinburgh, 1945, Ph.D., 1947, D.Sc., 1951; m. Ann I. Alexander Dec. 23, 1957; 1 son, Ranald Ewen. Postdoctoral fellow U. Neuchatel (Switzerland), 1947-48; lectr. petrology U. Edinburgh, 1948-54; faculty Pomona Coll., Claremont, Calif., 1954—, prof. geology, 1957—; Distinguished lectr. Am. Assn. Petroleum Geologists, 1977-78. Guggenheim fellow, 1969-70. Mem. Royal Soc. Edinburgh, geol. socs. Am., London, Edinburgh, Sigma Xi. Home: 625 W 12th St Claremont CA 91711

MC INTYRE, DONALD FRANKLIN, city ofcl.; b. Chgo., May 12, 1930; s. Daniel Maxwell and Lucy Mae (Stickles) McI.; A.B., Millikin U., Decatur, Ill., 1952; M.A., Mich. State U., 1953; m. Nancy Elsa Todd, Sept. 10, 1955; children—Meribeth, Todd, Scott, Alex, Andrew. Town mgr., Los Gatos, Calif., 1960-67; city mgr. Oak Park, Mich., 1967-70, Vallejo, Calif., 1970-73, Pasadena, Calif., 1973—. Vice chmn. Calif. Peace Officers Standards and Tnng. Commn., 1974. Bd. dirs. Pasadena YMCA, 1973-75. Served as officer USNR, 1954-57. Recipient History award Millikin U., 52; named Outstanding Comm. Ser., Los Gatos, C. of C., 1963-64. Mem. Internat. City Mgmt. Assn., Am. Soc. Public Adminstrn., Millikin U. Alumni Assn. (chmn. No. Calif. 1960-67). Presbyterian (ruling elder 1966-67, 71-72). Club: University (Pasadena). Contbr. articles to profl. jours. Home: 1086 Armada Dr Pasadena CA 91103 Office: 100 N Garfield Ave Pasadena CA 91109

MC INTYRE, GORDON SCOTT, publisher; b. Vancouver, B.C., Can., May 13, 1944; s. Gordon Hugh and Helen Seton (Thompson) McI.; honours fine arts degree U. B.C., 1965; m. Lillian Hope Freedman, May 15, 1967; 1 son, David Eric. Asso. creative dir. Hayhurst Advt., Vancouver, 1966-67; advt. and promotion dir., trade div. McLelland and Stewart, Toronto, Ont., 1967-69; pres. McIntyre & Stanton, pubs. reps., Vancouver, 1972-76; pub. Douglas & McIntyre, Vancouver, 1977—. Mem. Assn. Can. Pubs. (mem. council 1978-79), Assn. Book Pubs. B.C. (chmn. 1978-79). Office: 1875 Welch St North Vancouver BC V7P 1B7 Canada

MCINTYRE, HENRY LANGENBERG, business exec.; b. St. Louis, Sept. 30, 1912; s. Joseph Shelby and Ida (Langenberg) McI.; A.B., Princeton, 1933; J.D., Northwestern U., 1936; m. Winifred Wheeler, Dec. 21, 1934; children—Robert W., Shelby H., Virginia H., Penelope T. Admitted to Ill. bar, 1936; practiced in Chgo., 1936-41; sec.-treas. Hiller Helicopters, 1946-52; partner McIntyre & Parker, real estate, mfr. devels., 1952-58; pres. Pacific Industries, San. Francisco, 1958-64; partner McIntyre & Gage, 1965-70; sec.-treas. Bangert & Co., San Francisco, 1971-75. Bd. dirs. Internat. Planned Parenthood Fedn., N.Y.C.; chmn. Population Resource Center, N.Y.C. and San Francisco, 1976—. Served as maj. F.A., AUS, 1942-45. Mem. Phi Beta Kappa, Phi Delta Phi, Order of Coif. Republican. Episcopalian. Clubs: Cottage (Princeton); Cypress Point, Burlingame (Calif.) Country. Home: 6 Fenwood Dr Atherton CA 94025 Office: 111 Pine St San Francisco CA 94111

MCINTYRE, JAMES CHARLES, life ins. co. exec.; b. St. Louis, June 5, 1922; s. James Francis and Ida Mae (Colestock) McI.; B.S. in Math., St. Louis U., 1943; m. June Margaret Trider, Oct. 30, 1943; children—Pamela Ann, Sandra Lee (Mrs. Richard John Foshage), Janice Marie. With Gen. Am. Life Ins. Co., St. Louis, 1946—, 2d v.p., 1966-74, actuary, 1972—, v.p., 1974-79, exec. v.p.-individual, 1979—. Served to 2d lt. USAAF, 1943-46. Fellow Soc. Actuaries; mem. Am. Acad. Actuaries (charter), St. Louis Actuaries Club (sec.-treas. 1958-59, chmn. 1961). Home: 1461 Crossett Dr St Louis MO 63138 Office: 700 Market St St Louis MO 63101

MCINTYRE, JAMES TALMADGE, JR., govt. ofcl.; b. Vidalia, Ga., Dec. 17, 1940; s. James T. McI.; B.S., J.D., U. Ga.; m. Maureen; 3 daus. Staff, U. Ga. Inst. Govt.; individual practice law, Athens, Ga.; gen. counsel Ga. Municipal Assn., 1966-70; dep. revenue commr. Ga., 1970-72; dir. Ga. Office Planning and Budget, 1972-76; dep. dir. Office Mgmt. and Budget, Exec. Office of Pres., Washington, 1977, acting dir., 1977-78, dir., 1978—. Office: Office Mgmt and Budget Old Exec Office Bldg Washington DC 20500*

MC INTYRE, JANE O'NEILL MAHADY, lawyer, govt. ofcl.; b. Latrobe, Pa., Feb. 18, 1922; d. James J. and Katharine (O'Neill) Mahady; B.A., Seton Hall Coll., 1942; LL.B., U. Pa., 1945; m. Carl M. McIntyre, Dec. 30, 1954; 1 son, James Joseph. Admitted to Pa. bar, 1946; law clk. Conlen, LaBrum & Beechwood, Phila., 1945-46; researcher Legis. Ref. Bur., Library of Congress, Washington, 1947; partner firm Mahady & Mahady, Greensburg, Pa. and Latrobe, 1947-62; chief devel. loans br. Office Gen. Counsel, SBA, Washington, 1961-64, chief interagy. br., 1964-65, atty. Office Congl. Relations, 1965-66, spl. asst. to adminstr., 1966-69; atty., adviser claims and litigation real estate div. Office C.E., Dept. Army, Washington, 1971-72, chief claims and litigation br., 1973-77, acting asst. chief counsel litigation, 1977-79, asst. chief counsel litigation, 1979—. Pres. Latrobe Civic Club, 1950-51, Quota Club, Greensburg, 1947-54, Hui O Wahine Officers Wives Club, Honolulu, 1959-60; Pa. nat. committeewoman Young Democratic Club Am., 1949-56; governing bd. Pa. Fedn. Dem. Women's Groups, 1950-56; exec. and policy com. Pa. Dem. Com., 1950-56; organizer Westmoreland County Young Dem. Group, 1948, past sec., v.p.; v.p. Young Dem. Clubs Am., 1951-55; alt. del. at large Dem. Nat. Conv., 1952. Named one of five top women qualified for high level presdl. appointment and D.C. Fedn. Bus. and Profl. Women. Mem. Am., Fed., Pa., Westmoreland, Phila. bar assns., Bus. and Profl. Women's Club (Latrobe dir.), Washington Forum, Women United (sec., bd. dirs.). Home: 12906 Crisfield Rd Silver Spring MD 20906 Office: Corps of Engineers Dept Army Washington DC 20314

MCINTYRE, JOHN ARMIN, educator; b. Seattle, June 2, 1920; s. Harry John and Florence (Armin) McI.; B.S., U. Wash., 1943; M.A., Princeton, 1948, Ph.D., 1950; m. Madeleine Forsman, June 15, 1947; 1 son, John Forsman. Mem. faculty elec. engring. Carnegie Inst. Tech., Pitts., 1943; radio engr. Westinghouse Elec. Co., Balt., 1944; research asso. Stanford, 1950-57; mem. faculty Yale, 1957-63, asso. prof., 1960-63; prof. physics Tex. A. & M. U., College Station, 1963—, asso. dir. Cyclotron Inst., 1965-70. Mem. council Oak Ridge Asso. Univs., 1964-71. Fellow Am. Phys. Soc.; mem. AAAS, Am. Sci. Affiliation (exec. council 1968-73). Presbyn. Research and publs. on scintillation counters for gamma ray spectroscopy; determination of nuclear charge distbns. by electron scattering; study of nuclear structure by neutron transfer reactions; devel. variable energy gamma ray beams, gamma ray cameras. Home: 2316 Bristol St Bryan TX 77801 Office: Dept Physics Tex A & M U College Station TX 77843

MCINTYRE, JOHN EDWARD, telephone co. exec.; b. Andover, Mass., Sept. 25, 1922; s. Clarence Edward and Christine Ann (Snyder) McI.; student Bentley Coll., Boston, 1946-48; m. Gloria Marie Manzelli, June 20, 1947; children—Lea (Mrs. Richard Wood), Nancy (Mrs. David Doda), Laura. Staff accountant New Eng. Bell Telephone Co., 1949-58, state accounting mgr., 1961-63; accountant Am. Tel. & Tel. Co., 1958-61, asst. comptroller, 1963-71; v.p., comptroller So. Bell Tel. & Tel. Co., Atlanta, 1971—. Served with USAAF, 1942-46. Mem. Financial Execs. Inst. Clubs: Commerce (Atlanta); Cherokee Town and Country. Home: 7030 Hunters Branch Dr NE Atlanta GA 30328 Office: Hurt Bldg Atlanta GA 30301

MCINTYRE, JOSEPH GEORGE, JR., chem. co. exec.; b. N.Y.C., Aug. 16, 1929; s. Joseph George and Eunice (Johnston) McI.; B.B.A., Manhattan Coll., 1953; M.B.A., N.Y. U., 1962; m. Elizabeth L.

Guida, June 26, 1954; 1 dau., Suzanne L. Tax cons. Haskins & Sells, C.P.A.'s, N.Y.C., 1953-55; sr. auditor Squires & Co., C.P.A.'s, N.Y.C., 1955-56; financial mgmt. positions with Gen. Foods Corp., White Plains, N.Y., 1956-67; asst. treas. Olin Corp., Stamford, Conn., 1967-72; treas. Richardson-Merrell, Inc., N.Y.C., 1972—; asso. dir. Union Trust Co., Wilton, Conn.; instr. accounting Iona Coll., 1957-58. Mem. Internat. Economic Policy Assn., Financial Execs. Inst., New Canaan Hist. Soc. Home: 1385 Smith Ridge Rd New Canaan CT 06840 Office: 10 Westport Rd Wilton CT 06897

MCINTYRE, LAMAR CALVERT, natural resources co. exec.; b. Jackson, Miss., Feb. 25, 1938; s. Elmer Stuart and Elizabeth (Calvert) McI.; B.S., Miss. State U., 1962; m. Margaret Ellen Price, July 4, 1969; children—Michele, Lee, Patricia. Tax mgr. Arthur Andersen & Co., Houston, 1962-68; v.p., treas. Zapata Corp., Houston, 1968—. Served with USNR, 1958-60. C.P.A., Tex. Mem. Am. Inst. C.P.A.'s, Tex. Soc. C.P.A.'s, Financial Execs. Inst. Baptist. Home: 14602 Bramblewood Dr Houston TX 77079 Office: Zapata Tower PO Box 4240 Houston TX 77001

MCINTYRE, OSWALD ROSS, physician; b. Chgo., Feb. 13, 1932; A.B. cum laude, Dartmouth Coll., 1953, postgrad 1953-55; M.D., Harvard U., 1957; m. Jean Geary, June 5, 1957; children—Margaret Jean, Archibald Ross, Elizabeth Geary. Intern, U. Pa. Hosp., 1957-58; resident in medicine Dartmouth Med. Sch. Affiliated Hosps., 1958-60; instr. medicine Dartmouth Coll., 1964-66; attending physician VA Hosp., White River Junction, Vt., 1964; asst. prof. medicine Dartmouth, 1966-69, asso. prof., 1969-75, prof., 1976—, dir. Norris Cotton Cancer Center, 1975—; cons. in hematology, oncology; individual practice medicine specializing in hematology-oncology, Hanover, N.H., 1964—. Served with USPHS, 1961-63. Mem. Am. Fedn. Clin. Research, AAAS, Am. Soc. Hematology, N.Y. Acad. Sci., Internat. Assn. Study Lung Cancer. Home: River Rd Lyme NH 03768 Office: Norris Cotton Cancer Center Hinman Box 7000 Hanover NH 03755

MCINTYRE, ROBERT MALCOLM, utility exec.; b. Portland, Oreg., Dec. 18, 1923; s. Daniel A. and Bessie W. (Earsley) McI.; B.A., UCLA, 1950; m. Marilyn Westcott, Aug. 27, 1949; 1 dau., Julie. With So. Calif. Gas Corp., Los Angeles, 1952—, sr. v.p., 1974—, dir., 1975—; dir. Pacific Lighting Service Co., 1975—; commnr. Los Angeles County Energy Commn.; mem. adv. com. Calif. Solar Energy Research Inst. Mem. Los Angeles Citizen's Olympic Com., Commn. Californias, Mayor Los Angeles Ad Hoc Com. City Finances; trustee Calif. Council Econ. Edn.; bd. dirs. Calif. Found. Environ. and Economy; chmn. citizens com. schs. Los Angeles Unified Sch. Dist. Served with USN, 1942-46. Mem. Am. Gas Assn., Pacific Coast Gas Assn. (dir.), Los Angeles C. of C., Phi Kappa Psi. Republican. Presbyterian. Office: 810 S Flower St Los Angeles CA 90017

MC INTYRE, ROBERT WALTER, ch. ofcl.; b. Bethlehem, Pa., June 20, 1922; s. Simon Jesse and Ruth (Young) McI.; student Miltonvale Wesleyan Coll., 1939-43; B.Religion, Marion Coll., 1944, B.A., 1959; postgrad. Ball State U., 1960-61; m. Elizabeth Norman, Nov. 6, 1953; children—Judith McIntyre Keilholtz, Joy McIntyre McCallum, John, James, June McIntyre Brannon. Ordained to ministry The Wesleyan Ch., 1945; pastor, Marengo, Ohio, 1944-47, Columbus, Ohio, 1947-52, Coshocton, Ohio, 1952-55; exec. sec. dept. youth The Wesleyan Ch., Marion, Ind., 1955-68; editor The Wesleyan Youth, Marion, 1959-68; gen. editor The Wesleyan Ch., editor The Wesleyan Adv., Marion, 1968-73; asso. editor The Preacher's Mag., Marion, 1973; gen. supt. The Wesleyan Ch., Marion, 1973—, mem. gen. bd. adminstrn., 1955—, mem. Commn. Christian Edn., 1959-73, mem. exec. bd., 1968—; chmn. Commn. on World Missions, 1973-76; denominational rep., bd. adminstrn. Nat. Assn. Evangelicals, 1973—, exec. com., 1978—; denominational rep. The Lord's Day Alliance, 1973-76; trustee Marion Coll., Asbury Theol. Sem., 1976—. Mem. Christian Holiness Assn. (chmn. social action commn. 1971-73, sec. 1973—), Wesleyan Theol. Soc., World Meth. Council. Author: Ten Commandments for Teen-Agers, 1965. Editor: Program Pathways for Young Adults, 1964; Mandate for Mission, 1970. Contbr. articles to religious jours. Home: 202 E North E St Gas City IN 46933 Office: PO Box 2000 Marion IN 46952

MCINTYRE, VONDA NEEL, author; b. Aug. 28, 1948; d. H. Neel and Vonda Barth (Keith) McI.; B.S., U. Wash., Seattle, 1970. Author: The Exile Waiting, 1976, Dreamsnake (Hugo award), 1978, Fireflood and Other Stories, 1979; editor: (with Susan Janice Anderson) Aurora: Beyond Equality, 1976. Recipient Nebula award, 1973, 78. Mem. Sci. Fiction Writers Am., Cousteau Soc., N.O.W., Authors Guild. Office: care Rodell-Collin Lit Agy 156 E 52d St New York NY 10022

MCISAAC, GEORGE SCOTT, govt. ofcl.; b. Auburn, N.Y., July 25, 1930; s. Robert Scott and Agnes Congalton (Aitchison) McI.; B.S., Yale U., 1952; M.S., U. Rochester, 1961; m. Betsy Roscoe Clark, Sept. 11, 1954; children—Ian Scott, Christopher Clark. In mfg. mgmt. Eastman Kodak Co., Rochester, N.Y., 1954-62; prin., dir. McKinsey & Co., Mgmt. Consultants, N.Y.C., Dusseldorf, Ger., Washington, 1962-78, dir., 1973-78; asst. sec. of energy for resource applications U.S. Dept. Energy, Washington, 1978—; cons. Dept. Def., U.S. Postal Service, HUD, German Agrl. Ministry, Govt. of Tanzania, various pvt. clients. Bd. dirs. Tisbury Gt. Pond Assn. Served to lt. USMC, 1952-54. Clubs: Met. (Washington); Yale (N.Y.C.). Contbr. articles to bus. jours. Home: 2814 Battery Pl NW Washington DC 20016 Office: US Dept Energy Washington DC 20545

MCISAAC, PAUL ROWLEY, elec. engr., educator; b. Port Washington, N.Y., Apr. 20, 1926; s. Robert Milton and June Zatella (Barrus) McI.; B.E.E., Cornell U., 1949; M.S.E., U. Mich., 1950, Ph.D., 1954; m. Mary Lou Heldenbrand, Sept. 10, 1949; children—Wendy Lee, Karen Jo, Hugh Paul, Kathleen Anne. Research engr. Microwave Tube div. Sperry Gyroscope Co., Great Neck, N.Y., 1954-59; asso. prof. elec. engring. Cornell U., 1959-65, prof., 1965—, asso. dean engring., 1975—. Served with USN, 1944-46. Rotary Found. fellow, 1951-52. Mem. IEEE, Am. Soc. Engring. Edn., AAAS, Sigma Xi. Home: 107 Forest Home Dr Ithaca NY 14850 Office: 241 Carpenter Hall Cornell University Ithaca NY 14853

MCKAIG, DIANNE L., lawyer, soft drink co. exec.; b. Massillon, Ohio, Nov. 17, 1930; d. Sherman J. and Kathryn (Shaidnagle) McKaig; B.A., U. Ky., 1952, J.D., 1954; LL.M., Harvard U., 1955. Admitted to Ky. bar, 1954, Mass. bar, 1956; law clk. Ky. Ct. Appeals, Frankfort, 1954; mem. firm Palmer, Dodge, Gardner & Bradford, Boston, 1955-56; individual practice law, Boston, 1956-58; atty. adviser Office of Solicitor, Dept. Labor, Washington, 1958-62, regional dir. Women's Bur., Atlanta, 1963-66, chief div. legis. and standards, Washington, 1966-68, dir. Office Consumer Services, 1968-69; spl. asst. for consumer interests to sec. HEW, Washington, 1968; exec. dir. Mich. Consumers Council, 1969-72; asst. v.p. consumer affairs Coca-Cola Co., Atlanta, 1972-74, v.p., 1976—; v.p. Coca-Cola U.S.A., 1974-76; mem. Maj. Appliance Consumer Action Panel, 1970-72; spl. lectr. Coll. Indsl. Mgmt., Ga. Inst. Tech., 1974. Bd. dirs. Nat. Council Family Fin. Edn.. 1970-72, Nat. Council Better Bus. Burs., 1971-72; chmn. pub. affairs com. Food Safety Council, 1977; dir. Indsl. Nat. Corp. Mem. Ky. Fed., Mass. bar assns., Soc. Consumer Affairs Profls. (dir. 1973-77, pres. 1975-76), U.S. C. of C. (consumer affairs com.), U. Ky. Alumni Assn. (pres. Washington 1962), Bus. and Profl. Women's Clubs, Order of Coif, Mortar Bd., Alpha Delta Pi (chpt. outstanding alumna 1965), Eta Sigma Phi, Phi Beta. Asso. editor Ky. Law Jour., 1953. Home: 4 Mooregate Sq NW Atlanta GA 30327

MCKAIG, GEORGE DAVID, restaurant chain exec.; b. Springfield, Ohio, Oct. 7, 1932; s. Frank E. and Ruthgail (Cowan) McK.; B.A., Wooster (Ohio) Coll., 1954; LL.B., Stanford U., 1957; m. Nancy Elizabeth Anderson, Aug. 25, 1950; children—David, Christopher, Bruce, Adam, Jennifer. Admitted to Calif. bar, 1957; asso. firm Cavalletto, Webster, Mullen & McCaughey, Santa Barbara, Calif., 1958-76; sr. v.p. corp. devel. Sambo's Restaurants, Inc., Santa Barbara, 1976—. Home: 2296 Las Tunas Rd Santa Barbara CA 93103 Office: 3760 State St Santa Barbara CA 93105

MCKAIN, WALTER CECIL, educator; b. Columbiana, Ohio, Oct. 12, 1912; s. Walter Cecil and Grace F. (Van Kirk) McK.; A.B. magna cum laude, Harvard, 1934, Ph.D., 1947; m. Elizabeth F. Seckerson, Sept. 30, 1939; children—Richard, Nancy, Walter, Douglas, Susan. With Dept. Agr., Upper Darby, Pa., 1938-41, Berkeley, Calif., 1941-47; prof. U. Conn. Coll. Agr., Storrs, 1947—. Mem. Conn. Commn. Aging, 1963-65, Cultural Exchange Program, USSR, 1965, 68, 72, 76. Mem. AAAS, Sociol. Assn., Gerontology Soc. Author: Ribbon of Hope, 1965; Retirement Marriage, 1969; Dignity for the Living, 1975. Home: RD 1 Northfield VT 05663

MC KAUGHAN, HOWARD PAUL, univ. dean; b. Canoga Park, Calif., July 5, 1922; s. Paul and Edith (Barton) McK.; A.B., U. Calif. at Los Angeles, 1945; M.Th., Dallas Theol. Sem., 1946; M.A., Cornell U., 1952, Ph.D., 1957; m. Barbara Jean Budroe, Dec. 25, 1943; children—Edith (Mrs. Daniel Skene Santoro), Charlotte (Mrs. Martin Douglas Barnhart), Patricia, Barbara (Mrs. Ronald Chester Bell), Judith. Mem. linguistic research team Summer Inst. Linguistics, Mexico, 1946-52; asso. dir. Summer Inst. Linguistics, Philippines, also asso. dir. summer sessions U. N.D., 1952-57, dir. Philippine br., 1957-61; research asst. prof. anthropology U. Wash., 1961-62, research asso. prof., 1962-63; asso. prof. linguistics U. Hawaii, 1963-64, prof. linguistics, 1964—, chmn. dept., 1963-66, dir. Pacific and Asian Linguistics Inst., 1964, 1966-69, asso. dean grad. div., 1965-72, dean grad. div., dir. research, 1972—, acting chancellor, 1979; lectr. linguistics U. Philippines, summers 1954, 60; Fulbright sr. lectr., Philippines, 1977; prin. Wycliffe Sch. Linguistics, summers 1953, 61; vis. prof. Australian Nat. U., Canberra, 1970. Sr. scholar East-West Center, Honolulu, 1964; NDEA Maranao-Philippines research grantee, 1963-65; Office of Edn. Hawaii English grantee, 1965-66; NSF Jeh Language of South Vietnam grantee, 1969-70, Maranao Linguistic Studies, 1971-72. Mem. linguistic socs. Am., Philippines, Hawaii, Linguistic Circle N.Y., Western Assn. Grad. Schs. (pres. 1978-79), Phi Beta Kappa, Phi Kappa Phi. Author: (with B. McKaughan) Chatino Dictionary, 1951; (with J. Forster) Ilocano: An Intensive Language Course, 1952; The Inflection and Syntax of Maranao Verbs, 1959; (with B. Macaraya): A Maranao Dictionary, 1967. Editor: Pali Language Texts: Philippines, 21 vols., 1971; The Languages of the Eastern Family of the East New Guinea Highlands Stock, 1973. Contbr. articles, chpts. to books, sci. jours. Home: 3670 Alani Dr Honolulu HI 96822

MC KAY, ALEXANDER GORDON, educator; b. Toronto, Can., Dec. 24, 1924; s. Alexander Lynn and Marjory Maud Redfern (Nicoll) McK.; B.A., U. Toronto, 1946; M.A., Yale, 1947; A.M., Princeton, 1948, Ph.D., 1950; m. Helen Jean Zulauf, Dec. 24, 1964; stepchildren—Julie Anne Stephanie Brott, Danae Helen Kremblewski. Mem. faculty classics Wells Coll., 1949-50, U. Pa., 1950-51, U. Man., 1951-52, 55-57, Mt. Allison U., 1952-53, Waterloo Coll., 1953-55; mem. faculty McMaster U., 1957—, prof., chmn. dept. classics, 1962-68, 76-79, dean humanities, 1968-73; Distinguished vis. prof. classics U. Colo., 1973; prof. in charge Intercollegiate Center for Classical Studies, Rome, 1975; mem. Inst. Advanced Study, Princeton, 1979; v.p., treas. Peers-McKay Prodns., Inc., 1972—. Pres., bd. govs. Hamilton Philharm. Orch., 1967—, Hamilton Chamber Music Soc., 1965-67, Hamilton br. Archtl. Conservancy Ont., 1965-67, Hamilton and Region Arts Council, 1971-72. Trustee, Hamilton Found., 1972-75; bd. govs. Art Gallery Hamilton. Woodrow Wilson fellow, 1947-48; Can. Council fellow, 1973-74; Killam research fellow, 1979-80. Fellow Royal Soc. Can. (hon. editor); mem. Vergilian Soc. (pres. 1972-74), Classical Assn. Middle West and South (pres. 1972-73), Classical Assn. Can. (v.p. 1970-72, 76-78, pres. 1978-80). Clubs: Princeton (N.Y.C.); Tamahaac (Ancaster); Canadian (Hamilton); Arts and Letters (Toronto). Author: Naples and Campania: Texts and Illustrations, 1962; Roman Lyric Poetry: Catullus and Horace, 1969; Vergil's Italy, 1970; Cumae and the Phlegraean Fields, 1972; Naples and Coastal Campania, 1972; Houses, Villas and Palaces in the Roman World, 1975; Roman Satire, 1976; Vitruvius, Architect and Engineer, 1978. Home: 1 Turner Ave Hamilton ON L8P 3K4 Canada

MCKAY, ALLAN L., machine tool co. exec.; b. Brainerd, Minn., Feb. 18, 1915; s. Charles Donald and Louise (White) McK.; ed. U. Minn.; m. Tennyse Willstumpf, Nov. 25, 1937; children—Bruce, Brian. Time study engr. Giddings & Lewis Machine Tool Co., Fond du Lac, Wis., 1937-42; gen. mgr. Kaukauna Machine Corp. (Wis.), 1942-46, pres., gen. mgr., 1946-55; with Cin. Bickford div. Giddings & Lewis Tool Co., 1956-60, v.p. mfg. and finance, 1961-62, exec. v.p., 1962-66; pres., gen. mgr., dir. Giddings & Lewis Machine Tool Co., Fond du Lac, 1966-70; pres., chief operating officer domestic operations Giddings & Lewis, Inc., 1970-72, pres., chief exec. officer, 1972-77, chmn. exec. com. of bd. dirs., 1977—; dir. Giddings & Lewis-Fraser, Ltd., Arbroath, Scotland, First Nat. Bank of Fond du Lac, Calumet Co., Algoma, Wis. Sec. Kaukauna Vocat. Sch., 1954-55; asst. sec.-asst. treas. Giddings & Lewis Found., Inc.; v.p. Kaukauna Hosp., 1954-55. Mem. Soc. Mfg. Engrs., Young Pres. Orgn. (pres. Wis. chpt. 1955), U.S. Power Squadron, Wis. C. of C. (dir.), Nat. Machine Tool Builders Assn. (past dir.), Am. Mgmt. Assn., N.A.M., Wis. Mfrs. and Commerce Assn. (dir.). Presbyn. Rotarian (pres. Kaukauna 1955). Clubs: Baudhuin Yacht Harbor (Sturgeon Bay, Wis.); Great Lakes Cruising, South Hills (past pres., past dir.). Home: The Birches Green Bay Rd Washington Island WI 54246 Office: 142 Doty St Fond du Lac WI 54935

MC KAY, ARTHUR FERGUSON, engring. co. exec.; b. Truro, N.S., Can., Dec. 1, 1916; s. John Ferguson and Mabel Florence (Thompson) McK.; came to U.S., 1971, naturalized, 1978; B.Sc., McGill U., 1937; M.Sc., Dalhousie U., 1941; Ph.D., U. Toronto, 1944; m. Kathryn Evelena Beals, Nov. 12, 1939; children—Arthur D., George R.A., Donald G., Peter S., Kathryn A. Ayerst, Am. Home Products, N.Y.C., 1937-38; asst. prof. chemistry Queen's U., Kingston, Ont., 1945-49; head organic chemistry div. Def. Research Bd., Ottawa, Ont., 1949-54; dir. research and devel. Monsanto, Montreal, Ont., 1954-55, v.p., 1958-66, also dir.; v.p. Norton Research Corp., Norton Co., Worcester, Mass. 1966-70; pres. Masury Columbia Co., Chgo., 1970-72, Ford-McKay, Inc., Vancouver, Wash., 1974—. Nat. Research Council fellow, 1943-44. Fellow AAAS, Chem. Inst. Can., Royal Soc. Can.; mem. Am. Mgmt. Assn., Am. Chem. Soc., Soc. Plastics Engrs., Ill. Acad. Sci. Christian Scientist. Contbr. articles to profl. jours. Patentee in field of chemistry. Home: 1201 NW 109th St Vancouver WA 98664

MCKAY, ARTHUR RAYMOND, clergyman; b. Waterbury, Conn., Feb. 16, 1918; s. Frank and Helen (Brennan) McK.; A.B., Albright Coll., 1942; B.D., Union Theol. Sem., 1945, S.T.M., 1946; Ph.D., U. Edinburgh (Scotland), 1951; D.D., Muskingum Coll., 1957; LL.D., Albright Coll., 1960; Litt. D., Coll. Idaho, 1963; m. Ann C. Usher, July 3, 1943; children—Deborah A., David A., James S. Ordained to ministry Presbyn. Ch., 1944; pastor Community Presbyn. Ch., Merrick, N.Y., 1943- 47; prof., chmn. dept. philosophy and religion Russell Sage Coll., 1947- 52; minister 1st Presbyn. Ch., Binghamton, N.Y., 1952-57; pres. McCormick Theol. Sem., Chgo., 1957-70; pres. Colgate Rochester Div. Sch./Bexley Hall/Crozer Theol. Sem., Rochester, N.Y., 1970-73; pres. Rochester Center for Theol. Studies, 1970-73; minister Knox Presbyn. Ch., Cin., 1973-77; sr. minister New York Ave. Presbyn. Ch., Washington, 1977—; chmn. Presbyn. Council Theol. Edn., 1961-64. Chmn. Broome County Council, N.Y. State Commn. Against Discrimination, 1953-57. Vice pres., trustee Lane Theol. Sem., Cin., 1957—; trustee Binghamton Pub. Library, 1953-57, Waynesburg Coll., 1957-70, Francis W. Parker Sch., 1959-69; dir. Westminster Found in N.Y. State, Inc., 1953-57. Kent fellow Nat. Council Religion in Higher Edn., 1949-51. Mem. Am. Philos. Assn., Am. Assn. Theol. Schs. (pres. 1968-70), Alpha Pi Omega, Tau Kappa Alpha. Club: University. Author: God's People in God's World, 1961; Servants and Stewards, 1963. Home: 379 N St SW Washington DC 20024

MCKAY, DEAN RAYMOND, bus. machines co. exec.; b. Seattle, Nov. 13, 1921; s. Joseph and Nora (MacDermitt) McK.; B.A., U. Wash., 1944; spl. course Harvard, 1955; m. Jean Davis, Dec. 26, 1942; children—Dean Brian, Bruce Thompson, Robert Joseph. With Internat. Bus. Machines Corp., Armonk, N.Y., 1946—, successively br. mgr., dist. mgr., asst. sales mgr., regional sales mgr., exec. asst. office of pres., dir. personnel of data processing div., dir. communications, 1957-61, v.p. communications, 1961-69, v.p. corporate ops. and services staff, 1969, mem. mgmt. com., 1970, sr. v.p., 1971, sr. v.p., group exec. data processing mktg. group, 1972—, sr. v.p. corp. ops. and services staffs, also mem. corp. mgmt. com., 1978—, also dir.; dir. Conoco, Inc., Nabisco, Inc., Sci. Research Assos. Mem. adv. council Nat. Urban Coalition. Served to lt. (s.g.) Intelligence Corps, USNR, 1942-46. Mem. Phi Beta Kappa. Clubs: Siwanoy (Bronxville, N.Y.); Ekwanok (Manchester, Vt.). Office: Old Orchard Rd Armonk NY 10504

MCKAY, DOUGLAS, JR., lawyer; b. Columbia, S.C., Aug. 12, 1917; s. Douglas McKay and Anne Lowndes Walker, B.A., U. of S.C., 1939; LL.B., S.C. Law Sch., 1941. Admitted to S.C. bar, 1941, U.S. Ct. Appeals bar, 1948, U.S. Sup. Ct. bar, 1971; asso. firm D. McKay, Columbia, 1941-46; partner firm McKay & McKay, Columbia, 1946-54, firm McKay, Sherrill, Walker & Townsend, and predecessors, Columbia, 1954—; chmn. advisory com. Improvement of Workmen's Compensation Laws, S.C. Mem. Am. Law Inst., Assn. RR Trial Counsel, Internat. Assn. Ins. Counsel, Am., S.C., Richland County (sec. 1945-46) bar assns. Office: McKay Sherrill et al 1340 Bull St PO Box 447 Columbia SC 29202

MC KAY, DOUGLAS WILLIAM, orthopedic surgeon; b. Howland, Maine, Mar. 10, 1927; s. Hugh Gordon and Elizabeth Mary (Jellison) Mc K; B.A. with distinction, U. Maine, 1951; M.D., Tufts U., 1955; m. Elinor Caswell, Mar. 31, 1950; children—Ann Elizabeth, Hugh Gordon, Heather Jean. Intern, Eastern Maine Gen. Hosp., Bangor, 1955-56; resident in orthopedic surgery McKinney VA Hosp., Dallas, 1956-59, Newington (Conn.) Hosp. for Crippled Children, 1959-60; practice medicine specializing in orthopedic surgery, Covington, Ky., 1960-61; chief surgeon Carrie Tingley Hosp. for Crippled Children, N.Mex., 1961-67; chief surgeon Shriner's Hosp. for Crippled Children, Shreveport, La., 1967-72; prof., head dept. orthopedic surgery La. State U., Shreveport, 1969-72; chmn. dept. pediatric orthopedic surgery, Children's Hosp., Nat. Med. Center, Washington, 1972—; prof. child health and devel., prof. orthopedic surgery George Washington U., 1972—; lectr. in field. Served with Maine Maritime Acad., 1944-46. Diplomate Am. Bd. Orthopedic Surgery. Mem. D.C. Med. Soc., Am. Acad. Orthopedic Surgeons, Pediatric Orthopedic Soc., Societe International de Chirurgie Orthopedique et de Traumatologie, Russell Hibbs Soc., Washington Orthopedic Soc., Western Orthopedic Assn. Clubs: Little Orthopedic, Rotary. Contbr. articles to med. jours. Home: 10616 Red Barn Ln Potomac MD 20854 Office: 111 Michigan Ave NW Washington DC 20010. *My professional goal is to improve the quality of life for children with orthopedic handicaps.*

MC KAY, GUNN, congressman; b. Ogden, Utah, Feb. 23, 1925; s. James Gunn and Elizabeth Catherine McKay; student Weber State Coll., 1958-60; B.S., Utah State U., 1962; m. Donna Biesinger; children—Gunn B., Mavis, Marl, Kolene, Carla, Ruston, Chad, Lon (dec.), Ruth, Rachel. Formerly businessman, tchr.; mem. Utah Ho. of Reps., 1962-66; adminstrv. asst. to Gov. of Utah, 1967-70; mem. 92d to 96th congresses from 1st Dist. Utah, chmn. mil. constrn. subcom. Appropriations Com. chmn. long range goals and planning com. Utah Legis. Council; mem. Legis. Task Force on Utah Reorgn. Com. Trustee David O. McKay Hosp.; chmn. United Dems. Congress; mem. exec. com. Rural Caucus, Congl. Campaign Com.; mem. exec. com. Steel Caucus. Served with USCGR, 1943-46. Mem. Am. Legion, Sons of Utah Pioneers. Democrat. Mem. Ch. of Jesus Christ of Latter-Day Saints (past stake pres.). Address: Huntsville UT 84317 Office: Room 2209 Rayburn House Office Bldg Washington DC 20515. *The McKay Family motto: "Don't sleep when you ought to be awake. Don't stay awake with eyes closed and hands folded. Work with your hands, think with your head, love with your heart, and never forget that character is capital."*

MCKAY, JIM, TV sports commentator; b. Phila., Sept. 24, 1921; s. Joseph F. and Florence (Gallagher) McManus; A.B., Loyola Coll., Balt., 1943; m. Margaret Dempsey, Oct. 2, 1948; children—Mary Edwina, Sean Joseph. Reporter, Balt. Eve. Sun, 1946-47; news and sports commentator sta. WMAR- TV, Balt., 1947-50; sports commentator CBS Network, 1950-61; sports commentator for Winter and Summer Olympics, 1960, 64, 68, 72, 76, 80; host Wide World of Sports, 1961—, This is New York, 1958-59. Served to lt. USNR, 1943-46. Recipient Emmy award, 1968, 70, 73, 74, 75, 76, George Polk Meml. award for journalism, 1973; Officer's Cross Order of Merit (Fed. Republic Germany), 1974; Olympic medal (Austria), 1977; Engelhard award Thoroughbreeders of Ky., 1978. Author: My Wide World, 1973. Office: ABC Sports 1330 Ave of Americas New York NY 10019

MC KAY, JOHN ARTHUR, rubber co. exec.; b. New Castle, Pa., Nov. 10, 1933; s. A. G. and Gladys M. (Downing) McK.; B.S. in Bus., Youngstown U., 1956; postgrad. Kent State U., 1959-62; grad. exec. program Stanford U., 1977; m. Sara K. Mikels, June 2, 1956; children—Mark A., Jeffrey S., Patricia A. Successively controller Vanderbilt div., mgr. lease dept. tire div., dir. field sales adminstrn., div. v.p. mktg. engineered systems div., div. pres., sr. v.p. BFG Engineered Products Group and v.p. B.F. Goodrich Co., Akron, Ohio; chmn. bd. Continental Conveyor & Equipment Co. subs. B.F. Goodrich Co. Mem. Rubber Mfrs. Assn. (exec. com.), Aerospace

Industries Assn. Am., Am. Mgmt. Assn., Transp. Assn. Am. Clubs: Portage Country, Masons, Shriners (Akron). Home: 1919 N Revere Rd Akron OH 44313 Office: 500 S Main St Akron OH 44318

MCKAY, JOHN G., JR., lawyer; b. Indpls., 1916; s. John G. and Margaret (Boomer) McK.; A.B., Rollins Coll., 1937; J.D., Yale, 1941; m. Kathleen Cary; children—Sandra Jean, John G. III (dec.). Admitted to Fla. bar, 1941; now mem. firm Bradford, Williams, McKay, Kimbrell, Hamann, Jennings & Kniskern, P.A., Miami, dir., treas., 1972—. Pres., Estate Planning Council Greater Miami, 1966-67. Trustee Everglades Sch. for Girls, 1955-74, 1st v.p., 1966-68, trustee emeritus Ransom Everglades Sch.; trustee Fla. State U. Found., 1964—, pres., 1965-68, 73-76; trustee Rollins Coll., 1966-69; trustee Embry-Riddle Aero. U., 1955—, chmn. bd., 1968-71; mem. Com. of 100; bd. dirs. Nat. Strategy Info. Center, 1967—, v.p., 1973-77; trustee Freedoms Found. at Valley Forge, 1972-75, bd. dirs., 1975—. Fellow Am. Coll. Probate Counsel, Am. Bar Found.; mem. Am. (chmn. adv. com. on edn. about communism 1962-74, 77-78, com. on law and nat. security 1978—), Dade County (past dir.) bar assns., Fla. Bar (chmn. com. on edn. against Communism 1964-68), Internat. Assn. Ins. Counsel, Nat. Assn. Coll. and Univ. Attys. Presbyn. Mason. Clubs: Two Hundred, Miami, Bath, Riviera. Home: Apt E 1208 1121 Crandon Blvd Key Biscayne FL 33149 Office: 9th Floor Dade Fed Savings Bldg 101 E Flagler St Miami FL 33131

MCKAY, JOHN HARVEY, football coach; b. Everettsville, W.Va., July 5, 1923; grad. U. Oreg.; m. Nancy Hunter; 4 children. Coach, U. Oreg., 1949-59; coach U. So. Calif., Los Angeles, 1959-76, head coach, 1960-76; coach Tampa Bay Buccaneers, NFL, Tampa, Fla., 1976—. Served with USAAF, World War II. Office: Tampa Bay Buccaneers 1 Buccaneer Pl Tampa FL 33607*

MCKAY, KENNETH GARDINER, physicist, electronics co. exec.; b. Montreal, Que., Can., Apr. 8, 1917; s. James Gardiner and Margaret (Nicholas) McK.; B.Sc., McGill U., 1938, M.Sc., 1939; Sc.D., Mass. Inst. Tech., 1941; m. Irene C. Smith, July 25, 1942; children—Margaret Craig, Kenneth Gardiner. Came to U.S., 1946, naturalized, 1954. Research engr. Nat. Research Council Can., 1941-46; with Bell Telephone Labs., 1946-66, 73—, dir. solid state device devel., 1957-59, v.p. systems engring., 1959-62, exec. v.p. systems engring., 1962-66, exec. v.p., 1973—; v.p. engring. AT&T, 1966-73; chmn. bd. Bellcomm Inc., 1966-72; dir. Bell Telephone Labs. Inc., Keuffel & Esser Co., Charles Stark Draper Lab., Sandia Corp. Trustee, Stevens Inst. Tech.; bd. govs. McGill U., 1972-77; mem. vis. com. for engring. Stanford. Fellow Am. Phys. Soc., IEEE; mem. Nat. Acad. Scis., Nat. Acad. Engring. (councillor 1970-73). Clubs: Baltusrol Golf (Springfield, N.J.); Weston (Conn.) Gun. Home: 200 E 66th St New York City NY 10021 Office: Bell Telephone Labs Murray Hill NJ 07974

MCKAY, MONROE GUNN, judge; b. Huntsville, Utah, May 30, 1928; s. James Gunn and Elizabeth (Peterson) McK.; B.S., Brigham Young U., 1957; J.D., U. Chgo., 1960; m. Lucile A. Kinnison, Aug. 6, 1954; children—Michele, Valanne, Margaret, James, Melanie, Nathan, Bruce, Lisa, Monroe. Admitted to Ariz. bar, 1961; law clk. Ariz. Supreme Ct., 1960-61; asso. firm Lewis & Roca, Phoenix, 1961-66, partner, 1968-74; asso. prof. Brigham Young U., 1974-76, prof., 1976-77; judge U.S. Circuit Ct. Appeals, 10th circuit, Denver, 1977—. Mem. Phoenix Community Council Juvenile Problems, 1968-74; pres. Ariz. Assn. for Health and Welfare, 1970-72; dir. Peace Corps, Malawi, Africa, 1966-68; bd. dirs., pres. Maricopa county Legal Aid Soc., 1972-74. Served with USMCR, 1946-48. Mem. Ariz., Maricopa County bar assns., Am. Judicature Soc., Am. Law Inst., Order Coif, Blue Key, Phi Kappa Phi. Mem. Ch. Jesus Christ of Latter-day Saints. Address: US Court of Appeals 6012 Federal Bldg 125 S State St Salt Lake City UT 84138

MCKAY, NEIL, banker; b. East Tawas, Mich., Aug. 9, 1917; s. Lloyd G. and Rose (McDonald) McK.; A.B., U. Mich., 1939, J.D. with distinction, 1946; m. Olive D. Baird, Nov. 11, 1950; children—Julia B., Lynn B., Hunter L. Admitted to Mich. bar, 1946, Ill. bar, 1947; with firm Winston, Strawn, Smith & Patterson, Chgo., 1946-63, partner, 1954-63; with First Nat. Bank of Chgo., 1963—, from v.p. charge heavy industry lending div., gen. mgr. London br., to exec. v.p., cashier, 1970-75, vice chmn. bd., 1976—, also dir.; exec. v.p., sec. First Chgo. Corp., 1970-75, vice chmn. bd., 1976—, also dir.; dir. Kerr-McGee Corp., Oklahoma City, Morton-Norwich Products Inc., Paxall, Inc., LaSalle Steel Co., Chgo. Bd. dirs. Student Loan Marketing Assn., Washington. Served with USNR, 1942-46. Mem. Am. Chgo., Ill. bar assns., Chgo. Hort. Assn. (dir.), Res. City Bankers Assn., Am. Bankers Assn., Assn. for Modern Banking in Ill. (dir.), Chgo. Assn. Commerce and Industry (dir.). Clubs: Chicago, Chicago Golf, Mid-Day (Chgo.); Geneva Golf. Staff Mich. Law Rev., 1942, 46. Home: 906 Sunset Rd Geneva IL 60134 Office: 1 First National Plaza Chicago IL 60670

MCKAY, ORVILLE HERBERT, clergyman, educator; b. Croswell, Mich., Oct. 9, 1913; s. Herbert W. and Iva (Perry) McK.; A.B. cum laude, Asbury Coll., Wilmore, Ky., 1934; B.D. summa cum laude, Drew Theol. Sem., 1937, Ph.D., 1941; Delaplaine-McDaniel fellow, Oxford (Eng.) U., 1949; D.D. (hon.), Adrian (Mich.) Coll., 1962; S.T.D., MacMurray Coll., 1965; LL.D., McKendree Coll., 1966; m. Mabel Coppock, Aug. 19, 1935; children—Gwendolyn (Mrs. Duane Wasmuth), Janeth Laura (Mrs. Amherst Turner, Jr.), Kathleen Evalyn (Mrs. William Gilbert). Ordained to ministry Meth. Ch., 1936; asst. minister, then asso. minister, Detroit, 1941-43, 46-47; minister in Highland Park, Mich., 1947-51, Midland, Mich., 1951-65; pres. Garrett Theol. Sem., Evanston, Ill., 1965-70; minister Cargill United Meth. Ch., Janesville, Wis., 1970—; vis. mission stas. Union S. Africa, Portuguese East Africa, 1957, Egypt, Holy Land, Greece, Italy, 1963, 65. Deacon Detroit Ann. Conf. Meth. Ch., 1936, elder, 1938; mem. Detroit Conf. Bd. Ministerial Tng. and Qualifications, 1948-65, chmn., 1958-65; mem. Wis. Ann. Conf. Bd. Edn., 1970-72, dean Pastor's Sch., 1972-76; del. N. Central Jurisdictional Conf., 1956, 64, Gen. and Jurisdictional Conf., 1960, 64, 68; mem. evaluating com. Detroit Ann. Conf., 1963-68; mem. gen. bd. edn. Meth. Ch., 1964-68; mem. Gen. Commn. on Ecumenical Affairs, 1965—; pres. Midland Ministerial Assn., 1953. Chmn. Detroit Conf. Bd. Hosps. and Homes, 1949-50; mem. Commn. Community Relations, Midland, 1964-65. Served as chaplain USAAF, 1943-46. Rotarian, Mason. Home: 48 S Harmony Dr Janesville WI 53545

MCKAY, ROBERT BUDGE, educator; b. Wichita, Kans., Aug. 11, 1919; s. John Budge and Ruth Irene (Gelsthorpe) McK.; B.S., U. Kans., 1940; J.D., Yale, 1947; LL.D., Emory U., 1973, Seton Hall U., 1975; L.H.D., Mt. St. Mary Coll., 1973; m. Sara Kate Warmack, Nov. 20, 1954; children—Kathryn Lee, Sara Margaret. Admitted to Kans. bar, 1948, D.C. bar, 1948, N.Y. State bar, 1973; with Dept. Justice, 1947-50; asst., then asso. prof. law Emory U., 1950-53; prof. law N.Y. U., 1953—, dean Sch. Law, 1967-75. Mem. exec. com. Assn. Am. Law Schs., 1964-65; mem. exec. com. Lawyers Com. for Civil Rights Under Law; chmn. N.Y. State Spl. Commn. on Attica, 1971-72; chmn. N.Y.C. Bd. Correction, 1973-74; dir. program on justice, society and individual Aspen Inst. for Humanistic Studies, 1975—. Chmn. bd. dirs. Citizens Union, 1971-77; pres. Legal Aid Soc. of N.Y.C., 1975-77; vice chmn. Nat. News Council, 1973—. Recipient award Am. Friends Hebrew U. Law Sch., 1972, William Nelson Cromwell medal New York County Lawyers Assn., 1973, Arthur T. Vanderbilt medal N.Y. U. Sch. Law, 1974, Albert Gallatin medal N.Y. U., 1975. Mem. Am. (chmn. commn. on correctional facilities and services 1974-78), N.Y. State bar assns., Assn. Bar City N.Y. (chmn. exec. com. 1975-76, v.p. 1976-77), Delta Upsilon. Presbyn. Author: Reapportionment: The Law and Politics of Equal Representation, 1965. Editor: Annual Survey of American Law, 1953-56; An American Constitutional Law Reader, 1958; Time-Life Family Legal Guide, 1971. Home: 29 Washington Sq W New York NY 10011

MCKAY, ROBERT JAMES, JR., pediatrician, educator; b. N.Y.C., Oct. 8, 1917; s. Robert James and Mary (Montgomery) McK.; grad. Lawrenceville (N.J.) Sch., 1934; A.B., Princeton U., 1939; M.D., Harvard U., 1943; m. Elizabeth Stewardson Foote, May 30, 1943; children—Robert James III, David Montgomery, Daniel Graham, Timothy Foote. Intern, Columbia-Presbyn. Med. Center, N.Y.C., 1943, asst. resident, 1947; chief resident Childrens Hosp. Med. Center, Boston, 1948; Milton fellow pharmacology Harvard Med. Sch., 1949; asst. prof. pediatrics U. Vt. Coll. of Medicine, 1950-52, asso. prof., 1952-55, prof., 1955—, chmn. dept., 1950—; chief pediatric service Med. Center Hosp. Vt.; sr. pediatric cons. Vt. Health Dept. Served from 1st lt. to capt. M.C., AUS, 1944-46. Decorated Bronze Star medal; recipient Jaycee Distinguished Service award, 1953. John and Mary Markle Found. scholar in med. sci., 1950-55; Fulbright lectr. U. Groningen (Netherlands), 1960. Mem. Am. Acad. Pediatrics (pres. 1970), Soc. for Pediatric Research, Am. Soc. Human Genetics, Am., New Eng. (past pres.), Canadian pediatric socs., Ambulatory Pediatric Assn., AMA, Assn. Am. Med. Colls., Assn. Med. Sch. Pediatric Dept. Chmn. (pres.), Sigma Xi, Alpha Omega Alpha. Co-editor Nelson Textbook of Pediatrics. Contbr. articles to profl. jours. Home: RD 1 Box 424 Williston VT 05495 Office: Med Center Hosp Burlington VT 05401

MCKAY, THOMAS, JR., mfg. co. exec., lawyer; b. Kearny, N.J., Sept. 26, 1920; s. Thomas and Mary (Paterson) McK.; A.B., Rutgers U., 1941; LL.B., N.Y. U., 1944; m. Rosemary T. LaMarra, Oct. 5, 1946; children—Thomas III, Barbara Anne, Robert Michael. Admitted to N.J. bar, 1945, Ill. bar, 1967; asso. to Arthur T. Vanderbilt, 1944-47; asso. firm Toner, Speakman & Crowley, Newark, 1947-50; with McGraw-Edison Co. and predecessor, 1950—, sec., gen. counsel, 1967—, v.p., 1973—; dir. Impco de Mexico. Home: 4N 123 Thornly Rd St Charles IL 60174 Office: 333 W River Rd Elgin IL 60120

MCKAY, VERNON, educator; b. Independence, Kans., Oct. 8, 1912; s. Peter Miller and Myrtle Ethyl (Pierson) McK.; A.B., Baker U., 1933, LL.D., 1961; M.A., Syracuse U., 1934; Ph.D., Cornell U., 1939; m. Lila Buck, Sept. 22, 1935; children—Margaret Ann, Patricia Louise. Instr. history Syracuse U., 1936-40, asst. prof., 1940-45; research asso. Fgn. Policy Assn., 1945-48; staff Dept. State, 1948-56, dep. dir. Office Dependent Area Affairs, 1956, also mem. U.S. delegations UN Gen. Assembly and Trusteeship Council; Frances P. Bolton prof. African studies Sch. Advanced Internat. Studies, Johns Hopkins, 1956-78; research, teaching trips to Africa. Mem. U.S. Nat. Commn. for UNESCO, 1960-66, exec. com., 1961-63; chmn. adv. council African affairs Dept. State, 1962-68. Mem. African Studies Assn. (pres. 1961-62), Internat. African Inst., Royal African Soc., Council Fgn. Relations, Am. Hist. Assn., Am. Polit. Sci. Assn., Internat. Inst. Differing Civilizations, South African Inst. Race Relations, African-American Inst. (trustee 1964-69). Club: Cosmos (Washington). Author: Africa in World Politics, 1963; African Diplomacy, 1966. Co-author: Southern Africa and the United States, 1968. Editor: Africa in United States, 1967. Contbr. articles on Africa to profl. and other jours. Home: 15503 Prince Frederick Way Silver Spring MD 20906

MCKEACHIE, WILBERT JAMES, psychologist, educator; b. Clarkston, Mich., Aug. 24, 1921; s. Bert A. and Edith E. (Welberry) McK.; B.A., Mich. State Normal Coll., 1942; M.A., U. Mich., 1946, Ph.D., 1949; LL.D., Eastern Mich. U., 1957, U. Cin.; Sc.D., Northwestern U., 1973, Denison U., 1975, Nat. Acad. Edn., 1977; m. Virginia Mae Mack, Oct. 30, 1942; children—Linda, Karen. Faculty, U. Mich., 1946—, prof. psychology, 1961—, chmn. dept., 1961-71, dir. Center for Research in Learning and Teaching, 1975—. Mem. nat. adv. mental health council NIMH, 1976—; mem. spl. med. adv. group VA, 1967-72. Trustee Kalamazoo Coll., 1964-77; trustee-at-large Am. Psychol. Found., Inc., 1974—, pres., 1979—. Served as officer USNR, 1943-45. Recipient Outstanding Tchr. award U. Mich. Alumni Assn.; ACT-AERA award for outstanding research on coll. students. Mem. Am. Psychol. Assn. (sec., dir., pres. 1976—), Am. Assn. Higher Edn. (dir. 1974—, pres. 1978), AAUP (pres. U. Mich. chpt. 1970-71), AAAS (chmn. sect. on psychology 1976-77), Sigma Xi. Baptist. Author: (with J.E. Milholland) Undergraduate Curricula in Psychology, 1961; (with Charlotte Doyle and Mary Margaret Moffett) Psychology, 1966, 3d edit., 1977 (also Spanish edit. and Instructors Manual); Psychology: The Short Course, 1972; Teaching Tips, 7th edit., 1978; Research on College Teaching: A Review, 1970. Cons. editor Jour. Higher Edn., Jour. Edn. Psychology, 1974-76. Home: 4660 W Joy Rd Dexter MI 48130 Office: Dept Psychology U Mich 580 Union Dr Ann Arbor MI 48109

MCKEACHIE, WILLIAM EUGENE, advt. exec.; b. N.Y.C., Feb. 10, 1904; s. William Stevenson and Adelaide Anna (Theriault) McK.; B.S., Franklin and Marshall Coll., 1926; postgrad. New Sch. Social Research, Columbia; m. Anne Amelia Noble, Apr. 16, 1938; 1 son, William Noble. Reporter, feature writer, asst. Sunday editor Lancaster (Pa.) News Jour., 1922-26; copywriter Patterson-Andress Co., N.Y., 1926-28; exec. J. Walter Thompson Co., Paris and London, 1928-29; copywriter McCann-Erickson, Inc., N.Y.C., 1929-40, creative dir., 1940-52, v.p., dir., 1942-52, supr. European operations, 1952-60; pres., chmn. McCann-Erickson, S.A., Brussels, 1952-60; mng. dir. chmn. McCann-Erickson Advt., Ltd., London, 1952-60; sr. v.p., dir. McCann-Erickson Corp. Internat., N.Y.C., 1955-60; pres. McCann-Marschalk, 1960-61, ret., now cons. on European-Am. bus.; pres., dir. Adjunt-to-Mgmt., Inc., 1962—; former chmn. and mng. dir. McCann-Erickson Europe S.A., Geneva; dir. McCann-Erickson Italiana S.A., Milan, Sodico, Sa., Paris, H.K. McCann Co., Frankfurt, Germany. Mem. Joint Com. on Grassland Farming, 1946-52. Mem. Internat. C. of C., Inst. Practitioners in Advt., Franklin and Marshall Met. Alumni Assn. (pres. 1940-52), Delaware Valley Protective Assn. (dir.), Farm Club of N.Y., Phi Sigma Kappa, Alpha Delta Sigma. Clubs: University (N.Y.C.); American, Farmers, Royal Automobile, Roehampton (London); New Cosmopolitan (Hamburg); American (Brussels). Address Carversville Bucks County PA 18913

MC KEAG, THOMAS BENEDICT OLIVER, lawyer; b. Belfast, No. Ireland, Mar. 21, 1928; s. Thomas and Margaret (McCaffrey) McK.; came to Can., 1952, naturalized, 1970; student St. Malachys Coll., Belfast, 1945; LL.B., Queen's U., Belfast, 1948; m. Marie Cooper, Dec. 8, 1956; children—Maura, Ellen, Siobhan, Kevin. Admitted to bar No. Ireland, 1950; barrister-at-law Inn of Court of No. Ireland, Belfast, 1950-52; solicitor, Ont., 1956, barrister, 1958, appointed Queen's counsel, 1972; with dept. law Shell Can. Ltd., Toronto, Ont., 1953—, gen. counsel, 1973—, sec., 1977—. Bd. govs., pres. research found., St. Joseph's Hosp., Toronto, 1977—. Mem. Can. (chmn. Ont. br. 1973-74, chmn. corporate lawyers sect. 1977-79, nat. exec. com. 1979—), Internat. bar assns., Law Soc. Upper Can. Club: Royal Can. Yacht. Home: 49 Sandringham Dr Toronto ON M5M 3G4 Canada Office: 505 University Ave Toronto ON M5G 1X4 Canada

MCKEAN, HUGH FERGUSON, educator, painter, writer; b. Beaver Falls, Pa., July 28, 1908; s. Arthur and Eleanor (Ferguson) McK.; A.B., Rollins Coll., 1930; M.A., Williams Coll., 1940; Dr. Space Edn., Fla. Inst. Tech., 1963; L.H.D., Stetson U. Coll. Law, 1961; LL.D., U. Tampa, 1970; D.F.A., Rollins Coll., 1972; m. Jeannette Genius, June 28, 1945. Instr. art Rollins Coll., Winter Park, Fla., 1932-35, asst. prof., 1935-37, asst. prof., asst. to dir. dept. art, 1937-41, asso. prof., 1941-45, prof. art, dir. Morse Gallery Art, 1942—, acting pres. coll., 1951-52, pres., 1952-69, chancellor, 1969-73, chmn. bd., 1969-75; pres. Charles Hosmer Morse Found., 1976—; works exhibited Second Nat. Exhbn. Am. Painting, N.Y.C., Soc. The Four Arts, Palm Beach, Fla., 1948, Allied Artists Am. Ann Exhbn., 1949, 4th Southeastern Ann., Atlanta, 1949, numerous ann. exhbns. Fla. Fedn. Art; collections Tol. Mus. Art U. Va. Bd. dirs. Edyth Bush Charitable Found., 1973—; trustee Louis Comfort Tiffany Found., 1959—. Served as lt. comdr. USNR, 1942-45. Recipient Decoration Honor, Rollins Coll., 1942; Cervantes medal Hispanic Inst. in Fla., 1952; John Young award Orlando Area C. of C., 1967; best work in show Fla. Fedn. Art Ann. Exhbn. 1931, 49, best Fla. landscape, 1949. Mem. Fla. Fine Arts Council, 1970-74. Mem. Am. Soc. Order of St. John, Nat. Soccer Coaches Am., Omicron Delta Kappa. Clubs: X, Century Assn. (N.Y.C.); Long Island Wyandanch (Eastport, L.I.); Orlando (Fla.) Country. Home: 930 Genius Dr Winter Park FL 32789

MCKEAN, JOHN ROSSEEL OVERTON, coll. ofcl.; b. Cortland, N.Y., July 31, 1928; s. Norman Dodge and Janet (Passage) McK.; B.A., Coll. William and Mary, 1951; M.Ed., Cornell U., 1956, Ed.D., 1961; m. Ruth MacDonald, July 2, 1955; children—Janet, Annalise. Tchr. Landon Sch. for Boys, Washington, 1952-53; tchr. Central Sch., Homer, N.Y., 1953-55; asst. prof. history, dean students Allegheny Coll., 1957-67; headmaster Kingswood Sch. for Girls, Cranbrook, Bloomfield Hills, Mich., 1967-68; dean Hobart Coll., 1968-72; v.p. Coll., Kenyon Coll., Gambier, Ohio, 1973-77; dean arts and scis. State U. N.Y. at Canton, 1977—. Mem. Am. Conf. Acad. Deans, Nat. Assn. Student Personnel Adminstrs. (pres. Pa. 1958-59, dir. 1959-61), Am. Assn. Higher Edn., Middle States Assn. Colls. and Secondary Schs., Direct Descs. Signers Declaration Independence, Geneva Hist. Soc., Geneva Concerts Assn. (dir. 1969-72), Am. Hist. Assn., Round Table, Phi Delta Kappa, Kappa Sigma. Rotarian. Home: 5 Fairlane Dr Canton NY 13617

MCKEAN, KEITH FERGUSON, educator; b. Beaver Falls, Pa., Aug. 18, 1915; s. Arthur and Eleanor (Ferguson) McK.; A.B. (Clark scholar), Williams Coll., 1938; M.A., U. Chgo., 1940; Ph.D. (Rackham fellow), U. Mich., 1949; m. Catherine Stevenson, Oct. 31, 1942 (div. 1965); children—Kevin, Bruce; m. 2d, Joan Sanford Canter, Sept. 26, 1969. Instr., U. Toledo, 1940-42; prof. N.C. State U., 1949-61; prof. Elmira Coll., 1961-68; prof. U. No. Iowa, Cedar Falls, 1968—. Served to 1st lt. USAAF, 1942-46. Ford Faculty fellow for postdoctoral study, 1954-55. Mem. AAUP, Delta Kappa Epsilon. Rotarian. Author: Cross Currents in the South, 1960; The Moral Measure of Literature, 1961; Critical Approaches to Literature, 1968; Informative and Persuasive Prose, 1971. Home: 824 Hudson Rd Cedar Falls IA 50613. *I am deeply impressed with the part that plain chance plays in one's success or failure. Everything I have achieved that is really desirable was, in large measure, an accident of such things as time or place. Indeed, I might have accomplished far less than I actually have or far more—depending on factors over which I had no control. We are all created equal, in one sense, because all men are created equally dependent on blind chance, and a full realization of this fact can temper foolish pride and guard against excessive self-abasement.*

MCKEAN, MICHAEL, actor; b. N.Y.C., Oct. 17; s. Gilbert and Ruth McKean; student Carnegie Inst. Tech., N.Y. U.; m. Susan McKean; 1 son, Colin Russell. Toured with satirical comedy group The Credibility Gap; TV appearances include More Than Friends, American Bandstand, The TV Show; regular on ABC-TV series Laverne and Shirley, 1976—; appeared in film 1941, 1979; rec. artist (with David Lander) Lenny and the Squiggtones. Office: care ABC Public Relations 1330 Ave of Americas New York NY 10019*

MCKEAN, ROLAND NEELY, economist, educator; b. Mulberry Grove, Ill., Oct. 30, 1917; s. John Vincent and Maude R. (Spradling) McK.; A.B., U. Chgo., 1939, A.M., 1948, Ph.D., 1948; m. Anne Webster, Mar. 28, 1944; children—Margaret Anne McKean (Mrs. John P. Peraza), John V. (dec.). Asst. prof. econs. Vanderbilt U., 1948-51; research economist RAND Corp., 1951-63; prof. econs. U. Calif. at Los Angeles, 1964-68; vis. prof. econs. and edn. Harvard, 1967; Commonwealth prof. econs. U. Va., Charlottesville, 1968—; vis. scholar in residence Washington U., St. Louis, 1976; mem. panels various govt. agencies, 1964—; mem. Legis. Task Force Natural Resources, 1964. Served as pilot USAAF, 1941-45. Decorated D.F.C. with oak leaf cluster. Mem. Center Advanced Studies, U. Va., 1968-71; Fulbright prof. U. Glasgow, 1962; grantee NSF, 1971-74, 76-78, Social Sci. Research Council, 1962. Mem. Am., So. (pres. 1972) econ. assns., Public Choice Soc. Author: Public Spending, 1968; Efficiency in Government Through Systems Analysis, 1958; co-author: Economics of Defense in the Nuclear Age, 1960; Teacher Shortages and Salary Schedules, 1962. Bd. editors Am. Econ. Rev., 1962-64. Contbr. articles to profl. jours. Home: 1719 Meadowbrook Heights Rd Charlottesville VA 22918. *In the end it's important to be able to laugh.*

MC KECHNIE, DONNA RUTH, actress, dancer, singer; b. Pontiac, Mich., Nov. 16, 1942; d. Donald Bruce and Carolyn Ruth (Johnson) McK.; student pub. schs., Pontiac; m. Michael Bennett, Dec. 4, 1976. Ballet concert work in Mich., 1958; Broadway debut in How to Succeed in Business, 1960; other Broadway shows include Promises, Promises, 1968, Company, 1970, A Chorus Line, 1975; appeared on numerous TV shows; appeared in motion picture The Little Prince; choreographer own one-woman shows and benefits. Recipient Tony award as best mus. actress for A Chorus Line, 1975. Mem. Actors Equity, Screen Actors Guild, AFTRA, Actors Fund Am. (life). Office: c/o Shulman Inc 510 Madison Ave New York City NY 10022*

MCKEE, ARTHUR, JR., museum ofcl., treasure diver; b. Bridgeton, N.J., Nov. 2, 1910; s. Arthur and Mable A. (Chain) McK.; grad. Bridgeton High Sch., 1931; m. Janet Gay Bodden; children—Wayne Norris (dec.), Patricia D., Richard A., Arthur III, Terry (dec.), Karen T., Kevin D. Recreational dir., Bridgeton, 1935-36; city recreation dir., Homestead, Fla., 1940-50; deep sea diver USNR pipe line, Fla., 1941-43; organizer McKee's Museum Sunken Treasure, Inc., Homestead, 1949; founder, operator McKee's Treasure Mus., Treasure Harbor, Plantation Key, Fla., 1950—; founder, 1960, since operator divers' tng. sch. underwater archaeology, Treasure Harbor; condr. 32 expdns., Bahamas, Fla. Keys, Caribbean, including McKee-Smithsonian Instn. expdn. to recover treasure from Spanish ships wrecked, 1733; excavated sunken city Port Royal with Link expdn., Kingston Harbor; guest appearances numerous TV shows. Named Mr. Treasure Hunter, Am. Treasure Trove Club, N.Y.C., 1966; Pioneer in Underwater Archaeology in Western Hemisphere,

Nat. Geog. Soc., 1973-74. Mem. Islamorada (pres. 1967-68), Upper Keys Fla. (dir. 1973-75, pres. 1976-78) chambers commerce. Clubs: Ocho Rios Reef (Jamaica); Caribbean Yacht (Grand Cayman); Elks (pres. 1976-77). Patentee underwater motion picture camera cases, underwater metal detector, system excavating wreck sites, others; recovered gold, silver bars, doubloons, Spanish coins and artifacts. Address: Treasure Harbor Plantation Key FL 33070. *Treasure is where you find it.*

MCKEE, CALVIN CHARLES, oil co. exec.; b. Tulsa, Aug. 29, 1923; s. Charles and Estelle Marie (Larrieu) McK.; B.S. in Petroleum Engring., U. Tulsa, 1948; divorced; children—Christopher C., Gary P., Kirk J., Anne M., Brian M., Lynn L. With Gulf Oil Corp. and affiliates, 1963-77, v.p. crude oil Gulf Oil Exploration & Prodn. Co., Houston, 1975-77; pres. Warren Petroleum Co., Tulsa, 1977—; v.p. Global Energy Ops. and Mgmt. Co., Columbian Gulf Oil Co., Gulf Kuwait Co., Gulf Oil Products Co.; dir. Nat. Butane Co. Mem. exec. bd. Indian Nations council Boy Scouts Am.; bd. dirs. Goodwill Industries Tulsa, Jr. Achievement Greater Tulsa, Blue Cross/Blue Shield Okla. Served with AUS, 1942-45, 52. Registered profl. engr., Tex., Okla. Mem. Tulsa C. of C. (dir.), Am. Petroleum Inst., Am. Gas Assn., Gas Processors Assn., Internat. Petroleum Exposition, Mid-Continent Oil and Gas Assn. Republican. Roman Catholic. Clubs: So. Hills County, Tulsa. Office: PO Box 1589 Tulsa OK 74102

MC KEE, EDWIN DINWIDDIE, geologist; b. Washington, Sept. 24, 1906; s. Edwin Jones and Ethel (Swope) McK.; student U.S. Naval Acad., 1924-27; A.B., Cornell U., 1929; postgrad. U. Ariz., 1930-31, U. Calif. at Berkeley, 1933-34, Yale, 1939-40; Sc.D. (hon.), No. Ariz. U., 1957; m. Barbara Hastings, Dec. 31, 1929; children—William Dinwiddie, Barbara (Mrs. John Lajoie), Edwin Hastings. Park naturalist Grand Canyon Nat. Park, 1929-40; asst. dir. charge research Museum No. Ariz., 1941-42, summers 1942-53; mem. faculty U. Ariz., 1942-53, prof. geology, 1950-53, chmn. dept., 1951-53; chief paleotectonic map sect. U.S. Geol. Survey, Denver, 1953-61, research geologist, 1962—. Research investigator in field, vis. prof., participant numerous symposia, 1931—; mem. U.S. Nat. Com. on Geology, 1968-72; vis. lectr. NRC of Brazil, 1970; USSR Acad. Scis., 1970; prin. investigator desert sand seas of world Earth Resources Tech. Satellite, 1972-73; discipline expert (deserts) sci. support team Skylab IV, 1973-74; leader expdn. to Namib Desert, 1977; cons. Research Inst., Dhahran, Saudi Arabia, 1978; geologist Nepal Inst. Ecotechnics, Kathmandu; cons. Research Inst., U. Petroleum and Minerals, 1978-79. Commr. Bow Mar (Colo.), 1962-63; trustee Mus. No. Ariz., 1953—; bd. dirs. S.W. Parks and Monuments Assn., 1958—. Recipient Distinguished Service award Dept. Interior, 1962; nine fossil species (3 trilobites, 1 nautiloid, 2 brachiopods, 1 reptile, 1 foraminifer, 1 ammonoid) named mckeei in his honor, 1935-68; John Wesley Powell Centennial Guidebook of Four Corners Geol. Soc. dedicated to him, 1969. Mem. Grand Canyon Natural History Assn. (exec. sec. 1937-39), Tucson Natural History Assn. (pres. 1944), AAAS (Powell lectr. 1950), Ariz. Geol. Soc. (pres. 1952-53), Geol. Soc. Am. (councilor 1953-55), Am. Commn. Stratigraphic Nomenclature (chmn. 1957), Am. Assn. Petroleum Geologists (distinguished lectr. 1957), Rocky Mountain Assn. Geologists (hon.), Soc. Econ. Paleontologists and Mineralogists (hon.; pres. 1967-68, Twenhofel award 1975), Sigma Xi (pres. Ariz. chpt. 1950). Author books, monographs, articles in field. Home: 4845 Redwood Dr Littleton CO 80123 Office: US Geol Survey Federal Center Denver CO 80225

MCKEE, FRAN, naval officer; b. Florence, Ala., Sept. 13, 1926; d. Thomas W. and Geneva (Lumpkins) McK.; B.S., U. Ala., 1950; M.S. in Internat. Affairs, George Washington U., 1970; D.Pub.Adminstrn. (hon.), Mass. Maritime Acad. Commd. ensign U.S. Navy, 1950, advanced through grades to rear adm., 1976; service in Morocco and Spain; dep. asst. chief for human goals, Bur. Naval Personnel, 1972-73; comdg. officer Naval Security Group Activity, Ft. Meade, Md., 1973-76; dir. naval ednl. devel. Staff of Chief Naval Edn. and Tng., Naval Air Sta., Pensacola, Fla., 1976-78; asst. dep. chief naval ops. for human resource mgmt., Washington, 1978—. Decorated Legion of Merit, Meritorious Service medal; elected to Ala. Acad. Honor. Episcopalian. Home: 7420 Adams Park Ct Annandale VA 22003 Office: Office Chief Naval Ops (OP-15) Navy Dept Washington DC 20350

MCKEE, FRANK SYLVESTER, union ofcl.; b. Seattle, Dec. 31, 1920; s. Thomas J. and Hannah J. (Jordan) McK.; student parochial schs., Seattle; m. Lois Jane Brandt, June 21, 1947; children—Thomas Scott, Carolyn Louise. With open hearth dept. Bethlehem Steel Co., Seattle, 1940-60; officer United Steelworkers Am., Local Unit 1208, Seattle, 1952-60, staff rep., 1960-71, dir. Dist. 38, 1971-77, internat. treas., Pitts., 1977—; v.p. Calif. AFL-CIO, mem. com. on polit. action, 1977—. Chmn. nat. nonferrous bargaining com. Social Security Ret. Workers Strike and Def. Fund, 1977—; active Golden Triangle YMCA. Served with inf., AUS, 1943-45. Decorated Purple Heart; recipient Spirit of Life award City of Hope, 1978. Research fellow City of Hope, 1978. Democrat. Roman Catholic. Club: Rolling Hills Golf. Home: 200 White Hampton Ln Apt 202 Pittsburgh PA 15236 Office: 5 Gateway Center Pittsburgh PA 15222. *I submit, that no picture of America can be complete without including in its historic framework the role of the working people. Stood alongside labor, every other element, every other hero is somewhat bland when considering what made this nation what it is and what contributed to its spectacular rise in world prominence.*

MCKEE, FRANK WRAY, physician, med. commn. exec.; b. Beaver, Pa., Feb. 18, 1915; s. Frank Wray and Grace Katherine (Walrad) McK.; A.B., Hamilton Coll., 1936; M.D. with honors, U. Rochester, 1943; m. Mary Mulligan, Dec. 27, 1943; children—Malcolm B., Margaret S. Instr. pathology U. Rochester, 1947-51; chief pathologist Genesee Hosp., Rochester, 1951-54; prof. pathology, dir. clin. labs. U. Calif. at Los Angeles, 1954-62; from asso. dean to acting dean U. Rochester Sch. Medicine and Dentistry, 1962-66; med. dir. Rochester Regional Hosp. Council, 1966-67; dir. div. physician manpower Bur. Health Manpower of NIH, Bethesda, Md., 1967-70; dean Sch. of Medicine, W.Va. U., Morgantown, 1970-73, prof. pathology, 1973-74; assoc. dir. Ednl. Commn. for Fgn. Med. Grads., Phila., 1974—. Served as lt. M.C., USNR, 1944-46; ETO, PTO. Mem. Am. Assn. Pathologists and Bacteriologists, Am. Soc. Exptl. Pathology, A.M.A., Phi Beta Kappa, Sigma Xi, Alpha Omega Alpha. Club: U. Pa. Faculty (Phila.). Home: 516 College Ave Haverford PA 19041 Office: 3624 Market St Philadelphia PA 19104

MCKEE, GORDON NORFOLK, JR., business exec.; b. Boston, July 18, 1930; s. Gordon Norfolk and G. Marion (Schneider) McK.; A.B. in Psychology and Sociology, Harvard U., 1951; m. Mary Brandt, July 21, 1951; children—Linda, Gordon, Pamela, Martha. With Texasgulf, Inc., Stamford, Conn., 1958—, asst. treas., 1960-64, treas., 1964—, v.p., 1972—. Served to lt. (j.g.) USNR, 1951-55. Asso. mem. Am. Inst. Mining Engrs. Clubs: Sky (N.Y.C.); Landmark (Stamford); Wee Burn (Darien, Conn.). Home: 110 Stephen Mather Rd Darien CT 06820 Office: Texasgulf Inc High Ridge Park Stamford CT 06904

MCKEE, JAMES, JR., banker; b. Utica, N.Y., Aug. 29, 1918; s. James and Marie Roze (Tuller) McK.; B.S., Syracuse U., 1940; m. Doris Elsie Nafis, June 28, 1947; children— James III, Nancy C. (dec.), Peter C., David R., John S. Exec. v.p., cashier First Nat. Bank, Richfield Springs, N.Y., 1940-56; with State Bank of Albany, N.Y., 1956—, v.p., cashier, 1969—. Co-chmn. United Fund, Clinton County, 1969; treas. Eastern Adirondack Econ. Devel. Commn., 1967-69. Treas., bd. mgrs. Albany Home for Children, 1971-78; mem. Plattsburgh Coll. Found.; bd. dirs. Champlain Devel. Corp., 1969, New Industries for Clinton County, 1969; trustee Champlain Valley Physicians Hosp., 1969. Served to maj. C.E., AUS, 1942-46; ETO. Decorated Bronze Star medal. Mem. State Bank Albany Quarter Century Club (pres. 1974-75), Alpha Kappa Psi, Delta Kappa Epsilon, Phi Kappa Phi, Beta Gamma Sigma, Beta Alpha Psi. Elk, Rotarian (pres. Albany 1974-75). Club: Fort Orange (Albany). Home: 21 Valencia Ln Clifton Park NY 12065 Office: 69 State St Albany NY 12201

MC KEE, JEWEL CHESTER, JR., elec. engr., educator, univ. adminstr.; b. Madison, Wis., Nov. 4, 1923; s. Jewel Chester and Carolyn Reid (Ezell) McK.; student Tulane U., 1943-44; B.S., Miss. State U., 1944; M.S., U. Wis., 1949, Ph.D. (Gen. Edn. Bd. fellow), 1952; m. Rachel McIntosh Magruder, Aug. 30, 1947 (dec. Sept. 1968); children—William M., George C., Catherine M., Jeanne Christopher McKee; m. 2d, Barbara Jo Sims, Nov. 1, 1969; 1 dau., Sarah Margaret. Instr., Miss. State U., 1946, asst. prof. elec. engring., 1949-52, asso. prof., 1952-56, prof., 1956-79, prof. emeritus, 1979—, head dept., 1957-62, dean Grad. Sch., 1962-77, v.p. research and grad. studies, 1969—, v.p. emeritus, 1979—; pres. Conf. So. Grad. Schs., 1973-74; mem. exec. com. Council Grad. Schs. in U.S., 1973-78, chmn., 1977; dir. associateships NRC, 1979—. Exec. dir. Miss. Gov.'s Emergency Council for Camille disaster, 1969-70; dist. chmn. Boy Scouts Am.; bd. dirs. Miss. Heart Assn. Served as engring. officer Naval Amphibious Force, 1944-46. Mem. Nat., Miss. socs profl. engrs., AAAS, Am. Soc. Engring. Edn., IEEE, Sigma Xi, Sigma Chi, Eta Kappa Nu, Omicron Delta Kappa, Tau Beta Pi, Phi Kappa Phi. Presbyn. Rotarian. Contbr. articles to profl. and ednl. jours. Home: 9753 Bruton Pl Vienna VA 22180

MC KEE, JOHN ANGUS, mfg. co. exec.; b. Toronto, Ont., Can., Aug. 31, 1935; s. John William and Margaret Enid (Phippen) McK.; student U. Toronto, 1954-58; m. Susan Elizabeth Harley, May 30, 1970; children—John Andrew, Mary Susan. With Dominion Securities Corp. Ltd., Toronto, 1958-61; v.p. Patino Mining Corp., Toronto and London, Eng., 1962-72; pres. J. Angus McKee & Assos. Ltd.; dir. Teradyne Can. Ltd., Stone & Webster Can. Ltd., Taro Industries, Ltd., Cullman Ventures Inc., Canadian Occidental Petroleum Ltd., others. Mng. dir. Consol. Tin Smelters Ltd., 1968-71. Bd. govs. Trinity Coll. Sch. Mem. Alpha Delta Phi. Clubs: Toronto, York, Badminton and Racquet; Knickerbocker (N.Y.C.). Home: 9 Dunloe Rd Toronto ON M4V 2W4 Canada Office: 94 Cumberland St Suite 803 Toronto ON M5R 1A3 Canada

MC KEE, JOHN WILLIAM, business exec.; b. Toronto, Ont., Can., Dec. 25, 1897; s. John Arnold and Christie Ann (McRae) McK.; student Univ. Schs., Toronto, 1912-16, Royal Mil. Coll., Kingston, Can., 1916-17, U. Toronto, 1920; m. Margaret Enid Phippen, Oct. 15, 1924; children—Margaret Ann (Mrs. Pattison), John Angus. Dir. Stone & Webster Canada, Ltd., Toronto, 1950—, chmn. bd. dirs., 1950-75, chmn. exec. com., 1975—; dir. Stone & Webster, Inc., N.Y.C., 1950-70; dir., past pres. Royal Agrl. Winter Fair, Toronto; hon. dir., mem. adv. bd. Royal Trustco., Royal Trust Corp. Adv. bd. Salvation Army; dir. Canadian Geriatrics Soc. Served as lt. Royal Arty. RFC and RAF, World War I; exec. asst. Master Gen. of Ordnance, also mem. Nat. War Finance Com. and chmn. North York War Finance Com., World War II. Mem. Alpha Delta Phi. Presbyn. Clubs: Toronto, York, Rosedale Golf, North York Hunt (Toronto); Knickerbocker (N.Y.C.); Ocean of Fla. (Delray Beach). Home: 345 Riverview Dr Toronto ON M4N 3C9 Canada Office: Yonge-Eglinton Centre 2300 Yonge St Toronto ON M4P 2W6 Canada

MCKEE, JOSEPH VINCENT, JR., appliance co. exec.; b. N.Y.C., Jan. 1, 1921; s. Joseph Vincent and Cornelia (Kraft) McK.; grad. Phillips Exeter Acad., 1938; A.B., Princeton, 1942; LL.B., Columbia, 1948; m. Phyllis Feldmann, May 1, 1948; children—Charlotte Cornelia McKee Worcester, Catherine Barbara McKee Donovan, Joseph Vincent III, Charles Russell. With N.Y. Supreme Ct., 1948-49, Henney Motor Co., Inc., N.Y.C., 1949-52; v.p. Oneida Products Corp., N.Y.C., 1952-53; v.p., treas., dir. Nat. Union Electric Corp., 1953-66, exec. v.p., dir., 1966-74, chmn. bd., pres., 1974-77, chmn., 1977—; dir. Lone Star Industries, Inc., St. Joe Minerals Corp., A.B. Electrolux, Stockholm. Bd. dirs. Greenwich (Conn.) Boys' Club Assn.; trustee Greenwich Hosp. Assn.; trustee Woods Hole Oceanographic Inst. Served with F.A., AUS, 1942-45. Decorated Air medal, Bronze Star. Roman Catholic. Clubs: Indian Harbor Yacht (Greenwich); N.Y. Yacht (N.Y.C.). Home: Field Point Park Greenwich CT 06830 Office: 66 Field Point Rd Greenwich CT 06830

MC KEE, KINNAIRD ROWE, navy officer; b. Louisville, Ky., Aug. 14, 1929; s. James H. and Kathleen (Sutton) McK.; B.S., U.S. Naval Acad., 1951; grad. Nuclear Power Tng., 1958; m. Betty Ann Harris, June 23, 1953; children—James Henry III, Anne Arnold. Commd. ensign U.S. Navy, 1951, advanced through grades to vice adm., 1978; served in Pacific fleet destroyer Marshall, Korean War; served in div. naval reactors AEC, 1964-66; comdg. officer nuclear attack submarine DACE, 1966-69; asst. to dir. program planning Office Chief of Naval Ops., Washington, 1969-70, exec. dir. Chief Naval Ops. Exec. Panel, 1970-73; comdr. U.S. and NATO submarine forces, 1973-75; supt. U.S. Naval Acad., Annapolis, 1975-78; comdr. U.S. Third Fleet, 1978-79; dir. ASW programs Chief of Naval Ops., Washington, 1979—. Mem. Internat. Inst. Strategic Studies, U.S. Naval Inst., Newcomen Soc. N.Am. Home: Quarters H Navy Yard Washington DC 20374

MC KEE, PATRICK ALLEN, physician; b. Tulsa, Apr. 30, 1937; s. Charles and Estelle Marie (Larrieu) Mc K.; student U. Tulsa, 1958, 62; M.D., U. Okla., 1962. Intern, Duke Hosp., Durham, N.C., U. Okla. Med. Center, Oklahoma City, 1967-68; asso. medicine dept. medicine Duke U. Med. Center, 1969-70, asst. prof., clin. investigator, 1970-71, asst. prof. medicine, 1971-72, asst. prof. biochemistry, 1971—, asso. prof. medicine, 1972-75, prof. medicine, 1975—, dir. outpatient clinic, 1975—, chief div. gen. medicine, 1976—; cons. thrombosis research Nat. Heart and Lung Inst., 1970-71; mem. hematology study sect. NIH, 1973-77; NIH grantee U. Okla. Med. Center, 1968-69, Duke U. Med. Center, 1972; diplomate Am. Bd. Internal Medicine. Fellow Am. Heart Assn.; mem. So., Am. socs. clin. investigation, Internat. Soc. Cardiology, Am. Fedn. Clin. Research, Internat. Soc. Thrombosis and Haemostasis, Am. Soc. Hematology, Am. Soc. Biol. Chemists, Alpha Omega Alpha, Phi Eta Sigma, Sword & Key (U. Tulsa), Sigma Xi. Roman Catholic. Contbr. numerous articles to profl. jours. Office: Box 3705 Duke Hosp Durham NC 27710*

MC KEE, RICHARD DONALD, II, opera and concert singer; b. Hagerstown, Md., Dec. 28, 1941; s. Charles and Frances (Burton) McK.; B.A., Yale U., 1964; Mus.M., U. Ill., 1969; m. Francine Fenn, Aug. 11, 1962; children—Carolyn Fenn, Janet Mason. Profl. debut as Leporello in Don Giovanni, Goldovsky Opera, 1971; European debut Wexford Festival, Ireland, 1973; N.Y.C. Opera debut, 1974; appeared with various U.S. opera cos. including N.Y.C. Opera; fellow Saybrook Coll., Yale U. Mem. Nat. Assn. Tchrs. of Singing, Am. Guild Mus. Artists (dir.). Episcopalian. Home: 182 Daniel Rd Hamden CT 06517 Office: care Tornay Mgmt Inc 1995 Broadway New York NY 10023

MCKEE, ROBERT SMITH, pipeline co. exec.; b. Martins Ferry, Ohio, Dec. 31, 1921; s. David S. and Ada M. (Smith) McK.; B.S. in Commerce, U. Va., 1948; LL.B., U. Houston, 1959; m. Margaret McGinley, Oct. 20, 1948; children—David, Patrick, Robert, Cathy, Becky, Phelps. Accountant, H.S. Hutzell, C.P.A., Wheeling, W.Va., 1948-50; treas. Compania Indsl. Comercial del Sur S.A., Montevideo, Uruguay, 1950-53; v.p., treas. Transcon Cos., Inc., Houston, 1953—. Mem. Am. Gas Assn. (chmn. tax com. 1973), Ind. Natural Gas Assn. Am. (treas. 1972-77), Nat. Tax Assn., Mid-Continent Oil and Gas Assn., Am. Bar Assn., State Bar Tex. Clubs: University, Houston (Houston). Home: 5214 Darnell Houston TX 77096 Office: PO Box 1396 Houston TX 77001

MCKEE, SETH JEFFERSON, ret. air force officer; b. McGehee, Ark., Nov. 6, 1916; s. William F. and Jeffie O. (Warrington) McK.; student Southeastern Mo. State Tchrs. Coll., 1934-37; B.S., U. Okla., 1947; grad. Air Command and Staff Sch., 1948; m. Sarah H. Parshall, June 7, 1941; children—Seth Jefferson, William B., Thomas J. Commd. 2d lt. USAAF, 1939, advanced through grades to gen. USAF, 1969; various operations and command positions, 1939-44; dep. comdr. 370th Fighter Group, Eng., 1944, comdr., France, Belgium, Germany, 1944-46; comdr. Air Force Radar Sch., Boca Raton, Fla., 1946; operations and tng. div. officer, later dir. plans Hdqrs. 12th Air Force, 1947-48, dir. Air Force Reserves, 1948-50; chief tech. adviser Italian Air Force, U.S. Mil. Assistance Adv. Group, Rome, Italy, 1950-51; chief tng. br., operations and tng. div. Hdqrs. USAF, Europe, 1951; comdr. 36th Fighter-Bomber Group, Europe, 1951-53; staff planning officer, policy div. Hdqrs. USAF, 1953-54; asst. sec. Air Force Council, Office Vice Chief Staff, 1954-56; comdr. 2d Bomb Wing, Hunter AFB, Ga., 1956-58; comdr. 823d Air Div., Homestead AFB, Fla., 1958-59; dep. dir. plans Hdqrs. SAC, Offutt AFB, Nebr., 1959-62, dir. plans, 1962-64; comdr. 821st Strat Aerospace div. SAC, Ellsworth AFB, S.D., 1964-65; dir. plans Office Dep. Chief Staff, Plans and Operations, USAF, Washington, 1965, asst. dept. chief staff Plans and Operations, 1965-66; comdr. U.S. Forces, Japan, also 5th Air Force, 1966-68; asst. vice chief staff U.S. Air Force, 1968-69; comdr.-in-chief N.Am. Air Def., Continental Air Def. commands, Ent AFB, Colo., 1969-73, ret., 1973; now bus. cons.; dir. numerous corps. Decorated D.S.M. with cluster, Legion of Merit with cluster, Silver Star, D.F.C., Air medal with 10 clusters, Outstanding Unit award, Presdl. Unit citation (U.S.); Croix de Guerre with palm (France and Belgium); Order Leopold with palm; Order Royal Crown (Thailand); Order Sacred Treasure (Japan); Nat. Security Merit (South Korea). Address: Litchfield Park AZ 85340

MCKEE, WILLIAM F., bus. exec., former air force officer; b. Va., Oct. 17, 1906; B.S., U.S. Mil. Acad., 1929; grad. Coast Arty. Sch., 1936; m. Gertrude S. McKee; children—Christopher Fulton, William St. John. Commd. 2d lt. U.S. Army, advanced through grades to gen., 1961; apptd. asst. vice chief of staff USAF, 1947; vice comdr. air material command Wright Patterson AFB, Ohio, 1953, comdr. Air Force Logistics Command, 1961-62, vice chief of staff USAF, 1962-64; asst. adminstr. for mgmt. devel. NASA, 1964-65; adminstr. FAA, 1965-68; pres. Schriever-McKee Assos., Arlington, Va., 1968-70, Shriever & Mckee, Inc., Washington, 1971—. Decorated D.S.M. with 2 oak leaf clusters. Home: 2410 S Lynn St Arlington VA 22202 Office: 1899 L St NW Suite 405 Washington DC 20036. *Advice from my father, a great country doctor, who died at 93: "Son, when you are sure in your heart and in your head that you are right, give no quarter to anyone regardless of position. If you are not sure, keep your big mouth shut."*

MCKEEFERY, WILLIAM J., educator; b. Phila., Dec. 29, 1918; s. William J. and Anna (Reichelt) McK.; B.S., U. Pa., 1941; M.Div., Princeton, 1945; Ph.D., Columbia, 1949; m. Ruth Franklin, June 6, 1948; children—Virginia Lou, Carol Ann, William James, III. Instr. engring. Princeton, 1943-45; prof. philosophy Alma (Mich.) Coll., 1948-50, dean, 1950-58; v.p. Washburn U., Topeka, 1958-61; dean acad. affairs So. Ill. U., Carbondale, 1961-69; exec. v.p. Va. Poly. Inst., Blacksburg, 1969-73; pres. William Paterson Coll. of N.J., Wayne, 1973-76; vis. prof. higher edn. Rutgers U., New Brunswick, N.J., 1976-77; ret., 1977; dir. Nat. Study Interinstnl. Cooperation, Am. Assn. State Colls. and Univs., Washington, 1977—; coordinator liberal arts study North Central Assn. Colls., 1951-58. Moderator, Presbytery of Saginaw, Presbyn. Ch. U.S.A., 1955-56. Served as chaplain USNR, 1945-46. Mem. Mich. Coll. Assn. (pres. 1955-57), Kappa Delta Pi, Tau Beta Pi. Rotarian. Author: Parameters of Learning-Perspectives in Higher Education Today, 1970. Contbr. articles to profl. publs. Home: 252A Doremus Dr Cranbury NJ 08512

MCKEEL, SAM STEWART, newspaper exec.; b. Wilson, N.C., Aug. 28, 1926; s. Henry Connor and Tryphenia (Mann) McK.; A.B., U. N.C., 1950; M.S., Columbia, 1952; m. Margarett Elizabeth Fields, June 14, 1952; children—Douglas, Karen, Stuart. Editor Northampton (N.C.) News, 1950-51; reporter Greensboro (N.C.) Daily News, 1952-54; reporter, personnel mgr. Charlotte (N.C.) Obs. and News, 1954-63; gen. mgr. Akron (Ohio) Beacon-Jour., 1964-71; pres. Philadelphia Inquirer and Daily News, dir., 1972—. Pres., Akron Art Inst., 1968-71; trustee, chmn. Phila. Coll. Art; trustee Friends Hosp., Pop Warner Little Scholars; elder Bryn Mawr Presbyterian Ch. Served with USNR, 1943-46. Mem. Phila. C. of C. (dir., exec. com.). Home: 1321 Pine Rd Rosemont PA 19010 Office: 400 N Broad St Philadelphia PA 19101

MC KEEN, CHESTER M., JR., helicopter co. exec.; b. Shelby, Ohio, Mar. 18, 1923; s. Chester Mancil and Nettie Augusta (Fox) McK.; B.S. in Mil. Sci., U. Md., 1962; M.B.A., Babson Coll., Wellesley, Mass., 1962; m. Alma Virginia Pierce, Mar. 1946; children—David Richard, Karin, Thomas Kevin. Enlisted in U.S. Army, 1942, commd. 2d lt., 1943, advanced through grades to maj. gen., 1973; service in Pacific Islands, Ger., Vietnam; dir. procurement Army Material Command, also comdr. Tank/Automotive Command, 1972-77; ret., 1977; dir. logistics Bell Helicopter Internat., 1977-79, v.p.-procurement Bell Helicopter Textron, Ft. Worth, 1979—. Decorated D.S.M., Legion of Merit (2), Commendation medal (3). Mem. Am. Def. Preparedness Assn. (v.p. S.W. region), Assn. U.S. Army, Sigma Pi. Clubs: Masons, Ridglea Country (Ft. Worth). Home: 2310 Woodsong Trail Arlington TX 76016 Office: PO Box 482 Fort Worth TX 76101. *Three bits of advice stand out: my father's, who said, "you serve yourself best by serving others first; an early teacher's, who maintained that you never need to worry if you always do your best; and finally, William Shakespeare's, who advised in Hamlet, "To thine own self be true. Thou canst not then be false to any man".*

MC KEEVER, HAROLD JAMES, editor; b. Manhattan, Kans., Oct. 30, 1900; s. William A. and Edith (Shattuck) McK.; B.S. in Civil Engring., U. Kans., 1922; postgrad. (research fellow) U. Ill., 1923; m. Austa Cross, 1924 (div.); m. 2d, Harriet Hayner, 1947; children—Marilyn (Mrs. J.A. Oeming), Anne (Mrs. Humberto Javier). Bridge designer I.C.R.R., Chgo., 1923-26; editor Armco Steel Corp., 1926-29; writer, account exec. Dyer-Enzinger Advt., 1929-34; advt. mgr. Portland Cement Assn., Chgo., 1934-42; editor Roads and Streets mag., 1942-72, World Construction mag., 1948-64, Rural and

Urban Rds. mag., 1970-75; editorial dir. Reuben H. Donnelley Corp. (now Tech. Pub. Pub. Co.), Chgo., 1958-72, cons. editor, 1972—. Vice pres. Chgo. Federated Advt. Club, 1938. Recipient Distinguished Service award Nat. Asphalt Pavement Assn., 1970. Life mem. ASCE (sec. hwy. exec. com. 1952-55); mem. Am. Rd. Builders Assn. (spl. award county div. for outstanding journalism 1975), Am. Concrete Inst., Constrn. Writers Assn. (past pres., Silver Hard Hat award 1970, Boger award for constrn. journalism 1973), Internat. Slurry Seal Assn. (hon.). Founder: World Constrn. mag., 1948; Rural Rds. mag., 1952; Street Engring. mag., 1955. Contbr. articles to profl. jours. Home: 2055 Commerce #221 Ann Arbor MI 40813 Office: 1301 S Grove St Barrington IL 60010. *Fortunate is the man or woman who has found a means of livlihood that is right for his or her talents and capabilities. Even more fortunate when it kindles "fire in the belly", leading to satisfying accomplishment in life.*

MCKEEVER, PORTER, orgn. exec.; b. Lenox, S.D., Nov. 8, 1915; s. George L. and Maye M. (McIlvenna) McK.; student New Coll., Columbia, 1933-37; LL.D., Springfield Coll., 1973; m. Susan Clark Lobenstine, Aug. 10, 1946; children—James Edwin, William Kevin, Mary Karen. Washington newspaper and radio corr., 1937-42; dir. OWI, Reykiavik, Iceland, 1942-44; chief Am. Psychol. Warfare Operations, N. Burma, hdqrs. S.E. Asia Command, 1944-45; press relations officer Dept. State, 1945-46, press officer U.S. delegation UN, 1946-47, dir. information U.S. Mission to UN, 1947-52; exec. dir. Chgo. Council Fgn. Relations, 1952-53; dir. office public reports Ford Found., 1953-56; dir. information Com. for Econ. Devel., 1956-65; pres. UN Assn. of U.S., 1965-73; asso. John D. Rockefeller 3d, v.p. JDR III Fund. Mem. nat. adv. com. Hampshire Coll. Mem. Council Fgn. Relations, Asia Soc. (trustee, exec. com.), Japan Soc. (trustee, exec. com.). Clubs: Nat. Press, Cosmos (Washington); Century Assn. (N.Y.C.). Assisted former Sec. State James F. Byrnes in writing book, Speaking Frankly, 1946. Contbr. to mags. Home: 318 Cliff Ave Pelham NY 10803 Office: 30 Rockefeller Plaza Room 5600 New York NY 10020

MC KEITHAN, DANIEL FRANKLIN, JR., brewery exec.; b. Abbottsburg, N.C., Nov. 8, 1935; s. Daniel Franklin and Kathryn (Ballentine) McK.; B.S., U. Okla., 1959; m. Gillian A. Uihlein, Dec. 28, 1957 (div.); children—Deborah, Catherine, Genevie. Geologist, Tamarack Petroleum Co., Inc., Henderson, Ky., 1959-61; mgr. Caspian Oil Co., Evansville, Ind., 1961-66; geologist, asst. mgr. Tamarack Petroleum Co., Inc., Evansville, 1966-71, v.p., Milw., 1971-73, pres., 1973-76, also dir.; chmn. bd. Jos. Schlitz Brewing Co., Milw., 1976—, chief exec. officer, 1977—; dir. First Wis. Corp. Bd. dirs. Greater Milw. Com., Jr. Achievement Southeastern Wis.; trustee Milw. Boys' Club. Home: 7975 N Range Line Rd Milwaukee WI 53209 Office: 235 W Galena St Milwaukee WI 53201

MCKELL, CYRUS MILO, agrl. scientist, orgn. exec.; b. Payson, Utah, Mar. 19, 1926; s. Robert Dewey and Mary (Ellsworth) McK.; B.S. in Biology, U. Utah, 1949, M.S. in Botany, 1950; Ph.D., Oreg. State U., 1956; m. Betty Marie Johnson, June 16, 1947; children—Meredith Sue, Brian, John. Prin., Tabiona (Utah) High Sch., 1952-53; teaching asst. botany Oreg. State U., 1953-55, instr., 1955-56; range plant physiologist Agr. Research Service, Dept. Agr., Davis, Calif., 1956-61; vice chmn., later chmn. agronomy dept. U. Calif. at Riverside, 1961-69; prof., head range sci. dept. Utah State U., 1969-71, dir. environment and man program, 1971-75; dir. Inst. for Land Rehab., 1975—; cons. in field, 1965—. Pres. Internat. Relations Council Riverside, 1967; spl. rep. Commn. of Californias, 1967-69; chmn. Cache County Planning Commn., 1974—; mem. adv. council Wasatch Nat. Forest; mem. Utah Energy Conservation and Devel. Council. Served to 1st lt. USAAF, 1944-45, USAF, 1951-52. Rockefeller fellow, 1964; Fulbright research fellow, 1967-68. Mem. Am. Soc. Range Mgmt. (pres. Cal. 1963), Agronomy Soc., Ecol. Soc. Am., Sigma Xi, Phi Sigma. Republican. Mem. Ch. of Jesus Christ of Latter-day Saints. Contbr. articles to profl. jours. Home: 1336 East 1700 North Logan UT 84321

MCKELVEY, JAMES MORGAN, univ. dean; b. St. Louis, Aug. 22, 1925; s. James Grey and Muriel (Morgan) McK.; B.S., U. Mo.-Rolla, 1945; M.S., Washington U., St. Louis, 1947, Ph.D., 1950; m. Edith Rothbauer, Dec. 28, 1957; children—James, Robert. Research engr. E.I. DuPont de Nemours & Co., Inc., 1950-54; asst. prof. chem. engring. Johns Hopkins, 1954-57; mem. faculty Washington U., St. Louis, 1957—, dean Sch. Engring. and Applied Sci., 1964—. Recipient Disting. Educator award Soc. Plastics Engrs., 1979. Home: 9861 Copper Hill Rd St Louis MO 63124

MCKELVEY, JEAN TREPP, educator; b. St. Louis, Feb. 9, 1908; d. Samuel and Blanche (Goodman) Trepp; A.B., Wellesley Coll., 1929; M.A., Radcliffe Coll., 1931 Ph.D., 1933; m. Blake McKelvey, June 29, 1934. Faculty Sarah Lawrence Coll., 1932-45; faculty N.Y. State Sch. Indsl. and Labor Relations, Cornell U., Ithaca, N.Y., 1946—, asst. prof., asso. prof., prof. indsl. relations, 1946—, vis. prof. Law Sch., 1977-78; pub. panel mem., hearing officer and arbitrator Nat. War Labor Bd., 1944-45; mem. N.Y. State Bd. Inquiry into Rochester Transit Dispute, 1952; pub. mem. adv. com. to sec. labor, 1953; mem. N.Y. State Bd. Mediation, 1956- 66; mem. pub. rev. bd. U.A.W., 1960—; presdl. Emergency Bd., Ry. Shopcrafts Dispute, 1964, Ry. Signalmen Dispute, 1971; mem. Fed. Service Impasses Panel, 1970—. Mem. Nat. Acad. Arbitrators (bd. govs., pres. 1970), Am. Fedn. Tchrs. (pub. rev. bd. 1969-73), Am. Arbitration Assn. (nat. panel), Indsl. Relations Research Assn., Phi Beta Kappa. Author: The Uses of Field Work in Teaching Economics, 1939; AFL Attitudes Toward Production, 1952; Dock Labor Disputes in Great Britain, 1953; Fact Finding in Public Employment Disputes, 1969; Sex and the Single Arbitrator, 1971. Editor several vols. on arbitration. Home: 53 Aberthaw Rd Rochester NY 14610 Office: Cornell U Ithaca NY 14853

MC KELVEY, JOHN CLIFFORD, research inst. exec.; b. Decatur, Ill., Jan. 25, 1934; s. Clifford Venice and Pauline Lytton (Runkel) McK.; B.A., Stanford U., 1956, M.B.A., 1958; children—Sean, Kerry, Tara. Research analyst Stanford Research Inst., Palo Alto, Calif., 1959-60, indsl. economist, 1960-64; with Midwest Research Inst., Kansas City, Mo., 1964—, v.p. econs. and mgmt. sci., 1970-73, exec. v.p., 1973-75, pres., chief exec. officer, 1975—; dir. Yellow Freight System, Inc.; mem. adv. com. Kerr Found., Oklahoma City, 1974; mem. external adv. com. Engring. Expt. Sta., Ga. Inst. Tech., 1976—. Mem. exec. bd. Heart of Am. council Boy Scouts Am., 1976—; mem. Civic Council of Greater Kansas City; bd. regents Rockhurst Coll., Kansas City, Mo., 1973—; bd. dirs. NCCJ, 1978, Oxford Park Acad., Carnegie-Mellon Inst., 1978—; trustee Avila Coll., 1974, Livestock Merchandising Inst., 1975; trustee, mem. exec. com. The Menninger Found., 1975; pres. Council on Edn., 1979. Mem. Nat. Assn. Bus. Economists, Travel Research Assn. Clubs: Carriage; Mission Hills. Home: 4925 Wornall Rd Kansas City MO 64112 Office: 425 Volker Blvd Kansas City MO 64110

MCKELVEY, JOHN JAY, JR., found. exec.; b. Albany, N.Y., July 16, 1917; s. John Jay and Louise E. (Brunning) McK.; A.B., Oberlin Coll., 1939; M.S., Va. Poly. Inst., 1941; Ph.D., Cornell U., 1945; m. Josephine G. Faulkner, June 28, 1941; children—John Jay III, Richard Drummond, Edward Faulkner, Laurence Brunning. Investigator, N.Y. State Agrl. Expt. Sta., 1942-45; with Rockefeller Found., 1945—, dep. dir. agrl. sci., 1966-68, asso. dir. agrl. scis., 1968—; cons. in field, 1959—. Mem. survey team natural resources No. Region Nigeria, FAO-ICA, 1960; cons. UN spl. fund project agrl. research, Thailand, 1964: study com. manpower needs and ednl. capabilities in Africa, Edn. and World Affairs, 1964-65; rev. commn. higher edn. Botswana, Lesotho and Swaziland, Overseas Devel. Ministry U.K., 1966; overseas liaison com. study team higher edn., Sierra Leone, 1968; mem. agrl. edn. mission to U.S. Pacific, Overseas Devel. Ministry of U.K., 1970; mem. Africa sci. bd. Nat. Acad. Scis., 1961-68, vice chmn., 1964-68, mem. sci. orgn. devel. bd., 1966-68, mem. bd. sci. and tech. internat. devel., also chmn. Africa sci. panel, 1968—, chmn. adv. panel on arid lands of sub-Saharan Africa, 1974; chmn. com. African agrl. research capabilities Nat. Acad. Scis./Agrl. Bd., 1971-74; mem. vis. com. for biology and related research facilities Harvard Coll., 1975—; mem. area adv. com. for Africa, Council for Internat. Exchange of Scholars, 1976—; mem. Chappaqua Internat. Exchange, 1976—; chmn. USAID/IBAR Task Force, 1978-79. Trustee Internat. Inst. Tropical Agr., Ibadan, Nigeria, 1971—; bd. govs. Inst. for Agrl. Research, Ahmadu Bello U., Zaria, Nigeria, 1971-74. Mem. AAAS, Entomol. Soc. Am., Am. Phytopathol. Soc., Assn. for Advancement Agrl. Sci. in Africa. Author: Man Against Tse-tse, 1973. Editor: (with R.L. Metcalf) The Future for Insecticides, 1976; (with H.H. Shorey) Chemical Control of Insect Behavior, 1977; (with Louis H. Miller and John A. Pino) Immunity to Blood Parasites of Animals and Man, 1977. Contbr. articles to profl. jours., chpt. in book. Home: 12 Barnes Terr Chappaqua NY 10514 Office: 1133 Ave of Americas New York NY 10036

MC KELVEY, VINCENT ELLIS, geologist; b. Huntingdon, Pa., Apr. 6, 1916; s. Ellis Elmer and Eva Rupert (Faus) McK.; B.A. with honors, Syracuse U., 1937, D.Sc., 1975; M.A., U. Wis., 1939, Ph.D., 1947; D.Sc., S.D. Sch. Mines and Tech., 1976; m. Genevieve Patricia Bowman, June 5, 1937; 1 son, Gregory Ellis. Jr. geologist Soil Conservation Service, part time 1938-40; asst. geologist Wis. Geol. and Natural History Survey, part time 1939-40; geologist U.S. Geol. Survey, 1941—, chief radioactive minerals investigations, Washington, 1950-53, asst. chief geologist for econ. and fgn. geology, 1960-65, sr. research geologist, 1969-71, 78—, chief geologist, 1971, dir., 1971-78. McKinstry Meml. lectr., 1971; J. Seward Johnson Meml. lectr., 1976; Donnel Foster Hewett Meml. lectr., 1976; U.S. adv. OECD energy com., 1965-67; U.S. rep. seabed com. UN, 1968-73; sr. sci. adv. U.S. del. UN Conf. Law of Sea, 1978—. Bd. dirs. Resources for the Future, 1978—. Recipient Distinguished Service award Interior Dept., 1963; award for sustained excellence Nat. Civil Service League, 1972; Rockefeller Pub. Service award, 1973; Alexander Winchell Distinguished Alumnus award Syracuse U., 1976; Distinguished Service award N.W. Mining Assn., 1977; Distinguished Service award Rocky Mountain Assn. Geologists, 1977; Mt. McKelvey, Antarctica, named in his honor, 1977. Fellow AAAS, Geol. Soc. Am. (mem. council 1969-72), Am. Geophys. Union; mem. Am. Geol. Inst. (bd. dirs. 1968-70), Soc. Econ. Geologists (council 1967-70), Econ. Geol. Pub. Co. (dir.), Geochem. Soc., Am. Inst. Mining Engrs. (Henry Krumb lectr. 1968), Am. Assn. Petroleum Geologists (Spl. award for meritorious service 1977, Human Need medal 1978), Soc. Exploration Geophysicists (hon.), Marine Tech. Soc., Sigma Xi. Club: Cosmos (Washington). Contbr. articles to profl. jours. Home: 6601 Broxburn Dr Bethesda MD 20034 Office: US Geol Survey National Center Reston VA 22092

MCKELVY, CHARLES LOCKHART, JR., banker; b. Toledo, Aug. 1, 1930; s. Charles Lockhart and Margaret (Gosline) M.; A.B., Williams Coll., 1956; m. Barbara B. McKelvy, July 27, 1974; children by previous marriage—Charles Lockhart, Taylor, Johnson. With Owens-Corning Fiberglas Corp., 1956-68, with personnel and rate structure areas, 1956-62, adminstrv. services mgr., 1962-64, asst. treas., 1964-65, treas., 1965-68; pres., chief exec. officer First Nat. Bank, Toledo, 1968—. Pres. bd. Maumee Valley Country Day Sch., Toledo, 1969; trustee U. Toledo, Jr. Achievement Northwestern Ohio, Toledo Community Chest, Toledo Hosp., Toledo Mus. Art. Served with USAF, 1951-54. Mem. Downtown Toledo Assos. (pres. 1969—). Home: 28503 E River Rd Perrysburg OH 43551 Office: First National Bank PO Box 1868 Toledo OH 43604

MCKENNA, ADRIENNE DELORES, hosp. adminstr.; b. Joliet, Ill., May 17, 1934; d. John J. and Anna Catherine (Hauser) Droney; B.S. in Nursing, St. Louis U., 1957; M.S. in Nursing, Washington U., St. Louis, 1967; children by previous marriage—Theresa, Daniel, Deborah, Patricia. Staff nurse St. Mary's Hosp., St. Louis, 1957, 60-64; nursery supr. Nix Meml. Hosp., St. Louis, 1957; staff nurse, asst. head nurse Barnes Hosp., St. Louis, 1958; exec. dir. sch. Kinder Prep. Gardens, St. Louis, 1964-65; asst. dir. Sch. Nursing, St. Johns Mercy Hosp., 1965-66; asst. dir. Sch. Nursing, St. Louis State Sch. and Hosp., 1966-68, dir. nursing edn., asst. dir. nursing, 1969-71; adminstr. clinic Springfield (Mo.) Regional Diagnostic Clinic, 1972; supt. Marshall (Mo.) State Sch. and Hosp., 1972—; cons. in field. Chmn. bd. Mo. Spl. Olympics, 1972-76; chmn. Work Activity Center Bd., 1974-77; bd. dirs. Saline County Sheltered Workshop; mem. St. Peter's Catholic Sch. Bd., 1973-75. Mem. Marshall C. of C., Nat. Assn. Supts. of Public Residential Facilities for Mentally Retarded (dir. 1978—), Am. Assn. Mental Deficiency. Home: Box 190 Marshall MO 65340 Office: Marshall State Sch and Hosp E Slater and Lincoln Box 190 Marshall MO 65340

MC KENNA, ALEX GEORGE, metals co. exec.; b. Crafton, Pa., Dec. 9, 1914; s. Charles H. and Jennie (Elliott) McK.; grad. Carnegie Inst. Tech., 1938; m. Wilma Fitzmaurice, June 1949; children—David, Linda, Mary Zan, Kim, Beth. Partner, McKenna Metals Co., Latrobe, Pa., 1940-43; v.p., dir. Kennametal, Inc., Latrobe, 1943-51, dir., exec. v.p., 1951-64, pres., dir., 1964—; pres., dir. Kennametal Inc., 1964-78, chmn. bd., chief exec. officer, 1978-79, chmn. bd., 1979—; pres., dir. Kennametal Internat., S.A., Latrobe, Pa., Kennametal Ltd., Toronto, Ont., Can., CA.ME.S., S.P.A., Milan, Italy, Kennametal Co. of Ohio; dir. Kennametal Holdings Ltd., Kennametal Ltd., Eng., Kennametal Can. Ltd., Kennametal Exports, Inc., Kenroc Western Ltd. Kennametal Australia Pty., Ltd., Kenroc Tools Ltd., Toronto, Kennamex, S.A., de C.V. Mexico, A.C. Wickman Ltd., Craig Bit Co. Ltd. Bd. dirs. Ltrobe Hosp. Assn. Mem. ASME, Am. Soc. Tool Engrs. Clubs: Rolling Rock (Ligonier); University (Pitts.); Latrobe Country. Home: Summit Dr Ligonier PA 15658 Office: 1 Lloyd Ave Latrobe PA 15650

MCKENNA, DAVID LOREN, univ. pres., clergyman; b. Detroit, May 5, 1929; s. William Loren and Ilmi E. (Matson) McK.; A.A., Spring Arbor Jr. Coll., 1949; B.A. magna cum laude in History, Western Mich. U., 1951; B.D., Asbury Theol. Sem., 1953; M.A., U. Mich., 1955, Ph.D. (Clifford Woody scholar), 1958; LL.D., Houghton Coll., 1974, Spring Arbor Coll., 1976; m. Janet Voorheis, June 9, 1950; children—David Douglas, Debra Lynn, Suzanne Marie, Robert Bruce. Ordained to ministry Free Methodist Ch. N.Am., 1950; dean of men Spring Arbor Jr. Coll., 1953-55, instr. psychology, 1955-60, acad. dean, 1955-57, v.p., 1958-60, pres., 1961-68; lectr. higher edn. U. Mich., 1958-60; asst. prof., coordinator Center for the Study of Higher Edn., Ohio State U., Columbus, 1960-61; pres. Seattle Pacific U., 1968—. Del. World Meth. Council, London, 1966; chmn. Mich. Commn. Coll. Accrediting, 1966-68; bd. dirs. Council Advancement Small Colls., 1964-67; pres. Assn. Free Meth. Colls., 1968-70; chmn. Christian Coll. Consortium, 1970-74; participant Internat. Congress World Evangelization, 1974. Pres. United Community Services, Jackson, Mich., 1968, Wash. Coll. Assn., 1970, 76. Bd. dirs. Jerry Lorentson Found., Crippled Children's Soc., 1965-67, Jr. Achievement, 1966-68, Land O'Lakes council Boy Scouts Am., 1965-68; mem. Wash. State Council Higher Edn., 1969-75, Pacific Sci. Center, 1969—, Seattle Found., 1975. Named One of Outstanding Young Men of Year, Jr. C. of C., 1965, Seattle Citizen of Yr., 1976. Mem. Assn. Am. Colls., Ind. Colls. Wash. (pres. 1969-71), Seattle C. of C., Wash. Friends of Higher Edn., Phi Kappa Phi. Rotarian (pres. Jackson 1966-67). Clubs: Washington Athletic, Rainier (Seattle); Diet. Author: The Jesus Model, 1976. Editor: The Urban Crisis, 1969. Contbr. articles to profl. jours. Office: Seattle Pacific U 3307 3d Ave West Seattle WA 98119*

MC KENNA, GERALD CLAIR, hotel co. exec.; b. Rochester, Pa., Aug. 6, 1925; s. Anthony H. and Carolyn (Tubetto) McK.; B.S., Duquesne U., 1949; m. Ruth Denner, June 9, 1951; children—Alexandria, Dennis, Terence, Mary, Timothy, James, Cathleen, Brigid. Auditor Harris, Kerr, Foster, 1949-50; field auditor Horwath & Horwath, 1950-55; auditor, controller Sheraton Hotels, 1956-64; resident mgr. Sheraton Royal Hawaiian, 1964-67; gen. mgr. Sheraton-Philippines Hotel, 1967-69, Huntington-Sheraton Hotel, Pasadena, Cal., 1969-71, Lucayan Beach Hotel and Casino, Freeport, Bahamas, 1972, St. Petersburg (Fla.) Hilton Hotel, 1972; regional mgr. Lucayan Hotel Corp., 1973—; gen. mgr. Beachcomer Oceanfront Inn, 1979. Lectr., U. Hawaii. Bd. dirs. So. Calif. Visitors Council, 1970. Served with USMC, 1943-46; PTO. Mem. Calif. (dir. 1970), Fla. (dir. 1978-79), St. Petersburg (v.p., pres. 1975) hotel-motel assns., St. Petersburg C. of C. (gov.), SKAL (pres. Fla. West Coast 1979-80). Address: 1926 N Atlantic Ave Daytona Beach FL 32018

MCKENNA, HUGH FRANKLIN, govt. ofcl.; b. Meriden, Conn., Jan. 10, 1907; s. Hugh and Augusta (Gode) McK.; A.B., Tufts U., 1929; m. Bettina O. Mears, July 14, 1934; children—Hugh Franklin, Alison Chase (Mrs. Anthony J. Dorn, Jr.). Advt. dept. Chase Brass & Copper Co., Waterbury, Conn., 1929-32; group ins. and pension rep. Prudential Ins. Co., Balt., 1932-35, Conn. Gen. Ins. Co., Phila., 1935-36; tech. adviser Social Security Bd., 1936-37; N.Y. regional rep. Social Security Adminstrn., 1938-43, dir. Bur. Dist. Office Operations, Balt., 1943-67, dir. Bur. Retirement and Survivors Ins., Balt., 1967-74, asso. commr. office program ops., 1974-75, mgmt. cons., 1975-; mem. 1st Brookings Conf. for Execs. in Fed. Service, 1958. Adv. council Baltimore County Sch. Bd., 1976-79, pres., 1978-79. Recipient Distinguished Service award HEW, 1956, Equal Opportunity Achievement award, 1974; Commr.'s citation Social Security Adminstrn. 1973; Presdl. Mgmt. Improvement award, 1975. Mem. Am. Soc. Pub. Adminstrn., Acad. Polit. Sci., Am. Acad. Polit. and Social Sci., Zeta Psi. Home: 10 Nightingale Way Lutherville MD 21093 Office: 6713 Collinsdale Rd Baltimore MD 21234

MCKENNA, J. FENTON, ednl. adminstr.; Ph.B., U. Santa Clara, 1928, J.D., 1933; postgrad. Stanford U., 1936-37, Northwestern U., 1938-39; LL.D., Loyola U., 1966; D.H.L., Alma Coll., 1967. Chmn. dept. speech and drama Santa Clara U., 1930-46; chmn. drama dept., dir. prodns. creative arts div. San Francisco State Coll., 1946-59, chmn. creative arts div., 1959-63, dean Sch. Creative Arts, 1963-76, dean emeritus, 1976—, asst. to pres., 1976-79; dir. Exptl. Theatre, Northwestern U., 3 summer sessions, mem. theatre faculty, guest dir. 12 summer sessions; dir. numerous coll. theatre prodns.; cons. Central Arts Program, Merced County (Calif.) Schs., Theatre sect. World Book Dictionary; regional chmn. Com. for Nat. Theatre Festival. Bd. dirs. San Francisco Boys' Chorus, Asian Arts Found., Cath. Theatre Conf., Community Music Sch., White Oaks Theatre, Carmel, Calif., Jr. Film Acad., Regional Theatre Council, San Francisco Ballet Guild; bd. regents Notre Dame Coll., Belmont, Calif.; bd. dirs., pres. Regional Arts Council; bd. govs. Bay Area Council. McKenna Theatre, San Francisco State U. named in his honor, 1972. Mem. Speech Assn. Am., ANTA (organizer, pres. Region I 1953-55, now chmn., dir. 1953—), Northwest Drama Conf., Am. Ednl. Theatre Assn., AAUP, Calif. State Employee's Assn., Assn. State Coll. Instrs., Western Speech Assn., Nat. Newman Club (hon.), Nat. Council Fine Arts Deans, Alpha Psi Omega (hon., adviser). Roman Catholic (adv. bd. Archdiocesan Council Cath. Men). Clubs: Bohemian, Family, Olympic, Faculty.

MCKENNA, JAMES ALOYSIUS, JR., lawyer, broadcasting exec.; b. Poughkeepsie, N.Y., July 1, 1918; s. James Aloysius and Eleanor Frances (Mahoney) McK.; student Manhattan Coll., 1934-35; B.S., Cath. U., 1938; LL.B., Georgetown U., 1942; m. Rebekah Ann Rial, Sept. 1, 1941; children—Michelle Marie McKenna Nassif, James Aloysius, Dennis M., Matthew M., Marc W., Aileen M. Admitted to D.C. bar, 1941, U.S. Supreme Ct., 1947; counsel Civil Aeronautics Bd., 1941-42; asst. to gen. counsel Office Alien Property Custodian, 1942-44; practicing lawyer, Washington, 1946—; now partner McKenna, Wilkinson & Kittner; pres., dir., owner radio stas. WCMB and WSFM, Harrisburg, Pa.; pres. and dir., owner radio stas. KQRS and KQRS-FM, Mpls., WWQM and WWQM-FM, Madison, Wis. Served as lt. (j.g.), USNR, active duty, 1944-46. Named Outstanding Alumni, Cath. U. Am., 1978; recipient DuBois medal Mt. St. Mary's Coll., 1966. Mem. FCC Bar Assn., Inst. Radio Engrs., Georgetown U. Alumni Assn., Delta Theta Phi. Clubs: Internat., Army and Navy (Washington); Broadcasters'. Home: 5219 Oakland Rd Chevy Chase MD 20015 Office: 1150 17th St NW Washington DC 20036

MCKENNA, JAMES EDWARD, naval officer; b. Bklyn., Mar. 15, 1926; s. James Francis and Frances (Courtney) McK.; B.A., Brown U., 1947; postgrad. Navy Postgrad. Sch., 1957-58, Naval War Coll., 1961-62; m. Claudia Fishburne Antrim, June 10, 1949; children—Claudia Anne, James Edward, Mary Courtney. Entered V-12/NROTC program, 1944; commd. ensign U.S. Navy, 1946, advanced through grades to rear adm., 1974; program officer Bur. Supplies and Accounts, Washington, 1958-61; storage dir. Naval Supply Center, Norfolk, 1962-65; supply officer U.S.S. Sylvania with 6th Fleet, 1965-67; asst. fleet supply officer U.S. Pacific Fleet, 1970-72; comdg. officer Naval Supply Depot, Subic Bay, Philippines, 1972-74, Navy Ships Parts Control Center, Mechanicsburg, Pa., 1974-77, Naval Supply Center, Norfolk, Va., 1977—. Chmn. fed. div. Tri-County United Way, Harrisburg; mem. exec. bd. Keystone Area council Boy Scouts Am. Decorated Legion of Merit with gold star, Meritorious Service medal. Mem. Harrisburg, Mechanicsburg chambers of commerce, Hampton Roads Maritime Assn. (hon.), Fed. Exec. Assn. Greater Tidewater of Va. (pres.). Club: Rotary. Home: 431 Dillingham Blvd Norfolk VA 23511 Office: Comdg Officer Naval Supply Center Norfolk VA 23512

MCKENNA, MALCOLM CARNEGIE, vertebrate paleontologist; b. Pomona, Calif., July 21, 1930; s. Donald Carnegie and Bernice Caroline (Waller) McK.; B.A., U. Calif., Berkeley, 1954, Ph.D., 1958; m. Priscilla Coffey, June 17, 1952; children—Douglas M., Katharine L., Andrew M., Bruce C. Instr. dept. paleontology U. Calif., Berkeley, 1958-59; asst. curator dept. vertebrate paleontology Am. Mus. Natural History, N.Y.C., 1960-64, asso. curator, 1964-65, Frick asso. curator, chmn. Frick Lab., 1965-68, Frick curator, 1968—; asst. prof. geology Columbia U., N.Y.C., 1960-64, asso. prof., 1964-72, prof. geol. scis., 1972—; research asso. U. Colo. Mus., Boulder, 1962—. Bd. dirs. Bergen Community (N.J.) Mus., 1964-67, pres., 1965-67; trustee Dwight-Englewood Sch., Englewood, N.J., 1968—; bd. dirs. Bergen

County council Girl Scouts U.S.A., 1968-70. Nat. Acad. Scis. exchange fellow, USSR, 1965. Fellow Geol. Soc. Am.; mem. Mongolia Soc. (dir. 1963-67), Grand Canyon Natural History Assn. (dir. 1972-76), AAAS, Soc. Systematic Zoology (council 1974—), Soc. Vertebrate Paleontology (v.p. 1975, pres. 1976), Am. Assn. Anatomists, Am. Geophys. Union, Am. Soc. Mammalogists, Am. Soc. Zoologists, Soc. for Study Evolution, Sigma Xi. Contbr. articles on fossil mammals and their evolution, the dating of Mesozoic and Tertiary sedimentary rocks, and paleogeography and plate tectonics to profl. jours. Home: 320 Walnut St Englewood NJ 07631 Office: Dept Vertebrate Paleontology Am Mus Natural History Central Park W at 79th St New York NY 10024

MCKENNA, QUENTIN CARNEGIE, tool co. exec.; b. Claremont, Calif., Sept. 2, 1926; s. George Alexander and Lillian Frances (Street) McK.; B.A. cum laude, Pomona Coll., 1948; postgrad. Stanford U. (Hewlett Packard fellow), 1948-50, U. So. Calif., 1951-53, UCLA, 1968-69; m. Barbara Louise Williamson, Sept. 12, 1948; children—Candace, Megan, Carl, Erin. Mem. tech. staff guided missile div. Hughes Aircraft Co., 1950-52; with Indsl. Electronics, 1952-55; with Hughes Aircraft Co., 1955-78, asst. group exec. missile systems group, 1977-78; pres. Kennametal, Inc., Latrobe, Pa., 1978-79, pres., chief exec. officer, 1979—. Mem. Los Angeles County Central Republican Com., 1953-58, mem. state central com., 1956-58, chmn. 46th Assembly Dist., 1956-58; bd. dirs. St. Paul's Cathedral, Los Angeles, 1975-78; bd. dirs. San Antonio Water Conservation Dist., 1974-75. Mem. Phi Beta Kappa, Sigma Xi. Episcopalian. Patentee in field. Office: 1 Lloyd Ave Latrobe PA 15650

MC KENNA, SIDNEY F., automobile mfg. co. exec.; b. Detroit, Nov. 27, 1922; s. Michael James and Elizabeth Josephine McK.; A.B., U. Mich., Ann Arbor, 1947; M.A., Wayne State U., 1948; m. Helen Mary Spiroff, Sept. 20, 1944; children—Lynn Marie McKenna Hoss, Dennis Michael, Patrick Conlon, Mary Elizabeth, Maureen Therese, Christopher John. With Ward Baking Co., Detroit, 1939-41; prodn. worker Cadillac Motor Co., div. Gen. Motors Corp., Detroit, 1941-42; mem. indsl. relations staff Ford Motor Co., Dearborn, Mich., 1942—, v.p., 1974—. Served with USN, 1942-46. Chmn. advisory bd. Providence Hosp., Detroit, 1972—; bd. dirs. Brighton (Mich.) Hosp., 1976—, Mercy Coll., Detroit, 1976—, United Found., Detroit, 1976—. Mem. Labor Policy Assn., Indsl. Relations Research Assn., Motor Vehicle Mfrs. Assn., Bus. Roundtable, Orgn. Resources Counselors, Commerce and Industry Council, Nat. Urban League. Roman Catholic. Clubs: Econ. (Detroit); Bloomfield Hills Country, Birmingham (Mich.) Athletic, K.C. Home: 3720 Lincoln Dr Birmingham MI 48010 Office: Ford Motor Co The American Rd Dearborn MI 48121

MC KENNA, TERENCE PATRICK, ins. co. exec.; b. Oldham, Lancashire, Eng., Sept. 3, 1928; s. Patrick A. and Mary F. McK.; came to U.S., 1929, naturalized, 1939; student St. Thomas Coll., Bloomfield, Conn., 1946-48; m. Patricia Buckley, Sept. 22, 1973. With John Hancock Mut. Life Ins. Co., Boston, 1951—, gen. agt., Cherry Hill, N.J., 1963-67, field v.p. gen. agy. dept., Atlanta, 1967-69, field v.p. dist. agy. dept., Boston, 1969-73, 2d v.p. mktg. ops. dept., 1973-74, v.p. dept., 1974-76, sr. v.p. dept., 1976—; v.p., dir. John Hancock Variable Life Ins. Co.; chmn. bd. Profesco; chmn. bd. mgrs. I.V.A.; dir. Maritime Life. Served with USMC, 1952-54. Mem. Am. Coll. Life Underwriters, Am. Soc. C.L.U.'s, Nat. Assn. Life Underwriters. Clubs: Univ. (Boston); Woods Hole Golf (Falmouth, Mass.). Office: John Hancock Pl PO Box 111 Boston MA 02117

MCKENNA, THOMAS JOSEPH, advt. exec.; b. Chgo., Oct. 20, 1929; s. Robert Emmet and Helen Elizabeth (Norton) McK.; B.A., Northwestern U., 1952; m. Geraldine M. Bednarz, May 23, 1953 (div. 1977); children—Terence Patrick, Kathleen Mary, Thomas Joseph. Dir. advt. and sales promotion Ency. Britannica, Chgo., 1956-61; v.p. creative, Marketways, Inc., Chgo., 1961-62; exec. v.p. Hefter-McKenna Advt., Chgo., 1962-64; v.p., account supr. Reach McClinton Advt., Chgo., 1964-69; sr. v.p. creative, pub. Odyssey Mag., Douglas Dunhill, Inc., Chgo., 1969—. Served with USAF, 1950-52. Mem. Chgo. 76 Com., 1976. Mem. Chgo. Assn. Direct Marketing, Direct Mail/Marketing Assn. Home: 4900 Marine Dr Chicago IL 60640 Office: 4225 Frontage Rd Oak Forest IL 60452

MC KENNA, WILLIAM EDWARD, restaurant exec.; b. Boston, Aug. 9, 1919; s. Alfred W. and Mary E.C. (Quigley) McK.; A.B., Holy Cross Coll., 1947; M.B.A., Harvard, 1949; children—William P., Kathleen M., Daniel J., Eileen F., Paul V., Mary Ellen; m. Mary N. Smith, Oct. 3, 1968. Staff accountant Touche, Niven, Bailey & Smart, N.Y.C., 1949-52; v.p., controller Monroe Calculating Machine Co., Orange, N.J., 1952-60, also dir.; v.p., treas., controller Litton Industries, Beverly Hills, Calif., 1960-63; sr. v.p. Litton Industries Bus. Equipment Group, Beverly Hills, 1964-67, also dir.; chmn., chief exec., dir. Hunt Foods & Industries, Inc., Fullerton, Calif., 1967-68; chmn., chief exec., dir. Norton Simon, Inc., Fullerton, 1968-69; bus. cons., 1969-70; chmn., dir. Technicolor, Inc., Hollywood, Calif., 1970-76, Sambo's Restaurants, Inc., Santa Barbara, Calif., 1979—; chmn. bd. Vencap, Inc.; dir. Midlantic Nat. Bank, LDB Corp., Tiger Internat., Inc., Rockwood Nat. Corp., Hydro-Mill Co., Precision Monolithics, Inc., N.J. Galvanizing & Tinning Works, Inc.; Mohawk Data Scis. Corp., Image Systems, Inc., Xcor Internat., Inc., Drexler Tech, Inc., Lehigh Valley Industries, Inc., Tech. Equities Corp., Manning Environ. Corp. Mem. pres.'s council, asso. trustee Coll. Holy Cross; trustee St. John's Hosp. Found. C.P.A., N.Y., Calif. Mem. Am. Inst. C.P.A.'s, Nat. Assn. Accts., Fin. Execs. Inst., Calif., N.Y., N.J. socs. C.P.A.'s, Delta Epsilon. Home and office: 912 Oxford Way Beverly Hills CA 90210 Office: 1888 Century Park E 20th Floor Los Angeles CA 90067

MCKENNA, WILLIAM J., textile products mfg. co. exec.; b. N.Y.C., Oct. 11, 1926; s. William T. and Florence (Valis) McK.; B.B.A., Iona Coll., 1949; M.S. (Univ. Store Service scholar), N.Y. U., 1950; m. Jean T. McNulty, Aug. 27, 1949; children—Kevin, Marybeth, Peter, Dawn. Vice pres. Hat Corp. Am., N.Y.C., v.p. mktg., 1961-63, exec. v.p., 1963-67; pres. Manhattan Shirt Co., N.Y.C., 1967-74; pres. Lee Co., Inc., Shawnee Mission, Kans., 1974—, also dir.; dir. VF Corp., Genovese Drug Stores, United Mo. Bank of Kansas City. Served with USN, 1944-46; PTO. Roman Catholic. Clubs: Carriage (Kansas City, Kans.); Milburn Country.

MC KENNEY, WALTER GIBBS, JR., lawyer, publisher; b. Jacobsville, Md., Apr. 22, 1913; s. Walter Gibbs and Mary (Starkey) McK.; Ph.B., Dickinson Coll., 1939; LL.B., J.D., U. Va., 1942; LL.D., Dickinson Sch. Law, 1964; m. Florence Roberta Rea, July 17, 1939. Admitted to Md. bar, 1942, since practiced in Balt.; partner firm McKenney, Thomsen & Burke; partner, gen. mgr., editor Taxes & Estates Pub. Co., Balt., 1946—; dir., chmn. trust com. Equitable Trust Co., Balt., 1968—; dir. Lutherville Supply & Equipment Co., Equitable Bancorp., Alban Tractor Co. Lectr. Southwestern Grad. Sch. Banking, 1966-77. Pres. Kelso Home for Girls; mem. bd. child care Balt. Conf. Meth. Ch., pres., 1961-64; pres. Balt. Estate Planning Council, 1963-64. Trustee Goucher Coll., Dickinson Coll., Lycoming Coll., Wesley Theol. Sem., Loyola Coll. at Balt., Franklin Sq. Hosp. Served to lt. USNR, 1942-45. Mem. Am., Md., Balt. bar assns. Republican. Methodist. Editor: Minimizing Taxes, 1946—; The Educator, 1965—; The Patron, 1968—. Home: 102 Estes Rd Baltimore MD 21212

MCKENNY, JERE WESLEY, geol. engring. firm exec.; b. Okmulgee, Okla., Feb. 14, 1929; s. Jere Claus and Juanita (Hunter) McK.; B.S. in Geol. Engring., U. Okla., 1951, M.S. in Geol. Engring., 1952; m. Anne Ross Stewart, May 4, 1957; children—Jere James, Robert Stewart. With Kerr-McGee Corp., Oklahoma City, 1953—, mgr. oil and gas exploration, 1968-69, v.p. oil and gas, 1969-74, v.p. exploration, 1974-77, vice chmn. bd., 1977—. Mem. alumni adv. council Sch. Geology and Geophysics U. Okla. Served with U.S. Army, 1953-55. Mem. Am. Assn. Petroleum Geologists, Am. Petroleum Inst., Houston Geol. Soc., Oklahoma City Geol. Soc., Sigma Xi, Sigma Gamma Epsilon. Episcopalian. Clubs: Oklahoma City Golf and Country, Whitehall. Home: 2932 Cornwall Pl Oklahoma City OK 73120 Office: 123 Robert S Kerr Oklahoma City OK 73125

MC KENZIE, ALLAN DOUGLAS, surgeon; b. Kelowna, B.C., Can., Mar. 19, 1917; s. George Simon and Jeanette R. (Auld) McK.; M.D., U. Alta., 1942; diploma in surgery McGill U., 1952; m. June Bowen Perry, Feb. 13, 1954; children—Michael, Paul. Intern, Montreal Gen. Hosp., 1942-43; resident McGill U. Hosps., then St. Vincent's Hosp., N.Y.C., 1946-52; with surgery dept. U. B.C., 1952-65, head dept., 1959-65, clin. prof. surgery, 1965—; practice medicine specializing in surgery, Vancouver, 1965—. Served with M.C., Royal Canadian Army, 1942-46. Decorated Mil. Cross. Fellow Royal Coll. Surgeons, A.C.S. (regent 1968-77); mem. James IV Surg. Assn., Western, Pacific Coast surg. assns., Assn. Surgeons Gt. Britain and Ireland (asso.), Internat. Surg. Group. Home: 2585 Point Grey Rd Vancouver BC V6K 1A1 Canada Office: 2525 Willow St Vancouver BC V5Z 3N8 Canada

MCKENZIE, GEORGE KENNETH, mgmt. cons.; b. Phillips, Maine, July 7, 1911; s. Charles Herbert and Mary (Bangs) McK.; LL.B., Suffolk Law Sch., 1932, D.Bus. Sci., 1961; m. Barbara Mitchell, Jan. 12, 1934; children—Jeffrey Allan, Jeremy Alec, Jamieson Angus. Salesman, asst. cashier C.H. McKenzie Co., Rumford, Maine, 1926-27; reporter Rumford Falls Times, 1927-28; with Flintkote Co., 1928-62, v.p., sec., 1945-58, exec. v.p., 1958-62, dir., 1956-62; v.p. mktg. and planning, dir. Nashua Corp., 1962-65; v.p. corp. planning U.S. Plywood Corp., N.Y.C., 1965-67, founder, mng. partner McKenzie & Co., 1967—; founder, pres., dir. McKenzie Mgmt. & Research Co., Inc., 1968—; sec. Patent & Licensing Corp., 1938-62; admitted to Maine bar, 1932; partner Fidelity Exchange Fund Inc.; dir. Magelian Fund, Fidelity Municipal Bond Fund, Fidelity Govt. Fund Ltd., Salem Fund, Congress St. Fund, Fidelity Trend Fund, Fidelity Ltd. Term Municipal Fund, Fidelity Capital Fund, Fidelity Fund, Inc., Puritan Fund, Inc. (Boston), Contra Fund, Inc., Fidelity Aggressive Income Fund, Fidelity Destiny Fund, Fidelity Bond-Debenture Fund, Fidelity High Yield Municipal Bond Fund, Fidelity Equity Income Fund; trustee Fidelity Daily Investment Trust, Fidelity Thrift Trust, Fidelity Asset Investment Trust, Fidelity Money Market Trust. Chmn., Town Meeting reps. Old Greenwich, Conn., 1948-49. Mem. Am. Bar Assn., Am. Soc. Corporate Sec.'s (past pres., chmn. securities com., dir.), Newcomen Soc., Assn. for Corporate Growth, SAR. Republican. Conglist. Clubs: Canadian, Metropolitan (N.Y.C.); Greenwich (Conn.) Country. Home and office: 114 E 72d St New York NY 10021

MC KENZIE, HAROLD CANTRELL, JR., utility co. exec.; b. Carrollton, Ga., Dec. 25, 1931; s. Harold Cantrell and Sue (Tanner) McK.; B.Indsl. Engring., Ga. Inst. Tech., 1953; LL.B., Emory U., 1955; m. Katherine Branch, Apr. 11, 1958; children—Ansley, Katherine, Harold Cantrell, III. Admitted to Ga. bar, 1955; law clk. to judge Fulton County (Ga.) Criminal Ct., Atlanta, 1955, to judge U.S. Dist. Ct., Atlanta, 1956; asso. firm Troutman, Sams, Schroder & Lockerman, Atlanta, 1957-61, partner, 1961-67; with Ga. Power Co., Atlanta, 1967—, sr. v.p., 1973-75, exec. v.p., 1975—, also dir.; dir. Columbus Foundries, Inc., So. Electric Generating Co. Bd. dirs. Fulton County unit Am. Cancer Soc., Keep America Beautiful, Inc., Ga. Motor Club; trustee Nat. Recreation and Park Assn.; mem. steering com. for devel. funds Georgia Agrirama, Tifton, Ga.; chmn. bd. trustees Bedford-Pine Child and Family Resource Center, Atlanta. Mem. State Bar Ga., Atlanta Bar Assn., Atlanta C. of C., Ga. Bus., Industry Assn. Episcopalian. Clubs: Rotary, Lawyers of Atlanta, Capital City (Atlanta); Piedmont Driving, Commerce. Home: 937 Buckingham Circle NW Atlanta GA 30327 Office: PO Box 4545 Atlanta GA 30302

MC KENZIE, HAROLD JACKSON, transp. and mgmt. cons.; b. Houston, Oct. 11, 1904; s. Phillip Alexander and Alice Julia (Hannon) McK.; B.S., Tex. A. and M. Coll., 1927; postgrad. Houston Engring. Coll., 1929-32, Advanced Mgmt. Course Harvard, 1950; LL.D., Shurtleff Coll., 1953; m. Jewel Ina Gatlin, Dec. 22, 1929; children—James Garrett, Marcella Ann. Engring. dept. S.P. Co., Tex., La., summer 1926, draftsman, constrn. insp., chief draftsman, asst. to chief engr., asst. chief engr., chief engr., 1927-45; exec. v.p. St. Louis Southwestern Ry. Co., 1951, pres. St. Louis Southwestern Ry. Co. Tex., 1951-69; former chmn. Southwestern Transp. Co., So. Pacific Transport Co., Houston; former pres. Bravo Oil Co., Houston, v.p. So. Pacific Co., Houston; transp. and mgmt. cons., Tyler, Tex., 1969—; dir. Citizens First Nat. Bank of Tyler; mem. adv. com. Houston Nat. Bank. Bd. regents Tex. Eastern U. Mem. Tex. Soc. Profl. Engrs. (past v.p.), Houston C. of C. (mem. ednl. com.), Tyler C. of C. (pres.), Am. Soc. Profl. Engrs., Am. Ry. Engring. Soc., Newcomen Soc., Tau Beta Phi. Republican. Baptist. Mason (Shriner). Clubs: Tyler, Willowbrook Country, Tyler Petroleum (Tyler); Engineers, Houston Country (Houston); City (Dallas). Contbr. articles to profl. jours. Home: 2800 Ridge Ln Tyler TX 75701 Office: 1517 W Front St Tyler TX 75701

MCKENZIE, JACK HARRIS, coll. dean; b. Springfield, Mo., Nov. 11, 1930; s. Fred F. and Thelma L. (Harris) McK.; student Southwest Mo. State U., 1948-50; B.Mus., U. Ill., 1954; M.A., Ariz. State U., 1956; m. Patricia L. Chrisman, Feb. 4, 1951; children—Janet, James, Judith, Jill, Julia, Jennifer. Tchr. dept. music Ariz. State U., Tempe, 1954-56; instr. Nat. Music Camp, Interlochen, Mich., summers 1954-66; instr. to prof. Sch. Music, U. Ill., Urbana, 1954-68, prof., 1968—, asso. dean Coll. Fine and Applied Arts, 1969-70, acting dean, 1971, dean, 1972—. Mem. Internat. Council Fine Arts Deans (chmn. 1976-77). Author: (with A. Payson) Music Educators Guide to Percussion, 1966, Percussion in the School Music Program, 1976. Composer: Introduction and Allegro, 1953, Rites, 1962, Pastorale, 1953, Paths I, 1967, Paths II, 1968, Nonet, 1954. Office: 110 Architecture Bldg Univ of Illinois Urbana IL 61801

MC KENZIE, JEREMY ALEC, food service co. exec.; b. Stamford, Conn., Sept. 27, 1941; s. George Kenneth and Barbara (Mitchell) McK.; B.S., N.Y. U., 1965; M.B.A. with distinction, Harvard U., 1967; m. Susan Hallaran, Mar. 30, 1963; children—Scott G., Kristin W., Jennifer K. Adminstrv. asst. to sales mgr. Owens Corning Fiberglas Corp., N.Y.C., 1962-65; dir. corp. planning Squibb Corp., N.Y.C., 1967-71; v.p. restaurant div. Dobbs Houses Inc., Memphis, 1971-75, exec. v.p. terminal and restaurant div., 1975-77; v.p. restaurant group W.R. Grace & Co., Costa Mesa, Calif., 1978—; dir. McKenzie Mgmt. and Research Co., N.Y.C. Served with USCGR, 1961-62. Conglist. Clubs: Met., Harvard, Can. (N.Y.C.). Home: 20912 Paseo Olma El Toro CA 92630 Office: PO Box 2350 Costa Mesa CA 92626

MCKENZIE, JOHN FITZGERALD, coll. pres.; b. Boston, Jan. 19, 1917; s. William and Kathryn (Blades) McK.; B.A., Harvard U., 1938; M.C.S., Boston U., 1940; m. Florence Boone Stevenson, Aug. 24, 1944; children—James Johnston, Thomas William. Dir. mens div. Fisher Jr. Coll., Boston, 1946-47; asso. prof. bus. adminstrn., chmn. dept. U. Mass., 1947-49; asst. to dean Grad. Sch., Boston U., 1949-52, acting dean, 1952-53, dean of men, 1953-59; program div. adminstr. Itek Corp., Boston, 1959-60, asst. to pres., dir. pub. and community relations, 1960-61; pres. Mass. Bay Community Coll., Wellesley Hills, 1961—; chmn. adv. bd., dir. Guaranty First Trust Co., Waltham, Mass. Mem. ednl. task force Boston Urban Coalition, 1967-69. Bd. dirs. YMCA; mem. adv. bd. Oblate Coll. and Sem.; mem. exec. com., ednl. adviser Nat. Interfraternity Conf. Served to 1st lt. AUS, 1942-46. Mem. Boston Execs. Assn., Nat. Assn. Student Personnel Adminstrs., Assn. Coll. and Univ. Housing Officers, AAUP, Am. Assn. Community and Jr. Colls. (commn. on legislation), Nat. Assn. Mgmt. Educators, Alpha Phi Omega, Sigma Phi Epsilon. Methodist. Contbr. articles profl. jours. Home: 34 Salisbury Dr Westwood MA 02090 Office: Mass Bay Community Coll 50 Oakland St Wellesley Hills MA 02181

MCKENZIE, JOHN LAWRENCE, educator; b. Brazil, Ind., Oct. 9, 1910; s. Harry James and Myra (Daly) McK.; Litt. B., Xavier U., Cin., 1932; M.A., St. Louis U., 1934; S.T.D., Weston (Mass.) Coll., 1942; Litt.D. (hon.), Bucknell U., 1969, Rosary Coll., 1972. Joined Soc. of Jesus, 1928, ordained priest Roman Cath. Ch., 1939; prof. O.T., West Baden (Ind.) Coll., 1942-60; prof. history Loyola U., Chgo., 1960-65; prof. O.T., U. Notre Dame, 1966-70; prof. theology DePaul U., 1970-78; vis. prof. O.T., U. Chgo., 1965-66. Mem. Cath. Bibl. Assn. (pres. 1963-64), Soc. Bibl. Lit. (pres. 1965-66), Am. Oriental Soc. Author: The Two-Edged Sword, 1956; Myths and Realities, 1963; The Power and the Wisdom, 1965; Dictionary of the Bible, 1965; Authority in the Church, 1966; The World of Judges, 1966; Second Isaiah, 1968; The Roman Catholic Church, 1969; Theology of the Old Testament, 1974. Address: 447 W 10th St Claremont CA 91711

MC KENZIE, LIONEL WILFRED, economist, educator; b. Montezuma, Ga., Jan. 26, 1919; s. Lionel Wilfred and Lida (Rushin) McK.; A.B., Duke, 1939; M.A., Princeton, 1946, Ph.D., 1956; B.Litt., Oxford (Eng.) U., 1949; postgrad. U. Chgo., 1950-51; m. Blanche Veron, Jan. 2, 1943; children—Lionel Wilfred, Gwendolyn Veron, David Rushin. Asst. economist WPB, 1942; instr. Mass. Inst. Tech., 1946; asst. prof., then asso. prof. Duke, 1948-57; prof. econs. U. Rochester, 1957-64, John Munro prof. econs., 1964-67, Wilson prof. econs., 1967—, chmn. dept., 1957-66. Mem. math. div. NRC, 1960-63, mem. behavioral scis. div., 1964-70; mem. math., social scis. bd. Center Advanced Study in Behavioral Scis., Palo Alto, Calif., 1964-70, chmn., 1969-70. Served to lt. (s.g.) USNR, 1943-45. Rhodes scholar Oriel Coll., Oxford U., 1939; Guggenheim fellow, 1973-74; fellow Center for Advanced Study in Behavioral Scis., 1973-74. Fellow Econometric Soc. (council 1973-78, pres. 1977), Am. Acad. Arts and Scis.; mem. Am. Econ. Assn., Royal Econ. Soc., Am. Math. Soc., Nat. Acad. Scis., Phi Beta Kappa (chpt. v.p. 1968-70, chpt. pres. 1972-73). Asso. editor Internat. Econ. Rev., 1964—, Jour. Econ. Theory, 1970-73, Jour. Internat. Econs., 1970—. Contbr. articles to profl. jours. Home: 225 Dorchester Rd Rochester NY 14610

MCKENZIE, LLOYD WILLIAM, JR., prefabricated bldgs. co. exec.; b. Delaware, Ohio, Aug. 4, 1937; s. Lloyd William and Lois (Brower) McK.; B.S., Purdue U., 1959; m. Anne Price, Aug. 31, 1958; children—Jennifer Anne, John Edward, James Douglas. Exec. v.p., constrn. coordinator Alexander Constrn. Co., Chgo., 1959-60; dist. sales mgr. Nat. Homes Corp., Lafayette, Ind., 1960-62, regional sales mgr., 1963-65, mgr. market devel., 1965-66, gen. sales mgr., Martinsville, Va. div., 1966, pres., 1967-70, exec. v.p. So. Modular Plants, 1971-72, exec. v.p. nat. accounts, Lafayette, 1972—, mem. corp. mgmt. com., mem. corp. mktg. com., 1970—. Chmn. indsl. contbns. United Fund, 1971; mem. P-man com. Red Mackey grants Purdue U., 1974-75. Named Ky. col.; Am. Airlines adm. of Flagship Fleet; col., aide-de-camp Gov.'s Staff Miss. Mem. Am. Mgmt. Assn., Men's Club (Purdue U.), Sigma Chi (chpt. dir.). Presbyn. (stewardship com.). Club: Golden Broncho (pres. 1974, dir.). Home: 50 Ash Ct Lafayette IN 47904 Office: PO Box 680 Lafayette IN 47902

MCKENZIE, ROBERT PALMER, naval officer; b. Marshall, Mich., June 2, 1924; s. Robert Palmer and Hortense (Hatch) McK.; B.S. E.E., U.S. Naval Acad., 1945; student U.S. Naval War Coll.; m. Annie Louise Stinchcomb, Oct. 10, 1953; children—Blair, Melinda. Commd. ensign U.S. Navy, 1945, advanced through grades to rear adm.; served in U.S.S. Kimberly, U.S.S. R.L. Wilson, in flight tng., with Fighter Squadron 74, aviation Advanced Tng. Command, Photo Squadron 61, Fleet Air Gunner Unit, mem. staff Car Div. 4; mem. Joint Strategic Target Planning Staff; comdg. officer Attack Squadron 46; mem. staff Chief Naval Ops., Washington; comdg. officer U.S.S. Cacapon; mem. staff 7th Fleet; comdg. officer Naval Air Sta., North Island; served with COMLIGHT Attack Wing, U.S. Pacific Fleet; chief of staff U.S. Forces Japan; instr. advanced flight tng. in jet, air to air weapon delivery. Decorated Legion of Merit (5), Bronze Star, Meritorious Service medal, Navy Commendation medal, Air Force Commendation medal, Air medal (3). Mem. U.S. Naval Acad. Assn., Naval Aviators Assn., Ret. Officer's Assn., Navy League, Navy Relief Assn., C. of C. Episcopalian. Club: Rotary. Home: PSC PO Box 2 APO San Francisco CA 93245 Office: Staff US Forces Japan APO San Francisco CA 93245*

MC KENZIE, WILLIAM H., banker; b. Blytheville, Ark., Aug. 5, 1918; s. William M. and Rose (Phillips) McK.; grad. Stonier Grad. Sch. Banking, Rutgers U., 1956; m. Louise Ogletree, Feb. 21, 1959 (dec. Aug. 1979); children—Pamela (Mrs. Ralph Bertella), Cynthia Anne (Mrs. Richard Scott), James Joseph, William Harold, Frank Phillips. With Union Bank & Trust Co., Montgomery, Ala., 1937-49; with Birmingham Trust Nat. Bank (Ala.), 1949—, v.p., cashier, 1960-63, v.p., sec., 1963-65, sr. v.p., sec., 1965-69, exec. v.p., sec., 1969-77; exec. dir. Ala. Automated Clearing House Assn., 1978—; exec. v.p., sec. So. Bancorp., 1969-77. Gen. co-chmn. United Appeal campaign, 1970-71; past pres., bd. dirs. Jefferson County Soc. Crippled Children and Adults; mem. exec. bd. Birmingham Area council Boy Scouts Am. Served with USAAF, 1943-46. Mem. Financial Execs. Inst., Am. Inst. Banking (past pres. Montgomery chpt.), U.S., Ala., Birmingham chambers commerce, Ala. Bankers Assn., Bank Adminstrn. Inst., Asso. Industries Ala. Home: Route 4 Box 1135 Pell City AL 35125 Office: Room 1820 John Hand Bldg 17 N 20th St Birmingham AL 35203

MC KEOUGH, RICHARD BLAIR, publishing co. exec.; b. Evanston, Ill., Dec. 23, 1927; s. John K. and Leone (O'Brien) McK.; B.A., Mich. State U., 1950; m. Barbara J. Widney, June 11, 1949; children—Richard Blair II, Mary, John (dec.), Susan. Auditor, Frazer & Torbert, Chgo., 1950-52; mem. staff comptroller's dept. Time, Inc., N.Y.C., 1952-54, asst. bus. mgr. internat. div., 1954-55, bus. mgr. internat. div., 1956-60, corporate asst. treas., 1961-68, treas., 1969-70, v.p. finance, treas., 1970-73, v.p. finance, chmn. finance Com., 1974—, also dir.; dir. Temple-Eastex, Inc., Inland Container Co., Am. TV & Communications; mem. adv. bd. Chem. Bank-Rockefeller Center.

Past pres. trustees King Sch., Stamford, Conn.; bd. govs. St. Joseph Hosp., Stamford, Conn. Served with AUS, 1946-47. Club: Woodway Country (bd. govs.) (Darien, Conn.). Home: 245 West Hill Rd New Canaan CT 06840 Office: Time Inc Time and Life Bldg Rockefeller Center New York NY 10020

MCKEOUGH, WILLIAM DARCY, gas co. exec.; b. Chatham, Ont., Can., Jan. 31, 1933; s. George Grant and Florence Sewell (Woodward) McK.; B.A., U. Western Ont., 1954; m. Margaret Joyce Walker, June 18, 1965; children—Walker Stewart, James Grant. Mem. Ont. Legislature, 1963-78, minister without portfolio, 1966, minister of mcpl. affairs, 1967-71, treas., minister of econs., chmn. Treasury Bd., 1971-72, parliamentary asst. to premier of Ont., 1973, 1st Ont. minister of energy, 1973-75, treas. and minister of econs. and intergovtl. affairs, 1975-78; pres., chief exec. officer Union Gas Ltd., Chatham, Ont., 1979—; dir. Algoma Central Ry., Can. Imperial Bank of Commerce, Consumers' Glass Co. Ltd., McKeough Sons Co. Ltd., Noranda Mines Ltd., Redpath Industries Ltd. Bd. govs. Ridley Coll., Stratford Shakespearean Festival; mem. Can. group Trilateral Commn. Anglican. Office: 50 Keil Dr N Chatham ON N7M 5M1 Canada

MC KEOWN, CLINTON BEGGS, rubber co. exec.; b. Springfield, Ill., Sept. 17, 1915; s. William Henry and Edistina (Beggs) McK.; B.S. in Chemistry, U. Ill., 1937; m. Betty Holland, Sept. 21, 1940; children—W.L., Lynne McKeown Phillippe. With B.F. Goodrich Co., Akron, Ohio, 1937—, gen. mgr. rubber products mfg., 1956-60, gen. mgr. aviation products div., 1960-69, pres. aerospace and def. products div., 1969-74, exec. v.p. engineered systems div., 1974-75, v.p. engring. and mfg. services div., 1975—. Bd. dirs. ARC. Mem. Am. Chem. Soc., Bus. Roundtable of No. Ohio. Club: Silver Lake Country (Stow, Ohio). Home: 3070 Kent Rd Stow OH 44224 Office: 500 S Main St Akron OH 44318

MCKEOWN, JAMES EDWARD, sociologist, educator; b. Detroit, Sept. 3, 1919; s. Francis Joseph and Grace Margaret (Ruddon) McK.; B.A., Wayne U., 1941, M.A., 1945; Ph.D., U. Chgo., 1949; m. Mary Elizabeth McNamara, Aug. 6, 1955. Instr. social sci. St. Xavier Coll., Chgo., 1945-48; asst. prof. sociology N.Mex. Highlands U., Las Vegas, 1948-52; asst. prof. sociology DePaul U., Chgo., 1952-55, asso. prof., 1955-57, prof. sociology, 1957-70, chmn. dept., 1962-70; prof. sociology U. Wis.: Parkside, Kenosha, Wis., 1970—; vis. prof. sociology Emory U., summer 1952, Escuela Nacional de Asistencia Publica, La Paz, Bolivia, 1958, Northwestern U., 1965, Concordia Tchrs. Coll., River Forest, Ill., 1965, 66, Universidad Catolica, Santiago, Chile, 1968; fellow Fund Advancement Edn., summer 1954; Smith-Mundt lectr., Bolivia, 1958; Fulbright Hays lectr., Chile, 1968. Social Sci. Research Council travel grantee, 1958. Mem. Am. Sociol. Soc., AAAS, Am. Acad. Polit. and Social Sci., AAUP, Pi Gamma Mu, Psi Chi, Phi Sigma Iota. Club: Quadrangle. Co-editor: The Changing Metropolis, 1964, 2d edit., 1971. Contbr. articles to profl. jours., also to Britannica Book of Year, 1968-72. Home: 1469 N Sheridan Rd Kenosha WI 53140

MCKEOWN, RAYMOND MERLL, physician, surgeon; b. Hibbing, Minn., May 22, 1902; s. Henry Joseph and Alberta May (Smith) McK.; B.A., U. Oreg., 1924; student Willamette U., summer 1924, U. Oreg. Med. Sch., 1924-26; M.D., U. Toronto (Ont., Can.), 1929; Licentiate Med. Council Can.; postgrad. Yale, 1929-36; m. Charlotte Elizabeth Van Cleve, Sept. 9, 1931; children—Michael John, Timothy Joseph. Davis and Geck research fellow surgery Yale, 1930-32; resident in surgery, gynecology, obstetrics Grace-New Haven Hosp., 1929-35, instr. obstetrics and gynecology, 1933-35; practice of medicine, Coos Bay, Oreg., from 1936. Past pres. Am. Med. Ednl. and Research Found., World Med. Assn., London, 1965. Mayor, City of Coos Bay. Mem. A.C.S., Am. Coll. Obstetrics and Gynecology, Am. Acad. Gen. Practice, AMA (trustee, sec.-treas.), Coos Bay C. of C. (pres.), Nat. Assn. Professions (pres.) Am. Profl. Practice Assn. (v.p.), Sigma Xi, Alpha Omega Alpha, Beta Theta Pi, Nu Sigma Nu. Mason (Shriner), Rotarian. Author articles on wound and fracture healing, med. ethics, socioecons. of medicine. Home and Office: 4399 Coast Hwy North Bend OR 97459*

MC KEOWN, TOM, poet; b. Evanston, Ill., Sept. 29, 1937; s. Thomas Shanks and Ruth Ann (Fordyce) McK.; A.B. in English, U. Mich., 1961, A.M. in English, 1962. Instr. Alpena Coll., 1962-64, Wis. State U. (now U. Wis.-Oshkosh), 1964-68; poet-in-residence Stephens Coll., 1968-74, U. Wis., Stevens Point, 1976—; reader Nat. Endowment for Arts in Mo., Kans., Mich.; active poet-in-the schs. program. Recipient Avery Hopwood award for poetry U. Mich., 1968; Yaddo Residence grantee; Wurlitzer Residence grantee; Ossabaw Island Project grantee. Mem. Psi Upsilon (pledge pres. 1957). Episcopalian. Author: The Luminous Revolver, 1974; Driving to New Mexico, 1974; The House of Water, 1974; Certain Minutes, 1978. Contbr. numerous poems to nat. and internat. lit. jours. and popular mags. Address: PO Box 82 North Beach Pentwater MI 49449. *Writing poetry is a continuous exploration. My work is beginning to approach the mythic and archetypal, the things that have been lost in the contemporary world. Beyond power, money and manipulation is the sea, the cave, the dry sticks, the open fire, the singing of man, the cries of animals, and the pale glowing of lights above the mountain. These things are close to the heart of man. In contemporary life we have lost our feelings for the earth and for ourselves: the music is gone. Poetry, in its highest form, is an attempt to bring this lost music back to the heart of man.*

MCKEOWN, WILLIAM TAYLOR, mag. editor, author; b. Ft. Collins, Colo., July 4, 1921; s. Stuart Ellison and Eunice Harris (Akin) McK.; A.B., Bowdoin Coll., 1942; student Columbia U. Grad. Sch., 1948; m. Lorraine Laredo; children—Elizabeth Ellison, Katherine, Suzanne. Editor, Fawcett Library Series, 1953-56; founding editor True's Boating Yearbook, 1955-56; founding editor Popular Boating mag., 1956, editor-in-chief, 1956-62; author weekly N.E.A. syndicated newspaper column, America Afloat, 1959—; contbr. fiction, non-fiction nat. mags., 1947—; travel editor Davis Publs.; outdoor editor Popular Mechanics. Served as test and fighter pilot USAAF, World War II; ETO. Mem. Am. Power Boat Assn., U.S. Power Squadrons. Clubs: New York Yacht, Overseas Press (N.Y.C.); Royal Danish Yacht (Copenhagen); Turtles Internat. Author: Boating Handbook, 1956; Boating in America, 1960. Internat. competitor power and sail racing events. also Darien CT

MC KETTA, JOHN J., JR., educator, chem. engr.; b. Wyano, Pa., Oct. 17, 1915; s. John J. and Mary (Gelet) McK.; B.S., Tri-State Coll., Angola, Ind., 1937; B.S.E., U. Mich., 1943, M.S., 1944, Ph.D., 1946; D.Eng. (hon.), Tri-State Coll., 1965, Drexel U., 1977; Sc.D., U. Toledo, 1973; m. Helen Elisabeth Smith, Oct. 17, 1943; children—Charles William, John J. III, Robert Andrew, Mary Anne. Group leader tech. dept. Wyandotte Chem. Corp. (Mich.), 1937-40, asst. supt. caustic soda div., 1940-41; teaching fellow U. Mich., 1942-44, instr. chem. engring., 1944-45; faculty U. Tex., Austin, 1946—, successively asst. prof. chem. engring., asso. prof., then prof. chem. engring., 1951-52, 54—, E.P. Schoch prof. chem. engring., 1970—, John J. McKetta prof., 1977—, asst. dir. Tex. petroleum research com., 1951-52, 54-56, chmn. chem. engring. dept., 1950-52, 55-63, dean Coll. Engring., 1963-69; vice chancellor acad. affairs U. Tex. System, 1969-70; editorial dir. Petroleum Refiner, 1952-54; pres. Chemoil Cons., Inc., 1957-73; dir. Big Three Co., Gulf Pub. Co., AID, Inc., Dallas, Houston Oil & Minerals Co., Howell Corp. (all Houston), San Antonio br. Fed. Res. Bank of Dallas, Marley Co., Kansas City, Vulcan Materials Co., Birmingham, Ala., KINARK Corp., Tulsa. Chmn. Tex. AEC, So. Interstate Nuclear Bd.; mem. Tex. Radiation Adv. Bd., 1978—; chmn. Nat. Energy Policy Com., 1970-72, Nat. Air Quality Control Com., 1972—; mem. adv. bd. Carnegie-Mellon Inst. Research, 1978—. Bd. regents Tri-State U., 1957—. Recipient Bronze plaque Am. Inst. Chem. Engrs., 1952, Charles Schwab award Am. Steel Inst., 1973; Lamme award as outstanding U.S. educator, 1976; Joe J. King Profl. Engring. Achievement award U. Tex., 1976, Gen. Dynamics Teaching Excellence award, 1979; Triple E award for contbns. to nat. issues on energy, environment and econs. Nat. Environ. Devel. Assn., 1976; Boris Pregal Sci. and Tech. award N.Y. Acad. Scis., 1978; named distinguished alumnus U. Mich Coll. Engring., 1953, Tri-State Coll., 1956; fellow Allied Chem. & Dye, 1945-46; distinguished fellow Carnegie-Mellon U., 1978; registered profl. engr., Tex., Mich. Mem. Am. Inst. Mining Engrs., Am. Chem. Soc. (chmn. Central Tex. sect. 1950), Am. Inst. Chem. Engrs. (chmn. nat. membership com. 1955, regional exec. com., nat. dir.; nat. v.p. 1961, pres. 1962, service to soc. award 1975), Am. Soc. Engring. Edn., Chem. Markets Research Assn., Am. Gas Assn. (adv. bd. chems. from gas 1954), Houston C. of C. (chmn. refining div. 1954, vice chmn. research and statistics com. 1954), Engrs. Joint Council (dir.), Engrs. Joint Countil Profl. Devel. (dir. 1963—), Nat. Acad. Engring., Sigma Xi, Chi Epsilon, Alpha Psi Omega, Tau Omega, Phi Lambda Upsilon, Phi Kappa Phi, Iota Alpha, Omega Chi Epsilon, Tau Beta Pi, Omicron Delta Kappa. Author series: Advances in Petroleum Chemistry and Refining. Chmn. editorial com. Petroleum Refiner; mem. adv. bd. Internat. Chem. Engring. mag.; editorial bd. Ency. of Chem. Tech.; exec. editor Ency. of Chem. Processing and Design. Home: 5227 Tortuga Trail Austin TX 78731

MC KHANN, CHARLES FREMONT, pediatrician; b. Cin., Dec. 21, 1898; s. Charles Fremont and Mary (Grassel) McK.; A.B., Miami U., 1918; B.S., U. Cin., 1920, A.M., 1921, M.D., 1923; m. Emily Priest, June 23, 1928 (dec. 1932); children—Charles Fremont, Guy Mead; m. 2d, Ileana Semenenko, Sept. 20, 1933 (dec. 1977); 1 son, Sergei Nicholas; m. 3d, Laura Dane, Apr. 9, 1979. Intern, Cin. Gen. Hosp., 1922-23; asst., instr. pediatrics Harvard Med. Sch., 1923-28, asst. prof. pediatrics, communicable diseases Med. Sch., Sch. Pub. Health, 1928-36, asso. prof., 1936-40; vis. prof. pediatrics Peiking (China) Union Med. Coll., 1935-36; prof., chmn. dept. pediatrics and communicable diseases U. Mich. Sch. Medicine, 1940-43; asst. to pres. in charge research and devel. Parke, Davis & Co., 1943-45; prof. pediatrics Western Res. U. Sch. Medicine, 1945-50, Jefferson Med. Coll. of Phila., 1952-56; dir. pediatrics Univ. Hosps., Cleve., 1945-50; med. dir. U.C.P.A., 1950-52; chmn. exec. com. Chemway Corp., 1954-71, chmn., pres., 1963-64. Vice chmn. Cleve. Health Council, 1947-49. Diplomate Am. Bd. Pediatrics (pres. 1947-50). Mem. Am. Pediatric Soc., Am. Soc. Clin. Investigation (emeritus), Am. Soc. for Pediatric Research (emeritus), A.M.A., Phi Beta Kappa, Sigma Xi, Alpha Omega Alpha, Delta Omega. Republican. Clubs: University (N.Y.C.); Wianno (Mass.). Home: 511 Seaview Ave Osterville MA 02655

MCKHANN, GUY MEAD, physician, educator; b. Boston, Mar. 20, 1932; s. Charles Fremont and Emily (Priest) McK.; student Harvard, 1948-51; M.D., Yale, 1955; m. Katherine E. Henderson, Nov. 30, 1957; children—Ian, James, Emily, Guy, Charles. Intern New York Hosp., 1955-56; asst. resident pediatrics Johns Hopkins Hosp., Balt., 1956-57; clin. asso. NIH, Bethesda, Md., 1957-60; resident neurology Mass. Gen. Hosp., Boston, 1960-63; asst. and asso. prof. pediatrics and neurology Stanford (Calif.) U., 1963-69; prof. neurology Johns Hopkins, Balt., 1969—, Kennedy prof. neurology, head neurology dept., 1969—; cons. NIH, 1969—. Served with USPHS, 1957-60. Markle scholar, 1964-69; Joseph P. Kennedy Jr. scholar, 1963-69. Mem. Am. Acad. Neurology, Am. Neurol. Assn., Soc. Pediatric Research, Am. Neurochem. Soc., Alpha Omega Alpha. Research on normal and abnormally developing nervous system. Home: 6526 Montrose Ave Baltimore MD 21212 Office: Dept Neurology Johns Hopkins Hosp Baltimore MD 21205

MCKIBBEN, WILLIAM TORREY, educator; b. Seattle, Sept. 30, 1916; s. Ernest Collet and Britannia (Torrey) McK.; A.B., Stanford, 1937, M.A., 1938; Ph.D., U. Chgo., 1942; m. Elizabeth Pence, June 25, 1944; children—Timothy Pence (dec. May 1968), Andrew William. Lectr. classics U. Utah, 1946-47, asst. prof., 1947-50; asso. prof. classical langs. Grinnell Coll., 1952-57, prof., 1958—, Benedict prof., 1961—. Fellow Am. Acad. in Rome, 1949-51; Fulbright grantee, 1950-51. Served with USNR, 1942-46. Mem. Am. Philol. Assn., Archaeol. Inst. Am., AAUP, Council Basic Edn., Classical Soc. Am. Acad. in Rome (pres. 1959), Ia. Fgn. Lang. Assn. (pres. 1960-61), Am. Council Teaching Fgn. Langs., Phi Beta Kappa. Home: 916 7th Ave Grinnell IA 50112

MCKIBBIN, JOHN MEAD, biochemist, educator; b. Tucson, Nov. 15, 1915; s. Clifford Worden and Ruth (Mead) McK.; B.S., Mich. State U., 1938; M.S., U. Wis., 1940, Ph.D., 1942; m. Virginia Rowland, Mar. 11, 1944; children—Janet B., John R., Douglas W., William K. Instr., asso. Harvard Schs. Medicine and Pub. Health, 1942-45; asst. prof. State U. N.Y. Med. Center, Syracuse, 1945-47, asso. prof., 1947-56, prof. biochemistry, 1956-61; prof. biochemistry, chmn. dept. U. Ala., Birmingham, 1961—. Recipient A.M.A. Golden Apple award, 1968. Mem. Soc. Biol. Chemists, Biochem. Soc., Soc. for Exptl. Biology and Medicine, Am. Chem. Soc., Ala. Acad. Sci. (treas. 1965-69), Soc. Complex Carbohydrates, Sigma Xi. Research in chemistry and metabolism of complex lipids in animal tissues. Home: 3 Montcrest Dr Birmingham AL 35213

MC KIE, JAMES WARREN, educator; b. Los Angeles, June 18, 1922; s. Clarence Gilmer and Clara (De Koster) McK.; B.A., U. Tex., 1943, M.A., 1947; Ph.D., Harvard, 1952; m. Alice Catherine Wharton, Dec. 25, 1947; children—David Glenn, Julia Kathryn, Ellen Elizabeth. Asst. prof. econs. Williams Coll., 1951-52, Harvard, 1952-54; faculty Vanderbilt U., Nashville, 1954-71, prof. econs., 1960-71, chmn. dept. econs. and bus. adminstrn., 1965-68; dean Coll. Social and Behavioral Scis., U. Tex., Austin, 1971-76, prof. econs., 1971—, chmn. dept., 1979—; sr. fellow Brookings Instn., 1970-71; vis. asso. prof. Harvard, 1959-60; vis. prof. U. Calif. at Berkeley, 1963-64; cons. to govt. and industry, 1960—; mem. com. on emergency energy capacity Nat. Acad. Scis., 1972-73, com. energy alternatives for P.R., 1979. Mem. Pres.'s Task Force on Antitrust Policy, 1967-68; chief economist Cabinet Task Force on Oil Import Controls, 1969-70; faculty Salzburg Seminar in Am. Studies, 1975. Served with USAAF, 1943-46. Mem. Am., So. (pres. 1970-71, editor jour. 1959-63) econ. assns., Internat. Assn. Energy Economists, Mont Pelerin Soc. Club: Cosmos (Washington). Author: Tin Cans and Tin Plate, 1959. Editor: Education and the Southern Economy, 1965; Social Responsibility and the Business Predicament, 1974. Contbr. articles to profl. jours. Home: 3607 Highland View Austin TX 78731

MCKIERNAN, JOHN SAMMON, judge; b. Providence, Oct. 15, 1911; s. John Francis and Loretta Mulvey) McK.; A.B. cum laude, Notre Dame U., 1934; LL.B., Boston U., 1937. Admitted to R.I. bar, 1937; asso. firm McKiernan, McElroy and Going, 1937—; first asst. city solicitor, Providence, 1942-43, 1946-47; elected lt. gov. of R.I., 1946, re-elected, 1948, gov., Dec. 1950-Jan. 1951, lt. gov., 1951-56; judge R.I. Superior Ct., 1956—. Chmn. Fair Fent Com., Providence, 1941; legal adviser Civil Service Commn., Providence, 1941—; mem. bd. govs., Univ. Notre Dame. Served with U.S. Army, World War II. Mem. Am. Vets., Am. Legion. K.C. Club: Notre Dame Alumni (past pres.). Home: 75 Hilltop Dr East Greenwich RI 02818

MCKIERNAN, JOHN WILLIAM, mech. engr.; b. Hannibal, Mo., Jan. 12, 1923; s. Charles and Anna Laura (Turner) McK.; B.S., U. Mo., 1947; M.S., Iowa State Coll., 1950; m. Jeannette Dorothy Hagen, Aug. 26, 1945; children—Kathleen J., Linda J., John E. With E.I. duPont de Nemours & Co., Inc., Richmond, Va., 1947-48; faculty Iowa State Coll., 1948-51; mech. engr. Sandia Labs., Albuquerque, 1951—. Served with USAAF, 1943-45. Decorated D.F.C., Air medal. Mem. ASME (v.p.). Mem. Christian Ch. Home: 1709 Cardenas St NE Albuquerque NM 87110 Office: Div 4542 Sandia Labs Kirtland AFB Albuquerque NM 87115

MCKILLOP, DAVID HOLMES, ret. fgn. service officer; b. Globe, Ariz., Feb. 2, 1916; s. Archibald Campbell and Helen (Holmes) McK.; A.B., Harvard U., 1937, M.A., 1939; m. Stratton Nicolson Griswold, Nov. 24, 1956. Tchr., N.Y. Inst. Edn. Blind, 1940; vice consul Am. Consulate Gen., Zurich, Switzerland, 1941; 3d sec. Am. Embassy, Berlin, Germany, 1941, Am. Legation, Stockholm, Sweden, 1941-45; vice consul Am. Consulate Gen., Hamburg, Germany, 1946-47; consul Am. Consulate, Basra, Iraq, 1947-48; fgn. affairs specialist Dept. State, 1948-51; consul Am. Consulate Gen., Hong Kong, 1951; assigned Nat. War Coll., 1954-55, Dept. of State, 1955-57; counselor Am. embassy, Tunis, Tunisia, 1957-62; dep. chief of mission and counselor of embassy, Brussels, Belgium, 1962-65; dir. Office Western European Affairs, Dept. State, 1965-66, country dir. Scandinavia, Iceland and Finland, 1966-68, inter-agy. coordinator Mid-Atlantic region Office Econ. Opportunity, Washington, 1968-69, Viet-Nam CORDS Program, 1969-71; mem. sec.'s planning and coordination staff Dept. State, Washington, 1971-73; fgn. affairs adviser to Senator Claiborne Pell of R.I., 1973-77; free-lance writer, cons. Meridian House Internat. Center for Def. Info., 1978. Mem. Am. Fgn. Service Assn. Episcopalian. Clubs: DACOR, Metropolitan, Nat. Press (Washington); Harvard (Boston and Washington). Home: 5169 Tilden St NW Washington DC 20016 also Smith Neck Ola Lyme CT 06371. *What happens to you in life is less important than how you take what happens to you.*

MCKILLOP, LUCILLE, coll. pres.; b. Chgo., Sept. 28, 1924; d. Daniel and Catherine (Hamill) McKillop; B.A., St. Xavier Coll., 1951; M.S., U. Notre Dame, 1959; Ph.D., U. Wis., 1965. Tchr. pub. schs., Chgo. and Ottawa, Ill., 1946-58; instr. Edgewood Coll., Madison, Wis., 1961-62; vis. prof. Ill. Inst. Tech., Chgo., 1969; faculty St. Xavier Coll., Chgo., 1958-59, 63-73; pres. Salve Regina Coll., Newport, R.I., 1973—; dir. Old Colony Coop. Bank, Providence, 1976—; mem. Gov.'s Adv. Commn. Ednl. TV, 1977—. Trustee Newport Hosp., 1976—; chmn. univ. dept. United Way S.E. New Eng., 1977. Mem. Nat. Cath. Ednl. Assn. (exec. com. coll. and univ. dept. 1977—). Address: Newport Coll Salve Regina Ochre Point Ave Newport RI 02840

MCKIM, PAUL ARTHUR, petroleum co. exec.; b. Milford, Conn., Feb. 1, 1923; s. Arthur Wheatley and Helen Agnes (Brennan) McK.; student Lamar Inst. Tech., 1940-42; B.S. in Chem. Engring., La. State U., 1943, M.S., 1947, Ph.D., 1949; grad. Advanced Mgmt. Program Harvard, 1959, Aspen Inst. Humanistic Studies Exec. Program, 1970; m. Daisy Flora Brown, June 18, 1945; 1 dau., Meredith Ann. With Ethyl Corp., 1949-62, asst. gen. mgr. research and devel. operations, 1958-62; v.p., gen. mgr. research and devel. Atlantic Refining Co., Phila., 1962-66; v.p. Atlantic Richfield Co., 1966—; v.p. comml. devel. Arco Chem. Co., 1966-69, v.p. nuclear operations and comml. devel., 1969-78; exec. v.p. Sinclair Koppers Co., 1973—; pres. Arco Polymers, Inc., 1974-78, Tex. Eastern Transmission Corp., 1978—. Vice chmn. U.S. com. for World Petroleum Congresses. Bd. mgrs. Spring Garden Inst.; vice chmn. bd. mgrs. Phila. Coll. Art; mem. lab. com. Franklin Inst. Research Labs.; bd. dirs. met. Phila. YMCA. Served to lt. (j.g.) USNR, 1944-46. Mem. Am. Inst. Chem. Engrs., Am. Petroleum Inst., Phila. C. of C., World Affairs Council Phila. (dir.), Alpha Chi Sigma, Omicron Delta Kappa, Tau Beta Pi, Phi Lambda Upsilon, Phi Kappa Phi, Delta Kappa Epsilon. Clubs: Union League, Phila. Racquet; Merion (Pa.) Cricket, Merion Golf. Home: 1015 Briarmead Houston TX 77057 Office: 1 Houston Center Houston TX 77002

MCKININ, LAWRENCE, artist, educator; b. Yukon, Pa., Aug. 24, 1917; s. Michael and Anna (Russakov) McK.; B.S. in Edn., Wayne State U., 1939; postgrad. Cranbrook Acad. Art, 1946-48; m. Emma Jean James, July 14, 1951 (div. 1976); children—Katherine, Nicholas. Package designer C.E. Jamieson Drug Co., Detroit, 1939-41; tchr. art Detroit Public Schs., 1941-42, 46; mem. faculty dept. art U. Mo., Columbia, 1948—, prof. art, 1959—, chmn. dept., 1955-59; art dir. Archaeology mag., 1954-55; exhbns. include: Springfield Art Mus. Ann., 1950-76, Mo. Arts Council, 1955-57, Nelson-Atkins Gallery, Kansas City, 1958, 59, 60, 65; represented in permanent collections: Nelson-Atkins Gallery, Springfield Art Mus., Mo. Hist. Soc., U. Mo. Served with USAAF, 1942-46. Mem. Mid-Am. Coll. Art Assn., NEA. Home: 1005 Belleview Ct Columbia MO 65201 Office: A126 Fine Arts U MO Columbia MO 65211

MC KINLEY, DAVID ALEXANDER, JR., architect; b. Spokane, Wash., Mar. 7, 1930; s. David Alexander and Irene Ann (Mueller) McK.; B.A., U. Wash., 1953; m. Cherrill Joyce Mayer, Mar. 18, 1950 (div.); children—Lauren Ann, Diana Marr, Teri Lynn; m. 2d, Jeannette R. Billings, June 25, 1971. Architect Paul Thiry, Seattle, 1953-54, Paul Hayden Kirk, Seattle, 1956-60; partner Kirk, Wallace, McKinley A.I.A. & Assos., Seattle, 1960-78; pres. The McKinley Architects, P.C., 1978—; asst. prof. architecture U. Wash., 1959-60; vis. design prof. Rice U., 1964. Served as 1st lt. C.E., AUS, 1954-56. Fellow A.I.A. (pres. Seattle chpt. 1966, mem. nat. future of profession com. 1967-69). Author: Ten Designs for Community Colleges, 1962; Architecture for the Community Mental Health Center, 1965. Home: 2010 Taylor Ave N Seattle WA 98109 Office: 2000 Fairview St E Seattle WA 98102

MCKINLEY, DOUGLAS WEBSTER, journalist; b. Bay City, Mich., May 26, 1917; s. Frank and Amelia Ingraham (Webster) McK.; B.A., Amherst Coll., 1939; m. Martha Slade, July 12, 1945; children—Judith Anne (Mrs. Kingman Penniman), Martha Webster (Mrs. Duane Kissick), Mary Slade, Jane Elizabeth. Reporter, Ann Arbor News, 1940-41, 46-47; staff AP, Detroit, 1947-53, Rome, 1953-57, chief of bur., Istanbul, 1957-60; chief Middle East services, Beirut, 1960-65, news editor world services, N.Y.C., 1965—. Served as maj. AUS, 1941-45. Mem. Phi Kappa Psi. Club: Overseas Press (N.Y.C.). Author: Trouble in the Middle East. Home: 47 Summit Ridge Rd Stamford CT 06902 Office: 50 Rockefeller Plaza New York City NY 10020

MC KINLEY, GORDON WELLS, former pub. co. exec.; b. New Harbor, Maine, Mar. 9, 1915; s. Alan Robertson and Florence (Wells) McK.; B.A., McMaster U., 1938; M.A., Ohio State U., 1940, Ph.D., 1948; m. Ruth Burkhalter, Jan. 4, 1943; 1 dau., Kathryn Sue. Instr., Lehigh U., 1938-40; instr., asst. prof. Ohio State U., 1946-51; with

Prudential Ins. Co. Am., 1951-61, exec. dir. econ. and investment research, 1957-61; v.p., chief economist F.W. Dodge Corp., 1961-63, dir., 1962-65; v.p. econs. McGraw-Hill, Inc., 1963-70, v.p., treas., 1968-70, sr. v.p. econs. and financial planning, 1970-80, also dir.; dir. Standard Poor's Corp., Howard Savs. Bank, Evlico Account One, NJB Prime Investors, Inc., St. Paul Securities, Inc., Newton Falls Paper Mill, Rock-McGraw, Inc. Served to lt., AC, USNR, 1941-45. Mem. Am. Econ. Assn., Am. Statis. Assn., Am. Finance Assn., Am. Assn. Bus. Econs. Episcopalian. Clubs: Canoe Brook Country (Summit, N.J.); Marshwood (Savannah, Ga.). Co-author: The Federal Reserve System, 1960. Contbr. articles to profl. jours. Home: 35 Magnolia Crossing Skidaway Island Savannah GA 31411

MC KINLEY, HUGH, city mgr.; b. Portland, Oreg., Mar. 6, 1919; s. Charles and Nellie Linda (Higgins) McK.; B.A., Reed Coll., 1941; m. Evelyn Griffin, July 2, 1944; children—Charles, Maria, Kirk. City mgr. Sutherlin, Oreg., 1953-56, Grants Pass, Oreg., 1956-60, Eugene, Oreg., 1960-75, San Diego, 1975-78, Glendale, Calif., 1978—; pres. League Oreg. Cities, 1963-64. Served with U.S. Army, 1942-46. Mem. Internat. City Mgmt. Assn. (v.p. western region 1968-69), Am. Soc. Pub. Adminstrn., Nat. Acad. Pub. Adminstrn. Home: 1227 Viscano Dr Glendale CA 91207 Office: 202 C St San Diego CA 92101

MC KINLEY, JOHN KEY, oil co. exec.; b. Tuscaloosa, Ala., Mar. 24, 1920; s. Virgil Parks and Mary Emma (Key) McK.; B.S. in Chem. Engring., U. Ala., 1940, M.S. in Organic Chemistry, 1941, LL.D. (hon.), 1972; grad. Advanced Mgmt. Program, Harvard U., 1962; LL.D. (hon.), Troy State U., 1974; m. Helen Heare, July 19, 1946; children—John Key, Mark Charles. With Texaco Inc., 1941—, asst. dir. research, Beacon, N.Y., 1957-59, asst. to v.p., 1959-60, mgr. comml. devel., 1960, gen. mgr. petrochem. dept., N.Y.C., 1960-67, v.p. petrochem. dept., v.p. in charge supply and distbn., 1967-71, sr. v.p. worldwide refining, petrochems., also supply and distbn., 1971, pres., dir., 1971—, chmn. bd. Texaco Devel. Corp., N.Y.C., 1971—; dir. Burlington Industries. Served as maj. AUS, 1941-45; ETO. Decorated Bronze Star; recipient George Washington Honor medal Freedoms Found., 1972; Andrew Wellington Cordier fellow Columbia U. Registered profl. engr., Tex. Fellow Am. Inst. Chem. Engrs.; mem. Am. Petroleum Inst. (dir.), Am. Chem. Soc., Sigma Xi, Tau Beta Pi, Gamma Sigma Epsilon, Kappa Sigma. Clubs: Wee Burn Country (Darien, Conn.); N.Y. Yacht, Brook (N.Y.C.); Blind Brook Country (Port Chester, N.Y.). Patentee chem. processing. Home: 26 Parsons Walk Darien CT 06820 Office: 2000 Westchester Ave White Plains NY 10650

MCKINLEY, LOREN DHUE, museum dir.; b. Tillamook, Oreg., Feb. 1, 1920; s. Henry Raymond and Flora (Phillips) McK.; student Oreg. State U., U. Oreg.; D.Sc., U. Portland, 1973; m. Mary Eileen Sessions, May 22, 1942; children—Candace Eileen, Scott Dhu, Kevin Loren, Laurie Lee, Maris Colleen. Advt. mgr. Headlight Herald, Tillamook, 1946; partner Kenwood Press, Tillamook, 1949; dir. Oreg. Mus. Sci. and Industry, Portland, 1960-78, chief exec. officer, 1978—. Pres., Assn. Sci. and Tech. Centers Am., 1973—. Mayor, Tillamook, 1954-60. Served with AUS, World War II; ETO, MTO. Decorated Bronze Star with oak leaf cluster; recipient Oreg. Mus. Sci. and Industry award, 1965, Elsie M.B. Naumberg award as outstanding sci. mus. dir., 1968, citation for outstanding service Oreg. Acad. Sci., 1971; Aubrey Watzek award Lewis and Clark Coll., 1973; named First Citizen of Oreg., 1961. Mem. League Oreg. Cities (past pres.), Kappa Sigma. Republican. Home: 11925 SW Belvidere Pl Portland OR 97225 Office: 4015 S W Canyon Rd Portland OR 97221

MC KINLEY, ROYCE BALDWIN, corp. exec.; b. Ann Arbor, Mich., Feb. 20, 1921; s. Earle B. and Leola (Royce) McK.; student Harvard, 1938-40; A.B., U. Mich., 1942; J.D., Harvard, 1948; LL.M., George Washington U., 1951; m. Roberta Schreck, Apr. 15, 1943; 1 dau., Martha Lee; m. 2d, Anne de Beixedon, July 7, 1973. Admitted to D.C. bar, 1949, Mo. bar, 1953, Ill. bar, 1959; practiced in Washington, 1948-52; counsel Ralston Purina Co., St. Louis, 1952-55; asso. McKinsey & Co., Inc., Chgo. and London, Eng., 1955-60; v.p., sec. Electro-Sci.-Investors, Inc., Dallas, 1960-63; v.p. finance and adminstrn. Space Gen. Corp., El Monte, Calif., 1963-66; asst. dir. mgmt. systems TRW, Inc., Redondo Beach, Calif., 1967-68; v.p. fin., sec.-treas. Santa Anita Consol., Inc., Los Angeles, 1968-73, exec. v.p., chief operating officer, 1973—; dir. Santa Anita Consol. Inc., Magnetic Head Corp., Glen Heads, N.Y., Los Angeles Turf Club, Arcadia, Calif., Robert H. Grant Corp., Santa Ana, Calif., Santa Anita Devel. Corp., Newport Beach, Calif. Served to lt. (j.g.) USNR, 1943-46. Mem. Fin. Execs. Inst. Club: California (Los Angeles). Home: 262 S Orange Dr Los Angeles CA 90036 Office: 1 Wilshire Bldg Los Angeles CA 90017

MCKINLEY, THEODORE DAVID, chem. products co. exec.; b. N.Y.C., May 19, 1914; s. Robert George and Elizabeth (Hunter) McK.; B.S., Worcester Poly. Inst., 1935; M.S., U. Del., 1942; m. Sue Elise Wootton, June 24, 1939. Research chemist Du Pont Co., Newport, Del., 1935-56, research supr., exptl. sta., Wilmington, Del., 1956—. Coordinator U.S. del. to adv. group aerospace research and devel. NATO, 1962-69. Mem. Am. Chem. Soc., Soc. Chem. Industry, Electrochem. Soc. (v.p. 1969-72, pres. 1972-73), ASTM, Sigma Xi, Tau Beta Pi, Theta Chi. Editor in chief The Electron Microprobe, 1966. Home: 1510 Barley Mill Rd Wilmington DE 19807 Office: Du Pont Experimental Station Wilmington DE 19898

MCKINLEY, WILLIAM A., educator, physicist; b. Dallas, Aug. 23, 1917; s. William A. and Nora (Richards) McK.; B.A., U. Tex., 1939; Ph.D., Mass. Inst. Tech., 1947; m. Georgia MacKinnon, Nov. 16, 1940 (div. 1969); children—William A. III, Kathryn; m. 2d, Hedi Freund, 1969. Fellow Inst. Neurology, Northwestern U. Med. Sch., 1940-42; staff mem. Radiation Lab., Mass. Inst. Tech., 1943-45; mem. faculty Rensselaer Poly. Inst., 1947—, prof. physics, 1955—. Mem. AAAS, Am. Phys. Soc., Am. Assn. Physics Tchrs., Phi Beta Kappa, Sigma Xi. Spl. research quantum scattering theory, quantum field theory, electrophysiology central nervous system. Home: PO Box 411 Altamont NY 12009 Office: Rensselaer Poly Inst Troy NY 12180

MC KINLEY, WILLIAM LESTER, mfg. co. exec.; b. Grant, Mich., Mar. 2, 1924; s. Robert B. and Susie (McInnis) McK.; student Alma (Mich.) Coll., 1942, U. Oreg., 1943; B.A., U. Mich., 1948, LL.B., 1950; m. Margaret Alice Sheller, Aug. 17, 1946; children—Richard, Michael, Cathleen. Trainee Auto Owners Ins. Co., Lansing, Mich., 1950; with Gerber Products Co., Fremont, Mich., 1950—, v.p., sec., 1965-68, gen. counsel, 1955-72, exec. v.p., 1971-78, vice chmn., 1978—, also dir.; dir. Old State Bank, Fremont. Mem. Fremont Pub. Sch. Bd., 1962-69, Gerber Meml. Hosp., 1959—. Served with AUS, World War II. Mem. Phi Alpha Delta. Conglist. Rotarian. Home: 406 Chippewa Dr Fremont MI 49412 Office: 445 State St Fremont MI 49412

MC KINNELL, ROBERT GILMORE, educator; b. Springfield, Mo., Aug. 9, 1926; s. William Parks and Mary Catherine (Gilmore) McK.; A.B., U. Mo., 1948; B.S., Drury Coll., 1949; Ph.D., U. Minn., 1959; m. Beverly Walton Kerr, Jan. 24, 1964; children—Nancy Elizabeth, Robert Gilmore, Susan Kerr. Research asso. Inst. for Cancer Research, Phila., 1958-61; asst. prof. biology Tulane U., New Orleans, 1961-65, asso. prof., 1965-69, prof., 1969-70; prof. zoology U. Minn., Mpls., 1970—, prof. genetics and cell biology, St. Paul, 1976—; vis. scientist Dow Chem. Co., Freeport, Tex., 1976; guest dept. zoology U. Calif., Berkeley, 1979; mem. secretariat Third Internat. Conf. Differentiation, 1978; mem. amphibian com. Inst. Lab. Animal Resources, NRC, 1970-73, mem. adv. council, 1974. Served to lt. USNR, 1944-47, 51-53. Recipient Outstanding Teaching award Newcomb Coll., Tulane U., 1970; Disting. Alumni award Drury Coll., 1979; Research fellow Nat. Cancer Inst., 1957-58, Sr. Sci. fellow NATO, 1974. Fellow Linnean Soc. (London); mem. Am. Assn. Cancer Research, Am. Soc. Zoologists, Am. Inst. Biol. Scis., Soc. for Devel. Biology, Internat. Soc. Differentiation (mem. exec. com., secretariat 1975—), Environ. Mutagen Soc., Am. Assn. for Lab. Animal Sci., AAAS, Sigma Xi. Club: Gown-In-Town. Author: Cloning: Amphibian Nuclear Transplantation, 1978; Cloning, A Biologist Reports, 1979. Mem. editorial bd. Differentiation, 1973. Contbr. articles to profl. jours. Home: 2124 Hoyt Ave W Saint Paul MN 55108 Office: Dept Genetics and Cell Biology U Minn Saint Paul MN 55108

MC KINNEY, ALEXIS, pub. relations cons.; b. Cin., Mar. 13, 1907; s. John Austin and Gertrude (Kofler) McK.; ed. pub. schs., Cin., Rocky Ford, Colo., and Tex.; m. Esther Ryker Simmons, Aug. 27, 1930; 1 dau., Eunice Christine. Enlisted in U.S. Navy, 1923, served aboard U.S.S. New Mexico, 1923-27; circulation agt. Pueblo (Colo.) Star-Jour., 1928; reporter Pueblo Chieftain, 1929, state editor, 1930, city editor, 1931-32; co-pub. and editor Rocky Ford Tribune, 1933-34; news editor Alamosa (Colo.) Daily Courier, 1934-42; statehouse reporter Denver Post, 1942-45; information officer U.S. Bur. Reclamation, Denver, 1945-46; asst. city editor Denver Post, 1946, city editor, 1946-47, mng. editor, 1947-49, asst. pub., 1949-63; project dir. Rio Grande-land, Durango, Colo., 1963-65; dir. pub. relations Denver & Rio Grande Western R.R. Co., 1965-73; pub. relations cons. Rio Grande Industries, Inc., 1973—. Trustee Colo. R.R. Hist. Found. and Mus. Mem. Pub. Relations Soc. Am., R.R. Pub. Relations Assn., Sigma Delta Chi. Conglist. Address: 855 Pennsylvania St 411 Denver CO 80203

MC KINNEY, DAVID E(WING), info. processing products co. exec.; b. Harriman, Tenn., Nov. 28, 1934; s. David Lloyd and Mattie (Ewing) McK.; student (Founders scholar) Vanderbilt U., 1952-53; B.S. in Mktg. (Gen. Electric scholar), U. Tenn., 1956; m. Kathryn Ann James, Nov. 21, 1956; children—Mary, John, James, Mark. With IBM, 1956—, br. mgr., New Orleans, 1966-68, exec. asst. to chmn. bd., Armonk, N.Y., 1971-73, pres. info. records div., Princeton, N.J., 1975-76, v.p. office products div., Franklin Lakes, N.J., 1976-77, v.p. personnel, Armonk, 1979—. Mem. adv. bd. T. J. Watson Found., Providence; elder First Presbyterian Ch., New Canaan, Conn.; pres. United Way of New Canaan, 1979-80; bd. dirs. Nat. Soc. Prevention Blindness, 1977—. Served to lt. U.S. Army, 1957-58. Mem. Bus. Roundtable, Orgn. Resources Counselors, Conf. Bd., Internat. Sponsors Council, Internat. Exec. Service Corps, Nat. Urban League. Club: Country of New Canaan. Office: IBM Old Orchard Rd Armonk NY 10504

MCKINNEY, DONALD LEE, mag. editor; b. Evanston, Ill., July 12, 1923; s. Guy Doane and Cora Redfield (Brenton) McK.; A.B., U. N.C., 1948; m. Mary Frances Joyce, Dec. 14, 1958; children—Jennifer Joyce, Douglas Guy. Salesman textbooks John Wiley & Sons, N.Y.C., 1949-52; freelance writer mostly comic books with some short articles and fiction, 1952-54; asst. mng. editor True mag., N.Y.C., 1955-62; editor articles Saturday Evening Post, 1962-69; spl. features editor N.Y. Daily News, 1969-70; mng. editor McCalls mag., N.Y.C., 1969—. Served with USNR, 1943-46. Democrat. Home: 152 E Rocks Rd Norwalk CT 06851 Office: 230 Park Ave New York NY 10017. *I learned early that it is important to speak up if you think you are being treated unfairly; sometimes it's true, and nobody else will complain if you don't. I also learned that in my business, and probably in most others, it is best to always say what you think. Truth is usually more helpful than any assortment of euphemisms, and it also saves a lot of worry over who you have lied to and just what you've said. Truth is not only the best policy—by all odds it's the easiest to keep track of.*

MC KINNEY, FRANK EDWARD, JR., banker; b. Indpls., Nov. 3, 1938; s. Frank Edward and Margaret Leonard (Warner) McK.; B.S., Ind. U., 1961, M.B.A., 1962; LL.D. (hon.), Butler U., Indpls., 1975; m. Katherine Berry, Aug. 18, 1962; children—Frank Edward, III, Katherine Marie, Margaret Leonard, Madeleine Warner, Robert Warner. Asst. cashier First Nat. Bank, Chgo., 1964-67; with Am. Fletcher Nat. Bank, Indpls., 1967—, exec. v.p., then pres., 1970-73, chmn. bd., 1973—; chmn. bd. Am. Fletcher Corp., 1974—; dir., mem. exec. com. Allied Bank Internat., N.Y.C.; dir., 2d vice-chmn., exec. [illegible] Fletcher Bank (Suisse) S.A., Geneva, Ind. Bell Telephone Co., Indpls. Water Co., Indpls. Power & Light Co., Am. United Life Ins. Co. Trustee, Butler U., Indpls.; bd. dirs. Indpls. Mus. Art, Children's Museum, Indpls., Exec. Council on Fgn. Diplomats; adv. council Coll. Bus., Notre Dame U. Served to 1st. lt. AUS, 1962-64. Named to Internat. Swimming Hall Fame, 1975, Ind. U. Acad. Alumni Fellows, 1973; recipient Distinguished Service award Indpls. Jaycees, 1974. Mem. Assn. Res. City Bankers, Am., Ind. bankers assns., Young Pres. Orgn., Ind. Soc. Chicago, Penrod Soc., Indpls. C. of C., 500 Festival Assos., Econ. Club Indpls. (pres. 1977), Am. Legion, Sigma Alpha Epsilon. Democrat. Roman Catholic. Clubs: Meridian Hill Country, Indpls. Athletic, Columbia, Notre Dame, K.C. (Indpls.). Address: Am Fletcher Nat Bank 101 Monument Circle Indianapolis IN 46277

MCKINNEY, FRED, psychologist, educator; b. New Orleans, Apr. 4, 1908; s. William Henry and Clara Edna (Schneider) McK.; A.B., Tulane U., 1928, M.A., 1929; Ph.D., U. Chgo., 1931; m. Margery Mulkern, Aug. 19, 1933; children—Megan (Mrs. Robert W. Whitfield, Jr.), Kent, Molly (Mrs. Carliss C. Farmer), Doyne (Mrs. William S. McKenzie). Clerk and advt. rep. Item-Tribune, New Orleans, 1923-29; instr. psychology John Marshall Law Sch., Chgo., 1930-31; psychologist Mo. Unemployment Compensation Com., Com. on Personnel, 1936; instr. psychology U. Mo., 1933-35, asst. prof., 1935-38, asso. prof., 1939-44, prof., 1944-78, emeritus, 1978—, chmn. dept. psychology, 1945-55, psychologist Student Health Service, 1938-58; vis. asst. prof. U. Ark., summer 1934; vis. prof. Miss. State Coll., summers 1948-49, U. Denver, summers 1950, 56, San Francisco State Coll., summer 1951, Tulane U., summer 1952; vis. lectr., cons. Stephens Coll., 1956-57; Fulbright prof. U. Ankara and Middle East U., Ankara, Turkey, 1958-59; prof. psychology U. Mid-Am., Ball State U. Overseas, 1978-79. Chmn. Conf. of State Psychol. Assns., 1956-57; asso. editor Edn. and Psychol. Measurement, editor and rep. Am. Coll. Personnel Assn., 1947-58; asso. editor Jour. Cons. Psychol. Recipient Distinguished Faculty award Univ. Alumni Assn., 1966, Distinguished Teaching award in psychology Am. Psychol. Found., 1977, commendation Mo. Senate, 1977. Former asso. and fellow Am. Psychol. Assn. (pres. Div. 2, teaching psychology 1958-59); diplomate Am. Bd. Examiners in Psychology; mem. Midwestern Psychol. Assn. (council mem. 1945-49), Mo. Psychol. Assn. (v.p. 1947-48; pres. 1948-49), AAUP, Mo. Assn. for Mental Hygiene (sec.-treas. 1936-38), Blue Key, U. of Mo. YMCA (chmn. faculty bd. advisors 1937-44), Midwestern Assn. Coll. Psychiatrists and Clin. Psychol. (sec.-treas. 1945-46; pres. 1946-47), Alpha Pi Zeta, Sigma Xi, Omicron Delta Kappa, Psi Chi (pres. Midwest div. 1930-32, nat. pres. 1932-34). Episcopalian. Author: Psychology of Personal Adjustment, 1941, rev., 1960; You and Your Life, 1951; Counseling for Personal Adjustment, 1958; Understanding Personality: Cases in Counseling, 1965; Psychology in Action: Basic Readings, 1967, rev. edit., 1973; Effective Behavior and Human Developments, 1976. Contbr. chpts. to Handbook for Child Guidance by E. Harms, 1947; An Introduction to Clinical Psychology by L.A. Pennington and I.A. Berg, 1948. Producer and performer: Not in Our Stars (TV program); producer for Stephens Coll., 13 TV kinescopes (ednl.), Live Your Life, 1958; also produced 31 ednl. television video tapes on gen. psychology, 8 tapes for Psychology of Personality. Research in psychotherapy, personality adjustment. Home: 710 Thilly Columbia MO 65201

MC KINNEY, GEORGE WESLEY, JR., banker; b. Amigo, W.Va., May 27, 1922; s. George W. and Charlotte (Ashworth) McK.; A.B., Berea Coll., 1942; M.A., U. Va., 1947, Ph.D., 1949; postgrad. Stonier Grad. Sch. Banking, 1958; m. Lucille Christian, Sept. 5, 1941; children—George Wesley III, Mary, Ruth. With Fed. Res. Bank Richmond (Va.), 1948-60, asst. v.p., 1958-60; with Irving Trust Co., N.Y.C., 1960—, sr. v.p., 1968—, head econ. research and planning div., 1968-78, chmn. econ. adv. com., 1978—. Served to capt. AUS, 1942-45. Fellow Nat. Assn. Bus. Economists (pres. 1965-66); mem. Phi Kappa Phi. Author: Federal Taxing and Spending in Virginia, 1949; Federal Reserve Discount Window, 1960; Management of Commercial Bank Funds, 1974. Contbr. to books. Office: 1 Wall St New York NY 10015

MC KINNEY, JAMES CARROLL, coll. dean; b. Minden, La., Jan. 11, 1921; s. William C. and Carolyn (Hilman) McK.; student La. Poly. Inst., 1938-41, Stanford, 1943-44; Mus.B., La. State U., 1949, Mus. M., 1950; D.Mus. Arts, U. So. Calif., 1969; m. Elizabeth Richmond, Aug. 28, 1949; children—James Carroll, Timothy Richmond, John Kevin. Grad. asst. La. State U., 1949-50; asst. prof. music theory Southwestern Baptist Theol. Sem., Ft. Worth, 1950-54, chmn. dept. music theory, composition, 1954-56, dean Sch. Ch. Music, 1956—; baritone soloist First Presbyn. Ch., Hollywood, Calif., 1957-58, First Methodist Ch., Ft. Worth, 1963-67; guest tchr. U. So. Calif., 1958; vis. lectr. Hong Kong Bapt. Coll., Hong Kong Bapt. Theol. Sem., 1971-72; presented solo recitals, appeared TV and choral prodns., Bangkok, Thailand, Hong Kong, Israel, Jordan, 1971-72. Bd. dirs. Ft. Worth Symphony Orch. Assn., Ft. Worth Civic Music Assn., Van Cliburn Internat. Piano Competition; bd. dirs., pres. So. Bapt. Ch. Music Conf. Served AUS, 1941-45. Mem. Music Tchrs. Nat. Assn., Music Educators Nat. Conf., Nat. Assn. Tchrs. Singing, Am. Choral Dirs. Assn., Tex. Assn. Music Schs., Ft. Worth Voice Tchrs. Forum, Phi Mu Alpha Sinfonia, Omicron Delta Kappa, Phi Kappa Phi, Pi Kappa Lambda. Baptist. Author: The Beginning Music Reader, 1958; The Progressing Music Reader, 1959; You Can Read Music, 1960; The Advanced Music Reader, 1961; Mastering Music Reading, 1964; Study Guide for Fundamentals of Music, 1964; Vocal Fundamentals Kit, 1976; Vocal Development Kit, 1977. Home: 5604 Wedgmont Circle Fort Worth TX 76133 Office: PO Box 22000-4D Fort Worth TX 76122. *The longer I live, the more certain I become that the basic value systems passed on to me by my parents are valid. Inherent in all their systems were personal integrity and abiding respect for the rights of others. My chief hope is that I may be as effective as they in transmitting these values to my own children and to the students with whom I come in contact.*

MCKINNEY, JAMES EDWARD, JR., educator; b. Emory, Tex., Feb. 28, 1927; s. James Edward and Agatha (Porter) McK.; B.A. cum laude, E. Tex. State U., 1948; M.A., Middlebury Coll., 1953; Ph.D., Purdue U., 1961; m. Virginia Kimmel, Aug. 22, 1951; children—Kimmel, Alma, Melanie. Tchr., Western Mil. Acad., Alton, Ill., 1948-54; tchr. Baytown (Tex.) Pub. Schs., 1954-56; instr. modern lang. Purdue U., 1956-61, asst. prof., 1961-63, asso. prof., 1963-66; prof., chmn. dept. fgn. langs. Western Ill. U., Macomb, 1966—; dir. fgn. study programs for U. Ind. and Purdue, Madrid, Spain, 1963-64. Mem. Pub. Sch. Bd., West Lafayette, Ind., 1962-64. Served with USNR, 1945-47. Mem. Modern Lang. Assn. Am., AAUP, Am. Council Teaching Fgn. Langs., Am. Assn. Tchrs. Spanish and Portuguese (chpt. pres.), Ill. Fgn. Lang. Tchrs. Assn. (v.p. 1970-72, pres. 1973-75, editor bull.), Assn. Depts. Fgn. Langs. (exec. bd. 1975-78), Alpha Chi, Sigma Delta Pi, Kappa Delta Pi. Author: (with E. Brenes) Learning Spanish the Modern Way, Level I, 1962; (with E. Brenes) Learning Spanish the Modern Way, Level II, 1963; (with others) Paginas de un Diario, 1966; (with others) Learning Spanish the Modern Way, Levels I and II, 1967. Contbr. articles profl. jours. Home: 620 S Lafayette St Macomb IL 61455

MC KINNEY, JAMES WILLIAM, broker; b. Pitts., July 19, 1913; s. James [illegible] 1932-35, N.Y.U., 1947-51; m. Winifred Shaffer, Jan. 15, 1938; 1 son, James Barclay II. Asst. in corporate research, credit and investment mgmt. J.P. Morgan & Co., N.Y.C., 1936-52; head portfolio div. Thomson & McKinnon, N.Y.C., 1952-56; v.p., trust investment officer Palmer First Nat. Bank & Trust Co., Sarasota, Fla., 1956-68; v.p., trust investment officer United Bancshares of Fla., 1968-71; v.p., trust investment officer Miami Beach (Fla.) First Nat. Bank, 1968-71, Pan Am. Bank Miami, 1971-77; v.p., trust officer Pan Am. Bank Sarasota (Fla.), 1977-79; account exec. Dean Witter Reynolds, Inc., 1979—; mem. faculty Fla. Bankers Assn. Trust Sch., U. Fla.; instr. Sarasota County Adult Evening Edn. Program, 1962-64. Treas., bd. dirs. Sarasota County Heart Assn., Sarasota-Manatee Assn. Mentally Retarded Children; bd. dirs. Sarasota County chpt. A.R.C. Served with Amphibious Corps, USNR, 1944-45; PTO. Mem. Fla. Bankers Assn. (com. chmn.). Mason (32 deg., Shriner). Home: 2750 Mall Dr 123 Sarasota FL 33581 Office: 3870 S Tamiami Trail Sarasota FL 33579

MC KINNEY, JOHN ADAMS, constrn. co. exec.; b. Huntsville, Tex., Nov. 9, 1923; s. Andrew Todd and Myra (Adams) McK.; B.S., U.S. Naval Acad., 1945; J.D., Georgetown U., 1951; m. Cleo Turner, Aug. 31, 1946; children—John Adams, Todd T. Admitted to D.C. bar, 1951, Colo. bar, 1976; examiner U.S. Patent Office, 1947-51; chief patent counsel Johns-Manville Corp., Denver, 1957-71, v.p. legal services, 1971-74, sr. v.p., corp. sec., dir., 1974-76, pres., dir., 1976—, chief exec. officer, 1977—, chmn. bd., 1979—; dir. Public Service Co. Colo. Served to ensign U.S. Navy, 1945-47. Mem. Am., D.C. bar assns., Am. Patent Law Assn., Licensing Execs. Soc. Home: 2042 Crestridge Dr Littleton CO 80121 Office: Ken-Caryl Ranch Denver CO 80217

MCKINNEY, JOSEPH CRESCENT, bishop; b. Grand Rapids, Mich., Sept. 10, 1928; s. Joseph Crescent and Antoinette (Theisen) McK.; student Seminaire de Philosophie, Montreal, Can., 1948-50; S.T.L., Collegio di Propaganda Fide, Rome, Italy, 1954. Ordained priest Roman Catholic Ch., 1953; high sch. prof. St. Joseph Sem., Grand Rapids, 1954-62; asst. pastor Sacred Heart Parish, Mt. Pleasant, Mich., 1962-65; pastor St. Francis Parish, Conklin, Mich., 1965-68; asst. chancellor Diocese of Grand Rapids, 1965-68; pastor St. Andrew Cathedral, Grand Rapids, 1968-69; ordained aux. bishop Grand Rapids, 1968; vicar gen. Diocese of Grand Rapids, 1968—; adminstr. Sede Vacante 1969; pastor St. Stephen's Ch., Grand Rapids, 1971-77, Sacred Heart Parish, Muskegon Hts., Mich., 1977—. Address: 150 E Summit St Muskegon Heights MI 49444

MCKINNEY, JOSEPH F., corp. exec.; b. Phila., 1931; B.S., St. Joseph's Coll., 1952; M.B.A., Harvard U., 1957; married. Mgr. Phila. research dept. Reynolds & Co., 1957-59; dir. research Warner, Jenkins, Mandel & Longstreth, 1959-60; founder, pres. ElectroSci. Investors Inc., Richardson, Tex., 1960-63; v.p. Brown, Allen & Co., 1963-64; dir. corporate fin. Ling & Co., 1964-65, Goodbody & Co., 1965-66; now pres., chief exec. officer, chmn. bd. Tyler Corp. (formerly Saturn Industries, Inc.), also dir. Home: 8601 Jourdan Way Dallas TX 75225 Office: Tyler Corp Southland Center Dallas TX 75201

MCKINNEY, LUTHER CASWELL, lawyer, food co. exec.; b. Dallas Center, Iowa, June 29, 1931; s. S. and Avis Florence (Dietrich) McK.; B.S. in Econs., Iowa State U., 1953; LL.B., U. Ill., 1959; m. Gloria Edson, July 22, 1950; children—Karyn Kay, Scott Edson, Beth Ann. Admitted to Ill. bar, 1959; pvt. practice, Chgo., 1959-73; sr. v.p. law, corp. sec. Quaker Oats Co., Chgo., 1974—. Served with AUS, 1953-55. Mem. Am., Ill., Chgo. bar assns. Lutheran. Clubs: Mid Day, Metropolitan (Chgo.). Home: 6119 N Route 47 Hebron IL 60034 Office: Quaker Oats Co Merchandise Mart Plaza Chicago IL 60654

MC KINNEY, MONTGOMERY NELSON, advt. exec.; b. Chgo., June 20, 1910; s. William Ayer and Roberta (Montgomery) McK.; B.A., Oberlin Coll., 1934; m. Virginia Dickey, Nov. 2, 1957; children by previous marriage—Jane (Mrs. Gordon M. McDonald), William; children—Beth, Robert. Sales, sales promotion, advt., treas. Kitchen Art Foods, Inc., Chgo., 1934-40; v.p. Earle Ludgin & Co., Chgo., 1940-55; account supr. Leo Burnett Co., Inc., 1956; v.p. Doyle-Dane Bernbach, Inc., Los Angeles, 1957-69, sr. v.p. client services, 1969-75; exec. v.p., dir. client services Chiat/Day, Inc., Los Angeles, 1975-76, chmn. bd., 1976—; faculty Inst. Advanced Advt. Studies, 1964-68. Chmn. campaign Winnetka (Ill.) Community Chest, 1950, pres., 1952. Trustee John Thomas Dye Sch., Bel Air, Calif., 1966-75, pres., 1973-75; trustee Oberlin Coll., 1971—. Served to lt. USNR, 1944-46. Mem. Am. Assn. Advt. Agys. (gov. So. Calif. council 1972-76, sec.-treas. 1972, vice chmn. 1973, chmn. 1974-75). Methodist (trustee, vice-chmn.). Clubs: Riviera Country (Pacific Palisades, Calif.), Los Angeles Athletic. Home: 11496 Orum Rd Bel Air Los Angeles CA 90049 Office: 517 S Olive St Los Angeles CA 90013

MCKINNEY, PETER STARKWEATHER, univ. dean; b. South Bend, Ind., Apr. 29, 1931; s. Charles F. and Mildred (Brown) McK.; m. Sylvia Sanborn, June 10, 1953; children—Pamela, Peter, Andrew, Alec. Chemist, asso. dean div. applied scis. Grad. Sch., Harvard U., Cambridge, Mass., 1973—. Served with USAF, 1953-57. Home: 11 Glenn Rd Belmont MA 02176 Office: Div Applied Scis Harvard U Cambridge MA 02138

MC KINNEY, ROBERT HURLEY, lawyer, bus. exec.; b. Indpls., Nov. 7, 1925; s. E. Kirk and Irene (Hurley) McK.; B.S., U.S. Naval Acad., 1946; J.D., Ind. U., 1951; m. Arlene Frances Allsopp, Nov. 28, 1951; children—Robert, Marni, Kevin, Kent, Lisa. Admitted to Ind. bar, 1951, since practiced in Indpls.; sr. partner Bose McKinney & Evans, 1963—; pres., chmn. bd. Jefferson Corp. and subs.'s, Indpls., 1961-70; chmn. First Fed. Savs. & Loan Assn. Indpls., 1961—; chmn. Fed. Home Loan Bank Bd., 1977-79; dir. Baker, McHenry & Welch, Inc., Jefferson Nat. Life Ins. Co. Bd. dirs. Indpls. Legal Aid Soc., Children's Mus. Indpls.; bd. dirs., mem. exec. com. Brebeuf Prep. Sch., 1970—; trustee Indpls. Community Hosp.; trustee, chmn. fin. com. Marian Coll., Indpls.; del. Democratic Nat. Conv., 1968, 76. Served to lt. comdr. USNR, 1946-49, 51-53. Mem. Am., Ind., Indpls. bar assns., Young Pres.'s Orgn. (nat. chmn. for econ. edn. 1968-69, pres. Ind. chpt. 1973-74). Office: Jefferson Corp One Virginia Ave Indianapolis IN 46204

MCKINNEY, ROBERT MOODY, newspaper pub.; b. Shattuck, Okla., Aug. 28, 1910; s. Edwin S. and Eva (Moody) McK.; A.B., U. Okla., 1932; LL.D., U. N.Mex., 1964; m. Louise Trigg, Apr. 30, 1943; 1 dau., Robin; m. 2d, Marie-Louise de Montmollin, May 7, 1970. Editor, pub. Santa Fe New Mexican; chmn. The New Mexican, Inc. and Taos Pub. Corp.; dir. Martin Marietta Corp., Martin Marietta Aluminum Corp., Surveyor Fund, Inc., Trans World Airlines. Pres. Robert Moody Found.; chmn. N.Mex. Econ. Devel. Commn. and Water Resources Devel. Bd., 1949-51; asst. sec. of Interior, 1951-52; chmn. panel to report to Congress on the Impact of the Peaceful Uses Atomic Energy, 1955-56; permanent U.S. rep. Internat. Atomic Energy Agy., Vienna, 1957-58; U.S. rep. 2d Internat. Conf. Peaceful Uses Atomic Energy, Geneva, 1958; U.S. ambassador to Switzerland, 1961-63; exec. officer Presdl. Task Force Internat. Investments, 1963-64; chmn. bd. visitors U. Okla., 1968-72; U.S. rep. Internat. Centre Settlement Investment Disputes, Washington, 1967-74; chmn. Presdl. Commn. on Travel, 1968. Served from lt. (j.g.) to lt. USNR, 1942-45. Mem. Am. Soc. Newspaper Editors, Council Fgn. Relations, Am. Newspaper Pubs. Assn., Phi Beta Kappa, Phi Gamma Delta. Democrat. Episcopalian. Clubs: Chevy Chase, F Street, Metropolitan (Washington); University, Brook, Century, Links, River (N.Y.C.). Author: Hymn to Wreckage: A Picaresque Interpretation of History, 1947, The Scientific Found. for European Integration, 1959; On Increasing Effectiveness of Western Sci. and Technology, 1959; The Red Challenge to Technological Renewal, 1960; Review of the International Atomic Policies and Programs of the United States, 1960. Home: Wind Fields Route 1 Box 64 Middleburg VA 22117 Office: PO Box 1705 Santa Fe NM 87501

MCKINNEY, ROSS ERWIN, educator; b. San Antonio, Aug. 2, 1926; s. Roy Earl and Beatrice (Saylor) McK.; B.A., So. Meth. U., 1948, B.S. in Civil Engring., 1948; S.M., Mass. Inst. Tech., 1949, Sc.D., 1951; m. Margaret McKinney Curtis, June 21, 1952; children—Ross Erwin, Margaret E., William S., Susanne C. San. scientist S.W. Found. for Research and Edn., San Antonio, 1951-53; asst. prof. Mass. Inst. Tech., 1953-58, asso. prof., 1958-60; prof. U. Kans., 1960-63, chmn. dept. civil engring., 1963-66, Parker prof. civil engring., 1966-76, N.T. Veatch prof. environ. engring., 1976—; v.p. Rolf Eliassen Assos., Winchester, Mass., 1954-60; pres. Environ. Pollution Control Services, Lawrence, Kans., 1969-73. Mem. Cambridge (Mass.) Water Bd., 1953-59, Lawrence-Douglas County Health Bd., 1969-76, Kans. Water Quality Adv. Council, 1965-76, Kans. Solid Waste Adv. Council, 1970-76, Kans. Environ. Adv. Bd., 1976—. Served with USNR, 1943-46. Recipient Harrison P. Eddy award, 1962, Water Pollution Control Fedn. Rudolph Hering award, 1964; U.S. Presdl. Commendation, 1971. Mem. ASCE, Am. Water Works Assn., Am. Pub. Works Assn., Am. Chem. Soc., Am. Soc. Microbiologists, AAAS, Am. Soc. Engring. Edn., Kans. Water Pollution Control Assn., Nat. Acad. Engring., N.Y. Acad. Sci., AAUP, Sigma Xi, Sigma Tau, Kappa Mu Epsilon, Chi Epsilon, Tau Beta Pi. Author: Microbiology for Sanitary Engineers, 1962. Editor Nat. Conf. on Solid Waste Research, 1964, 2d Internat. Symposium for Waste Treatment Lagoons, 1970. Patentee water treatment process. Home: 2617 Oxford Rd Lawrence KS 66044

MCKINNEY, STEWART B., congressman; b. Pitts., Jan. 30, 1931; grad. Kent Sch., 1949; student Princeton, 1949-51; B.A. in Am. History, Yale, 1958; m. Lucie Cunningham; children—Stewart B., Lucie, Jean, Libby, John. Mem. Conn. Ho. of Reps., 1966-70, minority leader, 1969-70; mem. 92d-93d congresses from Conn., 94th-96th Congresses from 4th Conn. Dist. Bd. dirs. Bridgeport (Conn.) Hosp., Bridgeport Child Guidance Clinic, Rehab. Center of Eastern Fairfield County. Served to sgt. USAF, 1951-55. Mem. Fairfield C. of C. (past v.p.). Republican. Club: Rotary. Address: 106 Cannon House Office Bldg Washington DC 20515*

MCKINNEY, THEOPHILUS ELISHA, bus. exec.; b. Charlotte, N.C., Jan. 20, 1933; s. Theophilus Elisha and Martha (Lloyd) McK.; A.B. cum laude in govt. and legal studies, Bowdoin Coll., 1954; A.M., Fletcher Sch. Law and Diplomacy (Tufts-Harvard), 1955, M.A. in Law and Diplomacy, 1957, Ph.D., 1963; m. Sarah Louise Evans, Aug. 17, 1957; children—Marie Alessandria, Margaret Celeste, Theophilus Elisha III, Linda Maureen. Instr. govt. Carver Coll., Charlotte, N.C., 1955-56, Tufts U., Medford, Mass., 1957-58; asso. prof. polit. sci. Fla. A. and M. U., Tallahassee, 1959-61; prof., chmn. dept. polit. sci. Southern U., Baton Rouge, 1961-65; prof. polit. sci. Sarah Lawrence Coll., 1968-69; exec. asso. Edn. and World Affairs, N.Y.C., 1965-69; v.p. for acad. affairs Howard U., Washington, 1969-70; dir. instl. services United Negro Coll. Fund, N.Y.C., 1970-75, chmn. premed. policy rev. and planning com., 1971-75, exec. sec. instl. services com., 1971, dir. Nat. Conf. Edn., 1974; pres. Research Industries, Pleasantville and White Plains, N.Y., Wilmington, Del., 1966—, chmn., 1974—; acad. dean, prof. history, polit. sci. Del. State Coll., Dover, 1975-78; pres. Forest Industries, Inc., Dover, 1978—; dir. Triple A Enterprises, Inc.; sr. cons. Phelps-Stokes Fund Mgmt. Devel. Survey, 1971-72, chmn. task force on study new occupations related to environment and ecology Phelps Stokes Fund, 1972; mem. Congl. Black Caucus Adv. Panel on Higher Edn., 1973-75; cons. numerous assns., colls., founds., govt. agys. and univs. U.S. and abroad. Guest lectr. U. Rangoon (Burma), 1958-59. Mem. N.Y. State Civil Service Bd. Examiners, 1974—. Mem. commn. on liberal learning Assn. Am. Colls., 1973-76; mem. adv. com. on Ralph Bunche awards UN Assn., 1973; mem. fathers' council Marymount Secondary Sch., Tarrytown, N.Y., 1972—, pres., 1975-76; mem. fathers' assn. Hackley Sch., Tarrytown, 1971-75, bd. dirs., 1973-75; mem. adv. com., research and resources div. NIH, 1971-72; mem. adv. com. Coll. Service Bur., 1971-72; mem. nat. bicentennial steering com. Assn. Study Afro-Am. Life and History, 1974-76; nat. health manpower adv. com. Nat. Med. Assn., 1974. Bd. dirs. Va. Community Devel. Orgn., 1970—, UN Assn., N.Y.C., 1969-70, Carver Center, White Plains, N.Y., 1968-69, Westchester (N.Y.) Legal Services, 1967-70, Pkwy. Homes Civic Assn., White Plains, 1967-69, Pleasantville (N.Y.) Fair Housing Com., 1966-67, Friends Fletcher Sch. Law and Diplomacy, 1973—, Nat. Assn. So. Poor, 1977—; bd. govs. Nat. Enquiry on Scholarly Communication, Am. Council Learned Socs., 1975—; chmn. bd. dirs. Del. Program for Minority Engrs., 1977-78, City of Refuge Farm, 1978—, Community Concerts Assn. Kent County, 1977—; chmn. steering com. Jacob Smith Meml. Trust. bd. dirs., steering com. Human Relations Council, Baton Rouge. Served to lt. AUS, 1954-55. Recipient Philo Sherman Bennett award, 1954. Bowdoin Alumni Fund scholar, also Edwards Fund scholar, 1950-54; Danforth fellow, 1954-58; Fulbright Research scholar, U. Rangoon (Burma), 1958-59; Danforth teaching fellow, 1958—; recipient Nathan W. Collier award meritorious and outstanding service Fla. Meml. Coll., St. Augustine, 1968. Fellow Soc. for Values in Higher Edn. (dir. 1970—); mem. Am. Acad. Polit. and Social Sci., Am. Econ. Assn., Am. Mgmt. Assn., Am. Polit. Sci. Assn., Am. Assn. for Higher Edn., Assn. for Study of Afro-Am. Life and History, Burma Research Soc., Internat. Platform Assn., Internat. Studies Assn., Ops. Research Soc. Am., NEA, Soc. Gen. Systems Research, World Future Soc., Common Cause, Met. Opera Guild, Greater Dover C. of C., Delta Sigma, Kappa Delta Pi, Pi Gamma Mu, Phi Alpha Theta, Omega Psi Phi. Presbyn. (ruling elder 1964—). Clubs: Bowdoin, Williams (N.Y.); Gov.'s Thursday Morning Breakfast (Dover). Author: The Black Revolt and the Student Revolt in Perspective, 1970; The Financial Problems of Private Negro Colleges, 1971; The Future of Black Higher Education, 1972; Management Data Collection and Analysis for Higher Education, 1972; The Expenditures of the United Negro College Fund Member Colleges, 1973; Student Financial Aid, 1973. Contbr. articles to profl. jours. Home: 726 Forest St Dover DE 19901 Office: Office of Pres Forest Industries Inc Dover DE 19901

MC KINNEY, THOMAS EARL, broadcasting exec.; b. Summerlee, W.Va., Aug. 24, 1942; s. Samuel and Louise (Wilder) McK.; B.S. in Mgmt., Fairfield (Conn.) U., 1972; M.B.A., Fordham U., 1976; m. Frances Elizabeth Maupin, Aug. 22, 1969; children—Thomas Earl, Nicole Elizabeth, Anthony Louis. Account exec. Westinghouse Broadcasting Co., 1972-76; v.p., gen. mgr. Sheridan Broadcasting Network, Washington, 1976-78, pres., Pitts., 1978—. Trustee, Fairfield U. Served with AUS, 1959-66. Mem. Nat. Assn. Broadcasters (dir.), M.B.A. Assn., Alumni Assn. Fordham U., Fairfield U. Alumni Assn. Office: 1811 Blvd of Allied Pittsburgh PA 15219

MC KINNON, ALAN LEO, banker; b. Boston, Feb. 13, 1928; s. Frederic W. and Helen L. (Cunningham) McK.; B.S. in Bus. Adminstrn., Boston U., 1950; student Bentley Coll., Columbia Grad. Bus. Sch.; m. Eleanor Hannigan, Aug. 13, 1955; children—Alan Leo, Brian, Ian. Pub. accountant Alexander, Grant & Co. (formerly Patterson, Teele & Dennis), Boston, 1953-61; tax and ins. mgr. United-Carr, Inc., Boston, 1961-69; sr. v.p. 1st Nat. Bank Boston, 1973—; v.p., comptroller First Nat. Boston Corp., 1972—; comptroller, dir. Bank of Boston Internat., N.Y.C., 1971—, Bank of Boston Internat., Miami, 1972—, Boston Overseas Financial Corp., 1971—, Bank of Boston Internat., Los Angeles, First of Boston Computeristics, Inc.; dir. Mortgage Corp. of the South, FNBC Acceptance Corp., Birmingham, Ala., Caribbean Am. Service Investment and Finance Co. Ltd. Bd. dirs., treas. Milton Hosp.; mem. Town Meeting, Milton, 1971—. Served with USNR, 1946-47. C.P.A., Mass. Mem. Fin. Execs. Inst., Tax Execs. Inst., Mass. Soc. C.P.A.'s. Clubs: Federal; Milton-Hoosic, Milton Town. Home: 12 Longwood Rd Milton MA 02187 Office: PO Box 2016 Boston MA 02106

MC KINNON, ALASTAIR THOMSON, educator; b. Hillsburgh, Ont., Can., May 25, 1925; s. Arnold Thomson and Ella (McKinnon) McK.; B.A., Victoria Coll., 1947; M.A., U. Toronto, 1948; Ph.D., Edinburgh (Scotland), 1950; B.D., McGill U., 1953; m. Mildred Mae Sutton, Sept. 13, 1947; children—Catherine, Christine, Angus. Mem. faculty McGill U., 1950—, lectr., 1950-53, asst. prof. philosophy, 1953-60, asso. prof., 1960-69, prof., 1969-71, MacDonald prof. moral philosophy, 1971—, chmn. dept., 1975—, mem. senate, 1976-79; hon. fellow Inst. for Advanced Studies in Humanities, U. Edinburgh, 1972-73. Served with Royal Canadian Navy, 1944-45. Rockefeller travelling fellow, 1961-62. Mem. Can. (pres. 1979-80), Am. philos. assns., Canadian Theol. Soc., Kierkegaard Akademiet. Mem. United Ch. of Can. Author: Kierkegaard in Translation/ en Traduction/ in Ubersetzung, 1970; Falsification and Belief, 1970; Fundamental Polygot Konkordans til Kierkegaards Samlede Vaerker, 1971; Ausgewählte Konkordanz zu Wittgensteins Philosophischen Untersuchungen, 1971; Index Verborum til Kierkegaards Samlede Vaerker, 1973; Computational Analysis of Kiekegaard's Samlede Vaerker, 1975; (with Hans Kaal) Concordance to Wittgenstein's Philosophischen Untersuchungen, 1975. Home: 3005 Barat Rd Montreal PQ H3Y 2H4 Canada

MC KINNON, ALLAN BRUCE, Canadian govt. ofcl.; b. Canora, Sask., Can., Jan. 11, 1917; s. Peter MacDonald and Belle (Stewart) McK.; student U. Victoria; m. Joan Elizabeth Menzies, Oct. 2, 1947; children—Ian Bruce, Peter Menzies. Served with Can. Army, ret., 1965; sch. tchr., 1965-72; trustee Greater Victoria Sch. Bd., 1968-70, chmn., 1970-72; mem. Parliament, 1972—; now minister nat. def. and vets. affairs. Decorated Mil. Cross. Mem. United Services Inst., Can. Legion. Progressive Conservative. Mem. United Ch. Can. Address: House of Commons Ottawa ON K1A 0A7 Canada*

MCKINNON, CLINTON D., editor, former congressman; b. Dallas, Feb. 5, 1906; s. John C. and Tennie Clifdell (Hawkins) McK.; A.B., U. Redlands (Calif.), 1930, L.H.D., 1967; postgrad. U. Geneva (Switzerland), 1930; m. Lucille Virginia McVey, Oct. 15, 1932; children—Clinton Dan, Michael, Connie. Reporter, editor, advt. mgr. on various So. Calif. newspapers, 1931-35; pres., gen. mgr. Valley News Corp., North Hollywood, Calif., 1935-43, established San Fernando Valley Times, 1935, Los Angeles Aircraft Times, 1940, Long Beach Shipyard Times, 1941; established San Diego Daily Jour., 1944, editor, pub. and owner, 1946-48; co-owner Coronado Jour., 1953-72, owner Radio Sta. KSDJ, Columbia affiliate, San Diego, 1945-48; pres., editor and pub. Los Angeles Daily News, 1954; pres., gen. mgr. Alvarado Television Co., Inc., KVOA-TV, Tucson and KOAT-TV, Albuquerque, 1955-63; chmn. San Diego North Shores Pub. Co., San Diego, 1953-72, Sentinel Savs. and Loan Assn., 1963-69, San Diego Transit Co., 1966-71; sec. South Tex. Telecasting Co. Inc. Chmn. Indsl. Devel. Commn., San Diego, 1964-66, Econ. Devel. Corp. San Diego County, 1966-67, San Diego Urban Coalition, 1967-69; mem. Gov.'s Bus. Adv. Council, Calif. Mem. 81st-82d congresses from Calif.; vice chmn. Democratic State Central Com. of Calif., 1952-54. Recipient San Diego Golden Man and Boy award, 1968; San Diego Mayor's award of merit, 1971. Rotarian. Club: San Diego Yacht. Home: 1125 Pacific Beach Dr Apt 401 San Diego CA 92109 Office: 1023 Grand St San Diego CA 92109. *I believe in the Golden Rule, and that service to mankind brings the highest rewards, both in personal happiness and material success.*

MC KINNON, CLINTON DAN, broadcasting exec.; b. San Bernardino, Calif., Jan. 27, 1934; s. Clinton Dotson and Lucille V. (McVey) McK.; B.A., U. Mo., 1956; children—Holly Jean, Sherri Lynn, Clinton Scott. Page boy U.S. Ho. of Reps., 1950-52; reporter, photographer, advt. salesman Sentinel Newspaper, San Diego, 1960-62; owner, pres. KSON Radio, San Diego, 1962—, KSON-FM, San Diego, 1964—; pub. La Jolla (Calif.) Light Jour., 1969-73; owner House of Hits, music pub., San Diego, 1972—, KIII-TV, Corpus Christi, Tex., 1964—, KBMT-TV, Beaumont, Tex., 1976—. Co-chmn. San Diego County Com. to Re-elect the Pres.; chmn. Californians for Lower Taxes; mem. exec. com. Republican State Central Com.; v.p. Rep. Assos.; alt. del. Rep. Nat. Conv., 1972; chmn. various congressional and city council races in San Diego; chmn. exec. com. Greater San Diego Billy Graham Crusade; bd. dirs. Youth for Christ; mem. adv. com. San Diego City Coll., Mesa Coll.; mem. Gov. Calif. Consumer Adv. Council; trustee Boys' Clubs San Diego; bd. dirs. Religious Youth Found. Served as aviator USNR, 1956-60. Set Navy helicopter rescue record, 1958; recipient Advt. Man of Year award San Diego Advt. and Sales Club, 1971; Radio Sta. Mgr. of Year award Billboard Mag., 1973; Good Guys award Leukemia Soc., 1973; Internat. Pres.'s award Youth for Christ, 1975; Man of Distinction award Mexican-Am. Found., 1976; Pub. Interest award Nat. Safety Council, 1976; George Washington Honor medal Freedoms Found., 1976. Mem. Country Music Assn. (pres.), C. of C. (dir.), Calif. Broadcasters Assn. (dir.), San Diego Advt. and Sales Club, Navy League. Club: Rotary (San Diego). Author: The Good Life, 1974. Office: KSON Radio College Grove Center San Diego CA 92115

MC KINNON, FRANCIS ARTHUR RICHARD, utility exec.; b. Delburne, Alta., Can., Mar. 5, 1933; s. John Donald and Ruth Rebecca (Sundberg) McK.; B. Commerce, U. Alta., 1954; m. Elma Lorraine Lebsack, June 1, 1957; children—Kenneth Richard, Stephen David, Karen Diane. With Alta. Gas Trunk Line Co. Ltd., Calgary, 1960-75, treas., 1971-75; dir. fin. Calgary Power Ltd., 1975—, treas., 1976—; dir. AEC Power Ltd. Bd. dirs. Foothills Gen. Hosp., Calgary. Mem. Canadian Inst. Chartered Accountants, Inst. Chartered Accountants Alta., Fin. Execs. Inst. Can. (dir. Calgary chpt.). Clubs: Calgary Petroleum, Canyon Meadows Golf and Country. Home: 1412 Windsor St Calgary AB T2N 3X3 Canada Office: 110 12th Ave SW Calgary AB T2P 2M1 Canada

MCKINNON, GEORGE EDMUND, journalist; b. Providence, Apr. 16, 1921; s. George Linus and Ann Marie (Sheridan) McK.; A.B., Boston Coll., 1943. With Boston Globe, 1943—, movie and theater critic, 1964-73, theater/arts columnist Marquee, 1973—. Roman Catholic. Home: 151 Tremont St 20C Boston MA 02111 Office: Boston Globe 135 Morrissey Blvd Boston MA 02107

MCKINNON, MICHAEL D., state legislator, TV broadcasting co. exec.; b. Los Angeles, June 12, 1939; s. Clinton D. and Lucille V. (Mevey) McK.; student Redlands U., 1957-59, Harvard Grad. Sch. Bus., 1968; m. Mar. 1962 (div. Dec. 1970); children—Michael Dean, Mark Daniel; m. 2d, Sandra Elaine Spickerman Gillis, May 1973. Photo editor N. Shore Sentinel, San Diego, 1957-59; pub. La Jolla (Calif.) Jour., 1962-64; co-owner KSON Radio, San Diego, 1962—; TV dir. KOAT-TV, Albuquerque, 1960-62; pres., gen. mgr. KIII-TV, Corpus Christi, Tex., 1964—. Mem. Tex. Senate. Mem. adv. council U. Tex. Sch. Communication, Austin, 1970—; mem. Com. of 100, Corpus Christi, 1969—, Urban Coalition Council, Corpus Christi, 1968—, Corpus Christi Arts Council, 1967—, Corpus Christi Tourist Bur., 1967—, S. Tex. Planned Parenthood League, 1967—; chmn. communications div. United Fund, 1969. Mem. Tex. Senate, 1973—. Bd. dirs. Salvation Army, Robert L. Moore Community Bur. Recipient Presdl. commendation for outstanding service to community following Hurricane Celia, 1971; named Outstanding Young Man of Year, Corpus Christi Jr. C. of C., 1971; Boss of Year, Coastal Bend chpt. Nat. Secs. Assn., 1971. Mem. Tex. (pres. 1971), Nat. assns. broadcasters, Broadcast Promotion Assn., Am. Advt. Fedn., Corpus Christi Ad Club, Television Bur. Advertisers, ABC Affiliates Orgn. Home: 4750 S Padre Island Dr Corpus Christi TX 78412 Office: PO Box 6669 Corpus Christi TX 78411

MCKIRAHAN, ROBERT ROY, aerospace co. exec.; b. Mt. Pleasant, Iowa, July 30, 1926; s. Joseph Ralph and Frieda Helen (Schumann) McK.; B.S., U. Iowa, 1949; m. Joan Elizabeth Smith, Aug. 31, 1947; children—Mark, Stephen (dec.), David, Paul, John. Accountant, asst. office mgr. J.C. White Co., Des Moines, 1949-50; indsl. engr. Hughes Aircraft Co., Culver City, Calif., 1954-55; dir. fin. ops. Lockheed Missiles & Space Co., Sunnyvale, Calif., 1955-72; v.p. fin. and adminstrn. Lockheed-Calif. Co., Burbank, Calif., 1972-75; v.p., treas. Lockheed Aircraft Corp., Burbank, 1975—. Served with U.S. Army, 1945-47, 50-52. Mem. Fin. Execs. Inst. Club: Oakmont Country (Glendale, Calif.). Home: 15761 Royal Ridge Rd Sherman Oaks CA 91403 Office: 2555 N Hollywood Way PO Box 551 Burbank CA 91520

MCKITRICK, ERIC LOUIS, historian, educator; b. Battle Creek, Mich., July 5, 1919; s. Fred Louis and Colleen (Hodges) McK.; B.S., Columbia, 1949, M.A., 1951, Ph.D., 1959; m. Edyth Carol Stevenson, Dec. 26, 1946; children—Frederick Louis II, Enid Lael, Charles Keith, Mary Caroline. Asst. prof. history U. Chgo., 1955-59; asst. prof. history Douglass Coll., Rutgers U., 1955-60; asso. prof. history Columbia, 1960-65, prof., 1965—; Pitt prof. Am. history and instns. Cambridge (Eng.) U., 1973-74; Harmsworth prof. Am. history Oxford

(Eng.) U., 1979-80. Served with AUS, 1941-45. Recipient Dunning prize Am. Hist. Assn., 1960. Ford Found. fellow, 1957-58; Rockefeller Found. fellow, 1962-63; Nat. Endowment for Humanities fellow, 1967-68; Guggenheim Found. fellow, 1970-71, 76-77. Fellow Am. Philos. Soc., Am. Council Learned Socs. Club: Century (N.Y.C.). Author: Andrew Johnson and Reconstruction, 1960; Slavery Defended: Views of the Old South 1963; Andrew Johnson: A Profile, 1969; The Hofstadter Aegis: A Memorial, 1974. Office: Grad Sch Arts and Scis Columbia U New York NY 10027

MCKNEW, THOMAS WILLSON, assn. exec.; b. Washington, July 6, 1896; s. Thomas Willson and Bertha Virginia (Fisher) McK.; D.Eng. (hon.), S.D. Sch. Mines and Tech., 1935; m. Virginia Chauncey Paff, Jan. 15, 1921 (dec. Sept. 1976); m. 2d, Lenore Knight Williams, Nov. 23, 1977. Constrn. engr. and v.p. James Baird Co., Inc., Washington (notable bldgs. include U.S. Internal Revenue Bldg., Washington, Folger Shakespeare Library, Washington, State Office Bldg., Charleston, W.Va., State Office Bldg., Harrisburg, Pa., R.J. Reynolds Tobacco Co. Office Bldg., Winston-Salem, N.C., Corcoran Gallery of Art, Washington, 1924-31; asso. with Nat. Geog. Soc., Washington, 1931—, asst. sec., 1932-45, sec., 1945, life trustee, 1949, became v.p., sec., 1955, exec. v.p., sec., 1958-62, vice chmn. bd., 1962-66, chmn. bd., 1966-67, adv. chmn. bd., 1967—. Recipient Distinguished Pub. Service awards U.S. Navy, 1957, 78; Exceptional Service award USAF, 1965. Episcopalian. Clubs: Chevy Chase Country, Alfalfa, Metropolitan, Alibi (Washington); Bohemian (San Francisco). Home: 4936 Lowell St Washington DC 20016 Office: 1145 17th St NW Washington DC 20036

MCKNIGHT, COLBERT AUGUSTUS, newspaper exec.; b. Shelby, N.C., Aug. 19, 1916; s. John Samuel and Norva (Proctor) McK.; B.S., Davidson Coll. 1938, LL.D., 1977; LL.D., Colby Coll., 1965; m. Margaret Henderson, Mar. 19, 1941 (div.); children—John Peter, Margaret C., David P.; m. 2d, Gail Oliver Ehle, Oct. 30, 1968; 1 dau., Colby A. Reporter, Charlotte (N.C.) News, 1939-42, news editor, 1944-48, mng. editor, 1948-49, editor, 1949- 54; editor San Juan (P.R.) World Jour., war corr. A.P., 1942-44; exec. dir. So. Edn. Reporting Service, 1954-55, mem. bd., 1954-69, chmn. bd., 1963-65; editor Charlotte Observer, 1955-76, asso. pub., 1976-78; dir. Knight Pub. Co. Pres., N.C. Fund, 1963-65. Bd. dirs. Civil Rights Documentation Project, Race Relations Information Center. Recipient Elijah Parish Lovejoy award Colby Coll., 1965. Mem. Am. Soc. Newspaper Editors (pres. 1972, project dir. 1977—), Nat., N.C. confs. editorial writers. Presbyn. Home: 1627 Beverly Dr Charlotte NC 28207 Office: 600 S Tryon St Charlotte NC 28202

MC KNIGHT, JOHN LACY, educator; b. Monroe, Mich., Sept. 13, 1931; s. Joseph Daniel and Esther (Lacy) McK.; A.B., U. Mich., 1953; M.S., Yale, 1954, Ph.D., 1957; m. Joyce Nunn, May 30, 1964; 1 son, Andrew. Mem. Faculty Coll. William and Mary, 1957—, prof. physics, 1968—. Pres. Va. Wilderness Com., 1969-70; bd. dirs. Conservation Council Va., 1969-71; trustee Va. chpt. Nature Conservancy, 1971-78, chmn. bd., 1975-77. Mem. Am. Phys. Soc., AAAS, Philosophy of Sci. Assn., History of Sci. Soc., Soc. History of Tech., Phi Beta Kappa, Sigma Xi, Phi Kappa Phi. Home: 701 College Terr Williamsburg VA 23185

MCKNIGHT, ROBERT KELLOGG, educator; b. Sendai, Japan, Jan. 10, 1924; s. William Quay and Mary (Kellogg) McK. (parents Am. citizens); B.A. cum laude in Psychology, Miami U., Oxford, Ohio, 1951; M.A. in Social Psychology, Ohio State U., 1954, Ph.D. in Anthropology, 1960; m. Veronica Margaret Schwartz, Nov. 7, 1947; children—William K., Victoria (Mrs. Timothy Labarge). Dist. anthropologist Trust Ter. Govt., Palau, Micronesia, 1958-63, community devel. officer, Saipan, Micronesia, 1963-65; asso. prof. anthropology U. Wis.-Milw., 1965-66; prof. anthropology Calif. State U., Hayward, 1966—, chmn. dept., 1969-74. Served with AUS, 1943-46, 51-52. Mem. Am., Southwestern anthrop. assns., Soc. Applied Anthropology, Am. Ethnol. Soc., Assn. Social Anthropology in Oceania, Internat. House (Japan), Volunteers Internat. Tech. Assistance. Author: (with J. Bennett and H. Passin) In Search of Identity, 1960. Contbr. profl. jours. Home: 25681 Barnard St Hayward CA 94545

MCKNIGHT, TOM LEE, geographer, educator; b. Dallas, Oct. 8, 1928; s. Alva Frank and Mary Wacil (Dees) McK.; B.A., So. Meth. U., 1949; M.A., U. Colo., 1950; Ph.D., U. Wis., 1955; m. Marian Lee Anderson, Sept. 5, 1953; children—Thomas Clinton, Jill Suzanne. Instr. geography So. Meth. U., 1953-55, U. Tex., 1955-56; asst. prof. geography UCLA, 1956-62, asso. prof., 1962-67, prof., 1967—. Mem. Assn. Am. Geographers, Assn. Pacific Coast Geographers, Calif. Council Geog. Edn., Los Angeles Geog. Soc., Can. Assn. Geographers, Inst. Australian Geographers, Geog. Soc. New South Wales, New Zealand Geog. Soc. Methodist. Author: The Camel in Australia, 1969; Australia's Corner of the World: A Geographical Summation, 1970; Regional Geography of Anglo-America, 1979. Home: 3240 Tilden Ave Los Angeles CA 90034 Office: Univ of Calif Los Angeles CA 90024

MC KNIGHT, WILLIAM WARREN, JR., publisher; b. Normal, Ill., June 9, 1913; s. William Warren and Isabel Alida (Travis) McK.; B.S. in Bus. Adminstrn., Northwestern U., 1938; m. Alice McGuire, Oct. 30, 1937; children—William Warren, III, Michael Joe, John James. With McKnight Pub. Co., Bloomington, Ill., 1938—, sec.-treas., 1949-56, pres., 1956-67, chmn. bd., 1968-79; dir. Gen. Telephone Co. Ill., Bloomington Fed. Savs. & Loan Assn. Mem. Ill. Commn. Higher Edn., 1956-60; chmn. Bloomington-Normal Airport Authority, 1965-70; chmn. CETA Pvt. Industry Council Ill. Balance of State, 1979—. Served with USNR, 1942-46. Recipient Distinguished Service award Bloomington Kiwanis Club, 1963, Normal C. of C., 1973; Good Govt. award Bloomington Jaycees, 1970; Edn. Constrn. award Edn. Council Graphic Arts Industry, 1974, Distinguished Alumni award Ill. State U., 1978. Mem. Graphic Arts Edn. Assn., Am. Indsl. Arts Assn., Nat. Assn. Indsl. and Tech. Tchrs. Educators, Ill. C. of C. (dir. 1964-69), Ill. Mfrs. Assn. (dir. 1954-62). Republican. Presbyterian. Clubs: Coll. Alumni, Bloomington Country. Home: 401 W Vernon Ave Normal IL 61761 Office: 808 Eldorado Rd Bloomington IL 61701

MC KONE, DON T., corp. exec.; b. Jackson, Mich., 1921; grad. U. Mich., 1947. Pres., chief exec. officer, dir. Libbey-Owens-Ford Co., Toledo; dir. Ohio Citizens Trust Co., Hayes-Albion Corp., Consumers Power Co., Nat. Bank Detroit. Office: Libbey-Owens-Ford Co 811 Madison Ave Toledo OH 43695

MCKOWN, ROBERTA ELLEN, polit. scientist, educator; b. Endicott, N.Y., Mar. 26, 1932; d. Robert Edward and Rubina (Cunningham) McK.; B.A. in Econs., U. Oreg., 1953, M.A. in Polit. Sci., 1965, Ph.D., 1968; children—Bruce Koplin, Mara Koplin Everett, Therese Koplin. Inst., U. Oreg., 1967-68; asst. prof. polit. sci. U. Alta., Edmonton, 1968-72, asso. prof., 1972-77, prof., 1977—, chmn. dept., 1976—. Can. Council Research grantee, 1971-72. Mem. Am. Polit. Sci. Assn., Can. Polit. Sci. Assn., Royal African Soc., Can. African Studies Assn., Internat. Studies Assn. Contbr. articles to profl. jours. Home: 9110 116 St Edmonton AB T6G 1P9 Canada Office: Dept Polit Sci Univ of Alberta Edmonton AB Canada

MC KOY, BASIL VINCENT CHARLES, theoretical chemist, educator; b. Trinidad, W.I., Mar. 25, 1938; came to U.S., 1960, naturalized, 1973; s. Allan Cecil and Doris Augusta McK.; B.Chem. Eng., N.S. Tech. Coll., 1960; Ph.D. in Chemistry (Univ. fellow), Yale U., 1964; m. Anne Ellen Shannon, Mar. 18, 1967; 1 son, Christopher Allan. Instr. chemistry Calif. Inst. Tech., 1964-66, asst. prof. chemistry, 1966-69, asso. prof., 1969-75, prof. theoretical chemistry, 1975—; cons. Lawrence Livermore Lab., U. Calif., Livermore, 1964—; vis. prof. Max Planck Inst., Munich, Ger., 1976—, U. Paris, 1968—, U. Campinas (Brazil), 1976—. Recipient medal Gov.-Gen. Can., 1960; Alfred P. Sloan Found. fellow, 1969-73; Guggenheim fellow, 1973-74. Mem. Am. Phys. Soc. Contbr. articles to Phys. Rev., Jour. Chem. Physics, Jour. Physics (London), Chem. Physics Letters; bd. editors Jour. Chem. Physics, 1977-79. Home: 3855 Keswick Rd Flintridge CA 91011 Office: Div Chemistry Calif Inst Tech Pasadena CA 91125

MCKUEN, ROD, poet, composer, author, singer; b. Oakland, Calif., Apr. 29, 1933. Appeared in numerous films, TV, concerts; composer motion picture scores, background music for TV, modern classical music; pres. Stanyan Records, Discus Records, New Gramaphone Soc., Mr. Kelly Prodns., Montcalm Prodns., Stanyan Books, Cheval Books, Biplane Books, Rod McKuen Enterprises; v.p. Tamarack Books; dir. Animal Concern. Mem. adv. bd. Market Theatre, Johannesburg, S. Africa, Fund for Animals. Bd. dirs. Am. Nat. Theatre of Ballet; bd. govs. Nat. Acad. Rec. Arts and Scis. Recipient Grande Prix du Disc, Paris, 1966, Golden Globes award, 1969, Motion Picture Daily award, 1969; Grammy award best spoken album, 1969 Entertainer of Year award Los Angeles Shrine Club, 1975; Freedoms Found. award, 1975; Horatio Alger award, 1976; Emmy award, 1977; Humanitarian award 1st Amendment Soc., 1977; Carl Sandburg Poetry award, 1978. Mem. ASCAP, Writer's Guild, Internat. Platform Assn., AFTRA, AGVA (hon. v.p.). Composer—lyricist: Jean (Acad. award nominee 1969); If You Go Away; Seasons in the Sun; Ally, Ally, Oxen Free; Doesn't Anybody Know My Name; I Think of You; The Lovers; A Man Alone; Stanyan Street; The Single Man; We; Natalie; Champion Charlie Brown; A Boy Named Charlie Brown; Joanna; I'll Catch the Sun; Kaleidoscope; A Cat Named Sloopy; Everybody's Rich But Us; The Ivy that Clings to the Wall; Listen to the Warm; The Beautiful Strangers; The Ever Constant Sea; Without a Worry in the World; Soldiers Who Want to be Heroes; The World I Used to Know; Love's Been Good to Me; I'm Not Afraid; Pastures Green; The Loner; Bend Down and Touch Me; Amsterdam; Miles to Go; Mr. Kelly; I've Been to Town, others; composer classical works including Symphony No. One; Concerto for Guitar & Orchestra; Concerto for Four Harpsichords; Concert No. 3 for Piano and Orch.; Adagio for Harp and Strings; Piano Variations; The City (Pulitzer prize nominee 1973); I Hear Am. Singing; The Ballad of Distances; Concerto for Balloon and Orch.; Concerto for Cello and Orch.; ballet Rod McKuen's America, 1979; numerous commns. including Symphony #3 for Menninger Clinic's 50th Anniversary, 1975, also works for various orchs. Film scores include Joanna, 1968; The Prime of Miss Jean Brodie, 1969; Me, Natalie, 1969; A Boy Named Charlie Brown, 1970; Come to Your Senses, 1971; Scandalous John, 1971; Wildflowers, 1971; The Seagull, 1972; Lisa, Bright and Dark, 1973; The Borrowers, 1973; The Unknown War, 1978. Author: (poetry) And Autumn Came, 1954; Stanyan Street and Other Sorrows, 1966; Listen to the Warm, 1967; Twelve Years of Christmas, 1968; In Someone's Shadow, 1969; With Love, 1970; Caught in the Quiet, 1970; Moment to Moment, 1971; Fields of Wonder, 1971; The Carols of Christmas, 1971; And to Each Season, 1972; Beyond the Boardwalk, 1975; Come to Me in Silence, 1973; America-An Affirmation, 1974; Seasons in the Sun, 1974; Alone, Moment to Moment, 1974; The McKuen Omnibus, 1975; Celebrations of the Heart, 1975; The Sea Around Me: The Hills Above, 1976; Finding My Father, 1976; Hand in Hand . . ., 1977; Coming Close to the Earth, 1977; Love's Been Good to Me, 1979; We Touch the Sky, 1979. Home: PO Box G Beverly Hills CA 90213 Office: 8440 Santa Monica Blvd Los Angeles CA 90069

MC KUSICK, VICTOR ALMON, physician, geneticist, educator; b. Parkman, Maine, Oct. 21, 1921; s. Carroll L. and Ethel M. (Buzzell) McK.; student Tufts Coll., 1940-43; M.D., Johns Hopkins, 1946; D.Sc., N.Y. Med. Coll., 1974, U. Maine, 1978, Tufts U., 1978; M.D. (hon.), Liverpool U., 1976; Sc.D. (hon.), U. Rochester, 1979, Meml. U. Nfld., 1979; D.Med.Sc., Med. U. S.C., 1979; m. Anne Bishop, June 11, 1949; children—Carol Anne, Kenneth Andrew, Victor Wayne. Tng. in clin. medicine, lab. research Johns Hopkins, USPHS, 1946-52; instr. medicine Johns Hopkins Sch. Medicine, 1952-54, asst. prof., 1954-57, asso. prof., 1957-60, prof. medicine, 1960—, chief div. med. genetics, dept. medicine, 1957-73, prof. epidemiology, biology, 1969-78, William Osler prof. medicine, 1978—, chmn. dept. medicine, 1973—; physician-in-chief Johns Hopkins Hosp., 1973—. Mem. research adv. com. Nat. Found., 1959-78; mem. med. adv. bd. Howard Hughes Med. Inst.; pres. Internat. Med. Congress, Ltd., 1972-78; mem. Nat. Adv. Research Resources Council, 1970-74; mem. bd. sci. advisers Roche Inst. Molecular Biology, 1967-71. Recipient John Phillips award A.C.P., 1972; Gairdner Internat. award, 1977. Fellow Am. Acad. Orthopedic Surgeons (hon.), Royal Coll. Physicians (London); mem. Nat. Acad. Sci., Am. Philos. Soc., Am. Soc. Human Genetics (pres. 1974, Wm. A. Allan award 1977), Assn. Am. Physicians, Am. Soc. Clin. Investigation, Académie Nationale Médecine (France) (corr.), Phi Beta Kappa, Alpha Omega Alpha. Presbyn. Author: Heritable Disorders of Connective Tissue, 1956, 60, 66, 72; Cardiovascular Sound in Health and Disease, 1958; Medical Genetics 1958-60, 1961; Human Genetics, 1964, 69; On the X Chromosome of Man, 1964; Mendelian Inheritance in Man, 1966, 68, 71, 75, 78; (with others) Genetics of Hand Malformations, 1978; Medical Genetic Studies of the Amish, 1978. Editor textbook. Home: 221 Northway Baltimore MD 21218 Office: Johns Hopkins Hosp Baltimore MD 21205

MC KUSICK, VINCENT LEE, state chief justice; b. Parkman, Maine, Oct. 21, 1921; s. Carroll Lee and Ethel (Buzzell) McK.; A.B., Bates Coll., 1943; S.B., S.M., Mass. Inst. Tech., 1947; LL.B., Harvard U., 1950; LL.D., Colby Coll., 1976, Nasson Coll., 1978, Bates and Bowdoin colls., 1979; L.H.D., U. So. Maine, 1978; m. Nancy Elizabeth Green, June 23, 1951; children—Barbara Jane McKusick Liscord, James Emory, Katherine, Anne Elizabeth. Admitted to Maine bar, 1952; law clk. to Chief Judge Learned Hand, 1950-51, to Justice Felix Frankfurter, 1951-52; partner Pierce, Atwood, Scribner, Allen & McKusick and predecessors, Portland, Maine, 1953-77; chief justice Maine Supreme Jud. Ct., 1977—; mem. Supreme Jud. Ct. Adv. Com. Maine Rules of Civil Procedure, 1957-59, chmn., 1966-75; commr. on uniform state laws, 1968-76, sec. nat. conf., 1975-77. Trustee, Bates Coll.; mem. overseers vis. com. Harvard Law Sch.; past trustee Kent's Hill Sch., Maine Hist. Soc., Portland YMCA. Served with AUS, 1943-46; Manhattan Project, Los Alamos, 1945-46. Fellow Am. Bar. Found. (dir. 1977—); mem. Am. (chmn. fed. rules com. 1966-71, bd. editors Jour. 1971—, chmn. bd. editors 1976-77, mem. study group to China 1978), Maine, Cumberland County bar assns., Am. Judicature Soc. (dir. 1976-78), Am. Law Inst. (council 1968—), Maine Jud. Council (chmn. 1977—), Inst. Judicial Adminstrn., Supreme Ct. Hist. Soc., Phi Beta Kappa, Sigma Xi, Tau Beta Pi. Republican. Unitarian. Clubs: Rotary (hon.; past pres. Portland), Harvard of N.Y. Author: Patent Policy of Educational Institutions, 1947; (with Richard H. Field) Maine Civil Practice, 1959, supplements 1962, 67, (with Richard H. Field and L. Kinvin Wroth) 2d edit., 1970, supplements, 1972, 74, 77, also articles in legal publs. Home: 1152 Shore Rd Cape Elizabeth ME 04107 Office: Cumberland County Courthouse PO Box 4910 Portland ME 04112

MC LACHLAN, IAN, educator, author; b. London, Oct. 20, 1938; s. William Nicol and Agnes Johnston (McMartin) McL.; B.A., Oxford U., 1960, M.A., 1963; m. Dominique Françoise Isabelle, Sept. 21, 1960; children—Stéphane, Jérôme, Gavin. Lectr., English Hong Kong U., 1960-66; sr. lectr., chmn. dept. European lit., 1967-70; asso. prof. English, Trent U., Peterborough, Ont., Can., 1970-76, prof., 1976—, chmn. comparative lit. program, 1973-76, master Peter Robinson Coll., 1976—; bd. dirs. Artspace. Recipient Books in Can. award, 1976; Ont. Arts Council grantee, 1976, 79. Mem. Writers Union Can. Author: The Seventh Hexagram, 1976. Home: Rural Route 1 Ennismore ON K0L 1T0 Canada Office: Peter Robinson Coll Trent Univ Peterborough ON Canada. *I write as a means of defining the revolution that will eventually overthrow the decadent culture of which I am myself a part.*

MCLAFFERTY, FRED WARREN, chemist, educator; b. Evanston, Ill., May 11, 1923; s. Joel E. and Margaret E. (Keifer) McL.; B.S., U. Nebr., 1943, M.S., 1947; Ph.D., Cornell U., 1950; m. Elizabeth E. Curley, Feb. 5, 1948; children—Sara L., Joel E., Martha A., Samuel A., Ann E. Postdoctoral fellow U. Ia., 1949-50; research chemist, div. leader Dow Chem. Co., 1950-56, dir. Eastern Research Lab., 1956-64; prof. chemistry Purdue U., 1964-68, Cornell U., 1968—. Bd. dirs. Framingham (Mass.) Union Hosp., 1962-64. Served with AUS, 1943-45; ETO. Decorated Purple Heart, Combat Inf. badge, Bronze Star medal with 4 oak leaf clusters; recipient Pitts. Spectroscopy award Spectroscopy Soc. Pitts., 1975. John Simon Guggenheim fellow, 1972. Fellow N.Y. Acad. Scis.; mem. Am. Chem. Soc. (chmn. analytical chem. div. 1969, chmn. Midland sect. 1956, Northeastern sect. 1964, award chem. instrumentation 1971), Am. Soc. Mass Spectroscopy (founder, sec. 1957-58), Chem. Soc. London, A.A.A.S., Sigma Xi, Phi Lambda Upsilon, Alpha Chi Sigma. Presbyn. Author: Mass Spectrometry of Organic Ions, 1963; Mass Spectral Correlations, 1963; Interpretation of Mass Spectra, 1966, 2d edit., 1973; Advances in Analytical Chemistry and Instrumentation (with C.N. Reilley), Vols. 4-7, 1967-70; Index and Bibliography of Mass Spectrometry (with J. Pinzelik), 1967; Atlas of Mass Spectral Data (with E. Stenhagen and S. Abrahamsson), 1969; (with E. Stenhagen and S. Abrahamson) Registry of Mass Spectral Data, 1974. Co-editor: Archives of Mass Spectral Data, 1969-72. Home: 110 The Parkway Ithaca NY 14850

MC LAGLEN, ANDREW VICTOR, film dir.; b. London, Eng., July 28, 1920; s. Victor Andre and Enid Mary (Lamont) McL.; student U. Va., 1939-40; m. Sally Pierce, July 13, 1957 (div. 1979); children—Sharon Zinneman, Andrew Victor, Josh, Mary. Prodn. asst. Republic Pictures, 1945; Batjac Prodns., Republic Pictures asst. dir., 1946-54; dir. for CBS TV, 1955-62; dir. numerous feature films various studios, Los Angeles, 1955—. Dir. films McLintock, 1963; Shenandoah, 1965; The Rare Breed, 1966; Monkeys Go Home, 1966; The Way West, 1967; Ballad of Josie, 1967; The Devil's Brigade, 1967; Bandolero, 1968; Hellfighters, 1968; The Undefeated, 1969; Chisum, 1970; Fools' Parade, 1971; Something Big, 1972; Cahill, 1973; Mitchell, 1975; The Last Hard Men, 1976; The Wild Geese, 1978; Breakthrough, 1978; Esther, Ruth & Jennifer, 1979; The Sea Wolves, 1979-80. Home: Box 1056 Friday Harbor WA 98250 Office: Suite 2270 Kaufman & Bernstein 1900 Ave of Stars Los Angeles CA 90067

MC LAIN, JOHN DAVID, JR., choreographer, educator, adminstr.; b. Brighton, Tenn., Dec. 29, 1931; s. John David and Elsie Leola (Burt) McL.; B.S. in Edn., U. Ark., 1953; M.A., Wayne State U., Detroit, 1962. Asst. to dir. Robert Joffrey Ballet Co., N.Y.C., 1962-63; mem. faculty Am. Ballet Center, N.Y.C., 1962-63; ballet master Dayton (Ohio) Civic Ballet, also mem. faculty Schwarz Sch. Dance, Dayton, 1963-66; artistic dir. Cin. Ballet Co., also prof. ballet U. Cin. Coll.-Conservatory Music, 1966—; mus. adviser Detroit Severo Ballet, 1955-62; guest tchr. Sch. Pa. Ballet, Phila., 1963, Chgo. Nat. Dance Masters Assn., 1968, 70, 73; artist-in-residence Utah State U., 1970; mem. dance adv. panel Ohio Arts Council, 1969-71, Ky. Arts Commn., 1975-76; choreographer: Ancient Dances and Airs, Lovers and Songs of Silence, 1967, Night Soliloquies, 1968, L'histoire du Soldat, 1968, Two x Two, 1968, Romanza, 1969, 12 x 9 in 5, 1969, Concerto, 1969, Morphosis and Clouds, 1971, Guitar Concerto, 1971, Winter's Traces, 1978, Lyric Waltz, 1972, Dilemmas Moderne, 1972. cons. in field. Named Outstanding Alumnus in Fine Arts, U. Ark., 1962; recipient Dolly Cohen award U. Cin., 1971; Samuel and Rose Sachs award Cin. Inst. Fine Arts, 1975. Mem. Assn. Am. Dance Cos., MacDowell Music Soc., Phi Mu Alpha Sinfonia, Kappa Kappa Psi, Phi Delta Theta. Home: 854 Rue de la Paix B-3 Cincinnati OH 45220 Office: Dance Div Univ Cin Coll-Coservatory Music Cincinnati OH 45221. *I agree with Dr. Karl Menninger who has stated that "attitudes are more important than facts." Any achievements I have had are largely attributable to those times in my life when I have been able to maintain a positive mental attitude and an imaginative view.*

MC LAIN, JOHN HOWARD, assn. exec.; b. Pitts., Jan. 21, 1919; s. T. Ray, Jr., and Marion Cora (Kidd) McL.; A.B. with honor, U. Pitts., 1947, M.A., 1954; student Northeastern Inst. Comml. and Trade Orgn. Execs., Yale U., 1956, 57; grad. with honors Inst. Orgn. Mgmt., Mich. State U., 1958; m. Patricia Ann O'Connor, Nov. 28, 1953; children—Wendy Ray, John Howard, Sarah Annabelle, Marion Kathleen. Lectr. history U. Pitts., 1947, lectr. English, 1954-57; asst. prof. English, Presbyn. Jr. Coll., Maxton, N.C., 1948; head English dept. Adm. Farragut Acad., St. Petersburg, Fla., 1949-50; grad. asst. English, Fla. State U., 1950; instr. English, St. Petersburg Sr. High Sch., 1951-52, Edgewood High Sch., Pitts., 1954-55; mgr. govtl. and ednl. affairs Greater Pitts. C. of C., 1956-58, staff dir., 1959, exec. dir., 1960-65, exec. v.p., 1965-72; mgmt. cons., 1972-77; dir. membership affairs Res. Officers Assn. U.S., 1978—. Co-sec. of Greater Pitts. Labor-Mgmt. Adv. Council; mem. Regional Export Expansion Council of U.S. Dept. Commerce; mem. nat. adv. council Employer Suport for Guard and Res., U.S. Dept. Def.; mem. Guard and Res. in the total force study group U.S. Def. Dept., 1974; chief project precise First U.S. Army, 1975; bd. dirs. Bus. and Job Devel. Corp. bd. dirs. Am. Wind Symphony Orch.; past pres. Allegheny County Easter Seal Soc.; bd. dirs., v.p. United Mental Health Services of Allegheny County; trustee Community Services Pa.; mem. exec. com. Allegheny Children and Youth Services Council; chmn. City of Hope Greater Pitts. Citizens' Council, 1970-74. Served with AUS, 1940-45, 52-53; brig. gen. Res. ret., dep. comdr. 99th U.S. Army Res. Command, 1971-77. Decorated Legion of Merit, Bronze Star medal, Meritorious Service medal; recipient Man of Year award Jaycees, 1962, cert. Goodwill Industries, 1971; Brace-for-Ace award Pa. Easter Seal Soc., 1971; named to Field Arty. Officer Candidate Sch. Hall of Fame. Mem. Am. Arbitration Assn. (mem. regional adv. council), Am., (dir.), Pa. (past pres.) chambers commerce execs., Mil. Order World Wars, Council of Chambers of Commerce of Western Pa. (past pres.), Res. Officers Assn., Assn. U.S. Army, Mil. Order World Wars, VFW, Am. Def. Preparedness Assn. (dir.), Sr. Army Res. Comdrs. Assn., Am. Legion, Kappa Phi Kappa, Pi Kappa Alpha. Episcopalian. Mason (32 deg., Shriner), Rotarian (past pres.). Club: Pittsburgh Press. Home: 218 Dewey St Pittsburgh PA 15218 also 1200 N Court House Rd

Arlington VA 22201. *Be prepared to assume the job you thought you would never get.*

MC LAIN, JOSEPH HOWARD, coll. pres.; b. Wierton, W.Va., July 11, 1916; s. Howard Storer and Elizabeth Agnes (Gray) M.; B.S., Washington Coll., Chestertown, Md., 1937; Ph.D., Johns Hopkins U., 1946; m. Margaret Ann Hollingsworth, Sept. 6, 1941; children—Elizabeth Ann, Susan Lynn. Tech. dir., sec. Kent Mfg. Corp., Chestertown, 1946-54; research liaison mgr. Olin Mathieson Corp., N.Y.C., 1954-55; prof. chemistry Washington Coll., 1946-73, pres., 1973—; dir. Balt. br. Fed. Res. Bank of Richmond; chmn. adv. bd. Md. Nat. Bank, Chestertown, 1963-78. Chmn., Water Pollution Control Commn., Annapolis, Md., 1947-53; mem. Kent County Bd. Edn., 1958-64, Gov.'s Sci. Adv. Council, 1974—, Bay Bridge Commn., 1966, Chesapeake Bay Grasses Com., 1975—. Served in U.S. Army, 1941-46. Mem. Am. Chemistry Soc., Am. Ordnance Assn., Am. Rocket Soc. (sr.), Faraday Soc., Chem. Soc. (London), N.Y. Acad. Sci., Combustion Inst., Phi Beta Kappa, Sigma Xi, Phi Lambda Upsilon. Democrat. Episcopalian. Club: Chester River Yacht Country. Contbr. articles on solid state chemistry to profl. jours. Home: 106 S Water St Chestertown MD 21620 Office: Washington Coll Chestertown MD 21620

MCLAIN, MAURICE CLAYTON, real estate services co. exec., lawyer; b. Hillsboro, Tex., Sept. 22, 1929; s. Otis Ogen and Rachel Elizabeth (Estes) McL.; student Hillsboro Jr. Coll., 1945-46, Tex. A&M Coll., 1946-47; B.A. in Math. North Tex. State U., 1951; J.D., So. Meth. U., 1962; m. Martha Orlana Gould, Sept. 25, 1953; 1 son, William Gould. Admitted to Tex. bar, 1962, U.S. Supreme Ct. bar, 1976; engring. contracts coordinator Vought Aerospace div. LTV Corp., Dallas, 1961-64; asso. firm Abney & Burleson, Dallas, 1964-66; counsel Fed. Nat. Mortgage Assn., Dallas, 1966-69; v.p., counsel USLIFE Real Estate Services Corp., Dallas, 1970—; chmn. real estate specialization adv. commn., Tex. Bd. Legal Specialization, 1979-80. Fellow Am. Coll. Mortgage Attys.; mem. State Bar Tex., Am. Bar Assn., Dallas Bar Assn., Tex. Bar Assn., Fed. Bar Assn., Am. Judicature Soc., Real Estate Fin. Execs. Assn., Acad. Real Estate Attys., Phi Delta Phi, Sigma Phi Epsilon. Republican. Episcopalian. Clubs: Dallas Scottish Soc., English Speaking Union, SAR. Home: 3908 Royal Ln Dallas TX 75229 Office: 6500 Harry Hines Blvd Dallas TX 75235

MC LANATHAN, RICHARD BARTON KENNEDY, author, cons., assn. exec.; b. Methuen, Mass., Mar. 12, 1916; s. Frank Watson and Helen (Kennedy) McL.; grad. Choate Sch., 1934; A.B., Harvard, 1938, Ph.D., 1951; m. Jane Fuller, Jan. 2, 1942. Instr. English and history Allen-Stevenson Sch., N.Y.C., 1938-43; asst. curator paintings Mus. Fine Arts, Boston, 1946-48, asst. curator decorative arts, 1949-54, sec. of museum, 1952-56, editor museum publs., 1952-57, asso. curator decorative arts, 1954, curator decorative arts, 1954-57; dir. Mus. Art, Munson-Williams-Proctor Inst., Utica, N.Y., 1957-61; exec. dir. Am. Assn. Museums, Washington, 1976-78; trustee, mem. exec. com. Boston Arts Festival, 1954-59; curator art exhbn., Moscow, 1959; Am. specialist to W. Germany, Poland and Denmark, 1959, Yugoslavia, 1961; mem. U.S. Nat. Commn. for UNESCO, 1976-79; mem. Corcoran Biennial Jury, 1960; mem. N.Y. State Council Arts, 1960-64; bd. advisers Albany (N.Y.) Inst. History and Art, 1958-70; cons. in field, 1961-75. Bd. advisers Boys Clubs Boston, 1950-57; trustee Boys' Club Utica, 1959-61, Brandywine River Mus., 1970-75; bd. dirs. St. Luke's Meml. Hosp. Center, Utica, 1957-61. Sr. fellow Am. Acad. Rome, 1947; recipient Distinguished Service award USIA, 1959; Prix de Rome, 1948-49; Rockefeller sr. fellow Met. Mus., 1975-76. Mem. Am. Assn. Museums, Asso. Council Arts. Author: Images of the Universe: Leonardo da Vinci, The Artists as Scientist, 1966; The Pageant of Medieval Art, 1966; The American Tradition in the Arts, 1968; A Guide to Civilisation, The Kenneth Clark Films on the Cultural Life of Western Man, 1970; The Brandywine Heritage, 1971; Art in America, 1973; The Art of Marguerite Stix, 1977; National Gallery of Art, East Building: A Profile, 1978; co-author: M. and M. Karolik Collection of American Paintings, 1815-1855, 1949. Editor: Catalogue of Classical Coins, 1955; cons. editor Art and Man, Nat. Gallery Art, 1969-76; adv. editor The Great Controversial Issues: The Arts, 1978; contbr.: Am. Foundation Philanthropy, 1967. Home: The Stone School House Phippsburg ME 04562

MCLANE, JOHN ROY, JR., lawyer; b. Manchester, N.H., Feb. 19, 1916; s. John R. and Elisabeth (Bancroft) McL.; grad. St. Paul's Sch., Concord, N.H., 1934; A.B., Dartmouth Coll., 1938; LL.B., Harvard U., 1941; m. Blanche Marshall, Feb. 15, 1935; children—John Roy III, Andrew M., Lyn, Blanche M., Angus; m. 2d, Elisabeth Deane, Dec. 30, 1960; children—Towner D., Virginia W., Kathryn E., Duncan C. Admitted to N.H. bar, 1941, since practiced in Manchester; dir. firm McLane, Graf, Greene, Raulerson & Middleton, P.A., 1941-42, 45—; dir. First Fin. Group N.H., Inc. (formerly Manchester Savs. Bank), Manchester Gas Co. Trustee Spaulding-Potter Charitable Trusts, 1958-72. Chmn., N.H. Advisory Commn. on Health and Welfare, 1965-68. Alderman, Manchester, 1952-53. Trustee, clk. St. Paul's Sch., 1952—; trustee N.H. State Hosp., 1949-62; trustee, sec. Norwin S. and Elizabeth N. Bean Found., 1967—; distbg. dir. N.H. Charitable Fund, 1962-69; bd. dirs. Council on Founds., 1968-74, chmn., 1970-72; bd. dirs. Child and Family Services N.H., 1946-71, pres., 1963-71; pres. N.H. Performing Arts Center, 1974-77; trustee Hurricane Island Outward Bound Sch., 1972—. Served to lt. USNR, 1942-45. Mem. Am., N.H., Manchester bar assns. Republican. Episcopalian (vestry 1963, 68). Home: 1595 N River Rd Manchester NH 03104 Office: 40 Stark St Manchester NH 03101

MCLAREN, DIGBY JOHNS, Can. govt. ofcl., geologist; b. Carrickfergus, No. Ireland, Dec. 11, 1919; student Queens' Coll., Cambridge U., 1938-40, B.A., 1941, M.A. (Harkness scholar), 1948; Ph.D., Mich. U., 1951; m. Phyllis Mary Matkin, Mar. 25, 1942; children—Ian, Patrick, Alison. Geologist, Geol. Survey Can., Ottawa, Ont., 1948—, dir. gen., 1973—; 1st dir. Inst. Sedimentary and Petroleum Geology, Calgary, Alta., Can., 1967-73; pres. Commn. on Stratigraphy, Internat. Union Geol. Scis., 1972-76; apptd. 14th dir. Geol. Survey Can., 1973; chmn. bd. Internat. Geol. Correlation Program, UNESCO-IGCP, 1976—. Served to capt. Royal Arty., Brit. Army, 1940-46. Fellow Royal Soc. Can., Royal Soc. London; fgn. asso. mem. U.S. Nat. Acad. Scis; mem. Geol. Soc. London, Paleontol. Assn., Geol. Soc. Am., Can. Paleontol. Soc., Geol. Assn. Can., Can. Soc. Petroleum Geologists. Contbr. memoirs, bulls., papers, geol. maps, sci. articles in field to profl. lit. Office: Office Dir Gen Geol Survey Can 601 Booth St Ottawa ON K1A 0E8 Canada

MC LAREN, JOHN ALEXANDER, hosp. exec.; b. Vancouver, B.C., Can., Mar. 21, 1919; s. Henry Moncrieff and Elizabeth Jean (Dingwall) McL.; came to U.S., 1948, naturalized, 1952; B.A., U. B.C., 1939; M.D., C.M., McGill U., Montreal, 1943; m. Valerie Jean Adams, June 24, 1944; children—John Alexander, Jeannie McLaren Martz, Duncan R., Laurie. Intern and resident Montreal Gen. Hosp.; resident Toronto Gen. Hosp., 1946-48; gen. practice internal medicine, Wilmette and Evanston, Ill., 1948-68; v.p. patient care services Evanston (Ill.) Hosp., 1968-74, v.p. mktg., 1976—; v.p. orgn., planning and staffing Glenbrook Hosp., Glenview, Ill., 1974-76; v.p., dir. Merced Industries Inc.; asst. prof. medicine Northwestern U. Med. Sch.; mem. Nat. Bd. Med. Examiners, 1975-78, long-term care council Joint Commn. Accreditation Hosps., 1971-78. Served with M.C., Canadian Army, 1943-46. Diplomate Am. Bd. Internal Medicine. Mem. Chgo. Soc. Internal Medicine, Inst. Medicine Chgo. Club: Mission Hills Country (Northbrook). Home: 1854 Mission Hills Ln Northbrook IL 60062 Office: 2650 Ridge Ave Evanston IL 60201

MCLAREN, LEROY CLARENCE, educator; b. Bishop, Calif., Jan. 18, 1924; s. Leroy Clarence and Amelia Ellen (Barlow) McL.; A.B., San Jose (Calif.) State Coll., 1949; M.A., UCLA, 1951, Ph.D. (fellow Nat. Tb Assn. 1952-53), 1953; m. Dorothy Louise Appleton, Aug. 14, 1945; children—Mark Douglas, David Leroy, Deborah Ellen. Instr. infectious diseases UCLA Sch. Medicine, 1953-55; mem. faculty microbiology U. Minn., 1955-64, asso. prof., 1959-64; prof. microbiology, U. N.Mex. Sch. Medicine, 1964—, chmn. dept., 1964-76; spl. research virology, med. microbiology; cons. virology Eli Lilly Co., 1964-70. Served as pilot USAAF, 1943-45. Recipient research career award USPHS at U. Minn., 1962-64. Decorated D.F.C., Air medal. Diplomate Am. Bd. Med. Microbiology. Fellow AAAS, Am. Acad. Microbiology; mem. Am. Soc. Microbiology, Am. Assn. Immunologists, AAUP, Soc. Exptl. Biology and Medicine, Tissue Culture Assn., Am. Bd. Med. Microbiology, Sigma Xi. Home: 7705 Palo Duro Ave NE Albuquerque NM 87110

MC LAREN, MALCOLM GRANT, IV, educator; b. Denver, July 22, 1928; s. George W. and Evelyn (Hodgson) McL.; B.S., Rutgers U., 1950, M.S., 1951, Ph.D., 1962; m. Barbara Stephen, Sept. 23, 1950; children—Malcolm Grant, George, Thomas, Michael. Research asst. Rutgers U., 1950-54; chief ceramist Paper Makers Importing Co., Easton, Pa., 1954-55, v.p., dir., 1957-62; mem. faculty Rutgers U., 1962—, prof. ceramics, 1969—, chmn. dept., 1969—; cons. WHO, also to industry. Dir. Ceramicmagnetics Corp., Del. Valley Indsl. Ceramics Co. Served to 1st lt. USAF, 1955-57. Recipient Gardner award Rutgers U., 1970; Man of Year award Associacão Brasiliera de Cerâmica, 1978; Ann. award Ceramic Assn. N.J. Fellow Am. Ceramic Soc. (v.p. 1974, pres. 1979—, Albert Victor Bleininger award 1979); mem. Am. Soc. Engring. Edn., Ceramic Ednl. Council (pres.), Sigma Xi, Phi Lambda Upsilon, Phi Gamma Delta, Keramos. Author articles in field. Home: RD 3 Milford NJ 08848 Office: Ceramics Dept Rutgers Univ New Brunswick NJ 08903

MC LARNAN, CHARLES WALTER, univ. dean; b. Mt. Vernon, Ohio, Mar. 13, 1928; s. John Walter and Cora Marie (Conard) McL.; B.A., Ohio Wesleyan U., 1951; B.M.E., Ohio State U., 1954, M.S., 1955, Ph.D., 1960; m. Marjorie Lucile Roseboom, June 15, 1952; children—Timothy, Linda, Margaret, Kenneth, William. Instr., Ohio State U., 1954-60, asst. prof., 1960-64, asso. prof., 1964-68, prof. mech. engring., 1968-72, exec. asst. to provost and v.p. acad. affairs, sec. univ. faculty, 1969-72; v.p., dir. instl. services Macalester Coll., St. Paul, 1972-73, v.p., exec. officer, 1973-74, interim pres., 1974-75, spl. asst. to the pres., 1975-76; dean sci. and engring. U. Tex. of Permian Basin, Odessa, 1976—; vis. scholar Columbia, 1965-66; cons. Nat. Cash Register, Western Electric, Bell Telephone Labs., Diamond Power Specialty Corp., Battelle Meml. Inst. Served with USAAF, 1946-47. NSF Sci. Faculty fellow, 1965-66; registered profl. engr., Ohio, Tex. Mem. ASME (exec. com. design engring. div.), Am. Soc. Engring. Edn., AAAS, Soc. Petroleum Engrs., Sigma Phi Epsilon. Methodist. Mason, Kiwanian. Tech. editor ASME transactions Jour. Mech. Design. Home: 3806 Blossom Ln Odessa TX 79762 Died Apr. 10, 1979.

MCLARNAN, DONALD EDWARD, banker, corp. exec.; b. Nashua, Iowa, Dec. 19, 1906; s. Samuel and Grace (Prudhon) McL.; A.B., U. So. Calif., 1930; grad. Southwestern U., 1933; m. Virginia Rickard, May 5, 1939; children—Marilyn, Marcia, Roxane. Trust appraiser, property mgr. Security-Pacific Nat. Bank, Los Angeles, 1935-54; regional dir. SBA for So. Calif., Ariz., Nev., 1954-61, area adminstr. Alaska, Western U.S., Hawaii, Guam, Samoa, U.S. Trust Terr., 1969-73; pres. Am. MARC, Inc., offshore oil drillers and mfr. diesel engines, 1961-63, Terminal Drilling & Prodn. Co., Haney & Williams Drilling Co., Western Offshore, 1961-63; v.p., dir. Edgemar Dairy, Santa Monica Dairy Co., 1954-70; founder, pres., chmn. bd. Mission Nat. Bank, 1963-67; pres. Mut. Trading Co.; dir. Coast Fed. Savs. & Loan; cons. numerous corps.; guest lectr. various univs. Chmn. fed. agys. div. Community Chest, 1956; nat. pres. Teachers Day, 1956; bd. councillors U. So. Calif.; founder, chmn., pres. Soc. Care and Protection Injured Innocent; adv. bd. Los Angeles City Coll.; bd. dirs. Calif. Easter Seal Soc. Recipient Los Angeles City and County Civic Leadership award, 1959. Mem. Skull and Dagger, Delta Chi. Mason (K.T., Shriner). Clubs: Los Angeles, Jonathan (Los Angeles). Contbr. articles on mgmt. and fin. to profl. jours. Home: 135 S Norton Ave Los Angeles CA 90004 Office: 1101 S Crenshaw Blvd Los Angeles CA 90019

MC LAUGHLIN, CHARLES WILLIAM, JR., surgeon; b. Washington, Iowa, Feb. 3, 1906; s. Charles William and Bessie (Hamilton) McL.; B.A., U. Iowa, 1927; M.D., Washington U., St. Louis, 1929; fellow U. Edinburgh (Scotland), 1935; m. Beatrice Reimers, Jan. 17, 1940; 1 son, Charles William. Intern, Montreal (Can.) Gen. Hosp., 1929-31; fellow surgery U. Pa. Hosp., 1931-34; mem. faculty U. Nebr. Sch. Medicine, 1935—, prof. surgery, 1954-72, sr. cons. surgeon, 1972—; pvt. practice, Omaha, 1935—; cons. SAC Hosp., Offutt AFB, 1946-73; surg. cons. USAF, 1968—; pres. staff Meth. Hosp., 1952, Children's Hosp., 1961; mem. Conf. Com. Grad. Tng. in Surgery in U.S., 1957-64. Served to comdr., M.C., USNR, 1941-45; PTO. Named King Aksarben, 1966. Mem. A.C.S. (chmn. bd. govs. 1968-69, regent 1969-74, pres. 1974-75); mem. Am., Central, Western, So. surg. assns., Douglas County Med. Soc. (past pres.). Contbr. articles to profl. jours. Home: 10085 Fieldcrest Dr Omaha NE 68114 Office: Doctors Bldg Omaha NE 68131

MC LAUGHLIN, DAVID THOMAS, mfg. co. exec.; b. Grand Rapids, Mich., Mar. 16, 1932; s. Wilfred P. and Arlene (Sunderlin) McL.; B.A., Dartmouth U., 1954, M.B.A., Amos Tuck Sch., 1955; m. Judith Ann Landauer, Mar. 25, 1955; children—William, Wendy, Susan, Jay. With Champion Internat. Co., 1957-70, v.p., gen. mgr. Champion packages div., 1957-70; pres., chief exec. officer Toro Co., Bloomington, Minn., 1970-77, chmn., chief exec. officer, Mpls., 1977—; dir. Dayton-Hudson Corp., Mpls., Westinghouse Electric Corp., Pitts. Chmn. bd. trustees Dartmouth Coll.; bd. dirs. United Way of Mpls. Area, Mpls. Soc. Fine Arts. Served with USAF, 1955-57. Mem. Nat. C. of C. (dir.). Episcopalian. Address: Toro Co 1 Appletree Sq 8009 34th Ave S Minneapolis MN 55420

MC LAUGHLIN, DONALD HAMILTON, mining geologist and engr.; b. San Francisco, Dec. 15, 1891; s. William Henry and Katherine (Hamilton) McL.; B.S., U. Calif. (with honorable mention for U. Calif. medal), 1914; A.M., Harvard U., 1915, Ph.D., 1917; D.Eng. (hon.), S.D. Sch. Mines and Tech., 1950, Mich. Coll. Mines and Tech., 1950, Mont. Sch. Mines, 1950, Colo. Sch. Mines, 1955; LL.D., U. Calif. at Berkeley, 1966; m. Eleanor Eckhart, Sept. 12, 1925; children—Donald Hamilton, Charles Capen; m. 2d, Sylvia Cranmer, Dec. 29, 1948; children—Jean Katherine, George Cranmer. Chief geologist Cerro de Pasco Copper Corp., Oroya, Peru, 1919-25; mem. faculty Harvard, 1925-41; dean Coll. Mining, U. Calif. at Berkeley, 1941-42, prof. mining engring., 1941-43, dean Coll. Engring., 1942-43, prof. emeritus, 1967—, Berkeley fellow, 1968—; pres. Homestake Mining Co., 1944-61, chmn., 1961-70, chmn. exec. com., 1970—, also dir.; dir. emeritus Western Air Lines; chmn. adv. com. on raw materials AEC, 1947-52, mem. plowshare adv. com., 1959-72; trustee Com. for Econ. Devel., 1960-62; mem. advisory com. U.S. Geol. Survey, 1950-65. Regent U. Calif., 1951-66, chmn. bd., 1958-60; mem. nat. sci. bd. NSF, 1950-60; mem. earth scis. advisory bd. Stanford U., 1969—; mem. overseers com. to visit dept. geol. scis. Harvard, 1972-79; trustee San Francisco Conservatory Music, 1964-73. Served as 1st lt., inf. U.S. Army, 1917-19. Rand medalist Am. Inst. Mining, Metall. and Petroleum Engrs., 1961; Monell medal and prize Columbia U., 1964; Golden Plate award Am. Acad. Achievement, 1972. Fellow Geol. Soc. Am. (councilor 1934-36), Am. Acad. Arts and Scis. (councilor 1939-42), Calif. Alumni Assn. (mem. council 1972-76, Alumnus of Year award 1977); mem. and sometime officer several profl. assns., Phi Beta Kappa, Sigma Xi, Tau Beta Pi, Kappa Sigma, Theta Tau. Clubs: Pacific Union, Bohemian, Engineers' (San Francisco); University, Century, (N.Y.C.); Cosmos (Washington). Contbr. articles to profl. jours. Home: 1450 Hawthorne Terr Berkeley CA 94708 Address: 650 California St San Francisco CA 94108

MCLAUGHLIN, EDWARD FRANCIS, JR., lawyer; b. Boston, Aug. 18, 1920; s. Edward Francis and Helen Celia (Kane) McL.; A.B., Dartmouth, 1942; LL.B., Northeastern U., 1949; m. Gerturde Elizabeth Drake, Apr. 14, 1945; children—Edward Francis III, Patricia Ann (dec.), Paul R., Robert D., Richard J., Elizabeth Ann. With agys. U.S. Govt., 1946-49; admitted to Mass. bar, 1949; asst. U.S. atty., 1950-53; pvt. practice, Boston, 1953—; councillor City of Boston, 1954-61, pres. council, 1959-60; lt. gov. Mass., 1960-63; gen. counsel Mass. Bay Transp. Authority, 1962-70; asso. firm Herrick & Smith, 1970—, partner, 1971—. Mem. civic com. President's People to People Program; hon. vice chmn. Mass. com. for project HOPE. Del. Democratic Nat. Conv., 1960. Served with USNR, 1942-45. Mem. Fed., Boston bar assns., Am. Legion, V.F.W., D.A.V., Dartmouth Alumni Assn. Greater Boston (past pres.), Northeastern U. Law Sch. Alumni Assn. (past pres.), Phi Sigma Kappa. K.C. Home: 41 Bayview Rd Little Island Osterville MA 02655 Office: 100 Federal St Boston MA 02110

MCLAUGHLIN, EMILY, actress; b. White Plains, N.Y., Dec. 1; B.A. in Am. Lit., Middlebury (Vt.) Coll.; m. Jeffrey Hunter (dec.); m. 2d, Robert Lansing (div.); 1 son, Robert. With Neighborhood Playhouse, N.Y.C.; appeared on Broadway in The Frogs of Spring, The Lovers, off-Broadway in Troilus and Cressida; tour of Plaza Suite, U.S. and Can.; regular TV series Gen. Hosp., 1963—; other TV appearances include: Studio One, Kraft Theater, Twilight Zone, The Eleventh Hour. Mem. AFTRA. Office: care ABC 1330 Ave of Americas New York City NY 10019*

MCLAUGHLIN, FRANCIS, psychoanalyst, psychiatrist; b. Syracuse, N.Y., Oct. 2, 1914; s. Thomas Flynn and Lillian (Baeder) McL.; student Johns Hopkins U., 1932-35; M.D., U. Md., 1939; m. Louise Polly Porter, Aug. 23, 1959; children—Thomas, Carol (Mrs. Stuart Miller). Intern, U. Hosp., Balt., 1939-41; staff psychiatrist Sheppard-Enoch Pratt Hosp., Balt., 1941-46; practice medicine specializing in psychoanalysis, Balt., 1946—; supr., tng. analyst, mem. faculty Inst. for Psychoanalysis, Balt., Washington, 1946—; mem. staff, faculty Johns Hopkins U. Med. Sch. and Hosp., 1962—. Fellow Am. Psychiat. Assn.; mem. Md. Psychiat. Assn. (pres. 1967-68), Internat. (sec. 1977—), Am. (chmn. bd. profl. standards 1970-73, pres. 1975-76) psychoanalytic assns., AAAS, Royal Soc. Health (Eng.), Home: 120 E Melrose Ave Baltimore MD 21212 Office: 829 Park Ave Baltimore MD 21201

MC LAUGHLIN, (ROBERT) FRED, farm coop. exec.; b. Fairfield County, Ohio, Jan. 30, 1916; s. Clarence Jefferson and Mary Ethel (Love) McL.; B.A., Otterbein Coll., 1937; m. Ruth Eileen Ridenour, Oct. 21, 1939; children—Thomas Jeffrey, John Richard. With Landmark Inc., Columbus, Ohio, 1937—, successively sales mgr., asst. gen. mgr., gen. mgr., now exec. v.p., chief exec. officer, gen. mgr.; dir. CF Industries, Internat. Energy Co-op Inc., Select Seeds, Inc., Energy Coop., Inc.; bd. dirs. Nat. Council Farmer Coops. Served with USN, 1943-46. Recipient hon. state degree Future Farmers Am. Mem. Gamma Sigma Delta. Presbyterian. Club: Masons. Office: 35 E Chestnut St PO Box 479 Columbus OH 43216

MCLAUGHLIN, (ROBERT) FRED, farm coop. exec.; b. Fairfield County, Ohio, Jan. 30, 1916; s. Clarence Jefferson and Mary Ethel (Love) McL.; B.A., Otterbein Coll., 1937; m. Ruth Eileen Ridenour, Oct. 21, 1939; children—Thomas Jeffrey, John Richard. With Landmark, Inc., Columbus, Ohio, 1937—, gen. mgr., 1976, exec. v.p., 1977, chief exec. officer, 1977—; dir. CF Industries, Mid-States Terminals, Internat. Energy Co-op., Select Seeds, Inc. Served with USN, 1943-46. Presbyterian. Club: Masons. Home: 561 Hallmark Pl Worthington OH 43085 Office: 35 E Chestnut St PO Box 479 Columbus OH 43216

MCLAUGHLIN, HARRY ROLL, architect; b. Indpls., Nov. 29, 1922; s. William T. and Ruth E. (Roll) McL.; student John Herron Art Sch., Indpls., 1936, 40, 41; m. Linda Hamilton, Oct. 23, 1954; 1 son, Harry Roll. Partner, pres., charge pub. relations, dir. James Assos., Architects and Engrs., Inc., Indpls., 1956—; sec., dir. James & Berger, Architects, Engrs., Planners, Economists; adv. bd. Pompeiiana Inc., Indpls.; specializing in restoration of historic bldgs. Past mem. Mayor's Progress Com., Arts and Culture Com. Chmn. bd. Historic Landmarks Found.; past bd. dirs. Carmel Clay Ednl. Found.; archtl. adviser, bd. advisers Historic Madison, Inc.; mem. adv. council Historic Am. Bldgs. survey Nat. Park Service, 1967-73; mem. Ind. Profl. Rev. Com. for Nat. Register Nominations; past adv. bd. Conner Prairie Mus., Patrick Henry Sullivan Found.; past adviser Indpls. Historic Preservation Commn., New Harmony Historic Dist.; past mem. preservation com. Ind. U.; architect mem. Meridian St. Preservation Commn., Indpls.; hon. mem. Ind. Bicentennial Commn. Bd. dirs. Park-Tudor Sch.; nat. bd. dirs. Preservation Action; bd. advisers restoration com. Northwood Inst. at West Baden, Ind. Served with USNR, 1943-45. Recipient awards including Ind. Gov.'s citation, 1967; Indpls. Mayor's citation for services in preservation archtl. heritage, 1972; U.S. Sec. Interior's citation, 1973; design and environment citations for work in preservation, 1975; registered architect, Ind., Alaska, D.C., Ohio, Ill., Md., Va., Nat. Council Registration Bds. Fellow AIA (mem. nat. com. historic bldgs.; chmn. historic resources com. 1970; mem. Ind. Soc. Architects (state preservation coordinator 1960—, biennial award 1972, Design award 1978), Constrn. League Indpls. (dir. 1969-71), Nat. Trust for Historic Preservation (past trustee, bd. advisers, Soc. Archtl. Historians (past dir.), Am. Assn. State and Local History, Indpls. Mus. Art, Assn. Preservation Tech., Zionsville C. of C. (hon. dir.), Ind. Conservation Council, U.S. Capitol (hon. trustee), Ind., Marion County (past v.p., dir.), Zionsville hist. socs., Victorian Soc. Am. (adv. bd.), Smithsonian Assos., East African Wildlife Soc., Navy League U.S. (life), Ind. State Mus. Soc. (charter), English Speaking Union (bd. dirs. Indpls.), Athenaeum Turners, Ind. Acad. Arts and Scis., Nat. Audubon Soc. Clubs: Woodstock, Literary, Portfolio, Amateur Movie, Athletic (Indpls.). Restorations include: Old State Bank State Meml., Vincennes, Old Opera House State Meml., New Harmony, Old Morris-Butler House, Indpls. (Merit award 1972), Market St. Restoration and Maria Creek Baptist Ch., Vincennes, Ind., Benjamin Harrison House, Old James Ball Residence, Lafayette, Ind. (1st Design award 1972), Lockerbie Sq. Master Plan and Park Sch.,

Indpls., Knox County Ct. House, Vincennes, 1972, J.K. Lilly House, Indpls., 1972, Waiting Station and Chapel, Crown Hill Cemetery, Indpls., 1972, Blackford-Condit several Indian houses Angel Mounds Archaeol. Site and Interpretative Center, nr. Evansville, Ind.; architect Glenn A. Black Mus. Archaeology, Ind. U., Bloomington; Restoration Morgan County Ct. House, Indpls. City Market, Hist. Scofield House, Madison, Ind., Ernie Pyle Birthplace, Dana, Ind. Contbr. articles to profl. jours. Illustrator: Harmonist Construction. Home: 950 W 116th St Carmel IN 46032 Office: 2828 E 45th St Indianapolis IN 46205

MCLAUGHLIN, HARRY ROLL, architect; b. Indpls., Nov. 29, 1922; s. William T. and Ruth E. (Roll) McL.; student John Herron Art Sch., Indpls., 1936, 40, 41; m. Linda Hamilton, Oct. 23, 1954; 1 son, Harry Roll. Partner, pres., charge pub. relations, dir. James Assos., Architects and Engrs., Inc., Indpls., 1956—; sec., dir. James & Berger, Architects, Engrs., Planners, Economists; adv. bd. Pompeiiana Inc., Indpls.; specializing in restoration of historic bldgs. Past mem. Mayor's Progress Com., Arts and Culture Com. Chmn. bd. Historic Landmarks Found.; past bd. dirs. Carmel Clay Ednl. Found.; archtl. adviser, bd. advisers Historic Madison, Inc.; mem. advisory council Historic Am. Bldgs. survey Nat. Park Service, 1967-73; mem. Ind. Profl. Rev. Com. for Nat. Register Nominations; past advisory bd. Conner Prairie Mus., Patrick Henry Sullivan Found.; past adviser Indpls. Historic Preservation Commn., New Harmony Historic Dist.; past mem. preservation com. Ind. U.; mem. Ind. Com. Preservation Archtl. Records; architect mem. Meridian St. Preservation Commn., Indpls.; hon. mem. Ind. Bicentennial Commn. Bd. dirs. Park-Tudor Sch.; nat. bd. dirs. Preservation Action; bd. advisers restoration com. Northwood Inst. at West Baden, Ind.; trustee Indpls. Mus. Art. Served with USNR, 1943-45. Recipient awards including Ind. Gov.'s citation, 1967; Indpls. Mayor's citation for services in preservation archtl. heritage, 1972; U.S. Sec. Interior's citation, 1973; design and environment citations for work in preservation, 1975; citation Huntington Coll., 1975, Masons, 1975, Ind. Gov., 1977. Registered architect, Ind., Alaska, D.C., Ohio, Ill., Md., Va., Nat. Council Registration Bds. Fellow AIA (mem. nat. com. historic bldgs.; chmn. historic resources com. 1970; mem. Ind. Soc. Architects state (preservation coordinator 1960—, biennial award 1972, 78), Constrn. League Indpls. (dir. 1969-71), Nat. Trust for Historic Preservation (past trustee, bd. advisers, Soc. Archtl. Historians (past dir.), Am. Assn. State and Local History, Indpls. Mus. Art, Assn. Preservation Tech., Zionsville C. of C. (hon. dir.), Ind. Conservation Council, U.S. Capitol (hon. trustee), Ind., Marion County (past v.p., dir.), Zionsville hist. socs., Victorian Soc. Am. (adv. bd.), Smithsonian Assos., East African Wildlife Soc., Navy League U.S. (life), Ind. State Mus. Soc. (charter), English Speaking Union (bd. dirs. Indpls.), Athenaeum Turners, Ind. Acad. Arts and Scis., Nat. Audubon Soc., Cadillac/LaSalle Owners Club, Packard Club Am., Milestone Car Soc. Clubs: Woodstock, Literary, Portfolio, Amateur Movie, Athletic (Indpls.). Restorations include: Old State Bank State Meml., Vincennes, Old Opera House State Meml., New Harmony, Old Morris-Butler House, Indpls. (Merit award 1972), Market St. Restoration and Maria Creek Baptist Ch., Vincennes, Ind., Benjamin Harrison House, Old James Ball Residence, Lafayette, Ind. (1st Design award 1972), Lockerbie Sq. Master Plan and Park Sch., Indpls., Knox County Ct. House, Vincennes, 1972, J.K. Lilly House, Indpls., 1972, Waiting Station and Chapel, Crown Hill Cemetery, Indpls., 1972, Blackford-Condit several Indian houses Angel Mounds Archaeol. Site and Interpretative Center, nr. Evansville, Ind.; architect Glenn A. Black Mus. Archaeology, Ind. U., Bloomington; Restoration Morgan County Ct. House, Indpls City Market. Contbr. articles to profl. jours. Illustrator: Harmonist Construction. Home: 950 W 116th St Carmel IN 46032 Office: 2828 E 45th St Indianapolis IN 46205

MCLAUGHLIN, JEROME MICHAEL, lawyer, shipping co. exec.; b. St. Louis, Jan. 11, 1929; s. John Thomas and Mary Adelaide (White) McL.; A.B., St. Louis U., 1950, J.D., 1954; m. Delphine M. McClellan, June 15, 1957; children—Margaret D., Mary Martha, Elizabeth O., Jerome Michael, John T. Admitted to Mo. bar, 1954, U.S. Supreme Ct. bar, 1972; v.p. Internat. Indemnity, St. Louis, 1955-56; asst. circuit atty. City of St. Louis, 1957-58; partner firm Willson, Cunningham & McClellan, St. Louis, 1958-78; v.p., gen. counsel Alexander & Baldwin, Inc., Honolulu, 1978-79; v.p. ops. Philippines, Micronesia & Orient Navigation Co., San Francisco, 1979—; instr. philosophy St. Louis U., 1955-60. Served to capt. USMC, 1951-53; Korea. Mem. Mo. Bar Assn., Am. Bar Assn., South Pacific Ports Assn. Republican. Roman Catholic. Club: Mo. Athletic. Home: 1225 Hillview Menlo Park CA 94025 Office: 181 Fremont St San Francisco CA 94105

MCLAUGHLIN, JOHN D., food mfg. co. exec., ret. army officer; b. San Francisco, Dec. 24, 1917; s. John and Lottie (Bruhns) McL.; ed. George Washington U.; grad. Armed Forces Staff Coll., 1956, Nat. War Coll., 1959, Advanced Mgmt. Program, Harvard U., 1963; m. Elizabeth Susan Stumper, July 11, 1946; children—John D., William F., Susan C. Commd. 2d lt. U.S. Army, 1942, advanced through grades to lt. gen.; staff asst. Office Sec. of Def., 1960-61; exec. officer Def. Supply Agy., 1961-63; chief of staff U.S. Army, VietNam, 1965-66; dir. supply U.S. Army, 1966-67; asst. chief of staff for logistics Pacific Command, 1967-69; comdg. gen. Quartermaster Center, comdt. U.S. Army Quartermaster Sch., Ft. Lee, Va., 1969-73; comdg. gen. U.S. Army Support Command, Europe, 1973-74; v.p. L.J. Minor Corp., Cleve., 1974—; pres. Food Am. Exports, Inc., Colonial Heights, Va.; regional dir. First & Mchts. Bank, Petersburg, Va. Mem. exec. council Richmond Boy Scouts Am. Chmn. Nat. Foodservice Edn. and Tng. Coordinating Council; chmn. advisory bd. Ednl. Inst. of Am. Culinary Fedn.; trustee, mem. exec. com. Culinary Inst. Am. Served with AUS, 1934-74. Decorated D.S.M. with oak leaf cluster, Legion of Merit with 4 oak leaf clusters, Bronze Star Medal with 2 oak leaf clusters, Air medal (U.S.), Distinguished Service Medal (Greece); recipient Silver Plate award Internat. Food Service Mfrs. Assn., 1973, others. Mem. Quartermaster Meml. Assn. Quartermaster Assn. (pres. Washington chpt. 1969-70), Harvard Bus. Sch. Alumni Assn., Nat. Research Council, Am. Culinary Fedn., Internat. Food Service Mfrs. Assn. (trustee Gold and Silver Plate Award Soc.), Am. Acad. Chefs (hon. life, chmn. advisory com.), Honorable Order Golden Toque. Clubs: Kiwanis of Petersburg (dir.), Harvard of Va. (Va.); Petersburg Country. Home: 411 Springdale Ave Colonial Heights VA 23834 Office: 436 Bulkley Bldg Cleveland OH 44115 also 3235 Boulevard Colonial Heights VA 23834. *Always take the time, no matter how busy you are, to assist, guide, and/or counsel people who come to you with their problems. Your support as a leader increases a thousandfold for each time you take time to listen, provide understanding, and help those in need.*

MC LAUGHLIN, JOHN FRANCIS, civil engr., educator; b. N.Y.C., Sept. 21, 1927; s. William Francis and Anna (Goodwin) McL.; B.C.E., Syracuse U., 1950; M.S. in Civil Engring., Purdue U., 1953, Ph.D., 1957; m. Eleanor Thomas Trethewey, Nov. 22, 1950; children—Susan, Donald, Cynthia, Kevin. Mem. faculty Purdue U., 1950—, prof. civil engring., 1963—, head Sch. Civil Engring., 1968-78, asst. dean engring., 1977—; cons. in field. Served with USAAF, 1945-47. Fellow ASCE; mem. Am. Concrete Inst. (bd. dirs., v.p. 1977-79, pres. 1979), Hwy. Research Bd., ASTM, Sigma Xi, Tau Beta Pi, Chi Epsilon, Theta Tau. Home: 112 Sumac Dr West Lafayette IN 47906 Office: Civil Engring Dept Purdue Univ Lafayette IN 47907

MC LAUGHLIN, JOSEPH MAILEY, lawyer; b. Los Angeles, July 10, 1928; s. James Aloysius and Cecilia Ann (Mailey) McL.; J.D., Loyola U., Los Angeles, 1955; m. Beverly Jane Walker, July 24, 1949; children—Stephen Joseph, Lawrence James, Suzanne Carol, Eileen Louise. Admitted to Calif. bar, 1955, U.S. Supreme Ct. bar, 1959; mem. firm McLaughlin & Irvin, Los Angeles, 1955—, San Francisco, 1969—; lectr. labor relations Loyola U., Los Angeles, 1958-60. Served to 1st lt. USAF, 1951-53. Mem. San Francisco, Long Beach, Los Angeles County, Fed., Am., Internat., Inter-Am. bar assns., State Bar Calif., Am. Judicature Soc., Am. Soc. Internat. Law. Clubs: California, Los Angeles Stock Exchange (pres. 1972). Contbg. author Labor Law for General Practitioners, 1960. Office: 800 W 6th St Suite 300 Los Angeles CA 90017 also One California St Suite 1935 San Francisco CA 94111

MC LAUGHLIN, JOSEPH THOMAS, lawyer; b. Boston, Mar. 30, 1944; s. James Francis and Madeline Louise (Hickman) McL.; B.A. magna cum laude, Boston Coll., 1965; J.D., Cornell U., 1968; m. Christine E. Mullen, Sept. 2, 1967; children—Amy Melissa, Caitlin Christine. Research asst. Brit. Council of Archaeology, Winchester, Eng., 1964, site supr., 1966; legis. asst. Rep. Thomas P. O'Neill, Washington, 1967; research asst. Cornell U., 1967-68; admittgd to Mass. bar, 1969, N.Y. State bar, 1968, U.S. Supreme Ct. bar, 1974; law clk. to chief justice Mass. Superior Ct., 1968-69; asso. firm Shearman & Sterling, N.Y.C., 1969-76, partner, 1976—. Exec. dir. Brooklyn Heights Draft Counseling Service, 1970-74; exec. dir. Presbyn. Task Force for Justice Counseling Service, 1973-75; v.p., dir. Brooklyn Heights Assn., 1973-77; dir. Willoughby Settlement House, Inc., Ingersoll-Willoughby Community Center, Inc., 1970-75; dir. United Neighborhood Houses, 1976-78. Mem. Assn. Bar City N.Y. (mem. com. on fed. cts. 1973-77), Am. Law Inst., N.Y. State Bar Assn. (chmn. com. on marijuana and drug abuse 1972-75). Clubs: Heights Casino, Broad Street. Author: Federal Class Action Digests, 1974; Federal Class Action Digests, 1976; contbr. articles to profl. jours. Home: 174 State St Brooklyn NY 11201 Office: 53 Wall New York NY 10005

MC LAUGHLIN, KATHLEEN, free-lance writer; b. Greenleaf, Kans.; d. John Charles and Mary (Loftus) McL.; student Mt. St. Scholastica Acad., Atchison, Kans. Reporter, Daily Globe, Atchison, Chgo. Tribune, 1925-33; women's editor Chgo. Tribune, 1933-35; reporter gen. news N.Y. Times, 1935-41, women's editor, 1941-43, Wash. corr., 1943-45, fgn. corr., 1945-51, N.Y. bur. UN Hdqrs., 1951-67, bus. news, 1967-68; free lance writer and researcher, 1968—. Recipient award for best reporting, 1938, for fgn. corr., 1948 (both N.Y. Newswomen's Club). Democrat. Roman Catholic. Clubs: Newswomen's, Overseas Press (N.Y.C.). Author: New Life in Old Lands, 1954; What's the U.N. Doing There?, 1961. Contbr. articles to mags. Home and office: 7264 W Peterson Ave C512 Chicago IL 60631

MC LAUGHLIN, LEIGHTON BATES, II, newspaper editor; b. Evanton, Ill., Apr. 10, 1930; s. Leighton Bates and Gwendolyn I. (Markle) McL.; student English lit. Kenyon Coll., Gambier, Ohio, 1948-50, Northwestern U., 1951, UCLA, 1955-56; m. Beverly Jean Jeske, May 5, 1962; children—Leighton Bates III, Jeffrey, Steven, Patrick. Copyboy, reporter, rewriteman City News Bur., Chgo., 1957-58; reporter, rewriteman Chgo. Sun-Times, 1958-62; rewriteman, asst. city editor Ariz. Jour., Phoenix, 1962; reporter Miami (Fla.) Herald, 1962-64; successively rewriteman, night city editor, 1st asst. city editor, telegraph editor Chgo. Sun-Times, 1964-74; dir. Chgo. Daily News/Sun-Times News Service (now Field News Service), 1974-79; editorial coordinator electronics newspaper div. Field Enterprises, 1975-79; adminstr. reference library and communications center Field Newspapers, 1976-79; editor Field Newspaper Syndicate, Irvine, Calif., 1979—; lectr., condr. seminars in field. Active local Cub Scouts, United Fund. Served to 1st lt. USMC, 1951-54. Recipient Stock-o-Type award for best feature story Chgo. Newspaper Guild, 1961, Best News story award Ill. AP and UPI, 1967. Mem. Soc. Profl. Journalists, Psi Upsilon. Author articles in field. Office: 1703 Kaiser Ave Irvine CA 92714. *Reporting the news is like any other intellectual activity in that it involves research, vertification, organization, and clarity of presentation. But news reporting is unique in that all this is done on a dead run, in time for the day's editions, for every breaking story.*

MCLAUGHLIN, MARVIN LOUIS, univ. dean; b. Centerville, Tex., Nov. 7, 1914; s. Robert A. and Margaret (Harrison) McL.; B.S., Sam Houston State U., 1935; M.Ed., U. Tex., 1940; Ed.D., U. Houston, 1955; m. Nell Turner, Dec. 22, 1939; 1 son, James Alan. Elementary sch. tchr., Corsicana, Tex., 1935-36; tchr.-prin. Voth-Rosedale Sch., Beaumont, Tex., 1936-40; prin. Livingston (Tex.) elementary and high schs., 1940-42; faculty Lamar U., Beaumont, 1946—, dean Grad. Sch., 1964-69, dean Coll. Edn., 1969—. Served with AUS, 1942-46. Mem. Tex. Assn. Coll. Tchrs., Tex. Tchrs. Assn., Tex. Assn. Colls. for Tchr. Edn. (sec. 1975-77), Phi Delta Kappa, Alpha Chi, Pi Gamma Mu, Phi Kappa Phi (pres. 1965-66). Methodist. Rotarian (pres. S. Park 1963-64). Home: 1150 Ivy Ln Beaumont TX 77706

MC LAUGHLIN, MATTHEW A., constrn. co. exec., lawyer; b. Washington, Aug. 30, 1936; s. Matthew Aloysius and Rose Adele (Molony) McL.; Honors A.B., Xavier U., 1958; LL.B., Columbia U., 1961; m. Kathleen Dee Kiely, June 27, 1964; children—Kathleen, Moira, Sheila, Regan. Admitted to N.Y. State bar, 1962; asso. firm Donovan, Leisure, Newton & Irvine, N.Y.C., 1962-66; with Davy Inc. (formerly The McKee Corp.), Cleve., 1966—, gen. counsel, 1969—, sec., 1974—, v.p., 1978—; chmn. gen. counsels com. Nat. Constructors Assn., 1975. Served with USAF, 1961-62. Mem. Assn. Bar City N.Y., Cleve., Am. bar assns. Home: 2758 Landon Rd Shaker Heights OH 44122 Office: 6200 Oak Tree Blvd Independence OH 44131

MCLAUGHLIN, MERLYN, ins. co. exec.; b. Salem, Ill., Sept. 7, 1901; s. Charles T. and Dorothy (Huff) McL.; A.B., Sterling Coll., 1927; A.M., U. Colo., 1937; Ph.D., 1951; m. Maurice Matthews, Jan. 2, 1935; children—Donn Charles, Robert Walter, John Scott. Athletic coach, Liberty High Sch., Pratt, Kan., 1927-37; head history dept., coach Pratt Jr. Coll., 1937-40; head history dept. Colo. Women's Coll., 1941-43; mem. faculty U. Denver, 1943-50, dir. Army Specialized Tng., 1943-44, dir. student personnel, 1944-46, dir. sch. aeros., 1946-50; chief liaison officer Br. A.F.R.O.T.C., H.Q. USAF, 1950; chief liaison div., asst. chief of staff, Res., H.Q. USAF; comdr. Iowa Air Res. Center, 1955-59; pres. Coll. Osteopathic Medicine and Surgery, Des Moines, 1959-66; v.p. Pioneer Ins. Co., 1969—; v.p. pub. relations Superior Equity Corp., 1970—. U.S. rep. Fedn. Aeronautique Internationale, 1953, 54, 58-59, 60. U.S. mem. UNESCO Aviation Edn. Council, 1947; chmn. Internat. Council for Aviation Edn.; mem. editorial adv. bd. Aviation Rev.; chmn. adv. com. on aviation edn. CAP. Mem. U. Aviation Assn. (dir.), Nat. Aeros. Assn., Internat. Soc. Aviation Writers, Air Force Assn., Res. Officers Assn., C. of C., Alpha Eta Rho, Sigma Chi, Phi Delta Kappa, Pi Kappa Delta, Delta Sigma Pi, Sigma Sigma Phi. Mason (32 deg., Shriner), Rotarian. Clubs: Lincoln, University, Omaha Press. Home: 6230 Sunrise Rd Lincoln NE 68510 Office: First Nat Bank Travel Div Box 81008 Lincoln NE 68501. *I have been so busy trying to manage my own life that I haven't had time to try to tell others how to manage theirs.*

MCLAUGHLIN, PETER JOSEPH, paper co. exec.; b. N.Y.C., July 21, 1928; s. Peter J. and Amelia (Greenochle) McL.; B.B.A., Pace Coll., 1954; J.D., Fordham U., 1960; m. Helen Ann Wollak, Jan. 20, 1951. With Union Camp Corp., N.Y.C., 1945—, asst. comptroller, 1962-65, comptroller, 1965-69, v.p. fin., comptroller, 1969-72, exec. v.p., 1972-77, pres., 1977—, also dir.; admitted to N.Y. bar, 1961; dir. Mut. Benefit Life Ins. Co. Served with AUS, 1954-56. Mem. Am. Bar Assn., Fordham U. Law Alumni Assn. (sec. Nassau-Suffolk 1964-65). Club: Upper Montclair Country. Office: 1600 Valley Rd Wayne NJ 07470

MCLAUGHLIN, ROBERT WILLIAM, architect; b. Kalamazoo, June 24, 1900; s. Robert William and Anna (Oggel) McL.; A.B., Princeton, 1921, M.F.A., 1926; Procter traveling fellow in Italy, France and England, 1926; m. Katherine Thurber, Oct. 21, 1933; children—Meredith (Mrs. Marcus P. Knowlton III), Robert. Began practice of architecture with H. Van Buren Magonigle; asso. with Charles Over Cornelius in archaeol. and restoration work, 1928-30; partner Holden, McLaughlin and Assos., 1930-53; pvt. practice as architect, 1953—; profl. adviser N.J. State Capitol Commn., 1964—; founded Am. Houses, Inc for mfr. of prefabricated houses, 1932, chmn. bd. until 1945; established research lab. Bedford Village, N.Y., for study of bldg. technique, 1940; prof. architecture, dir. Sch. Architecture, Princeton, 1952-65, prof. emeritus, 1965—; cons. architect Bahai World Centre, Mount Carmel, Haifa, Israel; profl. adviser Dept. of State, London embassy, Port of N.Y. Authority. Served as apprentice seaman, USN, 1918. Fellow A.I.A.; mem. Nat. Inst. for Archtl. Edn. (hon.), Soc. for Am. Archaeology, Archtl. League N.Y. (hon.), Soc. Preservation Historic Landmarks. Club: Century (N.Y.C.). Author: Architect, 1962; co-author: Curtain Walls, 1955; also archtl. monographs on brick architecture of Sweden and on San Gimignano. Editor: Architecture and the University, 1954. Home: Brixham RFD 1 Box 203 York ME 03909

MC LAUGHLIN, STUART BRUCE, real estate developer; b. Toronto, Ont., Can., Apr. 23, 1926; s. Stuart Wilson and Florence Beatrice (Hamilton) McL.; B.A., U. Toronto, 1957; LL.B., 1960; m. Patricia Elaine Morrison, Feb. 1, 1951; children—Laurel, Joanne, Stuart, Pamela, Julie. Called to Ont. bar, 1962; chmn., pres., chief exec. officer S.B. McLaughlin Assos. Ltd., and subs. and affiliated cos., Mississauga, Ont. Gen. campaign chmn. Peel Community Services, United Appeal, 1970; founding chmn. Mississauga Symphonic Assn.; bd. dirs. Council for Can. Unity, Que. Student Intra-Exchange Program, Can. Equestrian Team; bd. govs. Appleby Coll., Oakville, Ont.; chmn. Peel region Diabetic Assn. fund raising campaign, 1978; hon. dir. Cyclos Theatre Co., Mississauga; mem. governing council U. Toronto, 1978-80. Served with Royal Can. Air Force and Can. Inf. Corps, 1944-45. Recipient Can. Silver Jubilee medal. Mem. Law Soc. Peel Region, Can. Horse Council (past pres., founding dir.), Can. Equestrian Fedn. (life dir.), Can. Inst. Public Real Estate Cos. (dir.), Urban Devel. Inst. Clubs: Eglinton Hunt, Mississauga Golf, Chinguacousy Country (founding pres.). Author: One Hundred Million Canadians, 1973; 40 Million Places to Stand, 1975. Home: 1993 Mississauga Rd Mississauga ON L5H 2K5 Canada Office: 77 Centre Dr Mississauga ON L5B 1M6 Canada*

MCLAUGHLIN, TED JOHN, educator; b. Elkhart, Ind., Dec. 23, 1921; s. Frederick L. and Agnes (McBride) McL.; B.A., Manchester Coll., 1947; M.A., U. Wis., 1948, Ph.D., 1952; m. Helen F. Myers, Aug. 24, 1946. Instr. speech U. Wis., Milw., 1949-53, asst. prof., 1953-56, asso. prof., 1957-65, prof., 1965-67, prof. communication, 1967—, sec. faculty, 1956-59, asso. dean humanities and communication, 1962-65, 67-69, asso. dean Grad. Sch., 1971-76. Bd. dirs. U. Faculty Assn. Served with AUS, 1943-47. Mem. A.A.A.S., Friends of Art, Milw. Art Center, Central States Speech Assn., AAUP, Internat. Communication Assn., Speech Communication Assn., Wis. Acad. Scis., Arts and Letters (past v.p., sec.). Author: (with others) Communication, 1964; (with others) Cases and Projects in Communication, 1965. Home: 3073 N Hackett Ave Milwaukee WI 53211

MCLAUGHLIN, WALLACE ALVIN, civil engr., ednl. adminstr.; b. Calgary, Alta., Can., May 5, 1927; s. Benjamin Franklin and Mary (Krikau) McL.; B.Sc., U. Sask., 1951; M.S.C.E., Purdue U., 1958, Ph.D., 1965; m. Phyllis Victoria Coburn, Aug. 13, 1951; children—Dawn Theresa, Deborah Anne, Mari Lynne, Michael Wallace, Heather Janine. Project engr. Sask. Hwys., Regina, 1951-54, div. engr., 1955-57, sr. traffic engr., 1958-61; asst. prof. civil engring. U. Waterloo, Ont., Can., 1961-63, asso. prof., 1964-66, prof., chmn. dept., 1966-72, dean Faculty of Engring., 1974—. Mem. Kitchener (Ont.) Planning Bd., 1967-74. Internat. Rds. Fedn., Canadian Good Rds Assn. scholar, 1964; Can. Dept. Transport fellow, 1969. Mem. Assn. Profl. Engrs. Ont. Office: Univ Waterloo Waterloo ON N2L 3G1 Canada

MC LAUGHLIN, WILLIAM EARLE, banker; b. Oshawa, Ont., Can., Sept. 16, 1915; s. Frank and Frankie L. (Houlden) McL.; B.A., Queen's U., Kingston, Ont., 1936; m. Ethel Wattie, July 20, 1940; children—William, Mary. With Royal Bank of Can., 1936—, mgr. Montreal br., 1951-53, asst. gen. mgr., 1953-59, asst. to pres., 1959-60, gen. mgr., 1960—, pres., 1960, chmn., pres., 1962-77, chief exec. officer, 1977-79, chmn. bd., 1977—; chmn. bd. Sun Alliance Ins. Co.; dir. Adela Investment Co. S.A.; trustee Can. Staff Pension Plan; dir. Ralston Purina Can., Inc., Algoma Steel Corp., Ltd., Power Corp. Can., Ltd., Standard Brands, Inc., Genstar, Ltd., Met. Life Ins. Co., Continental Reins. Corp. (Bermuda) Ltd., Shawinigan Industries, Ltd., C.P. Ltd., Textron Can. Ltd., Allied Chem. (Can.) Ltd., Gen. Motors Corp., Trans-Can. Corp. Fund. Bd. govs. Royal Victoria Hosp.; trustee Queen's U. Clubs: Engineers, Royal Montreal Golf, Royal Montreal Curling, University, Mount Royal, Forest and Stream, St. James, Montreal; Seigniory (Montebello); Toronto, York (Toronto); Mt. Bruno Golf; Rideau (Ottawa, Can.); Canadian (N.Y.); Lyford Cay (Nassau); Mid-Ocean (Bermuda). Home: 67 Sunnyside Ave Westmount Montreal PQ Canada Office: Royal Bank of Can Bldg Montreal PQ H3C 3A9 Canada

MCLAURIN, JAMES W., physician; b. Natchez, Miss., July 1, 1910; s. Walter and Annie Wall (Whitaker) McL.; student Washington and Lee U., 1928-30; M.D., U. Ark., 1934; m. Lady Katharine Kretschmar, Sept. 28, 1935. Interne Mary's Help Hosp., San Francisco, 1934-35; resident Los Angeles Children's Hosp., 1935-36; pvt. practice otolaryngology, Baton Rouge, 1936—; instr. Eye, Nose and Throat Clinics, U. Ark. Sch. Medicine, 1934; instr. otolaryngology La. State U. Med. Sch., 1946-49; Otto Joachim prof. otolaryngology Tulane U. Sch. Medicine, 1949-69, clin. prof. otology, 1969—, chmn. dept. otolaryngology, 1949-58. Mem. nat. com. Deafness Research Found. Fellow A.C.S.; mem. A.M.A., Am. Acad. Ophthalmology and Otolaryngology, Am. Laryngol., Rhin., and Otol. Soc., Am. Broncho-Esophagol. Assn., Am. Otol. Soc. Presbyn. Clubs: Baton Rouge Camelot, Baton Rouge Country, Baton Rouge City. Contbr. articles to med. jours. Home: 2856 Reymond Ave Baton Rouge LA 70808 Office: 3888 Government St Baton Rouge LA 70806

MCLEAN, DON, singer, instrumentalist, composer; b. New Rochelle, N.Y., Oct. 2, 1945; s. Donald and Elizabeth (Bucci) McL.; student Villanova U., 1964; B.B.A., Iona Coll., 1968. Hudson River troubadour N.Y. State Council on Arts, 1968; mem. Hudson River Sloop Singers, 1969; solo concert tours, Australia, New Zealand, Japan, China, Eng., France, Israel, Germany, Ireland, Scotland, Holland, Sweden, Denmark, U.S. and Can.; appeared on TV spl. Till Tomorrow, 1973, Sounds of Summer, Sesame Street, Dinah Shore Show, Merv Griffith Show, Mike Douglas Show, Smothers Brothers Show, numerous others; composer film score Fraternity Row; pres. Benny Bird Corp., Inc. Mem. bd. Hudson River Sloop Restoration, World Hunger Yr., Advs. for Arts; fund raiser Scenic Hudson, Hudson River Fishermans Assn. Recipient 2 Gold records, 10 Gold records, Australia, 3 Gold records, Eng., 1 Gold record, Ireland, 4 Grammy award nominations. Author: Songs of Don McLean, 1972; The Songs of Don McLean, Vol. II, 1974; (songbook) Mummies Dreidles Babys and Laments. Editor: Songs and Sketches of the Clearwater Crew, 1969. Composer over 200 songs including Vincent (Starry Starry Night), Dreidle, And I Love You So, American Pie, Wonderful Baby, The Legend of Andrew McCrew, Empty Chairs, Castles in the Air, If We Try, Color TV Blues; Prime Time. Recordings include Tapestry, 1970; American Pie, 1971; Don McLean, 1972; Playin' Favorites, 1973; Homeless Brother, 1974, Solo, 1976; Prime Time, 1977, Chain Lightning, 1979.

MC LEAN, DONALD MILLIS, physician, educator; b. Melbourne, Australia, July 26, 1926; s. Donald and Nellie (Millis) McL.; B.Sc., U. Melbourne, 1947, M.B., 1950, M.D., 1954; married. Fellow Rockefeller Found., N.Y.C. and Hamilton, Mont., 1955; vis. instr. bacteriology U. Minn., Mpls., 1957; med. officer Commonwealth Serum Labs., Melbourne, 1957; virologist Research Inst., Hosp. for Sick Children, Toronto, Ont., Can., 1958-67; asso. prof. microbiology, asso. in pediatrics U. Toronto Med. Sch., 1962-67; prof. microbiology U. B.C. Med. Sch., Vancouver, Can., 1967—, head div. med. microbiology, 1968—. Fellow Royal Coll. Physicians (Can.), Royal Coll. Pathologists; mem. Am. Soc. Microbiologists, Canadian Pub. Health Assn., Am. Epidemiological Soc., Am. Soc. Tropical Medicine, Can. Med. Assn., Am. Soc. Microbiology, Canadian Soc. Microbiologists. Contbr. articles to profl. jours. Office: Div Med Microbiology U BC Vancouver BC V6T 1W5 Canada

MC LEAN, GEORGE FRANCIS, clergyman, educator; b. Lowell, Mass., June 29, 1919; s. Arthur and Agnes (McHugh) McL.; Ph.L., Gregorian U., Rome, 1952, S.T.L., 1956; Ph.D., Cath. U. Am., 1958. Joined Order Oblates of Mary Immaculate, 1949; ordained priest Roman Catholic Ch., 1955; prof. metaphysics, philosophy of religion Cath U. Am., Washington, 1958—; research scholar U. Madras, 1969, U. Paris, 1970. Mem. Am. Cath. Philos. Assn. (nat. sec. 1965—), World Union Cath. Philos. Socs. (sec. gen. 1973—), Internat. Soc. Metaphysics (gen. sec. 1974—), Internat. Fedn. Philos. Socs. (dir.), Cath. Learned Socs. and Scholars (sec. 1975-77). Author: Man's Knowledge of God According to Paul Tillich, 1958; Perspectives on Reality, 1966; An Annotated Bibliography of Philosophy in Catholic Thought, 1966; A Bibliography of Christian Philosophy and Contemporary Issues, 1966; Readings in Ancient Western Philosophy, 1970; Ancient Western Philosophy, 1971; Plenitude and Participation, 1978; editor numerous books including The Existence of God, 1972, Religion in Contemporary Thought, 1973, Traces of God in a Secular Culture, 1973, The Philosopher as Teacher, 1973, The Impact of Belief, 1974, The Role of Reason in Belief, 1974; New Dynamics in Ethical Thinking, 1974, Thomas and Bonaventure, 1976, Philosophy and Civil Law, 1975, Freedom, 1976, Ethical Wisdom East and/or West, 1977, Man and Nature, 1978, Immateriality, 1978, The Human Person, 1979; area editor New Cath. Ency. Home: 391 Michigan Ave NE Washington DC 20017 Office: Cath U Am Washington DC 20064

MCLEAN, HUGH, educator; b. Denver, Feb. 5, 1925; s. Hugh and Rosamond (Denison) McL.; grad. Taft Sch., 1942; B.A., Yale, 1947; M.A., Columbia, 1949; Ph.D., Harvard, 1956; m. Katharine Hoag, Feb. 2, 1957; children—Anna Scattergood, Clara Denison, Gregory Hugh. Instr. Russian lang. and lit. Harvard, 1953-56, asst. prof. Russian lit., 1956-59; asso. prof. U. Chgo., 1959-62, prof., 1962-68, chmn. Slavic dept., 1961-67; vis. prof. U. Calif., Berkeley, 1967-68, prof. 1968—, chmn. Slavic dept., 1970-72, 74-76, divisional dean of humanities, 1976—. Served to ensign USNR, 1943-46. Am. Council Learned Socs. fellow, Fulbright research grantee, U.K., 1958-59; Guggenheim fellow, 1965-66. Mem. Am. Assn. Tchrs. Slavic and East European Langs., Am. Assn. for Advancement Slavic Studies. Author: Nikolai Leskov: The Man and His Art, 1977. Co-editor: For Roman Jakobson, 1956; Russian Thought and Politics, 1957; The Year of Protest, 1956, 1961; Nervous People and Other Satires (M. Zoshchenko), 1963. Contbr. articles and revs. to profl. jours. Home: 827 Indian Rock Berkeley CA 94707

MCLEAN, HUGH JOHN, univ. adminstr.; b. Winnipeg, Man., Can., Jan. 5, 1930; s. Robert and Olive May (Smallwood) McL.; B.A., King's Coll., Cambridge (Eng.) U., 1954, Mus.B., 1956, M.A., 1958; m. Florence Anne Stillman, Aug. 18, 1979; children by previous marriage—Robert A., J. Stuart, Hugh D. Free-lance profl. musician, Vancouver, B.C., Can., 1957-67; asst. prof. Music U. Victoria (B.C.), 1967-69; asso. prof. U. B.C., Vancouver, 1969-73; prof., dean Faculty of Music, U. Western Ont., London, 1973—. Recipient Arnold Bax Commonwealth medal Festival of Commonwealth Youth, 1954, Harriet Cohen Bach medal, 1955; Can. Council grantee, 1960, 65, 72. Fellow Royal Coll. Organists, Royal Can. Coll. Organists, Royal Soc. Can.; mem. Am. Fedn. Musicians, Am. Musicological Soc., Can. Assn. Univ. Schs. Music, Can. Music Educators' Assn., Internat. Soc. Music Edn., Royal Musical Assn. Anglican. Clubs: Racquet (Victoria); Univ. of London (Ont.). Home: 1020 Maitland St London ON N5Y 2X9 Canada Office: Faculty of Music U Western Ont London N6A 3K7 Canada

MC LEAN, JOHN DOUGLAS, psychiatrist; b. Chatham, N.B., Can., July 9, 1935; s. Murdo L. and Edith M. (Martin) McL.; student St. Francis Xavier, 1952-55; M.D., Dalhousie U., 1960; m. Lynn Keating, May 20, 1960; children—Douglas, Elizabeth, Andrew, Stephen, Ann, Mary. Intern, St. John (N.B.) Gen. Hosp., 1959-60; resident in psychiatry Dalhousie U. Hosps., Halifax, N.S. and St. Johns, Nfld., 1960-64; pvt. practice psychiatry, St. John, N.B., 1966—; staff psychiatrist Hosp. for Mental and Nervous Diseases, St. John's, Nfld., 1964, dir. resident tng., 1965-66, acting supt., 1966; mem. staff St. John Gen. Hosp., 1966—, dir. psychiat. edn., 1972—; asso. prof. psychiatry Dalhousie U., Halifax, 1972—; vice chmn. N.B. Adv. Com. on Mental Health Services, 1966-68. Fellow Royal Coll. Physicians and Surgeons Can. (bd. examiners 1968-76, council 1979—), Am. Coll. Psychiatry; mem. N.B. Med. Assn., Can. (past pres.), Nfld. (past pres.), N.B. (past pres.) psychiat. assns. Home: 145 Bedell Ave Saint John NB Canada Office: 66 Waterloo St Saint John NB E2L 3P4 Canada

MC LEAN, JOHN WILLIAM, banker; b. Okmulgee, Okla., Apr. 2, 1922; s. Lawrence W. and Margaret (McGill) McL.; B.S., Okla. U., 1943; m. Eleanor Jane Johnson, May 8, 1943; children—Margo, Lawrence William, Scott Johnson. Account exec. Merrill Lynch, Pierce, Fenner & Beane, Tulsa, 1947-48; with First Nat. Bank & Trust Co., Tulsa, 1948-58, loan officer, v.p., 1951-58, also chmn. investment com., trust dept.; pres. Tex. Nat. Bank of Commerce, 1959-65; sr. v.p., mgr. internat. banking Bank of Am., Los Angeles, 1965-66, sr. v.p., dir. marketing, San Francisco, 1966-67; became pres., chief exec. officer Liberty Nat. Bank & Trust Co., Oklahoma City, 1967, now chmn. bd., chief exec. officer; founder, dir. Reading and Bates Offshore Drilling Co.; dir., vice chmn. Allied Bank Internat. Bd. govs. Rice U.; exec. com. Frontiers of Sci. Found. Okla.; mem. Fed. Adv. Council, 1977-79, pres., 1979. Served from pvt. to capt., F.A., AUS, 1942-46. Decorated Bronze Star; named Outstanding Young Man, Tulsa C. of C., 1951, Regional Banker of Year, Finance Mag., 1972; recipient Distinguished Service citation U. Okla., 1975. Named to Okla. Hall of Fame, 1976. Mem. Oklahoma City C. of C. (mem. corporate bd.), Am. Bankers Assn. (chmn. credit policy com. 1964-65, mem. exec. council, chmn. com. right of privacy), Res. City Bankers Assn., U.S. Golf Assn. (exec. com.), Sigma Alpha Epsilon, Beta Gamma Sigma. Presbyn. (deacon). Club: Oklahoma City Golf and Country (pres. 1973). Author, editor: Fundamental Principles of Sound Bank Credit, 1965; Cross-Selling Bank Services to Business, 1966; The Art (?) of Selling, 1969. Office: Liberty Nat Bank & Trust Co Oklahoma City OK 73102

MC LEAN, MALCOLM, coll. pres.; b. Duluth, Minn., Apr. 23, 1927; s. Charles Russell and Mildred (Washburn) McL.; B.A., Yale U., 1948; M.S. in Internat. Affairs, George Washington U., 1967; L.H.D., Coll. St. Scholastica, Duluth, 1973; m. Wendy Heaton, May 20, 1956; children—Ian, Hugh Heaton, Christopher Russell. Advt. mgr. H.B. Fuller Co., St. Paul, 1953-55; with USIA, 1955-71; br. pub. affairs officer, Pusan, Korea, 1955-57; information officer Consulate Gen., Sao Paulo, Brazil, 1958-60; officer-in-charge West Coast South Am. Affairs, Hdqrs. USIA, 1960-61; cultural affairs officer embassy, Santo Domingo, Dominican Republic, 1961-64, pub. affairs officer, 1964-65; with Office Dir. Gen. Fgn. Service, 1965-66; spl. asst. to dep. dir., 1967-69; pub. affairs officer, 1st sec. embassy, Guatemala, 1969-71; pres. Northland Coll., Ashland, Wis., 1971—; dir. Chippewa Industries, Lake Superior Dist. Power Co. Trustee, Lake Superior Assn. Colls and Univs., 1973—. Served with USNR, 1944-46, AUS, 1950-52. Decorated Bronze Star. Mem. Wis. Acad. Scis., Arts and Letters (dir.). Chmn. editorial bd. Fgn. Service Jour., 1968-69. Address: 1300 Ellis Ave Ashland WI 54806

MC LEAN, ROBERT JOSEPH, transp. co. exec.; b. Newark, Apr. 29, 1920; s. Robert and Bertha (Hecht) McL.; student Dartmouth Coll., 1938-40; A.B., Columbia U., 1942, LL.B., 1947; m. Claire Stroncer, May 21, 1949; children—Robert Paul, Barbara Claire. Admitted to N.Y. bar, 1948, Calif. bar, 1960; with S.P. Co., 1947—, exec. v.p. fin., 1976—; dir. Trailer Train Co., Am. Rail Box Car Co. Bd. dirs. Golden Gate chpt. ARC, 1969-75; trustee Golden Gate U., 1976—. Served with AUS, 1942-45. Mem. Assn. Am. R.R.'s (treasury div.), Am. Bar Assn. Republican. Roman Catholic. Clubs: Family, Bankers, Pacific Union (San Francisco); Burlingame Country (Hillsborough). Home: 530 Patrick Way Los Altos CA 94022 Office: One Market Plaza So Pacific Bldg San Francisco CA 94105

MC LEAN, ROBERT THOMAS, mathematician, educator; b. Westerville, Ohio, July 18, 1922; s. Earl H. and Angeline (Thomas) McL.; B.S., Otterbein Coll., 1946; M.A., Bowling Green State U., 1950; Ph.D., U. Pitts., 1961; m. E. Elizabeth Weaver, Dec. 26, 1953; 1 dau., Betty Carole (Mrs. Clifford B. James, Jr.). Instr. math. Upper Sandusky High Sch., 1945-49; prof., head dept. math., chmn. sci. div. Coll. of Steubenville, 1952-67; prof. math. Loyola U., New Orleans, 1967—, chmn. dept., 1967-73, 79—; dir. La. Transcribing Service; bd. dirs. Nat. Accreditation Council. Chmn. consumer advisory council Blind Services Program of La.; del. White House Conf. on Handicapped; mem. La. Gov.'s Advisory Council on Handicapped; chmn. Affiliated Leadership League; v.p. Am. Council Blind; trustee La. State Library; cons. Council on Ageing; bd. dirs., v.p. Lighthouse for Blind; pres. La. Council of Blind, Radio for the Blind and Print Handicapped, Greater New Orleans Council of Blind. Mem. Am. Math. Soc., Math. Assn. Am., Nat. Council Tchrs. Math., AAUP, AAWB, AEVH, Sigma Xi. Presbyterian (elder). Mason. Office: 6363 St Charles Ave New Orleans LA 70118

MC LEAN, THOMAS EDWIN, mgmt. cons.; b. St. Petersburg, Fla., Feb. 14, 1925; s. Annis and Grace (Bell) McL.; B.S. in Bus. Adminstrn., U. Fla., 1950; grad. Ind. U. Sch. Savs. and Loan, 1967, also Am. Savs. and Loan Inst.; m. Virginia Starr, Feb. 20, 1948; children—Brent Starr, Thomas Edwin, Lynn Elizabeth. Partner firm Gassner and McLean, C.P.A.'s, St. Petersburg, 1953-65; sr. v.p., sec. First Fed. Savs. & Loan Assn., St. Petersburg, 1965-69; exec. v.p. St. Petersburg Fed. Savs. & Loan Assn., 1969-71, pres., 1971-75, also dir.; pres. Abilities, Inc. of Fla., 1968-70; dir. Southeastern Suppliers Inc., Mfd. Housing Products. Pres., Jr. Achievement Pinellas County, 1968-71, St. Petersburg Relocation Assistance Corp., 1971-75; mem. bishop's finance com. Episcopal Diocese S.W. Fla.; chmn. Bishop's Com. on State of Ch., 1973-75; mem. Com. of 100, chmn., 1970; mem. Pinellas County Budget Commn., 1954-56; mem. Pinellas County Tourist Devel. Commn., 1978—. Bd. dirs. Anclote Psychiat. Center; bd. dirs. St. Petersburg Speech and Hearing Clinic, pres., 1968-69; bd. dirs. Pinellas Assn. Retarded Children, 1969-72, Police Athletic League, 1971-74, Community Alliance, 1972-74, Sunny Shores Villas, 1964-68, Suncoast Manor, 1969-75, Pinellas Horizon Mental Health Center and Hosp., 1977—. Served with AUS, 1943-45. Decorated Purple Heart; named Sertoman of Yr., 1957-58; Liberty Bell award St. Petersburg Bar Assn., 1975. Mem. Nat. League Insured Savs. Assns. (chmn. finance com. 1973, mem. exec. com. 1972-74), U.S., Fla. (chmn. advt. and pub. relations com. 1970-72) savs. and loans leagues, Sales and Mktg. Club (pres. 1968-69), St. Petersburg Area (dir., pres. 1975-76), Suncoast (dir.) chambers commerce. Republican. Episcopalian (treas., sr. warden). Clubs: Rotary; Bat Boys, Yacht (St. Petersburg); Dragon (dir.), Tiger Bay (pres.), Suncoasters, Golden Triangle, Quarterback. Home: 1339 43d Ave N Saint Petersburg FL 33703

MCLEAN, THOMAS NEIL, editor; b. Blythewood, S.C., July 30, 1938; s. Hudnalle Bridges and Helen (Allen) McL.; B.A., U. S.C., 1960; postgrad. Boston U., 1962; m. Margaret Ann McMurray, Mar. 3, 1962; children—Thomas Neil, Melanie Ann, Patrick David. With Columbia (S.C.) Newspapers Inc., 1964—, asst. mng. editor The State, 1972-73, editor The Columbia Record, 1973—. Mem. S.C. Consumer Affairs Commn.; trustee United Fund, Columbia. Served with USAF, 1961-64. Mem. Am. Soc. Newspaper Editors, AP Mng. Editors Assn., S.C. AP News Council (pres.), Sigma Delta Chi. Clubs: Summit, Kiwanis (dir. local club). Home: 505 Winston Rd Columbia SC 29209 Office: PO Box 1333 Columbia SC 29209

MC LEAN, VINCENT RONALD, mfg. co. exec.; b. Detroit, June 1, 1931; s. Frederick Ronald and Bernice Mary (Vincent) McL.; B.B.A., U. Mich., 1954, M.B.A., 1955; m. Joyce Adrienne Koch, July 23, 1960; children—Judith Adrienne, Bruce Ronald. Financial analyst Ford Motor Co., Detroit, 1954-55; with Mobil Oil Corp., 1958-69; treas. Mobil Chem. Co., 1966-69; asst. to v.p. fin. NL Industries, Inc. (formerly Nat. Lead Co.), N.Y.C., 1969-70, treas., 1970-72, v.p. fin., treas., 1972-76, exec. v.p. fin. and planning, 1976—, also dir., mem. exec. com.; dir. Titanium Metals Corp. Am., Toronto, Ohio, Can. Metals Co., Toronto, Ont. Enlisted man Biol. Warfare Labs., 1955-57. Mem. N.Y. Soc. Security Analysts, Canadian Soc. N.Y. Clubs: Economic N.Y.; University (Chgo.). Home: 702 Shackamaxon Dr Westfield NJ 07090 Office: 1230 Ave of Americas New York NY 10020

MC LEAN, W. F., packing co. exec.; b. Toronto, Ont., Can., 1916; ed. U. Toronto, 1938. Chmn., dir. Can. Packers Ltd., Toronto; v.p., dir. Canadian Imperial Bank Commerce; dir. Canadian Gen. Electric Co. Ltd., Steel Co. Can. Ltd. Home: 32 Whitney Ave Toronto ON M4W 2A8 Canada Office: 95 St Clair Ave W Toronto ON M4V 1P2 Canada

MCLEAN, WILLIAM BRUCE, advt. exec.; b. Toronto, Ont., Can., June 4, 1925; s. John and Edith Kate (Tallett) McL.; student bus. adminstrn. Ryerson Coll., Toronto, 1946; m. Pelma Violet Cook, Aug. 4, 1945; children—David Bruce, Douglas James. Tchr., Ryerson Coll., 1946-47; account supr. McKim Advt., Toronto, 1947-53; advt. mgr. Yardley of London, Toronto, 1953-54; chmn. Needham, Harper & Steers Can. Ltd., Toronto, 1954—; bd. dirs. Inst. Canadian Advt., Broadcast Exec. Soc. Served with Canadian Navy, 1942-45. Conservative. Anglican. Clubs: Mississauga Golf, Toronto Press, Mt. Stephen. Home: 1407 Royal York Rd Toronto ON M9P 3A6 Canada Office: 101 Richmond St W Toronto ON M5H 1T3 Canada

MC LEAN, WILLIAM HENRY, engr.; b. N.Y.C., Apr. 15, 1911; s. William and Ella (Powel) McL.; M.E., Stevens Inst. Tech., 1931; M.S., Harvard, 1933, M.B.A., 1934, D.C.S., 1938, D.Engring., 1976; m. Vesta Barbara Tittmann, Oct. 16, 1950; children—William Henry, Eugene Brown. Mem. faculty Harvard, 1931-40; treas. Nat. Can. Corp., 1940-41, Dewey & Almy Chem. Co., 1946-48; v.p. mktg. Merck & Co., Inc., 1948-54, v.p., gen. mgr. chem. div., 1954-55, pres. chem. div., 1955-63; dean Coll., sec. Stevens Inst. Tech., 1964, v.p., 1972-76; dir. Digital Equipment Corp., Econs. Lab., Inc., Nat. Aviation Corp., Titanium Industries. Mem. N.J. Bd. Higher Edn. Trustee Overlook Hosp., Union Coll. Served to lt. col. AUS, 1942-46. Decorated Legion of Merit. Mem. Am. Chem. Soc., Inst. Food Tech., A.A.A.S., Am. Soc. Engring. Edn., N.Y. Acad. Scis., Sigma Xi, Tau Beta Pi. Clubs: Union, Harvard (N.Y.C.); Baltusrol Golf (Springfield, N.J); Short Hills; St. Louis Country; Pilgrims. Home: 120 Knollwood Rd Short Hills NJ 07078 Office: 382 Springfield Ave Summit NJ 07901

MC LEAN, WILLIAM HUGH, banker; b. Little Rock, Nov. 21, 1916; s. Arthur Edward and Margaret (Crosby) McL.; B.A., Cornell U., 1939; postgrad. Sch. Banking of South, 1960; m. Marjorie Offenhauser, Oct. 26, 1940; children—Peggy (Mrs. Phillip Walker), Barbara (Mrs. Harry Ford), Jean (Mrs. Bruce Brookby). With Comml. Nat. Bank, Little Rock, 1958—, chmn. trust com., 1968—, vice chmn. bd., 1969-79, chmn. bd., 1979—; pres. Rob Roy Plantation Co., Little Rock, 1960—. Pres., Met. YMCA, 1957, Little Rock AFB Community Council, 1975-76; pres. United Fund Pulaski County, 1963, campaign chmn., 1962; commr. Little Rock Municipal Airport, 1969—, treas., 1970—, chmn., 1973—; treas. Metroplan, 1976-77, pres., 1978—. Served with AUS, World War II. Kiwanian. Club: Country (Little Rock). Home: 5114 Sherwood Little Rock AR 72207 Office: 200 Main St Little Rock AR 72201

MC LEAN, WILLIAM L., III, publisher; b. Phila., Oct. 4, 1927; s. William L., Jr. and Eleanor Ray (Bushnell) McL.; B.A., Princeton U., 1949; m. Elizabeth D. Peterson, Sept. 4, 1954; children—Elizabeth, William L., IV, Helen Brooke, Sandra, Warden. With The Bull., Phila., 1949—. v.p., 1969-74, sr. v.p., 1974-75, editor, pub., 1975—. Mem. Pa. Newspapers Pubs. Assn. (chmn. finance com., pres. 1964). Episcopalian. Club: Blooming Grove (Pa.) Hunting and Fishing. Home: 139 Cherry Ln Wynnewood PA 19096 Office: 30th and Market Sts Philadelphia PA 19101

MC LELLAN, W. ROBERT, mfg. co. exec.; b. Kearney, Nebr., Mar. 11, 1923; s. H.H. and Margaret (Calhoun) McL.; student Tex. Technol. Coll., 1944; B.S., Calif. State Coll., San Jose, 1949; postgrad. U. Santa Clara, 1950-52, Stanford, summer 1959; m. Helen Joyce Kidd, June 29, 1946; children—Margaret Ann McLellan Lolmaugh, Jennifer Sue McLellan Guy, William Robert, Katherine Marie. Sales engr. export dept. FMC Corp., San Jose, Calif., 1949-54, sales mgr., 1954-56, gen. mgr. machinery export dept. FMC Internat., 1956-60, v.p., 1960-69; asst. sec. for domestic and internat. bus. Dept. Commerce, Washington, 1969-71; v.p. FMC Corp., Chgo., 1971—; dir. several overseas corps., Chgo.-Tokyo Bank; co-chmn. Mid-Am. World Trade Conf., 1973, chmn., 1974; mem. U.S. Food Industry Research Team to USSR, 1960. Mem. Gov. Reagan's Task Force, Chile-Calif. Program, 1968-69; mem. adv. com. Sch. Bus., San Francisco State Coll., 1964-69; dir. Midwest Council Internat. Econ. Policy, mem. exec. com., 1977—; trustee Am. Grad. Sch. Internat. Mgmt., 1978—. Served with AUS, 1944-45. Mem. NAM (chmn. internat. trade subcom.), U.S. C. of C. (internat. investment subcom.), Mid Am.-Arab C. of C. (dir.), Chgo. Council Fgn. Relations (Chgo. com.), Mid-Am. Com. Congregationalist (past chmn. bd. trustees, past deacon). Clubs: Econ., Mid-Am. (Chgo.). Home: 546 Greenwood Ave Kenilworth IL 60043 Office: FMC Corp 200 E Randolph Dr Chicago IL 60601

MCLELLAND, JOSEPH CUMMING, educator; b. Scotland, Sept. 10, 1925; s. David and Jessie (Cumming) McL.; B.A., McMaster U., Hamilton, Ont., Can., 1946; M.A., U. Toronto, 1949; B.D., Knox Coll., Toronto, 1951; Ph.D., New Coll. U. Edinburgh (Scotland), 1953; m. Audrey Brunton, Aug. 23, 1947; children—Jonathan, Peter, Andrew, Margaret. Ordained to ministry Presbyn. Ch., 1949; minister in Val D'Or, Que., 1949-51, Bolton, Ont., 1953-57; prof. philosophy of religion and ethics Presbyn. Coll., Montreal, 1957-64; prof. philosophy religion McGill U., 1964—, dean faculty religious studies, 1975—. Chmn. Orthodox and Reformed Chs. Consulation N. Am., 1963—. Can. Council grantee and Am. Assn. Theol. Schs. fellow, 1968. Mem. Canadian Theol. Soc. (past pres.), Canadian Soc. Study Religion. Author: Visible Words of God, 1957; The Clown and the Crocodile, 1970; God the Anonymous, 1976. Asso. editor Studies in Religion, 1970-73, editor, 1973—; editorial bd. Theology Today, 1960—. Home: 121 Alston St Pointe-Claire PQ H9R 3E2 Canada Office: 3520 University St Montreal PQ H3A 2A7 Canada

MC LEMORE, ROBERT HENRY, petroleum engr., cons.; b. Dallas, Feb. 28, 1910; s. Edward Eugene and Margaret (Butler) McL.; B.S., Tex. A. and M. Coll., 1933; m. Ethel Ruth Ward, June 30, 1935; 1 dau., Mary Frances (Mrs. Guyton). Div. engr. Sun Oil Co., Dallas, 1933-41; exec. v.p., gen. mgr. Welex Jet Services, Ft. Worth, 1946-53; cons. engr., 1953-55; v.p., gen. mgr. Turbo Drill div. Dresser Industries, Dallas, 1955-57; pres. Otis Engring. Corp., 1957-75. Councilor, Tex. A. and M. U. Research Found.; trustee Tex. A. and M. U. Geoscis. and Earth Resources Found. Served from lt. to col., USAAF, 1941-45. Mem. Soc. Petroleum Engrs. (treas. 1960-63, pres. 1970, dir. 1969-72, DeGolyer Distinguished Service medal 1976), Mid Continent Oil and Gas Assn., Am. Petroleum Inst., Independent Producers Assn. Am., AIME (hon. mem.; dir. 1969—, v.p. 1971; Roger McConnell Engring. Achievement award 1975). Clubs: Petroleum; Engineers, Dallas (Dallas); Fort Worth; Northwood Country. Home: 11625 Wander Ln Dallas TX 75230

MCLENDON, CHARLES A., textile co. exec.; b. Raleigh, N.C., Feb. 6, 1923; s. Lennox Polk and Mary (Aycock) McL.; grad. Baylor Mil. Acad., 1940; A.B., U. N.C., 1944; student N.C. State Textile Sch.,

1945; m. Mary Stuart Snider; children—Stuart T. (Mrs. S. Kirk Materne), Mildred A. (Mrs. Charles King), Mary Davis (Mrs. Jeffrey Diff Ritchie), Charles A. With hosiery div. Burlington Industries, 1948—, So. personnel dir., 1952-54, N.Y. personnel dir., 1954-56, exec. asst. to pres. and chmn., 1956-58, v.p., 1958, v.p. charge personnel and indsl. relations North and South, 1970, sr. v.p., 1972-73, exec. v.p., 1973—, also dir., mem. policy com.; exec. dir. Burlington Industries Found., 1971—; dir. 1st Union Nat. Bank Greensboro, Key Co., Greensboro, First Union Corp. Bd. dirs. N.C. Citizens Assn., N.C. Outward Bound; trustee Guilford Coll., Greensboro, N.C.; trustee-at-large Ind. Coll. Funds Am. Served with AUS, 1943-45. Mem. Am. Mgmt. Assn. Episcopalian. Clubs: Greensboro Country; Country of North Carolina (Pinehurst). Home: 2318 Kirkpatrick Pl Greensboro NC 27408 Office: PO Box 21207 3330 W Friendly Ave Greensboro NC 27420

MC LENDON, HEATH BRIAN, securities investment co. exec.; b. San Francisco, May 24, 1933; s. Jesse Heath and Clara Martha (Nelson) McL.; B.A., Stanford U., 1955; M.B.A., Harvard U., 1959; m. Judith Nelson Locke, May 30, 1959; children—Laurie, Eric, Brian and Michael (twins). With Shearson Hayden Stone, and predecessors, N.Y.C., 1960—, exec. v.p., dir., 1971-77; chmn., pres. Shearson Mut. Funds, N.Y.C., 1971-78; pres. Bernstein Macaulay Inc., N.Y.C., 1977—. Pres. bd. trustees N.J. Shakespeare Festival, 1975-76; v.p., adv. bd. Summit (N.J.) YWCA, 1972-77; trustee Drew U., 1978—. Served to 1st lt. AUS, 1955-57. Mem. N.Y. Soc. Security Analysts, Money Marketeers. Presbyterian. Club: Beacon Hill. Home: 17 Lenox Rd Summit NJ 07901 Office: 767 Fifth Ave New York NY 10022

MCLENDON, JOHN AYCOCK, diversified co. exec.; b. Durham, N.C., Jan. 30, 1933; s. Lennox Polk and Mary Lilly (Aycock) McL.; B.S., U. N.C., 1954; M.B.A. (Love fellow), Harvard U., 1959; m. Barbara Lee Whittington, May 4, 1957; children—John A., Mark W., Lee. With Burlington Industries, Inc., 1959—, asst. v.p., 1967-69, treas., 1969-71, v.p., treas., 1971-76; v.p. fin. Insilco Corp., Meriden, Conn., 1976—; dir. Gilbert & Bennett Mfg. Co. Trustee Conn. Pub. Expenditure Council, Inc. Served with AUS, 1954-56. Mem. Beta Theta Pi, Beta Gamma Sigma. Episcopalian. Clubs: Greensboro Country; Harvard (N.Y.C.). Home: Haddam CT 06438 Office: 1000 Research Pkwy Meriden CT 06450

MCLENDON, RUTH ANN, fgn. service officer; b. Fort Worth, June 8, 1929; d. Chester Lee and Laura Anna (Johnson) McL.; B.A., Tex. Christian U., 1949; M.A., Fletcher Sch. Law and Diplomacy, 1950; postgrad. Nat. War Coll., 1969-70. Commd. fgn. service officer Dept. State; internat. relations officer Dept. State, 1955-58; consul, Adelaide, Australia, 1959-61; 2d sec., consul, Rangoon, Burma, 1962-66; tng. officer Fgn. Service Inst., 1967; internat. relations officer Dept. State, 1968-69; 1st sec. Bangkok, 1970-72; consul, Paris, 1973-75; consul, Mexico City, 1975-77; consul gen., Monterrey, Mex., 1977-79; dep. asst. Sec. of State for consular affairs, Washington, 1979—. Office: Dept of State Washington DC 20520

MCLENNAN, CHARLES EWART, obstetrician, gynecologist; b. Duluth, Minn., Dec. 26, 1909; s. Archibald James and Grace Jane (McLean) McL.; A.B., U. Minn., 1930, A.M., 1932, M.D., 1934, Ph.D., 1942; m. Margaret Jane Thomas, June 26, 1937; children—James Edward, Nancy Ann, Jane, Thomas. Teaching fellow in medicine U. Minn., 1936-38, instr. obstetrics and gynecology, 1938-40; Commonwealth Fund fellow, dept. medicine U. Va., 1940-41; asst. prof. obstetrics and gynecology U. Minn., 1941-43, asso. prof., 1943-44; prof. and head dept. obstetrics and gynecology Sch. Medicine, U. Utah, 1944-47; prof. obstetrics and gynecology, head dept. Stanford, 1947-75, prof. emeritus, 1975—; chief obstet. and gynecol. service Stanford Hosp., until 1975; gynec. cons. Menlo Med. Clinic, Menlo Park, Calif., 1975—. Diplomate Am. Bd. Obstetrics and Gynecology (dir.). Mem. Am. Coll. Obstetricians and Gynecologists, AMA, Am. Gynecol. Soc. (pres. 1972-73), AAAS, Am. Fedn. Clin. Research, Cal. Med. Assn., San Francisco Gynecol. Soc. (past pres.), Pacific Coast Obstet. and Gynecol. Soc. (pres. 1972-73), Soc. Gynecologic Investigation (past pres.), Phi Beta Kappa, Sigma Xi, Alpha Omega Alpha, Theta Chi, Nu Sigma Nu. Author: Synopsis of Obstetrics, 9th edit., 1974. Home: 39 Pearce Mitchell Pl Stanford CA 94305 Office: Stanford Med Center Stanford CA 94305

MCLENNAN, JAMES ALAN, JR., educator, physicist; b. Atlanta, Nov. 24, 1924; s. James Alan and Edith (Camp) McL.; A.B., Harvard U., 1948; M.S., Lehigh U., 1950, Ph.D., 1952; m. Elizabeth Jane Rohs, Aug. 16, 1952; children—William Ross, Marie Camp. With Gen. Electric Co., 1952-53; instr. Lehigh U., 1953-54, asst. prof., 1954-58, asso. prof., 1958-62, prof., 1962—, chmn. dept. physics, 1968-78. Cons. Los Alamos Sci. Lab., 1962—, Frankford Arsenal, 1955-58. Served to 1st lt. USAF, 1943-46. NSF fellow, 1960-61, AEC pre-doctoral fellow, 1950-52. Fellow Am. Phys. Soc.; mem. AAUP, Sigma Xi. Home: Route 1 Bethlehem PA 18017

MCLENNAN, KENNETH ALAN, cons. engr.; b. Walkerton, Ont., Can., Feb. 28, 1936; s. Kenneth Campbell and Ruth Evelyn (Hannan) McL.; B.A.Sc. with honors, U. Toronto, 1958; m. Ann Marie McGuire, Sept. 1, 1958; children—Karen, Michael, Katherine, Jacqueline. Design and adminstrv. engr. TransCanada PipeLines Ltd., 1958-61; with Marshall Macklin Monaghan Ltd., Don Mills, Ont., 1961—, chief mcpl. engr., 1966-72, partner, dir., 1969—, mgr. engrng. dept., 1972-75, v.p. engring., 1975—; dir. Macmarmon Ltd., Cansult Ltd. Recipient Sons of Martha medal Assn. Profl. Engrs. Ont., 1973, also other awards and commendations. Mem. Cons. Engrs. Ont. (pres. 1977-78), Assn. Cons. Engrs. Can. (dir., treas. 1978-79, v.p. 1979-80, pres. 1980-81), Assn. Profl. Engrs. Ont. (chmn. Scarborough chpt. 1969-70), Engring. Inst. Can., Can. Soc. Civil Engring., Am. Water Works Assn., ASTM, Pollution Control Assn. Ont., Water Pollution Control Fedn., Roads and Transp. Assn. Can. Club: Donalda. Home: 24 Kenmanor Blvd Agincourt ON M1W 1R7 Canada Office: 275 Duncan Mill Rd Don Mills ON M3B 2Y1 Canada

MCLEOD, DANIEL ROGERS, atty. gen. S.C.; b. Sumter, S.C., Oct. 6, 1913; s. D. Melvin and Bertie (Guyton) McL.; student Wofford Coll., 1931-32; LL.B., U. S.C., 1948; m. Ellen D. LaBorde, May 20, 1941 (dec.); children—Daniel R., Elizabeth Ann; m. 2d, Virginia B. Hart, July 29, 1962. Admitted to S.C. bar, 1948; asst. atty. gen. S.C., 1950-58, atty. gen., 1958—. Mem. Am., S.C. bar assns. Methodist (ofcl. bd.). Home: 4511 Landgrave Rd Columbia SC 29206 Office: Wade Hampton Office Bldg Columbia SC 29201

MCLEOD, JAMES CURRIE, clergyman, educator; b. Buffalo; s. Dugald and Mary Holmes (Currie) McL.; B.S., Middlebury Coll., 1926, D.D., 1950; B.D., Yale U., 1929; D.D., Alfred U., 1941; m. Emily Louise Johnson, Aug. 24, 1929; children—Mary Louise (Mrs. James S. Aagaard), Adrienne (Mrs. Craig Heatley), James Currie. Ordained to ministry Presbyn. Ch., 1929; univ. chaplain Alfred (N.Y.) U., 1929-40; minister to students Ohio State U., Columbus, 1940-43, univ. chaplain, prof. history and lit. of religion Northwestern U., 1946-50, prof., 1950-71, prof. emeritus, 1971—, dean students, 1952-67; research fellow Yale Div. Sch., 1963-64; vis. scholar Colgate-Rochester Div. Sch., 1967-68; guest preacher Presbytery of Glasgow, Scotland, 1950, also at Syracuse, Chgo., Rutgers, Lake Forest, Middlebury, Stanford, Howard, others. Pres., trustee Evanston (Ill.) Pub. Library; bd. dirs. Vis. Nurses Assn., Evanston. Served as lt. comdr., chaplain USNR, 1943-46. Mem. Nat. Acad. Religion, Nat. Assn. Student Personnel Adminstrs. (pres. 1963-64), Religious Edn. Assn. (v.p. 1963-64), Presbytery of Chgo., Delta Upsilon (internat. pres. 1972-73). Republican. Mason. Clubs: Rotary (past pres.); St. Andrew Soc. (pres. 1973-74); Yale (Chgo.). Author: Fruits of Faith (symposium); also articles various jours. Home: 422 5th St Apt 1W Wilmette IL 60091

MCLEOD, JOHN WISHART, architect; b. Edinburgh, Scotland, Mar. 24, 1908; s. Thomas and Catherine (Wishart) McL.; student archtl. schs. Columbia, N.Y. U., Beaux-Arts Inst. Design, Columbia Tchrs. Coll.; m. Helen G. Rath, July 11, 1936; children—Ian Wishart, Cathie Ann. Archtl. tng. in N.Y., N.J. area, 1930-36; partner firm McLeod, Ferrara & Ensign and predecessor firms, Elizabeth, N.J., 1936-41, Washington, 1946—; with WPB, 1941-46. Mem. U.S. del. UNESCO-IBE Conf. Sch. Bldg., Geneva, Switzerland, 1957; mem., vice chmn. U.S. del. UNESCO-UK Conf. Sch. Bldg., London, Eng., 1962; mem., co-chmn. constrn. adv. com. fallout shelters Dept. Def., 1962-76; mem. Bd. Examiners and Registrars Architects D.C., 1959-66. Fellow AIA (chmn. nat. com. ednl. facilities 1950-63; pres. Washington-Met. chpt. 1961); mem. Council Ednl. Facility Planners Internat. (Planner of Year 1975), Am. Assn. Sch. Adminstrs., Washington Bldg. Congress. Mem. Potomac Meth. Ch. Prin. works include ednl. facilities. Co-author: Planning America's School Buildings, 1960; author: Urban Schools in Europe, 1968. Home: 10805 Admirals Way Potomac MD 20854 Office: 5454 Wisconsin Ave NW Washington DC 20015

MCLEOD, LIONEL EVERETT, univ. dean; b. Wainwright, Alta., Can., Aug. 9, 1927; s. Frank Everett and Anne (Withnell) McL.; B.Sc., U. Alta., 1947, M.D., 1951; M.Sc., McGill U., 1956; m. Barbara A. Lipsey, Oct. 18, 1952; children—Laura, Bruce, Judy, Nancy. Intern U. Alta. Hosp., Edmonton, 1951-52; gen. practice medicine, Wainwright, 1952-53; from asst. prof. to prof. medicine U. Alta. Faculty Medicine, 1957-68; prof. medicine, head div. U. Calgary Faculty Medicine, 1968-73, dean, 1973—. Markle scholar med. sci., 1958-62. Mem. Royal Coll. Phys. and Surg. Can., Canadian Med. Assn., Canadian Soc. Clin. Investigation, Assn. Can. Med. Colls. (pres.), Can. Soc. Endocrinology, Can. Soc. Nephrology. Home: 6919 Livingstone Dr Calgary AB T3E 6J6 Canada Office: Faculty Medicine Univ Calgary Calgary AB 2TN 1N4 Canada

MCLEOD, NORMAN WILLIAM, civil engr.; b. Nichol Twp., Ont., Can., Nov. 26, 1904; s. William and Elizabeth Helen (Ewen) McL.; B.Sc. in Chem. Engring., U. Alta. (Can.), 1930, M.Sc. in Chem. Engring., U Sask. (Can.), 1936; Sc.D. in Civil Engring., U. Mich., 1938; m. Irene Marguerite Briggs, Feb. 10, 1931; children—Norman Barrie, Muriel Irene, Ruth Marilyn, Murray Graeme, Susan Eileen. In charge asphalt constrn. and maintenance Sask. Dept. Hwys., 1930-38; asphalt cons. responsible for asphalt mfg. and quality Imperial Oil Ltd., Toronto, Ont., 1938-69; v.p., asphalt cons. McAsphalt Engring. Services, Toronto, 1970—; internat. lectr. in field; adj. prof. civil engring. U. Waterloo, 1970—; mem. U.S. Hwy. Transp. Bd. Recipient awards, including Hwy. Research Bd. award, 1946, Disting. Alumnus citation U. Mich., 1953. Fellow Royal Soc. Can., AAAS; mem. Ont. Assn. Profl. Engrs., ASTM (Dudley medal 1952, D-4 Prevost Hubbard award 1978), Assn. Asphalt Paving Technologists (award 1952), Sigma Xi. Mem. United Ch. Can. Contbr. articles on soil engring., flexible pavement structural design, and design asphalt surfaces to profl. jours. Home: 41 Glenrose Ave Toronto ON M4T 1K3 Canada Office: PO Box 247 West Hill Toronto ON M1E 4R5 Canada

MCLEOD, WALTON JAMES, JR., lawyer; b. Lynchburg, S.C., Aug. 7, 1906; s. Walton James and Pauline (Mullins) McL.; grad. Porter Mil. Acad., 1923; A.B., Wofford Coll., 1926; LL.B., U. S.C., 1930; m. Rhoda Lane Brown, Feb. 2, 1935; children—Walton James III, Peden Brown, William Mullins, Thomas Gordon III. Admitted to S.C. bar, 1930, also U.S. Dist. Ct., Ct. Appeals, U.S. Supreme Ct., practice of law, Walterboro, 1930—; mem. firm McLeod, Fraser & Unger, 1976—; city atty., Walterboro. Mem., vice chmn. S.C. Hwy. Commn., 1946-50. Mem. nat. exec. com. Young Democrats, 1938-42; Dem. chmn. Colleton County, 1950-60; mem. S.C. Dem. Exec. Com., 1960—, temporary chmn. state conv., 1976; trustee Walterboro pub. schs., 1936-46, Wofford Coll., 1954-66. Served to lt. comdr. USNR, 1942-46. Mem. Am. Legion (comdr. S.C. 1949-50, mem. nat. exec. com. 1951-52), Am. (ho. of dels, 1950-76, bd. govs. 1964-67, chmn. resolutions com. 1961-62), S.C. (pres. 1969-70), Colleton County (pres. 1962) bar assns., Am. Coll. Probate Counsel, Am. Law Inst., Am. Judicature Soc., Am. Coll. Trial Lawyers, Kappa Alpha, Phi Delta Phi. Methodist. Mason (Shriner). Home: 109 Savage St Walterboro SC 29488 Office: 111 E Washington St Walterboro SC 29488

MC LEOD, WILLIAM EUGENE, army officer; b. Granite, Okla., Apr. 25, 1921; s. Howard Clifton and Ruby Ethel (Heasley) McL.; grad. Army War Coll., 1962; m. Dorothy Ann Davis, July 20, 1940 (dec. Dec. 1966); children—Sherril McLeod Stull, Patricia McLeod Sheller, Christie McLeod Medley, Bryhn, Leslie McLeod Thatcher; m. 2d, Sylvia H. Lunceford, Nov. 17, 1967; 1 dau., Lindee. Commd. 2d lt. U.S. Army, 1942, advanced through grades to maj. gen., 1971; mem. chmn.'s spl. studies group Office Joint Chiefs Staff, 1963-65; div. arty. comdr. 24th Inf. Div., Germany, 1965-67; corps arty. comdr. III Corps Arty., Ft. Sill, 1968; chief staff VII Corps, Germany, 1968-69; corps arty. comdr. VII Corps Arty., Germany, 1969-70; dep. dir. Office Dep. Asst. Sec. Def., 1970-71; dir. orgn. and unit tng. Office Asst. Chief Staff Force Devel., Hdqrs. Dept. Army, 1971-72; chief staff 8th U.S. Army, sr. UN Command rep. to Mil. Armistice Commn., 1973-74; dep. chief staff Hdqrs. Comdr.-in-Chief Pacific, 1975-79. Decorated D.S.M., Legion of Merit with two oak leaf clusters, Joint Services Commendation medal, Bronze Star with V, Army Commendation medal with oak leaf cluster, Purple Heart. Home: 7921 Folkstone Way Lawton OK 73505

MCLINDON, GERALD JOSEPH, univ. dean; b. Bathgate, Scotland, Aug. 27, 1923; s. Patrick J. and Anne (Sloan) MacL.; student Liverpool Coll. Tech. City and Guilds of London Structural Engring., 1948; B.Archs. with Honors, Dipl.C.D., U. Liverpool (Eng.), 1949, 51; M.L.A., Harvard, 1954; m. Agnes Helena Cooke, July 12, 1951; children—Michael, Christopher, Maureen, Ann, Andrew, John, Duncan. Asst. prof. U. Mass., Amherst, 1951-55; dir. Metroplan, Little Rock, 1955-58; planning dir. Cloverdale Corp., Little Rock, 1958-60; owner Gerald J. McLindon, planning consultants, Little Rock, 1960-63; dir. Market St. Devel. Project, San Francisco, 1963-66; dir. state planning State of La., 1968-70; dean La. State U. Sch. Environmental Design, Baton Rouge, 1966—; prin. Gerald J. McLindon & Assos., planning cons., 1960—; mem. bd. cons. for environ. concern C.E. Mobile Dist., 1971—, New Orleans dist., 1974-76; mem. Am. Council for Constrn. Edn., 1974—, mem. accreditation com., 1974, chmn. guidance com., 1975, sr. v.p., 1977, pres., 1978; mem. La. Gov.'s Com. on Waste Mgmt., also chmn. subcom. on recycling and reduction, 1976-78. Mem. La. Domed Stadium Adv. Bd., 1966-72, La. Health Planning Council, 1968-74, La. Health Planning Exec. Com., 1969-74, La. Mississippi River Crossing Adv. Com., 1971-72, Gov.'s Citizens Adv. Com. Transp. New Orleans, 1972-78, La. Deep Draft Harbor and Terminal Authority, 1972—, La. Trails Adv. Council mem. nat. air pollution manpower adv. com. EPA, 1971-76; mem. standards com. Found. for Interior Design Edn. Research, 1972-77, mem. accreditation com., 1977; mem. transp. com. La. Goals Program; mem. environ. adv. bd. chief engrs. Corps Engrs., Washington, 1977, chmn., 1978—. Served with Brit. Army, 1942-45. Fulbright scholar, 1950-51; Uriel M. Crocker scholar, 1950. Fellow Am. Inst. Constructors (com. on goals and objectives); mem. Am. Inst. Landscape Architects (hon.), Royal Inst. Brit. Architects, Am. Inst. Interior Designers (hon.), Am. Soc. Cost Engrs., Am. Soc. Landscape Architects, ASME (com. for safety and pollution prevention equipment used in offshore gas ops., mem. subcom. on certification and accreditation 1976-78), Royal Agrl. Soc. Eng., Am. Forestry Assn., Baton Rouge C. of C. (transp. com.). Contbr. articles to profl. publs. Home: 635 Riveroaks Pl Baton Rouge LA 70803

MCLINTOCK, PETER, editor; b. Glasgow, Scotland, Aug. 19, 1916; s. John and Jean (Stewart) McL.; ed. Regina, Sask., Can.; m. Ruth Inez Houston, Aug. 9, 1946; 1 dau., Barbara Jean. Reporter, Regina (Sask., Can.) Leader-Post, 1946-48, editorial writer, 1948-50, Ottawa (Can.) corr., 1950-54; with Winnipeg (Man., Can.) Free Press, 1954—, asso. editor, 1960-67, exec. editor, 1967—; free-lance commentator Canadian Broadcasting Corp., BBC. Served with Canadian Army, 1940-46; Europe. Club: Manitoba (Winnipeg, Can.). Home: 111 Wildwood Park Winnipeg MB Canada Office: 300 Carlton St Winnipeg MB Canada

MC LOUGHLIN, ELLEN VERONICA, editor; b. Utica, N.Y.; d. James Henry and Mary Frances (Riley) McL.; student Utica Free Acad.; A.B., Smith Coll., 1915; postgrad. Radcliffe Coll., 1921-22; L.H.D. (hon.), Lincoln Coll., 1949. Asst. editor woman's page Country Gentleman, 1915-17; circulation promoter Crowell Pub. Co., 1922-24; asst. advt. mgr. Grolier Soc., 1924-34, advt. mgr., 1934-41, editorial dir., 1947-59, v.p., 1956- 64; mng. editor Book of Knowledge, Children's Ency., 1936-42, editor Book of Knowledge Annuals, 1940-53, Book of Knowledge, 1942-60; editor Story of Our Time, 1947-53, L'Encyclopédie de la Jeunesse, 1948-60, Le Livre de l'Année, 1950-61, La Science Pour Tous, 1960-64; pres. Cragsmoor Free Library Assn., 1965-69. Roman Catholic. Author: The Murder of Doctor Casenova (with Lucile Rathbun, Anetia McLoughlin), 1934; contbr. verse to mags. Home: 500 Osceola Ave Apt 202 Winter Park FL 32789

MCLOUGHLIN, WILLIAM G., author, editor; b. Maplewood, N.J., June 11, 1922; s. William G. and Florence M. (Quinn) McL.; A.B., Princeton U., 1947; A.M., Harvard U., 1948, Ph.D., 1953; m. Virginia Ward Duffy; children—Helen, Gail, Martha. Author: Billy Sunday Was His Real Name, 1955; Modern Revivalism: Charles Grandison Finney to Billy Graham, 1958; Billy Graham: Revivalist in a Secular Age, 1960; Isaac Backus and the American Pietistic Tradition, 1967; The Meaning of Henry Ward Beecher, 1967; New England Dissent 1630-1833: The Baptists and the Separation of Church and State, 2 vols. (Frederic J. Melcher Book award) 1971; Revivals, Awakenings and Reform, 1978; Rhode Island: A Bicentennial History, 1978; editor: American Evangelicals, 1968; (with Robert N. Bellah) Religion in America, 1968; asst. dean Grad. Sch. Arts and Scis., Harvard U., 1950-53; asst. prof. history Brown U., Providence, 1954-60, asso. prof., 1960-63, prof., 1963—. Fulbright scholar, Eng., 1953-54; Guggenheim fellow, 1960-61; fellow Harvard Center for Study of History of Liberty, 1960-62; Nat. Endowment for Humanities sr. fellow, 1968-69. Mem. Am. Hist. Assn., Am. Studies Assn., AAUP, Phi Beta Kappa. Office: Dept History Brown U Providence RI 02912

MC LUCAS, JOHN LUTHER, corp. ofcl.; b. Fayetteville, N.C., Aug. 22, 1920; s. John Luther and Viola (Conley) McL.; B.S., Davidson Coll., 1941, D.Sc., 1974; M.S., Tulane U., 1943; Ph.D., Pa. State U., 1950; m. Patricia Knapp, July 27, 1946; children—Pamela (Mrs. Jeffrey O. Byers), Susan, John C., Roderick K. Vice pres., tech. dir. Haller, Raymond & Brown, Inc., State College, Pa., 1950-57; pres. HRB-Singer, Inc., State College, 1958-62; dep. dir. research and engring. Dept. Def., 1962-64; asst. sec.-gen. for sci. affairs NATO, Paris, France, 1964-66; pres., chief exec. officer Mitre Corp., Bedford, Mass., 1966-69; under sec. of air force, 1969-73, sec. of air force, 1973-75; adminstr. FAA, 1975-77; pres. Comsat Gen. Corp., Washington, 1977-79, exec. v.p. COMSAT, 1979—; mem. Def. Intelligence Agy. Sci. Advisory Com., 1966-69, U.S. Air Force Sci. Advisory Bd., 1967-69, 77—, Def. Sci. Bd., 1968-69. Bd. dirs. von Karman Inst., Brussels, 1966-69. Served with USNR, 1943-46. Recipient Distinguished Service award Dept. Def., 1964, 1st bronze palm, 1973, silver palm, 1975. Fellow IEEE, fellow Am. Inst. Aeros. and Astronautics; mem. N.Y. Acad. Scis., Operations Research Soc. Am., Am. Phys. Soc., Nat. Acad. Engring., Chief Execs. Forum, Sigma Xi, Sigma Pi Sigma. Contbr. articles to tech. lit. Patentee in field. Home: 6519 Dearborn Dr Falls Church VA 22044 Office: Comsat 950 L'Enfant Plaza Washington DC 20024

MCLUHAN, HERBERT MARSHALL, communications specialist, educator, writer; b. Edmonton, Alta., Can., July 21, 1911; s. Herbert Ernest and Elsie Naomi (Hall) McL.; B.A., U. Man. (Can.), 1932, M.A., 1934, Litt.D., 1967; B.A., Cambridge (Eng.) U., 1936, M.A., 1939, Ph.D., 1942; D.Litt. (hon.), U. Windsor (Ont., Can.), 1965, Assumption U., 1966, Simon Fraser U., 1967, St. John Fisher Coll., 1969, Grinnell Coll., 1967, U. Western Ont., 1972, U. Toronto, 1977; LL.D., U. Alta., 1971, Niagara U., 1978; m. Corine Keller Lewis, Aug. 4, 1939; children—Eric, Mary Colton, Teresa, Stephanie, Elizabeth (Mrs. Sean O'Sullivan), Michael. Faculty U. Wis., Madison, 1936-37; instr. English, St. Louis U., 1937-44; asso. prof. English, Assumption U., Windsor, 1944-46; faculty St. Michael's Coll., U. Toronto (Ont.), 1946—, prof. English, 1952—, dir. Centre for Culture and Tech., 1963—; Albert Schweitzer prof. humanities Fordham U., N.Y.C., 1967-68; Pound lectr. The Possum and the Midwife, 1978. Chmn. Ford Found. seminar on culture and communication, 1953-55; dir. media project U.S. Office Edn.-Nat. Assn. Ednl. Broadcasters, 1959-60. Consultor, Pontifical Commn. for Social Communications, 1973. Decorated companion Order of Can., 1970; recipient hon. award in culture and communications Niagara U., 1967; Molson award in social scis., 1967; Carl-Einstein-Preis, West Germany Critics award, 1967; Christian Culture award Assumption U., 1971; Gold medal Pres. Italian Republic, 1971; Pres.'s award Inst. Pub. Relations Gt. Britain, 1970; Pres.'s Cabinet award U. Detroit, 1972. Fellow Royal Soc. Can. Roman Catholic. Author: The Mechanical Bride: Folklore of Industrial Man, 1951; Selected Poetry of Tennyson, 1956; (with E.S. Carpenter) Explorations in Communications, 1960; The Gutenberg Galaxy: The Making of Typographic Man (Gov. Gen.'s literary award for critical prose 1963), 1962; Understanding Media, 1964; (with R.J. Schoeck) Voices of Literature, 3 vols., 1964, 65, 70; The Medium is the Massage, 1967; War and Peace in the Global Village, 1968; (with Harley Parker) Through the Vanishing Point: Space in Poetry and Painting, 1968; Literary Criticism of Marshall McLuhan 1943-62, 1969; Counterblast, 1969; Culture is Our Business, 1970; From Cliche to Archetype, 1970; (with B. Nevitt) Take Today: The Executive as Dropout, 1972; (with Eric McLuhan and Kathy Hutchon) The City as Classroom, 1977; Dóeil á oreille, 1977; (with P. Babin) Autre homme autre chrétien á l'âge électronique, 1977. Co-editor Explorations, 1953-59, editor, 1964—. Home: 3 Wychwood Park Toronto ON M6G 2V5 Canada

MC LURE, CHARLES E., JR., economist; b. Sierra Blanca, Tex., Apr. 14, 1940; s. Charles E. and Dessie (Evans) McL.; B.A., U. Kans., 1962; M.A., Princeton U., 1964, Ph.D., 1966; m. Patsy Nell Carroll, Sept. 17, 1962. Asst. prof. econs. Rice U., Houston, 1965-69, asso. prof., 1969-72, prof., 1972-79, Allyn R. and Gladys M. Cline prof. econs., 1973-79; exec. dir. for research Nat. Bur. Econ. Research, Cambridge, Mass., 1977-78, v.p., 1978—; sr. staff economist Council Econ. Advisers, Washington, 1969-70. Vis. lectr. U. Wyo., 1972; vis. prof. Stanford, 1973; cons. U.S. Treasury Dept., Labor Dept., World Bank, UN, Com. Econ. Devel., govts. Colombia, Malaysia, Panama, Jamaica, Bolivia. Ford Found. faculty research fellow, 1967-68. Mem. Am. Econ. Assn., Nat. Tax Assn. (dir., editorial bd. jour.), Beta Theta Pi. Author: Fiscal Failure: Lessons of the Sixties, 1972; (with N. Ture) Value Added Tax: Two Views, 1972; (with M. Gillis) La Reforma Tributara Colombiana de 1974, 1977; Must Corporate Income Be Taxed Twice?, 1979; also numerous articles on econs. and public finance. Home: 103 Kendall Rd Lexington MA 02173

MCLURE, WILLIAM PAUL, educator; b. Troy, Ala., Nov. 29, 1910; s. Samuel E. and Mary O. (White) McL.; A.B., U. Ala., 1931, M.A., 1932; Ph.D., Columbia Tchrs. Coll., 1946; m. Nola I. Deal, Aug. 18, 1933; 1 son, John William. Tchr. sci. Scottsboro (Ala.) High Sch., 1933-34, Citronelle (Ala.) High Sch., 1934-37; prin. Talladega (Ala.) High Sch., 1937-45; research asso. N.Y. State Dept. Edn., 1946-47; dir. bur. ednl. research, asso. prof. edn. U. Miss., 1947-48; asso. prof. edn. U. Ill., 1948-51, prof. edn., dir. bur. ednl. research, 1951—. Mem. Am., Ill. assns. sch. adminstrs., Nat., Ill. edn. assns., Am. Ednl. Research Assn., Phi Delta Kappa, Kappa Delta Pi. Author: The Effect of Population Sparsity on School Cost, 1947; Let Us Pay for the Kind of Education We Need, 1948; (with others) Financing Education in Efficient School Districts, 1949; (with James E. Stone) A Study of Leadership in School District Reorganization, 1955; The Intermediate Administrative School District in the United States, 1956; Vocational and Technical Education in Illinois, 1960; Fiscal Policies of the Great Cities in the United States, 1961; Federal Financing of Vocational Education, 1963; The Structure of Educational Costs in the Great Cities, 1964; A Study of the Public Schools of Illinois, 1965; Education for the Future of Illinois, 1966; Early Childhood and Basic Elementary and Secondary Education (with Audra May Pence), 1971; (with others) Special Education: Needs, Costs, Methods of Financing, 1975. Home: 203 W Delaware Ave Urbana IL 61801

MC LURG, CHARLES ERNEST, financial cons.; b. Sault Ste. Marie, Ont., Can., Feb. 7, 1909; s. Charles Laurin and Kathrine (Niebergall) McL.; B.Commerce, Queen's U., 1929, B.A., 1943; m. Marjorie Eileen Black, Dec. 23, 1938; children—Ian, Louise. Auditor, Price, Waterhouse & Co., Toronto, Ont., 1929-33; sec. Am. Watch Case Co., 1934-38; asst. comptroller Gutta Percha Rubber, Ltd., 1939-41, asst. gen. mgr., 1943-45, comptroller, 1945-50; comptroller Joint Insp. Bd., Ottawa, 1941-43; asst. comptroller Algoma Steel Corp., Sault Ste. Marie, 1950-54, treas., 1954-73; chmn., pres., treas. Sault Windsor Hotel Ltd., 1954-73; asst. sec., treas. Yankcanuck Steamships, Ltd., 1954-73; treas. Cannelton Industries, Inc. (Va.), 1954-73; sec.-treas., dir. Searchmont Valley Ski Resort, 1960—; financial cons., 1973—. Mem. Ont. Chartered Accountants Council, 1973-77. Dir. Ont. Ski Resorts Assn., 1970-75. Fellow Inst. Chartered accountants Ont., Inst. Chartered Secs.; mem. Sault Ste. Marie Assn. Chartered Accountants. Mem. United Ch. Can. Rotarian. Home: 524 Albert St E Sault Ste Marie ON Canada Office: PO Box 85 Sault Ste Marie ON P6A 5L2 Canada

MCMAHAN, FREDERICK JOSEPH, coll. provost; b. Wellesley, Mass., Sept. 18, 1914; s. Albert Francis and Lillian Marie (Kirmayer) McM.; A.B., St. Ambrose Coll., Davenport, Iowa, 1935; M.A., Cath. U. Am., 1940; Ph.D., State U. Iowa, 1951. Ordained priest Roman Cath. Ch., 1940; high sch. tchr., then asst. prin. St. Ambrose Acad., Davenport, 1940-49; mem. faculty St. Ambrose Coll., Davenport, 1951—, chmn. dept. edn., 1954-61, v.p., 1960-65, dean coll., 1960-74, provost, 1974—. Mem. AAUP, Nat. Cath. Edn. Assn., Am. Assn. Higher Edn., Soc. for Coll. and Univ. Planning, Assn. for Instnl. Research-Upper Midwest. Kappa Delta Pi, Phi Delta Kappa, Delta Epsilon Sigma. Address: St Ambrose Coll Davenport IA 52803

MC MAHAN, ROBERT CHANDLER, savs. and loan assn. exec.; b. Sevierville, Tenn., June 17, 1940; s. Homer Wright and Cathryn Alexander (Murphy) McM.; B.B.A., Ga. State U., 1972; grad. Sch. Savs. and Loan, U. Ind., 1977; m. Judith Ann Raymer, Dec. 23, 1963; children—Kellie Elizabeth, Alice Marie. Mgr., Credithrift Fin. Corp., Tenn., La., Tex. and Ga., 1961-69; with Decatur Fed. Savs. and Loan Assn. (Ga.), 1969—, sr. v.p., mgr. loan dept., 1974-75, exec. v.p., chief operating officer, 1975—; chmn. bd., dir. CorresponDecatur, Inc. Bd. dirs. Decatur-DeKalb YMCA, 1974-76, 79—, sec., 1976; bd. dirs., treas. Goals for DeKalb, 1977—; mem. leadership Atlanta, 1976-77. Served with AUS, 1962-63. Mem. Home Builders Assn. Met. Atlanta (dir.), DeKalb Bd. Realtors, DeKalb Developers Assn, Goals for DeKalb, Citizens for Better Govt., DeKalb C. of C. (dir. Leadership Ga. 1980—), Sigma Phi Omega. Mem. Ch. of Christ. Clubs: Rotary (pres. E. DeKalb 1975-76), Masons. Home: 1818 Bedfordshire Dr Decatur GA 30033 Office: 250 E Ponce de Leon Ave Decatur GA 30031

MCMAHEN, CHARLES EDWIN, bank holding co. exec.; b. McKamie, Ark., May 19, 1939; s. Carl E. and Mattie L. (Nations) McM.; B.B.A. in Accounting, U. Houston, 1962; m. Patricia L. Dixon, Aug. 14, 1965; children—Craig Randall, Dixon Andrew. Auditor, Phillips, Sheffield, Hopson, Lewis & Luther, Houston, 1962-63, Haskins & Sells, C.P.A.'s, Houston, 1963-66; from asst. auditor to v.p., controller Tex. Commerce Bank, Houston, 1966-70, sr. v.p., controller, 1972, exec. v.p., 1974-76; exec. v.p. Tex. Commerce Bancshares, Houston, 1975-76; exec. v.p., chief operating officer Southwest Bancshares, Inc., Houston, 1976—, also dir.; dir. Westbury Nat. Bank, Intercontinental Bank, First Nat. Bank, Brownsville, Tex., S.W. Bancshares Mortgage Co., S.W. Bancshares Leasing Co., S.W. Bancshares Life Ins. Co., Continental Nat. Bank, Ft. Worth, Baybrook Nat. Bank, Houston. Bd. dirs. Houston chpt. ARC, CBA Alumni Ednl. Found. of U. Houston. Served with AUS., 1963. C.P.A., Tex. Mem. Tex. Soc. C.P.A.'s, Am., Tex. bankers assns. Presbyterian. Clubs: Ramada, Forest, Houstonian (Houston). Home: 11513 Memorial Dr Houston TX 77024 Office: PO Box 2629 Houston TX 77001

MC MAHON, CHARLES JOSEPH, JR., educator; b. Phila., July 10, 1933; s. Charles Joseph and Alice (Schu) McM.; B.S., U. Pa., 1955; Sc.D., Mass. Inst. Tech., 1963; m. Helen June O'Brien, Jan. 31, 1959; children—Christine, Charles, Elise, Robert, David. Instr. metallurgy Mass. Inst. Tech., 1958-62, research asst., 1962-63; postdoctoral fellow U. Pa., 1963-64; asst. prof. dept. metallurgy and materials sci., 1964-68, asso. prof., 1968-74, prof., 1974—; cons. in field. Served with USN, 1955-58. Churchill Overseas fellow Churchill Coll., Cambridge (Eng.) U., 1973-74. Fellow Am. Soc. Metals, Inst. Metallurgists U.K.; mem. Am. Inst. Mining and Metall. Engrs., Instn. Metallurgists, Metals Soc. (U.K.), AAAS. Democrat. Roman Catholic. Editor: Microplasticity, 1968. Contbr. articles to profl. jours. Home: 7103 Sherman St Philadelphia PA 19119 Office: U Pa Philadelphia PA 19104

MC MAHON, DONALD AYLWARD, bus. exec.; b. N.Y.C., Feb. 20, 1931; s. William F. and Anne (Aylward) McM.; student Hofstra Coll., L.I. U., U. Pa., 1952-62; m. Nancy Lantz, Apr. 12, 1953; children—Gail, Brian, Lisa, Glenn, Ann, Carol, William, Douglas. With Dime Savs. Bank, Bklyn., 1952; salesman Monroe Calculating Machine Co., Bklyn., 1952-55, asst. br. mgr., Pitts., 1955-56, br. mgr., Phila., 1956-63, asst. gen. sales mgr., Orange, N.J., 1963-64, Eastern regional gen. sales mgr., 1964-65, v.p. mktg., 1965-66; pres. Monroe Calculator Co. div. Litton Industries, Inc., Orange, 1966-70, v.p. parent co., 1967-70; pres., chief operating officer Baker Industries, Inc., Parsippany, N.J., 1970-75; pres., chief exec. officer, dir. Royal Crown Cos., Inc., Atlanta, 1975—. Home: 1665 Winterthur Close NW Atlanta GA 30328 Office: 41 Perimeter Center East NE Atlanta GA 30346

MCMAHON, ED, TV announcer; b. Detroit; ed. Boston Coll.; B.A., Cath. U. Am.; m. Victoria, Mar. 6, 1976; children—Claudia, Michael, Linda, Jeffrey. TV announcer Tonight Show; appeared in films The Incident, Slaughter II, Fun with Dick and Jane; host TV series Whodunnit?, 1979; numerous other TV appearances; appeared on Broadway in The Impossible Years. Active Muscular Dystrophy Assn. Served in USMC. Address: care NBC-TV 3000 W Alameda Ave Burbank CA 91505*

MCMAHON, F. GILBERT, physician, med. educator; b. Kalamazoo, Sept. 10, 1923; s. Frank A. and Marion (Krueger) McM.; B.S. in Chemistry, U. Notre Dame, B.S. in Chemistry magna cum laude, 1945; M.S. in Pharmacology, U. Mich., 1950, M.D., 1953; m. Mary Ann Dunworth, July 24, 1954; children—Sean, Mary Christina, Ann Marie, Christopher. Dir. clin. research Upjohn Co., Kalamazoo, 1960-64; v.p. med. research CIBA, Summit, N.J., 1964-67; exec. med. dir. Merck Sharp & Dohme Co., West Point, Pa., 1967-68, cons., 1968—; prof. medicine, dir. clin. pharmacology Med. Sch., Tulane U., New Orleans, 1968—; pres. Clin. Research Center, Inc., New Orleans, 1969—; sr. vis. physician Charity Hosp., New Orleans. Served to capt. M.C., USAF, 1954-56. Mem. Am. Soc. Clin. Pharmacology and Therapeutics (pres.). Clubs: Plimsoll, So. Yacht, Metairie Country (New Orleans). Home: 1104 Falcon Rd Metairie New Orleans LA 70005 Office: 1430 Tulane Ave New Orleans LA 70112

MC MAHON, GEORGE JOSEPH, coll. ofcl.; b. N.Y.C., June 20, 1923; s. Martin Joseph and Mary (O'Connor) McM.; A.B., Woodstock Coll., 1946, Ph.L., 1947, M.A., 1948, S.T.L., 1954; M.A., Fordham U., 1951; Ph.D., Laval U., 1959. Joined Soc. of Jesus, 1940, ordained priest Roman Catholic Ch., 1953; instr. physics and Latin, Regis High Sch., N.Y.C., 1947-49; instr. philosophy St. Peter's Coll., Jersey City, 1958-60, asst. dean, dir. Sch. Bus. Adminstrn., 1961-62, also trustee; instr. philosophy Loyola Sem., Shrub Oak, N.Y., 1960-61; dean Fordham Coll., Fordham U., Bronx, N.Y., 1962-74, v.p. adminstrn. Fordham U., 1974—. Vice pres. Friends of U. Laval, Que., Can.; trustee Coll. of Holy Cross, Worcester, Mass.; chmn. bd. St. Peter's Coll., Jersey City, Marymount Sch. N.Y. Mem. Nat. Cath. Ednl. Assn. Author: The Order of Procedure in the Philosophy of Nature, 1958; The Proemium to the Physics of Aristotle, 1957. Address: Fordham Univ Bronx NY 10458

MC MAHON, GERALD J., lawyer; b. N.Y.C., Dec. 24, 1907; s. Jeremiah M. and Delia B. (Clifford) McM.; A.B., Coll. City N.Y., 1929; LL.B., Columbia, 1932; m. Jane Morley Williams, Nov. 27, 1943; children—Kevin C., Richard T., Jane Scott, Thomas Morley. Admitted to N.Y. bar, 1933; asso. Peaslee & Brigham, N.Y.C., 1932-36, partner Peaslee, Albrecht & McMahon and predecessors, 1936-73; asso. counsel for Am. claimants against Germany in sabotage cases, 1933-39; asst. sec. gen. Internat. Bar Assn., 1947-53, acting sec. gen., 1953-56, sec. gen., 1956-76. Dir. Can-Car, Inc., Agy. Can. Car & Foundry Co., Ltd., Corinth Machinery Co., Tree Farmer Equipment Co., Inc., Chip-N-Saw, Inc., Dosco Corp. Fellow Am. Bar Found.; mem. Legal Aid Soc., Internat. Law Assn., Am. Judicature Soc., Assn. Bar City N.Y., Am., Internat., Inter-Am., N.Y. bar assns., Am. Soc. Internat. Law, Nat. Legal Aid Assn., Selden Soc. Served as lt. col., staff Judge Adv. 9th Armored Div., AUS, 1943-46. Decorated Bronze Star medal. Clubs: Assn. Ex-Mems. Squadron A; Town, Scarsdale Golf (Scarsdale, N.Y.). Author: Restraints of Trade at Common Law, 1932; International Associations in United States Law, 1956. Home: 24 Walworth Ave Scarsdale NY 10583 Office: 180 E Post Rd White Plains NY 10601

MC MAHON, JOHN ALEXANDER, med. assn. exec.; b. Monongahela, Pa., July 31, 1921; s. John Hamilton and Jean (Alexander) McM.; A.B. magna cum laude, Duke U., 1942; student Harvard U. Bus. Sch., 1942-43, J.D., Law Sch., 1948; LL.D., Wake Forest U., 1978; m. Betty Wagner, Sept. 14, 1947 (div. Mar. 1977); children—Alexander Talpey, Sarah Francis, Elizabeth Wagner, Ann Wallace; m. 2d, Anne Fountain Willets, May 1, 1977. Admitted to N.C. bar, 1950; prof. pub. law and govt., asst. dir. Inst. Govt. U. N.C., 1948-59; gen. counsel, sec.-treas. N.C. Assn. County Commrs., Chapel Hill, 1959-65; v.p. spl. devel. Hosp. Saving Assn., Chapel Hill, N.C., 1965-67; pres. N.C. Blue Cross and Blue Shield, Inc., Chapel Hill, 1968-72, Am. Hosp. Assn., Chgo., 1972—; mem. Chapel Hill bd. N.C. Nat. Bank, 1967-72. Bd. govs. Blue Cross Assn., 1969-72. Mem. Orange County Welfare Bd., 1956-63; chmn. N.C. Comprehensive Health Planning Council, 1968-72; chmn. Health Planning Council of Central N.C., 1963-69; mem. President's Com. on Health Edn., 1971-72; mem. com. health services industry and health industry adv. com. Econ. Stablzn. Program, 1971-74; mem. adv. council Kate Bitting Reynolds Health Care Trust, 1971—; mem. adv. council Northwestern U.; mem. med. adv. com. VA.; mem. com. on nation's health care C. of C. U.S.; mem. commn. on cost med. care AMA. Mem. Orange County Democratic Exec. Com., also chmn. Kings Mill Precinct, 1964-68. Chmn. bd. trustees Duke, 1971—; bd. dirs. Research Triangle Found., Nat. Center for Health Edn.; bd. mgrs., mem. exec. com., pres. designate Internat. Hosp. Fedn., London. Served with USAAF, 1942-46; col. Res. (Ret.). Mem. N.C. Bar Assn., N.C. State Bar, N.C. Citizens Assn. (dir. 1972), Duke Alumni Assn. (pres. 1968-70), Nat. Acad. Sci. (Inst. Med.). Presbyn. Clubs: Chapel Hill Country; Hope Valley Country (Durham); Carlton (Chgo.). Author: North Carolina County Government, 1959; The North Carolina Local Government Commission, 1960. Editor N.C. County Yearbook, 1959-64. Contbr. articles to profl. jours. Home: 1150 N Lake Shore Dr Chicago IL 60611 Office: 840 N Lake Shore Dr Chicago IL 60611

MCMAHON, JOHN FRANCIS, social welfare exec.; b. Buffalo, Sept. 16, 1910; s. John Francis, and Rose Belle (Hayes) McM.; student U. Louisville, 1929-32, Marquette U., 1937, U. Wis., Milw.; m. Kyong Sun Paik, May 27, 1977. Program supr. Vols. of Am., East St. Louis, Ill., 1933-34; exec. dir., Milw., 1934-48, nat. field sec., 1948-58, gen. and comdr.-in-chief, 1958—, also pres. bd. dirs.; pres., chief exec. officer numerous non-profit housing corps., 1970—; mem. U.S. Dept. Labor adv. com. on sheltered workshops; pres. grand field council, nat. exec. bd. and nat. field bd. Nat. Soc. Vols. Am.; mem. gen. com., exec. com., various commns. Dept. Social Work, Nat. Council Chs.; mem. Pres.'s Com. Employment of Handicapped, Nat. Council on the Aging; v.p. Council Nat. Orgns. Children and Youth, 1972-75, pres., 1975—; v.p. Religion in Am. Life. Trustee Kiwanis Internat. Found., 1975—. Fellow Gerontol. Soc., Am. Protestant Correctional Assn.; mem. Nat. Assn. Social Workers, Acad. Certified Social Workers, Internat. Conf. Social Work, Am. Correctional Assn. (dir.), Am. Correctional Chaplains Assn., Nat. Conf. Social Welfare, N.Y. State Welfare Conf., Nat. Assn. Tng. Schs. and Juvenile Agys., Ch. Conf. Social Work (v.p. 1950-53), Am. Pub. Welfare Assn., Internat. Platform Assn., Newcomen Soc. N.Am. Presbyterian. Clubs: Masons, German Shepherd Dog, Kiwanis (pres. N.Y.C. club 1959, lt. gov. 1961, gov. N.Y. dist. 1964, internat. chmn. vocat. guidance 1966, internat. trustee 1966-70). Home: 12 Elaine Terr Bryn Mawr Park Yonkers NY 10701 Office: 340 W 85th St New York NY 10024

MCMAHON, JOHN FREDERICK, educator; b. Phila., Mar. 3, 1911; s. John and Kathryn (Stinson) McM.; B.A., Haverford Coll., 1933; M.A., U. Pa., 1935; Ph.D., Columbia U., 1962; student U. Bonn (Germany), 1937-38; m. Virginia Stockhausen, Mar. 24, 1943; 1 dau., Kathryn Kristine. Instr. German and Latin, Harrisburg (Pa.) Acad., 1938-42; asst. prof. German, Beloit Coll., 1946-47; mem. faculty Lawrence Coll., 1947—, prof. German, 1950—, Wing prof. German, 1962-76, prof. emeritus, 1976—, dir. German Study Center, Eningen, Germany, 1970. Mem. Modern Lang. Assn., Am. Assn. Tchrs. German (pres. 1974-76), AAUP, Wis. Modern Fgn. Langs. Tchrs. (pres. 1965-66), Phi Beta Kappa. Home: 1024 W 4th St Appleton WI 54911

MC MAHON, WILLIAM AMBROSE, ins. co. exec.; b. Lynn, Mass., June 12, 1917; s. Francis J. and Anna M. (O'Connell) McM.; B.S., Tufts U., Medford, Mass., 1941, Ed.M., 1942; LL.B., Boston U., 1949; m. Catherine Sylvia, Dec. 24, 1942; children—Cynthia McMahon Clancy, Thomas, Jill. Asst. to dean Tufts U., 1945-46; adminstrv. asst. War Assets Adminstrn., Boston, 1946-47; admitted to Mass. bar, 1950, Conn. bar, 1964; with Hartford Ins. Group (Conn.), 1947—, now gen. counsel and sec. Hartford Life and Accident Ins. Co., Hartford Variable Annuity Life Ins. Co., Hartford Life Ins. Co. Trustee Tufts U., Dean Jr. Coll., Franklin, Mass. Served with USNR, 1942-45. Recipient Disting. Service award Tufts U., 1966, Dean Jr. Coll., 1967. Mem. Conn., Hartford County bar assns., Assn. Life Ins. Counsel. Home: 124 Ridgewood Rd West Hartford CT 06107 Office: Hartford Ins Group Hartford Plaza Hartford CT 06115

MC MANAWAY, HERMAN BLAIR, holding co. exec.; b. Greenville, S.C., July 27, 1925; s. Herman Blair and Rawie (Jones) McM.; B.S., U. S.C., 1947; M.B.A., Wharton Sch., U. Pa., 1949; m. Olivia Fitts Conyers, July 15, 1949; children—Olivia, Mary, Elizabeth. Analyst investment dept. Prudential Ins. Co., Newark, 1949-52; v.p. Wachovia Bank, Charlotte, N.C., 1952-61; pres. Cardinas Capitol Corp., Charlotte, 1961-67; sr. v.p. A.C.V. Corp., Phila., 1967-73; fin. v.p. Ruddick Corp., Charlotte, 1973—; dir. Scope Inc., Stearns Mfg. Co., Versa-Technologies Co., Aldon Industries Inc., Piedmont R.E.I.T. Co. Served to lt. (j.g.) USNR, 1942-45. Republican. Episcopalian. Home: 3427 Seward Pl Charlotte NC 28211 Office: 2000 First Union Tower Charlotte NC 28282

MC MANN, RENVILLE HUPFEL, JR., broadcasting exec.; b. N.Y.C., Aug. 20, 1927; s. Renville H. and Helen (Murray) McM.; B.E., Yale U., 1950; m. Sheila S. Knott, July 3, 1968. Engr., Armstrong Lab., Columbia U., N.Y.C., 1950-52; project engr. NBC Research Lab., N.Y.C., 1952-55; with labs. div. CBS, N.Y.C., 1955—, v.p., dir. engring., 1963-72, pres., 1972-75; pres. Thomson-CSF Labs., 1975—; vis. prof. Hahnemann Med. Coll., Phila., 1972—. Served with USNR, 1945-46. Recipient Armstrong medal Radio Club Am., 1972, Emmy award Nat. Acad. TV Arts and Scis., 1969, 71, 78. Fellow Soc. Motion Picture and TV Engrs. (David Sarnoff gold medal 1977), Yale Engring. Soc.; mem. I.E.E.E., Royal TV Soc., Soaring Soc. Am. Patentee in field. Home: 963 Oenoke Ridge New Canaan CT 06840 Office: 37 Brown House Rd Stamford CT 06902

MC MANUS, CHARLES ANTHONY, JR., polit. and pub. relations exec.; b. Wilkes-Barre, Pa., June 4, 1927; s. Charles Anthony and Mary (Romanoski) McM.; student King's Coll., Wilkes-Barre, 1946-49, Wyo. Sem. Sch. Bus., Kingston, Pa., 1949-51, Temple U., 1953-59; m. Catherine P. Madison, Sept. 8, 1951; children—Patricia, Catherine, Mary, Charles, Susan, William, James. With Thiokol Chem. Corp., Trenton, N.J., 1951-52, U.S. Steel Corp., 1952-59; exec. dir. Americans for Constl. Action, Washington, 1959-69, pres., trustee, 1969-75; confidential asst. to dep. undersec. pub. and Congl. affairs Dept. Agr., Washington, 1976-77; dir. polit. action com. Republican Nat. Com., 1977-78; public and govt. affairs cons.; nat. dir. Nat. Draft Haig Com., 1979. Served with USNR, 1945-46. Mem. King's Coll. Alumni Assn. K.C. Republican. Roman Catholic. Clubs: Nat. Press, Capitol Hill; Boys and Girls (dir.) (Bowie, Md.); Off the Record. Home: 12907 Kendale Ln Bowie MD 20715 Office: 201 N Fairfax St Alexandria VA 22314

MCMANUS, EDWARD JOSEPH, U.S. judge; b. Keokuk, Iowa, Feb. 9, 1920; s. Edward W. and Kathleen (O'Connor) McM.; student St. Ambrose Coll., 1936-38; B.A., U. Iowa, 1940, J.D., 1942; m. Sally A. Hassett, June 30, 1948; children—David P., Edward W., John N., Thomas J., Dennis Q. Admitted to Iowa bar, 1942; gen. practice of law, Keokuk, 1946-62; city atty., Keokuk, 1946-55; mem. Iowa Senate, 1955-59; lt. gov. Iowa, 1959-62; chief U.S. judge No. Dist. Iowa, 1962—. Del Democratic Nat. Conv., 1956, 60. Served as lt. AC, USNR, 1942-46. Office PO Box 4815 Cedar Rapids IA 52407

MCMANUS, HAROLD LYNN, clergyman, educator; b. Sanford, N.C., Sept. 27, 1919; s. James Burch and Mary Elizabeth (Glass) McM.; A.B., Wake Forest Coll., 1941; Th.M., So. Bapt. Theol. Sem., 1944; S.T.M., Yale, 1948, Ph.D., 1953; m. Louise Virginia Paschall, Dec. 28, 1946; children—Harold Lynn, Kermit Neal, Marcia Louise. Ordained to ministry Baptist Ch., 1944; pastor in Conn. and Ga., 1944-48; instr. Wake Forest Coll., summer 1948; asso. prof. ch. history Roberts dept. Christianity, Mercer U., 1949-53, Roberts prof. ch. history, 1953—, chmn., 1963—. Served as chaplain USNR, 1944-46; capt. Res. Mem. Am. Hist. Assn., AAUP, Am. Soc. Ch. History, Blue Key, Scabbard and Blade, Omicron Delta Kappa, Delta Kappa Alpha, Pi Kappa Alpha. Club: Palaver (Macon). Home: 3308 Napier Ave Macon GA 31204

MCMANUS, JOHN B., JR., justice N.Mex. Supreme Ct.; b. 1919; grad. U. N.Mex.; LL.B., Georgetown U. Admitted to bar, 1947; now chief justice N.Mex. Supreme Ct. Office: Supreme Court of New Mexico Santa Fe NM 87501

MCMANUS, JOHN FRANCIS, III, advt. agy. exec.; b. Bklyn., Mar. 8, 1919; s. John Francis and Helen Jane (Cleary) McM.; B.A., N.Y. U., 1941; m. Regina Delores Smith, Feb. 22, 1942 (div. Sept. 1950); m. 2d, Sara Grace Scerra, Mar. 8, 1951 (dec. July 1970); m. 3d, Jane Caroline Lewis, Apr. 25, 1974; children—Stephan George, Kathleen Elizabeth, John Francis IV, Jane Frances. Advt. mgr., Thayer Inc., Gardner, Mass., 1948-52; account supr. ZKC, Detroit, 1952-57; group head McCann-Erickson, N.Y.C., 1957-58; v.p., mgmt. supr. DDB, N.Y.C., 1958-69; sr. v.p. Smith/Greenland, N.Y.C., 1969-70; pres. The McManus Co., Westport, Conn., 1970—; dir. Holiday Houseboats Inc., Homes U.S.A. Dir. Ashburnham (Mass.) CD, 1948-52; mem. Town Ashburnham Finance Com., 1948-50; active Larchmont (N.Y.) Fire Dept., 1960-64; bd. dirs. United Fund. Served from pvt. to capt., A.C., AUS; ETO, PTO. Recipient Gold medals Freedoms Found., 1948, 49, award Internat. Council Indsl.

Editors, 1949, Chgo. Art Dirs. award, 1970, N.Y. Ad Club award, 1970, Boston Ad Club award, 1971. Mem. Internat. Council Indsl. Editors (exec. v.p. 1950-51), Am. Mktg. Assn. (Effie, Cleo, Archie awards 1972), League Advt. Agys., Fairfield County Advt. Club, Westport Hist. Soc. Republican. Clubs: Cedar Point Yacht; Rotary (Westport). TV producer sports, contbr. articles on marketing, bus. to publs. Home: 16 High Point Rd Westport CT 06880 Office: The McManus Co Westport CT 06880

MCMANUS, JOSEPH FORDE ANTHONY, physician, educator; b. Blackville, N.B., Can., July 13, 1911; s. John Patrick Cantwell and Mary Clare Rose (Forde) McM.; came to U.S., 1938 naturalized, 1947; B.S., Fordham U., 1933; M.D., Queen's U., Kingston, Can., 1938; m. Norma Rose Shumway, Jan. 3, 1941; children—Anthony Edward Joseph, Terence Boe Timothy. Asst. pathologist Johns Hopkins U. Hosp., 1938-40; resident N.Y. Hosp., 1940; Beit Meml. fellow U. Mus. Oxford, Eng., 1945-46; asst. prof. to asso. prof. pathology U. Ala., 1946-50; asso. prof. pathology U. Va., 1950-53; prof., chmn. dept. pathology U. Ala., 1953-61; prof. pathology Ind. U., 1961-65; exec. dir. Fedn. Am. Socs. for Exptl. Biology, Bethesda, Md., 1965-70; prof. pathology Med. U. S.C., Charleston, 1970—, dean Coll. Med., 1970-74. Home: 129 Beaufain St Charleston SC 29401 Office: 171 Ashley Ave Charleston SC 29401

MC MANUS, PHILIP DANIEL, bus. exec.; b. Chgo., Apr. 15, 1916; s. Jackson B. and Isabelle (Lewis) McM.; B.A., U. Chgo., 1943, M.B.A., 1946; m. Arvada Belle Roche, July 6, 1935; children—Marilyn (Mrs. Jack Osborn), Bonnie (Mrs. Thomas Ruggles), Philip Daniel, Kerry. With A.O. Smith Corp., 1947-63, corporate controller, Milw., 1947-60, gen. mgr. meter and service sta. equipment div., Erie, Pa., 1960-63; v.p. Eagle-Picher Industries, Inc., Cin., 1963-69, group v.p., 1969-73, exec. v.p., 1973-79, also dir., pres. Ohio Rubber Co. div., Willoughby, 1965-69; chmn. bd. McDonough Co., Parkersburg, W.Va., 1979—; dir. LeBlond Co., Stearns & Foster Co., McDonough Co. Mem. Fin. Execs. Inst. Am. (past dir. Milw. chpt.). Clubs: Cin. Country, Queen City; Hyde Park Country; Parkersburg Country. Home: 51 Oakwood Estates Parkersburg WV 26101 Office: PO Box 1774 Parkersburg WV 26101

MC MANUS, SAMUEL PLYLER, chemist; b. Edgemoor, S.C., Oct. 29, 1938; s. Henry Plyler and Louise (Sanders) McM.; B.S. in Chemistry, The Citadel, 1960; M.S., Clemson U., 1962, Ph.D. in Chemistry, 1964; m. Nancy Fincher, Mar. 26, 1959; children—Samuel Plyler, Robert Adair. Research chemist Du Pont, Phila., 1964; asst. prof. chemistry U. Ala., Huntsville, 1966-68, asso. prof., 1968-73, prof., 1973—, chmn. dept. chemistry, 1970-72, 77-78; vis. faculty mem. U. S.C., 1974-75. Cons. to govt. and industry. Committeeman Tenn Valley council Boy Scouts Am., 1973-75; chmn. radio com. U.S. Power Squadrons, 1973-74. Served to capt. U.S. Army, 1964-66. Named Outstanding Educator, U. Ala., Huntsville, 1971, 74; Sigma Xi Researcher of Yr., 1978. Alumni fellow Clemson U., 1961; Petroleum Research Fund grantee, 1968—. Mem. Am. Chem. Soc. (councillor 1970-74, 78—, bd. dirs. 1966-74, 78—), Ala. Acad. Sci. (v.p. 1973-74, exec. com. 1967, 73-74), AAAS, Am. Assn. State Colls. and Univs. (subcom. fed. peer rev. bd. membership of com. sci. and tech. 1978), Sigma Xi (chpt. sec. 1967-69, pres. 1970-71, exec. com. 1967-72). Clubs: Lake Guntersville Yacht (treas. 1975, gov. 1974—, commodore 1977, chmn. bd. govs. 1978, chmn. exec. com. 1978-79), Yacht Club Assn. Ala. (pres., chmn. bd. commodores 1977). Author: Neighboring Group Participation. Editor: Organic Reactive Intermediates. Contbr. articles on chemistry to sci. jours. Home: 2513 Norman Terr Huntsville AL 35810 Office: Dept Chemistry U Ala Huntsville AL 35807. *At the beginning of my academic career I was fortunate to have realized that opportunity always exists. Success requires that one seize even the fleeting opportunity and to make do with the available resources. I suspect that all great men and women have closely followed a similar philosophy. Unfortunately, too many promising individuals have not.*

MCMANUS, WALTER LEONARD, investment exec.; b. N.Y.C., Apr. 27, 1918; s. Charles E. and Eva M. (Olt) McM.; student Barnard Sch. for Boys, N.Y.C., 1924-36, Harvard Bus. Sch.; B.S.F.S., Georgetown U., 1940; m. Lillian Ziegler, June 6, 1941; children—Walter Leonard, Peter David, Susan. With Crown Cork & Seal Co., Inc., Balt., 1940-60, became sec., 1945, v.p., 1949, sec.-treas., 1958-60; pres., dir. Cem Securities Corp.; chmn. bd. Castlewood Internat. Corp.; ltd. partner Holly Lakes Properties; asso. Castlewood Realty Co. Clubs: University, Merchants, Baltimore Country; Lighthouse Point Yacht (Pompano Beach, Fla.). Home: 2490 SE 7th Dr Pompano Beach FL 33062 Office: Towson Plaza Towson MD 21204

MCMANUS, WILLIAM EDWARD, clergyman; b. Chgo., Jan. 27, 1914; s. Bernard A. and Marie T. (Kennedy) M.; S.T.L., St. Mary Sem., Mundelein, Ill., 1939; M.A., Cath. U. Am., 1942. Ordained priest Roman Cath. Ch., 1939; asst. dir. dept. edn. Nat. Cath. Welfare Conf., 1945-57; supt. schs. Chgo. archdiocese, 1957-68; aux. bishop Chgo., 1967-76; bishop Diocese of Ft. Wayne-South Bend (Ind.), 1976—. Address: 1103 S Calhoun St PO Box 390 Fort Wayne IN 46801

MC MASTER, HOWARD MAXWELL, civil engr.; b. Omaha, July 31, 1921; s. Howard M. and Lila Violet (Lilly) McM.; student Harvard U., 1943; B.S., U. Nebr., 1948, M.S., 1949; cert. Oak Ridge Inst. Nuclear Study, 1950; m. Dorothy J. Robb, June 3, 1942; children—Patrick Howard, Douglas Mark. Prof., U. Nebr., 1946-57; v.p., regional mng. prin., dir. Woodward-Clyde Cons., Central region, Kansas City, Mo., 1957—. Served with C.E., AUS, 1941-46. Mem. ASCE, ASTM, Nebr., Kans. engring. socs., Nat., Mo. socs. profl. engrs., Cons. Engrs. Council, Internat. Com. on Large Dams. Author: (with A.R. Legault and R.R. Marlette) Surveying-An Introduction to Engineering Measurement, 1956; contbr. engring. articles to profl. jours. Home: 9901 El Monte Overland Park KS 66207 Office: 600 E 95th St Kansas City MO 64131

MCMASTER, ROBERT CHARLES, engring. educator; b. Wilkinsburg, Pa., May 13, 1913; s. Charles Royal and Pearl (Beaver) McM.; B.E.E., Carnegie Inst. Tech., 1936; M.S., Calif. Inst. Tech., 1938, Ph.D., 1944; m. Laura Elizabeth Gerould, Sept. 7, 1937; children—Leonard Royal, James Albert, Lois McMaster Bujold. Supr. dept. elec. engring. Battelle Meml. Inst., Columbus, Ohio, 1945-54; Regents prof. welding engring, elec. engring. and research supr. Engring. Experiment Sta. and Research Found., Ohio State U., Columbus, 1955-77, prof. emeritus, 1977—; dir. F.W. Bell, Inc., 1965-69; cons. industry. Recipient Nat. Reliability award 1966. Fellow Am. Soc. Nondestructive Testing (Coolidge award 1957, also De Forest award, Gold medal 1977; delivered Mehl hon. lectr. 1950; life mem.; nat. pres. 1952-53); mem. Am. Welding Soc. (Adams lectr. 1965), ASTM (Marburg lectr. 1952), Nat. Acad. Engring., IEEE (life), Am. Soc. Metals. Editor: Nondestructive Testing Handbook, 1959, 2d edit., 1970—; contbr. articles to profl. jours. Patentee in field. Home and Office: 6453 Dublin Rd Delaware OH 43015

MC MATH, SIDNEY SANDERS, lawyer; b. Magnolia, Ark. June 14, 1912; s. Hal P. and Nettie (Sanders) McM.; LL.B., U. Ark., 1936; m. Anne Phillips, Oct. 6, 1944; children—Sandy, Phillip, Bruce, Melissa, Patricia. Admitted to Ark. bar; prosecuting atty. 18th Jud. Dist., 1947-49; gov. State of Ark., 1949-53; sr. mem. firm McMath, Leatherman & Woods, Little Rock, 1953—. Served with USMC, 1940-46. Decorated Silver Star, Legion of Merit. Fellow Internat. Acad. Trial Lawyers (pres. 1977-78); mem. Am., Ark., Pulaski County bar assns., Assn. Trial Lawyers Am. (gov. 1960-62), Am. Coll. Trial Lawyers. Democrat. Episcopalian. Home: 22 E Palisades St Little Rock AR 72207 Office: 711 W Third St Little Rock AR 72201

MC MEEL, JOHN PAUL, newspaper syndicate, publishing exec.; b. South Bend, Ind., Jan. 26, 1936; s. James E. and Naomi R. (Reilly) McM.; B.S., U. Notre Dame, 1957; m. Susan S. Sykes, Apr. 16, 1966; children—Maureen, Suzanne, Bridget. Sales dir. Hall Syndicate, 1960-67; asst. gen. mgr., sales dir. Publishers-Hall Syndicate, 1968-70; co-founder Universal Press Syndicate, Mission, Kans., 1970, pres., 1970—; chmn. bd., exec. v.p. Andrews & McMeel, Inc. (formerly Sheed Andrews & McMeel, Inc.), 1973—. Bd. dirs. Johnson County Mental Health Assn. Served with AUS, 1958-59. Home: 2410 W 64th St Mission Hills KS 66208 Office: Universal Press Syndicate 6700 Squibb Rd Mission KS 66202

MC MENAMY, EDWARD L., food co. exec.; b. North Easton, Mass., Oct. 13, 1916; s. Frank J. and Mary (Schindler) McM.; ed. Dickinson Coll.; grad. Advanced Mgmt. Program, Harvard U.; m. Margaret Mary Cruise, June 13, 1943; children—Edward L., Mary Lou, Thomas, Joseph, Mark. Mktg. mgr. Wishbone, Inc., Kansas City, Mo., 1957; gen. product mgr. Thomas J. Lipton, Inc., Englewood Cliffs, N.J., v.p., 1964-75, exec. v.p. mktg., 1975-79; pres., chief exec. officer Summit Fin., Inc., 1979—. Served with USAAF, 1942-45. Home: 6 Colony Dr Summit NJ 07901

MC MENNAMIN, GEORGE BARRY, advt. agy. exec.; b. N.Y.C., May 23, 1922; s. Harold G. and Hazel F. (Stanbridge) McM.; B.S., Harvard, 1945; m. Marilynn L. Simon, Sept. 9, 1946; children—Marilynn Breeze, Karen Foster. With Doremus & Co., 1946—, exec. v.p., 1967-73, pres., 1973—, mem. exec. com., 1968—. Served to lt. (j.g.) USNR, 1944-46. Mem. Fin. Advt. and Mktg. Assn. Met. N.Y. (pres. 1967), Hasty Pudding Inst. 1770, Harvard Coll. Speakers Club. Republican. Episcopalian. Clubs: Harvard Fairfield County (dir.); Recess (N.Y.C.); New Canaan Field; Norwalk Yacht; Brook, Pilgrims of U.S. Home: 28 Cross Ridge Rd New Canaan CT 06840 Office: 120 Broadway New York NY 10005

MCMICHAEL, GEORGE, educator; b. Tulsa, Aug. 20, 1927; s. Joseph and Jane (Neves) McM.; B.S., Northwestern U., 1950, M.A., 1955, Ph.D., 1959; m. Barbara Wenner, July 12, 1952; 1 son, Steven. Prof. Am. lit., dean faculty Calif. State Coll. at San Bernardino, 1962-67; Fulbright lectr. Am. lit. U. Salonica, Greece, 1968-69; prof. Am. lit. Calif. State U. at Hayward, 1972—, dean arts, letters and social scis., 1972-77. Author: Journey to Obscurity, 1965. Editor: Shakespeare and His Rivals, 1962; Anthology of American Literature, 1974. Home: 5371 Crown Ct Castro Valley CA 94546 Office: 25800 Carlos Bee Ave Hayward CA 94542

MC MICHAEL, JANE PIERSON, polit. and legis. cons.; b. Elizabeth, N.J., Apr. 11, 1942; d. J. Earl and Eleanor (Morris) Pierson. Reporter, producer Sta. WNDC-TV, South Bend, Ind., 1965-71; exec. dir. Nat. Women's Polit. Caucus, Washington, 1971-79, dir. legis. and polit. affairs, 1979—. Mem. Am. Fedn. Govt. Employees, Nat. Women's Polit. Caucus, Nat. Coalition Labor Union Women, NOW, Common Cause, Ams. for Democratic Action (exec. bd.). Office: 1325 Massachusetts Ave NW Washington DC 20005

MC MICHAEL, ROBERT, art gallery adminstr.; b. Toronto, Ont., Can., July 27, 1921; s. Norman and Evelyn May (Kennedy) McM.; D.Litt., York U., 1970; m. Signe Kirsten Sorensen, Feb. 9, 1949. Co-founder Canadian High News, 1940; founder Robert McMichael Studios, 1946; founder, pres. Travel Pak Ltd., 1952, Robert McMichael, Inc., N.Y.C., 1959; founder, dir. McMichael Canadian Collection of Art, Kleinburg, Ont., 1964—. Served with Royal Canadian Navy, World War II. Decorated Order of Can.; recipient Connie award Am. Soc. Travel Writers. Anglican. Fellow Ont. Coll. Art. Office: McMichael Canadian Collection Kleinburg ON L0J 1C0 Canada

MC MILLAN, BROCKWAY, former communications exec.; b. Mpls., Mar. 30, 1915; s. Franklin and Luvena (Brockway) McM.; student Armour Inst. Tech., 1932-34; B.S., Mass. Inst. Tech., 1936, Ph.D., 1939; m. Audrey Wishard, Sept. 2, 1942; children—Sarah Linn (Mrs. D.J. Yim), Douglas Wishard, Gordon Brockway. Procter fellow Princeton, 1939-40, H.B. Fine instr., 1940-41; with Bell Telephone Labs., 1946-61, dir. mil. research, 1959-61; asst. sec. research and devel. USAF, 1961-63, under-sec. of Air Force, 1963-65; exec. dir. mil. research Bell Telephone Labs., Whippany, N.J. 1965-69, v.p. mil. devel., 1969-79. Mem. Bd. Edn. Summit (N.J.), 1958-61. Served with USNR, 1942-45. Fellow IEEE; mem. Soc. Indsl. and Applied Math. (pres. 1959-60), Am. Math. Soc., Math. Assn. Am., Inst. Math. Statistics, A.A.A.S., Nat. Acad. Engring. Home: 6 Hawthorne Pl Summit NJ 07901

MCMILLAN, CHARLES WILLIAM, trade assn. exec.; b. Fort Collins, Colo., Feb. 9, 1926; s. Charles and Margaret (Jennings) McM.; B.S., Colo. State U., 1948; m. Jardell Hollier, Feb. 12, 1951; children—Brett W., Kurt C., Scott P. Asst. 4-H agt., Denver, 1948; county agrl. agt., LaJara, Colo., 1949-50, Julesburg, 1950-53; faculty Colo. State U., 1954; div. head, agrl. research dept. Swift & Co., Chgo., 1954-59; exec. v.p. Am. Nat. Cattlemen's Assn., 1959-77; v.p. Nat. Cattlemen's Assn., 1977—; mem. sec.'s adv. com. on fgn. animal diseases U.S. Dept. Agr. Served to lt. (j.g.) USNR, World War II. Mem. Food Group of Washington, U.S. C. of C., Newcomen Soc. N.Am., Sigma Alpha Epsilon. Clubs: Nat. Press, Capitol Hill, Commodity, Nat. Capital Democratic (Washington). Home: 4003 Pine Brook Rd Alexandria VA 22310 Office: 425 13th St NW Washington DC 20004

MC MILLAN, CLAUDE, JR., educator; b. Ada, Okla., May 22, 1923; s. Claude and Zona (Cummings) McM.; B.E.E., U. Colo., 1948, M.B.A., 1949; Ph.D., Ohio State U., 1955; m. Shirley Sue Jackson, Oct. 8, 1949; children—Claude III, Diana, Clayton, Scott. Instr. Ohio State U., 1953-55; asst. prof. Mich. State U., 1955-58, asso. prof., 1958-63, prof., 1963-64, chief of party tech. assistance to Brazil, 1956-60; prof. computer sci., prof. mgmt. sci. U. Colo., 1964—. Served with USAAF, 1943-44, USAF, 1950-51. Mem. Inst. Mgmt. Sci., Am. Inst. Decision Sci. Author: (with R. Gonzales) Systems Analysis, 1965; International Enterprise in a Developing Economy, 1964; (with J. Demaree) The Management of Metal Inventories, 1966; Mathematical Programming, 1970; (with R. Gonzalez) Machine Computation, 1971; (with D. Plane) Discrete Optimization, 1971. Home: 485 Baseline Rd Boulder CO 80302

MC MILLAN, DANIEL ALEXANDER, III, publisher; b. Berkeley, Calif., July 2, 1931; s. Daniel Alexander Jr. and Mary Rosamond (Werner) McM.; A.B in Journalism, U. Calif. at Berkeley, 1953, M.A. in Journalism, 1956; m. Deborah Kay Geering, Sept. 5, 1953; children—Daniel Alexander IV, Benjamin B. With McGraw-Hill, Inc., N.Y.C., 1956-61, 69—, group v.p. publs., 1979—, pub. Electronics Mag., 1970—; With TRW, Inc., 1961-69; pres., dir. Thermal Exploration Co., San Francisco; lectr. electronics tech. and mktg. Served to 1st lt. inf. AUS, 1953-55. Established joint pub. venture with USSR, 1973. Home: 23 Hardwell Rd Short Hills NJ 07078 Office: 1221 Ave of Americas New York NY 10020

MCMILLAN, DONALD EDGAR, pharmacologist; b. Butler, Pa., Sept. 23, 1937; s. Chandler Burdell and Ruth Elizabeth (Beach) McM.; B.S., Grove City Coll., 1959; M.S., U. Pitts., 1962, Ph.D., 1965; m. Marjorie Ann Leavitt, Feb. 4, 1963; children—David Craig, Pamela Jean. Postdoctoral fellow Harvard U. Med. Sch., 1965-66; instr. in pharmacology SUNY Downstate Med. Center, N.Y.C., 1967-68, asst. prof., 1968-69; asst. prof. pharmacology U. N.C., 1969-72, asso. prof., 1972-76, prof., 1976-78; prof., chmn. dept. pharmacology U. Ark. for Med. Scis., 1978—; vis. lectr. Universidad Central, Caracas, Venezuela, 1974; mem. neurobiology rev. bd. NSF; bd. dirs. Chapel Hill (N.C.) Drug Action Com., 1977-78. NIMH grantee, 1971-74; Nat. Inst. Drug Abuse grantee, 1972—; Nat. Inst. Environ. Health Scis. grantee, 19—; N.C. Alcoholism Research Authority Grantee, 1975-77. Mem. AAAS, Behavioral Pharmacology Soc., Eastern Psychol. Assn., Am. Soc. Pharmacology and Exptl. Therapeutics, Internat. Narcotics Research Club, Elisha Mitchell Soc., N.Y. Acad. Sci. Author: Central Nervous System Pharmacology—A Self Instruction Text, 1979, 2d, rev. edit., 1979; research, numerous publs. in behavioral pharmacology and drug abuse; bd. editors Jour. Pharmacology and Exptl. Therapeutics, 1972—, Psychopharmacology, 1973—, Neurotoxicology, 1979—. Home: 814 Gillette Dr Little Rock AR 72207 Office: Dept Pharmacology Sch Medicine U Ark for Med Scis 4301 W Markham St Little Rock AR 72205

MCMILLAN, EDWIN MATTISON, physicist, educator; b. Redondo Beach, Calif., Sept. 18, 1907: s. Edwin Harbaugh and Anna Marie (Mattison) McM.; B.S., Calif. Inst. Tech., 1928, M.S., 1929; Ph.D., Princeton U., 1932; D.Sc. Rensselaer Poly. Inst., 1961, Gustavus Adolphus Coll., 1963; m. Elsie Walford Blumer, June 7, 1941; children—Ann B., David M., Stephen W. Nat. research fellow U. Calif. at Berkeley, 1932-34, research asso., 1934-35, instr. in physics, 1935-36, asst. prof. physics 1936-41, asso. prof., 1941-46, prof. physics, 1946-73, emeritus, 1973—; mem. staff Lawrence Radiation Lab., 1934—, asso. dir., 1954-58, dir., 1958-73, on leave for def. research at Mass. Inst. Tech. Radiation Lab., U.S. Navy Radio and Sound Lab., San Diego, and Los Alamos Sci. Lab., 1940-45; mem. gen. adv. com. AEC, 1954-58; mem. commn. high energy physics Internat. Union Pure and Applied Physics, 1960-67; mem. sci. policy com. Stanford Linear Accelerator Center, 1962-66; mem. physics adv. com. Nat. Accelerator Lab., 1967-69; chmn. 13th Internat. Conf. on High Energy Physics, 1966; guest prof. CERN, Geneva, 1974. Trustee Rand Corp., 1959-69. Bd. dirs. San Francisco Palace Arts and Scis. Found., 1968—; trustee Univs. Research Assn., 1969-74. Recipient Research Corp. Sci. award, 1951; (with Glenn T. Seaborg) Nobel prize in chemistry, 1951; (with Vladimir I. Veksler) Atoms for Peace award, 1963; Alumni Distinguished Service award Calif. Inst. Tech., 1966; Centennial citation U. Calif. at Berkeley, 1968. Faculty Research lectr. U. Calif. at Berkeley, 1955. Fellow Am. Acad. Arts and Scis., Am. Phys. Soc.; mem. Nat. Acad. Scis. (chmn. class I 1968-71), Am. Philos. Soc., Sigma Xi, Tau Beta Pi. Address: Lawrence Berkeley Lab Berkeley CA 94720

MC MILLAN, GEORGE DUNCAN HASTIE, JR., state ofcl., lawyer; b. Greenville, Ala., Oct. 11, 1943; s. George Duncan Hastie and Jean (Autrey) McM.; B.A. magna cum laude, Auburn U., 1966; LL.B. (Southeastern Regional scholar), U. Va., 1969; m. Ann Louise Dial, Nov. 20, 1971; children—George Duncan Hastie, III, Ann Dial. Admitted to Ala. bar, 1969; research asst. dept. agronomy Auburn U., summers 1963-65; law clk. firm Lange, Simpson, Robinson & Somerville, Birmingham, Ala., summers 1967-68; law clk. to judge U.S. Dist. Ct. No. Dist. Ala., 1969-70; instr. U. Ala. Law Sch., 1969-70; individual practice law, Birmingham, 1970-74; partner firm McMillan & Spratling, Birmingham, 1971—; mem. Ala. Ho. of Reps., 1973, Ala. Senate, 1974-78; lt. gov. Ala., 1978—; mem. Permanent Study Commn. on Ala.'s Jud. System, 1975-79. Chmn., Ala. Film Commn.; mem. Arts Task Force, Nat. Conf. State Legislatures; mem. Multi-State Transp. Adv. Bd.; mem., com. chmn. So. Growth Policies Bd.; bd. dirs. Campfire, Inc., Met. YMCA, Birmingham, Boys and Girls Ranches, Ala. Served to lt. USAR, 1969. Recipient award Ala. Nurses Assn., 1975; named Legislator of Year, Ala. Forestry Assn., 1978; Hardest Working Senator, Capitol Press Corps, 1976; 1 of 4 Outstanding Young Men, Ala. Jaycees, 1977; 1 of 10 Most Outstanding State Legislators, Assn. Govtl. Employees, 1978; award Birmingham Emancipation Assn., 1977; award Ala. Hist. Commn., 1978; James Tingle award, 1979. Mem. Birmingham Bar Assn., Ala. Bar Assn., Am. Bar Assn., Birmingham Jaycees, Ala. Jaycees (dir. 1970-72), Birmingham Urban League, United Negro Coll. Fund. Democrat. Mem. Ch. of Christ. Club: Rotary (Birmingham). Office: 1550 First Nat So Natural Bldg Birmingham AL 35203

MC MILLAN, JAMES, business exec.; b. Grosse Pointe Farms, Mich.; s. James Thayer and Anne Davenport (Russel) McM.; A.B., Yale, 1934; m. Virginia Cutting, Jan. 4, 1935; children—Francis Wetmore (Sandy), Virginia. With Detroit & Cleve. Nav. Co., supt., asst. gen. mgr., gen. mgr., pres., chmn. bd., 1934-48; pres. McMillan Packard, Inc.; pres., dir. Great Lakes-Oceanic Line, Inc.; security-ins. broker Multivest Financial Corp., Inc.; dir. Detroit Bank & Trust Co., Packard Motor Car Co., Studebaker Corp., Detroit Bank, Detroit Trust Co., Ferry-Morse Seed Co., Detroit & Cleve. Nav. Co., Am. Presidents Life Ins. Co., Grand Rapids, Mich.; v.p., dir., treas. Boyer-Campbell Co.; adminstrv. exec. asst. Am. Nat. Gas Service Co.; cons. Glover Assos., Inc., N.Y.C., Ordnance Tank Automotive Center, U.S. Army; mgmt. cons. Glover Assos. (Can.) Ltd. Exec. asst. United Found., 1964—. Bd. dirs. ARO; trustee Grosse Pointe War Meml. Assn., Detroit Hist. Assn., Mich. State Appellate Defender Commn., Grace Hosp., Grosse Pointe Country Day Sch., Detroit U., Sch. Corp., Estate James T. McMillan, Katherine K. Brookfield Trust. Village commr., police commr., Grosse Pointe Park. Mem. Detroit Bd. Commerce (dir. 1938-43), Mich. Hort. Soc. (trustee, treas.), Newcomen Soc. N.Am., Nat. Assn. Security Dealers. Mason. Republican. Presbyn. (elder, trustee). Clubs: St. Clair Flats Shooting, Yondotega, Detroit Country, Grosse Pointe (pres. 1953); Detroit (pres. 1962). Home: 46 Sunningdale Dr Grosse Pointe Shores MI 48236 Office: Free Press Bldg Detroit MI 48226

MCMILLAN, JAMES BRYAN, judge; b. Goldsboro, N.C., Dec. 19, 1916; s. Robert Hunter and Louise (Outlaw) McM.; grad. Presbyn. Jr. Coll., 1934; A.B., U. N.C., 1937; LL.B., Harvard, 1940; m. Margaret Blair Miles, Feb. 27, 1944; children—James Bryan, Marjorie Miles Rodell. Admitted to N.C. bar, 1941; mem. staff N.C. atty.-gen., 1940-42; partner Helms, Mulliss, McMillan & Johnston, Charlotte, 1946-68; U.S. dist. judge Western Dist. N.C., Charlotte, 1968—; judge pro tem Charlotte City Ct., 1947-51; mem. faculty Nat. Inst. Trial Advocacy, Boulder, Colo., 1973-77; instr. trial advocacy course Harvard Law Sch., 1975-78, U. N.C. Law Sch., 1976-78, U. Fla. Law Sch., 1978; mem. N.C. Cts. Commn., 1963-71. Pres., Travelers Aid Soc., 1957-59; bd. visitors Davidson Coll. Served from apprentice seaman to lt. USNR, 1942-46; ETO. Recipient Algernon Sydney Sullivan award St. Andrews Presbyn. Coll. Fellow Internat. Acad. Trial Lawyers; mem. Am., 26th Dist. (pres. 1957-58), N.C. (pres. 1960-61) bar assns., United World Federalists, Newcomen Soc., St. Andrews Coll. Alumni Assn. (pres. 1965-66), Order of Coif, Golden

Fleece, Omicron Delta Kappa. Democrat. Presbyn. Clubs: Charlotte City, Charlotte Country, Charlotte Philosophers. Home: 1930 Mecklenburg Ave Charlotte NC 28205 Office: US Dist Ct Charlotte NC 28231

MC MILLAN, JAMES THOMAS, fin. co. exec.; b. Alhambra, Calif., Aug. 5, 1925; s. James and Mary Wilhelmina (O'Hurley) McM.; B.C.E., U. So. Calif., 1951; J.D., UCLA, 1954; m. Jean Grunland, June 27, 1953; children—Suzanne, Brian, David, Kathryn, Mary. Engr., Calif. Div. Hwys., 1951-52, Calif. Div. Water Resources, 1953-54; admitted to Calif. bar, 1956; from patent engr. to v.p. fin. Douglas Aircraft Co., 1954-68; pres., dir. McDonnell Douglas Fin. Corp., Long Beach, Calif., 1968—; corp. v.p. McDonnell Douglas Corp., 1967—, dir., 1978—; pres. MDC Realty Co., 1974-78, dir., 1974—; dir. Douglas Aircraft Co., 1967—. Served with USNR, 1943-46. Mem. Am. Bar Assn., Nat. Def. Transp. Assn., Calif. Bar Assn., Los Angeles County Bar Assn., Los Angeles Area C. of C., Los Angeles World Affairs Council, Order of Coif, Sigma Alpha Epsilon, Tau Beta Pi, Theta Chi. Clubs: Los Angeles; Bel-Air Country. Home: 2416 Palm Ave Manhattan Beach CA 90266 Office: 3855 Lakewood Blvd Long Beach CA 90846

MC MILLAN, JOHN CLARK, banker; b. Glasgow, Scotland, Jan. 4, 1920; came to Can., 1923; s. Thomas Paton and Lily (Clark) McM.; student public schs., Peterborough, Ont.; m. Orma Margaret Lacheur, Apr. 17, 1946. With Royal Bank of Can., 1937—, v.p., gen. mgr. adminstrn., head office, Montreal, Que., 1974, sr. v.p., gen. mgr. corp. banking, 1974-78, exec. v.p., gen. mgr. nat. accounts div., 1978—; dir. RoyNat Ltd., J. & P. Coats (Can.) Inc. Pres. Can. Heart Found., 1979. Served with RCAF, 1940-45. Mem. Inst. Can. Bankers (gov. 1970). Presbyterian. Clubs: Royal Montreal Golf, St. James's of Montreal. Office: Royal Bank Plaza Toronto ON M5J 2J5 Canada

MC MILLAN, JOHN ROBERTSON, oil co. exec.; b. Burlington, Vt., Sept. 6, 1909; s. Trevelick A. and Jeanie Newton (Miller) McM.; student U. Calif. at Los Angeles, 1927-28; B.S., Calif. Inst. Tech., 1931; m. Eleanor Deacon, Sept. 30, 1933; children—Laurie Ann, Linda Joan. Petroleum engr., prodn. Barnsdall Oil Co., 1929-43; mgr. field ops. Fullerton Oil Co., Pasadena, Calif., 1943-47, v.p. charge exploration and prodn., dir., 1947-54, pres., dir., 1954; exec. v.p., dir. Monterey Oil Co., Los Angeles, 1954-61; pres., dir. Transwestern Pipeline Co., Houston, 1957-58, dir., 1957-61; pres. Monterey div. Humble Oil & Refining Co., 1961; pres., dir. Monterey Gas Transmission Co., Houston, 1961-63; partner Lacal Petroleum Co., Los Angeles, 1963; pres., dir. Fargo Oils, Ltd., 1967; chmn. bd., chief exec. officer, dir. Canadian Res. Oil & Gas Ltd., 1968-77, chmn. bd., 1977—; chief exec. officer, dir. Res. Oil & Gas Co., 1963-77, pres., 1963-73, chmn. bd., 1974—; dir. Am. Mut. Fund Inc. Bd. dirs. Assos. Calif. Inst. Tech., pres., 1968-70. Mem. Am. Inst. Mining, Metall. and Petroleum Engrs. (pres. 1968), Am. Assn. Petroleum Geologists, Am. Petroleum Inst. (dir.), Western Oil and Gas Assn. (pres. 1972-73), Theta Xi. Clubs: California, Petroleum (Midland); Gnome; Petroleum (Los Angeles); Ramada (Houston); Annandale Golf (Pasadena). Home: 1025 Hillside Terr Pasadena CA 91105 Office: 550 S Flower St Los Angeles CA 90071

MC MILLAN, KENNETH, actor; b. Bklyn., July 2, 1932; m. Kitty McDonald; 1 dau., Alison. Mem. resident acting co. Studio Arena Theatre, Buffalo and Milw. Repertory Theatre; appeared with N.Y. Shakespeare Festival in Kid Champion, Where Do We Go From Here?, Merry Wives of Windsor, Streamers; Broadway debut in Borstal Boy, 1970, also on Broadway in American Buffalo; appeared off-Broadway in Little Mary Sunshine and Moonchildren; films include: The Taking of Pelham 1, 2, 3, 1974, Serpico, 1974, The Stepford Wives, 1975, Bloodbrothers, Oliver's Story, Hide in Plain Sight, Little Miss Marker, Head Over Heels, Carny, Borderline, True Confessions; TV appearances include: Kojak, Love of Life, Ryan's Hope, Search for Tomorrow; TV movies: Salem's Lot, Stone in the River, Johnny, We Hardly Knew Ye, King; A Death in Canan; Starsky and Hutch; Rockford Files; Rhoda; nat. tour with The Last of the Red Hot Lovers. Office: 12636 Rye St Studio City CA 91604

MCMILLAN, R(OBERT) BRUCE, museum exec., archaeologist; b. Springfield, Mo., Dec. 3, 1937; s. George Glassey and Winnie Mae (Booth) McM.; B.S. in Edn., S.W. Mo. State U., 1960; M.A. in Anthropology, U. Mo., Columbia, 1963; Ph.D. in Anthropology (NSF fellow), U. Colo., Boulder, 1971; m. Virginia Kay Moore, Sept. 30, 1961; children—Robert Gregory, Michael David, Lynn Kathryn. Research asso. in archaeology U. Mo., 1963-65, 68-69; asso. curator anthropology Ill. State Mus., Springfield, 1969-72, curator anthropology, 1972-73, asst. mus. dir., 1973-76, mus. dir., 1977—; exec. sec. Ill. State Mus. Soc., 1977—; lectr. in anthropology Northwestern U., 1973; bd. dirs. Found. Ill. Archaeology, 1978-79. Mem. Ill. Spl. Events Commn., 1977-79, program chmn., 1977-78. NSF grantee, 1971, 72; Nat. Endowment for Humanities grantee, 1978. Fellow AAAS, Am. Anthropol. Assn.; mem. Am. Assn. Museums Midwest Museums Conf. (v.p.), Soc. Am. Archaeology, Soc. Profl. Archaeologists, Current Anthropology (asso.), Am. Quaternary Assn., Sigma Xi. Editor: (with W. Raymond Wood) Prehistoric Man and His Environments, 1976. Home: 2844 E Lake Dr Springfield IL 62707 Office: Ill State Mus Spring and Edwards Sts Springfield IL 62706

MCMILLEN, ALAN BOURNE, educator; b. Brookline, Mass., Feb. 12, 1918; s. Fred Ewing and Ruth (Burns) McM.; B.S., Hamilton Coll., Clinton, N.Y., 1939; M.A., Columbia, 1940; m. Phyllis Irene Brown, June 19, 1943; children—Peter Brown, Fred Ewing II. Intern English, George (Pa.) Sch., 1940-41, tchr. English, 1941-47; supr. student tchrs. Temple U., summers 1945-47; tchr. English, Shady Side Acad., Pitts., 1947-54, headmaster jr. sch., 1954-58, middle sch., 1958-64; headmaster Northampton (Mass.) Sch. for Girls, 1964-68; acting headmaster Avon Old Farms Sch., 1968-69; headmaster Cisqua Sch., Mt. Kisco, N.Y., 1969-73; test coordinator Rippowam-Cisqua Sch., Bedford, N.Y., 1973-76; tchr. English, reading Shady Side Acad., Pitts., 1976—. Mem. testing, measurements com. Ednl. Records Bur., 1966-70. Chmn. pvt. schs. com. Northampton Community Chest, 1966. Bd. overseers Williston Acad., 1966-68; chmn. bd. Pitts. Child Guidance Center, 1963-64. Pitts. Area Pvt. Sch. Tchrs. Assn. (exec. com. 1977—). Address: care Shady Side Acad Middle Sch 500 Squaw Run Rd Pittsburgh PA 15238

MCMILLEN, LOUIS ALBERT, architect; b. St. Louis, Oct. 24, 1916; s. Drury A. and Eleanor (Stockstrom) McM.; grad. St. George's Sch., Newport, R.I., 1935; B.F.A., Yale U., 1940; M.Arch., Harvard U., 1947; m. Persis White, Aug. 26, 1949; children—Michael Albert, Louis Stockstrom, Leander A.C. Vice pres., dir. Architects Collaborative Inc., Cambridge, Mass., 1947-70, pres., 1970—; pres. Architects Collaborative Internat. Ltd., Vaduz, 1959—. Architect in residence Am. Acad. Rome, 1968, 69; prin. works include master planning air bases in U.S., ednl. facilities in New Eng.; commd. to do U. Bagdad (Iraq), 1959, U. Mosul (Iraq), 1965, W.Va. State Parks, Hawks Nest, Canaan Valley, Pipestem/Bluestone and Twin Falls, office bldg. Kuwait Fund for Arab Econ. Devel., 1968, total tourist facilities Porto Carras, Sithonia, Greece, 1969. Mem. planning bd. Concord, Mass., 1958-60. Served to lt. USNR, 1942-46. Fellow AIA; mem. Boston Soc. Architects, Zeta Psi. Clubs: Bath (London, Eng.), Societa Romana della Caccia alla Volpe (Rome, Italy); Millwood Hunt (Framingham, Mass.); Somerset, Harvard (Boston). Home: Monument St Concord MA 01742 Office: 46 Brattle St Cambridge MA 02138

MCMILLEN, RUSSELL GROSS, metal products co. exec.; b. Bridgeville, Pa., June 27, 1918; s. Charles Robert and Hilda Marie (Gross) McM.; B.S. in Metall. Engring., Carnegie Mellon U., 1940; m. Josephine Lacy Portong, July 27, 1963; children—Jeffrey R., Stephanie A., Meridee S., Lois L. Asst. metallurgist Alcoa, Cleve., 1940-42; chief metallurgist Eastern Casting Corp., N.Y.C., 1942-45, pres., Newburgh, N.Y., 1945-48; mng. dir. Eastern Co., Naugatuck, Conn., 1948-62, exec. v.p., 1961-63, pres., chief exec. officer, 1963—; dir. Naugatuck, Colonial Bancorp, Waterbury, Conn. Mem. Malleable Founders Soc. (pres. 1970-71), Am. Soc. Metals, Am. Foundrymen's Soc. Republican. Clubs: Highfield; Waterbury; East Haddam. Home: 96 Crest Rd Middlebury CT 06762 Office: 112 Bridge St Naugatuck CT 06770

MC MILLEN, THOMAS ROBERTS, judge; b. Decatur, Ill., June 8, 1916; s. Rolla C. and Ruth (Roberts) McM.; A.B., Princeton, 1938; LL.B., Harvard, 1941; m. Anne Ford, Aug. 16, 1946; children—Margot F. (Mrs. James Roberson), Patricia R., Anne C. Admitted to Ill. bar, 1941; practiced in Chgo., 1946-66; mem. firm Bell, Boyd, Lloyd, Haddad & Burns, 1946-66; judge Cook County, Ill., 1966-71, U.S. Dist. Ct., No. Dist. Ill., Chgo., 1971—. Bd. govs. United Republican Fund Ill., 1950-66. Served to maj. CIC, AUS, 1941-45. Decorated Bronze Star medal; Croix de Guerre. Mem. Am., Chgo. (bd. mgrs.) bar assns., CIC Assn., Phi Beta Kappa. Clubs: University (Chgo.); Indian Hill Country (Winnetka, Ill.). Office: Everett M Dirksen Bldg S Dearborn St Chicago IL 60604

MC MILLEN, WHEELER, author; b. nr. Ada, Ohio, Jan. 27, 1893; s. Lewis D. and Ella (Wheeler) McM.; student Ohio No. U., LL.D. (hon.), 1940; D.Litt., Parsons Coll., 1953; m. Edna Doane, May 28, 1915; 1 son, Robert Doane. Reporter, Cin. Post, 1912; owner Covington (Ind.) Republican, 1914-18; farmer, Hardin County, Ohio, 1918-22; asso. editor Country Home (formerly Farm & Fireside), 1922-34, editor, 1934-37, editorial dir., 1937-39; editor-in-chief Farm Jour., 1939-55; v.p., dir. Farm Jour., Inc., 1955-63; dir. N.J. Bell Telephone Co., 1948-65, Bankers Nat. Life Ins. Co., 1955-71; pres., chmn. Nat. Farm Chemurgic Council, 1937-62, Am. Assn. Agrl. Editors, 1934-38. Mem. nat. exec. bd. Boy Scouts Am., 1938-63, v.p. nat. orgn., 1959-63; chmn. N.J. Pub. Health Council, 1947-49; mem. adv. com. Pres.'s Council on Youth Fitness, 1957-58; exec. dir. Pres.'s Commn. on Increased Indsl. Use Agrl. Products, 1956-57. Recipient Silver Buffalo, Antelope awards Boy Scouts Am.; Hon. Am. Farmer award Future Farmers Am.; citation Nat. 4-H Clubs; Louis Bromfield gold medal Malabar Farm Found., 1965; numerous Freedoms Found. awards for editorials, speeches. U.S. del. Internat. Congress Indsl. Chemistry, Milan, 1950. Mem. Phila. Soc. Promoting Agr. (pres. 1960-62), Kappa Tau Alpha, Alpha Zeta. Republican. Mem. Grange. Club: Cosmos (Washington). Author: The Farming Fever, 1924; The Young Collector, 1928; Too Many Farmers, 1929; New Riches from the Soil, 1946; Land of Plenty, 1961; Why the United States is Rich, 1963; Possums, Politicians and People, 1964; Bugs or People?, 1965; Fifty Useful Americans, 1965; Farmers in the United States, 1966; The Green Frontier, 1968; Weekly on the Wabash, 1969; Ohio Farmer, 1974; (books transl. 13 langs.); editor: Harvest: An Anthology of Farm Writing, 1964. Home: Route 1 Box 158B Lovettsville VA 22080. *All human experience has yielded no greater wisdom than the Golden Rule.*

MCMILLIAN, THEODORE, fed. judge; b. St. Louis, Jan. 28, 1919; B.S., Lincoln U., 1941; J.D., St. Louis U., 1949; H.H.D. (hon.), U. Mo., St. Louis, 1978; m. Minnie E. Foster, Dec. 8, 1941. Asst. circuit atty. U.S. Eighth Circuit, 1953-56, U.S. circuit Judge U.S. Ct. Appeals, 1978—; judge Circuit Ct. for City St. Louis, 1956-72; judge Eastern div. Mo. Ct. Appeals, 1972-78; asso. prof. adminstrn. justice U. Mo., St. Louis, 1970—; asso. prof. Webster Coll. Grad. Program, 1977—; mem. faculty Nat. Coll. Juvenile Justice, U. Nev., 1972—. Served to 1st lt. Signal Corps, U.S. Army, 1942-46. Recipient Alumni Merit award St. Louis U., 1965. Mem. Lawyers Assn., Mound City Bar Assn., Am. Judicature Soc., Phi Beta Kappa, Alpha Sigma Nu. Office: 1114 Market St Room 526 Saint Louis MO 63109*

MC MILLIN, MILES JAMES, editor, publisher; b. Crandon, Wis., Mar. 12, 1913; s. Rolland James and Lillian (Lutsey) McM.; LL.D., U. Wis., 1941; m. Elsie Rockefeller, Aug. 16, 1955; children—Nancy, Miles James. Admitted to Wis. bar, 1941; writer Progressive Pub. Co., 1941-45; editorial page editor Capital Times, Madison, Wis., 1945-66, asso. editor, 1966-67, exec. pub., 1967-70, editor, pub., 1970-78, pres. Capital Times Co., 1970-79; chmn. bd. Madison Newspapers, Inc., 1970—; v.p. Badger Broadcasting Co., 1970-78. Vice pres. William T. Evjue Found., Madison Kiddie Camp. Trustee, William T. Evjue Charitable Trust. Mem. Wis. Bar Assn., Am. Newspaper Pubs. Assn. Club: Madison. Home: Bay Pond Paul Smith's NY 12970 Office: 1901 Fishhatchery Rd Madison WI 53708

MC MILLION, JOHN MACON, newspaper pub.; b. Coffeyville, Kans., Dec. 25, 1929; s. John Dibrell and Mattie Anna (Macon) McM.; student Vanderbilt U., 1947-49; B.S. in Journalism, U. Kans., 1956; m. Virginia Johanna Stumbaugh, Feb. 12, 1956; children—John Thomas, Johanna, Jennifer. Police reporter Amarillo (Tex.) Globe-News, 1956; sports editor, telegraph editor Grand Junction (Colo.) Daily Sentinel, 1956-58; mng. editor Alliance (Nebr.) Times-Herald, 1958-59, Clovis (N.Mex.) Jour., 1959-62; gen. mgr. Pasadena (Tex.) Citizen, 1962; bur. mgr. UPI, 1962-66; exec. editor Albuquerque Jour., 1966-69; bus. mgr. Albuquerque Pub. Co., 1971-75; pub. Herald and News-Tribune, Duluth, Minn., 1975—; campaign mgr. gubernatorial campaign, 1969-71. Served with USN, 1950-54. Office: 424 W 1st St Duluth MN 55801

MCMORRIS, DONALD LESTER, trucking co. exec.; b. Weldon, Iowa, Apr. 28, 1919; s. Wm. Fred and Eliza (Bunch) McM.; grad. Chillicothe Bus. Coll., 1941; B.S., Kans. U., 1948; m. Asenath Breece Evans, Dec. 4, 1944; children—Asenath Marie, Sandra Jane, Linda Kay. With H.R. McMorris, C.P.A., 1946-48; auditor, controller, treas. Riss & Co., Inc., Kansas City, 1948-54; controller Yellow Freight System, Inc., Kansas City, Mo., 1954-57, v.p., 1957-63, exec. v.p., dir., 1963-68, pres., 1968—; dir. Leawood Nat. Bank. Served to 1st lt. AUS, 1942-46. Methodist. Club: Mission Hills (Kans.) Country; Kansas City (Mo.). Home: 8609 Mohawk St Leawood KS 66206 Office: 10990 Roe Ave Shawnee Mission KS 66207

MC MORROW, RICHARD MARK, utility exec.; b. Boston, Aug. 8, 1941; s. J. Edward and Marie L. (Martine) McM.; student Northeastern U., 1959-61, Bentley Coll., Waltham, Mass., 1962-65; J.D., New Eng. Sch. Law, Boston, 1968; m. Ursula M. Rodgers, Apr. 24, 1965; children—Ethan Rodgers, Juliet Marie. Admitted to Mass. bar, 1971; with New Eng. Gas & Electric Assn., Cambridge, Mass., 1969-76, sec., 1973-76; sec. Columbus & So. Ohio Electric Co., Columbus, 1976-79, v.p. law and risk mgmt., 1979—. Trustee, Columbus Zoo. Served with USCGR, 1963-68. Mem. Am., Mass., Middlesex, Boston bar assns., Am. Judicature Soc., Am. Soc. Corp. Secs., Edison Electric Inst., Am. Mgmt. Assn., Ohio Electric Utility Inst., Columbus C. of C. Club: Rotary (Columbus). Home: Columbus OH 43221 Office: 215 N Front St Columbus OH 43215

MCMULKIN, FRANCIS JOHN, steel co. exec.; b. Sault Ste. Marie, Ont., Can., Dec. 7, 1915; s. George Alexander and Leanora Augusta (Zryd) McM.; B.S. in Metallurgy, Mich. Coll. Mining and Tech., 1937; D.Engring. (hon.), Mich. Tech. U.; m. Margaret Lilian Winch, Sept. 21, 1946; children—John Bruce, Mary Diane. Formerly metallurgist Algoma Steel Corp., Sault Ste. Marie; then research fellow Ont. Research Found., Mississauga, until 1947; research and devel. engr. Dominion Foundries & Steel Ltd., Hamilton, Ont., Can., from 1947, then dir. research, until 1964, v.p. research, 1964—; dir. Dofasco/Eveleth Corp.; Howe Meml. lectr., 1973. Recipient Disting. Alumnus award Mich. Tech. U., 1976. Fellow Am. Soc. Metals (William Hunt Eisenman award 1968); mem. CIM (H.T. Airey Meml. Ann. Conf. Lecture award 1965), AIME (award 1963; charter disting. mem. Iron and Steel Soc. 1976), Engring. Inst. Can. (John Galbraith prize 1945), Iron and Steel Inst., U.K. Mem. United Ch. of Canada. Clubs: Hamilton, Hamilton Golf and Country. Contbr. articles to profl. publs. Home: 270 Roseland Burlington ON L7N 1S3 Canada Office: PO Box 460 Hamilton ON L8N 3J5 Canada

MC MULLAN, DOROTHY, nurse educator; b. Bloomfield, N.J., June 19, 1911; d. Samuel H. and Anne (Gardiner) McMullan; diploma Cornell U.-N.Y. Hosp. Sch. Nursing, 1935; B.S., N.Y. U., 1948, M.A., 1950, Ed.D., 1962. Pub. health nurse Henry St. Vis. Nurse Service, N.Y.C., 1935-39; pvt. duty nurse, N.Y.C., 1939-41; instr. N.Y. Hosp.-Cornell U. Sch. Nursing, 1947-55; supr. N.Y. Hosp.-Cornell Med. Center, 1947-50, asst. dept. head, 1950-53, adminstrv. asst. nursing services for methods improvements, 1953-55, dir. Sch. Nursing, prof. nursing Russell Sage Coll., 1955-61; dean, prof. Ind. State U. Sch. Nursing, Terre Haute, 1962-71; dir. div. nursing Nat. League for Nursing, N.Y.C., 1971-77, chmn. dept. baccalaureate and higher edn. N.Y. League, 1960-62; mem. Nat. Commn. on Allied Health Edn., 1977—; cons. on nurse edn., 1977—; cons. Council on Postsecondary Accreditation, 1977-78; v.p. N.Y. Nurses Assn., 1960-61; pres., Vigo County Coordinating Council, 1966-69; mem. advisory bd. Ind. Regional Med. Planning, 1966-71; sec.-treas. exec. com. Ind. Comprehensive Health Council, 1967-71; mem. advisory com. on women in services U.S. Dept. Def., 1971-73; mem. nursing adv. com. Am. Cancer Soc., 1975—; mem. com. on health manpower Nat. Health Council, 1974-77. Bd. dirs. Vigo County Cancer Soc., Vigo County Cerebral Palsy Assn., Goodwill Industries Terre Haute, Community Found. Wabash Valley, 1964-71. Served to 1st lt. Nurse Corps, AUS, 1942-46; ETO. Mem. Cornell U.-N.Y. Hosp. Sch. Nursing Alumnae Assn. (pres. 1950-52), Ind. League for Nursing (pres. 1966-71), Nat. Assembly Constituent League Nursing (chmn. Gt. Lakes Regional Assembly 1969-71), Nat. League Nursing, Am. Pub. Health Assn., Assn. Higher Edn., Kappa Delta Pi. Republican. Episcopalian. Author: (with Hayt, Groeschel) Law of Hospital and Nurse, 1958; The Role of the Nurse as Employee: A Case of Mutual Responsibilities, 1976; Preparation of the Nurse Specialist, 1977. Home: 233 E 69th St New York NY 10021

MCMULLEN, CHARLES HAYNES, educator; b. Tarkio, Mo., Mar. 3, 1915; s. Charles Bell and Lille (Haynes) McM.; A.B. cum laude, Centre Coll. Ky., 1935; B.S. in Library Sci., U. Ill., 1936, M.S., 1940; Ph.D., U. Chgo., 1949; m. Jane Koch, Aug. 25, 1938 (dec. July 1964); children—David Koch, Joel Haynes; m. 2d, Sun Hauk Chong, Aug. 3, 1978. Reference asst. U. Ill. Library, Urbana, 1936-41; librarian Western State Coll. of Colo., 1941-43, Madison Coll., Harrisonburg, Va., 1945-51; asso. prof. to prof. library sci. Ind. U., 1951-72; prof. U. N.C. at Chapel Hill, 1972—. Cons. Inst. Pub. Adminstrn., Thammasat U., Bangkok, Thailand, spring 1961; library advisor Kabul (Afghanistan) U., fall 1969. Mem. Am., Ind., Southeastern, N.C. library assns., Assn. Am. Library Schs., Popular Culture Assn. Am., Beta Phi Mu. Home: 1306 Willow Dr Chapel Hill NC 27514

MCMULLEN, FRANK DAY, JR., naval officer; b. Kansas City, Mo., Sept. 19, 1924; s. Frank Day and Lora Catherine (Weber) McM.; B.S., U.S. Naval Acad., 1946; M.B.A., George Washington U., 1954; m. Ruth Wheeler Hubbard, Apr. 27, 1951; children—Frank Day, Christine Day, Charles Hubbard. Commd. ensign USN, 1946, advanced through grades to vice adm., 1976; dep. asst. to Sec. Def., Washington, 1967-69; comdr. Submarine Squadron 14, Holy Loch, Scotland, 1970-72, Submarine Force, U.S. Pacific Fleet, 1972-75; vice dir. Strategic Target Planning, Offutt AFB, Nebr., 1976—. Decorated Legion of Merit with 2 stars. Home: Quarters 3 Offutt AFB NE 68113 Office: JSTPS Offutt AFB NE 68113

MCMULLEN, JAMES ERNEST, JR., bank exec.; b. Macon, Ga., Apr. 28, 1924; s. James Ernest and Marilu (Ellis) McM.; student Mercer U., 1947-50; auditor's cert. U. Wis.; m. Theresa Gallagher, Nov. 15, 1945; children—James Ernest III, Karen Jean, Terence V., Helen Marie. With 1st Nat. Bank & Trust Co., Macon, 1941-66, Montclair Nat. Bank & Trust Co. (N.J.), 1966-70; auditor Am. Nat. Bank & Trust Co., Montclair, 1970-72, Princeton Am. Bankcorp., 1973—, Horizon Bancorp., 1974-77; chmn. bd., chief exec. officer Mortgage Investment Securities, Inc., 1977—. Served with USNR, 1943-46. Mem. Bank Adminstrn. Inst., Inst. Internal Auditors. Home: 1697 McKay Creek Dr Largo FL 33540 Office: 1321 US Hwy 19 S Clearwater FL 33516

MC MULLEN, THOMAS HENRY, air force officer; b. Dayton, Ohio, July 4, 1929; s. Clements and Adelaide Palmer (Lewis) McM.; student St. Mary's U. Tex., 1945-47; B.S. in Mil. Engring., U.S. Mil. Acad., 1951; M.S. in Astronautics, Air Force Inst. Tech. 1964; M.S. in Adminstrn., George Washington U., 1971; student Indsl. Coll. Armed Forces, Ft. McNair, Washington, 1970-71; m. Clara Faye Kirkwood, Mar. 28, 1956; children—Susan Marie, Thomas Clements, John Kirkwood. Commd. 2d lt. U.S. Air Force, 1951, advanced through grades to maj. gen., 1978; flight trainee Hondo AB, Tex., Bryan AFB, Tex. and Nellis AFB, Nev., 1951-52; fighter pilot/flight comdr. K-13 AB, Suwn, Korea, 1952-53; flight test maintenance officer Kelly AFB, Tex., 1953-59; Air Force flight acceptance test pilot at Gen. Dynamics Inc., Ft. Worth, 1959-62; project officer, Gemini Launch Vehicle Program, officer Space Systems Div., Los Angeles, 1964-66; air liaison officer 25th Inf. Div., Cu Chi, South Vietnam, 1967-68; asst. mission dir. Apollo Program Hdqrs. NASA, Washington, 1968-70; B-1 dep. system program dir. Wright Patterson AFB, Ohio, 1971-73, A-10 System program dir., 1973-74; vice comdr. Tactical Air Warfare Center, Eglin AFB, Fla., 1974-75, comdr., 1975-76; dep. chief of staff/requirements Hdqrs. Tactical Air Command, Langley AFB, Va., 1976-79; dep. chief of staff/systems Hdqrs. Air Force Systems Command, Andrews AFB, Md., 1979—. Decorated D.S.M., Silver Star, Legion of Merit, D.F.C. with oak leaf cluster, Bronze Star, Meritorious Service medal with oak leaf cluster, Air Force Commendation medal with oak leaf cluster, Air medal with 18 oak leaf clusters, Purple Heart, (U.S.); Cross of Gallantry with palm (Vietnam); recipient Exceptional Service medal NASA, 1969, Group Achievement award, 1969, 71. Fellow AIAA (asso.); mem. Air Force Assn., Order Daedalians, Tau Beta Pi. Presbyterian. Home: 4782 Command Ln Andrews AFB MD 20335 Office: DCS/Systems Hdqrs AFSC Andrews AFB MD 20334. *The key to success is a combination of fortunate circumstance, hard work, and a willingness to accept responsibility. Few people get ahead without some combination of all three.*

MCMULLIAN, AMOS RYALS, food co. exec.; b. Jackson County, Fla., Aug. 28, 1937; s. Andrew Jackson and Willie Ross (Ryals) McM.; B.S., Fla. State U., 1962; m. Jackie Williams, Aug. 27, 1960; children—Amos Ryals, Britton Jackelyn. Successively asst. controller, data processing coordinator, adminstrv. asst. to gen. mgr., asst. plant mgr., plant mgr. Flowers Industries Inc., Thomasville, Ga., 1963-70; pres. Atlanta Baking Co. div. Flowers Industries Inc., 1970-72, regional v.p. parent co., 1972-74. pres., chief operating officer bakery div., 1974-76, pres., chief operating officer industry, 1976—, also dir. Served with USMC, 1958-61. Mem. Atlanta Bakers Club (past ores.). Atlanta Commerce Club, Thomasville C. of C. (dir.), Thomasville Landmarks Soc. Episcopalian (vestry). Home: 329 Tuxedo Dr Thomasville GA 31792 Office: PO Drawer 1338 US Hwy 19 S Thomasville GA 31792

MCMULLIN, CARLETON EUGENE, city adminstr.; b. Hutchinson, Kans., Feb. 17, 1932; s. Cloys E. and Beatrice (Jennings) McM.; B.A., U. Okla., 1954; M.P.A., U. Kans., 1958; m. Beth Becker; children—Lucinda Lou, Charis Ann. Asst. city mgr. City of Corpus Christi (Tex.), 1957-58; city mgr. City of McAlester (Okla.), 1958-62, City of Oak Ridge, 1962-73, City of Little Rock, 1973—; pres. Keystone Enterprises Inc.; v.p., treas. Devonian Corp.; sec. Precision Tune Franchise Adv. Council; cons. in field; mem. intergovtl. sci. engring. tech. adv. panel U.S. Office Sci. and Tech. Policy; mem. NSF Adv. Council; chmn. Urban Tech. System Adv. Bd. Served with Signal Corps, U.S. Army, 1954-56. Mem. Internat. City Mgmt. Assn., Ark. City Mgmt. Assn., Ark. Mcpl. League. Episcopalian. Club: Rotary. Home: 7112 Rockwood Rd Little Rock AR 72207 Office: City Hall Markham and Broadway Sts Little Rock AR 72201

MC MULLIN, ERNAN VINCENT, educator; b. Donegal, Ireland, Oct. 13, 1924; s. Vincent Paul and Carmel (Farrell) McM.; B.Sc., Maynooth (Ireland) Coll., 1945, B.D., 1948; postgrad. theoretical physics Dublin (Ireland) Inst. Advanced Studies, 1949-50; B.Ph., U. Louvain (Belgium), 1951, L.Ph., 1953, Ph.D., 1954; D.Litt., Loyola U. Chgo., 1969. Came to U.S., 1954. Ordained priest Roman Catholic Ch., 1949; faculty U. Notre Dame, 1954-57, 59—, asso. prof. philosophy, 1964, prof. philosophy, 1966—, chmn. dept., 1965-72; postdoctoral fellow Yale U., 1957-59; vis. prof. Georgetown U., summer 1963, U. Minn., 1964-65, U. Cape Town, summers 1972, 73, U. Calif., Los Angeles, 1977; exec. bd. Council for Philos. Studies, 1970-75; cons. history and philosophy of sci. div. NSF, 1963-65, Vatican Secretariate for Non-Believers, 1966—; chmn. philosophy of sci. div. Internat. Congress Philosophy, 1968, 73. NSF research grantee Cambridge U., 1968-69; vis. research fellow Cambridge U., 1973-74, U. Pitts., 1979. Fellow AAAS (chmn. sect. L, 1977); mem. Am. Cath. Philos. Assn. (chmn. nominating com. 1962-64, pres. 1966-67), Philosophy of Sci. Assn. (governing bd. 1969-73, pres. 1980—), Metaphys. Assn. Am. (exec. council 1968-72, pres. 1973-74), Am. Philos. Assn. (exec. council 1978—), Soc. for Values in Higher Edn., Sigma Xi. Editor: The Concept of Matter, 1963; Galileo, Man of Science, 1967; Newton on Matter and Activity, 1978; The Concept of Matter in Modern Philosophy, 1978; Death and Decision, 1978; cons. editor New Scholasticism, 1964—, Philosophy of Sci., 1972—, Philosophy Research Archives, 1974—; Isis, 1975, Jour. Medicine and Philosophy, 1977—, Nature and System, 1978—. Address: Box 36 Notre Dame IN 46556

MC MUNN, EARL WILLIAM, farm mag. editor; b. Lore City, Ohio, May 14, 1910; s. Orval Clark and Alice (Baird) McM.; B.S., Ohio State U., 1934; m. Wilma L. Shane, May 5, 1934. County supr. U.S. Dept. Agr., Farmers Home Adminstrn., 1934-36; asst. editor Ohio Farmer, 1936-48, editor, 1948-75, dir. pub. affairs Harvest Pub. Co., 1975-78; dir. public relations Robinson Hybrids, Inc., 1978—. Mem. Ohio Air Pollution Control Bd., 1968-72; pres. Ohio Farm and Home Safety Com., 1968-70; mem. Ohio Agrl. Tech. Inst. Adv. Com., Sec. Agr. Hog Cholera Adv. Com., 1970-76, Ohio Extension Adv. Com. Bd. dirs. Agrl. Relations Council, 1972-74; mem. Ohio Student Loan Commn., 1976—; alt. del. Republican Nat. Conv., 1976. Recipient Coll. Agr. Centennial award Ohio State U.; Pfizer Nat. Agrl. Communications award; DeKalb Oscar in Agr.; Agrl. Communications award Am. Feed Mfrs. Assn.; Conservation award Nat. Plant Food Council; Am. Forestry Assn. award; Reuben Brigham award Am. Assn. Agrl. Coll. Editors, 1974; Distinguished Service award Ohio Farm Bur. Fedn.; Ohio 4-H Alumni award; meritorious Service in Communications award Am. Soc. Farm mgrs. and Rural Appraisers, 1976; named Hon. State Farmer, Ohio Future Farmers Am.; named to Ohio Agrl. Hall of Fame; named hon. Am. farmer Future Farmers Am. Mem. Am. Agr. Editors Assn. (past pres.), Ohio C. of C. (dir.), Ohio Forestry Assn. (pres. 1968-70, chmn. bd. 1971-73), Agrl. Communicators in Edn. (dir. 1978—), Gamma Sigma Delta, Sigma Delta Chi. Methodist. Home: 3760 Waldo Pl Columbus OH 43220 Office: 1350 W 5th Ave Columbus OH 43212. *Anything you do can lead to a new opportunity. But you have to start by doing something.*

MC MURRAY, PAUL RAY, nuclear co. exec.; b. Emporia, Kans., July 23, 1923; s. Guy Ray and Clara Esther (Simcox) McM.; B.S. in Engring., U.S. Naval Acad., 1946; m. Betty Churchill, June 7, 1946; children—Philip Ray, David Ruel, Daniel Paul, Mary Ann, James Emmett, Julie Diane. Various supervisory and managerial positions in nuclear ops. Gen. Electric Co., Richland, Wash., 1947-58, mgr. Purex Chem. Separations Plant, 1958-63, corp. mgmt. devel. cons., W. Lynn, Mass., 1963-66, bus. sect. mgr., 1966 68, mgr. mfg. Aerospace Instruments, Wilmington, Mass., 1968-70; v.p., gen. mgr. fuel reprocessing dept. Exxon Nuclear Co., Bellevue, Wash., 1970-77, dir., 1977—, exec. in charge mktg. and uranium ops., 1978—. Pres., Tri-City YMCA, Richland, 1956-57; v.p. Pacific N.W. Area Council YMCA, Seattle, 1960-62; chmn. Richland Jr. Achievement, 1954-56. Served with USN, 1943-47. Mem. Atomic Indsl. Forum (chmn. nuclear waste mgmt. subcom. 1977—), Am. Nuclear Soc. Methodist. Home: 6115 133d Ave NE Kirkland WA 98033 Office: 777 106th Ave NE C-00777 Bellevue WA 98009

MC MURRAY, ROBERT, bus. exec.; b. Brooklyn, Iowa, Aug. 31, 1931; s. Arthur Robert and Harriet Campbell (Ray) McM.; A.B., Harvard U., 1956, M.B.A., 1958; m. Ann Wood, Apr. 28, 1962; children—Locke, Mary Elizabeth. Budget mgr. Meredith Pub. Co., Des Moines, 1958-61; fin. analyst McCall Corp., N.Y.C., 1961-62; budget mgr. Leesona Corp., Warwick, R.I., 1962-67, asst. treas., 1967-69, treas., 1969-71, v.p. fin., treas., 1971-76, sr. v.p., treas., 1976—, also dir.; dir. Old Stone Bank, Providence. Co-chmn. univs. and colls. United Way, 1976-78; bd. dirs. Meeting Street Sch., 1975-79, treas., 1977-78. Served with U.S. Army, 1951-53; Korea. Clubs: Harvard (N.Y.C. and Boston); Hope, Dunes. Home: 277 Kenyon Ave East Greenwich RI 02818 Office: 333 Strawberry Field Rd Warwick RI 02887

MCMURREN, WILLIAM HENRY, constrn. co. exec.; b. Ontario, Oreg., Oct. 20, 1927; s. Serene Elbert and Louise (Baker) McM.; B.S. in Civil Engring., Tex. A & M U., 1950; m. Carlyn Dorothy Stenberg, Oct. 17, 1953; children—Catherine Lynn, John Henry. With Morrison-Knudsen Co., 1955—, exec. v.p., 1969-72, pres., chief exec. officer, 1972—, also dir.; dir. H.K. Ferguson Co., Cleve., Idaho. 1st Nat. Bank, Boise, Nat. Steel & Shipbldg. Co., San Diego, Internat. Engring. Co., Inc., San Francisco, Emkay Devel. Co., Inc., Newport Beach, Calif. Served with AUS, 1945-46, 50-53. Mem. Am. Inst. Contractors, Soc. Am. Mil. Engrs. (dir.), Newcomen Soc. N.Am., Moles, Beavers (dir.), Pub. Works Hist. Soc. (trustee). Clubs: Houston; Hillcrest Country (Boise); Internat., Georgetown, Capitol Hill (Washington). Home: 4902 Roberts Rd Boise ID 83705 Office: One Morrison-Knudsen Plaza Boise ID 83729

MC MURRIN, LEE RAY, ednl. adminstr.; b. Ind., June 29, 1930; s. Albert R. and Myrtle E. (Brickley) McM.; B.S. in Secondary Edn., Olivet Coll., Kankakee, Ill., 1952; M.Ed., U. Cin., 1955; postgrad. Miami U., Oxford, Ohio, 1955, Kent State U., 1957, Ohio State U., 1958-65; Ph.D., U. Toledo, 1971; m. Frances, Aug. 19, 1956; children—Michelle, Marianne, Marshall. Elem. tchr. Sharonville (Ohio) Schs., 1952-55; prin., elem. supr. Leetonia (Ohio) Schs., 1955-58; asst. supt. Dover City (Ohio) Schs., 1958-60, South-Western City Schs., Grove City, Ohio, 1960-65; asst. supt. Toledo Pub. Schs., 1965-71, dep. supt., 1971-75; supt. schs. Milw. Pub. Schs., 1975—. Mem. corporate bd. Milw. Symphony Orch.; bd. dirs. United Fund, Milw., Jr. Achievement Southeastern Wis.; active Boy Scouts Am. Served with inf. U.S. Army, 1953-55. Mem. Am. Assn. Sch. Adminstrs., Wis. Assn. Sch. Dist. Adminstrs., Assn. Supervision and Curriculum Devel., NAACP, NCCJ; Phi Delta Kappa. Methodist. Clubs: Rotary, Kiwanis. Home: 3435 N Lake Dr Milwaukee WI 53211 Office: 5225 W Vliet St PO Drawer 10K Milwaukee WI 53201

MCMURRIN, STERLING MOSS, educator; b. Woods Cross, Utah, Jan. 12, 1914; s. Joseph W. and Gertrude (Moss) McM.; A.B., U. Utah, 1936, M.A., 1937, LL.D., 1961; Ph.D., U. So. Calif., 1946; LL.D., U. So. Calif., Clark U., Del. State Coll., 1962; Pepperdine Coll., 1967; D.Litt., U. Puget Sound, 1963; m. Natalie Barbara Cotterel, June 8, 1938; children—Gertrude Ann, Joseph Cotterel, Sterling James, Natalie Laurie, Melanie. Asst. prof. philosophy U. So. Calif., 1946-48; prof. philosophy U. Utah, Salt Lake City, 1948—, dean Coll. Letters and Sci., 1954-60, acad. v.p., 1960-61, Ericksen distinguished prof. philosophy, provost, 1965—, dean Grad. Sch., 1966—, prof. philosophy edn., 1968—, prof. history, 1970—; vis. scholar Columbia U., 1952-53, Union Theol. Sem., 1952-53; U.S. commr. edn., 1961-62; cons. to Am. Tel. & Tel. Co., IBM Corp., Com. for Econ. Devel., Fund Advancement Edn., D.C. Commn. Licensure, Office Sci. and Tech. Exec. Office Pres. Mem. U.S. Commn. UNESCO, 1961-62; mem. Bd. Fgn. Scholarships, 1961-62; exec. bd. Nat. Cultural Center; chmn. Fed. Commn. on Instructional Tech.; adviser, chancellor U. Teheran, 1958-59; v.p. 25th Internat. Congress on Edn., Geneva, Switzerland, 1962; mem. U.S. dels. on edn. and cultural affairs to Washington, Chile, Japan, 1962; chmn. Mountain States and Midcontinent manpower adv. coms. U.S. Dept. Labor, 1965-68; mem. higher commn. Northwest Assn. Secondary and Higher Schs., 1964-73; sr. commr. Western Assn. Schs. and Colls., 1974-77; mem. Grad. Record Exam. Bd., 1974-79. Bd. dirs. Agy. for Instrnl. Television, 1974-78; trustee Carnegie Found. Advancement Teaching, Am. U., Rome; adv. com. for philosophy Princeton U.; mem. nat. bd. fellowships and assocrateships NRC, 1974-77; exec. dir. Tanner Lecture Trust, 1977—. Bd. dirs. Utah Humanities Endowment, 1977—. Ford fellow, 1952-53. Mem. Am. (v.p.), Mountain Plains (pres.) philos. assns., Phi Beta Kappa, Phi Kappa Phi. Author: (with B.A.G. Fuller) A History of Philosophy, 2 vols., 1955; (with James L. Jarrett) Contemporary Philosophy, 1954; editor: The Schools and the Challenge of Innovation, 1969; Functional Education for Disadvantaged Youth, 1971; The Conditions for Educational Equality, 1971; Resources for Urban Schools: Better Use and Balance, 1971; On the Meaning of the University, 1976; also monographs, articles, revs. on philosophy, religion and edn. Home: 2969 Devonshire Circle Salt Lake City UT 84108

MC MURRY, IDANELLE SAM, sch. adminstr.; b. Morganfield, Ky., Dec. 6, 1924; d. Sam Anderson and Aurelia Marie (Robertson) McMurry; B.A., Vanderbilt U., 1945, M.A., 1946. Tchr. English Abbot Acad., Andover, Mass., 1946-50, Hockaday Sch., Dallas, 1951-54, San Jacinto High Sch., Houston, 1954-55; dean of girls Kinkaid Sch., Houston, 1955-63; headmistress Harpeth Hall Sch., Nashville, 1963-79, Hockaday Sch., Dallas, 1979—. Mem. Nat. Nat. Study Sch. Evaluation (dir. 1979—), Ednl. Records Bur. (dir. 1979—), (dir. 1974—, acad. com. 1974—, sec. 1978-80, chmn. 1980—), So. (pres. 1974-75), Tenn. (pres. 1967-68), Mid-South (pres. 1972-73) assns. ind. schs., Nat. Assn. Prins. Schs. for Girls (sec. 1970-72, pres. 1975-77), Nat. Assn. Secondary Schs. Prins., Country Day Sch. Headmasters Assn., So. Assn. Colls. and Schs. (adminstrv. council 1974-77, central reviewing com. 1972-77, vice chmn. secondary commn. 1975-76, chmn. 1976-77, dir. 1976—), Ladies Hermitage Assn., Vanderbilt Aid Soc. (sec. 1971-73, trustee 1976—), Nashville Symphony Soc., Phi Beta Kappa, Pi Beta Phi. Republican. Presbyn. Clubs: Belle Meade, Richland, Centennial. Office: Hockaday Sch 11600 Welch Rd Dallas TX 75229

MC MURRY, ROBERT NOLEMAN, mgmt. cons.; b. Chgo., Dec. 19, 1901; s. Oscar Lincoln and Sadie (Adelaide) McM.; Ph.B., U. Chgo., 1925, M.S. in Psychology, 1932; Ph.D. (fellow Inst. Internat. Edn.), U. Vienna, 1934; m. Doris Baird, Oct. 3, 1936 (dec. Oct. 1965); children—Michael Baird, Sara Lou; m. 2d, Katherine Miller, Apr. 29, 1966. With Fed. Electric Co., Chgo., 1925-27, Yellow Cab Co., 1927-28, Transit Mixers, Inc., Chgo., 1928-31; charge Chgo. office Psychol. Corp., 1935-43; cons. service personnel, indsl. relations, market research Robert N. McMurry & Co., Chgo., 1943-53, McMurry, Hamstra & Co., Chgo. (name changed to McMurry Co., Oct. 1958), 1943—; chmn. John Wareham Internat., N.Y.C., 1978. Diplomate Am. Bd. Examiners Profl. Psychology. Fellow Am Psychol. Assn.; mem. Indsl. Relations Research Assn., Am. Mgmt. Assn., Am. Statis. Assn., Chgo. Psychoanalytic Assn., Am. Marketing Assn., Inst. Mgmt. Scis. Author: Handling Personality Adjustment in Industry, 1944; Tested Techniques of Personnel Selection, 1955; McMurry's Management Clinic, 1960; How to Recruit, Select and Place Salesmen, 1964; How to Build a Dynamic Sales Organization, 1968; 101 Business Problems and their Solutions, 1973; The Maverick Executive, 1974. Home: 505 N Lake Shore Dr Chicago IL 60611 Office: 645 N Michigan Ave Chicago IL 60611

MCMURTRY, R. ROY, Canadian govt. ofcl.; b. Toronto, Ont., Can., May 31, 1932; s. Roland Roy and Doris Elizabeth (Belcher) McM.; B.A. with honors, U. Toronto, 1954; LL.B., Osgoode Hall Law Sch., 1957; m. Ria Jean Macrae, Apr. 18, 1957; children—Janet, James, Harry, Jeanie, Erin, Michael. Called to bar, later created queen's counsel; partner firm Benson, McMurtry, Percival and Brown; mem. Provincial Parliament for Aglinton, 1975—; atty. gen. for Ont., 1975—, solicitor gen. for Ont., 1978—; instr. bar admission course; lectr. continuing edn. program Law Soc. Vice pres. Met. Toronto Housing Authority; chmn. Ont. Folk Arts Council. Recipient Brotherhood award Beth Shalom, Promises of Hope award Canadian Save the Children; named Metro Morning Newsmaker of Yr., CBC. Mem. Law Soc. Upper Can. (lectr. continuing edn. program), Advs. Soc., Canadian Bar Assn., Thomas More Lawyers Guild, Criminal Lawyers Assn. Progressive Conservative. Mem. United Ch. of Can. Columnist, Toronto Sun. Office: 18 King St E Toronto ON M5C 1C5 Canada

MCNAB, ALLAN, museum dir., artist; b. Swaythling, Eng., May 27, 1901; s. Duncan K. and Florence S. (McLeod) McN.; grad. Westminster, London, 1917, Royal Mil. Coll., Sandhurst, 1918; M.A., Royal Coll. Art, London, 1929; student Ecole des Beaux-Arts, Paris, France, 1929-30; m. Dorothy Cumming, 1933 (div. 1949); m. 2d, Marjorie Kreilick, 1973. Came to U.S., 1938, naturalized, 1943. Art dir. Gaumont Brit. Pictures Corp., 1930-38; design dir. Norman Bel Geddes, 1939-41; art dir. Life mag., 1941-48: dir. Lowe Gallery, U. Miami, 1949-55, trustee, 1950-55; tech. adviser Nat. Mus., Havana, Cuba, 1955-59; dir. Soc. Four Arts, Palm Beach, Fla., 1955-56; asst. dir. Art Inst. Chgo., 1956-57, asso. dir., 1957-58, dir. adminstrn., 1959-66; dir. Telfair Acad., Savannah, Ga.; chmn. trustees Miami Art Center, trustee Miami Arts Council, also mus. cons., 1966—; cons. on bldg. mus. City of Oakland (Calif.), 1962—; art cons. Mayo Found., 1967—; art adv. panel Internal Revenue Service, 1966-69. Chmn. bd. suprs. Town La Pointe, 1967—. Exhibited paintings Beaux Art Gallery, London, 1930, St. Georges Gallery, London, 1932, Print Club, Phila., 1932, Royal Acad., London, 1928-31, English Soc. Wood Engravers, 1929-31, Royal Soc. Painter-Etchers, 1929-31, Royal Scottish Acad., 1930, Art Inst. Chgo., 1930, City Art Gallery, Leeds, Eng., 1931, Melbourne (Australia) Mus., 1930; works in permanent collections Brit. Mus., Nat. Gallery (Edinburgh), City Art Gallery (Leeds), Rosenwald Collection, Balt. Mus., also collections Duke of Windsor, Crown Prince of Sweden, Edwin Marsh, Sir Frank Crowinshield. Trustee Minn. Mus. Art, Allentown Mus. Art; adviser Met. Mus. of Manila, 1976—; hon. trustee Allentown Art Mus., Lincoln Acad. Ill. Decorated Order Vasa 1st class. Mem. So. Art Mus. Dirs. Assn. (chmn. emeritus), S.E. Mus. Conf. (council 1953-54), Assn. Art Mus. Dirs., Am. Assn. Mus., Am. Inst. Decorators. Clubs: Tavern, Arts (Chgo.). Address: 2713 Chamberlain Ave Madison WI 53705

MC NAB, JAMES ALEXANDER, hosp. adminstr.; b. Vancouver, B.C., Can., June 6, 1927; s. William Boyd and Eva Meredith (Shirley) McN.; B. in Commerce, U. B.C., 1949; diploma in hosp. adminstrn. U. Toronto, 1951; m. Grace Elizabeth Bruce, Dec. 22, 1951; children—William Bruce, James Ross, David Boyd. Hosp. cons. B.C. Hosp. Ins. Service, Victoria, 1951-54; adminstr. Port Arthur (Ont., Can.) Gen. Hosp., 1954-60; dir. planning Ont. Hosp. Service Commn., Toronto, 1960-64; partner Woods, Gordon & Co., Toronto, 1964-70; pres. Toronto (Ont.) Gen. Hosp., 1970—; sec. Toronto Gen. Hosp. Found. Fellow Am. Coll. Hosp. Adminstrs.; mem. Canadian Coll. Health Service Execs. (past pres.), Assn. Canadian Teaching Hosps. (past pres.), Ont. Inst. Mgmt. Cons. (certified mgmt. cons.), Alpha Delta Phi. Mem. United Ch. of Canada. Club: Granite. Home: 536 Blythwood Rd Toronto ON M4N 1B3 Canada Office: 101 College St Toronto ON M5G 1L7 Canada

MC NAB, MAXWELL DOUGLAS, profl. sports exec.; b. Watson, Sask., Can., June 21, 1924; s. Peter McIntyre and Dorcas Delilah (Thompson) McN.; came to U.S., 1966; student U. Sask., 1942-43, 45-46; m. June Cleone Ness, June 23, 1951; children—Peter Maxwell, Michael Ian, David Martin. Profl. hockey player Omaha Knights, 1946-48, Detroit Redwings, 1948-52, New Westminster (B.C.) Royals, 1952-59; coach San Francisco Seals, 1961-62; gen. mgr., coach Vancouver (B.C.) Canucks, 1962-66; v.p., gen. mgr. San Diego Gulls, 1966-74; pres. Central Hockey League, 1974-75; gen. mgr. Washington Capitals, 1975—. Mem. Parks and Recreation Bd., New Westminster, 1960-61; mem. New Westminster Library Bd., 1963-65. Served with Royal Can. Air Force and Can. Army, 1943-45. Named Most Valuable Player Western Hockey League, 1958; recipient Outstanding Contribution award Breitbard Athletic Found., San Diego, 1974. Club: Tantallon Golf and Country. Home: 113 Chartsey St Upper Marlboro MD 20870 Office: 1 Harry S Truman Dr Landover MD 20870

MCNABB, FREDERICK WILLIAM, JR., diversified mfg. exec., lawyer; b. Lowell, Mass., Nov. 24, 1932; s. Frederick William and Katherine Moore (Flanagan) McN.; A.B., U. Rochester, 1954; LL.B., Yale U., 1959; m. Elizabeth Ann Coleman, May 12, 1956; children—Frederick William III, Mary E., Mark C., Robert O., Patricia A. Admitted to N.Y. bar, 1959; asso. firm Nixon, Hargrave, Devans & Doyle, Rochester, N.Y., 1959-64; partner firm Goldstein, Goldman, Kessler & Underberg, Rochester, 1964-71; v.p., gen. counsel, sec. Continental Investment Corp., Boston, 1971-74, GAF Corp., N.Y.C., 1974—; lectr. Cornell U., 1968. Bd. dirs. Rochester Legal Aid Soc., 1969-71, St. Martin DePorres Center, Rochester, 1968-71. Served to 1st lt. USAF, 1955-57. Mem. Am., N.Y. State bar assns., Am. Soc. Corp. Secs., Phi Beta Kappa. Democrat. Roman Catholic. Clubs: N.Y. Athletic, Yale (N.Y.C); Oak Hill Country (Rochester). Home: 578 Valley Rd New Canaan CT 06840 Office: 140 W 51st St New York City NY 10020

MCNAGNY, PHIL MCCLELLAN, JR., U.S. judge; b. Ft. Wayne, Ind., July 16, 1924; s. Phil McClellan and Lucy (Cole) McN.; LL.B., Ind. U., 1950; m. Patricia Gates, Feb. 24, 1951; children—Julia, Elizabeth, Carolyn, Marcia. Admitted to Ind. bar, 1950; asst. U.S. atty., 1953-55; U.S. atty. No. Dist. Ind., 1955-59; partner firm Gates, Gates & McNagny, Columbia City, Ind., 1960-76; U.S. dist. judge No. Ind., 1976—. Served with USMCR, 1942-45. Mem. Am. Coll. Trial Lawyers, Am., Ind., Whitley County bar assns., Phi Delta Phi. Episcopalian. Club: Rotary (pres. Columbia City chpt. 1962). Address: 507 State St Hammond IN 46320

MCNAIR, BARBARA, singer, actress; b. Racine, Wis., Mar. 4, 1939; d. Horace and Claudia (Taylor) McN.; student U. So. Calif.; m. Rick Manzie, 1972. Formerly night club singer; theatrical appearances include The Body Beautiful, 1958, The Merry World of Nat King Cole, 1961, No Strings, 1962; films include Spencer's Mountain, 1962, Stiletto, 1969, Change of Habit, 1969, Venus in Furs, 1970, They Call Me Mister Tibbs, 1970; star weekly TV show Barbara McNair Show, 1969-70. Mem. AGVA, Stage Artists Guild, AFTRA, Actors Equity Guild. Address: care Moss Agy Ltd 113 N San Vicente Blvd Beverly Hills CA 90211*

MCNAIR, CHAMPNEY ADAMS, banker; b. Sanford, N.C., Oct. 30, 1924; s. John Nelson and Jesse (Chamberlain) McN.; B.S., Davidson Coll., 1949; M.B.A., Harvard, 1951; m. Catherine Gilliam, Sept. 21, 1946; children—Champney Adams, William Alfred, John Edward, Robert Gilliam. With Trust Co. Ga., Atlanta, 1951—, sr. v.p., 1961-67, exec. v.p., 1967-74, vice chmn., 1977—, also dir.; pres. Trust Co. Bank, 1974-77, also dir.; dir. Adair Mortgage Co., Trust Co. Ga. Assos. Pres. Ga. Safety Council, 1969-70, Atlanta Area council Boy Scouts Am., 1973-75; active fund raising United Way. Bd. dirs. Columbia Theol. Sem.; trustee Rabun Gap-Nacoochee Sch. Served with AUS, 1943-46. Mem. Atlanta, DeKalb County chambers commerce, Harvard Bus. Sch. Club Atlanta, Davidson Coll. Alumni Atlanta Club (pres. 1967-68). Presbyterian (elder 1967—). Rotarian. Clubs: Atlanta Athletic, Capital City (Atlanta). Home: 2139 Black Fox Dr NE Atlanta GA 30345 Office: Trust Co Ga PO Drawer 4418 Atlanta GA 30302

MC NAIR, ROBERT EVANDER, lawyer, former gov. S.C.; b. Cades, S.C., Dec. 14, 1923; s. Daniel Evander and Claudia (Crawford) McN.; A.B., U. S.C., 1947, LL.B., 1948; m. Josephine Robinson, May 30, 1944; children—Robert Evander, Robin Lee, Corinne Calhoun, Claudia Crawford. Admitted to S.C. bar, 1948, practiced in Allendale; mem. S.C. Ho. of Reps. from Allendale County, 1951-62, chmn. labor, commerce and industry com., 1953-54, judiciary com., 1955-62; lt. gov. S.C., 1962-65, gov., 1965-71; sr. partner law firm McNair, Konduros, Corley, Singletary & Dibble, Columbia, S.C., 1971—; dir.

Investors Heritage Life Ins. Co. South, AIRCO, Inc., So. Ry. System, Ga.-Pacific Corp., Crum & Forster, R.L. Bryan Co., Bankers Trust S.C.; chmn. So. Regional Edn. Bd., 1967-68, Edn. Commn. States, 1968-69; states' co-chmn. Coastal Plains Regional Commn., 1967, Appalachian Regional Commn., 1970; chmn. Nat. Conf. Lt. Govs., 1965, So. Govs. Conf., 1968-69; chmn. Nat. Dem. Govs. Conf., 1968-69; vice chmn. Dem. Nat. Com., 1969-70; Dem. Govs.' rep. to Dem. Nat. Conv., 1971-72. Bd. visitors Presbyn. Coll.; trustee Baptist Coll. at Charleston. Served with USNR, 1942-46; PTO. Mem. Am. Legion, Farm Bur. Democrat. Clubs: Masons, Shriners, Lions. Home: Route 2 Box 310 Columbia SC 29210 Office: Suite 1820 Bankers Trust Tower Columbia SC 29202 also PO Box 11390 Columbia SC 29211

MCNAIRY, PHILIP FREDERICK, bishop; b. Lake City, Minn., Mar. 19, 1911; s. Harry Doughty and Clara (Moseman) McN.; A.B., Kenyon Coll., Gambier, 1932, D.D. (hon.). 1951; B.D., Bexley Div. Sch., 1934; Dr. Laws and Letters, Lake Erie Coll., 1962; S.T.D., St. John's Coll., Winnipeg, Can., 1963; D.D., Seabury Western Sem., 1970; m. Cary Elizabeth Fleming, Nov. 29, 1935; children—Philip Edward, Judith, Patricia. Ordained to ministry of Protestant Episcopal Ch., 1935; in charge of St. Andrew's Mission, Columbus, Ohio, and St. Stephen's parish, Cincinnati, 1934-40; rector Christ Ch., St. Paul, 1940-50; dean St. Paul's Cathedral, Buffalo, 1950-57; suffragan bishop Diocese of Minn., Mpls., 1958-68, coadjutor, 1968-70; bishop of Minn., 1971-78. Pres. Buffalo Council of Chs., 1954-55; protestant chaplain Buffalo Trades and Labor Assembly, 1955-57; pres. Province Midwest, Episcopal Ch., 1970-73, mem. nat. exec. council, 1970-73. Bd. dirs. St. Paul Community Chest Bd., 1947-50, hon., 1950; bd. dirs. Buffalo Community Chest, 1952-57; mem. Council Social Agencies (past pres.), St. Paul Council Human Relations (past pres.). Mem. Sigma Pi. Mason. For contbn. to community and civic work was named outstanding young man of St. Paul by Jr. C. of C., 1946. Author: Family Story, 1960. Contbg. author: Confirmation: History Doctrine and Practice, 1962. Home: 1632 Comstock Ln Wayzata MN 55391

MCNALLY, ANDREW, III, printer, publisher; b. Chgo., Aug. 17, 1909; s. Andrew and Eleanor (Vilas) McN.; A.B., Yale U., 1931; m. Margaret Clark MacMillin, Nov. 20, 1936; children—Betty Jane, Andrew, Edward Clark. With Chgo. factory Rand McNally & Co., 1931, N.Y. sales office v.p., dir., 1933, pres., 1948-74, chmn. bd., 1974—; dir. Nat. Ry. Publ. Co., N.Y.C., Harvey Hubbell Inc. Past pres. Graphic Arts Tech. Found., now bd. dirs. Served as capt., C.E. Army Map Service, 1942-45. Mem. Chgo. Hist. Soc. (past pres., trustee). Office: PO Box 7600 Chicago IL 60680

MC NALLY, ANDREW, IV, pub. co. exec.; b. Chgo., Nov. 11, 1939; s. Andrew and Margaret C. (MacMillin) McN.; B.A., U. N.C., 1963; M.B.A., U. Chgo., 1969; m. Jeanine Sanchez, July 3, 1966; children—Andrew, Carrie, Ward. Bus. mgr. edn. div. Rand McNally & Co., Chgo., 1967-70, exec. v.p., sec., 1970-74, pres., 1974—, chief exec. officer, 1978—, also dir. Mem. fin. com. Printing Industries Am., 1970—; mem. edn. com. Graphic Arts Tech. Found., also mem. tech.-econ. forecasting com. Trustee Hill Sch., Latin Sch., Newberry Library; mem. vis. com. of library U. Chgo.; mem. aux. bd. Art Inst. Chgo. Mem. Air Force N.G., 1963-69. Mem. Chgo. Forum, Young Presidents Orgn., Chgo. Map. Soc. Clubs: Chicago, Saddle and Cycle, Commonwealth (Chgo.); Glen View Golf. Home: 16 Canterbury Ct Wilmette IL 60091 Office: PO Box 7600 Chicago IL 60680

MC NALLY, ARTHUR JEROME, clergyman; b. Holyoke, Mass., Apr. 6, 1931; s. Howard Jerome and Anna (Warecki) McN.; B.S. in Sci., St. Francis Xavier U., Antigonish, N.S., Can., 1953; postgrad. U. Notre Dame. Joined Congregation of Passion, Roman Cath. Ch., 1954, ordained priest, 1961; asso. editor Sign mag., Union City, N.J., 1961-75, editor, 1975-78. Home: 148 Monastery Ave Pittsburgh PA 15203

MC NALLY, EDWARD THOMAS, mfg. co. exec.; b. Pittsburg, Kans., May 28, 1914; s. Thomas Joseph and Mary Agnes (Henneberry) McN.; Ph.B. in Commerce, U. Notre Dame, 1936; postgrad. London U., 1936-37; m. Edythe Clare Williams, May 30, 1940; children—Eileen, Peggy, Thomas, Timothy, Michael, Anne. With McNally Pittsburg Mfg. Corp., 1937-43, 46—, treas., 1946-55, pres., 1955-76, chmn. bd., 1976—; dir. Commerce Bancshares Corp., Kansas City, Mo., Kansas City So. Industries Inc. (Mo.), McNally Bharat Engring. Co., Calcutta, India, Monarch Cement Co., Humboldt, Kans.; occasional lectr. bus. Pittsburg State U. Mem. adv. bd. Sch. Bus., Pittsburg State U.; trustee Mt. Carmel Hosp., Pittsburg. Served to lt. (j.g.) Supply Corps, USN, 1943-46. Named Disting. Alumni, Mo. Mil. Acad., 1969, Kans. Businessman of Year, 1974, Kansan of Year, 1975. Mem. Am Mining Congress (pres. mfrs. div. 1960-61), Soc. Mining Engrs., Pittsburg C. of C. (pres. 1952-54). Republican. Roman Catholic. Clubs: K.C., Crestwood Country. Contbr. articles on coal to profl. publs.

MCNALLY, FRANK J., bus. exec.; b. 1916, A.B., Manhattan Coll.; LL.B., Columbia; married. With SEC, 1940-42; with Ethyl Corp., 1946—, dir. finance dept., 1960-67, treas., 1967—, v.p., 1977—. Served with USNR, World War II. Address: 330 S 4th St Richmond VA 23219

MCNALLY, FRANK MICHAEL, signal mfg. co. exec.; b. Phila., Aug. 4, 1943; s. Frank M. and Marguerite L. (Smith) McN.; B.S. in Mech. Engring., Drexel U., 1966; M.B.A., Rochester Inst. Tech., 1971; J.D. (Constl. Law award 1974), Temple U., 1974; m. Ann C. Melone, June 24, 1967; 1 son, Kevin Paul. Design engr. Eastman Kodak Co., Rochester, N.Y., 1966-69; adminstrv. asst. Xerox Corp., Rochester, 1969-71; counsel, v.p. CPI Corp., Phila., 1971-79; admitted to Pa. bar, 1974; gen. counsel Leeds & Northrop Co., North Wales, Pa., 1977-79, Gen. Signal Corp., Stamford, Conn., 1979—. Mem. Am. Bar Assn. Roman Catholic. Home: 1037 Valley View Rd New Canaan CT 06840 Office: Gen Signal Corp High Ridge Park Stamford CT 06905

MCNALLY, H(ORACE) VINCENT, JR., lawyer; b. N.Y.C., Apr. 14, 1941; s. Horace Vincent and Rita Louise (Wintrich) McN.; B.A., Loyola U., Los Angeles, 1963, LL.B., 1966; m. Colleen Marie Cashen, Apr. 20, 1963; children—Maureen Ann, Peter Vincent. Admitted to Calif. bar, 1967; with firm Bodkin, Breslin & Luddy, Los Angeles, 1966-69; asst. gen. counsel A.J. Industries, Inc., Los Angeles, 1969-70, gen. counsel, sec., 1970-71; with firm Montgomery, Bell, Harper & Bottum, Los Angeles, 1972; partner firm Montgomery, Bottum, Regal & McNally, Inc., Los Angeles, 1973—. Home: 263 S Van Ness Ave Los Angeles CA 90004 Office: 1100 Glendon Ave Suite 1800 Los Angeles CA 90024

MCNALLY, TERRENCE, playwright; b. St. Petersburg, Fla., Nov. 3, 1939; s. Hubert Arthur and Dorothy Katharine (Rapp) McN.; B.A., Columbia U., 1960. Recipient Obie award for distinguished play, 1974. Guggenheim fellow, 1966, 69. Mem. Am. Acad. Arts and Letters. Author: (plays) And Things That Go Bump in the Night, 1965, Next, 1969, Sweet Eros, 1969, Noon, 1969, Where Has Tommy Flowers Gone, 1971, Bad Habits, 1973, The Ritz, 1974, The Golden Age, 1975, Broadway, Broadway, 1978. Home: 218 W 10th St New York NY 10014

MCNALLY, THOMAS CHARLES, III, lawyer, mfg. co. exec.; b. San Francisco, Dec. 5, 1938; s. Thomas Charles and Claire Marie (Egan) McN.; B.S., U. San Francisco, 1960; J.D., Hastings Coll. Law, U. Cal. at San Francisco, 1963; m. Paula Ann Berger, Sept. 3, 1960; children—Megan, Martin, J. Tevis. Admitted to Calif. bar, 1964; dep. atty. gen. State Calif., 1964; asso. firm Bohnert, Flowers & McCarthy, San Francisco, 1965-68; asst. sec., counsel DiGiorgio Corp., San Francisco, 1968-73, sec., counsel, 1974-75; sec., gen. counsel Consol. Fibres, Inc., San Francisco, 1975—, also dir.; lectr. McGeorge Bar Rev., 1964-65, Continuing Edn. of Bar, U. Calif., 1975-76; judge moot ct. U. San Francisco, 1974—. Co-chmn. Mill Valley Citizens Adv. Com., 1974-76; mem. pub. affairs com. San Francisco Assn. Mental Health, 1965-69. Mem. Am., San Francisco bar assns., State Bar Calif., Am. Soc. Corporate Secs. Republican. Roman Catholic (lector). Clubs: Olympic; Commercial; Scott Valley Tennis (founder, dir. 1971-76). Home: 3 Midhill Dr Mill Valley CA 94941 Office: 50 California St San Francisco CA 94111

MC NAMARA, EDWARD HOWARD, mayor Livonia (Mich.); b. Detroit, Sept. 21, 1926; s. Andrew Kurcina and Ellen Gertrude (Bennett) McN.; Ph.B., U. Detroit, 1959, postgrad. in law; m. Lucille Yvonne Martin, June 26, 1948; children—Colleen, Michael, Nancy, Kevin, Terence. Councilman, City of Livonia, 1962-70, pres. council, 1968-70, mayor, 1970—; pres. Dearborn Twp. Sch. Bd., 1954; mem. Wayne County Bd. Suprs., 1964; mem. Mich. Gov.'s Spl. Com. Land Use, 1971; pres. Mich. Conf. Mayors, 1975-76; chmn. South Eastern Mich. Transp. Authority, 1978; pres. Mich. Mcpl. League, 1974-75; mem. Livonia Meadows Civic Assn.; chmn. Sunset dist. Detroit Area council Boy Scouts Am.; mem. Mich. Dem. Com. Served with USN, 1944-46. Club: K.C. Home: 16501 Park Dr Livonia MI 48154 Office: Office of Mayor City Hall Livonia MI 48150

MC NAMARA, FRANCIS JOSEPH, JR., lawyer; b. Boston, Nov. 30, 1927; s. Francis Joseph and Louise (English) McN.; A.B., Georgetown U., 1949, LL.B., 1951; m. Noreen E. O'Connor, June 18, 1953; children—Francis Joseph III, Moira Patricia, John Allen, Kathleen Louise, Martha Jeanne, Mark Jeffrey. Admitted to Conn. bar, 1952; asso. firm Pullman, Comley, Bradley & Reeves, 1953; asst. U.S. Atty., dist. Conn., 1953-57; asso. firm Cummings & Lockwood, Stamford, Conn., 1957—, partner, 1959—. Trustee Fairfield (Conn.) U., 1968—, Charles E. Culpeper Trust; chmn. bd. Charles E. Culpeper Found. Served with USNR, 1946, 51-53. Fellow Am. Bar Found.; mem. Am., Fed. bar assns., Conn. Bar Assn. (chmn. fed. judiciary com. 1976—, mem. ho. of dels., bd. govs. 1978—), Navy League U.S., Knights of Malta, Phi Delta Phi. Roman Catholic. Republican. Clubs: Univ. (N.Y.C.); Yacht, Midtown, Landmark (Stamford); Noroton Yacht, Wee Burn Country (Darien, Conn.). Home: 16 Allwood Rd Darien CT 06820 Office: 1 Atlantic St Stamford CT 06904 also 866 United Nations Plaza New York NY 10017

MC NAMARA, FRANCIS TERRY, fgn. service officer; b. Troy, N.Y., Nov. 2, 1927; s. John Francis and Ellin Frances (Fennelly) McN.; B.A., Russell Sage Coll., 1953; postgrad. McGill U., 1953-54, Syracuse U., 1954-56; M.A., George Washington U., 1972; m. Margaret Clarkson, June 1954 (div. May 1967); children—Catherine, Ellin, Anne, Jane, Patricia; m. 2d, Cong Tang Ton Nu Nhu De, Dec. 1976; 1 son, Terry Patrick. Joined U.S. Fgn. Service, 1956; vice consul, Salisbury, Rhodesia, 1957-59; research analyst Dept. State, 1959-61; consul, Elizabethville, Congo, 1961-63; 2d sec. embassy, Dar-Es-Salaam, Tanzania, 1963-67; assigned Armed Forces Staff Coll., 1967; chief rural devel., Vinh Long, Vietnam, 1968; dep. province sr. adviser, Quang Tri, Vietnam, 1968-69; consul, Da Nang, Vietnam, 1969-71; assigned Naval War Coll., 1971-72; dep. chief mission Am. embassy, Dahomey, 1972-74; consul gen., Can Tho, Vietnam, 1974-75; asso. dir. Inter-Agy. Task Force for Resettlement of Indochinese Refugees, 1975; consul gen., Que., Can., 1975-79; mem. Exec. Seminar for Nat. and Internat. Affairs, Washington, 1979—. Vice pres. Vietnamese-Am. Children's Aid Soc., 1971—. Served with USNR, 1944-46, 50-51. Decorated Vietnam Armed Forces Honor medal 1st Class, Civic Action medal 1st Class, Humanitarian medal; recipient Dept. State Meritorious Honors award, 1965, 70, Superior Honors award, 1968, 77, 79. Clubs: Army-Navy, Am. Fgn. Service, George Washington U. (Washington); Cercle Universitaire (Quebec City); Mt. Stephan (Montreal). Home: 362 5th Ave Troy NY 12182 also Lone Pine Manchester VT 05254 Office: care Dept State Washington DC 20520

MC NAMARA, J(OHN) DONALD, lawyer; b. Bridgeport, Conn., Feb. 28, 1924; s. John T. and Agnes (Keating) McN.; B.A., Dartmouth, 1945; M.A. in Govt., Harvard, 1947, LL.B., 1950; m. Shirley Addison Holdridge, Nov. 5, 1960. Admitted to N.Y. and Conn. bars, 1951; asso. firm Hall, Haywood, Patterson & Taylor, N.Y.C., 1951-53, 55-56; asst. U.S. atty., So. Dist. N.Y., 1953-55; asso. firm Wickes, Riddell, Bloomer, Jacobi & McGuire, N.Y.C., 1956-57; asso., then partner firm Nottingham & McEniry, and successor, N.Y.C., 1957-59; sec., gen. counsel Interpub. Group of Companies, Inc., N.Y.C., 1960—, dir., 1965—, sr. v.p., 1966-73, exec. v.p., 1973—, mem. exec. com., 1967—. Chmn. U.S. Nat. Tennis Championships, 1965. Served to lt. (j.g.) USNR, 1943-46. Mem. Am. (com. fgn. and internat. bus. law 1971—), Internat. bar assns. Clubs: River, University, Metropolitan Opera (N.Y.C.); West Side Tennis (pres. 1964-66, bd. govs. 1962-66, 78—); Internat. (Washington). Home: 350 E 57th St New York NY 10022 also Ethan Allen Rd Peru VT 05152 Office: 1271 Ave of Americas New York NY 10020

MC NAMARA, JOHN J(OSEPH), advt. agy. exec.; b. Yonkers, N.Y., Mar. 7, 1934; B.S., Yale U., 1956; M.B.A., N.Y. U., 1963; m. Patricia A. Widmann, Sept. 14, 1963; children—Mary, John. Exec. v.p., eastern regional dir. Young & Rubicam, N.Y.C., 1979—. Pres. United Way, Pelham, N.Y.; mem. Pelham Manor (N.Y.) Zoning Bd. Served to 1st lt. USMC, 1956-58. Clubs: Pelham Country, Union League. Home: 1316 Pelhamdale Ave Pelham Manor NY 10803 Office: 285 Madison Ave New York NY 10017

MCNAMARA, JOSEPH MARTIN, insurance co. exec.; b. Jersey City, Apr. 6, 1919; s. Martin Joseph and Mary Ellen McN.; A.B., Villanova U., 1940; J.D., Fordham U. Sch. Law, 1946; m. Mar. 20, 1943; children—Stephen, Ruth Ann, Elizabeth. Admitted to N.Y. State bar, 1946, N.J. bar, 1948; claims mgr. Am. Surety Co., 1946-52; with Gen. Accident, Fire & Life Assurance Corp. Ltd., Phila., 1952—, exec. v.p., 1972-76, sr. exec. v.p., 19—; mem. Claims Exec. Council, Villanova U. Devel. Program. Mem. Phila. Crime Commn. Served with USCG, 1942-45. Mem. Am. Bar Assn., Internat. Assn. Ins. Counsel (v.p.). Clubs: Down Town (dir.), Skytop. Office: 414 Walnut St Philadelphia PA 19106

MC NAMARA, LAWRENCE J., bishop; b. Chgo., Aug. 5, 1928; s. Lawrence and Margaret (Knusman) McN.; B.A., St. Paul Sem., 1949; S.T.L., Catholic U. Am., 1953. Ordained priest Roman Catholic Ch., 1953; parish priest, tchr. Kansas City-St. Joseph Diocese, 1953-57; dir. diocesan Refugee Resettlement, 1957-60; chaplain Jackson County Jail, 1957-64; exec. dir. Campaign for Human Devel., 1973-77; bishop of Grand Island (Nebr.), 1978—. Recipient award Cath. Relief Services. *

MC NAMARA, PAUL JAMES, hotel exec.; b. Elmira, N.Y., July 15, 1912; s. James P. and Harriet (Lynch) McN.; B.S., Cornell U., 1935; m. Betty Waters, Jan. 11, 1947; children—Susan, Joan, Paul James, William Burke. With Castleton Hotel, New Castle, Pa. 1935-38, Van Curier Hotel, Schenectady, 1938-40, Roosevelt Hotel, Pitts., 1940-42; staff Warwick Hotel (Phila. Warwick Corp.), Phila., 1946—, gen. mgr., 1950—, also v.p.; v.p. Independence Motor Inn, Brandywine Motor Inn Corp., Prussia Motor Inn Corp., Airport Motor Inn Corp., Kulpesville Motor Inn Corp.; partner Holiday Inn franchise for Phila. area. Bd. dirs. Eagleville Hosp., United Way, Nat. Council Alcoholism. Served as maj. AUS, World War II. Mem. Phila. C. of C. (past dir.), Am., Pa. (sec.), Phila. hotel assns., Friendly Sons St. Patrick, Phi Delta Theta. Clubs: Cornell, Racquet, Phila. Country (Phila.). Home: 237 Ladbroke Rd Bryn Mawr PA 19010 Office: 1305 Walnut St Philadelphia PA 19107

MCNAMARA, RIEMAN, JR., banker; b. Richmond, Va., July 25, 1928; s. Rieman and Selina (Heyward) McN.; B.S., Va. Poly. Inst. and State U., 1948; Chartered Fin. Analyst, U. Va., 1966; m. Merrily Brooks, Aug. 2, 1958; children—Brooks, Daniel Heyward. Field rep. Burroughs Corp., 1950-52; asst. trust officer Central Nat. Bank, Richmond, 1952-58; v.p., trust officer So. Bank & Trust Co., Richmond, 1958-65, sr. v.p., 1965-68, exec. v.p., 1968, exec. v.p., dir., 1969, pres., 1972-79, vice chmn., 1977—; exec. v.p., dir. So. Bankshares, Inc.; dir. Carmine Foods, Inc., Petroleum Marketers, Inc. Trustee Grace and Holy Trinity Endowment Fund, Inc. Served to 2d lt. inf. AUS, 1948-50. Mem. Richmond Soc. Fin. Analysts (past pres.), Bond Club Va. (past pres.), SR, Descs. Signers Declaration Independence. Episcopalian. Clubs: Va. Creepers, Focus, Commonwealth, Country of Va. (Richmond). Office: So Bank & Trust Co 2d and Grace Sts Richmond VA 23260*

MC NAMARA, ROBERT STRANGE, banker; b. San Francisco, June 9, 1916; s. Robert James and Clara Nell (Strange) McN.; A.B., U. Calif., 1937, M. B.A., Harvard, 1939; LL.D., Harvard, U. Calif., U. Mich., Columbia U., George Washington U., Princeton, Amherst, Williams Coll., U. Ala., Ohio State U., N.Y. U., Notre Dame U., U. Philippines, Aberdeen U.; m. Margaret Craig, Aug. 13, 1940; children—Margaret Elizabeth, Kathleen, Robert Craig. Asst. prof. bus. adminstrn. Harvard, 1940-43; exec. Ford Motor Co., 1946-61, controller, 1949-53, asst. gen. mgr. Ford div., 1953-55, v.p., gen. mgr. Ford div., 1955-57, group v.p. car divisions, 1957-60, pres. co., 1960-61, co. dir. 1957-61; U.S. sec. of defense, 1961-68; pres. World Bank, 1968—. Dir. pub. and pvt. instns. including Ford Found., Brookings Instn., Calif. Inst. Tech. Spl. cons. War Department, 1942. Served as lt. col. USAAF, 1943-46. Decorated Legion of Merit, Medal of Freedom, D.S.M. Mem. Phi Beta Kappa. Author: The Essence of Security, 1968; One Hundred Countries-Two Billion People. Home: 2412 Tracy Pl Washington DC 20008

MCNAMARA, WILLIAM ALBINUS, utility exec.; b. Superior, Wis., Mar. 1, 1909; s. Bartlett M. and Mary J. (Carpenter) McN.; B.A. in Commerce, U. Wis., 1930, M.A., 1931, LL.B., 1934; m. Irene G. Chaltre, June 8, 1935; children—William B., Thomas J., John M. Admitted to Wis. bar, 1934; accountant Frazer and Torbett, C.P.A.'s, Chgo., 1934-35; sec. bondholders com. Chgo. Title & Trust Co., 1935-36; corp. sect. Curt G. Joa, Inc., Sheboygan Falls, Wis., 1936-37, dir., 1936—; partner firm Cavanaugh & McNamara, Madison, Wis., 1937-42, Rieser, Mathy, McNamara & Stafford, Madison, 1942-58; fin. v.p., then v.p. fin. Madison Gas and Electric Co., 1958-77, chmn. bd., 1977—, dir., 1958—; dir. First Fed. Savs. & Loan Assn., Madison, 1966—. Mem. president's council Edgewood Coll., Madison, 1969-72; adv. bd. St. Mary's Hosp. Nursing Sch., Madison, 1965-66. Mem. Am. Gas Assn., Wis. Utility Assn., Am. Bar Assn., State Bar Wis. (chmn. taxation sect. 1950-51), Dane County Bar Assn., Greater Madison C. of C. (pres. 1962), Wis. Bus. Econs. Assn. Republican. Roman Catholic. Clubs: Maple Bluff Country, Madison, K.C. Home: 112 N Roby Rd Madison WI 53705 Office: 100 N Fairchild St Box 1231 Madison WI 53701

MC NAMEE, MAURICE BASIL, educator; b. Montello, Wis., June 5, 1909; s. James Patrick and Ida (Griffith) McN; A.B., St. Louis U., 1933, A.M., 1934, S.T.L., 1941, Ph.D., 1945. Joined Soc. of Jesus, 1927, ordained priest Roman Cath. Ch., 1940; instr. Creighton U. High Sch., 1936-37; faculty St. Louis U., 1944—, prof. English, 1960—, dir. dept., 1956-70, dir. honors program, 1950-61. Lectr. fgn. workshops, 1957-60. Mem. Cath. Commn. Intellectual and Cultural Affairs, 1971—; exec. dir. Samuel Cupples House Found., 1974; mem. Mayor's Council Cultural Affairs, 1979. Recipient Nancy McNeir Ring Outstanding Faculty award, 1973. Research grantee St. Louis U., 1955, Ford Found. Jesuit Faculty Fund, St. Louis U., 1966; Fulbright research follow, Belgium, 1966; research grantee in humanities Am. Philos. Soc., 1966, 78. Mem. Modern Lang. Assn., Renaissance Soc. Am., Amici Thomae Mori, Soc. Art Historians (pres. 1962-64), Coll. Art Assn., Medieval Acad. Am., Phi Beta Kappa. Democrat. Club: Knights St. Columba (London, Eng.). Author: Literary Decorum in Francis Bacon, 1950; Reading for Understanding, 1958, 68; Honor and the Epic Hero, 1960; (with J. Cronin, J. Rogers) Literary Types and Themes, 1960, 70; Essays by the Masters, 1968; Essays in Exposition, 1969; Bacon's Inductive Method and Humanistic Grammar, 1971; The Origin of the Vested Angel as a Eucharistic Symbol in Flemish Painting, 1972. Address: 3601 Lindell Blvd Saint Louis MO 63108

MC NAUGHT, JOHN J., fed. judge; b. 1921; A.B., J.D., Boston Coll. Admitted to Mass. bar, 1949; asso. justice Superior Ct. Mass.; judge U.S. Dist. Ct. for Mass., 1979—. Mem. Am. Bar Assn. Office: care US Dist Ct McCormack PO and Courthouse Bldg Boston MA 02109*

MCNAUGHTON, ROBERT FORBES, JR., educator; b. Bklyn., Mar. 13, 1924; s. Robert Forbes and Helen (Brown) McN.; student Bklyn. Coll., 1942-43, 46; B.A., Columbia, 1948; Ph.D., Harvard, 1951; m. Ann Gerardo, Dec. 20, 1948 (div. 1957); children—Nicholas F., Sarah E.; m. 2d, Vivien Leonard, June 23, 1974. Tchr. philosophy Ohio State U., 1951-52, U. Mich., 1953-54, Stanford, 1954-57; tchr. computer sci. and elec. engring. Moore Sch. Elec. Engring., U. Pa., 1957-64, Mass. Inst. Tech., 1964-66; prof. computer sci., math. Rensselaer Poly. Inst., Troy, N.Y., 1966—. Research, Office Naval Research, 1952-53, RCA, Moorestown, summer 1960, RCA, Princeton, summer 1963. Served with AUS, 1943-46. Recipient Levy medal Franklin Inst., 1956. Mem. Assn. Symbolic Logic, Assn. Computing Machinery, Am. Math. Soc., Math. Assn. Am., Phi Beta Kappa. Home: 2511 15th St Troy NY 12180

MC NAUGHTON, WILLIAM HUGH, banker; b. Washington, May 23, 1916; s. John and Minnie Maud (Price) McN.; B.C.S., Columbus U., Washington, 1937, M.C.S., 1938; m. Virginia Pauline Russell, Sept. 9, 1942 (dec. Jan. 2, 1969). With Nat. Assn. Securities Dealers and predecessor orgn., Washington, 1934-57, comptroller, 1954-57; treas. Internat. Bank, Washington, 1957-62, v.p., 1962-72, sr. v.p.-financial, 1972—; pres., dir. Financial Services, Inc.; v.p. Internat. Gen. Industries; dir. IB Credit Corp.; dir. AICC Life Ins. Co., Globe Industries, Inc., Chgo., Gen. Services Life Ins. Co., United Services Gen. Ins. Co., Washington, Washington Internat. Bank & Trust (Cayman Island), Avis Indsl. Corp., Upland, Ind. Served from ensign to lt. comdr. USNR, 1942-46. C.P.A., Md. Mem. Fin. Execs.

Inst. Clubs: Manor Country (Rockville, Md.); International (Washington). Home: 1916 Norvale Rd Silver Spring MD 20906 Office: 1701 Pennsylvania Ave NW Washington DC 20006

MC NAUGHTON, WILLIAM JOHN, bishop; b. Lawrence, Mass., Dec. 7, 1926; s. William John and Ruth Irene (Howe) McN.; student Maryknoll Venard Coll., Clarks Summit, Pa., 1944-46; B.A., Maryknoll Maj. Sem., 1948, B.S.T., M.R.E., 1953; student Maryknoll Novitiate, 1948-49, Fgn. Lang. Inst. Yale, 1953-54. Joined Maryknoll Order, Catholic Fgn. Mission Soc. Am., 1944, ordained priest Roman Catholic Ch., 1953; missionary Chung Chong Pouk To, Korea, 1954-61; consecrated bishop, 1961; 1st vicar apostolic of Inchon, Korea, 1961-62, bishop of Inchon, 1962—. Address: Bishop's Residence PO Box 19 Tap Tong Inchon Korea 160-00

MC NEAL, ARCHIE LIDDELL, ret. librarian; b. Ruleville, Miss., Sept. 3, 1912; s. Archibald Walter and Amelia (Thompson) McN.; B.S., Memphis State Coll., 1932; B.L.S., George Peabody Coll., 1936; Ph.D., U. Chgo., 1951; m. Billie Irene Cornett, Feb. 11, 1946 (dec. Apr. 1968); m. 2d, Dorothy M. Johnson, June 11, 1969. Reference asst. Cossitt Library, Memphis, 1932-34; librarian Millington (Tenn.) High Sch., 1934-36, East Tenn. State Coll., 1936-43, 46-48; chief readers services div. U. Tenn., 1948-52; dir. libraries U. Miami (Fla.), 1952-79; vis. prof. Fla. State U. Library Sch., summers 1954, 55, 57, U. N.C. Sch. Library Sci., 1959, 61, Columbia, summer 1964, 67, 69. Mem. Fla. State Library and Hist. Commn., 1966-69, chmn. commn., 1968-69; cons. libraries, gen. edn. Dept. State, India, 1957; mem. adv. council on library resources U.S. Office Edn., 1966-70. Served to 1st lt. AUS, 1943-46; Mem. A.L.A. (council 1955-65, pres. library adminstrn. div. 1960-61, chmn. intellectual freedom com. 1959-64, exec. bd. 1961-65, 68-69, 2d v.p. 1968-69 chmn. legislation com. 1969-71), Assn. Coll. and Research Libraries (pres. 1964-65), Southeastern (pres. 1964-66), Fla. (pres. 1958-59), Tenn. (pres. 1940-42) library assns., Assn. Caribbean U. and Research Libraries (exec. council 1970-75, pres. 1973-74), Phi Kappa Phi. Democrat. Conglist. Home: 8445 SW 108th St Miami FL 33156

MC NEAL, HARLEY JOHN, lawyer; b. Birmingham, Ala.; s. John Harley and Alfretta (Frederick) McN.; A.B., U. Mich., 1932, student Law Sch., 1934, student Med. Sch., 1936; LL.B., Western Res. U., 1936, LL.M., 1966, student Case Sch. Applied Sci., 1938-39, student Med. Sch., 1940; student U. Wis. Law Sch., 1935, Cleve. Coll., 1938; m. Virginia Marie Hutzel, Feb. 8, 1936; children—Virginia Marie (Mrs. Thomas Woodard), Sandra Jean (Mrs. Robert Keavy). Admitted to Ohio bar, 1935; mem. firm John H. McNeal and Harley J. McNeal, Cleve., 1935-45; partner firm Burgess, Fulton & Fullmer, Cleve., 1945-50; partner firm McNeal & Schick, Cleve., 1950-69, sr. partner, 1969—; lectr. Western Res. U. Med. Sch., also Dental Sch., 1945-62, Cleve. Marshall Law Sch., 1958-60, Western Res. U. Law Sch., 1958-62; mem. Nat. Bd. Trial Advocacy, 1979—. Mem. council Bay Village, Ohio, 1950-52; mem. center com. on law and environment World Peace Through Law Center, Belgrade, Yugoslavia, 1971. Mem. adminstrn. justice adv. com. Greater Cleve. Asso. Found.; mem. com. for justice Greater Cleve. Growth Assn.; bd. dirs. Def. Research Inst. Served to capt. JAG Dept., USAAF, 1942-45; ETO. Fellow Am. Coll. Trial Lawyers (chmn. com. on procedures and preservation oral argument), Internat. Acad. Trial Lawyers, Am. Acad. Forensic Scis., Am., Ohio bar founds.; mem. Am. Bd. Profl. Attys. (trustee), Internat. Assn. Ins. Counsel (pres. 1966-67), Fedn. Ins. Counsel Assn., Am. (chmn. rules and procedure and trial technique coms. ins. sect., co-chmn. profl. liability com. litigation sect., mem. council litigation sect. 1978—), Internat., Fed., Inter-Am., Ohio (chmn. individual rights and responsibilities com.), Cleve. (chmn. modern jud. system com., trustee, pres. 1980), Cyahoga County bar assns., World Peace Through Law (maritime com., chmn. litigation sect.), Seldon Soc. (Eng.), Am. Judicature Soc., Ohio Jud. Conf. (rules adv. com.), Maritime Law Assn. U.S., Nat. Assn. R.R. Trial Lawyers, Am. Soc. Internat. Law, Internat. Acad. Law and Sci., Greater Cleve. Growth Assn., Phi Delta Phi, Sigma Alpha Epsilon, Druids. Republican. Presbyn. Mason (32, K.T.). Clubs: Clifton, Westwood Country (Rocky River, Ohio); Union, Nisi Prius, Hermit, Mid Day (Cleve.); Coquille (Lantana, Fla.); Lotos (N.Y.C.). Author numerous articles profl. jours. Co-author: Personal Injury Litigation in Ohio. Asso. editor The Forum, 1965-69. Home: 26828 W Lake Rd Bay Village OH 44140 Office: Williamson Bldg Cleveland OH 44114

MCNEAL, JAMES HECTOR, JR., mfg. co. exec.; b. Dover, Del., Nov. 22, 1927; s. James Hector and Elizabeth Vickers (Hodgson) McN.; B.S., U. Del., 1951; m. Lucy Cooper Finn, June 16, 1951; children—James Hector, Edwin Howell, Sarah Elizabeth. With Budd Co., 1951—, v.p. mfg. services, Troy, Mich., 1972-73, group v.p. automotive products, 1973-74, pres., chief operating officer, 1974—, also dir.; dir. Automotive Co. of Can. Ltd. Bd. dirs. Detroit Area council Boy Scouts Am. Served with USNR, 1945-46. Mem. Newcomen Soc. N.Am., Econ. Club Detroit. Clubs: Bloomfield Hills Country; Oakland Hills Country; Detroit Athletic. Office: 3155 W Big Beaver Rd Troy MI 48084*

MC NEALY, RAYMOND WILLIAM, JR., business exec.; b. Chgo., Nov. 21, 1927; s. Raymond William and Mary Sarina (Kinney) McN.; B.A., Harvard, 1950, M.B.A., 1952; m. Marmalee Doris Noffke, Jan. 10, 1952; children—Raymond William III, Scott, Barry, Susan. Dir. purchasing Cummins Engine Co., Columbus, Ind., 1956-59; pres. Berliana Corp., Rockford, Ill., 1959-60; dir. material Vendo Co., Kansas City, Mo., 1960-62; vice chmn., dir. Am. Motors Corp., Detroit, 1962-77; pres., chief operating officer, dir. AMF Inc., White Plains, N.Y., 1978—. Club: Stanwich (Greenwich, Conn.). Home: 60 E Middle Patent Rd Greenwich CT 06830 Office: 777 Westchester Ave White Plains NY 10604

MCNEAR, DENMAN KITTREDGE, transp. co. exec.; b. San Francisco, July 20, 1925; s. E. Denman and Mary H. (Kittredge) McN.; B.S. in Civil Engring., Mass. Inst. Tech., 1948; M.B.A., Stanford U., 1950; m. Susan L. Anderson, Jan. 27, 1962; children—Denman K., Stephen A., George D. With So. Pacific Transp. Co., San Francisco, 1948—, asst. to pres. and v.p., 1963-75, v.p. operations, 1975-76, pres., 1976—; pres. St. Louis Southwestern Ry. Co., 1975—, dir., 1969—; mem. of corp. Mass. Inst. Tech., Cambridge, 1977-82. Served with USN, 1944-46. Registered profl. engr., Calif., Ariz., N.M., Tex. Mem. ASCE, Calif. Council Economic Edn. (pres. 1975—, trustee 1972—). Republican. Clubs: Bohemian, Pacific-Union, Stock Exchange. Office: So Pacific Bldg 1 Market Plaza San Francisco CA 94105*

MCNEE, ROBERT BRUCE, geographer, educator; b. Big Timber, Mont., Aug. 20, 1922; s. William Wooldridge and Nina Lucy (Gates) McN.; B.A. with high honors, Wayne U., 1949; M.A., Syracuse U., 1950, Ph.D., 1953; m. Gilberta Lyons, Sept. 20, 1949 (annulled Sept. 1954); 1 son, Robert Andrew; m. 2d, Doris Smithers, Dec. 11, 1954; children—Margaret Ann, William Smithers. From lectr. to asso. prof. City Coll. N.Y., 1952-63; prof. geography U. Cin., 1963-73, 76—, chmn. dept., 1963-69; dir. Am. Geog. Soc., N.Y.C., 1973-76; summer tchr. St. Lawrence U., Wayne State U., So. Ill. U.; cons. Ford Found., 1962-63. Mem. Assn. Am. Geographers (chmn. N.Y.-N.J. div. 1960-62; regional councilor), Am. Geog. Soc., Nat. Council Geog. Edn. Methodist. Author: A Primer on Economic Geography, 1971; also articles in field. Home: 3500 Banning Rd Cincinnati OH 45239

MC NEELA, EDWARD PHILIP, lawyer; b. Chgo., Jan. 7, 1928; s. Thomas and Ellen (Mc Gowan) McN.; student U. Ill., 1948-49; J.D., DePaul U., 1952; m. L. Germaine Harnish, Nov. 30, 1963; children—Teresa, Daniel, David, Laura, Jennifer, Thomas. Admitted to Ill. bar, 1952; partner firm McNeela & Griffen, Ltd., Chgo., 1964—. Served with U.S. Army, 1946-48. Mem. Am., Ill., Chgo. bar assns., Internat. Assn. Ins. Counsel. Roman Catholic. Home: 1404 Royal Oak Ln Glenview IL 60025 Office: 209 S LaSalle St Chicago IL 60604

MC NEELEY, HARRY DRAKE, bank exec.; b. Orlinda, Tenn., Feb. 23, 1914; s. H.W. and Lemma (Drake) McN.; B.S., Carson-Newman Coll., 1935; m. Murray Lee Stone, Mar. 6, 1940; children—William S., Susan Brooke, With Tenn. Eastman Co., Kingsport, 1935—, exec. v.p., 1959-63, pres., 1963-74; pres. Carolina Eastman Co., 1966-77, Ark. Eastman Co., 1974-77; chmn. Tex. Eastman Co., 1969-73, chmn. Eastman Chem. Products, Inc., 1969-73, Holston Def. Corp., 1966-73, v.p. Eastman Chem. Inter-Am. Ltd., 1962-73; dir., mem. exec. com. Eastman Kodak Co., 1967-79, v.p., 1968-72; exec. v.p., gen. mgr. Eastman Chems. div., 1972-79; dir. Conwood Corp.; chmn. bd. First Nat. Bank Sullivan County. Bd. dirs. Holston Valley Community Hosp., Kingsport Community Chest; chmn. bd. trustees Carson-Newman Coll. Mem. Am. Chem. Soc., Kingsport C. of C. Democrat. Baptist. Club: Ridgefields Country (Kingsport). Home: 4527 Preston Ct Kingsport TN 37664 Office: PO Box 889 Kingsport TN 37662

MC NEELY, E.L., merchandising co. exec.; b. Pattonsburg, Mo., Oct. 5, 1918; s. Ralph H. and Viola (Vogel) McN.; student Central Bus. Coll., Kansas City, Mo., 1935-36, U. Mo., 1936-37; A.B., No. Mo. State U., Kirksville, 1940; student Rockhurst Coll., Kansas City, Mo., 1942; m. Alice Elaine Hall, Sept. 18, 1948; children—Sandra (Mrs. Ronald Gessl), Gregory, Mark, Kevin. With Montgomery Ward & Co., 1940-64, divisional mdse. mgr., 1961-64; dir. marketing Wickes Corp., Saginaw, Mich., 1964-65, sr. v.p., 1965-69, pres., 1969-74, chief exec. officer, chmn., 1974—, also dir.; dir. Dayco Corp., Fed. Mogul Corp., Mich. Nat. Corp., Mich. Nat. Bank Detroit, Transam. Corp. Bd. dirs. YMCA, City of Hope; trustee Scripps Clinic and Research Found., Boys Clubs Am. Served as officer USNR, 1942-46; PTO. Mem. Beta Gamma Sigma, Alpha Phi Omega. Republican. Presbyterian. Clubs: Saginaw; Union League, Metropolitan (Chgo.); La Jolla Country; Cuyamaca (San Diego). Home: 1020 La Jolla Rancho Rd La Jolla CA 92037 Office: 1010 2d Ave San Diego CA 92101

MC NEELY, JERRY CLARK, educator, dramatist; b. Cape Girardeau, Mo., June 20, 1928; s. Archie Harris and Ida Mildred (McKee) McN.; student Westminster (Mo.) Coll., 1945-47; B.A., S.E. Mo. State Coll., 1949; M.S., U. Wis., 1950, Ph.D., 1956; m. Priscilla Grant, June 8, 1952; children—Melissa, Joel, Elizabeth. Instr., U. Wis., 1956-57, asst. prof., asso. prof., 1957-64, prof. communication arts, 1964-75. Writer plays produced on tv shows, including Hallmark Hall of Fame, Studio One, Climax, Twilight Zone, Dr. Kildare, Eleventh Hour, Mr. Novak, The Man From U.N.C.L.E., The Girl From U.N.C.L.E., The Virginian, Marcus Welby, M.D., Streets of San Francisco, Sandburg's Lincoln, Legend in Granite, Love Story, 1957—; co-creator, exec. story cons., writer-dir. TV series Owen Marshall, Counselor at Law; series creator, writer-dir. Lucas Tanner; writer-producer world premier Lucas Tanner; series creator, exec. producer Three for the Road, 1975—; writer-producer Something for Joey, MTM Enterprises, 1976—, The Critical List, 1978; exec. producer The Boy Who Drank Too Much, 1980. Served with AUS, 1951-53. Named Outstanding Young Tchr. Speech, 1959. Mem. Writers Guild Am., Dirs. Guild Am., A.S.C.A.P., Speech Assn. Am., Producers Guild Am., Beta Theta Pi. Presbyn. (elder, trustee). Author: (play) The Staring Match, 1957; (screen play) Owen Marshall, 1970. Writer song lyrics: What is Different About Today, 1964; Smiles from Yesterday; The First Day of Your Life, 1972. Office: CBS Studio Center 4024 Radford Ave Studio City CA 91604

MC NEER, CHARLES SELDEN, utility exec.; b. Gilbert, W.Va., Apr. 8, 1926; s. Richard Mason and Bertie May (Sparks) McN.; student Berea Coll., 1943-44, 46-47, U.S. Mcht. Marine Acad., 1944-46; B.S. in Elec. Engring., Northwestern U., 1950; m. Ann Campbell Bishop, Mar. 20, 1949; children—Charles William, Robert Lee, Thomas Richard. With Wis. Electric Power Co., Milw., 1950—, mgr. elec. engring., 1961-65, research engr. Operating Research Bur., 1965-67, asst. v.p., 1967, v.p. adminstrn., 1968, sr. v.p., 1969-73, exec. v.p., 1973-75, pres., 1975—; pres., dir. Wis. Natural Gas Co., Badger Service. Mem. exec. com. Wis.-Upper Mich. Systems, Mid-Am. Interpool Network; mem. council Operation ACTION UP; bd. dirs. United Way Greater Milw., Wis. Mfrs. and Commerce, Wis. Electric Utilities Research Found., Milw. Area Goodwill Industries, Inc., Greater Milw. Com., Wis. State Council Econ. Edn., YMCA of Met. Milw., Wis. Soc. to Prevent Blindness; mem. adv. council U. Wis. Sch. Bus. Adminstrn.; mem. council Med. Coll. Wis.; bd. govs. Jr. Achievement. Served with USNR, 1946-47. Registered profl. engr., Wis. Mem. IEEE, Engrs. and Scientists of Milw., Wis. Utilities Assn. (dir.), Met. Milw. Assn. Commerce (dir.), Assn. Edison Illuminating Cos., Edison Electric Inst. (dir., policy com. on nuclear power, policy com. on research), Wis., Nat. socs. profl. engrs., Sigma Xi, Eta Kappa Nu, Tau Beta Pi, Sigma Pi Sigma, Pi Mu Epsilon. Kiwanian. Home: 6520 Washington Circle Wauwatosa WI 53213 Office: 231 W Michigan St Milwaukee WI 53201

MCNEES, JAMES LAFAYETTE, JR., lawyer; b. Dallas, Oct. 25, 1916; s. James Lafayette and Elsie Mae (Holbert) McN.; student U. Tex., Arlington, 1936; J.D., Cumberland U., 1939; grad. U.S. Army Command and Gen. Staff Coll., 1960, Indsl. Coll. Armed Forces, 1979. Admitted to Tex. bar, U.S. Supreme Ct. bar; partner firm McNees & McNees, Dallas, 1940—; dir. Trinity Valley Bldg. Center Inc., Oilchem Corp., A.P.C. Foods Inc. Formerly pres. Greenway Parks Homeowners Assn.; mem. USO Council; formerly nat. v.p., mem. exec. com., nat. trustee Leukemia Soc. Am. Precinct chmn. Democratic Party; mem. Dallas County Dem. Exec. Com.; mem. exec. com. Dems. for Responsible Govt.; mem. Dallas Dem. Forum; Dem. candidate for lt. gov. Tex., 1978. Served with inf. U.S. Army, World War II; ETO; col. Res. (ret.). Decorated Bronze Star, Combat Infantrymen's Badge. Mem. Am., Tex., Dallas bar assns., Dallas C. of C., Am. Legion (formerly post comdr.), U. Tex. at Arlington Alumni Assn. (past pres.), Sigma Alpha Epsilon. Methodist (formerly pres. Men's Bible Class, now lay speaker, adminstrv. bd.). Mason (32 deg.), K.P. Clubs: Gaiete, Dervish, Calyx, Willow Bend Polo and Hunt. Home: 7705-C Eastern Ave Dallas TX 75209 Office: 1309 Main St Dallas TX 75202

MC NEESE, AYLMER GREEN, JR., banker; b. Hubbard, Tex., June 4, 1911; s. Aylmer G. and Maude (Carter) McN.; B.A., U. Tex., 1933, LL.B., 1937; m. Catherine Elsbury, Sept. 19, 1938; children—Thomas Dwyer, Margaret Carter. Admitted to Tex. bar, 1937; with Fulbright, Crooker & Jaworski, 1939-43; v.p., gen. counsel McCarthy Oil & Gas Corp., 1943-51; adminstrv. asst. to pres. Houston Oil Co. of Tex., 1951-53; asst. pres. Second Nat. Bank of Houston, 1953-56; pres., chief exec. officer Bank of Southwest, Houston, 1956-67, chmn. bd., 1967—, pres. S.W. Bancshares, Inc., 1970-76, chmn. exec. com., 1976—, also dir.; dir. Nat. Airlines, Inc., Long Point Nat. Bank, Temple-Eastex, Inc., Village Nat. Bank, Bank of Woodlake, Bank of Southwest Nat. Assn.; mem. adv. bd. Continental Nat. Bank, Ft. Worth. Bd. dirs. Tex. Med. Center, Inc., 1964—; bd. regents U. Tex., 1956-62, 71-76, chmn., 1973-74; trustee M.D. Anderson Found. Decorated knights cross Order of Crown (Belgium). Mem. State Bar Assn. Tex., Army Athletic Assn., Sons Republic Tex., S.A.R. Episcopalian. Mason (Shriner). Clubs: Ramada; Houston Country, Coronado, Forest, Houston; Metropolitan (N.Y.C.); Balboa (Matzalon, Mexico). Home: 603 W Friar Tuck Ln Houston TX 77024 Office: PO Box 2629 Houston TX 77001

MC NEICE, JOHN AMBROSE, JR., investment co. exec.; b. Quincy, Mass., Sept. 28, 1932; s. John Ambrose and Gladys Lydia (Starratt) McN.; B.A. magna cum laude, Boston Coll., 1954; M.B.A., Northeastern U., Boston, 1960; m. Margarete Emma Aust, Apr. 2, 1956; children—Gabriele S., Margarete Anne. With Colonial Mgmt. Assos., Inc., Boston, 1956—, v.p., 1968-74, exec. v.p., 1974, pres., 1975—. Trustee Wentworth Inst. Served with AUS, 1954-56. Chartered fin. analyst. Roman Catholic. Clubs: Union, Milton-Hoosic, Wollaston Golf. Home: 47 Green St Canton MA 02021 Office: 75 Federal St Boston MA 02110

MC NEIL, CLARID F., social worker, educator; b. nr. Hillsboro, Ohio, Jan. 19, 1908; s. Charles F. and Mary Anne (Tannehill) McN.; A.B., Ohio State U., 1931, M.A., 1947; m. Frances C. Dugan, Aug. 7, 1937; children—Jean Ann McNeil Martin, Patricia Lynn. Asso. sec. Community Welfare Council, Omaha, 1932-33; sec. Douglas County Emergency Relief Com., 1933-34, dir. relief div. Douglas County Relief Adminstrn., 1934-35, adminstr., 1935-36; dir. Omaha Community Chest, exec. v.p. Community Welfare Council, 1936-44; dir. personnel Community Chests and Councils Am., Inc., N.Y.C., 1944-47; prof., dir. sch. social adminstrn. Ohio State U., 1947-54; exec. dir. Health and Welfare Council, Inc., Phila., 1954-66; exec. dir. Nat. Assembly for Social Policy and Devel., Inc., N.Y.C., 1966-73; cons. Nat. Center Vol. Action, 1973-74, bd. dirs., 1974-79; asso. Century 21 Anderstokes, Rehoboth Beach, Del., 1976—; mem. 501(C)(3) Group, chmn., 1972-73. Recipient Centennial Achievement award Ohio State U., 1970, Centennial Distinguished Service award Coll. Adminstrv. Scis., 1970. Author: Community Orgn. for Social Welfare, monograph, 1951, 1954; Principles of Community Orgn., 1960; The Dynamics of Health and Welfare Planning Structures and and Processes, 1964; contbr. articles and papers to profl. publs. Home: 21 Sussex Dr Lewes DE 19958

MCNEIL, CLAUDIA MAE, actress; b. Balt., Aug. 13, 1917; d. Marvin and Annie Mae (Anderson) McN.; ed. pub. schs., N.Y.C. Debut as singer at Black Cat, N.Y.C., 1933; program coordinator, entertainer Jamaican Broadcasting Co., 1951-52; theatrical appearances: Raisin In the Sun, 1959, Tiger, Tiger Burning Bright, 1962; Member of the Wedding, 1964, The Amen Corner, 1965, Something Different, 1968, Her First Roman, 1968, The Wrong Way Light Bulb, 1969, Contributions, 1970; TV appearances include Simply Heavenly, 1952, Member of the Wedding, 1958, The Nurses, 1963, To Be Young, Gifted and Black, 1971, The American Woman, 1976; appeared in motion pictures The Last Angry Man, 1958, Black Girl, 1972, There Was a Crooked Man, 1970. Vol. worker Harlem Hosp., St. Vincent's Hosp. Nominee Tony award, 1962, Emmy award, 1963; recipient award Am. Jewish Congress, 1959. Mem. Negro Actors Guild. Address: care Negro Actors Guild 1674 Broadway New York NY 10019*

MCNEIL, EDGAR WILLIAM, lawyer; b. Boone, Iowa, Aug. 12, 1903; s. William H. and Alice R. (Pittman) McN.; student Staunton Mil. Acad., 1918-20, Muhlenberg Coll., Pa., 1922, U. Iowa, 1925; m. Margaret P. Gordon, July 3, 1926; children—Mary Margaret (Mrs. William Harry), Norma Jean (Mrs. James J. Williamson). Admitted Ia. bar, 1925, since practiced in Montezuma; dir. Peoples Savs. Bank, Montezuma, Gibson (Iowa) Savs. Bank. Pres. bd. edn., Montezuma; state chmn. United Def. Fund. Bd. dirs. Iowa State Bar Found., 1947—. Served as lt. col. USAAF, 1942-45. Mem. Am. Bar Assn., Iowa Bar Assn. (gov., 1948—; pres. 1952-53; chmn. com. on scope and correlation work 1954—; Award Merit 1959), Nat. Conf. Uniform Laws (commn.), Am. Coll. Probate Counsel, Am. Legion, V.F.W., Res. Officers Assn., League Iowa Rep. Vets. (state chmn. 1948-50). Presbyn. Mason (Shriner), Lion. Home: 206 N 10th St Montezuma IA 50171 Office: 105 N 4th St Montezuma IA 50171

MC NEIL, FREDERICK HAROLD, banker; b. Saskatoon, Sask., Can., Nov. 17, 1916; s. Harold and Jean (Swan) McN.; student U. Man., U. Sask.; m. Marian Doreen Williams, Jan. 16, 1943; children—Marie (Mrs. L.Y. Aiken), Ronald, Bruce. Journalist, 1945-54; with Braun & Co., Vancouver, B.C., 1954-56, Powell River Co., Vancouver, 1956-60, Ford Motor Co. Can., 1960-65; with Bank of Montreal, 1966—, exec. v.p., gen. mgr., chief operating officer, 1971-73, pres., chief operating officer, dir., 1973-75, dep. chmn., 1975, chmn., chief exec. officer, 1975—; dir. Can. Canners Ltd., MICC Investments Ltd., Mortgage Ins. Co. Can., Dominion Life Assurance Co., Bank of Montreal (Calif.), Seagram Co. Ltd., Internat. Resources and Fin. Bank, S.A., Luxembourg; trustee BM-RT Realty Investments. Life gov. Montreal Gen. Hosp.; mem. adv. bd. Salvation Army, U. Western Ont. Bus. Sch.; hon. vice chmn. Que. Provincial council, hon. mem. Nat. council Boy Scouts Can.; mem. Bus. Council on Nat. Issues, Conf. Bd.; bd. dirs. Can. Exec. Service Overseas, Can. Assn.-Latin Am., Can. Cancer Soc.; mem. bd. Can. Council Christians and Jews; hon. patron Montreal Jr. Symphony Soc.; hon. vice chmn. Que. council St. John Ambulance; mem. adv. com. Ecole des Hautes Etudes Commerciales; bd. govs. Olympic Trust Can.; life gov. Douglas Hosp. Served as squadron leader RCAF, World War II. Decorated Air Force Cross. Clubs: Forest and Stream, Badminton and Squash, Mount Royal, Mt. Bruno Country, St. Denis, Laval sur-le-Lac St. James's (Montreal); Toronto. Home: 36 Surrey Gardens Westmount PQ H3Y 1N6 Canada Office: 129 St James St W Montreal PQ H2Y 1L6 Canada

MC NEIL, GEORGE JOSEPH, painter; b. Bklyn., Feb. 22, 1908; s. James Henry and Julia Anna (Kenney) McN.; student Pratt Inst., 1927-29, Art Students League, 1930-31, 32-33, Hans Hofmann Sch. Fine Art, 1933-36; B.S., Columbia Tchrs. Coll., 1943, M.A., 1946, Ed.D., 1952; m. Dora Tamler, Feb. 8, 1936; children—Helen, James. One man exhbns. include Lyceum Gallery, Havana, Cuba, 1941, Egan Gallery, N.Y.C., 1950, 52, 53, 54, De Young Mus., San Francisco, 1956, Poindexter Gallery, N.Y.C., 1957, 59, Howard Wise Gallery, N.Y.C., 1960, 62, 64, 67, Univ. Art Mus., Austin, Tex., 1965, Great Jones Gallery, N.Y.C., 1966, Des Moines Art Center, 1969, Pratt Manhattan Center, 1973, Landmark Gallery, 1975, Berman Gallery, 1977, Terry Dintenfass Gallery, 1979; group exhbns. include Am. Abstract Artists exhbns., 1935-56, Art Inst. Chgo., 1948, Mus. Modern Art, 1951, Whitney Mus., 1953, 57, 61, 65, Carnegie Internat. exhbns., 1953, 55, 58; rep. permanent collections Bundy Art Gallery, Waitsfield, Vt., Mus. Modern Art, N.Y.C., Nat. Mus., Havana, Newark Mus., Walker Art Center, Mpls., U. Mich. Art Mus., U. Tex. Art Mus., Whitney Mus., 1953, 57, 61, 65; asst. prof. U. Wyo., 1946-48; asso. dean, prof. Pratt Inst., 1948-74, prof. emeritus, 1974—; guest prof. U. Calif. at Berkeley, 1956-57; artist-in-residence Tamarind Inst., 1971, 75, 76. Served with USNR, 1943. Recipient Ford Found. purchase, 1963, Nat. Council on Arts award, 1966. Guggenheim fellow, 1968. Home: 195 Waverly Ave Brooklyn NY 11205

MC NEIL, GOMER THOMAS, engr.; b. Kingston, Pa., Nov. 27, 1917; s. Roy Leslie and Elizabeth (Thomas) McN.; B.Civil Engring., Syracuse U., 1939; m. Myrtie Mae Erwin, Sept. 28, 1940; children—Myrtie Mae (Mrs. James B. Cummins), Dianne Leslie (Mrs. R. Wayne Loekle). Staff asst. Bell Aircraft Corp., 1943-44; civil engr. TVA, 1946-48; head photogrammetry dept. U.S. Naval Photog. Interpretation Center, 1948-52; pres. Photogrammetry, Inc., Rockville, Md., 1952-69, Photogrammetry div. Data Corp., Rockville, 1969-72, Mitchell Photogrammetry, Inc., Rockville, 1972, McNeil Engring., 1953—; Mass. Inst. Tech. cons. to Navy Deep Submergence, 1973, Naval Photog. Center for underwater optical imaging systems, 1974—. Served with USNR, 1944-46. Registered profl. engr., Md., D.C. Mem. Am. Soc. Photogrammetry (pres. 1965; Talbert Abrams award 1969, Fairchild Photogrammetric award 1971; hon. mem. award 1975), Nat. Soc. Profl. Engrs., Soc. Photo-Optical Instrumentation Engrs., Soc. Photog. Scientists and Engrs. Mason (32 deg.). Author: Photographic Measurements, 1953; Optical Fundamentals of Underwater Photography, 1968, also articles. Patentee in field. Home: 10252 Hatherleigh Dr Bethesda MD 20014. *An Ode to my Wife—Mankind is involved with the nature of the survival role within the life content but few are involved with the background, substance, and appreciation of the survival role with a performance that is uniquely sprinkled with the spicy seasoning of dignity that reflects to the nature of life the initiating role of art and culture.*

MC NEIL, HENRY SLACK, pharm. co. exec.; b. Phila., Apr. 22, 1917; s. Robert Lincoln and Grace F. (Slack) McN.; B.Sc., Yale, 1939; LL.D., Phila. Coll. Pharmacy and Sci.; m. Lois A. Fernley, Oct. 4, 1941; children—Henry Slack, Barbara Joan McNeil Jordan, Marjorie Fernley McNeil Findlay, Robert Douglas. Dir., McNeil Labs., Inc., Phila., 1940-79, pres., 1955-60; pres., dir. McNeil Labs. (Can.) Ltd., Toronto, 1956-61; v.p., dir. Johnson & Johnson, 1959-77; dir. Penquin Industries, Inc., S. Eleuthera Properties; chmn. Claneil Enterprises, Inc. Mem. Nat. Multiple Sclerosis Adv. Council; mem. spl. fine arts com., chmn. fin. com. Dept. State Diplomatic Reception Rooms; mem. Nat. council Boy Scouts Am.; pres., trustee Pa. Acad. Fine Arts; mem. Yale Devel. Bd.; bd. dirs. Nat. Trust for Hist. Preservation; trustee Henry Francis du Pont Winterthur Mus.; asso. trustee U. Pa.; mem. council Am. Mus. in Britain. Mem. St. Andrew's Soc. Phila., Hist. Soc. Phila., Am. Pharm. Assn. (life), Clan Macneil Assn. Am. (pres. 1962-72), Newcomen Soc. N.Am., Confrerie des Chevaliers du Tastevin, Omicron Delta Kappa (hon.). Clubs: Racquet, Yale, Philadelphia, Cricket, Sunnybrook, Union League, Aviation Country, Corinthian Yacht (Phila.); St. Elmo (New Haven); Metropolitan (N.Y.C.); Metropolitan, Capitol Hill (Washington); Royal Danish Yacht (Copenhagen). Home: Plymouth Meeting PA 19462 Office: Suite 511 One Plymouth Meeting Plymouth Meeting PA 19462

MC NEIL, NEIL VENABLE, educator; b. Houston, Oct. 24, 1927; s. Marshall and Blanche (Venable) McN.; student U. Tex., 1945; A.B. with distinction, George Washington U., 1948; postgrad. Columbia U., 1948-49; M.A., Northwestern U., 1965; m. Doris Rounder Matthews, Sept. 9, 1950; children—Jenny, Pitt Taylor Nieman. Reporter El Paso (Tex.) Herald-Post, 1949-52; reporter, desk man Washington Daily News, 1952-56; Washington corr. El Paso Herald-Post, Houston Press, Ft. Worth Press (Scripps Howard Newspapers), 1956-61; instr. Medill Sch. Journalism, Northwestern U., Evanston, Ill., 1961-62, asst. prof., 1962-68, asso. prof., 1968—; founder, dir. Medill News Service, 1966—. Nieman fellow, 1959-60. Mem. Nat. Assn. Profl. Bureaucrats (v.p., acad. chmn.), Am. Acad. Polit. and Social Sci., Nat. Aero. Assn., AAUP, Assn. Edn. in Journalism, Phi Beta Kappa. Clubs: Nat. Press, Harvard. Author articles, revs. Home: 3723 T St NW Washington DC 20007 Office: 806 15th St NW Washington DC 20005

MC NEIL, ROBERT LINCOLN, JR., pharm. mfg. co. exec.; b. Bethel, Conn., July 13, 1915; s. Robert Lincoln and Grace (Slack) McN.; B.S., Yale U., 1936; B.Sc., Phila. Coll. Pharmacy and Sci., 1938, D.Sc., 1970; postgrad. Temple U., 1938; m. Nancy McKinney Jones, Nov. 24, 1956; children—Collin Farquhar, Mary Victoria, Joanna Phelps, Robert Lincoln III. With McNeil Labs., Phila., 1936-66, chmn. bd., 1956-64, dir., 1941-66, corp. devel., 1966—; dir. Resco Products, Island Gem Enterprises, Peter A. Frasse & Co., Merrimac Clearance, Pa., Botfield Refractories, Crescent Brick Co., Chattanooga Pharmacal Co. Past mem. Pa. Drug, Device and Cosmetic Bd.; past pres., dir. Phila. Drug Exchange; lectr. Temple U. Grad. Sch. Pharmacy, 1953-59. Mem. pharm. adv. com. NPA, 1951-53. Mem. White House Preservation Commn., Mt. Vernon Adv. Commn.; trustee Phila. Mus. Art, Germantown Acad., Yale U. Art Gallery; gov., past chmn. exec. com. Nat. Vitamin Found.; commr. Nat. Portrait Gallery. Mem. Pharm. Mfrs. Assn., Am. Pharm. Assn. (past pres. Phila. br.), Am. Chem. Soc., AAAS, S.A.R. (past chpt. pres.), S.R. (bd. mgrs.), St. Andrew's Soc. Presbyn. (elder). Clubs: Philadelphia, Walpole Soc., St. Elmo, Academy, Yale, Union League, Cricket (Phila.); Circus Saints and Sinners of Am. (dir.). Office: 805 E Willow Grove Ave Wyndmoor PA 19118

MC NEILL, ANDREW JOHN, rubber, chem. and plastics mfg. co. exec.; b. Boston, Feb. 2, 1921; s. Andrew J. and Joanna C. (Murphy) McN.; B.S. in Chem. Engring., Northeastern U., Boston, 1947; m. Helen V. Jewell, Feb. 22, 1946; children—Keith A., J. Scott, Paul. With Uniroyal, Inc., 1947—, prodn. supt., Naugatuck, Conn., 1947-50, asst. purchasing agt., 1959-61, div. purchasing agt., 1961-63; materials supt., Painesville, Ohio, 1950-52, Baton Rouge, 1952-59; dir. purchases, N.Y.C., 1963-65, v.p. purchasing, 1965-66, v.p. materials and purchasing, 1966-72, pres. Uniroyal Chem., 1972-75; group v.p., Oxford, Conn., 1975-77, exec. v.p., 1977, ret., 1977; pres., chief exec. officer Mansfield Tire and Rubber Co., also dir.; pres., chmn. bd. Pa. Tire; dir. Rubicon, Monochem., Texus Chem. Co. Bd. dirs. Northeastern U. Served with USAF, 1942-44. Mem. Mfg. Chemists Assn. (dir.), Soc. Plastics Industry, Rubber Mfs. Assn., Am. Inst. Chem. Engrs. Clubs: Patterson, Princeton. Home: 11 Bayberry Ridge Westport CT 06880 Office: Oxford Mgmt and Research Center Middlebury CT 06749

MC NEILL, CHARLES JAMES, bus. exec.; b. Newton, Kans., Dec. 1, 1912; s. Hugh Andrew and Elizabeth (Sheehan) McN.; A.B., St. Benedict's Coll., 1933, L.H.D., 1956; postgrad. U. Denver, 1934-36; B.J., Register Coll. Journalism, Denver, 1935, M.J., 1937, D.Journalism, 1939; m. Mary Elizabeth O'Neill, Nov. 6, 1935; 1 dau., Mary Sharon McGlynn. Librarian, Sacred Heart Jr. Coll., 1933; exec. sec. Cath. Action Com. of Men, Wichita, Kans., 1933-34; staff Cath. Advance, Wichita, 1934; asso. editor Register System of Cath. Newspapers, 1934-43; staff Geo. A. Pflaum, Pub., Inc., Dayton, Ohio, 1946-49, asst. to pres., 1949-51, gen. mgr., 1951-57; asst. European dir. Radio Free Europe, Munich, Germany, 1957-61; treas. Internat. Television Devel. Corp., N.Y.C., 1961-63; treas. Inter Tel N.V., Amsterdam, 1961-63; v.p. Kane, McNeill, Inc., N.Y.C., 1963-72; v.p. Cath. Lists, Inc., Mt. Vernon, N.Y., 1965-72, pres., 1972—; dir. Intertel (Prodns.) S.A., Brussels, Belgium, 1961-63. Ofcl. del. Internat. Union Cath. Press ECOSOC, 1952-56; nat. council USO, 1956; bd. advisers Nat. Fund Raising Conf., 1968-69; trustee Our Sunday Visitor, Inc. Served with AUS, 1943-46. Mem. Classroom Periodical Pubs. Assn. (chmn. 1950-57), Cath. Press Assn. (pres. 1954-56), Cath. Assn. Internat. Peace (v.p. 1953-59), Nat. Cath. Edn. Assn., C. of C. Democrat. K.C. Club: Nat. Press (Washington). Author: The Sacramentals, 1938; Prayers, 1939; Catholic Church in Colorado, 1943; (with Gregory Smith) Divine Love Story, 1941. Home: 860 Grand Concourse Bronx NY 10451 Office: 3 N West St Mount Vernon NY 10550

MC NEILL, DAVID, psychologist, educator; b. Santa Rosa, Calif., Dec. 21, 1933; s. Glenn H. and Ethel G. (Little) McN.; A.B., U. Calif. at Berkeley, 1953, Ph.D., 1962; m. Nobuko Baba, Dec. 17, 1957; children—Cheryl Yumi, Randall Baba. Research fellow Harvard, 1962-65; asst. prof. psychology U. Mich., 1965-66, asso. prof., 1966-68; prof. behavioral scis. and linguistics U. Chgo., 1969—, chmn. com. cognition and communication, 1975—; vis. fellow Center Humanities, Wesleyan U. Middletown, Conn., 1970; mem. Inst. Advanced Study, Princeton, 1973-75. Hon. trustee Japan Assn. Coll. English Tchrs. Guggenheim fellow, 1973-74; NSF grantee, 1969-75; NIMH grantee, 1975—; Spencer Found. grantee, 1979—. Mem. AAAS, Linguistic Soc. Am., Medieval Acad. Am., Violoncello Soc., Phi Beta Kappa, Sigma Xi. Author: The Acquisition of Language, 1970; The Conceptual Basis of Language, 1979; editorial bd. Cognition, 1976—; adv. bd. Jour. Child Lang., 1973—. Home: 4820 S Greenwood Ave Chicago IL 60615

MCNEILL, ISHMAEL EUGENE, univ. dean; b. Ervin, Okla., July 18, 1920; s. Joseph A. and Mary (Christian) McN.; A.B., Howard Payne Coll., 1943; M.B.A., U. Tex., 1947, Ph.D., 1953; m. Edith Richards, Sept. 7, 1943; children—Amanda, Mary Lu, Laurie Nell. Asst. prof. accounting U. Tex., 1948-53; asso. prof. accounting U. Houston, 1953-55, prof., 1955-76, chmn. dept., 1955-60, 63-66; dean Coll. Bus. and Econs., Houston Baptist U., 1976—; developed materials, tchr. accounting on open-broadcast TV, 1955. Pres., dir. Mineral Resource Corp. Am., 1958-59; v.p., dir. Indsl. TV, Inc., 1958; v.p., treas. Houston Oil Producers Corp., 1962. Cons. to comptroller Houston Ind. Sch. Dist., 1960-62. Served as statis service officer, USAAF, 1944-45; col. Res. C.P.A., Tex. Mem. Am. Accounting Assn., Tex. Soc. C.P.A.'s, Tex. Assn. U. Instrs. Accounting (past pres.), Am. Inst. C.P.A.'s, Financial Execs. Inst., Phi Kappa Phi, Beta Gamma Sigma, Beta Alpha Psi, Sigma Iota Epsilon. Baptist (deacon). Author: Accounting Demonstration Problems and Notes, 2 vols., 1958; Projector Transparencies for Teaching Accounting, 2 sets, 1958; Basic Accounting Procedures, 1966; Financial Accounting: A Decision Information System, 1971; A Programmed Introduction to Financial Accounting, 1971; Demonstration Problems and Notes for Financial Accounting, 1971; co-author: Business Review for Secretaries, 1960. Home: 4359 Graduate Circle Houston TX 77004

MCNEILL, K(ENNETH) G(ORDON), med. physicist; b. Cheshire, Eng., Dec. 21, 1926; s. Ferguson and Elizabeth (Stevenson) McN.; B.A., Oxford (Eng.) U., 1947, M.A., 1950, D.Phil. (Harmsworth Sr. scholar), 1950; m. J. Ruth S. Robertson, Nov. 6, 1959; 1 dau., Diane E.S. Sir John Dill Meml. fellow Yale U., 1950-51; Nuffield research fellow Glasgow (Scotland) U., 1951-52, lectr., 1952-57; mem. faculty U. Toronto (Ont., Can.), 1957—, prof. physics, 1963—, prof. medicine, 1969—; spl. staff mem. Toronto Gen. Hosp., 1974—; mem. adv. com. radiation protection to Ministry Nat. Health and Welfare, 1964-68. Fellow Instn. Nuclear Engrs. (U.K.); mem. Canadian Assn. Physicists, Soc. Nuclear Medicine, Am. Phys. Soc. Author: (with J. Maclachlan, J. Bell) Matter and Energy, 1963, 2d edit., 1978; contbr. numerous articles to profl. jours. Research on low energy nuclear physics and med. physics. Home: 227 St Leonards Ave Toronto ON M4N 1K8 Canada

MC NEILL, ROBERT EUGENE, cons. elec. engr.; b. Detroit, Dec. 11, 1921; s. Chester A. and Mildred Elizabeth (Carr) McN.; B.Engring. in Elec. Engring., Johns Hopkins U., 1947; m. Vivian Florence Foote, June 27, 1942; children—Michael L., Jeffrey S. Design engr. Henry Adams, Inc., Balt., 1947-51; chief elec. engr. McNeill & Baldwin, Inc., Glen Burnie, Md., 1951-63, pres., 1963—; pres. Baldwin-McNeill Corp.; dir. Gibson Island Yacht Yard. Served with AUS, 1942-45. Registered profl. engr., Md., Pa., N.J., Del., W.Va., N.C., D.C. Fellow Cons. Engrs. Council; mem. Nat. Soc. Profl. Engrs., IEEE, Engring. Soc. Balt. Republican. Presbyn. Clubs: Annapolis (Md.) Yacht; Gibson Island; Sailing of the Chesapeake, Windjammers. Home: 226 McKinsey Rd Severna Park MD 21146 Office: 7300 Ritchie Hwy Glen Burnie MD 21061. *The engineering profession, with some vital political assistance, has allowed its image to become tarnished. I am distressed with myself, not because I contributed in any way to the tarnish but because I didn't do enough soon enough to help prevent it. Remedies are not easy or apparent but they must be established. I shall do my part.*

MCNEILL, ROBERT L., trade ofcl.; b. Cambridge, Mass., Oct. 29, 1924; s. Walter Leonard and Alice (Mitchell) McN.; A.B., Northeastern U., 1952; M.A., Fletcher Sch. Law and Diplomacy, 1953, Ph.D., 1956; m. Josephine Piwcio, Jan. 25, 1947; children—Robert Fletcher, Craig Foster; m. 2d, Martha Weirich, Feb. 27, 1970; children—David Robert, Timothy Clark. Sr. internat. economist Exec. Office Pres., Bur. Budget, 1959-61; exec. sec. President's Trade Policy Com., 1961-62; dep. asst. sec. commerce for trade policy, 1963-67; dir. internat. affairs Ford Motor Co., 1967-69; exec. vice chmn. Emergency Com. for Am. Trade, Washington, 1969—; instr. Tufts U., 1953-56; lectr. soc. sci. U. P.R., 1956-57. Served with USNR, 1943-46. Recipient Profl. Achievement award Bur. Budget, 1961; Gold medal award U.S. Dept. Commerce, 1967. Mem. Council on Fgn. Relations. Home: 2 Hitching Post Pl Rockville MD 20852

MC NEILL, WILLIAM HARDY, educator; b. Vancouver, B.C., Can., Oct. 31, 1917; s. John Thomas and Netta (Hardy) McN.; B.A., U. Chgo., 1938, M.A., 1939; Ph.D., Cornell U., 1947; four hon. degrees; m. Elizabeth Darbishire, Sept. 7, 1946; children—Ruth Netta, Deborah Joan, John Robert, Andrew Duncan. Faculty, U. Chgo., 1947—, prof. history, 1957—, chmn. dept., 1961-67, Robert A. Millikan Distinguished Service prof., 1969—. Served with AUS, 1941-46; lt. col. Res. ret. Fulbright Research scholar Royal Inst. Internat. Affairs, Eng., 1950-51; Rockefeller grantee, 1951-52; Ford Faculty fellow, 1954-55; Carnegie grantee, 1957-62, 63-64; Guggenheim fellow, 1971-72. Fellow Am. Philos. Soc., Am. Acad. Arts and Scis.; mem. Am. Hist. Assn. (council, del. Am. Council Learned Socs.). Author: Greek Dilemma, War and Aftermath, 1947; History Handbook of Western Civilization, rev. and enlarged, 1969; America, Britain and Russia, Their Cooperation and Conflict, 1941-46, 1954; Past and Future, 1954; Greece: American Aid in Action, 1947-56, 1957; Rise of the West, a History of the Human Community (Nat. Book award, Gordon J. Laing prize), 1963; Europe's Steppe Frontier, 1964; A World History, 1967; The Contemporary World, 1967; The Ecumene: Story of Humanity, 1973; Venice, the Hinge of Europe, 1081-1797, 1974; The Shape of European History, 1974; Plagues and Peoples, 1976; Metamorphosis of Greece since World War II, 1978. Editor: (with others) Readings in World History, Vols. I-X, 1968-73; Human Migration, 1978; Jour. Modern History, 1971—; contbr. articles to publs. Office: Dept History U Chgo 1126 E 59th St Chicago IL 60637

MC NEILLY, JOHN J., state justice; b. Feb. 16, 1918; A.B., Duke U.; J.D., U. Pa. Admitted to Del. bar, 1949; dep. atty. gen. Del., 1951-55; resident judge Del. Superior Ct. for Sussex County, 1963-74; asso. justice Del. Supreme Ct., 1974—. Mem. Am. Bar Assn. Office: Courthouse Georgetown DE 19947*

MCNEILY, PETER WILLIAM G., finance co. exec.; b. St. Johns, Nfld., Can., Jan. 17, 1919; s. James Alexander William Whiteford and Margaret Elizabeth (Potts) McN.; naturalized Am. citizen, 1950; student Leys Sch., Cambridge, Eng.; m. Margaret A. Goodbody, Oct. 5, 1946; children—Susan Margaret, Alexander Peter, Kathleen Collett. With Canadian Bank of Commerce, N.Y.C., 1935-49; asst. to treas. Singer Co., N.Y.C., 1949-64, Mack Truck Co., Montvale, N.J., 1964-68; sr. asst. treas. Am. Express Co., 1970-71; pres., dir. Am. Express Credit Corp., Wilmington, Del., 1971—. Served to capt., arty. Brit. Army. Episcopalian. Clubs: Knickerbocker Country (Tenafly, N.J.); Kennett Square (Pa.) Golf and Country. Home: 22 Turkey Hollow Rd RD 2 Kennett Square PA 19348 Office: 2200 Concord Pike Wilmington DE 19803

MCNENNY, HAROLD FRANCIS, lawyer; b. Sturgis, S.D., Nov. 9, 1904; s. James and Kate C. (Halbert) McN.; student Vanderbilt U., 1922; J.D., Nat. U., 1928, M.Patent Law, 1928; m. Anna Mary Hunter, Aug. 2, 1928 (dec. Jan. 1947); children—Patrick J. Shelby, Barbara K. (Mrs. John Tierny Noonan), Margaret A. (Mrs. James Allison English), James Hunter; m. 2d, Hazel Susan Williams, Oct. 29, 1947. Admitted to D.C. bar, 1928, Ohio bar, 1957, also fed. bars; examiner U.S. Patent Office, Washington, 1924-29; patent atty. Willys-Overland Co., Toledo, 1929; asso. Richey & Watts, Cleve., 1929-33, mem. firm, 1933-51; mem. firm. McNenny, Pearne, Gordon, Gail, Dickinson & Schiller, and predecessor firms, Cleve., 1951-79; counsel firm Pearne, Gordon, Sessions, McCoy and Granger, 1979—. Mem. World Peace Through Law Center, Geneva, Switzerland, 1966—. Mem. Am. Bar Assn., Am. Patent Law Assn. Republican. Mason (Shriner). Home: 1911 Camino de La Costa Redondo Beach CA 90277 Office: 1200 Leader Bldg Cleveland OH 44114

MC NERNEY, WALTER JAMES, assn. exec.; b. New Haven, June 8, 1925; s. Robert Francis and Anna Gertrude (Shanley) McN.; B.S., Yale U., 1947; M.H.A., U. Minn., 1950; m. Shirley Ann Hamilton, June 26, 1948; children—Walter James, Peter Hamilton, Jennifer Allison, Daniel Martin, Richard Hamilton. Research asst. Labor-Mgmt. Center, Yale U., 1947; instr. advanced math. Hopkins Prep. Sch., New Haven, 1947-48; adminstrv. resident R.I. Hosp., Providence, 1949-50; asst. to coordinator Hosp. and Clinics of Med. Center, U. Pitts., 1950-53, also instr., then asst. prof. hosp. adminstrn. at univ., then asst. prof. hosp. and med. adminstrn., 1953-55; asso. prof., dir. program hosp. adminstrn. Sch. Bus. Adminstrn., U. Mich., 1955-58, prof., dir. Bur. Hosp. Adminstrn., 1958-61; pres. Blue Cross Assn., Chgo., 1961-77; pres., chief exec. officer Blue Cross and Blue Shield Assns., Chgo., 1977—; mem. Nat. Council on Health Planning and Devel., HEW, 1976—; pres. Health Services Found., 1963—; mem. bd. dirs. Nat. Health Council, 1963-77, pres., 1972-73; bd. dirs. Nat. Center for Health Edn.; bd. govs. Health Service, Inc., Chgo.; mem. nat. health policy study group Nat. Chamber Found.; mem. nat. commn. on cost of med. care AMA, 1977, mem. com. on pvt. philanthropy, 1977-78; mem. council mgmt. Internat. Fedn. Vol. Health Service Funds; nat. chmn. maj. and spl. gifts com. Campaign for Yale U.; trustee Nat. Exec. Service Corps; chmn. task force on Medicaid and related programs HEW, 1969-70; charter mem. council Inst. Medicine-Nat. Acad. Scis., mem. fin. com., mem. gov.'s council; vice chmn. Pres.'s Com. on Health Edn., 1972-73. Served to lt. (j.g.) USNR, 1943-46. Named 1 of 100 most important young men and women in U.S. by Life Mag., 1962; recipient Justin Ford Kimball award, 1967; Outstanding Achievement award U. Minn., 1970; Nuffield Provincial Hosps. Trust-Kings Fund (Eng.) fellow, 1970. Fellow Am. Pub. Health Assn., Am. Coll. Hosp. Adminstrs.; mem. Am. Coll. Health Assn., Am. Mgmt. Assn. (dir., trustee), Assn. Tchrs. Preventive Medicine, Internat. Hosp. Fedn., U.S. C. of C., Royal Soc. Health, Group Health Assn. Am. (dir.), Mgmt. Execs. Soc., Assn. Yale Alumni, Sigma Xi, Delta Sigma Pi. Clubs: Chgo. Commonwealth, Chgo., Mid-Am. (Chgo.); Yale (N.Y.C.); Cosmos (Washington). Author: Hospital and Medical Economics, 1962; Regionalization and Rural Health Care, 1962; contbr. articles to profl. jours. Home: 675 Blackthorn Rd Winnetka IL 60093 Office: 840 N Lake Shore Drive Chicago IL 60611

MC NEW, BENNIE BANKS, univ. dean; b. Greenbrier, Ark., Nov. 12, 1931; s. Roland H. and Stella (Avery) McN.; B.S., Ark. State Tchrs. Coll., 1953; M.B.A., U. Ark., 1954; Ph.D., U. Tex., 1961; m. Bonnie Lou Stone, Mar. 31, 1956; children—Bonnie Banks, Mary Kathleen, William Michael. Asst. nat. bank examiner, 1954-56; indsl. specialist U. Ark. Indsl. Research and Extension Center, 1956-59; lectr. finance U. Tex., 1959-61; prof. banking U. Miss., University, 1961-65, dean Sch. Bus. Adminstrn., 1965—; asst. dir. Sch. Banking of South, La. State U., 1966—. Served with AUS, 1950-51. Mem. Am., So., Southwestern finance assns., So. Econ. Assn., Fin. Execs. Inst., Beta Gamma Sigma, Delta Pi Epsilon, Delta Sigma Pi, Omicron Delta Kappa, Phi Kappa Phi. Lion (pres. Oxford, Miss. 1964-65). Author: (with Charles L. Prather) Fraud Control for Commercial Banks, 1962; contbg. author Money and Banking Casebook, 1966; The Bankers Handbook, 1966; A History of Mississippi, 1973. Home: 128 Lakeway Gardens Oxford MS 38655

MCNICHOL, KRISTY, actress; b. Los Angeles, Sept. 9; d. Carollyne McN. Appeared on TV commls.; regular on TV series: Apple's Way, 1974, Family, 1976—; other TV appearances include: Love, American Style; The Bionic Woman, Starsky and Hutch, Fawn Story, Me and Dad's New Wife, The Pinballs, Challenge of the Network Stars; film appearances include: Black Sunday, The End. Winner Emmy awards for best supporting actress, 1976-77, 78-79; recipient Gold medal Photoplay, 1976. Office: care ABC Public Relations 1330 Ave of Americas New York NY 10019*

MC NICHOLAS, JOHN PATRICK, III, trial lawyer; b. Los Angeles, Aug. 18, 1936; s. John Patrick and Rosemary Helen (Hurley) McN.; B.A., U. Calif. at Los Angeles, 1958; postgrad. Loyola U. Law Sch., Los Angeles, 1958-62; m. Diane Sawaya, Aug. 25, 1956; children—Erin, Brigid, Patrick, Courtney, Monica, David, Matthew. Admitted to Calif. bar, 1962, since practiced in Los Angeles; asso. firm Hagenbaugh, Murphy & Meifert, Assos., Los Angeles, 1963-64, Morgan, Holzhauer, Burrows & Wenzel, Los Angeles, 1964-69; asso. firm Morgan, Wenzel & McNicholas, 1969—, sr. partner, 1969—; arbitrator Los Angeles Superior Ct. Spl. Arbitration Program, 1973—; hearing officer disciplinary proceedings State Bar Calif., 1974—; arbitrator Am. Arbitration Assn., 1969—. Diplomate Am. Bd. Trial Advs. Mem. Bus. Trial Lawyers Assn., So. Calif. Def. Counsel, Am. Judicature Soc., Am., Fed., Los Angeles County bar assns., Right to Life League, Speakers Forum, Phi Kappa Sigma, Phi Delta Phi. Republican. Roman Catholic. Clubs: Jonathan (Los Angeles); Crockford's (London). Home: 516 S Hudson Ave Los Angeles CA 90020 Office: 1545 Wilshire Blvd Los Angeles CA 90017

MC NICHOLAS, JOSEPH ALPHONSUS, bishop; b. St. Louis, Jan. 13, 1923; s. Joseph Alphonsus and Mary Blanche (Tallon) McN.; B.A., Cardinal Glennon Coll., St. Louis, 1945; student Kenrick Theol. Sem., St. Louis, 1949; M.A. in Social Work, St. Louis U., 1957. Ordained priest Roman Cath. Ch., 1949, consecrated bishop, 1969; parish priest, St. Louis, 1949-69; sec. Cath. Charities, St. Louis, 1957-75; cath. chaplain St. Louis Juvenile Ct., 1957-70; aux. bishop

Archdiocese St. Louis, 1969-75; bishop of Springfield, Ill., 1975—. Vice chmn. Human Devel. Corp. Met. St. Louis, 1967-75. Named Mo. Citizen of Year, Mo. Assn. Social Welfare, 1968. Mem. Acad. Certified Social Workers, Nat. Assn. Social Workers, Child Welfare League Am. (v.p.). Address: 524 E Lawrence Ave Springfield IL 62704

MC NICHOLS, RAY, U.S. judge; b. Bonners Ferry, Idaho, June 16, 1914; s. Michael T. and Kathleen (Clyne) McN.; LL.B., U. Idaho, 1950; m. Mary Katherine Riley, Aug. 1, 1938; children—Michael E., Kathleen (Mrs. John Dreps). Admitted to Idaho bar, 1950, U.S. Supreme Ct. bar; practice, Orofino, Idaho, 1950-64; U.S. dist. judge Dist. Idaho, Boise, 1964—. Served as officer AC, USNR, World War II. Mem. Phi Delta Theta, Phi Alpha Delta. Roman Catholic. Home: 3110 Crescent Rim Dr Boise ID 83706 Office: US Ct Bldg 550 W Fort St Boise ID 83724

MC NICHOLS, WILLIAM HENRY, JR., mayor Denver; b. Denver, Apr. 11, 1910; s. William H. and Catherine F. (Warner) McN.; student U. Colo., 1932-33, U. Ala., 1930-31; m. Laverne Peterson, Oct. 24, 1947; 1 son, Stephen Charles. Engaged in ins. and automobile bus., 1954-56; exec. sec. to Gov. Colo., 1956-62; mgr. pub. works City and County of Denver, 1963-69, dep. mayor, 1963-69, mayor, 1969—. Served with 4th Armored Inf., AUS, 1944-46. Decorated Purple Heart, others. Mem. Nat. League Cities (mem. com. on transp.), U.S. Conf. Mayors (pres., trustee, mem. urban econ. affairs com.), Nat. Conf. Dem. Mayors (regional chmn.), Am. Pub. Works Assn., CAP, Am. Legion. Home: 754 Krameria St Denver CO 80220 Office: 350 City and County Bldg Denver CO 80202

MC NICOL, DONALD EDWARD, lawyer; b. Kew Gardens, N.Y., Aug. 11, 1921; s. William J. and Margaret (McGirr) McN.; A.B., Harvard U., 1943, LL.B., 1948; m. Doris C. Egues, Apr. 3, 1943; children—Elaine McNicol Postley, Janet McNicol Barton, Donald Edward, Paul Mansfield. Admitted to N.Y. bar, 1949, since practiced in N.Y.C.; asso. atty. Davis, Polk, Wardwell, Sunderland & Kiendl, 1948-54; asso. firm Hall, McNicol, Hamilton, Murray & Clark, and predecessor, 1954-56, partner, 1956—; dir. Am. Maize-Products Co., Thomson McKinnon Securities, Inc., Gt. Island Holding Corp., Thomas Pub. Co., Heritage Quilts, Inc., Jon. H. Swisher & Son, Inc., S.A. Schonbrunn & Co., Inc., Boyer Bros., Inc. Mem. bd. Union Free Sch. Dist. 5, Cold Spring Harbor, N.Y., 1953-55; mem. nat. bd. Boys' Clubs Am., Inc.; trustee Leo N. Levi Meml. Hosp. Served with AUS, 1942-46. Mem. N.Y. State Bar Assn., Assn. Bar City N.Y. Club: Harvard (bd. mgrs. 1967-69) (N.Y.C.). Home: 82 Linden Ln Upper Brookville NY 11545 also 530 Park Ave New York NY 10021 Office: 330 Madison Ave New York NY 10017

MCNIFF, PHILLIP JAMES, librarian; b. Cambridge, Mass., Feb. 10, 1912; s. Patrick J. and Catherine (Gralton) McN.; A.B., Boston Coll., 1933; postgrad. Columbia U., 1940; D.H.L. (hon.), Boston Coll., 1969; m. Mary M. Stack, Nov. 28, 1935; 1 son, Brian S. Asst., Newton Free Library, 1933-35, head catalog dept., 1940-42; librarian West Newton Library, 1935-40; reference asst. Harvard Coll. Library, 1942-43, supt. reading room, 1943-48, librarian Lamont Library, 1948-56, asst. librarian Harvard Coll. Library, 1949-56, asso. librarian, 1956-65, mem. faculty arts and scis., 1954-65, Archibald Cary Coolidge bibliographer, 1962-65; dir., librarian Boston Pub. Library, 1965—. Bd. dirs. Newton Jr. Coll., Inst. Medieval Canon Law, Newton Coll. of Sacred Heart, Boston Coll. Library. Mem. Assn. Coll. and Research Libraries (pres. 1969-70), Am., Cath., New Eng., Mass. library assns., Mass. Hist. Soc. Democrat. Roman Catholic. Clubs: St. Botolph, Odd Volumes (Boston). Author: Catalogue of the Lamont Library, 1963; Freedom and Responsibly; Independence Day Oration, City Boston, 1966. Office: Boston Pub Library Copley Sq Boston MA 02117*

MCNISH, CHARLES OTIS, publishing co. exec.; b. South Sioux City, Nebr., Sept. 8, 1918; s. Tom Lamar and Lena May (Winn) McN.; student U. Tenn., 1946-47; m. Sarah Harwood, Oct. 2, 1942; children—Charles Kent, Granville Neal. With Meth. Pub. House, 1941, 46; sales rep. Abingdon Press, Nashville, 1957-63, mgr. ch. supplies, 1963-66, asst. mgr., 1966-71, mgr., 1971—. Served with AUS, 1941-46, 51-52. Decorated Bronze Star, Purple Heart, Combat Inf. badge with star. United Methodist (adminstrv. bd. 1958—). Home: 2108 Dearborn Dr Nashville TN 37214 Office: 201 8th Ave S Nashville TN 37202

MC NITT, WILLARD CHARLES, corp. exec.; b. Chgo., June 6, 1920; s. Willard C. and Louise (Richardson) McN.; B.A., Amherst Coll., 1942; A.M. with honors, Harvard Grad. Sch. Bus. Adminstrn., 1942; student Northwestern Grad. Sch. Bus. Adminstrn., U. Chgo. Sch. Bus. Adminstrn., 1947; m. Charlotte D. Boyd, Sept. 14, 1946; children—Willard Charles, James D., Jeffrey B. Asst. market planning and research Foote, Cone & Belding Co., Chgo., 1946-47; asst. sales promotion and advt. Bell & Gosset Co., Morton Grove, Ill., 1947-48; v.p. sales and mktg. Bowes Industries, Inc., Chgo., 1948-54; gen. mgr. sales and mktg. Clayton Mark & Co., Evanston, Ill., 1954-58; pres., dir. Bowey's, Inc., Chgo., 1958-62, H.M. Byllesby Co., Chgo., 1962-63; group v.p., dir., mem. exec. com. Consol. Foods Corp., Chgo., 1963-67; exec. v.p. consumer products group W.R. Grace & Co., N.Y.C., 1967-72; exec. v.p., dir., mem. exec. com. Ward Foods, Inc., Wilmette, Ill., 1972-73, chief operating officer, pres., dir., mem. exec. com., 1973-76; pres., chief exec. officer, dir. Westgate-Calif. Corp., and Sun Harbor Industries, San Diego, 1977—; dir. Air Calif. Troop head local Boy Scouts Am., 1957-67. Served to lt. (s.g.) USNR, 1942-46. Mem. Chi Psi. Republican. Congregationalist. Clubs: Execs., Amherst (Chgo.); Harvard Bus. Sch. (Chgo. and N.Y.C.); Indian Hill Country (Winnetka); Dairymen's (Boulder Junction, Wis.); Ponte Vedra (Fla.); Rancho Santa Fe (Calif.) Country; Cuyamaca (San Diego). Office: 1010 2d Ave Suite 1200 San Diego CA 92101

MC NOWN, JOHN STEPHENSON, engring. educator; b. Kansas City, Kans., Jan. 15, 1916; s. William Coleman and Florence Marie (Klahr) McN.; B.S., U. Kans., 1936; M.S., U. Iowa, 1937; Ph.D., U. Minn., 1942; D. ès Sc., U. Grenoble (France), 1951; m. Miriam Leigh Ellis, Sept. 6, 1938 (div. Nov. 1971); children—Stephen Ellis, Robert Neville, Cynthia Leigh, Mark William. Instr. math. and mechanics U. Minn., 1937-42; research asso. div. war research U. Calif., San Diego, 1942-43; asst. prof. mechanics and hydraulics, Coll. Engring., U. Iowa, 1943-47, asso. prof., 1947-52, prof., 1952-54, research engr. Iowa Inst. Hydraulic Research, 1943-51, asso. dir., 1951-54; Fulbright research scholar, Grenoble, France, 1950-51; prof. engring. mechanics U. Mich., 1954-57; prof. engring. mechanics U. Kans., 1957-65, Albert P. Learned prof. civil engring., 1965—, dean Sch. Engring. and Architecture, 1957-65, exec. dir. Center for Research in Engring. Sci., 1959-62, dir. engring. sci. div., 1962-65; on leave as dir. overseas liaison com. Am. Council Edn., 1967-69; tech. edn. specialist IBRD, 1972-73; hydraulic research cons. Bur. Pub. Roads, 1949-68; expert cons. engr. dept. U.S. Army, St. Paul dist., 1952-54, Waterways Expt. Sta., 1959-65; cons. Sandia Corp., Albuquerque, 1954-62; trustee U. Kans. Center for Research, Inc., 1962—; cons. engring. edn. in Africa, Ford Found., 1963-67, 70; trustee Rocky Mountain Hydraulic Lab., 1963-73; spl. tech. lectr. Colo. A. and M. Coll., 1949, U. Mich., 1950, Univs. Lille, Grenoble, Toulouse, and Poitiers, France, 1951, U. Bogotá (Colombia), 1952, Ecole Polytechnique, Montreal, 1953, U. Nebr., 1958, Purdue U., 1959, N.Mex. State U., 1966, Calif. Inst. Tech., 1967, U. Karlsruhe, 1976, U. Aachen, U. Luleå, 1978; on leave at Chalmers U., Goteborg, Sweden, 1977-78, Royal Inst. Tech., Stockholm, 1978; mem. adv. panel, engring. scis. div. NSF, 1957-60, cons., 1960-62; mem. engring. accreditation com. Engrs. Council for Profl. Devel., 1960-65; cons. higher edn. Bell Telephone Labs., 1964; planning com. World Congress Engring. Edn., 1964-65, 73-75; mem. Commn. on Engring. Edn., 1961-65; coordinator Kumasi Conf. Engring. Edn., 1967; cons. Internat. Bank Reconstrn. and Devel., 1965, 70, 74; mem. internat. study commn. engring. edn. Nigeria, 1963, 77, Zambia, 1967, Cameroon, 1968, Zaire, 1968, Ethiopia, 1969, Singapore, 1973, Haiti, 1978; cons. to UNESCO at U. Lagos (Nigeria), 1968-69, staffing engring. faculties in developing countries, 1972-75, mem. planning com. Dar es Salaam Congress, 1974, New Delhi Congress, 1976; cons. State Power Bd., Sweden, 1977-78; mem. univ. grants com. U. East Africa, 1967, U. Zambia, 1969-73; cons. Am. Council on Edn., 1970, 75; vis. mem. bd. govs. U. Guyana, 1967-72. Registered profl. engr., Kans. Recipient J.C. Stevens award, 1946, research program prize, 1949, J. Jas. R. Croes medal ASCE, 1955. Fellow ASCE (chmn. exec. com. Engring. Mechanics div. 1957-58, chmn. adv. com. 1960), Am. Acad. Mechanics; mem. Nat. Conf. Engring. Edn. (coordinator 1961), Internat. Assn. Hydraulic Research (council 1955-59), Am. Soc. Engring. Edn. (exec. com., vice chmn. internat. div. 1975-77), Com. Engring. Edn. Middle Africa, AAAS, Permanent Internat. Assn. for Nav. Congresses, AAUP, Am. Canal Soc., Sigma Xi, Theta Tau, Phi Delta Theta, Tau Beta Pi, Phi Kappa Phi, Chi Epsilon. Conglist. Author: Technical Education in Africa; also tech. papers on fluid mechanics, inland waterways, history of hydraulics, and engring. edn. Address: Dept Civil Engring U Kans Lawrence KS 66045

MC NULTY, ALBERT JOSEPH, former utility exec.; b. Salem, Mass., Nov. 13, 1913; s. Patrick J. and Margaret (Cassidy) McN.; B.S. in Bus. Adminstrn. cum laude, Boston U., 1937; m. Frances E. Finnegan, Aug. 10, 1940; children—Albert F., Jane E. With Boston Edison Co., 1937—, controller, 1952-78, asst. to v.p., 1975-78. Asst. treas. New Eng. Power Pool, 1970—; mem., dir. Mass. Bus. Task Force for Sch. Mgmt. Mem. merit com. Marblehead (Mass.) council Boy Scouts Am., 1949-50; bus. adviser Boston Jr. Achievement, 1953-58. Mem. Am. Mgmt. Assn., Edison Electric Inst., Electric Council New Eng. (treas. 1956-78), Boston U. Alumni Assn., Beta Gamma Sigma. Roman Catholic. Club: Tedesco Country (Marblehead). Home: 14 Mohawk Rd Marblehead MA 01945

MC NULTY, CARRELL STEWART, JR., mfg. co. exec., architect; b. Newark, Dec. 4, 1924; s. Carrell Stewart and Marjorie (Yaegerlehner) McN.; student Emory U., 1941-43, U. N.C., 1943-44; B.Arch., Columbia U., 1950, M.S. in Urban Planning, 1964; m. Barbara Brokaw, June 21, 1952; children—Peter Carrell, Susan Abigail. Asso., SMS Architects, Stamford, Conn., 1950-58, gen. partner, 1958-73; pvt. practice architecture, Weston, Conn., 1973-76; pres. CMW Co., Weston, 1975-77, NB Instruments, Inc., mfrs. flow measurement instrumentation, Horsham, Pa., 1977—, NB Products, Inc., mfrs. pipe stoppers and air test equipment; Weston rep. Southwestern Regional Planning Agy., 1962-76, chmn., 1967-68, 75; mem. Conn. Gov.'s Commn. on Environment, 1970, Conn. Gov.'s Task Force on Housing, 1971-72; chmn. Southwestern Regional Housing Task Force, 1972. Mem. Norwalk (Conn.) Housing Fund, 1971-75; vice chmn. Democratic Town Com., Weston, 1975-76; v.p. Bucks County (Pa.) Choral Soc., 1977—; chmn. bd. deacons United Ch. Christ, Weston, 1965-69. Served to lt., j.g., USNR, 1944-46. Recipient Honor ward 6th Biennial HUD Design Program, 1974. Fellow AIA (chmn. urban planning and design com. 1971); mem. Conn. Soc. Architects (pres. 1969), Urban Land Inst., Water Pollution Control Fedn., Sigma Nu. Home: 49 Oak Dr Doylestown PA 18901 Office: 935 Horsham Rd Horsham PA 19044

MCNULTY, CHESTER HOWARD, bank holding co. exec.; b. Melbourne, Fla., Dec. 12, 1935; s. Chester H. and Jennie (Larson) McN.; B.S. in Bus. Adminstrn., U. Fla., 1957, J.D., 1964; m. Sylvia Maxwell, July 20, 1957; children—Thad, Laurie, Paul, Shannon. Vice pres. Fla. State Bank of Sanford, 1957-60, pres., 1966-74; pres. 1st State Bank of Ft. Meade (Fla.), 1960-62; admitted to Fla. bar, 1965; asso. firm Bentley, Miller, Sinder, Carr, Chiles & Ellsworth, Lakeland, Fla., 1965; pres. Flagship Banks, Inc., Miami Beach, Fla., 1974-76, vice chmn., 1976-77, exec. v.p., 1977—. Home: PO Box 698 Lake Mary FL 32746 Office: PO Box 6727 Orlando FL 32803

MC NULTY, FREDERICK CHARLES, architect; b. Soochow, Kiangsu, China, Oct. 6, 1919; s. Henry Augustus and Edith (Piper) McN.; B.A. (Edwin Gould Found. scholar), Princeton, 1942, M.F.A., 1949; grad. Kent Sch., 1938; m. Sara Gene Farny, June 18, 1947; 1 dau., Margaret Piper. Draftsman, Robert Stanton, Carmel, Calif., 1949-52; designer Butner, Holm & Waterman, Salinas, Calif., 1952-57; asso. Wallace Holm & Assos., Monterey, Calif., 1957-64, sr. asso., 1964-72; v.p. Wallace Holm, Archictects, Inc., Monterey, 1973—; designer adminstrn. bldg., library, creative arts center, engring.-physics bldg. Monterey Peninsula Coll., 1956-64; instr. adult edn. program Monterey Peninsula Coll., 1958-59; owner Piper Paper and Plastics, Carmel, 1967—. Mem. Mayor's Adv. Com. for Master Plan of Carmel-by-the Sea, 1955-56. Past bd. dirs. New Monterey Property Owners' Assn., Monterey County Citizens' Planning Assn. Served with AUS, 1942-45; ETO. Decorated Legion of Merit; recipient Alexander Guthrie McCosh prize, 1942. Mem. A.I.A. (past chpt. bd. dirs.), White Pine Soc., Sigma Alpha. Republican. Episcopalian. Editor: Monterra, a Planned Residential Community General Development Plan Phase Environmental Reconnaissance. Home: PO Box 2504 Carmel CA 93921 Office: Hacienda Saucito 2999 Monterey-Salinas Hwy Monterey CA 93940

MCNULTY, JAMES JOSEPH, aviation co. exec.; b. N.Y.C., July 15, 1912; s. Joseph John and Catherine (Clancy) McN.; student Manhattan Coll., 1930-32, Columbia Sch. Bus. Adminstrn., 1962; m. Florence E. Wirth, Sept. 4, 1938; 1 son, Paul James. Auditor, Acme Fast Freight, Inc., N.Y.C., 1936-43; treas. Emery Air Freight Corp., N.Y.C., 1946-52, v.p. operations, 1952-62, pres., 1962-68, chmn., 1968—; dir. Bangor Punta Corp. Bd. dirs. Transp. Center, Northwestern U. Served to capt. AUS, 1943-46. Mem. Air Freight Forwarders Assn. (pres. 1962-64), U.S. C. of C. (v.p. transp. and communications com.), Transp. Assn. Am. (dir.). Clubs: Lost Tree (North Palm Beach, Fla.); Brooklawn Country; Traffic (N.Y.C.). Home: Harbour House Southport CT 06490 Office: Old Danbury Rd Wilton CT 06897

MC NULTY, JOHN BARD, educator; b. Mokanshan, China, July 13, 1916 (parents Am. citizens); s. Henry Augustus and Edith (Piper) McN.; B.S., Trinity Coll., Hartford, 1938; M.A., Columbia U., 1939; Ph.D., Yale U., 1944; m. Marjorie Mead Grant, May 23, 1942; children—Henry Bryant, Sarah Bard. Faculty, Trinity Coll., 1939—, prof. English, 1960—, chmn. dept., 1966-72, James J. Goodwin prof., 1967—. Trustee Antiquarians and Landmarks Soc. Conn. Mem. MLA, AAUP. Author: Older Than the Nation-a History of the Hartford Courant, 1964; Modes of Literature, 1977. Contbr. articles to profl. jours. Home: 8 Little Acres Rd Glastonbury CT 06033

MC NULTY, JOHN C., lawyer; b. Mpls., Dec. 24, 1924; s. John C. and Mildred (Marran) McN.; B.A., U. Minn., 1954, J.D., 1957; m. Loranda Dinham, Feb. 28, 1950; children—John Craig, Charlotte McNulty McCabe, Loranda Elizabeth. Mgr., Westwoods Hills Country Club, 1947-57; admitted to Minn. bar, 1957, since practiced in Mpls.; partner McNulty & Cox, 1957-60; partner Malson, Kaplan, Edelman, Borman, Brand & McNulty and predecessor law firms, 1960—; municipal judge City St. Louis Park, Minn., 1960-64; mem. jud. planning commn. Minn. Supreme Ct., 1976—; mem. adv. com.-model peer rev. Am. Law Inst.-Am. Bar Assn., 1978—. Bd. dirs. UN Assn. Minn., 1966-72. Recipient award of merit Minn. Bar Assn. Jr. Bar sect., 1963, Outstanding Community Service award County of Hennepin, 1966; Phi Delta Phi Man of Year, 1957. Fellow Am. Bar Found.; mem. Am. Judicature Soc. (chmn. bd. dirs. 1977-79), Am. (mem. com. on membership 1970-73, com. profl. disciple 1973—, chmn. com. 1976-79; task force advt. 1977, past mem. ho. of dels.), Minn. (gov. 1962-76, chmn. jud. adminstrn. com. 1974-77), Hennepin County (pres. 1967) bar assns., Phi Delta Phi. Home: 5304 E Bald Eagle Blvd White Bear Lake MN 55110 Office: Midwest Plaza Bldg Minneapolis MN 55402

MCNULTY, JOHN KENT, lawyer, educator; b. Buffalo, Oct. 13, 1934; A.B. with high honors, Swarthmore Coll., 1956; LL.B., Yale U., 1959. Admitted to Ohio bar, 1961, U.S. Supreme Ct. bar, 1964; law clk. Justice Hugo L. Black, U.S. Supreme Ct., Washington, 1959-60; vis. prof. Sch. Law, U. Tex., summer 1960; asso. firm Jones, Day, Cockley & Reavis, Cleve., 1960-64; prof. law Sch. Law, U. Calif., Berkeley, 1964—; of counsel firm Baker & McKenzie, San Francisco, 1974-75. Guggenheim fellow, 1977. Mem. Am. Bar Assn., Am. Law Inst., Internat. Fiscal Assn. (council U.S. br.), Order of Coif, Phi Beta Kappa. Author: (with Kragen) Federal Income Taxation of Individuals, 3d edit., 1979; Federal Income Taxation of Individuals, 2d edit., 1978; Federal Estate and Gift Taxation, 2d edit., 1979. Home: 620 Spruce St Berkeley CA 94707 Office: 389 Boalt Hall Sch of Law U Calif Berkeley CA 94720. *Apart from the personal sphere, where spouse and children take greatest importance, teaching and learning have given the greatest satisfactions in my life. The life of the mind leads one rewardingly into the lives and minds of others, a most satisfying path to travel.*

MC NULTY, KNEELAND, museum curator; b. Soochow, China, Oct. 25, 1921 (parents Am. citizens); s. Henry Augustus and Edith Clara (Piper) McN.; A.B., Princeton, 1943; postgrad. Harvard, 1946-47; M.L.S., Columbia, 1952; m. Anne Louise Rissmann, June 3, 1946; children—David Kneeland, Claudia Marshall. Asst. librarian N.Y. Pub. Library, 1949-52; mem. staff Phila. Mus. Art, 1952—, curator prints, drawings and photographs, 1964—; disting. vis. prof. U. Tex. at Austin, spring 1978. Bd. govs. Print Council Am., 1960—. Served to 1st lt. USAAF, World War II. Decorated D.F.C., Air medal (3), Purple Heart. Mem. Drawing Soc. (nat. com. 1964—), Print Club Phila. (bd. govs. 1955—). Author: The Collected Prints of Ben Shahn, 1967; Foreigners in Japan, Yokohama and Related Woodcuts, 1972; Peter Milton/Complete Etchings 1960-76, 1977. Contbg. editor Artist's Proof, 1963-71; editor The Lithographs of Jean Dubuffet, 1964; Alfred Bendiner: Lithographs, 1965; Marino Marini: Graphics and Related Works, 1965; The Art of Philadelphia Medicine, 1965; Eugene Feldman: Prints, 1965; Joan Miro: Prints and Books, 1966; Mauricio Lasansky: The Nazi Drawings, 1967; Master E.S.: Five Hundreth Anniversary, 1967; Suzuki Haronobu: Two Hundreth Anniversary, 1970; The Theatrical World of Osaks Prints, 1973. Home: 2130 Cherry St Philadelphia PA 19103 Office: Phila Museum Art PO Box 7646 Philadelphia PA 19101

MCNULTY, PAUL JAMES, educator; b. Elmira, N.Y., Feb. 10, 1931; s. Francis James and Marion Agnes (Good) McN.; B.A., Hobart Coll., 1959; Ph.D., Cornell U., 1965; m. Marian Adella Stever, July 16, 1960 (div. 1977); children—Michael James, Gregory Paul, Clare Elizabeth. Research asst. N.Y. State Div. of the Budget, Albany, 1960-61; instr. Cornell U., Ithaca, N.Y., 1964-65; asst. prof. Grad. Sch. of Bus., Columbia U., N.Y.C., 1965-68, asso. prof., 1968-73, prof. Grad. Sch. of Bus., 1973—. Trustee Jersey City State Coll.; vice chmn. bd. trustees Columbia Jour. World Bus. Served with U.S. Army, 1951-53. Woodrow Wilson fellow, 1958-59. Mem. Am. Econs. Assn., Hist. Econs. Soc., Assn. Evolutionary Econs., Phi Beta Kappa, Phi Kappa Phi, Beta Gamma Sigma. Contbr. articles to profl. jours. Home: 206 Watchung Ave Upper Montclair NJ 07043 Office: Grad Sch of Business Columbia Univ New York NY 10027

MC NUTT, DOLLY HITE, mayor, state legislator; b. Henderson, Ky., June 22, 1917; d. Leslie P. and Mary Gladys (Flaherty) Hite; student Paducah Jr. Coll., 1936, Am. Acad. Dramatic Arts, 1938; m. Houston McNutt, Feb. 25, 1941. Partner, Royal Crown-Nehi Bottling Co., Paducah, Ky., 1941-73; commr., mayor pro-tem City of Paducah, 1968-70, mayor, 1972—; mem. Ky. Ho. of Reps., 1977-78, 78-80; dir. Paducah Bank & Trust Co., Lakeland Wesley Village, Benton, Ky.; exec. com. econ. devel. Commonwealth of Ky., 1976. Vol. ARC, Paducah; seal chmn. McCracken County Tb Assn., 1969-71; chmn. civic beautification bd. City of Paducah, 1965-66; mem. steering com. Gov.'s White House Conf. on Libraries and Info., 1978; mem. Gov.'s Task Force on Welfare Reform, 1978; mem. adv. bd. Ky. Ednl. TV, 1978; mem. Home and Neighborhood Devel. Soc. Recipient Distinguished Woman award Fraternal Order of Eagles, 1972, Citizen of Yr. award Southside Kiwanis Club, 1972, Woman of Yr. award Bus. and Profl. Women's Club, 1971, Meritorious Service award Greater Paducah C. of C., 1974, Community Service award Midway (Ky.) Coll., 1977. Mem. Jackson Purchase Hist. Soc., Bus. and Profl. Women's Club, Greater Paducah C. of C. (v.p. 1976), Internat. Platform Assn. Democrat. Roman Catholic. Clubs: Paducah Garden, Paducah Country. Home: 105 Country Club Ln Paducah KY 42001 Office: PO Box 891 Paducah KY 42001

MCPARTLAND, JOHN WILLIAM, corp. exec.; b. N.Y.C., Sept. 26, 1917; s. Philip Maurice and Beatrice Ann (Kenney) McP.; B.B.A., St. John's U., 1941; m. Mary Adele Hollenstein, July 7, 1945; children—Maureen, John, Patricia, Daniel. Staff auditor Price Waterhouse & Co., N.Y.C., 1945-51; asst. to v.p. Deep Rock Oil Corp., Tulsa, 1951-54; v.p., treas. Great No. Oil Co., St. Paul, 1954-71; treas. Koch Industries, Inc., Wichita, Kans., 1971—, also dir., officer numerous subs. Served to lt. comdr. USNR, 1941-45. C.P.A., N.Y. Mem. Am. Inst. C.P.A.'s, N.Y. State Soc. C.P.A.'s. Home: 1601 N Woodlawn Blvd Wichita KS 67208 Office: PO Box 2256 Wichita KS 67201

MCPHAIL, ANDREW TENNENT, chemist, educator; b. Glasgow, Scotland, Sept. 23, 1937; s. Archibald Donaldson and Mary (Tennent) McP.; B.S. with honors, U. Glasgow, 1959, Ph.D., 1963; m. Annette Carson Paton, Aug. 4, 1961; children—Neil Andrew, Donald Robert. Asst. lectr. chemistry U. Glasgow, 1961-64; research asso. dept. chemistry U. Ill., 1964-66; lectr. chemistry U. Sussex (Eng.), 1966-68; asso. prof. chemistry Duke U., 1968-73, prof., 1973—; cons. Schering Research Corp., Burroughs Wellcome Co., Research Triangle Inst. Fellow Chem. Soc. (London), Am. Crystallographic Assn.; mem. Inst. Physics, Sigma Xi, Phi Lambda Upsilon. Contbr. articles to profl. jours. Home: 331 Smith Dr Durham NC 27712 Office: Paul M Gross Chemical Lab Duke U Durham NC 27706

MC PHEE, BRUCE GORDON, transp. co. exec.; b. Oakland, Calif., June 27, 1934; s. Douglas Gordon and Frieda Katrina (Heineman) McP.; B.A. in Polit. Sci., Stanford U., 1956; M.B.A., Harvard U., 1961; m. Elizabeth Sudgen Shaw, Sept. 28, 1957 (div. Oct. 1974);

children—Douglas H., Scott B.; m. 2d, Mary Jo Halsted, Oct. 18, 1975 (div. June 1979). With So. Pacific Co. and So. Pacific Transp. Co., and predecessors, San Francisco, 1961—, asst. v.p., 1972—, asst. treas., 1972-76, treas., 1976—. Bd. dirs. Golden Gate chpt. ARC. Served as officer USN, 1956-59; comdr. Res. Mem. Assn. Am. Railroads (advisory com. treasury div.), Nat. Assn. Bus. Economists. Clubs: Harvard Bus. Sch. No. Calif.; Commercial (San Francisco). Home: 1072 Del Norte Ave Menlo Park CA 94025 Office: So Pacific Co 1 Market Pl San Francisco CA 94105

MC PHEE, HENRY ROEMER, lawyer; b. Ames, Iowa, Jan. 11, 1925; s. Harry Roemer and Mary (Ziegler) McP.; A.B. cum laude, Princeton U., 1947; LL.B., Harvard U., 1950; m. Joanne Lambert, May 19, 1956; children—Henry Roemer III, Joanne, Larkin, Charles. Admitted to N.J. bar, 1951, Ill. bar, 1961, D.C. bar, 1966; asst. to gov. N.J., 1950-51, exec. asst., asso. counsel, 1951-52. pvt. practice law, New Brunswick and Princeton, N.J., 1952-54; gen. atty. Office Gen. Counsel, FTC, 1954; spl. asst. to Pres.'s econ. adviser White House, 1954-57; asst. spl. counsel Pres., 1957-58, asso. spl. counsel, pres., 1958-61; partner Hamel, Park, McCabe & Saunders, 1961—, also mem. mgmt. com.; dir. Clayton & Lambert Mfg. Co., Buckner, Ky. Sec., N.J. Commn. on Interstate Cooperation, 1952-54; v.p. Republican Club, Princeton, 1952-54; gen. counsel Rep. Nat. Fin. Com., 1968-76. Served from ensign to lt. (j.g.) USNR, 1943-46. Mem. Am., D.C., N.J. bar assns., Lincoln's Inn Soc. Harvard Law Sch. Presbyn. Clubs: Tower (Princeton U.); Princeton (pres. 1970-72), Metropolitan, Capitol Hill (Washington). Home: Partridge Run Ln Potomac MD 20854 Office: 1776 F St NW Washington DC 20006

MCPHEE, JOHN ANGUS, writer; b. Princeton, N.J., Mar. 8, 1931; s. Harry Roemer and Mary (Ziegler) McP.; A.B., Princeton U., 1953; postgrad. Magdalene Coll., Cambridge (Eng.) U., 1953-54; Litt.D. (hon.), Bates Coll., 1978; m. Pryde Brown, Mar. 16, 1957; children—Laura, Sarah, Jenny, Martha; m. 2d, Yolanda Whitman, Mar. 8, 1972; stepchildren—Cole, Andrew, Katherine, Vanessa Harrop. TV playwright for Robert Montgomery Presents, N.Y.C., 1955-56; contbg. editor, asso. editor Time mag., 1957-64, staff writer New Yorker mag., 1965—; Ferris prof. journalism Princeton, 1975, 76, 78. Author: A Sense of Where You Are, 1965; The Headmaster, 1966; Oranges, 1967; The Pine Barrens, 1968; A Roomful of Hovings, 1968; Levels of the Game, 1969; The Crofter and the Laird, 1970; Encounters with the Archdruid, 1971; The Deltoid Pumpkin Seed, 1973; The Curve of Binding Energy, 1974; Pieces of the Frame, 1975; The Survival of the Bark Canoe, 1975; Coming into the Country, 1977. Recipient award in lit. Am. Acad. and Inst. Arts and Letters, 1977. Address: care New Yorker 23 W 43d St New York NY 10036*

MCPHEETERS, EDWIN KEITH, architect; b. Stillwater, Okla., Mar. 26, 1924; s. William Henry and Eva Winona (Mitchell) McP.; B.Arch., Okla. State U., 1950; M.F.A., Princeton U., 1956; m. Patricia Ann Foster, Jan. 29, 1950; children—Marc Foster, Kevin Mitchell, Michael Hunter. Instr. architecture U. Fla., 1949-51; asst. prof. Ala. Poly. Inst. (Auburn U.), 1951-54; fellow Princeton U., 1955; from asst. prof. to prof. U. Ark., 1956-66; prof. Rensselaer Poly. Inst., 1966-69, dean, 1966-69; prof. Auburn U., 1969—, dean Sch. of Architecture and Fine Arts, 1969—; mem. Ala. State Bd. Registration for Architects, 1978-79; profl. adviser South Central Bell Telephone Co., 1977-79. Served to 2d lt. USAAC, 1943-45. Fellow AIA (pres. Ala. council 1978, recipient Merit award 1976; mem. Assn. Collegiate Schs. of Architecture (dir. 1970-77), Internat. Council of Fine Arts Deans. Democrat. Home: 221 Kimberly Dr Auburn AL 36830 Office: 202 Fine Arts Center Auburn AL 36830. *As a teacher and an architect I have been under constant pressure to endorse or become committed to a variety of movements, causes, philosophies, styles, and "truths of the moment." I've preferred the role of iconoclast and to stay with those basic principles which have endured the fickleness of stylistic change in the arts.*

MC PHEETERS, THOMAS S., JR., lawyer; b. St. Louis, Jan. 2, 1912; s. Thomas S. and Madeleine (Taussig) McP.; A.B., Princeton, 1933; LL.B., Washington U., St. Louis, 1936; m. Carroll W. Jones, Oct. 4, 1939; children—Thomas S. III, Hugh, John C., Peter G.; m. 2d, Martha B. Legg, Sept. 24, 1960 (dec. Nov. 1968); stepchildren—John C., Louisa O. Deland, Martha S.; m. 3d, Gladys McRee, Feb. 23, 1973. Admitted to Mo. bar, 1936, since practiced in St. Louis; asso. firm Bryan, Williams, Cave & McPheeters, and successor firm Bryan, Cave, McPheeters & McRoberts, 1936—, partner, 1951—. Mem. Ladue (Mo.) City Council, 1950-60; trustee David Ranken, Jr. Tech. Inst., Westminster Coll. Served with Am. Field Service, 1944-45; CBI. Democrat. Presbyn. Clubs: St. Louis Country, Racquet, Noonday, Log Cabin (St. Louis). Home: 9752 Litzsinger Rd Saint Louis MO 63124 Office: 500 N Broadway Saint Louis MO 63102

MC PHERSON, ALICE RUTH, ophthalmologist; b. Regina, Sask., Can., June 30, 1926; d. Gordon and Viola (Hoover) McPherson; came to U.S., 1938, naturalized, 1958; B.S., U. Wis., 1948, M.D., 1951. Intern, Santa Barbara (Calif.) Cottage Hosp., 1951-52; resident anesthesiology Hartford (Conn.) Hosp., 1952; resident ophthalmology Chgo. Eye, Ear, Nose and Throat Hosp., 1953, U. Wis. Hosps., 1953-55; ophthalmologist Davis and Duehr Eye Clinic, Madison, Wis., 1956-57; clin. instr. U. Wis., 1956-57; fellow retina service Mass. Eye and Ear Infirmary, 1957-58; ophthalmologist Scott and White Clinic, Temple, Tex., 1958-60; practice medicine specializing in ophthalmology and retinal diseases, Houston, 1960—; mem. staff Methodist, St. Luke's, Tex. Children's hosps., Houston; clin. asst. prof. Baylor Coll. Medicine, Houston, 1959-61, asst. prof. ophthalmology, 1961-69, clin. asso. prof., 1969-75, clin. prof., 1975—, chief retina service dept. ophthalmology, 1959—; lectr. ophthalmology U. Tex., 1959—; cons. retinal diseases VA Hosp., Houston, 1960—, Ben Taub Hosp., Houston, 1960—. Diplomate Am. Bd. Ophthalmology. Fellow Am. Acad. Ophthalmology and Otolaryngology, A.C.S.; mem. AMA, Tex., Pan-Am. med. assns., Internat. Coll. Surgeons, Am. Med. Women's Assn., Pan-Pacific Surg. Assn., Am. Assn. Ophthalmology, Assn. Research Ophthalmology, Assn. Am. Physicians and Surgeons, Retina Soc., Soc. Eye Surgeons, French Ophthal. Soc., Harris County Med. Soc., Houston Ophthal. Soc., Internat. Med. Assembly S.W. Tex., Jules Gonin Club. Author: New and Controversial Aspects of Retinal Detachment, 1968; editor: New and Controversial Aspects of Vitreoretinal Surgery, 1977. Office: 6500 Fannin Suite 2100 Houston TX 77030

MCPHERSON, DONALD J., metallurgist; B.S., M.S., Ph.D., Ohio State U., D.Sc. (hon.), 1975; married; children—Marjorie, Linda. Asso. metallurgist Argonne Nat. Lab. to 1950; research metallurgist, asst. div. mgr., div. mgr., v.p. IIT Research Inst., 1950-69; v.p., dir. tech. Kaiser Aluminum and Chem. Corp., Oakland, Calif., 1969—. Mem. numerous govt. coms. on devel. titanium for def. applications. Bd. dirs. Ohio State U. Research Found. Recipient Outstanding Young Men award Chgo. Jr. Assn. Commerce and Industry, 1956, Distinguished Alumnus and Centennial Achievement awards Ohio State U. Fellow Am. Soc. Metals (trustee, Campbell Meml. lectr. 1974, hon. mem.); mem. Am. Inst. Mining, Metall. and Petroleum Engrs. (chmn. titanium com.; chmn. Inst. of Metals div.; bd. dirs. Metall. Soc.), Inst. Metals London, Am. Ceramic Soc. AAAS. Contbr. numerous articles on titanium and its alloys to profl. jours. Home: 1180 Monticello Rd Lafayette CA 94549 Office: 300 Lakeside Dr Oakland CA 94643

MC PHERSON, FRANK ALFRED, corp. exec.; b. Stillwell, Okla., Apr. 29, 1933; s. Younce B. and Maurine Francis (Strauss) McP.; B.S., Okla. State U., 1957; m. Nadine Wall, Sept. 10, 1955; children—David, Craig, Mark, Rebecca. With Kerr-McGee, 1957—, gen. mgr. Gulf Coast Oil and gas ops., Morgan City, La., 1969-73, pres. Kerr-McGee Coal, 1973-76, pres. Kerr-McGee Nuclear, 1976-77, vice chmn. Kerr-McGee Corp., responsible for chem., coal, nuclear and refining corps. and engring. services div., 1977—. Mem. adv. bd. Salvation Army, Oklahoma City; bd. dirs. YMCA of Oklahoma City. Served to capt. USAF, 1957-60. Mem. Soc. Mining Engrs., Am. Mining Congress (dir., exec. com., adv. council), Atomic Indsl. Forum (dir.), Oklahoma City C. of C. (bd. dirs.). Democrat. Baptist. Patentee in field. Office: PO Box 25861 Oklahoma City OK 73125

MC PHERSON, HARRY CUMMINGS, JR., lawyer; b. Tyler, Tex., Aug. 22, 1929; s. Harry Cummings and Nan (Hight) McP.; B.A., U. South, 1949, D.C.L. (hon.), 1965; student Columbia, 1949-50; LL.B., U. Tex., 1956; m. Clayton Read, Aug. 30, 1952; children—Courtenay, Peter B. Admitted to Tex. bar, 1955; asst. gen. counsel Democratic policy com. U.S. Senate, 1956-59, asso. counsel, 1959-61, gen. counsel, 1961-63; dep. under sec. internat. affairs Dept. Army, 1963-64; asst. sec. state ednl. and cultural affairs, 1964-65; spl. asst. and counsel to Pres. Johnson, 1965-66, spl. counsel, 1966-69; pvt. practice law, Washington, 1969—. Chmn. task force on domestic policy Dem. Adv. Council Elected Ofcls., 1974-76; mem. Pres.'s Commn. on Accident at Three Mile Island, 1979; vice chmn. John F. Kennedy Center for Performing Arts, 1969-76, gen. counsel, 1977—; bd. mem. Woodrow Wilson Internat. Center for Scholars, 1969-74. Served to 2d lt. USAF, 1950-53. Recipient Distinguished Civilian Service award Dept. Army, 1964; Arthur S. Flemming award as one of the ten outstanding young men in govt. in 1968. Mem. D.C., Tex. bar assns., N.Y. Council on Fgn. Relations (dir. 1974-77). Democrat. Episcopalian. Author: A Political Education, 1972. Home: 30 W Irving St Chevy Chase MD 20015 Office: 1660 L St NW Washington DC 20036

MC PHERSON, JAMES ALAN, writer; b. Savannah, Ga., Sept. 16, 1943; s. James and Mable (Smalls) McP.; B.A., Morris Brown Coll., 1965; LL.B., Harvard, 1968; M.F.A., U. Iowa, 1971; m. Sarah Charlton, 1973; 1 dau., Rachel Alice. Asst. prof. lit. U. Calif., Santa Cruz, 1969-76; asso. prof. English, U. Va., Charlottesville, 1976—; contbg. editor Atlantic Monthly, Boston, 1969; mem. lit. panel Nat. Endowment for Arts, 1977—. Atlantic grantee 1968; recipient award in lit. Nat. Inst. Arts and Letters, 1970; Guggenheim fellow, 1972-73. Mem. Authors League, ACLU. Author: (short stories) Hue and Cry, 1969; Railroad, 1976; Elbow Room, 1977 (Pulitzer prize 1978); stories selected for O'Henry Collection and Best American Short Stories, 1969, 73.

MCPHERSON, JAMES MUNRO, educator; b. Valley City, N.D., Oct. 11, 1936; s. James Munro and Miriam (Osborn) McP.; B.A., Gustavus Adolphus Coll., 1958; Ph.D., Johns Hopkins, 1963; m. Patricia Rasche, Dec. 28, 1957; 1 dau., Joanna Erika. Mem. faculty Princeton, 1962—, prof. history, 1972—; cons. Ednl. Research Council Am., 1967—. Danforth fellow, 1958-62; Guggenheim fellow, 1967-68; Huntington-Nat. Endowment for Humanities fellow, 1977-78. Mem. Am., So. hist. assns., Orgn. Am. Historians, Phi Beta Kappa. Author: Struggle for Equality (Anisfield-Wolf award race relations 1965), 1964; The Negro's Civil War, 1965; Marching Toward Freedom; The Negro in the Civil War, 1968; Blacks in America: Bibliographical Essays, 1971; The Abolitionist Legacy: From Reconstruction to the NAACP, 1975. Home: 15 Randall Rd Princeton NJ 08540

MC PHERSON, JOHN BARKLEY, aerospace cons., ret. air force officer; b. Virginia, Minn., Oct. 4, 1917; s. Barkley John and Anna (Holmgren) McP.; B.C.E., U. Ariz., 1940; m. Leota Irene Wilson, July 16, 1940; children—Kenneth, Sue McPherson Cain, Shirley McPherson Curs, Robin McPherson Rohrback. Commd. 2d lt., cav. U.S. Army, 1940, advanced through grades to lt. gen. USAF, 1968; assigned B-29s, World War II, PTO; comdr. Walker AFB, Roswell, N.Mex., 1950-52; dir. faculty Air War Coll., 1955-56; dep. comdr. 5th Air Div. Morocco, 1956-58; comdr. 379th Bomb Wing, Homestead AFB, Fla., 1958-59, 823d Air Div., Homestead AFB, 1959-62, 810th Air Div., Minot AFB, N.D., 1962-64; vice dir. ops., joint staff Joint Chiefs Staff, 1964-67, vice dir. joint staff, 1967-68, asst. to chmn. Joint Chiefs Staff, 1968-70; comdt. Nat. War Coll., 1970-73; ret., 1973; cons. Martin Marietta Aerospace, 1973—. Decorated D.S.M. with 2 oak leaf clusters, Legion of Merit, Bronze Star, Joint Service Commendation medal; named Outstanding Young Man of Year, Roswell, 1951. Mem. Am. Inst. Aeros. and Astronautics, Air Force Hist. Found. (pres. 1974—), Air Force Assn., Nat. Space Club, Order of Daedalians, Theta Tau, Kappa Sigma. Address: 250 S Reynolds St Apt 1407 Alexandria VA 22304

MC PHERSON, JOHN DALLAS, investment co. exec.; b. Inglewood, Calif., Sept. 18, 1922; s. John and Hazel (Mitchell) McP.; B.S., U. Calif. at Berkeley, 1941; m. Ida Morgan, May 17, 1959; children—Dallas B., John Gordon; m. 2d, Ann Autry, Feb. 7, 1970. Exec. tng. Gen. Electric Corp., Schenectady, 1941-42; tng. officer VA, 1946; founder, pres. Airborne Freight Corp., San Francisco, 1946-69, now dir.; founder, pres. Ralston Investment Corp., 1969—; pres. Am. Orient Travel Corp., Personal Security Life Ins. Co.; chmn. bd. Star Airline Catering, Inc., Albertsen Travel Service, Inc., Portal Travel Service, Inc., Dipaco, Inc., S & S Ice Vending Machine Co., Inc.; dir. Mediacast, Inc. Pres. Medic Alert Found. Internat., 1975—. Bd. dirs. Med. Problem Welfare Assn., Inc., Medic Alert Found. Internat., Inc., U. Calif. Internat. House, Meals for Millions Found. Served to lt. comdr. USNR, 1942-46. Mem. San Francisco C. of C., San Francisco Art Assn., World Bus. Council (pres. 1974-75, dir. 1975—), Newcomen Soc. N.Am., Air Force Assn., Confrerie de la Chaine des Rotisseurs, Sonoma County Trail Blazers. Club: Commonwealth of Calif. (San Francisco). Home: 85 Fagan Dr Hillsborough CA 94010 Office: Ralston Investment Corp 1275 California Dr Burlingame CA 94010

MCPHERSON, MARY PATTERSON, coll. pres.; b. Abington, Pa., May 14, 1935; d. John B. and Marjorie Hoffman (Higgins) McP.; A.B., Smith Coll., 1957; M.A., U. Del., 1960; Ph.D., Bryn Mawr Coll., 1969; LL.D. (hon.), Juniata Coll., 1975. Instr. in philosophy U. Del., 1959-61; asst., fellow and lectr. dept. philosophy Bryn Mawr Coll., 1961-63, asst. dean, 1964-69, asso. dean, 1969-70, dean Undergrad. Coll., 1970-78, asso. prof., 1970—, acting pres., 1976-77, pres., 1978—; bd. dirs. Agnes Irwin Sch., 1971—, Shipley Sch., 1972—, Phillips Exeter Acad., 1973-76, Wilson Coll., 1976-79, Greater Phila. Movement, 1973-77, Internat. House of Phila., 1974-76, Josiah Macy, Jr. Found., 1977—, Carnegie Found. for Advancement Teaching, 1978—, Univ. Museum, Phila., 1977-79, Univ. City Sci. Center, Phila., 1979—, Am. Council on Edn., 1979—; dir. Provident Nat. Bank of Phila., Provident Nat. Corp., Bell Telephone Co. Pa.; mem. commn. on women in higher edn. Am. Council on Edn. Mem. Soc. for Ancient Greek Philosophy. Clubs: Fullerton, Cosmopolitan. Office: Office of Pres Bryn Mawr Coll Merion Ave Bryn Mawr PA 19010

MC PHERSON, PAUL FRANCIS, publishing co. exec.; b. Boston, Apr. 30, 1931; s. William Andrew and Margaret Frances (Rice) McP.; B.S.B.A., Boston Coll., 1952; M.B.A., Babson Coll., 1955; m. Mary Loretta Sanders, June 10, 1953; children—Paul, Kevin, Gary, Scott. With McGraw Hill, Inc., N.Y.C., 1955—, advt. sales mgr. McGraw-Hill Publs. Co., 1963-67, group v.p., 1973-76, exec. v.p., 1976-79, pres. McGraw-Hill Info. Systems Co., 1979—, McGraw-Hill Pub. Co., 1979—; dir. Nikkei-McGraw-Hill. Served with U.S. Army, 1952-54. Mem. Am. Bus. Press (dir., vice chmn.), Mag. Pubs. Assn. (dir.), Manhattan Bus. Group (chmn.). Clubs: Hemisphere (dir.), Roxbury Swim and Tennis (dir.). Home: 10 Drumhill Ln Stamford CT 06902 Office: 1221 Ave of Americas New York NY 10020

MC PHERSON, ROBERT DONALD, lawyer; b. Madison, Wis., Dec. 21, 1936; s. Clifford James and Alice Irene (Peterson) McP.; B.A., U. Tex., El Paso, 1960; J.D., S. Tex. Coll. Law, Houston, 1969; m. Nancy Joann Buenzli, Aug. 17, 1957; children—Sean Kelly, Eileen Patricia, Maureen Teresa, Cathleen Marie. Tchr. English schs., El Paso and Menomonie, Wis., 1960-62; claims rep. Employers Casualty Co. Tex., 1962-66; staff claims rep. Transp. Ins. Co., Tex., 1966-68; admitted to Tex. bar, 1969; partner firm Bousquet & McPherson, Houston, 1969-76; individual practice law, Houston, 1976—; instr. history and govt. South Tex. Jr. Coll., 1969-71; adj. prof. law South Tex. Coll. Law, 1972—. Served with AUS, 1953-56. Mem. State Bar Tex., Am. Bar Assn., Assn. Trial Lawyers Am., Tex. Trial Lawyers Assn., Order of Lytae. Home: 3419 Audubon Pl Houston TX 77006 also PO Box 546 Waller TX 77484 Office: 3401 Louisiana Suite 250 Houston TX 77002

MCPHERSON, ROBERT GRIER, educator; b. Athens, Ga., July 23, 1923; s. John Hanson Thomas and Margaret Virginia (Bonney) McP.; A.B., U. Ga., 1943, M.A., 1948; Ph.D., Johns Hopkins, 1957; m. Margaret Hibbard Lore, Dec. 23, 1947; children—Margaret Lore, Robert Grier, Jean Hibbard. Dir. U.S. Army Edn. Program Sch., Kobe, Japan, 1946-47; faculty history U. Ga., Athens, 1952—, prof., 1969—, head dept., 1969-77. Trustee Oconee Hill Cemetery, Athens. Served with AUS, 1943-46; PTO. Mem. Inst. Hist. Research U. London, Conf. Brit. Studies, Am. Hist. Assn., Phi Alpha Theta. Author: Theory of Higher Education in Nineteenth Century England, 1959; The Journal of the Earl of Egmont, 1962. Contbr. articles to profl. jours. Home: 145 Tallassee Farms Dr Athens GA 30606

MC PHERSON, ROLF KENNEDY, clergyman, ch. ofcl.; b. Providence, Mar. 23, 1913; s. Harold S. and Aimee Elizabeth (Semple) McP.; student So. Cal. Radio Inst., 1933; D.D. (hon.), L.I.F.E. Bible Coll., 1944; m. Lorna De Smith, July 21, 1931; children—Marlene (dec.), Kay Boyd. Ordained to ministry Internat. Ch. Foursquare Gospel, 1940; pres., dir. Internat. Ch. Foursquare Gospel, 1944—. Pres., dir. Echo Park Evangelistic Assn., L.I.F.E. Bible Coll., Inc.; bd. adminstrn. Pentecostal Fellowship N.Am., 1948—. Office: 1100 Glendale Blvd Los Angeles CA 90026

MCPHERSON, WILLIAM ALEXANDER, writer; b. Sault Sainte Marie, Mich., Mar. 16, 1933; s. Harold Agnew and Ruth (Brubaker) McP.; student U. Mich., 1951-55, Mich. State U., 1956-58, George Washington U., 1960-62; m. Elizabeth Mosher, July 7, 1959 (div. 1979); 1 dau., Jane Elizabeth. With Washington Post, 1958-66, 69—, staff writer, 1959-63, writer, editor, 1963-66, book critic, 1969-72, contbg. editor Book World, 1969-72, editor, 1972-78, critic, 1978—; sr. editor William Morrow & Co., Pubs., N.Y.C., 1967-69; lectr. Am. U., 1971-72, adj. prof., 1975. Mem. N.Y. County Democratic Com., 1969; trustee Washington Ednl. TV Sta., 1977—; trustee Jenny McKean Moore Fund for Writers, 1977—, v.p., 1979—; nat. adv. bd. Library of Congress Center for Book, 1978—. Recipient Pulitzer prize for disting. criticism, 1977. Mem. Nat. Book Critics Circle (dir. 1975—), PEN. Office: Washington Post Book World 1150 15th St NW Washington DC 20071

MC QUADA, QUADE, WALTER, author; b. Port Washington, N.Y., May 1, 1922; s. Walter P. and Theresa (Dwyer) McQ.; B.Arch., Cornell U., 1947; m. Ann Aikman, Nov. 25, 1950; children—Molly Elizabeth, Benjamin Barr, Kate Maud. Writer, Archtl. Forum mag., 1947-64; architecture and design critic The Nation, 1959-65, Life mag., 1970-74; bd. editors Fortune mag., 1964—; vis. critic Yale U. Sch. Architecture, 1962; mem. N.Y.C. Planning Commn., 1967-72; mem. Mayor N.Y.C. Task Force Design, 1967; author: Schoolhouse, 1958; Cities Fit To Live In, 1971; Stress, 1975; The Longevity Factor, 1979. Served with AUS, 1942-46. Ford Found. fellow, 1960; co-recipient Grand prize Milan Trennale, 1960; recipient Howard Blakeslee award Am. Heart Assn., 1972; Penney award U. Mo., 1972. Fellow AIA (Architecture Critics' medal 1974); mem. Municipal Arts Soc. N.Y. Roman Catholic. Home: 3 Grosvenor Pl Great Neck NY 11021 Office: care Fortune Magazine Time and Life Bldg Rockefeller Center New York NY 10020

MC QUADE, HENRY FORD, state justice; b. Pocatello, Idaho, Oct. 11, 1915; s. M. Joseph and Mary E. (Farnon) McQ.; A.B., U. Idaho, 1940, LL.B., 1943; m. Mary E. Downing, Apr. 11, 1942; children—Sharon McQuade Grisham, Michael, Frances McQuade Horan, Robert, Joseph, Peter, William. Admitted to Idaho bar, 1946; practice in Pocatello, 1946-51; pros. atty. Bannock County (Idaho), 1946-50; judge 5th Jud. Dist. Idaho, 1951-56; justice Idaho Supreme Ct., 1957-76, chief justice, 1972-75; dep. adminstr. Law Enforcement Assistance Adminstrn., U.S. Dept. Justice, Washington, 1976; adminstrv. law judge Occupational Safety and Health Rev. Commn., Washington, 1976—; mem. Nat. Commn. on Criminal Justice Standards and Goals, 1971-73, Nat. Commn. Hwy. Traffic Safety, 1971—. Chmn., Idaho Gov.'s Com. Traffic Safety, 1958-59, Idaho YMCA Youth Legislature, 1958-69, Boise chpt. ARC, 1970-71. Mem. Am. Bar Assn., Am. Judicature Soc., Idaho State Bar. Home: 420 Center St N Vienna VA 22180 Office: 6525 Belcrest Rd Hyattsville MD 20782

MC QUADE, LAWRENCE CARROLL, lawyer, corp. exec.; b. Yonkers, N.Y., Aug. 12, 1927; s. Edward A. and Thelma (Keefe) McQ.; B.A. with distinction, Yale U., 1950; B.A. (Rhodes scholar), Oxford (Eng.) U., 1952, M.A., 1956; LL.B. cum laude, Harvard U., 1954; m. de Rosset Parker Morrissey, Aug. 3, 1968 (dec. Oct. 1978); 1 son, Andrew Parker. Admitted to N.Y. State bar, 1955, D.C. bar, 1968; asso. firm Sullivan & Cromwell, N.Y.C., 1954-60; spl. asst. to asst. sec. for internat. security affairs Dept. Def., Washington, 1961-63; dep. asst. sec. Dept. Commerce, Washington, 1963-64, asst. to sec., 1965-67, asst. sec., 1967-69; pres. Procon Inc., Des Plaines, Ill., 1969-75, chief exec. officer, 1971-75, also dir.; v.p. Universal Oil Products Co., 1972-75; v.p. W. R. Grace & Co., N.Y.C., 1975-78, sr. v.p., 1978—; dir. Chemed Corp. Bd. dirs. Internat. House, U. Chgo., 1972-73, trustee, 1976—; bd. dirs. Fgn. Bondholders Protective Council, N.Y.C., 1978—. Served with AUS, 1946-47. Mem. Assn. Am. Rhodes Scholars, Council Fgn. Relations N.Y., Chgo. Council Fgn. Relations (dir. 1969-75), Nat. Fgn. Trade Council (dir. 1979—), Atlantic Council U.S. (dir. 1969—), Internat. Mgmt. and Devel. Inst. (dir. 1970—), Overseas Devel. Council (dir. 1974—), Phi Beta Kappa. Clubs: Harvard, Century, Pilgrims (N.Y.C.); Met. (Washington); Chgo. Author: (with others) The Ghana Report, 1959; contbr. articles to profl. jours. Office: Grace Plaza 1114 Ave of Americas New York NY 10036

MC QUAID, FRANK JOHN, mfg. co. exec.; b. Brewster, N.Y., July 20, 1929; s. Frank John and Jane (O'Connor) McQ.; B.B.A., Pace Coll., 1952; m. Gladys Johnson, May 3, 1952; children—Frank, Jonathan, Lauren. Controller, Gen. Precision Equipment Corp., Pleasantville, N.Y., 1954-67; div. controller Kearfott Group, Singer Co., L.I., 1967-69; sr. v.p. fin., treas. Dataproducts Corp., Woodland Hills, Calif., 1969—, also dir. Served with U.S. Army, 1952-54. Republican. Roman Catholic. Home: 24307 Long Valley Rd Hidden Hills CA 91302 Office: 6200 Canoga Ave Woodland Hills CA 91365

MC QUARRIE, DONALD ALLAN, chemist; b. Lowell, Mass., May 20, 1937; s. Allan Daniel and Dorothy Belle (Luce) McQ.; B.S., Lowell Tech. Inst., 1958; M.A., Johns Hopkins U., 1960; Ph.D., U. Oreg., 1962; m. Carole Ann Harper, Aug. 15, 1959; children—Allan Donald, Dawn Leslie. Asst. prof. chemistry Mich. State U., 1962-63; research scientist North Am. Aviation Co., Thousand Oaks, Calif., 1963-68; prof. Ind. U., 1968-78, U. Calif., Davis, 1978—. Guggenheim fellow, 1975-76. Mem. Am. Chem. Soc., Biophys. Soc., Sigma Xi. Author: Statistical Thermodynamics, 1973; Statistical Mechanics, 1976; editorial bd. Jour. Phys. Chemistry, 1979—. Office: U Calif Davis CA 95616

MC QUARRIE, GERALD H., savs. and loan exec.; b. Minersville, Utah, June 28, 1921; s. Herrick and Lucy Irene (Hall) McQ.; grad. Compton Coll., 1941; m. Oneida B. Martin, Feb. 22, 1946; children—Sandra Irene, Gerald Brent, Roger Scott. Pres., McQuarrie Realty Co.; chief exec. officer, exec. v.p. Prentz Southland Investment Corp.; co-founder, dir. Downey Savs. & Loan Assn. (Calif.); dir. Home Bank, Fed. Home Loan Bank. Served with USNR, 1945-46, USAF, 1950-52. Mem. Soc. Residential Appraisers (sr. residential appraiser, past pres.), Calif. Savs. and Loan League (dir.), U.S. Savs. and Loan League (dir. San Francisco chpt.). Mormon. Club: Rotary (past pres. Downey). Office: 3500 Bristol St Costa Mesa CA 92626*

MCQUARY, JOAN SUSAN, editor; b. South Bend, Ind., Feb. 20, 1922; d. George L. and Hazel H. (Haverstock) McQuary; B.A., U. Minn., 1943. Music librarian NBC, N.Y.C., 1943-48; with Columbia U. Press, N.Y.C., 1948—, asst. editor, 1950-55, editor, 1955-63, sr. editor, 1963-70, chief manuscript editor, 1970-75, mng. editor, 1975—; mem. music publ. com. Columbia Univ. Music Press, 1972—. Home: 1700 York Ave New York City NY 10028 Office: 562 W 113th St New York City NY 10025

MC QUEEN, JUSTICE ELLIS (ALSO KNOWN AS L.Q. JONES), actor, dir., writer, producer; b. Beaumont, Tex., Aug. 19, 1927; s. Justice Ellis and Paralee (Stevens) McQ.; student Lamar Jr. Coll., 1944, Lon Morris Coll., 1945, U. Tex., 1947-49; m. Neta Sue Lewis, Oct. 10, 1950; children—Marlin Randolph, Marilyn Helen, Steven Lewis. Actor numerous motion picture films, TV shows; dir. motion picture films including A Boy and His Dog (recipient Hugo award, Sci. Fiction achievement award for dramatic presentation), 1975; producer 4 films; author The Brotherhood of Satan, 1971. Served with USNR, 1945-46. Mem. Screen Actors Guild. Republican. Methodist. Home: 2144 1/2 N Cahuenga St Hollywood CA 90068 Office: 2144 N Cahuenga St Hollywood CA 90068

MCQUEEN, MARVIN DUNCAN, advt. agy. exec.; b. Superior, Wis., Apr. 19, 1914; s. Angus and Mary Louise (Reineccius) McQ.; student Superior State Teachers Coll., 1931; B. Journalism, U. Mo., 1936; m. Maria Luisa Ordonez, July 26, 1941; children—Augus Loren, Melissa. Advt. solicitor Superior Eve. Telegram, 1929-30; advt. mgr., reporter Canby (Minn.) Press, 1931; with D'Arcy Advt. Co., St. Louis, 1936-72, v.p., 1951-68, dir., 1957-72, adminstrv. v.p., N.Y.C., 1968-70, exec. v.p., 1970-72; pres. Ackerman Inc., Tulsa, 1972—. Chmn. Freedom of Info. Conf., Columbia, Mo., 1966; mem. Commn. on Ch. Papers Luth. Ch. in Am., 1967—. Bd. dirs. Ednl. Found., U. Wis., Superior, 1960—, Devel. Fund U. Mo., 1975—, Tulsa Philharmonic, 1976—; mem. exec. bd. Indian Nations council Boy Scouts Am., 1975—. Recipient Honor award for Distinguished Service in Journalism, U. Mo., 1967, Faculty/Alumni award U. Mo., 1970. Mem. St. Andrews Soc. N.Y., U. Mo. Alumni Assn. (pres. 1965-67), U. Mo. Sch. Journalism Alumni Assn. (pres. 1965). Republican. Lutheran. Clubs: Burns, Racquet (St. Louis); University (Mexico City and N.Y.C.); Tulsa. Home: 246 Center Plaza Tulsa OK 74119 Office: 123 E 5th St Tulsa OK 74103

MC QUEEN, ROBERT CHARLES, ins. co. exec.; b. Santiago, Chile, Jan. 23, 1921; s. Charles Alfred and Grace Juanita (Abrecht) McQ.; A.B., Dartmouth Coll., 1942; m. Donna Marie Ikeler, Oct. 6, 1945; children—Scott, Jerry, Monte, Donald. Mathematician, Equitable Life Assurance Soc., N.Y.C., 1945-49; group actuary Union Central Life Ins. Co., Cin., 1949-57; with Mut. Benefit Life Ins. Co., Newark, 1957—, exec. v.p., 1969-71, sr. exec. v.p., chief adminstrv. officer, 1971—, dir., 1978—; chmn. bd. Retirement Plans, Inc., Cleve., Mut. Benefit Fin. Service Co., Newark. Pres. Millburn Twp. (N.J.) Bd. Edn., 1969-71; chmn. Better Bus. Bur. Met. N.Y., 1978—. Served with OSS, 1943-45. Fellow Soc. Actuaries; mem. Am. Acad. Actuaries, Internat. Actuarial Assn. Republican. Episcopalian. Clubs: Essex, Canoe Brook Country; Quechee; Boca Lago. Home: 24 Tennyson Dr Short Hills NJ 07078 Office: 520 Broad St Newark NJ 07101

MC QUEEN, STEVE, actor. Race car, motorcycle racer and enthusiast; TV actor Wanted-Dead or Alive; motion pictures include The Great Escape, The Magnificent Seven, Love with the Proper Stranger, Baby, the Rain Must Fall, Soldier in the Rain, Cincinnati Kid, Nevada Smith, The Sand Pebbles, The Thomas Crown Affair, Bullitt, The Reivers, Le Mans, Junior Bonner, The Getaway, Papillon, The Towering Inferno, Enemy of the People. Served with USMC. Address: care Internat Creative Mgmt 8899 Beverly Blvd Los Angeles CA 90048

MC QUEENEY, HENRY MARTIN, SR., publisher; b. N.Y.C., Oct. 29, 1938; s. John Henry and Catherine Mary (Quigg) McQ.; B.B.A., St. Johns U., 1960; postgrad. U. Rochester, 1965-67; m. Elizabeth Bernino, May 14, 1960; children—Mary E., Henry Martin, John P., Matthew S. City sales rep. Curtis Circulation div. Curtis Pub. Co., 1960-62, asst. mgr., N.Y.C., 1962-63, field mgr., Rochester, N.Y., 1964-67, dept. mgr., account exec., Phila., 1968-74; v.p. sales, exec. v.p. mktg. Manor Books, Inc., N.Y.C., 1974—, pres., 1976—; rep. Western N.Y. Pubs.; cons. Bipad Ednl. Program. Pres. parish bd. Roman Catholic Ch., 1965, editor newspaper, Spencerport, N.Y., 1965, diocesan leader, mem. lay bd., Rochester, 1964-67; certified as tchr. Confraternity Christian Doctrine, Diocese of Rochester, 1964. Home: 12 Blenheim Ln Centerport NY 11721 Office: 45 E 30th St New York NY 10016

MC QUILKIN, JOHN HOWARD, engring. cons.; b. Washington, Ind., Aug. 20, 1913; s. Howard P. and Fannie May (Snyder) McQ.; B.S., U.S. Naval Acad., 1935; M.S., Mass. Inst. Tech., 1940; m. Diane LaSpada, Mar. 18, 1972; children by previous marriage—Sandra Gail (Mrs. Henry H. Tredwell III), Bruce Michael. Commd. ensign USN, 1935, advanced through grades to rear adm., 1963; various naval assignments afloat, with Constrn. Corps. and engring. div., 1935-43; mem. staff comdr. destroyers Pacific Fleet, 1943-45; with hull design br. Bur. Ships, 1946-50; asst. dir. standardization Office Chief Naval Ops., 1950; dep. chief devel. Field Command, Armed Forces Spl. Weapons Project, Albuquerque, 1950-54; repair and shipbldg. supt. Naval Shipyard, Vallejo, Calif., 1954-55; head preliminary design br., ship design div. Bur. Ships, 1955-57; comdg. officer, dir. navy radiol. def. lab. Naval Base, San Francisco, 1957-60; dir. ship design div. Bur. Ships, 1961-62, asst. chief research and devel., 1962-64; comdr. N.Y. Naval Shipyard, 1964-66; comdr. San Francisco Bay Naval Shipyard, 1966-68; ret., 1968; mgr. engring. and materials Bechtel Corp., San Francisco, 1968-76, mgr. Jubail project Saudi Arabian Bechtel Co., Dhahran, 1976-78; pvt. cons., 1978—. Decorated Bronze Star. Mem. Am. Soc. Naval Engrs. (pres. 1964), Soc. Naval Architects and Marine Engrs., Marine Tech. Soc., Sigma Xi. Club: St. Francis Yacht. Home and Office: 1 Half Moon Bend Coronado CA 92118

MC QUILKIN, WILLIAM WINTERS, ret. corp. exec.; b. San Jose, Calif., Apr. 5, 1907; s. Harmon Hudson and Elizabeth (Rhinehart) McQ.; B.A., Princeton, 1928, M.A., 1929; B.A., Balliol Coll., Oxford U., 1931, B.C.L., 1932; m. Eleanor Godwin Atterbury, Sept. 15, 1934; children—Robert Rennie, William Winters, John Atterbury, Michael Godwin. Admitted to N.Y. bar, 1933; atty. Rushmore, Bisbee & Stern, N.Y.C., 1932-38; sec., treas., v.p. Bausch & Lomb, Inc., Rochester, N.Y., 1938-57, dir., 1943-79, exec. v.p., 1957-59, pres., chief exec. officer, 1959-71, chmn. bd., 1969-71, chmn. exec. com., 1971-79; dir. Security N.Y. State Corp.; trustee Monroe Savs. Bank. Trustee Rochester Sch. for Deaf, David Hochstein Sch. Music, U. Rochester, Monroe Community Coll., Indsl. Mgmt. Council. Mem. Rochester C. of C., Am. Assn. Rhodes Scholars, Phi Beta Kappa. Club: Country of Rochester. Home: 777 Allens Creek Rd Rochester NY 14618

MC QUILLAN, JOSEPH MICHAEL, credit co. exec.; b. Meridian, Miss., Aug. 9, 1931; s. John Vincent and Florence (Hoban) McQ.; B.S., Creighton U., Omaha, 1956; m. Janet Holst, Aug. 30, 1952 (div.); children—Joseph Michael, James Vincent, Ann Marie, Tom Charles, Mary Clare, Tim Sean. Mgr., Arthur Andersen & Co., C.P.A.'s, Omaha, Los Angeles, 1956-63; comptroller Cudahy Co., Phoenix, 1963-66; sr. v.p., comptroller Asso. Corp. N.Am., N.Y.C., 1969—, Assos. Corp. N.Am., South Bend, Ind., 1966—. Served with USAF, 1951-55. Mem. Nat. Assn. C.P.A.'s, Financial Execs. Inst., Beta Alpha Si. Home: 604 Durango Circle S Irving TX 75062 Office: PO Box 222822 Dallas TX 75222

MC QUILLAN, MARGARET MARY, publishing co. exec.; b. N.Y.C.; d. John A. and Margaret (Higgins) McQuillan; A.B., Coll. New Rochelle, 1945; M.A., Columbia U., 1948. With Harcourt Brace Jovanovich Inc. (formerly Harcourt, Brace & World), N.Y.C., 1949—, asst. sec., 1960-70, sec., 1971—, v.p., 1975—, adminstrv. v.p., 1978—. Home: 125 Crestwood Ave Tuckahoe NY 10707 Office: 757 3d Ave New York NY 10017

MC QUINN, WENDELL JONES, oil co. exec.; b. Johnson County, Ind., Aug. 18, 1923; s. Thomas Wendal and Dorothy Ellen (Jones) McQ.; B.S. in Petroleum Engring., Colo. Sch. Mines, Golden, 1946; postgrad. Stanford U., 1958; LL.D. (hon.), Franklin (Ind.) Coll., 1978; m. Mary Bennett, Jan. 31, 1945; children—Douglas B., Paul B. With Standard Oil Co. Calif., 1946—, mgr. fgn. ops. staff, 1963-67, v.p. fgn., San Francisco, 1968—; dir. Arbian Am. Oil Co.; chmn. bd. Iran Chevron, Inc., Arabian Chevron, Inc. Recipient Disting. Achievement medal Colo. Sch. Mines, 1971; registered profl. engr., Calif. Mem. Am. Arbitration Assn., San Francisco Com. Fgn. Relations, World Trade Club San Francisco, Tau Beta Pi, Theta Tau, Phi Delta Theta. Clubs: Stock Exchange (San Francisco); Univ. (N.Y.C.); Meadow (Fairfax, Calif.). Office: Standard Oil Co Calif 225 Bush St San Francisco CA 94104

MC QUINN, WILLIAM PATRICK, corp. exec.; b. Waterbury, Conn., May 2, 1936; s. William and Bridget (Flynn) McQ.; B.S., Bryant Coll., 1956; m. M. Lorese Hucks, Apr. 17, 1964; children—Kathryn, Norah, Linda, Jennifer. Mgmt. auditor NASA, Washington, 1962-64; asst. controller Scovill Mfg. Co., Waterbury, 1964-67; controller C F & I Steel Co., Pueblo, Colo., 1967-71; v.p. financial services Loews Corp., N.Y.C., 1971-73; chief exec. officer Williams Hudson Am. subsidiary Williams Hudson Group Ltd. Eng., 1973-75, pres. Pegasus Design Group (formerly Williams Hudson Am.), 1975-78; controller M.W. Houck, Inc., Rye, N.Y., 1979—. Served with U.S. Army, 1959. C.P.A., Conn. Mem. Am. Inst. C.P.A.'s, Fin. Execs. Inst. Home: 8 Vista Ave Old Greenwich CT 06870. *If you don't speculate, you won't accumulate.*

MC QUISTAN, RICHMOND BECKETT, educator; b. West New York, N.J., June 12, 1927; s. Alistair C. and Jean (Beckett) McQ.; B.S. in Physics, Purdue U., 1950, M.S., 1952, Ph.D., 1954; m. Marilyn Masters, Aug. 25, 1951; children—Donald Douglas, Bruce Wallace. Supr. solid state physics sect. I T & T Lab., Ft. Wayne, Ind., 1954-56; supr. phys. electronics sec. Honeywell Research Center, 1956-60, prin. scientist, 1962-66; prof. U. Minn., 1960-62, vis. asso. prof., 1964; mem. faculty U. Wis., Milw., 1966—, prof. physics, 1966-68, chmn. dept., 1968-69, asso. dean Coll. Letters and Sci., 1969-71, asst. to vice chancellor, 1971-72, dean Grad. Sch., 1972-75, dir. lab. for surface studies, 1978—; vis. prof. U. Liverpool (Eng.), 1975-76. Served with USNR, 1944-46. Mem. Am. Phys. Soc., Am. Vacuum Soc. (chmn. Midwest sect. 1969), Sigma Xi, Sigma Pi Sigma. Author: Elements of Infrared Technology, 1962 Scalar and Vector Fields, 1964; Campos Escalares y Vectoriales, 1969. Home: 3556 N Murray Ave Shorewood WI 53211 Office: Univ Wis Milwaukee WI 53201

MC QUOWN, O. RUTH, educator; b. Lexington, Ky., July 28, 1920; d. Elam Boles and Omega (Smith) McQ.; B.A., U. Ky., 1942, M.A. (Hagin fellow), 1951; Fulbright scholar, Manchester (Eng.) U., 1954-55; Ph.D. (Arts and Scis. fellow 1958-59, So. Fellowship Fund fellow 1959-60), U. Fla., 1961. Legis planning analyst Dept. Agr., Washington, 1943-45; economist OPA, 1945-48; instr., research asso. polit. sci. U. Ky., 1948-61; asst. prof. U. Fla., Gainesville, 1961-65, asso. prof., 1965-74, prof., 1974—, asst. dean Coll. Arts and Scis., 1971-76, asso. dean, 1976—; cons. Legis. Research Com. State Ky., 1948-50, gov. Ky., Emergency Orgn. State Govt., 1957-58, vice chancellor SUNY, 1970, Conservation Found., 1972-73; vis. evaluator for accrediting of Boston U., New Eng. Assn. Schs. and Colls., 1979. Dept. Agr. grantee, 1962-63; Social Sci. Research Council grantee, 1965-66. Fellow AAUW, mem. Am. Polit. Sci. Assn., So. Polit. Sci. Assn. (sec.), Phi Beta Kappa, Phi Kappa Phi. Democrat. Episcopalian. Author: (with J. B. Shannon) Presidential Politics in Kentucky, 1953; (with J. E. Reeves) Legislative and Congressional Redistricting in Kentucky, 1959; (with G. Kammerer) The City Consultant, 1959; (with W. Hamilton and M. Schneider) The Political Restructuring of a Community, 1964; (with C. Feiss) A Study of the Social, Political and Administrative Setting of the Rookery Bay Ecosystem, 1973; contbr. articles to profl. jours. Home: 3720 SW 15th St Gainesville FL 32608

MC RAE, HAMILTON EUGENE, JR., lawyer; b. Arkadelphia, Ark., Feb. 9, 1905; s. Hamilton Eugene and Katherine (Old) McR.; student U. Ark., 1922-24; LL.B., U. Tex., 1928; m. Adrian Hagaman, Dec. 1, 1933; children—Mary Ann (Mrs. Tom M. Sloan), Hamilton Eugene III. Admitted to Tex. bar, 1928; practice in Eastland, 1928-36, Midland, 1936—; mem. firm Conner & McRae, 1928-32, McRae & McRae, 1932-36, Stubbeman, McRae & Sealy, 1936-57, Stubbeman, McRae, Sealy & Laughlin, 1957-70, Stubbeman, McRae, Sealy, Laughlin & Browder, 1970—. Dir. Depco, Inc. subsidiary DeKalb AgResearch, Inc., Santander Oil Co., Guanipa Oil Co. Pres., Midland Bd. Edn., 1943-44. Former trustee Austin (Tex.) Presbyn. Theol. Sem., Tex. Presbyn. Found.; past dir. Mus. of S.W.; bd. dirs. Permian Basin Petroleum Mus. Library and Hall of Fame, Midland Coll. Found.; fin. adv. com. United Way, Jr. League. Mem. Am., Tex., Midland, Fed. Energy bar assns., Midland C. of C., Sigma Chi, Phi Delta Phi. Democrat. Presbyn. (elder). Clubs: Petroleum, Midland Country (past pres., dir.), Racquet. Home: 406 South L St Midland TX 79701 Office: PO Box 1540 Midland TX 79702

MC RAE, KENNETH DOUGLAS, polit. scientist; b. Toronto, Ont., Can., Jan. 20, 1925; s. Douglas Archibald and Margaret Constance McR.; B.A., U. Toronto, 1946; A.M., Harvard U., 1947, Ph.D., 1954; postgrad. Oxford (Eng.) U., 1948-50; m. Dorothea Annette Simon, Aug. 4, 1950; children—Patricia, Sandra, Karen, Susan. Lectr. in polit. sci. U. Toronto, 1950-52; asst. prof. polit. sci. Carleton U., Ottawa, Ont., 1955-57, asso. prof., 1957-64, prof., 1964—; research supr. Royal Commn. on Bilingualism and Biculturalism, 1964-69. Fellow Royal Soc. Can.; mem. Can. Polit. Sci. Assn. (pres. 1978-79). Author: (with others) The Founding of New Societies: Studies in the History of the United States, Latin America, South Africa, Canada and Australia, 1964, French transl., 1968; Switzerland: Example of Cultural coexistence, 1964; editor: The Six Bookes of a Commonweale (Jean Bodin), 1962; editor and project dir. The Federal Capital: Governmental Institutions, 1969; editor, contbg. author Consociational Democracy: Political Accommodation in Segmented Societies, 1974. Office: Dept Polit Sci Carleton U Ottawa ON K1S 5B6 Canada

MC RAE, ROBERT MALCOLM, JR., U.S. dist. judge; b. Memphis, Dec. 31, 1921; s. Robert Malcolm and Irene (Pontius) McR.; B.A., Vanderbilt U., 1943; LL.B., U. Va., 1948; m. Louise Howry, July 31, 1943; children—Susan Campbell, Robert Malcolm III, Duncan Farquhar, Thomas Alexander Todd. Admitted to Tenn. bar, 1948; practiced in Memphis, 1948-64; partner firm Apperson, Crump, Duzane & McRae, 1955-59, Larkey, Dudley, Blanchard & McRae, 1959-64; judge Tenn. Circuit Ct., 1964-66; U.S. dist. judge Western Dist. Tenn., Memphis, 1966—, chief judge, 1979—. Served to lt. USNR, 1943-46. Mem. Beta Theta Pi, Phi Delta Phi, Omicron Delta Kappa. Episcopalian (pres. Episcopal Churchmen of Tenn. 1964-65). Home: 220 Baronne Pl Memphis TN 38117 Office: 167 N Main St Memphis TN 38103

MC RAE, THOMAS KENNETH, investment banker; b. Richmond, Va., July 7, 1906; s. Christopher D. and S. Alice (Lawrence) McR.; A.B., U. Richmond, 1927; grad. Am. Inst. Banking, 1931; grad. Sch. Banking, Rutgers U., 1938; m. Marion L. White, Sept. 11, 1937; children—Thomas K., John Daniel. With 1st & Mchts. Nat. Bank, 1927-71, asst. cashier, 1940-46, asst. v.p., 1946-49, v.p., 1949-63, sr. v.p., 1963-71; v.p. Davenport & Co. of Va., Inc., investment bankers, 1971—. Chartered fin. analyst. Mem. Richmond Soc. Financial Analysts, Va. Mus. Fine Arts, Phi Gamma Delta. Baptist. Mason, Rotarian. Clubs: Bond, Country of Virginia, Downtown (Richmond). Home: 9 Dahlgren Rd Richmond VA 23233 Office: Ross Bldg 8th and Main Sts Richmond VA 23219

MC RAVEN, DALE KEITH, TV writer and producer; b. Pulaski, Ill., Mar. 5, 1939; s. Raymond Leslie and Ella Marie (Palmer) McR.; student Phoenix Jr. Coll., 1956; m. 2d, Susan Bracken, Mar. 28, 1976; children—David, Renee, Michael, Cheryl. Producer, story editor Partridge Family, Screen Gems Studios, 1971; creator, exec. producer, head writer Texas Wheelers, Mary Tyler Moore Prodns., Studio City, Calif., 1974, producer Betty White Show, 1977; exec. producer, creator Angie, Paramount Studios, Hollywood, Calif., 1978; creator, producer, head writer Mork and Mindy, 1978-79. Recipient Best Comedy Series and Best New Comedy Series awards Peoples Choice award, 1979; honored for writing contbns. Dick Van Dyke Show, 1965; Emmy nomination for producing Mork and Mindy. Mem. Writers Guild Am. (award for Dick Van Dyke show 1965), Acad. Motion Picture Arts and Scis., Acad. TV Arts and Scis. (Emmy award, 1966). Office: 5451 Marathon Ave Los Angeles CA 90038

MC RORIE, ROBERT ANDERSON, JR., educator; b. Statesville, N.C., May 7, 1924; s. Robert Anderson and Helen Weedon (Deaton) McR.; B.S. in Biochemistry, N.C. State U., 1949, M.S., 1951; Ph.D., U. Tex., 1954; m. Deane Landis, Oct. 4, 1946; children—Susan Deane, Linda Kay, Donald Karl. Asst. prof. chemistry, asst. biochemist Coll. Expt. Sta., U. Ga., 1953-58, asso. prof. biochemistry, 1958-64, prof., 1964—, asso. dean Grad. Sch., 1959-68, dir. gen. research, 1959-71, asst. v.p. for research, 1968-71; research participant biology div. Oak Ridge Nat. Lab., summers 1957, 58; program dir. research mission to East Pakistan, USAID, 1971; mem. Ga. Nuclear Adv. Commn., 1963-64; mem. Ga. Sci. and Tech. Commn., 1964—, mem. exec. com., 1969—; mem. adv. bd. Chem. Abstracts Service, 1968-70. Served with USAAF, 1942-46. Lederle Research fellow N.C. State U., 1949-59; Research scientist Biochem. Inst., U. Tex., 1950-51; Eli Lilley Research fellow U. Tex., 1951-52, Rosalie B. Hite Cancer Research fellow, 1952-53. Mem. Am. Chem. Soc., Am. Soc. Biol. Chemists, Am. Soc. Microbiology, AAAS, Sigma Xi, Phi Kappa Phi, Phi Lambda Upsilon, Phi Sigma. Research in intermediary metabolism and enzymology, tetrahydrofolate function, methionine biosynthesis and uronic acid metabolism, biochemistry of reproduction, sperm enzymes. Home: 102 Cloverhurst Circle Athens GA 30606

MC ROSTIE, CLAIR NEIL, educator; b. Owatonna, Minn., Dec. 16, 1930; s. Neil Hale and Myrtle Julia (Peterson) McR.; B.S., Gustavus Adolphus Coll.; M.A., Mich. State U., 1953; Ph.D., U. Wis., 1964; m. Ursula Anne Schwieger, Aug. 29, 1968. Faculty, Gustavus Adolphus Coll., St. Peter, Minn., 1958—, chmn. dept. econs. and bus.; teaching asst. Sch. Commerce, U. Wis., 1960-62; lectr. European div. U. Md., 1966-67. Mem. adv. commn. Minn. Dept. Manpower Services, 1967-71; mem. North Central Regional Manpower Adv. Com. Bd. dirs. Midwest China Resource Study Center. Served with AUS, 1954-56. Research fellow Fed. Res. Bank of Chgo., 1962-63. Mem. Am., Minn. (dir.) econs. assns., Am. Finance Assn., Financial Execs. Inst., Sierra Club (exec. com. North Star chpt., Midwest regional conservation com.; 4th officer nat. council). Editor: Global Resources: Perspectives and Alternatives. Home: Rural Route 1 Saint Peter MN 56082

MCSHEA, JOSEPH, bishop; b. Lattimer, Pa., Feb. 22, 1907; s. Roger Aloysius and Jeanette (Beach) McS.; student St. Charles Sem., 1923-26; Ph.D., Pontifical Roman Sem., 1928, S.T.D., 1932. Ordained priest Roman Cath. Ch., 1931; prof. St. Charles Sem., Overbrook, Phila., 1932-35; ofcl. Sacred Oriental Congregation, Vatican City, 1935-38; sec. Apostolic Delegation, Washington, 1938-52; apptd. auxiliary bishop of Phila., 1952, bishop Allentown Diocese 1961, 1st bishop, 1961—. Home: 2920 Chew St Allentown PA 18104 Office: 202 N 17th St Allentown PA 18104

MC SHEFFREY, GERALD RAINEY, architect, city planner; b. Belfast, Ireland, Aug. 13, 1931; s. Hugh and Jane (Piggot) McS.; student Belfast Coll. Tech., 1950-56; Diploma in Architecture, Univ.

Coll., U. London, 1959; Diploma in Civic Design, U. Edinburgh (Scotland), 1963; m. Norma Isabella Lowry, June 4, 1956; children—Laurence, Niall, Aidan. Archtl. asst. various archtl. firms, Belfast, 1950-57; design architect Munce and Kennedy, Belfast, 1957-62; architect/planner Liverpool (Eng.) City Planning Dept. and Livingston New Town, 1963-65; asso. partner James Munc Partnership, Belfast, 1965-68; prin. planning officer (design) Belfast City Planning Dept., 1968-71; mem. faculty U. Kans., 1971-79, dir. archtl. studies, 1976-79; Belfast regional architect, dir. devel. No. Ireland Housing, 1973-76; prof. architecture, dean Coll. Architecture, Planning and Design, Ill. Inst. Tech., 1979—; external examiner in urban design and landscape studies U. Edinburgh, 1973-76. Fulbright scholar, 1965. Fellow Royal Inst. Brit. Architects, Royal Town Planning Inst. Episcopalian. Author: (with James Munce Partnership) Londonderry Area Plan, 1968. Office: 3360 S State St Chicago IL 60616

MCSHERRY, WILLIAM PATRICK, broadcasting exec.; b. Amatol, N.J., Sept. 16, 1918; s. Thomas Charles and Marie (Redmond) McS.; B.A., St. Peters Coll., 1940; m. Bobette Hope Ryan, Sept. 4, 1918; children—Patrice, Kevin, Sean. Writer, Blue Network, NBC, N.Y.C., 1941-49; writer ABC News, N.Y.C., 1949-58, producer John Daly and the News, N.Y.C., 1958-60, nat. news editor, asst. news dir. N.Y.C., 1960-64, western news dir., Los Angeles, 1964—; Mem. So. Calif. News Dirs. Assn. (dir. 1969), Radio and TV News Dirs. Assn., Cath. Press Counsel (dir.), Sigma Delta Chi. Clubs: Los Angeles Press, Nat. Press. Office: ABC TV Center 4151 Prospect Hollywood CA 90027

MC SHINE, KYNASTON LEIGH, curator; b. Port of Spain, Trinidad, Feb. 20, 1935; s. Austen H. Mc S.; A.B., Dartmouth Coll., 1958; postgrad. U. Mich., 1958-59, Inst. Fine Arts, N.Y. U., 1960-64. Asst. prof. art history Hunter Coll., 1968-69; lectr. in art history Sch. Visual Arts, N.Y.C., 1969-76; curator of painting and sculpture Jewish Museum, N.Y.C., 1965-68, acting dir. mus., 1967-68; asso. curator painting and sculpture Mus. Modern Art, N.Y.C., 1968-71, curator painting and sculpture, 1971—; mem. visual arts com. N.Y.C. Cultural Council, N.Y. State Council on Arts; mem. adv. com. Skowhegan Sch. Painting and Sculpture. Mem. Am. Fedn. Arts (trustee), Internat. Assn. Art Critics, Coll. Art Assn., Asm. Assn. Mus.'s. Author catalogs: Josef Albers: Homage to the Square, 1964; Primary Structures, 1966; Information, 1970; editor, contbg. author catalogs: Marcel Duchamp, 1973; The Natural Paradise: Painting in America 1800-1950, 1976; Jackie Winsor, 1979. Office: 11 W 53d St New York NY 10019

MC SORLEY, ARTHUR, constrn. co. exec.; b. Pitts., Nov. 19, 1928; s. Arthur and Dorothy (Jacob) McS.; B.S. in Civil Engring., Lafayette Coll., 1951; m. Nancy Jean Queer, Dec. 27, 1952; children—Arthur, Holly, Christine, Susan. Civil engr. John F. Casey Co., Pitts., 1955-65, mgr. sales, 1965-67, dir. purchases, 1968-69, pres., chief adminstrv. officer, 1969-70, pres., chief exec. officer, 1970; dir. Portec Inc., River Sand and Supply Co. Bd. dirs. Fox Chapel Sch. Authority, Western Pa. Safety Council. Served with USMCR, 1951-54. Mem. Gen. Contractors Assn. Pa. (gov.), Constructors Assn. Western Pa. (gov.). Clubs: Pitts. Field (dir.), Duquesne (Pitts.). Home: 300 Wildberry Rd Pittsburgh PA 15238 Office: Box 1888 Pittsburgh PA 15230

MC SPADDEN, GEORGE ELBERT, educator; b. Albuquerque, Feb. 25, 1912; s. Elbert Leonidas and Zoe Elizabeth (Faber) McS.; A.B., U. N.Mex., 1933, A.M., 1935; Ph.D., Stanford, 1947; m. Natalia Jane Allen, Oct. 11, 1941; children—Thomas Edward, Robert Allen, George David, John Steven. Tchr., Bernalillo County (N.Mex.) Pub. Schs., 1933-34, Santa Fe Pub. Schs., 1934-35; teaching asst. Stanford, 1935-39, sec. dept. Romance langs., 1937-39, instr. Spanish, 1941; instr. Spanish and Latin, U. Idaho, 1939-40; asso. prof. Spanish, U. B.C., 1946-54; vis. asso. prof. Spanish, U. Chgo., 1953-54, asso. prof., 1954-57; prof. George Washington U., 1957-67, exec. officer dept. Romance langs. and lit., 1957-61, coordinator grad. studies Romance langs., 1961-67, cons., 1967—; prof., head dept. Romance langs. U. N.C., Greensboro, 1967-75, dir. Latin Am. studies, 1976-79, emeritus, 1979—; vis. prof. applied Spanish linguistics NDEA Insts., Fairfield U., summers 1966, 68. Gen. chmn. Pacific N.W. Conf. Fgn. Lang. Tchrs., 1950-51, editor bull., 1952-53; mem. corp. Inter-Varsity Christian Fellowship, U.S., 1954—. Travel and study fellow Carnegie Corp. and Inst. Internat. Edn., 1938-39; first Pan Am. Airways travel fellow to S.Am., 1938-39. Served to lt. comdr. USNR, 1941-45. Mem. Am. Assn. Tchrs. Spanish and Portuguese (pres. Ill., v.p. Chgo. 1956-57, pres. elect 1957; 1st nat. v.p. 1966), Modern Lang. Assn., South Atlantic Modern Lang. Assn. (chmn. Spanish I sect. 1971), Am. Assn. Tchrs. French, South Atlantic Assn. Depts. Fgn. Langs. (pres. 1976-77), So. Humanities Assn., Mountain Interstate Fgn. Lang. Conf., Phi Kappa Phi, Sigma Delta Pi, Pi Delta Phi. Presbyn. (elder). Author: An Introduction to Spanish Usage, 1956; Spanish Spoken in Chilili, N.Mex.; The Spanish Prologue before 1700, 1977; Don Quijote and the Spanish Prologues, 1978-79; contbr. articles to profl. jours., bulls. Home: 3004 W Market St Greensboro NC 27403

MC SPADDEN, PETER FORD, advt. agy. exec.; b. Montclair, N.J., Oct. 2, 1930; s. Chester F. and Janet (Chase) McS.; A.B., Dartmouth, 1952; m. Barbara Dodds, June 30, 1956; children—Douglas Dodds, David Ford, Peter Chase. Account exec. McCann-Erickson, Inc., N.Y.C., 1956-59; with Dancer-Fitzgerald-Sample, Inc., N.Y.C., 1959—, v.p., account supr., 1965-68, sr. v.p., mgmt. supr., 1968-72, exec. v.p., 1972-74, pres., chief operating officer, 1974—, also dir.; dir. Broadstreet Communications, Inc.; bd. dirs. Am. Advt. Fedn.; mem. Nat. Advt. Rev. Bd. Pres. Greenwich (Conn.) Young Republican Club, 1966-67; campaign mgr. Congressman Lowell P. Weicker, 1968, Senator Weicker, 1970, 78; mem. Rep. Town Com., Greenwich, 1965-68. Served to lt. (j.g.) USNR, 1952-55. Clubs: Riverside (Conn.) Yacht; Greenwich Country. Home: Carriglea Dr Riverside CT 06878 Office: 405 Lexington Ave New York NY 10017

MCSURDY, ELMER BRAZIER, ednl., med. adminstr.; b. Pottsville, Pa., June 25, 1925; s. Elmer Frank and Edith (Shuttleworth) McS.; B.A., Pa. State U., 1948; m. Arlene Patricia Paul, July 26, 1946; children—Robert E., Gary M. Asst. mgr. retail sales S.S. Kresge Co., Pottsville, Pa., 1948-49; asst. supt. Schuykill County Instl. Dist. (Pa.), 1949-60; dir. adminstrn. Pennhurst State Sch. and Hosp., Spring City, Pa., 1960—. Mem. Humane Fire Co., Liberty Fire Co. Served with AUS, 1943-44. Mem. Am. Assn. Mental Health Adminstrs., Am. Legion. Lutheran. Elk, Rotarian (pres. Spring City-Royersford 1975-76). Home: 800 Church St Royersford PA 19468 Office: Pennhurst State Sch and Hosp Spring City PA 19475

MC SWAIN, ANGUS STEWART, JR., univ. dean; b. Bryan, Tex., Nov. 26, 1923; s. Angus Stewart and Lois (Pipkin) McS.; B.S. in Civil Engring., Tex. A. and M. U., 1947; LL.B., Baylor U., 1949; LL.M., U. Mich., 1951; m. Betty Ann McCartney, June 3, 1956; 1 son, Angus Earl. Admitted to Tex. bar, 1949; mem. faculty Baylor U. Law Sch., 1949—, prof. law, 1956—, dean, 1965—. Mem. panel arbitrators Fed. Mediation and Conciliation Service. Served to 1st lt., C.E., AUS, 1943-46. Mem. Am., Tex. (chmn. family law sect. 1967-69, chmn. com. on standards of admission 1972-73, 77-79) bar assns., Tau Beta Pi, Phi Alpha Delta Author: (with Wendorf) Cases and Materials on Texas Trusts and Probate, 1965; Supplementary Cases and Materials on Property, 1965, 78; (with Norvell and Simpkins) Cases and Materials for Texas Land Practice, 1968. Home: 4600 Kenny Ln Waco TX 76710

MC SWAIN, WILLIAM ADNEY, lawyer; b. Winston Salem, N.C., June 7, 1904; s. William A. and Caroline Thompson (Lee) McS.; B.S., U. S.C., 1925; LL.B., George Washington U., 1927; m. Marian Hartig, Oct. 4, 1941; children—Barbara Ann, Marian, Jane, Nan, Betty Lee. Admitted to D.C. bar, 1927, Ill., bar, 1931; with Eckhart, McSwain, Hassell & Silliman and predecessors, Chgo., 1931—. Dir. De Soto Securities Co. Life trustee Art Inst. Chgo. Mem. Am., Ill., Chgo. (pres. 1966), 7th Fed. Circuit Ct. (pres. 1965) bar assns. Presbyn. Clubs: Union League (Chgo.); Glenview (Ill.). Home: 1040 Sunset Rd Winnetka IL 60093 Office: One First Nat Plaza Chicago IL 60603

MC SWEEN, CIRILO ALEJANDRO, ins. broker; b. Panama City, Republic of Panama, July 8, 1932; s. Ernesto and Veronica (Lopez) McS.; came to U.S., 1950, naturalized, 1967; B.A. in Econs., U. Ill., 1954; m. Gwendolyn Amacker, Oct. 27, 1952. Pres. McSween Ins. Counselors and Brokers, Chgo., 1972—; v.p. Ind. Bank Chgo., 1966—, also dir.; pres. Cirilo-McDonald's, Inc., McDonald franchise, Chgo., 1969—. Vice-pres., nat. treas. SCLC, 1968—; v.p. Chgo. Econ. Devel. Corp., 1973—. Bd. dirs. Garrett-Evangel. Sem. Life, qualifying mem. Million Dollar Round Table, 1958. Home: 9205 S Parnell St Chicago IL 60620 Office: 230 S State St Chicago IL 60604

MC SWEENEY, EDWARD, mgmt. cons.; b. N.Y.C., May 23, 1900; s. Edward and Mary (McCarthy) McS.; Mass. Inst. Technology, 1923; m. Mary Hartzell, Feb. 24, 1931; children—Edward, III, Mary Denis, John. With Conde Nast, N.Y.C., 1923-31; founder, pres. Edward McSweeney Asso., management cons., 1933—; dir. Amerace Corp., Curtiss-Wright Corp., Lynch Corp., Mueller-Martinll Corp., Woodway Realty, Concord Fund. Former chmn. Westchester Charter Revision Com. Mem. Nat. Heart Com., Nat. Com. Against Mental Illness, Nat. Soc. Prevention Blindness. Bd. dirs. Printing Mgmt. Edn. Trust; trustee asso., former chmn. bd. trustees Bard Coll. Served with USN, World War I. Recipient Bard Coll. medal, Elmer Voight award, Friedman medal, Golden Keys award, Pres.'s medal Internat. Graphic Arts Edn. Assn., Westchester County Distinguished Service award. Fellow Brit. Inst. Printing; mem. Am. Mgmt. Assn. (all planning council), Am. Arbitration Assn., Printing Industries Am. (life). Clubs: Racquet & Tennis; Sky; Woods Hole Golf. Author: Organization for More Efficient Management; also numerous articles on mgmt. and marketing. Home and Office: 200 E 66th St New York NY 10021

MC SWINEY, JAMES WILMER, pulp and paper mfg. co. exec.; b. McEwen, Tenn., Nov. 13, 1915; s. James S. and Delia (Conroy) McS.; grad. Harvard Advanced Mgmt. Program, 1954; m. Jewel Bellar, 1940; children—Charles Ronald, Margaret Ann. Lab. technician, shipping clk. Nashville div. The Mead Corp., 1934-39, asst. office mgr. Harriman div., 1939, plant mgr., Rockport, Ind., 1940, asst. office mgr. Kingsport (Tenn.) div., 1941-44, exec. asst. to pres., Dayton, Ohio, 1954-57, v.p. devel., 1957-59, adminstrv v.p., 1959, group v.p., gen. mgr. Mead Bd. div., 1961-63, exec. v.p. corp., 1963-67, pres., 1968-71, chmn. bd., chief exec. officer, 1971-78, chmn. bd., 1978—, also dir.; accountant, office mgr., asst. sec.-treas. Brunswick Pulp & Paper Co. (Ga.), 1944-54, now dir.; dir. Ga. Kraft Co., Winters Nat. Bank & Trust Co., Dayton, Gem City Savs. Assn., Dayton, Northwood Pulp Ltd., Prince George, B.C., Vulcan Materials Co., Birmingham, Phillips Industries. Trustee, Sinclair Coll., Dayton. Served as aviation cadet USAAF, 1942-44. Home: 2300 Ridgeway Rd Dayton OH 45419 Office: Mead World Hdqrs Dayton OH 45463

MC TAGGART, LYNNE ANN, editor, writer; b. Yonkers, N.Y., Jan. 23, 1951; d. Robert Charles and Olga Cecelia (Gargiullo) McTaggart; student Northwestern U., 1969-71; B.A., Bennington Coll., 1973. With Playboy Mag., Chgo., 1971-72, Atlantic Monthly, Boston, 1972-73; asst. editor Sat. Review/World, N.Y.C., 1973-74; asso. editor Chgo. Tribune-N.Y. News Syndicate, N.Y.C., 1974-75, mng. editor, 1975-77. Recipient award of merit N.Y.C. Women's Press Club, 1976; 3d prize Nat. Coordinating Council of Lit. Mags., 1971-73. Mem. Alpha Lambda Delta. Author: The Baby Brokers: The Marketing of White Babies in America, 1980; editor-in-chief Bennington's lit. mag. Silo, 1971-73; contbr. articles to profl. jours. Home: 448 E 20th St New York NY 10009

MCTAGUE, PETER JAMES, utilities exec.; b. Bklyn., May 3, 1928; s. Peter and Margaret Ann (Rae) McT.; B.E.E., Cornell U., 1948; J.D., St. John's U., 1954; m. Virginia Mae Kane, Nov. 14, 1954; children—Lois Claire, Bruce Christian. Admitted to N.Y. bar, Conn. bar; various engring. and adminstrv. positions L.I. Lighting Co., Mineola, N.Y., 1948-57; asst. v.p. Citizens Utilities Co., Stamford, Conn., 1957-60; engring. fin. cons. W.C. Gilman Co., N.Y.C., 1960-63; mgmt. fin. cons. Gilbert Assos., Inc., Reading, Pa., 1963-74; pres., chief exec. officer Green Mountain Power Corp., Burlington, Vt., 1974—, also dir.; dir. Assn. Edison Illuminating Cos., Vt. Electric Power Corp. Bd. dirs. Electric Council of New Eng.; mem. exec. com. Electric Vehicle Council, 1975—. Mem. Edison Electric Inst. (policy com. on conservation and energy mgmt. 1975—, rate research com. 1967-70), Electric Power Research Inst. (research adv. com. 1980—, energy mgmt. and utilization task force 1977-79), Edison Elec. Inst./Elec. Power Research Inst. (com. on financing demonstration plants 1977—), Atomic Indsl. Forum (nuclear fuel financing com. 1973-75). Chmn. 1979 United Way of Chittenden Cty., Vt. Campaign; 1977-78 Vermont Savings Bond Drive. Voting mem. Shelburne Museum, Friend of University of Vt. Am. Bar Assn., Inst. Chartered Fin. Analysts, IEEE, Nat. Assn. Accts., N. Y. Soc. Security Analysts. Republican. Clubs: The Metropolitan Club (NYC); Downtown Executives Club (NYC); Ethan Allen Club (Burlington); contributing articles to various energy industry and gen. bus. publs. Home: Mount Philo Rd Charlotte VT 05445 Office: 1 Main St Burlington VT 05401*

MC TEER, MAUREEN ANNE, lawyer, wife of Can. prime minister; b. Cumberland, Ont., Can., Feb. 27, 1952; d. John J. McTeer; B.A., LL.B., U. Ottawa (Ont.); m. Charles Joseph (Joe) Clark, June 30, 1973; 1 dau., Catherine Jane. *

MC VAUGH, ROGERS, botanist, educator; b. Bklyn., May 30, 1909; s. Roy and Elizabeth (Skinner) McV.; A.B. with highest honors in Botany, Swarthmore Coll., 1931; Ph.D. in Botany, U. Pa., 1935; m. Ruth Beall, Sept. 8, 1937; children—Michael Rogers, Jenifer Beall (Mrs. Edgar Curtis Taylor, Jr.). From instr. to asst. prof. botany U. Ga., 1935-38; asso. botanist, div. plant exploration and introduction Dept. Agr., 1938-46; mem. faculty U. Mich., 1946—, prof. botany, 1951—, Harley Harris Bartlett prof. botany, 1974—, curator vascular plants univ. Herbarium, 1946—, dir. Herbarium, 1972-75. Program dir. systematic biology NSF, 1955-56; mem. adv. bd. Hunt Bot. Library, Pitts., 1961-64; research asso. Field Museum, Chgo., 1958—; mem. editorial com. Internat. Assn. Plant Taxonomy, 1964—, sec. com. spermatophyta, 1964-75, v.p., 1969-72, pres., 1972-75. Recipient merit award Bot. Soc. Am., 1977, Sociedad Botánica de México, 1978. Mem. Am. Soc. Plant Taxonomists (pres. 1956; editor Brittonia, 1959-63), Assn. Tropical Biology, Soc. Botánica de México (hon.). Contbr. articles to profl. jours. Home: 1925 Scottwood Ave Ann Arbor MI 48104

MCVAY, DONALD C., JR., food co. exec.; b. Trenton, Mo., Aug. 30, 1915; s. Donald C. and Beatrice (Bowne) McV.; A.B., U. Mo., 1936; postgrad. Princeton, 1936-38; M.B.A., Harvard, 1940. Cons. McKinsey & Co., N.Y.C., 1947-66; sr. v.p. corporate devel. H.J. Heinz Co., Pitts., 1966—, also dir. Mem. Sigma Nu. Episcopalian. Clubs: Duquesne, Pitts. Golf (Pitts); Rolling Rock. Home: 3955 Bigelow Blvd Pittsburgh PA 15213 Office: PO Box 57 Pittsburgh PA 15230

MCVAY, JOHN EDWARD, profl. football club exec.; b. Bellaire, Ohio, Jan. 5, 1931; s. John A. and Helen (Andrews) McV.; B.S. in Edn., Miami U., Oxford, Ohio, 1953; M.A. in Sch. Adminstrn., Kent (Ohio) State U., 1963; m. Eva Lee; children—John R., James P., Timothy G. Asst. football coach, instr. phys. edn. Mich. State U., 1962-65; head coach, dir. athletics U. Dayton, Ohio, 1965-74; head coach, gen. mgr. Memphis in World Football League, 1975-78; head football coach New York Giants, Nat. Football League, 1977-78; dir. player personnel San Francisco 49ers, Nat. Football League, 1979—. Exec. dir. Catholic Youth Council, Canton, Ohio, 1959-62. Named to Miami U. Athletic Hall of Fame. Mem. Sigma Chi, Phi Epsilon Kappa, Phi Delta Kappa. Office: c/o San Francisco 49ers 711 Nevada St Redwood City CA 94061

MCVERRY, THOMAS LEO, mfg. co. exec.; b. Pitts., Aug. 2, 1938; s. Thomas Leo and Anna Alberta McV.; B.B.A., U. Pitts., 1961, M.B.A., 1962; m. Jean Lee Smith, Apr. 29, 1961; children—Thomas Leo, III, Michael Scott, Amy Lynn. Sr. accountant Haskins & Sells, N.Y.C., 1962-66; controller Church & Dwight, N.Y.C., 1966-70, treas., 1970-73; v.p. fin. Rexham Corp., Charlotte, N.C., 1973—. Mem. Waldwick (N.J.) Bd. Edn., 1970-73, v.p., 1972-73; mem. Charlotte Catholic High Sch. Bd. Edn., 1977-80, chmn., 1979-80; chmn. fin. com. St. Gabriel's Catholic Ch., Charlotte, 1977-80. Recipient Bachrac, Sanderbac Acctg. award, 1961. Mem. Am. Inst. C.P.A.'s, N.Y. State Soc. C.P.A.'s, Fin. Execs. Inst. Republican. Clubs: Carmel Country, Charlotte Athletic. Office: 1201 Greenwood Cliff Charlotte NC 28204

MCVEY, JAMES WILLIAM, corp. exec.; b. Monmouth, Ill., Nov. 9, 1931; s. Richard Wright and Margaret (Foster) McV.; B.A., Monmouth Coll., 1953; m. Eleanor Louise Lauder, Nov. 15, 1953; children—Margret Lynne, Catherine Anne, Jane Louise, Mark Lauder. Various positions Oscar Mayer & Co., including sales mgr., Phila. and Chgo., regional sales mgr., gen. sales mgr., v.p. sales, v.p. mktg., now group v.p. mktg. provisions and procurement, Madison, Wis. Served with USN, 1953-56. Mem. Am. Meat Inst. Club: Maple Bluff Country. Office: 910 Mayer Ave Madison WI 53704

MC VEY, PHILLIP, educator; b. Wichita, Aug. 19, 1921; s. Hugh Given and Carolyn (English) McV.; B.A., U. Wichita, 1942; I.A., Harvard U., 1943, M.B.A., 1947; Ph.D., Ohio State U., 1954; m. Marian Elizabeth Crossen, Aug. 28, 1948; children—Carolyn, Bruce, Martha. Instr. mktg. Ohio U., 1947-51; asst. prof. engring. adminstrn. Case Inst., 1952-55; asso. prof. mktg. U. Nebr., 1955-61, prof., 1961—, chmn. dept., 1968-77; cons. marketing research, sales analysis, sales mgmt. Served with AUS, 1942-46; col. Res. (ret.). Mem. Am. Marketing Assn. (pres. Omaha-Lincoln chpt. 1958—), Beta Gamma Sigma, Delta Sigma Pi. Club: Rotary. Author: Retirement Income Plans for Outside Salesmen, National Sales Execs, Inc., 1953. Home: 3611 Van Dorn St Lincoln NE 68506 Office: Coll Bus Adminstrn U Nebr Lincoln NE 68588

MC VEY, WILLIAM MOZART, sculptor, educator; b. Boston, July 12, 1905; s. Silas R. and Cornelia (Mozart) McV.; grad. Cleve. Sch. Art, 1928; student Rice Inst., 1923-25, Academie Colarossi and Academie Scandinave, Paris, France, 1929-31; pupil of Despiau, Paris, 1929-31; m. Leza Marie Sullivan, Mar. 31, 1932. Tchr., Cleve. Mus., 1932, Houston Mus., 1936-38, U. Tex., 1939-46, Ohio State U., summer 1946, Cranbrook Art Acad., 1946-53; head sculpture dept. Cleve. Inst. Art, 1953-67; vis. sculptor Sch. Fine Arts, Ohio State U., 1963-64; sculpture in permanent collections IBM Collection, U. Mus., Pomona, Calif., Wichita (Kans.) Art Mus., Cleve., Houston, Syracuse and Cranbrook museums, Harvard Library, Smithsonian Instn., Washington, Nat. Cathedral, Washington, Ariana Mus., Geneva, Switzerland, others; publicly owned works include heroic reliefs and doors San Jacinto Monument, Tex., door FTC, Washington, doors and reliefs Tex. Meml. Mus. reliefs Lakeview Terrace Housing Project, Cleve., heroic grizzly Natural History Mus., figure Abercrombie Lab., Rice Inst., monument to David Crockett, Ozona, Tex., to James Bowie, Texarkana, Tex., 9 foot bronze of Winston Churchill, Brit. Embassy, Washington, St. Margaret of Scotland and Jan Hus at Washington Cathedral, St. Olga of Russia, Simon de Montfort, Churchill Bay, Stephen Langton, Churchill Bay, Sir Edward Coke, Churchill Bay, heroic U.S. shields Fed. Bldg., Cleve., Jennings Meml., University Circle, Cleve., granite hippo (with Victor Gruen) Eastgate Shopping Center, Detroit, 5 ton whale Lincoln Center, Urbana, Ill., bronze hippo Cleveland Heights Children's Library, Berry Monument bronze Cleve. Hopkins Airport, panels (with Eero Saarinen) Christ Luth. Ch., Mpls., bronze of George Washington at Washington Sq., Cleve., stainless steel and bronze B Clef logo Blossom Music Center, Senator Harry F. Byrd Meml., Capitol Grounds, Richmond, Va., relief portrait J. Edgar Hoover, FBI Acad., Quantico, Va., 65 foot O Bell tower for Hiram (Ohio) Coll. and Mt. Union Coll., Alliance, Ohio, bronze portrait Osborne Collection, Yale U. Library, numerous others. Chmn. nat. screening com. Fulbrights Grants, 1961-63. Mem. fine arts com. Cleve. City Planning Commn., 1963-69; art cons. Am. Soc. Metals; adv. bd. Cleve. Inst. Art. Recipient 1st award Nat. Sculpture Show, L.A. County Fair, 1941, $500 award Ceramic Nat., Syracuse, 1951, 52, $500 award Wichita Decorative Arts Nat., 1951, Ewald prize Detroit Inst. Art, 1952, Sculpture award Nat. Archtl. Ceramic, 1956, award of merit Mich. Acad. Sci., Arts and Letters, 1951, 1st Internat. Cultural Exchange Ceramic Exhibit, Geneva, 1960, Bernard award 7th ann. drawing and small sculpture show, Muncie, Ind., 1961, also 10 first awards Cleve. May shows; $500 Creative Fine Arts award Kulas Found., Cleve., 1964; Purchase award Butler Inst. Am. Art, 1967, 1st award Internat. Platform Assn., 1979, awards Internat. Soc. for Artificial Organs, Cleve. Clinic; Garfield fellow Hiram Coll. Served to maj. USAAF, W.W. II. Decorated Army Commendation medal. Fellow Nat. Sculpture Soc.; asso. NAD; mem. Coll. Arts Assn., Am. Soc. Aesthetics, Internat. Platform Assn. (gov.). Home and Office: 18 Pepper Ridge Rd Cleveland OH 44124

MC VICKER, CHARLES TAGGART, artist; b. Canonsburg, Pa., Aug. 31, 1930; s. Carl Walter and Mary Ruth (Washabaugh) McV.; B.A., Principia Coll., Elsah, Ill., 1952; B.F.A., Art Center Coll. Design, Los Angeles, 1957; m. Lucy Claire Graves, Mar. 20, 1954; children—Lauri, Bonnie, Heather. Staff artist Alexander Chaite Studios, 1957-58; freelance illustrator and painter, 1958—; asst. prof. Pratt Phoenix Sch. Art, N.Y.C.; one-man shows include: Thompson Gallery, N.Y.C., 1967; represented in permanent collections: U.S. Capitol, Am. Hist. Assn., Soc. Illustrators, USAF, Princeton U. Served with AUS, 1952-54. Mem. Soc. Illustrators (exec. com. 1972-74, pres. 1976-78), Am. Watercolor Soc., Graphic Artists Guild (v.p. nat. exec. com.), Princeton Art Assn. Home: 4 Willow St Princeton NJ 08540 Office: 230 E 44th St New York NY 10017

MC VICKER, JESSE JAY, artist, educator; b. Vici, Okla., Oct. 18, 1911; s. Jesse Allen and Clara Mae (Hendrick) McV.; B.A., Okla. State U., 1940, M.A., 1941; m. Laura Beth Paul, Aug. 20, 1938. Faculty, Okla. State U., Stillwater, 1941—, prof. art, 1959-77, prof. emeritus, 1977—, head dept., 1959-77. Exhbns. include Med. Mus. Art, Mus. Non-Objective Painting, Chgo, Art Inst., N.A.D., Library of Congress, San Francisco Mus. Art, Denver Art Mus., Pa. Acad. Fine Arts, Carnegie Inst., Print Club Phila., Salon Des Realities Nouvelles, Paris, France, Dallas, Mus. Fine Arts, Galleria Origine, Rome, Italy, Whitney Mus. Am. Art; represented in permanent collections Library of Congress, Seattle Art Mus., Dallas Mus. Fine Arts, Met. Mus. Art, Joslyn Meml. Art Mus. Served with USNR, 1943-46. Mem. Soc. Am. Graphic Artists, Audubon Artists, Print Club Phila., Pi Kappa Alpha. Home: 4212 N Washington Stillwater OK 74074

MC VIE, ALEXANDER MALCOLM, pharm. co. exec.; b. Liverpool, Eng., Nov. 4, 1919; s. Alexander M. and Nina (Coupe) McV.; came to U.S., 1920, naturalized, 1942; A.B., Wabash Coll., 1941; M.B.A., Harvard, 1947; m. Sue Anne Eveleigh, Mar. 19, 1943; children—Alexander Malcolm III, Susan E., Douglas S. With Ernst & Ernst, 1947-48; with Eli Lilly & Co., Indpls., 1948—, asst. treas., 1959-65, dir. prodn. planning, 1965-66, v.p. facilities and ops. planning, 1966-68, pres. Elanco Products Co. div., 1968-77, exec. v.p. parent co., 1976—, also dir.; dir. Indpls. Life Ins. Co., Ind. Nat. Corp. Hon. trustee Children's Mus. Indpls.; v.p. bd. trustees Wabash Coll., Crawfordsville, Ind.; trustee Meth. Hosp. Fund. Served to capt. USAAF, 1942-46. C.P.A., Ind. Mem. Am. Inst. C.P.A.'s, Ind. Assn. C.P.A.'s, Indpls. C. of C. (dir.), Beta Theta Pi. Episcopalian. Clubs: Crooked Stick Golf, University (Indpls.); Desert Forest Golf (Ariz.). Home: Rural Route 2 Box 108B Zionsville IN 46077 Office: 307 E McCarty St Indianapolis IN 46206

MCVIE, CHRISTINE PERFECT, musician; b. Eng., July 12, 1943; student art sch., pvt. student sculpture; m. John McVie (div.). Singer, keyboardist Fleetwood Mac, 1970—; composer songs including: Over My Head, Say You Love Me, You Make Lovin' Fun, Spare Me a Little of Your Love. Office: care Penguin Promotions 1420 N Beachwood Los Angeles CA 90028*

MCVIE, JOHN, musician; b. Eng., Nov. 26, 1946; m. Christine Perfect (div.); m. 2d, Julie Rubens, Apr. 16, 1978. Bass guitarist with John Mayall, 1963-67, with Fleetwood Mac, 1967—. Office: care Penguin Promotions 1420 N Beachwood Los Angeles CA 90028*

MC VITTY, EDMUND HUGH, ins. co. exec.; b. Toronto, Ont., Can., July 6, 1920; s. Charles Edwin and Maude (Houghton) McV.; B.A., U. Toronto, 1942; LL.B., Osgoode Hall Law Sch., Toronto, 1949; m. Diana M. DeGuerre, Sept. 12, 1952; children—Brian, Patricia, Susan, Catherine. Called to Ont. bar, 1949, apptd. Queen's Counsel, 1974; with Mfrs. Life Ins. Co., Toronto, 1949—, gen. counsel, 1966-70, legal. v.p., 1970—, sec., 1973—; bd. dirs. Ont. Safety League. Served with RAF and RCAF, overseas, 1942-45. Mem. Internat. Claim Assn. (past pres.), Canadian Bar Assn., Assn. Life Ins. Counsel, Toronto Bd. Trade. Conservative. Anglican. Club: Toronto Lawyers. Author: Life Insurance Laws of Canada, 1972. Home: 18 Foursome Crescent Toronto ON M2P 1W2 Canada Office: 200 Bloor St E Toronto ON M4W 1E5 Canada

MC VOY, JAMES DAVID, architect, govt. ofcl.; b. Joplin, Mo., Mar. 25, 1920; s. Edgar Cornelius and Ruth (Shartel) McV.; B.Arch. with honors, U. Fla., 1942, grad. study archtl. design; m. Lois Emmagene Stevens, Dec. 26, 1941; children—David Stevens, Cullen Shartel, Ruth Ellen, Michael Arthur. Archtl. designer Donald Deskey Assos., N.Y.C., 1945-46; chief draftsman, office mgr. Harry M. Griffin, architect, Daytona Beach, Fla., 1946-47; archtl. cons. Arthur D. McVoy, 1946, 48, asso. planner, 1954; partner Duncan, Stewart & McVoy, architects and engrs., Vero Beach, Fla., 1947-48, Stewart & McVoy, architects, 1948, 57; asst. prof. architecture Coll. Architecture and Allied Arts, U. Fla., 1948-50, asso. prof. architecture, chmn. and adminstr. Lower div. dept., 1950-54, chmn. Indonesian studies com., 1954-56, acting head dept. arch., 1957; USOM housing adviser Govt. Republic of Korea, chief aided self-help housing office, 1957-60; housing design, constrn. and finance adviser Korean Reconstrn. Bank, 1958-60, co-adminstr. Typhoon Reconstrn. program, 1959- 60, chief AID housing adviser Govt. So. Rhodesia, chief housing div. Office AID rep. to Rhodesia and Nyasaland, 1960-62, cons. AID Mission Tanganyika and Nat. Housing Corp., Govt. Tanganyika, 1962; housing adviser Govt. Eastern Nigeria, dep. chief housing div. AID Mission to Nigeria, 1963-65; ofcl. U.S. observer UN/ECA Housing Conf., Addis Ababa, 1964; dir. internat. programs Found. Coop. Housing, 1965-68; coop. devel. coordinator Office Pvt. Resources, AID, 1968-70, chief tech. programs div. Office for Pvt. Overseas Programs, 1970-72; chief Latin Am. operations Office Housing, AID, Washington, 1972-73; asst. dir. tech. services, 1973-77, acting dep. dir., asst. dir. for ops., 1977—. Served with USNR, 1942-45. Mem. AAUP, Fellowship So. Churchmen, Citizens Assn. Gainesville (v.p. 1955-56), Soc. Internat. Devel., Am. Fgn. Service Assn. Methodist. Home: 29 Biscayne Pl Sterling VA 22170 Office: AID Dept State Washington DC 20523

MCVOY, KIRK WARREN, physicist, educator; b. Mpls., Feb. 22, 1928; s. Kirk Warren and Phyllis (Farmer) McV.; B.A., Carleton Coll., 1950; B.A. (Rhodes scholar), Oxford U., Eng., 1952; Dipl., U. Gottingen, Germany, 1953; Ph.D., Cornell U, 1956; m. Hilda A. Van Der Laan, Aug. 15, 1953; children—Christopher, Lawrence, Annelies. Research asso. Brookhaven Nat. Lab., Upton, N.Y., 1956-58; asst. prof. Brandeis U., 1958-62; asso. prof. U. Wis., 1963-67, prof. physics, 1967—; vis. distinguished prof. physics Bklyn. Coll., 1970-71; vis. prof. Ind. U., 1971-72. Fulbright research grantee U. Utrecht (Netherlands), 1960-61. Fellow Am. Phys. Soc. Research, publs. on nuclear reaction theory. Address: Dept Physics U Wis Madison WI 53706

MC WHERTER, NED R., state legislator; b. Palmersville, Tenn., Oct. 15, 1930; s. Harmon R. and Lucille (Smith) McW.; children—Linda Ramsey, Michael Ray. Chmn. bd. Vol. Distb. Co. Inc., Eagle Distbrs., Inc., Vol. Express Inc., Hillview Nursing Homes Inc., Weakley Gas & Oil Co.; chmn. bd. Weakley County Mcpl. Electric System; dir. Weakley County Bank, Peoples Bank, Fed. Savs. & Loan; mem. Tenn. Ho. of Reps., 1968, speaker, 1973—. Bd. govs. Council State Govts.; exec. com. So. Legis. Conf.; chmn. So. Speakers' Conf. Democrat. Clubs: Elks, Moose, Eagles, Masons, Shriners, Lions. Office: Ho of Reps Office of Speaker State Capitol Nashville TN 37219 also 22 Bypass Dresden TN 38225

MC WHINNEY, EDWARD WATSON, educator, writer; b. Sydney, Australia, May 19, 1924; s. Matthew and Evelyn Annie (Watson) McW.; LL.B., U. Sydney, 1949; LL.M., Yale, 1951, Sc.Jur.D., 1953; diploma Acad. de Droit Internat., The Hague, 1950; m. Emily Ingalore Sabatzky, June 27, 1951. Called to Australian bar, 1949; apptd. Queen's counsel, Can., 1967; crown prosecutor, Sydney, 1949-50; lectr., then asst. prof. Law Sch. and Grad. Sch., Yale, 1951-55; prof. law, mem. Centre Russian Studies, U. Toronto (Ont., Can.), 1955-66; prof. law, dir. Inst. Air and Space Law, McGill U., Montreal, Que., Can., 1966-71; prof. law, dir. internat. and comparative legal studies U. Ind., Indpls., 1971-74; distinguished prof. law Simon Fraser U., Burnaby, B.C., 1974—; vis. prof. Ecole Libre des Hautes Etudes, 1952, Heidelberg and Max-Planck-Inst., 1960-61, N.Y. U., 1954, Faculté Internat. de Droit Compare, Luxembourg, 1959-60, U. San Antonio, 1963, U. Laval, Que., 1967, U. Paris, 1968, U. Madrid, 1968, U. Aix-Marseille, 1969, U. Nacional Autónoma de México, 1965, Institut Universitaire Luxembourg, 1972, 74, 76, Acad. Internat. Law, The Hague, 1973, Aristotelian U., Thessaloniki, Greece, 1974, 78, U. Nice, 1976-77, Jagellonian U., Cracow, Poland, 1976; legal cons. UN, 1953-54; cons. Japanese Commn. Constn., 1963; mem. prime minister Ont. Adv. Com. Confedn., 1964-71; cons. U.S. Naval War Coll., 1961-68; legal cons. Ministère de la Justice, Que., 1969-70; 74-75; constl. adviser to prime minister of Que., 1974-75; royal commr. Commn. Lang. Rights. Que., 1968-72; cons. U.S. Senate select com. presdl. campaign activities, 1973; spl. commr. inquiry Legislature B.C., 1974-75; chief adv. Fed. Govt.'s Task Force on Nat. Unity, 1978; commr. of enquiry City of Vancouver, 1979; constl. adv. Fedn. Can. Municipalities, 1978—. Served as officer Australian Air Force, 1943-45. Fellow Carnegie Endowment, 1951; Fulbright fellow, 1950-51; Sterling fellow Yale, 1950-51; Rockefeller fellow, 1960-61, 66-68; Can. Council fellow, 1960-61; fellow Am. Soc. Internat. Law, 1962-63. Mem. Australian Inst. Polit. Sci. (dir.), Internat. Law Assn. (pres. Toronto br. 1964-66, pres. Montreal br. 1970-71, chmn. exec. com. Canadian br. 1972-75), Canadian Bar Assn. (council Ont. 1956-58), Yale Law Sch. Assn. (pres. Can. 1964-69), Canadian Civil Liberties Assn. (v.p. 1965-67), Am. Soc. Internat. Law (council 1965-68), Am. Fgn. Law Assn., Inst. interamericano de Estudios Juridicos Internacionales (dir. 1965—); mem. Associé de l'Institut de Droit International, 1967, membre titulaire, 1975. Author: Judical Review, 4th edit., 1969; Canadian Jurisprudence, 1958; Föderalismus und Bundesverfassungsrecht, 1961; Constitutionalism in Germany, 1962; Comparative Federalism, 2d edit., 1965; Peaceful Coexistence and Soviet-Western International Law, 1964; Law Foreign Policy and the East-West Détente, 1964; Federal Constitution- Making for a Multi-National World, 1966; International Law and World Revolution, 1967; Conflit idéologique et ordre public mondial, 1970; (with M.A. Bradley) The Freedom of the Air, 1968; New Frontiers in Space Law, 1969; The International Law of Communications, 1970; Aerial Piracy and International Law, 1971; (with Pierre Pescatore) Federalism and Supreme Courts and the Integration of Legal Systems, 1973, Parliament and Parliamentary Power Today, 1976, The Executive and Executive Power Today, 1977; (with J-D Gendron and others) La situation de la lanque françaisé au Québec (3 vols.), 1973; The Illegal Diversion of Aircraft and International Law, 1974 Parliamentary Privilege and the Broadcasting of Parliamentary Debates, 1975; The International Law of Détente, 1978; The World Count and the Contemporary International Law-making Process, 1979; The Constitution and Quebec, 1979. Bd. editors Australian Quar., 1949-50, Canadian Yearbook of International Law, 1963—. Contbr. to Ency. Brit. Home: 1949 Beach Ave Vancouver BC V6G 1Z2 Canada Office: Simon Fraser U Burnaby 2 BC Canada

MC WHINNEY, RODNEY OWEN, investment co. exec.; b. Denver, Nov. 5, 1933; s. Leroy and Alice (Houston) McW.; B.A. cum laude, Williams Coll., 1955; LL.B., Stanford U., 1958; divorced; children—M. Seth, Margaret. Admitted to Colo. bar, 1958, Mo. bar, 1966; asso. firm Modestt & Shaw, Denver, 1958-66; sr. v.p., gen. counsel Waddell & Reed, Inc., Kansas City, Mo., 1966—; v.p., gen. counsel United Funds, Inc., Kansas City, 1966—; v.p., gen. counsel, dir. United Investors Life Ins. Co., Kansas City, 1975—; sec., treas., dir. Research Mgmt. Assos., Kansas City, 1975—. Served with AUS, 1961. Mem. Am., Mo., Colo. bar assns. Home: 3206 W 79 St Prairie Village KS 66208 Office: 1 Crown Center PO Box 1343 Kansas City MO 66141

MCWHIRTER, WILLIAM BUFORD, business cons.; b. Waco, Tex., Aug. 23, 1918; s. Buford and Katherine (McCollum) McW.; A.B.A., Glendale Jr. Coll., 1937; B.A. with honors, U. Calif. at Berkeley, 1939; m. Catherine Eugenia Forbes, Sept. 21, 1956. Br. mgr. IBM Corp., San Francisco, 1949-56, dist. mgr. N.Y. area, 1956-57, gen. mgr. supplies div., 1957-59, pres. data systems div., White Plains, N.Y., 1959-62, IBM dir. orgn., 1962-64, pres. indsl. products div., 1964-65; cons. to IBM, other firms, 1966—; dir. Itel Corp., San Francisco, MHC Corp., N.Y.C. Trustee, Mus. of No. Ariz. Mem. Phi Beta Kappa, Theta Xi. Clubs: San Francisco Sales Executives (pres. 1955-56); Siwanoy (Bronxville, N.Y.); Metropolitan (N.Y.C.); Army-Navy (Arlington, Va.); Phoenix Country; Desert Forest (Carefree, Ariz.); Pauma Valley (Calif.). Home: Carefree AZ 85331

MCWHORTER, ALAN LOUIS, elec. engr., physicist, educator; b. Crowley, La., Aug. 25, 1930; s. Arthur Walton and Andree (Genet) McW.; student Tulane U., 1947-48; B.S., U. Ill., 1951; Sc.D., Mass. Inst. Tech., 1955. Faculty, Mass. Inst. Tech., 1959—, head solid state div. Lincoln Lab., 1965—, prof. elec. engring., 1966—. Fellow Am. Phys. Soc., I.E.E.E. (David Sarnoff award 1971). Office: Lincoln Lab Mass Inst Tech PO Box 73 Lexington MA 02173

MCWHORTER, CLARENCE AUSTIN, physician; b. Wheatland, Wyo., July 19, 1918; s. Lester A. and Avis (Farrow) McW.; student Wayne State Tchrs. Coll., 1938-39; B.S., M.D., U. Nebr., 1944; m. Patricia Ethel Prott, Nov. 15, 1947; children—Lynne, Dianne, James. Intern Univ. Hosp., Omaha, 1944-45, resident Univ. Hosp., Omaha, Nebr., 1945-49: practice medicine, specializing in pathology, Omaha, 1949—; instr. dept. pathology and bacteriology Coll. Medicine, U. Nebr., 1949-51, asst. prof., 1951-55, asso. prof., asst. chmn. dept. pathology, 1955-65, prof., 1958, chmn. dept., 1965—, dir. Sch. Cytology, 1963—, mem. grad. faculty, 1965—. Served to capt., M.C., AUS, 1946-48. Fellow Am. Soc. Clin. Pathologists, Fellow Coll. Am. Pathologists (pres.); mem. Am. Soc. Cytology, Internat. Acad. Pathology, Alpha Omega Alpha. Home: 10711 Cedar St Omaha NE 68124

MC WHORTER, HEZZIE BOYD, educator; b. Cochran, Ga., May 8, 1923; s. Hezzie and Mary (Durham) McW.; B.S., U.S. Naval Acad., 1945; M.A., U. Ga., 1949; Ph.D., U. Tex., 1960; m. Marguerite Antley, Nov. 14, 1964; children—Carol (Mrs. Joel Pittard), William David Volk, Julie Volk Corona, Hamilton Boyd. Mem. faculty U. Ga., Athens, 1949-72, prof. English, dean Coll. Arts and Scis., 1968-72; commr. Southeastern Conf., 1972—. Served with USN, 1945-47, 51-53. Named to N. Ga. Coll. Disting. Alumni Hall of Fame, 1978, Ga. Sports Hall of Fame, 1980. Mem. Nat. Collegiate Athletic Assn. (dist. v.p., mem. nat. council, 1968—, sec. Southeastern conf. 1967-72), Phi Kappa Phi. Mem. Christian Ch. (elder). Home: 1608 Panorama Dr Birmingham AL 35216

MC WILLIAMS, CAREY, writer; b. Steamboat Springs, Colo., Dec. 13, 1905; s. Jerry and Harriet (Casley) McW.; LL.B., U. So. Calif., 1927; m. Iris Dornfeld, Sept. 10, 1941; children—Wilson Carey, Jerry Ross. Admitted to Calif. bar, 1927, practiced in Los Angeles, 1927-38, mem. firm Black, Hammack & McWilliams; commr. immigration and housing State of Calif., 1938-42; contbg. editor The Nation, N.Y.C., 1945-51, asso. editor, 1951-52, editorial dir., 1952-55, editor, 1955-75. Author: Ambrose Bierce: a Biography, 1929; Factories in the Field, 1939; Ill Fares the Land, 1942; Brothers Under the Skin, 1943; Prejudice, 1944; Southern California Country: An Island on the Land, 1946; A Mask for Privilege: Anti-Semitism in America, 1948; North from Mexico: The Spanish-Speaking People of the United States, 1949; California: The Great Exception, 1949: Witchhunt: The Revival of Heresy, 1950. Editor: The California Revolution, 1968; The Education of Carey McWilliams, 1979; contbr. to Dictionary of Am. Biography, numerous mags. Home: 601 W 115th St New York NY 10025

MC WILLIAMS, EDWIN JOSEPH, banker; b. Spokane, Washington, Aug. 11, 1919; s. Frank S. and Alice (Conlan) McW.; student U. Notre Dame, 1937-38, Marguette U., 1938-40; B.S. in Bus. Adminstrn., Gonzaga U., 1943: m. Betty J. Galbreath, Aug. 15, 1944; children—Lawrence, Barbara Anne, Marijoan, Peter. With Fidelity Mutual Savings Bank, Spokane, 1940—, exec. v.p., 1955-58, pres., 1958—; mem. adv. council Wash. State Dept. Commerce and Econ. Devel., 1977—. Pres. United Crusade Spokane County. 1966; past pres., mem. exec. bd. Inland Empire council, region 11 exec. com. Boy Scouts Am.; past pres. Spokane Unlimited; mem. adv. council Sch. Bus., Gonzaga U. Bd. dirs., mem. exec. com. Expo '74 World's Fair; past mem. bd. regents Ft. Wright Coll., Spokane; bd. regents Wash. State U. Served to lt. (j.g.) USNR, 1943-45. Mem. Nat. Assn. Mut. Savs. Banks (chmn. 1976-77), Mut. Savs. Banks Assn. State of Wash., Am. Savs. and Loan Inst. (past gov. dist. XI), Spokane C. of C. (pres. 1974-75). Roman Catholic. Clubs: Rotary of Spokane, K.C. Home: 1717 Upper Terrace Rd Spokane WA 99203 Office: 524 W Riverside Ave Spokane WA 99201

MC WILLIAMS, JOHN MICHAEL, lawyer; b. Annapolis, Md., Aug. 17, 1939; s. William J. and Helen (Disharon) McW.; B.S., Georgetown U., 1964; LL.B., U. Md., 1967; m. Frances Edelen McCabe, May 30, 1970; children—M. Edelen, J. Michael. Admitted to Md. bar, 1967, U.S. Supreme Ct. bar, 1970; law clk. Chief Judge Roszel C. Thomsen, U.S. Dist. Ct. Md., 1967-68; asso. firm Piper and Marbury, Balt., 1968-69; asst. atty. gen. State of Md., 1969-76; gen. counsel Md. Dept. Transp., Balt., 1971-76; partner firm Tydings and Rosenberg, Balt., 1977—; chmn. Md. adv. council to Nat. League Services Corp., 1975-78; commr. Gov.'s Com. to Revise Annotated Code of Md., 1973-78. Transition dir. Md. Gov.-Elect Harry Hughes, 1978-79. Served to 1st lt. U.S. Army, 1958-60. Mem. Am. Bar Assn. (mem. ho. of dels. 1976—), Md. State Bar Assn. (treas. 1973-78, bd. govs. 1971, 73—, mem. exec. com. 1973-78), Bar Assn. Balt. City, Am. Law Inst., Am. Judicature Soc. (dir. 1974—), Am. Acad. Jud. Edn. (dir. 1977). Democrat. Roman Catholic. Clubs: Center, Md., Rule; Sprat Bay (Water Island, V.I.). Home: 118 Hawthorne Rd Baltimore MD 21210 Office: 2300 Arlington Bldg Baltimore MD 21201

MC WILLIAMS, MARGARET ANN, home economist; b. Osage, Iowa, May 26, 1929; d. Alvin Randall and Mildred Irene (Lane) Edgar; B.S., Iowa State U., 1951, M.S., 1953; Ph.D., Oreg. State U., 1968; children—Roger, Kathleen. Asst. prof. home econs. Calif. State U., Los Angeles, 1961-66, asso. prof., 1966-68, prof., 1968—, chmn. dept., 1968-76; mem. Greater Los Angeles Nutrition Council, Calif. Liaison Council for Home Econs., Calif. Articulation for Home Econs., Orange County Nutrition Council; mem. home econs. adv. coms. East Los Angeles Coll., Harbor Coll., Los Angeles City Coll., Pasadena City Coll., Compton Coll.; home econs. edn. and bus. adminstrs. Interdeptl. Council Food and Nutrition in Calif. Recipient Alumni Centennial award Iowa State U., 1971, Profl. Achievement award, 1977; Phi Upsilon Omicron Nat. Founders fellow, 1964; Nat. Found. fellow, 1967; Outstanding Prof. award Calif. State U., 1976. Mem. Am. Home Econs. Assn., Am. Dietetic Assn., Inst. Food Technologists, Soc. Nutrition Edn., Nat. Council Home Econs. Adminstrs., Phi Kappa Phi, Phi Upsilon Omicron, Omicron Nu, Iota Sigma Pi, Sigma Delta Epsilon, Sigma Alpha Iota. Author: Food Fundamentals, 1966, 3d edit., 1979; Nutrition for the Growing Years, 1967, 3d edit., 1980; Experimental Foods Laboratory Manual, 1977; (with L. Kotschevar) Understanding Food, 1969; Illustrated Guide to Food Preparation, 1970, 3d edit., 1976; (with L. Davis) Food for You, 1971, 2d edit., 1976; The Meatless Cookbook, 1973; (with F. Stare) Living Nutrition, 1973, 2d edit., 1977; Nutrition for Good Health, 1974; (with H. Paine) Modern Food Preservation, 1977; Fundamentals of Meal Management, 1978. Tech. cons., abstractor Am. Home Econs. Assn. Jour. Home: PO Box 220 Redondo Beach CA 90277

MC WILLIAMS, RALPH DAVID, educator; b. Ft. Myers, Fla., Nov. 5, 1930; s. Ralph Leonard and Alma Louise (Jenny) McW.; B.S., Fla. State U., 1951, M.S., 1953; Ph.D., U. Tenn., 1957; m. Kathleen Dodge, May 23, 1959; children—Linda Louise, Martha Kay. Teaching asst. Fla. State U., 1951-53, asst. prof., 1959-63, asso. prof., 1963-69, prof., asso. chmn. dept. math., 1969—; teaching asst. U. Tenn., 1953-54; NSF fellow, 1954-56; instr. U. Tenn., 1956-57, Princeton, 1957-59. Mathematician, Aberdeen Proving Ground, summers 1953-54. Mem. Am. Math. Soc., Math. Assn. Am., AAAS, AAUP, Phi Beta Kappa, Sigma Xi, Phi Kappa Phi, Delta Tau Delta. Baptist. Contbr. articles to profl. jours. Home: 1704 Raa Ave Tallahassee FL 32303

MC WILLIAMS, ROBERT HUGH, judge; b. Salina, Kans., Apr. 27, 1916; s. Robert Hugh and Laura (Nicholson) McW.: A.B., U. Denver, 1938, LL.B., 1941; m. Catherine Ann Cooper, Nov. 4, 1942; 1 son, Edward Cooper. Admitted to Colo. bar, 1941; Colo. dist. judge, Denver, 1952-60; justice Colo. Supreme Ct., 1961-68, chief justice, 1969-70; judge 10th Circuit Ct. Appeals, 1970—. Served with AUS World War II. Mem. Phi Beta Kappa, Omicron Delta Kappa, Phi Delta Phi, Kappa Sigma. Republican. Episcopalian. Home: 137 Jersey St Denver CO 80220 Office: US Courthouse 1929 Stout St Denver CO 80294

MCWILLIAMS, WILLIAM JAMESON, oilfield supply co. exec.; b. Indian Head, Md., May 20, 1917; s. Francis DeSales and Emma Penn (Jameson) McW.; B.A., U. Md., 1938; m. Betty Hall Law, Oct. 19, 1940; children—Thomas F., Ann J., Susan L. With Dept. of State, Washington, 1946-54; with Republic Supply Co., Oklahoma City, 1954—, pres., 1958—, dir.; dir. Mut. Fed. Savs. & Loan Assn., Liberty Nat. Bank & Trust Co. (both Oklahoma City). Served to lt. col. AUS, 1941-46. Decorated Legion of Merit; Croix de Guerre (France). Mem. Am. Petroleum Inst., Petroleum Equipment Suppliers Assn., Ind. Petroleum Assn. Am. Democrat. Roman Catholic. Clubs: Petroleum, Oklahoma City Golf and Country. Home: 545 NW 38th St Oklahoma City OK 73118 Office: PO Box 1995 Oklahoma City OK 73101

MEACHAM, CHARLES HARDING, govt. ofcl.; b. Newman, Calif., Sept. 21, 1925; s. Vernon A. and Sara (Paulsen) M.; B.S., Utah State U., 1950; m. June Lorraine Yunker, June 22, 1946; children—Charles Paulsen, Bruce Herbert. Biologist, Calif. Dept. Fish and Game, 1950-56, Alaska Dept. Fisheries, 1956-59; regional supr. regions II and III, Alaska Dept. Fish and Game, 1959-68; dir. internat. fisheries Office Gov. Alaska, 1968-69; commr. U.S. Fish and Wildlife Service, Dept. Interior, 1969-70, spl. asst. to area dir., Alaska, 1971-74; dir. internat. affairs Office of Gov., Juneau, Alaska, 1975—; commr. U.S. North Pacific Fur Seal Commn.; mem. Pacific and North Pacific Fisheries Mgmt. Councils, 1976—. Served with USMCR, 1943-46. Mem. Am. Fisheries Soc., Wildlife Soc., Pacific Fisheries Biologists, Internat. Assn. Game, Fish and Conservation Commrs., Am. Legion. Club: Elks. Office: Office of Governor Juneau AK 99811

MEACHAM, STANDISH, JR., educator, historian; b. Cin., Mar. 12, 1932; s. Standish and Eleanor (Rapp) M.; B.A., Yale, 1954; Ph.D., Harvard, 1961; m. Sarah Shartle, Aug. 24, 1957; children—Edith, Louisa, Samuel. Asst. prof. history Harvard, 1962-67; mem. faculty U. Tex., Austin, 1967—, prof. history, 1970—. Served with AUS, 1955-57. Am. Council Learned Soc. fellow, 1965-66, 79-80; Guggenheim Found. fellow, 1972-73. Author: Henry Thornton of Clapham, 1964; Lord Bishop: The Life of Samuel Wilberforce, 1970; A Life Apart, 1977; (with R. Flukinger and Larry Schaaf) Paul Martin, Victorian Photographer, 1977. Editor: (Edward Bulwer) England and the English, 1970. Home: 1111 Red Bud Trail Austin TX 78746

MEACHAM, WILLIAM FELAND, neurol. surgeon, educator; b. Washington, Dec. 12, 1913; s. Marion H. and Mamie (Henderson) M.; B.S., Western Ky. State Coll., 1936; M.D., Vanderbilt U., 1940; m. Alice Marie Mathews, June 14, 1944; children—William Feland, Patrick, Barbara, Robert. Intern surgery Vanderbilt U. Hosp., Nashville, 1940-41, asst. resident surgery, 1941-43, resident surgeon, 1943-44, asst. vis. surgeon, 1944, asso. vis. surgeon Out- Patient Service, 1944; asst. in surgery Vanderbilt U. Sch. Medicine, 1941-43, instr. surgery, 1943-44, William Henry Howe fellow in neurol. surgery, 1945-47, asst. clin. prof. surgery, 1947-50, asso. clin. prof. surgery, 1950-53, asso. prof. neurol. surgery, 1953-54, prof. neurol. surgery, 1954-59, clin. prof. neurol. surgery, 1959—; vol. asst. Montreal Neurol. Inst., 1947; asst. clin. prof. neurol. surgery Meharry Med. Sch., 1947-50, clin. prof., 1950—; attending neurosurgeon Nashville Gen., St. Thomas, Mid-State Bapt. hosps., Riverside and Madison Sanitaria; cons. in neurosurgery Thayer Vets. Hosp., Murfreesboro (Tenn.) Vets. Hosp., Jr. League Home for Crippled Children. Chmn. Study Commn. on Stroke, Tenn. Mid South Regional Med. Program, 1968. Diplomate Am. Bd. Surgery, Am. Bd. Neurol. Surgery. Mem. Am. Acad. Neurol. Surgery, A.C.S. (chmn. adv. council for neurol. surgery 1959-63, bd. govs. 1964- 66, bd. regents 1966-75), AMA, Nashville Acad. Medicine (past pres., chmn. bd. dirs.), Nashville Surg. Soc. (past pres.), Am. Surg. Assn., Neurosurg. Soc. Am. (past pres., mem. exec. council), Neurosurg. Travel Club, Soc. Neurol. Surgeons (pres. 1971), Soc. Univ. Surgeons, Southeastern Surg. Congress, So. Med. Assn., So. Neurosurg. Soc. (past pres.), Tenn. Med. Assn., Am. Assn. Neurol. Surgeons (dir., past sec., past treas., pres. 1972), Am. Cancer Soc. (dir.), Sigma Xi, Alpha Omega Alpha. Methodist. Home: 3513 Woodmont Blvd Nashville TN 37215 Office: Vanderbilt U Hosp Nashville TN 37232

MEAD, BEVERLEY TUPPER, physician, educator; b. New Orleans, Jan. 22, 1923; s. Harold Tupper and Helen Edith (Hunt) M.; B.S., U. S.C., 1943; M.D., Med. Coll. S.C., 1947; M.S., U. Utah, 1958; m. Thelma Ruth Cottingham, June 8, 1947. intern, Detroit Receiving Hosp., 1947-48, resident, 1948-51; asst. prof. U. Utah, 1954-61; asso. prof. U. Ky., 1961-65; prof. psychiatry and behavioral sci. Creighton U. Sch. Medicine, Omaha, 1965—, chmn. dept., 1965-77. Home: 6731 Davenport Omaha NE 68132 Office: Creighton U Omaha NE 68131. *The approval of others does not concern me as much as my approval of myself.*

MEAD, CARL DAVID, educator; b. Cadiz, Ohio, May 4, 1913; s. Carl David and Neva Eloine (Walker) M.; student Washington and Jefferson Coll., 1932-34; B.S., Ohio State U., 1936, M.A., 1938, Ph.D., 1947; m. Lillian Martha Felton, Apr. 15, 1938; children—Susan Mead Maybee, Nancy Mead McKenzie. Instr. English, Denison U., 1938-39, Ohio State U., 1946-47; faculty Mich. State U., 1948—, prof. English, 1957—, head dept., 1959-66, cons., chief univ. adv. group to U. Ryukyus (Okinawa), 1955-57; Fulbright lectr., Philippines, 1964. Served with AUS, 1943-46. Decorated Legion of Merit. Mem. Modern Lang. Assn., Am. Studies Assn., A.A.U.P. Author: Yankee Eloquence in the Middle West, 1951; (with others) Prentice-Hall Handbook for Writers, 1951; The American Scholar Today, 1970. Adv. editor Dodd, Mead & Co., 1963-75; editor Centennial Review, 1966—. Home: 431 Kedzie Dr East Lansing MI 48823

MEAD, CARVER ANDRESS, educator, scientist; b. Bakersfield, Calif., May 1, 1934; s. James Arnold and Grace (Andress) M.; B.S. in Elec. Engring., Calif. Inst. Tech., 1956, M.S., 1957, Ph.D., 1959; m. Ingrid. Mem. faculty dept. elec. engring. and computer sci. Calif. Inst. Tech., 1958—, asso. prof., 1962-67, prof., 1967—. Recipient Electrochem. Soc. T.D. Callianan outstanding contbn. to lit. award, 1971. Fellow Am. Phys. Soc. Home: 2036 Pasadena Glen Rd Pasadena CA 91107

MEAD, CHESTER ALDEN, educator; b. St. Louis, Dec. 9, 1932; s. Chester Alden and Charlotte (Bowman) M.; B.A., Carleton Coll., 1954; Ph.D., Washington U., St. Louis, 1958. Research asso. Brookhaven Nat. Lab., 1957-58; faculty U. Minn., Mpls., 1958—, prof. phys. chemistry, 1966—. Vis. asso. chemist Brookhaven Nat. Lab., summer 1959; vis. research fellow Birkbeck Coll., London, 1964-65; vis. prof. Free U. Berlin (Germany), 1971-72. Mem. Am. Phys. Soc., Am. Chem. Soc., Fedn. Am. Scientists. Home: 5135 Belmont Ave Minneapolis MN 55419

MEAD, EDWARD JAIRUS, chemist; b. Cleve., Oct. 3, 1928; s. John Mendenhall and Sylvia (Cleland) M.; B.S. in Chemistry, Va. Mil. Inst., 1949; M.S. in Chemistry, Purdue U., 1952, Ph.D. in Chemistry, 1955; m. Pearl White Happer, Feb. 28, 1959; children—Janet, Joan. Research chemist E.I. duPont de Nemours & Co., Kinston, N.C., 1954-59, Wilmington, Del., 1959-63, research supr., 1964-65, product devel. mgr., 1965-73, lab. dir., 1974-78, new bus. devel. mgr., 1978—; instr. Va. Mil. Inst., 1945-50. Mem. Marshallton-McKean Sch. Dist. Sch. Bd., 1967—, pres., 1971-72, 75-76. Mem. Am. Chem. Soc. Contbr. articles to Jour. Am. Chem. Soc. Patentee in field. Home: 4 Leigh Ct Wilmington DE 19808 Office: DuPont Photo Products Dept 12th Floor Bank of Del Bldg Wilmington DE 19898

MEAD, EDWARD MATHEWS, newspaper exec.; b. Erie, Pa., Oct. 13, 1926; s. John James and Grace (Finerty) M.; student U. N.C., 1945-46; B.A. in History, Princeton U., 1949; m. Allene Steimer, Feb. 16, 1957; children—John James, Edward Mathews, Daniel Patrick. Trainee, Trenton Times, 1949-50; night editor Erie Times, 1950-54, Sunday editor, 1954-56, asst. to pub., 1956-64, asst. pub., 1964-73, pres., 1973—, also co-pub. Mem. Erie Conf. on Community Devel., 1971—, sec., 1980; bd. dirs. St. Vincent Hosp., 1974—, pres. 1980; bd. dirs. Villa Maria Coll., 1977—, pres., 1979. Served with USMC, 1945-46. Mem. Pa. Asso. Press (pres. 1977), Pa. Newspaper Pubs. Assn. (dir. 1977—). Roman Catholic. Office: 205 W 12th St Erie PA 16534

MEAD, EDWARD SHEPHERD, author; b. St. Louis, Apr. 26, 1914; s. Edward and Sarah (Woodward) M.; grad. St. Louis Country Day Sch., 1932; A.B., Washington U., 1936; m. Annabelle Pettibone, Sept. 18, 1943; children—Sally Ann, Shepherd, Edward. Script editor Benton & Bowles, Inc., N.Y.C., 1936-41, copy supr., v.p., TV copy chief, 1944-56; ret., 1956. Mem. Phi Beta Kappa, Omicron Delta Kappa, Kappa Alpha. Clubs: Hurlingham (London); St. George's Hill Lawn Tennis (Weybridge, Surrey, Eng.). Author: The Magnificent MacInnes, 1949; Tessie the Hound of Channel One, 1951; How to Succeed in Business Without Really Trying (also prod. as musical) (Pulitzer prize, N.Y. Drama Critics award), 1952; The Big Ball of Wax, 1954; How to Get Rich in TV Without Really Trying, 1956; How to Succeed with Women Without Really Trying, 1957; The Admen (Readers Digest Book Club selection), 1958; The Four Window Girl, or How to Make More Money than Men, 1959; Dudley, There is No Tommorow. Then How About this Afternoon?, 1963; How to Live Like a Lord Without Really Trying, 1964; The Carefully Considered Rape of the World, 1966; How to Succeed at Business Spying by Trying, 1968; 'ER, or The Brassbound Beauty, the Bearded Bicyclist, and the Gold-Colored Teenage Grandfather, 1969; How to Stay Medium-Young Practically Forever Without Really Trying, 1971; Free the Male Man! The Manifesto of the Men's Liberation Movement, 1972; How to Get to the Future Before It Gets to You, 1974; How to Succeed in Tennis Without Really Trying, 1977. Home: Flat B 3 W Eaton Pl London SW1X 8LU England

MEAD, FRANK SPENCER, author; b. Chatham, N.J., Jan. 15, 1898; s. Frank and Lillie (Spencer) M.; A.B., U. Denver, 1922; student Episcopal Theol. Sem. Va., 1922-23; B.D., Union Theol. Sem., 1927; Litt.D., Dickinson Coll., 1948; m. Judy Duryee, Oct. 24, 1927; children—Donald Duryee, Judy Spencer. Sec., 23d St. YMCA, N.Y.C., 1923-24; asst. pastor Reformed Ch., Harlem, N.Y., 1925-27; pastor Grace M.E. Ch., Newark, N.J., 1927-31, Kearny (N.J.) Ch., 1931-34; editor Homiletic Rev., 1934; exec. editor Christian Herald, 1942-48; editor-in-chief Fleming H. Revell Co., 1949—. Served in U.S. Army, 1917-18. Mem. Phi Beta Kappa, Beta Theta Pi. Author: The March of Eleven Men, 1932; 250 Bible Biographies, 1934; See These Banners Go, 1935; The Ten Decisive Battles of Christianity, 1937; Right Here at Home, 1939, The Handbook of Denominations, 1952 (rev. and pub. every 5 years); Rebels With A Cause, 1964; An Encyclopedia of Religious Quotations, 1965; (with Dale Evans Rogers) Let Freedom Ring, 1975, Hear the Children Crying, 1978; Talking With God, 1976. Editor: Tarbell's Teacher's Guide. Home: 6 McKinley St Nutley NJ 07110 Office: 184 Central Ave Old Tappan NJ 07675

MEAD, GEORGE WILSON, II, paper co. exec.; b. Milw., Oct. 11, 1927; s. Stanton W. and Dorothy (Williams) M; B.S., Yale, 1950; M.S., Inst. Paper Chemistry, Wis., 1952; m. Helen Patricia Anderson, Sept. 3, 1949; children—Deborah, David, Leslie. With Consol. Papers, Inc., Wisconsin Rapids, Wis., 1952—, v.p. operations, 1962-66, pres., chief exec. officer, 1966-71, chmn. bd., chief exec. officer, 1971—, also dir.; dir. Consol. Water Power Co., Consoweld Corp., First Nat. Bank, Soo Line R.R. Co-chmn. bldg. fund drive Riverview Hosp., Wisconsin Rapids, 1963-64, mem. bd., 1961-77. Bd. dirs. Consolidated's Civic Found., Nat. Council for Air and Stream Improvement; trustee Lawrence U., Inst. Paper Chemistry. Recipient Distingushed Service award Wisconsin Rapids Jr. C. of C., 1961. Mem. Am. Paper Inst. (dir. 1967-69), T.A.P.P.I. (dir. 1969-72), Wis. Paper Industry Information Service (gen. chmn. 1964-65), Wis. Paper and Pulp Mfrs. Traffic Assn. (exec. com. 1963-75, dir., pres. 1973). Elk (exalted ruler 1958), Rotarian. Home: N Biron Dr PO Box 966 Wisconsin Rapids WI 54494 Office: Consolidated Papers Inc Wisconsin Rapids WI 54494

MEAD, GILBERT D(UNBAR), geophysicist; b. Madison, Wis., May 31, 1930; s. Stanton Witter and Dorothy Elizabeth (Williams) M.; B.S., Yale U., 1952; Ph.D. in Physics, U. Calif., Berkeley, 1962; m. Jaylee Montague, Nov. 18, 1968; children—Elizabeth, Diana, Stanton, Robert. Tchr. sci. San Benito High Sch., Hollister, Calif., 1953-55; research asst. Lawrence Radiation Lab., Berkeley, 1957-62; physicist theoretical div. NASA Goddard Space Flight Center, Greenbelt, Md., 1962-74, head geophysics br., 1974—; dir., mem. audit com. Consol. Papers, Inc., Wisconsin Rapids, Wis., 1974—. Trustee, Beloit Coll., 1976—; mus. dir. Bowie (Md.) Barbershop Chorus. Recipient Outstanding Service award Goddard Space Flight Center, 1978. Mem. Am. Phys. Soc., Am. Geophys. Union (chmn. ann. meeting com. 1971-73), Seismol. Soc. Am. Republican. Editor: (with W. Hess) Introduction to Space Science, 1968; contbr. numerous articles to profl. jours. Home: 7724 Hanover Pkwy Greenbelt MD 20770 Office: Code 922 NASA Goddard Space Flight Center Greenbelt MD 20771

MEAD, GILES WILLIS, biologist, mus. adminstr.; b. N.Y.C., Feb. 5, 1928; s. G.W. and Elise (Graf) M.; A.B., Stanford U., 1949, A.M., 1952, Ph.D., 1953; children—Parry, Jane, Whit, Gale. Biologist U.S. Bur. Fisheries, Woods Hole, Mass., 1953-55; dir. ichthyological lab. U.S. Fish and Wildlife Service, Smithsonian Instn., 1955-60; curator of fishes Mus. Comparative Zoology, Harvard U., Cambridge, 1960-70; dir. Los Angeles County Mus. Nat. History, 1970—; mem. Smithsonian Council, 1971-77, Calif. Natural Areas Coordinating Council, 1971. Served with U.S. Army, 1954-55. Mem. Am. Assn. Museums (chmn. ethics com. 1974). Clubs: Calif., Bohemian. Home: 9317 A Burton Way Beverly Hills CA 90210 Office: 900 Exposition Blvd Los Angeles CA 90007

MEAD, GORDON V., corp. exec.; b. Thornton, Iowa, Apr. 6, 1906; s. Bert V. and Mary (Mahaffey) M.; B.S., U. Ill., 1929; m. Katie McRae, Mar. 24, 1934; children—Shirley (Mrs. Robert Stauffer), Marilyn (Mrs. G. Copeland), Gordon M. With Firestone Tire & Rubber Co., Akron, Ohio, 1929-56, mgr. retail stores, 1931-35, mgr. home & auto supply div., 1935-52, gen. merchandising mgr., 1952-56; pres., dir. Marshall-Wells Co., Duluth, Minn., 1956-58; chmn. Ace Hardware of Friendly Stores, Inc., Winter Haven, Fla., 1958—. Presbyn. Clubs: Lake Region Yacht and Country, Rotary (Winter Haven). Home: 1304 Lake Mirror Terr Winter Haven FL 33880 Office: 500 E Central Suite 248 Winter Haven FL 33880

MEAD, JEREMIAH, physiologist, educator; b. Madison, Wis., Aug. 30, 1920; s. Warren Judson and Bertha (Taylor) M.; S.B., Harvard, 1943, M.D., 1946; m. Dorothea Perry, Aug. 25, 1945; children—Jeremiah Putnam, Warren Perry, Andrew Washburn, Sarah Taylor. Intern Boston City Hosp., 1946-47, asst. resident, 1949-50; mem. faculty Harvard Sch. Pub. Health, 1950—, prof. physiology, 1965— Cecil K. and Philip Drinker prof. environ. physiology, 1976—. Served to capt., M.C., AUS, 1947-49. Mem. Am. Physiol. Soc., Am. Acad. Arts and Scis., Am. Inst. Biol. Scis., Harvard Musical Assn., Sigma Xi, Alpha Omega Alpha. Home: 56 Pine Ridge Rd Waban MA 02168 Office: 665 Huntington Ave Boston MA 02115

MEAD, JOHN MILTON, banker; b. Schenectady, Oct. 26, 1924; s. Milton Samuel and Jane (Drake) M.; B.S., U. Mo., 1950; postgrad. U. Wis., 1963-65; m. Marguerite Ann Stone, Jan. 3, 1948; children—Ann Elizabeth, Jane Stone, Mary Ames. Auditor, Schenectady Trust Co., 1950-51; v.p., auditor First Trust & Deposit Co., Syracuse, N.Y., 1955-77; v.p., compliance officer Key Banks, Inc., Albany, N.Y., 1977—. Treas., Marcellus Community Devel. Assn. Served with USAAF, 1943-46, USAF, 1951-55. Mem. Inst. Internal Auditors (pres. Central N.Y. chpt.), Am. Legion (past post comdr.). Republican. Presbyn. Clubs: Marcellus Optimist (past pres.), Skaneateles Country (dir. 1973). Home: RD 1 Yorkshire Dr Glens Falls NY 12801 Office: 60 State St Albany NY 12207

MEAD, STANTON WITTER, paper co. exec.; b. Rockford, Ill., Sept. 2, 1900; s. George W. and Ruth E. (Witter) M.; A.B., Yale U., 1922; m. Dorothy E. Williams, Sept. 1, 1926 (dec.); children—George W. II, Gilbert D., Mary M. La Mar; m. 2d, Elvira Jens Schulz, Oct. 1968. Pres., Consol. Papers, Inc., Wisconsin Rapids, Wis., 1950-66, now dir.; dir. Consol. Water Power Co., Consoweld Corp., Wisconsin Rapids, First Nat. Bank, Wisconsin Rapids. Home: 730 1st Ave S Wisconsin Rapids WI 54494

MEAD, WAYLAND MCCON, ins. holding co. exec.; b. Roxbury, N.Y., Nov. 25, 1931; s. Irvin John and Dorothy (Seablom) M.; B.S., Cornell U., 1953, J.D., 1958; m. Barbara Jean Wales, Aug. 24, 1958; children—Michael John, David Scott, Deborah Ellen. Admitted to N.Y. bar, 1958; asso. firm Sage, Gray, Todd & Sims, N.Y.C., 1958-59; atty. Mut. Ins. Rating Bur., N.Y.C., 1959-62, Continental Ins. Co., N.Y.C., 1962-65; atty., then sec., counsel Am. Home Assurance Co., N.Y.C., 1965-75; sec., counsel Nat. Union Fire Ins. Co., N.Y.C., 1968-75; asst. v.p., counsel Am. Internat. Group, Inc., N.Y.C., 1969-75, v.p., gen. counsel, 1975—; dir. Transatlantic Reins. Co., N.Y.C., AIU Ins. Co., N.Y.C., Commerce and Industry Ins. Co., N.Y.C., Birmingham Fire Ins. Co. of Pa., N.Y.C.; chmn. ad hoc com. property and casualty ins. industry, N.Y.C., 1976. Served with U.S. Army, 1953-55. Mem. Am. Bar Assn. Home: 22 Lucille Ct Massapequa NY 11758 Office: 70 Pine St New York NY 10005

MEAD, WILLIAM RAMEY, ins. co. exec.; b. Lincoln, Nebr., Oct. 10, 1919; s. William D. and Lita (Ramey) M.; B.B.A., U. Minn., 1942; m. Audrey Jane Williams, June 5, 1943; children—Sandra Lynn (Mrs. Ronald L. McIntire), Susan Gayle (Mrs. Marc C. Wigley), William Ramey, Robert Dwight. Investment research analyst Glore Forgan & Co., Chgo., 1946-48; account exec., investment analyst Moody's Investors Service, Chgo., 1948-56; formerly investment analyst, mgr. securities dept., treas., v.p. investment div. Gen. Am. Life Ins. Co., St. Louis; dir. Mark Twain Bancshares, St. Louis. Served with USNR, 1942-45. Chartered financial analyst. Mem. St. Louis Soc. Financial Analysts (past pres., dir.). Home: 708 Turtle Cove Manchester MO 63011

MEADE, EDWIN BAYLIES, lawyer; b. Danville, Va., Oct. 30, 1896; s. Julian and Bessie Edmunds (Bouldin) M.; student Danville Sch. for Boys; LL.B., U. Va., 1920; m. Madeline Merle Read, June 23, 1923; children—Edwin Baylies, Frank Opie, Elizabeth Lyne. Admitted to Va. bar, 1919; practiced in Danville, 1920—; mem. firm Meade, Tate, Meade & Daniel. Mem. Va. Constl. Conv., 1945; mem. Va. Bd. Law Examiners, 1947-50; guest lectr. U. Va. Law Sch., 1951-54, also mem. Bd. Law Rev. Bd. dirs. YMCA, 1951-54, past pres. Served as ensign USNRF, 1918-19. Fellow Am. Bar Found., Am. Coll. Trial Lawyers, Am. Law Found.; mem. U. Va. Alumni Assn. (pres. 1954-55), Va. (pres. 1956-57), Danville (past pres.) bar assns., Order of Cincinnati, Order of Coif, Sigma Nu. Episcopalian. Club: Danville Golf. Home: 260 Hawthorne Dr Danville VA 24541 Office: 116 S Ridge St Danville VA 24541

MEADE, EVERARD KIDDER, JR., corp. exec.; b. Tappahannock, Va., Oct. 3, 1919; s. Everard Kidder and Della (Wright) M.; grad. Va. Episcopal Sch., 1937, Millard Prep. Sch., 1938; B.S., U.S. Mil. Acad., 1943; m. Alice Amory Winslow, Sept. 1944; children—Mary Devereux, Everard Kidder III, Susanna Fitzhugh. Mem. Hoover Commn., U.S. Depts. Def. and State, 1946-53; v.p. Colonial Williamsburg, Inc., 1953-55; asso. Earl Newsom & Co., 1955-57; v.p. CBS Inc., 1957—. Served from 2d lt. to lt. col. U.S. Army, 1939-46. Mem. Fgn. Policy Assn., Chamber of Commerce and Industry Assn. N.Y. (vice chmn. mems.' council). Episcopalian. Clubs: Century Assn. (N.Y.C.); Nat. Press, Army and Navy (Washington); Bar Harbor (Me.) Yacht. Home: 45 E 62d St New York NY 10021 Office: 51 W 52d St New York NY 10019

MEADE, GORDON MONTGOMERY, physician, educator; b. Rochester, N.Y., Dec. 9, 1905; s. George and Adelaide (Ostrander) M.; A.B., U. Rochester, 1928, M.D., 1935; m. Jane Bullard, Oct. 2, 1943; children—Susan Bullard, Anne Harris. Intern, Strong Meml. Hosp., 1935-36, asst. dir., 1938-43; resident Tb Mt. Morris Hosp., 1936-37; dir. Tb control U. Rochester Sch. Medicine, 1943-46, asst. prof. medicine 1947-54, U. Vt., 1949-54; asso. med. dir. Trudeau (N.Y.) Sanatorium, 1946-50, med. dir., 1950-53; exec. dir. Trudeau-Saranac Inst., 1953-54; clin. dir. Miner's Meml. Hosp. Assn., 1956-63; dir. med. edn. Am. Thoracic Soc. and Nat. Tb and Respiratory Disease Assn., N.Y.C., 1964-71; clin. asso. prof. medicine, spl. asst. to dean and exec. sec. Med. Alumni Assn., U. Rochester Sch. Medicine, 1971—, dir. Office Continuing Profl. Edn., 1976—. Diplomate Am. Bd. Preventive Medicine. Fellow Am. Coll. Chest Physicians, A.C.P.; mem. Am. Thoracic Soc., Med. Adminstrs. Conf., Am. Clin. and Climatol. Soc., Am. Ornithologists Union, Sigma Xi, Alpha Omega Alpha, Alpha Delta Phi. Editor: Clin. Notes on Respiratory Diseases, 1964-73. Contbr. articles to profl. jours. Home: 27 Mill Valley Rd Pittsford NY 14534 Office: 601 Elmwood Ave Rochester NY 14642

MEADE, JULIA (MRS. OLIVER WORSHAM RUDD, JR.), actress; b. Boston; d. Adam and Caroline (Meade) Kunze; student Yale Drama Sch.; m. Oliver Worsham Rudd, Jr., May 17, 1952; children—Caroline Meade, Alice Diane. Made mus. comedy debut in Plain and Fancy, Detroit, then Flint, Mich.; appeared summer stock theaters in Tea and Sympathy, Love of Four Colonels, Oh Men, Oh Women; appeared feature role The Tender Trap, Broadway, also Double in Hearts, Roman Candle, 1960, Mary, Mary, 1962-63; featured in motion picture Pillow Talk, 1959, co-star Tammy Tell Me True, 1961, Zotz, 1962; former TV saleswoman on Ed Sullivan Show, Playhouse 90; hostess TV talk shows Dear Julia Meade, Triangle TV Network, 1969-71, Julia Meade and Friends, Cable TV, 1972. Recipient Sarah Siddons award for performance in Mary, Mary. Address: 1010 Fifth Ave New York NY 10028

MEADE, RICHARD ANDREW, educator; b. Sutherland, Va., Dec. 13, 1911; s. John Andrew and Cora (Spain) M.; A.B., Randolph-Macon Coll., 1931; M.A., U. Va., 1936, Ph.D., 1941; postgrad. U. Chgo., summers 1935, 39; m. Mildred Broocks Lipscomb, June 9, 1937; children—Betsy Barrington, Andrew Lipscomb. Tchr. English, Greensville County High Sch., Emporia, Va., 1931-34; tchr. English, Lane High Sch., Charlottesville, Va., asst. prof. secondary edn. and teaching of English, U. Va., 1934-50; asso. prof. edn. U. Va., Charlottesville, 1950-57, prof. edn., 1957—, chmn. curriculum and instrn. dept., 1967-71; cons. Va. Dept. Edn. Chmn. Charlottesville Sch. Bd., 1962-63. Recipient Distinguished Achievement award Alpha Beta chpt. Phi Delta Kappa, 1947. Mem. Nat. Council Tchrs. English (past mem. commn. on English curriculum), Conf. on English Edn. (past mem. exec. com.), Va. Assn. Tchrs. English (mem. exec. com.), Phi Beta Kappa, Phi Delta Kappa, Omicron Delta Kappa, Tau Kappa Alpha, Sigma Phi Epsilon. Clubs: Colonnade (U. Va.); Greencroft Country (Charlottesville). Author: Better English, 1945; Effective English, 1961; Fifth-Year and Five-Year Programs for the Education of Teachers of English, 1965; Literature for Adolescents: Selection and Use, 1973. Contbr. to National Interest and the Teaching of English, 1961, Ends and Issues, 1966. Contbr. articles to profl. jours. Home: 38 University Circle Charlottesville VA 22903

MEADE, RICHARD HARDAWAY, physician; b. Richmond, Va., May 10, 1897; s. Richard H. and Nellie Prior (Atkins) M.; student Va. Mil. Inst., 1913-14, Richmond Coll., 1915; B.S., U. Va., 1917; M.D., Harvard, 1921; m. Mary Frazier, June 14, 1924; children—Richard Hardaway III, Charles H. Frazier, James Gardiner, David Everard; m. 2d, Mary A. Martin, Nov. 30, 1946. Med. missionary, China,

1924-27; asst. prof. surgery, gynecology U. Va., 1927-31; asso. in surgery U. Pa., 1931-42; asso. in surgery Northwestern U., 1946-48; attending chest surgeon VA Hosp., Hines, Ill., 1946-48; hon. cons. thoracic surgeon Blodgett Meml. Hosp.; cons. thoracic surgery VA. Served from maj. to lt. col., M.C., AUS, 1942-45. Decorated Legion of Merit. Fellow A.C.S.; mem. Internat. Soc. Surgery, Am. Assn. Thoracic Surgery (sec. 1935-47, pres. 1955-56), Soc. Cincinnati, Am. Broncho-Esophagological Assn., Central Surg. Assn., Mich. State Med. Soc., A.M.A., Am. Assn. History Medicine, Am. Coll. Chest Physicians, Raven Soc., Delta Psi. Episcopalian. Rotarian. Club: Kent Country. Author: A History of Thoracic Surgery, 1961; An Introduction to the History of General Surgery, 1968; In the Sunshine of Life: A Biography of Dr. Richard Mead 1673-1754, 1974. Contbr. articles to profl. jours. Home: 750 San Jose Dr SE Grand Rapids MI 49506

MEADE, ROY HAMPTON, brick co. exec.; b. Pound, Va., Dec. 25, 1916; s. John R. and Winnie Meade; diploma Johnson City (Tenn.) Bus. Coll., 1936; m. Myrtle Linville, Sept. 4, 1937; children—Sandra, Judith. With Gen. Shale Products Corp., Johnson City, 1936—, fin. v.p., 1966-78, pres., 1978—, also dir. Republican. Clubs: Johnson City Country, Ponte Vedra, Elks. Address: Gen Shale Products Corp 3209 N Roan St Johnson City TN 37601

MEADER, JONATHAN GRANT, artist; b. Orange, N.J., Aug. 29, 1943; s. William Granville and Audrey M.; One-man shows: Corcoran Dupont Center, 1969, Lunn Gallery, Washington, 1972, Pyramid Gallery, Washington, 1973, 74, Plum Gallery, Md., 1976, 78, Klein-Vogel Gallery, Mich., 1976, Harlan Gallery, Tucson, 1977; Swearingen Gallery, Ky., 1977; group shows include: Corcoran Gallery Art, Washington, 1972, Balt. Mus. Traveling Show, 1972, Phillips Collection, Washington, 1972, Iowa U. Mus., 1975, Plum Gallery, 1975; represented in permanent collections: Whitney Mus. Am. Art, N.Y.C., Met. Mus. Art, N.Y.C., Nat. Gallery, Washington, Hirshhorn Mus., Washington. Wurlitzer Found. grantee, 1967; Stern Family grantee, 1970; Nat. Endowment Arts grantee, 1974. Address: PO Box 21146 Washington DC 20009

MEADER, RALPH GIBSON, med. adminstr.; b. Eaton Rapids, Mich., Sept. 6, 1904; s. Robert Eugene and Jennie Editha (Gibson) M.; A.B., Ohio Wesleyan U., 1925; student U. Mich., summers 1926, 27, 28; A.M., Hamilton Coll., 1927; Ph.D., Yale U., 1932; LL.D., Phila. Coll. Osteopathy, 1956; Sc.D., Ohio Wesleyan U., 1958; m. Olive Myrle Root, June 16, 1928; 1 dau., Mary Batcheller. Instr. biology Hamilton Coll., 1925-27; part-time instr. biology Wesleyan U., 1928-29; asst. prof. biology Hamilton Coll., 1927-28; fellow in neuroanatomy Blossom Fund, Yale U. Sch. Medicine, 1929-31; instr. anatomy Yale U. Sch. Medicine, 1931-37, asst. prof., 1937-45, asso. prof. anatomy, 1945-48; asst. dir. bd. sci. advisors Jane Coffin Childs Meml. Fund for Med. Research, 1942-48; spl. cons. USPHS, as sci. dir. cancer research grants br. Nat. Cancer Inst., 1947-48, chief of br., 1948-60, asso. dir. grants and tng., 1960-65; exec. sec. Nat. Adv. Cancer Council, 1947-65; dep. dir. for research adminstrn. and exec. sec. com. on research Mass. Gen. Hosp., Boston, 1965-76, cons. as asst. to asso. gen. dir., 1976-77, cons. grants and contracts, 1977—, also mem. Com. on Research; spl. cons. Nat. Cancer Inst., 1965—; biologist N.Y. State Biol. Survey, 1929-30; mem. biomed. library rev. com. Nat. Library Medicine, 1974-76, chmn., 1975-76, cons., 1976—; cons. Lovelace Med. Found., Albuquerque, 1980—; Rockefeller Found. fellow in neurology U. Amsterdam (Netherlands), 1938-39. Incorporator, trustee Eunice Kennedy Shriver Center for Mental Retardation, Waltham, Mass., 1969—, pres. bd. trustees, 1977—; incorporator, trustee Spaulding Youth Center, Tilton, N.H., 1967—, pres. bd. trustees, 1972-75. Recipient Superior Service award HEW, 1959. Fellow AAAS; mem. Am. Assn. Anatomists, Am. Assn. Cancer Research, Soc. Study of Devel. and Growth, Corp. of Bermuda Biol. Sta. for Research, Inc., Phi Beta Kappa, Sigma Xi. Home: Calef Farm Route 1 Franklin NH 03235 Office: Mass Gen Hosp Boston MA 02114

MEADMORE, CLEMENT LYON, sculptor; b. Melbourne, Australia, Feb. 9, 1929; s. Clement Robert Webb and Mary Agnes (Ludlow) M.; student Royal Melbourne Inst. Tech., 1947-49; m. Enid Jean Cameron, 1950 (div.); 1 son, Clement Quentin. Came to U.S., 1963, naturalized. One-man shows at Melbourne, 1954, 59, 62, Sydney, Australia, 1960, 62, Byron Gallery, N.Y.C., 1967, 68, Canberra, Australia, 1968, Max Hutchinson New York, Ltd., 1970, 71, 72, Richard Feigen Gallery, Chgo., 1971, Gallery A, Sydney, 1972, Donald Morris Gallery, Detroit, 1972, 73, Galerie Denise René/Hans Mayer, Düsseldorf, 1974, Rice U., 1975, U. Tex., Austin, 1975, La. Gallery, Houston, 1976, Kingpitcher Gallery, Pitts., 1976, Olympia Galleries, Phila., 1976, Hamilton Gallery Contemporary Art, N.Y.C., 1978; exhibited in group shows at Riverside Mus., N.Y.C., 1968, Rockefeller Collection, Mus. Modern Art, 1969, Whitney Mus. Am. Art, N.Y.C., 1969, Mexican Olympic Outdoor Sculpture, 1969, Max Hutchinson New York Ltd., 1970, Monumental Art, Cin., 1970, 7 Outside, Indpls., 1970, Monumental Sculpture, Boston, 1971, Sculpture in the Parks, N.J., 1971, Internat. Sculpture Symposium, Burlington, Vt., 1971, Washington Heights Outdoor Sculpture Project, N.Y.C., 1972, Fine Arts Gallery, San Diego, 1973, Sculpture off the Pedestal, Grand Rapids, Mich., 1973, Monumenta, Newport, R.I., 1974, Invitational Sculpture Show, Bethlehem, Pa., 1974, sculpture show, N.Y.C., 1975, outdoor show, Houston, 1975, Super Sculpture, New Orleans, 1976; represented in permanent collections at Nat. Gallery Victoria, Davenport (Ohio) Mcpl. Art Gallery, Columbus (Ohio) Gallery Fine Arts, Art Gallery N.S.W., Nat. Gallery of Australia, Columbia U., Australian Mut. Provident Soc., Atlantic Richfield Oil Co., Nelson A. Rockefeller, Bradley Collection, N.Y. State, Albany, Chase Manhattan Bank, Chgo. Art Inst., J.B. Speed Mus., Ky., Princeton U., Portland (Oreg.) Art Inst., U. Houston, Hale Boggs Fed. Bldg., New Orleans, numerous others. Trustee, New York Jazz Mus., 1973-74. Recipient award and citation Am. Acad. Arts and Letters; Guggenheim fellow, 1975; Creative Artists Public Service Program grantee, 1976. Mem. Archtl. League New York (v.p. for sculpture 1970-72). Address: 800 West End Ave New York NY 10025

MEADOR, CLIFTON KIRKPATRICK, physician, educator; b. Selma, Ala., Sept. 7, 1931; s. Daniel John and Mabel (Kirkpatrick) M.; B.A. (Walter O. Parmer scholar), Vanderbilt U., 1952, M.D., 1955; children—Clifton Kirkpatrick, Aubrey Allen, Ann Graham, Elizabeth Garrett. Intern, Presbyn. Hosp., N.Y.C., 1955-56, asst. resident in medicine, 1956-57; asst. resident in medicine Vanderbilt U. Hosp., 1959-60; fellow in endocrinology Vanderbilt U., 1960-61, instr. dept. medicine Sch. Medicine, 1960-61; practice medicine specializing in endocrinology, Selma, 1961-62; asst. prof. medicine Sch. Medicine, U. Ala., 1962-64, asso. prof., 1964-66, prof., 1966-73; asst. chief of staff U. Ala. Hosp., 1966-68; dean Sch. Medicine, U. Ala., 1968-73; prof. medicine Sch. Medicine, Vanderbilt U., 1973—; chief medicine St. Thomas Hosp., Nashville, 1973—. Served as capt. M.C., AUS, 1957-59. Recipient Founders medal for scholastic honors Vanderbilt Sch. Medicine, 1955. John and Mary R. Markle scholar, 1963. Fellow A.C.P.; mem. Am. Diabetes Assn., Am. Fedn. Clin. Research, Endocrine Soc., N.Y. Acad. Sci., Phi Beta Kappa, Sigma Xi, Alpha Omega Alpha. Mem. editorial bd. So. Med. Jour., 1969—; contbr. articles to profl. jours. Home: 865 Bellevue Rd Nashville TN 37221

MEADOR, DANIEL JOHN, lawyer, educator; b. Selma, Ala., Dec. 7, 1926; s. Daniel John and Mabel (Kirkpatrick) M.; B.S., Auburn U., 1949; J.D., U. Ala., 1951; LL.M., Harvard, 1954; m. Janet Caroline Heilmann, Nov. 19, 1955; children—Janet Barrie, Anna Kirkpatrick, Daniel John. Admitted to Ala. bar, 1951, Va. bar, 1961; law clk. to U.S. Supreme Ct. Justice Hugo L. Black, 1954-55; asso. firm Lange, Simpson, Robinson & Somerville, Birmingham, 1955-57; faculty U. Va. Law Sch., 1957-66, prof. law, 1961-66; prof., dean U. Ala. Law Sch., 1966-70; James Monroe prof. law U. Va., Charlottesville, 1970—; asst. atty. gen. U.S., 1977-79; Fulbright lectr. U.K., 1965-66. Chmn., Southeastern Conf. Assn. Am. Law Schs., 1964-65; chmn. Cts. Task Force Nat. Adv. Commn. on Criminal Justice, 1971-72; dir. appellate justice project Nat. Center for State Cts., 1972-74; mem. Adv. Council on Appellate Justice, 1971-75. Served to 1st lt. AUS, 1951-53. Decorated Bronze Star. Mem. Am. Law Inst., Am., Ala., Va. bar assns., Am. Judicature Soc. (dir. 1975-77), Soc. Pub. Tchrs. Law, Am. Soc. Legal History (dir. 1970-75), Order of Coif, Raven Soc., Phi Delta Phi, Omicron Delta Kappa, Kappa Alpha. Presbyn. Author: Preludes to Gideon, 1967; Criminal Appeals—English Practices and American Reforms, 1973; Mr. Justice Black and His Books, 1974; Appellate Courts: Staff and Process in the Crisis of Volume, 1974; also articles in legal periodicals. Editor: Va. Bar News, 1962-65. Home: Flordon Dr Charlottesville VA 22901 Office: U Va Law Sch Charlottesville VA 22901

MEADOW, LYNNE (CAROLYN) ELIZABETH, theatrical producer and dir.; b. New Haven, Nov. 12, 1946; d. Frank and Virginia R. Meadow; B.A. cum laude, Bryn Mawr Coll., 1968; postgrad. (Herbert Brodkin fellow) Yale Drama Sch., 1968-70. Artistic and exec. dir. Manhattan Theatre Club, N.Y.C., 1972—; guest dir. Nat. Playwrights Conf., Eugene O'Neill Theatre Center, 1975-77, Phoenix Theatre, 1976; dir. Ashes for Manhattan Theatre Club and N.Y. Shakespeare Festival, 1977; adj. prof. SUNY, Stony Brook, 1975-76, Yale U., Circle in the Sq., 1977-80; theatre and music/theatre panelist Nat. Endowment for Arts, 1977—; dir. Theatre Communications Group, 1978—. Recipient Citation of Merit, Nat. Council Women, 1976; Outer Circle Critics award, 1977; Drama Desk award, 1977; Obie award for Ashes, 1977. Office: 321 E 73d St New York NY 10021

MEADOWS, AUDREY, television actress; b. Wu Chang, China; m. 2d, Robert F. Six, 1961. Broadway prodn. Top Banana; on road 2 yrs. with nat. co. of High Button Shoes; lead role in Honeymooners, Jackie Gleason Show; appeared Bob and Ray Show, Colgate Comedy Hour, Ed Sullivan Show, Dinah Shore Show, Jack Benny Show, Alfred Hitchcock Show, Wagon Train, Checkmate, Play of the Week; co-star Sid Ceasar in eight CBS spectaculars, Dean Martin Spls.; appeared on Starsky and Hutch, The Love Boat; dir. First Nat. Bank Denver; adv. dir. Continental Airlines, Inc.; motion pictures include: Touch of Mink, Take Her She's Mine, Rosie. Bd. dirs. Continental Airlines Found.; trustee Pearl Buck Found. Recipient Emmy award for best supporting actress in regular series, 1955; Sylvania award for outstanding contbn. TV techniques. Address: care Val Irving Assos 527 Madison Ave New York City NY 10022

MEADOWS, CLYDE W., ret. bishop; b. Appomattox County, Va., Jan. 3, 1901; B.A., Huntington Coll., 1925, D.D., 1940; B.D., S.T.M., Gettysburg Luth. Theol. Sem.; m. Mabel F. Mumma, 1924; 1 dau., Una Joyce (Mrs. William H. Elder). Ordained to ministry United Brethren Ch., 1927; student pastor, Alexandria, Ind., 1921-23, Van Buren, Ind., 1923-25; pastor, New Dundee, Ont., 1925-27; conf. supt. United Brethren Ch., Va., 1927-28; pastor King St. Ch., Chambersburg, Pa., 1928-61; bishop Eastern area U.S. and Can., 1961-69; Eastern area, Western area U.S. and Can., 1968-69, bishop emeritus, 1969—; pastor Prince St. United Brethren Ch., Shippensburg, Pa., 1975-77. Trustee Milton Wright Meml. Home, Huntington Coll. Mem. Pa. (past chmn.), Franklin County (councilor), World's (pres. 1962-74, hon. pres. 1974—) Christian endeavor unions, Internat. Soc. Christian Endeavor (past pres.), Pa. Sabbath Sch. Assn. (dir., past pres., dir. dept. evangelism 1969—), Franklin County Sunday Sch. Assn. (supt. adminstrn.). Rotarian. Author: Why We Choose Christ; Music in Christian Education; A Christian and His Church; also numerous pamphlets. Editor: United Brethren Hymnal, United Brethern Hymnal Rev. Home: 2120 Philadelphia Ave Chambersburg PA 17201 Office: 1221 E Broad St Columbus OH 43216 also 900 S Arlington Ave Room 211 Harrisburg PA 17109. *My goal in life has been to serve the Lord Jesus Christ faithfully and leave the world better than I found it.*

MEADOWS, DANIEL THOMAS, dentist; b. Salem, Ala., June 5, 1917; s. Daniel Porter and Gemmie Bruce (Browning) M.; B.S., Auburn U., 1939; D.M.D., U. Ala., 1953; m. Agatha Joan Fischer, Mar. 31, 1944; children—Gemma Meadows Sanford, Daniel Thomas. Pvt. practice dentistry, Birmingham, Ala., 1953; resident in prosthodontics U. Ala., 1955-57; staff dentist Birmingham VA Hosp., 1954-55, 57-62, chief dental service, 1962-68, 69—; prof. clin. dentistry U. Ala., Birmingham, 1968—. Served to col. Dental Corps, U.S. Army, 1942-46, 68-69. Decorated Army Commendation medal with oak leaf cluster; recipient Disting. Service medal of Ala., 1973. Fellow Am. Coll. Dentists; mem. Am. Prosthodontic Soc., ADA, Ala. Dental Assn., Am. Legion, Southeastern Acad. Prosthodontics, Birmingham Dist. Dental Soc. (exec. council 1968-72), Phi Kappa Phi, Gamma Sigma Delta, Kappa Delta Pi, Xi Psi Phi. Editor Ala. Farmer, 1939. Home: 4309 Corinth Dr Birmingham AL 35213 Office: 700 S 19th St Birmingham AL 35233. *Approach each situation with enthusiastic personal dedication and perform in a manner reflecting concern for fellow man, credit to one's self, and glory to god and country.*

MEADOWS, DONALD FREDERICK, librarian; b. Regina, Sask., Can., Jan. 13, 1937; s. Frederick John and Doris Eileen (Willock) M.; B.A., U. Sask., 1964; B.L.S., U. B.C., 1968; m. Ruth Susan Cochran, June 10, 1960; children—Scott Frederick, George Edward. Library cons. Sask. Provincial Library, Regina, 1968-69, asst. provincial librarian, 1969-70, provincial librarian, 1970—. Mem. Canadian, Am., Sask. (past pres.) library assns. Mem. United. Ch. Can. Office: 1352 Winnipeg St Regina SK S4R 1J9 Canada*

MEADOWS, JACK EDWARD, paper co. exec., publishing co. exec.; b. Tulsa, Sept. 2, 1919; s. Noel Etter and Nellie (Connolly) M.; B.S. in Chem. Engring., U. Tex., 1941; postgrad. Harvard U., 1960; m. Jane Worthington Duls, Mar. 10, 1944; children—Jack Edward, William Noel. Asst. to supt. power and recovery Crossett Paper Mills (Ark.), 1945-49, asst. to mgr., 1949-52, asst. prodn. mgr., 1952-56, asst. mgr., 1956-62; asst. mgr. paper ops. Ga.-Pacific Corp., Crossett, 1962-64, mgr. paper ops., Toledo, Oreg., 1964, Crossett, 1964-69, sr. v.p., gen. mgr. Crossett div., 1969-75; pres. Pubs. Paper Co., Oregon City, Oreg., 1975—; v.p. Times Mirror Co., Los Angeles, 1975—; mem. adv. com. Oreg. State U. Forest Research Lab.; chmn. Oreg. Forest Industries Council. Bd. dirs. Oreg. Ind. Coll. Found., Portland (Oreg.) C. of C.; trustee George Fox Coll. Served to comdr. USNR, 1941-45. Recipient C.E. Palmer award for disting. service to Ark., 1953. Mem. U.S. Jr. C. of C. (Ark. pres. 1951-52, nat. v.p. 1952-53), Ark. C. of C. (v.p. 1973, dir. 1969-75), So. Forest Inst. (v.p. 1972, pres. 1973), Pi Kappa Alpha. Democrat. Methodist. Office: 419 Main St Oregon City OR 97045

MEADOWS, JAYNE, actress; b. Wu Chang, China, Sept. 27, 1926 (parents U.S. citizens); d. Francis James M. and Ida Miller (Taylor) Cotter; grad. St. Margaret's Boarding Sch., Waterbury, Conn.; m. Steve V.P.W. Allen, July 31, 1954; 1 son, William Christopher; stepchildren—Steve, Brian, David. Broadway appearances include Spring Again, 1942-43, Another Love Story, 1943-44, Kiss Them For Me, 1944-45, The Gazebo, 1958; motion picture appearances include Undercurrent, Lady in the Lake, Dr. Kildare, Thin Man, Luck of the Irish, Enchantment, David and Bathsheba, The Fat Man, College Confidential, Norman, Is That You?, 1976; TV appearances all major dramatic, panel and variety shows, 1952—; regular panel mem. TV show I've Got a Secret, 1952-58; author column for Carte Blanche mag., also N. Am. Newspaper Alliance, 1960-65; mem. cast Medical Center, CBS, 1969-76; appeared in night clubs Las Vegas, others; rec. artist for RCA, Dot and Coral. Chmn. fund raising dr. Nat. Assn. Mental Health, 1960-61. Address: care Contemporary-Korman Artists Ltd 132 Lasky Dr Beverly Hills CA 90212*

MEADOWS, PAUL, sociologist; b. Herrin, Ill., June 19, 1913; s. William C. and Mae (McCree) M.; A.B., McKendree Coll., 1935; M.A., Washington U., St. Louis, 1936; Ph.D., Northwestern U., 1940; m. Mary Nell Gouldin, Aug. 17, 1941; children—Michael, Peter. Instr., Western Mich. U., Kalamazoo, 1940-41, Northwestern U., 1941-44; asst. prof. Mont. State U., also research asso. Mont. Study, 1944-47; asso., then prof. U. Nebr., 1947-59; prof. sociology, chmn. dept. sociology Syracuse U., 1959-69; chmn. dept. sociology State U. N.Y. at Albany, 1969-72, research prof., 1972—; dir. research Diocese of Albany, 1970-73; sr. staff cons. Inst. on Man and Sci., Rensselaerville, N.Y. Pres. bd. Family Welfare Assn. Lincoln, 1951-53. Co-recipient Weatherly award Am. Unitarian-Assn., 1957; recipient Brotherhood award NCCJ, 1959. Mem. Midwest (pres. 1957-58, editor jour. 1953-56), Eastern sociol. socs., Phi Beta Kappa. Author: The Culture of Industrial Man, 1950; (with Reinhardt and Gillette) Social Problems and Social Policy, 1951; John Wesley Powell: Frontiersman of Science, 1949; Tecnologia y el Orden Social, 1957; El Proceso Social de la Revolucion, 1961; Marcos para el Estudio de los Movimentos Sociales, 1961; The Masks of Change, 1965; Industrial Man: Profiles of Developmental Society, 1965; The Rhetoric of Sociology, 1966; The Many Faces of Change: Explorations in the Theory of Social Change, 1971. Editor: (with E.H. Mizruchi) Urbanization, Urbanism and Change, 1968, 76; (with LaGory, Leue, Meadows) Bibliographical Guide to the Literature on Recent Immigration, 1977; Policy and Practice: The Interface between the Social Sciences and Urban Planning, 1978. Contbr. to The New Sociology, 1964; Fact and Value in Social Sciences, 1964; Development Administration, 1965; Sociological Theory, 1966; Among the People, 1968; Alienation: Concept and Meaning, 1973; Alienation and Contemporary Society: A Multidisciplinary Examination, 1975; American Communities, 1972; Essays on the Sociology of T. Parsons, 1977; The New Immigration, 1979; also publs. in field. Office: State U NY 1400 Washington Ave Albany NY 12222

MEADOWS, PAUL DWAIN, oil co. exec.; b. Niotaze, Kans., Oct. 22, 1926; s. Lowell G. and Georgia (Henderson) M.; B.S., N.Mex. Inst. Tech., 1952; m. Jimmie Loree Starkey, Jan. 28, 1950; 1 dau., Paula Jean. Various engring. positions Honolulu Oil Corp., Midland, Tex., 1952-59, mgr. engring., San Francisco, 1959-61; v.p. James A. Lewis Engring., Dallas, 1961-66, Res. Oil & Gas Co., Dallas, 1966-68; pres., dir. Canadian Res. Oil and Gas Ltd., Calgary, Alta., Can., 1968—; vice chmn., chief exec. officer, 1977—; dir. Res. Oil and Gas Co., Denver, 1970—, pres., 1974—, pres., chief exec. officer, 1977—. Del. State Dem. Conv., Tex., 1966. Served with USAAF, 1944-45. Mem. Am. Petroleum Inst., Indsl. Petroleum Assn. Am., Am. Inst. Petroleum Engrs. Home: 44 Sedgwick Dr Englewood CO 80110 Office: PO Box 5568 Denver CO 80217

MEADOWS, ROBERT MERLE, communication, wire, cable and equipment co exec.; b. Berwick, Ill., Feb. 5, 1917; s. Arlien Aden and Eva Lena (Byram) M.; student Brown's Bus. Coll., 1935, 46, Internat. Accountants Soc., 1949, Alexander Hamilton Inst., 1950; m. Shirley Sue Hallman, June 18, 1949; children—Robert Byram, Joan Adele. Order clk. Abingdon Potteries (Ill.), 1936-41; sec., asst. treas. Hyalyn Porcelain, Inc., Hickory, N.C., 1946-58; chief accountant Superior Continental Corp., Hickory, 1958-60, sec.-treas., 1961-75; v.p. finance Pepsi-Cola Bottling Co. of Hickory, Pepsi Cola Bottling Co. of Asheville (N.C.), Pepsi Cola Bottling Co. of Spruce Pine (N.C.), 1975—. Treas., Hickory Landmarks Soc., 1968—. Served with USAAF, 1941-45. Mem. Am. Mgmt. Assn. Mem. Ch. of Christ (deacon 1964-70). Moose. Club: Lake Hickory Country. Home: Route 10 Box 602 Hickory NC 28601 Office: 2640 Main Ave NW Hickory NC 28601

MEADS, DONALD EDWARD, bus. and fin. exec.; b. Salem, Mass., Sept. 23, 1920; s. Laurence Granville and Gertrude Francis (Hay) M.; A.B., Dartmouth Coll., 1942; M.B.A. in Fin., Harvard U., 1947; m. Jane Lightner, June 15, 1943; children—Edward G., Robert C., Laurence G., Judith C., Suzanne M., Clifford L., Nancy E. With N.Y. Life Ins. Co., 1947-61, v.p. investment dept., vice chmn. investment com., 1960-61; v.p. fin., chmn. investment com. Investors Diversified Services, Inc., 1961-65; pres., chief exec. officer, dir. Internat. Basic Economy Corp., N.Y.C., 1965-68, chmn., 1969-71; exec. v.p., chief fin. officer, dir. INA Corp., Phila., 1971-74; chmn., chief exec. officer, dir. CertainTeed Corp., Valley Forge, Pa., 1974-78; chmn., pres. Carver Assos., Inc., Plymouth Meeting, Pa., 1978—; dir. INA Corp, Kaneb Services Inc., Quaker Oats Co., The Singer Co., Perdue Inc., Western Savs. Fund Soc. Phila., Penjerdel Corp., Phila. Bd. dirs. Independence Hall Assn., World Affairs Council; chmn. Internat. House Phila.; trustee Thomas Jefferson U., Phila.; mem. Brit. N.Am. Com., N.Y.C. and London; mem. exec. com. Pa. Acad. Fine Arts. Served as capt. USMCR, 1942-45. Decorated D.F.C., six air medals. Mem. Nat. Planning Assn., Phila. Com. Fgn. Relations. Clubs: Econ., Harvard, Rockefeller Center (N.Y.C.); Phila. Aviation Country, Peale, Sunday Breakfast, Union League (Phila.). Office: One Plymouth Meeting Plymouth Meeting PA 19462

MEADS, MANSON, med. sch. adminstr.; b. Oakland, Calif., Mar. 25, 1918; s. Albert Manson and Romilda (Paroni) M.; A.B., U. Calif. at Berkeley, 1939, M.D., Temple U., 1943, D.Sc. (hon.), 1956; m. Helen Wheeler Belding, May 26, 1945; 1 dau., Elizabeth Manson. Intern, U. Calif. Hosp., San Francisco, 1943; resident medicine Permanente Found. Hosp., 1943-44; research fellow Thorndike Meml. Lab., Harvard, 1944-46, resident, 1945-46; asst. medicine Boston City Hosp., 1944-46, asst. bacteriology, 1946-47; Ernst fellow bacteriology Harvard, 1946-47; faculty Bowman Gray Sch. Medicine, Winston-Salem, N.C., 1947—, prof. preventive medicine, chmn. dept., 1955-57, prof. medicine, 1957—, exec. dean, 1959-63, dean, 1963-67, v.p. med. affairs, dean, 1967-71, v.p. health affairs, 1971—; dir. Med. Center, Bowman Gray Sch. Medicine - N.C. Bapt. Hosp., 1974—. Mem. adv. med. council N.C. Bd. Mental Health, 1964-67; adv. com. on med. edn. N.C. Bd. Higher Edn., 1970-72; cons. rev. com. constrn. schs. medicine USPHS, 1964-67, mem., 1967-70; mem. Gov.'s Adv. Council on Comprehensive Health Planning, 1974-76. Bd. dirs. Goodwill Industries, Winston-Salem, 1960-65, mem. exec. com., 1963-65; bd. dirs. N.C. Regional Med. Program, 1965-70; mem. Joint Conf. Com. on Med. Care in N.C., 1968—. Sr. surgeon USPHS, 1953-55. Markle scholar, 1947-52. Diplomate Am. Bd. Internal

Medicine. Fellow A.C.P.; mem. Am. Assn. Med. Colls. (distinguished service mem.), AMA, N.C., Forsyth County med. socs., Assn. Acad. Health Centers (bd. dirs. 1978—), Am. Soc. Clin. Investigation, C. of C. Winston-Salem and Forsyth County (dir. 1967-70, 73—, v.p. 1975, pres. 1976, chmn. found. bd. 1977—), Newcomen Soc. N.Am., Sigma Xi, Alpha Omega Alpha, Phi Chi. Home: 1855 Meadowbrook Dr Winston-Salem NC 27104

MEADS, WALTER FREDERICK, inst. exec.; b. Ft. Wayne, Ind., Mar. 11, 1923; s. Frederick C. and Minnie E. (Stephenson) M.; B.S., Kent State U., 1948; M.A., Fairfield U.; m. Mary E. Smith, Mar. 21, 1975; children by previous marriage—Kenneth W., Catherine L. With Norman Malone & Assos., Akron, Ohio, 1946-48; with Griswold-Eshleman Co., Cleve., 1949-53; with Fuller, Smith & Ross, Cleve., 1953-55; sr. v.p., mgmt. supr., mem. mgmt. com., vice chmn. plans and rev. bds. J. Walter Thompson Co., N.Y.C., 1955-72; with Walter F. Meads & Assos., 1972-77; mem. faculty Fla. A. and M. U., Tallahassee, 1975-77; pres. Meads Inst., Inc., Lakeland, Fla., 1977—. Served with USAAF, 1943-45. Recipient numerous nat. and local advt. industry awards. Mem. Pub. Relations Soc. Am. Unitarian-Universalist. Home: 4420 Orangewood Loop E Lakeland FL 33803 Office: 58 Lake Morton Dr Lakeland FL 33801. *Creative freedom is probably the core concept at the heart of my life—not only for myself but for others. Life is never static; it either deteriorates or grows. All growth, to me, springs from the creative doers of the world. The rest of humanity goes along for the ride. And creative growth, in any field or endeavor, demands an attitude of freedom to shake off the shackles of habit and find new and better ways of doing things.*

MEAGHER, CYNDI (MAZA, CYNTHIA NASH), journalist; b. Detroit, Dec. 24, 1947; d. Frederick Copp and Carolyn (Coffin) Nash; B.A., U. Mich., 1970; m. Michael William Maza, Apr. 10, 1972; 1 dau., Lydia Anne. With Detroit News, 1970—, sports columnist, 1975-77, lifestyle columnist, 1977-79, lifestyle editor, 1979—. Mem. Women in Communications, Sigma Delta Chi. Club: Women's Econ. (Detroit). Office: 615 W Lafayette Detroit MI 48231

MEAGHER, MARK JOSEPH, communication co. exec.; b. Balt., July 9, 1932; s. Harry Royce and Maria Paula (Demarco) M.; student U. Notre Dame, 1950-51; B.S., U. Md., 1954; m. Patricia Ann Essex, Aug. 8, 1951; children—Mark P., Terance S., Timothy B., Kathleen, Robert S., Christopher M., Bridget, Colleen O. Accountant, auditor Price Waterhouse & Co., Balt., 1954-57; systems analyst IBM, Balt., 1957-58; mgmt. cons. McKinsey Co., Washington, 1958-61; exec. v.p. McGraw Hill Book Co., N.Y.C., 1961-70; v.p. fin. and adminstrn. Washington Post Co., N.Y.C., Washington, 1970-74, exec. v.p., gen. mgr., 1974-76, pres. newspaper div., 1976-77, pres., chief operating officer co., 1977—, dir., 1970—; dir. Bowaters Mersey Paper Co., Maple Press. Trustee, Fed. City Council; dir. Met. Washington Bd. Trade; v.p. Urban League New Brunswick (N.J.), 1967-69; chmn. housing com. Metuchen/Edison (N.J.) unit NAACP, 1968; trustee Washington Hosp. Center; bd. dirs. Fgn. Policy Assn. C.P.A. Mem. Nat. Alliance Businessmen (exec. com. 1976), Hon. Accounting Soc., Am. Inst. C.P.A.'s, Am. Newspaper Pubs. Assn. Republican. Roman Catholic. Home: 2769 Unicorn Ln NW Washington DC 20015 Office: care Washington Post Co 1150 15th St NW Washington DC 20071

MEAGHER, WILLIAM R., lawyer; b. N.Y.C., 1903; A.B., Fordham U., 1924, LL.B. cum laude, 1927. Admitted to N.Y. State bar, 1928, U.S. Supreme Ct. bar, 1934; mem. firm Skadden, Arps, Slate, Meagher and Flom, N.Y.C.; spl. asst. atty. gen. N.Y. State, Amen investigation, Bklyn., 1938-42; lectr. law Fordham Law Sch., 1928-44, adj. prof. law, 1974-78. Mem. Assn. Bar City N.Y., N.Y. State Am. bar assns., Am. Law Inst., Am. Judicature Soc. Office: 919 3d Ave New York NY 10022

MEAKIN, JOHN DAVID, univ. research exec., educator; b. Nottingham, Eng., Feb. 11, 1934; s. Claude Edwin and Hilda May (Storer) M.; came to U.S., 1958, naturalized, 1972; B.Sc. in Metallurgy, Leeds (Eng.) U., 1955, Ph.D., 1957; m. Katharine Sadie Glover, July 21, 1956; children—Robert Nicolas, David Harry, Ian James, William Edwin, Andrew John. Vis. asso. Franklin Inst., Phila., 1958-59; research fellow U. Durham (Eng.), 1960-62, sr. research scientist, 1962-65, prin. scientist, 1965-70, mgr. lab., 1970-74; prof. mech. and aerospace engring., asso. dir. Inst. Energy Conversion, U. Del., 1974—. Pres. Home and Sch. Assn. Lower Merion High Sch., Ardmore, Pa., 1971, Penn Valley Sch., Narberth, Pa., 1973; chmn. cub pack 243 Valley Forge council Boy Scouts Am., 1971-73. Yorkshire Copper Works (Eng.) Research scholar, 1955; Dept. Sci. and Indsl. Research scholar, 1956-57; Imperial Chem. Industries Sr. Research fellow, 1961, 62. Mem. Electron Microscope Soc., Solar Energy Soc. Co-editor proceedings Cadmium Sulfide Solar Cells, 1975. Contbr. articles to profl. jours. Home: 905 Baylor Dr Newark DE 19711

MEANEY, DONALD VINCENT, television news exec.; b. Newark, N.J., June 3, 1920; s. Vincent I. and Marion R. (Blimm) M.; B.A. in Journalism, Rutgers U., 1947; m. Ruth Virginia Donegan; children—Christopher Ambrose, Andrea Comerford. News dir. Sta. WNJR, Newark, N.J., 1949-51; program dir. Sta. WCTC, New Brunswick, N.J., 1951-52; news producer NBC Radio, 1952-59, nat. news editor, 1959-62, dir. news documentaries NBC, 1962-67, v.p. news programming, N.Y.C., 1967-74, v.p. news, bur. chief NBC Television, Washington, 1974—. Mem. council, North Plainfield, N.J., 1958-61. Served with USNR, 1942-46. Mem. N.Am. Nat. Broadcasters Assn. (vice chmn.). Office: 4001 Nebraska Ave NW Washington DC 20016

MEANOR, H. CURTIS, judge; b. Cleve., Oct. 6, 1929; s. Homer and Helen (Hager) M.; B.A., Rutgers U., 1952, LL.B., 1955; m. Geraldine Strangio, Dec. 22, 1951. Admitted to N.J. bar, 1956, U.S. Supreme Ct. bar, 1961; law clk. to chief judge U.S. Dist. Ct., N.J., 1955-56; asso. firm Emory, Langan, Lamb & Blake, Jersey City, 1956-59; acting exec. sec. to N.J. Gov. Meyner, 1959-60; partner firm Lamb, Blake, Hutchinson & Dunne, and predecessor, Jersey City, 1960-69; judge Essex County Ct., Newark, 1969-72, law div. Superior Ct. of N.J., 1972-73, appellate div., 1973-74, U.S. Dist. Ct. for Dist. of N.J., Newark, 1974—; adj. asst. prof. law Fordham U. Sch. Law, 1964-68. Mem. Am. Law Inst., Am., N.J., Essex County bar assns., Mountainside Hosp. Assn. Republican. Club: Arcola Country (Paramus, N.J.). Asso. editor Rutgers Law Rev., 1954-55, N.J. Law Jour., 1961-69; author: New Jersey Digest Affecting Hospitals, 1956. Home: 280 Ridgewood Ave Glen Ridge NJ 07028 Office: 311 US Courthouse Newark NJ 07101

MEANS, CHARLES FRANKLIN, army officer; b. East Liverpool, Ohio, Mar. 22, 1928; s. Charles F. and Clara E. (Miller) M.; B.S., U.S. Mil. Acad., 1950; M.S.E., U. Mich., Ann Arbor, 1959; grad. U.S. Command and Gen. Staff Coll., 1964, Army War Coll., 1969; m. Anna Chan, June 6, 1950; children—Janis, Michael, Vincent, Lynn, John, Sherri. Commd. 2d lt. U.S. Army, 1950, advanced through grades to maj. gen., 1972; charge NIKE-X ops. div. and range ops. div., Kwajalein Test Site, 1964-65; charge advanced weapons br., plans and ops. div., dir. plans Office Dep. Chief of Staff for Logistics, U.S. Army Air Def. Command, 1965-67; comdg. officer 3d Bn., 59th Arty., Milw., 1967-68; charge ground combat div. U.S. Army Concept Team, Vietnam, 1969-70; comdg. officer 24th Arty. Group, Coventry, R.I., 1970-71; Army mem. Weapons System Evaluation Group, Office Sec. Def., Washington, 1971-72; asst. dep. chief of staff plans and programs NORAD, Ent AFB, Colo., 1972-73; project mgr. SAM-D/PATRIOT Missile System, Redstone Arsenal, Ala., 1973-77; comdg. gen. U.S. Army Missile Research and Devel. Command, 1977, 32d Army Air Def. Command, Germany, 1978—. Decorated Legion of Merit with 2 oak leaf clusters, Army Commendation Medal with oak leaf cluster; named one of 26 people recognized for outstanding contbns. to aerospace Aviation Week and Space Tech., 1975. Mem. Am. Def. Preparedness Assn., Assn. U.S. Army. Address: 32d AADCOM-Germany APO New York NY 09175. *A young soldier once said, "If you want success in life you cannot walk, you must run." Hard work, sacrifice and dedication are essential to success. So also is the right balance between work and family. Finally, when one realizes that most, if not all, problems in life begin with "me," then success will come.*

MEANS, DAVID HAMMOND, advt. exec.; b. Lebanon, Pa., Dec. 15, 1928; s. W. Horace and June (Zimmerman) M.; B.A., Amherst Coll., 1950; m. Nancy N. Downes, June 21, 1952; children—Elizabeth N., Susan Z., Emily M., David H. With CIA, 1950-53; with N.W. Ayer ABH Internat., Inc., 1953—, exec. v.p., 1976—, also dir. Mem. alumni exec. com. Taft Sch., 1967—; trustee Phila. Coll. Textiles and Sci.; bd. dirs. Phila. chpt. Care/Medico. Served to 1st lt. USAF, 1953. Mem. Bus. Profl. Advt. Assn., Psi Upsilon. Episcopalian. Clubs: Merion (Pa.) Golf; Amherst (N.Y.C.); Country of New Canaan (Conn.). Home: Wahackme Ln New Canaan CT 06840 Office: NW Ayer ABH Internat 1345 Ave of Americas New York NY 10019

MEANS, FLORENCE CRANNELL, author; b. Baldwinsville, N.Y., May 15, 1891; d. Philip Wendell and Fannie Eleanor (Grout) Crannell; student Henry Read Sch. Art, 1910-11; spl. student Kansas City Bapt. Theol. Sem., 1912, U. Denver, 1923-24, McPherson (Kans.) Coll., summers 1922-29; m. Carleton Bell Means, Sept. 19, 1912 (dec. Oct. 1973); 1 dau., Eleanor Crannell (Mrs. Angus C. Hull, Jr.). Lectr. Writers' Conf. of Rocky Mountains, U. Colo., 1947, 48, Colo. Woman's Coll. Writers' Workshop in Children's Lit., 1965. Mem. Authors' League Colo., Internat. Inst. Arts and Letters (asso.), Delta Kappa Gamma (hon.), Zeta Tau Alpha. Recipient ann. nat. award Child Study Assn., 1945, Nancy Bloch award, 1957; Florence Crannell Means Meml. Library dedicated 1975. Baptist. Clubs: Denver Woman's Press, Soroptimist International Club. Author: Rafael and Consuelo (with Harriet Fullen), 1929; A Candle in the Mist, 1931 (reprinted in Riverside Reading Series); Children of the Great Spirit (with Frances Somers Riggs), 1932; Ranch and Ring, a Story of the Pioneer West, 1932; Dusky Day, 1933; A Bowlful of Stars, 1934; Rainbow Bridge, 1934; Penny for Luck, 1935; Tangled Waters, 1936; The Singing Wood, 1937; Shuttered Windows, 1938; Adella Mary in Old New Mexico, 1939; Across the Fruited Plain, 1940; At the End of Nowhere, 1940; Children of the Promise, 1941; Whispering Girl, 1941; Shadow Over Wide Ruin, 1943; Teresita of the Valley, 1943; Peter of the Mesa, 1944; The Moved Outers, 1945; Great Day in the Morning, 1946; Assorted Sisters, 1947; The House Under the Hill, 1949; The Silver Fleece (with Carl Means), 1950; Hetty of the Grande Deluxe, 1951; Carvers' George, 1952; Alicia, 1953; The Rains Will Come, 1954; Sagebrush Surgeon, 1956; Knock At the Door, Emmy, 1956; Reach for a Star, 1957; Borrowed Brother, 1958; Emmy and the Blue Door, 1959; Sunlight on the Hopi Mesas, 1960; But I Am Sara, 1961; That Girl Andy, 1962; Tolliver, 1963; It Takes All Kinds, 1964; Us Maltbys, 1966; Our Cup Is Broken, 1969; (audiotape) Biography of Frederick Douglass, 1970; Smith Valley, 1973; (cassettes) The Author Speaks, 1973. Contbr. articles and verse to mags. Home: 595 Baseline Rd Boulder CO 80302

MEANS, GEORGE ROBERT, orgn. exec.; b. Bloomington, Ill., July 5, 1907; s. Arthur John and Alice (Johnson) M.; B.Ed., Ill. State U., 1930; A.M., Clark U., 1932; H.H.D. (hon.), Rikkyo U., Tokyo, Ill. Wesleyan U., Ky. Wesleyan Coll.; m. Martha Cowart, Aug. 5, 1950. Cartographer, map editor, 1932-35; with Rotary Internat., 1935—, beginning as conv. mgr., successively head Middle Asia office, Bombay, India, asst. gen. sec., 1935-52, gen. sec., 1953-72; sec. Rotary Found., 1953-72; dir. Washington Nat. Corp., Hertzberg-New Method, Inc. Mem.-at-large nat. council Boy Scouts Am.; bd. dirs. Four-Way Test Assn. Served as comdr. USNR, 1942-46. Decorated Legion of Honor (France); Chilean Order Merit; Japanese Order Rising Sun; Italian Order of Merit. Recipient Distinguished Service award Geog. Soc. Chgo., 1972. Fellow Am. Geog. Soc.; mem. Evanston Hist. Soc., Gamma Theta Upsilon (founder). Clubs: Rotary (Evanston, Bloomington, Ill.; Sydney, Australia; Kyoto, Osaka and Tokyo, Japan, Seoul, Korea, Cape Town, South Africa; Ituzaingo, Saavedra, Argentina). Author: Rotary's Return to Japan, also numerous articles in Rotary mags. Home: 1067 Smock Dr Greenwood IN 46142

MEANS, JOHN BARKLEY, educator, assn. exec.; b. Cin., Jan. 2, 1939; s. Walker Wilson and Rosetta Mae (Miller) M.; B.A., U. Ill. at Urbana, 1960, M.A., 1963, Ph.D., 1968. U.S. Govt. research analyst on Latin Am., Washington, 1962-64; asso. prof. Portuguese, Temple U., Phila., 1971—, co-chmn. dept. Spanish and Portuguese, 1971-75, dir. Center Critical Langs., 1975—; exec. dir. Nat. Assn. Self Instructional Lang. Programs, Phila.; cons. on Portuguese and self-instructional fgn. lang. edn., 1968—. Served to 1st lt. AUS, 1960-61. NDEA fellow, 1962, 64; scholar State Dept. diplomat seminar, 1970. Mem. Modern Lang. Assn., Latin Am. Studies Assn., Middle Atlantic Council Latin Am. Studies, Am. Assn. Tchrs. Spanish and Portuguese, Nat. Assn. Self-Instructional Lang. Programs, Am. Council Teaching Fgn. Langs., AAUP, Brazilian-Am. Soc., Am. Friends of the Middle East, S.R., Pi Kappa Phi (chmn. nat. future policy com.), Phi Lambda Beta, Sigma Delta Pi. Presbyterian. Editor: Essays on Brazilian Literature, 1971; contbr. articles to mags. Home: 1936 William Penn Annex Philadelphia PA 19105 Office: Humanities Bldg Temple Univ Philadelphia PA 19122. *The fundamental objective of an educator, in the context of the liberal arts, must be the enhancement of each student's capacity to develop both intellect and skills to the limits of one's potential. Distinguishing between the significant (i.e., the essential) and the trivial in the pursuit of the foregoing is supremely important in protecting and sustaining the quality of true liberal arts education.*

MEANS, MARIANNE HANSEN, polit. columnist; b. Sioux City, Iowa, June 13, 1934; d. Ernest Maynard and Else Marie Johanne (Andersen) Hansen; B.A., U. Nebr., 1956; J.D., George Washington U., 1977; m. Warren Weaver, Jr. Copy editor Lincoln (Nebr.) Jour., 1955-57; woman's editor No. Va. Sun, Arlington, 1957-59; Washington bur. corr. Hearst Headline Service, 1959-61, White House corr., 1961-65; polit. columnist King Features Syndicate, 1965—; commentator Spectrum, CBS radio. Mem. D.C. Woman's Savs. Bond Com., 1959-62. Recipient Front Page award N.Y. Newspaper Women, 1962; Tex. Headliners award, 1976. Mem. White House Corrs. Assn., Women in Communications, Phi Beta Kappa, Delta Delta Delta. Clubs: Washington Press, Federal City, Gridiron, City Tavern. Author: The Woman in the White House, 1963. Home: 1521 31st St NW Washington DC 20007 Office: 1701 Pennsylvania Ave Washington DC 20006

MEARA, ANNE, actress; b. Bklyn.; d. Edward Joseph and Mary (Dempsey) Meara; student Herbert Berghoff Studio, 1953-54; m. Gerald Stiller, Sept. 14, 1954; children—Amy, Benjamin. Apprentice in summer stock, Southold, L.I. and Woodstock, N.Y., 1950-53; off-Broadway appearances include Ulysses in Nighttown, 1958, Maedchen in Uniform (Show Bus. Off-Broadway award), 1955, A Month in the Country, 1954, The House of Blue Leaves, 1970; mem. Shakespeare Co., Central Park, N.Y.C., 1957; film appearances include The Out-of-Towners, 1968, Lovers and Other Strangers, 1969, Nasty Habits, 1976, The Boys From Brazil, 1978, Fame, 1979; comedy act (with husband Jerry Stiller), 1963—, syndicated TV series Take Five With Stiller and Meara, 1977-78; appearances include Happy Medium and Medium Rare, Chgo., 1960-61, Village Gate, Phase Two and Blue Angel, N.Y.C., 1963, The Establishment, London, 1963; numerous appearances on TV game and talk shows, also spls. and variety shows; rec. numerous commercials for TV and radio; star TV series Kate McShane, 1975, Archie Bunker's Place, 1979. Co-recipient Voice of Imagery award Radio Advt. Bur., 1975. Address: care Janice S Morgan Communications 250 W 57th St New York NY 10019

MEARS, WALTER ROBERT, journalist; b. Lynn, Mass., Jan. 11, 1935; s. Edward Lewis and Edythe Emily (Campbell) M.; B.A., Middlebury Coll., 1956, Litt.D. (hon.), 1977; m. Sally Danton, Dec. 28, 1956 (dec. Dec. 1962); children—Pamela (dec.), Walter Robert (dec.); m. 2d, Joyce Marie Lund, Aug. 4, 1963; children—Stephanie Joy, Susan Marie. Newsman, AP, Boston, 1956, corr., Montpelier, Vt., 1956-60, state house corr., Boston, 1960-61, newsman, Washington, 1961-69, chief polit. writer, 1969-72, asst. chief Washington bur., 1973-74, spl. corr., 1975, chief Washington bur., 1977—, v.p., 1978—; chief Washington bur. Detroit News, 1974-75. Recipient ann. award AP Mng. Editors Assn., 1973; Pulitzer prize for Nat. Reporting, 1977. Mem. Nat. Press Club, Phi Beta Kappa, Delta Kappa Epsilon. Clubs: Gridiron, Internat., Burning Tree. Home: 1338 Potomac School Rd McLean VA 22101 Office: Associated Press 2021 K St NW Washington DC 20006

MEASON, GEORGE HOLLINGSWORTH, chem. and natural gas co. exec.; b. Terrell, Tex., Oct. 23, 1916; s. George Hollingsworth and Sarah Elizabeth (Scott) M.; B.S. with honors in Chem. Engring., U. Tex., 1940; m. Martha Grissett, June 18, 1941; children—George Hollingsworth III, Barbara Meason Green. Mem. refining dept. Humble Oil & Refining Co., Baytown, Tex., 1940-56; chief engr. Tenneco Oil Co., Houston, 1956-59, v.p. refining, 1959-62, sr. v.p. refining and mktg., 1962-66, exec. v.p., 1966-70, pres., 1970-74, exec. v.p. Tenneco Inc., Houston, 1974—; mem. Engring. Found. adv. council Coll. Engring., U. Tex., Austin. Episcopalian. Clubs: Houston, Lakeside Country, Horseshoe Bay Country. Home: 8 Chuckanut Ln Houston TX 77024 Office: PO Box 2511 Houston TX 77001

MEATHE, PHILIP JAMES, architect; b. Grosse Pointe, Mich., Jan. 26, 1926; s. William J. and Mary (Spears) M.; B.Arch., U. Mich., 1948; m. Jeanne Marie Munger, Oct. 14, 1950; children—Mary C., Lawrence P., James B., Carol A. Prin., Meathe, Kessler & Assos., Inc., Grosse Pointe, 1955-69; exec. v.p. Smith, Hinchman & Grylls Assos., Inc., Detroit, 1969-71, pres., 1971—. Chmn., Detroit Urban League, 1978-79; mem. Econ. Growth Corp. Detroit, 1979. Recipient 24 archtl. awards, including Edward C. Kemper award, 1969. Mem. AIA (pres. Detroit chpt. 1961-62, nat. dir. 1965-68; recipient Gold medal Detroit chpt. 1967, chancellor coll. of fellows 1977), Mich. Soc. Architects (recipient Gold medal 1969), Greater Detroit C. of C. (chmn. 1979). Home: 329 Grosse Pointe Blvd Grosse Pointe Farms MI 48236 Office: 455 W Fort St Detroit MI 48226

MEBANE, JOHN HARRISON, editor; b. Greensboro, N.C., Sept. 20, 1909; s. Cornelius and Minnie (Clark) M.; A.B., U. N.C., 1930; m. Hannah Price Kallam, July 22, 1944; children—David Clark, Betty Carolyn, John Spencer. Mng. editor High Point (N.C.) Enterprise, 1930-42; editorial writer Atlanta Jour., 1942-51; mgr. Atlanta office Dudley-Anderson-Yutzy, 1951-68; editor The Antiques Jour., Dubuque, Iowa, 1968-78; tchr. course antiques Emory U., 1965; propr. Dixie Galleries, Atlanta, 1967-69. Mem. Atlanta Indsl. Bur., 1958. Recipient Southwide award So. Assn. Sci. and Industry, 1951. Mem. Authors League Am. Author: Treasure at Home, 1964; New Horizons in Collecting, 1966; The Coming Collecting Boom, 1968; The Poor Man's Guide to Antique Collecting, 1969; What's New That's Old, 1970; The Complete Book of Collecting Art Nouveau, 1970; Collecting Nostalgia, 1972; Best Sellers in Antiques, 1974; The Poor Man's Guide to Trivia Collecting, 1975; Collecting Brides' Baskets and Other Table Glass Fancies, 1976. Address: Box 88129 Dunwoody GA 30338

MEBANE, WILLIAM BLACK, assn. exec.; b. Vernon, Tex., Dec. 15, 1927; s. David Mitchell and Ida Virginia (Black) M.; B.B.A., Tex. A. and M. U., 1952; M.B.A., Harvard U., 1954; m. Joan Hebbard Dumper, Nov. 24, 1956; children—David Alexander, Virginia Ann. Mem. treas.'s office staff Gen. Motors Corp., N.Y.C., 1954-70; sec.-treas. Alfred P. Sloan Found., N.Y.C., 1971-78; dir. fin. and adminstrn. Am. Diabetes Assn., N.Y.C., 1979—. Vol. Essex Council Boy Scouts Am., 1967—. Served with USAAF, 1946-49. Republican. Episcopalian. Clubs: Harvard Bus. Sch., Univ. (N.Y.C.). Home: 36 Haddonfield Rd Short Hills NJ 07078 Office: 600 Fifth Ave New York NY 10020

MEBUST, WINSTON KEITH, surgeon, educator; b. Malta, Mont., July 2, 1933; s. Hans G. and Anna C. (Leiseth) M.; student U. Wash., 1951-54, M.D., 1958; m. Lora June Peterson, Sept. 15, 1955; children—Leanne, Kevin, Kreg, Kari. Intern, King County Hosp., Seattle, 1958-59; resident Virginia Mason Hosp., Seattle, 1959-63, Kans. U. Med. Center, 1963-66; practice medicine, specializing in urology, 1966—; instr. surgery and urology U. Kans. Med. Center, Kansas City, 1966-69, asst. prof., 1969-72, asso. prof., 1972-76, chmn. urology sect., 1974—, prof., 1977—; chief urology service VA Hosp., Kansas City, Mo., 1966-75. Served with U.S. Army, 1961-63. Diplomate Am. Bd. Urology. Mem. Am. Cancer Soc., Am. Bd. Surgery, Kansas City Urol. Soc., Assn. for Acad. Surgery, Am. Urol. Assn., Wyandotte Med. Soc., Kans. Med. Assn., A.C.S., Soc. Univ. Urologists, Am. Assn. Genitourinary Surgeons, Sigma Xi, Alpha Omega Alpha. Republican. Contbr. articles, chpts. to med. jours. and texts. Home: 309 Apache Trail W Lake Quivira KS 66106 Office: 39th and Rainbow Blvd Kansas City MO 66103

MECH, ROBERT, assn. exec.; b. Brantford, Ont., Can., Apr. 28, 1936; s. Thomas and Anne (Neziol) M.; B.Com., Assumption U.; m. Lois Jean Rosehart, Nov. 15, 1964; children—Michelle, Lisa, Thomas. Former salesman Gen. Foods, Gumperts Food Products; former adminstrv. asst. McMaster U.; now exec. dir. Real Estate Inst. Can., Don Mills, Ont. Mem. Am. Soc. Assn. Execs. Club: Mt. Hope Curling. Home: 16 Berku Ave Hamilton ON L8V 2R1 Canada Office: 99 Duncan Mill Rd Toronto ON M3B 1Z2 Canada

MECHANIC, DAVID, educator; b. N.Y.C., Feb. 21, 1936; s. Louis and Tillie (Penn) M.; B.A., Coll. City N.Y., 1956; M.A., Stanford, 1957, Ph.D., 1959; children—Robert Edmund, Michael Alexander. Faculty U. Wis., Madison, 1960—, prof. sociology, 1965-73, John Bascom prof., 1973-79, dir. Center for Med. Sociology and Health Services Research, 1971-79, chmn. dept. sociology, 1968-70; prof. social work and sociology Rutgers U., New Brunswick, N.J., 1979—; mem. panel on health services Pres.'s Sci. Adv. Com., 1971-72; coordinator panel Pres.'s Commn. Mental Health, 1977-78; dir.

Coordinating Council for Study of Health and Health Care, 1979—. Fellow Center for Advanced Study in the Behavioral Scis., 1974-75; NIMH research fellow, 1965-66; Ford Behavioral Sci. fellow, 1956-57; recipient Ward medal Coll. City N.Y., 1956; Guggenheim fellow, 1977-78. Fellow AAAS; mem. Am. Sociol. Assn. (governing council 1977-78, chmn. med. sociol. sect. 1969-70), Inst. Medicine-Nat. Acad. Sci. (governing council 1972-74), Phi Beta Kappa. Author: Students Under Stress, 1962, 2d edit., 1978; Medical Sociology, 1968, rev. edit., 1978; Mental Health and Social Policy, 1969, rev. edit., 1980; Public Expectations and Health Care, 1972; Politics, Medicine and Social Science, 1974; (with Charles E. Lewis and Rashi Fein) A Right to Health, 1976; Growth of Bureaucratic Medicine, 1976; Future Problems in Health Care, 1979. Office: Grad Sch Social Work Rutgers U New Brunswick NJ 08903

MECHEM, CHARLES STANLEY, JR., broadcasting exec.; b. Nelsonville, Ohio, Sept. 12, 1930; s. Charles Stanley and Helen (Hall) M.; A.B., Miami U., Oxford, Ohio, 1952; LL.B., Yale, 1955; m. Marilyn Brown, Aug. 31, 1952; children—Melissa, Daniel, Allison. Admitted to Ohio bar, 1955; practice in Cin., 1955-67; partner Taft, Stettinius & Hollister, 1965-67; chmn. bd. Taft Broadcasting Co., Cin., 1967—; dir. First Nat. Bank of Cin., Wald Mfg. Co., Myers Y. Cooper Co., Eagle Picher Industries, Mead Corp., Ohio Nat. Life Ins. Co., Cin. Bell, Inc., Kinder Care Learning Centers, Inc. Bd. dirs. Childrens Home, Family Service, Bethesda Hosp., all Cin.; chmn. Seven Hills Sch. Served to 1st lt., Judge Adv. Gen. Corps, U.S. Army, 1956-59. Mem. Cin. C. of C. (pres. 1977). Club: Commercial (Cin.). Home: 477 Tee Dr Mason OH 45040 Office: 1906 Highland Ave Cincinnati OH 45219

MECHEM, EDWIN LEARD, judge; b. Alamogordo, N.Mex., July 2, 1912; s. Edwin and Eunice (Leard) M.; student N.Mex. State U., 1930-35, LL.D., 1974; LL.B., U. Ark., 1939; m. Dorothy E. Heller, Dec. 30, 1932 (dec.); children—Martha, John, Jesse (dec.), Walter; m. 2d, Josephine D. Galloway, May 28, 1976. Admitted to N.Mex. bar, 1939; practice law, Las Cruces N.Mex., 1939-70; spl. agt. FBI, 1942-45; U.S. Dist. judge Dist. of N.Mex., Albuquerque, 1970—; mem. N.Mex. Ho. of Reps., 1947-48; gov. of N.Mex., 1951-54, 57-58, 61-62; mem. U.S. Senate, 1963-64. Mem. N.Mex. Bar Assn., Am. Bar Assn., Judicature Soc., Am. Law Inst. Republican. Office: 500 Gold SW PO Box 97 Albuquerque NM 87103

MECHLIN, GEORGE FRANCIS, elec. mfg. co. exec.; b. Pitts., July 23, 1923; s. George Francis and Ruth (Butler) M.; B.S. in Physics, U. Pitts., 1944, M.S. in Physics, 1949, Ph.D. in Physics, 1951; m. Mary Louise Megaffin, June 25, 1949; children—Thomas Walker, Ann Louise. With Westinghouse Electric Corp., 1949—, gen. mgr. astronuclear/oceanic div., Balt., 1971-72, v.p. astronuclear lab., oceanic and marine divs., Balt., 1972-73, v.p. research and devel., Pitts., 1973—; bd. dirs. Sta.-WQED, public broadcasting, Pitts., Forbes Health Maintenance Plan; chmn. marine bd. NRC. Recipient Meritorious Public Service award U.S. Navy, 1961, John J. Montgomery award Nat. Soc. Aerospace Profls. and San Diego Aerospace Mus., 1961; Order of Merit award Westinghouse Electric Corp., 1961. Mem. Am. Phys. Soc., AIAA, Nat. Acad. Engring., Sigma Xi. Home: 1134 Fox Chapel Rd Pittsburgh PA 15238 Office: 1310 Beulah Rd Pittsburgh PA 15235

MECIMORE, CHARLES DOUGLAS, educator; b. Belmont, N.C., Aug. 20, 1934; s. John Edgar and Hattie (Bolick) M.; B.S., Pfeiffer Coll., 1958; M.S., U. N.C., 1962; Ph.D., U. Ala., 1966; m. Barbara Jean Chiddie, June 7, 1959; children—Laura Jean, Charles D. Jr., John Amos. Asst. prof. U. Ala., Tuscaloosa, 1966-67; asso. prof. U. Ga., Athens, 1967-71; prof. U. Cin., 1971-79; prof acctg. Sch. Bus. and Econs., U. N.C., Greensboro, 1980—, head dept., 1980—. Served with USAF, 1951-55. Univ. scholar, 1963-66; Haskins and Sells fellow, 1963-64. C.P.A., N.C., Ohio. Mem. Am. Inst. C.P.A.'s, Ohio Soc. C.P.A.'s, Nat. Assn. Accountants, Am. Accounting Assn., Inst. Mgmt. Accounting. Home: 1312 Westridge Rd Greensboro NC 27410 Office: Coll Bus and Econs U NC Greensboro NC 27410

MECKE, THEODORE HART MCCALLA, JR., orgn. exec.; b. Phila., Mar. 6, 1923; s. Theodore Hart McCalla and Genevieve (Loughney) M.; student LaSalle Coll., Phila., 1941, LL.D. (hon.), 1964; m. Mary E. Flaherty, July 14, 1956; children—William Moyn, Theodore Hart III, John Chetwood, Stephen Campbell. Mng. editor Germantown (Pa.) Courier, 1942-43, 46-49; with Ford Motor Co., Dearborn, Mich., 1949-80, gen. public relations mgr., 1957-63, v.p. public relations, 1963-69, v.p. public affairs group, 1969-80; pres. Econ. Club Detroit, 1980—. Adv. mem. Arts Commn. City Detroit; trustee Univ.-Liggett Sch.; v.p., bd. dirs. Detroit United Found. Served with AUS, 1943-45. Mem. Mil. Order Loyal Legion, Am. Legion, Pub. Relations Soc. Am. Roman Catholic. Clubs: Country of Detroit, Detroit Athletic, Detroit, Yondotega. Home: 296 Cloverly Rd Grosse Pointe Farms MI 48236

MECKLING, WILLIAM HOWARD, coll. dean; b. McKeesport, Pa., Sept. 20, 1921; s. William Howard and K. Elizabeth Meckling; B.B.A., Westminster Coll., 1942; M.B.A., U. Denver, 1947; postgrad. U. Chgo., 1949-52; m. Rebecca Ely; children—William, Nancy, Bruce, Gregory, Scott. Asst. prof. Butler U., Indpls., 1952-53; lectr. U. Calif., Los Angeles, 1961-62; asst. dir. Bur. Govtl. Research, Indpls., 1953-55; econ. analyst The RAND Corp., Santa Monica, Calif., 1955-62; dir. naval warfare analysis group Center for Naval Analyses, Arlington, Va., 1963-64; pres. Center for Naval Analyses, U. Rochester (N.Y.), 1967; exec. dir. Pres.'s Commn. on All Vol. Armed Force, 1969-70; prof. bus. adminstrn. Grad. Sch. Mgmt., U. Rochester, 1964—, dean, 1964—; past mem. Nat. Sci. Bd.; dir. Superba Cravats, Inc., Rochester; past mem. N.Y. State Council Econ. Advisers. Co-recipient Leo Melamed prize U. Chgo., 1979. Mem. Mont Pelerin Soc., Beta Gamma Sigma. Contbr. articles to sci. and econ. revs. Office: Grad Sch Mgmt U Rochester Rochester NY 14627

MECKSTROTH, JOHN ROBERT, lawyer; b. Cin., Mar. 31, 1931; s. Ralph Walter and Ann Marie (Vonderhaar) M.; B.A., Xavier U., Cin., 1953; LL.B., U. Cin., 1956; m. Barbara A., Dec. 29, 1978; children by previous marriage—John Robert, Laura Ann, Steven G., Nancy M., James J. Admitted to Ohio bar, 1956, since practiced in Cin.; partner firm Meckstroth, Schwierling & Monnie Co. LPA; dir. Keystone Savs. & Loan Assn., Cin., Handy Window Shade Co.; solicitor Green Twp. Bd. Trustees. Mem. Ohio Bd. Edn., 1965—, pres., 1970, 73, 74; v.p. Nat. Assn. State Bds. Edn., 1974. Mem. Am. Bar Assn., Am. Judicature Assn., Ohio Bar Assn., Cin. Bar Assn., Lawyers Club Cin., Greater Cin. Sch. Found. Republican. Roman Catholic. Clubs: K.C., Bankers (Cin.). Office: 8 W 9th St Cincinnati OH 45202

MECOM, JOHN W., JR., oil exec., profl. football team exec.: b. Tex.; ed. U. Okla., U. Tex.; m. Katsy Mullendore, 1962; children—John III, Katsy Mullendare, Mary Elizabeth, Kathleen Boren. Active oil bus., La.; pres. New Orleans Saints profl. football team; also exec. auto and boat racing. Bd. regents Loyola U., New Orleans; bd. mgrs. Rose-Hulman Inst. Tech., Terre Haute, Ind. Address: care New Orleans Saints 944 St Charles Ave New Orleans LA 70130

MECUM, DUDLEY CLARKE, II, business exec.; b. Chgo., Dec. 21, 1934; s. Dudley Clarke and Ruth Ann (Fellman) M.; B.A., Ohio Wesleyan U., 1956; M.B.A., Harvard U., 1961; m. Harriet Zahn, 1959; children—Dudley, Scott, Lynne. With IBM, Columbus, Ohio, 1956-59, charge design and installation computer-based prodn. planning and control systems, Cambridge, Mass., 1961-63; with Mgmt. Systems Corp., Boston, 1963-66, v.p., 1965-66; prin. Peat, Marwick, Mitchell & Co., C.P.A.'s, Washington, 1966-71, sr. mgmt. group, 1969-71, partner-in-charge cons. dept., Los Angeles, 1974-77, vice chmn., 1977—; asst. sec. army for installation and logistics, Washington, 1971-73; asst. dir. mgmt. and orgn. Office Mgmt. and Budget, Exec. Office President, 1973-74. Home: 121 N Rockingham Ave Los Angeles CA 90049

MEDAK, HERMAN, educator, researcher; b. Vienna, Austria, Apr. 26, 1914; s. Ignaz and Ella (Medak) M.; student U. Vienna, 1932-38; B.S., U. Toledo, 1943; D.D.S., Northwestern U., 1946, M.S., 1946; Ph.D., U. Ill., 1959; M.D., U. Vienna, 1973; m. Vivian H. Fried, Dec. 22, 1945; children—Ruth Ellen, Joanne Marie, Susan Lee, Alan Walter. Came to U.S., 1939, naturalized, 1944. Med. technician lab. Flower Hosp., Toledo, 1939-43, Wesley Meml. Hosp., Chgo., 1943-47; research asst. U. Ill., 1948-51, instr. oral pathology, 1953-61, asso. prof., 1961-64, prof., 1964—, acting head dept. oral pathology, 1964-67, chief clin. oral pathology, 1967—, head dept. oral diagnosis, 1978—, staff appointment, research and edn. hosp., prof. dept. preventive medicine and community health Coll. Medicine, 1966—; mem. staff Luth. Gen. Hosp.; practice dentistry, part-time 1946—. Served with M.C., AUS, 1951-53. Diplomate Am. Bd. Oral Pathology. Fellow Am. Coll. Dentists; mem. Am. Dental Assn., Internat. Assn. Dental Research, Am. Acad. Oral Pathology, Internat. Coll. Dentists, A.A.A.S., Am. Soc. Cytology, Omicron Kappa Upsilon, Sigma Xi. Author: Atlas of Oral Cytology, 1971. Research in oral radiation, cancer. Home: 6820 N Kostner Ave Lincolnwood IL 60646 Office: 801 S Paulina St Chicago IL 60680 also 5850 N Clark St Chicago IL 60660

MEDALIE, JACK HARVEY, physician; b. Buhl, Minn., Jan. 8, 1922; s. Barney Joshua and Sarah (Klaff) M.; B.Sc., U. Witwatersrand, (South Africa), 1941, M.B.Ch.B., 1945; M.P.H. cum laude, Harvard U., 1958; m. June Girdy, May 27, 1948; children—Ilan, Karin, Ron. Dir. health center Hadassah U., Jerusalem, 1953-62; prof. family medicine Tel Aviv U., 1966-75; Dorothy Jones Weatherhead prof., chmn. dept. family medicine Case Western Res. U., Cleve., 1976—; cons., vis. prof. numerous univs.; mem. Inst. Medicine, Nat. Acad. Scis.; mem. Nat. Bd. Med. Examiners, 1979—. Served with Brit. Army, Israeli Army, World War II. Mem. Acad. Family Practice, Soc. Tchrs. Family Medicine, Am. Soc. Epidemiology. Author books in field; contbr. articles to profl. jours. Home: 2990 Keswick Rd Cleveland OH 44120 Office: 2119 Abington Rd Cleveland OH 44106

MEDALIE, RICHARD JAMES, lawyer; b. Duluth, Minn., July 21, 1929; s. William Louis and Mona (Kolad) M.; B.A. summa cum laude, U. Minn., 1952; certificate U. London, 1953; A.M., Harvard, 1955, J.D. cum laude, 1958; m. Susan Diane Abrams, June 5, 1960; children—Samuel David, Daniel Alexander. Admitted to D.C. bar, 1958, N.Y. bar, 1962; law clk. to judge U.S. Ct. Appeals, Washington, 1958-59; asst. solicitor gen. U.S., 1960-62; asso. firm Kaye, Scholer, Fierman, Hays & Handler, N.Y.C., 1962-65; dep. dir. Ford Found. Inst. Criminal Law and Procedure, Georgetown U. Law Center, 1965-68; partner firm Friedman and Medalie, and predecessors, Washington, 1968—; adj. prof. adminstrv. and criminal law Georgetown U. Law Center, 1967-70. Mem. D.C. Law Revision Commn., 1975—, chmn. Criminal Law Task Force; mem. exec. com. panel arbitrators Am. Arbitration Assn., 1964—. Bd. dirs. alumni assn. Expt. in Internat. Living, Brattleboro, Vt., 1961-64, pres., 1962-63. Fulbright scholar, 1952-53; Ford fellow, 1954-55. Mem. Am. Law Inst., Am., N.Y. State bar assns., D.C. Unified Bar, Assn. Bar City N.Y., Harvard Law Sch. Assn. D.C. (pres. 1976-77, nat. v.p. 1977-78), Phi Beta Kappa, Phi Alpha Theta. Club: Harvard of D.C. (v.p. 1979—). Author: From Escobedo to Miranda: The Anatomy of a Supreme Court Decision, 1966; co-author: Federal Consumer Safety Legislation, 1970. Contbr. to legal jours. Co-editor: Crime: A Community Responds, 1967; staff Harvard Law Rev., 1956-58, case editor, 1957-58. Home: 3113 Macomb St NW Washington DC 20008 Office: 1899 L St NW Washington DC 20036

MEDARIS, JOHN BRUCE, clergyman, ret. army officer; b. Milford, Ohio, May 12, 1902; s. William Roudebusch and Jessie (LeSourd) M.; student Ohio State U., 1919-21; Sc.D., Rollins Coll., 1958, U. Ala., 1958, N.Mex. State U.; LL.D., Pa. Mil. Coll., 1958, U. Chattanooga, 1958; D.Space Sc., Fla. Inst. Tech., 1963; m. Gwendolyn Hunter, May 19, 1920 (div. 1930); 1 dau., Marilyn C. (Mrs. Eugene Stillings), m. 2d, Virginia Rose Smith, Aug. 29, 1931; children—Marta Virginia (Mrs. Charles G. Smith, Jr.), John Bruce. Began career as enlisted man USMC, 1918-19; commd. lt. inf. U.S. Army, 1921, advanced through grades to maj. gen., 1955; attached 29th and 33d Inf. Regts., 1921-26, Ordnance Corps, 1926-27; res. officer, 1927-39; exec. officer Cin. Ordnance Dist., then asst. dist. control officer Office Chief of Ordnance, exec. contract distbn. sect. Office Under Sec. War, 1938-42; bn. comdr., ordnance officer II Corps, Tunisia, Sicily; ordnance officer 1st Army, Eng., also organized, operated Field Army Ordnance Service, 1st U.S. Army in Europe; ordnance officer 5th Service Command, also Army Ground Forces; chief U.S. Army Mission to Argentina, 1949-52; exec., asst. chief ammunition br., indsl. div. Office Chief Ordnance, 1953, asst. chief ordnance, chief indsl. div., 1953-55; comdg. gen. Army Ballistic Missile Agy., Huntsville, Ala., 1955-58; comdg. gen. U.S. Army Ordnance Missile Command, 1958-60, ret.; pres., chief exec. officer Lionel Corp., 1960-62, vice chmn. bd., 1962-63; chmn. bd. Electronic Teaching Labs. Washington, 1960-61; mem. bd., chmn. exec. com. All-State Devel. Corp., Miami, 1962-63; pres. Medaris, Cruger & Patterson (co. name changed to Medaris Mgmt., Inc. 1966), 1963-70, chmn. bd., 1970-78. Ordained deacon Episcopal Ch., 1969, priest, 1970; asso. rector Episcopal Ch. of Good Shepherd, Maitland, Fla., 1973-79; priest Anclican Ch., 1979—; rector Anglican Ch. of Incarnation, Maitland, 1979—; chaplain, missioner Internat. Order St. Luke, 1972—; priest Asso. Commn. St. Mary, 1976—; mem. Planning Commn. Diocese Central Fla., 1973-76. Fla. chmn. Radio Free Europe, 1963-64; v.p., dir. Pan Am. Funds, 1965-73; pres., dir. Chapel of Astronauts, Inc., 1969-72, dir., mem. exec. com., 1972-73; dir. World Center for Liturgical Studies, 1972-73, chmn. bd., 1973-74; mem. sci. adv. com. state Ala., adv. bd. Dallas Health and Sci. Mus. Councilman, Maitland, 1965-68. Decorated D.S.M. (with oak leaf cluster); Order de Coronne de Chene Luxembourg; Legion of Merit (with 2 oak leaf clusters), Soldiers Medal, Bronze Star Medal (U.S.), Legion of Honor (France); recipient Freedoms Found. awards, 1959, 60; John Young award, 1977; named to Ordnance Hall of Fame, 1973. Bd. pres. Pershing Commn. for Tacna-Arica Plebiscite, 1925. Rated army aviator, 1956. Fellow Am. Inst. Aeros. and Astronautics; mem. IEEE (sr.), Explorers Club, Am. Ordnance Assn. (life), Am. Legion (life), Mil. Chaplains Assn. (life), Soc. of Holy Cross, Assn. Ordnance-Industry Physicians, Scabbard and Blade, Sigma Tau. Clubs: Country of Orlando (Fla.); Wildcat Cliffs Country (hon.) (Highlands, N.C.). Author: Countdown for Decision, 1960. Home: 1050 Cottontail Ln Maitland FL 32751 Office: Anglican Church of Incarnation PO Box 1426 Maitland FL 32751

MEDBERRY, CHAUNCEY JOSEPH, III, banker; b. Los Angeles, Oct. 9, 1917; s. Chauncey Joseph, Jr. and Geneva (Raymond) M.; B.A., UCLA, 1938; postgrad. U. Munich (Germany), 1939; m. Thirza Cole Young, Mar. 14, 1958; children—Julie Ann Young (Mrs. G.E. Pendergast), Ralph D. Young III, Deborah D. Young, Chauncey Joseph Medberry IV. With Bank of Am., Los Angeles, 1939—; chmn. bd. Bank Am. Corp.; dir. Getty Oil Co. Trustee Com. for Econ. Devel., Industry Edn. Council; bd. dirs. Los Angeles Philharmonic Assn.; bd. overseers Huntington Library; chmn. bd. visitors Grad. Sch. Mgmt., UCLA; mem. Brit.-N.Am. Com. Mem. Assn. Res. City Bankers (dir.), Los Angeles Clearing House Assn. (past pres.), Am. Bankers Assn. Clubs: Bohemian, Bankers (San Francisco); Calif., Los Angeles Country (Los Angeles); Sky, Links (N.Y.). Office: Bank of Am 555 S Flower St Los Angeles CA 90071

MEDEARIS, DONALD NORMAN, JR., physician, educator; b. Kansas City, Kans., Aug. 22, 1927; s. Donald Norman and Gladys (Sandford) M.; A.B., U. Kans., 1949; M.D., Harvard, 1953; m. Mary Ellen Marble, Aug. 25, 1956; children—Donald Harrison, Ellen Sandford, John Norman, Mary Jennifer Marble. Intern internal medicine Barnes Hosp., St. Louis, 1953-54; resident pediatrics Children's Hosp., Cin., 1954-56; research fellow pediatrics Harvard research div. infectious diseases Children's Med. Center, Boston, 1956-58; asst. prof. pediatrics Johns Hopkins Sch. Medicine, 1958-63, asso. prof., 1963-65, asst. prof. microbiology, 1959-63, asso. prof., 1963-65; Joseph P. Kennedy, Jr. Meml. Found. Sr. Research scholar in mental retardation, 1960-65; prof. pediatrics U. Pitts. Sch. Medicine, 1965-74, chmn. dept., 1965-69, dean, 1969-74; med. dir. Children's Hosp., Pitts., 1965-69; prof. pediatrics Case Western Res. U., Cleve., 1974-77; dir. pediatrics Cleve. Met. Gen. Hosp., 1974-77; Charles Wilder prof. pediatrics Harvard U. Med. Sch., 1977—; chief children's service Mass. Gen. Hosp., Boston, 1977—. Adv. com. gen. research support program div. research resources NIH, 1971-74; adv. com. gen. clin. research centers div. research resources NIH, 1975-79; mem. Pres.'s Commn. Study of Ethical Problems in Medicine and Biomed. and Behavioral Research, 1979—; mem. Task Force Grad. Med. Edn., Assn. Am. Med. Colls., 1977—. Served with USNR, 1945-46. Diplomate Am. Bd. Pediatrics. Mem. Am. Acad. Pediatrics, Nat. Assn. Retarded Children (research adv. bd. 1966-69), Assn. Univ. Pediatric Dept. Chairmen, Am. Fedn. Clin. Research, Soc. for Pediatric Research (council 1967-70), Am. Pediatric Soc., Am. Assn. Immunologists, Soc. for Exptl. Biology and Medicine, Infectious Disease Soc. Am., Alpha Omega Alpha. Asso. editor Am. Jour. of Epidemiology, 1963-73; mem. editorial bd. Pediatrics, 1966-72, Jour. Med. Edn., 1978—; contbr. articles to profl. jours., texts. Office: Massachusetts Gen Hosp Fruit St Boston MA 02114

MEDEARIS, KENNETH GORDON, research cons., educator; b. Peoria, Ill., Aug. 5, 1930; s. Harold Oscar and Ferol Mae (Rowlett) M.; B.S., U. Ill., 1952, M.S., 1953; Ph.D., Stanford, 1962; m. Mary Genevieve Barlow, June 28, 1953; children—Mark Allen, Mary Lynne, Terry Gordon. Stress analyst Sandia Corp., Albuquerque, 1957-58; asst. prof. civil engring. U. N.Mex., 1958-62; asso. prof. engring. Ariz. State U., 1962-63; engr., computer cons., Sunnyvale, Calif., 1963-66; dir. Computer Center, prof. civil engring. Colo. State U., Ft. Collins, 1966-69, adj. prof., 1969—. Cons., Kenneth Medearis Assos.; research engring. Computer Cons., Ft. Collins, 1969—; chmn., Larimer County Computer Com., 1974—. Mem. Stanford Regional Cabinet. Served to 1st lt. USAF, 1953-56. Recipient Outstanding Engring. Achievement award No. Colo. Profl. Engrs., 1974, Outstanding Engring. Achievement award Profl. Engrs. of Colo., 1974. Registered profl. engr., Calif., Colo., N.Mex., Pa. Mem. Colo. Earthquake Research Soc. (v.p.), Univs. Council for Earthquake Engring. Research, Internat. Orgn. for Standardization (tech. com.), ASCE, Seismol. Soc. Am., Sigma Xi, Chi Epsilon, Sigma Tau. Methodist (chmn. bd. trustees 1958-60). Rotarian. Author: Numerical-Computer Methods for Engineers and Physical Scientists, 1974. Contbr. articles profl. jours. Home: 1901 Seminole Dr Fort Collins CO 80525 Office: 1413 S College Ave Fort Collins CO 80524

MEDEIROS, HUMBERTO SOUSA, archbishop; b. Arrifes, Sao Miquel, Azores, Oct. 6, 1915; s. Antonio Sousa and Maria de Jesus Sousa Massa (Flor) M.; came to U.S., 1931, naturalized, 1940; M.A., Catholic U. Am., 1942, S.T.L., 1946, S.T.D., 1952; LL.D., Stonehill Coll., Mass., 1959. Ordained priest Roman Catholic Ch., 1946; asst. St. John of God Parish, Somerset, Mass., 1946, St. Michael's Parish, Fall River, Mass., 1946-47, Our Lady of Health Parish, Fall River, 1947, St. Vincent de Paul Health Camp, 1948-49, Mt. Carmel Ch., New Bedford, Mass., 1949; research N.Am. Coll., Rome, 1949-50; asst. Holy Name Ch., Fall River, 1950-51; sec., asst. chancellor, chaplain Sacred Hearts Acad. and Vicar for Religious, 1951-53; vice-chancellor, chancellor Fall River (Mass.) Diocese, 1953-66; named domestic prelate, 1958; pastor St. Michael's Parish, 1960-66; consecrated bishop, 1966; bishop Diocese Brownsville, Tex., 1966-70. archbishop archdiocese Boston, 1970-73; elevated to cardinal, 1973. Mem. U.S. Cath. Conf., Nat. Conf. Cath. Bishops. Home: 2101 Commonwealth Ave Brighton MA 02135

MEDENBACH, MILTON HERMAN, ednl. adminstr.; b. Balt., Dec. 31, 1907; s. Herman and Bertha (Hildenbrand) M.; A.B., Johns Hopkins, 1929; certificate in Philology, U. Marburg (Germany), 1930; diploma, Konsularakademie, Vienna, Austria, 1931; diploma Sch. Mil. Govt., U. Va., 1944; diploma Civil Affairs Tng. Sch., Yale, 1944; Ped.D., Gettysburg Coll., 1952; m. Helen Carolyn Clarke, Sept. 28, 1935, children—Philip Clarke, Mary Louise. Instr. ancient and modern langs. Valley Forge Mil. Acad. and Jr. Coll., Wayne, Pa., 1932-33, adj., 1934-38, exec. officer, 1938-41, comdt. cadets, asst. supt., 1946-70, supt., 1970-71, supt. emeritus, 1972—. Mem. exec. com. Pa. Inaugural Com., 1963; v.p., sec. Chapel of St. Cornelius, Centurion Found., 1972—. Served from capt. to col. U.S. Army, 1941-46; to maj. gen. Pa. N.G., 1955-64, ret., 1971. Decorated Legion of Merit, Army Commendation medal with 2 oak leaf clusters; recipient Pa. Meritorious medal for excellence in field edn. and for outstanding service with Pa. Inaugural Com., 1963. Austro-Am. Exchange fellow Inst. Internat. Edn., 1929-31. Mem. Boarding Schs. Headmasters Assn. Phila. (pres. 1955), Assn. U.S. Army (pres. Valley Forge chpt. 1972), Mil. Order World Wars, Old Guard City of Phila., Centennial Legion of Hist. Mil. Commands. Republican. Episcopalian. Club: Johns Hopkins. Home: 15 Fariston Rd Wayne PA 19087 Office: Valley Forge Military Acad and Junior Coll Wayne PA 19087. *I have always believed that a man can achieve success and become a credit to his generation if he builds his life upon a firm belief in the traditional values which form the warp and woof of the American "dream", an habitual and a dedicated pursuit of excellence; an understanding of the requirements of duty to God, Country, and Family; and the constant adherence to fitness, as it pertains to one's association with one's fellowman.*

MEDHUS, SIGURD DUANE, pharm. co. exec.; b. Leeds, N.D., Mar. 1, 1929; s. Sigurd and Cora (Nordhougen) M.; B.S. in Bus. and Tech., Oreg. State U., 1950; m. Dolores Estella Samuelson, Nov. 4, 1949; children—Susan Mary, Mark Steven, Karen Dolores, Eric Sigurd, Nancy Carol, Margaret Joyce, Patricia Louise, Olaf Andrew. With Gen. Electric Co. and subsidiary companies, various locations, 1950—, v.p. finance Canadian Gen. Elec. Co. Ltd., Toronto, 1971-73, v.p., gen. mgr. consumer financing, bus. dept. Gen. Electric Credit Corp., Stamford, Conn., 1973—; v.p. fin., treas., dir., mem. exec. com.

Hoffmann-LaRoche, Inc., Nutley, N.J., 1976—. Bd. dirs. Vis. Nurses Assn., Stamford, 1967-69, Urban Redevel. Commn., Stamford, 1971. Mem. Fin. Execs. Inst. Home: 285 Gregory Rd Franklin Lakes NJ 07417 Office: 340 Kingsland Rd Nutley NJ 07110

MEDICI, PAUL THOMAS, coll. dean; b. N.Y.C., May 10, 1919; s. Salomone and Caroline (Frabbito) M.; B.S., St. John's U., 1942, B.S in Pharmacy, 1948, M.S. in Biology, 1951; Ph.D., N.Y. U., 1956; m. Elizabeth Schulte, Apr. 4, 1943; children—Paul Joseph, Elizabeth, Marie. Mem. faculty St. John's U., Jamaica, N.Y., 1948-68, prof., 1960-68, also chmn. dept. biology, 1965-68, dean Grad. Sch. Liberal Arts and Scis., 1969—. Served to capt. M.C., AUS, 1942-46; col. Res. (ret.). Fellow A.A.A.S., N.Y. Acad. Scis.; mem. Am. Soc. Hematology, Am. Soc. Zoologists, Am. Ins. Biol. Sci., AAUP, Assn Mil. Surgeons, Res. Officers Assn., Nat. Geog. Soc., Sigma Xi, Phi Sigma Kappa, Rho Chi, Tau Pi Lambda. Home: 89-14 89th St Woodhaven NY 11421 Office: St John's Univ Jamaica NY 11439

MEDINA, HAROLD R., judge, author; b. Bklyn., Feb. 16, 1888; s. Joaquin A. and Elizabeth (Fash) M.; A.B., Princeton, 1909 (highest honors in French); LL.B., Columbia, 1912 (Ordronaux Prize); hon. degrees from 25 colls. and univs., 1947—; m. Ethel Forde Hillyer, June 6, 1911; children—Harold Raymond, Standish Forde. Admitted to N.Y. bar, 1912; practiced law, N.Y.C., prof. law, Columbia, 1915-40; apptd. judge U.S. Dist. Ct., So. Dist. N.Y., 1947-51, U.S. circuit judge Ct. Appeals for 2d Circuit, 1951-58, ret., 1958, now sr. circuit judge; presided in N.Y.C., over trial of 11 Communists charged with conspiracy to teach and advocate overthrow of the U.S. govt. by force and violence, Jan.-Oct. 1949. Charter trustee emeritus Princeton; life trustee emeritus Tchrs. Coll., Columbia U. Fellow Am. Acad. Arts and Scis.; mem. and sometime officer, chmn. coms. several profl. assns. and orgns.; hon. mem. several state bars. Awards and medals Freedom Found., Holland Soc., N.Y. Bd. of Trade, Nat. Inst. of Social Sci., Eleanor Van Rensselaer Medal by Nat. Soc. Colonial Dames, Am. Edn. award N.E.A., Bklyn. Coll., Nat. Soc. New Eng. Women, S.A.R., Am. Judicature Soc., including Justice award, 1971, Texas Bill of Rights Found., and others; Harold R. Medina Professorship of Procedural Jurisprudence established Columbia Law Sch., 1973; James Madison award Nat. Broadcast Editorial Assn., 1976; Distinguished Pub. Service award Ohio Newspaper Assn., 1976. Episcopalian. Clubs: University, Princeton U., Lawyers (pres. 1942-48), Westhampton Country, Century, Church. Author numerous legal books, 1922—; those since 1950 include: Judge Medina Speaks, 1954; The Anatomy of Freedom, 1959. Contbr. to legal reviews. Home: 14 E 75th St New York City NY 10021 also Westhampton NY 11977 Address: US Court House Foley Sq New York City NY 10007

MEDINA, JOSE ENRIQUE, dentist, educator; b. Santurce, P.R., May 1, 1926; s. Jose Wilfredo and Genoveva (de la Baume) M.; student Johns Hopkins, 1942-44; D.D.S., U. Md., 1948; m. Betty Lee Mansfield, June 5, 1948 (dec. Feb. 1975); children—Elizabeth Lee, Jose Enrique, Virginia Genoveva; m. 2d, Patricia Fay Pachler, Dec. 26, 1975. Instr. Berlitz Sch. Langs., 1944-48; instr. operative dentistry dept. U. Md. Sch. Dentistry, 1948-50, asst. prof., 1950-52, asso. prof., 1952-57, prof., head, 1957-66, asst. dean, 1964-67; prof. clin. dentistry, asso. dean Coll. Dentistry, U. Fla., Gainesville, 1967-69, prof. clin. dentistry, 1969—, dean, 1969-74, dir. health center planning and utilization, 1974-76, v.p. for facilities planning and ops. J. Hillis Miller Health Center, 1976—. Cons. USPHS, U.S. Naval Dental Sch., Bethesda, VA Hosp., Gainesville, VA Hosp., Miami. Pres. So. Conf. Dental Deans and Examiners, 1973; mem. nat. adv. dental research council Nat. Inst. Dental Research, NIH, 1973-76. Pres. Sunnybrook (Md.) Community Assn., 1963-65. Served with USNR, 1944-46. Recipient Distinguished Alumnus award R.I. Alumni Assn. U. Md., 1965; hon. prof. U. De San Carlos, Guatemala, 1960—. Fellow Internat. Coll. Dentists, AAAS, Acad. Gen. Dentistry (hon.); mem. ADA, Fla. Dental Assn. (Disting. Service award 1978), Am. Acad. Gold Foil Operators (editor 1958-63, pres. 1965), Am. Coll. Dentists, Internat. Assn. Dental Research, Acad. Operative Dentistry (charter), Health Edn. Media Assn. (dir.), Royal Soc. Health, N.Y. Acad. Sci., Guatemala Dental Soc. (hon.), Omicron Kappa Upsilon; hon. mem. Am. Acad. Oral Medicine, Fla. Acad. Dental Practice Adminstrn. Mason, Kiwanian. Club: Optimist (Md.). Home: 5002 NW 18th Pl Gainesville FL 32605

MEDINA, KATHRYN BACH, editor; b. Plainfield, N.J.; d. Francis Earl and Elizabeth (Evans) Bach; B.A., Smith Coll., 1965; m. Standish Forde Medina, Jr., Apr. 20, 1968. With Doubleday & Co., N.Y.C., 1965—, now exec. editor gen. books; editor: Jaws, 1974; Tennessee Williams: Memoirs, 1975; Mary Cassatt, 1975; The Three Marias: New Portuguese Letters, 1975; The Deep, 1976; Loose Change, 1977; A Captive of Time, 1978; The Island, 1979.

MEDINA, WILLIAM A., govt. ofcl.; b. Washington, Oct. 28, 1935; B.A., M.A., George Washington U.; Ph.D., Am. U., 1976. With C.E., 1960; staff personnel office NASA; with CSC, 1963-71; chief exec. devel. and tng. Office of Mgmt. and Budget. Washington, to 1977; asst. sec. for adminstrn. HUD, 1977—. Trustee Nat. Acad. Pub. Adminstrn., United Black Fund. Mem. Am. Soc. Pub. Adminstrn. (pres. Nat. Capital Area chpt.; nat. council), Fed. Exec. Inst. Alumni Assn. (treas., pres.). Founder, asso. editor Bureaucrat. Office: HUD 451 7th St SW Washington DC 20410*

MEDITCH, JAMES STEPHEN, elec. engr.; b. Indpls., July 30, 1934; s. Vladimir Stephen and Sandra (Gogeff) M.; B.S. in Elec. Engring., Purdue U., 1956; S.M., M.I.T., 1958; Ph.D., 1961; m. Theresa Claire Scott, Apr. 4, 1964; children—James Stephen, Sandra Anne. Staff engr. Aerospace Corp., Los Angeles, 1961-65; asso. prof. elec. engring. Northwestern U., 1966-67; mem. tech. staff Boeing Sci. Research Labs., Seattle, 1967-70; prof. U. Calif., Irvine, 1970-77; prof., chmn. dept. elec. engring. U. Wash., 1977—; chmn. bd. ORINCON Corp., La Jolla, Calif. Fellow IEEE; mem. AAAS. Author: Stochastic Optimal Linear Estimation and Control, 1969. Office: Dept Elec Engring FT-10 U Wash Seattle WA 98195

MEDITZ, WALTER JOSEPH, pub. co. exec.; b. Bklyn., June 4, 1917; s. Joseph and Marie (Gaspar) M.; B.C.E., Bklyn Poly. Inst., 1939, M.M.E., 1941; M.Indsl. Engring., Ga. Inst. Tech., 1951; m. Elizabeth M. Cagney, Jan. 9, 1944; children—Jeannette, Mary Beth. Research engr., lab. instr. Bklyn. Poly. Inst., 1939-40; civil engr., supt. Spencer, White & Prentice, 1940-41; asst. to design and prodn. mgr. Frederick R. Harris, 1941-43; chief indsl. engr. Naval Aircraft, Norfolk, Va., 1943-46; asst. chief engr., Boyle-Midway, N.Y.C., 1946-47, plant mgr., Atlanta, 1947-51, asst. to pres., N.Y.C., 1951-55; asst. to pres. Standard Packaging Corp., N.Y.C., 1955-57, v.p. for mfg., 1957-67; mgr. facilities Doubleday & Co., Inc., Garden City, N.Y., 1967—, J. Waldo Smith fellow Am. Soc. C.E., 1939; Bklyn. Poly. Inst. fellow, 1939. Served from ensign to lt. (s.g.) USNR, 1943-46. Mem. Soc. Advancement Mgmt., Alpha Pi Mu. Club: Englewood Field. Home: 268 Chestnut St Englewood NJ 07631 Office: 501 Franklin Ave Garden City NY 11530

MEDLAND, CHARLES EDWARD, investment banker; b. Toronto, Ont., Can., July 6, 1928; s. Robert Charles and Elizabeth Winifred (Parker) M.; B.A., U. Toronto, 1950; m. Julie Windsor Eby, Feb. 1, 1973; 1 dau., Virginia; stepchildren—Brian, Stephen. With Wood Gundy Ltd., Toronto, 1950—, dir., 1966—, pres., chief exec. officer, 1972—, chmn. bd., chief exec. officer, 1978—; chmn., dir. Clover Meadow Creamery Ltd.; dir. Abitibi Paper Co. Ltd., Internat. Thomson Orgn. Ltd., Interprovincial Pipe Line Ltd., Irwin Toy Ltd., Seagram Co. Ltd.; mem. policy com. Bus. Council on Nat. Issues. Bd. dirs. Donwood Inst., Wellesley Hosp.; co-chmn. fund raising New Massey Hall. Mem. Investments Dealers Assn. Can. (chmn. 1979-80), Alpha Delta Phi. Anglican. Clubs: Toronto, York, Toronto Golf, Rosedale Golf, Badminton and Racquet (Toronto); Mt. Royal (Montreal); Craighleith Ski. Home: 1 Doncliffe Pl Toronto ON M4N 2P9 Canada Office: Wood Gundy Ltd Royal Trust Tower PO Box 274 Toronto ON M5K 1M7 Canada

MEDLIN, JOHN GRIMES, JR., banker; b. Benson, N.C., Nov. 23, 1933; s. John Grimes and Mabel (Stephenson) M.; B.S. in Bus. Adminstrn., U. N.C., Chapel Hill, 1956; grad. Advanced Mgmt. Program, U. Va., 1965; m. Pauline Winston Sims, Aug. 3, 1957; children—Elizabeth Warfield, Paula Ridgely. With Wachovia Bank & Trust Co., Winston-Salem, N.C., 1959—, exec. v.p., 1971-74, pres., 1974—, chief exec. officer, 1977—, also dir.; pres., chief exec. officer Wachovia Corp., 1977—; dir. Summit Communications, Inc. Active numerous civic and service orgns. Trustee Darden Grad. Sch. Bus. Adminstrn. U. Va., U. N.C., Greensboro, Davidson Coll.; bd. visitors Wake Forest Coll.; bd. dirs. Bus. Found. of U. N.C.; trustee Salem Acad. and Coll.; mem. N.C. Gov.'s Council Mgmt. and Devel. Served as officer USNR, 1956-59. Mem. Assn. Res. City Bankers (dir. membership com., govt. relations com.), Am. Bankers Assn. (govt. borrowing com.), U.S. C. of C. Internat. Com., Order Holy Grail, Order Old Well, Phi Delta Theta. Rotarian (pres. Winston-Salem 1973—). Club: Old Town (Winston-Salem). Office: PO Box 3099 Winston-Salem NC 27102

MEDNICK, MURRAY, playwright; b. Bklyn., Aug. 24, 1939; s. Sol Joseph and Betty (Greenstein) M.; student Bklyn. Coll., 1957-60. First prodn. at Theatre Genesis, N.Y.C., 1966, now artistic dir.; v.p. N.Y. Theatre Strategy, 1972—. Grantee Rockefeller Found., 1968, 72, Guggenheim Found., 1973; recipient Poetry award Nat. Council Arts, 1968, Creative Artists Pub. Service award, 1973, Obie award for The Deer Will, 1970. Mem. Dramatists Guild, Writers Guild, Nat. Soc. Lit. and the Arts. Author: The Hawk, 1968; The Hunter, 1969; The Shadow Ripens, 1969; The Deer Kill, 1971; Are You Lookin?, 1973; The Last Resort, 1973; The Black Hole in Space, 1975; Taxes, 1975; also pub. in New Underground Theatre, The Off-Off Broadway Book, More From Off-Off Broadway; poems in Evergreen Rev., Transatlantic Rev., others. Office: care Bobbs-Merrill Co 4300 W 62d St Indianapolis IN 46206*

MEDNIS, EDMAR JOHN, chem. engr., chess expert; b. Riga, Latvia, Mar. 22, 1937; s. Edwin and Marita (Graudins) M.; came to U.S., 1950, naturalized, 1955; B. Chem. Engring., N.Y. U., 1959, M. Chem. Engring., 1962; m. Baiba Tobiss, May 30, 1964; children—Sari Lara, Mariss Mark. Sr. engr. Gen. Foods Corp., Tarrytown, N.Y., 1959-67; chem. engr. U.S. Govt., 1967-68; pvt. investor, N.Y.C., 1968—; adj. asst. prof. math. for chess Richmond Coll., N.Y.C., 1973-74. Mem. Lettonia Frat., Inc., 1956—. Chess player U.S. Olympiad team, 1962, 70; N.Y. State Chess champion, 1955, intercollegiate chess champion, 1955-56, U.S. sr. chess master, 1955—; mem. World Student Championship team, 1960; internat. chess master, 1974—. Registered profl. engr., N.Y. Mem. Am. Inst. Chem. Engrs., U.S. Chess Fedn., Marshall Chess Club (bd. govs. 1968—). Lutheran. Author: How to Beat Bobby Fischer; How Karpov Wins; Practical Endgame Lessons; How To Beat the Russians; columnist Chess Life & Rev., 1964—. Address: 41-42 73d St Woodside NY 11377

MEDOFF, MARK HOWARD, playwright; b. Mt. Carmel, Ill., Mar. 18, 1940; s. Lawrence Ray and Thelma Irene (Butt) M.; B.A., U. Miami (Fla.), 1962; M.A., Stanford U., 1966; m. Stephanie Thorne, June 29, 1972; children—Debra, Rachel, Jessica. Instr. in English and drama N.Mex. State U., 1966-79, dramatist in residence, 1974—, head dept. drama, 1978—, prof. drama, 1979—; author plays: When You Comin Back, Red Ryder?, 1974, The Wager, 1975, The Kramer, 1975, The Halloween Bandit, 1978, The Conversion of Aaron Weiss, 1978, Firekeeper, 1978, The Last Chance Saloon, 1979; film: When You Comin Back, Red Ryder, 1979. Recipient Obie award, 1974, Drama Desk award, 1974, Outer Critics Circle award, 1974; works appear in Best Plays, 1973-74, 74-75, Best Short Plays, 1975; Guggenheim fellow, 1974-75. Mem. Writers Guild Am. Home: 800 Conway Ave Las Cruces NM 88001 Office: PO Box 3072 Las Cruces NM 88003

MEDSGER, BETTY LOUISE, writer, photographer; b. Johnstown, Pa., Mar. 14, 1942; d. Richard Joseph and Alice Jean (Wilson) Medsger; B.A., Grove City Coll., 1964; m. Ben Bagdikian, Feb. 24, 1973. Reporter, Johnstown Tribune-Democrat, 1964-66; med. writer Temple Med. Sch., 1967; reporter Phila. Evening Bull., 1967-69, Washington Post, 1970-73; freelance writer, photographer, lectr., 1973—; asst. prof. journalism San Francisco State U., 1977—; founder Mind Openers, 1976. Researcher, producer, reporter two investigative news documentary series WRC-TV NBC, Washington. Formerly bd. dirs. Center for Study of Power and Peace, Washington. Named Young Woman of Year, Bus. and Profl. Women, Johnstown, 1966. Author, photographer: Women At Work, 1975 (two sets of Women at Work photog. exhibits touring U.S. 1975—; 6 sets of photog. exhibits from book on USIA tour in Latin Am., Asia, Africa, Middle East, Europe). Contbr. articles to popular mags. Address: 217 Gravatt Dr Berkeley CA 94705

MEDVECKY, ROBERT STEPHEN, lawyer; b. Bridgeport, Conn., Feb. 12, 1931; s. Stephen and Elizabeth (Petro) M.; A.B., Dartmouth, 1952; J.D., Harvard, 1955; m. Ellen R. Munt, Nov. 11, 1966; children—Allison L., Beth A., Craig R. Admitted to Ill. bar, 1955, Conn. bar, 1958, D.C. bar, 1972; asso. firm Lord, Bissell & Brook, Chgo., 1955-57; gen. atty. So. New Eng. Telephone Co., New Haven, 1957-71; v.p., gen. counsel, sec. Amtrak, Washington, 1971-75; partner firm Lord, Bissell & Brook, Washington, 1975-78, Reid & Priest, N.Y.C., 1978—. Clubs: Reston (Va.) Golf and Country; Univ. (Washington); Bay Hill (Orlando, Fla.). Home: 10115 Westford Dr Vienna VA 22180 Office: 1701 K St NW Washington DC 20036

MEE, JOHN F., educator; b. Ada, Ohio, July 10, 1908; s. R. Kirk and Helen F. (Hickernell) M.; A.B., Miami U., 1930, LL.D., 1964; A.M., U. Maine, 1932; Ph.D., Ohio State U., 1959; m. Muriel E. Collins, Apr. 5, 1941; children—Marcia Joan, Virginia Ann, Raymond Kirk. Teaching fellow U. Maine, 1930-32; dean Beal Coll., Bangor, Maine, 1932-34; placement dir., instr., Ohio State U., 1934-39; asst. prof., dir. placement Ind. Univ., 1939-41, 46—, prof. mgmt., chmn. dept., 1946-62, Mead Johnson prof. mgmt., 1962—, dean div. gen. and tech. studies, 1966—; Ford distinguished vis. prof. N.Y. U., 1962; vis. prof. Servico Nacional de Aprendizagem Comercial, Brazil, 1978; cons. Ford Found., 1956-59; cons. personnel mgmt. and indsl. relations. Pres. Mee Farms, Inc., 1965—; pres. Richard D. Irwin Found., 1975—; dir. Richard D. Irwin, Inc. Mem. arbitration panel of gov. Ind.; staff dir. Ind. Study Commn. Intergovtl. Relations, 1954; arbitrator Fed. Mediation and Conciliation Service. Chmn. Am. Mgmt. Seminar Team to France, 1952. Chmn. adv. com. Ind. Exec. Devel. Program, 1951-70. Chmn. adv. com. Mead Johnson Inst., 1957-68. Served as col. USAAF, 1941-46. Commr. Ind. Dept. State Revenue, 1948; cons. Exec. Office, Pres. of U.S., 1950; staff dir. Pres. Com. on Presdl. Appointments, 1950; mem. Sec. Navy's Adv. Bd. Edn. and Tng., 1972-73; exec. dir. Ind. Tax Study Commn. Bd. advisers Indsl. Coll. Armed Forces. Named Ind. Sagamore of Wabash, 1964, Ky. col., 1966. Licensed psychologist, Ind. Fellow Internat. Acad. Mgmt.; mem. Acad. of Mgmt. (pres. 1951, bd. govs.), Soc. Advancement Mgmt. (v.p. 1964; Taylor Key award 1972), Am. Inst. Mgmt., Am. Pyschol. Assn., C. of C. (dir.), Council Profl. Edn. Bus. (pres. 1956-57), S.A.R., Beta Gamma Sigma (nat. pres. 1970-71, nat. honoree 1978); named Distinguished Scholar 1973), Phi Beta Kappa, Delta Sigma Pi, Phi Delta Theta. Presbyn. Club: Explorer's. Author: Mgmt. Thought in a Dynamic Economy, 1963. Editor: Personnel Handbook, 1951; Irwin Industrial Engineering and Management Series; editor: Irwin-Dorsey Series in Behavioral Sci.; cons. editor Advanced Management (1951-52); chmn. editorial bd. Business Horizons, 1957—; adv. bd. Mgmt. Internat., 1964. Home: 600 Soutar Dr Quail Ridge Bloomington IN 47401

MEE, LOWELL EDISON, petroleum refining co. exec.; b. St. Helena, Calif., Sept. 7, 1922; s. James Garfield and Olive Augusta (Martinelli) M.; B.S. with honors, U. Calif., Berkeley, 1948; m. Mariajane Clarke, Feb. 18, 1956; children—James K.K., Caroline M. Staff auditor Young, Lamberton & Pearson, C.P.A.'s, Honolulu, 1948-51; from asst. treas. to v.p., treas. Honolulu Gas Co., Ltd., 1951-71; v.p., treas. Pacific Resources, Inc., Honolulu, 1971—; dir. Enerco, Inc., Pacific Resources Terminals, Inc., Hawaiian Internat. Shipping, Inc., Pacific Resources (Liberia). Trustee, Hawaii Tax Found., 1965—, pres., 1970. Served with USNR, 1944-46. C.P.A., Hawaii. Mem. Am. Inst. C.P.A.'s, Fin. Execs. Inst., Am. Gas Assn., Pacific Coast Gas Assn., Hawaii Inst. C.P.A.'s. Republican. Office: 1060 Bishop St Honolulu HI 96813

MEECH, CHARLES BRADDOCK, mfg. exec.; b. Mpls., Oct. 24, 1915; s. Robert Lyon and Rose Estelle (Baldwin) M.; B.A., Princeton, 1936; m. Nanette Harrison, Apr. 6, 1940; children—Julia Baldwin, Charles Edward, Laurie, Christopher Harrison. With Mpls.-Honeywell Regulator Co. (name changed to Honeywell, Inc.), Mpls., 1936—, successively sales engr., mem. staff Toronto office, mgr. Honeywell A.G. and Internat. div. Europe, Zurich, Switzerland, mgr. Internat. div., Mpls., 1936-56, v.p. Internat. div., 1956-64, v.p. Far East, Honeywell, Inc., 1964-70, v.p. internat., 1970—. Served 2d lt. CAC to maj. AUS, 1941-46. Recipient Bronze Star and arrowhead. Episcopalian. Clubs: Minneapolis, Woodhill. Home: 1916 Knox Ave S Minneapolis MN 55403 Office: Honeywell Plaza Minneapolis MN 55408

MEECH, RICHARD CAMPBELL, lawyer; b. Portsmouth, Hampshire, Eng., Sept. 16, 1921; s. Richard George and Elizabeth (Campbell) M.; B.A., U. Toronto (Ont., Can.), 1946; postgrad. Osgoode Hall Law Sch., Toronto, 1950; LL.M., Harvard U., 1951; m. Carol Crockett, Oct. 6, 1951; children—Susan Crockett, Richard George, Peter, Sarah Elizabeth, Nancy Bingham. Admitted to Ont. bar, 1950; named Queen's counsel, 1960; mem. firm Borden & Elliot, Toronto, 1951—, sr. partner, 1957—; hon. consul Thailand, Toronto; dir. Barclays Can. Ltd., Budd Can. Inc., Harvey Hubbell Can. Ltd., Howden Group Ltd., Howden Group Am. Inc., RC Cola Can. Ltd., Stanton Pipes Ltd., Personal Ins. Co. Can.; dir., v.p., sec. Textron Can. Ltd.; dir., vice-chmn. Brown Boveri Howden Inc.; dir., vice chmn. Howden Group Can. Ltd.; dir., mem. exec. com. Slater Steel Industries Ltd.; sec., dir. Canabam Ltd.; sec. Can. Securities Inst., Nat. Contingency Fund, Can. Depository for Securities Ltd. Mem. advisory council Ridley Coll.; pres. Wellesley Coll. Can. Found.; trustee Sunnybrook Med. Centre, Toronto, Can. Hemophilia Soc.; trustee Havergal Coll. Found., Toronto, chmn., 1972-74; nat. chmn. Queen's U. Parents' Assn.; mem. Met. Toronto advisory bd. Salvation Army. Served with RCAF, 1942-46. Mem. Internat. Bar Assn. (sec. bus. sect.). Clubs: York, Badminton and Racquet, Nat. (1st v.p.), Toronto Golf, Harvard Law Sch. Assn. Ont. (pres. 1973-75), Lawyers, Can. (pres. 1974-75), Empire, St. George's Soc. (Toronto); Glenmajor Angling, Harvard (N.Y.C.); Garden of the Gods (Colorado Springs, Colo.); Coral Beach and Tennis (Bermuda). Home: 40 Stratheden Rd Toronto ON M4N 1E4 Canada Office: 250 University Ave Toronto ON M5H 3E9 Canada

MEECHAN, CHARLES JAMES, bus. exec.; b. Usk, Wash., Aug. 7, 1928; s. Robert John and Katherine B. (Battick) M.; student Eastern Wash. Coll., 1946-47; B.A. in Physics, Oreg. State U., 1951; m. Carmen Pauline Given, Sept. 15, 1951; children—Debbie, Susan, Craig, Nancy, Kevin, Brian. Research physicist Atomics Internat. div. N.Am. Rockwell, Canoga Park, Calif., 1951-62, dir. research, corp. offices, exec. dir. tech., v.p. indsl. systems, v.p. tech., 1962-70; v.p. Rockwell Internat. Sci. Center, 1971-72; v.p. corp. research and engring. Rockwell Internat. Corp., El Segundo, Calif., 1972-78, exec. v.p. energy systems group, Canoga Park, Calif., 1978—; chmn. evaluation panel Inst. Materials Research, Nat. Acad. Sci., 1975—, mem. exec. com. Nat. Acad. Sci.; mem. indsl. panel on sci. and tech. NSF, 1975—. Mem. adv. bd. Carnegie-Mellon Inst.; mem. adv. com. WINCON, 1975—. Recipient Distinguished Service award Oreg. State U., 1977. Fellow Am. Phys. Soc.; mem. Am. Inst. Aeros. and Astronautics, Research Engring. Soc. Am., Geophys. Union, Am. Soc. Oceanography, IEEE, Indsl. Research Inst., Soc. Automotive Engrs. (gen. chmn. aerospace and mfg.), Am. Nat. Metric Council, Phi Kappa Phi, Phi Eta Sigma, Sigma Pi Sigma. Contbr. articles to profl. jours. Patentee in field. Home: 5166 Kelvin Ave Woodland Hills CA 91364 Office: 8900 De Soto Ave Canoga Park CA 91304

MEEDER, WILLIAM GEORGE, vending machine mfg. co. exec.; b. Pitts., Feb. 22, 1925; s. Clair E. and Lydia C. (Trippel) M.; B.S., Hofstra Coll., 1948; m. Jeanne A., Oct. 16, 1949; children—Bill, Bob, Patti, Jeff. Successively area sales mgr., product mgr., group product mgr., div. sales v.p., internat. v.p. and mktg. dir., pres. internat. div., exec. v.p. Vendo Corp., now exec. v.p. mktg. and internat. div., Overland Park, Kans. Served with USAAF, 1943-45. Mem. Nat. Automatic Merchandising Assn. Lutheran. Home: 8016 Granda St Prairie Village KS 66208 Office: 10500 Barkley St Overland Park KS 66212

MEEHAN, FRANCIS J., ambassador; b. East Orange, N.J., Feb. 14, 1924; M.B., U. Glasgow, 1945; M.P.A., Harvard U., 1957. Adminstrv. asst. Econ. Coop. Adminstrn., 1948-51; fgn. service officer, Frankfurt, Hamburg and NATO, 1951-56; intelligence research specialist Dept. State, Washington, 1957-59; polit. officer, Moscow, 1959-61; econ. officer, polit. officer, Berlin, 1961-66; dir. Ops. Center, Dept. State, 1966-67, dep. exec. sec., 1967-68; dep. chief of mission, Budapest, 1968-72; counselor for polit. affairs, Bonn, 1972-75; dep. chief of mission, Vienna, 1975-77, Bonn, 1977-79; ambassador to Czechoslovakia, 1979—. Office: US Embassy Czechoslovakia c/o Amcongen APO New York NY 09757*

MEEHAN, JOHN EDWIN, cosmetic mfg. co. exec.; b. Los Angeles, Oct. 9, 1927; s. James Leo and Jeannette Stratton (Porter) M.; B.S., Loyola U., 1952; m. Paula Jane Kent, Apr. 26, 1973; children by previous marriage—Christopher James, Matthew Porter. Pub.'s rep. Don Harway & Co., Los Angeles, 1954-57; dist. mgr. Vance Pub. Corp., Chgo., 1957-69; pres., chief exec. officer Redken Labs., Canoga Park, Calif., 1969—; mem. bd. regents Loyola U., Los Angeles. Served with Maritime Service, 1945-47. Mem. Thalian's President Club. Republican. Roman Catholic. Clubs: Lakeside Golf, Pips. Office: 6625 Variel Ave Canoga Park CA 91303

MEEHAN, JOHN FRANCIS, ballet dancer, choreographer; b. Brisbane, Australia, May 1, 1950; came to U.S., 1977; s. Joseph and Dulcie Marie (Weis) M.; student Australian Ballet Sch., Melbourne, 1968-69. Mem. corps de ballet Australian Ballet Co., 1970-72, soloist, 1972-74, prin. dancer, 1974-76; guest artist Am. Ballet Theatre, N.Y.C., spring 1977, prin. dancer, 1977—; choreographer ballets, including: Night Episode, 1974. Recipient Choreography award Ballet 74, Canberra (Australia) Times. Office: care Am Ballet Theatre 888 7th Ave New York NY 10019

MEEHAN, JOHN PATRICK, educator; b. San Francisco, May 22, 1923; s. John Patrick and Rosa Hope (Barnitz) M.; student Calif. Inst. Tech., 1945; M.D., U. So. Calif., 1948; m. Frances Pauls, Aug. 19, 1949; children—John Patrick III, Woerner Pauls, Rosa Hope, Elizabeth Frances. Instr. dept. physiology U. So. Calif. Sch. Medicine, 1947-49, asst. prof., 1949-51, 54-57, asso. prof., 1957-63, acting chmn., prof. physiology, 1963-66, chmn., prof., 1966—; investigator NASA Biosatellite III Project, 1969; cons. NRC com. on bioastronautics. Served to capt. USAF, 1951-54. Mem. A.M.A., A.A.A.S., Am. Physiol. Soc., Aerospace Med. Assn., Ballistograph Research Soc., Calif., Los Angeles County (dir.) heart assns., Sigma Xi. Author: (with J.P. Henry) The Circulation: An Integrative Physiologic Study, 1971. Home: 460 W Walnut Ave Arcadia CA 91006 Office: 2025 Zonal Ave U So Cal Med Sch Los Angeles CA 90033

MEEHAN, PAULA KENT, cosmetic co. exec.; b. West Los Angeles, Calif., Aug. 9, 1931; d. Richard Moorehead and Lois Evelyn (Martin) Bear; extension student UCLA; m. John Edwin Meehan, Apr. 25, 1963; children—Michael D. Miller, Chris Meehan, Matthew Meehan. Founder, 1960, since pres., chmn. bd. Redken Labs. Inc., Canoga Park, Calif.; dir. Union Bank, Los Angeles, Amcord Co. Bd. regents Loyola U., Los Angeles. Mem. Cosmetic Toiletry Fragrance Assn., Nat. Beauty and Barber Mfrs. Assn. Republican. Address: 6625 Variel Ave Canoga Park CA 91303

MEEHAN, THOMAS EDWARD, writer; b. Ossining, N.Y., Aug. 14, 1929; s. Thomas Edward and Helen Cecille (O'Neill) M.; B.A., Hamilton Coll., 1951; m. Karen Termohlen, June 22, 1963; children—Joseph, Katharine. Staff writer The New Yorker mag., N.Y.C., 1956-66. Served with U.S. Army, 1951-53. Winner, Emmy for comedy writing, 1970; Writers Guild award, 1971; Antoinette Perry (Tony) Award for best book of a musical, Annie, 1977. Mem. Writers Guild Am., Dramatists Guild. Democrat. Clubs: The Coffee House, The Players. Contbr. short stories, parodies and factual articles various mags. including The New Yorker; author: Annie, 1977; author: Yma, Ava; Yma, Abba; Yma, Aga; Yma Ida . . . And Others (collection of humor pieces from The New Yorker), 1967.*

MEEHAN, WILLIAM P., electronics mfg. co. exec.; b. Boston, June 16, 1935; s. James T. and Elizabeth (Sullivan) M.; A.B., Harvard U., 1958; M.B.A., U. Chgo., 1972; m. Clara Richey, Dec. 19, 1970; children—William P., Sarah E. With First Nat. City Bank, N.Y.C., 1958-65, Inter-Am. Devel. Bank, 1965, AID, 1965-68, Dept. Treasury, 1968-69; v.p., treas. Motorola, Inc., Schaumburg, Ill., 1969—. Bd. dirs. Chgo. Boys Clubs. Served with Air N.G., USAFR. Clubs: Econ., Harvard (Chgo.). Home: 3027 Indianwood Rd Wilmette IL 60091 Office: 1303 E Algonquin Rd Schaumburg IL 60196

MEEHL, PAUL EVERETT, educator, psychologist; b. Mpls., Jan. 3, 1920; s. Otto John and Blanche Edna (Duncan) Swedal; A.B., U. Minn., 1941, Ph.D., 1945; m. Alyce M. Roworth, Sept. 6, 1941 (dec. 1972); children—Karen, Erik; m. 2d, Leslie Jane Yonce, Nov. 17, 1973. Teaching asst. psychology U. Minn., 1941-43, asst. neuropsychiatry, instr., asst., asso. prof., chmn. dept. psychology, 1951-57, prof., 1952—, prof. dept. psychiatry Med. Sch., 1952—, regents' prof. psychology, 1968—, also adj. prof. law; prof. Minn. Center for Philosophy of Sci., 1953-56, 69—, prof. philosophy, 1971—; acting chief clin. psychology VA Hosp., Mpls., 1947-49; participant Dartmouth conf. on behavior theory, 1950; mem. panel on criminal deterrence Nat. Acad. Sci., 1975-77; practice of psychotherapy, 1951—; staff Nicollet Clinic, 1970—. Diplomate in clin. psychology Am. Bd. Examiners in Profl. Psychology (mem. bd. 1957-62). Fellow Inst. for Advanced Study in Rational Psychotherapy; mem. Am. (pres. 1961-62, Distinguished Contbr. award clin. div. 1967, Distinguished Sci. Contbr. award 1958, Distinguished Scientist award 1976), Midwestern (pres. 1954-55) psychol. assns., Am. Acad. Arts and Scis. (Bruno Klopfer Disting. Contbn. award 1979), Psychonomic Soc., Psychometric Soc., Classification Soc., Am. Acad. Psychotherapists, Am. Psychology-Law Soc., Soc. Polit. and Legal Philosophy, Philosophy Sci. Assn., Sigma Xi, Phi Beta Kappa, Psi Chi. Libertarian. Author: (with S.R. Hathaway) Atlas for Clinical Use of MMPI, 1951; (with others) Modern Learning Theory, 1954; Clinical Versus Statistical Prediction, 1954; (with others) What, Then, Is Man?, 1958; Psychodiagnosis, 1973. Contbr. articles to profl., legal and philos. jours. Home: 1544 E River Terr Minneapolis MN 55414

MEEK, DAVID FELMLEY, utilities exec.; b. Carrollton, Ill., May 19, 1916; s. Alva Brace and Ruth (Felmley) M.; B.S., U. Ill., 1937, m. Rosemary Elizabeth Reid, June 20, 1942; children—David Reid, Richard Felmley. With Ill. Power Co., Decatur, 1937—, asst. sec., 1954-59, treas., 1956—, sec., 1959—; dir. Soy Capital Bank & Trust Co., Purity Baking Co. Mem. grad. dirs. council Decatur Meml. Hosp. Served with inf. AUS, 1942-46. Mem. Phi Delta Theta. Clubs: Decatur, Decatur Country (past pres.), Kiwanis (past pres.). Home: 7 Allen Bend Pl Decatur IL 62521 Office: 500 S 27th St Decatur IL 62525

MEEK, DEVON WALTER, educator; b. Johnson County, Ky., Feb. 24, 1936; s. Don C. and Willa M. (Walters) M.; B.A., Berea Coll., 1958; M.S. in Chemistry, U. Ill., 1960, Ph.D. in Inorganic Chemistry, 1961; m. Violet I. Imhof, Aug. 21, 1965; children—Brian Philip, Karen Ann. Asso. analytical chemist Oak Ridge Nat. Lab., summers 1957-59; teaching, research asst. U. Ill., Urbana, 1958-60, research fellow, 1960-61; mem. faculty dept. chemistry Ohio State U., Columbus, 1961—, asso. prof., 1966-69, prof., 1969—, chmn. dept., 1977—. Vis. scholar Northwestern U., Evanston, Ill., 1967; cons. Argonne (Ill.) Nat. Lab., 1968-69, Shepherd Chem. Co. (Ohio), 1975—, Procter & Gamble Co., 1979—; vis. sr. research fellow U. Sussex, Brighton, Eng., 1974. Gen. Electric Found. grad. fellow, 1960-61. Mem. Am. Chem. Soc., The Chem. Soc. (London), Sigma Xi. Author: (with W.T. Lippincott and F.H. Verhoek) Experimental General Chemistry, 1970, 2d edit., 1974. Home: 209 W Beechwold Blvd Columbus OH 43214

MEEK, EDWARD STANLEY, pathologist; b. Bristol, Eng., Oct. 9, 1919; s. Alfred Edward and Ann Mary Margaret (James) M.; M.B., Ch.B. cum laude, U. St. Andrews, Scotland, 1951, M.D., 1955; children—Pamela Ann, Patricia Susan. Intern, U. St. Andrews Hosps. and Clinics, Dundee, 1951-52; resident in pathology U. Bristol (Eng.) Hosps. and Clinics, 1952-56; practice medicine specializing in pathology U. Bristol, 1956-70; prof. microbiology U. Iowa, Iowa City, 1970—, prof. pathology, prof. ophthalmology, 1973—; cons. VA Hosp., Iowa City, 1970—; panel mem. NSF; cons. Travenol Labs., Costa Mesa, Calif. Served with Brit. Army, 1940-46. Fellow Am. Acad. Microbiologists, Royal Coll. Pathologists, Inst. Biologists, Sigma Xi; mem. AMA, AAAS, Am. Assn. Immunologists, Am. Soc. Microbiologists, Brit. Med. Assn., Path. Soc. Gt. Britain, N.Y. Acad. Scis. Author books and articles in field. Home: 614 E Jefferson St Iowa City IA 52240 Office: Dept Pathology U Iowa Iowa City IA 52242

MEEK, PAUL DERALD, oil and chem. co. exec.; b. McAllen, Tex., Aug. 15, 1930; s. William Van and Martha Mary (Sharp) M.; B.S. in Chem. Engring., U. Tex., Austin, 1953; m. Betty Catherine Robertson, Apr. 18, 1954; children—Paula Marie, Kathy Diane, Carol Ann, Linda Ray. Mem. tech. dept. Humble Oil & Refining Co., Baytown, Tex., 1953-55; with Cosden Oil & Chem. Co., 1955—, pres., 1968—; v.p. parent co., dir. Am. Petrofina, Inc., Dallas, 1968-76, pres., chief operating officer, 1976—. Chmn. chem. engring. vis. com. U. Tex., 1975-76; chmn. adv. council Coll. Engring. Found., U. Tex., Austin, 1979—. Named Disting. Engring. Grad., U. Tex., Austin, 1969. Mem. Am. Petroleum Inst., Am. Inst. Chem. Engrs., Mfg. Chemists Assn., Tex. Chem. Council (chmn. 1976). Contbg. author: Advances in Petroleum Chemistry and Refining, 1957. Office: Box 2159 Fina Plaza Dallas TX 75221

MEEK, PETER GRAY, ret. health agy. exec.; b. Bellefonte, Pa., Apr. 15, 1911; s. George Reuben and Ellen Downing (Valentine) M.; A.B., Pa. State U., 1932, M.A., 1933; postgrad. Carnegie Inst. Tech., 1934-35; m. Lucile Rasin, Oct. 4, 1941; children—Susan Gray (Mrs. Malcolm Landess), Katharine Rasin (Mrs. Gregg K. Jones), Ellen Downing (Mrs. Gregory Vaut). With Bur. Pub. Assistance FSA, 1938-49; asst. dir. Commn. Chronic Illness, Chgo., Balt., 1949-56; regional dir. Nat. Soc. Crippled Children and Adults, N.Y.C., 1956-61; exec. dir. Nat. Health Council, N.Y.C., 1961-73. Lectr., Johns Hopkins Sch. Hygiene and Pub. Health, 1952-56, Columbia Sch. Pub. Health, 1962-70; mem. Nat. Commn. Community Health Services, 1962-66; participant guest program Parliament Fed. Republic Germany, 1963; v.p. Nat. Council for Homemaker-Home Health Aide Services, 1967—; adviser Nat. Com. on Pvt. Philanthrophy and Pub. Needs, 1974. Bd. dirs. Pub. Affairs Com., Nat. Council on Aging; chmn. Nat. Vol. Orgns. for Ind. Living of the Aging, 1975-80. Served to lt. (s.g.) USNR, 1943-46. Fellow Am. Public Health Assn.; mem. Am. Assn. World Health (v.p. 1968-74), Phi Gamma Delta. Episcopalian. Author: (play) The Fourth Generation, 1935; Self-Regulation in Philanthropy, 1974; author, editor (with others) Chronic Illness in the United States, 1957. Home: 210 Fairmount Rd Ridgewood NJ 07450

MEEK, PHILLIP JOSEPH, publisher; b. Los Angeles, Nov. 17, 1937; s. Joseph Alcinus and Clara Amy (Phillips) M.; B.A. cum laude, Ohio Wesleyan U., 1959; M.B.A., Harvard U., 1961; m. Nancy Jean LaPorte, June 25, 1960; children—Katherine Amy, Brian Joseph, Laurie Noel. Fin. analyst Ford Motor Co., 1961-63, supr. capacity planning, 1963-66, supr. domestic scheduling, 1966, controller marketing services, 1966-68, on loan as pres. Econ. Devel. Corp. Greater Detroit, 1968-70; pres., pub. Oakland Press Co., Pontiac, Mich., 1970-77; exec. v.p., gen. mgr. Fort Worth Star-Telegram, 1977-79, pres., edn. chmn., 1980—. Past mem. Pontiac Stadium Bldg. Authority; pres. United Way Pontiac-N. Oakland, 1977. Mem. Tex. Daily Newspaper Assn. (dir.), Phi Beta Kappa, Omicron Delta Kappa, Pi Delta Epsilon, Phi Gamma Delta. Presbyterian. Clubs: Orchard Lake Country (Mich.); Rivercrest (Tex.) Country; Fort Worth, Petroleum of Fort Worth. Office: 400 W 7th St PO Box 1870 Fort Worth TX 76101

MEEK, RUSSELL CHARLES, prison cons.; b. Springfield, Ill., Sept. 9, 1937; s. Albert Jackson and Josephine (Snowden) M.; student Millikin U., Nat. U., 1959, LaSalle U., 1960; D.D., Universal Life Ch., 1975; D.Religious Humanities, Ednl. Life Coll., Modesto, Calif.; div.; 1 dau., Fredericka Patricia Shaolin Ssu. Cons. Cook County Dept. Corrections, 1966—; pres. Search for Truth, Inc., 1966—; dir. West Side Art and Karate Center, Inc., 1968—; producer, host Radio Sta. WVON, 1970—; dir. Black & Brown Communicators, Inc., 1970—; minister Universal Life Ch., 1970—. Instr., Malcolm-X Coll., 1970-72, spl. projects dir., exec. dir. ednl. tng. program, 1978—; exec. dir. Title 6 ednl. tng. program U. Ill. Circle Campus, 1977-78; producer, host WBEE Jazz Radio; mem. blue ribbon panel Citizens for Police Reform, 1973-75; rehab. ednl. specialist Northeastern Ill. U., 1974-75; co-chmn. Citizens Involvement Workshop, 1973—; lectr. Nat. Black Writers Workshop, 1973—; hearing coordinator Study Com. for Residential Schs., 1974—. Bd. dirs. Parents Without Partners. Mem. community adv. com. Malcolm X City Coll.; tech. adviser Malcom X Day Care Center. Recipient Humanitarian of Year award, 1972, 74, Community Integrity award, 1973, Champion of Imprisoned award, 1974, Community Service award, 1977; named Westside Citizen of Year, 1972-73. Democrat. Author: Poems For Peace Justice and Freedom, 1968; (song) My Love, You and Shadows in the Night, 1969. Office: PO Box 24066 Chicago IL 60624.
Only one who had lost his or her senses would fail to provide for the only future that we have: our children—the children of the world!

MEEK, SAMUEL WILLIAMS, bus. exec.; b. Nashville, Sept. 22, 1895; S. Samuel W. and Williea (Pierce) M.; student Phillips Exeter Academy, 1913; A.B., Yale, 1917; m. Priscilla Mitchel, Oct. 14, 1921; children—Elizabeth, Samuel, Priscilla, Susan. With J. Walter Thompson Co., 1925-63, vice chmn., dir.; chmn. bd. Walker Pub. Co., 1962—; pres., dir., pub. Rome Daily Am., Italy, 1964-69; dir. Time, Inc., 1922-70, adv. dir., 1970-74; chmn. bd. Walker & Co., N.Y.C., 1975—; dir. State Nat. Bank, Greenwich Pub. Co.; publisher Brussels Times, Brussels, Belgium; dir., treas. Episcopalian mag.; trustee Empire Savs. Bank (N.Y.), 1932-68; bd. govs. Yale U. Press. Nat. gov. A.R.C., 1959-65; hon. trustee Presbyn. Hosp., Am. Hosp., Paris; trustee Sch. Advanced Internat. Studies, Johns Hopkins; bd. dirs. Seabury House of P.E. Ch. in U.S., Episcopal Ch. Found.; mem. Yale Council and Yale devel. bd. Yale U.; pres. bd. trustees Greenwich Country Day Sch. Served as capt. USMC, 1917-19; mem. Navy civilian adv. com., World War II. Decorated Croix de Guerre with palm, Silver Star, Purple Heart with oak leaf cluster. Recipient of the Medal for Merit, Navy Distinguished Pub. Service award, World War II. Mem. English-Speaking Union (dir.), Atlantic Council (dir.). Republican. Episcopalian. Home: 88 Dolding Rd Greenwich CT 06830 Office: 720 Fifth Ave New York City NY 10019

MEEKER, DAVID BOWYER, elec. equipment co. exec.; b. Troy, Ohio, Sept. 19, 1925; s. David Anderson and Laura (Bowyer) M.; B.A., Dartmouth, 1948; M.B.A., U. Mich., 1950; m. Helen Sanders Nelson, June 30, 1948; children—David Nelson, George Nelson, Laura Jane (Mrs. James M. Johnson), Susan Sanders. With Hobart Corp., 1949—, sales mgr. br. and agy. div., 1955-63, treas., 1963-66, v.p., treas., 1966-67, exec. v.p., 1967-68, pres., 1968—, chief exec. officer, 1970—, also dir.; dir. Armco Inc., Phillips Petroleum Co., R.R. Donnelley & Sons Co., Dayton Power & Light Co., Winters Nat. Bank & Trust Co., Dayton. Trustee Hollins Coll., Nat. Inst. Foodservice Industry, Chgo., Lincoln Community Center, Troy; bd. dirs. Boy Scouts of Am., Dayton, Ohio, Jr. Achievement Dayton. Pres. Neil Armstrong Air and Space Mus. Assn., Wapakoneta, Ohio; founding v.p. Brukner Nature Center, Miami County, Ohio. Served with USNR, 1943-46. Mem. NAM (chmn. 1975, hon. life vice chmn.), Ohio Mfrs. Assn. (v.p.), Conf. Bd., Phi Delta Theta. Republican. Presbyterian. Clubs: Rotary, Troy Country; Dayton Racquet; Leland (Mich.) Country, Leland Yacht; Chgo. Yacht. Home: 420 S Market St Troy OH 45373 Office: World Hdqrs Bldg Troy OH 45374

MEEKER, DAVID OLAN, JR., architect, urban planner, cons.; b. Clifton Springs, N.Y., May 19, 1924; s. David Olan and Estelle (Niemann) M.; B.Arch., Yale U., 1950; grad. certificate U. Copenhagen, Royal Acad. Art Copenhagen, 1962; m. Martha J. Cantwell, July 19, 1948 (div. Mar. 1967); children—Scott C., Stone S., Brett L., Ann S.; m. 2d, Sarah M. Merriman, July 1, 1967 (div. Feb. 1974); 1 dau., Elizabeth; m. 3d, Laura Kuitunen, Aug. 6, 1977. With R.E. Bishop, Indpls., 1952-54; pvt. practice architecture, Indpls., 1954-56; partner, architect James Assos., Inc., Indpls., 1956-70; dir. Indpls. Model Cities Program, 1968-70; dir. Indpls. Dept. Met. Devel., 1970-71, dep. mayor, 1971-73; asst. sec. for community planning and devel. HUD, Washington, 1973-76, dir. urban coordination, 1973-76; Albert A. Levin prof. urban studies and pub. service Cleve. State U., 1977-78; exec. v.p. AIA, Washington, 1978—; pvt. practice as David Olan Meeker, Jr., urban devel. cons., Washington, 1976—; vis. lectr. Hollins Coll., 1965, Ind. U., 1965-67, Ball State U., 1971-73; mem. Water Resources Council, 1973-76, Pennsylvania Ave. Corp., 1974-76, Adv. Council on Historic Preservation, 1974—; chmn. Fed. Agy. Bi-Centennial Task Force subcom. Domestic Council, 1974—, chmn. Long Range Econ. Disaster Recovery Task Force, 1974—; chmn. com. II U.S. del. Habitat, UN Conf. Human Settlements, 1976; chmn. Joint U.S.A.-USSR com. Built Environment, 1975-76, com. New Communities, 1976; mem. architects adv. commn. Met. Plan Commn., Indpls., 1956—; mem. Mayor's Task Force on Housing and Relocation, Mayor's Task Force on Black Capitalism, Mayor's Task Force on Model Cities, Community Shelter Plan Council; mem. regional health adv. com. region V, Health Services and Mental Health Adminstrn., 1972-73; mem. adv. com. on sch. house planning Ind. Supt. Edn.; mem. exec. adv. bd. Ind. Limestone Inst. Am., 1968-71; Ind. project dir. Joint Ind.-Calif. State Univs. Acad. Bldg. Constrn. Systems Devel.; mem. constrn. action council U.S. C. of C., 1970. Trustee Housing Advocates, Inc.; bd. dirs. Rapid Recovery, Inc., Cleve., 1977—. Served with AUS, 1943-45, to cpl., 1950-52; lt. col. Res., ret. Recipient awards Ind. Soc. Architects, 1959, 65, Guild for Religious Architecture, 1958; Good Govt. award Indpls. Jaycees, 1971; named Man of Year in Constrn., Ind. Sub-Contractors Assn., 1969; recipient Dedicated Service and Profl. Guidance award Ind. Limestone Inst., 1971; Royal Danish fellow, 1961-62; Fulbright fellow, 1961-62. Fellow AIA (urban planning and design com., dir. Ind., Indpls. chpts.); mem. Newcomen Soc. N.Am., Assn. U.S. Army, Soc. Am. Mil. Engrs., Indpls. C. of C. (edn. com.), Ind. Soc. Architects (dir.), Nat. Assn. Housing and Redevel. Ofcls. (bd. dirs. Ind. chpt., exec. com. N. Central regional council, nat. renewal com. 1972), Guild for Religious Architecture, Council Ednl. Facility Planners, Urban Am., Am. Pub. Works Assn., Nat. Trust for Historic Preservation, Am. Soc. Pub. Adminstrn. (chpt. council). Republican. Presbyterian (deacon). Editorial adv. bd. Housing and Devel. Reporter, 1976—. Home: 2311 Connecticut Ave NW Apt 502 Washington DC 20008 Office: 1735 New York Ave NW Washington DC 20006

MEEKER, JAMES JULIAN, oil and gas producer; b. Ft. Worth, Dec. 20, 1935; s. Julian Robertson and Edna (Hill) M.; student Dartmouth, 1954-58, Stanford Law Sch., 1958-60, Grad. Sch. English, 1960-61. Art critic Ft. Worth Star Telegram, 1963—; adviser Kimbell Art Found., 1968—; partner Meeker Co., Ft. Worth, 1967—; owner Meeker Investments, 1972—; chmn. bd. Meeker-Gill Film Prodns., 1971—. Pres., Peacemaker Found.; founding mem., sec. bd. trustees Ft. Worth Country Day Sch.; bd. dirs. Ft. Worth Art Center, Ft. Worth Opera, Ft. Worth Symphony. Van Cliburn Internat. Piano Competition. Festival of Two Worlds, Spoleto, Italy. Mem. Sigma Alpha Epsilon. Clubs: Knickerbocker (N.Y.C.); Fort Worth, Rivercrest Country, Ridglea Country, Steeplechase Bachelor (Ft. Worth). Office: 1214 Ridglea Bank Bldg Fort Worth TX 76116

MEEKER, LEONARD CARPENTER, lawyer, govt. ofcl.; b. Montclair, N.J., Apr. 4, 1916; s. Irving Avard and Elizabeth Louise (Carpenter) M.; grad. Deerfield Acad., 1933; A.B., Amherst Coll., 1937, LL.D., 1967; LL.B., Harvard, 1940; m. Christine Rhoda Halliday, Sept. 27, 1947 (dec. Feb. 1958); children—Richard Halliday, Charles Carpenter, Sarah Louise; m. 2d, Beverly Joan Meeker, June 14, 1969; children—Eliza Ann Hunt, James Edward Weeks, Benjamin Chester Gilman. Admitted to D.C. bar, 1940, Calif. bar, 1941. With Office Gen. Counsel, Treasury Dept., Washington, 1940-41, Office Solicitor Gen., Dept. Justice, Washington, 1941-42; with Office Legal Adviser, Dept. State, Washington, 1946-51, asst. legal adviser, 1951-61, dep. legal adviser, 1961-65, legal adviser, 1965-69; U.S. ambassador to Romania, 1969-73; mem. Center for Law and Social Policy, 1974—. Trustee Potomac Sch., 1959-67, chmn., 1960-63. Mem. Am., Fed. bar assns., Am. Soc. Internat. Law (v.p. 1976—), St. Nicholas Soc. of City of N.Y. Home: 3000 Chain Bridge Rd NW Washington DC 20016 Office: 1751 N St NW Washington DC 20036

MEEKER, THOMAS GEORGE, lawyer, former govt. ofcl.; b. Orange, N.J., Sept. 30, 1919; s. John Harbeck and Adeline (Medinger) M.; B.A., Wesleyan U., 1941; LL.B., Yale, 1948; m. Mary Palmer Hankinson, June 14, 1952; children—Ann Ogden, Jane Stanton, Susan Dayton, Kenneth Hankinson. Clk. trainee Surplus Mktg. Adminstrn., Dept. Agr., 1941; intern Nat. Inst. Pub. Affairs, Washington, 1941-42; jr. adminstrv. asst. Bd. Econ. Warfare, 1942; teaching asst. govt. Wesleyan U., also instr. Jr. Coll. Commerce, New Haven, and lectr. law Quinnipiac Coll., 1947-54; vis. lectr. law Duke, 1960-61; law clk. U.S. Dist. Ct., Conn., 1947-49; admitted to Conn. bar, 1949; asso. firm Gumbart, Corbin, Tyler & Cooper, 1949-54; asst. gen. counsel SEC, 1954-55, asso. gen. counsel, 1955-56, acting exec. dir., 1955, gen. counsel, 1956-60; partner firm Schnader, Harrison, Segal & Lewis, Phila., 1960-70, Townsend, Elliott and Munson, Phila., 1971-73; pvt. practice, 1973; partner firm Stassen, Kostos & Mason, Phila., 1973—. Mem. corp. Phila. Crime Commn.; counsel New Haven Citizens Com. for Counsel Charter, 1953-54; pres. Citizens Com. on Pub. Edn. for Phila., 1966-68; mem. Radnor Twp. Municipal Authority, 1969—, chmn. Govt. Study Commn., 1974-76. Treas. Lella Day Nurseries, New Haven, 1952-54; dir. Vis. Nurse Assn., New Haven, 1952-54. Served to maj. USMCR, 1942-45. Recipient Arthur S. Flemming award, 1958. Mem. Am. (sec. Jr. Bar Conf. 1953-54, alternate del. Fed. Bar Assn. 1957), Fed. (pres. 1959-60), Pa., New Haven County, D.C., Phila. bar assns., State Bar Assn. Conn., Nat. Conf. Bar Presidents, Am. Judicature Soc., Inst. Jud. Adminstrn., Jud. Council Conn. (sec. 1954-61), Phi Beta Kappa, Phi Delta Phi, Delta Tau Delta, Delta Sigma Rho. Episcopalian. Clubs: Lawn, Graduates (New Haven); Yale (N.Y.C. and Phila.); Urban (Phila.); Army Navy, National Lawyers, Capitol Hill (Washington); St. David's Golf. Home: 205 S Aberdeen Ave Wayne PA 19087

MEEKER, WILLIAM EVERETT, zoo dir.; b. Phoenix, Aug. 2, 1937; s. Russell Youle and Lucy Helen (Axline) M.; B.S. in Zoology, U. Ariz., Tucson, 1959; m. Shirley Rae Kirts, Dec. 27, 1961; children—Eric David, Julie Ann. Curator, Ariz.-Sonora Desert Mus., Tucson, 1960-62; curator mammals Phoenix Maytag Zoo, 1962-64; asst. dir. Cheyenne Mountain Zoo, Colorado Springs, 1964-70; asst.

dir. Sacramento Zoo, 1970-72, dir., 1972—; cons. in field. Mem. Am. Assn. Zool. Parks and Aquariums (dir. 1972-76, pres. 1977—; President's award 1972, Bean award for most notable captive animal birth 1974), Soc. Prevention Cruelty to Animals. Presbyterian. Editor various zoo publs. Home: 636 Ironwood Way Sacramento CA 95831 Office: 3930 W Land Park Dr Sacramento CA 95822

MEEKS, CURTIS LEO, fin. holding co. exec.; b. Dallas, Mar. 10, 1913; s. Walter Tucker and Myrtle Elizabeth (Gantz) M.; A.A. in Acctg., John Tarleton Coll., Stephenville, Tex., 1936; postgrad. U. Tex. Law Sch.; m. Janie Marie Shirey, Nov. 25, 1939; children—Janis Shirey, Claudia Jill. With Sears, Roebuck & Co., 1939-75, operating mgr. Central Fla. region, Orlando, 1958-75; co-founder, sr. v.p. fin./adminstrn., sec., dir., mem. exec. com. Southland Equity Corp., Orlando, 1975—; realtor-asso. J.Rolfe Davis Real Estate, Orlando, 1979—; developer Holiday Inn motels, 1958—. Past pres. local United Appeal. Served to lt. comdr. A.C., USNR, World War II. Mem. Internat. Auditors Assn., Realtors Assn. Orlando, Winter Park Bd. Realtors. Democrat. Methodist. Clubs: Orlando Country, Citrus, Orlando Lions (past sec.). Home: 629 Lakeview St Orlando FL 32804 Office: CNA Tower Suite 1450 Orlando FL 32802

MEEKS, EVERETT R., dairy products co. exec.; b. N.Y.C., Aug. 2, 1915; s. Alfred and Mathilda (Joost) M.; B.S., Coll. City N.Y., 1937; m. Madeline Sweeney, Aug. 18, 1940; children—Lynn, Robert, William; m. 2d, Phyllis Mieinski, 1974. Jr. auditor McGarry, Christma & Ludgate, N.Y.C., 1937-38; analyst Peck & Durham, N.Y.C., 1938-39; salesman Sheffield Condensed Milk Co., N.Y.C., 1939-41; asst. sales mgr. Dairy Products Sales Co., N.Y.C., 1941-43; with Midwest Producers Creameries Inc. (name changed to Valley Lea Dairies, Inc., 1972), South Bend, Ind., 1946—, gen. mgr., chief exec. officer, 19—; mem. adv. bd. 1st Bank & Trust Co., South Bend. Mem. fin. com. TriValley Council Boy Scouts Am. Served with USAAF, 1943-46. Mem. Am. Dry Milk Inst. (dir.), Nat. Milk Producers Fedn. (dir.), Am. Butter Inst. (dir.), S.A.R. Republican. Episcopalian. Clubs: Elks, Masons, Knife and Fork. Home: 321 Rue Flambeau South Bend IN 46615 Office: 54501 N Ironwood Rd South Bend IN 46635. *Be interested in and learn all possible about everything from every source, including people. Ask when you don't know, for once answered you are no longer stupid about the subject. Knowledge in any field finds application in many fields. Be unselfish in doing for others for he who serves best profits most.*

MEEKS, JAMES EDWIN, lawyer, coll. adminstr.; b. Morgantown, W.Va., Nov. 8, 1938; s. Voras D. and Frankie E. (Wolfe) M.; A.B., Oberlin Coll., 1960; LL.B., Columbia U., 1963; m. Priscilla Lohr, Aug. 9, 1969; children—Kathryn Leslie, Jeffrey David. Admitted to Ohio bar, 1963, Iowa bar, 1969; law clk. to Judge Carl McGowan, U.S. Ct. Appeals for D.C., 1963-64; asst. prof. law U. Iowa, 1964-67, asso. prof., 1967-71, prof., 1971-78, asso. dean Coll. Law, 1973-76; vis. prof. U. Va., 1976-77; dean Ohio State U. Coll. Law, 1978—; vis. prof. Northwestern U., 1968-69. Mem. Am. Bar Assn., Columbus (Ohio) Bar Assn., Iowa State Bar Assn., Am. Law Inst. Contbr. articles to law jours. Home: 4459 Shire Mill Rd Columbus OH 43220 Office: 1659 N High St Columbus OH 43210

MEEKS, WILKISON WINFIELD, educator; b. Pitts., Apr. 4, 1915; s. Ralph and Ruby Katherine (Wagener) M.; A.B. magna cum laude, Maryville Coll., 1937; M.S., Northwestern U., 1939, Ph.D., 1941; m. Esther Belle McBain, Feb. 23, 1946; children—Katherine, Loretta. Physicist, Naval Ordnance Lab., Washington, 1941-44, Haskins Labs., N.Y.C., 1944-46; asso. prof. Western Md. Coll., 1946-47, So. Ill. U., 1947-48; asst. prof. Western Res. U., 1948-55; physicist B.F. Goodrich Research Lab., 1955-58; asso. prof. Rose Hulman Inst., Terre Haute, Ind., 1958-60, prof., 1960—, chmn. physics dept., 1960-68, recipient Dean's Outstanding Teaching award 1970-71. Mem. Am. Phys. Soc., Acoustical Soc. Am., Am. Assn. Physics Tchrs., Sigma Xi. Contbr. articles to tech. jours. Home: 2911 Oak St Terre Haute IN 47803 Mailing Address: Rose Hulman Institute Terre Haute IN 47803

MEEM, JAMES LAWRENCE, JR., nuclear scientist; b. N.Y., Dec. 24, 1915; s. James Lawrence and Phyllis (Deaderick) M.; B.S., Va. Mil. Inst., 1939; M.S., Ind. U., 1947. Ph.D., 1949; m. Buena Vista Speake, Sept. 5, 1940; children—James, John. Aero. research sci. NACA, 1940-46; dir. bulk shielding reactor Oak Ridge Nat. Lab., 1950-53, in charge nuclear operation aircraft reactor expt., 1954-55; chief reactor sci. Alco Products, Inc., 1955-57; in charge startup and initial testing Army Package Power Reactor, 1957; prof. nuclear engring., dir. reactor facility U. Va., 1957—; vis. cons. nuclear fuel cycle programs Sandia Labs., Albuquerque, 1977-78; vis. staff mem. Los Alamos Sci. Lab., 1967-68; mem. U.S.-Japan Seminar Optimization of Nuclear Engring. Edn., Tokai-mura, 1973. Fellow Am. Nuclear Soc. (sec. reactor ops. div. 1966-68, vice chmn. 1968-70, chmn. 1970-71); mem. Am. Phys. Soc., Am. Soc. Engring. Edn. Author: Two Group Reactor Theory, 1964. Home: Mount Airy RFD 2 Charlottesville VA 22901

MEEM, JOHN GAW, architect; b. Pelotas, Brazil, Nov. 17, 1894 (parents Am. citizens); s. John Gaw and Elsa (Krischke) M.; Sc.B., Va. Mil. Inst., 1914; M.A. hon., Colo. Coll., 1936; A.F.D. (hon.), U. N.Mex.; m. Faith Bemis, May 20, 1933; 1 dau., Nancy (Mrs. John Wirth). Began practice, 1924, specializing in Spanish pueblo architecture, ret. from active practice, now cons.; designer La Fonda Hotel and Anthropology Lab., Santa Fe, main bldgs. U. N.Mex., Albuquerque, Colorado Springs Fine Arts Center (Silver medal 5th Pan-Am. Congress Architects), 1st Presbyn. Ch., Santa Fe, Santa Fe County Ct. House Municipal Bldg., Mus. Internat. Folk Art, St. Vincent Hosp.; cons. architect St. John's Coll., Santa Fe. Fellow Sch. Am. Research. Served as capt. inf. World War. Fellow AIA; asso. mem. NAD. Episcopalian. Home: PO Box 1924 Santa Fe NM 87501

MEERKAMPER, BEAT, chemist, mfg. co. exec.; b. Davos, Switzerland, Aug. 24, 1923; s. Emil and Lina (Lendi) M.; came to U.S., 1955, naturalized, 1960; Chem. Eng., Swiss Fedn. Inst. Tech., Zurich, 1947, Dr. Sc. Tech., 1953; m. Ruth Meyer, Aug. 23, 1951; children—Gabriele, Roy B. Chemist in charge of tech. ops. Elox A.G., Baden, Switzerland, 1951-55; tchr. chemistry Gewerbeschle, Zurich, 1953-55; with photo products dept. E.I. duPont De Nemours & Co., Parlin, N.J., 1955-67, 74—, research mgr., 1966-67, dir. research lab., 1974—, tech. mgr. magnetic tape, Wilmington, Del., 1967-70; dir. research Du Pont (Deutschland) GmbH, Frankfurt, W. Ger., 1970-74. Mem. Soc. Photog. Sci. and Engring. Contbr. articles on photo chemistry, applied photog. tech. to profl. publs.; patentee in field. Home: 66 Briarwood Rd Fair Haven NJ 07701 Office: EI duPont De Nemours & Co Inc Research Lab Parlin NJ 08859

MEEROVITCH, EUGENE, parasitologist; s. Boris and Raisa (Zoreva) M.; B.Sc., St. John's U., 1947; M.Sc., McGill U., 1955, Ph.D., 1957; m. Carlota Pedroso, May 16, 1961; children—Sandra and Karen (twins). Asst. prof. parasitology McGill U., Montreal, Que., Can., 1960-66, asso. prof., 1966-70, prof., 1970—, dir. Inst. Parasitology, 1978—; cons. WHO, 1969—. Donner postdoctoral fellow, 1958-59. Mem. Can. Soc. Zoologists, Am. Soc. Parasitologists, Am. Soc. Tropical Medicine and Hygiene, Royal Soc. Tropical Medicine and Hygiene, Can. Soc. Tropical Medicine and Internat. Health, Assn. Microbiologistes du Que., Sigma Xi. Contbr. chpts. to books; contbr. articles to profl. jours. Office: Inst Parasitology McGill Univ Sainte Anne de Bellevue PQ H9X 1C0 Canada

MEERS, HENRY W., investment banker; b. Joliet, Ill., July 12, 1908; s. Robert and Mary (Cullen) M.; A.B., U. Ill., 1930; m. Evelyn Huckins; children—Henry Weber, Albert Huckins, Robert. With Halsey, Stuart & Co., Chgo., 1930-35, Harriman, Ripley & Co., 1936-42; resident partner White, Weld & Co., 1946-72, vice chmn., 1972-78; mng. dir. Merrill Lynch White Weld Capital Markets Group, Chgo., 1978—; dir. Reliance Ins. Co., Internat. Minerals & Chem. Corp., Ill. Tool Works, DuKane Corp., Kroehler Mfg. Co., Reliance Group, Inc. Chmn. bd. govs. Assn. Stock Exchange Firms, 1968-69; bd. govs. Midwest Stock Exchange 1957-60, N.Y. Stock Exchange, 1970-71. Mem. Chgo. Crime Commn.; chmn. Modern Cts. Ill., 1970; chmn. Met. Crusade Mercy, 1967-68. Trustee U. Chgo., Lake Forest Acad.; chmn. Chgo. Ednl. TV WTTW; bd. dirs. Children's Meml. Hosp., chmn., 1970-75; pres. bd. trustees Latin Sch. Chgo., 1956-58; mem. citizens bd. Loyola U.; chmn. Chgo. council Boy Scouts Am., 1952-56; trustee Nat. Recreation and Park Assn. Served to comdr. USNR, 1942-46. Recipient Man of Year award Nat. Conf. Christians and Jews, 1969. Mem. Investment Analysts Soc., Phi Beta Kappa. Clubs: University, Commercial, Casino (Chgo.); Links (N.Y.C.); Onwentsia, Old Elm; Seminole Golf; Shore Acres, Bohemian (San Francisco); Capitol Hill (Washington). Home: 89 East Deer Path Lake Forest IL 60045 Office: 5500 Sears Tower Chicago IL 60606

MEESE, WILLIAM GILES, utility co. exec.; b. Rugby, N.D., Aug. 27, 1916; s. William Gottlieb and Emma (LaPierre) M.; B.S. in Elec. Engring., Purdue U., 1941, D.Eng. (hon.), 1972; m. Mary Edith Monk, Apr. 4, 1942; children—Elizabeth Ann, Stephen William, Richard Edward. With Detroit Edison Co., 1941—, asst. v.p., 1967, v.p., 1967-69, exec. v.p. prodn., 1969-70, pres., 1970-75, chief exec. officer, 1971—, chmn., chief exec. officer, 1975—, also dir.; dir. Eaton Corp., Ex-Cell-O Corp., Mfrs. Nat. Bank Detroit, Mfrs. Nat Corp., Pub. Utilities Reports, Inc. Trustee Detroit Renaissance, Rackham Engring. Found., New Detroit, Inc.; bd. dirs. United Found. Served to maj. F.A., AUS, 1941-45. Decorated Bronze Star medal; recipient Distinguished Alumnus award Purdue U., 1969; Internat. B'nai B'rith Humanitarian award, 1977; registered prof. engr., Mich. Fellow Engring. Soc. Detroit; mem. IEEE, Conf. Internationale des Grands Reseaux Electriques, Newcomen Soc. N.Am., Tau Beta Pi, Eta Kappa Nu. Clubs: Economic of Detroit (dir.), Detroit Athletic, Detroit. Home: 570 Rudgate Rd Bloomfield Hills MI 48013 Office: 2000 2d Ave Detroit MI 48226

MEFFEN, JAMES DOUGLAS, sch. pres.; b. N.Y.C., Aug. 7, 1927; s. James Douglas and Edith (Anderson) M.; A.B., Gordon Coll., 1949; S.T.B., Harvard, 1951; M.A., Suffolk U., 1957; Ed.D., Calvin Coolidge U., 1959; H.H.D., Arubaanse Handels Academie, 1970; m. Ruth Freer, 1948; children—James Douglas III, David Mark, Melodee Joy, LaMarre Cherie; m. 2d, Janet Searles, 1960; children—Faith, Martha, Scott, Alison; m. 3d, Jean Mutschler, 1972; children—Philip, Steven, Christine. Ordained to ministry Christian Ch. (Congl. Christian), 1951; minister Christian chs., West Mansfield, Mass., 1950-51, Hallandale, Fla., 1954-55, Boston, 1955-56; chaplain S. Fla. State Hosp., West Hollywood, 1957-58; prin. Deerborne Sch., Coral Gables, Fla., 1959-63; adminstr. Coral Gables Acad. and Inst. Reading, 1961-70; pres. Gables Acads., Miami, Fla., Atlanta, New Orleans, St. Petersburg, Ft. Lauderdale, Baton Rouge, Mobile, Ala., 1970—. Cons. United Cerebral Palsy; field cons. Commn. on High Quality Tchr. Edn. of Internat. Reading Assn., 1971. Served from 1st lt. to capt., chaplain, USAF, 1951-54. Fellow Am. Orthopsychiat. Assn.; mem. Nat. Assn. for Retarded Children, Assn. for Children with Learning Disabilities, Am. Assn. on Mental Deficiency, Am. Personnel and Guidance Assn., Nat. Vocational Guidance Assn., Assn. for Measurement and Evaluation in Guidance, Nat. Rehab. Assn., Assn. for Supervision and Curriculum Devel., Am. Sch. Counsellor Assn., Internat. Reading Assn., Nat. Assn. Pvt. Schs. for Exceptional Children (pres. 1972), Am. Pub. Health Assn., Acad. Orthomolecular Psychiatry (asso.), Internat. Platform Assn., Am. Coll. Personnel Assn., Nat. Assn. Secondary Sch. Prins., Council for Exceptional Children, Assn. Christian Therapists, Am. Assn. Sex Educators, Counselors and Therapists, Old Colony Ministerial Assn. Mass., Am. Legion, D.A.V., Phi Delta Tau. Democrat. Home: 7700 Miller Rd Miami FL 33155 Office: 10700 Caribbean Blvd Miami FL 33189

MEFFERD, GEORGE W., business exec.; b. 1927; B.S., U. Calif., 1952; married. Auditor, John F. Forbes & Co., 1952-54; asst. div. controller Tidewater Oil Co., 1954-63; v.p. finance Rexall Chem. Co., 1963-67; v.p., controller Evans Products Co., Portland, Oreg., 1967-74; sr. v.p. fin., dir. Fluor Corp., Irvine, Calif., 1974—. Bd. dirs. Ind. Colls. of So. Calif.; trustee Greater Los Angeles Zoo Assn., UCLA Found. Served with AUS, 1946-48. C.P.A., Calif. Mem. Fin. Execs. Inst. Phi Gamma Delta. Club: Big Canyon Country. Office: Fluor Corp Irvine CA 92730

MEGAHAN, JOHN BRUCE, natural gas transmission co. exec.; b. Wilkinsburg, Pa., May 27, 1919; s. George W. and Florence (Beltz) M.; A.B., Allegheny Coll., 1940; LL.B., Columbia, 1943; m. Billie Jean Hightower, June 9, 1951; children—Sandra Lee, Carol Elise. Admitted to N.Y. bar, 1947; spl. agt. FBI, 1943-47; atty., asst. sec. Allied Chem. Corp., 1947-57; with El Paso Co. (formerly El Paso Natural Gas Co.), 1957—, sec., 1966—, v.p., 1978—. Mem. adv. bd. Booth Meml. Home, Salvation Army, El Paso, 1964-78. Pres. Family Service El Paso, 1972. Mem. Am. Bar Assn., Am. Soc. Corp. Secs., El Paso C. of C. (dir. 1973-76), Phi Beta Kappa, Phi Gamma Delta. Presbyn. Home: 10114 Briar Dr Houston TX 77042 Office: PO Box 2185 Houston TX 77001

MEGAN, THOMAS IGNATIUS, judge; b. Chgo., Dec. 24, 1913; s. Charles P. and May M. (Magan) M.; A.B., U. Ill., 1935; J.D., U. Chgo., 1938; m. Lucyanne Flaherty, Apr. 17, 1948; children—Anne, Thomas, Jane, Sarah, William, Molly. Admitted to Ill. bar, 1939, N.Y. bar, 1941; mem. firm Pruitt & Grealis, Chgo., 1939-40, Pruitt, Hale & MacIntyre, N.Y.C., 1941; atty. U.S. Ordnance Dept., Chgo., 1941-42; asst. gen. atty. C., R.I. & P. Ry., Chgo., 1945-51, gen. atty., 1951-61, asst. gen. counsel, 1961-70, gen. counsel, 1970—, v.p., 1973-75; adminstrv. law judge ICC, Washington, 1975—. Served to maj. AUS, 1942-45. Mem. Am., Fed. bar assns., Assn. ICC Practitioners (chmn. Chgo. chpt. 1961-62), Soc. Trial Lawyers Chgo., Chgo. Law Club, Phi Kappa Tau, Phi Delta Phi. Clubs: Union League (Chgo.); Nat. Lawyers (Washington). Home: 11108 Waycroft Way Rockville MD 20852 Office: 1900 L St NW 5th Floor Washington DC 20036

MEGARR, EDWARD JOHN, marine corps officer; b. Bklyn., Mar. 20, 1927; s. John Charles and Violet (Currinan) M.; B.A., Adelphi Coll., 1950; grad. Army War Coll., 1972; m. Jane Gulbransen, July 22, 1950; children—Claudia Jane Megarr Summers, Maureen Ellen. Served as enlisted man U.S. Marine Corps., 1945-46, commd. 2d lt. U.S. Marine Corps Res., 1950, integrated into Regular Marine Corps, 1955, advanced through grades to maj. gen., 1977; served with 1st Marine Div., Korea, 1951-52, guard officer Marine Barracks, Keyport, Wash., 1952-53, comdg. officer Hdqrs and Service Co., 2d Service Regt., 2d Marine Div., Camp Lejeune, N.C., 1955-56; served with Marine Corps Recruit Depot, Parris Island, S.C., 1956-59; comdr. 2d Landing Support Co., 3d Service Bn., 3d Marine Div., Okinawa, Japan, 1959-60; insp.-instr. 52d Rifle Co., New Bedford, Mass., 1960-62; marine aide and adminstrv. asst. to Adm. Claude Richetts and Adm. Horacio Rivero, Vice Chief Naval Ops., Washington, 1963-65; exec. officer Camp Lejeune, comdg. officer 2d Shore Party Bn., 2d Marine Div., 1965-67; J-3 staff officer Current Plans, I Corps, Hdqrs. Mil. Assistance Command, Saigon, Vietnam, 1967-68; J-4 staff officer Hdqrs. U.S. European Command, Stuttgart, Germany, 1968-71; head facilities dept. Marine Corps Devel. and Edn. Command, Quantico, Va., 1972, chief of staff, 1972-73, comdr. Officer Candidate Sch., 1973-75; asst. div. comdr. 3d Marine Div., Okinawa, Japan, 1975-76; comdg. gen. Force Troops, Pacific/Marine Corps Base, Twentynine Palms, Calif., 1976-78; dep. chief of staff for ops. and tng. Hdqrs. Marine Corps, Washington, 1978—; bd. dirs. Los Angeles Area USO, 1976-78. Decorated Bronze Star medal with combat V and gold star, Joint Service Commendation medal, Purple Heart medal with gold star, UN medal. Mem. Marine Corps Assn. Democrat. Roman Catholic. Club: Rotary (hon.). Home: 1416 S 20th St Arlington VA 22202 Office: Hdqrs USMC Washington DC 20380*

MEGARRY, A. ROY, publisher; b. Belfast, No. Ireland, Feb. 10, 1937; s. Andrew Blain and Barbara (Bennett) M.; ed. U. Western Ont. (Can.); grad. mgmt. devel. course Princeton U.; m. Barbara Todd Bird Bennett, May 31, 1959; children—Andrew, Kevin, Lianne. Controller, Honeywell Ltd., Toronto, Ont., 1957-64; v.p. Daystrom (Heathkit) Ltd., Toronto, 1964-66; sr. cons. Urwick, Currie, Coopers & Lybrand Ltd., Toronto, 1966-69; v.p. fin. Internat. Syscoms Ltd., Toronto, 1969-71; v.p., gen. mgr. Blackwoods Beverages Ltd., Winnipeg, Man., Can., 1971-73; v.p. Charterways Co. Ltd., 1974; v.p. Torstar Corp., Toronto, 1974-78; pub., chief exec. officer Globe and Mail, daily newspaper, Toronto, 1978—; dir. F.P. Publs. (Eastern) Ltd.; mem. edn. bd. Cost and Mgmt. mag.; mem. planning com. TV Ont. Mem. Soc. Indsl. Accts. Can. (past dir.), Soc. Indsl. Accts. Ont. Roman Catholic. Clubs: Donalda, Nat. Office: 444 Front St W Toronto ON M5V 2S6 Canada

MEGAW, ROBERT NEILL ELLISON, educator; b. Ottawa, Can., Oct. 7, 1920; s. John Wesley and Eileen (Ellison) M.; came to U.S., 1925, naturalized, 1936; student Duke, 1937-40; M.A., U. Chgo., 1947, Ph.D., 1950; m. Ann Barber, Dec. 20, 1947; children—Peter Kenneth McNeill, Margaret McNeill, Laura McNeill. Faculty, Williams Colls., 1950-69, prof. English, 1965; Carnegie intern Harvard, 1955-56; prof. English, chmn. dept. U. Tex., Austin, 1969-71. Cons. acad. planning, 1962—; mem. nat. bd. consultants Nat. Endowment for Humanities, 1974—; Nat. Humanities Faculty, 1969—. Served to 1st lt. USAAF, 1942-45. Mem. Modern Lang. Assn., Am. Ednl. Theatre Assn., A.A.U.P. (chmn. com. coll. and univ. teaching research and publ. 1965-71, pres. Tex. conf. 1976-78, chmn. assembly state confs. 1979—), Tex. Assn. Coll. Tchrs., Common Cause, ACLU, NAACP, Phi Beta Kappa. Democrat. Office: Dept English U Tex Austin TX 78712

MEGGERS, BETTY J(ANE), anthropologist; b. Washington, Dec. 5, 1921; d. William Frederick and Edith (Raddant) Meggers; A.B., U. Pa., 1943; M.A., U. Mich., 1944; Ph.D., Columbia, 1952; m. Clifford Evans, Sept. 13, 1946. Instr. anthropology Am. U., Washington, 1950-51; research asso. Smithsonian Instn., 1954—. Recipient award for sci. achievement Washington Acad. Sci., 1956; gold medal 37th Internat. Congress of Americanists, 1966; Order Al Merito, Govt. Ecuador, 1966. Fellow Am. Anthrop. Assn. (exec. sec. 1959-61), Assn. Tropical Biology (councilor 1976-78), AAAS; mem. Soc. Am. Archaeology (exec. bd. 1962-64), Am. Ethnol. Soc., Anthrop. Soc. Wash. (treas. 1955-60, v.p. 1965-66, pres. 1966-68), Phi Beta Kappa, Sigma Xi. Author: Environmental Limitation on the Development of Culture, 1954; Ecuador, 1966; Amazonia, 1971; Prehistoric America, 1972; (with Clifford Evans) Archeological Investigations at the Mouth of the Amazon, 1957; Archeological Investigations in British Guiana, 1960; Early Formative Period of Coastal Ecuador, 1965; Archeological Investigations on the Rio Napo, Eastern Ecuador, 1968. Home: 1227 30th St NW Washington DC 20007 Office: Smithsonian Inst Washington DC 20560

MEGGITT, MERVYN JOHN, educator; b. Warwick, Australia, Aug. 20, 1924; s. Reginald Arthur and Susan (Brodie) M.; B.A., U. Sydney, 1953, M.A., 1955, Ph.D., 1960; m. Joan Alice Lillistone, Jan. 1, 1949. Lectr., sr. lectr. anthropology U. Sydney, 1956-65; Simon fellow U. Manchester, 1963; prof. anthropology U. Mich., 1965-67; prof. anthropology City U. N.Y., 1967—. Served with Royal Australian Navy, 1942-46. Fellow Royal Anthrop. Inst. Gt. Britain; mem. Brit. Assn. Social Anthropologists. Author: Desert People, 1962; The Lineage System of the Mae Enga of New Guinea, 1965; (with P. Lawrence) Gods, Ghosts and Men in Melanesia, 1965; Gadjari Among the Walbiri of Central Australia, 1967; (with R.M. Glasse) Pigs, Pearlshells and Women, 1969; Studies in Enga History, 1974; Blood is Their Argument, 1976. Home: 241 Central Park W New York City NY 10024

MEGGS, BROWN MOORE, writer; b. Los Angeles, Oct. 20, 1930; s. Charles Winfield and Margarette (Brown) M.; student Calif. Inst. Tech., 1948-49, Harvard U., 1949-51; m. Nancy Bates Meachen, June 16, 1954; 1 son, Brook Meachen. Story analyst Warner Bros. Pictures Corp., Burbank, Calif., 1951; writer Jam Handy Orgn., Detroit, 1955-57; merchandising mgr. Capitol Records Inc., Hollywood, 1958, dir. pub. relations, 1959-62, eastern operations, N.Y.C., 1963-64, v.p. merchandising, Hollywood, 1964-67, v.p. internat. and classics, 1967-70, v.p. and asst. to pres., 1970-71, v.p. mktg., 1971-73, exec. v.p., 1973, chief operating officer, 1974-76; v.p., asst. to pres. Capitol Industries-EMI, Inc., Hollywood, 1976; writer, pres. Nanbrook Corp., Pasadena, Calif., 1976—. Served with AUS, CIC, 1953-54; PTO. Recipient Western Heritage award Nat. Cowboy Hall of Fame and Western Heritage Center, 1962. Mem. Authors Guild and Mystery Writers Am. Author: Saturday Games, 1974; The Matter of Paradise, 1975; Aria, 1978. Contbr. articles to popular mags. Home and office: 1450 El Mirador Dr Pasadena CA 91103

MEGHREBLIAN, ROBERT VARTAN, mfg. co. exec., physicist; b. Cairo, Sept. 6, 1922; s. Vahan V. and Mary (Kurkjian) M.; came to U.S., 1923, naturalized, 1946; B.Engring. (Gotshall-Powell scholar), Rensselaer Poly. Inst., 1943; M.S. (Guggenheim fellow), Calif. Inst. Tech., 1950, Ph.D. (Guggenheim fellow), 1953; m. Mary J. Walton, Apr. 16, 1955; children—David V., Susan L. Lectr., Oak Ridge Nat. Lab., 1952-55, asso. project mgr., 1955-58; chief sect. physics jet propulsion lab Calif. Inst. Tech., 1958-60, mgr. space scis. div., 1960-68, dep. asst. lab dir., 1968-71, asso. prof. applied mechanics, 1960-61; v.p. research and engring. Cabot Corp., Boston, 1971—; pres. Distrigas Corp., 1979—. Served to lt. (j.g.) USN, 1941-46; PTO. Fellow Am. Nuclear Soc., AIAA (asso.); mem. Indsl. Research Inst., Sigma Xi. Author: Reactor Analysis, 1960. Home: 1530 Beacon St Brookline MA 02146 Office: Cabot Corp 125 High St Boston MA 02110

MEGOWN, JOHN WILLIAM, agrl. business exec.; b. New London, Mo., Apr. 27, 1931; s. William P. and Fannie (Palmer) M.; Asso. Sci., Hannibal-LaGrange Coll., 1951; A.B., U. Mo., 1953, M.S., 1955; postgrad. Northwestern U., 1957; m. Dorothy Astrid Wiebust, Apr. 6, 1957; 1 son, Jeffrey William. Animal nutritionist Moorman Mfg. Co., Quincy, Ill., 1955; asso. biologist Hales & Hunter Co., Chgo., 1955-56; asst. coordinator research and sales Peter Hand Found.,

Chgo., 1956-59; mgr. nutritional services Morton Salt Co., Chgo., 1959-67, product mgr. custom and pvt. agrl. salt and mineral products, 1963-67, dir. agrl. coll. relations program, 1964-67; mgr. research communications Allied Mills, Inc., Chgo., 1967-68; asst. v.p., pub. relations dir. Vigortone Products Co. div. Beatrice Foods Co., Cedar Rapids, Iowa, 1968-70, v.p., dir. communications, 1970-72, v.p., dir. mktg. and pub. affairs, 1972-77, v.p. public affairs and govtl. relations, 1977—, also dir. Vice chmn. Nat. Agrl. Communications Bd., 1972-73; nat. coordinator Pub. Affairs Council for Am. Agr., 1969-70; chmn. Cedar Rapids Agrl. Exec.'s Forum, 1969-70; mem. Agribus, Coordinating Group, Dept. Agr., 1969-71; mem. Gov. Iowa Agr. Promotion Bd., 1970—, chmn., 1971—; mem. Curtis-Mahon Congl. Study Com., 1971-72; mem. agr. bus. adv. com. Joliet Jr. Coll., 1966-70; mem. Council Agr. and Sci. Tech., 1973—. Active Cedar Rapids YMCA; mem.-at-large Hawkeye Area council Boy Scouts Am., 1969-72; mem. Linn County Rural Devel. Com., 1971—; Iowa chmn. Nat. Future Farmers Am. Found., 1970. Mem. Republican Nat. Agr. and Food Com., 1968. Bd. dirs. Rolling Meadows (Ill.) Community Chest, 1968, Cedar Rapids Jr. Achievement, 1972-73, Self Help, Inc., Waverly, Iowa, 1976-77. Recipient award for filmstrip Nat. Agrl. Advt. and Marketing Assn., 1968, Best Pub. Relations Performance of Year award Midwest Feed Mfrs. Assn., 1974, hon. Am. farmer degree Future Farmers Am., 1973; Boss of Year award Marabwa chpt. Am. Bus. Women's Assn., 1975; named Eagle Scout; col. Ia. N.G., aide Gov. Iowa mil. staff. Mem. Nat. Feed Ingredients Assn. (dir. 1966-72, pub. relations dir. 1966-69, 1st v.p. 1969-70, pres., chief exec. officer 1970-71), Future Farmers Am. Alumni Assn., Animal Nutrition Research Council, Agrl. Relations Council, Nat. Agrl.-Mktg. Assn. (Iowa Farm Mktg. Man of Year 1975), Cedar Rapids C. of C. (exec. com. agr. bur., 1969—, congl. action com. 1972-76), Nat. Eagle Scout Assn., Phi Theta Kappa, Alpha Phi Omega. Rotarian (bd. dirs. Marion-East Cedar Rapids 1970-71, pres. 1974-75; Rotarian of Yr. award 1973), Elk. Clubs: Cedar Rapids Advertising, Cedar Rapids Grain and Feed; Elmcrest Country. Co-author: Beef Science Handbook, Vol. 4, 1967. Contbr. articles to tech. jours. Editorial adv. com. Animal Health Inst., 1967-73. Home: 2190 Northview Dr Marion IA 52406 Office: Box 1230 Cedar Rapids IA 52406

MEHEGAN, JOHN FRANCIS, jazz musician; b. Hartford, Conn., June 6, 1920; s. John James and Margaret (Egan) M.; student Hartford Fed. Coll., 1937-38, Julius Hartt Music Sch., Hartford, 1938-39; m. Doris Crowley, Dec. 3, 1940 (div. July 1956); children—Carey, Gretchen; m. 2d, Terry Adelstein, Feb. 17, 1957 (div. 1961); m. 3d, Gay Griscom, June 27, 1961 (div. Nov. 1978); children—Tara, Sean, Eben. Asst. to Teddy Wilson, Met. Mus. Sch., N.Y.C., 1945-46, head jazz dept., 1946-56; instr. jazz Juilliard Sch. Music, 1947-64, Columbia Tchrs. Coll., 1958-62, U. Bridgeport (Conn.), 1968-77; European jazz tour sponsored by State Dept., 1961; lectr. jazz Brandeis U. Art Festival, 1952, Union S. Africa, 1959, Music Educators Nat. Conf., Atlantic City, 1960, Yale U., 1974—; jazz critic N.Y. Herald Tribune, 1957-60; founder Sch. Jazz, 1963; conducted Jazz Seminar Syracuse U., summer 1964; jazz clinics in Denmark, Sweden and Norway, 1974, 75; recs. for Savoy, Perspective, Victor, T.J., Epic records. Author: Jazz Improvisation, 1959, vol. II, 1960, vol. III, 1963, vol. IV, 1964; jazz study books for children, 1962; contbr. articles to Metronome, Down Beat, Saturday Rev. Address: 72 Morningside Dr S Westport CT 06880

MEHLINGER, HOWARD DEAN, educator; b. Hillsboro, Kans., Aug. 22, 1931; s. Alex and Alice Hilda (Skibbee) M.; B.A., McPherson (Kans.) Coll., 1953; M.S. in Edn., U. Kans., 1959, Ph.D., 1964; m. Carolee Ann Case, Dec. 28, 1952; children—Bradley Case, Barbara Ann, Susan Kay. Tchr., coach Lawrence (Kans.) High Sch., 1953-63; co-dir. social studies project Pitts. pub. schs., 1963-64; asst. dir. fgn. relations project North Central Assn. Schs. and Colls., Chgo., 1964-65; mem. faculty Ind. U., Bloomington, 1965—, prof. history and edn., 1974—; social studies adviser Houghton Mifflin Pub. Co.; cons. U.S. Office Edn. STAG grantee Dept. State, 1975. Mem. Nat. Council Social Studies, Am. Edn. Research Assn., Am. Hist. Assn., Am. Polit. Sci. Assn., NEA, AAAS, Phi Beta Kappa, Phi Alpha Theta, Pi Sigma Alpha, Phi Delta Kappa. Co-author: American Political Behavior, 2d edit., 1977; Count Witte and the Tsarist Government in the 1905 Revolution, 1972; Toward Effective Instruction in the Social Studies, 1974. Editorial bd. Geschichtsdidaktik, History Tchr. Home: 3606 Park Ln Bloomington IN 47401 Office: 513 N Park St Bloomington IN 47401

MEHLMAN, FREDERICK GORDON, life ins. co. exec.; b. St. Paul, Alta., Can., July 21, 1918; s. Mileage Frederick and Rosemond Claire (Hamm) M.; came to U.S., 1920, naturalized, 1935; J.D., Boston U., 1941; m. Wanda M. Winfrey, Jan. 11, 1944; children—William M., Thomas W. Admitted to Vt. bar, 1941; pvt. practice, St. Johnsbury, Vt., 1946-47, 52-56; dep. atty. gen. Vt., 1947-52; with Nat. Life Ins. Co., Montpelier, Vt., 1956—, v.p., gen. counsel, 1974—. Chmn. Vt. Water Resources Bd., 1965—; trustee St. Johnsbury Acad., 1972—. Served with AUS, 1942-46. Mem. Am., Vt. bar assns. Home: 52 Clarendon Ave Montpelier VT 05602 Office: National Life Dr Montpelier VT 05602

MEHN, W. HARRISON, surgeon; b. Monroe, Wis., Nov. 25, 1918; s. William Herman and Hedwig Gertrude (Butenhoff) M.; B.A., N. Central Coll., Naperville, Ill., 1940; B.S., Northwestern U. Med. Sch., 1944, M.D., 1944, M.S. in Pathology, 1944; m. Jean Belle Dorr, Sept. 23, 1945; children—Mary Ann, Judith Susan. Intern, Passavant Meml. Hosp., Chgo., 1944, resident in surgery, 1947-50; resident in pathology Children's Meml. Hosp., Chgo., 1945, Alexian Bros. Hosp., Chgo., 1946-47; resident in surgery Cook County Hosp., Chgo., 1949-53; clin. asst. dept. surgery Northwestern U., 1948-52, instr. in surgery, 1952-53, asso. in surgery, 1953-58, asst. prof. surgery, 1958-73, asso. prof., 1973-74, prof. clin. surgery, 1974—; practice medicine, specializing in surgery, Chgo.; mem. staff Northwestern Meml. Hosp., VA Lakeside Hosp.; med. dir. Commonwealth Edison Co., Chgo., 1955—; mem. accident prevention com. Edison Electric Inst., N.Y.C., 1960—; participant profl. research task forces Electric Power Research Inst., Palo Alto, Calif., 1973—. Bd. dirs. NCCJ, 1968—; mem. bd. ruling elders Presbyn. Ch., Evanston, Ill., 1971—, bd. dirs. Presbyn. Home, Evanston. Served to lt., M.C., USN, 1945-46, to lt. comdr., 1953-55. Diplomate Am. Bd. Surgery. Mem. A.C.S. (Chgo. com. on trauma 1970—), Chgo. Heart Assn., Western, Chgo. surg. socs., Soc. Surgery Alimentary Tract, Collegium Internationale Chirurgiae Digestivae, Inst. Medicine, AMA, Ill., Chgo. med. socs., Indsl. Med. Assn., Am. Trauma Soc., McGraw Wildlife Found., Sigma Xi, Pi Kappa Epsilon, Phi Beta Pi. Clubs: Westmoreland Country (Wilmette, Ill.) (pres.); Internationale, Anglers, Campfire (Chgo.). Contbr. articles to profl. publs. Home: 3033 Normandy Pl Evanston IL 60201 Office: 707 N Fairbanks Ct Chicago IL 60611

MEHOS, CHARLES ARTHUR, consumer products co. exec.; b. Malden, Mass., Oct. 14, 1920; s. Arthur J. and Stella (Booras) M.; B.A., Boston U., 1942; I.A., Harvard, 1943; m. Rita Zoukee, May 10, 1959; children—Harris, Arthur, Stephen, Lia. With Loomis-Sayles & Co., Boston, 1946-50; with Am. Brands, Inc., N.Y.C., 1950—, treas., 1967, v.p., v.p. finance, 1973-79, exec. v.p., 1979—, also mem. exec. com., dir. Home: 54 Nearwater Lane Darien CT 06820 Office: 245 Park Ave New York NY 10017

MEHR, ROBERT IRWIN, educator; b. Phila., June 24, 1917; s. Charles Nathaniel and Elizabeth (Williams) M.; B.S., U. Ala., 1938, M.S., 1939; Ph.D., U. Pa., 1943; m. Margaret Louise Cochrun, Jan. 20, 1959; 1 son, James Lawrence. Instr., U. Ala., 1938-41; asst. prof. U. N.C., 1943-45; asso. prof. Butler U., Indpls., 1945-47; prof. finance U. Ill., Urbana, 1947—. Recipient Elizur Wright awards for outstanding original contbn. to lit. of ins., 1956, 64. Mem. Am. Risk and Ins. Assn. (past pres.), Am. Finance Assn. (past dir.), Pacific Ins. Conf. (co-founder, past chmn., mem. exec. com.), InterAm. Ins. Forum (co-founder, mem. exec. com.). Author: Modern Life Insurance, 3d edit., 1961; Risk Management in the Business Enterprise, 1963; Principles of Insurance, 7th edit., 1980; Life Insurance Theory and Practice, 1970, rev. edit., 1977; Inflation, Technology and Growth: Long-Range Implications for Insurance, 1972; Principles of Insurance—Self Review, 1973, rev., 1977; Risk Management: Concepts and Applications, 1974; Life Insurance—Self Review, 1979; editor Jour. Risk and Ins. Home: 101 W Windsor Rd Apt 1102 Urbana IL 61801

MEHREN, GEORGE LOUIS, business exec., govt. ofcl., economist; b. Sacramento, July 6, 1913; s. Gale Thomas and Faye Laura (Swain) M.; student Coll. Pacific, 1937; A.A., Sacramento Jr. Coll., 1931; A.B., U. Calif., 1938, Ph.D., 1942; m. Jean Dorothy McMurchy, June 26, 1938; children—Peter William, Elizabeth Jean; m. 2d, Ingeborg E. Hitchcock, 1968; 1 son, George Louis. Research asso. Giannini Found. Agrl. Econs., Agrl. Expt. Sta., U. Calif., 1942, dir., 1957-62, instr. to asso. prof., 1946-51, prof. agrl. econs., 1951-71, prof. emeritus, 1971, chmn. dept. agrl. econs., chmn. dept. agrl. bus., Berkeley, Davis and Los Angeles, 1957-62, exec., adv., coordinating coms. Wild Lands Research Center, Water Resources Center, 1957-62, chmn. statewide curriculum agrl. bus. mgmt., 1957-62, exec. coms. Sch. Bus. Adminstrn., Inst. Internat. Studies, Inst. Indsl. Relations, 1958-62, mem. Legislative Assembly, 1960-62; asst. sec. agr. U.S. Dept. Agr., Washington, 1963-68, dir. sci. and edn., 1965-68; spl. U.S. ambassador (spl.) to Panama, 1968; pres. Agribusiness Council Inc., 1968-71; gen. mgr. Asso. Milk Producers, Inc., 1972-76; exec. cons., 1976—; v.p. Hitchcock GmbH, W. Ger., 1976—, Overseas Mktg., Inc., 1977—. Mem. Fed. Council on Sci. and Tech., 1965-68, Fed. Interagy. Com. on Edn., 1966-68, Nat. Adv. Council on Extension and Continuing Edn., 1966-68; mem. President's Com. on Consumer Interests, 1964-67; bd. dirs. Commodity Credit Corp., 1963-68; mem. adv. panel AEC, 1966-68; mem. adminstrv. com. Center for Specialization and Research in Agrl. Econs. and Statistics, U. Naples, Portici, Italy, 1956-59. Dir. food and restaurant div. OPS, Washington, 1951, acting dir. price operations, 1952, cons. to dir., 1952-53; cons. Mut. Security Agy., Fgn. Operations Adminstrn., 1952-53; adviser Brit. minister agr. and fisheries, and sec. of state for Scotland, London, 1952-53; cons. Ministry of Agr. for Venezuela, Caracas, 1952-53, 70, Consejo de Bienestar Rural, Venezuela, 1953-54, OCDM, 1956-58, USOM to Korea, Republic of Korea, Seoul, U.S. Office Emergency Planning, AID, to govts. Pakistan, Iran, Mexico, Morocco, Indonesia, 1968-71; adviser Ministry Agr. and Forestry for Italy, Rome, 1956; cons. div. econs. FAO, Rome, 1956-57; dean, vis. prof. Internat. Center for Tng. Agrl. Econs. and Statistics, Govt. Republic of Italy, U. of Rome, FAO, 1956; contract collaborator U.S. and Calif. depts. agr. for appraisal European promotion programs, 1962; mem. gen. editorial bd. Jour. Marketing, Am. Marketing Assn., 1952-55, mng. editor, 1955-57, editor-in-chief, 1957-58. Chmn. Calif. exec. com. U.S. Food for Peace Program, 1961. Served to lt. USNR, 1942-45. Mem. Western Agrl. Econs. Research Council, Am. Farm Econs. Assn., Am. Marketing Assn., Western Farm Econs. Assn., Alpha Zeta. Contbr. to profl. jours. Home: 406 Country Ln San Antonio TX 78209 Office: 1006 Holbrook Rd San Antonio TX 78209. *I have always been deeply grateful to have been born a human being with human capacity to question, to think, to measure and to analyze, to experience joy and sorrow, to laugh and to sing, to work with hands and mind, and to cherish family and friends. Were there 10,000 such lives for each of us, every one of those lives could be fruitful and joyous. The one life given must be lived with full respect for all humanity. It must be used fully and well. If there be a touch of divinity in human existence, this I believe to be the way to realize it.*

MEHRTENS, WILLIAM OSBORNE, dist. judge; b. Savannah, Ga., Jan. 24, 1905; s. Leo W. and Cornelia (Millen) M.; J.D., U. Fla., 1932; m. Jaime H. Hancock, Nov. 4, 1936; 1 son, William Osborne. Admitted to Fla. bar, 1932; mem. firm Mershon, Sawyer, Johnston & Simmons, 1933-42, partner Mershon, Sawyer, Johnston, Dunwody, Mehrtens & Cole, and predecessor, Miami, Fla., 1942-65; U.S. dist. judge, 1965—. Mem. permanent adv. com. on appellate rules Fla. Supreme Ct., 1958—. Bd. dirs. Miami Heart Inst. Served from lt. (j.g.) to lt. comdr. USNR, 1942-45. Fellow Internat. Acad. Trial Lawyers, Am. Coll. Trial Lawyers, Acad. Fla. Trial Lawyers; mem. Fla. Bar (bd. govs. 1955-65, past pres. jr. sect., past dir.), Am., Fed., Internat., Dade County bar assns., Internat. Law Assn., Am. Trial Lawyers Assn., Internat. Oceanographic Assn. (dir.), Phi Beta Kappa, Sigma Alpha Epsilon, Phi Kappa Phi, Phi Delta Phi, Blue Key. Clubs: Riviera Country (Coral Gables, Fla.); Coral Reef Yacht (Miami); Palm Bay; Bermuda Anglers; Miami Beach Rod and Reel; Panama Marlin. Home: 1441 SW 11th St Miami FL 33135 Office: PO Box 2379 Miami FL 33101

MEHTA, ZUBIN, musician, condr.; b. Bombay, India, Apr. 29, 1936; s. Mehli Nowrowji and Tehmina (Daruvala) M.; student St. Xavier's Coll., Bombay, 1951-53, State Acad. Music, Vienna, Austria, 1954-60; LL.D., Sir George Willimas U., Montreal, 1965; D.Mus. (hon.), Occidental Coll., Cal.; m. Nancy Diane Kovack; children—Zarina, Merwan. Came to U.S., 1961. Music dir. Montreal (Can.) Symphony Orch., 1961-67, Los Angeles Philharmonic Orch., 1962-78, N.Y. Philharmonic, 1978—; guest condr. Met. Opera, Salzburg (Austria) Festival, Vienna Philharmonic, Berlin Philharmonic, La Scala, Milan, Italy; mus. dir. to Israel Philharmonic, 1969—; music dir. Maggio Musicale Florence (Italy), 1969; rec. artist for Decca Records. Decorated Order of Lotus (India), 1967, commendatore of Italy; recipient 1st prize Liverpool (Eng.) Condrs. Competition, 1958. Address: care NY Philharmonic Avery Fisher Hall Broadway and 65th St New York NY 10023

MEHUS, OSCAR MYKING, educator; b. Brinsmade, N.D., May 15, 1894; s. Mikkel Knutson and Anne (Myking) M.; A.B., Augsburg Coll., Mpls., 1916; A.M., U. N.D., 1920, Ph.D., 1931; postgrad. U. Chgo., summer 1917, U. Minn., 1924-26; m. Emma Hille, Aug. 25, 1920 (dec. Jan. 1941); children—Dorothy Jeannette, Donald Vincent, Orion Myking; m. 2d, Jewell Ross Davis, Sept. 9, 1945; 1 stepdau., Elizabeth Lou Davis. High sch. prin., Fessenden, N.D., 1916-17, supt., 1917-18; prin., Harvey, N.D., 1918-19; supt. schs., Spring Grove, Minn., 1920-21; prof. State Tchrs. Coll., Mayville, N.D., 1921-24; instr. sociology U. Minn., 1924-26; asst. prof. edn., Wittenberg Coll., Springfield, Ohio, 1926-28; prof. sociology and tchr. tng. State Tchrs. Coll., Maryville, Mo., 1928-39; pres. Winona (Minn.) State Tchrs. Coll., 1939-43; chief vocational rehab. and edn. div. VA Regional Office, Kansas City, Mo., 1943-60, St. Louis, 1960-63; dean student work program Sch. of Ozarks, Point Lookout, Mo., 1965, 66. Mem. Mayor's Com. on Juvenile Delinquency, Kansas City. Dir. Unitarian Forum (K.C.), 1944-60. Served with U.S. Army, 1918. Decorated Medal of Liberation (Denmark); recipient spl. commendation award Adminstr. Vets. Affairs, 1960; Distinguished Alumnus citation Augsburg Coll., 1975. Mem. Am. Scandinavian Found.; mem. Urban League of K.C., Mo. Assn. for Social Welfare, Kansas City Council on World Affairs (gov.), Nat. Rehab. Assn., Mo. Assn. Adult Edn., Westport-Roanoke Community Council (pres.), Mo., Kansas City assns. mental hygiene, Am. Humanist Assn., Soc. Advancement Scandinavian Study, League of Norsemen, Am. Legion (comdr. 1974-76), Last Men's Club (pres.), Hallinglaget of Am. (pres. 1960-65), Am. War Dads, Phi Delta Kappa, Pi Gamma Mu, Kappa Phi Kappa. Unitarian. Mason, Clubs: Masons, Rotary (chmn. public relations com.), Kansas City Farmers, Scandinavian of Greater Kansas City (pres., Norseman award 1977). Co-author: Extra-Curricular Activities at the U. of Minn., 1929. Contbr. articles to ednl. and religious periodicals. Home: Route 1 Box 389 Branson MO 65616 Office: Old Shepherd's Book Shop Branson MO 65616

MEIDER, ELMER CHARLES, JR., pub. co. exec.; b. Buffalo, Feb. 7, 1946; s. Elmer Charles and Marie (Gress) M.; B.B.A., Cleve. State U., 1971; m. July 8, 1967; children—Lisa Marie, Elmer Charles III. Advt. research analyst Meldrum & Fewsmith, advt., Cleve., 1967-69; sales promotion supr. ESB Inc., Cleve., 1969-72; sr. market research analyst, consumer products group Miles Labs., Elkhart, Ind., 1972-74; v.p., dir. market planning World Book-Childcraft Internat. Inc., Chgo., 1974—; cons. mktg. research and mktg. Mem. Am. Mktg. Assn. Republican. Episcopalian. Home: 6 S 345 New Castle St Naperville IL 60540 Office: World Book-Childcraft Internat Inc 500 Merchandise Mart Chicago IL 60654

MEIER, AUGUST, educator; b. N.Y.C., Apr. 30, 1923; s. Frank A. and Clara (Cohen) M.; A.B., Oberlin Coll., 1945; A.M., Columbia, 1949; Ph.D., 1957. Asst. prof. history Tougaloo (Miss.) Coll., 1945-49; research asst. to pres. Fisk U., 1953, asst. prof. history, 1953-56; asst., asso. prof. history Morgan State Coll., Balt., 1957-64; prof. history Roosevelt U., Chgo., 1964-67; prof. history Kent (Ohio) State U., 1967-69, univ. prof., 1969—. Sec., Newark br. N.A.A.C.P., 1951-52, 56-57; chmn. Balt. chpt. Ams. for Democratic Action, 1960-61, mem. nat. bd., exec. com., 1960-61; active Newark chpt. CORE, 1963-64, Balt. chpt. SNCC, 1960-63. Advanced grad. fellow Am. Council Learned Socs., 1952; Guggenheim fellow, 1971-72; Nat. Endowment for Humanities fellow, 1975-77; Center for Advanced Study in Behavioral Scis. fellow, 1976-77. Mem. Am., So. hist. assns., Assn. Study Negro Life and History, Orgn. Am. Historians (del. to Am. Council Learned Socs. 1979—). Unitarian. Author: Negro Thought in America, 1880-1915, 1963; (with Elliott Rudwick) From Plantation to Ghetto, 1966, 3d edit., 1976, Black Detroit and the Rise of the UAW, 1979; CORE: A Study In The Civil Rights Movement, 1942-68, 1973; Along the Color Line: Explorations in the Black Experience, 1976; editor: (with Francis Broderick) Negro Protest Thought in the Twentieth Century, 1966, rev. edit. renamed Black Protest Thought in The Twentieth Century (with Broderick and Elliott Rudwick), 1971; (with E. Rudwick) The Making of Black America, 1969; (with John H. Bracey, E. Rudwick) Black Nationalism in America, 1970. Gen. editor Atheneum Pubs. for Negro in Am. Life Series, 1966-74, U. Ill. Press for Blacks in the New World Series, 1972—; editorial bd. Booker T. Washington Papers, 1967—, Civil War History, 1970—; editorial adv. bd. Jour. Am. History, 1974-77, Marcus Garvey Papers, 1978—. Home: 122 N Prospect St Kent OH 44240

MEIER, BEN, sec. state N.D.; b. Napoleon, N.D., Aug. 1, 1918; s. Bernhardt and Theresia (Hilzenderger) M.; student Dakota Bus. Sch., 1943, U. Wis. Sch. Banking, 1947-48; m. Clara Kaczynski, Dec. 30, 1944; children—Lynn, Bernie. Asst. cashier Stock Growers Bank, Napoleon, 1945-47, Gackle State Bank (N.D.), 1947-49; pres. Bank of Hazelton (N.D.); pres., dir. Mandan Security Bank (N.D.), 1959-70; sec. state N.D., Bismarck, 1955—. Crusade chmn. N.D. Heart Assn., 1969, N.D. Cnacer Soc., 1970. Recipient N.D. Nat. Leadership Excellency award. Mem. N.D. Bankers Assn., Nat. Assn. Secs. State (pres. 1967), Nat. Assn. State Contractors Licensing Agys. (v.p. 1969-70), Sons of Norway. Republican. Office: Office Sec State ND State Capitol Bldg Bismarck ND 58501*

MEIER, DAVID EDWARD, religious assn. ofcl.; b. Muskegon, Mich., Feb. 17, 1918; s. Edward E. and Helen T. (Schelhas) M.; B.S., U. Detroit, 1941; M.A., St. Louis U., 1949; S.T.L., West Baden (Ind.) Coll., 1954. Joined Soc. of Jesus, 1942, ordained priest Roman Cath. Ch., 1953; treas. St. Ignatius High Sch., Cleve., 1955-58; treas. U. Detroit, 1958-66, v.p. bus. affairs, 1963-66, also trustee; treas. Creighton U., Omaha, 1966-69; sec. for finance Jesuit Conf., Washington, 1970—. Trustee St. Louis U., 1979—. Mem. Alpha Sigma Nu, Beta Alpha Psi. Address: 1717 Massachusetts Ave NW Washington DC 20036

MEIER, EDWARD KINDT, lawyer, container co. exec.; b. Chgo., Sept. 22, 1914; s. Edward and Florence (Kindt) M.; student Northwestern U., 1932-33; B.A., Denison U., 1936; J.D., DePaul U., 1940; m. Jean Billington Egelhof, Mar. 27, 1944; children—Marjorie L., Nancy J. Staff trust and probate dept. Harris Trust & Savs. Bank, Chgo., 1936-41; admitted to Ill. bar, 1940; atty. Container Corp. Am., Chgo., 1946-77, asst. sec., 1954-60, sec., asst. gen. counsel, 1960-77; practice law, Wilmette, Ill., 1977—. Mem. Chgo. Crime Commn. Served to lt. comdr. USNR, 1941-46. Mem. Am. Soc. Corp. Secs., Am., Ill., Chgo. bar assns., Beta Theta Pi. Home: 325 Washington Ave Wilmette IL 60091

MEIER, GERALD MARVIN, economist, educator; b. Tacoma, Feb. 9, 1923; s. Max and Bessie (Nagle) M.; B.A., Reed Coll., 1947; B.Litt. (Rhodes scholar), U. Oxford (Eng.), 1952, Ph.D., Harvard U., 1953; m. Gilda Slote, Oct. 23, 1954; children—David, Daniel, Jeremy, Andrew. Instr., Williams Coll., 1952-54; faculty Wesleyan U., Middletown, Conn., 1954-63, prof. econs., 1958-63, Chester D. Hubbard prof. econs., social sci., 1959-63; prof. internat. econs. Grad. Sch. Bus., Stanford, 1963—; resident in law and social sci. Russell Sage Found., Yale U., 1976-77. Vis. prof. Yale, 1959-61, Stanford U., 1962, Brookings Nat. Research prof. Stanford, 1961-62. Guggenheim fellow, 1957-58. Mem. Am. Assn. Rhodes Scholars, Am. Econ. Assn., Royal Econ. Soc., Phi Beta Kappa. Author: Economic Development, 1957; International Trade and Development, 1962; Leading Issues in Development Economics, 1964, 2d edit., 1970; International Economics of Development, 1968; Leading Issues in Economic Development, 1970, 3d edit., 1976; Problems of Trade Policy, 1973; Problems of World Monetary Order, 1974; Problems of Cooperation for Development, 1975; Employment, Trade, and Development, 1977. Home: 774 Santa Ynez Stanford CA 94305

MEIER, GERHARD J., library devel. cons.; b. Zwickau, Germany, May 12, 1927; s. Erich George and Erna Frieda (Wunderlich) M.; student U. Jena (Germany), 1945-46. Came to U.S., 1956, naturalized, 1962. Head German dept. B.H. Blackwell Ltd., Oxford, Eng., 1950-55; with Walter J. Johnson, Inc., N.Y.C., 1956-69; v.p. Maxwell, Meier & Holmes, Inc., N.Y.C., 1960-61; co-founder, v.p. Internat. Univ. Booksellers, Inc., N.Y.C., 1962-74; pres. Holmes & Meier Pubs., Inc., 1969-74; cons. internat. library devel., 1974—. Mem. A.L.A., Am., German pub. assns., Antiquarian Booksellers Assn. Home: 60 E 8th St New York City NY 10003 Office: 101 Fifth Ave New York City NY 10003

MEIER, JOHANNA THEODORA, soprano; b. Chgo., Feb. 13, 1938; d. Josef Johannes and Margery Clare (Hume) Meier; student U. Miami (Fla.), 1955-58; B. Music, Manhattan Sch. Music, N.Y.C., 1960; m. Guido Della Vecchia, Jan. 10, 1962. Mem. cast Black Hills Passion Play, 1938-56; debut Miami Opera Guild, 1957, N.Y.C., Little Orch. Soc., 1964, N.Y.C. Opera, 1969, N.Y. Philharmonic, 1975, Cleve. Orch., 1972, Boston Symphony Orch., 1972, Pitts. Symphony Orch., 1972, Can. debut, Nat. Arts Center, Ottawa, Ont., 1973, Met. Opera, 1976, Casals Festival, 1976, Israel Philharmonic, 1977; tchr. body movement for stage Manhattan Sch. Music, 1962-63; mem. Turneau Opera, U.S. tour, 1963-67. Recipient Young Artists award, 1957, Nat. Arts Club award, 1964, Pan Am Music Festival award, 1955. Mem. Sigma Alpha Iota. Appeared in world premiere operas The Sisters, 1960, The Maletroit Door, 1959, The Questions of Abraham, CBS TV award winner, 1974, on recording, The Stronger, 1972. Office: care Ludwig Lustig & Florian Ltd 111 W 57th St New York NY 10019*

MEIER, MARK FREDERICK, glaciologist; b. Iowa City, Dec. 19, 1925; s. Norman Charles and Clea (Grimes) M.; B.E.E., U. Iowa, 1949; M.S. in Geology, 1951; Ph.D., Calif. Inst. Tech., 1957; m. Barbara McKinley, Sept. 16, 1955; children—Lauren Gale, Mark Stephen, Gretchen Ann. Geol. engr. U.S. Bur. Reclamation, Coulee Dam, Wash., summers, 1948, 1949; geologist U.S. Geol. Survey, Big Delta, Alaska, summer, 1951; instr. geology Occidental Coll., 1952-55; leader Crevasse Study Expdn., North Greenland Ice Cap, 1955; glaciol. research (Fulbright grant), Innsbruck, Austria, 1955-56; project chief U.S. Geol. Survey, Tacoma, Wash., 1956—; vis. prof. dept. geology Dartmouth Coll., 1964; research prof. geophysics U. Wash., 1965—; mem. U.S. Nat. Com. for Internat. Hydrol. Decade, 1964-66; panel on glaciology Nat. Acad. Scis., 1957-68; chmn. working group on combined glacier basins Internat. Hydrol. Decade; pres. Internat. Commn. Snow and Ice, 1969-71; dir. World Data Center A: Glaciology, 1970-75. Recipient Distinguished Service award U.S. Dept. Interior, 1970; U.S. Antarctica Service medal, 1970, others. Fellow Geol. Soc. Am., Arctic Inst. N.Am., AAAS, Am. Geophys. Union (chmn. com. on glaciers 1958-64, 72-74); mem. Glaciological Soc. (v.p. 1966-69). Research on glacier flow, snow and ice hydrology and meteorology, geomorphology, structural geology. Home: 6815 Cascade Gig Harbor WA 98335 Office: US Geol Survey 1201 Pacific Ave Suite 850 Tacoma WA 98402

MEIER, RICHARD ALAN, architect; b. Newark, Oct. 12, 1934; s. Jerome and Carolyn (Kaltenbacher) M.; B. Arch., Cornell U., 1957; m. Katherine Gormley, Jan. 21, 1978. Architect with Frank Grad & Sons, N.J., 1957; Davis, Brody & Wisniewski, N.Y.C., 1958-59, Skidmore, Owings & Merrill, N.Y.C., 1959-60, Marcel Breuer & Assos., N.Y.C., 1960-63; prof. archtl. design Cooper Union, 1962-73; architect Richard Meier & Assos., N.Y.C., 1963—; resident architect Am. Acad. in Rome, 1973-74; vis. critic Pratt Inst., 1960-62, 65, Princeton, 1963, Syracuse U., 1964; William Henry Bishop vis. prof. architecture Yale U., 1975, 77, vis. critic, 1967, 72, 73, 77; vis. prof. Harvard, 1977; mem. adv. council Cornell U. Coll. Art, Architecture and Planning; mem. Jerusalem Com. Exhbns.: XV Triennale, Milan, Italy, 1973, Biennale, Venice, Italy, 1976; Cooper Union, N.Y.C., 1976, Cooper-Hewitt Mus., N.Y.C., 1976-77, Rosa Esman Gallery, N.Y.C., N.J. State Mus., 1978. Recipient Honor awards from AIA, 1964, 65, 68, 69, 70, 71, 72, 73, 74, 75, 76, 77, 78; Arnold Brunner Meml. prize Nat. Inst. Arts and Letters, 1972; Albert S. Bard Civic award City Club of N.Y., 1973, 1st honor award for excellence in architecture and urban design, 1977; R.S. Reynolds Meml. award, 1977; Archtl. Record award of excellence for design, 1977. Registered profl. architect, N.Y., N.J., Conn., Mich., Va., Fla. Fellow AIA (jury for medal of honor N.Y.C. chpt. 1974-76, nat. design com. 1972-74); asso. NAD; mem. Conf. Architects for Study Environment, Inst. Architecture and Urban Studies (trustee). Prin. works include: Westbeth Artists Housing, N.Y.C., Bronx (N.Y.) Developmental Center, Smith House, Darien, Conn., House in Old Westbury, N.Y., Monroe Developmental Center, Rochester, N.Y., Douglas House, Harbor Springs, Mich., Twin Parks N.E. Housing, N.Y.C., Atheneum, New Harmony, Ind., N.Y.: State of Art Exhbn., Cultural Edn. Center, Albany, Sarah Campbell Blaffer pottery shed, New Harmony, Ind., house in Palm Beach, Fla. Author: Richard Meier Architect, 1976. Contbr. articles profl. jours. Address: 136 E 57th St New York NY 10022

MEIER, RICHARD LOUIS, planner, futurist, behavioral scientist; b. Kendallville, Ind., May 16, 1920; s. Walter A. and Mary (Lottman) M.; student No. Ill. State Tchrs. Coll., 1936-39; B.S., U. Ill., 1940; M.A., U. Calif. at Los Angeles, 1942, Ph.D., 1944; m. Gitta Unger, May 20, 1944; children—Karen Reeds, Andrea Meier Whitmore, Alan. With Calif. Research Corp., 1943-47; exec. sec. Fedn. Am. Scis., 1947-48; with Petrocarbon, Ltd., 1949-50; Fulbright scholar Manchester U., Eng., 1949-50; asst. prof. program of edn. and research in planning U. Chgo., 1950-56; research social scientist Mental Health Research Inst., U. Mich., Ann Arbor, 1957—, asso. prof. conservation, 1960-65, prof., 1965-67; prof. environ. design U. Calif., Berkeley, 1967—. Vis. lectr. Harvard, 1959-60; vis. prof. Grad. Sch. Ekistics, Athens, 1962, U. Calif. at Berkeley, 1966. Indsl. planner P.R. Planning Bd., 1952; cons. on social planning and resources planning Joint Center for Urban Studies, Mass. Inst. Tech., Harvard, in Venezuela, 1963-65. Mem. Am. Chem. Soc., Am. Sociol. Assn., Am. Geog. Assn., Soc. for Gen. Systems Research, Regional Sci. Assn., Marine Tech. Soc., Fedn. Am. Scis., AAAS. Author: Science and Economic Development, 1956; Modern Science and the Human Fertility Problem, 1959; A Communications Theory of Urban Growth, 1962; Developmental Planning, 1965; Resource-Conserving Urbanism for South Asia, 1968; Planning for an Urban World, 1974. Contbr. numerous articles to profl. jours. Home: 7 San Mateo Rd Berkeley CA 94707

MEIER, WILBUR LEROY, JR., educator; b. Elgin, Tex., Jan. 3, 1939; s. Wilbur Leroy and Ruby (Hall) M.; B.S., U. Tex., 1962, M.S., 1964, Ph.D., 1967; m. Judy Lee Longbotham, Aug. 30, 1958; children—Melynn, Marla, Melissa. Planning engr. Tex. Water Devel. Bd., Austin, 1962-66, cons., 1967-72; research engr. U. Tex., Austin, 1966; asst. prof. indsl. engring. Tex. A. and M. U., College Station, 1967-68, asso. prof., 1968-70, prof., 1970-73, asst. head dept. indsl. engring., 1972-73; prof., chmn. dept. indsl. engring. Iowa State U., Ames, 1973-74; prof., head sch. of indsl. engring. Purdue U., West Lafayette, Ind., 1974—. Cons. Indsl. Research Inst., St. Louis, 1979, Environments for Tomorrow, Inc., Washington, 1970—, Water Resources Engrs., Inc., Walnut Creek, Calif., 1969-70, Computer Graphics, Inc., Bryan, Tex., 1969-70, Kaiser Engrs., Oakland, Calif., 1971, Tracor, Inc., Austin, 1966-68; cons. div. planning coordination Tex. Gov.'s Office, 1969. Named Outstanding Young Engr. of Year, Tex. Soc. Profl. Engrs., 1966. USPHS fellow, 1966. Mem. Am. Inst. Indsl. Engrs. (dir. ops. research div. 1975, pres. Ind. chpt. 1976, program chmn. 1973-75, editorial bd. Transactions, publ. chmn., newsletter editor engring. economy div. 1972-73, v.p. region VIII 1977—), Ops. Research Soc. Am., Inst. Mgmt. Scis. (v.p. S.W. chpt. 1971-72), Am. Soc. C.E. (sec.-treas. Austin br. 1965-66, chmn. research com., tech. council water resources planning and mgmt. 1972—), Nat., Ind. socs. profl. engrs., Am. Soc. for Engring. Edn. (chmn. indsl. engring. div. 1978—, pres. Tex. A. and M. U. chpt. 1971-72), Sigma Xi, Tau Beta Pi, Alpha Pi Mu (asso. editor Cogwheel 1970-75, regional dir. 1976-77, exec. v.p. 1977—), Phi Kappa Phi, Chi Epsilon. Rotarian. Contbr. articles to profl. jours. Home: #368 Overlook Dr West Lafayette IN 47906

MEIERHENRY, MARK V., state atty. gen.; b. Gregory, S.D., Oct. 29, 1944; s. Vernon and Mary (Casey) M.; B.A., U. S.D., 1966, J.D., 1970; m. Judith Knittel, May 14, 1961; children—Todd, Mary. Admitted to Nebr. bar, 1970, S.D. bar, 1971; asso. firm Camerer, Meierhenry and Tabor, Scottsbluff, Nebr., 1970-71; dir. S.D. Legal Services, Mission, 1971-74; partner firm Meierhenry, DeVany, & Krueger, Vermillion, S.D., 1974-78; atty. gen., State of S.D., Pierre, 1978—. Mem. Sch. Bd., Vermillion, S.D., 1976-78. Mem. S.D. State Bar Assn., S.D. Trial Lawyers Assn. Republican. Home: 218 Lakeside Ln Pierre SD 57501 Office: State Capitol Pierre SD 57501

MEIERHENRY, ROY ALBERT, energy co. fin. exec.; b. Norfolk, Nebr., Sept. 3, 1938; s. Albert Henry and Esther Miriam (Strate) M.; B.S.B.A., U. Nebr., Lincoln, 1960; M.B.A., Creighton U., 1966; grad. exec. edn. program for gas industry U. Colo., 1970, univ. exec. program Stanford U., 1976; m. Jill McKibben, Sept. 24, 1960; children—Kelly, Amy. With No. Natural Gas Co., Omaha, 1960-67, 71—, asst. treas. and mgr. treasury dept., 1973-78, treas., 1978—; mgr. employee relations Peoples Natural Gas, Omaha, 1967-68, mgr. adminstrn. and mktg., Council Bluffs, Iowa, 1968-71; mgr. adminstrn. and mktg. Plateau Natural Gas, Colorado Springs, Colo., 1971; bd. dirs. Coll. Bus. Adminstr. Adv. Council, U. Nebr., Omaha; trustee Nebr. Council on Econ. Edn., U. Nebr., Lincoln. Bd. dirs. Gt. Plains council Girls Scouts U.S.A., Girls Club, Omaha, Omaha Symphony Assn. Served to capt. U.S. Army, 1960-61. Mem. Fin. Execs. Inst., Ak-Sar-Ben. Republican. Methodist. Office: 2223 Dodge St Omaha NE 68102

MEIERHENRY, WESLEY CARL, educator; b. Arlington, Nebr., Nov. 12, 1915; s. Carl H. and Anna (Niederdeppe) M.; student Western Union Coll., 1932-34; B.Sc., Midland Coll., 1936; M.A., U. Nebr., 1941, Ph.D., 1946; m. Delsie Boschult, June 10, 1936; children—Dwight, Kent, Redge. Tchr. high sch., coach, supt. schs., Republican City, Nebr., 1936-43; supr. corr. study, extension div. U. Nebr., Lincoln, 1943-46, asst. prof. sch. adminstrn. Tchrs. Coll., 1946-52, asso. prof., 1952- 57, prof. edml. adminstrn., history and philosophy of edn., 1957—, asst. dean Tchrs. Coll., 1959-68, chmn. dept. adult and continuing edn., 1968—; vis. prof. San Jose (Calif.) State Coll., 1950-51, U. Mass., Amherst, 1961, U. P.R., Rio Piedras, 1966, U. Colo., Boulder, 1968, Colo. State U., Fort Collins, 1969, 70, 71. Mem. UNESCO Nat. Commn., 1968-73, exec. com., 1969-70, 70-71; mem. Nat. Adv. Com. for Deaf, 1970-74; mem. adv. com. Model Secondary Sch. for Deaf, 1970-76; mem. publs. bd. U. Wis./Sears Roebuck Found. IGE Tchr. Edn. Project, 1973-76; trustee Midland Coll., 1946-49. Recipient Midland Coll. Alumni Citation award, 1959; Disting. Service award Adult and Continuing Edn. Assn. Nebr., 1978. Mem. NEA (TEPS commn. 1969-72), Assn. Ednl. Communications and Tech. (pres. 1967-68), Am. Ednl. Research Assn., Neb. State Ednl. Assn., Midland Lutheran Coll. Alumni Assn. (pres. 1970-71), Phi Delta Kappa. Presbyn. (trustee 1956-59). Kiwanian. Editor: Enriching the Curriculum through Motion Pictures, 1952; Media and Educational Innovation, 1966; Planning for Evaluation of Special Education Programs, 1970; Co-editor: Trends in Programmed Instruction, 1964; Educational Media Theory into Practice, 1969. Home: 2920 William St Lincoln NE 68502

MEIEROTTO, LARRY EDWARD, govt. ofcl.; b. Dallas, Oreg., Oct. 8, 1945; s. Gervase F. Meierotto and Genevieve (Patterson) M.; B.A. in Polit. Sci., U. Portland, 1967. Asst. to dir. Idaho Dept. Adminstrn., Boise, 1971-73; spl. asst. to Idaho Budget Dir., Boise, 1973—; spl. asst. to Idaho Gov. Cecil D. Andrus, Boise, 1976; spl. asst. to Cecil D. Andrus, sec. Dept. Interior, Washington, 1977, dep. asst. sec. policy, budget and adminstrn., 1977-78, asst. sec. policy, budget and adminstrn., 1979—; sec. bd. Trans-Alaska Pipeline Liability Fund. Bd. dirs. United Cerebral Palsy of Idaho, Inc.; v.p. bd. dirs. Idaho Vols. in Corrections; v.p., bd. dirs. Central Vol. Bur., Inc. of Idaho. Recipient Dow Jones Outstanding Sr. award U. Portland, 1967. Democrat. Office: Dept of Interior 18th and C Sts NW Washington DC 20240

MEIGHAN, CLEMENT WOODWARD, archaeologist; b. San Francisco, Jan. 21, 1925; s. Charles Woodward and Lucille Christine (Mellin) M.; B.A., U. Calif., Berkeley, 1949, Ph.D., 1953; m. Joan Seibert, June 1, 1960; 1 dau., Maeve. Faculty anthropology U. Calif., Los Angeles, 1952—. Served with U.S. Army, 1943-47. Fellow Am. Anthropol. Assn., AAAS, Am. Geog. Soc. Field research, publs. on archaeology of Calif., Western U.S., Mexico, Chile. Home: 2727 Marquette Dr Topanga CA 90290 Office: Dept Anthropology U Calif Los Angeles CA 90024

MEIGHEN, MAXWELL CHARLES GORDON, investment exec.; b. Portage la Prairie, Man., Can., June 5, 1908; s. Arthur and Jessie Isabel (Cox) M.; B.A.Sc., U. Toronto, 1931; m. Catherine Jane McWhinnie, Sept. 15, 1934. Dir. Canadian Gen. Investments Ltd., 1946—, pres., 1950-70, chmn. bd., 1970—; chmn. exec. com., dir. Domtar Inc.; dir., mem. exec. com. Algoma Steel Corp. Ltd., Dominion Stores Ltd., Hollinger Mines Ltd., v.p., dir. Canada Trust Co., Can. Trusco Mortgage Com.; dir. Ravelston Corp. Ltd., Argus Corp. Ltd., Canadian Gen. Electric Co. Ltd., C.F.R.B., Massey-Ferguson Ltd. (London), Labrador Mining & Exploration Co. Ltd., Canadian Gen. Electric Co. Ltd., Standard Broadcasting Corp. Ltd. Chmn. advisory bd. Salvation Army; bd. mgmt. Grace Hosp., Toronto. Served to col. Canadian Army, 1939-45. Decorated Order Brit. Empire. Mem. United Ch. Can. Conservative. Club: Toronto. Home: 102 Binscarth Rd Toronto ON M4W 1Y4 Canada Office: 110 Yonge St Toronto ON M5C 1T4 Canada

MEIGS, WALTER BERKELEY, educator; b. Kansas City, Mo., Oct. 29, 1912; s. James B. and Alma (Jones) M.; B.S. in Bus. Adminstrn., U. Kans., 1935, M.B.A., 1938; postgrad. Harvard Grad. Sch. Bus. Adminstrn., 1939; Ph.D., U. So. Calif., 1944; m. Helen Finley, Apr. 4, 1936; children—Helen B., Robert F. Asso. prof. accounting U. So. Calif., 1945-50, prof. accounting, 1950—, head dept., 1955-64; prof. finance and control Instituto Post-Universitario Per Lo Studio Dell'Organizzazione Aziendale, Turin, Italy, 1958. Commr., C.P.A. exams. Calif. Bd. Accountancy, 1955-69. C.P.A., Calif. Mem. Am. Inst. C.P.A.'s, Calif. Soc. C.P.A.'s, Phi Beta Kappa, Kappa Sigma, Beta Alpha Psi. Author: Principles of Auditing, 1953, 6th edit., 1977; Accounting, The Basis for Business Accounting, 1962, 4th edit., 1977; (with others) Intermediate Accounting, 1963, 4th edit., 1978, Advanced Accounting, 1966; Financial Accounting, 1970, 3d edit., 1979; Modern Advanced Accounting, 3d edit., 1979. Contbg. editor: Handbook of Auditing Methods, 1953; editor profl. exams. dept. Accounting Rev., 1952-65. Home: 2881 Forrester Dr Los Angeles CA 90064

MEIJER, PAUL HERMAN ERNST, educator, physicist; b. The Hague, Netherlands, Nov. 14, 1921; s. Herman Willem and Elisabet (Kossmann) M.; Ph.D., U. Leiden (Netherlands), 1951; m. Marianne Anita Schwarz, Feb. 17, 1949; children—Onko Frans (dec.), Miriam, Daniel, Mark, Corinne. Came to U.S., 1953, naturalized, 1959. Research asso. U. Leiden, 1952-53, Duke, 1954-55; vis. lectr. Case Inst. Tech., 1953-54; asst. prof. U. Del., 1955-56; asso. prof. Cath. U., Washington, 1956-60, prof. physics, 1960—; vis. prof. U. Paris, 1964-65, 72, 78; part-time cons. Nat. Bur. Standards, Naval Ordnance Lab., Livermore Radiation Lab., Naval Research Lab., Night Vision Lab., Ft. Belvoir. Fulbright grantee, 1953-55, 77-78; Guggenheim grantee, 1964-65. Mem. Am., European phys. socs., Phys. Soc. Netherlands, Washington Philos. Soc., Fedn. Am. Scientists, AAUP, Fulbright Alumni Assn., Sigma Xi. Author: (with E. Bauer) Group Theory, 1962. Editor: Group Theory and Solid State Physics, 1964. Research, publs. statis. mechanics solids and liquids, other fields. Home: 1438 Geranium St NW Washington DC 20012 Office: Physics Dept Cath U Am Washington DC 20064

MEIKLE, THOMAS HARRY, JR., med. educator; b. Troy, Pa., Mar. 24, 1929; s. Thomas H. and Elizabeth (MacMorran) M.; A.B., Cornell U., 1951, M.D., 1954; m. Jane T. Germer, Aug. 26, 1966; children—David Andrew, Sarah Elizabeth. Intern Jefferson Hosp., Phila., 1954-55; clin. fellow Inst. Neurology, London, Eng., 1957-58; research fellow Inst. Neurol. Scis., U. Pa., 1958-61; asso. prof. anatomy Cornell U., 1961—, dean Cornell Grad. Sch. Med. Scis., 1969-76, acting dean Med. Sch., 1976-77, dep. dean, 1977—; spl. cons. Josiah Macy Jr. Found., 1979—; Career scientist Health Research Council, N.Y.C., 1969-71; scholar acad. medicine Markle Found., 1963-68. Served to capt., M.C., AUS, 1955-57; Korea. Mem. Am. Physiol. Soc., Soc. Neuroscis. Home: 333 E 69th St New York NY 10021

MEIKLEJOHN, DAVID SHIRRA, fin. exec.; b. N.Y.C., Oct. 4, 1908; s. David and Florence (Pickens) M.; B.A., Williams Coll., 1931; m. Mary Jeanne Faulkner, July 21, 1945; 1 dau., Shirra Belvoir Wilson. Clk., Emigrant Savs. Bank, 1932-33; credit analyst Bankers Trust Co., 1933-36; asst. to pres. Dorr Co., 1936-40; dir. dept. commerce N.Y.C., 1940-42; exec. sec. Mayor LaGuardia, 1945- 46; asst. treas. Am. Machine & Foundry Co., 1946-51, treas., 1951-70, dir., 1954-70, v.p., 1958-70; exec. v.p. finance, dir. Integrated Resources, Inc., N.Y.C., 1970—. Served to lt. comdr. USNR, 1942-45. Mem. St. Andrews Soc. Clubs: Williams, Union League (N.Y.C.); Stanwich Golf; Belle Haven Beach (Greenwich, Conn.). Home: 23 Clapboard Ridge Rd Greenwich CT 06830 Office: 295 Madison Ave New York NY 10017

MEIKLEJOHN, DONALD, educator; b. Providence, June 1 1909; s. Alexander and Nannine (LaVilla) M.; A.B., U. Wis., 1930; Ph.D., Harvard, 1936; m. Betty Moore, Aug. 25, 1941; children—Alexander M., Douglas, Elizabeth, Donald Stuart. Instr. philosophy Dartmouth, 1936-38; asso. prof. philosophy Coll. William and Mary, 1938-46; asso. prof. U. Chgo., 1946-59, prof., 1959-63, chmn. Coll. Social Sci. Group, 1958-61; prof. philosophy and social sci. Syracuse U., 1963—, dir. pub. affairs and citizenship Maxwell Sch., 1963-75, emeritus, 1975—. Served from pvt. to 1st lt., AUS, 1942-46. Mem. ACLU (dir. Ill.), AAUP, Phi Beta Kappa. Club: Hyde Park Neighborhood (dir.). Author: Freedom and the Public, 1965; also articles in field. Home: 822 Maryland Ave Syracuse NY 13210

MEILING, RICHARD LEWIS, physician, educator; b. Springfield, Ohio, Dec. 21, 1908; s. Lester L. and Matilda (Lobenherz) M.; A.B., Wittenberg U., 1930, D.Sc. (hon.), 1950; M.D., U. Munich (Germany), 1937; D.H.L. (hon.), Ohio State U., 1977; m. Ann Elizabeth Lucas, June 21, 1940; 1 son, George. Prof. obstetrics and gynecology Ohio State U., 1947-74, emeritus, 1974—, dean coll. of medicine, 1961-70, v.p., 1970-74, emeritus, 1974—, dir. Univ. Hosp., 1961-72; hon. staff Univ. Hosp., St. Ann's Hosp., Mt. Carmel Hosp. (all Columbus, Ohio), Riverside Hosp., Grant Hosp. (both Columbus); v.p. Lucas Supply Co., Newark, Ohio, Nutrition Today Soc., Inc., Annapolis, Md.; dir. Pharmacy Systems Co., Bishop Enterprises Co.; dir. emeritus City Nat. Bank & Trust Co., Columbus; chmn. bd. Medicon Co., Columbus. Dir. med. services of Dept. of Def., 1949-51; asst. to Sec. of Def., 1949-51; chmn. Armed Force med. policy council, 1951. Trustee Children's Hosp., Columbus. Maj. gen. USAF, ret. Diplomate Am. Bd. Obstetrics and Gynecology, Am. Bd. Preventive Medicine. Fellow Am. Coll. Obstetricians and Gynecologists, A.C.S., Aerospace Med. Assn., S.E. Surg. Congress; mem. AMA, Ohio Med. Assn. (pres. 1956-57), Central Assn. Obstetrics and Gynecology, Columbus Acad. Medicine. Episcopalian. Author med. articles. Cons. med. editor Ohio State Med. Jour. Home: 91 N Columbia Ave Columbus OH 43209

MEILY, HARRY S., banker; b. 1924; A.B., Occidental Coll., 1945; M.B.A., Stanford Grad. Sch. Bus., 1947; married. With Security Pacific Nat. Bank, Los Angeles, 1947—, now vice chmn. Address: PO Box 209 Terminal Annex 333 S Hope St Los Angeles CA 90051*

MEIMA, RALPH CHESTER, JR., fgn. service officer; b. Chgo., Mar. 29, 1927; s. Ralph Chester and Grace Georgine (Larson) M.; B.A., U. Americas, Mexico City, 1952; M.B.A., Am. U., 1964; m. Barbara M. Hughes, Aug. 6, 1955; children—Ralph Chester III, Stephen H. With Carborundum Co., Perth Amboy, N.J., 1952-53, Johns-Manville Corp., N.Y.C., 1953-58, Security Storage Co., Washington, 1958-61, Dept. Commerce, 1961-68; joined U.S. Fgn. Service, 1968; now consul gen., Marseille, France. Served with USN, 1945-46.

MEINCKE, PETER PAUL MAX, univ. adminstr.; b. Winnipeg, Man., Can., Jan. 21, 1936; s. Paul Henry and Marie (Winther) M.; student Royal Mil. Coll.; B.Sc., Queen's U., Kingston, Ont., Can., 1959; M.A., U. Toronto (Ont.), 1960, Ph.D., 1963; m. Donna Pauline Mallinson, June 28, 1958; children—Thomas, Carolyn. Mem. faculty Royal Mil. Coll., 1962-65; mem. tech. staff Bell Telephone Labs., Murray Hill, N.J., 1965-67; asst. prof. physics Erindale Coll., U. Toronto, 1967-69, asso. prof., 1969-70, asso. dean coll., 1970-72, vice provost univ., 1972-76, prof. physics U. Toronto, 1977-78; pres. U. P.E.I. (Can.), Charlottetown, 1978—. Chmn. bd. Inst. Man and Resources; bd. dirs. Holland Coll. Served with RCAF, 1962-65. Recipient Sword of Honour, Royal Mil. Coll., 1958. Mem. Soc. Gen. Systems Research. Club: Rotary. Contbr. articles to profl. jours. Office: U PEI University Ave Charlottetown PE C1A 4P3 Canada

MEINDL, JAMES DONALD, elec. engr.; b. Pitts., Apr. 20, 1933; s. Louis M. and Elizabeth F. (Steinhauser) M.; B.S., Carnegie Mellon U., 1955, M.S., 1956, Ph.D., 1958; m. Frederica Ziegler, May 21, 1961; children—Peter James, Candace Ann. Engr., Autonetics Co., Downey, Calif., 1957, Westinghouse Co., Pitts., 1958-59; head sect. microelectronics U.S. Army Electronics Command, Ft. Monmouth, N.J., 1959-62, chief br. semicondr. and microelectronics, 1962-65, dir. div. integrated electronics, 1965-67; asso. prof. elec. engring. Stanford U., 1967-70, prof., 1970—, dir. integrated circuits lab., 1967—, Stanford Electronics Lab., 1972—; dir. Telesensory Systems Inc., Palo Alto, Calif., 1971—; cons. to govt., industry. Served to 1st lt. AUS, 1959-61. Recipient Arthur S. Fleming Commn. award Washington Jr. C. of C., 1967. Fellow IEEE (editor Jour. Solid State Circuits 1966-71, Internat. Solid-State Circuits Conf. Outstanding Paper award 1970, 75, 76, 77, 78), AAAS; mem. Nat. Acad. Engring., Electrochem. Soc., Biomed. Engring. Soc. (co-editor Annals of Biomed. Engring. 1976—), Am. Inst. Ultrasound in Medicine, Assn. Advancement of Med. Instrumentation, Sigma Xi, Tau Beta Pi, Eta Kappa Nu, Phi Kappa Phi. Author: Micropower Circuits, 1969; contbr. numerous articles to profl. publs.; patentee integrated circuit field. Home: 1250 Montclaire Way Los Altos CA 94022 Office: 118 AEL Bldg Stanford U Stanford CA 94305

MEINERT, JOHN RAYMOND, corp. exec.; b. White Cloud, Mich., Aug. 11, 1927; s. Raymond and Mildred (Berg) M.; student U. Mich., 1944-45; B.S., Northwestern U., 1949; C.P.A., Ill., 1952; m. Joyce Macdonell, Nov. 5, 1955; children—Elizabeth Joyce, Pamela Anne. Treas., dir. Posto-Photo Co., Chgo., 1948-49; with Hart Schaffner & Marx, Chgo., 1949—, asst. treas., 1962-65, comptroller, 1965-69, v.p., 1966-69, sr. v.p., 1969-74, treas., 1970-72, exec. v.p., 1975—. dir., 1974—; instr. accounting Northwestern U., 1949. Bd. dirs. Duncan YMCA, Chgo., 1967—. Served with AUS, 1945-46. Mem. Am. Inst. C.P.A.'s (council mem. 1971—, chmn. fin. mgmt. com. 1974-75, dir. 1975-78, audit com. 1975-78, chmn. adv. com. industry and govt. 1975-78, chmn. spl. com. bylaws 1979—), Ill. Soc. C.P.A.'s (bd. dirs. 1966-67, v.p. 1967-68). Presbyn. (elder). Clubs: University (Chgo.); Rolling Green Country (Arlington Heights), Rotary. Home: 634 Ironwood Dr Arlington Heights IL 60004 Office: 36 S Franklin St Chicago IL 60606

MEININGER, LEIGH RICHARD, consumer fin. co. exec.; b. West Seneca, N.Y., Sept. 8, 1936; s. Alfred Frederick and Mildred (Lave) M.; B.S., SUNY, Buffalo, 1960; m. Joan R. Heintz, Dec. 15, 1956; children—Stephen, Tamara, John, Susan, Amy, Todd. Audit mgr. Arthur Andersen & Co., C.P.A.'s, Balt., 1960-71; v.p., controller Assos. Corp. N.Am., S. Bend, Ind., 1971-74; controller Aristar, Inc., Coral Gables, Fla., 1974-77, exec. v.p., chief fin. officer, dir., 1977—; chmn. bd., chief exec. officer John Alden Life Ins. Co., Coral Gables, 1979—. Served with USMCR, 1954-57. C.P.A., D.C. Mem. Am. Inst. C.P.A.'s, Nat. Assn. Accts., Fla. Inst. C.P.A.'s. Republican. Club: Riviera Country (Coral Gables). Office: 300 Sevilla Ave Coral Gables FL 33134

MEINKE, WILLIAM WAYNE, chemist; b. Elyria, Ohio, June 27, 1924; s. William Carl and Marian Ella (McRoberts) M.; A.B., Oberlin Coll., 1947; Ph.D., U. Calif. at Berkeley, 1950; m. Marilynn Hope Hayward, July 12, 1947; children—Sue Anne, David William. Mem. faculty U. Mich., 1950-63, prof. chemistry, 1962-63; chief analytical chemistry div. Nat. Bur. Standards, 1963-73, chief Office Standard Reference Materials, 1964-69; head radiation applications KMS Fusion, Inc., Ann Arbor, 1973-76, asst. to chmn., 1976—; chmn. subcom. radiochemistry, com. nuclear sci. NRC, 1958-62; mem. adv. com. to analytical and inorganic chemistry div. Nat. Bur. Standards, 1960-63; adv. com. to analytical div. Oak Ridge Nat. Lab., 1959-63; adv. com. isotopes and radiation devel. AEC, 1961-64, mem. subcom. physiochem. standards Nat. Acad. Scis., NRC, 1963—; rep. Am. Chem. Soc. on Am. Standards Assn. sect. com. N2 on gen. standards nuclear energy, 1960-68; geochemistry panel Apollo adv. com. NASA, 1963-65; cons. div. internat. affairs AEC and Internat. Atomic Energy Agy., 1961-64; titular mem. commn. on analytical radiochemistry and nuclear materials, 1965-71, commn. on data and standards Internat. Union Pure and Applied Chemistry, 1965-69, mem. U.S. nat. com., 1970—, sec. applied chemistry div., 1971-73; chmn. steering panel on characterization pure materials OECD, 1969-72; mem. sci. adv. bd. Center Radiochemistry and Activation Analysis, U. Pavia, Italy, 1970-73. Served to lt. (j.g.) USNR, 1943-46. Recipient Hevesy medal for radioanalytical chemistry, 1968; Rosa award Nat. Bur. Standards, 1968; Distinguished Service awards Am. Nuclear Soc., 1968, Fed. Exec. Inst., 1968; Gold Medal award U.S. Commerce Dept., 1971. Fellow A.A.A.S.; mem. Soc. Analytical Chemistry (hon.), Am. Chem. Soc. (chmn. nuclear chemistry and technology div. 1968, sec. analytical chemistry div. 1972-73; Fisher award in analytical chemistry 1972), Am. Phys. Soc., Am. Nuclear Soc. (exec. com. isotopes and radiation div., 1963-66), Am. Soc. Testing and Materials, Phi Beta Kappa, Sigma Xi, Gamma Alpha, Phi Lambda Upsilon, Alpha Chi Sigma. Editor series monographs on radiochemistry of the elements, 1961; regional editor The Analyst; adv. bd. Analytical Chemistry, 1968-71; co-editor Trace Characterization, Chemical and Physical; Analytical Chemistry: Key to Progress on National Problems. Home: 1351 Glendaloch Circle Ann Arbor MI 48104 Office: 3941 Research Park Dr PO Box 1567 Ann Arbor MI 48106

MEINSCHEIN, WARREN G., univ. dean; b. Slaughters, Ky., Nov. 12, 1920; s. Tim and Carrie (Poole) M.; B.S., U. Mich., 1948; Ph.D., U. Tex., 1951; m. Mary Elizabeth Williams, Feb. 5, 1944; children—Sherryl Elizabeth, Warren Gamaliel Jr., Tim Allan. Research asso. Magnolia Field Research Labs., Socony-Mobil Co., Dallas, 1951-58, Esso Research and Engring. Co., Linden, N.J., 1958-66; prof. geochemistry Ind. U., Bloomington, 1966—, asso. dean acad. affairs Sch. Pub. and Environ. Affairs, 1975—, univ. rep. Inst. Ecology, 1971-78, acting chmn. dept. geology, 1971-73; mem. Lunar Sci. Sample Rev. Bd., 1970-72; chmn. nat. com. geochemistry Nat. Acad. Sci.-NRC, 1970-72; J. Clarence Karcher lectr. chemistry U. Okla., 1978-79; cons. in field. Served to lt. comdr. USNR, 1940-46. Sun Oil Co. fellow, 1948-51; grantee NSF, 1968-76, 77—, NASA, 1969-76. Fellow Geol. Soc. Am., Am. Inst. Chemists, Explorers Club; mem. Geochem. Soc. (chmn. organic geochemistry div. 1968-69, chm. Clarke medalist com. 1979—), Am. Soc. Polit. and Social Sci., Soc. Environ. Geochemistry and Health, AAAS, Am. Geophys. Union, Am. Soc. Pub. Adminstrn., Ind. Acad. Sci., Am. Chem. Soc. Club: Rotary. Author papers in field. Home: 4418 Sheffield Dr Bloomington IN 47401 Office: Geology Dept Ind Univ Sch Pub and Environ Affairs Bloomington IN 47401

MEINWALD, JERROLD, chemist, educator; b. Bklyn., Jan. 16, 1927; s. Herman and Sophie (Baskind) M.; Ph.B., U. Chgo., 1947, B.S., 1948; M.A., Harvard, 1950, Ph.D., 1952; m. Yvonne Chu, June 25, 1955; children—Constance Chu, Pamela Joan. Mem. faculty Cornell U., 1952-72, 73—, prof. chemistry, 1961—, research dir. Internat. Centre Insect Physiology and Ecology, Nairobi, 1970-77; prof. chemistry U. Calif. at San Diego, 1972-73; vis. prof. Rockefeller U., 1970; cons. to industry; mem. vis. com. chemistry Brookhaven Nat. Lab., 1969-72, chmn., 1972; mem. med. A chemistry study sect. NIH, 1963-67, chmn., 1965-67; mem. adv. bd. Petroleum Research Found., 1971-73; mem. adv. council chemistry dept. Princeton U., 1978—; mem. adv. bd. Research Corp., 1978—; mem. adv. bd. chemistry div. NSF, 1979—. Sloan fellow, 1958-62; Guggenheim fellow, 1960-61, 76-77; NIH spl. postdoctoral fellow, 1967-68. Mem. Am. (chmn. organic div. 1969), Swiss chem. socs., A.A.A.S., Nat. Acad. Sci., Am. Acad. Arts and Scis., Chem. Soc. (London), Phi Beta Kappa, Sigma Xi. Bd. editors Jour. Organic Chemistry, 1962-66, Organic Reactions, 1968-78, Organic Synthesis, 1968-72, Jour. Chem. Ecology, 1974—, Insect Sci., 1979—; contbr. articles profl. jours. Office: Baker Lab Cornell U Ithaca NY 14850

MEIROSE, LEO HARRY, library adminstr.; b. Cin., Oct. 25, 1922; s. Leo and Clara (Barde) M.; A.B., Xavier U., 1945; M.S.L.S., Case Western Res. U., 1951; m. Ruth Meirose, Jan. 24, 1948; children—Leo, Mary, JoAnn, Martha, John, Judith. Instr., Xavier U., 1945-64, asst. librarian, 1947-51; with Cin. Public Library, 1951-64; dir. Fort Lauderdale (Fla.) Public Library, 1964-72; dir. Tampa-Hillsborough County (Fla.) Public Library System, 1972—. Mem. ALA, Southeastern Library Assn., Fla. Library Assn. Roman Catholic. Home: 1412 Moss Laden Ct Brandon FL 33511 Office: 900 N Ashley St Tampa FL 33602

MEIROVITCH, LEONARD, educator; b. Maxut, Rumania, Nov. 28, 1928; s. Carol and Adelle (Schoenfeld) M.; B.Sc. summa cum laude, Technion-Israel Inst. Tech., 1953; M.S. in Engring., U. Calif. at Los Angeles, 1957, Ph.D., 1960; m. Jo Anne Reifer, Oct. 15, 1960. Came to U.S., 1956, naturalized, 1964. Structural engr. Water Planning for Israel, Tel Aviv, 1953-55, asst. sect. head, 1955-56; asst. research engr., asso. in engring. U. Calif. at Los Angeles, 1956-60; staff engr. IBM, Endicott, N.Y., 1960-62; asso. prof. Ariz. State U., 1962-66; prof. U. Cin., 1967-71; prof. Va. Poly. Inst. and State U., Blacksburg, 1971-79, Reynolds Metals prof., 1979—. Cons., Goodyear Aerospace, Phoenix, 1962-63, C.S. Draper Labs., Cambridge, Mass., 1976—, Naval Research Lab., Washington, 1977—. Served with Israeli Army, 1948-49. Am. Soc. Engring. Edn.-NASA fellow, 1964; Nat. Acad. Scis. sr. research asso. Langley Research Center, Hampton, Va., 1966-67. Mem. Am. Inst. Aeros. and Astronautics, Am. Soc. M.E., Sigma Xi, Tau Beta Pi, Author: Analytical Methods in Vibrations, 1967, Methods of Analytical Dynamics, 1970; Elements of Vibration Analysis, 1975; also articles. Asso. editor Jour. Spacecraft and Rockets, 1971-76; editor Mechanics: Dynamical Systems; mem. internat. editorial bd. Journal de Mécanique Appliquée. Home: 303 Neil St Blacksburg VA 24060

MEISCH, ADRIEN FERDINAND JOSEPH, ambassador, lawyer; b. Luxembourg, Apr. 8, 1930; s. Aloyse and Mariette (Moutrier) M.; B. Litt. in Modern and Contemporary History, U. Paris, France, 1953; LL.D., Oxford (Eng.) U., 1956; m. Solange Pregermain, Sept. 28, 1963; adopted children—Yves, Patrick. Admitted to Luxembourg bar, 1953; attache of legation in Ministry Foreign Affairs, Luxembourg, Luxembourg, from 1956; dep. permanent rep. of Luxembourg to UN, N.Y.C., 1958-59, to European Communities, Brussels, Belgium, 1960, to NATO and OECD, Paris, 1961-67; polit. dir. Ministry Foreign Affairs in Luxembourg and permanent rep. of Luxembourg to European Council in Strasbourg (France), 1968-70; ambassador of Luxembourg to USSR and Poland, Moscow, USSR, 1971-74; accredited ambassador of Luxembourg to Finland, 1972-74; ambassador of Luxembourg to U.S., Mex., Can., Washington, 1974—. Home: 3933 Fordham Rd NW Washington DC 20016 Office: 2200 Massachusetts Ave NW Washington DC 20008

MEISEL, JOHN, polit. scientist; b. Vienna, Austria, Oct. 23, 1923; s. Fryda and Ann M.; B.A., U. Toronto, 1948, M.A., 1950; Ph.D. in Polit. Sci., London Sch. Econs., 1959; m. Murie. Mem. faculty dept. polit. sci. Queen's U., Kingston, Ont., Can., 1949—, Hardy prof. polit. sci., 1964—. Recipient Killam award Can. Council, 1968, 73. Author: The Canadian General Election of 1957, 1962; Papers on the 1962 Election, 1964; Ethnic Relations in Canadian Voluntary Assocations, 1972; Working Papers on Canadian Politics, 1975. Home: Colimaison Tichborne ON K0H 2V0 Canada Office: Queen's Univ Kingston ON K7L 3N6 Canada

MEISELMAN, DAVID ISRAEL, educator; b. Boston, May 21, 1924; s. Samuel and Sarah (Bovarnick) M.; A.B., Boston U., 1947; M.A., U. Chgo., 1951, Ph.D., 1961; m. Winifred Charm, Jan. 24, 1966; children—Ellen, Nina, Samuel Adam. Instr., Ill. Inst. Tech., Chgo., 1952-55; lectr. econs. Coll. City N.Y., 1957-58; asst. prof. econs. U. Chgo., 1958-62; economist Office Sec. Treasury, Washington, 1962-63; sr. economist com. on banking and currency U.S. Ho. of Reps., Washington, 1963; lectr. polit. economy Johns Hopkins U., 1963-64; sr. economist OAS Inter-Am. Devel. Bank Fiscal Mission to Peru, 1964; sr. economist, asso. editor Nat. Banking Rev., Office Comptroller Currency, U.S. Treasury Dept., Washington, 1964-66; Frederick R. Bigelow prof. econs., dir. bur. econ. studies Macalester Coll., St. Paul, 1966-71, acting chmn. dept. econs., 1968-69; prof. econs., dir. grad. econs. program, research asso. Center for Pub. Choice, Va. Poly. Inst. and State U., 1971—; adj. scholar Am. Enterprise Inst. for Pub. Policy Research, 1976—; econ. cons., sr. cons. IBRD, 1966; econ. cons. Republican Senatorial Campaign Com., 1974, Planning Research Corp., 1970, ICC, 1972, Commodity Futures Trading Commn., 1975, Labor Dept., 1976, Norman B. Ture, Inc., 1972— Sec. Treasury, 1969-76, Coopers & Lybrand, 1976, Bache Halsey Stuart, Inc., 1976-77, Wainwright Securities, Inc., 1977-78, Law and Econs. Center, U. Miami Sch. Law, 1977—, N.Y. Stock Exchange, 1979; dir., sec.-treas. Internat. Center for Econ. Policy Studies of N.Y., 1977—; chmn. Presdl. Task Force on Inflation, 1968-69. Served with AUS, 1942-46. Winner Ford Found. Doctoral Dissertation competition, 1960; named Miles B. Lane lectr. Ga. Inst. Tech., 1968; named to Collegium Distinguished Alumni Boston U., 1974. Mem. Am. Econ. Assn., Royal Econs. Soc., Am. Fin. Assn., Econometric Soc., Phila. Soc. (pres. 1973-75), Mont Pelerin Soc. Jewish. Author: The Term Structure of Interest Rates, 1962; (with Eli Shapiro) The Measurement of Corporate Sources and Uses of Funds, 1964; editor: Varieties of Monetary Experience, 1970; co-editor: The Phenomenon of Worldwide Inflation, 1975; Welfare Reform and The Carter Public Service Employment Program: A Critique; mem. adv. bd. Jour. Money, Credit and Banking, 1968-71; chmn. editorial bd. Policy Rev., 1977—; contbr. articles to profl. jours. Home: 2346 Centreville Rd Herndon VA 22070

MEISER, ROBERT NEWMAN, lawyer; b. Kendallville, Ind., May 2, 1935; s. Wesley H. and Ima L. (Bray) M.; A.B., Ind. U., 1957, LL.B., 1959; m. Hala Ansari, Sept. 4, 1964; children—Ramsey David, Rhenda Lynn. Admitted to N.Y. State bar, 1961, D.C. bar, 1967; with firm Cahill, Gordon, Reindel & Ohl, N.Y.C., 1960-64; counsel routes and agreements, also subsidy divs. CAB, 1964-66; with firm Ginsburg & Feldman, Washington, 1966-69; partner firm Haffer & Meiser, Washington, 1969-75; individual practice, Washington, 1975—. Exec. dir. Internat. Air Freight Agts. Assn. Dir. govt. affairs in U.S., Alia-Royal Jordanian Airlines Corp. Pres. Fairhill Elementary Sch. PTA, Fairfax County, Va., 1972-73; vice chmn. bipartisan com. for a referendum on Elected Sch. Bd. in Fairfax County, 1973. Parliamentarian, Fairfax County Republican Com., 1970-71; Rep. candidate for Va. Senate, 1971. Served with USAF, 1959-60. Recipient Moffat award in econs. Ind. U., 1956; Krannert fellow, 1957; Edwards fellow, 1958-59. Mem. Fed., D.C. bar assns., Phi Beta Kappa. Mem., contbg. author Ind. Law Jour. Home: 8700 Lothbury Ct Fairfax VA 22031 Office: 1300 Connecticut Ave NW Washington DC 20036. *My experience has been that success usually comes from a combination of hard work, proper motivation, the establishment of the right priorities, good personal relations, judicious risk taking and a dose of just plain good luck. Bad luck can be overcome in almost all cases by increasing the other factors. However, I do not believe that success as usually defined should be blindly pursued. I try to do that which gives me an inner peace.*

MEISER, ROBERT NEWMAN, lawyer; b. Kendallville, Ind., May 2, 1935; s. Wesley H. and Ima L. (Bray) M.; A.B., Ind. U., 1957, LL.B., 1959; m. Hala Ansari, Sept. 4, 1964; children—Ramsey David, Rhenda Lynn. Admitted to N.Y. State bar, 1961, D.C. bar, 1967; with firm Cahill, Gordon, Reindel & Ohl, N.Y.C., 1960-64; counsel routes and agreements, also subsidy divs. CAB, 1964-66; with firm Ginsburg & Feldman, Washington, 1966-69; partner firm Haffer & Meiser, Washington, 1969-75; individual practice, Washington, 1975—. Exec. dir. Internat. Airforwarder and Agts. Assn. Dir. govt. affairs in U.S., Alia-Royal Jordanian Airlines Corp. Vice chmn. bipartisan com. for a referendum on Elected Sch. Bd. in Fairfax County, 1973. Parliamentarian, Fairfax County Republican Com., 1970-71; Rep. candidate for Va. Senate, 1971. Served with USAF, 1959-60. Recipient Moffat award in econs. Ind. U., 1956; Krannert fellow, 1957; Edwards fellow, 1958-59. Mem. Fed., D.C. bar assns., Phi Beta Kappa. Mem., contbg. author Ind. Law Jour. Home: 8700 Lothbury Ct Fairfax VA 22031 Office: 910 17th St NW Washington DC 20006. *My experience has been that success usually comes from a combination of hard work, proper motivation, the establishment of the right priorities, good personal relations, judicious risk taking and a dose of just plain good luck. Bad luck can be overcome in almost all cases by increasing the other factors. However, I do not believe that success as usually defined should be blindly pursued. We should try to do whatever gives us inner peace.*

MEISLICH, HERBERT, educator; b. Bklyn., Mar. 26, 1920; s. Isidore and Bessie (Rose) M.; A.B., Bklyn. Coll., 1940; A.M., Columbia, 1947, Ph.D., 1950; m. Estelle Kalechstein, July 1, 1951; children—Mindy, Debrah, Susan. With Edgewood Arsenal (Mo.), 1942-44; asst. prof. chemistry Coll. City N.Y., 1946-62, asso. prof., 1963-68, prof., 1969—. Mem. New Milford (N.J.) Bd. Edn., 1967—. Served to lt. (j.g.) USN, 1944-46. Sloan Kettering fellow, 1956. Mem. Am. Chem. Soc. (past chmn. N.Y. sect., councilor). Author: Introduction to Organic Chemistry, 1960; Fundamentals of Chemistry, 1966, 3d edit., 1975; Introduction to Chemistry, 1968; Schaum's Organic Chemistry, 1977. Home: 338 Lacey Dr New Milford NJ 07646 Office: Dept Chemistry City Univ New York Convent Ave 138th St New York NY 10031

MEISLIN, BERNARD JOSHUA, lawyer; b. N.Y.C., Nov. 10, 1927; s. Aaron and Rose (Grayzel) M.; B.A., U. Mich., 1948; LL.B., Harvard, 1951; LL.M., N.Y. U., 1954; m. Zelda Joan Prussack, Dec. 24, 1950; children—Amy Deborah (Mrs. Martin Pollack), Nancy Ellen (Mrs. Warren Siegel), Warren Lowell. Admitted to N.Y. State bar, 1951, N.J. bar, 1976; asso. firm Orr & Brennan, Bklyn., 1951-60; partner firm Bressler, Meislin & Lipsitz, N.Y.C., 1960-77; counsel firm Bressler, Lipsitz & Rothenberg, 1977—. Dir. Electro-Protective Corp. Am., Technimetrics Inc. Author: (with others) Tax Annotations Nichols Ency. Forms, 1954-59; Jewish Law in American Tribunals, 1976. Editor: (with B. Bressler) New York Lawyers Manual, 1962. Contbr. to Stock Market Handbook, 1970. Contbr. articles to profl. jours. Home: 73 Athens Rd Short Hills NJ 07078 Office: Bressler Lipsitz & Rothenberg 90 Broad St New York City NY 10004

MEISSNER, CHARLES F., economist, govt. ofcl.; b. Milw., Jan. 11, 1941; B.S., U. Wis., 1964, M.S., 1966, Ph.D. in Agrl. Econs., 1969. Acad. analyst and spl. asst. to asst. sec. for internat. affairs, Dept. Treasury, Washington, 1971-73; mem. staff U.S. Senate Fgn. Relations Com., also staff dir. subcom. on fgn. assistance, 1973-77; dep. asst. sec. for internat. fin. and devel. Dept. State, Washington, 1977—. Served with U.S. Army, 1969-70. Decorated Bronze star. Office: Dept of State Econ and Business Affairs Bur 2201 C St NW Washington DC 20520

MEISSNER, DAVID GIFFORD, editorial writer; b. Milw., Sept. 30, 1937; s. Charles David and Harriet Elenore (Fellman) M.; B.S., U. Wis., 1960; M.A. (Woodrow Wilson fellow), U. Calif. at Berkeley, 1961; m. Judith Grant Abert, Aug. 6, 1960; children—Linda Beth, Donald Charles. Bus. trainee The Journal Co., Milw., 1961; reporter, copy editor Milw. Jour., 1965-70, editorial writer, 1970—; v.p., dir. Charles Meissner & Asso. Advt., Milw., 1965-73, pres., 1973-75. Bd. dirs. World Affairs Council of Milw., 1969-72; bd. dirs. Milwaukee County Hist. Soc., Historic Walkers Point, Inc., 1973-79; trustee Wis. Meml. Union. Served to lt. (j.g.) USNR, 1962-65. Stanford Profl. Journalism fellow, 1968-69, vis. fellow Harvard Center Sci. and Internat. Affairs, 1977. Mem. Inter-Am. Press Assn. (dir. 1975—). Clubs: Milwaukee Country, Milwaukee Athletic. Home: 9211 N Regent Rd Milwaukee WI 53217 Office: The Milwaukee Jour Journal Sq Milwaukee WI 53201

MEISSNER, DORIS MARIE, govt. ofcl.; b. Milw., Nov. 3, 1941; d. Fred and Hertha Borst; B.A., U. Wis., 1963, M.A. in Public Policy and Polit. Sci., 1969; cert. French lang., Lavalle U., Quebec, Can., 1962; m. June 8, 1963; children—Christine Marie, Andree David. Asst. dir. student fin. aids U. Wis., 1963-68; exec. dir. Nat. Women's Polit. Caucus, Washington, 1971-73; White House fellow, spl. asst. to atty. gen. U.S., 1973-74; asst. dir. Office Policy and Planning, then exec. dir. cabinet com. illegal aliens Dept. Justice, 1974-76, dep. asso. atty. gen., 1977—, mem. dept. women's adv. bd., 1979; nat. adv. bd. U.S.-Mex. Border Research Council, 1977—, Nat. Women's Polit. Caucus, 1976—, Nat. Assn. Pretrial Services Agencies, 1975-77; exec. com. White House Fellows Alumni Assn., bd. dirs. White House Fellows Found., 1979—. Mem. Mortar Board, Phi Kappa Phi. Home: 4619 DeRussey Pkwy Chevy Chase MD 20015 Office: Dept Justice 10th and Constitution Ave Washington DC 20530*

MEISSNER, EDWIN BENJAMIN, JR., real estate broker; b. St. Louis, Dec. 27, 1918; s. Edwin B. and Edna R. (Rice) M.; B.S., U. Pa., 1940; m. Nina Renard, Dec. 17, 1946; children—Edwin Benjamin III, Wallace, Robert, Donald. Joined St. Louis Car Co., 1934, asst. to pres., v.p., exec. v.p., 1950-56, pres., gen. mgr., 1956-61; pres. St. Louis Car div. Gen. Steel Industries, Inc., 1961-67; sr. v.p., dir. Gen. Steel Industries, Inc., 1968-74; real estate broker, v.p. Bakewell Corp., St. Louis. Mem. pres.'s council St. Louis U.; treas., bd. dirs. Washington U. Med. Center; trustee Govtl. Research Inst., Austen Riggs Center, Stockbridge, Mass.; bd. dirs. St. Louis Symphony Soc.; hon. v.p., bd. dirs. Humane Soc. Mo.; bd. dirs., pres. Barnard Free Skin and Cancer Hosp.; asso. trustee U. Pa.; bd. mgrs. Central Inst. for Deaf. Mem. St. Louis Flood Assn. (dir.), Am. Ordnance Assn. (life), Beta Gamma Sigma. Clubs: Mo. Athletic, Westwood Country, Bridlespur Hunt, Saint Louis. Home: 40 Roan Ln Saint Louis MO 63124 Office: Bakewell Corp 8820 Ladue Rd Saint Louis MO 63124

MEISSNER, WILLIAM WALTER, psychiatrist, clergyman; b. Buffalo, Feb. 13, 1931; s. William Walter and Mary Emma (Glauber) M.; B.A., St. Louis U., 1956, Ph.L., 1957, M.A., 1957; S.T.L., Woodstock Coll., 1962; M.D., Harvard, 1967. Joined Soc. Jesus, 1951; intern Mt. Auburn Hosp., Cambridge, Mass., 1967-68; resident Mass. Mental Health Center, Boston, 1968-71; mem., instr. Boston Psychoanalytic Inst., 1971—; staff psychiatrist Mass. Mental Health Center, 1971—, Cambridge (Mass.) Hosp., 1971-76; asst. clin. prof. psychiatry Harvard Med. Sch., 1971-76, asso. clin. prof., 1976—. Mem. No. New Eng. Psychiat. Soc., Am. Psychiat. Assn., Am. Psychoanalytic Assn., Sigma Xi. Author: Annotated Bibliography in Religion and Psychology, 1961; Group Dynamics in the Religious Life, 1965; Foundations for a Psychology of Grace, 1966; The Assault on Authority-Dialogue or Dilemma, 1971; Basic Concepts in Psychoanalytic Psychiatry, 1973; The Paranoid Process, 1978. Address: 6 Sumner Rd Cambridge MA 02138

MEISTER, ALTON, biochemist, educator; b. N.Y.C., June 1, 1922; s. Morris and Florence (Glickstein) M.; B.S., Harvard, 1942; M.D., Cornell U., 1945; m. Leonora Garten, Dec. 26, 1943; children—Jonathan Howard, Kenneth Eliot. Intern, asst. resident N.Y. Hosp., N.Y.C., 1946; commd. officer USPHS, NIH, 1946-55; prof. biochemistry, chmn. dept. Tufts U. Sch. Medicine, 1955-67; prof., chmn. dept. biochemistry Cornell U. Med. Coll., N.Y.C., 1967—; biochemist-in-chief N.Y. Hosp., 1971—. Vis. prof. biochemistry U. Wash., 1959, U. Calif. at Berkeley, 1961; cons. USPHS, 1964-68, chmn. physiol. chemistry study sect.; cons. com. on growth NRC, 1954; cons. biochemistry study sect. USPHS, 1955-60, cons. biochemistry tng. com., 1961-63; cons. Am. Cancer Soc., 1958-61, 71-74. Recipient Paul-Lewis award enzyme chemistry Am.

Chem. Soc., 1954. Fellow Am. Acad. Arts and Scis.; mem. Nat. Acad. Scis., Inst. of Medicine, Biophys. Soc., Biochem. Soc. London, Chem. Soc. London, AAAS, Am. Chem. Soc. (chmn. div. biol. chemistry 1965), Am. Assn. Cancer Research, Am. Soc. Biol. Chemists (pres. 1977), Japanese Biochem. Soc. (hon.), Harvey Soc. (hon.), Sigma Xi, Alpha Omega Alpha. Author: Biochemistry of Amino Acids. Mem. editorial bd. Jour. Biol. Chemistry, 1958-64, asso. editor, 1977—; mem. editorial bd. Biochem. Preparations, 1957-64, Biochemistry, 1962-71, 80—, Methods in Biochem. Analysis, 1963—, Biochimica et Biophysica Acta, 1965-77; mem. editorial bd. Ann. Rev. Biochemistry, 1961-65, asso. editor, 1965—. Editor: Advances in Enzymology, 1969—. Contbr. chpts. to books, articles to sci. jours. Address: 1300 York Ave New York NY 10021

MEISTER, CHARLES WALTER, educator; b. Chgo., Jan. 23, 1917; s. Arnold Paul and Hulda (Grossmann) M.; A.B., Central YMCA Coll., Chgo., 1941; M.A., U. Chgo., 1942, Ph.D., 1948; m. Eleanor Lillian Koeneke, Jan. 9, 1943; children—Marilyn Louise, Charles John. Statistician, Commonwealth Edison Co., Chgo., 1934-41; instr. Roosevelt Coll., Chgo., 1948-49; asst. prof., asso. prof. Ariz. State Coll., 1949-52, prof., 1953-65, dean instrn., 1957-65; pres. Eastern N.Mex. U., Portales, 1965-75, prof., 1975-79. Examiner, commr. North Central Assn. Colls. Vice chmn. A.R.C. chpt., 1952-54. Bd. dirs. Community Concert Assn.; pres. N.M. Council Pres., 1965-70. Served from pvt. to capt. AUS, 1942-46. Mem. Nat. Council Tchrs. English, Kappa Delta Pi, Alpha Psi Omega, Phi Eta Sigma, Phi Kappa Phi, Phi Delta Kappa. Contbr. articles to profl. jours. Home: PO Box 6219 Pine AZ 85544

MEISTER, STEVEN GERARD, cardiologist; b. Boston, Sept. 13, 1937; s. Harry and Edith (Segal) M.; B.A., Bowdoin Coll., 1958; M.D., Tufts U., 1962; m. Carol Anne Ross, Jan. 28, 1966; children—Laura Ilise, Elizabeth Lee. Intern in medicine Ind. U. Med. Center, Indpls., 1962-63; asst. resident in medicine Boston VA Hosp., 1965-66, resident in medicine, 1966-67; research fellow in medicine Boston City Hosp., 1967-68; research fellow in medicine Peter Bent Brigham Hosp., Boston, 1968-70; research fellow in cardiology Tufts U., 1967-68, Harvard U., 1968-70; practice medicine specializing in cardiology, Phila., 1970—; dir. cardiac catheterization lab. Med. Coll. Pa. and Hosp., 1973—, acting dir. div. cardiology, 1978-79; asst. prof. medicine U. Pa., Phila., 1970-73; asso. prof. medicine Med. Coll. Pa. and Hosp., 1973-78, prof., 1978—; cons. cardiology VA hosps. Served to capt. U.S. Army, 1963-65. Diplomate Am. Bd. Internal Medicine. Fellow A.C.P., Am. Coll., Cardiology; mem. Am. Fedn. Clin. Research, Am. Heart Assn. (Upper Atlantic research com. 1977—), Phila. Acad. Cardiology. Contbr. numerous articles on cardiology to profl. jours.

MEITES, LOUIS, educator, chemist; b. Balt., Dec. 6, 1926; s. Louis and Gertrude (Harand) M.; B.A., Middlebury Coll., 1945; M.A., Harvard, 1946, Ph.D., 1947; m. Thelma Steinberg, June 10, 1947 (div. 1979); children—Judith Ann, Norman Louis, Robin Leslie; m. 2d, Ruth Schwartz Schaefer, Jan. 10, 1979. Instr. Princeton, 1947-48; faculty Yale, 1948-55, asst. prof., 1952-55; faculty Poly. Inst. Bklyn., 1955-68, prof. chemistry, 1962-68; chmn. dept. chemistry Clarkson Coll. Tech., Potsdam, N.Y., 1968—. Mem. Am. Chem. Soc. (alternate councilor N.Y. sect. 1963-65), Internat. Union Pure and Applied Chemistry. Author: Polarographic Techniques, 1955, 2d edit., 1965; (with Henry C. Thomas) Advanced Analytical Chemistry, 1958; (with Petr Zuman, others) Electrochemical Data, 1974; CRC Handbook Series in Organic Electrochemistry, Vols. 1 and 2, 1977, Vol. 3, 1978, Vol. 4, 1979; CRC Handbook Series in Inorganic Chemistry, Vol. 1, 1980; also numerous articles; contbg. author, editor Handbook of Analytical Chemistry, 1963. Editorial adv. bd. Chem. Analysis Series, 1965-76, Talanta, 1966—, Analysis Letters, 1979—; editor Critical Revs. Analytical Chemistry, 1970-74; co-editor: Pergamon Series in Analytical Chemistry, 1978—; Research thermoanalytical and electroanalytical chemistry, controlled—potential electrolysis and coulometry, differential thermometry and ebulliometry, rates and mechanisms chem. reactions in solutions, theory potentiometric, other titration curves, data-handling techniques, machine interpretation of chem. data. Home: 22 Circle Dr Potsdam NY 13676

MEITZEN, MANFRED OTTO, educator; b. Houston, Dec. 12, 1930; s. Otto Hugo and Laura Emma (Munsch) M.; B.A., Rice U., 1952; M.Div., Wartburg Sem., 1956; Ph.D., Harvard, 1961; m. Fredrica Haden Kilmer, May 16, 1970. Asso. prof. religious studies Rocky Mountain Coll., Billings, Mont., 1961-65; prof. religious studies, chmn. dept. W.Va. U., Morgantown, 1965—, chmn. program humanities Coll. Arts and Scis., 1972-77; mem. senate, 1968-74, 76—. Vis. scholar Christ Ch. Coll. Oxford (Eng.) U., 1973; columnist Morgantown Dominion-Post, 1975-76. Harvard Div. Sch. scholar, 1957, fellow, 1958; Rockefeller fellow, 1959-60; Sheldon Traveling fellow, 1961; W.Va. U. Study grantee, 1970. Mem. Am. Guild Organists, Am. Acad. Religion, W.Va. Assn. for Humanities (pres. 1976-77), Harvard Alumni Assn., Univ. Profs. for Acad. Order (nat. 1st v.p. 1977—), Am. Rifle Assn., Rice U. Alumni Assn., Harvard Found. for Advanced Study and Research, Delta Phi Alpha. Episcopalian. Contbr. articles to profl. jours. Home: 119 Forest Dr Morgantown WV 26505

MEIXNER, JOHN, educator, author; b. Queens, N.Y., June 6, 1925; s. John Albert and Lena (Magenheimer) M.; student Columbia, 1943-45; A.B., Coll. City N.Y., 1951; A.M., Brown U., 1953, Ph.D., 1957; 1 son, John Reed. Reporter, N.Y. Times, 1947-48; instr. Brown U., 1953-56, Clark U., 1956-57; instr. U. Kans. at Lawrence, 1957-60, asst. prof., 1960-63, asso. prof., 1963-68; prof. English, Rice U., 1968—. Mem. Modern Lang. Assn., Am. Assn. U. Profs. Author: Ford Madox Ford's Novels, 1962; (play) Leaves, 1970 (produced in Houston 1977); (play) Women and Men, 1972 (produced in Houston 1979). Home: 4655 Wild Indigo 295 Houston TX 77027

MEKEEL, HERBERT SURFACE, clergyman; b. Dayton, Ohio, Feb. 14, 1904; s. Herbert Simeon and Octavia (Surface) M.; A.B., U. Mich.; student Andover Newton Theol. Sch., New Coll., U. Edinburgh, Scotland. Ordained, 1935; minister First United Ch., Swampscott, Mass., 1933-35; asst. and asso. minister of First Presbyn. Ch., Edmonton, Alberta, Can., 1935-36; interim minister St. Andrews Ch., Ottawa, Can., 1936-37, First Presbyn. Ch., Schenectady, 1937—; asso. prof., dean Fuller Theol. Sem., Pasadena, Cal., 1949-50. Pres., trustee Albany Bible Inst., N.Y., 1946-79; trustee Camp Pattersonville, 1948—, Gordon Coll., 1948-57; bd. dirs. Schenectady County Humane Soc., 1977—. Mem. Nat. Assn. Evangelicals (pres. 1958-60), N.Y. State Assn. Evangelicals (dir. 1979—). Home: Ennis Farm Route 3 Ennis Rd Schenectady NY 12306 Office: 115 Union St Schenectady NY 12305

MEKKA, EDDIE, actor; b. Worcester, Mass., June 14, student Worcester State Coll., Boston Conservatory Music. Broadway debut in Jumper; other stage appearances include The Magic Show, The Lieutenant, Kiss Me Kate, Sugar, Damn Yankees; regular on ABC-TV series Laverne and Shirley, 1976—; other TV appearances include: Happy Days, Blansky's Beauties, Dinah, The Merv Griffin Show, The $20,000 Pyramid, Love Boat, Fantasy Island. Office: care ABC Public Relations 1330 Ave of Americas New York NY 10019*

MELADY, THOMAS PATRICK, univ. pres., author, former ambassador; b. Norwich, Conn., Mar. 4, 1927; B.A., Duquesne U., 1950; M.A., Cath. U. Am., 1952, Ph.D., 1954; hon. doctorates from 10 univs.; m. Margaret Judith Badum; children—Christina, Monica. Former mem. faculties Fordham and St. John's Univs.; founder Inst. African Affairs Duquesne U., 1957; cons. to founds., govts., corps., 1959-67; pres. Africa Service Inst.; prof. Afro-Asian affairs, chmn. dept. Asian studies and NonWestern civilization Seton Hall U., South Orange, N.J., 1967-69, prof. Afro-Asian affairs, dir. Office of Internat. Studies, 1973-74; exec. v.p., prof. politics St. Joseph's Coll., Phila., 1974-76; pres. Sacred Heart U., Bridgeport, Conn., 1976—, prof. polit. sci., 1976—; ambassador to Burundi, 1969-72; ambassador to Uganda, 1972-73; sr. adviser to U.S. del. to 25 UN Gen. Assembly, 1970. Formerly adviser to African heads of state. Knighted by Pope Paul VI, 1968. Author 11 books including House Divided, Family of Man, Development: Lessons for the Future, Burundi: The Tragic Years; Uganda: Asian Exiles; Idi Amin Dada: Hitler in Africa. Office: Sacred Heart U Box 6460 Bridgeport CT 06606

MELAND, BERNARD EUGENE, educator, theologian; b. Chgo., June 28, 1899; s. Erick Bernhard and Elizabeth (Hansen) M.; A.B., Park Coll., 1923, D.D., 1956; student U. Ill., 1918, 23-24, McCormick Theol. Sem., 1924-25; B.D., U. Chgo., 1928. Ph.D., 1929; postgrad. U. Marburg, Germany, 1928-29; m. Margaret Evans McClusky, Aug. 6, 1926 (dec.); children—Bernard Eugene (dec.), Richard Dennis. Ordained to ministry Presbyn. Ch., 1928; prof. religion and philosophy Central Coll., Fayette, Mo., 1929-36; asso. prof. religion, head dept. Pomona Coll., Claremont, Calif., 1936-43, prof. religion, 1943-45, Clark lectr., 1947; prof. constructive theology U. Chgo., 1945-64, prof. emeritus Div. Sch., 1964, vis. prof. theology, 1965-68, pastors inst. lectr. Div. Sch., 1945; vis. prof. philosophy of religion Union Theol. Sem., N.Y.C., 1968-69; Hewitt vis. prof. humanities Ottawa U. (Kans.), 1971; Barrows lectr., Calcutta and Bangalore, India, Rangoon, Burma; vis. lectr. Serampore Coll. (India), 1957-58; Burrows lectr. U. Calcutta, Poona, 1964-65. Served with U.S. Army, 1918. Mem. Am. Theol. Soc. (v.p. 1951-52, pres. Midwest div. 1960-61). Author: Modern Man's Worship, 1934; (with H.N. Wieman) American Philosophies of Religion, 1936; Write Your own Ten Commandments, 1938; The Church and Adult Education, 1939; Seeds of Redemption, 1947; America's Spiritual Culture, 1948; The Reawakening of Christian Faith, 1949; Higher Education and the Human Spirit, 1953; Faith and Culture, 1953; The Realities of Faith: The Revolution in Cultural Forms, 1962; The Secularization of Modern Cultures, 1966; co-editor: Jour. Religion, 1946-64; The Future of Empirical Theology, 1969; Fallible Forms and Symbols, 1976. Home: 5842 Stony Island Ave Chicago IL 60637

MELAUGH, EDWARD GERARD, razor co. exec.; b. Boston, Feb. 3, 1917; s. John A. and Mary (Gately) M.; B.B.A., Boston U., 1941; m. Juliette Fauroux, Dec. 23, 1944; children—Michael G., Anne Marie, Patricia D. With Gillette Co., Boston, 1954—, controller, v.p., treas. Gillette Safety Razor Co. subs., 1960-65, asst. corporate controller and controller Gillette Products group, v.p., 1965-68, v.p. control and mgmt. services parent co., 1968-70, sr. v.p. fin., 1970—; dir. Shawnut Needham Bank N.A. Bd. dirs. Mass. Taxpayers Found. Served to maj. AUS, 1941-45, 50-52. Decorated Silver Star, Bronze Star; C.P.A., Mass. Mem. Am. Inst. C.P.A.'s, Fin. Execs. Inst., Mass. Soc. C.P.A.'s, Nat. Assn. Accountants. Clubs: Charles River Country, Algonquin (Boston). Home: 19 Cimino Rd Needham Heights MA 02194 Office: Prudential Tower Bldg Boston MA 02199

MELBIN, MURRAY, sociologist; b. N.Y.C., Sept. 26, 1927; s. Hyman and Anna (Boiucaner) M.; student CCNY, 1947-48; B.A., N.Y. U., 1951; M.S., Cornell U., 1954; Ph.D., U. Mich., 1959; m. Nina vonEggers Frank, Mar. 27, 1965; children—Laura, Anna. Extramural lectr. Ibadan U., Nigeria and Makerere Coll., Uganda, 1954; instr. Harvard U. Med. Sch., 1960-61, lectr. univ., 1961-65; asst. sociologist Mass. Gen. Hosp., 1966-69; prof. sociology Boston U., 1969—; vis. prof. U. London, 1975-76; cons. Ga. Dept. Health, N.J. Dept. Health, VA Mass., U.S. Mental Health Study Center, HEW. Active, ACLU, Council for a Livable World, Common Cause. Served with U.S. Army, 1945-46. Russell Sage Found. residency fellow, 1959-61; research grantee NSF, 1959-61, NIMH, 1963-66, 72-80, NIH, 1967-69. Mem. Am. Sociol. Assn., AAAS (Socio-Psychol. prize 1978), Internat. Soc. for Study of Time. Author: Alone and With Others: A Grammar of Interpersonal Behavior, 1972. Asso. editor, Am. Sociol. Rev., 1978—. Office: Dept Sociology Boston U Boston MA 02215

MELBO, IRVING ROBERT, educator; b. Gully, Minn., June 20, 1908; s. Hans H. and Hilda J. (Bergdahl) M.; A.B., N.Mex. State Tchrs. Coll., Silver City, 1930, M.A., 1932; Ed.D., U. Calif. at Berkeley, 1934; postgrad. Columbia Tchrs. Coll., 1936-37; LL.D., U. So. Calif., 1975, Pepperdine U., 1975; m. Lucile Hays, May 30, 1931; 1 son, Robert Irving; m. 2d, Virginia Archer, May 15, 1970. Prin. pub. elementary schs., Minn., 1927-28; research asst. to pres. N.Mex. State Tchrs. Coll., 1928-30, instr. social sci., supr. student tchrs., 1930-33; staff mem. div. textbooks and publs. Calif. Dept. Edn., Sacramento, 1934-35; dir. dept. research and curriculum Oakland (Calif.) Pub. Sch., 1935-38; dept. supt. and dir. curriculum Alameda Co. Schs., Oakland, 1938-39; prof. ednl. adminstrn. U. So. Calif., Los Angeles, 1939—, dean Sch. Edn., 1953-73, dir. sch. surveys, 1946—; Distinguished prof. edn. Pepperdine U., Los Angeles, 1975—. Vis. prof. edn. Kan., 1937, 38, U. Utah, 1951, U. Wis., 1953, U. Hawaii, 1956, 60. Pres. Melbo Assos., Inc.; dir. Founders Savs. and Loan Assn., Los Angeles. Mem. Calif. Bd. Edn. Accreditation Com., 1953-63, chmn., 1960-61; mem. adv. council Ednl. Policies Commn.; mem. citizens mgmt. rev. com. Los Angeles City Schs., 1975. Bd. dirs. S.W. Regional Lab. Ednl. Research; trustee Flintridge Prep. Sch. for Boys, La Canada, Calif. Served as lt. USNR, 1943-44; ETO, MTO. Recipient Spl. Freedom Leadership award Freedom Found. at Valley Forge, 1965; Exceptional Service medal USAF, 1968; Irving R. Melbo endowed professorship established in his honor, 1974. Mem. Am. Assn. Sch. Adminstrs., Calif. Congress Parents and Tchrs. (hon. life), Gen. Alumni Assn. U. So. Calif. (hon. life), Phi Delta Kappa. Author: Our America, rev. edit., 1948; Social Psychology of Education, 1937; The American Scene, 1942; Young Neighbors in South America, 1944; Our Country's National Parks, vols. 1 and 2, 1941, 50, 61, 64, 73; (with S.P. Poole and T.F. Barton) The World About Us, 1949. Home: 918 Afton Rd San Marino CA 91108 also 4100 Maritime Dr Palos Verdes Peninsula CA Office: U So Calif Los Angeles CA 90015

MELBY, EDWARD CARLOS, JR., veterinarian; b. Burlington, Vt., Aug. 10, 1929; s. Edward C. and Dorothy H. (Folsom) M.; student U. Pa., 1948-50; D.V.M., Cornell U., 1954; m. Jean Day File, Aug. 15, 1953; children—Scott E., Susan J., Jeffrey T., Richard A. Practice veterinary medicine, Middlebury, Vt., 1954-62; instr. lab. animal medicine Johns Hopkins U. Sch. Medicine, Balt., 1962-64, asst. prof., 1964-66, asso. prof., 1966-71, prof., dir. div. lab. animal medicine, 1971-74; prof. medicine, dean Coll. Veterinary Medicine, Cornell U., Ithaca, N.Y., 1974—; cons. VA, Nat. Research Council, NIH. Served with USMC, 1946-48. Diplomate Am. Coll. Lab. Animal Medicine. Mem. Am., N.Y. State, So. Tier, Vt. veterinary med. assns., Am. Assn. Lab. Animal Sci., Am. Coll. Lab. Animal Medicine, Am. Assn. Accreditation Lab. Animal Care, AAAS, Phi Zeta. Author: Handbook of Laboratory Animal Science, Vols. I, II, III, 1974-76. Home: 625 Highland Rd Ithaca NY 14850

MELBY, JAMES CHRISTIAN, physician, educator; b. Duluth, Minn., Feb. 14, 1928; s. Leonard and Frances (Sullivan) M.; B.S., U. Minn., 1951, M.D., 1953; m. Mary E. O'Brien, June 25, 1955; children—Christian Leonard, Elizabeth Ann. Intern dept. medicine U. Minn. Hosps., Mpls., 1953-54, resident, 1955-58; part-time practice medicine specializing in internal medicine, endocrinology and metabolism Univ. Hosp., Boston, 1962—; instr. U. Minn., 1958-59; asst. prof. U. Ark., 1959-62, asso. prof., 1961-62; asso. prof. medicine Boston U., 1962-69, prof., 1969—; head sect. endocrinology and metabolism Univ. Hosp., Boston U. Med. Center; vis. physician Boston City Hosp., Univ. Hosp.; mem. VA merit rev. bd. in endocrinology. Served with AUS, 1946-48. Diplomate Am. Bd. Internal Medicine. Mem. AMA, Assn. Am. Physicians, Am. Diabetes Assn., Am. Soc. Clin. Investigation, Endocrine Soc., Am. Fedn. Clin. Research, Central Soc. Clin. Research, AAAS, Am. Coll. Clin. Pharmacology, AAUP, Sigma Xi, Alpha Omega Alpha. Mem. editorial bd. Jour. Clin. Endocrinology and Metabolism; cons. editor Am. Jour. Medicine; editor Jour. Steroid Biochemistry; contbr. articles to profl. jours. Home: 26 Meredith Circle Milton MA 02186 Office: Univ Hosp 75 E Newton St Boston MA 02118

MELBY, ORVILLE ERLING, banker; b. Butte, Mont., Oct. 9, 1921; s. Ole and Esther (Jacobsen) M.; B.A. magna cum laude, U. Wash., 1949; m. Arvilla L. Underland, Nov. 24, 1956; children—Steve E., James E., Ann-Margaret. Treas., Boeing Co., 1956-66; sr. v.p. fin. Continental Airlines, Los Angeles, 1966; v.p. Bank of Am., San Francisco, 1967; treas. Bendix Corp., Detroit, 1968; v.p., treas. Vought Aeronautics, Dallas, 1969-70; v.p., treas. Bonanza Internat., Dallas, 1971-74; exec. v.p. world banking div. Rainier Nat. Bank, Seattle, 1974—; dir. Kings County Med. Blue Shield, Hillhaven Inc. Served with USAAF, 1942-46. C.P.A., Wash., Oreg. Mem. Fin. Execs. Inst., Phi Beta Kappa. Presbyterian. Mason. Home: 1453 86th Ave Bellevue WA 98004 Office: Rainier Nat Bank PO Box 3966 Seattle WA 98124

MELCHER, GEORGE W., JR., physician; b. Portsmouth, Va., Aug 24, 1922; s. George W. and Estelle (Rea) M.; B.A., Colo. Coll., 1943; M.D., Columbia U., 1946; children—Merrick, Paula, Ellen, Laura, George, John G. Practice medicine specializing in internal medicine, N.Y.C.; formerly instr. Columbia U. Sch. Pub. Health, now asso. clin. prof. internal medicine; asso. attending physician Presbyn. Hosp., N.Y.C.; pres. Health Care Inst. N.Y.C.; pres. Group Health, Inc., N.Y.C.; pres. Grough Health Ins. of N.J., N.Y.C. Pres. Nat. Genetics Found., Council of Mgmt., Internat. Fedn. Health Service Funds, Dublin, Ireland; dir. West Side Assn. Commerce, N.Y.C. Bd. dirs. Health Systems Agy. of N.Y.C. Served to capt. AUS, 1947-49. Diplomate Am. Bd. Internal Medicine. Fellow N.Y. Acad. Medicine; mem. A.C.P., N.Y. County, N.Y. (del.) med. socs., AMA. Clubs: N.Y. Athletic, N.Y. U. (N.Y.C.). Contbr. articles to med. jours. Home: 230 W 41st St New York NY 10036 Office: 326 W 42d St New York NY 10036

MELCHER, JAMES RUSSELL, educator; b. Giard, Iowa, July 5, 1936; s. Melvin Charles and Opal Maxine (Getty) M.; B.S. in Elec. Engring., Iowa State U., 1957, M.S. in Nuclear Engring., 1958; Ph.D., Mass. Inst. Tech., 1962; m. Janet Louise Damman, June 15, 1957; children—Jennifer, Eric, Douglas. Mem. faculty Mass. Inst. Tech., 1962—, asst. prof., 1962-66, asso. prof., 1966-69, prof. elec. engring., 1969—; Guggenheim fellow Churchill Coll., Cambridge, Eng., 1972; cons. to industry 1962—. Recipient first Mark Mills award Am. Nuclear Soc., 1958, Western Electric Fund award New Eng. sect. Am. Soc. Engring. Edn., 1969, Young Alumnus Recognition Ia. State U., 1971. Fellow IEEE, Am. Soc. Engring. Edn., Am. Phys. Soc., Am. Chem. Soc., Sigma Xi, Tau Beta Pi. Author: Field-Coupled Surface Waves, 1963; (with H.H. Woodson) Electromechanical Dynamics, 1969. Research and publ. in continuum electromechanics, continuum feedback control, energy conversion, electrohydrodynamics, air-pollution control, electromech. precipitation and coalescence of particles, electromechanics of electrochem. and biol. systems. Patentee: maker films for Nat. Com. Elec. Engring. Films. Home: 29 Fairlawn Ln Lexington MA 02173 Office: Mass Inst Tech Cambridge MA 02139

MELCHER, JOHN, U.S. senator; b. Sioux City, Iowa, Sept. 6, 1924; student U. Minn., 1942-43; D.V.M., Iowa State U., 1950; m. Ruth Klein, Dec. 1, 1945; children—Terry, Joan, Mary, Robert, John. Partner Yellowstone Valley Vet. Clinic, Forsyth, Mont., also operator cattle feed lot; alderman, Forsyth, 1953-55, mayor, 1955-61; mem. Mont. Ho. of Reps. from Rosebud County, 1961-62, 69, Mont. Senate, 1963-67; mem. 91st-94th congresses from 2d Mont. Dist.; U.S. senator from Mont., 1977—. Former mem. Mont. Legis. Council. Democratic candidate for U.S. Ho. of Reps., 1966. Served with AUS, 1943-45; ETO. Decorated Purple Heart. Democrat. Home: Forsyth MT 59327 Office: Senate Office Bldg Washington DC 20515

MELCHER, JOHN HENRY, JR., lawyer; b. Cleve., May 19, 1928; s. John Henry and Marian Louise (Clark) M.; B.A., Williams Coll., 1952; J.D., Harvard, 1955; m. Eleanor Ruth Dowling, July 23, 1955; children—Marian, Elisabeth, Cynthia, John Henry III. Admitted to Ohio bar, 1955; asso. with firm Thompson, Hine & Flory, Cleve., 1955-73, partner, 1966-73; gen. counsel Am. Shipbldg. Co., Cleve., 1967—, exec. v.p., 1973—, also dir. Bd. dirs. Health Hill Hosp., Cleve. Mem. Am., Cleve. bar assns. Episcopalian (vestryman 1967-71). Clubs: Kirtland Country (Ohio); Union, Tavern (Cleve.). Home: 19700 Shaker Blvd Shaker Heights OH 44122 Office: 1 Erieview Plaza Cleveland OH 44114

MELCHERT, JAMES FREDERICK, artist; b. New Bremen, Ohio, Dec. 2, 1930; s. John Charles and Hulda Lydia (Egli) M.; A.B., Princeton U., 1952; M.F.A., U. Chgo., 1957; M.A., U. Calif., Berkeley, 1961; m. Mary Ann Hostetler, June 18, 1954; children—Christopher, David, Renee. Instr. art Carthage (Ill.) Coll., 1957-59; head ceramics dept. San Francisco Art Inst., 1961-65; prof. art U. Calif., Berkeley, 1965-76; dir. Visual Arts Program, Nat. Endowment for Arts, Washington, 1977—; exhibited in one man shows at San Francisco Art Inst., 1970, San Francisco Mus. Modern Art, 1975; exhibited in group shows at Biennale de Paris, 1963, Whitney Mus., N.Y.C., 1966, 68, 70, Documenta 5, Kassel, Germany, 1972, Sydney (Australia) Biennal, 1976. Recipient Adaline Kent award San Francisco Art Inst., 1970; Woodrow Wilson fellow, 1960-61, Louis Comfort Tiffany fellow, 1964, Nat. Endowment for Arts artist fellow, 1973. Home: 3125 Adams Mill Rd NW Washington DC 20010 Office: Visual Arts Program Nat Endowment for Arts Washington DC 20506

MELCHIOR, KURT WERNER, lawyer; b. Essen, Germany, Oct. 30, 1924; s. Rudolf and Anna (Meyer) M.; came to U.S., 1938, naturalized, 1943; Ph.B., U. Chgo., 1943, M.A., 1949; LL.B., Yale U., 1951; m. Suzanne Ellen Sabin, Feb. 27, 1959; children—Karen Anne, Katherine Sabin. Admitted to D.C. bar, 1951, Ill. bar, 1951, Calif. bar, 1957, U.S. Supreme Ct. bar, 1956; asst. counsel U.S. Senate Preparedness Subcom., 1951-52; atty. Office Price Stblzn., 1952-53; spl. asst. to U.S. atty. gen. Tax Div., Dept. Justice, 1953-56; practice law, San Francisco, 1956-60; asso., mem. firm Severson, Werson, Berke & Melchior and predecessors, San Francisco, 1960—; lectr. Golden Gate Law Sch., 1960-68. Mem. Calif. Gov.'s Com. on Family, 1966; bd. dirs. Nat. Assn. Mental Health, 1967-73, chmn. pub. affairs com., 1972; v.p., bd. dirs. San Francisco Home Health Service, 1969, 72-75; bd. dirs. San Francisco Assn. for Mental Health, 1959-72, pres., 1960-61; former bd. dirs. Calif. Assn. Mental Health; pres. San Francisco Suicide Prevention, 1967-70, French Am. Bilingual Sch. of San Francisco, 1973-75; past trustee Wright Inst.; mem. human research com. Presbyn. Hosp., Pacific Med. Center, 1973-75. Served with AUS, 1943-46. Mem. Am. (ho. of dels. 1978—), San Francisco (dir. 1973-75, past chmn. various coms.) bar assns., State Bar Calif. (bd. govs. 1975-78, v.p. 1977-78, bd. legal specialization 1979—, jud. nominees evaluation com. 1978—). Home: 159 Miraloma Dr San Francisco CA 94127 Office: 1 Embarcadero Center San Francisco CA 94111

MELCHIOR, LOUIS G., retail exec.; b. Chgo., Dec. 31, 1919; s. William A. and Laura (Stern) M.; B.S. in Law, Northwestern U., 1941, LL.B., 1947; M.B.A., U. Chgo., 1953; m. Bertha Katz, Sept. 4, 1947; children—Paul W., Alan L. Admitted to Ill. bar, 1947; with firm Sonnenschein, Berkson, Lautman, Levinson & Morse, Chgo., 1947-50; with Goldblatt Bros., Inc., Chgo., 1950-63, financial v.p., 1959-63; v.p., treas. City Stores Co., N.Y.C., 1964-68, exec. v.p., treas., 1968-75, also dir.; v.p.-fin., treas. Edison Bros. Stores, Inc., St. Louis, 1975—, also dir.; dir. Mark Twain Bancshares, Inc., St. Louis. Bd. dirs. Ill. Retail Mchts. Assn., 1959-63, Nat. Retail Mchts. Assn., 1970-75. Served to capt., Signal Corp, AUS, 1941-45. Mem. Northwestern U. Law Alumni Assn. (dir. 1948-55), Order of Coif. Home: 5 Coach 'n Four Lane Saint Louis MO 63131 Office: 400 Washington Ave Saint Louis MO 63102

MELCZER, JOSEPH TREUHAFT, JR., lawyer; b. Phoenix, Nov. 13, 1912; s. Joseph T. and Hazel (Goldberg) M.; A.B., Stanford, 1934, J.D., 1937; m. Mary Alicia Farrell, Sept. 9, 1947; children—Joseph Treuhaft III, Patricia Ann Kaufman. Admitted to Ariz. bar, 1938, since practiced in Phoenix; partner firm Snell & Wilmer, 1947—; dir. Valley Nat. Bank Ariz. Sec. Phoenix Thunderbirds, 1946. Bd. dirs. Barrow Neurol. Found., Theodore Roosevelt council Boy Scouts Am. Bd. dirs. Ariz. Hist. Found., Tracy Found.; bd. regents emeritus Brophy Coll. Prep.; bd. visitors Stanford U. Law Sch., 1970-72, 79—. Served to maj. USAAF, 1942-46. Mem. Am., Ariz., Maricopa County bar assns., Am. Judicature Soc. Clubs: Phoenix 20-30 (pres. 1941), Phoenix Country, Paradise Valley Country, Kiva, Arizona (Phoenix). Home: 317 E Glenn Dr Phoenix AZ 85020 Office: 3100 Valley Center Phoenix AZ 85073

MELDRUM, ALAN HAYWARD, educator; b. Lethbridge, Alta., Can., May 24, 1913; s. William and Phyllis (Hayward) M.; B.Sc., U. Alta., 1938; B.S., U. Okla., 1946, M.S., 1947; Ph.D., Pa. State U., 1954; m. Erma Goodwin, May 31, 1947. Coke oven chemist Algoma Steel Corp., Sault Ste. Marie, Ont., Can., 1938-44; refinery chemist Brit. Am. Oil Refining Co., Clarkson, Ont., 1944-45; research asso. Pa. State U., 1947- 54; mem. faculty U. N.D., Grand Forks, 1954—, prof. petroleum engring., 1959-62, prof. indsl. engring., 1962—, chmn. dept., 1967—. Registered profl. engr., N.D. Mem. Am. Inst. Indsl. Engrs., Am. Assn. U. Profs., N.D. Acad. Sci., N.D. Soc. Profl. Engrs. (pres. 1972), Nat. Soc. Profl. Engrs., Sigma Xi, Sigma Tau. Episcopalian. Mason (Shriner), Elk, Lion. Home: Box 8144 University Sta Grand Forks ND 58202

MELENDEZ, JOSE CUAUHTEMOC, animator, production co. exec.; b. Mexico, Nov. 15, 1916; s. Romon Melendez Rodriguez and Sarah Vasquez Freaner; came to U.S., 1924, naturalized, 1945; student Chouinard Art Sch., 1938-41; m. Helen Huhn, Sept. 1, 1940; children—Rodrigo, Steven. Animator, Walt Disney, 1938-41, Warner Bros., 1942-49, U.P.A., 1949-51, John Sutherland Prodns., 1951-55, Playhouse Pic's, 1955-63; pres. Bill Melendez Prodns., Los Angeles, 1964—. Served with inf., AUS, 1945. Mem. TV Acad., Assn. Internat. au Film D'Animation, Motion Picture Acad., Nat. Cartoonists Soc. Office: 439 N Larchmont Blvd Los Angeles CA 90004

MELENDY, HOWARD BRETT, educator, historian; b. Eureka, Calif., May 3, 1924; s. Howard Burton and Pearl Marjorie (Brett) M.; student Humboldt State Coll., 1942-45; A.B. in English, Stanford, 1946, M.A. in Edn., 1948, Ph.D. in History, 1952; m. Marian Ethel Robinson, Mar. 29, 1952; children—Brenda Dale, Darcie Brett, Lisa Marie. Tchr., Theodore Roosevelt High Sch., Fresno, Calif., 1950-54; instr. Fresno City Coll., 1954-55; faculty San Jose State Coll., 1955-69, prof. history, 1961-69, head dept., 1958-65, chmn. dept., 1965-69, asst. v.p., 1968-69, acting acad. v.p., 1969, dean undergrad. studies, 1979—; interim dean for acad. devel. U. Hawaii, Honolulu, 1970, v.p. for community colls., 1970-73, prof. history, 1970-79; reader in Am. history advanced placement exam. Ednl. Testing Service, 1961-74; chmn. Hawaii Com. for Humanities, 1977-79. Grantee Am. Philos. Soc. 1962, 74; Am. Council Edn. fellow in acad. adminstrn., 1967-68; Nat. Endowment for Humanities Edn. Planning grantee, 1975-76, 76-78. Mem. Am. Hist. Assn., NEA. Presbyterian (ruling elder). Author: (with Benjamin F. Gilbert) Governors of California, 1965; Oriental Americans, 1972; Asians in America, 1977. Contbr. Ency. Americana, Ency. Brit., hist. jours.; contbr. chpts. to books. Office: San Jose State U Washington Sq San Jose CA 95192

MELERVEY, ARTHUR CHARLES, food chain exec.; b. Jersey City, June 18, 1923; s. Arthur C., Sr., and Grace C. (Russo) M.; B.A., U. Va., 1944; J.D., Columbia U., 1948; m. Mabel G. Pedersen, Dec. 27, 1945; children—Kevin, Brian. Admitted to N.Y. State bar, 1949; asso. firm James Maxwell Fassett, N.Y.C., 1949, McLanahan, Merritt & Ingraham, N.Y.C., 1949-51; mem. legal staff Gt. Atlantic & Pacific Tea Co., Inc., N.Y.C., 1951-73, asst. gen. counsel, 1973-75, corp. sec., 1975—; officer, dir. various subsidiaries. Mem. Republican Town Com., Pelham, N.Y., 1946-48, Com. on Selection of Sch. Bd., Mamaroneck, N.Y., 1960-62. Served to lt. (j.g.), USNR, 1943-46. Mem. Assn. Bar City N.Y., N.Y. State Bar Assn., Am. Soc. Corp. Secs., U.S. Polo Assn. (del. 1975-76), Sigma Nu. Home: 136 N Chatsworth Ave Larchmont NY 10538 Office: 2 Paragon Dr Montvale NJ 07645

MELHORN, WILTON NEWTON, educator; b. Sistersville, W.Va., July 8, 1921; s. Ralph Wilton and Pauline (Jones) M.; B.S., Mich. State U., 1942, M.S., 1951; M.S., N.Y. U., 1943; Ph.D., U. Mich., 1955; m. Agnes Leigh Beck, Aug. 25, 1961; children—Kristina L., Kimberly M. Hydrogeologist Mich. Geol. Survey, Lansing, 1946-49; hydrologist U.S. Weather Bur., Indpls., 1949-50; asst., then asso. prof. engring. geology Purdue U., Lafayette, Ind., 1954-70, head dept. geoscis., 1967-70, prof., 1970—; vis. prof. U. Ill. at Urbana, 1960-61; vis. prof. U. Nev., Reno, 1971-72, adj. prof., 1973—; geol. cons. Cook County Hwy Commn., Chgo., 1955-56, Martin-Marietta Corp., Balt., 1964-66, Calif. Nuclear, Inc., Lafayette, 1966-68. Served to maj. USAAF, 1942-46. Fellow Geol. Soc. Am., AAAS; mem. Am. Assn. Petroleum Geologists, Soc. Econ. Geologists and Paleontologists, Speleological Soc., Ind. Acad. Scis., Mich. Acad. Arts, Sci. and Letters, Am. Meteorol. Soc., Clay Minerals Soc., Sigma Xi, Sigma Gamma Epsilon, Delta Chi. Contbr. articles to tech. jours. Home: 2065 S 9th St Lafayette IN 47905

MELICAN, JAMES PATRICK, JR., lawyer; b. Worcester, Mass., Sept. 8, 1940; s. James Patrick and Abigail Helen (Donahue) M.; B.A., Fordham U., 1962; J.D., Harvard U., 1965; M.B.A., Mich. State U., 1971; m. Debra A. Burns, Dec. 2, 1978; children—Marlane, James P., David. Admitted to Mich. bar, 1976; supervising atty. product liability sect. Gen. Motors Corp., Detroit, 1971-73, atty.-in-charge trade regulation, 1973-77, atty.-in-charge mktg. and purchasing, 1977—. Mem. Am. Bar Assn., Am. Law Inst. (chmn. research project com.). Roman Catholic. Home: 1039 Whittier Grosse Pointe Park MI 48230 Office: Gen Motors Corp 3044 W Grand Blvd Detroit MI 48202

MELICH, MITCHELL, lawyer, corp. exec.; b. Bingham Canyon, Utah, Feb. 1, 1912; s. Joseph and Mary (Kalembar) M.; LL.B., U. Utah, 1934; m. Doris M. Snyder, June 3, 1935; children—Tanya (Mrs. Noel L. Silverman), Michael, Nancy (Mrs. Timothy J. Funk), Robert A. Admitted to Utah bar, 1934; pvt. practice, Moab, 1934-63; city atty., Moab, 1934-55; county atty., Grand County, 1940-42. Sec., dir. Utex Exploration Co., Moab, 1953-62; pres., dir. Uranium Reduction Co., Moab, 1954-62; cons. to pres. Atlas Minerals, div. Atlas Corp., 1962-67; dir., treas. New Park Mining Co., 1962-65; partner firm Ray, Quinney & Nebeker, 1973—. Solicitor Dept. Interior, Washington, 1969-73. Mem. of Colorado River Com. of Utah, 1945-47; mem. Utah Water and Power Bd., 1947; chmn. Citizens Adv. Com. on Higher Edn., 1968; mem. nat. adv. council U. Utah, 1976—. Mem. Utah Senate, 1942-50, minority leader, 1949-50; mem. Utah Legislative Council, 1949-54; del. Republican Nat. Conv., 1952-72, mem. Rep. Nat. Com. for Utah, 1961-64; Rep. candidate for gov., 1964; cons. on staff Congressman Sherman P. Lloyd, Utah, 1967-68. Bd. dirs. St. Marks Hosp., 1973—; bd. regents U. Utah, 1961-65, also mem. devel. fund com., mem. nat. adv. council, 1968-73, 76—. Recipient Distinguished Alumni award U. Utah, 1969. Mem. Am. Bar Assn., Utah State Bar, Utah Mining Assn. (pres. 1962-63), Kappa Sigma. Republican. Mason (Shriner). Club: Alta Salt Lake Country (Salt Lake City). Home: 900 Donner Way Salt Lake City UT 84108 Office: 400 Deseret Bldg 79 S Main St Salt Lake City UT 84111

MELICK, DERMONT WILSON, surgeon; b. Williams, Ariz., Mar. 3, 1910; s. Prince Albert and Cora (Wilson) M.; B.S., U. Ariz., 1931; M.D., U. Pa., 1935, M.Sc., 1941, D.Sc., 1945; postgrad. surgery U. Wis., 1939-41, 42-45, U. Mich., 1941-42; m. Dorothy Helen Marvel, Jan. 1, 1943; children—Richard Wilson, John Wilson, Penelope Ann Wilson (dec.). Intern, Grad. Hosp., U. Pa., 1935-37; resident U. Wis., 1939-41, U. Mich., 1941-42; instr. surgery U. Wis., Madison, 1942-45; practice medicine, specializing in thoracic and cardiovascular surgery, Phoenix, 1945-67, 77—; prof. surgery, coordinator regional med. program U. Ariz. Coll. Medicine, Tucson, 1967-77. Chmn. Western Interstate Commn. Higher Edn., 1964. Chmn. bd. S.W. Blood Banks, Inc., 1955-67; pres. Sahuaro Med. Arts Found. Served to 1st lt., M.C., AUS, 1941. Recipient Merit medallion U. Ariz., 1960, Distinguished Service award Maricopa County Med. Soc., 1957, Distinguished Citizen award U. Ariz., 1966, Joseph Bank medal, 1967; named (with father) Pioneer Family in Medicine in Ariz., Phoenix Hist. Soc., 1977. Fellow A.C.S.; mem. AMA, Maricopa County (pres. 1951), Ariz. (pres. 1959) med. assns., Sigma Xi, Kappa Sigma, Alpha Kappa Kappa. Republican. Presbyn. Mason (32 deg.). Home: 1614 E Gardenia Ave N Phoenix AZ 85020

MELICK, GAIL, banker; b. Waterloo, Iowa, Jan. 11, 1928; s. Roy Elza and Mary Elizabeth (Quinn) M.; B.A., Carleton Coll., Northfield, Minn., 1952; M.B.A., U. Chgo., 1962; m. Nancy Eaton, Aug. 29, 1953; children—Daniel, Mary, Matthew. With Continental Ill. Bank, Chgo., 1952—, sr. v.p., from 1966, cashier, from 1970, now exec. v.p. ops. and mgmt. services dept.; dir. Tower Products Inc.; bd. dirs. Northwestern U. Banking Research Center. Trustee Lutheran Gen. Hosp.; bd. dirs. Chgo. Crime Commn. Served with USNR, 1946-48. Unitarian. Clubs: Chgo. Econs., Chgo. Bankers, Meadow, Metropolitan. Home: 909 Belle Plaine St Park Ridge IL 60068 Office: 231 S LaSalle St Chicago IL 60693

MELICK, WILLIAM FRANK, urologist; b. St. Louis, Nov. 9, 1914; s. William Grant and Elizabeth (Tweedy) M.; M.D., Washington U., St. Louis, 1939; M.Urology, St. Louis U., 1943; m. Margaret Franklin Rhodes, June 7, 1939 (dec. Dec. 1976); children—Carolyn (Mrs. Burton W. Noll), Margaret (Mrs. Aaron P. Scholnik), Frances (Mrs. Robert M. Slusher, Jr.), William Frank, Mary Katherine; m. 2d, Mary A. McElfresh, Mar. 17, 1979; stepchildren—Peter, Duncan, Stuart, Bruce. Intern, St. Lukes Hosp., St. Louis, 1939-40; resident St. Louis U Hosp., 1940-43; faculty St. Louis U. Sch. Medicine, 1943—, chmn. dept. urology, 1959-71, clin. prof., 1962—. Served with M.C., AUS, 1943-46. Diplomate Am. Bd. Urology. Fellow A.C.S.; mem. A.M.A., Am. Urol. Assn. (exec. com. 1972—; exec. com. central sect. 1964-67, sec. south central sect. 1967-70, pres. 1972, exec. com. 1974-75), Am. Acad. Pediatrics (sect. urology). Home: 302 Planthurst Rd Webster Groves MO 63119 Office: 9115 Brentwood Blvd Saint Louis MO 63105

MELILLO, LOUIS CHARLES, supermarket exec.; b. Somerville, Mass., Nov. 13, 1926; s. Pasquale and Constance (Bimbo) M.; student UCLA, 1960; div.; children—Delaine, Louis, Rodney, Jason. With Boys Market Inc., Pasadena, Calif., 1951—, dir. ops., 1967-70, v.p. ops., 1970-78, exec. v.p., 1978—; mem. faculty UCLA, 1974-78; mem. adv. bd. Job Placement, Pasadena City Coll., 1974-78. Served with USMC, 1944-47, 50-51. Mem. So. Calif. Grocers Assn. (vice chmn. 1974-79, chmn. bd. 1978-79), Western Assn. Food Chains, Food Mktg. Inst., VFW. Democrat. Home: 276 S Marengo Pasadena CA 91101 Office: 1030 S Arroyo Pkwy Pasadena CA 91109

MELIS, FRANCIS KENNETH, investment co. exec., import-export exec.; b. Spokane, Sept. 10, 1917; s. Frank and Ava (Thierman) M.; B.S., N.Y. U., 1948; m. Frances Inez Esson, Dec. 15, 1941; children—Jeanne Melis Mills, Richard K., Gerald K., Darleen D., Carole J. Partner, v.p. F. Eberstadt & Co., Inc., N.Y.C., 1945-62; founder, partner, chmn. N.Y. Securities Co., Inc., N.Y.C., 1962—; mng. trustee Asso. Mortgage Investors, Coral Gables, Fla.; pres. Parmel Import Export Co., Inc., 1979—; owner Melis Land & Cattle Co., 1967—. Trustee F. Kenneth Melis Found., 1966, Marlboro (Vt.) Coll. Served to capt. USAAF, 1940-45. Chartered financial analyst. Mem. N.Y. Soc. Security Analysts. Club: N.Y. Plaza. Home: Linden House Apt 39D 262 Glenbrook Rd Stamford CT 06906 Office: 1290 Ave of Americas New York NY 10019 also Wardsboro VT 05355

MELISSINOS, ADRIAN CONSTANTIN, physicist; b. Thessaloniki, Greece, July 28, 1929; s. Constantin John and Olympia (Abbott) M.; came to U.S., 1955, naturalized, 1970; student Royal Naval Acad., Greece, 1945-48; M.S., Mass. Inst. Tech., 1956, Ph.D., 1958; m. Mary Joyce Mitchell, June 7, 1960; children—Constantin John, Andrew William. Naval cadet Greek Navy, 1945-48, commd. ensign, 1948, advanced through grades to lt., 1951; ret., 1954; teaching and research asst. Mass. Inst. Tech., 1955-58; instr. U. Rochester (N.Y.), 1958-60, asst. prof. physics, 1960-63, asso. prof., 1963-67, prof., 1967—, chmn. dept. physics and astronomy, 1974-77; vis. scientist CERN European Center for Nuclear Research, 1968-69, 77-78; cons. Brookhaven Nat. Lab., 1970-72, 75-79. Decorated Swedish Order of Sword. Fellow Am. Phys. Soc.; mem. Greek Nat. Acad. (corr.). Author: Experiments in Modern Physics, 1966; (with F. Lobkowicz) Physics for Scientists and Engineers, 1975. Home: 177 Whitewood Ln Rochester NY 14618 Office: Dept Physics U Rochester Rochester NY 14627

MELKONIAN, EDWARD, nuclear scientist; b. Alexandria, Egypt, June 29, 1920; s. James and Mary (Chooljian) M.; came to U.S., 1921, naturalized, 1928; B.A., Columbia U., 1940, M.A., 1941, Ph.D. in Physics, 1949; m. Miriam Levin, May 26, 1954; children—David (dec.), Michael, Karen. Lab. asst. physics dept. Columbia U., 1940-41, research asso., 1949-63, prof. nuclear sci. and engring., 1963—; mem. staff Manhattan Project and predecessors at Columbia U. and Oak Ridge Lab., 1941-46; exchange scientist Atomic Energy Research Establishment, Harwell, Eng., 1958-60. Grantee, AEC, ERDA and Dept. Energy, 1946-79; Nat. Def. Research Council grantee, 1941-42; Dept. Energy grantee, 1979—. Fellow Am. Phys. Soc.; mem. Am. Nuclear Soc., AAAS, Sigma Xi. Republican. Research, numerous publs. in neutron physics and fission physics. Home: 35 Claremont Ave New York NY 10027 Office: Columbia U 520 W 120th St New YOrk NY 10027

MELLAM, LEO LESLIE, leasing co. exec.; b. Comstock, Nebr., July 1, 1906; s. Charles and Jennie Myrtle (Reynolds) M.; grad. high sch.; m. Laural Darlene Carey, May 1, 1926; 1 dau., Marilyn Darlene Mellam Rogers. Chmn. bd., chief exec. officer, dir. Flexi-Van Corp., N.Y.C., 1971—. Founder, Leo L. and Laural D. Mellam Found. Clubs: Westchester Country; New York Traffice, New York Athletic. Home: 425 E 58th St New York City NY 10022 Office: 330 Madison Ave New York City NY 10017

MELLEN, ARTHUR WILLIAM, III, bus. exec.; b. N.Y.C., May 28, 1930; s. Arthur William and Ethel (Donnelly) M.; B.Chem.Eng., Cornell U., 1953; grad. Advanced Mgmt. Program, Harvard U.; m. Mary Jane Lind, June 13, 1953; children—Arthur W., Mary Lynn, Robert Lind, Susan Stoddard, Michael Scott, Christopher. Engr., group head Esso Research and Engring. Co., 1956-59, econ. analyst, 1960; sales engr., mktg. mgr. Air Products and Chems., Inc., Allentown, Pa., 1960-69, pres. Cryogenic Systems div., 1969-78, group v.p. process systems group, 1978—; dir. Hopkington LNG Corp. Served with USAF, 1954-56. Mem. Am. Inst. Chem. Engrs. Republican. Roman Catholic. Home: 1800 W Union Blvd Bethlehem PA 18018 Office: PO Box 538 Allentown PA 18105

MELLEN, WILLIAM ROBERT, lawyer; b. Atlanta, Oct. 19, 1930; s. Seth Baldwin and Mary Frances (Brown) M.; B.A., U. Va., 1953; LL.B., U. Ga., 1956; LL.M., N.Y. U., 1960; m. Eleanor Randolph Ruffin, May 28, 1960; children—Eleanor Garnett, Frances Carrick, Lelia Randolph. Admitted to Ga. bar, 1955; partner firm McClain, Mellen, Bowling & Hickman, Atlanta, 1958—; lectr. in field. Pres., Atlanta Estate Planning Council, 1972-73. Served with USAF, 1955-58. Fellow Am. Coll. Probate Counsel; mem. Atlanta, Am. bar assns., State Bar Ga., Chi Phi, Phi Delta Phi, Omicron Delta Kappa. Episcopalian. Clubs: Piedmont Driving, Lake Lanier Sailing, Lawyers'. Author: Drafting of Wills, Georgia Lawyer's Basic Practice Handbook, 1968; contbr. articles to profl. jours. Home: 889 W Wesley Rd NW Atlanta GA 30327 Office: 300 Peachtree Center South 225 Peachtree St NE Atlanta GA 30303

MELLINK, MACHTELD JOHANNA, educator, archaeologist; b. Amsterdam, Holland, Oct. 26, 1917; d. Johan and Machteld (Kruyff) Mellink; B.A., U. Amsterdam, 1938, M.A., 1941; Ph.D., Utrecht (Netherlands) U., 1943. Came to U.S., 1949. Faculty, Bryn Mawr Coll., 1949—, prof. classical and Near Eastern archaeology, 1962—, chmn. dept., 1955—; staff mem. excavations, Tarsus, Turkey, 1947-49, Gordion, Turkey, 1950—; field dir. excavations, Karatas-Semayuk, Lycia, Turkey, 1963—; research asso. U. Mus., U. Pa., 1955—. Fellow Am. Acad. Arts and Scis.; mem. Archaeol. Inst. Am., German Archaeol. Inst., Am. Oriental Soc., Am. Philos. Soc.; corr. mem. Royal Netherlands Acad. Scis., Austrian Archaeol. Inst. (corr.). Contbr. articles to profl. jours. Home: 221 N Roberts Rd Bryn Mawr PA 19010

MELLINKOFF, SHERMAN MUSSOFF, med. sch. dean, physician; b. McKeesport, Pa., Mar. 23, 1920; s. Albert and Helen (Mussoff) M.; B.A., Stanford, 1941, M.D., 1944; m. June O'Connell, Nov. 18, 1944; children—Sherrill M., Albert J. Intern, asst. resident Stanford Hosp., 1944-45; asst. resident Johns Hopkins Hosp., 1947-49, resident, 1950-51, instr. medicine, 1951-53; fellow gastroenterology U. Pa., 1949-50; asst., asso. prof. medicine U. Calif. at Los Angeles Med. Sch., 1953-62, prof. medicine, dean Med. Sch., 1962—; attending cons. internal medicine Wadsworth Gen. Hosp., VA Center, Los Angeles; sr. attending physician Harbor Gen. Hosp., Torrance, Calif. Served to capt. M.C., U.S. Army, 1945-47. Diplomate Am. Bd. Internal Medicine. Mem. Am. Gastroent. Assn., A.C.P., Assn. Am. Physicians, Western Assn. Physicians, Nat. Acad. Scis. Inst. Medicine, A.M.A., Am. Soc. Clin. Nutrition, Western Soc. Clin. Research, Am. Fedn. Clin. Research, A.A.A.S. Contbr. numerous articles to med. jours. Editor: Differential Diagnosis of Abnominal Pain, 1959; Differential Diagnosis of Diarrhea, 1964. Office: U Calif at Los Angeles Med Center Los Angeles CA 90024

MELLIS, JOEL PAUL, communications co. exec.; b. Bronx, N.Y., July 23, 1934; s. Samuel and Yetta (Goldner) M.; B.S. cum laude, N.Y. U., 1956; J.D., Harvard U., 1959; m. Ellen Steinam, July 2, 1967; children—Jon Andrew, James Stephen, Elizabeth Gail. Admitted to N.Y. bar, 1960; sr. atty. SEC, Washington, 1961-63; corp. counsel Raytheon Corp., 1964-65; sr. atty. Gen. Telephone & Electronics Corp., Stamford, Conn., 1965-74, corp. sec., 1974—, also dir. subsidiaries. Served with U.S. Army, 1959-60. Mem. Am. Bar Assn., Assn. Bar City N.Y., Am. Soc. Corp. Secs., Westchester-Fairfield Corp. Counsel Assn., Beta Gamma Sigma. Home: 280 Barncroft Rd Stamford CT 06902 Office: 1 Stamford Forum Stamford CT 06904

MELLISH, DONALD LEROY, banker; b. Fairbanks, Alaska, Nov. 1, 1927; s. William and Monica (Hugg) M.; student U. B.C. (Can.), Vancouver, 1946-47; grad. Pacific Coast Banking Sch., 1963; m. Susan H. Schmelzer; children—Gabriele, John, Robert. With Nat. Bank of Alaska, Anchorage, 1953—, exec. v.p., 1962-65, pres., 1965-75, chmn. bd., 1975—; dir. Seattle br. Fed. Res. Bank San Francisco, 1978—; dir. Alascom Inc.; commr. Alaska Housing Authority, Yukon Taiya Project, 1973-74; mem. Nat. Export Expansion Council, Small Bus. Adv. Council, Regional Adv. Com. on Banking Policies and Practices, 1968-69. Chmn. Alaska Radio Free Europe, 1971-74. Mem. Am. Bankers Assn., Young Pres's. Orgn., Chief Execs. Forum, World Bus. Council, Alaska Nippon Kai. Club: Rotary (Anchorage). Home: 2200 Cliff Ct Anchorage AK 99503 Office: PO Box 600 Anchorage AK 99510

MELLMAN, WILLIAM JULES, geneticist, educator; b. Phila., May 7, 1928; s. Martin William and Freda (Haas) M.; A.B., U. Pa., 1948, M.D., 1952; m. Ruth Behnke, Aug. 30, 1963; children—Lewis Alfred, Andrea Kay. Intern, Phila. Gen. Hosp., 1952-53; resident Hosp. of U. Pa., 1955-58; prof. dept. pediatrics U. Pa., Phila., 1955-72, chmn. dept. human genetics, 1972—. Mem. genetics study sect. NIH, 1974-78. Served with AUS, 1953-55. Mem. Am. Pediatric Soc., Am. Soc. Human Genetics, Phi Beta Kappa. Editor-in-chief Am. Jour. of Human Genetics, 1975-78. Home: 25 University Mews Philadelphia PA 19104

MELLON, PAUL, art gallery exec.; b. Pitts., June 11, 1907; s. Andrew W. and Nora (McMullen) M.; A.B., Yale, 1929, L.H.D. (hon.), 1967; A.B., Cambridge (Eng.) U., 1931, M.A., 1938; Litt.D. (hon.), Oxford U., 1961; LL.D. (hon.), Carnegie Inst. Tech., 1967; m. Mary Conover, Feb. 2, 1935 (dec. Oct. 1946); children—Catherine Conover (Mrs. Ashley Carrithers) Timothy; m. 2d, Rachel Lambert

Lloyd, May 1, 1948. Pres. Nat. Gallery Art, Washington, to 1979, also trustee; trustee Va. Mus. Fine Arts, Richmond, A.W. Mellon Ednl. and Charitable Trust, Pitts.; trustee Andrew W. Mellon Found., N.Y. Asso. fellow Berkeley Coll., Yale; hon. fellow Clare Coll., Cambridge, Eng., St. John's Coll., Annapolis; Benjamin Franklin fellow Royal Soc. Arts, London, 1969. Served from pvt. to 1st lt. Cav., AUS, 1941-43, 1st lt. to maj. overseas service with OSS, 1943-45. Recipient Yale medal award, 1953; Horace Marden Albright Scenic Preservation medal, 1957; award for distinguished service to arts Nat. Inst. Arts and Letters, 1962; Benjamin Franklin medal Royal Soc. Arts, London, 1965; Skowhegan Gertrude Vanderbilt Whitney award, 1972; decorated hon. knight comdr. Order Brit. Empire, 1974. Mem. Scroll and Key Soc., Am. Philos. Soc.; hon. mem. English Jockey Club, London. Clubs: Metropolitan (Washington); Racquet and Tennis, Grolier, Links, Knickerbocker, Jockey, Nat. Steeplechase and Hunt Assn. (N.Y.C.); Society of the Dilettanti (London). Office: 1729 H St NW Washington DC 20006

MELLON, RICHARD PROSSER, charitable found. exec.; b. Chgo., May 19, 1939; s. Richard King and Constance Mary (Prosser) M.; student U. Pitts., 1958-60; A.A. (hon.), Valley Forge Mil. Jr. Coll., 1970; m. Gertrude Alice Adams, Apr. 28, 1962 (div. 1976); children—Richard Adams, Armour Negley; m. 2d, Katherine Woodward Hooker, Dec. 2, 1976. Vice chmn. Richard King Mellon Found., Pitts., 1970—; trustee Sarah Scaife Found., Inc.; v.p., trustee Rachelwood Wildlife Research Preserve. Bd. dirs. Ducks Unlimited Found.; trustee Brandywine Conservancy, Carnegie Inst.; nat. trustee, mem. nat. exec. com., life mem. Ducks Unlimited, Inc.; corporator Western Pa. Sch. for Blind. Served to 1st lt. U.S. Army Res., 1958-67. Episcopalian. Clubs: Duquesne (Pitts.); Laurel Valley Golf, Rolling Rock, Rolling Rock-Westmoreland Hunt (Ligonier); Links, Racquet and Tennis, Nat. Steeplechase and Hunt Assn. (N.Y.C.). Home: Ligonier PA 15658 Office: PO Box 187 Laughlintown PA 15655

MELLON, SEWARD PROSSER, investment exec.; b. Chgo., July 28, 1942; s. Richard King Mellon and Constance Mary (Prosser) Mellon Burrell; grad. Choate Sch., 1960, B.A., Susquehanna U., 1965; m. Karen Leigh Boyd, Sept. 10, 1966 (div. 1974); children—Catherine Leigh, Constance Elizabeth; m. 2d, Sandra Springer Stout, 1975. With Mellon Nat. Corp., Pitts., 1965-69; with T. Mellon & Sons, Pitts., 1969-71; pres. Richard K. Mellon & Sons, Ligonier, 1971—. Trustee, Rachelwood Wildlife Research Preserve, Richard King Mellon Family Found.; trustee, pres. Richard King Mellon Found.; nat. trustee, state sponsor Ducks Unltd.; bd. dirs. Ducks Unltd. Can.; chmn. real estate com., v.p., mem. fin. and exec. com. Valley Sch. Ligonier. Mem. Western Pa. Conservancy (life), LoyalHanna Assn. (pres.), Phi Mu Delta. Republican. Clubs: Duquesne (Pitts.); Laurel Valley Golf (Ligonier); Latrobe Country, Rolling Rock, Rolling Rock Hunt. Home: Rolling Winds Box K Ligonier PA 15658 Office: PO Box RKM Ligonier PA 15658

MELLOR, GEORGE LINCOLN, educator; b. Yonkers, N.Y., May 12, 1929; s. George L. and Elizabeth (Hoar) M.; S.B., Mass. Inst. Tech., 1952, S.M., 1954, Sc.D., 1957; m. Virginia Keegan, Sept. 11, 1954; children—James Keegan, Edward Lincoln. Engr., Pratt & Whitney Aircraft Corp., 1952-53, Curtiss-Wright Corp., 1957-58; mem. faculty Princeton, 1958—, prof. fluid mechanics, 1968—; cons. to industry, 1958—. Dir. cons., Dynalysis of Princeton Corp. Served with AUS, 1946-48. NSF fellow Cambridge (Eng.) U., 1962-63; Nat. Acad. Scis. sci. exchange fellow Inst. Oceanology, Moscow, USSR, 1970-71. Mem. Am. Soc. M.E. (Robert Knapp award 1959), Am. Geophys. Union, Am. Meterol. Soc., Sigma Xi, Pi Tau Sigma. Author papers in field. Home: Pheasant Hill Rd Princeton NJ 08540

MELLOR, JAMES ROBB, electronics co. exec.; b. Detroit, May 3, 1930; s. Clifford and Gladys (Robb) M.; B.S. in Elec. Engring. and Math., U. Mich., 1952, M.S., 1953; m. Suzanne Stykos, June 8, 1953; children—James Robb, Diane Elyse, Deborah Lynn. Mem. tech. staff Hughes Aircraft Co., Fullerton, Calif., 1955-58; pres. Data Systems div. Litton Industries, Van Nuys, Calif., after 1958; exec. v.p. Litton Industries, Inc., Beverly Hills, Calif.; pres., chief operating officer AM Internat., Inc., Los Angeles; dir. Bergen Brunswig Corp. Bd. councilors Grad. Sch. Bus. Adminstrn. and Sch. Bus., U. So. Calif.; mem. adv. council Coll. Bus. Adminstrn., Loyola Marymount U.; bd. dirs. Hollywood Presbyterian Med. Center Found. Served to 1st lt., Signal Corps, AUS, 1953-55. Mem. IEEE, Am. Mgmt. Assn., Armed Forces Communications and Electronics Assn. (dir.), Computer and Bus. Equipment Mfrs. Assn. (dir.), Sigma Xi, Tau Beta Pi, Eta Kappa Nu, Phi Kappa Phi. Club: Los Angeles Country. Contbr. articles to profl. publs. Patentee fields of storage tubes and display systems. Home: 541 Perugia Way Bel Air CA 90024 Office: 1900 Ave of Stars Los Angeles CA 90067

MELLOR, JOHN EDWARD, ret. diplomat; b. N.Y.C., Aug. 1, 1922; s. Charles Edward and Anita Constance (Ragone) M.; student Coll. City N.Y., 1938-39; B.A., George Washington U., 1942, M.A., 1951; m. Carol Helen Krause, June 19, 1948; children—Charles Edward, Thomas Andrew, Richard Joseph. Mem. staff Dept. State, 1945-55; 2d sec. Am. embassy, London, Eng., 1955-57; 1st sec., Warsaw, Poland, 1958-60; officer charge commodity control affairs Dept. State, 1960-63; assigned Indsl. Coll. Armed Forces, Washington, 1963-64; econ. counselor Am. embassy, Oslo, Norway, 1964-69; chief div. internat. bus. affairs Dept. State, 1969-71; comml. counselor Am. embassy, Ottawa, Can., 1971-75; comml. counselor Am. embassy, Tokyo, 1975-76; econ. counselor Am. embassy, Manila, 1977-78. Served with C.E., AUS, 1942-44. Presbyn. Home: 7044 Leestone St Springfield VA 22151

MELLORS, ROBERT CHARLES, pathologist; b. Dayton, Ohio, 1916; s. Bert S. and Clementine (Steinmetz) M.; Ph.D., Western Res. U., 1940; M.D., Johns Hopkins, 1944; m. Jane K. Winternitz, Mar. 25, 1944; children—Alice J., Robert Charles, William K., John. Intern Nat. Naval Med. Center, Bethesda, Md., 1944-45; research fellow medicine Meml. Center Cancer and Allied Diseases, N.Y.C., 1946-50, research fellow pathology, 1950-53, asst. attending pathologist, 1953-57, asso. attending pathologist, 1957-58; sr. fellow Am. Cancer Soc., 1947-50; sr. clin. research fellow Damon Runyon Meml. Fund, 1950-53; asst. attending pathologist Meml. Hosp., N.Y.C., 1953-57, asso. attending pathologist, 1957-58; asst. attending pathologist Ewing Hosp., N.Y.C., 1953-57, asso. attending pathologist, 1957-58; instr. biochemistry Western Res. U., 1940-42; asst. prof. biology Meml. Center Cancer and Allied Diseases, N.Y.C., 1952-53, asst. prof. pathology Sloan Kettering div. Cornell U., 1953-57, asso. prof., 1957-58, prof. pathology Med. Coll., 1961—; asso. attending pathologist N.Y. Hosp., 1961-72, attending pathologist, 1972—; pathologist-in-chief, dir. labs., 1958—, asso. dir. research Hosp. for Spl. Surgery, N.Y.C., 1958-69, dir. research, 1969—. Mem. research adv. com. NIH, 1962-66, adv. com. Nat. Inst. Environ. Health Sci., 1966-69; com. nomenclature and classification of disease Coll. Am. Pathologists, 1960-64. Served as lt. (j.g.), M.C., USNR, 1944-46. Recipient Kappa Delta award Am. Acad. of Orthopedic Surgeons, 1962. Diplomate Am. Bd. Pathology in path. anatomy. Fellow Royal Coll. Pathologists; mem. Am. Assn. Pathologists, Am. Assn. Immunologists, Am. Soc. Biol. Chemists, Am. Soc. Clin. Pathology, Am. Orthopedic Assn. Author: Analytical Cytology, 1955, 2d edit., 1959; Analytical Pathology, 1957. Home: 3 Hardscrabble Circle Armonk NY 10504

MELLOW, JAMES ROBERT, writer, editor; b. Gloucester, Mass., Feb. 28, 1926; s. James Robert and Cecilia Margaret (Sawyer) M.; B.S., Northwestern U., 1950. Mem. staff Arts mag., 1955-65, exec. editor, 1961, editor, 1961-65; editor Indsl. Design, 1965-68; art critic The New Leader, 1964-72, Art Internat., 1965-69, N.Y. Times, 1970-74. Served with USAAF, 1944-46. Author: Charmed Circle: Gertrude Stein & Co., 1974. Editor: The Best in Arts, 1962; New York: The Art World, 1963. Address: PO Box 297 Clinton CT 06413

MELLQUIST, PROCTOR, editor; b. Leavenworth, Kans., Aug. 14, 1915; s. Carl and Blanche (Thomas) M.; student U. Wash., 1933-37; m. Alice Stauffacher, Oct. 4, 1940; children—Susan Proctor, John Quincy. Copywriter, copy group head J. Stirling Getchell, Inc., N.Y.C., 1937-42; dir. visual research Cowles Mag., Inc., 1946; mng. editor Science Illustrated, McGraw Hill Pub. Co., 1947-49, asso. mng. editor Bus. Week, 1949-50; mng. editor Sunset Mag., Lane Pub. Co., Menlo Park, 1950-51, exec. editor, 1951-53, editor, 1954—; v.p. Lane Pub. Co. Planning commr. Los Altos Hills, 1956-64; adv. bd. Calif. Tomorrow, 1961-78, bd. dirs., 1978—. Served as 1st lt. AUS, 1943-46, psychol. warfare. Home: 12365 Stonebrook Rd Los Altos Hills CA 94022 Office: Lane Pub Co Menlo Park CA 94025

MELMAN, SEYMOUR, author, educator. Prof. indsl. engring. Columbia. Author: Dynamic Factors in Industrial Productivity, 1956; Decision Making and Productivity, 1958; Peace Race, 1961; Our Depleted Society, 1965; Pentagon Capitalism, 1970; The Permanent War Economy, 1974. Editor: Inspection for Disarmament, 1958; No Place To Hide, 1962; Disarmament: its Politics and Economics, 1962; In the Name of America, 1968; Conversion of Industry from a Military to Civilian Economy: A Series, 1970; The War Economy of the U.S., 1971. Home: 15 Claremont Ave New York City NY 10027

MELMON, KENNETH LLOYD, physician, biologist; b. San Francisco, July 20, 1934; s. Abe Irving and Jean (Kahn) M.; A.B. in Biology with honors, Stanford U., 1956; M.D., U. Calif. at San Francisco, 1959; m. Elyce Edelman, June 9, 1957; children—Bradley S., Debra W. Intern, then resident in internal medicine U. Calif. Med. Center, San Francisco, 1959-61; clin. asso., surgeon USPHS, Nat. Heart and Lung Inst., NIH, 1961-64; chief resident in medicine U. Wash. Med. Center, Seattle, 1964-65; chief div. clin. pharmacology U. Calif. Med. Center, 1965-68, chief sect. clin. pharmacology, 1968-78; chief dept. medicine Stanford U. Med. Center, 1978—; mem. sr. staff Cardiovascular Research Inst., 1973—; chmn. joint commn. prescription drug use Senate Subcom. on Health, Inst. Medicine and HEW-Pharm. Mfrs. Assn.; cons. to govt. Burroughs Wellcome clin. pharmacology scholar, 1966-71; Guggenheim fellow, 1971; vis. scientist Weizmann Inst., Israel, 1971-72; NIH spl. fellow, 1972. Mem. Am. Fedn. Clin. Research (pres. 1973-74), Am. Soc. Clin. Investigation (pres. 1978-79), AAAS, Assn. Am. Physicians, Western Assn. Physicians, Am. Soc. Pharmacology and Exptl. Therapeutics, Am. Physiol. Soc., Calif. Acad. Medicine, Phi Beta Kappa. Jewish. Author articles, chpts. in books, sects. encys. Editor: Clinical Pharmacology: Basic Principles in Therapeutics, 2d edit., 1978; Cardiovascular Therapeutics, 1974; asso. editor The Pharmacological Basis of Therapeutics (Goodman and Gilman), 1980. Research on cellular response to low molecular weight hormones. Home: 51 Cragmont Way Woodside CA 94062 Office: Stanford U Med Center Dept Medicine Stanford CA 94305

MELNER, SINCLAIR LEWIS, army officer; b. Reno, Nev., Apr. 6, 1928; s. A. H. and Carol Rachel (Myers) M.; B.S., U. Nev., 1949; M.S. in Internat. Affairs, George Washington U., 1969; m. Roma F. Garner, Dec. 26, 1949; children—Catherine, Michael, Joan. Commd. 2d lt. U.S. Army, 1949, advanced through grades to maj. gen.; formerly dep. comdg. gen. Allied Land Forces Southeastern Europe; now comdg. gen., Fort Benjamin Harrison, Ind. Decorated Legion of Merit with oak leaf cluster, Silver Star with oak leaf cluster. Home: Quarters 661 Lawton Loop Fort Benjamin Harrison IN 46216 Office: Comdg Gen Fort Benjamin Harrison IN 46216

MELNICK, DANIEL, motion picture producer; b. N.Y.C., Apr. 21, 1932; 1 son, Peter. Partner, Talent Assos.; v.p., then sr. v.p. charge worldwide prodn. M.G.M., 1972-76; ind. film producer, 1976-77, 79—; charge worldwide prodn. Columbia Pictures Industries Inc., 1977-78, pres. motion picture div., 1978; producer film Straw Dogs; exec. producer That's Entertainment and That's Entertainment Part 2. Recipient Nat. Acad. TV Arts and Scis. Emmy award for Death of a Salesman and The Ages of Man. Office: 300 Colgems Sq Burbank CA 91505*

MELNICK, JOSEPH L., educator, virologist; b. Boston, Oct. 9, 1914; s. Samuel and Esther (Melny) M.; A.B., Wesleyan U., 1936; Ph.D. (Univ. scholar), Yale, 1939; D.Sc., Wesleyan U., 1971; m. Matilda Benyesh, 1958; 1 dau., Nancy. Asst. in physiol. chemistry Yale Sch. Medicine, 1937-39, Finney-Howell Research Found. fellow, 1939-41, NRC fellow in med. scis., 1941-42, research asst. in preventive medicine with rank of instr., 1942-44, asst. prof., 1944-48, research asso., 1948-49, asso. prof. microbiology, 1949-54, prof. epidemiology, 1954-57; chief virus labs., div. biologics standards NIH, USPHS, 1957-58; prof. virology and epidemiology Baylor Coll. Medicine, Houston, 1958-74, distinguished service prof., 1974—, also dean for grad. studies, 1968—. Mem. com. on virus diseases WHO, 1957—, dir. WHO Internat. Center Enteroviruses, 1963-70, mem. cons. group on poliomyelitis vaccine, 1973—, dir. WHO Collaborating Center for Virus Reference and Research, 1974—; mem. com. on live poliovirus vaccines USPHS, 1959-61, virus reference bd. NIH, 1962-70; mem. human cancer virus task force Nat. Cancer Inst., USPHS, 1962-67, nat. adv. cancer council NIH, 1965-69; sec.-gen. Internat. Congresses Virology, 1968-71; chmn. Internat. Conf. Viruses in Water, Mexico City, 1974; mem. exec. bd. Internat. Assn. Microbiol. Socs., chmn. sect. on virology, 1970-75, mem. internat. commn. microbiol ecology, 1972—; mem. research council Am. Cancer Soc., 1971-75; mem. com. on hepatitis Nat. Acad. Sci./NRC, 1972-77; lectr. cons. Chinese Acad. Med. Scis., 1978, 79; mem. adv. com. Comparative Virology Orgn., 1978—. Recipient Internat. medal (with Dr. Herids von Magnus of Denmark); award Argentinian Found. Against Infantile Paralysis, for research in immunity to poliomyelitis, 1949; Humanitarian award Jewish Inst. Med. Research, 1964; Modern Medicine Distinguished Achievement award, 1965; Eleanor Roosevelt Humanities award, 1965; Indsl. Research-100 award (with Prof. Craig Wallis), 1971, 74; Inventor of Year award Houston Patent Law Assn., 1972; named to Nat. Found.'s Polio Hall Fame, 1958. Fellow A.A.A.S., Am. Pub. Health Assn., N.Y. Acad. Scis. (Freedman Found. award for research in virology 1973), Am. Acad. Microbiology; mem. Am. Soc. Microbiology, Soc. Exptl. Biol. and Medicine (mem. council, 1965-69), Am. Assn. Immunologists, Am. Epidemiological Soc., Am. Assn. Cancer Research (pres. S.W. sect. 1968), Microbiol. Soc. Israel (hon.), USSR Soc. Microbiologists and Epidemiologists (hon.), Phi Beta Kappa, Sigma Xi. Author: Textbook of Medical Microbiology; other sci. publs. Editor: Jour. Progress in Medical Virology, Monographs in Virology; editor-in-chief Intervirology, ofcl. jour. virology Internat. Assn. Microbiol. Socs. Home: 8838 Chatsworth Dr Houston TX 77024

MELNIKER, BENJAMIN, motion picture exec., lawyer; b. Bayonne, N.J., May 25, 1913; s. Hyman and Ida Lena (Yankeloff) M.; student Bklyn. Coll., 1928-31; LL.B., Fordham U., 1934; m. Shirley Gross, Feb. 20, 1944; children—Harvey David, Charles Neil. Admitted to N.Y. bar, 1936; pvt. practice, N.Y.C., 1936-42; with Loew's Inc. (now Metro-Goldwyn-Mayer), 1942—, v.p., gen. counsel, 1954-69, exec. v.p., 1968-70, v.p., 1970-71, also dir., mem. exec. com.; pres. Essex Enterprises Ltd.; adj. asso. prof. N.Y. Law Sch. Motion picture chmn. Anti-Defamation League, B'nai B'rith. Mem. Am., N.Y. State bar assns., Bar Assn. City N.Y., N.Y. County Lawyers Assn., Acad. Motion Picture Arts and Scis. Club: Engineers Country (Roslyn Harbor). Home: 14 Glenwood Rd Roslyn Harbor NY 11576 Office: 1350 Ave of Americas New York NY 10019

MELOAN, TAYLOR WELLS, ednl. adminstr.; b. St. Louis, July 31, 1919; s. Taylor Wells and Edith (Graham) M.; B.S. cum laude, St. Louis U., 1949; M.B.A., Washington U., St. Louis, 1950; D.B.A., Ind. U., 1953; m. Anna Geraldine Leukering, Dec. 17, 1944 (div. 1974); children—Michael David, Steven Lee; m. 2d, Jane Innes Bierlich, Jan. 30, 1975. Advt. mgr. Herz Corp., St. Louis, 1941-42; sales promotion supr. Liggett & Myers Tobacco Co., St. Louis, 1942-43; asst. prof. mktg. U. Okla., Norman, 1953; from asst. prof. to asso. prof. mktg. Ind. U., Bloomington, 1953-59; prof., chmn. dept. mktg. U. So. Calif., Los Angeles, 1959-69, interim dean Sch. Bus. Adminstrn., 1969-71; asso. v.p. for academic adminstrn. and research, 1971—, prof. mktg., 1959—; prof. bus. adminstrn. U. Karachi (Pakistan), 1962; vis. prof. mktg. Istituto Post U. Per Lo Studio Dell Organizzazione Aziendale, Turin, Italy, 1964; Disting. vis. prof. U. Witwatersrand, Johannesburg, 1978; editorial adviser bus. adminstrn. Houghton Mifflin Co., Boston, 1959-73; cons. to industry and govt., 1953—; mem. bd. dirs. Council Better Bus. Burs., Inc. Served with USNR, 1943-46. Mem. Newcomen Soc. N.Am., Am. Mktg. Assn. (pres. Los Angeles chpt. 1963-64), Order of Artus, Beta Gamma Sigma, Delta Pi Epsilon. Clubs: Rotary, Internat., Univ. (Los Angeles). Author: New Career Opportunities, 1978; Innovation Strategy and Management, 1979; co-author: Managerial Marketing, 1970; Internationalizing the Business Curriculum, 1968; Handbook of Modern Marketing, 1970; bd. editors Jour. Mktg., 1965-72. Home: 639 Burlingame Ave Los Angeles CA 90049 Office: U So Calif Los Angeles CA 90007

MELONE, JOSEPH JAMES, ins. co. exec.; b. Pittston, Pa., July 27, 1931; s. Dominick William and Beatrice Marie (Pignone) M.; B.S., U. Pa., 1953, M.B.A., 1954, Ph.D. in Econs., 1961; C.L.U., 1963, C.P.C.U., 1964; m. Marie Jane DeGeorge, Jan. 23, 1960; children—Lisa, Carol. Asso. prof. ins. U. Pa., 1959-66, mem. pension research council, 1961-66; research dir. Am. Coll. Life Underwriters, 1966-68; v.p. Prudential Ins. Co., Boston, 1968-76, sr. v.p., Newark, 1976—. Bd. advisers Suffolk U., Boston. Served with U.S. Army, 1955-57. Gen. Electric scholar, 1952; Huebner Found. fellow, 1957-59. Mem. Am. Risk and Ins. Assn., Am. Soc. C.L.U.'s (mem. continuing edn. com.), Alpha Tau Omega. Clubs: Essex (Newark); Morris County Country (Convent, N.J.). Author: Collectively Bargained Multi-Employer Pension Plans, 1961; co-author: Risk and Insurance, 1963; Pension Planning, 1966. Home: 281 Hartshorn Dr Short Hills NJ 07078 Office: Prudential Plaza Newark NJ 07101

MELOY, GUY STANLEY, III, army officer; b. Washington, May 16, 1930; s. Guy S. and Catherine Louise (Cahill) M.; B.S., U.S. Mil. Acad., 1953; grad. Nat. War Coll., 1969; m. Harriet Grizzard, June 12, 1954; children—Guy Stanley, Sharon Elizabeth, Catherine Irene. Commd. 2d lt., U.S. Army, 1953, advanced through grades to maj. gen., 1977; platoon leader and co. comdr. 86th Inf. Regt., Fort Riley, Kans. and 10th Inf. Div., Schweinfurt, Germany, 1954-56, platoon leader 188th Airborne Inf. Regt., Augsburg, Germany, 1957-59, 187th Inf., 11th Airborne Div.; aide-de-camp to comdt. U.S. Army Inf. Sch., Fort Benning, Ga., 1960-61, co. comdr. 1st battle group, 8th cav., 1st cav. div., Korea, 1961-62; instr. joint airborne ops. U.S. Army Command and Gen. Staff Coll., Ft. Leavenworth, Kans., 1963-66; sr. adv. task force I, Vietnamese Airborne Div., 1966, bn. comdr. 1st bn. 27th inf., 25th inf. div., Vietnam, 1966-67; Vietnam desk officer Internat. Affairs Directorate, Office Dep. Chief of Staff for Ops., Dept. Army, Pentagon, Washington, 1967-68; G3, 8th inf. div., Germany, 1969-70, bn. comdr. 1st Bn., 12th Calvary, 1st Calvary Div., Vietnam, 1970-71; dep. dir. bn. ops. dept. U.S. Army Inf. Sch., Ft. Benning, Ga., 1971-72, chief tactics group, 1972-73; brigade comdr. 1st brigade, 82d Airborne Div., Ft. Bragg, N.C., 1973-74, chief of staff, 1974-75, asst. div. comdr. ops., 1975-76; asst. dep. chief of staff for ops. Hdqrs. U.S. Army Forces Command, Fort McPherson, Ga., 1976-78; comdg. gen. 82d Airborne Div., Fort Bragg, 1978—. Decorated D.S.C., Legion of Merit with two oak leaf clusters, D.F.C. with one oak leaf cluster, Purple Heart with one oak leaf cluster, Air medal with thirty one oak leaf clusters, Bronze Star with two oak leaf clusters; Cross of Gallantry with Palm, Cross of Gallantry with Silver Star, Cross of Gallantry with Bronze Star (Republic of Vietnam). Mem. Assn. of U.S. Army, 1st. Calvary Div. Assn., 25th Inf. Div. Assn., 82d Airborne Div. Assn. Roman Catholic. Office: Hdqrs 82nd Airborne Div Fort Bragg NC 28307

MELOY, HARRY, lawyer; b. Hoopeston, Ill., Mar. 24, 1908; s. John Templeton and Sarah (Wilson) M.; A.B., Monmouth Coll., 1931; J.D., DePaul U., 1935; m. Cordelia Buck, Sept. 4, 1937; children—John Buck, Sarah (Mrs. R. Kent Landmark), Alex James. Admitted to Ill. bar, 1935; atty., asso. gen. counsel Ill. Agrl. Assn., Bloomington, 1935-61; gen. counsel, sec. CF Industries Inc., Chgo., 1961-73, ret., 1973; of counsel McDermott Will & Emery, Chgo., 1973—; sec., counsel Cooperative Fertilizers Internat., 1966-73; counsel Nat. Livestock Producers Assn. Mem. Wilmette (Ill.) Village Bd., 1953-62. Bd. dirs. Association House of Chgo. Mem. Am., Ill., Chgo. bar assns., Am. Judicature Soc., Tau Kappa Epsilon. Presbyn. (elder 1949-52). Clubs: Tower; Sheridan Shore Yacht. Home: 427 8th St Wilmette IL 60091 Office: 111 W Monroe St Chicago IL 60603

MELOY, JOHN CALVIN, III, ins. co. exec.; b. Washington, Pa., Mar. 3, 1924; s. Robert Harry and Alice (Lambie) M.; student Bucknell U., 1943, Yale U., 1944; B.A., Washington and Jefferson Coll., 1947; m. Miriam Krout, July 5, 1945; children—John C., Judith M., Beth A., Lydia L. With Aetna Life & Casualty Co., Hartford, Conn., 1947—, v.p., 1974—. Exec. trustee Washington and Jefferson Coll.; active Big Brothers Am. Served with USMC, 1942-45. Mem. Scotch-Irish Soc. Am. Presbyterian. Clubs: Racquet, Overbrook Golf. Home: 728 Dodds Ln Gladwyne PA 19035 Office: 3 Penn Center Plaza Room 1108 Philadelphia PA 19102

MELSEN, JOHN P., paper co. exec.; b. 1924; ed. U. Wis., 1948; married. Tax auditor, accountant Wis. Dept. Taxation, 1948-50; with Internal Revenue Service, 1950-53; with Nekoosa Papers Inc., 1953—, treas., 1966—, v.p., 1969—. C.P.A., Wis. Address: 241 Monroe Ave Port Edwards WI 54469

MELSHEIMER, MEL P(OWELL), agri-bus., natural resources co. exec.; b. Los Angeles, July 9, 1939; s. Oscar Merrill M.; A.B. in Econs., Occidental Coll., 1961; M.B.A., U. So. Calif., 1965; m. Sara Sturdevant, Sept. 1, 1962; children—Heidi, Erich, Douglas. Lending officer United Calif. Bank, Los Angeles, 1962-66; sr. fin. analyst Ford Motor Co., Newport Beach, Calif., 1966-67; v.p., chief fin. officer Pepsi Cola Co. Pepsico, Inc., Purchase, N.Y., 1968-75; exec. v.p., chief fin. officer, treas. AZL Resources, Inc., 1975—. Served with U.S.

Army, 1961-62. Mem. Fin. Execs. Inst., Planning Execs. Inst. Office: 5025 E Washington St Phoenix AZ 85034

MELSON, WILLIAM HENRY, JR., communications specialist, educator; b. Elizabeth City, N.C., Aug. 18, 1927; s. William Henry and Maude Marion (Jackson) M.; A.B., U. N.C., 1950; Ph.D., 1969; m. Eva Pauline Bullard July 7, 1947; children—Diana Candace, Susan Dawn. With Jefferson Pilot Broadcasting Co., Charlotte, N.C., 1951-65, personnel mgr., 1956-63, asst. v.p., 1963-65; asso. prof. radio, TV, and motion pictures U. N.C., Chapel Hill, 1969-74, prof., 1974-76, chmn. dept. radio, TV, motion pictures, 1974-76, asso. dean. Grad. Sch., 1972-74; prof. U. Ala., University, 1976—, dean Sch. Communication, 1976—. Served with USN, 1945-46. Mem. Assn. for Edn. in Journalism, Broadcast Edn. Assn., Ala. Broadcasters Assn., Ala. Press Assn., Phi Beta Kappa, Sigma Delta Chi. Episcopalian. Contbr. articles to profl. jours. Home: Route 2 55 Four Winds Northport AL 35476 Office: PO Box 1482 University of Alabama University AL 35486

MELTON, ANDREW JOSEPH, JR., investment co. exec.: b. Bay Shore, N.Y., Mar. 4, 1920; s. Andrew J. and Alice (Lonergan) M.; B.S., Villanova U., 1942; m. Mary Ann Shanks, Sept. 18, 1943; children—Diana, Andrew, Robert, Karen, Marjorie, Sandra, Michaelle, Edward. With Smith Barney & Co., N.Y.C., 1946-72, chmn. exec. com., 1968-72; exec. v.p. Dean Witter & Co., Inc., N.Y.C., after 1972—; chmn., chief exec. officer Dean Witter Reynolds, Inc., N.Y.C., 1978—. Served with USMC, 1942-46, 51-53. Home: 848 Lakeside Dr North Palm Beach FL 33408 Office: Dean Witter Reynolds Inc 130 Liberty St New York NY 10006

MELTON, BUCKNER FRANKLIN, lawyer, mayor; b. Arlington, Ga., Oct. 24, 1923; s. Henry Martin and Mary (Layman) M.; student Norman Coll., 1941-42; A.B., Mercer U., 1949; LL.B., Walter F. George Sch. Law, 1949; m. Tommie Jean Beck, Oct. 24, 1954; children—Mary Leigh, Buckner Franklin. Admitted to Ga. bar, 1948; pvt. practice law, Macon, Ga., 1949-51, 53-64; sr. mem. firm Melton, McKenna & House, Macon, 1964-75; mayor City of Macon, 1975—; lectr. Inst. Continuing Edn. (Legal) in Ga., 1971; dir. Forest Services, Inc., Macon; city atty. Macon, 1959-63; atty. Middle Ga. Coliseum Authority, 1963-75, Macon Bibb County Indsl. Authority, 1964-75. Served with USN, 1942-46, 51-52. Recipient Lawyer of Year award Macon Bar Assn., 1972; Algernon Sydney Sullivan award Mercer U., 1975. Mem. Am., Macon (pres. 1961) bar assns., State Bar Ga., Greater Macon C. of C. (pres. 1971). Democrat. Baptist. Clubs: Macon Civic (pres. 1961), Idle Hour Golf and Country (pres. 1970), Elks. Contbr. articles in field to profl. jours. Home: 2710 Hilandale Circle Macon GA 31204 Office: 700 Poplar St Macon GA 31201

MELTON, CHARLES ESTEL, educator; b. Fancy Gap, Va., May 18, 1924; s. Charlie Glenn and Ella (Ayers) M.; B.A., Emory and Henry Coll., 1952, D.Sc., 1967; M.S., Vanderbilt U., 1954; Ph.D., U. Notre Dame, 1964; m. Una Faye Hull, Dec. 7, 1946; children—Sharon (Mrs. Lawrence Husch), Wayne, Sandra (Mrs. Glenn Allen). Physicist, Oak Ridge Nat. Lab., 1954-67; prof. chemistry U. Ga., Athens, 1967—, head dept., 1972-77. Served with USNR, 1943-46. Recipient DeFriece medal Emory and Henry Coll., 1959; numerous research grants. Fellow AAAS; mem. Am. Phys. Soc., Am. Chem. Soc., Ga. Acad. Sci. Presbyterian. Author: Principles of Mass Spectrometry and Negative Ions, 1970. Contbr. articles to profl. jours. Home: Route 2 Box 18 Hull GA 30646 Office: Dept Chemistry Univ Georgia Athens GA 30602

MELTON, HOWELL WEBSTER, judge; b. Atlanta, Dec. 15, 1923; s. Holmes and Alma (Combee) M.; J.D., U. Fla., 1948; m. Margaret Catherine Wolfe, Mar. 4, 1950; children—Howell Webster, Carol Anne. Admitted to Fla. bar, 1948; mem. firm Upchurch, Melton & Upchurch, St. Augustine, 1948-61; judge 7th Jud. Circuit of Fla., St. Augustine, 1961-77, U.S. Dist. Ct. Middle Dist. Fla., Jacksonville, 1977—. Past chmn. Fla. Conf. Circuit Judges, 1974. Trustee Flagler Coll., St. Augustine. Served with U.S. Army, 1943-46. Recipient Distinguished Service award St. Augustine Jaycees, 1953. Mem. Am., St. Johns County, Volusia County, Jacksonville, Fed. bar assns., Fla. Bar (past chmn. council bar pres.'s), Am. Judicature Soc., Blue Key, Phi Delta Theta, Phi Delta Phi. Methodist (chmn. bd. trustees). Clubs: Ponce de Leon Country (St. Augustine); Masons; Kiwanis (past pres.); Sawgrass (Ponte Vedra, Fla.); Fla. Yacht (Jacksonville). Home: 41 Carrera St Saint Augustine FL 32084 also 6208 Lake Lugano Dr Jacksonville FL 32216 Office: US Dist Ct 311 W Monroe St Jacksonville FL 32201

MELTON, JOHN DERREL, ins. co. exec.; b. Winnfield, La., Dec. 1, 1925; s. Lee Joseph and Clara Gertrude (Cupp) M.; B.B.A. in Acctg., So. Methodist U., 1949; m. Norma Jean Denton, Aug. 24, 1946; children—Derrel C., Joyce Lynn. Vice pres. Res. Life Ins. Co., Dallas, 1953-59, also dir.; pres. Am. Pacific Life Ins. Co., Honolulu, 1970-73; cons. ins., Dallas, 1973-77; pres., chief exec. officer Republic Nat. Life Ins. Co., Dallas, 1977—; dir. Richardson Heights Bank & Trust, Richardson, Tex. Served with USAAF, 1943-46, USAF, 1951-53. Decorated D.F.C., Air medal with 4 oak leaf clusters; C.P.A. Mem. Nat. Assn. Life Underwriters. Office: 3988 N Central Expy Dallas TX 75204

MELTON, NANCY LOPEZ, profl. golfer; b. Torrance, Calif., Jan. 6, 1957; d. Domingo and Marina (Griego) Lopez; student U. Tulsa, 1976-78; m. Tim Melton, Jan. 6, 1979. Profl. golfer, 1978—, first victor at Bent Tree Classic, Sarasota, Fla., 1978. Named AP Athlete for 1978. Mem. Ladies Profl. Golf Assn. (Player and Rookie of Yr. 1978). Republican. Baptist. Author: The Education of a Woman Golfer, 1979. Office: 1 Erieview Plaza Cleveland OH 44114

MELTSNER, MICHAEL C(HARLES), univ. adminstr., lawyer; b. N.Y.C., Mar. 29, 1937; s. Ira D. and Alice G. M.; A.B., Oberlin Coll., 1957; LL.B., Yale U., 1960; m. Heli Spiegel, Sept. 10, 1961; children—Jessica, Molly. Admitted to N.Y. bar, 1961; first asst. counsel NAACP Legal Def. and Ednl. Fund, N.Y.C., 1961-70; prof. law Columbia U., 1970-78; prof., dean law Northeastern U. Sch. Law, 1979—. Bd. dirs. Legal Action Center N.Y.C. Simon Guggenheim fellow, 1977-78. Mem. Assn. Bar City N.Y., Soc. Am. Law Tchrs. (dir.). Author: Cruel and Unusual: The Supreme Court and Capital Punishment, 1973; (with P. Schrag) Public Interest Advocacy, 1974. Office: 400 Huntington Ave Boston MA 02115

MELTZER, ALLAN HAROLD, economist; b. Boston, Feb. 6, 1928; s. George B. and Minerva I. (Simons) M.; A.B., Duke U., 1948; M.A., U. Calif. at Los Angeles, 1955, Ph.D., 1958; m. Marilyn Ginsburg, Aug. 27, 1950; children—Bruce Michael, Eric Charles, Beth Denise. Lectr. econs. U. Pa., Phila., 1956-57; mem. faculty Carnegie Mellon U. Grad. Sch. Indsl. Adminstrn., Pitts., 1957—, prof. econs., 1964—, Maurice Falk prof. econs. and social sci., 1970—, acting dean, 1972-73; vis. prof. U. Chgo., 1964-65; vis. fellow Hoover Instn., 1977-78; co-chmn. Shadow Open Market Com., 1974—; cons. U.S. Treasury, Joint econ. com. U.S. Congress, 1960, com. on banking and currency U.S. Ho. of Reps., 1963-64; bd. govs. Fed. Res. System, Fed. Deposit Ins. Corp., Nat. Assn. Home Builders. Social Sci. Research Council fellow, 1955-56; Ford Found. fellow, 1962-63. Mem. Am. Econ. Assn., Am. Fin. Assn. Author: (With G. von der Linde) A Study of the Dealer Market, 1960; (with Karl Brunner) An Analysis of Federal Reserve Monetary Policymaking, 1964; also articles. Research on relation of money and changes in monetary policy to nat. income, employment and prices. Home: 5830 Marlborough Ave Pittsburgh PA 15217

MELTZER, BERNARD DAVID, legal educator; b. Phila., Nov. 21, 1914; s. Julius and Rose (Welkov) M.; A.B., U. Chgo., 1935, J.D., 1937; LL.M., Harvard, 1938; m. Jean Sulzberger, Jan. 17, 1947; children—Joan, Daniel, Susan. Admitted to Ill. bar, 1938; atty., spl. asst. to chmn. SEC, 1938-40; asso. firm Mayer, Meyer, Austrian & Platt, Chgo., 1940; spl. asst. to asst. sec. state, also acting chief fgn. funds control div. div. State 1941-43; trial counsel U.S. staff Internat. Nuremberg War Trials, 1945-46; from professorial lectr. to prof. law U. Chgo. Law Sch., 1946—. Hearing commr. NPA, 1952-53; labor arbitrator; spl. master U.S. Ct. Appeals for D.C., 1963-64; bd. publs. U. Chgo., 1965-67, chmn., 1967-68; mem. Gov. Ill. Adv. Commn. Labor-Mgmt. Policy for Pub. Employees in Ill., 1966-67; cons. U.S. Dept. Labor, 1969-70. Bd. dirs. High Park Community Conf., 1954-56, S.E. Chgo. Commn., 1956-57. Served to lt. (j.g.) USNR, 1943-46. Decorated Army Commendation medal. Mem. Am. (co-chmn. com. devel. law under NLRA 1959-60; mem. spl. com. transp. strikes), Ill., Chgo. (bd. mgrs. 1972-73) bar assns., Nat. Acad. Arbitrators, Am. Law Inst., Am. Acad. Arts and Scis., Phi Beta Kappa, Order of Coif. Author: (with W.G. Katz) Cases and Materials on Business Corporations, 1949; Labor Law Cases, Materials and Problems, 1970, supplement, 1972, 75, 2d edit., 1977; also articles. Home: 1219 E 50th St Chicago IL 60615

MELTZER, BERNARD N(ATHAN), educator, sociologist; b. N.Y.C., Oct. 17, 1916; s. Philip and Anna (Kemper) M.; B.A., Wayne State U., 1943, M.A., 1944; Ph.D., U. Chgo., 1948; m. Ida Wasserman, June 11, 1944; children—Iris Jean, William Jay. Research asso. U. Chgo., 1948-49; asst. prof. sociology McGill U., 1949-51; mem. faculty Central Mich. U., Mt. Pleasant, 1951—, prof. sociology, 1955—, chmn. dept., 1959—. Chmn. Isabella County Civil Rights Com., 1959. Recipient citation Mich. Acad. Sci., Arts and Letters, 1969; Ascher fellow social sci. U. Chgo., 1944, Univ. fellow sociology, 1945, Marshall Field fellow sociology, 1946; grantee Canadian Social Sci. Research Council, 1950. Fellow Am. Sociol. Assn.; mem. Am. Acad. Polit. and Social Scis., A.A.U.P., Mich. (pres. 1961-62), North Central (v.p. 1971-72) sociol. assns., Soc. for Study Social Problems. Author: Education in Society: Readings, 1958; The Social Psychology of George Herbert Mead, 1959; Symbolic Interaction: A Reader in Social Psychology, 3d edit., 1978; Symbolic Interactionism: Genesis, Varieties and Criticism, 1975; also articles to profl. periodicals. Home: 318 E Cherry St Mt Pleasant MI 48858

MELTZER, DAVID, author, musician; b. Rochester, N.Y., Feb. 17, 1937; s. Louis and Roseamunde (Lovelace) M.; student Los Angeles City Coll., 1955-56, U. Calif. at Los Angeles, 1956-57; m. Christina Meyer, Apr. 1, 1958; children—Jennifer, Margaret, Amanda, Adam Benjamin ben David. Mem. cons. bd. Coordinating Council of Lit. Mags. Coordinating Council of Lit. Mags. grantee, 1973-74; Nat. Endowment of Arts grantee for creative writing, 1974, for pub., 1975; Calif. Arts Council grantee, 1979; author numerous books of poetry, including: Tens, Selected Poems, 1973; Six, 1976; Two-Way Mirror: Notebook on Poetry, 1977. Editor: The San Francisco Poets, 1971; Birth, 1973; The Secret Garden: Anthology of the Classic Kabbalah, 1977; editor, pub. Tree, bi-annual jour., also Tree Books; song-writer: Serpent Power, 1968; Poet Song, 1970; soundtrack for Chance, 1978. Bd. dirs. Before Columbus Found., 1977—. Office: PO Box 9005 Berkeley CA 94709

MELTZER, DONALD RICHARD, precision test equipment co. exec.; b. Boston, Sept. 1, 1932; s. Leo N. and Betty (Flesher) M.; A.B., Dartmouth Coll., 1954, M.B.A., 1955; m. Mary D. Seelye, Dec. 7, 1963; children—Kimberly Ann, Christopher Douglas. Mgr., Peat, Marwick, Mitchell & Co., Boston, 1955-67; asst. controller United Fruit Co., Boston, 1968-69, controller, 1969-70, v.p., controller, 1970-73; v.p. finance banana and diversified divs. United Brands Co., Boston, 1973, v.p., chief accounting officer, N.Y.C., 1973-74, v.p. adminstrn. and fin., 1974-76; v.p. fin., treas. Instron Corp., Canton, Mass., 1976—. Mem. fin. com. Town of Sudbury, Mass., 1967; mem. adv. com. Mass. Dept. Spl. Edn., 1976—; bd. dirs., v.p. Mass. Parents Assn. for Deaf and Hard of Hearing, 1973-75, pres., 1976-77; mem. publs. com. Alexander Graham Bell Assn. for Deaf, Washington, 1978—; mem. adv. bd. Multilevel Captioning project WGBH-TV, 1979—; chmn. bd. trustees First Parish Ch. of Sudbury, 1970-71. C.P.A., Mass. Mem. Am. Inst. C.P.A.'s, Mass. Soc. C.P.A.'s, Financial Execs. Inst., Treas.' Club. Home: 341 Old Lancaster Rd Sudbury MA 01776 Office: 100 Royall St Canton MA 02021

MELTZER, JACK, educator; b. Bayonne, N.J., Aug. 21, 1921; s. Louis and Debbie (Gold) M.; B.A., Wayne State U., 1941; M.A., U. Chgo., 1947; m. Rae Libin, June 26, 1944; children—Richard, Marc, Ellen. Dir. planning Michael Reese Hosp., Chgo., 1953-54; S.E. Chgo. Commn. and U. Chgo., 1954-58; propr. Jack Meltzer Assos., planners, 1958-63; acting dir. Am. Soc. Planning Ofcls., 1967-68; prof., dir. Center Urban Studies, U. Chgo., 1963-71, now prof. div. social scis., prof. Sch. Social Service Adminstrn.; cons. to govt. and industry, 1945—. Village trustee, Park Forest, Ill., 1950-52, mem. plan commn., 1949. Trustee Bettman Found. Served to capt. USAAF, World War II. Mem. Am. Soc. Planning Ofcls. (past treas.), Am. Inst. Planners (past v.p. pvt. practice dept.), Nat. Assn. Housing and Renewal Ofcls., Am. Soc. Pub. Adminstrn., Lambda Alpha. Author book revs., articles, books. Home: 1700 E 56th St Chicago IL 60637 Office: 969 E 60th St Chicago IL 60637

MELTZER, JAY H., health service co. exec.; b. Bklyn., Mar. 30, 1944; s. Solomon G. and Ethel L. (Kraft) M.; A.B., Dartmouth Coll., 1964; LL.B., Harvard U., 1967; m. Bonnie R. Rosenberg, June 27, 1965; children—Wendy, Elizabeth, Jonathan. Admitted to N.Y. bar, 1968, Mass. bar, 1978; law clk. to U.S. dist. judge, 1967-68; asso. firm Shearman & Sterling, N.Y.C., 1968-72; with Damon Corp., Needham Heights, Mass., 1972—, gen. counsel, sec., 1973—. Mem. Am. Bar Assn., Am. Soc. Corp. Secs., Internat. Wine and Food Soc., Phi Beta Kappa. Office: 115 4th Ave Needham Heights MA 02194

MELTZER, LEON, lawyer; b. Phila., Apr. 30, 1903; s. Alexander and Minnie (Epstein) M.; B.S., U. Pa., 1923, LL.B., 1926; m. Ruth Meyers, Dec. 20, 1936; children—Joan, Elaine. Admitted to Pa. bar, 1926, since practiced in Phila.; sr. partner Meltzer & Schiffrin. Chmn. bd. Congl. Life Co.; dir. Silo, Inc., Simkins Industries, Cine-Tel Communications Corp., Sonitrol Sers. Inc.; dir. Eagle Downs Racing. Trustee Pa. Coll. Podiatric Medicine. Mem. Am., Pa., Phila. bar assns., Am. Judicature Soc. Democrat. Clubs: Locust (Phila.); Philmont Country (Huntington Valley, Pa.). Home: 1349 Lindsay Ln Meadowbrook PA 19046 Office: 1500 Walnut St Philadelphia PA 19102

MELTZER, MILTON, author; b. Worcester, Mass., May 8, 1915; s. Benjamin and Mary (Richter) M.; student Columbia, 1932-36; m. Hilda Balinky, June 22, 1941; children—Jane, Amy. Author, cons. editor several pub. houses; adj. prof. history U. Mass., Amherst, 1977—. Served with USAAF, 1942-46. Nominee for Nat. Book award, 1969, 75, 77. Mem. Am. Hist. Assn., Orgn. Am. Historians, Authors Guild, P.E.N. Author: Mark Twain Himself, 1960; (with Walter Harding) A Thoreau Profile, 1962; Tongue of Flame: the Life of Lydia Maria Child, 1965; Thaddeus Stevens and the Fight for Negro Rights, 1967; Milestones to American Liberty, 1966; Light in the Dark: the Life of Samuel Gridley Howe, 1964; Langston Hughes: a Biography, 1968; In Their Own Words: a History of the American Negro, 3 vols., 1967; Bread and Roses, 1967; Brother, Can You Spare a Dime, 1968; Slavery: A World History, 2 vols., 1972; Hunted Like A Wolf: The Seminole War, 1972; The Right to Remain Silent, 1972; Underground Man, 1972; (with Langston Hughes and C. Eric Lincoln) A Pictorial History of Blackamericans, 1973; The Eye of Conscience, 1974; World of Our Fathers: The Jews of Eastern Europe, 1974; Remember the Days: A Short History of the Jewish American, 1974; Never to Forget: the Jews of the Holocaust, 1976; Taking Root: Jewish Immigrants in America, 1976; Violins and Shovels: The WPA Arts Projects, 1976; Dorothea Lange: A Photographer's Life, 1978. Editor: The Correspondence of Lydia Maria Child, 1977—. Address: 263 West End Ave New York City NY 10023

MELVILLE, DONALD BURTON, educator, biochemist; b. Netherton, Eng., Jan. 30, 1914; s. Donald and Hilda (Burton) M.; came to U.S., 1925, naturalized, 1932; B.S., U. Ill., 1936, M.S., 1937, Ph.D., 1939; m. Dorothy Robbin, July 20, 1940; children—Joan (Mrs. Walter Corcoran), Laura (Mrs. Roger Williams). Mem. faculty Cornell U. Med. Coll., 1939-60; prof. dept. biochemistry U. Vt. Coll. Medicine, 1960-79. Mem. Am. Soc. Biol. Chemists, Am. Chem. Soc., Sigma Xi, Phi Kappa Phi, Phi Lambda Upsilon. Contbr. articles to profl. jours. Home: 1 Fern St Burlington VT 05401

MELVILLE, DONALD ROBERT, abrasive mfg. co. exec.; b. Manchester, Eng., Nov. 18, 1926; s. Robert and Minnie (Veitch) M.; B.A., M.A., Queen's Coll., Cambridge (Eng.) U., 1951; M.B.A., Harvard, 1956; m. Mary Sutton, June 16, 1955; children—Wendy F., Jennifer K. Came to U.S., 1954, naturalized, 1966. Salesman, Dunlop Rubber Co., London, Eng., 1951-54; asst. to v.p. Continental Can Co., N.Y.C., 1956-60, sales mgr., 1962-67; Market analysis Mgr. Scott Paper Co., Phila., 1960-62; v.p. marketing Norton Co., Worcester, Mass., 1967-69, exec. v.p., 1969-79, pres., 1979—, also dir.; dir. Leesona Corp., Chemoplast, Inc. Chmn. Worcester Arts Council; mem. Mass. Council on Arts and Humanities; mem. Task Force on Public Financing of Arts and Humanities in Mass. Served with RAF, 1945-48. Mem. Am. Mktg. Assn., NAM (bd. dirs.). Club: Harvard. Home: 4 Paul Revere Rd Worcester MA 01609 Office: 1 New Bond St Worcester MA 01606

MELVILLE, ROBERT SEAMAN, govt. ofcl.; b. Worcester, Mass., Nov. 20, 1913; A.B., Clark U., 1937; Ph.D. in Biochemistry, U. Iowa, 1950; m., 1942; 5 children. Research chemist Mass. Gen. Hosp., Boston, 1939-42; clin. biochemist St. Luke's Hosp., Chgo., 1950-54; clin. biochemist VA Hosp., Iowa City, 1954-63, chief biochemist VA Central Office, Washington, 1963-65; scientist adminstr. automated clin. lab., sect. biomed. engring. program Nat. Inst. Gen. Med. Scis. HEW, Bethesda, Md., 1965, now chief automated clin. lab. program; chmn. adv. com. to chem. and chem.-tech. div. Nat. Acad. Scis.-NRC, 1966-68. Served with M.C. AUS, 1942-46. Fellow Assn. Clin. Chemistry (pres. 1969-70); mem. Am. Bd. Clin. Chemistry (cert. 1965, v.p. 1972-78, pres. 1978-79, dir.), AAAS, Am. Chem. Soc., Instrument Soc. Am. (sr.), Am. Assn. Clin. Sci. Research in clin. biochemistry, clin. chemistry methodology, instrumentation, tng. clin. chemists. Home: PO Box 56 11112 Kenilworth Ave Garrett Park MD 20766 Office: Nat Inst Gen Med Scis 5333 Westbard Ave Room 950 Bethesda MD 20014

MELVILL-JONES, GEOFFREY, physician, educator; b. Cambridge, Eng., Jan. 14, 1923; s. Benett and Dorothy Laxton (Jotham) Melvill J.; came to Can., 1961, naturalized, 1974; B.A., Cambridge U., 1942, M.A., 1947, M.B.,B.Ch., 1949; m. Jenny Marigold Burnaby, June 21, 1953; children—Katharine F., Francis H., Andrew, Dorothy. House surgeon Middlesex (Eng.) Hosp., 1950; sr. house surgeon in otolaryngology Addenbrooke's Hosp., Cambridge, 1950-51; sci. officer Med. Research Council Gt. Britain, 1955-61; asso. prof. physiology McGill U., Montreal, Que., Can., 1961-68, prof., 1968—, Hosmer research prof., 1978—, dir. aviation med. research unit, 1961—; vis. prof. Standord U., 1971-72, College de France, 1979. Served with RAF, 1951-55. Recipient SkyLab Achievement award NASA, 1974. Fellow Can. Aero. and Space Inst., Aerospace Med. Assn. (Harry G. Armstrong Lectureship award 1968, Arnold D. Tuttle award 1971), Royal Soc., Royal Soc. Can.; mem. U.K. Physiol. Soc., Can. Physiol. Soc., Royal Aero. Soc., Can. Soc. Aviation Medicine, Internat. Collegium Otolaryngology, Soc. Neurosci., Barany Soc. Author: Mammalian Vestibular Physiology, 1979; contbr. numerous articles-to profl. publs. Office: 3655 Drummond St Montreal PQ H3G 1Y6 Canada

MELVIN, BILLY ALFRED, clergyman; b. Macon, Ga., Nov. 25, 1929; s. Daniel Henry and Leola Dale (Seidell) M.; student Free Will Baptist Bible Coll., Nashville, 1947-49; B.A., Taylor U., Upland, Ind., 1951; postgrad. Asbury Theol. Sem., Wilmore, Ky., 1951-53; B.D., Union Theol. Sem., Richmond, Va., 1956; D.D., Azusa (Calif.) Coll., 1968; m. Marcia Darlene Eby, Oct. 26, 1952; children—Deborah Ruth, Daniel Henry II. Ordained to ministry Free Will Baptist Ch., 1951; pastor First Free Will Baptist Chs., Newport, Tenn., 1951-53, Richmond, 1953-57, Bethany Ch., Norfolk, Va., 1957-69; exec. sec. Nat. Assn. Free Will Baptists 1957-67; exec. dir. Nat. Assn. Evangelicals, 1967— Office: Nat Assn Evangelicals PO Box 28 Wheaton IL 60187*

MELVIN, MAEL AVRAMY, educator, physicist; b. Israel, Mar. 27, 1913 (parents Am. citizens); s. Abraham Elijah and Norma (Gottfried) M.; B.S., U. Chgo., 1933, M.S., 1935, Ph.D., 1938; m. Sophia Jean Brown, Sept. 18, 1946; children—Jonathan David, Paul Michael. Mem. faculty Columbia, 1938-48; prof. physics Fla. State U., 1952-66; prof. physics Temple U., Phila., 1966—; vis. prof. U. Uppsala (Sweden), 1957-58, Instituto di Fisica, Bariloche, Argentina, 1960. Sr. research asso. Nat. Acad. Sci.-NRC, 1971-72. Guggenheim Found. fellow, 1951-52, 57-58. Fellow Am. Phys. Soc.; mem. Phi Beta Kappa, Sigma Xi. Research, publs. on algebraic method for determining arrangement of atoms in crystals directly from x-ray data, theory of rates of transformation of phases of matter, method of applying symmetry to analyze phys. phenomena; (collaboration) prediction of non-strangeness changing neutral lepton current, proof that a magnetic field can exist stably all by itself without current to cause it, interpretation of properties of zero-mass infinite-spin particles, cosmology with an initial homogeneous radiation stream, metrics from symmetries of spatially homogeneous cosmologies.

MELVIN, NORMAN CECIL, railroad ofcl., lawyer; b. Balt., Aug. 21, 1916; s. Norman Cecil and Anna H. (Holzworth) M.; A.B., Johns Hopkins, 1939; LL.B., Harvard, 1942; m. Louise A. Gillen, Feb. 10, 1945 (dec. Oct. 1958); children—Leigh G., Norman Cecil III; m. 2d, Virginia Brown Lester, Nov. 2, 1959; 1 dau., Susan A. Admitted to Md. bar, 1942; practice in Balt., 1946—; mem. firm Brown & Brune, 1946-52; gen. atty. Western Md. Ry. Co., Balt., 1952-66, gen. solicitor, 1966-68, v.p., gen. counsel, 1968-75, dir., 1970-75; asst. peoples counsel Pub. Service Commn. Md., 1951-52; instr. U. Balt., 1957-66. Dir. Presbyn. Home Md. Served to capt. AUS, 1942-46. Recipient Erskine M. Ross essay award Am. Bar Assn., 1950. Mem. Am., Md., Balt. bar assns., Assn. ICC Practitioners, Soc. Colonial

Wars (council 1966-69), S.A.R., Johns Hopkins Alumni Assn. (pres. 1968-70). Clubs: Harvard, Johns Hopkins (Balt.). Home: 4202 Wickford Rd Baltimore MD 21210

MELZACK, RONALD, educator; b. Montreal, Que., Can., July 19, 1929; s. Joseph and Annie (Mandel) M.; B.Sc., McGill U., 1950, M.Sc., 1951, Ph.D., 1954; m. Lucy Birch, Aug. 7, 1960; children—Lauren, Joel. Lectr. McGill U., Montreal, 1953-54; lectr. Univ. Coll., London, Eng., 1957-58; asso. prof. Mass. Inst. Tech., 1959-63; prof. psychology McGill U., 1963—. Fellow Am., Canadian psychol. assns., AAAS. Author: Raven, Creator of the World, 1970; The Day Tuk Became Hunter, and Other Eskimo Stories, 1967; The Puzzle of Pain, 1973; Why the Mán in the Moon is Happy, and Other Eskimo Creation Stories, 1978. Home: 51 Banstead Rd Montreal W PQ Canada

MEMBERY, ROBERT EDWARD, petrochem. co. exec.; b. Toronto, Ont., Can., Feb. 6, 1925; s. Morris Howard and Ruth (Clark) M.; B. Commerce, McGill U., 1948; m. Isabel Hashim, Feb. 23, 1957; 1 dau., Jennifer. Indsl. accountant Canadian Industries Ltd., 1950-58; controller Anglo-Nfld. Devel. Co., 1959-61; controller Price Co. Ltd., Quebec, Can., 1962-1966, v.p. fin., 1967-76; v.p. fin. and adminstrn. Petrosar Ltd., Corunna, Ont., 1977—; v.p. Abitibi Paper Co. Ltd.; dir. Boise Cascade Can., Ltd. Served as pilot officer, RCAF, 1943-46. Chartered accountant, Que. Mem. Order Chartered Accountants Que., Delta Sigma Phi. Clubs; St. James (Montreal); Lake Louisa Country. Home: 1312 Maynard Rd Sarnia ON Canada Office: PO Box 7000 Corunna ON N0N 1G0 Canada

MENAKER, J. THOMAS, lawyer; b. Harrisburg, Pa., Sept. 30, 1938; s. Frank H. and N. Romaine (Sadler) M.; A.B., Duke U., 1960, J.D., 1963; postgrad. in labor relations Cornell U., 1966; m. Bonnie Douglass, June 18, 1960. Admitted to Pa. bar, 1963, D.C. bar, 1964, U.S. Supreme Ct. bar, 1970; asso. firm McNees, Wallace & Nurick, Harrisburg, 1963-67, partner, 1968—; solicitor Borough of Dauphin, 1964-67; gen. counsel Dickinson Coll., 1973—. Vice pres. ACLU of Pa., 1976—. Fellow Am. Bar Found.; mem. Am. Law Inst., Dauphin County Bar Assn. (dir. 1972-74), Pa. Bar Assn.(ho. of dels. 1968—, chmn. labor law sect. 1975-77), Am. Bar Assn. Office: PO Box 1166 Harrisburg PA 17108

MENARD, ALBERT ROBERT, JR., educator, lawyer; b. Macon, Ga., Apr. 10, 1918; s. Albert Robert and Margaret (Akerman) M.; A.B., U. Ga., 1938; J.D., Columbia U., 1941; postgrad. Harvard U., 1946; m. Laura E. McManus, Dec. 27, 1941; children—Albert Robert, Laura Suzanne Menard Wyckoff, John Tappan. Admitted to N.Y. bar, 1941, Colo. bar, 1952; atty. Assn. Casualty and Surety Cos., N.Y.C., 1941; instr. Wake Forest (N.C.) Coll., 1946-47, asso. prof., 1947-49; asso. prof. U. Colo. Sch. Law, 1949-55, prof., 1955-67; dean U. Idaho Coll. Law, Moscow, 1967-78, prof., 1978—; vis. faculty U. Fla., 1948, Ohio State U., 1956, Cornell U., 1959, U. Tex., 1961, U. Mo., 1966; counsel Joint Judiciary Com. of Colo. Gen. Assembly to Implement Jud. Reorgn., 1963-64; mem. Colo. Gov.'s Commn. on Mental Health and Mental Retardation, 1966-67. Served from 2d lt. to lt. col., AUS, 1941-46. Decorated Army Commendation medal; recipient award of merit Colo. Bar Assn., 1964; resolution of merit Idaho State Bar Assn., 1977. Mem. Am. Bar Assn., Order of Coif, Phi Beta Kappa, Phi Kappa Phi, Kappa Alpha Order, Phi Delta Phi. Episcopalian. Home: 602 Ridge Rd Moscow ID 83843

MENARD, HENRY WILLIAM, JR., geologist; b. Fresno, Calif., Dec. 10, 1920; s. Henry William and Blanche (Hodges) M.; B.S., Calif. Inst. Tech., 1942, M.S., 1947; Ph.D., Harvard U., 1949; m. Gifford Merrill, Sept. 21, 1946; children—Andrew O., Elizabeth M., Dorothy M. Geologist, Amerada Petroleum Corp., 1947; from asso. to supervisory oceanographer Navy Electronics Lab., 1949-55; asso. prof. marine geology Inst. Marine Resources, U. Calif., 1955-61, prof., 1961—, acting dir., 1967-68; prof. geology Scripps Inst. Oceanography, 1955-78; dir. U.S. Geol. Survey, 1978—. Mem. panel underwater swimmers Nat. Acad. Scis.-NRC, 1955, Pacific sci. bd., 1956-62, panel on ocean resources, 1958, mem. com. sci. and pub. policy; tech. asst. U.S. Office Sci. and Tech., 1965-66; oceanographic expdns. Mid-Pacific, 1949, No. Holiday, 1950, Cascadia, 1951, Capricorn, 1952-53, Chinook, 1956, Downwind, 1957-58, Aleutian Islands, Tonga, Fiji, Tahiti, S.A., others. Dir. Geol. Diving Cons., Inc., 1953-58. Served from ensign to lt. comdr., USNR, 1942-46. Decorated Bronze Star. Guggenheim Meml. Found. fellow, 1962-63; Overseas fellow Churchill Coll., 1970-71; Woods Hole Oceanographic Instn. fellow, 1973. Fellow Geol. Soc. Am., Am. Geophys. Union; mem. Nat. Acad. Scis., Am. Acad. Arts and Scis., Am. Assn. Petroleum Geologists, Royal Astron. Soc., Sigma Xi. Office: US Geological Survey 12201 Sunrise Valley Dr Reston VA 22092

MENCHEL, DONALD, TV exec.; b. N.Y.C., Oct. 26, 1932; s. Abraham and Tessie (Green) M.; B.A., Brandeis U., 1954; m. Barbara Winograd, Jan. 27, 1957; children—Pamela W., Terry G. Film booker ABC Films, N.Y.C., 1956; with Telcom Assos., N.Y.C., 1957-72, v.p., 1961, exec. v.p., 1972, also dir.; dir. mktg. Time-Life TV, N.Y.C., 1972-75; v.p., dir. sales MCA TV, N.Y.C., 1975-77, exec. v.p., 1977-78, pres., 1978—; bd. dirs. TV Bur. Advt., Internat. Radio and TV Found. Served with U.S. Army, 1954-56. Mem. Internat. Radio and TV Soc. Office: 445 Park Ave New York NY 10022

MENCHER, BRUCE STEPHAN, judge; b. Washington, May 21, 1935; s. Emanuel and Bertha Miriam (Robbin) M.; B.A., George Washington U., 1957, J.D. with honors, 1960; m. Janet Patricia Whitfield, Nov. 24, 1974; children by previous marriage—Sean Robbin, Marc Nadzo. Admitted to D.C. bar, 1960; gen. atty. Office Gen. Counsel, Dept. Agr., 1960-61; asst. corp. counsel for D.C., 1961-67; atty.-adviser Office Gen. Counsel, Bur. for Africa, AID, 1967-69; partner firm Wilkes & Artis, Washington, 1969-75; asso. judge Superior Ct. D.C., 1975—. Mem. gen. alumni gov. bd. George Washington U., 1972—, recipient Alumni Service award, 1975; life mem. Nat. Children's Center. Mem. Am., D.C. bar assns., Am. Judicature Soc., George Washington Law Assn. (exec. com. 1972-77), The Barristers, Phi Delta Phi (pres. Barrister Inn 1974-75). Home: 3821 Veazey St NW Washington DC 20016 Office: Room 1530 500 Indiana Ave NW Superior Ct DC Washington DC 20001. *While it may sound old-fashioned, I attribute my appointment to the bench, in large part, to hard work, dedication, a love of the law and respect for my fellow man. One should maintain his sense of balance, always try to understand the other person's position and, at all costs, maintain a sense of humor throughout.*

MENCHER, MELVIN, journalist, educator; b. Bklyn., Jan. 25, 1927; s. Peter and Theresa (Sherman) M.; student U. N.Mex., 1943-44; B.A., U. Colo., 1947; postgrad. (Nieman fellow), Harvard, 1952-53; m. Helen Chamberlain, Aug. 27, 1947; children—Thomas, Marianne, Nicholas. Reporter, UP, 1947-50; state polit. corr. Albuquerque Jour., 1951-54; reporter Fresno (Calif.) Bee, 1954-58; asst. prof. journalism U. Kans., Lawrence, 1958-62; asst. prof. Columbia, N.Y.C., 1962-65, asso. prof., 1965-75, prof., 1975—, asso. dir. summer program for journalism edn. of minorities, 1971. Served with USNR, 1945. Mem. Soc. Profl. Journalists, Nat. Council Coll. Pubs. Advisers, Kappa Tau Alpha. Contbg. author: Evaluating the Press, 1973; author: News Reporting and Writing, 1977; editor: The FNMA Guide to Buying, Financing and Selling Your Home, 1973; contbr. articles to profl. jours. Home: 450 Riverside Dr New York City NY 10027 Office: 705 Grad Sch Journalism Columbia U New York City NY 10027

MENCKE, JOHN BERNHARD, banker; b. Elizabeth, N.J., Feb. 19, 1926; s. J. William H. and Eleanor (Allsop) M.; B.S., U.S. Naval Acad., 1947; M.B.A., Harvard, 1956; m. Margaret Brady, June 28, 1952; children—Susan, Alice, John, Anne. Joined N.Y. Trust Co. (now Chem. Bank), 1956, asst. treas., 1957-59, asst. v.p., 1959, in charge mid-Manhattan br., 1959-68, v.p., 1963-69, met. marketing liaison officer, 1968-69, regional v.p., 1969-70, sr. v.p., 1970-79; pres., chief exec. officer Empire Nat. Bank, Newburgh, N.Y., 1979—. Served to lt. comdr. USNR, 1947-55. Clubs: Harvard (N.Y.C.); Army and Navy (Washington). Home: Van Beuren Rd Morristown NJ 07960 Office: 280 Broadway Newburgh NY 12550

MENDE, ROBERT GRAHAM, engring. assn. exec.; b. Newark, Dec. 4, 1926; s. Herman Ernest and Etta (Hillenbrand) M.; student Mass. Inst. Tech., 1944-45, N.Y. State Maritime Acad., 1945-47; B.S., Webb Inst. Naval Architecture, 1951; m. Joan B. Tamlyn, Apr. 12, 1958; children—Lisa Anne, Robert Graham. Project engr. Foster Wheeler Corp., N.Y.C., 1953-56; dist. mgr., naval architect Bird-Johnson Co., N.Y.C., 1956-62; sr. naval architect J.J. Henry Co., Inc., N.Y.C., 1962-69; sec., exec. dir. Soc. Naval Architects and Marine Engrs., N.Y.C., 1969—; mem. marine engring. council Underwriters Labs, Inc., 1969—; ad hoc vis. com. Engrs. Council for Profl. Devel., 1970-72. Served to lt. USNR, 1951-53. Fellow Royal Inst. Naval Architects; mem. Soc. Naval Architects and Marine Engrs. (chmn. N.Y. sect. 1968-69), Am. Soc. Naval Engrs., ASME, N.E. Coast Inst. Engrs. and Shipbuilders, Am. Soc. Assn. Execs., Council of Engring. and Sci. Soc. Execs., Webb Alumni Assn. (pres. 1970-72). Clubs: World Trade Center, Whitehall (N.Y.C.). Office: Suite 1369 One World Trade Center New York NY 10048

MENDEL, DENNIS DAVID, lawyer; b. Chgo., Apr. 2, 1940; s. Curt W. and Herta S. (Schoemann) M.; B.A., U. Chgo., 1961; M.A., U. Mich., 1962; J.D., U. Calif., Los Angeles, 1965; m. Janet Hoffman, Aug. 20, 1961; children—Lisa, Lara, Eden. Vice pres., sec., gen. counsel Beneficial Standard Corp., Los Angeles. Mem. Am., Calif., Los Angeles County bar assns. Office: 3700 Wilshire Blvd Los Angeles CA 90010

MENDELL, M(ORDECAI) LESTER, company dir.; b. N.Y., June 18, 1896; s. Abraham and Fannie (Weintraub) M.; student Coll. City N.Y., 1916-17, Sheffield Sci. Sch., Yale, 1918-19; m. Malvina Winifred Cohen, June 15, 1919; children—Edward, Oliver, Olga (Mrs. Wilbur Toll). Various positions mfg. and wholesale lumber firms, 1920-35; with liquidating com. N.Y. banks, 1933; dir., then chmn. Flushing Nat. Bank, 1940-50, merged into Bankers Trust Co. N.Y., 1950, v.p. banking dept., 1950-61; dir. mem. exec. com. Glen Alden Corp.; dir. Interstate Dept. Stores, Nat. Equipment Rental Corp., Palestine Econ. Corp., Bank Leumi, N.Y.C., First Nat. Bank Palm Beach. Bd. dirs. A.R.C., Palm Beach County (Fla.) Small Bus. Adminstrn., Nat. Jewish Welfare Bd., Mental Health Hosp., Palm Beach Habilitation Center, Fla. chpt. A.R.C., Civic Assn. Palm Beach; bd. govs. Good Samaritan Hosp.; bd. dirs., sec. Community Fund Palm Beach; trustee, mem. exec. com. United Jewish Appeal; trustee Fedn. Jewish Philanthropies N.Y.; founder L.I. Jewish Hosp.; chmn. lay bd. Queens Gen., Triboro hosp., N.Y.C.; nat. co-chmn. legacy com. Brandeis U. Served with U.S. Navy, 1917-18. Mem. Flushing Interfaith Soc. (gov.). Clubs: Harmonie, Lotos (N.Y.C.); Palm Beach Country (dir., past pres.). Address: 313 Dunbar Rd Palm Beach FL 33480

MENDELL, WAYNE, banker, industrialist; b. Moran, Kans., Dec. 22, 1886; s. Charles and Mary (Carmain) M.; ed. pub. and pvt. schs.; m. Marguerite Meeker, Apr. 29, 1910 (dec. 1939); children—Wayne, Donn, Nadine (Mrs. A. J. Lotito); m. 2d, Charlotte Knorr, Mar. 15, 1940. Pres., dir. hardware bus., Indian Ter., 1905-14; founder-dir. Bartlesville (Okla.) State Bank, Bartlesville Water Co., 1911-14; mem. advt. dept. Nat. Cash Register Co. (now NCR Corp.), Dayton, Ohio, 1914-16; founder NCR Mchts. Service Bur.; sales and advt. mgr. W.T. Grant Co., N.Y.C., 1916; with Am. Internat. Corp., 1918, exec. v.p. subsidiary, Internat. Steel Corp., 1919-21; assisted in reorganizing Brantford Computing Scale Co., 1922; with Allied Chem. Corp., 1923, sales mgr., v.p. Can. subs. Barrett Co., Ltd.; dir. gen. Canadian Asphalt Roofing Industry, 1926-28; v.p. U.S. Hoffman Machinery Corp., N.Y.C., 1928-33; dir. Fletcher Works, Inc., Phila.; pres., dir. Fletcher Machinery Corp., 1934-39; with Am. Machine & Metals, Inc. (name later changed to Ametek, Inc.), N.Y.C., 1939-48, v.p. charge sales, also pres., dir. Canadian subsidiary; pvt. cons. banks and indsl. corps., 1948-52; v.p. San Diego Fed. Savs. and Loan Assn., 1952-65. Republican. Presbyn. Clubs: Metropolitan, Bankers (N.Y.C.); Tavern (Chgo.); University, Cuyamaca (San Diego). Lectr. business tng. and fgn. trade, 1918-22. Author: The Steel Industry (with H.A. Knight); also numerous monographs on bus. management, notably, Appraisal of Intangibles. Home: Burton Pl 733 Kline St LaJolla CA 92037. *Strive for perfection though you never achieve it. Perfection is unattainable. Time itself is inexact. Nothing is absolute. Only God is absolute.*

MENDELOFF, ALBERT IRWIN, physician, educator; b. Charleston, W.Va., Jan. 29, 1918; s. Morris Israel and Esther (Cohen) M.; A.B., Princeton, 1938; M.D., Harvard, 1942, M.P.H., 1944; m. Natalie Lavenstein, Dec. 19, 1943; children—Henry, John, Katherine. Fellow in nutrition Rockefeller Found., 1943-44; nutrition cons. UNRRA mission to Greece, 1944-46; asst. prof. medicine and preventive medicine Washington U. Med. Sch., 1949-54, asso. prof., 1955; gastroenterology cons. Barnes Hosp., St. Louis, 1952-55; asso. prof. medicine Johns Hopkins Med. Sch., 1955-70, prof., 1970—; physician-in-chief Sinai Hosp., Balt., 1955—. Sr. surgeon Res. USPHS. Mem. Assn. Am. Physicians, Am. Soc. Clin. Investigation, Central Soc. Clin. Research, Am. Fedn. Clin. Research, Am. Gastroent. Assn., Phi Beta Kappa, Alpha Omega Alpha. Home: 2109 Northcliff Dr Baltimore MD 21209 Office: Sinai Hosp Baltimore MD 21215

MENDELOFF, HENRY, educator; b. N.Y.C., Jan. 1, 1917; s. Benjamin and Fannie (Levine) M.; B.S., CCNY, 1936, M.S. in Edn., 1939; Ph.D., Catholic U. Am., 1960. Tchr. secondary schs. in N.Y.C. and Washington, 1937-60; lectr. D.C. Tchrs. Coll., 1958, George Washington U., 1959; mem. faculty U. Md., 1960—, prof. Romance langs., 1968-74, emeritus, 1979—, chmn. dept., 1974-79; dir. seminar Fgn. Lang. Workshop, Cath. U. Am., 1961, asso. dir. NDEA summer lang. insts., 1961, 62, vis. prof., summers 1959-69. Served with USAAF, 1942-45. Grantee Gen. Research Bd., U. Md., 1963, 66. Mem. Am. Assn. Tchrs. Spanish and Portuguese (past pres. D.C. chpt.), MLA, AAUP, Md. Medieval Panel (past chmn.), Md. Fgn. Lang. Assn. (past pres.), Phi Beta Kappa, Sigma Delta Pi (past chpt. pres.). Author: The Evolution of the Conditional Sentence Contrary to Fact in Old Spanish, 1960, A Manual of Comparative Romance Linguistics: Phonology and Morphology, 1969; also articles. Home: 2014 Evansdale Dr Adelphi MD 20783 Office: Dept Spanish and Portuguese Univ Md College Park MD 20742

MENDELS, JOSEPH, psychiatrist; b. Capetown, South Africa, Oct. 29, 1937; s. Max and Lily (Turecki) M.; came to U.S., 1964, naturalized, 1975; M.B., Ch.B., U. Capetown, 1960; M.D., U. Witwatersrand, 1965; m. Ora Kark, June 17, 1960; children—Gilla Avril, Charles Alan, David Ralph. Intern U. Witwatersrand, 1961; resident in psychiatry U. Witwatersrand and U. N.C., 1962-67; chief depression research program, prof. psychiatry and pharmacology U. Pa. and VA Hosp., Phila., 1973—; ad hoc cons. NIMH; dir. Spectrum Publs.; lectr. univs. and hosps. Grantee NIMH, VA. Mem. Am. Psychiat. Assn. (Lester N. Hofheimer award 1976), Psychiat. Research Soc., Am. Coll. Neuropsychopharmacology, Congressium Internationale Neuropsychopharmacologia. Author, editor: Concepts of Depression, 1971; Biological Psychiatry, 1973. Contbr. articles to med. jours. Office: Veterans Administration Hospital 151E University and Woodland Aves Philadelphia PA 19104

MENDELSOHN, EVERETT IRWIN, educator; b. Yonkers, N.Y., Oct. 28, 1931; s. Morris H. and May (Albert) M.; A.B., Antioch Coll., 1953; postgrad. Marine Biol. Lab., Woods Hole, Mass., 1957; Ph.D., Harvard U., 1960; D.H.L., R.I. Coll., 1977; m. Mary B. Anderson, Sept. 14, 1974; children by previous marriage—Daniel Leeds, Sarah Ellicott, Joanna Moore; 1 Stepson, Jesse Marshall Wallace. Research asso. sci. and pub. policy Grad. Sch. Pub. Adminstrn. Harvard U., 1960-65, asso. prof. history of sci., 1965-69, prof. history of sci., 1969—, chmn. dept., 1971-78; overseas fellow Churchill Coll., U. Cambridge (Eng.); fellow Van Leer Jerusalem Found., Israel, 1978; vis. fellow Zentrum für Interdizsciplindre Forschung, Bielefeld, W. Ger., 1978; dir. research group on bio-med. scis. Program on Tech. and Soc., Harvard U., 1966-68, mem. Soc. Fellows, 1957-60. Trustee Cambridge Friends Sch., The Sanctuary; chmn. exec. com. Am. Friends Service Com. New Eng. regional office; chmn. Harvard-Radcliffe Child Care Council. Recipient Bowdoin prize, 1957. Fellow AAAS (v.p., chmn. sect. L), Am. Acad. Arts and Scis.; mem. Academie Internat. d'Historie des Scis., History Sci. Soc. (council), Internat. Acad. History Medicine, Internat. Council Sci. Policy Studies (v.p.). Author: Heat and Life: The History of the Theory of Animal Heat, 1964; Human Aspects of Biomedical Innovation, 1971; Topics in the Philosophy of Biology, 1976; The Social Production of Scientific Knowledge, 1977; The Social Assessment of Science, 1978. Editor: Jour. History Biology, 1967—; mem. editorial bd. Sci., 1965-70, Social Studies of Sci., 1970—, Ethics in Science and Medicine, 1973—, Philosophy and Medicine, 1974—, Sociology of Sciences, 1976—. Home: 26 Walker St Cambridge MA 02138

MENDELSOHN, HAROLD, sociologist, educator; b. Jersey City, Oct. 30, 1923; s. Louis and Bessie (Yulinsky) M.; B.S., Coll. City N.Y., 1945; M.A., Columbia, 1946; Ph.D., New Sch. Social Research, 1956; m. Irene Sylvia Gordon, Apr. 10, 1949; 1 dau., Susan Lynn. Sr. survey analyst U.S. Dept. State, Washington, 1951-52; research asso. Bur. Social Sci. Research, Am. U., Washington, 1951-56; asso. mgr. mktg. communications McCann-Erickson Advt., N.Y.C., 1956-58; asso. dir. Psychol. Corp., N.Y.C., 1958-62; prof. dept. mass communications U. Denver, 1962—, chmn., 1970-78; cons. Fed. Trade Commn., Denver Research Inst., U.S. Consumer Product Safety Commn., Ford Found., Fedn. Rocky Mountain States, CBS, Children's TV Workshop. Mem. Denver Council Pub. TV, 1970-78; mem. U.S. Surgeon Gen.'s Sci. Adv. Com. on TV and Social Behavior, 1969-71; bd. dirs. Nat. Safety Council, 1963-69; mem. pub. affairs adv. bd. Air Force Acad. Found., 1972—; mem. cancer control and rehab. adv. com. Nat. Cancer Inst., 1976; mem. adv. council, prevention div. Nat. Inst. Alcoholism and Alcohol Abuse, 1977—; trustee Colo. Med. Service, Inc., 1973-78. Recipient award TV Bur. Advt., 1962, Met. Life award Nat. Safety Council, 1967 Emmy award Nat. Acad. TV Arts Scis., 1968, Gold Camera award U.S. Indsl. Film Festival, 1972, Gold Eagle award, 1973, Silver award Internat. Festival Film and TV, 1974. Fellow Am. Psychol. Assn., Am. Sociol. Assn.; mem. Am. Assn. Pub. Opinion Research (pres. 1973-74), AAAS, Sigma Delta Chi, Omicron Delta Kappa. Club: Chicago Press. Author: Mass Entertainment, 1966; (with David H. Bayley) Minorities and the Police: Confrontation in America, 1969; (with Irving Crespi) Polls, Television and the New Politics, 1970; (with others) Television and Growing Up: The Impact of Televised Violence, 1972; (with Garrett O'Keefe) The People Choose a President, 1976. Editor: Mass Communications series, 1967-69. Contbr. articles to profl. jours. Home: 1451 E Cornell Pl Englewood CO 80110 Office: Dept Mass Communications U Denver 2490 S Gaylord Denver CO 80210

MENDELSOHN, JACK, clergyman, author; b. Cambridge, Mass., July 22, 1918; B.A., Boston U., 1939; S.T.B., Harvard, 1945; D.D. (hon.) Meadville Theol. Sch., 1962; m. Ruth P. Mendelsohn, Dec. 26, 1949 (div. 1969); children—Channing T., Deborah T., Kurt A.; m. 2d, Joan Silverstone Hall, Aug. 3, 1969: 1 stepdau., Lisabeth Hall. Ordained to ministry Unitarian Universalist Ch., 1945; minister in Rockford, Ill., 1947-54, Indpls., 1954-59, Arlington St. Ch., Boston, 1959-69; sr. minister First Unitarian Ch. Chgo., 1969-79; minister First Parish in Bedford (Mass.), 1979—; partner Halcyon House, 1979—; mem. adj. faculty Meadville Theol. Sch., U. Chgo., 1969-79. Vice pres. Unitarian Service Com., 1963-67; pres. Urban League Greater Boston, 1966-68; bd. dirs. World Affairs Council Boston, 1962-66; chmn. Alliance to End Repression, Chgo., 1970-76; mem. adv. council Comprehensive Health Planning, Chgo., 1969-79; pres. Hyde Park-Kenwood Council Chs. and Synagogues, Chgo., 1974-76; chmn. William Ellery Channing Bicentennial Celebration Com., 1979—. Pres. Abraham Lincoln Centre, Chgo., 1977-79, Binder Schweitzer Hosp. Found., N.Y.C., 1965—, Chgo. Meml. Assn., 1969-79. Mem. Internat. Inst. Boston (bd. dirs. 1962-68), NAACP, ACLU. Club: Harvard (Boston). Author: Why I Am a Unitarian, 1960; God, Allah and Ju Ju, 1962; The Forest Calls Back, 1965; The Martyrs, 1966; Channing, The Reluctant Radical, 1971; Alone Together, 1979. Address: 5 Ledgewood Dr Bedford MA 01730

MENDELSOHN, JOE, III, toy co. exec.; b. Cin., July 5, 1930; s. Simon and Marion (Lehman) M.; B.A. in History, Washington and Lee U., 1952. With Kenner Products Co., Cin., 1956—, sr. exec. v.p., 1977—, pres., 1978—; v.p. Gen. Mills, Inc.; bd. dirs. Jr. Achievement of Greater Cin.; trustee Cin. Better Bus. Bur.; mem. bus. adv. bd. U. Cin. Trustee Jewish Hosp., Cin.; bd. dirs. Dan Beard council Boy Scouts Am. Jewish. Clubs: Losantiville Country (pres.), Cin. Home: 1617 E McMillan St Apt 805 Cincinnati OH 45206 Office: 1014 Vine St Cincinnati OH 45202

MENDELSOHN, NATHAN SAUL, mathematician; b. Bklyn, Apr. 14, 1917; s. Samuel and Sylvia (Kirschenbaum) M.; B.A., U. Toronto (Ont., Can.), 1939, M.A., 1940, Ph.D., 1942; m. Helen Brontman, Oct. 26, 1940; children—Eric, Alan. Teaching fellow U. Toronto, 1939-42; lectr. Queen's U., 1945-46; asst. prof. math. U. Man. (Can.), Winnipeg, 1947, now prof., head dept. math.; participant Internat. Math. Union, Saltzobaden, Sweden, 1962, Dubna, USSR, 1966, Menton, France, 1970. Fellow Royal Soc. Can. (Can. del.); mem. Computing and Data processing Soc. Can. (dir. 1960-65). Contbr. numerous articles on geometry, group theory and combinational math. to profl. jours. Home: 364 Enniskillen Winnipeg MB R2V 0J3 Canada Office: U Man 343 Machray Hall Winnipeg MB R3T 2N2 Canada

MENDELSOHN, WALTER, lawyer; b. N.Y.C., Jan. 22, 1897; s. Sigmund and Paula (Stieglitz) M.; A.B., Yale, 1918, LL.B., 1921; m. Josephine Becker, Mar. 31, 1927; children—Sue (Mrs. Robert Mellins), Paul Richard. Admitted to N.Y. bar, 1921; partner

Proskauer Rose Goetz & Mendelsohn, and predecessor firms, N.Y.C., 1926—. Dir. Seligman & Latz, Inc., 150 Central Park S. Corp. Mem. bd. Surprise Lake Camp, Welfare and Health Council; exec., adminstrv. coms. Am. Jewish Com., 1942—; bd. visitors State Tng. Sch. for Boys; chmn. trustees, chmn. bd., past pres. Jewish Bd. Guardians; trustee, past chmn. com. communal planning Fedn. Jewish Philanthropies; hon. trustee, past pres. Camp Ramapo; past trustee Inst. Internat. Edn.; trustee, pres. Henry Kaufmann Found., Edward de Rothschild Found. Served as pvt. U.S. Army, World War I; from maj. to lt. col. AUS, World War II; liaison officer SSS to under sec. war. Mem. Yale Law Sch. Assn. N.Y. (mem. bd.), Assn. Bar City N.Y., N.Y. County Lawyers Assn., Am., N.Y. State bar assns., Am. Judicature Soc. Clubs: Yale, Harmonie (N.Y.C.). Home: 150 Central Park S New York City NY 10022 also High Up Purdy's Station NY 10578 Office: 300 Park Ave New York City NY 10022

MENDELSON, CURTIS LESTER, obstetrician, gynecologist; b. N.Y.C., Sept. 4, 1913; s. Lester and Elsa Aronheim (Robinson) M.; B.A., U. Mich., 1934; M.D., Cornell U., 1938; m. Marie Victoria Krause, 1941. Intern, N.Y. Hosp., N.Y.C., 1938-39; resident in obstetrics and gynecology N.Y. Lying-In Hosp., N.Y.C., 1939-41, N.Y. Polyclinic Hosp., N.Y.C., 1941-43; attending obstetrician and gynecologist N.Y. Hosp., 1945-59, N.Y. Polyclinic Hosp., 1950-59; dir. cardiac clinic N.Y. Lying-In Hosp., 1945-59; asso. prof. obstetrics and gynecology Cornell U., 1950-59; prof. N.Y. Polyclinic Med. Sch., 1950-59; obstetric cons. N.Y.C. Dept. Health, 1944-49; dir., cons. Green Turtle Cay Clinic, Abaco, Bahamas, 1958—. Fellow N.Y. Obstetrical Soc., N.Y. Acad. Medicine, A.C.S., Internat. Coll. Surgeons, AMA, Am. Pub. Health Assn., Am. Coll. Obstetricians, Gynecologists; mem. Internat. Tuna Tournament (chmn.), English Channel Swimming Assn., Flying Physicians Assn., Phi Beta Kappa, Alpha Omega Alpha, Phi Kappa Phi, Phi Sigma. Club: Sands Point Bath and Tennis. Author: Cardiac Disease in Pregnancy, 1960; contbr. numerous articles on heart disease in pregnancy to med. publs.; first to describe a pulmonary disease which now bears the name Mendelson's Syndrome. Home and Office: Green Turtle Cay Abaco Bahamas

MENDELSON, ELLIOTT, educator, mathematician; b. N.Y.C., May 24, 1931; s. Joseph and Helen (Bienstock) M.; A.B., Columbia U., 1952; M.A., Cornell U., 1954, Ph.D., 1955; m. Arlene Zimmerman, Jan. 25, 1959; children—Julia, Hilary, Peter. Instr., U. Chgo., 1955-56; jr. fellow Soc. Fellows, Harvard, 1956-58; Ritt instr. Columbia, 1958-61; mem. faculty Queens Coll., City U. N.Y., 1961—, prof. math., 1965—, dir., instr. NSF math. program for high sch. students, 1964-71. Mem. Am. Math. Soc., Math Assn. Am., Assn. for Symbolic Logic, Phi Beta Kappa. Author: Introduction to Mathematical Logic, 1964; Boolean Algebra and Switching Circuits, 1970; Number Systems, 1973; also articles. Research in axiomatic set theory and math. logic especially ind. various important propositions of axiomatic set theory; axiom of choice, axiom of restriction. Home: 10 Pinewood Rd East Hills Roslyn NY 11576 Office: Queens Coll Flushing NY 11367

MENDELSON, LEE M., writer, producer, dir.; b. San Francisco, Mar. 24, 1933; s. Palmer C. and Jeanette D. (Wise) M.; B.A., Stanford U., 1954; m. Deborah B. Muller, Nov. 10, 1973; children—Glenn, Linda, Jason. With Sta. KPIX-TV, 1961-63; chmn. bd., pres. Lee Mendelson Film Prodns. Inc., Burlingame, Calif., 1973—; producer Charlie Brown TV spls.; guest instr. in communications Stanford U. Served to 1st lt. USAF, 1954-57. Recipient Emmy award (4), Peabody award. Mem. Writers Guild Am., Dirs. Guild Am. Office: 1408 Chapin Ave Burlingame CA 94010

MENDELSON, MICHAEL, physician, hosp. adminstr.; b. N.Y.C., Mar. 24, 1909; s. Max and Ida (Eisenstein) M.; A.B., Coll. City N.Y., 1930; M.D., U. Vienna (Austria), 1936; m. Rose Kutner, Apr. 5, 1930; children—Neil Harland, Penny Sue. Intern Ideal Hosp., Endicott, N.Y., 1936-37; resident Binghamton (N.Y.) State Hosp., 1937-40, asst. physician, 1937-42; individual practice psychiatry and neurology, N.Y.C., 1946-55; asst. med. dir. Ancora State Hosp., Hammonton, N.J., 1955-58; dir. tng. N.J. Neuropsychiat. Inst., Skillman, N.J., 1958-68, med. dir., 1968-74; mem. staff Diagnostic Center, Menlo Park, N.J., 1974-75; asso. clin. prof. psychiatry Rutgers Med. Sch., 1972-77; cons. psychiatry N.Y.C. Dept. Welfare, 1946-55; cons. neurology Carrier Clinic, Belle Mead, N.J., 1962-75; cons. neurology and psychiatry Somerset Hosp., Somerville, N.J., 1960-77. Served with AUS, 1942-46. Diplomate neurology and psychiatry Am. Bd. Neurology and Psychiatry; certified mental hosp. adminstr. Fellow Am. Psychiat. Assn. (life); mem. Phi Beta Kappa. Club: K.P. Address: 63 Waterbury Ln Westbury NY 11590

MENDELSON, THEODORE R., ladies apparel mfg. co. exec.; b. Quincy, Ill., July 25, 1940; s. Lawrence and Leah Frances (Mestman) M.; B.S. in Mktg., Northwestern U., 1962; m. Susan Beth Komie, Sept. 9, 1962; children—Timothy R., Jill Lynn. Vice pres. merchandising Jack Winter, Inc., Milw., 1966-72, Salem Co., Winston-Salem, N.C., 1972-73; pres. Mr. Alex, Los Angeles, 1973-78, Alex Colman, Inc., Los Angeles, 1978—. Served with USAR, 1964. Home: 19359 Winged Fort Circle Northridge CA 91326 Office: 2100 S Figueroa St Los Angeles CA 90007

MENDELSON, WALLACE, educator; b. Dubuque, Iowa, Sept. 25, 1911; s. Morris and Marion (Humann) M.; B.A., U. Wis., 1933, Ph.D., 1940; LL.B., Harvard, 1936; m. Margery Rosen, Dec. 2, 1942; children—Wallace Brand, Roger Hugh. Instr., U. Mo. at Columbia, 1940-41, U. Ill. at Urbana, 1941-42; prof. U. Tenn., 1946-57, U. Tex. at Austin, 1957—; asst. to Justice Frankfurter, U.S. Supreme Ct., 1953-54; spl. asst. atty. gen. U.S., 1973. Dir. summer seminar Nat. Endowment for Humanities, 1977. Served with USAAF, 1942-46. Mem. So. Polit. Sci. Assn. (pres. 1968-69), Am. Polit. Sci. Assn. (mem. exec. council 1965-67). Author: The Constitution and the Supreme Court, 1958, rev. edit., 1961; Justices Black and Frankfurter, 1961, rev. edit., 1966; Discrimination, 1962; Supreme Court, Law and Discretion, 1967. Contbg. author: The Study of Comparative Government—Essays Written in Honor of Frederic Austin Ogg, 1949; The Commerce Clause, 1964. Editor: Felix Frankfurter: A Tribute, 1964; Felix Frankfurter: The Judge, 1964; John Marshall (by J.B. Thayer), 1974. Editor-in-chief ann. report U.S. Commn. Civil Rights, 1961. Contbr. articles to profl. jours. Home: 2605 Pecos St Austin TX 78703

MENDENHALL, EDWARD EMERSON, JR., realtor; b. Greensboro, N.C., June 24, 1909; s. Edward Emerson and Ida Martisha (Allred) M.; B.S. in Commerce, U. N.C., 1930; LL.D., High Point Coll., 1966; m. Annie Robbins, Oct. 20, 1934; children—Edward Emerson III, Martha (Mrs. John C. Braman). Sr. partner Mendenhall-Moore, realtors, High Point, N.C., 1931—; dir. emeritus Perpetual Savs. & Loan Assn.; dir. High Point Bank and Trust Co. Pres. High Point Community Chest, 1942, Downtown Devel. Corp., High Point, 1959-66. Trustee Guilford Coll. Named N.C. Realtor of Year, 1953. Mem. High Point C. of C. (past pres.), High Point Bd. Realtors (pres. 1935, 54), N.C. Assn. Realtors (pres. 1938, life mem. exec. com.), Nat. Assn. Realtors (v.p. 1941, pres., 1964, now dir., life mem. exec. com., pres. statutes com., mem. exec. com.), Internat. Real Estate Fedn. (council, pres. Am. chpt. 1972), Soc. Indsl. Realtors, Realtors Nat. Mktg. Inst. (pres. 1949), Am. Soc. Real Estate Counselors, Inst. Real Estate Mgmt. Quaker. Rotarian. Clubs: Emerywood Country, String and Splinter (High Point). Home: 1003 Parkwood Circle High Point NC 27260 Office: Box 2288 201 Church Ave High Point NC 27261

MENDENHALL, GEORGE EMERY, educator; b. Muscatine, Iowa, Aug. 13, 1916; s. George Newton and Mary Christine (Johnson) M.; B.A., Midland Coll., Fremont, Nebr., 1936, Litt.D., 1959; B.D., Gettysburg Sem., 1938; Ph.D., Johns Hopkins, 1947; m. Eathel Louise Tidrick, Dec. 6, 1943; children—George David, Lauri Philip, Stanley Theodore, Gordon Louis, Stephen Robert. Ordained to ministry Lutheran Ch., 1942-54; pastor in Laramie, Wyo., 1942-43; asst. prof. Hamma Div. Sch., 1947-50, asso. prof., 1950-52; asso. prof. U. Mich., 1952-58, prof., 1958—, chmn. com. studies religion Coll. Lit. Sci. and Arts, 1957-67, chmn. council grad. studies religion, 1964-66, dir. Euphrates archaeol. expdn. to Syria, 1971; ann. prof. Am. Sch. Oriental Research, Jerusalem, Jordan, 1955-56, dir., 1965-66; dir. Am. Center Oriental Research, Amman, Jordan, 1975; field supr. Brit. Sch. of Archaeology in Jerusalem in excavation Jericho, 1956. Pres. Lutheran Student Found., U. Mich., 1962-65. Trustee Chgo. Luth. Theol. Sem., 1956-69. Sr. fellow Nat. Endowment for Humanities, 1971. Served to lt. (j.g.) USNR, 1943-46; PTO. Mem. Am. Oriental Soc. (pres. Middle West br. 1950-51. asso. editor jour. 1954-59), Soc. Bibl. Lit. (pres. Midwest sect. 1960), Archaeol. Inst. Am., Am. Schs. Oriental Research, Bibl. Colloquium (pres. 1963-65), Phi Beta Kappa. Author: Law and Covenant in Israel and the Ancient Near East, 1955; The Tenth Generation: The Origins of the Biblical Tradition, 1973. Cons. editor, contbr. Interpreters Dictionary of the Bible, 1962. Contbr. Ency. Brit., profl. jours. Home: 1510 Cedar Bend Dr Ann Arbor MI 48105 Office: U Mich Ann Arbor MI 48109

MENDENHALL, ROBERT VERNON, educator; b. Geneva, Ind., Dec. 27, 1920; s. Carl and Lulu (Niswander) M.; B.A. summa cum laude, Ohio State U., 1947, M.A., 1949, Ph.D., 1952; m. Gay Dalrymple, Dec. 15, 1944; children—Lisa, Robin, Valerie. Instr., Ohio State U., 1951-53; sr. engr. N.Am. Aviation Corp., 1953-55; mathematician Vitro Labs., Inc., 1955; asst. prof. U. Miami, 1955-62; asso. prof. Ohio Wesleyan U., 1962-66, prof. math., 1966—; cons. math Benares Hindu U., 1965, Andhra (India) U., 1966, U. Roorkee (India), 1970. Served with AUS, 1942-46; ETO Mem. Am., Indian math. socs., Math. Assn. Am., A.A.A.S., Phi Beta Kappa, Sigma Xi. Author: (with Herman Meyer) Techniques of Differentiation and Integration, 1966. Home: 129 Oak Hill Ave Delaware OH 43015

MENDENHALL, RODGER EUGENE, hosp. exec.; b. Marietta, Ohio, Nov. 4, 1928; s. Glenn Travis and S. Gertrude (Wible) M.; B.S., Marietta Coll., 1952; M.S., U. Pitts., 1959; m. Barbara Gramkow Prunty, Dec. 29, 1973; children by previous marriage—Becky, Debbie, Rodger. Rep., Asso. Hosp. Service, Inc., Youngstown, Ohio, 1952-54; rowing coach Marietta Coll., 1953-57; acting adminstr. Marietta Meml. Hosp., 1954-57; adminstr. Woodside Receiving Hosp., Youngstown, 1959-61, Columbus (Ohio) State Hosp., 1961-64; dir. Highland View Hosp., Cleve., 1964-68; adminstr. Cuyahoga County Hosp., 1968-69, U. Cin. Gen. Hosp., 1969-75; asso. prof. hosp. adminstrn. U. Cin. Colls. Medicine and Pharmacy, 1969-75; exec. dir. Med. Center, Columbus, Ga., 1975-77; supt. Dayton Mental Health and Developmental Center, 1977—; clin. prof. Sch. Profl. Psychology, Wright State U., 1978—, asso. clin. prof. dept. psychiatry Sch. Medicine, 1978—; preceptor, adj. instr. hosp. adminstrn. U. Pitts., Xavier U., Cin. Welfare rep. Ohio Citizens Council for Health and Welfare, 1964-69; mem. com. on chronically ill Welfare Fedn.; mem. bd. Health Planning Assn. Hamilton County, Ohio, 1969-75; mem. advisory council Health Service div. Columbus Coll., 1975-77; mem. adv. council Girrard Clinic, 1975-77; mem. Med. Examiner Bd., 1975-76; trustee Blue Cross-Blue Shield of Ga., 1976-77; bd. dirs. Talbert House, 1969-75, sec., mem. exec. com., 1971; mem. bd. Ambulatory Patient Care, Inc., 1969-75, chmn. bd., 1970-72. Mem. Ohio Valley Regional Med. Program, 1969-75. Served with USN, 1946-48. Mem. Am., Ohio (chmn. S.W. dist. 1972-75, chmn. govt. relations com., 1972-75, trustee), Ga. (legis. com. 1976-77) Greater Dayton Area (sec. 1979—) hosp. assns., Cin. Hosp. Council, Soc. Hosp. and Med. Adminstrn. (pres. 1971-72), Assn. Mental Health Adminstrs., Alpha Tau Omega. Methodist. Contbr. articles to profl. publs. Home: 90 Lynn Rae Circle Centerville OH 45459 Office: Office of the Superintendent Dayton Mental Health and Developmental Center 2611 Wayne Ave Dayton OH 45420

MENDICINO, V. FRANK, lawyer; b. Denver, June 26, 1939; s. V. Flory and Helen Margaret (Armbrust) M.; B.S., U. Wyo., 1962, J.D. with honors, 1970; m. Barbara Jane Gilroy, Nov. 3, 1963; children—V. Frank, Michael Flory, Marlo Anne. Admitted to Wyo. bar, 1970, since practiced in Laramie; justice of peace, Albany County, 1971-72; asst. city atty. Laramie, 1970-75; mem. Wyo. Ho. of Reps. from Albany County, 1973-75; atty. gen. State of Wyo., 1975-78; vis. instr. U. Wyo., 1972—. Treas. Cathedral Home for Children, Laramie, 1971-75; pres. Laramie United Way, 1973. Served to capt. AUS, 1964-66. Recipient Distinguished Service award Wyo. Jr. C. of C., 1973. Mem. Am., Wyo., Albany County bar assns., Nat. Assn. Attys. Gen., Am. Legion. Democrat. Clubs: Elks, Rotary. Contbr. articles to mags. Home: 3711 Dover Rd Cheyenne WY 82001 Office: 2424 Pioneer Ave Suite 403 Cheyenne WY 82001

MENDONSA, ARTHUR ADONEL, city ofcl.; b. Wauchula, Fla., Apr. 5, 1928; s. Arthur Abner and Mamie (Swafford) M.; B.A., Emory U., 1952; M. City Planning, Ga. Inst. Tech., 1954; m. Beverly Glover, Sept. 6, 1951; children—Arthur Adonel, George Andrew. Planning dir. Gainesville-Hall County (Ga.) Planning Commn., 1954-56, 57-60; sr. planner Charleston (S.C.) County Planning Commn., 1956-57; exec. dir. Savannah-Chatham (Ga.) County Met. Planning Commn., 1960-62; city mgr. Savannah, 1962-67; 71—; dir. field services, asst. prof. Inst. Govt., U. Ga., Athens, 1967-69; exec. asst. to chmn. DeKalb County Bd. Commrs., Decatur, Ga., 1969-71; mem. Coastal Area Planning and Devel. Commn., 1972—, Ga. Gov.'s Adv. Council on Coastal Zone Mgmt., 1976-78, Ga. Coastal Mgmt. Bd., 1978—. Mem. Am. Inst. Planners (bd. examiners), Am. Soc. Pub. Adminstrn., Internat. City Mgrs. Assn., Ga. City-County Mgrs. Assn. (pres. 1974-75). Kiwanian. Author: Simplified Financial Management in Local Government, 1967. Home: 401-B Tattnall St Savannah GA 31401

MENEELEY, EDWARD STERLING, artist, pub.; b. Wilkes-Barre, Pa., Dec. 18, 1927; s. Edward Sterling and Louina Halter M.; student Murray Art Sch., Wilkes-Barre, 1947-50, Sch. Visual Arts, N.Y.C., 1952-53. One-man exhbs. include: Donovan Gallery, Phila., 1952, Parma Gallery, N.Y.C., 1962, Teuscher Gallery, N.Y.C., 1966, 68, Inst. Contemporary Arts, London, 1971, Victoria and Albert Mus., London, 1972, U. Sussex (Eng.), 1972, Whitechapel Art Gallery, London, 1973, Demos Gallery, Athens, Greece, 1976, Frank Marino Gallery, N.Y.C., 1978; vis. lectr. Belleville Coll., St. Louis, Art Students League, N.Y.C.; pres. ESM Documentations, N.Y.C.; fine arts cons. Arts Initiatives, Inc., N.Y.C. Served with USNR, 1945-47, 50-52. Nat. Endowment Arts grantee. Mem. Artist Club N.Y.C., Inst. Contemporary Arts London. Founder, Portable Gallery Press, 1957-67. Office: 114 Liberty St New York NY 10006

MENEELY, GEORGE RODNEY, physician; b. Hempstead, N.Y., Sept. 30, 1911; s. Charles D. and Emily F. (Gahn) M.; B.S., Princeton U., 1933; M.D., Cornell U., 1937; m. Mary Leslie Stewart, May 29, 1968; children by previous marriage—Judith, Denny Meneely Chapnick, George Rodney. James Gleason fellow medicine U. Rochester Sch. Medicine and Dentistry, 1940-41; asst. resident medicine Strong Meml. Hosp., also asst. medicine U. Rochester Sch. Medicine and Dentistry, 1939-40; fellow medicine U. Rochester Sch. Medicine and Dentistry, 1938-39; intern medicine Strong Meml. Hosp., 1937-38; instr. medicine La. State U. Sch. Medicine, 1941-43; vis. physician Charity Hosp., New Orleans, 1941-43, dir. lung sta., 1942-43; mem. faculty Vanderbilt U. Sch. Medicine, 1943-62, vis. physician Univ. Hosp., 1943-62, asso. prof. medicine, 1953-62; asso. prof. medicine Northwestern U. Med. Sch., also dir. dept. sci. assembly AMA, 1962-63; mem. staff U. Tex. M.D. Anderson Hosp. and Tumor Inst., 1963-66, acting head dept. biomath., 1964-65, internist, 1963-66, chief cardio-pulmonary function lab., 1963-66, cons., 1966—; prof. nuclear medicine U. Tex. Grad. Sch. Biomed. Sci. at Houston, 1963-66; prof. physiology, biophysics and medicine La. State U. Sch. Medicine, Shreveport, 1966—, asso. dean, 1966-73; cons. in field, 1943—; mem. sci. adv. com. United Health Founds., 1963-70, Grayson Found., 1965-75. Diplomate Am. Bd. Internal Medicine. Fellow A.C.P., Am. Coll. Cardiology (pres. 1957-58), Am. Coll. Nuclear Medicine, Council Clin. Cardiology, Council Clin. Epidemiology, Am. Heart Assn.; mem. Am. Physiol. Soc., Biophys. Soc., So. Soc. Clin. Investigation, Soc. Exptl. Biology and Medicine, Am. Fedn. Clin. Research, Am. Thoracic Soc., N.Y. Acad. Scis., Assn. Computing Machinery, Assn. Am. Med. Colls., AAUP, Pan Am. Med. Assns., Sigma Xi. Author numerous articles, chpts. in books. Office: LS U Med Center PO Box 33932 Shreveport LA 71130

MENEES, TIMOTHY RYAN, editorial cartoonist; b. Seattle, Nov. 15, 1943; s. Gerald Edwin and Marjorie Dean (Williams) M.; B.A. in Polit. Sci., U. Wash., Seattle, 1966; m. Katherine Julianna Determan, Aug. 24, 1968; children—Timothy Marion, Rebecca Katherine. Reporter, Bremerton (Wash.) Sun, 1966, Seattle Post-Intelligencer, 1972-76; editorial cartoonist Pitts. Post-Gazette, 1976—; syndicated comic script Wordsmith, 1976-78. Served with USAF, 1966-72. Decorated Air Force Commendation medal; recipient Best Weekly Cartoon of Year award Nat. Newspaper Assn., 1974. Mem. Assn. Am. Editorial Cartoonists. Episcopalian. Home: 5001 Highland Ave Bethel Park PA 15102 Office: 50 Boulevard of Allies Pittsburgh PA 15230

MENEGUS, ALFRED AURELIUS, publisher; b. Clifton, N.J., Jan. 20, 1914; s. Bortolo and Margaret (DeLotto) M.; student U. Fla., 1944; m. Marthe B. Menegus, Nov. 21, 1972. Mng. editor Clifton Jour., 1936-41; advt./pub. relations mgr. Link Radio Corp., N.Y.C., 1947-52; advt./sales promotion mgr. Sun Radio & Electronics Co., Inc., N.Y.C., 1952-60; sales promotion mgr. GPL div. Gen. Precision, Inc., Pleasantville, N.Y., 1960-63; advt./pub. relations mgr. Visual Electronics Corp., N.Y.C., 1963-67; pub. Electronic Technician/Dealer, N.Y.C., 1971—. Mem. Grand Jury, Passaic County, N.J., 1969. Served with USAAF, 1942-46. Mem. Radio Club Am., VFW. Republican. Roman Catholic. Home: 3B Linden Ct Old Bridge NJ 08857 Office: 757 3d Ave New York City NY 10017

MENEN, AUBREY (SALVATOR AUBREY CLARENCE MENON), author; b. London, Apr. 22, 1912; s. Kali Narain and Alice Violet (Everett) M.; student Univ. Coll., London, 1930-32. Dramatic critic The Bookman, London, 1934; dir. Exptl. Theatre, London, 1935-36; with Personalities Press Service, London, 1937-39; head English drama dept. (Allied war publicity) All India Radio, 1940-41; script editor info. films Govt. of India, 1943-45, staff polit. dept. 1946; head motion picture dept. J. Walter Thompson Co. (Eastern, Ltd.), 1947-48; author: The Prevalence of Witches, 1949; The Stumbling Stone, 1949; The Backward Bride, 1950; The Duke of Gallodoro, 1952; Dead Man in the Silver Market, 1953; The Ramayana, 1954; The Abode of Love, 1956; The Fig Tree, 1959; Rome for Ourselves, 1960; Speaking the Language Like a Native, 1962; Shela, 1962; A Conspiracy of Women, 1965; India, 1969; The Space Within the Heart, 1970; Upon this Rock, 1972; Cities in the Sand, 1973; Fonthill, 1974; (with Graham Hall) The Mystics, 1974; London, 1976; Venice, 1976; also numerous essays, articles. Roman Catholic. Address: Hotel Tramonto d'Oro 84010 Praiano (SA) Costiera Amalfitana Italy. *I have been a writer since I was sixteen. I am now sixty and I have spent the years between learning my craft. The hardest lesson to learn was that there is only one chair at a writer's desk. He works alone; nobody can advise him. If anybody tries, he must be completely ignored.*

MENETREY, LOUIS CHARLES, army officer; b. Hollywood, Calif., Aug. 19, 1929; s. Louis Charles and Bertha (Selzer) M.; B.A., UCLA, 1953; M.A., Georgetown U., 1967; m. Susan Steel Karabin, Oct. 27, 1979; children—Linda, Susan, Kathleen, Louis. Commd. 2d lt., U.S. Army, 1954, advanced through grades to maj. gen., 1977; asst. div. comdr. 2d Inf. div., 1975-76; asst. dep. comdr. U.S. Army Combined Arms Combat Devel. Activity, Ft. Leavenworth, Kans., 1976-77; dep. comdr., 1977-78; comdg. gen. Fort Carson and 4th Inf. div., Fort Carson, Colo., 1978—. Decorated D.S.C., D.F.C. with oak leaf cluster, air medal with 17 oak leaf clusters, Bronze star, others. Office: Comdg Gen Fort Carson and 4th Inf Div Fort Carson CO 80913

MENG, JOHN JOSEPH, educator; b. Cleve., Dec. 12, 1906; s. George Edward and Marie Louise (Gott) M.; A.B., Catholic U. Am., 1928, A.M., 1929, Ph.D., 1932, LL.D., 1975; student Ecole Libre des Sciences Politiques, Paris, 1930-31; LL.D., Manhattan Coll., 1960; L.H.D., Canisius Coll., 1961; D.Litt., Siena Coll., 1966; Pd.D., St. John's U., 1966; L.H.D., Wilberforce U., 1967; LL.D., Georgetown U., 1977, city U. N.Y., 1979; m. Marjorie F. Brunini, Aug. 18, 1937; children—Marie Louise, Marjorie Kathryn, John Joseph, George Edward, Alexander Brunini, Charles Frederick and Matthew Thomas (twins), Michael Richard. Asst. in politics Cath. U. Am., Washington, 1931, instr., 1932-38, asst. prof., 1938; instr. polit sci. Queens Coll., Flushing, L.I., N.Y., 1938-41, asst. prof., 1941-48, asso. prof., 1948, chmn. dept. polit. sci., 1941-44, 45-49, chmn. div. social scis., 1942-43, 47-48; lectr. Nazareth Coll., Rochester, N.Y., summer 1932; lectr. govt. Turner's Diplomatic Sch., Washington, 1937, 38; prof. history Hunter Coll., N.Y., 1949-52, prof. history, dean adminstrn., 1952-60, pres., 1960-67, emeritus, 1967—; exec. v.p. Fordham U., 1966-69; pres. Marymount Coll., Tarrytown, N.Y., 1969-75, emeritus, 1975—; exec. dir. Consortium Small Pvt. Colls., 1975-76, sr. staff adviser, 1976-78; pres. Meng Asso. Consultants, Inc., 1978—. Engaged in hist. research Carnegie Instn. Washington, 1936-54; sec. Coll. Arts and Scis., Cath. U. Am., 1937-38; chmn. bd. Taraknath Das Found.; grants com. Lois and Samuel Silberman Fund, Inc. Served with USMCR, 1929-30. Mem. Am. Cath. Hist. Assn. (exec. com.), Soc. Early N.Y. History (dir.), Cath. Commn. on Intellectual and Cultural Affairs, U.S. Cath. Hist. Soc., Institut Francais de Washington (trustee). Author: The Comte de Vergennes: European Phases of His American Diplomacy. 1932; Guide to Materials for American History in Libraries and Archives of Paris, Vol. II (with others), 1944; Christianity and America (with others), 1948. Editor: Despatches and Instructions of Conrad Alexandre Gerard, 1939. Home: 17 Heritage Ct Tarrytown NY 10591

MENGDEN, JOSEPH MICHAEL, investment banker; b. Houston, Sept. 28, 1924; s. Hippolyt Frederick and Amalie (Dittlinger) M.; Ph.B., U. Notre Dame, 1949; m. Suzanne Miner, Sept. 30, 1950; children—Anne Elise, Amanda Mary, Michael Joseph, Charles Louis, Melissa Mary, Mary Miner. Vice pres. Nat. Bank of Detroit, 1950-67; exec. v.p., dir. First of Mich. Capital Corp., Detroit, 1967. Served to 1st lt. USAAF, World War II. Decorated Air medal with 2 oak leaf clusters. Home: 87 Kenwood Rd Grosse Pointe Farms MI 48236 Office: 100 Renaissance Center 26th Floor Detroit MI 48243

MENGEL, CHARLES EDMUND, educator, physician; b. Balt., Nov. 29, 1931; s. Charles LeRoy and Anna (Apgar) M.; A.B. in Chemistry, Lafayette Coll., 1953; M.D., Johns Hopkins, 1957; m. Paula Padgett, June 5, 1978; children—Cheryl Lynn, Charles Edmund, Gregory John, Scott Alan, Carol Ann. Intern Johns Hopkins Hosp., 1957-58; resident Duke Hosp., 1958-59, 61-62; clin. asso. NIH, 1959-61; mem. faculty Duke Med. Sch., 1961-65; dir. hematology and oncology Ohio State U. Med. Sch., 1965-69; prof. medicine, chmn. dept. U. Mo. Med. Sch. at Columbia, 1969—. Served with USPHS, 1959-61. Markle scholar acad. medicine, 1963; Doan prof., 1965-69. Mem. A.C.P., Am. Fedn. Clin. Research, Am. Soc. Hematology, Am. Soc. Clin. Investigation. Author textbook, articles. Home: Route 9 Columbia MO 65201

MENGEL, ROBERT MORROW, ornithologist; b. Glenview, Ky., Aug. 19, 1921; s. Charles C. and Mary A. (Kelly) M.; B.S., Cornell U., 1947; M.A., U. Mich., 1950, Ph.D., 1958; m. Marion Anne Jenkinson, Dec. 21, 1963; 1 dau., Tracy Lynn. Research asso. U. Kans., Lawrence, 1953-62, mem. faculty, prof. systematics and ecology, 1972—, curator Mus. Natural History, 1972—; one-man exhbns. and group shows of paintings and watercolors include galleries in Lawrence, 1973, 76, 77, Norman, Okla., 1974, Wichita, 1978, Ithaca, N.Y., 1978, Wausau, Wis., 1979. Served with USAAF, 1942-46. Fellow Am. Ornithologists Union (editor jour. 1962-67, editor monograph series 1970-74, councillor 1972-74); mem. Cooper (councillor 1966-68), Wilson (asso. editor bull. 1953-54), Kan., Ky. ornithol. socs., Soc. Study Evolution, Am. Soc. Systematic Zoologists, Soc. Am. Naturalists, Brit. Ornithologists Union, Sigma Xi. Author, illustrator: The Birds of Kentucky, 1965; author: The Ellis Collection of Ornithological Books in the University of Kansas Libraries, Vol. 1, 1972; illustrator: Handbook of North American Birds, Vol. 1, 1962, Vols. 2 and 3, 1976; contbg. illustrator: The Birds of Colorado, 1965. Home: Route 4 Lawrence KS 66044 Office: Museum Natural History Univ Kansas Lawrence KS 66045

MENGER, CARL S., mfg. co. exec.; b. Tex., Dec. 12, 1909; s. Rudolph A. and Adella Menger; student U. Iowa, St. Mary's U.; children by previous marriage—Carl S., Joanne; m. Eleanor McAuliffe, 1945; children—John, Eugene, Adella. With Triangle Conduit & Cable, Inc. (name later changed to Triangle Industries, Inc.), Holmdel, N.J., 1945—, pres., 1960-70, chmn. bd., chief exec. officer, 1965—, chmn. exec. com., 1965—; chmn. bd. Plastic Wire & Cable Corp., 1965—, Rowe Internat., Inc., 1968—; chmn., pres. Triangle Exploration, Inc., 1968—; dir. First Nat. State Bank N.J., Newark. Trustee Wardlaw Country Day Sch., Plainfield, Franklin Coll., Switzerland; trustee, mem. exec. com. N.J. Safety Council. Mem. Am. Mgmt. Assn., Nat. Indsl. Conf. Bd., NAM, Nat. Elec. Mfrs. Assn., Am. Soc. Naval Engrs., U.S., N.J., New Brunswick chambers commerce. Clubs: Baltusrol Golf; Bay Head (N.J.) Yacht; Everglades, La Coquille (Palm Beach, Fla.); Williams Country (Weirton, W.Va.). Home: 1513 Ocean Ave Mantoloking NJ 08738 Office: Holmdel NJ 07733

MENGER, KARL, mathematician; b. Vienna, Austria, Jan. 13, 1902; s. Carl and Mina (Andermann) M.; Ph.D., U. Vienna, 1924; Sc.D. (hon.), Shimer Coll., 1970; m. Hilda Axamit, 1934 (div.); children—Karl, Rosemary, Fred, Eva. Came to U.S., 1937, naturalized, 1942. Docent, U. Amsterdam, 1925-27; prof. U. Vienna, 1927-37; vis. lectr. Harvard, Rice Inst., 1930-31; prof. U. Notre Dame, 1937-46; prof. Ill. Inst. Tech., Chgo., 1946-71, prof. emeritus, 1971—; devel. new approach to teaching math. under Carnegie Corp. of N.Y. grant, 1957-60; founder, editor Reports of a Mathematical Colloquium, 1st series: Vienna, 1932-37, 2d series: Notre Dame, 1938-47; vis. prof. Sorbonne, 1951; vis. lectr. Europe, 1961; vis. prof. U. Ariz., 1964, Ford Inst., Vienna, 1964, 65, Middle East Tech. U., Ankara, 1968. Vice pres. Internat. Congress Math., 1936. Decorated Austrian Cross Honor for Sci. and Art. Fgn. mem. Austrian Acad. Scis. Author: Dimensions Theorie, 1928; Kurven Theorie, 1932, 67; Morality, Decision and Social Organization, 1934, 74; Calculus: A Modern Approach, 1953, 57; Géométrie Générale, 1954; (with L.M. Blumenthal) Studies in Geometry, 1970; Selected Papers in Logic and Foundations, Didactics, Economics, 1979; numerous pamphlets and articles. Home: 5506 N Wayne Ave Chicago IL 60640

MENGERS, SUE, motion picture talent agt.; b. Hamburg, Germany, Sept. 2, 1938; s. Eugene and Ruth Sender; came to U.S., 1938; student public schs., N.Y.C.; m. Jean-Claude Tramont, May 5, 1973. Agent, Korman & Assos., N.Y.C., 1963-68; with Creative Mgmt. (name now Internat. Creative Mgmt.), Los Angeles, 1968—, sr. v.p., co-chmn. dept. motion pictures, 1977—; mem. bd. advisers Horizon Mag., Ladies Blue Ribbon 400. Office: Internat Creative Mgmt 8899 Beverly Blvd Suite 721 Los Angeles CA 90048

MENGES, CARL BRAUN, investment banker; b. N.Y.C., Sept. 17, 1930; s. Hermann and Alice (Braun) M.; B.A., Hamilton Coll., 1951; M.B.A., Harvard U., 1953; m. Cordelia Sykes, Apr. 24, 1965; children—James C., Benjamin W., Samuel G. Salesman, Owens Corning Fiberglass Corp., 1953-59, mktg. mgr., 1959-63; with instl. sales dept. Model Roland Co., N.Y.C., 1963-66; with Donaldson, Lufkin & Jenrette Inc., N.Y.C., 1966—, now dir., also mng. dir. Donaldson, Lufkin & Jenrette Securities Corp., 1972—, chmn. bd. Donaldson, Lufkin & Jenrette, A.G., Zurich. Treas., bd. dirs. Assn. Homemaker Services, N.Y.C., 1971-73; trustee Hosp. for Spl. Surgery, 1977—. Episcopalian. Clubs: Union, Maidstone, Madison Sq. Garden. Home: 215 E 72d St New York NY 10021 Office: 140 Broadway New York NY 10005

MENGUY, RENE, surgeon, educator; b. Prague, Czechoslovakia, Feb. 4, 1926; s. Auguste and Beatrice (Adam) M.; B.A., U. Hanoi (Indochina), 1944; M.D., U. Paris (France), 1951; Ph.D., U. Minn., 1957; m. Emilie Marie Rigacci, Aug. 10, 1950; children—Jean, Ghislaine. Came to U.S., 1951, naturalized, 1957. Fellow gen. surgery Mayo Clinic, 1952-57; mem. faculty U. Okla. Med. Sch., 1957-61, U. Ky. Med. Center, 1961-65; prof. surgery, chmn. dept. U. Chgo. Med. Sch., 1965-71; prof. surgery U. Rochester Med. Sch., 1971—; surgeon Genesee Hosp., 1971—. Mem. clin. research tng. com. NIH, 1965-69; cons. VA, 1964—. Recipient citation French Expeditionary Corps, Hanoi, 1946; Fulbright travel grantee, 1951-52; recipient Alumni award meritorious research Mayo Found., 1956; John and Mary R. Markle scholar med. scis., 1958-63. Mem. A.C.S., Am. Fedn. Clin. Research, N.Y. Acad. Scis., Soc. Exptl. Biology and Medicine, Am. Assn. Cancer Research, Am. Gastroenterol. Assn., Soc. Univ. Surgeons, Soc. Surgery Alimentary Tract, Am. Physiol. Soc., Internat. Soc. Surgery, Surg. Biology Club, Soc. Clin. Surgery, Am. Surg. Assn., Acad. Chir. (Paris), Surg. Research Soc. So. Africa (corr.), Congrès Francais de Chirurgie (hon.), Sigma Xi. Author: Peptic Ulcer, 1975. Mem. editorials bd. jours. in field. Contbr. articles to profl. jours. Home: 8 Highland Heights Rochester NY 14618

MENIHAN, JOHN CONWAY, artist, designer; b. Rochester, N.Y., Feb. 14, 1908; s. Jeremiah G. and May Louise (Conway) M.; student Phillips Exeter Acad., 1922-25; B.S. in Econs., U. Pa., 1930; m. Margaret Teresa Hickey, Sept. 26, 1936; children—Mary, John Conway, Tom, Pete. Oil painter, water colorist, printmaker of portraits, landscapes, genre; mem. faculty U. Rochester, 1946-65; represented in permanent collections Carnegie Inst., Library Congress, Rochester Meml. Art Gallery, Print Club of Rochester, St. John Fisher Coll., Rochester, Columbia Banking, Rochester, Keuka Coll., Pennyan, N.Y.; designer mural window of Nazarath Coll. Library, convent chapel St. John Evangelist, enamel tryptich St. Thomas Convent, Stations of the Cross for Our Lady of Lourdes Roman Cath. Ch. (all Rochester); St. Anthony Shrine, side altars St. Ambrose Ch.; triptych Life of St. Elizabeth Seton, St. Thomas the Apostle Ch., Rochester; murals, designed and executed Xerox Corp., Webster, N.Y., Rochester Tel. Co., Security Trust Co., R.T. French Co., Rochester, N.Y. and Fresno, Calif.; mural for Lowenthal-Tenn., Columbia, Tenn.; designer enamel shrine St. Joseph, Pittsford, N.Y., shrine Our Lady of Grapes, St. Januarius Ch., Naples, N.Y.; mural St. John Fisher Library; designed and executed windows, wall hangings, furnishings Notre Dame High Sch. Chapel, Elmira, N.Y.: 6 liturgical wall hangings St. Louis Ch. Bd. dirs. Rochester Meml. Art Gallery, 1968-73; Arts Council of Rochester, 1976. Recipient Lillian Fairchild award; Marion Stratton Gould award, 1946; 1st prize oil, watercolor drawing and print, Finger Lakes Show, Rochester, 1947. A.N.A. Fellow Rochester Museum and Sci. Center; mem. Am. Soc. Graphic Artists, Am. Watercolor Soc., Friends Rochester Pub. Library, Sigma Nu. Roman Catholic. Clubs: Art, Mask and Wig, The Group, Print (Rochester). Illustrator: How Scientists Find Out; designer, illustrator: Historic St. Mary's; St. Ann's of Hornell. Address: 208 Alpine Dr Rochester NY 14618

MENIST, STUART D., ins. co. exec.; b. P.R., Nov. 24, 1914; B.S. in Econs., U. Calif., 1934. With Marsh & McLennan, 1935-37; with Fireman's Fund Am. Ins. Co., San Francisco, 1937—, asst. sec. fidelity and surety, 1949-50, asst. sec., 1950-54, mgr. San Francisco br., 1954-58, resident v.p., mgr. Pacific dept., 1958-59, v.p., 1959-62, sr. exec. charge nationwide fidelity, surety and burglary ops., 1962-67, sr. v.p. adminstrn., 1967-69, exec. v.p., 1969-72, pres., dir., 1972-74, chmn. bd., dir., 1974-75; pres., chief exec. officer Mut. Ins. Co., 1977—; formerly chmn. bd., dir. Fireman's Fund Ins. Co., Am. Automobile Ins. Co., Am. Ins. Co., Asso. Indemnity Corp., Nat. Surety Corp.; chmn. bd. Shaw & Begg, Ltd., Can., Consol. Fire & Casualty Co., Fed. Fire Ins. Co., Wellington Fire Ins. Co. (all Can.); former dir. Crusader Ins. Co., Reigate and London, Eng. Chmn. bd. Nat. Automobile Club; bd. dirs., past chmn. Ins. Info. Inst. Campaign chmn. United Bay Area Crusade, 1973; chmn. Nat. Crime Prevention Assn., Washington; former bd. dirs. Golden Gate chpt. A.R.C.; bd. dirs. San Francisco Bay Area Council; bd. regents U. San Francisco; trustee San Domenico Sch. for Girls, Coll. Ins. Mem. Am. Ins. Assn. (exec. com.), Surety Underwriters Assn. No. Calif. (past pres.), Credit Mgrs. Assn. No. and Central Calif. (past pres.), Western Ins. Info. Service (past pres.), Calif. Bus. Adminstrn. Alumni Assn. (past pres.), Ins. Ednl. Assn. (past pres.), Greater San Francisco (past dir.), Calif. (past dir.) chambers commerce. Rotarian (dir. San Francisco). Clubs: Bankers, Olympic, Meadow, Commonwealth, Pacific Union. Home: 690 Goodhill Rd PO Box 7 Kentfield CA 94904 Office: One Market Plaza San Francisco CA 94105

MENIUS, ARTHUR CLAYTON, JR., univ. dean; b. Salisbury, N.C., Apr. 30, 1916; s. Arthur Clayton and Maud Edna (Webb) M.; A.B. in Physics and Math., Catawba Coll., 1937, D.Sc., 1969; Ph.D. in Physics, U. N.C., 1942; m. Lucille Clark Varner, Mar. 31, 1946; 1 son, Arthur Clayton III. Sr. physicist Applied Physics Lab., Johns Hopkins, 1944-46, head battery group for proximity fuse project, 1945-46; prof. physics Clemson Coll., 1946-48; mem. faculty N.C. State U., Raleigh, 1949—, prof. physics, 1949-55, head dept., 1956-60, dean Sch. Phys. and Math. Scis., 1960—; cons. govt. agys. pvt. bus., 1950—. Chmn. Gov. N.C. Sci. Adv. Com., 1961-69, Atomic Energy Adv. Com. N.C., 1963-71; mem. N.C. Sci. and Tech. Bd.; N.C. State council rep. Oak Ridge Asso. Univs., 1963-69, mem. bd., 1969-76; edn. rep. So. Interstate Nuclear Bd. Bd. govs. Research Triangle Inst. Fellow Am. Phys. Soc.; mem. N.C. Acad. Sci., Am. Inst. Physics, Sigma Xi, Phi Kappa Phi. Presbyn. Author numerous monographs, articles profl. jours. Home: 541 Hertford St Raleigh NC 27609

MENK, CARL WILLIAM, exec. search co. exec.; b. Montclair, N.J., Oct. 19, 1921; s. Carl William and Catherine Regina (Murray) M.; B.S.B.A., Seton Hall U., 1943; M.A. in Vocat. Guidance, Columbia U., 1950; m. Elizabeth Cullum, May 30, 1947; children—Carl, Elizabeth, Mary, Paul. Sr. v.p. P. Ballantine & Sons, Newark, 1946-69; pres. Boyden Assos., Inc., N.Y.C., 1969—; instr. N.J. Inst. Tech., Seton Hall U. Served as pilot, 2d lt. USAAF, 1943-46. Mem. Assn. Exec. Recruiting Cons. (dir.). Clubs: Glen Ridge Country (dir., v.p.), Spring Lake Golf (dir.), Sea View Country, Montclair Country, Union League of N.Y. Home: 546 Ridgewood Ave Glen Ridge NJ 07028 Office: 260 Madison Ave New York NY 10016

MENK, LOUIS WILSON, r.r. ofcl.; b. Englewood, Colo., Apr. 8, 1918; s. Louis Albert and Daisy Deane (Frantz) M.; student Denver U., 1937-38; grad. Advanced Mgmt. Program, Harvard, 1953, Transp. Sch., Northwestern U., 1959; LL.D., Drury Coll., 1965, Denver U., 1966, Monmouth Coll., 1967; m. Martha Jane Swan, May 30, 1942; children—David Louis, Barbara Ann. With U.P. R.R., 1936-40; with St. L.-S.F. R.R., 1940-65, telegrapher, 1940, chmn., pres., 1964-65; pres., dir. Burlington Lines, Chgo., 1965-66, No. Pacific R.R., St. Paul, 1966-70; pres. Burlington No. Inc., 1970-71, chmn., chief exec. officer, 1971-78, chmn. bd., 1978—, also dir.; dir. First Nat. Bank Chgo., Internat. Harvester, ASARCO Inc., Minn. Mut. Life Ins. Co., Gen. Mills, Inc., First Bank System, Ft. Worth & Denver Ry., C. & S. Ry. Co. Bd. lay trustees Loyola U., Chgo.; trustee U. Denver. Presbyterian. Clubs: Masons, Yellowstone Country (Billings, Mont.); Chicago (Chgo.); Minn.; Desert Forest Golf (Carefree, Ariz.). Home: 2751 Gregory Dr S Billings MT 59102 Office: 176 E 5th St St Paul MN 55101

MENKART, JOHN, cosmetic co. exec.; b. Prague, Czechoslovakia, Aug. 20, 1922; s. Rudolph J. and Milada (Fischer) M.; came to U.S., 1954, naturalized, 1961; B.Sc., U. Leeds (Eng.), 1943, Ph.D., 1946; m. Margaret White, Apr. 4, 1953; children—Andrew, Deborah; m. 2d, Edith L. Chandler, Aug. 2, 1968; stepchildren—Elizabeth, David. Research chemist, Eng., 1946-53; asst. dir. research Textile Research Inst., Princeton, N.J., 1954-58; with Gillette Co., 1958-71, pres. Gillette Research Inst., 1968-71; v.p. tech. Clairol Inc., Stamford, Conn., 1971-76, sr. v.p., 1977—. Mem. bd. mgmt. Stamford Hosp. Fellow Textile Inst. Gt. Britain; mem. Cosmetic, Toiletry and Fragrance Assn. (chmn. sci. adv. com. 1974-76), Am. Chem. Soc., Soc. Cosmetic Chemists, Fiber Soc. Clubs: Cosmos (Washington); Chemists (N.Y.C.). Author, patentee in field. Mem. editorial bds. profl. jours. Home: 157 Shelter Rock Rd Stamford CT 06903 Office: 2 Blachley Rd Stamford CT 06902

MENKE, ALLEN CARL, corp. exec.; b. Huntingburg, Ind., Feb. 16, 1922; s. William Ernest and Clara (Moenkhaus) M.; B.S. in Mech. Engring., Purdue U., 1943, M.S., 1948; m. Virginia Lee MacDonald, Apr. 14, 1944; children—Janet, William, Sarah. Instr., Purdue U., 1946-48; with Trane Co., 1948-68, v.p. sales, 1963-64, exec. v.p. sales, mfg. and engring., 1964-68, also dir.; v.p. Borg-Warner Corp., Chgo., 1969-76; pres. Artesian Industries, Mansfield, Ohio, 1976—; dir. Huntingburg Machine Works, Styline, Inc., Huntingburg, SPS Techs., Am. Air Filter. Pres. Met. Housing Devel. Corp. of Leadership Council; founder, pres. Winnetka Interch. Council. Bd. dirs., vice chmn. Presbyn. Home. Served to 1st lt. AUS, 1944-46. Named Distinguished Alumnus, Purdue U., 1965, mem. Purdue Hall of Fame. Mem. Sigma Chi. Presbyn. (elder). Mason. Home: 1420 Tower Rd Winnetka IL 60093 Office: Artesian Industries 20 N Wacker Dr Suite 1741 Chicago IL 60606

MENKES, JOSHUA, sci. adminstr.; b. Vienna, Austria, Aug. 14, 1925; s. Isidore and Valerie (Biber) M.; B.S., Bklyn. Poly. Inst., 1953, M.A., 1954; Ph.D., U. Mich., 1956; m. Diana Elise Davis, Aug. 7, 1962; children by previous marriage— Nina, Tinka. Came to U.S., 1950. Research scientist fluid physics sect. Jet Propulsion Lab., Pasadena, Calif., 1956-61; systems analyst Inst. Def. Analyses, Washington, 1961-69; prof. aerospace engring. scis. U. Colo., 1969-74; div. dir. Research Applied to Nat. Needs program (Rann) Research Applications Directorate, NSF, Washington, 1974-77, group leader for tech. assessment Policy Research and Analysis div., 1977—; cons. Plesset Assos., Nat. Acad. Sci., Def. Sci. Bd., Space Sci. Bd., Nat. Bur. Standards, Aerospace Corp., Office Def. Research and Engring., U.S. Dept. Transp. Served with Israeli Army, 1947-49. Vis. scholar U. Tokyo, 1966. Mem. AAAS, Sigma Xi, Tau Beta Pi. Editor of Re-entry Physics Series, 1966-68, of Computing, 1966-69. Contbr. articles to profl. jours. Home: 7510 Alaska Ave NW Washington DC 20012

MENN, JULIUS JOEL, scientist; b. Free City of Danzig, Feb. 20, 1929; s. David and Regina (Eisenstadt) M.; B.Sc., U. Calif., Berkeley, 1953, M.Sc., 1954, Ph.D., 1958; m. Alma Roma Zito, Aug. 31, 1952; children—Leslie Rona, David Vincent (dec.), Diana Marie (dec.). Research asst. U. Calif., Berkeley, 1953-57; head insecticide research Stauffer Chem. Co., Mountain View, Calif., 1957-66, sr. sect. mgr. insecticide research and biochemistry, 1966-73, mgr. biochemistry dept., 1973-79; dir. research Zoecon Corp., Palo Alto, Calif., 1979—; adj. prof. toxicology San Jose State U., 1979—. Recipient Burdick and Jackson internat. award pesticide chem. div. Am. Chem. Soc., 1978. Fellow Am. Chem. Soc.; mem. AAAS, N.Y. Acad. Scis., Am. Soc. Pharmacology and Exptl. Therapeutics, Soc. Toxicology, Entomol. Soc. Am., Sigma Xi. Editor 3 books; contbr. 75 articles to sci. jours.; editorial bd. Jour. Agrl. Food Chemistry, Jour. Toxicology and Environ. Health. Patentee in field. Office: Zoecon Corp 975 California Ave Palo Alto CA 94304

MENNEN, GEORGE JEFF, toiletries co. exec.; b. Orange, N.J., Dec. 10, 1940; s. George Schenk and Mary Elizabeth (Mahoney) M.; grad. Washington and Lee U., 1964; postgrad. Am. Inst. Fgn. Trade, 1965; m. Carolyn Burton Campbell, June 12, 1965; children—Mona Vance, George Jeff. Account mgr. Grey Advt., 1965-66; mktg. mgr. Petroleum Engr. Pub. Co., 1966; account mgr. Grey Advt., 1967-68; with Mennen Co., Morristown, N.J., 1968—, now pres. internat. Bd. dirs. Am. Heart Assn., 1974-79, YMCA, 1979—; active Boy Scouts Am. Served with U.S. Army, 1966. Episcopalian. Office: Mennen Co Morristown NJ 07960*

MENNIN, PETER, composer, music conservatory adminstr.; b. Erie, Pa., May 17, 1923; student Oberlin Conservatory, 1940-42; Mus.B., Mus.M., Eastman Sch. Music, 1945, Ph.D., 1947; studied with Howard Hanson; studied conducting with Serge Koussevitsky at Tanglewood, Mass., 1946; m. Georganne Bairnson, Aug. 28, 1947; children—Felica, Mark. Tchr. composition Juilliard Sch. Music, 1947-58, pres., 1962—; dir. Peabody Conservatory Music, Balt., 1958-62. Mem. adv. panel USIA, 1961; adv. com. arts State Dept., 1963—; mem. exec. com. Internat. Music Council, Paris, 1956, Nat. Fedn. Music Clubs Commn., 1957. Bd. dirs. Walter W. Naumburg Found. Served with USAAF, 1943. Recipient award Am. Acad. Arts and Letters; Guggenheim award; Bearns prize Columbia; First Gershwin Meml. award; Koussevitsky award; Dallas Symphony Commn.; Juilliard Found. commn.; Collegiate Chorale commn.; NBC Radio commn.; League of Composers commn.; Prot. Radio commn.; Columbia Record's Chamber Music award, 1952; Naumburg Found. Am. Composition award, 1952; Elizabeth Sprague Coolidge Found.-Library of Congress Chamber Music commn., 1952; Nat. Fedn. Music Clubs commn., 1956; Cleve. Symphony commn., 1957; others. Mem. League Composers (bd. dirs.). Composers' Forum (dir.), Nat. Music Council (pres. 1968—), Nat. Inst. Arts and Letters, Am. Music (dir.), Am. Soc. Composers, Authors and Pubs. (dir.), Phi Mu Alpha. Composer: First Symphony, 1942; String Quartet, 1942; Concertino for Flute, Strings and Percussion, 1945; Second Symphony, 1945; Folk Overture, 1945; Fantasia for Strings (Canzona and Tocata), 1946; Third Symphony, 1946; (for piano) Divertimento, 1947, Partita (5 movements), 1949; (for mixed chorus) The Gold-Threaded Robe, Crossing the Han River, In the Quiet Night, Song of the Palace, 1948; (for women's chorus) Tumbling Hair, Bought Locks, 1949; Fourth Symphony for Chorus and Orch., 1949; A Christmas Cantata for Chorus, Soloists and Chamber Orch., 1949; Second Quartet, 1950; Fifth Symphony, 1950; Concertato for Orch. (Moby-Dick), 1952; Sixth Symphony, 1953, Cello Concerto, 1955, Sonata Concertante for Violin and Piano, 1956, Piano Concerto, 1957, Canto for Orch., 1957, Symphony No. 7, 1964, Piano Sonata, 1964, Sinfonia for Orch., 1971, Cantata de Virtute, 1969, Symphony No. 8, 1973, Voices for Soprano and Chamber Ensemble, Reflections of Emily for Treble Voices and Ensemble, 1979, others. Works performed by N.Y. Philharmonic Soc., NBC Symphony Orch., Columbia Broadcasting Orch., Boston; Chgo., San Francisco, Nat., Cin. WOR, Rochester (N.Y.), Mpls., Dallas, Houston, Los Angeles, Phila., Pitts., Detroit orchs., Götesburg Symphony Orch. of Sweden, orchs. in Europe, S.A., Orient and Far East; in music festivals, Rochester, N.Y., Tanglewood, Mass., Yaddo (Saratoga Springs, N.Y.), Colorado Springs and Seattle. Office: Juilliard School Lincoln Center New York NY 10023

MENNINGER, KARL AUGUSTUS, psychiatrist; b. Topeka, July 22, 1893; s. Charles Frederick (M.D.) and Flora (Knisely) M.; student Washburn Coll., 1910-12, Ind. U., summer 1910; A.B., U. Wis., 1914, M.S., 1915, D.Sc., 1965; M.D. cum laude, Harvard, 1917; L.H.D., Park Coll., 1955, St. Benedict's Coll., 1963, Loyola U., 1972, DePaul U., 1974; LL.D., Jefferson Med. Coll., 1956, Parsons Coll., 1960, Kans. State U., 1962, Baker U., 1965, Pepperdine U., 1973, John Jay Coll. Criminal Justice, N.Y., 1978; D.Sc., Washburn U., 1949, Oklahoma City U., 1966; m. Grace Gaines, Sept. 1916 (div. Feb. 1941); children—Julia Menninger Gottesman, Robert Gaines, Martha Menninger Nichols; m. 2d, Jeanetta Lyle, Sept. 1941; 1 dau., Rosemary Jeanetta Karla. Chmn. bd. trustees Menninger Found.; prof. at large U. Kans.; distinguished prof. psychiatry Chgo. Med. Sch.; prof. Loyola U., Chgo., U. Cin.; vis. prof. U. Chgo.; cons. Ill. Dept. Mental Health, Ill. State Psychiat. Inst., 1967-73; founder Menninger Sch. Psychiatry, 1946, dean, 1946-69; cons. Topeka VA Hosp., Topeka State Hosp., Stormont-Vail Hosp., Kans. Reception and Diagnostic Center, Kans. Neurol. Inst., Fed. Bur. Prisons, Office

Vocat. Rehab., HEW, President's Task Force on Prisoner Rehab., 1969, Mt. Sinai Med. Center, Chgo., Am. Bar Assn. com. on correctional facilities and services, 1970-76, Com. on Penal Reform, Kans. Assn. Mental Health. Mem. spl. com. on psychiatry, OSRD, ETO, adv. to surgeon gen. U.S. Army, 1945; adviser on penology to Gov. Kans., 1966-75; mem. Nat. Council on Crime and Delinquency, Open Lands Project. Commd. lt. (j.g.) USNRF, 1918-21. Mem. adv. bd. Adult div. Ill. Dept. Corrections, Ill. State Psychiat. Inst.; med. adv. council Gov. Ill.; mem. adv. coms. many other civic, govtl. orgns. Bd. overseers Lemberg Center for Study Violence, Brandeis U.; bd. dirs. Chgo. Boys Club, John Howard Assn. Chgo., W. Clement and Jessie V. Stone Found., Chgo.; founder, chmn. bd. dirs. the Villages, Inc., Topeka. Recipient T.W. Salmon award N.Y. Acad. Medicine, 1967, Good Samaritan award Eagles Lodge, 1968, 69, Ann. Service award John Howard Assn., 1969, Good Shepherd award The Lambs, Chgo., 1969, award Am. Acad. Psychiatry and Law, 1974, Roscoe Pound award Nat. Council Crime and Delinquency, 1975, Spl. award Kans. Dept. Corrections, 1976, Sheen award AMA, 1978, numerous others. Life fellow Am. Psychiat. Assn. (Isaac Ray award 1962, 1st distinguished service award 1965, 1st Founders award 1977), A.C.P. (life master), Am. Coll. Psychiatrists, Am. Med. Writers Assn.; life mem. A.M.A., Am. Psychol. Assn., Chgo. Psychoanalytic Soc., Am. Orthopsychiat. Assn., Am. Psychoanalytic Assn. (founder; pres. 1941-43); hon. mem. Am. Assn. Suicidology, Internat. Assn. for Suicide Prevention, Sigmund Freud Archives; joint founder, charter mem. Central Neuropsychiat. Assn., Central Psychiat. Hosp. Assn., Med. Assn. for Research Nervous and Mental Diseases; mem. Am. Assn. for Child Psychoanalysis, Am. Soc. Criminology, Ill. Acad. Criminology, Assn. for Psychiat. Treatment Offenders, Am. Acad. Psychiatry and Law, Am. Justice Inst. (adv. com. sponsors), Assn. Clin. Pastoral Edn., Ill. Com. on Family Law, Internat. Psychoanalytic Assn., Kans. Med. Soc., Sigmund Freud Soc. Vienna, World Soc. Ekistics, Nat. Congress Am. Indians, Am. Hort. Council, AAAS, ACLU (nat. adv. council), NAACP, Sierra Club, Chgo. Orchestral Assn. (gov.), Am. Assn. Bot. Gardens and Arboreta, Friends of the Earth, Am. Indian Center (Chgo. Grand Council), Aspen Inst. for Humanistic Studies (former trustee, now hon. trustee), Am. Humanics Found., Nat. Commn. for Prevention of Child Abuse (co-chmn. hon. bd.), Save the Tallgrass Prairie Inc. (chmn. nat. hon. bd.), others. Presbyterian. Clubs: Masons; Univ. (Chgo.); Country (Topeka). Author: (with others) Why Men Fail, 1918; The Human Mind, 1930, rev., 1945; (with others) The Healthy-Minded Child, 1930; Man Against Himself, 1938; (with others) America Now, 1938; (with Mrs. Menninger) Love Against Hate, 1942; (with Devereux) A Guide to Psychiatric Books, 1950, 2d rev. edit., 1958, 3d rev. edit., 1972; Manual for Psychiatric Case Study, 1952; Theory of Psychoanalytic Technique, 1958, rev. edit. (with Holzman), 1973; (selected papers) A Psychiatrist's World, 1959; The Vital Balance, 1963; The Crime of Punishment, 1968; (with Lucy Freeman) Sparks, 1973; Whatever Became of Sin, 1974; also articles. Editorial bd. Bull. Menninger Clinic. Home: 1819 Westwood Circle Topeka KS 66604 Office: Menninger Found Box 829 Topeka KS 66601 also Topeka VA Hosp Topeka KS

MENNINGER, ROY WRIGHT, found. exec.; b. Topeka, Oct. 27, 1926; A.B., Swarthmore Coll., 1947; M.D., Cornell U., 1951; m. Beverly Menninger; children—Heather, Ariel, Bonar, Eric. Intern N.Y. Hosp., 1951-52; resident psychiatrist Boston State Hosp., 1952-53, Boston Psychopathic Hosp., 1953-56; from resident psychiatrist to asso. medicine (psychiatry) Peter Bent Brigham Hosp., Boston, 1956-61; teaching and research fellow Harvard Med. Sch., 1956-61; staff psychiatrist C.F. Menninger Meml. Hosp., Menninger Found., Topeka, 1961-63, co-dir. div. sch. mental health, 1963-67; dir. dept. preventive psychiatry Menninger Found., 1965-67, pres. found., 1967—. Mem. sponsoring com. Inst. Am. Democracy, 1967—; mem. adv. group Horizons '76 Am. Revolution Bicentennial Commn.; adv. bd. Parents Mag., 1966—; adv. group Topeka Inst. Urban Affairs, 1967-70, bd. dirs., Goals for Topeka, Topeka Inst. Urban Affairs, 1969—, v.p., 1972—; adv. bd. Highland Park-Pierce Neighborhood House, Topeka, 1966-70; med. adv. com. VA Hosp., Topeka, 1971—; mem. Gov.'s Com. on Criminal Adminstrn., 1971—; trustee People-to- People, Kansas City, Mo., 1967-69, Baker U., 1968-71; trustee Midwest Research Inst., 1967—, mem. exec. com., 1970—; bd. dirs. Shawnee council Campfire Girls, Topeka, 1962-69, A.K. Rice Inst., Washington, Sex Information and Edn. Council U.S., 1970-73, mem. edn. com., long range planning com., 1972-73; vis. lectr. Fgn. Service Inst., State Dept., 1963-66; chmn. social issues com. Group Advancement Psychiatry; community adv. bd. Kan. Health Workers Union, 1967-68. Adv. com. to bd. dirs. New Eng. Mut. Life Ins. Co., 1967-70. Diplomate Am. Bd. Psychiatry and Neurology. Fellow Am. Psychiat. Assn. (Joint Information Service exec. com.), A.C.P.; hon. mem. Northeastern Group Psychotherapy, Mass. Med. Soc., A.A.A.S., Physicians Social Responsibility, Kan. Psychiat. Soc., Am. Orthopsychiat. Assn., Greater Topeka C. of C. (dir.). Office: PO Box 829 Topeka KS 66601

MENNINGER, WILLIAM WALTER, psychiatrist; b. Topeka, Oct. 23, 1931; s. William Claire and Catharine Louisa (Wright) M.; A.B., Stanford U., 1953; M.D., Cornell U., 1957; m. Constance Arnold Libbey, June 15, 1953; children—Frederick Prince, John Alexander, Eliza Wright, Marian Stuart, William Libbey, David Henry. Intern, Harvard Med. Service, Boston City Hosp., 1957-58; resident in psychiatry Menninger Sch. Psychiatry, 1958-61; chief med. officer, psychiatrist Fed. Reformatory, El Reno, Okla., 1961-63; asso. psychiatrist Peace Corps, 1963-64; staff psychiatrist Menninger Found., Topeka, 1965—, coordinator for devel., 1967-69; clin. supr. Topeka State Hosp., 1969-70, sect. dir., 1970-72, asst. supt., clin., dir. residency tng., 1972—; syndicated columnist In-Sights, 1975—; adj. prof. Washburn U.; lectr., mem. mgmt. com. Menninger Sch. Psychiatry; mem. adv. bd. Nat. Inst. Corrections, 1975—; cons. U.S. Bur. Prisons; mem. Fed. Prison Facilities Planning Council, 1970-73. Mem. nat. health and safety com. Boy Scouts Am., 1970—; bd. dirs. Nat. Com. for Prevention Child Abuse, 1975—; mem. Kans. Adv. Council on Community Mental Health Centers, 1976—; mem. nat. adv. health council HEW, 1967-71; mem. Nat. Commn. Causes and Prevention Violence, 1968-69; mem. Kans. Gov.'s Penal Planning Council, 1970. Served with USPHS, 1959-64. Diplomate Am. Bd. Psychiatry and Neurology, Am. Bd. Forensic Psychiatry. Fellow A.C.P., Am. Psychiat. Assn.; mem. AMA, Group for Advancement of Psychiatry (chmn. com. mental health services 1974-77), Inst. Medicine Nat. Acad. Scis., Am. Psychoanalytic Assn., Am. Acad. Psychiatry and Law, AAAS. Author: Happiness Without Sex and Other Things Too Good to Miss, 1976; Caution: Living May Be Hazardous, 1978. Editor, Psychiatry Digest, 1971-74, mem. bd. editors, 1974-78. Contbr. chpts. to books, articles to profl. jours. Home: 1505 Plass St Topeka KS 66604 Office: Menninger Found Box 829 Topeka KS 66601

MENNIS, EDMUND ADDI, investment mgr.; b. Allentown, Pa., Aug. 12, 1919; s. William Henry and Grace (Addi) M.; B.A., Coll. City N.Y., 1941; M.A., Columbia, 1946; Ph.D., N.Y.U., 1961; m. Selma Adinoff, Sept. 25, 1945; children—Ardith Grace, Daniel Liam. Security analyst Eastman, Dillon & Co., N.Y.C., 1945-46; sr. research asst. Am. Inst. Econ. Research, Great Barrington, Mass., 1946-50; security analyst Wellington Mgmt. Co., Phila., 1950-61, dir. research, 1958-61, v.p., mem. investment com., 1958-66, economist, 1953-66; sr. v.p., chmn. trust investment com. Republic Nat. Bank, Dallas, 1966-72, sr. v.p., chmn. investment policy com. Security Pacific Nat. Bank, Los Angeles, 1972—; pres., dir. Bunker Hill Income Securities, Inc., 1973—; chmn. bd. Security Pacific Investment Mgrs., Inc., 1977—. Tech. cons. Bus. Council, Washington, 1962-66, 72-77, 79—; econ. adviser sec. commerce, 1967-68. Served to 1st lt. USAAF, 1942-45; to capt. USAF, 1951-53. Fellow Nat. Assn. Bus. Economists (council 1967-69), Fin. Analysts Fedn. (dir. 1970-72, Molodovsky award 1972); mem. Am. Econ. Assn., Am. Fin. Assn., Am. Statis. Assn., N.Y. Soc. Security Analysts, Los Angeles Soc. Fin. Analysts, Forecasters Club N.Y., Conf. Bus. Economists (vice chmn. 1977, chmn. 1978), Inst. Chartered Fin. Analysts (pres. 1970-72, trustee 1968-74, C. Stewart Sheppard award 1978). Asso. editor: Financial Analysts Jour., 1960—; editor C.F.A. Digest, 1971—. Home: 721 Paseo Del Mar Palos Verdes Estates CA 90274 Office: PO Box 60400 Terminal Annex Los Angeles CA 90060

MENOLASCINO, FRANK JOSEPH, psychiatrist, pediatrician; b. Omaha, May 25, 1940; s. Phillip Joseph and Annie Marie (Ferrante) M.; M.D., U. Nebr., 1957; m. Donna Colleen Potthoff, Dec. 28, 1956; children—Michelle, Cynthia, Michael, Scott, Mark, Amy. Staff psychiatrist Lincoln (Nebr.) Regional Center, 1961-62; mem. staff Nebr. Psychiat. Inst., Omaha, 1962—, prof. psychiatry and pediatrics, 1972—, asso. dir. inst., 1973—; prof. psychiatry and pediatrics U. Nebr. Coll. Medicine; mem. Pres.'s Com. Mental Retardation, 1977—; co-chmn. Nebr. Gov.'s Com. Mental Retardation, 1969, Douglas County Mental Health Com., 1972; pres. Nat. Assn. Retarded Citizens, 1976-77. Recipient Edward A. Strecker Meml. award, 1976. Fellow Am. Psychiat. Assn., Am. Assn. Mental Deficiency; mem. Am., Nebr. med. assns., Douglas County Med. Soc., Alpha Omega Alpha. Democrat. Roman Catholic. Club: K.C. Author: Beyond the Limits, 1970; Psychiatric Aspects of Mental Retardation, 1971; Challenges in Mental Retardation, 1977; also articles. Home: 2318 S 102d St Omaha NE 68124 Office: 602 S 45th St Omaha NE 68124

MENON, VIJAYA BHASKAR, phonograph records co. exec.; b. Trivandrum, India, May 29, 1934; s. Rama Krishna and Saraswathi Menon; B.A., U. Delhi, India, 1953; M.A., U. Oxford, Eng., 1956; m. Sumitra Paniker, Jan. 21, 1972; children—Siddhartha Shankar, Vishnu Shankar. Comml. mgr., mng. dir., chmn. A & R sales, mktg. and promotion divs. EMI Gramophone Co. of India, Ltd., 1957-70; mng. dir. EMI Internat. Services, Ltd., London, 1970-71; exec. v.p. Capitol Industries-EMI, Inc., Los Angeles, 1971, pres., chief exec. officer, 1971—; chmn., chief exec. officer Capitol Records, Inc., 1971—; chmn., chief exec. officer EMI Films, Inc., Los Angeles, EMI TV Programs, Inc., Los Angeles, Screen Gems/Colgems-EMI Music Inc., N.Y.C. and Los Angeles; chmn. Capitol/EMI Am./United Artists Records Group; chmn., chief exec. EMI Music; dir. EMI Ltd., London. Office: 1750 N Vine St Hollywood CA 90028

MENOTTI, GIAN CARLO, composer; b. Cadegliano, Italy, July 7, 1911; s. Alfonso and Ines (Pellini) M.; came to U.S. 1928; grad. in composition Curtis Inst. Music, 1933, Mus.B. (hon.), 1945. Writer chamber music, songs and operas; tchr. Curtis Inst. Music, 1941—; composer: (operas) Amelia Goes to the Ball (premiere Acad. Music, Phila., 1936, later performed at Met. Opera House and in various European cities); The Old Maid and the Thief (written for NBC, later performed by Phila. Opera Co.); The Island God (premiere Met. Opera House 1942); (ballet) Sebastian (premiere Ballet Internat., 1943); (opera) The Telephone (premiere Ballet Soc., 1947); Concerto in A Minor for Piano and Orch. (Firkusny and Boston Symphony 1945); (opera) The Medium (premiere 1946); The Consul (premiere 1950); Errand into the Maze (ballet), 1947; Apocalypse (orch.), 1951; (opera) Amahl and the Night Visitors (commd. by NBC, 1st performed on TV 1951), The Saint of Bleecker Street (premiere Broadway Theater, N.Y.C.); (ballet) The Unicorn, The Gorgon and The Manticore (premiere Washington 1956); (opera) Maria Golovin (premiere Brussels World Exposition 1958); (opera) The Last Savage (premiere Paris 1963); (cantata) The Death of the Bishop of Brindisi (premiere Cin. 1963); (TV opera) Labyrinth, 1963; (ch. opera) Martin's Lie (premiere Bristol, Eng. 1964); (song cycle) Canti della Lontananza, 1967; (opera) Help, Help, the Globolinks, 1968; (drama) The Leper, 1970; (symphonic piece) Triplo Concerto atre, 1970; (opera) The Most Important Man in the World, 1971; (opera) Arrival, 1973; (opera) Tamu-Tamu, 1973; writer own libretti. Recipient Guggenheim award, 1946, 47, Pulitzer prize, 1950; N.Y. Drama Critics Circle award, 1954; Pulitzer prize for music, 1954. Mem. ASCAP. Founder, Festival of Two Worlds, Spoleto, Italy, 1958. Office: care Thea Dispeker Artists Rep 59 E 54th St New York NY 10022*

MENSES, JAN, painter, draughtsman, etcher, lithographer; b. Rotterdam, Netherlands, Apr. 28, 1933; s. Jan and Elisabeth Wilhelmina (Schwarz) M.; came to Can., 1960, naturalized, 1965; student Acad. Fine Arts, Rotterdam, Officers Acad. Royal Dutch Air Force, 1953-55; m. Rachel Régine Kadoch, Dec. 7, 1958; children—Salomon, Nina Sarah, Nechamah Elisabeth. One-man shows: Montreal Mus. Fine Arts, 1961, 65, 76, Isaacs Gallery, Toronto, Ont., Can., 1964, Delta Gallery, Rotterdam, 1965, Galerie Godard Lefort, Montreal, 1966, Gallery Moos, Toronto, 1967, Rotterdam Art Found., 1974, Galerie Mira Godard, Toronto, 1977, Montreal, 1978; numerous group shows latest including Montreal World Exhbn., 1967, Salon Internat. Art, Basle, Switzerland, 1972, 74, Canadian Nat. Exhbn., 1972; represented in numerous permanent collections, including: Museo Ciani di Villa Caccia, Lugano, Switzerland, Museum Modern Art, N.Y.C., Phila. Mus. Art, Solomon R. Guggenheim Mus., N.Y.C., Bklyn., Mus., Art Inst. Chgo., Cleve. Mus. Art, Detroit Inst. Arts, Yale U., U. Montreal, Museum Boymans-van Beuningen, Rotterdam, Stedelijk Mus., Amsterdam, Rijksmuseum, Amsterdam, Nat. Gallery Can., Ottawa, Montreal Mus. Fine Arts, Musée d'Art Contemporain, Montreal, Art Inst. Ont., Que. Provincial Mus.; paintings include: Klippoth Series, 1963—, Kaddish Series, 1964—, Hechaloth Series, 1973—, mural for Montreal Holocaust Meml. Center; lectr. in fine arts Concordia U., Montreal, Que., 1973-76. Served with Royal Dutch Air Force Res., 1953-55. Recipient 5 1st prizes Nat. Art Exhbn., Quebec, Que., 1960-65; Grand prize Concours Artistiques de la Province de Que., 1975; prize X and XI Winnipeg (Man., Can.) Shows, 1966, 68; prize IX Internat. Exhbn. Drawings and Prints, Lugano, 1966; prize Ofcl. Centennial Art Competition, Toronto, 1967; 1st prize Hadassah, 1969, 71; award Reeves of Can., 1969; Tigert award Ont. Soc. Arts, 1970, Loomis and Toles award, 1972; J. I. Segal award J. I. Segal Fund Jewish Culture, 1975; Can. Council sr. arts fellow, 1969-70, 71-72, grantee, 1966-67, 67-68, travel grantee, 1968, 73. Mem. Royal Canadian Acad. Arts, Société des Artistes Professionnels du Que., Print, Drawing Council Can. Jewish.

MENTER, SANFORD, fgn. service officer; b. Middletown, N.Y., July 25, 1920; s. Max and Esther Miriam (Miller) M.; B.A., U. Tex., 1943; M.S. in Pub. Adminstrn., Syracuse U., 1947; m. Jeannette Corn, Jan. 14, 1946; children—Patricia Alison (dec.), Timothy Sanford. Joined U.S. Fgn. Service, 1944; vice consul, chief visa sect. consulate gen., Dublin, Ireland, 1944-47; orgn. and mgmt. analyst div. fgn. service planning State Dept., 1947-48, budget analyst, div. fgn. service budget, 1948-49, chief budget officer, div. fgn. service personnel, 1949-50; consul, adminstrv. officer consulate gen., Sydney, Australia, 1950-53; attache, consul, dep. adminstrv. officer embassy, Belgrade, Yugoslavia, 1953-55; mgmt. analyst, regulations and procedures staff Office Asst. Sec. State Adminstrn., 1955-58, dep. chief, regulations and procedures staff, 1958-59; 2d sec. embassy, consul, adminstrv. officer embassy, Accra, Ghana, 1959-61; 1st sec., consul, dep. adminstrv. officer embassy, Bonn, W. Germany, 1961-64; 1st sec., consul, adminstrv. officer embassy, Moscow, USSR, 1965-67, London, Eng., 1967-70, U.S. fgn. service insp., 1970-71; exec. dir. ACDA, 1971-73; exec. dir. Bur. Internat. Orgn. Affairs, Dept. State, 1973-77, dep. insp. gen. Dept. State, 1977—. Mem. Am. Soc. Pub. Adminstrn., Am. Fgn. Service Assn., Nat. Rifle Assn. Am. Home: 1157 Colonial Rd McLean VA 22101 Office: 2201 C St NW Washington DC 20520

MENTSCHIKOFF, SOIA, lawyer, univ. dean; b. Moscow, USSR (parents Am. citizens), Apr. 2, 1915; d. Roman S. and Eugenia A. (Ossipov) M.; B.A., Hunter Coll., 1934; LL.B., Columbia, 1937, LL.D., 1978; LL.D., Smith Coll., 1967, Lafayette Coll., 1974, Boston Coll., 1974, Boston U., 1974, Syracuse U., 1974, U. Puget Sound, 1976; m. Karl N. Llewellyn, 1946 (dec.). Admitted to N.Y. State bar, 1937, practiced in N.Y.C., 1937-49; asso. firm Scandrett, Tuttle & Chalaire, 1937-41; asso. mem. firm Spence, Windels, Walser, Hotchkiss & Angell, 1944-45; mem. firm Spence, Hotchkiss, Parker & Duryee, 1945-49; asso. chief reporter Uniform Comml. Code, 1944-54; vis. prof., cons. Harvard Law Sch., 1947-49, U. Chgo. Law Sch., 1951-74; dean U. Miami Law Sch., Coral Gables, Fla., 1974—. U.S. del. Hague Conf., 1964; commr. Uniform State Law, State of Ill., 1965-70; Trustee Rand Corp., 1972—. Mem. Commn. on Rights, Liberties and Responsibilities of Am. Indians, 1962-66; mem. exec. com. Council for Study Mankind, 1965-69. Mem. Am. Bar Assn., Am. Law Inst., Am. Judicature Soc., Am. Soc. Internat. Law, Internat. Faculty Comparative Law, Assn. Am. Law Schs. (pres. 1974). Author: (with Katzenbach) International Unification of Private Law, 1961; Commercial Transactions, 1970. Contbr. articles to profl. publs. Home: 1012 San Pedro Ave Coral Gables FL 33156 Office: U Miami PO Box 248087 Coral Gables FL 33124

MENUHIN, YEHUDI, violinist; b. N.Y.C., Apr. 22, 1916; s. Moshe and Marutha M.; educated by pvt. tutors; studied music under Sigmund Anker, Louis Persinger, San Francisco, Georges Enesco, Rumania and Paris, and Adolph Busch, Switzerland; Mus.D. (hon.) U. Oxford, 1962, Queen's U., Belfast, 1965, U. Leicester, 1965; LL.D., U. St. Andrews, 1963, U. Liverpool, 1963, U. Sussex, 1966, U. Bath, 1969; D.Litt., U. Warwick, 1968; Mus.D., U. London, 1969, U. Cambridge, 1970; m. Nola Ruby Nicholas, May 26, 1938; children—Zamira, Krov; m. 2d, Diana Gould, Oct. 19, 1947; children—Gerard, Jeremy. Played violin at age 4; at 7 was soloist with San Francisco Orch.; at 8 in recital at Manhattan Opera House; Carnegie Hall debut as child of 10, playing Beethoven Concerto with N.Y. Symphony Orch.; at 11 with Berlin Philharmonic Orch. (Bruno Walter conducting) playing in one orchestral concert Bach, Beethoven, and Brahms concertos; at 12 appeared with major symphony orchs. of Europe and Am., regularly playing 3 concertos with orchestral accompaniment; appeared with N.Y. Philharmonic at age of 15, also (Arturo Toscanini conducting), 1934; completed his first round-the-world concert tour, 1935, appearing in 110 concert engagements; ret. to 1937; has toured in Latin Am., S.Am., Australia, S.Africa and Pacific Islands; played 22 concerts during 12 day tour in Israel; filmed series of complete concert programs; opened Japan to world concert artists, 1951; concert tours in India, 1952, 54; also charity concerts various instns.; has own yearly summer festival in Gstaad, Switzerland, 1957—; debut as condr. symphony orch. in Am. with Am. Symphony Orch., Carnegie Hall, 1966; dir. Bath Festival, Eng., 1958-68 (Bath Fesival Orch. now the Menuhin Festival Orch.); presented his first festival at Windsor, 1969; established Yehudi Menuhin Sch. at Stoke D'Abernon, Eng.; pres. Internat. Music Council of UNESCO. Held over 500 concerts for armed forces, Red Cross, others; followed U.S. Army into France and Belgium; first artist to play in liberated Paris, Brussels, Bucharest, Budapest and Antwerp, also first in Moscow after cessation of hostilities. Decorated Officer Legion of Honor; Chevalier De L'Ordre Des Arts Et Des Lettres (France); Order of Leopold (Belgium); Ordre de la Couronne (Belgium); Order of Merit (West German Republic); hon. knight comdr. Order Brit. Empire (Gt. Britain); Royal Order Phoenix (Greece); Jawaharlal Nehru award for Internat. Understanding (India), 1968. Fellow World Acad. Art and Sci., mem. and/or officer numerous U.S., fgn. orgns. Author: The Violin: Six Lessons by Yehudi Menuhin, 1971; Theme and Variations, 1972; The Violin and Viola, 1976; (autobiography) Unfinished Journey, 1977; co-author: The Music of Man, 1979. Research expansion violin concert repertoire; introduced many rare and important works both classical and modern. Office: care Columbia Artists Mgmt Inc Cami Bldg 165 W 57th St New York NY 10019*

MENZIES, IAN STUART, newspaper editor; b. Glasgow, Scotland, Mar. 11, 1920; s. John S. and Gertrude (Mephius) M.; student Royal Tech. Coll., 1937-39; L.H.D., Salem State Coll., 1978; m. Barbara Edith Newton, June 16, 1945; children—Marla Ann, Gillian Jean, Alexa Stuart, Deborah Newton. Came to U.S., 1944, naturalized, 1948. Reporter, Boston Globe, 1948-57, sci. editor, 1957-63, financial editor, 1963-65, mng. editor, 1965-70, asso. editor, 1970—. Vis. asso. Joint Center for Urban Studies, Mass. Inst. Tech.-Harvard, 1970—. Mem. Hingham (Mass.) Sch. Com., 1962-68. Served to lt. comdr. Royal Naval Vol. Res., 1939-46. Decorated D.S.C.; recipient Pub. Service award Nat. Edn. Writers, 1961; Pub. Service award A.A.A.S., 1963; Heywood Broun award, 1961; Sevellon Brown award, 1959; Rudolph Elie award, 1959; A.P. Big City award, 1958; U.P.I. award, 1959. Nieman fellow Harvard, 1961-62. Mem. Nat. Assn. Sci. Writers, Am. Soc. Newspaper Editors. Home: 479 Main St Hingham MA 02043 Office: Morrissey Blvd Boston MA 02124

MERAHN, LAWRENCE WILBURN, media promotion and research specialist; b. Bklyn., Jan. 12, 1909; s. Samuel and Anne (Spada) M.; grad. Manual Tng. High Sch., N.Y.C., 1927, Coll. City N.Y., 1931; m. Rose Irene Acker, Sept. 1931; 1 son, Roger Noel. Promotion copy writer, N.Y. Evening Jour., 1931-36; promotion mgr. N.Y. Post, 1936-41; dir. promotion and research N.Y. Sun, 1941-50; promotion dir. N.Y. World-Telegram and Sun, 1950-64; dir. promotion and mktg. Bell-McClure Syndicate div. N.Am. Newspaper Alliance, 1964-65; advt. mgr. L.I. Press, Nassau-Suffolk, 1965-67; sales mgr. Mid-Atlantic region Newhouse Newspapers, 1967—; prof. media, advt. course Coll. City N.Y. Past pres. N.Y. Newspaper Promotion Mgrs. Assn. and Nat. Newspaper Promotion Assn. In charge press publicity U.S. Victory Waste Paper Campaign; chmn. press publicity div. U.S. Trade Mark Assn., 1957—. Top winner in Editor and Publisher Ann. Awards for nationwide newspaper circulation campaign, 1957, best newspaper direct mail campaign to advertisers, 1958, best newspaper sales presentation, 1959, nat. 1st prize audio-visual market presentation, 1965. Creator, writer radio program Food Forum of Air; creator, editor So Goes The Nation, monthly study of economic patterns of Am., 1944. Author: Standard Guide for Newspaper Promotion and Research (Nat. Newspaper Promotion Assn.). Home: 9701 Shore Rd Brooklyn NY 11209 Office: Newhouse Newspapers 485 Lexington Ave 22d Floor New York NY 10017

MERCER, CHARLES, writer; b. Stouffville, Ont., Can., July 12, 1917 (parents Am. citizens); s. Alfred and Alma (Hoover) M.; A.B., Brown U., 1939; m. Alma Sutton, Feb. 21, 1940. Reporter, Washington Post, 1939-42; reporter, feature writer, columnist A.P., N.Y.C., 1946-59; sr. editor G.P. Putnam's Sons, N.Y.C., 1966-79, v.p., 1975-79. Served to 1st lt. AUS, World War II, Korean War. Mem. Phi Beta Kappa, Alpha Delta Phi. Club: Overseas Press (N.Y.C.). Author: (novels) The Narrow Ledge, 1951; There Comes A Time, 1955; Rachel Cade, 1956; The Drummond Tradition, 1957; Enough Good Men, 1960; Pilgrim Strangers, 1961; The Reckoning, 1962; Gift of Life, 1963; Beyond Bojador, 1965; Promise Morning, 1966; The Minister, 1969; Revolt in April, 1971; The Castle on the River, 1975; Witch Tide, 1976; (nonfiction) Alexander The Great, 1963, Legion of Strangers, 1964; Miracle at Midway, 1977; Monsters in the Earth: The Story of Earthquakes, 1978; Statue of Liberty, 1979; also numerous short stories, articles. Address: PO Box 314 Sussex NJ 07461

MERCER, ELWYN JARVIS, mfg. co. exec.; b. Bone Gap, Ill., Apr. 4, 1911; s. Charles Lawrence and Chloe Alice (Hocking) M.; B.M.E., U. Idaho, 1936; m. Ione McPherson, Dec. 31, 1936. With Allis-Chalmers Mfg. Co., 1937-68, mng. dir., Eng., 1951-56, gen. mgr. constrn. machine div., 1956-57, v.p., gen., 1957-62, v.p., mng. dir. internat. div., 1962-68; gen. mgr.-owner Mercer Enterprises, Protem, Mo., 1968—. Staff WPB, Washington, 1942-43. Served to lt. USNR, 1943-45. Clubs: Masons (32 deg.), Shriners. Home: Hillcrest Subdiv Protem MO 65733 Office: Protem MO 65733

MERCER, JOHNNY (JOHN H.), musician; b. Savannah, Ga., Nov. 18, 1909; student Woodbury Forest Sch., Orange, Va.; m. Ginger Meehan; children—Amanda, John. Actor, bit player, N.Y.C., 1927-29, vocalist, master ceremonies, writer mus. sketches Paul Whiteman orch.; singer Benny Goodman orch. CBS network, 1938, Bob Crosby orch. NBC, 1939-40; master ceremonies Army-sponsored program Mail Call, also master ceremonies, singer Lucky Strike Hit Parade; organizer Capitol Records, Inc. (with Glenn Wallichs, Buddy DeSylva), 1942, past pres.; founder Heritage Music, Inc., 1970. Writer lyrics for songs including: Pardon My Southern Accent, Jeepers Creepers, You Must Have Been a Beautiful Baby, Too Marvelous for Words, Angels Sing, Blues in the Night, You Were Never Lovelier, Accentuate the Positive, Laura, Skylark, Lazybones, Fools Rush In, Autumn Leaves, Goody Goody, Day In, Day Out, One for My Baby, I Wanna Be Around, Come Rain or Come Shine, Satin Doll, I Remember You, That Old Black Magic, others; writer lyrics, music Something's Gotta Give, GI Jive, Dream, I'm An Old Cowhand; writer lyrics for motion pictures including: Daddy Long Legs, Here Comes the Waves, Star Spangled Rhythm, Ready Willing and Able, Harvey Girls, others; plays St. Louis Woman, Li'l Abner, Foxy, Life is What You Make It for film Kotch (Golden Globes award 1972). Recipient Acad. Award for lyrics Atchison, Topeka, and Santa Fe, 1946. Pres., Songwriter's Hall of Fame, 1967—. Mem. A.S.C.A.P. Office: 1209 N Western Ave Hollywood CA 90029 Died June 25, 1976.

MERCER, MARIAN, actress; b. Akron, Ohio, Nov. 26, 1935; d. Samuel Lewis and Nelle (Leggatt) M.; B.S., U. Mich.; m. Martin Joseph Cassidy, Nov. 9, 1964. Stage debut in The Happiest Millionaire, 1957, other stage appearances include: Holiday for Lovers, A Hole in the Head, The Ballad of Baby Doe, Show Boat, The Most Happy Fella, The Waltz of the Toreadors, 1958; Guys and Dolls, The Pajama Game, The Student Prince, Bells are Ringing, Hotel Paradiso, 1959; Greenwillow, Fiorello!, Little Mary Sunshine, 1960; New Faces of 1962, Bye Bye Birdie, Gypsy, 1962; Much Ado About Nothing, 1963; The Hostage, A Streetcar Named Desire, 1967; Your Own Thing, Promises, Promises, 1968; A Place for Polly, Othello, 1970; The Wanderers, The Taming of the Shrew, The Good and Bad Times of Cady Francis McCullum and Friends, 1971; Volpone, And Miss Reardon Drinks a Little, 1972; Tadpole, Lovers and Other Strangers, Nobody's Ernest, 1973; The Seagull, Travellers, Petrified Man, 1974; regular on The Dean Martin Show, 1972-73. Recipient Antoinette Perry award, Drama Desk award, Theatre World award. Address: care Susan Smith & Assos 850 7th Ave New York NY 10019*

MERCER, ROBERT LEE, trade assn. exec.; b. Alta., Can., July 8, 1926; naturalized U.S. citizen, 1974; s. James Lee and Catherine Ela (Coombs) M.; B.S., Brigham Young U., 1949, postgrad., 1952-53; M.S. (Univ. fellow), U. Maine, 1956; m. Beverley Knowlton, Sept. 2, 1953; children—Robin Lee, Cherie, Catherine Jo, Jeffrey Robert. Research asst. U. Maine, Orono, 1954-55; researcher U.S. Steel Corp., Provo, Utah, 1956-57; mgr. field dept. R.T. French Co., Shelley, Idaho, 1957-72; exec. v.p. Potato Bd., Denver, 1972—; mem. Idaho Gov.'s Potato Adv. Com., 1962-70; vice chmn., chmn. research and edn. com. Potato Commn. Idaho, 1970-72; pres. Potato Processors of Idaho, 1963-64. Recipient cert. highest merit Gov. Idaho, 1972, Key award Idaho Jaycees, 1960. Mem. Potato Assn. Am. (pres. 1975-76), United Fresh Fruit and Vegetable Assn., Produce Mktg. Assn. (dir.), AAAS. Republican. Mormon. Club: Lions (pres. local chpt. 1967-68). Author booklets on potatoes; contbr. numerous articles to profl. jours. Office: 1385 S Colorado St Denver CO 80222

MERCER, SAMUEL, JR., univ. dean; b. Phila., Sept. 4, 1920; s. Samuel and Sophia Elizabeth (Link) M.; B.S., Drexel U., 1943; M.S., Mich. State U., 1950; Ph.D., Purdue U., 1956; m. Deborrah Marie Sifkovitz, July 15, 1944; children—Mary Mercer Jewett, Catherine Mercer Credelle, John, Robert, Allyson, Louise Mercer DeNight, Irene, Thomas. Draftsman mech. design sect. Glenn L. Martin Co., Balt., 1946-47; mem. faculty Mich. State U., East Lansing, 1947-59; mem. faculty Drexel U., Phila., 1959—, prof., head mech. engring. dept., 1959-66, asso. dean Coll. Engring., 1966-70, dir. continuing profl. edn., 1971-72, dean continuing and coop. edn., 1972-77, dean continuing edn., 1977—. Mem. indsl. standards adv. bd. Pa. Dept. Labor and Industry, 1965-70. Served to 1st lt. USAAF, 1943-46; PTO. Mem. Am. Soc. M.E. (chmn. Phila. 1971-72), Am. Soc. Engring. Edn., Sigma Xi, Phi Kappa Phi, Tau Beta Pi, Pi Tau Sigma, Sigma Pi Sigma, Phi Eta Sigma, Delta Sigma Phi. Home: 308 Martin Lane Wallingford PA 19086 Office: Office Continuing Profl Edn Drexel Univ Philadelphia PA 19104

MERCER, WILLIAM CRAWFORD, telephone co. exec.; b. Phila., Jan. 13, 1919; s. Herbert C. and Wilhelmina (Manz) M.; A.B., Dartmouth, 1940; S.M. (Sloan fellow), Mass. Inst. Tech., 1956; m. Ramona Wells, Sept. 4, 1955; children—Lee William, Ray A., John G., Robert T. Salesman, IBM Corp., 1940-46; with Western Electric Co., 1947-58, works comptroller, North Andover, Mass., 1956-58; with New Eng. Tel. & Tel. Co., 1958-62, 72—, gen. mgr., N.H., 1959-60, v.p. personnel, Boston, 1960-62, pres. 1972—, also dir.; v.p. operations Ind. Bell Telephone Co., 1962-64; asst. v.p. personnel Am. Tel. & Tel. Co., N.Y.C., 1964-65, v.p. marketing, 1965-67, v.p. personnel, 1967-71; dir. John Hancock Ins. Co., First Nat. Boston Corp. Bd. dirs. United Way Mass.; bd. overseers Crotchet Mountain Rehab. Center, Tuck Sch. Bus. Adminstrn.; trustee Mass. Eye and Ear Infirmary; mem. corp. Mass. Gen. Hosp., Boston Museum Sci., Northeastern U., Babson Coll. Served to capt. USAAF, 1941-45. Mem. Soc. Sloan Fellows, Boston C. of C. (dir.). Clubs: Dartmouth (Charles River); Braeburn Country. Home: 11 Falmouth Rd Wellesley Hills MA 02181 Office: 185 Franklin St Boston MA 02107

MERCEREAU, JAMES EDGAR, educator, physicist; b. Sharon, Pa., Apr. 3, 1930; s. James T. and S. Francis (Festermaker) M.; B.A., Pomona Coll., 1953, Sc.D. (hon.), 1968; M.S., U. Ill., 1954; Ph.D., Calif. Inst. Tech., 1959; m. Gabriella Lengyel, Dec. 23, 1967; children—James A., Michael D., Steven F. Research physicist Hughes Research Lab., 1954-59; asst. prof. physics Calif. Inst. Tech., 1959-62, prof., 1969—; prin. scientist Ford Sci. Lab., 1962-65; mgr. Ford Cryogenic Labs., 1965-69. Dir. R.A.I. Corp. Mem. adv. com. NASA; mem. Nat. Acad. Com. Adv. to Nat. Bur. Standards. Named one of America's 10 Outstanding Young Men, U.S. Jr. C. of C., 1965; recipient achievement award in physics Am. Acad. Achievement, 1966. Fellow Am. Phys. Soc. Contbr. articles profl. jours. Patentee in field. Home: 218 Monarch Bay South Laguna CA 92677 Office: 1201 E California Blvd Pasadena CA 91109

MERCHANT, MYLON EUGENE, engr., physicist; b. Springfield, Mass., May 6, 1913; s. Mylon Dickinson and Rebecca Chase (Currier) M.; B.S. magna cum laude, U. Vt., 1936, D.Sc. (hon.), 1973; D.Sc., U. Cin., 1941; m. Helen Silver Bennett, Aug. 4, 1937; children—Mylon David, Leslie Ann Merchant Alexander, Frances Sue Merchant Jacobson. Research physicist Cin. Milacron, Inc., 1940-48, sr. research physicist, 1948-51, asst. dir. research, 1951-57, dir. phys. research, 1957-63, dir. sci. research, 1963-69, dir. research planning, 1969—; adj. prof. mech. engring. U. Cin., 1964-69; vis. prof. mech. engring. U. Salford (Eng.), 1973—. Bd. dirs. Dan Beard council Boy Scouts Am., 1967—. Fellow Am. Soc. Lubrication Engrs. (pres. 1952-53), Am. Soc. Metals, Ohio Acad. Sci.; mem. Nat. Acad. Engring., Soc. Mfg. Engrs. (pres. 1976-77), ASME (hon.), Internat. Instn. Prodn. Engring. Research (pres. 1968-69), Engring. Soc. Cin. (pres. 1961-62), Fedn. Materials Socs. (pres. 1974), Phi Beta Kappa, Sigma Xi, Tau Beta Pi. Contbr. articles to profl. jours. Research on systems approach to mfg. Home: 3709 Center St Cincinnati OH 45227 Office: 4701 Marburg Ave Cincinnati OH 45209

MERCIER, FRANCOIS, lawyer; b. Paris, France, Apr. 13, 1923; s. Oscar and Jeanne (Bruneau) M., B.A., Loyola Coll., Montreal, Que., Can., 1942; LL.B., U. Montreal, 1945; m. Lucile Rouleau, May 25, 1946; children—Genevieve, Madeleine, Jean Francois, Helene. Called to bar Que., 1945, since practiced in Montreal; sr. partner Stikeman, Elliott, Tamaki, Mercier & Robb, 1964—; lectr. ins. law U. Montreal, 1945-58. Dir. Citroen Can., Ltd., Mercanmor Corp., Popular Industries Ltd., Gen. Accident Assurance Co. Can., Scottish Canadian Assurance Corp., Canadian Pioneer Ins. Co., Campeau Corp., Ltd. Chmn. bd. Hôtel-Dieu Hosp., Montreal; pres. La Librairie Fernand Nathan Can. Ltée.; vice chmn. Société des Hôtels Méridien (Can.) Ltée. Decorated officer Order of Can. Mem. Can., Montreal bar assns. Home: One Spring Grove Crescent Outremont 153 PQ Canada Office: 1155 Dorchester St Montreal PQ Canada

MERCOURI, MELINA (MARIA AMALIA), actress; b. Athens, Greece, Oct. 18, 1925; d. Stamatis and Irene M.; ed. Acad. Nat. Theatre Greece; m. Jules Dassin, 1966. Films include: Stella, 1955, He Who Must Die, 1956, The Gipsy and the Gentleman, 1955, Never on Sunday, 1960, Topkapi, 1963, Les Pianos Mécaniques, 1964, 10:30 P.M. Summer, 1966, Phaedra, 1962, Gaily, Gaily, 1969, Once Is Not Enough, 1975, Promise at Dawn, Earthquake, 1974, A Dream of Passion, 1978; stage appearances include: Ilya, Darling, Lysistrata, 1972, Mourning Becomes Electra, A Streetcar Named Desire, Helen or the Joy of Living, The Queen of Clubs, The Seven Year Itch, Sweet Bird of Youth. Author: I Was Born Greek. Address: care Jules Dassin 25 rue du Montparnasse Paris 6e France*

MERCURE, ALEX P., govt. ofcl.; b. Lumberton, N.Mex., June 30, 1931; B.S. in Edn., U. N.Mex., 1958, now postgrad.; M.A. in Guidance, N.Mex. Highlands U., 1961. Tchr., Chama (N.Mex.) High Sch., 1958-62; counselor pub. schs., Los Lunas, N.Mex., 1962-64; exec. dir. home edn. livelihood program N.Mex. Council Chs., 1965-71; pres. N.Mex. Tech. Vocat. Sch., El Rito, 1971-74; v.p., asso. provost U. N.Mex., 1974-77; asst. sec. agr. for rural devel. Dept. Agr., Washington, 1977—, also dir. Rural Telephone Bank Bd. Mem. study group applied scis. and social change in rural areas Nat. Acad. Scis.; mem. Nat. Adv. Com. Adult Edn., Nat. Adv. Com. Minority Bus. Enterprise, White House Conf. Children and Youth, White House Conf. Food, Nutrition and Health, mem. Joint Commn. Mental Health for Children-N.Mex. Coop. Research and Study Council. Bd. dirs. Albuquerque Community Council, Spanish Colonial History Found., Santa Fe. Recipient N.Mex. Distinguished Pub. Service award, 1976.*

MERDINGER, CHARLES JOHN, civil engr., ednl. adminstr.; b. Chgo., Apr. 20 1918; s. Walter F. and Catherine (Phelan) M.; student Marquette U.; B.S., U.S. Naval Acad., 1941; B.C.E., Rensselaer Poly. Inst., 1945, M.C.E., 1946; D.Phil. (Rhodes scholar), Brasenose Coll., Oxford (Eng.) U., 1949; m. Mary McKelleget, Oct. 21, 1944; children—Anne, Joan, Susan, Jane. Commd. ensign U.S. Navy, 1941, advanced through grades to capt., 1959; served in USS Nevada, USS Alabama, 1941-44; design, constrn. pub. works, Panama, 1946-47, Washington, Bremerton, Wash., Adak, Alaska and Miramar, Calif., 1949-56; comdg. officer, dir. U.S. Naval Civil Engring. Lab., Port Hueneme, Calif., 1956-59; pub. works officer U.S. Fleet activities, Yokosuka, Japan, 1959-62; head English, history and govt. dept. U.S. Naval Acad., 1962-65; asst. comdr. operations and maintenance Navy Facilities Engring. Command, Navy Dept., 1965-67; pub. works officer NSA, DaNang, Vietnam, 1967-68; comdg. officer Western div. Naval Facilities Engring. Command, 1968-70; pres. Washington Coll., Chestertown, Md., 1970-73; v.p. Aspen (Colo.) Inst. Humanistic Studies, 1973-74; dep. dir. Scripps Instn. Oceanography, La Jolla, Calif., 1974—; dir. Avco Corp., Avco Community Developers. Mem. Md., Calif., Oreg. Selection Com. for Rhodes Scholars; exec. vol. Boy Scouts Am.; sec., mem. exec. com. Md. Ind. Coll. and Univ. Assn., 1971-72; mem. So. Regional Edn. Bd., 1971-73; mem. Nat. Com. History and Heritage of Am. Civil Engring., 1965-72. Alumni trustee U.S. Naval Acad., 1971-74; mem. council Rensselaer Poly. Inst., 1972—; trustee Found. for Ocean Research, 1976—. Decorated Legion of Merit with combat V, Navy Meritorious Service medal; named All-Am. in lacrosse, 1946. Registered profl. engr., Wis. Fellow ASCE (Nat. History and Heritage award 1972), Explorers Club; mem. Nat. Soc. Profl. Engrs., Soc. Am. Mil. Engrs. (Toulmin medal 1952, 57, 61), Soc. History Tech., Am. Soc. Engring. Edn., Brasenose Soc., Pearl Harbor Survivors Assn., Eagle Scout Alumni Assn., Phalanx, Sigma Xi, Tau Beta Pi, Chi Epsilon. Roman Catholic. Author: Civil Engineering Through the Ages, 1963; contbr. articles to Ency. Britannica, others. Home: Box 5294 321 Ski Way 190 Incline Village-Lake Tahoe NV 84590 Office: Scripps Instn Oceanography U Calif San Diego La Jolla CA 92093

MEREDITH, BURGESS, actor; b. Cleve., Nov. 16, 1909; s. William George and Ida (Burgess) M.; student Amherst Coll., 1927-28, hon. A.M., 1939; m. Helen Berrian Derby, 1932 (div. 1935); m. 2d, Margaret H. Frueauff (Margaret Perry), 1936 (div. July 1938); m. 3d, Paulette Goddard, May 21, 1944 (div.); m. 4th, Kaja Sundsten, 1950; children—Jonathan Sanford, Tala Beth. Reporter, salesman, seaman, 1928-29; first small part with Eva La Gallienne's Student Repertory Group, 1930; theatre appearances include: Little Ol' Boy, 1933, She Loves Me Not, 1933, The Barrets of Wimpole Street, Flowers of the Forest, (with Katherine Cornell), 1935, Winterset (Drama Critics award), 1936, High Tor (Drama Critics award), 1937, Star Wagon, 1937, Five Kings, 1939, Liliom, 1940, Candida, 1942, Lincoln Portrait, 1943, The Playboy of the Western World, 1946, Winterset, 1947, Harvey, 1950, Let Me Hear the Melody, 1951, Lo and Behold! (dir.), 1951, The Remarkable Mr. Pennypacker, 1953, 58, Macbeth (dir.), 1954, Teahouse of the August Moon, 1955, Major Barbara, 1956, Speaking of Murder (producer), 1956, Ulysses in Nighttown (dir.), 1958, 74, Enrico, 1958, God and Kate Murphy (dir.), 1959, The Vagabond King, 1959, A Thurber Carnival (dir.), 1960, An Evening with Burgess Meredith, 1960, Midgie Purvis (dir.), 1961, A Whiff of Melancholy (dir.), 1961, Blues for Mr. Charlie (dir.), 1964, motion pictures include: Winterset, 1936, There Goes the Groom, 1937; Spring Madness, 1938; Idiot's Delight, 1938; Of Mice and Men, 1939; Castle on the Hudson, 1940; Second Chorus, 1940; San Francisco Docks, 1941; That Uncertain Feeling, 1941; Tom, Dick and Harry, 1941; The Forgotten Village, 1941; Street of Chance, 1942; Welcome to Britain, 1943; Salute to France, 1944; The Yank Comes Back, 1945; Story of G.I. Joe, 1945; The Diary of a Chambermaid, 1946; Magnificent Doll, 1946; On Our Merry Way, 1948; Mine Own Executioner, 1948; Jigsaw, 1949; The Man on the Eiffel Tower, 1950; The Gay Adventure, 1953; Joe Butterfly, 1957; Universe, 1961; Advise and Consent, 1962; The Cardinal, 1963; In Harm's Way, 1965; Madame X, 1966; The Crazy Quilt, 1966; A Big Hand for the Little Lady, 1966; Batman, 1966; Hurry Sundown, 1967; Torture Garden, 1968; Stay Away Joe, 1968; Mackenna's Gold, 1968; There Was a Crooked Man, 1969; The Yin and the Yang (also writer, dir.), 1970; A Fan's Notes, 1970; The Clay Pidgeon, 1970; The Man, 1972; B for Murder, 1973; Golden Needles, 1973; Day of the Locust, 1974; The Hindenburg, 1974; 92 in the Shade, 1975; Burnt Offerings, 1976; Rocky (Acad. award nomination), 1976; The Sentinel, 1977; Foul Play, 1978; Magic, 1978; The Manitou, 1978; Rocky II, 1979; producer, writer Diary of a Chambermaid, 1946; producer, actor On Our Merry Way, 1947; dir. Man On The Eiffel Tower, 1948, The Latent Heterosexual, 1969; various TV appearances, including: Ah, Wilderness!, Waiting for Godot, 77 Sunset Strip, Batman, Wagon Train, The Invaders, Daniel Boone, The Bold Ones, Night Gallery; World of Disney, others; directed N.Y. Symphony, Carnegie Hall, 1969; exec. dir. Actors Studio West, 1972—; artistic dir. Merle Oberon Theatre, Los Angeles, 1972—; v.p. Actors Equity, 1938—, acting pres., spring 1938; chmn. adv. bd. Fed. Arts Projects, 1937. Served with AUS, 1942-44; ETO. Episcopalian. Club: Players (N.Y.C.). Office: care Jack Fields & Assos 9255 Sunset Blvd Suite 1105 Los Angeles CA 90069

MEREDITH, CHARLES EYMARD, psychiatrist, hosp. adminstr.; b. St. John, N.B., Can., Apr. 1, 1926; s. Charles H.G. and Catherine Ann (Collins) M.; B.A. magna cum laude, Loyola Coll., Montreal, Que., 1947; M.D., C.M., McGill U., 1951. Came to U.S., 1952, naturalized, 1956. Intern Montreal Gen. Hosp., 1951-52; resident psychiatry Conn. Valley Hosp., Middletown, 1952-54, 56-57, psychiatrist, 1957-59, clin. dir., dir. residency tng. program in psychiatry, 1959-61, asst. supt., 1961-63; pvt. practice, 1960-63; supt. Colo. State Hosp., Pueblo, 1963-76; dir. Augusta (Maine) Mental Health Inst., 1977; supt. St. Elizabeths Hosp., Washington, 1977—; hosp. dir. USPHS, 1977—; asso. clin. prof. psychiatry Sch. Medicine, U. Colo., 1963-76; prof. med. tech. U. So. Colo., Pueblo, 1964-76; cons. div. mental health service programs NIMH, 1975—. Served to lt. M.C., USNR, 1954-56; capt. Res. ret. Diplomate Am. Bd. Psychiatry. Fellow Am. Psychiat. Assn.; mem. Pueblo Navy League (past pres.), Am. Assn. Psychiat. Adminstrs. (exec. com. 1975-77), Psychiat. Soc. Washington. Address: St Elizabeths Hosp Washington DC 20032

MEREDITH, DON (JOSEPH DONALD), actor, sportscaster; b. Mt. Vernon, Tex., Apr. 10, 1938; s. Jeff B. and Hazel (White) M.; B.B.A., So. Meth. U., 1960; m. Susan Schloss, 1972; children—Mary Donna, Michael, Heather. Quarterback, Dallas Cowboys, 1960-69; sports commentator ABC Monday Night Football, 1970-73, 77—; sportscaster NBC, 1974-76; appeared numerous TV shows including Police Story, McCloud, Quest, Grandstand; appeared TV movies Terror on the 40th Floor, 1974, Sky Heist, 1975, Banjo Hackett, 1976, Mayday at 40,000 Feet, 1976, The Courage and the Passion, 1978, Kate Bliss and the Ticker Tape Kid, 1978. Recipient Emmy award.*

MEREDITH, EDWIN THOMAS, III, publishing co. exec.; b. Chgo., Feb. 7, 1933; s. Edwin Thomas, Jr. and Anna (Kauffman) M.; student U. Ariz., 1950-53; m. Katherine Comfort, Sept. 4, 1953; children—Mildred K., Dianna M., Edwin Thomas. With Meredith Corp., Des Moines, 1956—, dir., 1966—, v.p., 1968-71, pres., chief exec. officer, 1971-73, chmn. bd., 1973—; dir., mem. exec. com. Bankers Trust Co., Des Moines; dir. Mut. of Omaha. Bd. dirs. Nat. Merit Scholarship Corp., Evanston, Ill.; trustee Iowa Methodist Med. Center, Drake U., Des Moines, Iowa 4-H Found., Ames. Served with U.S. Army, 1953-56. Clubs: Chgo.; Wakonda, Des Moines (Des Moines). Home: 3650 Lincoln Pl Dr Des Moines IA 50312 Office: 1716 Locust St Des Moines IA 50336

MEREDITH, HENRY MCGAUGHY, banker; b. Longview, Tex., Dec. 10, 1934; s. David Sutton and Lois (McGaughy) M.; B.B.A., North Tex. State U., 1956; M.L.A., So. Methodist U., 1972; m. Sara Ann Parker, June 4, 1966; children—John McGaughy, Steven Parker. Vice-pres. First Nat. Bank, Dallas, 1964-69; sr. v.p. Nat. Bank Commerce, Dallas, 1969-74; exec. v.p., dir. Dallas Internat. Bank, 1974-75; v.p. First Main Capital Corp., 1975—; dir. Meredith Investment Corp., Transcontinental Oil Corp., Shreveport, Wil-Mc Oil Corp., Dallas. Served with AUS, 1957. Mem. Am. Inst. Banking, Ind. Petroleum Assn. Am., Tex. Mid-Continent Oil and Gas Assn., Kappa Sigma. Methodist. Club: Royal Oaks Country. Home: 3607 Euclid Dr Dallas TX 75205 Office: PO Box 2327 Dallas TX 75221

MEREDITH, HOWARD VOAS, physical growth specialist, human biologist; b. Birmingham, Eng. Nov. 5, 1903; s. Howard and Ada (Barker) M.; came to U.S., 1923, naturalized, 1937; A.A., Graceland Coll., Lamoni, Ia., 1929; B.A., U. Ia., 1931, A.M., 1932, Ph.D. 1935; m. Matilda Johnson, July 27, 1926; children—Leslie Hugh, Mavis Rogene. Research asst. Ia. Child Welfare Research Sta., 1931-35, research asso., 1935-39; asst. prof. Ia. Child Welfare Research Sta., U. Iowa, 1939-42, asso. prof., 1943-48, prof., 1948-49, prof., chmn., 1949; prof. phys. growth Sch. Health and Phys. Edn., U. Oreg., 1949-52; prof., cons. Ia. Child Welfare Research Sta. and Coll. Dentistry, 1952-56; prof. child somatology Inst. Child Behavior and Devel., U. Iowa, 1956-72, emeritus, 1972—; adj. research prof. Coll. Health and Phys. Edn., U. S.C., 1973—; exchange appointment Harvard, summer 1935; vis. lectr. U. So. Cal., summer 1948, vis. prof., 1951. Trustee Graceland Coll., 1953-58. Fellow Soc. Research Child Devel. (pres. 1953-55); mem. Am. Assn. Orthodontists (hon. mem.), Am. Assn. Phys. Anthropologists, AAUP, Internat. Assn. Human Biologists, Sigma Xi, Phi Epsilon Kappa, Lambda Delta Sigma. Club: Research. Author: The Rhythm of Physical Growth, 1935; Physical Growth of White Children, 1936; Physical Growth from Birth to Two Years: I Stature, 1943; Physical Growth Record, 1948; Height Weight Interpretation Chart, 1951; Concept of Physical Development, 1957; Methods of Studying Physical Growth, 1960; Change in Stature of American Boys During Last 80 Years, 1963; Body Size and Form in Childhood, 1966; Body Size of Contemporary Groups of Children Studied in Different Parts of the World, 1969; Compendium of Research Findings on Body Size, 1971; Childhood Changes of Head, Face and Dentition, 1973; Height-Weight Interpretation Folder,

1975; Height and Weight Charts for Black American Children and Youths, 1977; A Vignette on Human Body Growth from Infant to Adult, 1977; Human Body Growth in the First Ten Years of Life, 1978. Contbr. articles to Yearbook Physical Anthropology, Nat. Ency., Annals of N.Y. Acad. Sci., Colliers Ency., Ency. Americana, Ency. Ednl. Research med., dental, ednl., and anthropol. jours., other profl. publs. Specialist on body growth of the child. Home: 5225 Clemson Ave Columbia SC 29206

MEREDITH, HUGH STOCKDELL, lawyer; b. Virginia Beach, Va., Nov. 2, 1916; s. George Minor and Elizabeth (Morrison) M.; J.D., U. Va., 1940; m. Gwendolyn Maclin Simmons, Apr. 23, 1949; children—Hugh Stockdell, Ann Leighton, Robert Barret. Admitted to Va. bar, 1939; mem. firm Vandeventer, Black, Meredith, & Martin, Norfolk, Va., 1940—, partner, 1951—; gen. counsel, dir. MacArthur Meml. Found., 1974—. Mem. adv. com. Tulane Admiralty Law Inst., 1966—; trustee St. Paul's Coll., 1971-79; del. Gen. Conv. Episcopal Ch., 1973, 76, 79. Served to comdr. USNR, 1941-46. Fellow Am. Coll. Trial Lawyers; mem. Am. Bar Assn. (standing com. on admiralty and maritime law 1978—), Maritime Law Assn. U.S. (exec. com. 1967-70, 2d v.p. 1970-72), Average Adjusters Assn. U.S., Jud. Conf. 4th Circuit U.S. Ct. Appeals. Episcopalian (chancellor Diocese So. Va. 1971-78). Asso. editor Am. Maritime Cases, 1956—. Home: 1409 N Bay Shore Dr Virginia Beach VA 23451 Office: One Commercial Pl Norfolk VA 23510

MEREDITH, JAMES HARGROVE, U.S. judge; b. Wedderburn, Oreg., Aug. 25, 1914; s. Willis H. and Ollie (Hargrove) M.; A.B., Mo. U., 1935, LL.B., 1937; m. Dorothy Doke, Sept. 7, 1937 (dec. Feb. 1972); 1 son, James Doke; m. 2d, Susan B. Fitzgibbon, 1977. Admitted to Mo. bar, 1937; pvt. practice, New Madrid County, 1937-42, 46-49; spl. agt. FBI, 1942-44; partner Stolar, Kuhlman & Meredith, St. Louis, 1952-61, Cook, Meredith, Murphy & English, 1961-62, Stuart & Meredith, Washington, 1961-62; judge U.S. Dist. Ct., Eastern Dist. Mo., 1962-71, chief judge, 1971—; judge U.S. Fgn. Intelligence Surveillance Ct., 1979—; chief counsel Mo. Ins. Dept., Jefferson City, 1949-52. Past dir. Bank St. Louis, Comml. Bank St. Louis County, Gen. Bancshares, Inc., Investment Securities Co., Northland Bank; v.p., gen. counsel Nat. Underwriters, Inc. Mem. Mental Health Commn. Mo., 1961-62; trustee Friends U. Mo. Library, U. Mo. Law Sch. Found. Served with USNR, 1944-46. Recipient Patriots award SR, 1974. Mem. Jud. Conf. U.S. (exec. com. 1976, subcom. on improvement judiciary 1971—), Mo., D.C., St. Louis, Am. bar assns., Lawyers Assn. St. Louis, Mo. Squires, VFW, Am. Legion, Order of Coif, Sigma Chi (Significant Sig award), Phi Delta Phi. Presbyn. Mason (Shriner). Clubs: Old Warson Country, University, Missouri Athletic (St. Louis). Home: 108 Runnymede Dr Saint Louis MO 63105 Office: US Ct and Custom House Saint Louis MO 63101

MEREDITH, JAMES HOWARD, racial rights worker; b. Kosciusko, Miss., June 25, 1933; s. Moses Cap and Roxie (Patterson) M.; student Jackson (Miss.) State Coll., 1960-62; B.A. in Polit. Sci., U. Miss., 1963; student U. Ibadan, Nigeria, West Africa, 1964-65; student Columbia Law Sch., 1965; m. Mary June Wiggins, Dec. 16, 1956; children—John Howard, Joseph Howard, James Henry. Employed with stock brokerage firm; lectr. on racial problems at various univs. and colls.; active in voter registration campaigns. Served with USAF, 1951-60. Mem. Phi Alpha Delta. Author: Three Years in Mississippi, 1966. *

MEREDITH, JOHN, artist; b. Fergus, Ont., Can. One-man shows: Isaacs Gallery, Toronto, Ont., 1961, 63, 65, 67, 73, 77, Blue Barn Gallery, Ottawa, Ont., 1965, Gallery Contemporary Art, Toronto, Art Gallery Ont. travelling shows, 1974-75; asso. prof. art Guelph (Ont.) U., 1978—. Office: care Isaacs Gallery 832 Yonge St Toronto ON M4W 2H1 Canada*

MEREDITH, LEWIS DOUGLAS, utility exec.; b. Scranton, Pa., May 7, 1905; s. William S. and Carrie C. (Huff) M.; student Bucknell U., 1922-23; A.B. cum laude, Syracuse U., 1926, A.M., 1927; Ph.D., Yale, 1933; LL.D., Middlebury Coll., 1975; m. Laura J. Parker, Aug. 19, 1935. Instr. Syracuse (N.Y.) U., 1925-27; asst. prof. econs. U. Vt., 1927-35; univ. fellow Yale, 1930-31; instr. Milw. State Tchrs. Coll., summer 1932; Vt. commr. banking and ins., 1934-35; investment analyst Nat. Life Ins. Co., Montpelier, Vt., 1935-38, mem. finance com., 1938-68, asst. to pres., 1939-42, treas., 1940-44, v.p., 1943—, v.p., chmn. com. finance, 1944-47, exec. v.p., chmn. finance com., 1947-66, vice chmn. bd., chief financial officer, 1966-68, dir., 1950—; pres., chief exec. officer Central Vt. Pub. Service Corp., Rutland, 1968-72, chmn., dir., 1972—, chief exec. officer, 1972-73, dir., 1953—; chmn., dir. Conn. Valley Electric Co. Inc.; dir. emeritus Vt. Mut. Fire Ins. Co., North Security Ins. Co., Allegheny Airlines, Chittenden Trust Co.; dir. Vt. Elec. Power Co., Inc.; corporator Burlington Savs. Bank; lectr. S.S. Huebner Found., 1952, Sch. Banking, U. Vt., 1948, 50, 53, 56, various seminars. Cons. State Dept. AID Program, Ecuador, 1965; sec. Vermont Bankers Com., 1932-33; mem. residential real estate credit adv. com. Fed. Res. Bank, 1950-52; mem. Vt. Merit System Council, 1939-47, chmn., 1940-47; mem. Vt. Council Safety, 1941-46; vice chmn. Vt. War Finance Commn., 1945; mem. Gov.'s Housing Adv. Com., 1945; mem. Gov.'s Reapportionment Panel, 1964. Dir. Asso. Industries Vt., 1969-73; dir. New Eng. Council, 1944-50, v.p., mem. exec. com., 1954-58, pres., 1957-59, chmn. bd., 1959, chmn. com. to study question of taxation Vt., 1951-52; mem. Vt. Housing Authority 1972-74. Alumni trustee Syracuse U., 1950-56, 59-60; chmn. bd. trustees Middlebury Coll., 1967-75, trustee emeritus, 1975—; corporator Rutland Hosp.; bd. govs. Med. Center Hosp. Vt., 1969-73; trustee-at-large Syracuse U., 1966-72; trustee Vt. Arthritis Assn., 1974-77. Recipient Keystone Jr. Coll. Alumni Assn. 1949 honor award, LaPlume, Pa.; Arents medal Syracuse U., 1978; Meredith Wing of Starr Library at Middlebury Coll. named in his honor, 1979. Mem. Mortgage Bankers Assn. (gov. 1947-51), Am. Econ. Assn., Vt. Bankers Assn. (hon.), Tex. Mortgage Bankers Assn. (hon. life), Lake Champlain Regional C. of C. (dir. 1977—), Phi Beta Kappa, Kappa Phi Kappa, Delta Sigma Rho, Phi Kappa Phi. Republican. Conglist. Mason (32 deg. Shriner). Clubs: Lake Mansfield (Vt.) Trout; University (N.Y.C.); Metropolitan (Washington); Algonquin (Boston); Ethan Allen (Burlington, Vt.). Contbg. editor Burlington Free Press, 1933-35. Author: Merchandising for Banks, Trust Companies and Investment Houses, 1935; How to Buy a House, 1947; also articles financial mags. Home: 1500 Spear St South Burlington VT 05401 Office: 77 Grove St Rutland VT 05701. *Hard work, long hours, integrity, consideration of others, an abiding faith, and thrift—while trite—are, to my mind, the century-old ingredients of life's richest rewards and satisfactions.*

MEREDITH, MORLEY, baritone; b. Winnipeg, Man., Can.; studied with W.H. Anderson, Can., Boris Goldovsky, Tanglewood, Mass., Alfredo Martino, Melchiore Luise, U.S.A.; B.A., U. Man.; m. Erlene Meredith. Debut as Escamillo in Carmen at N.Y.C. Opera, 1957; Met. Opera debut in baritone roles in Tales of Hoffmann, 1962; sang with major cos. in Toronto, Can., Geneva, Switzerland, Glasgow, Scotland, Chgo., Ft. Worth, Kansas City, Milw. Florentine, New Orleans, New York Met. and City Opera, Phila. Lyric Opera, St. Paul, San Antonio, San Francisco Opera, Washington; appeared in operas Bluebeard's Castle, Fidelio, Wozzeck, Carmen, Peter Grimes, Flying Dutchman, Medea, Don Pasquale, Faust, Cavalleria Rusticana, Dernier Sauvage, Cosi fan Tutte, Contes d'Hoffmann, Carmina Burana, War and Peace, Boheme, Tosca, RosenKavalier, Elektra, Salome, Aida, Otello, Traviata, Lohengrin, Boris Godunof, others; recorded for Vanguard. Office: care Herbert Barrett Mgmt 1860 Broadway New York NY 10023*

MEREDITH, SCOTT, authors' rep.; b. N.Y.C., Nov. 24, 1923; s. Henry and Esta (Meredith); educated privately; m. Helen Kovet, Apr. 22, 1944; children—Stephen Charles, Randy Beth Meredith Sheer. Writer numerous mag. stories; established Scott Meredith Lit. Agy., Inc., N.Y.C., 1940, pres., 1942—. Served with USAAF, World War II. Clubs: Three Oaks Tennis, Spectator, Rare Book Soc. (N.Y.C.). Author: Writing to Sell, rev. edits., 1960, 74; Writing for the American Market, 1960; The Face of Comedy, 1961; George S. Kaufman and His Friends, 1974; The Science of Gaming, 1974; Louis B. Mayer and His Enemies, 1980; also stories, novelettes, serials and articles. Editor: The Best of Wodehouse, 1949; The Best of Modern Humor, 1951; Bar One Roundup, 1951; The Week-End Book of Humor, 1952; Bar Two Roundup, 1952; The Murder of Mr. Malone, An Anthology of Craig Rice Stories, 1953; Bar Three Roundup, 1954; Bar Four Roundup, 1955, 2d series, 1956; Bar Five Roundup, 1956; (with Ken Murray) The Ken Murray Book of Humor, 1957; Bar Six Roundup, 1957; (with Henry Morgan) The Henry Morgan Book of Humor, 1958; (with Sidney Meredith) The Best from Manhunt, 1958; The Bloodhound Anthology, 1960; The Fireside Treasury of Modern Humor, 1963; Best Western Stories, 1964; Best Western Stories For Young People, 1965; (with P.G. Wodehouse) The Best of Humor, 1965, A Carnival of Modern Humor, 1966. Contbr. articles on humor to Ency. Brit., 1954-59, articles on fiction writing to Oxford Ency., 1960-61. Frequent guest TV, radio shows; expert witness copyright cases. Home: Kings Point NY 11024 Office: 845 3d Ave New York NY 10022 also 44 Great Russell St London WC1 England

MEREDITH, WILLIAM (MORRIS), poet; b. N.Y.C., Jan. 9, 1919; s. William Morris and Nelley (Keyser) M.; A.B., Princeton, 1940, Woodrow Wilson fellow, 1946-47. Copy boy, reporter N.Y. Times, 1940-41; instr. English, creative writing Princeton, 1946, 47-48, 49-50; asst. prof. English, U. Hawaii, 1950-51; mem. faculty Conn. Coll., 1955—, prof. English, 1965—; mem. faculty Bread Loaf School English, 1958-62; dir. Conn. Coll. Humanities-Upward Bound program, 1964-68; poetry cons. Library of Congress, 1978—. Chancellor Acad. Am. Poets, 1964—; mem. Conn. Commn. Arts, 1963-65. Served with USAAF, 1941-42; to lt. USNR, 1942-46; PTO; to lt. comdr. USNR, Korea. Decorated Air medal with oak leaf cluster; recipient Loines prize Nat. Inst. Arts and Letters, 1966; Van Wyck Brooks award, 1971. Mem. Nat. Inst. Arts and Letters. Author: (poems) Love Letter From an Impossible Land, 1944; Ships and Other Figures, 1948; The Open Sea and Other Poems, 1958; Shelley, 1962; The Wreck of the Thresher and Other Poems, 1964; (translation) Alcools, 1964; Earth Walk: New and Selected Poems, 1970; Hazard, The Painter, 1975. Office: Connecticut College New London CT 06320

MERENESS, DOROTHY ANN, educator; b. Mo., Oct. 31, 1910; d. William Roy and Myrtle (Hoobler) Mereness; A.A., Colo. Woman's Coll., 1930; A.B., Colo. No. U., 1937; M. Nursing, Case-Western Res. U., 1941; M. Letters, U. Pitts., 1948; Ed.D., Columbia Tchrs. Coll., 1956; D.Social Sci. (hon.), Villanova U., 1978; Grade sch. tchr., pub. schs., Center and Las Animas, Colo., 1930-38; instr. psychiat. nursing Municipal Gen. Hosp., Cleve., 1941-46; ednl. dir. Jewish Hosp., Cin., 1946-47; asst. prof. psychiat. nursing U. Pitts. Sch. Nursing, 1948-52, Boston U. Sch. Nursing, 1952-53; part-time staff nurse N.Y. State Psychiat. Inst., 1953- 55; asso. prof. nurse edn. Sch. Edn., N.Y. U., 1955-63, also prof. edn., dir. grad. curriculum psychiat.-mental health nursing, 1955-65; prof. Sch. Nursing, U. Pa., 1965-79, prof. emeritus, 1979—, dean, 1965-77, dean emeritus, 1977—; mem. Pa. Bd. Nurse Examiners, 1970-77. Mem. subcom. nurse tng. com. NIMH, HEW, 1959-62; mem. nursing research study sect. NIH, HEW, 1964-67; pres. Am. Assn. Colls. Nursing, 1968-69; bd. dirs. nursing edn. alumni assn. Tchrs. Coll., Columbia, 1976, treas., 1978—; trustee Nurses' Ednl. Funds, Inc., 1966—, pres., 1970-76, exec. com., 1976—. Named Distinguished Alumni, Case-Western Res. U., 1968; recipient Dora Mathis award So. Pa. League for Nursing, 1975; Distinguished Achievement in Nursing Edn. award Nursing Edn. Alumni Tchrs. Coll., Columbia, 1976. Mem. Nat. League for Nursing (collegiate bd. rev. 1956-60), Pa. (trustee 1970-74), Southeastern Pa. (chmn. 1975-79) leagues nursing, Am., Pa. (chmn. psychiat. conf. group 1966-73, 76, chmn. joint practice commn. 1972-74, 79, mem. commn. on edn. 1976—, Disting. Service award 1978), Philadelphia County (trustee 1973—) nurses assns., N.Y. Acad. Sci., AAUP, AAUW, Coll. Physicians Phila., World Mental Health Assn., Pi Lambda Theta, Sigma Theta Tau, Kappa Delta Pi. Author (with Cecelia Taylor) Essentials of Psychiatric Nursing, 10th edit., 1978; A Survey of the Journey of the Pennsywania Nurses Assn. from 1903-1978. Editor: Psychiatric Nursing-Developing Psychiatric Nursing Skills, Vol. 1, 1970; Psychiatric Nursing-Understanding the Nurse's Role in Psychiatric Patient Care, Vol. 11, 1970; editorial bd. Perspective in Psychiatric Care, 1963-70; Nursing Forum, 1970-76. Home: Garden Court Apts 47th and Pine Sts Philadelphia PA 19143

MERGEN, FRANCOIS, educator, forester; b. Grand Duchy of Luxembourg, May 1, 1925; s. Aloyse and Marie (Arens) M.; certificat de fin d'etudes Luxembourg Coll., 1946; student Laval U., 1947; B.S., U. N.B., 1950; M.F. cum laude, Yale, 1951, Ph.D., 1954; m. Andree Bodson, Aug. 2, 1947; 1 son, John Francis. Mem. faculty Yale, 1954—, prof. forestry, 1963—, dean Sch. Forestry and Environmental Studies, 1965-75, also Pinchot prof. forestry. Hon. consul Grand Duchy of Luxembourg, 1974—. Mem. Soc. Am. Foresters (participant Vis. Scientist Program 1961-65; award for outstanding achievement in biol. research 1966), Sigma Xi. Contbr. numerous articles to profl. jours. Home: 86 Hill St Hamden CT 06514 Office: 370 Prospect St New Haven CT 06511

MERGEN, JOSEPH MICHAEL, aircraft co. exec.; b. Madison, Wis., Dec. 25, 1916; s. Michael Frank and Esther (Livesey) M.; B.S. in Mech. and Aero. Enginring., U. Wis., 1940; m. Margaret E. McLeod, May 28, 1941; children—Richard J., William J., Barbara J. With Curtiss-Wright Corp., 1940-60, pres. VTOL div., 1960-65; v.p., gen. mgr. Avco Lycoming Div., Charleston, S.C., 1965-69; pres., chief exec. officer Piper Aircraft Corp., Lockhaven, Pa., 1969-74, also dir.; now v.p. Starcraft Co., Goshen, Ind. Mem. Community Relations Commn., Charleston, 1967-69. Bd. dirs. Charleston Devel. Bd., 1967-69, exec. com., 1967-69; past bd. dirs. St. Francis Hosp., Charleston; past trustee Charleston Coll. Recipient Manley medal Soc. Automotive Engrs., 1951. Mem. Am. Inst. Aeros. and Astronautics, Beta Theta Pi. K.C. (4 deg.). Patents, publs. in field. Home: 301 Parmley Dr Goshen IN 46526 Office: Starcraft Co 2703 College Ave Goshen IN 46526

MERGENTIME, BERNARD CHARLES, stock broker; b. Chgo., June 21, 1898; s. Aaron and Rose (Goodman) M.; student Cornell Coll., 1916-17; m. Maxine Doris Stevens, Aug. 18, 1939; children—Charles Eric, Dian (Mrs. John Fatula). Clk. L.F. Rothchild & Co., 1919-22; office mgr. Straus & Co., 1922-27; with Ernst & Co., N.Y.C., 1927—, mng. partner, 1937—; dir. Mergentime Corp. Served with AUS, 1917-18. Decorated Silver Star. Mem. India House. Clubs: Downtown Athletic (N.Y.C.); Golden's Bridge Hounds (North Salem, N.Y.); Rombout Hunt (Salt Point, N.Y.); County Galway Hunt (Ireland). Home: North Salem NY 10560 Office: 100 Wall St New York NY 10005

MERGLER, HARRY WINSTON, educator; b. Chillicothe, O., June 1, 1924; s. Harry Franklin and Letitia (Walburn) M.; B.S., Mass. Inst. Tech., 1948; M.S., Case Inst. Tech., 1950, Ph.D., 1956; m. Irmgard Erna Steudel, June 22, 1948; children—Myra A. L., Marcia B. E., Harry F. Aero. research scientist NACA, 1948-56; mem. faculty Case Inst. Tech., 1957—, prof. engring., 1962—, Leonard Case prof. engring., 1973—, dir. Digital Systems Lab., 1959—; vis. scientist USSR, 1958; vis. prof. Norwegian Tech. U., 1962; cons. to industry, 1957—; editor Control Engring. mag., 1956—. Pres. Digital/Gen. Corp., 1968-72; cons. Exploratory Research div. NSF. Served with AUS, 1942-45. Fellow IEEE (pres. profl. group indsl. electronics 1977-79, recipient Lamme medal 1978), Cleve. Engring. Soc., N.Y. Acad. Sci., Sigma Xi, Tau Beta Pi, Theta Tau, Pi Delta Epsilon, Zeta Psi, Blue Key. Republican. Lutheran. Mason. Author: Digital Systems Engineering, 1961; also articles, chpts. in books. Home: 1525 Queen Anne's Gate Westlake OH 44145

MERHIGE, ROBERT REYNOLD, JR., U.S. judge; b. N.Y.C., Feb. 5, 1919; s. Robert Reynold and Eleanor (Donovan) M.; LL.B., U. Richmond, 1942, LL.D., 1976; m. Shirley Galleher, Apr. 24, 1957; childrenRobert Reynold III, Mark Reynold. Admitted to Va. bar, 1942; practice in Richmond, 1942-67; judge U.S. Dist. Ct., Richmond, 1967—; guest lectr. trial tactics U. Va. Law Sch.; adj. prof. U. Richmond Law Sch.; appeal agt. Henrico County Draft Bd., 1954-67. Mem. Richmond Citizens Assn.; mem. citizens adv. com. San. Dist. A, Henrico County. Served with USAAF, World War II. Decorated Air medal with 4 clusters; recipient Amara Civic Club award, 1968; spl. award, jud. council Nat. Bar Assn., 1972; citation City Richmond, 1967; named Citizen of Yr., 3d dist. Omega Psi Phi, 1972, Richmond Urban League, 1977; Disting. Alumni award U. Richmond, 1979. Mem. Am., Va., Richmond (pres. 1963-64) bar assns., Va. State Bar, Va. Trial Lawyers Assn. (chmn. membership com. 1964-65), Va. Trial Lawyers Assn. (distinguished service award 1977), Jud. Conf. U.S., Omicron Delta Kappa. Co-author: Virginia Jury Instructions. Home: 5 Kanawha Rd Richmond VA 23226 Office: Post Office Bldg Richmond VA 23219

MERIAM, JAMES LATHROP, educator; b. Columbia, Mo., Mar. 25, 1917; s. Junius Lathrop and Mary (Bone) M.; B.Engring., Yale, 1939, M.Engring., 1941, Ph.D., 1942; m. Julia Ellen Powers, Dec. 25, 1940; children—Mary Ellen (Mrs. George W. Seitz), Melissa Lee (Mrs. James E. Bullard). Asst. instrn. Yale, 1940-42; with Pratt and Whitney Aircraft Co., summer 1940, Gen. Electric Co., summer 1942; mem. faculty U. Calif. at Berkeley, 1942-63, prof. engring. mechanics, 1954-63, chmn. div. mechanics and design, 1959-61, chmn. faculty Coll. Engring., 1961-62, prof. engring. mech., Duke, 1963-72, dir. research and devel., dean Sch. Engring., 1963- 69; prof. mech. engring. Calif. Poly State U., San Luis Obispo, 1972—; cons. in field, 1946—. Served as lt. (j.g.) USCGR, 1944-45. Registered mech. engr., Calif.; registered profl. engr., N.C. Recipient award advancement basic and applied sci. Yale Engring. Assn., 1952; Outstanding Faculty award Tau Beta Pi, 1963. Fellow ASME; mem. Am. Soc. Engring. Edn. (chmn. grad. studies div. 1959-60, mem. council 1960-63, chmn. mechanics div. 1974-75, Outstanding Service award Southeastern sect. 1975, Disting. Educator award 1978), Engrs. Council for Profl. Devel. (1966-69), Sigma Xi, Tau Beta Pi, Pi Tau Sigma. Author: Mechanics, Part I, Statics, 2d edit., 1959; Mechanics, Part II, Dynamics, 2d edit., 1959; Dynamics, 1966, 2d edit., 1971; Statics, 1966, 2d edit., 1971; Statics SI-Version, Dynamics SI-Version, 1975; Mechanics, Vol. 1, Vol. 2, 1978. also numerous papers. Home: 4312 Marina Dr Santa Barbara CA 93110

MERIGAN, THOMAS CHARLES, JR., physician, med. researcher, adminstr.; b. San Francisco, Jan. 18, 1934; s. Thomas C. and Helen M. (Greeley) M.; B.A., U. Calif., Berkeley, 1955; M.D., U. Calif., San Francisco, 1958; m. Joan Mary Freeborn, Oct. 3, 1959; 1 son, Thomas Charles. Intern in medicine 2d and 4th Harvard med. services Boston City Hosp., 1958-59, asst. resident medicine, 1959-60; clin. asso. Nat. Heart Inst., NIH, Bethesda, Md., 1960-62, asso. Lab. Molecular Biology, Nat. Inst. Arthritis and Metabolic Diseases, NIH, 1962-63; practice medicine specializing in internal medicine and infectious diseases, Stanford, Calif., 1963—; asst. prof. medicine Stanford U. Sch. Medicine, 1963-67, asso. prof. medicine, 1967-72, head div. infectious diseases, 1966—, prof. medicine, 1972—, dir. diagnostic microbiology lab. Univ. Hosp., 1966-72, dir. Diagnostic Virology Lab., 1969—, hosp. epidemiologist; mem. microbiology research tng. grants com. NIH, 1969-73, cons. antiviral substances program Nat. Inst. Allergy and Infectious Diseases, 1970—, mem. Virology Task Force, 1976-78, bd. sci. counselors, 1974-78; mem. U.S. Hepatitis panel U.S. and Japan Cooperative Med. Sci. Program, 1979—. Recipient Borden award for Outstanding Research, Am. Assn. Med. Colls., 1973; Guggenheim Meml. fellow, 1972. Diplomate Am. Bd. Internal Medicine. Mem. Am. Assn. Physicians, Western Assn. Physicians, Am. Soc. Microbiology, Am. Soc. Clin. Investigation, Am. Assn. Immunologists, Am. Fedn. Clin. Research, Western Soc. Clin. Research, Soc. Exptl. Biology and Medicine, Infectious Diseases Soc. Am., AMA, Calif. Med. Assn., Santa Clara County Med. Soc., Calif. Acad. Medicine, Royal Soc. Medicine, AAAS, Alpha Omega Alpha. Contbr. over 220 articles on infectious diseases, virology and immunology to sci. jours.; editor: Antivirals with Clinical Potential, 1976, Antivirals and Virus Diseases of Man, 1979; Regulatory Functions of Interferon, 1980; asso. editor Virology, 1975-78; co-editor: monograph series-Current Topics in Infectious Diseases, 1975—; editorial bd. Archives Internal Medicine, 1971, Jour. Gen. Virology, 1972-77, Infection and Immunity, 1973—, Intervirology, 1973—, Virology, 1975-78, Proc. Soc. Expt. Biology and Medicine, 1978—, Reviews of Infectious Diseases, 1979—. Home: 148 Goya Rd Portola Valley CA 94025 Office: Div Infectious Diseases Stanford Univ Sch Medicine Stanford CA 94305

MERILAN, CHARLES PRESTON, dairy husbandry scientist; b. Lesterville, Mo., Jan. 14, 1926; s. Peter Samuel and Cleo Sarah (Harper) M.; B.S. in Agr., U. Mo., 1948, A.M., 1949, Ph.D., 1952; m. Phyllis Pauline Laughlin, June 12, 1949; children—Michael Preston, Jean Elizabeth. Mem. faculty U. Mo., Columbia, 1950—, prof. dairy husbandry, 1959—, chmn. dept., 1961-62, asso. dir. Mo. Agrl. Expt. Sta., 1962-63, asso. investigator space sci. research center, 1964-74, exec. sec., dir. grad. studies physiology area, 1969-72, chmn. univ. patent and copyright com., 1963—. Served with USMC, 1944-45. Decorated Purple Heart. Mem. AAAS, Am. Chem. Soc., Am. Dairy Sci. Assn., Am. Soc. Animal Sci, IEEE (profl. group biomed. electronics), Soc. Cryobiology, Sigma Xi, Alpha Zeta, Gamma Sigma Delta, Phi Beta Pi. Researcher on biol. material preservation. Home: 1509 Bouchelle Ave Columbia MO 65201 Office: Univ Missouri Columbia MO 65211

MERIVALE, PATRICIA, educator; b. Derby, Eng., July 19, 1934; d. Alexander and Elizabeth (Bier) Merivale; A.B., U. Calif. at Berkeley, 1955; B.A., Oxford (Eng.) U., 1958, M.A., 1962; Ph.D., Harvard, 1963. Mem. faculty U. B.C., Vancouver, Can., 1962—, prof. English, 1970—. Mem. Modern Lang. Assn., Am., Canadian comparative lit. assns. Author: Pan the Goat-God: His Myth in

Modern Times, 1969; also articles, revs. Office: English Dept U BC Vancouver BC V6T 1W5 Canada

MERIWETHER, CHARLES MINOR, retail and wholesale drug co. exec.; b. Memphis, Feb. 15, 1911; s. Charles Minor and Leslie Allen (Stevens) M.; student U. Tenn., 1932; LL.B., Cumberland U., 1933; J.D., Sanford U., 1969; m. Beverly Alston, June 7, 1939; children—Leslie Ann (Mrs. A.M. Shuler Jr.), Beverly (Mrs. Frank Lockridge, Jr.), Charles Minor. Engaged in ins. law and ins. mgmt., Memphis, 1933-42, in retail and wholesale drug bus., Birmingham, Ala., 1944-58; dir. finance, Ala., 1958-61; bd. dirs. Export-Import Bank Washington, 1961-66; pres. Dewberry Drug Co., Inc., Birmingham, 1966—; cons. Dewberry Drug Co., 1977—. Pres. Ala. Ednl. Authority, 1958-61, Ala. Hwy. Authority, 1958-61; chmn. investment com. Tchr. Retirement Fund and Employees Retirement Fund, Ala., 1958-61; dir. Ala. Adjustment Bd., 1958-61. Chmn. dirs. Ala. chpt. Nat. Multiple Sclerosis Soc., 1958-59. Served with U.S. Mcht. Marine, 1942-43. Mem. Phi Gamma Delta, Birmingham City Salesmen's Club. Methodist. Odd Fellow. Clubs: Nat. Press (Washington); Downtown, Relay House (Birmingham). Home: 4421 Corinth Dr Birmingham AL 35213 Office: City Fed Bldg Birmingham AL 35203

MERIWETHER, JAMES BABCOCK, educator; b. Columbia, S.C., May 8, 1928; s. Robert Lee and Margaret (Babcock) M.; B.A., U. S.C., 1949; M.A., Princeton, 1952, Ph.D., 1958; m. Nancy Anderson Callcott, July 29, 1955; children—Rebecca, Robert, George, Nicholas, Margaret. Asst. prof. English, U. Tex., Austin, 1958-59; asst. prof. U. N.C., Chapel Hill, 1959-62, asso. prof., 1962-64; prof. U. S.C., Columbia, 1964-70, McClintock prof. So. letters, 1970—, dir. So. studies program, 1974—; Fulbright prof. U. Paris (France), 1970-71. Served with U.S. Army, 1953-56. Am. Council Learned Socs. fellow, 1960-61, Guggenheim fellow, 1963-64. Mem. Modern Lang. Assn. Am., Bibliographical Soc. Am., Am. Studies Assn., French, Brit. assns. Am. studies, South Atlantic Modern Lang. Assn., Phi Beta Kappa. Club: N.Y. Athletic (N.Y.C.). Author: The Literary Career of William Faulkner, 1961. Editor: Essays, Speeches and Public Letters of William Faulkner, 1966; others. Contbr. articles to profl. jours. Home: 1400 Devonshire Dr Columbia SC 29204

MERIWETHER, LEE, actress; b. Los Angeles, May 27, 1935; student City Coll. San Francisco; studied drama with Lee Strasberg, Curt Conway; m. Frank Aletter (div.); children—Kyle, Lesley. Actress in stage plays A Hatful of Rain, Dial M for Murder; TV debut on Philco Playhouse, 1955; other TV appearances include Today Show, The FBI, Twelve O'Clock High, Perry Mason, The Man from U.N.C.L.E., Mission Impossible, Dragnet, The New Andy Griffith Show; regular on TV series Clear Horizon, 1960-62, The Young Marrieds, 1964-65, Time Tunnel, 1966-67, Barnaby Jones, 1973—; motion pictures include: The 4-D Man, 1959, The Courtship of Eddie's Father, 1963, Batman, 1966, Namu, the Killer Whale, 1966, The Legend of Lylah Clare, 1968, Angel in My Pocket, 1969, The Undefeated, 1969; TV movies Cruise into Terror, 1978, True Grit, 1978, Mirror, Mirror, 1979. Named Miss America, 1955.*

MERIWETHER, W. DELANO, physician, govt. ofcl., educator; b. Nashville, Apr. 23, 1943; s. Wilhelm Roscoe and Martha (Holland) M.; grad. Mich. State U., 1963; M.D., Duke U., 1967. Intern, U. Pa. Hosps., 1967-68; resident in medicine Ohio State U. Hosps., 1968-69; clin. researcher Nat. Cancer Inst., NIH, Balt., 1969-71; research and clin. fellow Thorndike Labs., Boston City Hosp., Harvard U. Med. Sch., 1971-73, instr. medicine, 1973, dir. Harvard Health Career Summer Program, 1972-73; spl. asst. to sec. HEW, Washington, 1973, spl. asst. to asst. sec. for health, 1974-79, dir. nat. influenza immunization program, 1976; asst. prof. Johns Hopkins Sch. Public Health, 1979—; mem. Greater Boston Sickle Cell Center, 1973. Sloan fellow, 1963-67; White House fellow, 1973-74; recipient J.D. Lane award research USPHS, 1971; Distinguished Med. Alumnus award Duke U., 1974; award excellence research Columbus (Ohio) Soc. Internal Medicine, 1969; Achievement award Black Grad. Caucus, Ohio State U. Grad. Sch. Edn., 1971. Fellow A.C.P.; mem. Phi Kappa Phi. Mem. Ch. of Brethren. U.S. nat. outdoor sprint track and field champion, 1971, nat. indoor champion, 1972. Home: 1301 Delaware Ave SW Washington DC 20024 Office: Room 729-H HEW Bldg South Portal Washington DC 20201

MERKEL, JOHN CONDON, lawyer; b. Seattle, Jan. 15, 1941; s. John C. and Marjorie (Cartwright) M.; B.A., George Washington U., 1965, J.D., 1968; m. Betty Joyce Adams, June 5, 1971; 1 dau., Carrie Jane. Admitted to Wash. bar, 1968; staff mem. Sen. Henry M. Jackson, 1960-68; dep. prosecutor, Kitsap County, Wash., 1968-69, pros. atty., 1971-77; asso. firm Arthur & Hanley, Bremerton, Wash., 1969-71; U.S. atty., Western Dist. Wash., Seattle, 1977—. Democratic precinct committeeman, 1968-77. Mem. Wash. Bar Assn. Democrat. Club: Kiwanis. Home: Seabeck WA 98310 Office: 1012 US Courthouse Seattle WA 98104

MERKER, FRANK FERDINAND, hosp. adminstr.; b. Bklyn., July 2, 1909; s. August and Mathilda (Schmidt) M.; student Balt. Poly. Inst., 1924-27; B.Engring., Johns Hopkins, 1931; M.D., Med. Coll. Va., 1943; postgrad. Menninger Sch. Psychiatry, 1946-49; m. Edith Marjorie Greer, Feb. 6, 1937; 1 dau., Mathilda Sue. With Balt. Gas & Electric Co., 1931; with Glenn L. Martin Aircraft Co., 1933-35; with Civilian Conservation Corps, 1935-40; intern U.S. Marine Hosp., Balt., 1944; resident psychiatry VA Hosp., Topeka, 1946-49, asst. sect. chief, 1949-51, sect. chief, 1952-54, asst. dir. profl. services, 1954-55, dir. profl. services, 1954-58; practice medicine specializing in psychiatry, Topeka, 1946-58, Salem, Va., 1958-60, Roseburg, Ore., 1960-66; dir. profl. services VA Hosp., Salem, 1958-60; dir. VA Hosp., Roseburg, Ore., 1960-66, VA Hosp., Coatesville, Pa., 1966-69, VA Hosp., Richmond, Va., 1969-72, Southwestern State Hosp., Marion, Va., 1972-78, med. dir. forensic unit, 1978—; asso. clin. prof. psychiatry Med. Coll. Va., 1969—. Served to capt. M.C., USAAF, 1944-46. Fellow AAAS, Am. Psychiat. Assn.; mem. AMA. Home: PO Box 52 Troutdale VA 24378 Office: Southwestern State Hosp Marion VA 24354

MERKES, EDWARD PETER, educator; b. Chgo., Apr. 14, 1929; s. Henry Peter and Catherine (Klemmer) M.; B.S., DePaul U., 1950, M.S., 1950; Ph.D., Northwestern U., 1958; m. Geraldine Carter, Sept. 1, 1956; 1 son, Fritz. Instr. DePaul U., Chgo., 1950-54, 56-58, Marquette U., Milw., 1959-62; asso. prof. math. U. Wis.-Madison, 1962-63; asso. prof. Cin. U., 1963-69, prof., 1969—. Served with AUS, 1954-56. Mem. Math. Assn. Am., Am. Math. Soc., Soc. Indsl. and Applied Math., Sigma Xi. Contbr. articles to profl. jours. Home: 3108 Hanna St Cincinnati OH 45211

MERKL, NEIL MATTHEW, lawyer, ins. co. exec.; b. N.Y.C., Apr. 18, 1931; s. Pierre Paul and Florence Cornelia (Callahan) M.; B.S., Georgetown U., 1952; LL.B., Fordham U., 1955; m. Jessica Marie Quirk, June 30, 1956; children—Neil, Thomas, Stephen, Daniel, Andrew, Eve, Nan. With Liberty Mut. Ins. Co., N.Y.C., 1959-60; admitted to N.Y. State bar, 1955; asso. firm Wood Werner France & Tully, 1960-62; atty. Manhattan Life Ins. Co., N.Y.C., 1962—, counsel, 1966-69, v.p., gen. counsel, 1972-74, sr. v.p., 1974—; v.p. Manhattan Life Corp., N.Y.C., 1974—. Served to lt. USCG, 1956-59. Mem. Am., N.Y. State bar assns., Assn. Bar City N.Y., Assn. Life Ins. Counsel. Roman Catholic. Home: 35-35 161st St Flushing NY 11358 Office: 111 W 57th St New York City NY 10019

MERKLIN, KENNETH EDWIN, mining and shipping co. exec.; b. Index, Wash., Jan. 6, 1920; s. Orlin R. and Roma E. (Carncross) M.; B.S. in Metall. Engring., U. Wash., 1944; m. Barbara Esther Daum, May 6, 1942; children—Roma, Rita. Engr., Boeing Aircraft Co., 1946-47; sales mgr. Western Machinery Co., 1947-56; chief metallurgist Pickands Mather & Co., Hibbing, Minn., 1956-63; successively v.p., sr. v.p., exec. v.p., pres. Marcona Corp., San Francisco, 1963-78, also dir.; pres. Merit Systems Inc., Sausalito, Calif., 1978—; dir. Marcona Ocean Industries, Wiapipi Iron Sands of N.Z. Served to lt. C.E., USNR, 1944-46. Mem. Am. Inst. Mining and Metall. Engrs., World Affairs Council, Pan Am. Soc., Japan-Calif. Soc., Pacific Basic Econ. Council, Conf. Bd. Home: 1805 Lagoon View Dr Tiburon CA 94920 Office: 3030 Bridgeway Sausalito CA 94965

MERKLING, FRANK, editor; b. Washington, Jan. 20, 1924; s. Frank and Marie (Judd) M.; B.A. cum laude, Harvard U., 1949; m. Erica Perl, Nov. 8, 1952; children—Melissa, Maria, Christian. Free-lance writer, 1949-54; asso. editor Opera News, 1954-57, editor, 1957-74; music and arts critic Danbury (Conn.) News-Times, 1978—. Chmn. New Milford (Conn.) Commn. Arts, 1977—. Served with USAAF, 1943-46. Author: English libretto of Carmen for Met. Opera Co., 1951; co-author: The Golden Horseshoe, 1965. Contbr. articles to profl. jours. Home: Route 3 116 Buckingham Rd New Milford CT 06776

MERLIN, JAN, writer, actor; b. N.Y.C., Apr. 3, 1925; m. Patricia Anne Datz, Aug. 17, 1951; 1 son, Peter. Broadway debut Mister Roberts, 1949; numerous TV appearances; appeared in feature films; lead role Rough Riders series, Tom Corbett, Space Cadet series; free-lance writer, novelist. Served with USN, 1942-46. Recipient Emmy award, 1975. Mem. Writers Guild Am. West, Screen Actors Guild, Actors Equity, AFTRA, AGVA. Office: care Damio Group Inc 225 E 47th St New York NY 10017*

MERLINO, MAXINE OLLIE SEELBINDER, artist; b. Portland, Oreg., July, 1912; d. Ernest August and Ollie (Shuey) Seelbinder; scholar Mus. Art Sch., Portland, 1933-36, Art Students League, N.Y.C., 1936-39; B.A., Long Beach (Calif.) State Coll., 1952, M.A., 1952; Ed.D., U. So. Calif., 1961; m. Dante R. Merlino, Nov. 23, 1936; 1 son, Dante R. Freelance artist, murals and illustrations, N.Y.C. and Washington, 1939-43, Long Beach, 1945-46; sci. illustrator USAAF, 1944-45; set designer and interior murals Preston Sturges, Hollywood producer and dir., 1946-52; prof. art, dean Sch. Fine Arts, Calif. State U., Long Beach, 1952-75, emeritus, 1975—; exhibited in group shows Eastern U.S., 1937-43, Western U.S., 1952—; illustrator, art cons. Teaching Tools (periodical), 1954-59. Active YWCA, Children's Theater. Mem. Art Students League N.Y.C. (life), AAUP. Contbr. illustrations to popular mags. Home: 359 Panama Ave Long Beach CA 90814

MERLO, HARRY ANGELO, forest products co. exec.; b. Stirling City, Calif., Mar. 5, 1925; s. Joseph Angelo and Clotilde (Camussa) M.; B.S., U. Calif. at Berkeley, 1949, postgrad., 1949; 1 son, Harry A. Vice pres. Rockport Redwood Co., Cloverdale, Calif., 1967; v.p. No. div. Ga.-Pacific Corp., Samoa, Calif., 1967-69, v.p. Western lumber div., Portland, Oreg., 1969-71, exec. v.p. Western timber, plywood and lumber operations, 1971-73; pres., chmn. bd. La.-Pacific Corp., Portland, 1973—. Formerly pres., dir. Redwood Inspection Service, formerly mem. exec. bd. Redwood Area council Boy Scouts Am.; trustee Oreg. Mus. Sci. and Industry, Jr. Achievement Council; bd. dirs. Western Forestry Center, Goodwill Industries; chmn. bd. Am. Acad. Achievement; mem. lay adv. bd. St. Joseph Hosp., Eureka, Calif.; mem. adv. bd. Forest Products Lab., U. Calif. Served to lt. USMCR. Named Man of Year, Ga.-Pacific Corp., 1969; recipient Golden Plate award Am. Acad. Achievement, 1974. Mem. Calif. Redwood Assn. (past pres., dir.), Nat. Forest Products Assn. (com. on internat. trade, bd. dirs., mem. exec. com.), Knights of the Vine. Clubs: Waverly Country, Arlington, Multnomah Athletic, Ingomar, West Hills Racquet. Home: 2141 SW Scholls Ferry Rd Portland OR 97221 Office: 1300 SW 5th Ave Portland OR 97201

MERMAN, ETHEL, singer, actress; b. Astoria, N.Y., Jan. 16, 1909; d. Edward and Agnes Zimmerman; student pub. schs. Long Island City, N.Y.; m. William B. Smith, Nov. 16, 1940 (div. Oct. 1941); m. 2d, Robert D. Levitt (div.); m. 3d, Robert F. Six (div. 1961); m. 4th, Ernest Borgnine, July 1964 (div.). Sec. to pres. B.K. Vacuum Booster-Brake Co.; night club singer, also singing with Jimmy Durante, Clayton and Jackson; made Broadway debut in Girl Crazy, 1930; other theatre appearances include: George White's Scandals, 1931-32; Take a Chance, 1932; Anything Goes, 1934; Red, Hot and Blue, 1936; Stars in Your Eyes, 1939; Dubarry Was a Lady, 1939; Panama Hattie, 1940; Something for the Boys, 1943; Annie Get Your Gun, 1946; Call Me Madam, 1950; Happy Hunting, 1956; Gypsy, 1959; Hello, Dolly!, 1970; radio program Rhythm at Eight, 1935; appearances in motion pictures include: We're Not Dressing, Kid Millions, 1934; The Big Broadcast, 1935; Strike Me Pink, 1936; Anything Goes, 1936; Happy Landing, 1938; Alexander's Ragtime Band, Straight, Place and Show, Stage Door Canteen, 1943; Call Me Madam, 1953; No Business Like Show Business, 1954; Gypsy, It's a Mad, Mad, Mad, Mad World, 1963; Won Ton Ton, 1976; numerous TV appearances, including Merv Griffin's Salute to Irving Berlin, 1976. Winner N.Y. Drama Critics award, 1943, 46, 59; Donaldson award, 1947; Tony award, 1951, 72; Barter Theatre of Va. award, 1957; Drama Desk award, 1969-70. Author: Merman, An Autobiography, 1978. Address: care Gus Schirmer 1403 N Orange Grove Ave Los Angeles CA 90046*

MERMEL, THADDEUS WALTER, engring. cons.; b. Chgo., Sept. 12, 1907; s. Stanley and Caroline (Stach) M.; B.S., U. Ill., 1930; student George Washington U., 1930-32, U. Colo., 1934-36; m. Lillian Loretta Sommers, Sept. 10, 1930; children—John Frederick, Marilyn Ann, Yvonne T. Engring. aide ICC, 1930-33; with Bur. Reclamation, 1933-73, beginning as engring. draftsman, Denver, successively jr. engr., asst. engr., asso. engr., engr., sr. engr., Washington, liaison rep., asso. engring. asst., asst. to commr. engring., 1933-54, engring. div. chief, 1954-64, asst. to commr. for research, 1964-71, asst. to commr. for sci. affairs, 1971-73; cons. to power ministry Govt. Iran, 1973; cons. to World Bank, 1973-79; mem. World Bank Mission to Pakistan, 1978, Indonesia, 1979; pvt. cons. engring. practice, 1976—; cons. govt. power procurement Saudi Arabia, 1976-77; Mem. U.S. com. Internat. Irrigation and Drainage Commn.; chmn. com. on world register of dams Internat. Commn. on Large Dams; mem. U.S. nat. com. tunneling tech. Nat. Acad. Scis. Nat. Acad. Engring.; mem. exec com., chmn. com. rev. and inspection dams U.S. Com. on Large Dams, 1964; mem. USCOLD Com. Model Legislation Dam Safety, Interagy. Com. Excavation Tech., 1972—; del. White House Conf. Natural Beauty, 1965. Recipient Distinguished Service award Dept. Interior. Fellow Am. Soc. C.E., Engring. Found. (mem. bd., mem. research com. 1966-78, confs. com., mem. constrn. research council; chmn. research conf. on common rights of way 1969, co-chmn. research conf. underground transmission 1971, chmn. conf. com. 1972—, co-chmn. conf. on converting existing dams to pump-storage); mem. C.I.G.R.E. (internat. conf. on large high tension electric systems), Nat. Acad. Scis., Fed. Constrn. Council, U.S. Nat. Com. on Tunnelling Tech., AAAS, IEEE, ASCE (life), Washington Soc. Engrs., D.C. Profl. Engrs., Internat. Com. World Register of Dams. Author: Register of Dams in U.S., 1958, 63, 66, 69, 72; also articles in periodicals; editorial cons. Water Power and Dam Constrn. mag., London, 1977—. Address: 4540 43d St NW Washington DC 20016

MERRELL, BROWNELL, JR., lawyer; b. Pasadena, Oct. 12, 1939; s. Brownell and Elizabeth Leigh (Wright) M.; student Stanford, 1957-59; B.A. with honors, Northwestern U., 1961, LL.B., 1964; m. Marian Ann Edmondson, July 2, 1960; children—Sharon Leigh, Victoria Ann, Rebecca Seymour. Admitted to Calif. bar, 1965, since practiced in Los Angeles and Long Beach; asso. firm Walker, Wright, Tyler & Ward, Los Angeles 1964-66; mem. firm Dietsch, Gates, Morris & Merrell, Los Angeles, 1966-78; individual practice law, Long Beach, 1978—; mem. hearing subcom. Calif. Commn. Bar Examiners; mem. Calif. Assn. Pub. Utility Counsel. Lockheed scholar, 1958. Mem. Am. Bar Assn., State Bar Calif., Long Beach Bar Assn., Phi Beta Kappa. Home: 2417 Via Sonoma Palos Verdes Estates CA 90274 Office: 400 Oceangate Long Beach CA 90808

MERRELL, DAVID JOHN, educator, geneticist; b. Bound Brook, N.J., Aug. 20, 1919; s. Edward Peterson and Elizabeth (Herder) M.; B.S., Rutgers U., 1941; M.A., Harvard, 1947, Ph.D., 1948; m. Jessie Clark, Mar. 19, 1945; children—Edward Clark, David Wilson, James Hart, Ann Elizabeth. Chemist, Am. Cyanamid Co., Bound Brook, 1941-42; teaching fellow Harvard, 1946-48; mem. faculty U. Minn., Mpls., 1948—, prof. genetics and ecology 1964—. Served with AUS, 1942-46. Mem. Genetics Soc. Am., Am. Genetics Assn., Soc. for Study Evolution, Am. Soc. Naturalists, AAAS, Behavior Genetics Assn., Phi Beta Kappa, Sigma Xi. Author: Evolution and Genetics, 1962; An Introduction to Genetics, 1975; also articles. Research in genetics of populations, ecol. genetics, behavior genetics. Home: 1511 Chelmsford St St Paul MN 55108 Office: U Minn Dept Ecology and Behavioral Biology Minneapolis MN 55455

MERRELL, JAMES LEE, editor, clergyman; b. Indpls., Oct. 24, 1930; s. Mark W. and Pauline F. (Tucker) M.; A.B., Ind. U., 1952; M.Div., Christian Theol. Sem., 1956; Litt.D., Culver-Stockton Coll., 1972; m. Barbara Jeanne Burch, Dec. 23, 1951; children—Deborah Lea Merrell Griffin, Cynthia Lynn Merrell Schrader, Stuart Allen. Ordained to ministry Christian Ch., 1956; asso. editor World Call, Indpls., 1956-66, editor, 1971-73; pastor Crestview Christian Ch., Indpls., 1966-71; editor The Disciple, St. Louis, 1974—; v.p. Christian Bd. Publ., 1976—. Chmn. bd. Kennedy Meml. Christian Home, Martinsville, Ind., 1971-73; trustee Christian Theol. Sem., 1978—. Mem. Asso. Ch. Press (award 1973, dir. 1974-75, 78—), Christian Theol. Sem. Alumni Assn. (pres. 1966-68), Religious Public Relations Council (award 1979), Sigma Delta Chi (award 1952), Theta Phi. Author: They Live Their Faith, 1965; The Power of One, 1976; Discover the Word in Print, 1979. Home: 5347 Warmwinds Ct Saint Louis MO 63129 Office: PO Box 179 Saint Louis MO 63166

MERRIAM, ALAN (PARKHURST), educator; b. Missoula, Mont., Nov. 1, 1923; s. Harold Guy and Doris (Foote) M.; B.A., Mont. State U., 1947; M. Music, Northwestern U., 1948, Ph.D. in Anthropology, 1951; m. Barbara Anne Williams, Aug. 29, 1947 (div. Sept. 1974); children—Virginia Claire, Paige Alison, Cynthia Williams; m. 2d, Valerie Ann Christian, May 6, 1977. Instr. anthropology Northwestern U., 1953-54, asst. prof., 1956-58, asso. prof., 1958-62; asst. prof. sociology and anthropology U. Wis.-Milw., 1954-56; asst. prof. anthropology and Am. studies U. Minn., summer 1957; prof. anthropology Ind. U., 1962—, chmn. dept., 1966-69, asso. chmn., 1978—; disting. vis. prof. U. Mont., summer 1965; vis. scholar UCLA, 1978; field research in Western Mont., Belgian Congo, Ruanda Urundi, Republic of Zaire. Mem. com. human resources in Central Africa, NRC, 1958; mem. President's Task Force for Africa, 1960; mem. joint com. African studies Social Sci. Research Council-Am. Council Learned Socs., 1960-66, chmn., 1962-65; adv. bd. Inter-Am. Inst. Musical Research, Tulane U., 1961-70; U.S. del. 1st Internat. Congress Africanists, Accra, Ghana, 1962, 2d Internat. Congress Africanists, Dakar, Senegal, 1967; bd. dirs. Com. on Research in Dance, 1975-76; U.S. del. Baghdad Internat. Conf. on Arabic Music, 1975. Served with USAAF, 1942-45. Grantee Mont. State U. Music Found., 1950, Grad. Sch. Northwestern U., 1958, Belgian Am. Ednl. Found. and Wenner Gren Found. Anthrop. Research, 1951-52, NSF-Belgian Am. Ednl. Found., 1959-60, African Studies Program, Ind. U. and joint African studies com. Social Sci. Research Council-Am. Council Learned Socs., 1973; Guggenheim fellow, 1969-70; Australian-Am. Ednl. Found. sr. scholar in anthropology U. Sydney (Australia), 1976. Fellow Am. Anthrop. Assn., AAAS; founding fellow African Studies Assn. (chmn. com. fine arts and humanities 1960-62, 65-66, dir. 1962-65); mem. Am. Folklore Soc. (councilor 1956-58, rev. editor jour. 1957-58), Internat. Folk Music Council (corr. 1956-60), Soc. Ethnomusicology (co-founder 1952; editor ofcl. publ. 1953-58, mem.-at-large exec. bd. 1956-65, 70-72, mem. council 1958-70, 71-74, 75-78, pres. 1962-64, editor spl. series 1972-77, 1st v.p. 1977-79), Central States Anthrop. Soc. (pres. 1960-61, exec. com. 1961-63, 78-80), Sigma Xi. Author: (with R.J. Benford) A Bibliography of Jazz, 1954; Congo: Background of Conflict, 1961; The Anthropology of Music, 1964; (with Frank Gillis) Ethnomusicology and Folk Music, 1966; Ethnomusicology of the Flathead Indians, 1967; African Music on LP: An Annotated Discography, 1970; An African World: The Basongye Village of Lupupa Nyge, 1974; Culture History of the Basongye, 1975. also monographs. Home: 511 Pleasant Ridge Rd Bloomington IN 47401

MERRIAM, CHARLES J., lawyer; b. Chgo., Feb. 4, 1903; s. Charles E. and Elizabeth (Doyle) M.; B.S., U. Chgo., 1922, J.D. cum laude, 1925; m. Kathryn Cheney, May 15, 1926; m. 2d, Ethelmae Sturgeon, Mar. 14, 1946; children—Dorothy (Mrs. Kenneth Venolia), Carol (Mrs. Theodore Bockman), Elizabeth (Mrs. Mason Thomas), Charles E., Robert C. Admitted to Ill. bar, 1925, since practiced in Chgo.; sr. partner firm Merriam, Marshall, & Bicknell, 1965-76, of counsel, 1976—; reporter Chgo. Daily News, 1978; dir., v.p. Pine Trees Inc., 1968—; dir. Continental Gas Transmission Co., Inc., Chemithon Corp. Mem. panel on patents, trademarks and copyrights Bur. Nat. Affairs, 1972—. Mem. Winnetka Sch. Bd., 1945-48, U. Ill. Citizens Com., 1965—. Dir., v.p. U. Ill. Found., pres., 1976-78. Mem. Am. Bar Assn., Chgo. Bar Assn., Order of Coif, Phi Beta Kappa, Sigma Xi. Republican. Clubs: Law, Chicago (Chgo.); Moon Valley (Phoenix); Desert Forest (Carefree, Ariz.). Home: 320 Baltusrol Circle W Phoenix AZ 85023 Office: 2 1st Nat Plaza Chicago IL 60603

MERRIAM, DANIEL F(RANCIS), geologist; b. Omaha, Feb. 9, 1927; s. Faye Mills and Amanda Frances (Wood) M.; B.S., U. Kans., 1949, M.S., 1953, Ph.D., 1961; M.Sc., Leicester U., 1969, D.Sc., 1975; m. Annie Laura Young, Feb. 12, 1946; children—Beth Ann Merriam Wissman, John Francis, Anita Pauline, James Daniel, Judith Diane. Geologist, Union Oil Co. of Calif., Rocky Mountains and W. Tex., 1949-51, summer 1952; asst. instr. U. Kans., 1951-53, instr., 1954, research asso., 1963-71; geologist Kans. Geol. Survey, 1953-58, div. head basic geology, 1958-63, chief geologic research, 1963-71; Jessie Page Heroy prof. geology, chmn. dept. Syracuse U., 1971—; vis. research scientist Stanford U., 1963; Fulbright-Hays sr. research fellow, U.K., 1964-65; chmn. supply-tech. adv. com. FPC, 1975-77; dir. Am. Geol. Inst.'s Internat. Field Inst. to Japan, 1967; vis. prof.

geology Wichita State U., 1968-70; Am. Geol. Inst. vis. geol. scientist, 1969; U.S. del. UNESCO-IUGS Internat. Geol. Correlations Program, Budapest, 1969; chmn. U.S. Nat. Com. for IGCP., 1976-79, participant project COMPUTE, Dartmouth Coll., 1974; Esso disting. lectr. Earth Scis. Found., U. Sydney (Australia), 1979. Served with USNR, 1945-46. Mem. Am. Assn. Petroleum Geologists bus. com. 1956-57, research com. 1964-67, chmn. field trip research and coordination com. 1964-73, asso. editor 1969-75, Matson award com. 1970, acad. adv. com. 1973-77, ho. of dels. 1974-76, computer applications in geology com. 1971—), Geol. Soc. Am. (gen. chmn. 10th ann. meeting Northeastern sect. 1975, publs. com. 1973-76), Soc. Econ. Paleontologists and Mineralogists (chmn. research group; in computer tech. com. 1970-75, nominating com. 1972-73), Classification Soc. Geology (chmn. membership com. 1968-71, bd. dirs. 1968-71, council 1968-72, sec.-gen. 1972-76, pres. 1976—), N.Y. State Geol. Assn. (exec. sec. 1972-77, pres. 1977-78, bd. dirs. 1978—), Rocky Mountain Assn. Geologists (research com. 1966-69), Kans. Acad. Sci. (program chmn. geology sect. 1959), Geologists Assn. (Eng.) (field trip dir. 1965), AAAS (nominating com. 1977—), Kans. Geol. Soc. (mem. coms., dir. 1964), Leicester Geol. Soc. (hon. life), Nat. Assn. Geology Tchrs., Sigma Xi, Sigma Gamma Epsilon (Alpha chpt. pres. 1952-53). Founder, editor-in-chief: Math. Geology, 1968-76, Computers & Geoscis., 1975—; editorial cons. Geosystems, 1971—; co-editor: Pacific Geology, 1971—; editor: Syracuse U. Geology Contbns., 1973—; editorial rev. bd. Colo. Sch. Mines Quar., 1974—; editorial com. Syracuse U. Press., 1978—; corr. Open Earth, 1978—; contbr. articles to sci. jours. Home: 12 Drumlins Terr Syracuse NY 13224 Office: Dept Geology Syracuse U Syracuse NY 13210

MERRIAM, EVE, writer; b. Phila., July 19, 1916; children—Guy Michel, Dee Michel. Tchr., Coll. City N.Y., N.Y. U., 1966-69; lectr. on sexism in edn., 1974—. Recipient Yale Younger Poets award, 1946; Collier's Star Fiction award, 1949; Obie award, 1977. Mem. Dramatists Guild Council, Am. Soc. Journalists and Authors. Author: Real Book About Franklin D. Roosevelt, 1952; The Voice of Liberty, 1959; Figleaf, 1960; Basics, 1962; After Nora Slammed the Door, 1964; (poems) Family Circle, 1946; Tomorrow Morning, 1951; Montgomery, Alabama, Money, Mississippi and Other Places, 1956; The Double Bed from the Feminine Side, 1958; The Trouble with Love, 1961; A Gaggle of Geese, 1960; Mommies at Work, 1961; There is No Rhyme for Silver, 1962; It Doesn't Always Have to Rhyme, 1964; Catch A Little Rhyme, 1965; Independent Voices, 1968; The Inner City Mother Goose, 1969; The Nixon Poems, 1970; Finding A Poem, 1970; Growing Up Female In America, 1971; Out Loud, 1973; Boys and Girls, Girls and Boys, 1973; A Husband's Notes About Her, 1976; Rainbow Writing, 1976; The Birthday Cow, 1978; Unhurry Harry, 1978; Ab to Zog, 1978; author, lyricist musicals Inner City, 1971, The Club, 1976, At Her Age, 1979. Co-editor: Male and Female Under 18, 1973. Contbr. to numerous mags., anthologies. Address: 101 W 12th St New York NY 10011

MERRIAM, JOHN FRANCIS, utilities exec.; b. Constableville, N.Y., July 1, 1904; s. Charles Edward and Hilda (Doyle) M.; Ph.B., U. Chgo., 1925, LL.B., Chgo. Kent Coll. Law, 1930; m. Lucy Lamon, Aug. 28, 1930; 1 son, James Alexander. With U. Chgo. bus. office, 1925-27, Hathaway & Co., 1927-30; with No. Natural Gas Co., Omaha, 1930-75, dir., 1946—, pres., 1950-60, chmn. bd., 1960-66, chmn. exec. com., 1966-75. Trustee U. Chgo., Com. Econ. Devel., Oakland (Calif.) Mus., 1974—; trustee Aspen (Colo.) Insts. Humanistic Studies, Mus. Soc. San Francisco (dir.). Mem. Beta Theta Pi, Phi Delta Phi. Home: 999 Green St San Francisco CA 94133

MERRIAM, ROBERT EDWARD, business exec.; b. Chgo., Oct. 2, 1918; s. Charles and Elizabeth Hilda (Doyle) M.; M.A., U. Chgo., 1940; m. Marguerite DeTernova, Feb. 4, 1950; children—Aimee M. Buch, Oliver, Monique. Dir. Met. Housing Council, Chgo., 1946-47; alderman City Chgo., chmn. com. on housing and emergency com. on crime, 1947-55; asst. dir. U.S. Bur. Budget, Washington, 1955-58, dep. dir., 1958; dep. asst. to Pres. U.S., 1958-61; pres. Spaceonics, Inc., 1961-64, Univ. Patents, Inc. of Ill., Chgo., 1964-70; exec. v.p. Urban Investment and Devel. Co., Chgo., 1971-76; chmn. bd. MGA Tech., Inc., Chgo., 1971—; partner Alexander Proudfoot, 1977—. Co-chmn. Ill. Commn. Urban Area Govt., 1969-72; chmn. Adv. Commn. Intergovtl. Relations, 1969-78. Republican candidate for mayor Chgo., 1955. Served from pvt. to capt. AUS, 1942-46. Mem. Am. Polit. Sci. Assn., Am. Soc. Pub. Adminstrn., Nat. Acad. Pub. Adminstrn. Clubs: Casino, Tavern (Chgo.). Author: Dark December: The Full Account of the Battle of the Bulge, 1947 (paper edit. titled Battle of the Bulge); (with Charles E. Merriam) The American Government: Democracy in Action, 1954; (with Rachel Goetz) Going Into Politics: A Guide for Citizens, 1957; also numerous mag. articles. Home: 2340 Lincoln Park W Chicago IL 60614

MERRIAM, WILLIAM RUSH, govt. relations cons.; b. Washington, Oct. 4, 1912; s. John H. and Rose (Wallach) M.; A.B., Lehigh U., 1933; m. Maria Teresa Ippoliti, Feb. 16, 1946; children—Rosemary D., Laura Elizabeth. Asst. to drama editor Washington Times, 1934; pub. relations account exec. John Price Jones Corp., N.Y.C., 1935-40, fund raising campaign dir., 1946-47; membership sec. Fedn. for Ry. Progress, Washington, 1948-49, dir. pub. relations, 1950-52, v.p., 1953, v.p., sec., treas., 1954-57; spl. asst. pub. relations Assn. Am. Railroads, Washington, 1957-60; asst. v.p., dir. Washington relations Internat. Tel. & Tel. Corp., 1961-67, v.p., dir. Washington relations, 1967-73, v.p., Rome, Italy, 1973-74, N.Y.C., 1975-76; govt. relations cons., Washington, 1976—. Bd. dirs. Washington Tennis Patrons Found., Internat. Rescue Com. Served to capt. Q.M.C., AUS, 1941-46. Decorated Commendatore della Repubblica d'Italia. Mem. Pub. Relations Soc. Am., Alpha Chi Rho. Episcopalian. Clubs: 1925 F Street, Metropolitan, Chevy Chase (Washington). Home: 1808 45th St NW Washington DC 20007 Office: 905 16th St NW Washington DC 20006

MERRICK, DAVID (DAVID MARGULIES), theatrical producer; b. St. Louis, Nov. 27, 1912; s. Samuel and Celia Margulies; B.A., Washington U., St. Louis; LL.B., St. Louis U.; m. Etan Aronson. Produced plays on Broadway: Fanny, 1954; The Matchmaker, 1955; Look Back in Anger, Romanoff and Juliet, Jamaica, 1957; The Entertainer, The World of Suzie Wong, La Plume de ma Tante, Epitaph for George Dillon, 1958; Destry Rides Again, Gypsy, Take Me Along, 1958; Irma La Douce, A Taste of Honey, Becket (Tony award), Do Re Mi, 1960; Carnival, 1961; Sunday in New York, 1961; Ross, 1961; Subways are for Sleeping, 1961; I Can Get It For You Wholesale, Stop the World—I Want to Get Off, Tchin Tchin, Oliver, 1962; Rehearsal, Luther (Tony award), 110 in the Shade, Arturo Ui, 1963; Hello Dolly (Tony award), Oh, What A Lovely War, 1964; The Roar of the Greasepaint—The Smell of the Crowd, Inadmissible Evidence, Cactus Flower, 1965; The Persecution and Assassination of Jean Paul Marat as Performed by the Inmates of the Asylum of Charenton Under the Direction of the Marquis de Sade (Tony award), 1965; Philadelphia, Here I Come, Don't Drink the Water, I Do I Do, 1966; Rosencrantz and Guildenstern Are Dead (Tony award) 1967; Forty Carats, 1968; Promises, Promises, Play it Again Sam, Private Lives, 1969; Child's Play, 1970; Four in a Garden, 1971; A Midsummer Night's Dream, The Philanthropist, Promises, Promises, 1971; Mack and Mabel, Dreyfus in Rehearsal, 1974; Travesties, Red Devil Battery Sign, Very Good Eddy, 1975; produced film The Great Gatsby, 1974. Office: 246 W 44th St New York NY 10036*

MERRICK, GEORGE BOESCH, aerospace co. exec.; b. Burlington, Iowa, Mar. 9, 1928; s. Dale McKeen and Marjorie May (Boesch) M.; B.S., U. Minn., 1949; m. Eleanor Gamble Moore, Sept. 1, 1951; children—Charles, Ellen, Elizabeth. With N. Am. Aviation, 1949—(name changed to Rockwell Internat.), dir. Apollo Command and Service Module, Space div., 1966-72, v.p., program mgr. Apollo Program, 1972-74, v.p., program mgr. Space Shuttle Orbiter Program, 1974-76, pres. space div. Rockwell Internat., Downey, Calif., 1976-78, pres. Space Systems Group, 1978—. Recipient Public Service award NASA. Fellow Am. Astron. Soc., AIAA. Office: 12214 Lakewood Blvd Downey CA 90241*

MERRICK, ROBERT GRAFF, banker; b. Balt., Nov. 18, 1895; s. Samuel K. and Mary Charlton (Graff) M.; A.B., Johns Hopkins, 1917, Ph.D., 1922; m. Anne McEvoy, Jan. 27, 1923; children—Anne McEvoy (Mrs. Walter D. Pinkard), Robert Graff. Pres. Equitable Trust Co., 1932-63, chmn. bd., 1963-67, chmn. exec. com., 1967-72. Former chmn. Balt. County Revenue Authority. Former pres. Balt. Mus. Art; mem. council Md. Hist. Soc. Trustee Johns Hopkins, Balt. Mus. Art, Peale Mus., Hammond-Harwood House Assn.; treas. Evergreen Found. Served as capt. 10th F.A., World War I. Decorated D.S.C.; Croix de Guerre. Mem. S.A.R., Soc. Cincinnati, Beta Theta Pi. Protestant Episcopalian. Clubs: Gibson Island (Md.) Yacht; Bachelors Cotillon, Maryland, Merchants, Elkridge Fox Hunting (gov.), Johns Hopkins, Center (Balt.). Author: Modern Credit Company, 1922. Sponsor book Md. Hist. Prints 1752-1889. Home: 201 Woodbrook Ln Baltimore MD 21212 Office: Munsey Bldg Baltimore MD 21202

MERRIDEW, REGINALD P., assn. exec.; b. S. Wales, June 28, 1916; s. Percy Charles and Sarah (Lewis) M.; came to U.S., 1921, naturalized, 1927; B.S. in Edn., Bucknell U., 1937; m. Doris Mae Long, July 5, 1938; children—Carole Mae (Mrs. George E. Van Lieu), Pamela Ann (Mrs. Robert F. Baker). Chief announcer radio sta. WKOK, Sunbury, Pa., 1937-42; with radio sta. WGAR, Cleve., 1942-56, dir. operations, 1954-56; mng. dir. radio sta. WJW, Cleve., 1957-59; program dir. radio sta. WJR, Detroit, 1959-65; exec. v.p. Display & Exhibit Co., Detroit, 1965-66; internat. sec. Kiwanis Internat., 1966—; speech instr. Western Res. U., nights 1943-52. Vice pres. trustees Cuyahoga County Library, 1954-55; bd. dirs. Cleve. Ch. Fedn., 1955, Goodwill Industries Chgo., 1967-70; mem. adv. com. Nat. 4-H Council, 1971—; mem. at large nat. council Boy Scouts Am., 1971—; pres. Cleve. Kiwanis Found., 1955-56; v.p. Goodwill Industries Detroit, 1965-66. Kiwanian (pres. Cleve. 1954, Detroit 1965), Mason (32 deg.). Mem. Am. Soc. Assn. Execs., Kappa Sigma. Methodist. Club: Chgo. Press. Home: 2885 Shannon Rd Northbrook IL 60062 Office: 101 E Erie St Chicago IL 60611

MERRIFIELD, DONALD PAUL, univ. pres.; b. Los Angeles, Nov. 14, 1928; s. Arthur S. and Elizabeth (Baker) M.; B.S. in Physics, Calif. Inst. Tech., 1950; M.S., U. Notre Dame, 1951; A.M., Ph.L. in Philosophy, St. Louis U., 1957; Ph.D., Mass. Inst. Tech., 1962; S.T.M., U. Santa Clara (Calif.), 1966; S.T.D. (hon.), U. So. Calif., 1969. Joined Soc. of Jesus, 1951, ordained priest Roman Cath. Ch. 1965; instr. physics Loyola U., Los Angeles, 1961-62; lectr. Engring. Sch., Santa Clara, 1965; cons. theoretical chemistry Jet Propulsion Lab., Calif. Inst. Tech., 1962-69; asst. prof. physics U. San Francisco, 1967-69; pres. Loyola Marymount U., Los Angeles, 1969—. Mem. Assn. Jesuit Colls. and Univs. (trustee), Assn. Ind. Calif. Colls. and Univs., Ind. Colls. So. Calif. (trustee), Sigma Xi. Home: Xavier Hall Loyola Marymount U Los Angeles CA 90045. *In today's world, we all stand in need of that pragmatic hope which allows us to see the possibilities for building a more just society and meeting the challenges before us. Without such hope we are paralyzed before our difficulties. With a less realistic hope, too idealistic, we are continually overwhelmed by failures. But with an openness to possibilities, we can move ahead with determination.*

MERRIFIELD, PHILIP RALPH, educator; b. Abilene, Kans., Apr. 12, 1921; s. Ralph Arthur and Julia (Brann) M.; A.B. in Math., Kenyon Coll., 1946; M.S. in Edn., U. So. Calif., 1953, Ph.D. in Psychology, 1959; m. N. Kathryn Butcher, Feb. 6, 1945; children—Signe Kathryn, Karla Jane. Meteorologist, Weather Service, Commerce Dept., Manila, P.I., 1947-49, Anchorage, 1950-52; mem. staff and faculty U. So. Calif., 1953-64, asst. dir. aptitudes research project, 1957-62, adj. asst. prof., 1962-64; human factors scientist System Devel. Corp., Santa Monica, Calif., 1962-64; asso. prof. edn. Kent (Ohio) State U., 1964-66, prof., 1966-68, dir. bur. ednl. research, 1964-68; prof. N.Y.U., 1968—, chmn. dept. ednl. psychology, 1968-74, head div. behavioral sci., 1970-72, mem. staff TTT project, 1969-73, COPES project, 1969-72, co-dir. model research tng. project, 1973-74, dir. doctoral program in psycho-ednl. research, evaluation and measurement, 1975—. Research dir. Northeastern Ohio Ednl. Research Council, 1966-68; cons. to Title 1, bd. edns., Alliance, O. and N.Y.C., 1966-69, to project pre-sch. aptitudes Merrill-Palmer Inst., Detroit, 1965-67, Ariz. State U., 1968-72, Research for Better Schs., Inc., Phila., 1969-72, Minn. research and evaluation project NSF, U. Minn., 1972—, Community Sexuality Info., Inc., N.Y.C., 1977—, Boys Harbor, N.Y.C., 1977—, Modes of Inquiry in the Arts, ESEA Title IV C, Troy, N.Y. Served with USAAF, 1942-46. Fellow Am. Psychol. Assn., AAAS; mem. Am. Ednl. Research Assn., Nat. Council Measurement in Edn., Psychometric Soc., Soc. Multivariate Exptl. Psychology, Eastern Ednl. Research Assn. (pres. 1979—), Sigma Xi, Psi Chi, Phi Delta Kappa. Contbr. profl. jours. Home: 14 Washington Pl New York City NY 10003

MERRIFIELD, ROBERT BRUCE, educator, biochemist; b. Ft. Worth, July 15, 1921; s. George E. and Lorene (Lucas) M.; B.A., U. Calif. at Los Angeles, 1943, Ph.D., 1949; m. Elizabeth Furlong, June 20, 1949; children—Nancy, James, Betsy, Cathy, Laurie, Sally. Chemist, Park Research Found., 1943-44; research asst. Med. Sch., U. Calif. at Los Angeles, 1948-49; asst. Rockefeller Inst. for Med. Research, 1949-53, asso., 1953-57; asst. prof. Rockefeller U., 1957-58, asso. prof., 1958-66, prof., 1966—. Recipient Lasker award biomed. research 1969, Gairdner award, 1970, Intra-Sci. award, 1970, Nichols medal, 1973. Mem. Am. Chem. Soc. (award creative work synthetic organic chemistry 1972), Nat. Acad. Scis., Am. Soc. Biol. Chemists, Sigma Xi, Phi Lambda Upsilon, Alpha Chi Sigma. Asso. editor Internat. Jour. Peptide and Protein Research. Contbr. aritcles sci. jours. Developed solid phase peptide synthesis; completed (with B. Gutte) 1st total synthesis of an enzyme, 1969. Home: 43 Mezzine Dr Cresskill NJ 07626 Office: Rockefeller U New York City NY 10021

MERRILL, AMBROSE POND, JR., physician, health services cons.; b. Provo, Utah, Dec. 14, 1909; s. Ambrose Pond and Lydia (Stephens) M.; A.B., Stanford, 1932, M.D., 1935; M.H.A. with distinction, Northwestern U., 1948; m. Elizabeth Call, Apr. 7, 1931. Intern, San Francisco County Hosp., 1934-35; surg. house officer Stanford U. Hosps., 1935-36; gen. practice medicine and surgery, 1936-40; surgeon San Francisco Emergency Hosp. Service, Dept. Pub. Health, 1936-38; asst. supt. San Francisco County Hosp., 1938-40; asst. dir. St. Luke's Hosp., Chgo., 1940-42, med. dir., 1942-45; exec. dir. St. Barnabas Hosp., N.Y.C., 1945-67; asst. dir. bur. hosp. certification N.Y. State Dept. Health, 1967-68; pres. A.P. Merrill, M.D. & Assos., Hosp. and Health Services Consultants, Delmar, N.Y., 1968—; asst. clin. prof. phys. medicine and rehab. N.Y. U., 1955-60; lectr. Sch. Hosp. Adminstrn., Columbia, 1946-53, preceptor, 1946-67. Pres., Middle Atlantic Hosp. Assembly, 1958-59, Hosp. Assn. N.Y. State, 1956-57, Greater N.Y. Hosp. Assn., 1953-54; mem. N.Y.C. Mayor's Adv. Com. for the Aged, 1955-60; del. Nat. Health Assembly, 1948, Nat. Conf. on Aging, 1950, Internat. Gerontological Congress, 1951, Nat. Conf. on Care of Long-Term Patient, 1954, White House Conf. on Aging, 1961; chmn. com. on chronic illness Welfare and Health Council of N.Y.C., 1949-55; chmn. med. adv. com. Fedn. of Protestant Welfare Agys., N.Y.C., 1956-59; mem. subcom. on aging and chronic illness Interdepartmental Health Council, N.Y.C., 1957-60. Bd. dirs. Bronx Bd. Trade, 1955-67; bd. mgrs. Bronx YMCA, 1955-67, Bronx div. Protestant Council N.Y.C., 1950-65. Recipient Brotherhood award NCCJ, 1967; Modern Hosp. award and medal, 1945, numerous others. Fellow N.Y. Acad. Medicine, Am. Coll. Hosp. Adminstrs., Am. Coll. Preventive Medicine; mem. N.Y. State, Bronx County med. socs., Am. Hosp. Assn. (life), Am. Pub. Health Assn., AAAS, Am. Geriatric Soc., N.Y. Acad. Scis., Am. Assn. Hosp. Consultants, Internat. Hosp. Fedn., World Med. Assn., AMA. Republican. Mem. Ch. of Jesus Christ of Latter-day Saints (high council N.Y. stake 1961-67, Hudson River stake 1969-72). Club: University (N.Y.C.). Contbr. chpt. to Functional Planning of Gen. Hospitals, 1969, also articles to hosp. and med. jours. Home: 73 Greenock Rd Delmar NY 12054

MERRILL, ARTHUR ALEXANDER, fin. analyst; b. Honolulu, June 17, 1906; s. Arthur Merton and Grace Graydon (Dickey) M.; B.S. in Elec. Engring., U. Calif., 1927; M.B.A., Harvard U., 1929; m. Elsie Louise Breed, Aug. 17, 1929; 1 dau., Anne Louise Merrill Breiling. Mem. engring., statistics, and mgmt. depts. Gen. Electric Co., Schenectady, also N.Y.C., 1927-61; fin. writer and analyst, pres. Merrill Analysis Inc., Chappaqua, N.Y., 1961—. Mem. Market Technicians Assn. (Ann. award 1977), Fin. Analysts Fedn., N.Y. Soc. Security Analysts, Harvard Bus. Sch. Alumni Assn., Mensa, Soc. Preservation and Encouragement Barber Shop Quartet Singing Am., Sigma Xi, Theta Chi, Tau Beta Pi, Eta Kappa Nu. Republican. Congregationalist. Club: Harvard. Author: How Do You Use a Slide Rule, 1961; Behavior of Prices on Wall Street, 1966; Battle of White Plains, 1975; Seasonal Tendencies in Stock Prices, 1975; Filtered Waves, Basic Theory, 1977; Bias in Hourly, Daily and Weekly Wave Patterns, 1979; editor Tech. Trends, 1961—. Home: 25 Commodore Rd Chappaqua NY 10514 Office: Box 228 Chappaqua NY 10514

MERRILL, ARTHUR JESSE, physician; b. Atlanta, Sept. 16, 1908; s. Arthur Jesse and Natalie (Heath) M.; student Ga. Sch. Tech., 1925-27; B.S., Emory U., 1930, M.D., 1933; m. Sarah Elizabeth Harrison, Nov. 25, 1938; children—Arthur J., William Harrison, Tinsley Randolph. Intern, asst. resident pathology and internal medicine Cin. Gen. Hosp., 1933-36; asst. resident internal medicine Vanderbilt U. Hosp., 1936-37; resident medicine Grady Meml. Hosp., 1937-38, dir. renal and electrolyte lab., 1943-55, now vis. physician; pvt. practice medicine, 1938-43, 45—; asst. prof. medicine Emory U. Med. Sch., 1943-49, asso. prof., 1949, now prof. clin. medicine; vis. physician Emory U., Piedmont, Crawford W. Long hosps. Recipient Golden-headed Cane award excellence, 1967, plaque distinguished service, 1973. Fellow A.C.P.; mem. Am. Fedn. Clin. Research (pres. 1942-43), So. Soc. Clin. Research (pres.), Am. Soc. Clin. Investigation, Southeastern Clin. Club (pres.), Am. Clin. and Climatol. Soc. (v.p. 1966-67), Am. (high blood pressure research council, pres. council circulation 1955-56, also dir.), Ga. heart assns., Atlanta Clin. Soc., A.M.A. (council drugs), Med. Assn. Ga., Fulton County Med. Soc., Emory Med. Alumni (pres. 1958-59, Distinguished Service award 1974), Sigma Xi, Alpha Omega Alpha, Sigma Alpha Epsilon. Clubs: Capital City, Piedmont Driving, University Yacht (Atlanta). Asso. editor: Practice of Medicine (by Meakin). Past mem. Editorial bd. Am. Heart Jour., Minerva Nephrologica. Home: 3601 Nancy Creek Rd NW Atlanta GA 30327 Office: 35 Collier Rd NW Atlanta GA 30309

MERRILL, BOB, composer; b. Atlantic City, 1922; ed. Phila. pub. schs. Began career as actor on the stage, protégé of Richard Bennett; stage and screen actor, motion picture dir., writer and TV producer; dialogue dir., dir. Columbia Pictures Corp.; supr. writers NBC Nat. Radio; composer, lyricist Broadway shows New Girl in Town, Carnival, Take Me Along, Funny Girl, Sugar; screenplays include: Mahogany, W.C. Fields and Me; TV spls. include: The Wonderful Christmas of Red Riding Hood, Mister Magoo's Christmas Carol; songs include: If I Knew You Were Comin' I'd've Baked a Cake, Sparrow in the Tree Top, My Truly Truly Fair, Belle, Belle, My Liberty Belle, How Much is That Doggie in the Window?, Pittsburgh, Pennsylvania, Mambo Italiano, Honeycomb, People, Love Makes the World Go Round, Don't Rain on My Parade, Take Me Along, It's Good to be Alive, She Wears Red Feathers. Recipient Anglo-Am. award, 1966, Drama Critics Circle award, others. Address: care ASCAP 1 Lincoln Plaza New York NY 10023

MERRILL, CHARLES MERTON, U.S. judge; b. Honolulu, Dec. 11, 1907; s. Arthur M. and Grace Graydon (Dickey) M.; A.B., U. Calif., 1928; LL.B., Harvard, 1931; m. Mary Luita Sherman, Aug. 28, 1931; children—Julia Booth Stoddard, Charles McKinney. Admitted to Calif. bar, 1931, Nev. bar, 1932; practice in Reno, 1932-50; judge Nev. Supreme Ct., 1951-59, chief justice, 1955-56, 59; judge U.S. Ct. of Appeals, 9th Circuit, San Francisco, 1959—. Gov. State Bar Nev., 1947-50. Mem. Am. Bar Assn., Am. Law Inst. (council 1960—). Home: 2243 North Point St San Francisco CA 94123 Office: US Ct of Appeals San Francisco CA 94101

MERRILL, DINA (MRS. CLIFF ROBERTSON), actress; b. N.Y.C.; d. E.F. Hutton and Marjorie Merriweather Post; ed. Mt. Vernon Sem.; student George Washington U., Am. Acad. Dramatic Arts, Am. Mus. and Dramatic Acad.; m. Stanley M. Rumbough, Jr., Mar. 23, 1946 (div. Dec. 1966); children—Stanley M. David, Nina; m. 2d, Cliff Robertson, Dec. 21, 1966; 1 dau., Heather. Broadway debut in The Mermaids Singing, 1945; star Angel Street, 1976; appeared off-Broadway plays My Sister Eileen, George Washington Slept Here, 1945; motion picture debut in Desk Set, 1957, co-starred movies including Don't Give Up the Ship, 1958, Operation Petticoat, 1959, The Sundowners, 1960, Butterfield 8, 1961, Courtship of Eddie's Father, 1963, I'll Take Sweden, 1964, Walking Major, 1970, Throw Out the Anchor, 1972, Run Wild, 1973, The Meal, 1975, The Greatest, 1976, A Wedding, 1978; Shakespeare debut with Helen Hayes Equity Group in Twelfth Night, Othello, 1960; summer theatre tours in Voice of the Turtle, 1961, Write Me a Murder, 1963, Shaw Festival Repertory, Major Barbara, Misalliance, 1965; guest star over 100 TV shows. Vice pres. N.Y.C. Mission Soc.; bd. dirs. N.Y. Com. Olympic Ski Team, Am. Mus. and Dramatic Acad., Juvenile Diabetes Found., Joslin Diabetes Found. Office: care Irv Schlechter Co 404 N Roxbury Dr Suite 800 Beverly Hills CA 90210*

MERRILL, EDWARD CLIFTON, JR., coll. pres.; b. Asheville, N.C., Jan. 29, 1920; s. Edward Clifton and Alice (Tiddy) M.; B.A., U. N.C., 1942; M.S., U. Tenn., 1948; Ph.D., George Peabody Coll., 1953; LL.D., Gallaudet Coll., 1969; m. Frances Bonkemeyer, June 2, 1946; children—Susan, Nancy, Ned, Ann. Instr., Asheville-Biltmore Coll., 1946- 47; tchr., dean Lee Edwards High Sch., Asheville, 1948-51;

instr. George Peabody Coll., also coordinator So. State Coop. Program Ednl. Adminstrn., 1953-55; asso. prof. edn. Auburn U., 1955-57; summer vis. asso. prof. edn. Coll. Edn., U. Fla., 1957; prof. edn., asso. dean grad. studies Coll. Edn., U. Rochester, 1957-60; prof. edn. Coll. Edn., U. N.C., 1960-61; dean Coll. Edn., U. Tenn., 1961-69; spl. asst. to pres. Gallaudet Coll., 1969, pres. coll., 1969—. Dir. N.Y. Statewide In-Service Program State Sch. Adminstrns., 1958-60; mem. N.Y. State Adminstrv. Council Leadership, 1957-60; dir. workshops and insts. U. Rochester, 1957-60; chmn. Asso. Orgns. Tchr. Edn., 1966; mem. bd. Appalachia Ednl. Labs., Inc., Washington Ednl. TV Assn. Bd. dirs. Nat. Assn. Hearing and Speech Agys. (pres. 1971). Served with AUS, World War II; ETO. Recipient Disting. Service award Nat. Assn. of Deaf, 1978; Décoration au Mérite Social, World Fedn. of Deaf, 1979. Mem. Am. Assn. Sch. Adminstrs., Nat. Conf. Profs. Ednl. Adminstrn., Am. Assn. Colls. Tchr. Edn., Iota Lambda Sigma, Phi Kappa Phi, Phi Delta Kappa. Co-author: Community Leadership for Public Education, 1955; The Deaf Child in the Public School, 2d edit., 1978. Editor: Better Teaching in School Administration, 1955. Contbr. articles to profl. jours., chpts. to books. Home: Gallaudet Coll Washington DC 20002

MERRILL, EDWARD WILSON, educator; b. New Bedford, Mass., Aug. 31, 1923; s. Edward Clifton and Gertrude (Wilson) M.; A.B., Harvard, 1945; D.Sc., Mass. Inst. Tech., 1947; m. Genevieve de Bidart, Aug. 19, 1948; children—Anne de Bidart, Francis de Bidart. Research engr. Dewey & Almy div. W.R. Grace & Co., 1947-50; mem. faculty Mass. Inst. Tech., 1950—, prof. chem. engring., 1964—, Carbon P. Dubbs prof., 1973—; cons. in field, 1950—; research asso. in surgery Beth Israel Hosp., Boston, 1969—. Pres. bd. trustees Buckingham Sch., Cambridge, 1969-74; trustee Browne and Nichols Sch., Cambridge, 1972-74, hon. trustee, 1974—. Fellow Am. Acad. Arts and Scis.; mem. Am. Chem. Soc., Am. Inst. Chem. Engrs., Am. Phys. Soc., Am. Soc. Artificial Internal Organs. Episcopalian (vestry 1960-69). Author articles on polymers, rheology, med. engring.; patentee chem. and rheological instruments. Home: 90 Somerset St Belmont MA 02178

MERRILL, EZRA, agribus. cons.; b. Misswa, Minn., Jan. 3, 1909; s. Ezra Birdette and Mabel (Brown) M.; A.B., Kalamazoo Coll., 1930; LL.B., Harvard, 1933, postgrad. econs., 1934-35; m. Eva L. Vandenbergh, Dec. 22, 1965. With H.P. Hood & Sons, Boston, 1934—, treas., 1962-66, pres., 1966-71, vice chmn. bd., 1971-74, also asso. Agribus. Assos., Boston, 1974—. Mem. corp. or bd. dirs. Boston Children's Service Assn., Mass. Correctional Assn., Mass. Half-way Houses; co-founder Flynn Houses Boston. Clubs: Harvard, Commercial (Boston). Home and office: 68 Chestnut St Boston MA 02108

MERRILL, HUGH DAVIS, state legislator; b. Anniston, Ala., Apr. 2, 1913; s. Hugh D. and Martha (Chitwood) M.; A.B., U. Ala., 1935, LL.B., 1937; m. Martha Elizabeth Holcombe, Dec. 28, 1951; children—Hugh Davis, David, Paul Speake, Nancy. Admitted to Ala. bar, 1937; sr. partner firm Merrill, Merrill & Vardaman, Anniston, 1937—; city atty., Anniston, 1939-46; mem. Ala. Ho. of Reps., 1955—, speaker pro tem., 1967-71, chmn. judiciary com., 1963-74, chmn. ways and means com., 1974—. Mem. Ala. Edn. Commn., Ala. Constl. Revision Commn.; del.-at-large Democratic Nat. Conv., 1944, 52, 56, 64. Chmn. bd. trustees, Jacksonville State U.; bd. dirs. Ala. Law Sch. Found. Served to lt. JAG AUS, 1943-45. Mem. Ala. State Bar, Ala. Bar Commn., Calhoun County bar Assn. (past pres.), Ala. Law Inst. (pres.), Anniston C. of C., Am. Legion, Sigma Alpha Epsilon, Kiwanis. Office: PO Box 1498 Anniston AL 36202

MERRILL, JAMES, author; b. N.Y.C., Mar. 3, 1926; s. Charles Edward and Hellen (Ingram) M.; B.A., Amherst Coll., 1947. Author: First Poems, 1951; (play) The Immortal Husband, 1956; The Seraglio, 1957; (poetry) The Country of a Thousand Years of Peace, 1959; (play) The Bait, 1960; (poetry) Water Street, 1962; The (Diblos) Notebook, 1965; (poetry) Nights and Days (Nat. Book award), 1967; (poetry) The Fire Screen, 1969, Braving the Elements, 1972, The Yellow Pages, 1974, Divine Comedies (Pulitzer prize), 1976, Mirabell: Books of Number, 1978. Recipient Bollingen prize in poetry, 1973; Nat. Book award for poetry, 1979. Mem. Nat. Inst. Arts and Letters. Served with AUS, 1944-45. Home: 107 Water St Stonington CT 06378

MERRILL, JAMES ALLEN, obstetrician, gynecologist; b. Cedar City, Utah, Oct. 27, 1925; s. Arthur L. and Thelma P. M.; A.B., U. Calif., Berkeley, 1945, M.D., San Francisco, 1948; m. Patricia Gallagher, June 19, 1949; children—Janet Lynn, Cynthia Ann, Elizabeth Lee, Rebecca Marie. Intern, U. Calif., San Francisco, 1948-49; resident in pathology Cleve. City Hosp., 1949-50, Boston Lying-In Hosp. and Free Hosp. for Women, Boston, 1950-51, in ob-gyn U. Calif. Med. Center, 1953-57; asst. prof. ob-gyn U. Calif., San Francisco, 1957-61, asst. clin. prof. pathology, 1959-61, research asst. Cancer Research Inst., 1957-61; prof. pathology U. Okla., 1961—, prof. cytotech. Coll. Health, 1970—, prof. ob-gyn, head dept. Coll. Medicine, 1961—; teaching fellow in pathology Harvard U. Med. Sch., 1950-51; mem. test com. Nat. Bd. Med. Examiners. Pres., Oklahoma City Ballet Soc., 1968-71. Served with USN, 1944-46, M.C., USAF, 1951-53. Recipient Aesculapian award U. Okla. Student Body, 1963, 69, Regents award U. Okla., 1969; Markle scholar, 1957-62. Diplomate Am. Bd. Ob-Gyn (sec.-treas.). Mem. Am. Gynecol. Soc., Soc. Gynecol. Investigation, Soc. Gynecol. Oncologists, Am. Soc. Cytology, Am. Fertility Soc., Internat. Soc. Advancement Humanistic Studies in Gynecology, Am. Cancer Soc., Am. Coll. Ob-Gyn, Am. Assn. Obstetricians and Gynecologists, Assn. Profs. Gynecology and Obstetrics, Central Assn. Ob-Gyn, Am. Assn. Cancer Research, Ovarian Tumor Registry, AMA (residency rev. com.), Am. Gynecologic Club. Contbr. numerous articles to med. jours.; editor: (with others) Gynecology and Obstetrics: The Health of Women, 1975. Office: 800 NE 13th St Oklahoma City OK 73104

MERRILL, JAMES MERCER, educator; b. Los Angeles, Apr. 25, 1920; s. Clarence Mercer and Helen Eugenia (Hillman) M.; B.A., Pomona Coll., 1947; M.A., Claremont Grad. Sch., 1949; Ph.D., U. Calif., Los Angeles, 1954; m. Ann Elizabeth McIntosh, July 7, 1945; children—Eugenia Louise, James McIntosh. Asst. prof. Whittier Coll., 1952-56, asso. prof., 1956-66; prof. history U. Del., Newark, 1966—; chmn. bd. U. Del. Press. Served to lt. (j.g.) USNR, 1942-46. Recipient John and Dora Haynes grant, 1958; Guggenheim research fellow, 1958-59, Mershon Nat. Security fellow, 1961-62. Mem. Am., So. hist. assns., Phi Kappa Phi. Author: Rebel Shore, 1958; Quarter-Deck and Fo'c'sle, 1962; Uncommon Valor, 1964; Target Tokyo, 1964; Spurs to Glory, 1966; Battle Flags South, 1970; William Tecumseh Sherman (Florence Roberts Head Meml. book award), 1972; The USA: History of the American Republic, 1975; A Sailors Admiral: William F. Halsey, 1976. Home: 100 Old Polly Drummond Hill Newark DE 19711

MERRILL, JEAN FAIRBANKS, writer; b. Rochester, N.Y., Jan. 27, 1923; d. Earl Dwight and Elsie (Fairbanks) Merrill; B.A., Allegheny Coll., 1944; M.A., Wellesley Coll., 1945. Feature editor Scholastic Mags., 1947-50; editor Lit. Cavalcade, 1956-57; publs. div. Bank St. Coll. Edn., 1964-65; Fulbright fellow, India, 1952-53; children's books include: Henry, the Hand-Painted Mouse, 1951; The Woover, 1952; Boxes, 1953; The Tree House of Jimmy Domino, 1955; The Travels of Marco, 1956; A Song for Gar, 1957; The Very Nice Things, 1959; Blue's Broken Heart, 1960; Shan's Lucky Knife (Jr. Lit. Guild selection), Emily Emerson's Moon (Jr. Lit. Guild selection), 1960; The Superlative Horse (Jr. Lit. Guild selection, Lewis Carroll Shelf award 1963), 1961; Tell About the Cowbarn, Daddy, 1963; The Pushcart War (Lewis Carroll Shelf award, Boys Club Am. Jr. Book award), 1964; High, Wide & Handsome (Jr. Lit. Guild selection), 1964; The Elephant Who Liked to Smash Small Cars, 1967; Red Riding, 1968; The Black Sheep, 1969; Here I Come—Ready or Not!, 1970; Mary, Come Running, 1970; How Many Kids are Hiding on My Block?, 1970; Please, Don't Eat My Cabin, 1971; The Toothpaste Millionaire (Dorothy Canfield Fisher Meml. award 1975-76, Sequoyah award 1977), 1972; The Second Greatest Clown in the World, 1972; The Jackpot, 1972; The Bumper Sticker Book, 1973; Maria's House, 1974; poetry books edited include: A Few Flies and I, 1969. Mem. N.Am. Mycol. Assn., Authors League, ACLU, Nat. Women in Arts, Vt. Arts Council, War Resisters League, Vt. Inst. Natural Sci., Audubon Soc., Phi Beta Kappa. Address: Angels Ark 29 S Main St Randolph VT 05060

MERRILL, JOHN CALHOUN, educator; b. Yazoo City, Miss., Jan. 9, 1924; s. John Calhoun and Jennie Irene (Hooter) M.; B.A., Miss. Delta State Coll., 1949; M.A., La. State U., 1950; Ph.D., U. Iowa, 1962; M.A., U. Mo., 1976; m. Dorothy Jefferson, Sept. 5, 1948; children—Charles, Judith, Jon, Linda, Deborah. Instr. English and journalism Southwestern Coll., Winfield, Kans., 1950-51; wire editor Clarion-Ledger, Jackson, Miss., 1951; asst. prof. Northwestern State Coll., Natchitoches, La., 1951-62; asso. prof. Tex. A. and M. U., 1962-64; prof. Sch. Journalism, U. Mo., Columbia, 1964-79; prof. Coll. Journalism, U. Md., 1979—; Disting. vis. prof. Calif. State U., Long Beach, 1977-78; reporter, columnist, feature and editorial writer Greenville (Miss.) Delta Democrat Times, Natchitoches (La.) Times, Shreveport (La.) Times, Bryan (Tex.) Eagle; corr. Corriere della Sera, Milan, Italy, Neue Zuercher Zeitung, Zurich, ABC, Madrid; vis. prof., Taipei, Taiwan, U. Va.; lectr. Berlin, Rome, Florence, Genoa, Turin, Trieste, Milan, Mexico City, La Paz, London, Reykjevik, Madrid, Pamplona, Athens, Vienna, Zurich, Seoul, Manila, Jakarta, Kuala Lumpur, Saigon, Lisbon, Kabul, Delhi, Bombay, Madras, Calcutta, Dacca, Santiago, Montevideo, Buenos Aires. Served with USNR, 1942-46. Mem. Inter. Am. Press Assn., Assn. Edn. Journalism, Sigma Delta Chi, Kappa Tau Alpha, Phi Kappa Phi, Omicron Delta Kappa, Delta Phi Alpha. Democrat. Baptist. Author: Handbook of the Foreign Press, 1959; Gringo, 1963; The Foreign Press, 1964; The Elite Press: Great Newspapers of the World, 1968; (with H.D. Fischer) International Communication, 1970, 76; (with D. Bell) Dimensions of Christian Writing; (with R. Lowenstein) Media, Messages and Men, 1971, 79; The Imperative of Freedom: A Philosophy of Journalistic Autonomy, 1974; (with R. Barney) Ethics and the Press, 1975; (with H.D. Fischer) International and Interpersonal Communication, 1976; Existential Journalism, 1977; (with Harold Fisher) The World's Great Dailies, 1979. Home: 4218 Wilton Woods Ln Alexandria VA 22310

MERRILL, JOHN OGDEN, JR., architect; b. Evanston, Ill., Aug. 27, 1923; s. John Ogden and Ross (MacKenzie) M.; student U. Wis., 1940-42, U. Minn., 1946; B.Arch., M.I.T., 1949; m. Elizabeth Martin, May 16, 1978; children by previous marriage—John Ogden, Alison, Jennifer, Lindsen, Charles, Katherine. With Skidmore, Owings & Merrill, 1949—, gen. partner, San Francisco, 1957—; prin. works include Portland Meml. Coliseum, Standard Ins. Bldg., Hilton Hotel (all Portland, Oreg.), Oakland (Calif.) Stadium, Alcoa Bldg., San Francisco, hdqrs. bldgs. for MCA, Inc., Beneficial Life Ins. Bldg. (both Los Angeles). Vice pres. San Francisco Planning and Urban Renewal Assn. 1969-71; chmn. bd. trustees San Francisco Art Inst., 1967-72; trustee Portland Art Inst., 1959-61, World Affairs Council Portland, 1958-60. Served to capt. USAAF, 1942-45. Mem. AIA (pres. No. Calif. 1976—), Urban Land Inst. (exec. group central city council 1965-67), Am. Soc. Mil. Engrs., Bldg. Research Inst., Calif., San Francisco (dir. 1970-73) chambers commerce, Phi Delta Theta, Lambda Alpha. Clubs: Family, Saint Francis Yacht, Univ. (San Francisco). Office: 1 Maritime Plaza San Francisco CA 94111

MERRILL, JOSEPH HARTWELL, assn. exec.; b. Norway, Maine, Jan. 16, 1903; s. Wiggin L. and Ella M. (Porter) M.; grad. high sch. Head retouching dept. Bachrach, Inc., photographers, Newton, Mass., 1937-61; sec. Mass. Assn. Spiritualists, 1953-61; exec. sec. Nat. Spiritualist Assn. Chs., Milw., 1961-71, v.p., 1971-73, pres., 1973—; v.p. Internat. Spiritualist Fedn.; lectr. social legislation for oldsters Townsend Orgn. Served with AUS, 1942-43. Address: 13 Cleveland Ave Lily Dale NY 14752

MERRILL, JOSEPH MELTON, physician, educator; b. Andalusia, Ala., Dec. 8, 1923; s. Walter C. and Mary (McLaney) M.; student U. Ala., 1942-43, Tex. A. and M. U., 1944; M.D., Harvard, 1948; m. Gudrun Wallgren, Sept. 16, 1962; children—Maria, Caroline. Intern Louisville Gen. Hosp., 1948-49; intern Vanderbilt U. Hosp., 1949-50, resident, 1950-51; fellow medicine VA Hosp., Nashville, also Hammersmith Hosp., London, Eng., 1954-56; asso. chief staff for research VA Hosp., Nashville, 1960-64; chief gen. clin. research centers br. NIH, Bethesda, Md., 1964-67; prof. medicine Baylor Coll. Medicine, Houston, 1967—, dean sci. affairs, 1967-70, exec. v.p., 1970-78. Diplomate Am. Bd. Internal Medicine. Fellow A.C.P. Home: 2234 Inwood St Houston TX 77019

MERRILL, KENNETH COLEMAN, automobile co. exec.; b. South Bend, Ind., Feb. 20, 1930; s. Kenneth Griggs and Helen Shapley (Coleman) M.; B.A., Cornell U., 1953; M.B.A., Ind. U., 1956; m. Helen Jean Tagtmeyer, June 10, 1956; children—Barry, Diane, John. With Ford Motor Co., Dearborn, Mich., 1956—, asst. controller, 1967-71, gen. asst. controller, 1971-73, controller N.Am. automotive ops., 1973-79, exec. dir. parts ops., 1979—. Pres., Plymouth (Mich.) Symphony Soc., 1969-70. Vice chmn. bd. dirs. Detroit Inner City Bus. Improvement Forum. Served with AUS, 1953-55. Mem. Detroit Econ. Club, Beta Gamma Sigma, Psi Upsilon. Episcopalian (treas. 1973-74). Clubs: Barton Hills, Round Table. Home: 1450 Maple St Plymouth MI 48170 Office: 3000 Schaefer Rd Dearborn MI 48121

MERRILL, LELAND GILBERT, JR., univ. adminstr.; b. Danville, Ill., Oct. 4, 1920; s. Leland Gilbert and May (Babcock) M.; B.S., Mich. State U., 1942; M.S., Rutgers U., 1948, Ph.D., 1949; m. Virginia Gilhooley, Sept. 14, 1949; children—Susan Jane, Alison Lee. Research asst. entomology Rutgers U., 1946-49; asst. prof. entomology Mich. State U., 1949-53; mem. faculty Rutgers-The State U., 1953—, research specialist entomology, 1960—, dean agr., 1961-71, dir. Inst. Environ. Studies, 1971-76, prof. central coastal and environ. studies, 1976—. Served to maj. AUS, 1942-46. Mem. AAAS, Entomol. Soc. Am., U.S. C. of C. (agrl. com.), Sigma Xi, Alpha Gamma Rho, Phi Kappa Phi, Alpha Zeta, Epsilon Sigma Phi. Home: 49 Gulick Rd Princeton NJ 08540 Office: Doolittle Bldg Rutgers-The State Univ New Brunswick NJ 08903

MERRILL, LINDSEY, music educator; b. Madisonville, Ky., Jan. 10, 1925; s. James E. and Della (Scott) M.; Mus.B., U. Louisville, 1949; Mus.M., Yale, 1950; Ph.D., U. Rochester, 1963; m. Martha Lynn Rowe, June 11, 1948; children—Jonathan Scott, Rebecca Rowe. Mem. faculty Queen's Coll., N.C., 1950-53, Smith Coll., 1953-56; prof. music Bucknell U., 1957-67, chmn. dept., 1966-67; prof., dir. Sch. Music, dir. Blossom Festival Sch., Kent State U., 1967-75; dean Conservatory Music, U. Mo.-Kansas City, 1975—. Music editor Merriam Webster 3d New Internat. Dictionary; cons. in field. Served with AUS, 1943-46. Mem. Pi Kappa Lambda. Violinist, composer electronic music. Home: 5318 Locust St Kansas City MO 64110 Office: Conservatory of Music U Mo-Kansas City Kansas City MO 64111

MERRILL, MAURICE HITCHCOCK, lawyer, educator; b. Washington, Oct. 3, 1897; s. George Waite and Mary Lavinia (Hitchcock) M.; A.B., U. Okla., 1919, LL.B., 1922; S.J.D., Harvard, 1925; L.H.D., Okla. Christian Coll., 1974; m. Orpha Roberts, June 4, 1922 (dec. May 1971); 1 dau., Jean (Mrs. Donald Barnes). Admitted to Okla. bar, 1922; practice in Tulsa, 1922-26, Norman, 1936—; asst., later spl. instr. and instr. in govt. U. Okla., 1919-22; asso. prof. law U. Idaho, 1925-26; asst. prof. law, U. Nebr., 1926-28, prof., 1928-36; prof. law U. Okla., 1936-50, acting dean, 1945-46, research prof. law, 1950-68, George Lynn Cross research prof. law emeritus, 1968—; vis. prof. law Oklahoma City U., 1975-76, 77; atty. U. Okla. Research Inst., 1941-72; vis. tchr. law summer sessions law schs. U. Calif., 1927, Cornell U., 1928, U. Ia., 1931, U. Kans., 1934, U. Tex., 1937, U. Chgo., 1938, U. N.C., 1958, U. Mich., 1960, 62; lectr. Southwestern Legal Found. Center for Municipal Studies, 1969; gen. Counsel Okla. Assn. Municipal Attys., 1971—; spl. justice Supreme Ct. Okla., 1965-68. Mem. Okla. Spl. Com. on Constl. Revision, 1969-70; counsel, draftsman Tulsa Charter Revision Com., 1939; mem. Norman Charter Revision Com., 1940-45. Chmn. local examining bds. for Okla. under U.S. Bd. of Legal Examiners and Civil Service Commn., 1942-44; pub. panel mem. 8th Regional War Labor Bd., 1943-45; chmn. permanent trucking panel, 1943-45; mem. labor panel Am. Arbitration Assn., 1944—; mem. from Okla., Nat. Conf. Commrs. on Uniform State Laws, 1944—, v.p., 1963-67; mem., sec. Jud. Council, Okla., 1945-46; mem. Cleve. County Vets. Assistance Council, 1945-50; arbitrator F.M.C.S., 1946—; hon. mem. Jud. Council of Okla., 1947-65. Trustee Okla. Bar Found., 1970-74. Served with U.S. Army, 1918. Recipient Hatton W. Sumners award, 1964; Distinguished Service citation U. Okla., 1968; named to Okla. Hall Fame, 1970. Fellow Am. Bar Found.; mem. Nat. Acad. Arbitrators, Am. (numerous coms.), Okla. (asso. editor Jour. 1940-71; President's award 1972), Cleveland County (pres. 1952-53) bar assns., Southwestern Soc. Sci. Assn., Am. Acad. Polit. and Social Sci., Acad. Polit. Sci., Indsl. Relations Research Assn., Okla. Hist. Soc., Cleveland County Hist. Soc. (pres. 1978—), Am. Judicature Soc., Am. Rose Soc., Phi Beta Kappa, Order of Coif, Alpha Kappa Psi, Phi Delta Phi. Author or co-author several books; latest publ.: Cases and Materials on Administrative Law, 1950; Law of Notice, 3 vols., 1952, and supplements, 1957; Administrative Law, 1954; Covenants Implied in Oil and Gas Leases Supplement, 1964; The Public's Concern with the Fuel Minerals, 1960. Home: 800 Elm Ave Norman OK 73069 Office: 300 W Timberdell Rd Norman OK 73019

MERRILL, OLIVER BOUTWELL, lawyer; b. Summit, N.J., Nov. 13, 1903; s. Oliver Boutwell and Kitty Earl (Lyall) M.; grad. Phillips Acad., Andover, Mass., 1921; B.A., Amherst Coll., 1925, LL.D., 1976; LL.B. (bd. editors Law Rev.), Columbia, 1928; m. Laura Gardner Provost, Sept. 1, 1928; 1 dau., Barbara Louise (Mrs. Kenneth R. Huggins). Legal sec. to U.S. Supreme Ct. Justice Stone 1928-29; admitted to N.Y. bar, 1930, since practiced in N.Y.C.; partner firm Sullivan & Cromwell, 1937-74. Counsel, Nat. War Fund, 1941-46; govt. appeal agt. local SSS, 1942-45. Dir. Am. Water Works Co., Inc., 1947-51. Bd. dirs. Peoples Symphony Concerts, 1951—; trustee Brearley Sch., 1943-53; trustee Amherst Coll., 1953—, chmn. bd., 1969-73. Decorated comdr. Order Brit. Empire. Mem. Am. Bar Assn. Clubs: University, Century Assn. (N.Y.C.). Home: Mead St Waccabuc NY 10597

MERRILL, PHILIP, publisher; b. Balt.; student Cornell U., Harvard Bus. Sch.; m. Eleanor Merrill; children—Douglas, Catharine, Nancy. Publisher, Annapolis (Md.) Evening Capital, Balt. Mag., Washingtonian Mag. Home: 312 Rugby Cove Rd Arnold MD 21012 Office: 213 West St Annapolis MD 21401

MERRILL, REED MILLER, educator, psychologist; b. Salt Lake City, Oct. 25, 1919; s. Daniel R. and Nettie Merrill; B.A., U. Utah, 1941, M.A., 1946; Ph.D., U. Wash., 1953; m. Maurine Wright, Nov. 4, 1937; children—Robert W., Roger G., Lynne, Shelley. Clin. psychologist U.S. Army, 1941-46; dir. counseling center U. Wash., 1947-54; dir. counseling center, prof. ednl. psychology U. Utah, 1954—, head dept., 1962-70. Mem. Am., Western, Utah (past pres.) psychol. assns., AAAS, AAUP (past pres. local chpt.). Author articles in field. Home: 1741 E 3150 South Salt Lake City UT 84106

MERRILL, RICHARD AUSTIN, lawyer; b. Logan, Utah, May 20, 1937; s. Milton Rees and Bessie (Austin) M.; A.B., Columbia U., 1959, LL.B., 1964; B.A. (Rhodes scholar), Oxford (Eng.) U., 1961, M.A., 1965; m. Elizabeth Duvall, Aug. 26, 1961; children—Patricia, John. Admitted to N.Y. bar, 1964, D.C. bar, 1965; law clk. to Hon. Carl McGowan, U.S. Ct. Appeals for D.C., 1964-65; asso. firm Covington & Burling, Washington, 1965-69; asso. prof. law U. Va., 1969-72, prof., 1972-75, Daniel Caplin prof. law, 1977—; gen. counsel FDA, Washington, 1975-77; cons. in field. Mem. Inst. Medicine, Nat. Acad. Scis., 1977—. Democrat. Author: (with Jerry L. Mashaw) Introduction to American Public Law System, 1975. Office: U Va Sch Law Charlottesville VA 22901

MERRILL, RICHARD GLEN, banker; b. Anaheim, Calif., Feb. 23, 1931; s. Howard Glen and Ann (Clark) M.; B.S., U. Calif., Los Angeles, 1953; m. Grace Marilyn Hansler, Aug. 29, 1959; children—Thomas Glen, Ann Adelia, Elizabeth Mary, John Richard. Group sales rep. Prudential Ins. Co. Am., Los Angeles, Seattle, San Francisco, 1956-66, dir. group sales and service, Newark, 1966-68, v.p. group ins., 1968-70, v.p. group annuity dept., 1970-72, sr. v.p. in charge, Houston, 1972-78; pres. First City Nat. Bank, 1978—. Mem. exec. bd. Sam Houston council Boy Scouts Am., 1973—, v.p. fin., chmn. council campaign fund, 1974, pres. council, 1975-76; bd. dirs., mem. exec. com. Houston Symphony Soc.; bd. dirs. U. St. Thomas, 1977—; mem. bd. visitors M.D. Anderson Hosp. Cancer Found.; bd. dirs. Rice Center for Research and Design, 1979; campaign chmn. United Fund Houston and Harris County, 1978. Served to 1st lt. U.S. Army, 1954-56. Mem. Houston C. of C. (dir., chmn. research com. 1974), Alpha Tau Omega. Clubs: Ramada, Houston Country, Met. Racquet, Houstonian, City (Houston). Home: 605 E Friar Tuck Houston TX 77024 Office: First City Nat Bank 1001 Main St Houston TX 77002

MERRILL, RICHARD JAMES, educator; b. Milw., Apr. 15, 1931; s. Henry Baldwin and Doris (Lucas) M.; B.S., U. Mich., 1953; M.A., Columbia, 1957, Ed.D., 1960; m. Kathleen Emden Keely, June 14, 1953 (dec. Jan. 1974); children—Wendy Ann, Vicki Louise, Robin Kay, Christina Suzanne; m. 2d, Terry Bradley Alt, Aug. 10, 1974 (div. 1976); m. 3d, Shannon Ann Lynch, June 19, 1977. Tchr. sci. Ramona High Sch., Riverside, Calif., 1958-62; secondary sci. coordinator Riverside city schs., 1960-62; exec. dir. chem. edn. material study Harvey Mudd Coll. and U. Calif. at Berkeley, 1962-65; cons. curriculum Mt. Diablo Unified Sch. Dist., Concord, Calif., 1965—; tchr. extension courses Calif. State Coll., Hayward, St. Mary's Coll., Moraga, Calif.; cons. ednl. policies commn. NEA. Mem. adv. bd. Lawrence Hall Sci.; bd. dirs. San Francisco Bay Area Sci. Fair. Served from ensign to lt. (j.g.), USN, 1953-56. Mem. Nat. Sci. Tchrs. Assn. (past pres., past mem. exec. com.), Calif. Math. Council, Elementary Sch. Sci. Assn. (council 1975-78), Calif. Sci. Tchrs. Assn., Acacia, Phi Delta Kappa. Author: (with David W. Ridgway) The CHEM Study Story, 1969; co-author: Guidelines for Self-Assessment of Secondary Science Programs, 1975, Science Framework for California Public Schools, 1977. Home: 1862 2d Ave Walnut Creek CA 94596 Office: 1936 Carlotta Dr Concord CA 94519

MERRILL, RICHARD THOMAS, pub. co. exec.; b. Chgo., June 26, 1928; s. Thomas William and Mary Ann (Colvin) M.; B.A., U. Mo., 1950, B.J., 1951; m. Lisi Y. Snyder, June 7, 1952; children—T. William II, James R., Stephen J. With Commerce Clearing House, Chgo., 1953—, v.p., 1962-76, exec. v.p., 1976—, also dir.; dir. CCH Australia, CCH Canadian Ltd., CCH N.J., Nat. Quotation Bur., CT Corp. System, Computax, State Capitol Info. Service, CCH Products Co., Facts on File, Investment Dealers Digest. Served to capt. USAF, 1951-53. Home: 2940 Lake Placid Ln Northbrook IL 60062 Office: 4025 W Peterson Ave Chicago IL 60646

MERRILL, ROBERT, baritone; b. Bklyn., June 4, 1919; s. Abraham and Lillian (Balaban) M.; ed. New Utrecht High School; Mus.D. (hon.), Gustavus Adolphus Coll., St. Peter, Minn., 1971; m. Marion Machno, May 30, 1954; children—David Robert, Lizanne. Singer in concert, opera and on radio and TV; winner Met. Auditions of the Air, 1945; debut in opera, 1945; operatic roles include Escamillo in Carmen; Germont in La Traviata; Valentine in Faust; Amonasro in Alda; Marcello in La Boheme; Don Carlo in La Forza del Destino; Sir Henry Ashton in Lucia de Lammermoor; sang in La Traviata, condr. Arturo Toscanini, over NBC network; singer with NBC, 1946—; opened Met. Opera season, Rodrigo in Don Carlo, 1950; appeared in Toscanini's final opera performance and recording as Renato in Un Ballo in Maschera; opened Met. season as Valentine in Faust, 1953, as Figaro in Barber of Seville, 1954, Rigoletto in Rigoletto, Barnaba in Giocanda, Scarpia in Tosca, Renato in Un Ballo, in Maschera, Iago in Otello, Count di Luna in Il Trovatore, Tonio in Pagliacci; opened Met. season as Gerard in Andrea Chenier, 1962, as Sir Henry in Lucia, 1964, as Valentine in Faust, 1965, as Germont in La Traviata, 1966, as Amonasro in Aida, 1969, also opened Met. Opera season, 1971; opened Royal Opera House-Covent Garden season as Germont in La Traviata, 1967; opened in La Traviata in Met. Opera visit to Japan, Tokyo, 1975; debut at Teatro Colon as Escamillo in Carmen, 1968; appeared in concerts, London, Bournemouth, Geneva, Israel, 1975; rec. artist RCA-Victor, Angel, London, Columbia; stage debut as Tevye in Fiddler on the Roof, 1970. Appearances for Presidents Roosevelt, Truman, Eisenhower, Kennedy and Johnson; only singer at Roosevelt Meml. before both houses of U.S. Congress. Mem. Nat. Council of the Arts, 1968—; 1st Am. opera singer to sing 500 performances at Met. Opera, N.Y.C., 1973. Recipient Music Ann. award, 1946, for rec., Ah, Dite Alla Giovine; best opera rec. award Nat. Acad. Rec. Arts and Scis., 1962, 64; Harriet Cohen Internat. Music award, Opera, medal, 1961; Handel medal City N.Y., 1970. Mem. Opera Guild, Am. Fedn. Radio Artists, Am. Guild Variety Artists, Actors Equity. Club: Friars (monk 1968—). Author: Once More From the Beginning; Between Acts; The Divas. Office: CAMI 165 W 57 St New York NY 10019. *If you honestly feel that you are doing your best, it makes good criticism even sweeter and bad criticism less painful.*

MERRILL, WALTER JAMES, lawyer; b. Anniston, Ala., Sept. 30, 1912; s. Walter B. and Lilla (Jones) M.; A.B., U. Ala., 1931, LL.B., 1934; m. Polly McCarty, Sept. 6, 1941; children—Martha, Mary. Admitted to Ala. bar, 1934, since practiced in Anniston; mem. firm Merrill, Jones & Merrill, 1934-42, Knox, Jones, Woolf & Merrill, 1946-75, Merrill, Porch, Doster & Dillon, 1975—. Dir. Wilmer Bldg. Corp., Howell Realty Co., Inc., Comml. Nat. Bank. Mem. adv. com. on appellate practice rules Ala. Supreme Ct. Mem. Ala. Democratic Exec. Com., 1946-52. Mem. adv. com. Ala. Med. Center, 1955-64; chmn. trustees Anniston Meml. Hosp. Sch. Nursing. Served to lt. col. USAAF, 1942-46. Mem. Anniston C. of C. (bd. dirs.), Am. Coll. Trial Lawyers, Am. Legion, Phi Beta Kappa, Omicron Delta Kappa. Baptist. Rotarian. Club: Anniston Country. Home: 226 Crestview Rd Anniston AL 36201 Office: 1st Nat Bank Bldg Anniston AL 36201

MERRILL, WALTER MCINTOSH, educator; b. Evanston, Ill., May 26, 1915; s. Frank E. and Eunice M. (McIntosh) M.; B.S.L., Northwestern U., 1937; A.M., Harvard, 1941, Ph.D., 1946; m. Anna Gardner Montgomery; 1 son, Scott M.; m. 2d, Adeline Godfrey Pringle; children—Adeline Godfrey, Margaret Buist; m. 3d, Rhona Hoover Brockett; 1 dau., Cinda Hoover. Master jr. and sr. English, Loomis Sch., 1942-43; instr. English, Amherst Coll., 1943-45, Temple U., 1945, Swarthmore Coll., 1945-47, Northwestern U., 1947-51; postdoctoral fellow Am. Council Learned Socs., 1951-53; asst. prof. Bowdoin Coll., 1953-54; dir. Essex Inst., Salem, Mass., 1954-59; prof. English, chmn. dept. Wichita State U., 1959-69; prof. English, Drexel U., 1969—, chmn. dept. lit. and lang., 1969-71. Chmn. tourist promotion com., Salem, 1955-57; pres. Essex County Tourist Council of Mass., Inc., 1956-58. Bd. dirs. Wichita Art Mus., 1964-69, treas., 1967-69; bd. dirs. Wichita Community Theatre, 1960-68, Wichita City Library, 1961-62; mem. Mid-Atlantic Film Bd., 1970—; juror Internat. Festival Short Films, Phila., 1971; mem. film com. Walnut St. Theatre, 1972-73; dir. Phila. Art Alliance, 1973-76, pres., 1973-75. Nat. Endowment for Humanities grantee, 1970-79; Am. Philos Soc. grantee, 1978, Pa. Abolition Soc. grantee; Claremont Found. grantee. Mem. Modern Lang. Assn. Am., Colonial Soc. Mass., Fellows in Am. Studies (v.p. 1973), Sigma Chi. Author: From Statesman to Philosopher, A Study of Bolingbroke's Deism, 1949; Against Wind and Tide, A Biography of Wm. Lloyd Garrison, 1963; also articles, book revs. Editor: Behold Me Once More: The Memoirs of James Holley Garrison, Brother of William Lloyd Garrison, 1954; I Will Be Heard, The Letters of William Lloyd Garrison, 1971; No Union with Slaveholders, Letters of Wm. Lloyd Garrison, Vol. III, 1974; Let The Oppressed Go Free, Letters of Wm. Lloyd Garrison, Vol. V, 1979; contbr. Ency. Brit., Dict. Am. Negro Biography. Paintings shown in various exhbns.; one man exhbns.: Gallery 252, Phila., 1972, Arts Center, Widener Coll., Chester, Pa., 1973, Phila. Art Alliance, 1974, Wallnuts Gallery, Phila., 1976. Address: 2043 Wallace St Philadelphia PA 19130

MERRILL, WILLIAM MCGILL, utility exec.; b. Des Moines, Aug. 25, 1923; s. Albert W. and Helen (McGill) M.; B.S., Iowa State U., 1947; m. Dorothy Glasener, Dec. 16, 1944; children—James, Thomas, Barbara. With Phillips Petroleum Co., 1947-50; with Iowa Power & Light Co., Des Moines, 1950—, treas., 1966-71, v.p., 1971—. Served with AUS, 1943-46. Home: 4019 45th St Des Moines IA 50310 Office: 823 Walnut St Des Moines IA 50303

MERRILL, WILLIAM MEREDITH, geologist; b. Detroit, Dec. 1, 1918; s. Frederick I. and Isobel (LaBombard) M.; B.S., Mich. State U., 1946; M.A. (John A. Bowncker fellow 1948-50), Ohio State U., 1948, Ph.D., 1950; m. Gypsie V. Smith, Feb. 23, 1943 (div. Oct. 1973); children—Russell B., William W., Douglas G.; m. 2d, Mary Jo Forsyth, Dec. 29, 1973; children—David J. Forsyth, Timothy M. Geologist, Geol. Survey Ohio, 1946-50; from instr. to asso. prof. geology U. Ill., 1950-58; prof. geology, chmn. dept. Syracuse U., 1958-63; prof. geology U. Kans., 1963—, chmn. dept., 1963-72; geologist, party chief Geol. Survey of Nfld., 1954; research asso. Ohio State U. Research Found. group to Red Rock Lake, Greenland, 1955-57; geologist Research Council Alta. (Can.), summers 1958-62; chmn. Geo-study Panel on Preparation of Secondary Sch. Earth Sci. Tchrs., 1964-67; mem. Council Edn. in Geol. Sci., 1965-67; mem. steering com. Earth Sci. Curriculum Project, 1965-70, mem. writers conf., 1966. Served from 2d lt. to maj., cav. and armored force, AUS, 1941-46; N. Africa, ETO. Mem. Internat. Assn. Sedimentologists, Geol. Soc. Am. (mgmt. bd. S. Central sect. 1967-71, vice chmn. S. Central sect. 1968-69, chmn. 1969-70), AAAS (council del. sect. E 1974-78), Am. Assn. Petroleum Geologists, Soc. Econ. Paleontologists and Mineralogists, Internat. Assn. Sedimentologists, Internat. Assn. Math. Geologists, Sigma Xi. Contbr. articles to profl. jours. Home: Rural Route 1 Box 135-A Overbrook KS 66524

MERRIMAN, HEMINWAY, lawyer, bus. exec.; b. N.Y.C., Nov. 2, 1912; s. Merritt Heminway and Sally Mallory (Betts) M.; B.A., Yale U., 1934, J.D., 1937; m. Natalie Smith Rowbottom, Feb. 3, 1945; children—Mallory Betts Merriman Constantine, M. Heminway, Natalie Smith. Admitted to Conn. bar; asso. firm Carmody & Torrance, Waterbury, Conn., 1938-42, 46-48; with Scovill Mfg. Co. (now Scovill Inc.), Waterbury, 1948—, sec., gen. counsel, treas., v.p.; dir. Banking Center, Waterbury. Bd. dirs. ARC; trustee Watertown Found., Woodward Fund, Evergreen Cemetery Assn.; mem. zoning bd. appeals Watertown Fire Dist. Served with USN, 1942-46. Mem. New Haven Bar Assn., Litchfield County Bar Assn., Conn. Bar Assn., Conn. State Srs. Golf Assn., Phi Delta Phi. Republican. Episcopalian. Clubs: Waterbury, Country of Waterbury; Weekapang (R.I.) Yacht; Univ. of Litchfield County. Office: 500 Chase Pkwy Waterbury CT 06720

MERRIMAN, JOE JACK, insurance co. exec.; b. Kansas City, Mo., Nov. 9, 1926; s. Jack Dawson and Sarah Elizabeth (Bryant) M.; B.S. in Civil Engring., Northwestern U., 1946; m. Elaine Atha, Feb. 14, 1953; children—Mark, Marybeth, Michael. With Merriman Mortgage Co., Kansas City, Mo., 1946-69, v.p., 1952-69, past dir.; pres., dir. United Investors Life Ins. Co., 1961-69, Waddell & Reed, Inc., 1965-69, Kansas City Securities Corp., 1964-69; past dir. United Funds, Inc.; pres. Continental Bankers Life Ins. Co., Mpls., 1971-; chmn. bd. Home Office Reference Lab., Lenexa, Kans., 1972-, Fin. Assurance Inc., Denver, 1976-. Bd. govs. Kansas City (Mo.) Art Inst.; dir., exec. com. Kansas City council Boy Scouts Am. Mem. ASCE, Sigma Alpha Epsilon. Episcopalian. Office: 300 W 11th St Kansas City MO 64105

MERRITT, ARTHUR DONALD, educator, physician; b. Shawnee, Okla., June 11, 1925; s. Arthur B. and Frances (Harris) M.; student U. Md., 1946-47; A.B., George Washington U., 1949, M.D., 1952; m. Doris Honig, May 5, 1953; children—Kenneth Arthur, Christopher Ralph. Rotating intern D.C. Gen. Hosp., 1952-53; asst. resident medicine George Washington U. Hosp., 1953-54, clin. instr., 1959-60; asst. resident medicine Duke Hosp., 1954-55, fellow medicine, 1955-56, chief resident, 1956-57, instr. medicine, 1956-57; clin. asso. Nat. Inst. Arthritis and Metabolic Diseases, Bethesda, Md., 1957-58; chief med. investigation sect. Nat. Inst. Dental Research, Bethesda, 1958-60; asso. prof. medicine and biochemistry Ind. U. Sch. Medicine, 1961-65, chmn. med. genetics program Grad. Sch., 1962-66, chmn. dept. med. genetics, 1966-78, prof. medicine and med. genetics, 1966-79; with Lister Hill Nat. Center for Biomed. Communications, Nat. Library Medicine, NIH, Bethesda, Md., 1978—; cons. Indpls. VA Hosp., 1961-79. Med. adviser, bd. dirs. Ind. Cystic Fibrosis Found., 1961-77. Served with AUS, 1943-46, USPHS, 1957-60. Diplomate Am. Bd. Internal Medicine. Fellow A.C.P.; mem. William Beaumont Med. Soc., Smith-Reed-Russell Med. Soc., George Washington U. Med. Soc., Duke Med. Alumni Soc., Am., Ind. med. assns., Marion (Ind.) County Med. Soc., N.Y. Acad. Scis., Am. Fedn. Clin. Research, Central Soc. Clin. Research, Am. Soc. Human Genetics (treas. 1964-67, 67-70), Behavior Genetics Assn., Genetics Soc. Am., Sigma Xi, Nu Sigma Nu, Alpha Omega Alpha. Home: 4977 Battery Ln Bethesda MD 20014

MERRITT, DORIS HONIG, pediatrician, univ. dean; b. N.Y.C., July 16, 1923; d. Aaron and Lillian (Kunstlich) Honig; B.A., City U. N.Y., 1944; M.D., George Washington U., 1952; children—Kenneth Arthur, Christopher Ralph. Pediatric intern Duke Hosp., 1952-53; teaching and research fellow pediatrics George Washington U., 1953-54; pediatric asst. resident Duke U. Hosp., 1954-55, cardiovascular fellow pediatrics, 1955-56, instr. pediatrics, dir. pediatric cardiorenal clinic, 1956-57; exec. sec. cardiovascular study sect., gen. medicine study sect. div. research grants NIH, 1957-60; dir. med. research grants and contracts Ind. U. Sch. Medicine, 1961-62, asst. prof. pediatrics, 1961-68, asst. dean med. research, 1962-65, asst. dir. med. research, aerospace research application center, 1963-65, asso. dir. med. research, 1965-68, asst. dean for research, office v.p. research and dean advanced studies, 1965-67, dir. sponsored programs, asst. to provost, 1965-68, asso. dean for research and advanced studies, office v.p. and dean for research and advanced studies, 1967-71, asso. prof. pediatrics, 1968-73, prof., 1973—; spl. asst. to dir. NIH, 1978—; cons. USPHS, NIH div. research grants, Div. Health Research Facilities and Resources, Nat. Heart Inst., 1963-78, Am. Heart Assn., 1963-67, Ind. Med. Assn. Commn. Vol. Health Orgns., 1964-67, Bur. Health Manpower, Health Profession's Constrn. Program, 1965-71, Nat. Library Medicine, Health Center Library Constrn. Program, 1966-72; dir. office sponsored programs Ind. U.-Purdue U. Indpls. Office Chancellor, 1968-71, dean research and sponsored programs, 1971-79; mem. Nat. Library Medicine biomed. communications rev. com., 1970-74. Chmn. Indpls. Consortium for Urban Edn., 1971-75; v.p. Greater Indpls. Progress Com., 1974-79; mem. Community Service Council, 1969-75; bd. dirs. Bd. for Fundamental Edn., 1973-77, Ind. Sci. Edn. Found., 1977-78, Community Addiction Services Agy., Inc., 1972-74; trustee Marian Coll., 1977-78; exec. com. Nat. Council U. Research Adminstrs., 1977-78; bd. regents Nat. Library Medicine, 1976-80; chmn. adv. screening com. for life scis. Council Internat. Exchange of Scholars, 1978—. Served to lt. (j.g.), USNR. Diplomate Nat. Bd. Med. Examiners, Am. Bd. Pediatrics. Fellow Am. Acad. Pediatrics; mem. AAAS, George Washington U., Duke U. med. alumni assns., Phi Beta Kappa, Alpha Omega Alpha. Contbr. articles to profl. jours. Office: Bldg 1 Room 118 NIH Bethesda MD 20014. *The era in which I have lived and worked has been one of transition for women entering traditional male fields. What recognition and advancement I have achieved, have been due to maintaining high standards of performance on equal terms with my professional peers without compromising the fundamental femininity of my own character. I consider the three essential ingredients of success to be competence, optimistic tenacity of purpose and an enduring sense of humor.*

MERRITT, EVELYN CAROLINE, seafood co. exec.; b. Plentywood, Mont., Mar. 1, 1932; d. Idwal and Evelyn Nettie (Kellar) Jones; grad. Lincoln High Sch., Seattle, 1948; m. Richard R. Merritt, Nov. 27, 1970; children by previous marriage—Patricia Ann Brier, Edward David Brier. Various secretarial and adminstrv. positions in mortgage loan, constrn., importing/exporting, Seattle, 1948-59; adminstrv. asst. to sr. officer Seattle World's Fair, 1959-62; adminstrv. asst. to sr. legal officer Western Internat. Hotels, Seattle, 1962-68, asst. corporate sec., 1968-72; corporate sec. New Eng. Fish Co., Seattle, 1972—. Mem. budget com. Seattle/King County Conv. and Visitors' Bur., 1974-76, mem. nominating com., 1975, dir., 1975-79. Mem. Am. Soc. Corporate Secs. (regional group pres. 1974-75, nat. v.p. 1975-76, nat. dir. 1976-79). Methodist. Home: 507 N 169th St Seattle WA 98133 Office: 4th and Vine Bldg 7th Floor Seattle WA 98121. *A favorite thought - "I'd rather be criticized for doing something than for doing nothing."*

MERRITT, GILBERT STROUD, fed. judge; b. Nashville, Jan. 17, 1936; s. Gilbert Stroud and Angie Fields (Cantrell) M.; B.A., Yale U., 1957; LL.B., Vanderbilt U., 1960; LL.M., Harvard U., 1962; m. Louise Clark Fort, July 10, 1964 (dec.); children—Stroud, Louise Clark, Eli. Admitted to Tenn. bar, 1960; asst. dean, instr. Vanderbilt Law Sch., 1960-61, lectr., 1962-76, asso. prof. law, 1969-70; asso. dir. law Nashville Met. Govt., 1963-65; U.S. dist. atty. for Middle Tenn., 1966-69; partner firm Gullett, Steele, Sanford, Robinson & Merritt, Nashville, 1970-77; judge U.S. Ct. of Appeals for 6th Circuit, Nashville, 1977—. Del., Tenn. Constl. Conv., 1965. Mem. Vanderbilt Law Alumni Assn. (pres. 1979-80), Am. Law Inst., Order of Coif. Episcopalian. Mng. editor Vanderbilt Law Rev., 1959-60. Contbr. articles to law jours. Home: 612 Fair St Franklin TN 37064 Office: 736 US Courthouse Nashville TN 37203

MERRITT, HIRAM HOUSTON, educator, physician; b. Wilmington, N.C., Jan. 12, 1902; s. Hiram Houston and Dessie (Cline) M.; A.B., Vanderbilt U., 1922; M.D., Johns Hopkins, 1926; A.M. (hon.) Harvard, 1942; Sc.D. (hon.), N.Y. Med. Coll., 1967, Columbia, 1971; m. Mabel Carmichael, Aug. 2, 1930. Intern New Haven Hosp., 1926-27; various hosp. and univ. assignments, study and fellowships, 1927-42; asso. prof. neurology Harvard Med. Sch. 1942-44; vis. neurologist Boston City Hosp., 1934-42; cons. neurologist Peter Bent Brigham Hosp., 1939-44; cons. in neuropsychiatry U.S. Marine Hosp., 1937-44; dir. neuropathol. labs. Boston Psychopathic Hosp., 1943-44; mem. med. adv. bd. No. 12 SSS, 1940-44; prof clin. neurology Columbia Med. Sch., 1944-68, chmn. dept., 1948-68, Moses prof. neurology, 1963-70, emeritus, 1970-79, dean faculty medicine, v.p. charge med. affairs, 1958-70, dean, v.p. emeritus, 1970-79; chief neuropsychiat. service Montefiore Hosp., 1944-48; dir. service of neurology Neurol. Inst., Presbyn. Hosp., 1948-68; cons. various govtl. agys. Decorated grand officer Portuguese Order of Santiago; recipient George W. Jacoby award Am. Neurol. Assn., 1965; Bronze Hope Chest award Nat. Multiple Sclerosis Soc., 1967; Lennox award Am. Epilepsy Soc., 1967; North Carolina award, 1967; Golden Anniversary medal Assn. for Research in Nervous and Mental Disease, 1970; Thomas W. Salmon Distinguished Service award in psychiatry and mental hygiene, 1973. Diplomate Am. Bd. Psychiatry and Neurology (dir. 1942-50, pres. 1950). Mem. A.M.A., various other gen. and spl. med. and profl. assns. and orgns. Author: Cerebrospinal Fluid, 1937; Neurosyphillis, 1946; also textbooks; articles in profl. jours. Died Jan. 9, 1979.

MERRITT, JACK NEIL, army officer; b. Lawton, Okla., Oct. 23, 1930; s. Theodore Wood and Lovell (Draughon); stepson Earle Merritt; B.S., U. Nebr., Omaha, 1959; M.B.A., George Washington U., 1965; grad. F.A. Officer Advance Course, 1961, Air Command and Staff Coll., 1965, Indsl. Coll. Armed Forces, 1970; m. Rosemary Ralston, Oct. 31, 1953; children—Stephen Cahill, Grover Wood, Roger William. Commd. 2d lt. U.S. Army, 1953, advanced through grades to maj. gen., 1977; served in various command and staff assignments, U.S., Korea, Germany, 1953-65; served with Army Gen. Staff, Pentagon, 1965-66; mem. staff Asst. Sec. Def. for Systems Analysis, Washington, 1966-68; bn. comdr. Riverine Arty., Vietnam, 1968-69; staff asst. to Asst. to Pres. for Nat. Security Affairs, White House, 1970-73; div. arty. comdr. Ft. Hood, Tex., 1973-74, chief of staff, 1974-75, asst. div. comdr. 1st Calvary Div., 1975-77; comdg. gen. U.S. Army F.A. Center and comdt. U.S. Army F.A. Sch., Ft. Sill, Okla., 1977—; chmn. mil. profl. devel. com. West Point Study, 1977. Decorated Silver Star, Legion of Merit, D.F.C., Soldiers medal, Bronze Star, Air medal, Joint Commendation medal, Navy Commendation medal, Army Commendation medal. Mem. Internat. Inst. Strategic Studies, Assn. U.S. Army, F.A. Assn., 1st Cavalry Div. Assn., 9th Inf. Div. Assn. Home: 422 Hamilton Rd Fort Sill OK 73503 Office: US Army FA Center Fort Sill OK 73503

MERRITT, JAMES HARMER, trade assn. exec.; b. St. Clairsville, Ohio, Sept. 30, 1923; s. William Lodge and Emma Jean (Lyle) M.; B.S. in Bus. Adminstrn., Ohio State U., 1947; m. Delores Corder, Sept. 11, 1943; children—Rebecca Lynne, Bonita Jane, Judith Anne. Edn. dir. Ohio Assn. Ins. Agts., Columbus, 1947-50; exec. sec. Ohio Pharm. Assn., Columbus, 1950-57; sec. Proprietary Assn., Washington, 1957-61; exec. v.p. Nat. Assn. Chain Drug Stores, Washington, 1961-67; pres. Cosmetic, Toiletry and Fragrance Assn., Washington, 1967—. Served with USAAF, 1943-45. Decorated Air medal with 2 oak leaf clusters. Mem. Am. Soc. Assn. Execs., Ohio Trade Assn. Execs. (pres. 1954), Washington Soc. Assn. Execs., 22d Bomber Group Assn. Methodist. Club: Kenwood. Home: 5133 Westpath Way Bethesda MD 20016 Office: 1133 15th St NW Washington DC 20005

MERRITT, LYNNE LIONEL, JR., chemist, univ. dean; b. Alba, Pa., Sept. 10, 1915; s. Lynne Lionel and Pauline (Brown) M.; B.S., Wayne U., 1936, M.S., 1937; Ph.D., U. Mich., 1940; m. Lucille E. Widman, Dec. 18, 1937; children—Margaret Merritt Bowen, Lucille Merritt Williams, Lynn (dec.), Linda Merritt Marler. Teaching fellow U. Mich., 1937-39; instr. chemistry Wayne U., 1939-42; asst. prof. Ind. U., 1942-47, asso. prof., 1947-53, prof., 1953—, asso. dean Coll. Arts and Scis., 1959-62, asso. dean faculties, 1962-65, v.p., dean research and advanced studies, 1965-75, spl. asst. to pres., dean for research coordination and devel., 1975—, dir. Bur. Instl. Research, 1960-65; vis. prof. Calif. Inst. Tech., 1949, research asso., 1955-56. Pres., dir. Ind. Instrument & Chem. Corp., Bloomington, 1959—. Guggenheim fellow, 1955-56; Fulbright fellow C.N.R.S., Paris, France, 1963; recipient distinguished alumni award Wayne State U., 1959. Fellow AAAS; mem. Am. Chem. Soc., Am. Crystallographic Assn., Soc. Internat. Devel., Soc. Research Adminstrs., Am. Inst. Chemists, Ind. Acad. Sci., Phi Beta Kappa, Sigma Xi, Phi Kappa Phi, Phi Lambda Upsilon, Alpha Chi Sigma. Club: Cosmos (Washington). Author: (with H.H. Willard and John A. Dean) Instrumental Methods of Analysis, 5th edit., 1974. Home: 916 S Highland Ave Bloomington IN 47401

MERRITT, PAUL EUGENE, educator; b. Watertown, N.Y., Oct. 23, 1920; s. Thomas Henry and Myrtle Mae (Brady) M.; B.A., State U. N.Y. at Albany, 1942, M.A., 1947; Ph.D., Rensselaer Poly. Inst., 1954; m. Shirley Mildred Coddington, June 29, 1946; children—Kathaleen, Mark, Katheryn. Line foreman Gen. Chem. Corp., Point Pleasant, W.Va., 1942-43; tchr. sci. Pine Bush (N.Y.) Central Sch., 1947-48; instr. Rensselaer Poly. Inst., 1953-54; asst. prof. chemistry St. Lawrence U., 1954-58, asso. prof., 1958-63; prof. chemistry State U.N.Y. at Potsdam, 1963—, chmn. dept., 1970-73. Radiol. chief St. Lawrence County (N.Y.) Civil Def., 1960—. Bd. dirs. Central St. Lawrence Health Services, 1976-77; bd. dirs. Potsdam Coll. Devel. Fund, 1973-78, pres. bd., 1975-78; mem. Potsdam Central Sch. Dist. Sch. Bd., 1975—. Served with USNR, 1943-46, 51-53. NSF Ednl. Equipment grantee, 1964. Fellow Am. Inst. Chemists, N.Y. Acad. Sci.; mem. Am. Chem. Soc. (pres. No. N.Y. sect. 1957), Sigma Xi, Phi Lambda Upsilon, Kappa Phi Kappa, Kappa Delta Rho, Gamma Sigma Epsilon. Rotarian (pres. 1974-75, dist. gov. dist. 704 1978-79). Author: Quantitative Analysis, 1964. Home: 15 Leroy St Potsdam NY 13676

MERRITT, ROBERT LLOYD, lawyer; b. N.Y.C., Sept. 24, 1919; s. Irving and Ida (Ellen) M.; B.S. cum laude, Coll. City N.Y., 1939; J.D. (James Kent scholar), Columbia, 1942; m. Cynthia Lloyd, Feb. 17, 1952 (dec. June 1973); children—Ethan Allen, Andrew Lloyd, Elizabeth Ellen; m. 2d, Catherine Crowe Dickman, July 27, 1977. Admitted to N.Y. bar, 1942, Ohio bar, 1951, U.S. Supreme Ct. bar, 1952; spl. atty. U.S. Dept. Justice, 1942; asso. Milbank Tweed, Hope, Hadley & McCloy, N.Y.C., 1946-50; practiced in Cleve., 1951—; partner firm Guren, Merritt, Sogg, & Cohen and predecessors, 1958—; dir., asst. sec. First Bank Nat. Assn., 1974—. Trustee Cleve. Pub. Library, 1968-74, pres., 1970-71, v.p., 1972-74; trustee Free Med. Clinic Greater Cleve., 1972—. Served with AUS, 1942-46. Mem. AAAS, Archaeol. Inst. Am., Am., Greater Cleve. (trustee 1968-71) bar assns., Phi Beta Kappa. Contbr. articles to legal, archaeol. and other profl. jours. Home: 2645 Fairmount Blvd Cleveland Heights OH 44106 Office: 650 Terminal Tower Cleveland OH 44113

MERRITT, STANLEY S., advt. exec.; b. Bklyn., Aug. 7, 1929; s. Louis and Rose (Berne) M.; diploma in advt., City U. N.Y., 1949; B.A. in English, L.I. U., 1954; m. Louise Horowitz, June 4, 1955; children—Jodi Eve, William Robert. With J. Walter Thompson, N.Y.C., 1946-51, B.B.D.O., 1951-58, Gray Advt., 1958-59; v.p., creative dir. William Esty Co., 1961-67; sr. v.p. Lennen & Newell, 1967-70; pres., creative dir. Stan Merritt, Inc., N.Y.C., 1971—. Founder, co-owner Syosset Racquet Club (N.Y.). Served with AUS, 1947-49. Recipient Starch's Best Read Ad award, 1964, Comml. Film Festival award, 1970; numerous art dir. show awards, others. Club: Huntington Racquet. Author: (movie script) Run For Your Money Stanley Lewis, 1972. Home: Glenby Ln Brookville NY 11545 Office: 261 Madison Ave New York City NY 10016

MERRITT, WALTER DAVIS, JR., newspaper editor; b. Roanoke Rapids, N.C., Oct. 29, 1936; s. Walter Davis and Elizabeth Byrd (Suiter) M.; A.B. in Journalism (Morehead scholar 1954-58), U. N.C., 1958; m. Elizabeth Ann Little, June 5, 1958; children—Walter Davis, III, Robert Charles, Anna Elizabeth. With Knight Newspapers, 1958-75, news editor Washington bur., 1972-75; exec. editor Wichita (Kans.) Eagle and Beacon, Knight-Ridder Newspapers, 1975—; vis. editor Kans. U. Mem. Morehead Award Com., 1963-69. Mem. Am. Soc. Newspaper Editors, Kans. Press Assn. Home: 21 Cypress St Wichita KS 67206 Office: 825 E Douglas St Wichita KS 67201

MERRIWETHER, DUNCAN, ret. mfr.; b. Greenville, Ala., June 9, 1903; s. Jacob and Claudia (Robinson) M.; B.S., Columbia, 1928, M.S., 1938; m. Asenath Kenyon, Feb. 9, 1929; children—Duncan Charles, Virginia Ann (Mrs. L.B. Disharoon), Julia Elizabeth (Mrs. E.G. Granger, III), Jacob Douglass. Asst. to mgr. indsl. dept. Peat, Marwick, Mitchell & Co., C.P.A.'s, N.Y.C., 1929-33; various assignments Irving Trust Co., 1933-39; chief accountant Rohm & Haas Co., Phila., 1939-41, asst. treas., 1941-43, treas., dir., mem. exec. com., 1943-48, exec. v.p., 1948, vice chmn., 1953-58, past dir., mem. exec. com. Dir. Haas Community Fund, 1943-70; trustee Mt. Holyoke Coll., 1958-68, chmn. emeritus, 1968—. Mem. Columbia U. Assos. (Distinguished Alumni Service medal 1949), Am. Inst. C.P.A.'s, Alpha Kappa Psi, Beta Gamma Sigma. Episcopalian. Mason. Clubs: Merion Cricket, Rittenhouse (Phila.); Marco Island (Fla.) Country. Home: Sunset House N Apt 611 Marco Island FL 33937

MERRYMAN, HOLT WALLACE, finance co. exec.; b. Los Angeles, Nov. 26, 1927; s. Emmett and Annette (Wallace) M.; B.S., U. Calif. at Los Angeles, 1952; postgrad. U. Hawaii, 1962; m. Fantine Elizabeth Holley, Apr. 24, 1949; children—Lloyd, Elizabeth (Mrs. Bruce W. Lorber), Craig. With Seaboard Finance Co., Los Angeles, 1956-67, pres., 1969-71; pres. Avco Fin. Services, Inc. (merger Seaboard Fin. Co. and Avco Delta Corp.), Newport Beach, Calif., 1971—, chmn. bd., 1975—; dir. Collins Foods Internat., Inc. Mem. Chancellor's club, also community adv. council Grad. Sch. Adminstrn., U. Calif., Irvine. Bd. dirs. Orange County council Boy Scouts Am.; trustee U. Calif. at Irvine Calif. Coll. Medicine. Served with USNR, 1945-48. C.P.A., Calif. Clubs: Big Canyon Country; Balboa Bay. Office: 620 Newport Center Dr Newport Beach CA 92660

MERRYMAN, JAMES HAROLD, army officer; b. Hot Springs, Ark., Apr. 3, 1929; s. Jim and Edith Agnes (Dyer) M.; B.A., Henderson State Coll., 1951; m. Jane Frantz, Dec. 22, 1950; 1 son, Lee James. Commd. 2d lt. U.S. Army, 1951, advanced through grades to maj. gen., 1977; service in Vietnam, Korea and Europe; dep. chief staff combat devels. U.S. Tng. and Doctrine Command, Ft. Monroe, Va., 1977; comdg. gen. U.S. Army Aviation Center, Ft. Rucker, Ala., 1978—. Decorated Legion of Merit with oak leaf cluster, D.F.C. with 2 oak leaf clusters, Bronze Star, Meritorious Service medal, Air medal (25), Army Commendation medal with 2 oak leaf clusters; Cross of gallantry with gold star and palm (S. Vietnam). Presbyterian. Club: Masons. Home: 45 Red Cloud St Ft Rucker AL 36362 Office: Comdg Gen US Army Aviation Center Fort Rucker AL 36362

MERRYMAN, JOHN HENRY, legal educator; b. Portland, Oreg., Feb. 24, 1920; s. Joseph M. and Bertha (Hale) M.; B.S., U. Portland, 1943; M.S., U. Notre Dame, 1944, J.D. (editor-in-chief N.D. Lawyer), 1947; LL.M., N.Y.U., 1950, J.S.D., 1955; m. Nancy Dyer, Apr. 1, 1953; stepchildren—Leonard Perry Edwards, Samuel Dyer Edwards, Bruce Haven Edwards. Mem. faculty U. Santa Clara (Calif.), 1948-53; mem. faculty Stanford Sch. Law, 1953—, prof., 1960—, Nelson B. and Marie B. Sweitzer prof., 1971—; vis. prof. law schs. N.Y. U., 1950, U. Rome (Italy), 1963-64; vis. research prof. Center Planning and Econ. Research, Athens, Greece, 1962, 64; mem. Internat. Faculty Comparative Law, Strasbourg, France, 1964, 69, Mexico, 1965; Fulbright research scholar, vis. research prof. Max Planck Institut für ausländisches und internationales Privatrecht, Hamburg, Germany, 1968-69. Mem. Atty. Gen. Calif. Adv. Com. on Civil Rights, 1960-63. Bd. dirs. No. Calif. chpt. ACLU, 1955-68, chmn., 1957-61. Recipient Silver medal U. Rome, 1964; decorated officer Order Merit Italian Republic. Author: The Civil Law Tradition, 1969, Spanish edit., 1971, Italian, 1973; (with M. Cappelletti and J. Perillo) The Italian Legal System; An Introduction, 1967; Some Problems of Greek Shoreland Development, in Greek, 1966, in English, 1965; (with D. Clark) Comparative Law: Western Europe and Latin Am. Legal Systems, 1978; also articles. Home: 835 Pine Hill Rd Stanford CA 94305

MERSEREAU, HIRAM STIPE, wood products co. exec.; b. Portland, Oreg., Aug. 4, 1917; s. E.W. and Ruth (Stipe) M.; student George Washington U., 1939, Harvard, 1959; m. Margaret Daggett, Dec. 25, 1937; children—Hiram Stipe, John Bradford, Timothy Daggett. With Weyerhaeuser Timber Co., 1937-38, Alexander-Yawkey Lumber Co., 1938-52; gen. mgr. lumber div. Crossett Co. (Ark.), 1954-62; corp. sr. v.p., gen. mgr. So. div. Ga.-Pacific Corp., 1963—; v.p. Ga. Steamship Corp.; dir. Citizens & So. Nat. Bank, Augusta, Appalachian Hardwood Mfrs. Inc., Merry Cos., Inc., Augusta. Mem. Richmond County Transp. Authority. Past Bd. dirs. Young Life; bd. dirs. Ga. Conservancy, Jr. Achievement Augusta, Augusta br. Boys Clubs Am., Augusta Cancer Fund; trustee Paine Coll., Augusta. Mem. Nat. Forest Products Assn. (exec. com., dir.). Republican. Presbyterian (elder). Home: 758 Tripps Ct Augusta GA 30904 Office: PO Box 909 Augusta GA 30903

MERSHEIMER, WALTER LYON, surgeon, educator; b. N.Y.C., Mar. 25, 1911; s. Christian Henry and Catherine (Vogel) M.; B.S., Norwich U., 1933, D.Sc. (hon.), 1962; M.D., N.Y. Med. Coll., 1937, M.Med. Sc. in Surgery, 1942; m. Janet Angeline Stanley, Dec. 26, 1941; children—Carol Janet (Mrs. Werner J. Roeder), Walter Henry, Joan Elizabeth (Mrs. Charles A. Taylor), Chris Lyon. Intern Flower and Fifth Av. Hosps., N.Y.C., 1937-39; resident surgery Met. Hosp., N.Y.C., 1940-42; fellow surgery N.Y. Med. Coll., 1939-40, mem. faculty, 1942—, coordinator cancer edn. program, 1948-61, 62-72, prof. surgery, 1962—, chmn. dept., 1962-76; dir. surgery Flower and Fifth Ave. Hosps., also Met. and Bird S. Coler Hosps., 1962-76, attending surgeon, 1950—; attending surgeon Westchester County Med. Center, Valhalla, N.Y., 1970—, chmn. div. surgery, 1970-76; cons. U.S. Naval Hosp., St. Albans, N.Y., 1947-59, VA Hosp., Lyons, N.J., 1951-64, Bronx VA Hosp., 1956-66, Yonkers Gen. Hosp., 1966—, Victory Meml. Hosp., 1966—, Holy Name Hosp., Teaneck, N.J., 1967—, Italian Hosp., N.Y.C., 1967—, S.I. Hosp., 1967—, Hackensack (N.J.) Hosp., 1969—, Lawrence Hosp., Bronxville, N.Y., 1969—, Mt. Vernon Hosp., 1971—, Stamford Hosp., 1974—, VA Hosp., Castle Point, N.Y., 1976—, St. John's Riverside Hosp., Yonkers, N.Y., 1976—. Dir. N.Y.C. cancer com. Am. Cancer Soc., 1966—; mem. results com. Nat. Cancer Inst., 1956—. Trustee Pace U., N.Y., Norwich U., Northfield, Vt. Served to capt. M.C., USNR, 1942-46. Decorated Bronze Star; recipient Alumni medal N.Y. Med. Coll., 1960, 72. Diplomate Am. Bd. Surgery. Fellow A.C.S., Am. Coll. Gastroenterology; mem. AMA, N.Y. State, N.Y. County med. assns., N.Y. Acad. Medicine, N.Y. Acad. Sci., Harvey Soc., N.Y. Cancer Soc., N.Y. Surg. Soc., Assn. Am. Med. Colls., AAAS, Soc. Exptl. Biology and Medicine, Am. Assn. Surgery Trauma, Allen O. Whipple Surg. Soc., Soc. Surgery Alimentary Tract, Soc. Surg. Chmn., Am. Assn. Cancer Edn., Assn. Med. Schs. Greater N.Y. (mem. regional med. program), Westchester Acad. Medicine, Westchester Surg. Soc., Med. Soc. County Westchester, Sigma Alpha Epsilon, Alpha Kappa Kappa, Alpha Omega Alpha. Contbr. med jours. Home: 7 Polly Park Rd Rye NY 10580 Office: 1249 Fifth Ave New York City NY 10029

MERSKEY, CLARENCE, physician; b. S. Africa, July 20, 1914; s. Bernard and Hilda (Solomon) M.; came to U.S., 1959, naturalized, 1965; B. Med., B. Surgery, U. Capetown (S.Africa), 1937, M.D., 1947; m. Marie G. Fine, Oct. 8, 1939; children—Hilary Pamela, Susan Heather, Joan Margaret. Intern, Groote Schuur Hosp., Capetown, 1938, City Hosp. for Infectious Diseases, Capetown, 1939; gen. med. practice, Tabankulu, Cape Province, Union S.Africa, 1939-40; 1st asst. dept. medicine, vis. asst. physician Groote Schuur Hosp., 1947-48, vis. asst. physician, 1951, vis. physician, cons. hematologist, 1951-59; part-time lectr. physiology U. Capetown, 1947-48, 1st asst., sr. lectr. medicine, 1951-59; vis. fellow hematology Radcliffe Infirmary, Oxford, Eng., 1949-50; practice internal medicine, Capetown, 1951; fellow in biochemistry Harvard U. Med. Sch., Boston, 1957; asst. prof. medicine Albert Einstein Coll. Medicine, N.Y.C., 1959-66, asso. prof., 1967-72, prof. medicine, 1972—, asst. prof. pathology, 1966-68, asso. prof., 1968-74, prof. lab. medicine, 1974—. Served to capt. M.C., South African Army, 1940-46. Mem. Am., N.Y., Bronx County med. assns., Royal Coll. Physicians London (Eng.), Coll. Physicians and Surgeons South Africa, Am. Physiol. Soc., Soc. Exptl. Biology and Medicine, Assn. Am. Physicians, Internat. Com. Thrombosis and Haemostasis, Am., Internat. socs. hematology, Soc. Study Blood. Contbr. articles to profl. jours. Home: 316 S Barry Ave Mamaroneck NY 10543 Office: 1300 Morris Park Ave Bronx NY 10461

MERSMAN, SCUDDER, JR., banker; b. Tahiti, Mar. 29, 1921 (parents Am. citizens); s. Scudder and Marguerite (Riddell) M.; B.A., U. Cal. at Berkeley, 1942; m. Nita Bolin, June 28, 1947; children—Joan Mary, Scudder Gordon. With internat. dept. Bank of Am., San Francisco, 1949—, regional v.p. France, Spain, Portugal at London, Eng. office, 1958-60, Paris, France office, 1960-68, sr. v.p. for Europe, Africa, Middle East, head office, San Francisco, 1968—, head mcht. banking and affiliates World Banking div., 1976—, now sr. v.p., liaison officer Hdqrs. World Banking div. Home: 1950 Ralston Ave Hillsborough CA 94010 Office: Bank of Am 555 California St San Francisco CA 94120

MERSZEI, ZOLTAN, oil co. exec.; b. Budapest, Hungary, Sept. 30, 1922; Architecture degree Fed. Poly. Inst. Zurich (Switzerland), 1944; LL.D. (hon.), Northwood Inst., 1976; Dr.Sci., Albion Coll., 1978; m. Ilona Eisele, May 22, 1946; children—Leslie G., Geoffery E., Karen G. With Dow Chem. Co. and subs's., 1949-79, v.p. Dow Chem. Internat. Ltd., 1961-65, pres. Dow Chem. Europe, 1965-75, mem. exec. com. Dow Chem. Co., Midland, Mich., 1971-79, exec. v.p., 1975-76, pres., chief exec. officer, 1976-79, chmn., 1978-79; vice-chmn. Occidental Petroleum Corp., Los Angeles, 1979—. Decorated Grand Cross of Order of Merit (Spain); comdr. Order Oranje Nassau (Netherlands). Clubs: Met.; Midland Country; Canadian (N.Y.C.). Office: Occidental Petroleum Corp 10889 Wilshire Blvd Los Angeles CA 90024

MERTE, HERMAN, JR., educator, mech. engr.; b. Detroit, Apr. 3, 1929; s. Herman and Anna Marie (Mitterer) M.; B.S. in Marine Engring., U. Mich., Ann Arbor, 1950, B.S. in Mech. Engring., 1951, M.S., 1956, Ph.D., 1960; m. Bernice Marie Brant, Sept. 17, 1952; children—Kenneth Edward, James Dennis, Lawrence Carleton, Richard Brant, Robert Paul. Mem. faculty U. Mich., 1959—, prof. mech. engring., 1967—; vis. prof. Tech. U. Munich (Germany), 1974-75. Served to lt. (j.g.) USNR, 1952-55. NSF sr. postdoctoral fellow, 1967-68. Mem. ASME, Am. Soc. Engring. Edn., Am. Assn. U. Profs. Home: 3480 Cottontail Ln Ann Arbor MI 48103

MERTINS, CHRISTA, ballerina; b. Guatemala City, Guatemala, Mar. 17, 1936; d. Heinz and Marie (Hammer) Mertins; student Am. Sch., Ecuador, 1953; m. Peter Spatz, Feb. 5, 1960 (dec. June 1963). Soloist, asst. dir. Guatemalan Ballet, 1956; exchange student scholarship Dept. State to Met. Opera Ballet Sch., N.Y.C., 1957; first dancer Ballet Guatemala, tchr. Nat. Ballet Sch., 1958; soloist Ballet Cuba, 1959; prima ballerina Guatemalan Ballet, dir. Nat. Sch., 1962-64; scholarship Harkness Found., Watch Hill, R.I., summer 1964; leading dancer Les Grands Ballet Canadien, Montreal, Que., 1964—; first appearance as Giselle, Guatemala, spring 1965; first appearance in U.S. as prima ballerina Jacobs Pillow, Mass., 1965; free lance ballerina, dance tchr., 1968—; ballerina Ballet Guatemala; owner, dir. Terpsichore Inst., Guatemala City. Recipient Gold medal of merit Bellas Artes Republic Guatemala, 1963. Address: Terpsichore Inst 11 Calle 10-28 Zone 1 Guatemala City Guatemala

MERTON, ROBERT K., educator, sociologist; b. Phila., July 5, 1910; A.B., Temple U., 1931, LL.D., 1956; M.A., Harvard, 1932, Ph.D., 1936; L.H.D., Emory U., 1965, Loyola U., Chgo., 1970, Kalamazoo Coll., 1970, Cleve. State U., 1977, U. Pa., 1979; Dr. honoris causa, U. Leyden, 1965; LL.D., Western Res. U., 1966, U. Chgo., 1968, Tulane U., 1971; Litt.D., Colgate U., 1967; Dr. Social Sci., Yale, 1968; D.Sc. in Econ., U. Wales, 1968; m. Suzanne Carhart, 1934 (separated); children—Stephanie (Mrs. Thomas A. Tombrello), Robert C., Vanessa H. (Mrs. John K. Carroll). Asst., tutor sociology Harvard, 1934-36, instr., tutor, 1936-39; asso. prof. Tulane U., 1939-40, prof., chmn. dept., 1940-41; asst. prof. Columbia, 1941-44, asso. prof., 1944-47, prof., 1947-63, Giddings prof., 1963-74, univ. prof., 1974-79, Univ. prof. emeritus and spl. service prof., 1979—; asso. dir. Bur. Applied Social Research, 1942-71; adj. prof. Rockefeller U., 1979; adv. editor sociology Harcourt Brace Jovanovich; Gilman lectr. Johns Hopkins, 1962, NIH lectr., 1964, Paley lectr. Cornell Med. Sch., 1975, Trumbull lectr. Yale, 1976, Karl Compton lectr. Washington U., 1976; Fulbright lectr. U. Kyoto, 1967—, Phi Beta Kappa-Sigma Xi lectr. AAAS, 1968; Geary lectr., Dublin, Ireland. Ednl. adv. bd. Guggenheim Found., 1963-79, chmn., 1971-79. Past pres. Community Service Council, Hastings. Trustee Center Advanced Study Behavioral Scis., 1952-75, Temple U., 1964-68, Inst. Sci. Info. Recipient prize distinguished scholarship humanities Am. Council Learned Socs., 1962; Guggenheim fellow, 1962. Fellow Am. (Talcott Parsons award 1979), World acads. arts and scis.; mem. Am. Philos. Soc., Sociol. Research Assn. (pres. 1968), Nat. Acad. Edn., Nat. Acad. Scis., Nat. Inst. Medicine, Am. (pres. 1957), Eastern (pres. 1969) sociol. socs., History Sci. Soc., Soc. Social Studies of Sci. (pres. 1975), Royal Swedish Acad. Scis. (fgn.). Club: Century Assn. (N.Y.C.). Author: Science Technology and Society in 17th Century England, 2d edit., 1978; Mass Persuasion, 2d edit., 1971; Social Theory and Social Structure, rev. edit., 1968; On The Shoulders of Giants, 1965; On Theoretical Sociology, 1967; The Sociology of Science, 1973, 79; Sociological Ambivalence, 1976; Sociology of Science: An Episodic Memoir, 1979; co-author: The Focussed Interview, rev. edit., 1956; Freedom to Read, 1957. Co-editor, co-author: Continuities in Social Research, 1950; Social Policy and Social Research in Housing, 1951; Reader in Bureaucracy, 1952; The Student-Physician, 1957; Sociology Today, 1959; Contemporary Social Problems, 4th edit., 1976; The Sociology of Science in Europe, 1977; Toward a Metric of Science, 1978; Qualitative and Quantitative Social Research: Papers in Honor of Paul F. Lazarsfeld, 1979; Sociological Traditions from Generation to Generation, 1979. Office: Fayerweather Hall Columbia U New York NY 10027

MERTZ, EDGAR THEODORE, food co. exec.; b. Reading, Pa., Sept. 15, 1927; s. Edgar Garfield and Carrie Virginia (Weidenhammer) M.; B.S. in Indsl. Engring., Lehigh U., 1952; M.B.A., N.Y. U., 1954; grad. Advanced Mgmt. Program, Harvard U., 1975; LL.B., LaSalle U., 1976; m. Patricia Schearer, Sept. 12, 1953, children—Howard Randall, Karen Elizabeth. Factory mgmt. with Procter & Gamble Co., 1952-70; asst. to pres. Texize Chems. Co., Greenville, S.C., 1970-73; exec. v.p. H.J. Heinz Co., Pitts., 1973-77; group v.p. Pillsbury Co., Mpls., 1977—. Bd. dirs. Pitts. chpt. Planned Parenthood, 1974-77, Opportunity Indsl. Center, 1975-77; individual gifts chmn. Mpls. United Way, 1979. Served with AUS, 1946-48. Mem. Am. Arbitration Assn. Home: 1820 Fox St Wayzata MN 55391 Office: 608 2d Ave S Minneapolis MN 55402

MERTZ, EDWIN THEODORE, biochemist, educator; b. Missoula, Mont., Dec. 6, 1909; s. Gustav Henry and Louise (Sain) M.; B.A., U. Mont., 1931, M.S. in Biochemistry, 1933, D.Sc. (hon.), 1979; Ph.D. in Biochemistry, U. Ill., 1935; D.Agr. (hon.), Purdue U., 1977; m. Mary Ellen Ruskamp, Oct. 5, 1936; children—Martha Ellen, Edwin T. Research biochemist Armour & Co., Chgo., 1935-37; instr. biochemistry U. Ill., 1937-38; research asso. pathology U. Iowa, 1938-40; instr. agrl. chemistry U. Mo., 1940-43; research chemist Hercules Powder Co., 1943-46; prof. biochemistry Purdue U., West Lafayette, Ind., 1946-76, emeritus, 1976—; vis. prof. U. Notre Dame, South Bend, Ind., 1976-77; cons. in field. Recipient McCoy award Purdue U., 1967; John Scott award City of Phila., 1967; Hoblitzelle Nat. award Tex. Research Found., 1968; Congressional medal Fed. Land Banks, 1968; Distinguished Service award U. Mont., 1973; Browning award Am. Soc. Agronomy, 1974; Pioneer Chemist award Am. Inst. Chemists, 1976. Mem. AAAS, AAUP, Nat. Acad. Scis., Am. Soc. Biol. Chemists, Am. Inst. Nutrition (Osborne-Mendel award 1972), Am. Chem. Soc. (Spencer award 1970), Am. Assn. Cereal Chemists. Presbyterian. Co-discoverer high lysine corn, 1963. Author: Elementary Biochemistry, 1969. Home: 143 Tamiami Trail West Lafayette IN 47906 Office: Dept Biochemistry Purdue U Lafayette IN 47907

MERTZ, GEORGE HENRY, surgeon; b. El Paso, Tex., Feb. 13, 1926; s. Henry William and Linda (deLeon) M.; B.S., U. N.Mex., 1949; M.D., U. Colo., 1953; m. Gisa Marie Neuhaus, Sept. 7, 1947; children—David G., Steven W. Intern, Wayne County Gen. Hosp., Eloise, Mich., 1953-54, resident, 1954-58; individual practice medicine specializing in surgery, Phoenix, 1958-76; chief surgery Dr.'s Hosp., Phoenix, 1956-58, chief staff, 1958-59; chief exec. officer Good Samaritan Hosp., Phoenix, 1976-79; adj. asso. prof. surgery U. Ariz. Coll. Medicine, 1979—; chief surgery VA Med. Center, Phoenix, 1979—; dir. Phoenix Integrated Surg. Residency Program, 1979—; pres. Southwestern Surg. Congress, 1974-75. Served to capt., M.C., USNR. Diplomate Am. Bd. Surgery. Mem. A.C.S., Western Surg. Assn., Pan Pacific Surg. Assn., U. N.Mex. Alumni Assn. (dir. 1968-69), Phi Rho Sigma, Kappa Sigma. Republican. Roman Catholic. Clubs: Phoenix Country, Arizona, Kiva. Contbr. articles to profl. jours. Home: 217 Glenn Dr E Phoenix AZ 85020 Office: VA Med Center 7th St at Indian School Rd Phoenix AZ 85012

MERTZ, STUART MOULTON, landscape architect; b. Wayne, Pa., Dec. 4, 1915; s. Walter Smith and Elizabeth Armenia (Day) M.; B.S. in Landscape Architecture, Pa. State U., 1937; B.Landscape Architecture, Cornell U., 1938; travelling fellow Am. Acad. Rome, 1938-40, fellow, 1940; m. Constance Coulter Buck, June 27, 1942; children—Stuart Moulton, Maurice Walter. With John Noyes, St. Louis, 1940-41; chief designer Harland Bartholomew & Assos., St. Louis, 1941-49; pvt. practice landscape architecture, St. Louis, 1949—; prin. work includes 15 parks and playgrounds for City St. Louis, St. Louis County, St. John's Hosp., St. Luke's Hosp.-West, Visitation Acad., St. Louis County Library Hdqrs. Bldg., Charter Nat. Life Ins. Bldg., Florissant Valley Community Coll., Bettendorf Stores, Meramec Community Coll., Barnwell Art and Garden Center, Shreveport, La.; lectr. nurserymen's short course Tex. A. and M. Coll., landscape architecture Iowa State U., also S.W. Park Tng. Inst., U. Kans., U. Ga., Mich. State U., U. Ill., Kans. State U., Washington U., St. Louis. Pres. People's Art Center Assn., 1960-62, mem. bd., 1959-63; mem. bd. Spirit of St. Louis Fund, 1960-62; advisory council U. Mo. Sch. Forestry, Fisheries and Wildlife, 1974—. Served to 2d lt. USAAF, 1943-45. Fellow Am. Soc. Landscape Architects (chmn. St. Louis 1960-63, trustee Mo. Valley chpt. 1954-60, nat. sec.-treas. 1963-67, nat. 2d v.p. 1967-69; bd. soc. found. 1965-69, 71-75, sec.-treas. 1967-69); mem. Mo. Assn. Landscape Architects (pres. 1966-80), Chi Phi. Presbyn. (trustee 1960-63, 76-78, ruling elder 1971-74). Clubs: Cornell (pres. 1955-56), Engineers (St. Louis); Clayton (Mo.), Penn State. Home: 13 Lindworth Dr Ladue Saint Louis MO 63124 Office: 9430 Manchester Rd Saint Louis MO 63119

MERWIN, CHARLES EDWARD, constrn. co. exec.; b. Kittanning, Pa., May 26, 1923; s. Paul D. and Pearl C. (Mobley) M.; 1941; student Kittanning pub. schs.; m. Helen Lou Booher, Aug. 30, 1941; children—Mary Lee, Charles Edwin, Connie Lynn, Becky Ann. Supt. Darin & Armstrong, Inc., Detroit, 1949-56, gen. supt., 1957-72, v.p., 1972, exec. v.p., 1973, pres., 1974-76, chmn., 1976—, also dir.; dir. Mich. Mutual Ins. Co., Asso. Gen. Ins. Co., Asso. Gen. Life Co. Chmn. United Fund., Detroit, 1976-77. Served with CE U.S. Army, 1943-45. Mem. Assn. Iron and Steel Engrs., Engring. Soc. Detroit. Clubs: Recess, Fairlane, Elks. Office: 23999 Northwestern Hwy Southfield MI 48075

MERWIN, CHARLES LEWIS, economist; b. East Palestine, Ohio, June 30, 1912; s. Charles Lewis and Estella (Meek) M.; B.A. cum laude, Ohio Wesleyan U., 1934; M.A., U. Pa., 1936, Ph.D., 1942; m. Elizabeth Jane Quay, Sept. 6, 1939; 1 son, Grier Humphrey. Instr. Muhlenberg Coll., 1936-37; economist Dept. Commerce, 1938-42, Nat. Bur. Econ. Research, 1938, 40-41, Mission for Econ. Affairs, Am. embassy, London, 1943-46; with IMF, Washington, 1946-77, successively sr. economist, asst. chief balance of payments div., chief Western European div., 1946-55, asst. dir. European dept., 1955-64, dep. dir. African dept., 1964-77; adj. prof. Am. U., 1977—; professorial lectr. Am. U., 1947-53. Mem. ECA Mission to France, 1948. Mem. Am. Econ. Assn., Royal Econ. Soc., Phi Beta Kappa. Methodist. Club: Cosmos (Washington). Author: Financing Small Corporations in Five Manufacturing Industries, 1942. Home: 4113 49th St NW Washington DC 20016

MERWIN, DAVIS UNDERWOOD, newspaper exec.; b. Chgo., June 22, 1928; s. Davis and Josephine (Underwood) M.; A.B., Harvard U., 1950; m. Nancy Snowden Smith Tailer, Nov. 14, 1958; children—Davis Fell, Laura Howell, James B. Tailer. Pres. Evergreen Communications, Inc., Bloomington, Ill., 1950—; pub. Daily Pantagraph; v.p., dir. WJBC Communications Conf., 1230 Communications Corp., dir. Newspaper Advt. Bur., Wood Canyon Corp., Tucson, State Farm Mut. Funds, Corn Belt Bank, Radio Stas. WJBC, WBNQ, WGOW, WSKZ; dir. adv. bd. UPI. Pres., Bloomington-Normal YMCA, 1959-64, chmn. Capital Fund Drive, 1968; bd. dirs. Daily Pantagraph Found.; pres. United Fund, United Community Funds and Councils Am.; bd. dirs., mem. exec. com. Adlai E. Stevenson Lectures; trustee, mem. exec. com. Ill. Wesleyan U.; pres., trustee Inland Daily Press Found.; pres. Bloomington Unltd. Served to capt. USMCR, 1950-53. Recipient Distinguished Service award U.S. Jr. C. of C., 1959. Mem. Am. Newspaper Pubs. Assn. (mem. newsprint com., chmn. subcom. quality and test standards), Internat. Press Assn., Ill. Daily Newspaper Markets (pres. 1967-69), Inland Daily Press Assn. (pres. 1977, chmn. bd. 1978), So. Newspaper Pubs. Assn. Republican. Unitarian. Rotarian. Clubs: Harvard (Chgo.); Phoenix-SK; Hasty Pudding, Bloomington Country. Home: Hopewell Rural Route 1 Bloomington IL 61701 Office: 301 W Washington St Bloomington IL 61701

MERWIN, JACK CLIFFORD, educator; b. Woodstock, Ill., July 9, 1925; s. Clifford Laverne and Helen Margaret (Boyce) M.; B.S., U. Ill., 1949, M.S., 1950, Ed.D., 1955; m. Betty Lou Dunning, Feb. 25, 1945; children—Margaret (Mrs. Charles Reich), Darcy (Mrs. David M. Ross). Tchr. math. Moline (Ill.) Pub. Schs., 1949-52; asst. to asso. prof. edn. Syracuse (N.Y.), U., 1955-60; staff dir. Nat. Assessment of Ednl. Progress, 1965-67; asso. to full prof. edn. U. Minn., Mpls., 1960—, dean, prof. Coll. Edn., 1970-76. Mem. bd. Midwest Univs. Consortium on Internat. Activities, 1972-76. Served with A.C., AUS, 1943-45. Fellow Am. Psychol. Assn.; mem. Am. Ednl. Research Assn. (v.p. 1967-69), Nat. Council on Measurement in Edn. (pres. 1971-72), Nat. Soc. Study Edn., Phi Delta Kappa. Author: (with others) Counseling and the Use of Tests, 1962; Stanford Achievement Tests, 1965, 73. Home: 3419 Glenarden Rd St Paul MN 55112 Office: Coll Edn U Minn Minneapolis MN 55455

MERWIN, JOHN DAVID, lawyer, former gov. V.I.; b. Frederiksted, St. Croix, V.I., Sept. 26, 1921; s. Miles and Marguerite Louise (Fleming) M.; student U. Lausanne (Switzerland), 1938-39, U. P.R., 1939-40; B.Sc., Yale, 1943; LL.B., George Washington U., 1948; m. Ludmila D. Childs, Nov. 8, 1958. Admitted to Conn. bar, V.I. bar, 1949; practice law, St. Croix, V.I., 1949-50, 1953-57, 67—; gen. counsel, v.p. Robert L. Merwin & Co., Inc., 1953-57; senator-at-large V.I. Legislature, 1955-57; govt. sec. for V.I., 1957-58; gov. V.I., 1958-61; rep. Chase Manhattan Bank, Nassau, Bahamas, 1961-65; exec. v.p. Equity Pub. Corp. Orford, N.H., 1965-67. Chmn., V.I. Port Authority, 1972-75. Served from 2d lt. to capt. F.A., AUS, 1942-46, 50-53. Decorated Bronze Star; Croix de Guerre with silver star. Mem. Internat., Conn., N.H., V.I. bar assns., Phi Delta Phi. Clubs: St. Croix (V.I.) Country; Yale (N.Y.C.). Home: PO Box 216 Frederiksted St Croix VI 00840 Office: PO Box 216 Frederiksted St Croix VI 00840

MERWIN, WILLIAM STANLEY, poet; b. N.Y.C., Sept. 30, 1927; A.B., Princeton, 1947. Tutor in France and Portugal, 1949, to Robert Graves' son, Majorca, 1950; translator, London, Eng., 1951-54; playwright for Poets' Theater, Cambridge, Mass., from 1956; asso. Theatre de la Cite, Lyons, France, 1964-65. Kenyon Review fellow in poetry, 1954; Rockefeller fellow, 1956; Nat. Inst. Arts and Letters grantee, 1957; Arts Council Gt. Britain bursary, 1957; Rabinowitz Found. grantee, 1961; Ford Found. grantee, 1964-65; Chapelbrook Found. fellow, 1966. Author: A Mask for Janus (poems), 1952; The Dancing Bears (poems), 1954; Green With Beasts (poems), 1956; (with Dido Milroy) Darkling Child (play), 1956; Favor Island (play), 1957; The Drunk in the Furnace (poems), 1960; The Gilded West (play), 1961; The Moving Target (poems), 1963; The Lice (poems), 1967; (poems) The Carrier of Ladders (Pulitzer prize 1971), 1970; The Miner's Pale Children: A Book of Prose, 1970; Writings to an Unfinished Accompaniment, 1973; The Compass Flower (poems), 1977; Houses and Travellers, 1977. Mem. Nat. Inst. Arts and Letters. Editor: West Wind: Supplement of American Poetry, 1961; poetry editor The Nation, 1962. Translator numerous Spanish, French works. Contbr. articles to lit. mags. Address: care Atheneum Publishers 122 E 42d St New York NY 10017*

MERZBACHER, EUGEN, physicist, educator; b. Berlin, Germany, Apr. 9, 1921; s. Siegfried and Lilli (Wilmersdoerffer) M.; licentiate U. Istanbul, 1943; A.M., Harvard, 1948, Ph.D., 1950; m. Ann Townsend Reid, July 11, 1952; children—Celia Irene, Charles Reid, Matthew Allen, Mary Letitia. Came to U.S., 1947, naturalized, 1953. High sch. tchr., Ankara, Turkey, 1943-47; mem. Inst. Advanced Study, Princeton, N.J., 1950-51; vis. asst. prof. Duke, 1951-52; mem. faculty U. N.C., Chapel Hill, 1952—, prof., 1961—, acting chmn. physics dept., 1965-67, 71-72, Kenan prof. physics, 1969—, chmn. dept., 1977—; vis. prof. U. Wash., 1967-68. NSF Sci. Faculty fellow U. Copenhagen (Denmark), 1959-60; recipient Thomas Jefferson award U. N.C., 1972; Humboldt sr. scientist award U. Frankfurt (Germany), 1976-77. Fellow Am. Phys. Soc. (chmn. Southeastern sect. 1971-72; mem.-at-large council 1972-76, chmn. div. electron and atomic physics 1978-79); mem. Am. Assn. Physics Tchrs., AAAS, AAUP, Sigma Xi. Author: Quantum Mechanics, 2d edit, 1970; also articles. Editorial bd. Am. Jour. Physics, 1965-70, Atomic Data and Nuclear Data Tables, 1970—. Research on applications of quantum mechanics to study atoms and nuclei. Home: 1396 Halifax Rd Chapel Hill NC 27514

MESCHAN, ISADORE, radiologist, educator; b. Cleve., May 30, 1914; s. Julius and Anna (Gordon) M.; B.A., Western Res. U., 1935, M.A., 1937, M.D., 1939; m. Rachel Farrer, Sept. 3, 1943; children—David, Eleanor Jane, Rosalind, Joyce. Instr. Western Res. U., 1946-47; prof., head dept. radiology U. Ark., Little Rock, 1947-55; prof., dir. dept. radiology Bowman Gray Sch. Medicine, Wake Forest U., Winston-Salem, N.C., 1955-77. Fellow mem. Am. Coll. Radiology (com. chmn., Gold medal 1978); mem. Am. Roentgen Ray Soc., AMA, Radiology Soc. N.Am., N.C. Radiol. Soc., So. Med. Assn., Soc. Nuclear Medicine, Assn. U. Radiologists, Sigma Xi, Alpha Omega Alpha. Author: Atlas of Normal Radiographic Anatomy, 1951; Roentgen Signs in Clinical Diagnosis, 1956; (with R. Meschan) Synopsis of Roentgen Signs, 1962; Roentgen Signs in Clinical Practice, 1966; Radiographic Positioning Related Anatomy, 1969, 2d edit., 1978; Analysis of Roentgen Signs, 3 vols., 1972; Atlas of Anatomy Basic to Radiology, 1975; Synopsis of Analysis of Roentgen Signs, 1976; Synopsis of Radiographic Anatomy, 1978. Editor: The Radiologic Clinics of North America, 1965. Contbr. articles to profl. jours. Home: 2716 Bartram Rd Winston-Salem NC 27106

MESCON, HERBERT, physician, educator; b. Toronto, Ont., Can., Apr. 3, 1919 (parents Am. citizens); s. Morris and Bella (Paleschuck) M.; B.S., Coll. City N.Y., 1938; M.D., Boston U., 1942; m. Barbara Jeanne McKenzie, Sept. 15, 1946; children—Susan Lee, Gary Lawrence, Robin Lenore, Stanley Richard. Resident pathology Mallory Inst. Pathology, Boston City Hosp., 1942-43, med. intern Tufts U. med. service, 1947-48; rotating intern Lebanon Hosp., Bronx, N.Y., 1946-47; fellow dept. dermatology Hosp. U. Pa., 1948-51, Damon Runyon cancer research fellow, 1949-51; asst. instr. dermatology U. Pa. Med. Sch., 1948-50, instr., 1950-51, asso., 1951-52, instr. dermatology Grad. Sch. Medicine, 1952; attending physician VA Hosp., Wilmington, Del., 1950-51, cons., 1951-52; cons. Skin and Cancer Hosp., Phila., 1951-52; prof. Boston U. Sch. Medicine, 1952—, also head dept. dermatology, 1952—; dir. genito-infectious diseases clinic of Univ. Hosps., 1958-74, asst. mem. Robert Dawson Evans Meml. dept. clin. research and preventive medicine, 1952, asso. mem., 1954-60, mem., 1960—; dir. dermatology Boston City Hosp., 1974—; cons. dermato-pathology and dermatology VA Hosp., Boston, 1955—, area VA 1960-66; sr. cons. dermatology Lemuel Shattuck Hosp., Boston, 1955—. Served to lt. col. M.C., AUS, 1943-46. Diplomate Am. Bd. Dermatology and Syphilology, Am. Bd. Skin Pathology. Mem. Am. Assn. Paththologists and Bacteriologists. Soc. Investigative Dermatology (pres.), Boston (pres.), New Eng. (pres.) dermatol. socs., Am. Acad. Dermatology and Syphilology (dir. 1972-74, v.p., 1974), AMA, Histochem. Soc., Am. Dermatol. Assn. Home: 155 Lake Ave Newton MA 02158 Office: 80 E Concord St Boston MA 02109

MESELSON, MATTHEW STANLEY, educator, biochemist; b. Denver, May 24, 1930; s. Hymen Avram and Ann (Swedlow) M.; Ph.B., U. Chgo., 1951, D.Sc. (hon.), 1975; Ph.D., Calif. Inst. Tech., 1957; Sc.D. (hon.), Oakland Coll., 1964, Columbia, 1971; m. Sarah Page; children—Zoe, Amy Valor. From research fellow to sr. research fellow Calif. Inst. Tech., 1957-60; mem. faculty Harvard, 1960—, prof. biology, 1964—. Recipient prize for molecular biology Nat. Acad. Scis., 1963, Eli Lilly award microbiology and immunology, 1964, Alumni medal U. Chgo., 1971; Pub. Service award Fedn. Am. Scientists, 1972; Lehman award N.Y. Acad. Scis., 1975; Alumni Distinguished Service award Calif. Inst. Tech., 1975; Leo Szilard award Am. Phys. Soc., 1978. Mem. Am. Acad. Arts and Scis., Council Fgn. Relations, Accademia Santa Chiara, Nat. Acad. Scis., Inst. Medicine. Address: Biol Labs Harvard U Cambridge MA 02138

MESERVE, ROBERT WILLIAM, lawyer; b. Chelsea, Mass., Jan. 12, 1909; s. George Harris and Florence Elizabeth (Small) M.; A.B., Tufts Coll., 1931; LL.B., Harvard, 1934; LL.D., Villanova U., 1972, Drury Coll., 1972, Suffolk U., 1972, St. Michael's Coll., 1972, Wm. Mitchell Law Sch., 1977, Tufts U., 1979; m. Gladys E. Swenson, Oct. 17, 1936; children—Roberta Ann (Mrs. Gordon Weil), William George, Richard Andrew, John Eric, Jeanne-Marthe. Admitted to Mass. bar, 1934; asst. U.S. atty., Boston, 1936-41; lectr. Boston Coll. Law Sch., 1938-40, Harvard Law Sch., 1957-61; asso., then partner firm Nutter, McClennen & Fish, Boston, 1934-36, 41-43, 46-73; partner firm Newman & Meserve, 1973-78, Palmer & Dodge, 1978—; Mem. Mass. Bd. Bar Examiners, 1961-71, sec., 1964-71; chmn. Mass. Bd. Bar Overseers, 1974-77. Mem. sch. com., Medford, Mass., 1936-40, chmn., 1940. Mem. bd. aldermen, Medford, 1941-43. Trustee Tufts Coll., 1955—, chmn., 1965-70. Served to lt. (s.g.) USNR, 1943-46. Mem. Am. (past chmn. standing com. fed. Judiciary, pres. 1972-73), Mass., Boston (past pres.) bar assns., Am. Bar Found. (pres. 1978—), Am. Acad. Arts and Sci., Am. Coll. Trial Lawyers (regent, pres. 1968-69), Phi Beta Kappa. Democrat. Unitarian. Editor: Harvard Law Rev., 1933-34. Home: 109 Worcester Lane Waltham MA 02154 Office: 1 Beacon St Boston MA 02108

MESHII, MASAHIRO, metall. engr.; b. Amagasaki, Hyogo, Japan, Oct. 6, 1931; s. Masataro and Kazuyo M.; came to U.S., 1956, naturalized, 1976; B.S., Osaka U., 1954, M.S., 1956; Ph.D. (Fulbright grantee 1956, Japan Soc. fellow 1958), Northwestern U., 1959; m. Eiko Kumagai, May 21, 1959; children—Alisa, Erica. Lectr. dept. materials sci. and engring. Northwestern U., 1959-60. asst. prof., 1960-64, asso. prof., 1964-67, prof., 1967—, dept. chmn., 1978—; vis. scientist Nat. Research Inst. for Metals, Japan, 1970-71; vis. prof. Osaka U., 1971. Mem. AIME, Am. Soc. Metals (Henry Marion Howe medal 1968), Am. Phys. Soc., Electron Microscope Soc. Am., Am. Soc. Engring. Edn., Phys. Soc. Japan, Japan Inst. Metals (Kosekisho 1972), Sigma Xi, Alpha Sigma Mu, Tau Beta Pi. Editor: Lattice Defects in Quenched Metals, 1965; Martensitic Transformation, 1978; Fatigue and Microstructure, 1979. Contbr. articles to tech. jours. Home: 3051 Centennial Ln Highland Park IL 60035 Office: Northwestern U Dept Materials Sci and Engring Evanston IL 60201

MESIROV, LEON I., lawyer; b. Phila., Jan. 19, 1912; s. Isaac and Zippa (Robbins) M.; A.B., U. Pa., 1931, LL.B., 1934; m. Sylvia W. Portner, June 25, 1935; children—Joan C. (Mrs. Thomas Rondell), Judy Lynn (Mrs. Hans B. Greenberg), Jill P. (Mrs. Jerry L. Kazdan). Admitted to Pa. bar, 1934, since practiced in Phila.; partner firm Mesirov, Gelman, Jaffe, Cramer & Jamieson, 1960—. Dir. Steel Heddle Mfg. Co., H. Freeman & Son, Inc. Commnr., Phila. Civil Service, 1952-70; pres. Jewish Community Relations Council, 1952-55, hon. pres., 1955—; commnr. Phila. Fellowship Commn., 1952—, counsel, 1959—; sec. Jewish Y's and Centers, 1967-71. Trustee Fedn. Jewish Agencies, 1960-71, Com. of Seventy, 1972—. Mem. Am., Pa., Phila. bar assns., Am. Judicature Soc., Order of Coif, Beta Sigma Rho. Jewish. Clubs: Racquet, Peale (Phila.). Home: 2131 St James Pl Philadelphia PA 19103 Office: Fidelity Bldg Philadelphia PA 19109

MESKILL, THOMAS J., judge; b. New Britain, Conn., Jan. 30, 1928; s. Thomas J. Meskill; B.S., Trinity Coll., Hartford, Conn., 1950, LL.D., 1972; J.D., U. Conn., 1956; postgrad. Sch. Law, N.Y.U.; LL.D., U. Bridgeport, 1971, U. New Haven, 1974; m. Mary T. Grady; children—Maureen Meskill Heneghan, John, Peter, Eileen, Thomas. Admitted to Conn., Fla., Fed. bars, also U.S. Supreme Ct. bar; former mem. firm Meskill, Dorsey, Sledzik and Walsh, New Britain; mem. 90th-91st Congresses 6th Conn. Dist.; gov. Conn., 1971-75; judge U.S. Circuit Ct., 1975—. Pres. New Britain Council Social Agys. Asst. corp. council City of New Britain, 1960-62, mayor, 1962-64, corp. counsel, 1965-67; mem. Constl. Conv., Hartford, 1965. Served to 1st lt. USAF, 1950-53. Recipient Distinguished Service award Jr. C. of C., 1964. Mem. Conn., Hartford County, Fla., New Britain bar assns., New Britain Jr. C. of C. (pres.). Republican. Clubs: K.C., Elks. Home: 84 Randeckers Ln Kensington CT 06037

MESKILL, VICTOR PETER, coll. pres.; b. Albertson, N.Y., May 9, 1935; s. James Joseph and Ida May (Pfalzer) M.; B.A., Hofstra U., 1961, M.A. (grad. scholar), 1962; Ph.D., St. John's U., 1967; postgrad. insts. Ohio State U., 1968, Harvard U., 1972, N.Y. U., 1973; m. Lynn Drewe Walsh, Aug. 16, 1975; children—Susan Ann, Janet Louise, Gary James, Glenn Thomas, Kenneth John. Lab. asst., instr. biology Hofstra U., 1960-62; N.Y. State teaching fellow St. John's U., 1962-63; instr. biology Nassau (N.Y.) Community Coll., 1963-64; tchr. sci. Central High Sch. Dist. 2, Floral Park, N.Y., 1963-64; lectr. biology C.W. Post Coll., Greenvale, N.Y., 1963-64, instr. biology, 1964-67, asst. prof., 1967-68, asso. prof., 1968-74, asso. dir. Inst. for Student Problems, supr. student tchrs., 1967-68, asst. dean Coll., dean summer sch., coordinator Admissions Office, coordinator adult and continuing edn. programs, 1968-69; dean adminstrn. C.W. Post Center of L.I. U., 1969-70, v.p. adminstrn., 1970-77, prof. biology, 1975-77; pres. Dowling Coll., Oakdale, L.I., 1977—; cons. in edn. and biology. Bot. field worker Asplundh Tree Expert Co., 1954-58; chem. technician, detective Tech. Research Bur., Nassau County Police Dept., 1958-63, mem. sci. advisory com., 1970; mem. adv. council Aerospace Edn. Council Inc. N.Y., 1968; mem. evaluation teams Middle States Assn., 1971—; mem. legis. com. Commn. on Ind. Colls. and Univs.; founding mem., vice chmn. bd. trustees Nassau Higher Edn. Consortium; chmn. bd. trustees L.I. Regional Adv. Council Higher Edn.; trustee L.I. Mid Suffolk Businessmen's Action; bd. dirs. L.I. Forum for Tech. NSF Research grantee, 1967-69. Named Tchr. of Year, Aesculapius Med. Arts Soc., C.W. Post Coll. of L.I. U., 1967; Distinguished Faculty Mem. of Year, C.W. Post Center L.I. U., 1977; George M. Estabrook award Hofstra U., 1978. Mem. AAAS, Council Advancement and Support of Edn., Am. Assn. Collegiate Registrars and Admissions Officers, Am. Assn. Higher Edn., Am. Inst. Biol. Scis., Am. Soc. Zoologists, Am. Assn. Univ. Adminstrs. Nat. Assn. Biology Tchrs., Nat. Sci. Tchrs. Assn., Soc. Protozoologists, N.Y. Acad. Scis., Met. Assn. Coll. and Univ. Biologists (founder, mem. steering com.), Oakdale C. of C. (founding mem., dir.), Sigma Xi. Beta Beta Beta. Author book; contbr. articles to profl. jours. Home: 178 Connetquot Dr Oakdale NY 11769 Office: Dowling Coll Office of Pres Oakdale NY 11769

MESKIN, LAWRENCE HENRY, educator, dentist; b. Detroit, July 21, 1935; s. Monte J. and Susan (Hayman) M.; student U. Mich., 1953-57; D.D.S., U. Detroit, 1961; M.S.D., U. Minn., 1963, M.P.H., 1964, Ph.D., 1966; m. Estelle Ring, Aug. 23, 1959; children—Scott, Sarah. Hill research prof. delivery of dental health services U. Minn. Sch. Dentistry, 1970—, prof., chmn. div. health ecology, 1966—, prof., dir. dental health program, 1967—; lectr. pediatrics U. Minn. Sch. Medicine; epidemiol. cons. Cleft Palate Clinic, U. Ill. WHO traveling fellow, 1968; recipient award of spl. merit Am. Assn. Orthodontists, 1970. Mem. Am. Dental Assn., Am. Pub. Health Assn., Am. Acad. Oral Pathology, Internat. Assn. Dental Research, Internat. Soc. Cranial Facial Biology, Omicron Kappa Upsilon. Contbr. articles to profl. jours. Home: 4724 Gaywood Dr Minnetonka MN 55343 Office: U Minn Minneapolis MN 55455

MESLER, RUSSELL BERNARD, chem. engr.; b. Kansas City, Mo., Aug. 24, 1927; s. James Elmer and Catherine Lena (Knaack) M.; B.S., U. Kans., 1949; M.S., U. Mich., 1953, Ph.D., 1955; m. Jenny-Lea Elizabeth McGowan, June 9, 1951; children—Diane Lee, Scott Owen, Douglas Bernard, Sandra Jennings. Process engr. Colgate Palmolive Co., Kansas City, Kans., 1949-51; project engr. Ford Nuclear Reactor Co., Ann Arbor, Mich., 1955-57; asst. prof. chem. engring. U. Mich., Ann Arbor, 1955-57; prof. chem. engring. U. Kans., Lawrence, 1961—, Warren S. Bellows prof., 1970—; mem. generating bd. Berkeley (Eng.) Nuclear Labs., 1975-76. Served with USNR, 1945-46. Danforth asso., 1965-69. Fellow Am. Inst. Chem. Engrs.; mem. ASME (Robert T. Knapp award 1967), Am. Chem. Soc., Am. Nuclear Soc., Am. Soc. Engring. Edn., Sigma Xi. Lutheran. Contbr. articles to profl. jours. Home: 1629 Dudley Ct Lawrence KS 66044 Office: 102 Nuclear Reactor Center Lawrence KS 66045

MESROBIAN, ARPENA SACHAKLIAN, publisher, editor; b. Boston, Nov. 11; d. Aaron Harry and Eliza (Der Melkonian) Sachaklian; student Armenian Coll. of Beirut (Lebanon), 1937-38; A.A., Univ. Coll., Syracuse (N.Y.) U., 1959, B.A. magna cum laude, 1971; m. William John Mesrobian, June 22, 1940; children—William Stephen, Marian Elizabeth (Mrs. Bruce MacCurdy). Editor, Syracuse U. Press, 1955-58, exec. editor, 1958-61, asst. dir., 1961-65, acting dir., 1965-66, editor, 1968—, asso. dir., 1968-75, dir., 1975—. Pres. Syracuse chpt. Armenian Relief Soc., 1972-74; sponsor Armenian Assembly, Washington, 1975. Mem. Women in Communications, Soc. Armenian Studies (adminstrv. council 1976-78, sec. 1978), Syracuse U. Library Assos., Am. Univ. Press Services (dir. 1976-77), Armenian Lit. Soc., Sierra Club, Armenian Community Center, Assn. Am. Univ. Presses (v.p. 1976-77), Phi Kappa Phi, Alpha Sigma Lambda. Mem. Armenian Apostolic Ch. (trustee). Club: Zonta of Syracuse (pres. 1979-80). Book rev. editor Armenian Rev., 1967-75; publs. bd. Courier, 1970—. Contbr. numerous articles, revs. to profl. jours. Home: 4851 Pembridge Circle Syracuse NY 13215 Office: 1011 E Water St Syracuse NY 13210

MESSAC, MAGALI ERNESTINE JOSEPHINE, ballerina; b. Toulon, France, Nov. 10, 1951; came to U.S., 1978; d. Robert Leopold Joseph and Georgette Marie Simone (D'Esmenard) M.; grad. Taneeff Ballet Sch., Toulon, 1968; m. Lars G.O. Söderström, July 29, 1978. Apprentice, Hamburg (W. Ger.) State Opera Ballet, 1969-70, from group dancer to prin. dancer, 1970-78; prin. dancer Phila. Ballet, Phila., 1978—; tours throughout Europe, U.S. and Israel. Recipient Oberdörfer Culture award City of Hamburg, 1971. Office: Pennsylvania Ballet 2333 Fairmount Ave Philadelphia PA 19130

MESSEMER, GEORGE J., banker; b. N.Y.C., Feb. 3, 1901; s. Paul John and Anna (Miller) M.; student pub. schs., N.Y.C.; m. Alberta Genova, Oct. 11, 1927; children—Dolores (Mrs. Oswald Lenhard), George Anthony. With Irving Trust Co., N.Y.C., 1918-66, asst. sec., 1937-44, asst. v.p., 1944-57, v.p., 1957-66; founder, dir. Chinese Am. Bank, N.Y.C., 1967—; adv. com. Export-Import Bank, Washington, 1959-61; pres., dir. Patchogue Properties Inc., East Patchogue, N.Y., 1967—. Mem. Com. on Internat. Banking N.Y. (chmn. 1942-44), Bankers Assn. Fgn. Trade (pres. 1959-60). Home: 12 S William St East Patchogue NY 11772

MESSENKOPF, EUGENE JOHN, investment co. exec.; b. N.Y.C., Jan. 26, 1928; s. John Philip and Helen Bessie (Holden) M.; B.B.A., Iona Coll., 1950; M.B.A., N.Y. U., 1956; m. Martha Ann Crane, Jan. 29, 1955; children—Diane, Nancy, Eugene John, Susan. Sec.-treas. KLM Process Co., N.Y.C., 1952-54; accountant Am. Tobacco Co., N.Y.C., 1954-56; sr. accountant Peat, Marwick & Mitchell, N.Y.C., 1956-60; exec. v.p. Donaldson, Lufkin & Jenrette, Inc., N.Y.C., 1960-77, pres., chief exec. officer real estate div., 1977—; pres., chief exec. officer Meridian Investing and Devel. Corp., 1977—. Chmn. Wall St. Tax Com., 1969-70. Served as sgt. AUS, 1950-52: Korea. Decorated Combat Infantryman's badge. C.P.A., N.Y. Mem. Assn. Stock Exchange Firms (bd. govs. accounting div. 1965-79). Club: Bonnie Briar Country (bd. govs. 1971-73) (Larchmont, N.Y.). Home: 54 Park Rd Scarsdale NY 10583 Office: 140 Broadway New York NY 10005

MESSERLI, JONATHAN CARL, univ. pres.; b. Albany, Oreg., Feb. 14, 1926; s. Henry Conrad and Lilly (Rietz) M.; B.S., Concordia Tchrs. Coll., River Forest, Ill., 1947; M.A., Washington U., St. Louis, 1952; Ph.D., Harvard U., 1963; m. Vi L. Rabey, Aug. 15, 1948; children—Timothy, Martha, Hannah. Coppersmith, Williamette Iron & Steel Co., Portland, Oreg., 1941-44; biology tchr. Lutheran High

Sch., St. Louis, 1947-52; gen. sci. tchr. St. Louis Country Day Sch., 1952-57; asst. prof. history and edn. U. Wash., 1963-64; asst. prof., asso. prof. history and edn. Tchrs. Coll., Columbia U., 1964-68; dean Sch. Edn., Hofstra U., Hempstead, N.Y., 1968-73, Fordham U., N.Y.C., 1973-77; pres. Susquehanna U., Selinsgrove, Pa., 1977—; mem. faculty Sarah Lawrence Coll., spring 1967, Yale U., summer 1967, N.Y. U., summer 1970, U. Hawaii, summer 1968; coordinator Internat. Tchr. Devel. Program, Harvard U.; fellow Hudson Inst., 1975—; mem. advisory com. on tchr. edn. N.Y. State Regents, 1975-77. Mem. Am. Assn. Colls. Tchr. Edn. (pres. N.Y. State chpt. 1972-73), Susquehanna Valley C. of C. (dir. 1977—), Kappa Delta Pi, Phi Delta Kappa. Author: Horace Mann, A Biography, 1973; editorial bd. Harvard Ednl. Rev., 1958-61, editorial chmn., 1960-61; editorial bd. N.Y. U. Edn. Quar., 1975-77; contbr. articles to profl. jours., books. Home: RD 1 Liverpool PA 17045 Office: Susquehanna U Selinsgrove PA 17870

MESSERSMITH, JOHN ALEXANDER, baseball player; b. Toms River, N.J., Aug. 6, 1945; ed. U. Calif. at Berkeley. With Calif. Angels, 1968-73, Los Angeles Dodgers, 1973-76, 79—, Atlanta Braves, 1976-79.*

MESSICK, DALE, cartoonist; b. South Bend, Ind., 1906; d. Cephas and Bertha M.; student Art Inst. Chgo.; m. Oscar Strom; 1 dau. by previous marriage, Starr. Designer greeting cards, Chgo. firm; creator comic strip Brenda Starr, Reporter, appearing Sunday newspapers Chgo. Tribune-N.Y. News Syndicate, 1940—, daily feature, 1945—. Office: Chgo Tribune-NY News Syndicate 220 42d St New York NY 10017*

MESSING, FREDERICK ANDREW, JR., bus. lobbyist; b. N.Y.C., Sept. 29, 1946; s. Frederick Andrew and Anne M.; B.S., U. Md., 1972; m. Susanne Marie Christian, Nov. 28, 1970; children—Camilla Beth, Frederick Andrew III. Commd. 2d lt. U.S. Army Res., 1967, advanced through grades to maj., 1979; inf. platoon leader 1st Air CAV, RVN, 1967; spl. forces officer, 1969-74; Congl. liaison for Army as G-13, 1974 77, resigned, 1977; exec. dir. Am. Conservative Union, Washington, 1977-79; pres. Nat. Def. Council, Washington, 1979—; cons. Am. Security Council. Decorated Meritorious Service medal, Sr. Airborne badge, Combat Inf. badge, Can. Airborne badge, Air medal, German Airborne badge, Purple Heart with oak leaf cluster, Vietnamese Cross of Gallantry; recipient Leadership award Am. Conservative Union, 1979. Mem. Res. Officers Assn. Home: 1008 Croton Dr Alexandria VA 22309 Office: Nat Def Council Capitol Hill Box 1807 Washington DC 20013

MESSING, GORDON MYRON, educator; b. Toledo, Mar. 4, 1917; s. Samuel Meyer and Selma (Silberberg) M.; A.B., Harvard, 1938, A.M., 1940, Ph.D., 1942; m. Florence Evelyn Hope, Mar. 16, 1946; children—Hope Candida (Robbins), Faith Erica (Winters), Daniel Peregrine, Seth Jeremy. Asst. prof. classics, chmn. dept. comparative philology U. Wis.-Madison, 1946-47; mem. diplomatic staff State Dept., various internat. locations, 1947-65, attache Am. embassy, Athens, Greece, 1955-60, attache, polit. officer Am. embassy, Reykjavik, Iceland, 1962-65; asso. prof. classics Cornell U., N.Y., 1967-71, prof. classics and linguistics, 1971—. Served with AUS, 1942-46; ETO. Decorated Bronze Star. Nat. Endowment Humanities sr. fellow, 1973-74. Mem. Linguistic Soc. Am., Am. Philol. Assn. Editor: Smyth's Greek Grammar, 1956. Contbr. articles to profl. jours. Home: 135 Graham Rd Ithaca NY 14850

MESSINGER, SHELDON L(EOPOLD), educator; b. Chgo., Aug. 26, 1925; s. Leopold J. and Cornelia (Eichel) M.; Ph.D. in Sociology, U. Calif. at Los Angeles, 1969; m. Mildred Handler, June 30, 1947; children—Adam J., Eli B. Asso. research sociologist Center Study Law and Soc., U. Calif. at Berkeley, 1961-69, research sociologist, 1969-70, vice chmn., 1961-69, prof. criminology, 1970-77, acting dean criminology, 1970-71, dean criminology, 1971-75, prof. law (jurisprudence and social policy program), 1977—. Author, co-author numerous books, articles. Home: 860 Indian Rock Ave Berkeley CA 94707

MESSINGER, WILLIAM CLIFFORD, mfg. co. exec.; b. Milw., Jan. 22, 1915; s. Charles Raymond and Mildred (Hart) M.; B.S., Yale U., 1939; m. Mary Douglass, June 24, 1940; children—Anne Messinger Hazelwood, William Frye, Joseph Douglass, Mary Catherine, Robert Hart. Apprentice Sivyer Steel Casting Co., 1939-42; prodn. clk. Rexnord Inc., Milw., 1942-43, prodn. mgr., 1943-46, supt. plant, mgr. factory, 1946-52, mgr. sales constrn. machinery sect., 1952-58, v.p. constrn. machinery sect., 1958-62, v.p. research, planning, 1962-63, pres., 1963-67, chmn., 1967—, chmn. exec. com. of bd. dirs.; dir. First Wis. Corp., First Wis. Nat. Bank, Sivyer Steel Corp., Square D Co., Wis. Gas. Co., Sandusky Foundry & Machine Co., Wis. Securities of Delaware; trustee Northwestern Mut. Life Ins. Co. Vice pres. Greater Milw. Com., 1971—; bd. dirs. YMCA, Milw. Found., Columbia Hosp.; pres. Affiliated Hosps. Milw. Mem. Yale Engring. Assn. Clubs: Milw. Country, Milw. Athletic, Milw., Univ. of Milw.; Yale of N.Y.C.; Univ. of Chgo. Home: 1470 E Bay Point Rd Milwaukee WI 53217 Office: 3500 First Wisconsin Center Milwaukee WI 53202

MESSINGER, WILLIAM HENRY, lawyer; b. Fulton, Ind., Sept. 9, 1897; s. Henry and Mary E. (Stingley) M.; A.B., U. Mich., 1921, J.D., 1923; m. Vera M. Felder, Oct. 1, 1923; children—Paul Raymond, Philip William, Mary Joan (Mrs. Chisato Kitagawa). Admitted to Mich. bar, 1923, Ariz. bar, 1943; practice law, Grand Rapids, Mich., 1923-43, Phoenix, 1944—; mem. firm Cunningham, Carson, Messinger & Carson, 1947-56, Cunningham, Carson & Messinger, 1956-62, Carson, Messinger, Elliott, Laughlin & Ragan, 1963—. Mem. Bd. Edn. Scottsdale, Ariz., 1948-54. Mem. Am., Mich., Ariz., Maricopa County, Grand Rapids (pres. 1942) bar assns. Republican. Conglist. Mason (32 deg.). Clubs: Arizona (Phoenix); Kiwanis (pres. Scottsdale 1948). Home: 4033 Miller Rd Scottsdale AZ 85251 Office: United Bank Bldg Phoenix AZ 85012

MESSNER, ROBERT THOMAS, retail co. exec.; b. McKeesport, Pa., Mar. 27, 1938; s. Thomas M. and Cecilia Mary (McElhinny) M.; A.B., Dartmouth Coll., 1960; LL.B., U. Pa., 1963; m. Anne Margaret Lux, Dec. 3, 1966; children—Megan Anne, Michael Thomas. Admitted to Pa. bar, 1965; with firm Rose, Schmidt & Dixon, Pitts., 1965-68; with G.C. Murphy Co., McKeesport, 1968—, sec., 1974—, gen. counsel, 1975—, v.p., 1976—; sec. Mack Realty Co., Spotsylvania Realty Co.; dir. G.C. Murphy Found. Bd. dirs. McKeesport YMCA; adv. bd. Pa. Human Relations Commn., 1968, 69; chmn. Republican registration Allegheny County, Pa., 1967; Rep. candidate for Pa. Legislature, 1966. Served to 1st lt. U.S. Army, 1963-65. Decorated Commendation medal. Mem. Am., Pa., Allegheny County bar assns., Am. Soc. Corp. Secs. (pres. Pitts. regional group), Am. Mgmt. Assn., McKeesport C. of C. (dir.), Theta Delta Chi. Clubs: Dartmouth Western Pa.; University (Pitts.); Nat. Lawyers (Washington). Home: 1061 Blackridge Rd Pittsburgh PA 15235 Office: 531 5th Ave Pittsburgh PA 15132

MESTER, JORGE, orch. condr.; b. Mexico City, Apr. 10, 1935; s. Victor and Margarita (Knöpfler) M.; B.S., Juilliard Sch. Music, 1957, M.S., 1958; studied conducting with Jean Morel, Leonard Bernstein. Came to U.S., 1946, naturalized, 1968. Faculty, Juilliard Sch. Music, 1956-68, also condr. Juilliard Theatre Orch.; mus. dir. Louisville Orch., Greenwich Village Symphony, 1961-62; mus. dir., condr. Louisville Orch., 1967—; artistic adviser Kansas City Philharmonic, 1971-72, music dir., 1973-77; music dir. Aspen Music Festival, 1970—, Festival Casals, 1980; prin. guest condr. St. Paul Chamber Orch., 1978-79; guest condr. Orquesta Sinfonica Nacional de Mexico, Philharmonica Triestina, Spoleto Festival Orch., Japan Philharmonic, Yomiuri Nippon Symphony, Boston Symphony, Pitts. Symphony, New Orleans Philharmonic, Indpls. Symphony, N.Y.C. Opera, Phila. Orch., London Royal Philharmonic, Denver Symphony, Bach Aria Group, Cin. Orch., Rochester Philharmonic, others; condr. dance season Spoleto Festival, Grant Park, Chgo., Tanglewood (Mass.), Harkness Dance Festival, 1964, Cosi Fan Tutte, 1964, L'Elisir D'Amore; rec. with Columbia, Vanguard, Mercury, Desto, CRI, Cambridge records, also Louisville 1st Edit. Recs. Named Ky. col., 1967; recipient Naumburg award, 1968. Office: 333 W Broadway Louisville KY 40202

MESTHENE, EMMANUEL GEORGE, educator, philosopher; b. N.Y.C., Aug. 19, 1920; s. Emmanuel P. and Georgette (Anzolinou) M.; B.S., Columbia, 1948, M.A., 1949, Ph.D. in Philosophy, 1964; m. Ruth Allgeier, Jan. 29, 1944; children—Laura, Donna, James E. Sales engr. Am. Viscose Corp., N.Y.C., 1939-42; lectr. philosophy Columbia, 1948-51, Adelphi Coll., Garden City, N.Y., 1948-51; editor Bantam Books, N.Y.C., 1951-53; research staff mem. Rand Corp., Santa Monica, Calif., 1953-64; dir. program on tech. and soc. Harvard, 1964-73, faculty Bus. Sch., 1964-73; dean Livingston Coll., Rutgers U., New Brunswick, N.J., 1974-77, distinguished prof. philosophy Rutgers U., 1974—. Cons. Office of Spl. Asst. to Pres. on Sci. and Tech., 1960, U.S. Senate subcom. nat. policy machinery, 1961, Sec. Ministerial Meeting on Sci., OECD, 1962-64, NSF, 1967-73, Exec. Office Pres., 1967-69, U.S. Office Edn., 1967-68, Rand Corp., 1964—. Served with AUS, 1942-46. Mem. Am. Philos. Assn., AAAS. Author: How Language Makes Us Know, 1964; Technological Change, 1970. Editor: Ministers Talk About Science, 1965; Technology and Social Change, 1967; also articles. Home: 12 Lafayette St New Brunswick NJ 08901

MESZAR, FRANK, pub. exec., former army officer; b. East Chicago, Ind., Sept. 5, 1915; s. Frank Rach and Julia (Labois) M.; B.S. in Civil Engring., U.S. Mil. Acad., 1940; grad. Army War Coll., 1955; M.B.A., Ga. So. Coll.; m. Carla Ruth Jorgensen, May 21, 1965; children—Frank, Sarah. Commd. 2d lt. U.S. Army, 1940, advanced through grades to brig. gen., 1965; chief aviation affairs Dept. Army, 1959-62; asst. dep. chief staff operations U.S. Army Europe, 1962-65; asst. dep. chief staff Continental Army Command, Ft. Monroe, Va., 1965-67; comdg. gen. Army Flight Tng. Center, Hunter AFB, Ga., 1967-68; asst. comdg. gen. 1st Cav. Div., 1969-70; ret., 1970; v.p. finance U.S. Medicine, Inc., Washington, 1970—; treas. Profl. Lithography, Inc., Washington. Pres. Savannah (Ga.) West Point Soc., 1970-79, Savannah Symphony Soc.; trustee Ga. Infirmary; hon. judge Chatham County, Ga.; vestryman St. John's Episc. Ch. Decorated D.S.M. with oak leaf cluster, Legion of Merit, D.F.C., Silver Star with oak leaf cluster, Bronze Star with 3 oak leaf clusters, Purple Heart with oak leaf cluster; Legion of Honor, Croix de Guerre (France). Club: Oglethorpe. Home: 302 E 46th St Savannah GA 31405 Office: 1601 18th St NW Washington DC 20009

METCALF, ARTHUR GEORGE BRADFORD, corp. exec.; b. Boston, Nov. 1, 1908; s. Franklin B. and Emma A. (Maclachlin) M; student Mass. Inst. Tech., 1932; S.B., Boston U., 1935, LL.D., 1974; S.M., Harvard U., 1939; S.D., Franklin Pierce Coll., 1966; m. Mary G. Curtis, Feb. 22, 1935; children—Anne C., Helen C., Mary Lee, Arthur G.B., Hope S. Engring. test pilot, 1930—; prof. math., physics Boston U., 1935; pres., chmn. bd. Electronics Corp. Am., Cambridge, Mass., 1954—. Cons. engr., research physics, electronics. Chmn. bd. trustees, exec. com. Boston U.; trustee Symmes Hosp.; bd. overseers, visitor research lab. com. Mus. Fine Arts, Boston mem. trustee council Boston U. Med. Center; chmn. U.S. Strategic Inst., Washington; mem. nat. bd. internat. security studies program Fletcher Sch. Law and Diplomacy. Served to lt. col. AUS, World War II. Decorated Legion of Merit, Commendation medal. Benjamin Franklin fellow Royal Soc. Arts London, 1972. Asso. fellow Royal Aero. Soc. (London), Inst. Aero. Scis.; mem. Internat. Inst. Strategic Studies, Am. Def. Preparedness Assn. (dir.), Clubs: Harvard (Boston, N.Y.C.); Algonquin (Boston); Athletic; Edgartown (Mass.) Yacht; Army and Navy (Washington); Wings; Winchester (Mass.) Country; Royal Canadian Yacht (Toronto, Can.). Author articles to profl. jours. Mil. editor: Strategic Rev. Home: 45 Arlington St Winchester MA 01890 Office: 1 Memorial Dr Cambridge MA 02142

METCALF, CHARLES WILLIAM, banking cons.; b. Dennison, Ohio, Dec. 31, 1909; s. George W. and Anne (Rutter) M.; student Cleve. Inst. Tech., 1927, Internat. Accountants Soc., 1935-37, Carnegie Inst. Tech., 1957; m. Louise Kitchen, Oct. 30, 1931; children—Judith, Kathleen Simons, Charles Evan. With Dennison Nat. Bank, 1926-29; with First Nat. Bank, Pitts., 1929-37; examiner Fed. Deposit Ins. Corp., 1937-49; with Equibank N.A., and predecessor, Pitts., 1949-75, ret. as exec. v.p.; v.p. Equimark; banking cons., writer, 1975—. Served with Alien Properties Custodian, World War II. Mem. Bankers Club Pitts. (past pres.), Nat. Assn. Bank Auditors and Comptrollers (past pres. Pitts.), C. of C. Greater Pitts. (past pres., chmn. bd.). Republican. Presbyn. Mason (Shriner). Clubs: Duquesne (Pitts.); Saint Clair Country (Upper St. Clair). Home: 1616 Seegar Rd Upper St Clair PA 15241

METCALF, FREDERIC THOMAS, educator; b. Oak Park, Ill., Dec. 28, 1935; s. Frederic Thomas and Alice (Henderson) M.; B.A., Lake Forest Coll., 1957; M.A., U. Md., 1959, Ph.D., 1961; m. Marilyn Ann Smale, June 22, 1957; children—Karen Ann, Thomas Robert. Engr., Westinghouse Elec. Corp., Balt., 1957-58; mathematician U.S. Naval Ordnance Lab., White Oak, Md., 1960-63; research asst. prof. Inst. for Fluid Dynamics and Applied Math., U. Md., 1963-66; asso. prof. U. Calif., Riverside, 1966-69, prof., 1969—, chmn. dept. math., 1968-70. Bd. govs. Pacific Jour. Math. Mem. AAAS, Am. Math. Soc., Math. Assn. Am., Sigma Xi, Kappa Sigma. Contbr. articles to profl. jours. Home: 5201 Stonewood Dr Riverside CA 92506 Office: Dept Math U Calif Riverside CA 92502

METCALF, FREDERICK THOMAS, cable television exec.; b. Toronto, Ont., Can., Mar. 17, 1921; s. Charles Edward and Mable (Atkinson) M.; student N. Toronto Collegiate Inst., 1935-39; m. Kathleen May Adams, Oct. 3, 1940; children—Diane Kathleen (Mrs. James King), Cheryl Lynne (Mrs. Douglas Seaver), Douglas Frederick, David Edward, Charles Arthur. Pres., dir. Metro Home Theatre Inc., Detroit, Peterborough Cable TV Ltd.; pres., chief operating officer Maclean-Hunter Ltd., Toronto, 1977—; chmn. bd., dir. Suburban Cablevision, N.J.; dir. Clubs: Guelph Country, Guelph Curling; Cutten. Home: Box 78 Puslinch ON N0B 2J0 Canada Office: 481 University Ave Toronto ON Canada

METCALF, JOSEPH, III, naval officer; b. Holyoke, Mass., Dec. 20, 1927; s. Joseph and Alice Folger (Conrad) M.; B.S., U.S. Naval Acad., 1951; B.S., U.S. Naval Postgrad. Sch., 1964; postgrad. U.S. Army War Coll., 1971; m. Ruth Daniels, June 13, 1951; children—Joseph, David, Elizabeth. Commd. ensign, U.S. Navy, 1951, advanced through grades to rear adm., 1977; comdr. Destroyer Squadron 33, 1974-75; comdr. Destroyer Group Mid-Pacific, 1975; asst. chief naval personnel for fin. mgmt. and mgmt. info., 1976-78; dir. total force mgmt. control and analysis div. Office Chief Naval Ops., Washington, 1978-79, comdr. cruiser destroyer group 8, 1979—; v.p. bd. dirs. Navy Fed. Credit Union, Washington. Decorated Bronze Star, Legion of Merit. Episcopalian. Home: 453 Dillingham Blvd Norfolk VA 23511 Office: Navy Dept Washington DC 20370

METCALF, KEYES DEWITT, library cons.; b. Elyria, Ohio, Apr. 13, 1889; s. Isaac Stevens and Harriet (Howes) M.; A.B., Oberlin Coll., 1911, Litt.D., 1939; certificate and diploma Library Sch., N.Y. Pub. Library, 1914; L.H.D., Yale, 1946; LL.D., Harvard, 1951, Toronto, 1954, Marquette U., Milw., 1958, St. Louis U., 1959, Grinnell Coll., 1959, Notre Dame, 1964, Ind. U., 1974; Litt.D., Brandeis U., 1959, Bowdoin, 1965, Hamilton Coll., 1972; m. Martha Gerrish, June 16, 1914 (dec. 1938); children—Margaret (Mrs. Maxwell M. Small), William Gerrish; m. 2d, Elinor Gregory, July 12, 1941. Student asst. Oberlin Coll. Library, 1905-11, exec. asst., 1912, acting librarian, 1916-17; chief of stacks, N.Y. Pub. Library, N.Y.C., 1913-16 and 1917-18, exec. asst., 1919-27, chief of reference dept., 1928-37; librarian Harvard Coll. and dir. of Harvard U. Library, 1937-55, prof. bibliography, 1945-55, librarian emeritus, 1955—; adj. prof. library service Rutgers Univ., 1955-58, cons. library adminstrn. and bldg. planning, 1955—; library cons., Australian univs., 1958, 61, 63, 65, 68, India, S. Africa, 1959, Ireland, 1960, Japan, 1961, Can., 1960—, Costa Rica, 1964. U.K., 1972—, Venezuela, 1973, Libya, Abu Dhabi, Saudi Arabia, 1975, Iran, 1976; cons. Nat. Capital Devel. Commn., Canberra, Australia, 1961-68; Fulbright lectr. to Australia, 1958-59; lectr. Inst. Advanced Archtl. Studies, York, Eng., 1966. Exec. sec. Assn. Research Libraries, 1938-41; v.p. New Eng. Deposit Library, 1942-55. Trustee Radcliffe Coll., 1939-45, Mass. State Library, 1942-60; mem. Com. to Aid Nat. Library of Peru, 1943-50. Recipient 50th Anniversary medal N.Y. Pub. Library, 1961, Academic/Research Librarian of Year award, 1978. Fulbright scholar Queen's U., Belfast, 1966. Mem. Am. Library Assn. (pres. 1942-43), Am. Library Inst., Bibliog. Soc. of Am., Am. Antiquarian Soc., Mass. Hist. Soc., Bibliog. Soc. (London), Am. Acad. Arts and Scis. Congregationalist. Clubs: Century (N.Y.C.); Odd Volumes (Boston). Contbr. numerous articles to profl. publs. Home: 68 Fairmont St Belmont MA 02178. *I was fortunate enough to decide my profession (Librarianship) in 1905 and have never regretted it and am still active in it 75 years later, consulting, traveling, and speaking.*

METCALF, LAWRENCE EUGENE, educator; b. Dennison, Ohio, Sept. 30, 1915; s. George Madison and Oma (Cotter) M.; B.S., Ohio State U., 1940, M.A., 1945, Ph.D., 1948; m. Barbara May Stanberry, Aug. 22, 1951; children—Janet Elaine, Alan Edward, Lawrence Andrew. Tchr., Boys Indsl. Sch., Lancaster, Ohio, 1941, Midvale (Ohio) High Sch., 1941-43; tchr., prin. Lexington (Ohio) High Sch., 1943-44; research asst. Ohio State U., 1944-46; instr. Goddard Coll., Plainfield, Vt., 1946-47; asst. prof. edn. U. Ga., 1947-49; asst. prof. edn. U. Ill. at Urbana, 1949-55, asso. prof., 1955-61, prof., 1961—. Cons. econ. edn. Joint Council Econ. Edn., also curriculum dir.; cons. Orgn. Econ. Coop. and Devel., U.S. Office Edn., Ednl. Testing Service, Sociol. Resources for Secondary Schs.; tchr. summer sessions Northwestern U., Syracuse U., N.Y. U., Temple U., Kent State U., U. So. Calif. Sr. fellow Inst. for World Order, 1975—. Mem. John Dewey Soc., Philosophy Edn. Soc., Nat. Soc. Coll. Tchrs. Edn., Nat. Council Social Studies (dir.), Assn. Supervision and Curriculum Devel., Am. Fedn. Tchrs., Nat. Soc. Study Edn., AAUP, Social Sci. Edn. Consortium (dir.), Phi Delta Kappa. Author: (with Maurice P. Hunt) Teaching High School Social Studies, 1968. Editor: Progressive Education, 1955-56; (with John J. DeBoer, Walter Kaulfers) Secondary Education: A Textbook of Readings, 1966. Editor: sect. 41st yearbook Nat. Council Social Studies, 1971; asso. editor: Educational Theory, 1953-54; editor-in-chief High Sch. Publs., World Law Fund, 1967-72. Home: 1501 Western Ave Champaign IL 61820 Office: Edn Bldg U Ill Urbana IL 61801

METCALF, LAWRENCE VINCENT, investment mgr.; b. Berkeley, Calif., Sept. 20, 1919; s. John Brockway and Elizabeth Vincent Huntington M.; B.S., U. Calif. at Berkeley, 1940; postgrad. Stanford, 1941; m. Susan Stimmel, Jan. 27, 1950; children—Elsie, John Brockway. Auto dealer, 1947-76; partner Tecolote Fund, San Francisco, 1966—; v.p. Alpine Meadows of Tahoe, Inc., Tahoe City, Calif., 1971—, also dir. Pres. San Francisco Symphony Assn., 1974—; chmn. bd. trustees Town Sch. Boys, 1969-75; trustee U. Calif. Berkeley Found.; bd. dirs. San Francisco Ballet, San Francisco Opera. Served to lt. comdr. USNR, 1941-45. Clubs: Pacific Union, San Francisco Golf, Burlingame Country. Office: 311 California St San Francisco CA 94104

METCALF, MICHAEL PIERCE, newspaper publishing exec.; b. Providence, Sept. 1, 1933; s. George Pierce and Pauline Pumpelly (Cabot) M.; B.A., Harvard U., 1955; M.B.A., Stanford U., 1959; m. Charlotte L. Saville, Jan. 30, 1971; children—Hannah, Jesse, Lucy. Reporter, Charlotte Observer, 1959-60; sales exec. Phila. Bull., 1960-61; asst. to pres. Providence Jour. Co., 1962-71, exec. v.p., 1971-74, pres., 1974—, pub., 1979—, also dir.; pres., dir. Providence Jour. Broadcasting Corp., 1978—; dir. Colony Communications, Providence Gravure, Inc., Virginia Gravure, Inc., Tex. Color Printers, Inc. Trustee Ocean States Performing Arts Center, Providence Found., R.I. Sch. Design. Served to lt. (j.g.) USN, 1955-57. Mem. Inter-Am. press insts., Gravure Research Inst., Am. Newspaper Pubs. Assn. Clubs: Brook; Agawam Hunt and Hope. Office: 75 Fountain St Providence RI 02902

METCALF, ROBERT LEE, entomologist, educator; b. Columbus, Ohio, Nov. 13, 1916; s. Clell Lee and Cleo Esther (Fouch) M.; B.A., U. Ill., 1939, M.A., 1940; Ph.D., Cornell U., 1943; m. Esther Jemimia Rutherford, June 22, 1940; children—Esther Lee (Mrs. James Sims), Robert Alan, Michael Rutherford. Entomologist, TVA, 1943-46; mem. faculty U. Calif. at Riverside, 1946-68, prof. entomology, 1952-68, chmn. dept., 1950-63, vice-chancellor, 1963-66; prof. entomology, biology, agrl. entomology, vet. physiology and pharmacology, also research prof. environ. studies U. Ill., Urbana, 1968—, head dept. zoology, 1969-73; prin. scientist Ill. Natural History Survey, 1970—. Recipient Order Cherubini, U. Pisa (Italy). Mem. Nat. Acad. Scis., Am. Acad. Arts and Scis., Entomol. Soc. Am. (pres. 1958), Am. Chem. Soc. (Charles F. Spencer award, 1966 pesticide chemistry, 1972), Phi Beta Kappa, Sigma Xi, Phi Kappa Phi, Phi Sigma. Clubs: Dial; Urbana Country. Author: Organic Insecticides, 1955; Destructive and Useful Insects, 2d edit., 1962; co-author: Introduction to Insect Pest Management, 1975. Co-editor: Advances in Environmental Sciences and Technology, 1968. Home: 1902 Golfview Dr Urbana IL 61801

METCALF, WILLIAM HENRY, JR., architect; b. Memphis, Feb. 9, 1928; s. William Henry and Mary Myrtle (Tittle) M.; B.A., Yale U., 1949, B.Arch., 1951. M.Arch., 1952; m. Barbara Ann Keller, Oct. 8, 1955; children—Ramsay Katherine, Anne Louis. Fellow div. archtl. studies Nuffield Found., London, 1957-58; pvt. practice architecture, Washington, 1958-66; partner firm Metcalf and Assos., Washington, 1966—; vis. archtl. critic/lectr. Carnegie Inst. Tech., Howard U., Catholic U. Am., George Washington U., Tex. A. and M. U.; prin. works include Health Centers, Lagos, Nigeria, 1964, Anne Arundel Gen. Hosp., Annapolis, Md., 1966, Fairfax Hosp., Falls Church, Va.,

1967, Andrew Meml. Hosp., Tuskegee Inst., Ala., 1968, Montgomery Gen. Hosp., Olney, Md., 1969, Concentrated Care Center, Georgetown U., 1976, Am. embassy residence, also Cairo Am. Coll., Cairo, Egypt, 1977, St. Joseph's Hosp., Parkersburg, W.Va., 1977, Wilmington (Del.) Med. Center, 1977. Served with USAF, 1953-56. Hopper fellow, 1951. Fellow AIA (Rehmann fellow 1957); mem. Am. Assn. Hosp. Planning, Internat. Hosp. Fedn. Presbyterian. Clubs: City Tavern, Washington Golf and Country. Home: 2525 N 10th St Arlington VA 22201 Office: 3222 N St NW Washington DC 20007

METCALFE, BURTON DENIS, television producer, dir.; b. Sask., Can., Mar. 19, 1935; s. Louis and Esther (Goldman) M.; came to U.S., 1949; B.A., UCLA, 1955. Stage and film actor, 1958-65; TV exec. Screen Gems, Los Angeles, 1965-70; asso. producer TV show MASH, 20th Century Fox, Los Angeles, 1971-75, producer, 1976—. Served with USN, 1956-57. Office: 20th Century Fox 10201 W Pico Blvd Los Angeles CA 90046

METCALFE, DARREL SEYMOUR, educator, agronomist; b. Arkansaw, Wis., Aug. 28, 1913; s. Howard Lee and Mabel (De Marce) M.; tchr. certificate, U. Wis. at River Falls, 1931; B.S. in Agronomy, U. Wis., 1941; M.S., Kans. State U., 1942; Ph.D., Ia. State U., 1950; m. Ellen Lucille Moore, May 16, 1942; children—Dean Darrel, Alan Moore. From instr. to prof. agronomy Ia. State U., 1946-56, asst. dir. student affairs, 1956-58; asso. dean, dir. resident instrn., asst. dir. agrl. expt. sta., agronomist U. Ariz., Tucson, 1958—, dean, dir. extension, 1978—. Chmn. resident instrn. sect., div. agr. Nat. Assn. State Univs. and Land Grant Colls., 1958-59; mem. com. edn. agr. and natural resources Nat. Acad. Sci., 1966-70; U.S. rep. OECD Conf. Higher Edn. in Agr., Paris, 1963-65; mem. AID missions to Brazil, 1962, 64, 66, 69, 71, 72, 73. Served with AUS, 1942-46; PTO. Fellow Am. Soc. Agronomy (Agronomic edn. award 1958; chmn. student activities sect. 1950-53, edn. div. 1956; editorial bd., tech. editor jour. 1961-65), Nat. Assn. Colls. and Tchrs. Agr. (E.B. Knight award 1967, pres. 1970-71), Sigma Xi, Phi Kappa Phi, Phi Eta Sigma, Gamma Sigma Delta, Alpha Tau Alpha, Delta Theta Sigma, Acacia (medallion of merit 1966). Kiwanian. Co-author: Forages, 3d edit., 1973; Crop Production, rev. edits., 1957, 72. Home: 5811 E 9th St Tucson AZ 85711

METCALFE, TOM BROOKS, educator; b. Smithville, Tex., Feb. 26, 1920; s. Joseph Franklin and Ethel Louise (Taylor) M.; B.S., U. Tex., 1941, M.S., 1947; Ph.D., Ga. Inst. Tech., 1953; m. Gwendolyn Imogene Soward, July 3, 1944; children— Gwendolyn Jean (Mrs. Rodger T. Ellis), Linda Gail (Mrs. John Patrick Rogers), Marilyn Louise, Carolyn Marguerite. Chemist Dow Chem. Co., Freeport, Tex., 1941-43; research scientist U. Tex., 1947-50; research engr. Ga. Inst. Tech., 1951-52, Shell Oil Co., Houston, 1952-62; asst. prof. U. Houston, 1953-56; head dept. chem. engring. W.Va. Inst. Tech., 1962-63, U. Southwestern La., 1963—; founder, pub. Pinehill Pub. Co.; cons. U.S. Bur. Pub. Rds.; U.S. Dept. Interior Office of Saline Water. Pres. Edgewood Civic Corp., 1954, 57, 59. Mem. Houston Mayor's Com. Zoning, 1958-60. Chmn. bd. U. Southwestern La. Wesley Found., 1966—. Served to lt. USNR, 1943-46; PTO. Fellow Am. Inst. Chem. Engrs. (nat. chmn. acad. dept. heads 1967-69); mem. Am. Soc. Engring. Edn., Sigma Xi, Phi Eta Sigma, Omega Chi Epsilon, Phi Lambda Upsilon, Tau Beta Pi. Methodist (ofcl. bd.). Mason. Author: Radiation Spectra of Radionuclides, 1970; Chemical Engineering as a Career, 1966; Safe Handling of Radioactive Materials, 1964. Contbr. articles to profl. jours. Home: 109 Juanita Dr Lafayette LA 70506. *Seek good and not evil; bless them who curse you; with God, all things are possible.*

METHOD, HAROLD LAMBERT, educator, surgeon; b. Duluth, Minn., July 22, 1918; s. Harold S. and Irene (Lambert) M.; B.S., Northwestern U., 1940, B.M., M.D., 1944, M.S., 1949; m. Margaret Elizabeth Nelson, May 3, 1943. Intern, Cook County Hosp., Chgo., 1944, resident, 1949-52; resident Passavant Meml. Hosp., Chgo., 1947-48; mem. attending staff Passavant Meml. Hosp., Chgo., 1952—, Cook County Hosp., Chgo., 1950-52, VA Research Hosp., Chgo., 1953—; faculty Northwestern U. Med. Sch., 1949—, asso. prof. surgery, 1973-75, prof. surgery, 1975—; pres. med. staff Passavant Meml. Hosp., 1965-67. Served to lt. M.C., USNR, 1944-46. Recipient Service award Northwestern U., 1959; All-Am. Football award Sports Illustrated 25th Anniversary, 1964. Diplomate Am. Bd. Surgery. Mem. AMA., Ill., Chgo. (award excellence and originality in research in art and sci. surgery 1947) med. socs., Chgo. Surg. Soc., A.C.S., Western Surg. Assn., Soc. Surgery Alimentary Tract, James IV Surg. Assn., Am. Fedn. Clin. Research, Northwestern U. Alumni Assn. (council med. div. 1952-54, v.p. charge activities 1954-55, pres. 1957-59, bd. dirs. 1956-58). Clubs: Tavern of Chgo. (pres. 1974-76); Lake Zurich Golf (pres. 1976-77). Contbr. articles to med. jours. Asso. editor Surgery, Gynecology and Obstetrics, 1970—. Home: 230 E Delaware Pl Chicago IL 60611 Office: 707 N Fairbanks Ct Chicago IL 60611

METRAKOS, ROBERT ARTHUR, assn. exec.; b. Wellington, Kans., Feb. 9, 1927; s. Arthur P. and Fern B. (Cook) M.; B.S., U. Nebr., 1949, postgrad., 1950-53; postgrad. U. N.C., 1961, U. Ga., 1963, 68; m. Pauline Basil Carellas, Dec. 3, 1961. Adminstrv. asst. dist. sales office Ford Motor Co., Omaha, 1954-55; indsl. mgr. Lincoln (Nebr.) C. of C., 1955-59; sec., mgr. Lincoln Indsl. Devel. Corp., 1956-59, exec. dir. Chester County Bd. Commerce and Devel., Chester, S.C., 1959-62; exec. v.p. Greater Orangeburg (S.C.) C. of C., 1962-70; exec. dir. Orangeburg County Planning and Devel. Commn., 1962-70; exec. v.p. Portsmouth (Va.) C. of C., 1970—; dir. Locksley Hall, Inc., furniture mfrs.; v.p. Global Travel Agy., 1974-77. Tchr., Inst. for Orgn. Mgmt. U. Ga., Athens, 1964-66; dir. Piedmont Area Devel. Council, 1960-61; sec. Portsmouth Indsl. Found., 1974—; exec. dir. Portsmouth Indsl. Devel. Authority, 1974—, Portsmouth Port and Indsl. Commn., 1973—. Unit chmn. United Fund, 1956-58, allocations com., 1976-77; sec. Lincoln Mayor's Com. for Employment Handicapped; mem. Orangeburg Area Mail Users Council, Va. Air Pollution Control Adv. Com., 1976—; pres. elect Interfrat. Advisers Alumni Council U. Neb.; mem. adv. com. Adult Edn. Program; mem. SACCE, Task Force Tomorrow, 1974-75. Bd. dirs. Chester County Library, Bi-County Trade and Indsl. Sch. Served with USAAF, 1943-46. Recipient 3 Oscars United Fund for going over goal, 1956-58; Top Program of Work award U.S. C. of C., 1961. Mem. So. (dir., 1st v.p. 1975, pres. 1976-77), S.C. (pres. 1965-66), Va. (2d v.p. 1974) assns. C. of C. execs., Am. Indsl. Devel. Council (Certified Indsl. Developer award 1971, chmn. membership com. 1956, 66), Am. C. of C. Execs. (Certified Chamber Exec. award 1966, ambassador 1963-65, dir. 1977-80), C. of C. U.S. (adv. com.), Automobile Assn. Am., Travelers Protective Assn., Am. Legion, Tau Kappa Epsilon. Elk, Moose, Rotarian (dir. Portsmouth 1978). Home: 2413 Sterling Point Dr Portsmouth VA 23703 Office: 524 Middle St Mall Portsmouth VA 23704. *Whatever success I now enjoy, much of it must be contributed to my philosophy that in everyday life I must: be true to myself as well as to every other man and woman; adhere to the devotion I have for my family and religion; profess my loyalty to my organization and friends; never exploit my associates or association for my own advantage; and always admit an error readily and face the consequences without hesitation.*

METTER, BERTRAM MILTON, advt. exec.; b. N.Y.C., Aug. 14, 1927; s. Harry W. and Rosella (Fischbein) M.; B.A., Bklyn. Coll., 1949; M.A., Columbia, 1952; m. Roslyn H. Reiser, Jan. 11, 1952; children—Joel, Lawrence, Daniel. Copy chief N.Y. Mirror, 1953-56, Newsweek mag., N.Y.C., 1956-59; with J. Walter Thompson Co., N.Y.C., 1959—, v.p., 1965-73, sr. v.p., 1973-78, creative dir., 1974—, exec. v.p., 1978—. Club: Baliwick (Greenwich, Conn.). Home: 41 Nutmeg Dr Greenwich CT 06830 Office: 420 Lexington Ave New York NY 10017

METTLER, FREDERICK ALBERT, educator, physician; b. N.Y.C., June 13, 1907; s. Frederick and Anne (Mathews) M.; A.B., Clark U., 1929, Sc.D., 1951; A.M., Cornell U., 1931, Ph.D., 1933; M.D., U. Ga., 1937. Asst. in anatomy Cornell Med. Coll., 1930-31, instr. anatomy, 1931-33; instr. physiology U. St. Louis Med. Coll., 1933-34; asst. prof. anatomy U. Ga. Sch. Medicine, 1934-36, asso. prof., 1936-38, prof., 1938-42; asso. prof. anatomy Coll. Phys. and Surg. Columbia, N.Y.C., 1941-51, prof., 1951-75, emeritus, 1975—; distinguished prof. Uniformed Services U. Med. Sch., 1978—; Commonwealth Fund vis. prof. L.I. Med. Coll., 1943-44; research cons. N.J. State Hosp., Greystone Park, 1947-71; coordinator research N.Y. Dept. Mental Hygiene, 1948-49, dir. research, 1949; lectr. Rutgers U., 1948; cons. VA, 1949-71, Research Center, Rockland State Hosp., Orangeburg, N.Y., 1974-76. Chmn. psycho-surg. com., div. mental hygiene Nat. Adv. Mental Health Council USPHS, 1949; med. adv. bd. Law-Medicine Research Inst., Boston U.; mem. adv. bd. Yerkes Reg. Primate Research Center, Emory U., Am. Coll. Toxicology. Fellow N.Y. Acad. Medicine, N.Y. Zool. Soc.; mem. Am. Assn. Anatomists, Am. Physiol. Soc., Assn. Phys. Anthropology, Soc. Exptl. Biology, Harvey Soc., Assn. Research Nervous and Mental Disorders (editorial bd. 1943), Am. Neurol. Soc., Soc. Neurology France, Acad. Neurology, Nat. Acad. Sci. Norway, Assn. Eastern Electroencephalographers, Ga. Med. Soc., Med. Soc. N.J., N.Y. Acad. Scis. (asso.), Am. Coll. Toxicology. Editorial bd. Jour. Comparative Neurology, 1948-71, Psychiat. Quar., 1958-75, Jour. Neuropathology and Exptl. Neurology. Home: Pippin Hill Blairstown NJ 07825 Office: Uniformed Services U Med Sch 4301 Jones Bridge Rd Bethesda MD 20014 also Pippin Hill Experimental Area Box 376 Blairstown NJ 07825

METTLER, RUBEN FREDERICK, electronics and engring. co. exec.; b. Shafter, Calif., Feb. 23, 1924; s. Henry Frederick and Lydia Mettler; student Stanford, 1941-43; B.S. in Elec. Engring., Calif. Inst. Tech., 1944, M.S., 1947, Ph.D. in Elec. and Aero. Engring, 1949; m. Donna Jean Smith, May 1, 1955; children—Matthew Frederick, Daniel Frederick. Asso. div. dir. systems research and devel. Hughes Aircraft Co., 1949-54; spl. cons. to asst. sec. def., 1954-55; asst. gen. mgr. guided missile research div. Ramo-Wooldridge Corp., 1955-58, pres., dir. Space Tech. Labs., Inc., Los Angeles, 1962-68; exec. v.p., dir. TRW Inc. (formerly Thompson Ramo Wooldridge, Inc.), 1965, asst. pres., 1968-69, pres., 1969-77, chmn. bd., chief exec. officer, 1977—; dir. Bank Am. Corp., Goodyear Tire & Rubber Co., Merck & Co.; past vice-chmn. Ind. adv. council Dept. Def. Adv. com. United Negro Coll. Fund, nat. campaign chmn., 1980; mem. bd. advisers Council for Fin. Aid to Edn., Case Western Res. U.; chmn. Pres.'s Sci. Policy Task Force, 1969; mem. Emergency Com. for Am. Trade; nat. chmn. Nat. Alliance Businessmen, 1978-79; bd. dirs. Greater Los Angeles Urban Coalition; trustee Calif. Inst. Tech., 1969—, mem. Caltech Assos., 1963—; mem. council Rockefeller U.; trustee, research policy com. Com. Economic Devel.; trustee Nat. Safety Council, Cleve. Clinic Found., Nat. Fund Minority Engring. Students; aerospace chmn. U.S. Ind. Payroll Savs. Commn.; mem. bd. Smithsonian Nat. Assos. Named 1 of ten Outstanding Young Men of Am., U.S. Jr. C. of C., 1955; So. Calif.'s Engr. of Year, 1964; recipient Meritorious Civilian Service award Dept. Def., 1969. Served with USNR, 1943-46. Registered profl. engr., Calif.; recipient Nat. Human Relations award NCCJ, 1979; Excellence in Mgmt. award Industry Week mag., 1979. Fellow IEEE, AIAA; mem. Sci. Research Soc. Am., Calif. Inst. Tech. Alumni Assn. (dir.), Nat. Acad. Engring., James Smithson Soc., Sigma Xi, Eta Kappa Nu (named nation's outstanding young elec. engr. 1954), Tau Beta Pi, Theta Xi. Clubs: Cosmos (Washington); Union, 50 (Cleve.). Author reports airborne electronic systems. Patentee interceptor fire control systems. Office: 1 Space Park Redondo Beach CA 90278 also 23555 Euclid Ave Cleveland OH 44117

METTRICK, DAVID FRANCIS, zoologist; b. London, Feb. 29, 1932; s. Francis and Marjorie (Palmer) M.; B.Sc. with honors, U. Wales, 1954; Ph.D., U. London, 1957, D.Sc. 1973. Lectr., U. Coll. Rhodesia and Nyasaland, 1957-61; sr. lectr. dept. zoology U. W.I., Jamaica, 1961-67; asso. prof. U. Toronto (Ont., Can.), 1967-71, prof. zoology, 1971—, chmn. dept. zoology, 1975—; mem. adv. bd. sci. publs. Nat. Research Council Can. Recipient Queen's Silver Jubilee medal, 1978. Fellow Royal Soc. Arts, Royal Soc. Can.; mem. Biol. Council Can. (pres. 1975-79), Assn. Sci., Engring. and Tech. Community Can. (v.p. life scis.), Am. Soc. Parasitology, Brit. Soc. Parasitology, Helminthological Soc. Washington, Can. Soc. Zoology, Can. Com. Univ. Biology Chmn. (exec. com.). Editorial bd. Exptl. Parasitology, 1975-78, Jour. Parasitology, 1976—; asso. editor Can. Jour. Zoology, 1977—. Home: 28 Admiral Rd Townhouse 3 Toronto ON M5R 2L5 Canada Office: Dept Zoology U Toronto Ramsay Wright Zool Labs Toronto ON M5S 1A1 Canada

METZ, CHARLES BAKER, educator, biologist; b. N.Y.C., Dec. 27, 1916; s. Charles W. and Blanche S. (Stafford) M.; A.B., Johns Hopkins, 1939; Ph.D., Calif. Inst. Tech., 1942; m. Mary Ethel Bucheimer, July 3, 1940; children—Rinda Margaret, Richard Stafford. Instr. biology Wesleyan U., Middletown, Conn., 1942-46; NRC fellow Ind. U., 1945-46; instr., then asst. prof. zoology Yale, 1947-52; asso. prof. zoology U. N.C., 1952-53; asso. prof. zoology Fla. State U., 1953-57, prof. zoology, 1957-62, prof. biology Inst. for Space Bioscis., 1962-64; prof. zoology Inst. Molecular Evolution, U. Miami, 1964—. Gosney fellow Calif. Inst. Tech., spring 1950; vis. asst. prof. U. Calif. at Berkeley, spring 1952. Instr., Marine Biol. Lab., Woods Hole, Mass., 1947-52, F.R. Lillie fellow, 1952, mem. corp., dir. fertilization and gamete physiology tng. program, 1962-74, trustee, 1956-64, 66-73, Fellow AAAS; mem. Am. Soc. Zoologists (sec. 1961-64), Soc. Gen. Physiologists, Soc. Exptl. Biology and Medicine, Am. Soc. Naturalists, Soc. Developmental Biology, Soc. Study Fertility, Am. Soc. Cell Biology, Soc. Study Reprodn. (bd. asso. editors 1971-73), Internat. Soc. Developmental Biologists, Am. Soc. Andrology, Bermuda Biol. Assn., Sigma Xi. Home: 7220 SW 124th St Miami FL 33156 Office: Inst Molecular and Cellular Evolution 521 Anastasia Ave U Miami Coral Gables FL 33134

METZ, GEORGE HAROLD, electronics co. exec.; b. Phila., Aug. 30, 1917; s. George Harold and Marie (Cummiskey) M.; A.B magna cum laude, La Salle Coll., 1939; M.A., U. Pa., 1945, Ph.D., 1968; m. Mary Caldevilla, June 27, 1941; children—Mary Ellen (Mrs. Frederick Symmes Johnston III). Elizabeth Ann (Mrs. Louis J. Casella), George Harold III, Thomas More, Clare (Mrs. Bruce Horvath), Marie, Catharine, Regina, Teresa. With RCA, 1944-65, div. v.p. ednl. services, 1959-63, personnel dir., 1963-65; v.p. personnel AMBAC Industries, Inc. (formerly Am. Bosch Arma Corp.), Carle Place, N.Y., 1965—; dir. Packard Instrument Co. Mem. Pres.'s Com. on Handicapped, 1965-77. Mem. Greenwich (Conn.) Representative Town Meeting, 1972—, chmn. edn. com. Mem. Am. Mgmt. Assn., Am. Arbitration Assn. Clubs: University, Union League (N.Y.C.); Burning Tree Country (Greenwich); Seaview Country (Absecon, N.J.). Compiler: (with Matthew W. Black) A Supplemental Bibliography to the New Variorum Edition of The Life and Death of King Richard II, 1977. Contbr. articles to scholarly jours. Home: 10 Taconic Rd Greenwich CT 06830 Office: 195 Farmington Ave Farmington CT 06032

METZ, GEORGE WILLIAM, banker; b. Ashland, Pa., Oct. 26, 1916; s. George W. and May A (Maurer) M.; student State Tchrs. Coll., Mansfield, Pa., 1936-37; grad. Wharton Evening Sch. Accounts and Finance, U. Pa., 1951; grad. Stonier Grad. Sch. Banking, Rutgers U., 1958; m. Eddena May Christine, Mar. 19, 1949; children—Pamela Ann, Judith May. Teller, gen. bookkeeper Ashland Nat. Bank, 1938-41; loan mgr., asst. mgr. Northeast Nat. Bank Phila., 1951; with Fed. Res. Bank Phila., 1951—, gen. auditor, 1963—, v.p., 1966—. Faculty, Inter-Agy. Bank Exam. Sch., Washington, 1956-63. Chmn. standing com. Conf. Gen. Auditors Fed. Res. Banks, 1969-70. Chmn. group edn. Community Leadership Seminar Fels Inst., 1968-69; active United Fund. Served with AUS, 1942-46. Mem. Bank Adminstrn. Inst. (pres. 1974-75), Inst. Internal Auditors (certified), Gen. Alumni Soc. U. Pa. Baptist (ch. moderator, pres., tchr. men's class). Home: 3234 Brighton St Philadelphia PA 19149 Office: 100 N 6th St Philadelphia PA 19106

METZ, JOHN A., lawyer; b. Dormont, Pa., May 1, 1909; s. John Alfred and Anna (Murray) M.; A.B., Princeton, 1930; LL.B., U. Pitts., 1933; m. Margaret Ritchey, Dec. 6, 1934; children—Margaret (Mrs. Alexander Ogle), Sandra Ann (Mrs. Mohsin Qureshi), John R. (dec.). Gen. practice law, Pitts., 1933—, now sr. partner Metz, Cook, Hanna & Kelly; instr., asst. prof., then asso. prof. law U. Pitts. Law Sch., 1933-58. Dir., vice chmn., chmn. exec. com. Link-Belt Co., Chgo., 1957-67. Mem. civil procedural rules com. Supreme Ct. Pa., 1958—, vice chmn., 1969—; dist. rationing atty., dist enforcement atty., regional enforcement exec. N.Y. region OPA, 1942-46. Mem. Am., Pa., Allegheny County bar assns., Am. Judicature Soc., Am. Coll. Trial Lawyers, Phi Beta Kappa, Order of Coif. Clubs: Duquesne, University (Pitts.); Somerset (Pa.) Country; Princeton (N.Y.C.); Union League (Chgo.). Home: LeGrande Apts Pittsburgh PA 15211 Office: Grant Bldg Pittsburgh PA 15219 also 127 W Union St Somerset PA 15501

METZ, LAWRENCE ANTHONY, lawyer; b. Chgo., July 26, 1941; s. Florian Lawrence and Angeline M.; B.S.C., DePaul U., 1963, J.D. 1967; m. Lorraine Kutz, Aug. 14, 1965; children—Robert, Kathleen, Sandra, Diane, Jeanne. Admitted to Ill. bar, 1967; atty. City Products Corp., Des Plaines, Ill., 1967-70; atty. Jewel Cos., Inc., Chgo., 1970-75, asst. sec., 1975-79, asst. gen. counsel, 1979—. Bd. dirs. United Way of Suburban Chgo., 1977-79. Served with U.S. Army, 1963. Mem. Chgo. Bar Assn., Ill. State Bar Assn. Roman Catholic. Home: 804 S Ridge Ave Arlington Heights IL 60005 Office: 5725 N East River Rd Chicago IL 60631

METZ, MARY CLARE, educator; b. Perry, Okla., Jan. 27, 1907; d. John Joseph and Julia (Sommars) M.; B.A., Our Lady of the Lake Coll., 1928; M.A., Cath. U. Am., 1931; Ph.D., 1934. Prof. biology, chmn. dept. Our Lady of Lake Coll., San Antonio, 1934-55, comptroller, 1955-60, acad. dean, 1961-72, dir. alumni assn., 1972-76. Mem. Pan-Am. Scholarship Found., 1964-66; mem. career opportunities program bd. trustees Edgewood Ind. Sch. Dist., San Antonio, 1969-71; mem. Minnie Stevens Piper Scholarship Com., San Antonio, 1962-78; bd. dirs. San Antonio Ballet Co., 1971-78, pres., 1977-78; bd. dirs. Alamo Regional Sci. Fair, 1977; trustee Our Lady of the Lake U., 1977—; mem., sec. St. Mary's Sch. Bd., San Antonio, 1978—. Fellow Tex. Acad. Sci.; mem. Am. Bot. Soc., Internat. Taxonomic Soc., Sigma Xi. Mem. Congregation Divine Providence. Address: 1147A Cupples Rd San Antonio TX 78226. *A combination of many elements have entered into the past years of my life: 1) concern for people and their mental, emotional and spiritual growth; 2) recognition of the good in other persons even when one worked to my detriment; 3) belief in respect for honesty, sincerity, courtesy, and kindness toward others; 4) the objectivity I was able to bring to the solution of problems; 5) membership in the Congregation of the Sisters of Divine Providence where women share equal opportunity and are given occasion to develop and use their talents and abilities.*

METZ, ROBERT ROY, editor; b. Richmond Hill, N.Y., Mar. 23, 1929; s. Robert Roy, Sr. and Mary (Kissel) M.; B.A., Wesleyan U., Middletown Conn., 1950; children—Robert Sumner, Christopher Roy. Copyboy, N.Y. Times, 1951, asst. fgn. news desk, 1952; rewriteman cable desk I.N.S., 1953, overnight cable editor, 1954-56, asst. feature editor, 1956-58; asst. news editor Newspaper Enterprise Assn., 1958, news editor, 1959-63, mng. editor, 1963-66, exec. editor, 1966-68, v.p., 1967-71, editorial dir., 1968-71, pres., editor, dir., 1972—; dir. Berkeley-Small Inc., 1974-77, chmn., 1976-77; v.p., dir. United Feature Syndicate, 1976-77, pres., editor, 1978; pres., editor, dir. United Media Enterprises, 1978—. Mem. Sigma Delta Chi, Sigma Nu. Lutheran. Club: Union League (N.Y.C.). Home: 54 E 83d St New York NY 10028 Office: 200 Park Ave New York NY 10017

METZENBAUM, HOWARD MORTON, U.S. senator; b. Cleve., June 4, 1917; s. Charles I. and Anna (Klafter) M.; B.A., Ohio State U., 1939, LL.D., 1941; m. Shirley Turoff, Aug. 8, 1946; children—Barbara Jo, Susan Lynn, Shelley Hope, Amy Beth. Chmn. bd. Airport Parking Co. Am., 1958-66, ITT Consumer Services Corp., 1966-68; chmn. bd. ComCorp, 1969-74, after 1975; U.S. senator from Ohio, 1974, 77—. Mem. War Labor Bd., 1942-45, Ohio Bur. Code Rev., 1949-50, Cleve. Met. Housing Authority, 1968-70, Lake Erie Regional Transit Authority, 1972-73. Mem. Ohio Ho. of Reps., 1943-46, Ohio Senate, 1947-50; mem. Ohio Democratic Exec. Com., 1966—; mem. Ohio Dem. Finance Com., 1969—. Trustee Mt. Sinai Hosp., Cleve., 1961-73, treas., 1966-73; bd. dirs. Council Human Relations, United Cerebral Palsy Assn., Nat. Council Hunger and Malnutrition, Karamu House, St. Vincent Charity Hosp., Cleve., St. Jude Research Hosp., Memphis; nat. co-chmn. Nat. Citizens' Com. Conquest Cancer; vice-chmn. fellows Brandeis U. Mem. Am., Ohio, Cuyahoga, Cleve. bar assns., Am. Assn. Trial Lawyers, Order of Coif, Phi Eta Sigma, Tau Epsilon Rho. Office: 347 Russell Senate Office Bldg Washington DC 20510*

METZGER, BRUCE MANNING, educator, clergyman; b. Middletown, Pa., Feb. 9, 1914; s. Maurice Rutt and Anna Mary (Manning) M.; A.B., Lebanon Valley Coll., 1935, D.D., 1951; Th.B., Princeton Theol. Sem., 1938, Th.M., 1939; A.M., Princeton, 1940, Ph.D., 1942; L.H.D., Findlay Coll., 1962; D.D., St. Andrews U., Scotland, 1964; D.Theol., Münster (Germany) U., 1970; m. Isobel E. Mackay, July 7, 1944; children—John Mackay, James Bruce. Ordained to ministry Presbyn. Ch., 1939; teaching fellow N.T., Princeton Theol. Sem., 1938-40, mem. faculty, 1940—, prof. N.T. lang., lit., 1954-64, George L. Collord prof. N.T. lang., lit., 1964—. Vis. lectr. Presbyn. Theol. Sem. South, Campinas, Brazil, 1952, Presbyn. Theol. Sem. North, Recife, Brazil, 1952; mem. Inst. Advanced Study, Princeton, 1964-65, 73-74; scholar-in-residence Tyndale House, Cambridge, 1969; vis. fellow Clare Hall, Cambridge, 1974; vis. fellow Wolfson Coll., Oxford U., 1979. Mem. mng. com. Am. Sch. Classical Studies, Athens, Greece. Mem. Standard Bible com. Nat. Council Chs., 1952—, chmn., 1975—; mem seminar N.T.

studies Columbia U., 1959—; mem. Kuratorium of Vetus-Latina Inst., Beuron, Germany, 1959—; advisory com. Inst. N.T. Text Research, U. Münster, 1961—, Thesaurus Linguae Graecae, 1972—; Collected Works of Erasmus, 1977—, chmn. Am. com. versions Internat. Greek N.T., 1950—; participant internat. congresses scholars Aarhus, Aberdeen, Bangor, Bonn, Brussels, Cairo, Cambridge, Exeter, Heidelberg, Frankfurt, London, Louvain, Munich, Münster, Newcastle, Nottingham, Oxford, St. Andrews, Stockholm, Strasbourg, Tübingen; mem. Presbytery New Brunswick. Recipient certificate Distinguished Service, Nat. Council Chs., 1957; Distinguished Alumnus award Lebanon Valley Coll. Alumni Assn., 1961; prize lit. competition Christian Research Found., 1955, 62, 63. Mem. Soc. Bibl. Lit. (pres. 1970-71, past del. Am. Council Learned Socs.), Am. Acad. Religion, Am. Bible Soc. (bd. mgrs. 1948—, chmn. com. transls. 1964-70), Am. Philol. Assn., Studiorum Novi Testamenti Societas (pres. 1971-72), Cath. Bibl. Assn., N.Am. Patristic Soc. (past pres.), Ch. History Soc. Am., Am. Soc. Papyrologists; hon. fellow, corr. mem. Higher Inst. Coptic Studies, Cairo; corr. fellow Brit. Acad. Republican. Author: The Saturday and Sunday Lessons from Luke in the Greek Gospel Lectionary, 1944; Lexical Aids for Students of New Testament Greek, 1946, enlarged edit., 1955; A Guide to the Preparation of a Thesis, 1950; An Introduction to the Apocrypha, 1957; Chapters in the History of New Testament Textual Criticism, 1963; The Text of the New Testament, Its Transmission, Corruption, and Restoration, 1964; (with H.G. May) The Oxford Annotated Bible with the Apocrypha, 1965, The New Testament, Its Background, Growth, and Content, 1965; Index to Periodical Literature on Christ and the Gospels, 1966; Historical and Literary Studies, Pagan, Jewish and Christian, 1968; Index to Periodical Literature on the Apostle Paul, 1970; A Textual Commentary on the Greek New Testament, 1971; The Early Versions of the New Testament, 1977. Editorial com. Critical Greek New Testament, 1956—; chmn., Am. com. Internat. Greek New Testament Project, 1970—; sec. com. translators Apocrypha (rev. standard version); editor: New Testament Tools and Studies, 9 vols., 1960-69; Oxford Annotated Apocrypha, 1965, enlarged edit., 1977; co-editor: United Bible Societies Greek New Testament, 1966. Compiler: Index of Articles on the New Testament and the Early Church Published in Festschriften, 1951, supplement, 1955; Lists of Words Occurring Frequently in the Coptic New Testament (Sahidic Dialect); Annotated Bibliography of the Textual Criticism of the New Testament, 1955; (with Isobel M. Metzger) Oxford Concise Concordance to the Holy Bible. Contbr. articles to jours. Address: 20 Cleveland Ln Princeton NJ 08540

METZGER, H(OWELL) PETER, essayist, publicist; b. N.Y.C., Feb. 22, 1931; s. Julius Radley and Gertrude (Fuller) M.; B.A., Brandeis U., 1953; Ph.D., Columbia U., 1965; m. Frances Windham, June 30, 1956; children—John, James, Lisa, Suzanne. Mgr. advanced programs Ball Bros. Research Corp., Boulder, 1968-70; research asso. Dept. Chemistry, U. Colo., Boulder, 1966-68; sr. research scientist N.Y. State Psychiat. Inst., N.Y.C., 1965-66; syndicated columnist N.Y. Times Syndicate, 1972-74; syndicated columnist Science Critic, Newspaper Enterprise Assn., 1974-76; sci. editor Rocky Mt. News, Denver, 1976—; mgr. public affairs planning Public Service Co. Colo., Denver; cons. Environ. Instrumentation, 1970-72; dir. Colspan Environ. Systems, Inc., Boulder, Colo., 1969-72. Pres. Colo. Com. for Environ. Info., Boulder, 1968-72; mem. Colo. Gov.'s Adv. Com. Underground Nuclear Explosions, 1971-74. Bd. dirs. Wildlife-2000, 1970-72, Colo. Def. Council, 1972—. USPHS fellow, 1959-65, prin. investigator, 1968. Mem. ACLU (state bd. 1968-71), Sigma Xi, Phi Lambda Upsilon. Clubs: Denver Athletic, Denver Press; Am. Alpine (N.Y.C.). Author: The Atomic Establishment, 1972. Contbr. articles in field to profl. jours., nat. mags. Address: 2595 Stanford Ave Boulder CO 80303

METZGER, SAMUEL, lawyer; b. N.Y.C., Nov. 16, 1939; s. Miles and Matty (Remez) M.; B.A., Coll. William and Mary, 1961; LL.B., N.Y. U., 1964; m. Tricia Sembera, Dec. 11, 1977. Admitted to N.Y. bar, 1965; labor relations mediator N.Y.C. Dept. Labor, 1964-65; asso. firm Fellner & Rovins, N.Y.C., 1965; partner firm Metzger & Metzger, N.Y.C., 1966-75; v.p., gen. counsel, dir. Flagstaff Corp., N.Y.C., 1975-78; pvt. practice, N.Y.C., 1978—; dir. Third Colony Corp. Co-op, 1972-77. Mem. personal gifts com. United Cerebral Palsy, 1976—. Mem. N.Y.C. Bar Assn. Club: Le Club. Home: Stoneridge NY Office: 650 Fifth Ave New York NY 10019

METZGER, SIDNEY, elec. engr.; b. N.Y.C., Feb. 1, 1917; s. Julius and Molly (Gottesman) M.; B.S. in Elec. Engring., N.Y. U., 1937; M.E.E., Poly. Inst. Bklyn., 1950; m. Miriam Marsha Lipstein, Dec. 3, 1944; children—David J., Sally Ann Metzger Fasman, Philip C. Chief radio relay br. U.S. Army Signal Corps Labs., Ft. Monmouth, N.J., 1939-45; div. head radio relay div. ITT Labs., Nutley, N.J., 1945-54; mem. tech. staff RCA Labs., Princeton, N.J., 1954-58; mgr. communications engring. div. astro electronics RCA, Princeton, 1958-63; asst. v.p., chief scientist Communications Satellite Corp., Washington, 1963—; cons. Arthur S. Flemming Awards, 1975-77. Fellow IEEE (Electronics award 1975, award in internat. communications 1976), AIAA (asso.; mem. joint telecommunications adv. com. IEEE 1971-79, chmn. joint com. 1975-77); mem. Nat. Acad. Engring., Sigma Xi, Tau Beta Pi. Designer early radio relay systems in U.S., Can., Mexico, Belgium; designer mil. radio relay systems; communications engring. for early satellites; patentee in field. Office: 950 L'Enfant Plaza SW Washington DC 20024

METZKER, RAY K., photographer; b. Milw., Sept. 10, 1931; s. William Martin and Marian Helen (Krueger) M.; B.A., Beloit Coll., 1953; M.S., Inst. Design, Ill. Inst. Tech., 1959. Mem. faculty photography-film dept. Phila. Coll. Art, 1962—, prof., chmn. dept., 1978—; vis. asso. prof. U. N.Mex., 1970-72; vis. adj. prof. R.I. Sch. Design, spring 1977; one-man exhbns. include: Art Inst. Chgo., 1959, Mus. Modern Art, N.Y.C., 1967, Milw. Art Center, 1970, The Picture Gallery, Zurich, Switzerland, 1974, Marion Locks Gallery, Phila., 1978, Internat. Center Photography, N.Y.C., 1978, Light Gallery, N.Y.C., 1979; represented in permanent collections: Mus. Modern Art, N.Y.C., Art Inst. Chgo., Smithsonian Inst., Washington, Met. Mus. Art, N.Y.C., Phila. Mus. Art, Bibliotheque Nat., Paris. Served with U.S. Army, 1954-56. Guggenheim fellow, 1966, 79; Nat. Endowment Arts fellow, 1974. Home: 733 S 6th St Philadelphia PA 19147 Office: Phila Coll Art Broad and Spruce Sts Philadelphia PA 19102

METZLER, DWIGHT FOX, state ofcl., civil engr.; b. Carbondale, Kans., Mar. 25, 1916; s. Ross R. and Grace (Fox) M.; B.S., U. Kan., 1940, C.E., 1947; S.M., Harvard, 1948; m. Lela Ross, June 20, 1941; children—Linda Diane, Brenda Lee, Marilyn Anne, Martha Jeanne. Asst. engr. Kans. Bd. Health, 1940-42, san. engr., 1946-48, chief engr., Topeka, 1948-62; asso. prof. civil engring. U. Kans., 1948-59, prof., 1959-66; exec. sec. Kans. Water Resources Bd., Topeka, 1962-66; dep. commr. N.Y. State Dept. Health, Albany, 1966-70; dep. commr. N.Y. State Dept. Environ. Conservation, Albany, 1970-74; sec. Kans. Dept. Health and Environment, Topeka, 1974—. Cons. san. engring. Fed. Pub. Housing Authority, USPHS, 1943-46; housing cons. Chgo.-Cook County Health Survey, 1946; cons. water supply and water pollution control USPHS, 1957-66; adviser Govt. India, 1960; mem. ofcl. exchange to USSR on environ. health research and practice, 1962; adviser WHO, 1964—; mem. Water Pollution Bd., Internat. Joint Commn., 1967-74, Assembly of Engring. Nat. Research Council, 1977—. Chmn., Kans. Bible Chair Bd., 1957-66; chmn. com. for new bldg. U. Kans. Sch. Religion. Recipient Distinguished Service award U. Kans., 1970. Registered profl. engr., Kans., N.Y. Diplomate Am. Acad. Environ. Engrs. Fellow Royal Soc. Health Gt. Britain (hon.), Am. Pub. Health Assn. (Centennial award 1972, governing council exec. bd., pres., chmn. action bd.), ASCE (sec. 1959-61, chmn. san. engring. div. 1963); mem. Am. Am. Water Works Assn. (Fuller award 1954, Purification div. award 1958), Water Pollution Control Fedn. (Bedell award 1963), Kans. (Pub. Health Assn. (Crumbine award 1965), Kans. Engring. Soc., Nat. Acad. Engring., Sigma Xi, Tau Beta Pi. Contbr. articles to profl. jours. Home: 3219 MacVicar Ave Topeka KS 66611 Office: Kansas Dept of Health and Environment Topeka KS 66620

METZLER, OWEN EUGENE, corp. exec.; b. nr. Hitchcock, Okla., Aug. 5, 1929; s. Henry G. and Helen L. (Haas) M.; B.A., San Diego State Coll., 1951; m. Bevis Ann Ellis, Dec. 2, 1951; children—Susan, Sally. Sr. v.p. Avco Corp., Greenwich, Conn., 1960—. Past mem. bd. dirs., former treas. Newport Harbor Art Mus.; former bd. dirs. Canyon Hills Assn. Served to capt. AUS, 1953-55. C.P.A., Calif. Mem. Fin. Execs. Inst., Am. Inst. C.P.A.'s, Calif. Soc. C.P.A.'s. Home: 21 Stepping Stone Ln Greenwich CT 06830 Office: 1275 King St Greenwich CT 06830

METZNER, A.W. KENNETH, profl. assn. exec.; b. Germany; B.A. in Math., Corpus Christi Coll., Oxford (Eng.) U., also M.A.; M.S., Ph.D. in Physics, Cornell U.; m. Judith Metzner; children—Marc, Michael. Came to U.S., 1956, now naturalized citizen. Formerly teaching asst. Cornell U., Ithaca, N.Y.; mem. staff Lincoln Labs., Mass. Inst. Tech., Cambridge; mem. staff phys. sci. study com. project Ednl. Services Inc., Watertown, Mass.; asst. prof. physics San Diego State Coll.; co-editor The Physical Rev., now dir. publs. Am. Inst. Physics, N.Y.C. Mem. Am. Phys. Soc., Am. Assn. Physics Tchrs., AAAS, N.Y. Acad. Scis., Fedn. Am. Scientists, Acoustical Soc. Am. Contbr. articles to profl. jours. Home: Scarsdale NY Office: 335 E 45th St New York City NY 10017

METZNER, ARTHUR BERTHOLD, educator; b. Can., Apr. 13, 1927; s. Reinhold Berthold and Lillian (Bredis) M.; B.Sc., U. Alta., 1948; Sc.D., Mass. Inst. Tech., 1951; D.A.Sc. (honoris causa), Katholieke U. te Leuven, Belgium, 1975; m. Elisabeth Krieger, May 9, 1948; children—Elisabeth L., Arthur P., Rebecca. With Def. Research Bd., Ottawa, 1947-48, Colgate Palmolive Co., Jersey City, 1951-53; instr. Mass. Inst. Tech., 1950-51, Bklyn. Poly. Inst., 1951-53; mem. faculty U. Del., 1953—, H. Fletcher Brown prof. chem. engring., 1962—, chmn. dept., 1970-77; vis. prof. Stanford, 1967; Lacey lectr. Calif. Inst. Tech., 1968; vis. prof. U. Cambridge (Eng.), 1968-69. Recipient Wilmington Sect. award Am. Chem. Soc., 1958; Colburn award Am. Inst. Chem. Engrs., 1958, Walker award, 1970; Lewis award, 1977; Bingham medal Soc. Rheology, 1977. Guggenheim fellow, 1968. Mem. Soc. Rheology, Nat. Acad. Engring., Am. Inst. Chem. Engrs. Home: 713 Greenwood Rd Wilmington DE 19807 Office: U Del Newark DE 19711

METZNER, CHARLES MILLER, judge; b. N.Y.C., Mar. 13, 1912; s. Emanuel and Gertrude (Miller) M.; A.B., Columbia U., 1931, LL.B., 1933; m. Jeanne Gottlieb, Oct. 6, 1966. Admitted to N.Y. bar, 1933; pvt. practice, 1934; mem. Jud. Council State N.Y., 1935-41; law clk. to N.Y. supreme ct. justice, 1942-52; exec. asst. to U.S. atty. Gen. Herbert Brownell, Jr., 1953-54; mem. firm Chapman, Walsh & O'Connell, 1954-59; judge U.S. Dist Ct. for So. Dist. N.Y., 1959—. Mem. Law Revision Commn. N.Y. State, 1959; chmn. com. adminstrn. magistrates system U.S. Jud. Conf. Chmn., Columbia Coll. Council, 1965-66. Pres., N.Y. Young Republican Club, 1941. Trustee Columbia U., 1972—. Recipient Columbia U. Alumni medal, 1966. Mem. Am. Law Inst., Fed. Bar Assn. Mem. B'nai B'rith. Club: Lawyers. Home: 36 Sutton Pl S New York City NY 10022 Office: US Courthouse Foley Sq New York City NY 10007

MEUSER, FREDRICK WILLIAM, sem. pres., ch. historian; b. Payne, Ohio, Sept. 14, 1923; s. Henry William and Alvina Maria (Bouyack) M.; A.B., Capital U., 1945, B.D., 1948; S.T.M., Yale U., 1949, M.A., 1953, Ph.D., 1956; postdoctoral Heidelberg U., 1961-62; m. Jeanne Bond Griffiths, July 29, 1951; children—Jill Martha, Douglas Griffiths. Ordained to ministry Am. Lutheran Ch., 1948; asst. pastor 1st Luth. Ch., Galveston, Tex., 1948, Christ Luth. Ch., North Miami, Fla., 1949-51; campus minister Yale U., 1951-53; prof. ch. history Luth. Theol. Sem., Columbus, Ohio, 1953-78, dean grad. studies, 1963-69, pres., 1971-78; pres. Trinity Luth. Sem., 1978—; exec. sec. div. theol. studies Luth. Council in U.S.A., 1969-71; del. World Council Chs., 1968, Luth. World Fedn., 1970. Recipient Distinguished Churchman's award Tex. Luth. Coll., 1972; named Outstanding Alumnus, Capital U., 1977; Am. Assn. Theol. Schs. fellow, 1961-62. Mem. Am. Soc. Ch. History. Author: The Formation of the American Lutheran Church, 1958; (with others) Church in Fellowship, 1963, Lutherans in North America, 1975; translator: What Did Luther Understand by Religion, 1977; The Reconstruction of Morality, 1979; editor: Interpreting Luther's Legacy, 1967. Home: 2402 Berwick Blvd Columbus OH 43209 Office: 2199 E Main St Columbus OH 43209

MEW, THOMAS (TOMMY) JOSEPH, III, painter, educator; b. Miami, Fla., Aug. 15, 1942; s. Thomas Joseph and Maude Edith (Perry) M.; B.S., Fla. State U., 1962, M.A., 1964; Ph.D., N.Y. U., 1966; m. Mary Ann Kelley, June 17, 1966; 1 son, Thomas Joseph. Grad. instr. Fla. State U., 1963; asst. prof. art Troy State U., 1966-68, Jacksonville U., 1968-70; prof., chmn. dept. art Berry Coll., 1970—; exhibited in one-man shows: Parkway Gallery, Miami, 1962-63, 319 Gallery, N.Y.C., 1968, Meridian (Miss.) Mus., 1976, C.D.O. Gallery, Parma, Italy, 1978, Calif. State U., Sacramento, 1979, Miss. Mus. Art, Jackson, 1979; group shows include: High Mus., Atlanta, 1971, 72, 74, New Reform Gallery, Aalst, Belgium, 1975, U. Guelph (Ont., Can.), 1975, Neuberger Mus., Purchase, N.Y., 1978, Arte Fiera, Bologna, Italy, 1979; represented in permanent collections: Kansas City Art Inst., Mildura Art Centre, Australia, Wichita Art Mus., Jacksonville (Fla.) Art Mus.; juror art shows: vis. artist; lectr. in field; host Art: The Mew View, Cable TV show, 1978—; cons. art. Mem. bd. mgmt. YMCA, 1974—; mem. adminstrv. bd. 1st United Methodist Ch., 1974—. Recipient Gellhorn award N.Y. U., 1966; Cowperthwaite grantee, 1972; Lilly Found. grantee, 1976; Gulf Life grantee, 1978. Mem. Southeastern Coll. Art Conf., Coll. Art Assn. Am., Am. Fedn. Arts, Nat. Art Edn. Assn. Filmmaker 1966-69; contbr. articles to profl. jours.; pres. bd. dirs. Contemporary Art/S.E. Mag. Home: 414 Pheasant Run Rome GA 20161 Office: Art Dept Berry Coll Mount Berry GA 30149

MEWBORN, ANCEL CLYDE, mathematician; b. Green County, N.C., Sept. 22, 1932; s. Titus George and Mary Elizabeth (Moye) M.; A.B., U. N.C., 1954, M.A., 1957, Ph.D., 1959; m. Sylvia June McCoy, Jan. 30, 1954; children—Timothy Titus, Melissa June. Instr. math. Yale U., 1959-61; mem. faculty dept. math. U. N.C., Chapel Hill, 1961—, prof., 1970—. Served with USN, 1954-56. Mem. Am. Math. Soc., Math. Assn. Am. Methodist. Home: 413 Landerwood St Chapel Hill NC 27514 Office: Math Dept Univ of NC Chapel Hill NC 27514

MEWBORNE, WILLIAM BURKE, JR., textile co. exec.; b. Durham, N.C., Dec. 15, 1935; s. William Burke and Carlotta A. (Satterfield) M.; A.B., Duke, 1958; m. Elizabeth Leigh Jordan, July 19, 1958; children—William Burke III, Margaret Elizabeth, Virginia Jordan. Asso. partner Roxboro Lumber Co. (N.C.), 1960-64; v.p. Wachovia Bank & Trust Co., Winston-Salem, N.C., 1965-70; v.p. Wachovia Corp., Winston-Salem, 1970; dir., exec. v.p. Adams-Millis Corp., High Point, N.C., 1970-74, pres., chief operating officer, 1974—; dir. Reliance Universal, Inc., Louisville. Served with USNR, 1958-60. Mason. Home: 1312 Westminster Dr High Point NC 27260 Office: 225 N Elm St High Point NC 27261

MEYAART, PAUL JAN, distilling co. exec.; b. Berchem, Belgium, Mar. 6, 1943; came to U.S., 1965; s. Joseph and Leonie (Devreese) M.; B.Commerce, U. Antwerp (Belgium), 1965; M.B.A. (Ford internat. fellow 1965-67, Fulbright grantee 1965-67), U. Chgo., 1967; m. Mary-Ann Mota, Mar. 18, 1967; children—Peter, Antoine, Danielle. Fin. planning mgr. Sinclair Belgium S. A., Brussels, 1967-70; controller-treas. Knoll Internat. Inc., N.Y.C., 1971-74; v.p. fin. Boyle Midway div. Am. Home Products Co., N.Y.C., 1974-78, treas., 1977-78; v.p. fin. and adminstrn., treas. Am. Distilling Co. Inc., N.Y.C., 1978—. Mem. Fin. Execs. Inst. Home: 2 Pace Dr Wyckoff NJ 07481 Office: 245 Park Ave New York NY 10017

MEYBURG, ARNIM HANS, transp. engr.; b. Bremerhaven, W. Ger., Aug. 25, 1939; s. Friedel and Auguste (Kleeberg) M.; came to U.S., 1965; student U. Hamburg, 1960-62, Free U. Berlin, 1962-65; M.S. (Fulbright travel grantee), Northwestern U., 1968, Ph.D., 1971; m. Lee Denise Stollerman, June 18, 1967. Research asso. Transp. Center, Northwestern U., 1968-69; asst. prof. transp. engring. Cornell U., 1969-75, asso. prof., 1975-78, prof., 1978—, acting dept. chmn., 1977-78; vis. mem. faculties U. Calif., Irvine, Tech. U. Munich (Germany); Humboldt Found. research fellow Tech. U. Munich, 1978-79; mem. Transp. Research Bd., 1970—, Transp. Research Forum, 1972—; prin. investigator projects Dept. Transp., NSF Nat. Coop. Hwy. Research Program. NSF Research Initiation grantee, 1973. Mem. ASCE, Ops. Research Soc. Am., Regional Sci. Assn. Author: (with others) Urban Transportation Modeling and Planning, 1975, Transportation Systems Evaluation, 1976, Survey Sampling and Multivariate Analysis for Social Scientists and Engineers, 1979. Co-editor: Behavioral Travel-Demand Models, 1976. Home: 30 St Joseph Ln Ithaca NY 14850 Office: 305 Hollister Hall Cornell U Ithaca NY 14853

MEYER, ADOLPH CONRAD, JR., savs. and loan exec.; b. Oakland, Calif., Aug. 29, 1924; s. Adolph Conrad and Hazel Georgianna (Hanley) M.; student U. Calif. at Berkeley, 1943-44, 46-49; m. Patricia Ann Lewis, Jan. 19, 1974. Pres., chief exec. officer Fidelity Savs. & Loan Assn., San Francisco, 1963—; pres. Fidelity Financial Corp., San Francisco, 1969—. Served to ensign USNR, 1944-46. Mem. Zeta Psi. Republican. Clubs: Orinda Country; Olympic, Merchants Exchange (San Francisco). Office: 260 California St San Francisco CA 94111

MEYER, ALBERT JULIUS, educator; b. Hawarden, Iowa, May 14, 1919; s. Albert Julius and Susan (French) M.; A.B., U. Calif. at Los Angeles, 1941, M.A., 1942; Ph.D., Johns Hopkins, 1951; M.A. (hon.), Harvard, 1960; m. Anne Avantaggio, Dec. 23, 1950; children—Barbara, Peter, Stephen. Asso. prof. econs., exec. asst. to pres. Am. U., Beirut, Lebanon, 1947-55; mem. faculty Harvard, 1955—, prof. Middle Eastern studies, 1964—, lectr. econs., 1955—, asso. dir. Center Middle Eastern Studies, 1956—; cons. corps., philanthropic founds., govt. agys., 1955—. Dir. Indsl. Bank of Japan Trust Co. Head spl. U.S. econ. mission to Saudi Arabia, 1962. Trustee Rhinelander Found., 1964—, Am. Friends of Middle East, 1969—, Near East Found., 1970—. Served to lt. USNR, 1942-45. Fulbright-Hays vis. scholar Middle East, 1966-67. Mem. N.Y. Council Fgn. Relations, Middle East Inst. Author: Middle Eastern Capitalism; Nine Essays, 1959; The Economy of Cyprus, 1962. Home: 1010 Memorial Dr Cambridge MA 02138

MEYER, ALFRED GEORGE, educator; b. Bielefeld, Germany, Feb. 5, 1920; s. Gustav and Therese (Melchior) M.; came to U.S., 1939, naturalized, 1942; A.M., Harvard, 1946, Ph.D., 1950; m. Eva Ruth Apel, Jan. 24, 1946; children—Stefan Garris, Vera Ellen. Research fellow Russian Research Center, Harvard, 1950-53, asst. to dir., 1951-52, asst. dir., 1952-53; acting asst. prof. U. Wash., 1953-55; dir. research program on history of Communist Party, Columbia, 1955-57; mem. faculty Mich. State U., 1957-66, prof., 1959-66; prof. polit. sci. U. Mich., Ann Arbor, 1966—, dir. Center Russian and E. European Studies, 1969-72. Served with AUS, 1941-45. Decorated Bronze Star; Rockefeller fellow, 1947-48; Ford fellow, 1954-55; Guggenheim fellow, 1963-64. Author: (with Gustav Hilger) The Incompatible Allies, 1953; Marxism-The Unity of Theory and Practice, 1954; Leninism, 1957; Communism, 1960; The Soviet Political System, 1965. Home: 4081 E Huron River Dr Ann Arbor MI 48104

MEYER, ALVIN EARL, lawyer; b. New Albany, Ind., Apr. 1, 1923; s. Henry W. and Hallie (Leach) M.; B.S., Ind. U., 1944, LL.B. with distinction, 1946; m. Joanne Warvel, Feb. 12, 1949; 1 son, John C. Admitted to Ind. bar, 1946; practiced in New Albany, 1946-48, Indpls., 1948; prof. law U. Louisville, Ind. U., 1946-47; partner firm Stewart, Irwin, Gilliom, Fuller & Meyer, Indpls., 1955—. Home: 755 Braeside Dr S Indianapolis IN 46260 Office: 300 Mchts Bank Bldg Indianapolis IN 46204

MEYER, ANDRE, banker; b. Paris, France, Sept. 3, 1898; m. Bella Lehman, Dec. 23, 1922; children—Philippe, Francine. Sr. partner Lazard Frères & Co., N.Y.C.; dir. Lazard Bros. & Co., Ltd., London. Trustee Mt. Sinai Hosp. Decorated grand officer Legion of Honor. Home: 35 E 76th St New York City NY 10021 Office: 1 Rockefeller Plaza New York City NY 10021

MEYER, ARMIN HENRY, ret. diplomat, author, educator; b. Ft. Wayne, Ind., Jan. 19, 1914; s. Armin Paul and Leona (Buss) M.; student Lincoln (Ill.) Coll., 1931-33; A.B., Capital U., 1935, LL.D., 1957; M.A., Ohio State U., 1941, LL.D., 1972; LL.D., Wartburg Coll., S.D. Sch. Mines and Tech., 1972; m. Alice James, Apr. 23, 1949; 1 dau., Kathleen Alice. Faculty, Capital U., Columbus, Ohio, 1935-41; staff OWI, Egypt, Iraq, 1942-46; U.S. pub. affairs officer, Baghdad, Iraq, 1946-48; pub. affairs adviser U.S. Dept. State, 1948-52; sec. Am. embassy, Beirut, Lebanon, 1952-55; dep. chief mission, Kabul, Afghanistan, 1955-57; dep. dir. Office South Asian Affairs, Dept. State, 1957-58, dep. dir. Office Near Eastern Affairs, 1958-59, dir., 1959-61, dep. asst. sec. of state for Nr. Eastern and South Asian Affairs, 1961; U.S. ambassador to Lebanon, 1961-65, Iran, 1965-69, Japan, 1969-72; spl. asst. to sec. state, chmn. Cabinet Com. to Combat Terrorism, 1972-73; vis. prof. Am. U., 1974-75; dir. Ferdowsi project Georgetown U., 1975-79, adj. prof. diplomacy, 1975—; Woodrow Wilson vis. fellow, 1974—; cons. Middle East, 1975—. Hon. mem. Lincoln Sesquicentennial Commn., 1959. Recipient Meritorious service award Dept. State, 1958, Superior Honor award, 1973. Mem. Sigma Psi. Lutheran. Author: Assignment Tokyo: An Ambassador's Journal, 1974. Home: 4610 Reno Rd NW Washington DC 20008

MEYER, ARTHUR B., govt. ofcl., forester, b. Jamestown, Mo., Mar. 27, 1916; s. Arthur Bismark and Mary (Moore) M.; B.S. in Forestry, Mich. State Coll., 1938; m. Carolyn Stivers Larkin, Feb. 9, 1940; children—Arthur Stivers, George Stivers; 1 stepson, Robert Larkin. Dist. forester Mo. Conservation Commn., 1938-42, asst. state forester, 1945-47, 49-52; engaged in pvt. bus., 1947-49; editor Jour. Forestry, Soc. Am. Foresters, 1952-68, Pub. Land Law Rev. Commn., Washington, 1968-70; with div. environment Bur. Mines, Dept. Interior, 1970—. Served with USNR, 1942-45. Mem. Soil Conservation Soc. Am., Soc. Am. Foresters, Am. Forestry Assn., Xi Sigma Pi. Co-editor: Forestry Handbook, 1955; American Forestry: Six Decades of Growth, 1960. Contbg. author: Careers in Conservation, 1963; Origins of American Conservation, 1966; co-author: The World of the Forest, 1965. Staff editor History of Public Land Law Development, 1968; One Third of the Nation's Lands, 1970. Home: 502 Dennis Ave Silver Spring MD 20901

MEYER, AUGUST CHRISTOPHER, lawyer, television exec.; b. Brookport, Ill., Oct. 28, 1900; s. Gus and Ida (Pierce) M.; grad. So. Ill. U., 1922; J.D., U. Ill., Urbana, 1928; m. Clara Rocke, Feb. 2, 1929; 1 son, August Christopher. Banker, Brookport, 1917-28; admitted to Ill. bar, 1928; practice law, Champaign, 1928—; mem. firm Leonard & Meyer, 1928-34, Meyer & Franklin, 1934-54, Meyer & Capel, 1954-65; atty. Ill. Press Assn., 1946-54; organizer Midwest Televison, Inc., 1952, pres., 1952-76, chmn. bd., 1976—; chmn. bd. dirs. Bank of Ill. (formerly Trevett-Mattis Banking Co.), Champaign, 1962—. Mem. CBS-TV affiliates adv. bd., 1960-63, 66-69. State of Ill. rep. in negotiations for procurement airport for U. Ill., 1943-45; mem. com. to study future devel. Sch. of Aeros. and devel. of aviation, U. Ill. Past pres., bd. dirs. Burnham City Hosp., Champaign; trustee Lincoln Acad. Ill. Mem. Def. Orientation Conf. Assn., Nat. Assn. Broadcasters, Assn. of Maximum Service Telecasters (dir.), Ill., Champaign County bar assns., Phi Alpha Delta, Alpha Kappa Psi. Republican. Presbyn. Clubs: President's (U. Ill.); Burning Tree (Bethesda, Md.); Cuyamaca (San Diego); Champaign Country; La Jolla Country, Torrey (La Jolla, Calif.). Assisted in procuring publ. Dyess Story, which told of Bataan Death March. Home: 1208 Waverly Dr Champaign IL 61820 Office: 509 S Neil St Champaign IL 61820. *Conduct every conference or finish each transaction with others as if you expected to do business with them tomorrow.*

MEYER, AUGUST CHRISTOPHER, JR., broadcasting co. exec., lawyer; b. Champaign, Ill., Aug. 14, 1937; s. August C. and Clara (Rocke) M.; A.B. cum laude, Harvard U., 1959, LL.B., 1962; m. Karen Haugh Hassett, Dec. 28, 1960; children—August Christopher, Elisabeth Hassett. Admitted to Ill. bar, 1962; partner firm Meyer, Capel, Hirschfeld, Muncy, Jahn and Aldeen, Champaign, Ill., 1962—; dir., officer Midwest Television, Inc., owner Sta. KFMB-TV-AM-FM, San Diego, Sta. WCIA-TV, Champaign, Ill., Sta. WMBD-TV-AM, WKZW, Peoria, Ill., 1968—, pres., 1976—; dir. Bank of Ill.; spl. asst. atty. gen. Ill., 1968-76. Trustee Carle Found. Hosp., Urbana, Ill.; bd. dirs. McKinley, YMCA. Mem. Ill., Champaign County bar assns. Club: Champaign Country. Home: 106 Greencroft Champaign IL 61820 Office: 509 S Neil Champaign IL 61820

MEYER, AXEL, educator; b. Copenhagen, Denmark, Mar. 3, 1926; s. Fred and Anna Elizabeth (Olsen) M.; B.M.E., Coll. City N.Y., 1948, B.E.E., 1950; M.S. in Physics, Ga. Inst. Tech., 1952; Ph.D. in Physics, Ill. Inst. Tech., 1956; m. Cecile Paul, Dec. 17, 1950; children—Carla, Linda, Frederick. Asst. prof. U. Fla., 1955-58, asso. prof., 1958-59; physicist neutron physics and solid state divs. Oak Ridge Nat Lab, 1959-67, research participant, summers 1956, 57; asso. prof. physics No. Ill. U., DeKalb, 1967-69, prof., 1969—, mem. Univ. Council, 1971-72. Served with USNR, 1944-46. Research Corp. grantee U. Fla., 1958; Brit. Sci. Research Council grantee, summers 1971, 73, 79; Can. NRC grantee, summer 1975. Fellow Inst. Physics London; mem. Am. Phys. Soc., A.A.U.P., Sigma Xi. Contbr. articles to profl. jours. Home: 739 Hillcrest Dr DeKalb IL 60115. *I have been fortunate to have had the opportunity to engage in research abroad in England and Canada. In general I work toward a perspective on events that reflects on me as a member of the human species and not as a citizen of a particular country. I am seriously concerned about nuclear war, over-population, energy and resource depletion and environmental deterioration.*

MEYER, BEN FRANKLIN, journalist, Latin Am. specialist; b. San Antonio, Aug. 18, 1903; s. Ben Franklin and Emily (Peters) M.; student Baylor U., 1923-26; m. Christine Richardson, Feb. 8, 1927. With San Antonio Light, 1918-19, San Antonio Express, 1919-21, Cuero Daily Record, 1921-23, Waco News-Tribune, 1923-24; gen. mgr. Electra (Tex.) News, 1926; corr. A.P., Atlanta, 1927-38, chief bur., Mexico City, 1938-41, exec. rep. for Caribbean, Havana, Cuba, 1941-43, 48-54, chief bur., Santiago, Chile, 1943-45, exec. rep. for N.C. and S.C., 1946, exec. rep., Ill., Ind., 1947, Latin Am. affairs specialist, Washington, 1954-68; U.S. corr. domestic and Latin Am. newspapers, 1968-69, Latin Am. columnist, 1971—; chief press div. OAS, 1969-70. Lectr., Georgetown U., Cath. U., Baylor U., U. Tex. Mem. Club de Dialogo, Overseas Writers, State Dept. corrs. assns. Democrat. Episcopalian. Address: 2632 S Grant St Arlington VA 22202

MEYER, BERNARD STERN, lawyer; b. Balt., June 7, 1916; s. Benjamin and Josephine M.; B.S., Johns Hopkins U., 1936; LL.B., U. Md., 1938; m. Elaine Strass, June 25, 1939; children—Patricia, Susan; m. Edythe Birnbaum, Apr. 18, 1975. Admitted to Md. bar, 1938, D.C., N.Y. bars, 1947; practiced in Balt., 1938-41, N.Y.C., 1948-58; with Office Gen. Counsel Treasury Dept., Washington, 1941-43; justice N.Y. State Supreme Ct., 1958-72; mem. firm Meyer, English & Cianciulli, P.C., Mineola, N.Y., 1975—; counsel firm Fink, Weinberger, Fredman & Charney, P.C., N.Y.C., 1974-79; asso. judge N.Y. Ct. Appeals, Albany, 1979—; spl. dep. atty. gen. N.Y. State in charge spl. Attica investigation, 1975. Asso. counsel, spl. counsel Moreland Commn. to Study Workmen's Compensation Adminstrn. and Costs. Founder United Fund L.I.; mem. adv. bd. Commn. Law and Social Action, Am. Jewish Congress; bd. dirs Health and Welfare Council Nassau County, Nassau-Suffolk region NCCJ, Nassau County council Boy Scouts Am., Nat. Center for State Cts. Recipient Disting. services award L.I. Press. Served to lt. USNR, World War II. Mem. Am. Law Inst., Scribes, Am., N.Y. State (chmn. jud. sect.), Nassau County bar assns., a Trial Judges (exec. com., past chmn.), Nat. Coll. State Judiciary (dir.), Assn. Supreme Ct. Justices (past pres., com. chmn.), Nassau County Lawyers Assn. (recipient award), Order of Coif, Omicron Delta Kappa. Contbr. articles to profl. jours. Office: Ct Appeals Hall Albany NY 12207 also 6 W 44th St New York NY 10038

MEYER, BRUD RICHARD, pharm. co. exec.; b. Waukegan, Ill., Feb. 22, 1926; s. Charles Lewis and Mamie Olive (Broom) M.; B.S., Purdue U., 1949; m. Betty Louise Stine (dec. 1970); children—Linda (Mrs. Gary Stillabower), Louise, Janet (Mrs. J. Cockrell), Jeff, Karen, Blake, Amy; m. 2d, Barbara Ann Hamilton, Nov. 26, 1970. With Eli Lilly & Co., 1949—, indsl. engr., 1949-56, supr. indsl. engr., 1956-59, sr. personnel rep., 1960-64 (all Indpls.), personnel mgr., Lafayette, Ind., 1964-67, asst. dir., 1967-69, dir. adminstrn., 1969—. Bd. dirs. Lafayette Home Hosp., 1977—, bd. dirs. United Way Tippecanoe County, 1970—, pres., 1974; bd. dirs. Legal Aid Soc. Tippecanoe County, 1973—, Jr. Achievement; bd. dirs. Lilly Credit Union, 1969-75, pres., 1973-74; mem. Citizen's Com. on Alcoholism, 1966-72; bd. dirs. Greater Lafayette Community Centers, 1975—, pres., 1977—. Served with USAAF, 1943-45. Mem. Pi Tau Sigma, Lambda Chi Alpha, C. of C. Greater Lafayette (bd. dirs., v.p. 1969-73), Battleground Hist. Soc. Methodist. Home: 4217 Trees Hill Dr Lafayette IN 47905 Office: PO Box 685 Lafayette IN 47902

MEYER, CARL EDWIN, JR., aviation co. exec.; b. Flushing, N.Y., Aug. 6, 1928; s. Carl Edwin and Eunice Clifton (Taylor) M.; B.A., Amherst Coll., 1950; M.B.A., N.Y.U., 1955; m. Ruth Leslie Oddy, Sept. 21, 1957; children—Jeffrey S., William D. Mgr., Harris, Kerr, Forster & Co., N.Y.C., 1953-65; asst. treas. Eastern Air Lines, 1965-68; pres., chief airline exec. Trans World Airlines, 1968—, also dir.; dir. Hilton Internat., Canteen Corp.; trustee Empire Savs. Bank. Trustee Midwest Research Inst. Served with AUS, 1950-53. Mem. Am. Inst. C.P.A.'s, Air Transport Assn. (dir.). Clubs: Sky, Wings (N.Y.C.). Home: 51 Hawthorne Pl Manhasset NY 11030 Office: 605 3d Ave New York City NY 11016

MEYER, CHARLES APPLETON, retailing exec.; b. Boston, June 27, 1918; s. George von Lengerke and Frances (Saltonstall) M.; student Phillips Acad.; B.A., Harvard, 1939; m. Suzanne Seyburn, June 15, 1940; children—Brooke M. Franzgen, Nancy M. Hovey. With Sears, Roebuck & Co., 1939-69, beginning in New Haven store, successively mail order buyer, Boston, asst. buyer hdqrs. orgn., staff asst. fgn. stores, mgr. fgn. adminstrn., pres. Sears subsidiary, Bogota, Colombia, 1939-55, v.p., 1955-60, v.p., dir. southwestern ty., 1960-66, v.p., dir. Eastern ty., 1966-69, v.p. corporate planning, 1973-78, sr. v.p. pub. affairs, 1978—; asst. sec. state for inter-Am. affairs, 1969-73; dir. Dow Jones Inc., Gillette Co., Sears Roebuck and Allstate Ins. cos. Bd. dirs. Childrens Meml. Hosp. Chgo.; trustee Phillips Acad., Andover, Mass., Art Inst. Chgo., Lake Forest (Ill.) Coll. Served as capt. AUS, World War II. Clubs: Harvard, Brook (N.Y.C.); Racquet (Chgo.); Old Elm (Ft. Sheridan, Ill.); Shoreacres (Lake Bluff, Ill.); Philadelphia; Metropolitan (Washington); Chevy Chase (Md.). Home: 1320 N Sheridan Rd Lake Forest IL 60045 Office: Sears Tower Chicago IL 60684

MEYER, CHARLES EDWARD, art historian, educator; b. Detroit, Sept. 7, 1928; s. Heinz Adolph and Anna (Blunck) M.; B.F.A., Wayne State U., 1950, M.A., 1952; postgrad. Freie U., Berlin, Germany, 1952-54, U. Wurzburg, Germany, 1958-59; Ph.D., U. Mich., 1967; m. Marjorie Ellen Keilholz, June 14, 1952; children—Heidi Anna, Katrina Ellen, Karl Victor. Curator, faculty Detroit Inst. Arts, 1957-58; asst. prof., asso. prof. art history Mich. State U., 1959-66, dir. div. fine arts, 1960-61, acting head art dept., 1960-62; head art dept. Western Mich. U., Kalamazoo, 1966-77, prof. art history, 1977—. Juror exhbns. of art. Served with AUS, 1952-54. Recipient Distinguished Alumni award Wayne State U., 1967. Mem. Coll. Art Assn., Midwest Coll. Art Conf., Nat. Assn. Schs. of Art (dir. Div. II schs. 1976—, accrediting officer 1974-80), Ann Arbor Potters Guild (pres. 1954-57). Home: 1116 Bronson Circle Kalamazoo MI 49008

MEYER, DANIEL JOSEPH, machinery co. exec.; b. Flint, Mich., May 31, 1936; s. John Michael and Margaret (Meehan) M.; B.S., Purdue U., 1958; M.B.A., Ind. U., 1963; m. Bonnie Harrison, June 22, 1963; children—Daniel P., Jennifer. Mgr., Touche, Ross & Co., Detroit, 1964-69; controller Cin. Milacron, Inc., 1969-77, v.p. finance, treas., 1977—. Served with U.S. Army, 1959. C.P.A., N.Y. Mem. Am. Inst. C.P.A.'s. Club: Kenwood Country (Cin.). Home: 8010 Peregrine Ln Cincinnati OH 45243 Office: 4701 Marburg Ave Cincinnati OH 45209

MEYER, DONALD BURTON, historian; b. Lincoln, Nebr., Oct. 29, 1923; s. Clifford C. and Maude (Myers) M.; student Deep Springs (Calif.) Coll., 1940-41; B.A., U. Chgo., 1947; Ph.D., Harvard U., 1953; m. Jean Shepherd, July 1, 1965; 1 son, William Shepherd; step-children—Rebecca, Sarah, Jeffrey, Rachel. Instr. history Harvard U., 1953-55; from asst. prof. to prof. U. Calif. at Los Angeles, 1955-67; prof. history Wesleyan U., Middletown, Conn., 1967—, dir. Am. studies, 1967, chmn. history dept., 1968-69. Served with AUS, 1943-46. Mem. Am. Hist. Assn., Orgn. Am. Historians, Am. Studies Assn. Author: The Protestant Search for Political Realism, 1960; The Positive Thinkers, 1965. Home: Norwich Rd East Haddam CT 06423 Office: History Dept Wesleyan U Middletown CT 06457

MEYER, DONALD GORDON, educator; b. St. Louis, Nov. 5, 1934; s. William Gordon and Grace Frances (Picraux) M.; B.A., Blackburn Coll., 1956; M.A., Northwestern, 1959, Ph.D., 1965; m. Marilyn Lee Nathan, June 9, 1956; children—Wayne, Kathleen. Instr. econs. Oberlin (Ohio) Coll., 1959-60; lectr. Northwestern U., spring 1960; mem. faculty Loyola U., Chgo., 1961—, asso. prof. mktg., 1967-70, prof., chmn. dept., 1970—, dir. Grad. Sch. Bus., 1975-77, dean Sch. Bus. Adminstrn., 1977—; research cons. Lerner Newspapers, 1964-72. Mem. adv. bd. regional econ. seminars Ill. Bell Telephone Co., 1968-69. Trustee Blackburn Coll., Carlinville, Ill., 1973—. Scholar, Northwestern U., 1956-57, fellow, 1957-58, research fellow, 1958-59; recipient Wall St. Jour. award, 1956. Mem. Am. Mktg. Assn., Am. Econs. Assn., Am. Inst. Decision Scis. (editor Mktg. Insights, 1969). Home: 2306 Grant St Evanston IL 60201 Office: Grad Sch Bus Loyola Univ Chicago IL 60611

MEYER, DUANE GILBERT, coll. pres.; b. Carroll, Iowa, June 29, 1926; s. Ronald John and Dena Regina (Huendling) M.; B.A., U. Dubuque, 1950; M.A., State U. Iowa, Ph.D., 1956; m. Marilyn Hansen, May 20, 1951; children—Paul Christian, Mark Lincoln, James Stephen, Andrea Lynn. Teaching asst. State U. Iowa, 1953-55; asso. prof. history S.W. Mo. State Coll., Springfield, 1955-60, prof., 1960—, dean instruction and admissions, 1961-67, dean faculties and provost, 1967-71, pres., 1971—; pres. Mo. Intercollegiate Athletic Assn., 1966-71. Pres., Springfield Area Council Chs., 1961-62; mem. exec. com., bd. dirs. Greene County chpt. ARC, 1961-62; mem. Nat. Bd. Christian Edn., U.P. Ch., 1968-71, mem. gen. assembly mission council, 1971-75, vice moderator Synod of Mo., 1969—. Served with USNR, 1944-46, Republican. Presbyterian. Author: The Highland Scots of North Carolina, 1732-1776, 1961; The Heritage of Missouri, 1962. Home: 1515 S Fairway St Springfield MO 65804

MEYER, EDMOND GERALD, univ. ofcl.; b. Albuquerque, Nov. 2, 1919; s. Leopold and Beatrice (Ilfeld) M.; B.S. in Chemistry, Carnegie Mellon U., 1940, M.S., 1942; Ph.D. (research fellow), U. N.Mex., 1950; m. Betty F. Knobloch, July 4, 1941; children—Lee Gordon, Terry Gene, David Gary. Chemist Harbison Walker Refractories Co., 1940-41; instr. Carnegie Mellon U., 1941-42; asst. phys. chemist Bur. Mines, 1942-44; chemist research div. N.Mex. Inst. Mining and Tech., 1946-48; head dept. sci. U. Albuquerque, 1950-52; head dept. chemistry N.Mex. Highlands U., 1952-59, dir. Inst. Sci. Research, 1957-63, dean Grad. Sch., 1961-63; dean Coll. Arts and Sci., U. Wyo., 1963-75, v.p., 1974—; dir. First Wyo. Bank, Laramie. Sci. adviser Gov. Wyo.; cons. Los Alamos Sci. Lab., NSF, HEW, GAO; contract investigator Research Corp., Dept. Interior, AEC, NIH, NSF, Dept. Energy, Office of Edn. Fulbright exchange prof. U. Concepcion, Chile, 1959. Served with USNR, 1944-46. Recipient Disting. service award Jaycees. Fellow AAAS, Am. Inst. Chemists; mem. Asso. Western Univs. (chmn. 1973-74), Am. (councillor), Chilean chem. socs., Biophys. Soc., Council Coll. Arts and Scis. (pres. 1971, sec.-treas. 1972-75, dir. Washington office 1973), C. of C. (dir.), Sigma Xi. Co-author: Chemistry-Survey of Principles, 1963; Legal Rights of Chemists and Engineers, 1977. Contbr. articles to profl. jours. Home: 1058 Colina Dr Laramie WY 82070 Office: Old Main Bldg U Wyo Laramie WY 82071

MEYER, EDWARD C., army officer; b. St. Marys, Pa., Dec. 11, 1928; B.S., U.S. Mil. Acad., 1951. Commd. 2d lt. inf. U.S. Army, 1951, advanced through grades to gen. U.S. Army; served with 40th Inf. Div., Korea; comdr. inf. co., staff officer bn.; instr. Inf. Sch., Ft. Benning, Ga.; comdr. airborne co. 101st Airborne Div., Ft. Campbell, Ky.; served on Allied Staff at Supreme Hdqrs., Allied Powers, Europe Hdqrs.; served on Dept. Army staff in Office Chief of Staff, Washington; with 1st Cavalry Div., Vietnam, div. chief of staff; with Joint Staff, Washington; Fed. Exec. fellow Brookings Inst., Washington; asst. div. comdr. 82d Airborne Div.; dep. comdt. Army War Coll.; dep. chief of staff for ops. and plans U.S. Army, Europe; comdg. gen. 3d Inf. Div., Germany; asst. dep. chief of staff for ops. and plans Dept. Army, Washington, 1975-76, dep. chief staff for ops. and plans, 1976-79, chief of staff U.S. Army, 1979—. Office: Office of Chief of Staff Dept of Army Washington DC 20310*

MEYER, EDWARD HENRY, advt. exec.; b. N.Y.C., Jan. 8, 1927; s. I.H. and Mildred (Driesen) M.; B.A. with honors in Econs., Cornell U., 1949; m. Sandra Raabin, Apr. 26, 1957; children—Margaret Ann, Anthony Edward. With Bloomingdale's div. Federated Dept Stores, 1949-51, Biow Co., agy., 1951-56; with Grey Advt., Inc., N.Y.C., 1956—, exec. v.p., 1963-68, pres., chief exec. officer,, 1968—; dir. May Dept. Stores Co., Merrill Lynch Ready Assets Trust, Merrill Lynch Spl. Value Fund, Trans Lux Corp. Trustee Asso. Y's of N.Y., Am. Health Found. Served with USCGR, 1945-47. Clubs: Univ., Cornell, Harmonie, Economic (N.Y.C.); Century Country. Home: 580 Park Ave New York NY 10021 Office: 777 3d Ave New York NY 10017

MEYER, FREDERICK RAY, mfg. co. exec.; b. Highland Park, Ill., Dec. 30, 1927; s. Raymond Thorne and Marian Catherine (Anderson) M.; B.S., Purdue U., 1949; M.B.A., Harvard, 1958; m. Barbara Spreuer, Oct. 24, 1953; children—Cheryl L., Amy Sue, Bradley A. Treas., Aladdin Industries, Nashville, 1958-67; pres. Crescent Dallas div. Tyler Corp., 1967-68, v.p. corporate staff, 1968-70, sr. v.p., 1970-77, exec. v.p., 1977—, dir., 1967—, mem. exec. com., 1971—; dir. Aladdin Industries, Inc. Chmn., Rep. Alan Steelman's campaigns, 1972, 74; chmn. Dallas County Rep. Party. Trustee, Inst. for Aerobics Research, Tex. Outward Bound. Served with U.S. Army, 1953-55. Registered profl. engr., Tex. Mem. Dallas Petroleum Club. Republican. Presbyn. (elder). Mason. Home: 5830 Averill Way Dallas TX 75225 Office: 3121 Southland Center Dallas TX 75201

MEYER, GEORGE GOTTHOLD, physician; b. Frankfurt, Germany, Nov. 13, 1931; s. Hans and Hilda (Lesser) M.; came to U.S., 1941, naturalized, 1946; B.A., Johns Hopkins U., 1951; M.D., U. Chgo., 1955; m. Paula Saslaw, June 17, 1953; children—Bruce Alan, Brian Lee, Barry Dale. Intern, USPHS Hosp., S.I., N.Y., 1955-56; resident in psychiatry U. Chgo. Hosps. and Clinics, 1958-60, chief resident, 1960-61, chief psychiat. inpatient service, 1966-69; mem. faculty U. Chgo. Med. Sch., 1961-69, asso. prof. psychiatry, 1968-69; asso. prof. U. Tex. Med. Sch., San Antonio, 1969-71; prof. U. Tex. Health Sci. Center, San Antonio, 1971—; dir. N.W. San Antonio Mental Health Center, 1969-74; mem. exec. bd. Crisis Center, San Antonio, 1971-75; cons. VA Hosp., San Antonio and Kerrville, Tex., Kerrville State Hosp., San Antonio State Hosp., Santa Rosa Med. Center; psychiat cons. Dallas Office, NIMH, also psychiatry edn. br.; vis. lectr. psychiatry U. Edinburg (Scotland) Med. Sch., 1966; vis. prof. psychiatry U. Man. (Can.), Winnipeg, 1977; mem. med. adv. bd. for driver licensing Tex. Dept. Health, 1973-78; bd. dirs. Ecumenical Center Religion and Health San Antonio, 1974-77. Served with USPHS, 1955-58. NIMH career tchr. grantee, 1961-63; recipient Okie award Gov. Okla., 1969. Diplomate Am. Bd. Psychiatry and Neurology. Fellow Am. Psychiat. Assn., Am. Orthopsychiat. Assn.; mem. Am., Tex., Bexar County med. assns., Tex., Bexar County, World psychiat. assns., Am. Group Psychotherapy Assn., San Antonio Group Process and Group Psychotherapy Soc., Am. Assn. Med. Colls., Am. Coll. Psychiatrists, Am. Assn. Geriatric Psychiatry, Sigma Xi, Alpha Omega Alpha, Phi Lambda Upsilon. Contbr. numerous articles to med. jours. Home: 2907 Marlborough Dr San Antonio TX 78230

MEYER, GEORGE HERBERT, lawyer; b. Detroit, Feb. 19, 1928; s. Herbert M. and Agnes F. (Eaton) M.; A.B., U. Mich., 1949; J.D., Harvard, 1952; certificate Oxford (Eng.) U., 1955; LL.M., Wayne State U., 1962; m. Carol Ann Jones, June 28, 1958; children—Karen Ann, George Herbert. Admitted to D.C. bar, 1952, Mich. bar, 1953; asso. firm Fischer, Franklin & Ford, Detroit, 1956-63, mem. firm, 1963-74; established firm George H. Meyer, 1974-78; sr. mem. firm Meyer and Kirk, 1978—. Chmn. Birmingham (Mich.) Bd. Housing Appeals, 1964-68; vice chmn. Birmingham Bd. Zoning Appeals, 1966-69; mem. Birmingham Planning Bd., 1968-70; trustee Bloomfield Village, Mich., 1976—, pres., 1979—; mem. exec. bd. Detroit Area council Boy Scouts Am., 1976—, asst. counsel, 1979—; chmn. Detroit area council Eagle Scout Recognition Dinner Com., 1978. Served as 1st lt. JAG, USAF, 1952-55; maj. Res. ret. Recipient William Jennings Bryant prize in polit. sci. U. Mich., 1949. Mem. Am., Detroit, Oakland County bar assns., State Bar Mich., Harvard Law Sch. Assn. Mich. (dir. 1959—, pres. 1970—), Detroit Sci. Mus. Soc. (pres. 1961-74, chmn. 1974—), Phi Beta Kappa, Alpha Phi Omega. Republican. Unitarian. Clubs: Masons, Rotary, Detroit Boat, Scarab, Harvard of N.Y.C. Author: Equalization in Michigan and Its Effect on Local Assessments, 1963. Home: 1228 Sandringham Way Birmingham MI 48010 Office: 100 W Long Lake Rd Suite 100 Bloomfield Hills MI 48013

MEYER, HARRY M., JR., pediatrician; b. Palestine, Tex., 1928; M.D., U. Ark., 1953. Intern Walter Reed Army Hosp., 1953-54; asst. resident pediatrics N.C. Meml. Hosp., Chapel Hill. 1957-59; chief lab. viral immunology, div. biologics standards NIH (transferred to Food and Drug Adminstrn.), 1959-72, dir. Bur. Biologics, 1972—. Served to capt. M.C., AUS, 1953-57. Diplomate Am. Bd. Pediatrics. A pioneer in devel. German measles vaccine. Address: Bur Biologics FDA 8800 Rockville Pike Bethesda MD 20205

MEYER, HOWARD RAYMOND, architect; b. N.Y.C., Feb. 17, 1903; s. Emile and Estelle (Freund) M.; A.B., Columbia, 1923, B.Arch., 1928; m. Schon Landman, Oct. 16, 1928; 1 son, Paul Emile. With office William Lescaze, architect, N.Y.C., 1926, Bertram G. Goodhue Assos., architects, N.Y.C., 1929-30; travel in Europe, 1930-31; supr. constrn. Albanian-Am. Inst. of Nr. East Found., Kavaja, Albania, for Thompson & Churchill, architects, N.Y.C., 1932; partner firm Morris B. Sanders & Howard R. Meyer, architects, N.Y.C., 1933-34; pvt. practice architecture, Dallas, 1935-42, 46—; prin. works include 13th Ch. of Christ Scientist, N.Y.C., 1934, Temple Beth El, Tyler, Tex., 1938, Hillel Found. at U. Tex., 1950, bldgs. Red River Arsenal and Longhorn Ordnance Works, 1951-53, 2 pub. housing projects, Dallas, 1953, Burnet Elementary Sch., Dallas, 1955, 3525 Turtle Creek apt. bldg., Dallas, 1957, Temple Emanu El, Dallas, 1957, Dallas Rehab. Center, 1960, Turtle Creek Village, 1962, Dallas Home and Hosp. Jewish Aged, 1963, 1st Presbyn. Ch., Denton, Tex., 1966, Nogales Bldg., Vicksburg, Miss., 1966, McKinney (Tex.) Job

Corps Center for Women, 1967, Aircraft Instrument Trainer Bldg., Ft. Wolters, Tex., 1968, bachelor officer's quarters Ft. Hood, Tex., 1969, officer family housing Bergstrom AFB, Tex., 1969, U.S. P.O. and Fed. Bldg., Rockwall Tex., 1970, St. Paul Luth. Ch., Denton, 1972, Adminstrv. Tng. Bldg. for Big Brown Steam Electric Sta., Tex., 1972, Byer Sq. at Dallas Home for Jewish Aged, 1974, Dallas West Br. Library, 1974, Ruth W. and Milton P. Levy Bldg., Dallas, 1977, Denton Area Tchrs. Credit Union, 1978, others; cons. to PHA; archtl. advisory panel Office Chief Engrs., Dept. Army; cons. architect student chapel Tex. A. and M. Coll., 1956. Chmn. architects adv. com. Dallas Hist. Monuments Commn., 1961; mem. design com. Greater Dallas Planning Council. Served to maj. C.E., AUS, 1942-46. Recipient grand prize Matico competition Mastic Tile Corp. Am., 1959. Fellow AIA (award merit 1959, chmn. com. on housing 1966); mem. Tex. Soc. Architects (medal merit 1950, award merit 1958), Guild Religious Archtecture, Zeta Beta Tau. Jewish. Home: 4433 Belclaire Dallas TX 75205 Office: Lee Park Center 3141 Hood St Dallas TX 75219

MEYER, HUGO BARDILL, mfg. exec.; b. Highland, Ill., Mar. 2, 1911; s. Adolph and Clara (Bardill) M.; A.B. with great distinction, Stanford, 1932; M.B.A. with honors, Harvard, 1934; m. Elizabeth B. Hyde, Nov. 2, 1939; children—Katherine H., Stephen B., John B., Peter B., Anne F. With investment dept. Continental Ins. Co., 1934-37, Schroder-Rockefeller Co., Inc., investment bankers, 1937-45; pres. U.S. Fiber & Plastics Corp., 1946—, Bardill Land & Lumber Co., 1951—; dir. Piggly-Wiggly-Southern, Inc.; dir., mem. exec. com. Pet Inc., 1949-78. Chmn., Summit Community Chest, 1950. Trustee Overlook Hosp., 1953-59, gen. chmn. hosp. bldg. fund, 1957; bd. dirs. Summit YMCA, 1957-61, pres., 1961-63; chmn. bd. trustees Union Coll., Cranford, N.J., 1965-69; bd. dirs. Vt. Natural Resources Council, treas., 1975. Clubs: Mountain View (Greensboro, Vt.); Baltusrol Golf (Springfield, N.J.). Home: Cabot Rd Woodbury VT 05681 Office: Woodbury VT 05681

MEYER, JAMES HENRY, univ. ofcl.; b. Fenn, Idaho, Apr. 13, 1922; s. Carl A. and Anita (de Coursey) M.; B.S. in Agr., U. Idaho, 1947; M.S. in Nutrition (fellow Wis. Alumni Research Found.), U. Wis., 1949, Ph.D., 1951; m. Margaret Hickman, Aug. 21, 1947; children—Stephen J., Susan T., Gary C., Joan K., Teresa A. Research asst. U. Wis., 1949-51; faculty U. Calif. at Davis, 1951—, prof. animal husbandry, 1960—, chmn. dept., 1960-63, dean Coll. Agr. and Environment, 1963-69, chancellor univ., 1969—. Mem. Commn. Undergrad. Edn. in Biology, 1964-69. Served with USMCR, 1942-46. Recipient Am. Feed Mfr.'s award in nutrition, 1960. Mem. AAAS, Am. Soc. Animal Prodn., Nat. Assn. State Univs. and Land Grant Colls., Western Coll. Assn. (exec. com. 1971-74), Sigma Xi. Editorial bd. Jour. Animal Sci., 1961-65. Home: 16 College Park Davis CA 95616

MEYER, JANET KATHERINE, journalist; b. Kansas City, Mo., Dec. 10, 1947; d. Lawrence Edward and Mary Jane (Sanders) M.; B.J., U. Mo., 1969; postgrad. U. Mo., Kansas City, 1975—; m. Marshall Miller, July 18, 1976. Fin. writer Kansas City Star, 1969-73, asst. fin. editor, 1973-78; fin. editor Kansas City Star and Times, 1978-79, fin. Kansas City Times, 1979—. Co-chmn. Internat. Womens Year, Kansas City, 1975; trustee Kansas City Art Inst. Mem. Am. Soc. Bus. and Econ. Writers. Roman Catholic. Home: 701 E 45th St Kansas City MO 64110 Office: 1729 Grand Ave Kansas City MO 64108

MEYER, JEFFERY WILSON, chem. mktg. co. exec.; b. San Francisco, June 22, 1923; s. Wilson and Mabel (Wilson) M.; B.S. in Agr., U. Calif., 1948; m. Janet Busse, Jan. 28, 1945; children—Pamela Wilson, Elizabeth Ruth. With Wilson & Geo. Meyer & Co., San Francisco, 1948—, v.p., 1951-59, pres., chief exec. officer, 1959—, chmn., 1973—; dir. Security First Group. Trustee Calif. Acad. Scis. Served to 1st lt., inf., U.S. Army, 1945-48, with Chem. Corps, U.S. Army, 1951-52. Decorated Bronze Star. Mem. Calif. Fertilizer Assn. (pres. 1975), Internat. Super phosphate and Compound Mfrs. Assn. Ltd., Norwegian Am. C. of C., Fertilizer Inst., Chem. Industry Councl. Clubs: Bohemian, Pacific-Union, Menlo Country, San Francisco Yacht, St. Francis Yacht, Cercle de l'Union. Home: 3880 Ralston Ave Hillsborough CA 94010 Office: 270 Lawrence Ave S San Francisco CA 94080

MEYER, JOHANNES HORST, physicist; b. Berlin, Germany, Mar. 1, 1926; s. Kurt Heinrich and Gertrude (Hellwig) M.; B.Sc., U. Geneva, 1949; Ph.D., U. Zurich, 1953; m. Ruth Mary Hunter, Mar. 28, 1953; children—Richard, Christopher. Came to U.S., 1957. Nuffield fellow Oxford (Eng.) U., 1953-57; lectr. Harvard U., 1957-59, asst. prof., 1959-60, asso. prof., 1960-64; prof. physics Duke U., 1964—; vis. prof. Technische Hochschule, Munich, Germany, fall 1965; vis. fellow Japanese Soc. Promotion Sci., 1971, 79; vis. scientist Institut Laue-Langevin, Grenoble, France, 1974, 75; cons. NSF, mem. materials scis. and physics panels, 1972-76. Served with Swiss Army, 1946-56. Alfred P. Sloan fellow, 1960-64. Fellow Am. Phys. Soc. Contbr. numerous articles on low temperature physics to sci. jours. Home: 2716 Montgomery St Durham NC 27705 Office: Dept Physics Duke U Durham NC 27706

MEYER, JOHN EDWARD, nuclear engr.; b. Pitts., Dec. 17, 1931; s. Albert Edward and Thelma Elizabeth (Brethauer) M.; B.S., Carnegie Inst. Tech., 1953, M.S., 1953, Ph.D. (ASME Student award 1955), 1955; m. Gracyann Lenz, June 13, 1953; children—Susan Meyer Heydon, Karl, Karen, Thomas. Engring. and mgmt. positions Westinghouse Bettis Atomic Power Lab., West Mifflin, Pa., 1955-75; vis. lectr. U. Calif., Berkeley, 1968-69; prof. nuclear engring. M.I.T., 1975—; cons. in field. Recipient Bettis Disting. Service award, 1962, Outstanding Tchr. award nuclear engring. M.I.T., 1979. Fellow Am. Nuclear Soc.; mem. ASME, Sigma Xi. Author papers in field. Office: Room 24-208 77 Massachusetts Ave Cambridge MA 02139

MEYER, JOHN EDWARD, oil co. exec.; b. Hoisington, Kans., Aug. 23, 1926; s. John J. and Helen W. (McIllwaine) M.; B.S., U. Kans., 1950; grad. Advanced Mgmt. Program Harvard, 1966; m. Margaret Jean Lutz, June 9, 1948; children—Cynthia Sue (Mrs. Caputo), Winifred Jan (Mrs. McAtee), Elizabeth Anne (Mrs. McCollam), John Edward. Various oil field jobs, 1942-50; joined Cities Service Oil Co., 1950, with purchasing dept., Bartlesville, Okla., 1951-54, head purchasing, Chgo., 1954-56, engr. marine dept., N.Y.C., 1956-58, fgn. flag mgr., 1958-60, asst. to gen. supt., 1960-62, asst. to gen. mgr., 1962-63, v.p., gen. mgr. Cities Service Tankers, 1963-66, project coordinator Cities Service Co., N.Y.C., 1966-67, staff v.p. indsl. relations, 1967-68, v.p. Natural Gas Liquids Group, Tulsa, 1969-71, group v.p. internat., 1971, exec. v.p., 1972-78, v.p., 1978—; pres. Cities Service Tankers, 1968-69. Served with USNR, 1944-46. Registered profl. engr., Okla. Mem. Am. Petroleum Inst., 25 Year Club Petroleum Industry, Soc. Naval Architects and Marine Engrs., Delta Upsilon, Tau Beta Pi, Pi Tau Sigma, Sigma Tau. Methodist. Mason. Club: So. Hills Country (Tulsa).

MEYER, JOHN ROBERT, educator, economist; b. Pasco, Wash., Dec. 6, 1927; s. Philip Conrad and Cora (Kempter) M.; student Pacific U., 1945-46; B.A., U. Wash., 1950; Ph.D. (David A. Wells prize), Harvard U., 1955; m. Lee Stowell, Dec. 17, 1949; children—Leslie Karen, Ann Elizabeth, Robert Conrad. Jr. fellow Harvard, 1953-55, asst. prof., 1955-58, asso. prof., 1958-59, prof. econs., 1959-68; prof. Yale, 1968-73; 1907 prof. Harvard U., 1973—; dir. Dun & Bradstreet, Union Pacific Corp., Charles River Assos., Dominion Bridge Ltd., AMCA Internat., Canellus Inc.; trustee Mut. Life Ins. Co. N.Y. Pres., Nat. Bur. Econ. Research, 1967-77; mem. Presdl. Task Force on Transp., 1964, Presdl. Commn. on Population Growth and Am. Future, 1970-72. Served with USNR, 1946-48. Guggenheim fellow, 1958. Fellow Am. Acad. Arts and Scis., Econometric Soc.; mem. Am. Econ. Assn. (exec. com. 1971-73), Am. Statis. Assn., Council Fgn. Relations, Econ. History Assn. Co-author: The Investment Decision-An Empirical Inquiry, 1957; Economics of Competition in the Transportation Industry, 1959; The Economics of Slavery and Other Essays on the Quantitative Study of Economic History, 1964; The Urban Transportation Problem, 1965; other books. Contbr. articles to several profl. jours. Home: 138 Brattle St Cambridge MA 02138 Office: Harvard Business School Morgan 322 Boston MA 02163

MEYER, KARL ERNEST, journalist; b. Madison, Wis., May 22, 1928; s. Ernest Louis and Dorothy (Narefsky) M.; B.A., U. Wis., 1951; M.P.A., Princeton U., 1953, Ph.D., 1956; m. Sarah Nielsen Peck, Aug. 12, 1959 (div. 1972); children—Ernest, Heather, Jonathan. Reporter, N.Y. Times, N.Y.C., 1952, mem. editorial bd., 1979—; editorial writer Washington Post, 1956-65, chief London bur., 1965-70, N.Y.C. corr., 1970-71; Washington corr. New Statesman, 1961-65; sr. editor, TV critic Saturday Rev., N.Y.C., 1975-79; corr. in residence Fletcher Sch. Law and Diplomacy, Tufts U., 1979; mem. bd. judges Rockefeller Public Service Awards, 1972-75, George Foster Peabody Broadcasting Awards, 1977—. Recipient citation for excellence Overseas Press Club, 1960; Bronze medal Sigma Delta Chi, 1963. Mem. PEN Club Internat. Clubs: Fed. City (Washington); Princeton of N.Y.C. Author: The New America, 1961; (with Tad Szulc) The Cuban Invasion, 1962; Fulbright of Arkansas, 1963; The Pleasures of Archaeology, 1971; The Plundered Past, 1973; Teotihuacán, 1975; The Art Museum: Power, Money, Ethics, 1979. Home: 96 Eleven O'Clock Rd Weston CT 06883 Office: NY Times 229 W 43d St New York NY 10036

MEYER, KARL WILLIAM, coll. pres.; b. Ft. Wayne, Ind., May 8, 1925; s. K.W. and L. (Hofacker) M.; A.B., Valpariaso U., 1948; M.F.S., U. Md., 1949; Ph.D., U. Wis., 1953; postgrad. U. Basel (Switzerland), 1948-49; postdoctoral fellow U. Mich., 1958-59; m. Margery R. Hamman, Apr. 15, 1949; children—Mary, William, Frederick, Ann, Jean. Faculty, Valparaiso U., 1952-53, Augustana Coll., 1953-55, Wis. State U., 1955-58; dean instrn., dir. grad. studies Wayne State Coll., 1959-63; asst. dir. bd. regents Wis. State Colls., Madison, 1963-64; pres. U. Wis.-Superior, 1964—. Served with USAAF, 1943-46; ETO. Author: Karl Liebknecht: Man Without a Country, 1957. Contbr. articles to profl. jours. Home: Route 1 Box 406 Lake Nebagamon WI 54849

MEYER, KERSTIN, singer, mezzo soprano; b. Stockholm, Apr. 3, 1928; d. J.O. and Anna (Eriksson) M.; student Royal Conservatory, Stockholm, Accademia Chigiana, Siena, Italy, Mozarteum, Salzburg, Austria; m. Bjorn Bexelius. Debut in Il Trovatore, Stockholm, 1952; appears with opera cos. in Buenos Aires, Salzburg, Vienna, Brussels, Vancouver, Copenhagen, Helsinki, Paris, London, Glyndebourne, Bayreuth, Berlin, Hamburg, Tokyo, Munich, Glasgow, Mexico City, Milan, Rome, Oslo, Edinburgh Festival, Moscow, N.Y.C., San Francisco, Santa Fe, also maj. orchs. in U.S., Europe, Australia, New Zealand, Far East. Royal Court singer. Awards include Swedish Wasa Order, medal Litteris et Artibus, Italian Order of Merit. Mem. Royal Acad. Music. Home: Valhallavägen 46 11422 Stockholm Sweden Office: care Thea Dispeker 59 E 54th St New York NY 10022

MEYER, KURT WERNER, architect; b. Zurich, Switzerland, June 3, 1922; s. Max E. and Elizabeth (Stadler) M.; M.A., Swiss Fed. Inst. Tech., 1948; children—Susanne, Randolph, Richard. Designer, Lacy, Atherton & Davis, Harrisburg, Pa., 1948-49; chief archtl. designer Bechtel Corp., Los Angeles, 1949-53; designer Kistner, Wright & Wright, 1953-55; pvt. practice architecture, Los Angeles, 1956—. Chmn., Community Redevel. Agy., Los Angeles, 1976—; bd. dirs. YMCA. Recipient Design award City of Los Angeles, 1967. Fellow AIA; mem. Los Angeles C. of C., Urban Land Inst. Important works include Liberty Office Bldg., Los Angeles, Civic Center Huntington Beach (Calif.) (AIA Design award 1977), San Bernardino County Govt. Center. Home: 2702 Westshire Dr Los Angeles CA 90068 Office: 2690 Beachwood Dr Los Angeles CA 90068

MEYER, LEONARD B., educator, musician; b. N.Y.C., Jan. 12, 1918; s. Arthur S. and Marion (Wolff) M.; student Bard Coll., 1936-37; B.A., Columbia, 1940, M.A., 1948; Ph.D., U. Chgo., 1954; L.H.D., Grinnell Coll., Loyola U., Chgo., Bard Coll.; m. Janet M. Levy; children—Marion L., Carlin, Erica Cecile. Faculty, U. Chgo., 1946-75, head humanities sect., 1958-60, prof. music, 1961-75, chmn. music dept., 1961-70, Phyllis Fay Horton distinguished service prof. humanities, 1972-75; Benjamin Franklin prof. music and humanities U. Pa., 1975—. Ernest Bloch prof. music, Berkeley, Calif., 1971. Fellow Center for Advanced Studies, Wesleyan U., Middletown, Conn., 1960-61; Guggenheim fellow, 1971-72. Fellow Am. Acad. Arts and Scis.; mem. Am. Musicological Soc., Am. Soc. Aesthetics, Soc. Music Theory, AAUP, Phi Beta Kappa. Author: Emotion and Meaning in Music, 1956; The Rhythmic Structure of Music, 1960; Music, the Arts and Ideas, 1967; Explaining Music: Essays and Explorations, 1973. Contbr. articles to profl. jours. Office: Dept of Music Univ of Pa Philadelphia PA 19174

MEYER, LEONARD HERMAN, utility exec.; b. Evansville, Ind., Mar. 31, 1917; s. John Henry and Ruth Fern (Meeks) M.; grad. Lockyear Coll. Bus., Evansville, 1936; student U. Evansville, evenings 1938-39; m. Agnes Louise Rainwater, Dec. 30, 1949; 1 son, James Gale. With So. Ind. Gas & Electric Co., Evansville, 1936—, sec., asst. treas., 1954-59, sec., treas., 1959-78, v.p. fin., 1978—. Asso. gen. chmn. fund drive United Way Southwestern Ind., 1974-75, 1st v.p., chmn. advance corporate gifts div. fund drive, 1975-76; treas., mem. exec. com. Raintree council Girl Scouts U.S.A., 1974-78. Bd. dirs. United Fund Evansville and Vanderburg County, 1964-70, treas., 1964-69; pres. United Way Southwestern Ind., 1976; bd. dirs., exec. council Buffalo Trace council Boy Scouts Am., 1965-68. Served to maj., 4th Inf. Div., AUS, 1941-46; ETO. Decorated Bronze Star. Mem. Evansville C. of C., Nat. Assn. Accountants (v.p. 1955-56), Ind. Elec. Assn. and Ind. Gas Assn. (chmn., sec. joint accounting com. 1962-63). Elk, Eagle. Clubs: Petroleum, Kennel. Home: 209 Camden Ct Evansville IN 47715 Office: 20 NW 4th St Evansville IN 47741

MEYER, LOUIS, JR., investment banker; b. Los Angeles, Dec. 22, 1900; s. Louis and Lillie (Newman) M.; student U. Calif. at Berkeley, 1918-20; m. Bertha Guggenheim, Dec. 28, 1921; children—Patricia (Mrs. Geoffrey M. Berman), Eleanor (Mrs. Emil J. Rothenberg). With Union Bank, Los Angeles, 1926-34; with Stern, Frank, Meyer & Fox, Inc., Los Angeles, 1934—, chmn. bd., from 1967; v.p., Drexel, Burnham, Lambert, Inc. Bd. govs. N.Y. Stock Exchange, 1962-65. Bd. dirs. Caltech. Assos., Pasadena, 1975—, Bel Air Assn., Los Angeles, 1978—. Mem. Investment Bankers Assn. Am. (bd. govs. 1967-69). Clubs: Los Angeles, Stock Exchange. Home: 266 N Bentley Ave Los Angeles CA 90049 Office: 1901 Ave of Stars Suite 1100 Los Angeles CA 90067

MEYER, MARGARET ELEANOR, microbiologist; b. Westwood, Calif., Feb. 8, 1923; d. Herman Henry and Eleanor (Dobson) M.; B.S., U. Calif., Berkeley, 1945; Ph.D., U. Calif., Davis, 1961. Pub. health analyst USPHS, Bethesda, Md., 1945-46; swine Brucellosis control agt. Dept. Agr., Davis, 1946-47; bacteriologist, U. Calif., Davis, 1947-61; research microbiologist Sch. Vet. Medicine, 1961-77, prof. veterinary pub. health and microbiologist exptl. sta., 1977—; research microbiologist U. Calif. Med. Sch., Los Angeles, 1961-77; supr. Brucella identifications lab. WHO, U. Calif., Davis, 1964—, prof. vet. pub. health, 1973—; cons. subcom. on Brucella, Internat. Com. Bacterial Taxonomy, 1962—, mem., 1966—; mem. 5th Pan Am. Congress Veterinary Medicine, Venezuela, 1966, Internat. Congress Microbiology, Moscow, 1966, Mexico City, 1970, Internat. Congress Microbiology, Munich, Ger., 1978; mem. advisory com. to Bergey's Manual Determative Bacteriology, 1967; Internat. Conf. Culture Collections, Tokyo, 1968; cons. in resident Pan Am. Health Orgn., Zoonoses Lab., Buenos Aires, 1968; mem. brucellosis tech. adv. com. U.S. Animal Health Assn., 1977; cons. Alaska Dept. Fish and Game, 1976. Bd. dirs. Carmichael (Calif.) Park and Recreation Dist., 1975. Recipient Research Career Devel. award USPHS-NIH, 1963. Fellow Am. Pub. Health Assn., Am. Acad. Microbiology; mem. Soc. Am. Microbiologists, N.Am. Conf. Animal Disease Research Workers, Am. Coll. Veterinary Microbiologists (hon. affiliate), U.S. Animal Health Assn. (chmn. brucellosis tech. advisory com. 1978-79), Internat. Assn. Microbiol. Socs. (mem. 1st intersect. congress 1974), AAUW, No. Calif. Women's Golf Assn., U. Calif. Alumni Assn., Sigma Xi. Clubs: U. Calif. Faculty (Davis); El Dorado Royal Country (Shingle Springs, Calif.); Reno Women's Golf. Contbr. articles to profl. jours. Home: 5611 Fair Oaks Blvd Carmichael CA 95608 Office: Dept Epidemiology and Preventive Medicine Sch Veterinary Medicine U Calif Davis CA 95616

MEYER, MAX BERNHARDT, mfg. co. exec.; b. Far Rockaway, N.Y., Oct. 8, 1916; s. Bernhardt and Birdie (Marqusee) M.; A.B., Harvard, 1938; m. Edith Marjorie Meyers, Mar. 16, 1941; children—Elizabeth Ann, Peter Bernhardt. Mem. tng. squad, asst. buyer R.H. Macy & Co., N.Y.C., 1939-41; with Gen. Cigar Co., Inc., Hatfield, Mass., 1941-42; with tobacco tng. program Gen. Cigar Co., Inc., Cuba and P.R., 1945-47, mgr. Cuban and P.R. operations, 1947-49, v.p. charge various segments of operations, 1949-65, v.p., sec., 1965-75, also dir.; v.p., gen. mgr. Ex-Lax, Inc., Humaco, P.R., 1975-76, pres., 1976—. Served with USCGR, 1942-45. Mem. Cigar Mfrs. Assn. Am. (pres. 1969-75, dir.). Home: Rural Box 6238 Rd 914 Bo Tejas Humacao PR 00661 Office: Ex-Lax Inc Box AL Humacao PR 00661

MEYER, MAYNARD WILLIAM, architect; b. Milw., Dec. 10, 1913; s. Arnold Frederick and Isabelle Anna (Fiebing) M.; B.A., Yale U., 1938, M.F.A., 1940; m. Mary Helen Nagler, Mar. 15, 1941; children—Michael Wilhelmina, John Forrest, Susan Elizabeth. Instr., design critic Yale U., 1940-43; dir. planning City of New Haven, 1940-43; propr. Maynard W. Meyer & Assos., architects and planners, Milw., 1946—. Served with USNR, 1943-46. Decorated Bronze Star, Air medal. Fellow AIA; mem. Am. Inst. Planning, Am. Soc. Planning Ofcls., Antique Automobile Club Am., Classic Car Club, Lincoln Owners Club, Inland Lake Yachting Assn., U.S. Yacht Racing Union. Lutheran. Clubs: Pewaukee (Wis.) Yacht; Milw. Yacht. Home: 1843 Rocky Point Rd Pewaukee WI 53072 Office: 797 N Jefferson St Milwaukee WI 53202

MEYER, MILTON EDWARD, JR., lawyer; b. St. Louis, Nov. 26, 1922; s. Milton Edward and Jessie Marie (Hurley) M.; B.S. in Bus. Adminstrn., Washington U., 1943; LL.B., St. Louis, U., 1950; LL.M., N.Y. U., 1953; m. Mary C. Kramer, Nov. 5, 1949; children—Milton E. III, Melanie M., Daniel K., Gregory N. Admitted to Mo. bar, 1950, Colo. bar, 1956; trust adminstr. Mississippi Valley Trust Co., St. Louis, 1946-50; asso. firm Burnett, Stern & Liberman, St. Louis, 1953-56; founding partner firm Hindry & Meyer, Denver, 1956-79, chmn. bd., 1970-79; spl. counsel Thomas & Esperti P.C., 1979—; sec. C.A. Norgren Co., Littleton, Colo., 1960-78, dir., 1971-78; dir. Ruwart-Rubenstein Chevrolet, Inc., Denver. Bd. dirs. Nat. Club Assn., 1971—, pres., 1976-78; bd. dirs., pres. Denver Community Concert Assn., 1960-64; bd. dirs. Sewall Rehab. Center, Denver, 1965-68, Carl A. Norgren Found., Denver, 1960-70. Served with U.S. Airborne Inf., 1943-46, 50-52. Mem. Am., Colo., Denver bar assns., Greater Denver Tax Counsels Assn. (founder, chmn. 1957), Denver Estate Planning Council (founder, pres. 1958), Am. Coll. Probate Counsel, Phi Eta Sigma, Beta Gamma Sigma, Omicron Delta Kappa, Beta Theta Pi. Republican. Roman Catholic. Clubs: Denver Athletic, N.Y. U., Cherry Hills Country, Pinehurst Country, Denver Executive. Contbr. articles to profl. jours. Home: 17 Carriage Ln Littleton CO 80121 Office: 821 17th St 600 Denver CO 80202

MEYER, NICHOLAS, author; b. N.Y.C., Dec. 24, 1945; s. Bernard Constant and Elly (Kassman) M.; B.A. in Theatre and Film, U. Iowa, 1968. Asso. publicist Paramount Pictures, N.Y.C., 1968-69; story editor Warner Bros., N.Y.C., 1970-71; writer, dir. film Time After Time, 1979. Mem. Authors Guild, Writers Guild. Democrat. Author: The Seven-Per-Cent Solution, 1974; Target Practice, 1974; The West End Horror, 1976; co-author: Black Orchid, 1977. Home: 2109 Stanley Hills Dr Los Angeles CA 90046

MEYER, PETER, educator, physicist; b. Berlin, Germany, Jan. 6, 1920; s. Franz and Frida (Lehmann) M.; Dipl.Ing., Tech. U., Berlin, 1942; Ph.D., U. Goettingen (Germany), 1948; m. Luise Schützmeister, July 20, 1946; children—Stephan S., Andreas S. Came to U.S., 1952, naturalized, 1962. Faculty, U. Goettingen, 1946-49; fellow U. Cambridge (Eng.), 1949-50; mem. sci. staff Max-Planck Inst. fuer Physik, Goettingen, 1950-52; faculty U. Chgo., 1953—, prof. physics, 1965—, dir. Enrico Fermi Inst., 1978—. Cons. NASA, NSF. Mem. cosmic ray commn. Internat. Union Pure and Applied Physics, 1966-72; mem. space sci. bd. Nat. Acad. Scis., 1975-78. Fellow Am. Phys. Soc. (chmn. div. cosmic physics 1972-73), AAAS; mem. Am. Astron. Soc., Am. Geophys. Union, Max Planck Inst. fuer Physik und Astrophysik (fgn.), Sigma Xi. Home: 2626 Park Dr Flossmoor IL 60422 Office: 933 E 56th St Chicago IL 60637

MEYER, RABBAN, educator; b. Pitts., July 1, 1918; s. Saul and Dora (Rosen) Rabinovitz; B.A., U. Pitts., 1939; M.A., Columbia, 1948, Ph.D., 1950; postgrad. William Alanson White Inst. Psychiatry, 1949-50, Coll. City N.Y., 1948-49; m. Elana Ghitman, July 13, 1948; children—David, Miriam, Jessica. Mem. psychology dept. Sarah Lawrence Coll., Bronxville, N.Y., 1949—. Lectr. child devel. Adelphi Coll., 1950-54, 56, Bank St. Coll. Edn., N.Y.C., 1950-60; group discussion leader Bklyn. Child Guidance League, 1950-53, Child Study Assn., 1954-55; asso. in parent edn. Guidance Center New Rochelle (N.Y.), 1955-59; dir. Windward Sch., White Plains, N.Y., 1955-61; group therapist Tappan Zee Mental Health Center, North Tarrytown, N.Y., 1963—, Scarsdale (N.Y.) Family Service, 1968-73; asso. Tavistock Centre, London, Eng., 1967-68, 73-74; research asso. div. community and social psychiatry Albert Einstein Coll. Medicine, 1960-69; dir. Camp Rainbow Croton-on-Hudson, N.Y., 1960-78. Served to capt. AUS, 1942-46; ETO. Decorated Bronze Star. Fellow Am. Psychol. Assn., Soc. Research Child Devel.; mem. Sigma Xi. Home: 123 Brite Ave Scarsdale NY 10583 Office: Dept Psychology Sarah Lawrence Coll Bronxville NY 10708

MEYER, RANDALL, oil co. exec.; b. Mt. Union, Iowa, Jan. 19, 1923; s. Carl Henry and Edythe (Stuck) M.; B.S. in Mech. Engring., U. Iowa, 1948; LL.D. (hon.), Iowa Wesleyan Coll., 1977; m. Barbara Swetman, Nov. 29, 1958; children—Warren, Gretchen, Kirsten. With Exxon Co. U.S.A. (formerly Humble Oil & Refining Co.) div. Exxon Corp., 1948—, with tech. and mgmt. depts., Baton Rouge, Houston, 1948-66, exec. asst. to pres. Exxon Corp., N.Y.C., 1966-67, sr. v.p., dir. Exxon Co. U.S.A., Houston, 1967-72, pres., 1972—; dir. 1st City Bancorporation Tex., Inc., Nat. Chamber Found.; chmn. bd. trustees Found. for Bus. Politics Economics. Bd. dirs., mem. exec. com. U. Iowa Found. Mem. C. of C. of U.S. (dir.), Am. Petroleum Inst. (dir., mgmt. com.), Tex. Research League (dir.), Tex. Assn. Taxpayers (dir., mem. exec. com.), Sigma Xi, Tau Beta Pi, Omicron Delta Kappa, Pi Tau Sigma. Methodist. Home: 407 Shadywood St Houston TX 77057 Office: 800 Bell Ave Houston TX 77002

MEYER, RAYMOND JOSEPH, univ. basketball coach; b. Chgo., Dec. 18, 1913; s. Joseph E. and Barbara (Hummel) M.; A.B., U. Notre Dame, 1938; m. Margaret Mary Delaney, May 27, 1939; children—Barbara (Mrs. Gerald Starzyk), Raymond Thomas, Patricia (Mrs. Thomas Butterfield), Meriann (Mrs. James McGowan), Joseph, Robert. Asst. coach U. Notre Dame, 1941-42; basketball coach DePaul U., Chgo., 1942—. Named Coach of Year, Chgo. Basketball Writers, 1943, 44, 48, 52, Nat. Assn. Basketball Coaches, 1978-79; Sportwriters Coach of Year, 1978; recipient Marine Corps Sportsman of Yr. award, 1979; named to Basketball Hall of Fame, 1979. Mem. Nat. Basketball Coaches Assn. Roman Catholic. Author: How To Play Winning Basketball, 1960; Basketball as Coached by Ray Meyer, 1967. Home: 2518 Cedar Glen Dr Arlington Heights IL 60005 Office: 1011 W Belden Ave Chicago IL 60614

MEYER, RICHARD CHARLES, microbiologist; b. Cleve., May 2, 1930; s. Frederick Albert and Tekla Charlotte (Schrade) M.; B.Sc., Baldwin-Wallace Coll., 1952; M.Sc., Ohio State U., 1957, Ph.D., 1961; m. Carolyn Yvonne Patton, Apr. 6, 1963; children—Frederick Gustav, Carl Anselm. Teaching and research asst. Ohio State U., 1956-61, research asso., 1961-62; microbiologist Nat. Cancer Inst., NIH, Bethesda, Md., 1962-64; asst. prof. vet. pathology and hygiene and microbiology U. Ill., Urbana-Champaign, 1965-68, asso. prof., 1968-73, prof., 1973—. Served with C.E., U.S. Army, 1952-54. Mem. Am. Acad. Microbiology, AAAS, Am. Inst. Biol. Sci., Am. Soc. Microbiology, Gamma Sigma Delta, Phi Zeta. Republican. Lutheran. Office: Dept Vet Pathology and Hygiene U Ill at Urbana-Champaign Urbana IL 61801

MEYER, RICHARD E(DWARD), fragrance and cosmetics mfg. co. exec.; b. Cin., May 8, 1939; s. Joseph H. and Dolores C. (Daley) M.; A.B. with honors in Journalism, Advt. and Mktg., U. Mich., 1961; m. Judith A. Shoup, Sept. 1, 1973; children—Donna, Valerie. Mgr. auto staff advt. dept. Chgo. Tribune, 1961-63; account supr., v.p. London & Assos., advt., Chgo., 1963-64; founder, pres., chmn. bd. Richard E. Meyer, Inc., advt. (name changed to Meyer & Rosenthal, Inc. 1970), Chgo., 1965-74; exec. v.p., gen. mgr. Jovan Inc., Chgo., 1974-75, pres., chief operating officer, 1975—, also dir.; dir. Fragrance Found. Recipient numerous awards N.Y. Advt. Club, Designers and Art Dirs., U.S. TV Comml. Awards, Communication Arts Awards, Printing Industry Am., Print Casebook, First Advt. Agy. Network awards. Mem. Chgo. Advt. Club (various awards 1965-79), Broadcast Advt. Club, Nat. Assn. Chain Drugstores, Cosmetics, Toiletries and Fragrance Assn. (dir.), Delta Upsilon (trustee 1971—). Clubs: U. Mich. of Chgo., Carlton. Patentee product design. Office: 875 N Michigan Ave Chicago IL 60611

MEYER, RUSS, film producer, dir.; b. Oakland, Calif., 1922; m. Betty Meyel; m. 2d, Eve Meyer (div.); m. 3d, Edy Williams (div.). Former photographer Playboy Mag.; film producer, dir., 1959—; partner RM Films Internat. Inc. Films include: Vixen, 1969; The Immoral Mr. Teas, 1958; The Seven Minutes, 1971; Cherry, Harry and Racquel, 1970; Beyond the Valley of The Dolls, 1970; Blacksnake, 1973; The Super Vixens, 1975; Up!, 1976; Beneath the Valley of the Ultravixens, 1979. Office: care RM Films Internat PO Box 3748 Los Angeles CA 90051*

MEYER, RUSSEL WILLIAM, JR., aircraft co. exec.; b. Davenport, Iowa, July 19, 1932; s. Russell William and Ellen Marie (Matthews) M.; B.A., Yale U., 1954; LL.B., Harvard U., 1961; m. Helen Scott Vaughn, Aug. 20, 1960; children—Russell William, III, Elizabeth Ellen, Jeffrey Vaughn, Christopher Matthews, Carolyn Louise. Admitted to Ohio bar, 1961; mem. firm Arter & Hadden, Cleve., 1961-66; pres., chief exec. officer Grumman Am. Aviation Corp., Cleve., 1966-74; exec. v.p. Cessna Aircraft Co., Wichita, Kans., 1974-75, chmn. bd., chief exec. officer, 1975—; dir. 4th Nat. Bank, Wichita. Bd. dirs. Cleve. Yale Scholarship Com., 1962-74; chmn. bd. trustees 1st Baptist Ch., Cleve., 1972-74; bd. dirs. United Way Wichita and Sedgwick County, Wichita State U. Endowment Assn.; trustee Wesley Hosp. Endowment Assn. Served with USAF, 1955-58. Mem. Am., Ohio, Kans., Cleve. bar assns., Gen. Aviation Mfrs. Assn. (chmn. bd. 1973-74), Wichita C. of C. (dir.). Clubs: Wichita, Wichita Country. Home: 600 Tara Ct Wichita KS 67206 Office: 5800 Pawnee Rd Wichita KS 67218

MEYER, SAMUEL JAMES, educator, opthalmologist; b. Centralia, Ill., Dec. 3, 1896; s. Peter and Rose (Born) M.; B.S., U. Chgo., 1917; M.D., Rush Med. Coll., Chgo., 1923; m. Dorothy W. Asher, Oct. 14, 1938; 1 dau., Patricia E. Intern, Cook County Hosp., Chgo., 1923-24, resident ophthalmology, 1925; asst. German U. Eye Clinic, Prague, 1925-26; extern Allgemeines Krankenhaus, Vienna, 1927; attending opthalmologist Michael Reese Hosp., Chgo., 1928—, chmn. dept., 1938-50; attending Ill. Eye and Ear Infirmary, Chgo., 1933-52, Cook County Hosp., 1952—; prof. ophthalmology, chmn. dept. Chgo. Med. Sch., 1952—; cons. Highland Park (Ill.) Hosp., 1945—, Weiss Meml. Hosp., Chgo., 1955—. Served as ensign USN, 1917-19. Diplomate Am. Bd. Ophthalmology. Fellow A.C.S., Am. Acad. Ophthalmology (hon. key 1950); mem. Assn. Research Ophthalmology, Ill. Med. Soc. (chmn. eye sect. 1936), Soc. Eye Surgeons, Assn. U. Profs. Ophthalmology, Chgo. Ophthal. Soc. (chmn. 1944), Phi Beta Kappa, Sigma Xi, Alpha Omega Alpha, Phi Delta Epsilon. Republican. Jewish religion. Clubs: Standard (Chgo.); Northmoor Country (Highland Park). Author: Glaucoma Manual, 1964. Contbr. articles to profl. jours. Home; 2600 Sheridan Rd Highland Park IL 60035 Office: 111 N Wabash Ave Chicago IL 60602

MEYER, SANDRA W., travel co. exec.; b. N.J., Aug. 20, 1937; student U. Mich.; B.A. cum laude, Syracuse (N.Y.) U., 1957; postgrad. London Sch. Econs., 1958; divorced; children—Jenifer Anne Schweitzer, Samantha Boughton Schweitzer. Advt. account exec. London Press Exchange, 1959-63; product mgr. Beecham Products Inc., Clifton, N.J., 1963-66; with Gen. Foods Co., White Plains, N.J., 1966-76, dir. corp. mktg. planning, 1975-76; sr. v.p. travel related services group Am. Express Co., N.Y.C., 1976—; dir. A.D.R. Inc., Warner/Amex Cable Communications Co. Trustee New Canaan (Conn.) Library, 1973-76. Mem. Mktg. Sci. Inst. (dir.). Office: American Express 125 Broad St New York NY 10004

MEYER, SHELDON, publisher; b. Chgo., June 8, 1926; s. Arthur Christof and Hester Truslow (Sheldon) M.; student Lawrenceville Sch., 1942-44; A.B. summa cum laude, Princeton U., 1949; m. Margaret Mary Kirk, July 29, 1964; children—Arabella Cristina, Andrew Kirk. With Funk & Wagnalls Co., 1951-55; asso. editor Grosset & Dunlap, 1955-56; with Oxford Univ. Press., N.Y.C., 1956—, editor, 1956-70, exec. editor Trade Books, 1970—, v.p., 1974-79, sr. v.p., 1979—. Mem. Assn. Am. Univ. Presses (dir. 1969-71, v.p. 1979-80), P.E.N., Am. Center, Am. Hist. Assn., Orgn. Am. Historians. Clubs: Princeton N.Y., Dutch Treat, Century. Home: 180 Riverside Dr New York NY 10024 Office: 200 Madison Ave New York NY 10016

MEYER, SUSAN E., editor; b. N.Y.C., Apr. 22, 1940; d. Ernest L. and Dorothy (Narefsky) Meyer; B.A., U. Wis., 1962. Asst. editor Collier Books, N.Y.C., 1962; mng. editor Watson-Guptill Publs., N.Y.C., 1963-70; editor-in-chief Am. Artist mag., N.Y.C., 1971-79; editorial dir. Am. Artist, Am. Art and Antiques, Interiors, Residential Interiors, 1979—. Dir. Ednl. Solutions, Inc., 1969-70; draft counselor Village Peace Center, 1967-70; tutor Empire State Coll., 1975-76; adj. prof. Union Grad. Sch., 1976—. Trustee Artists Fellowship, 1978—. Author: Three Generations of the Wyeth Family, 1975; James Montgomery Flagg, 1974; 40 Watercolorists and How They Work, 1976; America's Great Illustrators, 1978; You Can Renovate Your Own Home, 1978; (with Kent) Watercolorists at Work, 1972. Editor: (with Guptill) Watercolor Painting Step-by-Step, 1966; (with Kent) 100 Watercolor Techniques, 1968; (with Kinstler) Painting Portraits, 1971; (with Craig) Designing with Type, 1971; (with Guptill) Rendering in Pen and Ink, 1976; (with Guptill) Rendering in Pencil, 1977; 20 Landscape Painters and How They Work, 1977; 20 Oil Painters and How They Work, 1978; 20 Figure Painters and How They Work, 1979. Photographer: (with Buchman) Stage Makeup, 1971, Film and Television Makeup, 1973. Home: New York NY 10003 Office: 1515 Broadway New York NY 10036

MEYER, SYLVAN HUGH, editor, mag. exec.; b. Atlanta, Oct. 7, 1921; s. David Norman and Ray (Levinsohn) M.; A.B. in Journalism, U. N.C., 1943; D.H.L. (hon.), Oglethorpe U., 1973; m. Annemie Heineman, Jan. 19, 1947; children—Erica, David, Jason. Editor, The Times, Gainesville, Ga., 1950-69; editor Miami (Fla.) News, 1969-73; editor, pres. Miami Mag.; distinguished vis. prof. Fla. Internat. U., Miami, 1973—; project dir. Commn. on Future of South, 1974; chmn. 3d Century U.S.A., Bicentennial Commn. Dade County, 1973—. Chmn., Ga. adv. com. U.S. Commn. Civil Rights, 1958-65; mem. nat. com. ACLU, 1959—; mem. adv. bd. Pulitzer prize, 1968-73. Served to lt. USNR, 1943-46. Nieman fellow, Harvard, 1951. Recipient award Sidney Hillman Found., 1961; Dept. of Army Patriotic Civilian Service award, 1961. Mem. Am. Soc. Newspaper Editors (dir. 1966-73), Am. Council on Edn. in Journalism, Greater Miami C. of C. (bd. govs. 1970-74), U. N.C. Alumni Assn. (dir. 1973), Sigma Delta Chi (Distinguished Service award for editorial writing 1957), Tau Epsilon Phi. Clubs: Miami, Standard (pres. 1978—), Ocean Reef. Home: 248 W Rivo Alto Dr Miami Beach FL 33139. *In small city and urban journalism, I found people respond to fundamental American principles of freedom and individualism even when those tenets uphold ideas and movements with which they disagree. It sounds anachronistically Jeffersonian, but Americans do believe in their country and can handle disagreement, hardships and sacrifice in its name if they trust the fairness of the demands on them.*

MEYER, WALTER, nuclear engr.; b. Chgo., Jan. 19, 1932; s. Walter and Ruth (Killoran) M.; B.Chem. Engring., Syracuse (N.Y.) U., 1956, M.Chem. Engring., 1957; postgrad. (NSF Sci. Faculty fellow) M.I.T., 1962; Ph.D. (NSF Sci. Faculty fellow), Oreg. State U., 1964; m. Jacqueline Miscall, May 8, 1953; children—Kim, Holt, Eric, Leah, Suzannah. Prin. chem. engr. Battelle Meml. Inst., Columbus, Ohio, 1957-58; instr., then asst. prof. Oreg. State U., 1958-64; research engr. Hanford Atomic Labs., Richland, Wash., 1959-60, Lawrence Radiation Lab., Livermore, Calif., 1964; from asst. prof. to prof. nuclear engring. Kans. State U., Manhattan, 1964-72; prof., chmn. nuclear engring. U. Mo., Columbia, 1972—, Robert Lee Tatum prof. engring., 1974—, co-dir. energy systems and resources program, 1978; dir. summer insts. NSF-AEC, 1969, NSF, 1972; co-dir. summer instr. AEC, 1972, dir. workshop, 1973; dir. ERDA workshops, 1975-79; mem. Columbia Coal Gasification Task Force, 1977; mem. Gov. Kans. Nuclear Energy Council, 1971-72; cons. to govt. and industry. Mem. Manhattan Human Relations Orgn., 1966-72; active local Boy Scouts Am. Grantee NSF, 1965-67, 73-75, 77-80, AEC, 1969-71, 73-74, Dept. Def., 1969-72, ERDA, 1975, 77—; NRC, 1977-80; registered profl. engr., Calif. Mem. Am. Inst. Chem. Engrs. (chmn. nuclear engring. div. 1977-78), Am. Chem. Soc., Am. Nuclear Soc. (chmn. pub. info. com. 1975-79, nat. spl. award 1974), Am. Soc. Engring. Edn. (chmn. nuclear div. 1976-77), Am. Wind Soc., Sigma Xi, Tau Beta Pi. Congregationalist. Author, patentee in field. Home: 206 Devine Ct Columbia MO 65201 Office: Dept Nuclear Engring Univ Missouri Columbia MO 65201

MEYER, WALTER FREDERICK, mining co. exec.; b. N.Y.C., June 15, 1925; s. Herman William and Anna (Kahrs) M.; B.S. in Accounting, N.Y.U., 1948; m. Jeannette Emma Anna Neiswender, Aug. 9, 1952; 1 son, Jan Stephen. Staff accountant Alexander Grant & Co., N.Y.C., 1948-50; sr. accountant Peat, Marwick, Mitchell & Co., N.Y.C., 1950-56; staff accountant Singer Mfg. Co., N.Y.C., 1956-57; with Texasgulf, Inc., N.Y.C., 1957—, asst. controller, 1960-62, controller, 1962—, v.p., 1972—. Served with inf. AUS, 1943-45. C.P.A. N.Y. Mem. Am. Inst. C.P.A.'s, N.Y. State Soc. C.P.A.'s, Fin. Execs. Inst. Mason. Home: 280 Winton Rd Fairfield CT 06430 Office: High Ridge Park Fairfield CT 06904

MEYER, WALTER LESLIE, educator, chemist; b. Toledo, Feb. 28, 1931; s. Walter D. and Vera I. (Kilburn) M.; B.S., U. Mich., 1953, M.S., 1955, Ph.D., 1957; m. Ann Margaret Weaver, June 26, 1954; children—Janet Elaine, Robert Leslie, Barbara Kay. NSF postdoctoral fellow U. Wis., 1957-58; instr. chemistry Ind. U., 1958-60, asst. prof., 1960-65; asso. prof. chemistry U. Ark., 1965-68, prof., 1968—, chmn. dept., 1967-73. NSF fellow, 1954-58. Mem. Am. Chem. Soc., Chem. Soc. London, AAAS, Phi Beta Kappa, Sigma Xi, Phi Lambda Upsilon, Phi Kappa Phi. Home: Route 2 Fayetteville AR 72701

MEYER, WAYNE EUGENE, naval officer; b. Brunswick, Mo., Apr. 21, 1926; s. Eugene Clarence and Nettie Elizabeth (Gunn) M.; B.S. in Elec. Engring., Kans. U., 1946, U.S. Naval Postgrad. Sch., 1960; B.S. in Elec. Engring., Mass. Inst. Tech., 1947; M.S. in Aeros., 1961. Enlisted in U.S. Navy, 1943, commd. ensign, 1946, advanced through grades to rear adm., 1975; service in Mediterranean, Western Pacific; dir. engring. surface missile systems Navy Dept., 1973; project mgr. shipboard anti air warfare systems, 1970—; project mgr. Aegis system, 1970—. Decorated Meritorious Service medal. Mem. Am. Soc. Naval Engrs. (Gold medal 1976), Am. Inst. Aeros. and Astronautics, U.S. Naval Inst. Contbr. mil. jours. Address: (PMS400) Naval Sea Systems Command Navy Dept Washington DC 20362

MEYER, WILLIAM DANIELSON, dept. store exec.; b. Mpls., May 5, 1923; s. J.A. and Florence (Danielson) M.; B.S., U. Calif. at Los Angeles, 1947; m. Betty Ann McBride, May 28, 1950; children—Patricia Ann, Janet Elizabeth, Jean Louise. With actuarial dept. Prudential Ins. Co. Am., Los Angeles, 1948-53; with Carter Hawley Hale Stores, Inc., Los Angeles, 1953—, asst. sec., 1962-64, sec., 1964-73, dir. employee benefits, asst. sec., 1973—. Bd. dirs. Profit Sharing Council, Travelers Aid Soc. Los Angeles, pres., 1976-77; trustee Profit Sharing Research Found. Served to lt. (j.g.) USNR, 1943-46. Mem. Am. Soc. Corp. Secs., Personnel and Indsl. Relations Assn., Los Angeles C. of C., Sigma Pi, Alpha Kappa Psi, Phi Phi, Gold Key. Republican. Presbyterian. Home: 1725 Durklyn Ct San Marino CA 91108 Office: 550 S Flower St Los Angeles CA 90071

MEYERAND, RUSSELL GILBERT, JR., scientist; b. St. Louis, Dec. 2, 1933; s. Russell Gilbert and Elsa Louise (Gebhardt) M.; B.S. in Elec. Engring., M.I.T., 1955, M.S. in Nuclear Engring., 1956, Ph.D. in Plasma Physics, 1959; m. Mary Grace Guillemin, June 16, 1956; 1 dau., Mary Elizabeth. Cons. to atomic power equipment dept. Gen. Electric Co., Schenectady, 1955-56; research asst. M.I.T., 1956-58; prin. scientist plasma physics United Technologies Research Center, East Hartford, Conn., 1958-64, chief research scientist, 1964-67, dir. research, 1967-79, v.p. research and devel., 1979—. Mem. vis. com. dept. physics M.I.T., 1977—; mem. adv. com. U. Hartford Sch. Arts and Scis., 1966—; mem. engring. adv. com. Rensselaer Poly. Inst., 1965—. Recipient Eli Whitney award Conn. Patent Law Assn., 1979. Fellow AIAA; mem. Nat. Acad. Engring., IEEE, Am. Phys. Soc., Sigma Xi. Contbr. articles to profl. jours., chpts. to books; patentee in field. Office: Silver Ln East Hartford CT 06108

MEYERHOF, WALTER ERNST, physicist, educator; b. Kiel, Germany, Apr. 29, 1922; s. Otto Fritz and Hedwig (Schallenberg) M.; Ph.D., U. Pa., 1946; m. Miriam G. Ruben, Aug. 21, 1947; children—Michael O., David L. Came to U.S., 1941, naturalized, 1946. Asst. prof. U. Ill., Urbana, 1946-49; faculty physics Stanford (Cal.), 1949—, prof., 1959—, acting exec. head, 1962-63, chmn. dept. physics, 1970-77. Fellow Am. Phys. Soc. Home: 213 Blackburn Ave Menlo Park CA 94025 Office: Physics Dept Stanford Stanford CA 94305

MEYERHOFF, ARTHUR EDWARD, advt. exec.; b. Chgo., Mar. 12, 1895; s. Emanuel and Jennie (Lewin) M.; student pub. schs.; m. Madelaine H. Goldman, 1921; m. 2d, Elaine Clemens, Jan. 27, 1945; children—Jane, Arthur E., Joanne, William, Judith Lynn. With Hood Rubber Co., 1914-22; classified advt., circulation mgr. Wis. News, Milw., 1922-29; with Neisser & Meyerhoff, Chgo., advt. and merchandising, 1929-41; pres. Arthur Meyerhoff Assos., Inc. (formerly Arthur Meyerhoff & Co.), Chgo., 1941-65, chmn., 1965—; organized Gibraltar Industries, Inc., 1958; pioneered comic page advt.; dir. Santa Catalina Island Co., Chgo. Nat. League Ball Club, Inc.; developer Myzon products; organized Myzon, Inc., 1951; advisory bd. KBIG-KBRT, Los Angeles. Served with AEF, World War I. Received 1st prize Marshall Field candid div. 6th ann., 3d internat. competition and salon, 1939; George Washington Honor medal award Freedoms Found. Valley Forge, 1967. Mem. Am. Assn. Advt. Agys., C. of C. Author: Strategy of Persuasion, 1965. Office: 410 N Michigan Ave Chicago IL 60611

MEYERHOFF, JACK FULTON, fin. exec.; b. Joliet, Ill., May 15, 1926; s. Charles F. and Helen M. Ferguson) M.; B.S., Miami U., Oxford, Ohio, 1947; postgrad. Ohio Wesleyan U., 1944-45; grad. Advanced Mgmt. Program Harvard, 1968; m. Mary Margaret Williams, Jan. 2, 1949; children—Keith F., Greg H., Deborah S., Todd C. Mgr., Arthur Andersen & Co., Chgo., Cin., Cleve., 1947-59; treas. MacGregor Sports, Cin., 1959-63; v.p., corporate controller Brunswick Corp., Chgo., 1963-77, chief fin. officer, 1972-77, v.p. corporate affairs, 1977—; dir. Sherwood Med. Industries, Inc., Old Orchard Bank & Trust Co. Treas., bd. dirs. Cove Schs.; bd. dirs., pres. Skokie Valley Community Hosp., No. Ill. Indsl. Assn.; v.p., bd. dirs. Jr. Achievement; advisory council Miami U., Georgetown U., U. So. Fla. Served with USNR, 1944-46. Mem. Am. Inst. C.P.A.'s, Ohio, Ill. socs. C.P.A.'s, Financial Execs. Inst., Nat. Assn. Accountants, Harvard Bus. Sch. Alumni Assn., Miami U. Exec. Alumni Council, Sigma Alpha Epsilon, Delta Sigma Pi, Beta Alpha Psi, Beta Gamma Sigma. Presbyterian. Mason. Clubs: Mid America, Economic, Mission Hills Country, East Lakes Woodlands Country. Home: 326 S Stratford Rd Arlington Heights IL 60004 Office: 1 Brunswick Plaza Skokie IL 60077

MEYERHOFF, JOSEPH, philanthropist; b. Russia, Apr. 8, 1899; s. Oscar and Hannah (Gurewitz) M.; brought to U.S., 1906, naturalized, 1913; LL.B., U. Md., 1920; D.H.L. (honoris causa), Balt. Hebrew Coll., Dropsie U., 1974; Ph.D., Tel Aviv U., 1973; Ph.D. (hon.), Hebrew U., Jerusalem, 1977, Weizmann Inst., 1979; m. Rebecca Witten, Aug. 21, 1921; children—Peggy (Mrs. Jack Pearlstone, dec.), Harvey M., Eleanor (Mrs. Herbert D. Katz). With Monumental Properties, Inc. (formerly Joseph Meyerhoff Corp.), Balt., and predecessor cos., 1933—, pres., 1933-72, chmn. bd., 1972-75, chmn. exec. com., 1973-78; trustee Monumental Properties Trust, 1978-79; chmn. bd. Magna Properties, Inc., 1979—; dir. PEC-Israel Econ. Corp. (formerly Palestine Econ. Corp.), N.Y.C., 1950—, pres., 1957-63, chmn. bd., 1963—; dir. Indsl. Devel. Bank Israel, Discount Investment Corp. Mem. bd. Md. Bd. Pub. Welfare, 1953-57, Technion-Israel Inst. Tech., Hebrew U. Jerusalem, Tel Aviv U., U. Negev, Weizmann Inst., Tel Aviv Museum. chmn. Md. Planning Commn., 1957-63; gen. chmn. United Jewish Appeal, 1961-64; pres., chmn. Balt. Symphony Orch. Assn., 1965—, Jewish Welfare Fund of Balt., 1951-53, Asso. Jewish Charities of Balt., 1959-62, bd., 1953—; bd. dirs. Balt. Mus. Art, Balt. Opera Co.; exec. com. Peabody Conservatory of Music. Mem. Nat. Assn. Home Builders U.S. (pres. 1946-47, dir.). Club: Center (pres. 1964-74) (Balt.). Home: 1 Slade Ave Baltimore MD 21208 Office: 28 S Charles St Baltimore MD 21201

MEYEROWITZ, WILLIAM, artist; b. Russia, July 15, 1893; s. Gershon and Sophia (Midleman) M.; came to U.S., 1905; art edn. N.A.D.; m. Theresa F. Bernstein, Feb. 1918. Painter, etcher; work rep. numerous pub., pvt. collections. Recipient Modern Jury first prize and gold medal for painting Exodus; 1st prize for etching N.Y., Am. Color Print Soc., 1950; 1st anonymous prize Audubon Artists, 1955; best painting prize N. Shore Arts Assn., 1957, 1st prize, 1968; Peterson Allied Arts prize, 1958; hon. mention for still life Ogunquit Art Assn., 1959; Eric Hudson prize for painting Cavalcade, 1960; Layton prize Allied Artists, 1962; Vavana Meml. Painting prize, 1965; H. Register prize Rockport Art Assn., 1964, Rothenberg prize 1967; Ellin P. Speyer prize N.A.D.; 1965; Nat. Acad. prize for painting, 1965; W.F. Schrafft award for best painting exhbn. Rockport Art Assn., 1965, prize, 1967, gold medal honor award painting, 1970; Vayana Meml. award Ogonquit Art Center, 1973; Carl Matson meml. prize portrait painting, 1964, Iver Rose Meml. award Rockport Art Assn., 1975, E. Schllem award for excellence in painting North Shore Arts Assn., 1976, Gold medal honor Rockport Art Assn., 1978. Mem. arts council Gloucester Arts Festival; v.p., hon. life mem. N. Shore Art Assn. N.Am. Mem. Bklyn. Soc. Etchers, Conn. Acad. Fine Arts, Gloucester Soc. Art, Phila. Soc. Etchers, Cape Ann Art Soc., Boston Print Makers, Soc. Am. Etchers, Audubon Soc. Artists, Rockport Summer Artists, Internat. Inst. Arts and Letters, Allied Artists Am., Rockport Art Assn. (Gold medal of honor 1978). Home: 54 W 74th St New York NY 10023 summer studio: 44 Mt Pleasant Ave East Gloucester MA 01930

MEYERS, ARTHUR CHRISTIAN, JR., educator, economist, clergyman; b. St. Louis, May 16, 1914; s. Arthur Christian and Bertha (Weitz) M.; B.C.S., St. Louis U., 1936, M.C.S., 1937, Ph.D., 1950;

postgrad. U. Chgo., 1937-38; M.Div., Eden Sem., St. Louis, 1975; m. Myoma Rupp, Apr. 8, 1939 (dec.); children—Arthur Christian III, James C., Thomas C., Robert C., Joan R., Susan R.; m. 2d, Olive Davies, Oct. 18, 1968. Faculty, St. Louis U., 1936—, prof., 1960—, acting dir. dept. econs., 1962-68, dir., 1968-74; ordained to ministry Methodist Ch., 1976, elder, 1976. Faculty, Am. Inst. Banking, 1950—; cons. statistics, econs. St. Louis Bd. Police Commrs., 1946—. Active Boy Scouts Am. Served with AUS, 1942-46; CBI; maj. to col. Q.M.C., Res., 1945-69. Mem. Am. Econ. Assn., Am. Statis. Assn., Municipal Finance Officers Assn., AAAS, Res. Officers Assn., Def. Supply Assn., Mil. Order World Wars, Alpha Sigma Nu, Sigma Lambda Upsilon, Delta Sigma Pi, Beta Gamma Sigma. Contbr. articles to profl. jours. Home: 6481 Kinsey Pl St Louis MO 63109

MEYERS, CAL YALE, chemist, educator; b. Utica, N.Y., Nov. 14, 1927; s. Max and Anna (Bernstein) M.; B.A., Cornell, 1948; M.S., U. Ill., 1949, Ph.D., 1951; postgrad. Princeton, 1951-53; m. Vera Kolb, Sept. 7, 1976. Research chemist Union Carbide Corp., Bound Brook, N.J., 1953-56, project leader, 1956-60; vis. research prof. U. Bologna (Italy), 1960-63; vis. chemistry scholar U. Calif. at Los Angeles, 1963-64; asso. prof. So. Ill. U., Carbondale, 1964-68, prof., 1968—. Cons. Heliodyne Corp., 1964, Scripps Clinic and Research Found., 1964—, Toni Co., 1966-68; vis. prof. Kyoto, Kyushu univs., Japan, 1973; vis. lectr. Polish Acad. Sci., 1978. NSF Internat. Travel grantee, 1961, 70, 71, 73. Recipient Intra-Sci. Research Found. award, 1964; Petroleum Research Found. Internat. Research awards, 1961, 62. Mem. Am., Italian chem. socs., N.Y. Acad. Scis., Sigma Xi, Phi Lambda Upsilon. Inventor: Poly Phenolic Sulfones, 1957. Contbr. to numerous research publs. Co-editor Chemistry of Organic Sulfur Compounds, 4 vols., 1966—; mem. editorial bd. Internat. Jour. Sulfur Chemistry, 1971—, Jour. Phosphorous and Sulfur, 1975—. Home: 112 Hewitt St Carbondale IL 62901

MEYERS, CHARLES JARVIS, lawyer, educator; b. Dallas, Aug. 7, 1925; s. Percy Avery and Katherine (Jarvis) M.; B.A., Rice U., 1949; LL.B., U. Tex., 1949; LL.M., Columbia, 1953, J.S.D., 1964; m. Pamela Adams, Aug. 4, 1954; children—George Frederick, Katherine. Admitted to Tex. bar, 1949; asst. prof. law U. Tex., Austin, 1949-52, asso. prof., 1952-54; asso. prof. Columbia, 1954-57, prof., 1957-62; prof. law Stanford, 1962—, Charles A. Beardsley prof., 1971-76, Richard E. Lang prof. and dean, 1976—; vis. prof. U. Minn., 1953-54, Cornell U., 1961, U. Mich., 1963, U. Utah, 1965, U. Chile, Santiago, 1968-69; dir. Pub. Advs., Inc., San Francisco, 1971—; sr. prof. Chile Law Program, Santiago, 1968-69; asst. gen. counsel Nat. Water Commn., 1970-73; pres. Assn. Am. Law Schs., 1975; vice chmn. Gov.'s Commn. to Study Calif. Water Rights Law, 1977-79. Served to lt. (j.g.) USNR, 1945-46; PTO. Mem. Am. Law Inst., Am., Tex. bar assns., Nat. Acad. Engring. (com. pub. policy 1970-73), Order of Coif, Phi Beta Kappa, Phi Delta Phi. Republican. Author: (with H.R. Williams) Oil and Gas Law, 1959, 64; Cases on Oil and Gas Law, 4th edit., 1978; Report to President's Task Force on Communications Policy, Market Exchange of Spectrum Rights, 1968; (with Tarlock) Water Resource Management, 2d edit., 1979; Legal-Economic Aspects of Environmental Protection, 1971. Home: 730 Frenchmans Rd Stanford CA 94305

MEYERS, DALE (MRS. MARIO COOPER), artist; b. Chgo., Jan. 24, 1922; d. Walter Herman and Gertude (Pettee) Wetterer; student Glendale Coll., 1940-41, Corcoran Gallery Sch. Art, Washington, 1962-63, Art Student's League, N.Y.C., 1964-78; m. Mario Cooper, Oct. 11, 1964; children—Dale (Mrs. John F. Hellegers), Steven R. One woman exhbns. include West Wing Gallery, Ringwood (N.J.) State Park, 1970, Manor Club, Pelham Manor, N.Y., 1970, Apollo Art Gallery, Oklahoma City, 1972, Quadrangle Gallery, Dallas, 1972, Galveston Center for Arts, 1974, Fla. Gulf Coast Art Center, 1977, Okura Hotel, Tokyo, Japan, 1977, others; exhbn., artist-in-residence Galveston Arts Center, 1974; group exhbns. include Two Hundred Years of Watercolor Painting in Am., Met. Mus. Art, 1966, Eyewitness to Space, Nat. Gallery Art, Washington, 1969, Smithsonian Instn., 1961-63, Corcoran Gallery, 1963, Museo de la Acuarela, Mexico City, 1968, London (Ont., Can.) Mus. Art, 1971-72, Art Gallery Hamilton (Ont., Can.), 1971-72, Ont. Inst. Edn., 1971-72, Butler Inst. Art, 1962—, Frye Mus., 1962—, Am. Watercolor Soc., 1962—, N.A.D., 1964—, Allied Artists Am., 1964—, also Cheyenne Artists Guild, Muckenthaler (Calif.) Cultural Center, McMurry Coll., Columbia (S.C.) Mus., Fla. Mus. Arts and Scis., others; represented in permanent collections N.A.D., Avon Products Fine Arts Collection, NASA, Environmental Protection Agy., Museo de la Acuarela, Schumacher Gallery, Columbus, Ohio, Slater Mus., Norwich, Conn., Portland (Maine) Mus., U. Utah Fine Arts Collection, Frye Mus., Seattle. Recipient bronze medal honor award Am. Watercolor Soc., 1968, Famous Artists Sch. award, 1970, Paul B. Remmey award, 1972; Henry W. Ranger award Nat. Acad. Design, 1968, Samuel F.B. Morse medal, 1973; Anna Hyatt Huntington bronze medal, 1971; Knickerbocker Artists award, 1968; Allied Artists Am. award, 1969; gold medal honor Nat. Arts Club, 1972; Anna Hyatt Huntington Gold medal, 1974; Adolf and Clara Obrig award Nat. Acad., 1974, Walter Biggs award, 1976, Emily Lowe award Am. Watercolor Soc., 1978. Fellow Royal Soc. Arts; mem. Am. Watercolor Soc. (editor jours. 1962-74, hon. pres.), Nat. Acad. (academician), Allied Artists Am. (pres. 1975-78), Knickerbocker Artists, Art Student's League N.Y., La. Watercolor Soc., Watercolor Soc. Mex., Audubon Artists. Contbr. Eyewitness to Space, also Am. Artist mag. Address: 1 W 67th St New York NY 10023

MEYERS, EDWARD, magazine editor; b. Flushing, N.Y., Nov. 2, 1934; s. Gerson G. and Hester (Noble) M.; B.F.A., Rochester (N.Y.) Inst. Tech., 1957; m. Marcia Rothman, June 29, 1958; children—Beth, Adam, Rosemarie. Tech. editor Modern Photography mag., N.Y.C., 1957-66; photographer-writer, N.Y.C., 1966-70; exec. editor Popular Photography mag., N.Y.C., 1971—; lectr. Sch. Visual Arts, 1968—. Served with U.S. Army, 1957-58. Recipient Alumni Achievement award Rochester Inst. Tech., 1972. Mem. Soc. Photog. Scientists and Engrs., Soc. Photog. Edn., Indsl. Photographers N.Y., Am. Soc. Bus. Press Editors. Editor: Modern Photography Photo Almanac, 1967, 69; co-editor: The Official Depth of Field Tables, 1962. Home: 61-68 77th St Middle Village NY 11379 Office: 1 Park Ave New York City NY 10016

MEYERS, GEORG NELSON, newspaperman; b. Kansas City, Mo., July 1, 1915; s. Cary Monroe and Mabel (French) M.; student Bakersfield Jr. Coll., 1933-35; B.A., Coll. of Pacific, 1939; m. Dallas Helen Higdon, Aug. 9, 1941; children—Janine, Troy Clinton. Reporter, Inglewood (Calif.) Californian, 1931-33, Bakersfield (Calif.) Californian, 1933-35, Stockton (Cal.) Record, 1935-39; reporter Fairbanks (Alaska) Daily News-Miner, 1939-42, editor, 1946-49; reporter Seattle Times, 1949-56, sports editor, 1956—. Dir. Fairbanks Sch. Bd., 1947-48; mem. citizens adv. com. YMCA, Seattle, 1960. Served with USAAF, 1942-46. Recipient Wash. State Press award for distinguished reporting, 1951, 53, 55, for distinguished sports writing, 1957, 59, 61-68, 70-78; Nat. Headliners' Club award, 1944; Nat. Sportswriters and Sportscasters award, 1960-62, 67, 70, 72, 77. Mem. Sigma Delta Chi. Contbr. articles, fiction to popular mags. Home: 2609 26th Ave W Seattle WA 98199 Office: Seattle Times Fairview Ave N and John St Seattle WA 98111

MEYERS, GERALD CARL, automobile co. exec.; b. Buffalo, Dec. 5, 1928; s. Meyer and Berenice (Meyers) M.; B.S., Carnegie Inst. Tech., 1950, M.S. summa cum laude, 1954; m. Barbara Jacob, Nov. 2, 1958. With Ford Motor Co., Detroit, 1950-51, Chrysler Corp., Detroit and Geneva, 1954-62; with Am. Motors Corp., Detroit, 1962—, v.p., 1967-72, group v.p. product, 1972-75, exec. v.p., 1975-77, pres., 1977—, chief operating officer, 1977, chief exec. officer, 1977—, chmn., 1978—. Trustee Carnegie Mellon U.; bd. dirs. Detroit Renaissance, Inc., Detroit Symphony Orch. Served as 1st lt. USAF, 1951-53. Mem. Econ. Club Detroit (dir.), Soc. Automotive Engrs., Hwy. Users Fedn. (dir.), Motor Vehicle Mfrs. Assn. (dir.), Internat. C. of C. (trustee U.S. council). Automotive Orgn. Team, Greater Detroit C. of C., Conf. Bd., Tau Beta Pi, Phi Kappa Phi, Omicron Delta Kappa. Home: Bloomfield Hills MI 48013 Office: Am Center 27777 Franklin Rd Southfield MI 48034

MEYERS, ISHMAEL ALEXANDER, lawyer, U.S. atty.; b. St. Thomas, V.I., Feb. 3, 1939; s. H. Alexander and Elvera Lawrencena (Matthias) M.; B.S., Morgan State U., 1962; M.B.A., Am. U., 1964; J.D., George Washington U., 1972; m. Gwendolyn L. Pate, Apr. 1, 1972; children—Ishmael, Micheline, Michael. Acct., ICC, Washington, 1963-64; asst. commr. housing and community renewal, St. Thomas, V.I., 1964-69; dep. asst. atty. gen., V.I. Dept. Law, St. Thomas, 1972-73; asst. U.S. atty., 1973-78, U.S. atty., 1978—; mem. Jud. Conf., U.S. Ct. Appeals for 3d Circuit; mem. Jud. Conf., V.I.; mem. Law Enforcement Planning Commn., V.I. Mem. Meml. Moravian Ch. Sch. Bd., 1977-78. John Hay Whitney Found. fellow. Mem. V.I. Bar Assn., D.C. Bar Assn., Am. Bar Assn., Alpha Phi Alpha. Democrat. Club: Lions. Office: PO Box 1441 St Thomas VI 00801*

MEYERS, JOHN ALLEN, mag. publisher; b. Winnetka, Ill., Feb. 21, 1929; s. Fred W. and Ruth B. (Burras) M.; B.A., Mich. State U., 1951; postgrad. Columbia, 1965; m. Jane Bowers, Sept. 18, 1931; children—Jennifer, Katherine, John. Trainee, McCann-Erickson, Chgo., 1953-54; sales rep. Curtis Pub. Co., Chgo., 1954-55; salesman Time mag., 1955-60, mgr. Time Clevc., 1960 63, Time Chgo., 1963-65, Time N.Y.C., 1965-68, U.S. sales dir., 1968, worldwide advt. sales dir., 1968-72, asso. publisher, dir. advt., 1972; v.p. Time, Inc., publisher Sports Illustrated mag., 1972-78, pub. Time mag., 1978—. Trustee Pop Warner Jr. League Football, Boys Club N.Y.; bd. dirs. Found. Children with Learning Disabilities. Served with USMC, 1951-53. Decorated Purple Heart; recipient Pop Warner Service to Youth award, 1974, Distinguished Alumni award Mich. State U., 1974. Mem. Am. Mgmt. Assn., Mich. State Alumni Assn. (exec. bd.). Clubs: Stanwich Golf (Greenwich, Conn.); Jupiter Hills Country (Jupiter, Fla.); Pine Valley Golf; Mid-Ocean (Bermuda). Home: 12 Winterset Rd Greenwich CT 06830 Office: Time Mag Rockefeller Center New York City NY 10020

MEYERS, JOHN FRANCIS, ednl. assn. exec.; b. Altoona, Pa., July 26, 1930; s. George and Magdalene (Keller) M.; A.B., Pontifical Coll. Josephinum, Columbus, Ohio, 1952, M.Div., 1975, D.Litt. (hon.), 1976; M.A., Catholic U. Am., 1959; postgrad. N.Y. U., summers 1961-62; Ed.D., North Tex. State U., 1964. Ordained priest Roman Catholic Ch., 1956; asst. pastor Holy Name Parish, Ft. Worth, 1956-58; dean students, lectr. U. Dallas, 1959-61; asst. supt. schs. Diocesan Schs. Dallas, 1960-61, diocesan supt. schs., 1961-67; pastor Immaculate Conception Parish, Tyler, Tex., 1967-68; exec. sec. dept. chief adminstrs. Cath. edn. Nat. Cath. Ednl. Assn., Washington, 1968-74, v.p. div. fundamental edn., 1970-74, acting pres., 1972-74, pres., 1974—; trustee Pontifical Coll. Josephinum, 1973—; bd. dirs. Internat. Cath. Ednl. Assn., 1978—, Confederacion Interamericana de Education Catolica, 1977—. Served to lt. USNR, 1963-69. Mem. Am. Assn. Sch. Adminstrs., Religious Edn. Assn., Phi Delta Kappa. Author: (with Thomas Sullivan) Focus on American Catechetics: A Commentary on the General Catechetical Directory, 1972; exec. editor: Criteria for the Evaluation of Religious Education Programs, 1970; A Curriculum Guide for Continuous Progress in Religious Education, 1973; The Qualities and Competencies of the Religion Teacher, 1973; co-editor: Boards of Education: A Primer, 1972; contbr. articles to profl. pubs. Office: Nat Cath Ednl Assn One Dupont Circle Suite 350 Washington DC 20036

MEYERS, MICHAEL (OZZIE), congressman; b. Phila., May 4, 1943; s. Mark and Margaret (Sullivan) M.; student Phila. pub. schs.; m. Ethel Sutherland; children—Michael, Kelly Ann, Kevin. Mem. Pa. Ho. of Reps., 1970-76; mem. U.S. Ho. of Reps., 1976—. Roman Catholic. Home: 2636 S 6th St Philadelphia PA 19148 Office: 1217 Longworth Bldg Washington DC 20515

MEYERS, PHILIP MITCHELL, corp. exec.; b. Cin., June 25, 1899; s. Mitchell and Bess (Jaffe) M.; A.B., D.C.S., U. Cin., 1922; m. Lucille Goldberg, Dec. 18, 1929; children—Philip M., Lynne, Susan. With Fashion Frocks, Inc., Cin., 1922—, pres., 1938-64; chmn. Meyers Enterprises, Inc., Meyers Devel. Corp., Workum Constrn. Co.; dir., emeritus 1st Nat. Bank, Cin. Mem. adv. council Three Rivers council Girl Scouts U.S.A. Past trustee U. Cin., chmn. budget and finance com.; past trustee, treas. Cin. Zoo; past pres. Jewish Hosp. Cin. Adv. council Citizens Sch. Found.; mem. bd. fellows Brandeis U.; past mem. exec. com. Greater Cin. Hosp. Council; founding mem., past v.p. Health Careers Assn. Mem. Nat. Assn. Direct Selling Cos. (past pres.), Cin. Better Bus. Bur. Clubs: Losantiville Country, Cincinnati. Home: Ridge Acres 230 W Galbraith Rd Cincinnati OH 45215 Office: 200 W Galbraith Rd Cincinnati OH 45215. *From earliest childhood I learned from my parents the importance of truthfulness and honesty. Later, at public school here in Cincinnati, I was greatly influenced by the eight McGuffey Readers, one for each of the eight grades of primary school. Somewhere in that period I was required to memorize Longfellow's "A Psalm of Life" which I can still recite from memory at age 79. This poem made a profound impression upon me. At any time that I became discouraged I would recite it—when I felt that the possible gain wasn't worth the effort, I recited the poem—whenever the "going was tough" I breathed the poem softly to myself.*

MEYERS, SHELDON, govt. ofcl.; b. N.Y.C., Sept. 6, 1929; s. Charles and Charlotte (Farb) M.; B.Engring., SUNY, 1952; M.S.E., U. Mich., 1955; M.B.A., N.Y. U., 1967; m. Anne Catherine Dietzel, Apr. 14, 1962; children—James, John, Catherine, Peter, Paul. Engr., Cities Service Oil Co., N.Y.C., 1952-54; engr. Westinghouse Co., Pitts., 1955-56; engr. Argonne (Ill.) Nat. Lab., 1956-58; engr., div. dir. AEC, N.Y.C., 1958-69; office dir., dep. asst. adminstr. EPA, 1969-77; dir. Office of Nuclear Waste Mgmt., Dept. Energy, Washington, 1977—. Princeton U. fellow, 1964-65. Mem. ASME. Home: 3506 Dundee Dr Chevy Chase MD 20015 Office: US Dept Energy Washington DC 20545

MEYERSON, MARTIN, univ. pres., urbanist; b. N.Y.C., Nov. 14, 1922; s. S.Z. and Etta (Berger) M.; A.B., Columbia, 1942; M.C.P. (Wheelwright fellow), Harvard, 1949; LL.D. (hon.), U. Pa., 1970; numerous other hon. degrees univs. U.S. and abroad including Queen's U., Can., 1968, Pahlavi U., 1973, U. Edinburgh, 1976; m. Margy Ellin Lazarus, Dec. 31, 1945; children—Adam, Laura, Matthew. Mem. staff Am. Soc. Planning Ofcls., 1943-44, Phila. City Planning Commn., 1944-45, Michael Reese Hosp., Chgo., 1945-47; asst. prof. coll. and social scis. U. Chgo., 1948-52; asso. Com. on Nat. Policy, Yale U., New Haven, 1948; asso. prof. city and regional planning, asso. research prof. urban studies U. Pa., Phila., 1952-56, prof., 1956-57; exec. dir., research dir. Am. Council to Improve Our Neighborhoods, 1955-56, vice chmn. bd., 1961-66; Frank Backus Williams prof. city planning and urban research Harvard U., Cambridge, Mass., 1957-63, acting dean Grad. Sch. Design, 1963; 1st dir. Joint Center for Urban Studies, Mass. Inst. Tech. and Harvard U., 1959-63; dean, prof. urban devel. Coll. Environ. Design, U. Calif., Berkeley, 1963-66, acting chancellor, 1965; pres., prof. public policy State U. New York, Buffalo, 1966-70; pres., prof. U. Pa., 1970—. Dir. Real Estate Research Corp., 1961-67, Marine Midland Bank, 1966-70, Fidelity Bank, 1971—, Scott Paper Co., 1972—, Penn Mut. Life, 1974—, Certain Teed, 1978—. Cons. to govts., pvt. firms U.S. and abroad, UN missions to Japan, Indonesia, Yugoslavia, 1958-65; cons. Arthur D. Little, Inc., 1958-66, Sears Roebuck Found., 1958-69; chmn. bd. Western N.Y. Nuclear Research Center, 1966-70; adv. com. U.S. Census, 1958-61, NASA, 1960-65, panel White House Office Sci. and Tech., 1962-66, White House task forces, 1960-69; mem. council Electric Power Research Inst., 1973-77; mem. U.S. del. UN Conf. on Sci. and Tech. for Less Developed Areas, 1963; mem. Air Conservation Commn., 1962-66, Bay Area Conservation and Devel. Commn., 1965-66; chmn. Assembly Univ. Goals and Governance, 1969-73; commr. N.Y. State Commn. on Post-Secondary Sch. Edn., 1976-77; hon. prof. Nat. U. Paraguay, 1969—. Bd. dirs. Phila. Bicentennial Corp., 1970-76, Greater Phila. Partnership, 1973—, Park Sch., 1966-70, Afro-Am. Film Found., 1966-70 Niagara U., 1968-70, Center for Community Change, 1968-72, Acad. Religion and Mental Health, 1970-78, Center for Ednl. Devel., 1967-70, Phila. Mus. Art, 1974—, Nat. Urban Coalition, 1969-78, Inst. for Internat. Edn., 1971—, Internat. Council Ednl. Devel., 1971—, Am. Council Financial Aid to Edn., 1975—, Open Univ. Found., 1979—; chmn. council pres.' Nat. Accelerator Lab., 1972-73; co-chmn. Images (French TV), 1976—, Salzburg Seminar Bd., 1978—, Marconi Fellowship Council, 1978—. internat. gov. Center Environ. Studies, London, 1966—; exec. council Conf. Bd., 1970-77; spl. adv. Aspen. Inst. Humanistic Studies, 1976—. Recipient Einstein medal Am. Technion Soc., 1976. Fellow AAAS, Am. Acad. Arts and Scis., Royal Soc. Arts, Am. Philos. Soc. Nat. Acad. Edn.; mem. Am. Soc. Planning Ofcls. (past dir.), Am. Inst. Planners (past gov., award winner) Internat. Assn. Univs. (Am. dir. 1975—), Council Fgn. Relations, Phi Beta Kappa Assos. Clubs: Philadelphia, Rittenhouse (Phila.); Cosmos (Washington); Century (N.Y.C.). Author: (with E. C. Banfield) Politics, Planning and the Public Interest, 1955; Housing, People and Cities, 1962; Face of the Metropolis, 1963; Boston, 1966; Gladly Learn and Gladly Teach, 1978. Editor: Conscience of the City, 1970; Housing and Community Development Series, McGraw-Hill; author various reports, articles and monographs; editorial bd. Daedalus. Office: 100 Coll Hall Univ Pa Philadelphia PA 19174

MEYNER, ROBERT BAUMLE, lawyer; b. Easton, Pa., July 3, 1908; s. Gustave Herman and Mary Sophia (Baumle) M.; A.B., Lafayette Coll., 1930, LL.D., 1954; LL.B., Columbia, 1933; LL.D., Rutgers U., 1954, Princeton, 1956, L.I. U., 1958, Fairleigh Dickinson U., 1959, Syracuse U., 1960, Lincoln U., 1960, Colo. Coll., 1961; m. Helen Stevenson, Jan. 19, 1957. Admitted to N.J. bar, 1934, also U.S. Supreme Ct. bar; practice in Pohatcong Twp., N.J.; county lawyer Warren County, 1942; elected to N.J. State Senate, 1947, minority leader, 1950; gov. N.J., 1954-62; now partner firm Meyner, Landis, Newark; dir. Engelhard Minerals & Chems. Corp., Phillipsburg Nat. Bank & Trust Co. (N.J.), First Nat. State Bank Newark, First Nat. State Bancorp., Newark, Del. & Bound Brook R.R. Former civilian aide for N.J. to sec. army; co-chmn. Interracial Council Bus. Opportunity, Newark. Served to comdr. USNR, 1942-45. Mem. Lafayette Coll. Alumni Assn., Am., N.J., Hudson County, Essex County, Warren County bar assns., Phillipsburg (past pres.), Greater Newark chambers commerce, Grange, Columbia U. Law Sch. Alumni Assn. (v.p.), Alpha Chi Rho. Democrat. Elk, Eagle, Odd Fellow, Moose, Rotarian. Clubs: Essex (Newark); River (N.Y.C.); Pomfret. Home: 372 Lincoln St Phillipsburg NJ 08865 also 16 Olden Lane Princeton NJ 08540 Office: Suite 2500 Gateway I Newark NJ 07102 also 83 S Main St Phillipsburg NJ 08865

MEYVAERT, PAUL JEFFREY, historian; b. Wallasey, Cheshire, Eng., Nov. 12, 1921; s. Fernand and Jessie (Ledger) M.; student St. Teresa Coll. (Ireland), 1934-38; m. Ann Freeman, Feb. 4, 1967; 1 dau., Jenny Louisa. Benedictine monk Ft. Augustus Abbey, Scotland, 1938-40, Quarr Abbey, Isle of Wight, Eng., 1940-65; lectr., art history librarian Duke, 1967-71; exec. sec. Mediaeval Acad. Am., also editor of Speculum, 1971—. Mem. bd. scholars Dumbarton Oaks Research Library, 1973-75; mem. Inst. Advanced Study Princeton, 1976-77; vis. fellow All Souls Coll., Oxford, 1980-81. Recipient grants, Coop. Program in Humanities, Duke, 1970, Am. Council Learned Socs., 1970, 73. Editor: Anglo-Saxon England, 1970—; Benedict, Gregory, Bede and Others, 1977. Contbr. articles to profl. jours. Home: 8 Hawthorne Park Cambridge MA 02138 Office: Mediaeval Academy of America 1430 Massachusetts Ave Cambridge MA 02138

MEZERA, JAMES ALLEN, mfg. co. exec.; b. Two Rivers, Wis., Feb. 5, 1930; s. John W. and Alice (Skorch) M.; B.S., Marquette U., 1952, M.B.A., 1959; m. Marian Grimm, Sept. 12, 1953; children—Kathryn Jean, Keith James, Thomas Robert, Anne Marie. Accountant, Oxnard, Calif., 1953-55; asst. controller Harnischfeger Corp., Milw., 1955-58, controller, 1958-64, v.p. adminstrn., 1964-67, group v.p. constrn. and mining equipment, 1967-73, exec. v.p., 1973—, also dir. Served to lt. Supply Corps, USNR, World War II. C.P.A., Wis. Mem. Am. Inst. C.P.A.'s, Fin. Execs. Inst., Constrn. Industry Mfrs. Assn. (dir.). Home: 15460 Santa Maria Dr Brookfield WI 53005 Office: 4400 National Ave Milwaukee WI 53214

MICA, DANIEL A., congressman; b. Binghamton, N.Y., Feb. 4, 1944; s. John and Adeline M.; student U. Fla., Gainesville, 1961; B.A., Fla. Atlantic U., Boca Raton, 1966; m. Martha Fry, 1967; children—Christine, Andrew, Caroline, Paul. Tchr. public schs., Palm Beach County, Fla., Montgomery County, Md., 1967-68; staff mem. U.S. Rep. Paul G. Rogers of Fla., 1968-78; mem. 96th Congress from 11th Fla. dist. Bd. dirs. Goodwill Industries; past bd. dirs. Community Mental Health Center, Public Television Found. of S. Fla. Mem. Fla. Atlantic U. Alumni Assn. (past pres.). Democrat. Roman Catholic. Clubs: Jaycees, Kiwanis, Forum of Palm Beaches. Office: 512 Cannon House Office Bldg Washington DC 20515*

MICALI, THOMAS AGATINO, mfg. co. exec., lawyer; b. Chgo., Dec. 2, 1914; s. Carmel and Concettina (Cannavo) M.; A.B., U. Ill., 1936, J.D., 1939; m. Mary Alice Zielinski, Aug. 23, 1941; children—Thomas Kent, Mark Allan. Admitted to Ill. bar, 1939; pvt. practice, 1939-41; with legal div. Chgo. Ordnance Dist., 1941-43; with Pullman-Standard Car Mfg. Co., subs. Pullman, Inc., 1947—, gen. counsel, 1953—, sec., 1955—, also gen. counsel Pullman, Inc., 1957—, v.p., 1959—, v.p., gen. mgr. Trailmobile div., 1969-70, pres., 1971—; dir. Pullman, Inc. Served as 1st lt. Judge Adv. Gen. Dept., AUS, 1943-46. Mem. Am., Ill., Chgo. bar assns., Phi Beta Kappa. Home: 1301 Plum Tree Ln Winnetka IL 60093 Office: 200 E Randolph Dr Chicago IL 60601

MICCIO, JOSEPH V., educator, cons.; b. Bklyn., May 1, 1915; s. Salvatore and Marian (Lauro) M.; B.B.A. cum laude (econ. award), St. John's U., 1938; M.A. cum laude, N.Y. U., 1940, Ed.D., 1965; LL.D.,

Fairleigh Dickinson U., 1963; m. Lillian Pratt, Oct. 12, 1957. Accountant, Rockwood & Co., Bklyn., 1932-39; controller Lightfoot, Schultz Co., N.J., 1939-42; controller, asst. to financial v.p. Republic Aviation Corp., L.I., 1942-45; controller-treas. Air-cooled Motors, Inc., Syracuse, N.Y., 1945-50; gen. mgr. electronics div. Curtiss-Wright Corp., 1951-54, v.p. corp., 1953-64, pres., gen. mgr. Wright Aero. div., Wood-Ridge, N.J., 1954-64, sr. v.p., 1964-66, gen. mgr. plastics div., 1953-54; gen. mgr., exec. v.p. Columbia Protektosite Co. (wholly-owned subsidiary), 1951-54; chmn. bd. Redel Corp., Anaheim, Calif.; adj. prof. Fairleigh Dicknson U.; instr. N.Y. U.; prof. mgmt. and bus. policy U. Hawaii 1966-69, prof., 1969—, chmn. Grad. Sch. Bus., 1966-69, asso. dean Coll. Bus. Adminstrn., 1966-69; dir. Cosco Supply Inc., Oahu Industries Inc., Central Pacific Supply Inc., Tiki Gems Inc., Arvak Inc. Mem. aero. ednl. commn. N.Y.C. Bd. Edn.; adviser SBA; Hawaii del. Pres.'s Conf. Small Bus., 1980. Trustee, N.J. Symphony; bd. fellows Fairleigh Dickinson U.; mem. council St. John's U.; mem. finance com. bd. trustees Chaminade Coll., Honolulu. Recipient award of merit Aircraft War Prodn. Council; Founders award N.Y. U.; Profl. Mgr. award Soc. Advancement Mgmt., 1975. C.P.A., N.Y. Mem. N.Y. State Soc. C.P.A.'s, Fin. Execs. Inst., Am. Arbitration Assn., Am. Mgmt. Assn., Aerospace Industries Assn., Acad. Mgmt., Am. Inst. C.P.A.'s, Am. Inst. Aeros. and Astronautics, Navy League U.S., Soc. for Advancement Mgmt., Soc. Automotive Engrs., Conquistadores del Cielo, Honolulu C. of C., Phi Delta Kappa, Phi Delta Epsilon, Beta Gamma Sigma (adv. com. to Hawaii Crime Com.). Club: Economic (N.Y.C.). Contbr. articles to profl. jours. Address: 2943 Kalakaua Ave Honolulu HI 96815

MICHAEL, DONALD NELSON, social scientist, educator; b. Chgo., Jan. 24, 1923; s. Albert Abraham and Jean (Lewis) M.; S.B., Harvard, 1946, Ph.D., 1952; M.A., U. Chgo., 1948; D.Sc. (hon.), Marlboro Coll., 1964; m. Margot Jean Murphy, Apr. 7, 1956; 1 son, Geoffrey William. Staff social scientist Weapons Systems Evaluation Group U.S., Joint Chiefs Staff, Washington, 1953-54; adviser Office Spl. Studies NSF, Washington, 1954-56; sr. research asso. Dunlap & Assos., Stanford, Conn., 1956-59; sr. staff mem. Brookings Instn., Washington, 1959-61; dir. Peace Research Inst., Washington, 1961-63; resident fellow Inst. Policy Studies, Washington, 1963-66; prof. planning and pub. policy, program dir. Center Research Utilization Sci. Knowledge Inst. Social Research, prof. psychology U. Mich. at Ann Arbor, 1966—, NIMH spl. research fellow, 1968-70; vis. fellow Inst. Internat. Studies U. Cal. at Berkeley, 1972-73. Lectr. John Dewey Soc., 1967; mem. Commn. Study Orgn. Peace, 1965-74; co-vice-chmn. nat. bd. U.S. Assn. for Club of Rome, 1978—; mem. nat. bd. Citizen Involvement Network, 1975. Mem. nat. bd. Girl Scouts Am., 1969-72. Served with AUS, 1943-46. Fellow Inst. Soc. Ethics Life Scis., AAAS, Am. Psychol. Assn., Soc. Psychol. Study Social Issues; mem. Club Rome, N.Y. Acad. Sci., Sigma Xi. Club: Cosmos. Author: Proposed Studies on the Implications of Peaceful Space Activities for Human Affairs, 1961; Cybernation: The Silent Conquest, 1962; The Next Generation, 1965; The Unprepared Society, 1968; On Learning to Plan — And Planning to Learn, 1973. Office: U Mich Dana Bldg Ann Arbor MI 48109

MICHAEL, ERNEST ARTHUR, educator; b. Zürich, Switzerland, Aug. 26, 1925; s. Jakob and Erna (Sondheimer) M.; came to U.S., 1939; B.A., Cornell U., 1947; M.A., Harvard, 1948; Ph.D., U. Chgo., 1951; m. Colette Verger Davis, 1956 (div. 1966); children—Alan, David, Gerard; m. 2d, Erika Goodman Joseph, Dec. 4, 1966; children—Hillary, Joshua. Mem. faculty dept. math. U. Wash., Seattle, 1953—, asst. prof., 1953-56, asso. prof., 1956-60, prof., 1960—; mem. Inst. for Advanced Studies, Princeton, 1951-52, 56-57, 60-61, 68; mem. Math. Research Inst., E.T.H., Zürich, 1973-74. Served with USNR, 1944-46. Grantee AEC, Office Nav. Research, NSF, Guggenheim Found., Humboldt Found., 1978-79. Mem. Am. Math. Soc., Math. Assn. Am., ACLU, Amnesty Internat. Jewish. Editor: Procs. Am. Math. Soc., 1968-71; Gen. Topology and its Applications. Contbr. to profl. jours. Home: 16751 15th Ave NW Seattle WA 98177

MICHAEL, FLOYD DONALD, banker; b. Columbus, Ind., Sept. 13, 1921; s. Louis Edward and Martha (Armuth) M.; A.B., Franklin Coll., 1943; J.D., Ind. U., 1949; m. Helen White, Nov. 4, 1944; children—John William, Donald Louis, Martha Sue. Claims cons. ARC, Indpls., 1946-47; trust asst., asst. sec., trust officer Ind. Trust Co., Indpls., 1947-53; trust officer, v.p. Mchts. Nat. Bank & Trust Co., Indpls., 1953-61; sr. v.p., trust officer Gary (Ind.) Nat. Bank, 1961—. Am. Inst. Banking instr. negotiable instruments Ind. U., Indpls., 1960-61; instr. advanced estate planning Valparaiso U. Sch. Law, 1965; pres. Indpls. Estate Planning Council, 1960. Mem. Jr. Probate Code Study Commn., 1950-52, Ind. Probate Code Study Commn., 1972—; advanced gifts chmn. United Fund Greater Gary Area, 1964; mem. regional campus adv. com. N.W. Campus Ind. U., 1964-72. Bd. dirs. Ogden Dunes Homeowners Assn. Served to lt. (j.g.) USNR, 1943-46. Mem. Ind., Gary bar assns., Gary C. of C., Am., Ind. (past com. chmn.) bankers assns., Ind. Conf. Bankers and Lawyers, Order of Coif, Phi Delta Theta, Sigma Delta Kappa. Republican. Kiwanian. Home: Box 418 Ogden Dunes Portage IN 46368 Office: 8585 Broadway Box 209 Gary IN 46402

MICHAEL, GARY LINN, architect; b. Portland, Oreg., Apr. 27, 1934; s. Donald Glenn and Ida Marie (Luoto) M.; B.Arch., U. Oreg., 1957; M.Arch., Yale U., 1965; m. Sandra Ann Schori, Sept. 16, 1956; children—Brian Russell, Laura Joy, Jesse Daniel. Designer, mgr. br. office Wilmsen, Endicott & Unthank, Portland, 1961-64; partner Campbell, Michael, Yost, Portland, 1965-68; prin. Gary L. Michael, Architects & Planners, Portland, 1969-74; pres. Michael, Mann & Lakeman, Architects, Planners & Urban Designers, Portland, 1974—; mem. Oreg. Bd. Architect Examiners, 1978—; guest archtl. design critic Portland State U., U. Oreg.; guest lectr. pub. schs., colls., tchr. tng. seminars. Mem. Portland Sch. Dist. Eco-Aesthetics Bd., 1972-74; mem. citizens coordinating com. Oreg. Hwy. Div., 1973; chmn. Sensible Transp. Options for People, Portland, 1974; chmn. for architects and landscape architects United Way Campaign, Portland area, 1977; mem. Downtown Housing Adv. Com., 1978-79. Ion Lewis Traveling fellow, 1957. Fellow AIA (10 local design awards 1960-78, nat. design award 1973, pres. Portland chpt. 1972). Works include Basic Sci. Bldg., U. Oreg. Med. Sch., 1967, additions to Sch. Architecture and Allied Arts, U. Oreg., 1968, Zach Studio and Residence, Elmira, Oreg., 1969, Columbia Gorge Center, Cascade Locks, Oreg., 1973, Waverly Children's Home, Portland, 1973, Cowles Bldg., Portland, 1973, Unthank Plaza Pub. Housing, Portland, 1977, Drummond Residence, Lake Oswego, 1978. Home: 1615 SW Ford St Dr Portland OR 97201 Office: 430 SW Morrison St Portland OR 97204

MICHAEL, HENRY N., geographer; b. Pitts., July 14, 1913; s. Anthony M. and Albina (Dubska) M.; B.A., U. Pa., 1948, M.A., 1951, Ph.D., 1954; m. Ida Nemez, June 8, 1943; children—Susan Shelley, Richard Carleton, Andrew Paul. Instr. geography U. Pa., 1948-54; faculty Temple U., 1958—, prof. geography, chmn. dept., 1965-73, prof., 1965—; research asso. Univ. Mus., Phila., 1959—, Radiocarbon Lab., U. Pa., 1960—; mem. Bi-Nat. Commn. on Social Scis. and Humanities, Am. Council Learned Socs./Acad. Scis. USSR, 1975—. Served to 1st lt. AUS, 1942-45. Decorated Purple Heart. Fellow Am. Anthrop. Assn.; mem. Phila. Anthrop. Soc. (council 1954—), Delaware Valley Assn. Geographers, Arctic Inst. N.Am., Assn. Am. Geographers, Sigma Xi. Contbr. articles to profl. jours.; editor: Anthropology of the North, 1959—; editor, author Dating Techniques for the Archaeologist, 1971, 73. Home: 2712 Pine Valley Ln Ardmore PA 19003 Office: Dept Geography Temple U Philadelphia PA 19122

MICHAEL, I. E., physician; b. Clinton County, Ind., Feb. 10, 1915; s. Generous C. and Ina (Blanche) M.; B.S. in Physiology, U. Chgo., 1938, M.S., 1940, M.D., 1942; m. Kathleen McGauley, June 18, 1953; children—Judith Lynne, Maureen, John Patrick. Intern, Presbyn. Hosp., Chgo., 1942-43; pvt. practice, Frankfort, Ind., 1946-50; fellow internal medicine Mayo Clinic, 1950-54; instr. internal medicine Ohio State U. Med. Sch., 1954-57; pvt. practice, Indpls., 1957—; chmn. dept. internal medicine Meth. Hosp., 1965-68; asst. prof. medicine Ind. U. Med. Sch., 1964—. Served to maj. M.C., AUS, 1943-46. Decorated Bronze Star, Combat Med. badge. Diplomate Am. Bd. Internal Medicine. Fellow A.C.P.; mem. A.M.A., Am. Soc. Internal Medicine, Marion County Med. Soc. (pres. 1974-75). Home: 5208 Roland Dr Indianapolis IN 46208 Office: 2010 W 86th St Indianapolis IN 46260

MICHAEL, JERROLD MARK, public health specialist, univ. dean, educator; b. Richmond, Va., Aug. 3, 1927; s. Joseph Leon and Esther Leah M.; B.C.E., George Washington U., 1949; M.S.E., Johns Hopkins U., 1950; M.P.H., U. Calif., Berkeley, 1957; m. Lynn Y. Simon, Mar. 17, 1951; children—Scott J., Nelson L. Commd. ensign USPHS, 1950, advanced through ranks to rear adm., asst. surgeon gen., 1966; ret., 1970; dean, prof. public health Sch. Public Health, U. Hawaii, Honolulu, 1971—. Bd. dirs. Nat. Health Council, 1967-78, Nat. Center for Health Edn., 1977—; mem. nat. adv. council on health professions edn., 1978-81. Served with USNR, 1945-47. Recipient J.S. Billings award for mil. medicine, 1964. Fellow Am. Public Health Assn.; mem. Am. Acad. Health Adminstrn., Am. Soc. Cert. Sanitarians, Nat. Environ. Health Assn., Am. Acad. Environ. Engrs. Democrat. Jewish. Club: Masons. Contbr. articles to profl. jours.; asso. editor Jour. Environ. Health, 1958—. Office: 1960 East-West Rd Honolulu HI 96822

MICHAEL, LUDWIG ALEXANDER, educator, otolaryngologist; b. N.Y.C., July 20, 1919; s. Maximilian J. and Flora (Weiss) Furchtgott; B.A., N.Y.U., 1939, M.D., 1943; m. Carmen Miller, Aug. 2, 1956; children—Andrew, Susan. Intern, St. Louis City Hosp., 1943; resident Barnes Hosp., St. Louis, 1944-45; pvt. practice, Dallas, 1948—; chief otolaryngology Baylor U. Med. Center, 1963—; prof. Southwestern Med. Sch. U. Tex., 1956—. Cons. audiology VA, 1948—. Served with USAAF, 1945-47. Fellow A.C.S., Am. Acad. Otolaryngology and Ophthalmology, Am. Laryng., Rhinol. and Otol. Soc. Clubs: Columbian (Dallas); Town and Gown (So. Meth. U.). Home: 5329 Royal Crest Dr Dallas TX 75229

MICHAEL, MAX, JR., physician, educator; b. Athens, Ga., Feb. 14, 1916; s. Max and Cecilia (Solomons) M.; B.S., U. Ga., 1935; M.D., Harvard, 1939; m. Barbara Siegel, July 20, 1944 (dec. Nov. 1976); children—Max III, Robert, Paul, Lloyd, Stephen. Intern, Peter Bent Brigham Hosp., Boston, 1939-41; resident Johns Hopkins Hosp., Balt., 1941-42; chief med. services Atlanta VA Hosp., 1947-54; asso. prof. internal medicine Emory U., Atlanta, 1947-54; dir. med. services Maimonides Hosp., Bklyn., 1954-58; prof. internal medicine State U. N.Y., 1954-58; prof. internal medicine U. Fla., Gainesville, 1958—, asst. dean Coll. Medicine, 1967—. Exec. dir. Jacksonville Hosps. Ednl. Program, 1958—. Mem. research coms. Am. Cancer Soc., 1956-62; mem. Nat. Acad. Scis. Inst. Medicine, 1971—. Bd. regents Nat. Library Medicine, 1968-72. Served to capt. M.C., AUS, 1942-45. Fellow A.C.P.; mem. Am., So. socs. for clin. investigation, Am. Clin. and Climatol. Assn., Assn. Hosp. Med. Edn. (sec.-treas. 1969-72, pres. 1972-74), Phi Beta Kappa, Alpha Omega Alpha. Contbr. articles to profl. jours. Home: 3649 Montclair Dr Jacksonville FL 32217

MICHAEL, R. KEITH, educator; b. Muncy, Pa., Nov. 16, 1930; s. James R. and Lena (Snyder) M.; B.S., Indiana (Pa.) U., 1952; M.F.A., U. Iowa, 1958; Ph.D., U. Bristol (Eng.), 1970; m. Marion B. Bankert, Oct. 30, 1954. Dir. theatre, chmn. dept. theatre St. Cloud (Minn.) State Coll., 1960-71; prof., chmn. dept. theatre and drama, Ind. U., Bloomington, 1971—; co-founder, artistic dir. Theatre L'Homme Dieu, Alexandria, Minn., 1960-70; pres. Brown County Playhouse, Inc., Nashville, Ind., 1972—; cons. theatrical architecture; mem. adv. bd. Minn. Theatre Co., 1965-67; mem. theatre adv. bd. Minn. Arts Council, 1968-70; mem. adv. bd. Ind. Arts Commn., 1972-73, 75-77. Pres. Alexandria-St. Cloud State Coll. Performing Arts Found., 1965-66. Served with USNR, 1952-56. Mem. Nat. Theatre Conf., Am. (dir. 1975-77), N. Central (pres. 1965-66) theatre assns., Univ. and Coll. Theatre Assn. (pres. 1978), AAUP. Home: 2218 N Dunn St Bloomington IN 47401

MICHAEL, SHERWOOD ALBERT, retail clothing chain exec.; b. Plainfield, N.J., Sept. 17, 1920; s. Julius E. and Adelaide N. M.; student pub. schs., Richmond, Va.; m. Pearl Rothenberg, Oct. 26, 1941; children—Sandra, Paula, Alan. With Thalhimer Bros., Inc., 1938-42, 45—, v.p., gen. mgr. all N.C. stores, Winston-Salem, 1956-69, sr. v.p., corporate gen. mdse. mgr., Richmond, 1969-74, exec. v.p., gen. mdse. mgr., 1974—, mem. exec. com., 1969—, also dir. Bd. dirs. Better Bus. Bur., Winston-Salem, 1960, Goodwill Industries, Winston-Salem, 1962-65. Served with USN, 1942-45. Mem. Retail Mchts. Assn. Winston-Salem (N.C.) (pres. 1960-61), Richmond C. of C. (dir.). Jewish. Home: 330 Greenway Ln Richmond VA 23226 Office: Thalhimer Bros Inc 6th and Broad Sts Richmond VA 23219

MICHAEL, THOMAS HUGH GLYNN, assn. exec.; b. Toronto, Ont., Can., May 20, 1918; s. John Hugh and Hilda (Clarke) M.; B.A. with honors in Chemistry, U. Toronto, 1940; m. Ruth Vivian Dexter, June 20, 1942; children—Margaret (Mrs. J.H. Tait), Barbara (Mrs. D.W. Drew), John Hugh. With Ont. Research Found., 1940-41, NRC Can., 1941-46; chief chemist Woburn Chems. Ltd., Toronto, 1946-53; research dir. Howards & Sons Can. Ltd., Cornwall, Ont., 1953-57; exec. dir. Chem. Inst. Can., Ottawa, Ont., 1958—. Treas., Youth Sci. Found., 1960-71. Bd. dirs. Canadian Bus. Press. Recipient Centennial medal of Can. Govt., 1967; Queen's Silver Jubilee medal, 1977. Fellow Chem. Inst. Can., Chem. Soc. London; mem. Societé de Chimie Industrielle de France (hon.), Council Engring. and Sci. Soc. Execs. (pres. 1969-70), Inst. Assn. Execs. (pres. 1971-72), Soc. Chem. Industry. Clubs: Rideau (Ottawa); Le Cercle Universitaire D'Ottawa. Home: 295 Clemow Ave Ottawa ON KIS 2B7 Canada Office: 151 Slater St Ottawa ON KIP 5H3 Canada

MICHAEL, WILLIAM HERBERT, JR., ofcl. NASA; b. Richmond, Va., Dec. 10, 1926; s. William Herbert and Alice (Anderson) M.; B.S., Princeton U., 1948, Ph.D., 1967; M.S., U. Va., 1951; M.A., Coll. William and Mary, 1962; m. Marjorie May Boswick, June 28, 1952; children—Alice Caroline, Cynthia Boswick. With Langley Research Center, NASA, Hampton, Va., 1948—, head lunar and planetary scis. br., 1969-70, chief environ. and space scis. div., 1970—, also head radio sci. team Viking project, 1970—; mem. working group artificial satellites Com. on Space Research, 1967—; mem. com. on moon Internat. Astron. Union, 1970—. Served with USNR, 1944-46. Recipient Exceptional Service award NASA, 1967, Spl. Achievement award, 1969, 77, medal for Exceptional Sci. Achievement, 1977. Registered profl. engr., Va. Asso. fellow AIAA; mem. Am. Geophys. Union. Contbr. articles to profl. jours. Home: 29 Haughton Ln Newport News VA 23606 Office: NASA Langley Research Center Hampton VA 23365

MICHAELIDES, CONSTANTINE EVANGELOS, architect; b. Athens, Greece, Jan. 26, 1930; s. Evangelos George and Kalliopi Constantine (Kefallonitis) M.; came to U.S., 1955, naturalized, 1964. Diploma in Architecture Nat. Tech. U., Athens, 1952; M.Arch., Harvard U., 1957; m. Maria S. Canellakis, Sept. 3, 1955; children—Evangelos Constantine, Dimitri Canellakis. Practice architecture, Athens, 1954-55, St. Louis, 1963—; asso. architect Carl Koch, Jose Luis Sert, Hideo Sasaki, Cambridge, Mass., 1957-59, Doxiadis Assos., Athens and Washington, 1959-60, Hellmuth, Obata & Kassabaum, St. Louis, 1962; instr. Grad. Sch. Design Harvard U., 1975-59, Athens Inst. Tech., 1959-60; asst. prof. architecture Washington U., St. Louis, 1960-64, asso. prof., 1964-69, prof., 1969—, asso. dean Sch. Architecture, 1969-73, dean, 1973—; vis. prof. Sch. Architecture, Ahmedabad, India, 1970; counselor Landmarks Assn. St. Louis. Mem. Municipal Commn. on Arts, Letters, University City, Mo. Served to lt. Greek Army Res., 1952-54. Mem. AIA (dir. St. Louis chpt. 1977-79, research award 1963-64), Tech. Chamber of Greece, Soc. Archtl. Historians, Modern Greek Studies Assn. Author: Hydra: A Greek Island Town: Its Growth and Form, 1967. Home: 735 Radcliffe St University City MO 63130 Office: Sch Architecture Washington U Saint Louis MO 63130

MICHAELIS, JOHN HERSEY, army officer; b. San Francisco, Aug. 21, 1912; s. Otho E. and Louise E. (Haas) M.; B.S., U.S. Mil. Acad., 1936; grad. Command and Gen. Staff Sch., 1942, Armed Forces Staff Coll., 1949, Brit. Sr. Officers Course, 1944; LL.D., Franklin and Marshall Coll., 1964, Chungang U., 1970; m. Mary Wadsworth, Dec. 28, 1937; children—Maurene L., Marie A. Commd. 2d lt., inf. U.S. Army, 1936, advanced through grades to gen., 1969; assigned U.S., P.I., C.Z., 1936-44; comdr. 502d Parachute Inf., 101st Airborne Div., 1944; chief staff 101st Airborne Div., 1944-45; assigned Gen. Staff, War Dept., 1945; sr. aide to Gen. Eisenhower, 1947-48; asst. chief staff operations 8th Army, 1949-50; comdg. officer 27th Inf. Regt., Korea, 1950; asst. div. comdr. 25th Inf. Div., 1950-51; dep. for tng. SHAPE, 1951-52; comdt. cadets U.S. Mil. Acad., 1952-54; readiness officer Hdqrs. Allied Forces So. Europe, 1954-55; comdg. gen. So. European Task Force, 1955-56; chief legislative liaison Office Sec. Army, 1956-59; comdg. gen. U.S. Army, Alaska, 1959-62, V Corps, 1962-63, ALFSEE, 1963-66, Fifth U.S. Army 1966-69; dep. comdg. gen. Eighth U.S. Army, 1969; comdr. in chief UN Command, also comdr. USFK and 8th U.S. Army, 1969-72; ret., 1972; mgmt. cons. Hanjin Internat. Inc., 1972—. Decorated D.S.M. with 2 oak leaf clusters, D.S.C., Silver Star with oak leaf cluster, Legion of Merit with 3 oak leaf clusters, Bronze Star with V device and 2 oak leaf clusters, Air medal, Purple Heart with oak leaf cluster (U.S.); Croix de Guerre with palm (France); Croix de Guerre with palm (Belgium); Bronze Lion (Netherlands); comdr. Order of Merit (Italy), Philippine Legion of Honor); Ulchi Distinguished Mil. Service medal with gold star, Tong-Il medal 1st class Order Nat. Security Merit (Korea); Army Mil. medal 1st class (Chile); grand comdr. Royal Order of King George I (Greece); 1st knight grand cross Exalted Order White Elephant (Thailand); Home: 5130 Brittany Dr S St Petersburg FL 33715

MICHAELIS, MICHAEL, mgmt. and engring. cons.; b. Berlin, Germany (Brit. subject), June 8, 1919; s. George and Martha (Bluth) M.; B.Sc., U. London, 1941; m. Diana Ordway Tead, Sept. 11, 1954; children—Ordway Peter, David Tead; m. 2d, Cintra McIlwain Williams, Mar. 19, 1966 (div. Nov. 1975). Research asst., group leader research labs. Gen. Electric Co., Ltd., Eng., 1935-45, staff physicist and cons., 1945-49; dir. physics div. Radiochem. Centre, Brit. Atomic Energy Authority, 1949-51; cons. Arthur D. Little, Inc., Cambridge, Mass., 1951-52, staff cons., 1952—, sr. asso., 1957-61, head nuclear mgmt. cons. services, 1956-61, internat. bus. devel. services, 1959-61, policy adviser to several large corps, 1954-61, mgr. Washington operations, 1963-72, sr. cons., 1972—. Cons. to Pres.'s Spl. Asst. Sci. and Tech., 1961-63; exec. sec. White House Panel on Civilian Tech., 1961-63; exec. dir. research mgmt. advisory panel, com. on sci. and tech. U.S. Ho. of Reps., 1963—; dep. coordinator then Pres.-elect Carter's Task Force on Sci. and Tech. Policy, 1976; mem. tech. adv. bd. to U.S. Sec. Commerce, 1978—; mem. nat. com. Am. goals and resources Nat. Planning Assn., 1964-67, mem. advisory com. sci., tech. and economy, 1966-68. Vice chmn. com. internat. affairs Atomic Indsl. Forum, 1958-60; asso. with Anglo-Am. radar research project. World War II; dir. Interdisciplinary Communications Assos., Inc., 1969—. Mem. Sci. Film Assn. (founder 1943, council, sec. 1943-48, v.p. 1948-51), IEEE, (sr.), Am. Nuclear Soc., AAAS (chmn. engring. sect. 1980—), Boston Com. Fgn. Relations, Royal Inst. Physics, Phys. Soc., Soc. Internat. Devel., Royal Instn. Elec. Engrs., Assn. Hosp. Physicists, Nat. Planning Assn., World Future Soc. (dir. 1966—), U.S. C. of C. (chmn. com. on govt.-industry relations in sci. and tech. 1963-64), Am. Econ. Assn., Am. Soc. Cybernetics, Am. Soc. for Pub. Adminstrn., Atlantic Council U.S. Clubs: Federal City, Cosmos (Washington); Harvard Faculty (Cambridge). Editor, project dir.: Federal Funding of Civilian Research and Development, 1976. Contbr. articles to publs., periodicals. Home: 3001 Veazey Terr NW Washington DC 20008 Office: 1735 I St NW Washington DC 20006. *The Constitution of the U.S. diffuses power so as to better secure liberty. But it also intends that practice will integrate the dispersed powers into a workable government. It confers upon its branches autonomy but also reciprocity, separateness but also interdependence. It is incumbent on each of us to help make this system work, and to make it responsive to the human needs of our country and the world.*

MICHAELIS, PAUL CHARLES, engring. physicist; b. Bronx, N.Y., June 18, 1935; s. Paul Fredrick and Rose (Landsbury) M.; B.S. in Elec. Engring., Newark Coll. Engring., 1964, M.S. in Physics, 1967; m. Geraldine A. DeCuollo, June 29, 1958; 1 son, Paul Charles. With Bell Telephone Labs., Murray Hill, N.J., 1953—, asso. mem. tech. staff, 1963-67, mem. tech. staff, 1967—; lectr. USSR Acad. Scis., 1972. Mem. IEEE (Morris N. Liebmann award 1975), Am. Phys. Soc., AAAS, U.S. Naval Inst. Club: Watchung Lions (past pres.). Contbr. articles to profl. jours. Patentee single wall domain memory tech., electronics, magnetics and mechanics. Home: 103 High Tor Dr Watchung NJ 07060 Office: 600 Mountain Ave Murray Hill NJ 07974

MICHAELS, DAVID DORY, publishing cons.; b. N.Y.C., Feb. 22, 1919; s. Harry C. and Virginia (Banks) M.; B.A., U. Rochester, 1942; m. Carol F. Hughson, May 5, 1943; children—David H., Thomas F.,

Laurie F. With New Yorker mag., 1947—, mem. staff, 1947-66, advt. dir., 1966-69, pub., 1969-73, also dir.; v.p. Gourmet mag., 1973-75, advt. dir., 1979—; advt. dir. Harvard Bus. Rev., 1979—; pub. cons., 1975-79. Served with USAAF, 1943-45. Home: Church St Roxbury CT 06783 Office: 777 3d Ave New York NY 10017

MICHAELS, JAMES WALKER, editor; b. Buffalo, June 17, 1921; s. Dewey and Phyllis (Boasberg) M.; B.S. cum laude, Harvard, 1942; m. Frances Matthews, June 6, 1947; children—Robert Matthews, James Walker, Anne Phyllis. Ambulance driver Am. Field Service, India, Burma, 1943-44; with USIS, New Delhi, India, also Bangkok, Thailand, 1944-46; fgn. corr. United Press, bur. mgr. New Delhi, 1946-50; with Forbes mag., 1954—, mng. editor, 1956-61, editor, 1961—. Contbr. articles to mags. Home: Brookside Dr Greenwich CT 06830 Office: Forbes Inc 60 Fifth Ave New York NY 10011

MICHAELS, LEONARD, educator; b. N.Y.C., Jan. 2, 1933; s. Leon and Anna (Czeskies) M.; B.A., N.Y. U., 1953; M.A., U. Mich., 1956, Ph.D., 1967; m. Priscilla Drake Older, June 9, 1966 (div.); children—Ethan, Jesse; m. 2d, Brenda Lynn Hillman, Aug. 8, 1976; 1 dau., Louisa Alice. Prof. English, Paterson (N.J.) State Coll., 1961-62, U. Calif. at Davis, 1966-68, U. Calif. at Berkeley, 1969—. Recipient award Nat. Found. on Arts and Humanities, 1967, Am. Nat. Acad. Arts and Letters, 1972. Guggenheim fellow, 1970. Author: Going Places, 1969; I Would Have Saved Them If I Could, 1975. Editor various lit. mags. Co-editor: (with Christopher Ricks) The State of the Language, 1979. Contbr. short stories, book reviews, critical essays to various publs. Office: English Dept U Calif Berkeley CA 94720

MICHAELS, LORNE, TV producer and writer; b. Toronto, Ont., Can., Nov. 17. Writer, producer comedy spls. and dramas CBC, Canadian TV, 1969-72; contbg. writer TV shows: Rowan and Martin Laugh-In, 1968-69; producer, writer Saturday Night Live, NBC, 1975—; writer, producer 4 Lily Tomlin Spls., 1972, 73, 74, 75; producer, writer TV spls.: Rutles' All You Need is Cash, 1978, Paul Simon, 1977, Beach Boys, 1976, Flip Wilson, 1974, Perry Como, 1974. Recipient Emmy awards as writer for Lily, 1973, Lily Tomlin, 1975; 2 Emmy awards as writer and producer for Saturday Night Live, 1976, 1 Emmy award as writer, 1977; Emmy award for Paul Simon Spl., 1978; San Francisco Film award, 1976; 4 awards Writers Guild; Winner award Nat. Acad. TV Arts and Scis. (2). Office: care NBC Press Dept 30 Rockefeller Plaza New York City NY 10020

MICHAELS, WILLARD A., broadcasting co. exec.; b. Omaha, May 13, 1917; s. Gus M. and Bessie (Kerstine) M.; B.A., U. San Antonio, 1940; m. Helen Louise Mintel, Nov. 20, 1938; children—Marcella (Mrs. Lawrence Pickell), Lawrence Richard, Betty (Mrs. Robert Westbrook). Asst. sports editor San Antonio Express, 1937-40; sports announcer, sales mgr., gen. mgr. KABC, San Antonio, 1940-53, v.p. WJBK-TV, Detroit, 1955-61; dir. Storer Broadcasting Co., Miami Beach, Fla., 1960—, TV v.p., 1961-66, exec. v.p., 1966-67, pres., 1967-74, chmn., 1974—; chmn. New Boston Garden Corp. (Boston Bruins), 1972-75; dir., mem. exec. com. Northeast Airlines, 1965-72, pres., 1970-72; dir. Delta Air Lines, Inc. Bd. dirs. Storer Found., Miami Heart Inst., Miami Heart Assn. Home: 11 La Gorce Circle Miami Beach FL 33141 Office: 1177 Kane Concourse Miami Beach FL 33154

MICHAELSEN, EDWARD HUGO, mining and mfg. co. exec.; b. Copenhagen, Denmark, Oct. 2, 1917; s. Hugo and Carolyn (Kappel) M.; B.B.A., Danish English Comml. Coll., Ealing, Eng.; m. Fritze Pihl, Jan. 7, 1941; children—John E., Carol Ann Michaelsen Owens, Linda Pihl. With Phelps Dodge Industries, 1940—, v.p. Phelps Dodge Copper Products Co., 1959-62, pres. Phelps Dodge Internat. Co., 1962-68, pres. Phelps Dodge Industries, Inc., 1968—, chief exec. officer, 1969—; dir. Consol. Aluminum Corp., Christiana Gen. Ins., Switzerland Gen. Ins., ACF Industries, J. Henry Schroder Bank. Mem. Econ. Devel. Council of N.Y. Served to lt. AUS. Mem. Elec. Mfrs. Club, Copper Devel. Assn., Greater N.Y. C. of C. Clubs: Board Room; Innis Arden Golf (Old Greenwich, Conn.); Blind Brook (Portchester, N.Y.). Home: Cove Rd Lucas Point Old Greenwich CT 06870 Office: 300 Park Ave New York NY 10022

MICHAELSON, JULIUS, physician; b. Bessemer, Ala., July 8, 1920; s. Bernard Leon and Sarah (Heinberg) M.; B.S., La. State U., 1942, M.D., 1944; m. Allison Barclay, Nov. 14, 1978; children by previous marriage—Jeffry, Frederic, Julius, Eric Blake. Intern, USPHS Marine Hosp., S.I., N.Y., 1944-45; gen. practice family medicine, Foley, Ala., 1947—; clin. asso. prof. family practice Med. Coll. Ala., 1965—; preceptor dept. family practice U. S.Ala., 1975—; active numerous profl. coms. Past chmn. bd. trustees Foley Pub. Schs.; mem. human rights com. Ala. Prison System, 1976—. Served with U.S. Army, 1945-47. Named Outstanding Alumnus La. State U., 1942; recipient John Walsh award Am. Acad. Family Physicians, 1976. Fellow Am. Coll. Sports Medicine; mem. Am. Acad. Gen. Practice (pres. 1964-65, chmn. bd. 1961-63, treas. 1967-71), AMA, Am. Assn. Med. Assts. (Outstanding Service award 1969, hon. life mem.), Am. Bd. Family Practice (charter dir., founding v.p. 1965), Family Health Found. Am. (pres. 1975—), Ala. Sheriffs Assn. (hon.), Phi Eta Sigma, Pi Mu, Omicron Delta Kappa. Republican. Episcopalian. Clubs: Lions, Optimist (past pres.), Masons. Contbr. articles in field to med. jours. Home: Sunset Rd Foley AL 36535 Office: PO Box 910 Foley AL 36535. *I am a firm exponent of the premise of latter-day noblesse oblige. Those who have the intellectual capacity, the physical stamina, the moral and mental integrity are obligated to assume positions of leadership. All of our capabilities and talents accrue to us, only as a gift, and through the grace of God. Our economic assets, our physical attributes, our motivation are all His gift to us. What we do with our God-given talents is our obligation and gift to Him.*

MICHAELSON, JULIUS C., former state atty. gen.; b. Salem, Mass., Jan. 26, 1922; s. Carl and Celia (Cooley) M.; LL.B., Boston U., 1948; M.A., Brown U., 1967; m. Rita Caslowitz, Nov. 26, 1950; children—Mark, Jeffrey. Admitted to Mass. bar, 1947, R.I. bar, 1948; mem. R.I. Senate, 1962-74, dep. majority leader, 1969-72, chmn. Senate Judiciary Comm., Senate Steering Com.; atty gen. R.I., 1974-79. Served with U.S. Army, 1943-46. Recipient Outstanding Service award, Jewish War Vets., 1977. Mem. Fed., R.I. (pres. 1973, mem. bd. of bar examiners, 1973-75), Mass. bar assns., Nat. Assn. Atty. Gens. Democrat. Jewish. Home: 78 Lorraine Ave Providence RI 02906 Office: 220 S Main St Providence RI 02903

MICHALOS, JAMES, educator, cons. engr.; b. Milw., Sept. 12, 1912; s. Peter and Angeline (Metros) M.; B.S., U. Wis., 1938; M.Engring., Yale, 1945; Ph.D., Northwestern U., 1949; m. Claire Pappas, June 4, 1939; children—Kiki, Peter. Designer, Chas. S. Whitney, cons. engr., Milw., 1938; project engr. Chas. W. Cole & Son, Gary, Ind., 1938-40; civil engr. Michael Pontarelli & Sons, Chgo., 1940; asso. structural engr. TVA, 1940-43; designer Carnegie-Ill. Steel Corp., Gary, Ind., 1943; asst. prof. Mont. State Coll., 1944-46, Syracuse U., 1946-47; asso. prof. Iowa State Coll., 1947-52, prof., 1952-54; prof. civil engring., chmn. dept. N.Y. U., 1954-73; prof. civil engring. Poly. Inst. N.Y., 1973—. Engring. cons., 1945—. NSF sr. postdoctoral fellow U. Cambridge (Eng.), 1963. Mem. ASCE, Am. Ry. Engring. Assn., Am. Concrete Inst., ASTM, Am. Soc. Engring. Edn., Internat. Assn. Bridge and Structural Engring., AAUP, Am. Inst. Cons. Engrs., Sigma Xi, Chi Epsilon. Author: Theory of Structural anlysis and Design, 1958; Structural Mechanics and Analysis, 1965; also papers in field. Editor civil engineering sect. Sci. Ency., 1958. Home: Riverview Terr Irvington-on-Hudson NY 10533 Office: Poly Inst NY 333 Jay St Brooklyn NY 11201

MICHALS, DUANE STEVEN, photographer; b. McKeesport, Pa., Feb. 18, 1932; s. John Ambrose and Margaret Cecilia (Matik) M.; B.A., U. Denver, 1953. Comml. photographer with works appearing in Vogue, Esquire mags., N.Y. Times and others; comml. clients include Eli Lilly Co., Revlon, Elizabeth Arden; represented in permanent collections: Mus. of Modern Art, N.Y.C., Chgo. Art Inst., George Eastman House, Folkwang Mus., Essen, W.Ger. Served with U.S. Army, 1953-55. Nat. Endowment for the Arts grantee, 1976. Author: Sequences, 1970; The Journey of the Spirit After Death, 1971; Things Are Queer, 1973; Take One and See Mt. Fujiyama, 1976; Real Dreams, 1977. Office: care Sidney Janis Gallery 6 W 57th St New York NY*

MICHALS, GEORGE FRANCIS, multi-industry co. exec.; b. Hungary, Sept. 14, 1935; immigrated to Can., 1956, naturalized, 1961; s. Todor and Ilona (Sinkovich) Mihalcsics; B.Comm., Sir George Williams U., Montreal, 1961; chartered accountant, McGill U., Montreal, 1963; m. Patricia Elizabeth Hoffman, June 18, 1971; children—Kathrine, Julie, Elizabeth, Georgina. Accountant, Coopers & Lybrand, Montreal, 1963-68; from treas. to exec. v.p. knit div. Dominion Textile Co. Ltd., 1969-74; v.p. fin., sr. v.p., then exec. v.p. Genstar Ltd., Montreal, 1974—. Mem. Council Fin. Execs., Fin. Execs. Assn. Clubs: St. James's, Mt. Royal Tennis (Montreal). Home: 215 Round Hill Rd Tiburon CA 92920 Office: 3 Embarcadero Center Suite 2500 San Francisco CA 94111

MICHANOWSKY, GEORGE, research found. exec., author; b. Yalta, Russia, Mar. 9, 1920 (Am. citizen); s. Ilya and Eleonora M.; student Mont. Coll., Rome U. Founder, pres. Amazonia Found., N.Y.C., 1952. Originator prep. research, leader Amazonia Found. expdns. to unexplored Andes and Upper Amazon areas, resulting in mapping of legendary River of Writing and prehistoric roads; discoverer of new data on ancient scripts; organizer dir. 1st aerophotog. reconnaissance of pre-historic Tihuanacu ruins; originator ultraviolet reconnaissance technique for clear air turbulence detection approved for investigation by U.S. Navy Dept. and Air Transport Assn. Am. Dir. spl. ultraviolet flight safety project, Kennedy Internat. Airport, N.Y.; dir. ultraviolet study of jet engine pollutants, FAA, cons. Aviation Rev. Conf. Dir. spl. ultraviolet research project on wake turbulence, U.S. Nat. Aviation Facilities Exptl. Center. Decorated Comdr. Order of Condor of the Andes (Bolivia); recipient spl. citation inter-Am. Hist. Municipal Congress, spl. avalanche research citation Peru, citation from Bolivian Govt. and Parliament in fields of photogrammetry, flight safety, cultural activities and historical research; 100th Anniversary citation for contbn. to ency. Funk & Wagnalls. Hon. mem. Archeol. Soc. Bolivia; mem. U.S. Naval Inst., Saint-Georges de Bourgogne, Am. Inst. Aeros. & Astronautics. Club: Explorers (mem. sci. adv. bd.). Author: (book) The Once and Future Star, 1977, updated paperback edit., 1979, Brit., French, Italian edits., 1980. Author articles on archeology in Funk & Wagnalls New Ency.; author Special Ultraviolet Effect as Clear Air Turbulence Detector, The Potential of Ultraviolet Reconnaissance as a Remote Detector of Invisible Nitric Oxide; Ultraviolet Reconnaissance as a Remote Detector and Tracker of Wake Turbulence; Cuneiform Clues to an Ancient Starburst, 1975; Ankh Linked to Supernova: The Real Riddle of Tutankhamun, 1978; A Star Clue to Imhotep's Tomb; New Light on Egypt's Mysterious Scorpion King, 1979; contbr. article The Remote Detection of Air Pollutants to Ency. of Environmental Sci. and Engring. Initiator concept infrared and ultraviolet aerophotography for archeol. purposes and gen. Andean studies. Discoverer of references to Vela X supernova explosion in Sumero-Akkadian cuneiform and Egyptian hieroglyphic texts. Address: Box 651 New York NY 10023

MICHAUX, HENRY MCKINLEY, JR., U.S. atty.; b. Durham, N.C., Sept. 4, 1930; s. Henry M. and Isadore M. (Coates) M.; B.S., N.C. Central U., 1952, J.D., 1964; m. Joyce M. Millett, July 2, 1966; 1 dau., Jocelyn Winston. Exec. v.p. Union Ins. & Realty Co., Durham, N.C., 1955-77, Washington Terr. Apts., Inc., Durham, 1956-77, Glenview Meml. Park, Durham, 1956-77; admitted to N.C. bar, 1966, U.S. Supreme Ct. bar, 1970; asst. dist. atty. for Durham County (N.C.), 1969-72; mem. N.C. Ho. of Reps., 1972-77; U.S. atty., Greensboro, 1977—; mem. Durham com. on affairs of Black people Nat. Assn. Real Estate Brokers, 1970-77. Served with U.S. Army, 1952-54. Mem. George H. White Bar Assn. Democrat. Mem. African Methodist Episcopal Ch. Home: 1722 Alfred St Durham NC 27713 Office: PO Box 1858 Greensboro NC 27402

MICHEJDA, OSKAR, civil engr.; b. Trzyniec, Czechoslovakia, May 19, 1922; s. Oskar and Paula (Grycz) M.; C.E., M.Sc., U. Wroclaw (Poland), 1950, Dr. Engring., 1961; m. Irena M. Neyman, July 14, 1948; 1 son, John A. Came to U.S., 1966, naturalized, 1971. Research and teaching asst. U. Wroclaw, 1948-51; asst. prof. U. Czestochowa (Poland), 1951-65, dean mech. engring. faculty, 1956-61, head chair of mechanics, 1955-65; sr. lectr. U. Khartoum (Sudan), 1965-66; asso. prof. Cooper Union Sch. Engring. and Sci., N.Y.C., 1966-68; prof. civil engring. Ind. Inst. Tech., Ft. Wayne, 1968-74; engring. specialist Burns & Roe, Paramus, N.J., 1974—; dir. Uni-World Industries, Inc., N.Y.C.; cons. engr. Named Outstanding Educator, 1972. Ford Found. scholar U. Sheffield (Eng.), Mass. Inst. Tech., 1959-60. Registered profl. engr., Ind. Mem. ASCE. Contbr. articles to profl jours. Patentee in field. Home: 278 Brook St Harrington Park NJ 07640 Office: 650 Winters Ave Paramus NJ 07652

MICHEL, DONALD CHARLES, editor; b. Ventura, Calif., Nov. 17, 1935; s. Charles J. and Esther Caroline (Heilert) M.; B.A., UCLA, 1958, M.S., 1959; m. Loretta Perron, May 4, 1963; children—Edwin, Robert, Christopher. Editor, San Fernando (Calif.) Sun, 1958-60; successively reporter, weekend editor, mng. editor Valley Times Today, North Hollywood, Calif., 1960-63; feature editor Houston Chronicle, 1963-68; asst. mng. editor features Chgo. Daily News, 1968-77; v.p., editor Chgo. Tribune-N.Y. News Syndicate, 1977—. Mem. Am. Assn. Sunday and Feature Editors, Comics Council, Sigma Delta Chi. Home: East Ln Revonah Woods Stamford CT 06905 Office: 220 E 42d St New York NY 10017

MICHEL, F. CURTIS, educator, physicist; b. La Crosse, Wis., June 5, 1934; s. Frank and Viola (Knudsen) M.; B.S., Calif. Inst. Tech., 1955, Ph.D., 1962; m. Beverly Muriel Kaminsky, Oct. 4, 1958; children—Jeffrey Bryan, Alice Elizabeth. Research fellow Calif. Inst. Tech., 1962-63; asst. prof. space sci. Rice U., Houston, 1963-64, asso. prof., 1964-70; prof., 1970—, chmn. space physics and astronomy dept., 1974-79, Andrew Hays Buchanan prof. astrophysics, 1974—; astronaut NASA Manned Spacecraft Center, Houston, 1965-69. NASA cons. on lunar atmospheres, 1965. Served with USAF, 1955-58. Guggenheim fellow, France, 1979. Fellow Am. Phys. Soc.; mem. Am. Geophys. Union, Am. Astron. Soc., Internat. Astron. Union. Home: 2101 University Blvd Houston TX 77030

MICHEL, HARDING BOEHME OWRE (MRS. JOHN F. MICHEL), educator; b. Louisville, Aug. 17, 1924; d. Henry Oscar and Mary Cornell (Inman) Boehme; B.S., Duke U., 1946; Ph.D., U. Mich., 1957; m. Oscar T. Owre, Aug. 4, 1948 (div. Dec. 1967); 1 dau., Caroline Harding; m. 2d John F. Michel, Nov. 24, 1970. Mem. faculty U. Miami (Fla.), 1952—, asso. prof. Rosenstiel Sch. Marine and Atmospheric Sci., 1967-70, prof., 1970—. Teaching fellow U. Mich., 1950-52; research grantee NSF, NIH, Office Naval Research. Mem. Marine Biol. Assn. U.K., Soc. Systematic Zoology, Phi Beta Kappa, Sigma Xi. Club: Key Biscayne Yacht. Author: Copepods of the Florida Current, 1967; (with F. M. Bayer) The Free-Living Lower Invertebrates, 1968; (with M. Foyo and D.A. Haagensen) Caribbean Zooplankton, 1976. Home: 5000 Hammock Lake Dr Miami FL 33156*

MICHEL, HENRY LUDWIG, civil engr.; b. Frankfurt, Germany, June 18, 1924; came to U.S., 1938, naturalized, 1943; s. Maximilian Frederick and Loschka (Hepner) M.; B.S. in Civil Engring., Columbia U., 1949. Chief engr. and gen. mgr. Panero-Weidlinger-Salvadori, cons. engrs., Rome, 1960-62; pres., chief engr. Engring. Cons., Internat., Rome, 1962-65; partner Parsons Brinckerhoff Quade & Douglas, N.Y.C., 1965-75, sr. v.p., 1965-75, pres., 1975—, chief exec. officer, 1975—, dir., 1969—; dir. Parsons Brinckerhoff Internat., Inc., Parsons Brinckerhoff CENTEC; guest lectr. Grad. Sch. Mgmt., Colo. State U., 1975-76. Registered profl. engr., Colo., N.Y., Ohio, Pa., Va., Mass., Conn., N.J., Mont. Mem. ASCE (endowment fund com. 1978), Am. Cons. Engrs. Council (civil works com. 1976), Internat. Road Fedn. (dir. 1977), N.Y. Soc. Profl. Engrs., Soc. Am. Mil. Engrs. (dir. N.Y. post 1977, scholarship com. 1972), Columbia U. Engring. Council (indsl. adv. com. 1978), Am. Water Works Assn., Am. Inst. Mgmt. (pres.'s council 1976-79), Newcomen Soc. N. Am., Agribus. Council (dir. 1977-78), Drug and Chem. Club. Contbr. numerous articles on water and waste engring., environ. impact and design to engring. jours.; instrumental in devel. and design of numerous water and sewage treatment systems in U.S. and abroad. Home: 45 East End Ave New York NY 10028 Office: Parsons Brinckerhoff Quade & Douglas Inc One Penn Plaza 250 W 34th St New York NY 10001

MICHEL, KENNETH GEORGE, packaging co. exec.; b. N.Y.C., Mar. 25, 1928; s. John F. and Elsie (Anhorn) M.; B.S. in Bus. Adminstrn. and Mech. Engring., Newark Coll. Engring., 1952; m. Marilynne Laura Kunze, Oct. 4, 1975; children—Terry L., Koren R. Vice Pres. Bradley Sun div. Am. Can Co., Union, N.J. 1952-64; with Continental Can Co., 1964—, group v.p. diversified products, N.Y.C., 1974-75, pres. Continental Diversified Industries, 1975-77; pres. Continental Plastics Industries, 1978—. Served in U.S. Army, 1946-48. Clubs: Sky, Pinnacle. Patentee plastic tubes, closures. Office: 633 Third Ave New York City NY 10017

MICHEL, LESTER ALLEN, chemist, educator; b. Mexico, Ind., Mar. 5, 1919; s. Otto Walter and Octa (Eller) M.; A.B., Taylor U., 1941; M.S., Purdue U., 1944; Ph.D., U. Colo., 1947; m. Martha Lilly Brown, Nov. 1, 1942; children—James Wesley, Janet Elaine, Barbara Louise, Kenneth Wayne, Stephen Lee. Faculty, Colo. Coll., Colorado Springs, 1947—, prof., 1960—, chmn. dept. chemistry, 1961-70; research chemist Marathon Oil Co., 1962. Mem. Am. Chem Soc., AAAS. Methodist. Club: Colorado Mountain (past pres.). Home: 309 Yucca Circle Colorado Springs CO 80906

MICHEL, PAUL REDMOND, lawyer, govt. ofcl.; b. Phila., Feb. 3, 1941; s. Lincoln Mattheus and Dorothy (Kelley) M.; B.A., Williams Coll., 1963; LL.D., U. Va., 1966; m. Sally Ann Clark, June 19, 1965; children—Sarah Elizabeth, Margaret Kelley. Admitted to Pa. bar, 1967, U.S. Supreme Ct. bar, 1970; dep. dist. atty. City of Phila., 1967-74; mem. Watergate Spl. Prosecution Force, 1974-75, Senate Select Com. on Intelligence, Washington, 1975-76; dep. chief sect. public integrity, criminal div. Dept. Justice, Washington, 1976-78, asso. dep. atty. gen. Dept. Justice, 1978—. Served with USAR, 1966-72. Mem. State Pa. Bar, Phila. Bar Assn. Home: 1853 Massachusetts Ave McLean VA 22101 Office: Dept Justice 10th and Constitution Ave NW Washington DC 20530

MICHEL, ROBERT HENRY, congressman; b. Peoria, Ill., Mar. 2, 1923; s. Charles and Anna (Baer) M.; B.S., Bradley U., 1948; L.H.D., Lincoln Coll.; m. Corinne Woodruff, Dec. 26, 1948; children—Scott, Bruce, Laurie, Robin. Adminstrv. asst. to Congressman Harold Velde, 1949-56; mem. 85th-96th Congresses, 18th Dist. Ill., house minority whip 94th-96th Congresses. Active YMCA. Del., Republican Nat. Conv., 1964, 68, 72, 76; chmn. Nat. Rep. Congl. Com., 1973-74. Served with inf. AUS. World War II: ETO. Decorated Bronze Star, Purple Heart; recipient Alumnus award Bradley U., 1961. Mem. Am. Legion, V.F.W., D.A.V., Amvets, Ill. State Soc., Cosmopolitan Internat. Rotarian. Home: 1029 N Glenwood St Peoria IL 61606 Office: House Office Bldg Washington DC 20515

MICHELA, BERNARD JOSEPH, physician; b. Iron Mountain, Mich., Dec. 6, 1924; s. Dominic A. and Anne (Giachino) M.; m. Barbara Trundy, June 24, 1950; children—Barton, Douglas, Kathryn, Patrick. Cons. phys. medicine and rehab., bur. maternal and child health D.C. Dept. Health, 1955-57; med. dir. Davis Meml. Goodwill Industries Rehab. Center, Washington, 1956-57; asst. dir., chief phys. medicine and rehab. Rehab. Inst. Chgo., 1957-58, dir. inst., 1958-61; cons. phys. medicine Chgo. Bd. Edn., 1959-60; asst. prof., acting chmn. dept. phys. medicine and rehab. Northwestern U., 1960-61; chief phys. medicine and rehab. Long Beach VA Hosp., 1961-64, cons., 1964—; dir. dept. rehab. Meml. Hosp., Long Beach, 1964—; asst. prof. phys. medicine U. So. Calif., 1961-65, asso. prof., 1965-66; asst. prof. phys. medicine and rehab. U. Calif. at Irvine, 1966-68, asso. prof., 1968-73, prof., 1973—; cons. Desert Hosp., Palm Springs, 1976—. Bd. dirs. Long Beach Heart Assn., 1967—, pres., 1968; bd. dirs. Calif. HT Assn., pres., 1974. Diplomate Am. Bd. Phys. Medicine and Rehab. Mem. Am. Acad. Phys. Medicine and Rehab. Home: 3175 Armourdale Av Long Beach CA 90808 Office: 2865 Atlantic Ave Long Beach CA 90808

MICHELI, FRANK JAMES, lawyer; b. Zanesville, Ohio, Mar. 23, 1930; s. John and Theresa (Carlini) M.; student John Carroll U., Cleve., 1947-48, Xavier U., Cin., 1949-50; LL.D., Ohio No. U., Ada., 1953; m. Doris Joan Clum, Jan. 9, 1954; children—Michael John, James Carl, Lisa Ann, Matthew Charles. Admitted to Ohio bar, 1953, since practiced in Zanesville; partner Leasure & Micheli, 1953-65, Kincaid, Micheli, Geyer & Ormond, 1965-75, Kincaid, Micheli, Geyer, Ormond, Zinn, Cultice & Miller, 1975—. Instr. bus. law Meredith Bus. Coll., Zanesville, 1956. Dir. Pub. Service for City of Zanesville, 1954. Mem. Internat. Assn. Ins. Counsel, Def. Research Inst., Ohio Def. Assn., Am. Ohio bar assns., Am. Judicature Soc., Am. Arbitration Assn. (mem. nat. panel). Elk. Home: 160 E Willow Dr Zanesville OH 43701 Office: 50 N 4th St Box 1307 Zanesville OH 43701

MICHELMAN, HERBERT, pub. co. exec.; b. Harrisburg, Pa., Mar. 26, 1913; s. David I. and Sara (Robbin) M.; B.A., Bklyn. Coll., 1934; m. Blanche Krainin, May 14, 1941; children—Faith Michelman Lennon, Frances. With Gimbel Bros. Co., N.Y.C., 1929-41, book buyer, 1938-41; asst. to pres. World Pub. Co., Cleve., 1941-42; with Crown Pubs. Inc., N.Y.C., 1943-79, v.p., editor-in-chief, 1952-59; pub. Herbert Michelman Books, N.Y.C., 1979—; lectr. adult edn. City

Coll. N.Y. Editor, Laurelton (N.Y.) Civic News. Served with U.S. Army, 1943-46. Jewish. Co-author: Body Control, 1964; International Guide to Physical Fitness, 1973. Office: 1 Park Ave New York NY 10016

MICHELS, AGNES KIRSOPP LAKE (MRS. WALTER C. MICHELS), educator; b. Leiden, Netherlands, July 31, 1909; came to U.S., 1914, naturalized, 1924; d. Kirsopp and Helen (Forman) Lake; student St. Paul's Girls' Sch., London, 1925-26; B.A., Bryn Mawr Coll., 1930, M.A., 1931, Ph.D., 1934; fellow Am. Acad., Rome, 1931-33; m. Walter Christian Michels, June 4, 1941; 1 stepdau., Leslyn Jane (Mrs. Charles H. Goodrich), Instr., Bryn Mawr Coll., 1934-38, asst. prof. Latin, 1938-46, asso. prof., 1946-55, prof., 1955-75, chmn. dept., 1964-74, Andrew W. Mellon prof. humanities, 1970-75, prof. emeritus, 1975—; vis. Paddison prof. Latin, U. N.C., Chapel Hill, 1977—; Martin lectr. Oberlin Coll., 1969. Recipient Goodwin award merit, 1970. Faculty fellow Found. for Advancement Edn., 1953-54; Guggenheim fellow 1960-61. Mem. Am. Philol. Assn. (pres. 1972), Soc. Promotion Roman Studies (Eng.), Internat. Archaeol. Assn., Soc. Fellows Am. Acad. Rome, Bryn Mawr Coll. Alumnae Assn. Mem. Soc. Friends. Author: The Calendar of the Roman Republic, 1967. Home: 143 Carol Woods Chapel Hill NC 27514

MICHELS, EUGENE, phys. therapist; b. Cin., May 16, 1926; s. Joseph and Anna (Bauer) M.; B.S., U. Cin., 1950; Certificate Phys. Therapy, U. Pa., 1951, M.A., 1965; m. Genevieve Wilma Readinger, June 28, 1947; children—Karen, Timothy, Donald, Marian, Monica, Martha, David, Ann. Phys. therapist Grad. Hosp., U. Pa., Phila., 1951-58, mem. faculty dept. phys. therapy, 1965—, asst. prof., 1969-75, asso. prof., 1975-77; dir. phys. therapy Magee Meml. Hosp., Phila., 1958-65; asso. exec. dir. Am. Phys. Therapy Assn., 1977—. Served with USNR, 1944-46. Recipient Dorothy Briggs Meml. sci. inquiry award, 1971, Lindback Found. distinguished teaching award, 1972. Mem. Pa. (past pres.), Am. (past pres., Golden Pen award 1977) phys. therapy assns., World Confedn. for Phys. Therapy (pres. 1974—). Democrat. Roman Catholic. Home: 7608 Wellesley Dr College Park MD 20740

MICHELS, ROBERT, psychiatrist; b. Chgo., Jan. 21, 1936; s. Samuel and Ann (Cooper) M.; B.A., U. Chgo., 1953; M.D., Northwestern U., 1958; m. Verena Sterba, Dec. 23, 1962; children—Katherine, James. Intern, Mt. Sinai Hosp., N.Y.C., 1958-59; resident in psychiatry Columbia Presbyn.-N.Y. State Psychiat. Inst., N.Y.C., 1959-62; mem. faculty Coll. Physicians and Surgeons, Columbia U., N.Y.C., 1964-74, asso. prof., 1971-74; psychiatrist student health service Columbia U., 1966-74; supervising and tng. analyst Columbia U. Center for Psychoanalytic Tng. and Research, 1967—; attending psychiatrist Vanderbilt Clinic, Presbyn. Hosp., N.Y.C., 1964-74; Barklie McKee Henry prof. psychiatry, chmn. dept. psychiatry Cornell U. Med. Coll., NY.C., 1974—; psychiatrist-in-chief N.Y. Hosp., 1974—; attending psychiatrist St. Luke's Hosp. Center, N.Y.C., 1966—. Served with USPHS, 1962-64. Mem. Am. Psychiat. Assn., Am. Coll. Psychiatrists, N.Y. Psychiat. Soc., Royal Medico-Psychol. Assn., Psychiat. Research Soc., Assn. Research in Nervous and Mental Diseases, Assn. Acad. Psychiatry, Am. Assn. Chairmen Depts. Psychiatry, Am. Psychoanalytic Assn., Internat. Psychoanalytic Assn., Center Advanced Psychoanalytic Studies, N.Y. County Health Services Rev. Orgn., N.Y. Acad. Scis., Alpha Omega Alpha. Co-author: The Psychiatric Interview in Clinical Practice, 1971; contbr. articles to profl. jours. Office: 525 E 68th St 525 E 68th St New York NY 10021

MICHELSON, EDWARD J., newspaper corr.; b. Northampton, Mass., Apr. 3, 1915; s. Isadore Henry and Fannie (Avrich) M.; B.A., Williams Coll., 1937; m. Dorothea Adair Pohlman, Feb. 3, 1938; children—Kathleen (Mrs. Frederick D. Meloan), Paul, Emily (Mrs. Thomas D. Crews). Reporter, St. Louis Post-Dispatch, 1937-38; writer pub. relations div. Westinghouse Electric Co., 1939-40; day editor, internat. shortwave news div. CBS, 1941-44; spl. asst. Office Sec. War, 1946; mem. hist. sect. strategic services unit War Dept., 1946, asso. Robert S. Allen, syndicated columnist, 1946-50; Washignton corr. N.Am. Newspaper Alliance, also New Eng. dailies, 1946—; Washington editor Forbes, mag., 1956-63, Printer's Ink mag., 1958-63; mag. editor Ocean Sci. News, 1968-mag., 1958-63; Washington editor Sci. and Tech. mag., 1969—. Exec., Enterprises Publs. Research dir. pub. works subcom. on water resources U.S. Ho. of Reps., 1951. Served with OSS, AUS, 1944-46. Mem. Aviation/Space Writers Assn., White House Corrs. Assn., Washington Soc. Investment Analysts, Gargoyle Soc. Clubs: Williams (N.Y.C.); Cosmos, Nat. Press (Washington). Contbr. to gen., financial, spl. bus. periodicals. Editor: (Wright Patman) Our American Government, 1948. Home: 2153 Florida Ave NW Washington DC 20008 Office: Nat Press Bldg Washington DC 20045

MICHELSON, IRVING, scientist; b. Jersey City, Jan. 4, 1922; s. Eli J. and Sadie H. (Ginsberg) M.; student George Washington U., 1938-41, 46; B.S., Ga. Sch. Tech., 1943; postgrad. Brown U., 1943-44; M.S., Calif. Inst. Tech., 1947, Ph.D. in Aero. and Math., 1951; m. Sonia D. Saeta, Apr. 4, 1954; children—Ann Michelson Shoham, Louis, Linda, Julia, Elise, Eliot, Jack. Lectr., U. Calif. at Los Angeles, 1951-54; research scientist ODIN Assos., Pasadena, Calif., 1954-57; prof. aero. engring., head dept. Pa. State U., 1957-60; prof. aerospace engring. Ill. Inst. Tech., also Faculté des Scis. de Nancy (France), 1960—; cons. to govt., industry, 1950—; writer newspaper column Prof. at the Breakfast Nook, 1970—, Scientifically Speaking, 1974—. Mem. adv. bd. Com. Pan Am. Policy, 1970—. Served to lt. (j.g.) USNR, 1944-46. Mem. Am. Astron. Soc., Am. Inst. Aeros. and Astronautics (chmn. edn. com. 1959-61), Am. Soc. Engring. Edn., AAUP, AAAS, Royal Soc. N.S.W., Sigma Xi, Kappa Kappa Psi. Club: Chgo. Press. Author: World Understanding, 1965; Man on the Moon, 1969; The Science of Fluids, 1970; Tides, 1976. Discovered interrelationship of earth-moon-sun distances and their mass ratios, 1964; introduced reciprocity concept in planetary mechanics, explanation of earth's rotational speed value, 1965-66; new formulation of ocean tide theory, 1965. Home: 6709 N Mozart St Chicago IL 60645

MICHELSON, MAX, JR., publisher; b. N.Y.C., June 7, 1921; s. Max and Ida Rose (Landau) M.; B.A., Lafayette Coll., Easton, Pa., 1941; m. Virginia Seames, Oct. 22, 1950; children—Gail Ida, Eric Seames, Bradley Maxwell. Advt. bus. mgr. R.K.O. Radio Pictures, N.Y.C., 1946-57; maj. nat. account mgr. Reuben H. Donnelley Corp., N.Y.C., 1958-65; Eastern dist. sales mgr. Sch. Products News, N.Y.C., 1965-69; publisher Am. Sch. and Univ., N.Y.C., 1970—; v.p. N.Am. Pub. Co., 1970—, pres. ednl. div., 1979—; mem. adv. council Ednl. Facilities Planners. Active local Little League. Served with AUS, 1943-46. Mem. Am. Mktg. Assn., Assn. Sch. Bus. Ofcls., Am. Assn. Sch. Adminstrs., Assn. Ednl. Communications Technology, Assn. Phys. Plant Adminstrs., Ednl. Industries Assn., Am. Mgmt. Assn., Assn. Curriculum Devel., Assn. Media Producers Club: Masons. Home: 482 Warren St Westbury NY 11590 Office: 545 Madison Ave New York NY 10022

MICHELSON, RICHARD ALBERT, mfg. co. exec.; b. Akron, Ohio, Oct. 25, 1926; s. Albert Sidney and Ellen Velora (Getz) M.; student Oberlin Coll., 1944-46, Kenyon Coll., 1947-49; m. Joan Helen Gleason, Aug. 8, 1949; children—Richard A., Jr., John Robert, Susan Ellen. With McNeil Corp., Akron, 1950, sales mgr., 1958-60, v.p. sales, 1960-64, pres., chief exec. officer, 1964—; dir. First Nat. Bank of Akron, 1968—. Trustee Akron City Hosp., 1965—. Served with USNR, 1944-46. Republican. Lutheran. Clubs: Portage Country, Ottaw Shooting, Sharon Golf. Office: 96 E Crosier St Akron OH 44311*

MICHENER, CHARLES DUNCAN, educator, entomologist; b. Pasadena, Calif., Sept. 22, 1918; s. Harold and Josephine (Rigden) M.; B.S., U. Calif. at Berkeley, 1939, Ph.D., 1941; m. Mary Hastings, Jan. 1, 1941; children—David, Daniel, Barbara, Walter. Tech. asst. U. Cal. at Berkeley, 1939-42; asst. curator Am. Mus. Natural History, N.Y.C., 1942-46, asso. curator, 1946-48, research asso., 1949—; asso. prof. U. Kans., 1948-49, prof., chmn. dept. entomology, 1949-61, 72-75, Watkins distinguished prof. entomology, 1959—, acting chmn. dept. systematics, ecology, 1968-69, Watkins distinguished prof. systematics and ecology, 1969—; dir. Snow Entomol. Museum, 1974—, state entomologist, 1949-61. Guggenheim fellow, vis. research prof. U. Paraná, Curitiba, Brazil, 1955-56; Fulbright fellow U. Queensland, Brisbane, Australia, 1958-59; research scholar U. Costa Rica, 1963; Guggenheim fellow, Africa, 1966-67. Served from 1st lt to capt. San. Corps, AUS, 1943-46. Fellow Am. Entomol. Soc., Am. Acad. Arts and Scis., Royal Entomol. Soc. London; mem. Nat. Acad. Scis., Linnean Soc. London, Soc. for Study Evolution (pres. 1967), Soc. Systematic Zoologists (pres. 1969), Am. Soc. Naturalists (pres. 1978), Internat. Union for Study Social Insects, Bee Research Assn., Kans. Entomol. Soc., Brazilian Acad. Scis. (corr.), Entomol. Soc. Am. Author: (with Mary H. Michener) American Social Insects, 1951; (with S.F. Sakagami) Nest Architecture of the Sweat Bees, 1962; The Social Behavior of the Bees, 1974; also articles; editor Evolution, 1962-64; Am. editor: Insectes Sociaux, Paris, 1954-55, 62—; asso. editor Ann. Rev. of Ecology and Systematics, 1970—. Home: 1706 W 2d St Lawrence KS 66044

MICHENER, CHARLES THOMSON, editor, writer; b. Cleve., Nov. 13, 1940; s. Jesse Hamor and Virginia Marie (Callinan) M.; A.B., Yale, 1962; M.S., Columbia, 1965; m. Fay Morgan Padelford, Aug. 5, 1967; 1 dau., Amanda Morgan; m. 2d, Diana Chatfield Geary, Sept. 13, 1975. Lectr., Haile Selassie I U., Addis Ababa, Ethiopia (with U.S. Peace Corps), 1962-64; staff writer Seattle mag., 1965-67, mng. editor, 1967-70; asso. editor Newsweek mag., N.Y.C., 1970-72, gen. editor, 1972-75, sr. editor, 1975—. Lectr., New Sch. for Social Research, 1975; mem. selection com. N.Y. Film Festival, 1975—. Bd. dirs. Allied Arts of Seattle, 1967-70. Served with AUS, 1966-71. Recipient Gavel award Am. Bar Assn., 1971. Mem. Zeta Psi. Club: Yale (N.Y.C.). Home: 850 Park Ave New York City NY 10021 Office: Newsweek 444 Madison Ave New York City NY 10022

MICHENER, JAMES ALBERT, author; b. N.Y.C., Feb. 3, 1907; s. Edwin and Mabel (Haddock) M.; A.B. summa cum laude, Swarthmore Coll., 1929; A.M., U. No. Colo., 1937; research study U. Pa., U. Va., Ohio State U., Harvard U., U. St. Andrews (Scotland), U. Siena (Italy), Brit. Mus. London (Lippincott Traveling fellow), 1930-33; numerous hon. degrees; m. Patti Koon, July 27, 1935 (div.); m. 2d, Vange Nord, Sept. 2, 1948 (div.); m. 3d, Mari Yoriko Sabusawa, Oct. 23, 1955. Tchr., Hill Sch., 1929-31, George Sch., Pa., 1933-36; prof. Colo. State Coll. Edn., 1936-41; vis. prof. Harvard U., 1939-40; asso. editor Macmillan Co., 1941-49; mem. adv. com. on arts State Dept., 1957; mem. U.S. Adv. Commn. on Info. 1971. Sec., Pa. Constl. Conv., 1967-68. Served with USNR, 1944-45; PTO. Mem. Phi Beta Kappa. Democrat. Mem. Soc. of Friends. Author: Unit in the Social Studies, 1940; Tales of the South Pacific (Pulitzer prize), 1947; The Fires of Spring, 1949; Return to Paradise, 1951; The Voice of Asia, 1951; The Bridges at Toko Ri, 1953; Sayonara, 1954; Floating World, 1955; The Bridge at Andau, 1957; Rascals in Paradise (with A. Grove Day), 1957; Selected Writings, 1957; The Hokusai Sketchbook, 1958; Japanese Prints, 1959; Hawaii, 1959; Report of the County Chairman, 1961; Caravans, 1963; The Source, 1965; Iberia, 1968; Presidential Lottery, 1969; The Quality of Life, 1970; Kent State, 1971; The Drifters, 1971; A Michener Miscellany, 1973; Centennial, 1974; Sports in America, 1976; Chesapeake, 1978. Editor: Future of Social Studies for N.E.A., 1940. Home: PO Box 250 Pipersville PA 18947

MICHENER, ROLAND, lawyer, former gov. gen. and comdr.-in-chief Can.; b. Lacombe, Alta., Can., Apr. 19, 1900; s. Edward and Mary Edith (Roland) M.; B.A. (Rhodes scholar), U. Alta., 1919; B.A., Oxford U., 1922, B.C.L., 1923, M.A., 1929; LL.D., U. Ottawa, 1948, Queen's U., 1958, U. Laval, 1960, U. Alta., 1967, St. Mary's U., Halifax, U. Toronto, 1968, Royal Mil. Coll. Can., Mt. Allison U., Brock U., 1969, U. Man., McGill U., York U., 1970, U. B.C., 1971, Jewish Theol. Sem. Am., U. N.B., 1972, Dalhousie U., 1974; D.C.L., Bishop's U., Lennoxville, 1968, U. Windsor, 1969, Oxford U., 1970; m. Norah Evangeline Willis, Feb. 26, 1927; children—Joan (Mrs. Donald Rohr), Diana (Mrs. Roy Edward Schatz), Wendy (Mrs. Leslie G. Lawrence, dec.). Barrister, Middle Temple (Eng.), 1923, Ont., 1924; created King's counsel, 1943; practice law, Toronto, 1924-57; mem. firm Lang, Michener & Cranston; mem. Ont. Legislature for St. David, Toronto, 1945-48; provincial sec. Ont., 1946-48; mem. Ho. of Commons, 1953-62, speaker, 1957-62, sworn Privy Council, 1962; Canadian high commr. to India, 1964-67, also ambassador to Nepal; gov. gen., comdr.-in-chief Can., 1967-74; chancellor Queen's U., 1976—; chmn. bd. Met. Trust Co., 1974-76, hon. chmn. bd., 1976—; chmn. Teck Corp. Ltd., 1974—; pub. gov. Toronto Stock Exchange, 1974-76; asso. counsel Lang, Michener, Cranston, Farquharson & Wright, 1974—; hon. dir. E.L. Fin. Corp.; dir. Pamour Porcupine Mines Ltd. Past pres. Bd. Trade Club. Gen. sec. for Can. Rhodes Scholarships, 1936-64. Past hon. counsel Ont. div. Red Cross; past gov. Toronto Western Hosp. Served with RAF, 1918. Chancellor prin. companion Order of Can., 1967; chancellor, comdr. Order Mil. Merit, 1972; prior for Can., knight justice Most Venerable Order Hosp. St. John of Jerusalem 1967; hon. fellow Hertford Coll., Oxford, 1961, Trinity Coll., Toronto, 1968, Frontier Coll., Toronto, 1972. Hon. fellow Royal Archtl. Inst. Can., Royal Coll. Physicians and Surgeons Can., Acad. Medicine Toronto, Royal Soc. Can., Royal Can. Mil. Inst., Heraldry Soc. Can.; mem. Canadian Inst. Internat. Affairs (pres.), Canadian Assn. Adult Edn. (past chmn. exec. com.), Canadian Med. Assn. (hon. mem.), Law Soc. Upper Can. (hon. bencher, life mem.). Clubs: Lawyers (past pres.), Empire (past pres.). Address: PO Box 10 1st Canadian Pl Toronto ON M5X 1A2 Canada

MICHIE, DANIEL BOORSE, JR., lawyer; b. Phila., July 28, 1922; s. Daniel Boorse and Mae (Mueller) M.; B.S., Harvard U., 1943; LL.B., U. Va., 1948; m. Barbara F. Maddox, Aug. 29, 1970. Admitted to Pa. bar, 1949; practiced law, Phila., 1949—; asso. firm Harry J. Alker, Esq., 1949, Kephart & Kephart, 1950-51; asso. firm Fell & Spalding, 1952-53, partner, 1954-68; partner firm Fell, Spalding, Goff & Rubin, 1969—; spl. master U.S. Ct. Appeals for 3d Circuit, 1970—; solicitor Twp. Abington, Pa., 1958-78. Pres. Phila. Council Internat. Visitors, 1957-60, chmn., 1979—; pres. Phila. Crime Commn., 1960-63, Phila. Fellowship Commn., 1970-71; chmn. Pa. Adv. Com. on Probation, 1966—, Bd. Phila. Prisons, 1968-71; pres. Nat. Assn. Citizens Crime Commns., 1961-62; pres. Unitarian Universalist Service Com., 1969-72; regional co-chmn. NCCJ, 1967-71, nat. bd. govs. 1971—; vice chmn. Southeastern Pa. chpt. ARC, 1978—; bd. dirs. Valley Forge council Boy Scouts Am., 1955—. Served to lt. USNR, 1943-46. Mem. Phila. Bar Assn. (gov. 1970-72), Pa. Bar Assn. (ho. of dels. 1971—), Am. Bar Assn. (chmn. organized crime com. 1964-65), Fed. Bar Assn., Am. Judicature Soc., Navy League (dir. Phila. 1967-73, v.p. 1973-76, pres. 1976-78, nat. dir. 1977—), St. Andrew's Soc., Friendly Sons of St. Patrick, SAR. Unitarian Universalist (ch. pres. 1961-62, dist. pres. 1966-69). Republican. Clubs: Huntingdon Valley Country, Down Town, Union League (Phila.). Home: 1129 Wrack Rd PO Box 8 Meadowbrook PA 19046 Office: 510 Walnut St Philadelphia PA 19106. *The most important standard of conduct I have attempted to follow is to respect the individuality and dignity of every person—including myself. Early in the practice of law I learned I could best represent my client in a business matter by gaining an understanding of the motivations and needs of the persons on the other side. Only then could I determine whether an agreement or settlement was feasible—as it almost invariably was. I found this same approach invariably helpful in other human endeavors.*

MICHTOM, BENJAMIN FRANKLIN, mfg. co. exec.; Bklyn., July 13, 1901; s. Morris and Rose (Katz) M., B.S., U. Pa., 1921; m. Hadassah Feil, June 14, 1925; children—William A., Mark Feil. With Ideal Toy Corp., Holis, 1923—, exec. v.p., chmn. bd., 1938-78, chmn. emeritus, 1978—; exec. v.p., chmn. Ideal Plastics Corp., Hollis, 1939—; v.p., dir. U.S.-Israel Plastics Corp., 1952-67; chmn. Kamiro Trucking Co., Ideal Wares, Inc.; dir. Ideal Toy Corp. (Can.), Ideal Toy Corp. (Japan), Ideal Toy Corp. S.A. (France), Ideal Toy Corp. (Gt. Brit.). Trustee Phi Sigma Delta Found.; bd. dirs. Am. ORT Fedn., Am. Jewish Com.; fellow Brandeis U. Mem. Am. Arbitration Assn. (arbitrator, panelist), Toy Mfrs. U.S. (dir., treas.), Benjamin Franklin Soc. (U. Pa.), Zeta Beta Tau. Clubs: Metropolis Country, Fifth Avenue, Sales Executives, Advertising (N.Y.C.). Home: 414 Sterling Rd Harrison NY 10528 Office: 200 Fifth Ave New York NY 10010. *What you can do, or think you can, begin it. Begin it, and the mind becomes more heated. Begin it, and the work will be completed.*

MICKEL, ERNEST PRESTON, pub. co. exec.; b. Cedar Rapids, Ia., Jan. 31, 1910; s. William Ernest and Jennie (Hayford) M.; student Coe Coll., Cedar Rapids, 1928-30; m. Muriel Lorraine Fairbanks, Aug. 16, 1947; children—Thomas Dean, Steven Hayford, Alan Ernest. Corr., Des Moines Register and Tribune, 1931-43; with F.W. Dodge Corp. (merged into McGraw-Hill, Inc., 1963), 1946—, Washington editor Dodge Daily Newspapers, 1946—; Washington editor Archtl. Record mag., 1970-75; Washington corr. twice-monthly newsletter Legal Briefs for Architects, Engrs. and Contractors. Dir. pub. relations Coe Coll., 1937-42. Editorial cons. Bldg. Research Adv. Bd., Bldg. Research Inst., 1970—; industry adviser Constrn. Specifications Inst., 1963, 69. Served with AUS, 1943-45. Recipient Presdl. citation Producers' Council, 1962, hon. membership, 1974; F. Stuart Fitzpatrick Meml. award, 1970. Mem. Nat. Press Club, Constrn. Writers Assn. (dir.), A.I.A. (hon.). Republican. Unitarian. Home: 6209 Poe Rd Bethesda MD 20034 Office: Nat Press Bldg Washington DC 20004

MICKELSEN, OLAF, educator, scientist; b. Perth Amboy, N.J., July 29, 1912; s. Frederick and Marie (Nielsen) M.; B.S., Rutgers U., 1935; M.S., U. Wis., 1937, Ph.D. (Nat. Livestock and Meat Bd. fellow), 1939; m. Edith Louise Nielsen, Dec. 1, 1939 (dec.); children—Elizabeth Karen, Margaret Louise; m. 2d, Clarice Helene Lewerenz. Research chemist E.I. duPont de Nemours & Co., Inc., 1936; chemist U. Minn. Hosp., 1939-41, research asso. Lab. Physiol. Hygiene, 1941-45, asso. prof., 1945-48; chief chemist, nutrition br. USPHS, 1948-51; chief lab. nutrition and endocrinology Nat. Inst. Arthritis and Metabolic Diseases, NIH, 1951-61; prof. nutrition Mich. State U., East Lansing, 1962—, Distinguished prof., 1974; vis. prof. Inst. Nutrition Sci. and Food Tech., Tehran, Iran, 1977—; scientist dir. USPHS, 1951-62. Mem. Am. Inst. Nutrition (pres. 1973-74), Am. Soc. Biol. Chemists, Brit. Nutrition Soc., Soc. Exptl. Biology and Medicine, Phi Beta Kappa, Sigma Xi, Omicron Nu. Author: The Biology of Human Starvation, 2 vols., 1950; Nutrition Science and You, 1964; Nutrition Self Studies, 1975; also numerous articles, chpts. in profl. publs. Home: 4412 Tacoma Blvd Okemos MI 48864 Office: Inst Nutrition Sci and Food Tech PO Box 3234 Tehran Iran

MICKELSON, ARNOLD RUST, church exec.; b. Finley, N.D., Jan. 8, 1922; s. Alfred B. and Clara (Rust) M.; B.A., Concordia Coll., Moorhead, Minn., 1943, LL.D. (hon.), 1972; m. Marjorie Arveson, June 8, 1944; 1 son, Richard. Owner, mgr. Luther Book Store, Decorah, Iowa, 1946-48; credit supr. Gen. Motors Acceptance Corp., Fargo, N.D., 1948-53; mgr. Epko Film Service, Fargo, 1953-58; asst. to pres. No. Minn. dist. Evang. Luth. Ch., 1958-61; asst. to pres. No. Minn. dist. Am. Luth. Ch., 1961-66; gen. sec. The Am. Luth. Ch., Mpls., 1967—; councilor Luth. Council in U.S.A., 1966—, sec., 1969-72, pres., 1973-76; mem. U.S.A. Nat. Com. Luth. World Fedn., 1966—, sec., 1966-69, 72-75; mem. Consultation on Luth. Unity, 1970-76, sec., 1970-73, chmn., 1974-76; mem. Com. on Luth. Unity, 1976—; del. 4th Assembly World Council Chs., Uppsala, Sweden, 1968, 5th Assembly, Nairobi, Kenya, 1975; chmn. Faith-in-Life Dialogue, Fargo-Moorhead, 1964, observor-trainer, Duluth, 1965. Mem. Conf. on Inflation, 1974, Mpls.-St. Paul Town Meeting Council, 1968-76; bd. govs. Midwest League, 1979—; bd. mgrs. Am. Bible Soc., 1979—. Served with AUS, 1943-46. Recipient Civic Service award Eagles, 1965. Mem. Ch. Staff Workers Assn. (past pres.), Concordia Coll. Alumni Assn. (past pres.), Alpha Phi Gamma, Zeta Sigma Pi. Club: Mpls. Athletic. Home: 6815 Harold Ave N Golden Valley MN 55427 Office: 422 S 5th St Minneapolis MN 55415

MICKELSON, GEORGE SPEAKER, lawyer, state legislator; b. Walworth, S.D., Jan. 31, 1941; s. George Theodore and Madge Ellen (Turner) M.; B.A., U. S.D., 1963, J.D., 1965; m. Linda Jane McCahren, Aug. 10, 1963; children—Mark, Amy, David. Admitted to S.D. bar, 1965; spl. asst. atty. gen. State of S.D., 1967-68; partner firm McCann, Martin & Mickelson, Brookings, 1969—; mem. S.D. Ho. of Reps., 1974—, speaker pro tem, 1977-78, speaker, 1979—; spl. prosecutor for S.D. atty. gen., 1972—; states atty. Brookings County, 1970—. Chmn. Brookings County Republican Central Com., 1970; chmn. Com. to Re-Elect the Pres., 1972; mem. commn. on missions, mem. adminstrn. bd. Methodist Ch., 1972—. Served to capt. U.S. Army, 1965-67. Decorated Army Commendation medal with oak leaf cluster. Mem. Brookings C. of C., Phi Delta Phi, Lambda Chi Alpha. Clubs: Masons, Shriners, Elks, Kiwanis. Mem. bd. editors U. S.D. Law Rev., 1964-65. Home: 1911 Lincoln Ln Brookings SD 57006 Office: 317 7th Ave Brookings SD 57006

MICKELSON, MERLYN FRANCIS, mfg. co. exec.; b. Minn., 1927. Formerly engaged as radio-sta. engr., broadcaster and electronics technician; joined Remington Rand Corp., 1953; now founder, chmn., pres., chief exec. officer Fabri-Tek Inc., mfr. memory systems for computers. Address: 5901 S County Rd 18 Minneapolis MN 55436

MICKELSON, SIG, broadcasting exec., educator; b. Clinton, Minn., May 24, 1913; s. Olaf and Harriet (Reinholdson) M.; B.A., Augustana Coll., 1934; M.A., U. Minn., 1940; m. Maybelle Brown, June 8, 1940; children—Karen Ann (Mrs. Christiaan De Brauw), Alan. With CBS, N.Y.C., 1943-61, pres. CBS News, 1954-61; v.p., dir. Time-Life Broadcast, Inc., N.Y.C., 1961-70; v.p., dir. Ency. Brit. Ednl. Corp.,

Chgo., 1970-72; prof., chmn. editorial dept. Medill Sch. Journalism, Northwestern U., Evanston, Ill., 1972-75; pres. RFE/RL, Inc., Washington, 1975-78; Disting. vis. prof. San Diego State U., 1978-79, exec. dir. Center for Communications, 1979—. Dir. CBS Found., 1957-61; founder, mem. adv. council Aspen Program on Communications and Soc., 1970—; advisor Nat. News Council, 1973—; ex-officio Bd. Internat. Broadcasting, 1975-78. Mem. Radio TV News Dirs. Assn. (founder; v.p. 1946-48, pres. 1948-49), Internat. Broadcast Inst. (founder; chmn. 1970-71, chmn. exec. com. 1967-70, 71-73), Chgo. Ednl. TV Assn. (dir. 1974-75), Council on Fgn. Relations, Soc. Profl. Journalists, Sigma Delta Chi. Clubs: Century Assn. (N.Y.C.); Cosmos (Washington). Author: The Electric Mirror, 1972. Home: 6443 Pasatiempo San Diego CA 92120

MICKELWAIT, LOWELL PITZER, lawyer; b. Glenwood, Iowa, Nov. 15, 1905; s. Wilbur W. and May I. (Pitzer) M.; A.B., U. Wash., 1928, LL.B. cum laude, 1930; m. Alice Semmes, July 18, 1936; children—Anne Nelson, John Semmes, Christie Betz. Admitted to Wash. bar, 1930, also U.S. Supreme Ct.; practice in Seattle, 1930—; with firm Holman, Mickelwait, Marion, Black & Perkins, 1930-62, mng. partner, 1954-62, of counsel, 1972—; v.p. indsl. and pub. relations Boeing Co., Seattle, 1962-72, also dir.; dir. Puget Sound Power & Light Co. Campaign chmn. Seattle-King County Community Chest, 1950, pres., 1953; pres. United Good Neighbour Fund, 1956, 61; chmn. Seattle-King County 1976 Bicentennial Commn., King County Design Commn., 1968—; chmn. bd. Pacific Sci. Center Found., 1964, 65; chmn. bd. mgrs. Norman Archibald Charitable Found., 1976—. Served to maj. USAAF, 1943-45. Mem. Am., Wash., Seattle bar assns., Seattle C. of C. (pres. 1972-73), Order of Coif, Phi Delta Phi, Phi Gamma Delta. Episcopalian. Clubs: Rainier, University, Golf, Yacht (Seattle). Home: 1551 NW 195th St Seattle WA 98177 Office: 1900 Washington Bldg Seattle WA 98101

MICKEN, RALPH ARLINGTON, educator; b. Mpls., Jan. 26, 1907; s. Hiram and Lillian (Hiller) M.; B.A., Intermountain Union Coll., Helena, Mont., 1929; postgrad. U. N.D., 1931; M.A., Mont. State U., 1936, Ph.D., Northwestern U., 1947; m. Lavina Morken, June 10, 1931 (dec. May 1964); children—Marguerite, Patrick H.; m. 2d, Doris Meagher, Aug. 28, 1965. Prin., Cut Bank (Mont.) High Sch., 1931-36; dir. forensics Gt. Falls (Mont.) High Sch., 1936-39; instr., then asst. prof. Mont. Sch. Mines, 1939-44; asst. prof., then asso. prof. Iowa State U., 1944-47, chmn. speech staff, 1948-49; grad. lectr. Northwestern U., 1947-48; sales speech counselor Banker's Life Ins. Co., 1947-49; prof. speech, dir. forensics Ill. State Normal U., 1949-57; chmn. speech dept. So. Ill. U., Carbondale 1957—. Moderator, World Affairs Forum, Bloominton, Ill., 1952-57. Mem. Central States (adv. council 1961-62), Ill. (pres. 1960-61) speech assns., Speech Communication Assn. Am. (legislative council 1961-63), Pi Kappa Delta (gov. Ill. province 1954-55), Delta Sigma Rho. Author: Speaking for Results, 1958; America in Controversy, 1973; Where a Man Is, 1973. Editor: Cicero on Oratory and Orators, 1969; editorial bd. Landmarks in Rhetoric Series, 1962. Home: 16 St Thomas Rd St Annes-on-Sea Lancashire England

MICKEY, PAUL FOGLE, lawyer; b. Winston-Salem, N.C., Sept. 3, 1914; s. Edward Timothy and Ada Eugenia (Fogle) M.; A.B., U. N.C., 1935, LL.B., 1937; m. Margaret Snowden Stanley, Dec. 4, 1943; children—Margaret Snowden, Paul Fogle, Frank Tayloe. Admitted to N.C. bar, 1937, U.S. Supreme Ct. bar, 1941, D.C. bar, 1947; asst. to attny. gen. of N.C., 1937-39; spl. atty. tax div. U.S. Dept. Justice, 1939-45, 46; mem. Office of Military Govt., Berlin, 1945; mem. firm Steptoe & Johnson, Washington, 1947-78, partner, 1950-78; gen. counsel, dir. Hamilton Watch Co., 1963-68. Mem. Am. Bar Assn., Am. Law Inst., N.C. Bar Assn., D.C. Bar Assn. Episcopalian. Clubs: Met., Chevy Chase (Washington). Home: Pine Island Kitty Hawk NC 27949

MICKLE, JACK PEARSON, city ofcl.; b. Auburn, Ala., Nov. 14, 1925; s. John Flemuel and Fannie (Cook) M.; m. Joyce Fields, Apr. 28, 1948; children—Jack P., Cassandra Joy, Kelli Sue. With Columbus Mfg. Co. (Ga.); lab. technician Swift Spinning Mills, Columbus; mem. advt. dept. Sears. Roebuck and Co., Columbus; with Columbus Bank and Trust Co., 1947-69; mem. congl. staff Rep. Jack T. Brinkley of Ga., 1969-74; mayor of Columbus, 1975—. Pres. Bruce Wilder chpt. Muscular Dystrophy Assn. Served with USNR, 1943-46. Mem. Assn. U.S. Army. Democrat. Mem. Assembly of God Ch. Clubs: Masons, Shriners. Office: PO Box 1340 Columbus GA 31902

MICKLEY, HAROLD SOMERS, chem. co. exec.; b. Seneca Falls, N.Y., Oct. 14, 1918; s. Harold Franklin and Marguerite Gladys (Somers) M.; B.S., Calif. Inst. Tech., 1940, M.S., 1941; Sc.D., Mass. Inst. Tech., 1946; m. Margaret W. Phillips, Dec. 21, 1941; children—Steven P., Richard S. Process engr. Union Oil Co. Calif., 1941-42; civilian project dir. torpedo research U.S. Navy, World War II; mem. faculty Mass. Inst. Tech., 1946-71, Ford prof. engring., 1961-71, dir. Center Advanced Engring., 1963-71; dir. Stauffer Chem. Co., Westport, Conn., 1967—, v.p., 1971-72, exec. v.p., 1972—; dir. Montrose Chem. Corp., SWS Silicones Corp. Trustee Norwalk (Conn.) Hosp. Recipient Naval Ordnance Devel. award, 1946; Distinguished Alumni award Calif. Inst. Tech., 1973. Fellow Am. Inst. Chem. Engrs.; mem. Nat. Acad. Engring., AAAS, Am. Chem. Soc., Am. Acad. Arts and Scis., Soc. Chem. Industry, N.Y. Acad. Scis., Conn. Acad. Sci. and Engring., Sigma Xi, Tau Beta Pi. Clubs: Country of Darien (Conn.); Pinnacle (N.Y.C.). Co-author: Applied Mathematics in Chemical Engineering, 1957; Recent Advances in Heat and Mass Transfer, 1961. Contbr. articles to profl. jours. Home: 11 Pequot Trail Westport CT 06880 Office: Stauffer Chem Co Westport CT 06880

MICKS, DON WILFRED, biologist, educator; b. Mt. Vernon, N.Y., Nov. 23, 1918; s. Wilfred Wallace and Bernice (Barbour) M.; B.S., N. Tex. State U., 1940, M.S., 1942; Sc.D., Johns Hopkins, 1949; m. Martha Millican, Feb. 15, 1944; children—Donald Frederick, Stephen Alan, Marjorie Ellen, Carol Jeanne. Faculty, Med. Br. U. Tex., Galveston, 1949—, prof., chmn. preventive medicine, community health, 1966—. Scientist-biologist div. Environmental Health, WHO, Geneva, Switzerland, 1958-59; cons. WHO, Pakistan, 1969. Chmn. bd. St. Vincent's House, 1969-70; mem. adv. bd. Tex. Air Control Bd. Served to lt. USNR, 1942-45; PTO. Named Distinguished Alumnus, N. Tex. State U., 1970. Fulbright sr. research scholar U. Pavia, Italy, 1953-54. Fellow Am. Pub. Health Assn., Royal Soc. Tropical Medicine and Hygiene, AAAS; mem. Assn. Tchrs. Preventive Medicine, Soc. Exptl. Biology and Medicine, Am. Soc. Tropical Medicine and Hygiene, Internat. Soc. Toxinology, Entomol. Soc. Am., Am. Mosquito Control Assn., Sigma Xi. Episcopalian (vestryman 1968-70, 74-76). Contbr. articles to profl. jours. Home: 1302 Ball St Galveston TX 77550

MIDDAUGH, ROBERT BURTON, artist; b. Chgo., May 12, 1935; s. John Burton and Mae Knight (Crooks) M.; student U. Chgo., 1960-64, B.F.A., Art Inst. Chgo., 1964. One-man shows include: Kovler Gallery, Chgo., 1965, 67, 69, Martin Schweig Gallery, St. Louis, 1970, 72, 79, U. Wis., 1976, Fairweather Hardin Gallery, Chgo., 1977; numerous group shows, including: Art Inst. Chgo., 1964, 66, 78, Cranfill Gallery, Dallas, 1971, Evanston (Ill.) Art Center, Three Man Show, 1966, Joslyn Art Mus., Omaha, 1968, U. Notre Dame, 1969, Va. Mus. Fine Arts, Richmond, 1966; represented in permanent collections: Art Inst. Chgo., Boston Mus. Fine Arts, Fine Art Mus. of South, Mobile, Ala., Los Angeles County Mus., Phoenix Art Mus., Worcester (Mass.) Art Mus.; curator art collection First Nat. Bank Chgo., 1971—; designed, executed permanent ednl. disply: Prehistoric Project at Oriental Inst. of U. Chgo., 1968; mem. artists com. Art Rental and Sales Gallery, Art Inst. Chgo. Served with U.S. Army, 1958-60; Mem. Arts Club Chgo. Home: 1318 W Cornelia St Chicago IL 60657

MIDDENDORF, JOHN HARLAN, educator; b. N.Y.C., Mar. 31, 1922; s. George Arlington and Margaret (Hofmann) M.; A.B., Dartmouth, 1943; A.M., Columbia, 1947, Ph.D., 1953; m. Beverly Bruner, July 14, 1943; children—Cathie Jean (Mrs. Robert B. Hamilton Jr.), Peggy Ruth (Mrs. Lawrence J. Brindisi). Lectr. English, Coll. City N.Y., 1946, Hunter Coll., 1946-49; faculty Columbia, 1947—, prof. English, 1965—, dir. grad. studies, 1971-74, vice-chmn., 1976—; chmn. English test com. Coll. Entrance Exam. Bd., 1967-69. Served to lt. (j.g.) USNR, 1943-46. Faculty fellow Fund Advancement Edn., 1951-52; grantee Council Research Humanities, 1958-59, Am. Philos. Soc., 1962, Am. Council Learned Socs., 1962, Nat. Endowment for Humanities, 1976—. Mem. Johnsonians (sec.-treas. 1958-68, chmn. 1969, 79), Univ. Seminar on 18th Century European Culture (chmn. 1973-75), Oxford Bibliog. Soc., Grolier Club, English Inst. (mem. supervisory com. 1963-66), Modern Lang. Assn., Conf. Brit. Studies, Econ. History Soc., Am. Soc. 18th Century Studies, AAUP, Phi Beta Kappa. Contbr. articles, revs. to profl. jours. Editor: English Writers of the Eighteenth Century, 1971; asst. editor Johnsonian News Letter, 1950-58, co-editor, 1958-78, editor, 1978—; asso. editor Yale edit. Works Samuel Johnson, 1962-66, gen. editor, 1966—. Home: 404 Riverside Dr New York NY 10025 Office: Dept English Columbia U New York NY 10027

MIDDENDORF, WILLIAM HENRY, educator; b. Cin., Mar. 23, 1921; s. William J. and Mary J. (Frommeyer) M.; B. Elec. Engring., U. Va., 1946; M.S., U. Cin., 1948; Ph.D., Ohio State U., 1960; m. Evelyn B. Taylor, Nov. 20, 1946; children—Judy (Mrs. Michael L. Marlowe), Mark E., Jeffrey W., Craig A., Susan A. Mem. faculty U. Cin., 1948—, prof. elec. engring., 1960—; with Wadsworth Elec. Mfg. Co., Covington, Ky., 1966—, dir. engring. and research, 1966—; dir. research Cin. Devel. and Mfg. Inc., 1960-66. Pres. Diocese of Covington Bd. Edn., 1972-73; trustee St. Elizabeth Hosp., Covington, 1967—, pres. bd., 1977-79. Served with USNR, 1943-46. Recipient Herman Schneider award, 1978. NSF fellow, 1958-59. Fellow IEEE; mem. Am. Soc. Engring. Edn. Author: Electric Circuit Analysis, 1956; Introductor Network Analysis, 1966; Engineering Design, 1969; co-author: Product Liability, 1979; editor book series Marcel Dekker, Inc.; contbr. to profl. publs. in field; patentee in field. Home: 1941 Provincial Ln Fort Mitchell KY 41011 Office: Loc 30 Univ Cin Cincinnati OH 45221

MIDDLEBROOK, ROBERT DAVID, electronics engr.; b. Eng., May 16, 1929; B.A., Cambridge (Eng.) U., 1952, M.A., 1956; M.S., Stanford U., 1953, Ph.D., 1955; m. Frances Christie. Came to U.S., 1952. Sr. tech. instr. Radio Sch. 3, RAF, 1947-49; research asst. Stanford U., 1953-55; faculty Calif. Inst. Tech., 1955—, prof. div. engring. and applied sci., 1965—; lectr., cons. in field. Recipient Tait Physics prize Peterhouse, Cambridge U., 1951. Fellow IEEE; mem. Sigma Xi. Author: An Introduction to Junction Transistor Theory, 1957; Differential Amplifiers, 1963. Office: Div Engring and Applied Sci Calif Inst Tech Pasadena CA 91125

MIDDLEBROOK, ROBERT WARD, pharmaceutical co. exec.; b. Pomona, Kans., July 8, 1916; s. Robert and Julia McPherson (Ward) M.; A.B., Princeton, 1937; LL.B., Columbia, 1940; m. Georgianna Shephard Leslie, May 10, 1947; children—Leslie, Julia. Admitted to N.Y. bar, 1940; with firm Mudge, Stern, Williams & Tucker, N.Y.C., 1940-49; vice consul, Calcutta, India, 1940-44; sec., gen. counsel Huylers, N.Y.C., 1949-51; v.p., dir. Pfizer Internat., 1951-63; v.p. Olin Mathieson Chem. Corp., N.Y.C., 1963-66; gen. mgr. Olin Internat., 1963-66; pres., dir. Squibb Internat. Co., 1966-67; sr. v.p., dir. Richardson Merrell, Inc., 1967—; dir. Reins. Corp. N.Y. Served to lt (j.g.) USNR, 1944-46. Mem. Assn. Bar City N.Y. Clubs: Pinnacle (N.Y.C.); Washington (Conn.); Princeton. Home: Nettleton Hollow Rd Washington CT 06793 Office: 10 Westport Rd Wilton CT 06897

MIDDLEBROOK, STEPHEN BEACH, ins. co. exec.; b. Hartford, Conn., Jan. 30, 1937; s. Louis Frank and Eugenia Gertrude (Caravatt) M.; B.A., Yale U., 1958, LL.B., 1961; m. Patricia Niles, June 9, 1964. Admitted to Conn. bar, 1961; with Aetna Life & Casualty Co., Hartford, 1962—, counsel, 1969-71, asst. gen. counsel, 1971—, corp. sec., 1973—, gen. counsel, 1978—. Trustee, v.p., treas. Wadsworth Atheneum, Hartford; v.p., bd. dirs. Legal Aid Soc. Hartford. Served to 1st lt. AUS, 1961-67. Mem. Assn. Life Ins. Counsel, Am., Conn. bar assns., Am. Soc. Corp. Secs. Club: Farmington (Conn.) Country. Home: 21 Guernsey Ln Avon CT 06001 Office: 151 Farmington Ave Hartford CT 06156

MIDDLEBROOKS, EDDIE JOE, environmental engr.; b. Crawford County, Ga., Oct. 16, 1932; s. Robert Harold and Jewell LaVerne (Dixon) M.; B.C.E., U. Fla., 1956, M.S., 1960; Ph.D., Miss. State U., 1966; m. Charlotte Linda Hardy, Dec. 6, 1958; 1 dau., Linda Tracey. Asst. san. engr. USPHS, Cin., 1956-58; field engr. T.T. Jones Constrn. Co., Atlanta, 1958-59; grad. teaching asst. U. Fla., 1959-60; research asst. U. Ariz., 1960-61; asst. prof., asso. prof. Miss. State U., 1962-67; research engr., asst. dir. San. Engring. Research Lab., U. Calif., Berkeley, 1968-70; prof. Utah State U., Logan, 1970—, dean Coll. Engring., 1974—; cons. EPA, UN Indsl. Devel. Orgn., Calif. Water Resources Control Bd., also numerous indsl. and engring. firms; mem. editorial adv. bd. Ann Arbor Sci. Pubs., Inc. Spl. fellow Fed. Water Pollution Control Adminstrn., 1967. Registered profl. engr., Ariz., Miss., Utah; registered land surveyor, Fla. Diplomate Am. Acad. Environmental Engrs. Fellow ASCE; mem. AAAS, Water Pollution Control Fedn. (Eddy medal 1969, dir. 1979—), Assn. Environ. Engring. Profs. (pres. 1974), Utah Water Pollution Control Assn. (pres. 1976), Internat. Assn. on Water Pollution Research, Am. Soc. Engring. Edn., Am. Soc. Limnology and Oceanography, Sigma Xi, Tau Beta Pi, Sigma Tau. Author: Modeling the Eutrophication Process, 1974; Statistical Calculations-How To Solve Statistical Problems, 1976; Biostimulation and Nutrient Assessment, 1976; Water Supply Engineering Design, 1977; Lagoon Information Source Book, 1978; Industrial Pollution Control, Vol. 1: Agro-Industries, 1979; Wastewater Collection and Treatment: Principles and Practices, 1979; contbr. tech. articles to profl. jours. Home: 1737 E 1400 N Logan UT 84321 Office: Coll Engring Utah State U Logan UT 84322

MIDDLEBROOKS, EVANN, JR., coll. dean; b. Winsted, Conn., May 16, 1925; s. Evann and Effie (Waldron) M.; student Ohio State U., 1945-46; B.A., Yale, 1949, M.A., 1950, Ph.D., 1957; m. Constance Mary Simmers, Sept. 4, 1948; children—Richard Evann, Stephen William. From instr. to asso. prof. psychology New Haven State Tchrs. Coll., 1952-59; dean coll. So. Conn. State Coll., New Haven, 1959-67, v.p. acad. affairs, 1967-78, exec. v.p., 1978—; chmn. com. licensing and accreditation Conn. Commn. Higher Edn., 1968-73; faculty cons. engrs. and degrees Conn. Bd. Acad. Awards, 1974—. Bd. dirs. Hopkins Grammar Sch., 1972-75, Community Health Care Plan, 1961—. Served with USNR, 1943-46. Mem. Assn. Higher Edn., N.E.A., Am. Assn. U. Profs. (pres. New Haven 1957-58), Conn. Edn. Assn. Kiwanian. Home: 277 McKinley Ave New Haven CT 06515 Office: 501 Crescent St New Haven CT 06515

MIDDLETON, CHRISTOPHER, poet, educator; b. Truro, Cornwall, Eng., June 10, 1926; s. Hubert Stanley and Dorothy May (Miller) M.; B.A., Merton Coll., Oxford (Eng. U.), 1951, D.Philosophy, 1954. Lectr. dept. English, U. Zurich, 1952-55; asst. to sr. lectr. U. London, 1955-65; prof. Germanic langs. U. Tex., Austin, 1966—. Served with RAF, 1944-48. Nat. Translation Center grantee, 1966, 67, 69-70; Guggenheim poetry fellow, 1974-75. Mem. West German Akademie der Kunste. Author: (poetry) Torse 3, 1962; Nonsequences, 1965; Our Flowers and Nice Bones, 1969; The Lonely Suppers of W.V. Balloon, 1975; (prose) Pataxanadu, 1977; Carminalenia, 1979. Home: 2314 River Hills Rd Austin TX 78746

MIDDLETON, DAVID, physicist, applied mathematician, educator; b. N.Y.C., Apr. 19, 1920; s. Charles Davies Scudder and Lucile (Davidson) M.; A.B. summa cum laude, Harvard U., 1942, A.M., 1945, Ph.D., 1947; m. Nadea Butler, May 26, 1945 (div. 1971); children—Susan Terry, Leslie Butler, David Scudder Blakeslee, George Davidson Powell; m. 2d, Joan Bartlett Reed, 1971. Teaching fellow electronics Harvard U., 1942, spl. research asso., radio research lab., 1942-45, NSF predoctoral fellow physics, 1945-47, research fellow electronics, 1947-49, asst. prof. applied physics, 1949-54; cons. physicist, Cambridge, Mass., 1954—, Concord, Mass., 1957-71, N.Y.C., 1971—, also Johns Hopkins U., Rand Corp., Air Force Cambridge Research Center, Communication Satellite Corp., Lincoln Lab., NASA, Raytheon, Sylvania, Sperry-Rand Inst. Def. Analyses, Office Naval Research, Applied Research Lab. U. Tex., Gen. Electric Co., Honeywell, Transp. Systems Center of Dept. Transp., Dept. Commerce Office Telecommunications, NOAA, Office Telecommunications Policy of Exec. Office Pres., Nat. Telecommunication and Info. Adminstrn., others; adj. prof. elec. engring. Columbia U., 1960-61; adj. prof. applied physics and communication theory Rensselaer Poly. Inst., Hartford Grad. Center, 1961-70; adj. prof. communication theory U. R.I., 1966—; adj. prof. math. scis. Rice U., 1979—; mem. exploitation adv. bd. USN Office Chief Naval Ops. Recipient award (with W.H. Huggins) Nat. Electronics Conf., 1956; Wisdom award of honor, 1970; several prize paper awards. Fellow Am. Phys. Soc., IEEE, AAAS, Explorers Club; mem. Acoustical Soc. Am., Optical Soc. Am., Am. Math. Soc., Soc. Indsl. and Applied Math., AAUP, N.Y. Acad. Sci., Authors Guild Am., Inst. Math. Stats., Phi Beta Kappa, Sigma Xi. Clubs: Harwich Port Tennis Assn., Stone Horse Yacht (Harwich Port, Mass.); Concord Country; Harvard (N.Y.C.); Cosmos (Washington). Author: Introduction to Statistical Communication Theory, 1960; Russia edit. Soviet Radio Moscow 2 vols., 1961, 62, Topics in Communication Theory, 1965 (Russian edit. 1966); tech. editor English edit. Statistical Methods in Sonar (by V.V. Ol'shevskii), 1978; mem. editorial bd. Info. and Control, Advanced Serials in Electronics and Cybernetics; contbr. articles to tech. jours.; research in radar, telecommunications, underwater acoustics, oceanography, seismology, systems analysis, communication theory. Home: 127 E 91st St New York NY 10028 Office: 127 E 91st St New York NY 10028 also 35 Concord Ave Cambridge MA 02138

MIDDLETON, DREW, author; b. N.Y.C., Oct. 14, 1913; s. Elmer Thomas and Jean (Drew) M.; B.S. in Journalism, Syracuse U., 1935, LL.D. (hon.), 1963; m. Estelle Mansel-Edwards, Mar. 31, 1943; 1 dau., Judith Mary. Sports editor Poughkeepsie (N.Y.) Eagle News, 1936; reporter Poughkeepsie Evening Star, 1936-37; sports writer, N.Y.C. office AP, 1939; war corr. attached to Brit. Expeditionary Force in France and Belgium, 1939-40; attached as corr. RAF, Brit. Home Army, 1940-41, U.S. Army and Navy as corr. in Iceland, 1941-42; Allied Forces, London, 1942; mem. staff N.Y. Times, London, 1942; corr. in Tunisia, Algeria and Mediterranean area and Allied Hdqrs., Algiers, 1942-43; with U.S. 8th Air Force and Bomber Command, RAF, 1943-44; accredited U.S. First Army and Supreme Hdqrs. Allied Expeditionary Force, 1944-45; at Frankfurt, Berlin and at Internat. Mil. Tribunal trials, Nuremberg, Germany, 1945-46; chief corr. N.Y. Times, to USSR, 1946-47, chief corr., Germany, 1947-53, London, 1953-63, Paris, 1963-65, UN, 1965-68, European affairs corr., 1968-70, mil. corr., 1970—. Recipient Headliners Club award fgn. corr., 1943; Internat. News Service medal for Dieppe coverage, 1942; U.S. Navy Certificate of Merit, 1945; U.S. Medal of Freedom, 1948; Order Brit. Empire (mil. div.), 1947. Mem. Am. Corr. Assn., London Anglo-Am. Corr. Assn., Moscow, Arras and Louvain Marching Soc., Delta Upsilon, Phi Kappa Alpha. Clubs: Garrick, Beefsteak (London); Overseas Press, Brook, Century (N.Y.C.); Travellers (Paris). Author: Our Share of Night, 1946; The Struggle for Germany, 1949; The Defense of Western Europe, 1952; These Are the British, 1957; The Sky Suspended, 1960; The Supreme Choice, 1963; The Atlantic Community, 1965; Retreat From Victory, 1973; Where Has Last July Gone?, 1974; Can America Win The Next War, 1975; Submarine, 1976; The Duel of the Giants: China and Russia in Asia, 1978. Office: care New York Times 229 W 43d St New York NY 10036

MIDDLETON, EDWIN GHEENS, mem. Republican Nat. Com., lawyer; b. Louisville, June 11, 1920; s. Charles G. and Anita (Gheens) M.; B.A., U. Va., 1941; LL.B., U. Louisville, 1948; m. Mary Jane Lampton, July 11, 1942; children—Edwin Gheens, Anita G., Huntley L. Admitted to Ky. bar, 1948; partner firm Middleton, Reutlinger & Baird, Louisville, 1948—; gen. counsel, dir. Am. Life & Accident Ins. Co.; vice chmn., dir. Capital Projects Corp., 1978—. Mem. Republican Nat. Com. for Ky., 1965—, state central com., 1972; chmn. Rep. county exec. com., 1958-63; del., mem. platform com. Rep. Nat. Conv., 1964, chmn. com. contests, 1972, vice-chmn. site selection com., 1976; chmn. bd., dir. Louisville and Jefferson County Children's Home, 1952-62, Louisville Park Theater Assn., 1956-68; trustee, sec. Louisville Country Day Sch., 1957-64; trustee Louisville Collegiate Sch.; chmn. bd. trustees U. Louisville, 1964-74, bd. overseers, 1975—. Served to maj. USMC, 1941-46. Decorated Bronze Star with V, Purple Heart; recipient Faculty Senate Disting. Service award U. Louisville Middleton Theatre, 1975, John Sherman Cooper award Lincoln Club, 1979. Mem. Am., Ky., Louisville bar assns. Episcopalian. Clubs: Filson, Salmagundi, Pendennis, Louisville County (pres. 1966-68, dir. 1964-69). Home: Transylvania Ave Harrods Creek KY 40027 Office: 501 S 2d St Louisville KY 40202

MIDDLETON, FRANK WALTERS, JR., lawyer; b. Texarkana, Tex., July 13, 1919; s. Frank Walters and Marian (Hodges) M.; B.S. in Bus. Administrn., La. State U., 1948, J.D., 1947; m. Jane Lobdell Porter, Jan. 12, 1944; children—Frank Walters III, Vernon Porter, Jayne Lobdell. Admitted to La. bar, 1947, since practiced in Baton Rouge; partner firm Taylor, Porter, Brooks & Phillips, 1952—; dir. Capital City Press, La. TV Broadcasting Co., Inc., Baton Rouge Water Works Co., La. Nat. Bank Baton Rouge. Chmn. adv. bd. Baton Rouge Salvation Army, 1949-50; mem. exec. bd. Istrouma area council Boy Scouts Am., 1950—, pres. council, 1964-67, mem. S.W. regional exec. com., 1967—. Vice pres. trustees Episcopal High Sch., Baton Rouge, 1964-75; mem. La. State U. Found., 1965-76; adv. bd. Our Lady of Lake Hosp., 1961-70; pres. Capitol area United Way, 1976. Served to maj. USAAF, 1941-46. Recipient Silver Beaver, Silver Antelope awards Boy Scouts Am., 1967. Mem. Am., La., Baton Rouge (pres. 1974) bar assns., Baton Rouge Assembly, Baton Rouge C. of C. (v.p. 1965), Phi Delta Phi, Sigma Alpha Epsilon, Omicron Delta Kappa.

Episcopalian (past sr. warden, vestryman). Rotarian. Clubs: Baton Rouge Country, City (Baton Rouge). Home: 917 Steele Blvd Baton Rouge LA 70806 Office: La Nat Bank Bldg Baton Rouge LA 70821

MIDDLETON, GERARD VINER, geologist; b. Capetown, South Africa, May 13, 1931; s. Reginald Viner Cecil and Doris May (Hutchinson) M.; B.Sc., Imperial Coll., London U., 1952, Ph.D., Diploma Imperial Coll., 1954; m. Muriel Anne Zinkewich, Apr. 4, 1959; children—Laurence, Teresa, Margaret. Geologist, California Standard Oil Co., Calgary, (Alta., Can., 1954-55; mem. faculty dept. geology McMaster U., Hamilton, Ont., Can., 1955—, asso. prof., 1962-67, prof., 1967—, chmn. dept. geology, 1959-62, 78—; vis. prof. Calif. Inst. Tech., 1964-65, Oxford (Eng.) U., 1971, Stanford U., 1978; cons. oil cos. Fellow Royal Soc. Can.; mem. Geol. Assn. Can., Am. Assn. Petroleum Geologists, Internat. Assn. Sedimentologists (v.p. 1972—), Soc. Econ. Paleontologists and Mineralogists, Can. Soc. Petroleum Geologists. Roman Catholic. Club: Dundas Valley Curling. Author: (with H. Blatt and R. Murray) Origin of Sedimentary Rocks, 1972; editor: Primary Sedimentary Structures, 1965; contbr. numerous articles on sedimentology to profl. jours.; editor Geosci. Can., 1974-78. Home: 90 Saint Margaret's Rd Ancaster ON L9G 2K9 Canada Office: Dept Geology McMaster U Hamilton ON L8S 4M1 Canada

MIDDLETON, HARRY JOSEPH, library adminstr.; b. Centerville, Iowa, Oct. 24, 1921; s. Harry J. and Florence (Beauvais) M.; student Washburn U., 1941-43, La. State U., 1946-47; m. Miriam Miller, Oct. 29, 1949; children—Susan, Deborah, James Miller, Jennifer. Reporter, AP, N.Y.C., 1947-49; news editor Archtl. Forum mag., N.Y.C., 1949-52; writer March of Time, N.Y.C., 1952-54; free lance writer, author, film dir., 1954-66; staff asst. to Pres. Lyndon B. Johnson, Washington, 1967-69, spl. asst., Austin, Tex., 1966-70; dir. Lyndon Baines Johnson Library, U. Tex., Austin, 1970—. Mem. Am. Battle Monuments Commn., 1968—. Served with AUS, 1943-46, 50-52. Mem. Sigma Delta Chi. Author: Compact History of the Korean War, 1965. Home: 2201 Exposition Blvd Austin TX 78703 Office: Lyndon Baines Johnson Library Austin TX 78705

MIDDLETON, ROBERT, educator, composer; b. Diamond, Ohio, Nov. 18, 1920; s. Elgin Joel and Alice (Roth) M.; A.B., Harvard, 1948, A.M., 1954; student mus. composition with Nadia Boulanger, Walter Piston, piano with Marie Waller, Beveridge Webster, Karl Ulrich Schnabel; m. Polly Alden Braun, Feb. 24, 1951. Instr., Harvard, 1950; faculty Vassar Coll., 1953—, prof., 1966—. Served with AUS, 1942-46. John Knowles Paine fellow Harvard, 1948-50; Guggenheim fellow, 1965. Author: Harmony in Modern Counterpoint, 1967. Composer (one act opera) Life Goes to a Party, 1947; String Quartet, 1950; Piano Sonata, 1957; (four act opera) Command Performance, 1958-60; Concerto di Quattro Duetti, 1962; Variations for Piano and Orchestra, 1965; Sinfonia Filofonica, 1969; also choral, chamber music. Home: 33 Sunrise Ln Poughkeepsie NY 12603

MIDGLEY, LESLIE, broadcasting exec., b. Salt Lake City, Jan. 18, 1915; s. J. George and Anna (Grant) M.; student Latter-Day Saints Coll., U. Utah; m. Jean Burke, Oct. 13, 1943; children—Leslie Rand, Andrea, Peter Jedediah; m. 2d, Betty Furness, Aug. 1967. Reporter, Salt Lake City Deseret News, 1935, city editor, 1937-40; reporter, rewriteman Denver Post, Louisville Courier-Jour., Chgo. Times, 1936-37; rewriteman N.Y. World Telegram, 1940; rewriteman, asst. city editor N.Y. Herald Tribune, 1941-44, night editor Paris (France) edit., 1944-49; asso. editor Colliers mag., 1949; fgn. editor Look mag., 1950-52, mng. editor, 1952-53; staff producer CBS News, 1954-67, exec. producer, 1967-80; v.p. spl. programs NBC News, 1980—. Recipient Peabody and Nat. Acad. TV Arts and Scis. award for program Face of Red China, 1958, Nat. Acad. award for the Senate and the Watergate Affair, 1974; Peabody award for The American Assassins, 1976. Club: Nat. Press (Washington). Home: 14 Old Farm Ln Hartsdale NY 10530 Office: NBC News 30 Rockefeller Plaza New York NY 10020

MIDKIFF, ROBERT RICHARDS, banker; b. Honolulu, Sept. 24, 1920; Frank E. and Ruth (Richards) M.; B.A., Yale, 1942; m. Evanita Sumner, July 24, 1948; children—Mary L., Robin S., Shelley S., Robert Richards, David W. Asst. sec. Hawaiian Trust Co., 1951-56, asst. v.p., 1956-57, v.p., 1957-65; dir. Am. Factors, Ltd., 1954-65; v.p. Amfac, Inc., 1965-68; exec. v.p., dir. Am. Security Bank, Honolulu, 1968-69, pres., dir., 1969-71; pres., dir. Am. Trust Co. Hawaii, Honolulu, 1971—; dir. Persis Corp., Helumba Co. Ltd. Co-chmn. Gov.'s Archtl. Adv. Com. on State Capital, 1960-65; co-chmn. Gov.'s Adv. Com. on Fine Arts for State Capitol, 1965-69. Past chmn. bd., bd. dirs. Hawaii Visitors Bur.; past pres., bd. dirs. Downtown Improvement Assn.; bd. dirs. Lahaina Restoration Found., Friends Jolani Palace, Samuel N. and Mary Castle Found., Atherton Family Found.; chmn. Profit Sharing Research Found. Served to 1st lt. AUS, 1943-46. Mem. Honolulu C. of C., Phi Beta Kappa. Home: 4477 Kahala Ave Honolulu HI 96816 Office: 1203 Davies Pacific Center Honolulu HI 96813

MIDLER, BETTE, singer, entertainer; b. Honolulu, 1945; student U. Hawaii, 1 year. Debut as actress film Hawaii, 1965; mem. cast Fiddler on the Roof, N.Y.C., 1966-69, Salvation, N.Y.C., 1970, Tommy, Seattle Opera Co., 1971; now nightclub concert performer on tour U.S., 1972-73; appearance Palace Theatre, N.Y.C., 1973; TV appearances include David Frost Show, Tonight Show; appeared revue Clams on The Half-Shell Revue, N.Y.C., 1975; rec. The Divine Miss M, 1972; Bette Midler, 1973; Broken Blossom, 1977, Thighs and Whispers, 1979; star motion picture The Rose, 1979. Recipient After Dark Ruby award, 1973, Grammy award, 1973, spl. Tony award, 1973, Emmy award for NBC Spl., Ol' Red Hair is Back, 1978. Address: care Miss M Prodns Inc PO Box 900 Beverly Hills CA 90213

MIECHUR, THOMAS FRANK, union ofcl.; b. Martins Creek, Pa., Jan. 25, 1923; s. Adam and Sophia (Buczek) M.; student Princeton, 1943-44; m. Lorraine Wesolowski, Oct. 19, 1957. Dist. rep. United Cement, Lime and Gypsum Workers Internat. Union, Easton, Pa., 1957-59, asst. to pres., Chgo., 1959-71, pres., 1971—; mem. gen. bd. AFL-CIO, also mem. exec. bd. indsl. union dept., maritime trades dept. Served with AUS, 1943-45. Mem. Indsl. Relations Research Assn., Chgo. Council Fgn. Relations, Smithsonian Assos. Democrat. Roman Catholic. Clubs: Moose, K.C. Home: 141 S Iroquois Trail Wood Dale IL 60191 Office: 7830 W Lawrence Ave Chicago IL 60656

MIEDÉL, RAINER, conductor; b. Regensburg, West Germany, June 1, 1938; s. Karl and Marga (Zippelinski) M.; came to U.S., 1970; m. Cordelia Wikarski; 1 son, Florian. Prin. cellist Stockholm Philharmonic, 1965; music dir. Gavleborg (Sweden) Symphony Orch., 1968; asst. condr. Stockholm Philharmonic, 1968; asst. condr. Balt. Symphony Orch., 1969, asso. condr., 1970-73; music dir. Seattle Symphony Orch., 1976—. German Govt. grantee, 1962; Swedish Govt. scholar, 1965. Mem. Nordiska Råd. Home: 2340 Magnolia Blvd Seattle WA 98199 Office: 305 Harrison St Seattle WA 98109

MIEDEMA, SYLVIA ANN, savs. and loan assn. exec.; b. Chgo., June 19, 1904; d. Celestin and Julia (Kropacek) Serp; student pub. schs.; m. Charles L. Klima, Jr., June 28, 1924 (dec. Sept. 1951); children—Carol L. (Mrs. Thomas J. Martin). Charles L. III; m. 2d, Jacob A. Miedema, Oct. 24, 1953 (dec. Oct. 1966). Dir., asst. sec. Clyde Savs. & Loan Assn., North Riverside, Ill., 1927-33, co-mgr., 1933-51, mgr., pres., dir., 1951—, chmn. bd., 1974—; dir. Clyde Service Corp., North Riverside, 1971—; chartering dir., cashier, dir. Bank for Savs. & Loan Assns., Chgo., 1968—; chartering dir. Darien Bank (Ill.), 1972—; dir. Home Loan Assos. Chmn. adv. com. to bd. dirs. Ill. Savs. and Loan League, 1971-73, bd. dirs., mem. exec. com., 1975-76, mem. polit. liaison com., legis. sect. league com. 1976—; mem. com. internal ops. U.S. Savs. and Loan League, 1973, mgmt. com., 1974-75; mem. com. on industry devel. Ill. savs. and loan commr., 1974; mem. legis. com. U.S. League of Savs. Assns., 1979. Founder, past pres. Burnham PTA; past pres. Cicero Edn. Council; bd. govs. Cicero Community Chest, 1970-75; bd. sponsors Evang. Hosp. Assn., Oak Brook, Ill., 1977—; bd. dirs. Central Suburban unit Ill. div. Am. Cancer Soc., 1972-75, Berwyn-Cicero Council on Aging, 1977—; adv. bd. South Suburban Home Health Service, Inc., North Riverside, 1975—. Recipient Spike Club designation Nat. Home Builders, 1956; recipient citation U.S. Treasury Dept., 1943. Mem. Ill. Fedn. Bus. and Profl. Womens Clubs (Woman of Achievement award Dist. 1, 1970), Nat. Home Builders, Lyric Opera Guild. Clubs: Ill. Fedn. Women's, West Suburban exec. Breakfast Cicero Woman's (life mem., past pres.); Berwyn Women's Civic (Berwyn, Ill.). Office: 7222 W Cermak Rd North Riverside IL 60546

MIEHER, ROBERT LEE, physicist; b. Scottsville, Ill., Oct. 10, 1932; s. Clyde Dean and Esther Eva M.; B.S. U. Ill., 1954, M.S., 1956, Ph.D., 1960; m. Waltraud Julie Boekle, Nov. 10, 1961; children—Walter, Michael, David. Post-doctoral research asso. U. Ill., 1959-60; vis. scientist II Phys. Inst., U. Stuttgart (W. Ger.), 1960-61; asst. prof. physics Columbia U., N.Y.C., 1962-65; asso. prof. Purdue U., West Lafayette, Inc., 1965-70, prof. physics, 1970—, head dept., 1977—. Alfred P. Sloan Found. fellow, 1963-67. Mem. Am. Phys. Soc., AAAS, AAUP. Home: 1915 Wea School Rd Lafayette IN 47905 Office: Dept Physics Purdue U West Lafayette IN 47907

MIELCKE, WILLIAM FREDERICK, JR., hotel exec.; b. Trenton, July 26, 1936; s. William Frederick and Jane Marie (Pergola) M.; B.S., Fairleigh Dickinson U., 1959; m. Marilyn Joyce Mielcke, Oct. 13, 1963; children—Julia Anne, William Frederick III. Teaching fellow Fairleigh Dickinson U., 1959-60; with Inter Island Resorts Ltd., Honolulu, 1960—; food and beverage controller Kauai Surf, 1960-61; food and beverage mgr. Kona Inn, 1961-63, mgr., 1963-65; interim mgr. Naniloa Surf, 1965-66, mgr. Kona Inn, 1966-70; gen. mgr. Kona Surf Resort, 1970—. Pres. Hawaii Island Visitor Industry Assn.; chmn. Hawaii County Planning Commn.; bd. dirs. Am. Cancer Soc. Mem. C. of C. of Hawaii (v.p. 1969), Hawaii Hotel Assn. (dir.), Keauhou Kona Resort Assn. (pres.), Confrérie de la Chaîne des Rotisseurs (chargé de presse Hawaii). Clubs: Masons (Shriner), Keauhou Kona Country. Home: Kona Sunshine Estates Kailua-Kona HI 96740 Office: 78-128 Ehukai St Kailua-Kona HI 96740

MIELE, ALFONSE RALPH, govt. ofcl.; b. N.Y.C., Jan. 6, 1922; s. Angelo and Alesia (Laudadio) M.; A.B. with honors in Litteris Gallicis, Fordham U., 1942; postgrad. U. Nancy (France), 1945; M.A., Columbia, 1947, Ph.D., 1958; m. Gloria I. Litrento, Nov. 22, 1942 (dec. Dec. 1977); children—Richard Lynn, Barbara Jo, Steven Arnold; m. 2d, Ann Carlino Valerio, Mar. 31, 1979. Commd. 2d lt. U.S. Army, 1942, advanced through grades to col. USAF, 1961; assigned 377th Automatic Weapons Bn., 1942-45; instr. French and public speaking Fordham Prep. Sch., N.Y.C., 1946-47; asst. prof. French and Russian, U.S. Naval Acad., 1949-52; exec. officer to NATO comdrs., 1953-55; teaching asst. Columbia, 1955-58; asso. prof. French, USAF Acad., 1958-60, prof., head dept. fgn. langs., 1960-67, asso. dean, chmn. div. humanities, 1967-68; exec. v.p. Loretto Heights Coll., Denver, 1968-70; pres. Coll. St. Rose, Albany, N.Y., 1970-72; prof. gen. edn. Schenectady County Community Coll., Schenectady, 1972-73; dep. asst. adminstr. internat. aviation affairs FAA, Washington, 1973-75, edn. specialist, 1976—; asst. dir. pub. affairs U.S. Dept. Interior, Washington, 1975-76; chief negotiator civil aviation tech. agreement with USSR, 1973-75; project dir. Nat. Aviation Edn. Plan for Am. Indians, 1978. Decorated Bronze Star, Legion of Merit; chevalier Palmes Academiques (France); recipient Encaenia award Fordham Coll., 1962. Home: 715 Dartmoor Westfield NJ 07090

MIELE, ANGELO, educator, author; b. Formia, Italy, Aug. 21, 1922; s. Salvatore and Elena (Marino) M.; D.Civil Engring., U. Rome (Italy), 1944, D.Aero. Engring., 1946. Came to U.S., 1952. Asst. prof. Poly. Inst. Bklyn., 1952- 55; prof. Purdue U., 1955-59; dir. astrodynamics Boeing Sci. Research Labs., 1959-64; prof. astronautics, math. scis. Rice U., Houston, 1964—. Cons. Douglas Aircraft Co., 1956-58, Allison div. Gen. Motors Corp., 1956-58. Pres., Italy in Am. Assn., 1966-68. Decorated knight comdr. Order Merit Italy; recipient Levy Medal Franklin Inst. of Phila., 1974. Fellow Am. Inst. Aeros. and Astronautics (asso.), Am. Astronautical Soc.; mem. Internat. Acad. Astronautics (corr.), Acad. Scis. Turin (corr.). Author: Flight Mechanics, 1962; editor Theory of Optimum Aerodynamic Shapes, 1965; also numerous research papers in aerospace engring., math. programming, optimal control theory and computing methods. Editor: Mathematical Concepts and Methods in Science and Engineering, 1974—; editor-in-chief Jour. Optimization Theory and Applications, 1966—; asso. editor Jour. Astronautical Scis., 1964—, Applied Mathematics and Computation, 1975—, Optimal Control Applications and Methods, 1979—. Home: 5330 Beverly Hills Ln 3 Houston TX 77056

MIELE, ANTHONY WILLIAM, librarian; b. Williamsport, Pa., Feb. 12, 1926; s. Harry John and Louise Casale (Troyano) M.; B.S. in Bus. Adminstrn., Marquette U., Milw., 1951; M.L.S., U. Pitts., 1966; m. Ruth Cassidy, Jan. 29, 1955; children—Terri Ann, Anthony William, Robert John, Elizabeth Ann. Partner, mgr. restaurant, Williamsport, 1960-66; dir. Elmwood Park (Ill.) Pub. Library, 1967-68; asst. dir. Oak Park (Ill.) Pub. Library, 1968-70; asst. dir. tech. services Ill. State Library, Springfield, 1970-75; dir. Ala. Pub. Library Service, Montgomery, 1975—; exec. dir. Ill. Nat. Library Week, 1970, ALA Nat. Library Commn., 1971-74; mem. Pub. Printer's Adv. Council Depository Libraries, 1975-78, vice chmn., 1977-78; asso. editor Govt. Publs. Rev., 1974—; reader Nat. Endowment for Humanities. Served with USNR, 1944-46. Mem. Am. (chmn. govt. documents round table 1974-76), Ill., Ala. library assns., Nat. Microfilm Assn., Spl. Library Assn., Internat. Fedn. Libraries, Chief Officers State Library Agys. (sec. 1978—), Beta Phi Mu. Roman Catholic. Club: Kiwanis. Author articles in field. Home: 103 Saccapatoy Dr Montgomery AL 36117 Office: 6030 Monticello Dr Montgomery AL 36130

MIELE, RALPH, JR., financial mktg. co. exec.; b. Newark, July 11, 1932; s. Ralph and Jeannette (Brock) M.; B.B.A., N.Y. U., 1959; m. Dorothy A. Jasones, Oct. 26, 1962; children—Pamela, Douglas. Sales rep. Plus Mktg., Inc., N.Y.C., 1959-61, Fed. Warehouses, Newark, 1961-62; account exec. Kennedy Sinclaire, Inc., Wayne, N.J., 1962-66, asst. v.p., 1966-70, v.p., 1970-73, exec. v.p., 1973-78, also dir., tchr. tng. programs; dir. mktg. D.M. Group, Inc., N.Y.C., 1979—. Served with M.C., USN, 1952-56. Mem. Am. Mktg. Assn., Advt. Club Am. Presbyterian. Club: Fairway Mews Racquet (Spring Lake, N.J.). Home: 4 Kinkaid Ct Roseland NJ 07068 Office: 477 Madison Ave New York NY 10022

MIELKE, DONALD CRAIG, mfg. co. exec.; b. Wampum, Pa., Jan. 4, 1943; s. Frank August and Nellie (Truby) M.; B.S. in Accounting and Fin., Pa. State U., 1964; m. Carol Lee Hoover, June 26, 1964; children—Julie, Kristin. With Diamond Shamrock Corp., 1964—, asst. treas., Cleve., 1974-76, treas., 1976—. Served with USNG, 1966. Mem. Cleve. Treas's. Club. Home: 17102 Preston Bend Dr Dallas TX 75248 Office: 2300 Southland Center Dallas TX 75201

MIELKE, FREDERICK WILLIAM, JR., utility co. exec.; b. N.Y.C., Mar. 19, 1921; s. Frederick William and Cressida (Flynn) M.; A.B., U. Calif., 1943; J.D., Stanford U., 1949; m. Lorraine Roberts, 1947; children—Bruce Frederick, Neal Russell. Admitted to Calif. bar, 1950; law clk. to Asso. Justice John W. Shenk, Calif. Supreme Ct., 1949-51; with Pacific Gas and Electric Co., San Francisco, 1951—, exec. v.p., 1976-79, chmn. bd., chief exec. officer, 1979—, also dir.; dir. Pacific Gas Transmission Co., Alta. and So. Gas Co., Eureka Energy Co., Natural Gas Corp. Calif., Edison Electric Inst. Trustee, Stanford U., Golden Gate U.; bd. dirs. Calif. C. of C., 1979, San Francisco C. of C., 1977, Ind. Colls. No. Calif., 1969-79. Served with USN, 1943-46. Mem. Am. Bar Assn., Calif. Bar Assn., Pacific Coast Elec. Assn., Pacific Coast Gas Assn. Club: Electric of San Francisco. Office: 77 Beale St San Francisco CA 94106

MIGDEN, CHESTER L., labor union exec.; b. N.Y.C., May 21, 1921; s. Albert and Louise (Jawer) M.; B.A., Coll. City N.Y., 1941; LL.B., Columbia, 1947; m. Dina Vohl, July 22, 1944; children—Barbara, Ann, Amy. Admitted to N.Y. State bar, 1947; atty. NLRB, N.Y.C., 1947-51; various positions Screen Actors Guild Inc., Hollywood, 1952—, nat. exec. sec., 1973—; v.p. Internat. Fedn. Actors, 1973—, Calif. Labor Fedn., 1974—, Asso. Actors and Artistes Am., 1973—, Hollywood Film Council, 1973—. Vice-chmn. Cal. State Film Devel. Council, 1974—; officer, trustee Producers-Screen Actors Guild pension, welfare plans, 1960—. Bd. dirs. Motion Picture and TV Fund. Served with AUS, 1942-46; PTO. Mem. Acad. Motion Picture Arts and Scis., Partnership for Performing Arts (dir. 1974—). Democrat. Contbr. articles to profl. jours. Home: 3539 Cody Rd Sherman Oaks CA 91403 Office: Screen Actors Guild Inc 7750 Sunset Blvd Hollywood CA 90046

MIGEON, CLAUDE JEAN, medical educator; b. Lievin, Pas-De-Calais, France, Dec. 22, 1923; s. André and Pauline (Descamps) M.; M.D. Sch. Medicine, U. Paris, 1950; m. Barbara Lou Ruben, Apr. 2, 1960; children—Jacques, Jean-Paul, Nicole. Came to U.S., 1950, naturalized, 1967. Fellow dept. pediatrics Sch. Medicine, Johns Hopkins, 1950-52, asst. prof., 1954-60, asso. prof., 1960-71, prof., 1971—; instr. biochemistry U. Utah, 1952-54; pediatrician Johns Hopkins Hosp., 1954—. Mem. diabetes, metabolism tng. grants com. NIH, 1963-67, gen. clin. research centers com., 1968-71, mem. endocrinology study sect., 1974-78; cons. Med. Research Council Can., 1969-79. Fulbright fellow, 1950, Am. Field Service fellow, 1950-51, Andre and Bella Meyer fellow, 1951-52; recipient research career award NIH, 1964—. Mem. Endocrine Soc. (council chmn. pub. affairs com. 1974—), Soc. Pediatric Research, Am. Fedn. Clin. Research, Johns Hopkins Med. Soc., Am. Soc. Clin. Investigation, AAAS, Am. Physiol. Soc., Am. Pediatric Soc., Soc. Francaise d'Endocrinologie (fgn. corr. mem.), Perinatal Research Soc., Lawson Wilkins Pediatric Endocrine Soc. (founding pres. 1972—), European Soc. Pediatric Endocrinology (corr. mem.). Mem. editorial bd. Johns Hopkins Med. Jour., 1970-72, Jour. Clin. Endocrinology and Metabolism, 1971-77. Contbr. profl. jours. Home: 502 Somerset Rd Baltimore MD 21210 Office: CMSC 3-110 Johns Hopkins Hosp Baltimore MD 21205

MIGHELL, KENNETH JOHN, lawyer, govt. ofcl.; b. Schenectady, Mar. 17, 1931; s. Richard Henry and Ruth Aline (Simon) M.; B.B.A., U. Tex., 1952, J.D., 1957; m. Julia Anne Carstarphen, Aug. 24, 1961; children—Thomas L., Elizabeth A. Admitted to Tex. bar, 1957; individual practice law, Dallas, 1957-61; asst. U.S. Atty., Justice Dept., Dallas, 1961-77, 1st asst., No. Dist. Tex., 1972-77, U.S. Atty., No. Dist., Tex., 1977—. Chmn. bd. mgmt. Downtown Dallas YMCA, 1974-76. Served with USN, 1952-54, to capt. USNR, 1954—. Mem. Am., Dallas, Dallas Jr. (pres. 1961) bar assns., State Bar Tex., State Jr. Bar Tex. (dir. 1962), Phi Alpha Delta, Phi Gamma Delta. Methodist. Home: 11081 Lawn Haven Rd Dallas TX 75230 Office: Room 16G28 1100 Commerce St Dallas TX 75242

MIGUE, JEAN LUC, economist; b. Montreal, Que., Can., Apr. 13, 1933; s. Joseph Alfred and Marie Laurence (Venne) M.; B.A. in Econs., U. Montreal, 1953, M.A., 1956; Ph.D. in Econs., Am. U., 1968; m. Renee Caron, Sept. 13, 1958; children—Paule, Pascal, Nicolas. Researcher, Bank of Can., 1957-58; prof. Laval U., 1962-70; prof. econs. Nat. Sch. Public Adminstrn., Quebec, 1970—; mem. staff Econ. Council Can., 1973-74. Massey Found. fellow, 1956. Fellow Royal Soc. Can.; mem. Am. Econ. Assn., Can. Econ. Assn., Public Choice Soc. Roman Catholic. Author: (with G. Belanger) The Price of Health, 1974; Le Prix du Transport, 1978; Nationalisms in Canada, 1979; L'Economiste et La chose Publique, 1979. Editor Le Quebec D'aujourd'hui, 1971. Office: 625 St Amable Quebec PQ G1R 2G5 Canada

MIHALAS, DIMITRI MANUEL, scientist; b. Los Angeles, Mar. 20, 1939; s. Emmanuel Demetrious and Jean (Christo) M.; B.A. with highest honors, U. Calif. at Los Angeles, 1959; M.S., Calif. Inst. Tech., 1960, Ph.D., 1964; m. Alice Joelen Covalt, June 15, 1963 (div. Nov. 1974); children—Michael Demetrious, Genevieve Alexandra; m. 2d, Barbara Ruth Rickey, May 18, 1975. Asst. prof. astrophys. scis. Princeton U., 1964-67; asst. prof. physics U. Colo., 1967-68; asso. prof. astronomy and astrophysics U. Chgo., 1968-70, prof., 1970-71; adj. prof. astrogeophysics, also physics and astrophysics U. Colo., 1972—; sr. scientist High Altitude Obs., Nat. Center Atmospheric Research, Boulder, Colo., 1971—; vis. prof. dept. astrophysics Oxford (Eng.) U., 1977-78; vis. prof. dept. physics and astronomy Univ. Coll., London, 1978; mem. astronomy adv. panel NSF, 1972-75. NSF fellow, 1959-62; Van Maanen fellow, 1962-63; Alfred P. Sloan Found. Research fellow, 1969-71. Mem. Internat. Astron. Union (pres. commn. 36 1976-79), Am. Astron. Soc. (Helen B. Warner prize 1974), Astron. Soc. Pacific (dir. 1975-77). Author: Galactic Astronomy, 1968; Stellar Atmospheres, 1970, 2d edit., 1978; Theorie des Atmospheres Stellaires, 1971; asso. editor Astrophys. Jour., 1970-79. Home: 3225 Dover Dr Boulder CO 80303

MIHALAS, NICHOLAS MICHAEL, watch and clock co. exec.; b. Norfolk, Va., June 23, 1937; s. Michael and Vivian (Pitsikoulis) M.; B.Sc., Va. Poly. Inst., 1959; M.B.A., Pepperdine U., 1975; m. Elaine Zelinsky, July 2, 1966; children—Michael Joseph, Christina. Engring. mgr. Gen. Electric Co., Phila., 1960-69; cons. Aerospace Corp., Los Angeles, 1970; pres. Timex Corp., Waterbury, Conn., 1971—, dir.; dir. TMX Ltd., Conn. Econ. Devel. Corp. Trustee St. Margaret's Sch. Served with USAF, 1959. Mem. Am. Mgmt. Assn., Conf. Bd., Western Conn. Indsl. Council, Waterbury C. of C. (dir.). Republican. Waterbury Country, Copper Valley. Office: Timex Corp Waterbury CT 06720

MIHALIK, EMIL JOHN, bishop; b. Pitts., Feb. 7, 1920; s. William and Mary (Jubic) M.; student Catholic Inst. Pitts., 1938-40, St. Procopius Sem., 1940-45. Ordained priest Roman Catholic Ch., 1945, bishop, 1969; pastor Sts. Peter and Paul Chs., Struthers, Ohio, 1945-55, Endicot, N.Y., 1955-61, St. Thomas Ch., Rahway, N.J., 1961-69; dir. vocations Diocese of Passaic, mem. Diocesan Tribunal, chancellor of Diocese, 1968; mem. Diocesan Bd. Consultors, 1968; bishop of Parma, Ohio, 1969—. Mem. Nat., Ohio confs. Cath. bishops. Home: 1900 Carlton Rd Parma OH 44134*

MIHALY, EUGENE BRAMER, cons., exec., writer; b. The Hague, Netherlands, Nov. 11, 1934 (mother Am. citizen); s. Eddy and Cecile (Bramer) Kahn; stepson Eugene Mihaly; A.B. magna cum laude, Harvard U., 1956; Ph.D., London Sch. Econs. and Polit. Sci., 1964; m. Linda Davis DuBrow, Oct. 7, 1978; children—Lisa Klee, Jessica. Aviation/space editor Hartford (Conn.) Courant, 1960-61; internat. economist AID, Washington, 1964-65; dep. dir. Peace Corps, Tanzania, 1966, dir., 1967-68, dir. Office Program Devel., Evaluation and Research, Washington, 1969-70; asso. dir. Inst. Internat. Studies, U. Calif., Berkeley, 1970-72; pres. Mihaly Assos., Inc., 1972—. Bd. dirs. Internat. Vol. Services Inc., San Francisco Young Profls. Orch.; trustee World Affairs Council No. Calif., Urban Sch. San Francisco. Served to lt. (j.g.) USNR, 1956-59. Mem. Am. Polit. Sci. Assn., Soc. Internat. Devel. (dir. San Francisco), Amnesty Internat., Signet Soc., Com. Fgn. Relations. Clubs: Harvard (N.Y.C.); Harvard, Commonwealth (San Francisco). Author: Foreign Aid and Politics in Nepal: A Case Study, 1965; contbr.: Political Development in Micronesia, 1974; Management of the Multinationals, 1974; also articles to various publs. Home: 1 Heuter Ln Mill Valley CA 94941

MIHANOVICH, CLEMENT SIMON, educator; b. St. Louis, Apr. 3, 1913; s. Philip and Kate (Mihanovich) M.; B.S. in Edn., St. Louis U., 1935, M.A., 1936, Ph.D., 1939; m. Erma E. Schleicher, June 6, 1942; children—Ann Marie, Michael Gerard, Mark Jerome, David Francis. Instr., St. Louis U., 1938-42, sec. dept. sociology, 1940-46, asst. prof., 1942-45, asso. prof., 1945-47, dir. dept., 1946-64, prof., 1947—. Mem. Am. Cath., Am. sociol. socs., AAUP, Phi Beta Kappa, Alpha Sigma Nu, Alpha Kappa Delta, Pi Gamma Mu. Author: Current Social Problems, 1950; Principles of Delinquency, 1950; Marriage and the Family, 1952; Social Theorists, 1953; Papal Pronouncements on Marraige and Family, 1956; Glossary of Sociligical Terms, 1957. Contbr. articles to profl. jours. Home: 6214 Devonshire St Louis MO 63109

MIKALSON, ROY GALE, coll. pres.; b. Eureka, Mont., July 21, 1921; s. Lawrence Merton and Barbara Margaret (Patterson) M.; student Mont. State Coll.; B.A., U. Wash., 1947, M.A., 1948; Ph.D., U. Calif., Berkeley, 1964; m. Eva Marie Johnson, July 31, 1949; children—Steven A., Barbara G., Jeffrey R., Thomas L. Instr., Mont. State U., 1948-49; instr., chmn. English dept. Lower Columbia Coll., Longview, Wash., 1950-62; dean Coll. Marin, Kentfield, Calif., 1964-66; pres. Clackamas Community Coll., Oregon City, Oreg., 1966-68, Modesto Jr. Coll., Modesto, Calif., 1968-71; supt., pres. Santa Rosa (Calif.) Jr. Coll., 1971—. Bd. dirs. Drs. Hosp., Modesto, United Way, YMCA, Family Info. Center. Served with AUS, 1940-45. Decorated Silver Star, Purple Heart with 2 oak leaf clusters. Mem. C. of C., Phi Beta Kappa. Elk, Rotarian. Home: 4050 Alta Vista Santa Rosa CA 95404

MIKESELL, RAYMOND FRECH, economist; b. Eaton, Ohio, Feb. 13, 1913; s. Otho Francis and Josephine (Frech) M.; student Carnegie Inst. Tech., 1931-33; B.A. cum laude, Ohio U., 1935, M.A., 1935, Ph.D., 1939; m. Desyl DeLauder, July 6, 1937 (div.); children—George DeLauder and Norman DeLauder (twins); m. 2d, Irene Langdoc, Feb. 18, 1956. Asst. prof. econ. U. Wash., 1937-41; economist OPA, Washington, 1941-42, U.S. Treasury Dept., 1942-46, rep. in Cairo, Egypt, 1943-44, cons. 1946-47; cons. U.S. State Dept., 1947-53, on Middle East affairs FOA, 1953; chief fgn. minerals div. Pres.'s Materials Policy Commn., 1951-52; mem. staff Fgn. Econ. Policy Com. (Randall Com.), 1953-54; mem. U.S. Currency Mission to Saudi Arabia, 1948; spl. U.S. rep., Israel, summer 1952; mem. U.S. mission to Israel, Ethiopia, summer 1953; prof. econs. U. Va., 1946-57; W.E. Miner prof. econs. U. Oreg., 1957—, dir. Inst. Internat. Studies and Overseas Adminstrn., 1958-60, asso. dir., 1960-68; vis. prof. Grad. Inst. Internat. Studies, Geneva, 1964; sr. staff mem. Council Econ. Advisers, Exec. Office of Pres., 1955-56, cons. council, 1956-57; cons. Pan Am. Union, 1954-63, Dept. State, 1947-53, 63-67, 71—, Ford Found., 1962, Dept. Commerce, 1962-64, ICA, 1952-53, 61-62, OAS, 1963-73, AID, 1964-71; mem. UN Econ. Commn. for Latin Am. working group on regional market, 1958; cons. Senate Fgn. Relations Com., 1962, 67, World Bank, 1968, Inter-Am. Devel. Bank, 1968—; mem. panel advisers Sec. Treasury, 1965-69; sr. fellow Nat. Bur. Econ. Research, 1972-73. Mem. Econ. Assn., Pi Kappa Alpha, Alpha Kappa Psi. Unitarian. Author: U.S. Economic Policy and International Relations, 1952, Foreign Exchange in the Postwar World, 1954; The Emerging Pattern of International Payments, 1954; Foreign Investments in Latin Am., 1955; Promoting United States Private Investment Abroad, 1957; Agricultural Surpluses and Export Policy, 1958; (with H. Chenery) Arabian Oil, 1949; (with M. Trued) Postwar Bilateral Payments Agreements, 1955; (with J. Behrman) Financing Free World Trade with the Sino-Soviet Bloc, 1958; Public International Lending for Development, 1966; (with R.W. Adler) Public External Financing of Devel. Banks, 1966; Public Fgn. Capital for Private Enterprises in Developing Countries, 1966; The Economics of Foreign Aid, 1968; Financing World Trade, 1969; (with others) Foreign Investment in the Petroleum and Mineral Industries, 1971. Editor: U.S. Private and Government Investment Abroad, 1962; (with H. Furth) Foreign Dollar Balances and the International Role of the Dollar, 1974; Foreign Investment in the Copper Industry, 1975; The World Copper Industry, 1979; New Patterns of World Mineral Development, 1979; mem. editorial adv. bd. Middle East Jour., 1947-58; mem. bd. editors Am. Econ. Rev., 1953-55. Home: 2290 Spring Blvd Eugene OR 97403

MIKIC, BORIVOJE, mech. engr.; b. Loznica, Yugoslavia, Mar. 1, 1932; s. Budimir and Darinka (Zlatic) M.; came to U.S., 1964, naturalized, 1973; Dipl.Ing., U. Belgrade, 1957; Sc.D., M.I.T., 1966; m. Ljubica Milinovic, Apr. 7, 1957; children—Yelena, Borjana. Research scientist Aero-Tech. Inst., Belgrade, 1957-60; instr. U. Belgrade, 1960-61; lectr. Khartoun Tech. Inst., 1961-64; research asst. M.I.T., 1964-66, asst. prof., 1966-69, asso. prof., 1969-74, prof. mech. engring., 1974—. Sr. fellow U. Oxford, 1975-76. Mem. ASME, Geothermal Resources Council, Sigma Xi, Pi Tau Sigma. Research on heat transfer, energy, fluid mechanics, thermodynamics, biomedical scis. Home: 4 Ames St Cambridge MA 02139 Office: Mass Inst Tech Dept Mech Engring Cambridge MA 02139

MIKITA, JOSEPH KARL, broadcasting co. exec.; b. nr. Richmond, Va., Oct. 3, 1918; s. John and Catherine (Wargofcak) M.; B.S., Fordham U., 1939; M.S., Columbia U., 1940; m. Mary Therese Benya, Nov. 26, 1942; children—Patty-Jane Mikita Cashman, Michael, M. Noël Mikita Garagiola. Treas., controller Capital Cities Broadcasting Co., Albany, N.Y., 1955-58; controller Westinghouse Broadcasting Co., Inc., N.Y.C., 1958-60, v.p. fin., 1960-64, v.p. fin. and adminstrn., 1964-65, sr. v.p., 1965-69, sr. v.p., 1975—, also dir., exec. v.p. Westinghouse Electric Corp. for Broadcasting, Learning and Leisure Activities, N.Y.C., 1969-75; sr. v.p. Westinghouse Broadcasting Co., Inc., 1976—; dir. Sutro Tower, Inc. Bd. dirs. Fordham U. Council, Albany County Workshop, Albany County Heart Assn., Archdiocese of N.Y.; chmn. bd. Instructional TV. Served to maj. AUS, 1940-45; ETO. Recipient Order of Merit-Silver, Westinghouse Electric Corp., 1965; Distinguished Service Alumni award Fordham U., 1969. Mem. Internat. Radio and TV Soc., Am. Inst. C.P.A.'s, N.Y. Soc. C.P.A.'s, Fin. Execs. Inst. (dir., past pres. Manhattan chpt.), Inst. Broadcasting Fin. Mgmt. Clubs: Rotary (dir. N.Y.C.); Town (Scarsdale, N.Y.); Westchester Country (Harrison, N.Y.); Boca Raton (Fla.) Country; M.G.A. (N.Y.C.). Author: (with others) The Business of Broadcasting, 1964. Home: 3125 NE 7th Dr Boca Raton FL 33431 Office: 90 Park Ave New York NY 10016

MIKITA, STANLEY, profl. hockey player; b. Sokolee, Czechoslovakia, May 20, 1940; s. Juraj and Emilia (Mikita) Gvoth; grad. St. Catherines Collegiate Sch. (Can.), 1958; m. Jill Kathleen Cerny, Apr. 27, 1963; children—Margaret Anne, Scott Michael, Jane Elizabeth, Christopher Stanley. Player, Chgo. Blackhawks Hockey Team, 1958—. Recipient Hart trophy, 1967, 68, Lady Byng trophy, 1967, 68, Art Ross trophy, 1964, 65, 67, 68. Author: I Play to Win, 1969; Inside Hockey, 1971. Office: 1840 W Madison St Chicago IL 60612*

MIKKELSEN, HENNING DAHL, cartoonist; b. Skive, Denmark, Jan. 9, 1915; s. Jens Peder and Thora (Dahl) M.; came to U.S., 1948, naturalized, 1954; m. Jessie Anna Andersen, Oct. 2, 1949; children—Betty Ann, Mary Louise, Sally Jean, Eric Dahl. Creator animated cartoons for films, 1933-35; chief animator Anglia Films, London, 1935-36; creator comic strip Ferd'nand, 1937—, also comic strip based on old Nordic myths in Danish weeklies, 1940-45.

MIKLOS, JACK C., fgn. service officer; b. Moscow, Idaho, July 16, 1926; s. Jack D. and Mildred (Gossett) M.; student advanced econs. Stanford, 1959-60; m. Rhoda Virginia Knudten, Feb. 15, 1947; children—Stephen D., Shari J., Melpomene I. Joined U.S. Fgn. Service, 1946; assigned Yokohama, Japan, 1946-49, Tangier, Morocco, 1949-55, Istanbul, Turkey, 1955-57; 2d sec. embassy, Tehran, Iran, 1957-59; internat. economist Nr. East and S. Asian affairs State Dept., 1960-63; consul, Bombay, India, 1963; dep. chief mission to Ceylon, 1967-69; country dir. State Dept., 1969-74; minister-counselor Am. embassy, Tehran, Iran, 1974-78; dep. asst. sec. State, 1978—. Served with AUS, 1944-46; PTO. Decorated Bronze Star, Purple Heart. Mem. Am. Fgn. Service Assn. Address: 5407 Uppingham St Chevy Chase MD 20015

MIKLOWITZ, JULIUS, educator, scientist; b. Schenectady, May 22, 1919; s. Henry and Rebecca (Wolf) M.; B.S. in Mech. Engring., U. Mich., 1943; M.S. in Engring. Mechanics, 1948, Ph.D., 1949; m. Gloria Elaine Dubov, Aug. 28, 1948; children—Paul Stephen, David Jay. Research engr. plasticity Westinghouse Research Labs., 1943-46, 49; asso. prof. engring., head dept. N.Mex. Inst. Mining and Tech., 1949-51; research engr., cons. solid mechanics Naval Ordnance Test Sta., 1951-56; faculty Calif. Inst. Tech., Pasadena, 1956—, prof. applied mechanics, 1962—. Cons. to industry, govt., 1956—; W.W. Clyde prof. engring. U. Utah, 1970. Mem. U.S. Nat. Com. on Theoretical and Applied Mechanics, 1976—. Westinghouse Research Labs. grad. fellow, 1946-49; NSF sr. postdoctoral fellow, 1964-65. Fellow ASME (exec. com. applied mechanics div. 1971-76, chmn. div. 1975-76); mem. AAAS, AAUP. Author: Theory of Elastic Waves and Waveguides, 1978. Research and publs. on wave propagation in solids, yielding, fracture metals, polymers. Home: 5255 Vista Miguel Dr La Canada CA 91011 Office: Calif Inst Tech Pasadena CA 91125

MIKLOZEK, FRANK LOUIS, assn. exec.; b. Terre Haute, Ind., Aug. 22, 1914; s. Stanley and Nellie Sophia (Meyer) M.; A.B., Ind. State U., 1936; J.D., Ind. U., 1939; m. Louise Stoffers, Nov. 29, 1945; children—Frank Louis, Candace L., Meredith A. Admitted to Ind. bar, 1939; practiced in Terre Haute, 1939-41; engaged in corp. law, 1945-50; asst. city atty., Terre Haute, 1948-50; postmaster, Terre Haute, 1950-73, mgr. sectional center and postmaster, 1972-74; pres. Nat. Assn. Postmasters, Washington, 1972-73, exec. dir., 1974-77; dir. Postmasters of Am., Nat. Assn. Postmasters Credit Union. Pres. Vigo County Young Democrats, 1949-50. Bd. dirs. Terre Haute Jr. C. of C., Polio Found. Served with AUS, 1941-45. Named Outstanding Distinguished Alumnus, Ind. State U., 1974; Citizen of Day, Terre Haute, 1972; recipient numerous certificates of merit and appreciation. Mem. Ind., Terre Haute, Vigo County bar assns., Nat. Assn. Postmasters (past pres. Ind. chpt.; Order of Vest award 1970), Am., Washington soc. assns. execs., Terre Haute C. of C., Am. Legion, VFW, Pi Gamma Mu, Gamma Eta Gamma, Theta Chi, Blue Key. Elk, Rotarian. Author articles, inventor games. Home: 7414 Hallcrest Dr McLean VA 22101 Office: 1616 N Ft Myer Dr Arlington VA 22209

MIKOLJI, BORIS HRVOJE, educator; b. Visoko, Yugoslavia, Jan. 24, 1926; s. Vincent and Helena (Vrbica) M.; came to U.S., 1951, naturalized, 1956; student Karl Franzens U., Graz, Austria, 1947-51; M.A., Western Res. U., 1955, Ph.D., 1961; m. Adele Christine Tacher, Nov. 28, 1952; children—Helen, Dorothy, Vera-Marie. Research and adminstr. staff mem. McDowell-Wellman, Inc., Cleve., 1955-63; asst. prof. sociology Concord Coll., 1963-64, Nazareth Coll., 1964-67; asso. prof. urbanization and sociology Rochester Inst. Tech., 1967, chmn. social sci. 1970-72, chmn. sociology, 1976—, prof. sociology, 1977—; vis. lectr. several European univs.; cons. govtl. and social agys. Trustee Diocesan Charities. Recipient Eisenhart award for outstanding teaching, 1977; NSF research fellow, 1973-74. Mem. Am. Sociol. Assn., N.Y. Sociol. Assn. (pres. 1976-77), Pi Gamma Mu, Delta Tau Kappa. Author: Ethnicity and Politics in Urban Community, 1971; contbr. articles to profl. publs. Home: 20 Sunset Trail Fairport NY 14450 Office: 06-1311 Rochester Inst Tech 1 Lomb Meml Dr Rochester NY 14623

MIKULAK, DANIEL, JR., hotel cons.; b. N.Y.C., Aug. 8, 1937; s. Daniel and Mary (Nemec) M.; A.A., Prince George Coll., 1959; B.S., U. Denver, 1961; m. Anna Marie Dixon, July 19, 1958; children—Ruth Ann, Daniel III. Exec. asst. mgr. Rainbow Hotel, Great Falls, Mont., 1962-63; cons. Western Internat. Hotels Co., 1963-64; area controller St. Francis Hotel, San Francisco, 1965-66; exec. asst. mgr. Continental Plaza Hotel, Chgo., 1967; gen. mgr. Fairmont-Roosevelt Hotel, New Orleans, 1967-75; prin. Dan Mikulak & Assos., 1975—; pres. N.O. Assos., Inc., 1975—; v.p. Grand Hotel Corp., New Orleans, 1977—; pres. Sports Devel. Corp., Columbia, S.C., 1977-78. Past pres., dir., mem. exec. com. Greater New Orleans Tourist and Conv. Commn. Mem. career advisement com. Tulane U., Mardi Gras com. City New Orleans; past v.p. Boys Club Greater New Orleans; chmn. emeritus Mayor's Super Bowl Task Force; mem. New Orleans Coastal Zone Mgmt. Com., Upper Pontalbo Commn. Past bd. mgrs. Delgado Coll. Mem. Greater New Orleans (past pres.), La. (past v.p.), Am. (nat. adv. council career devel. div., vice chmn. com. hotel-motel mgmt. cos., airlines inter-industry com.) hotel and motel assns., Internat. Soc. Hotel Motel Mgmt. Cos. (v.p.), Vols. Am., Urban League Greater New Orleans, Internat. Wine and Food Soc. New Orleans, Confrerie de la Chaine des Rotisseurs, Greater New Orleans C. of C. (past dir., com. of 50, com. mgmt., mems. council, dir.). Club: Tulane Green Wave, Manions Cove, Fountain Bay. Address: Dan Mikulak & Assos 4040 Tulane Ave New Orleans LA 70119

MIKULKA, CHARLES, photog. co. exec.; b. N.Y.C., Mar. 1, 1914; s. Justin and Anna (Bielaus) M.; B.S. in Mech. Engring., Cooper Union, 1936; LL.B., St. John's U., 1939; m. Elinor Palmer Allen, Jan 27, 1940; children—Mary Anne, Joan M., Donald J., Christine J., James R., Michael C., Steven M. Admitted to N.Y. bar, 1940; with firm F. Bascom Smith, N.Y.C., 1936-42; with Polaroid Corp., Cambridge, Mass., 1942—, patent counsel, 1957-60, v.p. patents, 1960—, v.p., 1970-75, sr. v.p., 1975—; dir. Omark Industries, Portland, Ore. Mem. Am. Patent Law Assn. Home: 105 Garfield St Watertown MA 02172 Office: 549 Technology Sq Plaza Cambridge MA 02139

MIKULSKI, BARBARA ANN, congresswoman; b. Balt., July 20, 1936; d. William and Christina Eleanor (Kutz) Mikulski; B.A., Mt. St. Agnes Coll., 1958; postgrad. Loyola Coll. at Balt., 1961; M.S.W., U. Md., 1965; LL.D., Goucher Coll., 1973. Caseworker, Asso. Cath. Charities, 1958-61; asst. chief community relations Balt. Dept. Social Services, 1961-63, 66-70; tchr. Vista Tng. Center, 1965-70, Mt. St. Agnes Coll., 1969, Community Coll. Balt., 1970-71, St. Mary's Sem., 1971; city councilwoman 1st dist. Balt., 1971-76; mem. 95th-96th Congresses from 3d Md. Dist., cons. Nat. Center Urban Ethnic Affairs, HUD, U.S. Senate Com. on Aging, and numerous other orgns. Chmn. commn. community devel. Archdiocese Urban Commn.; mem. nat. com. Muskie for Pres., 1971-72; chmn. commn. on del. selection and party structure Democratic Nat. Com.; nat. bd. dirs. Urban Coalition; bd. dirs. Valley House. Mem. Polish Women's Alliance, Polish Am. Congress, Citizen Planning and Housing Assn., S.E. Community Orgn., Am. Fed. Tchrs., Nat. Assn. Social Workers, League of Women Voters. Contbr. articles to N.Y. Times, U.S. Steelworker Jour., Redbook, other mags. Office: 1414 Federal Office Bldg Baltimore MD 21201

MIKULSKY, JOAN MARILYN, educator; b. Dobbs Ferry, N.Y., Feb. 27, 1932; d. Fred and Helen (Henshaw) de Serres; B.A., Hunter Coll., 1953, M.A., 1963; m. Walter Mikulsky, Aug. 5, 1956 (div. Aug. 1967). Chmn. art dept. Hendrick Hudson High Sch., Montrose, N.Y., 1953-61; instr. art Hunter Coll., City U. N.Y., 1961-65, asst. prof., 1965-66, asst. prof., asst. dean for campus planning Grad. Div City U. N.Y., 1966-67, asso. prof., asst. dean, 1968-70, prof., dean adminstrn. Grad. Sch. and Univ. Center, 1973-76, dir. campus planning and facilities, prof. art Baruch Coll., City U. N.Y., 1977—, design cons. Grad. Center, Computer Facility, 1967-74. Recipient various awards and certificates. Mem. Am. Soc. Interior Designers. Home: 345 E 69th St New York City NY 10022

MIKUS, ELEANOR ANN, artist; b. Detroit, July 25, 1927; d. Joseph and Bertha (Inglot) M.; student Mich. State U., 1946-49, U. Mex., summer 1948; B.F.A., U. Denver, 1957, M.A., 1967; postgrad. Art Students League, 1958, N.Y. U., 1959-60; m. Richard Burns, July 6, 1949 (div. 1963); children—Richard, Hillary, Gabrielle. Exhibited in twelve one person shows at Pace Gallery, N.Y.C. and O.K. Harris Gallery, N.Y.C.; represented in permanent collections including: Mus. Modern Art, N.Y.C., Whitney Mus., N.Y.C., Los Angeles County Mus., Cin. Mus., Birmingham (Ala.) Mus. Art, Indpls. Mus. Art, Victoria and Albert Mus., London, Library of Congress, Washington; asst. prof. art Monmouth Coll., West Long Branch, N.J., 1966-70; vis. lectr. painting Cooper Union, N.Y.C., 1970-72, Central Sch. Art and Design, London, 1973-77, Harrow (Eng.) Coll. Tech. and Art, 1975-76; now asst. prof. art Cornell U., Ithaca, N.Y. Guggenheim fellow, 1966-67; Tamarind fellow, summer 1968; MacDowell fellow, summer 1969. Mem. AAUP. Office: Dept Art Franklin Hall Cornell U Ithaca NY 14853

MIKUTA, RUDOLF, architect, publisher; b. Nydek, Czechoslovakia, Mar. 24, 1907; s. Thomas and Marie (Toulcova) M.; came to U.S., 1950, naturalized, 1955; student U. Dijon (France), 1924; M. Structural Engring. and Architecture, Charles Tech. U., Prague, Czechoslovakia, 1934; postgrad. Graphic Arts Sch., Leipzig, Ger., 1936, Acad. Arts, Rome, 1937; m. Marie Hruskova, Dec. 18, 1959; stepsons—Michael Rohacek, Jerry Rohacek. Univ. tchr. archtl. design and graphics, Prague, 1930-36; gen. dir. Czechoslovak Christian Party's Printing and Pub. Complex, Prague, 1937-41; owner Ing. R. Mikuta, printing and pub., Prague, 1942-48; interned in refugee camps, Germany and Italy, 1948-50; chief designer Lorimer Rich & Robbins, Conn., N.Y.C., 1950-55; chief designer Morris Lapidus and F. L. Vann, Miami, Fla., 1956-63; project designer Adrian Wilson, Los Angeles, 1963-64; chief designer Albert C. Martin, Los Angeles, 1964-67; prin. architect, chief designer Ralph M. Parsons Co., Pasadena, Calif., 1967-77, Rudolf Mikuta, AIA, Cons. and Devel., Alhambra, Calif., 1977—; founder Free World Pub. Co., N.Y.C., 1953, Architects and Arts Book Club, 1959, Royal Bohemian Club, 1977. Mem. AIA, Czechoslovak Soc. Arts and Scis. Numerous archtl. works include: U. Syracuse bldgs., dormitories, 1952-53, S.W. Chgo. Supplementary Fuel Processing Plant, 1976 (Most Outstanding Engring. Achievement in 1976 award), Fla. Hotel, Miami Beach, 1956, U.S. Navy and Air Force hosps., Camranh Bay, Vietnam, 1966, airport terminals, Hawaii, Tunisia, Panama, 1968-73, indsl. complexes, Saudi Arabia, Bahrain, Iran, Algeria, 1974-77, housing project, Egypt, 1978. Office: 1120 W Alhambra Rd Alhambra CA 91801

MIKVA, ABNER JOSEPH, U.S. judge; b. Milw., Jan. 21, 1926; s. Henry Abraham and Ida (Fishman) M.; J.D. cum laude, U. Chgo., 1951; m. Zoe Wise, Sept. 19, 1948; children—Mary, Laurie, Rachel. Admitted to Ill. bar, 1951; law clk. to U.S. Supreme Ct. Justice Sherman Minton, 1951; partner firm Devoe, Shadur, Mikva & Plotkin, Chgo., 1952-68, D'Ancona, Pflaum, Wyatt & Riskind, 1973-74; lectr. Northwestern U. Law Sch., Chgo., 1973-75; mem. Ill. Gen. Assembly from 23d Dist., 1956-66; mem. 91st-92d congresses from 2d Dist. Ill., 94th-96th congress from 10th Ill. Dist., mem. Ways and Means com., Judiciary com., chmn. Dem. Study Group; resigned from Congress, 1979; judge U.S. Circuit Ct. of Appeals for D.C., 1979—; chmn. Ill. Bd. Ethics, 1973. Served with USAAF, World War II. Recipient Page One award Chgo. Newspaper Guild, 1964; Best Legislator award Ind. Voters Ill., 1956-66; named One of Ten Outstanding Young Men in Chgo., Jr. Assn. Commerce and Industry, 1961. Mem. Am. (com. on individual rights and responsibilities 1973-77), Chgo. (bd. mgrs. 1962-64) bar assns., Phi Beta Kappa, Order of Coif. Democrat. Office: US Ct Appeals 3d and Constitution Ave NW Washington DC 20001

MILANDER, HENRY MARTIN, community coll. pres.; b. Northampton, Pa., Apr. 17, 1939; s. Martin Edward and Margaret Catherine (Makovetz) M.; B.S. summa cum laude, Lock Haven (Pa.) State Coll., 1961; M.A., Bowling Green (Ohio) State U., 1962; Ed.S. (Future Faculty fellow 1964), U. No. Iowa, 1965; Ed.D., Ill. State U., Normal, 1967; m. Joan Mary Ziegler, June 3, 1961; children—Martin Henry, Beth Ann. Instr., Wartburg Coll., Waverly, Iowa, 1962-64; asst. prof. Ill. State U., 1966-67; dean instrn. Belleville (Ill.) Area Coll., 1967-69; v.p. acad. affairs Lorain County Community Coll., Elyria, Ohio, 1969-72; pres. Olympic Coll., Bremerton, Wash., 1972—. Pres. Kitsap County Comprehensive Health Planning Council, 1975-76. Recipient Faculty Growth award, Wartburg Coll., 1963, Community Service award, 1975. Mem. Am. Assn. Higher Edn., Am. Assn. Community and Jr. Colls., Am. Assn. Univ. Adminstrs., Am. Assn. Sch. Adminstrs., Am. Tech. Edn. Assn., N.W. Assn. Community and Jr. Coll., Wash. Assn. Community Colls., Bremerton Area C. of C. (pres. 1977-78), Kappa Delta Pi, Phi Delta Kappa. Lutheran. Club:

Bremerton Central Lions. Contbr. articles to profl. jours. Home: 5145 NW El Camino Blvd Bremerton WA 98310 Office: Olympic Coll 16th and Chester Sts Bremerton WA 98310

MILBANK, JEREMIAH, found. exec.; b. N.Y.C., Mar. 24, 1920; s. Jeremiah and Katharine (Schulze) M.; B.A., Yale U., 1942; M.B.A., Harvard U., 1948; L.H.D., Ithaca (N.Y.) Coll., 1976; m. Andrea Hunter, July 19, 1947; children—Jeremiah, III, Victoria Milbank Doelger, Elizabeth, Joseph H. With J.M. Found., N.Y.C., pres., 1971—; pres. Cypress Woods Corp., 1972—; dir. Internat. Minerals and Chems. Corp. Vice pres. Boys Clubs Am.; pres. ICD Rehab. and Research Center; trustee, treas. Robert A. Taft Inst. Govt.; fin. chmn. Republican Nat. Com., 1969-72, 75-77. Served to lt. USNR, 1943-46. Republican. Episcopalian. Clubs: Racquet Tennis, Madison Sq. Garden, River, University (N.Y.C.); Round Hill (Greenwich). Author: First Century of Flight in America, 1942. Home: 620 Round Hill Rd Greenwich CT 06830 Office: 60 E 42d St New York NY 10017

MILBANK, SAMUEL ROBBINS, investment banker; b. N.Y.C., Mar. 16, 1906; s. Albert G. and Marjorie (Robbins) M.; A.B., Princeton U., 1927; m. Molly Wetmore, Jan. 9, 1934 (div.); children—Marjorie, Elenita, Samuel Livingston; m. 2d, Marilyn O. Baker, Sept. 9, 1969. With Brown Bros. & Co., investment bankers, N.Y.C., 1929-31; with Wood, Struthers & Winthrop, Inc., investment bankers and brokers, 1931—, gen. partner, 1936-69, chmn. bd., 1969-71, cons., 1972—; pres., dir. Pine St. Fund, 1949-72, dir., 1972—; chmn. bd. Rosario Resources Corp., 1964-77, chmn. exec. com., 1977—, also dir. Chmn. N.Y. State Citizens Com. 100 for Children and Youth, 1950-51; bd. mgrs. N.Y. State Charities Aid Assn., 1936-71, pres., 1949-59, chmn., 1959-61; chmn. bd. trustees Barnard Coll., 1956-67, now trustee; chmn. Milbank Meml. Fund; pres. Memton Fund; trustee Kirkland Coll., Internat. Center Photography; v.p. Flower Fifth Ave. Hosp., 1933-36; trustee Coll. Retirement Equities Fund (TIAA), 1952-72, Community Service Soc. N.Y., 1939-71. Served with USNR, 1941-45. Fellow Royal Numis. Soc., Am. Numis. Soc. (pres.); mem. Mass. Soc. Mayflower Descs., Phi Beta Kappa. Clubs: Union, Century Assn., Broad St., Pilgrims, Princeton (N.Y.C.); Hidden Valley Country (Reno); Met. (Washington). Author numis. monograph. Home: 68 Lovers Ln Princeton NJ 08540 Office: 1 E 75th St New York NY 10021

MILBOURNE, WALTER ROBERTSON, lawyer; b. Phila., Aug. 27, 1933; s. Charles Gordon and Florie Henderson (Robertson) M.; A.B., Princeton U., 1955; LL.B., Harvard U., 1958; m. Georgena Sue Dyer, June 19, 1965; children—Gregory Broughton, Karen Elizabeth, Walter Robertson. Admitted to Pa. bar, 1959; asso. firm Pepper, Hamilton & Sheetz, Phila., 1959-65; asso. firm Obermayer, Rebmann, Maxwell & Hippel, Phila., 1965-67, partner, 1968—; dir. Pa. Lumbermen's Mut. Ins. Co., 1972—, Phila. Reins. Corp., 1976—. Chmn. mental health budget sect. Phila. United Fund, 1967-70. Served with Army N.G., 1958-69. Fellow Am. Coll. Trial Lawyers; mem. Am. Bar Assn., Pa. Bar Assn., Phila. Bar Assn., Internat. Assn. Ins. Counsel, Assn. Def. Counsel. Republican. Clubs: Union League (Phila.); Merion Cricket, Princeton, Idle Hour Tennis (pres. 1968-69), Phila. Lawn Tennis Assn. (pres. 1969-70). Home: 689 Fernfield Circle Strafford PA 19087 Office: 14th Floor Packard Bldg 15th and Chestnut Sts Philadelphia PA 19102. *In litigation, and I suspect most business endeavors, the essential factor is to establish credibility with the person with whom one is dealing, whether that be the judge, the jury, your partners, or your clients. This requires not only integrity, but also hard work and attention to detail, and a willingness to face head-on the "tough spots."*

MILBRATH, ROBERT HENRY, petroleum mktg. exec.; b. Apr. 17, 1912; s. Paul and Mabel (Volkman) M.; B.S., U.S. Naval Acad., 1934; m. Margaret Ripperger, Jan. 19, 1940; children—Robert S., Constance, Susan Lopez Pelliza. With Standard Oil Co., 1934—, v.p., gen. mgr. Esso Sociedad Anonima Petrolera Argentina, 1938-42, 45-50, area contact East Coast South Am., mktg. coordination, 1950-52, dir. Internat. Petroleum Co., 1954—, v.p., 1956; v.p., dir. Esso Export Corp. N.Y., 1957-59, exec. v.p., dir., 1959-61; chmn. bd. Esso Export Ltd., London, 1958; pres., dir. chmn. exec. com. Esso Internat., Inc. (formerly Esso Export Corp.), 1961-66; exec. v.p. Esso Europe, 1966-68; logistics coordinator Standard Oil Co. (N.J.) (now Exxon Corp.), 1968-69, dir., v.p., 1969-70, dir., sr. v.p., 1970-73; cons. Boys Clubs Am., 1978—. Served to lt. comdr. USNR; asst. naval attache, Buenos Aires, 1942; chief Latin Am. sect. Army-Navy Petroleum Bd., Washington, 1943-45. Mem. U.S. Naval Acad. Alumni Assn., Navy League. Republican. Clubs: University (N.Y.C.); Pine Orchard (Conn.). Home: 117 Wingate Rd Guilford CT 06437 also Johnson VT 05656 Office: 1 Rockefeller Plaza New York NY 10020

MILBURN, RICHARD HENRY, educator; b. Newark, June 3, 1928; s. Richard Percy and Lucy Elizabeth (Karr) M.; A.B., Harvard, 1948, A.M., 1951, Ph.D., 1954; m. Nancy Jeannette Stafford, Aug. 25, 1951; children—Sarah Stafford, Anne Douglas. Instr. Harvard, 1954, 56-57, asst. prof., 1957-61; asso. prof. physics Tufts U., 1961-65, prof., 1965—. Served with AUS, 1954-56. Sheldon travelling fellow, 1948-49; NSF fellow, 1952-53; Guggenheim fellow, 1960. Fellow Am. Phys. Soc. (past chmn. New Eng. sect.); mem. Am. Assn. Physics Tchrs., AAAS, AAUP. Research on high energy and elementary particles physics. Home: 1 Plymouth Rd Winchester MA 01890 Office: Tufts Univ Medford MA 02155

MILCH, HAROLD CARLTON, art gallery dir.; b. N.Y.C., Jan. 2, 1908; s. Albert and Lillian (Smalls) M.; student Coll. City N.Y., 1924-26, Dwight Sch., 1926-27, N.Y. Stock Exchange Inst., 1935; m. Harriet Greenwald, Dec. 24, 1938; children—Peter and Roger (twins). With A. Aleon's Sons, oriental rug importers, N.Y.C., 1927-29; pres., dir. Milch & Vogel, Inc., 1929-34; with Ungerleider & Co., 1935-37, Newman Bros. and Worms Broad St., 1937-41; dir., pres. E. & A. Milch, Inc. (The Milch Galleries), specializing in Am. art, N.Y.C., 1941—; co-executor estates of artists Willard L. Metcalf, Thomas Moran and Childe Hassam. Mem. Am. Art Dealers Assn. (pres. 1968-70 dir. 1971—). Home: 140 E 72d St New York City NY 10021 Office: 1014 Madison Ave New York City NY 10021

MILES, A. STEVENS, banker; b. Louisville, Nov. 30, 1929; s. Algene Stevens and Edna May (Rietze) M.; B.A., Washington and Lee U., 1951; postgrad. Stonier Grad. Sch. Banking, Rutgers U., 1962-64; m. Ann Berry Houston, Nov. 6, 1954; 1 dau., Elizabeth. With First Nat. Bank of Louisville, 1954—, pres., dir., 1972—, chief exec. officer, 1975—; pres., dir. First Ky. Trust Co., 1973—, chief exec. officer, 1975—; pres., dir. First Ky. Nat. Corp., 1974—, chief exec. officer, 1975—. Bd. dirs. Norton-Children's Hosps., 1974-78; bd. overseers U. Louisville, 1972—; trustee James Graham Brown Found., 1975-78; pres. Louisville Central Area, Inc., 1976-79, Old Ky. Home council Boy Scouts Am., 1975-77, Greater Louisville Fund for Arts, 1978-79. Served to 2d lt. U.S. Army, 1951-53. Episcopalian. Clubs: Louisville Country, Pendennis, River Valley. Home: 394 Mockingbird Valley Rd Louisville KY 40207 Office: 101 S 5th St Louisville KY 40202

MILES, ERNEST PERCY, JR., educator; b. Birmingham, Ala., Mar. 16, 1919; s. Ernest Percy and Ida (Duke) M.; B.S., Birmingham So. Coll., 1937; M.A., Duke, 1939, Ph.D., 1949; m. Audrey Adair Vicknair, June 13, 1945; children—Duke, Vick Adair. Tchr. math. Ramsay High Sch., Birmingham, 1938-39; instr. math. N.C. State Coll., Raleigh, 1940-41; asso. prof. math. Ala. Poly. Inst. (now Auburn U.), Auburn, 1949-58; vis. research asso. prof. Inst. Fluid Dynamics and Applied Math., U. Md., 1957-58; asso. prof. math. Fla. State U., Tallahassee, 1958-61, cons. Computing Center, 1960-61, dir. Computing Center, 1961-71, prof. math., 1961—. Mem. applied math. lab. David Taylor Model Basin, summer 1957; profl. staff mem. NSF, summer 1958; vis. prof. U. N.Mex., 1959; cons. NSF, 1959-63, 65-72, U.S. Office Edn., 1966-71; task force chmn. Fla. Space Era Edn. Study, 1962-63; mem. com. computers and computer sci. So. Regional Edn. Bd., 1962-67, com. computing centers, 1968-71; vis. scientist Fla. Acad. Sci., 1963, 65-76; mem. council EDUCOM-Inter-Univ. Communications Council, 1965-74; local services coordinator nat. curricular revision project Center for Research in Coll. Instrn. Sci. and Math., 1967-70; dir. NSF/Fla. State U. Computer Augmented Modules for Sci. and Math., 1976—. Served to lt. comdr. USNR, 1941-46. Recipient 1st Place Nat. Sigma Xi competition for sci. edn. crisis plan, 1956. Fellow AAAS; mem. Am. Math. Soc., Math. Assn. Am., Soc. Indsl. and Applied Math., Nat. Council Tchrs. Math., World Future Soc., Assn. Computing Machinery (chmn. N.W. Fla. chpt. 1966-68, chmn. spl. interest group univ. computing centers 1968-71, rep. to Conf. Bd. Math. Socs. 1974—, nat. lectr. 1978—), AAUP (pres. Auburn chpt. 1953-54, pres. Ala. 1954-55), Sigma Xi, Pi Mu Epsilon. Author: (with Dr. Hartford) A Study of Administrative Uses of Computers in Colleges and Universities of the United States, 1962; (with others) Guidelines for Planning Computing Centers in Universities and Colleges, 1963; also articles. Home: 2804 St Leonard Dr Tallahassee FL 32303

MILES, FRANKLIN EVERETT, adj. gen. N.Mex.; b. Tucumari, N.Mex., Jan. 4, 1923; s. John Esten and Susie Carmen (Wade) M.; B.B.A., U. N.Mex., 1950; grad. numerous service schs.; m. Patricia Maes, Dec. 13, 1973; children—Donna, John, Jeff, Larry, Carl, Karin. Joined Enlisted Res. Corps, U.S. Army, 1942, active duty as officer in PTO, 1943-46; mem. N.Mex. N.G., 1948--, commd. 1st lt., 1949, advanced through grades to maj. gen., 1975, adj. gen. N.Mex., 1974—; exec. v.p. N.Mex. Sch. Book Depository, Inc., 1957-74. Decorated Legion of Merit, Meritorious Service medal. Mem. Am. Legion, VFW, N.G. Assn., Sigma Chi. Democrat. Clubs: Kiwanis, Shriners. Home: PO Box 5061 Santa Fe NM 87501 Office: PO Box 4277 Santa Fe NM 87501. *Every man has his dignity. Treat him with such.*

MILES, JEANNE PATTERSON, artist; b. Balt.; d. Walter and Wdna (Webb) M.; B.F.A., George Washington U.; student Philips Meml. Gallery Sch., Atelier Gromaire, Grand Chaumiere, Paris; m. Frank Curlee, Dec. 31, 1935 (dec.); m. 2d, Johannes Schiefer, Feb. 11, 1939 (div.); 1 dau., Joanna. One-woman shows include: Betty Parsons Gallery, N.Y.C., 1945, 52, 56, Grand Central Moderns, N.Y.C., 1968, Wesbeth Galleries, N.Y.C., 1972; group shows include: N.Y. Rome Found., 1957, Walker Art Gallery, Mpls., 1954, Corcoran Biennial, Yale U. Mus., 1957, Chateau Gagnes, France, 1938, Whitney Mus., 1963, Nat. Fedn. Am. Art, 1963, Mus. Modern Art, 1966, Riverside Mus., N.Y.C., 1964, Guggeheim Mus., 1965-66, Geodok Am. Women Show, Hamburg and Berlin, 1972, Springfield (Mass.) Art Mus., 1975, Hunterton Art Center, Clinton, N.J., 1975, Betty Parsons Gallery, 1977; represented in permanent collections; N.Y. U., Santa Barbara (Calif.) Mus., Muson Proctor Mus., Utica, N.Y., Rutgers Coll., U. Ariz., Guggenheim Mus., Cin. and Newark museums, White Art Mus., N.Y. State U. at Purchase, Cornell U., Ecumenical Inst., Garrison, N.Y., Graymoor, Garrison, Springfield Art Mus., Weatherspoon Art Mus., U. N.C.; also pvt. collections N.Y.C. and France. Charles C. Ladd painting scholar, Tahiti, 1938, 56; traveling scholar, France, 1937-48; grantee Am. Inst. Arts and Letters, 1968, Mark Rothko Found., 1970, 73, Pelham von Stoeffler Art Fund, 1974. Mem. Abstract Artists Am. Address: Wesbeth Apt A 1103 463 West St New York NY 10014. *My paintings, I find, come out successfully when I keep a steady grip on an interior focus.*

MILES, JOANNA, actress; b. Nice, France, Mar. 6, 1940; d. Johannes and Jeanne Paterson (Miles) Schiefer; came to U.S., 1941, naturalized, 1941; grad. Putney (Vt.) Sch., 1958; m. William Burns, May 23, 1970 (div. 1977); m. 2d, Michael Brandman, Apr. 29, 1978. Mem. Actors Studio, N.Y.C., 1966; appeared in motion pictures The Way We Live Now, 1969, Bug, 1975, The Ultimate Warrior, 1975, Golden Girl, 1978; appeared in numerous television films, including In What America, 1965, My Mothers House, 1968; Glass Menagerie (2 Emmy awards), 1974, Born Innocent, 1974, Aloha Means Goodbye, 1974, The Trial of Chaplain Jensen, 1975, Harvest Home, 1977, Fire in the Sky, 1978, Sophisticated Gents, 1979, episodes in numerous TV series including Medical Center, Caribe, Mannix, Kojak, Barnaby Jones, Most Wanted, The Magician, Eddie Capra Mysteries, Secret Storm, Edge of Night, All My Children, Kaz, The Incredible Hulk, Runaways; appeared in stage plays Walk-Up, 1962, Once in a Life Time, 1963, Cave Dwellers, 1964, Drums in the Night, 1968, Dracula, 1968, Home Free, 1964, One Night Stands of Angisy Passenger, 1972, Dylan, 1973, Dancing for the Kaiser, 1976. Recipient Am. Women in Radio and Television award, 1974. Mem. Acad. Motion Picture Arts and Scis., Acad. TV Arts and Scis. Home: 2062 N Vine St Hollywood CA 90068 also 35 E 67th St New York NY 10021 Office: care STE 211 S Beverly Dr Beverly Hills CA 90212 also STE 888 7th Ave New York NY 10019

MILES, JOHN BRUCE, educator; b. St. Louis, Feb. 2, 1933; s. Aaron Jefferson and Annabelle (John) M.; B.S., U. Mo., 1955, M.S., 1957; Ph.D., U. Ill., 1963; m. Beverly Jean Bartlett, Feb. 8, 1958; children—John David, Andrea. Asst. prof. applied sci. So. Ill. U., 1958-63; asso. prof. mech. engring. U. Mo., 1963-68, prof., 1968—; research engr. Gen. Elec. Co., 1965-66, NASA, 1971; vis. prof. Stanford, 1971; cons.; dir. NSF Summer Inst. Fluid Dynamics, U. Mo., 1971. Served with AUS, 1957. Recipient U. Mo. Faculty/Alumni award, 1978; A.P. Green fellow, 1955; NSF faculty fellow, 1960, 62; NASA-Am. Soc. Engring. Edn. sci. faculty fellow, 1965, 68; Ford Found. fellow, 1965; NRC fellow, 1970; research grantee NSF, NASA, USAF. Mem. AIAA, ASME, Am. Soc. Engring. Edn., Sigma Xi, Tau Beta Pi, Theta Tau, Pi Tau Sigma, Phi Kappa Phi. Contbr. articles to tech. jours. Home: 102 Westridge Dr Columbia MO 65201

MILES, JOHN WILDER, educator; b. Cin., Dec. 1, 1920; s. Harold M. and Cleopatra (Morton) M.; B.S., Calif. Inst. Tech., 1942, M.S., 1943, Aero. Engr., 1944; Ph.D., 1944; m. Herberta Blight, June 19, 1943; children—Patricia Marie, Diana Catherine, Ann Leslie. With research lab. Gen. Electric Co., Schenectady, 1942; instr. Calif. Inst. Tech., 1943-44; with radiation lab. Mass. Inst. Tech., 1944; with Lockheed Aircraft Co., Burbank, Calif., 1944-45; asst. prof. U. Calif., Los Angeles, 1945-49, asso. prof., 1949-55, prof., 1955-61; prof. applied math. Australian Nat. U., 1962-64; prof. applied mechanics and geophysics U. Calif. at San Diego, 1965—, chmn. applied mechanics and engring. sci., 1968-73; cons. Northrop Aircraft Co., 1946-49, N.Am. Aviation Co., 1948-51, U.S. Naval Ordnance Test Sta., 1948-51, Douglas Aircraft Co., 1952-54, Ramo Wooldridge Corp., 1955-60, NASA, 1959-60, Aerospace Corp., 1961-68, Gulf Gen. Atomic Corp., 1965-68, Systems Sci. & Software, 1972-75, Sci. Applications, 1978—, Gas Centrifuge Theory Cons. Group, 1978—. Recipient Fulbright awards U. New Zealand, 1951, Cambridge U., 1969; vis. lectr. Imperial Coll., London, 1952; Guggenheim fellow, 1958-59, 68-69. Fellow Am. Inst. Aeros. and Astronautics, Am. Acad. Arts and Scis., Am. Acad. Mechs.; mem. Nat. Acad. Scis., AAAS, N.Y. Acad. Scis., Fedn. Am. Scientists, Am. Geophys. Union, Sigma Xi. Asso. editor Jour. Soc. Indsl. and Applied Math., 1958-61, Jour. Fluid Mechanics, 1966—; co-editor Cambridge Monographs on Mechanics and Applied Math., 1963—, Math. Tools for Engrs. Series, 1967-70; bd. editors U. Calif. Press, 1955-58, Ann. Rev. of Fluid Mechanics, 1967-73; Fluid Mechanics-Soviet Research, 1972—; reviewer Applied Mechanics Revs., 1947—, Math. Revs., 1946—. Home: 8448 Paseo del Ocaso La Jolla CA 92037

MILES, JOSEPHINE, educator, poet; b. Chgo., June 11, 1911; d. Reginald Odber and Josephine (Lackner) Miles; B.A., U. Calif. at Los Angeles, 1932; M.A., U. Calif. at Berkeley, 1934, Ph.D., 1938; D.Litt., Mills Coll., 1965. Mem. faculty dept. English, U. Calif. at Berkeley, 1940—, prof. English, 1952—, Univ. prof., 1973—. Recipient Shelley Meml. award for poetry, 1935; Nat. Inst. Arts and Letters award for poetry, 1956; award for poetry Nat. Commn. Arts, 1966 MLA Lowell award for literary scholarship., 1974. Phelan fellow, 1937-38, AAUW fellow, 1939-40, Guggenheim fellow, 1948-49, Am. Council Learned Socs. fellow, 1965, Acad. Am. Poets fellow, 1978; Berkeley fellow, 1979. Mem. Modern Lang. Assn., Am. Acad. Arts and Scis., Am. Soc. Aesthetics, Phi Beta Kappa, Chi Delta Phi. Author: Lines at Intersection, 1939; Poems on Several Occasions, 1941; Local Measures, 1946; The Vocabulary of Poetry (3 studies), 1946; The Continuity of English Poetic Language, 1951; Prefabrications, 1955; Eras and Modes in English Poetry, 1957, rev. edit., 1964; Renaissance, Eighteenth Century and Modern Language in Poetry, 1960; Poems 1930-60, 1960; House and Home (verse play), 1961; Emerson, 1964; Style and Proportion, 1967; Kinds of Affection, 1967; Civil Poems, 1966; Fields of Learning Poems, 1968; To All Appearances: Poems New and Selected, 1974; Poetry and Change, 1974; Coming to Terms, 1979; Working Out Ideas, and Other Essays on Composition; co-editor anthology: Criticism, Foundations of Modern Judgment, 1948; Idea and Experiment, 1950-54; editor: The Poem, 1959; The Ways of the Poem, rev. edit., 1972; Classic Essays in English, rev. edit., 1965. Contbr.: Fifteen Modern American Poets, 1956; Poets' Choice, 1963; Modern Hindi Poetry, 1965; Voyages, 1968; Norton Anthology of Modern Poetry, 1975; contbr. articles, poems to critical revs.; recs: 12 Contemporary Poets, 1966, Todays Poets, vol. II, 1967. Home: 2275 Virginia St Berkeley CA 94709

MILES, LELAND WEBER, univ. pres.; b. Balt., Jan. 18, 1924; s. Leland Weber and Marie (Fitzpatrick) M.; A.B. cum laude, Juniata Coll., 1946; M.A., U. N.C., 1947, Ph.D., 1949; postgrad. Duke U., 1949; D.Litt., Juniata Coll.; L.H.D., Rosary Hill Coll.; LL.D., Far East U., 1979; m. Mary Virginia Geyer, July 9, 1947; children—Christine Marie, Gregory Lynn. Asso. prof. English, Hanover Coll., 1949-50, prof., chmn. English dept., 1950-60; asso. prof., asst. to head English dept. U. Cin., 1960-63, prof., 1963-64, founder humanities reading program for engrs., 1961; dean Coll. Arts and Scis., U. Bridgeport (Conn.), 1964-67; pres. Alfred U., 1967-74, U. Bridgeport, 1974—; dir. United Illuminating; bd. counselors Peoples Savs.; founder Shakespeare Inst., Bridgeport-Stratford, 1965; Danforth scholar Union Theol. Sem., summer 1956; Lilly fellow Sch. Letters Ind. U., summer 1959; Am. Council Learned Socs. fellow Harvard, 1963-64; Sr. Fulbright Research scholar Kings Coll. U. London, 1964, vis. scholar, 1972; cons. Middle States Assn., 1971-74; seminar leader, deans and presidents insts. Am. Council on Edn., 1973—; chmn. bd. Academic Collective Bargaining Info. Service, Washington, 1977—; producer, moderator Casing the Classics WHAS-TV, Louisville, 1958-61; moderator Aspen (Colo.) Inst. for Humanistic Studies, 1969-70; lectr. Keedick Lecture Bur., N.Y.C.; speaker Detroit Town Hall, Indpls. Town Hall, So. Lit. Festival, N.Y.; sec.-treas. Commn. Council Ind. Colls., 1977—. Trustee Western N.Y. Nuclear Research Center, 1967-73, Carborundum Mus. Ceramics, Niagara Falls, N.Y., 1973-74, N.Y. State Commn. on Ind. Colls., 1972-74; chmn. bd. Coll. Center Finger Lakes, 1968-71; vice chmn. bd. Empire State Found., 1969-71, chmn., 1971-73. Served to 1st lt. USAAF, 1944-45; capt. USAF Res. ret. Decorated D.F.C. with oak leaf cluster; Crown Decoration of Honor 3d Order (Iran); recipient Rosa and Samuel Sachs prize Cin. Inst. Fine Arts, 1961; Nat. Medal (Thailand), 1979. Fellow Royal Soc. Arts; mem. Royal Soc. Lit., Modern Humanities Research Assn. (del. Diamond Jubilee Congress, Cambridge U. (Eng.) summer 1968), Renaissance Soc. Am., Conf. British Studies, English Speaking Union, Internat. Assn. Univ. Pres.'s (chmn. N.Am. council 1976, mem. internat. exec. com. 1977—, pres.-elect 1978), Conn. Conf. Ind. Colls. (sec.-treas. 1977-79, vice-chmn. 1979—), Phi Kappa Phi. Episcopalian. Clubs: University (N.Y.C.); Algonquin, Brooklawn; Country of Fairfield (Conn.). Author: John Colet and the Platonic Tradition, 1961. Editor: St. Thomas More's Dialogue of Comfort Against Tribulation, 1966; sr. editor (with Stephen B. Baxter) Studies in British History and Culture, 1965-79. Contbr. articles to learned jours. Office: Univ of Bridgeport Bridgeport CT 06602

MILES, RUFUS EDWARD, JR., cons., writer; b. Cin., June 14, 1910; s. Rufus Edward and Mabel Veazie (Arnold) M.; A.B., Antioch Coll., 1932; m. Nelle Mary Petrowski, Aug. 11, 1938; children—Barbara, Mary (Mrs. Joseph Patten). Ohio supr. of selection for CCC, 1935-36; administr. asst. to dir. CCC Selection, Washington, 1936-41; budget examiner U.S. Bur. Budget, 1941-42, budget examiner and budget group chief, 1945-48, chief labor and welfare br., 1948-50; asst. adminstr. for def. activities FSA, 1950-52, asst. adminstr. for program, 1952-53; dir. adminstrn. HEW, 1953-55, 56-61, adminstrv. asst. sec., 1961-65, comptroller, 1955; lectr. pub. affairs and dir. Mid-Career Program, Woodrow Wilson Sch. Pub. and Internat. Affairs, Princeton, 1966-70, sr. fellow, 1975—; pres. Population Reference Bur., 1970-71; cons., writer, 1971—. Mem. Pres.'s Adv. Council on Mgmt. Improvement, 1970-73. Served in USNR, 1942-45. lt. comdr. Res. Recipient Rockefeller Pub. Service award, 1956; Nat. Civil Service League award, 1960; Louis Brownlow award Am. Soc. Pub. Adminstrn., 1966, 74. Mem. Am. Soc. for Pub. Adminstrn., Nat. Acad. Pub. Adminstrn., AAAS. Club: Cosmos (Washington). Author: The Department of Health, Education and Welfare, 1974; Awakening from the American Dream, 1976. Address: 136 Randall Rd Princeton NJ 08540

MILES, SARAH, actress; b. Ingatestone, Essex, Eng., Dec. 31, 1943; studied at Royal Acad. Dramatic Art, London; m. Robert Bolt, 1967 (div.); 1 son, Thomas. Appeared in play Vivat! Vivat Regina!; films include: The Servant, 1964, The Ceremony, 1963, Six-Sided Triangle, Those Magnificent Men in Their Flying Machines, 1965, Blow-Up, 1967, Ryan's Daughter, 1970, Lady Caroline Lamb, 1972, The Man Who Loved Cat Dancing, 1973, The Hireling, 1973, The Sailor Who Fell from Grace with the Sea, 1976, The Big Sleep, 1978. TV films include: Great Expectations, 1974, Requiem for a Nun, 1975, James A. Michener's Dynasty, 1976. Office: care Internat Creative Mgmt 8899 Beverly Blvd Los Angeles CA 90048*

MILES, TICHI WILKERSON, publisher; b. Los Angeles, May 10, 1932; d. Albert Clarence and Beatrice (Velderrain) Noble; ed. Sacred Heart Convent, Mexico, U. Mexico; H.H.D., Columbia Coll., 1976; m. William Miles, Nov. 13, 1965; children—William Wilkerson, Cynthia Wilkerson. Publisher, editor-in-chief Hollywood Reporter,

1962—, pres. Hollywood Reporter Corp.; dir. Imperial Bank. Mem. exec. com. Los Angeles Mayor's Com. Internat. Visitors and Sister Cities, 1966—; founder, Internat. Festival Adv. Council, 1971—; named ofcl. hostess, Los Angeles, 1974; bd. dirs. Friends of U. So. Calif. Libraries, Inst. Advance Planning, Bd. Edn. for Sr. Adults, Los Angeles Music Center; exec. bd. dirs. Bilingual Children's TV; sponsor Make It on Your Own, 1976, Hollywood Reporter Key Art awards; active Motion Picture Country Home, Motion Picture and TV Relief Fund, Los Angeles Orphanage. Recipient award Treasury Dept., 1966; Nat. Theatre Owners award, 1967; certificate Am. Women in Radio and TV, 1968; also award distinguished philanthropic service Nat. Jewish Hosp., Denver; citation Will Rogers Hosp., O'Donnell Meml. Research Labs., Montague Library and Study Center; letter Program Youth Opportunity Hubert H. Humphrey, 1968; Golden Flame award Calif. Press Women, 1970, Women of Year award Girl Fridays of Show Bus., 1972, Personal Mgrs. Industry, 1976; Bronze plaque Mayor Los Angeles, 1972; citation Los Angeles City Council; award of excellence Imperial Bank; Star on Wall, Hollywood C. of C., 1975; Shofar award United Jewish Appeal, 1976; ShoWest commendation, 1977, 78, 79. Mem. Printing Industry Am., Cinema Circulus (dir.), Women of Motion Picture Industry (chmn.) Am. Women in Radio and TV (dir.), Calif. Press Women, Nat. Acad. TV Arts and Scis., UN Assn., Internat. Newspaper Promotion Assn., Western Publs. Asssn., Dames des Champagne, Calif. Thoroughbreeders Assn., Hollywood C. of C. (dir. 1972—), Women in Film (founder, pres.), Los Angeles Film Industry Council (dir.), Delta Kappa Alpha. Office: Hollywood Reporter 6715 Sunset Blvd Hollywood CA 90028

MILES, VERA, actress; b. Boise City, Okla., Aug. 23, 1930; d. Thomas and Burnice (Wyrick) Ralston; div.; children—Debra, Mrs. Kelley Essoe, Michael, Erik. Film roles include: For Men Only (debut), 1952, Rose Bowl Story, Backstreet, Charge at Feather River, 1954, Pride of the Blue Grass, Wichita, 1955, The Searchers, 1956, 23 Paces to Baker St., 1956, Autume Leaves, 1956, The Wrong Man, 1957, Beau James, 1957, Web of Evidence, 1959, F.B.I. Story, 1959, Psycho, 1960, The Man Who Shot Liberty Valance, 1962, Gentle Giant, 1967, Kona Coast, 1968, Hellfighters, 1969, Mission Batangos, Wild Country, 1971; TV appearances include: Pepsi Cola Playhouse, Schlitz Playhouse, Ford Theater, Movie of the Week, Medical Center, Marcus Welby M.D., Cannon, Streets of San Francisco, others; TV movies include: Judge Horton and the Scottsboro Boys, 1976, McNaughton's Daughter, 1976, State Fair, 1976, Runaway!, 1973, The Underground Man, 1974, The Strange and Deadly Occurrence, 1974, Smash-Up on Interstate 5, 1976. Address: care Contemporary-Korman Artists Ltd 132 Lasky Dr Beverly Hills CA 90212*

MILES, VIRGINIA, (Mrs. Fred C. Miles), mktg. cons.; b. N.Y.C., Apr. 20, 1916; d. Samuel and Jeanette (Shalet) Goldman; B.A., Wellesley Coll., 1936; M.A., Columbia, 1938, Ph.D., 1940; m. Fred C. Miles, Mar. 24, 1940; 1 dau., Erica. Asso. dir. research R.H. Macy & Co., N.Y.C., 1940-46; instr. dept. psychology Coll. City N.Y., 1946-48; advt. research dir. Alexander Smith & Co., Yonkers, N.Y., 1948-50; v.p., research dir. McCann-Erickson Advt. Agy., N.Y.C., 1950-60; v.p. spl. planning Young & Rubicam, Inc., N.Y.C., 1960-71, sr. v.p. new product devel., 1971-75; mktg. cons., Englewood, N.J., 1975—. Active Urban Coalition. Mem. Advt. Women of N.Y., Am. Assn. Pub. Opinion Research, Am. Mktg. Assn., Internat. Advt. Assn., Sigma Xi. Contbr. articles to profl. jours., trade mags. Home and Office: 91 Glenbrook Pkwy Englewood NJ 07631. *I am often asked whether it was very difficult to succeed in the advertising profession as a woman. The answer is "no," though I started in 1940 when there were very few women executives in the business. I did not look on myself as a pioneer. I simply worked harder than anybody else and proved my abilities, as I was determined to be the best at anything I did. Promotions followed. I had great self-confidence and was not afraid of success. Being called "aggressive" bothered me, but I learned to ignore it as a male put-down to women.*

MILES, WENDELL A., fed. judge; b. Holland, Mich., Apr. 17, 1916; s. Fred T. and Dena Del (Alverson) M.; A.B., Hope Coll., 1938; M.A., U. Wyo., 1939; J.D., U. Mich., 1942; m. Mariette Bruckert, June 8, 1946; children—Lorraine Miles Rector, Michelle Miles Kopinski, Thomas Paul. Admitted to Mich. bar; partner firm Miles & Miles, Holland, 1948-53, Miles, Mika, Meyers, Beckett & Jones, Grand Rapids, Mich., 1961-70; pros. atty. County of Ottawa (Mich.), 1949-53; U.S. dist. atty. Western Dist. Mich., 1953-60, U.S. dist. judge, 1974—; circuit judge 20th Jud. Circuit Ct. Mich., 1970-74; instr. Hope Coll., 1948-53, Am. Inst. Banking, 1953-60; mem. Mich. Higher Edn. Commn., 1978—. Pres., Holland Bd. Edn., 1952-63. Served to capt. U.S. Army, 1942-47. Mem. Am., Mich., Fed., Ottawa County bar assns., Am. Judicature Soc. Clubs: Rotary, Torch, Masons. Office: US Dist Ct 482 Fed Bldg 110 Michigan St NW Grand Rapids MI 49503

MILETI, NICK JAMES, profl. sports exec.; b. Cleve., Apr. 22, 1931; s. Joseph and Josephine (Parisi) M.; B.A., Bowling Green (Ohio) State U., 1953, D.Bus. (hon.), 1975; J.D., Ohio State U., 1956; m. Gretchen Garnes, June 12, 1954; 1 son, James. Admitted to Ohio bar, 1957; pvt. practice, Cleve., 1958-64; pros. atty. City of Lakewood, Ohio, 1960-62; pres. Sr. Housing Cons., Inc., 1965—; pres., owner Cleve. Arena/Cleve. Barons, 1968-72, Cleve. Crusaders Prof. Hockey Team, 1972-75, Sta. WWWE, 1972-77, Sta. WWWM, 1972—; gen. partner Cleve. Indians Profl. Baseball Team, 1972—; chmn. bd., builder Ohio Sports Center, Inc., Cleve., 1974-76; pres., prin. owner Cleve. Cavaliers Profl. Basketball Team, 1970—. Bd. dirs. USO, 1977—, Cleve. Conv. Bur., 1974—, Lakewood Hosp., 1972-74. Served with AUS, 1956-58. Recipient key to City of Bowling Green, 1969; Distinguished Alumnus award Bowling Green State U., 1971; Sportsman of Year award Brith Emeth, 1971; Dir. and Bus. Citizen award Greater Cleve. Growth Asns., 1974; Constrn. citation Cleve. Engring. Soc., 1974; named Hqn. Big Brother, 1970; life mem., recipient Gold medal Dante Alighieri Soc. Mass., 1972. Mem. Young Presidents Orgn. Address: 2923 Streetsboro Rd Richfield OH 44286*

MILEY, GEORGE HUNTER, educator; b. Shreveport, La., Aug. 6, 1933; s. George Hunter and Norma Angeline (Dowling) M.; B.S. in Chem. Engring., Carnegie-Mellon U., 1955; M.S., U. Mich., 1956, Ph.D. in Chem.-Nuclear Engring., 1959; m. Elizabeth Burroughs, Nov. 22, 1958; children—Susan Elizabeth, Hunter Robert. Nuclear engr. Knolls Atomic Power Lab., Gen. Electric Co., Schenectady, 1959-61; mem. faculty U. Ill., Urbana, 1961—, prof., 1967—, chmn. nuclear engring. program, 1975—. Vis. prof. U. Colo., summer, 1967, Cornell U., 1969-70, Lawrence Livermore Lab., summers 1973-74. Served with C.E., AUS, 1960. Recipient Western Electric Teaching-Research award, 1977; NATO sr. sci. fellow, 1975-76. Fellow Am. Nuclear Soc.; mem. Am. Soc. Engring. Edn. (chmn. energy conversion com. 1967-70, pres. U. Ill. chpt. 1973-74, chmn. nuclear div. 1975-76, Outstanding Tchr. award 1973), Am. Phys. Soc., Sigma Xi. Presbyn. Kiwanian. Author: Direct Conversion of Nuclear Radiation Energy, 1971; Fusion Energy Conversion, 1976. Patentee direct energy conversion devices. Research on fusion, energy conversion, reactor kinectics. Home: 912 W Armory St Champaign IL 61820 Office: 214 Nuclear Engring Lab U Ill Urbana IL 61801

MILGRAM, JEROME H., marine and ocean engr.; b. Phila., Sept. 23, 1938; s. Samuel J. and Fannie M.; B.S. in Elec. Engring., M.I.T., 1961, B.S. in Naval Architecture and Marine Engring., 1961, M.S., 1962, Ph.D. in Hydrodynamics, 1965. With Scripps Instn. Oceanography, San Diego, summer 1961; project engr. Block Assos., Cambridge, Mass., 1961-67; asst. prof. M.I.T., 1967-70, asso. prof., 1970-77, prof. ocean engring., 1977—; research asso. biophysics Harvard U. Med. Sch., 1974-76; tech. dir., cons. Offshore Devices, Inc., Peabody, Mass., 1974—; cons. Kennecott Exploration, Inc., Exxon Prodn. Research, Inc. Recipient Am. Bur. Shipping award, 1961. Registered profl. engr., Mass. Mem. Soc. Naval Architects and Marine Engrs. (life). Contbr. articles to profl. jours. Patentee in field. Home: 321 Harvard St Cambridge MA 02138 Office: Room 5-320 MIT 77 Massachusetts Ave Cambridge MA 02139

MILGRAM, STANLEY, social psychologist; b. N.Y.C., Aug. 15, 1933; s. Samuel and Adele (Israel) M.; A.B., Queens Coll., N.Y.C., 1954; Ph.D., Harvard U., 1960; m. Alexandra Menkin, Dec. 10, 1961; children—Michele Sara, Marc Daniel. Asst. prof. psychology Yale U., 1960-63; asst. prof. social psychology Harvard U., 1963-67, exec. dir. comparative internat. program dept. social relations, 1966-67; faculty Grad. Center, City U. N.Y., N.Y.C., 1967—, prof. psychology, 1967-79, Disting. prof. psychology, 1980—; cons. Polaroid Corp., 1977. Guggenheim fellow, 1972-73. Fellow AAAS (Ann. Socio-Psychol. prize 1965), Am. Psychol. Assn.; mem. Assn. Ind. Video and Filmakers. Author: Obedience to Authority (Nat. Book award nomination 1975), 1974, Television and Antisocial Behavior, 1973, The Individual In A Social World, 1977; films: Obedience, 1965, The City and the Self, 1974, Conformity and Independence, 1974, Invitation to Social Psychology, 1974, Human Aggression, 1976, Nonverbal Communication, 1976. Office: Grad Center City U NY 33 W 42d St New York NY 10036. *As a social psychologist, I look at the world not to master it in any practical sense but to understand it and to communicate that understanding to others.*

MILGRIM, FRANKLIN MARSHALL, merchant; b. N.Y.C., Aug. 24, 1925; s. Charles and Sally (Knobel) M.; grad. Woodmere (N.Y.) Acad., 1943; B.S. in Econs. with honors, Wharton Sch. U. Pa., 1949; m. Carol E. Kleinman, Sept. 2, 1945; children—Nancy Ellen, Catherine. Asst. mgr. Milgrim, Cleve., 1949-50; merchandiser, buyer H. Milgrim Bros., Inc., N.Y.C., 1950-52, v.p., dir., gen. merchandiser, 1952-57, pres., dir. Milgrim, Inc., Cleve. and Columbus, Ohio, 1957—; v.p., dir. Milgrim, Inc. (Mich.), Detroit, 1962-66, The 9-18 Corp., Cleve., 1969—; pres., treas., dir. Milgrim Suburban, Inc., 1963—, Milo, Inc., Columbus, 1966—, The Milgrim Co., Cleve., 1966—; pres., dir. Franklin Paul Bailey Inc., Cleve., 1965—. Pres. Severance Center Mchts. Assn., Cleveland Heights, 1963-66. Pres., bd. dirs. Greater Cleve. Area chpt. Nat. Council on Alcoholism, 1973—; chmn. bd. Alcoholism Services of Cleve., 1977—; fin. chmn. adv. council Salvation Army Harbor Light Complex, 1976—. Served with USNR, 1943-46. Dir., v.p. M and M Receivers Assn., Cleve., 1959-68. Clubs: Oakwood Country, Cleveland Mid-Day, City (Cleve.); Cleveland Playhouse. Home: 1 Bratenahl Pl Bratenahl OH 44108 also 2801 NE 183d St North Miami Beach FL 33160 Office: 1310 Huron Rd Cleveland OH 44115

MILGROM, FELIX, educator, immunologist; b. Rohatyn, Poland, Oct. 12, 1919; s. Henryk and Ernestina (Cyryl) M.; student U. Lwow, 1937-41, U. Lublin, 1945; M.D., U. Wroclaw, 1947; M.D. (hon.), U. Vienna, 1976, U. Lund, 1979; m. Halina Miszel, Oct. 15, 1941; children—Henry, Martin Louis. Came to U.S., 1958, naturalized, 1963. Prof., head dept. microbiology Sch. Medicine Silesian U., Zabrze, Poland, 1954-57; research asso. Service de Chime Microbienne Pasteur Inst., Paris, France, 1957; research asso., prof. dept. bacteriology, immunology U. Buffalo Sch. Medicine, 1958-62; asso. prof., prof. and chmn. dept. microbiology State U. N.Y. Sch. Medicine, Buffalo, 1962—. Mem. Am. Assn. Immunologists, Transplantation Soc. (v.p. 1976-78), Am. Acad. Microbiology, Coll. Internat. Allergology (v.p. 1970-78, pres. 1978—), Sigma Xi. Author: Studies on the Structure of Antibodies, 1950; co-editor: International Convocation on Immunology, 1969, 75, 79, Principles of Immunology, 1973, 79; editor-in-chief Internat. Archives of Allergy and Applied Immunology, 1965—; contbg. editor Vox Sanguinis, 1965-76, Transfusion, 1966-73, Cellular Immunology, 1970—, Transplantation, 1975-78; contbr. numerous articles to profl. jours. Research, serology of syphillis, Tb and rheumatoid arthritis, organ and tissue specificity including blood groups, transplantation and autoimmunity. Home: 474 Getzville Rd Buffalo NY 14226

MILHOLLAND, JAMES, JR., publisher; b. Pitts., May 11, 1921; s. James and Frances Braden (Harman) M.; A.B., Pa. State U., 1947; M.A., Johns Hopkins U., 1951; m. Pamela Maude Burden, Oct. 2, 1959; children—James, III, Peter Burden. Editor, Harcourt, Brace & Co., N.Y.C., 1951-60; chmn. bd., pres. Harvest Pub. Co., Cleve., 1961-68, chmn., 1968—, also dir.; sr. v.p. Harcourt Brace Jovanovich, Inc., 1968—, also dir.; chmn. Harvest Life Ins. Co., 1968—, also dir.; dir. Knox, Lent & Tucker Co., J.M. Riehle & Co., Nebr. Farmer Pub. Co.; founding mem. Postmaster Gen.'s Tech. Adv. Com., 1962-69; pres. bd. dirs. Episcopalian mag., 1976. Trustee Western Res. Acad. Served with USNR, 1942-46. Mem. Am. Hist. Assn., Am. Council Learned Socs., Agrl. Pubs. Assn. (chmn. 1962-66; 3 awards), Am. Bus. Press (chmn. 1972-73; 5 awards), Audit Bur. Circulations (dir. 1966-70). Democrat. Episcopalian. Clubs: University (N.Y.C.); Union (Cleve.); Chagrin Valley Hunt. Address: 9800 Detroit Ave Cleveland OH 44102

MILHORAT, THOMAS HERRICK, neurosurgeon; b. N.Y.C.. Apr. 5, 1936; s. Ade Thomas and Edith Caulkins (Herrick) M.; B.S., Cornell U., 1957, M.D., 1961; children—John Thomas, Robert Herrick. Intern, then asst. resident gen. surgery N.Y. Hosp., 1961-63, asst., then chief resident in neurosurgery, 1965-68; clin. asso. NIH, 1963-65, staff neurosurgeon (lt. comdr. USPHS), 1968-71; chief neurosurgery Children's Hosp. Nat. Med. Center, Washington, 1971—; prof. neurosurgery George Washington U. Med. Sch., 1974—; cons. in field. Recipient Charles L. Horn prize Cornell U. Med. Sch., 1961. Diplomate Am. Bd. Neurol. Surgeons. Mem. Nat. Council Scientists of NIH, AAAS, Internat. Soc. Pediatric Neurosurgery, Am. Assn. Neurol. Surgery, Am. Acad. Pediatrics, Soc. Pediatric Research, Washington Soc. Medicine. Republican. Author: Hydrocephalus and the Cerebrospinal Fluid, 1972; Pediatric Neurosurgery, 1978; also articles. Home: 1324 35 St NW Washington DC 20007 Office: 111 Michigan Ave Washington DC 20010

MILHOUSE, PAUL WILLIAM, clergyman; b. St. Francisville, Ill., Aug. 31, 1910; s. Willis Cleveland and Carrie (Pence) M.; A.B., Ind. Central U., 1932, D.D., 1950; B.D., Am. Theol. Sem., 1937, Th.D., 1946; L.H.D., Westmar Coll., 1965; S.T.D., Okla. City U., 1969; D.D., So. Meth. U., 1969; m. Mary Frances Noblitt, June 29, 1932; children—Mary Catherine (Mrs. Ronald L. Houswald), Pauline Joyce (Mrs. Arthur Vermillion), Paul David. Ordained to ministry United Brethren Ch., 1931; pastor, Birds, Ill., 1928-29, Elliott, Ill., 1932-37, Olney, Ill., 1937-41, 1st Ch., Decatur, Ill., 1941-51; asso. editor Telescope-Messenger, 1951-58; exec. sec. gen. council Evang. United Brethren Ch., 1959-60, bishop, 1960-68; bishop United Meth. Ch., 1968—; pres. Council United Meth. Bishops, 1977-78. Trustee Southern Methodist U., Oklahoma City U., Meth. Home, Francis E. Willard Home, Meth. Manor, Boys Ranch, Last Frontier council Boy Scouts Am. Recipient Disting. Alumnus award Ind. Central U., 1978, Disting. Friendaward Oklahoma City U., 1979. Mem. Nat. (past dir., mem. gen. assembly), World (gen. assembly) councils chs., Mark Twain Writers Guild, Epsilon Sigma Alpha. Author: Enlisting and Developing Church Leaders, 1946; Come Unto Me, 1946; Lift Up Your Eyes, 1955; Doorways to Spritual Living, 1950; Except the Lord Build the House, 1949; Christian Worship in Symbol and Ritual, 1953; Laymen in the Church, 1957; At Life's Crossroads, 1959; Phillip William Otterbein, 1968; Nineteen Bishops of the Evangelical United Brethren Church, 1974; also articles. Editor: Facing Frontiers, 1960. Home: 2213 NW 56th Terr Oklahoma City OK 73112 Office: 2420 N Blackwelder Oklahoma City OK 73106

MILIC, LOUIS TONKO, educator; b. Split, Yugoslavia, Sept. 5, 1922; s. Tonko L. and Helen (Gross) M.; came to U.S., 1936; naturalized, 1946; A.B., Columbia, 1948, M.A., 1950, Ph.D., 1963; m. Patricia A. Langwell, May 27, 1950 (div. Sept. 1960); 1 dau., Barbara; m. 2d, Ann Mulford Boyer, Sept. 24, 1960 (div. Oct. 1970); children—Pamela, Antonia, Byrd Jones; m. 3d, Jan Louise Lundgren, Nov. 20, 1970. Instr. Mont. State Coll., 1952-54; lectr. Columbia, 1955-58, instr. 1958-63, asst. prof., 1963-67, asso. prof. Tchrs. Coll., 1967-69; prof. English, Cleve. State U., 1969—, chmn. dept., 1969-78. Served with USAAF, 1943-46. Am. Council Learned Socs. and IBM fellow, 1967. Mem. Internat. Assn. U. Profs. English, Modern Lang. Assn., Linguistic Soc. Am., Modern Humanities Research Assn., Assn. Computational Linguistics, Am. Soc. 18th Century Studies, Midwest Modern Lang. Assn. (exec. com. 1972-75). Author: A Quantitative Approach to the Style of Jonathan Swift, 1967; Style and Stylistics: An Analytical Bibliography, 1967; Stylists on Style, 1969; co-author The English Language: Form and Use, 1974. Editor: Modernity of the Eighteenth Century, 1971; gen. editor New Humanistic Research series, 1972—; book rev. editor Computers and the Humanities, 1966-72. Home: 311 Chelsea Dr Cleveland Heights OH 44118. *The world is a lucky accident. Its chance opportunities for the inquisitive mind are limitless. I have always found it hard to avoid studying everything, because of this richness, which is tantalizing and yet without permanent meaning.*

MILITZER, WALTER ERNEST, educator; b. Arlington Heights, Ill., Aug. 20, 1906; s. Theodore and Caroline (Demmerle) M.; B.A. in Chemistry, U. Wis., 1932, Ph.D. in Biochemistry, 1936; m. Clementine Newman, Aug. 20, 1939; children—John W., Susan A. Mem. faculty U. Nebr., 1936—, prof., 1948—, dean Coll. Arts and Scis., 1952-67. Mem. Am. Soc. Biol. Chemists, AAAS, Phi Beta Kappa, Sigma Xi, Alpha Chi Sigma, Sigma Alpha Epsilon. Methodist. Club: Sertoma. Author articles biochemistry bacteria. Home: 3141 Sheridan Blvd Lincoln NE 68502. *The hardest lesson I had to learn in my life was working for superiors who I felt truthfully were of lesser abilities than I—and particularly so when they were not honest with me. Another lesson I had to learn from experience was that things I wanted too desperately often turned out not to be very desirable after I had gained them.*

MILIUS, JOHN FREDERICK, film writer and dir.; b. St. Louis, Apr. 11, 1944; s. William Styx and Elizabeth (Roe) M.; ed. U. So. Calif.; m. Renée Fabri, Jan. 7, 1967; children—Ethan Jedediah, Marco Alexander; m. 2d, Celia K. Burkholder, Feb. 26, 1978. Writer films: Devil's 8, 1969, Evel Knievel, 1971, Dirty Harry, 1971, Jeremiah Johnson (Heritage Wrangler award), 1972, Magnum Force, 1973, Purvis FBI (TV), 1974, Apocalypse Now, 1978; writer, dir. films: Dillinger, 1973, The Wind and the Lion (Nat. Bell Ringer ednl. award), 1975, Big Wednesday, 1978; instr. motion pictures script analysis U. So. Calif., fall 1973, advanced motion picture script analysis, spring 1974. Recipient Nat. Student Film Festival award U. So. Calif., 1968; numerous gun shooting awards; honored by Winchester for The Wind and the Lion. Office: Burbank Studios 4000 Warner Blvd Burbank CA 91522

MILK, BENJAMIN LECHTMAN, mgmt. specialist, govt. ofcl.; b. Queens County, N.Y., Oct. 5, 1938; s. Albert and Henrietta (Lechtman) M.; A.B., Antioch Coll., 1961; M.P.A., U. Pitts., 1965; m. Leslie Deborah Berg, Mar. 24, 1968; children—Jeremy, Meredith. Mgmt. analyst Port of N.Y. Authority, 1963-68, asst. mgr. bus terminal, 1968-70; mgr. orgn. planning Western Union Corp., N.Y.C., 1970-72; exec. dir. SEC, Washington, 1972—. Mem. Am. Soc. Public Adminstrn. Office: SEC 500 N Capitol St Washington DC 20549

MILKIS, EDWARD KENNETH, motion picture and television producer; b. Los Angeles, July 16, 1931; s. Sam and Minnie (Satnick) M.; student Los Angeles City Coll., 1949-50, U. So. Calif., 1952-56; m. Bette Jean Miller, July 17, 1954; children—Steven, Gary, Chuck. Film shipper, asst. film editor ABC-TV, Hollywood, Calif., 1952; asst. film editor Walt Disney Prodns., MGM, Los Angeles, 1954-60; film editor MGM, 1960-65; asso. producer Star Trek, 1966-69; exec. in charge post-prodn. Paramount Television, 1969-72; partner Miller-Milkis Prodns., Inc., Hollywood, Calif., 1972—; partner Milkis/Milkis/Boyett Prodns. Inc., Hollywood, 1979—; exec. producer Happy Days, Laverne and Shirley, Petrocelli, Angie TV series, 1972—; co-producer feature films Silver Streak, 1976, Foul Play, 1977. Served with USAF, 1950-52. Mem. Acad. Motion Picture Arts and Scis., Acad. TV Arts and Scis., Producers Guild Am., Dirs. Guild Am., Film Editors Guild. Office: 5451 Marathon St Hollywood CA 90038

MILLAND, RAY(MOND ALTON), motion picture actor, dir.; b. Neath, Glamorganshire, Wales, Jan. 3, 1908; s. Alfred and Elizabeth (Truscott-Jones), M.; came to U.S., 1930, naturalized, 1938; ed. pvt. schs., Wales and Eng., then Monks Prep. Sch.; student Kings Coll., U. Wales; m. Muriel Weber, Sept. 30, 1932; children—Daniel David, Victoria Francesa. Served with Household Cav., Brit. Army, 1926-30. Appeared in approximately 145 motion pictures including: The Jungle Princess, 1936, Beau Geste, 1939, Reap the Wild Wind, 1942, Arise My Love, 1941, The Major and the Minor, 1942, Lady in the Dark, 1944, The Lost Weekend (Acad. award Best Actor), 1945, Kitty, 1945, California, 1946, Golden Earrings, 1947, Alias Nick Beal, 1949, It Happens Every Spring, 1949, The Thief, 1952, Dial M for Murder, 1954, Lisbon (also dir.), 1956, A Man Alone (also dir.), 1955, The Safecracker (also dir.), 1958, Panic in the Year Zero (also dir.), 1962, Hostile Witness (also dir.), 1969, Love Story, 1970, The House in Nightmare Park, 1973, The Last Tycoon, 1976, Slavers, 1977, Oliver's Story, 1978, The Swiss Conspiracy, 1979; TV series Markham, 1959, Rich Man, Poor Man, 1976; appeared on legitimate stage Eng. and U.S. Author: Wide-Eyed in Babylon: An Autobiography, 1974; contbr. numerous articles and short stories under own and other names to various publs. Address: care Contemporary-Korman Artists Ltd 132 Lasky Dr Beverly Hills CA 90212*

MILLAR, CHARLES GORDON, communications co. exec.; b. Montreal, Que., Can., Sept. 28, 1926; s. Gordon Eric and Jennie Kathleen (Mitchinson) M.; B.Sc., McGill U., 1947; m. Leonora Mary DeMers, Oct. 4, 1952; children—Jennifer Gail, Andrea Mary. With No. Electric Co. Ltd., 1947-77, v.p., 1972-73, exec. v.p. ops., Montreal, 1973-77; chmn., pres., chief exec. officer No. Telecom Can. Ltd., Montreal, 1977-78, exec. v.p. ops. No. Telecom Ltd., 1978—; dir. No. Telecom Can. Ltd., No. Telecom Systems Corp., Intersil, Inc., No. Telecom Inc., No. Telecom Internat.,' Bell-No. Research. Registered profl. engr., Que. Mem. Elec. and Electronic Mfrs. Assn.

Can. (dir., vice-chmn.), Order Engrs. Que., Assn. Profl. Engrs. Ont. Home: 39 Old Mill Rd PH 4 Old Mill Towers Toronto ON M8X 1G6 Canada Office: 33 City Centre Dr Mississauga ON L5B 2N5 Canada

MILLAR, GORDON HALSTEAD, mech. engr., agrl. machinery mfg. co. exec.; b. Newark, Nov. 28, 1923; s. George Halstead and Dill E. (McMullen) M.; B.M.E., U. Detroit, 1949, D.Sc. (hon.), 1977; Ph.D., U. Wis., 1952; m. Virginia M. Jedryczka, Aug. 24, 1957; children—George B., Kathryn M., Juliet S., John G., James H. Supr. new powerplants Ford Motor Co., 1952-57; engring. mgr. Meriam Instrument Co., Cleve., 1957-59; dir. new products McCulloch Corp., Los Angeles, 1959-63; with Deere & Co., 1963—, v.p. engring., Moline, Ill., 1972—; mem. Fed. Adv. Com. Indsl. Innovation, 1979; chmn. West Central Ill. Ednl. Telecommunications Corp. Chmn. Quad Cities chpt. United Way, 1976-77, bd. dirs.; adv. council Bradley U. Coll. Engring. and Tech.; mem. exec. com. Illowa council Boy Scouts Am., 1977-79. Served with U.S. Army, World War II. Decorated Purple Heart; recipient Alumnus of Year award U. Detroit, 1976. Mem. Nat. Acad. Engring., Soc. Automotive Engrs., Engrs. Council Profl. Devel., Engrs. Joint Council, Indsl. Research Inst., Engring. Soc. Detroit, ASME, Am. Soc. Agrl. Engrs., Ill. Soc. Profl. Engrs., Moline C. of C., Aviation Council. Contbr. numerous articles to profl. publs.; patentee in field. Home: 3705 39th St Ct Moline IL 61265 Office: John Deere Rd Moline IL 61265

MILLAR, GREGORY, conductor; b. Prince Albert, Sask., Can., June 9, 1929; s. Spiro A. and Dorothea M. (Trombley) M.; A.B., U. B.C., 1949; A.M., U. Calif., Berkeley, 1951; A.M. in Composition, Mills Coll., Oakland, Calif., 1953; m. Roslyn Frantz, Jan. 20, 1955; children—Denise Yvonne, Jason Spiro, Daphne Elizabeth, Damon Gregory. Founder, condr. San Francisco Little Symphony, 1951-60; asst. condr. N.Y. Philharm., 1960-62; dir. orchtl. studies Manhattan Sch. Music, 1960-65; music dir. Kalamazoo Symphony, 1961-68, Lansing (Mich.) Symphony, 1962-65; music adv. Ft. Wayne (Ind.) Philharm., 1966-67, Grand Rapids (Mich.) Symphony, 1968-73; resident condr. Tucson Symphony, 1966-77; artistic dir. Nat. Opera Mex., 1973-75; music dir., condr. Regina (Sask.) Symphony, 1978—; tenor; debut Austin (Tex.) Symphony, 1976; guest condr. symphonies in U.S. and Can., 1958—; rec. artist Fantasy and Columbia records, Mahler Soc.; pres. Gregory Millar Music Found., 1968-75. Grantee Rockefeller Found., 1955-58, Rosenberg Found., 1955, Ford Found., 1967, Nat. Endowment Arts, 1970-77.

MILLAR, JEFFERY LYNN, journalist; b. Pasadena, Tex., July 10, 1942; s. Daniel Lynn and Betty Ruth (Shove) M.; B.A., U. Tex., 1964; m. Lynne McDonald, Dec. 21, 1963. Reporter, Houston Chronicle, 1964-65, film critic, 1965—, columnist, 1972—; author Tank McNamara, comic strip, Universal Press Syndicate, Kansas City, 1974—. Author: And I'm Tank McNamara with the Norts Spews, 1975; Tank McNamara, 1975; If I Quit Baseball, Will You Still Love Me?, 1976; Shoot, Tank, Shoot!, 1976; All Blond Boys Should Be Quarterbacks, 1977; The Tank McNamara Chronicles, 1978. Home: 1301 Spring Oaks Circle Houston TX 77055 Office: 801 Texas Ave Houston TX 77002

MILLAR, JOHN DONALD, govt. ofcl.; b. Newport News, Va., Feb. 27, 1934; s. John and Dorothea Virginia (Smith) M.; B.S., U. Richmond, 1956; M.D., Med. Coll. Va., 1959; D.T.P.H., London Sch. Hygiene and Tropical Medicine, 1966; m. Joan M. Phillips, Aug. 17, 1957; children—John Stuart, Alison Gordon, Virginia Taylor. Intern, U. Utah Affiliated Hosps., Salt Lake City, 1959-60, asst. resident in medicine, 1960-61; asst. chief Epidemic Intelligence Service, Center for Disease Control, USPHS, HEW, Atlanta, 1961-62, chief Epidemic Intelligence Service, 1962-63, dep. chief surveillance sect., 1962-63, chief smallpox unit, 1963-65, dir. smallpox eradication program, 1966-70, dir. Bur. State Services, 1970—, acting dir. Nat. Inst. Occupational Safety and Health, 1978; cons. on smallpox, smallpox eradication and immunization programs WHO, Pan Am. Health Orgn.; mem. sci. group on smallpox eradication WHO. Recipient Surgeon Gen's. Commendation medal, 1965, Okeke prize London Sch. Hygiene and Tropical Medicine, 1966, Presdl. award for mgmt. improvement, 1972, Center for Disease Control medal of excellence, 1977. Contbr. articles to profl. jours. Home: 3243 Wake Robin Trail NE Atlanta GA 30341 Office: 1600 Clifton Rd NE Atlanta GA 30333

MILLAR, KENNETH (PSEUDONYM ROSS MACDONALD), author; b. Los Gatos, Calif., Dec. 13, 1915; s. John M. and Anne (Moyer) M.: B.A., U. Western Ont., 1938; postgrad. U. Toronto, 1938-39; M.A., U. Mich., 1942, Ph.D., 1951; m. Margaret Ellis Sturm, June 2, 1938; 1 dau., Linda Jane (Mrs. Joseph J. Pagnusat) (dec.). Tchr., English and history Kitchener (Ont.) Collegiate Inst., 1939-41; fellow, spl. instr. English dept. U. Mich., 1941-44; free lance writer, 1946—. Author: The Dark Tunnel, 1944; Trouble Follows Me, 1946; Blue City, 1947; The Three Roads, 1948; The Moving Target, 1949; The Drowning Pool, 1950; The Way Some People Die, 1951; The Ivory Grin, 1952; Meet Me at the Morgue, 1953; Find a Victim, 1954; The Name is Archer, 1955; The Barbarous Coast, 1956; The Doomsters, 1958; The Galton Case, 1959; The Ferguson Affair, 1960; The Wycherly Woman, 1961; The Zebra-Striped Hearse, 1962; The Chill, 1964; The Far Side of the Dollar, 1965; Black Money, 1966; The Instant Enemy, 1968; The Goodbye Look, 1969; The Underground Man, 1971; Sleeping Beauty, 1973; The Blue Hammer, 1976. Served to lt. (j.g.) USNR, 1944-46. Mem. Mystery Writers Am. (pres. 1965, recipient Edgar A. Poe scrolls 1962, 63, Grand Master award 1974), Crime Writers Assn. London (Silver Dagger award 1965, Golden Dagger award 1966), Writers Guild of Am., Authors League, ACLU, Phi Beta Kappa. Clubs: Sierra, Coral Casino (Santa Barbara). Address: 4420 Via Esperanza Santa Barbara CA 93110

MILLAR, MARGARET ELLIS, author; b. Kitchener, Ont., Can., Feb. 5, 1915; d. Henry William and Lavinia (Ferrier) Sturm; student U. Toronto, 1933-36; m. Kenneth Millar (pseudonym Ross Macdonald), June 2, 1938; 1 dau., Linda Jane (dec.). Author: The Invisible Worm, 1941; The Weak-Eyed Bat, 1942; The Devil Loves Me, 1942; Wall of Eyes, 1943; Fire Will Freeze, 1944; The Iron Gates, 1945; Experiment in Springtime, 1947; It's All in the Family, 1948; The Cannibal Heart, 1949; Do Evil in Return, 1950; Vanish in an Instant, 1952; Rose's Last Summer, 1952; Wives and Lovers, 1954; Beast in View, 1955; An Air That Kills, 1957; The Listening Walls, 1959; A Stranger in My Grave, 1960; How Like an Angel, 1962; The Fiend, 1964; The Birds and the Beasts Were There, 1968; Beyond This Point Are Monsters, 1970; Ask for Me Tomorrow, 1976; also writer short stories and TV plays. Recipient Edgar award for Beast in View, Mystery Writers Am., 1956. Mem. Mystery Writers Am. (pres. 1957). Home: 4420 Via Esperanza Santa Barbara CA 93110

MILLAR, RICHARD WILLIAM, business exec.; b. Denver, Jan. 8, 1899; s. Edward Richard and Marguerite Manitou (Atcheson) M.; student Occidental Coll., Los Angeles, 1917-18; B.A., U. Calif., 1921; m. 2d, Catherine Claiborne Armes, Feb. 25, 1934; children—Richard W. Jr., Roger James. Student security salesman Blair & Co., 1922, advancing to v.p., later v.p. successor Bancamerica-Blair Corp.; pres. Bankamerica Co., 1930-32; pres. Vultee Aircraft, 1939-43; chmn. Avion, Inc.; chmn. Northrop Aircraft, 1947-49; past vice chmn. Glore, Forgan, William R. Staats, Inc.; past vice chmn. investment banking bd., now vice-chmn. bd., chmn. exec. com. Northrop Corp.; dir. Quotron Systems, Inc. Hon. trustee Occidental Coll., Webb Sch. Calif. mil. instr., later Central Inf., Officers Tng. Camp, Waco, Tex., World War I. Mem. Owl and Key (Occidental Coll.), Phi Kappa Psi. Episcopalian. Clubs: Calif. (Los Angeles); Valley Hunt (Pasadena); Bohemian (San Francisco). Home: 480 S Orange Grove Blvd Pasadena CA 91105 Office: Northrop Corp 1800 Century Park E Los Angeles CA 90067

MILLARD, CHARLES E. F., corp. exec.; b. Paterson, N.J., Sept. 4, 1932; s. James C.B. and Mary (Orr) M.; A.B., Coll. Holy Cross, 1954; m. Marylou Slattery, Sept. 25, 1954; children—Marylou, Charles, Christopher, Maureen, Margaret, Suzanne, Kathleen, Gregory. Vice pres., account supr. Benton & Bowles, Inc., 1958-64, William Esty Co., Inc., 1964-66; sr. v.p., dir. client services Gilbert Advt. Agy., Inc., 1966-67; v.p., mgmt. supr. Benton & Bowles, Inc., 1967; pres. Coca-Cola Bottling Co., N.Y., Inc., 1967-68, chief exec. officer, chmn. bd., 1968—, also dir.; gov. Coca-Cola Bottlers Assn. Past pres., bd. dirs. N.Y. Urban League; trustee Nat. Urban League; mem. N.Y. indsl. adv. council Opportunities Industrialization Center; exec. com. Nat. Council Crime and Delinquency; mem. chief exec. officers council Com. to Reform Double Taxation of Investment; mem., chmn. exec. com. Newark Archbishop's Com. of Laity; chmn. bd. trustees Coll. Holy Cross; trustee Nat. Council on Alcoholism. Clubs: N.Y. Athletic, River, Sky (N.Y.C.); Arcola Country (N.J.); Seaview Country (Absecon, N.J.); Muirfield Village (Ohio); Windham Mountain. Home: 908 Mohawk Rd Franklin Lakes NJ 07417 Office: 411 Hackensack Ave Hackensack NJ 07601

MILLARD, CHARLES WARREN, III, museum curator; b. Elizabeth, N.J., Dec. 20, 1932; s. Charles Warren and Constance Emily (Keppler) M.; A.B., magna cum laude, Princeton U., 1954; M.A., Harvard U., 1963, Ph.D., 1971. Asst. to dir. Fogg Art Mus., Harvard U., 1963-64; asst. to dir. Dumbarton Oaks, Washington, 1965-66; dir. Washington Gallery Modern Art, 1966-67; curator 19th century European art Los Angeles County Mus. Art, 1971-74; chief curator Hirshhorn Mus. and Sculpture Garden, Smithsonian Instn., 1974—; teaching fellow Harvard U., 1968-69; chmn. vis. com. to art history dept. Boston U., 1977—. Served with USN, 1956-59. Author: The Sculpture of Edgar Degas, 1977; art editor Hudson Rev., 1972—; contbr. articles to profl. jours. Home: 2853 Ontario Rd NW Washington DC 20009 Office: Hirshhorn Mus 8th St and Independence Ave SW Washington DC 20560

MILLARD, DAVID RALPH, JR., plastic surgeon; b. St. Louis, June 4, 1919; s. David Ralph and Florence Nightegale (Hamilton) M.; B.A., Yale U., 1941; M.D., Harvard U., 1944; m. Barbara L. Smith, Apr. 7, 1956; children—David Ralph, III, William Bond, Meleney G. Practice medicine specializing in plastic surgery, Miami, Fla., 1955—; Light-Millard prof. plastic surgery U. Miami Med. Sch., 1974—. Served to lt. (j.g.) USNR, World War II; as maj. M.C., USMCR, 1953-55. Decorated Letter of Commendation; recipient 1st prize ednl. essay contest Ednl. Found. Plastic and Reconstructive Surgeons, 1965, 68; Herbert Lipschultz award, 1976; R.R. Hawkins book award, 1976; Jamaican Order of Distinction, 1976; Asheville Sch. Merit award, 1978. Diplomate Am. Bd. Plastic Surgery, vice chmn., 1978-79. Mem. Am. Soc. Plastic and Reconstructive Surgery (pres. ednl. found., asso. editor jour.), A.C.S., Am. Brit. assns. plastic surgeons. Republican. Episcopalian. Clubs: Bath, Palm Bay. Author: Cleft Craft, The Evolution of Its Surgery, 1976; co-author: Principles of Art of Plastic Surgery, 1957. Contbr. med. jours. Home: 4501 Lake Rd Bay Point Miami FL 33137 Office: 1444 NW 14th Ave Miami FL 33125

MILLARD, GEORGE RICHARD, bishop; b. Dunsmuir, Calif., Oct. 2, 1914; s. George Ellis and Constance (Rainsberry) M.; A.B., U. Calif. at Berkeley, 1936; B.D., Episcopal Theol. Sch., Cambridge, Mass., 1938; S.T.M., Pacific Sch. Religion, 1958; D.D., Ch. Div. Sch. Pacific, 1960; m. Mary Louise Gessling, June 29, 1939; children—George, Martha, Joseph. Ordained priest Episc. Ch., 1938; asst. in N.Y.C., 1938-39, Waterbury, Conn., 1930-40; rector in Danbury, Conn., 1940-50, Alameda, Calif., 1951-59; suffragan bishop Episc. Diocese Calif., 1960-76; bishop of San Jose, 1969-76; exec., venture in mission program, exec. council Episc. Ch., 1977-78; bishop in charge Am. Chs. in Europe, 1978—; dean Convocation of Oakland (Calif.), 1957-60; chmn. dept. missions Diocese Calif., 1958-60; mem. Joint Commn. on Structure, Episc. Ch., dir. office parish and clergy devel. Diocese Calif. Mem. pres.'s council San Jose State Coll.; chmn. Maria Kip Orphange; chmn. devel. program U. Calif. at Berkeley Student Coop. Assn., 1966; v.p. bd. trustees Ch. Div. Sch. Pacific; bd. dirs. Episc. Ch. Pension Fund, Ch. Life Ins. Co., Ch. Fire Ins. Co. Home: 23 Ave George V 75008 Paris France

MILLDYKE, JOHN WILLIAM, broadcasting co. exec.; b. Kearney, Nebr., Apr. 10, 1937; s. John William and Myra Irene (Dow) M.; B.A., Nebr. State Coll., 1958; postgrad U. Nebr., 1959-60; m. Doris Helen Evans, Aug. 28, 1960; children—Sonja Lynne, Michelle Marie. News dir. Sta. KHGI-TV, Kearney, 1960-62; news dir. Sta. WOI-AM-FM-TV, Ames, Iowa, 1962-68; asso. prof. journalism Iowa State U., 1963-68; assignment editor, producer news ABC, Washington, 1968-71, producer news, London, 1971-77, mgr. news coverage-Europe, 1977—. Mem. Assn. Am. Corrs. in London (dir. 1977-79), Brit. Acad. Film and TV Arts, Overseas Press Club Am., Internat. Press Inst., Radio-TV News Dirs. Assn. Home: 66 High St Amersham Bucks HP7 ODS England Office: 8 Carburton St London W1P 7DT England

MILLEN, FLOYD H., state legislator; b. Watertown, S.D., May 17, 1919; s. Homer E. and Pearle (Wright) M.; student Iowa State U., 1937-38, Nev. Sch. Mines, 1939-41; m. Betty Coffin, Feb. 15, 1942. Pres. Valley Limestone & Gravel, Inc., 1946—; mem. Iowa Ho. of Reps., 1963—, majority floor leader, 1967-68, speaker pro tem, 1969-73, minority floor leader, 1975-76, speaker of house, 1979—. Served to 2d lt. AUS, 1942-46. Mem. Am. Mil. Engrs., Nat. Limestone Inst., Am. Roadbuilders Assn., Iowa Limestone Producers Assn., AM. Legion, VFW, Izaak Walton League. Methodist. Clubs: Masons, Shriners. Home: Farmington IA 52626 Office: Ho of Reps Office of Speaker State Capitol Des Moines IA 50319

MILLER, A. EDWARD, publishing and communications cons.; b. N.Y.C., Aug. 28, 1918; s. Joseph and Sara (Miller) M.; B.B.A., Coll. City N.Y., 1939, M.B.A., 1942; m. Mary-Susan Morris, Nov. 19, 1949; children—Christopher, Eric Booth, Amy Katherine. Accountant, Ernst & Ernst, 1945-47; dir. research Life mag., Time Inc., N.Y.C., 1947-54, asst. to pub., 1955-59, pub. McCall's mag., 1959-64; pres. Alfred Politz Research, Inc., subsidiary of Computer Sciences Corp., 1964-68, also dir.; pres., chief exec. officer, dir. World Pub. Co., subsidiary Times-Mirror Corp., 1968-70; v.p., dir. McCall Corp.; pres., dir. Berlitz Schs. of Langs., subsidiary Crowell Collier and MacMillan, Inc., 1970-72; pres. Berlitz Travel Services, Inc., 1970-72; exec. v.p., dir. Downe Publishing, Inc. subs. Charter Co., 1972-74, pres., chief operating officer, dir., 1974-79, pres. Downe Communications, Inc. div., 1972-74; adj. prof. psychology Baruch Sch., Coll. City N.Y., 1953—; lectr. N.Y. U. Sch. Continuing Edn., 1979—; dir. U/Stat Inc., Community Nat. Bank; cons. in communications to U.S. and internat. cos., 1979—. Chmn. Mayor's Com. Indsl. Leaders Youth, N.Y.C.; mem. citizens adv. com. N.Y. Pub. Library; pres., dir. N.Y.C. Youth Bd. Research Inst.; adv. com. Center for Advancement Human Communication, Fairfield U.; adv. bd. manpower research study U.S. Office of Edn., NSF; mem. exec. com., treas., sec. Nat. Book Com.; chmn. Nat. Library Week Steering Com.; mem. Nat. Marketing Adv. Com. to Sec. of Commerce. Trustee Center for Urban Edn.; bd. dirs., vice chmn. Advt. Research Found., 1974—. Recipient Alumni award U. City N.Y., 1969. C.P.A. Mem. Market Research Council, Am. Mktg. Assn. (dir.), Grad. Bus. Alumni N.Y.U. (v.p.), Am. Statis. Assn., Am. Econ. Assn., Am. Sociol. Assn., Am. Assn. Pub. Opinion Research, Alpha Delta Sigma. Club: New York University. Mem. bd. editors Jour. Mktg. Home: Box 55 Green Pond Sherman CT 06784 Office: 345 E 52d St New York NY 10022

MILLER, ALAN B., hosp. mgmt. co. exec.; b. N.Y.C., Aug. 17, 1937; s. Manuel and Mary (Blumenthal) M.; B.A., William and Mary Coll., 1958; M.B.A., Wharton Sch., U. Pa., 1960; m. Jill K. Stein, Oct. 5, 1968; children—Marc Daniel, Marni Elizabeth, Abby Daniele. Vice pres. Young & Rubicam, Inc., N.Y.C., 1964-69; sr. v.p. Am. Medicorp., Inc., Los Angeles, pres., chief exec. officer, Phila., 1973-77, chmn. bd., 1977; chmn. bd. Hosp. Underwriting Group, 1977-78; founder, pres. Universal Health Services, Bala Cynwyd, Pa., 1978—; health care adviser Fed. Mediation and Conciliation Service. Served to capt. U.S. Army, 1960. Mem. Phila. C. of C. (dir.). Home: 45 Raynham Rd Merion Station PA 19066 Office: One Presidential Blvd Bala Cynwyd PA 19004

MILLER, ALBERT JAY, librarian, educator; b. Beaver Falls, Pa., Dec. 7, 1928; s. Joseph Jefferson and Alberta Fae (Shaffer) M.; B.S., Geneva Coll., 1952; M.L.S., Rutgers U., 1958; postgrad. U. Chgo., 1960-61, U. Pitts., 1963-68, U. Mich., 1969. Librarian, West Allegheny Jr. High Sch., Imperial, Pa., 1959-60, Butler (Pa.) Area Sr. High Sch., 1962-67; librarian Pa. State U., New Kensington, 1969—, tchr.-librarian continuing edn. dept., 1970—. Instr. water safety ARC, New Kensington, 1969—, Citizens Gen. Hosp., New Kensington, 1971-72; active Boy Scouts Am., 1970—. Bd. dirs. Westmoreland County, Butler County mental health assns.; mem. Allegheny-Kiski Human Relations Council, 1976-77; bd. dirs. Allegheny-Kiski Sr. Citizens Center, 1976-77. Mem. Pa., Nat. edn. assns., ALA, Pa. Library Assn. Presbyn. (Sunday sch. tchr. 1970—). Democratic. Author: A Selective Bibliography of Existentialism in Education and Related Topics, 1969; Confrontation, Conflict and Dissent, 1972; Death: A Bibliographical Guide, 1977; book and media rev. editor Learning Today, 1978—. Home: 417 Charles Ave New Kensington PA 15068 Office: 3550 7th St Rd New Kensington PA 15068

MILLER, ALLAN JOHN, lawyer; b. Beachwood, Ohio, Oct. 17, 1921; s. Carl Frederick and Rhoda (Warren) M.; B.B.A., Fenn Coll., 1946; LL.B., Western Res. U., 1948; m. Marjorie Hewitt Pirtle, Aug. 10, 1946; children—James W., Patricia Anne. Admitted to Ohio bar, 1948; with Standard Oil Co. (Ohio), 1948-77, treas., 1967-77; mem. firm Kiefer, Knecht, Rees, Meyer & Miller, Cleve., 1977—; dir. United Screw & Bolt Corp. Chmn. bd. dirs. Lutheran Med. Center, Cleve., 1967—; pres Luth. Med. Center Med. Staff Found., 1979—; chmn. bd. dirs. Christian Residencies Found., 1972-77, St. Luke's Hosp. Assn., 1973—; chmn. bd. trustees Dyke Coll., Cleve., 1971—. Served with AUS, 1943-46; PTO. Mem. Cleve. Treas.'s Club, Cleve. Soc. Security Analysts. Methodist. Clubs: Mid-day, Hermit (Cleve.); Meadow Wood Recreation (Lyndhurst, Ohio). Home: 5183 Meadow Wood Blvd Lyndhurst OH 44124 Office: 1126 Terminal Tower Cleveland OH 44113

MILLER, ANDREW PICKENS, lawyer; b. Fairfax, Va., Dec. 21, 1932; s. Francis Pickens and Helen (Hill) M.; A.B. magna cum laude, Princeton, 1954; postgrad. New Coll., Oxford (Eng.) U., 1954-55; LL.B., U. Va., 1960; m. Dorothy Andrews Brown, Aug. 14, 1954; children—Julia Lane, Andrew Pickens, Elise Givhan. Admitted to Va. bar, 1960, U.S. Supreme Ct. bar, 1967, D.C. bar, 1979; asso.. firm Penn, Stuart & Stuart, 1960-62; partner firm Penn, Stuart & Miller, Abingdon, Va., 1963-69; atty. gen. Va., 1970-77; partner firm Mays, Valentine, Davenport & Moore, Richmond, Va., 1977-78, Dickstein, Shapiro & Morin, Washington, 1979—. Pres. Young Democratic Clubs Va., 1966-67; chmn. Washington County Dem. Com., 1967-69; Dem. nominee for U.S. Senate from Va., 1978. Bd. dirs. Barter Found., 1962-69; trustee King Coll., 1966-74; mem. adv. bd. Ams. for Effective Law Enforcement, 1973-77, Center for Oceans Law and Policy, 1975—; Served to 1st lt. AUS, 1955-57. Fellow Am. Bar Found.; mem. So. Conf. Attys. Gen. (vice chmn. 1972-73, chmn. 1973-74), Nat. Assn. Attys. Gen. (exec. com. 1973-74, chmn. antitrust com. 1971-76, Wyman Meml. award 1976), Am. (ho. dels. 1971-76, mem. action commn. to reduce ct. costs and delay 1979—), Va. (chmn. young lawyers sect. 1967-68) bar assns., Am. Judicature Soc. (dir. 1973-76, exec. com. 1974-76), Phi Beta Kappa, Omicron Delta Kappa. Presbyn. Home: 506 Summers Ct Alexandria VA 22301 Office: 2101 L St NW Washington DC 20037

MILLER, ANGELA, editor; b. Chester County, Pa., Jan. 15, 1947; d. William Harris and Elizabeth Ann (Cosgrove) Miller; 1 dau., Samantha Miller Skolnik. Asst. editor Oxford U. Press, N.Y.C., 1968-70; v.p. Arbor House Pub. Co., Inc., N.Y.C., 1972-76; sr. editor Stein & Day/Pubs., Briarcliff Manor, N.Y., 1976-77; exec. editor A & W Pubs. subs. Reed Holdings, N.Y.C., 1977—. Home: 801 West End Ave New York NY 10025 Office: A & W Publishers 95 Madison Ave New York NY 10016

MILLER, ANN (LUCILLE ANN COLLIER), actress, dancer, singer; b. Houston, Apr. 12; d. John Alfred and Clara Emma (Birdwell) Collier; student Lawlors Profl. Sch., Los Angeles, 1937. Appeared in numerous motion pictures, including; You Can't Take It With You, 1939, Room Service, 1939, Easter Parade, 1949, Kiss Me Kate, 1956, On the Town, 1950, Hit the Deck, 1952, That's Entertainment, 1976, Won Ton Ton, 1976; star stage show Mame on Broadway, 1969-70, also in Los Angeles, Fla., Ohio, Ga., 1970-71; star Broadway show Sugar Babies, 1979; appeared TV shows including: Perry Como, 1961, Xmas Spl., 1968, Bob Hope Show, 1961, Jonathan Winters Show, 1969, Ed Sullivan Show, 1958, 59, Palace Shows, 1966-68, also Heinz Soup Comml., 1971; appeared in Hello Dolly in Ohio and Indpls., 1971; tour with Anything Goes, Cactus Flower, 1978-79; TV spl. Dames at Sea, 1971, Can Can, 1972. Author: Miller High Life, 1972. Home: 618 N Alta Dr Beverly Hills CA 90210 Office: care Contemporary Korman Agy 132 Lasky Dr Beverly Hills CA 90212

MILLER, ARCHIBALD MCARTHUR, sculptor; b. Shawinigan, Que., Can., Feb. 18, 1930; s. Archibald McArthur and Jean Blyth (Morrison) M.; B.A. in French and English, McGill U., 1951; M.F.A., Cranbrook Acad., 1960. Tchr. French and English, Vaviore High Schs., Quebec; prof., chmn. fine arts U. Rochester (N.Y.), coordinator for fine arts dept. Sch. Visual Arts, N.Y.C. Office: Fine Arts Dept U Rochester Rochester NY 14627

MILLER, ARJAY, univ. dean; b. Shelby, Nebr., Mar. 4, 1916; s. Rawley John and Mary Gertrude (Schade) M.; B.S. with highest honors, U. Calif. at Los Angeles, 1937; postgrad. U. Calif. at Berkeley, 1938-40; LL.D., U. Calif. at Los Angeles, 1964, Whitman Coll., 1965, U. Nebr., 1965; m. Frances Marion Fearing, Aug. 18, 1940; children—Kenneth Fearing, Ann Elizabeth (Mrs. James Olstad). Teaching asst. U. Calif. at Berkeley, 1938-40; research technician Calif. State Planning Bd., 1941; economist Fed. Res. Bank San Francisco, 1941-43; asst. treas. Ford Motor Co., 1946-53, controller,

1953-57, v.p., controller, 1957-61, v.p. finance, 1961-62, v.p. of staff group, 1962-63, pres., 1963-68, vice chmn., 1968-69, now dir.; dean Grad. Sch. Bus., Stanford U., 1969-79, emeritus, 1979—; dir. Ford Motor Co., Trans World Corp., Wells Fargo Bank, Utah Internat. Inc., Levi Strauss & Co., So. Pacific Corp., Washington Post Co.; mem. Trilateral Commn., Econ. Policy Council UNA. Former chmn. Automobile Mfrs. Assn., Econ. Devel. Corp. Greater Detroit. Trustee, The Conf. Bd.; past chmn., life trustee Urban Inst.; mem. Public Adv. Commn. on U.S. Trade Policy, 1968-69, Pres.'s Nat. Commn. on Productivity, 1970-74; trustee Andrew W. Mellon Found., Eisenhower Exchange Fellowship, Brookings Instn., Internat. Exec. Service Corps; bd. dirs. Wm. and Flora Hewlett Found., S.R.I. Internat.; former pres. Detroit Press Club Found. Served from pvt. to capt. USAAF, 1943-46. Recipient Alumnus of Year Achievement award U. Calif. at Los Angeles, 1964; Distinguished Nebraskan award, 1968; Nat. Industry Leader award B'nai B'rith, 1968. Presbyterian. Mem. Am. Econ. Assn., Am. Fin. Assn., Beta Gamma Sigma, Alpha Kappa Psi. Clubs: Pacific Union, Bohemian. Home: 225 Mountain Home Rd Woodside CA 94062. *Everyone desires a better world, but desire alone will not bring it about. One must also acquire the necessary skills and training, and be willing to work hard.*

MILLER, ARNOLD RAY, labor union ofcl.; b. Leewood, W.Va., Apr. 25, 1923; s. George Matt and Lulu (Hoy) M.; student pub. schs., Leewood; m. Virginia Ruth Brown, Nov. 26, 1948; children—Larry Allen, Vickie Lynn. Bituminous coal miner, 1939-42, 50-70; pres. Black Lung Assn., 1970-72; v.p. spl. projects Designs For Rural Action, Inc., 1970-72; pres. United Mine Workers Am., Washington, 1972—, co-organizer Miners for Democracy, 1969; v.p. Miners Internat. Fedn., 1975—. Bd. dirs. Appalachian Research and Def. Fund, 1970-72; trustee United Mine Workers Am. Welfare and Retirement Fund, 1972-73. Served with AUS, 1942-46. Decorated Purple Heart. Democrat. Office: 900 15th St NW Washington DC 20005

MILLER, ARTHUR, playwright, author; b. N.Y.C., Oct. 17, 1915; s. Isadore and Augusta (Barnett) M.; A.B., U. Mich., 1938, L.H.D., 1956; m. Mary Grace Slattery, Aug. 5, 1940 (div.); children—Jane Ellen, Robert; m. Marilyn Monroe, June 1956 (div.); m. Ingeborg Morath, Feb. 1962; 1 dau. Playwright: Man Who Had All the Luck, 1944; Situation Normal, 1944; All My Sons (N.Y. Drama Critics award), 1948; Death of a Salesman (later motion picture) (N.Y. Drama Critics Circle award, Pulitzer prize 1949), 1949; The Crucible (Tony award), 1953; View from the Bridge (later motion picture), 1955; Collected Plays, 1958; After the Fall, 1963; Incident at Vichy, 1964; A Memory of Two Mondays, 1955; The Price, 1956; Up From Paradise; The Archbishop's Ceiling; I Don't Need You Anymore (story collection), 1967; author novels: Focus, 1945; The Misfits (later screenplay), 1960; The Price, 1968; The Creation of the World and Other Businesses, 1972; In Russia, 1969; also stories; author: (with Inge Morath) Chinese Encounters, 1979; asso. prof. drama U. Mich., 1973-74. Recipient Hopwood award for Playwriting U. Mich., 1936, 37; Theatre Guild Nat. Award, 1938; Antoinette Perry Award, 1953; Gold Medal for drama Nat. Inst. Arts and Letters, 1959; Anglo-Am. award, 1966; Creative Arts award Brandeis U., 1970. Address: care ICM 40 W 57th St New York NY 10019*

MILLER, ARTHUR LARUE, steel co. exec.; b. Kokomo, Ind., 1909; s. John E. and Emma (Coppock) M.; B.M.E., Purdue U., 1931; m. Genevieve Elvin, Aug. 18, 1933; children—Eleanor Jane, Sarah Elizabeth, Marjorie Diane. With Continental Steel Corp., Kokomo, 1933—, mech. engr., machine shop supt., constrn. engr., asst. chief engr., asst. gen. supt., gen. supt., 1954-56, v.p. ops., 1956-64, exec. v.p., 1964-65, pres., 1965-71, cons., 1971—. Chmn. Ind. Statewide Health Coordinating Council, 1977-78. Mem. Am. Iron and Steel Inst. (past dir.), Assn. Iron and Steel Engrs., Theta Chi. Rotarian. Home: 200 Forest Dr Kokomo IN 46901 Office: 1109 S Main St Kokomo IN 46902. *Do your best in every endeavor—the results will be the best ever.*

MILLER, ARTHUR LEONARD, educator; b. Saginaw, Mich., Apr. 28, 1907; s. Gustave August and Sophie (Haase) M.; student Concordia Tchrs. Coll., River Forest, Ill., 1922-27; Ph.B., U. Chgo., 1932, M.A., 1942, Ph.D., 1951; Litt.D., Concordia Tchrs. Coll., Seward, Nebr., 1965; m. Irene Ann Setzke, June 30, 1945; 1 son, John Arthur. Tchr., Nazareth Lutheran Sch., Chgo., 1927-35, teaching prin., 1935-46; exec. sec. Bd. Parish Edn., Lutheran Ch.-Mo. Synod, 1946-72; dir. placement Basic Inst. Tech., 1973-76; ednl. sales rep. Ency. Britannica, 1976—; lectr. Sch. Grad. Studies, Concordia Sem., St. Louis. Chmn. div. parish edn. and services Council Adminstrs., 1960-72. Participant White House Conf. on Children and Youth, 1950, White House Conf. on Edn., 1955, 60. Mem. Luth. Edn. Assn. Author: Curriculum in Arithmetic, 1946; Train Up a Child, 1946; Educational Administration and Supervision of Lutheran Schools, 1951; Handbook for Local Boards of Parish Education, 1959. Editor: Tests and Measurements in Lutheran Schools, 1957. Contbr. to Church and State Under God, 1964; Legal Aspects of Lutheran Education, 1964; America's Schools and Churches, 1965. Home: 5625 Rosa Ave St Louis MO 63109

MILLER, BARRY, dept. store exec.; b. N.Y.C., May 19, 1936; s. Mortimer Lawrence and Dora (Libow) M.; B.A., Ind. U., 1957; m. Elaine Regina Bassler, June 17, 1958; children—Andrea, Robert, Charles. Trainee to divisional mdse. mgr. F. & R. Lazarus Co., Columbus, Ohio, 1957-69; br. v.p., then v.p. and gen. mdse. mgr. Sanger Harris Co., Dallas, 1969-75; pres., chief merchandising officer Elder Beerman Stores, Dayton, Ohio, 1976—, also dir.; pres., owner Gidding-Jenny Splty. Dept. Store, Cin., 1977. Trustee, Miami Valley Sch., Dayton; bd. dirs. Temple Israel, Dayton. Recipient Retailing award Am. Mktg. Assn., 1974. Home: 6720 Beechlands Dr Cincinnati OH 45237 Office: 3155 Elbee Rd Morraine OH 45401

MILLER, BEN NEELY, physician; b. Smyrna, S.C., Dec. 20, 1910; s. Benjamin Neely and Addie Jane (Whitesides) M.; B.S., M.D., Duke U., 1935; m. Ruth Elizabeth Gambill, Dec. 27, 1938; children—Elizabeth Gambill, Jane Adelaide, Ben Neely. Med. resident Duke Hosp., Durham, N.C., 1935-37; instr. U. Ala. Med. Sch., 1937-38; practice of internal medicine, Columbia, S.C., 1938—; vis. lectr. U. S.C. Sch. Medicine, 1967-70, clin. prof. medicine, 1977—; past chief staff Providence, Baptist, Columbia hosps.; med. cons. S.C. State Hosp., S.C. Dept. Vocat. Rehab. Bd. dirs. United Community Services, 1959-62, public-at-large trustee, 1963-66; med. adv. com. United Health and Med. Research Found. S.C.; mem. S.C. Pollution Control Authority, 1970—; trustee Duke U. Diplomate Am. Bd. Internal Medicine. Fellow A.C.P., Am. Coll. Allergists, Am. Acad. Allergy; mem. AMA, Southeastern Allergy Assn. (pres. 1955-56), Duke Alumni Assn. (pres. 1960-61), Duke Med. Alumni Assn. (pres. 1955-61), S.C. Med. Assn. (sec. 1962-68, pres. 1970-71), S.C. Soc. Internal Medicine (past pres.), Columbia Med. Soc. (pres. 1950). Presbyterian (elder). Club: Forest Lake Country (Columbia). Home: 766 Spring Lake Rd Columbia SC 29206 Office: 1433 Gregg St Columbia SC 29201

MILLER, BEN ROBERTSON, lawyer, b. Sulphur Springs, Tex., July 18, 1905; s. Hollis Henry and Grace Gilbert (Robertson) M.; A.B., La. State U., 1927, LL.B., 1927, A.M., 1932; Rhodes scholar elect, 1927; m. Mary Margaret Terry, May 23, 1933; children—Ben Robertson, Terry Hollis. Admitted to La. bar, 1927, since practiced in Baton Rouge; co-founder firm Sanders, Miller, Downing & Kean, now ret. from firm; interim judge 20th Jud. Ct., 1976, Baton Rouge City Ct., 1976-77, 21st Jud. Ct., 1978; asst. atty. gen. State of La., 1977, 78, 79; vice consul of Norway, 1953-58; chmn. bd. emeritus Baton Rouge Savs. & Loan Assn.; dir. Comml. Securities Co., Inc., Audubon Ins. Co., Audubon Life Ins. Co. Former mem. exec. council Boy Scouts Am. Served as lt. comdr. USNR, 1943-46. Decorated knight Order of Saint Olav (Norway). Fellow Am. Bar Assn. (chmn. 1957, bar activities sect.; ho. of dels. 1952-68, 70-79, fed. jud. com. 1949-58; chmn. uniform rules of evidence com., 1958; mem. non-partisan selection of fed. jud. com. 1959-62, chmn. 1961-62; gov. 1963-66; mem. individual rights sect. council 1966-70, mem. criminal law sect. council 1969-76, chmn. 1974-75), Am. Coll. Probate Counsel (regent 1968-74); mem. Criminal Justice Inst. (chmn. 1977), Am. Judicature Soc. (dir. 1958-62), Scibes, Internat., Inter-Am., La. (gov. 1942, 52, vice chmn. law reform com. 1960-77, chmn. jud. selection com. 1968-74), Baton Rouge (pres. 1949) bar assns., Am., La. (council) law insts., Internat. Soc. Barristers, Jameston Soc., Barons of Magna Charta, English Speaking Union, Selden Soc., Soc. of Cincinnati, C. of C., Order of Coif, Phi Delta Phi, Kappa Alpha. Presbyn (elder). Clubs: Boston (New Orleans); Baton Rouge Golf and Country. Author: The Louisiana Judiciary, 1932; Louisiana Corporations and Forms, 1970; Memoirs of a Southern Lawyer, 1974. Contbr. articles to profl. jours. Home: 3125 McCarroll Dr Baton Rouge LA 70809 Office: Dept Justice State Capitol Box 44005 Baton Rouge LA 70804

MILLER, BENNETT, physicist, govt. ofcl.; b. N.Y.C., Jan. 18, 1938; s. Meyer Leon and Henrietta (Abramowitz) M.; A.B. magna cum laude (U.S. Rubber Co. scholar), Columbia, 1959, M.A. (Eugene Higgins fellow), 1961, Ph.D., 1965; m. Patricia Dawn Schoenhut, June 3, 1961; children—Beth Ann, Jeffrey Martin. Research asso. plasma physics lab. Columbia U., 1965-69, adj. asst. prof. physics, 1969; adj. asso. prof. physics Fairleigh Dickinson U., 1967-69; asst. prof. nuclear engring. Ohio State U., cons. Battelle Meml. Inst, Columbus, Ohio, 1969-70; physicist div. controlled thermonuclear research U.S. Dept. Energy (formerly AEC and ERDA), Washington, 1970-74, dep. asst. dir. for research, acting chief exptl. plasma research br., 1974-75, asst. dir. research, 1975-76, dir. Office Plans, Budget and Program Implementation Solar, Geothermal and Advanced Energy Systems, 1976-78, program dir. solar, geothermal, electric and storage systems, 1978—. Pres., Columbia Coll. Class of 1959 Alumni, 1965-69; v.p. Watkins Mill Elementary Sc. PTA, Gaithersburg, Md., 1970-71, pres., 1972-73. Finalist, White House Fellows Program, 1966; recipient Spl. Achievement certificate AEC, 1973. Hon. Woodrow Wilson fellow, 1960. Mem. Am. Phys. Soc. Contbr. articles to profl. jours. Home: 7512 Hackamore Dr Potomac MD 20854 Office: Solar Geothermal Electric and Storage Systems US Dept Energy Washington DC 20545

MILLER, BRUCE LOUIS, meat packing co. exec.; b. Cin., Apr. 6, 1942; s. Wayne D. M.; B.A. in Econs., Cornell U., 1964; M.B.A. in Mktg., Wharton Grad. Sch. Bus. Adminstrn., 1966; m. Susan Backus, Sept. 11, 1965; children—Lisa, Bruce Louis. Sr. mgmt cons. McKinsey & Co., Inc., Chgo., 1966-71; dir. bus. devel. dept. Pet, Inc., St. Louis, 1973-75, pres. St. Louis ops. grocery group, 1975-76; pres. Old El Paso Mexican Foods (Tex.), 1976-77; pres., chief exec. officer Glover, Inc., Roswell, N.Mex., 1977—. Co-founder, co-chmn. planning com. Minority Enterprise Small Bus. Investment Co., Chgo., 1970-71. Episcopalian. Contbr. chpt. to Minority Economic Development: A Resolution for the Seventies, 1973. Home: 38 Clermont Ln Saint Louis MO 63124

MILLER, C. ARDEN, physician, educator; b. Shelby, Ohio, Sept. 19, 1924; s. Harley H. and Mary (Thuma) M.; student Oberlin Coll., 1942-44; M.D. cum laude, Yale, 1948; m. Helen Meihack, June 26, 1948; children—John Lewis, Thomas Meihack, Helen Lewis, Benjamin Lewis. Intern, then asst. resident pediatrics Grace-New Haven Community Hosp., 1948-51; faculty U. Kans. Med. Center, 1951-66, dir. childrens rehab. unit, 1957-60, dean, provost, 1965-66, dean Med. Sch., dir. Med. Center, 1960-65; prof. pediatrics and maternal and child health U. N.C., Chapel Hill, 1966—, vice chancellor health scis., 1966-71, chmn. dept. maternal and child health, 1977; cons., UNICEF, HEW, World Bank; chmn. exec. com. Citizens Bd. Inquiry into Health Services for Am., 1968—; cons. United Mine Workers Welfare and Retirement Fund, 1973—; mem. adv. com. on nat. health ins. U.S. Ho. of Reps. Ways and Means Com., 1974—. Trustee Appalachian Regional Hosps., 1974, Alan Guttmacher Inst., Planned Parenthood Fedn. Am. Markie scholar in med. scis., 1955-60. Recipient Robert H. Felix Distinguished Service award St. Louis U., 1977. Hon. fellow Royal Soc. Health; mem. Am. Pub. Health Assn. (chmn. action bd. 1972—, pres. 1974-75), Soc. Pediatric Research, Assn. Am. Med. Colls. (v.p. 1965-66), Sigma Xi, Alpha Omega Alpha, Delta Omega. Mem. editorial bd. Jour. Med. Edn., 1960-66. Author numerous articles in field. Home: 908 Greenwood Rd Chapel Hill NC 27514

MILLER, C(HARLES) PHILLIP, JR., physician; b. Oak Park, Ill., Aug. 29, 1894; s. Charles Phillip and Louise (Pebbles) M.; B.S., U. Chgo., 1916; M.D., Rush Med. Coll., 1919; M.S., U. Mich., 1920; m. Florence Lowden, Oct. 20, 1931; children—Phillip Lowden, Warren Pullman. Intern Presbyn. Hosp., Chgo., 1918-19; vol. research asst. pathology U. Mich., 1919-20, asst. prof., 1920; asst. resident physician Hosp. of Rockefeller Inst. for Med. Research, 1920-24, asst. pathology and bacteriology, 1924-25; vol. research assistant Institut für Infektionskrankheiten Robert Koch, Berlin, 1926; asst. prof. medicine U. Chgo., 1925-30, asso. prof., 1930-41, prof., 1941-60, prof. emeritus, 1960—; cons. to Sec. of War, 1941-49; mem. Commn. Meningitis and Commn. on Air Borne Infection, Army Epidemiol. Bd., 1941-45; sr. sci. officer Office Sci. and Tech., Am. Embassy, London, 1948. Mem. NRC, mem. med. fellowship bd. 1947-53, exec. com. 1957-62; mem. Streptococcal Commn., Armed Forces Epidemiology Bd., 1949-54, mem. Commn. Radiation and Infection, 1963-68, mem. com. epidemiol. survey, 1968—; mem. divisional com. Biol. and Med. Scis., NSF, 1955-60; Neisseria subcom. Nomenclature Com. Internat. Assn. Microbiologists. Trustee Farm Found., 1943-64. Master A.C.P.; fellow Am. Acad. Microbiology; mem. Conf. Bd. Asso. Research Councils, Com. Internat. Exchange of Persons 1950-53, Radiation Research Soc. (councilor 1957-60), Am. Forest Assn., Am. Clin. and Climatol. Assn., A.M.A., A.A.A.S., Am. Assn. Immunologists, Am. Soc. Exptl. Pathology (sec.-treas. 1930-34, councillor 1934-36, v.p. 1936, pres. 1937), Am. Soc. Clin. Investn. (v.p. 1938), Assn. Am. Phys. (pres. 1956-57), Nat. Acad. Sci., Am. Soc. Exptl. Biology (sec. 1933), Chgo. Inst. Medicine, Am. Acad. Arts and Scis., Am. Soc. Microbiology, Soc. Exptl. Biology and Medicine (editorial bd. 1953-58), Soc. Gen. Microbiology (Gt. Britain), Soc. Mayflower Descs., Sigma Xi. Episcopalian. Clubs: Quadrangle, Wayfarers, Casino, Arts, Tavern (Chgo.); Cosmos (Washington). Home: 5757 Kimbark Ave Chicago IL 60637

MILLER, CARROLL LEE LIVERPOOL, educator; b. Washington, Aug. 20, 1909; s. William and Georgie E. (Liverpool) M.; B.A. magna cum laude, Howard U., 1929, M.A., 1930; Ed.D., Columbia Tchrs. Coll., 1952. Instr., Miles Coll., 1930-31; mem. faculty Howard U., 1931—, prof. edn., 1957—, chmn. dept., 1961-68. asso. dean Coll. Liberal Arts, 1961-64, acting dean Grad. Sch., 1964-66, dean Grad. Sch., 1966-74, prof. higher edn., 1974—, dir. summer session, 1964-70; instr. social studies D.C. pub. schs., evenings 1933-40; summer 1934; research asst. Commonwealth Va., 1938-39. Mem. adv. com. Nat. Conf. Problems Rural Youth Okla., 1963; participant conf. Commn. Civil Rights, 1962. Mem. exec. council Episcopal Diocese Washington, 1964-66, mem. dept. coll. work, 1957-67, mem. standing com., 1967-68, chmn. Interracial Task Force, 1969-70, mem. Commn. on Ministry, 1971-72, mem. Rev. Bd., 1973-76; mem. Episcopal Council Overseas Students and Visitors, 1960-63. Mem. Grad. Record Exams. Bd., 1965-70; exec. com. Council Grad. Schs. U.S., 1968-71; mem. com. grad. deans African-Am. Inst. Bd. dirs. D.C. Tb Assn., 1953-59, 65-71, D.C. Episcopal Center for Children, 1964-76, New Ednl. Ways, 1977—; trustee Absalom Jones Theol. Inst. Mem. Am. Personnel and Guidance Assn. (del. assembly 1963-65, 68-69, bd. dirs. 1972), Consortium of Univs. of Washington Met. Area (adminstrv. com. 1971—), Am. Assn. Colls. Tchr. Edn. (liaison rep. D.C. 1963-65), Am. Coll. Personnel Assn., Nat. Vocational Guidance Assn., Student Personnel Assn. Tchr. Edn. (pres. 1971-72), Nat. Soc. Study Edn., Assn. Higher Edn., Soc. Advancement Education, Assn. Tchr. Educators, A.A.A.S., Assn. for Gen. and Liberal Edn., Nat. Soc. Coll. Tchrs. of Edn., Am. Ednl. Studies Assn., Am. Acad. Polit. and Social Scis., Soc. Profs. Edn., Phi Delta Kappa, Kappa Delta Pi. Contbr. ednl. jour. Home: 1301 Delaware Ave SW Washington DC 20024

MILLER, CHARLES EDMOND, library adminstr.; b. Bridgeport, Conn., Aug. 3, 1938; s. Edmond and Irene Ovelia (Boudreaux) M.; student U. Hawaii, 1957-58; B.A., McNeese State U., 1964; M.S. in L.S., La. State U., 1966; m. Alice Ann Phillips, June 2, 1962; children—Alison, Charles Edmond, Catherine, Susan. Tchr. Lake Charles (La.) High Sch., 1964-65; mem. staff La. State U. Library, Baton Rouge, 1966-69; asso. dir. Tulane U. Library New Orleans, 1969-73; dir. Fla. State U. Library, Tallahassee, 1973—. Vis. coms. So. Assn. Colls. and Schs.; cons. in field. Adv. coms. State Library Fla. Served with USMCR, 1956-59. Mem. Fla., Southeastern library assns., A.L.A., Phi Kappa Phi, Beta Phi Mu, Sigma Tau Delta. Asst. editor La. Library Assn. Bull., 1967. Home: 2911 Shamrock S Tallahassee FL 32308

MILLER, CHARLES LESLIE, engr., planner, cons.; b. Tampa, Fla., June 5, 1929; s. Charles H. and Myrle Iona (Walstrom) M.; B.C.E., Mass. Inst. Tech., 1951, M.C.E., 1958; m. Roberta Jean Pye, Sept. 9, 1949; children—Charles Henry, Stephen, Jonathan, Matthew. Successively field engr., project engr., exec. engr. Michael Baker, Jr., Inc., cons. engrs., Rochester, Pa., 1951-55; asst. prof. surveying, dir. photogrammetry lab. Mass. Inst. Tech., 1955-59, asso. prof. civil engring., head data engring. div., 1959-61, prof. civil engring., 1961-77, head dept., 1961-70, dir. urban systems lab., 1968-75, dir. civil engring. systems lab., 1961-65, dir. inter-Am. program civil engring., 1961-65, asso. dean engring., 1970-71; cons. engr., 1955—; chmn. bd., sr. cons., pres. CLM Systems, Inc.; originator of DTM, COGO and ICES computer systems; adviser Commonwealth of P.R; dir. Geo-Transport Found. Chmn. Pres.-elect's Task Force on Transp., 1968-69. Recipient Outstanding Young Man of Greater Boston award; registered profl. engr., Mass., Fla., Tenn., N.H., R.I., P.R. Fellow Am. Acad. Arts and Scis.; mem. ASCE, N.Y. Acad. Scis., Am. Inst. Cons. Engrs., Am. Soc. Engring. Edn. (George Westinghouse award), Am. Soc. Photogrammetry, Am. Congress Surveying and Mapping, Am. Rd. Builders Assn., Transp. Research Bd., Assn. Computing Machinery, Sigma Xi, Chi Epsilon, Tau Beta Pi. Author tech. papers. Home: Hillside Farm Hill Rd Boxboro MA 01719 Office: 234 E Davis Davis Islands FL 33606

MILLER, CHARLES O., cons.; b. Cleve., Aug. 7, 1924; s. Richard Charles and Mildred (Bloomberg) M.; B.S., Mass. Inst. Tech., 1949; M.Systems Mgmt., U. So. Cal., 1967; m. Ilene Falls, Oct. 8, 1950; children—Sandra Lee (Mrs. Peter Koeller), Cheryl Ann (Mrs. Richard Davis), Deborah Susan (Mrs. Craig Rylant), Janice Ilene (Mrs. Charles Grimes), Kenneth Bartlett. Flight test engr. Douglas Aircraft Co., 1949-50; test pilot, engr. Chance Vought Corp., 1950-62; asst. to dir. Flight Safety Found., 1962-63; dir. research, lectr. Inst. Aerospace Safety and Mgmt., U. So. Calif., 1963-68; dir. bur. aviation safety Nat. Transp. Safety Bd., Washington, 1968-74; pres., prin. cons. System Safety, Inc., 1974—; lectr. U. So. Calif. Served with USNR, 1942-44, USMCR, 1944-46. Mem. Am. Inst. Aero. and Astronautics, Soc. Automotive Engrs., Soc. for Exptl. Test Pilots, Aerospace Med. Assn., Soc. Air Safety Investigators, System Safety Soc. (pres. 1967). Author 2 books on aerospace safety; contbr. articles to profl. jours. Home: 7722 Bridle Path Ln McLean VA 22102 Office: 6800 Fleetwood Rd Suite 905 McLean VA 22101. *Think as men of action. . .act as men of thought.*

MILLER, CHARLES WILLIAM, county mgr.; b. New Castle, Colo., Jan 4, 1922; s. William J. and Dubie Rose (Rogers) M.; B.S., U. Denver, 1947, M.S., 1948; m. Suzanne B. Tornow, Aug. 24, 1947; children—Clint Charles, Sue Anne. Research dir. Maricopa Tax Council, Phoenix, 1948-50; research cons. Ariz. Tax. Research Assn., Phoenix, 1950-53; finance dir. Maricopa County, 1953-56, county mgr., 1960-64, 69—; asst. v.p. Valley Nat. Bank, Phoenix, 1956-60, controller, 1964-69. Pres., clk. Washington Elementary Sch. Bd. Trustees, 1956-61. Served with Q.M. Corps, AUS, 1941- 45. Decorated Bronze Star; recipient award distinguished pub. service Maricopa County Med. Soc.; Superior Services award Ariz. chpt. Am. Soc. Pub. Adminstrn., 1973. Mem. Nat. Assn. County Adminstrs. (pres., dir.), Nat. Assn. Counties (dir.), Phoenix C. of C. (chmn. local govt. com. 1964-69), Budget Execs. Inst. (pres. 1968-69), Delta Sigma Pi. Methodist (chmn. stewardship and finance com. 1963, ofcl. bd. 1952-68, trustee 1969—). Mason, Kiwanian. Clubs: Phoenix Country, University (Phoenix). Home: 911 W Las Palmaritas Dr Phoenix AZ 85021 Office: Maricopa County Adminstrn Bldg 111 S 3d Ave Phoenix AZ 85003

MILLER, CHARLES WILLIAMS, educator; b. Detroit, July 18, 1908; s. Joseph A. and Hallye (Williams) M.; student U. Detroit, 1926-30; B.S., Marquette U., 1949; M.A. in Econs., U. Minn., 1950, Ph.D. in Bus. Adminstrn., 1952; Ford fellow Harvard, 1955; m. Leone Steidl, Jan 20, 1940; 1 son, David B. Mem. faculty Coll. Bus. Adminstrn., Marquette U., 1952-60, prof. marketing. 1957-60, chmn. dept., 1957-60; treas. Miller Brewing Co., Milw., 1960-65, chief exec. officer, pres., 1966-70; v.p. consumer products group W.R. Grace & Co., N.Y.C., 1965-66; prof. Coll. Bus. Adminstrn., Marquette U., 1970—; dir. W.R. Grace Co., Marshall & Isley Bank, Milw. Bd. dirs. pub. Expenditure Survey Wis., 1966-70, Met. Milw. Assn. Commerce, 1966-71, Milw. World Festival, 1966-70, Miller High Life Found., 1966-71, Grace Found., 1966—; bd. regents Marquette U., 1967-70; trustee Citizens Govtl. Research Bur., 1967-70; dir. Crusade for Family Prayer, Albany, N.Y., 1979—, Family Rosary, Albany, 1979—. Made Knight of Malta, 1979. Served to lt. USNR, 1943-64; capt. Res. ret. Home: 1020 Lone Tree Rd Elm Grove WI 53122 Office: Coll Bus Adminstrn Marquette U Milwaukee WI 53201

MILLER, CLARENCE E., Congressman; b. Lancaster, Ohio, Nov. 1, 1917; D.Pub. Service (hon.), Rio Grande (Ohio) Coll. m. Helen M. Brown; children—Ronald, Jacqueline Miller Williams. Formerly elec. engr. Ohio Fuel Gas Co.; mem. Lancaster City Council, 1957-63, mayor, 1963-65; mem. 90th-96th Congresses from 10th Ohio Dist., mem. appropriations com.; past mem. legis. com. Nat. League Cities; past mem. Ohio Municipal League; past mem. exec. com. Mayors

Assn. Ohio. Hon. mem. Ohio Valley Health Services Found., Ohio Mental Health Assn.; bd. dirs. Fairfield County chpt. ARC, YMCA; co-chmn. Fairfield County Kidney Found. Named Hon. Alumnus, Ohio U., Athens. Methodist. Republican. Club: Elks. Address: Rayburn House Office Bldg Washington DC 20515

MILLER, CLARENCE HARVEY, educator; b. Kansas City, Mo., Aug. 4, 1930; s. Clarence C. and Theresa (Woess) M.; A.B., St. Louis U., 1951; A.M., Harvard, 1952, Ph.D., 1955; m. Jeanne Catherine Zimmer, Sept. 5, 1959; children—Lucy, Paula, Christopher, Bartholomew. Instr. English, St. Louis U., 1957-60, asst. prof., 1960-63, asso. prof., 1963-66, prof., 1966-79, Dorothy Orthwein prof. English, 1969-79; exec. editor Project for Complete Edit. of Works of St. Thomas More, Yale U., New Haven, 1979—; Fulbright exchange prof. U. Würzburg, Germany, 1960-61; guest prof. Ruhr-U. Bochum, W.Ger., 1976-77; vis. prof. Yale U., 1979—. Guggenheim fellow, 1966-67. Editor: Praise of Folly, 1965, translator, 1979; St. Thomas More's De Tristitia Christi, 1976. Address: Univ Tower 129 York St New Haven CT 06511

MILLER, CLAUDE RUE, lawyer; b. Bowie, Tex., Nov. 9, 1906; s. Irad O. and Katherine (Lively) M.; LL.B., So. Methodist U., 1931; m. Irene Elizabeth Risser, Dec. 19, 1931; children—Anna Carolyn (Mrs. Andrew D. Cosby), Ralph Irad. Admitted to Tex. bar, 1931, Ill. bar, 1941; partner firm Strasburger, Price, Kelton, Miller & Martin, and predecessor, Dallas, 1931-66; engaged in individual practice of law, Dallas, 1967-72; mem. firm Miller, Blankenship & Potts, Dallas, 1972-76. Gen. counsel Mars, Inc., Chgo., 1943-49, Grant Advt. Inc., 1940-56; sec., dir. Morten Investment Co., 1934-63; chmn. bd. Comet Rice Mills, 1955-57; pres., chmn. bd. Comet Rice Mills, Inc. and subsidiaries, 1957-65; exec. v.p. Gulfco Corp., 1961-65; owner Southern Boat Co., 1949-65, Springwood Co., 1949—. Founding pres. Rice Council for Market Devel., 1957-60. Trustee Menninger Found., 1962—, Mangold Trusts. Mem. Am., Dallas bar assns. Methodist. Club: Dallas Country. Author: Practice of Law, 1946. Home: 4243 Fairfax Ave Dallas TX 75205

MILLER, D(AVID) THOMAS, TV exec.; b. Chgo., July 13, 1925; s. William Henry and Doris Marie (Jones) M.; B.S., Loyola U., Chgo., 1950; postgrad. U. Chgo., 1950-51; L.H.D., St. John's U., 1974; m. Miriam Therese Koenig, May 16, 1953; children—Thomas, William, Mary, Jill, Lawrence. Asst. research dir. ABC, Chgo., 1950-51; sales service mgr. CBS-TV Network, Chgo., 1951-53; account exec. CBS-TV, N.Y.C., 1954-61; v.p., gen. mgr. WLS-TV, Chgo., 1961-66; asst. to pres. Broadcast Group, CBS-TV, N.Y.C., 1967-70, pres. TV Stas. div., 1970-77, v.p. CBS Broadcast Group, 1977—. Bd. dirs. Big Bros., 1971—, Catholic Communications Found., 1972—. Served to 2d lt. USAAF, 1943-46. Mem. Internat. Radio and TV Soc. (dir. 1970), TV Bur. Advt. (dir. 1970), Advt. Council (dir. 1973—). Roman Catholic. Clubs: Siwanoy Country (Bronxville, N.Y.); Winged Foot Golf (Mamaroneck, N.Y.). Home: 25 Ridge Rd Bronxville NY 10708 Office: 51 W 52d St New York NY 10019

MILLER, DALE ALWORTH, community coll. pres.; b. Waterbury, Nebr., Aug. 13, 1932; s. Aaron William and Susie Evelyn (Endsley) M.; B.A., Calif. State U., Los Angeles, 1955, M.A., 1960; Ed.D., Stanford U., 1965; m. Carol June Procter, June 15, 1952; children—Terry Lee, Julie Marie, Lisa Louise. Dean coll. affairs Golden West Coll., Huntington Beach, Calif., 1965-73; adminstrv. asst. public info. and research, then elementary and jr. high sch. tchr. Inglewood (Calif.) Unified Sch. Dist., 1956-63; pres., dist. supt. Shasta Coll., Redding, Calif., 1973—; cons. in field. Bd. dirs. Shasta County Manpower Commn., 1976—, Haven Humane Soc., 1976—, Lutheran Council Huntington Beach, 1969-71, Shasta County United Way, 1974—, March of Dimes, 1968-73. Served with USN, 1953-55; Korea. Recipient various service awards. Mem. Assn. Calif. Community Coll. Adminstrs., Greater Redding C. of C. (dir. 1975—), Phi Delta Kappa. Club: Redding Rotary (dir. 1975—). Office: 1065 N Old Oregon Trail Redding CA 96001

MILLER, DANIEL NEWTON, JR., geologist; b. St. Louis, Aug. 22, 1924; s. Daniel Newton and Glapha (Shuhardt) M.; B.S. in Geology, Mo. Sch. Mines, 1949, M.S., 1951; Ph.D., U. Tex., 1955; m. Esther Faye Howell, Sept. 9, 1950; children— Jeffrey Scott, Gwendolyn Esther. Intermediate geologist Stanolind Oil and Gas Co., 1951-52; sr. geologist Pan Am. Petroleum Corp., 1955-60, Monsanto Chem. Co., 1960-61; cons. geologist Barlow and Haun, Inc., Casper, Wyo., 1961-63; prof. geology, chmn. dept. So. Ill. U., 1963-69; state geologist, exec. dir. Wyo. Geol. Survey, 1969—; adj. prof. geology U. Wyo., 1969—. Mem. Interstate Oil Compact Commn., 1969—. Served with USAAF, 1943-46. Decorated Air medal; recipient award merit So. Ill. U., 1967. Mem. Am. Assn. Petroleum Geologists (chmn. govt. liaison com. 1970-71), Am. Inst. Profl. Geologists, Assn. Am. State Geologists (pres. 1979-80). Co-editor: Overthrust Belt of Southwestern Wyoming, 1960; gen. editor Geology and Petroleum Production of the Illinois Basin, 1968. Contbr. articles to profl. jours. Patentee exhaustoport for automobiles. Home: 1017 Sheridan St Laramie WY 82070 Office: Geol Survey Wyo Laramie WY 82071. *Use everything you know, in everything you do, all the time.*

MILLER, DANIEL WEBER, physicist, educator; b. Omaha, Jan 24, 1926; s. Merritt Finley and Flora Grace (Ernst) M.; B.S. in Elec. Engring., U. Mo., 1947; Ph.D. in Physics (AEC predoctral fellow), U. Wis., 1951; m. Carolyn Leigh Hunt, Dec. 26, 1947; children—Debra Leigh, Douglas Hunt. Mem. faculty Ind. U., 1951—, prof. physics, 1962—, asso. dean Coll. Arts and Scis. 1962-64, acting chmn. physics dept. 1964-65, asso. dean research and advanced studies, 1972-73, faculty rep. to Big Ten Conf., 1973-78, co-prin. investigator nuclear reactions research, asso. dir. cyclotron facility, 1968-79, co-dir., 1979—; cons. Los Alamos Sci. Lab., 1959-64, Sabbatical visitor, spring 1979; Sabbatical visitor Lawrence Berkeley Lab., spring 1972; spl. research exptl. nuclear physics. Del. Argonne Univs. Assn., 1966—. Bd. dirs. Midwestern Univs. Research Assn., 1964-71. Served with USNR, 1944-46. Fellow Am. Phys. Soc. (chmn. publs. com. div. nuclear physics 1975-77, mem. council publs. com. 1977-79); mem. AAAS, Sigma Xi, Tau Beta Pi, Eta Kappa Nu. Author profl. articles. Home: 1030 S High St Bloomington IN 47401

MILLER, DAVID, lawyer, advt. exec.; b. Fort Worth, Dec. 12, 1906; s. Max and Tillie (Hoffman) M.; A.B. cum laude, U. Tex., 1926; LL.B. cum laude, Harvard, 1929; m. Rosalie Agress, Jan 31, 1929; children—Allan David, Martha Sally. Admitted to N.Y. State bar, 1931, with law firm of Jones, Clark & Higson, N.Y. City, 1929-33; pvt. practice with Harold W. Newman, Jr., 1937-44; mem. law firm of Engel, Judge & Miller, 1944-74; counsel RFC, Washington, 1933-34; asst. gen. counsel Md. Casualty Co., Balt., 1934-36; with Office of Gen. Counsel, Securities & Exchange Commn. 1936-37; v.p. and gen. counsel Young & Rubicam, Inc., Advt. agy., 1951-71, sec., dir., sr. v.p., 1971—; counsel Squadron, Ellenoff & Plesent, 1974—; v.p., sec., gen. counsel The Music Project for TV, Inc., 1973—. Trustee Motion Picture Players Welfare Fund, Am. Fedn. TV & Radio Artists Pension and Welfare Fund. Cons. joint policy com. Am. Assn. Advt. Agys.-Assn. Nat. Advertisers. Mem. Am. Bar Assn., Assn. Bar City N.Y., N.Y. County Lawyers' Assn., Am. Assn. Advt. Agencies (cons. broadcast business affairs com.), Phi Beta Kappa. Lecturer on radio and TV law for professional groups. Editor: Harvard Law Review, 1927-29. Club: Harvard (N.Y.). Home: 30 Arleigh Rd Great Neck NY 11021 Office: 551 Fifth Ave New York NY 10017

MILLER, DAVID HEWITT, sci. educator; b. 1918; A.B. cum laude, U. Calif. at Los Angeles, 1939, M.A., 1944; Ph.D., U. Calif., Berkeley, 1953; D.Litt. (hon.), U. Newcastle, 1979; m. Enid Woodson Brown. Meteorologist, U.S. Corps Engrs., 1941-43; forecaster Trans World Airlines, 1943-44; meteorologist, hydrologist Coop. Snow Investigations, San Francisco, 1946-53; geographer U.S. Natick (Mass.) Labs., 1953-59; meteorologist, hydrologist U.S. Forest Service, 1959-64; prof. atmospheric scis. U. Wis.-Milw., 1964—; climatologist Q.M. Gen. Office, 1944-46; Fulbright lectr., Australia, 1966, 71, 79; exchange scientist Acad. Scis., Moscow, 1969; mem. adv. com. climatology Nat. Acad. Scis., 1958-64. NSF fellow, 1952-53. Mem. Am. Geophys. Union (transl. bd. 1972-76), Am. Meteorol. Soc., Ecol. Soc. Am., Soc. Am. Foresters, Assn. Am. Geographers, Inst. Australian Geographers, Phi Beta Kappa, Sigma Xi. Author: Snow Cover and Climate, 1955; (with others) Snow Hydrology, 1956; Heat and Water Budget of Earth's Surface, 1965; Water at the Surface of the Earth, 1977; editor: Climate and Life (M.I. Budyko), 1974. Office: Dept Geol Scis U Wis-Milw Milwaukee WI 53201

MILLER, DAVID PHILIP, pub. exec.; b. Warwick, N.Y., Nov. 29, 1921; s. Howard Pierson and Katherine M. (Avery) M.; B.S., Rutgers U., 1949; m. Carol A. Lovell, May 10, 1952; children—Dean, Mark, Keith, Kevin, Alan. With McGraw-Hill Co., N.Y.C., 1950-52; asst. v.p. W.B. Saunders Co., Phila., 1952-69; pub. med. dept. Harper-Row, Pubs., Hagerstown, Md., 1969—, v.p., 1976—. Served with USAAF, 1942-46. Ky. Col. Mem. Rutgers Rowing Assn., Nat. Rifle Assn., Delta Kappa Epsilon. Home: 131 E Potomac St Williamsport MD 21795 Office: 2350 Virginia Ave Hagerstown MD 21740

MILLER, DEAN EDGAR, lawyer; b. Caldwell, Idaho, Sept. 26, 1922; s. Dean Wilson and Mary A. (Meek) M.; LL.B., U. Idaho, 1949; m. Josephine Ney, Aug. 20, 1945; children—Dean J., Nicholas G., Thomas F., Mary M., Patrick J. Admitted to Idaho bar, 1949; gen. practice law, Caldwell, 1949—; partner firm Gigray, Miller, Downen & Weston, 1976—. Active Democratic Party, including del. Nat. Conv., 1968. Served with U.S. Army, 1942-46; PTO. Recipient award of legal merit U. Idaho Coll. Law, 1978. Mem. Am. Bar Assn., Am. Trial Lawyers Assn., Idaho State Bar (pres. 1977). Roman Catholic. Club: Elks (pres. Idaho 1965). Contbr. articles to law revs. Home: 2201 Washington St Caldwell ID 83605 Office: 9th and Dearborn Sts Caldwell ID 83605

MILLER, DEAN HAROLD, flutist; b. Fremont, Ohio, Mar. 25, 1940; s. Harold Tucker and Elma Catherine (Perrin) M.; Mus.B., Curtis Inst. Music, Phila., 1963; artist's diploma (Fulbright scholar), Vienna Acad. Music (Austria), 1965; m. AnnMarie Louise Boldt, May 29, 1971; children—Christa Elizabeth, Catherine Dorothea, Angela Marie. Instr. music Ball State U., Muncie, Ind., 1965-66; 1st flutist Que. Symphony Orch., 1966-68; asst. 1st flutist Minn. Orch., 1968-69; 1st flutist New Orleans Philharmonic Symphony Orch., 1969—. Prin. flutist, Sante Fe Opera Orch., summers, 1969-72; ednl. concerts in schs. Young Audiences, Inc.; performer Festival of the Two Worlds, Spoleto, Italy, 1963. Home: 8216 Spruce St New Orleans LA 70118

MILLER, DELMAS FERGUSON, coll. dean; b. McMechen, W.Va., Feb. 26, 1907; s. Francis B. and Sarah Ann (Wilson) M.; A.B., West Liberty State Coll., 1931; M.A., W.Va. U., 1934; Ph.D., U. Pitts., 1943; m. Myrtle Conner, June 7, 1932; children—Priscilla (Mrs. Charles Haden II), Bette Jo (Mrs. David Hobbs.). Prin. Moundsville (W.Va.) Jr. High Sch., 1930-38; prin. Moundsville (W.Va.) High Sch., 1938-50; prin. University High Sch., Morgantown, W.Va., 1950-56; dir. tchr. edn. W.Va.. U., 1957-68, dean 1969—. Mem. W.Va. Edn. Assn. (pres. 1953-54), Nat. Assn. Secondary Sch. Prins. (pres. 1968-69). Mason, Rotarian (pres. 1945-46). Author (with J. L. Trump) Secondary School Curriculum Improvement, 1969; contbg. author to Harl Douglas' The High School Curriculum, 1966, Alexander's The Changing Secondary School Curriculum, 1967. Home: 1289 Jacobs Dr Morgantown WV 26505

MILLER, DON ROBERT, surgeon; b. Highland, Kans., July 6, 1925; s. Pleasant V. and Lucy Anna (Hammond) M.; A.B., Westminster Coll., 1944; M.D., U. Kans., 1948; m. Geraldine Ellen Nelson, Sept. 6, 1947; children—Don R., Laurie, Todd, Marcia, Kristen, Felicia. Mem. faculty U. Kans., Kansas City, 1957-73, prof. surgery, 1970-73; prof. surgery U. Calif. at Irvine, 1973—; dir. surgery Orange County (Calif.) Med. Center, 1973—. Served with USNR, 1943-45, 50-52. Spl. research fellow Zurich, Switzerland, 1965-66. Fellow A.C.S., Am. Coll. Cardiology; mem. Am. Soc. Univ. Surgeons, Soc. Vascular Surgery, Am. Assn. Thoracic Surgery, Am., Central, Western surg. assns., Internat. Cardiovascular Soc., Sigma Xi, Alpha Omega Alpha. Research extracorporeal circulation, myocardial function; contbr. articles to profl. jours. Home: 1211 Starboard St Corona Del Mar CA 92625 Office: Dept Surgery U Calif Irvine CA 92664

MILLER, DONALD BALDWIN, advt. exec.; b. Phila., Jan. 3, 1926; s. Herbert Luther and Jeannette (Baldwin) M.; B. Journalism, U. Mo., 1949; student, U. Kans., 1943; m. E. Jean Duross, Nov. 1, 1951; children—Patricia, James. With radio sta. WRNY, 1949-50, J.B. Haines Advt. Co., Phila., 1950-51; with Rumrill Co., Rochester, N.Y., 1951-67, v.p. mktg. and sales, 1960-64, exec. v.p., dir., 1964-67; pres. Rumrill-Hoyt, Inc., N.Y.C., 1967-70, chmn. bd., 1970—; dir. Compton Advt. Inc., Lexington Growth Fund, Inc., Onondago Litho Supply Co., Lexington Research Fund. Bd. dirs., exec. com., regional v.p. Asso. Industries N.Y. State; past bd. dirs. Rochester YMCA. Mem. Bus. and Profl. Advt. Assn., Am. Assn. Advt. Agys. (past chmn. Eastern region, past chmn. N.Y.C. council), Advt. Council. Home: 48 Silver Ridge Rd New Canaan CT 06840 Office: 635 Madison Ave New York NY 10017

MILLER, DONALD CALVIN, banker; b. Geneseo, Ill., Mar. 31, 1920; s. Otto H. and Mary (Erdman) M.; A.B., U. Ill., 1942, A.M., 1943, Ph.D., 1948; m. Marjorie Grace Morgan, Dec. 18, 1943; children—Barbara Grace, Donald Calvin, Douglas Morgan. Asst. prof. econs. U. Calif. at Los Angeles, 1949-51; economist, chief govt. fin. sect. Bd. Govs. FRS, 1951-58; 2d v.p. Continental Ill. Nat. Bank & Trust Co., Chgo., 1958-59, v.p., 1959-68, sr. v.p., 1968-72, exec. v.p., 1972—, vice chmn. bd. dirs., 1976—; public gov. Chgo. Merc. Exchange, 1979—; dir. Royal Globe Ins. Co., A.E. Staley Mfg. Co.; mem. faculty adminstrv. com., asso. dir. Grad. Sch. Banking, U. Wis., Madison. Bd. dirs. U. Ill. Found. Served with AUS, 1943-46. Mem. Am. Bankers Assn. (govt. borrowing com.), Assn. Res. City Bankers, Nat. Tax Assn. (treas. 1961—), U.S. C. of C. (dir. 1979—), Phi Beta Kappa, Beta Theta Pi. Author: Taxes, The Public Debt and Transfers of Income, 1950. Home: 415 N Adams St Hinsdale IL 60521 Office: 231 S LaSalle St Chicago IL 60693

MILLER, DONALD HERBERT, JR., pub. exec.; b. N.Y.C., Apr. 7, 1914; s. Donald Herbert and Blanche Theola (Gray) M.; A.B., Dartmouth, 1937; m. Constance Hoague, June 21, 1939 (div. 1949); children—Linda, Geoffrey; m. 2d, Claire Strauss, Feb. 25, 1949; children—Meredith, Donald, Bruce, Sheila. Asst. mgr. circulation Honolulu Star Bull., 1937-40; Honolulu Advertiser, 1940-41; exec. asst. to dir. gen. Can. Dept. Munitions and Supply, Washington, 1941-45; asso. Handy Assos., Inc., Mgmt. Cons., N.Y.C., 1945-46; organizer (with Gerard Piel and Dennis Flanagan) v.p., sec., dir., gen. mgr., pub. Sci. Am., N.Y.C., 1946-79, now dir.; dir. AEL Industries, Inc., Lansdale, Pa., W.H. Freeman & Co., San Francisco, Ednl. Found. Nuclear Sci., Inc., pub. Bull. Atomic Scientists, Chgo. Club: University (N.Y.C.). Home: 31 Seneca Dr Chappaqua NY 10514 Office: 415 Madison Ave New York NY 10017

MILLER, DONALD LANG, banker; b. Winchester, Mass., Mar. 21, 1922; s. Francis Warren and Viola (Lang) M.; B.A., Dartmouth Coll., 1943; m. Lillian Hake Lary, June 17, 1954; children—John, Janette Miller Kaufman, Barbara Miller Ewell, Susan, Steven. With First Nat. Bank Boston, 1964—, v.p., 1965-66, sr. v.p., 1966-67, exec. v.p. comml. banking, 1967—; dir. First Capital Corp., Boston, First Bank Fin. Corp. Mem. Hamilton (Mass.) Sch. Com., 1955-63, chmn., 1959-63; commr. Hamilton Bd. Pub. Works, 1969—; chmn. fin. com. Children's Cancer Research, Boston. Served to lt. (s.g.) USNR, 1943-46. Mem. Phi Gamma Delta. Episcopalian. Clubs: Masons, Union (Boston). Home: 351 Bay Rd South Hamilton MA 01982 Office: 100 Federal St Boston MA 02110

MILLER, DONALD PETER, former newspaper pub.; b. Allentown, Pa., Mar. 17, 1906; s. David Aaron and Blanche (Berkemeyer) M.; A.B., Muhlenberg Coll., 1928; grad. student Oxford (Eng.) U., 1929; M.B.A., Harvard, 1931; m. Marjorie Wright, June 21, 1935 (dec. Feb. 1977); children—Joan (Mrs. David Moran), Alice, Edward. Editor, pub. Call Chronicle Newspapers, Allentown, 1934—, editor, 1941-68, exec. v.p., 1968—, pub., 1967-79, emeritus, 1979—; dir. Park & Shop, Inc., 1946—. Mem. Pa. German Soc., Inst. Newspaper Controllers and Finance Officers. Mem. United Ch. Christ. Club: Livingston (Allentown). Home: 2324 Lehigh Pkwy N Allentown PA 18103 Office: 101 N 6th St Allentown PA 18105

MILLER, DONALD SPENCER, geologist; b. Ventura, Calif., June 12, 1932; s. Spencer Jacob and Marquerite Rachael (Williams) M.; B.A., Occidental Coll., 1954; M.A., Columbia U., 1956, Ph.D., 1960; m. Carolyn Margaret Losee, June 12, 1954; children—Sandra Louise, Kenneth Donald, Christopher Spencer. Asst. prof. Rensselaer Poly. Inst., Troy, N.Y., 1960-64, asso. prof., 1964-69, prof., 1969—, chmn. dept. geology, 1969-76; research asso. geology Columbia U., 1960-63; research fellow geochemistry Calif. Inst. Tech., Pasadena, summer 1963; NSF Sci. Faculty fellow U. Bern (Switzerland), 1966-67; sci. guest prof. Max-Planck Inst. Nuclear Physics, Heidelberg, W. Ger., 1977-78, vis. prof., summer 1979; vis. prof. Isotope Geology Lab., U. Berne, summer 1979. Pres., treas. Troy Rehab. and Improvement, Inc., 1968-74; mem. Troy Zoning Bd. Appeals, 1970—. Fellow Geol. Soc. Am.; mem. Am. Geophys. Union, Geochem. Soc., Nat. Assn. Geol. Tchrs., Sigma Xi, Sigma Pi Sigma. Home: 2198 Tibbits Ave Troy NY 12180

MILLER, DONALD WILLIAM, librarian; b. Cornwall, Ont., Can., July 19, 1933; s. William Laurence and Jessie Munro (MacDermid) M.; B.A., U. Toronto (Ont.), 1957; M.L.S., U. B.C. (Can.), Vancouver, 1964; m. Patricia Marie Kirk, Mar. 27, 1965; children—Michael, Alison. Library asst. Scarborough Public Library, 1961-62; head reference dept. Calgary (Alta.) Public Library, 1964-66; asst. dir. London (Ont.) Public Library, 1966-71; dir. Greater Victoria (B.C., Can.) Public Library, 1971—. Pres., Art Gallery Greater Victoria, 1976-78. Mem. Can. Library Assn. (chmn. sect. adult services 1970-71), B.C. Library Assn. (pres. 1974-75), Instn. Victoria Librarians. Home: 339 Foul Bay Rd Victoria BC V8S 4G6 Canada Office: 794 Yates St Victoria BC V8W 1L4 Canada

MILLER, DONN BIDDLE, lawyer; b. Gallipolis, Ohio, July 10, 1929; s. Harry M. and Ernestine (Biddle) M.; B.A., Ohio Wesleyan U., 1951; J.D., U. Mich., 1954; grad. Advanced Mgmt. Program, Harvard, 1974; m. Margaret P. Sibert, Nov. 6, 1959; children—Robin, Karen, Arthur. Admitted to Ohio bar, 1954, Calif. bar, 1960; with firm Squire, Sanders & Dempsey, Cleve., 1956-59, O'Melveny & Myers, Los Angeles, 1959-74, 77—; exec. v.p. Carter Hawley Hale Stores, Inc., Los Angeles, 1974-77, also dir.; dir. Pacific Mutual Life Ins. Co., Edgington Oil Co., Pearson Sibert Oil Co. Tex. Mem. Los Angeles County Pub. Commn. on County Govt., 1975-76; pres. Conf. Calif. Pub. Utility Counsel, 1969. Trustee Ohio Wesleyan U., 1975-78, Sch. Theology at Claremont (Calif.), 1976-78; bd. dirs. United Way; mem. com. visitors U. Mich. Law Sch., 1971-74. Served with USAF, 1954-56. Rotary Found. fellow, 1951. Mem. Am. (mem. council pub. utilities sect. 1962-65, chmn. com. partnerships and inc. bus. orgns. 1970), Calif., Ohio, Los Angeles, Cleve. bar assns., Los Angeles C. of C. (v.p. 1976, dir. 1973-78), Phi Beta Kappa, Order of Coif, Sigma Chi, Omicron Delta Kappa, Delta Sigma Rho, Pi Sigma Alpha, Phi Delta Phi. Methodist (trustee ch.). Clubs: California, Stock Exchange, Los Angeles Country, Chancery (Los Angeles). Home: 308 Loring Ave Los Angeles CA 90024 Office: 611 W 6th St Los Angeles CA 90017

MILLER, DUANE LEON, ins. co. exec.; b. Oskaloosa, Iowa, July 31, 1937; s. Marvin L. and Cora Mae (Ver Steeg) M.; student Central Coll., Pella, Iowa, 1955-57; B.A. in Math., U. Iowa, 1959; M.B.A., Ill. State U., Normal, 1972; m. Suzanne Schoon, May 1, 1958; children—Debra, Jeffrey. With Ill. Agrl. Assn. and its affiliate, 1959-79, asst. v.p. fin., asst. treas., Bloomington, 1971-72, v.p. fin., treas., 1972-74; exec. v.p., chief exec. officer Country Life Ins. Co., Country Mut. Ins. Co., Country Ins. Co., Country Casualty Ins. Co., Country Capital Mgmt. Co., CC Services, Inc. and 3 related mut. funds, Bloomington, 1974—; pres. Ill. Ins. Info. Service, 1978-79; mem. governing bd. Property Loss Research Bur. Bd. dirs. Brokaw Hosp., Normal, 1976—; pres. United Way of McLean County (Ill.), 1977. C.P.A., Ill. Mem. Nat. Assn. Ind. Insurers (governing bd.), Conf. Casualty Ins. Cos. (past dir.), Nat. Assn. Ind. Insurers Safety Assn. (gov.), Am. Inst. C.P.A.'s. Presbyterian. Office: 1701 Towanda Ave Bloomington IL 61701

MILLER, DWIGHT CAMERON, art historian; b. St. Louis, Nov. 4, 1923; s. Charles Russell and Pearl (High) M.; B.A., U. Rochester, 1949; M.A., Harvard U., 1951; Ph.D., U. Chgo., 1959; m. Marion Elaine Benedict, June 15, 1950; children—David, Angela, Dwight, Alicia. Mem. faculty dept. art history U. Kans., Lawrence, U. Ill., Champaign, prof. art history Stanford U., 1965—. Served with USAAF, 1943-46. Mem. Coll. Art Assn. Contbr. articles to profl. jours. Home: 2210 Page Mill Rd Palo Alto CA 94304 Office: Art Dept Stanford Univ Stanford CA 94305

MILLER, E. WILLARD, geographer; b. Turkey City, Pa., May 17, 1915; s. Archie Howard and Tessie Bernella (Master) M.; M.A., U. Nebr., 1939; Ph.D., Ohio State U., 1942; m. Ruby Skinner, June 27, 1941. Instr., Ohio State U., 1941-43; asst. prof. geography and geology Western Res. U., 1943-44; asso. prof. geography Pa. State U., University Park, 1945-49, prof., 1949—, chief div. geography, 1945-53, head dept. geography, 1954-63, asst. dean for resident instrn. Coll. Earth and Mineral Scis., 1964-72, asso. dean, 1972—, asst. dean for resident instrn. and continuing edn., 1967-69; dir. Acad. Year Inst., Earth Scis., NSF, 1967-71; geographer OSS, Washington, 1944-45; spl. research onArctic environ. problems for Q.M. Gen., U.S. Army, 1947-50; geographic adviser Thomas Y. Crowell Co. Recipient certificate of merit from OSS; Whitback award Nat. Council Geog. Edn., 1950; Pa. Gov.'s citation for contbn. to Commonwealth,

1975; Pa. Dept. Commerce Sec.'s Meritorious Services award, 1975. Fellow Explorers Club, Am. Geog Soc., AAAS, Nat. Council Geog. Edn.; mem. Am. Inst. Mining, Metall. and Petroleum Engrs., Am. Soc. Profl. Geographers (pres. 1948), Assn. Am. Geographers, Pa. Acad. Sci. (pres. 1966-68, Spl. Services award 1976), Am. Geophys. Union, Sigma Xi, Pi Gamma Mu. Author: Careers in Geography, 1948 (rev. 1955); (with others) The World's Nations—An Economic and Regional Geography, 1958; chpt., Mineral Fuels, in Our Natural Resources and Their Conservation, 1950, rev. edits., 1958, 65, 71; A Geography of Manufacturing, 1962; An Economic Atlas of Pennsylvania, 1964; (with G. Langdon) Exploring Earth Environments: A World Geography, 1964; Energy Resources of the United States, 1968; Mineral Resources of the United States, 1968; A Geography of Industrial Location, 1970; A Socio-Economic Atlas of Pennsylvania, 1974; Manufacturing: A Study of Industrial Location, 1977; Industrial Location: A Bibliography, 1978; (with Ruby M. Miller) Economic, Political and Regional Aspects of the World's Energy Problems, 1979; editor: Global Geography, 1957; editorial dir. Earth and Mineral Scis. Bull., 1967-69; asso. editor The Pennsylvania Geographer; contbg. editor Producers Monthly Mag. Contbr. articles to sci. jours. Home: 845 Outer Dr State College PA 16801

MILLER, EDWARD AUGUST, bus. exec.; b. Bklyn., Aug. 28, 1915; s. August and Sophie (Van Axen) M.; C.E., Cornell U., 1943, M.C.E., 1943; m. Dorothy Shaver, Nov. 1, 1943; children—Edward August, Greta Katherine, William Van Axen, Douglas MacRae. With Fenestra, Inc., Detroit, 1943-61, successively research engr. bldg. panel div., chief engr., mgr., v.p. bldg. products div. 1943-59, exec. v.p., 1959, pres., 1959-62; acting dir. Thyssen Bauelemente Gmbh, Dusseldorf, Germany, 1962; mgr. fabricated sheet products Am. Bridge div. U.S. Steel, 1962-63; sec.-treas. Metal Roof Deck Tech. Inst., 1945-55, pres., 1957-58; pres. Albert Pick Co., Inc., Chgo., also Hobb Electric Supply Co., N.Y.C., subsidiaries Straus Duparquet, Inc., N.Y.C., 1964-65; pres. Hill Electronics, Inc., Mechanicsburg, Pa., 1965-69, also dir.; gen. mgr. Erie Frequency Control, Carlisle, Pa., 1969—. Chmn., Cumberland County Redevel. Authority. Mem. bd. Sir Edward Coke Found. Registered profl. engr., N.Y., Mich. Mem. ASTM, ASCE, Engring. Soc. Detroit, Cumberland County Redevel. Authority, Sigma Xi, Delta Chi, Tau Beta Pi, Chi Epsilon. Clubs: Detroit Athletic, Economic (Detroit); Ill. Athletic; Cornell (N.Y.C.). Holder patents light-gauge structural sects. Home: 6 Creekside Ln Camp Hill PA 17011 Office: 453 Lincoln St Carlisle PA 17013

MILLER, EDWARD B., lawyer; b. Milw., Mar. 26, 1922; s. Edward A. and Myra (Munsert) M.; B.A., U. Wis., 1942, LL.B., 1947; student Harvard Bus. Sch., 1942-43; m. Anne Harmon Chase Phillips, Feb. 14, 1969; children by previous marriage—Barbara Miller Anderson, Ellen Miller Gerkens, Elizabeth, Thomas; stepchildren—T. Christopher Phillips, Sarah Phillips. Admitted to Wis. bar, 1947, Ill. bar, 1948; with firm Pope, Ballard, Shepard & Fowle, Chgo., 1947-51, 52-70, partner, 1953-70, 75—; exec. asst. to industry mems. Regional Wage Stblzn. Bd., Chgo., 1951-52; chmn. NLRB, Washington, 1970-74; dir. Chgo. Wheel & Mfg. Co., 1965-70, 75—, Andes Candies, Inc., 1965-68, 75—. Mem. Gov. Ill. Commn. Labor-Mgmt. Policies for Pub. Employees, 1966-67; chmn. Midwest Pension Conf., 1960-61; mem. labor relations com. Ill. C. of C., 1953-70. Bd. dirs. Am. Found. Continuing Edn., 1960-69. Served to lt. USNR, 1943-46. Mem. Am. (NLRB practice and procedures com.), Ill., Wis. bar assns., Order of Coif. Republican. Conglist. Clubs: Legal, Law, Cliff Dwellers (Chgo.). Home: 632 Chatham Rd Glenview IL 60025 Office: 69 W Washington St Chicago IL 60602

MILLER, EDWARD DAVID, editor, pub.; b. Allentown, Pa., Apr. 25, 1942; s. Donald Peter and Marjorie (Wright) M.; student Williams Coll.; m. Elizabeth Mest, Apr. 7, 1979; children—Grace Mest, Julie Mest, Christina Miller, Hillary Miller. Copy editor internat. edit. N.Y. Herald Tribune, Paris, 1964-66; exec. editor, sec. Call-Chronicle Newspapers Inc., Allentown, 1966-79, editor, pub., 1979—. Trustee, Cedar Crest Coll.; active United Fund of Lehigh County (Pa.), Allentown Nat. Alliance Businessmen; founder, pres. Allentown Housing Devel. Corp. Served with Army N.G., 1963-64. Mem. First Amendment Coalition of Pa. (a founder), AP Mng. Editors Assn. (exec. com.), Am. Soc. Newspaper Editors (dir.). Mem. United Chs. of Christ. Office: PO Box 1260 Allentown PA 18105

MILLER, EDWARD KIRKBRIDE, investment co. exec.; b. Balt., July 27, 1917; s. Edward Kirkbride and Maude Elizabeth (Turner) M.; B.S., Mass. Inst. Tech., 1941; M.B.A., Harvard, 1950; m. Ann Renshaw Hoffman, Apr. 2, 1948; children—Pamela K. (Mrs. Michael Gisriel), Daniel K. Spl. rep. N.C. Shipbuilding Co., 1941-42; treas. Moldcraft, Inc., 1946-48; spl. rep. Western Md. Ry. Co., Balt., 1950-52; vice chmn. T. Rowe Price Assos., Inc., Balt., 1952—, chmn. bd., 1976—; chmn. bd. T. Rowe Price Growth Stock Fund, Inc. Bd. dirs. Balt. Symphony Orch.; v.p., bd. dirs. Balt. Council for Internat. Visitors; trustee Balt. Mus. Art. Served to lt. USNR, 1942-46. Home: 307 Overhill Rd Baltimore MD 21210 Office: 100 E Pratt St Baltimore MD 21202

MILLER, EDWARD SPENCER, railroad exec.; b. Springfield, Vt., Apr. 23, 1908; s. Edward Whitney and Grace Agnes (Spencer) M.; A.B., Dartmouth Coll., 1931; J.D., Harvard U., 1934; m. Juanita G. Fownes, May 20, 1938; children—Edward F., Anne G., Charles S. Admitted to Mass. bar, 1934, Maine bar, 1940, U.S. Supreme Ct. bar, 1946; gen. practice law, Lowell, Mass., 1934-38; commerce counsel Boston & Maine R.R., 1938-40; gen. atty. Maine Central R.R. Co., Portland, 1940-46, gen. counsel, 1946-52, pres., 1952-77, chmn. bd., 1968—; dir. Portland Terminal Co., Maine Nat. Bank; hon. dir. First Nat. Boston Co., First Nat. Bank of Boston; cons. dir. Gt. No. Nekoosa Co. Mem. Assn. Am. Railroads (dir. 1962-77), Eastern R.R. Assn. (pres. 1969-76), Greater Portland C. of C. (pres. 1952-53), Maine State C. of C. (dir. 1952-58). Republican. Congregationalist. Clubs: Union (Boston); Portland Country, Cumberland, Masons, Shriners. Author: History of Maine Central Railroad 1940-1979, 1979. Home: 15 Chadwick Portland ME 04102

MILLER, EDWARD STANLEY, mining co. exec.; b. N.Y.C., Nov. 14, 1930; s. Nathan and Amelia (Kapel) M.; B.A., Syracuse U., 1951; postgrad. Grad. Sch. Bus., N.Y. U., 1955-57; grad. Advanced Mgmt. Program, Harvard, 1964; m. Joyce Iris Trepel, Aug. 17, 1952; children—Susan Elizabeth, Thomas Ross. Economist-statistician AMAX, Inc., N.Y.C., 1951-54, portfolio and exchange mgr., 1955-57, asst. treas., 1961-65, dir. corp. devel., 1966-69, v.p., 1970-73, v.p., treas., 1973—, sec. finance and investment coms., 1961—, chmn. portfolio com., 1976—, sec. capital allocation com., also v.p. numerous subsidiaries; dir. Alumax Inc., Lehman Multi-Currency Assets Fund, Inc.; pres. Amax Credit Co.; chmn. bd., dir. Confifinance SA, Luxembourg. Served with AUS, 1952-54. Mem. Am. Mining Congress (chmn. fin. adv. council 1976—), Conf. Bd., Council Fin. Execs., Phi Beta Kappa, Pi Gamma Mu. Clubs: Sky, Dolphin Cove. Home: 235 Dolphin Cove Quay Stamford CT 06902 Office: AMAX Center Railroad Ave Greenwich CT 06830

MILLER, EDWIN FREDERICK, lawyer; b. Balt., Jan. 21, 1943; s. Charles C.H. and Edith H. Miller; B.A., U. Md., 1964, J.D., 1969; m. Sherry L. Taggart, June 19, 1964; 1 son, Joshua Taggart. Claims adjuster Liberty Mut. Ins. Co., 1964-67; with PHH Corp., Hunt Valley, Md., and predecessor, 1967—, v.p., sec., mgr. corp. legal div. Mem. Am. Soc. Corp. Secs., Am. Bar Assn., Md. Bar Assn. Methodist. Home: 413 Whitaker Mill Rd Fallston MD 21047 Office: 11333 McCormick Rd Hunt Valley MD 21031*

MILLER, ELFER BUEL, former banker; b. Cleve., Jan. 25, 1921; s. Clifford Buel and Clara (Elfer) M.; grad. Sch. Bank Auditors and Comptrollers, U. Wis., 1957; m. Angela Rizzo, Oct. 1, 1942. With Fed. Res. Bank Cleve., 1939-79, gen. auditor, 1960-79; past chmn. steering com. gen. auditors Fed. Res. Banks, past chmn. standing com. on electronic data processing auditing. Served with USMCR, 1942-45; PTO. Decorated Purple Heart. Mem. Inst. Internal Auditors (bd. govs. Cleve. chpt. 1963-64, 73-75), Bank Adminstrn. Inst. (past pres., past dir. Cleve. chpt). Home: 106 Fountain Head Peachtree City GA 30269

MILLER, ELIZABETH CAVERT, med. educator; b. Mpls., May 2, 1920; d. William Lane and Mary Elizabeth (Mead) Cavert; B.S., U. Minn., 1941; M.S., U. Wis., 1943, Ph.D., 1945; m. James Alexander Miller, Aug. 30, 1942; children—Linda Ann, Helen Louise. Instr. dept. oncology U. Wis. Med. Center, 1946-48, asst. prof., 1948-58, asso. prof., 1958-69, prof., 1969—, asso. dir. McArdle Lab. for Cancer Research, U. Wis., Madison, 1973—. Recipient (with J.A. Miller) Langer-Teplitz award for cancer research Ann Langer Cancer Research Found., 1962, Lucy Wortham James award for cancer research James Ewing Soc., 1965, Bertner award M.D. Anderson Hosp. and Tumor Inst., 1971, Wis. div. award Am. Cancer Soc., 1973, Outstanding Achievement award U. Minn., 1973, Papanicolau award for cancer research Papanicolaou Cancer Research Inst., Miami, 1975; Rosenstiel award for basic med. scis. Brandeis U., 1976, Nat. award Am. Cancer Soc., 1977, Bristol-Myers award in cancer research, 1978, Gairdner Found. Ann. award, 1978, Founders award Chem. Industry Inst. Toxicology, 1978, Prix Griffuel Assn. pour Developpement de Recherche sur Cancer, 1978, 3M Life Sci award Fedn. Am. Socs. Exptl. Biology, 1979. Mem. Nat. Acad. Sci., Am. Assn. for Cancer Research, Am. Soc. Biol. Chemists. Asso. editor Cancer Research, 1957-62; contbr. numerous articles on chem. carcinogenesis and microsomal oxidations to profl. jours. Home: 5517 Hammersley Rd Madison WI 53711 Office: University of Wisconsin McArdle Lab Madison WI 53706

MILLER, EMANUEL, lawyer, banker; b. N.Y.C., Jan. 22, 1917; s. Mayer and Helen (Stein) M.; B.A., Bklyn. Coll., 1937; LL.B., St. Lawrence U., Bklyn., 1941; m. Ruth Marcus, Jan. 3, 1942; children—Linda Alice, Henry Ward, Marjorie Joan. Admitted to N.Y. bar, 1942; with Harold W. Zeamans, Flushing, N.Y., 1950-51, firm White & Case, N.Y.C., 1951-53; with Bankers Trust Co., N.Y.C., 1953—, v.p., counsel, 1976—, dir. various affiliates; lectr. in field. Served with U.S. Army, 1942-45. Mem. Am., N.Y. State bar assns., Iota Theta. Contbr. legal publs. Home: 23 Saxon Way New Rochelle NY 10804 Office: 280 Park Ave New York NY 10017

MILLER, EUGENE, financial exec.; b. Chgo., Oct. 6, 1925; s. Harry and Fannie (Prosterman) M.; B.S., Ga. Inst. Tech., 1945; A.B. magna cum laude, Bethany Coll., 1947, LL.D., 1969; diploma Oxford (Eng.) U., 1947; M.S. in Journalism, Columbia, 1948; M.B.A., N.Y. U., 1959; postgrad. Pace U., 1973—; m. Edith Sutker, Sept. 23, 1951 (div. Sept. 1965); children—Ross, Scott, June; m. 2d, Thelma Gottlieb, Dec. 22, 1965; stepchildren—Paul Gottlieb, Alan Gottlieb. Reporter, then city editor Greensboro (N.C.) Daily News, 1948-52; S.W. bur. chief Bus. Week mag., Houston, 1952-54, asso. mng. editor, N.Y.C., 1954-60; dir. pub. affairs and communications McGraw-Hill, Inc., 1960-63, v.p., 1963-68; sr. v.p. pub. relations and investor relations, exec. com. N.Y. Stock Exchange, N.Y.C., 1968-73; sr. v.p. CNA Fin. Corp., Chgo., 1973-75; chmn. Eugene Miller & Assos., Glencoe, Ill., 1975-77; v.p. U.S. Gypsum Co., 1977—; adj. prof. mgmt. Grad. Sch. Bus. Adminstrn., N.Y.U., 1963-75; prof. bus. adminstrn. Fordham U., N.Y.C., Grad. Sch. Bus. Adminstrn., 1969-75; chmn., prof. fin. Northeastern Ill. U., 1975—; lectr. econs., pub relations to bus. and sch. groups; author syndicated bus. column, 1964—; dir. Tabb, Inc., Ann Arbor, Mich., Tech. Advisors, Inc., Wayne, Mich.; cons. to Sec. Commerce, 1961—. Trustee Bethany Coll.; mem. alumni bd. Columbia Sch. Journalism. Served to ensign USNR, World War II; comdr. Res. Recipient Outstanding Achievement award Bethany Coll., 1963; 50th Anniversary award Columbia U. Sch. Journalism, 1963; Honors award Ohio U. Sch. Journalism, 1964. Mem. Am. Econs. Assn., Am. Finance Assn., Nat. Assn. Bus. Economists, Soc. Am. Bus. Writers (founder), Pub. Relations Soc. Am., Newcomen Soc., Sigma Delta Chi, Alpha Sigma Phi. Clubs: Mid-Am. (Chgo.); Green Acres Country (Northbrook, Ill.); N.Y. University. Author: Your Future in Securities, 1974; Barron's Guide to Graduate Business Schools, 1977. Contbg. editor: Public Relations Handbook, 1971. Home: 376 Sunrise Circle Glencoe IL 60022 Office: 101 S Wacker Dr Chicago IL 60606 also 3280 Spanish Moss Terr Lauder Hill FL

MILLER, EUGENE ALBERT, banker; b. Detroit, Sept. 21, 1937; s. George Walter and Bernice (Johnston) M.; B.B.A., Detroit Inst. Tech., 1964; grad. Sch. Bank Adminstrn., Wis., 1968; m. Lois Sterk. With Detroit Bank & Trust Co., Detroit, 1955—, v.p., 1970-74, controller, 1971-78, sr. v.p., 1974-78, exec. v.p., 1978—; exec. v.p., treas. Detroit Bank Corp., 1978—; treas. Detroit bank Corp., 1973—. Vice pres. Met. Detroit council Girl Scouts U.S.A., 1978; past chmn. bd. dirs. SE Mich. Travel and Tourist Assn.; bd. dirs. Health Care Inst., 1974—. Mem. Nat. Assn. Accountants (past pres. Detroit), Bank Adminstrn. Inst., Fin. Execs. Inst., Assn. Res. City Bankers. Clubs: Detroit Athletic, Oakland Hills Country. Office: 211 W Fort St Detroit MI 48231

MILLER, EUGENE LESLIE, engine mfg. exec.; b. Tulsa, Apr. 23, 1919; s. Joseph G. and Flora (Shorten) M.; B.S. in Engring., Okla. A. and M. Coll., 1941; m. Doris Cooley, May 6, 1942; children—Melinda Miller Powell, Matthew, Melissa Miller Rush. With Mid Continent Petroleum Corp., Tulsa, summers 1937-40; project engr. Cooper-Bessemer Corp., Mt. Vernon, Ohio, 1946-54, asst. gen. mgr., 1954-56, gen. mgr. 1956-57, pres. and gen. mgr. 1957-65, pres., chief exec. officer, from 1965, chmn., from 1967; now chmn. bd. Cooper Industries; dir. Hydrotech Internat., Varo, Inc. Served as lt. col. C.E. AUS, 1942-46. Mem. Blue Key, Pi Tau Sigma, Sigma Tau. Presbyn. Office: Cooper Industries Inc Two Houston Center Suite 2700 Houston TX 77002

MILLER, EWING HARRY, architect; b. Toledo, Ohio, Oct. 5, 1923; s. Ewing Harry and Esther Alice (Graves) M.; B.A., U. Pa., 1947, M.A., 1948; m. Gladys Jacquelyn Good, Dec. 18, 1948; children—Victoria Alice, Paul Ewing. Draftsman, Harbeson, Hough, Livingston & Larson, Phila., 1948; designer Nolen & Swinburne, Phila., 1950-52; project architect Gilboy & O'Malley, London, 1953; partner Miller, Vrydagh & Miller, Terre Haute, Ind., 1954-65; pres. Ewing Miller Partnership, Terre Haute, 1965-70; pres. Archonics Corp., Terre Haute, 1970-76, chmn. bd. 1976-79; sr. partner for design, chmn. partners Archonics Design Partnership, Indpls., Fort Wayne, Terre Haute, 1977—; partner Lockereie Devel., 1978—. Mem. Ind. Gov.'s Commn. on Aging, 1959-62; pres. Gov.'s Commn. on Comprehensive Health Planning, Ind., 1970-75, Behavioral Research Found.; sec., bd. mgrs. Sheldon Swope Art Gallery, 1965—, pres., 1965-73; bd. dirs. Center for Exploration of Values and Meaning, 1978—. Recipient citation biennial awards program Ind. Soc. Architects, also Merit and Honor awards triennial design awards program; Archtl. award of excellence Am. Inst. Steel Constrn.; 1st Honor award and winner Internat. Competition for Housing, Indpls. Fellow AIA (mem. com. on design, chmn. com. on architecture for edn.); mem. Ind. Soc. Architects. Contbr. articles to profl. jours. Major archtl. works include: residence halls and power center at Ind. State U. at Evansville. Home: Rural Route 23 Terre Haute IN 47802 also Riley Tower 1 Apt 3002 225 E North St Indianapolis IN 46204 Office: 156 E Market 1000 Inland Bldg Indianapolis IN 46204

MILLER, FLORENCE LOWDEN (MRS. C. PHILLIP MILLER), civic worker; b. Chgo., May 4, 1898; d. Frank O. and Florence (Pullman) Lowden; student Oriental Inst., U. Chgo., 1929-34; m. Charles Phillip Miller, Oct. 20, 1931; children—Phillip Lowden, Warren Pullman. Owner and operator Upland Farms, Oregon, Ill., 1959—; operator Sinnissippi Exptl. Forest, Oregon, 1943-73, owner, 1959-73, partner, 1973-79. Trustee Florenden Plantation, Osceola, Ark., 1943-72. Mem. Ill. Nature Preserves Commn., 1968-74. Mem. bd. Southeast Chgo. Commn., 1955-70; mem. exec. com. Chgo. Community Trust, 1958-70; pres. George M. Pullman Ednl. Found., 1949-78; trustee Westover Sch., 1958-67; Shimer Coll., 1951-58. Recipient Westover award, 1964, U. Chgo. medal for disting. service, 1976, Heritage Conservation and Recreation Service Cultural Achievement award U.S. Dept. Interior, 1979. Fellow Met. Mus.; mem. Ill., Chgo. (dir.) hist. socs., Chgo. Hearing Soc. (dir.), Soc. Mayflower Descs., Nat. Soc. Colonial Dames, Orchestral Assn. Chgo., Antiquarian Soc. of Art Inst. Chgo. (pres. 1939-45, 49-51), Art Inst. Chgo. (life trustee, past pres., mem. women's bd.), Womens' Bd. U. Chgo., Republican. Episcopalian. Clubs: Casino (past dir.), Friday, Fortnightly, Woman's Athletic, Arts (Chgo.); Colony (N.Y.C.). Home: 5757 Kimbark Ave Chicago IL 60637

MILLER, FLOYD HARRY, JR., naval officer; b. Bklyn., Dec. 19, 1931; s. Floyd Harry and Harriet Alice (McMonigle) M.; B.S., SUNY, 1953; grad. Naval War Coll., 1966; m. Gale Walter, Dec. 27, 1958; children—Nancy Gale, Scott Walter. Joined U.S. Navy, 1953, advanced through grades to rear adm.; comdg. officer USS Voge, 1969-71, USS Calif., 1971-76; program coordinator Office of Chief of Naval Ops., 1976-77; comdr. Cruiser-Destroyer Group 1, San Francisco, 1977—. Mem. U.S. Naval Inst., N.Y. State Maritime Coll. Alumni Assn. Republican. Home: 109 Rendova Circle Coronado CA 92118 Office: Comdr Cruiser Destroyer Group 1 FPO San Francisco CA 96601

MILLER, FOIL ALLAN, educator, chemist; b. Aurora, Ill., Jan. 18, 1916; s. Fred Allen and Bertha (Milliren) M.; B.S., Hamline U., 1937; postgrad. U. Neb.; Ph.D., Johns Hopkins, 1942; m. Ruth Naomi Zeller, Sept. 4, 1941; children—Bruce Allan, Craig Foil. Fellow chemistry U. Minn., 1942-44; asst. prof. chemistry U. Ill., 1944-48; head spectroscopy div. Mellon Inst., Pitts., 1948-58, sr. fellow in ind. research, 1958-67, adj. sr. fellow, 1967-74; lectr. in chemistry U. Pitts., 1952-64, adj. prof. chemistry, 1964-67, univ. prof., dir. Spectroscopy Lab., 1967—; vis. prof., Sendai, Japan, 1977. Mem. IUPAC Commn. on Molecular Spectroscopy, 1967-75, sec., 1969-75. Co-recipient Pitts. Spectroscopy award, 1964, Hasler award Soc. Applied Spectroscopy, 1973; Guggenheim fellow, Zurich, 1957-58. Mem. Am. Chem. Soc. (Pitts. award 1965), Optical Soc. Am., Pitts. Acad. Sci. and Art (v.p. 1973-79), Coblentz Soc. (pres. 1959-60), Soc. Applied Spectroscopy (hon.). Contbr. articles on infrared and Raman spectra, far infrared spectroscopy to profl. jours. Home: 960 Lakemont Dr Pittsburgh PA 15243

MILLER, FRANCENA LOUNSBERY NOLAN, educator; b. Ithaca, N.Y., Jan. 29, 1919; d. Frank Granger and Vienna (Hunt) Lounsbery; B.S., Cornell U., 1942, M.S., 1949; Ph.D., Pa. State U., 1954; m. Paul A. Miller, Jan. 15, 1965; 1 son by previous marriage, Michael F. Nolan; stepchildren—Paula Kay Miller, Thomas Ausborn Miller. Mem. faculty Pa. State U., University Park, 1949-61, asso. prof. rural sociology, 1958-61; dir., asst. dean Coll. Agr., Forestry and Home Econs., U. W. Va., Morgantown, 1961-64; dean Sch. Home Econs., U. Conn., Storrs, 1964-65; asso. dir. Am. Assn. U. Women, 1966-67, gen. dir., 1967-68; prof. Queens Coll., Charlotte, N. C., 1968-69; research asso. Rochester (N.Y.) Inst. Tech., 1970-72, prof., 1972—; sr. program cons. W.K. Kellogg Found.; trustee Rochester Savs. Bank, Rochester Telephone Corp. Reviewer community-family-consumer work Coop. State Expt. Sta. Service, U.S. Dept. Agr., 1963, reviewer research Sch. Homes Econs., Ohio State U., 1965, reviewer coop. extension service Fed. Extension Service, 1966; mem. pres. study com. Coll. Home Econs., Cornell U., 1966. Pres. bd. dirs. Family Service of Rochester; trustee Keuka Coll., 1973. Mem. Phi Kappa Phi, Omicron Nu, Gamma Sigma Delta. Contbr. articles to profl. jours. Home: 30 Hillock Rd Rush NY 14543

MILLER, FRANCIS DON, ret. army officer, Olympics orgn. exec.; b. Racine, Wis., Apr. 9, 1920; s. Frank Gerhardt and Louise Mary (Kosterman) M.; B.S. in Phys. Edn., U. Wis., 1943; postgrad. U. Md., 1965; m. Katherine Rose Julian, Apr. 18, 1947; children—Patricia Ann (Mrs. Michael Wagner), Donna Louise (Mrs. Lawrence Blume). Mem. phys. edn. staff U. Wis.-Madison, 1942-43; commd. lt. U.S. Army, 1943, advanced through grades to col., 1966; comdr. combat inf. co., Europe, 1943-45; adminstr. army sports program, 1949-52; sr. instr. sports Spl. Services Schs., Ft. Monmouth, N.J., 1947-49; chmn. Inter-service Sports Council, 1967-68; dir. Army Edn. and Morale Support Directorate, 1968-69; ret., 1969; asst. exec. dir., dir. fund raising U.S. Olympic Com., N.Y.C., 1969-73, exec. dir., 1973—. Decorated Legion of Merit, Silver Star medal, Bronze Star medal (2), Purple Heart (2) (U.S.); Croix de Guerre, Fourgerre (France); recipient Medal of Honor Council Internat. Du Sport Militaire, 1968. Roman Catholic. Clubs: N.Y. Athletic, Knights of Malta. Contbr. articles to sports publs. Home: 35 1st St Broadmoor Colorado Springs CO 80906 Office: 1750 E Boulder St Colorado Springs CO 80909

MILLER, FRANCIS MARION, educator, chemist; b. Central City, Ky., Dec. 28, 1925; s. David Green and Mary (Griffin) M.; B.S., Western Ky. State Coll., 1946; Ph.D., Northwestern U., 1949; postdoctoral fellow Harvard, 1948-49; m. Marjorie Rickman, Mar. 22, 1947; children—Daniel, Jennifer, John; m. 2d, Clara Whang, Feb. 26, 1971. Mem. faculty U. Md., College Park, 1949-68, prof., chmn. dept. pharm. chemistry, 1961-68; prof., chmn. dept. chemistry, No. Ill. U., DeKalb, 1968-77, prof., 1977—; guest research prof. Chemische Inst., Heidelberg, Germany, 1958-59; vis. prof. U. Baghdad (Iraq), 1963; vis. scholar U. Va., 1977; cons. to govt. and industry, 1955—. Mem. Am. Chem. Soc. (chmn. Md. sect. 1966), Chem. Soc. (London, Eng.), AAUP, Sigma Xi. Unitarian. Author: (with Ward C. Sumpter) Heterocyclic Compounds with Indole and Carbazole Systems, 1954. Patentee local anesthetic. Home: 1219 Elizabeth St DeKalb IL 60115

MILLER, FRANK WILLIAM, lawyer; b. Appleton, Wis., May 15, 1921; s. Frank Paul and Ruth Margaret (Arft) M.; B.A., U. Wis., 1946, LL.B., 1948, S.J.D., 1954; m. Lucille Gloria Rinnan, Sept. 8, 1945; children—Deborah Lynn, Patrica Elizabeth. Admitted to Wis. bar, 1948; mem. faculty Washington U., St. Louis, 1948—, Coles prof. criminal law and adminstrn., 1962-64, James Carr prof. criminal jurisprudence, 1964—; summer vis. prof. law U. Ark., 1952, 54, 56, Stetson U., 1955, U. Wis., 1957, U. Tex., 1975; vis. prof. law So. Ill. U. at Carbondale, 1973-74, summers 1976-79; chmn. round table council criminal law Assn. Am. Law Schs., 1961; chmn. Pub.

Defender Adv. Com. St. Louis County, 1962. Served with AUS, 1942-45. Recipient citation for outstanding teaching Washington U. Alumni Fedn., 1965. Mem. Am. Bar Assn., Am. Law Inst. (Guttmacher award 1977), Wis. Bar Integrated, Order of Coif. Democrat. Author: (with A.C. Becht) Factual Causation in Negligence and Strict Liability Cases, 1961; Prosecution: The Decision to Charge a Suspect with a Crime, 1969; editor: (with R.O. Dawson, George E. Dix, Raymond I. Parnas) Criminal Justice Adminstration, 1976; (with Dawson, Dix, Parnas) The Police Function, 1971; Sentencing and The Correctional Process, 1976; The Juvenile Justice Process, 1976; The Mental Health Process, 1976. Office: Sch Law Washington U Saint Louis MO 63105

MILLER, FRED HUNTER, mining co. exec.; b. Cowen, W.Va., Apr. 8, 1933; s. William Edward and Hazel Helen (Jarvis) M.; B.S. in E.M., W.Va. U., 1956; m. Mary Myers, June 1, 1952; children—Anna, Daniel, Hunter, Elizabeth, Rebecca, Sarah. Vice pres. ops. NACCO Mining Co., Cleve.; v.p. adminstrn., dir. Florence Mining Co.; pres., dir., gen. mgr. Oneida Mining Co.; gen. mgr., gen. supt. Clinchfield Coal Co.; successively sect. foreman, maintenance foreman, asst. supt., supt. Christopher Coal Co. Served with C.E., AUS, 1968. Mem. Am. Inst. Mining Engrs., Soc. Mining Engrs., W.Va. U. Sch. Mines Alumni Assn. Democrat. Baptist. Clubs: Kiwanis, Masons, Eastern Star. Home: RD #1 Deer Haven Wheeling WV 26003 Office: Powhatan Point OH 43942

MILLER, FREDERICK, pathologist; b. N.Y.C., Apr. 5, 1937; s. Alex and Sarah M.; B.S., U. Wis., 1956; M.D., N.Y. U., 1961; m. Emilie J. Kronish, June 2, 1962; children—David, Allison. Intern, Bellevue Hosp., N.Y.C., 1961-62, resident, 1962-63; practice medicine specializing in pathology, 1965—; clin. asso., attending physician Nat. Inst. Arthritis and Metabolic Diseases, 1963-65, resident chief pathology dept. N.Y. U. Med. Center, 1965-67; attending pathologist Bellevue and Univ. Hosps., N.Y.C., 1967; asst. prof. pathology N.Y. U., 1967-70, asso. prof., 1970; asso. prof. SUNY, Stony Brook, 1970-75, prof., 1975—, acting chmn. dept. pathology, 1977—, dir. lab. for arthritis and related diseases, 1976—; dir. labs. Univ. Hosp., Stony Brook, 1978—, pathologist-in-chief, 1979—. Served with USPHS, 1963-65. Recipient Bausch & Lomb medal for research, 1961; Am. Soc. Clin. Pathologists award, 1961; NIH grantee, 1963—; diplomate Am. Bd. Pathology. Mem. Harvey Soc., Am. Soc. Exptl. Pathology, Reticuloendothelial Soc., AAAS, Am. Assn. Pathol. Bacteriology. Contbr. articles to med. jours.; hort. authority on roses. Home: 46 Manchester Ln Stony Brook NY 11790 Office: Dept Pathology HSC-SUSB Stony Brook NY 11794

MILLER, FREDERICK BYERS, educator; b. Cleve., Apr. 6, 1913, s. Hervey Eugene and Elva Blanche (Slaughenhaupt) M.; B.S., Baldwin-Wallace Coll., 1934; M.B.A., Ohio State U., 1940, Ph.D., 1952; m. Ruth Roberta Alton, Dec. 26, 1936; children—Frederick, Timothy. Tchr. high sch., Berea, O., 1934-39; asst. Ohio State U., Columbus, 1939-41; price economist Va. Bur. Labor Statistics, 1942; asso. dist. price exec. OPA, 1942-43; bus. cons. Bur. Fgn. and Domestic Commerce, 1944; asso. prof. U. Richmond (Va.), 1941-42, acting dean, dean eve. sch. bus. adminstrn., 1946-49, 1st dean sch. bus. adminstrn., 1949-56; pres., exec. dir. Bank Adminstrn. Inst., Chgo., 1956-76; faculty asso. Ariz. State U., 1976—; cons. marketing numerous business orgns., U.S. Army; dir. Security Fed. Savs. & Loan Assn. Field adviser Small Bus. Adminstrn.; former mem. research com. markets and marketing Gov.'s Adv. Council Va. Economy. Chmn., Park Ridge City Transp. Com. Served as lt. (j.g.), U.S. Navy, 1944-45. Mem. Nat. Sales Execs. Assn., Am. Marketing Assn., So. Econ. Assn., A.I.M., Controllers Inst. of Am., Park Ridge C. of C. (dir.), Beta Gamma Sigma, Pi Kappa Alpha, Pi Kappa Delta, Theta Alpha Phi. Club: Sales Executives (pres. 1950-51), Scottsdale Country (Scottsdale, Ariz.); Phoenix Country. Contbr. articles to profl. publs. Home: 7904 E Pecos Ln Scottsdale AZ 85253

MILLER, FREDERICK ROBESON, banker; b. Oakland, Calif., Oct. 11, 1927; s. Charles Lennon and Juliet Robeson (Chamberlain) M.; B.A., Yale U., 1952; m. Nancy McDaniel, July 19, 1952; children—Susan Chase Miller Clark, Stephen Robeson, Elizabeth Rockwell. With J.P. Morgan & Co., Inc., 1952-54; v.p. Phila. Nat. Bank, 1954-69; pres. Waterbury Nat. Bank (Conn.), 1969-71; pres. City Nat. Bank, Bridgeport, Conn., 1971-72; pres. Conn. Nat. Bank, Bridgeport, 1973—, also chief exec. officer; dir. CNB Equity Corp. Dir. United Way of Eastern Fairfield County, Am. Shakespeare Theater; trustee Bridgeport Hosp. Served with U.S. Army, 1946-47. Mem. Bridgeport C. of C. (dir.). Republican. Episcopalian. Clubs: Yale (N.Y.C.); Golf (Aspetuck, Conn.); Highfield. Home: Painter Hill Rd Woodbury CT 06798 Office: 888 Main St Bridgeport CT 06602

MILLER, FRITZ HENRY, r.r. exec.; b. Wykoff, Minn., Sept. 21, 1916; s. Paul Alvin and Amanda Marie (Horstman) M.; diploma, Mankato Comml. Coll., 1939; student Northwestern U., 1961-64; m. Dorothy Ruth White, Sept. 14, 1940; children—David, Roger, Linda, Verne, Dean, Mark. With C.M.St.P.&P. R.R. Co., Chgo., 1939—, spl. asst. to v.p. finance and accounting, 1969, asst. comptroller, 1970-71, comptroller, 1971; auditor Mpls. Eastern Ry. Co., 1974—. Mem. fin. com. Village of Bartlett (Ill.), 1973-74, mem. compensation com., 1975-77. Served with AUS, 1945-46. Mem. Assn. Am. R.S.'s, Western Ry. Club, Chgo. Assn. Commerce and Industry, Am. Legion, Chgo. R.R. Accounting Conf., Ill. Ry. Mus., Field Mus. Natural History, Internat. Lutheran Laymen's League, Smithsonian Assos. Lutheran. Home: 128 N Chase Ave Bartlett IL 60103 Office: Union Sta Chicago IL 60606

MILLER, G. WILLARD, JR., stock broker; b. Sacramento, Nov. 3, 1919; s. G. Willard and Ednah Miller (Simmons) M.; student Dartmouth Coll., 1936-40; m. Nancy Shurtleff, Aug. 24, 1940; children—Sandra Miller Rowe, Stephen R., Nancy L., Roy S. Vice pres., br. mgr. Dean Witter & Co., investment brokers, San Francisco, 1946-58, gen. partner, 1958—, mgr. San Francisco office, 1961-64, asst. mgr. No. div., 1964-67, mgr. No. div., 1967-72, pres., 1972—. Active United Bay Area Crusade; asso. mem. for fund-raising St. Francis Meml. Hosp. Served with USAAF, 1942-45. Decorated D.F.C. with three clusters, Air medal with six clusters. Mem. Nat. Assn. Securities Dealers (dist. chmn. 1967, gov. 1971-74), San Francisco Bond Club, Mchts. Exchange Club (pres. 1974). Clubs: Street (founding mem.) (San Francisco); Bohemian, Pacific-Union, Four Leaf Clover, Claremont Country. Home: 30 Las Cascadas Rd Orinda CA 94563 Office: 45 Montgomery St San Francisco CA 94106

MILLER, G(EORGE) WILLIAM, govt. ofcl.; b. Sapulpa, Okla., Mar. 9, 1925; s. James Dick and Hazle Deane (Orrick) M.; B.S. in Marine Engring., U.S. Coast Guard Acad., 1945; J.D., U. Calif. at Berkeley, 1952; D.B.A. (hon.), U. R.I., 1968, Bryant Coll., 1969; m. Ariadna Rogojarsky, Dec. 22, 1946. Admitted to Calif. bar, 1952, N.Y. bar, 1953; asso. firm Cravath, Swaine & Moore, N.Y.C., 1952-56; with Textron Inc., Providence, 1956-78, v.p., 1956-57, pres., chief operating officer, dir., 1960-67, pres., 1968-74, chief exec. officer, dir., 1968-78, chmn., chief exec. officer, dir., 1974-78; chmn. Fed. Res. Bd., Washington, 1978—. Chmn. adv. council Pres.'s Com. EEO, 1963-65; mem. council Nat. Found. Humanities, 1966-67; bd. dirs. USCG Acad. Found., 1969-78, pres., 1973-77, chmn., 1977-78; chmn. U.S. Indsl. Payroll Savs. Bond Com., 1977, Pres.'s Com. HIRE; co-chmn. Polish-U.S. Econ. Council. Served with USCG, 1945-49. Mem. State Bar Calif., Nat. Alliance Businessmen (dir. 1968-78, chmn. 1977-78), Conf. Bd. (trustee 1972-78, chmn. 1977-78), Bus. Council, Order of Coif, Phi Delta Phi. Clubs: Agawam Hunt; University, Hope, Turks Head, Squantum (Providence); Lyford Cay (Nassau); Acoaxet (Westport, Mass.); Brook (N.Y.C.). Office: Federal Reserve Bd Washington DC 20551

MILLER, GAVIN, lawyer; b. N.Y.C., Mar. 8, 1926; s. George Gavin and Catherine (Schurman) M.; A.B., Harvard U., 1950, LL.B., 1953; m. Camilla Congreve Strong, Aug. 15, 1959; children—Emily, Louise, Catherine. Admitted to N.Y. State bar, 1955, Calif. bar, 1962; practiced in N.Y.C., 1955-61, Los Angeles, 1962—; asso. firm Davis Polk & Wardwell, N.Y.C., 1953-61; asso. firm Kindel & Anderson, Los Angeles, 1961-63, mem. firm, 1963-66; mem. firm Agnew, Miller & Carlson, Los Angeles, 1966—. Dir. Denny's Restaurants Inc., 1st Newport Mortgage Investment Trust, Sovereign Corp., Sovereign Life Ins. Co. Calif., Piedmont Mgmt. Co. Inc. Served with AUS, 1944-46. Mem. Nature Conservancy (trustee So. Calif. chpt. 1974—), State Bar Calif. Am., Los Angeles County (trustee 1978—), N.Y. State bar assns., Phi Beta Kappa. Clubs: California; University (N.Y.C., Los Angeles). Home: 435 S Rimpau Blvd Los Angeles CA 90020 Office: 700 S Flower St Los Angeles CA 90017

MILLER, GENE EDWARD, newspaper reporter; b. Evansville, Ind., Sept. 16, 1928; s. Paul E. and Irene (Hudson) M.; A.B. in Journalism, Ind. U., 1950, LL.D. (hon.), 1977; Nieman fellow, Harvard U., 1967-68; m. Electra Sonia Yphantis, Apr. 13, 1952; children—Janet Irene, Theresa Jean, Thomas Raphael, Roberta Lynn. Reporter, Jour.-Gazette, Ft. Wayne, Ind., 1950-51, Washington Bur. Wall St. Jour., 1953-54, Richmond (Va.) News Leader, 1954-57, Miami (Fla.) Herald, 1957—. Served with AUS, 1951-53. Recipient Pulitzer prize for local reporting, 1967, 76. Author: 83 Hours Till Dawn; Invitation To A Lynching. Home: 8831 SW 20th St Miami FL 33165 Office: 1 Herald Plaza Miami FL 33101

MILLER, GENE WALKER, educator; b. Pleasant Grove, Utah, Dec. 21, 1925; s. George Lewis and Leah (Harris) M.; B.S., Utah State U., 1950, M.S., 1954; Ph.D., N.C. State U., 1957; m. Edeltraut Ruth Bark, Aug. 5, 1953; children—Cynthia, Patricia, Wayne, Michael, Elke. Research asst. N.C. State U., 1954-57; asst. prof. Utah State U., 1957-61, asso. prof., 1961-65, acting head dept. botany, 1965-66, acting dean Coll. Sci., 1967-68, dir. Pollution Center, 1968-69; dean Huxley Coll., Western Wash. State U., 1969-74; head biology dept. Utah State U., Logan, 1974—; exchange prof. Acad. Scis., Czechoslovakia, summer 1970; postdoctoral work Radioisotope Inst., U. Hawaii, 1962, in biochemistry U. Muenster (Germany), 1961, Electron Microscopy Inst. Pharmacognosy, 1967. Served with AUS, 1944-46. NSF grantee, NIH grantee, AEC grantee, EPA grantee. Mem. Am., Japanese socs. plant physiologists, Am. Inst. Biol. Sci., AAAS, Biochem. Soc., Air Pollution Control Assn., AAUP, Internat. Soc. Fluoride Research, Sigma Xi. Rotarian, Kiwanian. Contbr. articles to sci. jours. Home: 935 S 4th E Providence UT 84332

MILLER, GEORGE, congressman; b. Richmond, Calif., May 17, 1945; s. George and Dorothy (Rumsey) M.; B.A., San Francisco State Coll., 1968; J.D., U. Calif., Davis, 1972; m. Cynthia Caccavo, 1964; children—George, Stephen. Legis. counsel Calif. senate majority leader, 1969-73; mem. 94th-96th Congresses from 7th Calif. Dist. Chmn., Contra Costa County (Calif.) Democratic Central Com., 1969-70. Mem. Calif. Bar Assn., Common Cause. Democrat. Club: Martinez Democratic (past pres.). Home: Martinez CA Office: 1531 Longworth House Office Bldg Washington DC 20515

MILLER, GEORGE ARMITAGE, psychologist, educator; b. Charleston, W.Va., Feb. 3, 1920; s. George E. and Florence (Armitage) M.; B.A., U. Ala., 1940, M.A., 1941; Ph.D., Harvard, 1946; Doctorat honoris causa, U. Louvain, 1976; D.Social Sci., Yale U., 1979; m. Katherine James, Nov. 29, 1939; children—Nancy, Donnally James. Instr. psychology U. Ala., 1941-43; research fellow Harvard Psycho-Acoustic Lab., 1944-48, asst. prof. psychology, 1948-51, asso. prof., 1955-58, prof., 1958-68, chmn. dept psychology, 1964-67; prof. Rockefeller U., N.Y.C., 1968-79, adj. prof., 1979—; prof. psychology Princeton (N.J.) U., 1979—; vis. Inst. for Advanced Study, Princeton, fall 1950, 70-76; asso. prof. psychology Mass. Inst. Tech., 1951-55, vis. prof., 1976-79, group leader Lincoln Lab., 1953-55; fellow Center for Advanced Study in Behavioral Scis., Stanford, 1958-59; Fulbright research prof. Oxford (Eng.) U., 1963-64. Mem. Am. (pres. 1968-69), Eastern (pres. 1961-62) psychol. assns., Acoustical Soc. Am., Linguistic Soc. Am., Am. Statis. Assn., Am. Philos. Soc., Am. Physiol. Soc., Psychometric Soc., Soc. Exptl. Psychologists, Am. Acad. Arts and Scis., Psychonomic Soc., Nat. Acad. Sci., AAAS, Sigma Xi. Author: Language and Communication, 1951; (with Galanter and Pribram) Plans and the Structure of Behavior, 1960; Psychology, 1962; (with Johnson and Laird) Language and Perception, 1976; Spontaneous Apprentices, 1977. Home: 478 Lake Dr Princeton NJ 08540 Office: Dept Psychology Green Hall Princeton U Princeton NJ 08540

MILLER, GEORGE DAVID, air force officer; b. McKeesport, Pa., Apr. 5, 1930; s. George G. and Nellie G. (Cullen) M.; B.S., U.S. Naval Acad., 1953; M.S. in Aerospace Engring., Air Force Inst. Tech., 1966; postgrad. Nat. War Coll., 1970-71; m. Elizabeth Louise Hawk, June 6, 1953; 1 son, George David. Commd. 2d lt., U.S. Air Force, 1953, advanced through grades to maj. gen. 1977; ops. officer, comdr. 22d spl. ops. squadron, Nakhon Phanom Royal Thai AFB, Thailand, 1970-71; dep. comdr. for ops., vice comdr., comdr. 55th Strategic Reconnaissance Wing, Offutt AFB, Nebr., 1971-74; comdr. 17th Air div., 307th Strategic wing, U-Tapao Airfield, Thailand, 1974-75; comdr. 57th air div. Minot AFB, N.D., 1975-76; asst. dep. chief staff ops. Hdqrs. SAC, Offutt AFB, Nebr., 1976-77, dep. chief staff ops. plans, 1977-79, dep. dir. single integrated operational plan Joint Strategic Target Planning Staff, Joint Chiefs of Staff, 1977-79; dir. plans, dep. chief of staff ops., plans and readiness Hdqrs. USAF, Washington, 1979—. Decorated D.S.M., Legion of Merit, D.F.S. with 3 oak leaf clusters, air medal with 18 oak leaf clusters, others. Mem. Air Force Assn., Am. Legion. Republican. Lutheran. Clubs: Masons, Scottish Rite. Home: Quarters 72 Westover Ave Bolling AFB Washington DC 20336 Office: HQ USAF Pentagon Washington DC

MILLER, GERTRUDE NEVADA, biologist, educator; b. Newark, Del., July 6, 1919; d. Luther Pollard and Minnie Pearl (Shreve) Miller; B.S., W. Va. U., 1941, M.A., 1943; Ph.D., Cornell U., 1953. Tchr. Morgantown (W. Va.) Jr. High Sch., 1941-42, Univ. Demonstration High Sch., Morgantown, 1942-44, Wells Coll., Aurora, N.Y., 1947-50, South Appalachian State Tchrs., Boone, N.C., 1952, Hollins (Va.) Coll., 1953-54; asst. prof. No. State Coll., Aberdeen, S.D., 1954-57, asso. prof., acting chmn. div. sci. and math., 1958-59, prof. biology, 1960—, chmn. div. sci. and math., 1960-73, chmn. dept. math., natural scis. and health professions, 1974—. Mem. Aberdeen Environ. Action Com., 1972—. Mem. Assn. of Midwest Coll. Biology Tchrs., Nat. Assn. Biology Tchrs., Am. Inst. Biol. Scis., Nat. Sci. Tchrs. Assn., S.D. Acad. Sci., Central Assn. Advisers for Health Profession, Wilderness Soc., Nat. Wildlife Soc., Zonta Internat. (gov. dist. VII). Club: Zonta of Aberdeen (pres.). Home: 1105 N 4th St Aberdeen SD 57401 Office: S Jay St Aberdeen SD 57401. *My goal has been: (a) to achieve competence in my field (b) to keep informed on recent development (c) to build a program for students that, on completion, will allow them to compete anywhere or anyplace. I believe that no task is impossible if one is willing to spend whatever time is needed.*

MILLER, GLADYS, decorator; b. Franklin, Nebr., Apr. 10, 1896; d. George Owen and Carrie Lou (Graves) M., B.S., Oreg. State Coll.; M.A., N.Y. U., 1957; A.F.D., Moore Inst. Art, Sci. and Industry, 1957. Instr. interior decorating Phoenix High Sch. and Jr. Coll., 2 years; decorator Frederick & Nelson, Seattle, 4 years; 6 mos. study abroad; asst. mdse. mgr. Gimbel, Pitts., 2 years; in field promotion work F. Schumacher & Co., 3 years; instr. N.Y. U., 6 years; decorating editor Mademoiselle, 1938-42; decorating cons. Pub. Bldgs., Adminstrn. for dormitories, recreation bldgs., infirmaries, 1941-45; decorator diplomatic guest houses Blair House and Blair Lee; in bus. as decorating cons., 1937-58, decorating editor Family Circle Mag., 1946-55; weekly columns on decorating syndicated by N.A. Newspaper Alliance, 1946-53; decorating cons. lamp div. G.E., 1952-57; cons. U.S. Army, Q.M.G., and Research and Devel. Command, 1946-58; editor, New Homes Guide and Home Modernizing Guide, 1955-63; asso. pub. Bldg. Products Guide, 1964-73; now environmental cons. to builders; tchr. interior design seminar Oreg. State U., summer 1963. Fellow Am. Inst. Interior Designers; mem. Nat. Home Fashions League (awarded Third Nat. Trailblazer award 1968), The Fashion Group (charter, life), Illuminating Engring. Soc., Decorators Club N.Y. (hon.), Phi Kappa Phi, Kappa Kappa Gamma (recipient nat. achievement award 1956), Eta Mu Pi, Theta Sigma Phi. Democrat. Author: Decoratively Speaking, 1939; Room Make-up, 1941; Your Decorating A-B-C, 1946; Furniture for Your Home, 1946. Home: 735 Geary St San Francisco CA 94109

MILLER, HARBAUGH, lawyer; b. Wilkinsburg, Pa., July 23, 1902; s. Charles Shively and Ella (Harbaugh) M.; B.S., U. Pitts., 1922, J.D., 1925; m. Ruth M. Davis, Nov. 8, 1952. Admitted to Pa. bar, 1925, since in gen. practice; partner Miller, Entwisle & Duff, Pitts. Pres. Goodwill Industries, 1958-61, YMCA Pitts., 1956-58. Trustee U. Pitts., 1945-60, 66-72, trustee emeritus, 1973—; trustee Western Theol. Sem., 1955-58. Fellow Am. Bar Found., Am. Coll. Probate Counsel; mem. Am. Law Inst., Am. Judicature Soc., Am. (ho. dels.), Pa., Allegheny County (pres. 1955) bar assns., Pitts. Council Chs. (pres. 1951-53), SAR (pres. Pitts. 1940), U. Pitts. Alumni Assn. (pres. 1940), Phi Delta Theta, Omicron Delta Kappa, Beta Gamma Sigma, Phi Delta Phi. Presbyn. (elder). Mason. Clubs: Duquesne, Longue Vue, Seaview, Pitts. Athletic Assn., Automobile (pres. 1960-62) (Pitts.). Home: 154 N Bellefield Ave Pittsburgh PA 15213 Office: Frick Bldg Pittsburgh PA 15219

MILLER, HAROLD, advt. firm exec.; b. N.Y.C., Aug. 28, 1924; s. Harry and Nettie M.; B.B.A., Coll. City N.Y., 1949; m. Florence Miller, Apr. 13, 1946; children—Norman, Howard. Mgr. media research Biow Co., 1946-54; v.p., mgr. media dept. Benton & Bowles, Inc., N.Y.C., 1954-60; sr. v.p., media and programming dept. Grey Advt. Inc., 1960-69; sr. v.p. media and network programming S.S.C. & B., Inc., N.Y.C., 1969—, also dir. Lectr. Baruch Sch. Bus., Coll. City N.Y., N.Y. Inst. Tech.; asso. prof. Pace U. Mem. Media Dirs. Council (past pres.), Radio/TV Research Council (past pres.), 4A's Broadcast Policy Commn., Internat. Radio and TV Soc., Audit Bur. Circulation (dir.). Office: One Dag Hammarskjold Plaza New York City NY 10017

MILLER, HAROLD ALLEN, univ. dean; b. Powell, Wyo., July 12, 1931; s. James Lewis and Mary (Berryman) M.; B.A., Northwestern Coll., 1955; M.A., U. Minn., 1957, Ph.D., 1962; m. Patsy Ruth Reimann, Sept. 16, 1950; children—Christopher Lee, Sheree Suzanne, James Patrick Christian. Asst. dean summer session U. Minn., 1967-70, asso. dean summer session and gen. extension div., 1970-71, dean continuing edn. and extension, 1971—, prof. speech communication, 1967—. Mem. Nat. Univ. Extension Assn. (dir., chmn. Region IV 1975-77, nat. sec. 1978—), Nat. Assn. State U. and Land Grant Colls. Office: 150 Wesbrook Hall U Minn Minneapolis MN 55455

MILLER, HAROLD EDWARD, mfg. conglomerate exec.; b. St. Louis, Nov. 23, 1926; s. George Edward and Georgenia Elizabeth (Franklin) M.; B.S.B.A., Washington U., St. Louis, 1949; m. Lilian Ruth Gantner, Dec. 23, 1949; children—Ellen Susan, Jeffrey Arthur. Vice pres. Fulton Iron Works Co., St. Louis, 1968-71, pres., 1971-79, chmn. bd., 1979—; v.p. Katy Industries Inc., Elgin, Ill., 1976-77, exec. v.p., 1977—, also dir.; dir. W.J. Smith Wood Preserving Co.; mem. Sudan-U.S. Bus. Council, U.S.-Republic of China Bus. Council. Served with U.S. Army, 1945-46. Mem. Sugar Equipment and Service Exporters Assn., Internat. Machine Tool Builders Assn., Cutting Tool Mfr.'s Assn. Presbyterian. Clubs: Barrington Tennis, Mo. Athletic. Office: 853 Dundee Ave Elgin IL 60120

MILLER, HAROLD JOSEPH, metals mfg. co. exec.; b. Winstead, Conn., Feb. 23, 1923; s. Lee K. and Theresa (Quinn) M.; student Sch. Engring., DePaul U., 1942-43; B.S. in Bus. Adminstrn., Rutgers U., 1950; m. Betty Haggerty, Nov. 26, 1946; children—Colleen, Maureen. With Peat, Marwick, Mitchell & Co., C.P.A.'s, Newark, N.J., 1950-54; with Dixon Chem. Co., Bloomfield, N.J., 1955-61; financial cons. Hardy & Co., mem. N.Y. Stock Exchange, N.Y.C., 1962-65; founder, chmn., pres. Athlone Industries, Inc., Parsippany, N.J., 1965—. Served with AUS, 1941-44. C.P.A., N.J. Mem. Beta Gamma Sigma. Clubs: Cat Cay Yacht, Mountain Lakes. Office: 200 Webro Rd Parsippany NJ 07054

MILLER, HAROLD T., pub. co. exec.; b. New Paltz, N.Y., Jan. 5, 1923; s. Harold F. and Grace (Taylor) M.; B.S., Franklin and Marshall Coll., 1947; M.Ed., Columbia U., 1948; m. Marcheta Novak, 1947; 1 son, Harold F. Tchr. high sch., Plainfield, N.J., 1948-50; with Houghton Mifflin Co., 1950—, text book salesman, 1950-57, editor-in-chief test dept., 1957-62, asst. mgr. Midwestern regional office, 1962-65, mgr. Midwestern regional office, 1965-71, 1965-71, v.p. ednl. div., 1971-73, pres., chief exec. officer, 1973-79, pres., chmn., 1979—, also dir.; dir. SCA Services, New Eng. Mchts. Nat. Bank, Book Industry Study Group. Mem. corp. Babson Coll.; trustee Franklin and Marshall Coll. Mem. Assn. Am. Publishers (dir., chmn. bd. 1977-78), Kappa Sigma. Clubs: Union, Algonguin, St. Botolph, Comml. (Boston). Address: Houghton-Mifflin Co One Beacon St Boston MA 02107

MILLER, HARRIET EVELYN, mgmt. cons.; b. Council, Idaho, July 4, 1919; d. Colwell and Vera (Crome) Miller; B.A. magna cum laude, Whitman Coll., 1941; M.A., U. Pa., 1949. Chemist, Atlantic Refining Co., Phila., 1944-50; student personnel adminstr. U. Mont., Missoula, 1950-54, acting asso. dean students, 1954-55, asso. dean students, 1955-56; supt. pub. instrn., Mont., 1956-69; pres. Harriet Miller Assos., mgmt. cons., Helena, Mont., 1969-75; asso. dir. Am. Assn. Ret. Persons/Nat. Ret. Tchrs. Assn., 1975-76, exec. dir., 1976-77; mgmt. cons., 1977—; dir. Intertech Solar Corp. Bd. dirs. Nat. Council Homemaker-Home Health Aide Services, Ednl. Facilities Lab. Mem. Am. Assn. Sch. Adminstrs., P.E.O., Mont. Congress Parents and Tchrs. (life), AAUW, Phi Beta Kappa, Delta Kappa Gamma, Phi Kappa Phi, Psi Chi, Alpha Chi Omega. Methodist. Address: PO Box 19053 Washington DC 20036

MILLER, HARRY CHARLES, JR., physician; b. Ridgewood, N.J., Sept. 22, 1928; s. Harry Charles and Ruth G. (McDermott) M.; A.B., Amherst Coll., 1950; M.D., Yale U., 1954; m. Kari L. Palmer, June 14, 1969; children—Harry C., Carolynn A., Barbara J., Janet E., Jennifer T., Sandra L. Intern, Duke U. Hosp., Durham, N.C., 1954-55; resident U. Rochester Med. Group, 1959-62; practice medicine, specializing in urology, Washington, 1973—; asst. prof. urology U. Rochester Health Sci. Center, 1962-71; asso. prof. U. Okla. Health Sci. Center, 1971-73; prof., chmn. dept. urology George Washington U. Med. Center, 1973—. Served with U.S. Army, 1955-57. Mem. AMA, Am. Urol. Assn., A.C.S., Am. Trauma Assn., Western Trauma Assn., Am. Acad. Pediatrics, Société Internationale d'Urologie, Soc. Pediatric Urology, Soc. Univ. Urologists, Beekeepers Assn. No. Va. Clubs: Great Falls Grange; River Bend Golf and Country. Office: George Washington U Med Center 2150 Pennsylvania Ave NW Washington DC 20037

MILLER, HARRY GEORGE, educator; b. Waukesha, Wis., Feb. 15, 1941; s. Harry Fricke and Ethel Ruth (D'Amato) M.; B.A., Carroll Coll., 1963; M.Ed., U. Nebr., 1967, Ed.D., 1970; m. Mary Frances Shugrue, June 20, 1964; children—Alicia, Michael, Anne, Deirdre. Tchr., Westside Community Schs., Omaha, 1964-68; demonstration tchr. East Edn. Complex, Lincoln (Nebr.) Pub. Schs., 1967-68; instr. curriculum research Tchrs. Coll., U. Nebr., Lincoln, 1968-70; faculty So. Ill. U., Carbondale, 1970—, asso. prof. edn., dept. secondary edn., 1972—, chmn. dept. secondary edn., 1973-75, prof., chmn. dept. ednl. leadership, 1975—; research prof. Ministry Edn., Bangkok, Thailand, 1978; cons. to various orgns. and instns., 1969-74. Mem. Ill. Migrant Council, 1974. Adv. bd. Evaluation and Devel. Center, Rehab. Inst., Carbondale, 1974—. Mem. Pub. Adult and Continuing Edn. Assn., Rural Edn. Assn., Ill. Council for Social Studies (hon.), Greater Cleve. Council for Social Studies (hon.), Ednl. Council of 100 Inc., Phi Delta Kappa, Kappa Delta Pi. Democrat. Roman Catholic. K.C. Author: Strong Confrontation as an Educational Technique, 1973; Beyond Facts: Objective Ways to Measure Thinking, 1976; Drill Re-examined: A Taxonomy for Drill Exercises, 1975; Adults Teaching Adults, 1977; Responsibility Education, 1977; Instructional Planning Approaches for Better Learning Achievement in the Middle School, 1977; The Adult Educator: A Handbook for Staff Development, 1978; An Introduction to Adult and Continuing Education, 1979. also monographs. Mem. editorial bd. Training, 1976. Home: 2908 W Kent Dr Carbondale IL 62901

MILLER, HASBROUCK BAILEY, financial and travel services co. exec.; b. Gloversville, N.Y., Aug. 1, 1923; s. Edward Waite and Lorraine (Taylor) M.; B.A., Hamilton Coll., 1944; postgrad. U. Lausanne (Switzerland), 1946, Sch. Advanced Internat. Studies, Washington, 1947, Stanford Grad. Sch. Bus., 1961; m. Elizabeth J. Wilson, Jan. 5, 1949; children—Kimberly Elizabeth, Stacey Wilson, Hasbrouck Bailey, Sloan Taylor. With Am. Express Co., and subsidiaries, 1948—, v.p., sec., 1964-65, sr. v.p., 1965-68, exec. v.p., 1968—; exec. v.p. Am. Express Internat., Inc., 1960—. Served with OSS, AUS, 1942-45. Clubs: Recess (N.Y.C.); Morris County Golf (Convent Station, N.J.). Home: Fox Hollow Rd Convent Station NJ 07961 Office: Am Express Plaza New York City NY 10006

MILLER, HELEN MAY, librarian; b. Conway, Mo., Sept. 13, 1918; d. Lloyd Schmalhorst and Olive Frazier (Smith) Miller; A.B., Drury Coll., 1940; B.S. in L.S., U. Denver, 1941. Engring. librarian U. Ark., 1941-43; circulation librarian Springfield (Mo.) Pub. Library, 1943-45; librarian U.S. Army, Ft. George G. Meade, Md., 1945-46, Cole County Library, Jefferson City, Mo., 1947-49, Jefferson City and Cole County libraries, 1949-55, USAF libraries in Kaufbeuren and Furstenfeldbruck, Germany, also Lakenheath, Eng., 1955-58; pub. library cons. W. Va. Library Commn., 1959-61; librarian Idaho State Library, Boise, 1962—. Mem. steering com. for Nat. Library Week, Nat. Book Com., 1969-71. Mem. Am. Library Trustee Assn. (2d v.p. 1965-66), Am. (council 1952-53, 63-67, chmn. Nat. Library Week com. 1969-71), Pacific N.W., Idaho (exec. bd.), Mo. (pres. 1952-53), W.Va. (exec. bd. 1960-61) library assns., Am. Assn. State Librarians (sec. 1962-63, exec. bd. 1973-76). Editor: W. Va. Library Commn. Newsletter, 1960-61, The Idaho Librarian, 1962-69. Contbr. articles to profl. jours. Home: 4023 Whitehead St Boise ID 83703 Office: Idaho State Library Boise ID 83702

MILLER, HENRY (VALENTINE), author; b. N.Y.C., Dec. 26, 1891; student Coll. City N.Y., 1909; m. Beatrice Sylvas Wickens, 1917 (div. 1924); 1 dau., Barbara; m. 2d, June Smith, 1924 (div. 1934); m. 3d, Janina Lepska, Dec. 18, 1944 (div. 1952); children—Valentin, Tony; m. 4th, Eve McClure, Dec. 1953 (div. 1962); m. 5th, Hoki Tokuda, Sept. 10, 1967. Various odd jobs in U.S. until 1930; lived in Paris, 1930-39, in Greece, 1939; while living in Paris was mem. editorial staff lit. rev. Booster, also contbg. editor French rev. Volontes; living in U.S., 1940—; author: Tropic of Cancer, 1934; Topic of Capricorn, 1939; Black Spring, 1936; Max and the White Phagocytes, 1938; Money and How It Gets That Way, 1938; The Cosmological Eye, 1939; The Wisdom of the Heart, 1941; The Colossus of Maroussi, 1941; (with M. Fraenkel) Hamlet: a Philosophic Correspondence, 2 vols., 1939-41; Sunday After the War, 1944; The Air-Conditioned Nightmare Remember to Remember, 1945-47; The Smile at the Foot of the Ladder, 1948; Sexus, 1949; Plexus, 1949; The Books in My Life, 1952; Quiet Days in Clichy, 1956; Nexus, 1957; Big Sur and the Oranges of Hieronymus Bosch, 1958; Stand Still Like the Hummingbird, 1962; Watercolors, 1962; Lawrence Durrell and Henry Miller: A Private Correspondence, 1963; Greece, 1964; World of Sex, 1965; Plight of the Creative Artist in the United States of America, 2d edit., 1969; My Life and Times, 1971; Books Tangent to Circles, 1963; First Impressions of Greece, 1973; Henry Miller's Book of Friends, 1976; Gliding into the Everglades and Other Essays, 1977; My Bike and Other Friends, 1978, Joey, 1979, many others; exhibited paintings, Los Angeles, 1966. Decorated Legion of Honor (France), 1975. Mem. Nat. Inst. Arts and Letters. care Capra Press 631 State St Santa Barbara CA 93101•

MILLER, HENRY CHALFANT, mfg. co. exec.; b. Pitts., July 18, 1923; s. Henry Chalfant and Grace Adelia (Kelly) M.; B.A., Coll. Wooster, 1943; B.S., Case Inst. Tech., 1948; M.B.A., Harvard U., 1951; m. Virginia Clark, July 29, 1945; children—Patricia Lee, Torrence Clark, David Clark. Exec. v.p., gen. mgr. Chem-Therm Mfg. Co., Inc., Los Angeles, 1959-61; pres., owner, Mag Enterprises, Inc., Los Angeles, 1961-64; with Borg-Warner Corp., 1964-78, v.p. mfg. Borg and Beck div., Detroit, 1966-70, group v.p. Transp. Equipment Group, Detroit, 1970-78; pres., dir. Western Gear Corp., Lynwood, Calif., 1978—. Served to lt., USNR, 1943-46. Mem. Nat. Ocean Industries Assn., World Affairs Council, Soc. Automotive Engrs., Nat. Mgmt. Assn., Nat. Assn. Mfrs., Exec. Forum of Calif. Inst. Tech. Episcopalian. Clubs: California, Los Angeles Country. Home: 1253 Roberto Ln Los Angeles CA 90224 Office: 2600 E Imperial Hwy Lynwood CA 90262

MILLER, HENRY KNIGHT, educator; b. Bklyn., Apr. 25, 1920; s. Henry Knight and Jessie (Jewell) M.; student Western Md. Coll., 1938-40; B.A., Oberlin Coll., 1949; Ph.D., Princeton, 1953; m. Bertha Mercedes DeGraw, Sept. 10, 1949. Mem. faculty Princeton, 1953—, prof. English, 1969—, dir. grad. studies, 1970-73. Served with USCG, 1941-46. Mem. Modern Lang. Assn., Internat. Assn. Univ. Profs. English, Am. Soc. Eighteenth Century Studies, Johnsonians, Phi Beta Kappa. Author: Essays on Fielding's Miscellanies, 1961; Henry Fielding's Tom Jones and the Romance Tradition, 1976. Editor: Fielding's Miscellanies, 1972. Co-editor: Bibliography of Eighteenth-Century Literature, 1958-64; The Augustan Milieu, 1971; asso. editor: Wesleyan Edition of the Works of Henry Fielding, 1967—. Home: 135 McCosh Circle Princeton NJ 08540

MILLER, HENRY LOUIS, ret. naval officer, real estate exec.; b. Fairbanks, Alaska, July 18, 1912; s. Frank and Mary (Merhar) M.; B.S., U.S. Naval Acad., 1934; grad. Indsl. Coll. Armed Forces, 1953; LL.D. (hon.), U. Alaska; m. Margaret Lucille Dean, May 17, 1939; children—Henry Louis, Richard Brian. Commd. ensign U.S. Navy, 1934, advanced through grades to rear adm., 1960; trained Gen. Doolittle's Tokyo Raiders in aircraft carrier take-offs, 1942; comdr. Fighting Squadron, 23, 1942-44, Air Group 23, 1943-44, Air Group 6, 1944-45, Air br. Office Naval Research, 1946-48; comdr. Fleet Air, Philippines; comdr. Naval Air Bases, Philippines; comdg. officer Naval Sta., Sangley Point, Philippines, 1955-57; dir. Progress Analysis Group, Office of Chief Naval Operations, Washington, 1957-59; comdg. officer U.S.S. Hancock, 1959-60; chief staff Com. NAVAIRPAC, 1960-61; comdr. Carrier Div. 15, 1961-62; asst. chief staff, plans staff CINCPAC, 1962-64; comdr. Carrier Div. 3, 1964-66; launched first aircraft carrier strikes on North Vietnam, 1965; engaged first nuclear-powered Aircraft Carrier Task Group (USS Enterprise and USS Bainbridge) in combat in Vietnam, 1965; chief of info. Dept. Navy, Washington, 1966-68; comdr. Naval Air Test Center, Patuxent River, Md., comdr. Fleet Air, Patuxent, and Naval Air Systems Command test and evaluation coordinator, 1968-71; ret., 1971; real estate exec., 1973—. Dir. bd. control Naval Inst., 1966-71. Decorated Legion of Merit with V and 3 stars, Bronze Star, D.F.C. with 4 stars, Air medal with 5 stars, Army Commendation medal, Navy Commendation medal. Mem. U.S. Naval Acad. Alumni Assn., Naval Hist. Found., U.S. Naval Acad. Athletic Assn. Roman Catholic. Home: 153 Gunston Dr Lexington Park MD 20653

MILLER, HERBERT ELMER, accountant; b. DeWitt, Iowa, Aug. 11, 1914; s. Elmer Joseph and Marian (Briggs) M.; A.B., State U. Iowa, 1936, M.A., 1937; Ph.D., U. Minn., 1944; m. Lenore Snitkey, July 1, 1938; 1 dau., Barbara Ruth. Accounting prof. U. Minn., U. Mich., Mich. State U., 1938-70; partner Arthur Andersen & Co., Chgo., 1970-78; dir. Sch. Accounting, U. Ga., Athens, 1978—. C.P.A., Iowa, Ga., Ill. Mem. Am. Accounting Assn. (pres. 1965-66), Am. Inst. C.P.A.'s (dir. 1968-70), Beta Gamma Sigma, Beta Alpha Psi (nat. pres. 1961-62). Co-author: Finney-Miller accounting series, 1950-70; editor, contbr. C.P.A. Rev. Manual, 1951-79. Home: 12 S Stratford Dr Athens GA 30605 Office: Coll Bus Adminstrn U Ga Athens GA 30602

MILLER, HERBERT JOHN, JR., lawyer; b. Mpls., Jan. 11, 1924; s. Herbert John and Catherine (Johnson) M.; student U. Minn., 1941-43; B.A., George Washington U., 1948, LL.B., 1949; m. Carey Kinsolving, Apr. 3, 1948; children—John Kinsolving William Grady. Admitted to D.C. bar, 1949; asso. Kirkland, Fleming, Green, Martin & Ellis, Washington, 1949-58; partner Kirkland, Ellis, Hodson, Chaffetz and Masters, 1958-61; asst. atty. gen., criminal div. Dept. Justice, 1961-65; partner Miller, Cassidy, Larroca & Lewin, Washington, 1965—. Chmn. U.S. del. Conferees Attys. Gen. Ams., Mexico City, Mexico, 1963, Ministers of Govt., Interior and Security of Central Am., Panama, and U.S., 1964, 65; past v.p., trustee Bur. Social Sci. Research; chmn. Pres.'s Commn. on D.C. Crime, 1965-67. Served from pvt. to capt. AUS, 1943-46. Mem. Am., Fed., D.C. (pres. 1970-71), Fed. Communications bar assns., Order of Coif, Phi Delta Phi, Alpha Delta Phi. Club: Congressional (Washington). Home: 10600 River Rd Potomac MD 20854 Office: 2555 M St NW Washington DC 20037

MILLER, HERMAN, engring. co. exec.; b. St. Paul, Dec. 16, 1919; s. Ruben and Fae (Powell) M.; B.S., Calif. Inst. Tech., 1943, M.S., 1945, A.E., 1948; m. Joane Soss, Dec. 5, 1943; children—Stacey, Loren, Kris. Chief aerodynamic devel. So. Calif. Coop. Wind Tunnel, Calif. Inst. Tech., 1941-51, blackliner, computer, technician, crew chief, data analysis supr., aeronautics lectr. Aero. Grad. Sch., 1948-49; dep. chief propulsion wind tunnel Arnold Engring. Devel. Center, 1951-53; mgr. Idaho Engring. ANP dept. Gen. Electric Co., 1953-55, mgr. design and projects sect., 1955-60, mgr. spl. purpose nuclear systems operation Atomic Products div., 1960-64, gen. mgr., 1964-65; pres. Herman Miller Co., Palo Alto, Calif., 1966—, Nat. Nuclear Corp., Redwood City, Calif., 1967-78, Inet Corp., Palo Alto, 1978—. Mem. Caltech Mgmt. Club (bd. founder), Electric Automobile Assn. (dir. 1973—), Inst. Nuclear Materials Mgmt. (chmn. public info. com.), Am. Nuclear Soc., Sigma Xi. Contbr. articles to pubs. Home: 1788 Oak Creek Dr Palo Alto CA 94304 Office: 3150 Spring St Redwood City CA 94063

MILLER, HIRAM AUGUSTUS, glass co. exec.; b. Olean, N.Y., Oct. 21, 1920; s. Edward L. and Marie T. (Kreamer) M.; B.B.A., St. Bonaventure U., 1943; m. Pearl J. Levis, May 6, 1977; children—Kathleen M., Sharon L., Diane L. Auditor Graef Cutting & Coit, Buffalo, 1947-58; mgr. accounting dept. Knox Glass Co., Inc. (Pa.), 1958-62, controller, 1962-68; asst. controller Glass Containers Corp., Fullerton, Calif., 1968-70, controller, 1970—. Served with USNR, 1943-46; PTO. Mem. Nat. Assn. Accountants. Home: 1481 Skyline Dr Fullerton CA 92631 Office: 535 N Gilbert Ave Fullerton CA 92632

MILLER, HOPE RIDINGS, author; b. Bonham, Tex.; d. Alfred Lafayette and Grace (Dupree) Ridings; B.A., U. Tex.; M.A., Columbia; D.Litt., Austin Coll.; m. Clarence Lee Miller (dec.). Society editor Washington Post, 1938-44; Washington corr. Town and Country mag., 1944-46, The Argonaut mag., 1945-49; Washington columnist Promenade mag., 1945-51; syndicated column McNaught, 1946-48; asso. editor Diplomat mag., 1952-55, editor in chief, 1956-66; television prodn. staff Metromedia, Inc., 1966-70; Washington editor Antique Monthly, 1975—; mem. editorial adv. bd. Horizon mag., 1978—. Mem. Nat. Council U.S.O. Mem. Washington Press Club (past pres.), Am. Newspaper Women's Club, Soc. Am. Travel Writers, Nat. Communications Club, Smithsonian Assos., UN Assos., Author's Guild, Nat. Trust Historic Preservation, Phi Mu. Clubs: Sulgrave; Internat., Overseas Press. Author: Embassy Row; The Life and Times of Diplomatic Washington, 1969; Great Houses of Washington, 1969; Scandals In The Highest Office: Facts and Fictions in the Private Lives of Our Presidents, 1973; Circling Lafayette Square, 1976. Home: 1868 Columbia Rd NW Washington DC 20009

MILLER, HOWARD C., food co. exec.; b. Erie, Pa., 1926; s. Howard C. and Elsie M. (Hays) M.; B.S., U. Pa., 1950; m. JoAnne D. DeGraw, Sept. 8, 1948. Instr. U. Pa., Phila., 1950-51; sales engr. E.F. Houghton & Co., 1951-58; tech. sales div. mgr. Lubrizol Corp., Euclid, Ohio, 1958; asst. to pres. Dairy Pak Butler Inc., Cleve., 1958-61; cons. Robert Heller & Assos., Cleve., 1961-63; mgr. organizational devel. ITT, N.Y.C., 1963, mgr. indsl. products, 1964, product line mgr. consumer services, 1965-67, v.p., group exec. consumer services, 1967-72; pres., chief exec. officer Canteen Corp., Chgo., 1972—; dir. TWC, Lake Shore Nat. Bank. Mem. exec. bd. U.S. Olympic Com. Served to 1st lt. USAAF, 1945-46. Office: 1430 Merchandise Mart Chicago IL 60654

MILLER, HOWARD RAYMOND, credit assn. exec.; b. Ashland, Ohio, July 17, 1923; s. M. H. and Hazel P. (Harper) M.; student public schs., Ashland; m. Jean Oney, July 12, 1947; children—Linda, Karen, LuAnn, Sandra. Owner, operator farm, Ashland, Ohio, 1945-53; with Farmers Prodn. Credit Assn., 1953—, v.p., Ashland, 1968-75, pres., 1975—. Mem. Madison Local Sch. Bd., Mansfield, Ohio, 1968-78. Served with U.S. Army, 1942-45. Office: Farmers of Ashland Route 250 E Ashland OH 44805

MILLER, IRMA GANZ, publishing co. exec., journalist; b. Scranton, Pa., Dec. 25, 1916; d. Jacob and Dora (Weinberger) Ganz; B.A., Pa. State U., 1938; m. Milton Miller, Sept. 3, 1939 (dec. Dec. 15, 1969); children—Jeffrey Harold, Lee James. Mng. dir. Soccer Assos., New Rochelle, N.Y., 1948—; bus. mgr. Jeffrey Lee News Syndicate, New Rochelle, 1953—; pres. Sport Shelf, pub., New Rochelle, 1953—; mng. editor Soccer News, New Rochelle, 1968-77; columnist L.I. Press, 1969-73; soccer journalist Reuter's, 1967-77; dir. Wide World Book Centre Ltd., New Rochelle 1966—. Mem. Soccer Writers Assn. Am. (pres. 1969-77), Nat. Sportscasters and Sportswriters Assn., Internat. Platform Assn., Nat. Recreation Assn., AAHPER, Nat. Parks and Recreation Assn., Am. Booksellers Assn., Pa. State Alumni Assn. Contbr. articles to newspapers, mags. Office: PO Box 634 New Rochelle NY 10802

MILLER, IRVING FRANKLIN, educator, univ. dean; b. N.Y.C., Sept. 27, 1934; s. Sol and Gertrude (Rochkind) M.; B.S. in Chem. Engring., N.Y. U., 1955; M.S., Purdue U., 1956; Ph.D., U. Mich., 1960; m. Baila Hannah Milner, Jan. 28, 1962; children—Eugenia Lynne, Jonathan Mark. Research scientist United Aircraft Corp., Hartford, 1959-61; asst. prof. to prof., head chem. engring. Poly. Inst. Bklyn., 1961-72; prof., head bioengring. program U. Ill., Chgo. 1973-79, acting head systems engring. dept., 1978-79, dean Grad. Coll., 1979—, asso. vice chancellor for research, 1979—; cons. Nat. Acad. Scis., NIH. Mem. Am. Inst. Chem. Engrs., (industry mem.), Am. Chem. Soc., Am. Soc. Engring. Edn., AAAS, Biomed. Engring. Soc., Electrochem. Soc., N.Y. Acad Scis. Editor: Electrochemical Bioscience and Bioengineering, 1973. Contbr. articles profl. jours. Home: 2600 Orrington Ave Evanston IL 60201 Office: Box 4348 Chicago IL 60680

MILLER, IRWIN, cons.; b. July 3, 1928; s. Samuel C. and Cele M.; B.A., Alfred U., 1950; M.S., Purdue U., 1952; Ph.D., Va. Poly. Inst., 1956; m. JoAnn Schiff, Sept. 7, 1952; children—Dianne L., David G., Paul S. Mem. research staff applied research lab. U.S. Steel Co., Monroeville, Pa., 1956-58; asso. prof. math. Ariz. State U., 1958-64, prof. stats., 1964-65; sr. profl. staff mem. Arthur D. Little, Inc., Cambridge, Mass., 1965-73, v.p., 1973—; chmn. bd. Opinion Research Corp., Princeton, N.J.; adj. prof. stats. Coll. Bus. Adminstrn., Boston U., 1968-69; dir. acad. computer center, adj. prof. math. Wesleyan U., 1969-71. Served with Ordnance Corps, U.S. Army, 1953-54. Mem. Am. Statis. Assn., Inst. Math. Stats., Biometrics Soc. Author: Manual of Experimental Statistics, 1960; A Primer on Statistics for Business and Economics, 1968; Algebra and Trigonometry, 1962, 2d rev. edit., 1970; Probability and Statistics for Engineers, 1965, 2d rev. edit., 1977. Home: 33 Sanderson Rd Lexington MA 02173 Office: Arthur D Little Inc Acorn Park Cambridge MA 02130

MILLER, IRWIN ROBERT, lawyer; b. Mt. Vernon, N.Y., May 19, 1942; s. Hyman A. and Sylvia (Lash) M.; B.B.A., Woodbury Coll., 1964; J.D., U. Cin., 1968; m. Arlene Samuel, Aug. 26, 1964; children—Jeffrey Brian, Daniel Stewart. Admitted to Calif. bar, 1969, since practiced in Los Angeles; propr. Irwin R. Miller, P.C., 1976—. Mem. Los Angeles County, Hollywood (pres. 1978) bar assns., Calif., Los Angeles trial lawyers assns., Calif. State Bar (com. on maintenance of profl. competence). Contbr. to legal jours. Address: 6255 Sunset Blvd 20th Floor Hollywood CA 90028

MILLER, ISRAEL, clergyman, ednl. adminstr.; b. Balt., Apr. 6, 1918; s. Tobias and Bluma (Bunchez) M.; B.A. magna cum laude, Yeshiva Coll., 1938, D.D., 1967; M.A., Columbia, 1949; m. Ruth Joan Goldman, Oct. 16, 1945; children—David, Michael, Deborah, Judith. Rabbi, 1941; rabbi Kingsbridge Heights Jewish Center, Bronx, 1941-68, rabbi emeritus, 1968—; asst. to pres. Yeshiva U., N.Y.C., 1968-70, v.p., 1970—; counselor B'nai B'rith Hillel Found., Hunter Coll., Bronx, 1951-60; lectr. homiletics Yeshiva U., 1954-55. Vice pres. Bronx council Am. Jewish Congress, 1954-60, Bronx Council Jewish Edn., 1964-68; pres. Rabbinical Council Am., 1964-66, hon. pres., 1966-68; mem. exec. com. World Zionist Orgn., 1971-76; chmn. Am. Jewish Conf. on Soviet Jewry, 1965-67, Am. Zionist Council, 1967-70; pres. Am. Zionist Fedn., 1970-74, hon. pres., 1974—; v.p. Religious Zionists Am., 1966-68; religious cons., retreat master Dept. Def. in Europe, 1954, 63-64, Alaska, 1958, Japan, 1960. Vice chmn. Conf. Pres.'s Am. Jewish Orgns., 1969-74; chmn. Conf. Pres.'s Major Am. Jewish Orgns., 1974-76; vice chmn. N.Y. Jewish Community Relations Council, 1976—; exec. com. Bronx council Boy Scouts Am., 1951-58; mem. Nat. Citizens Com. Community Relations, 1946—. Bd. dirs. Nat. Jewish Welfare Bd., v.p., 1969—, chmn. Commn. Jewish Chaplaincy, 1962-65; bd. dirs. Bd. Jewish Edn. N.Y.C., Nat. Jewish Community Relations, United Israel Appeal, Conf. on Jewish Material Claims Against Germany, 1968—; sec. Meml. Found. for Jewish Culture, 1973—; bd. govs. Jewish Agy. for Israel, 1971-76. Served as chaplain USAAF, 1945-46. Recipient Bernard Revel award Yeshiva Coll. Alumni Assn., 1961, Nat. Rabbinic Leadership award Union of Orthodox Jewish Congregations, 1966, Shofor award Boy Scouts Am., 1965, Frank L. Weill award Nat. Jewish Welfare Bd., 1972; Man of Year award Nat. Council Young Israel, 1976; Dr. Harris J. Levine award B'nai Zion, 1979, others. Mem. Jewish War Vets. (nat. chaplain 1962-63), Assn. Jewish Chaplains Armed Forces (pres. 1955-56), Rabbinic Alumni Yeshiva U. (pres. 1960-62). Editor: Sermon Manual, 1951. Home: 2619 Davidson Ave Bronx NY 10468 Office: Yeshiva U 2540 Amsterdam Ave New York NY 10033

MILLER, IVAN LAWRENCE, lawyer; b. Cleve., Feb. 2, 1914; s. Ralph and Sarah (Kichler) M.; B.A., Case Western Res. U., 1936, LL.B., J.D., 1938; postgrad. Grad. Sch. Bus. Adminstrn., Harvard, 1943, Inns of Ct. (Middle Temple), London, Eng., 1945. Admitted to Ohio bar, 1938, U.S. Supreme Ct., 1960; practiced in Cleve., 1938—; partner Ziegler, Metzger, Miller & Hoppe, 1968—; consul of Belgium (Ohio), 1962—; legal adviser Brit. Consulate Gen., 1958—, Canadian Consulate and Trade Commn., 1964—. Vice pres., trustee Maison Francaise; bd. overseers Case Western Res. U. Served to maj., Judge Adv. Gen. Dept., AUS, 1941-46. Decorated Bronze Star medal, Exec. Order Ohio Commodore, Belgian Mil. Cross 1st Class, Knight Order Crown (Belgium); officer Order of Brit. Empire; named Consul of Year, 1974. Fellow Royal Soc. Arts (Brit.); mem. Am., Fed. (sec. 1973, pres. 1974-75, dir.), Ohio, Cleve. (past trustee) bar assns., Newcomen Soc., English Speaking Union (past pres., nat. dir.), Consular Corps Coll., Sch. of Law Alumni Assn. (past pres.), Nat. Alumni Assn. Case Western Res. U. (past pres.), Cleve. Dist Golf Assn. (counsel), World Trade Assn., Assn. Ohio Commodores, Inst. Dirs. (Eng.), Soc. Benchers. Rotarian. Clubs: Union; Lake Forest Country (Hudson, Ohio); Commerce, Mid-day, Ohio Commodores, Rowfant, Harvard, Harvard Graduate School (Cleve.); Wig and Pen, Link (Eng.). Home: 2482 Derbyshire Rd Cleveland Heights OH 44106 Office: 1670 Union Commerce Bldg Cleveland OH 44115

MILLER, J. DUANE, surgeon; b. Bangor, Mich., June 5, 1899; s. John James and Pearl A. (Snyder) M.; B.S., U. Mich., 1922, M.D., 1924; postgrad. U. Vienna (Austria), 1930-31; m. Josephine G. Frost, Sept. 2, 1933; 1 son, John Gregory. Teaching asst. anatomy U. Mich., 1921-23, teaching asst. pharmacology, 1923-24; intern Blodgett Meml. Hosp., Grand Rapids, Mich., 1924-25, preceptorship surgery, 1925-30; practice medicine specializing in surgery, Grand Rapids, 1931—; asso. clin. prof. surgery Mich. State U.; cons. surgeon Blodgett Meml., Butterworth, Ferguson-Droste-Ferguson, St. Mary's hosps. Pres. Kent County Health Council, 1958-62. Bd. dirs. Grand Rapids YMCA, 1936-57, United Community Service Grand Rapids, 1964-67, Kent County chpt. A.R.C., 1965-69. Served with U.S. Army, 1918; with USNR, 1942-46. Diplomate Am. Bd. Surgery. Fellow Am., Internat. (regent for Mich. 1954-60, v.p. U.S. sect. 1965-70) colls. surgeons; mem. Chgo. Surg. Soc., Mich. Soc. Obstetrics and Gynecology, Am. (exhibit award 1934), Indsl. (pres. Mich. 1946-47) med. assns., Assn. Mil. Surgeons, Am. Med. Soc. Vienna (life), Mich. (chmn. sect. gynecology and obstetrics 1936-37, councilor 5th dist. 1946-56), Kent County (pres. 1952) med. socs., U. Mich. Emeritus Club, Alpha Omega Alpha, Alpha Epsilon Mu. Republican. Episcopalian. Mason. Club: U. Mich. President's, Kent Country. Contbr. articles to med. jours. Devised technique for and performed first amniocentesis, 1930 (award exhibit Am. Roentgen Ray Soc.). Home: 439 Lakeside Dr NE Grand Rapids MI 49503 Office: Suite 240 Blodgett Profl Bldg 1900 Wealthy St SE Grand Rapids MI 49506

MILLER, J(AMES) GORMLY, librarian; b. Rochester, N.Y., Jan. 5, 1914; s. James Billings and Marian (Robinson) M.; A.B., U. Rochester, 1936; B.S. in L.S., Columbia U., 1938; m. Mildred Catharine Bevan, Sept. 6, 1939; children—Susan Miller Milligan, James Gormly, Paul B. Asst. librarian Rochester Pub. Library, 1938-42; research asst. Bur. Adult Edn., N.Y. State Dept. Edn., 1946; librarian Cornell U.-N.Y. State Sch. Indsl. and Labor Relations, 1946-62, asso. prof., then prof., 1949-70, 74-77, asst. dir. personnel and budget univ. libraries, 1962-70, libraries dir., 1975-79, librarian, 1979—; dep. chief central library and documentation br. ILO, Geneva, 1970-74; trustee Finger Lakes Library System, 1967-69; cons. in field. Alderman, Ithaca (N.Y.) Common Council, 1959-63, 68; commnr. Ithaca Civil Service Commn., 1964-67. Served with U.S. Army, 1943-46. Mem. Am., N.Y. State library assns., Indsl. Relations Research Assn., Internat. Indsl. Relations Assn. Democrat. Anglican. Author profl. articles, reports. Home: 7-D Wildflower Dr Eastwood Commons Ithaca NY 14850 Office: 331 Ives Hall Cornell Univ Ithaca NY 14853

MILLER, J. PHILIP, television producer, dir.; b. Barberton, Ohio, July 10, 1937; s. Cloy M. and Mary (Yoder) M.; B.A., Haverford Coll., 1959; Ed.M., Harvard U., 1960; children—Kimberly Lowell, Marc Cloy. Tchr. public schs., Newton and Lexington, Mass., 1959-63; dir., lead guitarist profl. folksinging trio, Boston, 1963-66; prodn. coordinator, prodn. asst. Candid Camera, N.Y.C., 1966-67; unit mgr., asso. producer NBC-TV, N.Y.C., 1967-73; free lance producer, dir., N.Y.C., 1973—; programs include: Go Show, 1973-75, Spl. Treat, 1975, 77, First Tuesday, 1970-71, Tonight Show, 1969; instr. TV prodn. N.Y. U. Recipient Emmy award, 1976; Peabody award, 1975. Mem. Dirs. Guild Am., Writers Guild Am., Nat. Acad. TV Arts and Scis., Assn. Ind. Video and Filmmakers. Home: 182 Scribner Ave Norwalk CT 06854 Office: Care Tapper Prodns Inc 150 E 52d St New York NY 10022

MILLER, JACK BARNETT, physician; b. Winslow, Ind., June 17, 1918; s. Lawrence R. and Bess Ellen (Barnett) M.; A.B., Ind. U., 1939, M.D., 1943; m. Jeanne Pierson, June 5, 1943; children—John Ross, Jeffrey Allen. Intern, Indpls. City Hosp., 1943-44; fellow in otolaryngology Cleve. Clinic Found., 1946-49; chief dept. otolaryngology Med. Clinic, Portland, Oreg., 1949—; mem. staffs Emanuel Hosp., Portland, Shrine Hosp., Portland, Portland Adventist Hosp., Physician and Surgeons Hosp., Portland, City of Roses Hosp., Portland, Dwyer Meml. Hosp., Milwaukie, Oreg.; clin. instr. U. Oreg., 1950-61; otolaryngology preceptor for intern-resident tng. program Emanuel Hosp., 1955—; cons. Shriner Hosp., 1954—. Served to capt. M.C. AUS, 1944-46, 51-51. Decorated Combat Med. badge, Bronze Star medal; recipient certificate of acknowledgement Shriners Hosp. for Crippled Children, 1962, certificate of appreciation Chiron Club Phi Beta Pi, 1955, Physicians Recognition award AMA, 1969—; certificate for participation as active tchr. Am. Acad. Family Physicians; diplomate Am. Bd. Otolaryngology. Mem. AAAS, AMA, Am. Assn. Study Headache, Am. Thoracic Soc., Internat. Corr. Soc. Ophthalmologists and Otolaryngologists, Oreg. Acad. Ophthalmology and Otolaryngology (pres. 1970-71), Oreg. lfed. Assn., Pacific Coast Soc. Otolaryngology and Ophthalmology, Pan-Pacific Surg. Assn., Am. Acad. Otolaryngology and Ophthalmology, Am. Laryngol., Rhinol., Otolaryn. Soc., Pan-Am. Assn. Oto-Rhinol., Laryngol. and Broncho-Esophageal, Pan-Am. Med. Assn., Am., Internat. rhinologic socs., Am. Council Otolaryngology, Delta Upsilon. Republican. Mem. Christian Ch. (Disciples of Christ). Clubs: Masons, Internat. Active (appreciation certificate 19—, chmn. com. hearings 1954-55), Portland Active (pres. 1952-53), Multnomah Athletic. Contbr. articles to profl. jours. Home: 325 NW Royal Blvd Portland OR 97210 Office: 4212 NE Broadway Portland OR 97213

MILLER, JACK DAVID R., physician; b. Johannesburg, South Africa, Apr. 15, 1930; s. Harold Lewis and Inez (Behrman) M.; B.Sc., M.B., Ch.B., U. Witwatersrand (Johannesburg), 1956. Intern Coronation Hosp., Johannesburg, 1957-58; resident radiology Passavant Meml. Hosp., Chgo., 1959-62, Wesley Meml. Hosp., Chgo., 1959-62; fellow radiology Northwestern U. Med. Sch., 1962-63; chmn. dept. radiology U. Hosp., Edmonton, Alta., Can., 1971—; clin. prof. radiology U. Alta., 1971—. Diplomate Am. Bd. Radiology. Fellow Royal Coll. Physicians Can. Office: U Alberta Dept Radiology Edmonton 7 AB Canada

MILLER, JACK RICHARD, judge; b. Chgo., June 6, 1916; s. Forest W. and Blanche Miller; A.B. cum laude, Creighton U., 1938, LL.D. (hon.), 1966; M.A., Cath. U., Washington, 1939; J.D., Columbia, 1946; postgrad. State U. Iowa Coll. Law, 1946; LL.D. (hon.), Loras Coll., 1967, Iowa Wesleyan Coll., 1969, Yonsei U., Korea, 1976; m. Isabelle M. Browning, Aug. 1, 1942; children—Janice Lee (Mrs. John Flanagan), Judy Ann (Mrs. Robert Flyn), James Forrest, Jaynie Kay. Admitted to Iowa, Nebr. bars, 1946, D.C. bar, 1949; atty. Office Chief Counsel, IRS, Washington, 1947-48; lectr. taxation George Washington U., 1948; asst. prof. law U. Notre Dame, 1948-49; practice tax law, Sioux City, Iowa, 1949-60; mem. Iowa Ho. of Reps., 1955-56, Iowa Senate, 1957-60; U.S. senator from Iowa, 1961-73; judge U.S. Ct. Customs and Patent Appeals, Washington, 1973—. Served from lt. to lt. col. USAAF, 1942-46; brig. gen. USAF Res. (ret.). Mem. Am., Iowa, Nebr., D.C. bar assns., Am. Law Inst. (life), Am. Patent Law Assn., Am. Legion, VFW, Amvets. K.C., Rotarian. Contbr. articles on tax and patent law to legal periodicals. Home: 5417 Kirkwood Dr Washington DC 20016 Office: 717 Madison Pl NW Washington DC 20439

MILLER, JACK WAYNE, service co. exec.; b. Duncan, Okla., Oct. 29, 1926; s. James Nicholas and Lilly E. (Small) M.; B.B.A., U. Okla., 1952; m. Carol Jean Morin, Oct. 29, 1954; children—Michael Wayne, Johnson Keith, Darrell Glen. With Halliburton Co., 1952—, asst. treas., 1967-70, treas., 1970-78, v.p., 1973-78, v.p. fin., 1978—. C.P.A., Tex., Okla. Mem. Financial Execs. Inst., Am. Inst. C.P.A.'s, Tex. Soc. C.P.A.'s. Baptist. Clubs: Chaparral, Las Colinas Country. Home: 3988 Courtshire Dr Dallas TX 75229 Office: 2600 Southland Center Dallas TX 75201

MILLER, JAMES ALEXANDER, oncologist; b. Dormont, Pa., May 27, 1915; s. John Herman and Emma Anna (Stenger) M.; B.S. in Chemistry, U. Pitts., 1939; M.S., U. Wis., 1941, Ph.D. in Biochemistry, 1943; m. Elizabeth Cavert, Aug. 30, 1942; children—Linda Ann, Helen Louise. Finney-Howell fellow in cancer research U. Wis., Madison, 1943-44, instr. oncology, 1944-46, asst. prof., 1946-48, asso. prof., 1948-52, prof., 19S2—; mem. advisory coms. Nat. Cancer Inst., Am. Cancer Soc., 1950—. Recipient awards (with E.C. Miller) Langer-Teplitz award Ann Langer Cancer Research Found., 1962, Lucy Wortham James award James Ewing Soc., 1965, G.H.A. Clowes award Am. Assn. Cancer Research, 1969, Bertner award M.D. Anderson Hosp. and Tumor Inst., 1971, Papanicolaou award Papanicolaou Inst. Cancer Research, 1975, Rosenstiel award Brandeis U., 1976, award Am. Cancer Soc., 1977, Bristol-Myers award in cancer research, 1978, Gairdner Found. ann. award, Toronto, 1978, Founders award Chem. Industry Inst. Toxicology, 1978, 3M Life Sci. award Fedn. Am. Socs. Exptl. Biology, 1979. Mem. Am. Assn. for Cancer Research, Am. Soc. Biol. Chemists, AAAS, Am. Chem. Soc., Soc. Toxicology, Soc. for Exptl. Biology and Medicine, Nat. Acad. Scis. Contbr. numerous articles on chemical carcinogenesis and microsomal oxidations to profl. jours. Home: 5517 Hammersely Rd Madison WI 53711 Office: McArdle Laboratory University of Wisconsin Madison WI 53706

MILLER, JAMES ALVIN, mfg. co. exec.; b. Bainbridge, Ga., Feb. 11, 1924; s. Robert E. and Tiercy (Cook) M.; student Gordon Mil. Coll., Barnesville, Ga., 1941-42, Wayne State U., Detroit, 1942-50; grad. Advanced Mgmt. Course, Princeton, 1965; m. Grace Marie Palermo, Mar. 11, 1944; children—James Alvin, Carol Lynn (Mrs. Bruce A. Nadler), Jerome Charles. Mgr. engring., constrn. and machinery div., also gen. mgr. Cedar Rapids (Iowa) plant Allis Chalmers Mfg. Co., 1963-66; v.p., gen. mgr. ry. div. Budd Co., Phila., 1966-70; dir. mfg. companies, automotive group ITT Corp., N.Y.C., 1970-73; chmn. bd., chief exec. officer, pres. Portec, Inc., Oak Brook, Ill., 1973—. Mem. Soc. Automotive Engrs., Engrs. Club Phila., Presidents Assn. Mason. Clubs: Metropolitan (N.Y.C.); Mid-Am. (Chgo.); Hinsdale (Ill.) Golf. Home: 47 Briarwood S Oak Brook IL 60521 Office: 300 Windsor Dr Oak Brook IL 60521

MILLER, JAMES EDWIN, JR., educator; b. Bartlesville, Okla., Sept. 9, 1920; s. James Edwin and Leona (Halsey) M.; B.A., U. Okla., 1942; M.A., U. Chgo., 1947, Ph.D., 1949; m. Barbara Anderson, July 3, 1944; children—James E. III, Charlotte Ann. Asst. prof. English, U. Nebr., Lincoln, 1953-56, prof., chmn. dept., 1956-62, Charles J. Mach Regents prof. English, 1961-62; prof. English, U. Chgo., 1962—, chmn. dept., 1978—; vis. prof. Northwestern U., 1962, U. Hawaii, 1964; Fulbright lectr., Italy, 1958-59, Kyoto, Japan, 1968, Australia, 1976. Served to capt. AUS, 1942-46, U.S. Army, 1950-52. Recipient Walt Whitman award Poetry Soc. Am., 1958, Poetry Chap Book award, 1961; Distinguished Service award Nat. Council Tchrs. English, 1975. Guggenheim fellow, 1969-70; Nat. Endowment for Humanities sr. fellow, 1974-75. Mem. Modern Lang. Assn., Nat. Council Tchrs. of English (editor Coll. English 1960-66, pres. 1970), Am. Studies Assn., AAUP (council 1964-67), Midwest Modern Lang. Assn. (pres. 1961-62), Phi Beta Kappa. Author: A Critical Guide to Leaves of Grass, 1957; (with Bernice Slote and Karl Shapiro) Start with the Sun, 1960; Walt Whitman, 1962; Reader's Guide to Herman Melville, 1962; F. Scott Fitzgerald: His Art and His Technique, 1964; J.D. Salinger, 1965; Quests Surd and Absurd: Essays in American Literature, 1967; Word Self, Reality: The Rhetoric of Imagination, 1972; T.S. Eliot's Personal Waste Land, 1977; The American Quest for a Supreme Fiction: Whitman's Legacy in the Personal Epic, 1979. Editor: Complete Poetry and Selected Prose of Walt Whitman, 1959; Myth and Method: Modern Theories of Fiction, 1960; (with Bernice Slote) Dimensions of Poetry, 1962; Dimensions of the Short Story, 1964; Whitman's Song of Myself: Origin, Growth, Meaning, 1964; Dimensions of Literature, 1967; The Arts and The Public, 1967; Theory of Fiction: Henry James, 1972. Home: 5536 S Blackstone Ave Chicago IL 60637

MILLER, JAMES ELWOOD, newspaper editor; b. Jersey Shore, Pa., Nov. 16, 1918; s. Raymond Luther and Winifred (Ritter) M.; B.S., Bucknell U., 1949; m. Barbara Louise Lenox, Apr. 17, 1952; children—James, Richard. Sports editor Jersey Shore Herald, 1949-51; asso. editor Sports Age mag., N.Y.C., 1951-54; with Del. State News, Dover, 1954—, exec. editor, 1964—. Dir. Del. State Fair. Served with USAAF, 1939-45. Author: Start the Press, 1978. Home: 54 Huntly Circle Dover DE 19901 Office: Del State News Webbs Lane Dover DE 19901

MILLER, JAMES FRANCIS, investment banker; b. Portland, Oreg., Feb. 20, 1905; s. James Francis and Ann (Grant) M.; student U. Wash., 1925-26; m. Marion Look, Nov. 18, 1929; 1 dau., Jacqueline (Mrs. Daniel Rice). Asso. Blyth & Co. Inc. (now Blyth Eastman Dillon & Co Inc.), N.Y.C., 1921—, sr. v.p., 1959-63, exec. v.p., 1963-66, pres., 1966-70, chmn. exec. com., 1970-71, vice chmn. mgmt. com., 1971—, former dir.; dir. Ethyl Corp., Maine Central R.R. Co., Portland, La. Pacific Corp. Trustee Lewis and Clark Coll. Republican. Clubs: Metropolitan, The Links (N.Y.C.); Blind Brook (Westchester, N.Y.); Arlington, Multnomah Athletic (Portland); Eldorado Country, Indian Wells (Calif.). Home: 700 Park Ave New York NY 10021 Office: 1221 Ave of Americas New York NY 10020

MILLER, JAMES FRANKLIN, ret. assn. exec., chemist; b. Lancaster, Pa., July 18, 1912; s. John Jay and Mary Louella (Stoutsenberger) M.; B.S., Franklin and Marshall Coll., 1935; M.S., Pa. State U., 1937, Ph.D., 1939; m. Nellie Virginia Weadon, Aug. 24, 1938; 1 dau., Caryl Jean. Instr. chemistry Undergrad. Center Pa. State U., Altoona, 1939-42; asst. prof. The Citadel, 1942; post-doctorate fellow (Manhattan Project fellow) Purdue U., Lafayette, Ind., 1943-44; fellow Mellon Inst., Pitts., 1944-46, sr. fellow, 1946-51, head analytical chem. sect. research service, 1951-59; lab. dir., gen. chemistry Central Research & Engring. div. Continental Can Co., Inc., 1959-64, mgr. applied research chem. and phys. labs., corporate research and devel., 1964-68; grand recorder, grand editor, exec. sec.-treas. Alpha Chi Sigma, editor Hexagon, Indpls., 1968-79, trustee, sec.-treas. Alpha Chi Sigma Ednl. Found. Pres., Profl. Interfraternity Council, 1975-76; pres. Coll. Fraternity Editors Assn., 1978-79. Mem. Am. Chem. Soc., Artisans Order Mut. Protection, Am. Inst. Chem. Engrs., Phi Beta Kappa, Sigma Xi, Alpha Chi Sigma (chmn. nat. profl. activities com. 1958-62, grand master alchemist 1966-68), Phi Lambda Upsilon, Phi Kappa Phi. Mason. Contbr. articles to profl. jours. Patentee in field. Home: 6004 Linton Ln Indianapolis IN 46220

MILLER, JAMES GRIER, univ. ofcl., psychiatrist, psychologist; b. Pitts., July 17, 1916; s. Earl Dalton and Mary Rebecca (Grier) M.; student Columbia (S.C.) Bible Coll., U. S.C., 1933-34, U. Mich., 1934-35; A.B. summa cum laude, Harvard, 1937, A.M., 1938, M.D. cum laude, 1942, Ph.D., 1943; m. Jessie Louise Luthi, Sept. 3, 1938; children—John Grier, Thomas Christian. Asst. and tutor psychology Harvard, 1937-38, mem. Soc. Fellows, 1938-44, asst. psychiatry Med. Sch., 1943-44; intern medicine Mass. Gen. Hosp., 1942-43, asst. resident, resident in psychiatry, 1943-44; Lowell lectr., Boston, 1944; mem. and chief assessment program OSS, 1944-46; asst. prof. clin. psychology Harvard (on leave), 1946-47; chief clin. psychology sect. VA, 1946-47; prof., chmn. dept. psychology U. Chgo., 1948-55; clin. instr. in psychiatry U. Ill. Med. Sch., 1952-55; lectr. Northwestern U. Med. Sch., 1953-55; prof. psychiatry and psychology, dir. Mental Health Research Inst., U. Mich., Ann Arbor, 1955-67; exec. dir., sec. EDUCOM (Inter-univ. Communications Council), 1964-66, v.p., prin. scientist, 1966-70, trustee, 1970—, chmn. bd., 1976; v.p. for acad. affairs Cleve. State U., 1967-70, provost, 1970-71; v.p. Acad. Ednl. Devel., Washington, 1971-73; lectr. psychiatry and behavioral scis. Johns Hopkins U., 1971-73; fellow Internat. Inst. Applied Systems Analysis, Vienna, summers 1973, 74; pres. U. Louisville, 1973—. Served from 1st lt. to capt. M.C., AUS; with OSS in U.S., ETO. Diplomate in clin. psychology Am. Bd. Examiners Profl. Psychology, in psychiatry Am. Bd. Neurology and Psychiatry. Fellow Am. Psychol. Assn. (pres. div. clin. psychology, 1958-59), Am. Psychiat. Assn., Am. Coll. Neuropsychopharmacology (charter), Am. Coll. Psychiatrists (charter), Am. Coll. Clin. Pharmacology and Therapeutics (charter); mem. AAAS, AMA, Am. Soc. for Cybernetics (charter), Soc. for Gen. Systems Research (pres. 1973-74), Group for Advancement Psychiatry, Operations Research Soc., Assn. Computing Machinery, Phi Beta Kappa, Sigma Xi. Episcopalian. Clubs: Century, Cosmos, Metropolitan (Washington); Harvard (N.Y.C.). Author: Unconsciousness, 1942; Living Systems, 1978; co-author: Assessment of Men, 1948. Editor: Behavioral Science, 1956—; dept. editor in psychology Ency. Brit., 1952-58; co-editor: Drugs and Behavior, 1960. Contbr. articles to profl. jours., revs. Address: University of Louisville Louisville KY 40208

MILLER, JAMES HALYBURTON, chem. co. exec.; b. Asheville, N.C., Feb. 22, 1940; s. Herbert Pinkney, Jr. and Lily Wingo (Jones) M.; A.B. in History, U. N.C., 1961; J.D., So. Methodist U., 1964; m. Sharon Ann Austin, Aug. 12, 1963; children—Meredith Austin, Brandon Fletcher. Admitted to Tex. bar, 1964, D.C. bar, 1965; atty. Chief Counsel's Office, IRS, 1964-67, asst. to commr., 1967-68; asso. firm Bogan & Freeland, Washington, 1968-71; asst. treas., then asst. controller Akzona, Inc., Asheville, N.C., 1971-76; treas. Am. Enka Co., Enka, N.C., 1977—. Bd. dirs., treas. Pisgah council Girl Scouts U.S., 1976; bd. govs. Jr. Achievement Western N.C., 1978, Western N.C. Health Systems Agy., 1978. Republican. Episcopalian. Office: Am Enka Co Enka NC 28728

MILLER, JAMES HUGH, JR., utility co. exec.; b. New Orleans, Oct. 14, 1922; s. James Hugh and Helen (Piguet) M.; B.E.E., Tulane U., 1943; m. Juliet deVilliers, Nov. 22, 1945; children—Juliet (Mrs. Walter McFarland Beale), James Hugh III, Robert Boyd, Mary Ashley. Exec. v.p. Ga. Power Co., Atlanta, 1975—; also dir.; dir. So. Electric Generating Co. Served with USNR, 1943-46; Korea, 1950-52. Registered profl. engr., Ala. Mem.. Assn. Edison Illuminating Cos., Southeastern Electric Exchange, Edison Electric Inst. Roman Catholic. Home: 2170 Mt Paran Rd NW Atlanta GA 30327 Office: PO Box 4545 Atlanta GA 30327

MILLER, JAMES JAY, utilities exec.; b. Nanuet, N.Y., Apr. 15, 1924; s. Edward A. and Gwendolyn (Mitchell) M.; B.E.E., Bucknell U., 1948; m. Dorothy Walker, Aug. 11, 1945; children—James Jay, Jeffery Craig. Designer, Niagara Mohawk Power Corp., Syracuse, N.Y., 1948-51, jr. engr., 1951-53, sta. designer, 1953-56, asst. to chief engr. Western div., 1956-69, mgr. system design engring., 1969-73, v.p., gen. mgr. Central div., 1973-76, sr. v.p., 1976—; pres. St. Lawrence Power Co., Cornwall, Ont., Can., 1975—, Beebee Island Corp., 1975—, NM Uranium, 1976—. Served with USNR, 1943-46. Licensed profl. engr., N.Y. Mem. IEEE (chmn. membership com. Niagara Frontier sect. 1962-63), Nat., N.Y. (treas. Central N.Y. chpt. 1971-73) socs. profl. engrs. Clubs: Limestone Pony, U.S. Pony Clubs, Inc. Home: 113 Draycott Rd Fayetteville NY 13066 Office: 300 Erie Blvd West Syracuse NY 13202

MILLER, JAMES MONROE, educator; b. Lancaster, Pa., Aug. 7, 1933; s. James M. and Ruth Hess (Ober) M.; B.S., Elizabethtown Coll., 1955; M.S., Purdue U., 1958, Ph.D., 1960; m. Elva Jean Lehman, Dec. 26, 1955; children—Gregory, Robert. Vis. asst. prof. Purdue U., 1960; asst. prof. chemistry Drew U., 1959-64, asso. prof., 1964-69, prof., 1969—, chmn. dept., 1972—, on leave at U. Ill., 1964-65, U. Amsterdam, 1971; cons. to industry. Asso. trustee Elizabethtown Coll., 1972-78. Named outstanding young man of Am., Jaycees, 1964; Danforth asso. Mem. Am. Chem. Soc., AAUP, N.J. Acad. Sci., AAAS. Methodist. Author: Experimental Gas Chromatography, 1965; Separation Methods in Chemical Analysis, 1975. Home: 8 Oxford Ln Madison NJ 07940

MILLER, JAMES ROGERS, JR., fed. judge; b. Montgomery County, Md., June 15, 1931; s. James Rogers and Mary Ada (Cecil) M.; B.A., Wesleyan U., 1953; LL.B., Georgetown U., 1955; m. Jo Anne Trice, Apr. 27, 1957; children—James Rogers III, Andrew Cecil, Merrie H., Katherine T. Admitted to D.C. bar, 1955, Md. bar, 1956; practiced in Rockville, 1956-70; mem. firm Miller, Miller & Canby, 1956-70; judge U.S. Dist. Ct. Md., Balt., 1970—. Mem. ho. of dels. Md. Gen. Assembly, 1962-66; mem. Legislative Council Md., 1963-66; chmn. Montgomery County del. Md. Gen. Assembly; chmn. Republican Central Com. for Montgomery County, 1966-67; mem. Jud. Conf. Com. To Consider Standards of Admission To Practice in Fed. Cts., 1977-79. Trustee Landon Sch. for Boys, Bethesda, Md., 1966-69. Mem. Am., Md., Montgomery County (pres. 1969-70) bar assns., Alpha Delta Phi. Office: US Courthouse Baltimore MD 21201

MILLER, JAMES ROLAND, soil chemist; b. Millington, Md., May 19, 1929; s. Roland and Edith (Judefind) M.; B.S., U. Md., 1951, M.S., 1953, Ph.D., 1956; m. Katherine Patricia Melvin, Dec. 18, 1954; children—Karla Patricia, Marcia Susan. Soil scientist Agrl. Research Service, Dept. Agr., 1956-58; mem. faculty U. Md., 1958—, prof. soils, 1964—, head dept. agronomy, 1963—; mem. N.E. Soil Research Com., 1961—, sec., 1973-74, vice chmn., 1975-76, chmn., 1977-78; mem. Potash and Phosphate Inst. Adv. Council, chmn., 1978. Named Hon. State Farmer, 1960. Fellow Soil Sci. Soc. Am., Am. Soc. Agronomy (dir. 1965-68, 77—, sec.-treas. Northeastern br. 1968, v.p. 1969, pres. 1970); mem. Del.-Md. Plant Food Assn. (v.p. 1972, pres. 1973), Am. Soc. Agronomy, Soil Conservation Soc. Am., Sigma Xi, Phi Kappa Phi. Methodist (ofcl. bd. 1965-68, adminstrv. bd. 1971-73, 1978—). Author articles in field. Address: care Dept Agronomy U Md College Park MD 20742

MILLER, JAMES RUMRILL, III, educator; b. Phila., Dec. 21, 1937; s. James Rumrill and Elizabeth Pleasants (King) M.; A.B., Princeton U., 1959; M.B.A. (Woodrow Wilson fellow), Harvard U., 1962; Ph.D., M.I.T., 1966; m. Sally Stinson Vaughn, May 14, 1975; children—Elizabeth, Katharine, Kerry. Systems analyst MITRE Corp., Bedford, Mass., 1962-67; asst. prof. bus. adminstrn. Stanford U., 1967-69, asso. prof., 1970-73, prof., 1973—, Walter and Elise Haas prof. bus. adminstrn., 1977—, asso. dean Bus. Sch., 1974-76; cons. in field. Mem. Phi Beta Kappa. Republican. Episcopalian. Author: Professional Decision Making, 1970; contbr. numerous articles to profl. jours. Home: 1068 Vernier Pl Stanford CA 94305 Office: Stanford U Bus Sch Stanford CA 94305

MILLER, JAMES VINCE, univ. pres.; b. Waynetown, Ind., July 16, 1920; s. J. Vince and Hazel B. (Spore) M.; B.A. in Philosophy and English, Ind. Central Coll., 1942; B.D. in History and Lit., United Sem., Dayton, Ohio, 1945; postgrad. Earlham Coll., 1945-46; Ph.D. in Philosophy, Boston U., 1955; LL.D. (hon.), Otterbein Coll., 1971, Ind. Central U., 1979; m. Mildred Mae Hockersmith, June 13, 1943; children—Maryllyn Jean, Rachel Katherine. Ordained to ministry Evang. United Brethren Ch., 1945; pastor, Greensfork, Ind., 1944-46, Stow, Mass., 1946-48; faculty dept. philosophy and religion Bates Coll., Lewiston, Maine, 1950-64, prof., 1960-64, chmn. dept., 1958-64; acad. dean Otterbein Coll., Westerville, Ohio, 1964-68, v.p. for acad. affairs, acad. dean, 1968-71; pres. Pacific U., Forest Grove, Oreg., 1971—. Adj. prof. Union Grad. Sch., 1970-78, San Francisco Theol. Sem., 1979—; chmn. NW Assn. Pvt. Colls. and Univs., 1974-76; treas. Oreg. Ind. Coll. Assn., 1974-75, 76-78, chmn., 1978-79; adv. com. Oreg. Ednl. Coordinating Commn., 1976-79; chmn. council for higher edn. United Ch. Bd. Homeland Missions, 1975-76. Mem. or former mem. Newcomen Soc. N.Am., Acad. Religion, Am. Philos. Assn., Danforth Assos. (co-chmn. New Eng. assos. 1960), Torch and Key, Phi Eta Sigma. Methodist. Rotarian. Home: 3010 NW Lavina Dr Forest Grove OR 97116 Office: Pacific U Forest Grove OR 97116

MILLER, JANE BEACHY, artist; b. Cumberland, Md., Nov. 17, 1906; d. John Stewart and Emma (Beachy) Miller; student Md. Inst. Fine Arts and Design, 1924-28; pvt. art study, France, 1928; m. Cameron F. MacRae, Dec. 24, 1935; 1 son, Cameron F. III. Free-lance illustrator, fashion artist, 1930—; fashion, instl. advt. illustrator, nat. advertisers, also dept. stores, Chgo., N.Y.C., St. Louis, Pitts., Washington, Phila., 1930—; story, fashion illustrator nat. mags., 1937—; cover artist Ladies Home Jour., 1937, This Week mag., 1952-54, Jr. League mag., 1964-65; one-man show: Sagittarius Gallery, N.Y.C., 1959, Bodley Gallery, N.Y.C., 1961. Recipient gold medal Art Directors Club, N.Y.C., 1938. Episcopalian. Clubs: Cosmopolitan, River (N.Y.C.); Island (Hobe Sound, Fla.); Mill Reef (Antigua, W.I.). Author, illustrator: Mogo Mouse, 1932; Lulu, 1941; Miss Lizzie, 1943; The Ill-Tempered Tiger, 1957; Pure Nuisance, 1977. Illustrator: A Dog of His Own, 1941; Thirty Three Bunn Street, 1952; A Dance for Susie, 1953; Susie and the Dancing Cat, 1954; Susie and the Ballet Family, 1955; On Your Toes Susie, 1958; Andrew the Lion Farmer, 1959; Scrappy the Pup, 1960; Flower Girl, 1961; Henrietta and the Hat, 1962; Someone Else, 1962; Mercy Percy; Dumb Stupid David; The Wet World; others. Home: 200 E 66th St New York NY 10021

MILLER, JARRELL ETSON, radiologist, educator; b. San Antonio, Nov. 14, 1913; s. Etson Lee and Mabel (Braddock) M.; B.A., St. Mary's U., 1934; M.D., Baylor U., 1938; m. Virginia Edith Gallagher, June 24, 1939; children—Gwen Janet, Dwight Leigh, Beverly Diane, Pamela Anne. Intern, Robert B. Green Meml. Hosp., San Antonio, 1938-39; resident radiology Cleve. City Hosp., 1939-42; practice medicine specializing in radiology, 1942—; radiologist Parkland Hosp., Dallas, 1946-49, Children's Med. Center, Dallas, 1947-65, Baylor U. Med. Center, Dallas, Tex., 1949-66, St. Paul Hosp., Dallas, 1967—; cons. VA Hosp., Lisbon, Tex., 1946-57, Vets. Hosp., McKinney, Tex., 1946-57; mem. faculty Southwestern Med. Sch. of U. Tex., Dallas, 1947—, clin. prof. radiology, 1956—; lectr. med. br. U. Tex., Galveston. Vice pres. med. activities Dallas Citizens Traffic Commn., 1960-67; v.p. pub. health com. Dallas C. of C., 1964, mem. legislative com., 1965—. Bd. dirs. Dallas County unit Am. Cancer Soc., 1950-70, pres., 1956-57, exec. com., Tex. div., 1957-70, pres., 1963; bd. dirs. Dallas Tb Assn., 1953-68, pres., 1960-61; bd. dirs. Tex. Tb Assn., 1961-63, Dallas Heart Assn., 1954-60; bd. govs. St. Mary's U., 1958-63. Served with M.C., AUS, 1942-46; ETO. Recipient Alumnus of Year award St. Mary's U., 1961. Diplomate Am. Bd. Radiology (guest examiner 1965, 69, 71). Mem. AMA (del. 1973), Tex. Med. Assn. (chmn. council sci. advancement 1959-68, exec. bd. 1959-73, Distinguished Service award 1971), Dallas County (pres. 1965, chmn. bd. 1966), Collin County (pres. 1948) med. socs., Am. Coll. Radiology (chmn. bd. chancellors, 1966, pres. 1967), Dallas-Ft. Worth, (pres. 1953, sec. 1956-58), Rocky Mountain radiol. socs., Radiol. Soc. N.Am., Am. Roentgen Ray Soc., Dallas So. Clin. Soc. (Marchman award 1962), Flying Physicians Assn., Aircraft Owners and Pilots Assn., Theta Kappa Psi, Alpha Pi Alpha. Contbr. articles to med. jours. Home: 6115 D Averill Way Dallas TX 75225. *The practice of medicine has changed; the principles have not changed. These principles should remain unchanged and unchanging. Holding to proper principles can bring one many honors; one may also feel lonesome, isolated or ostracized by strict adherence to principles. The world will not survive as we know it today unless enough people adopt proper principles and live by them.*

MILLER, JARVIS ERNEST, univ. ofcl.; b. Orange Grove, Tex., May 30, 1929; s. Richard Cook and Ethel (DuBose) M.; B.S., Tex. A&M U., 1950; M.S., Purdue U., Ph.D., 1954; m. Alma Scott Howell, June 20, 1952; children—Susan, Kathleen, Margaret, Carolyn. Chief of party Tex. A&M U. Internat. Programs, Santo Domingo, Dominican Republic, 1965-67, asst. dir. Tex. Agr. Expt. Sta., Tex. A&M U., College Station, 1967-71, asso. dir., 1971-72, dir., 1972-77, pres. univ., 1977—. Served with USAF, 1953-55. Mem. AAAS, Am. Agrl. Econ. Assn. Methodist. Club: Rotary. Home: 1 Circle Dr College Station TX 77840 Office: Office of Pres Tex A&M U College Station TX 77843*

MILLER, JASON, playwright; b. Long Island City, N.Y., Apr. 22, 1939; s. John and Mary Miller; student Cath. U.; B.A., U. Scranton, 1961; m. Linda Gleason, 1963; children—Jennifer, Jason, Jordan. Playwright: Circus Lady; Nobody Hears a Broken Drum; Lou Gehrig Did Not Die of Cancer; That Championship Season (Pulitzer prize 1973, also Tony awards), 1971; It's a Sin to Tell a Lie; appeared films: The Exorcist, 1973; The Nickel Ride, 1975; TV movie The Dain Curse, 1978; A Home of Our Own, Vampire, Henderson Experiment. Recipient N.Y. Drama Critics Circle award for best play of 1971-72, also Best Play citation. Address: care Earl Graham Graham Agy 317 W 45th St New York NY 10036

MILLER, JEAN ROGER, univ. pres.; b. Dollville, Ill., July 16, 1927; s. Everett John and Agnes (Dowdy) M.; B.Mus., Ill. Wesleyan U., 1949, M.Mus. (grad. fellow), 1950, LL.D., 1973; Ph.D. (grad. fellow), U. Wis., 1956; postgrad. (Carnegie postdoctoral fellow) U. Mich., 1966-67; m. Arlene Phyllis Truscott, Mar. 25, 1949; children—Gregory Kent, Deborrah Jean, John Thomas, Charles Frederick. Teaching asst. Ill. Wesleyan U., 1949-50; asst. prof. music Kan. Wesleyan U., 1950-52; teaching asst. U. Wis., 1952-54; asst. prof. music, head dept. music edn. Hardin-Simmons U., Abilene, Tex., 1954-59; faculty Millikin U., Decatur, Ill., 1959—, prof., dean Sch. Music, 1960-67, v.p. acad. affairs, dean univ., 1967-70, exec. v.p., 1970-71, pres., 1971—. Cons. in field, 1950—; cons.-examiner Commn. Colls. and Univs., North Central Assn. Colls. and Secondary Schs., 1971—. Trustee YMCA Decatur, Inst. European Studies. Served with USMCR, 1944-46. Mem. Assn. Higher Edn., Assn. Colls. Ill. (v.p.), Fedn. Ind. Ill. Colls. and Univs. (exec. bd.), Presbyn. Coll. Union, Central States Coll. Assn. (dir.), Blue Key, Phi Mu Alpha, Phi Kappa Phi, Pi Kappa Lambda, Alpha Kappa Psi. Clubs: Union League (Chgo.); University (N.Y.C.); Decatur, Commodore Decatur Yacht, Decatur Country. Spl. research in audio frequency sweep spectrum analysis of musical tones. Home: 2 Montgomery Pl Decatur IL 62522

MILLER, JESSE EDWARD, savs. and loan exec.; b. Graceville, Fla., June 24, 1925; s. Jesse Edward and Annie Lou (Knapp) M.; student Emory U., 1943-44; B.A. in Forestry, Duke U., 1947, M.F., 1948; grad. Sch. Savs. and Loan, Ind. U., 1964; m. Jean Hodo, July 29, 1950; children—Leslie, Mark, Jesse Edward. Forester land dept. U.S. Steel Corp., Birmingham, Ala., 1948-51; chief forester U.S. Pipe & Foundry Co., Birmingham, 1951-57, chief forester Arthur Brown & Sons, Decatur, Ala., 1957-59; with City Fed. Savs. & Loan Assn., Birmingham, 1959—, pres., 1966—, chmn. bd., 1974—, also chief exec. officer; dir. So. United Life Ins. Co., Montgomery. Bd. dirs. Birmingham chpt. United Appeal, Birmingham Football Found., Birmingham Better Bus. Bur., Operation New Birmingham, Personal and Family Counseling, Birmingham adv. bd. Salvation Army, Carraway Meth. Med. Center, Birmingham; Ala. Motorists Assn. Served with USNR, 1944-46. Mem. Ala. Savs. and Loan League (pres. 1968-69), Inst. Fin. Edn., U.S. League Savs. Assns. (dir. 1973). Republican. Presbyterian. Clubs: Birmingham Country, Mountain Brook, Redstone, Exchange (pres. 1969-70). Home: 4032 Old Leeds Circle Birmingham AL 35213 Office: 2030 2d Ave N Birmingham AL 35203

MILLER, JOAN VITA, art gallery exec.; b. L.I., N.Y., Jan. 22, 1946; d. Dominick Paul and Anne (Mavellia) Vita; B.A., Syracuse U., 1968, M.A., 1971. Asst. dir. Michael C. Rockefeller Art Gallery, State U. N.Y., Fredonia, 1971-72; dir. C.W. Post Art Gallery, C.W. Post Coll., L.I. U., Greenvale, N.Y., 1973—, prof. museum mgmt. C.W. Post Coll. Mem. Am. Assn. Museums, L.I. Mus. Assn. (pres.), Coll. Art Assn., Gallery Assn. N.Y. State, Contemporary Print Soc. N.Y. Office: CW Post Art Gallery CW Post Coll LI U Greenvale NY 11548

MILLER, JODY, recording artist, entertainer; b. Phoenix, Nov. 29, 1941; d. John and Fay (Harper) M.; m. Monty Brooks, Jan. 2, 1962; 1 child, Robin. Recording artist, 1964—; recorded numerous albums including: Wednesday's Child Is Full of Woe, Queen of the House, He's So Fine, Home of the Brave, There's a Party Goin' On, Good News, Here's Jody Miller, Look at Mine, Will You Love Me Tomorrow; owner Jody Miller Music Pub. Co. Recipient Grammy award for Queen of the House, 1965; 3 ASCAP awards, 1971, 73. Mem. AFTRA, Country Music Assn., Nat. Acad. Rec. Arts and Scis. Democrat. Baptist.

MILLER, JOE LEON, mfg. co. exec.; b. Lyons, Kans., May 23, 1931; s. William Alexander and Jenny Marie (Chapin) M.; B.A. in Econs. with honors, San Jose (Calif.) State U., 1958; M.B.A., U. Hartford, 1973; m. Katheryn Patricia Brent, Nov. 16, 1966; children—Sean Peter, Timothy Alexander. Dir. mgmt. info. systems Kaman Aerospace Corp., Bloomfield, Conn., 1967-74; pres. Aeronca, Inc., Pineville, N.C., 1974—; trustee Aeronca Found. Served with USAF, 1951-54. Mem. Nat. Assn. Accountants. Republican. Clubs: Union League (N.Y.C.); Carmel Country (Charlotte). Home: 4413 St Ives Pl Charlotte NC 28211 Office: 200 Rodney St Pineville NC 28134. *The most important aspect of life is the family. The parents should be the ethical model which continues through life as the inspiration for their children.*

MILLER, JOHN ADALBERT, life ins. co. exec.; b. Wilkes Barre, Pa., June 14, 1927; s. Joseph and Marie (Arenova) M.; B.A., Columbia U., 1948; postgrad. Cornell U.; m. Margaret Marie Hausler, Aug. 14, 1945; children—Cynthia Joan, Jeffrey Charles, John Joseph, Kristen Marie. Asst. adminstrv. personnel mgr. Willys Overland Motors Co., 1948-49; with Aetna Life & Casualty Co., 1948-58, acting gen. agt., Seattle, 1957-58; with Life Ins. Agy. Mgmt. Assn., Hartford, Conn., 1958-72, v.p. co. relations, 1968-72; v.p. sales, then sr. v.p. sales Provident Mut. Life Ins. Co., Phila., 1972-76, pres., 1976—, chief exec. officer, 1978—; dir. Phila. Nat. Bank. Bd. dirs. West Phila. Corp., Children's Hosp. Phila.; bd. dirs. Phila. YMCA, 1974—, vice chmn., 1976. Served with USMCR, 1945-46. C.L.U., 1954. Mem. Pa. Ins. Fedn. (dir.), Phila. C. of C. (dir. 1977—), Am. Coll. Life Underwriters. Republican. Presbyn. Club: Overbrook Golf. Author: What You Should Know About Permanent Life Insurance, 1962; Getting More Out of Life, 1968; others. Home: 1946 Montgomery Ave Villanova PA 19085 Office: PO Box 7378 Philadelphia PA 19101

MILLER, JOHN ALBERT, banker; b. Washington, July 30, 1923; s. Thomas Lorenzo and Alice Louise (Chapman) M.; B.C.S., Benjamin Franklin U., 1951; m. Kathryn Marie Auty, July 5, 1947; children—John Stephen, Diane Pegg, Judith Ann. With Liberty Nat. Bank, 1942-43, 45-56; with Citizens Bank & Trust Co. Md., Riverdale, 1956—, treas., 1969-71, v.p., treas., charge ops., 1971-73, exec. v.p., 1973—. Served with AUS, 1943-45; CBI. Clubs: K.C., Lions. Home: 12209 Galway Dr Silver Spring MD 20904 Office: 6200 Baltimore Blvd Riverdale MD 20840

MILLER, JOHN ELDON, state legislator; b. Melbourne, Ark., Mar. 2, 1929; s. Green Hightower and Annie Margaret (Gray) M.; B.S., Ark. State U., 1949; m. Ruby L. Robertson, Nov. 5, 1949; children—David Eldon, Martha Marie, Naomi. County and circuit clk. Izard County (Ark.), 1953-56; owner, operator John E. Miller Agy., real estate agy., Melbourne, 1957—, Izard County Abstract Co., Melbourne, 1957—; mem. Ark. Ho. of Reps., 1958—, speaker of house, 1979—; also engaged in farming. Chmn., Izard County chpt. ARC, 1960—; Ark. membership chmn. Easter Seals, 1976; pres. Delth Hills Health System Agy., Newport, Ark.; pres. White River Planning and Devel. Dist., 1969-70, also bd. dirs.; v.p. Ark. Mental Retardation and Devel. Disabilities; mem. Ark. Health Planning Council. Recipient awards, including state award Soil and Water Commn., 1976, Dist. award, 1975; Ark. Nurses Assn. award, 1979; City and Counties Orgn. award, 1978; Easter Seals award. Mem. Ark. Real Estate Assn., Ark. Ins. Assn., Registered Land Surveyor Assn., Nat. Assn. State Legislators. Democrat. Baptist. Clubs: Lions (pres. 1960-61) (Melbourne); Masons, Gideons. Home and Office: PO Box 436 Melbourne AR 72556

MILLER, JOHN ELVIS, U.S. dist. judge; b. nr. Aid, Mo., May 15, 1888; s. John Anderson and Mary K. (Harper) M.; student S.E. Mo. State Tchrs. Coll., Cape Girardeau, Valparaiso (Ind). U.; LL.B., U. Ky., 1912; LL.D. (hon.), U. Ark., 1949, Harding Coll., Searcy, Ark.; m. Ethel Lucile Lindsey, Oct. 21, 1914 (dec.); children—Mary Louise, John E.; m. 2d, Ethel L. Skinner, Dec. 27, 1956. Practiced law, Searcy, Ark, 1912—; mem. firm Miller & Yingling; pros. atty. 1st Jud. Circuit, Ark., 1919-22; mem. 72d to 75th congresses from 2d Ark. Dist.; U.S. senator from Ark., 1937-41; judge U.S. Dist. Ct. for Western Ark., 1941—, now sr. judge. Del., Ark. Constl. Conv., 1918. Recipient awards Sebastian County Bar Assn., 1961, Ark. Bar Assn., 1966, Internat. Acad. Trial Lawyers, 1977, Hatton W. Sumners award Southwestern Legal Found., 1973; named to Hall of Disting. Alumni, U. Ky.; Judge John E. Miller Scholarship Fund established by Ark. Bar Found. Mem. Ark. Bar Assn. Democrat. Methodist. Mason (32 deg., Shriner). Home: 1120 S Albert Pike Fort Smith AR 72901

MILLER, JOHN FRANCIS, social scientist; b. Canton, Ill., Aug. 3, 1908; s. Frank Lewis and Minnie Grace (Eyerly) M.; A.B., U. Ill., 1929, A.M., 1930; postgrad. Columbia, 1930-31, 34-35; German-Am. student exchange fellow U. Frankfurt on Main, 1931-33; m. Ruth Roby, May 29, 1937; children—Joan, Kent R., Dana R. Staff, Commn. Inquiry on Pub. Service Personnel, 1934-35, Regent's Inquiry Character and Cost Pub. Edn., 1936; cons. Pres.'s Com. on Adminstrv. Mgmt., 1936-37, Com. Civil Service Improvement, 1939, Inst. Pub. Adminstrn., 1937-38, Pub. Adminstrn. Clearing House, 1938; chief field service Nat. Resources Planning Bd., 1938-43; asst. dir. Nat. Planning Assn., 1943-50, asst. chmn., 1951-77, exec. sec., 1951-71, pres., 1971-79, vice chmn., 1977—; sec. Canadian-Am. Com., 1957-76; N.Am. sec. Brit.-N.Am. Com., 1969—. Trustee, mem. adv. com. Nat. Conf. on Family, 1946-49; mem. adv. council social security Senate Com. on Finance, 1947-48. Mem. Am. Econ. Assn., Am. Polit. Sci. Assn., Am. Hist. Assn., Am. Soc. Planning Ofcls., Am. Soc. Internat. Law, Am. Finance Assn., Am. Soc. Pub. Adminstrn., Phi Beta Kappa. Author: Veteran Preference in the Public Service, 1935. Home: 1515 Grassymeade Ln Alexandria VA 22308 Office: 1606 New Hampshire Ave Washington DC 20009

MILLER, JOHN GEORGE, educator, chemist; b. Phila., Oct. 18, 1908; s. Robert and Regina (Ramspacher) M.; A.B., U. Pa., 1929, M.Sc., 1930, Ph.D., 1932; m. Elizabeth Gregg Snyder, June 8, 1940; children—John Gregg, Margery Kampen. Research chemist Dermatol. Research Labs., 1929-30; mem. faculty U. Pa., Phila., 1930—, successively asst. chemistry dept., asst. instr., instr., asst. and asso. prof., prof., 1952—; cons. Minerals and Chems. Corp. Am. (now named Engelhard Minerals & Chems. Corp.), 1944—, Smith, Kline & French Labs., 1946-49, Pennwalt Corp., 1949-71, research and devel. labs. Franklin Inst., 1959-60, U.S. Dept. Agr. Eastern Utilization Research Br., 1953-57; project leader Thermodynamics Research Lab., U. Pa., 1945-51; vis. examiner in chemistry Swarthmore Coll., 1950-52. Fellow AAAS, Am. Inst. Chemists; mem. Am. Chem. Soc., Clay Minerals Soc., Metachem. Club, Am. Phys. Soc., Phi Beta Kappa, Sigma Xi, Pi Mu Epsilon, Alpha Chi Sigma, Phi Lambda Upsilon. Contbr. articles to chem. jours. Home: 7801 Lincoln Dr Philadelphia PA 19118 Office: Dept Chemistry U Pa Philadelphia PA 19104

MILLER, JOHN JOSE, judge; b. Savannah, Ga., July 28, 1932; s. Fred and Minnie (Edmond) M.; A.B., Talladega Coll., 1954; LL.B. (W.H.C. Brown fellow), Howard U., 1958; postgrad. (Walter Perry Johnson grad. research fellow in law) U. Calif., Berkeley, 1958-59; children—Duncan, Heather, Robin Hope. Admitted to Calif. bar, 1961; practiced in Berkeley, San Francisco, 1961-78; mem. Calif. Legislature, 1967-78, minority leader, 1970-71, chmn. judiciary com., 1974-78; asso. justice Calif. Ct. Appeals, 1st Appellate Dist., San Francisco, 1978—, mem. Jud. Council Calif., 1974-78. Pres., Berkeley Bd. Edn., 1966. Recipient Man of Year award Ch. by Side of Rd., Berkeley, 1965; Pub. Ofcl. of Year award Los Angeles Trial Lawyers Assn., 1975; Outstanding Service award Contra Costa Trial Lawyers Assn., 1976; Legislator of Year award Calif. Trial Lawyers Assn., 1976. Mem. Am. Judicature Soc., Am., Nat. bar assns., Alpha Phi Alpha. Democrat. Episcopalian. Club: U. Calif. Men's Faculty (Berkeley). Asso. editor: Howard Law Jour., 1957-58. Office: Ct Appeal 1st Appellate Dist State Bldg San Francisco CA

MILLER, JOHN OSCAR, ins. co. exec.; b. Marinette, Wis., Aug. 10, 1917; s. John Oscar and Lucy (MacMillen) M.; B.S., U. Wis., 1937, LL.D., 1941; m. Joan Cecile Swanson, Aug. 10, 1942; children—Carol K., John Oscar. With No. Trust Co., Chgo., 1941-42; claims Atty. Am. Family Mut. Ins. Co. (formerly Farmers Mut. Automobile Ins. Co.), Madison, Wis., 1945-51, dir. personnel, 1951-58, v.p. operations, 1958-62, exec. v.p., 1962-68, pres., 1968—, dir., 1959—, chmn. bd., 1977—; pres., dir., then chmn. bd. Am. Standard Ins. Co., Madison, 1961—, Am. Family Financial Services, Inc., Madison, 1969—; dir. First Wis. Nat. Bank of Madison; chmn. bd. Am. Family Life Ins. Co., 1977—. Dir., past pres. Conf. Mut. Casualty Cos., 1967. Trustee Madison Safety Council; mem. governing bd. Property Loss Research Bur. Served with Counter Intelligence Corps, AUS, 1942-45. Mem. Nat. Assn. Ind. Insurers (gov. 1972—), Health Ins. Assn. Am. (dir. 1977), Property-Casualty Ins. Council (charter). Republican. Presbyn. Lion. Home: 96 Oak Creek Trail Madison WI 53717 Office: 3099 E Washington Ave Madison WI 53701

MILLER, JOHN PEARSE, apparel corp. exec.; b. Kansas City, Mo., Feb. 22, 1914; s. Edwin L. and Faith A. (Pearse) M.; B.S., U. Mo., 1935; m. Joy F. Vencill, May 23, 1936 (dec. Oct. 1977); children—William Vencill, John Pearse; m. 2d, Betty G. Sayles, July 14, 1978. Acct., Ernst & Ernst, C.P.A.'s, Kansas City, Mo., 1935-43; with Spencer Chem. Co. (and former affiliate Pitts. & Midway Coal Mining Co.), Kansas City, Mo., 1943-64, sr. v.p., 1957-61, exec. v.p., 1961-64, also dir.; chmn. bd. Unitog Co., Kansas City, Mo., 1965-79, chmn. exec. com., 1979—. Police commr. Kansas City, 1964-65; mem. Kansas City Area Transp. Authority, 1966-70. Dir., gen. chmn. Heart Am. United Campaign, 1968. Mem. Am. Inst. C.P.A.'s, Mo. Soc. C.P.A.'s, Mo. C. of C., Beta Theta Pi. Clubs: University, Mission Hills Country; Tucson Country. Home: 40 Compton Ct Shawnee Mission KS 66208 also 2775 N Camino Valle Verde Tucson AZ 85715 Office: 101 W 11th St Kansas City MO 64105

MILLER, JOHN PERRY, educator, economist; b. Lynn, Mass., Mar. 26, 1911; s. Fred and Hilda Martha (Wagner) M.; B.A., Harvard, 1932, M.A., 1934, Ph.D., 1937; M.A. (hon.), Yale, 1950; LL.D., Claremont Grad. Sch., 1969; m. Dorothy Marie Willard, May 30, 1942; children—Perry Lowell, Ann Willard Kinder. Instr. econs. Princeton, 1935-37; instr., tutor econs. Harvard, 1937-39; asst. prof. econs. Yale, New Haven, Conn., 1939-45, asso. prof., 1946-50, prof. 1950—, Elizabeth S. and A. Varick Stout prof. social sci., 1969—, dir. grad. studies in econs., 1950-57, dir. social sci. div., 1959-61, dean of the Grad. Sch., 1961-69, dir. Inst. For Social and Policy Studies, 1969-73 chief exec. officer Campaign for Yale U., 1973-77, also corp. officer for instnl. devel., 1976—, dep. provost, 1977-78; vis. Walker-Ames prof. U. Wash., Seattle, 1960; dir. So. New Eng. Telephone Co. Prin. economist OPA, 1941-42; cons. Navy Dept., 1946-49, Munitions Bd., 1950- 51, Econ. Stblzn. Agy., 1951, Indian Statis. Inst., Calcutta, 1957, U.S. Treasury Dept., 1954, U.S. Dept. of Commerce, 1954, Conn. Devel. Commn., 1956; Am. specialist under cultural affairs program for India, Dept. State, 1960; cons. indsl. concentration study Brookings Instn. 1949-50; mem. com. experts on New Eng. econ., President's Council of Econ. Advisers, 1950-51; mem. Gov.'s Com. on Full Employment for Conn., 1950; mem. research adv. com. of com. on New Eng., NPA, 1952-54; mem. NRC Bd. on Grad. Edn., 1971-75; mem. N.Y. State Bd. Regents Commn. on Doctoral Edn., 1972-73. Bd. dirs. New Haven Coll., 1962-67; mem. adv. com. Kirkland Coll., 1967-69; mem. adv. bd. Conn. Mental Health Center, 1969-74. Served as lt. comdr. USNR, 1943-46. Social Sci. Research Council fellow, 1946, Guggenheim fellow, 1948. Fellow Am. Econ. Assn. (chmn. com. research and publs. 1953-60, 69-72), Assn. Grad. Schs. (pres. 1967-68), Council Grad. Schs. in U.S. (mem. exec. com. 1965-69), Social Sci. Research Council (dir. 1953-58, vice chmn. 1958), Nat. Inst. Social Scis., Royal Econ. Soc., Foote Sch. Assn. (dir. 1957-63, pres. 1957-60), Yale Grad. Sch. Assn. (Wilbur Lucius Cross medal 1969), Yale Engring. Assn. (award for meritorious service to Yale 1969), Phi Beta Kappa. Clubs: Graduates; Harvard (New Haven, N.Y.C.); Yale (New Haven and N.Y.C.); Elizabethan. Author: Unfair Competition, 1941; Pricing Military Procurements, 1949. Cartels Competition and Their Regulations, 1961. Co-author: The New England Economy, 1951; The Economic Outlook for the Naugatuck and Farmington River Valleys in Connecticut, 1956. Chmn. Index of Econ. Jours., 1961. Contbr. articles on edn. and econs. to publs. Home: 426 Prospect St New Haven CT 06511

MILLER, JOHN RICHARD, interior designer; b. Washington, Feb. 11, 1927; s. John Henry and Helen (Vermillion) M.; student Colbert Design Inst., Washington, 1950; m. Audrey Gene Owens, Nov. 6, 1946; children—Pamela Miller DeTurris, Felicity, Timothy. Designer, Hollidge Interiors, Washington, 1948-51; pres. Miller's Interiors, Marlow Heights, Md., 1951—; columnist Washington Star, 1970—; dir. C.B. Constrn. Co., Burgess Miller Properties Co. Mem. Pres.'s Commn. on Employment of Handicapped, 1972-78. Served with USN, 1944-46. Fellow Am. Soc. Interior Designers (White House design com. 1969-70, chmn. opportunity guidance council 1972-74, nat. dir. 1977-79, fellows selection com. 1977-78, pres. Potomac chpt. 1978-79, dir. 1979—). Democrat. Episcopalian. Club: Tantallon Country (Oxon Hill, Md.). Home: 13710 Piscataway Dr Oxon Hill MD 20022 Office: 4616 St Barnabas St Marlow Heights MD 20031. *The measure of mankind's removal from animalism is in the degree of his refinement, and that degree is judged by his compassion and consideration for others.*

MILLER, JOHN ROBINSON, JR., communications exec.; b. La Grange, Ill., Jan. 19, 1914; s. John Robinson and Helen Dora (Smythe) M.; student Goldey Bus. Coll., Wilmington, Del., 1933-34; m. Helen Elizabeth Fulton, June 14, 1935; children—Dale Dunlap, John Robinson III, Mark Fulton. With Hearst Mags., Inc., N.Y.C., 1934—, successively clk. circulation dept., agy. mgr., trade mgr., subscription sales dir., asst. treas., asst. gen. mgr., 1934-55, v.p., circulation dir., asst. gen. mgr., 1955-62, v.p., gen. mgr., 1962-67, exec. v.p., gen. mgr., 1967-73, also dir.; v.p. Internat. Circulation Co., N.Y.C., 1945-50; asst. treas. Hearst Corp., 1952-55, exec. v.p., 1973-74, pres., chief exec. officer, 1975-79, vice-chmn., 1979—; v.p., asst. treas., dir. Periodical Pubs. Service Bur., Inc., Sandusky, Ohio, 1953-55, pres., dir., 1963-70, chmn. bd., 1970-72; v.p., dir. Popular Mechanics Co., 1958-59, Science Digest Co., 1958-59, Good Housekeeping, Inc.; dir., chmn. Nat. Mag. Co., London, Eng.; mem. adv. bd. Mfrs. Hanover Trust Co.; dir. Southwest Forest Industries, Am. Home Products. Dir., vice chmn., sec. Audit Bur. Circulations, 1958-74, chmn. bd. central registry, 1957-58, dir., 1958; dir. Nat. Better Bus. Bur., 1961-70, chmn. bd., 1966-68; bd. dirs. ABBI, 1968-70; dir. Council of Better Bus. Burs., 1970-72. Trustee St. Paul's Sch., Garden City, Hearst Found., William Randolph Hearst Found. Recipient Human Relations award Anti-Defamation League, 1972; Lee C. Williams Pub. award for distinguished industry and community service, 1975; Henry T. Zwirner award Assn. 2d Class Mail Publs., 1976; Humanitarian award United Cerebral Palsy, 1978. Mem. Am. Arbitration Assn. Episcopalian. Clubs: Metropolitan (N.Y.C.); Cherry Valley Golf (Garden City). Home: 18 Wellington Rd Garden City NY 11530 also Falls Drive Buck Hill Falls PA 18323 Office: 959 8th Ave New York NY 10019

MILLER, JOHN STEPHEN, pub. relations exec.; b. Oakland, Calif., July 20, 1942; s. Vern Avon and Monnie Zula (Davis) M.; student journalism, U. Nev., 1960-61, 64-65; m. Jeannette Patterson, June 5, 1965; children—Mark, Brian, Caroline. Intern Fallon (Nev.) Eagle-Standard, 1965; reporter, advt. salesman Elko (Nev.) Daily Free Press, 1965-66; deskman Las Vegas Sun, 1966-69, Las Vegas Rev. Jour., 1969; editor Ely (Nev.) Daily Times, 1969-71, Nev. Appeal, Carson City, 1971-77; editorial page editor Reno Evening Gazette, 1977-78; pub. relations dir. Nev. Mines div. Kennecott Minerals Co., McGill, 1979—. Recipient Outstanding Young Journalist award Nev. Press Assn., 1970. Mem. Sigma Delta Chi. Home: PO Box 638 1 Steptoe Circle Ely NV 89301 Office: Nev Mines Div McGill NV 89318

MILLER, JOHN ULMAN, clergyman; b. N.Y.C., Dec. 9, 1914; s. Clarence James and Edythe Gladys (Shaffer) M.; B.A. cum laude, Taylor U., 1937; M.A., Butler U., 1942; D.D., Geneva (Wis.) Theol. Coll., 1968; m. Marcella E. Hubner, June 12, 1937; children—John U., Mark C. (dec.), Mary Kay (Mrs. Charles Bolin), Gretchen (Mrs. Ernest Micka). Ordained to ministry Bapt. Ch., 1937; pastor First Bapt. Ch., Bluffton, Ind., 1946-49, Boston, 1949-56, Tabernacle Ch., Utica, N.Y., 1956-63, United Ch. of Christ, Hagerstown, Ind., 1963-66, St. John's Evang. Ch., Louisville, 1967—. Participant Churchmen Weigh News, WNAC, Boston, 1953-56; preacher Meml. Chapel, instr. religion N.Y. Masonic Home, Utica, 1957-62; broadcast weekly services WKBV, Richmond, Ind., 1965-66; preacher Fellowship Chapel WHAS, Louisville, 1967-77; maintains 24 hour Dial-A-Prayer, Louisville, 1968-77; minister Royal Poinciana Chapel, Palm Beach, Fla., 1978—. Chmn. Campaigns Crippled Children, Tb, U.S.O., 1946-49. Served to capt. USAAF, 1942-45; PTO. Named Community Leader Am., News Pub. Co., 1969. Mem. Ind.-Ky. Conf. United Ch. of Christ, Bach Soc. Louisville. Home: 5200 N Dixie Apt 606 West Palm Beach FL 33402 Office: 60 Cocoanut Row Palm Beach FL 33480

MILLER, JOHN WADE, JR., mgmt. cons. exec.; b. Pitts., Apr. 9, 1920; s. John Wade and Margaret Elizabeth (Wallace) M.; A.B., Washington and Jefferson Coll., 1941; Ph.D., Mass. Inst. Tech., 1948; m. Margaret MacInnes, Apr. 19, 1952; children—Susan Elizabeth, Janice Lesley. Mem. indsl. relations staff Ford Motor Co., 1948-50; with Dewey & Almy chem. div. W.R. Grace & Co., 1950-63, v.p. central services, 1960-63; v.p. B.F. Goodrich Co., Akron, Ohio, 1963-74; exec. v.p. Orgn. Resources Counselors, Inc., N.Y.C., 1974—. Employer rep. Fed. Adv. Council Employment Security, 1957-61; mem. com. social ins. and taxes Pres.'s Commn. Status Women, 1963; mem. sec. of navy's adv. com. on manpower, 1966-68; mem. adv. council on mgmt. and personnel Conf. Bd., 1970-73. Mem. exec. bd. Akron Area council Boy Scouts Am., 1964-74. Trustee Litchfield Rehab. Center, Akron, 1967-73, Akron Child Guidance Center, 1968-73, Washington and Jefferson Coll., 1969-74, Old Trail Sch., Akron, 1970-74; dept. econs. vis. com. Mass. Inst. Tech. Served to lt. (s.g.), USNR, 1942-46; PTO. Mem. Am. Mgmt. Assn. (dir., v.p. personnel div. 1972-74), Phi Beta Kappa, Phi Delta Theta. Contbr. articles to profl. jours., books. Address: Orgn Resources Counselors Inc 1211 Ave of Americas Rockefeller Center New York City NY 10036 also 425 E 58th St New York City NY 10022

MILLER, JOHN WILLIAM, JR., bassoonist; b. Balt., Mar. 11, 1942; s. John William and Alverta Evelyn (Rodemaker) M.; B.S., Mass. Inst. Tech., 1964; Mus.M. with highest honors, New Eng. Conservatory, 1967, artist's diploma, 1969; m. Sibylle Weigel, July 12, 1966; children—Christian Desmond, Andrea Jocelyn, Claire Evelyn. Instr. bassoon Boston U., 1967-71, U. Minn., 1971—; prin. bassoonist, founding mem. Boston Philharmonia Chamber Orch., 1968-71; prin. bassoonist Minn. Orch., Mpls., 1971—; dir. Boston Baroque Ensemble, 1963-71. Recipient U.S. Govt. Fulbright award, 1964-65, Irwin Bodky award Cambridge Soc. Early Music, 1968. Mem. Internat. Double Reed Soc. Soloist on recs. for Cambridge and Musical Heritage Soc. Home: 706 Lincoln Ave Saint Paul MN 55105 Office: 1111 Nicollet Mall Minneapolis MN 55403

MILLER, JOHNNY LAURENCE, profl. golfer; b. San Francisco, Apr. 29, 1947; s. Laurence O. and Ida (Meldrum) M.; student Brigham Young U., 1965-68; m. Linda Strouse, Sept. 17, 1969; children—John Strouse, Kelly, Casi, Scott, Brent. Profl. golfer, 1969—; winner U.S. Open at Oakmont County Club, 1973, Lancome Trophy tournament, Paris, 1973; rep. U.S. in World Cup, 1973; winner Crosby Nat., Phoenix Open and Tucson Open tournaments, 1974; winner Heritage and Tournament of Champions, 1974, Westchester Classic, World Open and Kaiser Internat., 1974; winner Phoenix and Tucson Open, Hope Classic, Kaiser Open, 1975, Brit. Open, Bob Hope Classic, Tucson Open, 1976. Home: Napa CA 94558 Office: Suite 1200 2049 Century Park E Los Angeles CA 90067

MILLER, JON HAMILTON, mfg. co. exec.; b. Des Moines, Jan. 22, 1938; s. Victor George and Virginia Adelaine (Hamilton) M.; A.B. in Econs., Stanford U., 1959, M.B.A. in Mktg. and Finance, 1961; m. Sydney Gail Fernald, June 4, 1966; children—Emily, Sara. Asst. to pres. Boise Cascade Corp., 1961-62, prodn. service mgr., 1962-65, sr. v.p. bus. products and services and packaging, Portland, 1971-74, exec. v.p. paper and paper products, Boise, Idaho, 1974-76, exec. v.p. timber/wood products/bldg. materials, 1976-78, pres. and chief operating officer, 1978—, also dir.; dir. First Security Corp. Bd. dirs. Boise State U. Bronco Athletic Assn., St. Luke's Hosp. Served with U.S. Army, 1959-60. Mem. Greater Boise C. of C. (pres. 1977). Methodist. Clubs: Arid (Boise); Multnomah Athletic (Portland). Home: 3330 Mountain View Dr Boise ID 83704 Office: Boise Cascade Corp One Jefferson Sq Boise ID 83728

MILLER, JORDAN YALE, educator; b. Manhattan, Kans., Sept. 2, 1919; s. Edwin Cyrus and Della (Slye) M.; student Kans. State U., 1937-38; B.A., Yale U., 1942, postgrad., 1946-47; Ph.D., Columbia U., 1957; m. Elaine Elizabeth Graham, Dec. 31, 1945; children—Sherry Elaine, Adrienne Elizabeth. Mem. faculty Kans. State U., Manhattan, 1950-69, prof., 1967-69; prof., chmn. English dept. U. R.I., Kingston, 1969—; Fulbright lectr. drama and theatre Bombay, India, 1964-65; vis. exchange prof. Sch. English and Am. Studies, U. East Anglia, Norwich, Eng., 1977-78; cons. American Quar., Publ. Modern Lang. Assn., Nat. Endowment for Humanities. Served with AUS, 1942-45. Mem. Nat. Council Tchrs. English, Modern Lang. Assn. Am., AAUP, Popular Culture Assn. Unitarian-Universalist. Author: American Dramatic Literature, 1961; Eugene O'Neill and the American Critic, 1962, 2d edit., 1973; Playwright's Progress: O'Neill and the Critics, 1965; 20th Century Interpretation of A Streetcar Named Desire, 1971; Heath Introduction to Drama, 1976. Home: 23 Locust Dr Kingston RI 02881

MILLER, JOSEPH FREDERICK, JR., electronics co. exec.; b. nr. Tyrone, Pa., July 12, 1924; s. Joseph F. and Mary (Warburton) M.; B.S.E.E., Pa. State U., 1948; postgrad. U. Pitts., 1948-52; m. Jeanne Reichley, June 9, 1948; children—Timothy Irving, Thomas Warburton. With Motorola Inc., Schaumburg, Ill., 1952—, corp. v.p., 1971-76, gen. mgr. communications div., 1975-76, sr. v.p., 1976—, gen. mgr. communications group, 1976—. Served with USN, 1943-46; PTO. Mem. IEEE, SAR, Tau Beta Pi, Eta Kappa Nu, Phi Gamma Delta. Republican. Club: Inverness Country. Office: 1301 E Algonquin Rd Schaumburg IL 60196

MILLER, JOSEPH HILLIS, educator; b. Newport News, Va., Mar. 5, 1928; s. Joseph Hillis and Nell (Critzer) M.; B.A., Oberlin Coll., 1948; M.A., Harvard, 1949, Ph.D., 1952; M.A., Yale, 1972; m. Dorothy Marian James, Apr. 2, 1949; children—Robin Leigh, Matthew Hopkins, Sarah Elizabeth. Instr. English, Williams Coll., Williamstown, Mass., 1952-53; mem. faculty Johns Hopkins U., Balt., 1953-72, prof. English, 1963-68, prof. English and humanistic studies, 1968-72, chmn. dept. English, 1964-68; prof. English, Yale, New Haven, 1972-75, Gray prof. rhetoric, 1975-76, Frederick W. Hilles prof. English, 1976—, chmn. dept. English, 1976-79; summer tchr. U. Hawaii, 1956, Harvard, 1962, 72, U. Wash., 1971; Ward-Phillips lectr. U. Notre Dame, 1967; vis. prof. U. Va., 1969, U. Zurich (Switzerland), 1972, 78; fellow Wesleyan Center for the Humanities, 1971; vis. prof. and fellow Council of Humanities Princeton U., 1974; vis. prof. U. Calif. Sch. Criticism, Irvine. Trustee Keuka Coll., 1971—. Recipient E. Harris Harbison Distinguished Teaching award Danforth Found., 1968. Guggenheim fellow, 1959-60, 65-66; Nat. Endowment for Humanities sr. fellow, 1975. Fellow Soc. Religion in Higher Edn., Am. Acad. Arts and Scis., Conn. Acad. Arts and Scis.; mem. Modern Lang. Assn. (research com. 1968-69, exec. council 1970-73, PMLA 1975-77), Coll. English Assn. (dir. 1977-80), English Inst. (supr. com. 1968-70, chmn. 1970), New Eng. Coll. English Assn. (pres. 1975-76), Phi Beta Kappa (lectr. 1977-78). Author: Charles Dickens: The World of His Novels, 1958; The Disappearance of God; Five Nineteenth-Century Writers, 1963; Poets of Reality; Six Twentieth-Century Writers, 1965; The Form of Victorian Fiction, 1968; Thomas Hardy: Distance and Desire, 1970. Editor: Modern Lang. Notes, 1953-61, ELH, 1953—; mem. adv. bd. Diacritics, 1975—, Ga. Rev., 1975—, Critical Inquiry, 1974—, Poetics Today, 1979—, Oxford Lit. Rev., 1978—, Studies in English Lit., 1979—. Home: 28 Sperry Rd Bethany CT 06525

MILLER, JOSEPH IRWIN, automotive mfg. co. exec.; b. Columbus, Ind., May 26, 1909; s. Hugh Thomas and Nettie Irwin (Sweeney) M.; grad. Taft Sch., 1927; A.B., Yale U., 1931, M.A. (hon.), 1959, L.H.D. (hon.), 1979; M.A., Oxford (Eng.) U., 1933; LL.D., Bethany Coll., 1956, Tex. Christian U., Ind. U., 1958, Oberlin Coll., Princeton, 1962, Hamilton Coll., 1964, Columbia, 1968, Mich. State U., 1968, Dartmouth, 1971, U. Notre Dame, 1972, Ball State U., 1972; L.H.D. (hon.), Case Inst. Tech., 1966, U. Dubuque, 1977, Hum.D., Manchester U., 1973, Moravian Coll., 1976; m. Xenia Ruth Simons, Feb. 5, 1943; children—Margaret Irwin, Catherine Gibbs, Elizabeth Ann Garr, Hugh Thomas, II, William Irwin. Asso. Cummins Engine Co., Inc., Columbus, Ind., 1934—, v.p., gen. mgr., 1934-42, exec. v.p., 1944-47, pres., 1947-51, chmn. bd., 1951-77, chmn. exec. and fin. com., 1977—; pres. Irwin-Union Bank & Trust Co., 1947-54, dir., 1937—, chmn., 1954-75; chmn. exec. com. Irwin Union Corp., 1976—; dir. AT&T; mem. Commn. Money and Credit, 1958-61, Bus. Council, Conf. Bd., Pres.'s Com. Postal Reorgn. 1968, Pres.'s Com. Urban Housing, 1968; chmn. Pres.'s Com. on Trade Relations with Soviet Union and Eastern European Nations, 1965; chmn. Nat. Adv. Commn. on Health Manpower, 1966; vice chmn. UN Commn. on Multinat. Corps., 1974; adv. council U.S. Dept. Commerce, 1976; mem. U.S. Study Commn. on So. Africa. Pres. Nat. Council Chs. of Christ in U.S.A., 1960-63; mem. central and exec. coms. World Council Chs., 1961-68. Trustee Ford Found., Yale U., 1959-77, Urban Inst., 1966-76, Mayo Found.; asst. fellow Branford Coll., Recipient Rosenberger award U. Chgo., 1977; hon. fellow Balliol Coll., Oxford (Eng.) U.; Benjamin Franklin fellow Royal Soc. Arts. Served to lt. USNR, 1942-44. Fellow Am. Acad. Arts and Scis.; mem. Am. Philos. Soc., AIA (hon.), Phi Beta Kappa, Beta Gamma Sigma. Mem. Christian Ch. (elder). Clubs: Yale, Century, Links (N.Y.C.); Chicago; Indianapolis Athletic, Columbia (Indpls.). Home: 2760 Highland Way Columbus IN 47201 Office: 301 Washington St Columbus IN 47201

MILLER, JUDSON FREDERICK, army officer; b. Tulsa, Dec. 5, 1924; s. Herbert Frederick and Martha (Davidson) M.; B.S., U. Md., 1961; postgrad. Army War Coll., 1961-62; M.A., George Washington U., 1962; m. June Hirakis, Aug. 4, 1967; children by previous marriage—Kathleen, Shelley, Douglas, Judson Frederick. Commd. 2d lt. U.S. Army, 1943, advanced through grades to maj. gen., 1975; platoon leader, co. comdr. 4th Cav. Group, Europe, 1944-46, 82d Airborne Div., 1947-50; with 187th Airborne RCT and Hdqrs. 8th Army, 1950-52; instr. Armored Sch., 1953-56; bn. comdr. 14th Armored Cav., 1958-60; with Hdqrs. U.S. Strike Command, 1963-65; brigade comdr., chief of staff 4th Inf. Div., Vietnam, 1966-67; mem. gen. staff Dept. Army, 1967-68; dep. comdg. gen. Ft. Ord, Cal., 1968-69; asst. chief of staff Hdqrs. Allied Forces Central Europe, 1969-71; asst. comdr. 3d Inf. Div., Germany, 1971-73; chief of staff I Corps Group, Korea, 1973-75; dep. comdg. gen. VII Corps, Germany, 1975—. Decorated Silver Star, Legion of Merit, Bronze Star with V device and oak leaf cluster, Joint Service Commendation medal, Air medal with 8 oak leaf clusters, Purple Heart, Vietnamese Gallantry Cross with palm. Mem. Assn. U.S. Army. Address: 8009 75th St SW Tacoma WA 98498

MILLER, KENNETH EDWARD, educator, sociologist; b. N.Y.C., June 17, 1929; s. Joseph F. and Irene (Edersheim) M.; B.A., U. Ala., 1953, M.A., 1956; Ph.D., Duke, 1965; m. Andrée Nora Barthelemy, Feb. 14, 1959; children—Jennifer Andrée, Christopher Kenneth. Asst. to pres., dir. devel. Jacksonville (Fla.) U., 1957-60; dir. Health Council, asso. dir. Community Planning Council, Birmingham, Ala., 1960-62; asst. prof. sociology Emory U., Atlanta, 1966-70, acting chmn. dept., 1969-70; prof. sociology, chmn. dept. Drake U., Des Moines, 1970—. Research sociologist U. Ala., 1956-57; research asso. U.S. Civil Service Commn., summer 1968. Served with USN, 1946-48. Postdoctoral research fellow Duke, 1965-66. Mem. Am. Sociol. Assn., So., Midwest sociol. socs., AAUP. Home: 947 43d St West Des Moines IA 50265 Office: Dept Sociology Drake Univ Des Moines IA 50311

MILLER, KENNETH LYALL, computer co. exec.; b. South Hadley Falls, Mass., Oct. 27, 1927; s. George and Mabel R. (Murison) M.; B.S. in Elec. Engring. magna cum laude, Tufts U., 1951; J.D., George Washington U., 1957; LL.M., Wayne State U., 1968; m. Hiroko Otsuka, Dec. 23, 1974; children—Clifford, Tomoko. Admitted to Mich. bar; engr. Eastman Kodak Co., Rochester, N.Y., 1951-53; patent examiner U.S. Patent Office, 1953-56; with Burroughs Corp., 1956—, asst. v.p. legal, Detroit, 1969-70, sec., 1970—, v.p., 1979—. Served with USN, 1946-48. Mem. Am. Bar Assn., Am. Soc. Corp. Secs., Engring. Soc. Detroit, Licensing Execs. Soc., Mich. Patent Law Assn., Practising Law Inst., State Bar Mich., Tau Beta Pi. Home: 24108 E River Rd Grosse Ile MI 48138 Office: Burroughs Pl Detroit MI 48232

MILLER, KENNETH ROY, mgmt. cons.; b. Uniontown, Pa., Oct. 22, 1902; s. Franklin Pierce and Annabelle (Darby) M.; student Emerson Inst., 1922-23, George Washington U., 1923-25; LL.D., Lebanon Valley Coll., 1957, Fla. Atlantic U., 1975; m. Mary E. Hunnicutt, June 14, 1930; 1 son, Stephen Goodrich. Dir. conservation dept. Acadia Mut. Life Ins. Co., Washington, 1926-28; asst. supt. agencies Occidental Life Ins. Co., Raleigh, N.C., 1928-31; cons. Life Ins. Agy. Mgmt. Assn., Hartford, 1931-38; supt. agencies Atlantic Life Ins. Co., Richmond, Va., 1938-41; mng. dir. Nat. Fed. Sales Execs., N.Y.C., 1941-42; asst. to program vice chmn., dir. ops. analysis WPB, Washington, 1942-43; with NAM, N.Y.C., 1943-64, asst. to exec. v.p., asst. treas., treas., bus. mgr., sr. v.p., 1943-55, mng. dir., 1955-57, gen. mgr., 1957-62, group v.p., 1962-63, sr. v.p., adviser, 1963-64; prin. Kenneth R. Miller & Assos., mgmt. and fin. cons., Boca Raton, Fla., 1964—; adminstrv. bd. Boca Raton br. Sun Banks of Palm Beach County. Bd. dirs., immediate past pres., Fla. Atlantic U. Found., Boca Raton; pres. Caldwell Theatre Co.; chmn. adv. council Fla. Atlantic Music Guild. Mem. Friends of Caldwell Playhouse, Friends of the Library of Fla. Atlantic U., English-Speaking Union (pres. Boca Raton br.), Phi Sigma Kappa, Pi Delta Epsilon. Clubs: Deerfield Beach (Fla.) Country; Economic Roundtable (chmn.), Bankers. Address: 699 SW 5th St Boca Raton FL 33432

MILLER, LAMBERT H., lawyer; b. Groton, S.D., Aug. 31, 1907; s. William B. and Grace (Neff) M.; A.B., George Washington U., 1932, J.D., 1936, LL.M., 1937; m. Jane Brigham Cline, Oct. 8, 1938; children—Lambert H., Susan Carroll, Ann Sheldon, Margaret Neff. Admitted to D.C. bar, 1937, U.S. Supreme Ct. bar, 1941; practiced law, Washington, 1937—; asso. Hon. Royal C. Johnson, Washington, 1937-39; pvt. practice law, 1937-42; asso. counsel N.A.M., 1942-49, gen. counsel, 1949-69, sr. v.p., gen. counsel, 1969-72, also head assn. law dept., Washington; counsel Hamel, Park, McCabe & Saunders, 1972-79; adj. prof. trade assn. law Georgetown U. Grad. Sch. Law, 1957-59. Served as lt. USNR, 1944-46. Mem. Am., D.C. bar assns., Beta Theta Pi. Clubs: Washington Golf and Country, Metropolitan. Home: 610 N 11th St Falls Church VA 22046

MILLER, LAVERN ARCHIE, sci. cos. exec.; b. Sandwich, Ill., Jan. 14, 1925; s. Lavern Archie and Olive (Masear) M.; B.C.E., Ill. Inst. Tech., 1947; J.D., John Marshall Law Sch., 1951; m. Twilah Page, May 30, 1951 (div.); children—Melinda Susan, Douglas Page. Asst. staff engr. Standard Oil Co. (Ind.), Chgo., 1947-49; advt. mgr. Eugene Dietzgen Co., Chgo., 1949-51; asst. to pres., 1951-59; owner L.A. Miller & Assos., Chgo., 1951-53; exec. v.p. Cenco Inc., Chgo., 1959-76; owner, pres. Stoelting Co., Chgo., 1976—. Mem. Chi Epsilon. Republican. Clubs: Glen Oak Country (Glen Ellyn, Ill.); Union League (Chgo.). Home: 605 Carriage Hill Dr Glenview IL 60025 Office: 1350 S Kostner Ave Chicago IL 60623

MILLER, LELAND BISHOP, JR., food processing co. exec.; b. Bloomington, Ill., June 17, 1931; s. Leland Bishop and Nelle (Jolly) M.; B.S. in Chem. Engring., U. Ill., 1954, M.S. in Chem. Engring., 1955, M.B.A., 1978; m. Elene Schiermer, Apr. 5, 1958; children—Steven Robert, Susan Elizabeth. Research engr. Exxon Research & Engring., Linden, N.J., 1955-58; research asst. Purdue U., 1958-59; with A. E. Staley Mfg. Co., Decatur, Ill., 1959—, dir. corp. planning, 1971-73, asst. treas., 1973-77, corp. treas., 1977—; pres. Indsl. Devel. Research Council, 1973-74. State v.p. United Cerebral Palsy of Ill., 1971-72; pres. United Cerebral Palsy of Macon County (Ill.), 1972-73; bd. dirs. Progress Resource, Inc., Decatur. Served to 1st lt. U.S. Army, 1955-57. Mem. Corp. Planning Council, Planning Execs. Inst., M.W. Planning Assn., Fin. Mgmt. Assn., Alpha Chi Sigma, Phi Lambda Upsilon, Sigma Chi. Home: 2383 Florian Ave Decatur IL 62526 Office: 2200 E Eldorado St Decatur IL 62525

MILLER, LEONARD, real estate devel. co. exec.; b. New Bedford, Mass., Sept. 18, 1932; s. Jack and Ida (Freedman) M.; A.B., Harvard Coll., 1955; m. Susan Miller, June 18, 1955; children—Stuart Alan, Leslie Jane, Jeffrey Scott. Chmn. bd., pres. Lennar Corp., Lennar Mgmt. Corp., Miami, Fla., 1969—; chmn. bd. F & R Builders, Inc., Value Realty Co., Universal Am. Realty Corp., South Dade Utilities, Inc., Riviera Land Corp., 1st Atlantic Bldg. Corp., Lennar Ga., Inc., Franjo Devel. Corp., Bert L. Smokler & Co., Dreyfus Interstate Devel. Corp., Midwest Mgmt. Co., Standard Mortgage Corp., SMC Mortgage Corp., Womack Devel. Corp., Mastercraft Homes, Inc., Mastercraft Realty, Inc., Apache Springs Water Co., Miami Prefabricators, Inc., Quality Roof Truss Co., Builders Mart Components Corp., Supreme Lumber & Millwork Co., Holiday Unit Door Co., Inc.; dir. City Nat. Bank of Lauderhill (Fla.). Home: 23 Star Island Miami Beach FL 33139 Office: 9555 N Kendall Dr Miami FL 33176

MILLER, LEONARD DAVID, surgeon; b. Jersey City, July 8, 1930; s. Louis Abner and Esther (Levy) M.; A.B., Yale U., 1951; M.D., U. Pa., 1955; m. Adelaide C. Creveling; children—Steven Lawrence, Jason Lloyd. Intern, Hosp. of U. Pa., Phila., 1955-56, resident, 1956-57, 59-65; practice medicine, specializing in surgery, Phila., 1965—; vice chmn. dept. research and surgery U. Pa., 1972-75, acting chmn., 1975-78, John Rhea Barton prof., chmn. dept. surgery, 1978—; dir. Harrison Dept. Surgery. Served to capt., M.C., USAF, 1957-59.

Recipient Lindback award for disting. teaching, 1969, Student award for clin. teaching, 1965. Mem. Am. Surg. Assn., AAAS, Soc. for Surgery of Alimentary Tract, Nat. Soc. Med. Research (rep.), Soc. Univ. Surgeons, Am. Soc. Surgery of Trauma, Coll. Physicians of Phila., N.Y. Acad. Sci., Sigma Xi, Alpha Omega Alpha. Mem. editorial bd. Annals of Surgery, 1973—. Home: 4631 Pine St Philadelphia PA 19104 Office: Hosp of U Pa Dept Surgery 4 Silverstein 3400 Spruce St Philadelphia PA 19104

MILLER, LESLIE HAYNES, educator; b. Ironton, Ohio, Mar. 21, 1914; s. Thomas Jefferson and Mattie (Haynes) M.; B.S. in Edn., Ohio U., 1935, M.A., 1938; Ph.D., Ohio State U., 1943; m. Ethyl Rose, June 10, 1937; children—Joanne (Mrs. David Stichweh), Marilyn (Mrs. John Rehm). Tchr. pub. schs., Ironton, 1935-37; instr. Cedarville Coll., 1938-40; from instr. to asso. prof. math. Ohio State U., 1943-57, prof., 1957-79, prof. emeritus, 1979—, also mem. computer graphics research group. Served with USNR, 1943-44. Recipient awards for artistic carved gourds. Mem. Math. Assn. Am., Am. Gourd Soc. (dir., editor The Gourd jour.), Sigma Xi, Pi Mu Epsilon. Author: College Geometry, 1957; Fundamental Mathematics, 1957; Understanding Basic Mathematics, 1961; contbr. articles to profl. jours.; pioneer in computing and ednl. TV. Home: 1883 W Case Rd Columbus OH 43220

MILLER, LINDA B., polit. scientist; b. Manchester, N.H., Aug. 7, 1937; d. Louis and Helene (Chase) Miller; A.B. cum laude, Radcliffe Coll., 1959; M.A., Columbia U., 1961, Ph.D., 1965. Asst. prof. Barnard Coll., 1964-67; research asso. Princeton U., 1966-67; research asso. Harvard U., 1967-71, 76—, lectr. polit. sci., 1968-69; mem. faculty Wellesley (Mass.) Coll., 1969—, prof. polit. sci., 1975—. Internat. Affairs fellow Council Fgn. Relations, 1973-74; fellow internat. conflict Rockefeller Found., 1976-77; sr. fellow, guest investigator marine policy and ocean mgmt. program Woods Hole (Mass.) Oceanographic Instn., 1979-80. Mem. Am. Polit. Sci. Assn., AAUP, Inst. Strategic Studies. Author: World Order and Local Disorder: The United Nations and Internal Conflicts, 1967; Dynamics of World Politics: Studies in the Resolution of Conflicts, 1968; Cyprus: The Law and Politics of Civil Strife, 1968; also articles. Home: Box 415 South Wellfleet MA 02663 Office: Wellesley Coll Wellesley MA 02181

MILLER, LINDA KAY, ballet dancer; b. Washington, Sept. 7, 1953; d. James Thomas and Kay Ray (Luskey) Miller; diploma N.C. Sch. Arts, 1971. Soloist, N.C. Dance Theatre, Winston-Salem, 1971-74; singer, dancer, actress My Fair Lady, 1973, Merry Widow, 1973; prin. dancer Eliot Feld Ballet Co., N.Y.C., 1974—; guest tchr. Md. Sch. Ballet, 1974; guest artist Ballet Guild Lehigh Valley, 1974; performed in The Nutcraker Suite at White House, 1969. Ford Found. student, 1966-70. Mem. Am. Guild Mus. Artists. Home: 102 W 80th St Apt 47 New York NY 10024 Office: 890 Broadway New York NY 10003. *Harder than the rigorous repetition, self discipline, and unending struggle for perfection, is the realization that you'll always be in competition with yourself. But how lucky to earn your living at something you love.*

MILLER, LLOYD DANIEL, assn. exec.; b. Savannah, Mo., May 25, 1916; s. Daniel Edward and Minnie (Wiedmer) M.; B.S. in Agrl. Journalism, U. Mo., 1941; m. Mabel Gertrude Kurz, June 9, 1939; children—Sharon Gail (Mrs. A. E. Schumacher, Jr.), Donna Lynn (Mrs. Ronald L. Bodinson), Rosemary Rae, Jeffrey Lloyd. Reporter, feature writer, photographer, market editor Corn Belt Farm Dailies, Chgo., Kansas City, Mo., 1941-43; asst. agrl. editor U. Mo., 1946; dir. pub. relations Am. Angus Assn., Chgo., 1946-67, St. Joseph, Mo., 1967, asst. sec., dir. pub. relations, 1968, exec. sec., 1968-78, sr. cons., 1978—; dir. 1st Stock Yards Bank; mem. U.S. Agrl. Tech. Adv. Com. on Livestock and Livestock Products for Trade Negotiations, 1975-79; bd. govs. Am. Royal Livestock Show, Kansas City, Mo. Bd. dirs. Mo. Western State Coll. Found., 1976—, pres., 1978-79; past chmn. bd. Ashland Ave. United Methodist Ch., trustee Meth. Hosp. Assn. Served with AUS, 1943-45. Recipient Silver Anvil award Pub. Relations Soc. Am., 1962, Faculty-Alumni award U. Mo.-Columbia, 1975. Mem. Pub. Relations Soc. Am., Am. Soc. Assn. Execs., U.S. Beef Breeds Council (dir., pres. 1973-74), Nat. Soc. Livestock Record Assns. (dir. 1969-78), World Aberdeen-Angus Secretariat (sec.-treas. 1969-79), Nat. Cattlemen's Assn. (tech. adviser fgn. trade com. 1977—), Nat. Assn. Realtors, St. Joseph Area C. of C. (pres. 1969, dir., chmn. agri-bus. council 1971), Sigma Delta Chi. Mason (32 deg., Shriner), Kiwanian. Home: 3208 Miller Rd Saint Joseph MO 64505 Office: 3201 Frederick Blvd Saint Joseph MO 64506

MILLER, LLOYD IVAN, mfg. co. exec.; b. Cin., May 1, 1924; s. Lloyd Ivan and Louise (Ruscher) M.; student U. Chgo., 1943-44; LL.B., U. Cin., 1948; m. Catherine Marie Crider, Jan. 5, 1952; children—Lloyd Ivan III, Martin Gregg. Admitted to Ohio bar, 1948, since practiced in Cin.; stock broker, 1948-58; dir. Cin. Transit Co., 1950-73, chmn. 1956-72, pres., 1972-73; chmn. bd. Schaefers Bakery, Inc., Valley Industries, Inc., 1975—; chmn., chief exec. officer Vulcan Corp., 1975—; pres. Am. Controlled Industries, 1975—; dir. Super Food Services Inc., Central Bancorp., Central Trust Co. Mem. adv. com. internat. bus. problems State Dept., 1970-74; mem. U.S. Trade Mission, Yugoslavia and Poland, 1971, Regional Export Expansion Council, 1971-74; U.S. ambassador to Trinidad and Tobago, 1974-75. Served with inf. AUS, 1943-46. Mem. C. of C., Newcomen Soc. N.Am., Cin. Bar Assn. Mason (Shriner). Clubs: University, Queen City, Cincinnati Country, Racquet, Indian Creek Country. Home: 1244 Cliff Laine Dr Cincinnati OH 45226 Office: 6 E 4th St Cincinnati OH 45202

MILLER, LOUIS GERARD, editor, clergyman; b. Grand Rapids, Mich., Apr. 11, 1913; s. Wenzel and Margaret (Hyland) M.; student Redemptorist Sem., Oconomowoc, Wis., 1939; B.A., Marquette U., 1942. Ordained priest Roman Cath. Ch., 1939; asst. editor The Liguorian 1947-62, editor, 1962-78. Trustee Holy Redeemer Coll., Waterford, Wis. Served as chaplain AUS, 1943-46, 50-51. Mem. Cath. Press Assn. (dir. 1965, past pres.), Marquette U. Alumni Assn., Cath. Union of Sick in Am., UN Assn. Contbg. author Cath. Ency. Address: Box 6 Glenview IL 60025. *I believe that true peace of mind depends on our accepting the reality that the pattern of life remains incomplete in the few decades a man spends in this life; there is a life to come which alone can give meaning to this life's inevitable frustrations and vexations.*

MILLER, LOUIS RICE, corporate lawyer; b. Frankfort, Ind., Feb. 28, 1914; s. Louis A. and Josephine (Rice) M.; A.B., U. Chgo., 1935, J.D., 1937; m. Jean Preston Russell, Feb. 1, 1941; 1 dau., Mary Melissa. Admitted to Ill. bar, 1938; asso. firm Gardner, Carton & Douglas, Chgo., 1937-40; atty. Armour & Co. (now a subsidiary of Greyhound Corp.) Chgo., 1940-71, Phoenix, 1971-79, v.p., chief legal officer, 1967-79, v.p., chief legal officer Greyhound Corp., Phoenix, 1972-79. Served with AUS, 1941, USNR, 1942-45. Mem. Am. Bar Assn. (com. on corp. law depts.), Assn. Gen. Counsel. Clubs: Westmoreland Country (Wilmette, Ill.); Paradise Valley Country (Phoenix). Home: 7541 N Shadow Mountain Rd Paradise Valley AZ 85253 Office: Greyhound Tower Phoenix AZ 85077

MILLER, LOYE WHEAT, ret. newspaperman; b. Mt. Vernon, Ill., Jan. 18, 1899; s. Thomas Edward and Elsie (Wheat) M.; grad. high sch., Evansville, Ind., 1916; m. Sara Vance Davis, Apr. 3, 1929; children—Loye Wheat, Wayne Watson, Michael Van Hook. Reporter Evansville (Ind.) Press, 1916-20, Cleve. Press, 1920-21; mng. editor Knoxville (Tenn.) News, 1921-26, Knoxville News-Sentinel, 1926-41, editor, 1941-67. Mem. Tenn. Great Smoky Mountain Park Commn., 1958-76, chmn., 1973-76. Served in 4th U.S. F.A., U.S. Army, 1918-19. Mem. Am. Soc. Newspaper Editors, Tenn. Soc. SR (past pres.), Tenn. Press Assn. (pres. 1953-54), Am. Judicature Soc., Sigma Delta Chi. Presbyn. Rotarian. Club: Nat. Press. Author: Tennessee's Universal Registration Law, Enacted, 1951. Home: 2117 Manor Rd Knoxville TN 37920. *Died Nov. 30, 1979*

MILLER, LOYE WHEAT, JR., journalist; b. Knoxville, Tenn., Mar. 20, 1930; s. Loye Wheat and Sara Vance (Davis) M.; A.B., Dartmouth, 1951; M.S. in Journalism, Columbia, 1952; children—Lissa Wethey, Loye Wheat. Mem. staff Charlotte (N.C.) Observer, 1955-59, asst. city editor, 1959; corr. Washington bur. Time mag., 1959-64, 69-70; chief Midwest news bur. Time-Life mags., 1964-69; corr. Washington bur. Knight Newspapers, 1970-77; chief Washington bur. Chgo. Sun-Times, 1977-78; corr. Washington Bur., Gannett Newspapers, 1978—. Served to lt. (j.g.) USNR, 1952-55. Home: 2901 Connecticut Ave NW Washington DC 20008 Office: 1627 K St NW Washington DC 20006

MILLER, LYLE LESLIE, educator; b. Deer Lodge, Mont., Aug. 20, 1919; s. Birl O. and Anna (Oakley) M.; B.S., Mont. State Coll., 1940; M.S., U. So. Cal., 1944; Ph.D., Ohio State U., 1949; m. Grace Moore, Sept. 12, 1942; children—Thomas Oakley, Patricia Ann. Tchr., Gallatin County High Sch., Bozeman, Mont., 1940-42; indsl. personnel work Walter Butler Assos., Coeur d'Alene, Idaho, 1942-43, Douglas Aircraft & Calif. Flyers, Los Angeles, 1943-44; guidance coordinator Flathead County High Sch., Kalispell, Mont., 1944-46; asst. jr. dean Coll. Edn., Ohio State U., 1946-49; supr. student employment and study skills center U. Wyo., Laramie, 1949-53, prof. edn., chmn. guidance and spl. edn., 1953-65, prof., head dept. guidance and counselor edn., 1965-72, prof. guidance and counselor edn., 1972—, coordinator N.W. Regional Center Counselor Edn., 1969-71, dir. Reading Research Center, 1955—. Mem. exec. bd. Laramie United Fund, 1950-62; rep. nat. exec. bd. Boy Scouts Am., 1961—. Recipient Nat. Distinguished Service award in counselor edn., 1968. Mem. AAUP (chpt. pres. 1965-67), Am. Personnel and Guidance Assn. (nat. membership chmn. 1962-63), Am. Soc. for Group Psychotherapy and Psychodrama, NEA (life), Assn. Counselor Edn. and Supervision (nat. pres. 1963-64), Am. Psychol. Assn., Moreno Acad., Assn. Specialists in Group Work, Phi Delta Kappa. Presbyn. Author: Increasing Reading Efficiency, 4th edit., 1977; Maintaining Reading Efficiency, 4th edit., 1978; Developing Reading Efficiency, 4th edit., 1980; Counseling Leads, 2d edit., 1970; The Guidance Wheel, 1962; The Time Budget Sheet, 1962, 2d edit., 1970; Teaching Reading Efficiency, 1963; Accelerating Growth in Reading Efficiency, 1967; Challenge for Change in Counselor Education, 1968; Teaching Efficient Reading Skills, 1972; Personalizing Reading Efficiency, 1976. Video tape series on reading efficiency, 1974. Home: 1944 Sheridan Ave Laramie WY 82070. *An essay contest sponsored by IBM in my junior year in high school started me working on the theme "The Value of Time in Education." This interest in effective use of time in releasing human potential led to a long term interest in student personnel work and to research in effective study, efficient reading and interpersonal communication. The theme "seek the ideas behind the words" expresses a basic concern I have in all of these attempts to improve individual potential for success.*

MILLER, LYNN HARVEY, banker; b. Mpls., Mar. 4, 1927; s. Lynn Harvey and Mary (Johnson) M.; student Yale, 1944-48; m. Anne Carter Jeffris, Sept. 4, 1948; children—Marion, Roys, Lynn Harvey, Rufus, Jacqueline. Sr. v.p., head banking dept. No. Trust Co., Chgo., 1948—; exec. v.p. Merc. Trust Co., N.A., St. Louis, 1974-76, pres., 1977-78, also dir.; exec. v.p., adv. dir. Bank of S.W., Houston, 1978—. Vice chmn. bd. Webster Coll., Webster Grove, Mo.; bd. dirs. Boy Scouts Am., Met. YMCA; v.p., bd. dirs. Houston Ballet Found. Served with USMCR, 1945. Mem. Assn. Res. City Bankers. Clubs: Glen View (Golf, Ill.); Chgo. Home: 8840 Memorial Dr Houston TX 77024 Office: Bank of SW PO Box 2629 Houston TX 77001

MILLER, M. HUGHES, publisher; b. Phila., July 3, 1913; s. Samuel Maximillian and Sarah (Hughes) M.; A.B., Muhlenberg Coll., 1931; M.A., U. Pa., 1932; m. Doris Gloria Ross, Jan. 1, 1936 (div.); children—Bruce Hyatt, Stephen Hughes; m. 2d, Mala Powers, May 17, 1970. Editorial writer Phila. Pub. Ledger, 1929-32; editor Lehigh Valley Review, 1933; mgr. Nat. Advertising Service, 1933-36; mgr. coll. publishing Prentice-Hall, 1936-37; staff pub. relations Earl Newsom & Co., 1937-39; gen. mgr. book pub. Am. Edn. Press, publications dir. Current Sci. and Aviation, v.p., gen. mgr. Charles E. Merrill, also Wesleyan U. Press, 1939-56; v.p. new pub. Am. Book-Stratford Press, Inc., 1956-58; pres. Bobbs Merrill Co., Inc., 1959-63, Book Publishers Project, Inc., N.Y.C., 1963—, editor Dictionary of Basic Words; mem. edn. bd. Education mag.; governing, editorial bd. Mil. Pub. Inst.; pres. Hughes Miller Pubs. Projects, Inc., Four Seasons Estates Inc., Lake Tahoe, Calif.; chmn. bd. Inter-Assoc. Book Pub. Cons., 1966—; exec. com., dir. Devon Group, Inc. (formerly Gen. Edn. Services corp.). Founder Weekly Reader Children's Book Club, 1953. Mem. Am. Film Inst. (charter), Am. Childhood Assn. Nat. Council Social Studies, Profl. Bookmen Am. (past pres., founder mem.), Assn. Childhood Edn. Internat. (dir.), Am. Inst. Graphic Arts (chmn. textbook clinic), Am. Textbook Pub. Inst. (chmn. plans and program 1954-56, dir.), Am. Assn. Sch. Adminstrs., Assn. Supervision and Curriculum Devel., NEA, Am. Nat. Theatre Assn. (dir. 1973—, Ohio Soc. of N.Y., Internat. Reading Assn., Newcomen Soc. N.Am., Phi Beta Alpha, Kappa Beta Phi. Episcopalian. Mason. Clubs: Columbus (Ohio) Country: Dutch Treat, Metropolitan, Canadian (N.Y.C.); Siwanoy Country (Bronxville); University (Columbus). Home: 4317 Forman Ave North Hollywood CA 91602 Office: 1270 Ave of Americas New York NY 10020

MILLER, MAHLON ALBERT, coll. pres.; b. Verona, Pa., May 26, 1921; s. Albert Henry and Mildred (Ridgeway) M.; B.S. in Aero. Engring., U. Pitts., 1943; postgrad. Case Inst. Tech., 1943-45, Western Res. U., 1945-46; M.Div., Drew Theol. Sem., 1950, S.T.M., 1952; student U. Zurich (Switzerland), 1952-53, Tuebingen (Germany) U., 1953-55; D.D., Union Coll., Barbourville, Ky., 1959; LL.D., Morehead State U., 1975; m. Laura Jean Ritchey, Sept. 4, 1942. Aero. research NACA, 1943-47; instr. math. evening div. Fenn Coll., Cleve., 1946-47; instr. philosophy, religion Drew U., Madison, N.J., 1950-51; ordained ministry United Meth. Ch., 1950; asst. to pres. Union Coll., Barbourville, Ky., 1955-59, pres., 1959—. Pres., chmn. bd. Knox County Bowling Lanes, Inc., Barbourville, 1964-76; dir. Knoxco Improvement Co. Mem. exec. com. Ky. Ind. Coll. Found., 1959—, chmn. exec. com., 1969-70; pres. Mid-Appalachia Coll. Council, Inc., 1966-70, bd. dirs., 1966—; chmn. bd. Knox County Econ. Opportunity Council, 1964-66; bd. dirs. Council Ky. Ind. Colls. and Univs., 1964—, v.p., 1966, pres., 1967; bd. dirs. Henderson Settlement, 1966-73, Knox County Devel. Assn., 1963-66, Appalachia Ednl. Lab., 1968-78. Chmn. commn. Christian vocations Ky. Conf. United Meth. Church, 1963-68, mem. Interbd. Council, 1963-68, mem. Appalachian com. Ky. Conf., 1965-69, exec. com. Ky. Appalachian Devel. Com., 1969-73; mem. Appalachian devel. com. Nat. Div., 1968-73; mem. Area Commn. Higher Edn. and Campus Ministries, 1972—; mem. Wilderness Rd. Comprehensive Health Planning Council, 1967-69, exec. com., dir. S.E. Ky. Comprehensive Health Demonstration Corp., 1967-77, chmn. task force on finance, 1969-72, v.p., 1972-73, chmn. bd. dirs., 1973-75; mem. Cumberland Valley Comprehensive Health Planning Council, 1969-76, vice chmn., 1970-71, chmn., 1971-73; mem. exec. com. Ky. Devel. Council, 1961-62; chmn. Barbourville-Knox County Airport Bd., 1966-70; mem. adv. council Ohio Valley Regional Med. Program, 1971-76; mem. Health Facilities and Health Services Certificate of Need and License Bd. of Ky., 1973-76; chmn. SE Ky. Area Health Edn. System, 1973-75, 78—; mem. Eastern Ky. Health Professions Scholarship Program Council, 1974-76; mem. health scis. subcom. Council on Pub. Higher Edn., 1975-79. Recipient Community Service award Knox County C. of C., 1965, Citizen of Year award Barbourville-Knox County, 1966, Distinguished Service award S.E. Ky. Homecoming Assn., 1970. Fulbright scholar, Germany, 1953-54; Tipple traveling fellow Drew U., 1952-53. Mem. Am. Assn. UN (pres. Ky. div. 1962-64), Barbourville C. of C. (v.p., dir.), Newcomen Soc., Wesley Hist. Soc. Gt. Britain, Nat. Honor Soc., Internat. Assn. Univ. Presidents, Assn. Colls. and Univs. for Internat.-Intercultural Studies (dir.), Order Ky. Cols., Adm. Ky. Waterways, Sigma Tau, Pi Tau Sigma. Mason, Kiwanian. Clubs: Pendennis (Louisville); Lafayette (Lexington). Home: 302 College St Barbourville KY 40906

MILLER, MARVIN JULIAN, sports assn. exec.; b. N.Y.C., Apr. 14 1917; s. Alexander and Gertrude (Wald) M.; student Miami U., Oxford, Ohio, 1935-37; B.S. in Econs., N.Y.U., 1938; m. Theresa Morgenstern, Dec. 24, 1939; children—Peter D., Susan T. Economist, hearing officer, conciliator U.S. Govt. agys., 1939-40, 42-50; asso. dir. research United Steelworkers Am., 1950-60, asst. to pres., 1960-66; exec. dir. Major League Baseball Players' Assn., 1966—. Mem. Nat. Labor-Mgmt. Panel, 1963-67. Home: 211 E 70th St New York City NY 10021 Office: 375 Park Ave New York City NY 10022

MILLER, SISTER MARY AQUIN, coll. ofcl.; b. Kewaskum, Wis., Feb. 12, 1904; d. Edward F. and Margaret (Mueller) Miller; B.S. magna cum laude, Marquette U., 1936; Ph.D., Cath. U. Am., 1943. Joined Order of Sisters of St. Francis of Assisi, Milw., 1929; tchr. St. Mary's Acad., Milw., 1932-39; faculty dept. biology Cardinal Stritch Coll., Milw., 1942-62, prof. biology, 1952-63, pres., 1955-74, dir. instnl. research, 1974—. Mem. Delta Epsilon Sigma. Address: 6801 N Yates Rd Milwaukee WI 53217

MILLER, MAYNARD M., geologist; b. Seattle, Jan., 23, 1921; B.S., Harvard U., 1943; M.A., Columbia U., 1948; Ph.D. (Fulbright scholar 1951-53), Cambridge (Eng.) U., 1956. Asst. prof. naval sci. Princeton U., 1946; geologist Gulf Oil Corp., Cuba, 1947; research asso. Am. Geog. Soc., 1948-51; vis. staff mem. Swiss Fed. Inst. Snow and Avalanche Research, 1952; staff dept. geography Cambridge U., 1953-54; asso. producer, exec. dir. Cinerama Round-The-World Seven Wonders Expdn., 1955; research asso. Lamont Geol. Obs., Columbia U., 1955-57, sr. scientist dept. geology, 1957-58; lectr. Nat. Lecture Bur., 1958-59; dir. lunar field sta. simulation program Boeing Co., 1959-60; asst. prof. geology Mich. State U., East Lansing, 1959-61, asso. prof., 1961-63, prof., 1963-75; dean Coll. Mines and Earth Resources, U. Idaho, Moscow, 1975—; chief Idaho Bur. Mines and Geology, 1975—; dir. Glaciological and Arctic Scis. Inst., Juneau, Alaska, 1960—; exec. dir., pres. Found. Glacier and Environ. Research, Pacific Sci. Center, Seattle, 1955—; dir. Juneau Icefield Research Program, 1946—; chmn., exec. dir. World Center for Exploration Found., Explorers Club, N.Y.C., 1968-70; geol. cons. U.S. Forest Service, U.S. Nat. Park Service, Alaska Dept. Hwys., Nat. Geog. Soc., various industries, fgn. govt. agys., 1946—; geophys. cons. U.S. Navy Oceanographic Office, 1967, 70, 72, USAF, 1951-52, 1958-60, NASA, 1964, 72; oceanographer of Navy, 1972-74; charge numerous field activities govt. agys., univs., pvt. corps., geog. socs.; chief geologist Am. Mt. Everest Expdn., 1963; field leader Mt. Kennedy Yukon Meml. Mapping Expdn., 1965. Mem. nat. bd. Embry-Riddle Aero. U.; mem. nat. council, nat. expln. com. Boy Scouts Am.; bd. dirs. Idaho Research Found. Served with USNR, 1943-46; capt. Res., 1965—. Named Leader of Tomorrow Seattle C. of C., also Time Mag., 1953, one of 10 outstanding men of year U.S. C. of C., 1954; recipient Civilian commendation USAF, 1960, Hubbard medal Nat. Geog. Soc., 1963, Elisha Kent Kane gold medal Geog. Soc. Phila., 1964, Karo award Am. Soc. Mil. Engrs., 1966, Franklin L. Burr prize Nat. Geog. Soc., 1967, Boy Scouts Am. commendation, 1970, UN Assn. commendation, 1975, Outstanding Civilian Service medal Dept. Army, 1977. Fellow Geol. Soc. Am., Arctic Inst. N.Am., Royal Geog. Soc., Explorers Club; mem. Am. Geophys. Union, Assn. Am. State Geologists, Am. Inst. Mining, Metall. and Petroleum Engrs., Internat. Glaciological Soc. (past councillor), Am. (life; past councillor), London Alpine clubs, Brit. Mountaineering Assn. (hon. v.p.), UN Assn. (pres. Mich. div. 1970-73), Middle East Inst., Am. Amateur Rowing Assn. (life), Naval Res. Assn. (life), Sigma Xi, Phi Beta Kappa (pres. Epsilon chpt. Mich.), Phi Kappa Phi. Clubs: Rotary; Harvard (N.Y.C., Seattle); Central Mich. (past pres.); Circumnavigators (life), Adventurers (medalist); Himalayan (Calcutta, India); Appalachian (hon. corr.); Dutch Treat; Spokane. Contbr. numerous articles to nat. mags., books and sci. publs. Home: 514 E 1st St Moscow ID 83843 also 4533 19th St NE Seattle WA 98105 Office: Coll Mines and Earth Resources U Idaho Moscow ID 83843 also Found Glacier and Environmental Research Pacific Science Center 200 2d Ave N Seattle WA 98109

MILLER, MELVIN HULL, educator; b. Flushing, Mich., Apr. 19, 1920; s. Melvin Lyle and Dorothy (Hull) M.; A.B., Albion Coll., 1942; M.A., Mich. State U., 1949; Ph.D., U. Wis., 1957; postgrad. Oxford U., 1953, U. Birmingham (Eng.), 1952; m. Shirley Lou Mershon, Sept. 11, 1952; children—Pamela, Mark. Instr. speech Grinnell (Iowa) Coll., 1949-51; instr. speech U. Md. Overseas Program, 1951-54; instr. speech U. Wis.-Milw., 1956-58, asst. prof., 1958-63, asso. prof., chmn. dept., 1963-66, prof. communication, coordinator grad. studies, 1966—. Served to lt. comdr. USNR, 1943-47; PTO. Mem. Speech Communication Assn. (legislative assembly 1967-70), AAUP (chpt. pres. 1968-69), Central States Speech Assn., Wis. Acad. Sci., Arts and Letters. Author: Syllabus for Public Speaking, 1962; (with W.E. Buys) Creative Speaking, 1974. Contbr. articles to profl. jours. Home: 7332 Harwood Ave Wauwatosa WI 53213 Office: Univ Wis Milwaukee WI 53201

MILLER, MERLE, author; b. Montour, Iowa, May 17, 1919; s. Monte M. and Dora B. (Winders) M.; student State U. Iowa, 1935-38, 39-40, London Sch. Econs., 1938-39. Washington corr. Phila. Record, 1940-41; editor Yank mag., 1941-45; contbg. editor Time mag., 1945; editor Harpers mag., 1947-49. Author: Island 49, 1945; We Dropped the A-Bomb, 1946; That Winter, 1948; The Sure Thing, 1949; The Judges and the Judged, 1952; Reunion, 1954; A Gay and Melancholy Sound, 1961; A Day in Late September, 1963; Only You, Dick Daring, 1964; On Being Different, 1972; What Happened, 1973; Plain Speaking, An Oral Biography of Harry S. Truman, 1974; Lyndon, An Oral Biography of Lyndon Baines Johnson, 1980; contbr.: A Treasury of Great Reporting, 1949; The Best from Yank, 1945; Yank the GI Story of the War, 1947; Women Today, 1953; Highlights from Yank, 1953; author screen and TV plays. Mem. Authors Guild, Authors League. Home: Brewster NY 10509

MILLER, MERLE HAMILTON, lawyer; b. Middletown, Ind., Jan. 12, 1904; s. Clarence Harve and Lra (Carnefix) M.; A.B., Butler U., 1927; LL.B., Harvard, 1930; m. Dorthey Griggs, Oct. 10, 1930 (dec. Mar. 1946); 1 son, Merle Hamilton; m. 2d, Ophelia Lester, Aug. 28, 1948; children—Terry Ann, Lester Clarence. Admitted to Ind. bar, 1930; head interpretative div. Office Chief Counsel, Bur. Internal Revenue, 1938-40; now mem. firm Ice, Miller, Donadio & Ryan, Indpls.; chmn. Indpls. Lawyers Commn., 1969-71, Ind. Lawyers Commn., 1973—; dir. D & M Mfg. Co., Thrush Products; lectr. tax subjects. Pres. Central Ind. council Boy Scouts Am., 1953, United Cerebral Palsy Assn., 1956-59; v.p. Ind. Cancer Soc., 1946-50, pres. Marion County unit, 1948; chmn. Ind. United Negro Coll. Fund, 1955-59; bd. dirs. Regenstrief Found., 1970—; trustee Tougaloo Coll., 1963—. Mem. Fed., Am. (chmn. income tax com. 1943-45, mem. council taxation sect. 1946-50), Ind., Indpls. bar assns., Am., Ind. (pres. 1955-57) civil liberties unions, Am. Law Inst., Am. Bar Found., Tax Inst. (dir.). Contbr. articles on tax subjects to profl. publs. Home: 2888 W 44th St Indianapolis IN 46208 Office: 111 Monument Circle Indianapolis IN 46204

MILLER, MERTON HOWARD, educator; b. Boston, May 16, 1923; s. Joel L. and Sylvia F. (Starr) M.; A.B., Harvard U., 1943; Ph.D., Johns Hopkins U., 1952. With Treasury Dept., 1944-47, Fed. Res. Bd., 1947-49; asst. lectr. London Sch. Econs., 1952; asst. prof., then asso. prof. Grad. Sch. Indsl. Adminstrn., Carnegie Inst. Tech., Pitts., 1958-61; prof. banking and fin. Grad. Sch. Bus., U. Chgo., 1961—. Fellow Econometric Soc.; mem. Am. Fin. Assn. (pres. 1976), Am. Econ. Assn., Am. Statis. Assn. Co-author: Theory of Finance, 1972; Macroeconomics, 1974. Address: Grad Sch Business Univ Chgo 1101 E 58th St Chicago IL 60637

MILLER, MICHAEL SHAFFER, librarian; b. Hanover, Pa., Aug. 6, 1942; s. Wilton Raphael and Kathryn Johanna (Shaffer) M.; B.A., Duquesne U., Pitts., 1964; M.L.S., U. Pitts., 1966; m. Connie Lou Ferrier, Apr. 12, 1969; children—Eric Michael, Matthew Ferrier. Asst. librarian Pa. State Library, Harrisburg, 1961-62; asst. librarian Allegheny County Law Library, Pitts., 1967, dir., 1968-77; dir. Md. State Library, Annapolis, 1977—; lectr. U. Pitts.; cons. in field. Mem. Am. Assn. Law Libraries, Md. Library Assn., Law Library Soc. Washington. Democrat. Roman Cath. Editor: Spl. Libraries Assn. Directory Pitts. and Vicinity. Home: 932 Fall Ridge Way Gambrills MD 21054 Office: Courts of Appeals Bldg 361 Rowe Blvd Annapolis MD 21401

MILLER, MILDRED, opera singer, recitalist; b. Cleve.; d. William and Elsa (Friedhofer) Mueller; Mus.B., Cleve. Ins. Music 1946; artists' diploma New Eng. Conservatory Music, 1948, hon. doctorate, 1966; Mus.D. (hon.), Bowling Green State U., 1960; m. Wesley W. Posvar, Apr. 30, 1950; children—Wesley, Margot Marina, Lisa Christina. Operatic debut in Peter Grimes, Tanglewood, 1946; mem. N.E. Opera Theater, 1946-49, Stuttgart State Theater, Germany, 1949-50, Glyndebourne Opera, Edinburgh Festival, 1951; debut as Cherubino in Figaro, Met. Opera, 1951; radio debut Bell Telephone Hour; TV debut Voice of Firestone, 1952; appeared in films including Merry Wives of Windsor (filmed in Vienna), 1964; Vienna State Opera debut, 1963; appearances with San Francisco, Chgo. Lyric, Cin. Zoo, San Antonio, Berlin, Munich, Frankfurt, Pasadena, Ft. Worth, Kansas City, Pitts., Tulsa and St. Paul operas; founder, artistic dir. Pitts. Chamber Opera Theater, 1978—. Mem. adv. bd. music dept. Bowling Green State U.; mem. bd. Pitts. Ballet Theater, Pitts. Opera Inc., Mendelssohn choir, Gateway to Music. Recipient Frank Huntington Beebe Award for study abroad, 1949, 50; Grand Prix du Disque, 1965, Outstanding Achievements in Music award Boston C. of C., 1959; named one of outstanding women of Pitts., Pitts. Press-Pitts. Post-Gazette, 1968, Distinguished Daughter of Pa., 1972. Mem. Nat. Soc. Arts and Letters, Internat. Hugo Wolf Soc., Sigma Alpha Iota. Clubs: Tuesday Musical (Pitts.); Fortnightly Musical (Cleve.). Home: 718 Devonshire St Pittsburgh PA 15213 Office: Judd Concert Artist Bureau 127 W 69th St New York NY 10023

MILLER, MILTON HOWARD, psychiatrist; b. Indpls., Sept. 1, 1927; s. William and Helen L. (Lefkovits) M.; came to Can., 1971; B.S., Ind. U., 1946, M.D., 1950; diploma in psychiatry Menninger Sch., Topeka, 1953; m. Harriet Sanders, June 27, 1948; children—Bruce, Jeffrey, Marcie. Intern, Indpls. Gen. Hosp., 1950-51; resident Menninger Sch. Psychiatry, Topeka, 1951-53; with dept. psychiatry Univ. Hosps., U. Wis., Madison, 1955-71, prof., 1961-71, chmn., 1962-71, dir. Wis. Psychiat. Inst., 1962-71; vis. prof. Nat. Taiwan U., Taipei, 1969-70; prof. psychiatry U. B.C., Vancouver, 1972-78, head dept. psychiatry, 1972-78; dir. WHO-U. B.C. Mental Health Tng. Centre, Vancouver, 1976-78; dep. dir. Mental Health Services, Coastal Region, Los Angeles County, 1978—; prof., vice chmn. dept. psychiatry UCLA, 1978—; cons. in field. Fellow Am. Psychiat. Assn.; Royal Coll. Psychiatry; mem. Can. Psychiat. Assn., Royal Coll. Physicians and Surgeons (examiner 1973—), Can. Med. Assn., World Fedn. for Mental Health (mem. exec. bd. 1973—). Author: If the Patient is You (Or Someone You Love), 1977. Contbr. articles to profl. jours. Home: 535 Esplanade Redondo Beach CA 90277 Office: Dept Psychiatry Los Angeles County Harbor-UCLA Med Center 1000 W Carson St Torrance CA 90509. *For many years I worked hard for my parents and myself. Later I worked hard for my wife, children, friends and self. These last years I've been including strangers and it's better.*

MILLER, MITCH(ELL WILLIAM), musician; b. Rochester, N.Y., July 4, 1911; s. Abram Charles and Hinda (Rosenblum) M.; B.A., Eastman Sch. Music, U. Rochester, 1932; m. Frances Josephine Alexander, Sept. 10, 1935; children—Andrea, Margaret, Mitchell. Oboist with Rochester Philharmonic Orchestra, 1930-33, Met. Mus. Art Concerts, 1934; oboe soloist CBS Symphony, 1935-47, also with Saidenberg Little Symphony and the Budapest String Quartet; conducted CBS TV program; supr. classical recs., also dir. popular artists, and repertoire dir., Mercury Record Corp., 1947-50; head popular records div. Columbia Records, Inc., 1950-61; head Sing-Along With Mitch tv show on NBC, 1960-65; with MCA, 1965-67; music dir. Little Golden Records, 1966—. Conductor symphony orchs. in numerous major cities including Pitts., Phils., Detroit, Mpls., Miami, Chgo., Boston and Mexico City.*

MILLER, MORRIS FOLSOM, banker; b. Omaha, Mar. 17, 1919; s. Max Arnold and Phebe (Folsom) M.; A.B., U. Mich., 1940; m. Nancy Keegan, July 26, 1952 (dec. Jan. 1977); children—Joyce, Louise, Paul; m. 2d, Barbara Osborne Cunningham, Feb. 12, 1978. With Gering (Nebr.) Nat. Bank, 1946, Am. Nat. Bank, Kimball, Nebr., 1946-47, Boone (Iowa) State Bank, 1947-51; with Omaha Nat. Bank, 1951—, asst. v.p., 1953-54, v.p., 1954-58, exec. v.p., 1958-62, pres., 1962-70, chmn., 1969-77, vice chmn., 1977—, also dir.; dir. Omaha Nat. Corp., U.P. Corp., U.P. R.R. Co. Served with AUS, 1941-46, with USAF, 1951-52. Mem. Mid Am. Bankcard Assn. (past chmn., dir.), Omaha C. of C. (past pres.), Interbank Card Assn. (dir.), Assn. Bank Holding Cos., Omaha Bankers Assn. (past pres.). Home: 8415 Loveland Dr Omaha NE 68124 Office: Omaha Nat Corp 1700 Farnam St Omaha NE 68102

MILLER, MORTON DAVID, life ins. co. exec.; b. N.Y.C., Jan. 4, 1915; s. Samuel A. and Rhea R. (Loewenthal) M.; B.S. cum laude, Coll. City N.Y., 1937; m. Florence Louis, Feb. 14, 1949; 1 son, Jonathan David. With Equitable Life Assurance Soc. U.S., N.Y.C., 1937—, dir., 1971, exec. v.p., chief actuary, 1973—, vice chmn. bd., 1975—, dir. Health Ins. Assn. Am. Mem. nat. adv. council U. Pa. Leonard Davis Inst. Health Econs.; mem. actuarial adv. com. N.Y. State Dept. Audit and Control; Bd. dirs. N.Y. Urban Coalition, Point Lookout Civic Assn., City Coll. Fund; chmn. Nat. Med. Fellowships Inc., mem. Alumni Devel. Council City U. N.Y.; bd. overseers Sch. Medicine, Morehouse Coll.; mem. adv. council on Social Security, HEW, 1978-79; mem. select com. visitors Sch. Nursing, SUNY at Stony Brook; mem. Health Care Fin. Commn. Fellow Soc. Actuaries (pres. 1967-68, bd. govs. 1957-70); mem. Am. Acad. Actuaries (pres. 1973, bd. dirs.), Am. Arbitration Assn. (nat. panel arbitrators), Inst. of Medicine, Nat. Acad. Scis., Nat. Health Council (bd. dirs.), Washington Bus. Group on Health, Pilgrims of U.S. Club: Univ. Home: 35 Sutton Pl New York City NY 10022 also 128 Cedarhurst Ave Point Lookout NY Office: 1285 Ave of Americas New York City NY 10019

MILLER, NATHAN, author, journalist; b. Balt., May 26, 1927; s. David and Jennie (Miller) M.; B.A., U. Md., 1950; M.A., 1951; m. Jeanette Martick, Feb. 22, 1963. With Balt. Sun., 1954-69, corr. Latin Am., 1962-66, corr. Washington bur., 1966-69; asso. editor Editoral Research Reports, Washington, 1970-71, Kiplinger Washington Letters, 1971; profl. staff mem. Senate Com. on Appropriations, Washington, 1971-77; guest editor Washington Journalism Rev., 1977-78. Cons. to Nat. Park Service on naval history Am. Revolution, 1974-76. Served with USNR, 1945-46. Recipient award for pub. service reporting Am. Polit. Sci. Assn., 1961. Mem. Author's Guild, Washington Ind. Writers Assn. Author: Sea of Glory: The Continental Navy Fights for Independence 1775-1783, 1974; The Founding Finaglers: Corruption in American History, 1976; The U.S. Navy: An Illustrated History, 1977; The Roosevelt Chronicles, 1979. Contbr. to Inside the System, 1970, The Chesapeake Bay in the Era of the American Revolution, 1976. Home: 4916 Western Ave Chevy Chase MD 20016

MILLER, NEAL ELGAR, psychologist; b. Milw., Aug. 3, 1909; s. Irving E. and Lily R. (Fuenfstueck) M.; B.S., U. Wash., 1931; M.S., Stanford U., 1932; Ph.D., Yale U., 1935; D.Sc., U. Mich., 1965, U. Pa., 1968, St. Lawrence U., 1973, U. Uppsala (Sweden), 1977, LaSalle Coll., 1979; m. Marion E. Edwards, June 30, 1948; children—York, Sara. Social sci. research fellow Inst. Psychoanalysis, Vienna, Austria, 1935-36; asst. research psychologist Yale U., 1933-35, instr., asst. prof., research asst. psychol. Inst. Human Relations, 1936-41, asso. prof., research asso., 1941-42, 46-50, prof. psychology, 1950-52, James Rowland Angell prof. psychology, 1952-66, fellow Berkeley Coll., 1955—; prof. Rockefeller U., N.Y.C., 1966—; expert cons. Am. Inst. Research, 1946-62; spl. cons. com. human resources Research and Devel. Bd., Office Sec. Def., 1951-53; mem. tech. adv. panel Office Asst. Sec. Def., 1954-57; expert cons. Ops. Research Office and Human Resources Research Office, 1951-54. Chmn. bd. sci. dirs. Roscoe B. Jackson Meml. Lab., Bar Harbor, Maine, 1962-76; bd. sci. counsellors NIMH, 1957-61; fellowship com. Founds. Fund for Research in Psychiatry, 1956-61; mem. central council Internat. Brain Research Orgn., 1964; v.p. bd. dirs. Foote Sch., 1964-65; chmn. NAS/NRC Com. on Brain Scis., 1969-71; bd. sci. counsellors Nat. Inst. Child Health and Human Devel., 1969-72. Served as maj., U.S. A.C., 1942-46; officer in charge research, Psychol. Research Unit 1, Nashville, 1942-44, dir. psychol. research project Hdqrs. Flying Tng. Command, Randolph Field, Tex., 1944-46. Recipient Warren medal for exptl. psychology, 1954, Newcomb Cleveland prize, 1956; Nat. medal of Sci., 1964, Kenneth Craik Research award U. Cambridge, 1966, Wilbur Cross medal Yale U., 1967, Distinguished Alumnus award Western Wash. State Coll., Gold medal award Am. Psychol. Found., 1975; Mental Health Assn. research achievement award, 1978. Fellow Am. Acad. Arts and Scis. (council 1979—), Brit. Psychol. Soc. (hon. fgn.); mem. Am. Philos. Soc., N.Y. Acad. Scis. (hon. life), Spanish Soc. Psychology (hon.), Am. Psychol. Assn. (council reps. 1954-58, pres. exptl. div. 1952-53, pres. 1960-61, Disting. Sci. Contbn. award 1959), Eastern Psychol. Assn. (pres. 1952-53), NRC (div. anthropology and psychology 1950-53, chmn. 1958-60), Nat. Acad. Sci. (chmn. sect. psychology 1965-67), Soc. Exptl. Psychologists, AAAS, Soc. Neurosci. (pres. 1971-72), Biofeedback Soc. Am., Acad. Behavioral Medicine Research (pres. 1978-79), Sigma Xi (pres. Rockefeller U. chpt. 1968-69), Phi Beta Kappa. Club: Mory's, Lawn (New Haven). Author: Frustration and Aggression (with J. Dollard et al), 1939; (with Dollard) Social Learning and Imitation, 1941, Personality and Psychotherapy, 1950; Graphic Communication and the Crisis in Education, 1957; N.E. Miller: Selected Papers, 1971; contbr. chpts. to psychol. handbooks; editor: Psychological Research on Pilot Tng., 1947. Home: 500 E 77th St New York NY 10021 also Clapboard Rd Guilford CT 06437 Office: Rockefeller U New York NY 10021

MILLER, NEWTON EDD, JR., univ. adminstr.; b. Houston, Mar. 13, 1920; s. Newton Edd and Anastasia (Johnston) M.; B.S., U. Tex., 1939, M.A., 1940; Ph.D., U. Mich., 1952; LL.D., U. Nev., Reno. 1974; m. Edwina Whitaker, Aug. 30, 1942; children—Cathy Edwina, Kenneth Edd. Tutor U. Tex., Austin, 1940-41, instr., 1941-45, asst. prof. speech, 1945-47; research asst. Navy Conf. Research, 1947-52; Mem. faculty U. Mich., Ann Arbor, 1947-65, successively lectr., instr., asst. prof. speech, 1947-55, asso. prof., 1955-59, prof., 1959-65, asst. dir. summer session, 1953-57, asso. dir., 1957-63, asst. to v.p. acad. affairs, 1963-65; chancellor U. Nev., Reno, 1965-68, pres., 1968-73, pres. U. Maine, Portland-Gorham, 1973-78; chmn. communications program No. Ky. U., 1978—. Mem. adv. com. to commr. of edn. U.S. Office of Edn., Accreditation and Instl. Eligibility, 1976—, acting chmn., 1977-78; mem. Judicial Edn. Study Group Am. Univ. Law Inst., 1977-78. Pres. bd. dirs. Perry Nursery Sch., 1956-57. Mem. Ann Arbor Bd. Edn., 1959-65, Washtenaw County Bd. Edn. Mem. Mich. Assn. Sch. Bds. (dir.), N.W. Assn. Colls. and Secondary Schs. (chmn. higher commn. 1971-73), Am. Forensic Assn. (pres. Midwest sect. 1950-53), Central States (pres. 1958-59), Mich. (exec. sec. 1950-55) speech assns., Speech Assn. Am., AAUP, Assn. Western Us. (chmn. 1971-72), Delta Sigma Rho (nat. v.p. 1948-52), Phi Kappa Phi. Rotarian. Author: Post War World Organization, Background Studies, 1942; (with J.J. Villareal) First Course in Speech, 1945; (with W.M. Sattler) Discussion and Debate, 1951, Discussion and Conference, 2d edit., 1968. Co-editor: Required Arbitration of Labor Disputes, 1947. Address: 1058 Emerson Rd Park Hills KY 41011

MILLER, NORMAN CHARLES, JR., newspaperman; b. Pitts., Oct. 2, 1934; s. Norman Charles and Elizabeth (Burns) M.; B.A., Pa. State U., 1956; m. Mary Ann Rudy, June 15, 1957; children—Norman Charles, Mary Ellen, Teresa, Scott. Staff reporter Wall St. Jour., N.Y.C., 1956, San Francisco bur., 1960-63, N.Y.C., 1963-64, bur. chief, Detroit, 1964-66, congressional corr. Washington bur., 1966-74, chief Washington bur., 1974—. Served to lt. USNR, 1956-60. Recipient George Polk award met. reporting L.I. U., 1963; Pulitzer prize local reporting, 1964; Disting. Alumnus award Pa. State U., 1978. Mem. Sigma Delta Chi, Pi Kappa Alpha. Author: The Great Salad Oil Swindle, 1965. Home: 5604 Ontario Circle Washington DC 20016 Office: Wall St Jour Bur Suite 800 1025 Connecticut Ave Washington DC 20036

MILLER, NORMAN CLARK, oil co. exec.; b. Lyons, Kans., Feb. 23, 1920; s. William Alexander and Marie Jennie (Chapin) M.; student Kans. State U., 1937-39; B.S., Okla. U., 1947; m. Jean C. Hughes, Jan. 12, 1945; children—Marla Marie, Erik Clark, Valerie Jean, Lora Lea. Geologist Arkansas Fuel Oil Co., Shreveport, La., 1947-50, Wichita Falls, Tex., 1950-53; dist. geologist Ashland Oil & Refining Co., Oklahoma City, Okla., 1953-55; dist. geologist Delhi-Taylor Oil Corp., Oklahoma City, 1955-57, chief geologist, Dallas, 1957-60, exploration mgr., 1960-62, v.p. exploration, 1962-64; v.p. operations Delhi Internat. Oil Corp., Dallas, 1964-70, exec. v.p., 1970-74, pres., chief exec. officer, 1974—, also dir.; pres., chief exec. officer, dir. Delhi Colombian Oil Corp., 1974—; pres., chief exec. officer Delhi Oil Corp., Dallas, 1975—, DHL Gas Processing & Pipeline Co., Dallas, 1978—; chmn., chief exec. officer, dir. Cinco Drilling Co., Dallas, 1978—; dir. Tex. Am. Bank, Dallas. Served to capt. USAAF, 1942-45; ETO, NATOUSA, Middle Eastern Theater. Decorated D.F.C., Air medal with silver oak leaf cluster. Mem. Am. Assn. Petroleum Geologists, Dallas Geol. Soc. (v.p. 1964-65), Ind. Petroleum Assn. Am., Tex. Ind. Producers and Royalty Owners, Tex. Midcontinent Oil and Gas Assn., Sigma Gamma Epsilon. Clubs: Dallas Petroleum; University (Houston); Northwood. Home: 7048 Yamini Dr Dallas TX 75230 Office: 3500 First Internat Bldg Dallas TX 75270

MILLER, NORMAN RICHARD, diversified mfg. co. exec.; b. Balt., Mar. 7, 1922; s. Samuel and Tobie Hildreth (Engleman) M.; B.S. in Indsl. Engring., Ga. Inst. Tech., 1947; M.B.A., Harvard, 1950; m. Nancy Lee Rosenthal, 1967; children—Hilary S., Dana A. Indsl. cons. George S. Armstrong & Co., Inc., N.Y.C. 1950-51; ind. mgmt. cons., Italy, 1952-56; founder Italian Postgrad. Bus. Sch., Turin 1953-55; dir. analysis and bus. planning RCA, 1957-61, v.p. div. bus. planning, 1962-68, v.p., gen. mgr. Graphic Systems Div., 1968-71; cons. Office Sci. and Tech., 1971-72; pres., chief exec. officer, dir. Lynch Corp., N.Y.C., 1972-73; exec. v.p., dir. Radiation Dynamics, Inc., Westbury, N.Y., 1973-76; v.p. Diebold Group, N.Y.C., 1976—. Pres., Merce Cunningham Dance Found., 1976—; trustee Phila. Mus. Art. Served to 2d lt. AUS, 1943-46. Mem. Inst. Aero. Scis., Ga. Tech. Alumni Assn. (vice chmn. adv. bd.), Tau Beta Pi, Omicron Delta Kappa, Pi Delta Epsilon, Phi Epsilon Pi. Club: Harvard (N.Y.C.). Home: 170 E 79th St New York City NY 10021

MILLER, ORLANDO JACK, physician, educator; b. Oklahoma City, Okla., May 11, 1927; s. Arthur Leroy and Iduma Dorris (Berry) M.; B.S., Yale, 1946, M.D., 1950; m. Dorothy Anne Smith, July 10, 1954; children—Richard Lawrence, Cynthia Kathleen, Karen Anne. Intern St. Anthony Hosp., Oklahoma City, 1950-51; asst. resident in obstetrics and gynecology Yale-New Haven Conn.) Med. Center, 1954-57, resident, instr., 1957-58; vis. fellow dept. obstetrics and gynecology Tulane U. Service, Charity Hosp., New Orleans, 1958; hon. research asst. Galton Lab., Univ. Coll., London, 1958-60; instr. Coll. Physicians and Surgeons Columbia U., N.Y.C., 1960, asso. dept. obstetrics and gynecology, 1960-61, asst. prof., 1961-65, asso. prof., 1965-69, prof. dept. human genetics and devel., dept. obstetrics and gynecology, 1969—; asst. attending obstetrician, gynecologist Presbyn. Hosp., N.Y.C., 1964-65, asso., 1965-70, attending obstetrician and gynecologist, 1970—. Mem. sci. adv. com. on research Nat. Found. March of Dimes, 1967—, mem. sci. review com. Basil O'Connor starter grants, 1973-77; mem. human embryology and devel. study sect. NIH, 1970-74, chmn., 1972-74; mem. com. for study of inborn errors of metabolism NRC, 1972-74; mem. sci. adv. com. virology and cell biology Am. Cancer Soc., 1974-78. Served with AUS, 1951-53. James Hudson Brown Jr. fellow Yale U., 1947-48; NRC fellow, 1953-54; Population Council fellow, 1958-59; Josiah Macy Jr. fellow, 1960-61; NSF sr. postdoctoral fellow U. Oxford, 1968-69. Mem. AAAS, Am. Genetic Assn., Am. Soc. Cell Biology, Am. Soc. Human Genetics (bd. dirs. 1970-73), Genetics Soc. Am., N.Y. Obstet. Soc., Soc. of Sloane Alumni, Soc. Gynecol. Investigation, Tissue Culture Assn., Sigma Xi. Presbyn. Editor Cytogenetics, 1970-72; asso. editor Cytogenetics and Cell Genetics, 1972—; asso. editor Birth Defects Compendium, 1971—; mem. editorial bd. Cytogenetics, 1961-69, Am. Jour. Human Genetics, 1969-74, 79—, Gynecologic Investigation, 1970—, Teratology, 1972-74, Cancer Genetics and Cytogenetics, 1979—; mem. adv. bd. Human Genetics, 1978—; cons. Jour. Med. Primatology, 1977—; contbr. articles to med. and sci. jours., chpt. to textbooks. Home: 145 Pinewood Pl Teaneck NJ 07666 Office: 701 W 168th St New York NY 10032

MILLER, OSCAR LEE, JR., cell biologist; b. Gastonia, N.C., Apr. 12, 1925; s. Oscar Lee and Rose (Evans) M.; B.S., N.C. State Coll., 1948, M.S., 1950; Ph.D., U. Minn., 1960; m. Mary Rose Smith, Dec. 18, 1948; children—Sharon Lee, Oscar Lee, Ill. Comml. farm mgr., Horry County, S.C., 1950-56; mem. research staff biology div. Oak Ridge Nat. Lab., 1961-73; prof. Oak Ridge Grad. Sch. Biomed. Scis., U. Tenn., 1967-73; prof. biology U. Va., 1973—, chmn. dept. biology, 1973-79; Served with USN, 1943-46. USPHS postdoctoral fellow, 1960-61; NSF grantee, 1973-77; NIH grantee, 1973. Mem. Am. Soc. Cell Biology, AAAS, Soc. Devel. Biology, Nat. Acad. Sci. Contbr. numerous articles on ultrastructural aspects of genetic activity in prokaryotic and eukaryotic cells to profl. jours. Office: Dept Biology U Va Charlottesville VA 22901

MILLER, PAUL, newspaperman; b. Diamond, Mo., Sept. 28, 1906; s. James and Clara (Ranne) M.; student U. Okla., 1929-30; B.S., Okla. State U., 1931; D.Sc., Clarkson Coll., 1956; LL.D., Ursinus Coll., 1959; D.C.L., Union Coll., 1965; Litt.D., Westminster Coll., Niagara U., 1968; D.H.L., Transylvania U., 1974; D.L., Hobart and William Smith Coll., 1978; m. Louise Johnson, Oct. 19, 1932; children—Ranne Johnson, Jean Louise, Paul Talford, Kenper Wright. Reporter, editor various Okla. newspapers, including Pawhuska, Stillwater, Guthrie, Okemah and Oklahoma City, 1923-30; asst. dir., dir. Bur. Info. and Service, Okla. State U., 1930-32; with AP, 1932—, cable and gen. desk editor, N.Y.C., night news editor, Kansas City, chief bur., Salt Lake City, 1936, chief Pa. bur., Harrisburg and Phila., 1937-41, exec. asst. to gen. mgr., N.Y.C., 1941, chief Washington bur., 1942-47, asst. gen. mgr. AP, 1943-47, dir., 1950-58, 60—, pres., 1963-72, chmn., 1972-77; mem. exec. staff Gannett Newspapers, Rochester, N.Y., 1947-57, dir. Gannett Co., Inc., 1948—, pres., chief exec. officer, 1957-70, chmn., chief exec. officer, 1970-73, chmn. bd., 1973-79. mem. adv. bd. Sing-Tao Newspapers Inc., Hong Kong; dir. Hotel Waldorf-Astoria Corp. Mem. Pulitzer Prize Adv. Bd., 1956-68. Pres., chmn. Frank E. Gannett Newspaper Found., 1957—; adv. bd. Am. Press Inst., 1953-63, chmn., 1958-63; dir. New York World's Fair Corp., 1961; trustee N.Y. Racing Assn.; hon. trustee Rochester Inst. Tech., U. Rochester; chmn. Rochester chpt. ARC, 1958; bd. dirs. Boys' Clubs Am. Recipient William Allen White Found. award, 1963; NCCJ Brotherhood award, 1965; Hall of Fame award Okla. Heritage Assn., 1973; Journalism award Ohio U., 1979; Civic medal Rochester C. of C., 1979. Fellow Sigma Delta Chi (hon. pres. 1962); mem. C. of C. (trustee), Rochester Automobile Club (dir.), Internat. Press Inst., Inter Am. Press Assn., N.Y. State Pubs. Assn. (pres. 1954), Am. Soc. Newspaper Editors (del. Internat. Fedn. Editors and Pubs., Amsterdam 1949), Rochester Museum Assn. (dir.), Kappa Sigma. Presbyn. Mason (33). Clubs: Gridiron, National Press, Burning Tree Country (Washington); Rochester Country, Genesee Valley, Oak Hill Country (Rochester); Augusta National; Everglades. Office: Gannett Co Inc Lincoln Tower Rochester NY 14604

MILLER, PAUL A(LBERT), utility holding co. exec.; b. San Francisco, Oct. 30, 1924; s. Robert W. and Elizabeth (Folger) M.; A.B., Harvard U., 1948; children—Robert L., Charles B., Christian F., Gordon E. Staff aide So. Calif. Gas Co., Los Angeles, 1948-52; treas., dir. Pacific Lighting Corp., San Francisco, 1952-58, v.p., treas., 1958-66, exec. v.p., 1966-68, pres., chief exec. officer, 1968-72, chmn. bd., chief exec. officer, 1972—; dir. Wells Fargo & Co., Wells Fargo Bank; trustee Mut. Life Ins. Co. N.Y. Bd. dirs. Civic Light Opera Assn., Los Angeles World Affairs Council, United Way Los Angeles, Music Center Opera Assn. Los Angeles, Calif. Roundtable; trustee Am. Enterprise Inst., Washington, U. So. Calif.; bd. govs. United Way Am.; active Bus. Roundtable. Served with U.S. Army, 1943-46. Mem. Am., Pacific Coast gas assns., Calif. C. of C. (dir. 1968—). Clubs: Los Angeles, California (Los Angeles); Pacific Union, Bohemian (San Francisco); Brook, Racquet and Tennis (N.Y.C.). Office: Pacific Lighting Corp 810 S Flower St Los Angeles CA 90017

MILLER, PAUL A., govt. edn. ofcl.; b. Cin., July 6, 1913; s. Henry Aldine and Ethel May (Fisher) M.; B.S., Wilmington Coll., 1936; M.A., Miami U., Oxford, Ohio, 1941, LL.D., 1960; Ph.D., Ohio State U., 1951; m. Fay Curless, July 31, 1936; children—Linda Lee, Sherry Ann, Alan Paul. Tchr. elementary and high schs., Butler County, Ohio, 1934-39; asst. prin. sch., Seven Mile, Ohio, 1939-40, prin., supt. schs., 1942-45; prin., supt. schs., Okeana, Ohio, 1940-42, Wintersville, Ohio, 1945-47; research asst. Ohio State U., 1947-48; coordinator secondary edn., Cedar Rapids, Iowa, 1948-49; asst. supt. schs., Canton, Ohio, 1949-51; supt. schs., Warren, Ohio, 1951-55, Syracuse, N.Y., 1955-62, Omaha, 1962-67, Cin., 1967-71; sr. coordinator U.S. Office Edn., Washington, 1971—. Mem. Nat. Sch. Com. on Econ. Edn. Mem. Am. Assn. Sch. Adminstrs. (pres. 1972-73), Phi Delta Kappa. Contbr. articles to profl. jours. Home: 1201 Stable Gate Ct McLean VA 22101 Office: 400 Maryland SW Washington DC 20202

MILLER, PAUL AUSBORN, educator; b. East Liverpool, Ohio, Mar. 22, 1917; s. Harry A. and Elizabeth (Stewart) M.; B.S., U. W.Va., 1939; M.A., Mich. State U., 1947, Ph.D., 1953; m. Catherine Spiker, Dec. 9, 1939 (dec. Dec. 1964); children—Paula Kay, Thomas Ausborn; m. 2d, Francena Lounsbery Nolan, Jan. 15, 1966. County agrl. agt. in W.Va., 1939-42; extension specialist sociology and anthropology Mich. State U., East Lansing, 1947-55, asst. prof., 1947-52, asso. prof., 1953, prof., 1953-61, provost, 1959-61; pres. W.Va. U., Morgantown, 1962-66; asst. sec. for edn. HEW, 1966-68; distinguished prof. edn., dir. univ. planning studios U. N.C., Charlotte, prof. adult edn. N.C. State U. at Raleigh, 1968-69; pres. Rochester (N.Y.) Inst. of Tech., 1969-79, prof., 1979—; sr. program cons. W.K. Kellogg Found., 1979—. Mem. Colombian Commn. Higher Edn., 1960-61. Served as 1st lt. USAAF, 1942-46. Fellow Am. Sociol. Assn.; mem. Am. Acad. Polit. and Social Sci., Adult Edn. Assn. U.S.A., Rural Sociol. Soc., Am. Assn. Sch. Adminstrs., Phi Kappa Phi, Epsilon Sigma Phi. Author: Community Health Action, 1953. Contbr. to publs. in field. Home: 30 Hillock Rd Rush NY 14543

MILLER, PAUL FETTEROLF, JR., investment mgr.; b. Phila., 1927; s. Paul Fetterolf and Katharine Mills (Thompson) M.; ed. Wharton Sch., U. Pa., 1950, grad. Sch. Arts and Scis., 1952; m. Ella Warren Shafer, June 14, 1952; children—Ella Warren, Katharine Shafer, Paul Fetterolf III. Partner Miller, Anderson & Sherrerd, Bala-Cynwyd, Pa.; dir. Yarway Corp., First Pa. Bank, First Pa. Corp., Berwind Corp., Mead Corp., Phila. Suburban Corp., Rohm & Haas Co., Fidelity Mut. Life Ins. Co. Chmn. bd. trustees U. Pa.; trustee Coll. Retirement Equity Fund. Mem. Fin. Analysts Phila., Nat. Assn. Bus. Economists, Beta Theta Phi. Clubs: Merion Golf, Merion Cricket, Union League (Phila.). Home: 115 Maple Hill Rd Gladwyne PA 19035 Office: 2 Bala-Cynwyd Plaza Bala-Cynwyd PA 19004

MILLER, PAUL GEORGE, finance and ins. co. exec.; b. Louisville, Dec. 13, 1922; s. George Moore and Pauline Louise (Koob) M.; B.E.E., Purdue U., 1948; B.S., U.S. Naval Acad., 1946; B.S. in Electronics Engring., Mass. Inst. Tech., 1949, postgrad. in Nuclear Sci., 1949; m. Doris Kahl Ingram, Feb. 17, 1979; children—George, James, Randolph. Gen. mgr. control systems div. Daystrom (later acquired by Control Data Corp.), La Jolla, Calif., 1957-65; v.p., gen. mgr. communications and spl. systems group Control Data Corp., Mpls., 1965-67, v.p., group gen. mgr. computer systems and devel., 1967-69, sr. v.p., mktg. group exec., 1970-72, sr. v.p., 1973—, pres. Control Data Mktg. Co.; chmn. bd., pres., dir. Comml. Credit Co., Balt., 1975—; dir. Control Data Corp., Fed. Res. Bank, Richmond, Va. Served to lt. USN, 1946-57. Recipient Distinguished Alumnus award Purdue U., 1968. Mem. IEEE (sr.), Sigma Xi, Tau Beta Pi, Eta Kappa Nu, Delta Tau Delta. Home: Cedar Lane Farm Rd Annapolis MD 21401 Office: 300 Saint Paul Pl Baltimore MD 21202 Mailing Address: PO Box 9763 Annapolis MD 21012

MILLER, PAUL LUKENS, investment banker; b. Phila., Dec. 6, 1919; s. Henry C. L. and Elsie (Groff) M.; student William Penn Charter Sch., Phila., 1937; A.B., Princeton, 1941; m. Adele Olyphant, Nov. 4, 1950; children—Paul L., Hilary, Beverly, Leslie. With First Boston Corp., N.Y.C., 1946—, v.p., 1955-64, dir., 1959-78, pres., 1964-78; trustee Seamen's Bank for Savs.; dir. Cummins Engine Co., Aluminum Co. Am., Celanese Corp., Ogilvy & Mather Internat. Inc., Pullman, Inc. Served from 2d lt. to maj., F.A., AUS, 1941-46. Clubs: Ivy (Princeton); Links, Union, Recess (N.Y.C.); Duquesne (Pitts.). Home: Young's Rd New Vernon NJ 07976 Office: 20 Exchange Pl New York City NY 10005

MILLER, PHILIP R., judge; b. N.Y.C., Mar. 12, 1918; s. Louis and Minnie (Yatzkan) M.; B.B.A., Coll. City N.Y., 1937; LL.B., Columbia U., 1940; m. Eunice Rothenburg, Nov. 1, 1941; children—Carolyn Ann Uberman, Ellen. Admitted to N.Y. State bar, 1941, D.C. bar, 1942; asso. firm Covington & Burling, Washington, 1941-42, firm Fulton, Walter & Halley, N.Y.C. and Washington, 1951-52; atty. criminal div. Justice Dept., Washington, 1942-45, tax div., 1945-51, 52-59, asst. sect. chief tax div., 1959-67, sect. chief, 1967-72; trial judge U.S. Ct. Claims, 1972—. Mem. Am., Fed. bar assns. Home: 8502 Donnybrook Dr Chevy Chase MD 20015 Office: US Ct Claims 717 Madison Pl Washington DC 20005

MILLER, PLEASANT VOORHEES, JR., banker; b. Highland, Kans., June 11, 1922; s. Pleasant Voorhees and Lucyanna (Hammond) M.; B.A., Kans. U., 1947; m. Alice Rose Shankland, Feb. 8, 1947; children—Pleasant Voorhees III, David Wilson, Allison Elizabeth. With Commerce Bank Kansas City (Mo.), N.A., 1947—, pres., 1966-72, 73—, chmn. bd., from 1971, now vice chmn., dir.; dir. Commerce Bancshares, Inc., Atlas Mut. Ins. Co., Credit Bur. Greater Kansas City, Old Am. Inst. Co., Rival Mfg. Co. Mem. central gov. bd. Children's Mercy Hosp.; bd. dirs. Kansas City Assn. Trusts and Founds., Civic Council Kansas City; bd. advisers Sch. Bus., U. Kans.; adv. council U. Mo., Kansas City. Served as pilot USNR, 1942-45. Decorated D.F.C., Air medal. Mem. Assn. Res. City Bankers. Clubs: Kansas City, Mission Hills Country. Office: 922 Walnut St Kansas City MO 64106*

MILLER, RALPH DALE, educator, composer; b. Whitehall, Ill., Mar. 17, 1909; s. Clifford E. and Minnie (Poggenpohl) M.; B.Ed., Ill. State U., 1936; M.A., U. Iowa, 1939, M.F.A., 1941, Ph.D., 1942; m. Lucille Rynell, July 15, 1932 (div.); 1 son, Ralph D.; m. 2d, Charlene Peura, Dec. 17, 1947; children—Nicholas D., Lisa H. Tchr. public schs., Ill., 1936-41; asso. prof. music Duluth State Tchrs. Coll., 1942-47; asso. prof., chmn. div. fine arts U. Minn., Duluth, 1947-50, prof., 1950—, chmn. div. humanities, 1950-70. Mem. AAUP. Composer: Venus and Adonis, 1941; Suite Miniature, 1942; Twilight Sketches, 1942; Prelude to Autumn, 1942; Evening Fantasy, 1942; Quartet No. 1, 1942; Quartet No. 2, 1942; Lively Mood from Quartet No. 3, 1944; Canzonetta, 1944; Quiet Simplicity from Quartet No. 3, 1944; Martial Spirit from Quartet No. 3, 1944; Night Poem, 1945; Sinfonietta, 1946; Prelude and Scherzo, 1946; Three American Dances, 1948; Arabesque for Flute, 1963; Dance Poem, 1949; Symphony No. 1, 1949; Introduction and Allegro, 1949. Home: 2030 Lakeview Dr Duluth MN 55803 Office: U Minn Div Humanities Duluth MN 55812

MILLER, RALPH PAUL, banker; b. Chgo., Jan. 4, 1920; s. Henry and Elizabeth (Rocke) M.; grad. high sch.; m. Helen Chalpeck, July 10, 1943; children-Laura Miller Haule, Margaret Miller McNeill, Lois E. With Exchange Nat. Bank of Chgo., 1938—, exec. v.p., 1968-71, sr. cons., 1971-76, exec. v.p., 1976—. Served to capt. AUS, 1942-46. Clubs: Bankers, Union League (Chgo.). Home: 815 W Elm St Wheaton IL 60187 Office: 130 S LaSalle St Chicago IL 60603

MILLER, RANDOLPH CRUMP, educator, clergyman; b. Fresno, Calif., Oct. 1, 1910; s. Ray Oakley and Laura Belle (Crump) M.; student Harvard Sch., Los Angeles, 1921-27; A.B., Pomona Coll., 1931; postgrad. Episcopal Theol. Sch., 1935-36, D.D. (hon.), 1961; Ph.D., Yale, 1936; S.T.D. (hon.), Ch. Div. Sch. of Pacific, 1952; D.D. (hon.), Pacific Sch. Religion, 1952; m. Muriel Phyllis Hallett, June 9, 1938 (dec. May 1948); children—Barbara Hallett, Phyllis Muriel (Mrs. Victor A.B. Symonds), Carol Christine (Mrs. Laurance Blanchard Rand III), Muriel Randolph (Mrs. James E. Leahy); m. 2d, Elizabeth Rives Williams Fowlkes, June 16, 1950; children—Frank Vaughan Fowlkes, Elizabeth Rives Fowlkes (Mrs. Richard Cushman Carroll, Jr.). Ordained to ministry Episcopal Ch., 1935; instr. philosophy religion and Christian edn. Ch. Div. Sch. Pacific, 1936-40, asst. prof., 1940-45, asso. prof., 1945-50, prof., 1950-52; prof. Christian edn., div. sch. Yale, New Haven, 1952-63, Horace Bushnell prof. Christian nurture, 1963—. Vis. prof. Div. Sch. Harvard and Episcopal Theol. Sch., spring 1954, Union Theol. Sem., spring 1957, Andover Newton Theol. Sem., spring 1963, Berkeley Div. Sch., 1964, Theol. Coll., Serampore, West Bengal, India, 1966, Drew U. Div. Sch., 1968, Sch. Theology, Claremont, Calif., 1976; Episc. chaplain U. Calif., 1937-40; vicar St. Alban's Ch., Albany, Calif., 1940-51, rector, 1952. Chmn. dept. Christian edn. Diocese of Calif., 1944-47, 49-50; dir. ch. edn. Trinity Ch., N.H., 1961-71. Mem. Religious Edn. Assn. (chmn. bd. 1957-60, William Rainey Harper award 1978), Nat. Council P.E. Ch. (curriculum div. 1947-52, writer, cons. 1952-56), Hazen Pacific Coast Theology Group (chmn. 1945-52). Author: What We Can Believe, 1941; Challenge of the Church, 1945; Religion Makes Sense 1950; The Clue to Christian Education, 1950; A Symphony of the Christian Year, 1954; Education for Christian Living, 1956, rev. edit., 1963; Biblical Theology and Christian Education, 1956; Be Not Anxious, 1957; I Remember Jesus, 1958; Christian Nurture and the Church, 1961; Your Child's Religion, 1962, 75; Youth Considers Parents as People, 1965; The Language Gap and God, 1970; Living with Anxiety, 1971; Live Until You Die, 1973; The American Spirit in Theology, 1974; This We Can Believe, 1976. Editor: (with Henry H. Shires) Christianity and the Contemporary Scene, 1943; Church and Organized Movements, 1946; Religious Education (jour.), 1958-78; contbr. articles to profl. publs. Home: 15 Edgehill Rd New Haven CT 06511 Office: 409 Prospect St New Haven CT 06510

MILLER, RENE HARCOURT, educator, aero. engr.; b. Tenafly, N.J., May 19, 1916; s. Arthur C. and Elizabeth M. (Tobin) M.; B.A., Cambridge U., 1937, M.A., 1954; m. Marcelle Hansotte, July 16, 1948 (div. 1968); children—Christal L., John M.; m. 2d, Maureen Michael, Nov. 20, 1973. Aero. engr. G.L. Martin Co., Balt., 1937-39; chief aero. and devel. McDonnell Aircraft Corp., St. Louis, 1939-44; mem. faculty aero. engring. Mass. Inst. Tech., Cambridge, 1944—, prof., 1957—, now Slater prof. flight transp., head dept. aeros. and astronautics, 1968-78; v.p. engring. Kaman Aircraft Corp., Bloomfield, Conn., 1952-54; mem. tech. adv. bd. FAA, 1964-66; mem. aircraft panel Pres.'s Sci. Adv. Com., 1960-72, Army Sci. Adv. Panel, 1966-73; chmn. Army Aviation Sci. Adv. Group, 1963-73; mem. Air Force Sci. Adv. Bd., 1959-70, com. on aircraft aerodynamics NASA, 1960-70. Recipient U.S. Army Decoration for Meritorious Civilian Service, 1967, 70; recipient Klemin award Am. Helicopter Soc., 1968, Sylvanus Albert Reed award Am. Inst. Aeros. and Astronautics, 1969, I.B. Laskowitz award N.Y. Acad. Scis., 1976. Registered profl. engr., Mass. Hon. fellow Am. Helicopter Soc. (tech. dir. 1957-59; editor jour. 1957-59); fellow AIAA (pres. 1977-78), Royal Aeros. Soc. (Gt. Britain); mem. Nat. Acad. Engring. Contbr. articles to profl. jours. Home: 321 Beacon St Boston MA 02116 Office: Mass Inst Tech Cambridge MA 02139

MILLER, REUBEN GEORGE, educator; b. Phila., Mar. 28, 1930; s. George and Edna (Fuchs) M.; B.A., LaSalle Coll., 1952; diploma U. Stockholm, 1954; M.A., U. Mont., 1956; Ph.D., Ohio State U., 1966; m. Sylvia Raigla, June 9, 1955. Asst. instr. Ohio State U., 1954-57; acting asst. prof. Oberlin (Ohio) Coll., 1957-58; asst. prof. U. Mass., Amherst, 1959-67; asso. prof. econs. Smith Coll., 1967-70; Charles A. Dana prof. econs., chmn. dept. Sweet Briar Coll., 1970—, chmn. div. social scis.; sr. mem. tech. staff Computer Sci. Corp., Washington; cons. Dept. Def.; Fulbright-Hayes lectr. econs. Coll. Law, Nat. Taiwan U., Republic China, 1965-66. Am.-Scandinavian Found. fellow, 1952-53, Research Tng. fellow Social Sci. Research Council, 1958-59. Mem. Am. Econ. Assn., Am. Fin. Assn., Royal Econ. Soc. Contbr. articles to profl. jours. Office: Dept Econs Sweet Briar Coll Sweet Briar VA 24595

MILLER, RICHARD ALAN, paper co. exec.; b. Cleve., July 29, 1939; s. Joshua Spencer and Martha (Harris) M.; B.B.A., U. Mich., 1961, J.D., 1964; m. Virginia Bell McCully, June 23, 1962; children—Cynthia Lynn, Alexander James. Admitted to Ariz. bar, 1964; asso. Fennemore, Craig, von Ammon & Udall, Phoenix, 1964-69, partner, 1970-71; sr. v.p. corp. and legal affairs, sec. S.W. Forest Industries, Inc., Phoenix, 1972—. Mem. Am., Ariz. bar assns., Am. Soc. Corporate Secs. Clubs: Paradise Valley Country; Arizona. Office: PO Box 7548 Phoenix AZ 85011

MILLER, RICHARD AUSTIN, adj. gen. Oreg.; b. Albany, Oreg., Feb. 1, 1923; s. Algra Pete and Lela Marceil (Buckler) M.; B.S. in Edn., Oreg. State U., 1948, M.Ed., 1959; grad. various mil. schs.; m. Mary Ann Woods, Aug. 22, 1976; children by previous marriage—David, Anne Marie, Cathy Miller Hosmer, Janie. Tchr.-coach Grants Pass (Oreg.) High Sch., 1948-49, St. Helen's (Oreg.) High Sch., 1949-53, Hillsboro (Oreg.) High Sch., 1953-54; successively tchr.-coach, dir. athletics, vice prin., prin. David Douglas High Sch., Portland, Oreg., 1954-73; adj. gen. Mil. Dept. State of Oreg., 1973—. Bd. dirs. Willamette chpt. ARC, United Way, Marion-Polk Counties, Urban League of Portland; bd. trustees Oreg. State U. Found. Served with AUS, 1943-46; joined Oreg. N.G., 1947, advanced through grades to maj. gen., 1974, exec. officer, then dep. comdr. 41st Brigade, 1970-72. Decorated Bronze star, Legion of Merit, Meritorious Service medal, Combat Infantryman's badge, various N.G. medals. Mem. Multnomah County Schoolmasters (pres. 1959-60), Oreg. High Sch. Coaches Assn. (pres. 1961-62), Multnomah County Adminstrs. Assn. (pres. 1967-68), N.G. Assn. U.S. (treas. 1972-76, pres. 1976-78, N.G. Assn. Oreg. (dir. 1963-64), Oreg. Secondary Sch. Prins. Assn. (exec. bd. 1971-73), Assn. Secondary and High Schs. (permanent chmn. program com. 1971-72), Inter-League Council High Schs. in Portland Met. Area (pres. 1969-73), Oreg. Sch. Activities Assn. (mem. del. assembly 1970-73), Oreg. State U. Dad's Club (treas. 1968-69), David Douglas Edn. Assn., Air Force Assn., Assn. U.S. Army (adv. dir.), Phi Delta Theta. Presbyterian. Club: Kiwanis (pres. Greater S.E. club 1968-69), Elks. Home: Camp Withycombe Clackamas OR 97015 Office: Mil Dept Oreg 2150 Fairgrounds Rd NE Salem OR 97303

MILLER, RICHARD HAMILTON, lawyer, broadcasting co. exec.; b. Cleve., July 18, 1931; s. Ray Thomas and Ruth (Hamilton) M.; A.B., U. Notre Dame, 1953, J.D., 1955; m. Susan Elizabeth Klimcheck, June 27, 1953; children—James M., Suanne R., Elizabeth M., Judith K., William P., Matthew W. Admitted to Ohio bar, 1955, since practiced in Cleve. as mem. firm Miller & Miller; asst. prosecutor Cuyahoga County, 1957-60; pres. Cleve. Broadcasting, Inc., 1966-70, Searles Lake Chem. Corp., Los Angeles, 1966-69, Miller Broadcasting Co., Cleve., 1970—, Hollywood Bldg. Systems, Inc., Meridian, Miss., 1974—; mng. partner Miller & Co., Cleve., 1974—; owner, dir. Cleve. Profl. Basketball Co., Cleve. Baseball, Inc. Gen. chmn. N.E. Ohio March of Dimes, 1971-73; adv. council Catherine Horstman Home Retarded Children, 1969-73; mem. Cuyahoga Democratic Exec. Com., 1955-66. Served to capt. AUS, 1956-57. Mem. Ohio, Cuyahoga County, Cleve. bar assns., Cleve. Citizens League. Clubs: K.C., Variety, Notre Dame (pres. 1964-65), Cleve. Athletic (dir. 1971-74) (Cleve.); Shaker Heights (Ohio) Country. Home: 2245 Stillman Rd Cleveland Heights OH 44118 Office: 2021 Superior Bldg Cleveland OH 44114

MILLER, RICHARD IRWIN, ednl. adminstr.; b. Fairbury, Nebr., Feb. 1, 1924; s. Carl W. and Iva Mae (Wilburn) M.; B.S., U. Neb., 1947; M.Ed., Springfield Coll., 1948; Ed.D., Columbia, 1958; m. Peggy J. McLaren, June 25, 1955; children—Joan Marie, Diane Lee, Janine Louise. Instr. Pa. State U., 1957-58; observer UN, 1958-60; asso. dir. project on instrn. NEA, 1960-63, asso. dir. Center Study of Instrn., 1963-64; dir. program for ednl. change U. Ky., Lexington, 1964-69; dir. nat. evaluation of Elementary and Secondary Edn. Act Title III, 1967-68; exec. sec. Pres.'s Nat. Adv. Council Supplementary Centers and Services, 1968-69; chmn. dept. social philosophy Founds. in Edn., 1967-69, prof., 1964-69; v.p. acad. affairs, dean of coll. Baldwin-Wallace Coll., Berea, O., 1970-72; asso. dir. Ill. Bd. Higher Edn., Springfield, 1972-77; v.p. for ednl. services State U. N.Y., Brockport, 1977—; cons. Com. Econ. Devel; edn. cons. Mead Ednl. Service, Inc. div. Mead Corp., also coordinator spl. ednl. seminars; cons. U.S. Office Edn., 1967-70; mem. adv. bd. Center for Information on Am., 1965—; ednl. advisor Am. Bar Assn., 1959-63. Served with USAAF, 1942-43. Recipient Nat. Pacesetter award in edn. Nat. Council Supplementary Centers and Services, Mem. Am. Assn. Higher Edn. (nat. planning group), Nat. Council Social Studies (research council 1967-70), Am. Assn. Univ. Adminstrs. (dir. 1972), Phi Delta Kappa. Presbyn. Rotarian. Club: Cosmos (Washington). Author: Dag Hammarskjod and Crisis Diplomacy, 1961; Education in a Changing Society, 1963; (with Ole Sand) Schools for the Sixties, 1963; Teaching About Communism, 1966. Editor: ESEA Title III: Catalyst for Change, 1967; The Nongraded School, 1968; Perspectives on Educational Change, 1967; Evaluating Faculty Performance, 1972; Developing Programs for Faculty Evaluation, 1974; Assessment of College Performance, 1979. Home: 6 Old Elm Dr Brockport NY 14420

MILLER, RICHARD MCDERMOTT, sculptor; b. New Philadelphia, Ohio, Apr. 30, 1922; s. J. Harry and Clela Belle (McDermott) M.; student Cleve. Inst. Art, 1940-42, 49-51; m. Audrey F. Miller, 1942; 1 dau., Sue Ann (Mrs. Kenneth Hartz); m. 2d, Gloria B. Bley, Mar. 18, 1961. One man shows at Peridot Gallery, N.Y.C., 1964, 66, 67, 69, Washburn Gallery, N.Y.C., 1971, 74, 75, 77; represented in numerous pub. and pvt. collections. Tchr., Queens Coll., City U. N.Y., 1967—. Served with AUS, 1942-46. Mem. Sculptors Guild, NAD. Address: 53 Mercer St New York NY 10013

MILLER, RICHARD NATHAN, advt. agy. exec.; b. Mt. Vernon, Ohio, Dec. 19, 1925; s. LeRoy Curtis and Josephine Luvera (Griffin) M.; B.F.A., John Herron Art Inst., 1950; m. Virginia Ann Lee, Arp. 19, 1948; children—Johanne, Ann, Meredith, Amy, Richard. Art dir. William Polje Advt. Agy., Terre Haute, Ind., 1950-51, Ruben Advt., Indpls., 1951-52; pres. R.N. Miller Co., Indpls., 1953-61; pres. Handley & Miller, Inc., Indpls., 1961—. Served with USAF, 1943-45. Home: 7223 N Olney St Indianapolis IN 46240 Office: 1732 N Meridian St Indianapolis IN 46202

MILLER, ROBERT, chemist; b. Bklyn., Aug. 3, 1932; s. Irving and Lena (Weinzoff) M.; B.S. in Chemistry, U. Fla., 1954; M.S., Purdue U., 19S6, Ph.D., 1958; m. Enid Merlyn Artzt, Feb. 21, 1955; 1 dau., Sharon Lynn. With Uniroyal, Inc., 1958—, polypropylene research and devel. mgr. fiber and textile div., 1963-67, div. process and quality control mgr., 1967-69, research and devel. mgr. hose and expansion joints, indsl. div., 1969-73, dir. research and devel. indsl. div., 1973-74, corporate dir. research and devel., 1974-79, v.p. tire research and devel. Uniroyal Tire Co., 1979—. Mem. Am. Chem. Soc., Assn. Research Dirs., Indsl. Research Inst. Author, patentee in field. Address: Uniroyal Inc Benson Rd Middlebury CT 06749

MILLER, ROBERT, advt. exec.; b. N.Y.C., June 2, 1923; s. Samuel and Adele (Elswit) M.; student N.Y.U., 1940-42; m. Frances Fitzgerald, June 10, 1944 (dec. 1978); children—Marc Robert, William Fitzgerald, Daniel Bates, Ellen Minette. Newsroom employee N.Y. Daily Mirror, 1942; with Miller Advt. Agy., Inc., N.Y.C., 1946—, v.p., 1948-54, chmn. bd., 1954-57, pres., 1958—, pres. Miller Advt. Service Corp., 1956-62, pres. Miller Advt. Agy. Ill., Inc., 1965-73; founder Nat. Newspaper Classified Advt. Network, Inc., pres., 1958-60, sec., dir. Classified Mgmt., Inc., 1965-73; contbg. editor Madison Avenue mag., 1975—; contbr. Selling Travel. Bd. govs. Roslyn Democratic Club, 1957-61, 68-73; mem. Nassau County Dem. Com., 1958-61, 68-73. Bd. dirs. Shalom Peace Found. Served to 1st lt. USAAF, 1942-46. Mem. L.I. Builders Inst., Grand Street Boys Nat. Assn. Home Builders (asso.), Ednl. Alliance Alumni Assn., Am. Legion. Office: 850 3d Ave New York City NY 10022

MILLER, ROBERT BRANSON, newspaper publisher; b. Ottawa, Kan., June 25, 1906; s. Albert Laird and Louise (Branson) M.; B.A., Williams Coll., 1929; m. Jean Leonard, Apr. 28, 1934 (dec. Dec. 1976); children—Robert Branson, Allen L.; m. 2d, Olive T. Adams, Jan. 6, 1978. With Battle Creek (Mich.) Enquirer, 1929—, beginning as reporter, becoming pub., 1952—; v.p., dir. Federated Publs., 1944-54, pres., 1954-64, chmn. bd., 1964—, also exec. chmn. and dir.; sr. v.p., dir. Gannett Co. Inc., to 1979; dir. Peoples Home Life Ins. Co. of Ind., Riverside Ins. Co. Am. Pres., South Central Mich. Health Planning Council, 1969—; now pres. Albert and Louise B. Miller Found. Mem. Am. Newspaper Pubs. Assn., Inland Daily Press Assn., Chi Psi. Rotarian. Home: 300 Wah Wah Tay See Way Battle Creek MI 49015 Office: Federated Publs Inc Battle Creek MI 49016

MILLER, ROBERT BRANSON, JR., newspaper publisher; b. Battle Creek, Mich., Aug. 10, 1935; s. Robert Branson and Jean (Leonard) M.; grad. Hotchkiss Sch., Lakeville, Conn., 1953; student Hamilton Coll., 1953-55; B.A., Mich. State U., 1959; m. Joan Carter Bailey, Aug. 22, 1959; children—Melissa Ann, Gregory Allen, Jennifer Lynn, Jeffrey William. Advt. salesman State Jour., Lansing, Mich., 1959-61, circulation sales rep., 1961-62, reporter, 1962-65, nat. advt. mgr., 1965-66; asst. to pub. Idaho Statesman, Boise, 1966-69, pub., 1971-79; pub. Daily Olympian, Olympia, Wash., 1969-71, Enquirer & News, Battle Creek, 1979—. Bd. dirs. Battle Creek chpt. ARC; trustee Albert L. and Louise B. Miller Found., Battle Creek. Served with USNR, 1956-58. Mem. Chi Psi. Club: Rotary. Home: 60 Rambling Ln Battle Creek MI 49015 Office: 155 W Van Buren St Battle Creek MI 49016

MILLER, ROBERT CARL, librarian; b. Evanston, Ill., lMay 9, 1936; s. John and Mary Veronica (Maziarczyk) M.; B.S., Marquette U., 1958; M.S., U. Wis., 1962; A.M., U. Chgo., 1966; m. Ellen Condon Reynolds, June 28, 1958; children—John, Marcy, Elizabeth, Christopher, Charles, Catherine. Head telephone reference Library of Congress, Washington, 1959-60; acquisitions librarian Marquette U., Milw., 1960-66; coll. librarian Parsons Coll., Fairfield, Iowa, 1966-67; acquisitions librarian U. Chgo., 1967-71, asso. dir., 1971-75; dir. libraries U. Mo., St. Louis, 1975-78; dir. libraries U. Notre Dame, 1978—; instr. library sci. Marquette U., 1963-64; instr. Am. history Alverno Coll., Milw., 1965. Fellow Council on Library Resources, 1973. Mem. Am., Mo. library assns. Roman Catholic. Contbr. articles to profl. jours. Home: 857 Forest Ave South Bend IN 46616 Office: U Notre Dame Univ Libraries Notre Dame IN 46556

MILLER, ROBERT DEMOREST, educator; b. Omaha, Sept. 25, 1919; s. Merritt Finley and Grace (Ernst) M.; B.S. in Agr., U. Mo., 1940; M.S. in Agronomy, U. Neb., 1941; Ph.D., Cornell U., 1948; m. Beulah Wilson Cooper, Sept. 6, 1941; children—Leslie Grace (Mrs. David A. Browne), Anne Cosby (Mrs. Donald E. Karr), Melanie Randolph (Mrs. Stephen L. Little). Jr., then asst. soil physicist U. Calif. at Berkeley, 1948-52; mem. faculty Cornell U., Ithaca, N.Y., 1952—, prof. soil physics, 1956—, dean univ. faculty, 1967-71; cons. in field. Served to 1st lt. USAAF, 1942-45. Fulbright scholar and fellow Royal Norwegian Council Sci. and Indsl. Research, 1965-66. Fellow Am. Soc. Agronomy (dir.). Research on water and ice in porous and colloidal media. Home: 538 Cayuga Hts Rd Ithaca NY 14850

MILLER, ROBERT EARL, engr., educator; b. Rockford, Ill., Oct. 4, 1932; s. Leslie D. and Marcia V. (Jones) M.; B.S., U. Ill., 1954, M.S., 1955, Ph.D., 1959. Asst. prof. theoretical and applied mechanics U. Ill., Urbana, 1959-61, asso. prof., 1961-68, prof., 1968—; cons. in field to industry, U.S. Army; in various positions in industry, summers, 1963-68. Mem. AIAA, Am. Soc. Engring. Edn., Am. Acad. Mechanics. Contbr. articles to profl. jours. Home: 408 Mumford Dr Urbana IL 61801 Office: 216 Talbot Lab U Ill Urbana IL 61801

MILLER, ROBERT FRED, glass co. exec.; b. Detroit, Apr. 26, 1918; s. Irvin Edward and Johanna Adeline (Gerson) M.; student U. Me., 1941, U. W. Va., 1942; certificate Alexander Hamilton Inst., 1950; certificate Nat. Sales Execs. Sch., Grad. Sch., Rutgers U., 1954-55; m. Barbara Arnold, Sept. 7, 1946 (dec. 1960); 1 dau., Bonnie Jane; m. 2d, Joan Bates Parfet, Sept. 17, 1960; children—Jeffrey Scott, Sarah Elizabeth. With Owens-Ill. Inc., 1941—, v.p. glass container div., 1961-63, v.p., gen. mgr. Atlantic Coast region, 1964-68, group v.p., gen. mgr. consumer and tech. products div., 1968-72, exec. v.p., mgr. tech. products group, 1972-76, sr. v.p., 1976—, also dir.; dir. Fed. Mogul Corp., Ohio Citizens Trust Co. Chmn. paper and container group Greater N.Y. Fund, 1964. Nat. Adv. Council Ariz. Heart Inst., 1975. Served to 1st lt. USAAF, 1942-46. Clubs: Belmont Country, Toledo, Confrerie des Chevaliers du Tastevin (grand officier); River (N.Y.C.); Golf (Columbus, Ohio); Blind Brook (Port Chester, N.Y.). Home: 5700 E McDonald Dr Scottsdale AZ 85253 Office: PO Box 1035 Toledo OH 43666

MILLER, ROBERT FRIEND, lawyer; b. Cleve., Nov. 3, 1922; s. Leon W. and Helen (Friend) M.; A.B., Dartmouth Coll., 1944; LL.B., U. Ariz., 1950; widower; children—Michael D., Kim C. Admitted to Ariz. bar, 1950; practice in Tucson, 1950—; dep. county atty. Pima County, 1951-52, partner firm Miller, Pitt & Feldman, P.C., 1964—. Served as officer USNR, 1944-46. Fellow Am. Coll. Trial Lawyers, Internat. Acad. Trial Lawyers; mem. Am. Trial Lawyers Assn., State Bar Ariz., Pima County Bar Assn. (pres. 1973-74, exec. com. 1968-75). Democrat. Office: 111 S Church Ave Tucson AZ 85701

MILLER, ROBERT HARVEY, cosmetic co. exec.; b. Paterson, N.J., Mar. 22, 1940; s. David and Bertha (Harris) M.; B.S. cum laude, Rutgers U., 1960; m. Carole Gordon, June 11, 1960; children—Randi, Jill, Loren. Supr., Coopers & Lybrand, C.P.A.'s, N.Y.C., 1960-65; controller Manhattan Industries, Inc., N.Y.C., 1965-72; v.p. fin. and ops. Charles of the Ritz Group, Ltd., N.Y.C., 1972-74, pres. Internat. div., 1974—, also dir. Mem. Fin. Execs. Inst., Am. Mgmt. Assn., Am. Inst. C.P.A.'s, N.Y. Soc. C.P.A.'s, Beta Gamma Sigma. Home: 11 Woodbine Trail Parsippany NJ 07054 Office: 40 W 57th St New York NY 10019

MILLER, ROBERT HASKINS, state justice; b. Columbus, Ohio, Mar. 3, 1919; s. George L. and Marian Alice (Haskins) M.; A.B., Kans. U., 1940, LL.B., 1942; grad. Nat. Coll. State Trial Judges, Phila., 1967; m. Audene Fausett, Mar. 14, 1943; children—Stephen F., Thomas G., David W., Stacey Ann. Admitted to Kans. bar, 1943; practice in Paola, 1946-60; judge 6th Jud. Dist. Kans., Paola, 1961-69, U.S. magistrate Kans. Dist., Kansas City, 1969-75; justice Kans. Supreme Ct., 1975—. Served with AUS, 1942-46. Mem. Kans., Wyandotte and Shawnee County bar assns., Am. Judicature Soc., Am. Legion, Phi Gamma Delta, Phi Delta Phi. Presbyterian. Contbg. author: Pattern (Civil Jury) Instructions for Kansas, 2d edit., 1969. Home: 3440 Jardine Terr Topeka KS 66611 Office: Kans Jud Center Topeka KS 66612

MILLER, ROBERT HOPKINS, fgn. service officer; b. Port Angeles, Wash., Sept. 8, 1927; s. Hopkins Keith and Sarah Margaret (Harvey) M.; A.B., Stanford U., 1949; M.A., Harvard U., 1951; m. Catherine Antoniadis, Sept. 6, 1952; children—George Keith, Margaret Helen. Intern, State Dept., 1951-52, internat. relations officer Office European Regional Affairs, 1952-54; 2d sec. U.S. mission to NATO and European Regional Orgns., 1954-57; internat. relations officer Exec. Secretariat, State Dept., Washington, 1957-60; internat. relations officer Office Western European Affairs, 1960-62; 1st sec. embassy, Saigon, Vietnam, 1962-65; dir. Vietnam Working Group, Dept. State, 1965-67; assigned Imperial Def. Coll., London, 1968; sr. adviser U.S. Mission to Vietnam Peace Talks, Paris, 1968-71; dep. exec. sec., 1971-73; asst. dir. ACDA, 1973-74; dept. asst. sec. of state for East Asia and Pacific, 1974-77; ambassador to Malaysia, 1977—; staff mem. numerous U.S. dels. to internat. meetings. Served with AUS, 1945-47. Recipient Distinguished Service award Dept. State, 1967. Office: AIA Bldg Jalan Ampang PO Box 35 Kuala Lumpur Malaysia

MILLER, ROBERT JAMES, anthropologist; b. Detroit, Sept. 18, 1923; s. Robert Paul and Desdemona (Jelinek) M.; student India studies U. Pa., 1947; A.B. in Oriental Civilization, U. Mich., 1948; Ph.D. in Anthropology, U. Wash., 1956; m. Beatrice Diamond, Nov. 6, 1943; children—Karla M., Erik T., Terin T. Asia research fellow U. Wash., 1948-50, instr. in anthropology, 1950, fellow Inner Asia Project, 1951-52, research anthropologist Inner Mongolia Project, 1955-56; asst. prof. sociology-anthropology Washington U., St. Louis, 1956-59; asst. prof. anthropology U. Wis., Madison, 1959-61, asso. prof., 1962-64, prof., 1965—, chmn. dept. anthropology, 1965-69, 76-78, prof. South Asian studies, 1959—; resident dir. Am. Inst. Indian Studies, New Delhi, 1970-72; cons. in field; asso. dir. Qualitative Systems Analysis Co. Served with USCG, 1942-44. Social Sci. Research Council fellow, 1952-53; Ford Found. fellow, 1953-55; NSF grantee, 1963-64; Am. Inst. Indian Studies sr. fellow, 1963-64; Smithsonian fellow, 1970-72; Sloan Found. grantee, 1976. Fellow Am. Anthrop. Assn., AAAS, Sigma Xi; mem. Assn. Asian Studies, Am. Ethnol. Soc., Soc. Gen. Systems Research, Current Anthropology (asso.), AAUP, Council Anthropology and Edn., Indian Anthropol. Assn. (founding), Internat. Assn. Buddhist Studies (founding), World Future Soc., Bioelectromagnetics Soc., Am. Radio Relay League, Soc. Wireless Pioneers, Explorers Club. Author: Monasteries and Culture Change in Inner Mongolia, 1959; contbr. numerous articles to profl. publs.; editor: Religious Ferment in Asia, 1974. Home: 1227 Sweetbriar Rd Madison WI 53705 Office: U Wis 5329 Social Sci Bldg Observatory Dr Madison WI 53706

MILLER, ROBERT JAMES, coll. ofcl.; b. Dunn, N.C., Jan. 14, 1933; s. Robert James and Edith (Crockett) M.; B.S., N.C. State U., 1956; M.F., Yale, 1962, M.S., 1965, Ph.D., 1967; m. Rebecca L. Ballantine, Nov. 28, 1959; children—Patricia Ann, Susan Ballantine, Nancy Crockett. Forester, W.Va. Pulp & Paper Co., 1956-59, Tilghman Lumber Co., 1959-61; asst. in instrn. and research, Yale, New Haven, 1962-65; asso. prof. biology Radford (Va.) Coll., 1965-67, prof., chmn. biology dept., 1967-68, dean div. natural scis., 1968-71, v.p. for acad. affairs, 1971-73; academic dean St. Mary's Coll., Raleigh, N.C., 1973—. Ecol. cons. Registered land surveyor. Mem. Am. Soc. Plant Physiologists, Ecol. Soc. Am., Sigma Xi, Phi Kappa Phi, Xi Sigma Pi. Mason (Shriner). Episcopalian. Author: The Assimilation of Nitrogen Compounds by Tree Seedlings, 1957; Some Ecological Aspects of Dry Matter Production, 1962; Liberal Arts and the Individual, 1972; Liberal Arts: an Educational Philosophy, 1973; Laboratory Notebook: General Biology, 1976. Home: 4008 Brownstone Circle Raleigh NC 27609

MILLER, ROBERT L., coll. adminstr., educator; b. Chgo., Jan. 26, 1926; s. Sam P. and Ida (Reich) M.; Ph.B., U. Chgo., 1947; B.S., U. Chgo., 1949, M.S., 1951; Ph.D., Ill. Inst. Tech. (NSF Sci. faculty fellow), 1963; m. Virginia Southard, Oct. 26, 1947 (dec. Sept. 1973); children—Ruth, Stephen, Martin, Andrew; m. 2d, Bonnie Seay Berard, Nov. 28, 1975; children—Edouard, Derek. Mem. faculty U. Ill. Chgo. Circle Campus, 1953-67, asst. dean Coll. Liberal Arts and Scis., 1963-65, asso. dean 1965-67; prof. chemistry dean arts and scis. U. N.C. at Greensboro, 1968—; Am. Council Edn. adminstrv. intern State U. N.Y. at Binghamton, 1967-68. Mem. exec. com. of com. environ. affairs Piedmont Council Govts., 1971—; mem. Greensboro Task Force on Energy; mem. bd. edn., Oak Park, Ill., 1965-66. Bd. dirs. Gilbert Pearson Audubon Soc., Greensboro Civil Liberties Union, Weatherspoon Gallery. Served with AUS, 1944-46; ETO. Mem. AAAS, Am. Chem. Soc., Am. Phys. Soc., Sigma Xi (treas. U. N.C. at Greensboro). Home: 116 Homewood Ave Greensboro NC 27403

MILLER, ROBERT LAVELLE, educator; b. Struthers, Ohio, May 11, 1919; s. Albert Francis and Elizabeth Marie (Rudfors) M.; student Capital U., Columbus, Ohio, 1937-40; B.S., Ohio State U., 1941, M.B.A., 1950; m. Jean Marcella Meeker, Aug. 26, 1950; 1 dau., Kathy Ann. Instr. in accounting Capital U., 1939-41, Ohio State U., 1941-42, 1946; asst. prof. accounting Youngstown (Ohio) U., 1946-47, prof., 1959—, dean Sch. Bus. Adminstrn., 1947-78. Served to 1st lt. AUS, 1942-45; PTO. Mem. Am. Accounting Assn., Adminstrv. Mgmt. Soc., Beta Alpha Psi, Beta Gamma Sigma. Lutheran. Mason. Home: 2020 Volney Rd Youngstown OH 44511 Office: 410 Wick Ave Youngstown OH 44555

MILLER, ROBERT LEE, publisher; b. Atlanta, Nov. 10, 1910; s. Walter Grover and Mercedes Emily (Littlejohn) M.; B.A., U. Tex., 1932; B.J., U. lMo., 1933; m. Eva Marie McConnico, Aug. 19, 1953. Owner, Robert Lee Miller & Assos., advt., Houston, Washington, Richmond, Va., Mexico City, Panama and Lima, Peru, 1935-60; editor, pub. Pan-Am. Herald, English lang. newspaper, Lima, 1939-42; pres. Brit. Colonial Estates, Ltd., Nassau, Bahamas, 1958—; pres., pub. Travelog mag., Houston and Ft. Worth, 1960—. Mem. Sigma Delta Chi, Phi Gamma Delta. Clubs: Lawn Tennis (Lima); Union (Panama City); Fgn. Corrs. (Mexico City); American (Paris); Salatine (Karachi, Pakistan); Century II (Ft. Worth). Home: 4700 Ranch View Rd Fort Worth TX 76109 Office: PO Box 11156 Fort Worth TX 76109

MILLER, ROBERT MARTIN, musician, educator; b. Wichita, Kans., Jan. 3, 1922; s. Frank O. and Faye (Watkins) M.; B.Mus., Northwestern U., 1948, M.Mus., 1949; licence de concert in piano, Ecole Normale De Musique de Paris, 1951. Asso. prof. music Denison U., Granville, Ohio, 1949-50, 53-61; prof. music, piano Smith Coll., Northampton, Mass., 1961—, chmn. music dept., 1977 ; instr. Northwestern U., summer 1950; Paris debut, 1951, N.Y. debut, 1958. Served to 1st lt. USAF, World War II. Fulbright grantee, 1950-52. Mem. Pi Kappa Lambda. Home: 9 North Ln Hadley MA 01035 Office: Music Dept Smith Coll Northampton MA 01063

MILLER, ROBERT NEIL, profl. football coach; b. Macomb, Ill., Oct. 31, 1927; s. John Samual and Jennie Lola (Webster) M.; B.S., Western Ill. U., 1950, M.S., 1957; m. Nancy Sue Harris, June 21, 1952; children—Stephen Michael, Lana Sue. Off-line coach St. Louis Cardinals, Nat. Football League, 1966-70, Balt. Colts, Nat. Football League, 1971-72; off-line coordinator New Eng. Patriots, Nat. Football League, Foxboro, Mass., 1973-76; head coach Denver Broncos, Nat. Football League, 1977—. Chmn. United Way, Denver, 1978, Leukemia Soc. Colo., 1979. Served with U.S. N.G., 1947-48. Presbyterian. Office: 5700 Logan St Denver CO 80216

MILLER, ROBERT RICHEY CONKLIN, transp. co. exec.; b. Lincoln, Nebr., Apr. 1, 1925; s. Dwight R.C. and Cora E. (Conklin) M.; B.S. in Bus. Adminstrn., U. Nebr., 1943; M.B.A. with high distinction, Harvard U., 1948; m. Kappy S. Kellogg, Jan. 16, 1944; children—David K., Robert L. Adminstrv. asst. to dean Harvard U. Bus. Sch., Boston, 1948-49; exec. trainee Crossett Co. (Ark.), 1949-52; v.p. Ashley Drew & No. Ry. Co., Crossett, 1952-54, pres., gen. mgr., dir., 1954-59; v.p. planning and devel. Consol. Freightways, Inc., Menlo Park, Calif. and Portland, Oreg., 1959-61, v.p. spl. transp., 1961-63; pres., dir. Greyhound Van Lines, Inc. and subs., Chgo., 1963-70; cons. transp., 1970-71; exec. v.p. Atlas Van Lines, Inc., Evansville, Ind., 1971-74, pres., dir. chief operating officer, 1974—; dir. Union Fed. Savs. and Loan, Evansville. Conf. v.p. Am. Trucking Assn., 1977-79. Vice pres., bd. dirs. Buffalo Trace Council Boy Scouts Am., 1973-78; mem. Mayor's Spl. Commn. on Energy, Evansville, 1977. Served to capt. U.S. Army, 1943-46; PTO. Recipient Distinguished Service award U.S. Jr. C. of C., 1952; Silver Beaver award Boy Scouts Am., 1976. Mem. Am. Movers Conf. (treas. 1964-68, dir., exec. com. 1973—, vice chmn. 1978—), Harvard U. Bus. Sch. Club (pres. Oreg. chpt. 1962-63, Chgo. chpt. 1967-68), Ind. Soc. Chgo., Evansville C. of C. (dir., v.p. 1974-79), Alpha Kappa Psi, Phi Gamma Delta. Republican. Methodist. Clubs: Union League (Chgo.); Evansville Country, Petroleum (Evansville). Home: 416 Marlene Dr Evansville IN 47712 Office: 1212 Saint George Rd Evansville IN 47711

MILLER, ROBERT RUSH, ichthyologist; b. Colorado Springs, Colo., Apr. 23, 1916; s. Ralph Gifford and Lucy Bond (Robinson) M.; A.B., U. Calif., Berkeley, 1938; Ph.D., U. Mich., 1944; m. Frances V. Hubbs, Oct. 11, 1940; children—Frances, Gifford, Roger, Laurence, Benjamin. Research asst. U. Mich., 1939-44; asso. curator fishes Smithsonian Instn., 1944-48; asso. curator fishes Mus. of Zoology U. Mich., Ann Arbor, 1948-59, curator, 1960—, asst. prof. zoology U. Mich., 1948-53, asso. prof., 1954-59, prof. biol. scis., 1960—. Guggenheim fellow, 1973-74. Recipient award of excellence Am. Fisheries Soc., 1975. Fellow AAAS; mem. Am. Soc. Ichthyologists and Herpetologists (pres. 1965), Soc. Systematic Zoology, Soc. Study of Evolution, Am. Fisheries Soc., Mich. Acad. Sci., Arts and Letters, Assn. Tropical Biology, Southwestern Assn. Naturalists, Soc. Vertebrate Paleontology, Am. Quaternary Assn., Am. Inst. Biol. Scis., Am. Killifish Assn., Desert Fishes Council (past chmn.), Southeastern Fishes Council, Explorers Club. Contbr. numerous articles to profl. jours. Home: 1117 Brooks St Ann Arbor MI 48103 Office: Museum of Zoology Univ of Michigan Ann Arbor MI 48109

MILLER, ROBERT WILEY, ednl. found. exec.; b. Linden, Calif., June 8, 1928; s. Raymond Wiley and Florence Estelle (Burke) M.; B.A., Coll. of Pacific, Stockton, Calif., 1950; M.B.A., Harvard U., 1956; LL.D., Lincoln Meml. U., 1978; L.H.D., Samford U., 1978; m. Betty Ruth Brown, Nov. 15, 1953; children—Janet Ruth, Stephen Wiley. Exec. v.p. Pub. Relations Research Assos., and World Trade Relations, Ltd., Washington, 1956-60; dir. program in pub. relations Columbia U., 1960-65; dir. bus.-govt. relations program, dir. Center Study Pvt. Enterprise, Am. U., 1965-70; dir. Office Domestic Bus. Policy, Dept. Commerce, 1970-71; exec. dir. White House Conf. Indsl. World Ahead, 1971-72; asst. dir. Council Internat. Econ. Policy, White House, 1972-73; spl. asst. for Bicentennial affairs White House, 1973-74; sr. asst. adminstr. Am. Revolution Bicentennial Adminstrn., 1974-75; dep. asst. sec. edn. HEW, 1975; pres. Freedoms Found. at Valley Forge (Pa.), 1975—. Vice chmn. pub. relations com. Nat. council Boy Scouts Am., 1965-76; trustee Am. U., 1976—. Served with AUS, 1951-53. Recipient Medal of Honor, D.A.R., 1978; Silver Helmet Americanism award AMVETS, 1978; named Alumnus of Year, U. Pacific, 1976. Clubs: Cosmos (Washington); Masons. Author: Corporate Policies and Public Attitudes, 1965; Corporate Ambassadors to Washington, 1969. Editor: The Creative Interface I, The New Relationship Between Business and Government, 1969, The Creative Interface II, International Business-Government Relations, 1970, The Creative Interface III, Private Enterprise and the Urban Crisis, 1970. Address: Freedoms Found Valley Forge PA 19481

MILLER, ROGER DEAN, entertainer; b. Fort Worth, Jan. 2, 1936; s. Mr. and Mrs. Jean Miller, raised by E.D. and Armella Miller; student pub. schs., Erick; m. 2d, Mary Arnold, Feb. 14, 1978; children—Dean, Shannon, Alan, Rhonda, Shari. Composer, rec. artist songs including King of the Road, Chug-A-Lug, Dang Me, In the Summertime, England Swings, You Can't Roller Skate in a Buffalo Herd, Hey Little Star, Lock, Stock and Teardrops; albums include Return of Roger Miller, Dang Me, Roger Miller Golden Hits, Roger Miller-Off the Wall; TV program Roger Miller Show; personal appearances in U.S. and Eng., Australia, N.Z.; pres. Dang Me Prodns., Inc.; character voice for movie cartoon Robin Hood, 1973. Served with AUS, Korean conflict. Recipient 5 awards Nat. Assn. Rec. Arts and Scis., 1965, 6 awards, 1966. Office: care Management III 9744 Wilshire Blvd Beverly Hills CA 90212. *Some people feel the rain . . . and some just get wet.*

MILLER, ROLAND DREW, physician; b. Chgo., Mar. 16, 1922; s. Roland Bleeker and Fern (Drew) M.; A.B., DePauw U., 1943; M.B., Northwestern U., 1945, M.D., 1946; M.S., U. Minn., 1951; m. Elizabeth Lancaster, Dec. 18, 1943; children—Judith Lee, Cheryl Sue, Randall Scott. Intern U.S. Naval Hosp., San Diego, 1945-46; fellow medicine Mayo Found., 1948-51, asst. dir. found., 1959-61, asso. dir., 1961-73; cons. Mayo Clinic, 1952—; faculty U. Minn. Grad. Sch., 1953—, asso. prof. medicine, 1961-65, prof. medicine, 1966—. Pres. Rochester Council Chs., 1955-57. Served to lt. (j.g.) USNR, 1946-48; capt. Res. Diplomate Am. Bd. Internal Medicine (mem. bd. 1974—, chmn. pulmonary bd. 1974-77). Mem. AMA, A.C.P., Coll. Chest Physicians, Central Soc. Clin. Research, Am. Fedn. Clin. Research (Midwest chmn. nat. councilor 1960-61), Sigma Xi, Beta Theta Pi, Phi Beta Pi, Pi Kappa Epsilon, Alpha Omega Alpha. Methodist. Rotary. Contbr. articles on cardio-pulmonary diseases to profl. jours. Editorial bd. Minn. Medicine, 1956-60. Home: Route 1 Rochester MN 55901 Office: 200 SW 1st St Rochester MN 55901

MILLER, RONALD THOMAS, utility co. exec.; b. Burke, Idaho, Aug. 6, 1919; s. Dale D. and Mary E. (Dunphy) M.; B.S., Oreg. State U., 1941; m. Betty Loretta Bergman, Mar. 7, 1942; children—Mary L. (Mrs. John A. Rhine, Jr.), Margaret A. (Mrs. Jan E. Monroe). Insp. fed. diking project U.S. C.E., Deer Island, Oreg., 1941; with N.W. Natural Gas Co., Portland, 1947—, chief engr., 1968-71, v.p. engring. and gas control, 1971-73, exec. v.p., 1973-75, pres., chief exec. officer, 1975— also dir., chmn. exec. com.; v.p., dir. Asso. Oreg. Industries, Blue Cross Oreg. Pres., Lake Oswego (Oreg.) P.T.A., 1963, Am. Field Service, Lake Oswego, 1966-67; bd. dirs. Portland Better Bus. Bur., Columbia-Pacific council Boy Scouts Am. Served to capt. C.E. AUS, 1942-47; PTO. Registered profl. engr., Oreg. Mem. Am. Gas Assn. (chmn. liquefied natural gas com. 1972-73, dir. 1979—), Am. Soc. M.E., Nat. Soc. Profl. Engrs., Profl. Engrs. Oreg. (award of merit 1968, chpt. sec. 1968), Pacific Coast Gas Assn. (gen. chmn. operating sect. 1972-73, dir. 1976—, 2d vice chmn. 1979—), Portland C. of C. (dir. 1979—), Alpha Sigma Phi. Republican. Roman Catholic. Clubs: Waverley Country (Portland); Arlington; Rotary. Home: 99 SW Midvale Rd Portland OR 97219 Office: 200 SW Market St Portland OR 97201

MILLER, RONALD WILLIAM, film producer; b. Los Angeles, Apr. 17, 1933; s. John W. and Stella Miller; ed. U. So. Calif., 1951-54; m. Diane Marie Disney, May 9, 1954; children—Christopher, Joanna, Tamara, Jennifer, Walter, Ronald William, Patrick. With Walt Disney Prodns., Burbank, Calif., 1957—, v.p. in charge TV and exec. producer TV, from 1968, now exec. v.p. in charge prodn. and creative affairs, also mem. exec. com., dir. Served with U.S. Army, 1954-55. Mem. Acad. Motion Picture Arts and Scis., Nat. Acad. TV Arts and Scis., Motion Picture Pioneers, U. So. Calif. Assos., Frat. of Friends of Music Center. Republican. Episcopalian. Office: 500 S Buena Vista St Burbank CA 91521

MILLER, ROSS FRANKLIN, aircraft co. exec.; b. Seattle, Aug. 16, 1921; s. Ross Franklin and Lillian (Dickie) M.; student Seattle Pacific Coll., 1940-42; B.S. in Math., U. Wash., 1944, B.S. in Physics, M.A., 1948; m. Alice Millikan, Apr. 22, 1944; children—Ross A., Mark F., Dean E. With Northrop Corp., Hawthorne, Calif., 1950—, asst. mgr., dir. engring., 1961-62, v.p., mgr., 1962-69, v.p., gen. mgr., 1969-72, pres. subs. Page Communications Engrs.-Iran, 1972-74, group exec., sr. v.p. communications and electronics group, 1974-79, sr. v.p., group exec. aircraft group, 1979—. Served with U.S. Army, 1944-45. Mem. Armed Forces Communications and Electronics Assn. (bd. dirs.). Office: 3901 Broadway Hawthorne CA 90250

MILLER, ROSS HAYS, neurosurgeon; b. Ada, Okla., Jan. 30, 1923; s. Harry and Helen (Rice) M.; B.S., East Central State Coll., Ada, 1943; M.D., U. Okla., 1946; M.S. in Neurosurgery, U. Minn., 1952; m. Catherine Railey, May 2, 1943; children—Terry Hays, Helen Stacy. Intern, St. Luke's Hosp., Cleve., 1946-47; fellow in neurosurgery Mayo Clinic, Rochester, Minn., 1950-54, instr. in neurosurgery Mayo Med. Sch., 1954-63, asst. prof. neurosurgery, 1963-73, asso. prof., 1973-75, prof., chmn. dept. neurosurgery, 1975—. Trustee, East Central State U. Found. Served as capt., M.C., U.S. Army, 1947-49; Korea. Named to Okla. Hall of Fame, 1977. Diplomate Am. Bd. Neurol. Surgery (chmn. exam. com. 1978—). Mem. AMA, A.C.S., Am. Assn. Neurol. Surgeons (chmn. com. profl. practice 1976-79, dir. 1976-79, v.p. 1979), Congress Neurol. Surgeons (exec. com. 1963-65), Minn. Soc. Neurol. Scis., Neurosurg. Soc. Am. (v.p. 1975), Soc. Neurol. Surgeons, Sigma Xi. Contbr. numerous articles to med. publs. Office: Mayo Clinic Rochester MN 55901

MILLER, ROY ANDREW, educator; b. Winona, Minn., Sept. 5, 1924; s. Andrew and Jessie (Eickelberry) M.; B.A., Gustavus Adolphus Coll., 1946; M.A., Columbia, 1950, Ph.D., 1953; M.A. (hon.), Yale, 1964. Mem. faculty Internat Christian U., Tokyo, 1955-63, prof., 1961-63; mem. faculty Yale, 1962-71, prof., chmn. dept. Eastern and So. Asian langs. and lit., 1964-71, dir. Inst. Far Eastern Langs., 1962-71; prof. dept. Asian langs. and lit. U. Wash., Seattle, 1972—, chmn. dept., 1972-77. Dir. Inter-univ. Center for Japanese Studies, Tokyo, 1964-65. Served with USNR, World War II. Mem. Linguistic Soc. Am., Am. Oriental Soc., Societas Uralo-Altaica (Hamburg). Author: The Japanese Language, 1967; Japanese and the Other Altaic Languages, 1971; Footprints of the Buddha, 1975; Altaic Elements in Old Japanese, Part 1, 1975; Studies in the Grammatical Tradition in Tibet, 1976. Review editor Jour. Japanese Studies, 1974—. Home: 8001 Sandpoint Way NE Apt C-67 Seattle WA 98115

MILLER, RUBY SILLS (MRS. GLENN K. MILLER), assn. exec.; b. Montpelier, Ind.; d. Elijah Bert and Alma (Beeks) Sills; B.S. in Edn., Ball State Tchrs. Coll., 1957; M.B.A., U. Wis., 1958; m. Glenn Kenneth Miller, Mar. 26, 1966. Reporter, Montpelier Herald, 1937-41; reporter, soc. editor Hartford City (Ind.) News-Times, 1941-44, bus. office supr., 1945-57; asst. to dean, instr. U. Wis. Sch. Bus., 1958-60; exec. dir. Nat. Fedn. Bus. and Profl. Women's Clubs, 1960-64; asst. to nat. exec. dir. Girl Scouts U.S.A., 1964-66, spl. asst. to nat. exec. dir., N.Y.C., 1972-74; dir. exptl. project for adminstrv. trainees Camp Fire Girls, Inc. and Girl Scouts U.S.A., 1966-68; dir. regional confs. Nat. Assembly for Social Policy and Devel., Inc., 1968-71; project dir. Nat. Center for Vol. Action, 1971-72; cons. Nat. Council for Homemaker-Home Health Aide Service, Inc., 1972, 76; asst. dir. Gustavus Adolphus Community Lounge Sr. Center, 1977-78; Queens County community program officer N.Y.C. Dept. of Aging, 1978—. Sec., Hartford City Retailers Assn., 1951-54. Pres. Ind. Bapt. Youth Fellowship, 1944-46; adv. Two Together, Jewish Child Care Agy.; bd. dirs. Bellevue Day Care Bd., Bellevue Hosp. Center. Mem. Adult Edn. Assn. U.S.A., Nat. Assn. Social Workers, Nat. Council Aging. Home: 165 E 32d St New York NY 10016

MILLER, RUSSELL HAROLD, hosp. adminstr.; b. North English, Iowa, Aug. 19, 1924; s. Harold William and Annie (Long) M.; student U. Iowa, 1942-43, 48-49; B.A., Central Coll., 1948; M.H.A., U. Minn., 1951; m. Verna Mae Rozeboom, June 27, 1950; children—Candice, Kimberlee, Leslie. Adminstrv. resident Mary Hitchcook Meml. Hosp., Hanover, N.H., 1950-52; asst. adminstr. U. Kans. Med. Center, Kansas City, 1952-57, asso. dir., 1957-65, dir., 1965-72, dean for med. center adminstrn., 1972-74, vice chancellor med. center adminstrn., 1974—. Trustee Central Coll., Pella, Iowa. Served with USAAF, 1943-45; col. USAF Res. Decorated D.F.C., Air medal with four oak leaf clusters. Mem. Am. Coll. Hosp. Adminstrs., Am. (past mem. council on adminstrn.), Kans. (dir., past pres.), Midwest (past pres.), Kansas City Area (past pres.) hosp. assns. Presbyn. Rotarian. Home: 7221 Mastin St Shawnee Mission KS 66203 Office: University of Kans Medical Center 39th and Rainbow Blvd Kansas City KS 66103

MILLER, RUTH KELSEY, editor; b. Berkeley, Calif., Oct. 21, 1922; d. Henry Playman and Caroline (French) Melnikow; student U. Calif., Berkeley, 1939-41, U. So. Calif., 1953-54; children—Carol Marcuse, Robert Resner, Raymond Miller. With San Francisco Chronicle, 1944-45, 62—, women's editor, 1966-70, editor people sect., 1970—; public relations free-lancer, 1945-46, 51-53, 54-57; religion editor Honolulu Star-Bull., 1953-54; editor Davis Enterprise, Napa Jour. and Fairfield News, No. Calif., 1957-58; women's editor Santa Barbara (Calif.) News-Press, 1958-62. Bd. dirs. San Francisco unit Am. Cancer Soc.; mem. citizen's adv. com. Dominican Coll.; mem. Pinehurst aux. Salvation Army. Mem. Newspaper Guild, Am. Women for Internat. Understanding (v.p.), Women's Forum-West (dir.), Walden Soc. (rev. bd.). Democrat. Club: San Francisco Women's Press (pres.). Office: 901 Mission St San Francisco CA 94119

MILLER, S(EYMOUR) M(ICHAEL), educator; b. Phila., Nov. 21, 1922; s. Morris and Lena (Landau) M.; B.A., Bklyn. Coll., 1943; M.A., Columbia, 1945; M.A., Princeton, 1946, Ph.D., 1951; m. Jean Baker, Apr. 6, 1955; children—Jonathan Frank, Edward David. Instr. econs. Rutgers U., 1947-49; lectr. econs. to asso. prof. sociology Bklyn. Coll., 1949-61; prof. sociology Maxwell Sch., Syracuse U., 1961-65; prof. edn. and sociology N.Y. U., N.Y.C., 1965-72; chmn. dept. sociology Boston U., 1973—, prof. sociology and econs., 1976—. Program adviser in social devel. Ford Found., 1966-68; cons. Com. for econ. Devel., chmn. com. on problems census enumeration Nat. Acad. Scis., 1969-71. Chmn., Social Scientists' Com. on Welfare and Social Policy, 1969-70; chmn. bd. Nat. Com. for Employment of Youth, 1970-72. Mem. Eastern, (pres. 1970-71), Internat. (chmn. research com. on poverty, social welfare and social policy 1968-77), sociol. assns., Am. Sociol. Assn., Am. Econ. Assn., Soc. Study Social Problems (pres.), Assn. Evolutionary Econs. Author: (with C.H. Hession and C. Stoddard) The Dynamics of the American Economy, 1956; Comparative Social Mobility, 1960; (with Frank Riessman) Social Class and Social Policy, 1968; (with Pamela Roby) The Future of Inequality, 1970. Editor (with Alvin Gouldner) Applied Sociology, 1965; (with Bruno Stein) Incentives and Planning in Social Policy, 1973. Office: Boston U 100 Cummington St Boston MA 02215

MILLER, SAM SCOTT, lawyer; b. Ft. Worth, July 26, 1938; s. Percy Vernon and Mildred Lois (MacDowell) M.; B.A., Mich. State U., 1960; J.D., Tulane U., 1964; LL.M., Yale U., 1965; m. Mary Harrison FitzHugh, May 10, 1969. Admitted to La. bar, 1965, N.Y. bar, 1966, Minn. bar, 1969; asso. firm Simpson Thacher & Bartlett, N.Y.C., 1965-68; sr. counsel Investors Diversified Services, Mpls., 1968-73; partner firm Ireland Gibson Reams & Miller, Memphis, 1973-74; gen. counsel Paine, Webber, Jackson & Curtis Inc., N.Y.C., 1974—, sr. v.p., 1976—; dir. Arcturus Futures Corp.; adj. prof. Yale Law Sch. Mem. dean's council Tulane U. Law Sch., 1979—; bd. dirs. Guthrie Theatre Found., Mpls., 1971-74, Minn. Opera Co., Mpls., 1971-74. Mem. Assn. Bar City N.Y., Am. Bar Assn., Internat. Bar Assn., Securities Industry Assn. (chmn. fed. regulation com. 1976-78), Order of Coif, Omicron Delta Kappa. Democrat. Baptist. Club: Down Town Assn. Contbr. articles to profl. jours.; editor-in-chief Tulane Law Rev., 1964-65. Home: 510 E 86th St New York NY 10028 Office: 140 Broadway New York NY 10005

MILLER, SAMUEL CLIFFORD, museum dir.; b. Roseburg, Oreg., May 6, 1930; s. Loren and Blanche (Baron) M.; B.A., Stanford, 1951; postgrad. Inst. Fine Arts N.Y. U., 1962-64; m. Nell Schoellkopf Ely, 1966 (dec.); Rosetta Averill. Asst. to dir. Albright-Knox Art Gallery, Buffalo, 1964-67; asst. dir. Newark Mus., 1967, dir., 1968—. Mem. art com. Port Authority of N.Y. and N.J. Served with AUS, 1951-53. Mem. Am. Assn. Museums, Assn. Art Mus. Dirs., Museums Council N.J. Club: Essex (Newark). Home: 375 Mt Prospect Ave Newark NJ 07104 Office: Newark Museum 43 Washington St Newark NJ 07101

MILLER, SAMUEL MARTIN, apparel co. fin. exec.; b. N.Y.C., Jan. 31, 1938; s. Irving Nathiel and Estelle (Furman) M.; B.B.A. magna cum laude, CCNY, 1964; m. Kay Shapiro, Dec. 23, 1963; children—Jennifer, Suzanne. With Coopers & Lybrand, N.Y.C., 1964-72, supervising sr. acct., 1968-69, audit mgr., 1969-72; corp. controller Manhattan Industries, Inc., Glen Rock, N.J., 1972-74, v.p., corp. controller, 1974-76, v.p., treas., controller, 1976—. Served with USN, 1957-59. Recipient Haskin's award N.Y. State Uniform C.P.A. Exam. Mem. Fin. Execs. Inst., Nat. Assn. Accts., Am. Inst. C.P.A.'s, N.Y. State Soc. C.P.A.'s, Am. Apparel Mfrs. Assn. (chmn. fin. mgmt. com.), Am. Arbitration Assn., Beta Gamma Sigma, Beta Alpha Psi. Club: Long Ridge Swim and Tennis. Office: 25 De Boer Dr Glen Rock NJ 07452

MILLER, SANFORD ARTHUR, govt. ofcl., educator, biochemist; b. Bklyn., May 12, 1931; s. Howard and Lillian (Kenter) Epstein; B.S. in Chemistry and Biology, CCNY, 1952; M.S. in Physiology and Biochemistry, Rutgers U., 1956, Ph.D. in Physiology and Biochemistry, 1957; m. Judith W. Cohen, Aug. 17, 1958; children—Wallis Jo, Debra Lauren. Jr. chemistr electronics br. Army Chem. Center, Edgewood, Md., summer 1951, chemist applied research br., 1952; teaching asst. in physiology and biochemistry Rutgers U., 1955-57; research asso. dept. food tech. M.I.T., 1957-59, asst. prof. nutritional biochemistry, 1959-65, asso. prof., 1965-70, prof., dir. tng. program in oral sci., 1970—; dir. Bur. of Foods, FDA, Washington, 1978—; vis. lectr. in nutrition Tufts U. Sch. Dental Medicine, 1963—, Boston U. Sch. Medicine, 1963—, Harvard U. Sch. Medicine, 1963—; cons. to industry, food and drug cos., U.S. and abroad. Chmn. ad hoc com. Nat. Inst. Neurol. Diseases and Stroke, 1972-77; mem. expert com. on generally recognized as safe substances Fedn. Am. Socs. Exptl. Biology, 1972-78; mem. com. on maternal and child health and com. on contraceptive steroids Nat. Inst. Child Health and Human Devel., 1973-78; mem. adv. com. on nutrition Nat. Inst. Dental Research, 1973-78; bd. sci. advs. FDA, 1972-78; trustee Culinary Inst. Am., 1979—; mem. Food Update Bd. Govs., 1978—. Served with M.C., U.S. Army, 1953-54. Recipient Outstanding Tch. of Yr. award M.I.T., 1975; recipient numerous grants and fellowships, including: Nat. Acad. Scis., 1959, NIH, 1960-78, AEC, 1965. Fellow Mark L. Morris Animal Care Panel (hon.); mem. Am. Chem. Soc., AAAS, N.Y. Acad. Scis., Inst. Food Technologists (chmn. N.E. sect. 1970-71, nat. councilor 1966-69, nat. chmn. com. on nutrition edn. 1969-72), Animal Care Panel, Am. Inst. Nutrition (chmn. fellows com. 1977-78, program com. 1970-77), Soc. Teratology, Perinatal Research Soc., Am. Inst. Dental Research, Soc. Pediatric Research, Fedn. Am. Socs. Exptl. Biology (chmn. fedn. conf. 1974), Gordon Research Confs. on Food and Nutrition (chmn. 1973), Western Hemisphere Nutrition Congress (program com. 1978), Sigma Xi. Jewish. Clubs: Cosmos, New Century. Contbr. numerous articles, revs., chpts. to profl. publs. Office: 200 C St SW Washington DC 20204. *One of the most difficult skills for the young scientist to develop is the ability to recognize and then admit error. Science advances only on the ability of scientists to propose, challenge and modify ideas.*

MILLER, SAUL, editor; b. N.Y.C., Sept. 23, 1918; s. Louis and Kate (Zizmor) M.; B.S., N.Y.U., 1941; m. Beatrice Elbaum, Nov. 10, 1945; children—David, Kate, Judith, Jonathan. Reporter, Gazette & Daily, York, Pa., 1945-48; copy editor Richmond (Va.) Times-Dispatch, 1948-49; news editor Jamestown (N.Y.) Sun, 1949-51; dir. New Newspaper Service, Washington, 1951-55; asso. editor AFL News Reporter, 1955; mng. editor AFL-CIO News, 1955-58; dir. publs. AFL-CIO, 1958—. Served with AUS, 1942-45. Mem. Am. Newspaper Guild, Nat. Press Club (Washington). Home: 3410 Highview Ct Silver Spring MD 20902 Office: Dept Publications AFL-CIO 815 16th St Washington DC 20006

MILLER, SHELBY ALEXANDER, chem. engr., educator; b. Louisville, July 9, 1914; s. George Walter and Stella Katherine (Cralle) M.; B.S., U. Louisville, 1935; Ph.D., U. Minn., 1944; m. Jean Adele Danielson, Dec. 26, 1939; (div. May 1948); 1 son, Shelby Carlton; m. 2d, Doreen Adare Kennedy, May 29, 1952 (dec. Feb. 1971). Asst. chemist Corhart Refractories Co., Louisville, 1935-36; teaching, research asst. chem. engring. U. Minn., Mpls., 1935-39; devel. engr., research chem. engr. E.I. duPont de Nemours & Co., Inc., Wilmington, Del., 1940-46; asso. prof. chem. engring. U. Kan., Lawrence, 1946-50, prof., 1950-55; Fulbright prof. chem. engring. King's Coll. Durham U., Newcastle-upon-Tyne, Eng., 1952-53; prof., chem. engring. U. Rochester, 1955-69, chmn., 1955-68; asso. lab. dir. Argonne (Ill.) Nat. Lab., 1969-74, dir. Center Ednl. Affairs, 1969-79, sr. chem. engr., 1979—; vis. prof. chem. engring. U. Calif., Berkeley, 1967-68. Sec., Kans. Bd. Engring. Examiners, 1954-55. Treas., Lawrence (Kans.) League for Practice Democracy, 1950-52. Registered profl. engr., Del., Kans., N.Y. Fellow AAAS, Am. Inst. Chemists, Am. Inst. Chem. Engrs. (past chmn. Kansas City sect.), Am. Chem. Soc. (past chmn. Rochester sect.); mem. Soc. Chem. Industry, Am. Soc. Engring. Edn. (past chmn. grad. studies div.), Am. Nuclear Soc., AAUP, Triangle, Sigma Xi, Sigma Tau, Phi Lambda Upsilon, Tau Beta Pi, Alpha Chi Sigma. Presbyn. Editor: Chem. Engring. Edn. Quar. 1965-67; sect. editor 5th edit. Perry's Chem. Engring. Handbook, 1973, 6th edit., 1981; contbr. articles to tech., profl. jours. Home: 825 63d St Downers Grove IL 60515 Office: Chem Engring Div Argonne Nat Lab Argonne IL 60439

MILLER, SIDNEY, med. co. exec.; b. Newark, July 26, 1926; s. Samuel and Nina (Maidonick) M.; B.B.A., Coll. City N.Y., 1950; m. Constance Bernice Krauss, Apr. 4, 1954; children—Scott Michael, Nancy Beth. With Laventhol, Krekstein & Co., Phila., 1954-60; with Hoffman, Goldfine & Co., C.P.A.'s, Phila., 1960-63, partner, 1962-63; partner Bershad & Co., C.P.A.'s, Phila., 1963-67; partner Laventhol Krekstein Horwath & Horwath, Phila., 1967-68; v.p. Am. Medicorp, Inc., Bala Cynwyd, Pa., 1968-78, Universal Health Services, Inc., Bala Cynwyd Pa., 1978—. Served with USNR, 1944-46. Mem. Fin. Execs. Inst., Am., Pa. insts. C.P.A.'s, Hosp. Fin. Mgmt. Assn. Home: 7 Latham Pkwy Melrose Park PA 19126 Office: One Presdl Plaza Bala Cynwyd PA 19004

MILLER, STANFORD, ins. co. exec.; b. Kansas City, Mo., Nov. 15, 1913; s. Hugh and Gertrude Anna (Kraft) M.; B.A., U. Kans., 1934; J.D., U. Chgo., 1938; m. Gloria Goble, July 11, 1942 (div. 1958); 1 son, Hans Hugh; m. 2d, Beverly Breuer, Apr. 19, 1962; 1 son, Bradford Channing. Admitted to Mo. bar, 1938; pres., chief exec. officer ERC Corp. and Employers Reins. Corp., Kansas City, Mo.; chmn., dir. Nat. Fidelity Life Ins. Co., First Fidelity Equity Corp., First Systems Corp. (all Kansas City), Am. Defender Life Ins. Co., Raleigh, N.C., Centennial Life Ins. Co., Mission, Kans.; dir. Commerce Bank, Kansas City, Mo.; lectr. in field. Mem. exec. bd. Kansas City, Boy Scouts Am.; bd. dirs. Acad. Health Professions; trustee Kansas City Philharmonic Assn., U. Kansas City; bd. advisers U. Kans. Sch. Bus. Mem. Mo. Bar Assn., Reins. Assn. Am. (past chmn.), Health Ins. Assn. Am. (former sec., dir.), Am. Inst. Property and Liability Underwriters (trustee), Ins. Inst. Am. (trustee), Phi Alpha Delta, Alpha Tau Omega. Clubs: Rotary; Carriage, Kansas City, Profl. Men's; Mission Hills Country. Author: (with Robert D. Brown) Health Insurance Underwriting, 1962; also articles. Home: 2709 Tomahawk Mission Hills KS 66208 Office: Ins Exchange Bldg Kansas City MO 64105

MILLER, STANLEY CUSTER, JR., educator, physicist; b. Kansas City, Mo., July 30, 1926; s. Stanley Custer and Verda (Storer) M.; B.S. in Engring. Physics, U. Colo., 1948; Ph.D. in Physics, U. Calif. at Berkeley, 1953; m. Elene G. Josephson, Nov. 27, 1957; children—Gloria Diane, James Kenneth, Richard Eric. Mem. faculty U. Colo., Boulder, 1953—, prof. physics, 1961—. Served with USNR, 1944-46. Mem. Am. Phys. Soc., Am. Assn. Physics Tchrs. Author: Principles of Physics, 2 vols., 1966; Irreducible Representations of Space Groups, 1967; Principles of Modern Physics, 1970. Home: 207 Pine Brook Hills Boulder CO 80302

MILLER, STANLEY LLOYD, educator, chemist; b. Oakland, Calif., Mar. 7, 1930; s. Nathan Harry and Edith (Levy) M.; B.S., U. Calif. at Berkeley, 1951; Ph.D., U. Chgo., 1954; F.B. Jewett fellow Calif. Inst. Tech., 1954-55; asst. prof. biochemistry Columbia Coll. Physicians and Surgeons, 1955-60; mem. faculty U. Calif. at San Diego, 1960—, prof. chemistry, 1968—. Mem. Nat. Acad. Scis., Am. Chem. Soc., Am. Soc. Biol. Chemists, AAAS, Phi Beta Kappa, Sigma Xi. Co-author: The Origins of Life on Earth, 1974. Home: 1682 Torrey Pines Rd La Jolla CA 92037

MILLER, STEPHEN HERSCHEL, physician, educator; b. N.Y.C., Jan. 12, 1941; s. Morris Louis and Mildred Lily (Beller) M.; student U. Chgo., 1957-58, U. Ga., 1958-59, Tulane U., 1960-61; M.D. cum laude, UCLA, 1964; m. Carol Susan Shapiro, Dec. 18, 1965; children—Mark, David. Intern, UCLA, 1964-65, resident in gen. surgery, 1965-67; resident in gen. surgery U. Calif., San Diego, 1967-69; resident in plastic surgery U. Calif., San Francisco, 1969-71; research fellow in plastic surgery African Med. Research Found., Kenya, 1971-72; research fellow head and neck program Roswell Park, Buffalo, 1972; practice medicine specializing in plastic surgery, San Francisco, 1973-74, Hershey, Pa., 1974-79; asst. prof. surgery U. Calif., San Francisco, 1973-74, exec. head div. plastic surgery, 1973-74; chief plastic surgery San Francisco Gen. Hosp., 1973-74, VA Hosp., San Francisco, 1973-74; co-dir. burn unit San Francisco Gen. Hosp., 1973-74; asso. prof. surgery Pa. State U. Milton S. Hershey Med. Center, Hershey, 1974-78, prof., 1978-79, asso. chief div. plastic surgery, 1974-79, asso. mem. grad. faculty, 1975-79; cons. in plastic surgery Elizabethtown State Crippled Children's Hosp., 1976-79; prof. surgery, chief div. plastic and reconstructive surgery U. Oreg. Health Scis. Center, 1979—, prof. crippled children's div.; head plastic surgery Portland VA Hosp.; courtesy staff St. Vincent's Hosp., Emmanual Hosp., Good Samaritan Hosp., Providence Hosp. (all Portland). Recipient Physicians Recognition award AMA, 1976-79; Pacinian Corpuscle Regeneration study grantee, 1974-75; Am. Soc. Surgery of Hand grantee, 1974-75. Lic. physician, Pa., Calif., Oreg.; diplomate Am. Bd. Surgery, Am. Bd. Plastic Surgery. Mem. AMA, Am. Trauma Soc., Am. Soc. Plastic and Reconstructive Surgery, N.Y. Acad. Scis., Robert H. Ivy Soc., Assn. Am. Med. Colls., Am. Fedn. Clin. Research, Am. Burn Assn., Soc. Cryobiology, Plastic Surgery Research Council, Soc. Head and Neck Surgeons, Am. Soc. Aesthetic Plastic Surgery, Israel Assn. Plastic and Reconstructive Surgery, Assn. Acad. Surgery, Am. Assn. Plastic Surgeons, Am. Assn. Surgery of Trauma, Am. Soc. Surgery of Hand, Pan-Pacific Surg. Assn., Soc. Neurosci., Soc. U. Surgeons, Sigma Xi. Contbr. numerous articles to med. jours. Home: 2816 South Shore Blvd Lake Oswego OR 97034 Office: U Oreg Health Scis Center 3181 SW Sam Jackson Park Rd Portland OR 97201

MILLER, STEPHEN JOHN, univ. adminstr.; b. Secaucus, N.J., Sept. 11, 1936; s. George W. and Constance (Adamowicz) M.; B.S. in Sociology, St. Peter's Coll., Jersey City, 1958; Ph.D., St. Louis U., 1963; m. Robert M. Brahm, Sept. 17, 1960; children—Andrew S., Rodney J., Jessica A. Resident sociologist and research projects dir. Community Studies, Inc., Kansas City, Mo., 1962-64; asst. prof. social research Brandeis U., 1964-67, asso. prof. sociology Florence Heller Grad. Sch. Advanced Studies Social Welfare, 1967-72; asst. dir. Center Community Health and Med. Care, Harvard U. Med. Sch., also Sch. Public Health, 1968-69, asso. dean Urban affairs Med. Sch., 1969-72, asso. dean admissions, 1970-74, asso. prof. preventive and social medicine, 1973-76; v.p. Affiliated Hosps. Center, Boston, 1972-76; asso. provost Northwestern U., 1976—, prof. community medicine Med. Sch., 1976—, mem. bd. McGaw Med. Center, 1976—, exec. com., 1977—; cons. in field. Fellow Am. Sociol. Assn.; mem. Soc. Study Social Problems, Midwest, Eastern sociol. socs. Author: A Division of Nursing Labor, 1965; Prescription for Leadership: Training for the Medical Elite, 1970; dep. editor Jour. Health and Social Behavior, 1969-71. Home: 2116 Central Park Ave Evanston IL 60201 Office: Northwestern Univ Evanston IL 60201. *My objective as a member of the academic community has been to conduct myself as well as my teachers have conducted themselves. Whatever else I may have learned from them, I learned that the university, whether public or private, is a public trust. A university administrator, to be effective, must therefore assume along with any other responsibilities the responsibility for safeguarding and advancing its purposes on behalf of the public.*

MILLER, STEVE, musician; b. Dallas; student U. Wis., U. Copenhagen. Started group with Boz Scaggs, The Ardells, then with Barry Goldberg, The Goldberb/Miller Blues Band, now the Steve Miller Band; albums include: Children of the Future, 1968, Sailor, Brave New World, 1969, Your Saving Grace, 1969, Number Five, 1970, Rock Love, 1971, Recall the Beginning . . . A Journey from Eden, Anthology, The Joker, Fly Like an Eagle, Book of Dreams; appeared TV shows In Concert and The Midnight Spl. Recipient several Platinum Records. Office: care Howard Rose Agy 2029 Century Park E Los Angeles CA 90067*

MILLER, STEWART EDWARD, elec. engr.; b. Milw., Sept. 1, 1918; s. Walter C. and Martha L. (Ferguson) M.; student U. Wis., 1936-39; B.S., Mass. Inst. Tech., 1941, M.S., 1941; m. Helen Jeanette Stroebel, Sept. 27, 1940; children—Jonathan James, Stewart Ferguson, Chris Richard. With Bell Labs., N.Y.C., 1941-49, Holmdel, N.J., 1949—, dir. guided wave research, 1958—. Recipient Ballantine medal Franklin Inst., 1977. Fellow IEEE (Liebmann award 1972, Baker prize 1975), Optical Soc. Am.; mem. AAAS, Nat. Acad. Engring. Patentee in field. Home: 67 Wigwam Rd Locust NJ 07760 Office: Bell Labs Box 400 Holmdel NJ 07733

MILLER, TERRENCE BRENT, lt. gov. Alaska; b. San Francisco, Nov. 10, 1942; s. Con and Nellie W. Miller; B.A., U. Alaska, 1965; M.P.A., Harvard U., 1978; m. Janice I. Bowman, June 19, 1987; 1

dau., Jennifer. Part-owner retail and comml. interests in N. Pole, Alaska; mem. N. Pole City Council, 1963-66, Fairbanks N. Star Borough Assembly, 1964-66, Alaska Ho. of Reps., 1967-69; mem. Alaska Senate, 1969-77, majority leader, 1971-72, pres., 1973-75; lt. gov. Alaska, 1978—. Mem. Alaska Air N.G., 1966-73. Address: Pouch AA Juneau AK 99811*

MILLER, THEODORE ROBERT, physician, educator; b. Phila., Mar. 13, 1907; s. Robert and Regina (Ramspacher) M.; student Swarthmore Coll., Yale, Stockholm U.; M.D., Temple U., 1933; m. Helen E. Reiser, July 31, 1934. Intern Hackensack (N.J.) Hosp., 1933-34, resident, 1934-36, asst. attending surgeon, chief tumor clinic, 1936-39, adj. cons. neoplastic diseases, 1947-52, cons. in surgery, 1959—; asst. attending surgeon City Hosp., N.Y.C.; asst. resident, fellow Meml. Hosp., N.Y.C., 1939-42, clin. asst. surgeon gastric and mixed tumor services, 1947-49, asst. attending surgeon, gastric and mixed tumor services, 1949-59, asso. attending surgeon, 1959-64, attending surgeon chief bone tumor service, 1964-74, sr. attending surgeon, 1974—, chief spl. surgery service, 1964-70; fellow Am.-Scandinavian Found., 1946-47; asso. surgeon Pack Med. Group, N.Y.C., 1947-69, asso. radiotherapist, 1947-69; instr. in surgery Cornell U. Med. Coll., 1952-62, clin. asst. prof., 1962-64, clin. asso. prof. surgery, 1964-70, clin. prof. surgery, 1970—; clin. prof. surgery Rutgers U. Med. Coll.; attending surgeon Doctors Hosp., Med. Arts Center Hosp.; asst. clinician Sloan-Kettering Inst. Cancer Research; courtesy staff N.Y. Infirmary, Princeton Med. Center. Served from capt. to lt. col. M.C., AUS, 1942-46. Diplomate Am. Bd. Surgery. Fellow A.C.S., A.M.A., N.Y. Acad. Medicine, AAAS; mem. N.Y. State, County N.J. State, Middlesex County med. socs., Am. Radium Soc. (pres. 1959-60), N.Y. Cancer Soc., Del. Valley Ornithol. Club, N.Y. Surg. Soc., James Ewing Soc. (pres. 1967-68), N.Y. Acad. Scis., Academia Peruana de Cirguia (corr.), Sociedad Venezolana de Cirugia (corr.), Academia de Zulia (Venezuela) (corr.), Phi Sigma Kappa. Clubs: Yale, Cornell, Chemists (N.Y.C.). Contbr. articles to profl. publs. Home: 373-A New Bedford Ln Jamesburg NJ 08831 Office: 137 E 36th St New York NY 10016

MILLER, THOMAS BURK, state justice; b. Buffalo, May 4, 1929; s. Clarence Edwin and Helen Elizabeth (Burk) M.; A.B., U. Va., 1950; LL.B., W.Va. U., 1956; m. Vaughn Carol Nolte, Apr. 17, 1954; children—Kenneth L. Goudy, George H. Goudy, Brian D. Miller, Bradley R. Miller. Admitted to W.Va. bar, 1956; sr. partner firm Schrader, Miller, Stamp & Recht, Wheeling, 1959-76; justice W.Va. Supreme Ct. Appeals, 1977—. Served with USNR, 1950-53. Mem. Am., W.Va. bar assns., Assn. Trial Lawyers Am., W.Va. Trial Lawyers Assn. Democrat. Methodist. Home: 610 Burkewood Pl Charleston WV 25314 Office: Room E301 State Capitol Charleston WV 25305

MILLER, THOMAS GOSS, lawyer; b. 1914; B.S.L., Beloit Coll., 1936; J.D., Northwestern U., 1938; postgrad. law and accounting U. Wis., 1937. With tax and legal dept. Jos. T. Ryerson & Son Inc., Chgo., 1938—, asst. sec., 1949-50, sec., 1950—, v.p. tax and legal affairs, 1964-79; asst. sec., gen. counsel Inryco, Inc. 1969-79; v.p., gen. counsel Nat. Bur. Property Adminstrn. Home: 4021 Central Ave Western Springs IL 60558 Office: 1824 Prudential Plaza Chicago IL 60601

MILLER, THOMAS HULBERT, JR., former marine corps officer; b. San Antonio, June 3, 1923; s. Thomas Hulbert and Dora S. (Bartlett) M.; student U. Tex.; m. Ida Mai Giddings, May 11, 1943; children—Jacqueline Mai, Jo Ann. Commd. 2d lt. USMC, 1943, designated naval aviator, 1943, advanced through grades to lt. gen., 1975; service in Pacific, Korea; chief staff 3d Amphibious Force, Vietnam, 1970; comdg. gen. 2d Marine Aircraft Wing, 1972; dep. comdr., later comdg. gen. Fleet Marine Forces, Pacific, 1975; dep. chief staff aviation Hdqrs. USMC, 1975-79; ret., 1979. Decorated D.S.M., Legion of Merit (2), D.F.C. (4), Air medal (15), Navy Commendation medal. Mem. Soc. Exptl. Test Pilots, Marine Corps Aviation Assn., Assn. Naval Aviation, Daedalians, Golden Eagles, Am. Helicopter Soc., Am. Radio Relay League. Presbyterian. Club: Masons. Holder 500 kilometer closed course world speed record F4H-1 Phantom aircraft, 1960; first American to fly British Harrier aircraft, 1968. Home: 3689 N Harrison St Arlington VA 22207

MILLER, THOMAS J., atty. gen. Iowa; b. Dubuque, Iowa, Aug. 11, 1944; s. Elmer John and Betty Maude (Kross) M.; B.A., Loras Coll., Dubuque, 1966; J.D., Harvard U., 1969. Admitted to Iowa bar, 1969; with VISTA, 1969-70; legis. asst. to U.S. congressman, 1970-71; legal edn. dir. Balt. Legal Aid Bur., also mem. part-time faculty U. Md. Sch. Law, 1971-73; pvt. practice, McGregor, Iowa, 1973-78; city atty., McGregor, 1975-78; atty. gen. of Iowa, 1978—. Pres. 2d Dist. New Democratic Club, Balt., 1972. Mem. Am. Bar Assn., Iowa Bar Assn., Common Cause. Roman Catholic. Office: Hoover Bldg 2d Floor Des Moines IA 50319

MILLER, THOMAS LEE, motion picture and TV producer, writer; b. Milw., Aug. 31, 1940; s. Edward Allan and Shirley Annette (Plous) M.; B.S., U. Wis., 1962. Dir. devel. 20th Century Fox TV, 1967-68; v.p. devel. Paramount TV, 1968-72; partner Miller-Milkis-Boyett Prodns., Inc., Hollywood, Calif., 1972—; exec. producer Happy Days, Laverne and Shirley, Petrocelli, Blansky's Beauties, Mork and Mindy, Makin' It, Sweepstakes, Angie, Out of the Blue TV series; co-producer Silver Streak, Foul Play feature films. Mem. Writers Guild Am. West, Inc., Acad. Motion Picture Arts and Scis., Acad. TV Arts and Scis., Producers Guild Am. Co-creator TV series: Nanny and the Professor, 1967, Love American Style, 1968, Me and The Chimp, 1971, Sweepstakes, 1979, Out of the Blue, 1979. Office: 5451 Marathon St Hollywood CA 90038

MILLER, THOMAS MARSHALL, air line cons.; b. Mineral Wells, Tex., Oct. 19, 1910; s. Van Dorn and Ida (Crockett) M.; LL.B., Houston Law Sch., 1935; m. Edith Mae Blake, July 8, 1936; children—Kay (Mrs. Robert Amick), Thomas Marshall, Robert, Philp, James. Reporter, Dun & Bradstreet, Inc., Houston, Dallas and Ft. Worth, 1926-36, office mgr., Houston, 1936-42; v.p. traffic and sales Chgo. & So. Air Lines, Inc., Memphis, 1942-53; sr. v.p. mktg., dir. Delta Air Lines, Inc., Atlanta, until 1973, dir., mktg. cons., 1973—; dir. Citizens & So. Bank of Fulton County, East Point, Ga., Charter Med. Corp., Macon, Ga., Sea Pines Co., Hilton Head Island, S.C. Pres. Air Traffic Conf. Am., 1964. Mem. Am., Ga. bar assns., Inst. Certified Travel Agts. (vice chmn. emeritus). Republican. Episcopalian. Home: One Yonah Dr NE Atlanta GA 30309 Office: Delta Air Lines Inc Atlanta Airport Atlanta GA 30320

MILLER, THOMAS MILTON, banker; b. Corydon, Ind., Mar. 2, 1930; s. R. Earl and Catherine (Hudson) M.; B.S. in Bus., Ind. U., 1952; postgrad. U. Wis. Grad. Sch. Banking 1961; m. Kathryn Janet Owens, Aug. 28, 1954; children—Kimberleigh Kathryn, Thomas Milton, Jennifer Allen. With Ind. Nat. Bank, Indpls., 1954—, head Ind. div., 1964-68, sr. v.p., head met. 1968-71, exec. v.p., head comml. banking div., 1971-76, pres., 1976—, chmn. bd., 1979—, also dir.; vice chmn. Ind. Nat. Corp.; v.p., dir. Ind. Nat. Corp.; dir. Corydon Bank, Hook Drugs, Inc., State Life Ins. Co., London Interstate Bank, Euratlantis Maritime Bank. Bd. dirs. Historic Landmarks Found. Ind.; trustee, mem. exec. com. Methodist Hosp.; trustee Marian Coll., Indpls.; bd. dirs., mem. exec. com. Indpls. Conv. and Visitors Bur.; mem. adv. bd. Ind. U.-Purdue U., Indpls. Served to 1st lt. AUS, 1952-54. Mem. Am. Bankers Assn. (Ind. v.p. 1967-69, regional v.p. 1969-72), Ind. (citizenship com. 1969—, dir.), Indpls. (govtl. affairs com. 1968—) chambers of commerce, Ind. U. Alumni Assn. (exec. council), Ind. Soc. Chgo., Sigma Chi. Republican. Methodist. Clubs: Masons; Indiana University Varsity; Columbia (dir.), Meridian Hills Country (Indpls.). Home: 11809 Forest Dr Carmel IN 46032 Office: 1 Indiana Sq Indianapolis IN 46204

MILLER, THOMAS WILLIAMS, univ. dean; b. Pottstown, Pa., July 2, 1930; s. Franklin Sullivan and Margaret (Williams) M.; B.S. in Music Edn., West Chester (Pa.) State Coll., 1952; M.A., East Carolina U., Greenville, N.C., 1957; Mus.A.D. (Univ. fellow), Boston U., 1964; m. Edythe Edwards, Dec. 20, 1952; children—Theresa, Thomas, Christine, Stefanie. Dir. instrumental music Susquenita (Pa.) High Sch., 1955-56; instr. trumpet East Carolina U., 1957-61, asst. dean Sch. Music, 1962-68, dean, 1969-71; vis. prof. U. Hawaii, Honolulu, 1968; dean Sch. Music Northwestern U., Evanston, Ill., 1971—. Served with AUS, 1952-55. Named Distinguished Alumnus, West Chester State Coll., 1975. Mem. Music Educators Nat. Conf. (life), Nat. Assn. Schs. Music (grad. commr.), Music Tchrs. Nat. Assn., Coll. Music Soc., Pi Kappa Lambda (nat. pres. 1978), Phi Mu Alpha Sinfonia (hon.). Contbr. articles to profl. jours. Home: 2103 Orrington Ave Evanston IL 60201 Office: Northwestern U Sch of Music Evanston IL 60201

MILLER, THORMUND AUBREY, lawyer; b. Pocatello, Idaho, July 14, 1919; s. Roy Edmund and Lillian (Thordarson) M.; B.A., Reed Coll., 1941; LL.B., Columbia U., 1948; grad. Advanced Mgmt. Program, Harvard Bus. Sch., 1961; m. Hannah A. Flansburgh, Feb. 10, 1946; children—Karen Lynette, Christine Alison. Admitted to Calif. bar, 1949, D.C. bar, 1951; mem. firm McCutchen, Thomas, Matthews, Griffiths & Greene, San Francisco, 1948-50; atty. So. Pacific Transp. Co., Washington, 1950-56, asst. gen. atty., 1956-59, gen. atty., 1959-66, sr. gen. atty., San Francisco, 1966-75, gen. solicitor, 1975-79, gen. counsel So. Pacific Communications Co., San Francisco, 1970-79, gen. commerce counsel So. Pacific Transp. Co., 1979—; dir. So. Pacific Pipelines Co., So. Pacific Communications Co. Pres., Wood Acres Citizens Assn., Bethesda, Md., 1955-56; mem. exec. com. Holbrook Palmer Recreation Park Found., 1979—; mem. alumni bd. Reed Coll., 1971-72. Served with USNR, 1942-46. Mem. Am. Bar Assn., Calif. State Bar, Transp. Research Forum, Assn. of ICC Practitioners, Fed. Communications Bar Assn. Presbyterian. Clubs: University (Washington); San Francisco Comml. Home: 228 Polhemus Ave Atherton CA 94025 Office: 1 Market Plaza San Francisco CA 94105

MILLER, VICTOR CHARLES, educator; b. Stamford, Conn., Mar. 17, 1922; s. Walter Strong and Mary Priscilla (Gortner) M.; A.B., Columbia, 1943, M.A., 1948, Ph.D., 1953; children—Michelle, Denise. Photogeologist, Sinclair Oil Co., Denver, 1947-49; pres. Miller-McCulloch Ltd., cons. photogeologists, Calgary, Can., 1952-55, V.C. Miller & Assos. Photogeologists Ltd. Calgary, 1955-57, Miller & Assos., cons. photogeologists, Denver, 1957-62; chmn. dep. geology U. Libya, Tripoli, 1962-64; chmn. dept. geology C.W. Post Coll., Greenvale, N.Y., 1964-67; prof. dept. geography and geology Ind. State U., Terre Haute, Ind., 1967—. Served with USAAF, 1943-45; ETO. Fellow Geol. Soc. Am.; mem. Am. Assn. Petroleum Geologists, Am. Soc. Photogrammetry, Assn. Am. Geographers. Author: Photogeology, 1961. Home: 28 Heritage Dr Terre Haute IN 47803. *I've never derived any particular satisfaction from competing and winning for the sake of competing and winning. The building of empire is meaningless to me. The highways I follow are not those congested with gripping, grappling road-hogs, but silent country lanes through pastures where working and living are such a quiet joy that whatever success I achieve proves to be the product of appreciation and inner contentment, rather than of labor.*

MILLER, WALLACE, JR., lawyer; b. Macon, Ga., May 28, 1915; s. Wallace and Mary (Shewell) M.; B.S., U. Ga., 1938; m. Betsy, Oct. 4, 1939; children—Betsy, Judith, Mary Ann, Wallace III, Patricia. Admitted to Ga. bar, 1939, U.S. Supreme Ct. bar, 1950; partner firm Miller, Miller & Miller and predecessor, Macon, 1946-68, Jones, Cork, Miller & Benton, Macon, 1968—. Mem. Bibb County (Ga.) Bd. Edn., 1952-68, sec., 1964-67, pres., 1967-68; bd. dirs. Forward Macon. Served with USAAF, 1943-46; Guam. Fellow Am. Coll. Trial Lawyers; mem. Macon, Am. bar assns., State Bar Ga., Am. Judicature Soc., Ga. Def. Lawyers. Methodist. Clubs: Lions, Elks (Macon). Home: 5044 Wellington Dr Macon GA 31210 Office: 500 First Nat Bank Bldg Macon GA 31201

MILLER, WALTER NEAL, ins. co. exec.; b. N.Y.C., Nov. 26, 1929; s. Morton and Kathryn (Gersten) M.; B.A., Swarthmore Coll., 1951; m. Nancy Louise Clapp, Sept. 11, 1954; children—Scott, Timothy, David, Kathryn, Amy. With N.Y. Life Ins. Co., N.Y.C., 1951—, sr. v.p., actuary, 1979—. Mem. Soc. Actuaries, Am. Acad. Actuaries, Canadian Inst. Actuaries. Author: (with others) Analysis of Actuarial Theory for Variable Life Insurance, 1969; contbr. articles to profl. jours. Home: 4 Pine Ln Rye NY 10580 Office: NY Life Ins Co 51 Madison Ave New York NY 10010

MILLER, WARREN EDWARD, polit. scientist; b. Hawarden, Iowa, Mar. 26, 1924; s. John Carroll and Mildred Ovedia (Lien) M.; B.S., U. Oreg., 1948, M.S., 1950; Ph.D., Maxwell Sch. Citizenship and Public Affairs, Syracuse U., 1954; Ph.D. (hon.), U. Goteborg (Sweden), 1972; children by previous marriage—Jeffrey Ralph, Jennifer Louise. Asst. study dir. Survey Research Center, Inst. Social Research, U. Mich., 1951-53, study dir., 1953-56, research asso., 1956-59, program dir., 1959-68, research coordinator polit. behavior program, 1968-70, dir. Center Polit. Studies, Inst. Social Research, 1970—, asst. prof. polit. sci., 1956-58, asso. prof., 1958-63, prof., 1963—; asst. prof. polit. sci. U. Calif., Berkeley, 1954-56; fellow Center Advanced Study in Behavioral Scis., 1961-62; exec. dir. Inter-univ. Consortium for Polit. and Social Research, 1962-70; vis. prof. U. Tilburg (Netherlands), 1973, U. Geneva, 1973, European U. Inst., Florence, Italy, 1979; trustee Inst. Am. Univs., 1970—. Served with USAAF, 1943-46. Recipient Disting. Alumnus award Maxwell Sch. Citizenship and Public Affairs, Syracuse U., 1974, Disting. Faculty Achievement award U. Mich., 1977. Fellow Am. Acad. Arts and Scis.; mem. Am. Polit. Sci. Assn. (pres. 1979-80), Internat. Polit. Sci. Assn. (council 1969-73), M.W. Polit. Sci. Assn., Internat. Soc. Polit. Psychology, So. Polit. Sci. Assn., Social Sci. History Assn. (pres. 1979-80). Author books including: (with others) The American Voter, 1960; (with T.E. Levitin) Leadership and Change: Presidential Elections from 1952-1976, 1977; (with others) The American National Election Studies Data Sourcebook, 1952-1978, 1980; contbr. articles to profl. publs.; editorial bd. Am. Polit. Sci. Rev., 1966-71, Computers and the Humanities, 1969-71; editorial adv. bd. Sage Electoral Studies Yearbook, 1974—. Office: Center for Polit Studies Inst Social Research U Mich PO Box 1248 Ann Arbor MI 48106

MILLER, WAYNE CHARLES, educator; b. N.Y.C., Nov. 3, 1939; s. Charles Henry and Florence Violet (Keenan) M.; B.A. magna cum laude (Rand McNally Centennial scholar), St. John's U., Jamaica, N.Y., 1960; M.A. (N.Y State Regents fellow), Columbia U., 1961; Ph.D., N.Y. U., 1968; m. Patricia Clemens, Sept. 2, 1973; 1 son, Wayne Joshua; children by previous marriage—Alison Catherine, Heather, Mary. Asso. prof. English, SUNY, Oneonta, 1967-70; mem. faculty U. Cin., 1970—, prof. English, 1972—; producer TV series The Policeman: Images and Realities, 1973, Open Forum, 1974, Changing Cin., 1975, Religion Today, 1976, Decision Makers, 1977-78, for Sta. WCET-TV, Cin. Served to capt. USAF, 1962-67. Fellow SUNY, 1969, U. Cin., 1971, Taft Found., 1972; grantee Ohio Program in Humanities, 1973-77, Nat. Endowment for Humanities, 1976, 77, 79. Mem. MLA, Am. Acad. Polit. and Social Sci., Soc. Study Multi-Ethnic Lit. U.S., Delta Kappa Tau. Author: An Armed America—Its Face in Fiction: A History of the American Military Novel, 1970; A Gathering of Ghetto Writers: Irish, Italian, Jewish, Black and Puerto Rican, 1971; A Comprehensive Bibliography for the Study of American Minorities, 1976; A Handbook for the Study of American Minorities, 1976. Home: 343 Compton Hills Dr Cincinnati OH 45215 Office: Dept English Univ Cincinnati Cincinnati OH 45221

MILLER, WILBUR CASTEEL, univ. pres.; b. Des Moines, Aug. 26, 1923; s. Cecil S. and Laura M. (Kesterson) M.; student Drake U., 1941-43, St. Louis U., 1943-44; B.S. in Bus. Adminstrn., U. Denver, 1948, M.A., 1949, Ph.D., 1953, LL.D., 1972; m. Viretta A. Shaw, Mar. 30, 1946; children—W. Kent, Jill M. Faculty dept. psychology U. Denver, 1949-72, prof., 1963-72, dean Grad. Sch., 1964-65, vice chancellor acad. affairs, dean faculty, 1965-72, acting chancellor, 1966-67; pres. Drake U., Des Moines, 1972. Cons. USAF Acad., 1957; co-dir. research project in maladaptive behavior U. Colo. Med. Sch., 1960-72; Ford Found. cons. to Venezuela, 1968-69. Served with AUS, 1943-46. U. Mich. postdoctoral fellow, 1963-64. Fellow Am. Psychol. Assn.; mem. Colo. (past pres.), Rocky Mountain (past pres.) psychol. assns., Phi Beta Kappa, Sigma Xi. Author: Personality Social Class and Delinquency, 1966; contbg. author: New Viewpoints in the Social Sciences, 1958; Readings in Child Development and Personality, 1965. Home: 227 37th St Des Moines IA 50312

MILLER, WILLIAM CHRISTIAN, investment banker; b. N.Y.C., Oct. 7, 1905; s. William Christian and Virginia (Temple) M.; B.S., Rutgers U., 1926, LL.D., 1966; m. Caroline Burdett Mowry, Dec. 1, 1933; children—Carolyn (Mrs. Robert B. Knutson), William Christian, Sarah Kip. With Nat. City Co., 1926-29, Cassatt & Co., 1929-34; treas. Rustless Iron Co., 1934-35; with W.E. Hutton & Co., N.Y.C., 1936-74, partner, 1945-74; with Reynolds Securities Inc., N.Y.C., 1975-78; with Thomson McKinnon Securities Inc., N.Y.C., 1978—; dir. Consol. Refining Co., Dayton Malleable Inc., Scope, Inc., Econs. Lab., Inc. Trustee Rutgers Research and Edn. Found.; v.p., trustee Englewood Hosp.; trustee Rutgers U. Mem. Newcomen Soc., Pilgrims. Presbyn. Clubs: Recess, Stock Exchange Luncheon (N.Y.C.); Englewood Field, Englewood, Englewood (N.J.); Nantucket (Mass.) Yacht. Home: 214 Walnut St Englewood NJ 07631 Office: Thomson McKinnon Securities Inc One New York Plaza New York NY 10004

MILLER, WILLIAM FRANKLIN, physician; b. Stone Creek, Ohio, Jan. 16, 1920; s. Karl R. and Helen A. (Miller) M.; B.A., Wittenberg U., 1942; M.S., Case Western Res. U., 1945; m. Laura Barker, Nov. 22, 1942 (dec. Mar. 1957); children—Laura Leslie, Karla Jon, William Christopher, Lisa Diane; m. 2d, Jean Stevens, Jan. 12, 1958; 1 dau., Katy Cork. Intern, City Hosp., Cleve., 1945-56; resident VA Hosp., Dayton, Ohio, 1946-48; resident VA Hosp., Dallas, 1948-49, chief resident, 1949, 50, fellow, 1950-51; clin. instr. Southwestern Med. Sch., U. Tex., Dallas, 1951-53, asst. prof., 1953-57, asso. prof. medicine, 1957-67, prof., 1967—; dir. pulmonary div. Methodist Hosp., Dallas, 1967—; cons. staff Presbyterian, St. Paul, Baylor, VA hosps. (all Dallas); cons. Nat. Heart, Lung and Blood Inst.; med. dir. respiratory therapy tng. program El Centro Coll., Dallas, 1967-69, 78—. Mem. Tex. Area 5 Health Systems Agency Planning Bd., 1979—. Served to maj. M.C., AUS, 1946-48. Diplomate Am. Bd. Internal Medicine. Fellow ACP, Am. Coll. Chest Physicians (gov. Tex. 1970-74, chmn. respiratory therapy com. 1969-72), recipient best movie award 1967); mem. Am. Fedn. Clin. Research, So. Soc. Clin. Investigation, Central Soc. Clin. Research, AAAS, Tex. Thoracic Soc., Am. Thoracic Soc., Soc. Critical Care Medicine, AMA, Tex. Med. Assn. (award 1976), Assn. Schs. Allied Health Professions, Assn. Advancement Med. Instrumentation, Pan Am. Med. Assn., Am. Med. Writers Assn., Nat. Hospice Orgn. (N. Tex. adv. bd. 1978—), Am. Assn. Biofeedback Clinicians, Soc. Advancement Med. Systems, Am. Assn. Respiratory Therapy (Bird lit. award 1974, 78), Blue Key, Skull and Chain, Sigma Xi. Med. editor Respiratory Care jour. Am. Assn. Respiratory Therapy, 1966—; sr. editor Chest, 1971-74; contbr. over 130 articles to profl. jours. Home: 5533 Northaven Rd Dallas TX 75229 Office: PO Box 22 5999 Dallas TX 75265. *My greatest pleasures in life have come from my efforts to understand human nature and from service to others in their pursuit of health and happiness.*

MILLER, WILLIAM FREDERICK, educator; b. Vincennes, Ind., Nov. 19, 1925; s. William and Elsie M. (Everts) M.; student Vincennes U., 1946-47; B.S., Purdue U., 1949, M.S., 1951, Ph.D., 1956 D.Sc., 1972; m. Patty J. Smith, June 19, 1949; 1 son, Rodney Wayne. Mem. staff Argonne Nat. Lab., 1955-64, asso. physicist, 1956-59, dir. applied math. div., 1959-64; prof. computer sci. Stanford U., Palo Alto, Calif., 1965-79, Herbert Hoover prof. pub. and pvt. mgmt., 1979—, asso. provost for computing, 1968-70, v.p. for research, 1970-71, v.p., provost, 1971-78, mem. Stanford Assos., 1972—; pres., chief exec. officer SRI Internat., Menlo Park, Calif., 1979—; profl. lectr. applied math. U. Chgo., 1962-64; vis. prof. math. Purdue U., 1962-63; vis. scholar Center for Advanced Study in Behavioral Scis., 1976. Dir. Fireman's Fund Ins. Co., Ann. Revs. Inc., Boothe Fin. Co., Varian Assos. Inc. Mem. computer sci. and engring. bd. Nat. Acad. Sci., 1968-71; mem. corp. com. on computers in edn. Brown U., 1972—; mem. policy bd. EDUCOM Planning Council on Computing in Edn., 1974-79, chmn., 1974-76; bd. dirs. SIAM Inst. Math. in Society, 1977-79; ednl. adv. bd. Guggenheim Meml. Found., 1976—; com. postdoctoral and doctoral research staff NRC, 1977—; bd. dirs. RESOLVE, Center for Environ. Conflict Resolution, 1978—. Served to 2d lt. F.A., AUS, 1943-46. Mem. Am. Math. Soc., Am. Phys. Soc., AAAS, Assn. Computing Machinery, IEEE, Sigma Xi. Asso. editor Pattern Recognition Jour., 1968—, Jour. Computational Physics, 1970-74. Home: 821 San Francisco Ct Stanford CA 94305 Office: SRI Internat 333 Ravenswood Ave Menlo Park CA 94025

MILLER, WILLIAM H(OWARD), fin. public relations co. exec.; b. Cin., Jan. 27, 1941; s. Joseph R. and Elaine (Goldman) M.; student U. Pa., 1959-61; B.A., U. Cin., 1963, M.B.A., 1965; m. Karen Pilder, June 21, 1964; children—Bradley, Craig. Fin. analyst Ford Motor Co., Dearborn, Mich., 1965-67; fin. specialist Booz Allen Hamilton, Chgo., 1967-69; midwest fin. liaison Fin. Relations Bd., Chgo., 1969-71, v.p., 1971-73, sr. v.p., 1973-76, exec. v.p., 1976—. Clubs: Milw. Athletic, Union League (Chgo.). Home: 8837 Kenneth Terr Skokie IL 60076 Office: 150 E Huron St Chicago IL 60611

MILLER, WILLIAM HUGHES, theoretical chemist; b. Kosciusko, Miss., Mar. 16, 1941; s. Weldon Howard and Jewel Irene (Hughes) M.; B.S., Ga. Inst. Tech., 1963; A.M., Harvard U., 1964, Ph.D., 1967; m. Margaret Ann Westbrook, June 4, 1966; children—Alison Leslie, Emily Sinclaire. Jr. fellow Harvard U., 1967-69; NATO postdoctoral fellow Freiburg (Germany) U., 1967-68; asst. prof. chemistry U. Calif., Berkeley, 1969-72, asso. prof., 1972-74, prof., 1974—; fellow Churchill Coll., Cambridge (Eng.) U., 1975-76. Recipient Ann. prize

Internat. Acad. Quantum Molecular Sci., 1974; Alfred P. Sloan fellow, 1970-72; Camille and Henry Dreyfus fellow, 1973-78; Guggenheim fellow, 1975-76. Mem. Am. Phys. Soc., AAAS. Research, numerous publs. in field. Home: 617 Santa Rosa Ave Berkeley CA 94707 Office: Dept Chemistry U Calif Berkeley CA 94720

MILLER, WILLIAM JACK, educator; b. Nathan's Creek, N.C., Feb. 7, 1927; s. William Thomas and Virginia Juanita (Bledsoe) M.; B.S., N.C. State U., 1949, M.S., 1950; Ph.D., U. Wis., 1952; m. Marianna Morris, Dec. 21, 1950; children—Virginia Miller McGuffey, Nancy Miller Jones, Barbara, William Jack. Research asso. U. Ill., Urbana, 1952-53; asst. prof. animal and dairy sci. dept. U. Ga., Athens, 1953-58, asso. prof., 1958-64, prof., 1964-73, Alumni Found. Distinguished prof., 1973—, chmn. animal nutrition grad. faculty, 1963-66, 67—. Served in USNR, 1945-46. Calcium Carbonate Trace Mineral travel fellow, 1969; named Ga. Outstanding Scientist, Ga. Sci. and Tech. Commn., 1969; Outstanding Research Scientist, U. Ga. Agrl. Alumni Assn. Mem. Am. Inst. Nutrition, Am. Soc. Animal Sci. (Gustav Bohstedt award 1971), Fedn. Am. Socs. for Exptl. Biology, Am. Dairy Sci. Assn. (Am. Feed Mfg. research award 1963, Borden award 1971), Soc. Exptl. Biology and Medicine, Assn. So. Agrl. Workers, Am. Forage and Grassland Council, Soc. Environ. Geochemistry and Health, Sigma Xi (Excellence in Research award 1969), Gamma Sigma Delta (Distinguished Service award 1965, Internat. award 1970, Sr. Faculty Distinguished Service award 1970), Phi Kappa Phi. Contbr. articles in field to profl. jours. Home: 215 Harben Pl Athens GA 30606 Office: Dept Animal and Dairy Sci L-P Bldg U Ga Athens GA 30602

MILLER, WILLIAM JESSE, JR., ins. co. exec.; b. Columbus, Kans., Nov. 5, 1925; s. William Jesse and Mona Clare (Huffman) M.; B.S. in Bus., U. Kans., 1948; LL.B., U. Washburn, 1952; Advanced Mgmt. Program, Harvard U., 1975; m. Mary Louise Snook, May 10, 1946 (div. Feb. 1962); children—Marcia, Nancy, William H.; m. 2d, Betty J. Schreck; children—Melissa, Lisa, Mark Baber. Indsl. engr. John Morrel & Co., Topeka, 1948-51; admitted to Kans. bar, 1952; individual practice law, Sabetha, Kans., 1952; pres., dir. Security Benefit Life Ins. Co., Topeka, 1954—; dir. Security Equity Fund, Inc., Security Distbrs., Inc., Security Mgmt. Co., Inc., Security Bond Fund, Inc., Security Ultra Fund, Inc., Columbian Nat. Title Co.; adv. dir. 1st Nat. Bank Topeka. Chmn. United Way Campaign, 1977, pres., 1979. Served to lt. USNR, 1944-47, 52-54. Mem. Assn. Life Ins. Counsel, Kans. Life Assn. (pres. 1967-69), Kans. Life and Health Guaranty Assn. (chmn., dir.), Kans. Assn. Commerce and Industry (dir.), Am., Kans., Topeka bar assns., Am. Council Life Ins. (dir. 1979—), Topeka C. of C. (dir. 1973-76), Beta Theta Pi. Republican. Episcopalian. Clubs: Topeka Country (pres., dir. 1971-75), Cosmopolitan (Topeka). Home: 2322 Mayfair Pl Topeka KS 66611 Office: 700 Harrison St Topeka KS 66636

MILLER, WILLIAM KELLER, internat. orgn. exec., former fgn. service officer; b. Lancaster, Pa., Feb. 25, 1920; s. Robert Everts and Elizabeth (Keller) M.; A.B., Haverford Coll., 1941; M.A., Fletcher Sch. Law and Diplomacy, 1942; postgrad. Georgetown U., 1947-48; m. Margaret Lavin, June 29, 1947; children—Michael Robert, Mary Margaret, William Keller, Elizabeth Barbara. Requirements officer Fgn. Econ. Adminstrn., 1944-45; with State Dept., 1945-78; 1st sec., consul Am. embassy, Helsinki, 1957-58, counselor econ. affairs, 1959-61, assigned to NATO Def. Coll., Paris, France, 1961-62, counselor econ. affairs Am. embassy, Taipei, Taiwan, 1962-63; chief trade agreements div. State Dept., 1964; dep. dir. Office Internat. Finance and Econ. Analysis, 1964-65; dir. Office Maritime Affairs, 1965-68, Office Telecommunications, 1968-70; minister econ. affairs U.S. Mission, Geneva, Switzerland, 1971-74; minister econ. and comml. affairs Am. embassy, London, 1974-78; exec. dir. Internat. Sugar Orgn., London, 1978—. Mem. Phi Beta Kappa. Clubs: Reform, Hampstead Golf. Home: 6758 Towne Lane Rd McLean VA 22101 also 34 Devere Gardens London W8 England Office: Internat Sugar Orgn 28 Haymarket London England

MILLER, WILLIAM MICHAEL, cosmetics co. exec.; b. Istanbul, Turkey, Feb. 5, 1923; came to U.S., 1930; s. William Benson and Helen Agnes M.; student Princeton U., 1943-44; B.S. in Econs., Wharton Sch., U. Pa., 1947; m. Nevine Sirry, Dec. 21, 1973; children—Patricia, Lane, Peter, Hope. Buyer, L. Bamberger & Co., Newark, 1947-52; v.p. mktg. Brunswick Corp., Chgo., 1952-66; exec. v.p. Elizabeth Arden, Inc., N.Y.C., 1966-76, London, 1976—. Served with USMC, 1942-46, 50-52. Republican. Club: N.Y. Yacht. Office: 13 Hanover Sq London W1 England

MILLER, WILLIAM OWEN, lawyer; b. Atlanta, Sept. 2, 1925; s. Frank Alexander and Mary Jeanette (Rauschenberg) M.; B.S., U. S.C., 1946; LL.B., Atlanta Law Sch., 1949; LL.M., George Washington U., 1964, M.S., 1969; m. Jane Goolsby, June 20, 1945; children—Rebecca Jane Miller Chambers, William Owen, Lee St. Clair. Served as enlisted man U.S. Navy, 1943-46; commd. U.S. Navy, 1946, advanced through grades to rear adm., 1975; judge adv. gen. Navy Dept., 1976-78, ret., 1978; adminstr. firm Sutherland, Asbill & Brennan, Atlanta and Washington, 1978—. Decorated Navy Commendation medal, D.S.M. Mem. Am. Bar Assn., Fed. Bar Assn., Judge Advocates Assn., Phi Beta Kappa. Contbr. articles on internat. law to various publs. Home: 116 Elizabeth St Atlanta GA 30307 Office: 3100 1st Nat Bank Tower Atlanta GA 30303 also 1666 K St NW Washington DC 20006

MILLER, WILLIAM SCOTT, JR., lawyer; b. Williford, Ark., Apr. 15, 1921; s. William Scott and Thelma (Camp) M.; B.S. summa cum laude, Miss. State U., 1943; LL.B., Ark. Law Sch., 1949; m. Imogene Puckett, May 9, 1944; children-Gary Charles, Alan Scott. Admitted to Ark. bar, 1949; since practiced in Little Rock; mem. firm Eichenbaum, Scott & Miller, 1949—, partner, 1957—; lectr. Ark. Law Sch., Mo. Bar Assn., Central Ark. Estate Council. Adv. council to commr. internal revenue, 1973-74. Mem. exec. bd. Quapaw Area council Boy Scouts Am., 1967-77. Bd. dirs. Little Rock Boys Club; pres., trustee Ark. Bapt. Med. Center. Served to capt., inf., AUS. 1943-46; ETO. Decorated Silver Star medal, Bronze Star medal with oak leaf cluster, Purple Heart. Mem. Am., Ark. (past com. chmn.), Pulaski County (past pres.) bar assns., Am. Judicature Soc. Rotarian (past pres.). Home 3205 Shenandoah Valley Little Rock AR 72212 Office: Tower Bldg Little Rock AR 72201

MILLER, WILLIAM TAYLOR, educator, chemist; b. Winston-Salem, N.C., Aug. 24, 1911; s. William Taylor and Katie Jane (McMahan) M.; A.B., Duke, 1932, Ph.D., 1935; m. Betty Stewart Robb, July 1951. Mem. faculty Cornell U., Ithaca, N.Y., 1936—, prof. chemistry, 1947-77, prof. emeritus, 1977—; fluorocarbon research group leader Manhattan Project at Columbia U., Carbide & Carbon Chem. Corp., N.Y.C., 1943-46; cons. to govt. and industry. Fellow AAAS; mem. Am. Chem. Soc. (award for creative work in fluorine chemistry 1974), London Chem. Soc., Phi Beta Kappa, Sigma Xi. Author: Preparation of Fluorocarbons by Polymerization of Olefins, Vol. VII-I Nat. Nuclear Energy Series, 1951; also articles. Inventor organic fluorine products and chem. processes including chlorotrifluoroethylene polymers, oil and plastic utilized in the first gaseous diffusion plant for the separation of uranium isotopes during World War II. Home: 100 Sunset Park Ithaca NY 14850

MILLER, WILMER GLENN, chemist, educator; b. Mt. Orab, O., Aug. 28, 1932; s. Clarence William and Mary Leona (Klein) M.; B.S., Capital U., 1954; Ph.D., U. Wis., 1958; m. Caroline Harriet Tautges, July 23, 1976; 1 son, Peter Andrew. Research fellow Harvard, 1958-59; research fellow U. Minn., Mpls., 1959-60, asso. prof., 1967-70, prof. chemistry, 1970—; asst. prof. U. Ia., 1960-66, asso. prof., 1966-67. USPHS postdoctoral fellow, 1958, Guggenheim fellow, 1964, U.S.A.-USSR exchange scientist, 1973. Mem. Am. Chem. Soc., AAAS, Sigma Xi. Home: 2732 W River Rd Minneapolis MN 55406

MILLER, ZELL BRYAN, lt. gov. Ga.; b. Young Harris, Ga., Feb. 24, 1932; s. Grady Stephen and Birdie (Bryan) M.; student Young Harris Coll.; A.B., M.A., U. Ga.; m. Shirley Carver, Jan. 14, 1954; children—Murphy Carver, Matthew Stephen. Dir., Ga. Bd. Probation, 1965-67; dep. dir. Ga. Dept. Corrections, 1967-68; exec. sec. to gov. Ga., 1968-73; mem. State Bd. Pardons and Paroles, Atlanta, 1973-75; lt. gov. Ga., 1975—; prof. polit. sci. and history U. Ga., Young Harris Coll., 1959-64. Mem. Ga. Ho. of Reps., 1960; mem. Ga. Senate, 1962-64; mayor, Young Harris, 1959; exec. dir. Democratic Com. Ga., 1971-72; bd. dirs. Towns County Hosp. Authority. Served with USMCR, 1953-56. Mem. Ga. Sch. Food Services Assn. (life), Gridiron Soc. U. Ga., Blue Key. Methodist. Clubs: Masons, Lions. Office: 418 State Capitol Atlanta GA 30334*

MILLETT, JOHN DAVID, ednl. adminstr.; b. Indpls., Mar. 14, 1912; s. Grover Allan and Helen (Welch) M.; A.B. DePauw U., 1933, LL.D., 1950; A.M., Columbia U., 1935, Ph.D., 1938; LL.D. Fenn Coll., 1954, Xavier U., 1959, Ohio State U., 1961, Denison U., 1963, Kent State U., 1964, U. Akron, 1964, Ohio Wesleyan U., 1966; Litt.D., U. Toledo, 1966; L.H.D., Miami U., 1963, Findlay Coll., 1965, Waynesburg Coll., 1966; D.Ped., Youngstown U., 1964, U. Dayton, 1967; LL.D., U. Cin., 1967, Central Mich. U., 1968, Central State U., 1968, Mt. Union, 1969, Chase Coll., 1969, Urbana Coll., 1975; L.H.D., Marion Coll. 1968, D. Pub. Service, Garfield Coll., 1973; m. Catherine Letsinger, Sept. 2, 1934; children—Allan R., David P., Stephen M. Asst. Columbia, N.Y.C., 1935-38, asso. prof. pub. adminstrn., 1945-48, prof., 1948-53; pres. Miami U., Oxford, Ohio, 1953-64; chancellor, Ohio Board of Regents, 1964-72; v.p. Acad. for Ednl. Devel., Washington, 1972—. Mem. staff Pres.' Com. on Adminstrv. Mgmt., Washington 1936, Social Sci. Research Council, N.Y.C., 1939-41, Nat. Resources Planning Bd., 1941-42; asst. to exec. dir. Hoover Commn. on Orgn. Exec. Br. of Govt., 1948-49; exec. dir. Commn. on Financing Higher Edn., 1949-52; cons. U. of the Philippines, 1954. Trustee Education Testing Service, 1959-63, 66-70, chmn., 1962-63, 69-70; trustee Coll. Entrance Exam. Board, 1961-64, DePauw U., 1977—; chmn. Ohio Commn. Edn. Beyond High Sch., 1962-63; mem. Nat. Bd. Grad. Edn.; mem. of Nat. Commn. for UNESCO, 1965-70; del. Internat. Conf. Inst. Adminstrv. Sci., Bern, 1947. Served from maj. to col. AUS, 1942-46, 47. Decorated Legion of Merit. Postdoctoral fellow, London, 1938-39. Mem. Am. Polit. Sci. Assn. (exec. council), Am. Soc. Pub. Adminstrn. (pres. 1960-61), Nat. Assn. State Us. (sec. 1955-61), State UN Assn. (pres. 1961-63), Am. Legion, Nat. Acad. Pub. Adminstrn. (chmn. 1966-72), Inst. Am. Univs. (trustee 1963—), Phi Delta Theta (pres. 1972-74). Methodist. Club: Cosmos (Washington). Author: The Process and Organization of Government Planning, 1947; Financing Higher Education in the U.S., 1953; Management in the Public Service, 1954; Government and Public Administration, 1959; The Organization and Role of the Army Service Forces, 1959; The Academic Community, 1962; Organization for the Public Service, 1966; Strengthening Community in Higher Education, 1974; Politics and Higher Education, 1974; New Structures of Campus Power, 1978; others. Contbr. to periodicals. Home: 10444 Democracy Ln Potomac MD 20854 Office: 1414 22d St Washington DC 20037

MILLETT, KATHERINE MURRAY (KATE), feminist leader; b. St. Paul, Sept. 14, 1934; B.A. magna cum laude, U. Minn., 1956; postgrad. with 1st class honors, St. Hilda's Coll. Oxford (Eng.), 1956-58; Ph.D., Columbia, 1970; m. Fumio Yoshimura, 1965. Instr. English U. N.C. at Greensboro, 1958; sculptor, Tokyo, Japan, 1961-63; file clk., N.Y.C., then kindergarten tchr. N.Y.C.; tchr. Barnard Coll., 1964-68; formerly tchr. English Bryn Mawr (Pa.) Coll.; distinguished vis. prof. Sacramento (Calif.) State Coll., 1973—; co-producer, co-dir. film Three Lives, 1970; sculptor with one woman shows Minami Gallery, Tokyo, Judson Gallery, Greenwich Village, 1967, Noho Gallery, N.Y.C., 1976, 78, 80, Women's Bldg., Los Angeles, 1977. Mem. Congress of Racial Equality, 1965—; chmn. edn. com. N.O.W., 1966; active supporter women's liberation groups. Mem. Phi Beta Kappa. Author: Sexual Politics, 1970; The Prostitution Papers, 1973; Flying, 1974; Sita, 1977; The Basement, 1979. Address: Simon & Schuster New York NY 10017

MILLETT, RALPH LINWOOD, JR., newspaper editor; b. Memphis, Oct. 30, 1919; s. Ralph Linwood and Alice (Campbell) M.; student U. Wyo., 1938-40; B.J., U. Mo., 1942; m. Mary Virgina Smith, Dec. 10, 1944; children—Mary Jo, Alice Virginia, Jan Vasco, Ralph Linwood III. Copy reader, copy desk chief, news editor Knoxville (Tenn.) News-Sentinel, 1947-66, editor, 1967—. Served to lt. USNR, 1942-45. Mem. Am. Soc. Newspaper Editors, Sigma Chi, Sigma Delta Chi, Kappa Tau Alpha. Presbyn. Club: Cherokee. Rotarian. Home: 4168 Towanda Trail Knoxville TN 37919 Office: 204 Church St Knoxville TN 37901

MILLHISER, ROSS R., tobacco products co. exec.; b. Richmond, Va., 1920; B.A., Yale U, 1941; married. With Philip Morris Inc., N.Y.C., 1941—, exec. v.p., 1965-66, pres. Philip Morris U.S.A., 1966-73, pres., dir. Philip Morris Inc., 1973—, vice chmn., 1978—; dir. First & Mchts. Corp., Best Products Co., Seven-Up Co., Mission Viejo Co., Philip Morris Indsl. Co.; Trustee Ind. Coll. Funds Am., Va. Found. Ind. Colls.; mem. exec. com. Tobacco Inst., Washington; chmn. Va. Found. Ind. Colls. Served as maj. U.S. Army, 1942-45. Office: Philip Morris Inc 100 Park Ave New York NY 10017*

MILLICAN, CHARLES NORMAN, educator; b. Wilson, Ark., Oct. 9, 1916; s. Joe F. and Merle Margaret (Wiggins) M.; B.S., Union U., Jackson Tenn., 1941; M.A., George Peabody Coll., 1946; Ph.D., U. Fla., 1954; LL.D., Rollins Coll., 1968; m. Frances Elaine Hilliard, May 15, 1945. High sch. tchr., Miss., 1941-42; coordinator USAAF tng. program Union U., Jackson, Tenn., 1943-45, head commerce dept., 1946-48; lab. asst. physics Peabody Coll., 1945-46; asst., instr., asst. prof. and asst. dean U. Fla., Gainsville, 1948-56; dean Sch. Bus. Adminstrn., Hardin-Simmons U., Abilene, Tex., 1956-59; dean Coll. Bus. Adminstrn., U. So. Fla., Tampa, 1959-65; pres. Fla. Tech. U., Orlando, 1965-78, prof. fin., 1978—; bus. cons. Office: PO Box 25000 Orlando FL 32816

MILLICHAP, JOSEPH GORDON, neurologist; b. Wellington, Eng., Dec. 18, 1918 (came to U.S. 1956, naturalized 1965); s. Joseph P. and Alice (Flello) M.; M.B. with honors in Surgery, St. Bartholomew's Med. Coll., U. London (Eng.), 1946, M.D. in Internal Medicine, 1951, diploma child health, 1948; m. Mary Irene Fortey Feb. 25, 1946 (dec. Oct. 1969); children—Martin Gordon, Paul Anthony; m. 2d, Nancy Melanie Kluczynski, Nov. 7, 1970; children—Gordon Thomas, John Joseph. Intern, resident St. Bartholomew's Hosp., 1946-49, Hosp. Sick Children, London, 1951-53, Mass. Gen. Hosp., Boston, 1958-60; pediatric neurologist NIH, 1955-56; USPHS fellow neurology Mass. Gen. Hosp., Boston, 1958-60; cons. pediatric neurology Mayo Clinic, 1960-63; pediatric neurologist Children's Meml. Hosp., Northwestern Med. Center, Chgo., 1963—; prof. neurology and pediatrics Northwestern U. Med. Sch., 1963—. Cons. surgeon gen. USPHS, mem. med. adv. bds. Ill. Epilepsy League, Muscular Dystrophy Found., Cerebral Palsy Found. 1963—. Chmn. research com. med. adv. bd. Epilepsy Found., 1965—. Served with RAF, 1949-51. Named New Citizen of Year in Met. Chgo., 1965, recipient Americanism Medal D.A.R., 1972; USPHS research grantee, 1957. Diplomate Am. Bd. Pediatrics, Am. Bd. Neurology and Child Neurology, Am. Bd. Electroencephalography. Fellow Royal Coll. Physicians; mem. Am. Neurol. Assn., Am. Pediatric Soc., Am. Soc. Pediatric Research, Am. Acad. Neurology, Am. Soc. Pharmacology and Exptl. Therapeautics, Soc. Exptl. Biology and Medicine, Am. Bd. Psychiatry and Neurology (asst. examiner 1961—), A.M.A., Episcopalian. Author: Febrile Convulsions, 1967: Pediatric Neurology, 1967; Learning Disabilities, 1974; The Hyperactive Child with MBD, 1975. Contbr. articles to profl. jours., chpts. to books. Home: 229 E Lake Shore Dr Chicago IL 60611 Office: 720 N Michigan Ave Chicago IL 60611

MILLIGAN, FLOYD WILMER, life ins. co. exec.; b. Des Moines, Dec. 21, 1920; s. Leslie Mason and Bertha Janetta (Kilpatrick) M.; B.B.A., Drake U., Des Moines, 1947; m. Margaret Augusta Swaine, Oct. 18, 1941; children—Carol Ann, Lynn Marie. With Bankers Life Co., Des Moines, 1947—, asst. treas., 1962-71, treas., 1971—; treas. BLC Equity Mgmt. Co., BLC Growth Fund, Inc., BLC Income Fund, Inc., BLC Fund, Inc. Served with USMCR, 1943-46, 51-52. Mem. Des Moines Soc. Fin. Analysts. Republican. Presbyterian. Club: Des Moines Sertoma. Home: 2720 Patricia Dr Des Moines IA 50322 Office: 711 High St Des Moines IA 50307

MILLIGAN, FRANCIS JOSEPH, JR., lawyer; b. Chgo., Aug. 19, 1924; s. Francis J. and Julia (Ryan) M.; student Loyola U., Chgo., U. Notre Dame; J.D., Harvard, 1949; m. Catherine Jeanne Collopy, July 10, 1954; children—Mary Ellen, Catherine Marie, Francis Joseph III, Elizabeth Marie, Anne Mary. Trust officer Continental Ill. Nat. Bank & Trust Co., Chgo., 1949-58; admitted to Ill. bar, 1950; practiced in Chgo., 1958—; mem. firm Arnstein, Gluck, Weitzenfeld & Minow, 1965—. Pres. council Mundelein Coll., 1956-66, pres., 1963-66, trustee, 1967-73; trustee St. Marys Coll., Winona, Minn., 1969-73, Blue Army of Our Lady of Fatima, Chgo., 1975—; bd. dirs., exec. com. NCCJ, 1959—, co-chmn., 1964-69, nat. dir., 1966-74; bd. dirs. Scholarship Found., U. Notre Dame Club, Chgo., 1955—, sec., 1959-64, pres., 1965-73; bd. dirs. John G. Symons YMCA, 1969—, Inst. for Religious Life, 1978—; bd. dirs. Madonna Center, 1955—, v.p., 1966—; bd. govs. Thomas Aquinas Coll., Santa Paula, Calif., 1978—; mem. adv. bd. Apostolate for Family Consecration, 1978—, Cath. Charities Chgo., 1975—. Served to ensign USNR, 1943-46. Mem. Am., Ill., Chgo. bar assns., Chgo. Estate Planning Council, Harvard Law Sch. Assn., Notre Dame Law Assn., Cath. Lawyers Guild Chgo. (bd. dirs. 1955—, v.p. 1974—. Clubs: Serra, Legal, Notre Dame Alumni (pres. 1957-58), Metropolitan (Chgo.). Home: 1721 Wagner Rd Glenview IL 60025 Office: Sears Tower Chicago IL 60606

MILLIGAN, GLENN ELLIS, psychologist; b. Emporia, Kans., Nov. 12, 1919; s. Ellis S. and Clara (Kriete) M.; B.S., Kans. State Tchrs. Coll., 1941; M.S., U. Chgo., 1942; Ed.D., Colo. State Coll., 1951; m. Phyllis Eaton, Aug. 26, 1945 (div.); children—Douglas, Gregory, David; m. 2d, Janice Barron Dawes, Oct. 10, 1970; 1 step-dau., Virginia. Head dept. edn. Findlay (Ohio) Coll. 1946-55; psychologist Columbus (Ohio) Pub. Schs., 1955-56; asso. prof. edn. Ohio Wesleyan U., Delaware, 1956-60; exec. dir. Am. Assn. Mental Deficiency, Columbus, 1960-65: cons. mental retardation Vocat. Rehab. Adminstrn., HEW, 1965-67; psychologist spl. edn. Montgomery County Pub. Schs., Rockville, Md., 1967—. Lectr., Catholic U. Am. Fellow Am. Assn. Mental Deficiency; mem. Am. Psychol. Assn., NEA (life). Editor: (1st) Mental Retardation, 1963-64; (with others) Directory of Residential Facilities for the Mentally Retarded, 1965. Home: 5208 Elsmere Ave Bethesda MD 20014 Office: Area 2 Continuum Edn 11721 Kemp Mill Rd Silver Spring MD 20902

MILLIGAN, JOHN DRANE, historian, educator; b. N.Y.C., Oct. 11, 1924; s. Carl Glover and Hazel Gray (Drane) M.; B.A., U. Mich., 1952, M.A., 1953, Ph.D., 1961; m. Joyce Mary Jervis, Nov. 16, 1946; children—Jacqueline M., Paula J., Mary M., Elizabeth Y. Teaching asst. U. Mich., 1951-52, teaching fellow, 1954-56; from asst. prof. to prof. history SUNY, Buffalo, 1962—, dir. grad. programs in history, 1963-68, dir. undergrad. programs in history, 1979—, acting dept. chmn., summers, 1977, 78; vis. prof. McMaster U., Hamilton, Ont., Can., summers 1964, 69-70. Exec. bds. Ann Arbor chpt. NAACP, 1956-61, ACLU, 1959-61; mem. campaign coms. for various candidates for local and nat. office, 1960-76; mem. Buffalo Housing Opportunities Made Equal, Citizens Council on Human Relations; faculty chmn. United Fund dr., 1977; active Foster Parents Plan, 1955—. Served with USAAF, 1943-46. James B. Angell scholar U. Mich.; grantee Research Found. SUNY, U.S. Naval Inst. Mem. Am. Hist. Assn., Assn. Am. Historians, So. Hist. Assn., Buffalo and Erie County Hist. Soc., Buffalo Council for Responsibility in Fgn. Policy (founding), Soaring Soc. Am., Aircraft Owners and Pilots Assn., Niagara Soaring Club, Tau Sigma Delta, Phi Kappa Phi. Author: Gunboats Down the Mississippi, 1965; From the Fresh-Water Navy, 1861-1864, 1970; also chpts. in books, articles in jours., encys. Home: 21 Allenhurst Rd Buffalo NY 14214 Office: History Dept SUNY Buffalo NY 14216. *If an individual cannot influence for good the course of mankind, one can sometimes influence for good the life of another individual.*

MILLIGAN, JOHN THOMAS, lawyer; b. Detroit, Oct. 18, 1929; s. John and Helen (LaBurn) M.; B.A., Miami U., 1951; J.D., U. Mich., 1956; m. Carol J. Anderson, Feb. 8, 1952; children—Janet Sue, Marcy Jane. Admitted to Ohio bar, 1957; practice in Warren, 1956—; partner Hoppe, Day & Ford, 1956-70; mem. firm Hoppe, Frey, Hewitt & Milligan, 1970—; sec. Taylor-Winfield Corp., Denton Anderson Co.; dir. Trumbull Savs. & Loan Co., I.J. Investment Co., Inc., Reese Tool & Supply Co., Dray Co. Trustee Trumbull Meml. Hosp., First Presbyterian Ch. of Warren. Served to lt. USNR, 1951-54. Mem. Am., Mich., Ohio, Trumbull County bar assns. Clubs: Buckeye, Trumbull Country (dir.). Home: 266 Country Club Dr Warren OH 44481 Office: Second Nat Bldg Warren OH 44481

MILLIGAN, MANCIL WOOD, educator; b. Shiloh, Tenn., Nov. 21, 1934; s. Mancil Abernathy and Ivy (Wood) M.; B.S., U. Tenn., 1956, M.S., 1958, Ph.D., 1963; postgrad. U. Wash., 1958, Stanford, 1964; m. Arlys Joyce Cushman, Sept. 15, 1956; children—Mancil Wood, Matthew Wayne. Research engr. Boeing Co., Seattle, 1956-57, 58-59; instr. mech. engring. U. Tenn., Knoxville, 1957-58, prof. mech. and aerospace engring., 1959—, head mech. and aerospace engring., 1973—; cons. Union Carbide Nuclear Co., Oak Ridge, 1959—. Mem. ASME, Am. Soc. Engring. Edn., Tech. Soc. Knoxville, Am. Inst. Aeros. and Astronautics, Nat. Soc. Profl. Engrs., Pi Tau Sigma, Tau Beta Pi. Home: 3624 Cherrylog Rd Knoxville TN 37921

MILLIGAN, MICHAEL ROY, lawyer; b. Houston, Nov. 2, 1941; s. Gaymond Eugene and Hilda Frances (Vaughan) M.; student Southwestern U., 1959-60; B.B.A., U. Tex., 1964; J.D., U. Houston, 1968; m. Elaine Kocian, Dec. 28, 1968 (div. 1977); m. 2d, Linda Herman, Dec. 1978. Admitted to Tex. bar, 1968, since practiced in Houston; asso. firm Sigel & Simms, 1968-69; mem. firm Roane & Milligan, 1970-74, Johnson, Milligan & Donaho, 1974-76, Johnson & Milligan, 1976—. Candidate for Tex. legislature, 1974; v.p. Dist. 93 Democratic Com., 1975. Served with AUS, 1964. Mem. Tex., Houston bar assns., Soc. Preservation and Encouragement of Barber Shop Quartet Singing in Am. (treas. 1977-78, dir. 1979), Phi Delta Phi. Club: Houston Galleria Kiwanis (dir.). Asso. editor Houston Law Rev., 1967-68. Home: 777 N Eldridge St Apt 238 Houston TX 77079 Office: 707 Post Oak Bank Bldg Houston TX 77056

MILLIGAN, W(INFRED) O(LIVER), found. exec., chemist; b. Coulterville, Ill., Nov. 5, 1908; s. John Winfred and Millie Mae (McMillan) M.; A.B., Ill. Coll., Jacksonville, 1930, Sc.D., 1946; M.A., Rice Inst., 1932, Ph.D., 1934; D.Sc. (hon.), Tex. Christian U., 1960; LL.D. (hon.), Baylor U., 1979. Research chemist Harshaw Chem. Co., Cleve., 1934; prof. chemistry Rice U., Houston, 1934-63; dir. research Robert A. Welch Found., Houston, 1955—; Distinguished Research prof. chemistry Baylor U., 1965—; cons. Houdry Process Corp., 1936-45, Humble Oil & Refining Co., 1945-62, Oak Ridge Nat. Lab., 1950—. Chmn. Nat. Colloid Symposium, 1952-59; chmn. Nat. Acad. Sci.-NRC Coms. on application x-ray and electron diffraction, 1938-41, panel on permanent magnet materials, 1952—, clay mineralogy, 1953—, Tex. Adv. Com. Atomic Energy, 1955—; investigator OSRD, 1943-45. Pres. Tex. Christian U. Research Found., 1963-65. Recipient award of merit U. Tex., Arlington, 1975. Fellow Am. Inst. Chemists (honor scroll S.W. chpt. 1969), Am. Phys. Soc. mem. Am. Crystallographic Assn., Am. Chem. Soc. (dir. 1961-66, chmn. nat. def. com., chmn. com. future nat. meetings, chmn. com. awards and recognitions, S.W. regional award 1956, southeastern Tex. sect. award 1971), Faraday Soc., S.W. Sci. Forum (pres. 1977-79), Phi Beta Kappa, Sigma Xi, Phi Lambda Upsilon, Alpha Chi Sigma. Asso. editor Jour. Phys. Chemistry, 1952, editorial bd. 1952-58. Contbr. papers to tech. lit. Address: 2010 Bank of SW Bldg Houston TX 77002

MILLIKAN, CHARLES ENGLISH (BRAD), lawyer; b. Los Angeles, Sept. 2, 1925; s. Charles English and Gertrude Eileen (Pentland) M.; J.D., U. So. Calif., 1950; m. Barbara Lorraine Fulton, Dec. 20, 1946; children—Gregory Fulton, Linda Louise, Laurie Anne, Gary Pentland. Admitted to Calif. bar, 1951; partner firm Olson and Millikan, Pasadena, Calif. and San Marino, Calif., 1951-53, Millikan, Montgomery, Olafson and Hardy, Pasadena, 1954-76; chief exec. officer Millikan and Hardy Law Corp., Pasadena, 1977—; dir. S.T.D. Research Corp., The MacNeal Schwendler Corp. Mem. governing bd. La Canada (Calif.) Unified Sch. Dist., 1960-75, pres., 1967-69; bd. dirs. La Canada Edn. Found. Served to lt. (j.g.) USN, 1943-45. Recipient Les Tupper Community Service award, La Canada, 1970. Mem. Am., Los Angeles County (chmn. arbitration com.), Pasadena bar assns., Calif. Congress Parents and Tchrs. (hon. life), Order Coif. Republican. Methodist. Clubs: La Canada YMCA, Kiwanis. Contbr. articles to prof. jours. Home: 437 Woodfield Rd La Canada-Flintridge CA 91101 Office: 424 North Lake Ave Pasadena CA 91101

MILLIKAN, CLARK HAROLD, physician; b. Freeport, Ill., Mar. 2, 1915, s. William Clarance and Louise (Chamberlain) M.; student Parsons (Kans.) Jr. Coll., 1935; M.D., U. Kans., 1939; m. Gayle Margaret Gross, May 2, 1942 (div. Apr. 1966); children—Terri, Clark William, Jeffry Brent; m. 2d, Janet T. Holmes, July 21, 1966. Intern St. Luke's Hosp., Clev. 1939-40, asst. resident medicine, 1940-41; from resident neurology to asst. prof. neurology State U. Iowa, Ames, 1941-49; staff Mayo Clinic, Rochester, Minn., 1949—, cons. neurology; 1958—; dir. Mayo Center for Clin. Research in Cerebrovascular Disease, prof. neurology Mayo Sch. Medicine; physician-in-chief pro tem Cleve. Clinic, 1970; prof. neurology U. Utah Sch. Medicine, Salt Lake City, 1976—. Asst. chmn., editor trans. 2d Princeton Conf. Cerebrovascular Disease, 1957, chmn. confs. 1961, 64; chmn. com. classification and nomenclature cerebrovascular disease USPHS, 1955-69; mem. council Nat. Inst. Neurologic Diseases and Blindness, NIH, USPHS, 1961-65, div. regional med. program, 1965-68; A.O.A. lectr. Baylor U., Waco, Tex., 1952; James Mawer Pearson Meml. lectr. Vancouver, B.C., Can., 1958; Conner Meml. lectr. Am. Heart Assn. 1961; Peter T. Bohan lectr. U. Kans. 1965, 73. Recipient Outstanding Alumnus award U. Kans., 1973. Diplomate Kans., Bd. Psychiatry and Neurology (dir., chmn. exams. com.). Fellow A.C.P., Am. Acad. Neurology, Royal Soc. Medicine; mem. Assn. Research Nervous and Mental Disease (pres. 1961), Am. Neurol. Assn. (1st v.p. 1969-70, pres. 1973-74) Am., Minn. med. assns., Four County Med. Soc. South Minn., AAUP, Central Neuropsychiat. Assn., AAAS, N.Y. Acad. Scis., Am. Heart Assn. (chmn. council cerebrovascular disease 1967-68, Gold Heart award 1976), Sigma Xi. Editor, Jour. Stroke, 1970-76, asso. editor, 1976—. Home: 3617 Brighton Point Dr Salt Lake City UT 84121

MILLIKAN, ROGER CONANT, educator, chemist; b. Tiffin, Ohio, Jan. 27, 1931; s. Robert F. and Laura (Grosvenor) M.; A.B., Oberlin Coll., 1953; Ph.D., U. Calif. at Berkeley, 1957; m. Mary Clark Stickell, Dec. 28, 1953; children—Ross E., Polly S., Sandra K., Jane G., Clark F. NSF fellow U. Calif. at Berkeley, 1955-56; phys. chemist Gen. Electric Co., Schenectady, 1956-67; prof. chemistry U. Calif. at Santa Barbara, 1967—. Fellow Am. Phys. Soc., Optical Soc. Am. Publs. on 1st correct interpretation of formic acid infrared spectrum; discovered (with W.E. Kaskan) molecule B02 and showed it is responsible for green color of boron flames; 1st observation of pure vibrational fluorescence; determined rates of vibrational energy exchange for many gases. Home: 5475 Toltec Dr Santa Barbara CA 93111

MILLIKEN, CALLIE FAYE, librarian; b. Augusta, Tex., Aug. 13, 1917; d. Arthur Benjamin and Callie Hortense (McCullar) M.; B.A., Abilene Christian Coll., 1938; M.A., Tex. U., 1944; Advanced M.L.S., Fla. State U., 1972; postgrad. library studies Peabody Coll., 1945, U. Denver, 1964; Ph.D., Fla. State U., 1976. Tchr. English high schs., Weldon, Tex., 1938-39, Grapeland, Tex., 1939-42; librarian Gaston Jr. High School, Joinerville, Tex., 1942-43, pub. schs. of Houston, 1943-53; dir. libraries Abilene (Tex.) Christian U., 1953-76, asso. dir. libraries and head of resources, 1976—. Delta Kappa Gamma doctoral fellow Fla. State U., 1973-74. Mem. ALA, Texas Library Assn., AAUW, Delta Kappa Gamma. Home: 1134 Washington Blvd Abilene TX 79601

MILLIKEN, FRANK ROSCOE, mining engr.; b. Malden, Mass., Jan. 25, 1914; s. Frank R. and Alice (Gould) M.; B.S. in Mining Engring., Mass. Inst. Tech., 1934; m. Barbara Kingsbury, Sept. 14, 1935; children—Frank R., David C. Chief metallurgist Gen. Engring. Co., Salt Lake City, 1936-41; asst. mgr. Titanium div. Nat. Lead Co., 1941-52; v.p. charge mining ops. Kennecott Copper Corp., N.Y.C., 1952—, exec. v.p., 1958-61, dir., 1958—, pres., chief exec. officer, 1961-78, chmn., chief exec. officer, 1978-79; chmn. Fed. Res. Bank N.Y., 1976-77; dir. Procter & Gamble Co. Life mem. corp. M.I.T. Named Copper Man of Yr., Am. Mining Congress, 1973, recipient 1st Disting. award; recipient Disting. Service award U.S. Treasury, 1965, 68. Mem. Nat. Acad. Engring., Mining and Metall. Soc. Am., Am. Inst. Mining Metall. and Petroleum Engrs. (Robert H. Richards award of minerals beneficiation div. 1951), The Bus. Council. Clubs: Pinnacle, River (N.Y.C.); Wee Burn Country (Darien, Conn.); Blind Brook (Purchase, N.Y.). Home: Contentment Island Rd Darien CT 06820 Office: 161 E 42d St New York NY 10017

MILLIKEN, JOHN BARNES, lawyer; b. Lewisville, Tex., Dec. 10, 1893; s. William Dickerson and Margaret (Young) M.; A.B., Southwestern U., Georgetown, Tex., 1914; studied law, U. of Tex.; m. Maybelle Michael, 1951; children by previous marriage—Mollie, William Dickerson. Admitted to Tex. bar, 1916; began practice Phoenix; asst. dir. U.S. Vets. Bur., Washington, 1919-22; asst. counsel U.S. Shipping Bd., 1922-23; asst. solicitor U.S. Bur. Internal Revenue, 1923-26; mem. U.S. Tax Court, 1926-29; now in practice of law, Los Angeles. Capt., judge adv. gen. O.R.C. Mem. Am. Bar Assn. (mem. tax council), Kappa Alpha. Methodist. Mason (32 deg.). Home: 266 Wigmore Rd Pasadena CA 91105 Office: 333 S Hope St 27th Floor Los Angeles CA 90071

MILLIKEN, ROGER, textile co. exec.; b. N.Y.C., Oct. 24, 1915; s. Gerrish and Agnes (Gayley) M.; student Groton Sch., 1929-33; A.B., Yale, 1937; LL.D. (hon.) Wofford Coll., Rose-Hulman Inst. Tech.; D. Textile Industry (hon.), Clemson U.; m. Justine V. R. Hooper, June 5, 1948; children—Justine, Nancy, Roger, David, Weston. Pres. Milliken & Co., N.Y.C., 1947—; dir. Westinghouse Electric Corp., Citicorp, N.A., Merc. Stores Co., W. R. Grace & Co. Chmn. bd. Inst. Textile Tech., 1948—; bd. dirs. Am. Textile Mfrs. Inst., S.C. Textile Mfrs. Assn. Chmn. Greenville-Spartanburg Airport Commn. Trustee Wofford Coll., S.C. Found. Ind. Coll. Mem. Bus. Council, Bus. Roundtable (policy com.). Clubs: University, Union League, Links, Augusta Nat. Golf. Home: 627 Otis Blvd Spartanburg SC 29302 Office: PO Box 3167 Spartanburg SC 29304

MILLIKEN, WILLIAM GRAWN, gov. Mich.; b. Traverse City, Mich., Mar. 26, 1922; s. James Thacker and Hildegarde (Grawn) M.; A.B., Yale, 1946; LL.D., U. Mich., Eastern Mich. U., Central Mich. U., Detroit Inst. Tech., Western Mich. U., No. Mich. U., Adrian Coll., U. Detroit, Ferris State Coll., Hope Coll., Yale U.; m. Helen Wallbank, Oct. 20, 1945; children—Elaine, William Grawn. Pres., J.W. Milliken, Inc., dept. stores, Traverse City, Cadillac, Manistee, Mich., 1952-75; mem. Mich. Senate from 27th Dist., 1960-64, majority floor leader, 1963-64; lt. gov. Mich., 1965-69, gov., 1969—. Mem. Mich. Waterways Commn., 1947-55. Chmn., Grand Traverse County Republican Com., 1948-54. Bd. dirs. Greater Mich. Found. Mem. Traverse City C. of C. (past pres.). Rotarian. Office: State Capitol Bldg Lansing MI 48933*

MILLIKIN, JOHN HARRIMAN, banker; b. Flushing, L.I., N.Y., Nov. 12, 1909; s. Bryson Carter and Louise (Harriman) M.; B.A., Yale U., 1933; LL.D. (hon.), Pace U., 1973; m. Winifred Castle, Apr.18, 1936; children—Pamela Sands, Winifred Carter, John Castle. With Bankers Trust Co., N.Y.C., 1933-75, asst. sec., 1942-44, asst. v.p., 1944-47, v.p., 1947-60, sr. v.p., 1960-71, sr. v.p., chmn. adv. com., 1971-75; v.p. Tri-Continental Corp.; dir. Fed. Paperboard Co., Inc., Coalition Venture Capitol & Devel. Corp. Chmn. bd. trustees Morristown Meml. Hosp.; mem. adv. council Columbia U. Grad. Sch. Bus. Adminstrn., Pace Coll. Home: Leddell Rd Mendham NJ 07945 Office: 1 Bankers Trust Plaza New York NY 10006

MILLIMET, JOSEPH ALLEN, lawyer; b. West Orange, N.J., July 23, 1914; s. Morris and Dorothy (McBlain) M.; A.B., Dartmouth, 1936; LL.B., Yale, 1939; m. Elizabeth Gray Gingras, Jan. 10, 1942; children—Madlyn Ann (Mrs. Angus Deming), Lisa Gray (Mrs. Silas Little, III), Rebecca Allen, Peter Joseph (dec.). Admitted to N.H. Bar, 1939, since practiced in Concord and Manchester; sr. partner firm Devine, Millimet, Stahl & Branch, and predecessors, 1947—; with FCC, 1941-42. Mem. N.H. Bd. Bar Examiners, 1953-61; legislative counsel to gov. N.H., 1963-66; chmn. Commn. to Revise N.H. Constn., 1964, 74; mem. Commn. Uniform State Laws, 1965-73. Served with USCG, 1942-45. Fellow Am. Coll. Trial Lawyers; mem. N.H. (pres. 1962-63), Am. bar assns. Democrat. Home: 1655 N River Rd Manchester NH 03104 Office: 1850 Elm St Manchester NH 03105

MILLIN, HENRY ALLAN, ofcl. V.I.; b. St. Thomas, V.I., Mar. 17, 1923; grad. Nat. Sch. Real Estate Fin.; m. Graciela Millin; 5 children. Formerly exec. dir. V.I. Housing Authority; lt. gov. V.I., 1978—. Mem. St. Thomas-St. John C. of C. (past pres.). Democrat. Club: Rotary (St. Thomas). Office: Office Lt Gov State Capitol Charlotte Amalie VI 00801*

MILLION, ELMER MAYSE, educator; b. Pond Creek, Okla., Dec. 10, 1912; s. Elmer Joseph and Jozie May (Mayse) M.; A.B. magna cum laude, Southwestern Okla. State Coll., 1936; LL.B., U. Okla., 1935; J.S.D., Yale, 1938; m. Zenna Belle Clark, Sept. 7, 1937 (div. 1956); children—Elmer Zen, Kenneth Mayse, Earl Clark, Tedder Riley; m. 2d, Angela Carman de Carteret, Sept. 27, 1958; children—Heather Carteret, Stephen Murray. Admitted to Okla. bar, 1935; pvt. practice law, Weatherford and Norman, Okla., 1935-36; instr. law So. Meth. U., 1937-38; asst. prof. U. Idaho, 1938-44, asso. prof., 1944-46; sr. atty. U.S. Dept. Justice, Washington, 1943-46, on leave from U. Idaho; asso. prof. W.Va. U., 1946-47; asst. prof. N.Y. U., 1947-48, asso. prof., 1948-53, prof., 1953-70; prof. law U. Okla., 1970—; vis. prof. U. Mich., 1964-65; mem. faculty Inter-Am. Law Inst. of N.Y. U., 1948-68, Comparative Law Inst., N.Y. U., 1955-68. Pres. Fairlington (Va.) Civic Assn., 1944-45. Bd. dirs. Maternity Consultation Service, N.Y.C., 1949-55, Greenwich Village Montessori Sch., 1966-69, Burgundy Farms Country Day Sch., Va., 1945-46. Sterling fellow Yale, 1936-37. Mem. Am., Okla. bar assns., Phi Alpha Delta, Order of Coif. Democrat. Episcopalian. Author: (with R.D. Niles) Walsh, Niles and Million Cases on Property, 3 vols., 1951, 54, 57. Contbr. to Landmarks of Law, 1960, Open Occupancy vs. Forced Housing Under 14th Amendment, 1963, Annual Survey of American Law, 1947-69. Gen. editor Okla. Practice Methods, 1970—. Home: 2530 Beaurue Dr Norman OK 73069

MILLIS, JAMES H., mfg. co. exec.; b. High Point, N.C., 1923; grad. U. N.C.; married. With Adams-Millis Corp., High Point, 1946—, asst. treas., 1949-52, pres., 1953-77, chmn. bd., chief exec. officer, 1978—, also dir.; dir. Highland Yarn Mills, Inc., Wachovia Bank & Trust Co., Western Coca Cola Co.; chmn. pres. Hanes-Millis Sales Corp. Home: 923 Country Club Dr High Point NC 27261 Office: 400 English St High Point NC 27260

MILLIS, ROBERT LOWELL, astronomer; b. Martinsville, Ill., Sept. 12, 1941; s. Dwight L. and Buelah E. (Baird) M.; B.A., Eastern Ill. U., 1963; Ph.D., U. Wis., 1968; m. Julia Ann Drean, June 6, 1965; children—David Lowell, Daniel John. Astronomer, Lowell Obs., Flagstaff, Ariz., 1967—; co-discoverer rings of Uranus, 1977. Recipient Disting. Service award Eastern Ill. U., 1979; fellow Wis. Alumni Research Found., 1963-64. Mem. Internat. Astron. Union, Am. Astron. Soc., Astron. Soc. Pacific. Address: PO Box 1269 Flagstaff AZ 86002

MILLMAN, HERBERT, assn. exec.; b. Kiev, Russia, Dec. 25, 1909; s. Henry and Sadie (Sima) M.; brought to U.S., 1914, naturalized, 1921; B.S., Springfield Coll., 1937; M.Ed., Harvard, 1940; m. Susan Ruth Feinburg, Aug. 18, 1940; children—Ellen S., Lester J. Program dir. Springfield (Mass.) YM-YWHA, 1936-38, exec. dir. Brockton (Mass.), 1938-43; regional cons. Nat. Jewish Welfare Bd., Boston, 1943-49; exec. dir. Greater Boston Council Jewish Centers, 1946-49; nat. dir. field services Jewish Welfare Bd., N.Y.C., 1949-60; asso. exec. Nat. Jewish Welfare Bd., 1960-70, exec. v.p., 1970-76, exec. v.p. emeritus, 1976—; exec. dir. World Confedn. Jewish Community Centers, 1976—; pres. Internat. Conf. Jewish Communal Service, 1978—. Chmn. editorial com. Nat. Conf. Social Welfare, 1960-61; sec. Lavanburg Corner House Fund. Recipient Florence G. Heller award Jewish Welfare Bd., 1978. Mem. Nat. Assn. Jewish Center Workers (past pres.), Nat. Social Welfare Assembly (past chmn. field service com.), Nat. Assn. Social Workers, Acad. Certified Social Workers, Nat. Conf. Jewish Communal Service, Pi Gamma Mu. Jewish (past pres. synagogue). Contbr. articles profl. jours., also Am. Jewish Year Book. Home: 104 Hix Ave Rye NY 10580 Office: 15 E 26th St New York City NY 10010

MILLMAN, PETER MACKENZIE, astrophysicist; b. Toronto, Ont., Can., Aug. 10, 1906; s. Robert Malcolm and Edith Ethelwyn (Middleton) M.; B.A., U. Toronto, 1929; A.M. in Astronomy, Harvard U., 1931, Ph.D., 1932; m. Margaret Bowness Gray, July 10, 1931; children—Barry Mackenzie, Cynthia Gray Millman Floyd. Asst., Dominion Astrophys. Obs., Victoria, B.C., Can., summers 1927-29; asst. in astronomy Harvard U., 1929-31, Agassiz scholar in astronomy Harvard Coll. Obs., 1932-33, asso., 1955-75; lectr. in astronomy U. Toronto, 1933-45; chief stellar physics div. Dominion Obs., Ottawa, Ont., 1946-55; head upper atmosphere research Nat. Research Council Can., Ottawa, 1955-71, guest scientist Herzberg Inst. Astrophysics, 1971—; counsellor Smithsonian Inst., Washington, 1966-72. Fin. v.p. Ottawa Music Festival Assn., 1962-67; bd. dirs. Youth Sci. Found. Can., 1966-71. Served to squadron leader RCAF, 1941-46. Decorated Can. Vol. Service medal and clasp, War medal, Kings Commendation, Centennial medal, Queen's Silver Jubilee medal; recipient J. Lawrence Smith medal Nat. Acad. Scis., 1954. Fellow Royal Soc. Can., Can. Aeros. and Space Inst.; mem. Royal Astron. Soc. Can. (nat. pres. 1960-62), Can. Astron. Soc. (sec. 1971-77), AIAA, Can. Assn. Physicists, Meteoritical Soc. (pres. 1962-66), Internat. Astron. Union (pres. working group for planetary system nomenclature 1973—), Gamma Alpha. Anglican. Author: This Universe of Space, 1961; editor: (with L. Kresak) Physics and Dynamics of Meteors, 1968; Meteorite Research, 1969; (with C.L. Hemenway and A.F. Cook) Evolutionary and Physical Properties of Meteoroids, 1973. Office: Nat Research Council Can Ottawa ON K1A 0R6 Canada. *As a christian I believe that the universe did not evolve by chance, but under the guidance of its creator, God. From my father I learned a tolerance and respect for all great religions. Throughout my life I have attempted to stress the constructive aspects of international human relations, and to practise the golden rule.*

MILLNER, ARNOLD JOHN, editor; b. N.Y.C., Oct. 10, 1920; s. Max Samuel and Bessie (Cohen) M.; B.J., U. Mo., 1949; m. Janice Lyle, June 1, 1948; children—John, Susan. Copy, telegraph editor Champaign (Ill.) News-Gazette, 1949-50; makeup editor, news editor Columbus (Ga.) Ledger, 1950-53; copy editor, picture editor St. Louis Globe-Democrat, 1953-56; mem. staff St. Louis Post-Dispatch, 1956—, copy. editor, picture editor, 1976-77, met. editor, 1972—. Bd. dirs. Christian Hosp. N.E.-N.W., Florissant, Mo., 1972—. Served with inf. U.S. Army, 1938-45. Decorated Bronze Star, Purple Heart with 2 oak leaf clusters. Mem. Sigma Delta Chi. Clubs: St. Louis Press; Shriners, Bogey Hills Country. Home: 11851 Cato Dr Florissant MO 63033 Office: 900 N 12th Blvd St Louis MO 63101

MILLON, HENRY ARMAND, educator, archtl. historian; b. Altoona, Pa., Feb. 22, 1927; s. Henri Francois and Louise (de Serent) M.; B.A., Tulane U., 1947, B.S., 1949, B.Arch., 1953; A.M., Harvard, 1954, M.Arch., 1955, Ph.D., 1964; m. Judith Rice, Dec. 27, 1966; children—Henri, Hadrian, Phoebe, Aaron. Fulbright fellow, Italy, 1957; fellow Am. Acad. Rome, 1957-60; asst. prof. Mass. Inst. Tech., Cambridge, 1960-69, prof., 1969-80, pres. U. Film Study Center, 1970-72, trustee, 1967-73; dir. Am. Acad. in Rome, 1974-77, trustee, 1977—; prof.-in-charge Center for Advanced Study in the Visual Arts, Nat. Gallery Art, 1979—; dir. Archtl. Heritage, 1970-73. Mem. adv. council Sch. Architecture, Princeton, 1970-73, adv. council dept. art and archeology, 1972-73; mem. cons. com. Nat. Survey Historic Sites and Bldgs., Nat. Park Service div. U.S. Dept. Interior, 1969—; vice chmn. Boston Landmarks Commn., 1970-73. Bd. visitors Boston Mus. Fine Arts Sch., 1972-78. Served with USNR, 1944-46. Mem. Soc. Archtl. Historians (pres. 1968-70), Coll. Art Assn., Renaissance Soc., Am. Acad. Arts and Scis., Deputazione Subalpina di Storia Patria, Accademia delle Scienze di Torino. Author: Baroque and Rococo Architecture, 1961; Key Monuments of the History of Architecture, 1964; editor: (with Linda Nochlin) Art and Architecture in the Service of Politics, 1978. Home: 60 Pinckney St Boston MA 02114

MILLON, RENÉ anthropologist; b. N.Y.C., July 12, 1921; s. Henri Francois and Louise Genevieve (de Serent) M.; B.A., Columbia U., 1948, M.A., 1952, Ph.D., 1955; m. Clara Stern Hall, 1961; children—David, Marc, Michele. Asst. prof. U. Calif. at Berkeley, 1957-61; mem. faculty U. Rochester (N.Y.), 1961—, prof. anthropology, 1964—; field research in Mex., 1950, 56-57, 59, 62-72, 78. Served with AUS, 1942-46. Doherty fellow, Mex., 1955-56; NSF fellow, Mex., 1956-57; fellow Center Advanced Study Behavioral Scis., Stanford, 1962-63. Fellow Am. Anthrop. Assn.; mem. Soc. Am. Archaeology, Soc. Mexicana de Antropología, Phi Beta Kappa. Author: (with B. Drewitt and J. Bennyhoff) Pyramid of Sun at Teotihuacán, 1965; Urbanization at Teotihuacán, Vol. 1, 2 parts (part 2 with Drewitt and G. Cowgill), 1973. Office: Dept Anthropology U Rochester Rochester NY 14627

MILLONZI, ROBERT I., lawyer; b. Buffalo, July 12, 1910; s. Philip and Frances (Laduca) M.; B.A., U. Buffalo, 1932, LL.B., 1935; m. Eleanor Verduin, Jan. 27, 1940; children—Mary (Mrs. C. Victor Raiser II), Elizabeth J. (Mrs. Richard A. Levinson). Admitted to N.Y. bar, 1935, D.C. bar, 1979; counsel N.Y. State Dept. Agr., 1939-42; atty. Western N.Y. Savs. Bank, Buffalo, 1947; atty., dir. First Nat. Bank Buffalo, 1947-55; commr. SEC, Washington, 1951-52; cons. RFC, 1952-53; now sr. partner Diebold & Millonzi; dir., gen. counsel First Empire State Corp.; dir., mem. exec. com. Mfrs. & Traders Trust Co.; counsel Western N.Y. Savs. Bank, Buffalo. Pub. mem. U.S. del. UN, 1967. Pres., bd. dirs., mem. exec. com. Buffalo Philharmonic Soc.; bd. dirs. Buffalo Fine Arts Acad., Buffalo Council on World Affairs; trustee John F. Kennedy Center for Performing Arts, Washington, 1966, 68-78; co-chmn. adv. com.; chmn. governing com. Buffalo Found., 1976-77; trustee Power Authority State N.Y.; mem. council of trustees SUNY, Buffalo, 1977, chmn., 1978—. Fellow Am. Bar Assn.; mem. N.Y. State, Erie County bar assns. Democrat. Clubs: Buffalo, Country, Saturn (Buffalo); Burning Tree (Washington); Metropolitan (N.Y.C.). Home: 75 Meadow Rd Buffalo NY 14216 Office: Western NY Savs Bank Bldg Buffalo NY 14202

MILLS, BARRISS, translator, poet; b. Cleve., Jan. 26, 1912; s. Charles Wendell and Emma (Barriss) M.; A.B., Dartmouth, 1934; M.A., U. Chgo., 1936; Ph.D., U. Wis., 1942; m. Iola Jones, Aug. 7, 1937; children—John, Russell, William Barriss, Robert. Instr. English, Ia. State Coll., Ames, 1937-40, asst. prof., 1944-46, asso. prof., 1946-47; instr. English, Mich. State Coll., 1942-44; asso. prof., chmn.

dept. English, U. Denver, 1947-48, prof., chmn. dept., 1948-50; prof. English, Purdue, Lafayette, Ind., 1950-73, now prof. emeritus, head dept., 1950-62. Author: Minimum Essentials of Good Writing (with Huntress, Orlovich, Walker), 1952; The Black and White Geometry (poems), 1955; Parvenus and Ancestors (poems), 1959; The Idylls of Theokritos (verse transl.), 1963; Occasions and Silences (poems), 1964; Aftermath (poems), 1964; The Carmina of Catullus: A Verse Translation, 1965; Letter to Felix (poems), 1968; Epigrams from Martial: A Verse Translation, 1969; Domestic Fables: Selected Poems, 1971; (with George Mills) Broken Present (poems), 1972; (with Lazarus, Stefanile, Woodford) A Suit of Four (poems), 1973; The Soldier and the Lady: Poems of Archilochos and Sappho, 1975; (with others) Indiana Indiana (Poems), 1975; Roughened Roundnesses (poems), 1976; The Unheroic Muse: Essays on Five Classical Poets, 1978. Contbr. articles and poems to lit. jours. Home: 915 N Chauncey West Lafayette IN 47906

MILLS, BRADFORD, investment banker; b. N.Y.C., Dec. 16, 1926; s. Dudley Holbrook and Louise (Morris) M.; B.A. cum laude in Econs., Princeton U., 1948; postgrad. Oxford U. (Eng.), 1950-51; m. Elizabeth Leisk, June 26, 1950; children—Elizabeth Lee, Bradford Alan, Barbara Louise, Ross Dudley. Asst. to dir. overseas ters. div. ECA, Paris, 1948-50; F. Eberstadt & Co., N.Y.C., 1954-62, partner, 1960-62; mng. partner N.Y. Securities Co. 1962-70; chmn., dir. Specialized Services, Inc., Atlanta, 1968—; pres., chief exec. officer Overseas Pvt. Investment Corp., Washington, 1971-73, dir., 1971-75; chmn. bd., dir. F. Eberstadt & Co. Internat., 1973-74; chmn., dir. Bradford Ventures, Ltd., 1974—; dir. Trinwall Cash Res., Inc., Trinwall Bond Fund, Knowlton Bros., Moxie Industries, Inc., Diamond Glass Co., Easco Corp., Foothill Group, Inc., Xtra, Inc., Am. Pad and Paper; lectr. multinat. corps. Woodrow Wilson Sch. Pub. and Internat. Affairs, Princeton U., 1974. Pres., Mills Found.; trustee Millbrook (N.J.) Sch., 1978—; adv. Princeton Chapel, 1968-75. Served with USNR, 1944-46; to lt., 1952-55. Mem. Council Fgn. Relations. Clubs: Blooming Grove (Pa.); Links, Leash, Downtown Assn. (N.Y.C.); Chevy Chase (Washington); Anglers of N.Y. Home: Pretty Brook Rd 2 Princeton NJ 08540 Office: 22 Chambers St Princeton NJ 08540

MILLS, CARROL, newspaper editor; b. Granite City, Ill., Dec. 21, 1941; d. Earl Palmer and Grace Juanita (Gay) M.; B.A., U. Mo., 1963, M.A., 1970; m. Stankomir J. Eremia, June 22, 1975. Editorial asst. pub. relations dept. Loma Linda (Calif.) U., 1963-64; reporter Press-Enterprise Co., Riverside, Calif., 1966-68; reporter The Daily Review, Hayward, Calif., 1970-72, asst. city editor, 1972-74, city editor, 1974—; tchr. Osaka (Japan) Seventh-day Adventist Lang. Sch., 1968-69. Bd. dirs. Faith Family, Inc., Berkeley, Calif. Recipient first prize Am. Acad. Family Physicians contest, 1973; first prize feature category A.P. Calif.-Nev., 1972. Home: 32525 Gina Way Union City CA 94587 Office: Daily Review Box 3127 Hayward CA 94540

MILLS, CHARLES BRIGHT, ret. seed co. exec.; b. Marysville, Ohio, May 14, 1896; s. Dr. Charles Drake and Ella Ann (Stewart) M.; A.B., Ohio Wesleyan U., 1920; m. Rachel Long, June 25, 1924; children—Rachel, Mary, Charles. Chmn. bd. dirs. First Nat. Bank, Marysville. County chmn. War Fund Am. Red Cross, 1942-44; chmn. Central Ohio Heart Assn.; Alternate del. Republican Nat. Conv., 1936. Bd. dirs. Central Ohio Area Boy Scouts Am.; past chmn. bd., trustee Ohio Wesleyan U.; trustee Lakeside Assn., Ohio Meth. Theol. Sem. Mem. Am. Seed Trade Assn. (past pres., life dir.), Am. Legion, Ohio Soc. N.Y., Am. Newcomen Soc. (chmn. Columbus com.), Pi Delta Epsilon, Phi Gamma Delta, Omicron Delta Kappa. Methodist (trustee Ch.). Mason (33 deg., Shriner). Clubs: Kiwanis, Marysville Golf, University, Columbus, Scioto Country. Home: 614 W 7th St Marysville OH 43040

MILLS, CHARLES KENT, lawyer; b. Salem, Oreg., Nov. 9, 1921; s. Roy Henry and Beulah (Spaulding) M.; A.B., Willamette (Oreg.) U., 1949, LL.D. (hon.), 1964; LL.B., U. Calif. at Berkeley, 1954; m. Eileen I. O'Byrne, Aug. 25, 1967; 1 son, Mark. Admitted to Calif. bar, 1954; with O'Melveny & Myers, Los Angeles, 1954-58; chief counsel Textron, Inc., Providence, 1958-60, group v.p., 1960-63; pres. Textron Electronics, Inc., Providence, 1963-64, also dir.; sr. partner firm Mills, Wilcox & Thayer, and predecessors, San Francisco, 1965—. Served to 1st lt. AUS, 1940-46, 51-52. Mem. Phi Delta Theta, Phi Delta Phi, Tau Kappa Alpha. Club: Warwick (R.I.) Country. Contbr. articles to profl. jours. Home: 827 Marina Blvd San Francisco CA 94123 Office: 235 Montgomery St Suite 1060 San Francisco CA 94104

MILLS, DAVID HARLOW, psychologist; b. Marshalltown, Iowa, Dec. 26, 1932; s. Harlow Burgess and Esther Winifred (Brewer) M.; B.S., Iowa State U., 1955, M.S., 1957; Ph.D., Mich. State U., 1964; m. Janet Louise Anderson, June 15, 1957; children—Ross Harlow, Anne Louise, Postdoctoral fellow USPHS U. Ill., Champaign, 1964-65; asst. prof. psychology Iowa State U., Ames, 1965-68, asso. prof., 1968-69, asst. dir. Counseling Center, 1967-69; mem. faculty U. Md., College Park, 1969—, prof. psychology, 1972—, asst. dir. counseling center, 1969—; cons. Iowa Women's Reformatory, 1966-69, VA, Rockwell City, Iowa, 1966-69; research asso. Nat. Register Health Services Providers in Psychology. Pres., Woodmoor-Pinecrest Citizens Assn., Silver Spring, Md., 1973-74; mem. com. higher edn. Allied Civic Group Montgomery County, 1974. Served with U.S. Army, 1957-61. Fellow Am. Psychol. Assn.; mem. Internat. Assn. Counseling Services (accrediting bd., 1972-74, v.p. 1975-77, pres. 1977-79). Democrat. Unitarian. Contbr. articles to profl. jours. Home: 221 Williamsburg Dr Silver Spring MD 20901 Office: Shoemaker Bldg Counseling Center U Md College Park MD 20742

MILLS, DONALD CALVIN, health care exec.; b. Neillsville, Wis., Apr. 3, 1934; s. Calvin B. and Elnora (Uhlman) M.; B.B.A., U. Minn., 1958, M.H.A., 1962; m. Loretta G. Thorson, Nov. 24, 1954; children—Jan D., Julie D., Jolene D. Tax accountant First Trust Co., St. Paul, 1958-60; adminstrv. asst. Bethesda Luth. Hosp., St. Paul, 1961-62; adminstr. Moose Lake (Minn.) State Hosp., 1962-68, Mt. Carmel Nursing Home, Milw., 1968-70; v.p. Nat. Health Enterprises, Milw., 1970-72, pres., 1972-74; adminstr. Bethesda Luth. Med. Center, St. Paul, 1974—; preceptor program in hosp. and health care adminstrn. U. Minn., 1975—; hosp. bd. rep. Blue Cross/Blue Shield Minn., 1975—; bd. dirs. Bethesda/Univ. Family Physicians, P.A., 1975—; mem. pediatric task force Health Bd. Met. Council, 1975-76, mem. long term care task force, 1977, task force on econ. impact, 1978; dir. Health Manpower Mgmt. Inc., 1975-79, pres., 1977-78; bd. dirs. Council Community Hosps., 1974—, mem. policy and issues com., 1979; chmn. N.E. Minn. Regional Mental Health Retardation Coordinating Com., 1968. Mem. Moose Lake Planning Commn., 1965-68; chmn. St. Paul health facilities United Way, 1977; pres. dist. G-East, St. Paul Assn., 1975-76. Served with AUS, 1954-56. Fellow Am. Coll. Nursing Home Adminstrs.; mem. Minn. Hosp. Assn. (trustee 1978—, chmn. fin. com. 1977-79 rate rev. adv. subcom. 1978-79, cost containment coordinating com. 1979). Kiwanian. Home: 5854 W Bald Eagle Blvd White Bear Lake MN 55110 Office: 559 Capitol Blvd Saint Paul MN 55103

MILLS, EARL B., constrn. co. exec.; b. Sneedville, Tenn., Mar. 19, 1928; s. Robert Taylor and Mattie Bell (Sutton) M.; B.S., Carson-Newman Coll., 1947; M.B.A., U. Tenn., 1948; m. Farrell Lawson, Dec. 20, 1950; children—Robert Joseph, John Charles, Alan Douglas, Jeffrey Sutton, Zachary Taylor. Cost supr., dir. mgmt. systems, asst. controller, dir. bus. systems, dir. polyester project, dir. research and engring., pres. fabric services Monsanto Co., N.Y.C. and St. Louis, 1952-66; v.p. ops., dir. Phillips Fibers Corp., Greenville, S.C., 1966-69; v.p., gen. mgr., dir. Yeargin Constrn. Co., Inc., Greenville, 1969-78, pres., chief operating officer, 1978—. Bd. dirs. Blue Ridge council Boy Scouts Am. Served to 1st lt. USAF, 1950-52. Recipient Silver Beaver award Boy Scouts Am., 1974, Lybrand award for contbn. to field indsl. accounting, 1956. Mem. AIM (pres.'s council), Nat. C. of C., So. Indsl. Devel. Council, Asso. Builders and Contractors, Asso. Gen. Contractors, Piedmont Gen. Contractors, ASME, ASCE. Baptist. Club: Greenville Country. Contbr. articles to profl. jours. Home: Route 4 Box 330-A Simpsonville SC 29681 Office: McAlister Plaza Greenville SC 29606

MILLS, EDWIN SMITH, educator; b. Collingswood, N.J., June 25, 1928; s. Edwin Smith and Roberta (Haywood) M.; B.A., Brown U., 1951; Ph.D., U. Birmingham (Eng.), 1956; m. Barbara Jean Dressner, Sept. 2, 1950; children—Alan Stuart, Susan Dorinda; m. 2d, Margaret M. Hutchinson, Jan. 22, 1977. Asst. lectr. Univ. Coll. North Staffordshire (Eng.), 1953-55; instr. Mass. Inst. Tech., 1955-57; mem. faculty Johns Hopkins, Balt., 1957-70, prof. econs., 1963-70, chmn. dept. econs., 1966-69; prof. econs. and pub. affairs, Gerald L. Phillippe prof. urban studies Princeton U., 1970-75, prof. econs., 1975—, chmn. dept., 1975-77; vis. research fellow Cowles Found., Yale, 1961; sr. profl. staff Council Econ. Advisers, 1964-65. Served to 2d lt. AUS, 1946-48. Mem. Am. Econ. Assn., Royal Econ. Soc., Econometric Soc., Phi Beta Kappa. Author: Urban Economics, 1972. Home: 46 Sturges Way Princeton NJ 08540

MILLS, EUGENE SUMNER, coll. pres.; b. West Newton, Ind., Sept. 13, 1924; s. Sumner Amos and Lela (Weatherly) M.; A.B., Earlham Coll., 1948; M.A., Claremont Grad. Sch., 1949, Ph.D., 1952; postgrad. Harvard, 1958-59; m. Dorothy Frances Wildman, Oct. 22, 1945; children—David Walden, Sara Anne. Instr. psychology Whittier (Cal.) Coll., 1950, asst. prof., chmn. dept., 1952-55, asso. prof., chmn. dept., 1955-60, prof. psychology, chmn. dept., 1960-62; faculty U. N.H., Durham, 1962-79, prof. psychology, 1962-79, chmn. dept., 1962-65, dean Grad. Sch., coordinator research, 1963-67, dean Coll. Liberal Arts, 1967-70, acad. v.p., 1970-71, provost, 1971-74, provost, acting pres., 1974, pres., 1974-79; pres. Whittier (Calif.) Coll., 1979—, prof. psychology Sch. Law, 1979—; vis. prof. U. Victoria, B.C., summers 1958, 60; dir. Elderhostel, Inc. Danforth Found. grantee, NSF grantee. Fellow Am. Psychol. Assn.; mem. Eastern, N.H. (pres. 1969-70, dir. 1967-70) psychol. assns., Sigma Xi, Phi Kappa Phi. Author: George Trumbull Ladd: Pioneer American Psychologist, 1969. Contbr. articles to profl. jours. Home: 13952 Summit Dr Whittier CA 90602 Office: Office of Pres Whittier College 13406 Philadelphia St Whittier CA 90608

MILLS, GEORGE ALEXANDER, govt. ofcl., scientist; b. Saskatoon, Sask., Can., Mar. 20, 1914; s. George Robison and Leafa (Johnson) M.; B.Sc., U. Sask., 1934, M.Sc., 1936; Ph.D., Columbia U.; m. Roberta Walker Mills, June 15, 1940; children—Richard, Sandra, Marilyn, Janice. Instr., Dartmouth Coll., 1939-40; with U.S. Bur. Mines, 1940-75, chief coal div., 1968-75; dir. fossil energy research Energy Research and Develop. Adminstrn., 1975-77; dir. internat. programs fossil energy Dept. of Energy, Washington, 1977—. Mem. Nat. Acad. Engring., Am. Chem. Soc. (Storch award), AAAS, Am. Inst. Chem. Engring., Catalysis Soc. Presbyterian. Contbr. numerous articles to profl. jours.; patentee in field. Home: 6304 Poe Rd Bethesda MD 20034 Office: Dept Energy Washington DC 20545

MILLS, GEORGE HIILANI, physician; b. Pepeekeo, Hawaii, June 10, 1921; s. George K. and Elsie Justine (Off) M.; B.A., Colo. Coll., 1944, M.A., 1945; M.D., Boston U., 1950; m. Barbara Freeman, June 21, 1944; children—George Hiilani, Kilburn, James, Elsa. Intern, Queens Med. Center, Honolulu, 1950-51, resident in internal medicine, 1951-54; partner Alsup Clinic, Honolulu, 1954-70; med. dir. Kamehameha Sch., 1962-78, Manalani Hosp., 1960-78; mem. faculty U. Hawaii Med. Sch., 1978—. Mem. Hawaii Senate from 3d Dist., 1970-74; mem. Nat. Adv. Com. Juvenile Justice and Delinquency Prevention, 1975-77. Mem. Am. (trustee), Hawaii med. assns., Inst. Medicine, Assn. Hawaiian Civic Clubs. Republican. Home: 53-179 Kamehameha Hwy Hauula HI 96717 Office: Kamehameha Schs Kapalama Heights Honolulu HI 96817

MILLS, GLEN EARL, educator; b. Mpls., May 10, 1908; s. Albert William and Bertha (Erickson) M.; B.S., Eastern S.D. Tchrs. Coll., 1930; M.A., U. Mich., 1935, Ph.D., 1941; m. Ruth Arlene Pence, May 28, 1937; 1 son, Richard Pence. Instr. speech Tyndall (S.D.) High Sch., 1930-34, Yankton (S.D.) High Sch., 1934-35, Ann Arbor (Mich.) High Sch., 1935-40; teaching fellow U. Mich., 1940-41, instr. speech, 1941-42; instr. speech Northwestern U., Evanston, Ill., 1942, asst. dean Sch. Speech, 1956-64, prof. speech, 1957-68, asso. dean, 1964-68, coordinator grad. studies, 1965-68; prof. speech U. Calif. at Santa Barbara, 1968—, dept. chmn., 1971-75, emeritus, recalled, 1975-78. Cons. AMA, GM Electron. Recipient Outstanding Alumnus award Dakota State Coll., 1967. Mem. Speech Communication Assn., Am. Forensic Assn., Rhetoric Soc. Am., Calif., Western States speech assns., Pi Kappa Delta, Delta Psi Omega, Phi Sigma Pi, Delta Sigma Rho. Presbyn. Author: (with McBurney) Argumentation and Debate, 1951, rev., 1964; Composing the Speech 1952; Reason In Controversy, 1964, rev., 1968; (with Bauer) Guidebook for Student Speakers, 1966; Speech Preparation; Analysis and Structure 1966; Putting a Message Together, 1972; Legal Argumentation, 1976; former editor: Western Speech, Jour. Am. Forensic Assn.; Contbr. articles to profl. jours. Home: 5184 Calle Asilo Santa Barbara CA 93111

MILLS, GORDON T., editor, publisher; b. Walters, Okla., Apr. 20, 1922; s. Gordon Turner and Lilian (Mills) M.; student Central State Coll., Edmond, Okla., 1940-42, U. Tulsa, 1946; B.J., U. Mo., 1948; postgrad. U. Vt., 1958; m. Christena Violet McGuff, May 19, 1945; children—Judith Ann (Mrs. Richard Krauss), Janice Lee, Charles Kirkwood. City editor Enid (Okla.) Daily Eagle, 1950-52; mng. editor Southwest Times, Pulaski, Va., 1952-56; editor Burlington (Vt.) Free Press, 1960-76; editor, pub. Addison County Ind., Middlebury, Vt., 1976—; corporator Burlington Savs. Bank. Served with USNR, 1942-45. Mem. New Eng. Press Assn. (sec.-treas.), Kappa Tau Alpha, Sigma Delta Chi. Home: 38 Gorham Ln Middlebury VT 05753 Office: 20 1/2 Main St Middlebury VT 05753. *Unwillingness to change is one of the most common reasons for failure. It prevents many persons with highly-developed skills from realizing the benefits of years of training and experience.*

MILLS, HAWTHORNE QUINN, fgn. service officer; b. Beverly Hills, Cal., Mar. 27, 1928; s. Harry Quinn and Anna Mildred (Lamb) M.; A.B., Colo. Coll., 1950; postgrad. U. Innsbruck (Austria), 1950-51; M.A., U. Cal. at Berkeley, 1958; postgrad. Nat. War Coll. 1972-73; m. Erika Hildegard Maria Menschel, Oct. 12, 1953; 1 son, Nicholas Lamb. Staff announcer Armed Forces Radio Service, Salzburg, Austria, 1951-53; teaching asst. polit. sci. U. Calif., Berkeley, 1956-58; joined Fgn. Service, 1958; 2d sec., polit. officer Am. embassy, Athens, Greece, 1960-63; with Dept. State exec. secretariat, 1963-65; mem. U.S. delegation 19th session UN Gen. Assembly, 1964; 2d sec., econ. officer Am. embassy, The Hague, Netherlands, 1965-67; province sr. adviser, Vietnam, 1967-70; 1st sec., mission coordinator Am. embassy, Vietnam, 1970-72; staff dir. bd. examiners fgn. service Dept. State, Washington, 1973-74; counselor of embassy for polit. affairs, Tehran, 1974-76; dep. chief of mission Am. Embassy, Athens, 1976—. Bd. dirs., treas. U.S. Ednl. Found. (Fulbright), Greece, 1661 Corp. Served with USN, 1945-46; PTO. Decorated Purple Heart, Gallantry Cross with bronze star (Vietnam); recipient Dept. State Heroism award, 1970, Superior Honor award 1972. Mem. Am. Fgn. Service Assn., Phi Gamma Delta, Tau Kappa Alpha. Clubs: Royal Selangor Golf and Tennis (Kuala Lumpur, Malaysia); Ft. McNair Officers (Washington). Home: 1661 Crescent Pl NW Washington DC 20009 Office: Am Embassy Athens APO New York NY 09253

MILLS, JAMES SPENCER, author; b. Milw., May 20, 1932; s. Ralph Erskine and Elisabeth Amsden (Stevens) M.; student Erskine Coll., 1950-51; B.A., Princeton U., 1956. Reporter, Worcester (Mass.) Telegram and Evening Gazette, summer 1955, Corpus Christi (Tex.) Caller Times, 1958, UPI, 1959; reporter, corr., writer, editor Life mag., 1960-66. Served with USNR, 1956-58. Author: The Panic in Needle Park, 1966; The Prosecutor, 1969; Report to the Commissioner, 1972; One Just Man, 1974; On the Edge, 1975; The Seventh Power, 1976. Address: care Lynn Nesbit Internat Creative Mgmt 40 W 57th St New York City NY 14304

MILLS, JAMES THOBURN, bus. exec.; b. Balt., Nov. 30, 1923; s. Victor Garfield and Beatrice (Moore) M.; B.A., Princeton U., 1945; LL.B., Yale U., 1950; m. Frances Clagett Keller, June 16, 1951; children—Elizabeth R., Hilary F., Frances T., Margaret K. Admitted to N.Y. bar, 1951; asso firm Burke & Burke, N.Y.C., 1950-51; asso. firm Mudge, Stern, Baldwin & Todd, N.Y.C., 1951-56; with Sperry & Hutchinson Co., N.Y.C., 1956—, pres., 1978—, also dir. Trustee, Rutgers U. Served as 1st lt. AUS, 1943-46. Decorated Bronze Star medal, Purple Heart. Mem Am. Bar Assn., N.Y. State Bar Assn., Bar Assn. City N.Y. Clubs: Union League; Montclair Golf.

MILLS, JESSE COBB, librarian; b. Morristown, Tenn., Feb. 13, 1921; s. Isaac Columbus and Jessie Lee (Phillips) M.; S.B., Harvard, 1942; postgrad. summer 1951; M.A., U. Tenn., 1949; postgrad. U. Pa., 1951-54; M.S. in Library Sci., Rutgers U., 1960. Instr. in English, U. Tenn., Knoxville, 1946-51, librarian, 1966-69, lectr., 1966—; instr. in English U. Pa., Phila., 1951-54; librarian 1954-62, asst. dir. libraries, 1963-66; chief librarian TVA, Knoxville, 1969—; cons. in library bldg.; lectr. library sci. Drexel Inst. Tech., Phila., 1960-66; mem. So. States Coop. Library Survey, 1972-74; chmn. Tenn. Adv. Council on Libraries. Served with AUS, 1942-46. Regional Merit scholar, 1938-39; Shaw scholar, 1939-42. Mem. Southeastern Library Assn., Spl. Libraries Assn. (pres. So. Appalachian chpt.), Pa. Hist. Soc., Genealogical Soc. Pa., East Tenn. Hist. Soc. (pres.), East Tenn. Library Assn. (pres.). Kiwanian. Contbr. articles to profl. jours. Home: 2001 Emoriland Blvd Knoxville TN 37917 Office: 400 Commerce Ave Knoxville TN 37902

MILLS, JOHN VERNOR, assn. exec.; b. Windsor, Ont., Can., Feb. 13, 1924; s. Cecil V. and Rose-Ann (Johnston) M.; B.A., Western U., 1949; grad. Osgoode Hall Law Sch., 1953; m. Helen Elliott, July 20, 1946; children—Coulson V., Douglas A., Karen J., Elizabeth J. Called to Ont. bar, 1953; created Queen's counsel, 1963; mem. firm Rowland & Mills, Barristers and Solicitors, Toronto, 1953-57; exec. asst. to gen. mgr., gen. counsel Composers Authors and Pubs. Assn. of Can. Ltd., Toronto, 1957-66, asst. gen. mgr., 1966-68, gen. mgr., 1968—. Served with Royal Canadian Air Force, 1942-46. Mem. County of York Law Assn., Canadian Bar Assn., Law Soc. Upper Can. Mem. Anglican Ch. of Can. Clubs: Lawyers, Lambton Golf, Rideau. Home: 6 Cherry Post Crescent Etobicoke ON Canada Office: 1240 Bay St 9th Fl Toronto ON M5R 2C2 Canada

MILLS, JOHN WELCH, lawyer; b. Cleve., June 4, 1931; s. Thoburn and Margaret (Welch) M.; A.B., Princeton, 1953; LL.B., Harvard, 1958; m. Louise Cantwell Connell, Oct. 19, 1963; children—Carolyn, James, Jennifer. Admitted to N.Y. bar, 1959, Ohio bar, 1965, Ill. bar, 1974; asso. firm White & Case, N.Y.C., 1958-61; asst. U.S. atty. So. Dist. N.Y., 1961-64; asst. gen. counsel Republic Steel Corp., Cleve., 1964-72; v.p., gen. counsel Maremont Corp., Chgo., 1972-78; v.p., gen. counsel Tenneco Automotive, Deerfield, Ill., 1978—. Mem. sch. bd. Sears Sch., Kenilworth, Ill., 1975-79; trustee Univ. Sch., Cleve., 1970-72. Served to 1st lt. arty. AUS, 1953-55. Clubs: Kirtland Country (Cleve.); Indian Hill (Chgo.). Home: 211 Essex Rd Kenilworth IL 60047 Office: 200 Wilmot Rd Deerfield IL 60015

MILLS, JOSEPH WILLIAM, educator; b. Toronto, Ont., Can., June 9, 1917 (came to U.S. 1950, naturalized 1957); s. Joseph William and Marguerite (Houle) M.; B.A. in Geology and Mineralogy, U. Toronto, 1939; Ph.D. in Geology, Mass. Inst. Tech., 1942; m. Yola L. Radochia, May 16, 1942; children—Andrea L., Joseph W. Mine and exploration geologist Consol. Mining & Smelting Co., MicMac Mines Ltd., also O'Brien Gold Mines Ltd., 1942-50; mem. faculty Wash. State U., Pullman, 1950—, prof. geology, 1962-71, chmn. dept., 1961-71, acting chmn., 1977-78; geologist div. mines and geology Wash. Dept. Conservation, summers 1959-77; vis. prof. U. Ibadan (Nigeria), 1973-74. Mem. Geol. Assn. Can., Soc. Econ. Geologists, Northwest Sci. Assn., Northwest Mining Assn., Sigma Xi (pres. Wash. State U. chpt. 1964-65). Editor Northwest Sci., 1958-70. Home: NW 1450 Orion Dr Pullman WA 99163

MILLS, LEV TIMOTHY, artist; b. Wakulla County, Fla., Dec. 11, 1940; s. Clarence and Beatrice M.; B.A. in Art Edn., Fla. A. and M. U., 1962; M.A., U. Wis., Madison, 1968, M.F.A. in Printmaking, 1970; m. Joyce White, Aug. 13, 1966; 1 son, Lev-Kehmel. Tchr., Broward County (Fla.) Sch. System, 1962-68; asst. prof. art Clark Coll., 1973-78, Spelman Coll.; one-man and group shows of graphics, prints, sculpture: numerous galleries U.S. and abroad, including Fisk U., S.C. State Coll., San Jose Mus. Art, Peachtree Center Gallery, Atlanta, Handshake Gallery, Atlanta, High Mus. Art, Atlanta, Gallery, Bonn, W. Ger., Mus. African Am. Art, Pomona, Calif.; represented in permanent collections, including: Victoria and Albert Mus., London, Eng., Brit. Mus., London, Library Congress, Washington, Mus. Modern Art, N.Y.C.; works include Three Glass Mosaics for one of Atlanta's subway stations; bd. dirs. Atlanta Arts Festival; cons. Atlanta Bur. Cultural Affairs; Ford Found. study and travel grantee, Europe, 1970. Served with ROTC, 1958-60. Named Tchr. of Yr., Everglades Sr. High Sch., Ft. Lauderdale, 1966. Bronze Jubilee award City of Atlanta, 1977; U. Wis. fellow, 1969-70. Mem. Nat. Coll. Art Assn., Black Artist/Atlanta, NAACP, YMCA, Heritage Trust S.W. Atlanta. Democrat. Baptists. Author, illustrator: I Do: A Book of Etchings and Poems, 1971. Home: 3378 Ardley Rd SW Atlanta GA 30311

MILLS, LORNA HENRIETTA, savs. and loan assn. exec.; b. Long Beach, Calif., Feb. 4, 1916; d. James H. and Henrietta (Waller) M.; student Johnston's Bus. Inst., 1935-36. With Laguna Fed. Savs. & Loan Assn., Laguna Beach, Calif., 1936—, sec.-treas., 1947-57, pres., gen. mgr., 1957—. Mem. Nat. Def. Adv. Com. on Women in the

Services, 1973-76; mem. adv. bd. Disneyland Community Awards; unit treas. Salvation Army; mem. Calif. State Adv. Hosp. Council; mem. Calif. Regional Hosp. Planning Com.; mem. adv. com. Community Energy Conservation Assn., Newport Beach, Calif. Named Woman of Yr., Laguna chpt. Bus. and Profl. Women's Club, 1967. Mem. Calif. Savs. and Loan League (past dir.), United Savs. and Loan League, Savs. and Loan Found. (state trustee 1977-79), Conf. Fed. Savs. and Loan Assns. (past dir.), Orange County C. of C., Laguna Beach C. of C. (bd. dirs. 1958-61, treas. 1960). Clubs: Soroptimist (past pres.), DAR. Office: 260 Ocean Ave Laguna Beach CA 92651

MILLS, MARGARET MARY HOWARD, assn. exec.; b. Levenshulme, Eng., Dec. 16, 1921; came to U.S., 1953, naturalized, 1973; d. Leonard and Katharine (Howard) M.; student U. London, 1939-42, Colegio Superior de Vicosa, Minas Gerais, Brazil, 1943-45. Translator, writer O Observador Economico, Rio de Janeiro, 1945-47; researcher Brazilian embassy, London, 1948-53; asst. dir. purchasing commn. Brazilian Treasury del., N.Y.C., 1954-64; asst. Cheryl Crawford Prodns., 1965-67; asst. to dir. Am. Acad. Arts and Letters, N.Y.C., 1968-73, exec. dir., 1973—; adv. com. Am. Art Directory, 1978. Bd. advisers Community Environments, N.Y.C., 1978. Recipient various certs. merit. Democrat. Office: 633 W 155th St New York NY 10032

MILLS, PAUL CHADBOURNE, museum ofcl.; b. Seattle, Sept. 24, 1924; s. Reed C. and Lillian (Hoey) M.; student Reed Coll., 1945-48; B.A., U. Wash., 1953, M.A., U. Calif., 1961; Ph.D. (hon.), Calif. Coll. Arts and Crafts, 1971; m. Janet L. Dowd, Apr. 30, 1955; children—Katherine, Megan, Michael. Reporter, Bellevue (Wash.) Am., 1948-51; asst. curator Henry Gallery, U. Wash., Seattle, 1952-53; curator art Oakland (Calif.) Mus., 1953-70; dir. Santa Barbara (Calif.) Mus. Art, 1970; v.p. Western Mus. Conf., 1956, 59. Served with Signal Corps, AUS, 1942-45. Ford Found. fellow, 1960-61; Spanish-U.S. Cultural Exchange grantee, 1977, 79. Mem. Western Assn. Art Mus. (v.p. 1956-57, treas. 1971—), Assn. Art Mus. Dirs. (trustee 1972-73, 80, sec. 1973—), N.Am. Vexillogical Assn. Contbr. articles to catalogues, profl. jours. Home: 1042 Las Alturas Rd Santa Barbara CA 93103 Office: 1130 State St Santa Barbara CA 93101

MILLS, PAUL SWINTON, former assn. exec.; b. Clinton, Ind., Feb. 1, 1914; s. Benjamin and Rosamond (Swinton) M.; B.S., Ind. State Tchrs. Coll., 1935; Ed.M., Harvard, 1942; student Ind. U. Grad. Sch. Bus. and Econs., 1948-49; m. Carolyn Sprague, June 12, 1943; children—Richard Paul, Janet Lee, Marsha Jo, Nancy Sue. Tchr., Fayette Twp. High Sch., New Goshen, Ind., 1936-42; instr. U.S. Naval Tng. Sch., Ind. U., 1942-43; asst. prof. accounting and ins. Mich. State U., East Lansing, 1946-49; supr. Great-West Life Assurance Co., Winnipeg, Can., 1949-52, br. mgr., 1952-56, mgr. advanced tng., 1956-57; exec. v.p., mng. dir. Am. Soc. C.L.U.'s, 1957-79. Served to lt. (j.g.) USNR, 1943-46. C.L.U. Recipient Distinguished Alumni award Ind. State U., Terre Haute, 1976. Mem. Am. Soc. C.L.U.'s. Mason. Contbg. author: Life and Health Insurance Handbook, 1959. Home: 1006 Edmonds Av Drexel Hill PA 19026

MILLS, PETER RICHARD, advt. exec.; b. Nanango, Australia, Mar. 28, 1939; s. Frederick R. and Muriel E. M.; student York U., Toronto, Ont., 1964, 65; immigrated to Can., 1960; children—Duncan, David, Alexander. Copywriter, T. Eaton Co., Toronto, 1961-62; with Southam Bus. Publs., Toronto, 1962-66; with J. Walter Thompson Co. Ltd., 1966—, gen. mgr., Montreal, 1973-75, gen. mgr., Toronto, 1976-77, exec. v.p., dir. ops., 1978-79, exec. v.p., gen. mgr. N.Y. office, 1979—, also dir. Mem. Proprietary Assn. Home: 322 W 57 St #36T New York NY 10019 Office: 420 Lexington Ave New York NY 10017

MILLS, RALPH JOSEPH, JR., educator; b. Chgo., Dec. 16, 1931; s. Ralph Joseph and Eileen (McGuire) M.; B.A., Lake Forest Coll., 1954; M.A., Northwestern U., 1956, Ph.D., 1963; m. Helen Daggett Harvey, Nov. 25, 1959; children—Natalie, Julian, Brett. Tchr. English, Am. lit. U. Chgo., 1959-65; prof. English, U. Ill. at Chgo. Circle, 1965—. English Speaking Union fellow, 1956-57. Mem. Phi Beta Kappa, Phi Kappa Phi. Roman Catholic. Author: Theodore Roethke, 1963; Contemporary American Poetry, 1965; Richard Eberhart, 1966; Edith Sitwell, 1966; Kathleen Raine, 1967; Creation's Very Self, 1969; Door To The Sun-Poems, 1974; Cry of The Human, 1975; A Man to His Shadow: Poems, 1975; Night Road/Poems, 1978; Living with Distance: Poems, 1979. Editor: On the Poet and His Craft-Selected Prose of Theodore Roethke, 1965; Selected Letters of Theodore Roethke, 1968; The Notebooks of David Ignatow, 1973. Home: 1451 N Astor St Chicago IL 60610

MILLS, RAY JACKSON, ins. co. exec.; b. Hale, Iowa, June 8, 1893; s. William J. and Margaret (Inglis) M.; LL.B., J.D., U. Mich., 1916; m. Marie Breyman, Nov. 5, 1919; children—William J., Robert E. Admitted to Iowa bar, 1916; practice of law, Cedar Rapids, 1916-20; claims mgr. Iowa Nat. Mut. Ins. Co., 1920-36, sec., gen. mgr., 1936-41, pres. Cedar Rapids, Iowa, 1941-51, chmn., 1951-68, vice chmn., 1968—, hon. life dir., 1975—; hon. dir. Mchts. Nat. Bank. Served with U.S. Army, 1917-19. Mem. Delta Chi. Mason, Elk. Club: St. Petersburg (Fla.) Yacht. Home: Bldg 6 Apt 1506 4900 Brittany Dr S St Petersburg FL 33715 Office: 518 2d Ave SE Cedar Rapids IA 52401

MILLS, ROBERT HUGH, educator; b. Evanston, Ill., Sept. 5, 1925; s. Spafford John and Phoebe (Johnson) M.; B.S., U. Colo., 1949, M.S., 1955; Ph.D., U. Wis., 1960; m. June Alberta Pfeiffer, Nov. 21, 1953; children—Peggy, Alan; 1 foster dau., Cindy. Staff accountant Haskins & Sells, C.P.A.'s, Chgo., 1950-54; instr. U. Wis., 1955-60; asst. prof. U. Mich., Ann Arbor, 1960-64; prof. accounting, dir. grad. studies Coll. Bus. and Econs., Lehigh U., Bethlehem, Pa., 1964—. Bd. dirs. Bethlehem Area Council of Chs., Housing Opportunity Assn. Served with USN, 1943-46. C.P.A., Pa. Mem. Am., Pa. insts. C.P.A.'s, Am. Acctg. Assn., Beta Alpha Psi, Beta Gamma Sigma. Presbyterian. Contbr. articles to profl. jours. Home: 3595 Stafore Dr W Bethlehem PA 18017

MILLS, ROBERT LAURENCE, educator; b. Englewood, N.J., Apr. 15, 1927; s. Frederick Cecil and Dorothy Katherine (Clarke) M.; A.B., Columbia Coll., 1948; B.A., Cambridge (Eng.) U., 1950, M.A., 1954; Ph.D., Columbia, 1955; m. Elise Ackley, July 21, 1948; children—Katherine, Edward, Jonathan, Susan, Dorothy. Research asso. Brookhaven Nat. Lab., Upton, N.Y., 1953-55; mem. Sch. Math. Inst. for Advanced Study, Princeton, 1955-56; asst. prof. physics Ohio State U., Columbus, 1956-59, asso. prof., 1959-62, prof., 1962—. Mem. Am. Phys. Soc., AAUP, Fedn. Am. Scientists. Author: Propagators for Many-Particle Systems, 1969. Home: 3655 Weston Pl Columbus OH 43214

MILLS, ROBERT LEE, coll. chancellor; b. Erlanger, Ky., Nov. 13, 1916; s. John Clifford and Dixie Lee (Morris) M., A.B. in Math. and Physics, U. Ky., 1938, M.A. in Ednl. Adminstrn., 1941, Ed.D., 1951; m. Mildred Sizer, June 24, 1942; children—Robert Lee, Dixie Louise, Barbara Jean. Tchr., Covington (Ky.) pub. schs., 1938-41; head hydraulics br. Air Force Tech. Sch., Lincoln, Nebr., 1942-44; mem. supervisory staff electromagnetic plant, Oak Ridge, 1944-48; research asst. U. Ky., Lexington, 1948-51, dean admissions, registrar, 1954-57; dir. research, head bur. adminstrn. and finance Ky. Dept. Edn., 1951-54; chmn. dept. ednl. adminstrn. U. Tex., Austin, 1957-59; pres. Georgetown (Ky.) Coll., 1959-78, chancellor, 1978—. Exec. sec. Ky. Adv. Commn. Ednl. Policy, 1952-54; v.p. Ky. Assn. Colls. and Secondary Schs., 1962-63, exec. com., 1959-64, pres., 1963-64; chmn. exec. com. Ky. Ind. Coll. Found.; mem. Ky. Commn. on Higher Edn., 1967-70; mem. Ky. Govt. Council, 1968—; adviser Texas Assn. Sch. Bds., 1957-59; cons. Pres. Com. White House Conf. Edn., 1955; mem. Ky. Devel. Council, 1961-65; mem. Ky. Constn. Revision Assembly, 1964-66. Recipient Distinguished Alumni award U. Ky., 1963, Centennial award, 1964. Mem. Nat., Ky. edn. assns., Newcomen Soc., So. Assn. Bapt. Colls. (pres. 1965-66), Bapt. World Aliance (chmn. mens dept. 1965-67), So. Assn. Colls. and Schs. (commn. on colls. 1971-77), Kappa Delta Pi, Phi Delta Kappa, Phi Kappa Tau. Democrat. Baptist. Kiwanian. Contbr. articles to profl. jours. Home: Route 4 Elk Lake Shores Owenton KY 40359

MILLS, RUSSELL CLARENCE, univ. adminstr.; b. Milw., Nov. 13, 1918; s. Clarence A. and Edith (Parrett) M.; B.S., U. Wis., 1940, M.S., 1942, Ph.D., 1944; m. Margaret A. Muth, June 19, 1940; children—Randolph, Elizabeth, Russell Clarence, Peter, Melissa. Asst. prof. biochemistry U. Kans., Lawrence, 1946-48, asso. prof., 1948-51, prof., 1951—, chmn. dept., 1948-62, asst. dean Grad. Sch., 1962-64, asso. dean, 1964-70, asso. dean Med. Sch., 1964-72, asso. vice chancellor for health affairs, 1972-76, univ. dir. support services, 1976—. Alan Gregg Traveling fellow, 1970-71. Served with USNR, 1944-46. Mem. Am. Soc. Biol. Chemists, AAAS. Contbr. articles to profl. jours. Home: 2203 W 70 Terr Shawnee Mission KS 66208 Office: U Kans Med Center Kansas City KS 66103

MILLS, SHIRLEY COLLUM, assn. exec.; b. Shelbyville, Tex., Jan. 19, 1936; d. John Bailey and Ruby Ealine (Kay) C.; B.S., La. State U., Baton Rouge, 1971, M.S., 1972. Asst. librarian Raleigh County Public Library, Beckley, W.Va.; dir. Miracle Valley Regional Library Systems, City-County Public Library, Moundsville, W.Va., 1974-78; exec. sec. Public Library Assn., ALA, Chgo., 1978—; adv. com. Gov. W.Va. Conf. Libraries and Info. Services, 1978. Mem. ALA, Council Library Assn. Execs., Ill. Library Assn., W.Va. Library Assn. Democrat. Episcopalian. Mem. editorial staff Southeastern Libraries, 1975-77. Home: 2700 N Hampden Ct Apt 16C Chicago IL 60614 Office: 50 E Huron St Chicago IL 60611

MILLS, THEODORE MASON, sociologist, educator; b. Fairfield, Ind., May 6, 1920; s. Charles S., Sr., and Pearl (Mason) M.; A.B., Guilford Coll., 1941; M.A., Haverford Coll., 1942; Ph.D., Harvard, 1952; m. Mary Jane Seaman, June 21, 1947; children—Duncan Kimball, Peter Benjamin, Sarah Jane. Lectr. sociology, also research asso. Lab. of Social Relations of Harvard, 1952-55, asst. prof. sociology and gen. edn., 1956-60; asso. prof. sociology, dir. interaction lab. Yale, 1960-68; prof., chmn. dept. sociology State U. N.Y. at Buffalo, 1968-72, also dir. Center for Study Human Groups; cons. USN, Family Service N.Y., Niagara Internat. Inst., A.K. Rice Inst., Prentice-Hall pubs. Mem. Math. Seminar for Social Scientists, 1950; vis. Fulbright prof. U. Oslo, 1955-56; vis. prof. U. Oslo, 1973-74; fellow Center Advanced Study in Behavioral Scis., Stanford, Calif., 1964-65, Social Sci. Research Council, 1951-52. Mem. Guilford (Conn.) Dem. Com., 1962-65. Served with Am. Friends Service Com. China Convoy, 1942-46. Mem. Am. Sociol. Assn., Am. Anthrop. Assn., Soc. Exptl. Psychology, Am. Psychol. Assn., Social Research Assn., Eastern Sociol. Soc. Author: (with others) Group Structure and the Newcomer, 1957, Group Transformation: an Analysis of a Learning Group, 1964, The Sociology of Small Groups, 1967; (with Stan Rosenberg) Readings on the Sociology of Small Groups, 1970; (film) Fathers and Sons; A Study in Group Dynamics, 1972. Asso. editor Sociometry, 1963-66, Personality and Social Systems. Home: 331 Depew Ave Buffalo NY 14214 Office: Center Study Human Groups Ellicott Complex State U NY Buffalo Amherst NY 14261

MILLS, WILBUR DAIGH, lawyer, former U.S. congressman; b. Kensett, Ark., May 24, 1909; s. Ardra Pickens and Abbie Lois (Daigh) M.; student Hendrix Coll., 1926-30, Harvard Law Sch., 1930-33; m. Clarine Billingsley, May 27, 1934; children—Martha Sue, Rebecca Ann. Admitted to Ark. bar, 1933, began practice in Searcy; county and probate judge, White County, 1934-38; cashier Bank of Kensett, 1934-35; mem. 76th-94th Congresses from 2d Ark. Dist.; tax counsel firm Shea and Gould, N.Y.C., 1977—. Democrat. Methodist. Mason (33 deg.). Office: care Shea and Gould 330 Madison Ave New York NY 10017

MILLS, WILLIAM ANDREW, accountant; b. nr. Sandersville, Ga., Apr. 7, 1910; s. Oscar L. and Willie Mae (Griffin) M.; B.S., U. Ga., 1934; m. Ruth H. Waters, Aug. 31, 1940 (dec.). Staff accountant M. H. Barnes & Co., C.P.A.'s, Savannah, Ga., 1934-43, 46-47; partner Barnes, Askew, Mills & Co., C.P.A.'s Savannah, 1947-61; partner Deloitte, Haskins & Sells, C.P.A.'s, Savannah, 1961-73, now ret. Served to capt. AUS, 1943-46. C.P.A., Ga., La., N.C. Mem. Am. Inst. C.P.A.'s, Ga. Soc. C.P.A.'s, Beta Gamma Sigma, Phi Kappa Phi, Beta Alpha Psi. Kiwanian. Home: 802 E 41st St Savannah GA 31401 Office: Suite 618 Citizens & So Nat Bank Bldg Savannah GA 31402

MILLS, WILLIAM HAYES, lawyer; b. Gordo, Ala., Mar. 30, 1931; s Early S. and Bama (Cameron) M; LL.B., U. Ala., 1956. Admitted to Ala. bar, 1956, since practiced in Birmingham; partner firm Rogers, Howard, Redden & Mills, 1961-79, Redden, Mills & Clark, 1979—; arbitrator Fed. Mediation and Conciliation Service, Am. Arbitration Assn. Served with AUS, 1948-50, 50-51. Mem. Am., Ala., Birmingham bar assns., Am., Ala. trial lawyers assns., Am. Judicature Soc. Baptist. Club: Birmingham Optimist. Home: 1418 Sharpsburg Circle Birmingham AL 35213 Office: 1st Ala Bank Bldg Birmingham AL 35203

MILLS, WILLIS NATHANIEL, JR., architect; b. N.Y.C., Sept. 25, 1933; s. Willis Nathaniel and Esther Elizabeth (Stehle) M.; A.B. magna cum laude, Princeton, 1955, M.F.A., 1958; m. Elizabeth Wylie Case, Aug. 14, 1956; children—Willis Nathaniel III, Jonathan, Elizabeth, David. With Pedersen & Tilney, New Haven, 1960-62, Earl P. Carlin, New Haven, 1962-63; with SMS Architects, Stamford, Conn., 1963-, partner, 1969-; teaching fellow Princeton, 1956-57; prin. works include: residences, Tokeneke Club, Darien, Conn., Hudson River Museum, Yonkers, N.Y., St. Matthews Ch., Wilton, Conn., Waveny Care Center, New Canaan, Conn., New Canaan Library. Co-chmn. Council Environ. Planning, Wilton, Conn., 1969-71; mem. adv. bd. Wilton Youth Project, 1969-71; dir. Regional Ecumenical Project, 1967-69; bd. dirs. Wilton Hist. Soc., 1971-75. Mem. Wilton Bd. Selectmen, 1969-72; chmn. Council on Pub. Facilities, Wilton; pres. bd. Conn. Architecture Found. Served to 1st lt. USAF, 1958-60. Recipient Butler prize Princeton, 1955, AIA medal for design excellence Princeton, 1958, Record House awards, 1967, 71. Mem. AIA. Democrat. Episcopalian. Clubs: Silver Spring Country (Ridgefield, Conn.); Chatham (Mass.) Beach and Tennis. Author: (with Nolan Lushington) Libraries Designed for Users, 1979. Home: 115 Signal Hill Rd Wilton CT 06897 Office: 59 Grove St New Canaan CT 06840

MILLSAPS, FRED RAY, investor; b. Blue Ridge, Ga., Apr. 30, 1929; s. Samuel Hunter and Ora Lee (Bradshaw) M.; A.B., Emory U., 1951; postgrad. U. Wis. Sch. Banking, 1955-57, Harvard Bus. Sch., 1962; m. Audrey Margaret Hopkins, June 22, 1957; children—Judith Gail, Stephen Hunter, Walter Scott. Auditor, Fed. Res. Bank, Atlanta, 1953-58, dept. mgr., 1958-61, asst. cashier, 1962-63, asst. v.p., New Orleans br., 1964-65, v.p., Atlanta, 1965; fin. v.p. Fla. Power & Light Co., 1965-69; pres., dir. First Nat. Bank of Fort Lauderdale (Fla.), 1969-73; chmn., pres. Landmark Banking Corp. of Fla., Ft. Lauderdale, 1971-78; chmn. Landmark Union Trust Bank of St. Petersburg (Fla.), 1976-78; mem. adv. bd. Shipp Corp., Toronto, Ont., Golden Bear, Inc. Chmn. com. of 100 Broward County (Fla.) Indsl. Devel. Bd., 1972-77; chmn. S. Fla. Coordinating Council, 1976-78; chmn. WPBT Community TV Found. of South Fla., 1973-75, Fla. So. Coll., Lakeland, Gleason Inverrary Classic, Holy Cross Hosp.; mem. Fla. Council 100. Methodist. Clubs: Tower, Inverrary, Coral Ridge Country (Fort Lauderdale). Home: 2665 NE 37th Dr Fort Lauderdale FL 33308

MILLSAPS, KNOX, educator; b. Birmingham, Ala., Sept. 10, 1921; s. Knox Taylor and Millie Mae (Joyce) M.; B.A., Auburn U., 1940; Ph.D., Calif. Inst. Tech., 1943; m. Lorraine Marie Hartle, June 12, 1956; children—Melinda Marie, Mary Charmaine, Karla Marie, Knox Taylor. Asso. prof. aero. engring. Ohio State U., Columbus, 1946-48; mathematician Office Air Research, 1948-49; prof. physics Auburn (Ala.) U., 1949-50, 51-52; research physicist Flight Research Lab., Wright Air Development Center, 1950-51, chief mathematician Aero. Research Lab., 1952-55; prof. mech. engring. Mass. Inst. Tech., Cambridge, 1955-56; chief sci. Air Force Missile Devel. Center, 1955-60; exec. dir. Air Force Office Sci. Research, 1960-63; research prof. aerospace engring. U. Fla., Gainesville, 1963-68, chmn. dept. engring. sci., 1973—; head prof. mech. engring. Colo. State U., Fort Collins, 1968-73. Mem. Am. Phys. Soc., Am. Math. Soc., Math. Assn. Am., Soc. Indsl. and Applied Math., Soc. Engring. Sci., Am. Inst. Aeros. and Astronautics, Sigma Xi. Clubs: Cosmos; Gainesville Golf and Country. Home: PO Box 13857 Gainesville FL 32604

MILLSON, WARNER LEE, retail co. exec.; b. Seattle, May 4, 1937; s. Cyril Albert and Norma Lee Nettie (Cochran) M.; B.S. magna cum laude, Am. U., Washington, 1961; M.B.A., Harvard, 1963; m. Mary Louise James, Sept. 12, 1959; children—Warner Lee, Scott Allen, James Walter. Controller, Intercraft Industries, Chgo., 1967-70; controller Apeco Corp., Evanston, Ill., 1970-74; fin. v.p. Story Chem. Corp., Muskegon, Mich., 1974-75; pres. Millson Enterprises Inc., Orange Park, Fla., 1975—. Home: 21 Mitchell Ave Orange Park FL 32073 Office: 410 Blanding Blvd Orange Park FL 32073

MILLSTEIN, IRA MARTIN, lawyer; b. N.Y.C., Nov. 8, 1926; s. Harry and Birdie (Rosenbaum) M.; B.S., Columbia U., 1947, LL.B. (Harlan Fiske Stone scholar), 1949; m. Diane Greenberg, July 3, 1949; children—James Eliot, Elizabeth Jane. Admitted to N.Y. bar, 1949, U.S. Supreme Ct. bar; asso. firm Weil, Gotshal & Manges, N.Y.C., 1951-57, partner firm, 1957—; atty. antitrust div. Dept. Justice, Washington, 1949-51, spl. asst. to Atty. Gen., 1951; adj. prof. law N.Y. U. Law Sch., 1967—. Chmn. Com. on Ratemaking and Econ. Regulation, Adminstrv. Conf. of U.S., 1974—; chmn. Nat. Commn. on Consumer Fin., 1971-72; chmn. N.Y.C.'s Spl. Commn. of Inquiry into Energy Failures, 1977; co-founder, mem. bd. advisors Columbia U. Center for Law and Econ. Studies, 1976—; chmn. Columbia U. Law Sch. Continuing Legal Edn. Com., 1977—; bd. overseers Albert Einstein Coll. Medicine, Yeshiva U., Bronx, N.Y., 1977—. Mem. Am. (chmn. antitrust law sect. 1977-78), N.Y. State (past chmn. antitrust law sect.) bar assns., Assn. Bar of City of N.Y., Fed. Bar Council, Columbia U. Law Sch. Alumni Assn. (past dir.). Club: City Athletic. Contbr. articles to profl. jours. Home: 1240 Flagler Dr Mamaroneck NY 10543 Office: 767 Fifth Ave New York City NY 10022

MILLSTONE, ISADORE ERWIN, constrn. co. exec.; b. St. Louis, Jan. 6, 1907; s. Louis I. and Mary (Apter) M.; B.S. in Archtl. Engring., Washington U., St. Louis, 1927; m. Goldie G. Gollin, Aug. 24, 1930; 1 son, David S. Pres., Millstone Constrn., Inc., St. Louis, 1930—; dir. Merc. Trust Co., St. Louis. Pres., Millstone Charitable Found., Jewish Community Centers Assn., 1964-65, World Fedn. YMHA's and Jewish Community Centers; v.p. Nat. Jewish Welfare Bd. Bd. dirs. Jewish Fedn. St. Louis; trustee Washington U.; trustee, v.p. Hebrew Union Coll.-Jewish Inst. Religion. Mem. Tau Beta Pi, Sigma Alpha Mu. Jewish (dir. temple). Clubs: Mo. Athletic, St. Louis, Engrs., Westwood Country (St. Louis); Old Port Yacht (North Palm Beach, Fla.). Home: 801 S Skinker Blvd Saint Louis MO 63105 Office: 8510 Eager Rd Saint Louis MO 63144

MILMAN, DORIS HOPE, psychiatrist; b. N.Y.C., Nov. 17, 1917; d. Barnet J. and Rose (Smoleroff) M.; B.A., Barnard Coll., 1939; M.D., N.Y. U., 1942; m. Nathan Kreeger, June 15, 1941; 1 dau., Elizabeth Kreeger Goldman. Intern, then resident in pediatrics Jewish Hosp., Bklyn., 1942-47; resident in psychiatry Bellevue Hosp., N.Y.C., 1948-51; practice medicine specializing in child and adolescent psychiatry, Bklyn., 1950-64; mem. faculty Downstate Med. Center, Bklyn., 1964—, prof. pediatrics, 1973—, acting chmn. dept., 1973-75. Grace Potter Rice fellow, 1938-39. Diplomate Am. Bd. Pediatrics. Fellow Am. Acad. Pediatrics; mem. Am. Psychiat. Assn., Bklyn. Psychiat. Soc., Am. Pediatric Soc., N.Y. Pediatric Soc., Am. Orthopsychiat. Assn., Bklyn. Acad. Pediatrics, Phi Beta Kappa, Alpha Omega Alpha. Contbr. articles to profl. jours. Home: 126 Westminster Rd Brooklyn NY 11218 Office: Box 49 450 Clarkson Ave Brooklyn NY 11203

MILNE, DAVID SPENCER, educator; b. Ogden, Utah, Oct. 10, 1911; s. Erastus J. and Annie E. (Spencer) M.; A.B., U. Calif. at Los Angeles, 1932; M.A., U. So. Calif., 1939; Ph.D., U. Chgo., 1948; m. Thair Smart, June 17, 1938; children—David S., Terry Ann, Kenneth Smart, Keith Thomas. Case worker, then case supr. Los Angeles County Dept. Charities and State Relief Adminstrn., 1933-36; parole officer Whittier State Sch., 1936-45; parole officer Calif. Youth Authority, 1936-45, field rep., 1945-46; asst. prof., asso. prof. San Diego State U., 1946-52, prof. sociology, 1952-76, chmn. dept. sociology and anthropology, 1951-55, chmn. social scis. div., 1956-69. Pres. Calif. Community Councils, 1959-61; del. 1960 White House Conf. on Children and Youth; chmn. San Diego County Coordinating Councils, 1956-59; del. UN Congress on Crime and Delinquency, Stockholm, 1965; mem. Gov.'s Adv. Com. on Children and Youth. Mem. Am., Pacific sociol. socs., Nat., Calif. probation and parole assns., Nat., Calif. confs. social work, San Diego Social Worker Club (pres. 1948), Nat. Council Family Relations (pres. San Diego chpt. 1961-62). Home: 5118 Bixel Dr San Diego CA 92115 Office: Dept Sociology San Diego State University San Diego CA 92182

MILNE, DONALD GEORGE, pub. co. exec.; b. Oak Park, Ill., May 26, 1927; s. Alexander L. and Katherine (Diez) M.; student U. Utah, 1945-46; B.S., Northwestern U., 1949; postgrad. Loyola U., Chgo., 1952-55, Ill. Inst. Tech., 1957; M.B.A., U. Chgo., 1959; m. Marilynn W. Ruopp, May 5, 1951; children—Paul D., Susan Joan, Philip W. Salesman, IBM Corp., 1949-51; with World Book-Childcraft Internat., Inc., Chgo., 1951—, pres., chief exec. officer, 1978—, dir., 1965—, mem. exec. mgmt. com., 1964—; v.p., asst. sec.-treas., dir. World Book-Childcraft of Can. Ltd.; v.p., dir. World Book Life Ins. Co.; pres., dir., World Book Ency., Inc.; exec. v.p., sec., dir. Field

Enterprises Internat. Inc. Served with USNR, 1945-46. C.P.A., Ill. Mem. Ill. Soc. C.P.A.'s, Northwestern U. Alumni Assn. Presbyterian. Home: 1308 N Scott St Wheaton IL 60187 Office: Merchandise Mart Plaza Chicago IL 60654

MILNE, EMILE ANTONIO, journalist; b. Panama City, Panama, June 30, 1946; s. Cedric Antonio and Olga Madeline (Rose) M.; came to U.S., 1952, naturalized, 1957; B.A. (Ford Found. fellow, N.Y.C. Urban fellow), Pace U., 1978. Reporter, San Francisco Examiner, 1968, N.Y. Post, N.Y.C., 1969-72; exec. editor Community News Service, N.Y.C., 1972-75; sr. writer Continental Group, N.Y.C., 1977-78; sr. editor Black Enterprise mag., N.Y.C., 1978—. Mem. Internat. Assn. Bus. Communicators, Nat. Black Journalists Assn., NAACP (life). Home: 132-09 160th St Jamaica NY 11434 Office: Black Enterprise Mag 295 Madison Ave New York NY 10017

MILNE, ERIC NIGHTINGALE CAMPBELL, radiologist; b. Perth, Scotland, Feb. 8, 1929; s. Gordon and Margaret (Campbell) M.; came to U.S., 1975, naturalized Can. citizen, 1972; M.B.Ch.B., Edinburgh U., 1956; m. Norah Symington, Dec. 27, 1954; children—Alastair, Steven, Penelope, Peter, Christopher. Intern, Monmouth Meml. Hosp., Long Branch, N.J., 1956-57; resident Tulare/King County Hosp., Springville, Calif., 1957-58; sr. house officer Royal Infirmary, Edinburgh, Scotland, 1958-60; Med. Research Council fellow Edinburgh U., 1960-61; radiologist McKellar Gen. Hosp., Thunder Bay, Ont., Can., 1961-65; asst. prof. diagnostic radiology U. Western Ont., London, 1965-67, Gordon Richards Cancer Research fellow, 1966; asst. prof. radiology Peter Bent Brigham Hosp. and Harvard U. Med. Sch., Boston, 1967-69; prof., founding dir. radiol. research labs. U. Toronto (Ont.), 1969-75; prof., chmn. dept. radiol. scis. U. Calif., Irvine, 1975-79, dir. radiology residency tng. program, 1974—; fellow Cardiovascular Research Inst., U. Calif., San Francisco, 1966-67; Rigler scholar UCLA, 1973; Century Forum lectr. U. Vt., 1977; Silver Ann. speaker Sociedad de Radiologica del Atlantico, Barranquilla, 1977; chmn. nat. adv. com. Mayo Clinic Biotech. Research Resource, 1978-79; cons. at large radiology sect. Orange County (Calif.) Health Planning Council. Served with Brit. Army, R.A.M.C., 1946-47, Forces Broadcasting Service, 1947-49. Recipient Atkinson and Bickel Found. awards U. Toronto, 1969, Negotiated Devel. award Med. Research Council Can., 1969-72; Gordon Richards fellow, 1951. Mem. Assn. Univ. Radiologists, Soc. Chmn. Acad. Depts. Radiology, Soc. Photo-optical Instrumentation Engrs., Am. Coll. Radiology, Royal Coll. Radiologists (Eng.), Royal Coll. Physicians and Surgeons (Can.), Royal Coll. Physicians (Ont.), Fleischner Soc. (founding); hon. mem. Phila. Roentgen Ray Soc., No. Japan Radiologic Soc., Bavarian-Am. Radiol. Soc. Author video and audio-tape teaching presentations; contbr. numerous articles to profl. publs.; guest editor Radiol. Clinics No. Am., 1978. Home: 32322 Azores Laguna Niguel CA 92677 Office: Dept Radiol Scis U Calif Irvine Coll Medicine Irvine CA 92717. *The successful academic needs self-doubt more than intellect. The accolade of an audience provides continued stimulus for his work but their approval is never enough for long. For him success can only be measured against his own unattainable inner standards. The advantage is that such a person will not only never give up in the face of failure - he will never give up in the face of success!*

MILNE, GEORGE DAVIDSON, ins. co. exec.; b. Kansas City, Mo., Nov. 28, 1914; s. George and Elizabeth (Wilson) M.; A.A., Jr. Coll. of Kansas City, 1934; B.A., U. Mo., Kansas City, 1936; M.A., U. Kan., 1937; m. Mary Eloise Kelso, Dec. 20, 1941; children—John Kelso, Jean Elizabeth. Asst. treas. Bus. Men's Assurance Co., Kansas City, 1937-51; treas. United Benefit Life Ins. Co., Omaha, 1951-62; vice chmn., chief investment officer Franklin Life Ins. Co., Springfield, Ill., 1962—, also dir., mem. exec. com., chmn. finance com.; treas., dir. Franklin United Life Ins. Co. of N.Y., Franklin Fin. Services Corp.; dir. Am. Franklin Co.; chmn. bd. mgrs. Franklin Life Variable Annuity Funds A and B. Commr., treas. Pub. Bldg. Commn., Springfield, 1966-70; active United Charities Campaigns, YMCA, ARC, Boy Scouts Am., Art Assn., PTA, Symphony Orch. Assn., Dads Club. Served to capt. Finance Dept., AUS, 1942-46. Decorated Army Commendation medal; recipient Alumni Distinguished Achievement award U. Mo., 1969. Mem. Am. Council Life Ins., Investment Analysts Soc. Chgo., U. Mo. Alumni Assn., Alpha Phi Omega, Pi Mu Epsilon. Republican. Presbyn. Mason (32 deg., K.T., Shriner). Clubs: Illini Country, Sangamo. Home: 720 S 7th St Springfield IL 62703 Office: 1 Franklin Sq Springfield IL 62713

MILNE, LORUS JOHNSON, educator, naturalist, author; b. Toronto, Ont., Can., Sept. 12, 1912; s. Charles Stanley and Edna Shepard (Johnson) M.; B.A., U. Toronto, 1933; M.A., Harvard, 1934, Ph.D., 1936; m. Margery Joan Greene, Sept. 10, 1939. Prof. biology Southwestern U., 1936-37; asso. prof. biology Randolph-Macon Woman's Coll., Lynchburg, Va., 1937-43; war research vision in aviation med. Johnson Found. Med. Physics, U. Pa., Phila., 1942-47; asso. prof. zoology U. Vt., Burlington, 1947-48; prof. zoology U. N.H., Durham, 1948—, chmn. inter-dept. gen. biology, 1949-55; writer Bausch & Lomb Optical Co., Eastman Kodak Co.; screen-tour lectr. Nat Audubon Soc.; research asso. Cranbrook Inst. Sci.; cons. writer, biol. scis. curriculum study at U. Colo., 1960; vis. prof. Scripps Inst. Oceanography, U. Calif., 1957, Wesleyan U., 1961, Fla. Internat. U., 1974; mem. staff U. N.H. Writers Conf., 1961, Writers' Conf. in Rocky Mountains, U. Colo., 1962, 67, 71; cons. writer Nat. Geog. Soc., 1966; cons., leader UNESCO SE Asia-Australia Conf. on Biology, Auckland, N.Z., 1966; ecology leader Albert Schweitzer Found. Conf., 1977. Recipient Westinghouse-AAAS writing award, 1947, Nash Conservation award, 1954. Ford Found. fellow, 1953-54. Eugene F. Saxton Meml. fellow for distinguished writing, 1954; exchangee U.S.-South Africa Leader Exchange Program, 1959. Mem. Corp. Marine Biol., Animal Behavior Soc., AAAS, Am. Soc. Zoologists, Sigma Xi. Club: Explorers. Author: Machine Shop Methods, 1950; (with wife) Multitude of Living Things, 1947; Famous Naturalists, 1952; The Biotic World and Man, 1952; The Mating Instinct, 1954; The World of Night, 1956; Paths Across the Earth, 1958; Animal Life, 1959; Plant Life, 1959; The Balance of Nature, 1960; The Senses of Animals and Men, 1962; The Valley, Meadow, Grove and Stream, 1963; Because of a Tree, 1963; Water and Life, 1964; The Crab That Crawled Out of the Past, 1965; (with wife and Ralph and Mildred Buschsbaum) The Lower Animals: Living Invertebrates of the World, 1960; (With wife and editors of Life) The Mountains, 1962; (with wife) Gift from the Sky, 1967; Patterns of Survival, 1967; Living Plants of the World, 1967; The Ages of Life, 1968; The Phoenix Forest, 1968; The Nature of Animals, 1968; North American Birds, 1969; When the Tide Goes Far Out, 1970; The Nature of Life, 1970; The Cougar Doesn't Live Here Any More: Does The World Still Have Room for Wildlife?, 1971; The Nature of Plants, 1971; The Arena of Life: The Dynamics of Ecology, 1972; The How and Why of Growing, 1972; Invertebrates of North America, 1972; The Animal in Man, 1973; Because of a Flower, 1975; (with wife and Franklin Russell) The Secret Life of Animals, 1975; (with wife) Ecology Out of Joint, 1977; A World Alive: The Natural Wonders of a New England River Valley, 1977. Contbr. articles to periodicals, anthologies. Field studies Can., U.S., Latin Am., W.I., Equatorial, North and South Africa, Europe, Near and Far East, Australia, New Zealand. Home: 1 Garden Ln Durham NH 03824. *The unifying joy in my life stems from discoveries, both personal and from the observations of others, about the on-going interactions among all kinds of life; and from sharing my enthusiasm on these topics with others of all ages. A reverence for life and a delight in learning about plants and animals, I find, opens the way to friendly communication with people of all nations, regardless of language, education or economic status.*

MILNE, WILLIAM GORDON, educator; b. Haverhill, Mass., Mar. 17, 1921; s. Morton Russell and Lulu (Smith) M.; A.B., Brown U., 1941, A.M., 1947; Ph.D., Harvard, 1951. Instr. English, U. Kansas City (Mo.), 1947-48; lectr. Mass. Inst. Tech., 1951, Tufts U., summers 1951, 52; mem. faculty Lake Forest (Ill.) Coll., 1951—, prof., 1958—. Fulbright guest prof. U. Würzburg (Germany), 1958-59. Served to lt. comdr. USNR, 1942-46. Mem. AAUP, Modern Lang. Assn., Phi Beta Kappa. Author: George William Curtis and the Genteel Tradition, 1956; The American Political Novel, 1966; The Sense of Society: A History of the American Novel of Manners, 1977. Home: 501 Green Bay Rd Lake Bluff IL 60044 Office: Lake Forest Coll Lake Forest IL 60045

MILNER, BRENDA ATKINSON LANGFORD, psychologist; b. Manchester, Eng., July 15, 1918; came to Can., 1944; d. Samuel and Leslie (Doig) Langford; B.A., Cambridge (Eng.) U., 1939, M.A., 1949, Sc.D., 1972; Ph.D., McGill U., 1952. Exptl. officer U.K. Ministry of Supply, 1941-44; prof. agrégé Institut de Psychologie, Université de Montréal, 1944-52; research asso. psychology dept. McGill U., Montreal, 1952-53, lectr. dept. neurology and neurosurgery, 1953-60, asst. prof., 1960-64, asso. prof., 1964-70, prof. psychology, 1970—; head neuropsychology research unit Montreal Neurol. Inst., 1953—; Clothworkers fellow Girton Coll., Cambridge, 1972-73. Asso. Med. Research Council Can., 1964—; recipient Disting. Sci. Contbn. award Am. Psychol. Assn., 1973; Karl Spencer Lashley award Am. Philos. Soc., 1979. Fellow Royal Soc. London, Royal Soc. Can., Am. Psychol. Assn., AAAS, Can. Psychol. Assn.; mem. Am. Epilepsy Soc., Am. Neurol. Assn., Association de Psychologie Scientifique de Langue Française, Brit. Soc. Exptl. Psychology, Psychonomic Soc., Eastern Psychol. Assn., Internat. Neuropsychology Symposium, Soc. Neurosci., Nat. Acad. Scis. (fgn. asso.), Am. Acad. Neurology (asso.), Assn. Research in Nervous and Mental Diseases (asso.), Royal Soc. Medicine (affiliate), Sigma Xi. Mem. editorial bd. Neuropsychologia, 1973—. Office: Montreal Neurol Inst 3801 University St Montreal PQ H3A 2B4 Canada

MILNER, ERIC CHARLES, mathematician, educator; b. London, May 17, 1928; s. Frederick Charles and Anne Elizabeth (Kluth) M.; came to Can., 1967, naturalized, 1972; B.Sc., King's Coll., London U., 1949, M.Sc., 1950, Ph.D., 1962; m. Esther Stella Lawton, Aug. 19, 1954 (dec.); children—Suzanne, Mark, Paul, Simon; m. 2d, Elizabeth Forsyth Borthwick, July 2, 1979. Lectr. math. U. Singapore, 1951-61; lectr. U. Reading (Eng.), 1961-67; prof. U. Calgary, 1967—, head dept. math., 1977—; vis. prof. U. Oxford, 1978-79, U. Cambridge, 1971-72. NRC Can. grantee, 1967—. Mem. Can. Math. Soc., London Math. Soc., Am. Math. Soc., Am. Math. Assn., N.Y. Acad. Scis., Royal Soc. Can., Can. Soc. History and Philosophy of Sci. Research in set theory and combinatorics. Office: 2920 24th Ave NW Calgary AB T2N 1N4 Canada

MILNER, HAROLD WILLIAM, real estate trust and hotel exec.; b. Salt Lake City, Nov. 11, 1934; s. Kenneth W. and Olive (Schoettlin) M.; B.S., U. Utah, 1960; M.B.A., Harvard, 1962; m. Susan Emmett, June 19, 1959 (div. 1976); children—John Kenneth, Mary Sue, Jennifer Rebecca; m. 2d, Lois Friemuth, Aug. 14, 1977. Instr. Brigham Young U., Provo, Utah, 1962-64; v.p. Gen. Paper Corp., Mpls., 1964-65; dir. finance Amalgamated Sugar Co., Ogden, Utah, 1965-67; corp. treas. Marriott Corp., Washington, 1967-70; pres., chief exec. officer, trustee Hotel Investors, Kensington, Md., 1970-75; pres., chief exec. officer Pick Hotels Corp., Chgo., 1975—. Served as lt. AUS, 1960. Mem. Greater Chgo. Hotel Assn. (dir. 1977—), Young Pres.'s Orgn., Am. Hotel and Motel Assn. (industry adv. council). Mem. Ch. Jesus Christ Latter-day Saints. Author: A Special Report on Contract Maintenance, 1963. Home: 474 Butler Dr Lake Forest IL 60045 Office: 532 S Michigan Ave Chicago IL 60605

MILNER, MARTIN SAM, actor; b. Detroit, Dec. 28, 1931; s. Sam Gordon and Jerre (Martin) M.; student U. So. Calif., San Fernando Valley State Coll.; m. Judith Bess Jones, Feb. 23, 1957; children—Amy, Molly, Stuart, Andrew. Appeared in numerous films; star TV shows Route 66, Adam 12, Swiss Family Robinson; appeared in TV miniseries The Seekers, 1979. Served with AUS. Office: care Blake Agy Ltd 409 N Camden Dr Beverly Hills CA 90210*

MILNER, PETER MARSHALL, educator; b. Silkstone Common, Eng., June 13, 1919; s. David William and Edith Anne (Marshall) M.; B.S., Leeds U., 1941; M.S., McGill U., Ph.D., 1954; m. Susan Walker, Oct. 13, 1970; 1 son, David Elliot. Sr. sci. officer U.K. Ministry Supply, 1941-48; research asso. physics McGill U., 1948-50, research asst., prof. dept. psychology, 1950—. Fellow Am. Psychol. Assn.; mem. Canadian Psychol. Assn., Animal Behavior Soc., Psychonomic Soc., Sigma Xi. Author: Physiological Psychology. Home: 512 Clarke Ave Westmount PQ H3Y 3C9 Canada Office: Dept Psychology McGill U Dr Penfield Ave Montreal PQ H3A 1B1 Canada

MILNER, PHILIP H., former banker; b. Yonkers, N.Y., Nov. 19, 1912; s. Wilfrid W. and Marguerite (Todd) M.; student Washington and Lee U., 1932-34; grad. Sch. Banking Rutgers U., 1947; postgrad. N.Y. Inst. Credit, 1934-40; m. Marcia Wenzel, July 22, 1950; children—Jane G., Philip H. With Mfrs. Trust Co., 1934-61, v.p., 1951-61; with Mfrs. Hanover Trust (merger Mfrs. Trust Co. and Hanover Bank 1961), sr. v.p., 1963-66, exec. v.p. met. div., mem. gen. adminstrv. bd., 1966-76, exec. v.p., asst. to pres., 1976-77; ret., 1977; dir. Interboro Mut. Indemnity Ins. Co., N.Y.C., Reeves Bros., Inc., Sterling Nat. Bank, Rolls-Royce Motors Inc.; trustee Met. Savs. Bank. Bd. dirs. Vis. Nurse Service N.Y. Episcopalian. Clubs: Union League (N.Y.C.); Misquamicut (Watch Hill, R.I.); Key Largo Angler's, Ocean Reef (Key Largo, Fla.). Home: 8 Knoll Ln Ocean Reef Key Largo FL 33037 also Winona Ave Weekapaug RI 02891

MILNES, ARTHUR GEORGE, educator, elec. engr.; b. Heswall, Eng., July 30, 1922 (came to U.S. 1957, naturalized 1964); s. George and Marion (Teasdale) M.; B.Sc., U. Bristol (Eng.), 1943, M.Sc., 1947, D.Sc., 1956; m. Mary Laverne Wertz, Dec. 4, 1955; children—Sheila Rae, Brian George, John Teasdale. With Royal Aircraft Establishment, 1943-57, prin. sci. officer, 1952-57; mem. faculty Carnegie-Mellon U., Pitts., 1957—, prof. elec. engring., 1960—, asso. head dept., 1966-69, Buhl prof., 1973—; cons. to industry on semiconductor devices, 1957. FOA research fellow Nat. Acad. Scis.-Royal Soc. London, 1954. Fellow Instn. Elec. Engrs. (London), IEEE, Am. Phys. Soc.; mem. Electrochem. Soc. Author: Transductors and Magnetic Amplifiers, 1957; (with D.L. Feucht) Heterojunctions and Metal-Semiconductor Junctions, 1972; Deep Impurities in Semiconductors, 1973; Semiconductor Devices and Integrated Electronics, 1979; contbr. articles to profl. jours. Home: 1417 Iverness Ave Pittsburgh PA 15217

MILNES, HUMPHREY NEWTON, educator; b. Oneida, N.Y., Nov. 2, 1919; s. Paul and Adele (Noyes) M.; B.A., U. Toronto, 1941, M.A., 1947; Ph.D., Ohio State U., 1949; m. Lillian Brett, Oct. 4, 1941 (div. Jan. 1963); children—Paul, Beverly; m. 2d, Irma Laakso McDonough, Sept. 28, 1966. Instr. German, Ohio State U., 1946-48; lectr. German, U. Coll., U. Toronto, 1948-52, asst. prof., 1952-59, asso. prof., 1959-64, prof., 1964—, head dept., 1967—; vis. lectr. Marburg U. (Germany), 1954; vis. prof. U. Coll., London, Eng., 1959-60. Served with Canadian Army, 1943-46. Mem. Can. Assn. U. Tchrs., Can. Assn. U. Tchrs. German. Club: Faculty (U. Toronto). Contbr. articles to scholarly jours. U.S., Can., England. Home: 98 Willcocks St Toronto ON M5S 1C8 Canada

MILNES, ROGER FARNAM, naval officer, thoracic surgeon; b. Oneida, N.Y., Apr. 14, 1923; B.A., Cornell U., 1944; M.D., U. Rochester; m. June 10, 1950; children—Christopher, Peter, Scott, James, Jeffrey. Commd. officer U.S. Navy, advanced through grades to rear adm.; served as insp. gen. med. U.S. Navy, also asst. chief for human resources and ops. Dept. Navy, Washington; now comdg. officer Naval Aerospace and Regional Med. Center, Pensacola, Fla. Mem. AMA, Am. Coll. Chest Physicians, Am. Thoracic Soc., Assn. Acad. Surgery, Assn. Mil. Surgeons. Contbr. articles to med. jours. Office: Naval Aerospace and Regional Med Center Pensacola FL 32512

MILNES, SHERRILL EUSTACE, baritone; b. Downers Grove, Ill., Jan. 10, 1935; s. James Knowlton and Thelma (Roe) M.; student Coe Coll.; B.A., Drake U., 1957, M.A., 1958; postgrad. Northwestern U., 1958-61; hon. degree Ripon Coll.; children by previous marriage—Eric, Erin; m. 2d, Nancy Denise Stokes, Sept. 28, 1969; 1 son, Shawn. Operatic debut, 1960; leading baritone Goldovsky Opera Co., N.Y.C., 1960-65, N.Y.C. Opera Co., 1964-67, San Antonio Opera Co., 1964-70, Cin. Opera Co., 1963-70, Balt. Opera Co., 1961-70, Pitts. Opera Co., 1962-71, Houston Opera Co., 1963-69, Met. Opera Co., N.Y.C., 1965—; appearances major world opera cos. including Covent Garden, London, L'Opera, Paris, Vienna (Austria) Staatsoper, Teatro Colon, Argentina, LáScala, Milan, Hamburg, Munich, Frankfurt, Berlin, Zurich; also TV and concerts; recs. RCA. Mem. Am. Guild Mus. Artists (bd. govs. 1969—), Affiliate Artists, Inc. (past pres., chmn. devel. com. 1966—, now chmn. bd.), Phi Mu Alfa Sinfonia. Office: care Herbert Barrett 1860 Broadway New York NY 10023

MILNOR, WILLIAM ROBERT, physician; b. Wilmington, Del., May 4, 1920; s. William Robert and Virginia (Sterling) M.; A.B., Princeton U., 1941; M.D., Johns Hopkins U., 1944; m. Gabriella Mahaffy, Aug. 19, 1944; children—Katherine Alexander, William Henry. Intern, resident Johns Hopkins Hosp., 1944-46; research fellow Nat. Heart Inst., 1949-51; physician-in-charge heart sta. Johns Hopkins Hosp., 1951-60, physician, 1952—, mem. faculty Johns Hopkins Med. Sch., 1951—, prof. physiology, 1969—; vis. fellow St. Catherine's Coll., Oxford (Eng.) U., 1968; mem. med. adv. panel Am. Inst. Biol. Scis., 1971—; assessor Nat. Med. Research Council of Australia, 1976—. Served to capt. M.C., USAAF, 1946-48. Diplomate Am. Bd. Internal Medicine. Fellow A.C.P.; mem. Am. Physiol. Soc., Am. Fedn. Clin. Research, Biomed. Engring. Soc., Am. Heart Assn. (chmn. research com. 1966), Heart Assn. Md. (past pres.). Clubs: L'Hirondelle, Princeton. Contbr. articles to med. textbooks, med. jours. Office: Johns Hopkins Med Sch 725 N Wolfe St Baltimore MD 21205

MILOSZ, CZESLAW, poet, author, educator; b. Lithuania, June 30, 1911; came to U.S., 1960, naturalized, 1970; s. Aleksander and Weronika (Kunat) M.; M.Juris, U. Wilno (Lithuania), 1934; Litt.D. (hon.), U. Mich., 1977; m. Janina Dluska, Jan. 1, 1944; children—Anthony, John Peter. Programmer, Polish Nat. Radio, 1935-39; diplomatic service Polish Fgn. Affairs Ministry, Warsaw, 1945-50; vis. lectr. U. Calif., Berkeley, 1960-61, prof. Slavic langs. and lits., 1961-78, prof. emeritus, 1978—; author books: The Captive Mind, 1953, Native Realm, 1968, Post-War Polish Poetry, 1965, The History of Polish Literature, 1969, Selected Poems, 1972, Bells in Winter, 1978. Recipient Prix Littéraire Européen, Les Guildes du Livre, Geneva, 1953, Neustadt Internat. prize for lit. U. Okla., 1978; citation U. Calif., Berkeley, 1978; Nat. Culture Fund fellow, 1934-35; Guggenheim fellow, 1976. Mem. Polish Inst. Letters and Scis. in Am., PEN Club in Exile. Office: Dept Slavic Langs and Lits U Calif Berkeley CA 94720

MILSAP, RONNIE, singer, rec. artist; b. Robinsville, N.C., Jan. 16; s. James Lee and Grace (Calhoun) M.; A.A., Young-Harris Jr. Coll., 1964; m. Frances Joyce Reeves, Oct. 30, 1965; 1 son, Ronald Todd. Country music singer; recs. for RCA Records. Mem. Country Music Assn. (Male Vocalist of Yr., 1974, 76, 77, Album of Yr. 1975, 77, 78, Entertainer of Yr. 1977), Nat. Acad. Rec. Arts and Scis. (Country Male Vocalist of Year 1974, 76). Office: care Don Reeves 12 Music Circle S Nashville TN 37203. *Since I am blind, there have been obstacles in my life. But there are advantages, too. For instance, I can concentrate more intensely on my music or whatever I am doing, because I am not distracted visually. I sometimes can tell a lot about people just from shaking a hand, feeling vibration, or listening to expression in one's voice—things that some sighted people never notice. I cannot see a sunset, but I am aware of some things some people take for granted, like being outside in the morning feeling the breeze on your face, or the way the earth smells after a rain, or the sound of snow falling. I don't want to dwell on my blindness, because never having seen before, everything I do, to me, is normal. I thank God for the things I can do, and the things I can't, well they really don't cross my mind. I don't need to see to play and sing my music, and I don't need to see to feel the love of people.*

MILSOM, ROBERT CORTLANDT, banker; b. Butler, Pa., Dec. 15, 1924; s. Robert C. and M. Ethel (Leyland) M.; B.S., John Carroll U., 1948. With Pitts. Nat. Bank, 1948—, asst. sec., asst. cashier customer relations div., 1953-56, asst. v.p. loan div., 1956-60, v.p. charge comml. loan group, 1960-65, sr. v.p. charge comml. banking div., 1965-68, exec. v.p., 1968-72, pres., 1972—, dir., also dir. Pitts. Nat. Corp.; dir. H.H. Robertson Co., Visa U.S.A. Inc. Bd. dirs. Mercy Hosp., Pitts., United Way of Allegheny County, Pitts. Ballet Theatre, Pitts. Regional Planning Assn., Regional Indsl. Devel. Corp. Served to 1st lt. AUS, 1943-46. Mem. Greater Pitts. C. of C. (dir.). Clubs: Pitts. Athletic, Allegheny, Duquesne, Fox Chapel Golf (Pitts.); Laurel Valley Golf; Rolling Rock. Office: Pittsburgh National Bank 5th Ave and Wood St Pittsburgh PA 15222

MILSTEIN, MILTON, architect; b. N.Y.C., May 17, 1910; s. Samuel and Rebecca (Zimmerman) M.; B.Arch. (Univ. awardee), Syracuse U., 1934; m. Nan Levy, Oct. 11, 1936; children—Lynne Milstein Frost, Robert M. Chief designer various Syracuse (N.Y.) and Buffalo archtl. offices, 1934-50; prin. Milton Milstein & Assos., Architects, Buffalo, 1950-66; sr. partner Milstein, Wittek, Davis & Assos., Buffalo, 1966—; v.p. Buffalo & Erie County Planning Assos., 1961-62; mem. N.Y. State Bd. for Architecture, 1966-76, chmn., 1975-76; works include govt. office bldgs., coll. and sch. bldgs., banks, housing projects, dormitories. Founding dir. Community Planning Assistance Center, Buffalo; coordinator Downtown Redevel. City of Buffalo and Waterfront, 1961-64; trustee Damen Coll., Amherst, N.Y. Centennial honoree Syracuse U. Sch. Architecture, 1974. Fellow AIA (pres. chpt. 1962-64, nat. com. on aesthetics), mem. N.Y. State Assn. Architects (past dir.), Nat. Council Archtl. Registration Bds. (cert.; mem. bd. examiners 1973-74, nat. chmn. profl. examiners 1975-76), Buffalo C. of C. Jewish. Clubs: Masons, Shriners. Office: Buffalo NY

MILSTEIN, NATHAN, concert violinist; b. Odessa, Russia, Dec. 31, 1904; s. Miron and Maria (Bluestein) M.; came to U.S., naturalized, 1942; student of P. Stoliarsky, Odessa, of Leopold Auer at Conservatory Music St. Petersburg, of Eugene Ysaye at Brussels; m. Therese Weldon, 1945; 1 dau., Maria Bernadette. Extensive tours of native country, 1920-26; ann. tours all European countries since 1929, interrupted by World War, also of U.S. and Can., 1929—; several tours S.Am., Cuba, Mex., N.Africa. Recipient Cross of Honor (Austria); decorated chevalier Legion of Honor (France), 1955, officer, 1967; Grammy award for classical-instrumental soloist, 1975. Mem. Acad. St. Cecilia (Italy). Address: care Shaw Concerts Inc 1995 Broadway New York NY 10023

MILSTEIN, RICHARD SHERMAN, lawyer; b. Westfield, Mass., May 9, 1926; s. Abraham and Sarah M.; A.B., Harvard U., 1948; J.D. Boston U., 1952. Admitted to Mass. bar, 1952, U.S. Supreme Ct. bar, 1960; asso. firm Ely, King, Corcoran, Milstein & Beaudry, Springfield, Mass., 1954-59, partner, 1959—; instr. Western New Eng. Coll., 1962-65, 74-76; adminstr. com. continuing legal edn. Mass. Bar Assn., 1960-69; dir. Mass. Continuing Legal Edn., Inc., 1969-76; exec. dir. Mass. Continuing Legal Edn.-New Eng. Law Inst., Inc., 1976—; mem. Gov.'s Jud. Nominating Commn., 1975-78. Chmn. personnel policy bd. City of Westfield, Mass., 1962-67; trustee Horace Smith Fund, 1972—; bd. tribunes, v.p., mem. exec. com. Sta. WGBY, Public TV; trustee Westfield Acad.; bd. dirs. Stage West, 1978—; bd. dirs. Bus. Fund for the Arts, 1978—; corporator Springfield Symphony Orch.; mem. trustee com. Mus. of Fine Arts, Springfield, 1978—. Served to lt. comdr. USCGR. Mem. Am. Law Inst., Am. Bar Assn., Mass. Bar Assn. (edn. com., future planning com. 1976—, sec. corp. law sect. 1978—), Hampden Bar Assn. (sec. 1959-63, exec. com. 1963-70, grievance com. 1967-70), Boston Bar Assn., Am. Counsel Assn., Am. Bar Found., Mass. Bar Found., Springfield Library and Museums Assn. (life). Jewish. Clubs: Harvard (Springfield; pres. 1962-65), Boston, Colony, Masons. Editorial bd. Mass. Law Quar., 1960-77. Home: 47 Mattoon St Springfield MA 01105 Office: 1387 Main St Springfield MA 01103

MILSTEIN, SEYMOUR, food co. exec.; b. N.Y.C., July 21, 1920; s. Morris and Rose (Gordon) M.; B.S., N.Y. U., 1941; m. Vivian Leiner, June 3, 1945; children—Constance Jane, Philip Lloyd. Sec.-treas. Mastic Tile Corp. Am., N.Y.C., 1945-55, dir., 1945-60, pres., 1955-60; v.p., dir., exec. com. Ruberoid Co. 1960-62, sr. v.p., 1962-67; partner One Lincoln Assos., 1968—; mem. adv. bd. Chase Manhattan Bank, 1964—; now chmn. bd., chief exec. officer United Brands Co. Hon. pres., chmn. bd. Bronx-Lebanon Hosp. Center. Clubs: Metropolis Country (White Plains, N.Y.); Harmonie (N.Y.C.). Home: 35 Ogden Rd Scarsdale NY 10583 Office: 1271 Ave of Americas New York NY 10020

MILSTEN, DAVID RANDOLPH, lawyer; b. Coalgate, Okla., Sept. 29, 1903; s. Morris and Etta (Goldstein) M.; B.A., U. Okla., 1925, LL.B., 1928; postgrad. Yale Law Sch., 1926; m. Minnie Gottlieb, Nov. 16, 1930; children—Donald E., Suzanne (Mrs. Allen G. Parelman). Admitted to Okla. bar, 1928, since practiced in Tulsa; asst. county atty. Tulsa County, 1929. Pub. speaker, lectr. founder, chmn. Benevolent and Welfare Fund of Tulsa County Bar Assn.; mem. Will Rogers Commn. Okla.; chmn. bd. Tulsa Salvation Army, 1954-55; pres. Tulsa Opera, 1953-55, bd. dirs., 1951—; pres. Thomas Gilcrease Inst. Am. History and Art, Tulsa, 1967-68, chmn. bd., 1969-70, bd. dirs., 1954—, life dir. emeritus, 1972—. Recipient Commendation Okla. Hist. Soc. Mem. Sigma Alpha Mu. (past supreme prior). Jewish (bd. dirs., past pres. temple, hon. life pres.). Mason (33 deg., past potentate, Shriner). Club: Meadowbrook Country (past sec. Tulsa). Author: An Appreciation of Will Rogers, 1935; Howdy Folks, 1938; Before My Night, 1962; The Morning After (poetry), 1968; Thomas Gilcrease, 1969. Home: 3905 S Florence Pl Tulsa OK 74105 Office: The Tower Suite-Philtower Bldg Tulsa OK 74103. *Throughout my adolescent and adult life my credo has been that there is no right way to do a wrong thing and there is no wrong way to do a right thing, and there is no compromise with efficiency.*

MILSTEN, ROBERT B., lawyer; b. Tulsa, Nov. 6, 1932; s. Travis I. and Regina (Jankowsky) M.; B.S., Ind. U., 1954; LL.B., U. Okla., 1956; postgrad. So. Meth. U., 1959; m. Jane Herskowitz, June 24, 1956; children—Stuart Paul, Leslie Jane. Admitted to Okla. bar, 1956, also U.S. Ct. of Appeals, U.S. Tax Ct.; practiced in Oklahoma City, 1962—; govt. atty. Office Chief Counsel, IRS, 1958-62; atty. Fuller, Smith, Mosburg & Davis, 1962-63; atty. Andrews, Davis, Legg, Bixler, Milsten & Murrah, Inc., and predecessor firm, 1964—, mem. firm, 1966—, mem. exec. com. of bd. dirs., 1977—, also dir. Co-chmn. Oklahoma City Israel Emergency Fund drive, 1969-70; mem. devel. com. Baptist Med. Center, Oklahoma City. Served as lt., JAGC, USAF, 1956-58. Mem. Am. (com. civil and criminal tax penalties sect. taxation 1962—), Okla., Oklahoma County, Fed. (2d v.p. local chpt. 1976—) bar assns., Phi Delta Phi (treas. 1955-56). Jewish (trustee, past pres., 1st v.p., past treas., past sec. temple). Office: 1600 Midland Center Tower Oklahoma City OK 73102

MILTON, ARTHUR GREGORY, newspaper exec.; b. Bklyn., Jan. 24, 1911; s. Joseph and Elsie (Broedel) M.; m. Marie F. Landis, Apr. 5, 1942; children—Donald Landis, Patricia Ann. With N.Y. World, 1930-31, N.Y. Mirror, 1931-34, 40-63, N.Y. Am., 1934-37; exec. N.Y. Jour. Am., 1963-66, World Jour. Tribune, N.Y.C., 1966-67; asso. pub., v.p. El Tiempo, 1967-68; pres., pub. Levittown (N.Y.) Tribune, 1968-72; exec. L.I. Press, 1972-77, The Trib, 1977-78; pub. Dateline mag., 1959-79; exec. v.p. Mid Island Tribune Co., Inc., 1968-79. Mem. N.Y. State Fair Trial-Free Press Conf., 1968-79. Trustee Overseas Press Club Edward R. Murrow Found., 1963-68, 72-79, treas., 1972-75; trustee Bob Considine Scholarship Fund. Served as capt. AUS, World War II; ETO. Mem. Overseas Press Club (sec. 1965-66, gov. 1973-74, 77-79, v.p. 1974-76, award for meritorious service 1959-61, 76), Soc. Silurians, Banshees, 4th Inf. Div. Assn., N.Y. Press Assn., Sigma Delta Chi (exec. council 1968-78), Deadline Club (treas. 1975-79). Club: L.I. Athletic. Home: 18823 129th Ave Sun City West AZ 85375

MILTON, JOHN CHARLES DOUGLAS, nuclear physicist; b. Regina, Sask., Can., June 1, 1924; s. William and Frances Craigie (McDowall) M.; A.M. in Music, U. Man., 1942, B.Sc. with honors, 1947, M.A., Princeton U., 1949, Ph.D. in Physics, 1951; m. Gwendolyn Margaret Shaw, Oct. 10, 1953; children—Bruce F., Leslie J.F., Neil W.D., Theresa M. Asst. research officer Atomic Energy Can., Ltd., Chalk River, Ont., 1951-57, asso. research officer, 1957-62, sr. research officer, 1962-70, prin. research officer, 1970—, head nuclear physics br., 1967—; vis. scientist Lawrence Berkeley Lab., 1960-62, Centre de Recherches, Strasbourg & Bruyeres-le-Chatel, 1975-76; chmn. nuclear physics grants Natural Sci. and Engring. Research Council, 1977—. Fellow Royal Soc. Can., Am. Phys. Soc.; mem. Can. Assn. Physicists. Home: 3 Alexander Pl Deep River ON K0J 1P0 Canada Office: Chalk River Nuclear Lab Chalk River ON K0J 1J0 Canada

MILTON, JOHN RONALD, educator, author; b. Anoka, Minn., May 24, 1924; s. John Peterson and Euphamia Alvera (Swanson) M.; B.A., U. Minn., 1948, M.A., 1951; Ph.D., U. Denver, 1961; m. Leonharda Allison Hinderlie, Aug. 3, 1946; 1 dau., Nanci Lynn. Instr. English and philosophy Augsburg Coll., Mpls., 1949-57; mem. faculty Jamestown (N.D.) Coll., 1957-63, prof. English, chmn. dept., 1961-63; prof. English, U. S.D., Vermillion, 1963—, chmn. dept., 1963-65, editor S.D. Rev., 1963—, dir. writing program, 1965—; vis. prof. N.D. State U., summer 1966, Ind. State U., summer 1966, Bemidji (Minn.) State Coll., 1969; chmn. Dakota Press, publ. U. S.D., 1968—. Served with U.S. Army, 1943-46. Recipient Gov.'s award for achievement in arts, 1978; Wurlitzer Found. fellow, 1965; Hill Found. grantee, 1966, 69, 70; grantee Whitney Found., 1970, 72, S.D. Arts Council, 1969, 70, 74, U. S.D., 1963, 64; Nat. Endowment Arts writing fellow, 1976-77. Mem. Am. Studies Assn. (regional bd. 1957-59), Western Lit. Assn. (pres. 1971, editorial bd. 1966—), Western History Assn. Author: (poetry) The Loving Hawk, 1962, Western Plains, 1964, The Tree of Bones, 1965, This Lonely House, 1968, The Tree of Bones and Other Poems, 1973, The Blue Belly of the World, 1974; (novel) Notes to a Bald Buffalo, 1976; (biography) Oscar Howe, 1972, Crazy Horse, 1974; (history) South Dakota: A Bicentennial History, 1977; also interviews, essays, stories, revs., articles. Editor: The American Indian Speaks, 1969; American Indian II, 1971; The Literature of South Dakota, 1976. Home: 630 Thomas St Vermillion SD 57069 Office: Box 111 University Exchange Vermillion SD 57069. *Although I have a vision of accomplishment in the areas of arts and humanities, and have maintained an intellectual dependence which often puts me at odds with the fashionable and the popular in my fields of endeavor, I have nevertheless attempted to work within what I consider an intelligent and humane compromise between devotion to my work and an equal devotion to family and community. The balance is often precarious, but I consider it necessary to the wholeness of self as well as to the validity of the work.*

MILTON, PETER WINSLOW, artist; b. Lower Merion, Pa., Apr. 2, 1930; s. William Hammond and Lois (Preston) M.; B.F.A., Yale, 1954, M.F.A., 1962; m. Edith Hanna Cohn, June 3, 1961; children—Jeremy Lawrence, Naomi Helen. Tchr. art Md. Inst., Balt., 1961-68, Yale Summer Sch. of Music and Art, 1970; exhibited in numerous one man shows including: Balt. Mus., 1965, U. N.H., 1970, De Cordova Mus., Lincoln, Mass., 1970, Phillips Exeter Acad., 1971, Museo La Tertula, Cali, Colombia, 1972, Middlebury (Vt.) Coll., 1973, U. Nebr., 1974, Schenectady Mus., 1974, Asso. Am. Artists, N.Y.C., 1975, Galerie Bernier, Paris, 1975, Bibliteca Luis-Angel Arango, Bogota, Colombia, 1975, traveling exhbn. Internat. Exhbns. Found., U.S., 1977, Europe, 1978; exhibited in numerous group shows; represented in numerous permanent collections. Yale Traveling Fellowship grantee, 1954, Louis Comfort Tiffany Found. grantee, 1964; recipient numerous nat. and internat. awards and prizes. Home: PO Box 137 Francestown NH 03043

MIMS, LAMBERT CARTER, mayor, city ofcl.; b. Uriah, Ala., Apr. 20, 1930; s. Jeff C. and Carrie (Lambert) M.; student pub. schs.; m. Reecie Phillips, Aug. 17, 1946; children—Dale Phillips, Louis Daniel. Owner, Mims Brokerage Co., Mobile, 1958—; pub. works commr. Mobile, 1965—, mayor Mobile, 1968-69, 72-73, 76—. Mem. human resources com. Nat. League Cities; mem. transp. com. Ala. League Municipalities; past pres. Mobile County Mcpl. Assn. Deacon, past chmn. bd. Riverside Bapt. Ch.; past pres. Mobile Bapt. Brotherhood, Ala. Bapt. Brotherhood; past pres. Ala. Bapt. State Conv., also former 1st v.p.; past trustee Judson Coll., Marion, Ala.; speaker numerous chs., convs. and confs.; bd. dirs. Christian Businessmen's Com. Internat., Moblie Rescue Mission; mem., past pres. Mobile Camp Gideons. Mem. Am. Public Works Assn. (v.p., pres. 1979, past dir. region IV Ala. Public Works Assn. (past pres.), Mobile County Mcpl. Assn. (past pres.), Mobile C. of C. Clubs: Masons (32 deg.), Shrine, Kiwanis. Author: For Christ and Country, 1969. Home: 3008 Bryant Rd Mobile AL 36605 Office: 111 S Royal St Mobile AL 36601

MIMS, THOMAS JEROME, ins. co. exec.; b. Sumter, S.C., Dec. 12, 1899; s. Lazarus and Sarah Rebecca (White) M.; A.B., Furman U., 1921; m. Valma Gillespie, Dec. 14, 1926; children—Thomas Jerome, George Franklin. With Recording & Statis. Corp. of N.Y., Detroit, 1921-29, Detroit, N.Y., 1921-22, asst. mgr., Phila., 1922-25, mgr., Indpls., 1925-27, Boston, 1927-29; salesman Burroughs Adding Machine Co., Detroit, Boston, 1929-31; spl. agt. Morley Gen. Agy., Camden, N.J., 1931-32; mgr. William R. Timmons Agy., Greenville, S.C., 1933—; v.p., sec. Canal Ins. Co., Greenville, 1942-48, pres., dir., 1948—; pres., dir. Canal Indemnity Co. Mem. council Greenville Little Theatre, 1951—, v.p. 1956-57, 72-73, pres., 1957-58, 73-75. Bd. dirs. United Way Greenville, 1970—, chmn. campaign, 1976, v.p., 1977, pres., 1978; bd. dirs. S.C. Safety Council, pres., 1971-75; mem. adv. council Furman U.; bd. dirs., mem. bd. mgmt. Internat. Ins. Seminar. Mem. Nat., S.C., Greenville (past pres.) assns. ins. agts., S.C. Motor Transp. Assn. (chmn. ins. com. 1951-63), S.C. (dir. 1973-75), U.S. (ins. com.), Greenville (dir. 1969-75, pres. 1973) chambers commerce, Am. Mgmt. Assn. (pres.'s assn.), AIM (fellow pres.'s council), Truck and Heavy Equipment Claims Council (chmn. membership com.), Assn. S.C. Property and Casualty Ins. Cos. (pres. 1962-63, 72-73), Internat. Platform Assn. Baptist. Rotarian (dir. Greenville 1957-58, pres. 1963-64, pres. Rotary Charities, Inc. 1964-65). Clubs: Touchdown (pres. 1963), City (pres. 1965), Forum, Poinsett (Greenville); Palmetto, Summit (Columbia, S.C.). Home: Knollwood Dr Route 6 Greenville SC 29607 Office: 417 E North St Greenville SC 29601

MINAHAN, DANIEL FRANCIS, mfg. co. exec.; b. Orange, N.J., Dec. 3, 1929; s. Alfred A. and Catherine (Kelly) M.; A.B. magna cum laude, U. Notre Dame, 1951; J.D. magna cum laude, U. Conn., 1964; grad. Advanced Mgmt. Program, Harvard, 1975; m. Mary Jean Gaffney, May 2, 1953; children—Daniel Francis, John Alfred. Mgr. indsl. engring. Uniroyal, Inc., Naugatuck, Conn., 1952-59, mgr. indsl. relations, 1959-64, supr. labor relations, N.Y.C., 1964-66; v.p. indsl. relations and labor counsel Phillips Van Heusen Corp., N.Y.C., 1966-69; v.p. personnel-adminstrn. Broadway-Hale Stores, Inc., Los Angeles, 1969-70; v.p. employee relations, sec. Magnavox-N.Am., Philips Corp., 1970-73, sr. v.p. ops., group exec., dir., 1973—; admitted to Conn. bar, 1964, also U.S. Supreme Ct., Ct. of Appeals and Fed. Dist. Ct. of Conn. bars. Pres. Magnavox Found.; bd. dirs. Young Audiences Los Angeles. Served with USMCR. Mem. Assn. Bar City N.Y., Am., Conn. bar assns., NAM, Research Inst. Am., Harvard Advanced Mgmt. Assn., Bur. Nat. Affairs, Electronic Inst. Am. Clubs: Harvard, Pinnacle (N.Y.C.); International (Chgo.); Belfrey (London). Co-author: The Developing Labor Law, 1971. Home: 15 Mill Hill Ln Southport CT 06490 Office: 100 E 42d St New York NY 10017

MINAHAN, JOHN ENGLISH, author; b. Albany, N.Y., Apr. 30, 1933; s. John English and Constance Madeline (Langdon) M.; student Cornell U., 1955-57, Harvard U., 1957-58, Columbia U., 1958-60; m. Verity Ann Hill, Apr. 27, 1966. Staff writer Time mag., 1960-61; chief TV writer J. Walter Thompson Co., N.Y.C., 1961-65; freelance writer, N.Y.C., 1965-73, Los Angeles, 1976—; editor, pub. American Way mag., N.Y.C., 1973-76; contbg. editor Los Angeles mag., 1978—; author: (novels) A Sudden Silence, 1963, The Passing Strange, 1965, Jeremy, 1973, Sorcerer, 1977, 9/30/55, 1977, Almost Summer, 1978, Nunzio, 1978; The Complete American Graffeti, 1979; (biography) The Dream Collector, 1972; (translation from French) The Fabulous Onassis, 1972; (screenplays) A Sudden Silence, 1965, The Passing Strange, 1979; (TV play) First Flight, 1968; also articles in N.Y. Times, Sat. Rev., Time-Life Spl. Reports; cons. Universal-MCA Inc. Recipient Doubleday award, 1960. Mem. Nat. Soc. Lit. and Arts, Alpha Delta Phi. Club: Harvard of So. Calif. Address: 377 Pinney Rd New Canaan CT 06840. *When you have ambitions of being a writer, people call you a dreamer. They tell you to wake up and go to work for the telephone company. They tell you it's almost impossible to get a good education when you don't have any money. They tell you it's unrealistic to work nights for five years on a first novel that's been rejected by everybody. They were right, of course. Someday I'm going to stop all this nonsense and go to work for the telephone company.*

MINAHAN, ROGER COPP, lawyer; b. Green Bay, Wis., Feb. 13, 1910; s. Eben R. and Jessie (Copp) M.; Ph.B., U. Wis., 1932, LL.B., 1934, J.S.D., 1935; m. 2d, Myrna J. Knight; children by previous marriage—Barbara Minahan Low, William Stephens. Admitted to Wis. bar, 1934; practiced in Milw., 1943—; partner firm Whyte & Hirschboeck, 1943-78, Minahan & Peterson, 1978—; sec., gen. counsel, dir. Post Corp.; dir. Intercontinental Diversified Corp., Wrought Washer Mfg. Inc. Mem. Natural Resources Bd., 1969-75. Served to lt. (s.g.) USNR, 1944-46. Mem. Am., Wis., Milw. bar assns., Order of Coif. Home: 9566 N Sequoia Dr Milwaukee WI 53217 Office: 815 E Mason St Milwaukee WI 53202

MINAHAN, VICTOR IVAN, communications exec.; b. Green Bay, Wis., Apr. 28, 1921; s. Victor I. and Bertha (Bush) M.; A.B., Stanford, 1946; m. Marilee Heron, Aug. 31, 1946; children—Pauline Ann, Timothy Ivan, Thomas Owen. State editor Boise (Idaho) Statesman, 1946; reporter Sacramento Union, 1947, U.P.I., Sacramento, 1947-48; with Appleton (Wis.) Post-Crescent, 1948—, exec. v.p., editor, 1959-60, pres., editor, 1960-62, pres., pub., 1962—; pres. Post Corp. and subsidiaries including Twin City News-Record, Neenah-Menasha, Wis., Milw. Post Newspapers, West Bend (Wis.) Daily News, Granite City (Ill.) Press-Record, Collinsville (Ill.) Herald (all newspapers), Transcript Newspapers, Dedham, Mass., Sun Newspapers, Cleve., Polk Shopper, Lakeland, Fla., TV stas. KTVO, Kirksville, Mo. and Ottumwa, Iowa, WEAU-TV, Eau Claire, Wis., WLUC-TV, Marquette, Mich., WLUK-TV, Green Bay, Wis., WOKR-TV, Rochester, N.Y., radio stas. KBIZ, Ottumwa, WAXX-WAYY-FM, Chippewa Falls, Eau Claire, Wis., Post Printing Inc., Appleton and West Bend, Wis., Gowe Printing Co., Medina, Ohio. Vice chmn. Gov. Wis. Commn. on Human Rights, 1959-63; chmn. Appleton Redevel. Authority, 1972—; chmn. Appleton Community Fund drive, 1954, pres., 1956. Served to 1st lt. inf., AUS, World War II. Decorated Bronze Star, Purple Heart with cluster. Recipient Distinguished Service award Appleton Jr. C. of C. Mem. Appleton C. of C. (pres. 1957). Elk. Club: North Shore Golf (Appleton). Home: 1517 S Outagamie St Appleton WI 54911 Office: Post Corp Appleton WI 54911

MINAMI, WAYNE, atty. gen. Hawaii; b. Waipahu, Hawaii, Apr. 28, 1942; B.A., Yale U., 1964; LL.B., Stanford U., 1967; married; 3 children. Admitted to Hawaii bar, 1967; dep. atty. gen. State of Hawaii, 1970-72, asst. atty. gen., 1972-74, atty. gen., 1978—; dir. Hawaii Regulatory Agys., 1974-78. Mem. Hawaii Bar Assn., Am. Bar Assn., Nat. Assn. Attys. Gen. Democrat. Office: Office Atty Gen State Capitol 415 S Beretania St Honolulu HI 96813*

MINAR, EDWIN LEROY, JR., educator; b. Portland, Oreg., Apr. 17, 1915; s. Edwin LeRoy and Alma Inez (Jackson) M.; A.B., Reed Coll., 1936; Ph.D., U. Wis., 1940; m. Louise Padberg, 1937; m. 2d, Anne Marie Kelley, 1950 (div. 1962); children—Robert K., Jane E., Annette A.D. Asst. prof. fgn. langs. Dakota Wesleyan U., 1939-40; asst. to asso. prof. classics Conn. Coll., New London, 1940-51; asso. prof. classical langs. and lit. DePauw U., Greencastle, Ind., 1951-54, prof. classical langs., Greek, 1954—, head dept., 1951-78; vis. prof. Ind. U., spring 1961, summer 1963; faculty fellow Fund for Advancement Edn., 1954-55. Mem. Soc. Ancient Greek Philosophy (pres. 1966-68), Am. Philol. Assn., Classical Assn. Middle West and South, AAUP. Democrat. Author: Early Pythagorean Politics in Practice and Theory, 1942, reprinted 1979; translator: Lore and Science in Ancient Pythagoreanism (Burkert), 1972. Contbr. to classical jours. Home: 409 E Walnut St Greencastle IN 46135

MINCH, JOHN JOSEPH, newspaper exec.; b. Cleve., Apr. 2, 1927; s. Walter William and Anne Catherine (Culliton) M.; A.B., U. Ga., 1950; postgrad. Chgo.-Kent Coll. Law, 1960; m. Charlotte Frances Lucas, Feb. 17, 1955; children—Todd Bartley, Mary Katherine Alice, Charlotte Mariam, Culliton Frances Mary, John Jude, Christian Holton-Lucas, Bridget Morgan. Reporter, Cleve. Press, 1951-52, El Paso (Tex.) Herald-Post, 1952-53; feature writer, make-up editor Cin. Times-Star, 1953-55; feature writer Chgo. Daily News, 1955-60; chief editorial writer, editorial page editor Balt. News-Am.; founding exec. editor Country Beautiful mag., Milw., 1960-63; asso. editor Cleve. Plain Dealer, 1965-67; chief editorial writer Harrisburg (Pa.) Patriot-News, 1967-69; gen. mgr., exec. editor Chgo. Tribune-N.Y. News Syndicate, N.Y.C., 1969-76; mktg. mgr. United Feature Syndicate, N.Y.C., 1976—. Served to sgt.-maj. USAAF, 1945-46. Mem. Pi Kappa Phi. Club: Setauket Yacht (Port Jefferson, L.I., N.Y.). Office: United Feature Syndicate 200 Park Ave New York NY 10017

MINCHIN, MICHAEL M., JR., food co. exec.; b. Los Angeles, Sept. 5, 1926; s. Michael M. and Daisy (Salmon) M.; B.A. cum laude, Stanford, 1948, postgrad. Sch. Law, 1948-49; M.B.A. cum laude, Harvard, 1951; m. Carolyn Brown, June 1, 1961; children—Michael M. III, Montgomery. Asst. to Sec. of Def., Washington, 1951; asst. to pres. Emporium-Capwell, San Francisco, 1951-53; v.p. Erwin Wasey, Inc., Los Angeles, 1958-65, sr. v.p., gen. mgr., 1965-69, exec. v.p., also dir., chmn. exec. policy com., 1969-72; v.p. mktg. Collins Foods Internat., Los Angeles 1973—. Home: 15401 Mulholland Dr Los Angeles CA 90024 Office: 12731 W Jefferson Blvd Los Angeles CA 90066

MINCKLER, ROBERT ALAN, bus. exec.; b. Glendale, Cal., Mar. 7, 1932; s. Robert Lee and Marguerite Emma (Keys) M.; B.A., Stanford, 1954, M.B.A., 1958; m. Helen Patricia Lundquist, June 15, 1957; children—Kathryn Anne, Lawrence Lee, Mary Helen. Loan adminstr. Security First Nat. Bank, Los Angeles, 1958-61; project mgr. Great Lakes Properties, Los Angeles, 1961-64; dir. finance Janss Corp., Los Angeles, 1964-65; dir. finance Castle & Cooke, Inc., real estate mgmt. and finance, Honolulu, 1965-73, treas., San Francisco, 1973-78; v.p.-fin. Glorietta Foods, San Jose, Calif., 1978—; instr. extension courses real estate finance U. Calif. at Los Angeles. Served with AUS, 1954-56. Republican. Episcopalian. Clubs: Pacific (Honolulu); Menlo Circus (Atherton, Calif.). Home: 175 Britton St Atherton CA 94025

MINDE, STEFAN PAUL, condr.; b. Leipzig, Germany, Apr. 12, 1936; s. Karl and Ilse M.; abitur Thomasschule Leipzig; came to U.S., 1968, naturalized, 1971; m. Edith Halla, July 8, 1961; children—Mathias, Bernd. Asst. condr. Frankfurt (Germany) Opera, 1959-61, Wiesbaden (Germany) Opera, 1961-68; condr. Trier (Germany) Opera, 1968; asst. to Erich Leinsdorf at Tanglewood Festival, 1968-70; asst. condr. San Francisco Opera, 1970; gen. dir., condr. Portland (Oreg.) Opera. Mem. Orch. League. Office: Portland Opera Assn PO Box 8598 Portland OR 97207

MINDLIN, RAYMOND DAVID, educator, engr.; b. N.Y.C., Sept. 17, 1906; s. Henry and Beatrice (Levy) M.; student Ethical Culture Sch., N.Y.C., 1918-24; B.A., Columbia, 1928, B.S., 1931, C.E., 1932,

Ph.D., 1936; D.Sc. (hon.), Northwestern U., 1975; m. Elizabeth Roth, 1940 (dec. 1950); m. 2d, Patricia Kaveney, 1953 (dec. 1976). Research asst. dept. civil engring. Columbia U., N.Y.C., 1932-38, Bridgham fellow, 1934-35, instr. civil engring., 1938-40, asst. prof., 1940-45, asso. prof., 1945-47, prof. civil engring., 1947-67, Finch prof. applied sci., 1967-75, prof. emeritus, 1975—; cons. Bell Telephone Labs. Inc., N.Y.C., 1943-51; cons. physicist Dept. Terrestrial Magnetism, Carnegie Instn. of Washington, 1940-42; cons. Nat. Defense Research Com., 1941-42, sect. T, Office Sci. Research and Devel., Applied Physics Lab., Johns Hopkins U., Balt., 1942-45. Recipient Illig medal Columbia U., 1932, U.S. Naval Ordnance Devel. award, 1945, Presdl. medal for Merit, 1946, Class of 1889 Sch. Mines medal Columbia U., 1947, research prize ASCE, 1958, Great Tchr. award Columbia U., 1960, von Karman medal ASCE, 1961, Timoshenko medal ASME, 1964, ASME medal, 1976, C.B. Sawyer Piezoelectric Resonator award, 1967, Egleston medal Columbia U., 1971, Trent-Crede medal Acoustical Soc., Am., 1971, Frocht award Soc. Exptl. Stress Analysis, 1974. Fellow Acoustical Soc. Am., Am. Acad. Arts and Scis.; mem. Soc. Exptl. Stress Analysis (exec. com. 1943-50, v.p. 1946, pres. 1947), ASCE (sec. com. applied mechanics 1940-42, chmn. 1942-45), Eastern Photoelasticity Conf. (exec. com. 1938-41), Am. Phys. Soc., Nat. Acad. Engring., Nat. Acad. Sci., Conn. Acad. Sci. and Engring., U.S. Nat. Com. Theoretical and Applied Mechanics, Internat. Union Theoretical and Applied Mechanics, ASME (hon.), Tau Beta Pi, Sigma Xi, Columbia Varsity "C". Mem. adv. bd. Applied Mech. Reviews. Contbr. articles to tech. and sci. jours. Home: 89 Deer Hill Dr Ridgefield CT 06877

MINDLIN, RICHARD BARNETT, bus. exec.; b. Kansas City, Mo., Apr. 9, 1926; s. Harold Saul and Ann (Copeland) M.; student U. of South, 1943-46, Columbia, 1947-48; m. Susan Dorothy Weinberg, Feb. 6, 1954; children—Steven, Edward, Andrew. Mdse. mgr. Kaufmann's Dept. Store, Pitts., 1951-54; founder, pres. Coach House Stores, Kansas City, Mo., 1955-76, Richard B. Mindlin Assos., mktg. cons., Shawnee Mission, Kans., 1963-79; pres. Radnor Internat., Inc., 1979—. Chmn. bd. dirs. Bacchus Charity, 1960; bd. dirs. Kaw council Boy Scouts Am., 1964-66; pres. bd. trustees Kansas City Mus. History and Sci.; trustee Menorah Med. Center, Kansas City, Mo. Served to lt. (j.g.) USNR, 1943-45. Mem. Internat. Coffee Service Inst. (hon.), Nat. Coffee Service Assn. (cons., organizing bd. dirs., bd. dirs. 1972-73), Nat. Automatic Merchandising Assn. (cons). Club: Oakwood Country (Kansas City, Mo.). Author: Operating a CSV Business; contbr. articles to profl. jours. Home and Office: 4101 W 90th St Shawnee Mission KS 66207

MINEAR, LEON PIERSON, ednl. adminstr.; b. San Antonio, Mar. 20, 1915; s. Joseph H. and Monnie M. (Guin) M.; A.B. cum laude, San Francisco State Coll., 1938, M.A., 1941; Ed.D., Stanford, 1947; m. Dolores F. Goetzee, Aug. 20, 1939; 1 son, Roger Leon. Tchr. elementary, jr. and sr. high schs., Oakland, Calif., 1938-42; demonstration tchr. U. Calif., summers 1940-42, vice prin. secondary demonstration summer sch., 1946; flight radio officer Pan Am. World Airways, 1942-43, sr. communications rep. South Pacific, 1944, asst. supt. tng., 1944, supt. tng., 1945-46; vice prin. Carmel High Sch., Carmel-by-the-Sea, Calif., 1946-47; asst. to dean Denver Jr. Coll., 1947-49; asst. prof. edn. U. Denver, 1947-49, dir. summer sessions, 1949; pres. Stockton (Calif.) Jr. Coll., 1949-52; prin. Benson Poly. Sch., 1952-61; supt. pub. instrn. Oreg., Salem, 1961-68; dir. vocat. tech. edn. U.S. Office Edn., 1968-71, U.S. regional commnr. edn., Denver, 1971-78; dir. coop. activities Edn. Commn. of States and U.S. Office Edn., 1978—; nat. coordinator Bicentennial Conf. Series for Edn., 1975-76. Mem. U.S. Armed Forces Adv. Com., 1959-60; mem. Pres.'s White House Com. on Aging, 1960, Pres.'s Com. on Vocational Edn., 1960, White House Conf. on Edn., 1965, Gov.'s Com. on Children and Youth, 1961-68, Gov.'s Com. Natural Resources, 1961-68, Gov.'s Higher Ednl. Coordinating Council, 1961-68 (chmn. 1961, 63, 65), Gov.'s Cabinet Human Relations, 1961-68, Gov.'s Traffic Safety Com., 1961-63; dir. Ford Found. Study for Oreg. Ednl. Improvement, 1962-66; dir. U.S. Office Edn. Study for Nat. System of Regional Research Centers, 1962-63; research cons. U.S. Office Edn., 1962-68; adviser to U.S. commr. edn., 1964-68, Carnegie Found. Study Fed.-State Relations in Edn., 1965, Harvard-Lexington Sch. Project, Harvard, 1965-67; mem. adv. com. Stanford Sch. Edn., 1966-68, Nat. Indsl. Conf. Bd., 1968-70; steering com. Edn. Commn. of States, 1960-68; chmn. E.C.S. Vocational-Tech. Task Force, 1966-68; cons. U.S. Dept. State, 1967, Liberia, 1967, P.R., 1967, Fed. Republic Germany, 1963, various state govts. and univs. Condr., Monterey Regional Symphony, 1946-47, Denver Community Symphony, 1947; mem. Denver Symphony Bd., 1977—; adv. Denver Center for Performing Arts, 1972-78. Served to lt. (j.g.) USNR, 1942-46. Mem. Denver Businessmen's Assn. (pres. 1947-49), NEA, Am. Assn. Sch. Adminstrs., Oreg. Edn. Assn., C. of C. (edn. com.), Brico Symphony Soc. (pres. 1972-74), Phi Delta Kappa, Kappa Delta Pi, Sigma Alpha Eta. Club: Portland City. Co-author edn. texts. Contbr. articles to ednl. jours. Home: 7027B E Girard Ave Denver CO 80222 Office: Fed Office Bldg Office Edn 1961 Stout St Denver CO 80202

MINER, EARL HOWARD, banker; b. Donnellson, Iowa, Jan. 26, 1923; s. Timothy Ralph and Carrie T. (Talbot) M.; B.A., Iowa Wesleyan Coll., 1947; J.D., U. Iowa, 1948; m. Marian Aumann, May 30, 1944; children—Marcia, Susan, Scott. Admitted to Iowa bar, 1948, Mich. bar, 1965; atty., Mt. Pleasant, Iowa, 1948-55; trust officer Nat. Bank Burlington (Iowa), 1955-57; v.p. 1st Trust Co., St. Joseph, Mo., 1957-62; investment editor Trusts & Estates Mag., N.Y.C., 1962-64; v.p., trust officer Chem. Bank, Midland, Mich., 1964-70; v.p., sr. trust officer Old Kent Bank and Trust Co., Grand Rapids, Mich., 1970-72, sr. v.p., 1972-79; sr. v.p. Ann Arbor Trust Co. (Mich.), 1979—; instr. Iowa Wesleyan Coll., part time 1949-50. Dir., Henry County CD, 1950-55; county atty. Henry County (Iowa), 1951-55. Chmn. bd. dirs. Mary Free Bed Hosp., Grand Rapids. Served with USAAF, World War II. Decorated D.F.C., Air medal with 2 oak leaf clusters. Mem. Iowa Bar Assn., State Bar Mich., Mich. Bankers Assn. (chmn. trust div. 1970-71), Lambda Chi Alpha, Phi Alpha Delta. Republican. Presbyn. (elder). Mason (Shriner). Club: Barton Hills. Home: 3264 Alpine Dr Ann Arbor MI 48104 Office: 100 S Main St Box 6812 Ann Arbor MI

MINER, EARL ROY, educator; b. Marshfield, Wis., Feb. 21, 1927; s. Roy Jacob and Marjory M.; B.A. summa cum laude, U. Minn., 1949, M.A., 1951, Ph.D., 1955; m. Virginia Lane, July 15, 1950; children—Erik Earl, Lisa Lane. Instr. in English, Williams Coll., 1953-55; mem. faculty dept. English, UCLA, 1955-72, prof., 1964-72; prof. English, Princeton U., 1972-74, Townsend Martin prof. English and comparative lit., 1974—; Fulbright lectr. Kyoto U., Osaka U., Japan, 1960-61, Oxford U., 1966-67; Clark Library prof. UCLA, 1971-72; vis. prof. Columbia U., 1976. Am. Council Learned Socs. fellow, 1962-63; Guggenheim Found. fellow, 1977-78. Author numerous books in field including: The Japanese Tradition in British and American Literature, 1958; The Metaphysical Mode from Donne to Cowley, 1969; The Restoration Mode from Milton to Dryden, 1974; Japanese Linked Poetry, 1979; editor: Selected Poetry and Prose of John Dryden, 1969; English Criticism in Japan, 1972; Illustrious Evidence: Approaches to English Literature of the Early Seventeenth Century, 1975; asso. gen. editor Calif. edit. Works of John Dryden, 1964-72, editor vols. 3, 15, 17; contbr. articles to profl. jours. Office: 22 McCosh Hall Princeton Univ Princeton NJ 08544

MINER, HORACE MITCHELL, educator; b. St. Paul, May 26, 1912; s. James Burt and Jessie Leightner (Schulten) M.; A.B., U. Ky., 1933; A.M., U. Chgo., 1935, Ph.D., 1937; postgrad. (Yale Inst. Human Relations fellow), Colombia, 1941-42; m. Agnes Genevieve Murphy, June 12, 1936; 1 dau., Denise Allison. Asso. curator Mus. Anthropology, U. Ky., 1932-33; dir. archeol. field party TVA, 1934; instr. anthropology and sociology Wayne U., Detroit, 1937-39; dir. archeol. field party U. Chgo., summer 1938; sr. social sci. analyst, field research in Ia., Dept. Agr., 1939; cons. Nat. Resources Planning Bd., 1941; asst. prof. sociology U. Mich., Ann Arbor, 1946-47, asso. prof. sociology, anthropology, 1947-51, research asso. Mus. Anthropology, 1948—, prof. sociology, anthropology, 1951—; Fulbright lectr. Makerere U., Uganda, 1961-62; research North African Center, Morocco, 1967-68. Mem. com. experts on indigenous labor Internat. Labor Office, 1949-65, conf. on indigenous labor, La Paz, 1951, Geneva, 1954, 62; mem. divisional com. for social scis. NSF, 1962-67. Served to lt. col. AUS, 1942-45. Decorated Legion of Merit, Bronze Star. Recipient Social Sci. Research Council demobilization award, 1945. Soc. Sci. Research Council fellow 1936-37, 40; Ford Found. grantee, 1956; Rockefeller grantee, Nigeria, 1957-58; Fulbright research award, Horace Rackham grant for field research, Algeria, 1950; NSF grant for research Nigeria, 1970-71. Fellow Am. Sociol. Assn., Am. Anthrop. Assn., African Studies Assn.; mem. Am. Philos. Soc., Internat. African Inst. (governing body 1949-64), Soc. Applied Anthropology (pres. 1954-55), Phi Beta Kappa, Sigma Xi, Omicron Delta Kappa, Alpha Kappa Delta, Delta Tau Delta. Author: St. Denis, a French-Canadian Parish, 1939, 2d edit., 1963; Culture and Agriculture, 1949; Principles of Sociology (with others), 1952, 2d edit., 1956; The Primitive City of Timbuctoo, 1953, 2d edit., 1965; Oasis and Casbah: Algerian Culture and Personality in Change (with G. DeVos), 1960; Rorschachs of Arabs from Algiers and from an Oasis, 1961. Editor: Social Science in Action in Sub-Saharan Africa, vol. 19, no. 3 of Human Organization, 1960; The City in Modern Africa, 1967. Home: 26 Harvard Pl Ann Arbor MI 48104

MINER, JOHN RONALD, agrl. engr.; b. Scottsburg, Ind., July 4, 1938; s. Gerald Lamont and Alice Mae (Murphy) M.; B.S. in Chem. Engring., U. Kans., 1959; M.S.E. in San. Engring., U. Mich., 1960; Ph.D. in Chem. Engring. and Microbiology, Kans. State U., 1967; m. Betty Kathron Emery, Aug. 4, 1963; children—Saralena Marie, Katherine Alice, Frederick Gerald. San. engr. Kans. Dept. Health, Topeka, 1959-64; grad. research asst. Kans. State U., Manhattan, 1964-67; asst. prof. agrl. engring. Iowa State U., 1967-71, asso. prof., 1971-72; asso. prof. Oreg. State U., 1972-76, prof., head dept. agrl. engring., 1976—; internat. cons.; cons. to livestock feeding ops., agrl. devel. firms. Lic. profl. engr., Kans., Oreg. Mem. Am. Soc. Agrl. Engrs., Water Pollution Control Fedn., Am. Soc. Engring. Educators, Sigma Xi, Gamma Sigma Delta, Alpha Epsilon, Tau Beta Pi. Presbyterian. Contbr. numerous articles on livestock prodn., pollution control, control of odors associated with livestock prodn. to profl. publs. Office: Dept Agrl Engring Oreg State U Corvallis OR 97331

MINER, ROBERT GORDON, assn. exec.; b. Blue Island, Ill., Jan. 29, 1923; s. Glen Ernest and Catherine (Leytze) M.; student Knox Coll., 1941-42; M.B.A., U. Chgo., 1950; grad. U.S. Army Command and Gen. Staff Coll., 1968; m. Betty Anne Clegg, May 23, 1944; children—Patricia L. (Mrs. Vaughn E. Clark), Stephen C., David N. Payroll auditor Employers Group Ins. Cos., 1946-49; advt. salesman Cole & Mason, pubs. reps., 1949-54, partner, 1955-56; asst. pub. Flower Grower mag., Williams Press, 1956-61, pub., 1961-67; owner Media Design Assos., Westport, Conn., 1967-71; pres. Early Am. Soc., Inc., pub. Early Am. Life, Harrisburg, Pa., 1971—; chmn. Hist. Times Travel; dir. Mus. Edits., Ltd. Chmn., Mechanicsburg (Pa.) Planning Commn.; v.p. Mechanicsburg Hist. Com.; bd. dirs. Mechanicsburg Museum Assn. Served from 2d lt. to capt. AUS, 1942-46; col. Res. ret. Decorated Bronze Star. Mem. Cumberland County Hist. Assn. (dir.). Republican. Episcopalian. Club: Princeton. Author: Handbook of Gardening, 1966; Complete Gardening Guide, 1969. Contbr. articles to mags. Home: 74 W Main St Mechanicsburg PA 17055 Office: Telegraph Press Bldg Cameron and Kelker Harrisburg PA 17105

MINER, WALTER FRANCIS, physician, research adminstr., naval officer; b. Akron, Ohio, Feb. 9, 1932; s. Newman Chaffee and Ethel St. Clair (Toland) M.; A.B., Middlebury Coll., 1953; M.D., U. Vt., 1957; M.P.H., U. Calif., Berkeley, 1968, postgrad., 1968-69; m. Gwendal Ruth Roberts, Apr. 3, 1969. Intern, Henry Ford Hosp., Detroit, 1957-58, resident in pediatrics, 1958-60; commd. lt. M.C., U.S. Navy, 1960, advanced through grades to capt., 1972; pediatrician Sta. Hosp., Tongue Point Naval Sta., Astoria, Oreg., 1960-61; pediatrician, diving med. officer Naval Sta. Dispensary, Guam, Mariana Islands, 1962-63, U.S. Naval Hosp., Guam, 1963-64; squadron med. officer Submarine Squadron One, Pearl Harbor, Hawaii, 1965-67; comd. officer U.S. Naval Research Unit 1, Berkeley, 1968-69; officer in charge preventive medicine unit Naval Support Activity, DaNang, Vietnam, 1969-70; officer in charge environ. and preventive medicine un 7, Naples, Italy and staff preventive officer, comdr. in chief U.S. Naval Forces Europe, and comdr. 6th Fleet, 1970-74; comdg. officer U.S. Naval Med. Research Unit 3, Cairo, 1974-77; comd. officer Naval Med. Research Inst., Bethesda, Md., 1977—; bd. dirs. Gorgas Meml. Ins. Decorated Bronze Star with combat distinguishing device, Meritorious Service medal Navy Achievement medal (U.S.); Cross of Gallantry, Civic Action medal (Vietnam). Fellow Am. Coll. Preventive Medicine; mem. AMA, Assn. Mil. Surgeons, Underwater Med. Soc., Am. Soc. Tropical Medicine and Hygiene, Soc. Med. Cons. to Armed Forces (asso.). Author: Noxious and Obnoxious Marine Life in the Tropical Pacific, 1965; contbr. articles to profl. publs. Home: 9409 Corsica Dr Bethesda MD 20014 Office: Naval Med Research Inst Nat Naval Med Center Bethesda MD 20014. *With the discovery that the world held vast numbers of people who actively dislike their work, came the realization of my own good fortune. I am absolutely convinced that the major determinant of a happy life is deep personal satisfaction with one's work. And I am equally convinced of the corollary, that no salary paid for unsatisfying work would be high enough to buy happiness.*

MINER, WORTHINGTON C. (TONY), theatre and TV exec.; b. Buffalo, Nov. 13, 1900; s. Worthington Cogswell and Margaret (Willard) M.; grad. Yale U., 1922; postgrad. Cambridge U. (Eng.), 1922-24; m. Frances Fuller, Mar. 30, 1929; children—Peter, Margaret Miner Raulson, Mary Elizabeth. Asso. with legitimate stage, 1924-39; asst. to Guthrie McClintic prodns. including: Green Hat, Shanghai Gesture, Saturday's Children; dir. Uncle Vanya, Up Pops the Devil, Five Star Final, House Beautiful, I Loved You Wednesday, Her Master's Voice, Blind Alley, Reunion in Vienna, Both Your Houses (Pulitzer prize), Father Malachy's Miracle, On Your Toes, Bury the Dead, Excursion; mem. exec. bd. Theatre Guild, 1937-41; author, dir. RKO Pictures, summers 1933, 34; asso. with TV, 1939; creator, producer Toast of the Town, Studio One; producer The Golbergs, Mr. I. Magination; with NBC-TV, 1952—; exec. producer Medic, Frontier, Play of the Week; producer The Fool Killer, The Pawnbroker. Served with U.S. Army, 1918-19. Recipient Look awards, 1950-51, Emmy awards, 1949, 50; also Sylvania, Peabody awards, 1950, 51. Mem. Am. Acad. Dramatic Arts (chmn. bd.), Phi Beta Kappa. Home: Apt 12J The Meurice 145 W 58th St New York City NY 10019 Office: 120 Madison Ave New York City NY 10016

MINETA, NORMAN Y., congressman; b. San Jose, Calif., Nov. 12, 1931; B.S., U. Calif. at Berkeley; m. May Hinoki; children—David, K., Stuart S. Agt./broker, Mineta Ins. Agy., San Jose, 1956—; mem. adv. bd. Bank of Tokyo in Calif., 1961-75; mem. San Jose City Council, 1967-71; vice mayor San Jose, 1969-71, mayor, 1971-75; mem. 94th-96th Congresses from 13th Calif. dist. Chmn. fin. com. Santa Clara County Council Chs., 1960-62; commr. San Jose Human Relations Commn., 1962-64, San Jose Housing Authority, 1966—; precinct chmn. Community Theater Bond Issue, 1964; mem. spl. gifts com. Santa Clara County council Boy Scouts Am., 1967; sec. Santa Clara County Grand Jury, 1964; bd. dirs. Wesley Found., San Jose State Coll., 1956-58, Pacific Neighbors, Community Council Central Santa Clara County, Japan Soc., San Francisco, Santa Clara County chpt. NCCJ, Mexican-Am. Community Services Agy.; mem. exec. bd. No. Calif.-Western Nev. dist. council Japanese Am. Citizens League, 1960-62, pres. San Jose chpt., 1957-59; bd. regents Smithsonian Instn., 1979—. Served to lt. AUS, 1954-56. Mem. Greater San Jose C. of C., Nat., Calif., San Jose (dir. 1960-62), assns. ind. ins. agts., North San Jose Optimists Club (chpt. pres. 1956-58), Jackson-Taylor Bus. and Profl. Assn. (dir. 1963). Methodist. Home: 1564 Peregrino Way San Jose CA 95125 Office: 313 Cannon House Office Bldg Washington DC 20515

MING, SI-CHUN, educator, pathologist; b. Shanghai, China, Nov. 10, 1922; s. Sian-Fan and Jan-Teh (Kuo) M.; came to U.S., 1949, naturalized, 1964; M.D., Nat. Central U. Coll. Medicine, China, 1947; m. Pen-Ming Lee, Aug. 17, 1957; children—Carol, Ruby, Stephanie, Michael, Jeffrey, Eileen. Resident in pathology Mass. Gen. Hosp., Boston, 1952-56; asso. pathologist Beth Israel Hosp., Boston, 1956-67; asst. prof. pathology Harvard U. Med. Sch., 1965-67; asso. prof. U. Md., 1967-71; prof. Temple U., 1971—; Nat. Cancer Inst. sr. fellow Karolinska Inst., Stockholm, 1964-65. Mem. Internat. Acad. Pathology, Am. Assn. Pathologists, AAAS, N.Y. Acad. Scis. Author: Tumors of the Esophagus and Stomach, 1973. Office: 3400 N Broad St Philadelphia PA 19140

MINGAY, JOHN INMAN, oil co. exec.; b. Superior, Wis., Aug. 12, 1915; s. Frederic James and Minna (Inman) M.; B.S., U.S. Naval Acad., 1937; m. Eleonora W. Copp, Apr. 4, 1959; children—Susan, John Inman, David. With Texaco, Inc., 1937—, v.p. mktg., 1961-66, v.p. marine, 1966-71, sr. v.p., dir., 1971—; pres., chief exec. officer Texaco Can. Ltd., 1972-76. Served to comdr. USNR, World War II. Mem. Soc. Naval Architects and Marine Engrs. Club: Sea Pines. Home: 31 Baynard Park Rd Hilton Head Island SC 29928

MINGES, ROBERT JAMES, econ. adviser; b. La Porte, Ind., June 14, 1923; s. William Edward and Elsie Anna (Zach) M.; M.A. in Internat. Relations, U. Chgo., 1950; m. Lilia Rodriguez, Dec. 21, 1962; children—Michael Robert, Marielle. Econ. affairs officer UN Secretariat, 1950-51; with ICA, 1951-56, assigned Tehran, 1951-53, Royal Devel. Bank, 1953-56; chief field service div., Vientiane, Laos, 1956-58, Tunis desk officer, 1958-60, asst. program officer, Tunis, 1960-61, program officer, Bamako, Mali, 1961-62, program officer, Recife, Brazil, 1962, asst. dir. for program, Rio de Janeiro, Brazil, 1962-65, dir. AID program Honduras, 1966-69, dir. AID program Ecuador, 1969-71; U.S. adviser Entente Fund, Abidjan, Ivory Coast, 1971-76. Served with USAAF, 1942-45. Home: 52 Ave Joseph Giordan 06200 Nice France

MINGLE, JOHN ORVILLE, nuclear and chem. engr.; b. Oakley, Kans., May 6, 1931; s. John Russell and Beulah Amelia (Johnson) M.; B.S., Kans. State U., Manhattan, 1953, M.S., 1958; Ph.D., Northwestern U., 1960; postgrad. in law Washburn U., 1977—; m. Patricia Ruth Schmitt, Aug. 17, 1957; children—Elizabeth Lorene, Stephen Roy. Tng. engr. Gen. Electric Co., Schenectady, 1953-54; mem. faculty Kans. State U., 1956—, prof. nuclear engring., 1965—, Black & Veatch disting. prof., 1973-78, dir. Inst. Computational Research in Engring., 1969—; instr. Northwestern U., 1958-59; vis. prof. U. So. Calif., 1967-68; cons. to govt. and industry. Served as officer AUS, 1954-56. Registered profl. engr., Kans. Mem. Am. Nuclear Soc. (sect. pres. 1976-77), Am. Inst. Chem. Engrs., Am. Soc. Engring. Edn., Nat. Soc. Profl. Engrs., Profl. Engrs. in Edn. (vice chmn. 1978—), Kans. Engring. Soc. (past chpt. pres.), Sigma Xi (past chpt. pres., lectr.). Author: The Invarient Imbedding Theory of Nuclear Transport, 1973; also articles. Home: 2408 Buena Vista Dr Manhattan KS 66502 Office: Ward Hall Kans State Univ Manhattan KS 66506. *The "workaholic" doctrine has been highly chastised by our modern society which seems to place great emphasis upon leisure; however those who are most slothful appear to be its loudest critics. Yet, this doctrine still remains one of the most viable methods for the dedicated person to make a lasting contribution to our society.*

MINGO, JAMES WILLIAM EDGAR, lawyer; b. Halifax, N.S., Can., Nov. 25, 1926; s. Edgar Willard and Lila Theresa (McManus) M.; B.A., Dalhousie U., Halifax, 1947, LL.B., 1949; LL.M., Columbia U., 1950; m. Edith Peppard Hawkins, July 6, 1953; children—Sarah M., James A., Johanna E., Nancy S., Charles H. Admitted to N.S. bar, 1950; apptd. Queen's counsel, 1966; practiced in Halifax, 1950—; mem. firm Stewart, MacKeen & Covert, and predecessors, Halifax, 1950—, partner, 1958—; dir. Bank of Can., Ottawa, Ont., Montreal Trust Co. (Que.), Royfund (Equity) Ltd., Montreal, Minas Basin Pulp & Power Co. Ltd., Hantsport, N.S., Bowater Mersey Paper Co. Ltd., Liverpool, N.S., Canning Investment Corp. Ltd., Halifax, The Great Eastern Corp. Ltd., Charlottetown, P.E.I., Ben's Ltd., Halifax, Deuterium Can. Ltd., Glace Bay, N.S., ABCO Ltd., Lunenburg, N.S., Riversdale Lumber Ltd., Truro, N.S., Maritime Accessories Ltd., Halifax, Avon Foods Ltd., Hantsport; chmn. bd. Halterm Ltd., Halifax; dir. Halifax Internat. Containers Ltd., Halifax; trustee Royfund Income Trust, Calgary, Alta. Mem. Halifax-Dartmouth Port Commn., 1955—, chmn., 1960—; chmn. Halifax Grammar Sch., 1971-73; mem. Halifax Port Authority, 1972—; chmn. nat. treasury com. Liberal Party Can. Mem. Can. Bar Assn. (exec. com. 1973-76), N.S. Barristers Soc. (pres. 1975-76), Royal Can. Geog. Soc. (dir.). Clubs: Halifax, Saraguay, Royal N.S. Yacht Squadron. Home: 5860 Chain Rock Dr Halifax NS B3H 1A1 Canada Office: Box 997 1583 Hollis St Halifax NS B3J 2X2 Canada

MINGUY, CLAUDE, zoo dir.; b. Quebec, Can., Feb. 20, 1930; s. Joseph W. and Florence (Dugal) M.; B.Sc. in Biology, Laval U., Quebec, 1955; m. Doris Vezina, Apr. 21, 1956; children—Jean-François, Pierre, Helene. Biologist, then big game biologist Que. Provincial Govt., 1955-61; asst. dir. Que. Wildlife Service, 1962-67; dir. Que. Zool. Gardens, Charlesbourg, 1967—. Mem. Canadian (v.p.), Am. assns. zool. parks and aquariums, Que. Assn. Zool. Parks (pres. 1977). Address: 8173 Zoo Ave Charlesbourg PQ G1G 4G4 Canada

MINICUS, ROBERT GEORGE, advt. exec.; b. Bronxville, N.Y., May 2, 1931; s. George Cornelius and Anne Loretta (McAulliffe) M.; B.A., Rutgers U., 1953; m. Norma A. Mastrodi, July 11, 1954; children—Richard, Pamela, Robert, Kevin. Copywriter J. Walter Thompson Co., 1956-60; creative supr. Cunningham & Walsh, Inc., N.Y.C., 1960-69, v.p., group creative dir., 1969-73, sr. v.p., creative dir., 1973-77, exec. v.p. creative, media and sales promotion, 1977—. Pres. Armonk (N.Y.) Little League. Served to capt. USAF, 1954-56; active Res. Mem. Am. Assn. Advt. Agencies. Clubs: Copywriters

(N.Y.C.), Windmill, Stanwich. Office: Cunningham & Walsh Inc 260 Madison Ave New York City NY 10016

MINIKES, STEPHAN MICHAEL, lawyer, banker; b. Berlin, Aug. 28, 1938; came to U.S., 1949, naturalized, 1957; B.S., Cornell U., 1961; J.D., Yale U., 1964; married; 1 child. Admitted to N.Y. State bar, 1965, U.S. Supreme Ct. bar, 1973, D.C. bar, 1977; asso. firm Milbank, Tweed, Hadley & McCloy, N.Y.C., 1964-68, Borden & Ball, N.Y.C., 1968-72; counsel to spl. cons. for energy Pres. U.S., 1973; counsel to chief Naval Ops., Washington, 1972-74; sr. v.p. Export-Import Bank of U.S., Washington, 1974-77; resident partner firm Butler, Binion, Rice, Cook & Knapp, Houston and Washington, 1977—; counsel Nat. Com. for Responsible Health Care. Mem. exec. com. Yale U. Law Sch.; trustee, chmn. fin. com. Washington Opera. Mem. Am. Bar Assn., Fed. Bar Assn., D.C. Bar Assn., Assn. Bar City N.Y., Am. Soc. Internat. Law, Am. Arbitration Assn. (nat. panel), Cornell U. Alumni Assn., Yale U. Alumni Assn. (law sch. rep.). Clubs: Univ., Yale (Washington). Contbr. articles to profl. jours. Office: 1747 Pennsylvania Ave Washington DC 20006

MINIO, JOSEPH C(ARMELO), alcohol distillery exec.; b. Putnam, Conn., Aug. 12, 1943; s. Carmelo and Concetta M.; B.S., Bryant Coll., 1965; m. Cathy Jean McKinley, Oct. 23, 1965; children—Joseph, Christopher. Auditor, Price Waterhouse & Co., L.I., N.Y., 1966-69; controller Mallory Randall Corp., L.I., 1969-72; treas. Kaufman and Broad Homes, L.I., 1972-74; v.p. fin. Beker Industries, Inc., Greenwich, Conn., 1974-77; exec. v.p. Publicker Industries Inc., Greenwich, 1977—. C.P.A., N.Y. State. Mem. Am. Inst. C.P.A.'s, N.Y. State Soc. C.P.A.'s, Am. Inst. Corp. Controllers. Roman Catholic. Home: 73 Angus Rd N Greenwich CT 06830 Office: 777 W Putnam Ave Greenwich CT 06830

MINISH, JOSEPH GEORGE, congressman; b. Throop, Pa., Sept. 1, 1916; s. George and Angeline (Nardozzi) M.; ed. pub. schs.; m. Theresa LaCapra, June 15, 1943; children—George, James, Joyce. Polit. action dir. dist. 4, L.U.E., AFL-CIO, 1953-54; exec. sec. Essex W. Hudson Labor Council, 1954-61, exec. sec.-treas., 1961-62; mem. 88th-96th congresses from 11th N.J. Dist.; mem. banking and currency com. Domestic Fin. Subcom., chmn. subcom. on urban mass transp., subcom. on gen. oversight and renegotiation of House Adminstrn. Com. Served with Armed Forces, World War II. Roman Catholic. Club: K.C. Office: 2162 House Office Bldg Washington DC 20515*

MINK, JOHN ROBERT, educator; b. Peru, Ill., Sept. 8, 1927; s. Monte Franklin and Marcella (White) M.; B.A., Ind. U., 1951; D.D.S. with honors, 1956, M.S. in Pedodontics, 1961; m. Barbara Joanne Merrell, June 21, 1952; children—Sarah, Teresa, Kathleen, Mary, James, Elizabeth. Instr., Ind. U., Indpls., 1957-60, asst. prof., 1960-62; dir. dental Clinic Handicapped Children, James Whitcomb Riley Hosp. for Children, Indpls., 1957-62; mem. faculty U. Ky., Lexington, 1962—, chmn. dept. pedodontics, 1962-74, prof. pedodontics, 1966—, asst. dean clin. affairs Coll. Dentistry, 1974—; cons. pedodontics USPHS, 1969-72, U.S. Army, Ft. Knox, 1969—, ADA, 1972—. Pres. Vols. Bur. Lexington, Ky., 1972-73; bd. dirs. Voluntary Action Center, 1978—. Bd. dirs. Margaret Hall Sch., Versailles, Ky., chmn. bd. 1976—. Served with AUS, 1946-47. Diplomate Am. Bd. Pedodontics (bd. examiners). Fellow Am. Acad. Pedodontics, Internat. Coll. Dentists; mem. Am. Soc. Dentistry for Children (pres. 1967—), Ky. Assn. Pedodontists, Am. Assn. Dental Schs., Internat. Assn. Dental Research, Delta Upsilon. Home: 5411 Parkers Mill Rd Lexington KY 40511 Office: Coll Dentistry U Ky Lexington KY 40511*

MINK, LOUIS OTTO, JR., educator; b. Ada, Ohio, Sept. 3, 1921; s. Louis Otto and Helen (Arndt) M.; B.A., Hiram (Ohio) Coll., 1942; M.A., Yale, 1948, Ph.D., 1952; M.A. (hon.), Wesleyan U., Middletown, Conn., 1965; m. Helen Louise Patterson, June 24, 1944; children—Louis Otto III, Sarah Patterson, Stephen Dorrance. Instr. Yale, 1950-52; mem. faculty Wesleyan U., 1952—, prof. philosophy, 1965—, Kenan prof. humanities, 1979—; vis. prof. Carleton Coll., Northfield, Minn., 1963, Yale U., 1977. Kent fellow Nat. Council Religion Higher Edn. (now Soc. for Values in Higher Edn.), 1948, bd. dirs., 1953-56, 73—, v.p., 1974—. Served with AUS, 1942-46; PTO. Mem. Am. Philos. Assn., AAUP, ACLU. Conglist. Author: Mind, History and Dialectic: The Philosophy of R.G. Collingwood, 1969; A Finnegans Wake Gazetteer, 1978. Contbr. articles to profl. jours. Mng. editor Rev. of Metaphysics, 1950-52; asso. editor History and Theory, 1965—. Home: 73 Home Ave Middletown CT 06457

MINK, PATSY TAKEMOTO, orgn. exec., former congresswoman, lawyer; b. Paia, Maui, Hawaii, Dec. 6, 1927; d. Suematsu and Mitama (Tateyama) Takemoto; student Wilson Coll., 1946, also recipient hon. degree; student U. Nebr., 1947; B.A., U. Hawaii, 1948; LL.D., U. Chgo., 1951; hon. degrees Lindenwood (Mo.) Coll., Duff's Inst., Pa.; D.H.L., Chaminade Coll., 1975, Syracuse U., 1976; m. John Francis Mink, Jan. 27, 1951; 1 dau., Gwendolyn. Admitted to Hawaii bar; practiced in Honolulu, 1953-65; lectr. U. Hawaii, 1952-56, 59-62, 79-80; atty. Territorial Ho. of Reps., 1955; mem. Ter. Hawaii Ho. of Reps., 1956-58; mem. Ter. Hawaii Senate, 1958-59, State Hawaii Senate, 1962-64; mem. 89th-94th congresses from 2d Dist. Hawaii, mem. edn. and labor com., interior com., budget com.; asst. sec. for oceans, internat. environ. and sci. Dept. State, 1977-78; mem. U.S. del. to UN Law of Sea, 1975-76, Internat. Womans Yr., 1975, UN Environment Program, 1977, Internat. Whaling Commn., 1977. Charter pres. Young Democratic Club Oahu, 1954-56, Ter. Hawaii Young Dems., 1956-58; del. Dem. Nat. Conv., 1960, 72; nat. v.p. Young Dem. Clubs Am., 1957-59; v.p. Ams. for Dem. Action, 1974-76, nat. pres., 1978-80; mem. nat. adv. com. White House Conf. on Families, 1979-80; mem. nat. adv. council Federally Employed Women, Adv. Com. for Campaign for UN Reform; v.p. Women USA; exec. com. Progressive Alliance; bd. dirs. New Directions; past bd. dirs. Hawaii Assn. Help Retarded Children, UNA-Hawaii, Hawaii NAACP, Rural Oahu YMCA, Honolulu Symphony, ACLU. Recipient Leadership for Freedom award Roosevelt Coll., Chgo., 1968; Alii award 4-H Clubs Hawaii, 1969; Nisei of Biennium award; Freedom award Honolulu chpt. NAACP, 1971; Disting. Humanitarian award YWCA, St. Louis, 1972; Creative Leadership in Women's Rights award NEA; 1977; Human Rights award Am. Fedn. Tchrs., 1975. Mem. Bus. and Profl. Womens Club. Home: 94-1037 Maikai St Waipahu HI 96797

MINKER, JACK, computer scientist; b. Bklyn., July 4, 1927; s. Harry and Rose (Lapuck) M.; B.A. in Math. cum laude with honors, Bklyn. Coll., 1949; M.S. in Math., U. Wis., 1950; Ph.D. in Math., U. Pa., 1959; m. Rita Goldberg, June 24, 1951; children—Michael Paul, Sally Anne. Grad. teaching asst. U. Wis., 1949-50; tchr. math. Erasmus Hall High Sch., Bklyn., 1950-51; engr. Bell Aircraft Corp., Buffalo, 1951-52; mgr. info. teach. sect. RCA, Bethesda, Md., 1952-63; dir. tech. staff Auerbach Corp., Washington, 1963-67, tech. cons., 1967-72; mem. Faculty NIH Grad. Sch., 1965-66; vis. mem. faculty U. Md., 1967-68, asso. prof. computer sci., 1968-71, prof., 1971—, 1st chmn. dept. computer sci., 1974-79; cons., speaker, lectr. in field; cons. NSF, 1979—; vice-chmn. Com. Concerned Scientists; past mem. U.S. Nat. Com. for Fedn. Info. Documentalists. Served with U.S. Army, 1945-46. NASA grantee, 1969-80; Nat. Bur. Standards investigator, 1970-73, grantee, 1975-76; NSF grantee, 1971-74, 74-76, 76-80. Mem. Assn. Computing Machinery (program chmn. Jerusalem Conf. on Info. Tech. 1967, chmn. nat. program com. 1968-69), IEEE, AAAS, Soc. Indsl. and Applied Maths. Jewish. Author: (with others) An Overview and Introduction to Logic and Data Bases, 1978; contbr. numerous articles to profl. pubis.; editor: (with H. Gallaire) Logic and Data Bases, 1978; pubis. reviewer. Home: 6913 Millwood Rd Bethesda MD 20034 Office: U Md Dept Computer Sci College Park MD 20742

MINKO, PHILIP PETER, chem. and food co. exec.; b. Troy, N.Y., Dec. 27, 1929; s. Panko J. and Catherine (Symbolie) C.; B.S. magna cum laude, St. Michael's Coll., 1952; M.B.A., U. Detroit, 1954; m. Dolores I. Metcalfe, Oct. 22, 1955; children—Philip Peter, David James. With Ford and Chrysler Motor Co., Detroit, 1954-61; plant controller Am.-Standard Co., Detroit, 1961-63; group controller Glidden Co., Cleve., 1963-67; v.p., controller Glidden-Durkee div. SCM Corp., Cleve., 1968-76, v.p., asst. to pres. Durkee Foods div., 1976—; teaching fellow U. Detroit, 1952-54, lectr. econs., 1954-63; mem. adv. council dept. accounting Kent State U., 1968—; lectr. Am. Mgmt. Assn. Asso. trustee St. Michael's Coll. Vt.; bd. dirs., treas. Jr. Achievement, Inc.; mem. adv. com. Sch. Bus., John Carroll U.; mem. Greater Cleve. Growth Assn. Served with USN, 1948-49; mem. Res., 1949-55. Mem. Fin. Execs. Inst. (past pres. N.E. Ohio chpt.), Nat. Assn. Accountants, Am. Mgmt. Assn., Ohio C. of C., Delta Sigma Pi, Delta Epsilon Sigma, Beta Gamma Sigma. Roman Catholic. Clubs: Cleveland Athletic; Westwood Country. Office: Union Commerce Bldg Cleveland OH 44115

MINKOFF, JACK, educator; b. N.Y.C., Jan. 29, 1925; s. Isidore and Yetta (Fine) M.; A.B., Cornell U., 1948; A.M., Columbia 1950, Ph.D. (Ford Found. fellow), 1960; m. Anne B. Johnson, June 19, 1948; children—Ellen, Paul. Instr. econs. Western Res. U., 1952-53; instr. econs. Sarah Lawrence Coll., 1959-60; prof. econs., chmn. dept. social sci. Pratt Inst., Bklyn., 1960—. Served with USAAF. 1943-45. Fellow Social Sci. Research Council, 1950-51. Mem. Phi Beta Kappa. Home: 57 Ruxton Rd Great Neck NY 11023 Office: Pratt Inst Brooklyn NY 11205

MINNELLI, LIZA, singer, actress; b. Los Angeles, Mar. 12, 1946; d. Vincente and Judy (Garland) M.; m. Peter Allen, 1967 (div. 1972); m. 2d, Jack Haley, Sept. 15, 1974 (div.); m. 3d, Mark Gero, Dec. 4, 1979. Appeared in Off Broadway revival of Best Foot Forward, 1963; recorded You Are for Loving, 1963, Tropical Nights, 1977; appeared with mother at London Palladium, 1964; appeared in Flora, the Red Menace (Tony award), 1965, The Act, 1977; nightclub debut at Shoreham Hotel, Washington, 1965; films include: Charlie Bubbles, 1967; The Sterile Cuckoo, 1969; Tell Me That You Love Me, Junie Moon, 1970; Cabaret (Oscar award), 1972; Lucky Lady, 1975; A Matter of Time, 1976; New York, New York, 1977; appeared on TV in own spl. Liza With a Z, 1972. Recipient Antoinette Perry award, 1978. Address: care Creative Mgmt Assos 40 W 57th St New York NY 10022*

MINNELLI, VINCENTE, motion picture dir.; b. Chgo., Feb. 28, 1910; student Art Inst. Chgo.; m. Judy Garland (div.); 1 dau., Liza May; m. 2d, Georgette Magnani (div.); 1 dau., Christiana Nina.; m. 3d, Denise Gigante (div.). Child actor Minnelli Bros. Dramatic Tent Show; asst. stage presentations Balban & Katz, then N.Y.C. Paramount Theatre; stage Du-Barry, N.Y.; art dir. Radio City Music Hall; prod. At Home Abroad, Ziegfeld Follies, Very Warm for May; screen debut, 1943; dir. motion pictures: Cabin in the Sky, 1943; I Dood It, 1943; Ziegfeld Follies, 1944; Meet Me in St. Louis, 1944; The Clock, 1944; Madame Bovary, 1949; The Pirate, 1949; Father of the Bride, 1950; An American in Paris, 1951; The Bad and the Beautiful, 1952; The Bandwagon, 1953; The Long Long Trailer, 1954; Brigadoon, 1954; Kismet, 1955; Lust for Life, 1956; Tea and Sympathy, 1956; Gigi (Oscar for Best Dir.), 1958; Reluctant Debutante, 1958; Some Came Running, 1958; Home from the Hill, 1959; Bells are Ringing, 1960; Four Horsemen of the Apocalypse, 1962; The Courtship of Eddie's Father, 1963; Goodbye Charlie, 1965; The Sandpiper, 1965; On a Clear Day You Can See Forever, 1970; A Matter of Time, 1976. Author: I Remember It Well, 1974. Office: care William Morris Agy 151 El Camino Beverly Hills CA 90212*

MINNER, ROBERT SCHERMERHORN, advt. agy. exec.; b. Chgo., Oct. 29, 1927; s. Charles Fred and Isabel (Schermerhorn) M.; B.S. in Bus. Adminstrn., Northwestern U., 1949; m. Arleen Ruth Johnson, Feb. 3, 1951; children—Barbara Ann, Thomas Oliran. Asst. mgr. data processing Pure Oil Co., 1957-63, asst. to adminstrv. v.p., 1963-64, asst. sec.-asst. treas., 1965; asst. sec. Union Oil Co. Calif., 1966; asst. treas. Needham, Harper & Steers, Chgo., 1967, v.p., treas., 1967-72; dir. planning Lien Chem. Co., 1972, v.p., treas., 1972-74; asst. treas. Leo Burnett Co., 1974-75, treas., 1975—. Home: 306 MacArthur Dr Mt Prospect IL 60056 Office: Prudential Plaza Chicago IL 60601

MINNICH, JOHN HARVEY, civil engr.; b. Landisville, Pa., Feb. 6, 1905; s. Harvey Wissler and Lizzie Johnstin (Bossler) M.; B.S., Dartmouth, 1928, C.E., Thayer Sch. Engring., 1929; m. Charlotte La Bombard, Jan. 2, 1928. Insp., resident engr., design engr. N.H. Hwy. Dept., Concord, 1929-33, constrn. engr., supervising engr., acting bridge engr., 1935-37; constrn. engr. Kittredge Bridge Co., Concord, 1933-34; constrn. supt. Davison Constrn. Co., Manchester, N.H., 1934-35; resident engr. Pub. Works Adminstrn., Portsmouth, N.H., 1938-40; constrn. foreman USN Yard Portsmouth, 1940; office engr. power plant constrn. Stone & Webster Engring Corp., Boston, 1940-42; asst. prof. civil engring. Thayer Sch. Engring., 1942-45, prof., 1945-54; cons. civil engr., pvt. practice, 1944—; asso. engr., mem. A.T. Granger Assos., Hanover, N.H., 1944-52; cons. structural engr. Anderson-Nichols & Co., Boston, 1951—, dir. engring., 1954-56; cons. structural engr. Am. Bridge Co., Pitts., 1955-56, Metcalf & Eddy, Boston, 1955-56, Dartmouth Coll., Hanover, 1959—, Fleck & Lewis, Architects, Hanover, 1959—, Pier Luigi Nervi, Rome, 1961-63; mem. Bd. Registration Profl. Engrs. N.H., 1945-52. Registered profl. engr., N.H., Vt., Mass. Mem. ASCE, Am. Concrete Inst., Am. Soc. Engring. Edn., Dartmouth Soc. Engrs. Address: 39 S Park St Hanover NH 03755

MINNICH, VIRGINIA, hematologist; b. Zanesville, Ohio, Jan. 24, 1910; d. Rufus Humphrey and Ollie (Burley) M.; B.S. in Home Econs., Ohio State U., 1937; M.S. in Nutrition, Iowa State Coll., 1938; Sc.D. (hon.), Williams Woods Coll., Fulton, Mo., 1972. Research asst., then research asso. medicine, div. hematology Washington U. Sch. Medicine, St. Louis, 1939-58, mem. faculty, 1958—, prof. medicine, 1974—. Recipient Alumni award home econs. Ohio State U., 1975; named St. Louis Woman of Achievement, Group Action Council, 1947; Fulbright-Hays grantee, Turkey, 1964. Mem. Am. Fedn. Clin. Research, Soc. Exptl. Biology and Medicine, Internat., Am. socs. hematology, Sigma Xi, Omicron Nu, Phi Upsilon Omicron. Contbr. articles to profl. jours. Office: Dept Medicine Washington Univ Med Sch Saint Louis MO 63110. *I discovered at an early age that there are many obstacles on the road to success. My friends and family helped me over the hurdles and they were the ones who were instrumental in the achievement of my goals.*

MINNICK, WALTER CLIFFORD, bldg. materials co. exec.; b. Walla Walla, Wash., Sept. 20,1942; s. Walter Lawrence and Dorothy (Waldron) M.; B.A., Whitman Coll., 1964; M.B.A., Harvard U., 1966, J.D., 1969; m. Jo Anne Oliver, June 11, 1965; children—Amy Louise, Adam Wade. Admitted to Oreg. and Wash. bars; asso. firm Davies, Biggs, Strayer, Stoel & Boley, Portland, Oreg., 1969-70; staff asst. Domestic Council, Washington, 1971-72; dep. asst. dir. Office Mgmt. and Budget, Washington 1972-73; with Trus Jofst Corp., Boise, Idaho, 1974—, v.p. div. ops., 1976-79, pres., 1979—. Served with U.S. Army, 1970-72. Mem. Wash. State Bar Assn., Oreg. State Bar Assn., Idaho Conservation League, Nature Conservancy, Boise Fgn. Affairs Soc., Bogus Basin Recreation Assn. Republican. Unitarian. Office: 9777 Chinden Blvd Boise ID 83702

MINOR, CHARLES DANIEL, lawyer; b. Columbus, Ohio, May 28, 1927; s. Walter Henry and Helen Margaret (Bergman) M.; B.S. in Bus. Adminstrn., Ohio State U., 1950, J.D. summa cum laude, 1952; m. Mary Jo Klinker, Dec. 27, 1950; children—Elizabeth, Daniel, Amy. Admitted to Ohio bar, 1952; mem. firm Vorys, Sater, Seymour and Pease, Columbus, 1952—; dir. Inland Products, Inc., Liebert Corp., Nat. Graphics Corp., Tracy-Wells Co., Worthington Industries, Inc. Served with USNR, 1946-47. Mem. Am., Columbus, Ohio State bar assns. Republican. Clubs: Scioto Country, Golf, Athletic of Columbus. Home: 2691 Lear Rd Columbus OH 43220 Office: 52 E Gay St Columbus OH 43215

MINOR, CHARLES VENABLE, lawyer; b. University, Va., Sept. 3, 1900; s. Raleigh Colston and Natalie (Embra) (Venable) M.; student Episcopal High Sch., Alexandria, Va., 1913-18; B.S., U. Va., 1922, LL.B., 1925; m. Louise Warner Minetree, Apr. 9, 1932 (dec. July 1976); children—Louise Warner (Mrs. Roderick D. Sinclair), Raleigh Colston, Charles Venable, Betty Eppes (Mrs. Gardner E. Cobb, Jr.). Admitted to Va. bar, 1924, S.C. bar, 1926; legal asst. to gen. solicitor So. Ry., 1925-27; practice in Charleston, S.C., 1927-29, in Charlottesville, Va., 1929—; occasional lectr. U. Va. Law Sch. Mem. Am., Va., Charlottesville-Albemarle bar assns., Va. State Bar (pres. 1963), Beta Theta Pi, Phi Delta Phi, Omicron Delta Kappa. Episcopalian. Home: Arrow Point Redart VA 23142 Office: Court Sq Bldg Charlottesville VA 22901

MINOR, GEORGE GILMER, JR., distbn. co. exec.; b. Richmond, Va., Oct. 1, 1912; s. George Gilmer and Helen (Flippen) M.; B.S. in Chemistry, Va. Mil. Inst., 1934; m. Elizabeth Roddey Watkins, Oct. 1, 1938; children—George Gilmer, Claiborne Watkins. Vice pres. Owens Minor & Bodeker, Richmond, 1946-49, pres., 1949-78, chmn. bd., 1978—, chief exec. officer, 1949—; dir. Watkins-Cottrell Hardware Co., Richmond First & Mchts. Nat. Bank. Pres., Richmond Cerebral Palsy Center, 1955, bd. dirs., 1953—; pres. March of Dimes, Richmond, 1950-52. Mem. Nat. Wholesale Druggist Assn., Va. Pharm. Assn., Richmond C. of C. Republican. Episcopalian. Office: 4825 Bethlehem Rd Richmond VA 23230

MINOR, HUGH CALVIN, oil co. exec.; b. Wheeling, W.Va., June 26, 1924; s. Chalmer Harvey and Tillie (Kison) M.; B.A., Dartmouth Coll., 1950; m. Cynthia Polley, Sept. 26, 1953; children—Lesley Karen, Michael Ian, Kim. With Texaco Inc., 1950—, mgr. Texaco Brasil S.A., Rio de Janeiro, 1967-71, gen. mgr. adminstrn., internat. sales, N.Y.C., 1971, v.p. petroleum products-Latin Am./West Africa, Coral Gables, Fla., 1971—. Bd. dirs. Greater Miami (Fla.) Opera Assn.; trustee Fla. Internat. U. Found. Served with USN, 1944-46. Club: Riviera Country. Office: 2121 Ponce de Leon Blvd Coral Gables FL 33134

MINOR, JAMES BERYLL, lawyer; b. Fairmont, W.Va., June 1, 1919; s. J. Beryll and Nettie L. (Faust) M.; B.A., George Washington U., 1943, LL.B., 1945. Admitted to D.C. bar, 1945, Md. bar, 1974; asst. legis. counsel U.S. Senate, 1946-47; legis. counsel War Assets Adminstrn., Washington, 1947-49; dep. chief legis. div. USAF, Washington, 1949-61; dir. rules codification, asso. gen. counsel FAA, Washington, 1961-67; asst. gen. counsel Dept. Transp., Washington, 1967-70, dep. asst. sec., 1970-71; gen. counsel U.S. Price Commn., Washington, 1972-73; individual practice law, Chevy Chase, Md., 1973-77; pres. James B. Minor and Assos., Regulatory Advisers and Cons., Sanibel, Fla., 1977—; dir. Plain Talk, Inc., Washington; adj. prof. Antioch Sch. Law, 1974-77. Mem. Am. (chmn. standing com. on legal drafting 1975-78), D.C., Md., Montgomery County bar assns. Address: 9426 Arum Ct Sanibel FL 33957 also Route 1 Box 817 Kill Devil Hills NC 27948. *I have found that what we cherish as our freedoms are highly relevant to the times. As life becomes more compressed and complex—so do our freedoms. Our biggest challenge is to find ways to preserve them as we may—faced always with pressures to give them up for expediency in solving our social and economic problems.*

MINOR, RICHARD J., hosp. adminstr.; b. Cin., June 11, 1934; s. Daniel E. and Lorraine (Thinnes) M.; B.S. in Bus. Adminstrn., U. Dayton, 1969; M.B.A., Xavier U., 1971; m. Carol Sester, Oct. 15, Oct. 15, 1973; children—Linda, Richard, Lorraine, Mary. Tech. sales rep. Hyland Labs., Los Angeles, 1957-58; purchasing agt. Good Samaritan Hosp., Dayton, Ohio, 1958-61, asst. adminstr., 1961-68; adminstr. Grandview Hosp., Dayton, 1968-73, pres., 1973—. Mem. Miami Valley Health Systems Agy.; mem. Dayton Area Hosp. Council; mem. adv. com. Dayton Sch. Practical Nursing. Served with USMC. Mem. Osteo. Assn. Am., Am. Hosp. Assn., Am. Coll. Hosp. Adminstrs., Nat. Council Community Hosps., Am. Osteo. Hosp. Assn., Ohio Hosp. Assn., Dayton C. of C. Office: 405 Grand Ave Dayton OH 45405

MINOR, ROBERT WALTER, lawyer; b. Columbus, Ohio, Dec. 15, 1919; s. Walter Henry and Helen Margaret (Bergman) M.; B.A., Ohio State U., 1940, J.D., 1948; m. Joan Allen, Sept. 13, 1947; children—Robert Allen, Mary Ann, Emily, Julia. Asst. counsel Senate Investigating Com., 1948-49; admitted to Ohio bar, 1949, D.C. bar, 1977, U.S. Supreme Ct. bar, 1952; adminstrv. asst. U.S. Senator John W. Bricker, 1949-53; apptd. 1st asst. dep. atty. gen., Washington, 1953; apptd. commr. ICC, 1956; v.p. law N.Y. Central R.R., 1958-67, v.p. exec. dept., 1967-68; sr. v.p. Penn Central Co., 1968-70; counsel Vorys, Sater, Seymour & Pease, Columbus, 1971-73, partner, 1974—; dir. Kauffman-Lattimer Co., Duff Truck Line. Served as lt. col., inf., U.S. Army, 1942-46. Decorated Bronze Star, Purple Heart; recipient Centennial Achievement award Ohio State U., 1970. Mem. Am., Fed., Ohio bar assns., Motor Carrier Lawyers Assn., Empire State C. of C. (pres.), Ohio C. of C. (dir.), Phi Delta Phi, Beta Theta Pi, Order of Coif. Republican. Mem. Ref. Ch. Am. (deacon). Clubs: Carlton (Washington); Scioto Country, Columbus Country, Golf, Athletic (Columbus). Home: 2384 W Lane Ave Columbus OH 43221 Office: 52 Gay St Columbus OH 43215

MINOR, WILSON FLOYD (BILL), newspaper editor; b. Hammond, La., May 17, 1922; s. Jacob Arthur and Johanna Marie (Clement) M.; B.S. in Journalism, Tulane U., 1943; m. Gloria Ethelyn Marks, Sept. 13, 1943; children—Paul Stephen, Jeffrey Clement, Douglas Marchand. Gen. assignment reporter Times-Pivayune, New Orleans, 1946-47, capital corr., Jackson, Miss., 1947-76; editor Capital Reporter, Jackson, 1976—; instr. Jackson State U., 1976-77, Millsaps Coll., Jackson, 1977-78. Served with USNR, 1943-46. Recipient Louis Lyons award Nieman Fellows Assn., 1966, Silver em award Miss. Scholastic Journalism Assn., 1972, Elijah Lovejoy award So. Ill. U., 1978. Mem. Investigative Reporters and Editors Assn., Reporters Com. Freedom of Press, La.-Miss. AP Assn. (past pres.), Sigma Delta Chi (past pres. Miss. chpt.). Democrat. Roman Catholic. Contbr. articles to various publs. Home: 4766 Kings Hwy Jackson MS 39206 Office: 153 Wesley Ave Jackson MS 39202

MINOW, JOSEPHINE BASKIN, civic worker; b. Chgo., Nov. 3, 1926; d. Salem N. and Bessie (Sampson) Baskin; B.S., Northwestern U., 1948; m. Newton N. Minow, May 29, 1949; children—Susan Neil, Martha Louise, Mary Rose. Asst. to advt. dir. Mandel Brothers Dept. Store, Chgo., 1948-49; tchr. Francis W. Parker Sch., Chgo., 1949-50; vol. in civil and charitable activities, 1950—; co-chmn. spl. study on juvenile justice Chgo. Community Trust, 1978—; bd. dirs. Juvenile Protective Assn., Chgo., 1958—, v.p., 1970-72, pres., 1973-75. Founder, coordinator Children's div. Hospitality and Info. Service, Washington, 1961-63; mem. Caucus Com., Glencoe, Ill., 1965-69; bd. dirs. Chgo. Council Fgn. Relations, Know Your Chgo.; mem. women's bd. Field Mus., Chgo. Urban League, U. Chgo.; founding mem. women's bd. Northwestern U., 1978; bd. govs. Chgo. Symphony, 1966-73, 76—; mem. exec. bd. WTTW Ann. Auction, 1967-71; exec. com. Northwestern U. Library Council, 1974—. Recipient spl. award Chgo. Sch. and Workshop for Retarded, 1975. Democrat. Jewish. Clubs: Standard, Carlton (Chgo.); Northmoor Country (Highland Park, Ill.). Home: 375 Palos Rd Glencoe IL 60022 Office: 208 S LaSalle St Chicago IL 60611

MINOW, NEWTON NORMAN, lawyer; b. Milw., Jan. 17, 1926; s. Jay A. and Doris (Stein) M.; B.A., Northwestern U., 1949, J.D., 1950, LL.D., 1965; LL.D., U. Wis., Brandeis U., 1963, Columbia Coll., 1972; m. Josephine Baskin, May 29, 1949; children—Nell, Martha, Mary. Admitted to Wis., Ill. bars, 1950; with firm Mayer, Brown & Platt, Chgo., 1950-51, 53-55; law clk. to chief justice Fred. M. Vinson, 1951-52; adminstrv. asst. to Ill. Gov. Stevenson, 1952-53; spl. asst. to Adlai E. Stevenson in presdl. campaign, 1952, 56; partner firm Adlai E. Stevenson, Chgo., 1955-57, Stevenson, Rifkind & Wirtz, Chgo., N.Y.C. and Washington, 1957-61; chmn. FCC, 1961-63; exec. v.p., gen. counsel, dir. Ency. Brit., Chgo., 1963-65; partner Sidley & Austin and predecessor firms, Chgo., 1965—; trustee, former chmn. bd. Rand Corp.; former chmn. Chgo. Ednl. TV, now hon. chmn.; chmn. pub. review bd. Arthur Andersen & Co., 1974—; dir., gen. counsel Aetna Casualty and Surety Co. Ill., Aetna Life Ins. Co. Ill.; dir. Field Enterprises, Inc.; mem. internat. advisory bd. Pan Am. World Airways. Professorial lectr. Northwestern U. Medill Sch. Journalism. Trustee Notre Dame U., 1964-77, mem. arts and letters adv. council, 1979—; trustee Mayo Found., Northwestern U.; co-chmn. presdl. debates LWV, 1976; bd. govs. Pub. Broadcasting Service, chmn. bd., 1978—; chmn. bd. overseers Jewish Theol. Sem., 1974-77; trustee Chgo. Orchestral Assn. Served with AUS, 1944-46. Named One of Ten Outstanding Young Men in Chgo., Jr. Chamber Commerce and Industry, 1960; named 1 of Am.'s 10 Outstanding Young Men of 1961; recipient George Foster Peabody Broadcasting award, 1961. Fellow Am. Bar Found.; mem. Am., Ill., Chgo. bar assns., Northwestern U. Alumni Assn. (merit award 1963). Democrat. Clubs: Standard, Legal, Economic, Carlton, Law, Commercial (Chgo.); Century (N.Y.C.); Northmoor Country (Highland Park, Ill.); Federal City (Washington). Author: Equal Time: The Private Broadcasters and the Public Interest, 1964; co-author: Presidential Television, 1973; co-author: Tomorrow's American: Electronics and the Future, 1977; contbr. As We Knew Adlai. Home: 375 Palos Rd Glencoe IL 60022 Office: 1 First National Plaza Chicago IL 60603

MINSKER, ELIOT ALAN, publisher; b. Jamestown, N.Y., Aug. 25, 1933; s. Louis and Lillian M.; B.M.E., Cornell U., 1956; M.B.A., Harvard U., 1962; m. Doris Finke, Dec. 22, 1957; children—JoAnn, Karen, Adam. With Burnham & Co., 1962-64; market researcher N.Y. Telephone Co., 1964-65; dir. instrument div. Ednalite Corp., 1965-67; pres., founder, pub. Knowledge Industry Publs., Inc., White Plains, N.Y., 1967—. Dir. adult edn. Briarcliff (N.Y.), 1976—, pres. West Orange (N.J.) Young Republicans, 1964-65; bd. dirs. West Orange United Fund, 1964. Served with USNR, 1956-60. Named Young Man of Year, West Orange, 1964. Jewish. Office: 2 Corporate Park Dr White Plains NY 10604

MINSKY, MARVIN LEE, mathematician; b. N.Y.C., Aug. 9, 1927; s. Henry and Fannie (Reyser) M.; B.A., Harvard U., 1950; Ph.D., Princeton U., 1954; m. Gloria Anna Rudisch, July 30, 1952; children—Margaret, Henry, Juliana. Mem. Harvard Soc. Fellows, 1954-57; with Lincoln Lab., Mass. Inst. Tech., 1957-58, prof. math., 1958-61, prof. elec. engring., 1961—, Donner prof. sci., 1973, dir. artificial intelligence group MAC project, 1958—, dir. artificial intelligence lab., 1970—. Served with USNR, 1945-46. Recipient Turing award Assn. for Computing Machinery, 1970. Fellow I.E.E.E., Am. Acad. Arts and Scis., N.Y. Acad. Scis., Nat. Acad. Sci. Author: Computation, 1967; Semantic Information Processing, 1968; Perceptrons (with S. Papert), 1968. Home: 111 Ivy St Brookline MA 02146 Office: 545 Main St Cambridge MA 02139

MINTEER, EDWIN DILLIN, editor; b. Gallatin, Mo., Nov. 2, 1891; s. Joseph C. and Martha (Richardson) M.; B.A., U. Okla., 1912; m. Laura Estelle Enochs, Nov. 12, 1919; 1 son, Edwin Drew. Mng. editor Okla. News, Oklahoma City, 1920-23; editor, pres. Terre Haute (Ind.) Post, 1923-29; editorial staff Cleve. Press, 1929-30; editor Fort Worth Press, 1930-32, El Paso (Tex.) World News, 1933-36; editor, pub. Las Cruces (N.Mex.) Sun-News, 1937-39; mng. editor Rocky Mountain News, Denver, 1939-45; asso. editor, columnist Albuquerque Jour., 1945-64, editor, 1964-67, editorial counselor, 1967—. Home: Broadmoor Apt 134 1499 Sutter St San Francisco CA 94109

MINTENER, JAMES BRADSHAW, lawyer; b. Trempealeau, Wis., July 6, 1902; s. John William and Anna Balfour (Bradshaw) M.; A.B., Yale U., 1923; student Oxford U. (Eng.), 1923-26, Harvard Law Sch., 1926-27; J.D., U. Minn., 1929; LL.D., Macalester Coll., W.Va. Wesleyan U., Gallaudet Coll.; Dr. Pub. Service, Ohio Wesleyan U.; m. Eleanor Van Gilder White, Mar. 2, 1934; children—Anne Randolph (Mrs. Peter A. Heegaard), James Bradshaw, Susan Perine (Mrs. Michael S. Northrop). Admitted to Minn. bar, 1930; gen. practice law with firm Cobb, Hoke, Benson, Krause & Faegre, Mpls., 1929-33; instr. Minn. Coll. Law, 1929-35; asso. with Pillsbury Mills, Inc. and predecessor cos., 1933—, asst. gen. counsel Pillsbury Flour Mills Co., Mpls., 1933-46, asst. sec., 1935-46, v.p. and gen. counsel, 1946-54; became asst. sec. HEW, 1954; sr. partner Mintener and Mitchell, 1962-75; cons. Chocolate Mfrs. U.S., Am. Cocoa Research Inst.; gen. counsel Parenteral Drug Assn.; former Washington counsel Govt. of U.S. V.I.; bd. dirs. Group Hospitalization, Inc., Washington. Past vice chmn., hon. mem. bd. trustees Am. U.; past pres. bd. trustees Wesley Theol. Sem.; vice chmn. bd. trustees Gallaudet Coll.; trustee, exec. com., v.p. Sibley Meml. Hosp.; asso. trustee Hamline U.; bd. dirs., mem. exec. com. Consortium of Univs., Washington; bd. dirs. Wesley Found., George Washington U.; bd. dirs., hon. mem. exec. com. Wolf Trap Found., Washington; former chmn., mem. exec., now hon. v.p. Methodist Bd. Publ.; mem. Folke Bernadotte Meml. Found., Gustavus Adolphus Coll., St. Peter, Minn. Mem. several civic groups on edn., youth, govt., human relations. Active in youth groups local, state, nat. race relations groups, related activities; past pres., treas., exec. com. D.C. Hosp. Council; mem. Pres.'s Commn. on Registration and Voting; mem. 2d citizens adv. com. FDA; mem. Surgeon Gen.'s Adv. Council Hosp. Research Facilities; lay del. World Meth. Conf. Meth. Gen. and Jurisdictional Confs.; mem. bd. Meth. World Council; mem. Meth. Commn. to Study Ministry. Mem. many comml. and profl. assns. and orgns., exec. of several, including English-Speaking Union (exec. com. nat. council, v.p. Washington br.). Clubs: Chevy Chase, Capitol Hill, Cosmos (past dir., chmn. program com.), Met., Palaver (Washington). Contbr. Christian Century. Received Jewish war vets. human relations award B'nai B'rith; nat. Jr. C. of C. good govt. award Mpls. Jr. C. of C.; U. Minn. outstanding achievement award. Home and Office: 4763 Berkeley Terr NW Washington DC 20007. *Having inherited from a devoted religious mother the highest standards of morals, ethics, and personal conduct, I am grateful for this inheritance and cherish it deeply. The result has been that all my life I have been deeply interested and involved in the church and many youth, health, and other activities related to the church. My goal is to help my family, friends, and my country in every possible way.*

MINTER, CHARLES FLOYD, Sr., ret. air force officer; b. Columbus, Ga., Aug. 20, 1925; s. John Millard and Maude (Phillips) M.; B.S., U. Omaha, 1966; m. Cloie Faye Dumas, Mar. 17, 1945; children—Charles Floyd, Susan A. Commd. 2d lt., USAAF, 1945, advanced through grades to maj. gen., USAF, 1973—; exec. officer to dir. ops. 2d Air Force, 1960-61; aide-de-camp to 2d Air Force Comdr. Lt. Gen. John D. Ryan, 1961-63; ops. staff officer, Blytheville AFB, Ark., 1963-64, SAC, Offutt AFB, Nebr., 1964-66; exec. officer to dir. ops. Hdqrs. SAC, 1966-67; vice-comdr. 9th Strategic Reconnaissance Wing SAC, 1967-69, comdr., 1969-70; vice-comdr. Ogden Air Material Area, Hill AFB, Utah, 1971-72; dep. chief of staff for maintenance Hdqrs. Air Force Logistics Command, Wright Patterson AFB, Ohio, 1972-74; vice comdr. HQ 15AF March AFB, Calif., 1974; comdr. HQ 8AF Anderson AFB, Guam, 1974-75; dir. log plans and programs Hdqrs. USAF, Washington, 1975, asst. dep. chief of staff for systems and logistics, 1976-77, ret., 1977. Decorated D.S.M. with one oak leaf cluster, Legion of Merit, D.F.C., Air medal with 3 oak leaf clusters. Mason (Shriner). Home: 3236 Lakewood Dr Shreveport LA 71107

MINTER, JAMES GIDEON, JR., newspaper editor; b. Inman, Ga., Oct. 22, 1930; s. James Gideon and Sara (Harp) M.; student North Ga. Coll., 1947-49; A.B. in Journalism, U. Ga., 1951; m. Anne Taylor, Aug. 21, 1955; children—Richard Anthony, James Robert. With sports dept. Atlanta Jour., 1951-52, 53-70, exec. sports editor, until 1970; mng. editor Atlanta Constitution, 1971-78, Atlanta Jour., 1978—. Served to 1st lt. AUS, 1951-53. Home: McBride Rd Fayetteville GA 30314 Office: 72 Marietta St Atlanta GA 30301

MINTER, PHILIP CLAYTON, training co. exec.; b. Sydney, Australia, Aug. 9, 1928; s. Roy Dixon and Adeline Claire (Bradly) M.; came to U.S., 1957, naturalized, 1968; B.Sc. with honours, U. Sydney, 1951; M.S., U. Wyo., 1958; Ph.D., U. Wis., 1960; m. Mary Bashford Schettler, Jan. 24, 1959; children—Elizabeth C., Margaret S. Tchr., King's Sch., Parramatta, Australia, 1951-57; mng. dir. Motivational Research Assos., Sydney, 1960-62; dir. research Nat. Fund Raising Counsel, Sydney, 1962-65; project dir. U.S. Dept. Agr., Ft. Collins, Colo., 1965-67; chief info. pesticides program USPHS, Atlanta, 1967-68; mgr. data bases div. Pa. Research Assos., Phila., 1968-70; pres. Ednl. Communications Inc., King of Prussia, Pa., 1970—; chmn. Service Tng. Ltd., Kenilworth, Eng.; cons. Westinghouse Learning Corp., 1972. Mem. Soc. Automotive Engrs., Sci. Research Soc. Am. Republican. Episcopalian. Club: Brit. Officers (Phila.). Author: Handbook for Pesticide-Chemicals Program Coordinators, 1967. Home: RD 1 Box 353 Malvern PA 19355 Office: 761 5th Ave King of Prussia PA 19406

MINTON, DWIGHT CHURCH, chem. co. exec.; b. North Hills, N.Y., Dec. 17, 1934; s. Henry Miller and Helen Dwight (Church) M.; B.A., Yale U., 1957; M.B.A., Stanford U., 1961; m. Marian Haven Haines, Aug. 4, 1956; children—Valerie Haven, Daphne Forsyth, Henry Brewster. With Church & Dwight Co., Inc., N.Y.C., 1961—, asst. v.p., 1964-66, v.p., 1966-67, pres., 1967-69, pres., chief exec. officer, 1969—, dir., 1966—; trustee Williamsburgh Savs. Bank. Treas., trustee Atlanta U., 1971—; trustee Spelman Coll., 1971—, Morehouse Coll., 1971—. Served with U.S. Army, 1956-57. Clubs: Seawanhaka Corinthian Yacht, Racquet and Tennis, Piping Rock, Yale. Office: PO Box 369 20 Kingsbridge Rd Piscataway NJ 08854

MINTON, JERRY DAVIS, banker; b. Ft. Worth, Aug. 13, 1928; s. Robert Bruch and Anna Elizabeth (Davis) M.; B.B.A., U. Tex., Austin, 1949, J.D., 1960; grad. certificate Nat. Trust Sch., Northwestern U., 1960; m. Martha Drew Fields, Nov. 28, 1975; children—Marianne, Martha, John Morgan. Sr. v.p. 1st Nat. Bank Ft. Worth, 1965—; dir. State Nat. Bank, Odessa, Tex. Mem. Ft. Worth City Council Aviation Bd.; pres. bd. trustees All Saints Episcopal Hosp., Ft. Worth, Harris Coll. Nursing; trustee, treas. Hist. Ft. Worth; bd. dirs. Ft. Worth Art Assn. Served as pilot USAF, 1951-55, Tex. Air N.G., 1955-57. Decorated D.F.C., Air medal with 3 oak leaf clusters; named Outstanding Young Lawyer, Ft. Worth Ft. Worth-Tarrant County Jr. Bar Assn., 1967. Mem. State Bar Tex., Am., Ft. Worth-Tarrant County (pres. jr. bar assn. 1961) bar assns., Am. (exec. com. trust div.), Tex. (chmn. legislative com. 1968-70, 71-73, chmn. trust div. 1975-76) bankers assns., Air Force Assn., Tex. Christian U. Mgmt. Alumni Assn. (pres. 1975), Sigma Iota Epsilon, Phi Delta Phi. Episcopalian. Mason (Shriner). Clubs: Shady Oaks Country, Fort Worth, Breakfast, Fort Worth Boat (Ft. Worth). Home: 5404 El Dorado Fort Worth TX 76107 Office: PO Box 2260 Fort Worth TX 76113

MINTON, JOHN DEAN, educator, historian; b. Cadiz, Ky., July 29, 1921; s. John Ernest and Daisy Dean (Wilson) M.; A.B. in Edn., U. Ky., 1943, M.A. in History, 1947; Ph.D., Vanderbilt U., 1959; m. Betty Jo Redick, June 8, 1947; children—John Dean, James Ernest. Instr. history U. Miami (Fla.), 1951; tchr. Broward County Pub. Sch. System, U. Miami evening div., 1951-53; prin. Trigg County (Ky.) High Sch., 1953-58; prof. history Western Ky. U., Bowling Green, 1958—, dean Grad. Coll., 1964-71, v.p. for adminstrv. affairs, 1970—. Cons. in field. Lay speaker Louisville Conf. Meth. Ch., 1954—, mem. Bd. Laity, 1965—; mem. Louisville Area Commn. on Higher Edn., Meth. Ch., 1972—; mem. Bowling Green Meth. Dist. Lay Activity, 1960—. Served with USNR, 1943-46. Mem. Nat., Ky. edn. assns., So. Hist. Assn., Phi Alpha Theta, Kappa Delta Pi. Club: Civitan (pres. Cadiz 1956). Contbr. articles to profl. jours. Home: 645 Ridgecrest Dr Bowling Green KY 42101

MINTON, PAUL DIXON, univ. ofcl.; b. Dallas, Aug. 4, 1918; s. William and Evelyn (Croft) M.; B.S., So. Meth. U., 1941, M.S., 1948; Ph.D., N.C. State U., 1957; m. Mary Frances Hickman, June 5, 1943; children—George Raymond, Roland Bertram. Asst. prof. math. So. Meth. U., 1952-56, asso. prof., dir. computing lab., 1957-61, prof. statistics, chmn. dept., 1961-72; dean Sch. Arts and Scis., Va. Commonwealth U., 1972-79, dir. Inst. Stats., 1979—; asso. prof. Va. Poly. Inst., 1956-57; cons. in field. Fellow Am. Statis. Assn., Am. Soc. Quality Control, Tex. Acad. Sci. (dir. 1969-71); mem. Inst. Math. Statistics, Biometric Soc., Am. Math. Soc. Contbr. articles to profl. jours. Home: 2626 Stratford Rd Richmond VA 23225

MINTON, WALTER JOSEPH, former publishing co. exec.; b. N.Y.C., Nov. 13, 1923; s. Melville and Ida (Harris) M.; grad. Lawrenceville Sch., 1938-41; student Williams Coll., 1941-42; A.B., Harvard, 1947; m. Pauline Snyder Ehst, Mar. 19, 1949 (div. 1970); children—Pamela Minton Barkley, Andrew Ehst, David Ehst; m. 2d, Marion Joan Whitehorn, Feb. 15, 1970; children—Jennifer Whitehorn, William Whitehorn, Katherine Whitehorn. With G.P. Putnam's Sons, N.Y.C., 1947-78, pres. G.P. Putnam's Sons, Inc., 1955-78; chmn. bd. Berkley Pub. Corp., 1966-78; v.p. MCA, Inc., 1976-78. Republican. Methodist. Clubs: Ridgewood (N.J.) Country; Union League, Harvard, Tuxedo (N.Y.C.); Yacht of Stone Harbor (N.J.).

MINTON, YVONNE FAY, mezzo-soprano; b. Sydney, Australia; d. Robert Thomas and Alice Violet Minton; ed. Sydney Conservatorium of Music, 1960-61; m. William Barclay, Aug. 24, 1965; children—Malcolm Alexander, Alison Elizabeth. Mezzo-soprano with all maj. orchs. in Australia, 1958-61; moved to London, 1961; joined Royal Opera House, Covent Garden, 1965-70; guest artist Cologne (W. Ger.) Opera, 1969—; appeared with Met. Opera, N.Y.C., 1973, Lyric Opera Co., Chgo., 1970, San Francisco Opera, 1974, Paris Opera, 1974; sings regularly with maj. symphony orchs. throughout world, 1968—; recs. include: Rosenkavalier, 1970, Cosi Fan Tutte, 1971, Lulu, 1979, The Knot Garden, 1970; maj. vocal works include: Mahler songs with Chgo. Symphony. Hon. mem. Royal Acad. Music. Office: care Ingpen & Williams 14 Kensington Ct London W85DN England

MINTS, THOMAS M., JR., research co. exec.; b. Chgo., Sept. 8, 1927; s. Thomas M. and Marie (Pendergast) M.; B.A., Yale, 1950; m. Marilyn E. Dungan, Nov. 29, 1952; children—Mary Kathleen, Martha Anne, Thomas M. III. With E.H. Sargent & Co., Chgo., 1950-68, asst. sec., 1952-53, v.p., 1953-62, pres., 1962-68; pres. Sargent-Welch Sci. Co. (merger E.H. Sargent & Co. and Welch Sci.), Skokie, Ill., 1968-70, chief exec. officer, chmn., pres., 1969—; dir. Old Orchard Bank. Bd. dirs. Cath. Charities Chgo., St. Francis Hosp., Evanston, Ill. Served with USAAF, 1946-47. Mem. Am. Chem. Soc., Sci. Apparatus Makers Assn., Phi Gamma Delta. Roman Catholic. Clubs: Economic, Yale (Chgo.); Michigan Shores (Wilmette, Ill.); Glen View (Golf, Ill.). Home: 1020 Hill Rd Winnetka IL 60093 Office: 7300 N Linder Ave Skokie IL 60077

MINTY, GEORGE JAMES, mathematician, educator; b. Detroit, Sept. 16, 1929; s. George James and Williamina Webster (Goodall) M.; B.S., Wayne State U., 1949, M.A., 1951; Ph.D. U. Mich., 1959; m. Emiko Shibata, Dec. 23, 1959; 1 dau., Michiko. Operations research cons. ICA, 1958; instr. Duke, 1958-59, U. Washington, 1959-60; asst. prof. U. Mich., 1960-64; vis. mem. Courant Inst., N.Y. U., 1964-65; prof. math. Ind. U., Bloomington, 1965—. Vis. prof. U. Calif., Berkeley, 1971; U.S. sr. scientist awardee Alexander von Humboldt Found., 1973-74; vis. prof. U. Hamburg (West Germany), 1973-74. Served with Signal Corps, AUS, 1953-55. Alfred P. Sloan fellow, 1964-66. Mem. Am. Math. Soc., Math. Assn. Am., Soc. Indsl. and Applied Math., Ops. Research Soc. Am., AAAS, AAUP, Phi Beta Kappa, Sigma Xi, Sigma Pi Sigma. Contbr. articles to tech. jours. Home: 1210 Collinswood Bloomington IN 47401

MINTZ, ALBERT, lawyer; b. New Orleans, Oct. 19, 1929; s. Morris and Goldie (Goldblum) M.; B.B.A., Tulane U., 1948, J.D., 1951; m. Linda Barnett, Dec. 19, 1954; children—John Morris, Margaret Anne. Admitted to La. bar, 1951, since practiced in New Orleans; partner firm Montgomery, Barnett, Brown & Read; partner Hurwitz-Mintz Realty Cos., New Orleans. Mem. adv. bd. Law Sch. Tulane U.; bd. dirs. Jewish Community Center, New Orleans, 1965-72, Jewish Fedn., New Orleans, 1968-73, Home for Jewish Aged, New Orleans, 1968-71, Jewish Family Service New Orleans, 1968-72; trustee bd. mgrs. Touro Informary Hosp. Mem. Am., La. (lectr., publ. on corp., tax, real estate law), New Orleans (exec. com. 1971-74) bar assns., Am. Law Inst., New Orleans C. of C. (chmn. com. civic affairs and state legis. 1968-69), Phi Delta Phi, Omicron Delta Kappa, Zeta Beta Tau. Jewish. Home: 2017 Jefferson Ave New Orleans LA 70115 Office: 806 First Nat Bank Commerce Bldg New Orleans LA 70115

MINTZ, BERNARD, univ. adminstr.; b. N.Y.C., July 19, 1914; s. Louis and Sadie (Robinson) M.; B.S. in Social Sci., City Coll. N.Y., 1934; M.A., Columbia, 1938; student N.Y. U., 1951-53; m. Bess Odesser, Mar. 22, 1936; children—Steven William, Nancy Ann; m. 2d, Frances Weisman, Oct. 1, 1970. Asst. to pres. Ever Ready Label Corp., Belleville, N.J., 1944-46; instr., lectr. eve. and grad. divs. Bernard M. Baruch Sch. Bus. and Pub. Adminstrn., City Coll. N.Y., 1943-64, asst. bus. mgr. coll., 1953-64; asst. univ. dean bus. affairs City U. N.Y., 1965-66, univ. prof., vice chancellor bus. affairs, 1966-72; mgmt. cons., 1951-64; exec. v.p. Bernard M. Baruch Coll., City U. N.Y., 1972-76, acting pres., 1976-77; exec. asst. to pres. William Paterson Coll. of N.J., 1977—. Mem. Eastern Assn. Coll. and Univ. Bus. Officers. Author: Living with Collective Bargaining, 1979; contbr. articles to profl. jours. Home: 1725 York Ave New York NY 10028

MINTZ, HARRY, artist, educator; b. Warsaw, Poland, Sept. 27, 1909; s. Zysman and Rachel Sari (Milgram) M.; M.F.A., Warsaw Acad. Fine Arts, 1927; m. Rosabelle Truglio, Sept. 1, 1958; children—William Zysman, Sari Rachel. Tchr. art Evanston Art Center, 1940—, North Shore Art League, 1950-59; vis. prof. Washington U., 1954-55; faculty Art Inst. of Chgo., 1955—, now prof. advanced painting; one man shows Art Inst. Chgo., Heller Gallery, N.Y.C., Feingarten Galleries, Chgo., also Beverly Hills, Calif., 1961, others; exhibited local, nat., internat. shows Art Inst. Chgo., 1932—, also N.Y. World's Fair, 1940, Whitney Mus. Am. Art, N.Y.C., Pa. Acad. Fine Arts, Carnegie Internat., Pitts., Venice Biennale, Italy, Palace Legion of Honor, San Francisco, Mus. Modern Art, N.Y.C., others; represented in permanent collections: Art Inst. Chgo., Whitney Mus., Warsaw Acad. Fine Arts, Mus. Art Tel-Aviv, Mus. Modern Art Rio de Janeiro, Evansville (Ind.) Mus., Notre Dame U., others. Recipient awards Art Inst. Chgo., 1937, 39, 45, 46, 49, 52, 54, 55, 61, Palace Legion of Honor Nat. Exhbn., San Francisco, 1946, U. Chgo., 1953, Union League Exhibit, Chgo., 1959, Old Orchard, Chgo., 1958-73, Sarasota (Fla.) Nat. Exhibit, 1959, others. Mem. Renaissance Soc. Address: 429 W Briar Pl Chicago IL 60657

MINTZ, MORTON ABNER, newspaper reporter; b. Ann Arbor, Mich., Jan. 26, 1922; s. William and Sarah (Solomon) M.; A.B. in Econs., U. Mich., 1943; m. Anita Inez Franz, Aug. 30, 1946; children—Margaret Ruth, Elizabeth Diane (dec.), Roberta Joan, Daniel Robert. Reporter, St. Louis Star-Times, 1946-50; reporter, asst. city editor St. Louis Globe-Democrat, 1951-58; reporter Washington Post, 1958—. Recipient Heywood Broun, Raymond Clapper, George Polk awards for journalism, 1962, A.J. Liebling award, 1974, Worth Bingham Meml. award, 1976. Author: The Therapeutic Nightmare, 1965; By Prescription Only, 1967; The Pill: An Alarming Report, 1969; (with Jerry S. Cohen) America, Inc.: Who Owns and Operates the United States, 1971, Power, Inc.: Public and Private Rulers and How to Make Them Accountable, 1976. Home: 3022 Macomb St NW Washington DC 20008 Office: 1150 15th St NW Washington DC 20071

MINTZ, SAUL AARON, wholesale co. exec.; b. New Orleans, Oct. 26, 1931; s. Morris and Goldie (Goldblum) M.; B.Arch., Tulane, 1953; m. Jean Strauss, June 6, 1953; children—Morris F., Carolyn Rose, Sally Ann. Chmn. bd., sec., treas., dir. F. Strauss & Son, Inc., Tallulah, La., 1954—, New Orleans, 1961—, Strauss Distbrs., Inc., Monroe, La., 1954—, Shreveport, 1961—; chmn. bd. Gulf Inland Corp., Houston, 1959—; pres. S&D Corp., Little Rock, 1963—, Falstaff Distbrs., Inc., Monroe, 1954—, Northgate Devel. Corp., Monroe, 1964—, G.M.S. Devel. Corp., Monroe, 1966—; chmn. Strauss Distbrs., Inc., Little Rock, 1961—, Sunbelt Mfg. Inc.; dir. Central Bank Monroe. Pres., past bd. dirs. Greater Ouachita Port Commn., Monroe, 1970—; past bd. dirs. United Givers Fund, Carolyn Rose Strauss Found. Served to lt. USAF, 1953-54. Mem. Monroe C. of C. (pres., dir.), Boosters Club N.E. La. U. (dir., past pres.), AIA, Young Pres.'s Orgn., Beer Industry League La. (past dir.), Zeta Beta Tau. Jewish (past sec., treas., bd. dirs. temple). Clubs: Masons, Shriners, Bayou DeSiard Country (dir.). Home: 2767 Point Dr Monroe LA 71201 Office: PO Box 6058 Monroe LA 71201

MINTZ, SEYMOUR STANLEY, lawyer; b. Newark, Mar. 7, 1912; A.B., George Washington U., 1933, J.D., 1936. Admitted to D.C. bar, 1936; atty. Office of Undersec. of Treasury, 1937-38, Office of Chief Counsel, IRS, 1938-42; asso. firm Hogan & Hartson, Washington, 1946-49, partner firm, 1949—; dir. Republic Steel Corp., Cleve., Dynalectron Corp., Washington. Mem. Am. Bar Assn., Fed. Bar Assn., D.C. Bar Assn., Am. Law Inst., Order of Coif. Contbr. articles to profl. jours. Office: Hogan & Hartson 815 Connecticut Ave NW Washington DC 20006

MINTZ, SIDNEY WILFRED, anthropologist; b. Dover, N.J., Nov. 16, 1922; s. Solomon and Fromme Leah (Tulchin) M.; B.A., Bklyn. Coll., 1943; Ph.D., Columbia U., 1951; M.A., Yale U., 1963; m. June Mirken, May 1952 (div. Dec. 1962); children—Eric Daniel, Elizabeth Rachel; m. 2d, Jacqueline Wei, June 6, 1964. Mem. faculty dept. anthropology Yale U., New Haven, 1951-74, prof., 1963-74; prof. anthropology Johns Hopkins U., Balt., 1974—; vis. prof. anthropology Mass. Inst. Tech., 1964-65, Princeton U., 1975-76; directeur d'études associé E.P.H.E., Paris, 1970-71; editor Yale U. Press Caribbean Series, 1957-74; cons. Overseas Devel. Program for Latin Am., Ford Found., 1957-62, U.S.-P.R. Commn. on Status P.R., 1964-65; Lewis Henry Morgan lectr. U. Rochester, 1972; Christian Gauss lectr. Princeton U., 1979. Served with USAAF, 1943-46. Recipient William Clyde DeVane medal Yale U., 1972; Social Sci. Research Council Faculty Research fellow, 1958-59; Guggenheim fellow, 1957; Fulbright fellow, 1966-67, 70-71; Nat. Endowment for Humanities fellow, 1978-79; mem. Inst. for Advanced Study, 1974-75. Fellow Am. Anthrop. Assn.; mem. Am. Ethnol. Soc. (v.p., pres.-elect 1967-68), Royal Anthrop. Soc. Gt. Britain and Ireland, Sigma Xi. Author: (with others) People of Puerto Rico, 1956; Worker in the Cane, The Life History of a Puerto Rican Sugar Cane Worker, 1960; Caribbean Transformations, 1974; (with others) An Anthropological Approach to the Afro-American Past, 1976. Office: Dept Anthropology Johns Hopkins U Baltimore MD 21218

MINTZ, WALTER, investment co. exec.; b. Vienna, Austria, Feb. 23, 1929; s. Maximilian and Ilse (Schueller) M.; came to U.S., 1938, naturalized, 1945; B.A., Reed Coll., 1950; postgrad. in econs. Columbia, 1950-51, 53-54; m. Sandra Jane Earl, Aug. 27, 1971. Asso. editor Barrons mag., 1951-53, 54-56; with Shearson Hammill Co., 1956-70, dir. research, 1962-69, exec. v.p. charge investment div., 1965-70; partner Cumberland Assos., investment mgmt., 1970—. Trustee, Reed Coll., 1971—. Mem. N.Y. Soc. Security Analysts (bd. dirs. 1969-75). Home: 923 Fifth Ave New York NY 10021 Office: 522 Fifth Ave New York NY 10017

MINTZER, DAVID, educator; b. N.Y.C., May 4, 1926; s. Herman and Anna (Katz) M.; B.S. in Physics, Mass. Inst. Tech., 1945, Ph.D., 1949; m. Justine Nancy Klein, June 26, 1949; children—Elizabeth Amy, Robert Andrew. Asst. prof. physics Brown U., 1949-55; research asso. Yale U., 1955-56, asso. prof., dir. lab. marine physics, 1956-62; prof. mech. engring., astronautical scis. Northwestern U., Evanston, 1962—, prof. astrophysics, 1968, asso. dean Technol. Inst., 1970-73, acting dean, 1971-72, v.p. for research, dean sci., 1973—; mem. mine adv. com. Nat. Acad. Sci.-NRC, 1963-73; trustee EDUCOM (interuniv. communications council), 1975—, vice chmn., 1977-78, chmn., 1978—. Fellow Am. Phys. Soc., Acoustical Soc. Am.; mem. ASME, Am. Astron. Soc., Sigma Xi, Tau Beta Pi, Pi Tau Sigma. Home: 736 Central St Evanston IL 60201

MINTZER, OLIN WESLEY, III, civil engr.; b. Spokane, June 6, 1916; s. Olin Wesley, Jr. and Ruth (Sugg) M.; B.C.E., U. Tenn., 1942; M.C.E., Purdue U., 1949; m. Marion Elizabeth Head, June 11, 1941; children—Elizabeth Wesley Mintzer Herron, Michael Olin, Patricia Ruthellen Mintzer Hopkins. Engring. aide TVA, Chattanooga, 1938-39, Paris, Tenn., 1940; instr. civil engring., research engr. Purdue U., 1947-49, asst. prof. hwy. engring., 1949-52; asst. prof. Case Inst. Tech., 1952-56; prof. AID project in India, Punjab Engring. Coll., Chandigarh, 1956-58; mem. faculty Ohio State U., Columbus, 1958—, prof. civil engring., 1974—; vis. prof. Escola Superior de Agricultura, Sao Paulo, Brazil, summer 1973. Asst. scoutmaster Central Ohio Area council Boy Scouts Am., 1961-68; mem. bd. Trinity Methodist Ch., Columbus, 1965-66. Served with C.E., U.S. Army, 1940-46. Decorated Legion of Merit; fellow Deutscher Akademischer Austauschdienst, 1970. Registered profl. engr. and surveyor, Ind., Ohio. Mem. ASCE, Am. Soc. Engring. Edn., Nat. Soc. Profl. Engrs., Transp. Research Bd., Am. Soc. Photogrammetry, Res. Officers Assn., Sigma Xi, Chi Epsilon. Author: Manual of Highway Engineering Applications of Photogrammetry, 1959; (with others) Airphoto Interpretation of Soils and Rocks for Engineering Purposes, 1953; also articles, chpts. in remote sensing manuals. Developer terrain investigation techniques. Home: 2027 Indianola Ave Columbus OH 43201 Office: 2070 Neil Mall Columbus OH 43210

MINTZES, JOSEPH, internat. economist; b. Phila., Dec. 4, 1915; s. Abraham and Sarah (Lisker) M.; B.S. in Edn., Temple U., 1942; M.A., Am. U., 1949; m. Doris Ellen Levy, Oct. 1, 1948; children—Judith Anne, Barbara Jane. Labor economist (internat.) Bur. Labor Statistics, Washington, 1946-49; econ. adviser labor/manpower matters Office U.S. Spl. Rep. in Europe, Paris, 1949-51; labor economist, chief labor economics div. ICA, Washington, 1951-57; dir. labor and manpower div. U.S. Mission to European Regional Orgns., Paris. 1957-62; labor adviser Bur. European Affairs, State Dept., Washington, 1962-64, fellow sr. seminar on fgn. policy, 1964-65; dir. U.S. Mission, AID, also econ. counsellor Am. embassy, Zaire, 1965-67; dir. Office Econ. Research and Analysis, State Dept., Washington, 1967-71; cons., internat. economist, 1972—. Mem. Am. Econ. Assn., Soc. Internat. Devel., Nat. Economists Club. Home: 3530 Yuma St Washington DC 20008 Office: Suite 401 2010 Massachussetts Ave NW Washington DC 20036

MINZ, ALEXANDER ISAAKAVICH, ballet dancer; b. Minsk, USSR, June 3, 1940; came to U.S., 1973; s. Isaac Efimovich and Ester Mendelievna (Jluskina) M.; student Vaganova Sch., Leningrad, USSR, 1950-60, Petrozauodsk (USSR) Theatre of Opera and Ballet, 1960-62; m. Ravza Sabirova, Feb., 1962. Mem. Kirov (USSR) Ballet Co., 1962-72; prin. dancer Am. Ballet Theatre, N.Y.C., 1977—; tchr. ballet La Scala, 1973, Toronto (Ont., Can.) Sch. Nat. Ballet, 1974, Teatro Colon, Buenos Aires, Argentina, 1974-75, Royal Swedish Sch., 1977, Santiago de Chile, Chile, 1979; appeared in Dybuk, 1974, Nureyev & Friends, Duke in Margaurite & Armand, 1975; TV appearance: Nutcracker, 1977; movie appearance: The Turning Point, 1976. Mem. Am. Guild Mus. Artists. Home: 2020 Broadway New York NY 10023 Office: Am Ballet Theatre 888 7th Ave New York NY 10019

MIRABAL, GEORGE MOLINA, assn. exec.; b. Pitts., July 17, 1938; s. Ralph C. and Marian C. (Clark) M.; B.S. in Econs., Thiel Coll., 1960; postgrad. U. Mich., 1967, Mich. State U., 1966-73; m. Corrine Ruth Miller, Aug. 29, 1959; children—George Molina, Linda Lee. Asst. buyer Joseph Horne Co., Pitts., 1960-63; sales rep. Charles Pfizer & Co., Youngstown, O., 1963-66; asst. mgr. Twin Cities Area C. of C., Benton Harbor, Mich., 1966-68; exec. dir. Streator (Ill.) Assn. Commerce and Industry, 1968-71; exec. v.p. Schenectady County (N.Y.) C. of C., 1971—. Recipient Human Relations award Streator, 1970, Distinguished Service award Streator, 1970; named Outstanding Young Man of Am., 1971. Mem. Am., N.Y. State C. of C. execs., U.S. C. of C. Roman Catholic. Rotarian. Home: 34 Memory Ln Schenectady NY 12306 Office: 243 State St Suite 6 Schenectady NY 12305

MIRABELLA, GRACE, mag. editor; b. Maplewood, N.J., June 10, 1930; d. Anthony and Florence (Bellofatto) Mirabella; B.A., Skidmore Coll., 1950; m. William G. Cahan, Nov. 24, 1974. Mem. exec. tng. program Macy's, N.Y.C., 1950-51; mem. fashion dept. Saks Fifth Ave., N.Y.C., 1951-52; with Vogue mag., N.Y.C., 1952-54, 56—, asso. editor, 1965-71, editor-in-chief, 1971—; mem. pub. relations staff Simonetta & Fabiani, Rome, Italy, 1954-56. Recipient Outstanding Grad. Achievement award Skidmore Coll., 1972. Office: Vogue 350 Madison Ave New York NY 10017*

MIRABITO, PAUL S., computer and office equipment mfg. co. exec.; b. N.Y.C., June 7, 1915; s. Salvatore and Virginia (Marra) M.; B.A., Coll. City N.Y., 1935; student Columbia U., 1935-37; M.B.A., N.Y. U., 1938; m. Virginia Ellen Woodstock, May 25, 1940; children—Terrence, Maureen, Kent, Lynn. Accountant controllers div. N.Y.C., 1936-39, Haskins & Sells, C.P.A.'s, N.Y.C., 1939-42; controller, dir. contracts Control Instrument Co., Inc., subsidiary Burroughs Corp., 1942-51; asst. controller Burroughs Corp., Detroit, 1951-55, gen. mgr. def. contracts orgn., 1955-60, v.p., 1960-62, v.p. adminstrv., 1962-65, v.p., group exec. fed. and spl. systems group, 1965-68, exec. v.p., dir., 1968-73, pres., chief operating officer, 1973-77, chmn. bd., chief exec. officer, 1978—, pres., 1978-79; dir. Consumers Power Co., Warner-Lambert Co., Bendix Corp. Bd. dirs., v.p. Detroit Symphony Orch., United Found. Met. Detroit; bd. dirs. The Conf. Bd., Detroit Econ. Growth Council, Detroit Renaissance. C.P.A., N.Y. Mem. Computer Bus. Equipment Mfrs. Assn. Club: Econ. Detroit. Office: Burroughs Corp World Hdqrs Detroit MI 48232

MIRACLE, GORDON ELDON, educator; b. Olympia, Wash., May 28, 1930; s. Gordon Tipler and Corine Adriana (Orlebeke) M.; B.B.A., U. Wis., 1952, M.B.A., 1958, Ph.D., 1962; m. Christa Stoeter, June 29, 1957; children—Gary, Gregory, Glenn. Case officer, civilian intelligence analyst U.S. Army, W. Ger., 1955-57; instr. commerce Grad. Sch. Bus., U. Wis., Madison, 1958-60; instr., then asst. prof. mktg. U. Mich., Ann Arbor, 1960-66; asso. prof. advt. Mich. State U., East Lansing, 1966-70, prof. advt., 1970—, chmn. dept., 1974—; vis. prof. mktg. mgmt. N. European Mgmt. Inst., Oslo, 1972-73; cons., lectr. in field. Served with AUS, 1952-55. Fellow Ford Found., 1961-62, 64, Am. Assn. Advt. Agys., 1967. Mem. Am. Acad. Advt. (treas., exec. com. 1978-79), Acad. Internat. Bus. (sec., exec. com. 1973-75), Am. Econ. Assn., Am. Mktg. Assn., Soc. Internat. Devel., Assn. Edn. in Journalism. Author: Management of International Advertising, 1966; co-author: International Marketing Management, 1970; Advertising and Government Regulation, 1979; Instructor's Manual for International Marketing Management, 1971; contbr. articles to scholarly and profl. jours.; editor: Marketing Decision Making: Strategy and Payoff, 1965; Sharing for Understanding (Proc. Ann. Conf. Am. Acad. Advt.), 1977. Home: 1461 Cheboygan Rd Okemos MI 48864 Office: Dept Advt Mich State Univ East Lansing MI 48824

MIRAND, EDWIN ALBERT, cancer scientist; b. Buffalo, July 18, 1926; s. Thomas and Lucy (Papier) M.; B.A., U. Buffalo, 1947, M.A., 1949; Ph.D., Syracuse (N.Y.) U., 1951; D.Sc. (hon.), Niagara (N.Y.) U., 1970, D'Youville Coll., Buffalo, 1974. Successively undergrad. asst., grad. asst., instr. U. Buffalo, 1946-48; teaching fellow Syracuse U., 1948-51; instr. Utica (N.Y.) Coll., 1950; mem. staff Roswell Park Meml. Inst., Buffalo, 1951—, head W. Seneca labs., 1961—, asso. inst. dir., head dept. edn., 1967—, dir. cancer research, 1968-73, head dept. viral oncology, 1970-73, head dept. biol. recources, 1973—; research prof. biology Grad. Sch., prof. biochem. pharmacology Sch. Pharmacy, State U. N.Y., Buffalo, 1955—, dean Roswell Park Meml. Inst. grad. div., 1967—; research prof. biology Grad. Sch., dean Roswell Park Meml. Inst. grad. div. Niagara U.; mem. human cancer virus task force, clin. cancer edn. com. NIH; mem. U.S. nat. com. Union Internat. Contra Cancer; profl. edn. com. cancer control Nat. Cancer Inst; liaison mem. Pres.'s Nat. Cancer Adv. Bd.; mem. N.Y. State Health Research Council. Recipient Billings Silver medal AMA, 1963; award sci. research mammalian tumor viruses Med. Soc. State N.Y., 1963; citation award in sci. Coll. Arts and Scis., State U. N.Y., Buffalo, 1964. Life mem., fellow N.Y. Acad. Sci.; fellow AAAS; mem. Am. Cancer Soc., Assn. Gnotobiotics (pres. 1968-69, dir. 1975-78), Assn. Am. Cancer Insts. (sec.-treas. 1968—), Am. Assn. Cancer Research, Radiation Research Soc., Am. Soc. Zoologists, Soc. Exptl. Biology and Medicine, Buffalo Acad. Medicine, Animal Care Panel, Internat. Soc. Hematology, Pub. Health Cancer Assn. Am., Internat. Union Against Cancer (chmn. U.S. nat. com. 1979—, sec.-gen. 13th Internat. Cancer Congress), Hematology Soc., Am. Soc. Preventive Oncology, Buffalo Hist. Soc. (life), Buffalo Fine Arts Acad. (life), Sigma Xi. Author articles cancer research, endocrinology, hematology, virology. Editorial bd. Yearbook Cancer, Oncology News, Jour. Surg. Oncology. Home: S-6178 Hunters Creek Buffalo NY 14139 Office: 666 Elm St Roswell Park Meml Inst Buffalo NY 14263

MIRANDA, CONSTANCIO FERNANDES, educator; b. Raia-Goa, India, Dec. 4, 1926; s. Alex Fernandes and Maria Marcelina (Viegas) M.; student Karnatak Coll., Dharwar, 1944-46; B.Engring. (civil), U. Bombay, 1949; M.S. in Civil Engring., U. Notre Dame, 1962; Ph.D. in Structural Engring., Ohio State U., 1964, M.A. in Math., 1974; m. Joan Mary Menezes, Mar. 3, 1957; children—Steven Alex, Christopher Gerard, Kenneth Michael, Marie Lynn. Came to U.S., 1960, naturalized, 1966. With civil engring. projects Govt. Bombay, 1950-60; teaching asst., then instr. U. Notre Dame, 1960-62; instr., research asso. Ohio State U., 1962-64; mem. research staff U. N.Mex., 1964-65; mem. faculty U. Detroit, 1965—, prof. civil engring., 1966—, chmn. dept. 1965-72, asso. dean, acting dean Coll. Engring., 1972-73, dir. Profl. Adv. Service Center, 1973-75; staff engr. EPA, N.C., 1976-77. Named Engring. Tchr. of Year, Engring. Joint Council, U. Detroit, 1966, 76; Distinguished Alumnus, Ohio State U., 1973. Registered profl. engr., Ind., Ohio, Mich., Ill. Mem. Am. Soc. C.E., Am. Soc. Engring. Edn., Instn. Engrs. (India), Am. Inst. for Decision Sci., Sigma Xi, Chi Epsilon, Tau Beta Pi, Pi Mu Epsilon. Contbr. profl. jours. Home: 19330 Warrington St Detroit MI 48221

MIRES, MAYNARD HAROLD, JR., state ofcl.; b. Ithaca, N.Y., Mar. 18, 1924; s. Maynard Harold and Ethel Emeline (Coon) M.; student Hamilton Coll., 1941-43; M.D., U. Buffalo, 1946; M.P.H. cum laude, Harvard U., 1954; m. Ruth Agnes Bingham, June 22, 1946; children—Stephen Austin, Peter Bingham, Martha Lee, Amy Louise. Intern, U.S. Marine Hosp., Boston, 1946-48; dir. communicable disease control Vt. Health Dept., Burlington, 1952-57; dir. local health services Del. Div. Pub. Health, 1957-73; dir. div. pub. health N.H. Dept. Health and Welfare, Concord, 1973—; exec. sec. N.H. Bd. Registration in Medicine, 1973—. Pres. Friends of Old Dover (Del.), 1959-62. Served with USPHS, 1948-52. Diplomate Am. Bd. Preventive Medicine. Fellow Am. Pub. Health Assn., Royal Soc. Health; mem. Delta Omega, SAR (surgeon gen. nat. soc. 1978-79). Episcopalian. Clubs: Mason, Scottish Rite (hon. 33 deg.), Rose Croix (past officer). Home: RFD #1 Concord NH 03301 Office: Health and Welfare Bldg Hazen Dr Concord NH 03301

MIRICK, HENRY DUSTIN, architect; b. Washington, Aug. 6, 1905; s. Henry Brown and Blanche Mitchell (Swope) M.; B.A., Princeton, 1927; B. Arch., U. Pa., 1930, M. Arch., 1931; m. Marion Winsor, June 24, 1933; children—Marion (Mrs. Jouko A. Ilvonen), Henry Dustin, Heath (Mrs. Mark Kennedy), Richard. Partner Mirick, Pearson, Ilvonen, Batcheler, Phila., 1935—; works include monograph on large baths Hadrians Villa (Trivoli, Italy), Pennwalt, Nat. Bd. Med. Examiners bldgs., Friends Select Sch., Shipley Sch., Bryn Mawr Hosp., Medford Leas Retirement Community. Pres. Lower Merion Bd. Hist. Review, 1963-66; mem. Lower Merion Planning Commn., 1955-69. Trustee Acad. Natural Scis.; dir. Pa. Environmental Council, Phila. Zool. Soc., Harriton Assn., Wharton Center, 1951-63; pres. Montgomery Country Day Sch., 1965-67; mem. vestry Ch. of the Redeemer, Bryn Mawr, 1977—. Served as lt. col. AUS, 1942-45. Recipient Rome prize in architecture, 1930, A.I.A. merit citations; fellow Am. Acad. Rome, 1933. Fellow A.I.A. (pres. Phila. 1970); mem. Pa. Soc. Architects, Phila. C. of C. (dir.), Pa. Hort. Soc. (pres. 1959-62), Pa. Soc. Promoting Agr., Am. Arbitration Assn., Shakespere Soc., Tau Sigma Delta, Delta Psi. Clubs: Philadelphia, Rittenhouse, Art Alliance, Princeton, Pohoqualine Fish Assn. (Phila.); Quadrangle (Princeton). Home: 101 Cherry Lane Ardmore PA 19003 Office: 3 Parkway Philadelphia PA 19103

MIRISCH, MARVIN ELLIOT, motion picture producer; b. N.Y.C., Mar. 19, 1918; s. Max and Josephine (Urbach) M.; B.A., Coll. City N.Y., 1940; m. Florene Smuckler, Dec. 28, 1941; children—Donald, Carol, Lynn. With contract and print depts., then office mgr. Grand Nat. Films, Inc., N.Y.C., 1936-40; organized theatre concession bus. Theatres Candy Co., Inc., Milw., 1940; exec., corporate officer Allied Artists Pictures Corp., Hollywood, Calif., 1953-57; co-organizer Mirisch Co., Inc., motion picture producers, Hollywood, Calif., 1957, v.p., dir., 1957—; chmn., chief exec. officer Mirisch Prodns., Inc., 1968—. Chmn. permanent charities com. Motion Picture and TV Industries. Pres., Mirisch Family Found.; bd. adminstrs. Hebrew Union Coll., Calif.; young men's adv. bd. Cedars of Lebanon Hosp., Los Angeles. Recipient Best Picture of Year award Acad. Motion Picture Arts and Scis. for The Apartment, 1961, West Side Story, 1962, In the Heat of the Night, 1968; Producer of Year award Nat. Assn. Theatre Owners, 1972. Mem. Assn. Motion Picture and TV Producers Am. (dir., vice-chmn.), Los Angeles Art Inst., Acad. Motion Picture Arts and Scis. (bd. govs., 1st v.p.). Jewish. Clubs: Motion Picture Pioneers, Hillcrest Country. Home: 723 N Crescent Dr Beverly Hills CA 90210 Office: 100 Universal City Plaza Universal City CA 90046

MIRISCH, WALTER MORTIMER, motion picture producer; b. N.Y.C., Nov. 8, 1921; s. Max and Josephine (Urbach) M.; student Coll. City N.Y., 1938-40; B.A., U. Wis., 1942; I.A., Harvard, 1943; m. Patricia Kahan, Oct. 11, 1947; children—Anne, Andrew, Lawrence. Producer, exec. producer Allied Artists Pictures Corp., 1946-57; producer, v.p. charge prodn. Mirisch Co., Inc., Los Angeles, 1957—; pres.-exec. head prodn. Mirisch Corp., Inc., 1969—; prodns. include Magnificient Seven, Two for the Seasaw, Toys in the Attic, Hawaii, In the Heat of the Night (Acad. award for best picture of year 1968), The Hawaiians, The Organization, Mr. Majestyk, Midway, Gray Lady Down, Same Time Next Year. Pres., bd. dirs. dir. Motion Picture Permanent Charities, 1960-61; bd. dirs. Center Theatre Group Los Angeles, Cedars-Sinai Med. Center; adv. bd. Cal. State U., Northridge. Decorated L'Ordre des Arts et des Lettres (France). Mem. Acad. Motion Picture Arts and Scis. (pres. 1973-77, gov. 1964-70, 72—, treas. 1972—), Producers Guild Am. (pres., dir. 1959-62), Motion Picture Assn. Am. (dir. 1961—), Wis. Alumni Assn. (dir. 1967-73). Office: 100 Universal City Plaza Universal City CA 91608*

MIRKIN, ABRAHAM JONATHAN, surgeon; b. Flushing, N.Y., Aug. 17, 1910; s. Samuel and Anna (Jaffe) M.; A.B., Cornell U., 1931; M.D., N.Y. U., 1935; m. Miriam G. Klawan, Jan. 26, 1936; children—Sara Louise, Lawrence Stanley. Intern, then resident Sinai Hosp., Balt., 1935-41; mem. surg. staff Meml. and Sacred Heart hosps. (both Cumberland, Md); pres. med. staff Meml. Hosp., 1966-67; instr. Traffic Inst., Northwestern U., 1968, 72, 74, 76, 78; med. adv. bd. Fla. Motor Vehicle Adminstr.'s Office. Mem. Nat. Com. on Uniform Laws and Ordinances, 1969-72. Gen. chmn. Nat. Conf. on Aging Drivers, 1974. Served to maj. M.C., AUS, 1942-46. Diplomate Am. Bd. Surgery. Fellow A.C.S. (chmn. hwy. safety com. Md. chpt. 1967-68), Southeastern Surg. Congress; mem. AMA (past chmn. med. aspects automotive safety), Allegany County Med. Soc. (pres. 1947-48), Am. Assn. Automotive Medicine (bd. dirs. 1957-60, 79—, pres. 1957-59), Soc. Automotive Engrs. (com. on automotive safety), Med.-Chirurgical Faculty Md. (subcom. on traffic safety 1970—). Home: 1014 Lewis Cove Delray Beach FL 33444 Office: Route 1 Box 153 Flintstone MD 21530

MIRKIN, MELVIN J., govt. ofcl.; b. Phoenix, May 8, 1929; s. Ben and Nell (Cohen) M.; A.B., U. Chgo., 1949; postgrad. Columbia U., 1950; LL.B., Stanford, 1954; m. Charlotte A. McIntire, Nov. 3, 1956; children—Andrew S., R. Peter, Adam N., Chad A., Miya C. Admitted to Ariz. bar, 1954, U.S. Supreme Ct. bar, 1958; asst. atty. gen. Ariz., Phoenix, 1955-59; asst. city atty. for pub. works, Phoenix, 1964-67; with Peace Corps, 1967-71; columnist for various daily newspapers, 1974-78; mem. Bd. Appeals Surface Mining and Reclamation, Dept. Interior, Washington, 1978—. Nat. Program Ednl. Leadership fellow, 1972-74. Office: 4015 Wilson Blvd Arlington VA 22203

MIRMAN, IRVING R., scientific adviser; b. Syracuse, N.Y., July 29, 1915; s. Saniel I. and Rebecca (Raichlin) M.; B.E.E., N.Y. U., 1942; postgrad. Harvard-Mass. Inst. Tech., 1942-43, Poly. Inst. Bklyn., 1947-51, Air U., 1952, 56, 59, George Washington U., 1956, Colgate U., 1957, Syracuse U., 1958, Am. U., 1964-65; m. Beatrice Wolff, Aug. 14, 1942; children—Robert, Marsha, Kenneth. Elec. engr. Central N.Y. Power Co., Syracuse, 1937-41; project engr. Watson Labs., Red Bank, N.J., 1946-50; mem. tech. staff Rome Air Devel. Center (N.Y.) 1950-51, chief program staff, 1951-55, asst. sci. dir., 1955-57, asso. dir. research and devel., 1957-59; dir. tech. planning and operations Capehart Corp., N.Y., 1959-60, v.p., 1960-63; sci. cons. Anser Corp.,

Baileys Cross Roads, Va., 1963; sci. adviser, dep. chief staff research and devel. in sci. and tech. Dept. Air Force, Washington, 1963-66; spl. asst. to comdr. Hdqrs. Air Force System Command, 1966-76; dep. dir. SHAPE Tech. Center, The Hague, Netherlands, 1976—; sci. adviser S.E. Asia matters, 1967-72. Served to capt. USAF, 1942-46. Recipient Meritorious Civilian award Dept. Air Force, 1958, also Distinguished Civilian award, 1976. Registered profl. engr., Mass. Fellow A.A.A.S.; sr. mem. IEEE; mem. Am. Inst. Aeros. and Astronautics, N.Y. Acad. Sci., Research Engring. Soc. Am. Home: 9922 Brixton Ln Bethesda MD 20034 Office: US Research Devel Coordinator SHAPE Tech Center APO NY 09159

MIRSE, RALPH THOMAS, coll. pres.; b. Carrsville, Ky., Aug. 8, 1924; s. Ralph Thomas and Rubye Catherine (Morris) M.; B.A., Asbury Coll., Wilmore, Ky., 1945; Th.M., Asbury Theol. Sem., 1947; Ph.D., Boston U., 1962; L.H.D. (hon.), Lakeland Coll., Sheboygan, Wis., 1977; LL.D., Buena Vista Coll., Storm Lake, Iowa, 1978; m. Blanche Allen, May 10, 1945; children—Ralph Allen, Deborah Lynn, Sally Ann. Ordained to ministry United Methodist Ch., 1947; pastor Meth. Chs. in Ky., 1947-57; exec. sec. New Eng. conf. United Meth. Ch., 1960-65, nat. div., 1965-70; v.p. Baker U., Baldwin, Kans., 1970-74; pres. Lakeland Coll., 1974-77, Columbia (S.C.) Coll., 1977—; mem. president's adv. bd. Small Coll. Consortium; adv. Eli Lilly Endowment; cons. instl. devel. CASC Nat. Cons. Network; mem. Nat. Rotary Scholarship Com., Gov. S.C. Adv. Bd. Social Services, S.C. Adv. Council Pvt. Colls. Mem. Am. Assn. Higher Edn., Council Advancement and Support Edn., Am. Acad. Polit. and Social Sci., Nat. Conf. Small Colls. (pres., dir.), S.C. Found. Pvt. Colls., S.C. Coll. Council. Republican. Clubs: Rotary, Shriners; Univ. (N.Y.C.); Hyannis (Mass.) Yacht. Author: The Methodist Minister, 1960; The Self-Image of the Methodist Minister, 1962; The Changing Face of New England, 1964; Community Planning Studies, 1970. Office: Columbia Coll Columbia SC 29203

MIRSKY, JEANNETTE, author; b. Bradley Beach, N.J., Sept. 3, 1903; d. Michael David and Frieda (Ittelson) Mirsky; grad. Ethical Culture Sch., N.Y.C., 1921; B.A., Barnard Coll. Columbia, 1924, postgrad., 1935-38; m. Edward Bellamy Ginsburg, Feb. 14, 1942 (dec. 1959). Lectr. for USIA, India, Iran and Central Am., Africa; vis. fellow dept. Oriental Studies Princeton, 1964-67, dept. East Asian studies, 1970-71, 72-73, 73-74. Guggenheim fellow, 1947-48, 49-50; Rockefeller fellow, 1964-67; Nat. Endowment Humanities grantee, 1970-72; Lucius N. Littauer Found. grantee Mem. Soc. Women Geographers, P.E.N., Royal Central Asian Soc., Phi Beta Kappa. Author: To the North, 1934, rev. As To The Arctic, 1946, reissued, 1974; The Westward Crossings; Balboa, Mackenzie, Lewis and Clark, 1946, rev. edit., 1970; (with Allan Nevins) The World of Eli Whitney, 1952; Elisha Kent Kane and the Seafaring Frontier, 1954; Balboa, Discoverer of the Pacific, 1964; Houses of God, 2d edit., 1976; The Gentle Conquistadors, 1969; Sir Aurel Stein Archaeological Explorer, 1977, also intros. Editor: The Great Chinese Travelers, 1964, paperback edit., 1974; writer forewards to The Lady, 1970, rev. edit. On Ancient Central-Asian Tracks, 1974; contbr., conc. Ency. Brit., Ency. Americana. Home: 230 Nassau St Princeton NJ 08540

MIRVISH, ROBERT FRANKLIN, author; b. Washington, July 17, 1921; s. David and Anna (Kornhauser) M.; student U. Toronto, 1946-47; m. Lucille A. DeGiglio; children—Anthony David, John Richard. Producer play Like Father, Like Fun; author: A House of Her Own, 1953; The Eternal Voyagers, 1953; Texana, 1954; The Long Watch, 1954; Red Sky at Midnight, 1955; Woman in a Room, 1959; Two Women, Two Worlds, 1960; Dust on the Sea, 1960: Point of Impact, 1961; Cleared Narvik 2000, 1962; The Last Capitalist, 1963; Business is People, 1963; There You Are, But Where Are You?, 1964; Holy Loch, 1964. Served U.S. Mcht. Marine, 1942-45. Mem. Author's Guild Am., Am. Radio Assn. Address: 32 Salonica Rd Don Mills ON M3C 2L9 Canada. *People have a tendency to confuse Education with Schooling. Schooling is what you get in a classroom. Education is what you get in a poolroom.*

MISCH, HERBERT LOUIS, automobile co. exec.; b. Sandusky, Ohio, Dec. 7, 1917; s. William Albert and Ethel Alice (Haller) M.; student Miami U., Oxford, Ohio, 1935-38; B.S. in Mech. Engring., U. Mich., 1941; m. Caroline Jane Brinkerhoff, Oct. 7, 1939; children—Suzanne, Thomas A. Chief engr. Packard Motor Car Co., 1941-56; dir. advanced planning Cadillac div. General Motors Corp., 1956-57; with Ford Motor Co., 1957—, v.p. engring. and research, 1962—, v.p. engring. and mfg., 1970-72, v.p. environ. safety engring., 1972—. Mem. Am. Soc. Body Engrs., Nat. Acad. Engring. Coordinating Research Council (dir. 1973—), Soc. Automotive Engrs. (dir. 1965-68). Clubs: Grosse Pointe Yacht, Detroit Athletic. Home: 1411 Lochridge Bloomfield Hills MI 48013 Office: Ford Motor Co American Rd Dearborn MI 48121

MISCH, ROBERT JAY, author, columnist; b. N.Y.C., Nov. 19, 1905, s. Moses and Jennie (Reshower) M.; m. Janet W. Misch, June 23, 1938; children—Mary Janet Misch Newmann Smith, Katherine Wolff Misch Koritzinsky. Numerous positions with advt. agys., N.Y.C., 1925-68; mag. writer, columnist, 1925—; drink and wine editor House Beautiful, 1976, Carte Blanche, 1975; books include: At Daddy's Office, 1947; Quick Guide to Wine, 1965; Quick Guide to Cheese, 1969; Quick Guide to Spirits, 1970; Quick Guide to Wines of all the Americas, 1977. Mem. Overseas Press Club. Club: Dutch Treat.

MISCHAKOFF, MISCHA, (adopted name), violinist; b. Proskourov, Russia; s. Isaac and Massia Fishberg; grad. Imperial Conservatory, St. Petersburg, Russia, 1912 (gold medal, Rubinstein prize); Ph.D., Eastern Mich. U., 1965, m. Hortense Moritz, Sept. 30, 1937; children—Paul, Anne, Matthew. Came to U.S., 1921, naturalized, 1927. Debut as violinist at Lipetzk, 1905; prof. Govt. Conservatory, Nizhni-Novgorod, 1918-20; concert master Moscow Grand Opera, 1920-21, Warsaw Philharmonic Orch., 1921-22; appeared as soloist in Petrograd, Moscow, Warsaw, Berlin; soloist with leading orchs. in U.S.; winner N.Y. Stadium Audition, 1923; concertmaster N.Y. Symphony Orch., 1924-27, Phila. Orch., 1927-29; became concertmaster Chgo. Symphony Orch., 1930, head violin dept. Am. Conservatory Music, Chgo., 1930; concertmaster NBC Symphony under direction of Arturo Toscanini, 1937-52, also leader of NBC String Quartet; concertmaster Detroit Symphony Orch., 1952-68; dir.-founder Mischakoff String Quartet; head violin dept. Chautaugua Instn., N.Y., 1926-65; concertmaster, soloist Meadow Brook Festival; mem. faculty Juilliard Sch. Music, 1940-52; faculty Oakland U., 1965-68; now prof. Wayne State U.; guest prof. Aspen Music Festival, 1970-73, spl. guest concertmaster, 1973; spl. guest concertmaster Balt. Symphony, 1969-70; guest prof. U. Colo., U. Mich., Boston U., 1971; prof. Peabody Conservatory, 1969-70. Mem. Soc. Am. Musicians (Chgo.). Club: Bohemians (N.Y.C.). Home: 18695 Fairfield Ave Detroit MI 48221

MISCHEL, WALTER, psychologist; b. Vienna, Austria, Feb. 22, 1930; s. Solomon and Lola (Schreck) M.; B.A., N.Y. U., 1951; M.A., City Coll. N.Y., 1953; Ph.D., Ohio State U., 1956; m. Harriet Nerlove, June 10, 1960; children—Judith, Rebecca, Linda. Asst. prof. psychology U. Colo., 1956-58; asst. prof., lectr. Harvard U., 1958-62; mem. faculty Stanford U., 1962—, prof. psychology, 1966—, chmn. dept., 1977-78; cons. in field. Fellow Am. Psychol. Assn. Author: Personality and Assessment, 1968; Introduction to Personality, 2d edit., 1976; Essentials of Psychology, 1977. Address: Dept Psychology Stanford Univ Stanford CA 94305

MISCHER, DONALD LEO, TV dir. and producer; b. San Antonio, Mar. 5, 1940; s. Elmer Frederick and Lillian Alma (Hoey) M.; student Tex. Luth. Coll., 1957-59; B.A., U. Tex., 1961, M.A., 1963; m. Beverly Jean Meyers, Aug. 13, 1960; children—Jennifer Christine, Heather Kathleen. Mem. faculty U. Tex., 1962-63; producer/dir. USIA, Washington, 1965-68; with Charles Guggenheim Prodns., 1969-71; producer, dir. network TV programs, 1971—, including: The Great American Dream Machine, (Emmy award 1972), 1971-72, Laugh-In, 1976-77, Making Television Dance with Twyla Tharp, 1977, The Goldie Hawn Special, 1978, The Kennedy Center Honors, (Dirs. Guild Am. award 1979), 1978, Alan King's Final Warnings, A Salute to American Imagination, 1978, John Denver and the Ladies, 1978, The Third Barry Manilow Spl., 1979, Goldie Hawn and Liza Minelli Spl., 1979, Donna Summer Spl., 1979; pres. Don Mischer Prodns., Beverly Hills, Calif., Juniper TV, Inc., Pacific Palisades, Calif. Mem. Dirs. Guild Am., Nat. Acad. TV Arts and Scis. Office: 9350 Wilshire Blvd Suite 228 Beverly Hills CA 90212

MISCHKE, CHARLES RUSSELL, mech. engr., educator; b. Glendale, N.Y., Mar. 2, 1927; s. Reinhart Charles and Dena Amelia (Scholl) M.; B.S. in Mech. Engring., Cornell U., 1947, M.Mech. Engring., 1950; Ph.D., U. Wis., 1953; m. Margaret Bubeck, Aug. 4, 1951; children—Thomas, James, Asst. prof., then asso. prof. mech. engring. U. Kans., 1953-57; prof. mech. engring., chmn. dept. Pratt Inst., 1957-64; prof. mech. enging. Iowa State U., 1964—, Alcoa Found. prof., 1974—. Served as ensign USN, 1947-49; lt. comdr. Res. ret. Registered profl. engr., Kans., Iowa. Mem. ASME, Am. Soc. Engring. Edn., Scabbard and Blade, Sigma Xi, Pi Tau Sigma, Phi Kappa Phi. Author: Elements of Mechanical Analysis, 1963; Introduction to Computer-Aided Design, 1968; Introduction to Engineering, 1969; Introduction to Engineering Through Mathematical Model Building, 1973. Home: 1815 Maxwell Ave Ames IA 50010

MISCHKE, FREDERICK CHARLES, mfg. co. exec.; b. Benton Harbor, Mich., Sept. 21, 1930; s. Fred William and Clara Adeline (Ruhno) M.; A.A., Lake Michigan Coll., 1956; B.B.A., Western Mich. U., 1958; m. Kathleen Ann Schultz, Nov. 19, 1955; children—Stephanie, Michael, Eric. Sr. auditor Lybrand, Ross Bros. & Montgomery, C.P.A.'s, Chgo., 1958-63, supr., Niles, Mich., 1963-65; v.p., treas. Skyline Corp., Elkhart, Ind., 1965—. Past sec. Sch. Bd. Parish Edn. Bd.; past pres. Jr. Achievement, United Way; past pres. bd. dirs. Better Bus. Bur.; mem. Vocat. Adv. Council Elkhart. Served with USAF, 1951-55. C.P.A., Ind., Mich. Mem. Am. Inst. C.P.A.'s, Fin. Execs. Inst. (past pres.), Nat. Assn. Accountants. Clubs: Rotary (past pres.); Elcona Country (past pres.) (Elkhart). Home: 23322 Greenleaf Blvd Elkhart IN 46514 Office: 2520 By-Pass Rd Elkhart IN 46514

MISCHLER, HARLAND LOUIS, food machinery mfr.; b. Troy, Ohio, Feb. 21, 1932, s. James Jolly and Margaret (Fladd M.; B.Sc., Ohio State U., 1954; M.B.A., 1957; m. Jean Marie O'Connor, June 20, 1959; children—Marilyn West, Thomas O'Connor. Prin. Haskins & Sells, Cin., 1958-66; with Hobart Corp., Troy, 1966—, controller, 1968—, v.p., 1975—, treas., 1977—; dir. Hobart Mfg. Co. Ltd. (Toronto); treas., dir. Hobart Export Co., Troy; v.p., treas. Hobart Sales & Service, P.R.; treas. Troy Pattern Works. Bd. dirs. Diagnostic Clinic for Mentally Retarded Children, Cin., 1966. Bd. dirs. Troy Nursing Assn., Stouder Meml. Hosp., Troy; vice chmn. bd. trustees Camp Fire Girls, 1973-77. Served to capt. USAF, 1955-57. Mem. Am. Inst. C.P.A.'s, Ohio Soc. C.P.A.'s, Fin. Execs. Inst. (2d v.p., dir. Dayton chpt.), Troy C. of C. (bd. dirs., pres.). Alpha Kappa Psi, Sigma Alpha Epsilon. Republican. Episcopalian. Clubs: Troy Rotary, Troy Country; Bankers (Cin.). Home: 2192 Merrimont Dr Troy OH 45373 Office: World Headquarters Ave Troy OH 45374

MISCHLEY, WALTER ANTHONY, hosp. adminstr.; b. Alpena, Mich., Feb. 28, 1920; s. Anthony V. and Veronica (Panowicz) M.; B.S., Mich. State Coll., 1947; m. Ann F. Hard, Jan. 17, 1948; children—Walter A., Sally Jo. City mgr. Hart, Mich., 1948-49, Manistee, Mich., 1950-51; chief mcpl. br. AEC, Richland, Wash., 1952-56; hosp. adminstr. Middletown (Ohio) Hosp., 1957—; mem. faculty Xavier U., Cin.; chmn. adv. bd. Blue Cross So. Ohio. County commr., Oceana County, Mich.; dir. Ohio Hosp. Ins. Co. Trustee Central Ohio River Planning Assn., Cancer Soc., Tb Assn., Community Action Com. Served to 1st lt. AUS, 1943-46. Fellow Am. Coll. Hosp. Adminstrs. (state regent); mem. Cin. Hosp. Council (pres.), Ohio Hosp. Assn. (trustee, chmn.-elect), Am. Legion, Ohio Hosp. Mgmt. Assn. (pres.), Sigma Chi. Rotarian (past pres.). Clubs: Wildwood Country, Brown's Run Country. Home: 1629 Croydon St Middletown OH 45042 Office: 105 McKnight St Middletown OH 45042

MISCHO, OTHMER JOSEPH, labor union exec.; b. Mt. Calvary, Wis., Nov. 20, 1904; s. Frank and Mary (Harter) M.; student U. Wis., 1924-27; B.Ed., Milw. State Tchrs. Coll., 1932; m. Virginia B.; children—Ivan, Dennis, Jay, Alana. Mem. Amalgamated Transit Union, 1933—, internat. v.p., 1941-46, internat. sec.-treas., 1946—. Home: 317 W 66th St Jacksonville FL 32208 Office: 5025 Wisconsin Ave NW Washington DC 20016

MISENER, AUSTIN DONALD, educator; b. Tornoto, Ont., Can., Jan. 19, 1911; s. Austin Perley and Ethel Wanita (Gould) M.; B.A., U. Toronto, 1933, M.A., 1934; Ph.D., Cambridge U., 1938; m. Eleanor Christina Fairley, Aug. 21, 1971. With U. Bristol (Eng.), 1938-40, Nat. Research Council Can., 1942-45; with Critoph & Misener cons. engrs., 1945-49; head physics dept. U. Western Ont., London, 1949-61; dir. Ont. Research Found., 1961-66; dir. Great Lakes Inst. U. Toronto, 1966—. Fellow Royal Soc. Can.; mem. Canadian Assn. Physicists (pres. 1952-53), Engring. Inst. Can., Internat. Assn. Great Lakes Research (pres. 1969), others. Contbr. articles to profl. jours. Home: PO Box 2469 Picton ON K0K 2T0 Canada

MISH, CHARLES CARROLL, educator; b. Williamsport, Pa., June 27, 1913; s. Charles Carroll and Elizabeth Reeves (Rex) M.; B.A., U. Pa., 1936, M.A., 1946, Ph.D., 1951; m. Mary Frances Faulkner, Jan. 19, 1945 (dec. Sept. 1974). Mem. faculty U. Md., College Park, 1948—, asso. prof. English, 1958-61, prof., 1961—. Home: 6700 Brookville Rd Chevy Chase MD 20015 Office: Dept English U Md College Park MD 20740

MISHKIN, PAUL J., lawyer, educator; b. Trenton, N.J., Jan. 1, 1927; s. Mark Mordecai and Bella (Dworetsky) M.; A.B., Columbia, 1947, LL.B., 1950; M.A. (hon.), U. Pa., 1971; m. Mildred Brofman Westover, Jan. 7, 1975; 1 son, Jonathan Mills Westover. Admitted to N.Y. State bar, 1950, U.S. Supreme Ct. bar, 1958; mem. faculty U. Pa. Law Sch., Phila., 1950-73; prof. law U. Calif. at Berkeley, 1973-75, Emanuel S. Heller prof., 1975—. Cons., City of Phila., 1953; reporter study div. jurisdiction between state and fed. cts. Am. Law Inst., 1960-65; mem. faculty Salzburg Seminar in Am. Studies, 1974; Charles Inglis Thompson guest prof. U. Colo., 1975. Trustee, Jewish Publ. Soc. Am., 1966-75; mem. adv. bd. Project '87, 1978—; mem. permanent com. Oliver Wendell Holmes Devise, 1979—. Served with USNR, 1945-46. Rockefeller Found. research grantee, 1956; Center for Advanced Study in Behavioral Scis. fellow, 1964-65. Fellow Am. Acad. Arts and Scis., Am. Bar Found.; mem. Am. Law Inst., Order of Coif, Phi Beta Kappa. Author: (with Morris) On Law in Courts, 1965; (with Bator, Shapiro and Wechsler) Federal Courts and the Federal System, 2d edit., 1973, supplement, 1977. Contbr. articles to profl. jours. Home: 91 Stonewall Rd Berkeley CA 94705 Office: Boalt Hall Berkeley CA 94720

MISHLER, JACOB, U.S. judge; b. N.Y.C., Apr. 20, 1911; s. Abraham and Rebecca (Heller) M.; B.S., N.Y.C., 1931, J.D., 1933; m. Helen Shillet; children—Alan J., Susan R. Admitted to N.Y. State bar, 1934; practiced in Long Island City, N.Y., 1934-59; justice N.Y. Supreme Ct., 10th Jud. Dist., 1959-60; U.S. dist. judge Eastern Dist. N.Y., 1960-69, chief judge, 1969—. Mem. Electoral Coll., 1952. Bd. dirs. Boys Club Queens. Mem. Queens County Bar Assn. Mason. Office: Courthouse 225 Cadman Plaza E Brooklyn NY 11201*

MISHOE, LUNA ISAAC, univ. pres.; b. Bucksport, S.C., Jan. 5, 1917; s. Henry and Martha (Oliver) M.; B.S., Allen U., 1938; M.S., U. Mich., 1942; Ph.D., N.Y. U., 1953; postgrad. Oxford (Eng.) U., 1955-56. Prof. math. and physics Kittrell (N.C.) Coll., 1939-42; prof. math. and physics Del. State U., Dover, 1946-48, pres., 1960—; asso. prof. physics Morgan State Coll., Balt., 1948-54, prof., 1954-60, chmn. div. natural sci., 1956-60; research mathematician Ballistics Research Lab., Aberdeen (Md.) Proving Ground, summers 1952-57, cons., 1957-60. Mem. Edn. Commn. of the States, 1977—; bd. dirs. Am. Council Edn., 1978; trustee U. Del., Del. State Coll., 1977—; bd. dirs. University City Sci. Center, Phila. Mem. Am. Math. Soc., Math. Assn. Am., Del. Acad. Sci. (pres. 1967-68). Address: Office of Pres Delaware State U Coll Dover DE 19901

MISHTOWT, GEORGE ILLARION, physician, ret. fgn. service officer; b. N.Y.C., Feb. 13, 1917; s. Illarion Vikenty and Irene (Rimsky-Korsakoff) M.; B.S., Georgetown U., 1938, M.D., 1942; m. Jacoba Johanna Meyer-Ranneft, Apr. 20, 1947; 1 son, Alexis George. Intern. Georgetown U. Hosp., 1942-43, instr. medicine, 1950-55; med. resident D.C. Gen. Hosp., 1946-47; med. fellow Lahey Clinic, Boston, 1947-49; practice internal medicine, Washington, 1950-55, Chevy Chase, Md., 1972—; med. attache Fgn. Service U.S., Baghdad, Iraq, 1955-58, Manila, P.I., 1959-62; asst. med. dir. U.S. programs and clin. activities; 1st sec., regional med. officer Am. embassy, Bangkok, 1965-67; med. dir. Dept. State, 1967-69, dep. asst. sec. for med. services, 1969-72; asst. clin. prof. medicine Georgetown U. Served to capt. M.C., AUS, 1943-46. Fellow A.C.P. Address: 5454 Wisconsin Ave Chevy Chase MD 20015

MISKOVSKY, GEORGE, lawyer; b. Oklahoma City, Feb. 13, 1910; s. Frank and Mary (Bourek) M.; LL.B., U. Okla., 1936; m. Nelly Oleta Donahue, Dec. 30, 1932; children—George, Gary, Grover, Gail Marie. Admitted to Okla. bar, 1936, since practiced in Oklahoma City; sr. partner firm Miskovsky, Sullivan & Miskovsky, 1936—; pub. defender Oklahoma City, 1936; county atty. Oklahoma County, 1943-44; mem. Okla. Ho. of Reps., 1939-42; mem. Okla. Senate, 1950-60; pres., dir. Economy Square Inc.; exec. sec., dir. Penn 74 Mall Inc. Mem. Am., Okla., Oklahoma County bar assns., Am. Judicature Soc., Am. Trial Lawyers Assn., Nat. Assn. Criminal Def. Lawyers, U. Okla. Law Assn., Oklahoma City C. of C., Order of Coif, Pi Kappa Alpha, Phi Alpha Delta. Democrat. Episcopalian. Clubs: Lions, Oklahoma City Golf and Country, Sooner Dinner, Masons, Shriners, Baillid Okla., Confrerie de la Chaine des Rotisseurs. Home: 1511 Drury Ln Oklahoma City OK 73116 Office: Suite 830 Hightower Bldg Oklahoma City OK 73102

MISLOW, KURT MARTIN, chemist, educator; b. Berlin, Germany, June 5, 1923; s. Max and Ida (Bingen) M.; came to U.S., 1940, naturalized, 1946; B.S., Tulane U., 1944, D.Sc. (hon.), 1975; Ph.D., Calif. Inst. Tech., 1947; D. honoris causa, Free U., Brussels, 1974, Uppsala U., 1977; m. Jacqueline Ford, 1966; children—Christopher, John. Instr., N. Y. U., 1947-51, asst. prof., 1951-56, asso. prof., 1956-60, prof., 1960-64; Hugh Stott Taylor prof. chemistry Princeton, 1964—, chmn. dept. chemistry, 1968-74; vis. prof. Stanford U., 1960; Univ. lectr. U. London, 1965; J.A. McRae Meml. lectr. Queen's U., 1967; H.A. Iddles lectr. U. N.H., 1972; Solvay lectr. and medalist Free U. Brussels, 1972; E.C. Lee lectr. U. Chgo.; A.A. Vernon lectr. Northeastern U., 1976; PPG lectr. Ohio U., 1977; J. Musher Meml. lectr. Hebrew U. Jerusalem, 1978; North Country lectr., 1978; Churchill fellow Cambridge U., 1974-75. Mem. adv. panel chemistry NSF, 1963-66; mem. panel medicinal and organic chemistry NIH, 1963-66. Guggenheim fellow, 1957-58, 74-75; Alfred P. Sloan fellow, 1959-63. Fellow Am. Acad. Arts and Scis.; mem. Nat. Acad. Scis., Am. Chem. Soc. (James Flack Norris award 1975), Chem. Soc. London, AAUP, Phi Beta Kappa, Sigma Xi, Phi Lambda Upsilon. Author: Introduction to Stereochemistry, 1965; also numerous articles. Bd. editors Jour. Organic Chemistry, 1965-70; mem. editorial adv. bd. Topics of Stereochemistry, Bull. des Sociétés Chimiques Belges, Accounts of Chem. Research, Monatshefte für Chemie. Home: 38 Maclean Circle Princeton NJ 08540

MISSAR, RICHARD RUDOLPH, mfg. co. exec.; b. Chgo., July 3, 1930; s. Jerry and Rose Blanche (Pfeiffer) M.; student Herzl Jr. Coll., 1948-50, Ill. Inst. Tech., 1951, 54-56; student Advanced Mgmt. Program, Harvard U., 1975; m. Jacqueline Q. Voigt, Oct. 18, 1952; children—Connie, Karen, Kathy. Lab. technician DeSoto Inc., Des Plaines, Ill., 1950, salesman, 1956-60, product mgr., 1960-62, sales mgr., 1963-68, dir. mktg., 1968-70, gen. mgr., 1970-75, v.p. mktg., 1976, exec. v.p., 1977—, also dir. Served with USMC, 1951-53. Mem. Nat. Paint and Coatings Assn., Golfhurst Civic Assn. Presbyterian. Club: Harvard Bus. (Chgo). Home: 901 Golfview Pl Mount Prospect IL 60056 Office: DeSoto Inc 1700 S Mount Prospect Dr Des Plaines IL 60018

MISSEN, RONALD WILLIAM, chem. engr.; b. St. Catharines, Ont., Can., Feb. 26, 1928; s. Edward Lionel and Helen Harrison (Miller) M.; B.Sc., Queen's U., 1950, M.Sc., 1951; Ph.D., Cambridge U., 1956; m. Elizabeth Barbara Ward, July 28, 1951; children—Nancy Elizabeth, Kathryn Margaret, Brenda Carol, Lynne Patricia. Chem. engr. Polysar Corp., Sarnia, Ont., 1951-53; mem. faculty U. Toronto, 1956—, asso. prof. chem. engring., 1961-68, prof., 1968—, vice-provost profl. faculties, 1977—, asso. dean phys. scis. Sch. Grad. Studies, 1976-77, mem. governing council, 1975-77; dir. Chem. Engring. Research Cons. Ltd. Recipient Plummer medal Engring. Inst. Can., 1962. Fellow Chem. Inst. Can.; mem. Faraday Soc., Canadian Soc. Chem. Engring., Assn. Profl. Engrs. Ont., U. Toronto Faculty Assn. (pres. 1970-71). Contbr. articles to profl. jours. Home: 19 Didrickson Dr Willowdale ON M2P 1J7 Canada Office: Dept Chem Engring U Toronto Toronto ON M5S 1A4 Canada

MITAU, G. THEODORE, educator; b. Berlin, Germany, Apr. 4, 1920; s. Alexander and Rosel (Streim) M.; B.A., Macalester Coll., 1940; M.A., U. Minn., 1942, Ph.D., 1948; m. Charlotte Cutts, Sept. 7, 1941; children—Lee, Andrea Mitau Kircher. Mem. faculty Macalester Coll., St. Paul, 1940-68, James Wallace prof. polit. sci., 1963-68, chmn. dept. polit. sci., 1956-68; chancellor Minn. State U. System, St. Paul, 1968-76, distinguished service prof. polit. sci., 1976—. Adj. prof. pub. affairs U. Minn.; vis. prof. U. Nebr.; chmn. task force on innovation and change in higher edn. Am. Assn. State Colls. and Univs.; chmn. Middle States accreditation com. Empire State Coll., State U. N.Y.; nat. program chmn. ann. conf. Soc. Coll. and Univ. Planning; cons. intergovtl. relations U.S. CSC; research cons. Minn. Legislative Commn. on Election Laws, Minn. Hist. Soc.; mem. com. appeals N. Central Accrediting Assn.; adv. com. Edn. Commn. States; adv. com. higher edn. Midwestern Conf. Council State Govts.; higher edn. adv. council Minn. Higher Edn. Coordinating Commn.; mem. Minn. Council Econ. Edn., Minn. Coll. Govt. Council. Mem. Gov.'s Council on Exec. Reorgn.; mem. St. Paul Charter Commn. Bd. dirs. Fund for Improvement Post-Secondary Edn., Twin City Area Ednl. TV Corp., Minn. Edn. Computing Consortium, North Star Research and Devel. Inst., Dynamy Minn., United Hosps., St. Paul; bd. dirs., exec. council Nat. Center for Higher Edn. Mgmt. Systems. Served to capt. AUS, World War II. Recipient Thomas Jefferson award for distinguished teaching McConnel Found. Mem. Am. Council Edn. (sec., exec. com.), Minn. Hist. Soc. (council), Phi Beta Kappa. Author: Politics in Minnesota, 1960; Proximate Solutions, Case Problems in State and Local Government (with Harold W. Chase), 1964; Insoluable Problems, 1966; Decade of Decision: The Supreme Court and the Constitutional Revolution, 1967; State and Local Government: Politics and Processes, 1966. Book rev. editor Midwestern Jour. Polit. Sci. Home: 1787 Bohland Ave Saint Paul MN 55116

MITBY, NORMAN PETER, coll. pres.; b. Cashton, Wis., May 21, 1916; s. Chester M. and Margaret (Murray) M.; B.S., Whitewater (Wis.) State Coll., 1938; postgrad. U. Wis., 1947-48; M.S., Stout State U., 1949; m. Luvern J. Jensen, June 15, 1941; children—John C., Margaret N. Tchr. high sch., vocat. sch., Cornell, Wis., 1938-41, Antigo, Wis., 1941-46; asst. dir. LaCrosse (Wis.) Vocat. and Adult Schs., 1946-54; dir. vocat. and adult sch., Oshkosh, Wis., 1954-55, Green Bay, Wis., 1955-60, Madison, Wis., 1960-67; dist. dir. tech. and adult edn. dist. Madison Area Tech. Coll., 1967, pres., 1967—; prof. Stout State U. Grad. Sch., Menomonie, Wis.; mem. adv. council U. Wis. Schs. Edn., Madison and Milw., 1961-64; cons., examiner North Central Assn. Colls. and Secondary Schs., 1970—; mem. pres.'s adv. com. Assn. Community Coll. Trustees, 1978-79. Mem. Community Welfare Council Madison, 1960-63, mem. needs and priorities com., 1964; sponsor Wis. Heart Assn.; chmn. pub. employees div. Cancer Fund drive, 1963; mem. Mayor's Com. for Employment Handicapped, 1964-68, Nat. Adv. Com. on Health Occupations Tng., 1964-68; chmn. gov.'s adv. com. Title I, Higher Edn. Act, 1965-74; mem. adv. council Midwest Community Coll., Leadership Council, 1968-73; mem. Wis. Gov.'s Adv. Council on Vocat. Edn., 1969-74; mem. Wis. Gov.'s Health Planning and Policy Task Force, 1971-73; adv. com. Wis. State Bd. Nursing, 1972-74. Bd. dirs. Wis. Council Safety, 1960-73, Madison Civic Music Assn. Recipient Disting. Service Alumni award U. Wis.-Whitewater. Mem. Am. Assn. Community and Jr. Colls. (dir. 1975-78), Am. Vocat. Assn., Wis. Assn. for Vocat. and Adult Edn., Wis. Assn. Dirs. Vocat. and Adult Edn. (pres. 1960-61), Nat. Assn. Pub. Sch. Adult Educators, Nat. Council Local Adminstrs. Vocat. Edn. and Practical Arts, Am. Tech. Edn. Assn., Sigma Tau Gamma, Epsilon Pi Tau, Delta Pi Epsilon. Rotarian, Elk. Club: Nakoma Golf. Home: 4413 Waite Ln Madison WI 53711 Office: 211 N Carroll St Madison WI 53703

MITCHELL, ALLAN GILLETTE, financial cons., ret. utility exec.; b. Montclair, N.J., Oct. 10, 1905; s. Warren Smith and Katherine (Gillette) M.; B.S. in Civil Engring., Rutgers U., 1927; m. Florence D. Hukill, June 28, 1930; children—Robert Allan, Barbara Anne (Mrs. John W. Brock, Jr.), Helen Elizabeth (Mrs. William H. Eigabroadt). With Ala. Power Co., 1927-31; with Phila. Electric Co., 1931-73, statistician, 1942-56, comptroller, 1956-62, v.p. finance and accounting, 1962-71, sr. v.p., 1971-73; fin. cons., 1973—; asso. cons. Asso Utility Services, Inc., Phila., 1975—. Trustee, gov. Rutgers U., 1963-75; mem. exec. com. S.E. Pa. Devel. Fund, 1964-74; cons. Internat. Exec. Service Corps, 1974-75; bd. govs. Eastern div. Pa. Economy League; trustee Eagleville Hosp. and Rehab. Center, 1970; past trustee Phila. United Fund. Past mem. Edison Electric Inst. (past chmn. accounting prins. com., past chmn. investor relations com.), Fin. Analysts Phila. (past pres.), Fin. Execs. Inst.; mem. Acad. Natural Scis., Franklin Inst. Unitarian (past pres. bd. trustees). Home: 623 Westview St Philadelphia PA 19119 Office: 2301 Market St Philadelphia PA 19101

MITCHELL, ARTHUR, dancer, choreographer; b. N.Y.C., Mar. 27, 1934; s. Arthur and Willie Mae Mitchell; student Sch. Am. Ballet. Prin., N.Y. City Ballet, 1955—; dir.-choreographer Dance Theatre of Harlem; has appeared in Western Symphony, A Midsummer Night's Dream, Agon, Arcade, Modern Jazz, Variants, Pan America, Creation of the World, The Unicorn, the Gorgon and the Manticore, Piège de Lumière, The Nutcracker, The Figure in the Carpet, Four Saints in Three Acts, House of Flowers, Clarinade, Interplay, Ivesiana, Ebony Concerto, Allegro Brilliante, Divertimento No. 15, Four Temperaments, Episodes, Afternoon of a Faun, Orpheus, Bugaku, Carmen Jones, Kiss Me, Kate, others; with John Butler Co., 1955, William Dollar's Ballet Theatre Workshop; choreographer (with Rod Alexander) Shinbone Alley, Newport Jazz Festival; dancer, choreographer, actor Spoleto Festival of Two Worlds, 1960; tchr. dance Katherine Dunham Sch., Karel Shook Studio, Melissa Hayden Sch., Cedarhurst, L.I., Jones-Haywood Sch. Ballet, Washington. Office: Dance Theater of Harlem 466 W 152d St New York NY 10031

MITCHELL, ARTHUR HARRIS, mag. editor; b. St. John, N.B., Canada, Nov. 8, 1916; s. Stuart Campbell and Marjorie (Harris) M.; student London Radio Coll., 1939-40, Columbia Sch. Journalism, 1945-46; m. Mary Moliawko, Nov. 6, 1944; children—John Stuart, Marjorie Starr. Travelling free-lance writer various U.S., Can. mags., 1946-48; editor Mitchell Press Ltd., Vancouver, B.C., also founding editor Can. Pulp and Paper Industry mag. and Western Homes & Living mag., 1948-66; editor Can. Homes mag., Southstar Publs. Ltd., Toronto, 1967—; Canadian cons. Time-Life Books, N.Y.C., 1976—. Served with Brit. and U.S. Merchant Marine, 1940-45. Mem. Royal Astron. Soc. Can. Author: You Wanted To Know, 1971; Easy Furniture Finishing, 1974; The Basement Book, 1977. Home: TH28 270 Timberbank Blvd Scarborough ON M1W 2M1 Canada Office: 2180 Yonge St Suite 1702 Toronto 1 ON Canada

MITCHELL, BRUCE TYSON, lawyer; b. San Francisco, Nov. 6, 1928; s. John Robert and Lorraine C. (Tyson) M.; A.B. with great distinction, Stanford U., 1949, J.D., 1951; m. Adrienne Means Hiscox, Oct. 14, 1951; 1 son, Mark Means. Admitted to Calif. bar, 1952; estate adminstr. Crocker Nat. Bank, San Francisco, 1955-57; with Utah Internat. Inc., San Francisco, 1957—, sec., 1974—, sr. counsel, 1961—; dir. Orpheum Bldg. Co., San Francisco. Chmn. San Mateo County Republican Central Com., 1964-70; mem. Calif. Rep. Central Com., 1964-74, 77—; alt. del. Rep. Nat. Conv., 1968; co-chmn. San Mateo County Pres. Ford Com., 1976; exec. v.p., bd. dirs. San Francisco Jr. C. of C., 1961; bd. dirs. No. Calif. chpt. Arthritis Found. Served to lt. (j.g.) USNR, 1952-55; Korea. Mem. Am., Calif., San Francisco bar assns., Am. Judicature Soc., Am. Soc. Corp. Secs. (v.p. 1976-77, dir. 1976-79). Conglist. Clubs: Olympic, Commonwealth (pres. 1973, bd. govs. 1970-77) (San Francisco); Capitol Hill (Washington); Masons (Yokosuka, Japan). Home: 165 Redwood Dr Hillsborough CA 94010 Office: 550 California St San Francisco CA 94104

MITCHELL, BRYAN HENRY, marketing research co. exec.; b. Chgo., Apr. 5, 1929; s. Ernest and Lilly Mae (Hunt) M.; B.S., Northwestern U., 1952, M.B.A., 1959; m. Joan E. McKay, Sept. 6, 1952; children—Deborah, Susan, Michael. Comptroller, Chambers Corp., Rolling Meadows, Ill., 1959-61, Oppenheimer Casing Co., Chgo., 1961-65; asst. treas. A.C. Nielsen Co., Chgo., 1965-69, controller, 1969—; instr. effective mgmt. Continuing Edn. Program, High Sch. Dist. 211, Palatine, Ill., 1966—. Served with Finance Corps, U.S. Army, 1952-54. Mem. Nat. Assn. Accountants (past nat. dir.; past pres., past dir. Chgo. chpt.). Home: 11009 122d St Kenosha WI 53142 Office: Nielsen Plaza Northbrook IL 60062

MITCHELL, CAMERON (CAMERON MIZELL), actor; b. Dallastown, Pa., 1918; attended N.Y. Theatre Sch. Former radio announcer and sportscaster; appeared in films, including They Were Expendable, Command Decision, Death of a Salesman, How to Marry a Millionaire, Monkey on My Back, Pony Soldier, Tall Men, Hombre, Buck and the Preacher, Slaughter, The Midnight Man, The Klansman, Viva, Knievel!, The Swarm, The Toolbox Murders, Haunts; appeared on TV series High Chapparel, 1967-71, Swiss Family Robinson, 1975-76; numerous other TV appearances, including The Andersonville Trial, The Stranger, Ironside, Search, Mission: Impossible; also stage appearances. Served with USAAF, World War II.

MITCHELL, CHARLES, educator, historian; b. London, Jan. 25, 1912; s. Stanley and Mary (Garrard) M.; B.A. (St. John's Coll.), Oxford U., 1934, B.Litt., 1939, M.A., 1943; Litt.D., Bowdoin Coll., 1970; m. Prudence Yalden Thomson, 1935 (dec. 1940); 1 son, Simon; m. 2d, Jean Flower, 1944; 1 son, John B. Asst., Nat. Maritime Mus., Greenwich, Eng., 1935-45; lectr. Warburg Inst., U. London, 1945-60; Tallman vis. prof. Bowdoin Coll., 1956-57; Bernheimer vis. prof. history of art Bryn Mawr Coll., 1959-60, prof. history of art, 1960—, chmn. dept., 1962-75, Andrew W. Mellon prof. humanities, 1975—; Ryerson lectr. Yale U., 1957; Benjamin West lectr. Swarthmore Coll., 1957; Italian lectr. Brit. Acad., 1961; Whiton lectr. Cornell, 1963; Power lectr. Sydney (Australia) U., 1970; art historian in residence Am. Acad. in Rome, 1965; Kennedy vis. prof. Smith Coll., 1975; mem. painting and sculpture com. Phila. Mus. Art. Fellow Am. Council Learned Socs., 1965-66; Guggenheim fellow, 1970-71; recipient Disting. Teaching award Lindback Found., 1974. Served with Brit. Naval War Service, 1939-45, lt. comdr. R.N.V.R., 1944-45. Fellow Royal Hist. Soc., Accademia degli Incamminati, Modigliana (Italy) (hon.); mem. Walpole Soc., Renaissance Soc. Am., Coll. Art Assn. Am., Società di Studi Romagnoli, Lewis Carroll Soc. N.Am. Author: Seaman's Portrait, 1939; A Book of Ships, 1940; Hogarth's Peregrination, 1952; A Fifteenth Century Italian Plutarch, 1961; Felice Feliciano Antiquarius, 1962; (with E. Mandowsky) Pirro Ligorio's Roman Antiquities, 1963; (with E.W. Bodnar) Cyriacus of Ancona's Journeys in the Propontis and the Northern Aegean 1444-1445, 1976; also numerous articles; contbr. chpts. to books; editor: A.P. Oppé, Raphael, 1970; co-editor Oxford Studies in the History of Art and Architecture. Address: Bryn Mawr Coll Bryn Mawr PA 19010

MITCHELL, CLARENCE M., JR., lawyer; b. Balt., Mar. 8, 1911; s. Clarence M. and Elsie (Davis) M.; A.B., Lincoln U., Chester County, Pa., 1932, LL.D.; LL.B., U. Md.; postgrad. U. Minn., Atlanta U.; LL.D. (hon.), Morgan State Coll., Balt., Georgetown U., 1973, Western Md. Coll., Howard U., 1979, Boston U., 1979; m. Juanita Elizabeth Jackson, Sept. 7, 1938; children—Clarence M. III, Keiffer J., Michael B., George D. Admitted to Md. bar; newspaper reporter; various govt. posts including Fair Employment Com., 1943, War Manpower Commn., WPB; labor sec. NAACP, 1945-50, dir. Washington bur., 1950-78, ret., 1978, cons., 1978—; individual practice law, Balt., 1978—; chmn. Leadership Conf. Civil Rights. Mem. Pres. Truman's Com. to Employ Physically Handicapped; U.S. rep. 7th spl. session, 30th gen. assembly UN, 1975—. Recipient Spingarn medal NAACP, 1969. Methodist. Home: 1324 Druid Hill Ave Baltimore MD 21217 Office: Suite 3700 222 Saint Paul St Baltimore MD 21202. *Success usually comes from action based on facts rather than on vain hopes or groundless fears.*

MITCHELL, CLIFFORD ROBERT, savs. and loan exec.; b. Springfield, Mo., Sept. 21, 1908; s. Clifford Romain and Charlotte (Haseltine) M.; B.A., Drury Coll., 1930; m. Catherine Martha Burman, Sept. 10, 1934. Br. mgr. Green County Savs. & Loan Assn., Kansas City br., Springfield, Mo., 1931-36; Kansas City mgr. Mo. State Bur. Savs. & Loan, 1936-37; exec. v.p. Jackson County Savs. & Loan Assn., Kansas City, Mo., 1938-41; chmn. bd., pres. 1st Fed. Savs. & Loan Assn., Kansas City, Mo., 1941—; dir. Panama Canal Co., 1961-69, Chgo. Title & Trust Co. Pres., U.S. Savs. & Loan League, 1959—; dir. Des Moines Fed. Home Loan Bank Bd., 1941-42, 55; mem. Fed. Savs. and Loan Adv. Council, Washington, 1951-57. Trustee, Drury Coll. Served to lt. USNR, 1943-46. Mem. U.S. League Savs. Assns. (chmn. legis. com. 1963-70), Kansas City C. of C. (dir. 1962-68), Kappa Alpha. Clubs: Kansas City, University, Carriage. Office: 919 Walnut St Kansas City MO 64106 Mailing Address: 9641 Lee Blvd Leawood KS 66206

MITCHELL, DAVID IRA, theatrical designer; b. Honesdale, Pa., May 12, 1932; s. Amos David and Ruth Grace (Cole) M.; grad. Pa. State U., Kutztown, 1954; postgrad. Boston U., 1957-60; m. Emily Jon Fouts, Sept. 9, 1961; children—Jennifer Lee, David Nathaniel. Designer stage prodns.: Mefistofele, 1969, Colette, 1970, Steambath, 1970, Journeys, 1970, How The Other Half Loves, 1971, Manon, 1971, The Incomparable Max, 1971, Aida, 1972, Il Trovatore, 1973, Macbeth, 1973, Boris Godunov, 1974, The Wager, 1974, Enter a Free Man, 1974, The Steadfast Tin Soldier, 1974, The Italian Straw Hat, 1974, I Love My Wife, 1977, Annie (Tony award, Outer Circle Critics award), 1977, The Gin Game, 1977, Working (Tony nomination), 1978; scenic supr. N.Y.C. Ballet Ravel Festival, 1974; designer N.Y. Shakespeare Festival prodns.: Naked Hamlet, 1968, The Basic Training of Pavlo Hummel, 1971, The Cherry Orchard, 1972, Barbary Shore, 1973, Short Eyes (Drama Desk award), 1974, Little Black Sheep, 1975, Shoe Shine Parlor, 1975, Trelawney of The Wells (Tony nomination), 1976, Apple Pie, 1976, Mrs. Warren's Profession, 1976, Henry IV, 1976. Served with AUS, 1955-57. Mem. United Scenic Artists Union. Address: care Alvin Theatre 250 W 52d St New York City NY 10019

MITCHELL, DAVID LESTER, profl. investor; b. Kansas City, Mo., Sept. 15, 1919; s. Ralph Wallace and Esther (Clark) M.; B.A., De Pauw U., 1940; M.B.A., U. Chgo., 1954; m. Beatrice Alleen Sand, Dec. 20, 1941; children—David Clark, Karen Sandra (Mrs. Donald E. Gleash). Controller, asst. treas. Am. Bakeries Co., Chgo., 1940-63, fin. v.p., 1969-70, exec. v.p., 1970-72; treas., dir. Jewels Internat., 1972-77; fin. v.p. Gold Bond Stamp Co., Mpls., 1963-65; pres. First Nat. Bank Barron (Wis.), 1965-67. Served to capt. USMCR, 1941-46. C.P.A., Ill. Mem. Phi Delta Theta. Republican. Presbyn. Mason. Clubs: Tubac Valley Country (Tubac, Ariz.); Union League (Chgo.). Home and office: 5038 N Chiquita Ln Scottsdale AZ 85253

MITCHELL, DAVID W., bus. exec.; b. 1928; with Avon Products, Inc., N.Y.C., 1947—, v.p.-sales promotion, 1964-65, group v.p., 1965-67, sr. group v.p., 1967-68, exec. v.p., 1968-72, pres., 1972-77, chmn. bd., chief exec. officer, 1977—, also dir. Office: Avon Products Inc 9 W 57 St New York NY 10019*

MITCHELL, DEREK FENTON, oil co. exec.; b. Orford, Eng., Sept. 10, 1918; s. William Charles and Catherine Mary (Cunningham) M.; B.A. with honors, Cambridge U., 1940; m. Gertrude Irene Pfingst, July 10, 1946; children—Susan Joan, Betsy Anne. With Brit. Petroleum Group, 1946—, pres. BP N.Am., Ltd., N.Y.C., 1961-63, gen. mgr. central planning dept., London, 1963-66, dir. BP Trading, 1963; pres. BP Can., 1966-77, chmn., chief exec. officer, 1977—; dir. Canadian Internat. Paper Co. Ltd. Served with Brit. Royal Naval Res., 1939-46. Mem. Brit.-Can. Trade Assn., Brit.-N.Am. Com., Bus. Council on Nat. Issues. Anglican. Clubs: St. James's, St.-Denis, Mt. Royal, Mt. Bruno Golf and Country; Toronto Golf; Royal and Ancient Golf, Walton Heath Golf (Gt. Britain). Home: 637 Carleton Ave Montreal PQ H3Y 2Y3 Canada Office: 1245 Sherbrooke St W Montreal PQ H3G 1G7 Canada

MITCHELL, DONALD J., congressman; b. Ilion, N.Y., May 8, 1923; student Hobart Coll., 1946-47; B.S. in Optometry, Columbia, 1949, M.A. in Edn., 1950; m. Margaretta Wilson Levee, 1945; children—Gretchen, Cynthia, Allen. Optometrist; mem. 93d-96th congresses from N.Y. Councilman, Town of Herkimer, 1954-56; mayor, Village of Herkimer, 1956-59; pres. Mohawk Valley Conf. Mayors, 1959; apptd. to Herkimer Zoning Bd. of Appeals, 1963; mem. N.Y. State Assembly, 1965-72, majority whip, 1968-72. Bd. dirs. Herkimer chpt. A.R.C., Cancer Soc., Washburn Meml. Library, Boy Scouts Am., Cub Scouts. Served with USNR, 1942-45, 51-53. Recipient Pub. Service award, 1965; named Optometrist of Year, N.Y. State Optometric Assn., 1971. Mem. Nat. Soc. State Legislators (bd. govs. 1971), Am. Legion, V.F.W., C. of C., Herkimer County Extension Service. Republican. Methodist. Mason, Elk, Kiwanian. Club: Rod and Gun. Home: Herkimer NY Office: 2431 Rayburn House Office Bldg Washington DC 20515

MITCHELL, EDWARD JOHN, economist; b. Newark, Aug. 15, 1937; s. Edward Charles and Gladys (Werner) M.; B.A. summa cum laude, Bowling Green State U., 1960; postgrad. (Social Sci. Research Council fellow) Nuffield Coll., Oxford (Eng.) U., 1963-64, Ph.D. in Econs. (NDEA fellow 1960-63, NSF fellow 1964-65), 1966; m. Mary Josephine Osborne, June 14, 1958; children—Susan, Edward. Lectr. in econs. Wharton Sch., U. Pa., 1964-65; economist Rand Corp., 1965-68; mem. Inst. Advanced Study, Princeton, N.J., 1968-69; sr. economist Pres.'s Council Econ. Advs., Washington, 1969-72; vis. asso. prof. econs. Cornell U., 1972-73; asso. prof. bus. econs. U. Mich., 1973-75, prof., 1975—; dir. nat. energy project Am. Enterprise Inst., 1974-76. Mem. Am. Enterprise Inst. (adj. scholar), Internat. Assn. Energy Economists. Author: U.S. Energy Policy: A Primer, 1974; Dialogue on World Oil, 1974; Financing the Energy Industry, 1975; Vertical Integration of the Oil Industry, 1976. Contbr. articles to profl. jours. Home: 3 Westbury Ct Ann Arbor MI 48105 Office: Grad Sch Bus U Mich Ann Arbor MI 48109

MITCHELL, EDWARD LEE, physician, ins. co. exec.; b. Corning, N.Y., Sept. 26, 1932; s. Edward Henry and Bessie (Dail) M.; B.S., U. N.C., 1955, M.D., 1959; m. Doris McKinney, Aug. 23, 1958; children—Gregory, Ted. Intern, Moses H. Cone Hosp., Greensboro, N.C., 1959-60; practice medicine, Liberty, N.C., 1962-66; asst. med. dir. Jefferson Standard Life Ins. Co., Greensboro, N.C., 1967-70, asso. med. dir., 1970-77; v.p. new bus. adminstrn. Commonwealth Life Ins. Co., Louisville, 1972-77, exec. v.p. adminstrn., med. dir., 1977—. Active March of Dimes, Kidney Found., Heart Fund. Served with USAF, 1960-62. Certified Bd. Life Ins. Medicine. Mem. AMA, Ky. Med. Assn., Jefferson County Med. Soc., Assn. Life Ins. Med. Dirs., Home Office Life Underwriters Assn., Midwestern Med Dirs. Club. Republican. Presbyterian. Club: Hunting Creek Country. Home: 6110 Tidewater Ct Prospect KY 40059 Office: Commonwealth Life Ins Co Commonwealth Bldg Louisville KY 40201

MITCHELL, EHRMAN BURKMAN, JR., architect; b. Harrisburg, Pa., Jan. 25, 1924; s. Ehrman Burkman and Alice (DeCevee) M.; A.B., U. Pa., 1947, B. Arch., 1948; m. Hermine Strickler, Sept. 25, 1948; children—Eric Ehrman, Marianne. Asso. architect Bellante & Clauss, 1951-58; partner Mitchell/Giurgola, Assos., Phila., 1958—; dir. Harmony Savs. & Loan Assn., Phila. Lectr., Ohio State U., U. Ariz., U. Utah, Washington U., St. Louis, Dartmouth, U. Ky., U. Md., Temple U. Pres., Citizens Council Whitemarch Twp., Montgomery County, Pa., 1963-65, dir., 1963-67; mem. Del. Valley Citizens Transp. Com., 1964—; mem. Citizens Council Montgomery County, 1964—. Fellow U. Pa. Mus. Served with USNR, 1943-46. Recipient Gold medal Artists Guild Phila. Mem. AIA (chpt. dir. Phila. 1965-68, coll. fellows 1969—, nat. dir. 1973-75, v.p. 1977, 1st v.p. 1978, pres. 1979; recipient gold medal Phila. chpt. 1964, 72, 74, silver medal 1973, Nat. Honor award 1974, 75, archtl. firm award 1976); mem. Pa. Soc. Architects (dir. 1966—, sec. 1966, v.p. 1967, pres. 1968, silver medal 1974, 75, 77), AIM (pres.'s council 1967), Inst. Contemporary Arts, Pa. Acad. Fine Arts, Greater Phila. C. of C., Inst. Contemporary Art, Beta Theta Pi. Prin. works: Wright Bros. Nat. Meml. Visitors Center, Kitty Hawk, N.C., nat. hdqrs. Am. Coll. Life Underwriters, Bryn Mawr, Pa. also Adult Learning Research Center, office bldg. Penn Mut. Life Ins. Co., Phila., office bldg. Ins. Co. N.Am., Phila., U. Wash. Law Sch. and Library, Seattle, USIS Cultural Center, Brasilia, Brazil, A.B. Volvo Co. mfg. plant, Chesapeake, Va. Home: 850 Andorra Rd Lafayette Hill PA 19444 Office: 12 S 12th St Philadelphia PA 19107 also 170 W 97th St New York City NY 10025

MITCHELL, FREDERICK CLEVELAND, book publisher; b. Erie, Pa., Feb. 2, 1933; s. John Forrest and Catharine (Cleveland) M.; grad. Phillips Exeter Acad., 1951; B.A., Yale, 1955; M.A., Middlebury Coll., 1960; postgrad. U. Cal. at Berkeley, 1960-66; m. Margaretta Meyer Kuhlthau, May 23, 1959; children—Anne, Catharine, Julia. Publisher Ramparts mag., San Francisco, 1968-69; co-prop. Scrimshaw Press., San Francisco, 1969—. Served to lt. (j.g.) USNR, 1955-57. Home: 280 Hillcrest Rd Berkeley CA 94705 Office: 6040 Claremont Ave Oakland CA 94618

MITCHELL, GEORGE E., mfg. co. exec.; b. N.Y.C., Aug. 29, 1937; s. George E. and Margaret M.; B.A., Villanova U., 1959; m. Regina Mitchell, June 20, 1959; children—Robert, Diane, Aileen. With Owens-Corning Fiberglass, 1962-69; pres. interior products and systems div. Keene Corp., 1969-74; with CertainTeed Corp., Valley Forge, Pa., 1974—, now sr. v.p. indsl. and bldg. products and pres. insulation group. Bd. trustees Acad. Notre Dame. Served with USMC, 1959-62. Mem. Am. Mgmt. Assn. Pres.'s Assn. Republican. Roman Catholic. Home: 1108 Beech Rd Rosemont PA 19010 Office: PO Box 850 Valley Forge PA 19482

MITCHELL, GEORGE JOHN, lawyer, U.S. dist. judge; b. Waterville, Maine, Aug. 20, 1933; s. George J. and Mary (Saad) M.; B.A., Bowdoin Coll., 1950; LL.B., Georgetown U., 1960; m. Sally L. Heath, Aug. 29, 1959; 1 dau., Andrea J. Admitted to Maine bar, 1960, D.C. bar, 1960; trial atty. U.S. Dept. Justice, Washington, 1960-62; exec. asst. Senator Muskie, 1962-65; partner firm Jensen & Baird, Portland, Maine, 1965-77; U.S. atty. Maine, 1977-79; U.S. dist. judge, 1979—. Chmn. Maine Democratic Com., 1966-68; nat. committeeman, Maine, 1968—; mem. Nat. Commn. on Party Structure and Del. Selections, 1969—; chmn. Maine Commn. on

Party Structure and Del. Selection, 1969—. Served with U.S. Army, 1954-56. Home: 25 Channel Rd South Portland ME 04106 Office: US Dist Ct Portland ME 04112

MITCHELL, GEORGE WASHINGTON, JR., educator, physician; b. Balt., Apr. 30, 1917; s. George Washington and Katharyne Eugenia (Diggs) M.; A.B., Johns Hopkins, 1938, M.D., 1942; m. Anne Jenkins Shriver, Dec. 19, 1942 (div. 1954); children—Beverly Shriver, George Washington III, Anne Jenkins, Edward Diggs; m. 2d, Mary Elizabeth McKay, Sept. 14, 1957; children—Bruce McKay, Katharyne Wilcox. Intern Johns Hopkins Hosp., 1942, resident, 1946-49; gynecologist in chief New Eng. Med. Center Hosp., Boston, 1950—; prof. obstetrics and gynecology Tufts U. Sch. Med., 1954—, chmn. dept., 1956—; cons. Newton-Wellesley, Boston City, St. Margaret's, Cambridge, St. Elizabeth's, Carney hosps., Surgeon Gen. Navy. Served with USNR, 1943-46. Diplomate Am. Bd. Obstetrics and Gynecology (dir.). Recipient Public Service award USN, 1977. Fellow Am. Assn. Obstetricians and Gynecologists, Am. Gynecol. Soc., A.C.S., Am. Coll. Obstetricians and Gynecologists; mem. Am. Fertility Soc., Soc. Pelvic Surgeons, AMA, Mass. Med. Soc., Obstet. Soc. Boston, New Eng. Obstetrics and Gynecology Soc., Soc. Gynecol. Oncologists, So. Atlantic, Tex., N.Am., S.W. obstet. and gynecol. soc., Am. Soc. Cytology, Johns Hopkins Med. and Surg. Assn., Sigma Xi. Home 60 Rolling Ln Weston MA 02193 Office: 171 Harrison Ave Boston MA 02111

MITCHELL, HAMILTON BARNES, corp. exec.; b. LaGrange, Ill., Aug. 13, 1916; s. Herbert H. and Gertrude (Barnes) M.; B.A., Dartmouth, 1938; law study U. Mich., 1938-39; m. Betty Jane Ward, June 14, 1940; children—John H., Thomas W., William B. With Reuben H. Donnelley Corp., Chgo., 1939-68, v.p., 1954-60, pres., 1960-68; pres., chief exec. officer, dir. Dun & Bradstreet Corp., 1968-72, chmn., chief exec. officer, 1972-75, chmn. exec. com., dir., 1975—; dir. N.Am. Philips Corp., Irving Trust Co., Union Pacific Corp., Irving Bank Corp. Clubs: Links (N.Y.C.); Apawamis Country (N.Y.); Metropolitan (Washington); Blind Brook; Augusta Nat. Golf. Office: Dun & Bradstreet Corp 299 Park Ave New York NY 10017

MITCHELL, HERBERT HALL, univ. dean; b. New Market, Ala., Dec. 10, 1916; s. Walter Hall and Vera Pearl (Johnston) M.; B.S., U. Ala., 1939, M.S., 1950; Ph.D., U. N.C., 1954; m. Audrey Elizabeth Taylor, Oct. 30, 1942; children—William Hall, Robert Michael, Richard Lee, Mary Ann. Asst. to dean of men U. Ala., 1939-42, asst. dean of men, 1942-43, asst. to dean of students, 1946-48; instr. U. N.C., 1948-51; asst. prof. Ala. Poly. Inst., 1951-55, asso. prof., 1955-56; prof., head dept. bus. adminstrn. Miss State U., 1956-60, Va. Poly. Inst., 1960—, also dean Sch. Bus., 1961—; vis. prof. finance grad. program in England and Germany, U. Ark., 1972; mem. adv. bd. Intercollegiate Case Clearing House, Harvard U., 1973-76, 77-78; dir. First Nat. Exchange Bank of Montgomery County. Mem. spl. adv. bd. Small Bus. Inst. Rev. of SBA. for Econ. Edn. fellow Joseph T. Ryerson & Son, Inc., Chgo., summer 1956. Served from cpl. to capt., Transp. Corps, AUS, 1943-46; col. Res. Mem. So Bus. Adminstrn. Assn. (pres. 1968-69), Am. Fin. Assn., So. Fin. Assn., Am. Soc. Traffic and Transp., Am. Assembly Collegiate Schs. Bus. (dir. 1973—, v.p. 1977, pres. 1978), Phi Eta Sigma, Delta Sigma Pi, Beta Gamma Sigma, Omicron Delta Kappa, Jasons, Ala. Quadrangle. Methodist. Club: Rotary. Contbr. articles to jours. Home: 1406 Highland Ave Blacksburg VA 24060

MITCHELL, HOMER IRVING, lawyer; b. Los Angeles, Dec. 9, 1899; s. Irving Jefferson and Susan (Bingham) M.; A.B., Stanford, 1922, J.D., 1923; m. Katharine Reid, Oct. 18, 1927 (d. Aug. 6, 1977); m. 2d, Katharine Howard Robinson, Dec. 14, 1977. Admitted to Calif. bar, 1923; dep. dist. atty., Los Angeles County, 1924-26, dep. county counsel, 1926-28; with O'Melveny & Myers, Los Angeles, 1928—, partner, 1936-73, of counsel, 1974—. Bd. visitors Stanford Law Sch., 1958-63, 78-80. Fellow Am. Coll. Trial Lawyers; mem. Am., Los Angeles bar assns., Theta Delta Chi, Phi Delta Phi. Clubs: Calif.; Los Angeles Yacht; Annandale Golf. Home: 1500 Charlton Rd San Marino CA 91108 Office: 611 W 6th St Los Angeles CA 90017

MITCHELL, HOWARD, symphonic condr.; b. Lyons, Nebr., Mar. 11, 1911; s. George Cheever and Vera (Bundy) M.; student Peabody Conservatory, 1928-30; honor grad. Curtis Inst. Music, 1935; Mus. D., Am. U., 1950, Georgetown U., 1960, Howard U., 1960, Western Md. Coll., 1966, Peabody Conservatory, 1966, Catholic U., 1969; m. Alma Metcalf, June 2, 1931; children—Lorraine, Glenn, Martha, Gerard, Andrew John. First cellist Nat. Symphony Orch., Washington, 1933-46, asso. condr., 1946-49, full condr., 1949-70: music dir. nat. orch., Uruguay, 1970—. Recipient Nat. Cath. Music Educators and Nat. Music Council, Nat. Assn. for Am. Composers and Condrs., Alice M. Ditson award, 1957; Laurel Leaf, Am. Composers Alliance, 1959; Nat. Fedn. Music Clubs award, 1960; Nat. Music Council Condr. citation, 1951, 55, 57, 61, 64; citation and scroll of commendation Concert Artists Guild, 1959; Peabody Conservatory Distinguished Alumni award, 1963; Jean Sibelius medal, Finland, 1965; Hadassah Myrtle Leaf award, 1968; decorated Nat. Order Condor of Andes (Bolivia); comdr.'s cross Order of Merit (Fed. Republic Germany); Knight of St. Gregory (Vatican). Mem. Nat. Cultural Center Com. (adv. com. arts). Address: Charlotte VT 05445

MITCHELL, IRVING EUGENE, educator, clergyman; b. Lynn, Mass., June 18, 1912; s. Arthur Irving and Lillian Frances (Ward) M.; A.B., Gordon Coll., 1943; M.A., U. N.H., 1944; Ph.D., Boston U., 1957; m. Audrey Elizabeth Clark, Oct. 27, 1935. Ordained to ministry Disciples of Christ Ch., 1942; minister Main Street Christian Ch., 1942-44, First Christian Ch., Worcester, Mass., 1944-46, St. Louisville Ch. of Christ, 1950; vis. lectr. race relations Boston U., 1949; asso. prof. sociology and econs. Lynchburg Coll., 1946-49; lectr. family life U. Va. Extension Service, 1948-49; prof. sociology dept. Denison U., 1949-77, prof. emeritus, 1977—, chmn., 1949-62, 68-74; vis. prof. U. Alta., summer 1961, Indiana U. of Pa., summers, 1964-74. Mem. Nat. Council on Crime and Delinquency. Past chmn. bd. Moundbuilders Guidance Center Psychiat. Clinic, Newark, Ohio; mem. policy bd. Ohio Citizens' Council for Health and Welfare, 1972-77; past state rep. Ohio Disciples of Christ, Ohio Council of Chs.; pres. New Eng. Conv. Disciples of Christ, 1945-46. Mem. Am. Sociol. Soc., Eastern, North Central, So. sociol. assns., AAUP, U.S. Power Squadron, Navy League U.S., Alpha Kappa Delta, Pi Gamma Mu, Delta Upsilon. Mason, Kiwanian. Home: 8 Samson Pl PO Box 402 Granville OH 43023

MITCHELL, J. RONALD, broadcasting co. exec.; b. Winnipeg, Man., Canada, June 23, 1933; s. Clifford and Clarice (Way) M.; diploma in accounting U. Man., 1957; children—J. Clifford, Grant E., Donna G. Auditor, Deloitte, Plender, Haskins & Sells, Winnipeg, 1951-56, Haskins & Sells, Chgo., 1956-58; prin. Deloitte, Haskins & Sells, Toronto, 1958-60, Winnipeg, 1960-63; asst. to pres. Moffat Communications Ltd., Winnipeg, 1963-64, exec. v.p., 1964-70, pres., chief exec. officer, 1970—; dir. CTV TV Network Ltd., Sta. CHED. Registered indsl. accountant. Mem. Canadian Assn. Broadcasters, Major Mkts. Broadcasters., Inst. Chartered Accountants. Liberal. Mem. United Ch. Can. Clubs: St. Charles, Winnipeg Winter, Mason. Home: 6022 Southboine Dr Winnipeg MB R3R 0B6 Canada Office: CKY Bldg Polo Pk Winnipeg MB R3G 0L7 Canada

MITCHELL, JAMES FREE, JR., ins. co. exec.; b. Balt., Oct. 13, 1903; s. James Free and Lillian Ives (Wilcox) M.; B.S. in Econs., U. Pa., 1926; m. Mary F. Schoettle, Feb. 21, 1935; children—James Free III, Suzanne Schoettle. Pres., Seltzer, Mitchell, Coyle & Co., ins. brokers, 1966-71; exec. v.p. Parker & Co., Inc., div. Frank B. Hall & Co., internat. ins. brokers, Phila., 1971-74, v.p. Frank B. Hall & Co. of Pa. Inc., 1974—; dir. N.J. Natural Gas Co., Davis-Elliott, Inc., Natural Energy Systems, Inc.; dir. emeritus Wellington Fund., Inc., Windsor Fund, Inc., Gemini Fund, Exeter Fund, W.L. Morgan Growth Fund, Wellesley Income Fund. Trustee Methodist Hospital, Phila. Served to col. AUS, World War II. Decorated Legion of Merit. Mem. Mil. Order Fgn. Wars. Methodist (trustee). Clubs: Racquet (Phila.); Merion Cricket (Haverford); Merion Golf (Ardmore, Pa.). Home: Dunwoody Village CH-8 3500 W Chester Pike Newtown Square PA 19073 Office: 2700 Two INA Plaza 1622 Arch St Philadelphia PA 19103

MITCHELL, JAMES LOWRY, II, lawyer, former govt. ofcl.; b. Evanston, Ill., May 20, 1937; s. David B. and Sara (McGinn) M.; B.A., Cornell U., 1959; LL.B., Yale, 1962; m. Ann Elizabeth Stupple, June 6, 1962; children—Caitlin, Andrew. Admitted to Ill. bar, 1962, D.C. bar, 1977; asso. firm Mayer, Brown & Platt, Chgo., 1966-69, partner, 1969-72, 77—; spl. asst. to sec. for policy devel. U.S. Dept. Commerce, Washington, 1972-73; gen. counsel HUD, 1973-74, under sec., 1974-75; asso. dir. Office Mgmt. and Budget, 1975-77. Served with USN, 1962-66. Mem. Am., Ill., Chgo., D.C. bar assns., Maritime Law Assn. Clubs: Union League (Chgo.), Chgo., Capitol Hill. Home: 8307 Burning Tree Rd Bethesda MD 20034 Office: 888 17th St NW Washington DC 20005

MITCHELL, JOAN, abstract expressionist painter; b. Chgo., 1926; d. James Herbert and Marion (Strobel) Mitchell; student Smith Coll., 1942-44, M.F.A., Art Inst. Chgo., 1947; hon. degree, Western Coll. Ohio, 1972. One-person shows: Galerie Fournier, Paris, 1967-78, Everson Mus., Syracuse, N.Y., 1972, Whitney Mus., N.Y., 1974, Art Club, Chgo., 1974, Carnegie Mus., Pitts., 1974, Corcoran Gallery Art, Washington, 1975, others; group shows include: Pa. Acad. Fine Arts, Phila., 1966, Mus. Modern Art, N.Y.C., tour in Japan, India and Australia, 1967, U. Ill., 1967, Jewish Mus., N.Y.C., 1967, Mass. Inst. Tech.; represented in permanent collections, including: Basel (Switzerland) Mus., Albright-Knox Art Gallery, Buffalo, Art Inst. Chgo., Mus. Modern Art, Phillips Collection, Washington; exhibited regularly at Stable Gallery, N.Y.C., 1952-64. Recipient Creative Arts citation Brandeis U., 1973; Art Inst. Chgo. Traveling fellow, 1947. Office: care Xavier Fourcade 35 E 75th St New York NY 10021*

MITCHELL, JOHN ALBERT, psychiatrist; b. Santa Barbara, Calif., Mar. 31, 1907; s. John and Dora (Cavalliere) M.; A.B., U. Calif. at Berkeley, 1929, M.D., U. Calif. at San Francisco, 1942; m. Katherine Groff, Oct. 13, 1953; children—James D., Philip J. Intern So. Pacific Gen. Hosp., San Francisco, 1942-43; resident psychiatry St. Elizabeths Hosp., Washington, 1946-47; mem. Calif. Dept. Mental Hygiene, 1947-57, Calif. Dept. Corrections, 1957-60; supt. DeWitt State Hosp., Auburn, Calif., 1960-67; pvt. practice psychiatry, Sacramento, from 1967, now ret.; clin. instr. psychiatry Loma Linda Sch. Medicine, 1954-55, U. Calif. at Los Angeles Med. Sch., 1955-57. Served to 1st lt. M.C., USNR, 1943-46. Diplomate Am. Bd. Psychiatry. Mem. Am. Psychiat. Assn., Am., Calif. med. assns., Sacramento County Med. Soc., Tau Beta Pi. Rotarian. Office: PO Box 1885 Carmel CA 93921

MITCHELL, JOHN CLARK, II, found. exec.; b. Denver, May 8, 1917; s. Clark Goodell and Ida Hermine (Quentin) M.; B.A., Yale U., 1938; grad. Rutgers U. Grad. Sch. Banking, 1952; m. Nancy Kountze, Dec. 28, 1940; children—John Clark, Joan Mitchell Whitbeck, Clark Goodell. With Chase Nat. Bank, N.Y.C., 1938-39; v.p., dir. United Bank Denver (formerly Denver Nat. Bank), 1939-62; pres., exec. dir. Boettcher Found., Denver, 1962—; dir. Brown Palace Hotel Co., Downtown Denver, Inc.; bd. dirs. Inst. Internat. Edn. Pres. trustees Denver Botanic Gardens, 1968—; bd. dirs. Denver Area council Boy Scouts Am., Western Stock Show Assn., Denver Art Mus., Denver Symphony Assn., Denver Center Performing Arts. Served to lt. comdr. USNR, 1942-45. Recipient Silver Beaver award Boy Scouts Am. Mem. Assn. Colo. Founds., Council Founds., Rocky Mountain Wine and Food Soc., Denver Orchid Soc., Chevaliers du Tastevin, Phi Beta Kappa, Delta Kappa Epsilon. Episcopalian. Clubs: Denver Country, Mile High, Brown Palace (Denver); Berzelius, Elizabethan (Yale U.). Home: 6560 Lakeridge Rd Denver CO 80227 Office: 828 17th St Denver CO 80202

MITCHELL, JOHN EDWARD, machinery mfg. co. exec.; b. Lemont, Ill., Apr. 30, 1926; s. John Martialis and Laura Elizabeth (Wold) M.; student Chgo. campuses U. Ill., Northwestern U.; m. Lois Ann Bush, May 6, 1950; children—John Eric, Gary Alan, Gayle Ann, Lauren Marie. Indsl. engr. Johnson & Johnson Surg. Dressings Co., Chgo., 1943-44, 46-48; sales engr. Hyster Co., Chgo., 1948-49, dist. sales mgr., N.Y.C., 1949-51; gen. mgr. Field Machinery Co., Cambridge, Mass., 1951-57; gen. mgr. N.Y.C. br. Clark Equipment Co., gen. sales mgr., dir. sales, group dir. marketing mobile products, 1957-65, also v.p. subsidiary Clark Rental Corp.; v.p. indsl. and constrn. machinery Massey-Ferguson Ltd., Toronto, Ont., Can., 1965-66, group v.p. indsl. and constrn. machinery, 1966-72, exec. v.p. Americas, 1972-79, dir., 1971-79; pres. Massey-Ferguson Inc., 1969-78, chmn., 1978-79; pvt. investor, 1979—. Served with USN, World War II. Mem. NAM, Farm and Indsl. Equipment Inst. (dir., mem. exec. com.). Clubs: Masons, Shriners; Royal Palm Yacht and Country (Boca Raton, Fla.). Office: Suite 103 301 Crawford Blvd Boca Raton FL 33432

MITCHELL, JOHN FRANCIS, electronics co. exec.; b. Chgo., Jan. 1, 1928; s. William and Bridie (Keane) M.; B.S. in Elec. Engring., Ill. Inst. Tech., 1950; m. Margaret J. Gillis, Aug. 26, 1950; children—Catherine (Mrs. Edward Welsh III), John, Kevin. Exec. v.p., asst. chief operating officer Motorola Inc., Schaumburg, Ill., 1953—. Served to lt. (j.g.) USNR, 1950-53. Mem. I.E.E.E. (sr.). Club: Inverness (Ill.) Country. Patentee in field. Home: 510 Plymouth Dr Inverness IL 60067 Office: 1303 E Algonquin Rd Schaumburg IL 60196

MITCHELL, JOHN FULTON BERRIEN, mining co. exec.; b. N.Y.C., July 8, 1914; s. John F.B. and Therese (Hewitt) M.; A.B., Princeton, 1935; LL.B., Yale, 1938; m. Margot D. Finletter, Feb. 18, 1949; 1 son, Thomas Finletter. Admitted to N.Y. bar, 1940; asso. Hawkins, Delafield & Wood, N.Y.C., 1938-41, 46-51; asst. gen. counsel CIA, 1951-55; individual practice law, N.Y.C., 1955-57; partner Baker, Nelson, Williams & Mitchell, N.Y.C., 1957-72; pres. Metron Inc., iron ore miners, 1976-78. Trustee Home for Old Men and Aged Couples. Vice chmn. N.Y. Bus. Men for Stevenson, 1956. Served from lt. to maj., USAAF, 1941-46. Decorated Croix de Guerre with silver star (France); Croix de Guerre with palm (Belgium). Democrat. Clubs: Century (N.Y.C.); Bar Harbor Yacht (commodore 1971-73). Home: 25 Main St Stonington CT 06378

MITCHELL, JOHN H., TV cons.; b. N.Y.C., Apr. 27, 1918; s. Ralph and Lillian (Hiedelberg) M.; A.B., U. Mich., 1939; m. Patricia Mitchell, 1969; 1 dau., Joan E. Market researcher Erwin, Wasey Advt. Co., 1939-41; sales service mgr. MBS, 1941-48; v.p., gen. mgr. United Artists Television, 1948-51; exec. v.p., dir. Screen Gems, Inc., N.Y.C., 1951-68, pres. Columbia Pictures TV div., 1968-77, exec. v.p. Columbia Pictures Industries, 1973-77, also dir.; founder, prin. John H. Mitchell Co., Inc., TV programming and distbn. cons., Los Angeles, 1977—. Bd. dirs. Internat. Radio and TV Fund; trustee TV Conf. Found. Inc., N.Y.C. Served to lt. USNR, 1942-45. Mem. Nat. Acad. TV Arts and Scis. (1st v.p. 1978-79), Hollywood Radio and TV Soc. (pres. 1975-76), TV Acad. Forum (chmn. 1979-80), Internat. Radio and TV Soc. Home: 1039 Wallace Ridge Beverly Hills CA 90210 Office: 1888 Century Park E Los Angeles CA 90067

MITCHELL, JOHN MURRAY, JR., climatologist; b. N.Y.C., Sept. 17, 1928; s. John Murray and Lanier (Comly) M.; B.S., Mass. Inst. Tech., 1951, M.S., 1952; Ph.D., Pa. State U., 1960; postgrad. Nat. War Coll., 1970-71; m. Pollyanne Bryant, May 5, 1956; children—John Murray, Brian Harrison, Katherine Comly, Anne Stuart. Research meteorologist Weather Bur., Commerce Dept., Suitland, Md., 1955-65, project scientist environ. data service NOAA, Silver Spring, Md., 1965-74, sr. research climatologist, 1974—; mem. various coms. and panels Nat. Acad. Scis., NRC; vis. lectr., prof. U. Calif., U. Wash. Mem. Fairfax County Air Pollution Control Bd. Served with USAF, 1952-55. Recipient Silver and Gold medals Commerce Dept. Fellow AAAS, Am. Meteorol. Soc. (2d Half Century award), Washington Acad. Scis.; mem. Am. Geophys. Union, Royal Meteorol. Soc., Sigma Xi. Contbr. articles to books, encys., tech. jours.; editor: Meteorol. Monographs, 1965-73. Home: 1106 Dogwood Dr McLean VA 22101 Office: NOAA 8060 13th St Silver Spring MD 20910

MITCHELL, JOHN NEWTON, bus. cons.; b. Detroit, Sept. 5, 1913; s. Joseph Charles and Margaret Agnes (McMahon) M.; student Fordham U., 1932-34, LL.B., 1938; postgrad. law St. John's U., 1938-39; m. Martha Beall, 1957 (separated 1973) (dec.); children—John Newton III, Jill Elizabeth (Mrs. Edwin C. Reed), Martha. Mem. N.Y. State bar, 1938-75; asso. firm Caldwell & Raymond, N.Y.C., 1938-42; partner firm Caldwell, Trimble & Mitchell, 1942-66, Nixon, Mudge, Rose, Guthrie, Alexander & Mitchell, 1967-68; atty. gen. U.S., 1969-72. Campaign mgr for Richard M. Nixon. 1968; chmn. Com. to Re-elect Pres., 1972. Served with USNR, 1943-46. Mem. Am. Bar Assn. (local govt. sect.). Address: care of Simon & Schuster Inc 630 Fifth Av New York NY 10020*

MITCHELL, JOHN STEWART, mfg. co. exec., lawyer; b. San Francisco, Aug. 11, 1915; s. John James and Edith (Franks) M.; A.B., Stanford, 1936, LL.B., 1939; m. Beverly Pratt, Jan. 16, 1942; 1 son, John James. Admitted to Calif. bar, 1939; chief law sec. Calif. Dist. Ct. Appeal, 1940-46; asso. firm Thomas, Beedy, Nelson & King, San Francisco, 1946-49; asst. sec., then sec.-treas. Fibreboard Products Inc., San Francisco, 1949-57; company merged to become Fibreboard Corp., 1957, sec., gen. atty., 1957-74, v.p., sec., gen. counsel, 1974—. Served to lt. USNR, 1942-45; PTO. Mem. Am. Soc. Corporate Secs., State Bar Calif., Kappa Sigma, Phi Delta Phi. Clubs: Claremont Country (Oakland, Calif.); Pacific-Union (San Francisco).

MITCHELL, JONI (ROBERTA JOAN ANDERSON), singer, songwriter; b. Ft. Macleod, Alta., Can., Nov. 7, 1943; d. William A. and Myrtle M. (McKee) Anderson; student Atla. Coll; m. Chuck Mitchell, 1965 (div.). Albums include Song to a Seagull, Clouds, Ladies of the Canyon, Blue, For the Roses, Court and Spark, Miles of Ailes, Hissing of Summer Lawns, Hejira, Don Juan's Reckless Daughter, Mingus (Jazz Album of Year and Rock-Blues Album of Year, Downbeat mag. 1979); compositions include Both Sides Now, Michael from Mountains, Urge for Going, Circle Game. Address: care Elliot Roberts Lookout Mgmt 9120 Sunset Blvd Los Angeles CA 90069

MITCHELL, JOSEPH (QUINCY), journalist, author; b. Fairmont, N.C., July 27, 1908; s. Averette Nance and Elizabeth Amanda (Parker) M.; student U. N.C., 1925-29; m. Therese Dagny Engelsted Jacobsen, Feb. 27, 1931; children—Nora (Mrs. John L.R. Sanborn), Elizabeth (Mrs. Henry Curtis). Reporter, N.Y. World, N.Y.C., 1929-30, N.Y. Herald Tribune, 1930-31, N.Y. World Telegram, 1931-38; writer New Yorker mag., N.Y.C., 1938—. Mem. Am. Acad. and Inst. Arts. and Letters (sec. 1972-74), South Street Seaport Mus. (restoration com. 1972—), Soc. Archtl. Historians, Soc. Indsl. Archeology, Friends of Cast-Iron Architecture, James Joyce Soc., Gypsy Lore Soc. (Eng.). Club: Century Assn. (N.Y.C.). Author: My Ears Are Bent, 1938; McSorley's Wonderful Saloon, 1943; Old Mr. Flood, 1948; The Bottom of the Harbor, 1960; Joe Gould's Secret, 1965. Home: 44 W 10th St New York NY 10011 Office: The New Yorker 25 W 43d St New York NY 10036

MITCHELL, JOSEPH A., govt. ofcl.; b. Columbus, Ga., Mar. 6, 1942; s. Joseph A. and Charlotte (Berry) M.; B.S., Auburn U., 1965; M.S. in Indsl. Mgmt., U. N.D., 1968; postgrad. U. Ga., 1970-71; J.D., Woodrow Wilson Law Sch., 1976; m. Leslie Ann Buchanan, Sept. 6, 1962; children—Kimberly Leigh, Joseph Matthew. Mgmt. cons. Peat, Marwick, Mitchell & Co., 1969-70; with Office of Planning and Budget, State of Ga., adminstrv. asst. to gov. exec. sec. to gov., 1970-75, exec. dir. State Ethics Commn., 1975-76; congl. liaison White House, Washington, 1977; dir. Fed. Preparedness Agy., Washington, 1977—. Served to capt. USAF, 1965-69. Mem. Ga. State Bar Assn. Democrat. Episcopalian. Home: 6600 Melrose Dr McLean VA 22101 Office: 18th and F St NW Washington DC 20405

MITCHELL, JOSEPH NATHAN, ins. co. exec.; b. Winnipeg, Man., Can., Oct. 10, 1922; s. Edward David and Anna (Copp) M.; student UCLA, 1940-42; m. Beverly Edna Henigson, Oct. 27, 1946; children—Jonathan Edward, Jan Ellen, Karin Helene. Came to U.S., 1931, naturalized, 1936. With Beneficial Standard Life Ins. Co., Los Angeles, 1946—, dir., 1946—, exec. v.p., 1957-59, pres., 1959—, chmn. bd., 1969; chmn. Fidelity Interstate Life Ins. Co., Phila.; pres. Beneficial Standard Corp.; v.p., dir. Ampal-Am. Israel Corp., N.Y.C.; dir. Brit. Pacific Life Ins. Co., Vancouver, B.C.; chmn. exec. com. Transit Casualty Co., St. Louis; dir. Pacific Lighting Corp., Calif. Fed. Savs. and Loan, Beneficial Nat. Life Ins. Co., N.Y.C.; v.p. Jackson-Mitchell Pharms., Inc., Santa Barbara, Calif. Chmn. Los Angeles Appeal, State of Israel Bonds, 1967, also past mem. exec. com., cabinet; mem. Mayor's Steering Com. on Urban Coalition; mem. Dist. Atty.'s Adv. Council; past mem. bd. dirs., exec. com., nat. campaign cabinet United Jewish Appeal; bd. dirs., vice chmn. mem. exec. com., chmn. audit com. Cedars-Sinai Med. Center; past mem. exec. com. Jewish Fedn.-Council Greater Los Angeles; bd. dirs., past v.p., gen. chmn. United Jewish Welfare Fund, 1952; mem. Greater Los Angeles Urban Coalition; trustee, mem. adv. bd., past v.p. Jewish Community Found.; bd. dirs. ops. mgmt. council United Way, 1972-73; exec. com. United Way; chmn. United Crusade Los Angeles; trustee, sec., treas. Edward D. and Anna Mitchell Family Found. Served with AUS, 1942-46; ETO. Mem. Am. Technion Soc. (past nat. v.p., bd. govs.), U.S., Calif., Calif.-Israel, Los Angeles (pres.) chambers commerce. Clubs: Hillcrest Country (past treas., dir.), Los Angeles (Los Angeles); Tamarisk Country, Tennis (Palm Springs, Calif.). Office: 3700 Wilshire Blvd Los Angeles CA 90010

MITCHELL, JOSEPHINE MARGARET (MRS. LOWELL SCHOENFELD), educator; b. Edmonton, Alta., Can.; d. Benjamin Foster and Kate (Russell) Mitchell; came to U.S., 1938, naturalized,

1950; B.Sc. in Arts, U. Alta., 1934; M.A., Bryn Mawr Coll., 1941, Ph.D., 1942; m. Lowell Schoenfeld, Aug. 10, 1953. Mem. faculty various colls., 1942-47; asst. prof. Okla. State U., 1947-48, U. Ill., 1948-54; engr. Gen. Electric Co., 1955-56; research mathematician Westinghouse Research Lab., 1956-57; asso. prof. U. Pitts., 1957-58; faculty Pa. State U., University Park, 1958-68, prof. math., 1961-68; prof. math. State U. N.Y. at Buffalo, 1968—; sabbatical leave at U. Mich. and U. Calif. at Berkeley, 1974; mem. Inst. for Advanced Study, 1954-55. Vis. research prof. math. Math. Research Center, U. Wis., 1964-65, summer 1967; lectr. for Math. Assn. Am., 1965-72. Am. Philos. Soc. research grantee, 1948, NSF research grantee, 1952-53, 69-72, AAUW fellow, 1954-55, NSF sr. postdoctoral fellow, 1964-65, USAF Office Sci. Research research grantee, 1960-63. Fellow AAAS (mem.-at-large sect. A 1974-78); mem. Am. Math. Soc., Math. Assn. Am., N.Y. Acad. Scis., Audubon Soc., Sierra Club. Contbr. articles to profl. publs. Home: 1701 W River Rd Grand Island NY 14072 Office: State U NY at Buffalo 222 Diefendorf Buffalo NY 14214

MITCHELL, JULIA L., savs. and loan assn. exec.; b. Conyers, Ga., Mar. 1, 1933; d. Runie Marvin and Uri (Roebuck) Farmer; B.A., Ga. State Coll., 1962; grad. various profl. schs.; m. James Tillman Mitchell, Sept. 8, 1951. With U.S. Fidelity & Guaranty Ins. Co., 1951-53; with Decatur Fed. Savs. and Loan Assn. (Ga.), 1953—, asst. sec., 1956—, treas., 1965—; sec. Service, Housing and Real Estate, Inc., 1970—, Preferred Ins. Agy., Inc., 1971—; mgr. Decatur Fed. Savs. and Loan Assn. Employees Pension Plan, 1965—; mem. steering com. Optimal Program Edn. in DeKalb County, Ga. Mem. Fin. Mgrs. Soc. for Savs. Assns., Inst. Fin. Edn. (past pres. Atlanta, dir. Ga. 1976-77, dir. Dixie regional conf. 1975), Atlanta Women's, DeKalb chambers commerce, Bus. and Profl. Women (named Outstanding Woman of Achievement 1974-78), Atlanta Econs. Baptist. Home: 3508 Midvale Rd Tucker GA 30084 Office: 250 E Ponce de Leon Ave Decatur GA 30030

MITCHELL, LANSING LEROY, U.S. judge; b. Sun, La., Jan. 17, 1914; s. Leroy A. and Eliza Jane (Richardson) M.; B.A., La. State U., 1934, LL.B., 1937; m. Virginia Jumonville, Apr. 18, 1938; children—Diane Mitchell (Mrs. Donald Lee Parker), Lansing Leroy. Admitted to La. bar, 1937; pvt. practice, Pontchatoula, 1937-38; spl. agt. FBI, 1938-41; atty. SEC, 1941-42; asst. U.S. atty. Eastern Dist. La., 1946-53, also engaged in pvt. practice; partner firm Deutsch, Kerrigan & Stiles. New Orleans, 1953-66; U.S. dist. judge Eastern Dist. La., 1966—. Chmn. nat. security com. New Orleans C. of C., 1963-66; vice chmn. New Orleans Armed Forces Day, 1964, 65, New Orleans Heart Fund campaign, 1959-60; mem. New Orleans Municipal Auditorium Adv. Com., 1957-61, New Orleans Municipal Com. Finance, 1955-67, Small Bus. Adv. Council La., 1963-66; pres. Camp Fire Girls Greater New Orleans, 1965-67. La. chmn. Lawyers for Kennedy-Johnson, 1960. Served to lt. col. AUS, 1942-46; col. Res. (ret.). Decorated Royal Order St. George, Royal Order Scotland. Mem. Am., Inter-Am., La., New Orleans bar assns., Maritime Law Assn. U.S., Judge Adv. Assn., Soc. Former Spl. Agts. FBI, Am. Legion, Mil. Order World Wars, V.F.W., Navy League, Assn. U.S. Army (pres. La. 1964-65, pres. New Orleans 1961-64, v.p. 4th Army region 1963-66), Scabbard and Blade, S.A.R., S.R., Soc. War 1812 La., Pi Kappa Alpha, Phi Delta Phi, Theta Nu Epsilon. Mason (Shriner). Clubs: Press, Paul Morphy Chess, Southern Yacht, Bienville, Pendennis (New Orleans); Tchefuncta Country (Covington, La.). Home: 6027 Hurst St New Orleans LA 70118 Office: 500 Camp St New Orleans LA 70130

MITCHELL, LEONA PEARL, soprano; b. Enid, Okla., Oct. 13, 1949; s. Hulon and Pearl Olive (Leatherman) M.; B.A., Oklahoma City U., 1971, D.Music (hon.), 1979. With San Francisco Merola Program, 1971, Santa Fe Apprentice Program, 1972; European debut, Barcelona, Spain, 1974; Met. Opera debut, 1975; Australian Opera debut, 1977; with San Francisco Opera, spring, 1973, fall, 1974; appeared at Edinburgh (Scotland) Festival, 1977, Sacria Umbria Festival, Perugia, Italy, 1977; on concert tour, Australia, 1978; has sung with most maj. symphonies throughout U.S. Named Ambassadress of Enid, 1978; George London grantee, 1973-74; Rockefeller grantee, 1975-76; Sullivan Found. grantee, 1973-74. Mem. Am. Guild Musicians Assn., Sigma Alpha Iota, Alpha Kappa Alpha. Mem. Ch. of God in Christ. Performed for Pres. Ford, 1976, Pres. Carter, 1978, 79. Office: Columbia Artists 165 W 57th St New York NY 10019

MITCHELL, LOFTEN, playwright; b. Columbus, N.C., Apr. 15, 1919; s. Ulysses Sanford and Willia (Spaulding) M.; studied playwriting at Coll. City N.Y., 1937-38; grad., Talladega (Ala.) Coll., 1943; postgrad. in playwriting Columbia U., 1947-51; m. Helen Marsh, Sept. 30, 1948; 2 sons. Formerly social investigator Dept. Welfare, N.Y.C.; playwright: Blood in the Night, performed 1946, A Land Beyond the River, performed Greenwich Mews Theatre, N.Y.C., 1957; Star of the Morning (story of Black entertainer, Bert Williams); (with Irving Burgie) Ballad for Bimshire, musical, produced on Broadway, 1963-64; tchr. State U. N.Y., Binghamton. Produced plays: The Cellar and Bancroft Dynasty, Harlem Showcase. Served with USNR. Recipient Guggenheim award for creative writing, 1958-59; Rockefeller Found. grantee, 1961; Harlem Cultural Com. award, 1969. Mem. Dramatists Guild, Am. Soc. African Culture, NAACP. Author: Black Drama: The Story of the American Negro in the Theater, 1967; The Stubborn Old Lady, 1972; Voices of Black Theatre, 1975; Bubbling Brown Sugar, 1975. Contbr. radio scripts, screenplays, articles on theatre to mags., newspapers. Office: care Ann Elmo 60 E 42d St New York NY 10017

MITCHELL, LYDELL DOUGLAS, football player; b. Salem, N.J., May 30, 1949; B.A., Pa. State U., 1972. Running back Balt. Colts, 1972-78, San Diego Chargers, 1978—; played in Pro Bowl, 1975, 76, 77. Office: care San Diego Chargers San Diego Stadium PO Box 20666 San Diego CA 92120*

MITCHELL, MARION BONNER, educator; b. Livingston, Tex., Nov. 28, 1929; s. Jewell Clarence and Verna Lorena (Bonner) M.; B.A., U. Tex., 1949, M.A., 1951; postgrad. Sorbonne, 1951-52; Ph.D., Ohio State U., 1958. Mem. faculty U. Mo., Columbia, 1958—, prof. French and Italian, 1966—, chmn. dept. Romance langs., 1972-75. Served with AUS, 1952-54. Mem. Am. Assn. Tchrs. Italian, Modern Lang. Assn., Renaissance Soc. Am., Phi Beta Kappa. Author: Les Manifestes Litteraires de la Belle Epoque, 1966; Rome in the High Renaissance, 1973; Italian Civic Pageantry in the High Renaissance: A Descriptive Bibliography, 1979; co-author: A Renaissance Entertainment, 1968. Home: 508 S Garth St Columbia MO 65201 Office: Dept Romance Langs Univ Missouri Columbia MO 65211

MITCHELL, MARVIN GEORGE, steel constrn. co. exec.; b. Waycross, Ga., Dec. 24, 1916; s. Marvin G. and Minnie (Holland) M.; B.S. in Civil Engring. cum laude, Ga. Inst. Tech., 1939; m. Margaret V. Lovelady, Sept. 24, 1942; children—Marvin George III, Margaret Nelle. With CBI Industries, Inc., 1939—, sr. v.p., 1967-68, pres., 1969—, chmn. bd., 1973—, also dir.; dir. Horton CBI Ltd. (Can.), CBI Constructors Ltd. (Eng.), Mitchell-Stewart Hardware Co., Bliss & Laughlin Industries, McGraw-Edison Co., R.R. Donnelley & Sons Co., Continental Ill. Corp. Bd. dirs. Ga. Inst. Tech. nat. adv. bd., Atomic Indsl. Forum; bd. govs. Chgo. Heart Assn., Beavers, Inc.; mem. citizens bd. U. Chgo.; mem. nat. adv. bd. Goodwill Industries, Inc. Mem. Am. Petroleum Inst., Am. Water Works Assn., Am. Iron and Steel Inst., NAM (dir.). Clubs: Hinsdale (Ill.) Golf, Butler Nat. Golf (pres.); Economic, Chicago, Comml., Mid-Am. (Chgo.). Office: 800 Jorie Blvd Oak Brook IL 60521

MITCHELL, MAURICE B., publishing co. exec.; b. N.Y.C., Feb. 9, 1915; s. Jacob and Beatrice Mitchell; student N.Y. U., 1932-35; LL.D. (hon.), U. Denver, 1958, W.Va. Wesleyan U., 1978; L.H.D., Nat. Coll. Edn., 1969; Litt.D. (hon.), Colo. State U., 1971; m. Mildred Roth, Mar. 1937; 1 son, Lee Mark; m. 2d, Mary V. Rowles, Nov. 1951; children—Keith Edward, Deborah Irene. With N.Y. Times, 1935-36; editor Gouverneur (N.Y.) Press, 1936-37; asst. pub. Ogdensburg (N.Y.) Jour., 1938-39, Rochester (N.Y.) Times-Union, 1940; nat. advt. mgr. Albany (N.Y.) Knickerbocker-News, 1941-43; with CBS, Washington, also N.Y.C., 1945-48, Nat. Assn. Broadcasters, Washington, 1948-49; mng. dir. Broadcast Advt. Bur., N.Y.C., 1949-50; with NBC, 1953; v.p., asso. program service div. Muzak Corp., N.Y.C., 1950-53, dir., 1953-58; pres., dir. Ency. Brit. Films, Inc., 1953-62, Ency. Brit., Inc., Chgo. and all subsidiaries, 1962-67, dir. Ency. Brit. Ednl. Corp., 1977—; chancellor U. Denver, 1967-77; pres. Center for Study Democratic Instns./Fund for the Republic, 1977-78; owner, pub. Rocky Mountain Herald; chmn. Denver br. Fed. Res. Bank, 1971-76, dir. Kansas City br., 1976-77; dir. Teleprompter Corp., Colo. & So. Ry., Ency. Brit. Mem. U.S. Commn. on Civil Rights, 1968-74; chmn. Denver Community Edn. Council on Integration Pub. Schs., 1974-76; trustee Freedoms Found.; chmn. Colo. com. Rhodes Scholarship Trust, 1974-77, Calif. Commn., 1978—; citizens bd. U. Chgo.; mem. adv. com. U.S. Army Command and Gen. Staff Coll., Dept. Army, 1975-78; chmn. Western Regional Judges Truman Scholarships, 1976—; dir. Nat. Public Radio, 1977—; bd. asso. Nat. Coll. Edn.; trustee Com. Econ. Devel., 1957-62; bd. dirs. Fgn. Policy Assn., World Affairs Center and Nat. Citizens on Internat. Cooperation, 1966-71, Nat. Center for Resource Recovery, Inc., African Student Aid Fund. Recipient George Washington medal Freedoms Found., 1969; VFW Medal of Merit, 1970; Certificate of Recognition for distinguished service to edn. Phi Delta Kappa, 1971; Golden Plate award Am. Acad. Achievement, 1972; Civis Princeps award Regis Coll., Denver, 1973; Meritorious award Denver Met. NAACP, 1973; Malcolm Glenn Wyer award Adult Edn. Council Met. Denver, 1975; B'nai B'rith award, 1976; Human Relations award Beth Joseph Synagogue, Denver, 1976. Mem. Colo. State Hist. Soc. (dir.), Phi Beta Kappa, Beta Alpha Psi, Omicron Delta Kappa, Beta Gamma Sigma, Alpha Kappa Psi. Clubs: Nat. Press, Cosmos (Washington); Denver, Denver Country, Univ., (Denver); Chgo., Mid-Am. (Chgo.). Contbr. articles on edn. and communications to profl. jours. Home and office: 260 Eucalyptus Hill Dr Santa Barbara CA 93103

MITCHELL, NICHOLAS PENDLETON, educator; b. Seymour, Tex., Apr. 25, 1911; s. Nick P. and Maude Amanda (Head) M.; B.A., U. Tex., 1929, M.A., 1930; Ph.D., Duke, 1934; m. Gartha Lena Morgan, Nov. 11, 1930; children—Nicholas Pendleton, III, Morgan Head, Maude Amanda. Instr. in govt. La. State U., 1930-31; teaching fellow in govt. Duke, 1931-34, part time instr., 1934-35; acting prof. history and polit. sci. U. Richmond, 1935-36; prof., head dept. polit. sci. Furman U., 1936-46; chmn. grad. dept., 1942-46; prof. govt., extension dept. U. S.C., 1939-50, dir. news service, 1956, dir. extension, 1957-65, dean Coll. Gen. Studies, 1965-71, asso. provost, 1971-74, v.p., 1974-76, distinguished prof. adult and continuing edn., 1973-76, prof. emeritus, 1976—; asso. editor Greenville News, 1950-55; editor, pub. Fla. Keys Keynoter, 1955-57; editor Furman Univ. Press, 1940-45. Founder, pres. Greenville Town Hall; chmn. S.C. Com. on Humanities, 1971-77, adminstrv. officer, 1977—. Mem. Am. Polit. Sci. Assn., AAUP, So. Polit. Sci. Assn., Am. Soc. Internat. Law, Am. Assn. U. Adminstrs., S.C. Adv. Council on Adult Edn. (chmn. 1951-60), Nat. Univ. Extension Assn. (pres. 1969-70), Adult Edn. Assn. U.S., S.E. Adult Edn. Assn. (pres. 1953-55), Internat. Platform Assn., Sigma Alpha Epsilon, Phi Beta Kappa, Pi Sigma Alpha, Sigma Delta Pi, Alpha Epsilon Rho, Pi Gamma Mu. Democrat. Presbyn. Clubs: Rotary (gov. 1959-60), Thirty-nine, Poinsett. Author: Land Problems and Policies in the African Mandates of the British Commonwealth, 1931; State Interests in American Treaties, 1936. Co-author: Government in the City and County of Greenville, S.C., 1941. Radio news commentator, 1941—. Editor: Adult Leadership, 1957—. Home: 943 Hampton Hill Rd Columbia SC 29209 Office: 328 McCrory Bldg 2801 Devine St Columbia SC 29205

MITCHELL, ORLAN E., coll. adminstr.; b. Eldora, Iowa, Mar. 13, 1933; s. Frank E. and Alice G. (Brown) M.; B.A., Grinnell Coll., 1955; B.D., Yale U., 1959, M.Div., 1965; D.Min., San Francisco Theol. Sem., 1976; m. Verlene J. Huehn, June 10, 1952; children—Jolene R., Stephen M., Nadene A., Timothy M., Mark E. Ordained to ministry United Ch. of Christ, 1959; pastor chs., Sheridan Twp., Iowa, 1954-55, New Preston, Conn., 1956-59, Clarion, Iowa, 1959-69, Yankton, S.D., 1969-77; pres. Yankton (S.D.) Coll., 1977—; dir. Yankton Savs. and Loan. Mem. Sch. Bd., Clarion, Iowa, 1965-69; mem. Sch. Bd., Yankton, S.D., 1973-77, pres., 1976; bd. dirs. Lewis and Clark Mental Health Center. Mem. S.D. Found. Pvt. Colls., S.D. Assn. Pvt. Colls., Colls. of Mid-Am. Democrat. Clubs: Kiwanis, Masons. Home: 1201 Douglas Yankton SD 57078 Office: Yankton Coll 12th and Douglas Yankton SD 57078

MITCHELL, ORMOND GLENN, educator; b. Long Beach, Calif., Sept. 17, 1927; s. Allen G. and Mary Eva (Bryan) M.; A.B., San Diego U., 1949; M.S., U. So. Calif., 1952, Ph.D., 1957; m. Chung Ja Kim, Nov. 4, 1964; 1 son, Allen. Asst. prof. biology Calif. State Poly. Coll., Pomona, 1957-62; research asso. U. So. Calif., Los Angeles, 1962-63; prof., chmn. dept. biology Adelphi U., Garden City, N.Y., 1970-72; asst. prof. anatomy Coll. Dentistry N.Y. U., N.Y.C., 1963-70, asso. prof., 1972-75, prof., 1975—, chmn. dept. anatomy, 1973—, head Div. Anatomical Sci., 1977—. Served with USNR, 1945-46, 51-52. NSF grantee, 1969-72. Mem. Am. Assn. Anatomists, Am. Soc. Mammalogists, N.Y. Acad. Sci., AAAS, Am. Soc. Zoologists, Harvey Soc., Sigma Xi. Home: 99-01 Ascan Ave Forest Hills NY 11375 Office: 345 E 24th St New York NY 10010

MITCHELL, OTIS CLINTON, JR., historian; b. Spearville, Kans., Jan. 10, 1935; s. Otis Clinton and Joeanna Esther (Woodring) M.; A.B., Wichita U., 1957; M.A., Kans. State Coll., 1960; Ph.D., U. Kans., 1964; m. Darlene Foley, Aug. 20, 1966. Instr. history Wichita State U., 1963-64; mem. faculty U. Cin., 1964—, prof. history, 1975—. Dir. civic com., Hidden Valley Lake, Ind., 1975; bd. dirs. Hidden Valley Lake P.O.A., 1978-79. Served with AUS, 1957-59. Grantee Taft Fund Fellowship, 1969-74, 77. Mem. Am. Hist. Assn., AAUP, Phi Alpha Theta. Author: Two Totalitarians, 1965; The Western Cultural Way, 1965; A Concise History of Western Civilization, 2d edit., 1976; Fascism: An Introductory Perspective, 1978; The Great European Revolutionary Era of 1789-1815, 1979; co-author: The World Since 1919, 1971; editor, contbr.: Nazism and the Common Man, 1972. Home: RFD 2 Hidden Valley Lake Lawrenceburg IN 47025 Office: Dept History Univ Cin Cincinnati OH 45221

MITCHELL, P(HILLIP) M(ARSHALL), lit. historian; b. Syracuse, N.Y., Sept. 23, 1916; s. Oliver Wendell Holmes and Preston (Settle) M.; B.A., Cornell U., 1938; Ph.D., U. Ill., 1942; m. Merete Krag, Apr. 12, 1941; children—Preston Holm Nielsen, Vivian Yvonne Greene-Gantzberg, Erik Krag, Halldor Krag. Tutor, Cornell U., 1945-46; instr. Harvard U., 1946-49; asst. prof. Germanic langs. and lit. U. Kans., 1950-54, asso. prof., 1954-58; prof. Germanic langs. U. Ill., 1958—; vis. lectr. U. Wis., 1956; vis. prof. U. Aarhus, (Denmark), 1964. Mem. U. Ill. Ad Hoc Faculty Com. on Vietnam, 1965-71, chmn., 1968-71. Served with AUS, 1942-45. Decorated knight's cross Order of Dannebrog (Denmark); Det Danske Salskab stipendiary, 1949-50; Fulbright grantee, 1956-57, 64-65; Guggenheim fellow, 1978-79. Mem. MLA, Soc. Advancement Scandinavian Study (pres. 1958-60), AAUP, Royal Danish Acad. Scis. (corr.). Author numerous books. mng. editor Jour. English and Germanic Philology, 1959—; editorial bd. Orbis Litterarum, 1960—, Scandinavica, 1962—, Scandinavian Studies, 1971—. Home: 806 W Nevada St Urbana IL 61801 Office: Dept Germanic Langs U Ill Urbana IL 61801

MITCHELL, PARREN JAMES, congressman; b. Balt., Apr. 29, 1922; s. Clarence Maurice and Elsie (Davis) M.; B.A., Morgan State Coll., 1950; M.A., U. Md., 1952; postgrad. U. Conn., 1960. Instr. sociology Morgan State Coll., 1953-54, prof. sociology, asst. dir. Urban Studies Inst., 1968-70; probation officer, 1954-59; supr. domestic relations div. Supreme Ct. Balt., 1957-63; exec. dir. Md. Commn. on Interracial Problems and Relations, 1963-65; exec. dir. Community Action Agy., Balt., 1965-68; mem. 92d-96th Congresses from 7th Md. dist.; mem. banking, fin. and urban affairs com., small bus. com., joint econ. com.; chmn. Congl. Black Caucus. Served to 1st lt., inf., AUS, 1943-46. Decorated Purple Heart. Mem. NAACP (life), Nat. Assn. Community Devels., Alpha Kappa Phi. Author: Profile of the Domestic Relations Offender, 1958; (with R.G. Murdy) Signal Four-Family Trouble, 1960. Home: 1805 Madison Ave Baltimore MD 21217 Office: 414 Cannon House Office Bldg Washington DC 20515

MITCHELL, RALPH, microbiologist; b. Dublin, Ireland, Nov. 26, 1934; s. Samuel and Sara (Miller) M.; came to U.S., 1956; B.A., Trinity Coll., Dublin, 1956; M.S., Cornell U., 1959, Ph.D., 1961; M.A. (hon.), Harvard U., 1971; m. Muriel Harris, 1957; children—Susan, Tricia, Dara. Sr. scientist Weizmann Inst. Sci., Rehovot, Israel, 1962-65; asst. prof. applied biology, div. engring. and applied physics Harvard U., 1966-69, asso. prof., 1969-70, Gordon McKay prof. applied biology, div. applied scis., 1970—. Mem. AAAS, Am. Soc. Microbiology, Internat. Water Pollution Control Fedn. Editor: Water Pollution Microbiology, vol. 1, 1971, vol. 2, 1978; author: Introduction to Environmental Microbiology, 1974; editor-in-chief Microbial Ecology, 1976—. Office: Div Applied Sci Harvard U Pierce Hall Cambridge MA 02138

MITCHELL, RICHARD FRANK, dept. store exec.; b. Columbus, Ga., Sept. 22, 1931; s. Harry Frank and Esther (Davis) M.; B.S., Auburn U., 1955; grad. exec. program U. Va., 1968; m. Iris Faye Tarvin, Aug. 7, 1955; children—Alison, Bradley. Chief accountant Vulcan Materials Co., Birmingham, Ala., 1958-62, treas., 1965-70; gen. accounting mgr. Bigelow-Sanford Inc., Greenville, S.C., 1962-63; asst. controller Blount Bros. Corp., Montgomery, Ala., 1963-65; exec. v.p. Waddell & Reed, Kansas City, Mo., 1970-74; v.p. fin., treas. Rich's, Inc., Atlanta, 1974—, Zale Corp., 1976—. Past mem. fund raising com. Pembroke County Day Sch., Kansas City, Mo. Mem. bus. advisory council So. Meth. U. Served with AUS, 1957. Mem. Fin. Execs. Inst. (sec. Birmingham 1969, past dir. Kansas City chpt., program chmn.), Nat. Assn. Accountants (v.p. Birmingham 1970), Birmingham, Kansas City chambers commerce. Presbyterian. Clubs: Cherokee, Commerce (Atlanta). Office: Zale Corp 3000 Diamond Park Dr Dallas TX 75247

MITCHELL, RICHARD SCOTT, educator; b. Longmont, Colo., Jan. 28, 1929; s. Clarence Floyd and Margaret May (Hartman) M.; student Scottsbluff Jr. Coll., 1946-47, U. Nebr., 1947-48; B.S., U. Mich., 1950, M.S., 1951, Ph.D., 1956. Mem. faculty U. Va., Charlottesville, 1953—, acting chmn. dept. geology, 1964-69, prof. environ. scis., 1969—. Sesquicentennial asso. U. Ill., 1973. Fellow Geol. Soc. Am., Mineral. Soc. Am.; mem. Am. Crystallographic Assn., AAAS, Clay Minerals Soc., Mineral Assn. Can., Sigma Xi, Sigma Gamma Epsilon. Author: Mineral Names: What Do They Mean? Contbr. articles to profl. jours.; exec. editor Rocks and Minerals Mag. Home: 712 Nelson Dr Charlottesville VA 22901 Office: Clark Hall U Va Charlottesville VA 22903

MITCHELL, ROBERT ARTHUR, univ. pres.; b. N.Y.C., Jan. 19, 1926; s. George P. and Vera A. (Duffy) M.; A.B., Woodstock Coll., 1949, Ph.L., 1950; S.T.L., Facultes S.J. de Louvain (Belgium), 1957; Th.D., U. Strasbourg (France), 1965. Joined S.J., Roman Catholic Ch., 1943, ordained priest, 1956; instr. in philosophy LeMoyne Coll., 1950-53, asst. prof. theology, 1958-59, acad. dean, 1959-63, asso. prof. theology, acad. dean, 1965-66; pres. Loyola Coll., Shrub Oak, 1966; provincial N.Y. State Province, S.J., 1966-72; pres. Jesuit Conf., chmn. Am. Jesuit Provincials, Washington, 1972-76; dir. Woodstock Theol. Center, 1976-79; pres. U. Detroit, 1979—. Bd. dirs. Georgetown U., New Detroit, Inc.; trustee Boston Coll., LeMoyne Coll. Clubs: Econ. of Detroit (dir.), Detroit Athletic.

MITCHELL, ROBERT DALE, cons. engr.; b. Worthington, Minn., Aug. 2, 1910; s. Karl V. and Margaret Dumont (Steigleder) M.; B.S., S.D. State U., 1932; S.M. (grad. fellow), Harvard U., 1939; m. Carol Sherman Northrop, June 17, 1939; children—Constance Remington, Robert Brown. Engr., J. Emberg, Madison, S.D., 1932-35; instr. S.D. State U., 1935-37; engr. Malcolm Pirnie, N.Y.C., 1939-42, project engr., partner, 1945-70, sr. v.p., sec., chief engr., 1970-75, cons., 1975—. Served to maj. San. Corps, AUS, 1942-45. Recipient Distinguished Engr. award S.D. State U., 1977. Mem. ASCE, Am. Acad. Environ. Engrs. (diplomate), Am. Cons. Engrs. Council, New Eng. Water Works Assn. (Commemorative award 1963). Home: 487 Brackett Rd Rye NH 03870 Office: 2 Corporate Park Dr White Plains NY 10602

MITCHELL, ROBERT EDWARD, educator; b. Detroit, May 16, 1930; s. Arthur and Elizabeth (Wayne) M.; B.A. in Oriental Civilization, U. Mich., 1952; M.A., Harvard, 1955; Ph.D. in Sociology, Columbia, 1962; m. Sylvia Ann Sheppard, Aug. 26, 1950; children—Anthony Edward, Maude Wayne, Adam Arthur. Instr., project dir. Bur. Applied Social Research Columbia, 1956-62; coordinator internat. research program, research asso. Survey Research Center U. Cal. at Berkeley, 1962-66; dir. Hong Kong Urban Family Life Survey, dir. Social Survey Research Centre, Chinese U., Hong Kong, 1966-69; prof. urban and regional planning, dir. Survey Data Center Fla. State U., Tallahassee, 1969-78; behavioral sci. adv. urban devel. Nr. East Bur., Office Tech. Support, AID, Dept. State, Washington, 1978—; exec. dir. Fla. Gov.'s Task Force on Housing and Community Devel., 1971-73; mem. UN Ad Hoc Meeting Experts on Social Aspects of Housing in Urban Areas, 1970; mem. tech. mission to Jordan, Dept. State, 1973; cons. in field. Mem. Am. Sociol. Assn., Nat. Council Family Relations. Author: The Needs of Hong Kong Manufacturing Industry for Higher Level Manpower, 1968; Levels of Emotional Strain in Southeast Asian Cities: A Study of Individual Responses to the Stresses of Urbanization and Industrialization; Family Life in Urban Hong Kong, 1972; Pupil, Parent and School, 1972; Housing, Urban Growth, and Economic Development, 1972. Contbr. articles to profl. jours. Address: NE/TECH/SA AID Washington DC 20523

MITCHELL, ROBERT WATSON, publisher; b. Randolph, Vt., Oct. 11, 1910; s. Robert J. and Stella (Watson) M.; A.B., Dartmouth, 1932; postgrad. London Sch. Econs., 1933; m. Rita C. Morrissey, Mar. 15, 1935 (dec. Aug. 1945); children—Margaret (Mrs. William B. Mather, Jr.), Robert John; m. 2d, Virginia Wright Buckingham, Nov. 27, 1946; children—Thomas S., Mary R. Editor-pub., pres. Rutland (Vt.) Herald, 1942—; pres. Barre-Montpelier Times-Argus, 1964—; past pres. Rutland Indsl. Devel. Corp.; v.p. H-R Devel. Corp. Mem. Sigma Delta Chi. Club: Nat. Press. Home: 58 Temple St Rutland VT 05701 Office: 27 Wales St Rutland VT 05701

MITCHELL, ROGER LOWRY, educator; b. Grinnell, Iowa, Sept. 13, 1932; s. Robert T. and Cecil (Lowry) M.; B.S. in Agronomy, Iowa State Coll., 1954; M.S., Cornell U., 1958; Ph.D. in Crop Physiology, Iowa State U., 1961; m. Joyce Elaine Lindgren, June 26, 1955; children—Laura, Susan, Sarah, Martha. Mem. faculty Iowa State U., 1959-69, prof. agronomy, 1967-69, prof. charge farm operation curriculum, 1962-66; prof. agronomy, chmn. dept. U. Mo. at Columbia, 1969-72, dean extension, 1972-75: v.p. agr. Kans. State U., Manhattan, 1975—; exec. bd. div. agr. Nat. Assn. State Univs. and Land Grant Colls. Served to 2d lt. USAAF, 1954-56. Danforth fellow, 1956-61. Acad. Adminstrn. fellow Am. Council Edn., 1966-67. Fellow Am. Soc. Agronomy (pres. 1979-80), AAAS; mem. Crop Sci. Soc. (pres. 1976), Soil Sci. Soc. Am., Council Agrl. Sci. and Tech., Sigma Xi, Gamma Sigma Delta, Alpha Zeta, Phi Kappa Phi. Author: Crop Growth and Culture, 1970. Home: 2008 Arthur Dr Manhattan KS 66502

MITCHELL, ROSCOE EDWARD, musician, composer; b. Chgo., Aug. 3, 1940; s. Roscoe Edward and Ida (Carter) M.; ed. Wilson Jr. Coll., 1961-63; married; children—Lisa Jackson, Atala Nicole. Mem. Englewood High Sch. Dance Band, Chgo., 1954-58; prin. Roscoe Mitchell Sextet, 1965-66, Roscoe Mitchell Quartet, 1966-67, Roscoe Mitchell Art Ensemble, 1967-69; multi-instrumentalist, composer Art Solo and Ensemble Chgo., 1969—; tchr. in field; artist-in-residence U. Ill., 1977; Creative Music Studio, Woodstock, N.Y., 1979. Served with Band, U.S. Army, 1958-61. NEA composer/performer grantee, 1973, composition fellowship grantee, 1975. Mem. Assn. Advancement Creative Musicians, Creative Arts Collective (founder, pres.). Recs. include: People in Sorrow, 1970 (French Prix de l'Academie du Jazz 1970); NONAAH, 1978 (Downbeat Mag. Record of Yr. award 1978). Home: Cambridge WI 53523 Office: 5322 S Drexel St Chicago IL 60615

MITCHELL, TERENCE EDWARD, metallurgist, materials scientist; b. Haywards Heath, Sussex, Eng., May 18, 1937; s. Thomas Frank and Dorothy Elizabeth (Perrin) M.; came to U.S., 1963, naturalized, 1978; B.A. (Coll. Open scholar), St. Cathararine's Coll., Cambridge (Eng.) U., 1958, M.A., 1962, Ph.D. in Physics, 1962; m. Marion Wyatt, Dec. 5, 1959; children—Robin Norman, Jeremy Neil. Research fellow Cavendish Lab., Cambridge, 1962-63; asst. prof. metallurgy Case Inst. Tech., 1963-66; asso. prof. Case Western Res. U., 1966-75, prof., 1975—, dir. high voltage electron microscopy facility, 1970—; vis. scientist NASA at Ames Lab., Stanford U. and Electric Power Research Inst., Palo Alto, Calif., 1975-76; cons. in field. Pres., Cleve. Ethical Soc., 1970-72; bd. dirs. Am. Ethical Union, 1972-74. Electric Power Research Inst. fellow, 1975-76; NSF grantee, 1966—; Dept. Energy grantee, 1970—; NIH grantee, 1969-72; NASA grantee, 1974-77; USAF Office Sci. Research grantee, 1974—; U.S. Army Research Office grantee, 1970-75. Mem. Metall. Soc., Am. Ceramics Soc., ASTM, Electron Microscopy Soc. Am., Metals Soc. (U.K.). Contbr. numerous articles, revs. on metallurgy, ceramics, radiation damage, electron microscopy and others to profl. jours. Home: 3311 Avalon Rd Shaker Heights OH 44120 Office: Dept Metallurgy Case Western Res U Cleveland OH 44106

MITCHELL, ULYSS STANFORD, clergyman, sociologist: b. Marshfield, Mo., July 2, 1902; s. Robert Campbell and May (Edwards) M.; A.B., U. So. Calif., 1931, A.M., research student U. Philippines, 1931-32; Th.B., Central Bapt. Theol. Sem., Kansas City, Mo., 1928, B.D., 1931, Th.D. summa cum laude, 1934; Am. Research student in Orient; m. Viola Elizabeth Westlund, Sept. 16, 1924; children—Robert Louis, Marcia Ann, Ellen May. Dir. youth work White Temple, San Diego, 1929-31; pastor Atherton Bapt. Ch., Los Angeles, 1932-34, First Bapt. Ch. (City Temple), Sioux Falls, S.D., 1934-36; dir. adult and social edn. divs. Am. Bapt. Publ. Soc., Am. Bapt. Conv., Phila., 1936-43; nat. v.p. and Western exec. dir. NCCJ, Inc., 1943-47; Western exec. sec. Ch. World Service, Inc., 1947-48; pres. U.S. Mitchell Assos., Inc., Found. for Humanity, 1963—; mem. U.S. del. founding UN, 1945; del. World Conf. Freedom, Justice, and Responsibility, 1946. Pres. Sierra Vista Properties, Highlands Don Pedro, Inc. Past bd. dirs. No. Cal. Council Chs.; past mem. gen. council Am. Bapt. Conv., mem. ministers council, former chmn. social service com., chmn. world affairs com.; founder Council on Christian Social Progress; active Nat. Council Chs. of Christ in Am.; chmn. com. indsl. relations, coops., past mem. com. Am. home; leader, lectr. world affairs, human relations; lectr. for U.S. Army Office Information and Edn., USA, Alaska and Aleutian Islands, World War II; past chmn. edn. com. UNESCO: exec. chaplain counselor Heart Warmers visitation agy., 1972—. Recipient 1st awards, Collegiate International Forensics, Honolulu, Tokyo, 1931; Wisdom award of honor, 1970. Mem. Fedn. Am. Scientists, Am. Polit. Sci. Assn., Am. Sociol. Assn., Acad. Polit. Sci., Am. Assn. for UN, United World Federalists, Phi Chi Phi, Delta Sigma Rho, Pi Kappa Delta. Kiwanian. Club: Commonwealth (San Francisco). Author: Objectives of Religious Education; History Missions in China; Manchurian Situation; contbr. publs. Home: 550 Ventura Ave San Mateo CA 94403. *My efforts have been consistently to work for the removal of underlying causes that make for misunderstanding and war among the nations, and to set forth goals of brotherhood and peace. My life is "people" centered.*

MITCHELL, VIRGIL ALLEN, clergyman; b. Six Mile, S.C., Apr. 21, 1914; s. E.A. and Mozelle (Davis) M.; Th.B., Central (S.C.) Wesleyan Coll., 1943; postgrad. High Point (N.C.) Coll., 1946; D.D., Houghton Coll., 1964; m. Mary Parks, Mar. 24, 1937; children—Walter Allen, Marilyn (Mrs. Alton C. Hollingsworth), Martha Theresa (Mrs. James Funnell). Ordained to ministry Wesleyan Methodist Ch., 1939; pastor in Walhalla, S.C., 1937-39, Westminster, S.C., 1937- 40, Oakway, S.C., 1939-40, Cateeche and Central, S.C., 1940-46, Glenwood, S.C., 1946-49; tchr. Bible, Central Wesleyan Meth. Coll., 1943-44, 46-48; pres. S.C. conf. Wesleyan Meth. Ch., 1949-57; nat. asst. sec. home missions and ch. extension and evangelism Wesleyan Meth. Ch., 1957-59, nat. sec. ch. extension and evangelism, 1959-63; gen. supt. Wesleyan Meth. Ch. Am., 1963-68; gen. supt. Wesleyan Ch. (merger Wesleyan Methodist and Pilgrim Holiness Chs.), 1968—. Ofcl. visitor 9th World Meth. Conf., 1956; mem. S.C. Bd. Christian Action, 1949-57, S.C. Wesleyan Youth Soc., 1943-45, 47-49; pres. So. Area Youth, 1945-47; mem. World Meth. Council, 1968—, Meth. Council, 1971—; mem. 13th Meth. Conf., Dublin, Ireland, 1976. Bd. dirs. Central Wesleyan Coll., 1950-57, vice chmn., 1954-57. Mem. Nat. Assn. Evangelicals, Nat. Holiness Assn. (bd. dirs.). Home: 3921 S Landess St Marion IN 46952 Office: Box 2000 Marion IN 46952

MITCHELL, WILLIAM HAMILTON, stock broker; b. Chgo., Jan. 31, 1895; s. John J. and Mary Louise (Jewett) M.; student Harvard; m. Ginevra Fuller King, Sept. 24, 1918; m. 2d, Mrs. Anne Wood Tullis, Jan. 1, 1942. Mem. firm Paine, Webber, Mitchell, Hutchins, Inc., stock brokers, 1919—, now hon. chmn.; past dir. Texaco, Inc., Continental Ill. Nat. Bank & Trust Co. of Chgo. Bd. dirs. Field Mus. Natural History, Northwestern Meml. Hosp. Clubs: Chicago, Racquet, Saddle and Cycle, Casino, Shoreacres (Chgo.); Onwentsia (Lake Forest); Harvard (N.Y.C.). Home: 901 Rosemary Rd E Lake Forest IL 60045 Office: 2 1st Nat Plaza Chicago IL 60603

MITCHELL, WILLIAM LEROY, design cons.; b. Cleve., July 2, 1912; s. Guy S. and Hazel R. (Mann) M.; student Carnegie Inst. Tech., 1930, Art Student's League, N.Y., 1931-32; m. Marian Crocker, Sept. 14, 1963; children—Nancy Lynne, Wendelin L., Penelope. Comml. illustrator Barron G. Collier, 1931-35; With Gen. Motors Corp., 1935—, successively auto designer, chief auto designer, chief designer Cadillac, 1935-58, v.p. in charge design, 1958-77, also dir.; ret., 1977; pres., owner William L. Mitchell, design cons., Rochester, Mich., 1977—; v.p., dir. design Harley Earl Assos., 1949-53. Served from lt. (j.g.) to lt., USNR, 1942-45. Clubs: Bloomfield Hills (Mich.) Country; Lyford Cay (Nassau); Lost Tree (Palm Beach, Fla.). Home: 760 Kennebec Ct Bloomfield Hills MI 48013 also 11167 Beach Club Point Lost Tree Village North Palm Beach FL 33408 Office: 1858 Star-Batt Dr Rochester MI 48063

MITCHELL, WILLIAM S., food store chain exec.; b. 1914; B.A., U. Calif., 1935; m. With Safeway Stores, Inc., Oakland, Calif., 1936—. controller, 1953-56, v.p., 1956-66, exec. v.p., 1966-71, pres., 1971—, chief exec. officer, 1974—, now chmn. bd., chmn. exec. com. C.P.A. Office: Safeway Stores Inc 201 4th St Oakland CA 94660*

MITCHELL, WYLIE WHITFIELD, city ofcl., engring. soc. ofcl.; b. Lithonia, Ga., Oct. 18, 1912; s. Henry Whitfield and Sarah Celia (Smith) M.; grad. pub. high sch.; m. Iva Jean Roberts, June 12, 1937; children—Wylene (Mrs. Robert Lamar Whiting), Cheryl, Beverly (Mrs. Victor Jordan Bowers). Self employed, 1940-46; gen. supt. Whitehead Plumbing Co., Atlanta, 1946-50; chief plumbing insp. City of Atlanta, 1950—; cons. plumbing and air conditioning engr.; plumbing-heating code cons.; instr. code enforcements apprenticeship tng. programs U. Ga. Mem. Nat. Hosp. Standards Com., 1969—; mem. Ga. Examining Bd. Plumbers, 1970—. Recipient Phoenix award City of Atlanta, 1964, Georgian award Ga. Plumbing Inspectors, 1967. Registered profl. engr., Ga. Mem. Am. Soc. San. Engrs. (internat. pres. 1972-74; Henry B. Davis award 1970), Bldg. Ofcls. Am. Internat. (chmn. plumbing code 1968—; Walker S. Lee award 1973, exec. com. 1974), Ga. Plumbing Inspectors Assn. (founder 1964, pres. 1964-66, dir. 1966—). Mason. Home: 2081 Rainbow Dr Snellville GA 30278 Office: 902 City Hall Atlanta GA 30303

MITCHELL-BATEMAN, MILDRED, psychiatrist, state ofcl.; b. Cordele, Ga., Mar. 22, 1922; d. S.Q. and Ella (McLeod) Mitchell; student Barber-Scotia Co.; B.S., Johnson C. Smith U., 1941; M.D., Woman's Med. Coll. Pa., 1946; m. William L. Bateman, Dec. 25, 1947. Intern Harlem Hosp., N.Y.C., 1946-47; resident Menninger Sch. Psychiatry, Topeka, 1952-55; clin. dir., supt. Lakin (W.Va.) State Hosp., 1958-60; supr. profl. services W.Va. Dept. Mental Health, Charleston, 1960-62, acting dir. dept., 1962, dir., 1962-77; prof., chmn. dept. psychiatry Marshall U. Sch. Medicine, 1977—. Former mem. Def. Adv. Com. Women in Services; former med. adv. com. Vocat. Rehab. Adminstrn., HEW. Bd. dirs. Nat. Assn. Mental Health; trustee Menninger Found., Barber Scotia Coll. Mem. Am. Psychiat. Assn., AMA, W.Va. Med. Assn., Cabell County Med. Soc., Am. Coll. Psychiatry, Inst. Medicine of Nat. Acad. Scis., Group for Advancement of Psychiatry. Presbyterian. Office: Marshall U Sch Medicine and Health Scis Huntington WV 25701

MITCHELSON, MARVIN M(ORRIS), lawyer; b. Detroit, May 7, 1928; s. Herbert and Sonia M.; B.A., UCLA, 1953; J.D., Southwestern U., 1956; m. Marcella Ferri, Dec. 19, 1961; 1 son, Morgan. Admitted to Calif. bar, 1957, U.S. Supreme Ct., 1962; individual practice law, Beverly Hills, Calif., 1957-67, Century City, Calif., 1967—, Los Angeles, 1973—; numerous appearances as expert in family law on nat. TV, at bar assns. and law schs. Bd. dirs. Los Angeles Music Center Opera Assn. Served with USN, 1946-47. Mem. Am. Bar Assn., Am. Trial Lawyers Assn., Century City Bar Assn., Trial Lawyers Am., Calif. Trial Lawyers. Jewish. Club: Optimists (past pres. Hollywood club). Author: Made In Heaven, Settled in Court, 1976; The Marvin Handbook, 1980. Office: 1801 Century Park E Los Angeles CA 90067

MITCHUM, ROBERT (CHARLES), actor; b. Bridgeport, Conn., Aug. 6, 1917; ed. N.Y.C. pub. schs.; m. Dorothy Spencer, Mar. 16, 1940; children—Jim, Petrine, Chris. Motion picture debut in Hopalong Cassidy film, 1944; producer, actor Thunder Road; motion pictures include River of No Return, Track of Cat, Not as a Stranger, Night of the Hunter, Man with Gun, The Longest Day, Two for the Seesaw, Bandido, Heaven Knows Mr. Allison, Wonderful Country, Home From the Hill, Sundowners, Cape Fear, Man in The Middle, El Dorado, The Way West, Five Card Stud, Anzio, Secret Ceremony, Young, Billy Young, The Good Guys and The Bad Guys, Ryan's Daughter, The Friends of Eddie Coyle, Yakuza, Farewell My Lovely, Midway, The Last Tycoon, The Big Sleep, Breakthrough.

MITFORD, JESSICA, author; b. Batsford Mansion, Eng., Sept. 11, 1917; d. Lord and Lady Redesdale; m. Esmond Romilly, June 1937; 1 dau., Constancia; m. 2d, Robert Treuhaft, June 21, 1943; 1 son, Benjamin. Author: (autobiography) Daughters and Rebels, 1960; The American Way of Death, 1963; The Trial of Dr. Spock, 1969; Kind and Usual Punishment-The Prison Business, 1973; A Fine Old Conflict, 1977. Address: care Random House Inc 201 E 50th St New York NY 10022*

MITGANG, HERBERT, author, journalist; b. N.Y.C., Jan. 20, 1920; s. Benjamin and Florence (Altman) M.; LL.B., St. John's Law Sch., 1942; m. Shirley Kravchick, May 13, 1945; children—Esther, Lee, Laura. Sports stringer Bklyn. Eagle, 1938-39; admitted to N.Y. bar, 1942; screen writer Universal-Internat. Pictures, 1945; copy editor, reviewer N.Y. Times, N.Y.C., 1945-54, supervising editor Sunday Times drama sect., 1955-62, editorial writer, mem. editorial bd. N.Y. Times, 1963-64, 67-76, publishing corr., 1976—; asst. to pres., exec. editor CBS News, 1964-67; writer, producer film documentaries including Henry Moore: Man of Form, D-Day Plus 20 Years, Sandburg's Prairie Years, Anthony Eden on Vietnam; instr. English evening div. Coll. City N.Y., 1948-49; vis. lectr. English, guest fellow Silliman Coll., Yale, 1975-76. Mem. exec. bd. Newspaper Guild of N.Y., CIO, 1948-49. Served with counter-intelligence sect. 5th wing, USAAF, 1942-43; MTO; Army corr., mng. editor Stars and Stripes, Oran-Casablanca and Sicily edits., 1943-45. Decorated six battle stars. Fellow Soc. Am. Historians; mem. Authors League (council 1962—, pres. fund 1976—), Authors Guild (pres. 1971-75), Internat. P.E.N. (U.S. del. London). Jewish. Club: Century Assn. (N.Y.C.). Author: Lincoln as They Saw Him, 1956; (novel) The Return, 1959; The Man Who Rode the Tiger: The Life and Times of Judge Samuel Seabury (Gavel award Am. Bar Assn.), 1963; Working for the Reader, 1970; (novel) Get These Men Out of the Hot Sun, 1972; The Fiery Trial: A Life of Lincoln, 1974. Editor: Washington, D.C., in Lincoln's Time, 1958; Civilians Under Arms: Stars and Stripes, Civil War to Korea, 1959; The Letters of Carl Sandburg, 1968; America at Random, 1969; Spectator of America, 1971; Abraham Lincoln: A Press Portrait, 1971; The World of Abraham Lincoln (play), 1979. Contbr. to Am. Heritage, Atlantic, Harper's, The Nation, The Observer, The New Republic, Commonweal, Art News. Office: NY Times 229 W 43d St New York NY 10036

MITHOEFER, JOHN CALDWELL, physician, educator; b. Cin., Feb. 12, 1920; s. William and Florence (Shanks) M.; A.B., Brown U., 1941; M.D., Harvard, 1944; m. Olivia Procter McCullough, June 20, 1942 (div.); children—Michael C., C. Keith, Olivia Procter; m. 2d, Mary Whitaker Hager, 1972. Rotating intern Cin. Gen. Hosp., 1944-45, asst. resident medicine, 1945-46, fellow Cardiac Lab., 1947-49; research fellow Mary Imogene Bassett Hosp., Columbia, 1949-52, asso. physician 1957-68, dir. cardiopulmonary lab., 1952-68; research asso. physiology Faculte de Medecine, Paris, 1954; vis. colleague cardiology Hammersmith Hosp., London, 1963: asst. clin. prof. medicine Columbia Coll. Phys. and Surgeons, 1963-68; prof. medicine, chief cardiopulmonary div. Dartmouth Med. Sch., 1968-72; prof. medicine, dir. pulmonary div. Med. U. S.C., 1972—. Bd. dirs. Otsego County Heart Assn; 1959-61, 65-67, pres., 1961; mem. research com. N.Y. State Heart Assn., 1964-66; mem. research com. N.Y. State Tb and Respiratory Diseases Assn., 1965-68; mem. program com., council cardiology Am. Heart Assn., 1968-69; mem. sci. program com. Am. Coll. Chest Physicians, 1973; chmn. Nat. Heart and Lung Inst. Com. Nat. Research and Demonstration Centers, 1973-75; mem. S.C. Health Care Adv. Bd., 1973-78; mem. program com. Cardiopulmonary Council Am. Heart Assn., 1975. Served with M.C., AUS, 1946-47. Fellow Am. Coll. Cardiology (gov. 1970-72), Am. Coll. Chest Physicians (gov. 1971-72, 76—); mem. Am. Soc. Clin. Investigation, Am. Physiol. Soc., Am. Thoracic Soc., So. Soc. Clin. Investigation, Assn. U. Cardiologists, Am. Heart Assn. (fellow council clin. cardiology). Author articles in field. Office: Med Univ South Carolina 171 Ashley Ave Charleston SC 29403

MITHUN, RAYMOND O., advt. exec., banker, real estate and ins. exec.; b. Warren, Minn., Mar. 20, 1909; s. Louis and Alma (Anderson) M.; A.B., U. Minn., 1930; m. Doris Berg, Aug. 9, 1932; children—Lewis, John, Raymond, Jr. From printers devil to editor Buffalo Jour., 1922. bus. mgr., 1924; editor Minn. Daily, 1929; pub. Wright Co. Press, 1929-30; city editor Mankato (Minn.) Free Press, 1930; copywriter, radio dir., account exec. Batten, Barton, Durstine & Osborn, Inc., 1930-32; founder, chmn. Campbell-Mithun, Inc., Mpls., 1933; chmn. Mithun Enterprises; owner Wayzata Bank & Trust Co., Wayzata Ins. Co., Wayzata Real Estate, Crystal State Bank (Minn.). Mem. Delta Upsilon, Sigma Delta Chi (Journalism award 1930). Clubs: Minneapolis, Minikahda (Mpls.); Tavern (Chgo.); Minnesota (St. Paul); El Dorado, Thunderbird (Palm Desert). Home: 3630 Northome Rd Wayzata MN 55391 Office: 1000 Cargill Bldg Minneapolis MN 55402

MITNICK, SAMUEL ALEXANDER, editor; b. N.Y.C., Aug. 15, 1944; s. Lewis and Esther (Hurowitz) M.; B.A. (N.Y. State Regents scholar), Coll. City N.Y., 1966; Ph.D. (NDEA fellow), U. Wash., 1969. Acquisitions dir. Johnson Reprint Corp., N.Y.C., 1970-73; v.p., cons. micropub. projects Photomatic Microfilm, N.Y.C., 1973; editor-in-chief Da Capo Press, N.Y.C., 1973-75; editor-in-chief Delta/Laurel Paperbacks, Dell Pub., N.Y.C., 1975-77; editor-in-chief Harvest Paperbacks, Harcourt, Brace, Jovanovich, Inc., 1977-78; editorial dir. Paragon Books, G.P. Putnam's Sons, N.Y.C., 1978—; lectr. U. Wash., 1968, 69; free-lance cons. non-fiction and fiction manuscripts. Home: 455 W 34th St New York NY 10001 Office: 200 Madison Ave New York NY 10016. *Personal and professional success is a matter of mental discipline: one must learn to engage an emotion or desire and temper it with the detachment of humor and reason.*

MITOVICH, JOHN, assn. exec.; b. Youngstown, Ohio, Feb. 8, 1927; s. John and Xanthe (Elieff) M.; B.S. in Journalism, Ohio U., 1951; m. Rebecca E. Webb, Aug. 1, 1953; children—Jon, Rosemary, Victoria, Janet, Martha, Matthew. Advt. and pub. relations specialist Gen. Electric Co., Schenectady, 1955-57, Pittsfield, Mass., 1957-58, pub. affairs specialist, Lynn, Mass., 1958-62, mgr. community relations, Johnson City, N.Y., 1962-64, cons. community and govt. relations, N.Y.C., 1964-66; exec. v.p. Rockford (Ill.) C. of C., 1966-70; exec. pres., pres. Southwestern Area (Conn.) Assn. Commerce and Industry, 1970—. Mem. bd. selectmen North Reading, Mass., 1961-62, chmn. indsl. devel. commn., 1960-62; mem. Rockford Mayor's Urban Devel. Adv. Commn., 1966-68, Ill. Gov. Commn. on Urban Area Govt., 1969-70; founder-dir. Winnebago County (Ill.) Opportunities Industrialization Center, 1968-70, Met. Rockford Housing Devel. Corp., Forward Rockford, Inc., 1969-70; mem. Gov.'s Commn. Services and Expenditures, 1971. Served with USMC, 1952-54. Recipient Gen. Electric Mgmt. award, 1958, Asso. Industries Mass. award, 1958, Freedoms Found. distinguished service award, 1965, Rockford Community Leadership award, 1970, Distinguished Salesman's award Southwestern Conn. Sales and Mktg. Exec., 1974; Dwight B. Havens acad. Scholar Acad. Orgn. Mgmt., 1976. Mem. Conn. Assn. C. of C. Execs. (v.p. 1979). Republican. Methodist. Home: 1992 Shippan Ave Stamford CT 06902 Office: 1 Landmark Sq Stamford CT 06901. *A good man isn't good for everything. Knowing this is the best guide to the best application of one's self toward the pursuit of one's goals in life.*

MITROS, JOHN D., railroad exec.; b. N.Y.C., June 5, 1924; s. James and Xanthe (Poulangos) M.; grad. U. Chgo., 1950, U. Mich., 1970; m. Mary Von Brown, Nov. 4, 1954; children—Nancy E., James C., Jeanne V., Gregory J. Western editor Railway Age, 1960-67; asst. to pres. Ill. Central R.R., 1967-72; asst. v.p. Ill. Central Gulf R.R., 1972-74; staff v.p. Chgo. Rock Island and Pacific R.R., Chgo., 1974-78, exec. v.p., 1979—; dir. Ill. Terminal R.R. Co., Terminal Railway Assn. St. Louis; vice chmn. Council for Sound Waterway Policies, 1972—. Served with USAAF, 1942-46; PTO. Mem. Transp. Research Forum, Sierra Club, Public Relations Assn. Am. Democrat. Greek Orthodox. Clubs: Chgo. Athletic, Flossmoor Country, Cliffdwellers, Nat. Press, Western Ry. Office: 332 S Michigan Ave Chicago IL 60604

MITSEFF, CARL, lawyer; b. Detroit, Nov. 16, 1928; s. Frank H. and Katherine (Schaffer) M.; B.S., Wayne State U., 1952, LL.B., 1955; m. Phyllis Schlitters, June 28, 1952; children—C. Randall, Bradley Scott, Julie, Emily, Faye. Admitted to Mich. bar, 1956, since practiced in Detroit; staff atty. Burroughs Corp., Detroit, 1955-60; mem. firm LeVasseur, Mitseff, Egan & Capp, Detroit, 1960—; lectr. in field. Mem. State Bar Mich., Am. Bar Assn., Internat. Assn. Ins. Counsel, Pi Kappa Alpha, Delta Theta Phi. Clubs: Detroit Athletic, Lochmoor. Home: 612 N Brys Dr Grosse Pointe Woods MI 48236 Office: 2900 David Stott Bldg Detroit MI 48226

MITTELMAN, NORMAN, opera singer; b. Winnipeg, Man., Can., May 25, 1932; student Curtis Inst. Music, Phila., Music Acad. West, Santa Barbara, Calif.; m. Brenda, 5 children. Debut with Can. Opera Co. in La Boheme, 1958; appeared with major opera cos., N.Am., S.Am. and Europe, including Lyric Opera Chgo., San Francisco Opera, Met. Opera, N.Y.C., London Royal Opera, L'Opera de Que.; also recitals, performances with symphonies. Recipient Singing Stars award, Can.; Fisher award Met. Opera Nat. Council Auditions; Rockefeller Found. grantee.

MITTELSTADT, CHARLES ANTHONY, advt. exec.; b. Eau Claire, Wis., Mar. 19, 1918; s. Frederick William and Pearl (White) M.; B.S., U. Wis., 1942, postgrad., 1945-47; grad. Advanced Mgmt. Program, Harvard, 1960; m. Angelica Farber, Feb. 20, 1957; children—Nancy Lee, Charles Anthony II, Monica, Simone. Radio announcer sta. WIBA, Madison, Wis., 1945-47; account exec. Foote, Cone & Belding, Chgo., 1948-52, Campbell-Mithun, Chgo., 1953-54; mktg. dir. Tatham-Laird, Chgo., 1955-56; exec. v.p. McCann-Marschalk, N.Y.C., 1957-64, also dir.; chmn. plans bd., mgr. Inter-pub. Group Cos., Inc., Frankfurt, Germany, 1964-66; pres., chief operating officer Erwin Wasey, Inc., Los Angeles, 1967-69; sr. v.p. Interpub. Group of Cos., Inc., 1969—. Trustee, N.Y. Foundling Hosp., 1979—. Clubs: Wisconsin Alumni, Harvard Alumni, N.Y. Athletic (N.Y.C.); Westchester Country (Rye); Am. Yacht. Home: Griswold Rd Rye NY 10580 Office: 1271 Ave of Americas New York NY 10020

MITTEN, DAVID GORDON, classical archaeologist; b. Youngstown, Ohio, Oct. 26, 1935; s. Joe Atlee and Helen Louise (Boyd) M.; B.A., Oberlin Coll., 1957; M.A. in Classical Archeology (Woodrow Wilson fellow), Harvard U., 1958, Ph.D. in Classical Archaeology, 1962; children by previous marriage—Claudia Antonia Sabina, Eleanor Elizabeth. Instr. dept. fine arts Harvard U., 1962-64, Francis Jones asst. prof. classics, 1964-68, asso. prof., 1968-69, James Loeb prof. classical art and archaeology, 1969—, curator ancient art Fogg Art Museum, 1976—; Fulbright fellow Am. Sch. Classical Studies at Athens, 1959-60; asso. dir. Harvard-Cornell Sardis Expdn., 1976. Archaeol. Inst. Am. Olivia James fellow, 1976-77; John Simon Guggenheim Found. fellow, 1976-77. Mem. Archaeol. Inst. Am., Assn. Field Archaeology (co-founder), Am. Schs. Oriental Research, Brit. Sch. Archaeology (Athens, Greece), Royal Numismatic Soc. Author: (with S. F. Doeringer) Master Bronze from the Classical World, 1967; Classical Bronzes: Museum of Art, Rhode Island School of Design, 1975. Office: Fogg Art Mus Harvard U Cambridge MA 02138

MITTENTHAL, FREEMAN LEE, lawyer; b. Dallas, Dec. 29, 1917; s. Albert Harry and Rae (Goldstein) M.; student U. Tex., 1934-36; LL.B., So. Meth. U., 1940; m. Evelyn Naomi Gates, May 3, 1947; children—Richard Charles, Brian Lee. Admitted to Tex. bar, 1940, U.S. Supreme Ct. and U.S. Ct. Mil. Appeals bars, 1954; practice law, Dallas, 1940-42, 49—; chief enforcement atty. Office Price Adminstrn., Dallas, 1946-47; claims atty. VA, Dallas, 1947-49; dir., gen. counsel Purvin & Gertz Inc. Mem. Tex. Economy Commn., 1950. Mem. state exec. com. Tex. Young Democrats, 1940. Served to maj., USAAF, 1942-46. Mem. State Bar Tex., Dallas (chmn. bicentennial com. 1975), Am., Fed. bar assns. Mason (32 deg., Shriner), Elk. Clubs: Dallas Athletic, Metropolitan. Home: 820 Overglen Dr Dallas TX 75218 Office: 2560 Main Tower Dallas TX 75202

MITTLEMAN, MARVIN HAROLD, educator; b. N.Y.C., Mar. 13, 1928; s. Sol and Jennie (Bookstein) M.; B.S., Poly. Inst. Bklyn., 1949; Ph.D., Mass. Inst. Tech., 1953; m. Sondra Koslow, Aug. 21, 1955; children—Richard, Joshua, Daniel. Instr. Columbia, 1952-55; research physicist U. Calif. at Berkeley, 1955-68; prof. physics City U. N.Y., 1968—, exec. officer Ph.D. program, 1970-74; vis. prof. Cath. U. Louvain (Belgium), 1977, U. Erlangen (W. Ger.), 1979; vis. scientist FOM Lab., Amsterdam, 1978; cons. NASA, Inst. Def. Analyes, U. Calif. Lawrence Radiation Lab. Sandia Corp. Sci. and Indsl. Research fellow University Coll., London, 1962-63. Fellow Am. Phys. Soc. Contbr. articles profl. jours. Home: 74 George St Harrington Park NJ 07640 Office: Physics Dept City College New York New York NY 10031

MIWA, RALPH MAKOTO, ednl. adminstr.; b. Honolulu, Jan. 4, 1925; s. Nobuichi and Fuyu (Hashimoto) M.; B.A., U. Hawaii, 1948, M.A., 1950; Ph.D. (Laucheimer fellow 1951-52), Johns Hopkins, 1953; m. Hilda Odan, June 23, 1951; children—Colin, Lani, Marie. Ford Found. fellow St. Johns Coll., 1953-54, U.S. Govt., 1954-57. Asso. prof. polit. sci. U. Mo., Columbia, 1957-61; legislative asst. to Senator Inouye of Hawaii, Washington, 1963-64, adminstrv. asst., 1964-66; prof. polit. sci. U. Hawaii, 1961—, dean Coll. Continuing Edn. and Community Service, 1968-72; provost Leeward Community Coll., Pearl City, Hawaii, 1972-75; chancellor West Oahu Coll., 1975—. Dir. Bank Honolulu N.A. Commr., Hawaii Edn. Commn., 1970—. Vice chmn. Democratic Party Hawaii, 1968-70; del. Nat. Dem. Conv., 1968. Bd. dirs. Kukui Gardens Corp., Honolulu; trustee Clarence T.C. Ching Found., Honolulu. Served with AUS, 1944-46; PTO. Mem. Phi Beta Kappa, Pi Sigma Alpha. Contbr. profl. jours. Home: 3038 Waipuna Rise Honolulu HI 96822 Office: Newtown Sq 98-1247 Kaahumanu St Aiea Honolulu HI 96701

MIXON, ALAN, actor; b. Miami, Fla., Mar. 15, 1933; s. James E. and Matilda (Beers) M.; student U. Miami, 1951-52. Appeared in premiere prodn. play Sweet Bird of Youth, Miami, 1956, N.Y.C., 1956; appeared in View from the Bridge, Chgo. and San Francisco, 1957, 59, Royal Hunt of the Sun, Broadway and Hollywood, 1966; New York prodns. include Suddenly Last Summer, 1958, Desire Under the Elms, 1963, Trojan Women, 1963-64, The Alchemist, 1964, Sign in Sidney Brustein's Window, 1964-65, The Child Buyer, 1964-65, The Devils, 1965-66, A Whitman Portrait, 1966, Black Comedy, 1966-67, Unknown Soldier and His Wife, 1967, Iphegenia in Aulis, 1967 68, Love Suicide at Schofield Barracks, 1972, Small Craft Warnings, 1972, Mourning Becomes Electra, 1972, Equus, 1974-75, Benito Cereno, 1976; London prodn. Whitman Portrait, 1969; TV appearances include Play of the Week, Kraft Theatre, CBS Workshop, Dragon Country, Edge of Night, Andros Targets, End of Summer, Theatre in America. Served with AUS, 1953-54. Home: 210 W 16th St New York NY 10011

MIXSON, JOHN WAYNE, lt. gov. Fla., cattleman; b. Coffee County, Ala., June 16, 1922; s. Cecil Marion and Mineola (Moseley) M.; student Columbia U., 1944, U. Pa., 1945; B.S. in Bus. Adminstrn., U. Fla., 1947; m. Margie Grace, Dec. 27, 1947. Acct., So. Bell Telephone Co., Jacksonville, 1947-48; farmer, cattleman, Jackson County, Fla., 1948—; dir. orgn. Fla. Farm Bur., Gainesville, 1954-59; dir. field services So. region Am. Farm Bur., 1959-61; mem. Fla. Ho. of Reps., Tallahassee, 1967-78; lt. gov. Fla., 1979—. Served with USNR, 1942-46. Named Legislator of Yr., Fla. Assn. Community Colls., 1975, Man of Yr. in Fla. Agr., Progressive Farmer mag., 1976; recipient awards, many So. agrl. groups. Mem. Fla. Farm Bur., Fla. Cattlemen's Assn. Democrat. Methodist. Club: Rotary. Office: Lt Gov's Office The Capitol Tallahassee FL 32304

MIXTER, DAVID MASON, advt. exec.; b. Boston, Oct. 9, 1922; s. William Jason and Dorothy (Fay) M.; B.A., Yale, 1945; m. Stephanie Leonard, June 1951; children—David Ives (dec.), Valerie Ives (Mrs. Carroll Cavanagh), Peter Jason, Stephen Leonard. Vice pres. Benton & Bowles, Inc., 1946-50, 52-61; sr. v.p. Ted. Bates & Co., Inc., N.Y.C., 1961-70; partner North-Castle Partners, 1971—, now sr. v.p., dir.; dir. Am. Tri-Star, Inc., West Chicago, Ill. Trustee Hosp. for Spl. Surgery, N.Y. Assn. for Blind. Served with USMCR, 1943-46, 50-52. Clubs: Wee Burn Country (Darien); Yale (N.Y.C.); Mid-Ocean (Bermuda). Home: Indian Spring Trail Darien CT 06820 Office: 20 Bridge St Greenwich CT 06820

MIYA, TOM SABURO, pharmacologist, educator; b. Hanford, Calif., Apr. 6, 1923; s. Katsunosuke and Harue (Takeuchi) M.; B.S., U. Nebr., 1947, M.S., 1948; Ph.D., Purdue U., 1952; m. Midori Sakamoto, Aug. 14, 1948; 1 dau., Pamela Anne. Faculty, Purdue U., Lafayette, Ind., 1948-56, 58—, prof. pharmacology, 1958—, head dept. pharmacology and toxicology, 1961—; head dept. pharmacology U. Nebr., 1956-57; dean. prof. Sch. Pharmacy, U. N.C., Chapel Hill, also prof pharmacology Sch. Medicine, 1977—. Mem. rev. com. U.S. Pharmacopeia XVIII, XIX; mem. pharmacology-toxicology program com. Nat. Inst. Gen. Med. Scis., NIH, mem. program rev. com. div. research resources, 1973-77, chmn. chem. and biol. info. handling rev. com., 1975-76; mem. NRC-Nat. Acad. Scis. toxicology info. com., chmn., 1977—. Mem. Am. Assn. Colls. Pharmacy (chmn. sect. tchrs. biol. scis. 1965-66, pres. 1975-76), Am. Pharm. Assn. (Research Achievement award in pharmacodynamics 1964), Am. Soc. Pharmacology and Exptl. Therapeutics, Am. Chem. Soc., Soc. for Exptl. Biology and Medicine (pres. Ohio Valley sect. 1972-74), Soc. Toxicology (mem. council 1975-77, pres. 1979-80), N.Y. Acad. Scis., Acad. Pharm. Scis. (chmn. elect sect. pharmacology and biochemistry 1970), AAAS, Sigma Xi, Rho Chi, Phi Lambda Upsilon, Kappa Psi. Rotarian (dir. 1971-73). Author: (with Holck, Yim, Mennear and Spratto) Laboratory Guide in Pharmacology, 4th edit., 1973. Asso. editor Toxicology and Applied Pharmacology. Contbr. articles profl. jours. Office: Beard Hall U NC Chapel Hill NC 27514

MIYAMOTO, RICHARD ISAMI, justice; b. Pepeekeo, Hawaii, Nov. 25, 1924; s. Kichiemon and Koei (Yukawa) M.; B.A., U. Hawaii, 1967; J.D., Boston U., 1952; m. Filomena Toledo, Nov. 6, 1971; children—Philip Isami, Charmaine Wamar, Teresa Wamar, Matthieu Utaifeau. Admitted to Hawaii bar, 1952, Am. Samoa bar, 1976; dep. county atty. County of Hawaii, 1954-55; dist. magistrate, South Hilo, North Hilo and Puna, 1955-65; U.S. commr., Hawaii, 1956-65; atty. gen. Trust Ter. of Pacific Island, 1971-76; asso. justice High Ct. Am. Samoa, Pago Pago, 1976—, chief justice, 1978—. Served with AUS, 1944-46; to col. U.S. Army Res., 1948—. Mem. Am., Am. Samoa, Hawaii bar assns. Republican. Buddhist. Home: Utulei American Samoa 96799 Office: High Court Pago Pago American Samoa 96799

MIYARES, BENJAMIN DAVID, editor; b. Tampa, Fla., July 23, 1940; s. Benigno and Mary Carolyn (Dominguez) M.; B.A. in Journalism, St. Bonaventure U., Olean, N.Y., 1962; m. Martha Suzanne Urban, May 14, 1966; children—David, Jeffrey, Beth. News dir. radio sta. WSET, Glens Falls, N.Y., 1962-63; with Magazines for Industry, N.Y.C., 1963—, editor Food and Drug Packaging mag., 1968—, editorial dir. company, 1975—, corp. v.p., 1977—; cons. in field. Pres. council Nat. Packaging Week, 1975; editorial com. Am. Bus. Press, 1973-74; mem. industry adv. com. packaging sci. and engring. program Rutgers U. Served with AUS, 1963. Mem. Packaging Inst. (v.p. 1976-78, pres. 1978-79). Home: 87 Bellewood Ave Dobbs Ferry NY 10522 Office: 747 3d Ave New York NY 10017

MIYASAKI, GEORGE JOJI, artist; b. Kalopa, Hawaii, Mar. 24, 1935; s. Uichi Miyasaki; B.F.A., Calif. Coll. Arts and Crafts, 1957, M.F.A., 1958; children—Julie, Farrell, Michael. Asst. prof. art Calif. Coll. Arts and Crafts, Oakland, 1958-64; mem. faculty dept. art U. Calif., Berkeley, 1964—, now asso. prof. John Hay Whitney fellow, 1957-58; Tamarind printing fellow, 1961; Guggenheim fellow, 1963-64. Home: 1721 Beverly Pl Berkeley CA 94707 Office: Univ Calif 238 Kroeber Hall Berkeley CA 94720

MIYASHIRO, AKIHO, geologist; b. Okayama, Japan, Oct. 30, 1920; s. Tsuneshi and Hideyo (Shigemasa) M.; came to U.S., 1967; B.Sc., U. Tokyo, 1943, D.Sc., 1953; children—Yumiko, Keiko. Instr. in geology U. Tokyo, 1946-58, asso. prof. petrology, 1958-67; vis. prof. Lamont-Doherty Geol. Obs., Columbia U., 1967-70; prof. geology SUNY, Albany, 1970—. Recipient Geol. Soc. Japan prize, 1958. Fellow Geol. Soc. Am. (Arthur L. Day medal 1977), Mineral. Soc. Am.; hon. mem. Geol. Soc. London, Geol. Soc. France. Author: Metamorphism and Metamorphic Belts, 1973. Home: 14 Stonehenge Dr Albany NY 12203 Office: Dept Geol Scis SUNY Albany NY 12222

MIZE, JOE HENRY, indsl. engr., educator; b. Colorado City, Tex., June 14, 1934; s. Kelly Marcus and Birtie (Adams) M.; B.S. in Indsl. Engring., Tex. Tech. Coll., 1958; M.S. (Research Found. grantee) in Indsl. Engring., Purdue U., 1963, Ph.D., 1964; m. Betty Bentley, Mar. 16, 1966; 1 dau., Kelly Jean. Indsl. engr. White Sands Missile Range, N.Mex., 1958-61; grad. research asst. Purdue U., Lafayette, Ind., 1961-64; asso. prof. engring. Auburn (Ala.) U., 1964-69, dir. Computer Center, 1965-66; prof. engring. Ariz. State U., Tempe, 1969-72; prof., head Sch. Indsl. Engring. and Mgmt., Okla. State U., Stillwater, 1972—; cons. to Air War Coll., 1968-69, U.S. Army, Ops. Analysis Standby Unit, U. N.C., 1965-69, various mfg. firms, 1964—; program adv. Office of Mgmt. and Budget, Exec. Office of the President, Washington, 1974-79; adv. to NSF, 1974-79, Nat. Center for Productivity and Quality of Work Life, 1973-78; chmn. tech. adv. council So. Growth Policies Bd., 1975-77; accrediting visitor Engrs. Council for Profl. Devel., 1973-80. Recipient Disting. Engring. Alumnus award Purdue U., 1978; registered profl. engr., Ala., Okla. Mem. Am. Inst. Indsl. Engrs. (exec. v.p. 1978—, H.G. Maynard Innovative Achievement award 1977), Am. Soc. for Engring. Edn. (sec. govt. relations com. 1975-76), Nat. Soc. Profl. Engrs., Okla. Soc. Profl. Engrs. (Outstanding Engring. Achievement award 1977), Inst. Mgmt. Scis., Council Indsl. Engring. Acad. Dept. Heads (chmn 1975-76), Sigma Xi, Tau Beta Pi, Alpha Pi Mu. Author: (with J.G. Cox) Essentials of Simulation (translated into Japanese 1970), 1968; Prosim V: Instructor's Manual, 1971, Student's Manual, 1971; (with C.R. White and George H. Brooks) Operations Planning and Control, 1971; (with W.C. Turner and K.E. Case) Introduction to Industrial and Systems Engineering, 1978 (named Book of Yr., Am. Inst. Indsl. Engrs. 1979); contbr. articles in field to engring. jours.; co-editor International Series in Industrial and Systems Engineering, 1972—. Home: 1511 N Glenwood St Stillwater OK 74074 Office: School of Industrial Engring and Mgmt Oklahoma State Univ Stillwater OK 74074

MIZELL, MERLE, develop. biologist; b. Chgo., Apr. 25, 1927; s. Harry M.; B.S., U. Ill., 1950, M.S., 1952, Ph.D. in Zoology, 1957; m. Lorraine E. Busse, Oct. 26, 1958; children—L. Tracy, Michael Jon. Instr. in zoology Tulane U., 1957-60; asst. prof. biology, 1960-64, asso. prof. biology, 1964-70, asso. prof. anatomy, 1969-70, prof. biology and prof. anatomy, 1970—, dir. Chapman H. Hyams III Lab. of Tumor Cell Biology, 1969—; cons. Nat. Cancer Inst.; project site visitor Cancer Research Centers; coordinator WHO Lucke Tumor Herpes virus Team; bd. dirs., mem. research adv. bd. Cancer Assn. Greater New Orleans; mem. instrn. com. Marine Biol. Lab., Woods Hole, Mass.; reviewer grants NSF. Served with USNR, World War II. Am. Cancer Soc. grantee; Cancer Assn. Greater New Orleans grantee. Mem. Am. Inst. Biol. Scientists, AAUP, Soc. Exptl. Biology and Medicine (sec. So. sect.), Am. Soc. Microbiology, Am. Soc. Zoologists (sec. div. devel. biology), AAAS, Soc. Devel. Biology (div. sec.), S.E. Cancer Research Assn., Sigma Xi (Research Faculty award 1969). Editor-in-chief: Progress in Developmental Physiology and Immunology; editor: Biology of Amphibian Tumors, 1969; contbr. numerous articles to sci. jours. Office: Lab Tumor Cell Biology Tulane U New Orleans LA 70118

MIZELL, WALTER SHERMAN, psychiatrist; b. Corning, Ark., Jan. 8, 1915; s. Earl Leonard and Artie Belle (Scrivner) M.; B.S., Ouachita Coll., 1943; M.D., U. Ark., 1950; m. Mary Jo Lile, Dec. 26, 1942; children—Joe Lile, David Walter, Philip Lewis. Intern, Madigan Gen. Hosp., Tacoma, Wash., 1950-51; served as enlisted man U.S. Marine Corps, 1935-39, U.S. Army, 1943-46, commd. capt. U.S. Army, 1950, advanced through grades to lt. col., 1962; resident in psychiatry Fitzsimons Gen. Hosp., Denver, 1951-54; chief dept. psychiatry and neurology, Ft. Jackson, S.C., 1954-57; asst. chief dept. psychiatry and neurology Valley Forge Gen. Hosp., Phoenixville, Pa., 1957-60; asst. chief dept. psychiatry and neurology 2d Gen. Hosp., Landstuhl, W.Ger., 1960-63; chief dept. psychiatry and neurology Ireland Army Hosp., Ft. Knox, Ky., 1963-64; ret., 1964; med. dir. Benton (Ark.) Services Center, 1964—. Mem. Am., Ark. psychiat. assns., Ark., Saline County (Ark.) med. socs., Assn. U.S. Army, Ret. Officers' Assn., Nat. Assn. Uniformed Services. Baptist. Club: Kiwanis (pres. local club 1967-68) (Benton). Home: 1415 Pinewood Dr Benton AR 72015 Office: Benton Services Center Benton AR 72015

MIZENER, ARTHUR MOORE, educator; b. Erie, Pa., Sept. 3, 1907; s. Mason Price and Mabel (Moore) M.; grad. cum laude The Hill Sch., Pottstown, Pa., 1926; B.S. with highest honors, Princeton, 1930, Ph.D., 1934; M.A., Harvard, 1932; m. Elizabeth Rosemary Paris, July 16, 1935; children—Rosemary Moore (Mrs. Leonard B. Colt, Jr.), Arthur Paris (dec.). Instr. English, Yale, 1934-40; asst. prof. Wells Coll., 1940-44, asso. prof., 1944-45; prof., chmn. English dept. Carleton Coll., Northfield, Minn., 1945-51; Mellon Found prof. English, Cornell U., Ithaca, N.Y., 1951-73, prof. emeritus, 1973—. Fulbright lectr. Am. Studies, U. London, 1955-56; Guggenheim fellow, 1964-65; Proctor fellow in English,, Princeton, 1933-34; sr. fellow Nat. Endowment for Humanities, 1968. Mem. Phi Beta Kappa. Democrat. Presbyn. Club: Tower. Author: The Far Side of Paradise: A Biography of F. Scott Fitzgerald, 1951; The Sense of Life in the Modern Novel, 1964; Twelve Great American Novels, 1967; The Saddest Story: A Critical Biography of Ford Madox Ford, 1970; Scott Fitzgerald and His World, 1973. Editor: Afternoon of an Author, 1957; The Fitzgerald Reader, 1963; The Last Chronicle of Barset, 1964. Home: 105 Miller St Ithaca NY 14850

MIZRAHI, ABRAHAM MORDECHAY, physician, pharm. co. exec.; b. Jerusalem, Israel, Apr. 16, 1929; s. Solomon R. and Rachel (Haliwa) M.; came to U.S., 1952, naturalized, 1960; B.S., Manchester Coll., 1955; M.D., Albert Einstein Coll. Medicine, 1960; m. Suzanne Eve Glasser, Mar. 15, 1956; children—Debra, Judith, Karen. Intern, U. N.C., 1960-61; pediatric resident Columbia-Presbyn. Med. Center, N.Y.C., 1961-63, NIH fellow in neonatology, 1963-65; asso. dir. Newborn Service, Mt. Sinai Hosp., N.Y.C., also dir. Newborn Service, Elmhurst Med. Center, 1965-67; staff physician Geigy Pharm. Corp., N.Y.C., 1967-69, head cardio-pulmonary sect., 1969-71; sr. v.p. corp. med. affairs USV Pharm. Corp., Tuckahoe, N.Y., 1971-76; v.p. health and safety Revlon, Inc., N.Y.C., 1976—; asso. in pediatrics Columbia, 1963-67; cons. neonatology Misericordia-Fordham Med. Center, 1967—. Trustee Westchester (N.Y.) Jewish Center. Diplomate Am. Bd. Pediatrics, Nat. Bd. Med. Examiners. Mem. AMA, N.Y. State and County Med. Soc., Am., N.Y. acads. medicine, Am. Soc. Clin. Pharmacology and Therapeutics, Am. Pub. Health Assn., Am. Occupational Med. Assn. Contbr. articles to profl. jours. Home: 7 Jason Ln Mamaroneck NY 10543 Office: 767 Fifth Ave New York NY 10022. *The principles that have guided my life are old Biblical concepts. Firstly, that God had created Adam and Eve and all Men are, therefore, brothers and sisters. Secondly, God created Man and, therefore every human being has a spark of God in him. It, therefore, follows that killing diminshes God's presence on earth and saving of a human being increases His presence.*

MIZWA, TAD (THADDEUS) S(TEPHEN), publisher; b. Springfield, Mass., July 4, 1927; s. Stephen Paul and Katherine Regina (Twarog) M.; B.B.A., Amherst (Mass.) Coll., 1949; M.A., Columbia U., 1951; postgrad. U. Houston, 1962-63; m. Mary Jane House, Mar. 12, 1965; children—John Thomas, Michael Barnett, Michelle Jane, Stephen Reed. Student counselor Miami U., Oxford, Ohio, then Kans. State U., Manhattan, 1950-53; owner Tad's Saddlery and Western Store, Houston, 1954-63; editor Conroe (Tex.) Courier, 1963-67; advt. mgr. Horseman mag., Houston, 1966-76; founder, editor Western Outfitter, Houston, 1968-77, publisher, 1977—; publisher Horseman mag., Houston, 1977—. Bd. dirs. Kosciuszko Found.; deacon First Presbyn. Ch., Houston. Mem. Sigma Delta Chi. Author: Successful Western Merchandising, Vol. I, 1972, Vol. II, 1973. Home: 8427 Westview Dr Houston TX 77055 Office: 5314 Bingle Rd Houston TX 77092

MNICH, WILLIAM RICHARD, broadcasting exec.; b. Pleasant City, Ohio, June 10, 1926; s. Matt and Ann Mnich; B.F.A., Ohio U., Athens, 1950; m. Norma Jean Marchi, June 5, 1954; children—Louise, William Richard, II, Ann, Matthew, Mark. Gen. mgr. Sta. WBEX, Chilicothe, Ohio, 1951-55; asst. to mgr. Air Trails, 1955-57; founder, 1957, since pres., gen. mgr. N. Am. Broadcasting Co. (stas. WMNI and WRMZ), Columbus, Ohio; pres. So. Hotel, Columbus, 1974—; past pres. Mut. Afiliates Adv. Council. Past mem. bd. Ohio Commodores; trustee Rio Grande Coll., 1974—. Served with USNR, 1944-46. Mem. Nat., Ohio broadcasters assns., Columbus Area C. of C., Navy League, Stelson Found. Republican. Roman Catholic. Club: Columbus Athletic. Home: 4567 Ravine Dr Westerville OH 43081 Office: Southern Hotel Main and High Sts Columbus OH 43215

MNOOKIN, ROBERT HARRIS, lawyer; b. Kansas City, Mo., Feb. 4, 1942; A.B., Harvard U., 1964, LL.B., 1968. Admitted to D.C. bar, 1969, Calif. bar, 1970; asso. firm Howard, Prim, Smith, Rice & Downs, San Francisco, 1970-72, of counsel, 1972—; lectr. U. Calif., Berkeley, 1972, dir. childhood and govt. project, 1972-74, acting prof. law, 1973-75, prof. law, 1975—. Mem. overseer's com. to visit Law Sch., Harvard U., 1972-78; trustee Berkeley Pub. Library, 1973—, chmn., 1975-77, vice chmn., 1978—. Mem. Am., Calif., San Francisco bar assns., Am. Law Inst. Author: Child, Family and State, 1978. Contbr. articles in field to profl. jours. Home: 9 The Uplands Berkeley CA 94705 Office: 342 Boalt Hall U Calif Berkeley CA 94720

MOAKLEY, JOHN JOSEPH, congressman; b. Apr. 27, 1927; LL.B., Suffolk U., 1956; m. Evelyn Duffy, 1957. Admitted to Mass. bar, 1957; practiced in Boston, 1957-72; mem. 93d-96th congresses from 9th Mass. dist. Mem. Mass. Ho. of Reps., 1953-60, Democratic majority whip, 1957, chmn. subcom. on rules, at large majority whip; mem. Mass. Senate, 1964-70; mem. Boston City Council, 1971-72, chmn. com. on appropriations and finance. Served with USNR, 1943-46. Address: Cannon House Office Bldg Washington DC 20515

MOATE, LESTER THOMAS, corp. exec.; b. Gridley, Ill., Mar. 10, 1919; s. Thomas and Amelia (King) M.; B.S., U. Ill., 1941; m. Pauline Fitzgibbon, Dec. 23, 1944; children —Nancy K., Mary P. With Am. Steel Foundries, Chgo., 1941—, successively trainee, accountant, asst. controller, controller, 1954-60, v.p., treas., 1960-74, co. name changed to Amsted Industries, 1962, exec. v.p., 1974—, also dir. Served as lt. (j.g.) Supply Corps, USNR, 1944. Mem. Am. Inst. Accountants, Ill. Soc. C.P.A.'s. Mason. Clubs: Mid-America, Chicago, Knollwood, Economic (Chgo.). Home: 716 Dimmeydale Deerfield IL 60015 Office: 3700 Prudential Plaza Chicago IL 60601

MOBBERLEY, DAVID GEORGE, coll. dean; b. Cleve., Oct. 18, 1921; s. James Chadwick and Hilda (Dean) M.; B.S., Baldwin-Wallace Coll., 1948; M.S., U. Mich., 1950; Ph.D., Iowa State U., 1953; m. Marjorie Garfield, Dec. 25, 1946; children—Lynne Ellen, James Carlton. Instr. biology Simpson Coll., Indianola, Iowa, 1950- 52, prof. biology, chmn. div. sci., 1954-57; instr. botany Iowa State U., 1952-53; dean Lycoming Coll., Williamsport, Pa., 1958-64, prof. biology, chmn. dept., 1965-69; dean Am. Univ., Washington, 1964-65; pres. Greensboro (N.C.) Coll., 1969-72; asst. sec. bd. higher edn. and ministry United Meth. Ch., 1972-77; v.p., dean Fla. So. Coll., Lakeland, 1977—. Served to 1st lt. with USAAF, 1942-46. Mem. AAAS, Sigma Xi, Phi Kappa Phi. Mason. Author: Introduction to Science: A Directed Study Manual, 1957; the Deanship of the Liberal College; also monograph. Home: 947 Hollingsworth Rd Lakeland FL 33801

MOBERG, DAVID OSCAR, educator; b. Montevideo, Minn., Feb. 13, 1922; s. Fred Ludwig and Anna E. (Sundberg) M.; A.A., Bethel Jr. Coll., 1942; A.B., Seattle Pacific Coll., 1947; M.A., U. Wash., 1949; Ph.D., U. Minn., 1952; m. Helen H. Heitzman, Mar. 16, 1946; children—David Paul, Lynette, Jonathan, Philip. Asso. instr. U. Wash., Seattle, 1948-49; faculty Bethel Coll., St. Paul, 1949-68, prof. sociology, 1959-68, chmn. dept. social scis., 1952-68; prof. sociology Marquette U., Milw., 1968—, chmn. dept. sociology and anthropology, 1968-77. Cons., Nat. Liberty Found., 1970-71, Nat. Interfaith Coalition on Aging, 1973-75; adj. prof. San Francisco Theol. Sem., 1964-73, McCormick Theol. Sem., 1975—. Fulbright lectr. U. Groningen (Netherlands), 1957-58, Muenster U., West Germany, 1964-65. Fellow Am. Sci. Affiliation (editor jour. 1962-64), Gerontological Soc.; mem. A.A.U.P., Am., Internat. (sociology of religion research com. 1972—), Wis. (pres. 1969-71), Midwest (Wis. dir. 1971-73) sociol. assns., Assn. Humanist Sociology, Assn. Devel. Religious Information Systems (coordinator ADRIS, 1971—, editor ADRIS newsletter 1971-76), Religious Research Assn. (editor Rev. Religious Research 1968-72, contbg. editor 1973-77, dir. 1959-61, 68-72), Assn. for Sociology of Religion (exec. council 1971-73, pres. 1976-77), Soc. for Sci. Study Religion (exec. council 1971-74), Evangelicals for Social Action (planning com. 1973-75), Christian Sociologists (planning com. 1973—). Baptist. Author: The Church as A Social Institution, 1962; (with Robert M. Gray) The Church and the Older Person, 1962, 2d edit., 1977; Inasmuch: Christian Social Responsibility in the 20th Century, 1965; White House Conference on Aging: Spiritual Well-Being Background and Issues, 1971; The Great Reversal: Evangelism vs. Social Concern, 1972, 2d edit., 1977; also articles, chpts. in symposia. Editor: International Directory of Religious Information Systems, 1971; Spiritual Well-Being: Sociological Perspectives, 1979; Rev. Religious Research, 1968-72, Jour. Am. Sci. Affiliation, 1962-64, Adris Newsletter, 1971-76. Home: 2619 E Newberry Blvd Milwaukee WI 53211

MOBERLY, DAVID LINDSEY, supt. schs.; b. Irvine, Ky., Apr. 25, 1929; s. Earl and Blanche (Finney) M.; A.B., U. Ky., 1951; postgrad. Am. U., 1950; M.A., U. Ky., 1953; Ph.D., Kent State U., 1965; m. Peggy Compton, Dec. 30, 1951; children—Kent, Lynn. Tchr., Jefferson County Bd. Edn., Louisville, 1951-54, dean of boys, 1954-55, asst. prin., 1955-57; ednl. adv. AID, U.S. State Dept., Tripoli, Benghazi, Libya, 1957-61, edn. program officer, research and survey team, Nairobi, Kenya, 1961-62; instr., resident project coordinator in Tanzania, Kent State U., 1962-65; supt. schs. Bd. Edn., Tallmadge, Ohio, 1966-67, Warren, Ohio, 1967-71, Cleve. Heights, 1971-74, Evanston (Ill.) Twp. High Sch., 1974-76, Seattle Sch. Dist. 1, 1976—; spl. participant documentary on problems in edn. ABC-TV, 1976. Area chmn. Ohio's Right-to-Read project, 1969-71; chmn. alumni com. for edn. com. Kent State U., 1968-71; mem. nat. adv. bd. Corp. for Pub. Broadcasting; U.S. del. to World Orgn. of Teaching Profession in Rome, Italy, 1958. Mem. Seattle council Boy Scouts Am.; bd. dirs. Jr. Achievement; trustee Pacific Sci. Center Found., Seattle; mem. Pvt. Sector's Initiative Bd., Seattle. Mem. NEA, Am. Assn. Sch. Adminstrs., Wash. Assn. Sch. Adminstrs., Mcpl. League, Seattle C. of C., Kappa Delta Pi, Phi Delta Kappa. Rotarian. Home: 3045 44th Ave W Seattle WA 98199 Office: Seattle School District 1 815 4th Ave N Seattle WA 98109

MOBERLY, RALPH MOON, educator; b. St. Louis, Apr. 17, 1929; s. Ralph Moon and Nellie Besse (Roe) M.; A.B., with highest honors, Princeton U., 1950, Ph.D. (NSF fellow, Proctor fellow), 1956; m. Jean Marilyn Lawson, June 13, 1954; children—Elizabeth Joan, Ralph Moon III. Geologist, Standard Oil Co. Calif., Salinas and Ventura, 1956-59; faculty U. Hawaii, Honolulu, 1959—, prof. geology, 1970—, chmn. dept. geology and geophysics, 1975—; Vis. prof. U. Calif. at Berkeley, 1965, U. Calif. at Santa Barbara, 1965-66, Bryn Mawr Coll., 1973. Served with USNR, 1950-53. NSF grantee, 1965-72; Fellow Geol. Soc. Am., AAAS; mem. Am. Geophys. Union, Am. Assn. Petroleum Geologists, Soc. Econ. Paleontology and Mineralogy Internat. Assn. Sedimentologist, Marine Technol. Soc., Hawaii Acad. Sci., Sigma Xi. Home: 754 Kokomo Pl Honolulu HI 96825 Office: Hawaii Institute of Geophysics University Hawaii 2525 Correa Rd Honolulu HI 96822

MOBERLY, ROBERT BLAKELY, lawyer; b. Madison, Wis., Sept. 17, 1941; s. Russell Louis and Hildegarde (Reimer) M.; B.S., U. Wis., 1963, J.D., 1966; m. Jeanne Clinton, Dec. 30, 1962; children—Laura, Richard. Admitted to Wis. bar, 1966, Tenn. bar, 1977; law clk. Wis. Supreme Ct., 1966-67; arbitrator, trial examiner, mediator Wis. Employment Relations Commn., 1968-71; practice law, Milw., 1971-73; prof. U. Tenn. Coll. Law, Knoxville, 1973-77, U. Fla. 1977—; vis. prof. U. Louvain (Belgium), 1975; mem. arbitration panels Fed. Mediation and Conciliation Service, Am. Arbitration Assn., Nat. Mediation Bd. Mem. Nat. Acad. Arbitrators (chmn. S.E. region), Am. Bar Assn., Indsl. Relations Research Assn., Soc. Profls. in Dispute Resolution. Author: Public Employment Labor Relations, 1974; Arbitration and Conflict Resolution, 1979; contbr. articles to profl. jours. Office: U Fla Coll Law Gainesville FL 32611

MOBRAATEN, WILLIAM LAWRENCE, telephone co. exec.; b. Wendell, Minn., May 17, 1929; s. Charles S. and Lillie M. (Hoff) M.; A.B. in Engring., Harvard U., 1950; m. Cynthia Weston, Oct. 18, 1952; children—David W., Robert L., Sally F. With traffic and engring. dept. Pacific Tel. & Tel Co., 1952-62, gen. plant mgr., Los Angeles, 1962-65, v.p. staff, San Francisco, 1967-69, v.p. personnel, 1969-72, v.p. adminstrn., 1972-73; v.p., treas. AT&T, N.Y.C., 1973-76; pres., dir. Bell Telephone Co. Pa., also Diamond State Telephone Co., Phila., 1976—; dir. Rohm and Haas Co., Hershey Trust Co. (Pa.), Pitts. Nat. Corp.; trustee Penn Mut. Life Ins. Co. Bd. dirs. World Affairs Council, 1977—; bd. dirs. Greater Phila. Partnership, 1976—, exec. com., 1977—; bd. dirs. Afro-Am. Hist. and Cultural Museum, 1977—, treas., 1977—; bd. dirs. Pa. Ballet, 1977—, Center Phila. Area Devel., 1977—, Food Distbn. Center, 1977—; exec. com. Eastern div., bd. dirs. Pa. div. Pa. Economy League; 1976—; bd. mgrs. Milton Hershey Sch., 1976—; exec. bd. Phila. council Boy Scouts Am. mem. Phila. Orch. Council; mem., co-chmn. Bus. Council Pa.; trustee Internat. House Phila., 1977—. Served as officer USMCR, 1948-52; Korea. Mem. Middle States Assn. Colls. and Schs. (trustee 1977—), C. of C. of U.S., Pa. C. of C., Greater Phila. C. of C. (dir. 1976—). Clubs: Harvard, Cricket, Union League (Phila.); Harvard (N.Y.C.); Marines Meml., Sunday Breakfast. Home: 9507 Marstan Rd Philadelphia PA 19118 Office: One Parkway 18th Floor Philadelphia PA 19102

MOCCIA, ALFRED JOHN, mfg. co. exec.; b. Wilmington, Del., Dec. 2, 1917; s. John A. and Kathryn (Elliot) M.; B.S., U. Pa. Wharton Sch. 1940; LL.B., Temple U., 1949; m. Evelyn Hedelt, June 25, 1941; children—Donald J., Bruce P. Admitted to Pa. bar, 1950; with firm Drinker, Biddle & Reath, Phila., 1950; tax atty. E.I. duPont De Nemours & Co., Inc., 1950-52; exec. Gen. Aniline & Film Corp., 1952-58; v.p., treas. Am. Airlines. Inc., 1959-67; dir., vice chmn., chief fin. officer Sperry Rand Corp., 1967—; dir. Nicholson Muir Prodns., Inc., Larchmont, N.Y., European Am. Bank, European Am. Bank and Trust Co., Bekaert Steel Wire Corp., N.Y.C.; mem. faculty Pace Coll., N.Y.C., 1956—. Served to 1st lt. USAAF, 1942-45. Decorated D.F.C., Air medal with 5 oak leaf clusters. Mem. Pa., Phila. bar assns., Phi Alpha Delta. Clubs: Union League, Board Room, Links, University (N.Y.C.); River (N.Y.); Blind Brook (Port Chester, N.Y.); Winged Foot Golf (Mamaroneck, N.Y.); Clove Valley (N.Y.) Rod and Gun. Home: 23 Dante St Larchmont NY 10538 Office: 1290 Ave Americas New York NY 10019

MOCH, ROBERT GASTON, lawyer; b. Montesano, Wash., June 20, 1914; s. Gaston and Fleeta Belle (Metcalf) M.; B.A., U. Wash., 1936; J.D., Harvard, 1941; m. Barbara M. Kent, Sept. 2, 1940 (dec.); children—Marilynn A., Michael K., Robert M.; m. 2d, LaVerne I. Miller, May 29, 1968. Asst. crew coach U. Wash., 1936-39; head crew coach Mass. Inst. Tech., 1939-44; admitted to Mass. bar, 1941, Wash. bar, 1945; practiced in Boston, 1941-44, Seattle, 1945—; asso. Herrick, Smith, Donald, Farley & Ketchum, 1941-44; asso. Eggerman, Rosling & Williams, 1945-50, Weter, Roberts & Shefelman, 1950-53; partner Roberts, Shefelman, Lawrence, Gay & Moch, 1953—. Del., Nat. Conf. on Law and Poverty, 1965, Nat. Defender Conf., 1969; chmn. King County Pub. Defender Adv. Com., 1970. Mem. bd. rowing stewards U. Wash. Recipient Olympic Gold medal, 1936; named to Helms Rowing Hall of Fame, U. Wash. Hall of Fame. Mem. Am., Wash. (com. chmn.), Seattle-King County (past trustee, com. chmn.) bar assns., U. Wash. Alumni Assn. (pres. 1978-79), Phi Beta Kappa, Alpha Kappa Psi, Beta Gamma Sigma, Phi Delta Phi, Phi Gamma Delta. Mem. Christian Ch. Clubs: Rainier, Rotary (Seattle); Overlake Golf and Country (Bellevue). Mem. U. Wash. Crew, 1933-36. Home: 101 101st Ave SE Apt 202C Bellevue WA 98004 Office: IBM Bldg Seattle WA 98101

MOCHRIE, RICHARD DOUGLAS, educator; b. Lowell, Mass., Feb. 17, 1928; s. William Blair and Helen (Stephens) M.; B.S., U. Conn., 1950, M.S., 1953; Ph.D., N.C. State U., 1958; m. Helene Mary Buchanan, Aug. 19, 1950; children—Barbara Jean, Steven Howard, Lois Ann. Research technician U. Conn., 1950-53; grad. asst. N.C. State U., 1953-54, instr., 1954-58, asst. prof., 1958-61, asso. prof., 1961-72, prof. lactational physiology and nutrition, 1972—. Precinct com. chmn., county conv. del. Cary and Wake County (N.C.) Democratic Party, 1972—; past chmn. Cary Recreation Commn.; mem. Wake County Parks and Recreation Commn., 1977, chmn., 1978—; bd. dirs. Raleigh YMCA. Served with AUS, 1946-47. Recipient Upjohn Co. citation for contbn. to quality milk mgmt., 1978. Mem. Nat. Mastitis Council (dir. 1973—, v.p. 1975, pres. 1976, disting. service award 1978), Am. Dairy Sci. Assn., Assn. Ofcl. Analytical Chemists (asso. referee), Interstate Milk Shippers, Gamma Sigma Delta (cert. of merit 1978), Sigma Chi, Pi Alpha Sigma, Sigma Xi. Democrat. Presbyterian (deacon 1959-61). Clubs: Cary Exchange (pres. 1963-64), Dairy Shriner. Author: Lactation Laboratory Outline, 1971; contbr. numerous articles to sci. jours.; contbr. Ruminant Nutrition and Metabolism to Ency. Biochemistry, 1967. Home: 505 S Dixon Ave Cary NC 27511 Office: NC State U Raleigh NC 27650

MOCK, HENRY BYRON, lawyer; b. Greenville, Tex., Feb. 1, 1911; s. Henry Byron and Ellena (Edmonds) M.; A.B., U. Ariz., 1933; J.D., Georgetown U., 1939, George Washington U., 1940; m. Mary Morris, Nov. 11, 1949. Asst. sec. to Congresswoman Isabella Greenway of Ariz., 1934-35; office mgr., legal research asst., recreation div. WPA, Washington, 1935-38, asst. atty., 1938; legal adv. President's Adv. Com. on Edn., 1938-39; asst. solicitor Dept. Interior, 1939-41; chief counsel U.S. Grazing Service, Salt Lake City, 1941-42; adminstr. region IV, U.S. Bur. Land Mgmt., Colo., Utah, 1947-54, area adminstr., Idaho, Ariz., Utah, Nev., 1954-55; exec. mining cos., 1955—, mineral records cos. Chmn., Dept. Interior storm relief com. Western U.S., 1949; mem. U.S. Pub. Land Law Rev. Commn., 1964-70, vice chmn., 1965-70; mem. Interior Oil Shale Com., 1964. Served pvt. to capt. with AUS, 1942-46: MTO. Mem. D.C., Va., Utah bar assns., Bar Supreme Ct. of U.S., Am., Fed. bar assn., U.S. C. of C., Bar of Ct. Mil. Appeals, Am. Inst. Mining and Metall. Engrs., Am. Soc. Range Mgmt., Am. Soc. Pub. Adminstrn. (past Utah pres.), Western Polit. Sci. Assn., Am. Forestry Assn., Pi Kappa Alpha. Clubs: Rotary, Alta (Salt Lake City). Contbr. profl. publs. Home: 1282 Gilmer Dr Salt Lake City UT 84105 Office: Continental Bldg Salt Lake City UT 84101 also 45 E 4th S Salt Lake City UT 84111

MOCK, JESSE ALEXANDER, JR., editor; b. Forsyth County, N.C., Sept. 17, 1920; s. Julius Alexander and Edna Elizabeth (Walker) M.; A.B. in Journalism, U. N.C., 1947; m. Dorothy Jeane Moreland, Oct. 11, 1947; children—Jeffrey Arden, Deverie Jeane, Danci Noella, Jon Adlai. Electrician, Elec. Service Co., Winston-Salem, N.C., 1934-40; Washington corr. various newspapers and radio stas., 1947-51, McGraw-Hill Pub. Co., 1951—; successively asst. to editor, prodn. editor, sr. editor Elec. World mag., 1953-70; asso. editor to editor in chief Elec. Week newsletter, N.Y.C., 1970-79; editor books on engring. ethics, civil def., nat. security. Peace activist, draft counselor. Recipient Jesse H. Neal award for editorial excellence in bus. journalism, 1961. Mem. Nat. Press Club. Democrat. Quaker. Home: 419 Hollywood Ave Ho Ho Kus NJ 07423 Office: 1221 Ave of Americas New York NY 10020

MOCK, LAWRENCE EDWARD, govt. ofcl.; b. Zanesville, Ohio, May 2, 1917; s. Clay Madon and Frances Brush (Merrick) M.; B.S., Ohio State U., 1939; M.B.A., Harvard, 1943; m. Mary Ann McCoy, June 2, 1945; children— Lawrence Edward, Martha Ann (Mrs. Dennis M. Ryan), Nelson McCoy, Ann Lawrence. Auditor, Arthur Young & Company, Pitts., 1939-41, partner, 1947-49; controller Harbison-Walker Refractories Co., 1949-51, treas., 1951-68, v.p., 1959-68, dir., 1967-68; finance v.p. Royal Crown Cola Co., Columbus, Ga., 1968-76; fin. mgr. Fed. Energy Adminstrn., Washington, 1976-77; treas. Overseas Pvt. Investment Corp., Washington, 1977-79; controller Naval Petroleum and Oil Shale Reserves, Washington, 1979—. Served from 2d lt. to maj. AUS, 1942-46. C.P.A., Pa., Ill., Ga. Mem. Conf. Bd. (chmn. finance council 1971-72), Harvard Bus. Sch. Assn. (exec. council 1964-67), Am. Contract Bridge League (pres. Ga. unit 114, 1973, bd. govs. 1975-77), Tau Kappa Epsilon. Presbyterian (elder). Clubs: Duquesne (Pitts.); Bay Point (Fla.) Yacht. Home: 406 Normandy House 1701 N Kent St Arlington VA 22209 Office: 3344 Fed Bldg 1200 Pennsylvania Ave NW Washington DC 20461

MOCK, RICHARD M., mgmt. cons.; b. N.Y.C., July 28, 1905; s. Dudley and Sadie (Danneberg) M.; B.S., N.Y. U., 1927; m. Claire Gasper, Mar. 7, 1938; 1 dau., Barbara Joan (Mrs. Strona). With exptl. dept. Ware Radio Corp., N.Y.C., 1925, Loening Aero Engring. Corp., N.Y.C., 1926; tech. editor Aviation mag., 1927-28; project engr., asst. to pres. Bellanca Aircraft Corp., New Castle, Del., 1928-29; project engr. Heinkel Aircraft Co., Germany, 1929-30; tech. rep. Fokker Aircraft Co., Netherlands, with offices at Douglas Aircraft Co., Santa Monica, Calif., 1931-40; Lear, Inc., 1940-62, sales mgr. Calif. div., 1940-42, chief engr., 1942-45, mgr. electro-mech. div., 1945-47, exec. v.p., 1947-48, pres., 1948-59, chmn. exec. com., 1957-61, chmn. exec. com., dir., 1961-62; bus. cons., 1962—; v.p., gen. mgr. indsl. systems div. Bunker Ramo Corp., Canoga Park, Calif., 1964, v.p. planning, bus. and industry group, 1964-65; dir. Electrochimica Corp., 1965-72; dir., mem. exec. com., nominating com. and audit com., chmn. compensation and investment com. Aeronca Inc., 1965—, chmn. exec. com., 1979—; mem. So. Calif. adv. bd. Liberty Mut. Ins. Co., 1959—; mgmt. cons., 1962—; mem. Calif. Motor Vehicle Pollution Control Bd., 1963-67. Bd. dirs., mem. exec. com. Greater Los Angeles affiliate Am. Heart Assn., 1970-71, chmn. fund raising com., 1971-73, mem. research com., 1979—, treas., 1973-74 v.p. non-med., 1974-75, chmn. bd. 1976-77; mem. nat. fund-raising adv. policy com. Am. Heart Assn., 1973-75, chmn. audit com., 1977-78, mem. bd. dirs., 1970—, mem. nat. bd. dirs., 1977-79. Trustee, mem. exec. com. City of Hope, Duarte, Calif., 1960—, mem. research rev. com., 1972—; mem. bus. adv. council Internat. Student Center, U. Calif., Los Angeles. Profl. engr., Ohio. Mem. Am. Inst. Aeros. and Astronautics (asso. fellow), Soc. Automotive Engrs. (asso.), Nat. Panel Arbitrators, Am. Arbitration Assn., Soc. Aerospace Material and Process Engrs., Def. Orientation Conf. Assn., Tau Beta Pi. Address: 3029 Corda Dr Los Angeles CA 90049

MOCKLER, COLMAN MICHAEL, JR., mfg. co. exec., b. St. Louis, Dec. 29, 1929; s. Colman Michael and Veronica (McKenna) M.; A.B., Harvard, 1952, M.B.A., 1954; m. Joanna Lois Sperry, Dec. 28, 1957; children—Colman Michael III, Joanna Lois, Emily McKenna, Andrew Sperry. With Gen. Electric Co., 1954-55; mem. faculty Harvard Grad. Sch. Bus., 1955-57; with Gillette Co., Boston, 1957—, treas., 1965-68, v.p., 1967-68, sr. v.p., 1968-70, exec. v.p., 1970-71, vice chmn. bd., 1971-74, pres., chief operating officer, 1974-76, chief exec. officer, 1975—, chmn. bd., 1976—, dir., 1971—; dir. First Nat. Boston Corp., First Nat. Bank Boston, Fabreeka Products Co., John Hancock Mutual Life Ins. Co., Raytheon Co. Bd. dirs. Greater Boston YMCA, Boston Municipal Research Bur. Boston; chmn. corp. Simmons Coll.; trustee New Eng. Conservatory Music; overseer Boston Symphony Orch.; pres. bd. overseers Harvard Coll.; mem. corp. Mus. Sci., Mass. Gen. Hosp. Served with AUS, 1948-49. Club: Harvard (N.Y.C.). Home: 37 Draper Rd Wayland MA 01778 Office: Gillette Co Prudential Tower Bldg Boston MA 02199

MOCKRIDGE, NORTON, author, editor; b. N.Y.C., Sept. 29, 1915; s. Frank Walter and Fredricka (Apfel) M.; student public schs., Mt. Kisco, N.Y.; m. Margaret Gleason, 1946 (div. 1961); m. 2d, Valborg Palmer, 1963; children—Philip, Nancy Mockridge Miner, John. Journalist, Mt. Kisco (N.Y.) Recorder, 1933-36, White Plains (N.Y.) Daily Reporter, 1936-40; with World-Telegram & Sun, N.Y.C., 1940-66, city editor, 1956-63, humor columnist, 1963-66; with World Jour. Tribune, 1967; syndicated humor columnist Scripps-Howard newspapers and United Feature Syndicate, 1963—; editor Customized Communications div. Med. Econs. Co., Litton Publs., Oradell, N.J., 1971—; author books, including: This is Costello, 1951, The Big Fix, 1954, Costello on the Spot, 1957, Fractured English, 1965, A Funny Thing Happened, 1966, Mockridge, You're Slipping!, 1967, The Scrawl of the Wild, 1968, Eye on the Odds, 1976; contbr. numerous articles to mags.; author numerous film story outlines; tech. adviser film Teacher's Pet, 1957; lectr. Keedick Lecture Bur.; star daily radio show Sta.-WCBS, 1963-64, CBS radio network, 1964-70; judge Miss Am. Pageant, 1967-71, Maj. Armstrong FM Radio Awards, 1970—. Served to 1st lt. AUS, 1942-45. Recipient Christopher award The Christophers, 1949, Pulitzer prize (with World-Telegram city news staff), 1963. Mem. 7th Regt. Vets. Assn. (life), Silurian Soc., N.Y. Vet. Police Assn., Sigma Delta Chi. Episcopalian. Clubs: Players, Dutch Treat, River, Coffee House, Regency, Casino (Chgo.); Cuernavaca (Mexico) Racquet. Home: Beach Ln Wainscott NY 11975 also Casa Andrada Palmira y Privada del Rio Cuernavaca Mexico

MODELL, ARTHUR B., profl. football team exec.; b. Bklyn., June 23, 1925; m. Patricia Breslin, July 25, 1969; stepchildren—John, David. Owner, pres. Cleve. Browns football team, 1961—; pres. Nat. Football League, 1967-70. Office: Cleveland Stadium Cleveland OH 44114*

MODELL, JEROME HERBERT, medical educator; b. St. Paul, Sept. 9, 1932; s. William and Frieda (Singer) M.; B.A., U. Minn., 1954, B.S., 1957, M.D., 1957; m. Shirley Graves, Nov. 25, 1977; children—Charles, Jack, Julie. Intern U.S. Naval Hosp., St. Albans, N.Y., 1957-58, resident, 1958-60; practice medicine specializing in anesthesiology, Gainesville, Fla., 1969—; attending staff U.S. Naval Hosp., St. Albans, 1960-61; chief anesthesiology U.S. Naval Hosp., Pensacola, Fla., 1961-63; asso. prof. dept. anesthesiology U. Miami (Fla.) Sch. Medicine, 1963-69; prof., chmn. dept. anesthesiology U. Fla. Coll. Medicine, Gainesville, 1969—. Served to lt. comdr. USN, 1957-63. Recipient NIH Research Career Devel. award. Mem. Assn. U. Anesthetists, Am. Soc. Anesthesiologists, A.M.A., N.Y. Acad. Scis., Am. Coll. Chest Physicians, AAAS. Author: The Pathophysiology and Treatment of Drowning and Near-Drowning, 1971; (with others) Introduction to Life Support, 1973; also numerous scientific articles. Home: PO Box 13285 Gainesville FL 32604

MODELL, JOHN, historian; b. N.Y.C., June 3, 1941; s. Walter and Merriam (Levant) M.; A.B., Columbia U., 1962, M.A., 1963, Ph.D., 1969; postgrad. (Social Sci. Research Council research tng. fellow), U. Pa., 1969-70; m. Judith Schachter, June 2, 1963; children—Jennifer, Matthew Thelonious. Research asst. Bur. Applied Social Research, Columbia U., 1962-65; lectr. Kingsborough Community Coll., 1965-66; dir. research Japanese Am. Research Project, UCLA, 1966-69; asst. prof. history U. Minn., 1969-72, asso. prof., 1972-77, prof., 1977—; research asso. Phila. Social History Project, U. Pa., 1974—; mem. Minn. State Hist. Records Adv. Bd., 1976-78. John Simon Guggenheim Meml. fellow, 1978-79. Mem. Am. Hist. Assn., Orgn. Am. Historians, Social Sci. History Assn., Internat. Union Sci. Study Population. Jewish. Author: The Economics and Politics of Racial Accommodation: The Japanese of Los Angeles 1900-1942, 1977; editor, author introduction: The Kikuchi Diary: Chronicle of an American Concentration Camp, 1973. Home: 2610 Irving Ave S Minneapolis MN 55408 Office: Dept History U Minn Minneapolis MN 55455

MODER, JOSEPH JOHN, educator; b. St. Louis, Dec. 12, 1924; s. Joseph John and Elizabeth (Mock) M.; B.S. in Chem. Engring., Washington U., St. Louis, 1947; M.S., Northwestern U., 1949, Ph.D., 1950; m. Florence E. Delburn, Sept. 15, 1951; children—Frederick J., Christopher M., Jeffrey A., Maria M., Sampson A., Joseph J. Prof. indsl. engring. Ga. Inst. Tech., Atlanta, 1950-64; prof. dept. indsl. engring. and system analysis U. Miami (Fla.), 1964—, prof., chmn. dept. mgmt. sci., 1978—. NSF faculty fellow Iowa State U., 1960-61; sci. faculty fellow, vis. prof. Stanford, 1961-62; vis. prof. U. Birmingham (Eng.), 1973-74. Served with USNR, 1944-46. Mem. Ops. Research Soc. Am., Inst. Mgmt. Sci., Am. Inst. Decision Scis., Project Mgmt. Inst., Am. Statis. Assn., Am. Inst. Indsl. Engrs. Author: (with C.R. Phillips) Project Management with CPM and PERT, 1964,

2d edit., 1970; (with S.E. Elmaghraby) Handbook of Operations. Home: 7801 S W 133d Terr Miami FL 33156

MODERSOHN, ROBERT JOHN, III, photographer; b. Passaic, N.J., Oct. 22, 1949; s. Robert John and Olga (Mikula) M.; B.A. in Journalism, Drake U., 1971; m. Paula Georgette Johns, May 29, 1971; children—Seth David, Mark Jacob. Staff photographer Des Moines Register & Tribune, 1971-77, spl. projects photographer Des Moines Sunday Register, 1977—; instr. photography Drake U., 1974-77. Served with AUS, 1971-72. Mem. Iowa (pres. 1973-74, Photographer of Year 1975), Nat. (1st runner-up Newspaper Photographer of Year 1974) press photographers assns. Elk. Contbr. articles to Iowa, Nat. press photographers assns. publs. Home: 1424 41st Place Des Moines IA 50311 Office: 715 Locust St Des Moines IA 50304

MODIC, STANLEY JOHN, bus. editor; b. Fairport Harbor, Ohio, Dec. 29, 1936; s. Frank and Mary (Zakrajsek) M.; B.S. in Commerce, Ohio U., 1958; m. Albina DiMichele, May 27, 1961; children—Mark Francis, Laurel Marie. Reporter The Telegraph, Painesville, Ohio, 1960-63, city editor, 1964-65; asst. editor Steel Mag., Cleve., 1965-67, news editor, 1968-70; news editor Industry Week (formerly Steel Mag.), Cleve., 1970-72, exec. editor, 1972, editor, 1972—. Municipal clk., Fairport Harbor, 1960-61; mem. Fairport Harbor Village Council, 1962-63, pres., 1962-63. Mem. Am. Soc. Bus. Press Editors, Am. Fedn. Musicians, Sigma Delta Chi (pres. Cleve. chpt. 1975-76). K.C. Clubs: Press (pres. 1978-79) (Cleve.); Am.-Slovenian (Fairport Harbor). Home: 5842 Woodhill St Painesville OH 44077 Office: 1111 Chester Ave Cleveland OH 44114

MODIGLIANI, FRANCO, educator; b. Rome, Italy, June 18, 1918; s. Enrico and Olga (Flaschel) M.; D.Jurisprudence, U. Rome, 1939; D.Social Sci., New Sch. Social Research, N.Y.C., 1944; LL.D. ad honorem, U. Chgo., 1967; D. honoris causa, U. Louvain (Belgium), 1974, Istituto Universitario di Bergamo, 1979; m. Serena Calabi, May 22, 1939; children—Andrea, Sergio. Came to U.S., 1939, naturalized, 1946. Instr. econs. and statistics N.J. Coll. Women, New Brunswick, 1942; Instr., then asso. econs. and statistics Bard Coll., Columbia, 1942-44; lectr., asst. prof. math. econs. and econometrics New Sch. Social Research, 1943-44, 46-48; research asso., chief statistician Inst. World Affairs, N.Y.C. 1945-48; research cons. Cowles Commn. Research in Econs., U. Chgo., 1949-54; asso. prof., then prof. econs. U. Ill., 1949-52; prof. econs. and indsl. adminstrn. Carnegie Inst. Tech., 1952-60; vis. prof. econs. Harvard, 1957-58; prof. econs. Northwestern U., 1960-62; vis. prof. econs. Mass. Inst. Tech., 1960-61, prof. econs. and finance, 1962—, Inst. prof., 1970. Fellow polit. economy U. Chgo., 1948; Fulbright lectr. U. Rome, also Palermo, Italy, 1955. Fellow Econometric Soc. (council 1960, v.p. 1961, pres. 1962), Am. (v.p. 1975 pres. 1976), Internat. (v.p. 1977) econ. assns., Am. Acad. Arts and Scis.; mem. Nat. Acad. Scis. Co-author: National Incomes and International Trade, 1953; Planning Production, Inventories and Work Forces, 1960; The Role of Anticipations and Plans in Economic Behavior and Their Use in Economic Analysis and Forecasting, 1961; New Mortgage Designs for Stable Housing in an Inflationary Environment, 1975; Mercato del Lavoro, Distribuzione del Reddito e Consumi Privati, 1975. Home: 25 Clark St Belmont MA 02178 Office: Sloan Sch Mgmt Mass Inst Tech Cambridge MA 02139

MODLIN, GEORGE MATTHEWS, univ. chancellor; b. Elizabeth City, N.C., July 13, 1903; s. John William and Nannie E. (Matthews) M.; A.B., Wake Forest (N.C.) U., 1924, LL.D., 1947; M.A., Princeton, 1925, Ph.D., 1932; Dr. Laws, Stetson U., 1962, Hampden-Sydney Coll., 1971; U. Richmond, 1971; m. Virginia Pendleton Brinkley, June 2, 1928. Asst. econ. Princeton, 1927-28, instr., 1928-32, asst. prof., 1932-38; part- time lectr. econs. Rutgers U., 1936-38; prof. econs., dean Sch. Bus. Adminstrn. U. Richmond (Va.), 1938-46, pres., 1946-71, chancellor, 1971—. Mem. pub. panel War Labor Bd., 1943-45. Trustee Keesee Ednl. Fund, Va. Found. Ind. Colls. Mem. Richmond C. of C. (pres. 1951), So. U. Conf. (pres. 1955), So. Assn. Bapt. Schs. and Colls. (pres. 1952), Assn. Va. Colls. (pres. 1952), Assn. Am. Colls. (pres. 1962), Phi Beta Kappa, Kappa Alpha, Omicron Delta Kappa. Clubs: Country of Virginia, Commonwealth. Author: (with F.T. De Vyver) Development of Economic Society, 1936, rev., 1946; (with A.M. McIsaac) Social Control of Industry, 1938. Home: University of Richmond Richmond VA 23173

MODLIN, PHILIP HODGIN, govt. ofcl.; b. Jamestown, N.C., Oct. 9, 1926; s. Henry Romulus, Sr., and Lucy Corinna (Hodgin) M.; student U. Mich., 1943-45; A.B., High Point Coll., 1947; postgrad. Law Sch., George Washington U., 1948-49; J.D., U. N.C., 1950; m. Rosalind Robinson, Aug. 20, 1953; children—Melanie Ann, Jennifer Bryan, Ann Robinson. Admitted to N.C. bar, 1951, D.C. bar, 1951; various atty. and labor relations positions U.S. Govt. and pvt. corps., 1952-58; asst. to Dep. Atty. Gen., also dep. dir. Exec. Office for U.S. Attys. of U.S. Dept. Justice, 1958-70; dir. Exec. Office for U.S. Attys., Office Dep. Atty. Gen., U.S. Dept. Justice, Washington, 1970-75, exec. asst. to dep. atty. gen., 1975-77, dep. asso. atty. gen., 1977—; mem. U.S. Bd. Parole, 1975. Mem. Sigma Chi, Phi Alpha Delta. Republican. Methodist. Home: 1307 Kingston Ave Alexandria VA 22302 Office: 10th and Constitution Ave Dept of Justice Washington DC 20530

MODREY, JOSEPH, mech. engr.; b. N.Y.C., Jan. 24, 1916; s. Florian Modrovsky and Mary Maly; B.S., Columbia, 1937, M.S., 1938; D. Eng., Rensselaer Poly. Inst., 1963; m. Evelyn F. Tabery, June 2, 1944; children—Laurie, Jon. Test engr. Wright Aero. Corp., 1938-40, project engr., 1940-44, gas turbine design engr., 1944-47; grad. instr. Stevens Inst. Tech., 1944-47; prof. mech. engring., head machine design Poly. Inst. Bklyn., 1947-55; head dept. mech. engring. Union Coll., 1955-63; prof. mech. engring. Purdue Univ., Lafayette, Ind., 1965—. Cons. engr. Bergen Research & Engring. Corp., 1955—, Mid West Applied Sci. Corp.; dir. NASA doctoral engring. systems traineeships. NSF faculty fellow, 1959-60. Mem. Am. Soc. Engring. Edn. (nat. chmn. mech. engring. div.), Soc. Automotive Engrs., ASME, Sigma Xi. Patentee field highspeed machinery. Home: 1100 Ravinia Rd West Lafayette IN 47906

MODZELEWSKI, ERNEST F., savs. and loan assn. exec.; b. Chicago Heights, Ill., Nov. 29, 1936; s. Frank and Sophie M.; B.A., DePauw U., 1958; LL.B., U. Ill.; m. Nancy Caroline Lendrum, June 10, 1959; children—Lisa Caroline, Karen Frances, Melinda Beth, Pamela Ann. With 1st Fed. Savs. and Loan Assn., Phoenix, 1962—, now exec. v.p. Past pres. The Thunderbirds, Valley Big Bros. Mem. Ariz. State Bar Assn., Ariz. State C. of C. (chmn. bd.). Republican. Roman Catholic. Club: Sertoma. Home: 910 El Camino Dr Phoenix AZ 85021 Office: 3003 N Central Ave Phoenix AZ 85012

MOE, CHESNEY RUDOLPH, educator; b. Ont., Can., Oct. 6, 1908; s. Oscar and Edith (Miller) M.; A.B., Stanford, 1929, A.M., 1931; Ph.D., U. So. Calif., 1941; m. Berthe Newton, Aug. 24, 1935; (dec. Sept. 1950); 1 son, Ronald; m. 2d, Bernice Woolman, July 21, 1951; 1 dau., Donna. Asst. in physics San Diego State U., 1929-30, instr., 1931-35, asst. prof., 1935-39, asso. prof., 1939-45, prof. physics, 1945—, chmn. dept. physics, 1948-51, 53-56, 61-64, asso. chmn. div. phys. scis., 1956-61. Mem. bd. rev. Marine Phys. Lab., U. Calif., 1946-55; cons. Tracor, Inc., in acoustics Jet Propulsion Lab., Pasadena, Cal., 1968-70; dir. Electronics Investment Corp., 1959-63. Served as comdr. USNR, 1942-46, 1951-54; capt. Res. ret. Registered profl. engr., Cal. Fellow Acoustical Soc. Am.; mem. Sigma Xi, Phi Delta Kappa, Sigma Pi Sigma, Kappa Sigma. Kiwanian. Contbr. articles to Proc. Nat. Acad. Sci., Jour. Acoustical Soc. Am. Home: 4669 E Talmadge Dr San Diego CA 92116

MOE, EDWARD OWEN, educator; b. Provo, Utah, Aug. 31, 1914; s. Edward Owen and Nancy (Carter) M.; student Graceland Coll., 1934; B.S., Brigham Young U. , 1938; postgrad. Am. U., 1938-39, 46-47; Ph.D., Cornell U., 1951; m. Lois Gaustad, Aug. 9, 1947; children—Marylyn Kristen, Janet Nancy, Debra Kathleen. Mem. faculty Cornell U., Ithaca, N.Y., 1948-55, asso. prof. sociology, 1951-53, prof., 1953-55, vis. prof., 1971—; prof. Mich. State U., 1955-62; prof. sociology, dir. bur. community devel. U. Utah, Salt Lake City, 1962-73; prin. sociologist, coordinator rural devel. Coop. Research, Sci. and Edn. Adminstrn., U.S. Dept. Agr., Washington, 1972-78; cons. Office Urban Community Devel., Govt. Panama, AID, State Dept., 1968-72, OAS, 1957-59, YW-YMCA, A.R.C. Mem. exec. com. NTL Inst. for Applied Behavioral Sci., 1952-55, 65-68, Model Cities Bd., Salt Lake County, 1969-70; pres. Community Services Council Salt Lake Area, 1966-67; mem. Citizens' Adv. Com., Salt Lake City, 1969-73. Bd. dirs. A.R.C., Salt Lake City. Served with AUS, 1943-46. Recipient Distinguished service award Salt Lake Area Community Services Council, 1970, Distinguished Service award Utah Fedn. Women's Clubs, 1968, 69, Gold Key award City Cheyenne, Wyo., 1970. Mem. Rural Sociol. Soc. (council, pres. elect 1978-79, pres. 1979—), AAUP, Am. Sociol. Assn., Soc. Psychol. Study Social Issues, Phi Kappa Phi, Tau Kappa Alpha, Alpha Kappa Psi. Co-developer Nat. Community Leadership Labs., NTL Inst. Applied Behavioral Scis., 1960-72, Community Leadership program Western Can. and Northwest Territory, 1969-73. Contbr. several books; editorial bd. Jour. Family and Community Health, 1977—. Home: 1414 Sigsbee Ave Salt Lake City UT 84103. *The essence of living is being engaged with other people, one's wife, family, friends, colleagues, neighbors and fellow citizens in the pursuit of significant ends. Things seem to work best when one sensitively lives each day to the fullest and plans and aspires each day as if he were to live forever. Such a perspective is possible if one recognizes that time and change require engaging in relationships, then disengaging from some relationships, and engaging again in new ones. A sense of continuity, a sense of being and becoming dignifies the days and enriches the years.*

MOE, GORDON KENNETH, physiologist, educator; b. Fairchild, Wis., May 30, 1915; s. Sylvester and Ellen Mae (Hanson) M.; student Virginia (Minn.) Jr. Coll., 1932-34; B.S., U. Minn., 1937, M.S., 1939, Ph.D., 1940; M.D., Harvard, 1943; m. Janet Woodruff Foster, Aug. 6, 1938; children—Christopher, Melanie, Jonathan, Bruce, Sally, Eric. Instr. Physiology U. Minn., 1939-40; instr. pharmacology Harvard Med. Sch., 1941-44; asst. prof. pharmacology U. Mich. Med. Sch., 1944-46, asso. prof., 1946-50; prof. physiology, chmn. dept. State U. N.Y. Coll. Medicine, Syracuse, 1950-60; dir. Masonic Med. Research Lab., Utica, N.Y., 1960—. Chmn. physiol. test com. Nat. Bd. Med. Examiners, 1956-57; mem. WHO vis. scientists, Israel, Iran, 1951; cons. Walter Reed Army Med. Center. Mem. Nat. Heart and Lung Adv. Council, 1970-74. Recipient travel award Internat. Physiol. Congress Oxford, 1947; Outstanding Achievement award U. Minn., 1958; Merit award Am. Heart Assn., 1968; Am. Physiol. Soc. fellow, Western Res. U., 1940-41; USPHS fellow Instituto Nacional de Cardiologia, Mexico City, 1948. Fellow AAAS (chmn. sect. 1958), Am. Coll. Cardiology (hon.); mem. Am. Physiol. Soc., N.Y. Soc. Med. Research, Am. Heart Assn. (chmn. basic sci. council 1962-63, chmn. research com. 1959-60), Mexican Acad. Medicine (hon.), Sigma Xi, Alpha Omega Alpha. Mason (33 deg.). Office: Masonic Med Research Lab Utica NY 13501

MOE, JOHN HOWARD, orthopaedic surgeon, educator; b. Grafton, N.D., Aug. 14, 1905; s. Hans Jacob and Gunhild (Loseth) M.; B.S., U. N.D., 1923; M.B., Northwestern U., 1929, M.D., 1930; m. Marguerite Elizabeth Clough, 1936 (dec. 1969); children—Elizabeth Ann, Lawrence Dexter; m. 3d, Mary Lou Kruger Wood, Aug. 1, 1976. Mem. staff Med. Sch. U. Minn., Mpls., 1933—, prof. emeritus dept. orthopedic surgery, former prof., chmn. dept. orthopedic surgery, former chief staff Gillette Children's Hosp.; founder, dir. Twin Cities Scoliosis Center, Mpls.; founder Scoliosis Service Santa Casa Hosp., Sao Paulo, Brazil, 1969, Twin Cities Scoliosis Fund, John Moe Scoliosis fellowship of U. Minn. Dept. Orthopedic Surgery, Mpls.; dir. Savannah Scoliosis Center. Recipient Bernardo O'Higgins medal, Chile, 1969, Sioux award U. N.D., 1968. Diplomate Am. Bd. Orthopedic Surgery. Mem. A.C.S., Am. Acad. Orthopedic Surgery, Clin. Orthopedic Soc. (past pres.), Am. Orthopedic Assn. (pres., 1971-72), Hennepin County Med. Soc. (pres. 1958), Minn. Acad. Medicine Soc. Internat. Orthopedics and Surgery (U.S. del. 1971-75), Canadian Orthopedic Assn., Scoliosis Research Soc. (founder, pres.), Nat. Acad. Sci., Nat. Acad. Medicine (Brazil), Venezuelan Orthopedic Soc., Argentine Soc. Orthopedics and Traumatology (corr.), Brit. Orthopedic Assn. (cor.); hon. mem. Chilean, Brazilian, Colombian, Peruvian orthopedic socs., Jugoslavian Orthopedic Soc. Club: Interlachen. Co-author: The Milwaukee Brace in Scoliosis, Scoliosis and Other Spinal Deformities, 1978. Contbr. numerous articles to profl. jours. Home: 8441 Irwin Rd 207 Bloomington MN 55437 Office: Twin Cities Scoliosis Center Fairview-St Mary's Med Bldg Suite 500 606 24th Ave S Minneapolis MN 55454

MOE, LAWRENCE HENRY, educator, organist; b. Chgo., May 9, 1917; s. H. L. and Hannah (Westerlund) M.; B.Mus., Northwestern U., 1939, M.Mus., 1940; M.A., Harvard, 1952, Ph.D., 1956; m. Georgiana Lund, Aug. 18, 1946; children—Eric Hans, Charis. Tchr. music history and theory Central Wash. Coll., Ellensburg, 1941-50; organist-choirmaster St. Paul's Episcopal Cathedral, Boston, 1954-57; mem. faculty U. Calif. at Berkeley, 1957—, prof. music, 1963—, chmn. dept., 1964-69, 78—, univ. organist, 1957—; rec. artist for Unicorn, Kapp, Fantasy and Cambridge records. Recipient Alumni Merit award Northwestern U., 1965; Fulbright Research fellow, 1952, 53, 63; U. Calif. Humanities Inst. fellow, 1970, 77. Mem. Am. Guild Organist (dean), Am. Musicol. Soc., Hist. Organ Soc. Episcopalian. Home: 1120 Miller Ave Berkeley CA 94708

MOE, RICHARD, govt. ofcl.; b. Duluth, Minn., Nov. 27, 1936; s. Russell James and Virginia Mary (Palmer) M.; B.A., Williams Coll., 1959; LL.B., U. Minn., 1966; m. Julia Neimeyer, Dec. 26, 1964; children—Eric Palmer, Andrew Neimeyer, Alexandra Julia. Adminstrv. asst. to mayor City of Mpls., 1961-62, to lt. gov. State of Minn., 1963-66; fin. dir. Minn. Democratic Farmer-Labor Party, 1967-69, chmn., 1969-72; adminstrv. asst. to Sen. Walter F. Mondale of Minn., Washington, 1972-76, chief of staff Vice Pres. Walter F. Mondale, 1977—. Vice pres. Dem. State Chmn. Assn., 1971-72. Home: 3611 Underwood St Chevy Chase MD 20015 Office: Office of Vice Pres Exec Office Bldg Washington DC 20501

MOEDE, AUSTIN LYN, physician; b. Chelan, Wash., Aug. 23, 1934; s. Allyn L. and Margaret M. (Aust) M.; A.A., Sacramento Jr. Coll., 1957; A.B., U. Calif. at Berkeley, 1959; M.D., George Washington U., 1963; m. Sharon K. Walker, May 6, 1967; children—John, William. Intern D.C. Gen. Hosp., Washington, 1963-64; resident internal medicine D.C. Gen. Hosp., also George Washington U. Hosp., 1964-67; instr. medicine George Washington U. Sch. Medicine, 1967-68; fellow hematology D.C. Gen. Hosp., 1968-70; USPHS sr. research fellow in hematology U. Wash. Med. Sch., Seattle, 1970-71; regional med. officer Am. embassy, Kabul, Afghanistan, 1971-73, Am. embassy, Jakarta, Indonesia, 1974-75, Am. embassy, Panama City, 1975-77, Am. embassy, Athens, Greece, 1977—; mem. dept. internal medicine Gorgas Hosp., C.Z., 1975-77. Served with AUS, 1953-55. Mem. Am. Soc. Hematology, Am., Royal socs. tropical medicine and hygiene. Address: Am Embassy APO New York City NY 09253

MOEDE, GUSTAVE HERMAN, JR., telephone co. exec.; b. Kewaunee County, Wis., Nov. 25, 1916; s. Gustave Herman and Elizabeth (Tews) M.; Ph.B., U. Wis., 1939; m. Audrey Jane Maas, Feb. 18, 1937; children—Gustave Herman, III, Walter M. With Commonwealth Telephone Co., 1939-43; with Wis. Telephone Co., Milw., 1946-53, 54-59, 62-63, 67—, v.p. ops., 1967-73, pres., 1973—, also dir.; with AT&T Co., 1953-54, 61-62, 65-67; dir. First Wis. Corp., Rexnord, Inc., Oscar Mayer & Co., Square D Co., First Wis. Nat. Bank, Milw., Congoleum Corp. Bd. dirs. Milw. Children's Hosp., 1969—, Jr. Achievement Southeastern Wis., 1971—, Greater Milw. Com., 1973—, United Way Greater Milw., 1973—, YMCA Met. Milw., 1973—, Milw. Blood Center, 1973—, Wis. Council Econ. Edn., 1973—, Wis. Found. Ind. Colls., 1974—. Served with USNR, 1943-46. Mem. Met. Milw. Assn. Commerce (dir.). Clubs: Milw. Country, Milwaukee. Home: 8117 N Gray Log Ln Milwaukee WI 53217 Office: 722 N Broadway Milwaukee WI 53202

MOEHRING, HORST RUDOLF, historian of religions, educator; b. Goerlitz, Germany, July 27, 1927; s. Rudolf Paul and Lina (Krueger) M.; came to U.S., 1951, naturalized, 1970; student U. Minn., 1953; A.M., U. Ill., 1954; Ph.D. (Carnegie fellow), U. Chgo., 1957; A.M. ad eundem, Brown U., 1964; m. Constance Marie Correll, Nov. 11, 1951. Instr., Brown U., 1957-59, asst. prof. religious studies, 1959-64, asso. prof., 1964-70, prof., 1970—, chmn. dept. religious studies, 1970-73; vis. lectr. Yale U., 1964-65. Lilly fellow, 1965-66. Mem. Soc. Bibl. Lit. (chmn. group on Hellenistic Judaism 1978—), Societas Novi Testamenti Studiorum, Philo Inst., Inst. Antiquity and Christianity (corr.). Contbr. articles on Hellenistic Judaism and early Christianity to profl. jours. Office: Dept Religious Studies Brown U Providence RI 02912

MOELLEKEN, WOLFGANG WILFRIED, educator; b. Duisburg, Germany, Jan. 14, 1934; came to U.S., 1961, naturalized, 1979; s. August and Emmy (d'Oliva) M.; student U. Cologne, 1955-57; B.E., U. B.C., 1961; M.A., U. Wash., 1962, Ph.D., 1965; m. Melita Anne Hildebrandt, Dec. 27, 1958; children—Brent Roderick Wilfred, Alan Patrick Wilfred, Sonja Melita Clarice. Asst. prof. U. Calif., Riverside, 1964-67; asso. prof. U. Va., 1967-68; asso. prof. SUNY, Stony Brook, 1968-69; prof. U. Calif., Davis, 1969-77; prof. Germanic langs. and lits., head dept. fgn. langs. and lits. Purdue U., 1977-79; prof., chmn. dept. Germanic langs. SUNY, Albany, 1979—. Calif. Humanities Inst. grantee and fellow, 1965-72, Regents fellow, 1975-76; Am. Council Learned Socs. grantee, 1966-75, Am. Philos. Soc. grantee, 1972. Mem. MLA, Medieval Acad. Am., Am. Assn. Tchrs. German. Author several books and monographs. Editor: German Lang. and Lit. Monographs, 1976—; gen. editor, Purdue U Monographs in Romance Langs., 1977-79; founding editor, Davis Medieval Texts and Studies. Contbr. articles to profl. jours. Home: 14 N Loudon Heights Loudonville NY 12211 Office: Dept Germanic Langs and Lits State U NY Albany NY 12222

MOELLER, CHARLES, JR., life ins. co. exec.; b. N.Y.C., Aug. 1, 1916; s. Charles and Augusta (Veit) M.; B.S., N.Y. U., 1941, M.B.A., 1944, Ph.D., 1953; m. Julia F. Doolittle, Sept. 3, 1939; children—Anne M., Peter A., Mary V., Thomas J. With Met. Life Ins. Co., N.Y.C., 1941—, v.p., economist, 1962-72, sr. v.p., 1973—; lectr. real estate N.Y. U., 1953-64. Trustee, Am. Enterprise Inst., John A. Hartford Found. Mem. Am. Econ. Assn., Am. Statis. Assn., Econometric Soc., Am. Risk and Ins. Assn., N.Y. State, N.Y.C. councils for econ. edn., Nat. Assn. Bus. Economists, Beta Gamma Sigma, Pi Mu Epsilon. Club: Sky (N.Y.C.). Home: 288 Prospect Ave Little Silver NJ 07739 Office: 1 Madison Ave New York City NY 10010

MOELLER, DADE WILLIAM, environ. engr., educator; b. Grant, Fla., Feb. 27, 1927; s. Robert A. and Victoria (Bolton) M.; B.C.E., Ga. Inst. Tech., 1947, M.S. in Civil Engring., 1948; Ph.D., N.C. State U., 1957; m. Betty Jean Radford, Oct. 7, 1949; children—Garland Radford, Mark Bolton, William Kehne, Matthew Palmer, Elisabeth Anne. Commd. jr. asst. san. engr. USPHS, 1948, advanced through grades to san. engr. dir., 1961; research engr. Los Alamos Sci. Lab., 1949-52; staff asst. Radiol. Health Program, Washington, 1952-54; research asso. Oak Ridge Nat. Lab., 1956-57; chief radiol. health tng. Taft San. Engring. Center, Cin., 1957-61; officer charge Northeastern Radiol. Health Lab., Winchester, Mass., 1961-66; asso. dir. Kresge Center Environ. Health, Harvard Sch. Pub. Health, 1966—, prof. engring. in environmental health, head dept. environmental health scis., 1968—; cons. radiol. health Profl. Exam. Service, Am. Pub. Health Assn., 1960-62, WHO, 1965—. Chmn. Am. Bd. Health Physics, 1967-70; mem. Nat. Council Radiation Protection and Measurements, 1968—; mem. com. A, Internat. Commn. on Radiol. Protection, 1978—; chmn. nat. air pollution manpower devel. adv. com. U.S. Environ. Protection Agy., 1972-75; mem. adv. com. reactor safeguards U.S. Nuclear Regulatory Commn., 1973—, vice chmn., 1975, chmn., 1976. Fellow Am. Pub. Health Assn., Am. Nuclear Soc., mem. Am. Acad. Environ. Engrs. (bd. dirs. 1968-73), Nat. Acad. Engring., Health Physics Soc. (pres. 1971-72), AAAS. Contbr. articles to profl. jours. Home: 27 Wildwood Dr Bedford MA 01730 Office: 665 Huntington Ave Boston MA 02115

MOELLER, KARL DIETER, educator; b. Hamburg, Germany, June 15, 1927; s. Karl Rudolf and Emma (Madauss) M.; Diploma in Physics, U. Hamburg, 1954, Ph.D., 1957; postdoctoral fellow, Sorbonne, Paris, 1958-60; m. Sylvia Ellinor Freiin v. Hodenberg, June 30, 1959; children—Bettina, Beate, Barbara. Came to U.S., 1960, naturalized, 1977. Staff mem. U.S. Army Signal Corps Lab., Ft. Monmouth, N.J., 1960-63; prof. physics, dir. molecular spectroscopy lab. Fairleigh Dickinson U., Teaneck, N.J., 1963—; vis. prof. U. Buenos Aires, 1969; vis. scientist ESRIN, Frascati, Rome, 1970; research contract NIH, 1974-76, U.S. Army, 1977—; vis. prof. U. Paris VI, 1976; cons. NASA-ERC, Cambridge, 1966-68, U.S. Army, 1971-75. Mem. Optical Soc. Am. Author: Far Infrared Spectroscopy, 1971. Contbr. articles profl. jours. Home: 80 Glenwood Rd Upper Saddle River NJ 07458 Office: Fairleigh Dickinson U Teaneck NJ 07666

MOELLER, ROBERT CHARLES, III, curator; b. Providence, Jan. 22, 1938; s. Robert Charles, Jr. and Eleanor Frances (Dowling) M.; grad. Choate Sch., 1955; B.A., Washington and Lee U., 1959; M.A., Harvard, 1963; m. Dorothy Jean Westby, July 12, 1958 (div. 1974); children—Kristen Read, Robert Charles IV. With Collyer Insulated Wire Co., R.I., 1960-62; research asso. Duke, 1967, instr., 1968, dir. Art Mus., 1968-69, asst. prof., 1968-69; asst. curator dept. European decorative arts and sculpture Mus. Fine Arts, Boston, 1970, curator, 1971, curatorial rep., 1971—. Teaching fellow Harvard, 1964-65.

N.E.A. grantee, 1972-73. Mem. Mediaeval Acad. Am., Coll. Art Assn., Société Francaise d'Archeologie, Internat. Council Museums, Am. Assn. Museums. Home: 29 River Rd Wayland MA 01778 Office: Mus Fine Arts Huntington Ave Boston MA 02115

MOELLER, THERALD, chemist, educator; b. North Bend, Oreg., Apr. 3, 1913; s. Edward and Kate (Wickham) M.; B.S., Oreg. State Coll., 1934; Ph.D., U. Wis., 1938; m. Ellyn Clara Elizabeth Stephenson, May 17, 1935; children—Karlyn Ann (Mrs. Karlyn M. Coverdale), Kathryn Jean (Mrs. James J. Krause), Stephen Therald. Faculty, Mich. State Coll., East Lansing, 1938-40; faculty U. Ill., Urbana, 1940-69, prof. inorganic chemistry, 1953-69; prof. chemistry Ariz. State U., Tempe, 1969—, chmn. dept., 1969-75. Cons. Argonne Nat. Lab., various indsl. concerns; lectr. Mem. Am. Chem. Soc. (chmn. div. inorganic chemistry 1961), Chem. Soc. Author: Inorganic Chemistry, 1952; Qualitative Analysis, 1958; The Chemistry of the Lanthanides, 1963, 75; (with J.C. Bailar, J. Kleinberg) University Chemistry, 1965; (with D.F. Martin) Laboratory Chemistry, 1965; (with R. O'Connor) Ions in Aqueous Systems, 1972; (with Bailar, Kleinberg, Guss, Castellion, Metz) Chemistry, 1978. Editor: Inorganic Syntheses, Vol. 5, 1957. Home: 3629 N 49th St Phoenix AZ 85018 Office: Dept Chemistry Ariz State U Tempe AZ 85821

MOELLERING, ALFRED WILLIAM, county judge; b. Fort Wayne, Ind., Dec. 13, 1926; s. William C. and Hilda (Dreyer) M.; B.S. in Bus., Ind. U., 1951, LL.B., 1953; m. Carol L. Wortman, June 22, 1958; children—Caroline, David. Admitted to Ind. bar, 1953, also U.S. Supreme Ct.; pvt. practice, Fort Wayne, 1954-62; U.S. atty. No. Dist. Ind., 1962-70; judge Superior Ct. Allen County, Ind., 1971—; lectr. parliamentary procedure Ind. U., Fort Wayne, 1956-65. Pres., Festival Music Theatre, Fort Wayne, 1956-57. Democratic nominee for mayor Fort Wayne, 1955; regional dir. Young Dem. Am., 1955-56. Bd. dirs. Fort Wayne Philharmonic Orch., 1969-72. Served with AUS, 1945-46. Mem. Am., Ind., Allen County (sec. 1959-60) bar assns., Am. Judicature Soc., Lutheran Laymen's League. Home: 5120 DeRome Dr Fort Wayne IN 46815 Office: Allen County Courthouse Fort Wayne IN 46802

MOEN, DONALD PHILIP, mfg. co. exec.; b. Amherst, Wis., Feb. 19, 1921; s. Ole and Mabel (Engebretson) M.; student Lawrence Coll., 1946-47; B.B.A., U. Wis., 1949; grad. AMP, Harvard U., 1972; m. Harriet A. Dale, July 10, 1941; children—Daune, Lisa. Asst. treas. Delta Hardware Co., Escanaba, Mich., 1949-51; asst. controller Roddis Plywood Corp., Marshfield, Wis., 1951-60; v.p., treas. L.L. Felker Co., Marshfield, 1960-65; pres. Marathon Battery Co., St. Paul, 1965-71; sr. v.p. Marathon Mfg. Co., Houston, 1971-75; pres. Eta Engrs., Inc., Houston, 1975-77; v.p. fin. Utility/Energy Systems, Inc., Houston, 1977-78; pres. Nat. Exec. Search-Tex., Houston, 1978-79; exec. v.p. Zimmermann Bros. Inc., Marshfield, Wis., 1979—. Pres. bd. edn., Marshfield, 1955-60; alderman, Marshfield, 1952-55. Served to 2d lt. AUS, 1942-46; ETO. C.P.A., Tex., Wis. Mem. Wis., Tex. socs. C.p.a.'s, Am. Inst. C.P.A.'s. Mason. Home: 709 N Schmidt Marshfield WI 54449 Office: Zimmermann Bros Inc Marshfield WI 54449

MOEN, DONNE PHILIP, banker; b. Oak Park, Ill., Mar. 16, 1936; s. Marcus M. and Lois (Fairchild) M.; B.S.C., U. Iowa, 1958; M.B.A., U. So. Calif., 1965; m. Elizabeth Heuler, May 14, 1977; children—Mark, Kevin. Asst. cashier Bank Am., Los Angeles, 1958-61; registered rep. Francis I. duPont & Co., Los Angeles, 1961-63; exec. v.p. Union Bank, Los Angeles, 1963—. Served to 2d lt. AUS, 1959-60. Mem. Robert Morris Assos. Clubs: Stock Exchange (San Francisco, Jonathan. Home: 28737 Shire Oak Dr Rancho Palos Verdes CA 90274

MOENS, PETER B., biologist; b. Sukabumi, Indonesia, May 15, 1931; s. Peter B. and Anneke D. (RitsemavanEck) M.; B.S. in Forestry, U. Toronto, 1957, M.A., 1961, Ph.D., 1963; m. Marja Schroder, May 8, 1953; children—Richard, Theodore, Vivian, Cecilia, Francis. Lectr. biology York U., Downsview, Ont., Can., 1963-64, asst. prof., 1964-67, asso. prof., 1967-71, prof., 1971—. Fellow Royal Soc. Can.; mem. Genetic Soc. Am., Am. Soc. Cell Biology, Can. Soc. Cell Biology, AAAS, Genetic Soc. Can. (pres. 1979). Asso. editor Can. Jour. Genetic Cytology. Office: Dept Biology York Univ Downsview ON M3J 1P3 Canada

MOERSCH, HERMAN JOHN, physician; b. St. Paul, Mar. 14, 1895; s. Julius and Cecilia (Kiefer) M.; B.S., U. Minn., 1918, M.D., 1921, M.S., 1925; m. Charline Buck, Sept. 26, 1925 (dec. Apr. 11, 1971); children—Richard, Donald; m. 2d, Mrs. Howard K. Gray, Jan. 3, 1973. Intern, City and County Hosp., St. Paul, 1920-21; 1st asst. in medicine Mayo Clinic, Rochester, Minn., 1924-26, mem. staff dept. med., 1926—, head sect. med. and personal endoscopy, 1938—, chmn. medicine sect., 1948—, instr. medicine Mayo Found., U. Minn., 1925-28, asst. prof., 1928- 33, asso. prof., 1933-47, prof., 1947—. Recipient Great Cross Merit (W. German Republic); Rudolph Schindler award; Chevalier Jackson award; Gold medal Am. Coll. Chest Physicians, 1965. Mem. AMA, Am. Assn. Thoracic Surg., Am. Broncho-Esophagol. Soc., Am. Gastrocopic Soc., A.C.P., Am. Coll. Chest Physicians (dir. edn., research), Central Soc. Clin. Research, Am. Gastro-Enterol. Assn., Sigma Xi, Alpha Kappa Kappa, Alpha Omega Alpha. Republican. Contbr. articles to profl. jours. Home: 2221 Hillside Ln SW Rochester MN 55901

MOERTEL, CHARLES GEORGE, physician; b. Milw., Oct. 17, 1927; s. Charles Henry and Alma Helen (Soffel) M.; B.S., U. Ill., 1946-51, M.D., 1953; M.S., U. Minn., 1958; m. Virginia Claire Sheridan, Mar. 22, 1952; children—Charles Stephen, Christopher Loren, Heather Lynn, David Matthew. Intern, Los Angeles County Hosp., 1953-54; resident in internal medicine Mayo Found., Rochester, Minn., 1954-57; cons. Mayo Clinic, Rochester, 1957—, chmn. dept. oncology, 1975—, dir. Mayo Comprehensive Cancer Center, 1975—; prof. medicine Mayo Med. Sch., 1972-76, prof. oncology, 1976—; mem. oncologic drugs adv. com. FDA; mem. cancer adv. com. AMA; Walter Hubert lectr. Br it. Assn. Cancer Research, 1976; Ejnar Perman Meml. lectr. Swedish Surg. Assn., 1978. Served with U.S. Army, 1946-47. Mem. Am. Soc. Clin. Oncology (pres. 1979-80), Soc. Clin. Trials (dir.), Am. Assn. Cancer Research, Gastrointestinal Tumor Study Group (co-chmn.), A.C.P., Soc. Surg. Oncology, Am. Gastroenterologic Assn., Sigma Xi. Author: Multiple Primary Malignant Neoplasms, 1966; Advanced gastrointestinal Cancer, Clinical Management and Chemotherapy, 1969; editorial bd. Cancer, 1974—, Cancer Medicine, 1978—, Current Problems in Cancer, 1978—; research in treatment of gastrointestinal cancer, clin. pharmacology. Home: 48 Skyline Dr Rochester MN 55901 Office: 200 SW 1st St Rochester MN 55901

MOESER, JAMES CHARLES, musician, univ. dean; b. Colorado City, Tex., Apr. 3, 1939; s. Charles Victor and Virginia (James) M.; B.Mus., U. Tex. at Austin, 1961, M.M., 1964; postgrad. (Fulbright grantee), Hochschule fur Musik, Berlin, Germany, 1961-62; D.M.A. (Univ. fellow), U. Mich., 1966; m. Jesse Kaye Edwards, Jan. 26, 1963; children—James Christopher, Kathryn Carter. Chmn. dept. organ, asst. prof. organ U. Kans., 1966-69, asso. prof., 1969-74, prof., 1974—, dean Sch. Fine Arts, 1975—. Organist, choirmaster Plymouth Congl. Ch., Lawrence, Kans., 1967—; organist nat. conf. Music Tchrs. Nat. Assn., Portland, Oreg., 1972, Los Angeles, 1974; concert organist, on tour, W. Ger., 1977, Lisbon (Portugal) Festival, 1978. Kent fellow Danforth Found.; Danforth Asso. Mem. Am. Guild Organists (past dean chpt., nat. dir. student groups 1973-75). Democrat. Congregationalist. Rotarian. Home: 3037 Campfire St Lawrence KS 66044

MOESTA, RODMAN CHARLES, lawyer; b. Detroit, Oct. 3, 1923; s. Waldemar Charles and Elvera Louise (Frederick) M.; student U. Mich., 1941-43; B.A., U. Detroit, 1946, LL.B., 1949; m. Mary B. Corcoran, June 8, 1944; children—Maureen (Mrs. John Bruce), Anne (Mrs. William Schultz), Elizabeth. Admitted to Mich. bar, 1949; since practiced in Detroit; partner Johnson, Campbell & Moesta, 1966—. Served with AUS, 1943-46. Decorated Bronze Star, Combat Inf. Badge. Mem. Am., Detroit bar assns., State Bar Mich., Fedn. Ins. Counsels, Def. Research Inst., V.F.W. Club: Beach Grove Golf & Country (Windsor, Ont., Can.). Home: 1148 Grayton St Grosse Pointe Park MI 48230 Office: 912 Buhl Bldg Detroit MI 48226

MOEVS, ROBERT WALTER, composer, educator; b. LaCrosse, Wis., Dec. 2, 1920; s. Walter and Florence (Verchota) M.; A.B. cum laude, Harvard, 1942, A.M., 1952; postgrad. Conservatoire Nat., Paris, 1947-51; m. Mariateresa Marabini, Oct. 1, 1953; children—Marina, Christian. Fellow, Am. Acad., Rome, Italy, 1952-55; instr., asst. prof. music Harvard, 1955-63; asso. prof. music Rutgers U., New Brunswick, N.J., 1964-68, prof., 1968—, chmn. dept. music, 1974—. Mem. Cath. Commn. on Intellectual and Cultural Affairs, 1966—, chmn., 1973-74; chmn. Millstone Valley (N.J.) Preservation Soc., 1965-75. Guggenheim fellow, Rome, 1963-64. Served to 1st lt. USAAF, 1942-47. Mem. Internat. Soc. For Contemporary Music (mem. exec. com. Am. sect. 1967-70.), Am. Soc. U. Composers. Composer numerous works including 14 Variations for Orch., 1952; 3 Symphonic Pieces, 1955; String Quartet, 1957; Attis, for chorus and orch., I, 1958, II, 1963; Concerto for Pfte, Percussion and Orch. (Stockhausen Internat. prize), 1960-77; Variazioni, for viola and cello, 1961; Et Nunc, Reges, for women's Chorus, flute, clarinet, bass clarinet, 1963; Et Occidentem Illustra, for chorus and orch., 1964; Musica da Camera; 1965 Piece for Synket, 1967; A Brief Mass, 1968; Time, 1969; Bach es ist genug, for organ, 1970; Phoenix, for piano, 1971; Musica da Camera II, 1972; Main Travelled Roads, for orch., 1973; the Aulos Player for two choruses and two organs, 1975; Ludi Praeteriti for two pianos, 1976; Collana Musicale for Piano, 1977. Home: Blackwell's Mills Belle Mead NJ 08502 Office: Dept Music Rutgers U New Brunswick NJ 08903

MOFFAT, DONALD, actor; b. Plymouth, Eng., Dec. 26, 1930; s. Walter George and Kathleen Mary (Smith) M.; student Royal Acad. Dramatic Art, 1952-54; m. Anne Murray Elisperman, May 22, 1954 (div. Aug. 1968); children—Kathleen Wendy, Gabriel Robin; m. 2d, Gwen Arner, May 1969; children—Lynn Marie, Catherine Jean. Appeared in numerous plays throughout U.S. 1956—, latest being War and Peace, Peace, 1964, 66, Man and Superman, 1964, The Hostage, 1964, Judith, 1964, The Wild Duck, 1965, 66, You Can't Take It With You, 1965, 66, Krapp's Last Tape, 1965, Right You Are, 1966, School for Scandal, 1966, Above Repertory, 1967, Cherry Orchard, 1967, 68, Cock-a-Doodle Dandy, 1968, 69, Hamlet, 1968, 69, Chemin de Fer, 1969, Hadrian VII, 1970, Father's Day, 1970, 71, Trial Catonsville Nine, 1971, Hotel Paradiso, 1971, The Tavern, 1973, Childs Play, 1973, Forget-Me-Not Lane, 1973, The Miser, 1974, The Kitchen, 1975; Heartbreak House, 1976, Misalliance, 1976, Waiting for Godot, 1977, Terra Nova, 1979; films Rachel, Rachel, 1968, R.P.M., 1969, Great Northfield, Minnesota Raid, 1970, Showdown, 1972, Terminal Man, 1973, Eleanor and Franklin, 1977, Sgt. Matlovich vs. U.S. Air Force, 1977, On the Nickel, 1979, Strangers, 1979, Health, 1979; dir. Akron (Ohio) Shakespeare Festival, 1961; asso. artistic dir. Gt. Lakes Shakespeare Festival, 1963; dir. McCarter Theatre, Princeton, 1963, 66; dir. Playhouse-in-the-Park, Cin., 1964; dir. Assn. Producing Artists Repertory, 1966-67, 68-69, Father's Day N.Y., 1971; mng. artist Los Angeles Actors' Theatre, 1976-77. Served with Royal Arty., 1949-51. Home: 223 33d St Hermosa Beach CA 90254

MOFFAT, JAY P., govt. ofcl.; b. N.Y.C., Jan. 17, 1932; s. Jay Pierrepont and Lilla Cabot (Grew) M.; Grad. Groton Sch., 1949; A.B., Harvard, 1953; m. Pamela Mary Dawson, Dec. 28, 1953; children—Sarah, Matthew, Nathaniel. Fgn. service officer, 1956—; vice consul, Kobe-Osaka, Japan. 1958-60; 2d sec., Paris, 1961-65; 1st sec., Bern, Switzerland, 1969-70; counselor Port of Spain, 1971-74; detailed NATO Def. Coll., Rome, Italy, 1974; dep. exec. sec. Dept. State, Washington, 1974-76; minister-counselor, Rabat, Morocco, 1976—. Chmn. bd. English-Speaking Sch. of Berne, 1969-70. Served with AUS, 1953-56. Club: Metropolitan (Washington). Address: Dept State Washington DC 20521

MOFFAT, JOHN WILLIAM, educator; b. Copenhagen, Denmark, May 24, 1932; s. George William and Esther (Winther) M.; Ph.D., Trinity Coll., Cambridge (Eng.) U., 1958. Sr. research fellow Imperial Coll., London, Eng., 1957-58; scientist Research Inst. Advanced Studies, Balt., 1958-60, prin. scientist, 1961-64; scientist CERN, Geneva, Switzerland, 1960-61; asso. prof. dept. physics U. Toronto (Ont., Can.), 1964-67, prof., 1967—. Dept. Sci. and Indsl. Research fellow, 1958-60, Nat. Research Council Can. grantee, 1965. Fellow Cambridge Philos. Soc. (Eng.). Contbr. articles to profl. jours. Office: Dept Physics Univ Toronto Toronto ON Canada

MOFFATT, JOYCE A., performing arts exec.; b. Grand Rapids, Mich., Jan. 3, 1936; d. John Barnard and Ruth Lillian (Pellow) M.; B.A. in Lit., U. Mich., 1957, M.A. in Theatre, 1960. Stage mgr., lighting designer Off-Broadway plays, costume, lighting and set designer, stage mgr. stock cos., 1954-62; nat. subscription mgr. Theatre Guild/Am. Theatre Soc., N.Y.C., 1965-67; subscription mgr. Theatre, Inc.-Phoenix Theatre, N.Y.C., 1963-67, also cons.; subscription mgr. N.Y.C. Ballet and N.Y.C. Opera, 1967-70; asst. house mgr. N.Y. State Theater, 1970-72; dir. ticket sales City Center of Music and Drama, Inc., N.Y.C., 1970-72; prodn. mgr. San Antonio Symphony/Opera, 1973-75, gen. mgr., 1975-76; gen. mgr. 55th St. Dance Theater Found., Inc., N.Y.C., 1976-77; gen. mgr. Ballet Theatre Found., Inc./Am. Ballet Theatre, N.Y.C., 1977—; cons. Ford Found., N.Y. State Council on Arts, Kennedy Center for Performing Arts. Mem. Assn. Theatrical Press Agts. and Mgrs., Actors Equity Assn., United Scenic Artists Local 350. Club: Argyle (San Antonio). Office: American Ballet Theatre 888 7th Ave New York NY 10019

MOFFATT, KATHERINE LOUELLA, musician, vocalist, songwriter; b. Ft. Worth, Nov. 19, 1950; d. Lester Huger and Sue-Jo (Harrott) M.; student Sophie Newcomb Coll., 1968, St. John's Coll., 1969-70. Folksinger, Ft. Worth, 1967-68; musician, vocalist, songwriter, rec. artist for film Billy Jack, 1970; TV prodn. asst. Sta.-KIII, Corpus Christi, 1970; TV audio engr. Sta.-KRIS, Corpus Christi, 1970; musician, vocalist in blues band, Corpus Christi, 1970; receptionist, bookkeeping asst., copywriter, announcer, Sta.-KFWT, Ft. Worth, 1971; musician, vocalist, songwriter, Denver, 1971-72; musician, vocalist, songwriter, on tour, 1973, 75—; musician, vocalist, songwriter, Denver, 1974; albums include Katy, 1976, Kissin' In The California Sun, 1977; songs include The Magic Ring, 1971, Gerry's Song, 1973, Kansas City Morning, 1974, Take Me Back To Texas, 1975, (Waitin' For) The Real Thing, 1975, Didn't We Have Love, 1976, Kissin' in the Calif. Sun, 1977; pres. Left Field Pub., Inc., BMI. Named #4 Top New Female Vocalist, Cashbox Singles Awards, 1976, #3 Top New Female Vocalist, Record World Album Awards, 1976. Mem. Am. Fedn. Musicians, AFTRA.

MOFFET, ALAN THEODORE, educator, astronomer; b. St. Paul, Mar. 24, 1936; s. William Theodore and Dorothy (Pratt) M.; B.A., Wesleyan U., Middletown, Conn., 1957; Ph.D., Calif. Inst. Tech., 1961. Research fellow Cal. Inst. Tech., Pasadena, 1962-66, asst. prof. radio astronomy, 1966-68, asso. prof., 1968-71, prof., 1971—, dir. Owens Valley Radio Obs., 1975—. Vis. prof. U. Wash., Seattle, 1969, Max Planck Inst., Bonn, Germany, 1973. Recipient Fulbright scholarship, U. Bonn, Germany, 1961-62, Alfred P. Sloan fellowship, 1962-65. Mem. Am. Astron. Soc., Am. Phys. Soc., AAAS, Am. Radio Relay League, IEEE, Internat. Astron. Union, U.S. Commn. J Internat. Union Radio Sci. (chmn. 1978-81), AAUP, ACLU. Contbr. articles to profl. jours. Office: Owens Valley Radio Obs Calif Inst Tech Pasadena CA 91125

MOFFET, DONALD PRATT, computer co. exec.; b. St. Paul, Jan. 30, 1932; s. William Theodore and Dorothy (Pratt) M.; student Wesleyen U., 1949-50; B.B.A., U. Minn., 1953, M.B.A., 1954; m. Sally E. Hullsiek, June 1, 1955; children—Kerry, Kenneth, Mark. With Honeywell, Inc., 1957-72, dir. computer services, 1970-72; v.p. mktg. AM Internat., 1972-77, exec. v.p., chief operating officer Sycor, Inc., Ann Arbor, Mich., 1977-78, pres., 1978—; dir. Wells Electronics Corp., South Bend, Ind. Served with USAF, 1955-57. Presbyterian. Club: Barton Hills Country. Home: 2201 Belmont Rd Ann Arbor MI 48104

MOFFET, ERNEST BEVERIDGE, JR., mfg. co. exec.; b. St. Paul, July 13, 1926; s. E. B. and Lucille E. M.; B.S., U. Minn., 1946; m. Patricia Kepler Stone, Mar. 19, 1977; children—Gregory, Timothy. With 3M Co., St. Paul, 1947—, mng. dir. 3M A/S Denmark, 1966-69, mktg. dir. comml. tape div., 1969-72, div. v.p., 1972-77, v.p. consumer products group, 1977—. Served with USNR, 1943-46. Mem. Nat. Office Products Assn. (v.p. mfg. div.), Wholesale Stationers Assn. (v.p. mfg. div.). Club: Dellwood Hills Golf (St. Paul). Home: 1395 E County Rd E White Bear Lake MN 55110 Office: 3M Co 3M Center Saint Paul MN 55101

MOFFETT, ANTHONY TOBY, congressman; b. Holyoke, Mass., Aug. 18, 1944; s. Anthony John and Mary (Romenius) M.; student Syracuse U. in Florence, Italy, 1964; B.A. in Polit. Sci., Syracuse U., 1966; M.A. in Urban Affairs, Boston Coll., 1968; 1 dau. by previous marriage, Julia. Tchr. pub. schs., Boston, 1967-68; first dir. U.S. Office Students and Youth HEW, Washington, 1968-70; aide to U.S. Senator Walter Mondale, Washington, 1971; first dir. Conn. Citizen Action Group, Hartford, 1971-74; mem. 94th-95th congresses from 6th Conn. Dist.; mem. Interstate and Fgn. Commerce, Govt. Ops., Ad Hoc Energy coms. Mem. edn. bd. Kettering Found. Author: The Participation Put-On, 1971; Nobody's Business, 1973. Office: 127 Cannon House Office Bldg Washington DC 20515

MOFFETT, HARRY LEE, natural resources cons.; b. Cleve., June 27, 1912; s. Leon Wesley and Mildred (Hixson) M.; A.B., Am. U., Washington, 1933; LL.B., Am. Sch. Law, 1951; m. Annie Wright Parker, Apr. 7, 1934; 1 dau., Marianne Virginia (Mrs. Norman Willard Schulz). Dist. mgr. Washington Post, 1933-34; dir. pub. relations Planning and Coordinating Com. for Petroleum Industry, 1934-35; dir. pub. affairs Am. Mining Congress, 1935-66; asst. dir. pub. Land Law Rev. Commn., 1966-69; dir. Office Minerals and Solid Fuels, Office Asst. Sec. Interior for mineral resources, 1969-71, dep. asst. sec. mineral resources, 1971-73; asso. BKW and Assos., Washington, 1973—; Washington mgr. Dunn Geosci. Corp., Latham, N.Y., 1974—. Cons. interior and insular affairs. com. Ho. of Reps., 1966; v.p., dir. Francis Scott Key Hotel; dir., officer Spl. Indsl. Radio Services Assn. Pres., Woodrow Wilson High Sch. Home and Sch. Assn., 1946-47. Served to col. AUS, 1939-46; PTO. Decorated Legion of Merit. Recipient Distinguished Service awards Spl. Indsl. Radio Services Assn., 1964, 65. Mem. Mining and Metall. Soc., Nat. Press Club Washington, Alpha Tau Omega. Mason (32 deg., Shriner). Asso. editor: Mining Congress Jour., 1935-66. Contbr. articles to profl. jours. Home: 10201 Grosvenor Pl Rockville MD 20852 Office: 1522 K St NW Washington DC 20005

MOFFETT, JAMES DAVIS, fgn. service officer; b. Duluth, Minn., Mar. 11, 1921; s. John Henry and Nora Wilhelmina (Eastlund) M.; B.A., Jamestown Coll., 1941; m. Beverly Negus, Dec. 31, 1949; children—Beverly, James Negus. High sch. tchr., 1941-42; vice consul, Stuttgart, Ger., 1948-50, Liverpool, 1950-51; 2d sec., Kabul, Afghanistan, 1951-53, London, 1954-57; with Brit. Desk, Dept. of State, Washington, 1957-61; consul, Marseille, France, 1961-64; 1st sec., Khartoum, Sudan, 1964-67; dep. province sr. adviser, Viet Nam, 1967-69; with Dept. State, Washington, 1968-73; polit. adviser to CG U.S. Army, Europe, 1973-75; consul gen., Izmir, Turkey, 1975—. Served with U.S. Army, 1942-46. Recipient Meritorious Honor award State Dept., 1969; Vietnam medal, 1969. Mem. Am. Fgn. Service Assn., Assn. U.S. Army. Presbyterian. Address: care Dept of State Washington DC

MOFFETT, WILLIAM EARL, oil co. exec.; b. nr. Real County, Tex., July 5, 1930; s. Willaim Ester and Lois (Kelly) M.; B.A., U. Tex., 1957, postgrad., 1957-59; E.D. (Farmer Internat. scholar), Nat. U. Mexico, 1957-59; m. Jimmie Rowan, July 25, 1953; children—William Earl, Deborah Deloise, Leslie Suzzane. Oil prospector Humble Oil & Refining Co., 1951-54; lectr. finance, econs. and marketing U. Tex., 1957-59; internat. relations Port of Houston, 1959-60; dep. dir. Cultural Center, USIS, Monterrey, Mexico, 1960-61; dir. BUCARAMANGA, Colombia, 1961-63; dep. dir. Central Am., Caribbean programs Peace Corps, Washington, 1963-64, dir. Chile, 1964-66, dir. Latin Am., 1966-69, v.p. Gulf Oil Co.-Latin Am., 1969-73; gen. mgr. Mene Grande Oil Co., Santome, Venezuela, 1973-74; exec. v.p. Rio Blanco Oil Shale project Gulf Oil, Denver, 1974-75; v.p. Gulf Oil Corp., 1975—. Bd. dirs. Fund Multinat. Mgmt. Edn., Pa. Environ. Council; bd. advisers Partners of Ams. Served with USNR, 1947-49; with USMCR, 1949-51. Decorated Bronze Star with combat V, Navy Commendation with combat V, Purple Heart with oak leaf cluster. Mem. Am. Petroleum Inst., Council of Ams. (adv. com.). Ducks Unltd. (state chmn.), Delta Sigma Pi. Mason. Home: Rio Frio TX 78879 also 3048 Harts Woods Dr Allison Park PA 15101 Office: 439 7th Ave Pittsburgh PA 15230

MOFFITT, CHARLES WILLIAM, retail store exec.; b. Altoona, Pa., Mar. 24, 1932; s. Charles William and Beatrice Jeanette (Shellenberger) M.; B.A., Pa. State U., 1957; m. Virginia Colyer, July 21, 1956; children—Michelle A., Charles William III, Deborah K. Examiner, Pa. R.R., Buffalo, 1957-62; asst. to pres. White Cross Stores, Inc., Monroeville, Pa., 1962-65, sec., 1965-70, v.p. adminstrn., sec., 1970-72; dir. labor relations and legal affairs Revco D.S., Inc., Cleve., 1972-75, asst. v.p. personnel, 1974-75; pres. Fashion Wearhouse, Inc., Altoona, Pa., 1975—; owner Omega Advt. Co. Served with AUS, 1950-53. Republican. Roman Catholic. Home: 416 31st St Altoona PA 16602 Office: Pleasant Valley Shopping Center Altoona PA 16602

MOFFITT, DONALD EUGENE, transp. and mfg. co. exec.; b. Terre Haute, Ind., May 22, 1932; s. James Robert and Margaret Mary (Long) M.; B.A., Ind. State U., 1954; postgrad. Ind. U., 1956; grad.

Advanced Mgmt. Program, Harvard U., 1972; m. Phyllis A. Stepp, Mar. 8, 1953; children—David, Mitchell, Christopher, Michael. Accountant, Foster Freight Lines, Indpls., 1955-56; with Consol. Freightways Inc., San Francisco, 1956—, v.p. planning, 1969-73, v.p. fin. Consol. Freightways Corp. Del., motor carrier subs., 1974-75, v.p. fin., treas. parent co., 1976—, also dir., officer affiliated cos. and subsidiaries. Leader, mem. bd. Sea Scouts, Stanford Area council Boy Scouts Am. Mem. Am. Trucking Assn., Bay Area Commonwealth Club, Fin. Execs. Inst. Club: Islander Yacht. Contbr. articles in field. Home: 26307 Esperanza Dr Los Altos Hills CA 94022 Office: 601 California St San Francisco CA 94108

MOFFITT, GEORGE, JR., fgn. service officer; b. N.Y.C., June 18, 1918; s. George and Margaret (Buchanan) M.; student U. Wis., 1950-51; m. Lois Anderson, July 7, 1946; children—Katherine (Mrs. Robert Roy), Margaret. With indsl. firm, 1937-39; fgn. service officer in Haiti, Iraq, Can., Belgium, Burma, Netherland Antilles, Washington and Italy, 1939—; counselor of embassy, Brussels, 1966-71; polit. adviser to comdr.-in-chief Allied Forces, So. Europe, 1971—. Bd. dirs. Fulbright Found. for Belgium and Luxembourg. Vice chmn. Burlington Bi-Centennial Commn.; chmn. adv. council Area Agy. on Aging, 1978-79; chmn. Central Conn. Adv. Council on Aging, 1979-80. Mem. Burlington Library Assn. (hon. pres.). Home: 8 Village Ln Burlington CT 06085 Office: Allied Forces So Europe Naples Italy

MOFFO, ANNA, opera singer; b. Wayne, Pa.; d Nicholas and Regina (Cinti) Moffo; grad. with honors Curtis Inst.; m. Robert Sarnoff, Nov. 14, 1974. Appeared TV opera Madame Butterfly, Italy; singer opera houses, Paris, London, Salzburg, LaScala, Milan, numerous others abroad; Am. debut Lyric Opera Co., Chgo., 1957, Met. Opera Co., N.Y.C., 1959; appeared Voice of Firestone telecast, 1957; operatic roles (soprano) include LaBoheme, Mignon, Rigoletto, Falstaff, Madame Butterfly, Barber of Seville, La Traviata, Thais, Daughter of Regiment, Stiffelio, Tosca, Hansel & Gretel, Faust, Don Pasquale, Romeo & Juliette, Magic Flute, Turandot, La Juive, Marriage of Figaro; recital tour U.S.; appeared film versions La Traviata, Lucia, also films The Adventurers, A Love Story; also numerous TV appearances U.S. and Italy; numerous recorindgs RCA Victor. Decorated Order Merit Republic Italy; recipient Young Artists award Phila. Orchestra; Fulbright award for study in Europe; Silver Griffo award for A Love Story; Liebe Augistin award. Address: c/o Edgar Vincent Assos 156 E 52d St New York NY 10022

MOFFORD, ROSE, state ofcl.; b. Globe, Ariz., June 10, 1922; attended public schs. Sec. to Joe Hunt, Ariz. State Treas., 1941-43, Ariz. State Tax Commr., 1943-54, to Wesley Bolin, Ariz. Sec. of State, 1954-55; asst. sec. of state State of Ariz., Phoenix, 1955-79, sec. of state, 1979—. Democrat. Office: Office of Sec of State West Wing State Capitol Phoenix AZ 85007*

MOGABGAB, WILLIAM JOSEPH, physician, educator; b. Durant, Okla., Nov. 2, 1921; s. Anees and Maude (Jopes) M.; B.S., Tulane U., 1942, M.D., 1944; m. Joy Roddy, Dec. 24, 1948; children—Robert, Ann, Kay, Edward R., Jean. Intern Charity Hosp. La., New Orleans, 1944-45, resident, 1946-49, vis. physician, 1949-51, sr. vis. physician, 1971-75; cons., 1976—; mem. faculty Tulane U. Med. Sch., 1948—, prof. medicine, 1962—; vis. investigator, asst. physician Hosp. Rockefeller Inst. Med. Research, N.Y.C., 1951-52; chief infectious disease VA Hosp., Houston, 1952-53; asst. prof. medicine Baylor U. Coll. Medicine, 1952-53; head virology div. NAMRU 4, USNTC, Great Lakes, Ill., 1953-55; cons. infectious disease VA Hosp., New Orleans, 1956—. Asso. mem. commn. influenza Armed Forces Epidemiological Bd., 1959-71. Fellow Nat. Found. Infantile Paralysis, 1951-52. Diplomate Am. Bd. Internal Medicine, Am. Bd. Microbiology. Fellow A.C.P., Am. Acad. Microbiology; mem. Soc. Exptl. Biology and Medicine, So., Central socs. clin. research, Am. Fedn. Clin. Research, Am. Soc. Cell Biology, Am. Soc. Microbiology, Am. Soc. Clin. Investigation, Infectious Disease Soc. Am., Tissue Culture Assn., Am. Pub. Health Assn., Am. Soc. Internal Medicine, Am. Soc. Clin. Pharmacology and Therapeutics, So. Med. Soc., AMA. Research, publns. agts. of and vaccines for respiratory infections, viruses, mycoplasma, new antibiotics. Home: 39 Lark St New Orleans LA 70124 Office: Sect Infectious Disease Dept Medicine Tulane U Sch Medicine 1430 Tulane Ave New Orleans LA 70112

MOGEL, LEONARD HENRY, publisher; b. Bklyn., Oct. 23, 1922; s. Isaac and Shirley (Goldman) M.; B.B.A., Coll. City N.Y., 1947; m. Ann Vera Levy, Oct. 23, 1949; children—Wendy Lynn, Jane Ellen. Salesman, N.Y. Printing Co., N.Y.C., 1946-48; sales mgr. Pollak Printing Co., N.Y.C., 1948-52; advt. dir. Diners Club, Inc., N.Y.C., 1952-56, pub. Diners Club for Signature and Bravo mags., 1956-67; pres. Leonard Mogel Assos., Inc., nat. advt. reps., N.Y.C., 1952—; prin. owner San Francisco Warriors Profl. Basketball Team, 1963-64; pres. Twenty First Century Communications Inc., N.Y.C., 1967—, pub. Cheetah and Weight Watchers mags., 1967—; dir. Regents Pub. Co. div. Simon & Schuster, 1960-67; advt. cons. Harvard Lampoon, 1968; pub. Nat. Lampoon, 1970—, Liberty mag., 1971—, Ingenue mag., 1973—, Heavy Metal mag., 1977—; adj. prof. N.Y. U. Sch. Continuing Edn., 1973—; panelist Forum Mag. Pub. Conf., 1975-76. Sponsor Albert Einstein Med. Coll., Birch Wathen Sch., N.Y.C. Served with AUS, 1942-46; CBI. Mem. Soc. Illustrators. Author: Everything You Need to Know to Make It in the Magazine Business, 1979. Home: New York Office: 635 Madison Ave New York NY 10028

MOGEY, JOHN MCFARLAND, educator; b. Ballymoney, North Ireland, July 7, 1915; s. Alexander and Annie (MacFarlane) M.; B.A., Queen's U., Belfast, N. Ireland, 1936, M.A., 1939, D.Sc., 1949; M.A., Oxford (Eng.) U., 1950; m. Doreen Alice Holland, Dec. 23, 1940; children—Martin Oliver, James Alexander, Sara Honor. Came to U.S., 1960, naturalized, 1965. Research fellow Queen's U., 1937-39, asst. lectr. geology, 1945-47; research officer Nat. Council Social Service, Belfast, 1942-45; lectr. U. Reading (Eng.), 1947-50; univ. lectr. Oxford U., 1950-59; prof. sociology, chmn. dept. sociology and anthropology Vanderbilt U., 1960-63; prof. sociology Boston U., 1963—, chmn. dept. sociology and anthropology, 1963-68. Mem. Ancient Monuments Adv. Council, No. Ireland, 1945-55; sec. research com. Reading U., 1948-56; mem. edn. com. Nat. Marriage Guidance Council, London 1957-59; mem. council Le Play Soc., London, 1949-59. Rockfeller fellow, 1954-55, exchange scientist Nat. Acad. Scis., Romania, 1972. Mem. Am., Brit. (exec. com. 1952-54), So., Mass. (pres. 1971-72) sociol. assns., Royal Anthrop. Inst. (British ethnography com. 1952-59), Nat. Council Family Relations. Author: Rural Life in Northern Ireland, 1947; The Study of Geography, 1950; Family and Neighbourhood, 1956; (with R.N. Morris) Sociology of Housing, 1965; Sociology of Marriage and Family Behavior; Social Effects of Eminent Domain; also articles, reviews. Home: 249 Summit Ave Brookline MA 02146

MOGK, JOHN EDWARD, legal educator; b. Detroit, Feb. 10, 1939; s. Clifford Anthony and Evelyn Lenore (Paselk) M.; B.B.A., U. Mich., 1961, J.D. with distinction, 1964; diploma comparative law, U. Stockholm (Sweden), 1965; m. Lylas Heidi Good, Aug. 23, 1964; children—Marya, Tenley, Matthew. Admitted to N.Y. bar, 1966, Mich. bar, 1970; asso. atty. Shearman & Sterling, N.Y.C., 1964-68; mem. faculty Wayne State U. Sch. Law, 1968—, prof. law, 1971—; pres. Mich. Energy and Resource Research Assn., 1974—; chmn. Central Solar Energy Research Corp., 1977—; cons. urban devel. Founder, dir. Profl. Skills Alliance, 1970-74; chmn. Mich. TOP Task Force, 1972; vice chmn. Mich. Constrn. Code Commn., 1973; mem. exec. com. Southeastern Mich. Council Govts., 1970; chmn., adviser Jefferson-Chalmers Redevel. Program, 1971. Chmn. Detroit Sch. Boundary Commn., 1970; mem. Detroit Bd. Edn., 1970. Am.-Scandinavian fellow, 1965; named Outstanding Wayne State U. Asso. Prof., 1971, Outstanding Young Man in Detroit, 1972, One of Ten Outstanding Young Men in U.S., 1973; One of Four Outstanding Vols. in U.S., 1974; recipient Presdl. citation Wayne State U., 1977. Mem. Am., Mich. bar assns., Bar Assn. City N.Y. Contbr. articles to profl. jours. Home: 1315 Grayton Grosse Pointe Park MI 48230

MOGULL, ARTHUR, record co. exec.; b. N.Y.C., Mar. 26, 1927; s. Leo and Rose (Gerstel) M.; B.A., Columbia U., 1949; divorced; children—Andrea, Cathy, Alison. Vice pres. Warner Bros. Music Co., 1960-66, Capitol Records, 1969-71, MCA Records, 1973-74; pres., dir. United Artists Records Am., Los Angeles, 1976-78, co-chmn., 1978—. Served with USNR, 1944-46. Mem. Rec. Industry Assn. Am. (dir.). Democrat. Jewish. Club: El Caballero Country (Tarzana, Calif.). Home: 2720 Benedict Canyon Dr Beverly Hills CA 90210 Office: 6920 Sunset Blvd Los Angeles CA 90028

MOHAMMED, M. HAMDI ABDELHAKIM, dentist; b. Egypt, May 10, 1940; s. Abdelhakim Mohammed and Enayat Abdelhakim (Abdelsamed) El-tahawi; D.D.S., U. Alexandria, 1963, M.S., 1965; M.Sc., Northwestern U., 1967; Ph.D. (Grad. fellow), U. Mich., 1971; m. Assma Abdelwahab, Sept. 24, 1964; children—Karim, Eman. Came to U.S., 1965, naturalized, 1975. Oral surgeon, instr. oral surgery U. Alexandria (Egypt) Hosp. and Dental Sch., 1963-65; research asso. dental materials, instr. dental anatomy and occlusion U. Mich., 1969-71; asst. prof. gen. dentistry U. Conn., Farmington, 1971-72, asso. prof., 1972-74; prof. U. Fla., Gainesville, 1974—, chmn. dept., 1975—. Recipient UAR medal sci. achievement, 1963. Fellow Royal Soc. Health (London), Internat. Coll. Oral Implantology; mem. Internat. Assn. Dental Research, Am. Assn. Dental Research, Am. Assn. Dental Schs., ADA, Am. Soc. Metals, Soc. Biomaterials, Soc. Exptl. Stress Analysis. Contbr. to 3 textbooks, also articles to profl. jours. Office: Dept Dental Biomaterials Coll Dentistry U Fla Box J446 Gainesville FL 32610. *The variation in the levels of our achievements is primarily due to out willingness to work hard and efficiently rather than for being especially gifted. As such, human bias against us should never be permitted to interfere with our success. All we must do is to demonstrate that we are not only good but superior through our work achievements. It is a great misfortune that we tend to forget that "a single person on the side of justice is a dominating majority."*

MOHAN, ROBERT PAUL, clergyman, educator; b. Wilkes Barre, Pa., Oct. 25, 1920; s. John Augustus and Lucy (Riley) M.; A.B., Catholic U., 1942, M.A., 1943, Ph.D., 1949, S.T.L., 1953; postgrad. Sorbonne, Paris, 1947. Faculty, St. Mary Sem., Balt., 1947; faculty St. Edwards Sem., Seattle, 1948-50; prof. Sch. Philosophy, marshall of univ., dean summer session, dir. workshops, sec. acad. senate Catholic U. Am., Washington, 1950—. Mem. Nat. Assn. Summer Sessions (chmn. govt. relations com. 1965-70), AAUP, Am. Philos. Assn. Author: A Thomistic Philosophy of Civilization and Culture, 1948; Philosophy of History, 1970. Editor: Technology and Christian Culture, 1960. Address: Box 138 Catholic U Washington DC 20064

MOHLENBROCK, ROBERT HERMAN, JR., educator, botanist; b. Murphysboro, Ill., Sept. 26, 1931; s. Robert Herman and Elsie (Treece) M.; B.A., So. Ill. U., 1953; M.S., 1954; Ph.D., Washington U., St. Louis, 1957; m. Beverly Ann Kling, Oct. 19, 1957; children—Mark William, Wendy Ann, Trent Alan. With dept. botany So. Ill. U., Carbondale, 1957—, chmn. dept., 1966—, prof., 1966—. Trustee Ill. Nature Conservancy. Mem. Am. Fern Soc., Assn. So. Biologists, Ill. Acad. Sci., Internat. Assn. Plant Taxonomists, So. Appalachian Bot. Club. Author: A Flora of Southern Illinois, 1957; Plant Communities of Southern Illinois, 1963; Ferns of Illinois, 1967; Flowering Plants of Illinois: Flowering Rush to Rushes, 1970; Flowering Plants of Illinois: Lilies to Orchids, 1970; Grasses of Illinois, 1972, 73; Forest Trees of Illinois, 1973; Guide to the Vascular Flora of Illinois, 1975; Summer and Fall Wildflowers of Carlyle-Rend-Shelbyville Lakes, 1975; Sedges of Illinois, 1976; Hollies to Loasas in Illinois, 1978; Distribution of Illinois Vascular Plants, 1978; also articles. Home: 1 Birdsong Dr Carbondale IL 62901

MOHLER, DANIEL NATHAN, physician, educator; b. Charleston, W.Va., June 22, 1927; s. Daniel Nathan and Barbara Linn (Bryrne) M.; B.A., U. Va., 1950, M.D., 1953; m. Harriet Hill Hodges, Dec. 26, 1951; children—Marian McQueen, Margaret Austin, Martha Hodges, Daniel Nathan. Intern Mass. Meml. Hosp. Boston, 1953-54, resident, 1954-56; resident U. Va. Hosp., 1956-58; research fellow Barnes Hosp., St. Louis, 1958-60; practice medicine, specializing in internal medicine, Charlottesville, Va., 1960—; instr. medicine U. Va. Sch. Medicine, 1960-61, asst. prof., 1961-65, asso. prof., 1965-69, prof., 1969—, asso. dean, 1970—. Served with AUS, 1945-47. Diplomate Am. Bd. Internal Medicine (hematology). Fellow A.C.P.; mem. Va., Albemarle med. socs., AMA, Am. Fedn. Clin. Research, So. Soc. Clin. Investigation, Internat., Am. socs. hematology, Am. Clin. and Climatol. Assn., AAAS, SIgma Xi, Alpha Omega Alpha, Omicron Delta Kappa. Contbr. chpt. to Leavell & Thorup, 1976, also articles to profl. jours. Home: 1747 Lambs Rd Charlottesville VA 22901

MOHLER, HAROLD SHEAFFER, food co. exec.; b. Ephrata, Pa., Mar. 8, 1919; s. Milton Keller and Esther Landis (Sheaffer) M.; B.S. in Indsl. Engring., Lehigh U., 1948, LL.D., 1975; LL.D., Elizabethtown Coll., 1979; m. Melda Lorraine Artz, July 21, 1945; children—Jeffrey Lee, Susan Lorraine, Julie Lynn. With Hershey Chocolate Corp. (Pa.) (name changed to Hershey Foods Corp. 1968), 1948—, asst. to pres., 1957-62, v.p., 1962-65, pres., chief exec. officer, 1965-74, chmn. bd., pres., 1974-76, chmn. bd., chmn. exec. com., 1976—; chmn. bd., dir. Hershey Nat. Bank, Hershey Trust Co.; dir. Herco, Inc. (formerly Hershey Estates), Pa. Power & Light Co. Bd. dirs., mem. exec. com. Pa. Economy League; past chmn. Pennsylvanians for Effective Govt.; mem., past chmn. Bus.-Industry Polit. Action Com. bd. mgrs. Milton Hershey Sch., M.S. Hershey Found.; trustee Hershey Fund; trustee Lehigh U., pres., 1973—; bd. dirs. Tri-County United Fund. Served to 1st lt. navigator, USAAF, 1943-45. Decorated Air medal with 2 oak leaf clusters, Purple Heart. Registered profl. engr., Pa. Mem. ASME, Newcomen Soc., Am. Cocoa Research Inst. (chmn. bd. 1979-80), Chocolate Mfrs. Assn. U.S. (pres. 1979-80), Pa. C. of C. (chmn. 1978, dir.), Alpha Kappa Psi (hon.), Alpha Pi Mu. Republican. Presbyn. (elder). Mason, Rotarian. Clubs: Hershey Country; University (N.Y.C.); Saucon Valley Country; Garden of the Gods. Home: 226 E Caracas Ave Hershey PA 17033 Office: 19 E Chocolate Ave Hershey PA 17033

MOHLER, ORREN CUTHBERT, educator, astronomer; b. Indpls., July 28, 1908; s. Charles Mikesell and Mary Ann (Culp) M.; A.B., Mich. State Normal Coll., 1929; M.A. (State Coll. fellow 1929), U. Mich., 1930, Ph.D. (Lawton fellow 1930-33), 1933; D.Sc. (hon.), Eastern Mich. U., 1956; m. Helen Jean Beal, June 10, 1935; children—Alice Beal (Mrs. William George DeLana), Jane Radcliffe (Mrs. Jeffery Wessels Barry). Instr. astronomy Swarthmore Coll., 1933-40; astromomer Cook Obs., Wynnewood, Pa., 1933-40; observer McMath-Hulbert Obs., U. Mich., 1933, dir. Obs., 1961—, mem. faculty univ., 1940—, prof. astronomy, 1955—, chmn. dept. astronomy, dir. observatories, 1962-71; dir. Assn. Univs. Research Astronomy, Tucson, 1961-74, chmn. scientific com., 1965-73. Fulbright research scholar Inst. d'Astrophysique, Liege, 1960-61. Vice pres. U.S. Nat. Com. Internat. Astron. Union, 1962-65. Bd. govs. Cranbrook Inst. Sci., 1960—. Recipient USN award, 1946. Mem. Am., Astron. Soc., Royal Astron. Soc. Can., Phi Beta Kappa, Sigma Xi. Clubs: Univ., Research (pres. 1966-67), Sci. Research (pres. 1970-71), Ann Arbor Golf and Outing; Torch (Oakland County). Author: Photometric Atlas of the Near Infrared Solar Spectrum, 1950; Table of Solar Spectrum Wave Lengths, 1955; also articles. Home: 405 Awixa Rd Ann Arbor MI 48104

MOHLER, RONALD RUTT, educator; b. Ephrata, Pa., Apr. 11, 1931; s. David Wealand and Elizabeth (Rutt) M.; B.S. (scholarship), Pa. State U., 1956; M.S., U. So. Calif., 1958; Ph.D., U. Mich., 1965; m. Nancy Alice Strickler, May 6, 1950; children—Curtis Gene, Pamela Louise, Susan Lynn, Anita Marie, John Scott, Andrew Thomas, Jennifer Lee, Lisa Nancy. Designer, trainee, Textile Machine Works, N. Am. Rockwell Corp., Reading, Pa., 1949-56; staff mem. Hughes Aircraft Co., Culver City, Calif., 1956-58; staff mem. Los Alamos Sci. Lab., 1958-65; asso. prof. elec. engring. U. N.Mex., Albuquerque, 1965-69; prof. elec. engring. and aerospace mech. and nuclear engring. U. Okla., 1969-72, prof., chmn. info. and computing scis., 1970-72, dir. Systems Research Center, 1969-72; lectr., prof. elec. engring. and nuclear engring. U. N.Mex., Los Alamos Grad. Center, 1959-65; cons. Sandia Corp., Albuquerque, 1966-69, Aerojet-Gen. Corp., Sacramento, 1966; vis. asso. prof. system sci. U. Calif. at Los Angeles, 1968-69; cons. community health project OEO, Oklahoma City, 1970-71; prof., head elec. and computer engring. Oreg. State U., Corvallis, 1972—; vis. prof. U. Rome, 1973, 75, Imperial Coll., London, 1978-79; cons. Optimization Software, Los Angeles, 1973—, Bonneville Power Adminstrn., 1975—. Chmn. St. Stephens Sch. Bd., Norman, 1970-72. Research grantee NSF, 1966-80, Sandia Labs., 1966-68; AEC fellow, 1961-65; Hughes fellow, 1956-58. Mem. Am. Soc. Engring. Edn., IEEE (local chmn. 1975). Control System Soc., Sigma Xi, Tau Beta Pi, Pi Tau Sigma. Democrat. Author: Optimal Control of Nuclear Reactors, 1970; Bilinear Control Processes, 1973. Editor: Theory and Application of Variable Structure Systems, 1972; Variable Structure Systems with Application to Biology and Economics, 1975; Recent Developments in Variable Structure Systems, Economics and Biology, 1979. Asso. editor Annals of Nuclear Energy, 1973—. Contbr. jours. Pioneer work on bilinear systems. Home: 2050 NW Dogwood St Corvallis OR 97330

MOHLER, STANLEY ROSS, govt. research ofcl.; b. Amarillo, Tex., Sept. 30, 1927; s. Norton Harrison and Minnie Alice (Ross) M.; B.A., U. Tex., 1953, M.A., 1953, M.D., 1956; m. Ursula Luise Burkhardt, Jan. 24, 1953; children—Susan Luise, Stanley Ross, Mark Hallock. Intern USPHS Hosp., San Francisco, 1956-57; med. officer Center Aging Research, NIH, Bethesda, Md., 1957-61; dir. Civil Aeromed. Research Inst., FAA, Washington, 1961-66, chief aeromed. applications div., 1966-78; prof., vice chmn. dept. community medicine, dir. aerospace medicine Wright State U. Sch. Medicine, Dayton, Ohio, 1978—; research asso. prof. preventive medicine and pub. health U. Okla. Med. Sch., 1961—. Bd. dirs. Sr. Citizens Assn. Oklahoma City, 1962—, Flying Physicians Assn., 1961—. Served with AUS, 1946-48. Recipient Gail Borden Research award; Boothby award Aerospace Med. Assn., 1966; FAA Meritorious Service award, 1974. Diplomate Am. Bd. Preventive Medicine (vice chmn. 1978—). Fellow Geriatrics Soc., Aerospace Med. Assn. (v.p. 1962, Harry G. Moseley award 1974), Am. Coll. Preventive Medicine, Gerontol. Soc.; mem. AMA, Alpha Omega Alpha. Author articles in field. Home: 6539 Reigate Rd Centerville OH 45459 Office: Wright State U Sch Medicine PO Box 927 Dayton OH 45401

MOHLIE, RAYMOND EUGENE, food co. exec.; b. Waterloo, Iowa, May 23, 1928; s. John Raymond and Helen A. (Jones) M.; B.S. in Chem. Engring., Mich. State U., 1949; postgrad. Harvard Bus. Sch., 1967; m. Patricia B. Goodman, Aug. 27, 1949; children—Steven, Marcia, Ted. With Gen. Foods Corp., White Plaines, N.Y., 1949—, now logistics dir. Beverage and Breakfast Foods div. Clubs: Harvard Business School (N.Y.C.); Bailiwick (Greenwich). Patentee in field. Home: 3 Roger Dr Greenwich CT 06830 Office: 250 North St White Plains NY 10602

MOHLMAN, ROBERT HENRY, mfg. co. exec.; b. New Haven, May 29, 1918; s. Floyd William and Mary Franklin (Savage) M.; A.B., U. Chgo., 1939, J.D., 1941; M.B.A., Harvard, 1948; m. Ina Maria Meyer, Aug. 23, 1941; children—Robert Peter, David John. Admitted Ill. bar, 1941; mgmt. trainee Inland Steel Co., Chgo., 1941-42; with Inland Container Corp., Indpls., 1946-66; v.p. planning Ball Corp., Muncie, Ind., 1966-67, treas., 1967—, corp. v.p. fin. and adminstrn., 1968-78, sr. v.p. fin., 1978—, also dir.; dir. Mchts. Nat. Bank of Muncie, Ball Agrl. Systems, Kent Plastics U.K., Avery-Laurence Singapore Pty.; co-mng. dir. Ball AG Zug Switzerland. Served to 1st lt. AUS, 1943-46. Mem. Ind. Mfgs. Assn. (dir.), Phi Delta Theta, Phi Delta Phi. Unitarian Universalist. Rotarian. Home: 3405 N Vienna Woods Dr Muncie IN 47304 Office: Muncie IN 47302

MOHN, PAUL EUGENE, mech. engrng. cons.; b. Mohnton, Pa., Sept. 21, 1901; s. Irwin and Sarah (Fitterling) M.; B.S., Pa. State Coll., 1922, M.E., 1931; M.S., U. Ill., 1930; m. Elizabeth Mulkey, Apr. 6, 1926. Instr. mech. engring. Renesselaer Poly. Inst., 1922-25, U. Ill., 1925-28, asso., 1928-31, asst. prof., 1931-41, asso. prof., 1941-44, prof., 1944; prof. dept. mech engring. SUNY, Buffalo, 1944-72, chmn. dept., 1944-67, dean Sch. Engring., 1946-59; cons. engr., Buffalo, 1944-78; cons. engr. Victory J. Azbe, 1927-28, Langenberg Furnace Co., 1930. Fellow Am. Soc. M.E.; mem. Engring. Soc. Buffalo, Am. Soc. Engring. Edn., Army Ordnance Assn., Am. Soc. Metals, Soc. Automotive Engrs., N.Y. Soc. Profl. Engrs., Sigma Xi, Pi Tau Sigma. Author tech. articles. Home: 101 W Windsor Rd Apt 6110 Urbana IL 61801

MOHNEY, RALPH WILSON, clergyman; b. Paris, Ky., May 20, 1918; s. Silas Phillip and Clarine (Wilson) M.; B.A., Transylvania Coll., 1940; B.D., Vanderbilt U., 1943; S.T.M., Boston U., 1945; postgrad. Harvard, Garrett Bibl. Inst.; D.D., Emory and Henry Coll., 1959; m. Nell Marie Webb, Dec. 31, 1948; children—Richard Bentley, Ralph Wilson. Ordained elder Meth. Ch., 1944; pastor Winter Street Congl. Ch., Bath, Me., 1943-45, Manker Meml. Meth. Ch., Chattannoga, 1945-50, Washington Pike Meth. Ch., Knoxville, 1950-56; supt. Kingsport dist. Holston Conf. Meth. Ch., 1956- 59; pres. Tenn. Wesleyan Coll., 1959-65; sr. minister Centenary Meth. Ch., 1965-66, First Centenary United Meth. Ch., Chattanooga, 1967—; Staley Disting. lectr. Columbia Coll., 1973, Emory and Henry Coll., 1975, Pfeiffer Coll., 1976, Union Coll., 1977; del. World Conf. Christian Youth, Oslo, Norway, 1947; adult counselor Meth. Youth Caravan to Poland. 1947; chmn. Holston Conf. Commn. on World Peace, 1952-56; leader Annual Lenten Pilgrimage to Holy Land, 1973—; pres. Holston Council on Finance and Adminstrn., 1968-76; exec. com. Gen. Council Finance and Adminstrn., 1976-80; chmn. Commn. on Christian Higher Edn., 1956-59; res. del. Gen. Conf. Meth. Ch., del. jurisdictional conf. Meth. Ch. 1960, 68, del. Gen.

Am. Med. Assn. (med. ambassador goodwill, life mem. sect. on cancer), Med. Soc. N.Y. State (regional obstetrics chmn., subcom. Maternal and Child Welfare), Onondaga County Med. Soc., Am. Soc. Cytology, Pub. Health Council N.Y. State, Alpha Omega Alpha, hon. mem. Southwest, Fla. obstet. and gynecol. socs., others. Author: Perinatal Loss in Modern Obstetrics, 1957; also chpts. in anthologies; co-author: Infant, Perinatal, Maternal and Childhood Mortality in U.S., 1968; editor: sect. on obstetrics and gynecology Stedman's Medical Dictionary, 1958-64; sect. on fetus Funk and Wagnalls Universal Standard Ency., 1959; 1st guest editor: Clinics in Perinatology, 1974; 1st editor: Clinical Diagnosis Quiz for Obstetrics and Gynecology, 1976; contbr. to Attorneys' Textbook of Medicine. Research and publs. on cytologic, cytochem. and histochem. study of early cervical cancer, perinatal and placental pathology, cytologic and hormonal studies in normal and high-risk obstet. patiens, exptl. prodn. of abruptio placentae, reproductive endocrinology, animal experimentation, induced endocrine insults upon pregnant and nonpregnant ewes and hormonal influence on placentation, invitro placenta perfusion, fetal growth and devel., female urology. Home: 125 Old Liverpool Rd Liverpool NY 13088

NESBITT, ROSEMARY SINNETT (MRS. GEORGE R. NESBITT), educator; b. Syracuse, N.Y., Oct. 12, 1924; d. Matthew A. and Mary Louise (Kane) Sinnett; B.S. magna cum laude, Syracuse U., 1947, M.A., 1952; m. George R. Nesbitt, June 18, 1955; children—Mary, Anne, George R., Elizabeth. Instr. speech Wells Coll., Aurora, N.Y., 1949-52, Syracuse U., 1952-57; asso. prof. speech and theatre State U. N.Y. at Oswego, after 1965, prof., dir. children's theatre, 1969—, distinguished teaching prof., 1976—. Cons., lectr. pub. schs., N.Y., 1965—. Bd. dirs. Oswego YMCA, 1964-65, Newman Found., 1970-71, Oswego Heritage Found., 1963-69; mem. exec. bd. Syracuse Diocese Cath. Edn., 1968-71. Recipient Avila award Cath. Action, Syracuse U. Thomas More Found., 1956, N.Y. State Yorker award, 1969, Distinguished N.Y. State Author's award Friends of Reading of Syracuse Pub. Library, 1970, State U. N.Y. Chancellor's award, 1972, George R. Arents Outstanding Alumni award Syracuse U., 1975; named Woman of Year in Cultural Devel., Syracuse Post Standard, 1971, Citizen of Year, City of Oswego, 1974. Mem. Oswego County Hist. Soc. (dir. 1970-71), Zonta Club, AAUW, Alpha Psi Omega, Alpha Epsilon Rho, Zeta Phi Eta. Author: The Great Rope, 1968; Colonel Meacham's Giant Cheese, 1971. Home: 119 W 4th St Oswego NY 13126. *In the course of my life, I have been an actor, author, teacher, lover, wife, mother and neighbor. I would like to be remembered as one who never said no when asked a favor, never turned away from a cry for help, as one who never ran away. If asked to summarize my attitudes and thoughts on my life I would say, "Dad, I have always tried to do the best I could."*

NESBITT, TOM EDWARD, physician; b. Mangum, Okla., Apr. 14, 1923; s. Carl E. and A. Routh (Johnson) N.; M.D., U. Tex., Dallas, 1948; M.S., U. Mich., 1954; m. Elizabeth Nathan Nesbitt, June 25, 1949; children—Tom E., Mary L., Jonathan C., Elizabeth S. Intern, resident in urology U. Mich., 1948-54; practice medicine specializing in urological surgery, Nashville, 1957—; mem. staff Baptist, Park View, St. Thomas, Vanderbilt hosps., Nashville; bd. commrs. Joint Commn. on Accreditation of Hosps. Elder, First Presbyn. Ch., Nashville. Served to capt. M.C., USAF, 1948-50. Mem. AMA (vice speaker, then speaker ho. of dels. 1972-77, pres. 1978-79), Tenn. Med. Assn. (pres. 1970-71), Am. Hosp. Assn. (trustee), Am. Assn. Clin. Urologists (pres. 1971-72), A.C.S., Am. Urol. Assn., Soc. Pediatric Urology, Nashville Area C. of C. (gov.). Republican. Clubs: Belle Meade Country (Nashville); Farmington Country (Charlottesville, Va.). Contbr. articles to med. jours. Home: 250 Ensworth Ave Nashville TN 37205 Office: 1921 Hayes St Nashville TN 37203

NESHEIM, JOHN LAMSON, semicondr. co. exec.; b. Montevideo, Minn., Sept. 21, 1942; s. Arnold Joseph and Lorna Lee (Lamson) N.; B. Aero. Engring., U. Minn., 1965; M.B.A., Cornell U., 1967; m. Gisela Trolp, June 9, 1967; children—Britt Catherine, Kim Nicole. With Chase Manhattan Bank, N.Y.C., 1967-68, McKinsey & Co., N.Y.C., 1968-72; asst. treas. Joseph E. Seagram & Sons, Inc., N.Y.C., 1972-75; dep. treas. Martin Marietta Corp., Bethesda, Md., 1975-76; treas. Nat. Semicondr. Corp., Santa Clara, Calif., 1976—. Mem. Fin. Execs. Inst. Office: 2900 Semiconductor Dr Santa Clara CA 95051

NESMITH, RICHARD DUEY, clergyman, univ. adminstr.; b. Belleville, Kans., Jan. 9, 1929; s. Eugene Gordon and Edith Mae (Duey) N.; B.A., Nebr. Wesleyan U., 1950; M.Div., Garrett Evang. Sem., 1953; postgrad. Boston U., 1957; m. Barbara Ann Bowman, Dec. 28, 1955; children—Leslie Ann, Lisa Lorraine, Laurel Sue, Lana Louise. Ordained to ministry United Methodist Ch., 1953; dean students MacMurray Coll., Jacksonville, Ill., 1957-61; prof. sociology of religion St. Paul's Sch. Theology, Kansas City, 1961-67; dir. planning Nat. div. Methodist Bd. of Global Ministries, N.Y.C., 1967-73; pastor Trinity Ch., Lincoln, Nebr., 1973-77; dean Sch. Theology, Boston U., 1977—; dir. State Line Farms, Inc.; pres. Nesmith Inc. Bd. govs. Nebr. Wesleyan U.; mem. Bd. Edn., Wycoff, N.J., 1968-72. Mem. Soc. Sci. Study Religion, Nat. Council Chs. Office: 745 Commonwealth Ave Boston MA 02215

NESS, EVALINE (MRS. ARNOLD A. BAYARD), illustrator, writer; b. Union City, Ohio, Apr. 24, 1911; d. Albert and Myrtle Woods (Carter) Michelow; student Muncie (Ind.) State Tchrs. Coll., 1931, Chgo. Art Inst., 1933, Corcoran Art Sch., 1945, Art Students League, N.Y.C., 1947, Accademia de Belle Arti, Rome, Italy, 1950; m. Arnold A. Bayard, Nov. 1959. Tchr. children's art classes Corcoran Sch. Art, Washington, 1945-46, Parsons Sch. Design, N.Y.C., 1959-60; fashion illustrator Saks Fifth Ave., N.Y.C., 1946-49; mag. and advt. illustrator, 1946-49; illustrator numerous books, 1959—. Recipient 1st prize painting Corcoran Sch. Art, 1945, Caldecott medal childrens books, 1967. Author, illustrator: Josefina February, 1963; Gift for Sula Sula, 1963; Pavo and the Princess, 1964; Exactly Alike, 1964: A Double Discovery, 1965; Sam Bangs and Moonshine, 1966; The Girl and the Goatherd, 1969; Do You Have the Time, Lydia, 1971; Yeck Eck, 1973; Marcella's Guardian Angel; author, designer: American Colonial Paper House; Paper Palace; Four Rooms from the Metropolitan Museum; Victorian Paper House; Shaker Paper House. Address: 350 S Ocean Blvd Palm Beach FL 33480. *I depend on my instincts rather than on rationalization.*

NESS, FREDERIC WILLIAM, former assn. exec., educator; b. York, Pa., Feb. 2, 1914; s. Harry and Rosalyn Barbara (Eichelberger) N.; A.B., Dickinson Coll., 1933, LL.D., 1973; student Cin. Conservatory Music, 1930, 31, 33-35; A.M., U. Cin., 1935; Ph.D., Yale, 1940; Litt.D., Ursinus Coll., 1971, Coll. Idaho, 1972, Monmouth Coll., 1976; L.H.D., Beaver Coll., 1972, Millikin U., 1972, Coll. St. Scholastica, 1972, Ottawa U., 1976, York Coll., 1978; Ped. D., Hofstra U., 1975; H.H.D., Rider Coll., 1975; LL.D., Elizabethtown Coll., 1976; m. Dore Roberts, June 30, 1943 (dec. May 1959); children—Lynne, Diane, Merryl, Melanie Barbara; m. 2d, Eleanor H. Hedge, Sept. 1, 1962; 1 dau., Brook H. Instr. English, dean men Cin. Conservatory Music, 1938-39; instr. English, U. Cin., 1939; instr. English, Yale, 1939-42, fellow Berkeley Coll., 1940-42; asst. to vice chancellor, sec. N.Y. U., 1945-52; dean, prof. English, Dickinson Coll., 1952-60, acad. v.p., 1955-60, chmn. dept. English, 1956-59, William W. Edel prof. humanities, 1959-60; v.p., provost, dean Grad. Sch. L.I. U., 1960-62; v.p. Hofstra U., 1962-64; pres. Fresno (Calif.) State Coll., 1964-69, pres. emeritus, 1975—; pres. Assn. Am. Colls., Washington, 1969-78, pres. emeritus, 1978—; vis. prof. Poly. Inst., San German, P.R., 1955; mem. Pa. Gov.'s Com. Edn., 1958-60; pres. Western Colls. Assn., 1967-69. Chmn. bd. dirs. Community Chest, Carlisle, Pa., 1960; bd. dirs. Bklyn. Acad., 1960-62, Fresno Philharmonic Orch., 1965-69, Am. Council Edn., 1968-69, Change, 1970-72, Common Fund, 1970-76, Catalyst, 1974-78, Ind. Colls. Fund Am., 1976—, Moravian Coll., 1976—; bd. dirs., pres. Teaching Film Custodians, 1970-73; mem. acad. adv. bd. U.S. Naval Acad., 1978—. Served from lt. (j.g.) to lt. comdr., USNR, 1942-46. Mem. Phi Beta Kappa, Beta Gamma Sigma, Omicron Delta Kappa, Phi Mu Alpha, Beta Theta Pi. Presbyn. Clubs: Elizabethan (Yale); Yale (N.Y.C.); Cosmos (Washington); Casino (Nantucket); Officers (U.S. Naval Acad.). Author: The Use of Rhyme in Shakespeare's Plays, 1941; An Uncertain Glory, 1971; co-author: Graduate Study in the Liberal Arts College, 1961. Editor, author: The Role of the College in the Recruitment of Teachers, 1958; A Guide to Graduate Study, 1957, 61; A Regional Faculty Orientation Program, 1961. Office: 1818 R St NW Washington DC 20009

NESS, JULIUS B., justice Supreme Ct. S.C.; b. Manning, S.C., Feb. 27, 1916; s. Morris P. and Raye L. N.; B.S., U. S.C., 1938, LL.B., 1940, J.D., 1970; m. Katherine Rhoad, Jan. 25, 1946; children—Gail Ness Richardson, Richard B. Admitted to S.C. bar, 1940; practiced law, Bamberg, S.C., 1940-58; judge S.C. Circuit Ct., 1958-74; asso. justice S.C. Supreme Ct., 1974—; mem. S.C. Senate, 1957-58; instr. Nat. Coll. State Judiciary, 1971. Mem. S.C. Hwy. Commn., 1954-56, chmn., 1956. Served to capt. U.S. Army, 1941-45. Named S.C. Judge of Yr. Assn. Trial Lawyers Am., S.C. Trial Lawyers Assn., 1973, 79. Mem. S.C. Bar, Am. Bar Assn. Democrat. Office: County Courthouse Bamberg SC 29003

NESS, NORMAN FREDERICK, space scientist; b. Springfield, Mass., Apr. 15, 1933; s. Herman Hugo and Eva (Carlson) N.; B.S., Mass. Inst. Tech., 1955, Ph.D., 1959; children—Elizabeth Ann, Stephen Andrew. Space physicist, asst. prof. geophysics U. Calif. at Los Angeles, 1959-61; Nat. Acad. Sci.-NRC post doctoral research asso. NASA, 1960-61, research physicist in space scis. Goddard Space Flight Center, Greenbelt, Md., 1961—, head extraterrestrial physics br., 1968-69, chief Lab. for Extraterrestrial Physics, 1969—; lectr. math. U. Md., 1962-64, asso. research prof., 1965-67. Recipient John Adam Fleming award Am. Geophys. Union, 1965, Exceptional Sci. Achievement award NASA, 1966, Arthur S. Flemming award, 1968, Space Sci. award Am. Inst. Aero. and Astronautics, 1971. Fellow Am. Geophys. Union. Contbr. articles profl. jours. Research, exptl. studies of interplanetary and planetary magnetic fields by satellites and space probes. Home: 4321 Woodberry St University Park MD 20782 Office: NASA Goddard Space Flight Center Greenbelt MD 20771

NESS, ORDEAN GERHARD, educator; b. Buxton, N.D., Oct. 4, 1921; s. Ole Thomas and Gerda (Johnson) N.; B.A. with highest honors, U. N.D., 1942; M.A., U. Wis., 1947, Ph.D. (fellow), 1953. Instr., Syracuse U., 1947-49; cons., personnel policies officer Office of Sec. of Army, 1950-52; asst. prof. Pa. State U., 1953-55; asst. prof. U. Wis., Madison, 1955-59, asso. prof., 1959-61, prof. communication arts, theatre and drama, 1961—, asso. chmn. dept. speech, 1961-70, asso. dir. articulated instrnl. media program, 1964-66, prof. theatre and drama, 1973—, chmn. dept., 1973-75, chmn. dept. communication arts, 1975—, prof. dept. comparative lit., 1978—, chmn. faculty div. humanities, 1976-77; mem. U. Wis. System Adv. Task Force on Telecommunications; free-lance stage, TV and radio actor-dir.; patron Madison Civic Repertory Theatre, Madison Community Access Center; acad. program cons. Served to 1st lt. U.S. Army, 1942-46, capt., 1950-52. Mem. Speech Communication Assn., Nat. Collegiate Players, Nat. Assn. Ednl. Broadcasters, Broadcasting Edn. Assn., AAUP, Am. Council for Arts, Internat. Communication Assn., Am. Film Inst., Central States Speech Assn., Wis. Hist. Soc., Wis. Acad. Scis., Letters and Arts, Am., Wis. theatre assns., Wis. Speech Communication Assn., Consortium for Arts, Wis. Council for Arts, U. Wis., U. N.D. alumni assns., Bascom Hill Soc., Nature Conservancy, Center for Study of Dem. Instns., Friends of Channel 21, Wis. Public Radio Assn., Phi Beta Kappa, Delta Sigma Rho, Blue Key, Phi Eta Sigma, Phi Beta (hon. patron). Author: (with A.T. Weaver) The Fundamentals and Forms of Speech, 1957, 63; An Introduction to Public Speaking, 1961. Deptl. editor Speech Tchr., 1955-63. Contbr. articles to profl. jours. Home: PO Box 5452 Madison WI 53705. *Communication is a human being's rarest gift—but a gift with strings attached. Central to all human endeavors, communication in every person's responsibility. One of my first mentors in "speech" believed that "it is no wonder that communication fails; the wonder is that we communicate at all." Out of respect for the complexities of the process, I have devoted my career to its study and practice.*

NESS, WILLIAM GEORGE, mfg. co. exec.; b. Fusston, Minn., May 22, 1938; s. George A. and Lillian (Austin) N.; B.S.E.E., U. N.D., 1960; grad. Minn. Exec. Program. U. Minn., 1972; m. Henrietta Mae Goulette, Aug. 13, 1960; children—Gregory, Teresa, Jon, Jeffrey, Racheal. Test engr. Univac, St. Paul, 1960-61; dir. engring. Dow KEY Co., Thief River Falls, Minn., 1961-66; dir. engring. Arctic Enterprises, Inc., Thief River Falls, 1966-69, exec. v.p. corp. staff, 1969—, also dir.; dir. No. State Bank. Recipient Gonvick (Minn.) Am. Legion award, 1956, Outstanding Boss award (thief River Falls Jaycees, 1972; named Outstanding Young Man, Am. Legion. Mem. Internat. Snowmobile Industry Assn., Water Sports Vehicle Assn. Roman Catholic. Club: Elks. Patentee snowmobile components and design. Home: 2021 Nelson Dr Thief River Falls MN 56701 Office: PO Box 635 Thief River Falls MN 56701

NESSEN, MAURICE N., lawyer; b. Boston, Jan. 28, 1927; s. Samuel and Molly N.; A.B., Yale U., 1950, LL.B., 1953; m. Hermine Fuld, Feb. 1, 1953; children—Joshua Fuld, William Arthur, Elizabeth. Admitted to N.Y. State bar; law clk. to Judge Edward J. Weinfeld, U.S. Dist. Ct. for So. Dist. N.Y., 1953-54; asst. U.S. atty., head appeals com. So. Dist. N.Y., 1954-57; partner firm Kramer, Lowenstein, Nessen, Kamin & Soll, N.Y.C., 1957—; lectr. N.Y. U. Sch. Law; spl. lectr. Wyo. Law Sch.; adj. prof. N.Y. Law Sch.; adj. prof. Columbia U. Law Sch., later vis. prof.; bd. dirs. Manhattan Legal Services Corp., 1970-74. Bd. dirs., sec. City Walls, Inc., 1968—, Jewish Mus., 1974—. Served with USN, 1945-46. Named Scholar of House, Yale U. Law Sch. Mem. Am. Bar Assn., N.Y. State Bar Assn. (ho. of dels. 1977—), New York County Lawyers Assn. (dir. 1976—), City N.Y. Bar Assn., Phi Beta Kappa. Democrat. Author: Royal Flush, 1963; Orange Power, Black Juice, 1974; contbr. articles to law revs. Home: 27 W 86th St New York NY 10024 Office: 919 3d Ave New York NY 10022

NESSEN, ROBERT LEWIS, investment banker, lawyer; b. Brookline, Mass., Feb. 19, 1932; s. Saul O. and Edith Z. (Rosen) N.; B.A. magna cum laude, Dartmouth Coll., 1953; LL.B., Harvard U., 1956; m. Susan Weil, July 4, 1956; children—Julie, Betsy, Ethan. Admitted to N.Y. bar, 1957, Mass. bar, 1965; asso. firm Dewey, Ballantine, Bushby, Palmer & Wood, N.Y.C., 1958-65; founder, sr. partner firm Nessen & Csaplar, Boston, 1965-75; founder, chmn. bd. March Co., Inc., Boston, 1969-79; of counsel firm Fine & Ambrogne, Boston, 1979—; chmn. bd. March-Eton Corp., Concord, Mass., 1975—; trustee API Trust, Boston, 1971—; lectr. Grad. Sch. Bus., Suffolk U., 1974-75; lectr. real estate devel. and fin. Boston U. Sch. Law, 1976—; adj. asst. profl. historic preservation Sch. Am. Studies, 1977—. Served with U.S. Army, 1956-58. Mem. Boston Bar Assn. Democrat. Jewish. Contbr. articles to profl. jours., popular mags. Home: 67 Sudbury Rd Concord MA 01742 Office: 81 Middle St Concord MA 01742

NESTER, WILLIAM RAYMOND, JR., univ. adminstr.; b. Cin., Feb. 19, 1928; s. William Raymond and Evelyn (Blettner) N.; B.S., U. Cin., 1950, Ed.M., 1953, Ed.D., 1965; m. Mary Jane Grossman, August 21, 1950; children—William Raymond III, Mark Patrick, Brian Phillip, Stephen Christopher. Tchr. high sch. English and history, 1950-52; dir. Union, U. Cin., 1952-53, asst. dean men, 1953-60, asso. prof. edn., dean of men, 1960-67, dean of students, 1967-69, vice provost student and univ. affairs, 1969-76, prof. edn., 1970-78, asso. sr. v.p., asso. provost, 1976-78; v.p. student services Ohio State U., Columbus, 1978—, prof. edn., 1978—. Pres., Metro-Six Athletic Conf., 1975-76, Pi Kappa Alpha Meml. Found., 1978-79. Mem. Am. Personnel and Guidance Assn., Nat. Assn. Student Personnel Adminstrs., AAUP, Am. Assn. for Higher Edn., Nat. (past regional v.p., exec. com.), Ohio (past pres.) assns. student personnel adminstrs., Pi Kappa Alpha (nat. pres. 1978), Frat. Scholarship Officers Assn. (past pres.), Omicron Delta Kappa, Phi Delta Kappa. Episcopalian. Home: 3800 Beecham Ct Columbus OH 43220

NESTMANN-HUSHION, JACQUELINE INEZ, assn. exec.; b. Charleston, W.Va., Feb. 19, 1946; d. Obert Dale and Inez Elsie (Burgess) Coleman; grad. Davis and Elkins Coll., 1967; m. William. J. Hushion, Nov. 16, 1978; 1 son, Earle R. Nestmann. With Ginn and Co., Toronto, Ont., Can., 1968-70, Toronto, 1973-74; asso. dir. Can. Book Pubs. Council, Toronto, Ont., Can. 1968-70, Collier-MacMillan, Toronto, 1973-74; asso. dir. Can. Book Pubs. Council, Toronto, 1974-78, exec. dir., 1978—. Mem. Inst. Assn. Execs., Book Publs. Profl. Assn., Can. Copyright Inst. Office: 45 Charles St E 701 Toronto ON M4Y 1S2 Canada

NESVOLD, BETTY ANNE KRAMBUHL, polit. scientist; b. Pensacola, Fla., Aug. 12, 1922; d. Otto G. and Anne P. (Price) Krambuhl; B.A., San Diego State Coll., 1961, M.A., 1964; Ph.D. (NDEA fellow), U. Minn., Mpls., 1968; m. Alfred Ole Nesvold, Apr. 3, 1943; children—Alfred Ole, Stephen G., Thomas J., Deborah Nesvold Gaspar, Vikki L. Asst. prof. polit. sci. San Diego State U., 1967-70, asso. prof., 1970-73, prof., 1973—, chmn. dept., 1977—; chairperson Inter-Univ. Consortium Polit. Research Council, 1974—. NSF grantee, 1967-72. Mem. Am. Polit. Sci. Assn. (treas. 1974-76), Western Polit. Sci. Assn. (pres. 1975-76), Internat. Studies Assn., Women's Caucus in Polit. Sci. (pres.), NOW. Author: Macro-Quantitative Analysis, 1971; contbr. articles on cross-nat. study of polit. conflict for Nat. Commn. Causes and Prevention of Violence to profl. jours. Home: 6766 Deerwood Ct San Diego CA 92120

NETER, JOHN, statistician; b. Germany, Feb. 8, 1923; B.S., U. Buffalo, 1943; M.B.A., U. Pa., 1947; Ph.D., Columbia U., 1952; m. Dorothy Rachman, June 24, 1951; children—Ronald J., David L. Asst. prof. Syracuse (N.Y.) U., 1949-55, chmn. dept. bus. stats., 1952-55; prof. U. Minn., Mpls., 1955-75, chmn. dept. quantitative analysis, 1961-65; distinguished prof. mgmt. sci., stats. U. Ga., Athens, 1975—; supervisory math. statistician U.S. Bur. Census, 1959-60; cons. in field. Chmn. citizens adv. com. City of St. Louis Park, Minn., 1972, mem. planning commn., 1974-75. Served with AUS, 1943-45. Ford Found. faculty research fellow, 1957-58. Fellow Am. Statis. Assn. (council 1963-64, 67-70, dir. 1975—), AAAS; mem. Am. Inst. Decision Scis. (pres. 1978-79), AAUP (chpt. pres. 1969-70), Inst. Mgmt. Scis., Inst. Math. Stats, Am. Soc. Quality Control. Co-author: Statistical Sampling for Auditors and Accountants, 1956, Fundamental Statistics for Business and Economics, 4th edit., 1973, Applied Linear Statistical Models, 1974; Applied Statistics, 1978. Editor: Am. Statistician, 1976—; asso. editor Decision Scis., 1973-74. Contbr. articles in field to profl. jours. Home: 310 St George Dr Athens GA 30606 Office: Coll Bus Adminstrn U Ga Athens GA 30602

NETHERCOTT, JAMES WALTER, mfg. co. exec.; b. London, Ont., Can., Dec. 23, 1927; naturalized U.S. citizen, 1968; s. James P.S. and Frances J. (Tufford) N.; B.Commerce, U. Toronto (Ont.), 1949; m. Anne H. S. Templeton, Dec. 26, 1948; 1 dau., Sandra Frances Nethercott Waters. With Procter & Gamble Co., Cin., 1951—, v.p. fin, 1973-76, sec., 1975—, sr. v.p., 1976—, also dir.; mem. Fin. Acctg. Standards Adv. Council. Trustee, Bethesda Found., Cin.; bd. dirs. Cin. YMCA, Cin. Community Chest. Chartered acct., Can. Mem. Canadian Inst. Chartered Accts., Conf. Bd. (council fin. execs.), Fin. Execs. Inst. Club: Queen City (Cin.). Home: 8431 Concord Hills Circle Cincinnati OH 45243 Office: 301 E 6th St Cincinnati OH 45202

NETHERCUT, PHILIP EDWIN, assn. exec.; b. Indpls., Apr. 3, 1921; s. William Richard and Ruth Salome (Habbe) N.; B.S., Beloit Coll., 1942; M.S., Lawrence Coll., 1944, Ph.D., 1949; m. Leah Teresa Diehl, Apr. 9, 1949; children—Bruce Philip, Gail Ellen, Anne Louise. With Watervliet Paper Co. (Mich.), 1949-50; research mgr. Scott Paper Co., 1951-56; with TAPPI, N.Y.C., now Atlanta, 1957—, sec.-treas., 1959-60, exec. sec., 1960-75, treas., 1964-75, exec. dir., 1975—; hon. consul for Finland in Ga., 1976—; trustee Inst. Paper Chemistry, 1979—. Bd. dirs. Met. Atlanta Boys' Club, 1979—. Served to lt. (j.g.) USNR, 1944-46. Recipient Distinguished Service citation Beloit Coll., 1967; Clarke award Ga. Soc. Assn. Execs., 1979. Fellow TAPPI; mem. Am. Soc. Assn. Execs. (certified), Inst. Paper Chemistry Alumni Assn. (chmn. 1960), Council Engring. and Sci. Soc. Execs. (pres. 1968), Phi Beta Kappa, Beta Theta Pi. Mem. Disciples of Christ Ch. Clubs: Huntcliff, Mountain View. Home: 9240 Huntcliff Trace NE Atlanta GA 30338 Office: 1 Dunwoody Park Atlanta GA 30338

NETHERCUT, WILLIAM ROBERT, educator, baritone; b. Rockford, Ill., Jan. 11, 1936; s. Robert C. and Constance E. (Stanley) N.; A.B. magna cum laude, Harvard U., 1958; student New Eng. Conservatory of Music, 1959-60; M.A. (Henry Drisler fellow, Pres.'s fellow), Columbia U., 1961, Ph.D., 1963; m. Jane Lillian Swann, July 27, 1977; children—William Andrew, Amanda Jane. Instr., Greek and Latin, Columbia U., 1961-66, asst. prof., 1966-67, Lawrence H. Chamberlain fellow, 1967; asso. prof. classics U. Ga., Athens, 1967-72, prof., 1972-75; prof. classics U. Tex., Austin, 1975—, undergrad. adv., 1977—; announcer radio sta. WROK, Rockford, 1957-58; soloist New Eng. Opera Theatre, Boston, 1958-59, debut as Figaro in Barber of Seville, 1958; soloist recital Carnegie Hall, N.Y.C., 1966; soloist Atlanta Opera Co., 1968; cons. on Greece and Rome, Pathescope Ednl. Films, N.Y.C., 1965-66; appearance ednl. program TV sta. WGTV, Athens, 1970-72; lectr. 1st Internat. Conf. on Ovid, Constanta, Rumania, 1972, Internat. Soc. Homeric Studies, Athens, Greece, 1973, 74, 3d Internat. Congress S.E. European Studies, Bucharest, 1974, Conf. on Ancient Novel, Bangor, Wales, 1976. Am. Council Learned Socs. grantee, 1972. Mem. Am. Philol. Assn., Archaeol. Inst. Am. (pres. Athens chpt. 1972-74), Vergilian Soc. Am. (trustee 1974-79), Classical Assn. Southwestern U.S., Classical Assn. Middle West and South, Tex. Classical Assn. (pres. 1979—). Clubs: Harvard, University, Explorers of N.Y.C., Masons (K.T.). Translator: De Praestigiis Daemonum (Johan Weyer), 1964, Almanach

Perpetuum Celestium Motuum (Rabbi Abraham Zacuto), 1973. Editor: Tex. Classics in Action, 1976—; asso. editor The World and Its Peoples, Italy, 1964; Latina et Graeca, 1974; Helios, Jour. Classical Assn. Southwestern U.S., 1977—. Contbr. articles on classical lit., antiquity to profl. jours. Home: 1003 High Rd Austin TX 78746. *Dedication to work tunes the soul. In creative vision there is eager pride, exaltation. One is humbled in the face of rejection, then taught to behave nobly, choosing, in pain, not to quit the contest, but to serve the vision more effectively.*

NETSCH, WALTER ANDREW, JR., architect, ednl. planner; b. Chgo., Feb. 23, 1920; s. Walter Andrew and Anna C. (Smith) N.; B.Arch., Mass. Inst. Tech., 1943; D.F.A. (hon.), Lawrence U.; Ph.D. in Humanities (hon.), Miami U., Oxford, Ohio; m. Dawn Clark, Oct. 19, 1963. Partner, Skidmore, Owings & Merrill, architects-engrs., Chgo., 1955—; prin. works include numerous ednl. and instl. structures U.S. and North Africa., also Air Force Acad. Recipient Reynolds award for Air Force Acad. Chapel. Fellow A.I.A. Home: 1700 N Hudson St Chicago IL 60614 Office: 30 W Monroe St Chicago IL 60603

NETTELS, CURTIS PUTNAM, educator, historian; b. Topeka, Aug. 25, 1898; s. Charles Henry and Nannie Nesmith (Curtis) N.; A.B., U. Kans., 1921; A.M., U. Wis., 1922, Ph.D., 1925; m. Elsie Patterson, Dec. 21, 1923; 1 dau., Elsa. Asst. instr. history U. Wis., 1921-22, univ. fellow, 1922-23, Pres. Adams fellow, 1923-24, instr. history, 1924-26, asst. prof., 1926-31, asso. prof., 1931-33, prof., 1933-44, chmn. dept., 1939-40; prof. Am. history Cornell U., 1944-66, prof. emeritus, 1966—; lectr. Harvard U., 1937-38, Columbia U., 1938, Johns Hopkins U., 1941. Guggenheim Meml. Found. fellow, 1928; Social Sci. Research Council grantee, 1933. Mem. Am. Hist. Assn. (nominating com. 1939-40, chmn. program com. 1941), Miss. Valley Hist. Assn., Colonial Soc. Mass., Mass. Hist. Soc., Phi Beta Kappa, Beta Theta Pi. Unitarian. Author: The Money Supply of the American Colonies, 1973; The Roots of American Civilization, 1963; George Washington and American Independence, (hist. book club selection), 1977; The Emergence of a National Economy, 1775-1815, 1977; contbr. to numerous anthologies. Editorial bd.: A History of American Economic Life (8 vols.), 1945-62, Jour. Econ. History 1941-46, Am. Hist. Rev., 1943-49, William and Mary Quarterly, 1943-46, Presidential Studies Quarterly, 1977—. Contbr. to hist jours. Address: 303 Comstock Rd Ithaca NY 14850

NETTELS, GEORGE EDWARD, JR., engring. mfg. co. exec.; b. Pittsburg, Kans., Oct. 20, 1927; s. George Edward and Mathilde A. (Wulke) N.; B.S. in Civil Engring., U. Kans., Lawrence, 1950; m. Mary Joanne Myers, July 19, 1952; children—Christopher Bryan, Margaret Anne, Katherine Anne, Rebecca Jane. With Black & Veatch Engrs., Kansas City, Mo., 1950-51, Spencer Chem. Co., Kansas City, Mo., 1951-55, Freeto Constrn. Co., Pittsburg, 1955-57; pres. Midwest Minerals, Inc., Pittsburg, 1957—; chmn. bd. McNally Pittsburg Mfg. Corp., 1970-76, pres., chief exec. officer, 1976—; dir. Nat. Bank Pittsburg, First Fed. Savs. & Loan Assn., Pittsburg; past chmn. bd. Nat. Limestone Inst.; bd. advisers Kans. U. Sch. Engring., Center Bus. and Econ. Devel. of Pittsburg State U.; bd. dirs. Pittsburg Indsl. Devel. Com. Trustee Kans. 4-H Found.; bd. advisers Kans. U. Endowment Assn.; mem. Kans. U. Chancellor's Club; past pres. Bd. Edn. 250, Pittsburg; past chmn. bd. trustees Mt. Carmel Hosp., Pittsburg; past mem. Kans. Commn. Civil Rights; chmn. Kans. Republican Com., 1966-68, Kans. del. Rep. Nat. Conv., 1968, Kan. Bus. and Industry Com. for Re-election of the President, 1972. Served with AUS, 1946-47. Mem. ASCE, Am. Mining Congress (bd. govs. mfrs. div.), NAM (dir.), Kans. Assn. Commerce and Industry (dir.), Kans. Right to Work (dir.), Kans. Council Indsl. Harmony (dir.), Pittsburg C. of C. (past dir.), Kans. U. Alumni Assn. (pres. 1977), Kans. Leadership Com., Tau Beta Pi, Omicron Delta Kappa, Beta Theta Pi. Presbyterian. Clubs: Crestwood Country (Pittsburg); Wolf Creek Golf (Olathe). Home: 509 W Quincy St Pittsburg KS 66762 Office: 101 E 4th St PO Box 651 Pittsburg KS 66762

NETTER, ERIC MAX, banker; b. Goeppingen, Germany, Sept. 7, 1920; s. Henry and Alice (Rothschild) N.; B.B.A., City Coll. N.Y., 1954; M.B.A., N.Y. U., 1960, advanced profl. certificate in computer applications and info. systems, 1975; m. Marion R. Rothschild, Aug. 29, 1948; children—Edith M., Beatrice M. Came to U.S., 1946, naturalized, 1950. With Bank Leumi Trust Co., N.Y.C., 1961—, auditor, 1963—, comptroller, 1968—, v.p., 1973—, sr. v.p., 1979—; adj. asso. prof. Long Island U. Mem. Queens Democratic County Com. Chartered bank auditor, 1969. Mem. Bank Adminstrn. Inst., Inst. Internal Auditors. Club: Lawyers. Office: 579 Fifth Ave New York NY 10017

NETTERVILLE, JOHN THOMAS, educator, chemist; b. Nashville, Oct. 26, 1930; s. William Magruder and Lottie (Keele) N.; B.S., David Lipscomb Coll., 1951; M.A., George Peabody Coll., 1957; M.S., U. Miss., 1961; Ph.D., Vanderbilt U., 1964; m. Annie Ruth Johnson, Dec. 15, 1951; children—John Thomas, James Lee, Joseph David, Jeffrey Paul. Tchr., David Lipscomb High Sch., Nashville, 1951-55, chmn. dept. sci., 1956-59; tchr. Ketchikan (Alaska) pub. schs., 1955-56; mem. faculty David Lipscomb Coll., 1959—, prof. chemistry, 1965—, chmn. dept., 1963-78. Shell merit fellow Cornell U., 1957. Fellow Tenn. Acad. Sci. (Disting. Teaching award 1958; chemistry editor Jour. 1973—); mem. NEA, Tenn. Sci. Tchrs. Assn. (pres. 1956-57), Am. Chem. Soc., Sigma Xi. Author: (with others) Chemistry: A Brief Introduction, 1969; Chemistry: Man and Society, 1972, 3d edit., 1980; Chemistry and the Environment, 1973; also research articles ionic solutions, non-aqueous polarography. Home: Route 8 Brentwood TN 37027 Office: David Lipscomb Coll Grann White Pike Nashville TN 37203. *Human values that count are interpersonal relationships. When positive, such relationships feed the soul and stimulate hunger for a worthwhile eternal destiny. Faith in humankind and faith in the Divine results. But, ignorance can and does blunt the point of human existence. So, I will devote my life to learning, which will give rise to a reasoned faith, and I trust this faith will hold me warm and secure through all of life.*

NETTL, BRUNO, educator; b. Prague, Czechoslovakia, Mar. 14, 1930; s. Paul and Gertrud (Hutter) N.; A.B., Ind. U., 1950, Ph.D., 1953; M.A. in L.S., U. Mich., 1960; m. Wanda Maria White, Sept. 15, 1952; children—Rebecca, Gloria. Mem. faculty Wayne State U., Detroit, 1953-64, asst. prof., 1954-64, music librarian, 1958-64; mem. faculty U. Ill., Urbana, 1964—, prof. music and anthropology, 1967—, chmn. div. musicology, 1967-72, 75-77; vis. lectr., Fulbright grantee U. Kiel (Germany), 1956-58; cons. Ency. Britannica 1969—, also on ethomusicology to various univs. Fulbright grantee, Iran, 1968-69. Mem. Soc. Ethnomusicology (pres. 1969-71), Am., Internat. musicol. socs., Internat. Folk Music Council. Author numerous books including: Theory and Method in Ethnomusicology, 1964; Music in Primitive Culture, 1956; Folk and Traditional Music of the Western Continents, 1965, 2d edit., 1973; Eight Urban Musical Cultures, 1978; also articles. Editor: Ethnomusicology, 1961-65, Yearbook of the Internat. Folk Music Council, 1975-77. Home: 1423 Cambridge Dr Champaign IL 61820 Office: Sch Music U Ill Urbana IL 61801

NETTLES, BERT SHEFFIELD, lawyer; b. Monroeville, Ala., May 6, 1936; s. George Lee and Blanche (Sheffield) N.; B.S., U. Ala., 1958, LL.B., 1960; m. Elizabeth Duquet, Sept. 16, 1967. Admitted to Ala. bar, 1960; asst. atty. gen. Ala., 1960-61; asso. firm Johnston, Johnston & Nettles, Mobile, 1961-64, partner, 1964-69; pvt. practice, 1969-70; sr. partner Nettles & Cox, Mobile, 1971-73; partner Bryan, Nelson, Nettles & Cox, 1973-79; sr. partner Nettles, Cox & Barker, 1979—. Asst. commr. Mobile area council Boy Scouts Am., 1967-71. Vice chmn. Mobile County Republican Exec. Com., 1967-68; legal counsel Ala. Young Rep. Fedn., 1967; chmn. Ala. Rep. Conv., 1968; mem., minority leader Ala. Ho. Reps., 1969-74; mem. Ala. Rep. Exec. Com., 1970-77; pres. Ala. Presdl. Electors, 1972; bd. dirs. Mobile County chpt. ARC, 1968-70; bd. govs. Mobile Protestant Children's Home; pres. Mobile Family Counseling Center, 1976; pres. standing com. Epis. Diocese Central Gulf Coast, 1977. Recipient Algernon Sydney Sullivan medallion U. Ala., 1958. Mem. Am. (chmn. standing com. on legislation 1978-79), Ala. (chmn. young lawyers sect. 1966), Mobile (sec. 1965) bar assns., Ala. Def. Lawyers Assn., Am. Right of Way Assn. (sr.; chpt. v.p. 1970), U. Ala. Alumni Assn. (v.p. 1968), Omicron Delta Kappa, Alpha Tau Omega, Beta Gamma Sigma, Tau Kappa Alpha. Episcopalian. Home: 109 Ryan Ave Mobile AL 36607 Office: First Nat Bank Bldg Mobile AL 36602

NETTLES, JOHN BARNWELL, physician, educator; b. Dover, N.C., May 19, 1922; s. Stephen A. and Estelle (Hendrix) N.; B.S., U. S.C., 1941; M.D., Med. Coll. S.C., 1944; m. Eunice Anita Saugstad, Apr. 28, 1956; children—Eric, Robert, John Barnwell. Intern, Garfield Meml. Hosp., Washington, 1944-45; research fellow in pathology Med. Coll. Ga., Augusta, 1946-47; resident in obstetrics and gynecology U. Ill. Research and Ednl. Hosps., Chgo., 1947-51; instr. to asst. prof. obstetrics and gynecology U. Ill. Coll. Medicine, Chgo., 1951-57; asst. prof., asso. prof., prof. obstetrics, gynecology U. Ark. Med. Center, Little Rock, 1957-69; dir. grad. edn. Hillcrest Med. Center, Tulsa, 1969-73; prof. Coll. Medicine, U. Okla., Oklahoma City, 1969—; prof., chmn. dept. gynecology, obstetrics Coll. Medicine, U. Okla., Tulsa, 1975—, mem. council on residency edn. in obstetrics, gynecology, 1974-79; dir. Tulsa Obstet. and Gynecol. Edn. Found., 1969—. Coordinator med. edn. Nat. Def., Ark., 1961-69; mem. S.W. regional med. adv. com. Planned Parenthood Fedn. Am., 1974-78. Served as lt. (j.g.) M.C., USNR, 1945-46, as lt., 1953-54. Diplomate Am. Bd. Obstetrics and Gynecology. Fellow Am. Coll. Obstetricians and Gynecologists (dist. sec.-treas. 1964-70, dist. chmn. exec. bd. 1970-73, v.p. 1977-78), A.C.S. (bd. govs. 1969-71), Royal Soc. Health, Royal Soc. Medicine; mem. Ark. Obstet. and Gynecol. Soc. (exec. sec. 1959-69), Central Assn. Obstetrics and Gynecology (exec. com. 1966-69, pres. 1978-79), Internat. Soc. Advancement Humanistic Studies in Gynecology, Assn. Mil. Surgeons U.S., AMA (sect. council on obstetrics and gynecology 1975—), So. Med. Assn. (chmn. obstetrics 1973-74), Okla. Med. Soc., Tulsa County Med. Soc., Chgo. Med. Soc., Am. Assn. for Maternal and Infant Health, Assn. Am. Med. Colls., Am. Public Health Assn., Assn. Hosp. ed. Edn., Assn. Planned Parenthood Physicians, Am. Assn. Sex Edn. Counselors and Therapists (S.W. regional bd. 1976—), N.Y. Acad. Sci., Soc. for Gynecol. Investigation, AAAS, Am. Soc. for Study Fertility and Sterility, Internat. Soc. Gen. Semantics, Aerospace Med. Assn., So. Gynecol. and Obstet. Soc., Am. Cancer Soc. (pres. Okla. div. 1979—), Com. on In-Tng. Exam. in Obstetrics and Gynecology, Am. Coll. Nurse Midwives (governing bd. examiners 1979—), Sigma Xi, Phi Rho Sigma. Lutheran. Contbr. articles on uterine malignancy, kidney biopsy in pregnancy, perinatal morbidity and mortality, human sexuality sch. age pregnancy to profl. jours. Office: Suite 408 U Okla Tulsa Med Coll 2727 E 21st St Tulsa OK 74114. *To live life fully, with faith and trust in God and his people, working with others to make our world a little better, and willing to fill the gaps wherever they are.*

NETTLETON, LOIS, actress; b. Oak Park, Ill.; d. Edward L. and Virginia (Schaffer) N.; student Goodman Theater Sch., Actors Studio, 1951. Actress stage plays, films, television; film appearances include Period of Adjustment, 1962, Come Fly With Me, 1963, Mail Order Bride, 1964, Valley of Mystery, Bamboo Saucer, The Good Guys and the Bad Guys, Dirty Dingus Magee, The Sidelong Glances of a Pigeon Kicker, The Honkers, Echoes of a Summer; TV appearances include Medical Center, Barnaby Jones, Hawaii Five-O, Route 66, Gunsmoke, The Nurses, Alfred Hitchcock Show, Twlight Zone, Dupont Show, Eleventh Hour, Armstrong Circle Theatre, Naked City, Doctor Kildare, Portrait of Emily Dickinson, Emanuel, Duet for Two Hands, The Hidden River, The Woman in White, The Light That Failed, Incident of Love, No Hiding Place; made Broadway debut in The Biggest Thief in Town; stage appearances include Darkness At Noon, The Rainmaker, God and Kate Murphy, Silent Night, Lonely Night, The Merchant of Venus, Much Ado About Nothing, Elektra, Cat on a Hot Tin Roof, The Wayward Stork, A Streetcar Named Desire. Recipient Clarence Derwent award, 1959, Laurel award, 1963. Mem. AFTRA, Screen Actors Guild. Address: care William Morris Agy 151 El Camino Beverly Hills CA 90212*

NETZER, DICK, univ. dean; b. N.Y.C., May 14, 1928; s. Solomon and Sue (Dick) N.; B.A., U. Wis., 1946; M.A., M.P.A., Harvard, 1948, Ph.D., 1952; m. Carol Risika, Dec. 30, 1945; children—Jenny, Katherine. Successively economist, sr. economist, asst. v.p. Fed. Res. Bank Chgo., 1948-60; econ. cons. Regional Plan Assn., N.Y.C., 1960—; asso. prof. N.Y. U., 1961-64, prof. econs., 1964—, dean Grad. Sch. Pub. Adminstrn., 1969—; cons. in field, 1960—. Mem. Mayor N.Y.C. Fiscal Adv. Com., 1969-73; treas. Colony-South Bklyn. Houses, 1968-73; mem. Mcpl. Securities Rulemaking Bd., 1978—; bd. dirs. Municipal Assistance Corp. City N.Y., 1975—, Adolph and Esther Gottlieb Found., 1975—. Served with U.S. Army, 1953-55. Mem. Am. Econ. Assn., Regional Sci. Assn., Nat. Tax Assn., Omicron Delta Epsilon. Author: Economics of the Property Tax, 1966; Financing Government in New York City, 1966; Economics and Urban Problems, 1970, rev. edit., 1974; The Subsidized Muse, 1978; co-author: Public Services in Older Cities, 1968; Issues in Urban Economics, 1968; Economic Aspects of Suburban Growth, 1969; The Economics of Public Finance, 1974. Home: 227 Clinton St Brooklyn NY 11201 Office: 4 Washington Sq N New York City NY 10003

NETZER, DONALD LEO, educator; b. Lena, Wis., Oct. 18, 1914; s. Henry Nathan and Julia Mary (Niquette) N.; Ph.B., U. Wis., 1942; M.A., U. Ill., 1946, Ph.D., 1952; m. Bernadette Brazeau, Sept. 10, 1949; children—Donald, Henry, John, Mary, Philip, Julia. Mem. faculty Atlanta div. U. Ga., 1951-55, St. Cloud State Coll., 1956-63; asso. prof. geography Wis. State U., Oshkosh, 1963—. Active Twin Lakes council Boy Scouts Am., 1963-71. Mem. Nat. Council Geog. Edn., Assn. Am. Geographers, Sigma Xi. K.C. Clubs: Optimist, Conservation (Oshkosh). Home: 770 E Sunnyview Rd Oskosh WI 54901

NEU, CHARLES ERIC, historian; b. Carroll, Iowa, Apr. 10, 1936; s. Arthur Nicholas and Martha Margaret (Frandsen) N.; B.A., Northwestern U., 1958; Ph.D., Harvard U., 1964; m. Deborah Alcott Dunning, Sept. 2, 1961 (div. 1978); children—Hilary Adams, Douglas Bancroft. Instr. history Rice U., 1963-64, asst. prof., 1964-67, asso. prof., 1968-70; asso. prof. history Brown U., Providence, 1970-76, prof., 1976—; fellow Charles Warren Center for Studies in Am. History, 1971-72. Woodrow Wilson fellow, 1958-59; Nat. Humanities Endowment younger scholar, 1968-69; Am. Council Learned Socs. fellow, 1975-76; Howard Found. fellow, 1976-77. Mem. Am. Hist. Assn., Orgn. Am. Historians, Soc. Historians of Am. Foreign Policy, Phi Beta Kappa. Democrat. Clubs: Agawam Hunt (Providence); Brown U. (N.Y.C.). Author: An Uncertain Friendship: Theodore Roosevelt and Japan, 1906-1909, 1967; The Troubled Encounter: The United States and Japan, 1975. Home: 346 Rochambeau Ave Providence RI 02906 Office: Dept History Brown Univ Providence RI 02912

NEUBAUER, CHARLES FREDERICK, investigative reporter; b. Elmhurst, Ill., Feb. 13, 1950; s. Fred Charles and Dolores Jeanne (Pries) N.; B.S.J., Northwestern U., 1972, M.S.J., 1973; m. Sandra Carol Bergo, Oct. 4, 1975. Investigator, Better Govt. Assn., Chgo., 1971-73; investigative reporter Chgo. Today, 1973-74, Chgo. Tribune, 1974—. Recipient Pulitzer prize local reporting, 1976. Office: 435 N Michigan Ave Chicago IL 60611

NEUBAUER, JOSEPH, fin. and devel. exec.; b. Oct. 19, 1941; s. Max and Herta (Kahn) N.; B.S. in Chem. Engring., Tufts U., 1963; M.B.A. in Fin., U. Chgo., 1965; m. Antonia R. Brody, May 21, 1965; children—Lawrence, Melissa. Asst. treas. Chase Manhattan Bank, 1965-68, asst. v.p., 1968-70, v.p., 1970-71; asst. treas. Pepsico Inc., Purchase, N.Y., 1971-72, treas., 1972-76, v.p., 1973-76; v.p. fin. and control Wilson Sporting Goods Co., River Grove, Ill., 1976-77, sr. v.p., gen. mgr. team sports div., 1977-79; exec. v.p. fin. and devel., chief fin. officer, dir. ARA Services, Inc., Phila., 1979—. Treas., United Way of Westchester (N.Y.), 1974-75, bd. dirs., 1975-76. Mem. Fin. Execs. Inst., Treas's. Group. Home: 251 Cheswold Ln Haverford PA 19041 Office: ARA Services Inc Independence Sq W Philadelphia PA 19106

NEUBAUER, WALTER KENNETH, civil engr.; b. N.Y.C., June 16, 1924; s. Walter Martin and Mildred Elizabeth (Boye) N.; B.C.E. magna cum laude, Syracuse U., 1949; m. Diane R. Johnson, Feb. 23, 1974; children by previous marriage—Rory, Debra, Craig, Eric. Field engr. Frederick Snare Corp., Annapolis, Md., 1949-52; engr. Donald E. Stearns, Cazenovia, N.Y., 1952-53; engr. O'Brien & Gere, Syracuse, N.Y., 1954—, asso., 1955—, partner, 1961—, exec. v.p., 1971—, also dir.; dir. O'Brien & Gere Inc., Justin & Courtney, Inc.; chmn. bd. O'Brien & Gere Ltd. Served with AC, U.S. Army, 1943-46. Mem. Am. Water Works Assn. (chmn. N.Y. sect. 1976-77, chmn. concrete pressure pipe standards com. 1970-78, standards council 1979—), Am. Cons. Engrs. Council (pres. Central N.Y. chpt. 1968-69), ASCE (pres. Central N.Y. chpt. 1959-60), Water Pollution Control Fedn., Nat. Soc. Profl. Engrs., Tau Beta Pi, Theta Tau, Pi Mu Epsilon. Clubs: Natacion porra del Tiburón, Cazenovia Ski. Home: 7327 Highbridge Rd Fayetteville NY 13066 Office: 1304 Buckley Rd Box 4873 Syracuse NY 13221

NEUBERGER, KATHERINE (MRS. HARRY H. NEUBERGER), civic worker; b. N.Y.C., Apr. 30, 1907; d. Samuel and Elsie (Wallach) Kridel; B.A., Barnard Coll., 1927; postgrad. Columbia, 1932-33; LL.D. (hon.), Montclair State Coll., 1972, Monmouth Coll., 1973, Fairleigh Dickinson U., 1979; D.H.L. (hon.), Jersey City State Coll., 1978, Rutgers U., 1979; m. Harry H. Neuberger, Mar. 7, 1929; children—Susan (Mrs. Donald M. Wilson), Joan (Mrs. Henry M. Woodhouse). Mem., v.p. bd. mgrs. N.J. Reformatory for Women, 1940-57; mem. N.J. Law Enforcement Council, 1952-57, chmn., 1954-57; mem. bd. Monmouth County Orgn. Social Service, 1937-59; mem. bd. Family Service Soc. Monmouth County, 1959—; chmn. Home Service Corps, Monmouth County chpt. A.R.C., 1940-46; mem. bd. Assn. Aid Crippled Children, 1949-77; mem. N.J. Bd. Higher Edn., 1970—, vice chmn., 1972-75, chmn., 1975-78; Pres. N.J. Fedn. Republican Women, 1957-61, mem. exec. bd. Nat. Fedn., 1959-61; mem. Rep. Nat. Com. for N.J., 1961-76. Trustee Monclair State Coll., 1967-70, Fairleigh Dickinson U., 1973-74; warden Christ Episcopal Ch., Middletown, N.J., 1975—. Mem. AAUW. Episcopalian. Clubs: Cosmopolitan (N.Y.C.); Navesink Country (N.J.); Woods Hole Golf, Quissett Yacht (Mass.). Home: 628 Middletown-Lincroft Rd Lincroft NJ 07738 Office: 225 W State St Trenton NJ 08608

NEUBERGER, ROY R., stockbroker; b. Bridgeport, Conn., July 21, 1903; s. Louis and Bertha (Rothschild) N.; ed. N.Y. U., also U. Sorbonne; m. Marie Salant, June 29, 1932; children—Ann Marie Neuberger Aceves, Roy S., James A. Buyer, B. Altman & Co., 1922-25; art student, Paris, 1925-29; broker Halle & Stieglitz, N.Y.C., 1929-40; sr. partner Neuberger & Berman, N.Y.C., 1940—; pres. Guardian Mut. Fund, Inc., 1950-79; chmn. bd. Neuberger & Berman Mgmt., Inc., 1970—, Neuberger & Berman Pension Mgmt. Inc., 1975—, Guardian Mut. Fund, 1979—. Bd. dirs. City Center Music and Drama, N.Y.C., 1957-74, trustee, 1974—, finance chmn., 1971-74; trustee Whitney Mus. Am. Art, 1961-69, trustee emeritus, 1969—; mem. collector's com. Nat. Gallery Art, Washington, 1975—; trustee, mem. exec. com. New Sch. Social Research, 1967-75; hon. trustee Met. Mus. Art, N.Y.C., 1968—; council of friends Inst. Fine Arts, N.Y. U., 1961—; mem. president's council Mus. City N.Y.; trustee Purchase (N.Y.) Coll. Found., 1971—; chmn. Purchase Coll. Found., 1974—; donor Roy R. Neuberger Mus. State U. N.Y. at Purchase, 1969—. Recipient Artists Equity award, 1972; Benjamin Franklin fellow Royal Soc. Arts, 1970—. Fellow in perpetuity NAD; mem. Am. Fedn. Arts (pres. 1958-67, hon. pres. 1968—), N.Y. Soc. Security Analysts, Soc. Ethical Culture N.Y.C. (treas. 1956-64, pres. 1965-68). Art collector, collection exhibited museums throughout U.S. and abroad, 1936—. Home: 993 Fifth Ave New York NY 10028 Office: 522 Fifth Ave New York NY 10036

NEUBERT, GEORGE WALTER, JR., museum ofcl.; b. Mpls., Oct. 24, 1942; s. George W. and Jaunita Lois (Mohler) N.; student William Jewell Coll., 1962; B.S. in Painting/Edn., Hardin-Simmons U., 1965; postgrad. Adelphi U., 1966; spl. studies San Francisco Art Inst., 1966-67; M.F.A., Mills Coll. (Trefethen fellow), 1969; m. Eva Saenz, July 24, 1965; 1 dau., Evangeline Katherine. Student curator art dept. gallery Hardin-Simmons U., Abilene, Tex., 1963-65; instr. art West Babylon (N.Y.) pub. schs., 1965-66; teaching asst. San Francisco Art Inst., 1966-67; grad. teaching asst. Mills Coll. Gallery, Oakland, Calif., 1967-68; curator art Oakland (Calif.) Mus., 1969—. Mus. con., art historian, lectr., sculptor. Mem. Assn. Art Mus. Dirs., Western Assn. Art Museums (dir. 1970—), Smithsonian Inst.'s Archives of Am. Art (adv. bd. 1971—), Am. Assn. Museums. Office: Oakland Mus 1000 Oak St Oakland CA 94607

NEUBERT, THEODORE JOHN, educator, chemist; b. Rochester, N.Y., Jan. 10, 1917; s. John H. and Josephine B. (Eich) N.; B.S., U. Rochester, 1939; Ph.D., Brown U., 1942. Prof. chemistry Ill. Inst. Tech., Chgo., 1949—; cons. solid state sci. div. Argonne Nat. Lab., 1947-70. Recipient award for excellence in undergraduate teaching Ill. Inst. Tech., 1966. Mem. Am. Phys. Soc., Am. Chem. Soc., AAUP. Office: Ill Inst Tech Dept Chemistry Chicago IL 60616

NEUCE, EDWIN OLANDO, editor; b. Morgantown, W.Va., Sept. 3, 1922; s. Thornton Olando and Elizabeth (Gutherie) N.; student pub. schs., Morgantown; b. Nina Lynne Foltz, Mar. 24, 1943; 1 dau., Carol Lynne Neuce Davidson. Police officer, Front Royal, Va., 1950-58; office mgr. No. Va. Daily, Front Royal, 1958-59; feature editor Dominion-News, Morgantown, 1959-60; news editor Coin World, Sidney, Ohio, 1961-72; editor Linn's Stamp News, Sidney, 1972—; mem. mgmt. planning group Amos Press Inc., Sidney. Mem. Sidney City Council, 1973-74. Served with U.S. Army, 1940-45. Recipient Outstanding Citizen award Sidney Jaycees, 1966. Mem.

Am. Philatelic Soc., Soc. Philatelic Americans, Am. Numismatic Assn. Presbyterian. Clubs: Kiwanis, Moose. Author: Basic Knowledge for the Coin Collector, 1962; Price Guide for the Collector of U.S. Paper Money Errors, 1968; editor: Linn's World Stamp Almanac, 1976. Home: 1013 Juniper Way Sidney OH 45365 Office: 911 Vandemark Rd Sidney OH 45365

NEUENSCHWANDER, FREDERICK PHILLIP, business exec., former state ofcl.; b. Akron, Ohio, Mar. 19, 1924; s. Willis Lee and Esther (Mayer) N.; student Franklin and Marshall Coll., 1942-43, U. Akron, 1946-48. also Inst. Orgn. Mgmt., Syracuse U., Mich. State U., U. N.C.; m. Mary Jane Porter, Mar. 19, 1948; children—Carol, Frederick Phillip, Lynn, Dean Richard. Chief insp. Retail Credit Co., Akron, 1948-55; exec. v.p. Wadsworth (Ohio) C. of C., 1955-62, Wadsworth Devel Corp., 1955-62, Wooster (Ohio) C. of C., 1962-63, Wooster Expansion, Inc., 1962-63; dep. dir. devel. Ohio, 1963-64, dir. devel., 1964-70; exec. v.p. James A. Rhodes & Assos., 1971-75, F.P. Neuenschwander & Assoc., Columbus, 1975—; sec., dir. Jackson Iron & Steel Co. Exec. dir. Wadsworth United Fund, 1956-62; past chmn. Chippewa Watershed Conservancy Dist.; dist. committeeman Boy Scouts Am.; past chmn. Midwest Govs. Adv. Council; vice-chmn. Ohio Water Commn., Ohio Air Pollution Control Bd.; sec. Ohio Devel. Council, Ohio Devel. Finance Commn.; mem. Gt. Lakes States Indsl. Devel. Council, Am. Indsl. Devel. Council, Interstate Compact Commn., Ohio Expns. Commn.; first chmn. Ohio Hwy. Transp. Research Center. Bd. dirs., past chmn. Temple Hills, Inc.; bd. dirs. Wadsworth br. Kent (Ohio) State U., 1959-62; mem. adv. bd. Rio Grand Coll.; mem. nat. adv. council Small Bus. Adminstrn.; mem. world bd. ministries United Ch. of Christ. Served with AUS, 1943-46. Named Outstanding Young Man of Year, Wadsworth Jr. C. of C., 1958; recipient Gov. Ohio award, 1966, award outstanding devel. program N. Am., Soc. Indsl. Realtors 1967, 69. Mem. C. of C. Execs. Ohio, Huguenot Soc. U.S., Huguenot Soc. Ohio, Am. Legion, Ohio Soc. N.Y. (research v.p.). Home: 1155 Clubview St S Worthington OH 43085 Office: FP Neuenschwander & Assoc Columbus OH 43215

NEUFFER, FRANK RAMSEY, univ. dean; b. Cin., Oct. 12, 1909; s. Frank Ellis and Bert (Ramsey) N.; Comml. Engr., U. Cin., 1933; LL.D., Drexel U. Tech., 1958; m. Grace H. Brown, Apr. 12, 1954; m. 2d, Celeste E. Garner, May 8, 1971. Asst. dir., asst. prof. U. Cin. Eve. Coll., 1937-41, asst. dean, asso. prof., 1941-43, acting dean, 1943-45, dean, prof., 1945-75, dir. U. Cin. lecture programs, 1951-75, dean emeritus, 1975—; dir. Center for Study Liberal Edn. for Adults (sec. 1955-58, chmn. bd. 1957-58); indsl. engr., 1945-74. Vis. com. Johns Hopkins Eve. Coll., 1964-69; mem. Ohio com. humanities Nat. Endowment Humanities, 1971-74. Mem. Am. Soc. Engring. Edn. (chmn. eve. edn. com. 1945-47), Assn. U. Eve. Colls. (pres. 1949-50), Adult Edn. Council Cin. (dir. 1944-52), Nat. Office Mgmt. Assn. (pres. Cin. chpt. 1950-51), Ohio Coll. Assn. (pres. adult edn. sect. 1948-49), Ohio Assn. Adult Edn. (dir. 1949-51), Adult Edn. Assn. U.S.A., NEA, Nat. U. Extension Assn. (chmn. eve. coll. div., dir. 1963-65, 67-68), Alpha Kappa Psi, Beta Gamma Sigma, Delta Mu Delta (nat. councilor, nat. v.p. 1953-56), Mu Pi Kappa, Alpha Sigma Lambda (nat. councilor, nat. pres. 1952-55), Alpha Sigma Kappa. Home: 13559 16th Ave NE Seattle WA 98125

NEUGARTEN, BERNICE LEVIN, social scientist; b. Norfolk, Nebr., Feb. 11, 1916; d. David L. and Sadie (Segall) Levin; B.A., U. Chgo., 1936, Ph.D., 1943; m. Fritz Neugarten, July 1, 1940; children—Dail Ann, Jerrold. Research asst. dept. edn. U. Chgo., 1937-39; fellow Am. Council on Edn., 1939-41; instr. psychology Englewood Coll., Chgo., 1941-43; research asso. Com. on Human Devel., U. Chgo., 1948-50, asst. prof., 1951-60, asso. prof., 1960-64, prof., 1964—, chmn., 1969-73; mem. council U. Chgo. Senate, 1968-71, 72-75, 78—, chmn. council com. on univ. women, 1969-70. Mem. tech. com. research and demonstration White House Conf. on Aging, 1971; tech. advisory com. on aging research HEW, 1972-73; nat. advisory council Nat. Inst. on Aging, 1975-76, 78—, Fed. Council on Aging, 1978—. Recipient Am. Psychol. Found. Teaching award, 1975; Disting. Psychologist award Ill. Psychol. Assn., 1979. Fellow AAAS, Am. Psychol. Assn. (council reps. 1967-69, 73-76), Am. Sociol. Assn., Gerontol. Soc. (pres. 1968-69, Kleemeier award for research in aging 1971); mem. Internat. Assn. Gerontology (governing council 1975-78), Sigma Xi, Pi Lambda Theta. Author: (with R. J. Havighurst) American Indian and White Children: A Social-Psychological Investigation, 1955, Society and Education, 1957, rev., 1974, Personality in Middle and Late Life, 1964; co-author: Adjustment to Retirement, 1969; Social Status in the City, 1971. Editor: Middle Age and Aging, 1968. Asso. editor Jour. Gerontology, 1958-61, Human Devel., 1962-68. Contbr. chpts. to books, articles to profl. jours. Home: 5801 Dorchester Ave Chicago IL 60637

NEUGEBAUER, GERRY, astrophysicist; b. Gottingen, Germany, Sept. 3, 1932; s. Otto E. and Grete (Brück) N.; B.S., Cornell U., 1954; Ph.D., Calif. Inst. Tech., 1960; m. Marcia MacDonald, Aug. 26, 1956; children—Carol, Lee. Came to U.S., 1939, derivative citizen. Mem. faculty Calif. Inst. Tech., Pasadena, 1962—, prof. physics, 1970—, mem. staff Hale Obs., 1970—. Served with AUS, 1961-63. Mem. Nat. Acad. Scis., Am. Acad. Arts and Scis. Office: Calif Inst Tech Pasadena CA 91125

NEUHARTH, ALLEN HAROLD, newspaper pub.; b. Eureka, S.D., Mar. 22, 1924; s. Daniel J. and Christina (Neuharth) N.; B.A. cum laude, U. S.D. 1950; student Am. Press Inst., Columbia, 1956, 62, 63; m. Lori Wilson, Dec. 31, 1973; children by previous marriage—Daniel J. II, Janet Ann. Reporter, Rapid City (S.D.) Jour., 1948; sports writer Mitchell (S.D.) Daily Republic, 1949; staff writer A.P., Sioux Falls, S.D. 1950-52; editor, pub. S.D. Sports Weekly Sioux Falls, 1952-54; with Miami (Fla.) Herald, 1954-60, asst. mng. editor, 1958-60; asst. exec. editor Detroit Free Press, 1960-63; gen. mgr. Times-Union and Democrat and Chronicle, Rochester, N.Y., 1963—; exec. v.p. Gannett Co., Inc., 1966-70, pres., 1970—, chief exec. officer, 1973—, chmn., 1979—; dir. Gannett New Service, Inc., Marine Midland Banks, Inc., Buffalo. Bd. dirs. Frank E. Gannett Newspaper Found., Nat. Council Better Bus. Burs., Inc. Served with inf. AUS, 1943-46; ETO, PTO. Decorated Bronze Star. Mem. Rochester-Monroe County C. of C., N.Y. State Pubs. Assn. (past pres.), Am. Newspaper Pubs. Assn. (dir. 1968—, chmn., pres. 1978—), Sigma Delta Chi (past nat. regional dir. region I, Horatio Alger award 1975). Clubs: Carlton (Chgo.); Genesee Valley (Rochester); Internat. (Washington); Jockey (Miami); Ocean Reef (Key Largo, Fla.); Sky (N.Y.C.). Home: 333 S Atlantic Ave Cocoa Beach FL 32931 Office: 1 Lincoln First Sq 25th Floor Rochester NY 14604

NEUHAUS, JULIUS VICTOR, III, architect; b. Houston, Sept. 9, 1926; s. Julius Victor, Jr. and Vera Inez (Richardson) N.; B.Arch., U. Tex., 1951; m. Judith Ann Brown, Oct. 22, 1976; children—Nancy Park, Patricia Richardson, Edith Brownell. Co-founder, 3D/Internat., and predecessor Neuhaus & Taylor, Architects and Planning Cons., Houston, 1955, pres., chief exec. officer, 1971—; moderator panel central cities Gov. Tex. Conf. Urban and Community Affairs, 1969; mem. Citizens Adv. Com. Housing, Houston, 1966; mem. regional adv. panel GSA, 1971. Served with USNR, 1944-46. Fellow AIA; mem. Tex. Soc. Architects, Houston C. of C. Republican. Episcopalian. Clubs: River Oaks Country, University (Houston); Capitol Hill (Washington).

NEUHAUS, OTTO WILHELM, educator; b. Zweibrucken, Germany, Nov. 18, 1922; s. Clemens Jakob and Johanna Amalie (Schnorr) N.; came to U.S., 1927, naturalized, 1931; B.S., U. Wis., 1944; M.S., U. Mich., 1947, Ph.D., 1953; m. Dorothy Ellen Rehn, Aug. 30, 1947; children—Thomas William, Carol Alida, Joanne Marie. Research chemist Huron Milling Co., 1951-54; mem. faculty Wayne State U., Detroit, 1954-66, asso. prof., 1965-66; prof., chmn. dept. biochemistry, acting chmn. dept. physiology and pharmacology U. S.D., Vermillion, 1966-76, prof., chmn. div. biochemistry, physiology and pharmacology, 1976—. NATO Research fellow, 1961-62. Fellow AAAS; mem. Am. Chem. Soc., Am. Soc. Biol. Chemists, Sigma Xi, Phi Sigma, Phi Lambda Upsilon. Lutheran. Author: (with John Halver) Fish in Research, 1969; (with James Orten) Human Biochemistry, 1975; also research articles. Office: Div Biochemistry Physiology and Pharmacology Sch Medicine Univ South Dakota Vermillion SD 57069

NEUHAUS, PHILIP ROSS, investment banker; b. Houston, Dec. 25, 1919; s. Hugo Victor and Kate Padgitt (Rice) N.; grad. St. Mark's Sch., Southborough, Mass., 1938; B.A., Yale, 1942; m. Barbara R. Haden, Aug. 14, 1968; children—Philip Ross (dec.), Lacey Thompson, Elizabeth Rice, Joan Thompson. With Nat. City Bank of Cleve., 1946-47, McDonald & Co., Cleve., 1947, Neuhaus & Co., 1947; with Underwood, Neuhaus & Co., Inc., Houston, 1948—, now pres., dir. Trustee, treas. Tex. Childrens Hosp.; trustee Salvation Army, Houston; asso. Rice U. Served to capt., cav., AUS, 1942-45. Mem. Securities Industry Assn. Am. (bd. govs., chmn. Tex. dist. 1973, exec. com. 1975), Houston Soc. Financial Analysts (pres. 1959), Stock and Bond Club Houston (past pres.), Nat. Fedn. Financial Analysts (v.p. 1963, dir.). Clubs: Bayou, Houston Country, Houston, Ramada, Eagle Lake Rod and Gun. Home: 407 Thamer Ln Houston TX 77024 Office: 724 Travis St Houston TX 77002

NEUHAUS, WILLIAM OSCAR, financial cons.; b. Houston, Jan. 4, 1916; s. Herbert Edward and Ethel (Bartholomew) N.; B.A., Rice U., 1936; m. Betty Palmer Bosworth, Dec. 9, 1942; children—William Oscar, Laurence Bosworth, Edward Kessler. With Quintana Petroleum Corp., Houston, 1937—, treas., 1967-72, fin. adv., 1972—; v.p. Neuhaus Investment Co., Houston, 1946—; co-chmn. bd., dir. Cullen Center Bank & Trust, Houston, 1969-77, now dir.; pres., dir. Cullen Center Inc.; v.p. Marshall Oman Exploration Inc., Houston, 1975—; gen. partner Neuhaus Developers, Houston, 1976—; dir. Oman Mining & Co., Muscat. Vice pres. Armand Bayou Nature Center, 1977—; pres. Kiwanis Found. Houston, 1977-79; treas. San Jacinto Mus. History Assn., 1975—; trustee, pres. Episcopal Ch. Corp., 1964—, treas. local ch., 1957—; trustee Glenwood Cemetery Assn., 1975—; bd. dirs. Houston Housing Devel. Corp., 1973—, Tax Research Assn., Houston, 1952—; trustee Faith Home, Houston, 1975—; trustee, chmn. Harris County chpt. ARC, 1978—; trustee United Way, Houston, 1979—. Served to capt. USAAF, 1942-46. Mem. Ind. Petroleum Assn. Am. (chmn. tax com. 1958-60), Am. Petroleum Inst., Orton Soc. (pres., dir. Houston br. 1978—). Clubs: Houston Country, Petroleum, Tex. Corinthian Yacht, Bayou, Eagle Lake Rod and Gun, Kiwanis (Houston). Home: 3461 Piping Rock Ln Houston TX 77027 Office: PO Box 1600 Houston TX 77001

NEUHOFF, ROGER ALAN, broadcasting co. exec.; b. N.Y.C., Feb. 16, 1928; s. Jerome Carl and Betty (Green) N.; B.A., Amherst Coll., 1950; m. Louise Reeve Hoover, June 21, 1952; children—Geoffrey Houghton, Marion Gordon Tully, Eric Alan, Alexander Amory. With CIA, 1950-56; pres., chmn. bd. dirs. Eastern Broadcasting Corp., Washington, 1958—; chmn. bd., pres. Springfield Advt. Co., 1969—; chmn. bd. New Eng. Media Corp., 1974—; chmn. bd., pres. State Coll. Communications Corp., 1975—; chmn. bd., pres. Ohio Broadcasting Corp.; chmn. bd., pres. Penn Broadcasting Corp., 1979—; dir. Southeastern Pub. Inc., Clubs: Chevy Chase, Edgartown Yacht, Univ., N.Y. Athletic. Home: 5100 39th St Washington DC 20016 Office: 1875 Connecticut Ave Washington DC 20009 also 3518 W Cahuenga Blvd #205 Los Angeles CA 90068

NEUMAIER, JOHN JOSEPH, educator; b. Frankfort on Main, Germany, Oct. 30, 1921; s. Otto and Leonore (Schwarz) N.; came to U.S., 1940, naturalized, 1943; B.A. magna cum laude, U. Minn., 1947, Ph.D., 1954; m. Virginia Bratman, Mar. 25, 1944; children—Diane Leonore, Roger, John; m. 2d, Sara Lee Fletcher Luther, Sept. 2, 1969. Instr. humanities U. Minn., 1948-51; instr. philosophy and sociology Hibbing (Minn.) Jr. Coll., 1951-55, dean, 1955-58; pres. Moorhead (Minn.) State Coll., 1958-68, State U. Coll. at New Paltz, N.Y., 1968-72; prof. philosophy and social theory State U. N.Y. Empire State Coll., N.Y.C., 1972—; faculty exchange program SUNY/Sr. scholar Moscow State U., 1979. Past mem. Gov.'s Human Rights Commn.; past Minn. adv. com. U.S. Commn. on Civil Rights; past pres. Assn. Minn. Colls. Co-editor: Der Richter Und Sein Henker (Friedrich Duerrenmatt), 1960. Bldg. named in his honor at Moorhead State U. Home: 60 S Randolph Ave Poughkeepsie NY 12601

NEUMAN, DONALD BERNARD, educator; b. Milw., Sept. 17, 1934; s. Harry Morris and Ida (Nashinsky) N.; B.S., U. Wis., 1956; M.A. in Teaching, Mich. State U., 1966, Ph.D. in Sci. Edn., 1968; m. Barbara Heavenrich, Feb. 3, 1957; children—Phillip, Michael, Joel, Laura. Tchr. pub. schs., Milw., 1960-65; asst. instr. edn. Mich. State U., East Lansing, 1966-68; prof. curriculum and instrn., sci. edn. U. Wis.-Milw., 1968—, chmn. dept. curriculum and instrn., 1974—; cons. Head Start Program. Mem. sch. bd. Milw. Hillel Acad., 1971—. Served to 1st. lt. M.S.C., AUS, 1957-59. Acad. Year Inst. fellow NSF, 1965-66. Mem. A.A.A.S. (council), Phi Delta Kappa. Jewish. Author: Sciencing for Tots, 2d edit., 1972; Creative Activities for Young Children, 1975; Science Activities for Young Children, 1978. Home: 941 E Sylvan Ave Milwaukee WI 53217

NEUMAN, E(RNST) JACK, TV producer-writer; b. Toledo, Feb. 27, 1921; s. Ernst J. and Agnes Rose (Killgallon) N.; B.J., U. Mo., 1942; LL.B., U. Cal. at Los Angeles, 1952; m. Marian Collier Barbour, Sept. 27, 1970; children by previous marriage—Eric John, Zachary James, Victoria Anne, Claudia Jane. Freelance writer for radio shows, 1946-54, TV shows, 1954-60; writer TV pilots, Dr. Kildare, Sam Benedict, Mr. Novak, Shenandoah, Police Story, Blue Knight, Petrocelli, Kate McShane, 1960—; pres. P.A. Prodns., 1972—. Served with USMCR, 1942-46. Recipient Mystery Writers Am. award 1953, 71, Eisenhower Freedom award, 1961, Peabody award for Mr. Novak, 1964. Home: 1849 Rising Glen Rd Los Angeles CA 90069 Office: 3518 W Cahuenga Blvd Suite 205 Los Angeles CA 90068

NEUMAN, HOWARD JAY, financial exec.; b. St. Louis, July 28, 1942; s. Leo and Ida Strauss (Cohen) N.; B.S. in Bus. Adminstrn., Washington U., St. Louis, 1965; m. Joyce Gross, July 26, 1964; children—Craig Alan, Nanci Faye, Mark Jason. Staff accountant Kessler & Chervitz, C.P.A.'s, St. Louis, 1964-65; staff accountant, asst. controller Valley Steel Products Co., 1965-69; sec.-treas. Valley Industries, Inc., St. Louis, 1969—. Active membership com. St. Louis Regional Commerce and Growth Assn. Served with U.S. Army, 1960. Mem. Nat. Assn. Accountants. Jewish. Home: 7810 Delmar Blvd University City MO 63130 Office: PO Box 503 Saint Louis MO 63166

NEUMAN, JAMES VINCENT, JR., geologist, cons. engr.; b. Redwood City, Calif., Mar. 8, 1913; s. James Vincent and Ann D. (Barg) N.; A.B. in Geology, Stanford, 1934, E.M., 1938; m. Lillian M. Burgess, June 9, 1942; children—Dianne E., James V. Engr.-geologist King Solomon Mine, Calif., 1935-36, A.O. Smith Corp., U.S. Geol. Survey, H. J. Kaiser Co., Summitville Consol. Mines, 1938-40; geologist Permanente Corp., 1941; with U.S. Smelting and Refining and Mining Co., 1941-73, gen. mgr. oil div., 1951-66, v.p., gen. mgr. oil div., 1956-66, v.p. charge mining and oil operations, 1966-73; v.p., dir. U.S. Smelting & UV Industries, 1956-73, cons., 1973—; cons. mining and oil, 1973—. Mem. Am. Inst. Mining, Metall, and Petroleum Engrs., Am. Assn. Petroleum Geoglists. Home: 2450 Maywood Dr Salt Lake City UT 84109

NEUMAN, WILLIAM FREDERICK, educator, biophysicist; b. Petoskey, Mich., June 2, 1919; s. Reinhardt F. and Louise (Grauel) N., B.S., Mich. State U., 1940; Ph.D., U. Rochester, 1944; m. Margaret Wrightington, June 10, 1943; children—W. Russell, Carol Louise, Peter David. Mem. faculty U. Rochester, 1944—, prof. radiation biology and biophysics, chmn. dept., 1966-75, Joseph C. Wilson prof., 1972—, prof. biochemistry and pharmacology, 1952—; cons. in field, 1950—. Recipient Eli Lilly award biol. chemistry, 1955, Claude Bernard medal U. Montreal, 1962, Kappa Delta award, 1964, Biol. Mineralization award Internat. Assn. Dental Research, 1965. Mem. AAAS, Am. Chem. Soc., Am. Soc. Biol. Chemists, Am. Soc. Pharmacology and Exptl. Therapy, Radiation Research Soc., Urban League (dir.), Biophys. Soc., Sigma Xi, Phi Kappa Phi. Unitarian (trustee). Author: Chemical Dynamics of Bone Mineral, 1958; also numerous articles, Home: 29 Menlo Pl Rochester NY 14620 Office: Univ Rochester Med Center 460 Elmwood Ave Rochester NY 14642

NEUMANN, ALFRED ROBERT, univ. chancellor; b. Frankfurt am Main, Germany, Jan. 26, 1921; s. Bernhard and Jenny (Heidenheimer) N.; came to U.S., 1937, naturalized, 1943; A.B., Marshall Coll., 1940; M.A., U. Ky., 1941; A.M., Harvard U., 1948; Ph.D., U. Mich., 1951; LL.D., Marshall U., 1964; m. Selma Smith, Sept. 5, 1944; children—Bernard Stephen, Carolyn Joyce. Tchr. Latin and French, condr. orch. Beall High Sch., Frostburg, Md., 1941-42; instr. German and French, Tulane U., 1946; teaching fellow German, Harvard, 1946-48; instr. German, U. Mich., 1948-52; asst. prof. U. Houston, 1953-56, asso. prof. German, 1956-61, prof., 1961—, asst. to v.p. acad. affairs, 1956, asst. to pres., 1957-59, acting dean, 1958-59, dean Coll. Arts and Scis., 1959-72, chancellor U. Houston/Clear Lake City, 1972—; mem. Am. Council Edn. Commn. Leadership Tng., 1976-78; mem. nat. advisory council Council on Learning. Presented coll. courses in German, KUHT-TV, Houston, 1954-55; program annotator Houston Symphony Orch., 1958-75, chmn. search com. for mus. dir. 1978; program annotator Houston Grand Opera Assn.; cons. on accreditation SACS. Examiner, Coll. Entrance Exam. Bd., 1962-65. Pres., Houston Jewish Family Service, 1969-70, So. Humanities Conf., 1969-70; vice chmn. Houston Municipal Art Commn., 1972. Decorated Order Merit 1st class, Comdr.'s Cross (W. Ger.). Mem. Houston Contemporary Music Soc. (pres. 1962-63), Am. Council Learned Socs. (scholar 1952-53, past regional asso.), Houston Grand Opera Assn. (dir. 1956-67), Houston Friends of Music (pres.), Modern Lang. Assn. (chmn. commn. on trends in edn. 1968-71), Houston Council Fgn. Lang. Tchrs. (pres. 1967-68), Am. Assn. State Colls. and Univs. (chmn. com. internat. programs), Am. Assn. Tchrs. German, Stillwater Conf. Acad. Deans (chmn. 1965), South Central Modern Lang. Assn. (pres. 1965-66), Conf. Acad. Deans So. States (chmn. 1966-67); Clear Lake C. of C. (dir.). Rotarian. Mem. editorial bd. Forum mag., 1956-59. Bibliographer: Literature and Other Arts Sect., Modern Lang. Assn. Compiler: Literature and the Other Arts: A Select Bibliography, 1952-58, New York Pub. Library, 1959. Asso. TV editor German Quar. Contbr. articles to learned and popular jours. Home: 906 Forest Lake Dr Seabrook TX 77586

NEUMANN, ELLSWORTH TRAVER, found. exec.; b. Wappinger Falls, N.Y., Oct. 16, 1919; s. Frederic J. and Edythe (Traver) N.; B.A., Hobart Coll., 1940; M.D., N.Y.U., 1943; M.S. in Hosp. Adminstrn., Columbia U., 1949; m. Elaine M. Biesterfield, June 3, 1944 (dec. Feb. 1970); children—Lelaine Edythe, Chester Henry, Elise Joy, Frederic Jay; m. 2d, Virginia Lawrence, Aug. 1, 1970; 1 stepdau., Leslie A. Lawrence. Intern, Del. Hosp., Wilmington, 1943-44; adminstrv. resident Roosevelt Hosp., N.Y.C., 1948-49; asst. dir. staff Mass. Gen. Hosp., Boston, 1949-53, adminstr., 1953-73; v.p. adminstrn. Rockefeller Found., 1974—. Vice chmn. Mental Health Planning Com. Met. Boston, 1966-73. Served to capt. M.C., AUS, 1944-47. Mem. Am. Coll. Hosp. Adminstrs., Council Med. Adminstrn. Home: 25 Rectory Ln Scarsdale NY 10583 Office: 1133 Ave of Americas New York City NY 10036

NEUMANN, FORREST KARL, hosp. adminstr.; b. St. Louis, Oct. 7, 1930; s. Metz Earl and Ruth (McGhee) N.; B.S., Roosevelt U., 1953; M.S. in Hosp. Adminstrn., Northwestern U., 1955; m. Erika Stefanie Turkl, Feb. 11, 1955; children—Tracey, Karen, Scott, Lisa. Adminstrv. resident Louis A. Weiss Hosp., Chgo., 1954-55; mem. staff Edward W. Sparrow Hosp., Lansing, Mich., 1958—, dir., 1962-71, pres., trustee, 1971—; pres., bd. dirs. Mason (Mich.) Gen. Hosp., 1973—; dir. Am. Bank and Trust Co., 1973—. Chmn. hosp. div. United Community Chest, 1965-68, chmn. budget steering com., 1970-71, bd. dirs., mem. exec. com., 1969—; mem. adv. com. Capitol Area Comprehensive Health Planning Assn., 1969, bd. dirs., 1971—, treas., 1974—; mem., vice chmn. Mich. Arbitration Adv. Com., 1975—; bd. dirs. Grad. Med. Edn., Inc., 1971—, pres., 1972-73, treas., 1973—. Fellow Am. Coll. Hosp. Adminstrs.; mem. Southwestern Mich. Hosp. Council (trustee 1968-73, pres. 1970-71), Am. Hosp. Assn. (ho. of dels. 1979—), Mich. Hosp. Assn. (1st v.p. 1972-73, dir., exec. com., treas. 1974—, chmn. 1976-77; treas., bd. dirs., exec. com. Mut. Ins. Co. 1976—, chmn. bd. 1979—). Rotarian (dir. Lansing club). Office: 1215 E Michigan St Lansing MI 48909

NEUMANN, HARRY, educator; b. Dormoschel, Germany, Oct. 10, 1930; s. Siegfried and Frieda (Lion) N.: came to U.S., 1937, naturalized, 1948; B.A., St. Johns Coll., 1952; M.A., U. Chgo., 1954; Ph.D., Johns Hopkins U., 1962; postgrad. U. Heidelberg, Germany, 1956-58; m. Christine Sopher, Sept. 25, 1959. Mem. faculty Mich. State U., 1962-63, Lake Forest Coll., 1963-65; prof. philosophy, govt. Scripps Coll., Claremont, Cal., Claremont Grad. Sch., 1966—; research asso. Rockefeller Inst., N.Y.C., 1963. Served with AUS, 1954-56. Classical Philosophy fellow Center Hellenic Studies, Dumbarton Oaks, Washington, 1965-66; research fellow Salvatori Center for the Study of Individual Freedom in the Modern World, 1970, Earhart Found., 1973-74, 78. Mem. Soc. Ancient Greek Philosophy, Univ. Centers Rational Alternatives, Univ. Profs. for Acad. Order, John Brown Cook Assn. for Freedom (advisor). Contbr. articles profl. jours. Home: Scripps Coll Claremont CA 91711

NEUMANN, HARRY, JR., banker; b. Union City, N.J., July 23, 1921; s. Harry and Minnie (Eysel) N.; student Am. Inst. Banking, 1940-41, Grad. Sch. N.Y. U., 1947-49; m. Virginia G. Prauninger, Dec. 8, 1943; children—Russell H., Glenn A. With J.P. Morgan & Co., N.Y.C., 1939-59, asst. head accounting dept., 1950-55, auditor, 1955-59; asst. auditor Morgan Guaranty Trust Co. N.Y., N.Y.C., 1959-65, auditor, 1965—; auditor J.P. Morgan & Co., Inc., N.Y.C. Served with USAAF, 1942-45. Decorated D.F.C., Air medal with clusters. Home: 24 Rocklynn Pl Glen Rock NJ 07452 Office: 23 Wall St New York City NY 10015

NEUMANN, HENRY MATTHEW, educator; b. Mpls., July 15, 1924; s. Henry M. and Mary (Keller) N.; B.S., Coll. St. Thomas, 1947; Ph.D., U. Cal. at Berkeley, 1950. Instr. chemistry Northwestern U., 1950-54, asst. prof., 1954-56; asso. prof. Ga. Inst. Tech., Atlanta, 1956-60, prof. chemistry, 1960—. Served with AUS, 1943-46. Mem. Am. Chem. Soc., AAAS, Sigma Xi. Roman Catholic. Home: 622 Webster Dr Decatur GA 30033 Office: Ga Inst Tech Atlanta GA 30332

NEUMANN, ROBERT GERHARD, former ambassador; b. Vienna, Austria, Jan. 2, 1916; s. Hugo and Stephanie (Taussky) N.; diplome superieur, U. Rennes (France), 1936; diploma Consular Acad., 1937, Geneva Sch. Internat. Studies, 1937; student U. Vienna, 1938; M.A., Amherst Coll., 1940; Ph.D. (Shevlin fellow 1940-41), U. Minn., 1946; m. Marlen Eldredge, July 27, 1941; children—Ronald E., Gregory W. Instr., State Tchrs. Coll., Oshkosh, Wis., 1941-42; lectr. U. Wis., 1946-47; asst. prof. U. Calif. at Los Angeles, 1947-52, asso. prof., 1952-58, prof., 1958-70, dir. Inst. Internat. and Fgn. Studies, 1959-65, chmn. Atlantic and West European Program, 1965-66; U.S. ambassador to Afghanistan, Kabul, 1966-73, to Morocco, Rabat, 1973-76; sr. staff asso., cons. Center for Strategic and Internat. Studies, Georgetown U., 1976—; cons. to bus. and govt., 1977—; dir. Am. Seminar Polit., Econ. and Social Scis., Nice, France, 1957. Adviser to sec. def. on internat. security affairs, Am. delegation NATO Ministerial Conf., Paris, 1962; cons. policy planning council Dept. of State, Ford Found., Rand Corp., also sec. def. Chmn. internat. relations sect. Town Hall, 1956-62. Mem. Calif. Republican Central Com., 1954-60. Bd. dirs. Revista di Diritto Europeo; mem. council Johns Hopkins Center, Bologna, Italy, 1970—. Served from pvt. to lst lt., AUS, 1942-46. Haynes Found. fellow, 1950-51, Social Sci. Research Council fellow, 1950- 51, Fulbright fellow, France, 1954-55; recipient hon. medal U. Brussels, 1955; decorated Legion of Honor, France, 1957; officers cross Order of Merit (Fed. Republic of Germany), 1963, comdr.'s Cross, 1974. Order of the Star (Afghanistan), 1973; grand officier Order and Star of Ouissam Alaoui (Morocco), 1976. Mem. Atlantic Council U.S. (sponsor), Inst. Strategic Studies London, Am., Internat. polit. sci. assns., Internat. Law Assn. Roman Catholic. Author: The Government of the German Federal Republic, 1966; European and Comparative Government, 4th edit., 1968; Toward a More Effective Executive-Legislative Relationship in the Conduct of America's Foreign Policy, 1977; bd. editors Rivista di Diritto Europeo, Rome. Contbr. articles to jours. Editorial writer Los Angeles Times, 1952-59. Home: 4986 Sentinel Dr #102 Washington DC 20016. *The following thoughts and principles, forged on the ladder to success, took their roots earlier when I was a prisoner in Nazi concentration camps and then a penniless immigrant to America: 1. When in doubt, choose the road of courage. The dynamics of action will carry others with you and confound your opponents. 2. While action must be carefully considered, it is generally better to act then not to act. It is easier to correct the course of action than to move from inaction to action. 3. Dream big and without restraint. There will always be time afterwards to reduce the scope of your action in the light of confining realities. But if you start dreaming small, you shackle your imagination from the outset. 4. Have some reasonable and constant ideas as to what you will not put up with and examine your conscience from time to time to check the possible corrosion success might have wrought. It might keep you honest, or, at least—humble.*

NEUMEIER, JOHN, choreographer; b. Milw., Feb. 24, 1942; s. Albert and Lucille N.; B.A., Marquette U., 1961; student Stone-Camryn Ballet Sch., Milw., 1957-62, Royal Ballet Sch., London, 1962-63; student of Vera Volkova, Copenhagen, 1962-63. Dancer, Sybil Sherer Co., Chgo., 1960-62, Stuttgart (W. Ger.) Ballet, 1963-69; ballet dir. Frankfurt (W. Ger.)) Opera, 1969-73, Hamburg (W. Ger.) State Opera, 1973—; guest choreographer for various cos., including: Am. Ballet Theatre, Royal Ballet London, Royal Danish Ballet, Nat. Ballet Can., Royal Winnipeg Ballet, Stuttgart Ballet, Vienna Opera; guest opera dir.: Otello, Munich (W. Ger.) Opera, 1977, Orpheus and Eurydice, Hamburg State Opera, 1978, West Side Story, Hamburg State Opera, 1978; ballet dir. film: Rondo (Prix Italia 1972), 1971. Mem. Akademie der Kunste Hamburg, Akademie der Kunste Berlin. Roman Catholic. Office: Hamburg Opera Ballet Grosse Theaterstr 34 Hamburg 36 Federal Republic of Germany D-2000

NEUSCHEL, RICHARD FREDERICK, mgmt. cons.; b. Buffalo, Mar. 3, 1915; s. Percy J. and Anna (Becker) N.; student U. Colo., 1932-33; A.B., Denison U., 1936; M.B.A. cum laude, Harvard U., 1941; m. Jean Fuller, Oct. 16, 1943; children—Robin Fuller, Debra Jean. Gen. procedures dir. Sperry Gyroscope Co., Lake Success, N.Y., 1941-45; with McKinsey & Co., Inc., N.Y.C., 1945—, prin., 1954-59, dir., 1959—, mem. exec. com., 1959-73, mng. dir. N.Y. office, 1968-74. Trustee Denison U., 1971—. Recipient citation Denison U., 1970; named Systems Man of Year, Internat. Systems and Procedures Assn., 1965. Mem. Am. Mgmt. Assn. (life; planning council), Sigma Alpha Epsilon, Omicron Delta Kappa, Pi Delta Epsilon. Clubs: Sky, Harvard (N.Y.C.); Nassau Country (Glen Cove, N.Y.). Author: Streamlining Business Procedures, 1950; Management by System, 1960; Management Systems for Profit and Growth, 1976; The Chief Executive's Strategic Role and Responsibilities, 1977; contbg. author: Industrial Engineering Handbook, 1956, 63; The Arts of Top Management, 1971. Home: 14 Woodacres Rd Brookville Glen Head NY 11545 Office: 245 Park Ave New York City NY 10017. *Life has taught me that success in any calling is critically dependent on one's ability to write and speak with clarity and impact. Clear writing is a basic intellectual skill; it reflects the ability to think. Articulate speaking is a basic communications skill; it is a key to personal effectiveness in any field.*

NEUSCHEL, ROBERT PERCY, educator, former mgmt. cons.; b. Hamburg, N.Y., Mar. 13, 1919; s. Percy J. and Anna (Becker) N.; B.A., Denison U., 1941; M.B.A., Harvard U., 1947; m. Dorothy Virginia Maxwell, Oct. 20, 1944; children—Kerr Anne Ziprick, Carla Becker, Robert Friedrich. Indsl. engr. Sylvania Elec. Products Co., Inc., 1947-49; with McKinsey & Co., Inc., 1950-79, sr. partner, dir., 1967-79; dir. Butler Mfg. Co., Combined Ins. Co. Am., Norfolk & Western Ry. Co.; prof. corp. governance Grad. Sch. Mgmt., dir. Transp. Center, Northwestern U.; lectr. in field. Mem. McKinsey Found. Mgmt. Research, Inc. Pres., Bd. Edn., Lake Forest, Ill., 1965-70. Rep. Nat. council Boy Scouts Am., 1970—, mem. N.E. exec. council, 1969—; chmn. bd. Lake Forest Symphony, 1973; Bd. dirs. Loyola U., Chgo., Chgo. Boys Club, Nat. Center for Voluntary Action, Inst. Mgmt. Consultants; trustee N. Suburban Mass Transit, 1972-73; mem. adv. council Grad. Sch. Mgmt., Northwestern U. Served to capt. USAAF, World War II. Mem. Ry. Systems and Mgmt. Assn., Transp. Assn. Am. Presbyterian (ruling elder). Clubs: Harvard Bus. Sch. (pres. 1964-65), Economic, Executive, Chicago, Mid America, Mid-Day, Onwentsia (Chgo.). Contbr. profl. jours. Home: 890 Larchmont Ln Lake Forest IL 60045 Office: 2001 Sheridan Rd Suite G-160 Evanston IL 60201. *My observations and experiences with corporate executives convinces me that leadership is based less on sheer intelligence and more on fundamental qualities of character. By traits of character I would suggest such things as trust, staying power, guts, fairness, maturity, and the capacity to be "big." And the primary task of the individual leader is, above all else, to manage himself—his time, talents, emotions, sense of values, and priorities, as a living example to those who follow his leadership.*

NEUSNER, MILTON MICHAEL, shoe mfg. co. exec.; b. Phila., July 9, 1931; s. Harry I. and Norma (Nuhman) N.; B.B.A., U. Mass., 1953; m. Constance Movitz, Dec. 11, 1960; children—David, Julie, Susan. Vice pres. Brown Shoe Co., 1966-72; pres. Front Row div. U.S. Shoe Co., 1972-73, group v.p. ops., 1973-76; exec. v.p. Wolverine World Wide Inc., Rockford, Mich., 1976—, also dir. Served with AUS, 1953-55. Mem. Two/Ten Assn. Jewish. Home: 3208 Hall St SE Grand Rapids MI 49506 Office: 9341 Courtland St Rockford MI 49351

NEUSTADT, BARBARA MAE, artist, illustrator, etcher; b. Davenport, Iowa, June 21, 1922; d. David and Cora (Wollensky) Neustadt; B.A., Smith Coll., 1944; postgrad. U. Chgo., 1945-46, (Art Student's League scholar) Ohio U. Sch. Fine Arts, 1952; children—Diane Elizabeth Walbridge Wheeler, Laurie Barbara Meyer Horne. Art dir., designer Shepherd Cards, Inc., N.Y.C., 1956-63; dir., instr. Studio Graphics Workshop, Woodstock, N.Y., 1970—; one-man shows include: Ruth White Gallery, N.Y.C., 1958, Phila. Art Alliance, 1959, Portland (Maine) Mus. Art, 1965, L.I. U., Bklyn., 1973, Smith Coll., Northampton, Mass., 1974; group shows include: Mus. Modern Art, N.Y.C., 1958-59, Yale U. Art Gallery, New Haven, 1960; Soc. Am. Graphic Artists nat. and internat. exhbns., 1954, 55, 57, 59, 60, 61, 73, 75, 76, L'Antipoete Galerie Librairie, Paris, 1961; represented in permanent collections: Met. Mus. Art, N.Y.C., Library of Congress, Nat. Gallery Art, Washington, Phila. Mus. Art, USIA, Bonn, Germany; lectr. on printmaking; participant artist in schs. program N.Y. State Schs., 1972-74. Bd. dirs., editor bull. LWV of Woodstock, 1969-70. Recipient prize Boston Printmakers, 1957, Joseph Pennell Meml. medal Phila. Watercolor Club, 1972; Yasuo Kuniyoshi Meml. award, 1978; Am. the Beautiful Fund of N.Y. of Natural Area Council grantee, 1973. Mem. Soc. Am. Graphic Artists (prize 1954, 78), Phila. Water Color Club (prize 1956), Artists Equity Assn. N.Y. Illustrator: The First Christmas, 1960; contbr. etching edits to Collectors Am. Art, N.Y.C., 1956, 58, 61, Internat. Graphic Arts Soc., N.Y.C., 1960, N.Y. Hilton Art Collection, N.Y.C., 1961. Mailing Address: PO Box 715 Woodstock NY 12498

NEUSTADT, DAVID HAROLD, physician; b. Evansville, Ind., Dec. 2, 1925; s. Moses and Leah (Epstein) N.; student DePauw U., 1943-44, 46-47; M.D., U. Louisville, 1950; m. Carolyn Jacobson, June 15, 1952; children—Susan Miriam, Jeffrey Bruce, Robert Alan. Intern, Morrisania City Hosp., N.Y.C., 1950-51; resident in internal medicine Lenox Hill Hosp., N.Y.C., 1951-52, NIH trainee in rheumatic diseases, 1952-53, resident in gastroenterology, 1953-54; practice medicine specializing in rheumatic diseases, Louisville, 1954—; chief arthritis clinic Louisville Gen. Hosp., 1960-76; asst. prof. medicine Sch. Medicine, U. Louisville, 1963-67, asso. prof. clin. medicine, 1967-75, clin. prof. medicine, 1974—, head sect. rheumatic diseases, 1960-76; chief dept. medicine Jewish Hosp., Louisville, 1965-67, pres. med. staff, 1967-69; cons. in rheumatology VA, 1970—. Former pres., chmn. bd. med. sci. com. Ky. chpt. Arthritis Found. Served with AUS, 1944-46. Fellow Am. Med. Writers Assn.; mem. A.C.P., N.Y. Rheumatism Soc., Am. Rheumatism Assn., Ky. Rheumatism Assn. (pres. 1956-57), AMA, AAAS, N.Y. Acad. Scis., Internat. Soc. Internal Medicine. Jewish. Clubs: Masons (32 deg.), Shriners. Author: The Chemistry and Therapy of Collagen Diseases, 1963, (with other) Aspiration and Injection Therapy in Arthritis and Musculoskeletal Disorders, 1972. Editor: Arthritis Abstracts, References Indexes, 1970-75. Contbr. articles to profl. jours. Home: 216 Smithfiled Rd Louisville KY 40207 Office: Med Towers South Louisville KY 40202. *I believe the qualities necessary to achieve success include a combination of ability, commitment to hard work, enthusiasm or enjoyment of your work, plus a liberal chunk of optimism, faith, luck, and a supporting family and co-workers.*

NEUSTADT, RICHARD ELLIOTT, polit. scientist, educator: b. Phila., June 27, 1919; s. Richard Mitchells and Elizabeth (Neufeld) N.; A.B., U. Calif., Berkeley, 1939; M.A., Harvard U., 1941, Ph.D., 1951; m. Bertha Frances Cummings, Dec. 21, 1945; children—Richard Mitchells, Elizabeth Ann. Economist, OPA, 1942; staff mem. Bur. of Budget, 1946-50; staff mem. White House, 1950-53; prof. pub. adminstrn. Cornell U., 1953-54; prof. govt. Columbia, 1954-64; prof. govt. Harvard U., 1965-78, Lucius N. Littauer prof. public adminstrn., 1978—, asso. dean John Fitzgerald Kennedy Sch. Govt., 1965-75, dir. Inst. Politics, 1966-71; spl. cons. subcom. on nat. policy machinery U.S. Senate, 1959-61; mem. adv. bd. Commn. Money and Credit, 1960-61; spl. cons. to Pres.-elect Kennedy, 1960-61, to subcom. on nat. security staffing and ops. U.S. Senate, 1962-68; cons. to Pres. Kennedy, 1961-63, Pres. Johnson, 1964-66, Dept. of State, 1962-69, Bur. Budget, 1961-70, AEC, 1962-68, Rand Corp., 1964-79, Pres.'s Reorgn. Project, Office Mgmt. and Budget, 1977—; vis. lectr. Nuffield College, Oxford, Eng., 1961-62, asso. mem., 1965-67. Chmn. Democratic Platform Com., 1972; trustee Radcliffe Coll., 1976—. Served with USNR, 1942-46. Fellow Am. Acad. Arts and Scis.; mem. Am. Polit. Sci. Assn., Nat. Acad. Pub. Adminstrn., Council Fgn. Relations, Inst. Strategic Studies, Am. Philos. Soc. Democrat. Club: Cosmos (Washington). Author: Presidential Power, 1960; Alliance Politics, 1970; (with Harvey V. Fineberg) The Swine Flu Affair, 1978; articles to mags., revs. Home: Cambridge MA also Wellfleet MA Office: Kennedy Sch Govt Harvard U Cambridge MA 02138

NEUSTEIN, JOSEPH, business exec.; b. Pitts., Aug. 29, 1920; s. Solomon and Sadie (Roth) N.; B.S.M.E., U. Pitts., 1943; M.S.M.E., Case Inst. Tech., Cleve., 1946; Ph.D., Calif. Inst. Tech., Pasadena, 1957; m. Suzanne Osborne, Sept. 11, 1939; children—Ronald, Kristin. Successively v.p., mgr., advanced technologies and systems, asso. mgr. research and engring., asso. mgr. program mgmt. and systems engring., mgr. power systems Xerox Electro-Optical Systems, Pasadena, 1960-69; pres. Xerox Electro-Optical Systems, Pasadena, 1969-79; v.p. Reprographics Tech. Group, 1979—. Served with USAAFR, 1944-46. Mem. Am. Inst. Aeros. and Astronautics, Pasadena C. of C. (past dir.), Pasadena Hall of Sci., Sigma Xi, Pi Tau Sigma, Sigma Tau, Phi Eta Sigma. Office: 701 S Aviation Blvd El Segundo CA 90245

NEUSTEIN, JOSHUA OHO, artist; b. Danzig, Oct. 10, 1940; s. Alter Eliezer and Fela (Mariowich) N.; came to U.S., 1950, naturalized, 1956; B.A., CCNY, 1961; student Pratt Inst., 1960-61; m. Katherine Goetschel, Aug. 22, 1978. Painter, 1964—; photographer, 1968—; one-man exhbns. include Urdang Gallery, N.Y.C., 1973, Birch Gallery, Copenhagen, 1976, Tel Aviv Mus. retrospective, 1977, Mary Boone Gallery, N.Y.C., 1978; represented in permanent collections Mus. Modern Art, N.Y.C., Guggenheim Mus., Steadelijk Mus., Amsterdam, Netherlands, Isaeli Mus., Jerusalem; mem. fine arts com. UNESCO. Recipient Jerusalem prize, 1971, Willem Sandberg prize, 1974. Address: 300 W 108th St New York NY 10025

NEUTHALER, PAUL DAVID, editor, publisher; b. N.Y.C., Nov. 2, 1942; s. Jacob and Frances (Poses) N.; grad. Horace Mann Sch., 1960; B.A., Columbia, 1964, M.A., 1965, Ph.D., 1972; m. Paula Diane Wool, Nov. 20, 1965 (div. 1976); children—Mindy Sue, Howard Jacob. Advt. and promotion dir. Tchrs. Coll. Press, Columbia, 1965-67; mgr. selected acad. readings div. Simon & Schuster, Inc., 1968-69, asst. dir. ednl. div., 1969-71, editor Touchstone/Clarion Paperbacks, 1971-72; sr. editor, dir. coll. dept., dir. subs. rights Basic Books, Inc., N.Y.C., 1973-77; pres., pub. Gen. Health Pub. Corp., 1977—. Office: 530 Park Ave New York City NY 10021

NEUTRA, DION, architect; b. Los Angeles, Oct. 8, 1926; s. Richard Joseph and Dione (Niedermann) N.; student Swiss Inst. Tech., 1947-48; B.Arch. cum laude, U. So. Calif., 1950; m. Mari Gee, June 14, 1964; children—Gregory, Wendy, Haig, Nicholas. With Richard J. Neutra, architect, Los Angeles, 1942-55; asso. Neutra & Alexander, Los Angeles, 1955-60, Robert E. Alexander, Los Angeles, 1960-62, Richard Dorman, Los Angeles, 1962-63; prin. Dion Neutra and Assos., Los Angeles, 1963-65, Richard & Dion Neutra, Architects and Assos., Los Angeles, 1965—; pres. Richard J. Neutra, Inc., 1970—; works include various housing, ednl., religious, instnl. and other facilities, Am. embassy, Karachi, Pakistan, Gettysburg Meml., univ. libraries of Simpson and Adelphi colls., library resource center for City Huntington Beach, Calif.; cons. Survival Through Design Inst., Los Angeles; lectr. Calif. State Coll., 1968, Sacramento City Coll., 1969, Mira Costa State Coll., 1973, Cabrillo State Coll., 1974, Soka U., Tokyo, 1975, San Diego City Coll., 1976, Germany, Switzerland and Eng., 1977; vis. prof. Calif. State Coll. at Pomona, 1970. Mem. Silver Lake-Echo Park Dist. Plan Adv. Com., Master Plan City of Los Angeles, 1970-71; mem. Citizens to Save Silver Lake, 1973-76. Dir. Child Care and Devel. Services, 1970-71. Served with USNR, 1944-46. Mem. AIA, Alpha Rho Chi. Office: 2379 Glendale Blvd Los Angeles CA 90039

NEUTS, MARCEL F., educator, mathematician; b. Ostend, Belgium. Feb. 21, 1935; s. Achille J. and Marceline (Neuts) N.; Lic. Math., U. Louvain, 1956; M.S., Stanford, 1959, Ph.D., 1961; m. Olga Alida Topff, June 27, 1959; children—Christopher J., Myriam A., Catherine J., Deborah A. Came to U.S., 1962, naturalized, 1968. With Lovanium U., Leopoldville, 1956-57, instr., 1956-57; research asst. U. Louvain, Belgium, 1957-58, 60-62; mem. faculty Purdue U., 1962-76; prof. math., 1968-76; Unidel prof. statistics and computer sci. U. Del., 1976—; cons. Gen. Motors Research Labs., 1965-67; asso. editor Operations Research, 1965-72; editor for probability Mgmt. Sci., 1974—; asso. editor Communications in Stats.; editor Jour. of Applied Probability, 1979—. Commn. Relief in Belgium fellow, 1958-60. Fellow Inst. Math. Statistics; mem. Soc. Belge Math., AAUP, Am. Soc. Ops. Research, Internat. Statis. Inst., Math. Assn. Am., Bernoulli Soc., Sigma Xi. Research, publs. on theory of Queues and Semi-Markov processes; order statistics and numerical methods in stochastic processes. Home: 322 Wedgewood Rd Newark DE 19711 Office: Dept Math Scis U Del Newark DE 19711

NEUWIRTH, ROBERT SAMUEL, obstetrician, gynecologist; b. N.Y.C., July 11, 1933; s. Abraham Alexander and Phyllis N.; B.S., Yale U., 1954, M.D., 1958; m. Gloria Salob, June 9, 1957; children—Susan, Jessica, Laura, Michael. Intern, Presbyn. Hosp., N.Y.C., 1958-59, resident 1959-64; asst. prof. obstetrics and gynecology Columbia U., 1964-68, asso. prof., 1968-71, prof., 1972—, Babcock prof., 1977—; dir. obstetrics and gynecology Bronx Lebanon Hosp., N.Y.C., 1967-72; prof. Albert Einstein Coll. Medicine, 1971-72; dir. obstetrics and gynecology Woman's Hosp., N.Y.C., St. Luke's Hosp. Center, N.Y.C., 1974—; cons. WHO, NIH, U.S. AID, U.S. FDA. Mem. N.Y. Obstet. Soc., Soc. Gynecologic Investigation, Am. Assn. Profs. Obstetrics and Gynecology Am. Coll. Obstetricians and Gynecologists, Assn. Vol. Sterilization (chmn. biomed. com. 1971—). Author: Hysteroscopy, 1975. Contbr. articles in field to profl. jours. Office: 1111 Amsterdam Ave New York NY 10025

NEVA, FRANKLIN ALLEN, physician, educator; b. Cloquet, Minn., June 8, 1922; s. Lauri Albin and Anna (Lahti) N.; S.B., U. Minn., 1944, M.D., 1946; A.M. (hon.), Harvard, 1964; m. Alice Hanson, July 5, 1947; children—Karen, Kristin, Erik. Intern Harvard Med. Services, Boston City Hosp., 1946-47, resident, 1949-50; research fellow Harvard Med. Sch., 1950-53; asst. prof. U. Pitts. Med. Sch., 1953-55; mem. faculty Harvard Sch. Pub. Health, 1955-69, John LaPorte Given prof. tropical pub. health, 1964-69; chief Lab. Parasitic Diseases, Inst. Allergy and Infectious Diseases, NIH, 1969—; spl. research infectious diseases especially tropical, parasitic and virus infections. Mem. commn. parasitic diseases, asso. mem. commn. virus infections Armed Forces Epidemiological Bd., 1963-68; mem. Latin Am. sci. bd. Nat. Acad. Scis.-NRC, 1963-68; bd. sci. counselors Inst. Allergy and Infectious Diseases, NIH, 1966-69. Served to lt. (j.G.) USNR, 1947-49. Diplomate Am. Bd. Internal Medicine. Mem. Soc. Exptl. Biology and Medicine, Infectious Diseases Soc. Am., Am. Soc. Tropical Medicine and Hygiene (Bailey K. Ashford award 1965), Assn. Am. Physicians. Home: 10851 Glen Rd Potomac MD 20854 Office: Institute of Allergy and Infectious Diseases NIH Bethesda MD 20014

NEVELSON, LOUISE, sculptor; b. Russia; d. Isaac and Minna Sadie (Smolerank) Berliaswky; ed. Rockland, Maine, Europe, Mexico; studied with Hans Hoffman, Germany, 1931; hon. degrees Hamlin U., Mpls. Sch. Art and Design, Bowdoin Coll., Hobart and William Smith Coll.; husband dec.; 1 son, Myron Nevelson. One-woman shows Janis Gallery, The Bienniel, Venice, Italy, 1963, also in Germany, London, Paris, Documenta III, 1964, Pace galleries, N.Y.C., Columbus, 1969, 71, Museo Civico de Torino, 1969, Gal. Jeanne Bucher, Paris, 1969, Kroller-Muller Mus., Holland, 1969, Akron Art Inst., 1969, Museum Fine Arts, Houston, 1969, U. Tex., 1970; one-woman retrospective exhbn. Whitney Mus. Am. Art, 1970; represented permanent collections Juilliard Sch., Princeton, Whitney Mus. Am. Art, Bklyn. Mus., Neward Mus., Carnegie Inst., Sara Robi Found., Brandeis U., Birmingham Mus., Houston Mus., Riverside Mus., Mus. Modern Art, Met. Mus. Art, N.Y. U. Mus., Nebr. Mus.; also numerous pvt. collections. Recipient 1st award United Soc. Artists, 1959; award Chgo. Inst., 1959; Ford Found. gift for Tamarind Workshop, Norfolk Mus., 1963; Brandeis U. Creative Arts award sculpture; Skowhegan medal sculpture. Mem. Am. Acad. and Inst. Arts and Letters, Fedn. Modern Painters and Sculptors (v.p.), Artists Equity (past pres.), Am. Abstract Artists, Sculptors Guild (exec. bd.). Address: 29 Spring St New York NY 10012

NEVIASER, ROBERT JON, orthopedic surgeon, educator; b. Washington, Nov. 21, 1936; s. Julius Salem and Jane Frances (Gibbons) N.; grad. Phillips Acad., Andover, Mass., 1954; A.B., Princeton U., 1958; M.D., Jefferson Coll., 1962; m. Anne Maclean Shedden, Dec. 3, 1966; children—Jeanne Nicole, Robert Jon, Ian Maclean, Andrew Shedden. Intern, N.Y. Hosp., Cornell Med. Center, N.Y.C., 1962-63, asst. resident, 1963-64; asst. resident in orthopaedic surgery N.Y. Orthopaedic Hosp., Columbia-Presbyn. Med. Center, N.Y.C., 1964-66, resident, 1966-67; fellow in surgery of the hand Orthopaedic Hosp., Los Angeles, 1969-70; asst. prof. div. orthopaedic and hand surgery, chmn. dept., U. Conn., Storrs, 1970-71; asso. prof. orthopaedic surgery George Washington U., Washington, 1971-76, prof., 1976—. Served to lt. comdr. USNR, 1967-69. Diplomate Am. Bd. Orthopaedic Surgery. Fellow Am. Soc. Surgery of the Hand, Am. Acad. Orthopaedic Surgery, Eastern Orthopaedic Assn., Am. Orthopaedic Assn.; mem. Alpha Kappa Kappa. Republican. Clubs: Princeton (N.Y., Washington); Darnestown Swim and Racquet, George Washington U.; Potomac Tennis. Contbr. articles in field to profl. jours. Office: 2150 Pennsylvania Ave NW Washington DC 20037

NEVID, NORBERT, ins. co. exec.; b. Rochester, N.Y., Jan. 8, 1934; s. Manuel E. and Betty F. Nevid; B.B.A., U. Wis., 1955, M.B.A., 1966; m. Barbara J. Landgraf, Feb. 4, 1955; children—Nancy, Nathan, Nicholas. Ins. examiner Wis. Ins. Dept., Madison, 1955-60; v.p. research MGIC Investment Corp., Milw., 1960—. Pres., dir. Wis. Amateur Athletic Union. C.P.A., Wis. Mem. Am. Inst. C.P.A.'s, Wis. Soc. C.P.A.'s. Home: 650 Meadow Ln Elm Grove WI 53122 Office: MGIC Investment Corp 431 H MGIC Plaza Milwaukee WI 53201

NEVILL, WILLIAM ALBERT, chemist; b. Indpls., Jan. 1, 1929; s. Irwin Lowell and Mary Marie (Barker) N.; B.S. magna cum laude, Butler U., 1951; Ph.D., Calif. Inst. Tech., 1954; m. Nancy Neiman Roll, May 19, 1979; children—Paul David, John Michael, Steven Joseph, Anne Marie, Deborah Ruth. Research chemist Proctor-Gamble, Cin., 1954; prof. chemistry, chmn. dept. Grinnell Coll., 1956-67; prof. chemistry, chmn. dept. Ind. U.-Purdue U., Indpls., 1967-72, dean Sch. Sci., 1972-79; dir. grad. studies, 1979—; arbitrator, mediator Ind. Employment Relations Bd., 1975—; bd. dirs. Indpls. Sci. and Engring. Found., 1972-75, 79-82, Westminster Found., Lafayette, Ind., 1972-74. Served with U.S. Army, 1954-56; col. USAR. Grantee NSF, 1959-74, NIH, 1963-70, Office Naval Research, 1953. Mem. Ind. Acad. Sci., Am. Chem. Soc. (chmn. sect. 1972, counselor 1973-81). Presbyterian. Club: Kiwanis. Author: General Chemistry, 1967; Experiments in General Chemistry, 1968. Home: 11514 Dona Dr Carmel IN 46032 Office: UN 101A 1100 W Michigan St Indianapolis IN 46223

NEVILLE, EMILY CHENEY, author; b. Manchester, Conn., Dec. 28, 1919; d. Howell and Anne (Bunce) Cheney; A.B., Bryn Mawr Coll., 1940; J.D., Albany Law Sch., 1976; m. Glenn Neville; children—Emily Tam, Glenn H.H., Dessie, Marcy, Alec. Feature writer N.Y. Mirror, 1941-42; admitted to N.Y. bar, 1977. Recipient Newbery award for It's Like This Cat, 1964, Jane Addams award for Berries Goodman, 1966. Author books including: Seventeen Street Gang, 1966; Traveler from a Small Kingdom, 1968; Fogarty, 1969; Garden of Broken Glass, 1975. Address: Keene Valley NY 12943

NEVILLE, HOWARD RALPH, univ. pres.; b. Kankakee, Ill., Mar. 6, 1926; s. Harry Clay and Florence Edith (Devere) N.; B.S., U. Ill., 1948; M.B.A., La. State U., 1952; Ph.D., Mich. State U., 1956; m. Fredrica Jane Karber, Apr. 1, 1945. Mem. sales and advt. staff Procter & Gamble Co., St. Louis, 1948-51; mem. faculty Mich. State U., 1953-69, prof., dir. continuing edn. service, 1956-62, asst. provost, 1962-63, provost, 1963-69; pres. Claremont (Calif.) Men's Coll., 1969-70; vice chancellor for bus. and finance adminstrn. U. Nebr., 1970-71, exec. v.p., 1971-73; pres., prof. econs. U. Maine at Orono, 1973-79; pres., prof. bus. adminstrn. and econs. Alfred (N.Y.) U., 1979—; vis. lectr. U. Chgo., summer 1960; vis. prof. La. State U., 1960-61; dir. Mchts. Nat. Bank, Bangor, Maine, 1973—. Served with USAAF, 1944-45. Mem. Nat. U. Extension Assn. (pres. 1963-64), Nat. Assn. State Univs. and Land Grant Colls. (chmn. extension div. 1961-62, mem. exec. com. acad. affairs 1968-70), Am. Ceramic Soc., Beta Gamma Sigma, Phi Kappa Phi, Omicron Delta Kappa, Omicron Delta Epsilon, Phi Delta Theta, Delta Mu Delta (hon.). Author: The Detroit Banking Collapse, 1933; also articles. Home: President's House 71 Pine Hill Dr Alfred NY 14802

NEVILLE, JAMES FRANCIS, lawyer; b. Harrison, N.Y., Sept. 10, 1907; s. Denis and Annie (Hanratty) N.; grad. St. Johns Prep. Sch., Danvers, Mass., 1928; A.B., Georgetown U., 1932, J.D., 1938; m. Mary R. Gilroy, Nov. 8, 1935; children—James Francis, Thomas Joseph, Martha Ann, Gerald Denis, Kathleen Ann. Admitted to D.C. bar, 1938; with Dept. Agr., 1934-37; atty. legal div. FHA, 1938-46, asst. zone commr. Western U.S., 1947-48, dep. asst. commr. field ops., 1948-51, zone commr. Eastern U.S. 1951-54, then regional dir. Southwestern U.S., then dir. internat. div. FHA; dep. adminstr. Farms Home Adminstrn., Dept. Agr.; now nat. and internat. housing cons.; pres., dir. Indsl. Loan Corp. in Va.; v.p. realty holding and constrn. corps. in Ohio; mgr. Navy Dept. owned realty, Midwest, S.W., Western, Pacific areas; dir. Navy Dept. Capehart Housing Projects, 1958-59; dir. rental housing, mortgage fin. Nat. Assn. Home Builders, Washington, 1959-61; operating commr. FHA, Washington, 1961—; pres. Skyline Plaza Corp.; dir. various orgns. Trustee Man-Kan Trust. Recipient Merrick medal Georgetown U., 1932. Mem. D.C. Bar Assn., Gamma Eta Gamma. Club: Fairfax Country (Fairfax, Va.). Co-author: What Builders Should Know About Garden-Type Apartments; The Apartment Plan; also articles on mortgage financing. Home: 3705 S Geo Mason Dr Falls Church VA 22041

NEVILLE, JAMES MORTON, food co. exec.; b. Mpls., May 28, 1939; s. Philip and Maurene (Morton) N.; B.A., U. Minn., LL.B. magna cum laude, 1964; m. Judie Martha Proctor, Sept. 9, 1961; children—Stephen Warren, Martha Maurene. Admitted to Minn. bar, 1964; asso. firm Neville, Johnson & Thompson, Mpls., 1964-69, partner, 1969-70; asso. counsel Gen. Mills, Inc., Mpls., 1970-77, sr. asso. counsel, 1977—, asst. treas., 1971—, corp. sec., 1976—; lectr. bus. law. U. Minn., 1967-71. Mem. South Hennepin Human Services Council, 1977-78. Named Man of Year, Edina Jaycees, 1967. Mem. Am., Minn. Hennepin County bar assns., U. Minn. Law Alumni Assn., Am. Soc. Corp. Secs., Order of Coif, Phi Delta Phi, Psi Upsilon. Democrat. Episcopalian. Club: Minikahda. Home: 5908 View Ln Edina MN 55436 Office: 9200 Wayzata Blvd Minneapolis MN 55426

NEVILLE, RICHARD M., lawyer, bus. exec.; b. N.Y.C., Apr. 14, 1942; s. Maurice J. and Amelia E. (Bennett) N.; A.B., Columbia U., 1963, J.D. cum laude, 1966; m. Melba Halloran, May 27, 1966; 1 dau., Kathryn. Admitted to N.Y. State bar, Conseil Juridique of France; asso. firm Dewey, Ballantine, Bushby, Palmer & Wood, N.Y.C. and Paris, 1966-75; sec., corp. counsel Pittston Co., Greenwich, Conn., 1975—; mem. adv. bd. Internat. Oil and Gas Ednl. Center of Southwestern Legal Found. Mem. Am. Bar Assn., N.Y. State Bar Assn., Assn. City N.Y., Westchester-Fairfield Corp. Counsel Assn. Office: One Pickwick Plaza Greenwich CT 06830

NEVIN, CROCKER, investment banker; b. Tulsa, Mar. 14, 1923; s. Ethelbert Paul and Jennie Crocker (Fassett) N.; grad. with high honors, St. Paul's Sch., 1942; A.B. with high honors, Princeton, 1946; m. Mary Elizabeth Sherwin, Apr. 24, 1952; children—Anne, Paul, Elizabeth, Crocker. With Vick Chem. Co., 1949-50, John Roberts Powers Cosmetic Co., 1950-52; with Marine Midland Grace Trust Co. of N.Y., 1952—, exec. v.p., 1964-66, pres. 1966-70, chmn. bd., chief exec. officer, 1968-73. also dir.; vice chmn. bd. Evans Products Co., N.Y.C., 1974-76, Drexel Burnam Lambert Co., investment bankers, N.Y.C., 1976—; dir. Evans Product Co., Airco Inc., CF&I Steel Corp., Crum & Forster, SCM Corp. Chmn. exec. com. ACCION Internat. Bd. dirs. Lincoln Center Performing Arts. Served to lt. (j.g.) AC, USN, 1942-46. Clubs: Links, N.Y. Yacht, (N.Y.C.); Blind Brook. Home: 62 E 91st St New York NY 10028 Office: 60 Broad St New York NY 10022

NEVIN, JOHN ANTHONY, educator; b. N.Y.C., July 5, 1933; s. Walter Scott and Emy (Hofmann) N.; grad. Choate Sch., 1950; B.E., Yale, 1954; M.A., Columbia, 1961, Ph.D., 1963; m. Jane Hanne, July 9, 1960 (div. Aug. 1976); children—Martha, Sara, Scott, Barbara, Mark; m. 2d, Nora Ophuls, Nov. 24, 1977; children—Nicholas Ophuls, Hardy Ophuls. Asst. prof. psychology Swarthmore Coll., 1963-68; asso. prof. psychology Columbia, 1968-69, prof., 1969—, chmn. dept., 1970-72; prof. U. N.H., Durham, 1972—. Prin. investigator research grants concerned with reinforcement, punishment and discrimination NIMH, 1964-73, NSF, 1974—; mem. Psychobiology Rev. Panel NSF, 1977-78. Served as lt. (j.g.), USCG, 1955-59. Research fellow Harvard, 1966-67. Mem. Soc. Exptl. Analysis of Behavior (dir.). Editor: The Study of Behavior, 1973; asso. editor: Jour. Exptl. Analysis of Behavior, 1969-70, 72-76, editor, 1979—. Home: 69 Mill Rd Durham NH 03824

NEVIN, JOHN JOSEPH, electronics mfg. co. exec.; b. Jersey City, Feb. 13, 1927; s. Edward Vincent and Anna (Burns) N.; B.S., U. Cal., 1950; M.B.A., Harvard, 1952; m. Anna Filice, June 16, 1951; children—Stanley James, John Joseph, Richard Charles, Paul Edward, Gerald Patrick, Mary Anne. Various positions fin., product planning and mktg. Ford Motor Co., Dearborn, Mich., 1954-71, v.p. mktg., 1969-71; pres. Zenith Radio Corp., Chgo., 1971—, chmn., 1976—. Gen. chmn. Detroit United Found., 1970. Served with USNR, 1945-46. Home: 1136 Chestnut St Wilmette IL 60091 Office: 1000 N Milwaukee Ave Glenview IL 60025*

NEVINS, ALBERT J., publisher, editor, author; b. Yonkers, N.Y., Sept. 11, 1915; s. Albert J. and Bessie (Corcoran) N.; ed. Venard Coll., Clarks Summit, Pa., 1936, Maryknoll (N.Y.) Sem., 1942; L.H.D. (hon.), St. Benedict's Coll., Atchinson, Kans., 1963, Catholic U., Ponce, P.R., 1978. Ordained priest Roman Catholic Ch., 1942; v.p., pub., editor-in-chief Our Sunday Visitor, Inc., 1969—; dir. social communications Cath. Fgn. Mission Soc. Am., 1960—; editor Maryknoll mag., 1955-69, World Campus mag., 1958-67; dir. World Horizon Films, 1945- 68; cons. internat. visitors office U.S. Cath. Conf.; treas. Inter-Am. Tech. Center, 1972—. Treas. IAPA Tech. Center. Comdr. Westchester group Civil Air Patrol. Pres., Cath. Journalism Scholarship Fund; bd. dirs. Cath. League for Religious and Civil Rights, 1975—. Recipient Nat. Brotherhood award NCCJ, 1958; Maria Moors Cabot prize Columbia, 1961; St. Augustine award Villanova U., 1962. Mem. Inter-Am. (bd. dirs.), Cath. (pres. 1959-61, bd. dirs.; award 1961) press assns., Cath. Inst. Press (co-founder, mem. exec. bd. 1945-50), Latin Am. Studies Assn., Cath. Assn. Internat. Peace. Club: Overseas Press. Author: The Catholic Year, 1949; Adventures of Wu Han of Korea, 1951; Adventures of Kenji of Japan, 1952; Adventures of Pancho of Peru, 1953; Adventures of Ramon of Bolivia, 1954; St. Francis of the Seven Seas, 1955; The Adventures of Duc of Indochina, 1955; The Meaning of Maryknoll, 1956; Adventures of Men of Maryknoll, 1957; The Maryknoll Golden Book, 1956; The Making of a Priest, 1958; Away to Africa, 1959; The Maryknoll Book of Peoples, 1959; The Young Conquistador, 1960; Aways to the Lands of the Andes, 1962; Maryknoll Catholic Dictionary, 1964; Church in the Modern World, 1964; Away to Mexico, 1966; Away to Central America, 1967; Maryknoll Book of Treasures, 1968; Away to Venezuela, 1969; The Prayer of the Faithful, 1970; Our American Catholic Heritage, 1972; General Intercessions, 1977. Producer, author, photographer numerous films, 1946—, including The Story of Juan Mateo (Film Festival award), 1957; A Problem of People (Film Festival award), 1961; The Gods of Todos Santos (Film Festival awards 1966, 67). Address: Noll Plaza Huntington IN 46750

NEVINS, FRANCIS MICHAEL, JR., lawyer, author; b. Bayonne, N.J., Jan. 6, 1943; s. Francis Michael and Rosemary (Konzelmann) N.; A.B. magna cum laude, St. Peters Coll., 1964; J.D. cum laude, N.Y. U., 1967; m. Muriel Ann Walter, June 6, 1966 (div. 1978). Admitted to N.J. bar, 1967; staff atty. Middlesex County Legal Services Corp., New Brunswick, N.J., 1970-71; successively asst. prof., asso. prof., prof. law St. Louis U., 1971—; legal adviser to estate of mystery writer Cornell Woolrich, 1970—; vis. prof. Washington U. Sch. Law, summer 1976. Mem. N.J. Bar Assn., Mystery Writers Am. (Edgar award for Royal Bloodline 1975), Assn. Am. Law Schs. Author: Royal Bloodline, 1974; Publish and Perish, 1975; Corrupt and Ensnare, 1978. Editor: The Mystery Writer's Art, 1970; Nightwebs, 1971. Home: 4466 West Pine Blvd Saint Louis MO 63108 Office: 3642 Lindell Blvd Saint Louis MO 63108. *To create, to enjoy and to care seem to me the elements of a satisfying life. To the extent one's days and nights are rich in all three, the distinction between work and play tends to vanish, and living becomes an adventure, with stability and the novelty we all need cunningly interwoven. I can think of no happier way to live.*

NEVITT, MICHAEL VOGT, metallurgist, lab. exec.; b. Lexington, Ky., Sept. 7, 1923; s. Charles A. and Cecilia Jane (Vogt) N.; B.S., U. Ill., 1944, Ph.D., 1954; M.S., Va. Poly. Inst., 1951; m. Jean Meierdirks, Sept. 14, 1946; children—Carole Nevitt Davis, Michael, Timothy, Robert. Research metallurgist, project supr. Olin-Mathieson Chem. Corp., East Alton, Ill., 1946-48; asso. prof., head dept. metall. engring. Va. Poly. Inst., Blacksburg, 1948-51, 53-55; sr. metallurgist, dep. lab. dir. for research Argonne (Ill.) Nat. Lab., 1955—; mem. external adv. coms. U. Ill., 1973—, U. Calif., Berkeley, 1975, Lehigh U., 1976—, U. Ky., 1978—. Served with USN, 1943-46. Fellow Am. Soc. for Metals; mem. U. Ill. Alumni Assn. (bd. mem. 1974-75), Am. Nuclear Soc., Metall. Soc. of Am. Inst. Mining, Metall. and Petroleum Engrs., AAAS, Sigma Xi, Alpha Sigma Mu (past nat. pres.), Sigma Gamma Epsilon. Cons. editor Contemporary Physics (U.K.), 1977—; contbr. articles on metallurgy and materials sci. to books, profl. jours. Home: 1507 Center Ave Wheaton IL 60187 Office: Argonne Nat Lab 9700 S Cass Ave Argonne IL 60439

NEVIUS, BLAKE REYNOLDS, educator; b. Winona, Minn., Feb. 12, 1916; s. Blake Reynolds and Helena (McLean) N.; B.A., Antioch Coll., 1938; M.A., U. Chgo., 1941, Ph.D., 1947. Teaching asst. English dept. U. Ill., 1941-42; mem. faculty U. Calif. at Los Angeles, 1947—, prof. English, 1961—. Editor Nineteenth-Century Fiction, 1965-71; sr. adv. editor NCF, 1971. Served with AUS, 1942-45; ETO. Decorated Bronze Star. Recipient award Humanities Inst., U. Calif., 1967, 71; Fulbright lectr., Germany, 1953-54; Guggenheim fellow, 1962-63. Mem. Modern Lang. Assn., Internat. Assn. U. Profs. English (treas. 1971-74). Democrat. Episcopalian. Author: Edith Wharton, 1953; Robert Herrick, 1962; Ethan Frome: The Story with Sources and Commentary, 1968; The American Novel: Sinclair Lewis to the Present, 1970; Ivy Compton-Burnett, 1970; Cooper's Landscapes: An Essay on the Picturesque Vision, 1975. Home: 4009 Woodcliff Rd Sherman Oaks CA 91403 Office: Dept English U Calif Los Angeles CA 90024

NEW, JOHN CALHOUN, ret. aero. engr.; b. Warrensburg, Mo., Aug. 9, 1920; s. George Raymond and Alexa Calhoun (Sligh) N.; B.S. in Civil Engring., U.Mo., 1943; M.S. in Mech. Engring., U. Md., 1950; m. L. Mildred Estes, Sept. 17, 1944; children—Deborah Anne, Brian Andrew. Instr. mechanics U. Mo., 1943-44; engr. evaluation naval ordnance U.S. Naval Ordnance Lab., 1944-49, supr. environment simulation br., 1949-59; chief test and evaluation div. Goddard Space Flight Center, NASA, 1959-76. Served with USNR, 1944-45. Recipient Meritorious Civilian Service award U.S. Navy, 1950, Gold Medal for Exceptional Service NASA, 1969, Vigness award for shock and vibration technology, Inst. Environmental Scis., 1973. Fellow Inst. Environmental Scis.; mem. Soc. Exptl. Stress Analysis (pres. 1964- 65), ASTM, Research Soc. Am., Am. Mgmt. Assn., Md. Acad. Scis., Tau Beta Pi. Author: (with M. B. Tate) Selected Problems in Materials Testing, 1944. Patentee in field. Home: 6304 Martins Lane Lanham MD 20801

NEW, JOHN GABRIEL, educator; b. N.Y.C., Jan. 16, 1927; s. Gabriel B. and Margaret (Warshauer) N.; B.S., Cornell U., 1950, M.S., 1951, Ph.D., 1956; m. Helen Elizabeth Sharp, Dec. 22, 1950; children—Lois Ann, Nancy Alice, Kenneth Edward, Christopher John. High sch. biology tchr., 1951-53; mem. faculty State U. N.Y. at Oneonta, 1956—, prof. vertebrate ecology, 1960—. Chmn. Oneonta Environ. Adv. Bd.; active numerous local, state and nat. environ. orgns. Mem. AAAS, Am. Inst. Biol. Sci., Am. Ornithologists Union, Am. Soc. Ichthydogists and Herpetologists, Am. Soc. Mammalogists, Wildlife Soc., Sierra Club, Sigma Xi. Author papers in field. Home: 15 College Park Dr Oneonta NY 13820

NEW, NOAH CARROLL, marine corps officer; b. Atlanta, May 7, 1924; s. Noah Adolphus and Elizabeth (Miles) N.; M.S., Ga. Tech. Inst., 1950; M.S. in Elec. Engring., U.S. Navy Postgrad. Sch., 1960; D.Sc., Mass. Inst. Tech., 1963; M.A. in Internat. Affairs, George Washington U., 1968; m. Ellen Wiley, Mar. 15, 1947; children—Steven, Elizabeth, John. Commd. 2d lt. U.S. Marine Corps, 1947, advanced through grades to maj. gen., 1975; comdg. officer Marine Air Base Squadron 16, Okinawa, 1963-64; liaison officer U.S. Naval Ordnance Test Sta., China Lake, Calif., 1964-67; comdg. officer Marine Aircraft Group 36, Vietnam, 1968-69; head air weapons systems br. Hdqrs. Marine Corps, 1969-73; dir. Marine Corps Devel. and Edn. Command, Quantico, Va., 1973-75; dir. plans div. Hdqrs. Marine Corps, 1975-77; comdg. gen. III Marine Amphibious Force, 1977, 1st Marine Aircraft Wing, Japan, 1977-78, dep. comdr. Fleet Marine Force, Atlantic, 1978—. Decorated Legion of Merit, D.F.C., Air medal. Mem. Marine Corps Assn., Marine Corps Aviation Assn., Am. Helicopter Soc., U.S. Naval Instn. Baptist. Club: Army Navy Country. Home: 415 Dillingham Blvd Norfolk VA 23511

NEW, WILLIAM NEIL, physician, ret. naval officer; b. Atoka, Okla., Oct. 24, 1908; s. Robert Calvin and Nommar Bell (Willmore) N.; B.A., Central State Tchrs. Coll., Edmond, Okla., 1931; B.S. in Medicine, U. Okla., 1932, M.D., 1934; postgrad. Northwestern U. Med. Sch., 1947-48; m. Ruth Anderson Pride, Mar. 30, 1940. Intern, So. Pacific R.R. Hosp., San Francisco, 1934-35; commd. lt. (j.g.), M.C., U.S. Navy, 1935, advanced through grades to rear adm., 1963; resident dermatology and syphilology Naval Hosp., Phila., 1946-47; med. officer on gunboat and USMC Hosp., Shanghai, 1937-39; regtl. surgeon 7th Marines in Guadalcanal, later div. surgeon 5th Marine Div., Japanese occupation, 1945; established Naval Med. Field Research Lab., Camp Lejeune, 1943; chief dermatology services naval hosps., Great Lakes, Ill., 1948-51, Phila., 1951-53, San Diego, 1956-59; force surgeon Fleet Marine Force, Pacific, 1954-56; comdg. officer U.S. Naval Hosp., Yokusuka, Japan, 1959-62; dir. staff Office Dep. Asst. Sec. Def. for Health and Med., 1962-66; ret., 1966; pvt. practice dermatology Dallas Med. and Surg. clinic, 1966—. Diplomate Am. Bd. Dermatology and Syphilology. Fellow A.C.P.; mem. Am. Acad. Dermatology and Syphilology, Assn. Mil. Dermatologists (past pres.), Pacific Dermatol. Assn., Cutaneous Therapy Soc. Home: 3310 Fairmount The Park Towers Dallas TX 75201 Office: 4105 Live Oak St Dallas TX 75221. *Love and live today as we plan a rewarding tomorrow.*

NEWALL, JAMES EDWARD MALCOLM, mfg. co. exec.; b. Holden, Alta., Can., Aug. 20, 1935; B.Comm., U. Sask.; m. 1959; 3 children. With DuPont Can., Inc., 1957—, v.p. mktg., Montreal, Que., 1975, exec. v.p., 1975-78, dir., 1976—, pres., chief exec. officer, 1978—. Clubs: St. James's of Montreal, Forest and Stream, Mt. Royal (Montreal); Toronto; Rideau (Ottawa, Ont.). Office: PO Box 660 Montreal PQ H3C 2V1 Canada

NEWBAUER, JOHN ARTHUR, editor; b. Newport, R.I., Apr. 24, 1928; s. John Arthur and Theo Caroline (Trewhella) N.; B.A., U. Calif. at Berkeley, 1951; m. Marilyn Mahler, Oct. 14, 1956; children—April, Dana, Miranda. Sr. editor and writer sci. and engring., rocket devel. dept. U.S. Naval Ordnance Test Sta., China Lake, Calif., 1951-56; editor-in-chief Astronautics and Aeronautics jour., N.Y.C., 1963—; asso. editor Plain Wrapper Press, 1968—. Asso. fellow Am. Inst. Aeros. and Astronautics, Brit. Interplanetary Soc. Home: 356 Bay Ridge Ave Brooklyn NY 11220 Office: AIAA 1290 6th Ave New York City NY 10019

NEWBERRY, WILLIAM MARCUS, physician; b. Columbus, Ga., Nov. 13, 1938; s. William Marcus and Evelyn (Jones) N.; B.A., Northwestern U., 1960; M.D., Emory U., 1964; m. Nancy Elaine Harris, May 22, 1965; children—William Marcus, III, Thomas William, Judith Alison. Intern in medicine Ohio State U. Hosp., 1964-65; with epidemic intelligence service Center Communicable Disease, USPHS, Atlanta, 1965-67; resident in medicine Barnes Hosp., St. Louis, 1967-69; research fellow U. Tex. Med. Sch., Dallas, 1969-70, asst. prof. medicine, 1970-71; mem. faculty Med. U. S.C., Charleston, 1971—, prof. medicine, 1975—, dean Coll. Medicine, 1974—; mem. Deans' Com. Med. Doctor Edn. S.C.; mem. deans' com. Charleston VA Hosp.; health and safety com. Spoleto Festival. Mem. S.C. Med. Assn. (ho. dels.), Charleston County Med. Soc. (exec. com.), Reticuloendothelial Soc., Am. Fedn. Clin. Research, So. Soc. Clin. Investigation, Assn. Am. Med. Colls., S.C. Lung Assn. (med. edn. com.), Alpha Omega Alpha. Contbr. med. jours. Home: 1172 Farm Quarter Rd Mt Pleasant SC 29464 Office: 171 Ashley Ave Charleston SC 29403

NEWBOLD, HERBERT LEON, JR., physician, writer; b. High Point, N.C., Nov. 3, 1921; s. Herbert Leon and Mary Temperance (Sherrod) N.; student U. Chgo., 1941; student Coll. of William and Mary, 1941; B.S., Duke U., 1945, M.D., 1945; postgrad. Northwestern U., 1951, New Sch. Social Research, 1960-61; children—Lucile Newbold Corley, Susan Newbold Saunders. Intern, U. Chgo. Clinics, 1945-46, U. Minn., 1949-50; resident Woodlawn Hosp., Chgo., 1946; resident in internal medicine VA Hosp., Nashville, 1946-47; resident in psychiatry VA Hosp., Hines, Ill., 1955-58; practice medicine specializing in internal medicine, Newton, N.C., 1947-48, Chgo., 1950-55; practice medicine specializing in psychiatry, Chgo., 1958-60, Asheville, N.C., 1961-70, N.Y.C., 1970-76, specializing in med. nutrition, N.Y.C., 1976—; instr. neurology and psychiatry Sch. Medicine, Northwestern U., Chgo., 1958-61; free lance writer, 1950—; novels include 1/3 of an Inch of French Bread, 1961, Long John, 1979, Dr. Cox's Couch, 1979, others under pseudonym, 1950-60; sci. books include text Psychiatric Programming of People, 1972, Mega-Nutrients for Your Nerves, 1975, Dr. Newbold's Revolutionary New Discoveries about Weight Loss, 1977, Vitamin C Against Cancer, 1979; numerous appearances radio and TV. Served with U.S. Army, 1943-45, 46-47. Mem. Internat. Coll. Applied Nutrition, Soc. Clin. Ecology, N.Y. Acad. Scis. Address: 300 Mercer St Suite 29-N New York NY 10003

NEWBOUND, KENNETH BATEMAN, physicist, educator; b. Winnipeg, Man., Can., Mar. 12, 1919; s. Albert Everard and Bertha Beatrice (Bateman) N.; B.Sc. with honors in Physics and Math., U. Man., 1940, M.Sc. in Physics, 1941; Ph.D., Mass. Inst. Tech., 1948; m. Lyndell Hilda Edmonds, Aug. 16, 1947; children—Beatrice Elizabeth, Kenneth Randolph, Lawrence Douglas, Peter Edmonds.

Asst. prof. physics, U. Alta., Edmonton, Can., 1948-58, prof. physics, 1958—, asso. dean sci., 1964-76, dean sci., 1976—. Served to lt. Royal Canadian Vol. Res., World War II. Home: 8910 Windsor Rd Edmonton AB T6G 2A2 Canada

NEWBROUGH, EDGAR TRUETT, mgmt. cons.; b. Madison, Ill., June 22, 1917; s. Edgar M. and Iris M. (Webb) N.; B.A., San Diego State Coll., 1938; m. Muriel E. Amos, Nov. 26, 1936; children—Sherrill (Mrs. T.D. McIntyre), Sandra (Mrs. D. S. Cole), Arthur T. With Solar Aircraft Co., San Diego, 1937-43, supt., Des Moines plant, 1942-43; mem. staff Albert Ramond & Assos., Chgo., 1943-72, v.p., 1956-61, pres., 1962-72; spl. cons. Theodore Barry & Assos., Los Angeles, 1977—; ind. mgmt. cons., Ishpeming, Mich. Registered profl. engr., Pa., Mo., Ill., Mich. Mem. Am. Inst. Indsl. Engrs., Assn. Cons. Mgmt. Engrs. (dir. 1964-66), Am. Inst. Plant Engrs. Presbyn. (elder). Mason (Shriner). Club: Wawonowin Country (Ishpeming). Author: Effective Maintenance Management, also articles. Address: Michigan Northwoods Club Route 3 Box 576 Ishpeming MI 49849

NEWBURGER, FRANK L., JR., investment broker; b. Phila., Nov. 26, 1908; s. Frank L. and Helen (Langfeld) N.; A.B., Cornell U., 1929; m. Dorothy Hess, Nov. 7, 1946 (dec.); children—Patricia S., Frank L., III; m. 2d, Jane Berger, Aug. 19, 1973. Partner, Newburger, Loeb & Co., Phila., 1930-46, Newburger & Co., 1946-70, Advest Co. (mng. partner Newburger & Co. div.), 1970-77; sr. v.p., dir. Advest Inc., Phila., 1977—. Bd. govs. N.Y. Stock Exchange, 1959-62; bd. govs. Phila.-Balt. Stock Exchange 1946-56, pres., 1954-57. Vice chmn. United Fund, 1957-63; dir. Fedn. Jewish Agys., 1950—, pres., 1966, 67. Bd. dirs. Acad. Natural Scis. treas., 1973-74; trustee Albert Einstein Med. Center, treas., 1957-60; mem. council Cornell U., 1965-71, 74-77, emeritus, 1978—; mem. Health and Welfare Council, 1965-70. Mem. Bond Club Phila. (pres. 1966). Home: Rydal PA 19046 Office: 1401 Walnut St Philadelphia PA 19102

NEWBURGER, HOWARD MARTIN, psychologist; b. N.Y.C., May 16, 1924; s. Bernhard and Bertha (Travers) N.; B.A., N.Y. U., 1948, M.A., 1950, Ph.D., 1952; tng. in Jungian, Neo-Freudian and Horneyian psychoanalysis; m. Doris Schekter, July 3, 1949; children—Amy, Barry, Cary. Rotating intern N.J. Dept. Instns. and Agys., 1948-49; chief psychologist N.J. State Instn., Annandale, 1949-52; dir. psychoanalysis Div. Social Def. UN, 1952; pvt. practice in psychoanalysis and group psychotherapy, 1952—; research asso. Beth Israel Hosp., 1958-69; lectr., adj. asso. prof. N.Y. U., 1951-60, chmn. dept. exceptional child and youth, 1954-62, chmn. faculty and supr. treatment Inst. Applied Human Dynamics, 1960—; lectr., cons. in field; psychology coordinator Prelect John Jay Coll. Criminal Justice, 1969-72. Chmn. bd. dirs. Inst. Applied Human Dynamics, N.Y.C. and Westchester, N.Y., 1960—. Served with AUS, World War II: ETO; MTO. Recipient Outstanding Service to Humanity award Inst. Applied Human Dynamics for Handicapped, 1970. Mem. Am. Psychol. Assn., Am. Soc. Group Psychotherapy and Psychodrama (sec.-treas., 1954-55), Am. Assn. Mental Deficiency. Jewish (trustee temple). Co-author: Winners and Losers. Asso. editor Excerpta Medica, 1951-62. Contbr. articles and papers to tech. jours. Office: Timber Trail Rye NY 10580. *Our country affords tremendous opportunity. Through the development of our inner resources, and their assertion, we can all have happy and effective lives.*

NEWBURGH, ROBERT WARREN, educator, biochemist; b. Sioux City, Iowa, Mar. 22, 1922; s. Oscar and Ida (Kreutz) N.; B.S., State U. Iowa, 1949; Ph.D., U. Wis., 1953; m. Marilyn Jean Gould, Aug. 30, 1947; children—Kirk, Elizabeth. Research asso. Ore. State U., Corvallis, 1952-54, mem. faculty, 1954—, prof. chemistry, 1961—, chmn. dept. biochemistry and biophysics, 1966-76, asst. dir. Sci. Research Inst., 1962-76, dean Grad. Sch., 1976—; vis. asso. prof. U. Conn., Storrs, 1960-61; vis. prof. U. Calif. at San Diego Med. Sch., 1971-72. Scholar, Am. Cancer Soc., 1958-61. Mem. Am. Soc. Biol. Chemistry, Am. Chem. Soc., Soc. Developmental Biology, AAAS, Sigma Xi. Rotarian. Author: (with V.H. Cheldelin) The Chemistry of Some Life Processes, 1964; also numerous articles. Research on phospholipid and carbohydrate metabolism of insects; biochemistry of devel. Home: 630 Merrie Dr Corvallis OR 97330

NEWBURY, GEORGE ADELBERT, lawyer; b. Ripley, N.Y., Nov. 7, 1895; s. Clarence Rollin and Mary Catharine (Moore) N.; LL.B., Cornell U., 1917; LL.D., Keuka Coll., Lycoming Coll., Houghton Coll.; m. Laura Hildred, Sept. 16, 1922 (dec. Jan. 1924); 1 son, George Hildred; m. 2d, Eleanor Louise Murray, Apr. 4. 1931. Admitted to N.Y. bar, 1919; practice in Westfield 1919-24, Buffalo, 1924-46, 62—; mem. firm Babcock Newbury & Russ, 1924-45; with Blue Cross of Western N.Y., 1944-68, pres., 1944-55, chmn., 1955-67; joined Mfrs. & Traders Trust Co., Buffalo, 1946, exec. v.p., 1946-54, pres., 1954-63; counsel firm Hodgson, Russ, Andrews, Woods & Goodyear, 1962-75; v.p. Health Service, Inc. Chgo., 1950-58, dir., 1950-68. Dir. Nat. Health and Welfare Retirement Assn., 1960-68; dir., 1st pres. WNED-TV; dir. Legal Aid Soc., 1936-54; pres. Children's Aid Soc., 1942-49; campaign chmn. Community Chest, Buffalo and Erie County, 1950-52; v.p., dir. Child Welfare League America, 1950-52. Adv. bd. Rosary Hill Coll., Buffalo, 1955-65; trustee Keuka Coll., Keuka Park, N.Y., 1967-75, Buffalo Gen. Hosp., 1943-66; trustee Cornell U., 1959-69, trustee emeritus, presdl. counsellor, 1969—; chmn. men's adv. com. Children's Hosp. Buffalo; adv. bd. State U. Coll. at Fredonia. Recipient Justin Ford Kimball award Am. Hosp. Assn., 1959, hon. life mem., 1973; Silver Beaver award Boy Scouts Am.; honor Cult of White Buffalo, 1976. Mem. Buffalo C. of C. (pres. 1943-45), Buffalo Bd. Trade (pres. 1943-45), Am. (past v.p. N.Y. sect.), N.Y. State (chmn. legis. com.) bankers assns., Am., N.Y. (chmn. banking law sect., pres. 1961-62), Erie County bar assns., Cornell Law Assn., Newcomen Soc., Tau Kappa Epsilon. Presbyterian (elder, deacon, trustee, chmn., finance com.). Mason (33 deg., sovereign grand comdr. Ancient Accepted Scottish Rite, No. Jurisdiction, 1965-75, pres. internat. conf. supreme council 1975—). Clubs: Buffalo, Cornell (past pres.) (Buffalo); Cornell (N.Y.C.); Thursday. Home: Westbrook Apts 675 Delaware Ave Buffalo NY 14202 Office: 1 M & T Plaza Buffalo NY 14203. *I was fortunate in being reared according to old-fashioned standards encouraging respect for my elders, decency in my private life, faith in God, love of my Country, and loyalty to it. This provided a solid and stable foundation on which to build my future life. All that I have accomplished in life can be traced to that early training.*

NEWBY, IDUS ATWELL, educator, historian; b. Hawkinsville, Ga., Oct. 3, 1931; s. Idus A. and Nomie Bell (Floyd) N.; B.S., Ga. So. Coll., 1951; M.A., U. S.C., 1957; Ph.D., U. Calif. at Los Angeles, 1962. Asst. prof. history Western Wash. State Coll., 1962-63, Calif. State Coll., Fullerton, 1963-66; asso. prof. history U. Hawaii, 1966—, prof. history, 1970—. Served with USAF, 1951-55. Mem. Am., So. hist. assns., Orgn. Am. Historians, Assn., Study Negro History and Life. Author: Jim Crow's Defense, 1965; Challenge to the Court, 1967; The Development of Segregationist Thought, 1968; Black Carolinians, 1973; The South: A History, 1978. Editor: The Civil War and Reconstruction, 1971. Home: 2533 Ala Wai Blvd Honolulu HI 96815

NEWCOMB, DAVID ROYAL, steel fabrication co. exec.; b. Rochester, N.Y., Dec. 14, 1923; s. Cortland J. and Marguerite (Hahn) N.; B.S. in Administrv. Engring., Cornell U., 1948; m. Anne Marie Ruffing, Jan. 16, 1945; children—David Royal, William, Martha, Lucy, Elizabeth. With Buffalo Forge Co., 1948—, exec. v.p. 1964-66, pres., 1966—, also dir.; dir. Pratt & Lambert, Inc., Utica Mat. Ins. Co., Conax Corp., Marine Midland Bank-Western. Chmn. corporate gifts Buffalo United Fund. Vice pres. Sch. Bd. East Aurora, N.Y., 1964-67; alt. del. Republican Nat. Conv., 1960. Bd. dirs. United Fund Erie County, Buffalo Gen. Hosp., YMCA of Buffalo, Asso. Industries N.Y. Served with USAAF 1942-45. Mem. Am. Soc. Heating, Refrigerating and Air Conditioning Engrs., Am. Legion, Newcomen Soc. N. Am. Clubs: Buffalo, Cornell (Buffalo); Cragburn. Home: 250 Porterville Rd East Aurora NY 14052 Office: 490 Broadway Buffalo NY 14204

NEWCOMB, ELDON HENRY, educator; b. Columbia, Mo., Jan. 19, 1919; s. Ernest Henry and Ruby Josephine (Anderson) N.; student U. Kansas City, 1936-38; A.B., U. Mo., 1940, A.M., 1942; Ph.D., U. Wis., 1949; m. Joyce Bright Rieling, June 21, 1949; children—Norman Robert, Barbara Pauline, Cynthia Irma. Asst. prof. botany U. Wis.-Madison, 1949-54, asso. prof., 1954-58, prof., 1958—, dir. Inst. Plant Devel., 1979—; cons. Shell Devel. Co., 1954-59. Served with AUS, 1942-45. NRC predoctoral fellow U. Wis., 1946-49; Guggenheim Found. fellow U. Calif. at Berkeley, 1951-52; Sci. Faculty fellow Harvard, 1963-64; Fulbright Sr. Research scholar Australian Nat. U., Canberra, 1976. Mem. Am. Soc. Cell Biologists, Bot. Soc. Am., Am. Soc. Plant Physiologists, Soc. Developmental Biology, Phi Beta Kappa (pres. Wis. Alpha chpt. 1978-79), Sigma Xi. Sr. author: Plants in Perspective, 1963. Mng. editor Protoplasma, 1969-73; editorial bd. Ann. Review Plant Physiology, 1965-69. Contbr. articles profl. jours. Mem. expdn. to Great Barrier Reef, 1973. Home: 3108 Creek View Dr Middleton WI 53562

NEWCOMB, PAUL KERRY, author; b. Milford, Conn., Dec. 7, 1946; s. Paul Guy and Ann Marie (Reno) N.; B.A. in English, U. Tex., Arlington, 1969; M.F.A. in Theatre, Trinity U., 1974; m. Patricia Ellen Blackwell, July 26, 1971; 1 dau., Amy Rose. Held various jobs, including profl. actor, comml. writer, salesman, vol. tchr., 1965-74; author books including: Pandora Man, 1979; Matanza, 1979; Raven, 1978; Paxton Pride, 1976; Love's Wildest Fires, 1977; Tutus Gamble, 1977; Rafe, 1976. Mem. Authors Guild. Roman Catholic.

NEWCOMB, ROBINSON, cons. economist; b. Thompson, Ohio, Aug. 30, 1901; s. Ozro Robinson and Cora (Mead) N.; student U. Ohio, U.N.C.; A.B., M.A. summa cum laude, Oberlin Coll., 1924; Ph.D., Brookings Grad. Sch., 1928; m. Carolyn Jones, June 29, 1929; children—Anthony Mead, Sarah Robinson. Economist, Dept. Commerce, NRA, Dept. Agr., Dept. Interior, Home Loan Bank Bd., 1928-40; dir. constrn. research WPB, 1940-45; dir. office econ. research Fed. Works Agy., 1945-47; economist Pres.'s Council Econ. Advisers, 1947-50, 53-55, Office Sec. Commerce, 1950-51, ODM, 1951-53; mem. adv. com. constrn. statistics U.S. Census, 1959-65; prin. Robinson Newcomb Assos., Washington, cons. to Amman & Whitney, Standard Oil N.Y., 1961—, Battelle Meml. Inst., 1973—; cons. Dept. Interior, Dept. Commerce, AID; dir. transp. AID-TCR, Dept. State, 1964-66. Chmn. exec. com. bldg. research adv. bd., mem. com. urban tech. NRC-Nat. Acad. Scis. U.S. rep. for Acad. Scis. on U.S. nat. com. Internat. Council for Bldg. Research, 1968—. Recipient Ted V. Rodgers Journalism award, 1961. Mem. Nat. Assn. Bus. Economists (pres. Washington chpt. 1963), Am., D.C. statis. assns., Lambda Alpha (pres. Washington chpt. 1961). Clubs: Internat., Cosmos (Washington). Author: Construction (for Com. Econ. Devel.). Translator: Modern Economic Organization. Contbr. articles to profl. jours. Address: Cosmos Club 2121 Massachusetts Ave NW Washington DC 20008

NEWCOMB, THOMAS FINLEY, physician; b. Buffalo, June 22, 1927; s. Thomas Higgs and Naomi Elora (Finley) N.; B.S. magna cum laude, U. Pitts., 1949, M.D., 1951; m. Carol Frances Bielat, Mar. 26, 1978; children by previous marriage—John, Charles, Christopher. Intern, Hosp. of U. Pa., 1951-52, resident in hematology, 1952-53; resident in medicine VA Hosp., Seattle, 1953-54, research fellow in hematology, 1954-55; Fulbright Research scholar in medicine Rikshospitalet Coagulation Lab., Oslo, Norway, 1955-56; sr. asst. resident in medicine Peter Bent Brigham Hosp., Boston, 1956-57, jr. asso. in medicine, 1957-59; investigator Howard Hughes Med. Inst., Boston, 1957-59; instr. medicine Harvard Med. Sch., Boston, also asso. dir. Richard C. Curtis Hematology Lab., Peter Bent Brigham Hosp., 1958-59; faculty U. Fla. Coll. Medicine, Gainesville, 1959-78, prof. medicine, 1968-76, clin. prof. medicine, 1976-78, acting chmn. dept. biochemistry, 1969-71, prof. biochemistry, 1971-73, dir. clin. hematology labs., 1959-62, head div. hematology, 1959-68; cons. internal medicine VA Hosp., Lake City, Fla., 1964-68; asso. chief of staff for research and edn. VA Hosp., Gainesville, Fla., 1968-72; dir. research service VA Central Office, Washington, 1972-73, asst. chief med. dir. for research and devel., 1973-78; chief of staff Audie Murphy VA Med. Center, San Antonio, 1978—; prof. medicine U. Tex. Health Sci. Center, San Antonio; mem. Inter-agy. Tech. Com. on Heart, Lung and Blood Vessel Diseases, 1972-76; Nat. Heart, Lung and Blood Adv. Council, 1973-77, White House Com. on Human Resources, 1973; mem. Fed. Coordinating Council Sci., Engring., and Tech., 1976-78, vice chmn. com. health and medicine, 1976-78; mem. Nat. Cancer Adv. Bd., 1977-78. Served with USNR, 1945-47. Fellow A.C.P.; mem. Internat., Am. socs. hematology, Internat. Soc. for Hemostasis and Thrombosis, Am. Fedn. for Clin. Research, So. Soc. for Clin. Investigation.

NEWCOMB, WILLIAM WILMON, JR., anthropologist; b. Detroit, Oct. 30, 1921; s. William Wilmon and Esther Gladys (Matthews) N.; A.B., U. Mich., 1943, M.A., 1947, Ph.D., 1953; m. Glendora Estella Thielan, Aug. 24, 1946; children—Mary Elaine, William Andrew. Instr., U. Tex., Austin, 1947-50, 51-52, lectr. anthropology, 1961-62, prof., 1962—; teaching fellow U. Mich., 1950-51, 52-53; vis. asst. prof. anthropology and sociology Colgate U., 1953-54; curator anthropology Tex. Meml. Mus., Austin, 1954-57, dir. mus., 1957-78; dir. Tex. Archeol. Salvage Project, 1965-66. Served with inf., AUS, 1943-46. NSF grantee, 1965-66. Fellow Am. Anthrop. Assn., Tex. Hist. Assn.; mem. Tex. Inst. Letters, Am. Assn. Museums. Author: The Indians of Texas, 1961; The Rock Art of Texas Indians, 1967; The People Called Wichita, 1976; North American Indians: An Anthropological Perspective, 1974; German Artist on the Texas Frontier: Friedrich Richard Petri, 1978. Home: 6206 Shoal Creek Blvd Austin TX 78757 Office: Dept Anthropology 336 Burdine Hall U Texas Austin TX 78712

NEWCOMBE, HOWARD BORDEN, biologist; b. Kentville, N.S., Can., Sept. 19, 1914; s. Edward Borden and Mabel Elsie (Outerbridge) N.; B.S., Acadia U., Wolfville, N.S., 1935, D.Sc. (hon.), 1970; Asso., Imperial Coll. Tropical Agr., Trinidad, 1938; Ph.D., McGill U., 1939, D.Sc. (hon.), 1966; m. Beryl Honor Callaway, Feb. 14, 1942; children—Kenneth Donald, Charles Philip, Richard William. Sci. officer British Ministry of Supply, 1940-41; research asso. Carnegie Instn., Washington, 1946-47; with Atomic Energy of Can., Ltd., Chalk River, Ont., 1947-79, head biology br., 1949-70, head population research br., 1970-79; vis. prof. genetics Ind. U., 1963; mem. Internation Commn. on Radiol. Protection, 1965-77, chmn. com. on biol. effects, 1965-72. Served to lt. Royal Naval Vol. Reserve, 1941-46. Recipient Canadian Centennial medal, 1967. Fellow Royal Soc. Can.; mem. Genetics Soc. Am. (sec. 1956-58), Am. Soc. Human Genetics (pres. 1965), Genetics Soc. Can (pres. 1964-65), Radiation Research Soc. Contbr. articles in field to profl. jours. Home: 67 Hillcrest Ave Deep River ON K0J 1P0 Canada

NEWCOMBE, LEO RAYMOND, ret. publishing exec., educator; b. Faribault, Minn., Sept. 24, 1921; s. Sumner and Jane Loretta (Kane) N.; B.B.A. with distinction, U. Minn., 1942; M.B.A. with distinction, U. Mich., 1947; m. Marion Ann Lombard, May 1, 1948; children—Leo Raymond, Richard S., Robert M., Douglas L., Jerome T., Mary Ann, John J., Margaret Mary. Engaged as accounting instr. U. Mich., 1946-47; auditor Arthur Andersen & Co., Chgo., 1947-51; controller corporate div. Field Enterprises, Inc., pubs. Chgo. Sun-Times, Chgo. Daily News, 1951-53, v.p. finance, newspaper div., 1959—, controller Chgo. Sun-Times, 1953-59, bus. mgr., 1959, v.p., gen. mgr., 1965-78, sr. v.p., 1978-79; sec.-treas. Field Newspaper Syndicate; mem. faculty Coll. Commerce, DePaul U., Chgo., 1979—. Bd. dirs. St. Joseph Hosp., Catholic Charities. Served to lt. Supply Corps, USNR, 1942-46. C.P.A., Ill. Mem. Ill. Soc. C.P.A.'s, Am. Inst. C.P.A.'s, Beta Gamma Sigma, Beta Alpha Psi, Alpha Kappa Psi. Roman Catholic. Clubs: Chicago, Tavern (Chgo.); Indian Hill (Winnetka, Ill.). Home: 50 Woodley Rd Winnetka IL 60093

NEWCOMER, CLARENCE CHARLES, judge; b. Mount Joy, Pa., Jan. 18, 1923; s. Clarence S. and Marion Clara (Charles) N.; A.B., Franklin and Marshall Coll., 1944; LL.B., Dickinson Sch. Law, 1948; m. Jane Moyer Martin, Oct. 2, 1948; children—Judy (Mrs. Kenneth N. Birkett, Jr.), Nancy Jane, Peggy Jo (Mrs. Russell Pollack). Admitted to Pa. bar, 1950; practiced law, Lancaster, 1950-57; partner firm Rohrer, Honaman, Newcomer & Musser, Lancaster, 1957-60; with Office of Dist. Atty., Lancaster, 1960-64, 1st asst. dist. atty., 1964-68, dist. atty., 1968-72; partner Newcomer, Roda & Morgan, 1968-72; fed. dist. judge Eastern Dist. Pa., Phila., 1972—. Spl. dep. atty. gen. Pa. Dept. Justice, 1953-54. Served to lt. (j.g.) USNR, 1943-46; PTO. Home: 600 Pleasure Rd Lancaster PA 17601 Office: 13th Floor US Courthouse Independence Mall Philadelphia PA 19106

NEWELL, ALLEN, educator; b. San Francisco, Mar. 19, 1927; s. Robert R. and Jeannette (LeValley) N.; B.S. in Physics, Stanford, 1949; postgrad. Math., Princeton, 1949-50; Ph.D. in Indsl. Adminstrn., Carnegie Inst. Tech., 1957; m. Noel Marie McKenna, Dec. 20, 1947; 1 son, Paul Allen. Research scientist RAND Corp., Santa Monica, Cal., 1950-61; Univ. prof. Carnegie-Mellon U., Pitts., 1961—; U.A. and Helen Whitaker U. Prof. in Computer Sci., 1976—; cons. Xerox Corp. Recipient Harry Goode award Am. Fedn. Information Processing Socs., 1971; (with H.A. Simon) A.M. Turing award Assn. Computing Machinery, 1975. Fellow IEEE, AAAS; mem. Am. Psychol. Assn., Assn. Computing Machinery, Nat. Acad. Sci., Am. Acad. Arts and Sci. Inst. Mgmt. Sci. Author: (with G. Ernst) GPS, A Case Study in Generality, 1969; (with G. Bell) Computer Structures, 1971; (with H.A. Simon) Human Problem Solving, 1972; (with C.G. Bell and J. Grason) Designing Computers and Digital Systems, 1972. Office: Carnegie-Mellon Univ Schenley Park Pittsburgh PA 15213

NEWELL, BARBARA WARNE, former coll. pres., internat. orgn. exec.; b. Pitts., Aug. 19, 1929; d. Colston E. and Frances (Corbett) Warne; B.A., Vassar Coll., 1951; M.A., U. Wis., 1953, Ph.D., 1958; hon. degrees: L.H.D., Trinity Coll., Lesley Coll., 1978; LL.D., Central Mich. U., Williams Coll.; D.Litt., Northeastern U., Mt. Vernon Coll.; D.Adminstrn., Purdue U., 1976; D.Litt., Denison U., 1978; m. George V. Thompson, June 15, 1954 (dec. 1954); m. 2d, George S. Newell, June 9, 1956 (dec. 1964); 1 dau., Elizabeth Penfield. Govt. intern NLRB, 1948, Hudson Shore Labor Sch., 1949; research, teaching asst. U. Wis., 1951-54, asst. to chancellor, 1965-67; research, teaching asst., asso. U. Ill., 1954-59; asst. prof., then asso. prof. econs. Purdue U., 1959-65; asst. to pres., asso. prof. econs. U. Mich. at Ann Arbor, 1967-68, acting v.p. student affairs, asso. prof., 1968-70, spl. asst. to pres., asso. prof., 1970-71; prof. econs., asso. provost grad. study and research U. Pitts.; 1971-72; pres. Wellesley (Mass.) Coll., 1972-79; U.S. rep. with rank ambassador to UNESCO, Paris, 1979—. Sec. Community Action Com., Madison, Wis., 1965-66; chmn. Nat. Commn. Med. Care Women, Am. Acad. Obstetricians and Gynecologists, 1970-72; mem. presdl. selection and career devel. Assn. Am. Colls., 1974; adviser to bd. trustees Wesleyan U., Middletown, Conn., 1970-71; mem. steering com. Presidents to Assist Boston Sch. Dept., 1975—. Bd. dirs. Dane County Community Welfare Council, 1964-66, Carnegie Endowment Internat. Peace, 1972—, Brookings Instn., 1972—; bd. dirs. Am. Council Edn., 1972-76, vice chmn., 1975-76; mem. vis. com. dept. econs. Harvard Coll., 1973-74; bd. dirs. WGBH, 1972—; term trustee U. Pitts., 1973-76, Carnegie Found. Advancement Teaching, 1976—. bd. overseers Boston Symphony Orch., 1974—; mem. corp. M.I.T., 1979—; trustee Com. for Econ. Devel., 1979—. Wells fellow, 1951. Mem. Nat. Assn. Ind. Colls. and Univs. (dir. 1977—, treas. 1978—). Club: Seven Colleges (past pres. Champaign, Ill., past dir. Lafayette, Ind.). Author: Chicago and the Labor Movement, 1961; (with Lawrence Senesh) The Pulse of the Nation, 1961; Our Labour Force, 1962. Editorial bd. Labor History, 1975—. Contbr. articles and revs. to profl. jours. and mags. Home: UNESCO 7 Place de Fontenoy 75700 Paris France

NEWELL, ERIC JAMES, ins. co. exec.; b. Toronto, Ont., Can., Sept. 24, 1930; s. James and Anne (Brown) N.; came to U.S., 1959, naturalized, 1970; student U. Toronto, 1951-53; m. Essie Miskelly, Sept. 30, 1950; 1 son, Eric Wayne. Pub. accountant W.J. Wilcox & Co., Toronto, 1949-53; chief accountant Toronto Mut. Life Ins. Co., 1953-57; asst. sec. Holland Life Ins. Co., Toronto, 1957-59; with Penn Mut. Life Ins. Co., Phila., 1959—, asso. controller, 1965-70, 2d v.p., controller, 1970—; dir. Hotel Brunswick, Lancaster, Pa. Mem. Traffic and Transp. Bd., Cherry Hill, N.J., 1971-73, Zoning Bd., 1975—; vice chmn. Cherry Hill Econ. Devel. Bd., 1973-75; pres. Greater Kingston Civic Assn., Cherry Hill, 1970-76; Democratic committeeman, Camden County, 1976—; vice chmn. Dem. Party, Cherry Hill, 1976. Fellow Life Mgmt. Inst., Royal Commonwealth Soc.; mem. Fin. Execs. Inst., Am. Inst. Corporate Controllers, N.Y. Ins. Accountants Club (chmn.), Royal Black Knights of Ireland, Loyal Orange Assn. Presbyn. (deacon ch. 1969—). Home: 521 Garwood Dr Cherry Hill NJ 08003 Office: 530 Walnut St Philadelphia PA 19172

NEWELL, FRANK WILLIAM, ophthalmologist, educator; b. St. Paul, Jan 14, 1916; s. Frank John and Hilda (Turnquist) N.; M.D., Loyola U., Chgo., 1939; M.Sc., U. Minn., 1942; m. Marian Elizabeth Glennon, Sept. 12, 1942; children—Frank William, Mary Susan, Elizabeth Glennon, David Andrew. Intern, Ancker Hosp., St. Paul, 1939-40; teaching fellow U. Minn., 1940-42; research fellow, instr., asso. dept. ophthalmology Northwestern U. Med. Sch., 1946-53; now James and Anna Raymond prof., chmn. dept. ophthalmology U. Chgo. Med. Sch.; prof. extraordinario Autonomous U. Barcelona (Spain), 1972—; Montgomery lectr. Trinity Coll., Dublin Ireland, 1966; Dunphy lectr. Mass. Eye and Ear Infirmary, 1967; McPherson lectr. U. N.C., 1968; Wright lectr. U. Toronto, 1973; Irvine lectr. U. So. Calif., 1971; O'Brien lectr. Tulane U., 1974; Atkinson lectr. Internat. Soc. Eye Surgeons, 1975; Stein lectr. U. Calif. at Los Angeles, 1976; Townes lectr. U. Louisville, 1977; sci. counselor Nat. Inst. Neurol. Diseases and Blindness, 1959-62, chmn., 1961-62; mem. nat. eye council NIH, 1972-75; cons. U.S. Pharmacopeia Scope Panel Ophthalmology; mem. Internat. Council Ophthalmology, 1977—. Bd. dirs. Heed

Ophthalmic Found., chmn., 1975—; bd. dirs. Ill. Soc. Prevention Blindness; dir. Ophthalmic Pub. Co., sec.-treas., 1971—; trustee Loyola U., Chgo., 1977—. Served from 1st lt. to maj. M.C., AUS, 1943-46. Recipient Alumni Citation award Loyola U., 1962, Stritch medal, 1966; Howe prize medal in ophthalmology AMA, 1968, Outstanding Achievement award U. Minn., 1975; Lang medal Royal Soc. Medicine, London, 1974; medal honor Soc. Eye Surgeons, 1975; medallo Andrés Bello, U. Chile, 1977. Diplomate Am. Bd. Ophthalmology (chmn. bd. 1967-69, cons. 1971-74). Mem. Chgo. Soc. History Medicine, Soc. Med. Cons. Armed Forces, AAUP, Nat. Council Combat Blindness (sci. adv. bd.), Nat. Soc. Prevention Blindness (dir., chmn. research com. 1961-68, 70—, v.p. 1970—, Dunnington medal 1976), AMA (chmn. sect. ophthalmology 1964-65), Am. Acad. Ophthalmology and Otolaryngology (honor award 1953, 1st v.p. 1965, counselor 1969-72, pres. 1975), Inst. Barraguer (pres. 1970—), Assn. U. Profs. Ophthalmology (trustee 1966-69, pres., chmn 1967-69), Assn. Research Ophthal. (trustee 1963-68, chmn. bd. trustees 1967-68). Pan-Am. Assn. Ophthalmology (dir. 1969—, Gradle lectr. 1972), Am. (council 1977—), Chgo. (pres. 1957-58), Pacific Coast (hon.), Mont. (hon.), Central Ill. (hon.), Oxford (Eng.; hon.), Colombia, S. Am. (hon.), Hellenic (hon.) ophthal. socs., Academia Ophthalmologica Internationalis (1st v.p. 1976—), Soc. Exptl. Biology and Medicine, Soc. Franc d'ophth., Sigma Xi, Alpha Omega Alpha. Roman Catholic. Clubs: Literary, Quadrangle (Chgo.). Author: (with D. Syndacker) Refraction, 3d edit., 1971; Ophthalmology: Principles and Concepts, 4th edit., 1978; also articles. Editor-in-chief Am. Jour. Ophthalmology; editor Trans Glaucoma Conf., Vols. 1-5, 1955-61, Amblyopia and Strabismus, 1975; mem. editorial bd. Metabolic Ophthalmology, Annales del Instituto Barraquer, Palestra Oftalmologica, Survey Opthalmology. Home: 4500 N Mozart St Chicago IL 60625 Office: 950 E 59th St Chicago IL 60637

NEWELL, GUY RENE, govt. research adminstr.; b. Bogalusa, La., Sept. 21, 1937; s. Guy Rene and Marie (LeBlanc) N.; B.S., Tulane U., 1959, M.D., 1962; M.S. in Hygiene, Harvard U., 1969; m. Saidee Watson, July 9, 1966; children—Arthur Watson, Emily Marie. Intern in medicine Johns Hopkins U. Hosp., Balt., 1962-63, asst. resident in medicine, 1965-67; asst. resident in medicine Peter Bent Brigham Hosp., Boston, 1967-68; asst. prof. epidemiology and biostatics Tulane U., 1970-72, asso. prof., head sect. chronic diseases, 1972-73; dep. dir. Nat. Cancer Inst., Bethesda, Md., 1973-79; dir. div. cancer prevention, prof. epidemiology U. Tex. System Cancer Center, Houston, 1979—. Recipient Research Career Devel. award Nat. Cancer Inst.-NIH, 1972, Superior Service award HEW, 1975. Mem. Am. Acad. Polit. and Social Sci., AAAS, Am. Assn. Cancer Research, Am. Soc. Clin. Oncologists, Am. Fedn. Clin. Research, AMA, Am. Pub. Health Assn., Soc. Epidemiol. Research, Am. Epidemiology Soc., Delta Omega. Roman Catholic. Contbr. numerous articles to sci. jours. Home: 13518 Taylorcrest Houston TX 77079 Office: MD Anderson Hosp Tex Med Center Houston TX 77030

NEWELL, HUBERT M., clergyman; b. Denver, Feb. 16, 1904; s. Thomas J. and Nellie N.; Ph.B., Regis Coll., 1922-26, LL.D., 1948; student St. Thomas Sem., Denver, 1926-30; M.A., Cath. U., Washington, 1937. Ordained priest Roman Catholic Ch., 1930; supt. Cath. schs. in Colo., 1937-47; consecrated coadjutor bishop of Cheyenne with right of succession, Sept. 24, 1947, succeeded to See, Nov. 8, 1951, resigned, 1978. Home: St Joseph's Children's Home PO Box 1117 Torrington WY 82240

NEWELL, OSWALD, JR., oil co. exec.; b. New Orleans, Aug. 7, 1925; s. Oswald and Montine (Fryer) N.; B.S., Ga. Tech. Inst., 1946, M.S. in Chem. Engring., 1948; M.S. in Indsl. Mgmt., M.I.T., 1956; m. Virginia Anne Gordon, Aug. 28, 1948; children—Oswald, Mary Lynne, Virginia Leigh, Deborah Susan. With Continental Oil Co., 1948—, supt. refinery, Denver, 1958-63, v.p. mfg. Douglas Oil Co., Los Angeles, 1963-66, pres. Continental Carbon Co., Houston, 1966-75, exec. v.p. worldwide refining Conoco, Inc., Houston, 1975—; dir. Continental Carbon; mem. adv. mgmt. com. Conoco, Inc. Mem. Am. Petroleum Inst., Nat. Petroleum Refiners Assn., Houston C. of C. Methodist. Clubs: Champions Golf, Houston, Masons. Office: PO Box 2197 Houston TX 77001

NEWELL, PAUL HAYNES, JR., coll. pres.; b. Nashville, July 1, 1933; s. Paul Haynes Newell; B.M.E., U. Tenn., 1958, M.M.E., 1961; Mech.E., Mass. Inst. Tech., 1964, Ph.D., 1966; children—Paul Haynes III, Mike, Nan. Student asst. mech. engring. U. Tenn., 1957, instr. mech. engring., 1958-62; NSF Sci. faculty fellow Mass. Inst. Tech., 1962-65; asso. prof. mech. engring. U. Ala. Coll. Engring., 1966-69; prof. mech. engring. Tex. A. and M. U., 1969-72, asso. dean engring., 1972; prof. biomed. engring., dept. phys. medicine Baylor Coll. Medicine, 1969-74, prof. biomed. engring., dept. physiology, 1970-74, prof. biomed. engring., dept. community medicine, 1972-74, prof. biomed. engring., dept. rehab., 1972—, mem. grad. faculty, 1970-74; prof., head indsl. engring. dept. Tex. A. & M. U., 1972-74, prof., head combined programs of behavioral engring., bioengring., cybernetic engring., hygiene and safety engring., indsl. engring., 1972-74; pres., prof. Newark Coll. Engring., N.J. Inst. Tech., 1974—, prof. Administration Prostehtics Center, N.Y., 1973-75, VA Hosp., Houston, 1972-75, Baylor Coll. Medicine, Houston, 1971—; dir. N.J. Bell Telephone Co., Mid Atlantic Nat. Bank, Thomas-Betts Corp. Mem. NSF liaison com. Mem. Newark Transp. Council, N.J. Safety Council; sec. exec. com. council Boy Scouts Am., Birmingham, Ala., 1966-68; bd. dirs. N.J. State Opera, United Hosps. Newark. Served with USMCR, Korean Conflict. Recipient NSF Sci. Faculty fellowship. Registered profl. engr., Ala., Tenn., Tex., N.J. Mem. Am. Soc. Tool and Mfg. Engrs., N.Y., Ala. acads. scis., AAAS, Am. Congress Rehab. Medicine, Am. Heart Assn., Am. Inst. Indsl. Engrs., Am. Soc. Artificial Internal Organs, Am. Soc. Engring. Edn., ASME, Biomed. Engring. Soc., Inst. Engring. Deans, Internat. Soc. Prosthetics and Orthotics, Nat. Soc. Profl. Engrs., Soc. Advanced Med. Systems, Soc. Engring. Sci., Pres.'s Assn., Am. Fluid Power Soc., N.J. Soc. Engrs., Sigma Xi, Tau Beta Pi, Phi Kappa Phi, Pi Tau Sigma. Club: Rotary. Contbr. articles to profl. jours., chpts. to books. Address: 3204 Canter Ln Austin TX 78759

NEWELL, PETER CARROLL, radio exec.; b. San Francisco, Mar. 29, 1933; s. Joseph Carroll and Jean (Oliver) N.; B.S., U. Calif., 1955; m. Nancy Barbara Gwerder, Sept. 18, 1955; children—William, Thomas, John, Deborah. Account exec. radio sta. KABL, San Francisco, 1959-64; v.p., gen. mgr. sta. WPRO, Providence, 1964-66, WPRO-TV, 1967; v.p., radio sta. mgr. WPAT, N.Y.C., 1968; v.p., gen. mgr. radio sta. WKBW, Buffalo, 1968-71; gen. mgr. radio sta. KPOL, Los Angeles, 1971—. Bd. dirs. R.I. Philharmonic Orch., 1966-67, Better Bus. Bur., Buffalo, 1970-71. Served to lt. (j.g.) USNR, 1955-57. Mem. So. Calif. Broadcasters Assn. (dir. 1973—). Home: 15700 Royal Oak Rd Encino CA 91316 Office: 5700 Sunset Blvd Los Angeles CA 90028

NEWELL, REGINALD EDWARD, educator; b. Peterborough, Eng., Apr. 9, 1931; s. Harold Aubrey and Edith (Swiffin) N.; B.S. in Physics, U. Birmingham (Eng.), 1954; M.S., Mass. Inst. Tech., 1956, Sc.D., 1960; m. Maireen W. Lees, Sept. 6, 1954; children—Madeleine, Elizabeth, Oliver, Nicholas. Came to U.S., 1954, naturalized, 1969. With Brit. Meteorol. Office, 1947-50; successively research staff asst., asst. prof., asso. prof., prof. Mass. Inst. Tech., Cambridge, 1954—; cons. Lincoln Lab., N. Am. Rockwell Co., Environ. Research and Tech., Systems and Applied Scis. Corp. Mem. IUGG Internat. Commn. Meteorology Upper Atmosphere, 1967-75, mem. Internat. Commn. Atmospheric Chemistry and Global Pollution, 1971—; pres. Internat. Commn. Climate, 1977—. Served with RAF, 1950-51. Fellow Royal Meteorol. Soc., Am. Meteorol. Soc.; mem. Inst. Physics and Phys. Soc., Am. Geophys. Union, Sigma Xi. Joint author: The General Circulation of the Tropical Atmosphere, Vols. 1 and 2. Contbr. articles to profl. jours. Home: 45 Jason St Arlington MA 02174 Office: 54-1520 Mass Inst Tech Cambridge MA 02139

NEWELL, ROBERT LINCOLN, banker; b. Hartford, Conn., Dec. 2, 1922; s. Robert B. and Helen C. (Lincoln) N.; grad. Deerfield Acad., 1941; student Wesleyan U., Middletown, Conn.; m. Sally C. Erdman, July 28, 1944; children—Sally N. Huss, Helen N. Douglas, Robert Lincoln, Katharine Erdman, William Henry II. With Hartford Nat. Bank and Trust Co. (Conn.), 1946—, 1st exec. v.p., 1967-72, 1st exec. v.p., 1972-75, pres., 1975-78, chmn., 1978—, also dir.; dir., chmn. Hartford Nat. Corp.; dir. Allied Bank Internat., Kaman Aircraft Corp., N. Am. Philips Corp. Bd. dirs. Boys Clubs Hartford, Boys Club Am.; corporator Hartford Hosp., Mt. Sinai Hosp., Hartford Sem. Found.; bd. dirs., corporator St. Francis Hosp.; bd. dirs. Am. Sch. for the Deaf; trustee St. Joseph Coll., Mystic Seaport mus. Served to lt. USNR, 1943-46. Mem. Greater Hartford C. of C. (dir.). Home: 42 Mountain View Dr West Hartford CT 06117 Office: 777 Main St Hartford CT 06115

NEWELL, STERLING, JR., lawyer; b. Cleve., Sept. 1, 1921; s. Sterling Newell and Evelyn (Walker) N.; B.S., Haverford Coll., 1943; LL.B., N.Y. U., 1948; m. Frances Herne Brown, May 29, 1947; children—Evelyn, Peter, David, Margaret, Martha. Admitted to Ohio bar; practice in Cleve., 1948—; sr. partner firm Spieth, Bell, McCurdy and Newell; spl. asst. to atty. gen. serving as hearing officer in conscientious objector cases. Mem. Presiding Bishop's Com. on Investments in S. Africa; pres. trustees Youth Service, Cleve., 1966-67; sec. Ch. Home, Cleve., 1956—; sec., trustee Christian Residences Found., 1965—; trustee Karamu House, Cleve., Cleve Mus. Natural History, Ohio Conservation Found., Univ. Sch.; chancellor Episcopal Diocese of Ohio. Served with USNR, 1943-46. Mem. Am., Ohio, Cuyahoga County, Cleve. bar assns., Phi Delta Phi. Contbr. articles. Home: 2717 Leighton Rd Shaker Heights OH 44120 Office: Union Commerce Bldg Cleveland OH 44115

NEWEY, PAUL DAVIS, lawyer; b. Mpls., July 4, 1914; s. Paul S. and Mary (Yonan) N.; A.A., Central YMCA, 1935; J.D., John Marshall Law Sch., 1940; A.B., Detroit Inst. Tech., 1947; diploma U.S. Treasury Dept. Law Enforcement Sch., 1943; spl. courses U.S. Gov. and Mil. Intelligence Schs., 1951-53; m. Viola W. Raymond, Dec. 16, 1943; children—Paul Sarkhoshe II, David Raymond, Dean Alan, Arthur Tyler. Admitted to Ill. bar, 1946; squad leader Bur. Census, Dept. Commerce, 1940; officer Uniformed Force U.S. Secret Service, 1940-42; agt. Bur. Narcotics, Treasury Dept., 1942-47; individual practice law, real estate and ins. broker, Chgo., 1948-51; spl. rep. CIA, 1951-57; asst. state's atty.-investigator County of Cook, Ill., 1957-58, asst. state's atty.-chief investigator, chief state's atty.'s policy, 1958-60; individual practice law, Chgo., 1961-65; spl. investigator, Chgo., 1961—; partner firm Adamowski, Newey & Adamowski, Chgo., 1965—; sec., dir. Master Fishing Gear, Inc., 1956-57. Served as pvt. AUS, 1941, 1st lt. CIC, 1949-54. Recipient Medal of Merit and elected to Hall of Fame, Nat. Police Officers Assn. Am., 1960; Disting. Citizen award Assyrian-Am. Welfare Council, 1970; citation of merit John Marshall Law Sch., 1970. Mem. Am., Ill. Chgo. bar assns., Internat. Assn. Investigators and Spl. Police (chmn. bd. dirs.), N. Am. Inst. Police Sci. (bd. dirs.), N. Am. Detective Agy. (bd. dirs.), Spl. Agts. Assn. (3d v.p. 1977—), U.S. Treasury Agts. Assn. (pres. 1970-71), John Marshall Law Sch. Alumni Assn. (treas. 1973-75, bd. dirs.), Internat. Assn. Chiefs of Police, Am. Judicature Soc., Chgo. Assn. Commerce and Industry, Ill. Assn. Chiefs of Police. Mem. Ch. of East, also United Ch. of Christ. Clubs: Aramaic Bible Soc., Masons, Shriners, Chgo., Congregational (pres. 1963-64, bd. dirs., trustee 1962-65), Starcraft. Home: 1034 W Altgeld St Chicago IL 60614 Office: 11 S LaSalle St Chicago IL 60603. *Life is an interlude in eternity, and material gain, by itself, makes it a nullity. The Master's admonition, "whatsoever ye have done for the least of these thy brethren, ye have done it unto me!" demands pro bono conduct; or perish without paying your debt for existance. I know that "man does not live by bread alond!" and try to shape my sojourn here accordingly.*

NEWFIELD, MAYER ULLMAN, lawyer; b. Birmingham, Ala., Apr. 5, 1905; s. Morris and Leah (Ullman) N.; A.B., Samford U., 1927; postgrad Harvard Law Sch., 1928-29; LL.B., U. Ala., 1931; m. Bertha Lehman, June 8, 1938 (dec. 1973); children—Jane, Melanie (Mrs. Harvey Seigle); m. 2d, Loretta Schneiderman Ostrow, Nov. 29, 1978. Admitted to Ala. bar, 1931, also U.S. Supreme Ct.; asso. firm London, Yancey & Brower, Birmingham, 1931-34; supervising atty. HOLC, 1934-35; sr. trial atty., chief proxy unit, chief litigation and enforcement sect., asst. regional adminstr. SEC, Atlanta, Washington, Phila. and N.Y.C., 1935-47, co-author Rule 10b-5 1942; asst. atty. City of Birmingham, 1948-56; gen. practice, Birmingham, 1956—; mem. firm Newfield & Minisman, Birmingham, 1972-73; counsel to firm Sirote, Permutt, Friend, Friedman, Held & Apolinsky, P.A., 1972—. Vice pres., dir. N. Ala. Mineral Devel. Co. Pres. Civic Opera Assn., 1964-66; Ala. co-chmn. NCCJ, 1964-74, Ala. chmn., 1974-75, mem. nat. bd. govs., 1974—; nat. commr. Anti-Defamation League, 1956—, exec. com., 1957-71, now hon. life mem.; pres. Jewish Community Council, 1975. Bd. dirs. Jefferson-Shelby Lung Assn., 1958-76; pres. Jewish Community Center, 1970-71; bd. dirs. Urban League, 1967-74, Leo N. Levi Hosp., Hot Springs, Ark., 1968-74, Jewish Children's Home, New Orleans, 1968-74; mem. nat. com. Am. Israel Council Pub. Affairs Com., 1977—; pres. Temple Emanu-El, 1976-77. Mem. Am., Ala., Birmingham, Fed. Power bar assns., Com. Fgn. Relations. Democrat. Mem. B'nai B'rith (pres. Ala. 1949). Home: 2900 Thornhill Rd Birmingham AL 35213 Office: 2222 Arlington Ave Birmingham AL 35205

NEWHALL, BEAUMONT, historian; b. Lynn, Mass., June 22, 1908; s. Herbert William and Alice Lilia (Davis) N.; A.B. cum laude, Harvard, 1930, A.M., 1931, D. Art (hon.), 1978; postgrad. Harvard, U. Paris, U. London, 1933-35; m. Nancy Wynne Parker, July 1, 1936 (dec. 1974); m. 2d, Christie Weston, 1975. Lectr., Phila. Mus. Art, 1931-32; asst. Met. Mus. Art, 1932-33; librarian Mus. Modern Art, N.Y.C., 1935-42, curator photography, 1940-42, 45-46; curator Internat. Mus. Photography, George Eastman House, Rochester, N.Y., 1948-58, dir., 1958-71; vis. prof. art U. N.Mex., Albuquerque, 1971—; lectr. Black Mountain Coll., 1946-48, U. Rochester, 1954-55, Rochester Inst. Tech., 1956-69; vis. prof. art State U. N.Y. at Buffalo, 1969-71. Bd. dirs. Civic Music Assn., Rochester, 1963-71. Served to maj. USAAF, 1942-45; ETO. John Simon Guggenheim Found. fellow, 1947, 75. Fellow Royal Photog. Soc. Gt. Britain (hon.), Photog. Soc. Am., Am. Acad. Arts and Scis.; mem. Profl. Photographers Am. (hon. master of photography), Deutsche Gesellschaft für Photographie (corr.). Author: (with Nancy Newhall) Masters of Photography, 1958; The History of Photography, 1964; Latent Image, 1967; The Daguerreotype in America, 3d rev. edit., 1976; Airborne Camera, 1969. Home: Route 7 Box 126-C Santa Fe NM 87501

NEWHALL, DAVID SOWLE, educator; b. Burlington, Vt., July 26, 1929; s. Chester Albert and Nella Perry (Tillotson) N.; B.A., U. Vt., 1951; A.M., Harvard, Ph.D. (Charles Downer fellow), 1963; m. Edna Irene Newton, Mar. 25, 1952; children—Rebecca, John Newton, Jesslyn, Melissa, David Chester. Instr., U. Vt., Burlington, 1959-63, asst. prof., 1963-66; asst. prof. Centre Coll. Ky., Danville, 1966-67, asso. prof., 1967-70, prof. history, 1970—, chmn. div. social studies, 1968-74. Served with AUS, 1951-53; Korea. Mem. Boulder Soc., Am. Hist. Assn., Soc. for French Hist. Studies, Phi Beta Kappa, Phi Alpha Theta, Omicron Delta Kappa, Delta Psi. Presbyn. (elder 1971—). Home: 634 N 3d St Danville KY 40422

NEWHALL, JOHN BREED, lawyer; b. Salem, Mass., Nov. 26, 1932; s. Charles Boardman and Mary Moore (Nason) N.; A.B. cum laude, Harvard U., 1954, LL.B., 1959; m. Lynn Cynthia Latta, Apr. 23, 1960 (div. 1970); children—Mary Carlyle, Charles Latta; m. 2d, Katharine Pitcher Copeland, Dec. 1, 1973; children—Hannah Katharine, Rebecca Copeland. Admitted to Mass. bar, 1959; asso. firm Nutter, McClennen & Fish, Boston, 1959—, jr. partner, 1967-69, partner, 1970—; dir. Shawmut Corp. Vice pres., trustee New Eng. Home for Deaf; incorporator Salem Hosp.; active Soc. for Ministerial Relief. Served to 1st lt. USAF, 1955-57. Mem. Am., Fed., Mass., Boston bar assns., Soc. Colonial Wars, Breed Family Assn. Unitarian. Clubs: Appalachian Mountain, Harvard (Boston); D.U. (Cambridge); Eastern Yacht (Marblehead); Essex County, Manchester Yacht, Manchester Sailing (dir.), Manchester Harbor Boat. Home: Smith Point Manchester MA 01944 Office: 600 Atlantic Ave Boston MA 02210

NEWHALL, SCOTT, publisher; b. San Francisco, Jan. 21, 1914; s. Almer M. and Anna Nicholson (Scott) N.; student U. Calif., 1932-35; m. Ruth Waldo, Nov. 2O, 1933; children—X.X., Anthony, Jonathan. With San Francisco Chronicle, 1935-71, beginning as photographer, successively editor This World, Sunday editor, 1949, operations mgr., 1953, exec. editor, 52-70, editor, 1970-71; editor-in-chief San Francisco mag., 1971; past pres., pub. Newhall (Calif.) Signal, now editor; pres. Newhall Newspapers, Inc.; v.p. White Investment Co.; chmn. bd. gov. Irrawaddy Steam Nav. Co.; pres. Bacanora Internat.; dir. Newhall Land & Farming Co., Cal. Land Co. Mem. Calif. Sir Francis Drake Commn.; trustee emeritus San Francisco Maritime Mus.; trustee Mus. Arts and Scis., Cypress Lawn Cemetery Assn. Served as war corr. in Eng., World War II. Berkeley Fellow U. Calif. Mem. Soc. Calif. Pioneers (dir.). Home: Box 344 Piru CA 93040 also 1050 North Point St San Francisco CA 94109 Office: 1050 N Point St San Francisco CA 94109

NEWHARD, HARRY WALLACE, investment banker; b. St. Louis, Aug. 19, 1930; s. Chapin Slater and Anne Kennard (Wallace) N.; grad. Hotchkiss Sch., 1949; B.A., Brown U., 1953; m. Jeanne Hamilton, Sept. 1960 (div. 1969); children—Jean H., Pennock H. With Newhard, Cook & Co. Inc., St. Louis, 1957—, pres., 1971—. Served as aviator USN, 1953-56. Clubs: St. Louis Country, Noonday, Racquet (St. Louis); Union (N.Y.C.). Home: 2 Pebble Creek Rd St Louis MO 63124 Office: 300 N Broadway St Louis MO 63102

NEWHART, BOB, entertainer; b. Oak Park, Ill., Sept. 5, 1929; B.S., Loyola U., Chgo., 1952; m. Virginia Quinn, Jan. 12, 1963; 4 children. With U.S. Gypsum Co.; law clk., part-time C.P.A.; copywriter Fred Niles Film Co.; performed Dan Sorkin TV show, 1957; appeared Jack Paar Show, 1960; recorded albums Button-Down Mind of Bob Newhart, Button Down Mind Strikes Back, Behind the Button-Down Mind of Bob Newhart, Button Down Mind on TV; star Bob Newhart Show on TV, 1961, 72—; Royal command performance, London, Eng., 1964; numerous guest TV appearances, 1961—; films include Hot Millions, Catch 22, Cold Turkey. Served with AUS, 1952-54. Recipient Emmy award, 1961; Peabody award, 1961; Sword of Loyola award, 1976. Address: 315 S Beverly Dr Beverly Hills CA 90212

NEWHOUSE, EDWARD, author; b. Budapest, Hungary, Nov. 10, 1911; s. Samuel and Theresa N.; came to U.S., Nov. 1923; student Townsend Harris Hall Prep. Sch., 1926-29; m. Dorothy DeLay, Mar. 5, 1941; children—Jeffrey Hooker, Alison Osborn. Author: (novels) You Can't Sleep Here, 1934; This Is Your Day, 1937; The Hollow of the Wave, 1949; The Temptation of Roger Heriott, 1954; (short story collections) Anything Can Happen, 1941; The Iron Chain, 1946; Many Are Called, 1951. Contbr. to The New Yorker, and other mags. Served with AUS, 1942; served from pvt. to maj. USAAF, World War II. Decorated Legion of Merit, Conspicuous Service Cross. Club: The Coffee House. Home: Upper Nyack NY 10960 Office: care The New Yorker 25 W 43d St New York City NY 10036

NEWHOUSE, JOSEPH PAUL, economist; b. Waterloo, Iowa, Feb. 24, 1942; s. Joseph Alexander and Ruth Linnea (Johnson) N.; B.A., Harvard U., 1963, Ph.D., 1969; postgrad (Fulbright scholar), Goethe U., Frankfort, Germany, 1963-64; m. Margaret Louise Locke, June 22, 1968; children—Eric Joseph, David Locke. Staff economist Rand Corp., Santa Monica, Calif., 1968-72, dep. program mgr., health and biosci. research, 1971—, sr. staff economist, 1972—; lectr. UCLA, 1970—; mem. faculty Rand Grad. Inst., 1972—; investigator grants Nat. Center for Health Services Research and Devel., OEO, 1971—, prin. investigator, health ins. study grant HEW; mem. advisory com. nat. health ins. U.S. Ho. of Reps. Com. Ways and Means, 1975—; mem. Nat. Commn. on Cost of Med. Care, 1976-77, chmn. Task Force Med. Marketplace; mem. health services developmental grants study sect. HEW, 1978—; mem. Inst. Medicine Nat. Acad. Scis., 1978—. Mem. Am. Econ. Assn., Royal Econ. Soc., Econometric Soc. Author: The Economics of Medical Care, 1978; contbr. articles to profl. jours. Home: 1834 Old Orchard Rd Los Angeles CA 90049 Office: 1700 Main St Santa Monica CA 90406

NEWITT, BEN J., computer and electronics co. exec.; b. Ely, Nev., Dec. 25, 1924; s. Phillip E. and Georgiana (Gladding) N.; B.B.A., Armstrong Coll., 1947; postgrad. UCLA, 1950; children—Lynelle, Karen, Lisa, Julie. Staff acct. McLaren Goode, C.P.A.'s, Los Angeles, 1948-52; controller Western Design div. U.S.I., Santa Barbara, Calif., 1953-58, exec. v.p., 1958-63; controller Applied Magnetics Corp., Goleta, Calif., 1963-67, v.p., 1967-70, exec. v.p., 1970-79, pres., 1979—, also dir. Served with USN, 1948-49. Mem. Am. Electronics Assn. (dir. 1977-79, local pres. 1978-79). Republican. Office: 75 Robin Hill Goleta CA 93017

NEWKIRK, GORDON ALLEN, JR., astrophysicist; b. Orange, N.J., June 12, 1928; s. Gordon Allen and Mildred (Fleming) N.; B.A., Harvard U., 1950; M.A., U. Mich., 1952, Ph.D., 1953; m. Nancy Buck, Apr. 11, 1956; children—Sally, Linda, Jennifer. Research asst. Observatory, U. Mich., 1950-53; astrophysicist Upper Air Research Observatory, 1953; sr. research staff High Altitude Observatory, Boulder, Colo., 1955—, adj. prof. dept. astrogeophysics U. Colo., 1961-65, adj. prof. physics and astrophysics, 1965-76; dir. High Altitude Observatory, 1968—; cons. NASA, 1964—; mem. geophysics research bd. Nat. Acad. Sci., 1976—. Served with U.S. Army, 1953-55. Mem. AAAS, Am. Astron. Soc. (chmn. solar physics div. 1972-73), Internat. Astron. Union (pres. com. 10 1975—), Research Soc. Am., Commn. V Union Radio Sci. Internat., Am.

Geophysical Union, Sigma Xi. Contbr. articles on solar-interplanetary physics to profl. jours. Home: 3797 Wonderland Hill Ave Boulder CO 80302 Office: High Altitude Observatory PO Box 3000 Boulder CO 80307

NEWLAND, CHESTER ALBERT, educator; b. Kansas City, Kans., June 18, 1930; s. Guy Wesley and Mary Virginia (Yoakum) N.; B.A., N. Tex. State U., Denton, 1954; M.A., U. Kans., 1955, Ph.D., 1958. Social Sci. Research Council fellow, 1958-59; instr. polit. sci. Idaho State U., 1959-60; mem. faculty N. Tex State U., 1960-66, prof. govt., 1963-66, dir. dept. govt., 1963-66; vis. prof. pub. adminstrn. U. So. Calif., 1966-67, prof. pub. administration, 1968-71, 76—; prof. polit. sci. U. Houston, 1967-68, dir. Lyndon B. Johnson Library, 1968-70; mem. faculty Fed. Exec. Inst., 1971-76, dir., 1973-76; mgr. task force on fed. labor-mgmt. relations U.S. Personnel Mgmt. Project, Pres.'s Reorgn., Washington, 1977-78. Chmn. Municipal Research Council, Denton, 1963-64; city councilman, Denton, 1964-66; mem. Pub. Sector Commn. on Productivity and Work Quality, 1974-78. Mem. Nat. Acad. Pub. Adminstrn., Southwestern Social Sci. Assn. (chmn. govt. sect. 1964-65), Am. Soc. Pub. Adminstrn. (pres. Dallas-Ft. Worth chpt. 1964-65, nat. council 1976, 78—, editorial bd. jour. 1972-76, chmn. publs. com. 1975-79, program chmn. 1977), Am., Western polit. sci. assns., Internat. Personnel Mgmt. Assn. (program chmn. 1978), Midwest Conf. Polit. Scientists, Am. Acad. Polit. and Social Sci. Contbr. articles profl. jours. Office: Washington Pub Affairs Center U So Calif 512 10th St NW Washington DC 20004

NEWLAND, THOMAS WILLS, hosp. adminstr.; b. Mokpo, Korea, July 6, 1915 (parents Am. citizens); s. Leroy Tate and Sara Louise (Andrews) N.; B.A., Presbyn. Coll., Clinton, S.C., 1937; m. Ruth Josephine Huffman, Dec. 17, 1938; 1 son, Thomas Judson. With Hawaiian Ins. Agy., 1946-47; adminstr. Minnie G. Boswell Meml. Hosp., Greensboro, Ga., 1948-49, Athens (Ga.) Gen. Hosp., 1952-55; with Ft. Sanders Presbyn. Hosp., Knoxville, Tenn., 1955—, now pres.; preceptor Cornell U., George Washington U., Washington U., St. Louis, U. Ala. Mem. Tenn. Bd. Nursing. Bd. dirs. Knoxville Better Bus. Bur.; bd. dirs. Knoxville chpt. Am. Cancer Soc., Blue Cross-Blue Shield Tenn. Served with USNR, 1942-46, 50-52. Fellow Am. Coll. Hosp. Adminstrs. (bd. regents); mem. Royal Soc. Health, Internat. Hosp. Congress, Am., Tenn. (past pres., trustee; Distinguished Service award) hosp. assns., Southeastern Hosp. Conf. (pres. 1973). Kiwanian, Elk. Clubs: Fort Loudon Yacht, Cherokee Country. Home: 865 Cherokee Blvd Knoxville TN 37919 Office: 1909 Clinch Ave SW Knoxville TN 37916

NEWLEY, ANTHONY, actor; b. Hackney, Eng., Sept. 24, 1931; ed. London schs.; m. Ann Lynn, Aug. 3O, 1956; m. 2d, Joan Collins, May 26, 1963 (div.); 2 children. Motion picture appearances include Above Us the Waves, Cockleshell Heroes, Battle of the River Plate, Port Afrique, Fire Down Below, Good Companions, X The Unknown, How To Murder a Rich Uncle, High Flight, No Time To Die, The Man Inside, The Bandit of Zhobe, The Lady in a Square, Idle on Parade, The Killer of Kilimanjaro, Jazzboat, In the Nick, Let's Get Married, The Heart of a Man, The Small World of Sammy Lee, Dr. Dolittle, Can Hieronymous Merkin Ever Forget Mercy Humppe and Find True Happiness? (also producer and writer), Sweet November, Quilp; TV appearances include Vic Oliver Show, Alfred Marks Show, The Wharf Road Mob, Picture Parade, Cranks, Sammy, Sunday Night at the London Palladium, Focus on Youth, Saturday Spectacular, Shirley Bassey Show, Music Shop, The Tonight Show, Merv Griffin Show, also Anthony Newley Shows, 1960-61, The Strange World of Gurney Slade, 1960-61; stage appearances in Cranks, Anthony Newley Show; also Stop the World—I Want to Get Off (co-author, co-composer, co-dir.), 1961-62, Roar of the Greasepaint-The Smell of the Crowd (co-author, co-composer with Bricusse), The Good Old Bad Old Days, 1972-73; dir. film Summertree, 1971; co-composer play The Good Old Bad Old Days, 1972; rec. artists for United Artists, Los Angeles. Address: care Internat Creative Mgmt 8899 Beverly Blvd Los Angeles CA 90048*

NEWLIN, ALBERT CHAUNCEY, lawyer; b. Cin., Aug. 8, 1905; s. Edgar Christian and Elizabeth (Berwanger) N.; A.B., Centre Coll., Danville, Ky., 1925, LL.D., 1958; LL.B., Columbia U., 1928; D.Sc., Fla. Inst. Tech., Melbourne; m. Janet Bethell, Oct. 19, 1929 (dec.); children—George Christian, John Bethell, Carl Albert; m. 2d, Mary Carson Bass Gibson, Aug. 23, 1976. Admitted to N.Y. bar, 1928, since practiced in N.Y.C.; with White & Case, 1928-77, mem. firm, 1937-77, ret., 1977; dir. Tolten Corp., N.Y.C. Mem. bd. edn., Scarsdale, N.Y., 1947-52, pres., 1949-50. Pres., dir. Marshall H. and Nellie Alworth Meml. Fund, Duluth, Minn.; v.p., dir. Jessie Smith Noyes Found., Inc., Henry L. and Grace Doherty Charitable Found., N.Y.C.; bd. dirs. Met. Opera Assn., N.Y.C., Guild Hall, East Hampton, N.Y.; trustee Solomon R. Guggenheim Found., N.Y.C.; former chmn. bd., trustee Centre Coll. Mem. Am., N.Y. State bar assns., Assn. Bar City N.Y., N.Y. County Lawyers Assn., Phi Beta Kappa, Sigma Chi, Omicron Delta Kappa. Republican. Episcopalian. Clubs: University, Down Town Assn. (N.Y.C.); Maidstone (East Hampton). Home: 850 Park Ave Apt 7C New York NY 10021 Office: 14 Wall St New York NY 10005

NEWLIN, CHARLES WILLIAM, civil engr., educator; b. Terre Haute, Ind., Feb. 3, 1924; s. Charles Coulter and Mayme Aline (Terhune) N.; B.S. in Engring., Rose Poly. Inst., 1947; M.S., Harvard, 1949; Ph.D., Northwestern U., 1965; m. Judith Deane, Jan. 1, 1974; children by previous marriage—Robert C., Deborah S. (Mrs. Donald Beeman). From instr. to asst. prof. engring. Swarthmore (Pa.) Coll., 1949-61; from asso. prof. to prof. civil engring. Ariz. State U., Tempe, 1961-74, chmn. dept.; sr. engr. Dames and Moore; 1974—. Mem. U.S. Geol.' Survey, U.S. Soil Conservation Service, Harza Engring. Co., Moran Proctor, Mueser & Rutledge, Pa. Turnpke Commn. Mem. Ariz. State Bd. Tech. Registration, 1967-74, chmn., 1969. Served to 1st lt. C.E., AUS, 1943-46. NSF faculty grantee, Ford Found. faculty grantee. Registered profl. engr., Ariz., Pa., Calif. Mem. ASCE, Am. Soc. Engring. Edn., Ariz. (chpt. pres.), Nat. socs. profl. engrs., Nat. Council Engring. Examiners (nat. com.), Sigma Xi, Tau Beta Pi. Home: 7223 N 15th Pl Phoenix AZ 85020 Office: Dames and Moore 234 N Central Ave Suite 111A Phoenix AZ 85004. *Problems involving things either have been solved or can be solved relatively easily. I have come to the realization that people problems should be primary in the endeavors of educated man. How sad it is that man is so poorly prepared for and so little interested in this vital task.*

NEWMAN, ANDREW JOSEPH, JR., editor; b. N.Y.C., July 3, 1917; s. Andrew Joseph and Mary (Hess) N.; A.B., Dartmouth, 1939; student Harvard, 1939-41; m. Dorothy M. Ogden, July 26, 1947; children—Andrew, Jane. Financial editor Phila. Bull., 1968—. Served with Am. Field Service, 1945. Home: 535 Ballytore Rd Wynnewood PA 19096 Office: Phila Bull 30th and Market Sts Philadelphia PA 19101

NEWMAN, ARNOLD, photographer; b. N.Y.C., Mar. 3, 1918; s. Isidore and Freda (Perell) N.; student U. Miami, Coral Gables, Fla., 1937-38; m. Augusta Rubenstein, Mar. 6, 1949; children—Eric Allan, David Saul. Began photography, 1938, exptl. portraiture, 1941; opened N.Y.C. studio, 1946; exhibited and represented in collections of: Mus. Modern Art, N.Y.C., Met. Mus., N.Y.C., Chgo. Art Inst., Smithsonian Instn., Washington, Phila. Mus. Art, Internat. Mus. Photography at George Eastman House, Rochester, N.Y., Photography Gallery, London, Eng., Israel Mus., Jerusalem, Moderna Museet, Stockholm, Nat. Portrait Gallery, London, others; represented by Light Gallery, N.Y.C. Adj. prof. photography Cooper Union, N.Y.C., 1968-75, vis. prof., 1975—; lectr. U.S. and abroad. Recipient Photokina award, Cologne, Germany, 1951, Newhouse citation Syracuse (N.Y.) U., 1961, Gold medal 4th Biennale Internazionale della Fotagrafic, Venice, Italy, 1963, others. Mem. Am. Soc. Mag. Photographers (Life Achievement in Photography award 1975). Author: Bravo Stravinsky, 1967; One Mind's Eye—The Portraits and Other Photographs of Arnold Newman, 1974; Faces USA, 1978; The Great British, 1979. Contbr. to Life, Look, Holiday, Fortune, Esquire, Town and Country, Travel and Leisure, others, 1946—; subject of Nebr. Ednl. TV program The Image Makers—The Environment of Arnold Newman, 1977. Home: 33 W 67th St New York NY 10023 Office: 39 W 67th St New York NY 10023

NEWMAN, BARRY FOSTER, actor; b. Boston, Nov. 7, 1938; s. Carl Henry and Sarah (Ostrovsky) N.; ed. Brandeis U., 1958. Starred in films: Lawyer, Vanishing Point, Salzburg Connection, Fear Is The Key; star TV series, Petrocelli, 1974-76, TV movie Sex and the Married Woman, 1977. Nominee for Emmy award for best actor in TV series, Golden Globe award for best actor. Office: care Chasin-Park-Citron Agy 9255 Sunset Blvd Los Angeles CA 90069*

NEWMAN, BERNARD, judge; b. N.Y.C., Oct. 28, 1907; s. Isidor J. and Sarah C. (Berkowitz) N.; B.S., N.Y. U., 1928, LL.B., 1929: m. Kathryn Bereano, Apr. 3, 1933; children—Phyllis Newman Checkini Helene Newman Bernstein. Admitted to N.Y. bar, 1930; with firm Newman & Newman, intermittently, 1930-65; asst. corp. counsel City N.Y. 1936-42; law sec. to N.Y. Supreme Ct. Justice Samuel H. Hofstadter, 1942-48; ofcl. referee appellate div. N.Y. Supreme Ct., 1948-62, spl. referee, 1963-65; justice N.Y. Supreme Ct., 1962; judge Family Ct. N.Y., N.Y.C., 1965-68, U.S. Customs Ct., 1968—; lectr. motion practice N.Y. U. Law Sch., Practicing Law Inst.; speaker colls., univs., civic assns.; mem. spl. panel examiners N.Y. State Labor Relations Bd.; spl. panel arbitrators N.Y. State Mediation Bd.; govt. appeals agt. Selective Service. Pres. P.T.A. High Sch. of Sci., N.Y.C., 1953-56, Bentley High Sch., N.Y.C., 1955-56; mem. exec. com. Fedn. Jewish Philanthropies. Dist. leader Republican party, 1955-62; counsel N.Y. Rep. County Com., 1957- 58; chmn. N.Y. County Rep. Com., 1958-62, five county N.Y.C. Republican Party, 1958-62; mem. exec. com. N.Y. Rep. State Com., 1958-62; del. to jud., state, nat. convs. Bd. dirs. Met. adv. bd. Anti-Defamation League, LaGuardia Meml. Assn., Civic Center Synagogue, Community Synagogue Center, N.Y.C., patron Met. Opera Assn., 1962—. Served with USCG, World War II. Recipient Silver medal Nat. Essay Contest; named Merit Man for N.Y.C.; cited by Internat. Trade Bd., N.Y. U. Mem. Am., N.Y. State bar assns., Fed. Bar Council, Assn. Bar City N.Y., Nat. Legal Aid Assn., N.Y. U. Law Rev. Alumni Assn. (pres. 1958-61, gov. and dir. 1956—). Jewish (dir. congregations 1950—). Home: 25 E 9th St New York NY 10003 Office: 1 Federal Plaza New York NY 10007

NEWMAN, CHARLES, author, editor, educator; b. St. Louis, May 27, 1938; s. Charles H. and June (Toney) N.; B.A. summa cum laude, Yale, 1960; postgrad. Balliol Coll. Oxford (Eng.) U., 1960-62. Instr. English, Northwestern U., Evanston, Ill., 1964-65, asst. prof., 1965-68, asso. prof., 1968-73, prof., 1974-75; prof., chmn. The Writing Seminars, Johns Hopkins, 1975-77. Dir. Coordinating Council Lit. Mags., Nat. Endowment for the Arts, Washington, 1968-74; dir. P.E.N., 1976—. Recipient Midland Authors Soc. Distinguished Service award, 1973; Distinguished Service award Friends of Lit., 1973; Zabel prize innovative writing Nat. Inst. Arts and Letters, 1975. Woodrow Wilson fellow, 1960-61; Fulbright grantee, 1961-62; Rockefeller grantee for creative writing, 1967-68; Nat. Endowment Creative Writing fellow, 1973; Ingram Merrill grantee creative writing, 1974; Guggenheim fellow, 1974-75. Author: (novels) New Axis, 1968; The Promisekeeper, 1971; There Must be More to Love Than Death, 1976; (non-fiction) A Child's History of America, 1973; contbr. short stories to various mags. and anthologies including Best American Short Stories of 1971, 77. Editor: New Writing from East Europe, 1968; New American Writers Under Thirty, 1970; The Art of Sylvia Plath, 1970; Nabokov: Criticism and Reminiscences, Translations and Tributes, 1970; Literature in Revolution, 1972; Prose for Borges, 1974; founder, editor Tri Quar. Rev., 1964-75, adv. editor, 1975—. Contbr. numerous articles to profl. jours., mag., newspapers. Address: Box 65 Volney VA 24379

NEWMAN, DAVID, writer; b. N.Y.C., Feb. 4, 1937; s. Herman and Rose (Spatz) N.; B.A., U. Mich., 1958, M.A., 1959; m. Leslie Harris England, June 22, 1958; children—Nathan, Catherine. Editor, Esquire mag., 1960-64, contbg. editor, 1964—; free-lance writer, 1964—; columnist Mademoiselle mag., 1964-74. Recipient Avery Hopwood Fiction award, 1957, Hopwood Drama award, 1958, N.Y. Film Critics Best Screenplay award, 1967, Nat. Film Critics Best Screenplay award, 1967, award best drama and best original for Bonnie and Clyde, Writers Guild Am., 1967. Co-author: Bonnie and Clyde, 1967; There Was A Crooked Man, 1970; What's Up, Doc?, 1971; (screenplay) Papillon, 1971; (with Robert Benton) Bad Company, 1972; It's a Bird, It's a Plane, It's Superman, 1966; O, Calcutta, 1969; Extremism, 1966; Esquire World of Humor, 1964; Esquire Book of Gambling, 1963; (screenplay) Superman, 1978. Address: care Esquire Mag 488 Madison Ave New York NY 10022*

NEWMAN, EDWARD, social scientist, educator; b. N.Y.C., Mar. 13, 1934; s. Jerome J. and Mollie (Dressler) N.; B.A., Drew U., 1956; M.S. in Social Adminstrn., Western Res. U., 1958; Ph.D., Brandeis U., 1968; D.H.L., World U., 1970; m. Claire Dresner, June 9, 1957; children—Mark, Julie, Paul. Coordinator Mass. Mental Retardation Planning Project, Boston, 1964-66; exec. dir. Vocational Rehab. Planning Commn. Mass., Boston, 1966-68; asst. for program planning and coordination human resources programs div. Bur. Budget, Washington, 1968-69; commr. rehab. services adminstrn., social and rehab. service Dept. Health, Edn. and Welfare, Washington, 1969-72; v.p., sr. asso. Linton, Mields & Coston, Inc., 1973-74; dir. human services planning, prof. social adminstrn. Temple U., Phila., 1974—. Project dir., cons. various fed. and state programs in human services, 1963—; condr. Washington interagy. rev. com. Neighborhood Services Program, 1967-68; mem. Mass. Mental Retardation Adv. Council, 1967-68; mem. Pa. Gov.'s Council on Developmental Disabilities, 1974—; lectr. Boston U. Sch. Social Work, 1965-68; cons. Govt. of Israel, 1973—, HEW, 1979—; vis. prof., chmn. Center for Rehab., Haifa U., 1977—; chmn. Gov.'s Task Force on Developmental Disabilities, 1976. Mem. profl. adv. council Nat. Goodwill Industries of Am., 1972—; bd. dirs. Epilepsy Found. Am., 1976—. Recipient Distinguished Service award Stout State U., 1971, Annual Homebound Rehab. award, 1971, Nat. Goodwill award, 1970; citations N.J. Rehab. Assn., Mass. Assn. Retarded Children. Mem. Nat. Assn. Social Workers, Nat. Rehab. Assn., Am. Pub. Health Assn., Am. Soc. Pub. Adminstrn., Acad. Certified Social Workers. Jewish religion. Author: Helping All the Handicapped. Contbr. to profl. jours. Home: 534 Elkins Ave Elkins Park PA 19117 Office: Temple U Philadelphia PA 19122

NEWMAN, EDWIN HAROLD, news commentator; b. N.Y.C., Jan. 25, 1919; s. Myron and Rose (Parker) N.; B.A., U. Wis., 1940; postgrad. (fellow) La. State U., 1940; m. Rigel Grell, Aug. 14, 1944; 1 dau., Nancy (Mrs. Henry Drucker). With Washington bur. Internat. News Service, 1941, U.P., 1941-42, 45-46, N.Y. Daily PM, 1946-47, ind. Washington news bur., 1947; asst to Eric Sevareid at Washington bur. CBS, 1947-49; free lance writer, broadcaster, London, Eng., 1949-52, also worked for European Recovery Program, 1951-52; with NBC, 1952—, chief news bur., London, 1956-57, Rome, Italy, 1957-58, Paris, France, 1958-61, news commentator, N.Y.C., 1961—; narrator TV spls. including Japan: East is West, 1961, Orient Express, 1964, Who Shall Live?, 1965, Politics: The Outer Fringe, 1966, Pensions-The Broken Promise, 1972, Violence in America, 1977, I Want It All Now, 1978, Spying for Uncle Sam, 1978; moderator 1st Ford—Carter Debate, 1976; drama critic WNBC-TV, 1965-71. Served from ensign to lt. USNR, 1942-45. Decorated chevalier Legion of Honor (France); recipient awards Overseas Press Club, 1961, U. Wis. Sch. Journalism, 1967, U. Mo. Sch. Journalism, 1975, Emmy awards, 1966, 68, 70, 72, 73, 74, Peabody award, 1966. Mem. Assn. Radio-Television News Analysts (pres. 1966), A.F.T.R.A. Author: Strictly Speaking: Will America Be The Death of English?, 1974; A Civil Tongue, 1976; Sunday Punch, 1979. Contbr. articles and revs. to various periodicals, U.S. and Eng. Office: care NBC 30 Rockefeller Plaza New York NY 10020

NEWMAN, ELIAS, artist; b. Stashow, Poland, Feb. 12, 1903; s. Simon and Rebecca (Becker) N.; came to U.S., 1913, naturalized, 1928; student N.A.D., 1919-20, Edn. Alliance Art Sch., 1920-25; m. Lillian Judith Tesser, Feb. 26, 1945. One-man shows, 1927—, including Balt. Mus. Art, 1930, 41, Montross Gallery, N.Y.C., 1932, Md. Art Inst., Balt., 1935, 36, Maxwell Galleries, San Francisco, 1945, Phila. Art Alliance, 1946, Jewish Mus. N.Y.C., 1949, Babcock Galleries N.Y.C., 1947, 49, 51, 53, 60, Tel-Aviv Mus. Israel, 1934, 38, 49, 62, Werbe Galleries, Detroit, 1956, Doll, Richards Galleries, Boston, 1947, 50, 60; participated juried exhbns., including N.A.D., Am. Acad. Arts and Letters, Am. Watercolor Soc., Nat. Soc. Painters in Casein and Acrylics, Audubon Artists, Rockport Art Assn., Am. Soc. Contemporary Artists, Butler Mus. Art, Youngstown, Ohio, Cape Ann Soc. Modern Artists; works in permanent collections Nat. Collection Fine Arts of Smithsonian Instn., Jewish Mus., N.Y.C., San Francisco Mus., Balt. Art Mus., John Herron Mus. Art, Indpls., Denver Mus. Art, Tel-Aviv (Israel) Mus., Bklyn. Mus., Haifa Mus. Modern Art, Israel, Histadruth House, Tel Aviv, Israel, Butler Mus. Am. Art, Boston Mus. Fine Arts, Nebr. U. Gallery, Inst. Man and Sci., Rensselaerville, N.Y., Brandeis U., Boston U., Joslyn Mus., Omaha, Addison Gallery Am. Art, Andover, Mass., George Washington Carver Mus., Tuskegee, Ala., Arnot Art Mus., Elmira, N.Y., Everson Mus. Art, Syracuse, N.Y., Slater Meml. Mus., Norwich, Conn., Norfolk (Va.) Mus. Arts and Scis., Phoenix Mus. Art, Met. Ins. Co., Newark, others; art dir. Palestine Pavilion, N.Y. World's Fair, 1939-40. Chmn. Conf. Am. Artists, 1971—; exec. officer Artists Welfare Fund, 1975—. Served with C.A.C., AUS, 1942-43. Recipient Minnie R. Stern Meml. medal and prize Audubon Artists 18th Ann. Exhibit, N.Y., 1960, Pauline Mintz Meml. award at 28th Ann. Exhibit, 1970, Stanley Grumbacher Meml. medal and prize 35th Ann. Exhibit, 1977; awards Nat. Soc. Painters in Casein and Acrylics; Joseph Mayer Co. prize, 1966; Gramercy prize 1968; M.J. Kaplan Meml. prize, 1970; Today's Art mag. medal merit, 1971; Beatrice S. Katz prize Am. Soc. Contemporary Artists, 1971. Mem. Palestine Artist and Sculptors Assn. (organizer 1935), Am. Artists for Israel (chmn. 1949), Cape Ann Soc. Modern Artists (pres. 1958-59), Am. Soc. Contemporary Artists (dir. 1970), Artists Equity Assn. (nat. sec. 1954, exec. dir. 1959-60, pres. N.Y. chpt. 1960-62, v.p. 1963-64, 67, 68), Artists Equity Assn. N.Y. (pres. 1970-75, pres. emeritus, 1975—), Municipal Art Assn. N.Y., Audubon Artists (dir. 1971-74, treas. 1976-77, dir. 1977-78, v.p. 1978—), Conf. Am. Artists (chmn. 1971—), Nat. Soc. Painters in Casein (dir. 1963, chmn. ways and means com. 1966, pres. 1967-71, hon. pres. 1971—), Zionist Orgn. Am. Club: Overseas Press. Author: Art in Palestine, 1939. Home: 215 Park Row New York NY 10038 Studio: 32 Union Sq New York NY. *I have tried in the course of my life in art to be guided by the following concepts: Art is a continuum that expresses the time in which we live. I am involved with the phenomenon of nature, the changing scene and the life around me. I believe that each painting should be the result of an experience deeply felt. I try to absorb influences, refine them and recreate them in my own image. I believe great works of art always had affinity with humanity, nature, and the soul of mankind.*

NEWMAN, ERIC PFEIFFER, shoe chain store exec.; b. St. Louis, May 25, 1911; s. Samuel Elijah and Rose (Pfeiffer) N.; B.S., Mass. Inst. Tech., 1932; J.D., Washington U., St. Louis, 1935; m. Evelyn Edison, Nov. 29, 1939; children—Linda (Mrs. Peter Jay Solomon), Andrew Edison. Admitted to Mo. bar, 1935; practice in St. Louis, 1935-43; with Edison Bros. Stores, Inc., St. Louis, 1944, sec., 1951—, v.p., 1964-68, exec. v.p., 1968—. Pres., Community Sch., 1952-53, Mark Twain Summer Inst., 1963-67; treas. Jefferson Nat. Expansion Meml. Assn., 1970-77; chmn. U.S. Assay Commn., 1967—; chmn. coins and medals panel Am. Revolution Bicentennial Commn., 1972-74; trustee Harry Edison Found., 1959—. Recipient Farran Zerbe award, 1969, Archer M. Huntington medal, 1979. Mem. Eric P. Newman Numis. Soc. (pres. 1959—), Am. Numis. Soc. (council 1963—, Archer M. Huntington medal 1978), Am. Numism. Assn. (11 Heath Lit. awards), Am. Antiquarian Soc. Club: Explorers. Author: Coinage for Colonial Virginia, 1957; The Secret of the Good Samaritan Shilling, 1959; The Fantastic 1804 Dollar, 1962; The Early Paper Money of America, 1967, rev. edit., 1976; editor: Studies on Money in Early America, 1976. Home: 6450 Cecil Ave Saint Louis MO 63105 Office: 400 Washington Ave Saint Louis MO 63102

NEWMAN, FRANK, univ. pres.; b. Flushing, N.Y., Feb. 24, 1927; s. Frank and Dorothy (Lawlor) N.; student Bucknell U., 1944; A.B., Brown U., 1946, B.S., 1949; postgrad. Oxford (Eng.) U., 1949; M.S., Columbia, 1955; Litt.D., U. Dubuque, 1972; H.H.D., U. Redlands, 1972; LL.D., Elmira Coll., 1973; D.Sc., Lowell Technol. Inst., 1975; m. Lucile Pettibone Fanning, Oct. 13, 1951; children—Kenneth C., James L., Michael H. Market sales mgr. Mpls.-Honeywell Regulator Co., N.Y.C., 1949-55; div. mgr. Beckman Instruments, Inc., Richmond, Calif., 1955-66; asso. gen. sec. Stanford, 1967-70, asso. dir. univ. relations, 1970-72, dir., 1972-74; pres. U. R.I., Kingston, 1974—. Faculty mem. WACUBO Bus. Mgmt. Inst., Stanford U., Workshop on Liberal Arts, Colo. Coll.; chmn. task forces HEW, 1969-71, 71-73; mem. Carnegie Council on Policy Studies in Higher Edn., Council for Northeast Econ. Action. Bd. dirs. Am. Council on Edn., trustee Carnegie Found. for Advancement of Teaching, Barnard Coll., N.Y.C. Served with USNR, 1944-47. Mem. Am. Assn. Higher Edn., Am. Hist. Assn. Author: (with others) Report on Higher Education, 1971; (with others) National Policy and Higher Education, 1973. Home: 56 Upper College Rd Kingston RI 02881 Office: President's Office U RI Kingston RI 02881

NEWMAN, FRANK CECIL, state justice; b. Eureka, Calif., July 17, 1917; s. Frank J. and Anna (Dunn) N.; A.B., Dartmouth Coll., 1938; LL.B., U. Calif., 1941; LL.M., Columbia U., 1947, J.S.D. 1953; LL.D., U. Santa Clara, 1978; m. Frances Burks, Jan. 14, 1940; children—Robert, Julie, Carol. Admitted to Calif. bar, 1942; prof. law U. Calif. at Berkeley, 1946—, Jackson H. Ralston prof. internat. law emeritus, dean Sch. Law, 1961-66; vis. prof. law schs. Harvard U.,

1953-54, U. Wash., summer 1952, Salzburg Seminar in Am. Studies, Austria, summer 1954, 64, Strasbourg, France, summer 1970, 71, 75, 77, Center Advanced Study in Behavioral Scis., 1957-58; law book editorial bd. Little, Brown & Co., 1956-77; justice Calif. Supreme Ct., San Francisco, 1977—; atty. OPA, N.Y.C. and Washington, 1942-43, Office Gen. Counsel Dept. Navy, 1943-46; cons. OPS, 1951; counsel Gov. Calif. Commn. on Unemployment Compensation, 1952; cons. GAO, 1959, Calif. Agr. and Services Agy., 1975-76; dir. Fed. Home Loan Bank, San Francisco, 1962-70; mem. exec. com., chmn. drafting com. Calif. Constn. Revision Commn., 1964-72. Mem. nat. adv. council Amnesty U.S.A. Served from ensign to lt. USNR, 1943-46. Mem. Internat. Inst. Human Rights (v.p.). Author: (with Stanley S. Surrey) Newman and Surrey on Legislation, 1955; (with Richard B. Lillich) International Human Rights: Problems of Law and Policy, 1979. Bd. editors Human Rights Jour., Strasbourg, 1968—. Office: State Bldg San Francisco CA 94102

NEWMAN, GERALD, restaurant franchise co. exec.; b. Chgo., May 26, 1931; s. Morris and Sara (Glaser) N.; student Chgo. City Jr. Colls., 1949-51, U. Ill., 1949; B.S., Roosevelt U., 1957; m. Bobbi F. Greenblatt, Dec. 18, 1955; children—Marc, Jeffrey. Bookkeeper, Evans Fur Co., Chgo., 1951; controller Stacy Constrn. Co., Chgo., 1951-59; co-owner, accountant Met. Roofing Co., Chgo., 1959-61; with McDonald's Corp., Oak Brook, Ill., 1961—, v.p., controller, 1969-72, exec. v.p., 1972—, also dir.; dir. Family Foods of Holland; former chmn. bd. Golden Arches of Eng., 1976—. Mem. Am. Inst. Corp. Controllers. Office: 1 McDonald's Plaza Oak Brook IL 60521

NEWMAN, GORDON HAROLD, lawyer, food co. exec.; b. Sioux City, Iowa, Mar. 31, 1933; s. George I. and Esther (Goldman) N.; B.S.C., U. Iowa, 1955, J.D. with distinction, 1961; m. Toby M. Dunitz, Dec. 26, 1955; children—Debra Susan, Stacy Fae, Eric Scott. Asso. firm Gamble, Riepe, Martin & Webster, Des Moines, 1961-62; asst. counsel, asst. sec. Bell & Howell Co., 1962-67; asso. gen. counsel, asst. sec. Consol. Foods Corp., Chgo., 1967-70, sr. v.p., sec., gen. counsel, 1970—. Served to 1st lt. USAF, 1955-58. Mem. Chgo. Bar Assn., Ill. Bar Assn., Am. Bar Assn., Am. Soc. Corp. Secs. Club: Union League (Chgo.). Home: 58 Sheridan Rd Highland Park IL 60035 Office: 135 S LaSalle St Chicago IL 60603*

NEWMAN, GUY DOUGLAS, clergyman, univ. chancellor; b. Dorchester, Tex., Dec. 9, 1907; s. W. W. and Lois (Helvv) N.; A.B., Baylor U., 1941; Th.M., Southwestern Theol. Sem., Ft. Worth. 1946. Th.D., 1952; m. Estelle McKneely. May 29, 1938; children—Guy Douglas, Patricia (Mrs. Guy Garner), Charlotte (Mrs. Robert Harris), Bobbie (Mrs. Fred Strickland). Ordained to Ministry Bapt. Ch., 1933; pastor 1st Ch., Groom, Tex., 1933-34; asst. pastor 1st Ch., Amarillo, Tex., 1934-35, interim pastor, 1936; asst. pastor 7th and James Ch., Waco, Tex., 1936-39; pastor Meml. Ch., Temple, Tex., 1939-42. 1st Ch., Denison, Tex., 1942-48, 1st Ch., Brownwood, Tex., 1951-52; asst. to pres. Baylor U., Waco. 1949-50, promotional v.p., 1952-55; pres. Howard Payne Coll., Brownwood, 1955-73, chancellor, 1973—. Originator Democracy In Action, program to promote Americanism on coll. and high sch. campuses. Press Tng. Union Conv. of Tex., 1944-48; mem. exec. bd. Bapt. Gen. Conv. of Tex., 1944-52; mem. Pres.'s Nat. Com. Conf. Children and Youth, 1960; mem. Pres.'s Com. Selection White House Fellows, 1975. Bd. dirs. Tex. Youth Council, Tex. United Fund. Founder, Douglas MacArthur Acad. Freedom at Howard Payne Coll. Recipient Freedoms Found. award, 1960, Wisdom award of Honor, 1970. Mason, Rotarian. Club: Knife and Fork (roving reporter, speaker for nat. asso. clubs). Author: When God Invaded History, 1958. Home: 106 Brentwood Dr Brownwood TX 76801 Office: Newman Hall Acad Freedom Coggin Ave Brownwood TX 76801

NEWMAN, HAROLD W., JR., author; b. New Orleans, Dec. 22, 1899; s. Harold W. and Bellagie (Israel) N.; B.A., Tulane U., 1920; LL.B., Harvard, 1923; m. Gwyneth M. Orme, Dec. 2, 1953. Gen. practice law, N.Y.C., 1923-32; asst. gen. counsel RFC, 1932-35; v.p., gen. counsel Met. Casualty Ins. Co., Newark, 1935-37; gen. practice, N.Y.C., 1937-42; gen. counsel Office Civilian Def., 1942-43; European travel writer, 1949-68. Mem. Phi Beta Kappa. Author: Newman's European Travel Guide, 12th edit., 1968; Veilleuses, 1750-1860, 1967; (with George Savage) Illustrated Dictionary of Ceramics 1974; Illustrated Dictionary of Glass, 1977; Illustrated Dictionary of Jewelry, 1980; editor: Harvard Law Rev., 1922-23. Contbr. articles on ceramics to art periodicals. Home: New Orleans LA also (winter) 54 Cadogan Sq London SW1X-OJW England

NEWMAN, HARRY RUDOLPH, educator, urologist; b. Russia, Sept. 10, 1909; s. Abraham and Mary (Rudolph) N.; M.D., U. Toronto, 1935; M.S., U. Pa., 1940; m. Lillian Lear, Aug. 18, 1942; children—Nancy Ellen, Robert Lear, Suzanne Mary. Canadian citizen, 1919; came to U.S., 1935, naturalized, 1944. Resident urology U. Minn. Hosps., 1936-37, All Saints Hosp., London, Eng., 1937-38; sr. resident urology N.Y. Postgrad. Med. Sch. and Hosp., 1939-40, Boston Long Island Hosp., 1941-42; resident surgery N.Y. Postgrad. Hosp., 1942; resident gen. surgery Prince of Wales Hosp., Plymouth, Eng.; attending urologist Yale New-Haven Community Hosp.; attending univ. service Yale, also prof. urology; dir. urology Albert Einstein Coll. Medicine, also clin. prof. surgery, chief urology, 1957—, clin. prof. urology, 1957-62, prof. urology, 1963-65, 66—, chmn. dept., 1966—; chief urology Bronx Municipal Hosp., 1966—; chief urology community div. Grace New Haven Hosp., 1965-66; cons. urologist Stamford (Conn.) Hosp., St. Joseph Hosp., Stamford, 1965—; former asst. clin. prof. urology N.Y.U.; dir. urology City N.Y. Bronx Municipal Med. Center, 1954-65; cons. urologist Griffin Hosp., Derby, Conn. Served from capt. to maj., USAAF, 1942-46, chief urology Regional Hosp., Hunter Field, Savannah, Ga. Diplomate Am. Bd. Urology. Fellow A.C.S., N.Y. Acad. Medicine. Mason (32 deg., Shriner). Clubs: Yale (New Haven); Woodbridge (Conn.) Country. Home: 95 Broadfield Rd Hamden CT 06517 Office: 2 Church St S New Haven CT 06510

NEWMAN, HERBERT ELLIS, educator; b. Birmingham, Ala., Sept. 12, 1914; s. Herbert E. and Henrietta (Chiles) N.; A.B. summa cum laude, Birmingham-So. Coll., 1936; A.M., U. Va., 1938, Ph.D., 1940. Instr., U. Va., 1939-40; instr. U. Del., 1940-42, asst. prof., 1944-46, asso. prof., 1946-52, prof., 1952-58; prof., chmn. dept. econs. Dickinson Coll., 1958-66; prof. econs. Hood Coll., 1966-78, emeritus, 1978—, chmn. dept. econs., 1969-78, dir. grad. studies, 1971-74; economist with OPA, 1942-44. Research fellow Brookings Instn., 1938-39. Mem. Phi Beta Kappa. Author: An Introduction To Public Finance, 1968. Home: 15 Brooklawn Apts Frederick MD 21701

NEWMAN, HOWARD ARTHUR, corp. exec.; b. N.Y.C., Feb. 2, 1921; s. Jerome A. and Estelle (Reiss) N.; A.B. Cornell U., 1942; m. Maria Teisseire, 1973. Pres., Hopewell Internat. Corp., exporters, 1947-49; v.p., treas., dir. Graham-Newman Corp., investments, N.Y.C., 1949-55; pres. Phila. and Reading Corp., 1956-68; chmn. bd. Northwest Industries, Inc., 1968-69; chmn. bd., chief exec. officer Western Pacific Industries Inc., 1970—. Bd. dirs. Jewish Guild for Blind. Served to lt. USNR, 1942-46. Office: 345 Park Ave New York NY 10022

NEWMAN, JAMES BLAKEY, physicist, educator; b. Little Rock, Jan. 10, 1917; s. John William and Mattie (Ayres) N.; B.S., Va. Mil. Inst., 1939; Ph.D., Cornell U., 1951; m. Dorothy Elizabeth Heflin, June 27, 1942; children—Dorothy Ann (Mrs. Ted Harrison Brown), Carol Dell, Harriet Ayres. Instr. physics Va. Mil. Inst., Lexington, 1939-42, asst. prof., 1949-52, asso. prof., 1952-56, prof. physics, 1956—, chmn. dept., 1964-69. Served to capt. Signal Corps, AUS, 1942-45. Mem. Am. Phys. Soc., Am. Nuclear Soc., Am. Assn. Physics Tchrs., Am. Soc. Engring. Edn., Sigma Xi. Presbyn. Home: Route 1 Box 326 B Lexington VA 24450

NEWMAN, JAMES HEFLIN, univ. cons.; b. LaFayette, Ala., June 3, 1908; s. James Robert and Sara Dean (Mathews) N.; A.B., U. Ala., 1929, M.A., 1930, LL.D., 1957; m. Dixie Ann Jones, June 6, 1940; children—Ann Dickson, James Blair. Dir. student activities Ala. Union, U. Ala., 1930-32, asst. dean men, 1932-37, asso. dean men, 1937-38, dean men, 1938-42; dean students U. Va., 1946-50; dean adminstrn. U. Ala., 1950-56, interim pres., 1957-58, exec. v.p., 1958-65; pres. Longwood Coll., Farmville, Va., 1965-67; v.p. acad. affairs Samford U., 1968-70, asst. to pres. for planning and research, 1970-73, univ. cons., 1973—. Pres. Nat. Assn. Deans and Advisers of Men, 1948-49, Assn. Ala. Coll. Adminstrs., 1958-59. Trustee Phi Gamma Delta Ednl. Found. Served from lt. (j.g.) to lt. comdr., USNR, 1942-45. Recipient Algernon Sydney Sullivan award, 1930. Mem. Newcomen Soc., Phi Beta Kappa, Phi Kappa Phi, Phi Gamma Delta, Omicron Delta Kappa, Phi Eta Sigma, Alpha Phi Omega, Jasons, Ala. Quadrangle. Episcopalian. Rotarian. Home: PO Box 743 Pell City AL 35125 Office: Samford University 800 Lakeshore Dr Birmingham AL 35209

NEWMAN, JAMES WILSON, business exec.; b. Clemson, S.C., Nov. 3, 1909; s. Charles Carter and Grace (Strode) N.; B.S., Clemson U., 1931, also LL.D. (hon.); student Am. Inst. Banking, 1931-32; J.D., N.Y. U., 1937; m. Clara Collier, July 1934; children—Clare Adelaide, Mildred Bledsoe, James Wilson, Charles Carter II. Admitted to N.Y. bar, 1937; reporter R.G. Dun & Co., 1931-46; v.p. Dun & Bradstreet, Inc., 1946-52, pres. 1952-60, chmn., chief exec. officer, 1960-68, chmn. finance com., 1968—, dir.; dir. Chem. N.Y. Corp., Chem. Bank, Gen. Foods Corp., Internat. Paper Co.; trustee Atlantic Mut. Ins. Co., Mut. Life Ins. Co. Am. Chmn. Pres.'s Task Force on Small Bus., 1969; mem. Commn. on Bankruptcy Laws U.S., 1970-73; chmn. Nat. Bur. Econ. Research, 1974-78; trustee Com. Econ. Devel., Va. Mus. Fine Arts, 1978; mem. Price Commn., 1971-72. Chmn. Sweet Briar Coll., 1963-69. Mem. Am. Bar Assn., Phi Delta Phi. Clubs: University, Links, Downtown Assn., Economic (N.Y.C.); Baltusrol Golf. Home: 21 Lake Rd Short Hills NJ 07078 Office: 99 Church St New York NY 10007

NEWMAN, JOHN NICHOLAS, naval architect; b. New Haven, Mar. 10, 1935; s. Richard and Daisy (Neumann) N.; B.S., Mass. Inst. Tech., 1956, M.S., 1957, Sc.D., 1960; postgrad. Cambridge (Eng.) U., 1958-59; m. Kathleen Smedley Kirk, June 16, 1956; children—James Bartram, Nancy Kirk, Carol Ann. Research naval architect David Taylor Model Basin, Navy Dept., Washington, 1959-67; asso. prof. naval architecture Mass. Inst. Tech., Cambridge, 1967-70, prof., 1970—; vis. prof. U. New South Wales (Australia), 1973, U. Adelaide (Australia), 1974; cons. Navy Dept., Dept. Justice, pvt. firms. Recipient prize Am. Bur. Shipping, 1956, Walter Atkinson prize, 1973, Bronze medal, 1976; Guggenheim fellow, 1973-74; research grantee Office Naval Research, NSF. Mem. Royal Instn. of Naval Architects, Soc. Naval Architects and Marine Engrs., AAAS. Author: Marine Hydrodynamics, 1977. Contbr. articles to profl. jours., including Jour. Fluid Mechs., Jour. Ship Research, Sci. Am. Home: 60 Campbell Rd Wayland MA 01778 Office: Massachusetts Institute of Technology Cambridge MA 02139

NEWMAN, JOHN SCOTT, chem. engr., educator; b. Richmond, Va., Nov. 17, 1938; s. Clarence William and Marjorie Lenore (Saucerman) N.; B.S., Northwestern U., 1960; M.S., U. Calif., Berkeley, 1962, Ph.D., 1963; m. Nguyen Thanh Lan, June 30, 1973; children—Natalie Diane, Michael Alexander. Asst. prof. chem. engring. U. Calif., Berkeley, 1963-67, asso. prof., 1967-70, prof., 1970—; prin. investigator materials and molecular research div. Lawrence Berkeley Lab., 1963—; vis. prof. U. Wis., Madison, 1973; summer participant Oak Ridge Nat. Lab., 1965, 66. Recipient Young Author's prize Electrochem. Soc., 1966, 69. Mem. Electrochem. Soc., Am. Inst. Chem. Engrs. Author: Electrochemical Systems, 1973; contbr. articles to profl. jours. Home: 114 York Ave Kensington CA 94708 Office: Dept Chem Engring U Calif Berkeley CA 94720

NEWMAN, JOHN V., agriculturist, corp. exec.; b. Pomona, Calif., Apr. 25, 1910; s. Carl V. and Florence (White) N.; B.A., Pomona Coll., 1931; m. Ruth Tantlinger, May 6, 1933; children—Peter V., Michael J. Citrus grower, rancher, 1931—; dir. Utt Devel. Co., Oxnard, Calif., 1942—, pres., 1969-76; pres. C.B.S.-Sony Calif., Inc., Oxnard, 1976—; chmn. bd. Irvine Co., Newport Beach, Calif., 1972-77; chmn. bd. Sunkist Growers, Inc., Sherman Oaks, Calif., 1971-77; dir. So. Calif. Edison Co. Mem. Calif. Bd. Agr., 1947-62; Calif. rep., spl. farm adv. com. Dept. Labor, 1950-61; agrl. adviser Employer del. ILO, Geneva, 1952—; commr. Calif. Horse Racing Bd., 1968-76, chmn., 1972-75; dir. Hollywood Park, 1977—. Bd. dirs. James Irvine Found., Pomona Coll. Mem. Council Calif. Growers (pres. 1960-61), Seaboard Lemon Assn., (dir. 1942-62, pres. 1962-72, chmn. bd. 1972—), Ventura County Citrus Growers Com. (pres. 1962-68), U.S. C. of C. (agrl. com. 1952-57), Rancheros Vistadores (dir. 1957—, pres. 1967-69). Club: California. Home: 10175 Santa Ana Rd Ventura CA 93001 Office: 4300 Etting Rd Oxnard CA 93030

NEWMAN, JON O., U.S. judge; b. N.Y.C., May 2, 1932; s. Harold W., Jr. and Estelle L. (Ormond) N.; grad. Hotchkiss Sch., 1949; A.B. magna cum laude, Princeton, 1953; LL.B., Yale, 1956; m. Martha G. Silberman, June 19, 1953; children—Leigh, Scott, David. Law clk. to judge U.S. Ct. Appeals, 1956-57; admitted to Conn. and D.C. bars, 1956; sr. law clk. to Chief Justice Earl Warren, U.S. Supreme Ct., 1957-58; mem. firm Ritter, Satter & Newman, Hartford, Conn., 1958-60; counsel to majority Conn. Gen. Assembly, 1959; spl. counsel to gov. Conn., 1959-61; asst. to sec. HEW, 1961-62; adminstrv. asst. to U.S. senator, 1963-64; U.S. atty., Conn., 1964-69; pvt. law practice, 1969-71; U.S. dist. judge Conn., 1972-79; U.S. circuit judge 2d Circuit Ct. of Appeals, 1979—. Chmn. bd. dirs. Hartford Inst. Criminal and Social Justice; mem. bd. regents U. Hartford. Mem. Conn. Bar Assn. Democrat. Co-author: Politics: The American Way. Home: 20 Brookside Blvd West Hartford CT 06107

NEWMAN, JOSEPH H., advt. agy. exec.; b. N.Y.C., Dec. 1, 1928; s. Max A. and Tillie C. (Weitzman) N.; A.B., Bethany Coll. (W.Va.), 1949; M.S., Columbia Grad. Sch. Bus., 1956; m. Ruth Z. Marcus, Dec. 19, 1954; children—Deborah Lynn, David Alan, Mark Jonathan. With 20th Century Fox Film Corp., N.Y.C., 1949-53; media supr. Fred Wittner Advt. Agy. (now Hammond Farrell Inc.), 1953-56; media dir. O.S. Tyson & Co. (now Poppe Tyson div. DeGarmo, Inc.), 1956-64; v.p., media dir. Marsteller Inc., N.Y.C., 1965—. Mem. faculty Advt. Age Media Workshop, 1972. Past chmn. com. bus. media Am. Assn. Advt. Agencies. Served with AUS, 1950-52. Named Agy. Media Exec. of Year, N.Y. chpt. Bus./Profl. Advt. Assn., 1960, 66, 71, 73. Mem. Bus./Profl. Advt. Assn. (mem. media comparability council, media data form com.). Contbr. articles to profl. jours. Home: 251-10 Van Zandt Ave Little Neck NY 11362 Office: 866 3d Ave New York NY 10022

NEWMAN, JOSEPH HERBERT, bldg. and constrn. tech. co. exec.; b. Bklyn., Feb. 2, 1925; s. Carl and Eva (Goldberg) N.; B.S. in Chem. Engring., Poly. Inst. N.Y., 1945, M.S. in Chem. Engring., 1947, fellow, 1978; m. Doris Kleigman, Jan. 1, 1950; children—Jane Beth, Douglas Carl. Research engr. Flintkote Co., 1945-51; sect. head M.W. Kellogg Co., 1951-53; asst. div. mgr. aero. div. Curtiss Wright Co., Woodridge, N.J., 1953-59; gen. mgr. Tishman Research Corp., N.Y.C., 1959-65, v.p., 1966-72, sr. v.p., 1973-76, exec. v.p., 1976—; v.p. Tishman Realty & Constrn. Co., Inc., N.Y.C., 1967-73, 1st v.p., 1974-76, sr. v.p., 1978—; sr. v.p. Tishman Constrn. & Research Co., Inc., N.Y.C., 1976-78; chmn. energy and pub. utilities com. Real Estate Bd. N.Y.C., 1972—; mem. adv. panel to bldg. research sect. Nat. Bur. Standards, 1965-68; mem. panel on housing tech U.S. Dept. Commerce, 1968-70; mem. adv. com. HUD, 1969-73; mem. com. on urban tech. NRC, 1967-69; mem. Mayor's Fire Safety Adv. Com., N.Y.C., 1970-73. Mem. Nat. Acad. Engring. (chmn. com. on tech. transfer 1973-74), Nat. Acad. Scis. (chmn. bldg. research adv. bd. 1972-73, mem. commn. on sociotech. systems 1974-77), Nat. Inst. Bldg. Scis. (dir. 1976—, chmn. 1979—), Am. Inst. Chem. Engrs., Am. Chem. Soc. Columnist, Bldg. Tech., Nat. Real Estate Investor Mag., 1975—. Home: 51 Woodland Ave West Orange NJ 07052 Office: 666 Fifth Ave New York NY 10019

NEWMAN, JOYCE KLIGERMAN, sculptor; b. Atlantic City, N.J., July 7, 1927; d. Louis and Anne (Levine) Kligerman; B.A., Cornell U., 1948; Ph.D. in Biochemistry, U. Chgo., 1955; student Art Students League, N.Y.C., 1962; m. Melvin Micklin Newman, Sept. 11, 1949; children—Rebecca, Morris Henry. Research asso. biochemistry U. Colo. Med. Center, Denver, 1963-70; mem. temp. faculty dept. chemistry Met. State Coll., 1976-77; profl. sculptor, Denver, 1968—; sculpture installed Douglas County (Colo.) Pub. Library, 1971. Mem. Artists Equity Assn. (pres. Colo. chpt. 1970-72, nat. pres. 1973-75), U. Chgo. Alumni Assn. (pres. Denver club 1967—), U. Chgo. Alumni Cabinet (mem. 1968-78). Contbr. numerous articles on biochemistry, also artists' rights to profl. jours. Address: 1517 S Dexter Way Denver CO 80222

NEWMAN, LARAINE, comedienne; b. Los Angeles, Mar. 2; student Calif. Inst. Arts; studied mime with Marcel Marceau. Joined improvisational group The Groundlings, 1972; appeared TV spl. Lily, 1975; performer NBC's Saturday Night Live, 1975—; appeared in film American Hot Wax, 1978; TV spls, Things We Did Last Summer, Bob and Ray & Jane, Laraine and Gilda. Mem. AFTRA.*

NEWMAN, LEON THEOPHANE, foundry co. exec.; b. Winona, Minn., Nov. 30, 1916; s. Theophil and Sophia (Bonk) N.; B.B.A. with distinction, U. Minn., 1939; m. Irene Thomas, Sept. 20, 1941; children—Michael T., John G., Gregory L., Mary Jane (Mrs. Kasper). Accountant, Price Waterhouse & Co., C.P.A.'s, Chgo., 1939-46; with J.I. Case Co., Racine, Wis., 1946-62, asst. treas., 1954-56, sec., 1956-62, sec.-treas., 1960; sec.-treas., dir. Grede Foundries, Inc., Milw., 1962—, Coatings, Inc., Milw., 1968—. C.P.A., Ill. Mem. Am. Inst. C.P.A.'s, Beta Gamma Sigma, Beta Alpha Psi. Club: Racine Country. Home: 3401 N Wisconsin St Racine WI 53402 Office: 9898 W Blue Mound Rd Milwaukee WI 53226

NEWMAN, LOUIS BENJAMIN, educator, physician; b. N.Y.C.; s. Morris and Mollie (Banzuly) N.; M.E., Ill. Inst. Tech., 1921; M.D., Rush Med. Coll., 1931; m. Rose Manilow, Jan. 21, 1951. Intern Cook County Hosp., Chgo., 1932-33; practice of medicine, specializing rehab. medicine, Chgo., 1933—; prof. rehab. medicine Northwestern U. Sch. Medicine, 1946—; chief rehab. medicine VA Hosp., Hines, Ill., 1946-53, VA Research Hosp., Chgo., 1953-66; cons. rehab. medicine VA hosps. and several community hosps., Chgo., 1967—; professorial lectr. rehab. medicine Coll. Medicine, U. Ill., Loyola U. Stritch Med. Sch., U. Health Scis.-The Chgo. Med. Sch.; mem. drs. adv. com. Shaare Zedek Hosp. and Med. Center, Jerusalem, Israel; cons. Loyola U. Hosp. Mem. med. adv. and cons. bd. Armour Research Fedn. of Ill. Inst. Tech.; health div. com. on handicapped Welfare Council of Met. Chgo.; med. adv. bd. Research Project on Rehab. Met. Chgo., Vis. Nurse Assn., United Parkinson Found., Am. Rehab. Found., Nat. Found., Inc., Am. Assn. Rehab. Therapists, Assn. Phys. and Mental Rehab., Nat. Multiple Sclerosis Soc. Founding mem. Hebrew U. Jerusalem, 1970—; mem. Chgo. com Weizmann Inst. Sci., Rehovot, Israel, 1970—; mem. com. Israel Inst. Tech., Technion City, 1970—. Served as comdr. M.C., USNR, World War II; head dept. phys. medicine and rehab. Naval Hosps., Oakland, Calif., also Seattle. Recipient B'nai B'rith award in recognition services for rehab. hospitalized vets., 1952; commendation Pres.'s Com. on Employment of Physically Handicapped, 1956; John E. Davis award for outstanding service phys. medicine and rehab. Assn. Phys. and Mental Rehab., 1956; distinguished service award Ill. Inst. Tech., 1957; named Civil Servant of Year, Fed. Personnel Council Chgo., 1958; meritorious service award VA, 1958; Citation Pub. Service as Useful Citizen, U. Chgo., 1959; commendation from adminstr. vets. affairs for success Crusade of Mercy Drive at VA Research Hospital, Chgo., 1962; Distinguished Service key Am. Congress of Rehab. Medicine, 1963; Nat. Rehab. Citation for outstanding services Am. Legion, 1967; Distinguished Achievement award Assn. Med. Rehab. Dirs. and Coordinators, 1967. Diplomate Am. Bd. Phys. Med. and Rehab. Fellow Am. Geriatrics Soc.; mem. Am. Congress Rehab. Medicine (v.p.; chmn. midwestern sect. 1948-49), AMA (past chmn. sect. on phys. medicine), Ill. Soc. Phys. Medicine and Rehab. (founding mem., 1st pres.), Inst. Medicine Chgo. (rehab. com.), Nat. Multiple Sclerosis Soc. (med. adv. bd.), Internat. Soc. for the Rehab. of Disabled, World Med. Assn., Ill., Chgo. med. socs., Am. Acad. Phys. Medicine and Rehab. (pres.), Chgo. Heart Assn. (rehab. com.), Ill. Assn. Professions (charter mem.), Vis. Nurse Assn. (mem. med. adv. com. 1967—), Am. Assn. Electromyography and Electrodiagnosis, Am. Inst. Ultrasonics in Medicine. Contbr. articles med. jours. Address: 400 E Randolph St Chicago IL 60601

NEWMAN, M.W., journalist; b. N.Y.C., 1917; B.A. in Journalism, U. Wis., 1938; m. Nancy Newman. Formerly with Indpls. Times, Greensboro (N.C.) Daily News, Hoboken (N.J.) Observer; with Chgo. Daily News, 1945-78, successively copyreader, rewrite man, reporter, book editor, editor arts, amusements and Panorama mag.; spl. writer Chgo. Sun-Times, 1978—; editor Inland Architect mag., 1969—. Address: care Chicago Sun-Times 401 N Wabash Ave Chicago IL 60611

NEWMAN, MARCEL K., educator, engr.; b. Frankfurt, Germany, Apr. 29, 1903; s. Maximilian Joseph and Henrietta (Melmer) N.; Engring. Diploma in Elec. Engring., Poly. Inst. Hanover, 1928; B.S., U. Ky., 1930; M.S., U. Pitts., 1934; Ph.D., Columbia, 1950; m. Maria Ervens, May 11, 1932; 1 dau., Elizabeth Mary. Research engr., mechanics div. Research Labs., Westinghouse Elec. Corp., Pitts., 1930-34; develop. engr. Gulf Develop. Corp., 1934-36; instr. mechanics Pupin Physics Labs., Columbia, 1936-44; research engr. Walter Kidde & Co., Inc., Belleville, N.J., 1944-46; asso. prof. mech. engring. Coll. Applied Sci., Syracuse U., 1946-47; asso. prof. engring. U. Buffalo, 1947-50; prof., head dept. mech. engring., dir. nuclear engring. U. Notre Dame, 1950-61; prof. mech. engring. U. Tenn.

Space Inst. Tullahoma, Tenn., 1961-71, prof. emeritus, 1971—, also coordinator research; cons. U.S. Sugar Corp., Clewiston, Fla., 1943—, Arnold AF Center, 1961. Registered profl. engr., N.Y., Tenn. Mem. AAAS, ASME (Outstanding Engr. award St. Joseph Valley sect. 1961), Am. Inst. Aero. and Astronautics, Am. Nuclear Soc., Am. Phys. Soc., Am. Soc. Engring. Edn., Am. Assn. U. Profs., N.Y. Acad. Scis., Air Force Assn., Sigma Xi. Author articles vibrations, stress analysis, nuclear propulsion. Home: Route 2 Country Club Dr Tullahoma TN 37388

NEWMAN, MAX KARL, physician, educator; b. Malden, Mass., Jan. 19, 1909; s. Samuel Paul and Celia (Korn) N.; A.B., U. Mich., 1930, M.D., 1934; m. Sophia Rosenzweig, July 21, 1932; children—Martin, Phyllis, Steven, Donald, Geoffrey. Intern Grace Hosp., Detroit, 1934-35; resident internal medicine Herman Keifer Hosp., Detroit, 1935-36; spl. tng. Dr. Krusen at Mayo Clinic, then Dr. Coulter at Northwestern U., 1936-38, also U. Calif. at Los Angeles Sch. Engring., 1953; pvt. practice specializing phys. medicine and rehab., Detroit, 1938—; past dir. phys. medicine and rehab. Detroit Meml. Hosp., Sinai Hosp., Detroit; cons. Jewish Home for Aged, Carmel Hall, Detroit House Correction, Bay City Gen. Hosp.; area cons. 5 state VA area; med. dir. Muscular Dystrophy Clinic, Martin Place Hosp.; past asst. prof. phys. medicine and rehab. Wayne State U. Med. Sch.; lectr. Inst. Continuing Legal Medicine, U. Mich., 1962—; lectr. Law-Sci. Inst., U. Tex. Sch. Medicine, 1959; clin. prof. biomechanics Mich. State U. Colls. Medicine; spl. lectr. U. Mich., U. Ill., U. Tex. at Galveston; nat. cons. disability evaluation in phys. medicine and rehab. HEW; cons. rehab. medicine Oakland County Hosp., Pontiac, Mich., 1976—. Past v.p. Comml. Acceptance Corp., Electrozad Corp. Ltd. Can. Past bd. dirs. Mich. Welfare League, Mich. Rehab. Assn., Mich. Soc. Crippled Children and Adults; med. adv. bd. United Cerebral Palsy Assn., Nat. Found. Wayne County. Med. dir. USPHS, 1944. Recipient President's award Mich. Med. Soc., 1963; annual award Mich. Chiropedy Assn. Diplomate Am. Bd. Phys. Medicine and Rehab. Fellow A.C.P., Am. Acad. Phys. Medicine and Rehab. (pres. 1962), Am. Congress Phys. Medicine and Rehab., Am. Geriatrics Soc., Assn. Mil. Surgeons and Physicians, Assn. Res. Officers USPHS, Am. Acad. Cerebral Palsy, Am. Acad. Law-Sci. (v.p. 1961-62); founding mem. Am. Assn. Electromyography and Electrodiagnosis; asso. mem. Am. Acad. Neurology; asso. internal medicine Am. Coll. Legal Medicine; mem. Internat. Assn. Indsl. Accident Bds. and Commns., Pan Am. Med. Assn. (N.Am. co-chmn. sect. phys. medicine, mem. sec. neurology), Mich. Acad. Phys. Medicine and Rehab. (past pres.), Mexican Assn. Phys. Medicine and Rehab., President's Club U. Mich., Phi Beta Kappa, Alpha Omega Alpha, Phi Kappa Phi. Author numerous articles in field. Editorial bd. Chronic Disease Mgmt., Electroneyography. Home: 4787 Crestview Ct Birmingham MI 48075 Office: 17320 W 12 Mile Rd Southfield MI 48076

NEWMAN, MELVIN SPENCER, chemist, educator; b. N.Y.C., Mar. 10, 1908; s. Jacob K. and Mae (Polack) N.; B.S., Yale, 1929, Ph.D., 1932; D.Sc. (hon.), U. New Orleans, 1975; m. Beatrice N. Crystal, June 30, 1933; children—Kiefer, Susan, Beth, Robert. Instr., Ohio State U., 1936-39, Elizabeth Clay Howald scholar, 1939-40, asst. prof., 1940-44, prof. chemistry, 1944—, regents prof., 1966; Fulbright lectr. U. Glasgow, 1957, 67. Guggenheim fellow, 1951. Recipient award, 1961, E.W. Morley medal, 1969, Columbus (Ohio) award, 1976 (all Am. Chem. Soc.); W.L. Cross medal Yale U., 1970; Joseph Sullivant medal Ohio State U., 1976. Mem. Am., Brit. chem. socs., Nat. Acad. Sci., Sigma Xi. Asso. editor Jour. Am. Chem. Soc., Jour. Organic Chemistry and Organic Syntheses. Home: 2239 Onandaga Dr Columbus OH 43221

NEWMAN, MONROE, educator, economist; b. Bklyn., Jan. 31, 1929; s. David A. and Ida Mary (Leight) N.; B.A., Antioch Coll., 1950; M.A., U. Ill., 1953, Ph.D., 1954; m. Ruth Zielinski Feb. 6, 1951. Mem. research staff AFL, 1947-48; examiner NLRB, 1949-50; asst. U. Ill., 1950-54; research analyst Assn. Casualty and Surety Cos., 1954-55; mem. faculty Pa. State U., 1955—, prof. econs., 1961—, head dept., 1958-62, 78—, chmn. grad. program regional planning, 1971-72, dir. Center Study Environ. Policy, 1972-73; vis. research prof. econs. U. Pitts., 1964-65. Economist, Pres.'s Appalachian Regional Commn., 1964-65; research dir. Appalachian Regional Commn., 1965-66, spl. cons., 1966—. Mem. So. Regional Sci. Assn. (pres.), Am. Econ. Assn., Regional Sci. Assn. Co-author: Insurance and Risk, 1964, Acid Mine Drainage in Appalachia, 1969, Experiment in Appalachia, 1973; author: Political Economy of Appalachia, 1972; also articles. Home: 1629 Cherry Hill Rd N State College PA 16801 Office: Pennsylvania State University University Park PA 16802

NEWMAN, MURRAY ARTHUR, aquarium adminstr.; b. Chgo., Mar. 6, 1924; came to Can., 1953, naturalized, 1970; s. Paul Jones and Virginia (Murray) N.; B.Sc., U. Chgo., 1949; postgrad. U. Hawaii, 1950; M.A., U. Calif., Berkeley, 1951; Ph.D., U. B.C. (Can.), Vancouver, 1960; m. Katherine Greene Rose, Aug. 8, 1952; 1 dau., Susan. Curator fisheries UCLA, 1951-53, Ichthyology Museum, U. B.C., 1953-56; curator Vancouver Public Aquarium, 1956-66, dir., 1966—; pres. Mana Aquarium Cons.; mem. council Westwater Research Centre, U. B.C.; mem. adv. com. Western Can. Univs. Marine Biol. Soc. Served with USN, 1943-46. Decorated Order of Can.; recipient Man of Yr. award City of Vancouver, 1964, Centennial award Govt. Can., 1967, Harold J. Merilees award Vancouver Visitors Bur., 1976. Mem. Am. Assn. Zool. Parks and Aquariums, Internat. Union Dirs. Zool. Gardens, N.Y. Acad. Scis., Can. Assn. Zool. Parks and Aquariums (pres. 1978-79), Tynehead Zool. Soc. B.C. (dir.). Clubs: Vancouver, Univ., Round Table. Office: Vancouver Aquarium PO Box 3232 Vancouver BC V6B 3X8 Canada

NEWMAN, PAUL, actor; b. Cleve., Jan. 26, 1925; s. Arthur S. and Theresa (Fetzer) N.; B.A., Kenyon Coll., 1949; postgrad. Yale Sch. Drama, 1951; m. Jacqueline Witte, Dec. 1949; children—Scott, Susan, Stephanie; m. 2d, Joanne Woodward, Jan. 1958; children—Elinor, Melissa, Clea. Appeared on Broadway in Picnic, 1953-54, Desperate Hours, 1955, Sweet Bird of Youth, 1959, Baby Want a Kiss, 1964; motion pictures include Somebody Up There Likes Me, 1956, Cat on a Hot Tin Roof, 1958, From the Terrace, 1960, Exodus, 1960, The Hustler, 1961, Sweet Bird of Youth, 1962, Hud, 1963, The Outrage, 1964, The Prize, 1964, Lady L, 1965, Harper, Hombre, Cool Hand Luke, Winning, Butch Cassidy and the Sundance Kid, WUSA (also producer), Sometimes a Great Notion (also dir.), Pocket Money, the Life and Times of Judge Roy Bean, The Mac Intosh Man, The Sting, The Towering Inferno, Buffalo Bill and the Indians, Slap Shot; dir. Rachel, Rachel, The Effect of Gamma Rays on Man-in-the-Moon Marigolds. Served with AC, USNR, 1943-46. Nominated best actor Acad. Motion Picture Arts and Scis., 1959-61, 63; recipient Man of Year award Hasty Pudding Theatrical, Harvard, 1968; World film favorite male Golden Globe awards, 1967; named Best Motion Picture Producer of Year, Producers Guild Am., 1968. Address: care Rogers & Cowan Inc 9665 Wilshire Blvd Beverly Hills CA 90210

NEWMAN, PETER CHARLES, journalist; b. Vienna, Austria, May 10, 1929; s. Oscar C. and Wanda (Newman) N.; came to Can., 1940, naturalized, 1945; ed. Upper Can. Coll., 1948; M.A., U. Toronto, 1951; m. Camilla Turner, Aug. 1, 1978; 1 dau., Ashley. Ottawa editor Maclean's Mag., 1951-64; Ottawa editor Toronto Daily Star, 1964-69, editor-in-chief, 1969-71; editor Maclean's, Toronto, 1971—. Dep. chmn. for Can., Internat. Press Inst., 1970—; vis. asso. prof. polit. sci. McMaster U., Hamilton, Ont., 1970—; vis. prof. York U., 1979—. Served to lt. Royal Canadian Navy. Decorated Order of Can.; recipient Nat. Newspaper award for feature writing, 1964; Wilderness award Can. Broadcasting Corp., 1967; Quill award, 1979. Clubs: Rideau (Ottawa); Royal Can. Yacht (Toronto). Author: Flame of Power, 1959; Renegade in Power, 1963; The Distemper of Our Times, 1968; Home Country, 1972; The Canadian Establishment, 1975; Bronfman Dynasty, 1978. Home: 64 Admiral Rd Toronto ON Canada Office: 481 University Ave Toronto ON Canada

NEWMAN, PETER KENNETH, economist, educator; b. Mitcham, Eng., Oct. 5, 1928; s. Charles Francis and Harriet Anne (Newbold) N.; came to U.S., 1961, naturalized, 1970; B.Sc. in Econs., Univ. Coll. U. London (Eng.), 1949, M.Sc. in Econs., 1951, D.Sc. in Econs., 1962; m. Jennifer Mary Hugh-Jones Steed, Sept. 30, 1974; children by previous marriage—Jean Ellen, John Lincoln, Kenneth Richard, Alan Peter. Lectr. U. West Indies, Jamaica, 1957-59, sr. lectr., 1959-61; prof. econs. U. Mich., Ann Arbor, 1961-63; prof. polit. economy Johns Hopkins, 1964-65, 66—; sr. asso. Robert R. Nathan Assos., Washington, 1965-66. Mem. Royal Econ. Soc., Am. Econ. Assn., Econometric Soc. Author: British Guiana, 1964; Malaria Eradication and Population Growth, 1965; Theory of Exchange, 1965. Home: 325 Woodlawn Rd Baltimore MD 21210

NEWMAN, PHILIP FREEDMAN, lawyer; b. Phila., Sept. 21, 1896; s. Bernhardt and Pauline (Freedman) N.; LL.B., U. Pa., 1917; m. Helene E. Schaul, July 13, 1923; children—Paul F. and Margot Newman Stickley. Admitted to Pa. bar, 1920; partner firm Newman & Master, Phila., 1920-61; counsel, sr. partner firm Blank, Rome, Comisky and McCauley, and predecessor, Phila., 1961—; counsel for real estate developers; cons. counsel Phila. Redevel. Authority, 1961; dir. Fla. Palm-Aire Corp., Pompano Beach; mem. constrn. loan com. Continental Bank, Phila. Chmn. cash mobilization drive Allied Jewish Appeal, 1963; hon. mem. bd. dirs. Am. joint distbn. com. United Jewish Appeal; mem. steering com. Law Sch., U. Pa.; pres. fedn. found., mem. exec. com., lifetime hon. trustee Fedn. Jewish Agencies Greater Phila.; trustee Pop Warner Little Scholars. Recipient Humanitarian award Allied Jewish Appeal, 1965. Mem. Am., Pa., Phila. bar assns. Clubs: Socialegal, Masons, Locust. Past mem. editorial bd. U. Pa. Law Rev. Home: 220 W Rittenhouse Sq Philadelphia PA 19103 Office: 4 Penn Center 11th Floor Philadelphia PA 19103

NEWMAN, RACHEL, magazine editor; b. Malden, Mass., May 1, 1938; d. Maurice and Edythe Brenda (Tichell) N.; B.A., Pa. State U., 1960; certificate N.Y. Sch. Interior Design, 1963; m. Herbert Bleiweiss, Apr. 6, 1973. Accessories editor Womens Wear Daily, N.Y.C., 1964-65; designer, publicist Grandoe Glove Corp., N.Y.C., 1965-67; asso. editor McCall's Sportswear and Dress Merchandiser mag., N.Y.C., 1967; mng. editor Ladies Home Jour. Needle and Craft mag., N.Y.C., 1970-72; editor-in-chief Am. Home Crafts mag., N.Y.C., 1972-77; fashion dir. Good Housekeeping Mag., N.Y.C., 1977-78, home bldg. and decorating dir., 1978—; editor Good Housekeeping's Country Living Mag., 1978—. Mem. N.Y. Radical Feminists. Address: Good Housekeeping Mag 959 8th Ave New York NY 10019

NEWMAN, RALPH GEOFFREY, bookseller, historian; b. Chgo., Nov. 3, 1911; s. Henry and Dora (Glickman) N.; Litt.D., James Milliken U. (Lincoln Coll.), 1950, Knox Coll., Rockford Coll.; LL.D., Iowa Wesleyan Coll.; m. Estelle Hoffman, 1934 (div.); children—Maxine (Mrs. Richard G. Brandenburg), Carol (Mrs. Parry); m. 2d, Patricia Lyons Simon, 1972. Founder, pres. Abraham Lincoln Book Shop, Inc., Chgo., 1933—; pres. Americana House, Inc., 1959—, Lincoln's New Salem Enterprises, Inc., 1952—, Ralph Geoffrey Newman, Inc., 1967—. Chmn. Ill. com. N.Y. World's Fair, 1963-65; chmn. Ill. Sesquicentennial Commn., 1965-69; mem. Ill. Spl. Events Commn., 1969-73; past pres. Adult Edn. Council Greater Chgo.; bd regents Lincoln Acad. Ill.; city archivist City of Chgo., 1979-80; pres. bd. dirs. Chgo. Public Library, 1964-79; trustee Lincoln Coll.; past chmn. bd. dirs. Ford's Theatre Soc., Washington; mem. library council Notre Dame U.; pres. Urban Libraries Council, 1970-78. Served with USNR, 1944-45. Recipient diploma of honor Lincoln Meml. U., 1952; Am. of Year award Independence Hall Assn., 1958; Nevins-Freeman award, 1975. Mem. Civil War Round Table Chgo. (founder 1940), Royal Arts Soc. (London), Abraham Lincoln Assn. (dir.), Stephen A. Douglas Assn. (pres.), Ulysses S. Grant Assn. (pres.), Am., Ind., Ill., Iowa, Kans., Chgo. hist. socs., Am. Legion, ALA, Am. Booksellers Assn., bibliog. socs. Am., London, Phi Alpha Theta. Clubs: Arts, Caxton, Press (Chgo.); Sangamo (Springfield, Ill.). Author: (with Otto Eisenschiml) The American Iliad, 1947; Abraham Lincoln: An Autobiographical Narrative, 1970. Editor: The Diary of a Public Man, 1945; The Railsplitter, 1950; (with Otto Eisenschiml, E.B. Long) The Civil War, 1956; The Abraham Lincoln Story (radio series), 1958-59; Lincoln for the Ages, 1960; (with Otto Eisenchiml), Evewitness, 1960; (with E.B. Long) The Civil War Digest, 1960; Pictorial Autobiography of Abraham Lincoln, 1962; Abraham Lincoln: His Story in His Own Words, 1975; mem. editorial bd. Civil War History, 1955—. Home: 175 Delaware Pl Chicago IL 60611 Office: 18 E Chestnut St Chicago IL 60611. *I believe opportunity exists wherever you are if you are willing to work hard enough to achieve it. No goal is impossible. If you are willing to forego dependence on anyone else and realize that your own, and only your own, efforts will be bring success, you can be successful.*

NEWMAN, RANDY, singer, songwriter, musician; b. Los Angeles, Nov. 28, 1943; s. Irving and Adele Newman; m. Roswitha Newman; children—Amos, Eric, John. Arranger, songwriter various record firms, artists; singer, songwriter, musician; singer-composer Mama Told Me Not to Come, I Think It's Going to Rain Today, Love Story, Short People, Sail Away; albums include Randy Newman, 12 Songs, Randy Newman/Live, Sail Away, Good Old Boys, Little Criminals, Born Again; appeared TV and concert engagements. Address: care Renaissance Mgmt Corp 433 N Camden Beverly Hills CA 90210

NEWMAN, RICHARD ALAN, editor; b. Watertown, N.Y., Mar. 30, 1930; s. Gordon Leon and Belle (Burton) N.; B.A., Maryville Coll., 1952; M.Div., Union Theol. Sem., 1955; postgrad. Syracuse U., 1959-61, Harvard U., 1966; m. Peggy J. Hoyt, Oct. 23, 1964 (div. 1978); stepchildren—David W. Bauer, Paul W. Bauer, Nancy E. Bauer. Ordained to ministry Presbyn. Ch., 1955, demitted, 1977; minister Westminster Presbyn. Ch., Syracuse, N.Y., 1955-59; instr. religion Vassar Coll., Poughkeepsie, N.Y., 1962-63; prof., chmn. dept. social scis. Boston U., 1964-73; sr. editor G.K. Hall Co., Boston, 1973-79; exec. editor Garland Pub. Co., N.Y.C., 1979—. Democratic candidate for N.Y. State Assembly from Onondaga County, 1960. Danforth Found. asso. Mem. Am. Acad. Religion, Soc. for African Ch. History, Animal Protection Inst. Am. Author: Prayers of Faith; Black Apostles; Index to the Birthplaces of American Authors. Contbr. articles to profl. jours. Office: care Garland Pub Co 136 Madison Ave New York NY 10016

NEWMAN, RICHARD JOSEPH, wines and spirits distilling, importing co. exec.; b. N.Y.C., May 16, 1931; s. Joseph and Dorothy S. (Schultz) N.; B.S. in Econs., Wharton Sch. U. Pa., 1956; m. Nancy E. Brown, Apr. 3, 1955; children—Michael, Matthew, Julie. Asst. account exec. Benton & Bowles Advt. Co., N.Y.C., 1956-58; mgr. advt. and sales promotion Chock Full O Nuts, Inc., N.Y.C., 1958-64; brand mgr. Nat. Distillers Co., N.Y.C., 1964-70; mktg. dir. Heublein, Inc., Hartford, Conn., 1970-73; sr. v.p. mktg. Seagram Distillers Co., N.Y.C., 1973-74; pres., chief exec. officer Austin, Nichols & Co., Inc., N.Y.C., 1974—. Served with USMC, 1951-53. Decorated Purple Heart. Club: DAV. Office: 733 Third Ave New York NY 10017*

NEWMAN, RICHARD OAKLEY, utilities exec.; b. Enid, Okla., Aug. 30, 1920; s. O. B. and Grace E. N.; B.S. in Mech. Engring., Okla. State U., 1942; m. Betty Lou Bennett, Mar. 13, 1940; children—Linda Lou Newman Weathers, Richard Oakley, Mark B. With Pub. Service Co. of Okla., Tulsa, 1946—, exec. v.p., 1968-70, exec. v.p., dir., 1970-72, pres., chief exec. officer, dir., 1972—; chmn. bd., chief exec. officer, dir. Transok Pipe Line Co., Ash Creek Mining Co.; dir. 1st Nat. Bank & Trust Co., Williams Cos.; chmn. S.W. Power Pool; past chmn. S.W. Underground Distbn. Exchange; dir. Central & S.W. Corp., Conf. Bd.; trustee Nat. Electric Reliability Council. Past chmn. ofcl. bd., deacon, elder, trustee, Sunday Sch. supt. East Side Christian Ch.; dir. Tulsa Christian Found.; past pres. Tulsa Area Christian Missionary Soc.; mem. Gov.'s Energy Advisory Council, 1973—; bd. dirs., past chmn. Industries for Tulsa, Inc.; bd. dirs., past pres. Goodwill Industries of Tulsa; bd. dirs. Indian Nations council Boy Scouts Am., Goodwill Industries Am., Inc., Okla. State U. Devel. Found., Internat. Petroleum Expn.; trustee St. Francis Hosp., Phillips U.; mem. advisory bd. Downtown Tulsa Unlimited, Inc.; mem. advisory bd. Coll. Engring. and Phys. Scis., chmn. bd. trustees Deans Advisory Council Bus. Adminstrn., U. Tulsa. Served with AUS, 1942-46. Mem. IEEE, Am. Nuclear Soc., ASME, Nat., Okla. socs. profl. engrs., Okla. Petroleum Council, Mid-Continent Oil and Gas Assn., Tulsa C. of C. (pres., bd. dirs., exec. com.), Nat. Alliance Businessmen (past met. chmn.), Edison Electric Inst. (dir.), Mo. Valley Electric Assn. (exec. com., past pres.), Nat. Assn. Electric Cos. (dir.). Clubs: Masons (32 deg.), Shriners, Royal Order Jesters, So. Hills Country, Tulsa, Utica 21, Tulsa Press. Home: PO Box 129 Tulsa OK 74101 Office: PO Box 201 Tulsa OK 74102

NEWMAN, ROBERT BRADFORD, acoustical cons. co. exec.; b. Unkung, Kwangtung, China, Nov. 5, 1917; s. Henry Ware and Ethel Marian (Smith) N. (parents Am. citizens); B.A., U. Tex., 1938, M.A., 1939; M. Arch., M.I.T., 1949; Sc.D. (hon.) Lawrence Coll., 1963; m. Mary Louise Herod, Oct. 18, 1941 (div. 1954); m. 2d Mary Patricia Shaw, June 4, 1955; children—Catherine, Henry, Bradford. Partner, Bolt Beranek & Newman, Cambridge, Mass., 1949-53, v.p., 1953—, also dir.; asso. prof. architecture M.I.T., 1949-76, adj. prof., 1976—; vis. lectr. acoustics Harvard U., 1955-71, prof. architecture tech., 1971—. Bd. dirs. DeCordova Mus., Lincoln, Mass., 1968-78, pres., 1971-74. Recipient Franklin Inst. Brown medal, 1966. Fellow Acoustical Soc. Am. Episcopalian. Contbr. to Ency. Brit. and Time Saver Standards. Home: Wheeler Rd Lincoln MA 01773 Office: 50 Moulton St Cambridge MA 02138

NEWMAN, ROBERT JACOB, investor; b. New Orleans, Feb. 4, 1904; s. Harold Weil and Bellagie (Israel) N.; prep. edn. Newman Sch., New Orleans; student Tulane U., 1921-22; m. Claire Poe, July 3, 1948; children—Leslie Claire, Robert Jacob, Christopher David. Asst. treas. Ins. Securities Co., Inc., Union Indemnity Co., Inc., New Orleans, 1927-32; founder, sr. partner Newman, Harris & Co., investment bankers, New Orleans, 1932-41; asso. Newman, Brown & Co., Inc., investment bankers, New Orleans, 1942-66; gen. partner Kohlmeyer & Co., mems. N.Y. Stock Exchange, New Orleans, 1966-73; dir. Thomson & McKinnon Auchincloss Kohlmeyer, Inc., 1974—; pres. Carrollton Realty, Inc., New Orleans; dir. Royal St. Louis Hotel, Inc., New Orleans. Chmn. art com. La. Purchase Sesquicentennial, 1954. Bd. dirs., trustee New Orleans Museum Art, New Orleans, 1960-72; pres., 1962-63, 67-71. Decorated officer l'Orde l'Etoile Noire (France). Mem. Chevalier Confrerie du Chevaliers du Tastevin, Compagnons de Bontemps, Bordeaux, France, Commanderie de Bordeaux, France-Amerique Soc. Yachting Club Am. (charter). Clubs: Silver Snow Flake, Golden Ski Book, Kitzbuhel Golf, Kitzbuhel Ski (Kitzbuhel, Austria); Metairie Country, Plimsoll (charter), Internat. House (New Orleans); Pass Christian (Miss.) Yacht, Swiss Alpine; Arlberg Ski (Austria). Winner Hambletonian trotting race, 1946, Roosevelt 1 mile trot, 1947. Home: 1111 Falcon Rd Metairie LA 70005 Office: 919 Gravier St New Orleans LA 70130 also Tiemberg Kitzbuhel Austria

NEWMAN, SAMUEL RAPHAEL, pediatrician; b. Warsaw, Poland, June 23, 1890; s. Abraham Jacob and Sarah Rebecca (Sussman) N.; student Theol. Acads., Poland, 1900-09, U. N.C., 1912-15; U. Vienna (Austria), 1922-23, certificate Faculty of Medicine, 1923; D.H.L. (hon.), Hebrew Union Coll., 1954; M.D., U. Va., 1917; m. Ida Mae Greenberg, Dec. 25, 1917; children—Naomi (Mrs. Stanley Macht), Ruth (Mrs. Stanley Siegel). Intern, Sinai Hosp., Balt., 1917-18, Italian Hosp., N.Y.C., 1919, Willard Parker Hosp., N.Y.C., 1919; asst. health officer, city bacteriologist Danville (Va.) Dept. Health, 1919-20; hospitant Children's Clinic, U. Vienna, 1922; pvt. practice medicine, specializing in pediatrics, Danville, 1923—; clinician Child Health Clinic, Danville, 1923—, Charity League Children's Clinic, Martinsville, Va., 1924-68, Jr. Wednesday Club Clinic, (name changed to Samuel Newman Children's Clinic, 1954), Danville, 1931-70; pres. staff Meml. Hosp., Danville, 1934—. Mem. Med. Study Mission to Israel, 1970. Chmn., Israel Bond Orgn., State of Va., 1951. Bd. dirs. Faith Home, Va. Council Human Religions. Served as 1st lt. Officers Med. Res., U.S. Army, 1917. Recipient Award of Honor, State of Israel, 1954, 64, Charity League, Martinsville, 1955; award Danville Dept. Health, 1963; Outstanding Leadership award United Jewish Appeal, 1964; Golden Anniversary citation U. N.C., 1965; Certificate of Award, Danville sect. Nat. Council Negro Women, 1968; Certificate of Recognition, Nat. Council Catholic Men, 1970; Legion of Honor, Kiwanis Internat., 1971; Citizenship awards radio sta. WBTM, 1971, Danville Kiwanis, 1974. Diplomate Am. Bd. Pediatrics. Fellow Am. Acad. Pediatrics; mem. Am. Physicians Fellowship, Danville-Pittsylvania Acad. Medicine (life mem., past pres.), Am. Legion, 40 and 8, Phi Epsilon Pi (founder U. Va. chpt.). Mason (32 deg.), Kiwanian; mem. B'nai B'rith. Contbr. articles to med. and lay jours. Address: 770 Main St Danville VA 24541

NEWMAN, SYDNEY CECIL, film and TV cons.; b. Toronto, Ont., Can., Apr. 1, 1917; student Fine Arts Sch., Toronto, 1931-35; m. Margaret Elizabeth McRae, May 20, 1944; children—Deirdre, Jennifer, Gillian. Artist, photographer Toronto, 1935-40; exec. producer Nat. Film Bd., Ottawa, Ont., 1941-52; staff NBC-TV, N.Y.C., 1949-50; exec. producer sports, features CBC-TV, Toronto, 1952-54, supr. drama, 1954-58; head of drama ABC-TV, England, 1958-62; head of drama group BBC-TV, London, Eng., 1963-68; exec. producer Asso. Brit. Picture Corp., Eng., 1969-70; spl. adv. chmn. Can. Radio-TV Commn., 1970—; pres. Sydney Newman Enterprises Inc.; chief creative cons. Can. Film Devel. Corp.; govt. film commr., chmn. Nat. Film Bd. Can., 1970-75; spl. advisor on film Canadian sec. state, 1975-77, ex-officio dir. Can. Nat. Arts Centre, 1970-75. Can. Broadcasting Corp.; ex-officio dir. Can. Film Devel. Corp., chief story cons., 1978; pres. Sydney Newman Enterprises, 1977—. Recipient

Desmond Davis award Brit. Soc. Film and TV Arts, 1967; Pres.'s award Writers Guild Gt. Britain, 1969, Zeta award, 1970; spl. awards Soc. Motion Picture and TV Engrs., 1975, Film and TV Producers Gt. Britain, Canadian Picture Pioneers; named Knight of Mark Twain. Fellow Soc. Film and TV Producers Gt. Britain, Royal Soc. Art; mem. Dirs. Guild Can. (hon. life). Office: 3 Nesbitt Dr Toronto ON M4W 2G2 Canada

NEWMAN, THEODORE R., JR., judge; b. Birmingham, Ala., July 5, 1934; s. Theodore R. and Ruth L. (Oliver) N.; A.B., Brown U., 1955; J.D., Harvard U., 1958. Admitted to D.C. bar, 1958, Ala. bar, 1959; atty. civil rights div. Dept. Justice, Washington, 1961-62; practiced law in Washington, 1962-70; asso. judge D.C. Superior Ct., 1970-76; chief judge D.C. Ct. of Appeals, 1976—. Bd. dirs. Nat. Center for State Cts.; trustee Brown U. Served with USAF, 1958-61. Fellow Am. Bar Found.; mem. Am., Nat. (past pres. judicial council) bar assns., Am. Judicature Soc. Home: 7924 16th St NW Washington DC 20012 Office: DC Ct of Appeals 500 Indiana Ave NW Washington DC 20001

NEWMAN, THOMAS DANIEL, clergyman, sch. adminstr.; b. London, Eng., May 12, 1922; s. Frederick and Margaret (O'Leary) N.; student Glasgow Sch. Accounting, 1946, Unity Sch. Christianity, 1962-66, Harvard Div. Sch., 1967—; D.Sc., Alma Coll., 1975; m. Louise Johannah Albertano, Apr. 1, 1963; 1 dau., Susan (Mrs. Alan J. Rennie). Mng. dir. Thomas Newman (Printers) Ltd., 1945-49; mng. dir. H. & M.J. Pubs. Ltd., 1947-49; mng. dir. Forget-Me-Not Greeting Cards Ltd., 1949-61; mng. dir. Diplomat Greetings Ltd., 1957-61; mng. dir. Nevill's Ltd., 1955-57; ordained to ministry Christ's Ch., 1966; pastor Christ's Ch., Springfield, Mo., 1966-67, Christ's Ch., Longwood, Brookline, Mass., 1967—; adminstrv. dir. Am. Schs. Oriental Research, 1968, treas., 1970—, trustee, 1972—; founder Carthage Research Inst., Khereddine, Tunisia, 1975, Cyprus Archaeol. Research Inst., Nicosia, 1977; cons. Joint Archeol. Expdns. to Ai, 1969-73, to Tell-El-Hesi, 1970-73, to Idalion, 1970-73; mem. Joint Archeol. Expdn. to Caesarea Maritima, 1971, to Carthage, 1975; dir. Logistics Survey Qu'Rayyah, Saudi Arabia, 1973; pub. cons. Dead Sea Scrolls Com., 1968-73. Trustee, Allbright Inst. Archeol. Research, Jerusalem. Am. Center Oriental Research, Amman, Jordan. Served with RAF, 1940-45. Mem. Archeol. Inst. Am., Soc. Bibl. Lit., Soc. O.T. Studies. Mason. Clubs: Harvard Faculty; University (Boston). Home: Olde Grange House East Candia NH 03040 Office: 126 Inman St Cambridge MA 02139

NEWMAN, THOMAS RUBIN, lawyer; b. London, Sept. 7, 1933; B.A. cum laude, Hofstra U., 1957; LL.B., N.Y. U., 1960. Admitted to N.Y. bar, 1961, U.S. Supreme Ct. bar, 1964; since practiced in N.Y.C., law clk. to Asso. Judge Charles W. Froessel, N.Y. Ct. Appeals, 1960-62; partner firm Siff & Newman, 1971—; lectr. in field; mem. nat. panel arbitrators Am. Arbitration Assn., 1967—. Mem. Am., N.Y. State, N.Y.C. bar assns., Am. Law Inst., Def. Research Inst., Pi Gamma Mu. Editor N.Y. U. Law Rev., 1959-60; columnist on appellate practice N.Y. Law Jour. contbr. articles in field to profl. jours. Home: Glengary Rd Croton-on-Hudson NY 10520 Office: 233 Broadway St New York NY 10007

NEWMAN, WILLIAM, librarian; b. Cerne, Czechoslovakia, Feb. 18, 1937; came to U.S., 1948, naturalized, 1955; s. Leo and Rose N.; B.A., Bklyn. Coll., 1959; M.S. in L.S., Columbia U., 1960; m. Vivian M. Dowling, July 11, 1964; children—Alexander Lewis, Theodore Reuel. Adult services librarian Bklyn. Pub. Library, 1959-60, 62-63; serials cataloger Cornell U., 1963-65; head reference dept. U. Mont., 1965-67; librarian Faculty Adminstrv. Studies, York U., Toronto, Ont., Can., 1967-69, asst. dir. pub. services York U. Libraries, 1969-71, asso. dir. univ., 1972-78; univ. librarian Tulane U., New Orleans, 1978—. Served with U.S. Army, 1960-62. Mem. ALA, Am. Soc. for Info. Sci., Audubon Soc. Home: 722 Cherokee St New Orleans LA 70118 Office: Howard-Tilton Meml Library Tulane U Audubon and Freret St New Orleans LA 70118

NEWMAN, WILLIAM KINCAID, ret. ch. ofcl., lawyer; b. Bklyn., Aug. 26, 1910; s. Bernard J. and Kate (Kincaid) N.; A.B., Princeton U., 1931; J.D., U. Pa., 1934; LL.D., Rocky Mountain Coll., 1956; m. Cathelia E. Pollock, Sept. 21, 1940; children—James B. Katherine K., William Harley. Admitted to Pa. bar, 1934, N.Y. bar, 1939; practice law, Phila., 1934-37; staff church bldg. dept. Bd. Home Missions, Congl. and Christian Chs., N.Y.C., 1937-59, sec. corp. of bd., sec. ch. bldg. dept. charge adminstrv. bldg. fund, 1940-59; gen. sec. Annuity Fund for Congl. Ministers and Retirement Fund for Lay Workers, 1959-62, exec. v.p., 1962-75; exec. v.p. United Ch. Bd. Ministerial Assistance, 1962-75, Bd. Pensions and Relief Evang. & Reformed Ch., 1968-75. Former mem. stewardship council United Ch. Christ; sec. United Ch. Found., 1959-75; former chmn. pensions com. Nat. Council Chs. Christ U.S.A.; chmn. housing adv. com. Town of Montclair. Served to lt. USNR, 1943-46. Recipient Conover award Ch. Archtl. Guild Am., 1956. Mem. N.Y. County Lawyers Assn. Club: Princeton of N.Y. Home: 279 Park St Upper Montclair NJ 07043

NEWMAN, WILLIAM LOUIS, geologist; b. Rockford, Ill., July 14, 1920; s. Lyle Winfred and Carrie (Waterman) N.; B.S., Beloit Coll., 1942; student Mont. Sch. Mines, 1946, U. Mont., 1948-50; m. Lucille Mary Hagen, Feb. 21, 1946; children—William Dwight, Christopher. Geologist, Anaconda Mining Co., Butte, Mont., 1946-48; geologist U.S. Geol. Survey, 1950—, uranium exploration, Colo. Plateau, 1950-57, staff asst. to asso. dir., 1957-59, chief Metallogenic Map Project, 1959-62, staff asst. Office of Chief Geologist, 1962-63, staff geologist Office of Chief Geologist, 1963-67, chief nontech. reports Office of Chief Geologist, 1967-78, dep. chief Office Sci. Publs., 1978—. Served with AUS, 1942-46. Recipient Superior Performance awards, 1963, 70; Superior Service award, 1972. Fellow Geol. Soc. Am. A.A.A.S.; mem. Soc. Economic Geologists, Am. Assn. Petroleum Geologists (Capital dist. rep. 1966-68), Geochem. Soc., Fed. Editors Assn., Assn. Earth Sci. Editors, Am. Geol. Inst. (sec.-treas., dir. 1971-72), Geol. Soc. Washington (program chmn. 1963, sec. 1968-69), S.A.R., Sigma Chi. K.C. Home: 11125 Hunt Club Dr Potomac MD 20854 Office: US Geol Survey National Center Reston VA 22092

NEWMAN, WILLIAM STEIN, music educator, author, pianist, composer; b. Cleve., Apr. 6, 1912; B.S., Cleve. Inst. Music, 1933; B.S. in Mus. Edn. (Cleve. Pub. Sch. Music scholar), Western Res. U., 1933, M.A. in Musicology (grad. fellow), 1935, Ph.D., 1939; postgrad. in Europe, 1939, Columbia, 1940; m. Claire Louise Murray, Dec. 20, 1947; 1 son, Craig William. Pvt. tchr. piano and theory, 1926—; fed. relief adminstr., Cleve., 1933-34; asst. choral dir. Western Res. U., 1934-36, instr. undergrad., grad. music courses, summer 1942; music tchr. Wilson Jr. High Sch., Cleve., 1935-37, Collinwood High Sch., 1937-42, Cleve. Music Sch. Settlement, 1937-38; vocal coach, accompanist Juilliard Sch. Music, Chautauqua, summer 1937, lectr., recitalist, summer 1948; instr. music history Bennington Coll., summer 1940; instr. grad. courses Columbia Tchrs. Coll., summer 1941, asst. prof., summers 1946-48; asst. to librarian Cleve. Pub. Library System, 1941-42; asst. prof. U. N.C., 1945-46, mem. grad. faculty, 1946—, Carnegie research grantee, 1947, 48, asso. prof. music, chmn. piano instrn., 1949-69, prof., 1955-62, Alumni Distinguished prof., 1962—, dir. grad. studies in music, 1966—, prof. emeritus, 1977—; prof. music summers U. Colo., 1956, U. Mont., 1963, U. Oreg., 1965, 69, Harpur Coll., 1966, Northwestern U., 1974, U. Mo., 1978; piano recitals, lectrs. throughout U.S. Served with USAAF, 1943-45. Recipient ann. composition award Fortnightly Mus. Club, Cleve., 1935; scholarship Concord (Mass.) Sch. Music, 1935; Kenan research leave U. N.C., 1956; Ford Found.-U. N.C. research grantee, 1958; Ford Found. teaching grantee WUNC-TV, 1959; Guggenheim fellow musicology, 1960-61; Am. Council Learned Socs. grantee-in-aid, 1960, 61, 66-67; sr. fellow Nat. Endowment for Humanities, 1973, summer seminars, 1975, 79, dir. year-long seminar, 1977-78. Mem. Music Tchrs. Nat. Assn. (chmn. theory forum 1940, membership chmn. N.C., 1949, chmn. sr. piano com. 1950-53, exec. bd. 1952-56), Am. Musicological Soc. (exec. council 1955-57, nat. v.p., 1968-69, pres. 1969-70, program chmn. 1958, 66, editor jour. summer 1959), Internat. Musicol. Soc. (U.S. rep. on directorium 1971—), N.C. Music Educators, Music Library Assn., Coll. Music Soc. Author: The Pianists' Problems, rev. edit., 1956 (London 1952), 1974; Understanding Music, rev. edit., 1961, 67; The Sonata in the Baroque Era, rev. edit., 1966, 72, 80; Sonata in the Classic Era, 1963, 72, 80; The Sonata Since Beethoven, (vols. 1, 2, and 3 of a History of the Sonata Idea), 1969, rev. edit., 1972, 80; Performance Practices in Beethoven's Piano Sonatas, 1971. Editor: Thirteen Keyboard Sonatas of the 18th and 19th Centuries, 1947; Two-Part Inventions of J.S. Bach, 1957; A Chopin Anthology, 1957; Diabelli Variations, 16 Contemporaries of Beethoven on a Waltz Tune, 1958; Six Keyboard Sonatas from the Classic Era, 1965. Contbg. editor Piano Quar. Contbr. numerous articles to profl. jours., reference works. Home: 808 Old Mill Rd Chapel Hill NC 27514

NEWMAN-GORDON, PAULINE, educator; b. N.Y.C., Aug. 5, 1925; d. Bernard and Eva Newman; B.A., Hunter Coll., N.Y.C., 1947; M.A., Columbia U., 1948; Ph.D., Sorbonne, 1951; m. Sydney A. Gordon, Sept. 13, 1959. Instr. French, Wellesley Coll., 1952-53; mem. faculty Stanford U., 1953—, prof. French lit., 1969—. Scholar, Internat. Inst. Edn., 1948-51, MLA, 1956-57, AAUW, 1962-63, Am. Philos. Soc., 1970-71. Mem. MLA, Am. Assn. Tchrs. French, Soc. Friends Marcel Proust. Author: Marcel Proust, 1953, Eugene Le Roy, 1957, Corbiere, Laforgue and Apollinaire, 1964, Helen of Troy Myth, 1968; editor: Dictionary of Ideas in Marcel Proust, 1968; Articles on André Spire, 1975; Proust's Gardens, 1977; Proust and Sartre, 1978; Proust's Jewels, 1980; contbr. articles to profl. jours. Office: French and Italian Dept Stanford Univ Stanford CA 94305

NEWMAR, JULIE CHALANE, actress; b. Hollywood, Calif.; d. Donald Charles and Helen (Jesmer) Newmeyer; student U. Calif., Los Angeles. Appeared in movies Seven Brides for Seven Brothers, Silk Stockings, Little Abner, For Love or Money, Marriage-Go-Round (Perry award for Best Supporting Actress), 1959, Stop the World, I Want to Get Off, Damn Yankees, Irma LaDouce, McKenna's Gold. Recipient Perry award. Mem. Actor's Studio.*

NEWMARK, NATHAN MORTIMORE, educator, cons. engr.; b. Plainfield, N.J., Sept. 22, 1910; s. Abraham S. and Mollie (Nathanson) N.; B.C.E., Rutgers U., 1930, D.Sc. (hon.), 1955; M.S., U. Ill., 1932, Ph.D., 1934, D.Sc. (hon.), 1978; Dr. h.c., U. Liège, 1967; LL.D. (hon.), U. Notre Dame, 1969; m. Anne Mae Cohen, Aug. 6, 1932; children—Richard Alan, Linda Beth, Susan Adele. Mem. faculty U. Ill., 1930—, research asst. civil engring., research asso., research asst. prof., research prof. structural engring., 1943-56, prof., head dept. civil engring., 1956-73, prof. civil engring., mem. Center for Advanced Study, 1973—, emeritus, 1976—, chmn. digital computer lab. Grad. Coll., 1951-57. Cons. structural, machine analysis and design govt. agys., indsl. orgns.; editor series of texts, civil engring. and engring. mechanics Prentice Hall, Inc., 1949—; cons. antiseismic design Le Chateau Champlain, Montreal, Que., Can. and Latino Americana Tower, Mexico City, Mexico; prin. seismic Cons. trans-Alaska pipeline, Canadian Arctic pipeline, Bay Area Rapid Transit System, reconstrn. Managua (Nicaragua), others. Cons. NDRC, office field service OSRD, World War II; sci. adv. bd. USAAF, 1945-49; mem. U.S. Nat. Com. Theoretical and Applied Mechanics, 1953-58; tech. adv. bd. Dept. Commerce, 1963-64; mem. com. to form Nat. Acad. Engring., 1964; mem. Pres.'s Com. Nat. Medal of Sci., 1972-78, chmn., 1975-78. Recipient Presdl. Certificate of Merit; award Concrete Reinforced Steel Inst., 1956; Vincent Bendix award Am. Soc. Engring. Edn., 1961; Order of Lincoln, Lincoln Acad. Ill., 1965; Nat. Medal Sci., 1968; Washington award, 1969; John Fritz medal, 1979; named to Am. Soc. Engring. Edn. Hall Fame, 1968; Outstanding Civilian Service medal Dept. Army, 1971. Argentine Acad. Exact, Natural and Phys. Scis. fellow, 1971. Fellow Am. Acad. Arts and Scis., Internat. Assn. Earthquake Engring. (hon.), Am. Geophys. Union, AAAS; mem. ASME (hon., chmn. applied mechanics div. 1954), Nat. Acad. Scis., Nat. Acad. Engring. (charter), ASCE (J. James R. Croes medal 1945, Moisseiff award 1950, Norman medal 1958, E.E. Howard award 1958, Theodore von Karman award 1962, chmn. engring. mechanics div. 1953, hon.), Am. Ry. Engring. Assn., Research Council Bolted Structural Joints, Column, Welding, Reinforced Concrete research councils, Am. Concrete Inst. (bd. dirs. 1949-52, Wason medalist 1950, hon.), Internat. Assn. Bridge and Structural Engrs., Earthquake Engring. Research Inst. (hon.), Am. Soc. Engring. Edn., Seismol. Soc. Am., Phi Beta Kappa, Sigma Xi, Tau Beta Pi, Phi Kappa Phi, Chi Epsilon. Author: (with Emilio Rosenblueth) Fundamentals of Earthquake Engineering, 1971. Editor series of civil engring., engring. mechanics texts. Contbr. articles to profl. jours. Home: 1705 S Pleasant St Urbana IL 61801

NEWPORT, JOHN PAUL, educator, minister; b. Buffalo, Mo., June 16, 1917; s. Marvin Jackson and Mildred Dupont (Morrow) N.; B.A., William Jewell Coll., 1938, Litt.D., 1967; Th.M. So. Baptist Theol. Sem., 1941, Th.D., 1946; M.A., Tex. Christian U., 1968; Ph.D., U. Edinburgh, 1953; m. Eddie Belle Leavell, Nov. 14, 1941; children—Martha Ellen Bailey, Frank Marvin, John Paul. Ordained to ministry, 1939; minister in Miss., Okla., 1943-49; asst. prof. religion, dir. grad. studies in religion Baylor U., 1949-51; prof. N.T., philosophy of religion New Orelans Bapt. Theol Sem., 1951-52; prof. philosophy of religion Southwestern Bapt. Theol. Sem., Ft. Worth, 1952-76, v.p. for acad. affairs, 1979—; prof. religious studies Rice U., 1976-79; dir. field work Boston U. Sch. Theology, 1958-59; postdoctoral vis. fellow, Harvard, 1958-59, Union Theol. Sem., N.Y.C., 1965. Seatlantic fellow Rockefeller Found.; mem. Am. Acad. Religion (pres. Southwestern region 1964), Southwestern Philos. Assn., Am. Soc. Ch. Hist. Author: Theology and Contemporary Art Forms, 1971; Demons, Demons, Demons, 1972; Why Christians Fight Over the Bible, 1974; Christ and the New Consciousness, 1978; Christianity and Contemporary Art Forms, 1979. Home: 4421 Dunwick Ln Fort Worth TX 76109 Office: Southwestern Bapt Theol Sem Box 22000 Fort Worth TX 76122

NEWPORT, MARVIN GENE, univ. dean; b. Albion, Ill., May 18, 1935; s. Marvin Edward and Zola Irene (Smith) N.; B.S., Eastern Ill. U., 1957; M.S., U. Ill., 1961, Ph.D., 1963; m. Sandra Lea Hull, Aug. 30, 1958; children—Monty Gene, Bruce Todd, Brenda Lea. Mem. faculty U. Nebr. at Omaha, 1962-71, asso. prof. mgmt., 1965-68, prof., 1968-71; chmn. dept. bus. adminstrn. U. Ala., Birmingham, 1971-74, dean Sch. Bus., 1974—; cons. supervisory and mgmt. devel. Recipient Author award Am. Soc. Tng. Dirs., 1965, Great Tchrs. award U. Nebr. at Omaha, 1970, Distinguished Alumni award Sch. Bus., Eastern Ill. U., 1977. Mem. Acad. Mgmt., Phi Kappa Phi, Phi Sigma Epsilon, Pi Omega Pi, Sigma Iota Epsilon, Omicron Delta Epsilon, Delta Sigma Pi, Beta Gamma Sigma. Author: Labor Relations and the Supervisor, 1968; The Tools of Managing: Functions, Techniques, and Skills, 1972; Dental Organization Management: Tools, Technics and Skills, 1974; (with R. Trewatha) Management: Functions and Behavior, rev. edit., 1979; editor: Supervisory Management: Tools and Techniques, 1976. Home: 2237 Royal Crest Dr Birmingham AL 35216

NEWSOM, CARROLL VINCENT, ret. educator; b. Buckley, Ill., Feb. 23, 1904; s. Curtis Bishop and Mattie F. (Fisher) N.; A.B., Coll. Emporia, 1924, L.H.D., 1957; M.A., U. Mich., 1927, Ph.D., 1931, LL.D., 1974; recipient 25 hon. degrees; m. Frances J. Higley, Aug. 15, 1928; children—Jeanne Carolyn (Mrs. W.A. Challener, III), Walter Burton, Gerald Higley. Mem. faculties U. Mich., U. N.M., Oberlin Coll., 1927-48; asst. commr. for higher edn. State N.Y. 1948-50, asso. commr. for higher and profl. edn., 1950-55; exec. v.p. N.Y. U., 1955-56, pres., 1956-62; sr. v.p. Prentice-Hall, Inc., Englewood Cliffs, N.J., 1962-64, vice chmn. bd., 1962-65, pres., 1964-65; chmn. bd. Hawthorn Books, 1964-65; chmn. exec. com. Random House, Inc., 1967-70, dir., 1967-70; ednl. cons. RCA, 1965-66, v.p. edn., 1966-69, dir., 1961-71; edn. cons. instns. in France, Turkey, India, Ethiopia. Mem. and former mem. bds. several orgns. in field of edn., math. and internat. affairs; bd. dirs. Nat. Assn. Ednl. Broadcasters; mem., dir. N.Y. World's Fair Corp., 1959-64; bd. dirs. Guggenheim Found., 1962-76, chmn., 1974-76; mem. several other coms. and bds. Decorated chevalier Legion of Honor (France); recipient Pasteur medal. Fellow AAAS (pres. S.W. div. 1940-41, nat. council 1945-46); Benjamin Franklin fellow Royal Soc. Arts (London); mem. and sometime officer several, nat. profl. assns. and orgns. including Phi Beta Kappa. Clubs: N.Y. U. (N.Y.C.). Author or co-author several books in field math., gen. edn., latest being: (with Howard Eves) Foundations and Fundamental Concepts of Mathematics, 1958; Mathematical Discourses, 1964; The Roots of Christianity, 1979; also articles profl. jours. Contbr. yearbook Nat. Soc. for Study of Edn., 1952. Editor: A Television Policy for Education, 1952, Am. Math. Monthly, 1947-51. Home: PO Drawer N New Fairfield CT 06810

NEWSOM, DAVID DUNLOP, fgn. service officer; b. Richmond, Calif., Jan. 6, 1918; s. Fred Stoddard and Ivy Elizabeth (Dunlop) N.; A.B., U. Calif., 1938; M.S., Columbia, 1940; m. Jean Frances Craig, Nov. 17, 1942; children—John, Daniel, Nancy, David, Catherine. Pulitzer traveling scholar, 1940-41; pub. Walnut Creek (Calif.) Courier-Jour., 1946-47; 3d sec., information officer Am. embassy, Karachi, Pakistan, 1948-50; 2d sec., vice consul Oslo, Norway, 1950-51; pub. affairs officer Baghdad, Iraq, 1952-55; officer-in-charge Arabian peninsula affairs Dept. State, Washington, 1955-59; with Nat. War Coll., 1959-60; 1st sec. Am. embassy, London, Eng., 1960-62; dep. dir. Office No. African Affairs, Dept. State, Washington, 1962-63, dir., 1963-65; U.S. ambassador to Libya, 1965-69; asst. sec. state for African affairs, 1969-74; U.S. ambassador to Indonesia, 1974-77, to Philippines, 1977-78; under sec. state of polit. affairs, Washington, 1978—; spl. adviser U.S. del. UN Gen. Assembly, 1972. Served to lt. USNR, 1942-46. Recipient Commendable Service award USIS, 1955; Dept. State Meritorious Service award, 1958; Nat. Civil Service League award, 1972; Rockefeller Pub. Service award, 1973. Mem. U.S. Fgn. Service Assn., Council on Fgn. Relations. Presbyterian. Home: 3230 Woodley Rd NW Washington DC 20008

NEWSOM, LIONEL HODGE, univ. pres.; b. Wichita Falls, Tex., Nov. 11, 1919; s. Lawson J. and Georgia (McCullough) N.; A.B., Lincoln (Mo.) U., 1938, L.H.D., 1975; M.A., U. Mich., 1940; Ph.D., Washington U., St. Louis, 1956; LL.D. (hon.), Davidson Coll., 1972, Bowling Green State U., 1974, Western Mich. U., 1976; D.Hum. (hon.), Miami U., Oxford, Ohio, 1979; m. Jane M. Emerson, June 17, 1946; 1 dau., Jacqueline Newsom Peters. Instr., Lincoln U., 1946-47; asso. prof. sociology Stowe Tchrs. Coll., 1949-51; prof. So. U., Baton Rouge, 1951-55; supr. community services St. Louis Housing Authority, 1955-56; head dept. sociology So. U., 1956-60; prof., dir. Woodrow Wilson Scholarship Program, Morehouse Coll., 1960-64; pres. Barber-Scotia Coll., Concord, N.C., 1964-66; asso. project dir. So. Regional Edn. Bd., Atlanta, 1966-68; pres. Johnson C. Smith U., Charlotte, N.C., 1969-72, Central State U., Wilberforce, Ohio, 1972—; civilian aide to Sec. of Army, 1979—. Past mem. adv. council Danforth Assos.; mem. adv. bd. to com. nat. employment Am. Friends Soc.; chmn. Ga. Council Human Relations, 1963; mem. bd. nat. missions Presbyn. Ch. U.S.A., 1970-73; mem. Nat. Mus. Afro-Am. History and Culture Planning Council, 1973—. Bd. trustees Mint Museum, N.C. Leadership Inst., Boggs Acad., Ga.; bd. visitors Davidson Coll. Served with AUS, 1943-46. Recipient Alumni Achievement award Lincoln U., 1965, Alumni citation Washington U., 1973. Fellow Am. Sociol. Assn.; mem. AAUP (past pres. So. U. chpt.), Nat. Council Social Studies, Inter-Univ. Council Ohio (chmn. 1975-76), So. Sociol. Assn., Assn. Social Sci. Tchrs., Ohio Coll. Assn. (pres. 1976-77), Charlotte C. of C. (bd. dirs.), Alpha Kappa Delta, Pi Gamma Mu, Alpha Phi Alpha (nat. pres. 1964-69, award of merit 1979), Sigma Pi Phi. Rotarian. Author: The Negro in Higher Education in the South, 1967; also articles. Home: President's Residence Central State Univ Wilberforce OH 45384

NEWSOM, MELVIN MAX, research co. exec.; b. El Paso, Tex., Dec. 27, 1931; s. Melvin William and Dorthy Maxine (Kinnison) N.; B.S. in Elec. Engring., Tex. A. and M. U., 1955, M.S. in Elec. Engring. (Tex. Power & Light fellow), 1956; m. Rose Marie Neill, June 5, 1953; children—Terri Laine, Cherri Leigh, Michael Dirk, Thomas Cody. Mem. tech. staff Sandia Lab., Albuquerque, 1956—, sect. supr., 1961-64, div. supr., 1964-77, dept. mgr., 1977, now mgr. exploratory systems devel. Pres. Tex. Shrimp Unltd.; reviewer NSF; cons. Dept. Energy; mem. U.S. group on petroleum tech. Joint U.S./USSR Energy Program; participant several programs Nat. Acad. Engring. Pres. coaches council Young Am. Football League, 1975—, mem. bd., 1977—. Dist. chmn. Republican Party, 1960-61, asst., 1963-64. Served with USN, 1951-53. Decorated Am. Spirit Honor medal; Dept. Energy grantee. Mem. Am. Inst. Mining Engrs., Am. Rose Soc., Tau Beta Pi, Etta Kappa Nu. Presbyterian. Club: Coronado (chmn. bd. 1965-66, 69-70, 73-74, 76-79, dir.). Contbr. numerous articles to profl. jours. Research in improved drilling tech. for petroleum, geothermal and sci. drilling, and on high temperature well logging. Home: 1517 Eastridge Ct NE Albuquerque NM 87112 Office: Dept 5620 PO Box 5800 Albuquerque NM 87115

NEWSOM, WILL ROY, former coll. pres.; b. Rivera, Calif., Jan. 12, 1912; s. William Charles and Sarah Ann (Mitchell) N.; A.B., Whittier Coll., 1934; M.A., U. So. Calif., 1935, Ph.D., 1939; m. Alice Claire Morgan, Jan. 24, 1931; children—Herbert Charles, Janine, Nina Ann. Grad. fellow U. So. Calif., 1935-39; mem. faculty Whittier Coll., 1939—, prof. chemistry, 1940-63, chmn. dept., 1940-66, dean coll., 1963-71, v.p., 1971-75, pres., 1975-79, pres. emeritus, 1979—. Mem. Los Angeles County Air Pollution Adv. Commn., 1944-54. Mem. Whittier City Library Bd., 1954-62, pres., 1956-60; mem. Whittier City Hist. Com., 1969-72. Recipient Shirley Mealer Alumni Service award Whittier Coll., 1962; Honor Scroll award Am. Inst. Chemists, 1979. Mem. Am. Chem. Soc., Pacific S.W. Assn. Chemistry Tchrs. (pres. 1954-55), Whittier Area C. of C. (bd. dirs. 1958-61), Sigma Xi, Phi Lambda Upsilon. Mem. Soc. of Friends. Rotarian. Home: 7829 S Vale Dr Whittier CA 90602

NEWSOME, GEORGE LANE, JR., educator; b. Bessemer, Ala., Oct. 5, 1923; s. George Lane and Mary Viola (Mobbs) N.; B.S., U. Ala., 1949, M.A., 1950; Ph.D., Yale, 1956; m. Martha Cornelia Merchant, June 8, 1947; children—George Lane III, Mary Virginia, Elizabeth Ann. Asst. prof. edn. U. Bridgeport, 1955-57, asso. prof., 1957-58; asso. prof. philosophy of edn. U. Ga., 1958-63, prof., head dept., 1963—; guest prof. Philosophy Inst., No. Ill. U., U. Pacific, 1970; guest lectr. U. Bridgeport, 1954-55. Served with AUS, 1943-46. Mem. Philosophy of Edn. Soc. (sec.-treas. 1964-66), Southeastern Philosophy of Edn. Soc. (pres. 1962), Phi Kappa Phi, Kappa Delta Pi. Author: Philosophical Perspectives, 1961. Editor: Philosophy of Education, Proceedings, 1968; (with William T. Blackstone) Education and Ethics, 1969; mem. bd. editors of Ednl. Philosophy and Theory; mem. editorial bd. Ga. Rev., 1973-75, Ednl. Theory, 1976—; mem. bd. U. Ga. Press, 1976—. Home: 145 Tuxedo Rd Athens GA 30606

NEWSOME, JOHN CHARLES, investment banker; b. Anderson, Ind., May 6, 1902; s. Lee Charles and Emma N. (Forkner) N.; B.S., Yale, 1925; m. Eleanor R. Alexander, June 18, 1929; children—John Charles, Anne A. Newsome Davis. Mem. N.Y. Stock Exchange, 1928-54; with firm Tucker, Anthony & R.L. Day, Inc., N.Y.C., 1954—, now asso. dir. Trustee Village Old Brookville, N.Y., 1949-67. Served to lt. comdr. USNR, World War II. Episcopalian. Home: Cedar Swamp Rd Glen Head NY 11545 Office: 120 Broadway New York City NY 10005

NEWSOME, PAUL ALBERT, former pub. relations exec.; b. Coffeen, Ill., Sept. 12, 1906; s. William Edward and Isadora (Stokes) N.; B.S., Harvard, 1929; m. Ruth A. Taplin, Dec. 5, 1931; children—Patricia (Mrs. Clare C. Leiby, Jr.), Nancy C. (Mrs. Bruce G. Bailey). Reporter, feature writer Lorain (Ohio) Times-Herald, 1924-25; editor, bus. mgr. Weymouth (Mass.) Gazette, 1931-40; condr. N.E. info. program OPA, 1941-44; founder Newsome & Co., Inc., pub. relations, Boston, 1945, now chmn. emeritus, dir. Pub. relations chmn. Boston Jubilee; spl. events chmn. United Fund; dir. Harvard Student Agys., 1962-63; chmn. bd. govs. Redington Beach (Fla.) Assn. Mem. New Eng., Mass. (exec. sec. 1936-38) press assns., Boston C. of C., Pub. Relations Soc. Am., Advt. Fedn. Am. (dir. 1st dist. 1952-53). Republican. Conglist. Clubs: Advertising (dir. 1949—, pres. 1952-53), Publicity (pres. 1959-60), Harvard (Boston); Rotary (pres. Weymouth, Mass. 1937-38); Bath (Fla.). Author: Directory of Weekly Newspapers in New England, 1937. Contbr. articles mags. Home: 16004 4th St E Redington Beach FL 33708

NEWTON, ALEXANDER WORTHY, lawyer; b. Birmingham, Ala., June 19, 1930; s. Jeff H. and Annis Lillian (Kelly) N.; B.S., U. Ala., 1952, LL.B., 1957; m. Sue Aldridge, Dec. 22, 1952; children—Lamar Aldridge, Kelly McClure, Jane Worthy, Robins Jeffry. Admitted to Ala. bar, 1957, since practiced in Birmingham; mem. firm Hare, Wynn, Newell & Newton, 1957—; lectr., U. Ala. Law Sch., Ala. State Bar series Continuing Legal Edn. Served to capt. AUS, 1952-54. Mem. Ala. State Bar (chmn. practices and procedure subsect. 1965), Ala. Trial Lawyers Assn., Internat Soc. Barristers, Am. (dir. 1974-75, sec.-treas. 1976-77, v.p. 1977-78, pres. 1979-80), Birmingham (exec. com. 1967) bar assns., Assn. Trial Lawyers Am., Am. Coll. Trial Lawyers, Am. Judicature Soc., U. Ala. Law Sch. Found. (v.p. 1978-79, pres. elect 1978-80), Sigma Chi. Democrat. Presbyterian. Home: 2837 Canoe Brook Ln Birmingham AL 35243 Office: City Fed Bldg Birmingham AL 35203

NEWTON, BLAKE TYLER, JR., life ins. assn. exec.; b. The Hague, Va., Oct. 17, 1915; s. Blake Tyler and Bertha Effingham (Lawrence) N.; B.A., Coll. William and Mary, 1935, B.C.L., 1938; m. Anne Rodgers Walker, May 31, 1941; children—Blake Tyler III, Anne Rodgers, Julia Benedict. Admitted to Va. bar., 1937, practiced in Warsaw until 1939; asst. prof. Sch. Jurisprudence, Coll. William and Mary, 1938-39; dir. securities div. Va. Corp. Commn., Richmond, 1939-46, gen. counsel, 1946-48; atty. then gen. solicitor Chesapeake & Potomac Telephone Co., 1948-55, gen. atty., 1955; asst. v.p., atty. AT&T, Washington, 1955-56; dir. Shenandoah Life Ins. Co., Roanoke, Va., 1948-59, pres., 1957-59; exec. v.p. Inst. Life Ins. (merged Am. Life Ins. Assn. 1976, now Am. Council Life Ins.), N.Y.C., 1959-61, pres., 1962—; dir. N.Am. Philips Corp., Putnam Trust Co., Bank of Va. Co.; mem. governing com. U.S. Philips Trust. Trustee, Va. Theol. Sem.; mem. corp. Greenwich (Conn.) Hosp. Assn. Served to lt. USNR, 1942-46. Recipient Algernon Sydney Sullivan award Coll. William and Mary, 1974; John Newton Russell award Nat. Assn. Life Underwriters, 1974; Free Enterprise award Ins. Fedn. N.Y., 1974. Mem. Am., Va., D.C. bar assns., Am. Law Inst. (life), Nat. Inst. Social Scis., Pi Kappa Alpha, Omicron Delta Kappa. Episcopalian (vestry). Office: 1850 K St NW Washington DC 20006

NEWTON, CARL DAVIDSON, photo-finishing co. exec.; b. San Antonio, July 9, 1919; s. Carl D. and Ethel (Alford) N.; student Wharton Sch. Fin. and Commerce U. Pa., 1937-38, Duke U.; m. Mary Jane Lawrence, Sept. 16, 1944; children—Carl, John L., William S. With Fox-Stanley Photo Products, Inc., San Antonio, 1945—, chmn. bd., 1970-79, vice chmn. bd., 1979—; dir. Alamo Nat. Bank, San Antonio, 1974-78. Served with USN, 1941-45. Home: PO Box 21H Wetmore TX 78163 Office: Fox Stanley Photo Products 8750 Tesoro Dr San Antonio TX 78286

NEWTON, CARL ELBRIDGE, lawyer; b. Somerville, Mass., Aug. 22, 1898; s. Elbridge Ward and Adelaide Louise (Veazie) N.; student Tufts Coll., 1916-17; B.S., Dartmouth, 1920; B.A. in Jurisprudence, Oxford (Eng.) U., 1922, B.C.L. (Rhodes scholar), 1923, M.A. (hon.), 1968; postgrad. in law Harvard, 1924; m. Mary Barrow, June 12, 1926; children—Sallie Barrow Newton Calhoun, William Elbridge, Thomas Vesey. Admitted to N.Y. bar, 1927; asst. U.S. atty. So. Dist. N.Y., N.Y.C., 1925-27; barrister Inner Temple, London, 1924—; spl. asst. atty. gen. N.Y., N.Y.C., 1928; asso. firm White & Case, N.Y.C., 1929-33; mem. firm Donovan, Leisure, Newton & Irvine, N.Y.C. and Washington, 1934-42, 46—; pres. C. & O. Ry., Cleve., also Richmond, Va., 1942-46. Dep. U.S. coal Mines adminstr., 1943. Served as 2d lt. USA, 1918-19. Fellow Am. Coll. Trial Lawyers; mem. Am. Bar Assn., Bar Assn. City N.Y., S.A.R., Fed. Bar Council, Soc. Mayflower Descs., Phi Beta Kappa, Zeta Psi. Congregationalist. Mason. Clubs: Century Assn., Explorers, Church, River. Home: 1088 Park Ave New York City NY 10028 Office: 30 Rockefeller Plaza New York City NY 10020

NEWTON, CAROL MARILYN, biomathematician; b. Oakland, Calif., Nov. 26, 1925; d. Phillip S. and Effie Mae (Gillett) Newton; A.B., Stanford U., 1947, M.S., 1949, Ph.D. in Physics, 1956; M.D., U. Chgo., 1960. Intern, U. Chgo. Clinics, 1960-61; U. Chgo. research asso. Argonne (Ill.) Cancer Research Hosp. and Biol. Sci. Computer Center, 1961-63; asst. prof. dept. medicine, com. on math. biology Argonne Cancer Research Hosp., 1963-66; asso. prof. biomathematics, asst. dir. health scis. computing facility U. Calif., Los Angeles, 1967-74, asso. prof. radiology, 1972-74, prof. biomathematics and radiology, 1974—, chmn. dept. biomathematics, 1974—, asso. dir. health scis. computing facility, 1974; mem. commns. on internat. relations Nat. Acad. Scis., joint chmn. U.S./Yugoslavia Research Program; mem. coop. clin. investigation rev. com. Nat. Cancer Inst.; mem. com. on conservation lab. animals Assembly of Life Scis., NRC; mem. liaison subcom. on systems and decision scis. Nat. Acad. Sci. advisory com. on Internat. Inst. Applied Systems Analysis. Named Woman of Sci., U. Calif., Los Angeles, 1975. Mem. Assn. Computing Machinery (past chmn., adv. com. spl. interest group on biomed. computing), Soc. Math. Biology, Am. Statis. Assn. Contbr. articles on cancer treatment, computer supports to radiotherapy, interactive graphics, exploratory data analysis to profl. jours.; asso. editor Ann. Rev. Biophysics and Bioengring.; mem. editorial bd. Math. Bioscis., Computers, Mathematics with Applications. Office: U Calif Dept Biomathematics Los Angeles CA 90024

NEWTON, CHARLES MARTIN, basketball coach; b. Rockwood, Tenn., Feb. 2, 1930; s. Richard Yates and Adelia (Martin) N.; A.B., U. Ky., 1952, M.A., 1957; postgrad. U. Ala., 1964-65; m. Evelyn Davis, Dec. 22, 1951; children—Debbie, Tracy, Martin. Basketball coach, asst. prof. phys. edn. Transylvania U., 1952-53, 55-68; head basketball coach U. Ala., 1968—; condr. basketball clinics, U.S., Central Am., Japan, Europe; dir. 1st State Bank of Tuscaloosa. Bd. dirs. Black Warrior council Boy Scouts Am.; mem. basketball rules com. NCAA. Served with USAF, 1953-55. Recipient numerous Coach of Yr. awards, including Southeastern Conf., 1975, 76, NCAA Dist. III, 1973. Mem. Nat. Assn. Basketball Coaches (dir.), AAHPER. Republican. Presbyterian. Contbr. numerous articles to coaching publs.; also film: Motivating Young Players Through Ball Handling, 1976. Home: 1 Woodland Hills Tuscaloosa AL 35405 Office: Box K Athletic Dept U Ala University AL 35486

NEWTON, DEREK ARNOLD, educator; b. Richmond, Eng., Feb. 18, 1930; s. John Newton and Joan Maude (Garnett) Newton Wright; A.B., Wabash Coll., 1952; M.B.A., Harvard U., 1962, D. Bus. Adminstrn. (Ford Found. fellow), 1964. Sales mgr. R.H. Donnelley Corp., Washington, 1954-60; lectr. in bus. adminstr. Harvard U. Sch. Bus., 1964-70; prof. bus. adminstrn. U. Va., 1970-76, Elis and Signe Olsson prof. bus. adminstrn., 1976—; cons. in sales and gen. mgmt. to various U.S. corps.; fellow U. Va. Center for Study Applied Ethics, 1977—. Mem. Am. Mktg. Assn. Author: Cases in Sales Force Management, 1970; Sales Force Performance and Turnover, 1973; Think Like a Man, Act Like a Lady, Work Like a Dog, 1979. Home: 228 Harvest Dr Charlottesville VA 22901 Office: PO Box 6550 U Va Charlottesville VA 22906

NEWTON, DOUGLAS, museum curator; b. Malaysia, Sept. 22, 1920 (Brit. citizen); s. Joseph and Gladys (Duggan) N.; ed. in Eng.; m. Kathleen Haven, Oct. 18, 1964. Mem. staff Mus. Primitive Art, N.Y.C., 1957-75, curator, then dir., 1960-78, trustee, 1975-78; curator, then cons. chmn. dept. primitive art Met. Mus. Art, N.Y.C., 1973-75, chmn., 1975—; research asso. Australian Mus., Sydney, 1974; mem. exhbns. com. Am. Fedn. Art, 1975; advisor Nat. Gallery Australia, Canberra, 1974; organizer numerous mus. exhbns., mem. various field expdns.; author: Art Styles of the Papuan Gulf, 1961, Crocodile and Cassowary: Religious Art of the Upper Sepik River, New Guinea, 1971, Masterpieces of Primitive Art: The Nelson A. Rockefeller Collection, 1978; also mus. catalogues. Office: Met Museum Art Fifth Ave at 82d St New York NY 10028

NEWTON, FRANCIS JOHN, museum cons.; b. Butte, Mont., Dec. 27, 1912; s. Frank Robert and Freda (Schilling) N.; B.A., U. Idaho, 1936, M.A., 1939, L.H.D., 1974; Ph.D., U. Iowa, 1951; Hospitant, Royal Art Acad., Stockholm, 1938. Tchr., Lewiston (Idaho) State Normal Sch., 1939-40; curatorial asst. Worcester (Mass.) Art Mus., 1951-53; curator Portland Art Mus., 1953-60. dir., 1960-75, devel. cons., 1975—, also sec.; chief cons. art Portland High Sch. curriculum. 1959; vis. prof. art history U. Oreg., 1959. Mem. Gov.'s Planning Council for Arts and Humanities. Served from seaman to lt. (j.g.), USCGR, 1942-46. Decorated Order of No. Star (Sweden); recipient Distinguished Citizen award U. Oreg., 1970. Mem. Coll. Art Assn., Am. Assn. Museums, Assn. Art Mus. Dirs., Phi Beta Kappa. Home: 6805 S E 31st Ave Portland OR 97202

NEWTON, FRANK RICHARDS, JR., investment banker; b. San Antonio, Jan. 5, 1903; s. Frank Richards and Carrie Thomason (Boyle) N.; B.A., U. Tex., 1924; m. Llora Beach Stout, June 1, 1939; children—Cynthia (Mrs. William K. Gayden), Anne. Co-founder, former mng. partner firm Lentz, Newton & Co., mems. N.Y. Stock Exchange, San Antonio; account exec. Eppler, Guerin & Turner, Inc. Served to comdr. USNR, WW II. Mem. Beta Theta Pi. Presbyn. Clubs: San Antonio Country, Order Alamo (past pres.), German (past v.p.), Argyle. Home: 318 W Lynwood Ave San Antonio TX 78212 Office: 214 NE Loop 410 PO Box 32768 San Antonio TX 78284

NEWTON, GEORGE ADDISON, investment banker, lawyer; b. Denver, Apr. 2, 1911; s. George Addison and Gertrude (Manderson) N.; student Colo. State Prep. Sch.; A.B., U. Colo., 1933; LL.B., Harvard, 1936; m. Mary Virginia Powell, Sept. 18, 1937; children—George Addison IV, Nancy Ella, Virginia Powell. Admitted to Ill. bar, 1937, Mo. bar, 1946; asso. Scott, MacLeish & Falk, Chgo., 1936-42; partner G.H. Walker & Co., St. Louis, 1946-62, mng. partner, 1962-72; chmn. bd. Stifel Nicolaus & Co., Inc., St. Louis, 1973—, chief exec. officer 1974-78. Bd. govs. Greater St. Louis Community Chest; mem. Council on Civic Needs; bd. dirs. Episcopal Home for Children, St. Luke's Hosp., Goodwill Industries, U. Colo. Improvement Corp.; dir. devel. fund U. Colo., 1954-55, chmn., 1955; trustee Fontbonne Coll., chmn., 1974-77; trustee Govtl. Research Inst., Whitfield Sch. Served to maj. USAAF, 1942-45; trial judge adv. Western Flying Tng. Command, 1942-43; legal officer procurement div. Wright Field, 1944-45. Recipient C. Fobb award U. Colo., 1955, alumni recognition award, 1958; named to C Club Hall Fame, 1968; silver ann. All Am. award Sports Illustrated, 1957; Norlin award U. Colo., 1968. Mem. Investment Bankers Assn. Am. (pres. 1961), Nat. Assn. Securities Dealers (gov. 1954-56; vice chmn. 1956), Assn. Stock Exchange Firms (gov. 1969—), Sales Execs. Assn. (dir. 1955-60), U. Colo. Assn. Alumni (dir. 1965-67), Phi Beta Kappa, Phi Gamma Delta. Episcopalian (treas. diocese of Mo., 1958-69; sr. warden; trustee diocesan investment trust). Clubs: Racquet, Noonday, St. Louis, Bellerive Country, Media (St. Louis); Denver Country; Legal (Chgo.); Boulder (Colo.) Country; Links (N.Y.C.). Home: 6428 Cecil Ave Saint Louis MO 63105 Office: 500 N Broadway St Saint Louis MO 63102. *A reward of one's own accomplishment is realizing how help of others made it possible. Gratitude makes life so much more meaningful.*

NEWTON, JAMES QUIGG, JR., found. exec.; b. Denver, 1911; s. James Quigg and Nelle (Singleton) N.; grad. Philips Acad., Andover; A.B., Yale, 1933, LL.B., 1936; D.P.S., U. Denver, 1952; LL.D., Adams State Coll., 1960, Colo. Coll., 1962; m. Virginia Shafroth, June 6, 1942; children—Nancy Ellen, Nelle Grainger, Abby Staunton, Virginia Rice. Legal sec. to W.O. Douglas, SEC, 1936-37; admitted to Colo. bar, 1938, and practiced in Denver, 1938-42, 46-47; lectr. U. Denver, 1938-41; with Ford Found., N.Y.C., 1955-56, v.p., 1956; pres. U. Colo., 1956-63; pres. Commonwealth Fund, N.Y.C., 1963-75, vice chmn., 1975-76, dir., 1951-55, 57-78; sr. cons. Henry J. Kaiser Family Found., Palo Alto, Calif., 1978—; dir. N.Y. Life Fund, 1972—, Kaiser Found. Hosps./Health Plan, 1972—; trustee Dry Dock Savs. Bank. Mem. Western Interstate Com. Higher Edn., 1957-63; nat. adv. mental health council NIH, 1964-68; mem. Inst. Medicine, Nat. Acad. Scis., 1972—; mem. VA Spl. Med. Adv. Group, 1968-74. Mayor, City and County of Denver, 1947-55. Sec. bd. trustees U. Denver, 1938-42, pres., 1946-47; pub. trustee Nutrition Found.; chmn. bd. YMCA Greater N.Y., 1976-77. Served with USNR, 1942-46. Fellow Acad. Arts and Scis.; mem. Am. Municipal Assn. (pres. 1950), Am. Council Edn. (dir. 1959-62), Am. Arbitration Assn. (dir., exec. com.), Nat. Inst. Social Scis., Fgn. Bondholders Protective Council (dir. 1975—), Phi Delta Phi, Alpha Delta Phi. Home: 754 DeSoto Dr Palo Alto CA 94303 Office: 2 Palo Alto Sq Palo Alto CA 94304

NEWTON, JOHN SKILLMAN, engring. exec.; b. Oneonta, N.Y., Sept. 21, 1908; s. Charles E. and Elizabeth (Coats) N.; B.S., Oreg. State U., 1930; m. Catherine Strachan, Sept. 23, 1929; children—Ronald, Richard, Bette, Margaret; m. 2d, Wannetta Roth, Oct. 24, 1946; children—Barbara, Charles. Engr., Westinghouse Elec. Corp., 1930-48, asst. mgr. engring., steam div., 1944-48; v.p. charge engring. Baldwin Locomotive Works, 1948-51, v.p. locomotive div., 1951-53; v.p. Baldwin-Lima-Hamilton Corp., Eddystone, 1953, v.p. testing equipment div., 1954-55; v.p., then exec. v.p. Goodman Mfg. Co. (now Mangood Corp.), Chgo., 1955-63, pres., chief adminstrv. officer, 1963-65; v.p. Westinghouse Air Brake Co., 1965-66; pres., chief exec. officer Portec Inc., Chgo., 1966-74, also dir.; pres. Newton Engring. Co., 1976—; dir. Intercole Automation, Inc., Ill. State Bank, Goodwill Industries. Mem. ASME, Am. Inst. Mining, Metall. and Petroleum Engineers. Clubs: Mid-America (Chgo.); Glen Oak Country. Contbr. tech. articles profl. jours. Home: 22 W 450 Ahlstrand Dr Glen Ellyn IL 60137

NEWTON, MICHAEL, physician; b. Malvern, Eng., June 4, 1920; s. Frank Leslie and Alice (Henderson) N.; B.A., Cambridge (Eng.) U., 1942, M.B., B.Ch., 1944, M.A., 1946; M.D., U. Pa., 1943; m. Niles Polk Rumely, Mar. 27, 1943; children—Elizabeth Willoughby (Mrs. Robert M. Reed), Frances Lees (Mrs. Stephen C. Stuntz), Edward Robson, Warren Polk. Came to U.S., 1941, naturalized, 1949. House surgeon in English hosps., 1944-46; tng. physiology, surgery, obstetrics and gynecology U.Pa. Med. Sch., 1946-53; prof., chmn. dept. obstetrics and gynecology U. Miss. Med. Center, Jackson, 1955-66; dir. Am. Coll. Obstetricians and Gynecologists, Chgo., 1966-74; prof. obstetrics and gynecology Pritzker Sch. Medicine, U. Chgo., 1966-77, Northwestern U. Med. Sch., 1977—; dir. Nat. Bd. Med. Examiners, 1966-69. Rockefeller student, 1941. Diplomate Am. Bd. Surgery, Am. Bd. Obstetrics and Gynecology. Fellow Am. Assn. Obstetricians and Gynecologists, Am. Gynecol. Soc., Am. Coll. Obstetricians and Gynecologists, A.C.S.; mem. AMA, Am. Fertility Soc., Central Assn. Obstetricians and Gynecologists (life), Assn. Profs. Gynecology and Obstetrics (hon.), Chgo. Gynecol. Soc. Author articles, chpt. in books. Editor: (with E.E. Philipp and J. Barnes) Scientific Foundations of Obstetrics and Gynecology, 1970, 2d edit., 1977; editor Jour. Reproductive Medicine; editorial bd. Internat. Corr. Soc. Obstetricians and Gynecologists; internat. bd. editors Excerpta Medica. Home: 2440 N Lakeview Ave Chicago IL 60614 Office: 333 E Superior St Chicago IL 60611

NEWTON, NORMAN THOMAS (KING), landscape architect, educator; b. Corry, Pa., Apr. 21, 1898; s. John Peter and Jessie Bertha (King) N.; B.S., Cornell U., 1919, Master Landscape Design, 1920; fellow Am. Acad. in Rome, Italy, 1923-26; A.M. (hon.), Harvard, 1957; m. Lyyli E.E. Lamsa, July 20, 1966. Landscape architect with Bryant Fleming, Wyoming, N.Y., 1920-23; with Ferruccio Vitale, N.Y.C., 1926-31, asso. firm, 1930-31; ind. practice, N.Y.C., 1931-42; landscape architect for many parks, residences, instns., historic sites and other land devels.; asso. landscape architect U.S. Nat. Park Service, 1933-39, later cons.; asst. prof. landscape architecture Harvard Grad. Sch. Design, 1939-47, asso. prof., 1947-55, prof., 1955-66, Charles Eliot prof. landscape architecture, 1963-66, Charles Eliot prof. emeritus, 1966—, chmn. dept. archtl. scis., 1949-64, sec. faculty design, 1950-64; resident landscape architect Am. Acad. in Rome (Italy), 1967. Bd. dirs. Hubbard Ednl. Trust. Awarded Rome prize in landscape architecture, 1923. Served as aviation cadet USMCR, 1918; served to lt. col. USAAF, 1942-46; 330th Air Service Group, 1942-43; sr. monuments officer, Brit. 8th Army, through Italian campaign; later, dir. sub-commn. for Monuments, Fine Arts and Archives, Allied Commn., Italy. Decorated comdr. Sts. Maurice and Lazarus, grand officer Crown of Italy, 1946; Order Star of Solidarity (Italy), 1950. Fellow Am. Acad. Rome, Am. Soc. Landscape Architects (trustee; treas. 1940-43, 46-57, nat. pres. 1957-61, Bradford Williams medal 1975 ASLA medal 1979); mem. Alumni Assn. Am. Acad. in Rome, Accademia Fiorentina della Arti del Disegno, New Eng. Historic Geneal. Soc., Theta Delta Chi. Clubs: Century Assn. (N.Y.C.); Faculty (Cambridge). Author: Structure of Design, Preliminary Notes, 1949; An Approach to Design, 1951, rev. edit., 1973; Design on the Land, the Development of Landscape Architecture, 1971; King-Rice Notes, 1976; The Forebears of George Oscar King, 1978. Editor: State Park Master Planning Manual, 1937; War Damage to Monuments and Fine Arts of Italy, 1946; Uncle Johnny, a Soldier's Journal, 1974. Contbr. to profl. jours. Lectr.; critic in design at ateliers, 1927-38. Home: 20 Prescott St Cambridge MA 02138

NEWTON, ROBERT CHAFFER, geologist, educator; b. Bellingham, Wash., June 11, 1933; s. Leslie Charles and Esther Ann (Ferguson) N.; student U. Kans., 1951-53; A.B., U. Calif., Los Angeles, 1956, M.A., 1958, Ph.D., 1963; m. Sabron Louise Reynolds, July 16, 1967; children—Miriam Ruth, Benjamin Willard. Asst. prof. geology U. Chgo., 1963-68, asso. prof., 1968-71, prof., 1971—. NSF grantee, 1964—. Mem. Geol. Soc. Am., Mineral. Soc. Am., Am. Geophys. Union. Mem. Soc. of Friends. Contbr. articles to profl. jours. Home: 5406 University Ave Chicago IL 60615 Office: Dept Geophys Sci Univ Chgo Chicago IL 60637

NEWTON, ROBERT EUGENE, educator; b. St. Louis, Oct. 16, 1917; s. H. Melville and Lily C. (Peterson) N.; B.S. in Mech. Engring., Washington U., St. Louis, 1938, M.S., 1939; Ph.D., U. Mich., 1951; m. Dorothy M. Fairbank, Jan. 31, 1942; children—Peggy D. (Mrs. Alan L. Rector), Gary Fairbank. From asst. applied math. to asso. prof. Washington U., 1938-51; head structural methods unit Curtiss-Wright Corp., 1941-45; sr. engr. McDonnell Aircraft Corp., 1945; prof. mech. engring. Naval Postgrad. Sch., Monterey, Calif., 1951—, chmn. dept., 1953-67; vis. prof. U. Wales, Swansea, 1968-69; cons. to industry, 1938—. Trustee Carmel (Calif.) Unified Sch. Dist., 1961-68, pres., 1962-67. Gov., Community Theatre Monterey Peninsula, 1971-73. Recipient Distinguished Service award St. Louis County Jr. C. of C. Fellow ASME (Jr. award 1940); mem. Am. Soc. Engring. Edn., Soc. Exptl. Stress Analysis, Sigma Xi, Tau Beta Pi, Omicron Delta Kappa. Presbyn. Author articles, chpt. in book. Home: 3810 Whitman Circle Carmel CA 93923 Office: Naval Postgrad Sch Monterey CA 93940

NEWTON, ROBERT PARK, JR., engring. co. exec.; b. Jackson, Ga., Oct. 25, 1913; s. Robert Park and Bessie (Powell) N.; B.S. in Chem. Engring., Ga. Inst. Tech., 1935; m. Elizabeth Edwards, Aug. 11, 1936; children—Nancy, Elizabeth, Robert Park III, William Aris. Asst. chemistry instr. Ga. Inst. Tech., 1936; research chemist Swann & Co., Birmingham, Ala., 1936-39; plant design engr. Naval Stores, Valdosta, Ga., 1940; exec. v.p. Wannamaker Chem. Co., Orangeburg, S.C., 1941-45; pres., treas. Applied Engring Co., Orangeburg, 1946-74, chmn. bd., 1974-79; chmn. bd. Dynamatics, Inc., Tampa, Fla.; dir. 1st Nat. Bank, Orangeburg. Trustee Orangeburg Regional Hosp.; mem.

nat. adv. bd. Ga. Inst. Tech.; bd. dirs., mem. exec. com. U.S. Indsl. Council. Mem. Am. Chem. Soc., S.C. C. of C. (dir.), Phi Delta Theta, Tau Beta Pi, Alpha Chi Sigma. Rotarian. Clubs: Summit, Palmetto (Columbia); Orangeburg Country; Wildcat Cliffs Country (Highlands, N.C.); Green Boundary (Aiken, S.C.). Inventor engring. devices. Home: 1120 Moss Ave Orangeburg SC 29115 Office: Carolina Bldg Orangeburg SC 29115

NEWTON, ROGER GERHARD, educator, physicist; b. Landsberg, Germany, Nov. 30, 1924; s. Arthur and Margaret (Blume) Neuweg; came to U.S., 1946, naturalized, 1949; student U. Berlin (Germany); A.B. summa cum laude, Harvard, 1949, M.A., 1950, Ph.D., 1953; m. Ruth Gordon, June 18, 1953; children—Rachel, Julie, Paul. Teaching fellow Harvard, 1951-52; mem. Inst. Advanced Study, Princeton, 1953-55, 79; mem. faculty Ind. U., 1955-, prof. physics, 1960-78, disting. prof. physics, 1978—, chmn. dept., 1973—, chmn. math. physics program, 1965—; vis. prof. U. Rome (Italy), 1962-63, U. Montpellier (France), 1971-72. Pres., Bloomington Civil Liberties Union, 1968. Served with AUS, 1946-47. Recipient Bowdoin prize Harvard, 1949. Jewett fellow, 1953-55; NSF sr. postdoctoral fellow, 1962-63; C.N.R.S. fellow U. Montpellier, France, 1971-72. Fellow Am. Phys. Soc.; mem. N.Y. Acad. Scis., Fedn. Am. Scientists, AAUP, AAAS, Phi Beta Kappa, Sigma Xi. Author: Scattering Theory of Waves and Particles, 1966; The Complex j-Plane, 1964; also articles. Asso. editor Jour. Math. Physics, 1967-70, 73-76.

NEWTON, THOMAS HANS, physician, educator; b. Berlin, Germany, May 9, 1925; s. Rudolf and Kate (Silberstein) Neustadter; came to U.S., 1938, naturalized, 1945; B.A., U. Calif. at Berkeley, 1949; M.D., U. Calif. at San Francisco, 1952; m. Patricia Workman, July 31, 1949; children—Judith, Diane. Intern, U. Wis. Hosps., Madison, 1952-53; resident U. Calif. Med. Center, San Francisco, 1953-54, Peter Bent Brigham Hosp., Boston, 1955-58; prof. radiology, chief sect. neuroradiology U. Calif. Sch. Medicine, San Francisco, 1959—. Served with USNR, 1943-46. Mem. Am. Soc. Neuroradiology, Assn. Univ. Radiologists. Editor: Radiology of the Skull and Brain, Vol. I, 1971, Vol. II, 1974, Vol. III, 1977, Vol. IV, 1978. Home: 200 S Ridgewood Rd Kentfield CA 94904 Office: Dept Radiology U Calif Sch Medicine San Francisco CA 94122

NEWTON, WAYNE, entertainer, actor, rec. artist; b. Norfolk, Va., Apr. 3, 1942; s. Patrick and Evelyn (Smith) N.; m. Elaine Okamura, June 1, 1968. Appearances include Sands, Desert Inn, Flamingo and Frontier hotels, Las Vegas, Harrah's Club, Reno and Lake Tahoe, Americana Hotel, N.Y.C., Talk of the Town, London, London Paladium, Grand Ole Oprey House, Nashville, Astrodome, Houston, Hollywood (Calif.) Bowl, Melodyland, Anaheim, Calif., Circle Star, San Francisco, Sea World, Orlando, Fla., Sherman House, Chgo., Deauville and Eden Roc hotels, Miami Beach, Fla. Boardwalk Regency Hotel, Atlantic City, N.J.; TV appearances on shows of Jack Benny, Ed Sullivan, Lucille Ball, Joey Bishop, Jackie Gleason, Dean Martin, Bob Hope, Merv Griffin; other TV appearances include Tonight Show, Bonanza, Wayne Newton spls.: One More Time, Opreyland USA, Having a Good Time, Sea World, Country Portrait, UNICEF in Berlin, Red, White & Wow, A Christmas Card; film appearance in 80 Steps to Jonah, 1969. A supporter St. John's Indian Mission, Levene, Ariz.; recs. Capitol, MGM, Chelsea, 20th Century, Aries II. Recipient citation as distinguished recording artist and humanitarian, 1971; Lantern award North Ch., Boston, others. Address: care Waynco PO Box 856 San Luis Obispo CA 93406

NEWTON-JOHN, OLIVIA, singer; b. Cambridge, Eng., Sept. 26, 1948; d. Brin and Irene (Born) N.-J.; student pub. schs. Singer in Australia, Eng., U.S., 1965—; appeared in film Grease, 1978. Recipient awards Acad. Country Music, 1973, Country Music Assn. (U.K.), 1974, Country Music Assn., 1974, Grammy awards, 1973, 74, AGVA, 1974, Billboard, People's Choice, 1974, Record World, 1974, 75, 76, Nat. Assn. Retail Merchandisers. Address: care LK Prodns 9229 Sunset Blvd Los Angeles CA 90069

NEXON, HUBERT HENRY, pub. utility exec.; b. Boston, Mar. 4, 1917; s. Norman D. and Sadie (Sheppy) N.; A.B., Harvard, 1937, LL.B., 1940; m. Phyllis L. Goldstein, Aug. 3, 1942; children—David H., Norman D., Janet A. Admitted to N.Y. bar, 1941, Ill. bar, 1946; atty. with U.S. Govt., then engaged in pvt. practice, 1946-55; with Commonwealth Edison Co., Chgo., 1955—, sr. v.p., 1973—. Mem. Bd. Edn. Northbrook (Ill.) Elementary Schs., 1955-58. Bd. govs. Met. Housing and Planning Council Chgo. Served with AUS, 1942-45. Mem. Am., Chgo. bar assns. Clubs: Mid-Day, Economic (Chgo.). Home: 554 Oakdale Ave Glencoe IL 60022 Office: 1 First National Plaza PO Box 767 Chicago IL 60690

NEXSEN, JULIAN JACOBS, lawyer; b. Kingstree, S.C., Apr. 14, 1924; s. William Ivey and Barbara (Jacobs) N.; student The Citadel, 1941-43; B.S. magna cum laude, U. S.C., 1948, LL.B. magna cum laude, 1950; m. Mary Elizabeth McIntosh, Jan. 28, 1948; children—Louise Ivey (Mrs. Heyward H. Bouknight, Jr.), Julian Jacobs. Admitted to S.C. bar, 1950, U.S. Supreme Ct. bar, 1960; partner firm Nexsen, Pruet, Jacobs & Pollard, Columbia, S.C., 1950—; dir. Am. Sentinel Life Ins. Co., Lawyers Abstract Co. Bd. dirs. Columbia Music Festival Assn., Columbia Philharmonic Orch., 1967-70, ARC Richland-Lexington Counties (S.C.); chmn. bd. trustees Providence Hosp., Richland County Pub. Library. Served to lt., inf., AUS, 1943-46, to capt., 1950-51. Decorated Silver Star, Bronze Star. Mem. Am., S.C. (gov. 1974-79), Richland County (pres. 1974-75) bar assns., S.C. Bar Found. (pres. 1971-72), Am. Law Inst., Am. Coll. Probate Counsel (regent 1973—), Am. Judicature Soc., Phi Beta Kappa. Democrat. Presbyterian (elder 1967—, trustee Congaree presbytery 1967—, trustee Synod S.C. 1969-74). Clubs: Forest Lake Country, Palmetto, Summit, Kiwanis (dir. 1972-74, 77-79). (Columbia). Home: 2840 Sheffield Rd Columbia SC 29204 Office: 1200 First Nat Bldg Main at Washington Columbia SC 29201

NEY, EDWARD NOONAN, advt. exec.; b. St. Paul, May 26, 1925; s. John Joseph and Marie (Noonan) N.; B.A. (Lord Jeffrey Amherst scholar 1942), Amherst Coll., 1947; m. Suzanne Hayes, 1950 (div. 1974); children—Nicholas, Hilary, Michelle; m. 2d, Judith I. Lasky, May 24, 1974. Account exec. Batten, Barton, Durstine & Osborn, N.Y.C., 1947-51; with Young & Rubicam, Inc., N.Y.C., 1951—, v.p., 1959-63, sr. v.p., 1963-67, exec. v.p., 1967-68, pres. internat. div., 1968-70, chmn., chief exec. officer, 1970—; dir. Warner Communications Inc. Bd. dirs., mem. exec. com. Radio Free Europe, 1975—; trustee, mem. exec. com. Com. for Econ. Devel., 1973—; trustee Nat. Urban League, 1974—, Amherst Coll., 1979—, N.Y. U. Med. Center, 1979—. Served to lt. (j.g.) USNR, 1943-46. Mem. Council Fgn. Relations. Home: Pound Ridge NY 10576 Office: 285 Madison Ave New York NY 10017

NEY, EDWARD PURDY, physicist; b. Mpls., Oct. 28, 1920; s. Otto Frederick and Jessamine (Purdy) N.; B.S., U. Minn., 1942; Ph.D., U. Va., 1947; m. June Felsing, June, 1942; children—Judy, John, Arthur, William. Research asst., research asso. U. Va., 1940-46; cons. Naval Research Lab., 1943-44; asst. prof. U. Va., 1947; mem. faculty dept. physics and astronomy U. Minn., Mpls., 1947—, prof., 1955-74, U. Minn. regents prof., 1974—, chmn. dept. astronomy, 1974-78. Recipient NASA Exceptional Sci. Achievement medal, 1975. Mem. Am. Phys. Soc., Am. Geophys. Union, Am. Astron. Soc., Nat. Acad. Sci., Am. Acad. Arts and Sci., Internat. Astron. Union, Sigma Xi. Author: Electromagnetism and Relativity, 1962; contbr. articles to profl. jours. Home: 1925 Penn Ave S Minneapolis MN 55405 Office: Sch Physics and Astronomy 116 Church St SE Minneapolis MN 55455

NEY, JEROME M., dept. store exec.; b. Ft. Smith, Ark., Aug. 23, 1906; s. Rudolph and Marie (Baer) N.; grad. Culver Mil. Acad., 1924; m. Ione Sternberg, Nov. 26, 1936; children—Randolph J., Jerome M. Dept. store work, 1924—, stock boy, Chgo., salesman, 1925-26, asst. dept. mgr., 1926-28, dept. mgr., 1928-30, divisional mdse. mgr., 1930-32, gen. mdse. mgr., 1932-36; pres., gen. mgr. Boston Store Dry Goods Co., Fort Smith and Fayetteville, Ark., 1936-73, chmn. bd., 1973—; on leave with OPA, Washington, 1942-46, chief program planning br., 1943, dir. miscellaneous products rationing div., 1944, asst. dept. adminstr. for rationing, 1944, dir. counsumer goods price div., 1944-45, dep. adminstr. price, 1945-46; pres. Kerr's, Inc., Oklahoma City, 1953-61; v.p., dir. Daniels & Fisher Stores Co., Denver, 1954-57, Stix, Baer & Fuller, Inc. St. Louis, 1949-60; pres., dir. Lawrence Corp., Denver, 1957-61; pres. White House Dry Goods Co., Beaumont, Tex., 1950-61, chmn. bd., 1961—; chmn. bd. Balliet's, Inc., Oklahoma City, 1967—. Trustee, exec. com. Am. Retail Fedn., 1945-60, chmn. bd., 1947-48; mem. Emergency Econ. Stablzn. Retailing Industry Adv. Com., 1968-70. Trustee Sparks Meml. Hosp., Ft. Smith, 1963-65; lay adv. bd. St. Edward Mercy Hosp., 1967-70. Mem. Nat. Retail Mchts. Assn. (dir., v.p. 1960-61, 72-73, chmn. vendor relations com. 1959-70, silver plaque for service to retailing 1965, exec. com. 1966-69, dir. 1974-78). Home: 1010 S Albert Pike Fort Smith AR Office: 5111 Rogers Ave Fort Smith AR 72903

NEY, ROBERT LEO, physician; b. Brno, Czechoslovakia, May 22, 1933; s. Paul Ernst and Katherine Beatrice (Kroner) N., came to U.S., 1941, naturalized, 1946; B.A., Harvard U., 1954; M.D., Cornell U., 1958; m. Sally Sanford, June 24, 1956; children—Elizabeth Burrage, Sarah Alden, Peter Albert. Intern, Vanderbilt U., Nashville, 1958-59, resident in medicine, 1960-61, instr. medicine, 1961-63, asst. prof., 1965-67; resident in medicine Pa. Hosp., Phila., 1959-60; asso. prof. U. N.C., Chapel Hill, 1967-70, prof. medicine and physiology, 1970—, chmn. dept. medicine, 1972—. Served with USPHS, 1963-65. Mem. Am. Soc. Clin. Investigation, Assn. Am. Physicians, Am. Fedn. Clin. Investigation, Assn. Profs. Medicine, Am. Clin. and Climatol. Assn., A.C.P., Am. Physiol. Soc., Alpha Omega Alpha. Home: 1009 Highland Woods Chapel Hill NC 27514 Office: Dept Medicine U NC 3029 Old Clinic Bldg Chapel Hill NC 27514

NEYER, JOSEPH, educator; b. New Rochelle, N.Y., Mar. 8, 1913; s. Louis and Tillie (Berzon) N.; A.B. magna cum laude, Harvard, 1934, A.M., 1935, Ph.D., 1942; student U. Paris (France), 1936-37; m. Friderika Ginsberg, July 26, 1966. Asst. philosophy Harvard, 1937-38, 39-40; research asst. anthropology U. Chgo., 1938-39; instr. philosophy Vassar Coll., 1940-42; Rockefeller fellow, 1946-47; mem. faculty Rutgers U., 1947—, prof. philosophy, 1963—, chmn. dept., 1953-65. Served with AUS, 1942-46. Mem. Am. Prof. for Peace in Middle East (mem. nat. steering com.), Am. Acad. Assn. Peace in Middle East (vice-chmn. bd. dirs.), Am. Sociol. Assn., Am. Philos. Soc., Phi Beta Kappa. Author articles in social and polit. philosophy, sociology, psychoanalysis, recent Middle East history. Chmn. editorial bd. Middle East Review. Home: 55 W 11th St New York NY 10011 Office: Dept Philosophy Rutgers Univ New Brunswick NJ 08903

NEYLON, MARTIN JOSEPH, clergyman; b. Buffalo, Feb. 13, 1920; s. Martin Francis and Delia (Breen) N.; Ph.L., Woodstock Coll., 1944, Th.L., 1951; M.A., Fordham U., 1948. Ordained priest Roman Cath. Ch., 1950, bishop, 1970; mem. Soc. of Jesus; tchr. Regis High Sch., N.Y.C., 1952-54; master Jesuit novices, Poughkeepsie, N.Y., 1955-67; chaplain Kwajalein Missile Range, Marshall Islands, 1967-68; superior Residence for Jesuit Students, Guam, 1968-70; coadjutor bishop Caroline and Marshall Islands, 1970—, Vicar apostolic, 1971—. Address: Truk Caroline Islands Trust Territory Pacific Islands 96942

NEYMAN, JERZY, statistician; b. Bendery, Russia, Apr. 16, 1894; s. Czeslaw and Kazimiera (Lutoslawska) N.; ed. U. Kharkov (Russia), 1912-16; Ph.D., U. Warsaw (Poland), 1923, D.Sc. (hon.), 1974; postdoctoral study U. London, 1925-26, U. Paris, 1926-27; D.Sc. (hon.), U. Chgo., 1959, Indian Statis. Inst., 1974; LL.D. (hon.), U. Calif., Berkeley, 1963; Ph.D. (hon.), U. Stockholm, 1964; m. Olga Solodovnikova, May 4, 1920; 1 son, Michael John. Came to U.S., 1938. Lectr., Inst. Technology, Kharkov, 1917-21; statistician Inst. Agr., Bydgoszcz, Poland, 1921-23; lectr. Coll. Agr., Warsaw, 1923-24, U. Warsaw, 1928-34; spl. lectr. Univ. Coll., London, 1934-35, reader in statistics, 1935-38; spl. lectr. U. Paris, 1936, U. London, U. Paris, Universite Libre de Bruxelles, U. Warsaw, U. Amsterdam, U. Cambridge, U. Coll. London, U. Stockholm, U. Uppsala, 1950; prof. math. U. Calif., Berkeley, 1938-55, dir. Statis. Lab., 1938—, now prof., dir. statis. lab. emeritus, recalled to active status; statis. expert U.S. Mission to observe Greek elections, 1946; del. Internat. Statis. Conf., 1947, Internat. Congress Philosophy of Sci., Paris, 1949. Recipient Nat. Sci. medal, 1968. Fellow Royal Statis. Soc., London Math. Soc. (hon.); mem. U.S. Nat., Polish, Royal Swedish acads. scis., Inst. Math. Statistics (pres. 1949), London Math. Soc. Am., French, Polish (hon.) math. socs., Am. Statis. Assn. (v.p. 1947), Inst. Statistics, Biometric Soc., AAAS, Internat. Statis. Inst. (hon. pres. 1972—), Royal Soc. (fgn.). Author publs. on math. statistics and applications to astronomy, public health, weather modification; editor: Heritage of Copernicus: Theories More Pleasing to the Mind, 1974. Home: 212 Amherst Ave Berkeley CA 94708

NEZELEK, EDWARD LEWIS, constrn. co. exec.; b. Binghamton, N.Y., Sept. 6, 1918; s. Paul and Amelia (Gladysz) N.; grad. high sch.; m. Annette Evelyn Van Howe, Apr. 3, 1961; children—Richard, Paul, Deborah Nezelek Passionino. Gen. supt. Gen. Contractors, Miami and Tampa, Fla., 1940-48; custom home builder, Miami, 1948-50, Binghamton, N.Y., 1950-56; pres. Edward L. Nezelek, Inc., Johnson City, N.Y. and Fort Lauderdale, Fla., 1956—; dir. Landmark Bank North Ft. Lauderdale. Campaign dir. Broome County Nat. Found., 1967; bd. dirs. Found. Broome Community Coll. Served with USNR, 1944. Mem. Bldg. Industry Employers N.Y. (pres. 1966), Associated Bldg. Contractors Triple Cities (pres. 1968), Broome County C. of C. (dir. 1969-75). Clubs: Binghamton (N.Y.) Country (dir. 1968-71); Tamarac Country (Fort Lauderdale); Pres.'s (Miami). Home: 22 Hamton Rd Binghamton NY 13903 Office: 4733 Vestal Pkwy E Binghamton NY 13903 also 6061 NE 14th Ave Fort Lauderdale FL 33308

NGAI, SHIH HSUN, physician; b. Wuchang, China, Sept. 15, 1920; s. Chih F. and Shen (Shih) N.; M.B., Nat. Central U. Sch. Medicine, China, 1944; m. Hsueh-hwa Wang, Nov. 6, 1948; children—Mae, Janet, John. Came to U.S., 1946, naturalized, 1953. Mem. staff Presbyn. Hosp., N.Y.C., 1949—, attending anesthesiologist, 1965—; faculty Columbia Coll. Phys. and Surg., 1949—, prof. anesthesiology, 1965—, prof. pharmacology, 1974—, chmn. dept. anesthesiology, 1970-73; mem. com. on anesthesia NRC-Nat. Acad. Scis., 1961-70; cons. NIH, 1963-67, 78—. Mem. Am. Physiol. Soc., Am. Soc. Pharmacology and Exptl. Therapeutics, Assn. Univ. Anesthetists, Soc. Exptl. Biology and Medicine, Am. Soc. Anesthesiologists, Academia Sinica, Sigma Xi. Author: Manual of Anesthesiology, 1959, 62; Metabolic Effects of Anesthesia, 1962; Highlights of Clinical Anesthesiology, 1971; contbr. to Physiol. Pharmacology, 1963, Handbook of Physiology, 1964, Modern Trends in Anesthesia, 1966, Advances in Anesthesiology-Muscle Relaxants, 1967, Handbook of Experimental Pharmacology XXX, Modern Inhalation Anesthetics, 1972; Muscle Relaxants, 1975; Enzymes in Anesthesiology, 1978; Text Book of Anesthesiology, 1979; editor Anesthesiology, 1967-77. Home: 281 Edgewood Ave Teaneck NJ 07666 Office: 622 W 168th St New York NY 10032

NIBLEY, ROBERT RICKS, lawyer; b. Salt Lake City, Sept. 24, 1913; s. Joel and Teresa (Taylor) N.; A.B., U. Utah, 1934; J.D., Loyola U., Los Angeles, 1942; m. Lee Allen, Jan. 31, 1945; children—Jane, Annette. Accountant, Nat. Parks Airways, Salt Lake City, 1934-37, Western Air Lines, Los Angeles, 1937-40; admitted to Calif. bar, 1943; asst. mgr. market research dept. Lockheed Aircraft Corp., Burbank, Calif., 1940-43; asso. firm Hill, Farrer and Burrill, Los Angeles, 1946-53, partner, 1953-70, of counsel, 1971-78. Vice pres., sec., dir. Beacon Oil Co., Hanford, Calif. Served from ensign to lt. comdr., USNR, 1943-46. Mem. Am., Los Angeles bar assns., Phi Delta Phi, Phi Kappa Phi, Phi Delta Theta. Club: California (Los Angeles). Home: 4860 Ambrose Ave Los Angeles CA 90027 Office: 445 S Figueroa St Los Angeles CA 90071

NIBLOCK, WALTER RAYMOND, lawyer; b. Little Rock, Nov. 19, 1927; s. Freeman John Nellie (Wolfe) N.; student Tex. A. and M. Coll., 1945, Little Rock Jr. Coll., 1947; B.S., U. Ark., 1951, J.D., 1953; m. Marjorie Lee Hammond, Oct. 17, 1953; children—Fred William, George Hammond, Walter Lester, Raymond Lee. Field dir. ARC, 1953-59; asst. gen. mgr., dir. Industria de Pollos, S.A., Cali, Colombia, 1959-61; admitted to Ark. bar, 1953; practice in Fayetteville, 1961—; now sr. partner Niblock & Odom. Exec. sec. Ark. Judiciary Commn., 1963-65; U.S. commr. Fayetteville div. U.S. Dist. Ct., Western Dist. Ark.; mem. Jud. Ethics Com. State Ark., 1978—; mem. Com. on Supreme Ct. Profl. Conduct, 1979—, chmn., 1980; mem. com. on jud. ethics Gen. Assembly, 1979—. Bd. dirs. Washington County chpt. ARC. Served with AUS, 1945-47. Recipient Meritorious Service award ARC, 1963. Fellow Ark. Bar Found. (sec.-treas. 1973-74, chmn. 1975-76); mem. Assn. Trial Lawyers Am. (bd. govs. 1978—), Ark. Trial Lawyers Assn. (pres. 1974-76), Am., Ark. (pres. 1977—), Washington County (v.p. 1973-74, pres. 1974-75) bar assns., Inst. Jud. Adminstrn., Delta Theta Phi. Democrat. Home: Box 818 Fayetteville AR 72701 Office: Niblock Bldg 20 E Mountain St Fayetteville AR 72701

NICANDROS, CONSTANTINE STAVROS, oil co. exec.; b. Port Said, Egypt, Aug. 2, 1933; s. Stavros Constantine and Helen (Lianakis) N.; came to U.S., 1955, naturalized, 1963; Diplome HEC Ecole des Hautes Etudes Commerciales, 1954; license en droit Law Sch. U. Paris, 1954, doctorate in economic sci., 1955; M.B.A., Harvard U., 1957; m. Tassie Boozalis, May 24, 1959; children—Steve Constantine, Vicky Ellen. With planning dept. Continental Oil Co., Houston, 1957-61, N.Y.C., 1961-65, land acquisition internat. exploration-prodn. dept., N.Y.C., 1964-65, mgr. planning eastern hemisphere, N.Y.C., 1966-71, gen. mgr. supply and transp., eastern hemisphere, 1971-72, v.p. supply and transp. eastern hemisphere, 1972-74, exec. v.p. eastern hemisphere refining, mktg. and supply and transp., 1974-75, exec. v.p. worldwide supply and transp., Stamford, Conn., 1975-78, group exec. v.p. petroleum products, Houston, 1978—. Trustee Houston Ballet Found. Mem. Am. Petroleum Inst., Houston C. of C. (internat. bus. (com.). Greek Orthodox. Clubs: Landmark (Stamford); Univ., Petroleum, City (Houston). Office: PO Box 2197 Houston TX 77001

NICE, CHARLES MONROE, JR., educator, physician; b. Parsons, Kans., Dec. 21, 1919; s. Charles Monroe and Margaret (McClenahan) N.; A.B., U. Kans., M.D., 1943; M.Sc. in Medicine, U. Colo., 1948; Ph.D., U. Minn., 1956; m. Mary Ellen Cranmer, Dec. 21, 1940; children—Norma Jane Nice Murphy, Pamela, Deborah, Julianne, Charles Monrie III, Thomas, Mary Ellen, Rebecca. Intern Grasslands Hosp., 1943-44; resident in radiology U. Minn. Hosp., 1948-50; mem. faculty U. Minn. Hosp., Mpls., 1951-58; prof. radiology Tulane U. Med. Sch., New Orleans, 1958—, chmn. dept., 1960—; mem. staff Charity Hosp., New Orleans, 1958—; mem. tng. com. NIH, 1967; mem. NRC, 1969; chmn. tng. adv. com. Bur. Radiol. Health, 1970-72. Served with AUS, 1944-46; PTO. Fellow Am. Coll. Chest Physicians, Am. Coll. Radiologists, Royal Soc. Medicine (London). Author: Roentgen Diagnois of Abdominal Tumors in Childhood, 1957; Clinical Roentgenology of Collagen Disease, 1966; Differential Diagnosis of Cardiovascular Disease by X-ray, 1966; Cardiovascular Roentgenology; a validated program, 1967; Cerebral Computed Tomography; contbr. articles to profl. jours. Home: 508 Millandon St New Orleans LA 70118 Office: 1430 Tulane Ave New Orleans LA 70112

NICHOL, FRED JOSEPH, U.S. judge; b. Sioux City, Iowa, Mar. 19, 1912; s. Ralph Edwin and Florence (Young) N.; A.B., Yankton Coll., 1933; J.D., U. S.D., 1936; LL.D. (hon.), Dakota Wesleyan U., 1975; m. Evelyn Parrish, June 2, 1939; children—Allen H., Janet M. Admitted to S.D. bar, 1936; mem. firm Hitchcock, Nichol & Lasegard, Mitchell, 1938-58; mem. S.D. Ho. of Reps. from Davison County, 1951-52, 57-58; state's atty. Davison County, 1947-51; circuit judge 4th Jud. Circuit S.D., 1959-65; U.S. dist. judge for S.D., 1965-66, chief judge, 1966—. Mem. exec. com. Legis. Research Council, 1951; S.D. del. Nat. Trial Judges Conv., 1962, 63, 64. Mem. sch. bd. and library bd., Mitchell, 1958-64; del. White House Conf. on Aging, 1961. Sec. S.D. delegation Democratic Nat. Conv., 1956. Mem. corp. bd., also trustee Yankton Coll., 1954—. Served to lt. USNR, World War II. Mem. Am. Bar Assn., Am. Judicature Soc., Phi Delta Phi. Conglist. (past chmn.). Elk, Mason (32 Shriner, K.T.), Rotarian. Home: 1100 Tomar Rd Sioux Falls SD 57105 Office: US Court House Sioux Falls SD 57101

NICHOL, HENRY FERRIS, environ. cons., former govt. ofcl.; b. Charleston, S.C., Jan. 21, 1911; s. A. Ferris and Ella (Humphrey) N.; A.B., Davidson Coll., 1933; postgrad. Georgetown U. Law Sch., 1936-37; m. Elizabeth B. Holmes, Apr. 15, 1944; children—Susan (Mrs. William C. Thompson), Elizabeth, David, Peter. Clk., HOLC, 1934-37; adminstrv. asst. FSA, 1937-46; fgn. affairs specialist Dept. State, 1946-63, fgn. service officer, 1955-63; conf. attache, Geneva, Switzerland, 1952-58; consul, Liverpool, Eng., 1958-63, acting prin. officer, 1958-59; sec. U.S. delegations to numerous confs.; adviser U.S. delegations, exec. com. Internat. Refugee Fund, Geneva, 1956-57; asst. dir., asst. to adminstr. Rural Community Devel. Service, U.S. Dept. Agr., 1963-66; rep. to Pres.'s Recreation Adv. Council, 1963-66, vice chmn. staff, 1964-66; mem. staff Pres.'s Council on Recreation and Natural Beauty, 1966-69; asst. to asso. adminstr. Soil Conservation Service, 1966-70; environ. cons., 1970—. Liaison officer Dept. Agr. to White House Conf. Natural Beauty, 1965; sr. warden Am. Ch., Geneva, Switzerland; Eastern rep. Nat. Outdoor Leadership Sch.; chmn. Montgomery County Citizens Adv. Com. on Bikeways and Trails; chmn. Potomac Com. Bikeways and Trails; trustee Potomac Conservation Found., Wilderness Use Edn. Assn.; v.p. Potomac Appalachian Trail Club. Named Outstanding Citizen of Year Potomac C. of C., 1976. Served to lt. comdr. USNR, 1942-45.

Mem. Phi Beta Kappa. Episcopalian. Club: International (Washington). Home: 9616 Accord Dr Potomac MD 20854

NICHOLAS, ARTHUR SOTERIOS, mfg. co. exec.; b. Grand Rapids, Mich., Mar. 6, 1930; s. Samuel D. and Penelope A. (Kalapodes) N.; B.S. in Chem. Engring., U. Mich., 1953; B.A. in Indsl. Mgmt., Wayne State U., 1957; m. Bessie Zazanis, Aug. 25, 1957; children—Niki Lynn, Arthur S., Thomas. Project engr. B.F. Goodrich Co., 1953-54; plant mgr. Cadillac Plastics and Chem. Co., 1954-69; pres., chief exec. officer Leon Chem. and Plastics, Inc., Grand Rapids 1960-69; with U.S. Industries, Inc., 1969-73, pres., chief operating officer, 1973; pres., chief exec. officer Apeco Corp., Des Plaines, Ill., 1974—; dir. Sensormatic Electronic Corp. Trustee Olivet (Mich.) Coll.; judge Jr. Achievement, Chgo. Served with USNR, 1948-49. Recipient Distinguished Alumni award Grand Rapids Jr. Coll., 1970. Registered profl. engr., Mich. Mem. Young Pres. Orgn., Soc. Plastic Engrs., Mich. Acad. Sci., Arts and Letters, Chgo. Council Fgn. Relations. Mem. Greek Orthodox Ch. Clubs: Chgo. Athletic Assn., Executives (Chgo.). Patentee in field. Home: 655 Oak Rd Barrington IL 60010 Office: 2454 Dempster St Des Plaines IL 60016

NICHOLAS, LOUIS THURSTON, educator; b. Trimble, Tenn., Oct. 2, 1910; s. Jeff Thurston and Lottie (Dunivant) N.; A.B., Southwestern at Memphis, 1934; postgrad. Memphis Coll. Music, 1934-38; M.Mus., U. Mich., 1939; diploma, Columbia, 1952; m. Sarah Elizabeth Lacey, Mar. 27, 1942; children—Joel Edward, David Paul, Kevin Lacey. Tchr. pub. schs., Dyer County, Tenn., 1928-30, Memphis, 1936-41; instr. music N.Tex. State Tchrs. Coll., 1941-44; asst. prof. music George Peabody Coll. Tchrs., Nashville, 1944-51, asso. prof., 1951-68, prof., 1968-79; music editor and critic Nashville Tennessean, 1951-75; tenor soloist, dir. various chs. Bd. dirs., 1st v.p. Nashville Community Concert Assn. Served with AUS, 1942-43. Mem. Nat. Assn. Tchrs. Singing (past pres.), Am. Acad. Tchrs. Singing, Music Tchrs. Nat. Assn., Music Educators Nat. Conf., Phi Mu Alpha, Omicron Delta Kappa. Democrat. Mem. Disciples of Christ Ch. Home: 207 Craighead Ave Nashville TN 37205

NICHOLAS, NANCY, publishing co. exec.; b. N.Y.C., Oct. 15, 1939; d. Jesse David and Elizabeth (Hess) Wolff; student Radcliffe Coll.; m. Charles Simmons, Sept. 17, 1977. Tutorial dir. Harlem Edn. Program, N.Y.C., then writer Scholastic Press, N.Y.C., Scope mag., N.Y.C., editor Alfred A. Knopf, Inc., N.Y.C., 1967—. Office: 201 E 50th St New York City NY 10022

NICHOLAS, ROBERT BATES, ins. co. exec.; b. West Sayville, N.Y., Apr. 24, 1929; s. Robert C. and Jean (Bates) N.; B.A., Denison U., 1950; M.S., Sch. Bus., Columbia U., 1954; m. Sally Anne Macomber, June 24, 1955; children—John B., Paul M., Sally Anne. With Atlantic Richfield Co., N.Y.C., 1960-71, sec., 1965-66, mgr. fin. services, 1966-68, sec., exec. com., mgr. corporate planning, 1968-71; v.p. corporate planning Aetna Life & Casualty Co., Hartford, Conn., 1971-75, v.p. finance and planning, 1976—, also sec. corp. mgmt. com., mem. fin. policy com. Treas. Delaware County Vocat.-Tech. Sch. Authority, 1966-68; pres., bd. dirs., mem. fin. com. Hartford Dispensary; trustee Hartford Grad. Center; trustee Simsbury United Meth. Ch.; mem. bd. advs. bus. environ. and policy U. Conn. Sch. Bus. Adminstrn. Served to 1st lt. AUS, 1951-53. Club: Hopmeadow Country (dir., mem. exec. com. 1976-79). Home: 6 Apple Ln Simsbury CT 06070 Office: 151 Farmington Ave Hartford CT 06115

NICHOLAS, THOMAS ANDREW, artist; b. Middletown, Conn., Sept. 26, 1934; s. Michael and Lena (Sequenzia) N.; student of Ernst Lohrmann, 1949-53; scholarship student Sch. Visual Arts, N.Y.C., 1953-55; m. Gloria R. Spencer, Oct. 11, 1958; 1 son, Thomas Michael. One-man shows include Grand Central Galleries, N.Y.C., 1962, 64, 66, 68, 70, 78, I.F.A. Galleries, Washington, 1964—; rep. permanent collections Butler Inst. Am. Art, Youngstown, O., Ga. Mus., Athens, U. Utah, Adelphi U., Greenshields Mus., Montreal, Can., Farnsworth Mus., Rockland, Maine, Springfield (Mo.) Art Mus., Ranger Collection at NAD; instr. Famous Artists Schs., Inc., Westport, Conn., 1958-60; instr. painting, Rockport, Mass., 1963-66. Elizabeth Greenshields grantee, 1961, 62; recipient numerous awards, 1957—, including Emile Lowe award for watercolor Am. Watercolor Soc., 1961, watercolor prize, 1964, Gold medal honor, 1969, Clare Stout award, 1971, Mary S. Litt award, 1972; medal honor for watercolor Knickerbocker Artists, 1962; Purchase award watercolor Butler Inst. Am. Art, 1962; Henry Ward Ranger Fund purchase watercolor NAD, 1962, 71, Obrig prize watercolor, 1964; gold medal honor watercolor Allied Artists Am., 1962, Grumbacher prize, 1978; Today Mag. Art medal, 1970, 74; gold medal honor watercolor Am. Artists Profl. League, 1964, best landscape award, 1974, gold medal, 1978; Edwin S. Webster award honor watercolor Boston Soc. Watercolor, 1964; gold medal honor watercolor Hudson Valley Art Assn., 1964, DuMond Meml. award, 1971, Isabel Stinschneider Meml. award, 1972, Herman Wick Meml. award Salmagundi Club, N.Y.C., 1966, 2d prize, 1966, June Justin J. Impasto award, 1972, Arthur T. Hill prize, 1973, Arthur T. Hill Meml. prize, 1975, Louis Z. Seley prize, 1978, Gwynne Lennon prize, 1979; Gold medal honor oil Rockport Art Assn., 1967, 67, 76; cash award Wichita Centennial Watercolor, 1970; Providence Art Club prize, 1972; gold medal Franklin Mint Competition, 1974; Gold medal Honor Acad. Assn., 1976; others. Mem. Am., Boston, Conn. watercolor socs., Allied Artists Am., Knickerbocker Artists (dir.'s prize 1971), Boston Guild Artists, Hudson Valley Artists. (gold medal 1974), NAD. Club: Salmagundi (N.Y.C.). Author articles; commd. by Franklin Mint Gallery Am. Art to produce lithographs of Am. coastline, 1977. Home: 7 Wildon Heights Rockport MA 01966 Office: 8B Main St Rockport MA 01966

NICHOLL, DON, TV producer, writer; b. Sunderland, Eng., Aug. 9; s. James Girvan and Evelyn Pyet (Hopper) N.; came to U.S., 1969; ed. in Eng.; m. Gee Dore. Newspaper reporter, 1946; press relations officer J. Arthur Rank Orgn., 1952-55; music columnist London Daily Mail, also music trade papers, 1955-65; script writer, disc jockey BBC Sound Radio, 1964-68; writer feature movies and TV series, Eng., 1956-58; TV producer, writer, U.S., 1968—; TV series include All In The Family, The Jeffersons, The Dumplings, Three's Company, The Ropers. Served with Brit. Army, World War II. Recipient various commendations, nominations. Mem. Writers Guild Am. Author: Record Roundabout, 1955; (libretto) Xmas Carol, 1963; (films) Golden Disc, 1957, Emergency, 1959. Office: 5752 Sunset Blvd Los Angeles CA 90028*

NICHOLLS, CHARLES GEOFFREY WILLIAM, theologian, educator; b. Hitchin, Hertfordshire, Eng., Oct. 10, 1921; s. Albert Charles and Kathleen (Thornton) N.; naturalized Canadian, 1969; B.A., St. John's Coll., Cambridge U., 1947, M.A., 1949; m. Hilary McCallum, July 15, 1950; children—Elizabeth Helen, Paul Charles Alexander, Felicity Kathleen Mary. Travelling sec. World's Student Christian Fedn., Geneva, 1949-51; chaplain to Anglican students in Edinburgh, 1955-60; asso. prof. systematic theology St. John's Coll., U. Man. (Can.), 1960-61; prof. religious studies U. B.C., Vancouver, 1961—, head dept., 1964—. Served with Brit. Army, 1941-45. Can. Council fellow, 1966-67, 74-75. Mem. Canadian Soc. Study Religion, Am. Acad. Religion. Mem. New Democratic Party. Author: Ecumenism and Catholicity, 1951; Systematic and Philosophical Theology, 1969; co-author: I AMness: The Discovery of The Self Beyond The Ego, 1972; editor: Conflicting Images of Man, 1966. Home: 3670 W 34th Ave Vancouver BC V6N 2L1 Canada Office: 2075 Wesbrook Mall Vancouver BC V6T 1W5 Canada

NICHOLLS, RALPH WILLIAM, physicist; b. Richmond, Surrey, Eng., May 3, 1926; s. William James and Evelyn Mabel (Jones) N.; B.Sc., Imperial Coll., U. London, 1945, Ph.D., 1951, D.Sc. in Spectroscopy, 1961; m. Doris Margaret McEwen, June 28, 1952. Sr. demonstrator in astrophysics Imperial Coll., U. London, 1945-48; instr. U. Western Ont. (Can.), London, 1948-50, lectr., 1950-52, asst. prof. physics, 1952-56, asso. prof., 1956-58, prof., 1958-63, sr. prof., 1963-65; prof. York U., Toronto, Ont., 1965—, chmn. dept. physics, 1965-69, dir. Centre for Research in Exptl. Space Scis., 1965—; vis. scientist Nat. Bur. Standard, 1959; vis. prof. Stanford U., 1964, 68. Fellow Royal Soc. Can., Optical Soc. Am., Am. Phys. Soc., Can. Aero. and Space Inst. Author: (with B. H. Armstrong) Emission, Absorption and Transfer of Radiation in Heated Atmospheres, 1972. Home: 9 Pinevale Rd Thornhill ON L3T 1J5 Canada Office: CRESS York U 4700 Keele St Downsview ON M3J 1P3 Canada

NICHOLLS, ROBERT PERRY, univ. adminstr., architect; b. Nottingham, Eng., Nov. 26, 1930; s. Henry and Jessie Irene Elizabeth (Perry) N.; naturalized, 1971; B.Arch. with honors, U. Liverpool (Eng.), 1953; M.Civic Design, 1954; M.Land. Arch., U. Pa., 1957; m. Pauline Margaret Dickson, Aug. 6, 1955; 1 son, Peter Jeffrey. Architect, Cwmbran Devel. Corp., South Wales, 1954-55; asst. prof. U. Ga., 1957-59; planner Frobisher Bay Cons., Can., 1959-60; liason architect Govt. of Can. Dept. Pub. Works, 1960-61; asso. S.A. Gitterman Architects, Ottawa, Can., 1962-63; architect Minto Constrn. Co. Can., 1963-64; asso. prof. U. Ga., 1964-67, prof. Sch. of Environ. Design, 1968-72, dean Sch. of Environ. Design, 1973—; v.p. Designers Collaborative, Inc.; cons. HUD. Trustee Athens Town and Gown Community Theatre. Fulbright scholar, 1955-57. Mem. Am. Soc. Landscape Architects (chmn. com. guidance of new programs), Royal Archtl. Inst. Can., Royal Inst. Brit. Architects, Royal Town Planning Inst. Gt. Britain. Episcopalian. Office: Sch Environ Design U Ga Athens GA 30602

NICHOLS, ALAN HAMMOND, lawyer; b. Palo Alto, Calif., Feb. 14, 1930; s. John Ralph and Shirley (Charles) N.; B.A., Stanford U., 1951, J.D., 1955; children—Sharon Elizabeth, Alan Hammond, Shan Darwin. Admitted to Calif. bar, 1955; asso. firm Lillick, Geary, Wheat, Adams & Charles, San Francisco, 1955-61; pres. firm Nichols & Rogers, San Francisco, 1961-74; pres. Nichols Law Corp., San Francisco, 1974—; prof. forensic medicine Calif. Coll. Podiatric Medicine, 1975-77. Mem. San Francisco Library Commn., 1962-65; v.p. San Francisco Council Chs., 1965-68; pres. sch. bd. San Francisco Unified Sch. Dist., 1967-71; mem. exec. com. Council Great City Schs. of U.S.; del. Calif. Sch. Bds. Assn. Assembly; mem. Civil Grand Jury, San Francisco, 1975-76; pres. Young Republicans San Francisco, 1957, Calif., 1959; mem. Rep. Central Com., San Francisco, 1961—, pres., 1976; trustee City Coll. San Francisco, 1966-71, pres. trustees, 1970-71; trustee Cathedral Sch., Calif. Coll. Podiatric Medicine, Prescott Center Coll. Served to lt. AUS, 1951-54. Decorated Commendation medal with 4 clusters; named Young Man of Yr., San Francisco newspapers, 1961. Mem. State Bar Calif., Am., San Francisco bar assns., Am. Arbitration Assn. (arbitrator), Phi Beta Kappa, Phi Delta Phi, Sigma Nu. Club: Bohemian. Author: Water for California, 1967; (poetry) San Francisco Commuter, 1970; (play) Siddartha, 1977; A Gift from the Master, 1978; To Climb a Sacred Mountain, 1979; contbr. articles to profl. jours. Home: 10 Florence St San Francisco CA 94133 Office: 1032 Broadway San Francisco CA 94133

NICHOLS, ALEXANDER LOWBER, lawyer; b. Tularosa, N.M., Feb. 28, 1906; s. Henry Dodge and Adele (Lowber) N.; B.A., Haverford Coll., 1928; LL.B., U. Pa., 1931; m. Dorothy A. Ackart, Apr. 9, 1937; children—David A., Carolyn M., Alan B. Admitted to Del. bar, 1932; asso. Hugh M. Morris, 1932-40; partner Morris, Nichols, Arsht & Tunnell, Wilmington, Del., 1940-76, of counsel, 1977—. Mem. exec. com. United Community Fund No. Del., Inc., 1950-60; pres. Family Service No. Del., 1955-57. Bd. dirs., past v.p. Wilmington YMCA. With Citizens Mil. Tng. Camps, 1924-25. Fellow Am Bar Found.; mem. Am. (ho. dels. 1957-75, bd. govs. 1970-73), Del. bar assns., Phi Delta Phi. Republican. Episcopalian. Rotarian. Home: 2310 W 17th St Wilmington DE 19806 Office: Wilmington Tower Wilmington DE 19899

NICHOLS, BRUCE W., lawyer; b. N.Y.C., Jan. 3, 1930; s. Frederick Willis and Marjorie B. (Lyon) N.; A.B., Princeton U., 1951; LL.B., Harvard U., 1954. Admitted to N.Y. bar, 1954; asso. firm Davis Polk & Wardwell, N.Y.C., 1954-61, partner, 1961—. Mem. Assn. Bar City N.Y., Am. Bar Assn., N.Y. State Bar Assn., N.Y. Law Inst. (chmn. exec. com. 1973—). Republican. Episcopalian. Clubs: Princeton of N.Y., Wall St. Home: 799 Park Ave New York NY 10021 Office: 1 Chase Manhattan Plaza New York NY 10005

NICHOLS, CHARLES AUGUST, film dir.; b. Milford, Utah, Sept. 15, 1910; s. Herbert and Ruby (Thiessen) N.; student public schs., Milford and Salt Lake City; m. Marguerite Estella Fink, Dec. 16, 1930; children—Ruella Arlene, Myrna La Vonne, Lawrence August. Animator, Walt Disney Prodns., Burbank, Calif., 1935-46, animation and live action dir., 1946-61; sr. animation dir., v.p., exec. in charge of animated feature motion pictures Hanna-Barbera Prodns., Hollywood, Calif., 1961-79. Films directed include: Toot, Whistle, Plunk and Boom, 19— (Acad. Motion Picture Arts and Scis. award 1954); Last of the Curlews, 1972 (Acad. TV Arts and Scis. award 1973); Charlotte's Web, 1974 (Filmex Internat. Film Expn. cert. merit 1978). Home: 1890 Euclid Ave San Marino CA 91108 Office: 3400 W Cahuenga Blvd Hollywood CA 90068

NICHOLS, CHARLES WALTER, JR., engring. exec.; b. Bklyn., Dec. 23, 1911; s. Charles Walter and Adelaide (Batterman) N.; student Choate Sch., 1922-29, Williams Coll., 1929-32; m. Marjorie H. Jones, June 5, 1934 (dec.); children—Joan, Charles Walter III, David Huntington; m. 2d, Marguerite Prince Sykes, May 22, 1948. Salesman, Nichols Copper Co., Nichols Engring. and Research Corp., N.Y.C., 1933-72, chmn. bd.; chmn. exec. com. Neptune Internat. Corp., 1972-79; dir. Allied Chem. Corp.; adv. com. to bd. Chem. Bank N.Y. Trust Co., N.Y.C.; dir. Allegheny Power System, Inc., Allegheny Power Service Corp., Monongahela Power Co., Potomac Edison Co., West Penn Power Co., Wheelabrator-Frye Inc. Chmn. bd. mgrs. Coop. Social Settlement Soc. N.Y.C.; mem. bd. N.Y. U.; pres., dir. Nichols Found., 1953—; v.p., chmn. exec. com. N.Y. Zool. Soc.; corporator Putnam Meml. Hosp.; trustee Animal Med. Center, Am. Soc. Prevention Cruelty to Animals. Congregationalist. Clubs: River, Hemisphere, Links Golf, Pilgrims Soc. (N.Y.C.); Lahinch (Ireland); Kildare St., Univ. (Dublin); Ekwanok (Manchester, Vt.). Home: 45 Sutton Pl S New York NY 10022 Office: 630 Fifth Ave New York NY 10020

NICHOLS, DALE WILLIAM, artist, lectr.; b. David City, Nebr., July 13, 1904; s. John Dale and Edith Mae (Pollman) N.; student Chgo. Acad. Fine Arts, 1924, Chgo. Art Inst., 1924-25; student of Joseph Binder, Vienna, Austria, 1934; m. Lucille McIntosh, 1925; 1 dau., Joan Lucille; m. 2d, Frances Waller, 1947; m. 3d, Ruth Fehr, 1949; 1 dau., Caroline Dale; m. 4th, Marjorie Tolken, 1954; m. 5th, Maria Gandera, 1961. Fashion illustrator Crafton Studios, 1927-28, Chgo. Tribune, 1927-28; art editor Ency. Brit., 1941-49; Carnegie prof., artist in residence U. Ill., 1939-40; artist in residence No. Mich. Coll. Edn., 1954; numerous one-man shows, including Kroch Galleries, 1933, U. Ill., 1939, Corcoran Gallery, Washington, Dallas Mus. Fine Arts, Milw. Art Inst., Toledo Mus. Art; group shows include: Art Inst. Chgo., 1936, Carnegie Internat. Exhbn., 1938, 39, 40-48, N.Y. World's Fair, 1939, Worcester (Mass.) Mus. Art, 1941; represented in permanent collections, including: Art Inst. Chgo., Met. Mus. Art, N.Y.C., Joslyn Meml. Mus., Omaha; lectr. on psychology in art, architecture, design for printing; cons. dynamic numerology; art dir. Tucson City Planning Bd., 1940-47. Recipient numerous awards, including William Randolph Hearst 1st award for painting Art Inst. Chgo., 1935, Watson Blair Purchase award, 1939, Detroit Art Dirs. award, 1947. Mem. Soc. Typog. Arts Chgo. (life; pres. 1937-38), Grand Central Art Galleries, Brownsville (Tex.) Art League (life) Zoroastrian. Author: A Philosophy of Esthetics, 1938; The Mayan Mystery, 1976; Let There Be Light, 1968; also booklets; contbr. articles to profl. jours., popular mags. Home: La Antigua Guatemala Guatemala

NICHOLS, DAVID ARTHUR, state justice; b. Lincolnville, Maine, Aug. 6, 1917; s. George E. and Flora E. (Pillsbury) N.; A.B. magna cum laude, Bates Coll., 1942; J.D., U. Mich., 1949. Admitted to Maine bar, 1949, Mass. bar, 1949, U.S. Supreme Ct., 1954; practice in Camden, Maine, 1949-75; justice Maine Superior Ct., 1975-77, Maine Supreme Jud. Ct., 1977—. Mem. Maine Exec. Council, 1955-57; moderator Lincolnville Town Meeting, 1950-74; chmn. Maine Republican Com., 1960-64; mem. Rep. Nat. Com., 1960-68; chmn. Maine council Young Reps., 1950-54, New Eng. council Young Reps., 1952-54; trustee, past pres. Penobscot Bay Med. Center. Served with USAAF, 1942-45. Fellow Am. Bar Found., Am. Coll. Trial Lawyers; mem. Camden-Rockport C. of C. (past pres.), Maine, Camden (past pres.) hist. socs., Camden Bus. Men's Assn. (past pres.), Am. (bd. govs. 1960-63, ho. dels. 1957-78), Mass., Maine bar assns., Am. Judicature Soc. (dir. 1960-64), Bates Coll. Alumni Assn. (past pres.), Maine Trial Lawyers Assn. (past pres.), Phi Beta Kappa, Delta Sigma Rho. Clubs: Odd Fellow, Rotary (past pres.). Contbr. to legal and geneal. publs. Home: Box 76 Lincolnville ME 04849 Office: Knox County Courthouse Rockland ME 04841

NICHOLS, DONALD ARTHUR, economist; b. Madison, Conn., Dec. 20, 1940; s. Edward Charles and Ruth Olson N.; B.A., Yale U., 1962, M.A., 1963, Ph.D., 1968; m. Linda Powley, Aug. 19, 1962; children—Charles Spencer, Elizabeth Clarke. Mem. faculty dept. econs. U. Wis., Madison, 1966—, prof., 1977—; lectr. Yale U., 1970-71; sr. economist Senate Budget Com., Washington, 1975-76; dep. asst. sec. of labor for econ. policy and research Dept. Labor, Washington, 1977-79; cons. in field. NSF fellow, 1963-66, 70-72. Recipient William H. Kiekhofer Meml. Teaching prize U. Wis., 1973. Mem. Am. Econ. Assn., Econometric Soc., Royal Econ. Soc. Author: (with Clark Reynolds) Principles of Economics, 1970. Contbr. articles to profl. jours. Home: 1522 Vilas Ave Madison WI 53711 Office: 1180 Observatory Dr Madison WI 53706

NICHOLS, DONALD RICHARDSON, medical educator; b. Mpls., Feb. 22, 1911; s. Arthur R. and Agusta (Fisher) N.; A.B., Amherst Coll., 1933; M.D., U. Minn., 1938, M.S. in Medicine, 1942; m. Margery Spicer, Mar. 5, 1942 (dec.); children—Virginia (Mrs. James Leipold), John; m. 2d, Mary Jean Scholberg, Mar. 2, 1957 (div.); children—Arthur, Edwin, Mary Jean, Barbara. Intern, Milw. County Hosp., 1939; fellow medicine Mayo Found., 1939-42; mem. faculty Mayo Grad. Sch. Medicine, U. Minn., 1948-72, prof. clin. medicine, 1965-72; prof. medicine Mayo Med. Sch., 1972—; cons. medicine Mayo Clinic, 1942—, head, sect. infectious diseases 1963-69, chmn. div. infectious diseases, 1970-73, sr. cons. medicine, 1973—. Diplomate Am. Bd. Internal Medicine. Fellow A.C.P.; mem. Minn. State Med. Assn., Infectious Diseases Soc. Am., Central Soc. Clin. Research, Central Clin. Research Club, Minn., Internat. socs. internal medicine, Sigma Xi, Nu Sigma Nu, Theta Delta Chi. Methodist. Home: 207 5th Ave SW Rochester MN 55901 Office: Mayo Clinic Rochester MN 55902

NICHOLS, EDWIN JAMES, govt. ofcl.; b. Detroit, June 23, 1931; s. Edwin D. and Lena (Tarrée) N.; student Windsor U. (Can.), 1952-55, Tübingen (Germany) U., 1955-57; Ph.D. (Austrian Ministry Edn. fellow 1959), Innsbruck (Austria) U., 1961; m. Sandra Hann, Aug. 27, 1966; children—Lisa H., Edwin L. Chief clin. psychologist Meharry Med. Coll., Nashville, 1963-68; psychologist Am. Mgmt., Cleve., 1968; asst. dir., coordinator spl. services Cleve. Job Corps for Women, 1968-70; chief Center for Studies Child and Family Mental Health, NIMH, HEW, Rockville, Md., 1970—; operation exec. Nigerian Fed. Ministry of Econ. Devel. and Reconstrn., 1974-77; vis. prof., dir. child's clinic Inst. Edn., U. Ibadan, 1974-77; cons. Nigerian Centre for Mgmt. Devel., 1974-77; asst. prof. Fisk U., 1963-68; asso. prof. Cleve. State U., 1968-70; prof. D.C. U., 1970-74; pvt. practice psychotherapy; cons. for systems transfer of tech. and cross-cultural mgmt. Served with AUS, 1950-52; Europe. Mem. Am., D.C., Black psychol. assns. Home: 3038 Chestnut St NW Washington DC 20015 Office: NIMH 5600 Fishers Ln Rockville MD 20852

NICHOLS, EUGENE DOUGLAS, educator; b. Rovno, Poland, Feb. 6, 1923; s. Alex and Anna (Radchuk) Nichiporuk; came to U.S., 1946, naturalized, 1951; B.S., U. Chgo., 1949, postgrad., 1949-51; M.Ed., U. Ill., 1953, M.A., 1954, Ph.D. 1956; m. Alice Bissell Mar. 31, 1951. Instr. math. Roberts Wesleyan Coll., North Chili, N.Y., 1950-51, U. Ill., 1951-56; asso. prof. math. edn. Fla. State U., 1956-61, prof., head dept., 1961-73, dir. Project for Mathematical Devel. of Children, 1973-77, dir. math program NSF, summers, 1958-61, dir. Math. Inst. Elementary Tchrs., 1961—. Chmn., U. Ill. Com. on Sch. Math., 1954-55; cons. editor math McGraw-Hill Book Co., summer 1956. Named Fla. State U. Distinguished Prof., 1968-69; recipient Distinguished Alumni award U. Ill. Coll. Edn., 1970. Mem. Am. Math. Soc., Math. Assn. Am., Sch. Sci. and Math. Assn., Nat. Council Tchrs. Math., Council Basic Edn., Pi Mu Epsilon, Phi Delta Kappa. Co-author: Modern Elementary Algebra, 1961; Introduction to Sets, 1962; Arithmetic of Directed Numbers, 1962; Introduction to Equations and Inequalities, 1963; Introduction to Coordinate Geometry, 1963; Introduction to Exponents, 1964; Understanding Arithmetic, 1965; Elementary Mathematics Patterns and Structure, 1966; Algebra, 1966; Modern Geometry, 1968; Modern Trigonometry, 1968; Modern Intermediate Algebra, 1969; Analytic Geometry, 1973; Holt Algebra 1, 1974, 78; Holt Algebra 2, 1974, 78; Holt Geometry, 1974, 78; Holt School Mathematics, 1974, 78, Pre-Algebra Mathematics, 1980; author: Pre-Algebra Mathematics, 1970, College Mathematics for General Education, rev. edit., 1975, Introductory Algebra for College Students, 1971, Mathematics for the Elementary School Teacher, 1971; College Mathematics, 1975. Home: 3386 W Lake Shore Dr Tallahassee FL 32312

NICHOLS, FRANKLIN ALLEN, air force officer; b. Holderville, Okla., Apr. 18, 1918; s. Allen G. and Helen (Cansler) N.; student Washington and Lee U., 1936-40; grad. Armed Forces Staff Coll., 1950, Naval War Coll., 1952; m. Harriett Ann Rogers, Aug. 27, 1941; 1 son, Allen Rogers. Commd. 2d lt. USAAF, 1941, advanced through grades to maj. gen. USAF, 1970; wing comdr. 31st T.F. Wing, 1964-65; div. comdr. 833d Air Div., 1965-66; chief of staff 7th Air Force, Vietnam, 1966-67; comdr. Ground Electronics Engring. Agy.,

Griffis AFB, Rome, N.Y. 1967—. Vice pres. dist. and region 2 Boy Scouts Am.; bd. dirs. Armed Forces YMCA. Decorated D.S.M. with oak leaf cluster, Silver Star, Legion of Merit with oak leaf cluster, D.F.C. with 3 oak leaf clusters, Air medal with 2 oak leaf clusters. Recipient Distinguished Eagle Scout award Boy Scouts Am., 1970. Mem. El Paso C. of C. (armed forces com.), Air Force Assn., Mil. Order World Wars, Am. Legion, VFW, DAV, Order Daedalions, Quiet Birdmen, Phi Kappa Psi. Home: 3708 Scobey El Paso TX 79927

NICHOLS, FREDERICK DOVETON, educator; b. Trinidad, Colo., July 1, 1911; s. Wilbur Oliver and Harriet (Doveton) N.; student Colo. Coll., 1929-31; B.F.A., Yale U., 1935; m. Jane Root, May 23, 1942; children—Catherine, Allen, Frederick Doveton. Regional dir. Historic Bldgs. Survey, Nat. Park Service, 1935-41; head archtl. studies program U. Hawaii, 1946-50; asso. prof. art and architecture U. Va., 1950-61, prof., 1961—, Cary D. Langhorne prof., 1967—, chmn. div., 1965-70, chmn. div. archtl. history, 1972—; lectr. architecture, restoration and preservation. Mem. Monticello Restoration Commn., 1956—, Va. Hist. Landmarks Commn., 1965—; cons. restorations Christ Ch., Jefferson bldgs. U. Va.; mem. Fine Arts Commn., Washington, 1976, Drayton Hall Com., 1976. Bd. dirs. Thomas Jefferson Meml. Found., 1971—. Served with USAAF, 1943-45. Guggenheim fellow, 1963; Sesquicentennial fellow, 1971. Fellow AIA; mem. NAD, Archtl. Historians (dir. 1955-57, 70-71), Am. Assn. Archtl. Bibliographers (gov., dir. 1959—), The Raven Soc., Walpole Soc., Century Assn., Phi Gamma Delta. Clubs: The Colonnade; Farmington Country, Farmington Hunt. Author: Catalog of the Historic American Buildings Survey, 1941; Early Architecture of Georgia, 1957 (Hitchcock medal); Fiske Kimball, A Bibliography, 1959; Thos. Jefferson's Architectural Drawings, 1959; Monticello, 1967. Home: Sunnyside Barracks Rd Charlottesville VA 22901

NICHOLS, GEORGE A., paints and home furnishings co. exec.; b. 1913; B.S. in Chemistry, N.D. State U., 1934; married. With Arco Co., 1934-36; tech. dir. Barrett Varnish Co., 1937-48; with DeSoto Inc., 1948—, became tech. dir., 1948, v.p. research, 1956, v.p., gen. mgr. chem. group, 1969, pres., Des Plaines, Ill., 1970—, chief exec. officer, 1974—, chmn. bd., 1976—, also dir.; dir. Sears Bank & Trust Co. (Chgo.). Served to capt. AUS, 1942-46. Office: 1700 S Mt Prospect Rd Des Plaines IL 60018

NICHOLS, GUY W., utilities exec.; b. Colchester, Vt., Oct. 27, 1925; s. Guy W. and Gladys (Tomlinson) N.; B.C.E., U. Vt., 1947; postgrad. Worcester Poly. Inst. Sch. Indsl. Mgmt., 1953-56; M.S. in Bus. Adminstrn. (Sloan fellow), M.I.T., 1961; m. Shirley Hibbard, June 21, 1947; children—Pamela, Gail, Sally. With New. Eng. Electric System, Westborough, Mass., 1947—, exec. v.p., 1968-70, dir., 1968—, pres., 1970—, chief exec. officer, 1972—, chmn. bd., 1978—; pres., dir. New Eng. Power Service Co.; dir. Nashua Corp., Mass. Electric Co., First Nat. Bank Boston, State Mut. Life Assurance Co. Am., Narragansett Electric Co.; chmn., dir. Yankee Atomic Electric Co., mem. exec. com. New Eng. Power Pool, N.E. Power Coordinating Council; Trustee, Thomas Alva Edison Found.; mem. corp. Woods Hole Oceanographic Instn.; mem. corp. devel. com., energy lab. adv. bd., corp. vis. com. dept. elec. engring. M.I.T. Served with AUS, 1944-46. Recipient Albert J. Schwieger award for achievement Sch. Indsl. Mgmt., Worcester Poly. Inst., 1975. Home: 69 Wildwood Dr Needham MA 02192 Office: 25 Research Dr Westborough MA 01581

NICHOLS, HAROLD NEIL, pipeline co. exec.; b. Digby, N.S., Can., June 15, 1937; s. Harold A. and Lillian (Nielsen) N.; grad. high sch.; m. Doris E. Outhouse, Mar. 2, 1957; children—Michael, Dale, Sherri, Susan, Lori. Various financial positions TransCan. PipeLines Ltd., Toronto, Ont., 1956-74, corp. treas., 1974—, v.p., 1977—. Mem. exec. com. Rehab. Found. for Disabled, Toronto, 1974—, bd. dirs., 1975—, treas., 1976—, v.p., 1977—. Registered indsl. accountant. Mem. Fin. Execs. Inst., Bd. Trade of Met. Toronto. Home: 24 Bushcroft Grove Agincourt ON M15 3V9 Canada Office: PO Box 54 Commerce Ct W Toronto ON M5L 1C2 Canada

NICHOLS, HENRY LOUIS, lawyer; b. Collin County, Tex., Nov. 7, 1916; s. Jesse Cleveland and Leva (Stiff) N.; LL.B., So. Meth. U., 1940; m. Elaine Guentherman, May 17, 1949; children—David Michael, Martha Marie. Admitted to Tex. bar, 1939; asst. city atty., Dallas, 1946-50; individual practice, Dallas, 1951—. Research fellow Southwestern Legal Found., 1964, now bd. dirs.; mem. adv. bd. Center for Legal Municipal Studies. Served to lt. col. AUS, 1941-46; col. USAR ret. Fellow Am. Bar Found.; mem. Am., Dallas (pres. 1963-64) bar assns., State Bar Tex., Tex. Bar Found. (charter). Club: Lakewood Country. Home: 6914 Orchid Ln Dallas TX 75230 Office: Republic Bank Bldg Dallas TX 75201. *As an night-school graduate (Law School), I believe the opportunities in America are unlimited for anyone willing to work. Nowhere in the world are such opportunities available. We who live in the U.S.A. are blessed and the most fortunate of all people. We should strive to maintain that which our fathers preserved for us.*

NICHOLS, HORACE ELMO, state justice; b. Elkmont, Ala., July 16, 1912; s. William Henry and Lou Ella (Bates) N.; Mus.B., Columbia, 1933, postgrad. in constnl. law, 1937-38; LL.B., Cumberland Law Sch., 1936; m. Edith Bowers, Oct. 20, 1945; children—Nancy (Mrs. Lewis Glenn), Carol, Horace Elmo. Admitted to Ga. bar, 1935; practice in Canton, Ga., 1938-40, Rome, Ga., 1940-48; judge Superior Ct., Rome, 1948-54; mem. Ct. Appeals Ga., 1954-66; justice Supreme Ct. Ga., Atlanta, 1966—, chief justice, 1975—. Vocal soloist World's Fair, Chgo., 1933. Mem. Sigma Alpha Epsilon, Blue Key. Democrat. Presbyterian. Clubs: Elks, Coosa Country (Rome). Home: 13 Virginia Circle Rome GA 30161 Office: 28 Jud Bldg Atlanta GA 30334

NICHOLS, HUGH CONKLIN, lawyer; b. Batavia, Ohio, Nov. 21, 1901; s. Allen B. and Edna (Hulick) N.; A.B., Miami U., Oxford, Ohio, 1923, LL.D., 1976; LL.B., U. Cin., 1926; m. Winbourne Smith, Sept. 7, 1930; children—Thomas S., James G. Admitted to Ohio bar, 1926, since practiced in Batavia; of counsel firm Nichols, Speidel & Nichols. Past mem. bd. edn., Batavia. Del. Democratic Nat. Conv., 1952. Trustee Miami U., 1946-68, chmn., 1956-59, past mem. found. Mem. Am., Ohio, Clermont County bar assns., Order of Coif, Phi Kappa Tau, Phi Alpha Delta, Alpha Kappa Psi. Presbyterian (elder). Rotarian. Office: Hamilton Bldg Batavia OH 45103

NICHOLS, JAMES HASTINGS, educator, historian; b. Auburn, N.Y., Jan. 18, 1915; s. Robert Hastings and Marjorie Newton (Wallace) N.; A.B., Yale, 1936, Ph.D., 1941; A.M., Harvard, 1937; hon. degrees Franklin and Marshall, Monmouth, Keuka colls.; m. Judith Beach, 1940; children—Robert Hastings, Susan Mills (Mrs. Susan Nichols Miller), Barbara Wallace (Mrs. John E. Meeker), David Beach. Ordained to ministry Presbyn. Ch., 1943; asst. prof. religion Macalester Coll., St. Paul, 1940-43; faculty Div. Sch., mem. federated theol. faculty U. Chgo., 1943-62, prof. history Christianity, 1955-62; Mary McIntosh Bridge prof. modern ch. history Princeton Theol. Sem., acad. dean, 1970-79; exchange prof. U. Frankfort (Germany), 1949. Fellow Nat. Council Religion in Higher Edn.; Guggenheim fellow, 1956-57. Author: Primer for Protestants, 1947; Democracy and the Churches, 1951; Evanston: An Interpretation, 1954; History of Christianity, 1650-1950, 1956; Romanticism in American Theology, 1963; Corporate Worship in the Reformed Tradition, 1968; (with R.H. Nichols) Presbyterianism in New York State, 1963; (with J. T. McNeill) Ecumenical Testimony, 1974. Editor: Am. transl. with introduction: Force and Freedom (Jacob Burckhardt), 1943; Jour. Presbyn. History, 1962-68; The Mercersburg Theology, 1966. Co-editor: Church History, 1948-62. Contbr. The Challenge of Our Culture, 1946; Religion in America. Home: 9 Cherry Brook Dr Princeton NJ 08540

NICHOLS, JAMES RICHARD, civil engr.; b. Amarillo, Tex., June 29, 1923; s. Marvin Curtis and Ethel (Nichols) N.; B.S. in Civil Engring., Tex. A. and M. U., 1949, M.S. In Civil Engring., 1950; m. Billie Louise Smith, Dec. 24, 1944; children—Judith Ann, James Jr., John M. Partner, Freese & Nichols, Inc., Cons. Engrs., Fort Worth, 1950-76, pres., 1977—. Farm operator Chisholm, Tex., 1969—; dir. Continental Nat. Bank, Fort Worth. Bd. dirs. Panther Boys Club, Fort Worth, 1969—; trustee All Saints Episcopal Hosp., Fort Worth. Served with U.S. Army, 1943-46. Registered profl. engr., Tex., Okla., N.Mex. Fellow Am. Cons. Engrs. Council; mem. Cons. Engrs. Council, ASCE, Nat. Soc. Profl. Engrs. Methodist. Clubs: Masons, Rotary; Fort Worth, Colonial Country (Fort Worth). Home: 3024 Tanglewood Park E Fort Worth TX 76109 Office: 811 Lamar St Fort Worth TX 76102

NICHOLS, JEANNETTE PADDOCK, educator; b. Rochelle, Ill.; d. Hosea Cornish Savery and Janette (Styles) Paddock; A.B., LL.D. (hon.), Knox Coll.; A.M., Ph.D., Columbia; m. Roy F. Nichols, 1920. Instr. history extension div. Columbia, 1919-21; acting prof. Wesleyan Coll., Macon, Ga., 1922-23; asso. prof. U. Pa., 1957-61, chmn. Econ. History Group, 1961-63, collector Recollections, 1969—; assembled source material for biography of N.W. Aldrich, 1922-25; vis. lectr. U. Birmingham (Eng.), 1948; Fulbright lectr., India, also Japan, 1962. Cons. U.S. Treasury Dept., 1945; condr. sessions internat. econ. relations at triennial confs. of Internat. Fedn. U. Women, Toronto, 1947, Zurich, 1950, London, Eng., 1953. Fellow Am. Philos. Soc.; mem. Middle States Council Social Studies (pres. 1943-44), Am. Hist. Assn. (chmn. com. govt. publs. 1941-53), Soc. Am. Studies (pres. 1956-57), Miss. Valley Hist. Assn. (council 1950-53; editorial bd. 1953-56), A.A.U.W. (V.J. Hill fellow 1944), League of Women Voters, Phi Beta Kappa, Gamma Assn. Pa. (pres. 1947-48), Pi Gamma Mu, Phi Alpha Theta. Author: History of Alaska, 1924; Industrial History of N.J. (sect. of Kull's History of N.J.), 1920; James Styles of Kingston, N.Y. and George Stuart of Schoolcraft, Mich., 1936; (with Roy F. Nichols) Growth of American Democracy, 1939, The Republic of the United States, 1942, A Short History of American Democracy, 1943; Twentieth Century United States, 1943. Editor: Democracy in the Middle West (with James G. Randall), 1941; History in the High School and Social Studies in the Elementary School (with M. Wolf and A. C. Bining), 1944. Contbr. to Dictionary Am. Biography, scholarly jours. Home: Fairfax Apts 43d and Locust Sts Philadelphia PA 19104

NICHOLS, JOHN ALDEN, educator; b. Westerly, R.I., Feb. 28, 1919; s. Thomas Pitman and Jennie (Howland) N.; B.A., Wesleyan U., Middletown, Conn., 1941; M.A., Columbia, 1948, Ph.D., 1951; m. Barbara Searles Tuttle, June 8, 1946; children—Catherine Tyler (Mrs. William Boardman), David Alden, Margaret Foster. Instr. history Wesleyan U., 1948-50, asst. prof. history, mng. editor Daedalus, 1959-61; asst. prof. history Skidmore Coll., Saratoga Springs, N.Y., 1950-51; Ford Found. faculty fellow, 1951-52; editor coll. dept. Ginn & Co., Boston, 1952-59; asso. prof. history U. Ill., Urbana, 1961-67, prof., 1967—. Fulbright sr. research fellow, Germany, 1963-64. Mem. Am. Hist. Assn., AAUP, Phi Beta Kappa. Author: Germany After Bismarck: the Caprivi Era, 1890-1894, 1958. Contbr. Interpreting European History, 1967. Home: 505 W Pennsylvania Ave Urbana IL 61801. *I have worked hard at achieving a modus vivendi between respect for external reality and respect for myself.*

NICHOLS, JOHN HENRY, JR., propane gas co. exec.; b. Huntington, N.Y., Feb. 10, 1928; s. John Henry and Antoinette Frances (Trendelberg) N.; A.B., Bowdoin Coll., 1949; postgrad. Cornell Law Sch., 1949-50; M.B.A., Harvard, 1954; m. Jane Elizabeth Anton, Sept. 19, 1953; children—John Henry III, Peter Byron, Anne Elizabeth. With Suburban Propane Gas Corp., Whippany, N.J., 1954—, fin. v.p., dir., 1963-67, exec. v.p., 1967—, pres. propane div., 1971—; asso. dir. Peoples Trust of N.J. Mem. N.J. Adv. Council for Dept. Energy. Chmn., bd. dirs. Deafness Research Found., N.Y.C., 1968-76; trustee St. Marys Abbey, Morristown, N.J. Served as capt. USMCR, 1950-52. Decorated Silver Star medal, Bronze Star medal, Purple Heart. Mem. Nat. LP Gas Assn. (dir., treas. 1975-77, 1st v.p. 1978-79, pres., dir. 1979—), Morris County C. of C. (dir. 1978—). Roman Catholic. Clubs: Rock Spring (West Orange, N.J.); Baltusrol Golf (Springfield, N.J.); Mendham Valley Gun (Green Village, N.J.). Home: 121 Forest Dr Short Hills NJ 07078 Office: PO Box 206 Whippany NJ 07981

NICHOLS, KENNETH DAVID, ret. army officer, cons. engr. b. Cleve., Nov. 13, 1907; s. Wilbur Loren and Minnie May (Colbrunn) N.; B.S., U.S. Mil. Acad., 1929; C.E., Cornell U., 1932, M.C.E., 1933; student Technische Hochschule, Charlottenburg, Germany, 1934-35; grad. Engr. Sch., Ft. Belvoir, Va., 1937; Ph.D., U. Ia., 1937; m. Jacqueline Darrieulat, Dec. 15, 1932; children—K. David, Jacqueline Anne (Mrs. Anthony J. Thompson). Commd. C.E., U.S. Army, 1929, advanced through grades to temp. maj. gen.; instr. civil, mil. engring. U.S. Mil. Acad., 1937-41; area engr. Rome Air Depot (N.Y.), 1941-42, Williamsport (Pa.) Ordnance Works, 1942; dep. dist. engr. Manhattan Dist., 1942-43, dist. engr., 1943-47; prof. mech. U.S. Mil. Acad., 1947-48; chief Armed Forces Spl. Weapons Project, 1948-50; dep. dir. guided missiles Office Sec. of Def., 1950-53; chief research and devel., U.S. Army 1952-53; ret., 1953; gen. mgr. U.S. AEC, 1953-55; cons. engr., 1955—; chmn. Westinghouse Internat. Atomic Power Co., 1958-71; dir. Detroit Edison Co., Fruehauf Corp. Mem. mem.-at-large engring. and indsl. research div. NRC, 1954-58; mem. army sci. adv. panel Dept. Army, 1956-65; dir. Atomic Indsl. Forum, 1964-70. Trustee Thomas Alva Edison Found., 1963-76. Decorated D.S.M. with oak leaf cluster; Presdl. Medal of Merit (Nicaragua); comdr. Brit. Empire; recipient Collinwood prize Am. Soc. C.E.; Distinguished Service award AEC. Fellow Am. Nuclear Soc.; mem. ASME, Nat. Acad. Engring., Sigma Xi. Club: Army-Navy. Home: 16715 Thurston Rd Dickerson MD 20753

NICHOLS, MIKE, stage and film dir.; b. Berlin, Nov. 6, 1931; s. Nicholaievitch and Brigitte (Landauer) Peschowsky; student U. Chgo., 1950-53; student acting Lee Strasberg; m. Patricia Scott, 1957 (div.); m. 2d, Margot Callas, 1974 (div.). Partner with Elaine May in comedy act, first appeared at Playwrights Theatre Club, Compass Theatre, Chgo.; N.Y. debut An Evening with Mike Nichols and Elaine May, 1960; acted in A Matter of Position, Phila., 1962; dir. N.Y. plays Barefoot in the Park (Tony award), 1963, The Knack, 1964, Luv, 1964, The Odd Couple (Tony award for Best Dir.), 1965, The Apple Tree, 1966, The Little Foxes, 1967, Plaza Suite (Tony award), 1968, The Prisoner of 2d Avenue (Tony award), 1971, Uncle Vanya (co-adapted), 1973, Streamers, 1976, Comedians, 1976; The Gin Game, 1977; dir. films: Who's Afraid of Virginia Woolf?, 1966, The Graduate (Acad. award and N.Y. Film Critics award), 1967, Catch-22, 1970, Carnal Knowledge, 1971, The Day of the Dolphin, 1973, The Fortune, 1975; producer N.Y. musical Annie, 1977; performed at Pres. Johnson's Inaugural Gala, 1965; TV appearances include: The Jack Paar Show, The Fabulous Fifties, Perry Como Show, Dinah Shore Show, Today Show. Office: care Sam Cohn Internat Creative Mgmt 40 W 57 St New York NY 10019*

NICHOLS, MILLER, realtor; b. Kansas City, Mo., July 24, 1911; s. Jesse Clyde and Jessie Eleanor (Miller) N.; A.B., Kans. U., 1934; m. Jeannette Deweese, Mar. 28, 1979; children—Kay, Nancy, Ann, Lynn; stepchildren—John, Jeneffer. With J.C. Nichols Co., realtors, Kansas City Mo., 1934—, sales mgr., 1946-50, pres., after 1950, now chmn., chief exec. officer; dir. Commerce Trust Co., Business Mens Assurance Co. Am.; pres. Regency Bldg. Co., 1959—; dir. Kansas City Real Estate Bd., 1948-50. Bd. dirs. Kansas City Crime Commn., 1953—, pres., 1953-54, chmn. bd., 1960; gen. chmn. United Funds Kansas City campaign, 1956; chmn. annual giving fund Kansas City Philharmonic Assn., 1961, bd. dirs., 1950—, exec. v.p., 1961-62, pres., 1963-64, chmn. bd. trustees, 1964-65; bd. dirs. Civic Council, 1965—. Chmn. bd. trustee Kansas City U., 1962—; trustee Midwest Research Inst., 1950—, vice chmn., mem. exec. com., 1952—; bd. dirs. Starlight Theatre, 1951—, Am. Royal Assn, 1960—; bd. regents Rockhurst Coll., 1958—. Served to lt. comdr. USNR, 1942-46. Mem. Nat. Assn. Real Estate Brokers (regional v.p. 1961), Kansas City C. of C. (dir. 1950-52, 65—), Man of Month Club (hon.). Clubs: Mission Hills Country, Kansas City Country (Prairie Village, Kan.); River (Kansas City, Mo.). Home: 55 Le Mans Ct Shawnee Mission KS 66208 Office: 310 Ward Pky Kansas City MO 64112

NICHOLS, OWEN HARVEY, stock broker; b. Market Harborough, Eng., Feb. 7, 1926; s. Walter J. and Marguerite (Bull) N.; grad. high sch.; m. Dorothy Arthur, Oct. 7, 1949 (div.); 1 son, Stuart Arthur; m. 2d, Carol Camp, May 14, 1977. Came to U.S., 1948, naturalized, 1968. Trader, Balfour Guthrie & Co. Ltd., Dallas, Chgo., San Francisco, 1949-53; mgr. Pillsbury Co., Chgo., 1954-61; 1st v.p., dir. Mitchell, Hutchins, Inc., Chgo., 1961—. Chmn. bd. dirs. Chgo. Bd. Trade, 1971-73; chmn. bd. dirs. Chgo. Bd. Options Exchange, 1972-74, founding chmn., 1974—. Mem. Chgo. Merc. Exchange, Internat. Monetary Market, Kansas City Bd. Trade, Winnipeg Grain Exchange, N.Y. Coffee and Sugar Exchange, Commodity Exchange, N.Y. Cocoa Exchange, N.Y. Cotton Exchange, N.Y., Am., Midwest stock exchanges. Served with Brit. Army and Royal Navy, 1944-48. Clubs: Union League, Executives, Saddle and Cycle, Commodity (Chgo.); Evanston Golf. Home: 100 Bellevue Pl Chicago IL 60611 Office: 208 S La Salle St Chicago IL 60603

NICHOLS, PHILIP, JR., judge; b. Boston, Aug. 11, 1907; s. Philip and Mabel (Gibson) N.; A.B., Harvard, 1929, LL.B., 1932; m. Dorothy Jackson, Apr. 19, 1940; children—Donald, Patricia, Christopher. Admitted to Mass. bar, 1932, D.C. bar, 1954; practiced in Boston, 1932-38; atty. lands div. Dept. Justice, 1938-41, Office of Gen. Counsel, WPB, 1942-43; counsel Navy Price Adjustment. Bd., 1945-46; gen. counsel War Contracts Price Adjustment. Bd., 1946; chief counsel Bur. Fed. Supply, Treasury Dept., 1946-48, asst. gen. counsel Treasury Dept., 1948-51; gen. counsel Renegotiation Bd., 1951-54; individual practice, 1954-61; commr. customs Treasury Dept., 1961-64; judge U.S. Customs Ct., 1964-66, U.S. Ct. Claims, 1966—. Served from lt. (j.g.) to lt. comdr. USNR 1943-46. Mem. Fed., Am. bar assns. Home: 2801 New Mexico Ave Washington DC 20007 Office: 717 Madison Pl Washington DC 20005

NICHOLS, RICHARD MAURICE, lawyer, co. dir.; b. Peterborough, N.H., May 10, 1905; s. Maurice Herbert and Cora Belle (Wilkins) N.; A.B., Dartmouth, 1926; LL.B., Harvard, 1929; LL.D., Babson Coll., 1973; m. Ruth J. Killian, June 20, 1931; children—Andrew L. James R. Admitted to Mass. bar, 1929, since practiced in Boston; dir. Foxboro Co. Trustee, past pres. Boston Sci. Museum; former chmn. trustees Babson Coll. Mem. Am., Boston bar assns., Phi Beta Kappa. Club: Union (Boston). Home: 166 Benvenue St Wellesley MA 02181 Office: 28 State St Boston MA 02109

NICHOLS, ROBERT EDMUND, bank exec., journalist; b. Daytona Beach, Fla., Feb. 14, 1925; s. Joe D. and Edna A. (Casper) N.; student San Diego State Coll., 1942-43, St. John's Coll., 1944-45, George Washington U., 1948-49; m. Julia M. Salazar, Aug. 16, 1958 (div. June 14, 1973); children—Craig S., Kim S., Robin K.; m. 2d, R. Grosso, Sept. 1, 1973. Reporter, San Diego Union, 1942-44; with Washington bur. N.Y. Herald Tribune, 1945-48, CBS, 1948-51; with Time, Inc., 1951-61, contbg. editor bus. and finance, asst. edn. dir., N.Y.C., 1951-52, corr. representing Time, Life, Fortune, Sports Illus. mags., San Diego area, 1952-61; Sunday editor San Diego Union, 1952-61; fin. editor Los Angeles Times, 1961-68, mem. editorial bd., 1965-68; spl. asst. to bd. govs. Fed. Res. System, 1968-70; v.p. pub. relations, dir. editorial services Bank of Am., 1970-73, v.p., dir. pub. relations, 1973-78, v.p., dir. policy and program devel., 1978—; Writer dir. film and radio documentaries. Recipient Loeb Newspaper Spl. Achievement award, 1963, Loeb award distinguished financial reporting, 1964. Mem. Nat. Assn. Bus. Economists, Cal. Scholarship Fedn. (hon. life), Pub. Relations Soc. Am., Soc. Am. Bus. Writers (pres. 1967-68), Sigma Delta Chi. Clubs: South Polar Press (Little Am. Antarctic); Explorers (N.Y.C.); Press (San Francisco). Home: 38 Ord Ct San Francisco CA 94114 Office: PO Box 37000 Bank Am World Hdqrs San Francisco CA 94137

NICHOLS, ROBERT LEE, food co. exec.; b. Clarksburg, W.Va., Nov. 4, 1924; s. Clarence Garfield and Reatha Maude (Berry) N.; student Bus. Coll., 1944, U. Detroit, 1959; m. Vianne Hope Demaray, Oct. 21, 1973; children—Donna Beth, Michael Alan, Jeffrey Mark Sales rep. Kellogg Sales Co., Battle Creek, Mich., 1944-50, dist. mgr., 1950-61, asst. div. mgr., 1961-64, sales promotion dir., 1964-69, exec. v.p., gen. sales mgr., 1969-71, pres., 1976-78; pres. Fearn Internat., 1971-76, now dir.; group exec. v.p. Kellogg Co., Battle Creek, 1978—, also dir.; dir. Mrs. Smith Pie Co., Pure Packed Foods; bd. dirs. Cereal Inst., 1976-79; bd. govs. Acad. Food Mktg., St. Joseph U., 1976-79. Exec. v.p., bd. dirs. Jr. Achievement, Battle Creek, 1970-71. Mem. Battle Creek Area C. of C. Clubs: Battle Creek Country, Masons. Office: Kellogg Co 235 Porter St Battle Creek MI 49016

NICHOLS, ROBERT LEIGHTON, civil engr.; b. Amarillo, Tex., June 24, 1926; s. Marvin Curtis and Ethel N.; B.S.C.E., Tex. A&M U., 1947, M.S.C.E., 1948; m. Frances Hardison, June 8, 1948; children—Eileen, William C., Michael L. Grad. asst., instr. Tex. A&M U., 1947-48; asso. Freese & Nichols, and predecessors, Ft. Worth, 1948-50, partner, 1950-77, v.p., 1977—; dir. First State Bank; mem. Bldg. Standards Commn., 1956-62. Chmn., Horn Frog dist. Boy Scouts Am. Mem. Nat. Soc. Profl. Engrs. (pres. 1977-78), Tex. Soc. Profl. Engrs. (pres. 1965-66, Engr. of Year Ft. Worth chpt. 1966), ASCE, Am. Water Works Assn., Tex. Water Conservation Assn., Water Pollution Control Fedn., Tex. Water Pollution Control Assn. (pres. 1962-63), Am. Public Works Assn., Tex. Water Utilities Assn., Tex. Public Works Assn., Tau Beta Pi (hon.), Chi Epsilon (hon.). Methodist. Clubs: Ft. Worth, Masons. Office: 811 Lamar St Fort Worth TX 76102

NICHOLS, ROGER LOYD, physician; b. Waverly, Iowa, Apr. 29, 1926; s. Charles Quaife and Nellie (Fox) N.; student Baldwin-Wallace Coll., 1943-45, Columbia, 1945; A.B., Cornell Coll., 1948; postgrad. Oberlin Coll., 1948-49; M.D., State U. Iowa, 1953; m. Elinor Grace Potee, Aug. 7, 1949; children—Kathleen, Wendy, Quaife. Intern, resident Harvard, 1953-56, postdoctoral research fellow dept.

medicine Med. Sch., 1955-56; physician with Aramco, Saudi Arabia, 1956-70; postdoctoral research fellow Harvard Sch. Pub. Health, 1957-60, research asso., 1961-63, asst. prof., 1963-68, asso. prof., 1968-70, Irene Heinz Given prof. microbiology, 1970—, chmn. dept., 1970-77; pres. Univ. Assos. for Internat. Health, 1973—. Served to ensign USNR, 1943-46. Mem. Am. Epidemiological Soc., Am. Soc. Tropical Medicine and Hygiene, Infectious Diseases Soc. Am. Club: Explorers (N.Y.C.). Editor: Trachoma and Allied Diseases, 1970. Home: Baileys Island North Scituate MA 02060 Office: Dept Microbiology Harvard 665 Huntington Ave Boston MA 02115

NICHOLS, ROY CALVIN, clergyman; b. Hurlock, Md., Mar. 19, 1918; s. Roy and Mamie (Waters) N.; B.A., Lincoln (Pa.) U., 1941; B.D., Pacific Sch. Religion, Berkeley, Calif., 1947, D.D. (hon.), 1964; D.D., U. Pacific, 1959; D.Pub. Service (hon.), Ohio No. U., 1969; D.D. (hon.), Allegheny Coll., 1969, W.Va. Wesleyan Coll., 1970, Morningside Coll., Sioux City, Iowa, 1971, Mt. Union Coll., Alliance, Ohio, 1971; LL.D., Duquesne U., 1972; m. Ruth Richardson, July 23, 1944; children—Melisande Nichols Burnette, Allegra Nichols Lewis, Nathan. Minister S. Berkeley Community Ch., 1943-47; ordained to ministry United Methodist Ch., 1949; pastor Down Meml. Meth. Ch., Oakland, Calif., 1949-64, Salem Meth. Ch., N.Y.C., 1964-68; bishop, Pitts., 1968—. Pres., Berkeley Bd. Edn., 1963-64. Office: 223 4th Ave Pittsburgh PA 15222

NICHOLS, SHUFORD REINHARDT, corp. exec.; b. Des Arc, Ark., Jan. 26, 1909; s. Henry and Grace (Reinhardt) N.; B.A., Washington and Lee U., 1930; postgrad. Harvard, 1931; m. Laura Campbell, June 18, 1935; children—Henry Lee, Anne Robinson, Laura Patricia. Pres. So. Compress Co., North Little Rock, Ark., 1930—; chmn. bd. Farmer & Mchts. Bank. Trustee Ark. Coll., Presbyterian Found. Ark./Okla., Inc. Mem. Cotton Warehouse Assn. Am., Sigma Nu. Presbyn. Clubs: Little Rock, Little Rock Country, XV of Little Rock, Balboa Club de Mazatlan, Confrerié des Chevaliers du Tastevin. Home: 12 Sherrill Rd Little Rock AR 72202 Office: 1600 E Gregory St North Little Rock AR 72119

NICHOLS, STEPHEN GEORGE, JR., educator; b. Cambridge, Mass., Oct. 24, 1936; s. Stephen George and Marjorie (Whitney) N.; A.B. cum laude, Dartmouth, 1958; Rotary Found. fellow Université d'Aix-Marseilles, France, 1958-59; Ph.D., Yale, 1963; m. Mary Winn Jordan, June 22, 1957 (div. 1972); children—Stephen Frost, Sarah Winn; m. 2d, Edith Karetzky, 1972; stepchildren—Laura Natalie Karetzky, Sarah Alexander Karetzky. Asst. prof. French, U. Calif. at Los Angeles, 1963-65; asso. prof. comparative lit. U. Wis.-Madison, 1965-68, chmn. dept., 1967-68; prof. Romance langs. and comparative lit. Dartmouth, 1968—, chmn. dept. comparative lit., 1969-74, 78, 79-82, chmn. dept. Romance langs., 1975-77, asso. dir. fgn. study program, 1970-78, vis. prof. U. Tel Aviv, 1977, Exeter (Eng.) U., 1980; Nat. Endowment Humanities fellow, 1978-79. Mem. adv. bd. Institut d'Etudes francaises d'Avignon, Bryn Mawr Coll., 1965—; dir. seminar Nat. Endowment for Humanities, 1975, 78; sec.-treas. Acad. Lit. Studies, 1978—; exec. com. Eastern Comparative Lit. Conf. Fellow Inst. Research in Humanities, 1966-67. Mem. Acad. Lit. Studies (nominating com. 1974-78, sec.-treas. 1978—), Dante Soc., Internat. Comparative Lit. Assn., Modern Lang. Assn. (editorial com.), Medieval Acad. Am., Société Rencesvals (sec.-treas. Am. sect. 1964-69), Assn. Internat. des Etudes Francaises. Author: Formulaic Diction and Thematic Composition in the Chanson de Roland, 1961; The Songs of Bernart de Ventadorn, 1962; Comparatists at Work, 1968; The Meaning of Mannerism, 1972; Signs of Royal Beauty Bright: Word and Image in the Legend of Charlemagne, 1981; contbr. articles to profl. jours.; editorial bd. French Rev. 1968—; Medievalia et Humanistica, 1974—, Medievalia, 1974—, Oliphant, 1974—, Medievalia, 1975—. Home: Old Route 10-A Norwich VT 05055

NICHOLS, THOMAS S., chem. co. exec.; b. Cambridge, Md., May 8, 1909; s. John P. and Emma H. (Meredith) N.; student U. Pa., 1928; D.Sc. (hon.), Southwestern Coll.; LL.D., Poly. Inst. Bklyn.; children—Judith A., Thomas S.; m. 5th, Mrs. Bernice S. Potter, Aug. 28, 1957 (dec. Oct. 10, 1964); m. 6th, Tatiana A. McKenna, Mar. 12, 1971 (dec. 1979). With E.I. duPont de Nemours & Co., Inc., 1928-37; v.p., dir. Prior Chem. Corp., 1937-41, 45-48; pres., chmn. bd., dir. Mathieson Chem. Corp., N.Y.C., 1948-54; co. merged with Olin Industries, Inc. forming Olin Mathieson Chem. Corp. (now Olin Corp.), pres., 1954-57, chmn. bd., 1957-63, chmn. exec. com., 1963-74, now dir.; dir. U.S. & Fgn. Securities, N.Y.C., Fruehauf Corp., Detroit, Laurel Race Course; past gov. N.Y. Stock Exchange. Spl. asst. to adminstr. Nat. Prodn. Authority, 1951, dep. adminstr., 1951; served on chem. bur. WPB; mem. Harriman Mission to London, State Dept.; chmn. Sulphuric Acid Operating Com., 1941-45; mem. Tech.-Indsl. Disarmament Com. on Chems., 1945, World War II. Trustee Logistics Mgmt. Inst., Johns Hopkins; trustee Md. Hist. Soc.; bd. govs. Washington Coll., Chesterton, Md.; dir.-at-large nat. bd. Jr. Achievement. Mem. Mfg. Chemists' Assn. (past dir.). Episcopalian. Clubs: Maidstone, Devon (East Hampton, N.Y.); Metropolitan (Washington); Lyford Cay (Bahamas); Beach, Meadow, Nat. Golf Links, Southampton (N.Y.); Seminole Golf, Bath and Tennis, Everglades (Palm Beach, Fla.); Brook, River, Links (N.Y.C.); Greenspring Valley Hunt (Balt.). Home: PO Box 253 Owings Mills MD 21117 Office: 460 Park Ave New York NY 10022

NICHOLS, WADE HAMPTON, JR., editorial and publishing cons.; b. Charlotte, N.C., May 31, 1915; s. Wade Hampton and Ora (Calloway) N.; B.S., Northwestern U., 1936; m. Edith Lou Docekal, July 12, 1938 (dec. 1975); children—Wade Hampton III, Nancy Elizabeth. Staff mem. Radio Guide mag., 1936; editor Screen Guide, 1938, Stardom, 1941, Click mag., 1942; free-lance articles, 1946-48; editor Modern Screen mag. 1948, Good Housekeeping Mag., 1958-75; v.p., dir. editorial devel. Mags. div. Hearst Corp., 1975-76; asso. pub. Bluebook mags., 1953-55; editor Redbook, 1949-58, asso. pub., 1953-55, pub., 1955-58; v.p., dir. McCall Corp., 1955-58; editorial and pub. cons., 1976—; Served to 1st lt. AUS, 1943-46. Recipient Benjamin Franklin Gold medal, 1955. Member Mag. Pubs. Assn. (chmn. editorial com. 1956-57), Am. Council Edn. Journalism (accrediting com. 1957-60), Am. Soc. Mag. Editors (exec. council, past chmn.), Phi Gamma Delta, Sigma Delta Chi. Clubs: Bronxville Field. Author: Army Life, WAC Life (basic orientation handbooks for Army), 1944. Home and office: 55 Summit Ave Bronxville NY 10708

NICHOLS, WILLIAM, congressman; b. Amory, Miss., Oct. 16, 1918; B.S. in Agr., Auburn U., 1939, M.A., 1941; m. Carolyn Funderburk; children—Memorie (Mrs. Chris Mitchell), Margaret, Flynt. Vice pres. Parker Fertilizer Co., Sylacauga, Ala., 1947-66; pres. Parker Gin Co., Sylacauga, 1947-60; mem. Ala. Senate, 1963-66, chmn. mil. affairs com., also finance and taxation com.; mem. 90th-92d congresses 4th Dist. Ala., mem. armed services com., chmn. subcom. on mil. compensation, agr. com., chmn. house flag day com., 1971-76; mem. 93d-95th Congresses 3d Dist. Ala. Mem. Sylacauga Bd. Edn. Bd. govs. Nat. Hall of Fame; trustee Auburn U. Served to capt. AUS, 1942-47; ETO. Decorated Bronze Star, Purple Heart; named Outstanding Mem. Ala. Senate, Capitol Press Corps, 1965, Man of Year in Agr., Progressive Farmer mag., 1965. Mem. Am. Legion, V.F.W., D.A.V., Ala. Cattlemens Assn., U. Auburn Alumni Assn., Ala. Farm Bur., Blue Key, Scabbard and Blade, Gamma Sigma Delta. Democrat. Methodist (steward). Home: Sylacauga AL 35150 Office: House Office Bldg Washington DC 20515

NICHOLS, WILLIAM CURTIS, JR., psychologist; b. Fayette, Ala., Apr. 16, 1929; s. William Curtis and Eva Adele (Hargett) N.; A.B., U. Ala., 1953; Ed.D., Columbia U., 1960; m. Alice Louise Mancill, May 29, 1954; children—Alice Camille, William Mancill, David Paul. Asst. prof. sociology U. Ala., Birmingham, 1960-63; postdoctoral fellow Merrill-Palmer Inst., 1963-64, mem. psychotherapy faculty, 1965-69; prof. sociology Samford U., 1963-65; pvt. practice psychology and marriage therapy, Grosse Pointe, Mich., 1969-73, Birmingham, Mich., 1976—; prof. home and family life, dir. marriage and family counseling Fla. State U., 1973-76; adj. clin. prof. psychology U. Detroit, 1976—; cons. Northland Clinic. Mem. mental health and health coms. Mayor's Commn. on Children and Youth, 1966-69; bd. dirs. Family and Childrens Service, Oakland, Mich. Served with C.E., U.S. Army, 1948-49. Recipient Ala. Assn. for Mental Health Service award, 1962. Spl. award for outstanding contbns. Fla. Assn. Marriage and Family Counselors, 1976, 78; NSF fellow U. Colo., 1963. Fellow Am. Assn. Marriage and Family Therapy (dir. 1969-72, chmn. accreditation com. 1976—, founding editor Jour. of Marriage and Family Counseling 1974-76, co-chmn. Atlanta Multiregional Conf. 1975, 77, Spl. award 1976, pres. elect 1979-80), Am. Orthopsychiat. Assn.; mem. Am. Psychol. Assn., Am. Acad. Psychologists in Pvt. Practice, Mich. Inter-Profl. Assn. on Marriage, Divorce and Family (trustee 1977—, com. chmn. 1968-71, 76—), Mich. Assn. Marriage Counselors (pres. 1969-71, chmn. profl. liaison com. 1972-73), Nat. Council on Family Relations (pres. 1976-77, dir., mem. exec. com. 1969-78, editor The Family Coordinator 1970-75, asso. editor Jour. of Marriage and the Family 1976—). Democrat. Presbyterian. Asso. editor: Jour. of Divorce, 1976—; editorial adv. bd. Internat. Jour. Family Therapy, 1977—, Sage Family Studies Abstracts, 1977—. Contbr. chpt. to Klemer's Counseling in Marital and Sexual Problems, 1977. Editor: Marriage and Family Therapy, 1974. Contbr. articles to profl. jours. Home: 31829 Sheridan Dr Birmingham MI 48009 Office: 30400 Telegraph Rd Suite 379 Birmingham MI 48010

NICHOLS, WILLIAM FORD, JR., food co. exec.; b. Palo Alto, Calif., July 4, 1934; s. William Ford and Elizabeth (Woodyatt) N.; A.B., Stanford, 1956, M.B.A., 1958; m. Lynn Mitchell, July 20, 1956; children—Deborah, John, Andrew. With Price Waterhouse & Co., San Francisco, 1958-69, Sydney, Australia, 1966; asst. controller Saga Corp., Menlo Park, Calif., 1969-72, controller, 1972—. C.P.A., Calif. Mem. Am. Inst. C.P.A.'s, Calif. Soc. C.P.A.'s, Nat. Assn. Accountants (v.p. 1974—, dir.), Financial Execs. Inst. Home: 318 Tioga Ct Palo Alto CA 94306 Office: 1 Saga Ln Menlo Park CA 94025

NICHOLS, WILLIAM ICHABOD, editor, pub.; b. Bklyn., June 27, 1905; s. William I. and Minerva (Parker) N.; student Milton (Mass.) Acad., 1917-22; A.B. magna cum laude, Harvard, 1926; Rhodes scholar Balliol Coll., Oxford (Eng.) U., 1926-27; m. Mary Graveley Cutler, June 18, 1932; m. 2d, Marie Therese Brolova Pereire, Sept. 6, 1942. Dean freshman Harvard, 1927-29, dir. news office, 1932-34; advt., publicity mgr. Nat. Electric Power Co., N.Y.C., 1929-32; dir. elec. devel. TVA, 1934-37; editor Sunset mag., San Francisco, 1937-39; mng. editor This Week mag., N.Y.C., 1939-43, editor, 1943-55, editor-in-chief and publisher, 1955-65, pub. and editorial dir., 1965-68, sr. cons., 1969-70; pres. Am. Library in Paris, Inc., 1970-72; cons. TVA, 1940-41, Office War Utilities, W.P.B., 1942-45, State Dept., 1947, 48, 51; hon. cons. journalism and communications Library of Congress, 1970-73. Chmn. National Book Com.; a founder Nat. Library Week; mem. adv. council Columbia Sch. Internat. Affairs; mem. citizens adv. com. N.Y. Pub. Library; mem. adv. bd. Hoover Instn. War, Revolution and Peace. Nat. bd. dirs. Boys Clubs of Am. Recipient Freedom Found. public address award, 1962; Irita Van Doren book award, 1967. Mem. Council Fgn. Relations, Pilgrims of U.S., P.E.N., Phi Beta Kappa, Sigma Delta Chi (hon.). Clubs: Century, Dutch Treat (N.Y.C.); Nat. Press (Washington); Anglo-American Press Assn. (Paris). Editor: Words to Live By, 1948; A New Treasury of Words To Live By, 1962, On Growing Up (Herbert Hoover), Fishing for Fun (Herbert Hoover); contbg. Editor The Overseas American, London, 1974-75. Address: 21 rue de Verneuil Paris 75007 France. *During many years as an editor, dealing with words — and especially Words to Live By — I learned that the greatest thoughts are those which can be expressed most simply. For example: God is Love...or, Know Thyself...or, less well known, Lao Tse's: The Way to Do Is To Be.*

NICHOLSON, BEN, artist; b. Denham, Bucks, Eng., Apr. 10, 1894; s. William and Mabel (Pryde) N. One-man exhbns. include Lefevre, London, 1930, 32, 35, 37, 39, 45, 47, 48, 50, 52, 54, Stedilijk Mus., Amsterdam, 1954, Palais des Beaux Arts, Brussels, 1955, Gimpel Fils, London, 1955, 57, 59, 60, 63, 73, Kunsthalle, Bern, Switzerland, 1961, Tate Gallery, London, 1955, 69, Emmerich Gallery, N.Y.C., 1961, 65, 74, 75, Marlborough Gallery, London, 1963, 68; retrospective exhbns. Albright-Knox Gallery, Buffalo, 1978, Hirshhorn Mus., 1978, Bklyn. Mus., 1979; exhibited other galleries U.S., Can., Europe, S. Am.; group exhbns. Musee Nat. d'Art Moderne, Paris, 1946, Venice Biennale, 1954, Mus. Modern Art, N.Y.C., 1956, Nat. Gallery, Washington, 1970, Tate Gallery, 1977; works pub. collections in Eng., U.S., Can., Switzerland, Argentina, Australia, Italy, Belgium, Brazil, Japan. Decorated Order of Merit (Eng.); recipient 1st prize Carnegie Internat. Exhbn., 1952; Ulissi prize Internat. Jury Venice Biennale, 1954; Governor of Tokyo prize 3d Internat. Exhbn., Tokyo, Japan, 1955; grand priz 4th Internat., Lugano, 1956; U.S. 1st Guggenheim Internat. award, 1956; 1st prize for painting IV Biennial Sao Paulo, Brazil, 1957; Rembrandt prize Johann Wolfgang van Goethe Found., 1974. Subject of monographs: Ben Nicholson: Paintings, Reliefs, Drawings 1911-48 (by Sir Herbert Read) vol. 1, 1947-55, vol. 2; Penguin Modern Painters (by Sir John Summerson), 1948; The Meaning of His Art (by J.P. Hodin), 1957; BN 'Peintures' (by Sir Herbert Read) 1962; monograph, 1969; Drawings, Paintings and Reliefs, 1911-68 (by John Russell); Studio Internat., London, 1969 (edited by M. de Saumarez); Ben Nicholson: Fifty Years of His Art, 1978. Address: care Emmerich Gallery 41 E 57th St New York NY 10022 also care Waddington Galleries 2 Cork St London England

NICHOLSON, DONALD GRANT, utility exec.; b. Buffalo, Ohio, Aug. 12, 1926; s. Lowell R. and Alberta (Ross) N.; B.S. in Bus. Adminstrn. cum laude, Bowling Green State U., 1950; M.B.A., U. Toledo, 1962; m. Wilma Bentley, Oct. 2, 1951; 1 son, Brent B. With Toledo Edison Co., 1950—, asst. sec.-asst. treas., 1962-65, sec.-treas., 1965—, v.p. finance, 1972—, dir., 1973—. Mem. adv. bd. Inst. Public Utilities, Mich. State U.; vice chmn. budget com. Toledo Community Chest, 1965-69, chmn., 1970-72; treas., mem. adv. bd. Salvation Army, Toledo. Served with AUS, 1944-46. Mem. Fin. Analysts Soc. Toledo (pres. 1976-77), Fin. Execs. Inst., Edison Electric Inst., Toledo Area C. of C., Toledo Mus. Art, Toledo Zool. Soc.; Bowling Green State U. Alumni Assn. (trustee), Beta Gamma Sigma. Methodist (lay leader 1963-66). Rotarian. Clubs: Toledo, Heatherdowns Country, Toledo. Home: 711 Kumler Dr Maumee OH 43537 Office: 300 Madison Ave Toledo OH 43652

NICHOLSON, DONALD LEA ROY, union exec.; b. New Glasgow, N.S., Can., Oct. 18, 1917; s. Thomas Cullen and Mary Agnes (Meisener) N.; student New Glasgow pub. schs.; m. Doris Williams, July 13, 1944; children—Hugh Lea Roy, Donald Cullen. With Acadia Coal Co., 1936-40, 45-52, Canadian Congress Labour and Canadian Labour Congress, 1952-59; pres. Canadian Brotherhood Ry., Transport and Gen. Workers, Ottawa, 1959—; chmn. bd. Mut. Press. Served with Canadian Army, 1940-45. Nuffield Found. fellow, U.K., 1966-67. Mem. N.S. Fedn. Labour (v.p.), Canadian Congress Labour (ofcl.), Canadian Labour Congress (v.p.), Internat. Transport Workers Fedn. Mem. New Democratic Party. Presbyterian. Contbr. articles on labour and politics to newspapers and trade jours. Office: 2300 Carling Ave Ottawa ON K2B 7G1 Canada*

NICHOLSON, DOUGLAS ROBERT, accountant; b. Avon, N.Y., Dec. 4, 1921; s. Robert William and Ruth (Neff) N.; A.B., U. Rochester, 1942, M.S., 1948; m. Gertrude Jane Scott, Apr. 24, 1944; children—Laurie, Scott, Susan, Steven. Staff accountant Oliver & Clapp, 1948-49; sr. accountant Charles L. Clapp & Co., 1949-51; office mgr. Williams, Clapp & Co., 1951-53, partner, 1953-56; prin. Haskins & Sells, C.P.A.'s, Rochester, N.Y., 1956-59, partner, 1959-67, partner-in-charge Rochester office, 1967—. Tchr. accounting, income tax courses U. Rochester, 1949-61. Pres., Estate Planning Council Rochester; team capt. YMCA capital fund drive, 1961, Rochester Inst. Tech. new campus fund drive, 1964; chmn. spl. gifts com. U. Rochester, 1965, group leader 38 million capital fund campaign, 1966; mem. accounting adv. bd. Syracuse U., 1968; adv. com. M.S. program Rochester Inst. Tech. Bd. dirs., treas. Highland Hosp., Rochester; bd. dirs. Hosp. Computer Center Rochester, Rochester Regional Research Library Council; mem. deferred giving adv. council Rochester Inst. Tech.; mem. N.Y. State Bd. Pub. Accountancy, 1977. Served to lt. USNR, 1942-45. Recipient Gannett Newspapers award, 1956. Mem. Am. Inst. C.P.A.'s, N.Y. State Soc. C.P.A.'s (past pres. Rochester), Nat. Assn. Accountants, Am. Accounting Assn., Am. Mgmt. Assn., Rochester C. of C., Beta Alpha Psi. Democrat. Unitarian (trustee). Clubs: Oak Hill Country, University, Genesee Valley. Home: 663 Lake Rd Webster NY 14580 Office: Midtown Tower Rochester NY 14604

NICHOLSON, GEORGE ALBERT, JR., fin. analyst; b. Baldwin City, Kan., May 7, 1908; s. George Albert and Nellie May (Ruthrauff) N.; A.B., U. Mich., 1928; M.B.A., Harvard U., 1930; LL.D., Carthage Coll., 1972; m. Elizabeth Farnham, Sept. 1, 1933; children—George Albert III, Edwin F., John R., Elizabeth C. (Mrs. David D. Hamm). With Hudson Motor Co., 1930-31, Union Guardian Trust Co., 1931-33; financial analyst Whitlock, Smith & Co., Detroit, 1933-37, Am. Industries, Detroit, 1937-41, Inc. Investors, Boston, 1941; civilian renegotiator USAF, 1942-45; financial analyst Watling, Lerchen & Co., Detroit, 1945-58; research dir. Smith, Hague & Co. Inc., Detroit, 1958—; columnist Better Investing Mag. Chmn. Investment Edn. Inst., Internat. Investment Edn. Inst., World Fedn. Investment Clubs. Recipient Nicholson award for best ann. individual investors reports Nat. Assn. Investors, 1978. Mem. Fin. Analyst Soc. Detroit (pres. 1957), Nat. Assn. Investment Clubs (chmn. adv. bd.), Delta Kappa Epsilon. Republican. Episcopalian. Clubs: University, Country, Indian Village (Detroit). Home: 1017 Cadieux Rd Grosse Pointe MI 48230 Office: City Nat Bank Bldg Detroit MI 48226

NICHOLSON, GLEN IRA, educator; b. Blairsburg, Iowa, Apr. 21, 1925; s. Willis I. and Berneice (McDaniel) N.; B.A., U. Iowa, 1948, M.A., 1952, Ph.D., 1963; m. Phyllis J. Runge, Aug. 9, 1963; children—Marc, Jonathan, Elisabeth. Prin. high sch., Rowan, Columbus Junction and Marion, Iowa, 1948-61; research asst. U. Iowa, 1961-63; asst., then asso. prof. Wichita State U., 1963-67; asso. prof., head dept. ednl. psychology N.Mex. State U., 1967-69; prof. ednl. psychology U. Ariz., Tucson, 1969—, head dept., 1969-75. Mem. NEA, Am. Ednl. Research Assn., Phi Delta Kappa. Home: 9045 Calle Playa Tucson AZ 85715

NICHOLSON, GUNNAR WALFRID ENANDER, corp. dir.; b. nr. Växiö, Sweden, July 11, 1893; s. Alfred and Mathilda (Niklasson) N.; Chem.E., Chalmers Inst. Tech., Gottenburg, Sweden, 1916; hon. Dr. Engring.; m. Lillian Greenough, Nov. 22, 1928. Engr. various pulp and paper mills, Sweden, 1916-21; engr., supt. various mills, U.S. and Can., 1921-27; gen. supt. Bogalusa Paper Co., 1927-31; mgr. mills So. Kraft Corp., 1931-41; resident mgr. Union Bag and Paper Corp., Savannah, Ga., 1941-45, v.p., N.Y.C., 1945-52, exec. v.p., dir., 1952-56; pres., dir. Tenn. River Pulp & Paper Co., 1956-67; dir. Rising Paper Co. Trustee Norwich U., Am. Scandinavian Found. Decorated comdr. Order Wasa (Sweden); recipient Gold medal Am. Scandinavian Found. Mem. TAPPI (gold medal award 1954, v.p. 1944-45, pres. 1946), Newcomen Soc., Swedish Acad. Engring. Sci., Engring. Inst. Can. (life), Swedish Pulp and Paper Assn. (hon.). Episcopalian. Club: Union League (N.Y.C.). Home: 200 E 66th St New York NY 10021

NICHOLSON, HOWARD WHITE, educator, economist; b. Bklyn., Oct. 5, 1920; s. George Edward and Ada (White) N.; A.B. magna cum laude in History, Oberlin Coll., 1942; A.M. in Econs., Harvard, 1948, Ph.D., 1953; m. Gertrude Baldwin Colson, Dec. 20, 1942; 1 son, Howard White. Instr., then asst. prof. econs. U. Va., 1949-58; acting asst. prof. bus. adminstrn. U. Cal. at Berkeley, 1955-56; mem. faculty Clark U., 1958—, prof. econs., 1967—, chmn. dept., 1963-67. Program dir. econs. NSF, 1965-67; cons. commerce com. U.S. Senate, 1960-61, Dept. Commerce, 1961, 63-64, World Bank, 1961, New Eng. Tel. & Tel. Co., 1963-65; mem. econ. data panel Hwy. Research Bd., 1958-61. Served to capt. USAAF, 1942-46. Mem. Am. Econ. Assn., Econometric Soc., Worcester C. of C. (v.p. 1964-65, 73), Phi Beta Kappa. Baptist (past deacon). Kiwanian. Contbr. articles to profl. jours. Home: 65 Commons Dr Apt 602 Shrewsbury MA 01545

NICHOLSON, JACK, actor, dir., producer; b. Neptune, N.J., Apr. 28, 1937; s. John and Ethel May Nicholson; m. Sandra Knight, 1961 (div. 1966); 1 dau., Jennifer. Acting debut Hollywood stage prodn. Tea and Sympathy; screen debut Cry-Baby Killer, 1958; films include Ensign Pulver, 1964, Easy Rider, 1969, Five Easy Pieces, 1970, Carnal Knowledge, 1971, A Safe Place, 1971, The Last Detail (Cannes Film Festival prize), 1974, Chinatown (Acad. award, N.Y. Film Critics Circle award), 1974, Tommy, The Passenger, 1975, The Fortune, 1975, One Flew Over the Cuckoo's Nest (Golden Globe award, Acad. award, N.Y. Film Critics Circle award), 1975, The Missouri Breaks, 1976, The Last Tycoon, 1976; producer (films) Ride the Whirlwind; The Shooting; Head, 1968; dir. Drive, He Said, 1971; dir., actor Goin' South, 1978. Recipient Oscar award for best supporting actor Easy Rider, 1969. Address: care Bresler Wolff Cota & Livingston 190 N Canon Dr Beverly Hills CA 90210*

NICHOLSON, JAMES JOHN, food co. financial exec., lawyer; b. Flushing, N.Y., Aug. 19, 1926; s. James Aloysius and Ellen (Gilmore) N.; A.B., Dartmouth, 1948; J.D., St. John's U., 1955; m. Margaret Louise Cullen, Oct. 13, 1956; children—John Cullen, Louise Ellen, Jeanine Rose. With U.S./New Amsterdam Casualty Cos., beginning 1948; asso. firm Suozzi & Sordi, beginning 1955; with Corn Products Co. CPC Internat. Inc., 1957—, with tax dept., 1957-59, asst. to comptroller, 1959-62, asst. sec., 1962-67, mgr. personnel, 1967-69, asst. treas., 1969-74, corp. treas., Englewood Cliffs, N.J., 1974—; dir. corp. affiliates Argo State Bank. Chmn. Pelham Manor chpt. A.R.C., 1967-69; mem. bd. edn. UF Sch. Dist. #10-Greenburgh, 1969—; village co-chmn. United Fund, 1971; trustee Coll. New Rochelle, 1978—; bd. dirs. Graham-Windham Services to Families and

Children, N.Y.C., 1968—, pres., 1970-73. Served with USN, World War II. Mem. N.Y. Bar, Am. Bar Assn., Am. Soc. Corp. Secs. Democrat. Roman Catholic. Clubs: Union League; Stage Harbor Yacht (Chatham, Mass.). Home: 1056 Prospect Ave Pelham Manor NY 10803 Office: Internat Plaza Englewood Cliffs NJ 07632

NICHOLSON, JESSE THOMPSON, orthopaedic surgeon; b. Camden, N.J., Apr. 28, 1903; s. Joseph Lippincott and Elizabeth (Thompson) N.; B.S., U. Pa., 1925, M.D., 1928; m. Edith Rose, Apr. 8, 1942; children—Elizabeth Thompson, Edith Davis, Joseph Lippincott, Virginia. Intern Pa. Hosp., Phila., 1928-30, orthopaedic surgeon, 1938—; resident orthopaedic surgery Phila. Orthopaedic Hosp. and Infirmary for Nervous Diseases, 1930-32, Shriner's Hosp., Phila., 1932, Johns Hopkins Hosp., 1932, Mass. Gen. Hosp., 1933; orthopaedic surgeon Grad. Hosp., 1934—, Phila. Children's Hosp., 1935—, Lankenau Hosp., 1953—; prof., chmn. dept. orthopaedic surgery U. Pa. Grad. Sch. Medicine, 1946-68, prof. emeritus, 1969—; cons. Phila. Gen. Hosp., Naval Hosp., Phila., Atlantic City Seashore House. Research dir. N.Y. Cancer Research Inst., Inc., 1952-57; mem. orthopedic sect. NRC, 1946-49; med. adviser Phila. chpt. Nat. Found. Poliomyelitis, 1935-55. Served as capt. M.C., USNR, 1942-46. Diplomate Am. Bd. Orthopaedic Surgery, Pan Am. Med. Assn. Fellow A.C.S., Internat. Coll. Pediatrics; mem. Am. Rheumatism Assn., Phila. Acad. Surgeons, Aid Assn. Phila. County Med. Soc. (sec.-treas. 1947-57, v.p. 1958, pres. 1959-60), Phila. Coll. Physicians, Am. Acad. Orthopaedic Surgeons (treas. 1954-59), Am. Orthopaedic Assn. (pres. 1964-65), Am. Assn. Surgery Trauma, Internat. Soc. Orthopaedic Surgery and Traumatology, AMA (chmn. orthopedic sect. 1955); corr. mem. extraordinary Argentina de Ortopedia y Traumatologia. Republican. Mem. Soc. of Friends. Co-editor: Bone as a Tissue, 1959; asso. editor Jour. Bone and Joint Surgery, 1947-49, 57-60, 61-64. Contbr. med., surg. jours. Home: 516 Oakley Rd Haverford PA 19041 Office: 415 S 19th St Philadelphia PA 19146

NICHOLSON, JOHN BURTON, JR., librarian; b. Chgo., Dec. 28, 1912; s. John Burton and Florence Love (Bridgman) N., Sr.; A.B., Washington and Lee U., 1935, A.M., 1936; B.S.L.S., Columbia, 1937; postgrad. U. Chgo., 1940, Western Res. U., 1951—; m. Mildred Vivian May Livsey, June 7, 1941; 1 son, John Burton. Reference asst., Duke Library, 1937-38; reference librarian Dickinson Coll., Carlisle, Pa., 1938-43, librarian, Fenn Coll., Cleve., 1943-45, Kent (Ohio) State U., 1945-64, dir. library, 1945-66, librarian and head dept. library sci., 1946-66; asso. prof., dir. dept. library tech. Catonsville (Maryland) Community College, 1966-68; chief librarian U. Balt., 1968—; exec. dir. Congress Acad. Library Dirs. Mem. Am., Md. library assns., Assn. Coll. and Reference Libraries (v.p. tri-state chpt. 1953-54, pres. 1954-55), Ohio Library Assn., Ohio Library Assn. (pres. coll. library div., 1947-48, pres. Kent Research group, 1949), Phi Sigma Kappa. Republican. Episcopalian. Clubs: Wranglers Torch, Brotherhood of St. Andrew; Rowfant; Grolier; Balt. Bibliophiles. Contbr. articles to prof. jours. Home: 609 Brookwood Rd Baltimore MD 21229 Office: Langsdale Library Univ Balt 1420 Maryland Ave Baltimore MD 21201. *As a librarian I am committed to the freedom of every individual to have access to any and all information without limitation. Only so long as such freedom is possible will the kind of society which we live in survive.*

NICHOLSON, JOHN HARRIS, naval officer; b. Salt Lake City, May 18, 1924; s. John Chipman and Martha LaNona (Harris) N.; B.S. in Elec. Engring., U.S. Naval Acad., 1946; M.S. in Bus. Adminstrn., George Washington U., 1970; m. Patricia Kent Addison, July 12, 1946; 1 dau., Laurie Kent. Commd. ensign U.S. Navy, 1946, advanced through grades to vice adm., 1979; dep. comdr. fleet maintenance and logistics Naval Ship Systems Center, Washington, 1972-74; dir. strategic submarine div. Office Chief Naval Ops., 1974-75; comdr. Submarine Group 8, Naples, Italy, 1975-77; dep. asst. chief staff plans and policy Supreme Allied Command, Europe, 1977-79; vice dir. Strategic Target Planning, Offutt AFB, Nebr., 1979—. Decorated D.S.M., Legion of Merit (2), Bronze Star with combat V. Mem. U.S. Naval Inst. Address: Quarters 3 Offutt AFB NE 68113

NICHOLSON, MORRIS EMMONS, JR., educator, metallurgist; b. Indpls., Feb. 15, 1916; s. Morris Emmons and Jesse (Cox) N.; B.S., Mass. Inst. Tech., 1939, Sc.D., 1947; m. Norma Story, Aug. 21, 1943; children—Morris Emmons III, Robert A., Richard A. Sect. head engring. research dept. Standard Oil Co. (Ind.), 1947-50; asst. prof. Inst. Study Metals, U. Chgo., 1950-55; prof. metallurgy U. Minn., 1956—, head dept., 1956-62, dir. continuing edn. in engring. and sci., 1973—. Mem. Materials Adv. Bd., 1960-62. Active Boy Scouts Am., 1952—, dist. commr., 1961-64, recipient Silver Beaver, 1966. Trustee Ind. Dist. 623 Sch. Bd., 1959-65, treas., 1965-77; bd. dirs. 916 AVTI, 1976—; dir. Minn. Sch. Bd. Assn., 1973-79. Served from 2d lt. to capt., AUS, 1941-46. Registered profl. engr., Minn. Mem. Am. Soc. Engring. Edn. (chmn. 1957-58), Am. Soc. Metals (chmn. Minn. chpt. 1958), Am. Inst. Mining and Metall. Engrs., Nat. Assn. Corrosion Engrs., Sigma Xi, Theta Delta Chi, Tau Beta Pi, Alpha Chi Sigma. Conglist. Home: 1776 N Pascal Ave Saint Paul MN 55113 Office: U Minn Minneapolis MN 55455

NICHOLSON, PATRICK JAMES, univ. adminstr.; b. Houston, Nov. 28, 1920; s. John Joseph and Mary Ellen (Brennan) N.; B.A., Rice U., 1942; Indsl. Adminstr., Harvard, 1943, M.B.A., 1946; Ph.D., U. Houston, 1959; m. Anne Stevenson, Dec. 26, 1951 (div. 1962, annulled 1969); m. 2d, Barbara Mary Simmons, 1965; 1 son, Michael Patrick James. Personnel asst. Freeport Sulphur Co., New Orleans, 1946-47; cons. communications, various pub. relations firms, Houston, 1947-56; lectr. mgmt. U. Houston, 1951-56, exec. dir. devel., asst. to pres., 1956-57, v.p. univ. devel., 1957-78, v.p. public info. and univ. relations U. Houston System, 1978—, exec. dir., asst. sec. U. Houston Found., 1970—. Sec., dir. Buffalo Savs. & Loan Assn.; pres., dir. Mt. Vernon Pub. Co., 1962—. Pres., Inst. Ophthalmology, Tex. Med. Center, 1963-66, 72—. Bd. dirs., pres. Monsignor John T. Nicholson Fund; bd. dirs. Houston Community Welfare Planning Assn., Alley Theatre, Aquinas Inst.; chmn. bd. dirs. S.E. Tex. Info. Network Assn., 1969—; pres. Astronaut Fund for Sci. Scholarships, 1978—; v.p. Cecil Amelia Blaffer Found., 1972—. Served with AUS, 1943-46; lt. col. M.I. Res. Fellow Tex. Acad. Scis.; mem. Pub. Relations Soc. Am., Am., Tex., S.W. psychol. assns., Acad. Mgmt., Am. Coll. Pub. Relations Assn. (pres. 1965-66), N.Y. Acad. Scis., Houston Council World Affairs (dir., pres. 1966-68), Yeats Assn., Sigma Xi, Phi Kappa Phi, Alpha Tau Omega, Phi Eta Sigma, Omicron Delta Kappa. Roman Catholic. Kiwanian. Clubs: Houston Country, Houston, Plaza, University, Criterion (Houston); Harvard (N.Y.C.). Author: In Time, An Anecdotal History of the First Fifty Years of the University of Houston, 1977; editor: Social Directory of Houston, 1952—; contbr. articles to profl. jours. Home: 3723 Olympia St Houston TX 77019

NICHOLSON, ROBERT ARTHUR, coll. dean; b. Pepin, Wis., Oct. 13, 1923; s. Arthur W. and Ethel (Weedin) N.; B.S., Anderson (Ind.) Coll., 1944; M.A., N.Y.U., 1946, Ph.D., 1953; m. Dorothy Nelis, June 17, 1944; children—Paul, Gary. With Anderson Coll. 1945—, successively instr., asst. prof., asso. prof. music, chmn. dept., asst. to dean, 1945-58, dean, 1958—, v.p., 1964—. Mem. pub. bd. Church of God, 1955—, chmn. commn. higher edn., 1963-70, vice chmn., 1970—. Mem. Am. Assn. Acad. Deans, Am. Assn. for Higher Edn. Author: Handbook to the Hymnal of the Church of God, 1953. Editor: Hymnal of the Church of God, 1953, 71. Home: 721 Maplewood St Anderson IN 46012

NICHOLSON, ROY S., clergyman; b. Walhalla, S.C., July 12, 1903; s. Samuel Dendy and Beulah Young (Lindsay) N.; student Wesleyan Meth. Acad. and Coll., Central, S.C., 1918-24; D.D., Houghton Coll., 1944; Th.B., Central Sch. Religion, 1956; m. Ethel Macy, June 26, 1924; children—Roy S., Lee Huffman. Ordained to ministry Wesleyan Meth. Ch., 1925; tchr., N.C., 1924; pastor, East Radford, Va., 1925-26, Long Shoals, N.C., 1926-30, Kannapolis, N.C., 1930-35, Brooksville, Fla., 1969-74; supt. Wesleyan Youth Work, 1934-35, Sunday sch. sec. and editor, 1935-39, home missionary sec., 1939-43; mem. bd. adminstrn. Wesleyan Meth. Ch., 1935-59, 63-68, chmn., 1947-59; v.p. Wesleyan Meth. Ch. Am., 1939-47, pres., 1947-59, pres. emeritus, 1959-68; prof. Bible, Central Wesleyan Coll., 1959-68, chmn. div. religion, 1959-68. Editor, Wesleyan Meth., Wesleyan Youth, 1943-47; Am. counselor Immanuel Gen. Mission, Japan, 1964—; bd. dirs. Wesleyan Bible Conf. Assn., 1970—; gen. supt. emeritus Wesleyan Ch., 1972—. Chmn. bd. trustees Houghton, Central, Miltonvale and Marion colls., 1947-59; adv. council Ky. Mountain Bible Inst., World Gospel Mission. Recipient Distinguished Alumnus of Yr. award Central Wesleyan Coll. Alumni Assn., 1973. Mem. Nat. Holiness Assn. (bd. adminstrn. 1955-64, rec. sec. 1960-64). Author: Wesleyan Methodism in the South, 1933; History of the Wesleyan Methodist Church, 1951; Notes on True Holiness, 1952; Arminian Emphases, 1962; A Valid Theology for Our Day, 1963; Commentary on The Pastoral Epistles, 1965; Commentary on The First Epistle of Peter, 1969; Studies in Church Doctrine; also articles; contbr. to Aldersgate Doctrinal Series, 1963, other publs. in field. Home: Wesleyan Arms 1909-S N Centennial St High Point NC 27260

NICHOLSON, ROY STEPHEN, ednl. adminstr.; b. Radford, Va., Mar. 4, 1926; s. Roy S. and Ethel Dovie (Macy) N.; A.B., Marion Coll., 1950; M.A., Syracuse U., 1956; Ph.D., Mich. State U., 1971; m. Mary DeAnn Jan. 15, 1977; 1 dau., Kimberly Rienzo. Acad. dean Lansing Community Coll., 1966-69; pres. S.W. Coll., Chgo., 1969-71; pres. Clark County Community Coll., 1971-76; pres. Mt. Hood Community Coll. Dist., 1976—. Mem. Mayor's Manpower Adv. Council, 1972-76; bd. dirs. Portland (Oreg.) Involvement Corp., 1976-79; mem. exec. com. Explorer Olympic Program, 1979; chief investigator HEW small research project, 1970-71. Served with USN, 1943-46. Mem. Am. Assn. Community and Jr. Colls. Pres.'s Acad. (treas.), N.W. Assn. Community and Jr. Colls. (pres. 1976), Am. Sch. Adminstrs. Assn., Am. Sociology Assn., Am. Acad. Polit. and Social Scis., Gresham C. of C. (dir. 1977-79), Phi Delta Kappa. Club: Rotary. Home: 2150 NE Francis Ct Gresham OR 97030 Office: 26000 SE Stark St Gresham OR 97030

NICHOLSON, THOMAS DOMINIC, astronomer; b. N.Y.C., Dec. 14, 1922; s. Dominic J. and Catherine (Brown) N.; B.S., U.S. Mcht. Marine Acad.; B.A., St. John's U., 1950; M.S., Fordham U., 1953, Ph.D., 1962; m. Branca Costa, Dec. 26, 1946; children—Lester C., Diana C., Glen C., Gail C. Marine deck officer Moore-McCormack Lines, 1941-46; from instr. to asst. prof. nautical sci. and asst. to dept. head U.S. Mcht. Marine Acad., 1946-53; lectr., instr. dept. astronomy Hayden Planetarium, Am. Mus. Natural History, N.Y.C., 1952-53, asso. astronomer, 1953-57, astronomer, 1957-67, chmn., 1964-67, mus. asst. dir., 1967-68, dep. dir., 1968-69, dir., 1969—; TV weather forecaster sta. WNBC, N.Y.C., 1967-72; has lectured in astronomy U.S. Mil. Acad., Yale, N.Y. U.; geodetic surveying, Arctic, 1956, Greenland Ice Cap, 1958; mem. adv. council Astrophys. Obs., Princeton U.; mem. nat. adv. bd. Morrell Chem. Senses Center. Served with U.S. Merchant Marine, 1940-46; lt. (j.g.) USNR. Fellow A.A.A.S., Royal Astron. Soc., Am. Astron. Assn.; mem. Inst. Nav. (past pres.), Astron. Soc. Pacific, Am. Meteorol. Soc., Am. Assn. Museums (v.p.), Assn. Systematics Collections (pres.). Author: (with J. M. Chamberlain) Planets, Stars and Space, 1957; Adventure with Stars, 1958; also numerous articles. Editor: Astronomy Highlights, Curator. Contbg. editor: Natural History, Christian Sci. Monitor. Home: 10 Bedford Rd Woodcliff Lake NJ 07675 Office: Am Museum Natural History Central Park W at 79th St New York NY 10024

NICHOLSON, THOMAS LAURENCE, lawyer; b. Evanston, Ill., Nov. 19, 1923; s. Thomas Laurence and Nelle Braxton (Jones) N.; A.B., Princeton U., 1947; postgrad. (Woodrow Wilson fellow) U. Paris, 1948-49, (Ford Found. grantee) U. Hamburg Law Sch., (W. Ger.), 1958-59; J.D., U. Chgo., 1955, M. Comparative Law, 1959; m. Eleanor Ann Kuester, Sept. 11, 1954; children—Anne Lindsey, John Chester, Sarah Stoney, Martha Kenyon. Admitted to Ill. bar, 1955; asst. public affairs officer, then acting public affairs officer, U.S. Consulate Gen., Algiers, Algeria, 1949-51; asso. firm Isham, Lincoln & Beale, Chgo., 1954-61, partner, 1961-66; partner firm Mayer, Brown & Platt, Chgo., 1967—; research asso. U. Mich. Law Sch., 1959-60; vis. prof. law U. Ill., 1973; lectr. in law Northwestern U., 1974, 75; mem. vis. com. U. Chgo. Law Sch., 1975-78. Bd. dirs. Met. Housing and Planning Council, Chgo., 1962-66, pres., 1964-65; trustee Inst. for Psychoanalysis, Chgo., 1974—, pres., 1979—. Served to lt., j.g., USN, 1941-46. Named 1 of 10 Outstanding Chicagoans, Jr. C. of C., 1963; recipient Outstanding Citizen award U. Chgo., 1966. Mem. Am. Law Inst., Am. Bar Assn., Chgo. Council Lawyers, Law Club, Legal Club, Phi Beta Kappa. Editor (with Eric Stein) and contbg. author: American Enterprise in The European Common Market—A Legal Profile, vol. 1, 1960, vol. 2, 1960. Home: 7 Swift Ln Lakeside MI 49116 Office: 231 S LaSalle St Chicago IL 60604

NICHOLSON, WILL FAUST, JR., bank holding co. exec.; b. Colorado Springs, Colo., Feb. 8, 1929; s. Will Faust and Gladys Olivia (Burns) N.; S.B., M.I.T., 1950; M.B.A., U. Denver, 1956; m. Shirley Ann Baker, Nov. 26, 1955; children—Ann Louise Nicholson Naughton, Will Faust. Vice pres. Van Schaack & Co., Denver, 1954-66; partner N. G. Petry Constrn. Co., Denver, 1966-70; sr. v.p. Colo. Nat. Bankshares, Inc., Denver, 1970-75, pres., 1975—. Mem. Denver Urban Renewal Authority, 1958-59; mem. Denver Bd. Water Commrs., 1959-65, pres., 1963-65; bd. dirs. Boys' Clubs Denver; bd. mgrs. Presbyterian Med. Center, Denver. Served with USAF, 1950-53. Mem. Colo. Golf Assn. (bd. govs. 1973—), U.S. Golf Assn. (exec. com. 1974—, v.p. 1978—). Republican. Episcopalian. Clubs: Denver Country, Univ., Denver (Denver); Univ. (N.Y.C.); Royal and Ancient Golf (St. Andrews, Scotland). Home: 30 Cherry St Denver CO 80220 Office: PO Box 5168 Denver CO 80217

NICHOLSON, WILLIAM LLOYD, III, air force officer; b. St. Louis, Mar. 9, 1926; s. William L. and Irene Alma (Ramspott) N.; B.S. in Meteorology, St. Louis U., 1950; M.S. in Internat. Affairs, George Washington U., 1970; m. Wanda Loraine Loyd, June 14, 1947; children—Linda Radford, Beverley Anne, Diedre Kaye. Commd. 2d lt., U.S. Air Force, 1950, advanced through grades to maj. gen., 1976; vice comdr. 305th Air Refueling Wing, Grissom AFB, Ind., 1971-72; comdr. 301st Air Refueling Wing, Lockbourne AFB, Ohio, 1972; comdr. 97th Bomb Wing, Blytheville AFB, Ark., 1973-74; comdt. Air Command and Staff Coll., Maxwell AFB, Ala., 1976-78; vice comdr. 15th AF, SAC, March AFB, Calif., 1978-79; dir. Def. Mapping Agy., Washington. Mem. Calif. Inland Empire council Boy Scouts Am. Decorated D.F.C., Air medal with 1 oak leaf cluster, Legion of Merit with 2 oak leaf clusters. Mem. Air Force Assn., Order of Daedalians. Lutheran. Office: HQ DMA/D Bldg 56 NAVO BSY Washington DC 20305

NICHTERN, CLAIRE JOSEPH (MRS. HERBERT KALLEM), theatrical producer; b. N.Y.C.; d. Fred and Rebecca (Brumer) Joseph; student N.Y. U., 1951-52; m. Sol Nichtern, June 4, 1944 (div.); m. 2d, Herbert Kallem; children—Judith (Mrs. Donald Gelfer), David. Casting dir. Phoenix Theatre, 1955-58, prodn. coordinator, 1959-60; asst. to gen. mgr. Playwrights Co., 1958-59; producer The Banker's Daughter, 1961-62, The Typist and the Tiger, 1962-63, Luv, N.Y.C., 1964-67, co-producer, London, Eng., 1964-65; producer Jimmy Shine, 1968-69, The Trial of A. Lincoln, 1971; dir. admissions Am. Acad. Dramatic Arts, 1970, producer in residence, 1971-73; asso. dir. Circle-in-the-Square, 1973; producer Santa Anita 42, Chelsea Theatre Center, spring 1975; producer I Got a Song, fall 1974, House of Blue Leaves, summer 1976, Absent Friends, 1977, Cold Storage, 1977-78; dir. creative affairs Warner/Regency, 1978-79, William Morris Agy., 1979; dir. theatre projects Warner Communications Inc., 1979—. Recipient Antoinette Perry award 1965. Mem. League N.Y. Theatres, Assn. Theatrical Press Agts. and Mgrs., ANTA. Home: 61 W 9th St New York NY 10011

NICKEL, GEORGE DANIEL, finance co. exec.; b. Pasadena, Calif., Sept. 1, 1906; s. George Christian and Minnie (Kopp) N.; B.A., U. So. Calif., 1929; M.A. in Sociology and Econs., 1932; m. Helen Josephine Green, Aug. 10, 1933; 1 dau., Marilyn (Mrs. Robert Alvin Bonsack). Dir. unemployment relief Kern County (Calif.), 1932-35; dir. social service Calif. Relief Adminstrn., San Francisco, 1935-38; regional dir. pub. relations Beneficial Finance System, Morristown, N.J., 1938—, dir. consumer edn., 1963—. Co-founder Family Debt Counselors, Phoenix. Bd. dirs. Arcadia Unified Sch. Dist., 1945-55, pres., 1947-50, 52-55; bd. dirs. Family Service Los Angeles, 1962-72, pres., 1959-61; bd. dirs. Family Service Assn. Am., 1967—, pres., 1972-74; exec. com. Nat. Found. Consumer Credit, 1972—, treas., 1975—; mem. council Rose Inst. State and Local Govt., Claremont Men's Coll., 1975—. Mem. Nat. Conf. Social Welfare (dir. 1972—), Pub. Relations Soc. Am., Nat. Assn. Social Workers (past pres. Los Angeles chpt.), Consumer Credit Counselors Calif (dir., past pres.), Calif. Loan and Finance Assn. (dir., pres. 1973—), Phi Kappa Phi, Alpha Kappa Delta. Rotarian. Home: 1300 Ramona Rd Arcadia CA 91006

NICKEL, HANS ERICH, computer service bur. exec.; b. Berlin, Germany, June 23, 1928; s. Erich and Margarete (Oberpichler) N.; masters degree in law and criminology, univs. Berlin and Bonn (Germany), 1955; grad. student econs., Wharton Sch., U. Pa., 1957-59; m. Sara Antoinette Angle, July 23, 1955; children—R. Spencer, Maria Jane. Came to U.S., 1955, naturalized, 1961. Car salesman, 1955-56; systems analyst Ins. Co. N.Am., 1956-58; supr. systems and programming Standard Pressed Steel Co., Jenkintown, Pa., 1958-64; v.p., dir. application programming Nat. Computer Analysts, Princeton, N.J., 1964-66; pres. Internat. Computaprint Corp., Ft. Washington, Pa., 1966—; dir. Computaprint Ltd., London, Tristar, Inc., Graphcom, Inc. Mem. Codasyl Com., 1960-68. Served with German Army, 1945. Mem. Printing Industries Am. Assn., Research and Engring. Council Graphic Arts Industry. Co-author: Detab-X. Home: Kindle Hill Gwynedd Valley PA 19437 Office: International Computaprint Corp 475 Virginia Dr Fort Washington PA 19034

NICKELL, THOMAS PIERATT, JR., univ. exec.; b. Richmond, Ind., Dec. 6, 1920; s. Thomas Pieratt and Helen C. (Fitzgerald) N.; student Butler U., Indpls., 1942; B.S., U. So. Calif., 1948; D.B.A. (hon.), Upper Iowa U., 1962; LL.D. (hon.), Pepperdine U., Los Angeles, 1971; m. Annette Y. Rowley, Aug. 31, 1946; children—Susan, Mary (Mrs. John Black), Carrie (Mrs. Patrick Reeves), Thomas Pieratt III, Patrick William. Prodn. control supr. electro motive dept. Allison div. Gen. Motors Corp., Indpls., 1941-42; asst. dir. advt. and pub. relations Occidental Life Ins. Co., Los Angeles, 1948-50; dir. Alumni Fund, U. So. Calif., Los Angeles, 1950-57, dir. fund raising, 1957, dir. devel., 1957-60, dir. univ. planning, 1960-61, v.p. univ. planning, 1961-70, v.p. univ. affairs, 1971—. Cons., Ford Found., Nat. Financial Devel. Adv. Council for Urban Coalition, Hoffman Found.; dir. Republic Fed. Savs. & Loan Corp., Am. Med. Internat., Inc. Mem. Atty. Gen.'s Vol. Adv. Com., State of Calif.; past dir. Los Angeles Jr. C. of C. Trustee, Soc. Exptl. Test Pilots. Served to 1st lt. USAAF, 1942-45; PTO. Decorated Bronze Star medal. Mem. Pith Helmet Soc., Pub. Relations Soc. Am., Newcomen Soc. N.Am., Assn. Independent Colls. and Univs. (past trustee), Am. Alumni Council (past regional dir.). Clubs: Jonathan (Los Angeles); Lakeside Golf. Contbr. articles to profl. publs. Home: 10214 Oakpark St Northridge CA 91324 Office: University Park Los Angeles CA 90007

NICKELSON, DONALD EUGENE, broker; b. Emporia, Kans., Dec. 9, 1932; s. Harry and Mildred B. (Nicholson) N.; m. Barbara Ruth Fronterhouse, Jan. 7, 1950; children—Marta, Nancy, Donny, Dana, Harry, Margaret, Elizabeth, James, Douglas. Mgr., Bache & Co., Beverly Hills, Calif., 1956-64; partner A.G. Edwards & Sons, St. Louis, 1964-66; sr. v.p., dir. Paine Webber Jackson & Curtis, Los Angeles, 1967—; chmn. Pacific Stock Exchange; chmn. Pacific Depository Trust. Chmn. Harris County (Tex.) March of Dimes, 1968. Mem. Securities Industry Assn. Republican. Lutheran. Clubs: Jonathan, Stock Exchange, Ramada. Home: 503 Dartmouth Pl Flintridge CA 91011 Office: 555 S Flower St Los Angeles CA 90017

NICKELSON, HARRY EDWARD, market research co. exec.; b. Spring Lake, Wis., Sept. 24, 1915; s. Emil J. and Ellen (Christensen) N.; student Pere Marquette Normal Sch., 1933-34, U. Minn., 1934-35, LaSalle Extension U., 1936-39; m. Ruth G. Faust, Dec. 26, 1941; 1 dau., Jacqueline. Accountant, George Rossiter & Co., 1938-39; landscaping Nickelson Bros., 1939-41; with A.C. Nielsen Co., Northbrook, Ill., 1941—, now exec. v.p., dir.; with Universal Farm Sales, Inc., 1952—, now v.p., dir.; partner Riddick, Currie & Nickelson, 1955-69. Mem. Am. Mktg. Assn. Home: 1041 Timber Ln Lake Forest IL 60045 Office: Nielsen Plaza Northbrook IL 60062

NICKERSON, ALBERT LINDSAY, oil co. exec.; b. Dedham, Mass., Jan. 17, 1911; s. Albert Lindsay and Christine (Atkinson) N.; ed. Noble and Greenough Sch., 1926-29; B.S., Harvard U., 1933, LL.D. (hon.), 1976; LL.D. (hon.), Hofstra U., 1964; m. Elizabeth Perkins, June 13, 1936; children—Christine Morgen, Albert W., Elizabeth Davis, Victoria. Service station attendant Socony-Vacuum Oil Co., (now Mobil Oil Corp.) 1933, dist. mgr., 1940, div. mgr., 1941, asst. gen. mgr. Eastern marketing div., 1944; dir. Vacuum Oil Co., Ltd. (now Mobil Oil Co., Ltd.), London, Eng., 1945, chmn. bd., 1946; dir. Socony-Vacuum, 1946—, v.p., dir., 1951-55, pres., 1955-61, chmn. exec. com., chief exec. officer, 1958-69, chmn. bd., 1961-69; dir. Met. Life Ins. Co., State St. Investment Co., Federal St. Fund, Raytheon Co., Harvard Mgmt. Co.; gen. partner State St. Exchange Fund; dir. Fed. Res. Bank N.Y., 1961-66, chmn. bd., 1969-71. Dir. Placement Bur. War Manpower Commn., 1943; chmn. balance of payments adv. com. Commerce Dept., 1965-66; chmn. Bus. Council, 1967-68. Trustee Internat. House, 1952-62, Am. Mus. Nat. History, 1958-62, 64-69; bd. overseers Peter Bent Brigham Hosp., Boston, 1972—; trustee Affiliated Hosp. Center, Boston, 1977—, Boston Symphony Orch., 1974—, Rockefeller U., 1957—; mem. corp. Harvard, 1965-75, bd. overseers, 1959-65. Mem. Harvard Alumni Assn. (dir.), Bus.

Council. Republican. Episcopalian. Clubs: Harvard Varsity, Harvard, (N.Y.C.); 25-Year of Petroleum Industry (pres. 1965); Country (Brookline, Mass.); Thames Rowing (London); Cambridge Boat (Mass.). Home: Lexington Rd Lincoln MA 01773 Office: 150 E 42d St New York NY 10017

NICKERSON, DOROTHY, color technologist; b. Boston, Aug. 5, 1900; d. Jean Paul and Alice Jane (Getchell) Nickerson; student Boston U., 1919-20, Johns Hopkins U., 1923-24, Harvard U., summer 1924, U. Wis., summer 1929, George Washington U., 1928-29, Grad. Sch. Dept. Agr., 1927-28. Asst., Munsell Research Lab., asst. mgr. Munsell Color Co., Boston, N.Y.C., Balt., 1921-26; color technologist U.S. Dept. Agr., Washington, 1927-64; research color cons., Washington, 1965—. Trustee Munsell Color Found., 1942-79, trustee emeritus, 1979—, pres., 1973-75. Recipient Superior Service award U.S. Dept. Agr., 1951, Gold certificate Am. Hort. Council, 1957, Distinguished Achievement award Instrument Soc. Am., 1964, Deane B. Judd AIC Gold medal award Internat. Color Assn., 1975. Fellow Optical Soc. Am., Illuminating Engring. Soc. (Gold medal 1970), AAAS, Washington Acad. Sci.; mem. Inter-Soc. Color Council (sec. 1938-52, pres. 1954, hon. mem. 1968, Godlove award 1961), Internat. Commn. on Illumination. Club: Quota. Contbr. articles to profl. jours. Address: 4800 Fillmore Ave Alexandria VA 22311

NICKERSON, EUGENE H., judge; b. Orange, N.J., Aug. 2, 1918; A.B., Harvard U., 1941; LL.B. (Kent scholar), Columbia U., 1943; LL.D. (hon.), Hofstra U., 1970. Admitted to N.Y. bar, 1944, U.S. Supreme Ct. bar, 1948; law clk. to Judge Augustus N. Hand, 2d circuit U.S. Ct. Appeals, 1943-44, to Chief Justice Harlan F. Stone, U.S. Supreme Ct., 1944-46; county exec., Nassau County, N.Y., 1962-70; practice law, N.Y.C., 1946-61, 71-77; judge U.S. Dist. Ct., Bklyn., 1977—. Counsel, N.Y. Gov.'s Com. Pub. Employee Procedures, 1956-58; mem. N.Y. State Law Revision Commn., 1958-59, 77; mem. Met. Regional Council, 1962-70, chmn., 1969-70; mem. adv. council pub. welfare HEW, 1963-65; mem. pub. ofcls. adv. council OEO, 1968. Mem. Assn. Bar City N.Y. (com. fed. legislation 1971-74, com. on communication 1971-77, com. on judiciary 1974-77), Am., N.Y. State, Nassau County bar assns., Am. Law Inst., Phi Delta Phi. Address: US Courthouse 225 Cadman Plaza E Brooklyn NY 11201

NICKERSON, JAMES FINDLEY, coll. adminstr.; b. Gretna, Nebr., Dec. 16, 1910; s. Elmer Samuel and Lulu Perkins (Patterson) N.; B.S., Nebr. Wesleyan U., 1932; M.A., Columbia Tchrs. Coll., 1940; Ph.D., U. Minn., 1948; Sc.D. (hon.), Yankton (S.D.) Coll., 1971; m. Juanita M. Bolin, Mar. 3, 1934; children—Ann Rogers (Mrs. Patrick Lueck), Maria De Miranda (Mrs. Jim Barker). Tchr. public schs., Giltner, Nebr., 1932-35; sch. music supr., Gordon, Nebr., 1936-38, Bayshore, L.I., 1939-41, Grand Island, Neb., 1941-42; instr. Coll. Edn., music supr. high sch. U. Minn., 1942-46, vis. prof. Coll. Edn., summer 1948; asst. prof. music edn. U. Kans., 1946-48, asso. prof., 1948-53; research asso. dept. psychology U. So. Calif., assigned human factors div. U.S. Navy Electronics Lab., San Diego, 1953-54; dean edn., dir. summer quar., prof. psychology Mont. State U., 1954-64, head dept. psychology, 1954-56, research asso. Electronics Research Lab., 1958-64; v.p. acad. affairs N.D. State U., Fargo, 1964-66; pres. Mankato (Minn.) State U., 1966-73, Distinguished Service prof., 1973—; dir. Servicemen's Opportunity Coll., Am. Assn. State Colls. and Univs., Washington, 1973—. Dir. Northwestern Nat. Bank, Mankato, 1967-69. Cons. publ. edn. Office Gov. Wash., 1964; exec. sec., study dir. interim com. edn. Wash. Legislature, 1959-60; chmn. regional conf. womanpower Nat. Manpower Council and Mont. State Coll., 1957; mem. steering com. Pacific N.W. Conf. Higher Edn., 1942—; mem. nat. adv. com. sci. edn. NSF, 1968-71, chmn., 1970-71. Mem. vis. com. Harvard Grad. Sch. Edn., 1970-76. Recipient citation interim study Wash. Legislature and Gov., 1960; Outstanding Achievement award Bd. Regents U. Minn., 1968; Danforth Found. grantee, 1969. Mem. Nat. Assn. State Univs. and Land Grant Colls. (senate, chmn. div. tchr. edn. 1962-65, sec. council acad. officers 1965), Acoustical Soc. Am., Am. Assn. State Coll. and State Univs. (bd. dirs. 1966-71), Am. Assn. Colls. Tchr. Edn. (bd. dirs. 1969-71), Am. Inst. Physics, I.E.E.E., Am. Psychol. Assn., Music Educators Nat. Conf., Am. Assn. Higher Edn. (chmn. resolutions com. 1964), Assn. Minn. Colls. (pres. 1972), Edn. Commn. of States (commr. 1967-73, mem. task force on coordination, governance and structure of postsecondary edn. 1973), Sigma Xi, Phi Mu Alpha Sinfonia. Office: Am Assn State Colls and Univs One Dupont Circle Washington DC 20036

NICKERSON, JOHN LESTER, educator; b. Halifax, N.S., Can., Oct. 8, 1903; s. Obed. F. and Olivia A. (Mills) N.; A.B., Dalhousie U., Halifax, 1925, M.A., 1928; Ph.D., Princeton, 1935; m. Annie McL. Cook, Oct. 5, 1929 (dec.). Came to U.S., 1939, naturalized, 1945. Substitute prof. physics Meml. Coll., St. John's, Nfld., 1925-26; MacGregor fellow Dalhousie U., 1926-27; bursar Can. NRC, 1927-28; instr. physics Princeton, 1928-30, postgrad. 1930-31; asst. prof. physics Mt. Allison U., Sackville, N.B., Can., 1931-38, prof., 1938-39, dean men, 1936-39; asst. prof. physiology Columbia, 1939-45, asso. prof., 1945-50, prof., 1950-56; prof. chmn. dept. physiology and pharmacology Chgo. Med. Sch., 1956-62, prof., chmn. dept. physiology, dir. div. biophysics, 1962-70, acting dean grad. studies, 1968-70, dean, 1970-76, prof. physiology, 1976—. Cons. physicist Enamel & Heating, Ltd., Sackville; liaison officer, biophysicist U.S. Office Naval Research, London, 1952-53; responsible investigator USPHS, 1947-68. Mem. XVIII Internat. Physiol. Congress, Denmark, 1950, 1st Internat. Cardiological Congress, Paris, 1950; 3d Internat. Cardiological Congress, Brussels, 1958. Mem. bd. edn. Du Page County dist. 3, 1959-63. Fellow A.A.A.S., Royal Soc. Medicine, Inst. Medicine Chgo.; mem. N.Y. Acad. Sci., Assn. Am. Med. Colls., Research Def. Soc. Gt. Britain, Am. Phys. Soc., Am. Inst. Physics, Am. Physiol. Soc. (distinguished mem. circulation sect.), Harvey Soc., Soc. for Exptl. Biology and Medicine, Am. Heart Assn., Am. Ballistocardiograph Research Soc. (pres. 1962-65), Sigma Xi. Contbr. numerous articles to sci. jours. Mem. editorial bd. Am. Heart Jour., 1950-60. Home: 1502 Lehigh Rd Glenview IL 60025 Office: U Health Scis/Chgo Med Sch 2020 W Ogden Ave Chicago IL 60612

NICKERSON, RUTH, sculptor; b. Appleton, Wis., Nov. 23, 1905; d. Robert Wellington and Kate Mary (Ellis) Nickerson; ed. Simcoe Collegiate Inst., 1921-23, Nat. Acad. Schs., 1928-32; m. Edmund Greacen, Jr., Dec. 30, 1935; children—Elizabeth Ruth, Barbara Eleanor. Works represented in permanent collections Newark Mus., Cedar Rapids, Iowa, Art Assn., New Brunswick, N.J., Post Office, Leaksville, N.C., children's br. Bklyn. Pub. Library, New Rochelle City Hall, Grasslands Hosp., Valhalla, N.Y., Montclair (N.J.) Mus. Art, Interchurch Center, N.Y.C. Mem. White Plains Civic Arts Commn., 1948-60. Recipient Nat. Arts Club medal, 1933; Saltus Gold medal N.A.D., 1933; Montclair Mus. medal, 1936; Am. Artists Profl. League medal, 1947; Guggenheim fellow, 1946-47. Fellow Nat. Sculpture Soc.; mem. N.A.D. (dipl., council mem. 1978—), Audubon Artists. Address: 106 Woodcrest Ave White Plains NY 10604. *The principles I have tried to express in all my sculpture are simplicity, dignity and strength. My belief that the ultimate purpose of creation is to integrate wildly disparate elements into a unified and harmonious whole is the basis for all my ideas. My goal has been to use a God-given talent to give others a glimpse of that same concept through my use of human character and forms. My standard of conduct has been to act with integrity and forthrightness.*

NICKLAS, ROBERT BRUCE, cell biologist; b. Lakewood, Ohio, May 29, 1932; s. Ford Adelbert and Marthabelle (Beckett) N.; B.A., Bowling Green State U., 1954; M.A. (Eugene Higgins fellow), Columbia U., 1956, Ph.D., 1958; m. Sheila Jean Counce, Sept. 24, 1960. Instr. in zoology Yale U., 1958-61, asst. prof. zoology, 1961-64, asso. prof., 1964-65; asso. prof. Duke U., 1965-71, prof., 1971—; mem. NSF Postdoctoral Fellowship Panel, 1969-71; mem. Am. Cancer Soc. Sci. Adv. Com. for Virology and Cell Biology, 1975-78. Recipient award for disting. teaching Duke Alumni, 1975; Yale fellow in scis., 1963-64; John Simon Guggenheim fellow, 1972-73; grantee Inst. Gen. Med. Scis. USPHS, 1960—. Fellow AAAS; mem. Am. Soc. Cell Biology (exec. com. 1976-78, council 1975-78), Am. Soc. Naturalists, Am. Soc. Zoologists, Biophys. Soc., Genetics Soc. Am., Soc. Gen. Physiologists, Sigma Xi. Contbr. numerous articles to profl. publs.; editorial bd. Chromosoma, 1966—, Jour. Exptl. Zoology, 1970-72. Home: 3101 Camelot Ct Durham NC 27705 Office: Dept Zoology Duke U Durham NC 27706

NICKLAUS, JACK WILLIAM, profl. golfer; b. Columbus, Ohio, Jan. 21, 1940; s. Louis Charles, Jr. and Helen (Schoener) N.; student Ohio State U., 1957-62, hon. Dr. Athletic Arts, 1972; m. Barbara Bash, July 23, 1960; children—Jack William II, Steven Charles, Nancy Jean, Gary Thomas. Major tournaments won include Tournament of Champions, 1963, 64, 71, 73, 77, U.S. Amateur, 1959, 61, U.S. Open, 1962, 67, 72, U.S. Masters, 1963, 65, 66, 72, 75, Brit. Open, 1966, 70, PGA Championship, 1963, 71, 73, 74, Internat. Pro-Amateur, 1973, Atlanta Golf Classic, 1973, Walt Disney World Golf Classic, 1973, Hawaiian Open, 1974, Tournament Players Championship, 1974, Tournament Players Championship, Hawaii, 1975, Doral-Eastern Open, Heritage Classic, Masters, PGA championship, World Open, 1976, Australian Open, 1976, World Series Golf, 1977, Gleason Inverrary Classic, 1977, others; pres. Golden Bear, Inc.; course design cons. Harbour Town Golf Links, Hilton Head Island, S.C., also Kings Island, Cin., Muirfield, Columbus, Mayacoo Lakes, West Palm Beach, Fla. and courses in Japan and Europe. Chmn. Ohio div. Am. Cancer Soc., 1967; chmn. sports div. Nat. Easter Seal Soc., 1967. Named PGA Player of Year, 1967, 72, Dunlop Profl. Athlete of Yr., 1972, Golfer of Year, Profl. Golfers Assn., 1973; Byron Nelson award, 1964, 65, 72, 73, Bob Jones award, 1975; Sports Illus. Sportsman of Year, 1978. Mem. President's Club Ohio State U., Phi Gamma Delta. Author: My 55 Ways to Lower Your Golf Score, 1962; Take a Tip From Me, 1964; The Greatest Game of All, 1969; Golf My Way, 1974; The Best Way To Better Golf, Vols. 1-3, 1974. Home: 11397 Old Harbour Rd North Palm Beach FL 33048 Office: 321 Northlake Blvd North Palm Beach FL 33403*

NICKLIN, GEORGE LESLIE, JR., educator, physician; b. Franklin, Pa., July 25, 1925; s. George Leslie and Emma (Reed) N.; B.A., Haverford Coll., 1949; M.D., Columbia U., 1951; postgrad. psychoanalysis William A. White Inst., N.Y.C., 1962; m. Katherine Mildred Aronson, Sept. 30, 1950; children—Emily, David, Jane, Sarah. Resident, then chief resident Bellevue Psychiat. Hosp., N.Y.C., 1953-56; practice medicine specializing in psychiatry, N.Y.C., 1956—; staff Bellevue Hosp., 1956—; asst. clin. prof. psychiatry N.Y. U., Med. Sch., 1962-70, asso. clin. prof. psychiatry, 1970—; chmn. Inst. Psychoanalysis, Nassau County Med. Center Clin. Campus, SUNY, Stonybrook, 1978—. Founder Friends World Coll., 1958, trustee, 1968-79, chmn. com. on Friends Coll., 1960-65. Served with AUS, 1943-46. Decorated Purple Heart, Bronze Star. Fellow Am. Acad. Psychoanalysis, Am. Psychiat. Assn.; mem. AAAS, NAACP, Soc. Med. Psychoanalysts, White Psychoanalytic Soc., Assn. for World Edn. (charter trustee, treas. 1970-78). Club: Gardiner's Bay Country (Shelter Island, N.Y.). Home and Office: 6 Butler Pl Garden City NY 11530. *Education is essential to the future evolution of human society. But education alone is not enough. Integrity and creativity must accompany it for maximum benefit to the world.*

NICKLIS, JOHN OSBORNE, former mfg. co. exec.; b. Dunkirk, N.Y., Aug. 10, 1909; s. John D. and Jessie (Durell) N.; student Sheffield Sci. Sch., Yale, 1927-30; m. Katherine E. Clark, June 10, 1939 (dec. Oct. 1974); 1 dau., Cynthia Orchard Nicklis Neumann, Jr.; m. 2d, Margaret C. Andrews, Sept. 6, 1975. Mgr., Green Meadow Club, Harrison, N.Y., 1936-40, Woodway Country Club, Darien, Conn., 1940-43; accountant Stamford Rolling Mills, Springdale, Conn., 1943-45; with Pitney-Bowes, Inc., Stamford, Conn., 1945-73, v.p. fin., 1959-62, exec. v.p., 1962-63, pres., 1963-73, chief exec. officer, 1964-72, chmn., 1969-73, dir., 1962—; hon. dir. State Nat. Bank Conn.; dir. Stamford Water Co. Trustee Family and Children's Services of Stamford. Home: 10 Pride's Crossing New Canaan CT 06840

NICKOLEY, KEITH D., graphic arts exec.; b. Libertyville, Ill., Sept. 30, 1927; s. William E. and Emma K. (Meyers) N.; B.S. in Econs., Lake Forest (Ill.) Coll., 1949; m. Jean C. Baldwin, Nov. 15, 1952; children—Lynn, Jill, Jan, Sarah. With Roberts and Porter, Inc., 1950—, exec. v.p., Des Plaines, Ill., 1970-75, pres., 1975—, chmn. bd., chief exec. officer, 1978—; v.p. Ednl. Council Graphic Arts. Mem. Bannockburn (Ill.) Plan Commn., 1972—. Served with USNR, 1945-46. Mem. Nat. Printing and Supply Assn. (dir.), Metal Decorating Suppliers Guild (dir.), Nat. Assn. Printers and Lithographers (dir.), Graphic Arts Tech. Found., Lithographers Club Chgo., Printers Supplymen's Guild. Club: Exmoor Country. Office: 125 E Oakton St Des Plaines IL 60018

NICKON, ALEX, educator, chemist; b. Poland, Oct. 6, 1927; s. Steve and Maria (Nickon); came to U.S., 1955, naturalized, 1961; B.Sc., U. Alta., 1949; M.A., Harvard U., 1951, Ph.D., 1953; m. Beulah Monica Godby, Aug. 22, 1950; children—Dale Beverly, Linda Cheryl, Leanne Marie. Vis. lectr. Bryn Mawr Coll., 1953; postdoctoral fellow Birkbeck Coll., U. London (Eng.), 1953-54, NRC, Ottawa, Can., 1954-55; NSF sr. fellow Imperial Coll., London, 1963-64, U. Munich (Germany), 1971-72; mem. faculty Johns Hopkins, 1955—, prof. chemistry, 1964—, Vernon K. Krieble prof. chemistry, 1975—; vis. asso. Am. Chem. Soc. on Profl. Tng., 1975—. Mem. medicinal chem. panel NIH, 1966-70, postdoctoral panel NRC, 1968-69. Sloan Found. fellow, 1957-61. Fellow N.Y. Acad. Scis.; mem. Am. (nat. awards com. 1974-76), Brit. chem. socs. Sr. editor Jour. Organic Chemistry, 1965-71; Am. exec. editor Tetrahedron Reports, 1978—. Home: 1009 Painters Ln Cockeysville MD 21030 Office: Dept Chemistry Johns Hopkins U Baltimore MD 21218

NICKS, ORAN WESLEY, govt. ofcl.; b. Eldorado, Tex., Feb. 2, 1925; s. Oran Millow and Leona Salome (Stewardson) N.; A.A. in Aero. Engring., Spartan Coll., 1943; student U. Tex., 1946-47; B.M.E., U. Okla., 1948; postgrad. U. So. Calif., 1949-57; Fed. Exec. Inst., 1977; m. Phyllis Vivian Beadel, May 14, 1955; children—Toni Nicks Staplin, Janet Nicks Huff, Connie Jo, Colby Oran. Engr., N. Am. Aviation Inc., Los Angeles, 1948-58; mgr. advanced projects engring. Chance-Vought Aircraft, Inc., Dallas, 1958-60; head lunar flight systems NASA, Washington, 1960-61, dir. lunar and planetary programs, 1961-67, dep. asso. adminstr. for space sci. and applications, 1967-70, acting asso. adminstr. for advanced research and tech., 1970, dep. dir. Langley Research Center, Hampton, Va., 1970—; co-chmn. NASA-Dept. Def. Nat. Aero. Facilities, 1974-77. Served with USAAF, 1944-45. Recipient Exceptional Service medal NASA, 1964, Outstanding Leadership medal, 1965, Disting. Service medal, 1971; Disting. Citizens award M Club, U. Md., 1965; named to Engring. Hall of Fame, U. Okla., 1969; Paul E. Tuntland award Soaring Soc. Am., 1976; lic. pilot. Fellow Am. Astron. Soc.; mem. AIAA, Exptl. Aircraft Assn., Soaring Soc. Am., Pi Tau Sigma, Tau Omega. Editor: This Island Earth, 1970. Research and publs. in aerodynamics, supersonic propulsion, rocket vehicle design and devel., lunar and planetary exploration, space tech.; patentee air induction systems, total energy sensors. Home: 425 Elizabeth Lake Dr Hampton VA 23669 Office: Dep Dir NASA Langley Research Center Hampton VA 23665

NICKS, STEVIE, singer, songwriter; b. Calif., May 26, 1948; m. Lindsey Buckingham (div.). Singer, songwriter with Lindsey Buckingham; recorded album Buckingham and Nicks, 1975; joined group Fleetwood Mac, 1975; composer song Rhiannon. Co-winner, Billboard award for Album of Year, Group of Year, 1977. Office: care Seedy Mgmt 1420 Beachwood Los Angeles CA 90068*

NICKSON, JAMES JOSEPH, physician, educator; b. Portland, Oreg., Dec. 31, 1915; s. Delbert Harry and Elvira W. (Wallin) N.; B.S., U. Wash., 1936; postgrad. Harvard Med. Sch., 1936-38; M.D., Johns Hopkins, 1940; m. Margaret Jane Hofrichter, June 12, 1939 (div.); children—Robert Frazier, James Bridges; m. 2d, Elizabeth Gibson, Dec. 2, 1967; 1 son, Michael Andrew. Mem. metall. lab. U. Chgo., 1942-47; sr. fellow NRC, 1947-49, now cons.; dir. dept. radiation therapy Meml. Hosp., mem. Sloan-Kettering Inst., N.Y.C., 1950-65; prof. Sloan-Kettering div. Cornell Med. Sch., 1952-55; prof. Cornell U. Med. Coll., 1955-65; chmn. dept. radiation therapy Michael Reese Hosp., Chgo., 1965-72, mem. Michael Reese Med. Research Inst., 1965-72; prof. radiology Pritzker Sch. Medicine, U. Chgo., 1969-72; prof. radiation oncology U. Tenn. Med. Sch., 1972—; dir. Memphis Regional Cancer Center, 1974—. Cons. USPHS. Fellow Am. Coll. Radiology; mem. Radiation Research Soc., AAAS, AMA, Am. Soc. Therapeutic Radiologists (past pres.), Radiol. Soc. N.Am., N.Y. Acad. Scis., Am. Radium Soc., Chgo. Roentgen Soc., Chgo. Med. Soc., Am. Cancer Soc., Internat. Coll. Radiology, Pan Am. Med. Assn., Phi Beta Kappa, Sigma Xi. Editor: Symposium on Radiobiology, 1952. Contbr. articles to profl. jours. Home: 1764 Great Oaks Cove Germantown TN 38138 Office: U Tenn Med Sch 865 Jefferson Ave Memphis TN 38108

NICOL, JOSEPH ARTHUR COLIN, marine biologist; b. Toronto, Dec. 5, 1915; s. George and Marie Noelle (Petrie) N.; B.Sc., McGill U., 1938; M.A., U. Western Ont., 1940; D.Phil., Oxford U., 1947, D.Sc., 1961; m. Helen Wilhelmina Cameron, Oct. 22, 1941; 1 dau., Josephine Marie. Asst. prof. U. B.C., 1947-49; marine biologist Marine Biol. Assn. U.K., 1949-66; vis. prof. dept. zoology U. Tex., Austin, 1966-67, prof., 1967—. Fellow Royal Soc. London. Aughor: Biology of Marine Animals. Office: Marine Sci Lab U Tex Port Aransas TX 78373

NICOL, WILLIAM KENNEDY, ins. co. exec.; b. Hamilton, Ont., Can., July 20, 1922; s. William R. and Mae (Kennedy) N.; B.A., U. Toronto, 1949; m. Phyllis Bowie, Feb. 7, 1946 (dec. 1969); children—Frances Mae (Mrs. Ben H. Teague), Christine (Mrs. Recy L. Dunn), Catherine (Mrs. Joe Meyer); m. 2d, Jessie Helms, Jan. 18, 1974. Came to U.S., 1952. Asso. actuary Tchrs. Ins. and Annuity Assn., 1952-55; controller, actuary Commonwealth Life Ins. Co., Louisville, 1955-61; v.p., actuary Am. Nat. Ins. Co., Galveston, Tex., 1961-69, exec. v.p. ins. services, 1969-74, exec. v.p. research, 1974—; dir. Trans World Life Ins. Co. N.Y., Am. Nat. Property and Casualty Co., Mo.; v.p. Am. Nat. Fin. Corp. Del.; v.p., dir. Am. Nat. Life Ins. Co. Tex., Standard Life and Accident Ins. Co. Okla. Enrolled actuary. Fellow Soc. Actuaries; mem. Am. Acad. Actuaries, Actuaries Club S.W.; corr. mem. Canadian Inst. Actuaries. Home: 711 Holiday Dr #29 Galveston TX 77550 Office: Am Nat Ins Co One Moody Plaza Galveston TX 77550

NICOLAIDES, JOHN DUDLEY, educator, aerospace cons.; b. Washington, Feb. 13, 1923; s. Phidias John and Marie (Kelly) N.; B.A., Lehigh U., 1943; postgrad. Rensselaer Poly. Inst., 1943-44; M.S. in Engring., Johns Hopkins, 1953; Ph.D., Cath. U. Am., 1962; m. Virginia Driscoll, June 9, 1945; 1 dau., Kathleen Mary. Project engr. Gen. Electric Co., 1946-48; research scientist, ballistic research lab. Aberdeen Proving Ground, 1948-53; asst. aerodynamics, hydrodynamics and ballistics, then tech. dir. astronautics Bur. Naval Weapons, 1953-61; spl. asst. to asso. adminstr. space scis. and applications, then dir. program rev. and resources mgmt. NASA, 1961-64; chmn., prof. dept. aerospace engring. U. Notre Dame, 1964-74; pres. A-E-R-O, 1969—; head dept. aerospace engring. Calif. Poly. U., San Luis Obispo, 1975—. Cons. in field, 1964—. Served as officer USNR, 1943-46. Mem. Am. Inst. Aeros. and Astronautics, Am. Ordnance Assn. Author: Missile Flight Dynamics, 1957; Advances in Space Science and Technology, vol. 5, 1955. Designer parafoil Flying Wing, plus six golf ball, Nicolaides-Flyer, Flying Machine. Address: 2048 Skylark Ln San Luis Obispo CA 93401

NICOLAYSEN, PETER SMITH, publishing co. exec.; b. Los Angeles, Nov. 12, 1934; s. Frank Andrew and Helen Mary (Herrmann) N.; m. Claudia Venae Smith, Mar. 4, 1966; children—Tawny, Tara, Kyla, Britta. Account exec. Hixson & Jorgensen Advt., Los Angeles, 1956-59; dir. mktg. services Capitol Records, Hollywood, Calif., 1962-65; Western advt. sales mgr., then pub. Motorcyclist and Wheels Afield mag., Petersen Pub. Co., Los Angeles, 1966-74; v.p. Pinnacle Paradise Inc., Scottsdale, Ariz., 1974-75; exec. v.p., pub. Cycle Guide, Custom Bike, also Road Test mags., Quinn Publs., Compton, Calif., 1975—. Bd. dirs. Malibu Twp. Council, 1966-67; pres. Sycamores Park Property Owners Assn., 1966-72. Served with AUS, 1956, 60-61. Mem. Motorcycle Industry Council (past dir.), Los Angeles Advt. Club, Western Pubs. Assn. Republican. Club: Malibu Yacht. Home: 6300 Gayton Pl Malibu CA 90265 Office: 1440 W Walnut St Compton CA 90220

NICOLL, CHARLES SAMUEL, physiologist; b. Toronto, Ont., Can., Apr. 11, 1937; s. Robert Knox and Annie (Young) N.; came to U.S., 1951, naturalized, 1958; B.S., Mich. State U., 1958, M.S., 1960, Ph.D. (NIH fellow), 1962; m. Sharon M. Russell, Apr. 14, 1974; children—Katherin Ann, Eric Robert, Scott Frank. Am. Cancer Soc. postdoctoral fellow U. Calif., Berkeley, 1962-64, asst. prof. physiology, 1966-70, asso. prof., 1970-74, prof., 1974—; staff fellow NIH, Bethesda, Md., 1964-66. Recipient award for meritorious research Sigma Xi, 1960, City of Nice (France), 1977. Mem. Endocrine Soc., Am. Soc. Zoologists, Am. Physiol. Soc., AAAS. Research on hormones, growth and devel. Office: Dept Physiology and Anatomy U Calif Berkeley CA 94720

NIDA, EUGENE ALBERT, orgn. exec.; b. Oklahoma City, Nov. 11, 1914; s. Richard Eugene and Alma Ruth (McCullough) N.; A.B., U. Calif. at Los Angeles, 1936; M.A., U. So. Cal., 1939; Ph.D., U. Mich., 1943; D.D. (hon.), Eastern Baptist Sem., Phila., 1956, So. Calif. Bapt. Sem. 1959; Th.D., U. Muenster (West Germany), 1967; Litt.D., Heriot-Watt U., Scotland; m. Althea Lucille Sprague, June 19, 1943. Prof. linguistics Summer Inst. Linguistics, U. Okla., 1937-53; ordained to ministry Bapt. Ch., 1943; exec. sec. translations Am. Bible Soc., 1943—; coordinator research in translations United Bible Socs. Active Boy Scouts Am. Recipient Diamond Jubilee award Inst. Linguistic, London, 1976; Alexander Gode medal Am. Translators Assn., 1977.

Mem. Am. Assn. Applied Linguistics, Linguistic Assn. Can. and U.S., Linguistic Soc. Am. (pres. 1968), Internat. Assn. Semiotic Studies, Am. Anthrop. Assn., Soc. N.T. Studies, Soc. Bibl. Lit. and Exegesis, Phi Beta Kappa, Pi Gamma Mu. Author: Bible Translating, 1947; Morphology, 1949; Learning a Foreign Language, 1950; God's Word in Man's Language, 1952; Customs and Cultures, 1954; Message and Mission, 1960; Translator's Handbook of the Gospel of Mark, 1962; Toward a Science of Translating, 1964; Religion Across Cultures, 1968; Theory and Practice of Translation, 1969; Componential Analysis of Meaning, 1975; Exploring Semantic Structures, 1975; Language Structure and Translation, 1975; Good News for Everyone, 1977. Co-author: Translator's Handbook of the Acts of the Apostles, 1972; Translator's Handbook on the Epistle to the Romans, 1973; Translator's Handbook on Ruth, 1973; Translator's Handbook on 1-2 Thessalonians, 1975; Translator's Handbook on Galatians, 1976; Translator's Handbook on Philippians, 1977; Translator's Handbook on Colossians and Philemon, 1977; Translator's Handbook on First Peter, 1979; Editor: Book of One Thousand Tongues, 1972. Home: 33 Husted Ln Greenwich CT 06830 Office: 1865 Broadway New York NY 10023

NIDA, JANE BOLSTER (MRS. DOW HUGHES NIDA), librarian; b. Chgo., July 19, 1918; d. Chalmer A. and Elsie R. (Sonderman) Bolster; B.A., Aurora (Ill.) Coll., 1942; B.S. in Library Sci., U. Ill., 1943; m. Dow Hughes Nida, Sept. 1, 1946; 1 dau., Janice Beth (Mrs. Robert M. Michaels). Circulation librarian Aurora Pub. Library, 1943-44, reference librarian, 1946; program dir. A.R.C., Eng., France, 1944-46; order librarian Ohio U., Athens, 1947; head librarian Falls Church (Va.) Pub. Library, 1951-54; asst. dir. Arlington County Dept. Libraries, Arlington, Va., 1954-57, dir., 1957—, on loan to AID, 1979-80. Mem. Va. Adv. Legis. Council, Com. to Revise State Library Laws, 1968-69, Women's Joint Congl. Com., 1968—; vol. Am. Cancer Soc., 1971—, bd. dirs. Arlington chpt., 1974—; mem. exec. com. Regional Adv. Group, Va. Regional Med. Program, 1971-76; v.p., founder, dir. Cultural Laureate Found. Recipient Meritorious Service award A.R.C., World War II. Mem. AAUW, ALA, D.C., Va. (pres. 1969-70) library assns., Arlington Hist. Soc. Baptist. Club: Army-Navy Country. Home: 4907 29th St N Arlington VA 22207 also 1617 Bayhouse Ct Sarasota FL 33581 Office: 1015 N Quincy St Arlington VA 22201

NIDECKER, JOHN E., former govt. ofcl., bus. exec.; b. Phila., Mar. 30, 1913; s. Arnold W. and Anne J. (Williams) N.; student LaSalle U. extensions, 1948-49; m. Jeanne Kara Brodhead, Apr. 12, 1958; children—Arnold W., Stephen A. Various positions in marketing Sun Oil Co., Phila., 1934-47; various mgmt. positions Cities Service Co., Inc., 1947-69, corp. mgr. bus. devel., 1967-69; dep. spl. asst. to President Nixon, 1969-73, spl. asst., 1973-74; spl. asst. to President Ford, 1974-75; pres., owner John E. Nidecker & Co., 1975—; professed Brotherhood of St. Gregory, 1976, asst. superior, 1977. Active Detectives Crime Clinic N.Y., N.J. and Conn., 1965—; asst. pres. Internat. Bridge, Tunnel and Turnpike Assn., 1960-61; drama instr. Trinity Ch., N.Y.C., 1964-68. Mem. advance staff Dwight D. Eisenhower and Richard M. Nixon, 1956, 60, 62, 68. Served with USMCR, 1936-40. Named Citizen of Month, N.J. Detectives Crime Clinic, 1965. Episcopalian (lay reader 1929—). Mason (Shriner). Home: 642 Crocus Dr Rockville MD 20850. *In religion, I follow the motto of St. Gregory "Soli Deo Gloria"—to God alone the glory. In secular life I follow the motto "Credo in Meipsum"—I believe in myself. This is due to self education which, though frequently unrecognized, can lift a person to the same levels as those formally educated.*

NIDEN, GEORGE, mfg. co. exec.; b. Oshkosh, Wis., Apr. 7, 1917; s. Michael and Paraskeva (Krevchena) N.; B.S., U. Mass., 1938; postgrad. Northeastern U., 1941, Yale U., 1942, Boston U., 1950; m. Barbara C. Macdonald, Aug. 23, 1945; children—Martha C., George, Wilma Bates and Lucinda Hubbard (twins). With Am. Locker Co., Inc., 1939—, successively trainee, staff asst., dist. mgr. West Coast, dir. sales, 1950, asst. v.p. sales-service, 1957-62, v.p., 1962-64, exec. v.p., 1964-73, pres., 1973—, also dir.; exec. v.p. Canadian Locker Co., Ltd., 1966-73, pres., 1973—, also dir.; exec. v.p. Automatic Voting Machine Corp., 1973. Served from pvt. to maj. U.S. Army and USAAF, 1941-45. Mem. Am. Legion, Adelphia (v.p.), Am. Assn. Airport Execs., Am. Bus Assn., Can. Motorcoach Assn., Hocksters Internat. (pres. 3 years), Am. Operators Councils Internat., Kappa Sigma (pres.). Republican. Presbyterian. Clubs: Livingston (dir.), Town, Wellesley Country; Sportsmen of Western N.Y., Rod and Gun. Home: 1 Vista Way Lakewood NY 14750 Office: Jones and Gifford Ave Jamestown NY 14701

NIDETCH, JEAN, health service exec.; b. Bklyn., Oct. 12, 1923; d. David and May (Rodin) Slutsky; children—David, Richard. Founding pres. Weight Watchers Internat., Inc., Manhasset, L.I. Cons., N.Y. State Assembly Mental Hygiene Com. 1968; adviser Joint Legis. Com. on Child Care Needs, Legislature N.Y. Pres., Weight Watchers Found. Named Marketing Woman of Year, Hon. adm. Gt. Navy Neb.; Woman of Year, Forest Hills Youth Assn.; recipient Woman of Achievement award, Speakers award Sales Promotion Execs. Assn. Mem. Washington Sq. Bus. and Profl. Womens Club, A.F.T.R.A. Author: Jean Nidetch: Weight Watchers Cookbook, 1966; The Story of Weight Watchers, 1970; Program Cookbook. Office: 10880 Wilshire Blvd Los Angeles CA 90024

NIEBANK, C(ORNELIUS) GEORGE, JR., diversified industry co. exec.; b. Niagara Falls, N.Y., Oct. 21, 1925; s. Cornelius George and Rose Veronica (Murphy) N.; A.B., Yale U., 1947; J.D., U. Buffalo, 1950; grad. Advanced Mgmt. Program, Harvard U., 1969; m. Rosemarie Wrigley, June 17, 1947; children—Cornelius George, III, Cecily Scott Niebank Noelker, Justin Wrigley, Mary Agatha. Admitted to N.Y. bar, 1950, Ill. bar, 1953; law clk. to Supreme Ct. Justice Robert H. Jackson, 1950-52; commr. U.S. Ct. Mil. Appeals, Washington, 1952-53; with Santa Fe Ry., 1953-78, v.p. law, 1976-78; sr. v.p. law Santa Fe Industries Inc., 1979—; chmn. Ill. Jud. Inquiry Bd., 1975-79. Mem. Glencoe (Ill.) Caucus Nominating Com., 1972-76; trustee Ripon (Wis.) Coll.; asso. Northwestern U. Served to lt. (j.g.) USNR, 1944-47. Mem. Am. Bar Assn., Conf. R.R. and Airline Labor Lawyers, Ill. Bar Assn., Chgo. Bar Assn. Republican. Roman Catholic. Clubs: Chicago, Chgo. Athletic Assn., Economic (Chgo.); Green Lake (Wis.) Yacht; Internat. Citabria. Home: 110 Glencoe Rd Glencoe IL 60022 Office: 224 S Michigan Ave Chicago IL 60604

NIEBAUER, JOHN JOSEPH, JR., physician, educator; b. San Francisco, July 7, 1914; s. John Joseph and Frieda E. (Sauer) N.; B.A., Stanford, 1937, M.D., 1942; m. Jean A. Mackay, Jan. 9, 1943; children—John S., Patricia A., Douglas W., Peter B. Intern, Stanford U. Hosp., San Francisco, 1941-42, asst. resident, 1942-44, resident orthopedic surgery, 1944-45; Gibney fellow orthopedic surgery Hosp. for Spl. Surgery, N.Y.C., 1945-46; asst. clin. prof. orthopedic surgery Stanford Sch. Medicine, 1946-51, asso. clin. prof., 1951-57, adj. clin. prof., 1957—; clin. prof. orthopedic surgery U. Calif. Sch. Medicine, 1965—; chief staff Presbyn. Hosp., San Francisco, 1975-76; trustee Pacific Med. Center. Diplomate Am. Bd. Orthopedic Surgery. Mem. AMA, Calif., San Francisco County med. socs., Am., Western orthopedic assns., Am. Acad. Orthopedic Surgery, Internat. Soc. Orthopedic Surgery and Traumatology, Am. Soc. for Surgery of Hand, A.C.S., Am. Orthopedic Assn., Sigma Xi. Office: Pacific Med Center PO Box 7999 San Francisco CA 94120

NIEBELL, PAUL MILTON, SR., lawyer; b. Scranton, Pa., June 26, 1901; s. Augustus Charles and Nancy Zorah (Pyles) N.; student in Violin, Chgo. Conservatory Music, 1921-22; J.D., George Washington U., 1925; m. Eleanor Warrene Smallwood, June 30, 1955; children—Paula, Nancy, Paul Milton; stepchildren—Barbara Lee Sweeney, Dorothy Anne Burkholder. Admitted to D.C. bar, 1926, U.S. Supreme Ct. bar, 1929, U.S. Ct. Claims bar, 1930; individual practice law, Washington, 1930—. Pres. Seabrook (Md.) Civic Assn., 1971-73, dir., 1965-70. Mem. Am., Fed., D.C. bar assns., Luther Rice Soc. Republican. Presbyterian. Clubs: Optimists (pres. Washington club 1972-73, life mem. internat. 1952—), George Washington U., Masons, Shriners, Jesters. Home: 7825 Mary Cassatt Dr Potomac MD 20854 Office: 910 17th St NW Washington DC 20006

NIEDERGESES, JAMES D., bishop; b. Lawrenceburg, Tenn., Feb. 2, 1917; student St. Bernard Coll., St. Ambrose Coll., Mt. St. Mary Sem. of West, Athenaeum of Ohio. Ordained priest Roman Catholic Ch., 1944; pastor Our Lady of Perpetual Help, Chattanooga, 1962-73, Sts. Peter and Paul Parish, 1973-75; bishop of Nashville, 1975—; mem. personnel bd. Diocese of Nashville. Office: 2400 21st Ave S Nashville TN 37219*

NIEDERLEHNER, LEONARD, lawyer; b. Cin., Oct. 12, 1914; s. Louis William and Agnes (Clark) N.; LL.B., U. Cin., 1937; m. Helen Virginia Warfield, July 2, 1948; children—James, Barbara, John. Admitted to Ohio bar, 1937, Supreme Ct. bar, 1958, D.C. bar, 1967; practice law, Cin., 1937-40; sec. to congressman, 1938; with Office Gen. Counsel, FSA, 1941; counsel bur. yards and docks Navy Dept., 1946-47, munitions bd. Office Sec. Def., 1948-52, asst. gen. counsel, 1952-53, dep. gen. counsel Dept. Def., Washington 1953—. Served to lt. comdr. USNR, 1942-46. Recipient Dept. Def. Distinguished Civilian Service medal, 1961, medal with palm, 1969, medal with double palm, 1973; Rockefeller Pub. Service award, 1961; Nat. Civil Service League Service award, 1965; Pres. award for Disting. Fed. Civilian Service, 1979; Silver Beaver award Boy Scouts Am., 1967. Mem. Inter-Am., Fed. bar assns., Order of Coif. Methodist. Home: 3709 N Nelson St Arlington VA 22207 Office: Office Sec Def Washington DC 20301

NIEDERMAIR, JOHN CHARLES, naval architect; b. Union Hill, N.J., Nov. 2, 1893; s. John and Katherine (Riess) N.; grad. as marine engr. and naval architect Webb Inst. Naval Architecture, 1918; m. Ethel Victoria May Irwin, Apr. 2, 1923 (dec. 1973); children—William I., Marion E. (Mrs. R.A. Williams), Patricia E. (Mrs. G. E. Long), John C., Mary Ann (Mrs. M. Mallinoff), George Edward, Richard Michael, Frank Robert. Ship draftsman, also supr. N.Y. Navy Yard, 1917-29; assisted salvage ops. submarines S-51, 1926, S-4, 1928; spl. work on watertight integrity and ship stability, 1925-60; with preliminary design br. Bur. Ships (constrn. and repair), Navy Dept., 1929-58, tech. dir., sr. civilian naval architect, 1939-58, cons. naval architect, 1958-74; cons. naval architect numerous engring. cos., 1929-74; designer LST, other type ships, World War II; design and research postwar types including basic designs aircraft carrier Forrestal and Enterprise, nuclear propelled submarines Nautilus and Skate, guided missile ships and Polaris submarine. Mem. tech. and research panels Nat. Acad. Scis., 1959-63. Recipient Distinguished Civilian Service medal Navy Dept., 1945; named one of 10 most outstanding persons in fed. service Nat. Civil Service League, 1956; recipient David W. Taylor gold medal Soc. Naval Architects and Marine Engrs. 1958; Gibbs Bros. Gold medal Nat. Acad. Scis., 1976; William S. Owen award Webb Inst. Naval Architecture, 1967. Fellow, hon. mem. Soc. Naval Architects and Marine Engrs. (chmn. Chesapeake sect. 1946-47); mem. Am. Soc. Naval Engrs. (past mem. council, Harold E. Saunders award 1978), U.S. Naval Inst., Assn. Scientists and Engrs. U.S. Navy Dept. (hon.; past pres.). Address: 219 117th St Stone Harbor NJ 08247

NIEDERMAN, JAMES CORSON, physician; b. Hamilton, Ohio, Nov. 27, 1924; s. Clifford Frederick and Henrietta (Corson) N.; student Kenyon Coll., 1942-45; M.D., Johns Hopkins U., 1949; m. Miriam Camp, Dec. 12, 1951; children—Timothy Porter, Derrick Corson, Eliza Orton, Caroline Noble. Intern, Johns Hopkins Hosp., Balt., 1949-50; asst. resident in medicine Yale-New Haven Med. Center, 1950-51, asso. resident, 1953-55; practice medicine specializing in internal medicine and clin. epidemiology, New Haven, 1955—; instr. Yale U., 1955-59, asst. prof., 1959-67, asso. prof., 1967-76, clin. prof. medicine and epidemiology, 1976—; mem. herpes adv. team Internat. Agy. for Research in Cancer, WHO. Trustee Kenyon Coll.; bd. counselors Smith Coll. Served to 1st lt. M.C., U.S. Army, 1951-53. Fellow Silliman Coll., Yale U. Mem. AMA, Am. Fedn. Clin. Research, Assn. Tchrs. Preventive Medicine, Infectious Diseases Soc. Am., Am. Epidemiol. Soc., Sigma Xi. Democrat. Episcopalian. Clubs: Yale (N.Y.C.); New Haven Lawn. Research in med. epidemiology, 1955—. Home: 429 Sperry Rd Bethany CT 06525 Office: 333 Cedar St New Haven CT 06510

NIEDZIELSKI, HENRI ZYGMUNT, educator; b. Troyes, France, Mar. 30, 1931; s. Zygmunt and Anna (Pelik) N.; came to U.S., 1956, naturalized, 1963; B.A., U. Conn., 1959, M.A., 1963, Ph.D., 1964; children—Henri Zygmunt, Daniel Domenic, Robert Mikolaj, Anna-Pia Irene. Instr., U. Mass., 1962-64, asst. prof., 1965-66; free-lance interpreter, 1960-64; asst. prof. U. Laval, Quebec, Can., 1964-65; asso. prof. U. Hawaii, 1966-72, prof., 1972—, chmn. div. French, 1968-70. Linguistic specialist NDEA, Edn. Profl. Devel. Act, 1963-69; Fulbright lectr. linguistics and TESL, Krakow, Poland, 1972-74. Pres., Family Counseling Center Hawaii, 1968-70; chmn. bd. Family Edn. Centers Hawaii, 1969-72. Served with French Armored Cav., 1951-53. Mem. Hawaii Assn. Lang. Tchrs. (pres. 1968-69), Modern Lang. Assn., Polish Inst. Arts and Scis., Soc. Profs. Francais en Amérique, Mediaeval Acad. Am., Am. Anthrop. Assn., Internat. Sociol. Assn., Alliance Francaise Hawaii (pres. 1978—), Internat. Platform Assn., Am. Assn. Tchrs. French, Assn. Computational Linguistics, Am. Council Teaching Fgn. Langs. (dir.), Am. Soc. Adlerian Psychology, Phi Beta Kappa, Pi Delta Phi, Phi Kappa Phi, Sigma Delta Pi. K.C. (3 deg.). Author: Le Roman de Helcanus, 1966; Basic French: A Programmed Course, 1968; Handbook of French Structure; A Systematic Review, 1968; Intermediate French: An Individualized Course, 1972; The Silent Language of France, 1975; French Sound Visuals, 1976. Editor: Language and Literature in Hawaii, 1968-72; Jean Misrahi Memorial Volume: Studies in Medieval Languages and Literature, 1977. Home: 1890 East West Center Rd Honolulu HI 96822. *There is more than one way to help people but there is only one way to live: Help people!*

NIEFELD, JAYE SUTTER, advt. exec.; b. Mpls., May 27, 1924; s. Julius and Sophia (Rosenfeld) N.; certificate London U., 1945; B.A., U. Minn., 1948; B.S., Georgetown U., 1949; Ph.D., U. Vienna, 1951; m. Piri Elizabeth Von Zabrana-Szilagy, July 5, 1947; 1 son, Peter Wendell. Project dir. Bur. Social Sci. Research, Washington, 1952-54; research dir. McCann-Erickson, Inc., Chgo., N.Y.C., 1954-57; dir. marketing Keyes, Madden & Jones, Chgo., 1957-60; pres., dir. Niefeld, Paley & Kuhn, Inc., Chgo., 1961-71; exec. v.p., dir. Bozell & Jacobs, Inc., 1971—; pres. Glencoe Angus Farm. Cons. U.S. depts. State, Commerce, HEW, also Intertel, Inc.; lectr. Columbia, Northwestern U. Mem. adv. bd. Glencoe Family Service. Served to 1st lt. AUS, 1942-46. Decorated Bronze Star. Mem. Am. Assn. Pub. Opinion Research, Am. Marketing Assn., Am. Sociol. Assn. Author: (with others) Marketing's Role in Scientific Management, 1957; Advertising and Marketing to Young People, 1965; also articles. Home: 1011 Bluff Rd Glencoe IL 60022 Office: 222 S Riverside Plaza Chicago IL 60606

NIEHAUS, MYRON STANLEY, JR., ins. co. exec.; b. Jacksonville, Fla., Aug. 13, 1931; s. Myron Stanley and Lois Valentine (Silas) N.; B.A., U. Fla., 1953; M.S., U. Mich., 1955; postgrad. U. So. Calif., summer 1978; m. Janice Levsen, Dec. 28, 1957; children—Craig Stephen, Jeffrey Dale. With Aetna Life & Casualty Co., Hartford, 1957—, mgr. ins. services Aetna Life of Australia & New Zealand, Ltd., Sydney, Australia, 1969, dir. special underwriter services parent co., 1972-74, v.p. life underwriting, 1974—. Bd. dirs. Hartford Stage Co., 1974—. Served with USN, 1955-57. Fellow Soc. Actuaries; mem. Acad. Actuaries, Hartford Actuaries Club, Home Office Life Underwriters Assn., Inst. Home Office Underwriters. Home: 163 Cliffmore Rd West Hartford CT 06107 Office: 151 Farmington Ave Hartford CT 06156

NIEHAUS, ROBERT JAMES, bus. exec.; b. Ann Arbor, Mich., Jan. 6, 1930; s. Julius Herman and Mary Johanna (Koch) N.; B.B.A., U. Mich., 1951; M.B.A., U. Detroit, 1958; m. Aileen R. O'Neill, Feb. 24, 1954. Asst. sr. buyer Ford Motor Co., Dearborn, Mich., 1954-58; gen. purchasing agt. Hercules Motors Corp., Canton, Ohio, 1958-60; v.p. procurement and programming Schwitzer Corp., Indpls., 1960-66, v.p. adminstrn., 1968, v.p. corp. devel., 1969-70, v.p., gen. mgr. Schwitzer div., 1970-72; group v.p. Wallace Murray Corp., N.Y.C., 1972-79, sr. v.p., 1979—. Served with USN, 1951-54. Club: Greenwich (Conn.) Country. Home: 15 Queenslane Darien CT 06820 Office: 299 Park Ave New York NY 10017

NIEHM, BERNARD FRANK, mental health center adminstr.; b. Sandusky, Ohio, Feb. 7, 1923; s. Bernard Frank and Hedwick (Panzer) N.; B.A., Ohio State U., 1951, M.A., 1955, Ph.D., 1968; m. Eunice M. Patterson, Oct. 4, 1924; children—Julie, Patti, Bernie. Tchr. pub. schs., Sandusky, 1951-57; chief ednl., vocat. and occupational therapy services Vineland (N.J.) Tng. Sch., 1957-61; exec. dir. Franklin County Council Retarded Children, Columbus, Ohio, 1962-64; dir. Ohio Sheltered Workshop Planning Project Mental Retardation, 1964-66; coordinator mental retardation planning Ohio Bur. Planning and Grants, Div. Mental Health and Mental Retardation, 1966-68; project dir. Ohio Gov.'s Citizen Com. on Mental Retardation Planning, 1966-68; adminstr. Franklin County Program for Mentally Retarded, 1968-70; supt. Gallipolis (Ohio) State Inst., 1970-76; tchr. spl. edn. Ohio U., 1975—; dir. consultation and edn. Gallia-Jackson-Meigs Community Mental Health Center, Gallipolis, 1977—. Mem. Foster Grandparents Advisory Council Gallia County, 1974-76, Gallipolis State Inst. Parent Vol. Assn., 1970—; chmn. MGM dist. Tri-State Boy Scout council; mem. Franklin County Bd. Mental Retardation, 1967-68; pres. Gallipolis Girls Athletic Assn. Booster Club, 1976—; bd. dirs. United Cerebral Palsy Columbus, 1968-70. Served with U.S. Army, 1943-46. Mem. Am. Assn. Mental Deficiency (past chmn. Ohio chpt., chmn. Great Lakes region), Nat., Ohio rehab. assns., Ohio Assn. Retarded Children (2d v.p. 1974-76, dir.), Vocat. Rehab. Assn. Lutheran. Contbr. articles to profl. jours. Home: 260 Mill Creek Dr Gallipolis OH 45631 Office: PO Box 292 Gallipolis OH 45631

NIELSEN, ALDON DALE, govt. ofcl., economist; b. Mason City, Nebr., Jan. 13, 1922; s. Seren and Sena (Nielsen) N.; student Biaritz (France) Am. U., 1945; B.Sc., U. Nebr., 1948, postgrad., 1951; m. Vivian Leola Lee, Mar. 26, 1944; children—Carol Ann, Aldon Lynn, Dennis Lee, Brian Paige. With Bur. Reclamation, Dept. Interior, 1948—, successively economist, Grand Island, Nebr., 1948-60, regional agrl. economist, Denver, 1960-63, contract and repayment specialist, 1963-65, chief economics and program analysis br., Washington, 1965-77, asst. chief div. water and land, 1977-78, dir. operation and maintenance policy staff, Washington, 1978—. Mem. Internat. Commn. on Irrigation and Drainage. Pres. Nebr. Baptist Men, 1957-59; bd. mgrs. Nebr. Bapt. Conv., 1957-59; mem. Nebr. Bapt. Lay Devel. Com., 1957-58; bd. dirs. Colo. Bapt. Conv., 1960-63; sec. Colo. Bapt. Men, 1961-63; exec. v.p. Am. Bapt. Men, 1963-65, pres., 1965-67; mem. exec. bd. D.C. Bapt. Conv., 1964-72, 76-78. Active local Jr. C. of C., County 4-H Club, Community Chest, ARC, Boy Scouts, Am. Served with AUS, 1944-46; ETO. Decorated Bronze Star; recipient Superior Service award Dept. Interior, 1958, 59, 61, 66, Meritorius Service award, 1973, Spl. Achievement award, 1978. Mem. Am., Western agrl. econ. assns., Internat. Water Resources Assn. Home: 519 S Harrison St Arlington VA 22204 Office: Interior Bldg 19th and C Sts NW Washington DC 20240

NIELSEN, ALVIN HERBORG, coll. dean, physicist; b. Menominee, Mich., May 30, 1910; s. Knud and Maren (Nielsen) N.; B.A., U. Mich., 1931, M.S., 1932, Ph.D., 1934; m. Jane Ann Evans, Dec. 29, 1942; 1 dau., Margaret Arthur Wayne. Research fellow Ohio State U., 1934-35; faculty U. Tenn., 1935—, prof. physics, 1946—, head dept., 1956-69, dean Coll. Liberal Arts, 1963-77, Mace Bearer and Phi Kappa Phi distinguished faculty lectr., 1962-63. Research asso. for OSRD, Ohio State U. Research Found., 1944-46; cons. Oak Ridge Gaseous Diffusion Plant Labs. and Oak Ridge Nat. Lab., 1947—. Mem. adv. com. basic research U.S. Army Research Office, 1964-70; active vis. scientists program Am. Inst. Physics-Am. Assn. Physics Tchrs., 1964-71. Mem. Knoxville Symphony Soc. Bd., 1963—, v.p., 1965-68, 75-76, 77-80, pres., 1968-69, 76-77. NRC fellow elect, 1942; Fulbright research scholar Astrophys. Inst., U. Liege (Belgium), 1951-52; research grantee Tenn. Acad. Scis., 1942, Am. Acad. Arts and Scis., 1942, Research Corp. Am., 1946, 47, NSF, 1962, Office Ordnance Research, U.S. Army, 1952, Air Force Cambridge Research Center, 1957-67, Div. Radiol. Health USPHS, 1962-70. Bd. dirs. Greater Knox Council for the Arts, 1975—, v.p., 1975-77; asso. Am. Scandinavian Found. Fellow Am. Phys. Soc. (chmn. S.E. sect. 1953-54; exec. com. 1962-65), Optical Soc. Am. (mem. fin. and investment com. 1979-80), AAAS, mem. Am. Assn. Physics Tchrs., AAUP, Tenn. Acad. Sci. (exec. com. 1959-61) Coblentz Soc., Scientists and Engrs. for Appalachia (dir. 1970-76), Am. Nat. Rebild Com., Am. Inst. Physics, Am. Conf. Acad. Deans (dir. 1968-75, chmn. 1972), Nat. Assn. State Univs. and Land-Grant Colls. (commn. on arts and scis. 1970-77, sec. 1974), So. Conf. Acad. Deans, Council Colls. Arts and Scis., (dir. 1969-75), Tenn. Edn. Assn., Am. Assn. Higher Edn., NEA, Phi Beta Kappa (pres. Tenn. Epsilon chpt. 1974-75), Sigma Xi (pres. chpt. 1950), Phi Kappa Phi, Sigma Pi Sigma, Pi Delta Phi, Omicron Delta Kappa. Episcopalian. Clubs: Faculty, Irving. Author articles molecular spectroscopy. Asso. editor Jour. Chem. Physics, 1955-57. Home: 3605 Timberlake Rd Knoxville TN 37920

NIELSEN, ARTHUR CHARLES, business exec.; b. Chgo., Sept. 5, 1897; s. Rasmus and Harriet Burr (Gunn) N.; B.S. in Elec. Engring., U. Wis., 1918, D.Sc. (hon.), 1974; m. Gertrude B. Smith, June 15, 1918; children—Arthur Charles, Margaret Ann, Philip Robert, Barbara Harriet, Virginia Beatrice. Elec. engr. Isko Co., Chgo., 1919-20; engr. H.P. Gould Co., Chgo., 1920-23; pres. A.C. Nielsen Co., 1923-57, chmn., 1957-75, chmn. exec. com., 1976—, marketing research and bus. services, operators of the Neilsen Retail Index

Services, Nielsen TV Index services, Nielsen Coupon Clearing House, NEODATA Services, Petroleum Info. Corp., others; chmn. A.C. Neilsen Internat. Inc., A.C. Nielsen Co., Can., Ltd., A.C. Nielsen Pty., Ltd. (Australia and New Zealand), A.C. Nielsen Co. (Pty.) Ltd., Johannesburg, South Africa, A.C. Nielsen Nederland B.V., A.C. Nielsen (Argentina) S.A., A.C. Nielsen Co., G.m.b.H., Germany, A.C. Nielsen Mgmt. Services, Switzerland, A.C. Nielsen S.A., Switzerland, A.C. Nielsen Co., Ges. M.B.H. Austria, A.C. Nielsen Prodn. S.A., Switzerland, A.C. Nielsen Cos., France, Italy, Spain, Portugal, Japan, Mexico, A.C. Nielsen Co. Ltd. (Oxford), A.C. Nielsen Co. (Belgium) S.A., A.C. Nielsen of Ireland, Ltd. Served as ensign USNR, World War I. Recipient 1936 Silver medal Ann. Advt. Awards Com.; award Chgo. Federated Advt. Club, 1941; Paul D. Converse award Am. Marketing Assn., 1951, Marketing Man of Year award, 1970; named to Hall of Fame in Distbn., 1953, Nat. Lawn Tennis Hall of Fame, 1971; knight Order Dannebrog, 1961; Parlin Meml. award, 1963; ann. award Internat. Advt. Assn., 1966. Mem. Tau Beta Pi, Eta Kappa Nu, Sigma Phi. Clubs: West Side Tennis (Forest Hills, L.I., N.Y.); University (N.Y.C.); Indian Hill (Winnetka). Office: AC Nielsen Co Nielsen Plaza Northbrook IL 60062*

NIELSEN, ARTHUR CHARLES, JR., mktg. research exec.; b. Chgo., Apr. 8, 1919; s. Arthur Charles and Gertrude (Smith) N.; Ph.B., U. Wis., 1941; m. Patricia McKnew, June 24, 1944; children—Arthur Charles III, John Christopher, Elizabeth Kingsbury. Chmn., chief exec. officer A. C. Nielsen Co., Chgo.; dir. Marsh & McLennan Corp., Republic Capital Corp., Gen. Binding Corp., Motorola, Inc., Marcor Inc., Harris Trust & Savs. Bank, Walgreen Drug Co., Hercules, Inc., Internat. Execs. Service Corps. Dir. Fair Campaign Practices Com. Cons., U.S. Govt. mission to Italy, 1952, OEEC, France, 1953, Japan, 1955, Israel, 1958, India, 1960, Middle East, 1961; mem. nat. marketing adv. com. U.S. Dept. Commerce. Asso. Northwestern U., mem. bus. adv. council Grad. Sch. Bus.; mem. nat. adv. council Peace Corps; mem. Presdl. Adv. Council Minority Enterprise, Census Adv. Com. on Privacy and Confidentiality; mem. Pres.'s Com. Health Edn.; chmn. Nat. Health Council, 1975; mem. U.S. Advisory Commn. Info. Bd. dirs. Advt. Research Found., Ill. Children's Home and Aid Soc., Northwestern Meml. Hosp., Jr. Achievement, Chgo.; trustee U. Chgo., others. Served to maj. C.E., AUS, 1941-45. Mem. Mgmt. Execs. Soc. (exec. com., past pres.), Nat. Planning Council (trustee), U. Wis. Alumni Assn. (dir.), Phi Eta Sigma, Phi Kappa Phi, Beta Gamma Sigma, Sigma Phi. Clubs: Chicago, Chicago Commonwealth, Economic, Indian Hill, Racquet, Casino, Commercial (Chgo.). Office: AC Nielsen Co Nielsen Plaza Northbrook IL 60093

NIELSEN, CHARLES LESTER, JR., paper co. exec.; b. S.I., N.Y., Nov. 29, 1938; s. Charles Lester and Marion Louise (Traub) N.; B.S., U. Rochester, 1961; m. Beverly Baldwin, Jan. 28, 1960; children—Jan, Michael, Nancy. Accountant, Xerox Corp., 1960-61; mem. audit staff Coopers & Lybrand, N.Y.C., 1961-69; treas. APL Corp., Great Neck, N.Y., 1969—. Served with AUS, 1959-60. C.P.A., N.Y. Mem. Am. Inst. C.P.A.'s. Home: 18 Meudon Dr Locust Valley NY 11560 Office: 1 Linden Pl Great Neck NY 11021

NIELSEN, EINER, investment banker; b. Fremont, Nebr., Feb. 19, 1902; s. Niels and Louise Dorothy (Nielsen) N.; B.A., U. Nebr., 1924; m. 2d, Gay Parkes, Mar. 15, 1967; children by previous marriage—Einer Dale, Charles Norris, Partner, J.C. Bradford & Co., Nashville, mem. N.Y. Stock Exchange, 1948—; v.p., dir. J.C. Bradford & Co., Inc. Mem. Alpha Tau Omega. Clubs: Belle Meade Country, Cumberland. Home: 4215 Harding Rd Apt 1210 Nashville TN 3720: Office: 170 4th Av N Nashville TN 37219

NIELSEN, EMIEL THEODORE, JR., mfg. co. exec.; b. Cupertino, Calif., Dec. 3, 1914; s. Emiel Theodore and Bessie (Kimball) N.; A.B., Stanford U., 1936, M.B.A., 1938; m. Marjorie Bothwell, July 14, 1940; children—Philip B., John K. With Gen. Mills, Inc., 1938-42; with FMC Corp., Chgo., 1942—, now vice chmn., chief operating officer; dir. Varian Assos., Inc., Bank of the West, Talley Industries, Inc., Am. Fletcher Corp. Mem. Nat. Security Indsl. Assn. (trustee), Am. Def. Preparedness Assn., Soc. Automotive Engrs. Republican. Clubs: Sainte Claire, San Jose Country; Mid-Am. (Chgo.). Office: 200 E Randolph Chicago IL 60601

NIELSEN, JOHN PHILLIP, metallurgist; b. Cleve., Nov. 11, 1911; s. John and Pauline (Plevnik) N.; B.S. in Metall. Engring., Yale U., 1942, Ph.D., 1947; m. Dorothy May Lewis, Mar. 16, 1945. Research metallurgist Internat. Nickel Co., 1941-43; asso. physicist Philips Labs. Inc. 1943-45; prof. metal sci. N.Y. U., 1947-73, chmn. dept. metallurgy and materials sci., 1955-71, prof. dental materials sci., 1976—; prof. metal sci. Poly. Inst. N.Y., 1973-76, prof. emeritus, 1976—; cons., dir. research J.F. Jelenko & Co., New Rochelle, N.Y., 1957-76. Pres., Sniffen Ct. Assn., 1959-76, pres. emeritus, 1976—. Fellow NSF, 1945-47, Am. Soc. Metals, 1973—; recipient Thomas Young award Marquette U., 1966. Mem. Am. Inst. Mining and Metall. Engrs., Am. Soc. Metals, Internat. Precious Metals Inst. (exec. dir., founder 1975—), Metal Sci. Club N.Y., Alpha Sigma Mu (past nat. pres.). Club: Yale (N.Y.C.). Originator Shell-Nielsen shear test for metal-ceramic bond, 1961. Editor Metallurgy/Materials Edn. Yearbook, 1969-76. Patentee in field. Home: 1 Washington Square Village New York City NY 10012 Office: Coll Dentistry NY U New York City NY 10010

NIELSEN, LAWRENCE ERNIE, physicist; b. Pilot Rock, Oreg., Dec. 17, 1917; s. Hans Christian and Mable Esther (Galbreath) N.; A.B., Pacific U., Forest Grove, Oreg., 1940; M.S., Wash. State U., 1942; Ph.D., Cornell U., 1945; m. Deanne May Boss, June 27, 1942; 1 dau., Linda Carolyn Nielsen Hickel. Physicist, Monsanto Co., Springfield, Mass., 1945-63, distinguished sci. fellow, St. Louis, 1963-77; plastics cons., Redmond, Oreg., 1977—; affiliate prof. Washington U., St. Louis, 1965-76. Fellow Am. Phys. Soc.; mem. Am. Chem. Soc., Soc. Rheology (Bingham medal 1976), Internat. Glaciol. Soc., Am. Alpine Club. Author: Mechanical Properties of Polymers, 1962; Mechanical Properties of Polymers and Composites, 1974; Polymer Rheology, 1977; Predicting Properties of Mixtures, 1978; also articles. Patentee mech. properties and rheology plastics. Address: 3208 NW Lynch Way Redmond OR 97756

NIELSEN, LELAND C., judge; b. Vesper, Kans., June 14, 1919; s. Carl Christian and Christena (Larson) N.; B.A., Washburn U., 1946; J.D., U. So. Calif., 1946; m. Virginia Garland, Nov. 27, 1958; 1 dau., Christena. Admitted to Calif. bar, 1947; dep. city atty., Los Angeles, 1947-51; asso., partner firm Luce, Forward, Kunzel & Scripps, San Diego, 1951-58; partner Schall, Nielsen & Boudreau, San Diego, 1958-68; judge Superior Ct., San Diego, 1968-71; judge U.S. Dist. Ct., So. Dist. Calif., San Diego, 1971—. Served with AUS, 1941-46. Decorated D.S.C.; Air medal with four silver and oak leaf clusters, Purple Heart. Home: 438 Ravina St La Jolla CA 92037 Office: US Courthouse San Diego CA 92189

NIELSEN, NIELS CHRISTIAN, JR., educator; b. Long Beach, Calif., June 2, 1921; s. Niels Hansen and Frances (Nofziger) N.; B.A., George Pepperdine Coll., Los Angeles, 1942; B.D., Yale, 1946, Ph.D., 1951; m. Erika Kreuth, May 10, 1958; children—Camilla Regina, Niels Albrecht. Ordained to ministry Meth. Ch., 1946; instr. religion Yale, 1948-51; faculty Rice U., Houston, 1951—, now J. Newton Rayzor prof., chmn. dept. religious studies. Mem. Am. Acad. Religion, Am. Philos. Soc., Metaphys. Soc. Am., So. Soc. Philosophy of Religion, Am. Soc. Study Religions. Author: Philosophy and Religion in Contemporary Japan, 1957; Geistige Länderkunde USA, 1960; A Layman Looks at World Religions, 1962; God in Education, 1966. Editor: Religion and Science: Updating the Perimeters, 1972; Solzhenitsyn's Religion (Nelson), 1975; The Religion of Jimmy Carter, 1977; The Crisis of Human Rights, 1978. Contbr. articles to profl. jours. Home: 2424 Swift St Houston TX 77025

NIELSEN, NIELS OLE, veterinary pathologist; b. Edmonton, Alta., Can., Mar. 3, 1930; s. Ludvig and Maren Medom (Hansen) N.; D.V.M., U. Toronto, 1956; Ph.D., U. Minn., 1963; m. Marilyn Anne Wilson, Mar. 5, 1955; children—Margo Lynn, John David, Gordon Ludvig. Instr., then asst. prof. veterinary pathology U. Minn., St. Paul, 1957-64; mem. faculty Western Coll. Veterinary Medicine, U. Sask., Saskatoon, 1964—, prof., head dept. veterinary pathology, 1968-74, dean, 1974—; research asst. Brookhaven Nat. Lab., 1960-61; Med. Research Council Can. vis. scientist WHO Escherchia Center, Statens Serum Inst., Copenhagen, 1971-72; mem. Canadian Agrl. Services Coordinating Com., 1974—. Diplomate Am. Coll. Veterinary Pathology. Mem. Canadian (pres. 1968-69), Am., Sask. veterinary med. assns., AAAS, Canadian Assn. Lab. Animal Sci., Canadian Assn. Vet. Pathologists, Sask. Natural History Soc. (pres. 1975-76). Research on enteric disease, mercury poisoning. Home: 327 Poplar Crescent Saskatoon SK S7M 0A8 Canada Office: Western Coll Veterinary Medicine Univ Sask Saskatoon SK S7N 0W0 Canada

NIELSEN, OTTO R., cons., psychologist, educator; b. Omaha, Dec. 24, 1905; s. Peder and Marthina (Christiansen) N.; A.B., Tex. Christian U., 1933, B.D., 1937, A.M., 1940; postgrad. U. Chgo., 1933, U. Minn., 1939; Ph.D., U. Tex., 1942; m. Martha Jane Butts, June 15, 1935; children—Elizabeth Carol, Patricia Jean, David Howard. Asst. prof. psychology Tex. Christian U., 1938-40, dean of men, 1933-40, dir. personnel, 1936-40, exec. v.p., 1950-52, dean Sch. Edn., dir. tchr. edn., 1952-63; dir. research Hogg Fund, 1940-42; instr. ednl. psychology, asst. to dean Coll. Arts and Scis., U. Tex., 1940-42; prof. vocat. guidance East Tex. State Tchrs. Coll., summer 1942; dean, prof. psychology and personnel adminstrn. Tex. Coll. Arts and Industries, Kingsville, 1942-50; chief div. human resources devel. AID, Latin Am., 1962-67; prof. psychology U. Americas, Puebla, Mexico, 1967—, exec. v.p., 1967-74. Vis. asso. prof. U. Chgo., summers 1947-48; cons. in field. Fellow Am. Psychol. Assn.; mem. Tex., (past dir.), Corpus Christi (past exec. com.) personnel assns., Tex. Soc. Mental Hygiene (past dir.), N.E.A., So. Conf. Acad. Deans (past pres.), Am. Assn. Higher Edn., So. Assn. Colls. and Secondary Schs., Tex. Assn. Coordinators Vets. Coll. Edn. (past exec. com.), Am. Coll. Personnel Assn., Assn. Tex. Colls., Tex. Tchrs. Assn., Phi Delta Kappa Mem. Christian Ch. Rotarian (past bd. dir.). Club: Golf (Ft. Worth). Address: 516 Westwood Richardson TX 75080

NIELSEN, THOMAS HAROLD, real estate exec.; b. Fullerton, Cal., Nov. 7, 1930; s. Harold and Ellen (Lene) N.; B.S. in Civil Engring. magna cum laude, U. Wash., 1952; M.B.A., Stanford, 1957; m. Marilyn Oldroyd, Mar. 5, 1955; children—John Thomas, Peter Martin, Kirsten Ellen. Vice pres. White Investment Co., San Francisco, 1962-67; pres. Calif. Land Co., Valencia, 1962-67; asst. sec. for fin. mgmt. USAF, Washington, 1967-69; sr. v.p. U.S. Financial, San Diego, 1969-72; exec. v.p. Malone Devel. Co., La Jolla, Calif., 1972—; pres. T.H. Nielsen Corp.; sr. v.p. charge community devel. Irvine Co.; cons. Office Asst. Sec. Air Force for Fin. Mgmt., 1969—. Served with C.E., USNR, 1955-64. C.P.A., Calif. Recipient Exceptional Civilian Service award Sec. Air Force, 1969. Mem. Phi Beta Kappa, Sigma Xi, Beta Theta Pi, Tau Beta Pi. Democrat. Home: 2587 Ardath Rd La Jolla CA 92037 Office: 7343 Ronson Rd San Diego CA 92111

NIELSON, GLENN E., oil co. exec.; b. Aetna, Alta., Can., May 26, 1903; s. James E. and Margaret (Pilling) N.; B.Sc., U. Alta., 1933; LL.D., U. Wyo., 1954; D.Sc., Brigham Young U., 1957; m. Olive Wood, Dec. 25, 1928; children—Margaret Ruth, James Edward and Joanne (twins), Anna Marie, Glenn William. Came to U.S., 1935, naturalized, 1940. Sheep rancher, Cardston, Alta., 1928-35; salesman Cut Bank (Mont.) Refining Co., 1936-37; organized Husky Refining Co., 1937 (now Husky Oil Co.), pres., 1938-67; pres. Husky Oil Ltd., Calgary, Alta., 1947-67, chmn., 1967-79. Nat. chmn. Bus. Industry Polit. Action Com., 1966-67; trustee Honor Am. Com. Mem. Ind. Petroleum Assn. Am. (dir.), Nat. Petroleum Council, Am. Petroleum Inst. (dir.). Mem. Ch. of Jesus Christ of Latter-day Saints (mission pres. 1973-77, regional rep. Council of Twelve, 1977—). Clubs: 25-Year of Petroleum Industry (pres. 1970-71); Calgary Petroleum, Ranchman's (Calgary); Alta (Salt Lake City). Home: 625 Skyline Dr Cody WY 82414 Office: PO Box 370 Cody WY 82414

NIELSON, HOWARD CURTIS, math. statistician, educator; b. Richfield, Utah, Sept. 12, 1924; s. Herman Taylor and Zula May (Curtis) N.; B.S. in Math., U. Utah, 1947; M.S. in Math., U. Oreg., 1949; M.B.A., Stanford U., 1956, Ph.D. in Bus. Adminstrn. and Statistics, 1958; m. Julia Adams, June 18, 1948; children—Noreen (Mrs. Stephen Astin), Elaine (Mrs. Stanley Taylor), John, Mary Lee (Mrs. Paul Jackson), James, Jean, Howard Curtis. Statistician, C & H Sugar Refining Corp., 1949-51; research economist and statistician Stanford Research Inst., 1951-57; mem. faculty Brigham Young U., Provo, Utah, 1957—, prof. statistics, 1961—, chmn. dept., 1960-63, dir. Center for Bus. and Econ. Research, 1971-72; sr. statistician, acting field mgr. C-E-I-R, Inc., 1963-64, mgr., cons., 1964-65; prin. scientist GCA Corp., 1965-67; dir. econ. research Eyring Research Inst., 1974-75; asso. commr. higher edn. State of Utah, 1976—; econ. adviser Kingdom of Jordan, Ford Found., 1970-71; prof. Am. U., Beirut, 1970; prof. U. Utah, 1972-73. Mem. Utah Gov.'s Econ. Research Adv. Council, 1967—. Dir. bur. ch. studies Ch. of Jesus Christ of Latter-day Saints, 1958-63; research dir. Utah Republican Party, 1967-68; mem. Utah Ho. Reps., 1967-75, majority leader, 1969-71, speaker, 1973-75, mem. legis. budget-audit com., 1967-73, chmn., 1971-73, chmn. legis. council, 1973-75; mem. Utah Council Sci. and Tech., 1974-76; chmn. Utah County Rep. Com., 1979—. Mem. Am. Statis. Assn. (pres. Utah 1964-65, nat. council 1967-70), Sci. Research Soc. Am., Order of Artus, Phi Beta Kappa, Sigma Xi, Pi Mu Epsilon, Sigma Pi Sigma, Phi Kappa Phi. Author: The Efficiency of Certain Truncated Order Statistics in Estimating the Mean of Various Distributions, 1949; Population Trends in the United States Through 1975, 1955; The Hows and Whys of Statistics, 1963; Experimental Designs Used in industry, 1965; Membership Growth of the Church of Jesus Christ of Latter Day Saints, 1957, 67, 71, 75, 78; Evaluation of the Seven Year Plan for Economic Development in Jordan, 1971; Economic Analysis of Fiji, Tonga, Western and Am. Samoa, 1972; co-author The Newsprint Situation in the Western Region of North America, 1952; America's Demand for Wood, 1954; also reports. Home: 580 Sagewood Ave Provo UT 84601

NIELSON, JAMES EDWARD, oil co. exec.; b. Cardston, Alta., Can., Apr. 2, 1931; s. Glenn E. and Olive W. Nielson; came to U.S., 1936, naturalized, 1940; B.S. in Bus. Adminstrn., U. Wyo., 1954; m. Joanne Henry, Apr. 7, 1962; children—James R., Julia E., John W., Jeffrey G., Jay E. With Husky Oil Ltd., 1958—, exec. v.p. exploration and prodn., 1971-73, pres., chief exec. officer, 1973-79, also dir.; dir. Y-Tex Corp., Nielson Enterprises, Inc., Wyo. Indsl. Devel. Corp. Trustee Buffalo Bill Meml. Assn. Served with USNR, 1955-58. Mem. Am. Petroleum Inst. (dir.), Rocky Mountain Oil and Gas Assn. (exec. com.), U.S. C. of C. (joint Can./U.S. com.), Conf. Bd. Home: PO Box 370 Cody WY 82414 Office: PO Box 380 Cody WY 82414

NIELSON, JAMES MELVIN, educator, govt. ofcl.; b. Marysville, Kans., Dec. 30, 1921; s. James M. and Emma (Zybach) N.; B.S., Kans. State U., 1947; M.A. (Carnegie fellow), Harvard, 1951, Ph.D., 1953; m. Beverly May Howe, June 28, 1947; children—Noel Christopher, Douglas Craig. Asso. county agt. Extension Service, Alma, Kan., 1947-48; mem. faculty Mich. State U., 1951-65; prof. agrl. econs. Wash. State U., Pullman, 1965-71, chmn. dept., 1965-71, dir. agrl. research, 1971-77; dep. asst. sec. for conservation, research and edn. U.S. Dept. Agr., 1977, acting dir. sci. and edn., 1978, dep. dir. for joint planning and evaluation, sci. and edn. adminstrn., 1978—; cons. Farm Credit Adminstrn., 1975; mem. Gov. Wash. Council Econ. Advisers, 1969-77; cons. Wash. Dept. Ecology, 1970. Served from pvt. to capt., AUS, 1942-46. Mem. Am. (v.p. 1967-68, pres. 1974-75), Western (pres. 1968-69) agrl. econs. assns., Internat. Assn. Agrl. Economists, Am. Men and Women Sci., Gamma Sigma Delta, Alpha Gamma Rho. Episcopalian. Kiwanian (bd. dirs. Pullman 1968-70). Contbr. articles to tech. lit. Home: 2345 S Queen St Arlington VA 22202

NIEMANN, KURT MAX WALTER, orthopedic surgeon, educator; b. Bklyn., July 31, 1932; s. Walter George and Walburg (von Schmitz) N.; B.S., Trinity Coll., 1954; M.D., Med. Coll. Ala., 1960; m. Violet Theresa Humenik, Feb. 14, 1956; children—Susan Elizabeth, Kurt Max Walter, Rebecca Marie, Eric Andrew. Intern, Med. Coll. Va. Hosp., Richmond, 1960-61; resident U. Pitts. Hosp., 1962-65; asst. prof. orthopedic surgery U. Pitts., 1966-69; asso. prof. surg. dept. orthopedics U. Ala., Birmingham, 1969-71, prof., 1971—, John D. Sherrill prof., 1971—; dir. div. orthopedic surgery U. Ala. Med. Center, Birmingham, 1974—. Served with USAF, 1954-56. Diplomate Am. Bd. Orthopedic Surgery. Mem. Am. Acad. Orthopedic Surgery, So. Med. Assn., Clin. Orthopedic Soc., Alpha Omega Alpha. Lutheran. Home: 4223 Old Brook Ln Birmingham AL 35243 Office: 619 S 19th St Birmingham AL 35233

NIEMANN, LEWIS KEITH, lamp mfg. co. exec.; b. Alliance, Nebr., Dec. 10, 1930; s. William Grover and Vivian Zelma (Holloway) N.; B.S. in Mktg. with honors (Standard Oil grantee), San Diego State Coll., 1956; m. Elaine Marie Achtenhagen, Dec. 23, 1951; children—Randall Scott, Debra Lee and Denise Lee (twins). Mdse. mgr. Fed Mart Corp., San Diego, 1954-61; store mgr. GEX, Atlanta, 1961-63; mdse. mgr. J. C. Penney Co., Pitts., 1963-67; mgr. sales planning and product devel. RCA Sales Corp., 1967-70; spl. asst. to pres. Magnavox Consumer Electronics Co., 1970-73, v.p. internat. and comml. sales, 1973-74; v.p. mktg., div. mfg. Beatrice Foods Co., Chgo., 1974-75; v.p. mktg., div. luggage Samsonite Corp., Denver, 1975-78; pres. Stiffel Co., Chgo., 1978—. Bd. dirs. Jr. Achievement, Denver, 1976-78. Served with USMC, 1948-52; Korea. Recipient CLIO award for Best TV Comml. in class, 1978. Republican. Episcopalian. Office: Stiffel Co 700 N Kingsbury St Chicago IL 60610

NIEMANN, WILLIAM LOVEKAMP, lawyer, mfg. co. exec.; b. Jacksonville, Ill., July 25, 1920; s. Otto H. and Lila M. (Lovekamp) N.; A.B., Carthage Coll., 1941, LL.D. (hon.), 1976; J.D. cum laude, Northwestern U., 1947; m. Doris Elizabeth Greenstreet, Mar. 16, 1956; children—William Learned, John Justin. Admitted to Ill. bar, 1948, Calif. bar, 1953; asso. firm Snyder, Chadwell & Eagerburg, Chgo., 1947-50; atty. Montgomery Ward & Co., Chgo., 1950-52, regional atty., 1952-57, gen. atty., 1957-59; sec., gen. atty. Brunswick Corp., Skokie, Ill., 1959-73, sec., gen. counsel, 1973—. Served to 1st lt. U.S. Army, 1942-46, to capt. Ill. N.G., 1947-52. Mem. Am., Calif., Ill. bar assns., Am. Soc. Corp. Secs., Law Club Chgo., Order of Coif. Lutheran. Club: Michigan Shores (Wilmette, Ill.). Home: 1243 Forest Glen N Winnetka IL 60093 Office: 1 Brunswick Plaza Skokie IL 60076

NIEMEYER, GERHART, educator; b. Essen, Germany, Feb. 15, 1907; s. Victor and Kaethe (Ley) N.; student Cambridge U., 1925-26, Munich U., 1926-27; J.U.D., Kiel U., 1932; m. Lucie Lenzner, Sept. 18, 1931; children—A. Hermann, Lucian L., Paul V., Lisa M., Christian B. Came to U.S., 1937, naturalized, 1943. Lectr., asst. prof. Princeton, 1937-44; prof., head div. Oglethorpe U., 1944-50; fgn. affairs officer Dept. State, 1950-53; research analyst Council Fgn. Relations, 1953-55; prof. U. Notre Dame, 1955-76, emeritus, 1976—; vis. prof. Yale U., 1942, 46, 54-55, Columbia U., 1952, Vanderbilt U., 1962-66; faculty Nat. War Coll., 1958-59; Fulbright prof. U. Munich, 1962-63; Distinguished vis. prof. Hillsdale Coll., 1976—. Mem. task force on fgn. policy Republican Nat. Com., 1965-68. Bd. advisers Young Ams. for Freedom. Mem. Am. Polit. Sci. Assn., Am. Soc. Polit. and Legal Philosophy. Episcopalian (ordained deacon 1973). Author: Law Without Force. 1941; An Inquiry into Soviet Mentality, 1956; Facts on Communism, vol. 1: The Communist Ideology, 1959; Handbook on Communism, 1962; Between Nothingness and Paradise, 1971; Deceitful Peace, 1971. Home: 806 E Angela Blvd South Bend IN 46617

NIEMI, RICHARD GENE, polit. scientist; b. Green Bay, Wis., Jan. 10, 1941; s. Eugene H. and Dorothy M. (Stevens) N.; B.A., Lawrence Coll., 1962; Ph.D., U. Mich., 1967; m. Shirley A. Gill, Aug. 4, 1962; children—Nancy, Patricia, Jennifer, Julie. Asst. prof. U. Rochester, N.Y., 1967-71, asso. prof., 1971-75, prof. polit. sci., 1975—, chmn. dept., 1979—; Thord-Gray vis. prof. U. Lund, Sweden, 1974. NSF research grantee, 1975-77, NIMH research grantee, 1969-70, Ford Found. research grantee, 1972-73. Mem. Am. Polit. Sci. Assn., Pub. Choice Soc., Phi Beta Kappa. Lutheran. Author: (with M. Kent Jennings) The Political Character of Adolescence, 1974, Political Transitions, 1980; How Family Members Perceive Each Other, 1974. Editor: (with Herbert Weisberg) Controversies in American Voting Behavior, 1976. Home: 45 Boniface Dr Rochester NY 14620 Office: Dept Polit Sci U Rochester Rochester NY 14627

NIEMI, TAISTO JOHN, librarian; b. Aurora, Minn., Dec. 3, 1914; s. John and Edla (Kauppi) N.; A.A., Va. Jr. Coll., 1936; B.S., U. Minn., 1946; A.M., U. Mich., 1951, Ph.D., 1960; m. Catherine Bruflat, June 23, 1948; children—Marylee, Nancy, John, Paula, David. Tchr. adult edn., Aurora, 1938-41; library asst. Western Mich. U., 1947-53; librarian No. Mich. U., 1953-60, N.Y. State U. Coll., Buffalo, 1960-63; library dir. Le Moyne Coll., Syracuse, N.Y., 1963—. Second v.p. Mich. Library Assn., 1956-60; extension lectr. library sci. U. Mich., 1958-60, N.Y. State U. Coll., Geneseo, 1960-63. Served with AUS, 1942-45; PTO. Mem. Cath., N.Y. library assns., Spl. Libraries Assn., N.E.A., Central N.Y. Library Resources Council. Democrat. Roman Catholic. Contbr. articles to profl. jours. Home: 1234 Salt Springs Rd Syracuse NY 13214

NIEMIEC, EDWARD WALTER, stock brokerage co. exec.; b. Detroit, Nov. 1, 1936; s. Walter A. and Mary N.; B.S., U. Detroit, 1959, M.B.A., 1961; m. Nancy M. Bennett, Aug. 25, 1961; children—Lisa, Julie, Brenda. With Paine Webber Jackson & Curtis, N.Y.C., 1959—, exec. v.p., dir. adminstrv. div. Served with U.S. Army. Roman Catholic. Office: 25 Broad St New York NY 10004*

NIER, ALFRED OTTO CARL, physicist; b. St. Paul, May 28, 1911; s. August Carl and Anna J. (Stoll) N.; B.S., U. Minn., 1931, M.S., 1933, Ph.D., 1936; m. Ruth E. Andersen, June 19, 1937; children—Janet, Keith; m. 2d, Ardis L. Hovland, June 21, 1969. Nat. Research fellow, Harvard, 1936-38; asst. prof. physics U. Minn., 1938-40, asso. prof., 1940-43, prof., 1946—; physicist Kellex Corp., N.Y.C., 1943-45. Mem. A.A.A.S., Am. Phys. Soc., Minn., Nat. acads. scis., Geochem. Soc., Am. Geophys. Union, Am. Philos. Soc., Am. Assn. Physics Tchrs., Geol. Soc. Am., Am. Soc. Mass Spectrometry, Am. Vacuum Soc., Soc. Applied Spectroscopy, Sigma Xi. Research activities include devel. of mass spectrometer and its application to problems in physics, chemistry, geology, medicine, space sci.; first to separate rare isotope of uranium, U-235, 1940; with J.R. Dunning, E.T. Booth and A.V. Grosse of Columbia, demonstrated it was source of atomic energy when uranium is bombarded with slow neutrons. Home: 2001 Aldine St St Paul MN 55113

NIERENBERG, WILLIAM AARON, educator, univ. ofcl.; b. N.Y.C., Feb. 13, 1919; s. Joseph and Minnie (Drucker) N.; Aaron Naumberg scholar, U. Paris, 1937-38; B.S., Coll. City N.Y., 1939; M.A., Columbia U., 1942, Ph.D. (NRC predoctoral fellow), 1947; m. Edith Meyerson, Nov. 21, 1941; children—Victoria Jean (Mrs. Tschinkel), Nicolas Clarke Eugene. Tutor, Coll. City N.Y., 1939-42; sect. leader Manhattan Project, 1942-45; instr. physics Columbia, 1946-48; asst. prof. physics U. Mich., 1948-50; asso. prof. physics U. Calif. at Berkeley, 1950-53, prof., 1954-65; dir. Scripps Instn. Oceanography, 1965—; vice chancellor for marine scis. U. Calif. at San Diego, 1969—; dir. Hudson Labs., Columbia, 1953-54; asso. prof. U. Paris, 1960-62; asst. sec. gen. NATO for sci. affairs, 1960-62; spl. cons. Exec. Office Pres., 1958-60; spl. cons. White House Office Sci. and Tech. Policy, 1976—. E.O. Lawrence lectr. Nat. Acad. Sci., 1958; Miller Found. fellow, 1957-59, Sloan Found. fellow, 1958; mem. U.S. Nat. Commn. UNESCO, 1964-68, Calif. Adv. Com. on Marine and Coastal Resources, 1967-71; adviser-at-large U.S. Dept. State, 1968—; mem. Nat. Sci. Bd., 1972-78; mem. Nat. Adv. Com. on Oceans and Atmosphere, 1971-77, chmn., 1971-75; mem. sci. and tech. adv. Council Calif. Assembly; chmn. adv. council NASA, 1978—. NATO Sr. Sci. fellow, 1969. Decorated officer Nat. Order of Merit (France); recipient Golden Dolphin award Assn. Artistico Letteraria Internazionale, Compass award Marine Tech. Soc., 1975; Procter prize Sigma Xi, 1977. Fellow Am. Phys. Soc. (council, sec. Pacific Coast sect. 1955-64); mem. Am. Acad. Arts and Scis., Nat. Acad. Scis., Am. Philos. Soc., Am. Assn. Naval Architects, Navy League, Fgn. Policy Assn. (mem. nat. council), Sigma Xi (pres.-elect 1980—). Club: Explorers. Contbr. papers to profl. jours. Home: 9581 La Jolla Farms Rd La Jolla CA 92037 Office: Scripps Instn Oceanography Dir's Office A-010 U Calif San Diego La Jolla CA 92093

NIERMAN, LEONARDO MENDELEJIS, artist; b. Mexico City, Mexico, Nov. 1, 1932; s. Chanel and Clara (Mendelejis) Nierman; B.S. in Physics and Math., U. Mexico, also degrees in Bus. Adminstrn., 1959, and in Music, hon. degree, 1960; m. Esther Ptak, Feb. 16, 1957; children—Monica, Daniel, Claudia. One-man shows Proteo Gallery, 1958, 60, C.D.I. Gallery, 1956, Misrachi Gallery, 1964, Galeria Merkup, 1969, Mus. Modern Art, 1972 (all Mexico City), Galeria Sudamericana, N.Y.C., 1958, Hammer Galleries, N.Y.C., 1960, I.F.A. Galleries, Washington, 1952, 62, 65, 68, 71, Edgardo Acosta Gallery, Beverly Hills, Calif., 1961, Art Collectors Gallery, Beverly Hills, 1966, Main St. Gallery, Chgo., 1961, Doll & Richard Gallery, Boston, 1963, Pucker Safrai Gallery, Boston, 1969, El Paso (Tex.) Mus Art, 1964, 71, Wolfard's Gallery, Rochester, N.Y., 1964, Pub. Library Rockville Centre, N.Y., 1964, Little Gallery, Phila., 1964, Neusteters Gallery Fine Arts, Denver, 1965, Judah L. Magnes Meml. Mus., Berkeley, Calif., 1967, Galerie Katia Granoff, Paris, 1969, Little Gallery, Phila., 1970, Aalwin Gallery, London, 1970, Gallery Modern Art, Scottsdale, Ariz., 1971, Mus. Contemporary Arts, Bogota, Colombia, 1973, 74, Galerie Dresdnere, Ont., Can., Casa de la Cultura, Cucuta, Colombia, 1974, also mus., galleries Haifa, Israel, Rome, Italy, Toronto, Ont., Can., Paris, France, 1962—; exhibited group shows mus. Caracas, Venezuela, 1958, Mexico City, 1958—, Havana, Cuba, 1959, Tokyo, Japan, 1963, Paris, France, 1961, Nagoya, Japan, 1963, Kyoto, Japan, 1963, Osaka, Japan, 1963, Bogota, 1963, Santiago, Chile, 1963, Buenos Aires, Argentina, 1963, Rio de Janeiro, Brazil, 1963, Costa Rica, 1963, Panama, 1963, Oslo, Norway, 1965, Warsaw, Poland, 1965, Madrid, Spain, 1965, Stockholm, Sweden, 1966, Brussels, Belgium, 1966 (also exhibited Expo, 1958), also numerous mus., univs. Eastern and Western U.S., Can., 1958—; executed murals Sch. Commerce University City, Mexico, 1956, Bank San Francisco, 1965, physics bldg. Princeton, 1969; also executed stained glass windows Mexican synagogues, 1968-69; represented in permanent collections Mus. Modern Art in Mexico, Atlanta Mus., Mus. Modern Art Haifa, Gallery Modern Art, N.Y.C., Phoenix Art Mus., Pan Am. Union, Washington, Detroit Inst. Arts, Bogota Mus. Contemporary Arts, Mus. Contemporary Arts, Madrid, Acad. Fine Arts, Honolulu, Tucson Art Center, Tel-Aviv Mus., Israel Mus., Jerusalem, Kennedy Art Center, Washington, Boston Mus. Fine Arts, U. Va., No. Ill. Univ., Chgo. Art Inst., other mus. and galleries. Recipient 1st prize Mexican Contemporary Art, Art Inst. Mexico, 1964; Palme d'or Beaux Arts, Monaco, 1969; gold medal Tomasso Campanella Found., 1972. Life fellow Royal Soc. Arts (London, Eng.). Home: Amsterdam 43 PH Mexico City 11 Mexico Office: 160-701 Nuevo Leon Mexico City Mexico

NIESS, ROBERT JUDSON, educator; b. Mason City, Iowa, Aug. 25, 1911; s. George and Mary Anne (Thibodeau) N.; A.B. magna cum laude, U. Minn., 1933, A.M., 1934, Ph.D., 1937; m. Martha Isabelle Laing, June 18, 1938; children—Martha (Mrs. H. Gene Moss), Barbara (Mrs. John W. Buys, Jr.). Teaching fellow Romance langs. Washington U., St. Louis, 1936-37, instr., 1937-39; asst. prof. Romance langs. Mundelein Coll., Chgo., 1939-42; asso. prof. Romance langs. U. Ky., 1946-47; asst. prof. French, Harvard, 1947-49; from asso. prof. to prof. French, U. Mich. at Ann Arbor, 1949-72; prof. French, Duke, 1972—. Democratic candidate for state senate, 1952. Served to maj. USAAF, 1942-46. Grantee Am. Philos. Soc., 1956, 68, 74; recipient U. Mich. Press prize, 1970; Am. Council Learned Socs. fellow, 1951-52. Mem. AAUP, Modern Lang. Assn., South Atlantic Modern Lang. Assn., Am. Assn. Tchrs. French, Palmes Académiques, Phi Beta Kappa, Theta Chi, Phi Sigma Iota. Author: Julien Benda, 1952; Zola, Cézanne and Manet, 1968. Contbr. articles to profl. jours. Home: 2709 Spencer St Durham NC 27705

NIEZER, LOUIS FOX, lawyer; b. Ft. Wayne, Ind., Sept. 10, 1907; s. Charles M. and Rose M. (Fox) N.; A.B., U. Notre Dame, 1929; LL.B., Ind. U., 1937; LL.D., St. Francis Coll., 1965; m. Rosemary Callahan, Apr. 21, 1937; children—Mary F., Louise, John, Charles, Elizabeth, James, Margaret. Admitted to Ind. bar, 1936; practice law, Ft. Wayne, 1936-56; dir. Tokheim Corp., Ft. Wayne, 1936—, treas., 1941-44, gen. counsel, 1944-57, vice chmn. bd., 1947-60, pres., 1957-66, chmn. bd., 1960-72; practice law, Ft. Wayne, 1972—; dir. Ft. Wayne Nat. Bank; v.p., trustee Our Sunday Visitor, Inc., Huntington, Ind. Mem. Am. Bar Assn. K.C., Elk. Home: 1301 Sunset Dr Ft Wayne IN 46807 Office: 2400 Fort Wayne Nat Bank Bldg Ft Wayne IN 46802

NIGAM, BISHAN PERKASH, educator; b. Delhi, India, July 14, 1928; s. Rajeshwar Nath and Durga (Vati) N.; B.S., U. Delhi, 1946, M.S., 1948; Ph.D., U. Rochester (N.Y.), 1955; m. Indira Bahadur, Nov. 14, 1956; children—Sanjay, Shobhna, Ajay. Came to U.S., 1952. Research fellow U. Delhi, 1948-50; lectr. in physics, 1950-52, 55-56; postdoctoral fellow Case Inst. Tech., Cleve., 1954-55; postdoctoral research fellow NRC, Ottawa, Can., 1956-59; research asso. U. Rochester, 1959-60, asst. prof. physics, part-time 1960-61; prin. scientist Gen. Dynamics/Electronics, Rochester, N.Y., 1960-61; asso. prof. physics State U. N.Y. at Buffalo, 1961-64; prof. physics Ariz. State U., Tempe, 1964—; prof. physics U. Wis., Milw., 1966-67. Govt. of India scholar U. Rochester, 1952-54. Fellow Am. Phys. Soc. Author: (with R.R. Roy) Nuclear Physics, 1967; also articles. Office: Dept Physics Ariz State U Tempe AZ 85281

NIGH, GEORGE, gov. Okla.; b. McAlester, Okla., June 9, 1927; s. Wilber and Irene (Crockett) N.; student Eastern A. and M. Coll., 1946-47, 47-48; B.A., E. Central State Coll., 1950; m. Donna Mashburn, 1963; children—Mike, Georgeann. Partner, Nigh Grocery, McAlester, 1956-60; mem. Okla. Legislature, 1950-58; lt. gov. Okla., 1958-63, 67-79, gov., 1963, 79—. Chmn. Nat. Conf. Lt. Govs., 1970-71. Mem. Okla. Young Democrats (pres.), Okla. Jr. C. of C. (sec.), Am. Legion, V.F.W., Am. Vets. Baptist. Mason (32 deg., Shriner). Home: 8321 Picnic Ln Oklahoma City OK Office: State Capitol Bldg Oklahoma City OK 73102

NIGHTINGALE, DAVID JOHN, journalist; b. Chgo., Feb. 7, 1935; s. Vincent F. and Mary F. (Krueger) N.; B.S. in Journalism, U. Ill., 1956; m. Margot H. Allison, June 23, 1956; children—C. Van, Allison Howe. Sports editor Dixon (Ill.) Eve. Telegraph, 1956-59; sports writer Rockford (Ill.) Morning Star, 1959-61; sports writer, then sports columnist Chgo. Daily News, 1961-78; sports writer Chgo. Tribune, 1978—. Mem. Sigma Delta Chi, Sigma Pi. Clubs: Chgo. Press, Elks. Winner 1st pl. award Nat. Golf Writers Assn., 1973, Ill. AP Sports Writers, 1974. Office: 435 N Michigan Ave Chicago IL 60611

NIGHTINGALE, EARL CLIFFORD, radio commentator; b. Los Angeles, Mar. 12, 1921; s. Albert Victor and Gladys Fae (Hamer) N.; m. Mary Peterson, July 21, 1942 (div. 1960); children—David Alan, Pamela; m. 2d, Lenarda Certa, May 17, 1962; 1 son, Earl Clifford. Writer, announcer Radio Sta. KTAR, Phoenix, 1946-49, CBS, Chgo., 1949-50; formed own co. Earl Nightingale, Inc., Chgo., 1950, chmn. bd., 1950-59; writer, producer own radio program WGN, Chgo., 1950-56; merged with Lloyd Conant and Splty. Mail Services, Chgo., 1959, forming Nightingale-Conant Corp., Chgo., 1959, chmn. bd., 1959—. Writer, narrator daily radio program broadcast world-wide. Active various civic and cultural affairs. Hon. trustee Broward Community Coll., 1974-75. Served with USMC, 1938-46. Clubs: Tower, Lago Mar (Ft. Lauderdale, Fla.); Jockey (Miami). Author: This is Earl Nightingale, 1969. Home and Office: 11 Emerald Pointe Dr Punta Gorda FL 33950. *We become what we think about.*

NIGHTINGALE, STEPHEN EDWARDS, chem. co. exec.; b. Providence, Mar. 18, 1923; s. John Kewley Henshaw, Jr. and Helen Chace (Edwards) N.; A.B., Princeton, 1944; M.B.A., Columbia, 1949; m. Sally Aborn Lord, June 25, 1949; children—Stephen L., Peter E., David C. Research chemist J.T. Baker Chem. Co., 1946-47; with Union Carbide Corp., N.Y.C., 1949—, treas., 1971—. Served with USNR, 1943-46. Club: Noroton Yacht. Office: 270 Park Av New York City NY 10017

NIGRELLI, ROSS FRANCO, pathologist; b. Pittston, Pa., 1903; s. Castrenza and Emanuela (Franco) N.; B.S., Pa. State U., 1927; M.S., N.Y. U., 1929, Ph.D., 1936; m. Margaret Carrozza, 1927; 1 dau., Emanuela Dobrin. Teaching fellow biology, N.Y. U., 1927-31; resident fellow N.Y. Zool. Soc., 1931-32; pathologist Aquarium, N.Y. Zool. Soc., 1934—, dir. Lab. Marine Biochemistry and Ecology, 1958-63, founder, dir. Osborn Labs. of Marine Scis., 1964-73, sr. scientist, 1973—; dir. N.Y. Aquarium, 1966-70; instr. biology Coll. City of N.Y., 1936-42; vis. instr. biology N.Y. U., 1943-45, vis. asst. prof., 1945-49, adj. asso. prof. 1949-58, adj. prof. Grad. Sch. Arts and Scis., 1958—. Cons., U.S. Fish and Wildlife Service, 1943-48; sci. cons. Bingham Oceanographic Lab., Yale, 1943-60; cons. U.S. Pure Food and Drug Adminstrn., 1945—, USN Applied Sci. Lab., 1966-70; mem. tech. adv. com. Atlantic States Fisheries Commn., 1946-56; com. animals from nature Inst. Animal Resources, Nat. Acad. Sci., 1954—; mem. panel experts fisheries div. FAO; mem. subpanel on marine biology Panel Oceanographic Pres.'s Sci. Adv. Commn., 1965-66, adv. panel for sea grant Nat. Oceanic and Atmospheric Adminstrn. Dept. Commerce, 1971—; mem. Internat. Union Dirs. Zool. Gardens, 1968-70; mem. N.Y.C. Mayor's Oceanographic Adv. Com., 1969-73; adv. council Regional Med. Library program N.Y. Acad. Medicine, 1967; adv. com. Soc. for Zool. Edn., 1968—; extramural reviewer EPA, 1972—. Recipient Order Merit, Soc. d'Encouragement pour la Recherche et l'Invention. Hon. fellow N.Y. Zool. Soc., N.Y. Acad. Scis. (life mem., chmn., sec. biology 1946-47, councillor 1948-51, 70-73, rec. sec. 1954, v.p. 1955, pres. 1957, trustee 1959, bd. govs. 1971-73), A.A.A.S. (mem. council 1951-52, 56); fellow Conservation Found., Am. Acad. Microbiology (emeritus), Royal Soc. Tropical Medicine and Hygiene, Consular Law Soc.; mem. Am. Soc. Parasitologists (emeritus), Internat. Acad. Pathology (emeritus), Am. Micros. Soc. (hon. mem.; emeritus), Am. Soc. Zoologists (emeritus), Am. Assn. Pathologists and Bacteriologists (emeritus), Am. Soc. Tropical Medicine and Hygiene (emeritus), N.Y. Inst. Ocean Resources (treas.; gov. 1970-73), Hudson River Environ. Soc. (dir. 1970-71), Soc. Exptl. Biology and Medicine (hon. mem.), Am. Assn. Anatomists (emeritus), Harvey Soc. (hon.), Bermuda Biol. Sta., Inc., Soc. Protozoologists (hon. mem., pres. 1947-49, exec. com. 1952-53), Wildlife Disease Assn., Soc. Am. Microbiologists (emeritus), Am. Assn. Cancer Research (emeritus), Soc. Systematic Zoologists, Atlantic Fishery Biologists, Am. Soc. Ichthyology and Herpetology, Internat. Soc. Toxicology (founding mem.), Royal Soc. Medicine, Soc. for Preservation Old Fishes (charter), Soc. Invertebrate Pathology, Internat. Platform Assn., Sigma Xi. Club: Explorers. Editorial bd. Revue Internationale d'Oceanographie Medicale, Nice, France, 1967, Current Topics in Comparative Pathobiology, 1970—. Home: 27 Barracuda Rd East Quogue NY 11942 Office: Osborn Labs Marine Sciences N Y Aquarium Seaside Park Brooklyn NY 11224

NIGRO, FELIX ANTHONY, educator, author; b. Bklyn., Aug. 8, 1914; s. Vincent and Katherine (Tempone) N.; A.B., U. Wis., 1935, M.A., 1936, Ph.D. in Polit. Sci., 1948; m. Edna Helen Nelson, July 28, 1938; children—Lloyd G., Kirsten F. Various positions U.S. Govt. and UNRRA, 1937-46; mem. staff Griffenhagen & Assos., 1946-47; asst. prof. govt. U. Tex., 1948-49; vis. prof. pub. adminstrn. U. P.R., 1949-51, asso. prof. pub. adminstrn., 1955-56; asso. prof. pub. adminstrn. Fla. State U., 1951-52; pub. adminstrn. field cons. Inst. Inter-Am. Affairs, 1952-54; sr. asso. J.L. Jacobs & Co., mgmt. cons.'s, Chgo., 1954; lectr. UN Advanced Sch. Pub. Adminstrn., C.A., 1956-57; prof. govt. So. Ill. U., 1957-61; prof. polit. sci. San Diego State Coll., 1961-65; Charles P. Messick prof. pub. adminstrn. U. Del., 1965-69; prof. polit. sci. U. Ga., 1969—; numerous vis. professorships. Mem. personnel bd., New Castle County, Del., 1967-69, bd. ethics, Newark, Del., 1968-69. Mem. Nat. Acad. Pub. Adminstrn., Am. Polit. Sci. Assn., Am. Soc. Pub. Adminstrn., Internat. Personnel Mgmt. Assn. Author: Public Adminstration; Readings and Documents, 1951; Public Personnel Administration, 1959; Modern Public Administration, 1965, 5th edit. (with Lloyd G. Nigro), 1980; (with Lloyd G. Nigro) New Public Personnel Adminstration, 1976; Management-Employee Relations in the Public Service, 1969; also numerous articles. Home: 199 West View Dr Athens GA 30601

NIIZUMA, MINORU, sculptor; b. Tokyo, Japan, Sept. 29, 1930; s. Takeshi and Fumiko (Okada) N.; B.F.A., Tokyo U. of Arts, 1955; married; children—Andre Ta, Ko Christopher. Exhibited one-man shows Howard Wise Gallery, N.Y.C., 1966, 68, Rockefeller U., 1971, Gimpel and Weitzenhoffer Gallery, N.Y.C., 1972, 73, 74, 75, 76, 78, Gimpel and Hanover Galerie Zurich, Switzerland, 1973, Centre Internat. Art N.Y., 1976, Seibu Mus. Art, Tokyo, 1976, Contemporary Sculpture Center, Tokyo, 1979; exhibited in group shows Mus. Modern Art, N.Y.C., 1965, 66, Nat. Mus. Modern Art, Tokyo, 1965, Whitney Mus. Am. Art, N.Y.C., 1966, 68, Pitts. Internat.-Carnegie Inst., 1967, Nat. Mus. Modern Art, Tokyo and Kyoto, Japan, 1973-74; represented in permanent collection Mus. Modern Art, N.Y.C., Nat. Mus. Modern Art, Tokyo and Kyoto, Albright Knox Gallery, Buffalo, Rockefeller U., Des Moines Art Center, Guggenheim Mus., N.Y.C., Hirshhorn Mus. and Sculpture Garden, Smithsonian Instn., Washington. Instr., Bklyn. Mus. Art Sch., 1964-70; prof. Columbia U., 1972—. Home: 463 West St New York NY 10014 Office: 458 W 168th St New York NY 10032

NIJENHUIS, ALBERT, educator, mathematician; b. Eindhoven, Netherlands, Nov. 21, 1926; s. Hendrik and Lijdia (Koornneef) N.; Candidaat, U. Amsterdam (Netherlands), 1947, Doctorandus, 1950, Doctor cum laude, 1952; m. Marianne Dannhauser, Aug. 14, 1955; children—Erika, Karin, Sabien, Alaine. Came to U.S., 1952, naturalized, 1959. Asso., Math. Center, Amsterdam, 1951-52; asst. Inst. Advanced Study, 1955, mem., 1953-55, 61-62; instr., research asso. U. Chgo., 1955-56; faculty U. Wash., Seattle, 1956-63, prof., 1961-63; prof. math. U. Pa., Phila., 1963—; Fulbright lectr. U. Amsterdam, 1963-64; vis. prof. U. Geneva (Switzerland), 1967-68, Dartmouth Coll., 1977-78. Postdoctoral fellow Princeton, 1952-53; Fulbright grantee, 1952-53, 63-64; Guggenheim fellow, 1961-62. Mem. Am. Math. Soc., Math. Assn. Am., Netherlands Math. Soc., Soc. for Indsl. and Applied Math., Assn. for Computing Machinery, AAUP, Royal Netherlands Acad. Scis. (corr.). Co-author: Combinatorial Algorithms, 1975, 78; editor: Jour. Differential Geometry, Jour. Algorithms; research and publs. differential geometry, deformation theory in algebra, combinatorics, especially tensors, holonomy groups, graded lie algebras, algorithms. Office: Dept Math U Pa Philadelphia PA 19104

NIKIFORUK, GORDON, dentist, educator; b. Redfield, Sask., Can., Nov. 2, 1922; s. Andrew and V. (Lazorko) N.; student U. Sask., 1940-42; D.D.S., U. Toronto, 1947; M.S., U. Ill., 1950; m. Margaret Jordis Nokleberg, Dec. 23, 1950; children—Andrew, Christian. Asst. dir. dept. dentistry Hosp. for Sick Children, Toronto, 1952-64; chmn. div. dental research U. Toronto, 1954-64, prof. dept. preventive dentistry Faculty Dentistry, 1956-64, dean Faculty Dentistry, 1970—, also hon. staff Addiction Research Found.; chmn. div. pediatric dentistry U. Calif. Sch. Dentistry, Los Angeles, 1964-66; chmn. dental study sect. Div. Research Grants, NIH, 1967-68. Fellow Royal Coll. Dentists of Can., Royal Coll. Dental Surgeons of Ont.; mem. Canadian Dental Assn. (chmn. research com. 1956-58), Canadian Soc. Dentistry for Children (pres. 1959-60). Home: 55 St Leonards Ave Toronto ON Canada Office: 124 Edward St Toronto ON Canada

NIKIFORUK, PETER NICK, educator; b. St. Paul, Alta., Can., Feb. 11, 1930; s. DeMetro N. and Mary (Dowhaniuk) N.; B.Sc., Queen's U., Ont., Can., 1952; Ph.D., Manchester U., Eng., 1955, D.Sc., 1970; m. Eugenie F. Dyson, Dec. 21, 1957; children—Elizabeth, Adrienne. Engr., A.V. Roe Ltd., Toronto, Ont., 1951-52; def. sci. service officer Def. Research Bd., Quebec, Que., Can., 1956-57; systems engr. Canadair Ltd., Montreal, Que., 1957-59; asst. prof. U. Sask., Saskatoon, 1960-61, asso. prof., 1961-65, prof., 1965—, chmn. div. control engring., 1964-69, head mech. engring., 1966-73, dean engring., 1973—; cons. in field. Fellow Inst. Physics, Instn. Elec. Engrs.; mem. Assn. Profl. Engrs. Sask. (chmn. bd. examiners), Sask. Sci. Council (chmn.), Sask. Research Council, Engrs. Inst. Can., Can. Soc. Mech. Engrs. Contbr. articles to profl. jours. Home: 31 Bell Crescent Saskatoon SK S7J 2W2 Canada

NIKOLAIEFF, GEORGE ALEXANDER, writer, editor, syndicated columnist; b. Armavir, Caucusus, USSR, Nov. 19, 1938; s. Alexander and Zinaida (Nikitina) N.; B.A., Columbia, 1961; m. Rosalind Gay Mills, Aug. 26, 1961; children—Gregory Alexander, Peter Christian. Writer Scholastic mags., N.Y.C. 1963-65, dir. student opinion poll, author Scholastic Youth Poll, 1971-76; editor responsible for Sr. Scholastic and InSide, 1971-75; reporter Wall St. Jour., N.Y.C., 1965-71; speechwriter sr. execs. Avon Products, Inc., 1976-77; sr. editorial officer Bank Am. N.T. & S.A., San Francisco, 1977-78; public relations coordinator Kaiser Found. Health Plan, Inc., Oakland, Calif., 1978—. Club: Heights Casino (Bklyn.). Home: 53 Beach Rd Belvedere CA 94920 Office: One Kaiser Plaza Oakland CA 94612

NIKOLAIS, ALWIN, choreographer; b. Southington, Conn., Nov. 25, 1912; s. John and Martha (Heinrich) N.; student Bennington Coll., summers 1938-40; pupil of Hanya Holm, Martha Graham, Doris Humphrey, Charles Weidman and Louis Horst, 1946-48; pvt. music and art study; D.F.A. (hon.), Washington U., St. Louis, 1979. Dir. Nikolais Sch. Dance, Hartford, Conn., 1939-42; dir. dance dept. Hartford U., 1940-42, 46-48; dir. Henry St. Playhouse, N.Y.C., 1948-70, Alwin Nikolais Dance Co., N.Y.C., 1953—; faculty Sarah Lawrence Coll., 1952-54, Columbia Tchrs. Coll., 1953-54, Colo. Coll., summers 1946-49, Conn. Coll., summers 1956-57, U. Utah, summers 1961-63, 65-67; European tours, 1968, 69, 71, 74, 75, 76, 78, S.Am. tours, 1973, 75, 77, 79, Japan-Far East tours, 1976, 79. Mem. nat. screening com. dance Inst. Internat. Edn., 1966-68, chmn. 1967-68; cons. Asso. Council of Arts, 1966-67, 74—, theatre arts com. Com. Internat. Exchange Persons, 1967-68; mem. N.Y. State Council on Arts, 1967-77; hon. mem. Consul International de la Dance, UNESCO; dir. Centre Nationale de Danse Contemporaine d'Angers, France, 1978. Bd. dirs. Arts Councils Am., Advs. for Arts. Served with AUS, 1942-46. Recipient Dance mag. award, 1968, grand prix Paris Internat. Festival Dance, 1968, Emmy award, 1968, Bitef Theater award, Belgrade, Yugoslavia, 1968; Circulo de Criticos award, Chile, 1973, 75; honored with Alwin Nikolais Week by proclamation Gov. Wis., Dec. 1978; Nat. Council Arts grantee, 1966, 69-71, 73-75; Guggenheim fellow, 1964-68. Fellow Am. Acad. Arts and Scis.; mem. Assn. Am. Dance Companies (dir. 1966-67, pres. 1967-68), Nat. Soc. Lit. and Arts. Choreographer: Kaleidoscope, 1956; Prism, 1960; Imago, 1963; Sanctum, 1964; Galaxy, 1965; Runic Canto, 1957; Allegory, 1959; Totem, 1960; Vaudeville of the Elements, 1965; Somniloquy, 1967; Triptych, 1967, Tent, 1968; (film) Fusion, 1967; (TV) Limbo, 1968; Echo, 1969; Structures, 1969; Scenario, 1971; Foreplay, 1972; Grotto, 1973; Crossfade, 1974; (BBC-TV) The Relay, 1971; Temple, 1974; Tribe, 1975; Styx, 1976; Triad, 1976; Guignol, 1977; Arporisms, 1977; Castings, 1978; Gallery, 1978; Aviary, A Ceremony for Bird People, 1978; Count Down, 1979; (USIA) Nik: An Experience in Sight and Sound, 1974; WHA TV documentary Aviary, 1978. Office: 33 E 18th St New York NY 10003

NILAND, EDWARD JOHN, lawyer; b. Boston, Aug. 25, 1916; s. Edward John and Angela (O'Donnell) N.; J.D. cum laude, Boston Coll., 1947; m. Muriel Ball, Aug. 27, 1942; children—Janet Louise, Edward Leo, Joyce Carol (Mrs. Sidney J. Weiss), Judith Patricia. Research asst. Boston Pub. Library, 1935-42; instr. asso. prof. law U. Santa Clara (Calif.), 1947-52; admitted to Calif. bar, 1948; since practiced in San Jose; partner firm Boccardo, Lull, Niland & Bell, 1952—. Vis. lectr. U. San Francisco Law Sch., 1948-53; lectr. Calif. Continuing Edn. of Bar Program, 1966. Bd. fellows U. Santa Clara, 1974—. Served to 1st lt. A.C., AUS, 1942-45. Mem. Am. Bar Assn., State Bar Calif., Assn. Trial Lawyers Am., Am. Judicature Soc., Calif. Acad. Appellate Lawyers (1st v.p. 1973-77), Calif. Trial Lawyers Assn. Democrat. Roman Catholic. Optimist (lt. gov. Dist. 20 1957-58), K.C. Home: 14110 Douglas Ln Saratoga CA 95070 Office: Boccardo Lull Niland & Bell 111 W St John St San Jose CA 95113

NILES, HENRY EDWARD, ins. co. exec.; b. Balt., Jan. 20, 1900; s. Alfred S. and Mary (Waters) N.; A.B. cum laude, Johns Hopkins, 1920, postgrad., 1920-23; student univs. in Europe; m. Mary Cushing Howard, Sept. 15, 1923; children—Cushing (Mrs. Louis P. Dolbeare), Alice Lee (Mrs. Staughton Lynd). With Balt. Life Ins. Co., summers 1918-22, supt. agys., 1940, sec., 1940-42, v.p., 1943-57, pres., 1957-65, chmn. bd., 1965-70; research clk. Fed. Res. Bank, N.Y.C., 1923; asst. mgr. Life Ins. Sales Research Bur., Hartford, Conn., 1923-30; asso. Woodward, Fondiller & Ryan, 1930-31; mem. firm Henry E. Niles & M.C.H. Niles, 1931-39. Sr. mgmt. cons. OPA, Washington, 1942-43; dep. dir. U.S. Tech. Coop. Mission to India, 1952-53. Past mem. nat. council United World Federalists; nat. chmn. Bus. Execs. Move for New Nat. Priorities. Trustee Morgan State Coll., 1960-67. Recipient awards Ams. for Democratic Action, Md. Civil Liberties Com., Md. Vets. for Peace. Mem. Am. Mgmt. Assn. (past v.p.), Soc. Advancement Mgmt., Balt. Urban League. Mem. Soc. of Friends (past vice chmn. Am. Friends Service Com. Clubs: Center, 14 West Hamilton Street (Balt.); Cosmos (Washington). Author: (with Mrs. Niles and James C. Stephens) The Office Supervisor, rev. edit., 1960. Home: 13801 York Rd Cockeysville MD 21030 Office: 901 N Howard St Baltimore MD 21201

NILES, JOHN JACOB, composer, folklore collector, folk singer; b. Louisville, Apr. 28, 1892; s. John Thomas and Lula Sarah (Reisch) N.; student U. Lyon, 1919, Cin. Conservatory Music, 1920-22, Mus.D. (hon.), 1949; D.F.A. (hon.), Transylvania U., 1968; Litt.D. (hon.), Episcopal Theol. Sem. in Ky., 1970, U. Ky., 1973; H.H.D. (hon.), U. Louisville, 1971; m. Rena Lipetz, Mar, 21, 1936; children—Thomas Michael Tolliver, John Edward. Concerts Am. folk music, maj. cities U.S., Eng. Holland, France, Germany, Scandinavian countries, 1927—. Served to 1st lt. A.C., U.S. Army, 1917-19. Recipient nat. citation Fedn. Music Clubs, 1967. Mem. Am. Folklore Soc., Am. Dialect Soc., ASCAP. Episcopalian. Maj. compositions include Lamentation, Mary the Rose, Rhapsody for the Merry Month of May; best known songs include I Wonder As I Wander, Go 'Way from My Window, Black is the Color of My True Love's Hair, Venezuela, others; rec. artist for Tradition Everest Records, Folkways and RCA-Victor Records. Author: Singing Soldiers, 1927; Songs My Mother Never Taught Me, 1929; One Man's War, 1929; The Ballad Book of John Jacob Niles, 1961; Folk Ballads for Young Actors, 1962; Folk Carols for Young Actors, 1962; (poetry collection) Brickdust and Buttermilk, 1977. Home: Boot Hill Farm Route 10 Lexington KY 40511

NILES, WILLIAM ISAAC CAMPBELL, mfg. co. exec.; b. Calgary, Alta., Can., Dec. 28, 1929; s. Donald Campbell and Viva (Niven) N.; m. Sheila Lee Talbott, June 29, 1951; children—Laurie, Christopher, Alicia, Sara. Articled clk. George A. Young, chartered accountant, Lethbridge, Alta., 1948-56; sr. accountant Price Waterhouse & Co., C.P.A.'s, Caracas, Venezuela, 1956-58; asst. to controller Schlumberger Surenco, Caracas, 1958-63; treas. Schlumberger Ltd., N.Y.C., 1963-71; exec. v.p. finance Canron Inc., Toronto, Ont., Can., 1971—. Mem. Inst. Chartered Accts. Alta. and Que., Fin. Execs. Inst. Episcopalian. Home: 40 Hillcrest Dr Toronto ON M6G 2E3 Canada Office: 1 First Can Pl Suite 6300 PO Box 134 Toronto ON M5X 1A4 Canada

NILL, KENNETH WELLMAN, sci. instrument mfg. co. exec.; b. Hutchinson, Kans., Nov. 29, 1939; s. Kenneth A. and H. Coyle (Wellman) N.; B.S., Mass. Inst. Tech., 1961, M.S., 1963, Ph.D. (Howard Hughes doctoral fellow), 1966; m. Barbara Gale Hummel, Dec. 28, 1968; children—Katherine, Ashley, Jocelyn. Mem. research staff Lincoln Lab., Mass. Inst. Tech., Lexington, 1966-75; co-founder, sr. v.p., dir. Laser Analytics, Inc., Lexington, 1975—. Mem. IEEE, Am. Inst. Physics, Sigma Xi, Tau Beta Pi, Eta Kappa Nu. Home: 16 Bennington Rd Lexington MA 02173 Office: 25 Wiggins Ave Bedford MA 01730

NILSSON, BIRGIT, soprano; b. Karup, Sweden; d. Nils P. and Justina (Paulsson) Svensson; student Royal Musical Acad., Stockholm; Mus.D. (hon.), Amherst (Mass.) U.; m. Bertil Niklasson, Sept. 10, 1948. Appeared opera and concert houses in Europe, N.Am., S.Am., Japan and Australia; most famous roles include Bruennhilde, Isolde, Salome, Elektra, Turandot, Tosca, Lady Macbeth, Fidelio. Decorated 1st comdr. Order of Vasa (Sweden); Austrian and Bavarian Kammersaengerin; named Swedish Royal Court Singer. Hon. mem. Royal Acad. Music London, Royal Acad. Music Stockholm, Vienna State Opera. Address: PO Box 527 Stockholm Sweden

NILSSON, HARRY, singer, songwriter; b. Bklyn., June 15, 1941. In charge computer center Ops. Security Pacific 1st Nat. Bank, Van Nuys, Calif., 7 years; singer Everybody's Talkin' in movie Midnight Cowboy; rec. artist for RCA; albums include Pandemonium Shadow Show, Aerial Ballet, Skidoo (mus. sound track), Aerial Pandemonium Ballet, Harry, Nilsson Sings Newman, The Point, Nilsson Schmillson, Son of Schmillson, A Little Touch of Schmillson in the Night, Son of Dracula (film sound track), Pussycats, Duit on Mon Dei; composer: I Guess the Lord Must Be in New York City; Open Your Window; Bath; 1941; The Puppy Song; Don't Leave Me; I Said Goodbye to Me; One; Gotta Get Up; Driving Along; Down; Jump Into the Fire. Recipient Grammy awards for best popular rock vocal, 1969, 72; 3 Album of Year awards for prodn. Stereo Rev.; Thomas Alva Edison award for best album of year (Nilsson Schmillson); has 8 gold records; BMI awards; Montreaux Film Festival spl. bd. of merit award for The Point; Atlanta Film Festival spl. merit award for The Point. Address: care Bruce Grakal 9777 Wilshire Blvd Suite 1018 Beverly Hills CA 90212. *Pretty soon there'll be nothing left for everybody since everything is food.*

NIMETZ, MATTHEW, lawyer, govt. ofcl.; b. Bklyn., June 17, 1939; s. Joseph L. and Elsie (Botwinnik) N.; B.A., Williams Coll., 1960, LL.D. (hon.), 1979; B.A. (Rhodes scholar), Balliol Coll., Oxford (Eng.) U., 1962, M.A., 1966; LL.B., Harvard U., 1965; m. Gloria S. Lorch, June 15, 1975; children—Alexandra Elise, Lloyd. Admitted to N.Y. bar, 1966; law clk. to Justice John M. Harlan, U.S. Supreme Ct., 1965-67; staff asst. to Pres. Johnson, 1967-69; asso. firm Simpson Thacher & Bartlett, N.Y.C., 1969-71, partner, 1972-77; counselor Dept. of State, Washington, 1977—, acting coordinator refugee affairs, 1979—. Commr., Port Authority N.Y. and N.J., 1975-77. Mem. Council Fgn. Relations, Assn. Bar City N.Y. Club: Harvard (N.Y.C.). Office: Dept of State 2201 C St NW Washington DC 20520

NIMITZ, CHESTER WILLIAM, JR., mfg. co. exec.; b. Bklyn., Feb. 17, 1915; s. Chester William and Catherine V. (Freeman) N.; B.S., U.S. Naval Acad., 1936; m. Joan Leona Labern, June 18, 1938; children—Frances Mary, Elizabeth Joan, Sarah Catherine. Commd. ensign U.S. Navy, 1936, advanced through grades to rear adm., 1957; principally assigned submarines and destroyers; ret. 1957; with Tex. Instruments Co., 1957-61; with Perkin-Elmer Corp., Norwalk, Conn., 1961—, pres., chief exec. officer, 1965-73, chmn. bd., 1973—, chief exec. officer, 1973-78; dir. U.S. Trust Co., Atlantic Mut. Ins. Cos., Stauffer Chem. Co., Leesona Corp. Decorated Navy Cross, Silver Star (3). Home: 64 Michigan Rd New Canaan CT 06840 Office: Perkin-Elmer Corp Main Ave Norwalk CT 06856

NIMKIN, BERNARD WILLIAM, lawyer; b. N.Y.C., Apr. 15, 1923; s. Myron Benjamin and Anabel (Davidow) N.; B.S. cum laude, Harvard U., 1943, LL.B. cum laude, 1949; m. Jean Horowitz, Feb. 9, 1947; children—David Andrew, Margaret Lee, Katherine. Admitted to N.Y. State bar, 1949; asso. firm Carter, Ledyard & Milburn, N.Y.C., 1949-58; asso. and partner firm Kaye, Scholer, Fierman, Hays & Handler, N.Y.C., 1958—; lectr. Practising Law Inst., Banking Law Inst. Mem. Am. Law Inst. vis. com. U. Miami Law Sch.; mem. adv. bd. Rev. of Securities Regulation. Mem. Conservation Commn., Town of Mamaroneck (N.Y.), 1970-74. Served to 1st lt. U.S. Army, 1943-46. Mem. Am. Bar Assn. (mem. fed. regulation of securities com. 1975—), N.Y. State Bar Assn. (chmn. sect. banking, corp. and bus. law 1979—, chmn. corp. law com. 1976-79), Assn. Bar of City of N.Y. (chmn. uniform state laws com. 1962-65). Democrat. Jewish. Club: Harvard (N.Y.C.). Contbr. articles to profl. jours. Home: 116 E 63d St New York NY 10021 Office: 425 Park Ave New York NY 10022

NIMMONS, PHILLIP RISTA, composer, condr., clarinetist, educator; b. Kamloops, B.C., Can., June 3, 1923; s. George Rista and Hilda Louise (McCrum) N.; B.A., U. B.C., 1944; student (Scholar), Juilliard Sch. Music, 1945-47, Royal Conservatory Music, U. Toronto, 1948-50; m. Noreen Liese Spencer, July 5, 1950; children—Holly Jayne, Carey Jocelyn, Phillip Rista. Performances include CBC radio and TV spls., 1948-79, CBC drama, musical comedy, variety shows and own jazz program, 1953—; appearances include Royal Alexander Theatre, Crest Theatre, Toronto Symphony Orch., Expo 67, 1976 Olympics; co-founder Advanced Sch. Contemporary Music, 1960, dir., 1961-66; on tour of Canadian bases with CBC, 1965-72; tour of Atlantic Provinces, 1974, 77; dir. jazz programm, prof. U. Toronto, 1970—, U. N.B., summers 1967—, Banff Sch. Fine Arts, 1972, U. Western Ont., 1968—; leader Nimmon 'n Nine Plus Six jazz ensemble, 1953—; pres. Nimmons 'N Music, Ltd., 1975—; lectrs. to schs., colls. and community groups; cons. in field; adjudicator numerous festivals. Mem. adv. bd. Humber Coll., Banff Sch. Fine Arts; trustee, then chmn. York Edn. Clinic, 1968-74; mem. parents adv. bd. Thornlea Secondary Sch., 1967-72. Recipient cert. for music contbn. to Expo '67, Govt. of Can., 1967; cert. of honour BMI (Can.), 1968; cert. of recognition City of Fredericton (N.B.), 1975; Juno award Can. Soc. Recording Arts and Scis., 1976. Mem. Am. Fedn. Musicians, PRO Can., Canadian League Composers (charter), Canadian Music Centre. Club: Celebrity (Toronto). Composer numerous jazz works including: The Atlantic Suite, 1974, Transformations, 1975, Invocation, 1976; rec. artist. Home and Office: 114 Babcombe Dr Thornhill ON L3T 1N1 Canada

NIMOY, LEONARD, actor; b. Boston, Mar. 26, 1931; s. Max and Dora (Spinner) N.; student (drama scholar) Boston Coll., Pasadena (Calif) Playhouse, Jeff Corey, 1960-63; M.A., Antioch U., Austin, Tex.; m. Sandi Zober, Feb. 21, 1954; children—Julie, Adam. Operator drama studio San Fernando Valley; tchr. Synanon; appeared in movies, including Kid Monk Baroni, 1952, The Balcony, 1963, Deathwatch (co-producer), 1966, Valley of Mystery, 1967, Assault on the Wayne, 1970, Catlow, 1971, Invasion of the Body Snatchers, 1978, Star Trek: The Motion Picture, 1979; appeared on television programs Profiles in Courage, Virginian, Outer Limits, Man from Uncle, Rawhide, Eleventh Hour, Kraft Theatre, Dr. Kildare, others; star Star Trek, Mission: Impossible; host TV series In Search of . . . ; appeared in TV film Seizure: The Story of Kathy Morris, 1979; appeared on stage in Dr. Faustus, Stalag 17, Streetcar Named Desire, Cat on a Hot Tin Roof, Deathwatch, Monserrat, Irma La Douce, Visit to a Small Planet, Fiddler on the Roof, The Man in the Glass Booth, 6 Rms Riv Vu, Equus, others; owner Adajul Music Pub. Co.; producer, host TV documentary If the Mind is Free; dir. episode Death on a Barge, TV show Night Gallery. Writer, producer, dir. Vincent, 1980. Mem. ACLU; mem. sch. com. adv. bd. Parents for Peace Western Los Angeles. Del. Dem. Central Com., 1971, 72. Served with AUS, 1954-56. Composed, recorded albums including Leonard Nimoy Presents Mr. Spock's Music from Outer Space, Two Sides of Leonard Nimoy, The Way I Feel, The Touch of Leonard Nimoy, The New World of Leonard Nimoy; composer other songs. Author: (poetry and photography) You and I, Will I Think of You; (biography) I Am Not Spock, 1975; We Are All Children, 1977; Come Be With Me, 1979.

NIMS, ARTHUR LEE, III, fed. judge; b. Oklahoma City, Jan. 3, 1923; s. Arthur Lee and Edwina (Peckham) N.; B.A., Williams Coll., 1945; LL.B., U. Ga., 1949; LL.M. in Taxation, N.Y. U., 1954; m. Nancy Chloe Keyes, July 28, 1950; children—Chloe, Lucy. Admitted to Ga. bar, 1949, N.J. bar, 1955; practice law, Macon, Ga., 1949-51; spl. atty. Office Chief Counsel, IRS, N.Y.C. and Washington, 1951-55; asso. firm McCarter & English, Newark, 1955-61, partner, 1961-79; judge U.S. Tax Ct., Washington, 1979—. Mem. standing com. Episcopal Diocese of Newark, 1971-75; pres. Colonial Symphony Soc., Madison, N.J., 1975-78. Served to lt. (j.g.) USNR, 1943-46. Mem. Am. Bar Assn. (sec. sect. taxation 1977-79), N.J. Bar Assn. (chmn. sect. taxation 1969-71), Am. Law Inst., Internat. Fiscal Assn. Clubs: Morris County (N.J.) Golf, Essex, Morristown. Office: US Tax Ct 400 Second St NW Washington DC 20217

NIMS, JOHN FREDERICK, educator, writer; b. Muskegon, Mich., Nov. 20, 1913; s. Frank McReynolds and Anne (McDonald) N.; A.B., U. Notre Dame, 1937, M.A., 1939; Ph.D., U. Chgo., 1945; m. Bonnie Larkin, Sept. 11, 1947; children—John, Frank, George (dec.), Sarah Hoyt, Emily Anne. Mem. faculty U. Notre Dame, 1939-45, 46-52, 54-58, U. Toronto, 1945-46, Bocconi U., Milan, Italy, 1952-53, U. Florence (Italy), 1953-54, U. Madrid, 1958-60, Harvard U., 1964, 68-69, summer 1974, U. Ill. at Urbana, 1961-65, at Chgo., 1965—, Bread Loaf Writers Conf., 1958-71, Bread Loaf Sch. English, 1965-69, U. Fla., fall 1972, 73-77; Margaret Scott Bundy prof. lit. Williams Coll., fall 1975; mem. editorial bd. Poetry mag., 1945-48, vis. editor, 1960-61, editor, 1978—; Phi Beta Kappa poet Harvard U., 1978. Recipient Harriet Monroe Meml. award Poetry mag., 1942, Guarantors prize, 1943, Levinson prize, 1944; Fulbright grantee, 1952, 53; Smith Mundt grantee, 1958, 59; Nat. Found. Arts and Humanities grantee, 1967-68; award for creative writing Am. Acad. Arts and Letters, 1968; Creative Arts citation in Poetry Brandeis U., 1974. Democrat. Roman Catholic. Author: The Iron Pastoral, 1947; A Fountain in Kentucky, 1950; The Poems of St. John of the Cross, 1959, rev., 1979; Knowledge of the Evening, 1960; Of Flesh and Bone, 1967; Sappho to Valéry: Poems in Translation, 1971, 79; Western Wind, 1974. Contbr.: Five Young American Poets, 1944; The Complete Greek Tragedies, 1959; also anthologies, mags.; editor: Ovid's Metamorphoses, 1965, Harper Anthology of Poetry, 1979; asso. editor: The Poem Itself, 1960; editorial adviser Princeton U. Press, 1975—. Address: Dept English U Ill at Chgo Circle Box 4348 Chicago IL 60680

NIND, THOMAS EAGLETON WESTWOOD, univ. pres.; b. London, Eng., June 16, 1926; s. John Warwick and Amy Mary (Greatbatch) N.; student Cambridge U., Eng., 1943-45, 48-50, Royal Sch. Mines, Eng., 1950-51; m. Jean Helen Marriott, May 22, 1954; children—Christopher, Sarah, Andrew. Research hydrodynamicist Short Bros. Seaplane Co., Eng., 1945-46; lectr. dept. pure math. U. Capetown, South Africa, 1947-48; prodn., oil reservoir engr. Royal Dutch/Shell Group, Eng., Holland, Venezuela, Brit. Borneo, 1950-58; asst. prof., asso. prof., then prof. dept. geol. studies U. Sask. (Can.), 1958-66; prof. math., dean sci. Trent U., Peterborough, Ont., Can., 1966-67, dean arts and sci., 1967-71, acad. v.p., 1971-72, pres., vice-chancellor, 1972-79; vis. prof. U. Autonoma de Mex., 1972, U. West Indies, Trinidad, 1978; dir. Quaker Oats Co. Can. Ltd. Mem. Oil and Gas Conservation Bd., Sask., 1959-66; mem. hydrology subcom. NRC, 1964-68. Bd. govs. Sir Sandford Fleming Coll. Applied Arts and Tech., 1970-77. Registered profl. engr., Ont. Fellow Cambridge Philos. Soc., Am. Geophys. Union; mem. Canadian Inst. Mining and Metallurgy, Canadian Math. Congress. Author: Principles of Oil Well Production, 1964. Contbr. articles to profl. jours. Home: 29 Merino Rd Peterborough ON K9J 6M8 Canada

NININGER, HARVEY HARLOW, meteoriticist; b. Conway Springs, Kans., Jan. 17, 1887; s. James Buchanan and Mary Ann (Bower) N.; student Northwestern State Tchrs. Coll., Alva, Okla., 1907-09; A.B., McPherson Coll., 1914, D.Sc., 1937; A.M., Pomono Coll., 1916, D.Sc. (hon.), 1976; postgrad. U. Calif., 1915-18; LL.D., Ariz. State U., 1961; m. Addie N. Delp, June 5, 1914; children—Robert D., Doris Elaine, Margaret Ann. Tchr. rural schs., 1909; substitute prof. biology Northwestern State Tchrs. Coll., 1912-13; prof. biology La Verne Coll., 1914-18, Southwestern Coll., Winfield, Kans., 1919-20, McPherson Coll., 1920-30; began study and collection of meteorites, 1923; founder Nininger Lab. for Research on Meteorites (became Am. Meteorite Lab. 1937), Denver, dir., 1930-46; curator meteorites Colo. Mus. Natural History; cons. N.Am. Aviation Space Sci. Lab.; pres., founder Rocky Mountain Summer Sch., Palmer Lake, Colo. Established Am. Meteorite Mus., 1946; extensive research Ariz. Meteorite Crater, 1946-56; expdn. Australia, study meteorite craters, 1958-59; explored and surveyed new meteorite crater Western Australia, 1959; studied meteorite collections, Europe, 1960; meteorite expn., B.C., 1966. Spl. field agt. U.S. Bur. Entomology, 1918-19, in food conservation program. Established Nininger Meteorite award in 1961. Recipient Leonard medal on 80th birthday. Fellow AAAS, Soc. for Research on Meteorites (co-founder; sec. 1933-37, pres. 1937-41), Kans. Acad. Sci. (pres. 1924-25); mem. Am. Astron. Union. Conglist. Author: Our Stone-Pelted Planet, 1933; A Comet Strikes the Earth, 1942; Chips From the Moon, 1947; Nininger Collection of Meteorites, 1950; Out of the Sky, 1952; Arizona's Meteorite Crater, 1956; Ask a Question About Meteorites, 1962; Field Guide to Birds of Central Kansas; Published Papers of H.H. Nininger, 1971; Find a Falling Star, 1972; A Photographic Study of Surface Features of Meteorites, 1977; also numerous articles in sci. jours. Meteoritic mineral named niningerite in his honor. Address: PO Box 420 Sedona AZ 86336

NIPPES, ERNEST FREDERICK, educator, metallurgist; b. N.Y.C., Feb. 1, 1918; s. Ernest Frederick and Louise (Kueckes) N.; B.Chem. Engring., Rensselaer Poly. Inst., 1938, M.Metall. Engring., 1940, Ph.D., 1942; m. Margaret Louise Hutchens, Sept. 1939 (div.); children—Raymond Allan, Robert Ernest; m. 2d, Marilyn Lenore Schue, 1969; children—Deborah Lynne, Stephen Edward, Stuart Joseph. Mem. faculty Rensselaer Poly. Inst., 1938—, prof. metallurgy, 1954—, chmn. dept. materials engring., 1961-65, dir. research div., 1965-71, dir. office research and sponsored programs, 1971-74, duPont Year in Industry Program, 1962-63; pres. Rensselaer Research Corp., 1965-69; cons. in field, 1939—. Mem. Poestenkill (N.Y.) Zoning Commn., 1955-56. Recipient prize Resistance Welding Mfrs. Assn., 1950, 51, 52, 53. Registered profl. engr., N.Y. Mem. Am. Welding Soc. (bd. nat. dirs. 1960-63, nat. v.p. 1965-68, nat. pres. 1968-69; Ednl. Lecture series 1955, Adams lectr., 1958, Samuel Wylie Miller Meml. medal 1959, Adams Meml. membership award 1965), Am. Soc. Metals (chmn. Eastern N.Y. chpt. 1947), Am. Inst. Mining, Metall. and Petroleum Engrs., Am. Soc. Testing and Materials, Am. Soc. Engring. Edn., Sigma Xi, Tau Beta Pi, Phi Kappa Tau (nat. councilor 1947-53), Phi Lambda Upsilon. Kiwanian (pres. Poestenkill 1953-54). Contbr. numerous articles to profl. jours. Office: Rensselaer Polytech Inst Troy NY 12181

NIPSON, HERBERT, journalist; b. Asheville, N.C., July 26, 1916; s. John William and Annie (Moore) N.; B.A., Pa. State Coll., 1940; M.F.A., State U. Iowa, 1948; m. E. Velvin Campbell, Jan. 3, 1942; children—Herbert Edwin, Maria Felice. Editor, Brown Am. mag., Phila., 1940-41; asso. editor Ebony mag., 1949-51, co-mng. editor, 1951-68, mng. editor, 1963-67, exec. editor, 1967—. Mem. Joseph Jefferson Com., Chgo., 1971—, Ill. Arts Council, 1972—. Bd. govs. Urban Gateways; chmn. bd. dirs. Southside Community Art Center. Served with Q.M.C., AUS, 1941-45. Recipient Journalism award Capital Press Club, 1965; named Distinguished Alumnus, Pa. State U., 1973; named to U. Iowa Journalism Hall of Fame, 1977. Mem. NAACP, Urban League, Phi Eta Sigma, Sigma Delta Chi. Co-editor: White on Black, 1964. Home: 7724 Dr Martin Luther King Dr Chicago IL 60619 Office: 820 S Michigan Ave Chicago IL 60605

NIRENBERG, LOUIS, mathematician; b. Hamilton, Ont., Can., Feb. 28, 1925; s. Zuzie and Bina (Katz) N.; came to U.S., 1945, naturalized, 1954; B.Sc., McGill U., Montreal, 1945; M.S., N.Y. U., 1947, Ph.D., 1949; m. Susan Blank, Jan. 25, 1948; children—Marc, Lisa. Mem. faculty N.Y. U., 1949—, prof. math., 1957—, dir. Courant Inst., 1970-72; visitor Inst. Advanced Study, 1958. NRC fellow, 1951-52; Sloan Found. fellow, 1958-60; Guggenheim Found. fellow, 1966-67, 75-76; Fulbright fellow, 1965. Mem. Nat. Acad. Scis., Am. Acad. Arts and Scis., Am. Math. Soc. (v.p. 1976-78), M. Bôcher prize 1959). Author research articles. Home: 221 W 82d St New York NY 10024 Office: Courant Inst 251 Mercer St New York NY 10012

NIRENBERG, MARSHALL WARREN, biochemist; b. N.Y.C., Apr. 10, 1927; s. Harry Edward and Minerva (Bykowsky) N.; B.S. in Zoology, U. Fla., 1948, M.S., 1952; Ph.D. in Biochemistry, U. Mich., 1957; m. Perola Zaltzman, July 14, 1961. Postdoctoral fellow Am. Cancer Soc. at NIH, 1957-59; postdoctoral fellow USPHS at NIH, 1959-60; mem. staff NIH, 1960—, research biochemist, chief lab. biochem. genetics Nat. Heart, Lung and Blood Inst., 1962—; spl. research mechanism protein synthesis, genetic code, nucleic acids, regulatory mechanisms in synthesis macromolecules, neurobiology. Recipient Molecular Biology award Nat. Acad. Scis., 1962, award in biol. scis. Washington Acad. Scis., 1962, medal HEW, 1964, Modern Medicine award, 1963, Harrison Howe award Am. Chem. Soc., 1964, Nat. Medal Sci., Pres. Johnson, 1965, Hildebrand award Am. Chem. Soc., 1966, Research Corp. award, 1966, A.C.P. award, 1967, Gairdner Found. award merit, Can., 1967, Prix Charles Leopold Meyer, French Acad. Scis., 1967, Franklin medal Franklin Inst., 1968, Albert Lasker Med. Research award, 1968, Priestly award, 1968; co-recipient Louisa Gross Horowitz prize Columbia, 1968, Nobel prize in medicine and physiology, 1968. Fellow AAAS, N.Y. Acad. Scis.; mem. Am. Soc. Biol. Chemists, Am. Chem. Soc. (Paul Lewis award enzyme chemistry 1964), Am. Acad. Arts and Scis., Biophys. Soc., Nat. Acad. Scis., Washington Acad. Scis., Soc. for Study Devel. and Growth, Harvey Soc. (hon.), Leopoldina Deutsche Akademie der Naturforscher, Pontificial Acad. Scis. Office: Nat Heart Inst NIH Lab Biochem Genetics Bethesda MD 20014

NISBET, JERRY J., educator; b. Palisade, Colo., Nov. 8, 1924; s. George Allen and Rena May (Smith) N.; A.A., Mesa Coll., 1947; A.B., U. No. Colo., 1949, A.M., 1950; Ph.D., Purdue U., 1958; m. Janice Ann Hampton, Aug. 1, 1948; children—Caroline, Donald. Mem. faculty Ball State U., Muncie, Ind., 1950—, adminstrv. asst. to head sci. dept., 1958-65, chmn. biology dept., 1965-74, coordinater univ. evaluations, 1974-77, dir. Inst. Environ. Studies, 1974-78, chmn. Grad. Council, 1963-64, 66-68, 70-72, 76—, dir. sci. doctoral programs, 1965-74 vice chmn. Univ. Senate, 1968-69. Dir. NSF Summer Insts., 1960, 62-64, 66-68, NSF Acad. Year Insts., 1968-71; fund asso. nat. project on elevating coll. teaching, 1975-77; council rep. Central States Univs., Inc., 1967-72, vice chmn. council, 1970-71, chmn. council, 1971-72, mem. bd., 1969-76, sec. bd. and council, 1968-70, pres. elect bd., 1975, pres. bd., 1976. Vice chmn. Nat. Assn. Biology Tchrs.-Outstanding Biology Tchrs. Awards Program, 1964-65, dir., 1965-67; mem. sci. adv. council Ind. Dept. Pub. Instrn., 1972-76; mem. Ind. Lt. Gov.'s Sci. Adv. Com., 1973-77. Served with AUS, 1942-46; ETO. Fellow Ind. Acad. Sci. (sec. 1973-74, pres. 1978); mem. Ind. Coll. Biology Tchrs. Assn. (hon. pres.), Nat. Assn. Biology Tchrs. (dir. Region III 1966-68, state chmn. Outstanding Biology Tchr. Awards program 1963-65), AAAS, Am. Inst. Biol. Sci., Nat. Assn. Research in Sci. Teaching, Nat. Sci. Tchrs. Assn., Sigma Xi. Mason (K.T., Shriner), Kiwanian. Contbr. articles to profl. jours. Home: 2351 Warwick Rd Muncie IN 47304

NISBET, ROBERT A., historian, sociologist; b. Los Angeles, Sept. 30, 1913; s. Henry S. and Cynthia (Jenifer) N.; A.B., U. Calif., 1936, M.A., 1937, Ph.D., 1939; L.H.D., Hofstra U., 1974; m. Emily P. Heron (div.); children—Martha Rehrman, Constance; m. 2d, Caroline Burks Kirkpatrick; 1 dau., Ann. Instr. social instns. U. Calif. at Berkeley, 1939-43, asst. dean Coll. Letters and Sci., 1942-43, 46, asst. prof. social instns., 1943-48, asso. prof. sociology, 1948-52; prof. sociology U. Calif., Riverside, 1953-72, vice chancellor, 1960-63, dean Coll. Letters and Sci., 1953-63; vis. prof. Columbia U., 1949, Albert Schweitzer prof. humanities, 1974-78, emeritus, 1978—; resident scholar Am. Enterprise Inst., Washington, 1978—; prof. history and sociology U. Ariz., 1972-74; vis. prof. U. Bologna, Italy, 1956-57; Rieker lectr. U. Ariz., 1956; lectr. all univs. Calif., 1961; Guggenheim fellow, 1963-64; Cooper lectr. Swarthmore Coll., 1966; John Dewey lectr. John Dewey Soc., 1970; William A. Neilson research prof. Smith Coll., 1971-72; Blazer lectr. U. Ky., 1971; Phi Beta Kappa Nat. vis. scholar, 1971-72; vis. fellow Princeton U., 1963-64; Johns Hopkins Centennial scholar, 1975-76; W.G. Sumner lectr. Yale U., 1976. Mem. Nat. Council Humanities, 1975-78; mem. N.Y. Gov.'s Health Adv. Council, 1975-76; mem. Parkman Prize Com., 1978—; bd. dirs. Am. Council Learned Socs., 1974-79, Council Acad. Advisers, Am. Enterprise Inst., Washington, 1972—. Served with AUS, 1943-45; PTO. Decorated cavaliere ufficiale Order of Merit (Italy); recipient Berkeley citation U. Calif. at Berkeley, 1970. Rockefeller Found. grantee, 1975-78. Fellow Am. Acad. Arts and Scis. (councillor 1977-80), Am. Philos. Soc. (councillor 1977-80), Soc. Am. Historians; mem. Société Europèene de Culture, Columbia Soc. Fellows, Institut Internationale de Sociologie, Phi Beta Kappa. Clubs: Century Assn. (N.Y.C.); City Tavern (Washington). Author: The Quest for Community, 1953; Human Relations in Administration, 1956; Emile Durkheim, 1965; The Sociological Tradition, 1966; Tradition and Revolt, 1968; Social Change and History, 1969; The Social Bond, 1970; The Degradation of the Academic Dogma, 1971; The Social Philosophers, 1973; The Sociology of Emile Durkheim, 1974; Twilight of Authority, 1975; Sociology as an Art Form, 1976; History of the Idea of Progress, 1979; co-editor: Contemporary Social Problems, 1976; History of Sociological Analysis, 1978; bd. editors Am. Jour. Sociology, 1970-74; mem. publ. com. The Public Interest, 1976—; mem. editorial bd. The American Scholar, 1975—. Contbr. articles to profl. jours. Address: 2828 Wisconsin Ave NW Washington DC 20007

NISHIMURA, PETE HIDEO, oral surgeon; b. Hilo, Hawaii, Aug. 7, 1922; s. Hideichi and Satsuki N.; student U. Hawaii, 1940-44; D.D.S., U. Mo., 1947; M.S.D., Northwestern U., 1949; m. Tomoe Nishimura, June, 1949; children—Dennis Dean, Grant Neil, Dawn Naomi. Practice dentistry specializing in oral surgery, Honolulu, 1952—, pres. Oral Surgery Group, 1978—; mem. council Nat. Bd. Dental Examination; dir. Hawaii Dental Service, 1962-70, pres., 1970-72, 76-78; pres. State Bd. Dental Examiners. Served with U.S. Army, 1952-54. Fellow Am. Coll. Dentists; mem. Hawaii Dental Assn. (past pres.), Delta Dental Plans Assn. (dir.), Honolulu County Dental Soc., ADA, Hawaii Soc. Oral Surgeons, Am. Assn. Oral and Maxillofacial Surgeons, Am. Assn. Dental Examiners, Pierre Fauchard Acad. Democrat. Home: 494 Halemaumau St Honolulu HI 96821 Office: 848 S Beretania St Honolulu HI 96813

NISHITANI, MARTHA, dancer; b. Seattle, Feb. 27, 1920; d. Denjiro and Jin (Aoto) Nishitani; B.A. in Comparative Arts, U. Wash., 1958; studied with Eleanor King, Mary Ann Wells, Perry Mansfield, Cornish Sch., Conn. Coll. Sch. Dance, Long Beach State U. Dancer, Eleanor King Co., Seattle, 1946-50; founder, dir. Martha Nishitani Modern Dance Sch. and Co., Seattle, 1950—; dance dir. Helen Bush Sch. and Central YWCA, 1951-54; choreographer U. Wash. Opera Theater, 1955-65, Intiman Theater, 1972—; dance films Channel 9 Ednl. TV, 1967-68; dance instr. Elementary and Secondary Edn. Act Program, 1966; dance specialist spl. edn. program Shoreline Pub. Schs., 1970-72; condr. workshops and concerts King County Youth Correctional Instns., 1972-73; lectr., demonstrator numerous colls., festivals, convs., childrens theater. Dance adv. counsel Wash. Cultural Enrichment Program; dance adv. bd. Seattle Parks and Recreation. Recipient Beta Sigma Phi Matrix Table award, 1968. Trustee Allied Arts Seattle, 1967. Mem. Am. Dance Guild (exec. com. 1961-63), Com. Research in Dance, Seattle Art Mus., Smithsonian Assos., Progressive Animal Welfare Soc. Author articles on dance. Address: 4205 University Way NE PO Box 5264 Seattle WA 98105. *Until a fews years ago a compelling force within me would let nothing interfere with performing, teaching, and directing dance. My belief: "I must be selfish about that which means most to me." This dedication was in constant battle with loneliness, frugality and neglect of loved ones. My first solo dance was Credo in Conflict. I have earned a degree of success, satisfaction, joy and recognition. My thoughts are now that I have learned to pursue a balance in life as I battle. The scars of selfishness persist but the broader view brings validity to my beliefs.*

NISHKIAN, BYRON LEVON, cons. engr.; b. San Francisco, Jan. 28, 1916; s. Levon Hagop and Elsie Sarah (Adams) N.; B.S., U. Calif., Berkeley, 1940; m. Elvira Elizabeth Huenergardt, June 18, 1938; children—Bonnie Dale, Barry Levon, Levon Hall. With L.H. Nishkian, Cons. Engr., San Francisco, 1940-42, 1945-47; prin. Byron L. Nishkian, Cons. Engr., San Francisco, 1947-70; pres. Nishkian, Hammill & Assos., Cons. Engrs., San Francisco, 1970—; pres., co-ordinator, co-founder Alpine Meadows Ski Area, Tahoe City, Calif. Trustee World Affairs Council No. Calif., No. Calif. Soc. Prevention Cruelty to Animals; mem. Waterfront Adv. Com. San Francisco Bay; mem. U.S. Olympic Ski Games Com., 1961-68. Served with USN, 1942-45. Named to U.S. Ski Hall of Fame, 1976. Fellow ASCE, Am. Cons. Engrs. Council; mem. Structural Engrs. Assn. Calif., Seismol. Soc. Am., Engrs. Club, Internat. Assn. Bridge and Structural Engrs., Wine and Food Soc., Calif. Vintage Wine Soc. (pres.), U.S. (pres. 1965-68), Far West (pres. 1959-62) ski assns., Fedn. Internat. de Ski. Democrat. Clubs: The Family, Bohemian, Olympic, San Francisco Golf, World Trade. Home: 65 Saint Germain Ave San Francisco CA 94114 Office: 1 Holland Ct San Francisco CA 94103

NISKA, MARALIN, soprano; b. San Pedro, Calif., Nov. 16; d. William Albert and Vera Zoe (Stott) Dice; B.A. in Edn., Long Beach U.; M.A. in English Lit., UCLA; m. William Mullen, May, 1970; stepchildren—Robert, Stuart. Leading roles in maj. opera house include: Traviata, Manon Lescaut, Madame Butterfly, Tosca, Medea, Salome; appeared in opera houses, including: Met. Opera House, N.Y.C. Opera, San Francisco Opera, Lyric Opera Chgo., Boston Opera, Houston Opera, San Diego Opera, Ft. Worth Opera; appeared in live telecast of La Boheme, Met. Opera, 1977; created role of Emilia Marty in The Makropoulos Affair, N.Y.C. Opera, 1970; appeared as Minnie in radio broadcast of Fanciulla del West, N.Y. State Theatre. Named Woman of Yr., Los Angeles Times, 1967. Mem. Am. Guild Mus. Artists (bd. govs.), Young Audiences (exec. bd.). Office: care Tony Hartmann Assos 250 W 57th St Suite 1128A New York NY 10019

NISKA, MARALIN, soprano; b. San Pedro, Calif., Nov. 16; d. William Albert and Vera Zoe (Stott) Dice; B.A., U. Calif., Los Angeles; m. William Mullen, May 23, 1970; stepchildren—Robert, Stuart. Eight roles with Met. Nat. Co. including: Violetta in La Traviata, Cio-Cio San in Madama Butterfly, Susannah in Susannah, Frasquita in Carmen, Musetta in La Boheme, 1965-67; twenty-five roles with N.Y. City Opera including: Countess in Marriage of Figaro, Nedda in I Pagliacci, Governess in Turn of the Screw, Marquerite in Faust, Tosca in Tosca, 1967-77; roles with Met. Opera include Mussetta, Nedda, Salome, Elvira in Don Giovanni, 1972-77, opera houses throughout U.S., Europe, Israel, Mex.; bd. dirs. Young Audiences. Pres. Democratic Club, San Pedro, 1964-65. Mem. AFTRA, Screen Actors Guild, Am. Guild Musical Artists (bd. govs.), Actors Equity.

NISONOFF, ALFRED, biochemist, educator; b. N.Y.C., Jan. 26, 1923; s. Hyman and Lillian (Klein) N.; B.S. (State scholar), Rutgers U., 1942; M.A., Johns Hopkins U., 1948, Ph.D. (AEC fellow), 1951; m. Sarah Weiseman, July 17, 1946; children—Donald Michael, Linda Ann. Postdoctoral fellow Johns Hopkins Med. Sch., 1951-52; research chemist U.S. Rubber Co., Naugatuck, Conn., 1952-54; sr. cancer research scientist Roswell Park Meml. Inst., Buffalo, 1954-57, asso. cancer research scientist, 1957-60; asso. prof. microbiology U. Ill., Urbana, 1960-62, prof., 1962-66, prof. microbiology Coll. Medicine, Chgo., 1966-69, head dept. biol. chemistry, 1969-75; prof. biology Rosenstiel Research Center, Brandeis U., Waltham, Mass., 1975—. Mem. grant rev. bds. allergy and immunology study sect. NIH, 1965-67, 71-74, Nat. Multiple Sclerosis Soc., 1972-75, 77—; mem. organizing com. 1st Internat. Congress Immunology, 1970—; invited lectr. 100th Anniversary of Birth of Dr. Jules Bordet, Brussels, 1970. Served to lt. (j.g.) USNR, 1943-46. Recipient Research Career award NIH, 1962-69; Pasteur Inst. medal, 1970. Mem. Am. Assn. Immunologists, Am. Soc. Biol. Chemists, AAUP, Belgian Royal Acad. Medicine (fgn. corr.), Phi Beta Kappa, Sigma Xi, Phi Lambda Upsilon. Author: The Antibody Molecule, 1975. Editorial bd. Jour. Immunology, 1962-67, 69-74, sect. editor, 1971-74, sr. editor, 1975-79; editorial bd. Immunochemistry, 1964-70; Bacteriological Revs., 1968-70, Jour. Exptl. Medicine, 1974-78; contbr. articles to profl. jours. Home: 96 Booth St Needham MA 02194 Office: Dept Biology Rosenstiel Research Center Brandeis Univ Waltham MA 02154

NISSEN, CLYDE THEODORE, assn. mgmt. firm exec., lawyer; b. Chgo., Jan. 11, 1912; s. Paul P. and Johanna J. (Jensen) N.; B.S., Northwestern U., 1932, J.D., 1935; m. Doris B. Olson, July 11, 1942; children—Karen Elizabeth, David R. Asso. editor Am. Law Book Co., Bklyn., 1935-40; asst. dir. Limited Price Variety Stores Assn., N.Y.C., 1940-50; pres. Trade Group Assos., N.Y.C., 1950—; exec. dir. Builders Hardware Mfrs. Assn., Essential Oil Assn. U.S.A. Mem. bd. zoning appeals, Peekskill, N.Y., 1958-62, chmn., 1961-62. Served to capt. AUS, 1942-45, 50-52. Mem. Inst. Assn. Mgmt. Cos., Am., N.Y. (pres. 1964) socs. assns. execs. Home: 1110 Hudson Ave Peekskill NY 10566 Office: 60 E 42d St New York NY 10017

NISSIM, RUDOLF, assn. musical cons.; b. Vienna, Austria, Jan. 25, 1901; s. Alfred and Marie (Bermann) N.; came to U.S., 1940, naturalized, 1945; student in Music Theory and Piano Acad. of Music, Vienna, 1920-24; LL.D., U. Vienna, 1924, postgrad. in Musicology Faculty of Philosophy, 1925-27. Practice law, Vienna, 1925; legal cons. Austrian Soc. Authors, Composers and Music Pubs., 1928-31, mng. dir., 1931-38; with ASCAP, 1940—, founder, head dept. serious music, 1942-75, head fgn. dept., 1947-75, cons. for symphonic and concert music, 1975—. ASCAP-Rudolf Nissim Fellowships established by ASCAP, 1975. Editor Austrian Authors' Jour., 1929-38. Contbr. articles to Austrian Authors' Jour., ASCAP Today. Office: 1 Lincoln Plaza New York NY 10023

NISWONGER, C. ROLLIN, educator; b. Pitsburg, Ohio, Mar. 24, 1907; s. Clifford O. and Edith Rose (Vance) N.; S.B., Miami U., Oxford, Ohio, 1929, LL.D., 1973; S.M., U. Ill., 1931; Ph.D., Ohio State U., 1950; m. Sue Janes, Aug. 22, 1938; children—Cynthia Sue, Thomas Rollin. Asst. instr. accounting U. Ill. 1929-31; instr. accounting Wash. State U., 1931-35; asst. prof. accounting Miami U., 1935-41, asso. prof., 1941-47, prof., 1947-72, emeritus, 1972—, head dept., 1947-66, asst. dean Sch. Bus. Adminstrn., 1940-56, acting dean, 1954-55, dir. summer session, 1946-48; cons. Office of U.S. Comptroller Gen., 1955-58; accounting cons. OPA, 1943. Served as lt. Supply Corps, USNR, cost inspection service, 1944-46. C.P.A., Washington, Ohio. Mem. Am. Inst. of C.P.A.'s, Financial Execs. Inst., Am. Accounting Assn. (pres. 1958), Ohio Soc. C.P.A.'s, Phi Beta Kappa, Beta Gamma Sigma, Sigma Chi, Beta Alpha Psi (nat. pres. 1962-63), Delta Sigma Pi (Delta Sig of Year 1978), Omicron Delta Kappa. Co-author: Federal Tax Accounting, ann. edits., 1940-46; Income Tax Procedure, ann. edits., 1947-67; Accounting Principles, 6th thru 12th edits., 1953-77. Contbr. to jours. Home: 8 Robin Ct Oxford OH 45056

NITESCU, TRAJAN, oil co. exec.; b. Craiova, Rumania, Oct. 11, 1902; s. Ioan and Elena (Becheru) N.; petroleum engr., Poly. Inst. Bucharest, 1924; m. Florica Constantineanu, Sept. 29, 1929. Engr., Dept. Industry and Commerce of Rumania, 1924-26; petroleum engr. Concordia Oil Co., Rumanian subsidiary of Petrofina, 1926-46; with Romano-Americana, Rumanian subsidiary Standard Esso, 1946-48, mng. dir., 1948; pres., mng. dir. Canadian Fina Oil Ltd., Calgary, Alta., 1950-66, chmn. bd., chief exec. officer, 1966—. Apptd. Consul of Belgium in Calgary, 1958—. Served as flying officer Rumanian Air Force, 1940-42. Clubs: Ranchmen's, Petroleum, Golf and Country (Calgary). Home: 409 Rutland House 3316 Rideau Pl SW Calgary AB T2S 1Z4 Canada Office: Canadian Fina Oil Ltd 736 8th Ave SW Calgary AB Canada

NITOWSKY, HAROLD MARTIN, physician, educator; b. Bklyn., Feb. 12, 1925; s. Max and Fannie (Gershowitz) N.; A.B., N.Y. U., 1944, M.D., 1947; M.S., U. Colo., 1952; m. Myra Heller, Nov. 28, 1954; children—Fran Ellen, Daniel Howard. Intern, Mt. Sinai Hosp., N.Y.C., 1947-48; resident pediatrics U. Colo. Med. Center, 1948-50; USPHS postdoctoral fellow U. Colo., 1950-51; staff Sinai Hosp., Balt., 1953-67, dir. pediatric research, 1960-67; faculty Johns Hopkins Sch. Medicine, 1953-67, asso. prof. pediatrics, 1962-67; prof. pediatrics and genetics Albert Einstein Coll. Medicine, 1967—; cons., Nat. Inst. Child Health and Human Devel., 1966—. Sr. surgeon USPHS, 1951-53. Mem. Am. Pediatric Soc., Soc. Pediatric Research. Contbr. articles on nutrition, metabolism, genetics to profl. jours. Home: 25 Devonshire Rd New Rochelle NY 10804

NITSCHE, JOHANNES CARL CHRISTIAN, educator; b. Olbernhau, Germany, Jan. 22, 1925; s. Ludwig Johannes and Irma (Raecke) N.; diplom für Mathematik, U. Göttingen, 1950; Ph.D., U. Leipzig, 1951; Privatdozent, Tech. U. Berlin, 1955; m. Carmen Dolores Mercado Delgado, July 1, 1959; children—Carmen Irma, Johannes Marcos and Ludwig Carlos (twins). Came to U.S., 1956. Asst., U. Göttingen, 1948-50; research mathematician Max Planck Institut für Strömungsforschung Göttingen, 1950-52; asst., Privatdozent Tech. U. Berlin, 1952-56; vis. asso. prof. U. Cin., 1956-57; asso. prof. U. Minn., Mpls., 1957-60, prof. math., 1960—, head Sch. Math., 1971-78; vis. prof. U. P.R., 1960-61, U. Hamburg, 1965, Tech. Hochschule Vienna, 1968, U. Bonn, 1971, 75, 77, U. Heidelberg, 1979. Mem. Am. del. joint Soviet-Am. Symposium on Partial Differential Equations, Novosibirsk, 1963, U.S.-Japan Seminar on Differential Geometry, Tokyo, 1977. Recipient Lester R. Ford award for outstanding expository writing, 1975. Fulbright research fellow Stanford, 1955-56. Mem. AAAS, Am. Math. Soc., Circolo Matematico di Palermo, Deutsche Mathematiker-Vereinigung, Edinburgh Math. Soc., Gesellschaft für Angewandte Mathematik und Mechanik, Math. Assn. Am., Österreichische Mathematische Gesellschaft, Soc. Natural Philosophy. Author: Vorlesungen über Minimalflächen, 1975; mem. editorial bd. Archive of Rational Mechanics and Analysis, 1967—. Contbr. articles to profl. jours. Home: 2765 Dean Pkwy Minneapolis MN 55416

NITZE, PAUL HENRY, corp. exec.; b. Amherst, Mass., Jan. 16, 1907; s. William A. and Anina (Hilken) N.; A.B. cum laude, Harvard, 1928; LL.D., New Sch. Social Research, Pratt Inst., Johns Hopkins; m. Phyllis Pratt, Dec. 2, 1932; children—Heidi, Peter, William II, Phyllis. With Dillon, Read & Co., investment bankers, N.Y.C., 1929-37, v.p., 1939-41; pres. P.H. Nitze & Co., Inc., 1938-39; U.S. govt. fin. dir. Coordinator, Inter-Am. Affairs; chief metals and minerals br. Bd. Econ. Warfare; dir. fgn. procurement and devel. br., Fgn. Econ. Adminstrn; spl. cons. to War Dept., 1941-44; dir., then vice chmn. U.S. Strategic Bombing Survey, 1944-46; dep. dir. Office Internat. Trade Policy, Dept. State, 1946; dep. to asst. sec. state for econ. affairs, 1948-49; dir. policy planning staff Dept. State, 1950-53; pres. Fgn. Service Ednl. Found., Washington, 1953-61; asst. sec. def. for Internat. Security Affairs, 1961-63; sec. of Navy, 1963-67; dep. sec. of def., 1967-69; mem. U.S. del. Strategic Arms Limitation Talks, 1969-74. Chmn. bd. dirs. Aspen Skiing Corp.; dir. Schroder's Inc., 20th Century-Fox Corp., Atlantic Council, Potomac Assos., Am. Med. Bldgs. Chmn. adv. council Sch. Advanced Internat. Studies, Johns Hopkins U.; pres. Potomac Preservation Inc.; chmn. policy studies Com. on Present Danger; trustee emeritus Aspen Inst. for Humanistic Studies. Recipient Medal for Merit. Author: U.S. Foreign Policy 1945-1955. Home: 3120 Woodley Rd NW Washington DC 20008 Office: 1500 Wilson Blvd Suite 1500 Arlington VA 22209

NIVEN, CHARLES FRANKLIN, JR., research exec.; b. Clemson, S.C., July 22, 1915; s. Charles F. and Ida Ellington (Wiley) N.; B.S., U. Ark., 1935; Ph.D., Cornell U., 1939; m. Treva Landers, Sept. 10, 1939; children—Katherine (Mrs. Larry Howell), William, Robert, Margaret (Mrs. Brett Simpson). Mem. faculty Cornell U., 1939-46, asso. prof., 1943-46; with Am. Meat Inst. Found., Chgo., 1946-64, sci. dir., 1961-64; mem. faculty U. Chgo., 1950-64, prof. microbiology, 1960-64; dir. research Del Monte Corp., Del Monte Corp. Research Center, Walnut Creek, Cal., 1964—. Cons. FAO, 1960-64. Bd. dirs. Bergey's Manual Trust. Mem. Am. Soc. Microbiology, Am. Chem. Soc., AAAS, Am. Pub. Health Assn., Soc. Gen. Microbiology, Inst. Food Technologists (pres. 1974-75). Contbr. articles to sci. jours. Home: 330 El Divisadero Ave Walnut Creek CA 94598 Office: 205 N Wiget Ln Walnut Creek CA 94598

NIVEN, DAVID, actor; b. Kirriemuir, Scotland, Mar. 1, 1910; s. William Graham and Lady (Comyn Platt) Niven; student Sandhurst Coll.; m. Primula Rollo (dec. 1946) 2 sons; m. 2d, Hjordis Tersmeden. Successively lumberman, newspaper writer, laundry messenger, rep. London wine firm in U.S.; motion picture debut, 1935; pictures include Without Regret, Rose Marie, Dodsworth, Beloved Enemy, Charge of the Light Brigade, Dinner at the Ritz, Four Men and a Prayer, Three Blind Mice, Dawn Patrol, Bluebeard's Eighth Wife, Wuthering Heights, Raffles, Eternally Yours, Kiss in the Dark, Toast of New Orleans, Soldiers Three, Lady Says No, The Moon is Blue, Love Lottery, Tonight's the Night, Happy Go Lovely, Around the World in 80 Days, Separate Tables, Please Don't Eat the Daisies, Ask Any Girl, Happy Anniversary, Guns of Navarone, Best of Enemies, 55 Days at Peking, The Pink Panther, Bedtime Story, Lady L, Where the Spies Are, Eye of the Devil, Casino Royale, Murder by Death, 1975, Death on the Nile, Candleshoe, Escape to Athena, 1978, A Man Called Intrepid, 1979, others; formed Four Star TV 1952; host, actor David Niven Show, TV, 1959-64; star TV show The Rogues, 1964-65. Served Highland Light Infantry, Malta; gunnery instr. revolutionists in Cuba; served from 2d lt. to col., Brit. Army, 1939-45. Recipient Legion of Merit; N.Y. Film Critics award for best actor of year in Separate Tables, 1958, Academy award for Separate Tables, 1958, N.Y. Critics award, 1960. Author: Rounding the Rugged Rocks, 1951; The Moon's A Balloon, 1971; Bring on the Empty Horses, 1975. Address: care Jess S Morgan & Co Inc 6420 Wilshire Blvd 19th Floor Los Angeles CA 90048

NIVEN, LAURENCE VAN COTT, author; b. Los Angeles, Apr. 30, 1938; s. Waldemar Van Cott and Lucy Estelle (Doheny) N.; student Calif. Inst. Tech., 1956-58; B.A. in Math., Washburn U., 1962; m. Marilyn Joyce Wisowaty, Sept. 6, 1969—. Free-lance writer; contbr. numerous stories to mags., also TV scripts. Recipient Nebula award, Hugo award (5), Best Internat. Sci. Fiction award, Lens award. Mem. Sci. Fiction Writers Am., Los Angeles Sci. Fantasy Soc. Republican. Author: Gift from Earth, 1970; All the Myriad Ways, 1971; Neutron Star, 1968; World of Ptavvs, 1966; Ringworld, 1969; (with Jerry Pournelle) The Mote In God's Eye, 1974; Protector, 1973; The Flight of the Horse, 1973; Tales of Known Space, 1975; World Out of Time, 1976; The Magic Goes Away, 1978; (with Jerry Pournelle) Inferno, 1975, Lucifer's Hammer, 1977; (with David Gerrold) The Flying Sorcerers, 1971. Address: 136 El Camino Dr Beverly Hills CA 90620. *Do your homework. If you don't know what you're talking about, you should be listening. If you're talking anyway, don't treat your listener like an idiot. If he is an idiot, find someone else to talk to.*

NIVEN, ROBERT FORBES, ret. bus. exec.; b. Los Angeles, Dec. 10, 1909; s. John Crombie and Nora (Van Cott) N.; A.B. cum laude, Yale U., 1932; m. Barbara Haskins, June 11, 1935; children—Nicholas Van Cott, Janet Niven Swords. Joined Union Oil Co., 1932, asst. sec.

and asst. treas., 1940, sec., 1947-72, officer, dir. subsidiary and affiliated cos. Union Oil Co. Calif., until 1972; sec., dir. Community Television So. Calif. Fellow J. Pierpont Morgan Library; past pres. Los Angeles Psychiat. Service, Town Hall. Trustee Claremont Men's Coll., Hathaway Home for Children, Cate Sch.; bd. dirs. past pres. Los Angeles Civic Light Opera Assn. Clubs: Bohemian (San Francisco); Old Capital; Sunset; California, Country (Los Angeles); Cypress Point (Pebble Beach). Author: Sign of the 76; Origin of the Alphabet. Home: 134 Fremont Pl Los Angeles CA 90005

NIVEN, WILLIAM, educator; b. Dundee, Scotland, Jan. 18, 1916; s. James Smith and Christina (Anderson) N.; brought to U.S., 1920, naturalized, 1926; B.B.A., Armstrong Coll., 1936; B.S., U. Calif. at Berkeley, 1944, M.B.A., 1945; m. Edna Leda Johnson, June 26, 1948; 1 son. Kenneth William. Cost accountant Elec. Products Corp., 1935-36; accountant San Francisco Examiner, 1936-37, Skinner & Hammond, 1937-38, Robert Dollar Co., 1938-42; auditor State Calif., 1942; accountant East Bay Municipal Utility Dist., 1943; instr. Stockton (Calif.) Coll., 1948-59, head bus. div., 1950-59, coordinator bus. edn., 1950-59; asst. prof. Coll. Pacific, Stockton, 1948-59; prof. accounting San Francisco State Coll., 1959—, dean Sch. Bus., 1964-74. C.P.A., Cal. Mem. Am. Inst. C.P.A.'s, Calif. Soc. C.P.A.'s, Phi Beta Kappa, Beta Alpha Psi, Beta Gamma Sigma, Delta Sigma Pi. Co-author: Elementary Accounting, 2d edit., 1960; Basic Accounting Procedures, 3d edit., 1977. Home: 1865 Brentwood Rd Oakland CA 94602 Office: 1600 Holloway St San Francisco CA 94132

NIVISON, DAVID SHEPHERD, educator; b. Farmingdale, Maine, Jan. 17, 1923; s. William and Ruth (Robinson) N.; A.B. summa cum laude, Harvard, 1946, M.A., 1948, Ph.D., 1953; m. Cornelia Green, Sept. 11, 1944; children—Louise, Helen Thom, David Gregory, James Nicholas. Instr. Chinese, Stanford, 1948-52, Ford Found. faculty fellow, 1952-53, instr. Chinese and philosophy, 1953-54; Fulbright research scholar Kyoto, Japan, 1954-55; lectr. philosophy Stanford, 1955-58, asst. prof. Chinese and philosophy, 1958-59, asso. prof., 1959-66, prof., 1966—, chmn. dept. philosophy, 1969-72, 75-76. Served with AUS, 1943-46. Recipient Prix Stanislas-Julien, Inst. de France, 1967. Am. Council Learned Socs. fellow, 1973; John Simon Guggenheim fellow, 1973-74. Mem. Assn. for Asian Studies, Am. Philos. Assn. (v.p. Pacific div. 1978-79, pres. 1979—), Am. Oriental Soc. (Western br. v.p. 1964-65, sec. 1965-70, pres., 1971-72), Am. Assn. U. Profs. (pres. No. Cal. Conf. 1964-66), Phi Beta Kappa. Author: The Life and Thought of Chang Hsüeh-ch'eng, 1738-1801, 1966; editor, co-compiler Stanford Chinese Concordance Series, 1979; co-editor: Confucianism in Action, 1959. Contbr. articles profl. jours. Home: 1169 Russell Ave Los Altos CA 94022 Office: Stanford U Philosophy Dept Stanford CA 94305

NIVISON, WILLIAM, ret. naval officer; b. Gardiner, Maine, July 12, 1924; s. William and Ruth (Robinson) N.; B.S., U.S. Naval Acad., 1946; M.A. in Internat. Affairs, George Washington U., 1966; postgrad. Naval War Coll., 1965-66; m. Betty Joyce Leeper, Mar. 19, 1949; children—Michael, Nancy, Margaret, Janet, William. Commd. ensign U.S. Navy, 1946, advanced through grades to rear adm., 1975; comdr. USS Wiltsie, 1963-65, destroyer div. 152, 1967-69, naval communication sta., Greece, 1969-71, destroyer squadron 17, 1971-73, destroyer squadron 5, 1972; dir. naval communications, 1975; dep. comdr. Naval Res., New Orleans, 1975-76; dir. naval communications, Washington, 1976-77, dir. C-E (J-6) staff EUCOM, 1977-79, ret., 1979. Decorated Legion of Merit, Bronze Star with gold star, others. Mem. U.S. Naval Inst. Republican. Episcopalian. Address: 1756 Essex St San Diego CA 92103

NIX, EDMUND ALFRED, U.S. atty; b. Eau Claire, Wis., May 24, 1929; s. Sebastian and Kathryn (Keirman) N.; B.S., Wis. State U., 1951; LL.B., U. Wis., 1954, postgrad. in speech, 1956-57; m. Mary Kathryn Nagle Daley, Apr. 27, 1968; children—Kim, Mary Kay, Norbert. Admitted to Wis. bar, 1954; practice in Eau Claire, 1954-65; dist. atty. Eau Claire County, 1958-64; U.S. atty. Western Dist. Wis., Eau Claire, 1965—; dist. atty., La Crosse County, Wis., 1975—. Co-chmn. United Fund, Eau Claire, 1958. Pres., Young Democrats Wis., 1951-53; mem. adminstrv. bd. Wis. Dem. party, 1953-54, chmn. 10th Congl. dist., 1965; sec. Kennedy for Pres. Club Wis., 1959-60. Served with AUS, 1954-56. Mem. Fed., Wis. (state chmn. crime prevention and control com.), La Crosse County bar assns., Nat. Dist. Attys. Assn. Roman Catholic. K.C., Elk. Home: 2525 Main St La Crosse WI 54601 Office: 1206 Caledonia St La Crosse WI 54601

NIX, JAMES KELLY, state edn. ofcl.; b. Oak Grove, La., Oct. 6, 1934; s. T.J. and Lilly (O'Neal) N.; B.A., N.E. La. State Coll., 1961; M.A., La. State U., 1962; m. Jo Ann McCurdy, Aug. 24, 1958; children—Elizabeth Ann, Kevin Patrick, Emily Celeste, Jennifer Kathleen. Asst. prof. govt. and pub. adminstrn. N.E. La. State U., 1965-68; exec. dir. North Delta Econ. Devel. Council, Inc., 1968-72; exec. asst. to gov. La., 1972-74, chief exec. asst. and chief of staff, 1975-76; supt. edn. La., Baton Rouge, 1976—; liaison with Edn. Commn. of States; mem. Council State Govt., So. Growth Policies Bd. Served with U.S. Army, 1955-58. Prof. James Kimbrough fellow in govt. Mem. Am. Polit. Sci. Assn., La. Tchrs. Assn., Council of Chief State Sch. Officers, La. State U. Alumni Assn., Govtl. Research Assn., La. Indsl. Devel. Execs. Assn., So. Indsl. Devel. Council, Pi Sigma Alpha. Democrat. Episcopalian. Author: Louisiana Reapportionment, 1963; Educational Status of Louisiana's Adult Population, 1964; Changes in the Louisiana Tax Structure, 1964. Office: 419 North St Baton Rouge LA 70804

NIX, ROBERT NELSON CORNELIUS, JR., state justice; b. Phila., July 13, 1928; s. Robert Nelson Cornelius and Ethel (Lanier) N.; A.B., Villanova U.; J.D., U. Pa.; postgrad. bus. adminstrn. and econs., Temple U.; m. Dorothy Lewis, July 3, 1954; children—Robert Nelson Cornelius 3d, Michael, Anthony, Jude. Admitted to Pa. bar, 1956; dep. atty. gen. Pa., 1956-58; partner firm Nix, Rhodes & Nix, Phila., 1958-68; judge Common Pleas Ct., Philadelphia County, 1968-71; justice Supreme Ct. Pa., 1972—. Bd. dirs. U.S.O., 1969—, Germantown Boys Club, 1968—; mem. council president's assos. La Salle Coll., 1971—; adv. bd. LaSalle Coll. High Sch.; bd. consultors Villanova U. Sch. Law, 1973—. Served with AUS, 1953-55. Recipient First Pa. award; Guardian Civic League Achievement award. Mem. Omega Psi Phi. K.C. Home: 6640 Lincoln Dr Philadelphia PA 19119 Office: City Hall Philadelphia PA 19107. *America is slowly becoming aware of the vast potential she possesses because of the varied backgrounds and cultures of her citizens. When this fact is fully appreciated and full advantage is taken of this resource, she will reach an unprecedented level of civilization.*

NIX, WILLIAM HAWLEY, opera dir.; b. San Jose, Calif., Mar. 30, 1933; s. Berry James and Concelia Catherine (Presho) N.; student San Francisco State Coll., 1951-52, San Jose State Coll., 1952-54; prodn. stage mgr. Sante Fe Opera, summers 1963, 64, Washington Opera Soc., 1964-65; with Met. Opera Assn., N.Y.C., 1962—, mgr. Met. Opera Studio, 1965-72, dir. studio, 1972-75; dir. regional devel. Boston Opera Co., 1975—; now with Herbert Barrett Mgmt., 1976—; lectr. performing arts secondary schs., N.Y., N.J., Conn., Mass. Mem. Lincoln Center Council on Ednl. Programs, Met. Opera Guild Edn. Com. (adjudicator), Met. Opera Nat. Council (adjudicator), Nat. Opera Inst. Home: 134 W 93d St New York City NY 10025 Office: 1860 Broadway New York City NY 10023

NIXON, AGNES ECKHARDT, TV writer; student Sch. Speech, Northwestern U.; m. Robert Nixon; 4 children. Writer for radio and TV; freelance writer for TV programs Robert Montgomery Presents, Studio One, Hallmark Hall of Fame; creator, producer, head writer daytime TV series All My Children; creator, producer daytime TV series One Life to Live; co-creator daytime TV series As The World Turns; formerly head writer daytime TV series The Guiding Light, Another World. Address: care ABC 1330 Ave Americas New York NY 10019

NIXON, ALAN CHARLES, chemist, assn. exec.; b. Workington, Eng., Oct. 10, 1908; B.Sc., U. Saskatchewan, 1929, M.Sc., 1931; Ph.D. in Chemistry, U. Calif., Berkeley, 1934; married; 2 children; naturalized. Instr. chemistry U. Calif., 1934-36, research asso., 1936-37, 72—; research chemist Shell Devel. Co., Emeryville, Calif., 1937-54, research supr., 1954-70, cons., 1970—. Chmn. Com. Sci. Soc. Pres.'s, 1973-74. Mem. Am. Chem. Soc. (pres. 1973), AAAS, Am. Inst. Aeros. and Astronautics, Combustion Inst., Catalysis Soc., Am. Inst. Chemists, Sierra Club, Sigma Xi, Alpha Chi Sigma. Address: care Wells Fargo Bldg Room 511 2140 Shattuck Ave Berkeley CA 94704 also 2727 Marin Ave Berkeley CA 94708

NIXON, EUGENE RAY, educator, chemist; b. Mt. Pleasant, Mich., Apr. 14, 1919; s. William S. and Grace (Brookens) N.; Sc.B. summa cum laude, Alma Coll., 1941; Ph.D., Brown U., 1947; m. Phyllis R. Jones, June 10, 1945; children—Cynthia L., Emily E. Research chemist Manhattan Project, 1942-46; instr. chemistry Brown U., 1947-49; mem. faculty U. Pa., Phila., 1949—, prof. chemistry, 1965—, vice dean grad. sch., 1958-62, acting chmn. dept. chemistry, 1965-66, dir. materials research lab., 1969-72; vis. prof. U. London (Eng.), 1963-64; vis. lectr. Bryn Mawr Coll., 1957-58. Mem. Am. Chem. Soc., Am. Phys. Soc., Soc. Applied Spectroscopy (Jour. award 1965), Coblentz Soc. (bd. mgrs.), Sigma Xi. Research, publs. on phys. chemistry, molecular structure and molecular spectroscopy, properties of crystals, intermolecular interactions, laser spectroscopy and laser chemistry. Home: 36 Springhouse Lane Media PA 19063 Office: Dept Chemistry U Pa Philadelphia PA 19104

NIXON, FRANK LESLIE, publisher; b. Jersey City, Feb. 19, 1919; s. George Robert Bracken and Mary Leslie (Swenarton) N.; B.A., Wesleyan U., Middletown, Conn., 1949; m. Mary Jean Jacobsen, Jan. 2, 1971; children—Todd Charles, Laura Louise, Sabina Jane, Peter George. Med. advt. editor Lederle Labs., Pearl River, N.Y., 1953-57; sales mgr. Physicians' Desk Reference, Med. Econs. Co., Oradell, N.J., 1957-69, founder, pub. Med. Lab. Observer, 1969—, Clin. Lab. Reference, 1973; pub. Clin. Laboratorian, 1974, Lab 78, 1977—; pres. PHILCOM, Ridgewood, N.J., 1977—; founder, editor F&I News, Winter Park, Fla. Pres. Elmwood Community Playhouse, Nyack, N.Y., 1956, 60. Served with AUS, 1941-45. Mem. Biomed. Mktg. Assn., Sigma Nu. Club: Tuxedo. Home: 1129 Golfside Dr Winter Park FL 32792 Office: Finance Concepts Inc 1850 Lee Rd Winter Park FL 32789. *Business is people. Everything that happens in business is controlled by people. The computer is programmed by people. In truth, so goes the personnel; so goes the business. The next time you hire someone, you'll be making a critical decision. Treat it that way. You'll come out ahead.*

NIXON, JACK LOWELL, govt. ofcl.; b. Muskogee, Okla., Jan. 5, 1926; s. Andrew Jackson and Alpha (Garrard) N.; A.B. magna cum laude, San Jose State Coll., 1948; M.A., U. Calif., 1956; m. Genevieve Jacqueline Delord, Feb. 25, 1961; 1 dau., Alexandra Solange. Tchr. Montezuma Sch., Los Gatos, Calif., 1948-49; adminstrv. employee USIS, Lille, France, 1951-52; fgn. service res. officer AID, Laos, Tunisia, Chile, U.S., Ecuador, Haiti, and Chad, 1956—. Served with U.S. Army, 1953-54. Mem. Phi Kappa Phi, Tau Delta Phi, Sigma Delta Phi, Iota Delta Phi. Author: Adonis Smiling Blindly, 1972. Home: 6908 Lamont Dr Lanham MD 20801 Office: AFR/DR/SDP/AID Dept State Washington DC 20520. *I have never labored under the illusion that I had lessons to teach to others. Rather I have sought to learn for my happiness and the betterment of my nature the lessons which are contained in most experiences in life. At times my progress has been slow; yet time's passing has always been too swift. Most people in life are eager to find a listener rather than a teller, even when a teller is what they need and are subconsciously seeking. I take care to restrict my honest listening to those voices which it benefits me to hear.*

NIXON, JOHN ERSKINE, educator; b. Pomona, Calif., June 28, 1917; s. Eugene White and Edna Maude (Blair) N.; A.B., Pomona Coll., 1939; M.A., Claremont Coll., 1941; Ed.D., U. So. Calif., 1949; m. Julia Eveleth Haskell, Feb. 10, 1945; children—Sarah (Mrs. Kris Esslinger), John H. With VA, Washington, 1946-47; prof. edn. and phys. edn. Stanford, 1949—, dir. Profl. Phys. Edn. Program, 1949—; State Dept. cons. to Egypt, 1955-56; lectr. summers U. Colo., U. Hawaii, U. Wash., U. Oreg., Alaska Methodist U.; sr. Fulbright lectr., Austria, Finland, Denmark, 1956, Norway, Eng., Scotland, Wales, 1971. Vice pres. Hamnic Corp., Palo Alto, Calif., 1964-72. Bd. dirs. Moore Sch., Burlingame, Calif., 1962-64. Served to maj. AUS, 1941-46; CBI. Mem. Am. Acad. Phys. Edn., Calif. Assn. Health, Phys. Edn. and Recreation (pres. 1960-61), Nat. Soc. for Study Edn., Am. Ednl. Research Assn., Nat. Coll. Mens Phys. Edn. Assn. (pres. 1963-64), Phi Beta Kappa, Phi Delta Kappa. Author: (with Ann E. Jewett) Physical Education Curriculum, 1963, An Introduction to Physical Education, 1974; (with Lynn Vendien) The World Today in Health, Physical Education and Recreation, 1969; (with Celeste Ulrich) Tones of Theory, 1972. Editor: Foundations of Physical Education series, 1969. Home: 732 Alvarado Ct Stanford CA 94305

NIXON, MARNI, singer; b. Altadena, Calif., Feb. 22; d. Charles Nixon and Margaret (Wittke) McEathron; student opera workshop of Los Angeles City Coll., U. Cal. at Los Angeles, U. So. Calif., also Tanglewood, Mass.; m. Ernest Gold, May 22, 1950 (div. 1969); children—Andrew Maurice, Martha Alice, Melani Christine; m. 2d, Lajos Frederick Fenster, July 23, 1971 (div. July 1975). Played violin at 4 years; studied in youth orch., 10 years; studied voice at 10 years; child actress Pasadena (Calif.) Playhouse, 1940-45; soloist Roger Wagner chorale, 1947-53; appeared with New Eng. Opera Co., Los Angeles Opera Co., also Ford Found TV Opera, 1948-63, San Francisco Spring Opera, 1966, Seattle Opera, 1971, 72, 73; classical recitals and appearances with symphony orchs. throughout U.S., Can., also Eng., Israel, Ireland; appeared on Broadway in My Fair Lady, 1964, in motion picture Sound of Music, 1964, also in numerous TV shows and night clubs; star children's ednl. TV show Boomerang, ABC-TV, 1975—; voice dubbed in for musical motion pictures; rec. artist for Columbia, Capital, RCA Victor, Educational records; dir. vocal faculty Calif. Inst. Arts, Valencia, 1970-72; pvt. tchr.; formerly dir. opera workshop Cornish Inst. Arts, Seattle. Recipient 19 Emmy awards; 2 Action for Childrens TV awards, 1977; Chgo. Film Festival award, 1977, Grammy award nominee 1st rec. Cabaret Songs and Early Songs by Arnold Schoenberg, RCA, 1977. Home: 7323 Mercer Terr Dr Mercer Island WA 98040

NIXON, RAYMOND BLALOCK, educator; b. Live Oak, Fla., June 10, 1903; s. Thomas James and Leanora Alice (Blalock) N.; Ph.B., Emory U., 1925; A.M., U. Wis., 1934; Ph.D., U. Minn., 1942; m. Amy Quillian, Dec. 24, 1928; 1 dau., Leslie (Mrs. John Hollister). Successively reporter, sports editor, telegraph editor, editorial writer, city editor Tampa (Fla.) Daily Times, 1917-24; sec. to pres. Emory U., 1924-28, asst. to pres. 1928-38, instr. journalism, 1926-28, asst. prof., 1928-33, asso. prof., 1933-40, prof. journalism, dir. div., 1940-52, alumni sec., 1927-31, editor Emory Alumnus, 1927-38; grad. asst. journalism U. Wis., 1933-34; teaching asst. U. Minn., 1939-40, vis. prof., summer 1947, prof. journalism and internat. relations, 1952-71, emeritus prof. journalism and internat. communication, 1971—; vis. prof. Inst. Communications Research, U. Ill., 1948-49, U. Calif., summer 1949, Stanford, summer, 1952, U. Pitts., summer 1953; lectr. many fgn. univs., 1957—. Acad. dir. Fgn. Assignment Tour Europe, 1951; vis. staff mem. Time mag., 1952; mem. accrediting com. Am. Council Edn. Journalism, 1946-49; v.p. UNESCO Conf. Journalism Edn. in Latin Am., 1958; dir. communication research India and Latin Am., 1966-67; cons. mass. communication UNESCO, Paris, 1959—; specialist journalism Dept. State, Europe and Middle East, 1961, Latin Am., 1962. Ford fellow study in Asia and Europe, 1957, Latin Am., 1962, 64-65; Tinker Found. fellow in Latin Am., 1969-70, 73-76; 1st U.S.-USSR journalism exchange, 1978. Recipient Disting. Service award in journalism U. Wis., 1971; Honor award for distinguished service in journalism U. Mo., 1974. Mem. Assn. Edn. Journalism (v.p. 1938-40), Internat. Assn. Mass Communication Research (pres. 1960-64, exec. com. 1965-72), World Assn. Pub. Opinion Research, Inter-Am. Press Assn., Internat. Press Inst., Am. Polit. Sci. Assn., Phi Beta Kappa (pres. Minn. 1965-66), Pi Kappa Phi (supreme historian 1926-28), Pi Delta Epsilon, Sigma Delta Chi, Omicron Delta Kappa, Kappa Tau Alpha. Congregationalist. Club: Overseas Press (N.Y.C.). Editor: Problems of the Country Weekly, 1930; Public Opinion and the Press (with C.B. Gosnell), 1933. Author: Henry W. Grady; Spokesman of the New South, 1943; Education for Journalism in Latin America, 1970. Editor Journalism Quar., 1945-64, internat. editor, 1965-68, editorial adv. bd., 1969—. Contbr. articles to newspapers, profl. jours. Home: 1578 Burton St Saint Paul MN 55108

NIXON, RICHARD MILHOUS, former President of U.S.; b. Yorba Linda, Calif., Jan. 9, 1913; s. Francis A. and Hannah (Milhous) N.; A.B., Whittier Coll., 1934; LL.B. with honors, Duke U., 1937; m. Thelma Catherine Patricia Ryan, June 21, 1940; children—Patricia (Mrs. Edward Finch Cox), Julie (Mrs. Dwight David Eisenhower II). Mem. Calif. bar, 1937-74, U.S. Supreme Ct. bar, 1947-75, N.Y. State bar, 1963-69; practiced in Whittier, Calif., 1937-42; atty. Office Price Adminstrn., Washington, Jan.-Aug. 1942; mem. 80th-81st Congresses from 12th Calif. Dist.; U.S. senator from Calif., 1950-53; v.p. of U.S., 1953-61; Republican candidate for Pres. of U.S., 1960; Republican nominee for gov. Calif., 1962; counsel firm Adams, Duque & Hazeltine, Los Angeles, 1961-63; mem. firm Mudge, Stern, Baldwin & Todd, N.Y.C., 1963-64; partner firm Nixon, Mudge, Rose, Guthrie & Alexander, N.Y.C., 1964-67, Nixon, Mudge, Rose, Guthrie, Alexander & Mitchell, N.Y.C., 1967-68; elected 37th Pres. of U.S., 1968, 72, inaugurated 1969, 73, resigned, 1974. Hon. chmn. Boys' Clubs Am.; trustee Whittier Coll., 1939-68. Served to lt. comdr. USNR, 1942-46; PTO. Mem. Order of Coif. Mem. Soc. of Friends. Author: Six Crises, 1962; RN, 1978. Address: care Grosset & Dunlap 51 Madison Ave New York NY 10010*

NIXON, ROBERT JAMES, architect; b. Ontario, Oreg., Aug. 27, 1930; s. William James and Eva Jane (Wilson) N.; B.S., U. Idaho, 1953; m. Maralice Boland, Nov. 20, 1954; children—Lillian Alice, Paul James. With archtl. firms in Dallas, Spokane and Seattle, 1956—; partner firm McClure/Nixon, Seattle, 1969-73, McClure/Nixon/Farr, Seattle and Anchorage, 1973-77, Nixon/Farr, Seattle and Anchorage, 1977—; asso. partner TRA, 1979—; dir. Pacific Inland Airlines, Environ. Works Design Center, Nixon Inc. Ranches; past chmn. Mercer Island Design Commn.; prin. works include campus plans U. Wash., 1963-68, State Capitol plans, Olympia, 1967-68, classroom and auditorium U. Alaska, Anchorage, 1972-75, U.S. Navy bachelor housing, 1969-77, Airport Terminal, Doha, Qatar, 1977-78, facilities for Imperial Iranian Air Force, 1978. Chmn. Seattle Goals Task Force, 1972. Served to 1st lt. USAF, 1953-55. Fellow AIA. Lutheran. Home: 5053 84th St SE Mercer Island WA 98040 Office: 215 Columbia Seattle WA 98104

NIXON, ROBERT PLEASANTS, electric motor mfg. co. exec.; b. Rome, Ga.; s. George Felton and Eunice (Adamson) N.; A.B. with honors in econs., Duke U., 1935; m. Helen May Hill, June 4, 1942; children—Robert H., Edward H., James R. Treas., Bus. News Pub. Co., Detroit, 1935-48; asst. to v.p. Wachovia Bank & Trust Co., Winston-Salem, N.C., 1942; auditor Jacuzzi Bros., Inc., Richmond, Calif., 1948-52; v.p., sec.-treas. Franklin Electric Co., Inc., Bluffton, Ind., 1952—, also dir.; sec. Oil Dynamics, Inc., Tulsa, 1967—; dir. Quincy Post & Lumber Co. Bd. dirs. Caylor-Nickel Hosp., Bluffton, 1974-78; pres. Wells County Found., 1972. Served with USNR, 1941-45; lt. comdr. Res. C.P.A. Mem. NAM (environ. quality com.), Risk and Ins. Mgmt. Soc., Phi Beta Kappa. Republican. Presbyterian. Clubs: Wildwood Racquet, Summit (Ft. Wayne, Ind.). Home: 630 Elm Dr Bluffton IN 46714 Office: 400 E Spring St Bluffton IN 46714

NIXON, RUTH ELIZABETH, educator; b. Webster City, Iowa, Aug. 27, 1915; d. Carl Emil and Mabel (Hay) Anderson; B.S. (Hawley scholar), U. Minn., 1937; M.A., U. Iowa, 1946; Ph.D. (grantee), State Fla. U., 1968; postgrad. U. Mex., U. Guatemala, Purdue U., Middlebury Coll.; m. George Carol Nixon, July 15, 1950; children—Clark E., Jayne Nixon Williams. Tchr., Ft. Dodge (Iowa) High Sch., 1938-43; tchr. high sch. Grosse Pointe, Mich., 1943-45; instr. Wis. State U., LaCrosse, 1945-46, prof. Spanish, 1947—, chmn. fgn. lang. dept., 1965—, supr. fgn. langs, 1968—; asso. dir. Area Latin Am. studies, U. Wis., Milw., 1972—; govt. scholar, Mex., 1946; instr. Albion (Mich.) Coll., 1946-47; adviser Viterbo Coll., 1955-65; also speaker confs. Mem. AAUW (treas. found. 1966-68, pres. LaCrosse 1964-66), Am. Guild Organists (pres. LaCrosse 1950-51), Am. Council Teaching Fgn. Langs., Am. Assn. Tchrs. Spanish and Portuguese (sec. Wis. 1968-69, v.p. Wis. 1976-77, pres. Wis. 1977-78, exec. council Wis. 1978-79), Central State Conf. Lang. Teaching (adv. council), Modern Lang. Assn., North Central Council Latinamericanists, Caribbean Studies Assn., Nat. Assn. Bilingual Edn., Wis. Assn. Fgn. Lang. Tchrs. (exec. council 1977). Republican. Methodist. Clubs: Hispanoamericano (v.p. LaCrosse 1979-80), Music Study, Latin Am. Organist Handel Organ Concerto with Youth Symphony, 1975. Home: 338 S Losey Blvd LaCrosse WI 54601 Office: University of Wisconsin LaCrosse WI 54601. *If there has been success in my life, it has been because I have tried to improve myself, to beat my own record instead of competing with others. I have tried to gain knowledge for my career but with it understanding, especially of people, those with whom I work and play. Whether or not the others understand me is not important; I must understand and appreciate them.*

NIXON, STANLEY ELKIN, cons.; b. St. John, N.B., Can., Mar. 13, 1912; s. Clarence Pengilly and Nellie Keillor (Thorne) N.; grad. high sch.; m. Marie Elizabeth Wilson, July 12, 1941; children—Martha Elizabeth, David Brooks. With Dominion Securities Corp., Ltd., Montreal, Que., Can., 1928—, partner, 1946—, v.p., 1953-62, exec. v.p., 1962-69, vice chmn., 1969-70, cons., 1973—; dir. Celanese Can., Ltd., 1971—, chmn., 1972-74; chmn., dir. Bristol Aeroplane Co. Can., Ltd., 1964—; dir. Canadian Pacific Investments, Ltd., Cominco, Ltd., Canadian Pacific (Bermuda) Ltd., Continental Ill. (Can.) Ltd., Rolls Royce Holdings N.Am., Ltd., Trizec Corp. Ltd. Can. Pub. finance specialist Royal Commn. on Dominion-Provincial Relations, 1938-39;

vice chmn. Montreal Stock Exchange, 1956-57; mem. council Montreal Bd. Trade, 1966-68. Mem. Investment Dealers Assn. Can. (pres. 1968-69). Home: 3468 Drummond St Apt 606 Montreal PQ H3G 1Y4 Canada

NIXON, THELMA CATHERINE PATRICIA RYAN (MRS. RICHARD M. NIXON), wife of former Pres. of U.S.; b. Ely, Nev., Mar. 16, 1912; grad. cum laude U. So. Calif., 1937, L.H.D., 1961; m. Richard Milhous Nixon, June 21, 1940; children—Patricia (Mrs. Edward Finch Cox), Julie (Mrs. Dwight David Eisenhower II). X-ray techinician, N.Y.C., 1931-33; tchr. high schs., Cal., 1937-41; govt. economist, 1942-45. Promoter of world wide humanitarian service, volunteerism in U.S. Decorated grand cross Order of Sun for relief work at time of massive earthquake, 1971 (Peru); grand cordon Most Venerable Order Knighthood Pioneers (Liberia), 1972; named among most admired women George Gallop polls, 1957, 68, 69, 70, 71.

NIXON, WALTER LOUIS, JR., U.S. judge; b. Biloxi, Miss., Dec. 16, 1928; s. Walter L. and Hazel (Kornman) N.; student Marion (Ala.) Mil. Inst., 1946-47, La. State U., 1947-48; J.S.D., Tulane U., 1951; m. Barbara Gill, June 5, 1976; children—Karen Adair, Walter Louis III, Courtney Kathleen. Admitted to La. bar, 1951, Miss. bar, 1952; gen. practice, Biloxi, 1952-68; judge U.S. Dist. Ct., So. Dist. Miss., 1968—. Served with USAF, 1953-55. Mem. Biloxi C. of C. (past pres., dir.), Order of Coif, Phi Delta Phi. Clubs: Elks, K.C. Office: US Dist Ct PO Drawer A Biloxi MS 39533*

NIZEL, ABRAHAM EDWARD, dentist, nutritionist; b. Boston, July 27, 1917; s. Louis and Lizza (Kurlansky) N.; D.M.D., Tufts U., 1940, M.S.D., 1952; m. Jeannette Silverstein, Nov. 15, 1942; children—David, Jonathan. Intern, Worcester (Mass.) City Hosp., 1941; pvt. practice gen. dentistry, Boston, 1946—; vis. prof. nutrition and food sci. dept. Mass. Inst. Tech., Cambridge, 1967—; prof. nutrition and preventive dentistry Tufts U. Sch. Dental Medicine, Boston, 1967—; vis. prof. Forsyth Sch. Dental Hygiene, Boston, 1967—; cons. bur. dental health edn. ADA. Served with Dental Corps, U.S. Army, 1941-46. Fellow Am. Coll. Dentists; mem. Acad. Dental Sci. (pres. 1977), ADA (Preventive Dentistry awards 1973, 75), Internat. Assn. Dental Research, Am. Inst. Nutrition, Sigma Xi, Omicron Kappa Upsilon. Jewish. Author books and articles in field of dentistry and nutrition. Home: 537 Parker St Newton Centre MA 02159 Office: 75 Federal St Boston MA 02110

NIZER, LOUIS, lawyer, author: b. London, Eng., Feb. 6, 1902; s. Joseph and Bella (Bialestock) N.; A.B., Columbia U., 1922, LL.B., 1924; numerous hon. degrees; m. Mildred Mantel Wollins, July 1939. Admitted to N.Y. bar, 1924, since practice in N.Y.C.; sr. partner firm Phillips, Nizer, Benjamin, Krim & Ballon, N.Y.C. and Washington; gen. counsel Motion Picture Assn. of Am.; lectr. in field. Paintings exhibited Hammer Gallery, N.Y.C., Permanent Art Gallery Am. Bank & Trust Co., N.Y.C. Named Lit. Father of Year, 1974. Mem. Bar Assn. City N.Y., Am., N.Y. State bar assns., A.S.C.A.P. Odd Fellow. Club: Lotos. Author: New Courts of Industry, 1935; Thinking on Your Feet, 1940; What to Do With Germany, 1944; Between You and Me, 1948; My Life in Court, 1962; The Jury Returns, 1966; The Implosion Conspiracy, 1972; Reflections Without Mirrors, 1978; work Reputation presented as play A Case of Libel, Broadway, N.Y.C. Contbr. to law revs., also mags. Home: 180 W 58th St New York City NY 10019 Office: 40 W 57th St New York City NY 10019

NOAH, HAROLD JULIUS, educator; b. London, Eng., Jan. 21, 1925; s. Abraham and Sophia (Cohen) N.; B.Sc. in Econs., London Sch. Econs. and Polit. Sci., 1946; student King's Coll., U. London, 1948-49, 52-54; Ph.D., Columbia, 1964; m. Norma Mestel, Oct. 20, 1945; children—Deborah Ann Susan, Carolyn Anne Elizabeth; m. 2d, Helen Claire Chisnall, Oct. 14, 1966; children—Adam Pierre Michael, David Harold Michael. Came to U.S., 1960. Instr. econs. Southwest London Coll. Commerce, 1948-49; asst. master, head dept. econs. Henry Thornton Sch., London, 1949-60; asst. prof. Fairleigh Dickinson U., 1960-61; mem faculty Columbia Tchrs. Coll., 1962—, prof. econs. of edn., 1969—, dir. Inst. Philosophy and Politics Edn., 1974-76, dean Coll., 1976—; vis. prof. East European Inst., Free U. Berlin, 1964-65; vis. research fellow Max Planck Soc., Inst. Ednl. Research, 1964-65, sr. vis. research scholar Internat. Assn. for Evaluation of Ednl. Achievement, Stockholm, Sweden, 1971. Cons., OECD, 1971—. Mem. Comparative and Internat. Edn. Soc. (pres. 1973-74), Am. Econ. Assn., Royal Econ. Soc., Assn. Comparative Econs., Am. Assn. Advancement Slavic Studies. Author: Financing Soviet Schools, 1967; Toward a Science of Comparative Education, 1969; The Economics of Education in The Soviet Union, 1969; Germany: Review of National Policies for Education, 1972; The National Case Study: An Empirical Comparative Study of Twenty-One Educational Systems, 1976; Canada: Review of National Policies for Education, 1976. Editor Comparative Edn. Rev., 1966-71, Soviet Education, 1970-79. Home: 560 Riverside Dr New York NY 10027 also The Lower House Separate Rd Amenia NY 12501

NOAKES, EDWARD HENRY, architect; b. Toronto, Ont., Can., July 12, 1916; s. Bertram William and Ethel Mary (Hutchinson) N.; came to U.S., 1947, naturalized, 1955; B.Arch., U. Toronto, 1946; m. Romkje Anna Oostenbrug, Jan. 6, 1946. Designer, Sir John Burnet Tail & Lorne, London, 1946; asso. Thorshov & Cerny, Mpls., 1947-52; chief hosp. designer Sherlock, Smith & Adams, Montgomery, Ala., 1952-54; prin. White, Noakes & Neubauer, Washington, 1955-57; Noakes Assos. Architects, Washington, 1958—; mem. Pres.'s Com. on Employment of Handicapped. Served with Can. Army, 1941-45. Recipient E. B. Whitten award Nat. Rehab. Assn., Honor award Md. Soc. Architects. Fellow AIA (pres. Potomac Valley chpt. 1973-74, chpt. Disting. Service award); mem. Am. Hosp. Assn., Am. Assn. Homes for Aged. Democrat. Episcopalian. Archtl. designs include: Sailors' Snug Harbor, Sea Level, N.C.; archtl. editor: Planning Homes for the Aged. Home: 10212 Lloyd Rd Potomac MD 20854 Office: 8401 Connecticut Ave Suite 402 Washington DC 20015*

NOALL, ROGER, export commodities co. exec.; b. Brigham City, Utah, Apr. 1, 1935; s. Albert and Mabel (Sorensen) N.; B.S., Utah U., 1955; LL.B., Harvard U., 1958; LL.M., N.Y. U., 1959; m. Colleen Mannion. Admitted to N.Y. State bar, 1959; partner firm Olwine, Connelly, Chase, D'Donnell & Weyher, N.Y.C., 1965-68; exec. v.p. Bunge Corp., N.Y.C., 1968—. Address: 1 Chase Manhattan Plaza New York City NY 10005

NOBACK, CHARLES ROBERT, anatomist, educator; b. N.Y.C., Feb. 15, 1916; s. Charles Victor and Beatrice (Cerny) N.; B.S., Cornell U., 1936; M.S., N.Y.U., 1938; postgrad. Columbia, 1936-38; Ph.D., U. Minn., 1942; m. Eleanor Louise Loomis, Nov. 23, 1938; children—Charles Victor, Margaret Beatrice, Ralph Theodore, Elizabeth Louise. Asst. prof. anatomy U. Ga., 1941-44; faculty L.I. Coll. Medicine, 1944-49, asso. prof., 1948-49; mem. faculty Columbia Coll. Phys. and Surg., 1949—, asso. prof. anatomy, 1953-68, prof., 1968—, acting chmn. dept., 1974-75. Fellow N.Y. Acad. Scis. (past rec. sec.); mem. AAAS, Am. Assn. Anatomists, Histochem. Soc., Internat. Primatological Soc., Am. Soc. Naturalists, Cajal Club Am. Assn. Phys. Anthropologists, Harvey Soc., Am. Acad. Neurology, Soc. Neurosci., Sigma Xi. Author: The Human Nervous System, 1967, 75; Spinal Cord, 1971; The Nervous System Introduction and Review, 1972, 77. Editor: The Primate Brain, 1970; Sensory Systems of Primates, 1978; sr. editor Advances in Primatology; series editor Contbns. to Primatology. Contbr. articles to profl. jours., sect. to Ency. Brit. Home: 116 7th St Cresskill NJ 07626 Office: Columbia U Anatomy Dept New York NY 10032

NOBACK, RICHARDSON KILBOURNE, physician, educator; b. Richmond, Va., Nov. 7, 1923; s. Gustave Joseph and Hazel (Kilborn) N.; grad. Phillips Exeter Acad., 1942; student Columbia 1942-43; M.D., Cornell U., 1947; m. Nan Jean Gates, Apr. 5, 1947; children—Carl Richardson, Robert Kilbourne, Catherine Elizabeth. Intern N.Y. Hosp., 1947-48; asst. resident, then chief resident 2d med. div. Bellevue Hosp., N.Y.C., 1948-52; research fellow Nat. Heart Inst., 1949-50; instr. medicine Cornell U. Med. Coll., 1950-53, asst. dir. comprehensive care and teaching program, 1952-53; asst. prof. medicine, dir. Syracuse dispensary State U. N.Y., Upstate Med. Center, Syracuse, 1955-56; asst. dean Coll. medicine U. Ky. Med. Center, 1956-58, asso. prof. medicine, 1956-64, dir. univ. health service, 1958-63, coordinator patient care, 1961-63, coordinator clin. affairs, 1963-64; exec. dir. Kansas City (Mo.) Gen. Hosp. and Med. Center, 1964-69; prof. medicine Sch. Medicine, U. Mo. at Kansas City, 1964—, asso. dean, 1964-69, acting dean, 1969-71, dean, 1971-78; active med. staff Kansas City Gen. Hosp., 1970—; clin. asst. vis. physician Bellevue Hosp., N.Y.C., 1952-53; physician to outpatients N.Y. Hosp., 1952-53; asst. attending physician Univ. Hosp. Good Shepard, VA Hosp., Syracuse Dispensary 1955-56; asso. attending Univ. Hosp.; cons. St. Joseph's Hosp., Central Baptist Hosp. (all Lexington, Ky.), 1957-64; cons. U. Tenn. Med. Coll., John Gaston Hosp., 1955, Norfolk (Va.) Area Med. Center Authority, 1964-72, Tex. Tech. U. Sch. Medicine, 1969-72. Asso. dir. Mo. Regional Med. Program, Kansas City, 1968-69; project dir. Western Mo. Area Health Edn. Center; mem. med. edn. rev. com. Bur. Health Professions Edn. and Manpower Tng., 1970-73; mem. biomed. library rev. com. Nat. Library Medicine, 1974-78, chmn., 1976—; cons., external adv. com. U. Mich. Sch. Medicine and Coll. Lit., Arts and Scis., 1972-74. Bd. dirs. Kansas City Mental Health Found., 1965-70, Mo. League Nursing, 1966; 1st pres., bd. dirs. Greater Lexington Swim Assn., 1960-64; bd. mem., exec. com. OEO Neighborhood Health Center; bd. dirs. Kansas City Gen. Hosp. and Med. Center, 1973-78. Served with AUS, 1943-46, to capt. USAF, 1953-55. Recipient Medal of Honor, Avila Coll., 1968; Gen. Hosp. medal, 1970. Diplomate Am. Bd. Internal Medicine. Mem. Assn. Am. Med. Colls., N.Y. Acad. Scis., AMA, Mo. Med. Assn. (ho. dels. 1973—), Jackson County Med. Soc. (dir. 1974—), IEEE, Bellevue Alumni Assn., Alpha Omega Alpha. Home: 628 W 67th St Kansas City MO 64113

NOBE, KENNETH CHARLES, educator; b. Venedy, Ill., Oct. 26, 1930; s. Elmer F. and Alvina (Froekhe) N.; B.S., So. Ill. U., 1953; M.S., Cornell U., 1954, Ph.D., 1959; m. Hazel Leona McCullough, Oct. 22, 1949; children—Sandra, Jeffrey, Michael. Marketing agt. Dept. Agr., Ithaca, N.Y., 1954-55; instr. Cornell U., 1955-56; economist Dept. Agr., Washington, 1958-61, USPHS, Denver, 1961-63, Dept. Interior, Washington, 1963-64; econ. cons. Harza Engring. Co. Internat., Lahore, West Pakistan, 1964-65; asso. prof. econs. Colo. State U., Ft. Collins, 1966-69, prof. econs., chmn. econs. dept., 1969—, chmn. exec. council Environ. Resources Center, 1970-71. Econ. adviser to dir. Water and Power Devel. Authority West Pakistan, 1964-65; cons. U.S. State Dept., AID, 1966, 76, 78, 79; chmn. Western Agrl. Econs. Council, 1976-78; cons. Dept. Agr., Republic of Philippines, 1977. Served with USAF, 1948-50. Recipient Ill. State Farmer award Future Farmers Am., 1947, Disting. Service award Colo. State U., 1979. Mem. Am. Econs. Assn., Am., Western agrl. econs. assns., Soil Conservation Soc. Am., Western Social Sci. Assn., Internat. Assn. Agrl. Econs., Omicron Delta Epsilon. Home: 3510 Terry Ridge Rd Fort Collins CO 80521

NOBILE, ARTHUR, microbiologist; b. Newark, May 6, 1920; s. Silverio and Margaret Nobile; A.B., U. Calif., 1950; m. Anne C. Carbone, Jan. 8, 1955; children—Arthur, Francine, Maria. Microbiologist, Schering Corp., Bloomfield, N.J., 1950-68; tech. dir. Organon Inc., West Orange, N.J., 1970—. Served with AUS, 1942-45. Fellow Am. Inst. Chemists; mem. Am. Chem. Soc. Patentee product, process and use of pregnadienes. Home: 15 Whitaker Pl West Caldwell NJ 07006 Office: 375 Mt Pleasant Ave West Orange NJ 07052

NOBLE, CHARLES CARMIN, civil engr.; b. Syracuse, N.Y., May 18, 1916; s. Anthony and Julia (Samar) N.; B.S., U.S. Mil. Acad., 1940; M.S. in Civil Engring., Mass. Inst. Tech., 1948; M.A. in Internat. Affairs, George Washington U., 1964; grad. Army War Coll., 1957, Nat. War Coll., 1964; m. Edith Margaret Lane, Sept. 12, 1942; children—Jeanne Lane (Mrs. Richard Davey, Jr.), Robert Charles, Barbara Lynn (Mrs. James P. O'Looney), Carol Anne (Mrs. Matthew Short), Stephen Gary. Commd. 2d lt., C.E., U.S. Army, 1940, advanced through grades to maj. gen., 1969; comdr. engr. combat bn., Europe, World War II; exec. officer Manhattan Dist., Oak Ridge, 1946-47; mem. AEC staff, 1947, Army Gen. staff, 1948-51; planner Supreme Hdqrs., Allied Powers Europe, 1951-54; dep. dist. engr. N.Y., 1954-56; comdr. engr. combat group, Ft. Benning, Ga., 1957-58; dist. engr., Louisville, 1958-60; dir. Atlas and Minuteman ICBM Constrn. Program, 1960-63; theater engr. UNC/8th U.S. Army, Korea, 1964-66; dir. constrn. Office Sec. Def., 1966-67; dir. civil works Office Chief Engrs., U.S. Army, 1967-69; chief engr. U.S. Army Europe, 1969-70; chief engr. U.S. Army Vietnam, comdg. gen. U.S. Army Engr. Command, Vietnam, 1970-71; div. engr. Lower Mississippi River Valley, pres. Mississippi River Commn., 1971-74; mgr. spl. projects Chas. T. Main Engrs., Inc., Boston, 1974-75, v.p., 1975-77 group v.p., 1977-78, exec. v.p., 1978—, also dir.; engring. agt. Atlantic-Pacific Interoceanic Canal Study Presdl. Commn.; Dept. Def. rep. Mexico-U.S. Joint Com. Mut. Disaster Assistance; army rep. Water Resources Council; mem. indsl. com. Am. Power Conf.; govt. rep. governing bd. U.S. Power Squadrons; army liaison mem. Fed. Adv. Council Regional Econ. Devel., 1967-70; mem. Pres.'s Task Force Bridge Safety, 1968; pres. U.S. Army Coastal Engring. Research Bd.; def. mem. com. Multiple Uses of the Coastal Zone, 1969-70; chmn., fed. mem. Red River Compact Commn. Decorated D.S.M. with 2 oak leaf clusters, Legion of Merit with 2 oak leaf clusters, Bronze Star, Army Commendation medal. Registered profl. engr., D.C., La., Tex., N.Y., Va., Miss. Fellow Soc. Am. Mil. Engrs. (Wheeler medal 1962), Am. Cons. Engrs. Council; mem. Internat. Assn. Navigational Congresses (chmn. Am. sect. 1969), U.S. Com. Large Dams, ASCE, Nat. Soc. Profl. Engrs., Newcomen Soc., Sigma Xi. Home: Gloucester Apt 3-G 770 Boylston St Boston MA 02199 Office: Chas T Main Engrs Inc Prudential Center Boston MA 02199

NOBLE, DANIEL EARL, radio and TV corp. exec.; b. Naugatuck, Conn., Oct. 4, 1901; s. George and Emma (Talboy) N.; summer student Harvard; B.S., Conn. State Coll., 1929; postgrad. Mass. Inst. Tech.; D.Sc. (hon.), Ariz. State Coll., 1957; m. Doraise E. Remington, July 10, 1925; (div. 1963); children—Talboy, Tryon; m. 2d, Mary Louise Lynch, Oct. 2, 1965. Instr., asst. prof. elec. engring. U. Conn., 1923-40; radio engring. cons., Conn., 1930-40; with Motorola, Inc., Chgo., 1940—, founder 3 high-tech. divs., 1940-49, successively dir. research, gen mgr. communications and electronics div., v.p. charge communications and electronics div., exec. v.p., 1949—, vice chmn. bd., chief tech. officer, 1965-70, dir., 1949-72, chmn. Motorola sci. adv. bd., 1970—; founding dir. United Bank Financial Corp., to 1976. Mem. steering group Research & Engring. Adv. Panel, Office Asst. Seg. Def., 1957-59; mem. Army Sci. Adv. Panel, 1957-64, cons. to Panel, 1964-68; chmn. panel 13 Radio Tech. Planning Bd., 1944-48; mem. nat. TV systems com. which formulated color TV standards, 1952. Past pres. bd. Phoenix Symphony Assn., 1970-71. Bd. dirs. Ariz. State U. Found.; bd. visitors Mass. Inst. Tech. Recipient Certificate Commendation from USN and U.S. Signal Corps for service during World War II; medal Achievement, Western Electronic Mfrs. Assn., 1962; Stuart Ballantine medal Franklin Inst., 1972. Fellow IEEE (dir., Edison medal 1978); mem. Nat. Acad. Engring. Patentee electronic devices. Home: 4227 N Upper Ridge Way Scottsdale AZ 85253 Office: 3102 N 56th St Phoenix AZ 85018

NOBLE, DAVID WATSON, educator; b. Princeton, N.J., Mar. 17, 1925; s. Charles John and Agnes Catherine (Konow) N.; B.A., Princeton, 1948; M.A., U. Wis., 1949, Ph.D., 1952; m. Lois Marie Keller, Aug. 2, 1944; children—David Watson, Jeffrey, Douglas, Patricia. Instr., U. Minn., Mpls., 1952-55, asst. prof., 1955-58, asso. prof., 1958-65, prof., 1965—. Recipient Distinguished Teaching awards U. Minn., 1958, 68; Am. Council Learned Socs. fellow, 1951. Mem. Phi Beta Kappa. Episcopalian. Author: The Paradox of Progressive Thought, 1958; Historians Against History, 1965; The Eternal Adam and the New World Garden, 1968; The Progressive Mind, 1970; (with Peter N. Carroll) The Restless Centuries: A History of the American People, 1973, The Free and the Unfree, 1977. Home: 2089 Commonwealth Ave St Paul MN 55108 Office: Social Sci Bldg U Minn Minneapolis MN 55455

NOBLE, DONALD EDGAR, rubber and plastics mfg. co. exec.; b. Lansing, Mich., Jan. 21, 1915; s. Philip E. and Mary (Meichie) N.; B.B.A., Western Res. U., 1939; m. Alice M. Jackson, July 8, 1939; children—David, Richard, Jeanne, Nancy. With Nat. City Bank Cleve., 1933-41; with Rubbermaid Inc., Wooster, Ohio, 1941—, v.p. charge finance, 1956-58, exec. v.p. charge finance, 1958-59, pres., gen. mgr., 1959-74, chmn. bd., chief exec. officer, 1974—, also dir.; dir. Nat. City Corp., Nat. City Bank, Stanley Works, Libbey, Owens, Ford Co. Insilco Corp. Trustee Coll. of Wooster. Mem. NAM. Rotarian. Home: 1488 Morgan St Wooster OH 44691 Office: Rubbermaid Inc Wooster OH 44691

NOBLE, ERNEST PASCAL, physician, govt. exec.; b. Baghdad, Iraq, Apr. 2, 1929; s. N. and B. Babikian; came to U.S., 1946, naturalized, 1954; B.S., U. Calif., Berkeley, 1951; Ph.D., Oreg. State U., Corvallis, 1955; M.D., Western Res. U., 1962; m. Inga Birgitta Kilströmer, May 1956; children—Lorna, Katharine, Erik. Sr. instr. biochemistry Western Res. U., 1957-62; intern in medicine Stanford (Calif.) Med. Center, 1962-63; resident in psychiatry Stanford U. Sch. Medicine, 1963-66, research asso., asst. prof. psychiatry, 1965-69; asso. prof. psychiatry, psychobiology and pharmacology, then prof. and chief neurochemistry U. Calif. Med. Sch., Irvine, 1969-76; dir. Nat. Inst. Alcohol Abuse and Alcoholism, HEW, 1976—. Fulbright scholar, 1955-56; Guggenheim fellow, 1974-75; recipient Career Devel. award HEW, 1966-69. Fellow Am. Coll. Neuropsychopharmacology; mem. Internat. Soc. Neurochemistry, N.Y. Acad. Scis. Mem. editorial bds. med. jours. Address: Nat Inst Alcohol Abuse and Alcoholism 5600 Fishers Ln Rockville MD 20857

NOBLE, JAMES VAN PETTEN, lawyer; b. Las Vegas, N.Mex., Apr. 4, 1922; s. Merrill Emmett and Martha (Van Petten) N.; student U. N.Mex., 1940-43; LL.B., J.D., U. Colo., 1949; m. Sara Jane Crail, Sept. 10, 1948; children—James Van Petten, Sara Ann, Charles Fulton. Admitted to N.Mex. bar, 1949, Navajo Nation bar, 1973; asso. firm Noble & Spiess, Las Vegas, 1949-51; partner firm Noble & Noble and predecessor, Las Vegas, 1951-60; asst. chief counsel Las Vegas Savs. Bank, 1949-59, chief counsel, 1959-63; asst. chief counsel Found. Res. Ins. Co., 1949-57, chief counsel, 1957-63; asst. chief Counsel Lloyds N.Mex. Ins. Co., 1950-57, chief counsel, 1957-63; asst. city atty. City of Las Vegas, 1950-54, spl. asst. atty. gen., 1956-57; asst. dist. atty. 4th Jud Dist., 1957-59; city atty., Las Vegas, 1958-60; asst. atty. gen. State of N.Mex., 1963-68, 1st asst. atty. gen., 1968-70; chief counsel Merc. Investment Corp., 1970—, also dir.; spl. asst. atty. gen. State Hwy. Dept. N.Mex., 1970—; dir. Las Vegas Portland Cement Co., mem. Com. Rules for Criminal Procedures and Instrns. N.Mex. Supreme Ct.; mem. N.Mex. Bar Coms. Real Property, Land Titles. Mem. exec. com., bd. dirs. N.Mex. Soc. Crippled Children; mem. Mayor's Santa Fe Action Airport Com., 1972—; bd. dirs. Las Vegas Community TV, Inc., 1959-63, Las Vegas Devel. Corp. Served with AUS, 1942-43, to 2d lt. USAAF, 1943-45. Mem. Jr. C. of C. (internat. senator 1967—, pres. N. Mex. unit 1957-58), Am., N.Mex. (exec. com. 1957-58, commn. on publs. 1964-65), San Miguel County (N.Mex.) (pres. 1958-59) bar assns., Am. Judicature Soc. Author: (with Ben S. Galland) Re-statement of the Laws of Corporations, Colorado, 1949 Home: 615 E Barcelona Rd Santa Fe NM 87501 Office: State Hwy Dept PO Box 1149 Santa Fe NM 87501

NOBLE, JOSEPH VEACH, museum exec.; b. Phila., Apr. 3, 1920; s. Joseph Hadermann and Helen Elizabeth (Veach) N.; student U. Pa., 1942; m. Olive Ashley Mooney, June 21, 1941 (dec. Sept. 1978); children—Josette, Ashley, Laurence; m. 2d, Lois Cook Cartwright, Oct. 27, 1979. Cameraman, dir. DeFrenes and Co. Studios, Phila., 1939-41; studio mgr. WPTZ, Philco TV Sta., Phila., 1941-42; studio mgr. DeFrenes and Co. Studios, 1946-49; gen. mgr. Murphy-Lillis Prodns., N.Y.C., 1949-50; exec. v.p. Film Counselors, Inc., N.Y.C., 1950-56, dir., 1950—; operating adminstr. Met. Mus. Art, 1956-67, vice dir. adminstrn., 1967-70; dir. Mus. City N.Y., 1970—; photog. salon exhibitor, 1936—; lectr. Coll. City N.Y., 1949-51. Chmn., N.Y. State Bd. Hist. Preservation, 1972-76; co-chmn. Save Venice, Inc., 1972. Trustee Archeol. Inst. Am.; trustee Brookgreen Gardens, pres., 1976—; trustee Corning Mus. of Glass. Served with AUS, 1942-46. Recipient Venice Film Festival medal for photography in sci., 1948; Sigma Xi award, 1963; Maple Leaf award Maplewood, N.J., 1966; Gold medal for The Big Apple, N.Y. Film Festival, 1979. Mem. N.Y. State Assn. Museums (pres. 1970-72), N.A.D. (medal 1976), Nat. Sculpture Soc. (medal 1978), Artists' Fellowship (medal 1978), Archeol. Inst. Am. (treas. 1963-70), Museums Council N.Y.C. (chmn. 1965-67), Am. Assn. Museums (pres. 1975-78), Soc. Promotion Hellenic Studies, Internat. Inst. Conservation Hist. and Artistic Works, Vereinigung der Freunde Antiker Kunst. Methodist (pres. 1966-68). Clubs: Maplewood Country; Explorers, Century Assn. (N.Y.C.). Author: The Techniques of Painted Attic Pottery, 1965; The Historical Murals of Maplewood, 1961; Forgery of the Etruscan Terracotta Warriors, 1961. Contbr. Ency. Brit., 1970. Home: 107 Durand Rd Maplewood NJ 07040 Office: Museum City NY Fifth Ave at 103d St New York NY 10029

NOBLE, MARSHALL HAYS, cons., former fgn. service officer; b. Culver, Ind., Feb. 22, 1923; s. Howard Frank and Sue (Nabors) N.; A.B., Princeton, 1948; certificate Oriental langs. Yale, 1949; postgrad. Cornell U., 1952-53; m. Carolie Woods Hollingsworth, July 1, 1976. Joined U.S. Fgn. Service, 1949; now cons. in info. mgmt. Served with AUS, World War II. Home: Osbrook Point Pawcatuck CT 06379 Office: Dept State Washington DC 20520

NOBLE, MERRILL EMMETT, educator, psychologist; b. Las Vegas, N.Mex., July 25, 1923; s. Merrill Emmett and Martha (Van Petten) N.; B.A., N.Mex. Highlands U., 1947; M.A., Ohio State U., 1949, Ph.D., 1951; m. Joy Lind, July 18, 1953; children—Margaret Lind, Eric Severin. Research asso. Ohio State U., 1951-54, summers

1956, 58; mem. faculty Kans. State U., 1954-67, prof. psychology, 1961-67, chmn. dept., 1962-67; prof. psychology Pa. State U., 1967—, chmn. dept., 1967-77. Vis. scientist Inst. for Perception TNO, Soesterberg, Netherlands, 1973-74, 77-78, also NATO vis. lectr. several univs. Bd. dirs. Environ. Research Found., Topeka, 1965-68. Fellow Am. Psychol. Assn. (com. on adv. services for edn. and tng. 1967-70, accreditation com. 1979—), AAAS; mem. Psychonomic Soc., Midwestern Psychol. Assn. (mem. council 1967-70), Sigma Xi. Cons. editor Psychol. Bull., 1963-64, Jour. Exptl. Psychology, 1967—; editorial bd. Acta Psychologica, 1968—. Office: Pa State U University Park PA 16802

NOBLE, RICHARD LLOYD, lawyer; b. Oklahoma City, Oct. 11, 1939; s. Samuel Lloyd and Eloise Joyce (Millard) N.; A.B. with distinction, Stanford, 1961, LL.B. (Benjamin Harrison fellow), 1964. Admitted to Calif. bar, 1964; asso. firm Cooper, White & Cooper, San Francisco, 1965-67; asso., partner firm Voegelin, Barton, Harris & Callister, Los Angeles, 1967-70; partner firm Noble, Campbell & Uhler, Los Angeles, San Francisco, 1970—. Dir. Jan-U-Wine Foods, Los Angeles, Emerson Communications Co., Los Angeles; lectr. Tax Inst. U. So. Calif., 1970. Treas. Young Republicans Calif., 1960-62. Bd. govs. St. Thomas Aquinas Coll. Recipient Hilmer Oehlman Jr. award Stanford Law Sch., 1962. Mem. Am., Los Angeles, San Francisco bar assns., State Bar Calif., Pi Sigma Alpha, Delta Sigma Rho. Republican. Clubs: Commercial, Commonwealth (San Francisco), Stock Exchange, Jonathon (Los Angeles), Beach Tennis (Pebble Beach, Calif.); Capitol Hill (Washington). Contbr. articles to legal jours. Home: 2222 Ave of Stars Los Angeles CA 90067 Office: 523 W 6th St Los Angeles CA 90017

NOBLE, ROBERT LAING, physiologist; b. Toronto, Ont., Can., Feb. 3, 1910; s. Robert Thomas and Suzannah Harriet N.; student U. Aberdeen (Scotland), 1929-31; M.D., U. Toronto, 1934; Ph.D., U. London, 1937, D.Sc., 1946; D.S.C. (hon.), U. Western Ont., London, 1973; m. Mary Aimee Eileen Dillon, 1935; children—Michael, John, Richard, Robert. Ellen Mickle fellow Middlesex Hosp., London, 1934-35, Royal Coll. Surgeons Leverhulme fellow, 1935-39; asso. prof. endocrinology McGill U., Montreal, Que., Can., 1939-47; prof. med. research, asso. dir. Collip Lab., U. Western Coll., 1947-60; dir. cancer research centre U. B.C. (Can.), Vancouver, 1960-75, emeritus profl. physiology, 1975—. Recipient Comfort Cruickshank award for cancer research Middlesex Hosp., 1964, Centennial medal Can., 1967, Discoveries award Can., 1970, Queen's Silver Jubilee medal, 1977. Fellow Royal Soc. Can., N.Y. Acad. Scis.; mem. Am. Assn. Cancer Research, Can., Brit., Am. physiol. socs., Endocrine Soc., Soc. Exptl. Biology and Medicine, N.Y., B.C. med. socs. Contbr. numerous articles on endocrinology and cancer research to profl. jours.; discovered vinblastin alkaloids; developed Nb inbred strain of rats. Home and Office: 4746 W 2d Ave Vancouver BC V6T 1B9 Canada

NOBLE, ROBERT WARREN, architect; b. Calkins, Pa., Aug. 13, 1904; s. Mervin G. and Elva A. (Spencer) N.; B. Arch., U. Pa., 1926; m. Alice Marion Dibble, June 22, 1929; children—Ann, Robert Warren, Ruth. Archtl. designer Ernest J. Mathewson, 1929-32; asso. architect Resettlement Adminstrn., Dept. Agr., Washington, 1935-37; archtl. designer William Henley Deitrick, Raleigh, N.C., 1937-48; asso. with Sydney E. Martin, 1950; partner Martin, Stewart, Noble and Partners, Phila., 1955-70; pvt. practice, Ardmore, Pa., 1970—; cons. archtl. designs U.S. Pub. Housing Authority; prin. projects include Children's Seashore House for Invalid Children, Atlantic City, 1952, Merc. Library, br. Free Library Phila., 1954, Psychiat. Hosp. for Pa. Hosp., Phila., 1956, Willets Hall, Swarthmore Coll., 1959, other coll., hosp. bldgs., U.S. Court House and Fed. Office Bldg., Phila., 1970. Recipient Gold medal Phila. chpt. A.I.A. for design Merc. Library, 1954, award of merit Nat. Honor Awards competition, 1955. Fellow AIA; mem. Pa. Soc. Architects, Phila. Art Alliance, Sigma Xi, Tau Sigma Delta. Methodist. Home and office: 2106 Chestnut Ave Ardmore PA 19003

NOBLES, EDWARD BURGESS, judge; b. Amarillo, Tex., Aug. 26, 1925; s. Mack and Frances McLemore (Burgess) N.; B.B.A., U. Tex., 1949, LL.B., 1953; postgrad. Nat. State Coll. Judiciary, 1974; m. Shirley Scott, Sept. 22, 1950; children—Anne, Claire, Charles B. With First Southwest Co., Dallas, 1949-50; admitted to Tex. bar, 1953; with Dist. Atty.'s Office, Dallas, 1953-54, County Atty.'s Office, Amarillo, 1954-55, Field Solicitors Office, Interior Dept., Amarillo, 1955; practiced in Amarillo, 1956-70; county judge Potter County, Amarillo, 1970-73; judge 108th Dist. Ct., Amarillo, 1973—; dir. Gt. Plains Nat. Bank, Amarillo Legal Aid. Pres., Family Service of Amarillo, 1969; chmn. Panhandle Regional Planning Commn., 1972; dist. chmn. Explorer Scouts, 1974. Served with USAAF, 1943-46. Mem. Tex., Amarillo (sec.-treas. 1957-58) bar assns., State Judges Assn., Phi Delta Theta. Kiwanian. Home: 2701 Sunlite St Amarillo TX 79106 Office: Potter County Court House Amarillo TX 79101

NOBLES, LAURENCE HEWIT, univ. dean; b. Spokane, Sept. 28, 1927; s. Harry and Florence (Giffin) N.; B.S., Calif. Inst. Tech., 1949, M.S., 1949; Ph.D., Harvard, 1952; m. Barbara Joanne Smith, Aug. 28, 1948; children—Heather C., Laurence F. Instr. geology Northwestern U., 1952-55, asst. prof., 1955-61, asso. prof., 1961-67, prof., 1967—, also asst. dean Coll. Arts and Scis., 1966-67, asso. dean, 1968-70, acting dean, 1970-72, dean adminstrn., 1972—. Mem. Am. Assn. Petroleum Geologists, Am. Geophys. Union, AAAS, Geol. Soc. Am., Glaciol. Soc., Chgo. Acad. Scis. (pres. 1973-78, trustee), Sigma Xi. Home: 611 Milburn St Evanston IL 60201

NOBLES, LEWIS, coll. pres.; b. Meridian, Mjss.; B.S. in Pharm. Chemistry, M.S., U. Miss.; Ph.D., U. Kans.; m. Joy Ford; children—Sandra Nobles Nash, Suzanne (dec.). Mem. faculty U. Miss., 1948-68, prof. pharm. chemistry, until 1968, dean Grad. Sch., 1960-68, coordinator univ. research, 1964-68; pres. Miss. Coll., Clinton, 1968—; chmn. bd. grants Am. Found. Pharm. Edn.; bd. dirs. Miss. Found. Med. Care; mem. Miss. Health Improvement Corp. Trustee New Orleans Baptist Theol. Sem.; deacon, lay speaker Bapt. Ch., Clinton. Mem. Acad. Pharm. Scis. (past pres. medicinal chemistry sect.), Am. Pharm. Assn. (found. award stimulation research 1966), Am. Chem. Soc., AAAS, N.Y. Acad. Scis., Chem. Soc. London, Sigma Xi, Rho Chi, Kappa Psi. Co-author: Physical and Technical Pharmacy; editorial adv. bd. Jour. Pharm. Scis., 1966. Address: Office of Pres Miss Coll PO Box 4186 Clinton MS 39058

NOBLES, WILLIAM LEWIS, coll. pres.; b. Meridian, Miss., Sept. 11, 1925; s. Julius Sidney and Ruby Rae (Roper) N.; student Ursinus Coll., 1944-45; B.S. in Pharmacy, U. Miss., 1948, M.S., 1949; Ph.D., U. Kans., 1952; NSF postdoctoral fellow, U. Mich., 1958-59; m. Joy Ford, Aug. 29, 1948; children—Sandra Jeanne (Mrs. Ben Nash), Glenda Suzanne (dec.). Mem. faculty U. Miss., 1952-68, prof. pharm. chemistry, 1955-68, dean Grad. Sch., 1960-68, coordinator univ. research, 1964-68; pres. Miss. Coll., Clinton, 1968—. Chmn. regional adv. group Miss. Regional Med. Program; mem. nat. adv. council on regional med. programs HEW, 1976-79; bd. grants Am. Found. Pharm. Ed. Trustee New Orleans Baptist Theol. Sem.; exec. bd. Andrew Jackson council Boy Scouts Am. Served to lt. (j.g.) USNR, 1944-46. Am. Found. Pharm. Edn. fellow, 1949, Gustavus A. Pfeiffer Meml. Research fellow, 1955; recipient award for stimulation of research Am. Pharm. Assn. Found., 1966. Fellow AAAS; mem. Am. Chem. Soc., Chem. Soc. Gt. Britain, N.Y. Acad. Sci., Acad. Pharm. Scis. (chmn. medicinal chemistry sect. 1967-68), Am. Pharm. Assn., Internat. Platform Assn. Jackson C. of C. (dir.), Sigma Xi, Rho Chi, Kappa Psi, Phi Eta Sigma, Pi Kappa Pi. Baptist. Rotarian. Co-author: Physical and Technical Pharmacy; contbr. to books; editorial adv. bd. Jour. Pharm. Scis., 1966—. Home: Box 4186 Clinton MS 39058

NOCE, ROBERT HENRY, neuropsychiatrist; b. Phila., Feb. 19, 1914; s. Rev. Sisto Julius and Madeleine (Saulino) N.; A.B., Kenyon Coll., 1935; M.D., U. Louisville, 1939; postgrad. U. Pa. Sch. Medicine, 1947, Langley-Porter Neuropsychiat. Inst., 1949, 52; m. Norma Macleod Arcus, 1974; 1 dau., Lisa Marie. Rotating intern Hamot Hosp., Erie, Pa., 1939-40; resident psychiatrist Warren (Pa.) State Hosp., 1940-41, staff psysician, 1946-48; staff physician Met. State Hosp., Norwalk, Calif., 1948-50; dir. clin. services Pacific State Hosp., Spadra, Calif., 1950-52; dir. clin. services Modesto (Calif.) State Hosp., 1952-58, asst. supt. psychiat. services, 1958-64; pvt. practice medicine specializing in neuropsychiatry, 1965-73. Mem. faculty postgrad. symposiums in psychiatry for physicians U. Calif., 1958, 66. Served from lt. (j.g.) to lt. comdr. M.C., USNR, 1941-46. Recipient Albert and Mary Lasker award for integration reserpine treatment mentally ill and mentally retarded, 1957; Wisdom award of honor, 1970. Life fellow Am. Psychiat. Assn. (sec. 1954, 55); fellow Royal Soc. Health; mem. Western Soc. Electroencephalography, Phi Beta Kappa, Delta Psi. Episcopalian. Author: (film) Reserpine Treatment of Psychotic Patients. Contbr. articles to profl. jours. Home: Box 189 Arcadia FL 33821 Office: G Pierce Wood Meml Hosp Box 189 Arcadia FL 33821. *I was fortunate in being raised in a Christian home. My late father was an Episcopal priest, and my eldest brother follows the same profession. All of my achievements are due to God's guidance. I feel that one must lead a balanced life, between worship, work, and leisure. Ideals, rather than material goals, should prevail at all times. Love of God and one's fellowman are of cardinal importance. Daily exercise, with observation of the marvels of nature, such as walking on the beach, promote physical and mental health.*

NOCK, FRANK FOLEY, bishop; b. Toronto, Ont., Can., Feb. 27, 1916; s. David and Beatrice Esther (Hambidge) N.; B.A., Trinity Coll., 1938, B.D., 1946, D.D. (hon.), 1957; m. Elizabeth Hope Adams, May 30, 1942; children—Nora Esther, David Allan. Ordained to ministry Anglican Ch., 1940; consecrated bishop, 1975; curate St. Matthews Ch., Toronto, 1940-42; incumbent Christ Ch., Sault Ste. Marie, Ont., 1942-45; rector St. Thomas Ch., Bracebridge, Ont., 1945-48, Ch. of the Epiphany, Sudbury, Ont., 1948-57, St. Lukes Cathedral, 1957-74; dean Diocese of Algoma, 1957-74, bishop, 1974—. Bd. dirs. Sault Ste. Marie Group Health Centre, Community Concert Assn. Conservative. Club: Rotary. Home: 134 Simpson St Sault Ste Marie ON P6A 3V4 Canada Office: Box 1168 Sault Ste Marie ON P6A 5N7 Canada

NODINE, WILLIAM EDWARD, savs. and loan assn. exec., lawyer; b. Meadville, Pa., Oct. 27, 1929; s. Frank Ernest and Mildred L. (Hazen) N.; B.A. with high honors, U. Fla., 1950, J.D. with high honors, 1951; m. Christine Randall, May 2, 1953; children—Donald, Thad, Bruce, Admitted to Fla. bar, 1951; partner firm Richards, Nodine, Gilkey, Fite, Meyer & Thompson, P.A., Clearwater, 1951—; pres. Clearwater Fed. Savs. & Loan Assn., 1972—; dir. Fla. S & L Service Corp.; mem. jud. nominating com. 6th Jud. Dist. Fla., 1974—. Chmn. Clearwater Community Fund, 1955; bd. dirs. Morton Plant Hosp. Assn., Clearwater, 1957-66; chmn. Clearwater Citizen's Com. for Sch. Bond Issue, 1976; elder Peace Meml. Presbyterian Ch., Clearwater, 1955-70; trustee Presbyn. Found., 1970-75. Served to 1st lt. AUS, 1952-54. Mem. Am., Clearwater (past pres.) bar assns., Fla. Bar, U.S. League Savs. Assns., Fla.s Savs. and Loan League (dir.), Pinellas Suncoact C. of C. (dir. 1975—). Democrat. Clubs: Springtime City Kiwanis (pres. 1963); Carlouel Yacht (commodore 1977). Office: PO Box 4608 Clearwater FL 33518

NODINE-ZELLER, DORIS EULALIA, geologist, educator; b. Ohio, Ill.; d. Harvey and Cleo E. (Howe) Nodine; A.B., U. Ill., 1946; M.S., U. Wis., 1951, Ph.D., 1954. Tech. asst. areal and engring. geology div. Ill. State Geol. Survey, 1944-46; teaching asst. dept. geology U. Kans., 1946-48; lab. technician dept. geology, U. Wis., 1951-54; cons. Shell Oil Co., Madison, Wis., 1954-55; cons. paleontologist Petrobras, Belem, Brazil, 1955-56; research asso., dept. geology U. Kans., Lawrence, 1960-63, lectr. western civilization, 1963—, mng. editor bulls., 1963-71; research asso. State Geol. Survey of Kans., Lawrence, 1963-75, asso. scientist micropaleontology, subsurface geology sect., 1976—; co-chmn. Carboniferous Foraminifera Symposium, 9th Internat. Congress Stratigraphy and Geology, Urbana, Ill., 1977-79; coordinator Central Mid-Continent Correlation of Stratigraphic Units N.Am., 1978—. Mem. AAAS, Soc. Econ. Paleontologists and Mineralogists (mem. research group Paleozoic Forams 1969—, vice chmn. 1978-79, chmn. 1979-80), Paleontol. Soc., Kans. Geol. Soc., AAUW, Assn. Earth Sci. Editors (dir. 1967-70, nat. program chmn. 1970-71, membership recruitment com. 1970-71), Sigma Xi, Sigma Delta Epsilon. Asst. editor: Treatise on Invertebrate Paleontology, 1960-63. Club: Faculty (sec. 1967-68). Contbr. articles to profl. jours. Research micropaleontology, taxonomic and stratigraphic work on endothyrid foraminifera, rhyncholites, and other invertebrate fossils, subsurface correlation and age-dating Kans. Home: 1920 Stratford Rd Lawrence KS 66044 Office: U Kans Geol Survey Lawrence KS 66044

NODTVEDT, MAGNUS, ins. co. exec.; b. St. Paul, Oct. 9, 1924; s. Magnus and Selma (Peterson) N.; student U. Notre Dame, 1942-43; B.S., U. Colo., 1948; m. Lois Roseborough, Mar. 17, 1947; children—Paula, Scott, Craig, Cynthia. Accountant, United Pacific Ins. Co., 1954-58; operations mgr. Cascade Ins. Co., 1958-63; v.p. Pilot Fire & Casualty Ins. Co., Greensboro, N.C., 1964-68; v.p. ops. Nat. Grange Mut. Ins. Co., Keene, N.H., 1968-69, exec. v.p., 1970-71, pres., chief exec. officer, 1972—, also dir.; dir. NGM Fire & Casualty Ins. Co., NGM Corp., NGM Leasing Corp., Maine Fidelity Life; bd. govs. DEVCO. Trustee NGM Charitable Found. Served in USNR; lt. comdr. Res. Mem. Alliance Am. Insurers (dir.), Ret. Officers Assn. Am. Episcopalian. Home: 84 Kendall Rd Keene NH 03431 Office: 55 West St Keene NH 03431

NOE, JERRE DONALD, educator; b. McCloud, Calif., Feb. 1, 1923; s. Charles J. and Mae H. (Linebarger) N.; B.S., U. Calif., 1943; Ph.D., Stanford, 1948; m. Mary A. Ward, Oct. 20, 1943; children—M. Sherill (Mrs. Michael F. Roberts), Jeffrey W., Russell H. Research asso. Radio Research Lab. Harvard and Am. Brit. Lab., Malvern, Eng., 1943-45; devel. engr. Hewlett-Packard Co., Palo Alto, Calif., 1946-48; research engr. Stanford Research Inst., Menlo Park, Calif., 1948-53; asst. dir. engring. research, 1954-60, exec. dir. info. sci. and engring., 1961-68; prof. computer sci. U. Wash., Seattle, 1968—, chmn. dept., 1968-76. Lectr. Stanford, 1955-68. Mem. Assn. Computing Machinery, IEEE. (nat. chmn. profl. group electronic computers 1956-57), Sigma Xi, Eta Kappa Nu, Tau Beta Pi. Tech. dir., devel. 1st computer for banking industry Bank Am. ERMA system, 1950-56. Home: 3616 Perkins Ln W Seattle WA 98199 Office: Dept Computer Science FR35 U Wash Seattle WA 98195

NOEHREN, ROBERT, organist, organ builder; b. Buffalo, Dec. 16, 1910; s. Alfred H. and Juliet (Egelhoff) N.; student Inst. Mus. Art, N.Y.C., 1929-30, Curtis Inst. Music, Phila., 1930-31; B. Mus., U. Mich., 1948; D. Mus. (hon.), Davidson Coll., 1957; m. Eloise Southern, Aug. 27, 1938; children—Judith, Arthur. Instr., Davidson Coll., 1946-49; prof., univ. organist U. Mich., 1949—; propr. organ bldg. shop, Ann Arbor, Mich., 1954—; vis. prof. U. Kan., 1975; important instruments include organ in St. John's Roman Cath. Cathedral, Milw., 1st Unitarian Ch., San Francisco, 1st Presbyn. Ch., Buffalo, St. Andrew's Epis. Ch., Newport News, Va., Calvary Epis. Ch., Rochester, Minn.; designer, cons., 1954—; concert tours Europe, 1948—; rec. artist Lyrichord, Urania, Orion, Delos records; spl. research old organs Europe, 17th and 18th century organs in France. Recipient Grande Prix du Disque. Contbr. articles profl. jours. Composer pieces for organ, piano, voice, chorus. Patentee combination action for organs. Home: 14865 Gavan Vista Rd Poway CA 92064

NOEL, JAMES LATANE, JR., U.S. judge; b. Pilot Point, Tex., Oct. 28, 1909; s. James Latane and Ina (Bobbitt) N.; B.S. in Civil Engring., So. Meth. U., 1931, B.S. in Commerce, 1932, LL.B., 1937, LL.D., 1966; m. Virginia Grubbs, Apr. 21, 1942; children—James Latane III, Carol Annelle, Edmund Orr, William David, Robert Cornelius. Asst. budget officer Dallas County, Tex., 1935-37, asst. dist. atty., 1937-38; admitted to Tex. bar, 1937; asst. atty. gen. of Tex., Austin, 1939-42, 45-46; pvt. practice, Houston, 1946-61; U.S. dist. judge So. Dist. of Tex., 1961—. Mem. U.S. Commn. of Govt. Security, Washington, 1956-58; mem. com. on inter-circuit assignments of judges U.S. Judicial Conf. Dir. Camp Fire Girls. Bd. devel. Sam Rayburn Found.; trustee So. Meth. U. Mem. Am., Houston bar assns., State Bar Tex. Democrat. Methodist (ofcl. bd.). Clubs: Galveston (Tex.) Boat; Houston Country, Terpsichore (Houston); Terpsichorean, Idlewild (Dallas). Home: 2454 Pine Valley Dr Houston TX 77019 Office: 515 Rusk Ave Houston TX 77002

NOEL, LAURENT, bishop, educator; b. St. Just de Bretenieres, Que., Can., Mar. 19, 1920; s. Remi and Albertine (Nadeau) N.; B.A., Coll. de Levis, 1940; L.Th., Laval U., 1944, L.Ph., 1948; D.Th., Inst. Angelicum, Rome, 1951. Ordained priest Roman Catholic Ch., 1944; prof. theology Laval U., 1946-48, 52-63, prof. ethics Med. Sch., 1952-63, vice rector Grand Sem., Sch. Theology, 1961-63; aux. bishop Que., 1963-74; apostolic adminstr. Diocese of Hauterive, 1974-75; bishop Diocese of Trois-Rivieres, Que., 1975—. Provincial chaplain Assn. des Infirmieres Catholiques, 1958—; chaplain Syndicat Profl. des Infirmieres Catholiques, 1958-63. Author: Precis de morale medicale, 1962. Address: Bishop's House CP 879 Trois-Rivieres PQ G9A 5J9 Canada

NOEL, MICHAEL LEE, utility exec.; b. Rapid City, S.D., Apr. 5, 1941; s. Milton George and Merel Lyreen (Roth) N.; B.S. in Finance cum laude, Calif. State U., Long Beach, 1964; M.B.A., U. So. Calif., 1973; m. Kristin Arnold, Aug. 3, 1963; children—Christy Carole, Craig Arnold. With So. Calif. Edison Co., Rosemead, 1964—, mgr. corp. planning, 1974-75, asst. treas., 1975-76, treas., 1976—; guest lectr. U. So. Calif./Calif. State U., Fullerton and Long Beach. Chmn., bd. dirs. Los Angeles Jr. C. of C. Mem. Los Angeles Soc. Financial Analysts, Pacific Coast Eecl. Assn., Los Angeles Treasury Assos. Clubs: Linborg Racquet, Los Angeles Treasurers. Home: 3908 Montego Dr Huntington Beach CA 92649 Office: 2244 Walnut Grove Ave Rosemead CA 91770

NOEL, PHILIP JORDAN, JR., army officer; b. Louisville, Mar. 3, 1914; s. Philip Jordan and Anna (Shader) N.; B.S., Western Ky. U., 1937; M.D., U. Louisville, 1941; M.B.A., George Washington U., 1963; m. Mary Katherine Sledge, May 16, 1942; children—Linda Ann (Mrs. John Thomas Pessoney), Philip Jordan III, David Sledge. Intern Walter Reed Gen. Hosp., Washington, 1941-42, resident, 1962-64; resident Louisville Gen. Hosp., 1947-50; commd. 2d lt. U.S. Army Res. 1937, advanced through grades to col., 1956; instr., dept. dir. medicine Field Service Sch., Ft. Sam Houston, Tex., 1946-47; prof., dept. head med. mil. sci. U. Louisville, 1947-51; suregeon, Korea, 1952-53, chief surg. service Army Hosp., Ft. Dix, N.J., 1953-54, Ft. Carson, Colo., 1955-58, 98th Gen. Hosp., Germany, 1958-59, 97th Gen. Hosp., Germany, 1959-61; comdr. med. dept. agy. Ft. Sam Houston, Tex., 1964-65; dep. comdr. Tripler Army Med. Center, Honolulu, 1965-68; comdr. U.S. Army Hosp., Ft. Campbell, Ky., 1968-70; dep. comdr. 44th Med. Brigade, Vietnam, 1970; comdr. U.S. Army Med. Command, surgeon U.S. Army, Vietnam, 1970-71; dir. dept. in Office Surgeon Gen., 1971-72; dir. Met. Nashville Dept. Hosps., 1972-76; med. dir. emergency services, asso. prof. surgery Vanderbilt U. Med. Center, 1977—. Dir. United Services annual drive, Ft. Campbell, Ky., 1969-70. Decorated Bronze Star with 2 oak leaf clusters. Mem. Am., Tenn. med. assns., A.C.S., Am. Coll. Chest Physicians, Pan-Pacific Surg. Assn., Assn. Mil. Surgeons, Am. Thoracic Soc., Nashville Acad. Medicine, Nashville Surg. Soc., H. William Scott Surg. Soc. Home: 5909 Robert E Lee Ct Nashville TN 37215 Office: Vanderbilt U Med Center Nashville TN 37232. *Of the many factors influencing human relationships, four assumptions have been helpful to me. First, I believe every individual desires to perform his job to the best of his ability, however well or poorly he may actually perform it. Second, all people appreciate praise for their efforts, whether or not the effort is effective. Third, no one appreciates criticism or reprimand, whether or not it may be deserved. Fourth, a single confrontation may permanently damage a relationship between people.*

NOËL HUME, IVOR, antiquary; b. London, Eng., 1927; s. Cecil and Gladys Mary (Bagshaw Mann) Noël H.; student Framlingham Coll., Suffolk, 1936-39, St. Lawrence Coll., Kent, 1942-44; L.H.D. (hon.), U. Pa., 1976. Archaeologist, Guildhall Mus. Corp., London, 1949-57; chief archaeologist Colonial Williamsburg (Va.), 1957-64, dir. dept. archaeology, 1964-72, resident archaeologist, 1972—; research asso. Smithsonian Instn., 1959—; archaeol. cons. to Govt. Jamaica, 1967-69. Vice chmn. Gov.'s Adv. Com. for Va. Research Center for Hist. Archaeology, 1967-70, mem., 1971-76; mem. rev. Panel Nat. Endowment for the Humanities, 1973-77; mem. Council Inst. Early Am. History and Culture, 1974-77. Served with Indian Army, 1944-45. Recipient spl. award for hist. archaeology U. S.C., 1975. Fellow Soc. Antiquaries London, Zool. Soc. London; mem. Soc. For Hist. Archaeology, Soc. for Post-Medieval Archaeology (v.p. 1967-76), Kent Archaeol. Soc. (Gt. Britain), Am. Assn. Museums, Va. Archeol. Soc. (hon.), English Ceramic Circle, Glass Circle. Author: Archaeology in Britain, 1953; (with Audrey Noël Hume) Handbook of Tortoises, Terrapins and Turtles, 1954; Treasure in the Thames, 1956; Great Moments in Archaeology, 1957; Here Lies Virginia, 1963; 1775: Another Part of the Field, 1966; Historical Archaeology, 1969; Artifacts of Early America, 1970; All the Best Rubbish, 1974; Early English Delftware, 1977. Contbr. articles to profl. jours. Writer-dir. film Doorway to the Past, 1968; co-writer, narrator TV film The Williamsburg File, 1976; author pseudonymous novels, 1971, 72. Home: PO Box 1711 Williamsburg VA 23185

NOER, RUDOLF J., surgeon, educator; b. Menominee, Mich., Apr. 25, 1904; s. Peter Juul and Ellen Marion (Peabody) N.; A.B., U. Wis., 1924; M.D., U. Pa., 1927; m. Anita May Showerman, June 22, 1933; children—Richard Juul, Philip Douglas. Intern Germantown Dispensary and Hosp., Phila., 1927-29; gen. practice, Wabeno, Wis., 1929-32; asst. anatomy U. Wis., 1932-34, resident surgery, 1934-37; from fellow to prof. surgery Wayne U. Coll. Medicine, 1937-52, asst. dean 1949-52; prof. surgery chmn. dept. U. Louisville Sch. Medicine, 1952-70, emeritus, 1970—, chief dept. surgery Louisville Gen. Hosp.,

1952-70; surgeon in chief Childrens Hosp., Louisville, 1961-68; sr. cons. surgery Louisville VA Hosp., 1954-70, prof. surgery U. South Fla. Coll. Medicine, Tampa, 1970-75, emeritus, 1975—. Bd. dirs. Louisville Philharmonic Soc., president, 1966-69. Served to lt. col., M.C., AUS, 1942-46. Decorated Bronze Star. Diplomate Am. Bd. Surgery. Fellow A.C.S. (v.p. 1964-65), Am. (v.p. 1963-64), So. (pres. 1968) surg. assns.; mem. Western, Central (pres. 1955) surg. assns., Am. Assn. Surgery Trauma (pres. 1963-64), Am. Assn. Anatomists, Internat. Surg. Soc. Episcopalian. Author articles on intestinal obstruction, pancreatitis, diverticular disease colon, cancer of breast. Editor: Jour. of Trauma, 1960-68. Home: 10364 Carrollwood Ln Tampa FL 33618

NOERDLINGER, PETER DAVID, astrophysicist, educator; b. N.Y.C., May 3, 1935; s. Julius Peter and Helen Caroline (Jacobs) N.; A.B. magna cum laude (Harvard Coll. Hon. fellow), Harvard Coll., 1956; Ph.D. (U.S. Steel Found. fellow 1958-59, Howard Hughes fellow 1959-60, NSF fellow 1959), Calif. Inst. Tech., 1960; m. Carol Anne White, June 1957 (div. 1962); 1 dau., Lucy Anne; m. 2d, Judy Anne Nau, Nov. 4, 1964; children—Henry Clifford, Frederick Nicholas, Rachel Holly, Victor David. Instr., U. Chgo., 1960-63, asst. prof., 1963-66; asso. prof. U. Iowa, 1966-68; asso. prof. N.Mex. Inst. Mining and Tech., 1968-69, prof., 1969-71; vis. prof. U. Calif., Santa Cruz, 1971; prof. astronomy and astrophysics Mich. State U., 1971—, acting chmn. dept. astronomy and astrophysics, 1974-75; NSF sr. resident research asso. NASA, Ames Research Center, Moffett Field, Calif., summers 1974-75, NRC sr. resident research asso., 1979—; NASA-Stanford U. summer fellow, 1969-70; NRC sr. postdoctoral research asso., summer 1971; vis. scientist Smithsonian Astrophys. Obs., Harvard U., summer 1973, High Altitude Obs., Boulder, Colo., 1977-78; sr. research asso. Astron. Inst., U. Amsterdam, summer 1976; vis. research asso. U. Colo., 1977-78; lectr. U. N.Mex., 1978. Active, Council for a Livable World, 1963-66; campus rep. Fedn. Am. Scientists, 1973-77; mem. adv. bd. Am. Friends Service Com., Chgo., 1963-66, Lansing, Mich., 1972-75. Recipient hon. mention Gravity Research Found., 1971. NSF research grantee, 1977—. Fellow Am. Phys. Soc., Royal Astron. Soc.; mem. Am. Astron. Soc., AAAS, Am. Assn. Physics Tchrs., Fedn. Am. Scientists, Internat. Astron. Union, Am. Geophys. Union, Phi Beta Kappa, Sigma Xi (award for meritorious research 1974). Quaker. Contbr. articles to sci. jours. Home: 1003 Louise St Menlo Park CA 94025 Office: NASA Ames Research Center 245-3 Moffett Field CA 94035

NOETHER, EMILIANA PASCA, historian; b. Naples, Italy; d. Guglielmo and Bianca (Dramis) Pasca; A.B., Hunter Coll., N.Y.C., 1943; M.A., Columbia, 1944, Ph.D., 1948; m. Gottfried E. Noether, Aug. 1, 1942; 1 dau., Monica Gail. Instr., then asst. prof. history Douglass Coll., Rutgers U., 1949-52; research asso. Center Internat. Studies, Mass. Inst. Tech., 1952-54; from lectr. to prof. history Regis Coll., Weston., Mass., 1959-66; prof. history Simmons Coll., Boston, 1966-68, U. Conn., Storrs, 1968—; editor Italian sect. Am. Hist. Rev., 1958-75, Recently Published Articles, 1976—. Fellow AAUW, 1946-47, 62-63, Bunting Inst., 1961-62; sr. Fulbright scholar, Florence, Italy, 1965-66; research grantee Am. Philos. Soc., summer 1970, U. Conn. Research Found., 1969-71, 73-77. Mem. Am. Hist. Assn. (council 1975-78, chmn. com. women historians 1976), Soc. Italian Studies (chmn. prize award and citation com. 1968, adv. council 1979—), Berkshire Conf. Women Historians (sec. 1962-64, pres. 1967-71), Coordinating Com. on Women in Hist. Profession, AAUW, Pi Gamma Mu. Author: Seeds of Italian Nationalism, 2d edit., 1969; also articles. Co-editor, contbr.: Modern Italy: A Topical History Since 1861, 1974. Address: Wood Hall Univ Conn Storrs CT 06268

NOETHER, GOTTFRIED EMANUEL, educator; b. Karlsruhe, Germany, Jan. 7, 1915; s. Fritz and Regina (Wuerth) N.; B.A., Ohio State U., 1940; M.A., U. Ill., 1941; Ph.D., Columbia, 1949; m. Emiliana Pasca, Aug. 1, 1942; 1 dau., Monica Gail. Instr., N.Y.U., 1949-51; faculty Boston U., 1951-68, prof., 1958-68; prof., head dept. statistics U. Conn. at Storrs, 1968—. Fulbright lectr., Germany, 1957-58, Austria, 1965-66. Served to 1st lt. AUS, 1941-45. Fellow AAAS, Am. Statis. Assn. (dir. 1971-73), Inst. Math. Statistics; mem. Internat. Statis. Assn., Math. Assn. Am., Phi Beta Kappa, Sigma Xi, Pi Mu Epsilon. Author: Elements of Nonparametric Statistics, 1967; Introduction to Statistics—A Nonparametric Approach, 2d edit., 1976; also research articles on statistics. Home: 88 Hillyndale Rd Storrs CT 06268

NOETZEL, GROVER ARCHIBALD JOSEPH, educator; b. Greenwood, Wis., June 14, 1908; s. August Herman and Coralie Marie (Van Den Bossche) N.; A.B., U. Wis., 1929, Ph.D., 1934; certificate in Econs. U. London, 1930, U. Geneva, 1936; fellow Social Sci. Research Council, 1935-36; LL.D. (hon.), Embry-Riddle U., 1976; m. Anna B. Dobbins, June 11, 1953. Instr. econs. U. S.D., 1930-32, U. Wis., 1934-35; economist Nat. Bur. Econ. Research, 1936-37; asst. prof. Temple U., 1937-40, asso. prof., 1940-46; pvt. cons. econs. and investment counselor, Phila. and N.Y.C., 1939-46; prof. econs. U. Miami (Fla.), 1946-48, dean sch. bus. adminstrn., 1948-61, dean emeritus, 1961—, prof. econs., cons. economist, 1961-72. Dir., Am. Bankers Ins. Co. Fla.; dir., chmn. investment and budget coms. Coral Gables Fed. Savs. & Loan Assn. Bd. dirs. Goodwill Industries South Fla., Med. Service Bur. Miami; trustee emeritus Embry-Riddle U., Daytona Beach, Fla. Mem. Am. Econ. Assn., Am. Finance Assn., Econ. Soc. of South Fla. (dir., pres. 1956), Artus, Phi Kappa Phi, Alpha Phi Omega, Alpha Delta Sigma, Delta Sigma Pi, Beta Gamma Sigma. Clubs: Coral Gables Country, Rivieria Country, Century (past pres.) (Coral Gables). Author: Recent Theories of Foreign Exchange, 1934; Cooperation Entre L'Universite et Les Milieux Economiques, 1956; Objectives of a Management Center, 1956; Decisions That Affect Profits, 1957; Our Longest Peacetime BoomWhere Now?, 1966; Growth of the Investment Potential of Florida, 1966; What Price Pax Americana, 1967; Consequences of Imbalance In Our Maturing Boom, 1968; Approaching Maturing of The Florida Economy, 1968; The 1969 Economy—The Case for Discipline; Options Available to the U.S.A. in International Decision Making; The Boom of the 1960's Shapes 1970's Prospects; Keynes and Inflation: An Interpretation of the Early 1970's; The 1971 Economy: Prospects and Change; 1975-A Year of Economic Decline. Home and Office: 2845 Granada Blvd Apt 1-A Coral Gables FL 33134

NOFSINGER, CHARLES WILLIAM, engring. co. exec.; b. Kansas City, Mo., Apr. 26, 1901; s. Joseph L. and Lizzie K. N.; B.S. in Mech. Engring., U. Ill., 1922; children—William M., Rowland L. Process engr. Sinclair Refining Co., 1922-26; with M.W. Kellogg Co., 1926-44; cons. engr. Sinclair Refining Co., Stratford Engring. Co., 1946-50; founder, pres., gen. mgr. C.W. Nofsinger Co., Kansas City, Mo., 1950-78, chmn. bd., chief exec. officer, 1978—; mem. exec. com. Fractionation Research, Inc., Heat Transfer Research, Inc. Fellow ASME, Am. Inst. Chem. Engrs.; mem. Am. Chem. Soc., Am. Petroleum Inst., Nat. Soc. Profl. Engrs., Mo. Soc. Profl. Engrs. Christian Scientist. Clubs: Rotary, Shriners. Patentee in field. Home: 310 W 49th St Apt 508 Kansas City MO 64112 Office: 307 E 63d St PO Box 7239 Kansas City MO 64113

NOGUCHI, ISAMU, sculptor; b. Los Angeles, Nov. 17, 1904; s. Yonejiro and Leonie (Gilmour) N.; student Columbia, 1922-24, Leonardo da Vinci Art Sch., 1924; studied with Brancusi; studied drawing Peking, China; m. Yoshiko Yamaguchi, 1953 (div. 1955). One-man shows Eugene Shoen Gallery, N.Y.C., 1928, Marie Sterner Gallery, N.Y.C., 1929, Marie Harriman Gallery, N.Y.C., 1935, Arts Club, Chgo., 1929, 32, Becker Gallery, N.Y.C., 1931, 32, Demotte Gallery, N.Y.C., 1932, Mellon Galleries, Phila., 1933, San Francisco Mus. Art, 1942, Mitsukoshi Store, Tokyo, 1951, Mus. Modern Art, Kamakura, 1952, Stable Gallery, 1953, 55, 59, Cordier and Ekstrom Gallery 1963, 65, 67, 70, 71, Claude Bernard Gallery, Paris, 1964, Whitney Mus. Modern Art, 1966, 68, Gimpel Fils and Gimpel Hanover, 1972, Pace Gallery, 1975, numerous others; exhibited numerous group shows in U.S., fgn. countries; represented in permanent collections Whitney Mus. Am. Art, Met. Mus. Art, Mus. Modern Art, N.Y.C., 140 Broadway, N.Y.C. Seattle Art Mus., Western Wash. State Coll., Bellingham, Bayerische Vereinsbank, Munich, Germany, Cleve. Mus., Art Inst. Chgo., others; important works include mural in market Rodriguez, Mexico, bas-relief A.P. Bldg., N.Y.C., gardens Keio (Japan) U., UNESCO Bldg., Paris, Beinecke Rare Book and Manuscript Library, Yale U., New Haven, Conn., Chase Manhattan Bank Plaza, N.Y.C., Billy Rose Sculpture Garden, Israeli Mus., Jerusalem, fountains at Expo '70, Osaka, Japan; fountain and sculpture John Hancock Bldg., Chgo., GSA, Seattle, IBM, Armonk, N.Y., Pepsi Co., Purchase, N.Y., Detroit Civic Center Plaza; designed 20 sets for Martha Graham ballets Frontier, 1935, Herodiade, Appalachian Spring, 1945, Dark Meadow, 1946, Ballet Orpheus; designed sets and costumes King Lear, London, 1955; designer Akari lamps. Recipient 1st prize Nat. Competition for relief at entrance to A.P. Bldg., 1938; Logan medal 63d Exhbn. Painting and Sculpture Art Inst. Chgo., 1959; Gold medal N.Y. Archtl. League, 1966; Brandeis Creative Arts award, 1966; 2d prize Soc. Four Arts Competition, Palm Beach, Fla., 1974. Guggenheim fellow, 1927-29; Bollingen fellow, 1950. Mem. Am. Inst. Art and Sci., Am. Acad. Art and Letters, N.Y. Soc. Architects. Author: A Sculptor's World, 1968. Address: 33-38 10th St Long Island City NY 11106*

NOGUCHI, THOMAS TSUNETOMI, coroner, physician, educator; b. Fukuoka, Japan, Jan. 4, 1927; s. Wataru and Tomika (Narahashi) N.; came to U.S., 1952, naturalized, 1960; attended pre-med. curriculum Nippon Med. Sch., Tokyo, Japan, 1944-47, M.D., 1951; m. Hisako Nishihara, Dec. 31, 1960; 1 foster dau., Masako Kumamoto (Mrs. Patrick Eaton). Intern Tokyo U. Hosp., 1951-52, Orange County (Calif.) Gen. Hosp., Orange, 1952-53; resident Loma Linda U.-White Meml. Hosp., 1953, 56-60, Barlow Sanitarium, Los Angeles, 1954-55; resident in forensic pathology Los Angeles County Dept. Chief Med. Examiner, 1961-62; dep. med. examiner Los Angeles County, Los Angeles, 1962-65, supervising and med. examiner, 1965-67, chief med. examiner-coroner, 1967—; mem. faculty Loma Linda U., 1961—, clin. prof. pathology, 1968—; mem. faculty U. So. Calif., 1964—, asso. clin. prof. pathology, 1967-73, prof. forensic pathology, 1973—; prof. dept. criminal justice Calif. State U. at Los Angeles, 1971—. Chmn. wound ballistic com. Less Lethal Weapon Task Force; mem. com. definitions of death Calif. Atty. Gen. Diplomate Am. Bd. Pathology. Fellow Am. Acad. Compensation Medicine, Am. Acad. Forensic Scis., Am. Soc. Clin. Pathologists, Coll. Am. Pathologists; mem. Am., Calif., Los Angeles County med. assns., Aerospace Med. Assn., A.A.A.S., Assn. Am. Med. Colls., Calif. Assn. Criminalists, Calif., Los Angeles socs. pathologists, Marine Tech. Soc., N.Y. Acad. Scis., Pitts. Inst. Legal Medicine, Tissue Culture Assn., Undersea Med. Soc., Brit. Acad. Forensic Scis., Internat. Assn. Forensic Scis., medico-legal socs. Gt. Britain, Japan, Am. Mgmt. Assn., Calif. State Coroners' Assn. (pres. 1974-75), Internat. Assn. Coroners, Japan-Am. Soc., Japanese Am. Citizens League, Japanese C. of C. of So. Calif., Los Angeles-Nagoy Sister City Affiliation., Internat. Reference Orgn. in Forensic Medicine. Contbr. numerous articles to profl. jours. Office: Dept Chief Med Examiner 1104 N Mission Rd Room 200 Los Angeles CA 90033

NOHEL, JOHN ADOLPH, educator; b. Prague, Czechoslovakia, Oct. 24, 1924; s. Arthur John and Irene Helene (Hoenig) N.; came to U.S., 1939, naturalized, 1943; student U. Calif., 1942-43; B.E.E. with distinction, George Washington U., 1948; Ph.D., Mass. Inst. Tech., 1953; m. Vera Jordan Weisskopf, Sept. 17, 1948; children—Richard Philip, Audrey Elizabeth, Tom Andrew. Teaching asst., instr. Mass. Inst. Tech., 1948-53; from asst. prof. to prof. math. Ga. Inst. Tech., 1953-61; asso. prof. to prof. math. U. Wis., 1961—, chmn. dept., 1968-70, mem. Math. Research Center, 1978—; cons. Oak Ridge Nat. Lab., 1954-62, Lincoln Lab., 1958-63, North Central Assn., 1966—; vis. prof. Math. Research Center, U. Wis., 1958-59, U. Paris, 1965-66, 76, Ecole Polytechnique Fédérale, Lausanne, Switzerland, 1971-72, 76. Served with USN, 1943-46. Mem. Am. Math. Soc., Math. Assn. Am., Soc. Indsl. and Applied Math., AAUP, AAAS, Fedn. Am. Scientists, Sigma Xi, Pi Mu Epsilon. Author: Ordinary Differential Equations, 1967; Qualitative Theory of Ordinary Differential Equations, 1969; Linear Mathematics, 1970. Editorial bd. Soc. Indsl. and Applied Math. Jour. Applied Math., 1966—, Jour. Math. Analysis, 1973—. Contbr. articles to math. jours. Home: 5213 Burnett Dr Madison WI 53705

NOKES, JOHN RICHARD, newspaper editor; b. Portland, Oreg., Feb. 23, 1915; s. James Abraham and Bernice Alfaretta (Bailey) N.; B.S., Linfield Coll., 1936; m. Evelyn Junkin, Sept. 13, 1936; children—Richard Gregory, William G., Gail (Mrs. William M. Hulden), Douglas J., Kathy E. With The Oregonian, Portland, 1936—, city editor, 1950-65, asst. mng. editor, 1965-71, mng. editor, 1971-75, editor, 1975—. Bd. dirs. Portland U.S.O., 1968-72, U.S. Coast Guard Acad. Found., 1972-74, Portland Opera Assn., 1976-78; trustee Linfield Coll., 1977—. Served to lt. (j.g.) USNR, 1944-46; comdr. Res. (ret.). Mem. Navy League U.S. (pres. Portland council 1969-71), Linfield Coll. Alumni Assn. (pres. 1940), World Affairs Council Oreg. (pres. 1973-74), Portland C. of C., AP Mng. Editors Assn. (dir. 1973—), Am. Soc. Newspaper Editors, Sigma Delta Chi (pres. Willamette Valley chpt. 1975-76). Republican. Methodist. Club: Multnomah Athletic (Portland). Author: American Form of Government, 1939. Editor of Oreg. Edn. Jour., 1944. Home: 14650 SW 103d Ave Tigard OR 97223 Office: 1320 SW Broadway Portland OR 97201

NOLAN, HELEN DOROTHY, advt. exec.; b. Paterson, N.J., Aug. 4, 1936; d. Daniel Patrick and Helen (Singer) Nolan; B.A., Fairleigh Dickinson U., 1958; postgrad. N.Y. U., 1960, Nathaniel Branden Inst., 1966-68. Sec., editorial asst. Kenyon & Eckhardt, N.Y.C., 1958-59, Conde Nast Publs., N.Y.C., 1960-61; jr. writer Warwick & Legler, N.Y.C., 1962-63; sr. writer Young & Rubicam, N.Y.C., 1964, creative supr., 1971-72; copy group head Pritchard Wood, N.Y.C., 1965; copy chief Delehanty, Kurnit & Geller, N.Y.C., 1966-67, asso. creative dir., 1969-71; co-creative dir. Smith/Greenland Advt. Co., N.Y.C., 1968; creative supr. Carl Ally, Inc., N.Y.C., 1972-74; v.p., creative dir., partner Della Femina, Travisano & Partners, N.Y.C., 1974—; pres. The Magnificent Doll, Inc., 1975—. Bd. dirs. Andy Awards, 1971-72. Recipient advt. awards including Gold medal Andy Advt. Club N.Y., 1966, 76-77, N.Y. Art Dirs. Club, 1969; Clio, Am. TV Festival, 1969, 71, 72, 74, 75, 76, 77; Gold medals The One Show, 1973, 78, Silver medal, 1977; Golden Lion, Cannes Film Festival, 1973. Club: Copy (bd. dirs. 1976 N.Y.C.). Office: 625 Madison Ave New York NY 10022

NOLAN, JAMES FINDLEY, physician, educator; b. Chgo., Sept. 5, 1914; s. Joseph Deglan and Berenice (Furey) N.; A.B., U. Mo., 1935; M.D., Washington U., St. Louis, 1938; m. Ann Lawry, Sept. 9, 1936 (dec.); children—James Lawry, Julia Lynne (Mrs. Truman Parker Handy); m. 2d, Jane Davis, Apr. 8, 1978. Intern Barnes Hosp., St. Louis, 1938-39; intern St. Louis Maternity Hosp., 1939-40, asst. resident gynecology, 1940-41, resident, 1941-42, instr. gynecology, 1941-42; Nat. Cancer Inst. spl. fellow Meml. Hosp., 1942-43; practice medicine, specializing in obstetrics and gynecology, St. Louis, 1946-48, Los Angeles, 1948—; gynecologist Los Angeles Tumor Inst.; mem. active staff Calif. Hosp. Med. Center, Los Angeles; profl. staff Los Angeles County U. So. Calif. Med. Center; mem. courtesy staff Santa Fe Meml. Hosp.; mem. courtesy staff St. Vincent Med. Center, Los Angeles; cons. staff St. Johns Hosp. and Health Center, Santa Monica; courtesy staff Hosp. Good Samaritan, Los Angeles; chmn. radiation safety com. Calif. Hosp.; mem. cons. staff St. Joseph Med. Center, Burbank, Calif.; hon. staff Cedars-Sinai Med. Center, Los Angeles; asst. prof. obstetrics-gynecology Washington U. Sch. Medicine, 1946-48; instr. U. So. Calif., 1949-53, asst. clin. prof., 1953-59, asso. clin. prof., 1959-65, clin. prof. obstetrics and gynecology, 1965—, clin. prof. radiology, 1968—; med. dir. So. Calif. Cancer Center, Los Angeles, 1972—; Adv. Com. for Calif. Tumor Registry; civilian cons. AEC, 1946-48. Trustee, Albert Soiland Cancer Found., Friendly Sons St. Patrick. Served to capt. Manhattan Engring. Dist., AUS, 1943-46. Decorated Legion of Merit. Diplomate Am. Bd. Obstetrics and Gynecology. Mem. AMA, Calif., Los Angeles County med. assns., Am. Gynecol. Soc., Am. Assn. Obstetricians and Gynecologists, Am. Coll. Obstetricians and Gynecologists, Soc. Pelvic Surgeons, Pacific Coast, Los Angeles obstet. and gynecol. soc., Obstet. and Gynecol. Assembly So. Calif., A.C.S., Los Angeles Surg. Soc., Am. Radium Soc. (pres. 1970-71), Radiol. Soc. N.Am., James Ewing Soc., Western Assn. Gynecologic Oncologists (pres. 1972), Sigma Chi, Nu Sigma Nu. Republican. Roman Catholic. Contbr. articles to profl. jours. Home: 5889 Clinton St Los Angeles CA 90004 Office: 1414 S Hope St Los Angeles CA 90015

NOLAN, JAMES PARKER, investment banker; b. Washington, July 12, 1897; s. Walter and Mary (Parker) N.; student Georgetown Law Sch., 1917; m. Ellen DuBose Ravenel Peelle, Nov. 15, 1928 (dec.); children—James Paker, Stanton Peelle, Gaillard Ravenel; m. 2d, Florence Wetherill Walker, Dec. 9, 1978. With U.S. Dept. State, 1919-24, Nat. City Co., 1924-32; formed Folger, Nolan & Co., 1932; pres., treas. Folger, Nolan-W.B. Hibbs & Co., Inc., Washington 1953—; pres., treas., dir. Folger, Nolan, Fleming & Co., Inc., 1962—; Washington Stock Exchange, 1944-45; bd. govs. N.Y. Stock Exchange, 1958-61, allied mem.; asso. mem. Am. Stock Exchange; dir. Balt. & O. R.R. Co. Trustee Chestnut Lodge, Hosp., Bethesda, Md.; bd. dirs. Washington Inst. Fgn. Affairs. Served as lt. Tank Corps, AEF, 1918-19. Decorated Knight Malta. Mem. Nat. Assn. Security Dealers (mem. bd. 1943-46), Assn. Stock Exchange Firms (bd. 1948-54), Investment Bankers Assn. Am., Delta Theta Phi. Republican. Roman Catholic. Clubs: The Brook (N.Y.C.); Bond, Metropolitan, Alfalfa (Washington); Chevy Chase Country. Home: 3310 Connecticut Ave Washington DC 20008 Office: 725 15th St NW Washington DC 20005

NOLAN, JOHN EDWARD, JR., lawyer; b. Mpls., July 11, 1927; B.S., U.S. Naval Acad., 1950; J.D., Georgetown U., 1955. Admitted to D.C. bar, 1955, U.S. Supreme Ct. bar, 1959, Md. bar, 1961; law clk. to Jr. Justice Clark, U.S. Supreme Ct., 1955-56; adminstrv. asst. at Atty. Gen. Robert F. Kennedy, 1963-64; asso. firm Steptoe & Johnson, Washington, 1956-62, partner, 1962-63, 65—; mem. exec. com. Lawyers Com. on Civil Rights Under Law. Trustee, bd. dirs. Robert F. Kennedy Meml., 1969—. Mem. Am., D.C. (gov.) bar assns., Am. Law Inst. Home: 7830 Persimmon Tree Ln Bethesda MD 20034 Office: 1250 Connecticut Ave NW Washington DC 20036

NOLAN, JOHN FRANCIS, coll. pres.; b. Lawrence, Mass., Sept. 7, 1924; s. Timothy Joseph and Martha (Greene) N.; B.A., Boston U., 1952; M.S., Mass. Inst. Tech., 1953; postgrad. info. systems Harvard U., 1955, DeCordova Museum Sch., 1962-65, Impressions Workshop, 1964-65; m. Virginia Magner; childen—Nancy, Sean, Liam. Research engr. Mass. Inst. Tech., Cambridge, 1953-55, mgr. research programs in Computer Systems, Lincoln Lab., Lexington, 1955-69; pres. Mass. Coll. Art, Boston, 1969—. Founder, pres. Art and Tech., Inc., 1967-69. Mem. nat. com. cultural affairs Am. Assn. State Colls. and Univs., 1969—; chmn., 1974—; mem. task force environ. edn. Mass. Adv. Council Conservation Edn., 1971—; mem. Mass. Gov.'s Task Force Arts and Humanities, vice chmn. task force ednl. opportunities in arts, 1972-73; mem. Mass. Gov.'s Task Force Open Univ., 1973—. Mem. awards com. Wilhelmina Denning Jackson Scholarship Fund, 1969—. Served with USAAF, 1943-46. Author: Analytical Differentiation on a Digital Computer, 1953; On-Line Data Storage and Retrieval Systems, 1965. Contbr. articles to profl. jours. Office: Mass Coll Art 364 Brookline Ave Boston MA 02215*

NOLAN, JOHN LESTER, librarian; b. Concord, N.H., Apr. 14, 1909; s. Edmund P. and Grace (Heilbrun) N.; B.S. cum laude, Harvard, 1931; B.S. in L.S., Columbia, 1938; m. Dallas Fraser, June 20, 1935; children—David Fraser, Barbara Dallas. Librarian, Adams House Library, Harvard, 1931-34; sect. head, sr. reference librarian N.Y. Pub. Library, 1935-40; with Library of Congress, 1940-69, asst. dir. reference dept., 1954-58, asso. dir. reference dept., 1958-68, dir. reference dept., 1968-69, hon. cons., 1969—; prof. library studies U. Hawaii, 1969-70; library cons., 1970—; dir. library services in U.K. for USIS, 1952-54. Mem. Am., D.C., Brit. library assns. Clubs: Cosmos, Harvard (Washington). Editor: Library of Congress Quar. Jour. Current Acquisitions, 1945-51. Contbr. articles to profl. jours. Home: 4007 Dresden St Kensington MD 20795

NOLAN, JOHN STEPHAN, lawyer; b. Cin., Jan. 12, 1926; s. Edward Leroy and Florence (Wetterer) N.; B.S. in Commerce, U. N.C., 1947, A.B., 1947; LL.B. magna cum laude, Harvard U., 1951; m. Adeline J. Mosher, Sept. 5, 1949; children—Michael C., Joyce P., Matthew M., John G., Elizabeth A. Admitted to D.C. bar, 1951, Md. bar, 1959; asso. firm Miller & Chevalier, Washington, 1951-56, partner, 1957-69, 1972—; dep. asst. sec. tax policy Dept. Treasury, Washington, 1969-72; adj. prof. law Georgetown U., 1959-69, 72—; dir. The Rockport Fund. Served with USN, 1944-47, 52-54. Recipient Alexander Hamilton award Dept. Treasury, 1970. Mem. Am. Bar Assn., Fed. Bar Assn., Bar Assn. D.C., D.C. Bar Assn. Republican. Roman Catholic. Club: Met. (Washington). Home: 10904 Stanmore Dr Potomac MD 20854 Office: 1700 Pennsylvania Ave NW Washington DC 20006

NOLAN, JOHN THOMAS, JR., advt. agy. exec.; b. Cin., Mar. 21, 1918; s. John Thomas and Laura Mary (McJoynt) N.; A.B., U. Cin., 1940, M.A., 1942; postgrad. Xavier U., U.S. Marine Corps Command and Staff Coll., U.S. Naval War Coll., Air War Coll., Indsl. War Coll., Army War Coll. Pub. relations dir. Gruen Watch Co., Cin., 1944-46; pres. Nolan, Keelor & Stites Inc., advt. agy., Cin., 1947-79, chmn. bd., 1979—; pres. Campion Investment Co. Inc., Cin., 1959—. Chmn. men's com. Cin. Symphony Orch., 1965; bd. dirs. Cin. Mus. Festival Assn., 1962—, pres., 1961-64; trustee Pub. Library Cin. and Hamilton County, 1951—, pres., 1965—; past pres. Queen City Assn., 1949; bd. govs. St. Xavier High Sch., 1962-68; pres. Fenwick Club, 1963-65; chmn. council on camp study United Fund, 1962; chmn. basin area study com. Community Health and Welfare Council, 1964. Mem. pres.'s adv. council Xavier U., Cin., 1973—; mem. adv. council Navy Affairs, 1959—; hon. trustee Cin. Ballet Co., 1964—; bd. dirs. Bur. Govtl. Research. Recipient Meritorious Public Service citation Sec. of Navy, 1957, Founder's award Xavier U., 1979; named man of year Cin. Marine Corps League, 1965. Mem. Cin. Council Navy League (pres. 1962-68), Def. Orientation Conf. Assn. (dir. 1970—), Cin. Indsl. Advertisers Assn. (Man of Distinction award 1975), Cin. Advertisers Club, Hist. and Philos. Soc. Ohio (life), Men. of Milford Retreat League (dir. 1960-62). Republican. Roman Catholic. Clubs: University, Queen City. Home: 1321 Observatory Dr Cincinnati OH 45208 Office: Nolan Keelor & Stites Inc 318 Broadway St Cincinnati OH 45202

NOLAN, JOSEPH THOMAS, chem. co. exec.; b. Waterbury, Conn., Apr. 11, 1920; s. Thomas Francis and Mary Margaret (Gaffney) N.; A.B., Holy Cross Coll., 1942; M.A. in English, Boston U., 1945; Ph.D. in Econs., N.Y. U., 1972; m. Virginia Theodate Tappin, May 6, 1943; children—Carol Nolan Rigolot, David J. Washington corr. UPI, 1943-49; writer, editor N.Y. Times, N.Y.C., 1949-55; mgr. editorial and press services RCA Corp., N.Y.C., 1955-62; sr. v.p. corporate communications Chase Manhattan Bank, N.Y.C., 1962-74; prof. journalism and pub. affairs U. S.C., Columbia, 1974-76; v.p. pub. affairs Monsanto Co., St. Louis, 1976—. Bd. dirs. Regional Commerce and Growth Assn., St. Louis, United Way Greater St. Louis. Mem. Pub. Relations Soc. Am. Contbr. articles to various mags. Home: 2316 Putter Ln Saint Louis MO 63131 Office: Monsanto Co 800 N Lindberg Blvd Saint Louis MO 63166

NOLAN, KATHLEEN, actress; b. St. Louis, Sept. 27, 1933; d. Steve and Clara (Kennedy) Ellsworth; student Neighborhood Playhouse, N.Y.C., Actor's Studio, N.Y.C.; 1 son, Spencer Garrett. Worked in children's theatre; toured with musical It's All For You; appeared in plays including Wendy in Peter Pan, Broadway, Hide and See, Detective Story, Love in E Flat, Broadway, South Pacific, N.Y.C.; numerous TV appearances, including: Philco Playhouse, 1953, as Kate in Real McCoys series, ABC-TV (TV Guild and TV Editors Limelight award), Broadside series; TV film novels: Testimony of Two Men, The Immigrants; films include: Limbo, Wednesday Night Out, No Time to be Young; guest artist with numerous repertory cos., including prodns. of classics of Brecht, Shaw and Chekov and mus. leads in Carousel, The Unsinkable Molly Brown, Ready When You Are C.G., Period of Adjustment, On A Clear Day and Mary, Mary; lectr. on film, theatre, women's issues to colls.; participant Women's Directing Workshop at Am. Film Inst.; bd. dirs. Corp. Public Broadcasting; mem. Carnegie Commn. on Future Public Broadcasting; mem. Los Angeles Mayor's Citizens Adv. Council on Greek Theater Devel.; mem. Los Angeles Film Devel. Com.; mem. adv. council Calif. Confedn. of Arts; vice chmn. Com. for Am. Movie Prodn.; ad hoc chmn. Com. for Public Rights in Broadcasting. Mem. Democratic Nat. Com.; mem. Internat. Women's Yr. Continuing Com.; mem. steering com. Women's Action Alliance; mem. Nat. Women's Agenda; mem. exec. com. Project on Human Sexual Devel.; mem. bd. human relations City Los Angeles; chmn. Arts Plank for Nat. Polit. Platforms; bd. dirs. Nat. Citizens Communication Lobby; participant tour State Dept., Vietnam. Recipient Presdl. citation. Mem. Screen Actors Guild (dir., v.p., nat. pres. 1975—), AFTRA, Actors' Equity, Acad. Motion Picture Arts and Scis., Acad. TV Arts and Scis., Am. Film Inst., Women in Film, Hollywood Film Council, Common Cause, ACLU, Nat. Women's Polit. Caucus. Office: 7750 Sunset Blvd Los Angeles CA 90046

NOLAN, PATRICK JOSEPH, screenwriter, playwright, educator; b. Bronx, N.Y., Jan. 2, 1933; s. Patrick John and Catherine Katrina (O'Malley) N.; A.B., Villanova U., 1955; M.A., U. Detroit, 1961; Ph.D., Bryn Mawr Coll., 1973; m. Karen Ursula O'Connor, May 10, 1969; children—Patrick, Christian, Mark. Teaching fellow and mem. faculty dept. English, U. Detroit, 1959-62; instr. English, Villanova U., 1962—, prof., 1980—; TV screenplays: The Hourglass Moment, Nat. Ednl. TV, 1968, The Jericho Mile, ABC (Emmy award 1979). Served with USNR, 1955-59. Mem. Writers Guild Am.-West. Roman Catholic. Office: Villanova U Villanova PA 19085

NOLAN, PATRICK JOSEPH, furniture co. exec.; b. Glendale, N.Y., July 17, 1938; s. Daniel Patrick and Anne Margaret (Krautter) N.; B.S. in Accounting Fordham U., 1964; postgrad. Pace Coll., 1968; m. Carol Mirabel, Nov. 14, 1964; children—Daniel, Peter, Brian, Patrick. Fin. analyst W.R. Grace & Co., N.Y.C., 1964-68; asst. to v.p.-fin. Holly Sugar Corp., N.Y.C., 1968-70; sr. v.p., treas. Levitz Furniture Corp., Miami, Fla., 1970—; dir. Pan Am. Bank, N.A., Miami. Mem. Fin. Execs. Inst. Republican. Roman Catholic. Clubs: Coral Springs Country, Jockey, Fla. Home: 11051 NW 24th St Coral Springs FL 33065 Office: 1317 NW 167th St Miami FL 33169

NOLAN, PAUL THOMAS, educator; b. Rochester, N.Y., Apr. 4, 1919; s. John J. and Anna (Sweeney) N.; student Aquinas Inst. Rochester, 1933-37; B.A., Central Ark. U., 1947; M.A., Tulane U., 1949, Ph.D., 1953; m. Peggy Hime, June 1, 1947; children—John Michael, Peter Andrew, Elizabeth Anne. Instr. English, dir. News Bur., Central Ark. U., 1947; asst. prof. English, dir. pub. relations Centenary Coll. of La., 1948-54; Ford Found. vis. prof. Ark. State U., 1954-55; prof. English, Dupre prof. humanities U. Southwestern La., Lafayette, 1955—. Served with USAAF, 1942-45. Mem. Modern Lang. Assn., Playwrights' Theatre La., Am. Studies Assn. Democrat. Club: Lafayette Town House. Author: Round-The-World Plays, 1961; One-Act Plays of Lee Arthur, 1962; Chaucer for Children, 1963; Writing the One-Act Play, 1964; Death For The Lonely (Nat. Workshop Players award), 1964; Three Plays by John W. Crawford, 1965; Marc Connelly, 1969; Drama Workshop Plays, 1969; Describing People, 1970; The Loneliest Game, 1971; Hedda Gabler, South, 1972; Last Week I Was Ninety-Five, 1973; Squeak to Me of Love, 1973; Between Hisses, 1973; (with James Burke) The Highwayman, 1975; The Eavesdrop Theatre, 1976. Home: 219 Renee Ave Lafayette LA 70501 Office: Box 4-0552 USL Sta Lafayette LA 70504

NOLAN, RICHARD, congressman; b. Brainerd, Minn., Dec. 17, 1943; s. James Henry and Mary Jean (Aylward) N.; student St. John's U., 1962; B.A., U. Minn., 1966; postgrad. U. Md., 1967; m. Marjorie C. Langer, June 13, 1964; children—Michael, Leah, John, Katherine. Staff asst. to Senator Walter Mondale of Minn., 1966-68; dir. Project Headstart, Minn., 1968; curriculum coordinator adult basic edn. Little Falls (Minn.) Sch. Dist.; tchr. social scis., Royalton, Minn., 1968-69; project coordinator Center Study Local Govt., St. John's U., Collegeville, Minn., 1971; adminstrv. asst. to sr. v.p. Fingerhut Corp., 1973-74; mem. 94th-96th Congresses from 6th Minn. Dist. Mem. Minn. Ho. of Reps., 1969-73. Roman Catholic. Office: 214 Cannon House Office Bldg Washington DC 20515

NOLAN, RICHARD CHARLES, football coach; b. Pitts., Mar. 26, 1932; s. Vincent John and Agnes (Sharples) N.; B.A. in Bus. Adminstrn., U. Md., 1954; m. Elizabeth Ann Tullis, Apr. 19, 1954; children—Richard Charles, Nancy, Michael, Kelly, Lisa, James. Defensive back N.Y. Giants, 1954-57, safety, 1959-61; defensive back Chgo. Cardinals, 1958; player-coach Dallas Cowboys, 1962, asst. coach, 1963-67; head coach San Francisco 49'ers, 1968-75; personnel scout Oakland Raiders (Calif.), 1976; asst. coach New Orleans Saints, 1977, head coach, 1978—; participant Sugar Bowl, 1952, Orange Bowl, Sr. Bowl and Chgo. All-Star Game, 1954. Named Nat. Football Conf. Coach of Yr., Nat. Football Writers Assn., Minn. Minutemen and 101 Sportwriters Club Kansas City (Mo.), 1970; recipient Disting. Alumni award U. Md., 1971; inducted into Westchester Sports Hall of Fame, 1978. Mem. Md. Alpha, Phi Delta Theta. Republican. Roman Catholic. Club: U. Md. M. Office: New Orleans Saints 6928 Saint Dr Metairie LA 70003

NOLAN, RICHARD EDWARD, lawyer; b. N.Y.C., Nov. 28, 1928; A.B. cum laude, Holy Cross Coll., 1950; LL.B., Columbia U., 1957; m. Agnes F. Gilligan, Jan. 31, 1959; children—Anthony R.G., Christopher W.P., Timothy R.W., Mariana Celeste, Katherine H.L. Admitted to N.Y. bar, 1958, U.S. Supreme Ct. bar, 1962; asso. firm Davis Polk & Wardwell, N.Y.C., 1957-65, partner, 1966—; dir. Whitbread Nolan, Inc., N.Y.C. Bd. dirs. United Neighborhood Houses of N.Y., 1970—. Mem. Am., Fed., N.Y. bar assns., Assn. Bar City N.Y., Am. Law Inst. Home: 271 Central Park W New York NY 10024 also Bolton Landing NY 12845 Office: 1 Chase Manhattan Plaza New York NY 10005

NOLAN, THOMAS BRENNAN, geologist; b. Greenfield, Mass., May 21, 1901; s. Frank Wesley and Anna (Brennan) N.; Ph.B. in Metallurgy, Yale, 1921, Ph.D. in Geology, 1924; LL.D., U. St. Andrews, 1962; m. Mabelle Orleman, Dec. 3, 1927; 1 son, Thomas Brennan. Geologist, U.S. Geol. Survey, 1924-44, asst. dir., 1944-56, dir., 1956-65, research geologist, 1965—. Recipient Spendiaroff prize Internat. Geol. Congress, 1933; K. C. Li prize and medal Columbia, 1954; Rockefeller Pub. Service award Princeton, 1961; Silver medal Tokyo Geog. Soc., 1965. Fellow Geol. Soc. Am. (pres. 1961), Soc. Econ. Geologists (pres. 1950), Am. Geophys. Union, Mineral. Soc. Am., Royal Soc. Edinburgh (hon.); mem. Nat. Acad. Scis., Geol. Soc. Washington, Am. Philos. Soc., Tokyo Geog. Soc. (hon. mem.), Internat. Union Geol. Scis., Am. Acad. Arts and Scis., Geol. Soc. London (fgn. mem.), Am. Ornithologists Union, Mining and Metall. Soc. Am., Sigma Xi. Clubs: Cosmos (Washington); Yale. Contbr. numerous articles, reports, bulls. to profl. and govtl. jours. Home: 2219 California St NW Washington DC 20008 Office: US Geological Survey Reston VA 22092

NOLAN, VAL, JR., lawyer, zoologist; b. Evansville, Ind., Apr. 28, 1920; s. Val and Jeannette (Covert) N.; A.B., Ind. U., 1941, J.D., 1949; m. Susanne Howe, Dec. 23, 1946; children—Val, Ann Clare, William Alan. Dep. U.S. marshal, 1941; agt. U.S. Secret Service, 1942; admitted to Indiana bar, 1949; asst. prof. law Ind. U., 1949-52, asso. prof., 1952-56, prof., 1956—; research scholar in zoology, 1957-68, prof. zoology, 1968—, acting dean Sch. of Law, 1976. Served with USNR, 1942-46. Guggenheim fellow, 1957. Fellow Am. Ornithologists Union; mem. Brit. Onithologists' Union, Cooper Ornithological Soc., Wilson Ornithological Soc., Ecological Soc. Am., Animal Behavior Soc., Deutsche Ornithologen-Gesellschaft, Nederlandse Ornithologische Unie, AAAS, Sigma Xi, Order of the Coif, Phi Beta Kappa. Democrat. Editor: Ind. Law Jour., 1945-46. Author: (with F.E. Horack, Jr.) Land Use Controls, 1955; Ecology and Behavior of the Prairie Warbler, 1978. Home: 4675 Heritage Woods Rd Bloomington IN 47401 Office: Indiana U Bloomington IN 47401

NOLAN, WILLIAM FRANCIS, author; b. Kansas City, Mo., Mar. 6, 1928; s. Michael Cahill and Bernadette Mariana (Kelly) N.; student Kansas City Art Inst., 1946-47, San Diego (Calif.) State Coll., 1947-48, Los Angeles City Coll., 1953; D. (hon.) in Sci. Fiction, Am. River Coll., 1975; m. Marilyn Elizabeth Seal, Mar. 6, 1970. Greeting card designer and cartoonist Hall Bros., Kansas City, Mo., 1945; outdoor mural painter, San Diego, Calif., 1949-50; aircraft inspector Convair, San Diego, 1950-52; credit asst. Blake, Moffitt & Towne Paper Co., Los Angeles, 1953-54; employment interviewer Calif. State Dept. of Employment, 1954-56; free lance writer of fiction, non-fiction, screenplays and teleplays, 1956—; book reviewer Los Angeles Times, 1964-70; appeared as actor in (films): The Intruder, 1962, The Legend of Machine-Gun Kelly, 1975; narrator, co-author ednl. film A Dream of the Stars, 1953; author: (novels) (with G.C. Johnson) Logan's Run, 1967, Death is for Losers, 1968, The White Cad Cross-Up, 1969, Space for Hire (Edgar Allan Poe award 1972), 1971, Logan's World, 1977; (collections) Impact 20, 1963, Men of Thunder, 1964, Carnival of Speed, 1973, Alien Horizons, 1974, Wonderworlds, 1977; (biographies) Barney Oldfield, 1961, Phil Hill: Yankee Champion, 1962, John Huston, King Rebel, 1965, Dashiell Hammett: A Casebook (Edgar Allan Poe award 1970), 1969, Steve McQueen: Star on Wheels, 1972; Hemingway: Last Days of the Lion, 1974, The Ray Bradbury Companion, 1975; (screenplays) Burnt Offerings (Best Horror Film award 1977), 1976, Logan's Run (Best Sci. Fiction film award 1977), 1976, The Legend of Machine-Gun Kelly, 1975; (teleplays) Melvin Purvis, G-Man, 1974, The Turn of the Screw, 1974, others; creator/writer TV series Logan's Run, 1977-78; contbr. 600 short stories and feature articles to various mags.; editor Ray Bradbury Rev., 1952, Omnibus of Speed, 1958, Man Against Tomorrow, 1965, The Pseudo-People, 1965, A Wilderness of Stars, 1969, The Future is Now, 1970, others; selections from works included in over 100 textbooks and anthologies. Mem. adv. bd. First Printings of Am. Authors, 1977. Mem. Writers Guild Am., Science Fiction Writers Am., Mystery Writers of Am. (motion picture awards com. 1970), Dashiell Hammett Soc. San Francisco (co-founder 1978), Writers Guild Film Soc. Address: 22720 Cavalier St Woodland Hills CA 91364. *In achieving the positive state of mind necessary for success in life my main problem was to overcome a negative childhood—in switching from the basic "I can't and won't" attitude to the "I can and will" attitude which allowed me to reach my full potential as a writer.*

NOLAND, JAMES ELLSWORTH, U.S. judge; b. LaGrange, Mo., Apr. 22, 1920; s. Otto Arthur and Elzena (Ellsworth) N.; A.B., Ind. U., 1942, LL.B., 1948; M.B.A., Harvard, 1943; m. Helen Warvel, Feb. 4, 1948; children—Kathleen Kimberly, James Ellsworth, Christopher Warvel. Admitted to Ind. State bar, 1948, since practiced in Bloomington; partner law firm of Hilgedag and Noland, Indpls., 1955-66, 1st asst. city atty., Indpls., 1956-57; dep. atty. gen., Ind., 1952; spl. asst. U.S. atty. gen., 1953; appointed Ind. State Election Commr., 1954; U.S. judge So. Dist. Ind., 1966—. Mem. com. on magistrates system Jud. Conf. U.S., 1973. Mem. 81st (1949-51) Congress, 7th Ind., Dist.; sec. Ind. Democratic Com., 1960-66. Chmn. bd. visitors Ind. Law Sch., Indpls., 1974-76. Served as capt., Transp. Corps., AUS, 1943-46. Mem. Am., Ind. bar assns., Ind. Assn. Trial Lawyers (pres. 1956), Nat. Conf. Fed. Trial Judges (sec. 1978—), Phi Delta Phi, Phi Kappa Psi. Mem. Moravian Ch. Home: 8979 Pickwick Dr Indianapolis IN 46260 Office: Federal Bldg Indianapolis IN 46204

NOLAND, JAMES TERRY, banker; b. Richmond, Ky., Feb. 17, 1922; s. Harris William and Elizabeth (Hagan) N.; B.S. in Acctg., U. Ky., 1943; grad. Stonier Grad. Sch. Banking, 1963; m. Joan Emery Taylor, Dec. 20, 1942; children—Ann, James, John, Alexander. Accountant, Humphrey Robinson & Co., C.P.A.'s, Louisville, 1946-49; pvt. and mgmt. positions with Vrendenburgh Family, 1949-58; with First Nat. Bank, Birmingham, Ala., 1958—, v.p., 1964-75, comptroller, 1969-74, exec. v.p., head trust div., 1975—. Mem. exec. bd. Birmingham Area council Boy Scouts Am.; trustee, bd. dirs. Valley Christian (Disciples of Christ) Ch., Birmingham. Served with AUS, 1943-45. Decorated Bronze Star; C.P.A., Ky. Mem. Fin. Execs. Inst. Democrat. Office: PO Box 11426 Birmingham AL 35202

NOLAND, KENNETH CLIFTON, artist; b. Asheville, N.C., Apr. 10, 1924; s. Harry C. and Bessie (Elkins) N.; studied Black Mountain Coll., N.C., 1946-48. summers 1950, 51; student Ozzip Zadkine, Paris, 1948-49; m. Cornelia Langer (div.); children—Cady, William L., Lyndon. Tchr., Inst. Contemporary Arts, 1950-52, Cath. U., 1951-60; one man shows include Galerie Creuze, Paris, 1949, Tibor de Nagy Gallery, N.Y.C., 1957, 58, Jefferson Place Gallery, 1958, French & Co., N.Y.C., 1959, Bennington Coll., 1961, Andre Emmerich Gallery, N.Y.C., 1960-64, 66-67, 71-73, 75, 77-78, Zurich, Switzerland, 1973, 76, 79, David Mirvish Gallery, Toronto, 1965, 67, 74, 76, Jewish Mus., 1965, also galleries Milan, Paris, Zurich, Dusseldorf, Germany, London, Toronto; retrospective show Guggenheim Mus., 1977; group shows Kootz Gallery, N.Y.C. 1954, Norman Mackenzie Art Gallery, Regina, Sask., Can., 1963, Corcoran Gallery, Washington, 1956, 59, 63, 64, 67, 70, 75, Venice (Italy) Biennial, 1964, Fogg Art Museum, Cambridge, Mass., 1965, 72, Mus. Modern Art, N.Y.C., 1965, 68, Nat. Gallery, Washington, 1968, Whitney Mus., N.Y.C., U.S. Pavilion, Expo 67, Montreal, Que., Can., Art Inst. Chgo., 1962, 70, 72, 76, Balt. Mus., 1957, 70, 77, Jewish Mus., 1963, Tate Gallery, 1964, 74, Guggenheim Mus., N.Y.C., 1961, 66, 70, 73-74, 76-77, Los Angeles County Mus., 1964, Inst. Contemporary Art, Boston, 1964, 65, 67, Whitney Mus., N.Y.C., 1961-67, 69-73, 76, Met. Mus., N.Y.C., 1968, 70, Mus. Fine Arts, Boston, 1972. Recipient 1st prize Premio Nacional Internat., Instituto Torcuato de Tella, Buenos Aires, 1964; Creative Arts award Brandeis U., 1965, 4th prize Corcoran Biennale, 1967. Home: Box 125 South Salem NY 10590

NOLAND, LLOYD U., JR., corp. exec.; b. Newport News, Va., Apr. 15, 1917; s. Lloyd J. and Rena (Schofield) N.; B.A., Dartmouth Coll., 1939; LL.D. (hon.), William and Mary Coll., 1964; m. Jane Christine Kiefaber, Jan. 27, 1940; children—Lloyd U. III, Susan Christine, Anne Noland Edwards. Chmn. bd. Noland Co., Basic Constrn. Co., Newport News; dir. Tidewater Constrn. Corp., Norfolk, Va., United Va. Bankshares, Inc. Bd. dirs. Va. Peninsula Indsl. Com., Va. Indsl. Fin. Corp.; mem. Va. Indsl. Devel. Corp.; hon. dir. Atlantic Rural Expn., Inc.; chmn. Progress Com. Newport News; trustee Eastern Va. Med. Sch. Found., Va. Found. Ind. Colls., War Meml. Mus. Va., United Community Services Newport News; past trustee Grad. Sch. Bus. Adminstrn., U. Va.; mem. Fellows Va. Mus. Fine Arts; mem. advisory council naval affairs 5th Naval Dist.; mem. pres.'s council Coll. William and Mary. Mem. Va. Industrialization Group (exec. com.), Va. Bus. Council, Am. Supply Assn., So. Wholesales Assn. (dir.), U.S., Peninsula, Va. chambers commerce, Newcomen Soc. N.Am., Casqun and Gauntlet, Alpha Soc., Beta Gamma Sigma. Clubs: Duquesne (Pitts.); Farmington Country (Charlottesville, Va.); Cedar Point (Suffolk, Va.); Commonwealth, Deep Run Hunt (Richmond, Va.); Williamsburg (Va.) Country; James River Country, Propeller (Newport News). Home: 206 James River Dr Newport News VA 23601 Office: 2700 Warwick Blvd Newport News VA 23607

NOLAND, ROBERT LEROY, mfg. co. exec.; b. Lawrence, Kans., Sept. 7, 1918; s. Harry L. and Angela (Scola) N.; B.S. in Mech. Engring., Calif. Inst. Tech., 1941; m. Delpha Mae Mierndorf, June 16, 1962; children—Gary, Fabra Jeanine, Derice Elizabeth. Design and devel. rocket propelled devices Calif. Inst. Tech., 1941-45; supr. propulsions Naval Ordnance Test Sta., China Lake, Calif., 1945-46; asst. chief engr. Aerojet Gen. Corp., 1946-52; cons. engr. plastic components, rockets and missiles, 1952-54; exec. v.p. Riehold Engring. and Plastics Co., 1954-57, pres., 1957-59; exec. v.p. Haveg Industries, Wilmington, Del., 1959-66; exec. v.p. Ametek, Inc., Paoli, Pa., 1966-68, pres., 1968—, also dir. Home: PO Box 6419 Incline Village NV 89450 Office: 410 Park Ave New York NY 10022

NOLAND, ROYCE PAUL, assn. exec.; b. Walla Walla, Pa., Dec. 6, 1928; s. Homer Vernon and Mildred Bessie (Royce) N.; B.A., Whitman Coll.; m. April Lynn Hawkes, Feb. 10, 1979; children—Royce Paul, Richard Mitchell. Pvt. practice phys. therapy; exec. dir. Calif. chpt. Am. Phys. Therapy Assn.; exec. dir. Am. Phys. Therapy Assn., Washington. Bd. trustees Found. for Phys. Therapy. Mem. Pres.'s Com. on Employment of the Handicapped. Mem. Am. Soc. Assn. Execs., Am. Public Health Assn. Republican. Congregationalist. Clubs: University (Washington). Home: 5931 4th St S Arlington VA 22204 Office: 1156 15th St NW Suite 500 Washington DC 20005

NOLAND, WAYLAND EVAN, educator; b. Madison, Wis., Dec. 8, 1926; s. Lowell Evan and Ruth (Chase) N.; B.A., U. Wis., 1948; M.A. (Pepsi Cola fellow), Harvard, 1950, Ph.D. (Allied Chem. & Dye Corp. fellow), in Physico Organic Chemistry, 1952. Lab. asst. U. Wis., 1943-44, Wis. Alumni Research Found. undergrad. research apprentice, 1947-48, project asst. arboretum com., summer 1948; duPont postdoctoral fellow U. Minn., 1951-52, mem. faculty, 1952—, prof. chemistry, 1962—, acting chmn. dept., 1967-69; vis. instr. U. B.C., summer 1956; cons. in field, 1958-70; sec. bd. editors, Organic Syntheses, Inc., 1969-79, mem., sec. bd. dirs., 1969—. Sec.-treas. Grovers Investment Club, Mpls., 1965, chmn., 1966-67. Bd. dirs. Wis. Trout Stream Improvement Assn., 1946-47. Served with AUS, 1945. Recipient Distinguished Teaching award U. Minn. Inst. Tech., 1964. Mem. Am. Chem. Soc. (chmn. arrangements com. Minn. sect. 1956, chmn. Minn. sect. 1970, alt. councilor 1971-73, 79-81, councilor 1974-78), AAAS (life), Assn. Harvard Chemists (life), N.Y. Acad. Scis. (life), AAUP, Minn. Acad. Sci., Wis. Acad. Scis., Arts and Letters (life), Minn., Am. civil liberties unions, Phi Beta Kappa (pres. Alpha of Minn. chpt. 1969-70), Sigma Xi (life; pres. U. Minn. chpt. 1978-79), Phi Eta Sigma, Phi Lambda Upsilon, Phi Kappa Phi, Alpha Chi Sigma (vice chmn. bd. Twin City Alumni Assn. 1954-55), Gamma Alpha (faculty counselor 1955-59, del. U. Minn. 1955-59). Republican. Contbr. articles to profl. jours.; patentee in field. Home: 820 Washington Ave SE Minneapolis MN 55414 Office: Sch Chemistry U Minn 207 Pleasant St SE Minneapolis MN 55455

NOLEN, CALVIN CLEAVE, univ. pres.; b. Pueblo, Colo., Oct. 23, 1924; s. Elmer Decie and Selina Adeline (Williams) N.; B.A., U. Tex. at Austin, 1948, postgrad., 1948-51; LL.D. (hon.), Tex. Christian U., 1971; m. June Gregg Dameron, Oct. 23, 1949; children—Cynthia (Mrs. Kim A. Page), Nina Elyse (Mrs. David L. Holmes). Dir., Tex. Union, U. Tex., Austin, 1951-61; asst. dir. U. Tex. Devel. Bd., 1961-65, asso. dir., 1965-68; vice chancellor for devel. Tex. Christian U., Ft. Worth, 1968-71; pres. N. Tex. State U., Denton, 1971—; pres. Tex. Coll. Osteo. Medicine, Ft. Worth, 1975—; dir., Gen. Tel. Co., S.W., Dameron Land and Cattle Co. Pres., Denton County United Way, 1974-75. Bd. dirs. Longhorn council Boy Scouts Am., 1973—, Denton County Community Found., 1975; trustee Alpha Phi Omega Nat. Endowment Fund, 1970-76; mem. Christian Ch. (Disciples of Christ), elder 1967-75, mem. gen. bd. 1973-77, mem. bd. Nat. Benevolence Assn., 1977—. Served with USNR, 1943-46; PTO; comdr. Res. (ret.). Mem. Council Advancement and Support Edn. (dist. chmn. 1970-71), N. Tex. State Alumni Assn., Newcomen Soc., Denton C. of C. (dir. 1971—), Blue Key, Friar Soc., Alpha Phi Omega, Phi Kappa Sigma, Beta Gamma Sigma, Mu Phi Epsilon. Mason (Shriner). Clubs: Century II, Denton Country, Headliners. Home: 1930 Eagle Dr Denton TX 76201 Office: Box 13737 North Texas State University Denton TX 76203

NOLEN, WILLIAM ANTHONY, surgeon, author; b. Holyoke, Mass., Mar. 20, 1928; s. James Robert and Katherine Margaret (Dillon) N.; A.B., Holy Cross Coll., 1949; M.D., Tufts U., 1953; m. Joan Helene Scheibel, Nov. 28, 1953; children—James, Joan, William, Anna, Julius, Mary. Intern, Cornell surg. div. Bellevue Hosp., N.Y.C., 1953-54, resident in surgery, 1954-55, 57-60; surgeon Litchfield (Minn.) Clinic, 1960—; mem. staff Meeker County Hosp., Litchfield, Minn., chief dept. surgery, 1960-79; attending surgeon Hennepin County Hosp., U. Minn., Mpls., 1962-69; author: The Making of a Surgeon, 1970, A Surgeon's World, 1972, Healing: A Doctor in Search of a Miracle, 1974, Surgeon Under The Knife, 1976, The Baby in The Bottle, 1978; columnist McCall's Mag. Served as capt. M.C., USAR, 1955-57. Diplomate Am. Bd. Surgery. Fellow A.C.S. Home: 421 Marshall Ave N Litchfield MN 55355 Office: Litchfield Clinic Litchfield MN 55355

NOLL, CHARLES HENRY, profl. football coach; b. Cleve., Jan. 5, 1931; B.E., U. Dayton, 1953; m. Marianne Noll; 1 son, Chris. Football player Cleve. Browns, NFL, 1953-59; asst. coach San Diego Chargers, AFL, 1960-65, Balt. Colts, 1966-68; head coach Pitts. Steelers, NFL, 1969—. Named Am. Football Conf. Coach of Year, U.P.I., 1972. Address: care Pittsburgh Steelers 300 Stadium Circle Pittsburgh PA 15212*

NOLL, HANS, educator; b. Basle, Switzerland, June 14, 1924; s. Johannes Ernst and Hedwig (Staehelin) N.; Ph.D. in Organic Chemistry magna cum laude, U. Basle, 1950; m. Johanne Bindesboll, 1949; children—Kirsten, Lucas, Barbara, Elizabeth. Came to U.S., 1951, naturalized, 1957. Postdoctoral fellow State Serum Inst., Dept. Biol. Standardization, Copenhagen, Denmark, 1950-51; asst. Tb div. Pub. Health Research Inst., N.Y.C., 1951-53, asso. Tb div., 1954-56; vis. investigator Inst. de Biologie Physico-Chimique, Paris, 1954; mem. faculty U. Pitts., 1956-64, asso. prof. microbiology, 1960-64; prof. biol. scis. Northwestern U., 1964—; vis. prof. dept. genetics U. Hawaii, Honolulu, 1969; vis. prof. Basle Inst. Immunology, 1971. Pres., Molecular Instruments Co.; cons. European Molecular Biology Conf. Research Labs., Heidelberg, Germany, 1974. Sr. research fellow NIH, 1959-63, lifetime career award, 1964; recipient life career professorship award Am. Cancer Soc., 1966. Mem. Am. Chem. Soc., Am. Soc. Biol. Chemists, AAAS, Biochem. Soc., Am. Soc. Microbiology. Author articles. Home: 2665 Orrington Ave Evanston IL 60201

NOLL, J(OHN) DOUGLAS, speech pathologist; b. Joliet, Ill., Aug. 4, 1930; s. Erwin Edward and Evelyn E. (Colby) N.; B.S., U. Ill., 1952; M.A., U. Iowa, 1956, Ph.D., 1960; m. Patricia Saddoris, Aug. 19, 1951; children—David Thomas, Janet Kay, James Philip. Tchr., North Boone (Ill.) Consol. Pub. Schs., 1952-54; speech and hearing cons. U. Iowa Gen. Hosps., 1957-60; asst. prof. speech pathology and audiology Stanford U., 1960-62; prof. dept. audiology and speech scis. Purdue U., West Lafayette, Ind., 1962—, dept. head, 1973-77. Fellow Am. Speech and Hearing Assn.; mem. Ind. Speech and Hearing Assn., Am. Cleft Palate Assn., Acad. of Aphasia, Sigma Xi. Contbr. sci. articles to profl. jours. Home: 624 Avondale Dr West Lafayette IN 47906 Office: Dept Audiology and Speech Scis Purdue U West Lafayette IN 47907

NOLL, WALTER, educator; b. Berlin, Jan. 7, 1925; s. Franz and Martha (Janssen) N.; Diplom-Ingenieur, Technische U. Berlin, 1951; Lincencié ès Sciences, U. Paris, 1950; Ph.D., Ind. U., 1954; m. Helga I. Schönberg, Apr. 1, 1955 (dec. Jan. 1976); children—Virginia, Peter; m. 2d, Mary T. Strauss, Jan. 3, 1979. Came to U.S., 1955, naturalized, 1961. Sci. asst. Technische U. Berlin, 1951-55; instr. U. So. Calif., 1955-56; asso. prof. Carnegie-Mellon U., Pitts., 1956-60, prof., 1960—. Vis. prof. Johns Hopkins, 1962-63; vis. lectr. Soc. for Indsl. and Applied Math., 1969-71. Mem. Soc. for Natural Philosophy (founding, pres. 1973-75), Am. Math. Soc., Math. Assn. Am. Author: (with C. Truesdell) The Non-Linear Field Theories of Mechanics, 1965; (with B.D. Coleman, H. Markovitz) Viscometric Flows of Non-Newtonian Fluids, 1966; The Foundations of Mechanics and Thermodynamics, Selected Papers, 1974. Home: 308 Field Club Ridge Rd Pittsburgh PA 15238

NOLTE, HENRY R., JR., automobile co. exec.; b. N.Y.C., Mar. 3, 1924; s. Henry R. and Emily A. (Eisele) N.; B.A., Duke, 1947; LL.B., U. Pa., 1949; m. Frances Messner, May 19, 1951; children—Gwynne, Henry Reed III, Jennifer, Suzanne. Admitted to N.Y. bar, 1950, Mich. bar, 1967; asso. firm Cravath, Swaine & Moore, N.Y.C., 1951-61; asso. counsel Ford Motor Co., Dearborn, Mich., 1961, asst. gen. counsel, 1964-71, asso. gen. counsel, 1971-74, v.p., gen. counsel, 1974—; v.p., gen. counsel, sec. Philco-Ford Corp., Phila., 1961-64, Ford of Europe, Inc., Warley, Essex, Eng., 1967-69; gen. counsel finance and ins. subsidiaries Ford Motor Co., 1974—; mem. Ford Motor Co. Fund. Trustee, Cranbrook-Kingswood Schs., Bloomfield Hills, Mich.; vice chmn. adv. bd. Internat. and Comparative Law Center of Southwestern Legal Found.; mem. Pres.'s Assos. Duke, 1976. Served to lt. USNR, 1943-46; PTO. Mem. Am. (mem. com. corporate law depts. 1974), Mich. bar assns., Assn. Bar City of N.Y., Assn. Gen. Counsel. Episcopalian. Club: Orchard Lake (Mich.) Country. Office: Ford Motor Co The American Rd Dearborn MI 48121

NOLTE, JAMES ADAM, bldg. materials distbg. co. exec.; b. Skokie, Ill., Sept. 9, 1943; s. Arthur Harry and Helen (Grimes) N.; B.A. in Bus. Adminstrn., Principia Coll., Elsah, Ill., 1965; M.B.A. in Fin., Northwestern U., 1967; m. Kay Slaughter, June 20, 1967; children—James Adam, II, Jennifer, Kathleen. Fin. analyst Gates Radio Co., Quincy, Ill., 1967-68; instr. Principia Coll., 1968-70; with Slaughter Bros. Inc., 1970—, treas., then v.p., 1974-78, pres., Dallas, 1978—. Active local Jr. Achievement. Mem. N. Am. Wholesale Lumber Assn., Nat. Bldg. Material Distbrs. Assn. Club: Northwood. Home: 3805 Maplewood St Dallas TX 75205 Office: 11300 N Central Expressway Dallas TX 75231

NOLTE, JUDITH ANN, mag. editor; b. Hampton, Iowa, Sept. 17, 1938; d. Clifford P. and Sigrid M. (Johnson) Nolte; B.S., U. Minn., 1960; M.A., in English, N.Y. U., 1965; m. Randers H. Heimer, May 7, 1971. Tchr. English, Middletown (N.Y.) High Sch., 1960-62, High Sch. of Commerce, N.Y.C., 1962-64; merchandising editor Conde Nast Publs., N.Y.C., 1964-69; editor-in-chief Am. Baby mag., N.Y.C., 1969—. Mem. Mortar Bd., Delta Gamma. Office: 575 Lexington Ave New York City NY 10022

NOLTE, NICK, actor; b. Omaha; m. Sharon Haddad. Acted with repertory groups; appeared in play The Last Pad, Hollywood, Calif., 1973; TV movies include: Winter Kill, 1974, The California Kid, 1974, Death Sentence, 1974, Adams of Eagle Lake, 1975, The Treasure Chest Murder, 1975, The Runaways, 1975; starred on TV in ltd. dramatic series Rich Man, Poor Man, 1976; films: The Deep, 1977, Return to Macon County, 1975, Who'll Stop the Rain, 1978, North Dallas Forty, 1979, Heartbeat, 1980. Office: care Internat Creative Mgmt 8899 Beverly Blvd Los Angeles CA 90048*

NOLTE, RICHARD HENRY, corp. exec.; b. Duluth, Minn., Dec. 27, 1920; s. Julius Mosher and Mildred (Miller) N.; A.B., Yale, 1943, M.A., 1947; B.A. (Rhodes scholar), Oxford (Eng.) U., 1950, Inst. Current World Affairs fellow, 1948-54; D.Sc. (hon.), U. Wis., Milw., 1979; m. Jeanne McQuarrie, Mar. 27, 1945; children—Charles McQuarrie, Roger Reed, Douglas Mitchell, Jameson Jay. Asso. in Middle East, Am. Univs. Field Staff, 1953-58; asst. dir. humanities Rockefeller Found., Inc., N.Y.C., 1958-59; exec. dir. Inst. Current World Affairs, N.Y.C., 1959-78; exec. dir. Alicia Patterson Found., N.Y.C., 1965-78; exec. v.p. Hamilton, Johnston & Co., Inc., N.Y.C., 1978—; ambassador to Egypt, Cairo, 1967. Bd. dirs. AMIDEAST, Inst. Current World Youth Affairs. Served as pilot, USNR, 1943-45. Mem. Am. Geog. Soc. (pres. 1973—, dir.), Arctic Inst. N.Am., Internat. Inst. Communications, Council on Fgn. Relations, Middle East Inst., Middle East Studies Assn., N.Y. Acad. Sci., Phi Beta Kappa. Clubs: Yale, Cosmos, Century Assn., Mid-Atlantic. Editor: The Modern Middle East, 1963. Home: 50 Cat Rock Rd Cos Cob CT 06807 Office: 11 E 44th St New York NY 10017

NOLTE, ROGER EMERSON, engring. educator; b. Moville, Iowa, Aug. 9, 1922; s. Paul Ervin and Ina Agnes (Rogers) N.; B.E.E., Iowa State Coll., 1943, M.S., 1948, Ph.D., 1955; grad. studies Columbia, Bowdoin Coll., Mass. Inst. Tech., U. Ill., Mo. Sch. Mines, Stanford; m. Janet Amanda Hansen, July 2, 1944; children—Susan Marie, Marilyn Janet, Karen Louise, Paul Allen, David Roger. Instr. naval engring. Iowa State Coll., 1943-44, instr. elec. engring. dept., 1946-49, research, 1954-55; research engr. electronics Martin Aircraft Co., 1946; asst., then asso. prof. electronics servomechanisms and circuits Mo. Sch. Mines, 1949-54, prof. elec. engring., 1955-60, prof., chmn. dept., 1960-67; prof., chmn. dept. elec. engring. U. Miami, 1967-69; dean Herf Coll. Engring., dir. Inst. Engring. Research, Memphis State U., 1969-78, prof. elec. engring., 1978—; cons. evaluation electronic countermeasures equipment, summer, 1957. Served to lt. USNR, 1944-46. Registered profl. engr., Mo. Mem. Am. Inst. E.E., I.R.E., I.E.E.E., Am. Soc. Engring. Edn. (chmn. Mo.- Ark. sect. 1963-64, chmn. exec. council sects. West 1964-66; v.p., dir. 1964-66), Tenn. Soc. Profl. Engrs., Sigma Xi, Phi Kappa Phi, Tau Beta Pi, Eta Kappa Nu (bd. dirs. 1957-59), Sigma Pi Sigma, Pi Kappa Alpha. Methodist. Home: 1307 Brookfield Rd Memphis TN 38117

NOLTE, WALTER EDUARD, retirement home adminstr., found. exec., former banker; b. Joplin, Mo., Oct. 28, 1911; s. Ernest Henry and Clara (Meyer) N.; A.B., U. Nebr., 1934, J.D., 1936; m. Sara Elizabeth Mumford, Oct. 6, 1939; children—Walter Eduard, Craig R. Admitted to Nebr. bar, 1936, Tex. bar, 1952, also U.S. Supreme Ct.; with firm Beghtol, Foe & Rankin, Lincoln, Nebr., 1936-48; asst. atty. gen., Neb., 1948-50, dep. atty. gen., 1950-52; pres. Nolte Nat. Bank, Seguin, Tex., 1952-59; v.p. 1st Nat. Bank & Trust Co., Lincoln, 1959-60, exec. v.p., 1960-76; adminstr. Gateway Manor Retirement Apt.; dir. 1st Nat. Lincoln Corp., Holiday Life Ins. Co., Dallas, Walker Mfg. & Sales Co., St. Joseph, Mo. Pres., Lincoln Better Bus. Bur., 1964-65. Past pres. Lincoln Gen. Hosp. and Lincoln Hosp. Assn.; gen. chmn. Lincoln United Fund, 1973-74; bd. dirs. Lincoln Symphony Assn.; pres. Tb Assn., 1970. Served to lt. comdr. USNR, 1943-45. Mem. Nebr. Bar Assn., State Bar Tex., Lincoln C. of C. (pres. 1967—), Neb. Assn. Commerce and Industry (pres. 1975-76), Beta Theta Pi, Phi Delta Phi. Republican. Episcopalian. Elk. Clubs: Country of Lincoln, Nebraska (dir.), Ak-Sar-Ben, Lincoln University. Co-editor: Nebraska Restatement of Trusts, 1941. Home: 225 N 56th St Lincoln NE 68504 Office: 3835 Holdrege St Lincoln NE 68503

NOLTMANN, ERNST AUGUST, biochemist, educator; b. Gotha, Germany, June 27, 1931; s. Ernst Heinrich and Tela Adelheid (Hoecke) N.; student U. Münster (Germany), 1950-53, U. Freiburg, 1953-54; M.D., U. Düsseldorf (Germany), 1956; m. Lisel Ruth Voss, June 2, 1956; children—Ingo, Udo. Came to U.S., 1959, naturalized, 1971. Asst. biochemist U. Düsseldorf Med. Sch., 1956-59; postdoctoral fellow U. Wis. Inst. Enzyme Research, 1959-62; asst. prof. biochemistry U. Calif., Riverside, 1962-65, asso. prof., 1965-69, prof. biochemistry, 1969—, chmn. dept., 1971-72, 75-76, asso. dean biomed. scis., 1976—. USPHS research grantee, 1963—, NSF grantee, 1964-66, 79—. Mem. Am. Soc. Biol. Chemists, Am. Chem. Soc., Deutsche Gesellschaft für Biologische Chemie, Sigma Xi. Office: Div Biomed Scis U Calif Biochemistry Riverside CA 92521

NOMURA, MASAYASU, scientist, educator; b. Hyogo-Ken, Japan, Apr. 27, 1927; s. Hiromichi and Yaeko N.; Ph.D., U. Tokyo, 1957; m. Junko Hamashima, Feb. 10, 1957; children—Keiko, Toshiyasu. Asst. prof. Inst. Protein Research, Osaka (Japan) U., 1960-63; asso. prof. genetics U. Wis., Madison, 1963-66, prof., 1966—, prof. genetics and biochemistry, 1970—, co-dir. Inst. for Enzyme Research, 1970—. Recipient U.S. Steel award in molecular biology Nat. Acad. Scis., 1971; recipient Acad. award Japanese Acad. Arts and Sci., 1972. Mem. Am. Acad. Arts and Scis., Nat. Acad. Scis., Royal Danish Acad. Scis. and Letters. Home: 6429 Maywood Ave Middleton WI 53562 Office: Univ of Wis Inst for Enzyme Research 1710 University Ave Madison WI 53706

NOOJIN, RAY O., dermatologist; b. Birmingham, Ala., Nov. 29, 1912; s. Ray Oscar and Lillian (Dunnam) N.; A.B., U. Ala., 1933; M.D., U. Chgo., 1937; m. Martha Gunning, May 12, 1938; children—Barbara Dade (Mrs. Richard LeRoy Walthall), Ray O., Martha Elizabeth (Mrs. Robert McLester Ramsay, Jr.). Instr. pharmacology U. Chgo., 1937; intern in medicine Duke U., 1938-40, resident dermatology, 1941-44, instr. dermatology, 1945; prof. dermatology U. Ala. Sch. Medicine, Birmingham, 1945—, chmn. dept., 1945—. Chmn. task force for allied health profls. Nat. Program for Dermatology, 1970-71; chmn. Residency Rev. Com. for Dermatology, 1969-72. Chmn. bd. trustees Brooke Hill Sch. for Girls, 1961. Diplomate Am. Bd. Dermatology (mem. bd. 1964—, v.p. 1969-70, pres. 1970-71). Mem. AMA, Am. Dermatol. Assn. (dir. 1959-64), Am. Acad. Dermatology (chmn. membership com. 1954, dir. 1957-59, ednl. com. 1971-74, dir. 1975—), Ala. Dermatol. Soc. (pres. 1947, 51), Soc. for Investigative Dermatology, Southeastern Dermatol. Assn. (pres. 1955), So. Med. Assn. (chmn. dermatology sect. 1955), Assn. Profs. Dermatology (pres. 1974-75), Phi Beta Kappa, Alpha Omega Alpha, Gamma Sigma Epsilon, Alpha Epsilon Delta, Delta Kappa Epsilon. Rotarian (pres. Birmingham 1971-72). Editor: Dermatology for Students; Dermatology, A Practitioner's Guide, 1977. Home: 3425 Argyle Rd Birmingham AL 35213 Office: 2661 10th Ave South Birmingham AL 35205

NOON, THEODORE WOODS, JR., ret. investment co. exec.; b. Cambridge, Mass., Feb. 19, 1919; s. Theodore Woods and Winifred Edith (Dearborn) N.; S.B., Harvard U., 1940, M.B.A., 1951; m. Marjorie Spence Hill, Nov. 27, 1942; children—Nicholas Woods, Jonathan Douglas, Laura Lee Noon Alton. Geologist, engr. Texaco, Inc., Fort Worth, 1940-48; partner, v.p. Colonial Fund and Colonial Mgmt. Assos., Boston, 1951-60; gen. investment mgr. Prudential Ins. Co., Newark, 1960-65; v.p. Affiliated Fund, exec. v.p. Lord Abbett Income Fund, v.p. Lord Abbett Devel. Growth Fund, Lord, Abbett & Co. (all N.Y.C.), 1965-79; cons. in field. Mem. zoning com. City of Holliston (Mass.), 1958; trustee Holliston Library, 1956-59. Served to capt. AUS, 1941-45. Decorated D.S.C. Mem. Am. Assn. Petroleum Geologists, Am. Inst. Mining and Metall. Engrs., Chartered Fin. Analysts Assn., N.Y. Soc. Security Analysts. Republican. Congregationalist. Home: Hopkinton Village RD 1 Concord NH 03301

NOONAN, JOHN T., JR., educator, author; b. Boston, Oct. 24, 1926; s. John T. and Marie (Shea) N.; B.A., Harvard, 1946, LL.B., 1954; student Cambridge (Eng.) U., 1946-47; M.A., Cath. U. Am., 1949, Ph.D., 1951; LL.D., U. Santa Clara, 1974, U. Notre Dame, 1976, Loyola U. of South, 1978; m. Mary Lee Bennett, Dec. 27, 1967; children—John Kenneth, Rebecca Lee, Susanna Bain. Admitted to Mass. bar, 1954, U.S. Supreme Ct. bar, 1971; mem. spl. staff Nat. Security Council, 1954-55; practice law, Boston, 1955-60; prof. law U. Notre Dame Law Sch., 1961-66; prof. law U. Calif. at Berkeley, 1967—, chmn. religious studies, 1970-73, chmn. medieval studies, 1978-79; Oliver Wendell Holmes, Jr. lectr. Harvard Law Sch., 1972; chmn. bd. Games Research, Inc., 1961-76; Pope John XXIII lectr. Cath. U. Law Sch., 1973; Cardinal Bellarmine lectr. St. Louis U. Div. Sch., 1973. Chmn. Brookline (Mass.) Redevel. Authority, 1958-62; cons. Papal Commn. on Family, 1965-66, Ford Found., Indonesian Legal Program, 1968, NIH, 1973, Nat. Endowment Humanities, 1973—; expert Presdl. Commn. on Population and Am. Future, 1971; cons. U.S. Cath. Conf., 1979—; sec.-treas. Inst. for Research in Medieval Canon Law, 1970—; pres. Thomas More-Jacques Maritain Inst., 1977—. Trustee, Population Council, 1969-76, Phi Beta Kappa Found., 1970-76, Grad. Theol. Union, 1970-73, U. San Francisco, 1971-75; mem. com. theol. edn. Yale, 1972-77; exec. com. Cath. Commn. Intellectual and Cultural Affairs, 1972-75; bd. dirs. Center for Human Values in the Health Sciences, 1969-71, S.W. Intergroup Relations Council, 1970-72, Inst. for Study Ethical Issues, 1971-73. Recipient St. Thomas More award U. San Francisco, 1974, 78, Christian Culture medal, 1975; Guggenheim fellow, 1965-66, 79-80; Center for Advanced Studies in Behavioral Scis. fellow, 1973-74; Wilson Center fellow, 1979-80. Fellow Am. Acad. Arts and Scis.; mem. Am. Soc. Polit. and Legal Philosophy (v.p. 1964), Canon Law Soc. Am. (gov. 1970-72), Am. Law Inst., Phi Beta Kappa (senator United chpts. 1970-76, pres. Alpha of Calif. chpt. 1972-73). Author: The Scholastic Analysis of Usury, 1957; Contraception: A History of Its Treatment by the Catholic Theologians and Canonists, 1965; Power to Dissolve, 1972; Persons and Masks of the Law, 1976; The Antelope, 1977; A Private Choice, 1979; editor: Natural Law Forum, 1961-70, Am. Jour. Jurisprudence, 1970, The Morality of Abortion, 1970. Home: 2599 Buena Vista Way Berkeley CA 94708

NOONAN, PATRICK FRANCIS, conservation assn. exec.; b. St. Petersburg, Fla., Dec. 2, 1942; s. Francis Patrick and Henrietta (Donovan) N.; A.B., Gettysburg Coll., 1961-65; M.City and Regional Planning, Catholic U. Am., 1967; M.B.A., Am. U., 1971; m. Nancy Elizabeth Peck, Aug. 15, 1964; children—Karen Elizabeth, Dawn Wiley. Retail exec. Sears, Roebuck & Co., Lancaster, Pa., 1965; planner Md. Nat. Capitol Park and Planning Com., Silver Spring, 1965-68; investment counseler, real estate broker, appraiser, Washington, 1967-69; dir. ops. The Nature Conservancy, Arlington, Va., 1969-73, pres., 1973—. Exec. com. Natural Resources Council Am., 1973-75; mem. Appalachian Nat. Scenic Trail Adv. Council, 1974—; trustee Cath. Youth Orgn. of Washington, 1975—, Nat. Council on Philanthropy, 1977—, Gettysburg Coll., 1978—. Recipient Conservation award Am. Motors Corp., 1974; Horace Marden Albright Scenic Preservation medal, 1974. Mem. Am. Soc. Appraisers (sr.), Am. Inst. Planners, The Nature Conservancy (life), Sigma Alpha Epsilon. Club: Congressional (Washington). Home: 11901 Glen Mill Rd Potomac MD 20854 Office: 1800 N Kent St Arlington VA 22209

NOONAN, WILLIAM FRANCIS, public relations co. exec.; b. Irvington, N.J., Sept. 29, 1932; s. Thomas Leo and Rose Anna (O'Reilly) N.; B.A. in Journalism, U. Notre Dame, 1954; married; children—William J., Thomas M., Robert P., Carol J. Asst. promotion mgr. plastics div. Union Carbide Corp., N.Y.C., 1956-62; with Burson-Marsteller, N.Y.C., 1962—, account exec., account supr., group mgr., 1962-72, exec. v.p., gen. mgr. N.Y.C. office, 1972—. Served with U.S. Army, 1954-56. Roman Catholic. Club: Citicorp Center (N.Y.C.), Home: 601 St Marks Ave Westfield NJ 07090 Office: 866 3d Ave New York NY 10022

NOONAN, WILLIAM JAMES, investment firm exec.; b. St. Louis, Mar. 9, 1926; s. William Anthony and Margaret (McDonough) N.; student La. Tech. U., 1942-43, St. Louis U., 1946-48; m. Dorothy Noonan, Oct. 29, 1949. With Merrill Lynch Pierce Fenner & Smith, Inc., 1952—, dir. mgmt. tng., N.Y.C., 1964-68, resident v.p., Detroit, 1969-74, regional v.p., dir., Dallas, 1975—. Served to capt. USMC, 1943-46, 50-52. Roman Catholic. Home: 12216 Montego Plaza Dallas TX 75230 Office: 688 Campbell Centre Dallas TX 75206

NOONKESTER, JAMES RALPH, coll. pres.; b. Flatridge, Va., June 10, 1924; s. Reggie L. and Arcie (Parks) N.; B.A., U. Richmond, 1944, LL.D., 1968, Th.M. So. Bapt. Theol. Sem., 1947, Ph.D., 1949; m. Naomi Hopkins, June 10, 1947; children—Myron Craig, Lila. Minister edn. 1st Bapt. Ch., Charlottesville, Va., 1950-52; prof., head div. religion and philosophy William Carey Coll., Hattiesburg, Miss., 1952-53, acad. dean, 1953-56, pres., 1956—; pres. Miss. Found. Ind. Colls.; mem. Edn. Commn. So. Bapt. Conv. Chmn. bd. dirs. Am. Cancer Soc., Miss. div., 1966; campaign chmn. United Givers Fund, 1975-76, pres., 1976-77; council chmn. Boy Scouts Am. Recipient award Outstanding Grad. English, U. Richmond, 1944; named Hattiesburg's Outstanding Young Man of 1956. Mem. NEA, Miss. Edn. Assn., Hattiesburg Concert Assn. (dir.), So. Assn. Bapt. Colls. and Schs. (pres.), Miss. Assn. Colls. (pres.), Hattiesburg C. of C. (pres. 1966), Phi Beta Kappa, Phi Delta Kappa; Chi Beta Phi, Omicron Delta Kappa. Kiwanian. Home: President's House William Carey Coll Hattiesburg MS 39401

NOORDERGRAAF, ABRAHAM, educator, biophysicist; b. Utrecht, Netherlands, Aug. 7, 1929; s. Leendert and Johanna (Kool) N.; B.Sc., U. Utrecht, 1953, M.S., 1955, Ph.D., 1956; M.A. (hon.), U. Pa., 1971; m. Geertruida Alida Van Nee, Sept. 6, 1956; children—Annemiek, Gerrit Jan, Jeske Inette, Alexander Abraham. Teaching asst. U. Utrecht, 1949-50, asst. dept. physics, 1951-53, research asst. dept. med. physics, 1953-55, research fellow dept. med. physics, 1956-58, sr. research fellow dept. med. physics, 1959-65; tchr. math. and physics Vereniging Nijverheidsonderwijs, Utrecht, 1951; research asst. U. Amsterdam (Netherlands), 1952; vis. fellow dept. therapeutic research U. Pa., Phila., 1957-58, asso. prof. biomed. engring. Moore Sch. Elec. Engring., 1964-70, acting head electromed. div., 1968-69, prof. biomed. engring., 1970—, prof. vet. medicine, 1976—, asso. dir. biomed. engring. tng. program, 1971-76, asso. dir. sch., 1972-74, chmn. grad. group in biomed. electronic engring., 1973-75, chmn. dept. bioengring., 1973-76, chmn. grad. group bioengring., 1975-76, dir. systems and integrative biology tng. program, 1979—; vis. prof. biomed. engring. U. Miami, 1970-79, Erasmus U. Med. Sch., Rotterdam, Netherlands, 1970-71, Tech. U., Delft, 1970-71. Mem. spl. study sect. NIH, 1966-68; cons. sci. affairs div. NATO, 1973—; participant numerous internat. confs. in field. Vice pres. Haverford Friends Sch. PTA, 1968-70. Recipient Herman C. Burger award, 1978. Fellow IEEE (mem. adminstrv. com. engring. in medicine and biology group 1967-70, mem. edn. com. group biomed. engring. 1968-70, sec. Phila. chpt. 1974-75, mem. regional council profl. group engring. in medicine and biology 1974—), N.Y. Acad. Scis., AAAS, Explorers Club, Coll. Physicians Phila.; mem. Nederlandse Natuurkundige Vereniging, Ballistocardiograph Research Soc. U.S.A. (sec.-treas. 1965-67, pres. 1968-70), Biophys. Soc. (charter), Soc. for Ballistocardiographic Research Europe (co-founder 1960, sec.-treas. 1960-61, mem. com. on nomenclature 1960-61, officer 1961-62), Cardiovascular System Dynamics Soc. (pres. 1976—), Franklin Inst., John Morgan Soc., Spl. Interest Group on Biomed. Computing, Biomed. Engring. Soc. (founding mem., chmn. membership com. 1978-79, dir. 1972-75), Am. Heart Assn., Instrument Soc. Am. (sr. mem.), Soc. Math. Biology (charter mem.), Am. Physiol. Soc., Microcirculatory Soc., Sigma Xi. Presbyterian (deacon). Author: (with I. Starr) Ballistocardiography in Cardiovascular Research, 1967; Circulatory System Dynamics, 1978; contbg. author: Biological Engineering, 1969. Editor: (with G.N. Jager and N. Westerhof) Circulatory Analog Computers, 1963; (with G.H. Pollack) Ballistocardiography and Cardiac Performance, 1967, (with E. Kresch) The Venous System: Characteristics and Function, 1969; (with J. Baan and J. Raines) Cardiovascular System Dynamics, 1978; Biophysics and Bioengring. Series, 1976—; contbr. articles to profl. jours. Referee, Biophys. Jour., 1968—, Med. Research Engring., 1968—, Physics in Medicine and Biology, 1969—, Bull. Math. Biophysics, 1972—, Circulation Research, 1973—; mem. editorial adv. bd. Jour. Biomechanics, 1969—; asso. editor Bull. Math. Biology, 1973—. Home: 620 Haydock Ln Haverford PA 19041 Office: Dept Bioengring D2 Univ Pa Philadelphia PA 19104

NOOTER, ROBERT HARRY, govt. ofcl.; b. St. Louis, July 14, 1926; s. Harry and Flora (Schwarz) N.; B.S. in Indsl. Engring., U. Calif. at Berkeley, 1947; postgrad. Washington U., St. Louis, 1948-52, Harvard U., 1961; m. Nancy Lane Ingram, Sept. 12, 1947; children—Thomas, Anne, William, Robert, Mary. With Nooter Corp., St. Louis, 1947-62, gen. mgr. Mo. boiler div., 1955-58, v.p. for prodn., 1959-62; with AID, State Dept., various internat. locations, 1962-69, asst. adminstr. for Vietnam, 1970-71, asst. adminstr. for supporting assistance, Washington, 1972-74, asst. adminstr. for Near East and South Asia, 1974-77, dep. adminstr. AID, Washington, 1977—. Served to 1st lt. USMCR, 1944-46, 51-52. Home: 5020 Linnean Ave NW Washington DC 20008 Office: AID Dept State Washington DC 20523

NORBECK, EDWARD, educator, anthropologist, author; b. Prince Albert, Sask., Can., Mar. 18, 1915; s. Gabriel and Hannah (Norman) N.; came to U.S., 1923, naturalized, 1941; student Wash. State Coll., 1936-37; B.A. in Oriental Langs. and Lit., U. Mich., 1948, M.A. in Oriental Civilizations, 1949, Ph.D. in Anthropology, 1952; m. Jeanne Lewellen, Sept. 22, 1940 (dec. Oct. 14, 1944); m. 2d, Margaret Roberta Field, Feb. 18, 1950 (div. Nov. 8, 1976); children—Hannah Field, Edward Crosby, Seth Peter; m. 3d, Katherine Shannon, Oct. 6, 1977; children—George T. Shannon, David C. Shannon, Albert P. Shannon. Instr., then asst. prof. anthropology U. Utah, 1952-54; asst. prof. U. Calif. at Berkeley, 1954-60; mem. faculty Rice U., 1960—, chmn. dept. anthropology and sociology, 1960-71, 78-79, prof. anthropology, 1962—, dean humanities, 1965-67, dir. symposium on new world archaeology, 1962, dir. interdisciplinary symposium on study personality, 1966, dir. Center Research Social Change and Econ. Devel. 1966-69, dir. grad. program in behavioral sci., 1969—. Vice pres. Tourmaline Press, 1970—. Bd. dirs. S.W. Center for Urban Research, 1970-74, v.p., 1972-73. Served to 2d lt. AUS, 1943-47. Recipient Piper award for excellence in teaching and scholarship, 1972. Fellow Am. Anthrop. Assn. (vis. lectr. 1962-73, program dir. ann. meeting 1977), Explorers Club; mem. Am. Ethnol. Soc. (councilor 1972-75, pres. 1976, program dir. ann. meeting 1977), Soc. for Sci. Study Religion, AAAS, Japanese Soc. Ethnology, Assn. for Asian Studies, Houston Archeol. Soc., Assn. for Anthrop. Study of Play (mem. at large exec. bd. 1977-79), Phi Beta Kappa, Sigma Xi, Phi Kappa Phi. Author: Takashima, A Japanese Fishing Community, 1954; Pineapple Town-Hawaii, 1959; Religion in Primitive Society, 1961; Changing Japan, 1965, 2d edit., 1976; Religion and Society in Modern Japan, 1970; Religion in Human Life, 1974; From Country to City: Takashima Urbanized, 1978. Editor: Prehistoric Man in the New World, 1964; The Study of Personality: An Interdisciplinary Appraisal, 1968; The Study of Japan in the Behavioral Sciences, 1970; The Anthropological Study of Human Play, 1974; Ideas of Culture, Sources and Uses, 1976; Forms of Play of Native North Americans, 1979; Goodyear series regional anthropology, 1970—. Contbr. articles to profl. jours. Anthrop. field research, Ont., 1949, Japan, 1950-51, 58-59, 64-66, 74, Hawaii, 1956. Office: Dept Anthropology Rice Univ Houston TX 77001

NORBERG, CHARLES ROBERT, lawyer; b. Cleve., July 25, 1912; s. Rudolf Carl and Ida Edith (Roberts) N.; B.S. in Adminstrv. Engring., Cornell U., 1934; M.A. in Internat. Econs., U. Pa., 1937; LL.B., Harvard U., 1939; Admitted to Pa. bar, 1940, U.S. Supreme Ct. bar, 1946, D.C. bar, 1947; lab. research asst. Willard Storage Battery Co., Cleve., 1934-35; asso. firm Hepburn and Norris, Phila., 1939-42; with Office of Assn. Sec. State for Public Affairs, Dept. State, 1948-51; asst. dir. phychol. strategy bd. Exec. Office of the Pres., 1952-54; mem. staff U.S. Delegation to UN Gen. Assembly, Paris, 1951; adviser U.S. Delegation to UNESCO Gen. Conf., Montevideo, 1954; asso. firm Morgan, Lewis and Bockius, Washington, 1955-56; individual practice law, Washington, 1956—; treas., gen. counsel Inter-Am. Comml. Arbitration Commn., 1968—; chief Spl. AID Mission to Ecuador, 1961, spl. Aid Mission to Uruguay, 1961; mem. U.S. delegation to Specialized Inter-Am. Conf. on pvt. internat. law, Panama, 1975. Chmn. Internat. Visitors Info. Service, Washington, 1965-69; chmn. Mayor's Com. on Internat. Visitors, Washington, 1971-78; chmn., pres. Bicentennial Commn. of D.C., Inc., 1975—. Served with USAF, 1942-46. Mem. Phila. Bar Assn., Pa. Bar Assn., Inter-Am. Bar Assn., Washington Fgn. Law Soc. (pres. 1959-63), Am. Soc. Internat. Law, Am. Law Inst., Am. Bar Assn. (chmn. internat. legal exchange program 1974-79), Bar Assn. of D.C. (chmn. internat. law com. 1977—), Inter-Am. Bar Found. (founder, dir. 1957, pres. 1969—), Academia Colombiana de Jurisprudencia, Inter-Am. Acad. Internat. and Comparative Law, Colegio de Abogados de Quito. Clubs: Met. (Washington); Racquet (Phila.); Harvard (N.Y.C.). Home: 3104 N St NW Washington DC 20007 Office: 1819 H St NW Washington DC 20006

NORBERG, RICHARD EDWIN, educator, physicist; b. Newark, Dec. 28, 1922; s. Arthur Edwin and Melita (Roefer) N.; B.A., DePauw U., 1943; M.A., U. Ill., 1947, Ph.D., 1951; m. Patricia Ann Leach, Dec. 27, 1947 (dec. July 1977); children—Karen Elizabeth, Craig Alan, Peter Douglas; m. 2d, Jeanne C. O'Brien, Apr. 1, 1978. Research asso., control systems lab. U. Ill., 1951-53, asst. prof., 1953; vis. lectr. physics Washington U., St. Louis, 1954—, mem. faculty, 1955—, prof. physics, 1958—, chmn. dept. 1963—. Served with USAAF, 1943-46. Fellow Am. Phys. Soc. Home: 7134 Princeton St Saint Louis MO 63130

NORBY, MAURICE JOSEPH, hosp. cons.; b. Le Center, Minn., May 21, 1908; s. Joseph Gerhard and Minnie Annett (Johnson) N.; B.A., St. Olaf Coll., 1930; M.A., U. Minn., 1934; m. Ethel Catherine Magnus, Aug. 21, 1931; 1 dau., Nancy Ann. High sch. tchr. sci., Minn., 1930-36; organizer Blue Cross Commn., Chgo., 1937-38; organizer, dir. Blue Cross Plan, Western Pa., 1939-40; research dir. Blue Cross Commn., 1941-45; asso. dir. Commn. Hosp. Care, 1946-48; with Am. Hosp. Assn., Chgo., 1948-73, dep. dir., 1953-62, sec., 1959-64, dir. Western office, San Francisco, 1964-66, staff cons., 1967-73; hosp. adminstrn. cons., 1973—. Mem. adv. coms. HEW. Mem. Evanston (Ill.) Bd. Edn., 1943-48. Bd. dirs. Hacienda Community Assn., 1968-69. Mem. Nat. Assn. Exhibit Mgrs. (dir. 1959-60), Am. Pub. Health Assn. Club: Executives (Chgo.). Address: Hacienda Carmel Carmel CA 93921

NORBY, ROCKFORD DOUGLAS, fin. services co. exec.; b. Silver City, N.Mex., June 28, 1935; s. John Rockford and Alice (Simons) N.; B.A. magna cum laude, Harvard U., 1957, M.B.A. with distinction (Baker scholar), 1959; m. Katherine Lorraine Williams, June 17, 1957; children—John Rockford II, Katherine Alice Laidley, James Randall. Asso., McKinsey & Co., Inc., N.Y.C., 1960-63, San Francisco, 1963-67; v.p. fin. Itel Corp., San Francisco, 1968-73, exec. v.p., 1977—; v.p. First Chgo. Corp., 1973-74; v.p. fin. Fairchild Camer & Instrument Corp., Mt. View, Calif., 1974-77; dir. New Horizons Savs. & Loan Assn.; mem. Minority Bus. Cons. Group. Recipient Decur award Harvard Coll., 1956. Mem. Am. Mgmt. Assn., Sierra Club, Phi Beta Kappa. Democrat. Roman Catholic. Clubs: Olympic, Commonwealth, Harvard, Bankers (San Francisco); Harvard, Bd. Room (N.Y.C.); Harvard Bus. Sch. of No. Calif. Home: PO Box 1113 Ross CA 94957 Office: 1 Embarcadero Center San Francisco CA 94111

NORBY, WILLIAM CHARLES, investment exec.; b. Chgo., Aug. 10, 1915; s. Oscar Maurice and Louise (Godejohann) N.; A.B., U. Chgo., 1935; m. Camilla Edbrooke, June 12, 1943; children—Martha N. Fraundorf, Richard James. With Harris Trust & Savs. Bank, Chgo., 1935-70, v.p., 1953-64, sr. v.p., 1964-70; exec. dir. Financial Analysts Fedn., N.Y.C., 1970-72; sr. v.p., dir. Duff & Phelps, Inc., Chgo., 1973—; mem. Fin. Accounting Standards Adv. Council, 1975—. Mem. Bd. Edn., Elementary Sch. Dist. 102, La Grange, Ill., 1959-68, pres., 1965-68. Bd. dirs. Plymouth Place Retirement Home, La Grange, pres., 1976-79; trustee George Williams Coll., Downers Grove, Ill., 1963-74, chmn., 1968-72, hon. trustee, 1974—; bd. mgrs. YMCA Met. Chgo. Served to capt. USAAF, 1942-46. Mem. Investment Analysts Soc. Chgo. (pres. 1955-56), Financial Analysts Fedn. (pres. 1963-64, dir. 1962-68; Distinguished Service award 1973, Nicholas Molodovsky award 1979), Am. Inst. C.P.A.'s (mem. commn. auditors responsibilities 1975-78), U. Chgo. Alumni Assn. (citation for Pub. Service, 1961), Phi Beta Kappa. Congregationalist (trustee 1950-56, chmn. 1955-56). Clubs: Board Room (N.Y.C.); University (Chgo.). Home: 337 Blackstone Ave LaGrange IL 60525 Office: 55 E Monroe St Chicago IL 60603

NORCIA, STEPHEN WILLIAM, advt. exec.; b. N.Y.C., Jan. 21, 1941; s. William Matthew and Amelia (Marrone) N.; B.A., U. Conn., 1962. Media planner and buyer Sullivan Stauffer & Bayles, N.Y.C., 1965-66; regional account exec. McCann Erickson Co., Chgo., 1966-68, v.p., account dir. Milw., 1972, N.Y.C., 1972-74, sr. v.p., gen. mgr., Atlanta, 1974-78, mgmt. rep., N.Y.C., 1978-79, exec. v.p., gen. mgr. N.Y. Office, 1979—; account exec. Needham, Harper & Steers, Chgo., 1968-70; mktg. dir. product devel. workshop Interpub., N.Y.C., 1970-72; bd. dirs. Communication Counselors Network, 1974—. Served with U.S. Army, 1962-65. Republican. Home: 2 Beekman Pl New York NY 10022 Office: 485 Lexington Ave New York NY 10017

NORCOTT, ALFRED A., advt. exec.; b. Bklyn., July 13, 1918; s. Alex Fred and Isabella (MacLennan) N.; B.S., Rutgers U., 1952; m. Ruth Marie Jackson, May 15, 1943; children—Alfred A., Ellen M. (Mrs. Joseph S. Koczeniak, Jr.). With U.S. Lines Co., 1939-42, Gen. Motors Corp., 1946-47; with Kenyon & Eckhardt, Inc., 1947—, now v.p., sec. Served with USNR, 1935-39, 42-45. Home: 25 Morningside Rd Verona NJ 07044 Office: 200 Park Ave New York NY 10017

NORD, ALAN ANDREW, army officer; b. Faulkton, S.D., Aug. 7, 1928; s. Roy Alan and CAroline Otillia (Boller) N.; B.S. in Chemistry, S.D. State U., 1952; B.A. (Rhodes scholar), Oxford (Eng.) U., 1955, M.A. in Chemistry, 1958; M.S. in Internat. Affairs, George Washington U., 1969; m. Elizabeth Anne Hawks, May 19, 1967; children—Brian, Andrew, Kevin. Served as enlisted man U.S. Army, 1946-47, commd., 1952, advanced through grades to maj. gen.; project mgr. for Safeguard Munitions, 1972-73; mem. exec. sci. and tech. team Army Materiel Acquisition Rev. Com., 1973-74; comdr., 1975; dir. procurement and prodn. Armament Command, 1975-77; dep. comdr. Armament Materiel Readiness Command, 1977; dir. supply and maintenance Office of Dep. Chief of Staff for Logistics, Dept. of the Army, Washington, 1977—. Decorated Legion of Merit with oak leaf cluster, Bronze Star medal, Meritorious Service medal, Army Commendation medal with oak leaf cluster; recipient Disting. Alumnus award S.D. State U., 1979. Mem. Assn. U.S. Army, Am. Legion, Nat. Def. Preparedness Assn. Congregationalist. Club: Masons. Office: Room 2E 554 The Pentagon Washington DC 20310

NORD, HENRY J., transp. co. exec.; b. Berlin, Germany, May 1, 1917; s. Walter and Herta (Riess) N.; came to U.S., 1937, naturalized, 1943; student U. Oxford (Eng.), 1934, Northwestern U., 1938-40, Ill. Inst. Tech., 1942; J.D., De Paul U., 1949; children—Stephen, Philip. Apprentice in export, Hamburg, Germany, 1935- 37; with GATX Corp., Chgo., 1938—, comptroller, 1961—, v.p., 1967-71, exec. v.p., 1971-78, sr. v.p., 1978—, dir., 1964-78; dir. Planned Lighting, Inc. Trustee DePaul U. Served to 1st lt. AUS, 1944-46. C.P.A., Ill. Mem. Internat. Law Assn. Club: City (bd. govs.) (Chgo.). Home: 1000 Lake Shore Plaza Chicago IL 60611 Office: 120 S Riverside Plaza Chicago IL 60680

NORD, ROBERT W(ILLIAM), woodworking mfg. co. exec.; b. Anacortes, Wash., Dec. 11, 1921; s. Eric A. and Olga A. Nord; B.A. in Econs. and Bus., U. Wash., 1946; m. Bette J. Baisden, Nov. 5, 1949; children—Patricia Arness, Scott R., Pamela L. Nord McClure. With E.A. Nord Co. Inc., Everett, Wash., 1946—, gen. mgr., 1964-76, pres., 1976-77, chmn. bd., 1977—; dir. Olympic Bank, Everett, Land Title Co., Everett. Bd. dirs. Everett Gen. Hosp. Served with USAAF, 1943-45. Republican. Presbyterian. Clubs: Cascade, Everett Golf and Country (Everett).

NORDBY, GENE MILO, coll. adminstr.; b. Anoka, Minn., May 7, 1926; s. Bert J. and Nina Grace (Nordby) N.; B.S. in Civil Engring., Oreg. State U., 1948; M.S. in Civil Engring., U. Minn., 1949, Ph.D. in Civil Engring., 1955; m. Arlene Delores Anderson, Aug. 27, 1949 (dec. Nov. 1974); children—Susan Pamela, Brett Gene, Lisa Lea; m. 2d, Dusilla Anne Rycroft, July 8, 1975. Grad. asst. U. Minn., 1948-50; structural designer Pfeiffer and Shultz, engrs., Mpls., summer 1950; instr., then asst. prof. civil engring. U. Colo., 1950-56; asso. prof. civil engring., research engr. Joint Hwy. Research Project, Purdue U., 1956; engr. program dir. engring. scis. NSF, 1956-58; lectr. civil engring. George Washington U., 1956-58; prof. civil engring., head dept. U. Ariz., 1958-62, dir., then chmn. adv. com. Ariz. Transp. and Traffic Inst. at univ., 1959-62; prof. engring. U. Okla., 1962-77, dean Coll. Engring., 1962-70, v.p. for adminstrn. and fin., 1969-77; v.p. for bus. and fin., prof. civil engring. Ga. Inst. Tech., 1977—; pres. Tetracon Assos., Inc., 1968—; cons. structural engring., research financing and programming, ednl. facilities planning and constrn., reinforced concrete. Served with AUS, 1943-46. Registered profl. engr., Colo. Ariz., Okla. Fellow ASCE; mem. Am. Soc. Engring. Edn. (projects bd. 1969—), Nat. Soc. Profl. Engrs., Am. Arbitration Assn., Engrs. Council for Profl. Devel. (chmn. engring. edn. and accreditation com. 1970, dir. 1976—), Okla. Soc. Profl. Engrs. (dir. 1966-69), Nat. Assn. State Univs. and Land Grant Colls. (commn. edn. engring. profession 1966, 70-73), Engring. Colls. Adminstrv. Council (mem. exec. bd. 1966), Ga. Soc. Profl. Engrs. (treas. Atlanta chpt. 1978-79), Nat. Assn. Coll. and Univ. Bus. Officers (chmn. personnel com. 1977-79), Sigma Tau, Omicron Delta Pi, Tau Beta Pi, Chi Epsilon. Mason. Co-author: Introduction to Structural Mechanics, 1960. Cons. editor MacMillan Co., 1962-70. Home: 1567 Peachtree Battle Ave Atlanta GA 30327

NORDELL, HANS RODERICK, journalist; b. Alexandria, Minn., June 26, 1925; s. Wilbur Eric and Amelia (Jasperson) N.; A.B. magna cum laude, Harvard, 1948; B.Litt., U. Dublin, 1951; m. Joan Projansky, Apr. 30, 1955; children—Eric Peter, John Roderick, Elizabeth Sabin. With Christian Sci. Monitor, 1948—, arts editor, 1968-73, asst. chief editorial writer, 1973—; free-lance writer, 1957—. Bd. dirs. Community Music Center Boston, 1970—, Young Audiences, 1970—; trustee Berklee Coll. Music; mem. adv. bd. Berlin Jazz Festival, 1970—; mem. Com. for Harvard Theater Collection, 1977—. Served with USMCR, 1943-46. Decorated Commendation ribbon; Rotary Found. fellow, 1950-51. Mem. Phi Beta Kappa. Christian Scientist. Home: 25 Meadow Way Cambridge MA 02138 Office: 1 Norway St Boston MA 02115

NORDEN, CARL WILLIAM, physician; b. N.Y.C., June 25, 1935; s. Daniel and Hazel (Reisman) N.; A.B., Columbia U., 1956; M.D., Harvard U., 1960; m. Margaret Kanof, June 22, 1960; children—Daniel, Samuel. Intern, Peter Bent Brigham Hosp., Boston, 1960-61, resident, 1961-62; resident in medicine Univ. Hosp., Cleve., 1964-66; fellow in medicine Boston City Hosp., 1966-68; asst. prof. medicine U. Rochester, 1968-71; asso. prof. U. Pitts., 1971-78, prof., 1978—; head unit infectious diseases Montefiore Hosp., Pitts., 1971—; cons. in field. Served with USPHS, 1962-64. NIH grantee, 1971—. Mem. Am. Soc. Clin. Investigation, Infectious Diseases Soc. Am., Am. Soc. Microbiology, Central Soc. Clin. Research, Am. Thoracic Soc. Contbr. numerous articles, book chpts. to med. publs. Home: 5466 Fair Oaks St Pittsburgh PA 15210 Office: Montefiore Hosp 3459 5th Ave Pittsburgh PA 15213

NORDHAUSEN, AUGUST HENRY, artist; b. Hoboken, N.J., Jan. 25, 1901; s. Henry and Katherine (Schwarmann) N.; student N.Y. Sch. Fine and Applied Arts, 1920, 21, Royal Acad. Fine Art, Munich, Germany, 1922-24, 28-29, Kunst Geverbe Schule, Munich, summer 1923, Mass. Inst. Tech., 1943, New Sch. Social Research, 1946, 47; m. Mirian Nordhausen, Oct. 8, 1929; m. 2d, Ethel Williams, Nov. 1978. One-man exhbns., N.Y.C., Atlanta, Balt., Columbus, Ga., also Munich, Germany; exhbns. numerous nat. shows and galleries, including Glass Palace, Munich, Germany, Nat. Acad. Design, Chgo. Art Inst., Corcoran Gallery, Art Inst. Balt., Allied Artists Am., Audubon Artists, Atlanta Art Mus.; represented in permanent collections Cleve. Mus. Fine Art, New Britain (Conn.) Mus., Columbus Art Mus., Ga. Inst. Tech., U. S.C., Syracuse U., C.W. Post Coll., Archives Am. Art, Smithsonian Instn., others; painter numerous portraits of pres.'s, govt. ofcls., univ. and indsl. figures. Bd. dirs. Wall Street Art Assn.; trustee MacDowell Colony. Served to capt. C.E., AUS, World War II; CBI. Fellow Trask Found., Tiffany Found., MacDowell Colony; recipient gold medal Allied Artists Am., award Audubon Artists, awards Am. Water Color Soc., 8 awards Salmagundi Club, others. Mem. Am. Water Color Soc., Artists Fellowship (past v.p.). Clubs: Explorers, Salmagundi (pres.). Home: Hotel des Artistes 1 W 67th St New York NY 10023 also 1108 16th Ave Columbus GA 31906 Office: 303 12th St Columbus GA 31901

NORDIN, JOHN ALGOT, educator; b. Mpls., Mar. 18, 1916; s. John A. and Beda (Nelson) N.; B.A., U. Minn., 1935, M.A., 1937; Ph.D., 1941; m. Agnes June Leith, Apr. 8, 1944 (dec. June 1969); children—Karyn Frances (Mrs. John Palmer), Margaret Lynn (Mrs. David Ragle), Barbara Jean; m. 2d, Margaret N. Lahey, Mar. 30, 1970. Mem. faculty Iowa State U., 1941-61, successively asst. prof. econs., asso. prof., 1941-56, prof. charge instrn., 1956-61; prof. dept. econs. Kans. State U., 1961—. Served with USNR, 1942-45. Mem. Am. Agrl. Econ. Assn., Am. Econ. Assn., Phi Beta Kappa, Gamma Sigma Delta, Omicron Delta Epsilon. Episcopalian. Author: (with Virgil Salera) Elementary Economics, 1954. Contbr. articles to profl. jours. Home: 3024 Montana Ct Manhattan KS 66502

NORDIN, VIDAR JOHN, educator, cons.; b. Ratansbyn, Sweden, June 28, 1924; s. John Herman and Beda Catherina (Wahlen) N.; B.A., U. B.C., 1946, B.Sc.F., 1947; Ph.D., U. Toronto, 1951; m. Julianne Leona Zerr, Oct. 11, 1947; children—Christopher Eric, Katrin Anne. Officer in charge Forest Pathology Lab., Fredericton, N.B., Can., 1949-51; officer in charge, Calgary, Alta., Can., 1952-57; asso. dir. forest biology div. Fed. Agr. Dept., 1958-65; research mgr. Fed. Environment Dept., Ottawa, Ont., Can., 1965-71; prof., dean faculty Forestry, U. Toronto (Ont.), 1971—; chmn. bd. Algonquin Forestry Authority Corp., 1974—; hon. lectr. U. N.B., 1949-51. Co-chmn. U. Toronto United Way Campaign, 1973-74; mem. Provincial Parks Adv. Council, 1974-77. Registered profl. forester, Ont. Mem. Canadian Inst. Forestry (past pres.), Internat. Union Forestry Research Orgns. (past subject group chmn.), Ont. Forestry Assn. (dir.), Ont. Profl. Foresters Assn., Soc. Am. Foresters, Assn. U. Forestry Schs. Can. (pres.), Canadian Owners and Pilots Assn. Club: Canadian. Editorial bd. European Jour. Forest Pathology, 1970—. Contbr. articles to profl. jours. Home: 50 Clarendon Ave Toronto ON M4V 1J1 Canada

NORDLAND, GERALD JOHN, museum adminstr.; b. Los Angeles, July 10, 1927; s. Arthur Andre and Doris Monica (Johnston) N.; A.B., U. So. Calif., 1948, J.D., 1950; m. Mary Lou Lindstrom, Aug. 29, 1948 (div. 1972); children—Brady Lynn, Todd Jefferson. Art critic various mags. and newspapers, 1955-64; dean Chouinard Art Inst., Los Angeles, 1960-64; dir. Washington Gallery Modern Art, Washington, 1964-66, San Francisco Museum Art, 1966-72, Frederick S. Wight Art Gallery, UCLA, 1973-77, Milw. Art Center, 1977—. Commr. Calif. State Fair, 1974-76. Served with U.S. Army, 1953-55. Gaston Lachaise Found. grantee, 1973-74. Mem. Assn. Art Mus. Dirs. Clubs: Univ., Arts (Chgo.). Author: Paul Jenkins, 1972; Gaston Lachaise/The Man and His Work, 1974. Home: 18330 Elm Terrace Dr Brookfield WI 53005 Office: Milw Art Center 750 N Lincoln Memorial Dr Milwaukee WI 53202

NORDLINGER, ERIC ALLEN, educator; b. Frankfurt, Germany, Sept. 18, 1939; s. Leo and Kate (Levi) N.; came to U.S., 1946, naturalized, 1951; B.A. with honors, Cornell U., 1961; M.A., Princeton U., 1963, Ph.D., 1966; m. Carol Maurine Uhl, Jan. 7, 1978; 1 dau., Alexandra. Asst. prof. polit. sci. Brandeis U., 1965-70, asso. prof., 1970-71; research fellow Center for Internat. Affairs, Harvard U., 1968—, lectr. govt. Harvard U. Sch. Medicine, 1969-70; asso. prof. polit. sci. Brown U., 1971-73, prof., 1973—, chmn. dept. polit. sci., 1978—. NSF grantee, 1968, 74; Ford Found. grantee, 1970, fellow, 1971. Mem. Am. Polit. Sci. Assn., Phi Beta Kappa. Author: The Working Class Tories: Authority, Deference and Stable Democracy, 1967; Conflict Regulation in Divided Societies, 1972; Decentralizing the City, 1973; Soldiers in Politics: Military Coups and Governments, 1977; editor: Politics and Society, 1970; mem. editorial bd. Public Policy, Jour. Polit. and Mil. Sociology. Home: 21 Craigie St Cambridge MA 02138 Office: Brown University Providence RI 02912

NORDLUND, DONALD ELMER, mfg. exec.; b. Stromsburg, Nebr., Mar. 1, 1922; s. E.C. and Edith O. (Peterson) N.; A.B., Midland Coll., 1943; LL.B., U. Mich., 1948; m. Mary Jane Houston, June 5, 1948; children—Donald Craig, William Chalmers, Sarah, James. Admitted to Ill. bar, 1949; with Stevenson, Conaghan, Velde

& Hackbert, Chgo., 1948-55; with A.E. Staley Mfg. Co., Decatur, Ill., 1956—, v.p., dir., mem. exec. com., 1958-65, pres., dir., mem. exec. com., 1965—, also chmn., 1975—; dir. Ill. Bell Telephone Co., Amsted Industries, Inc., Citizens Nat. Bank Decatur, Sentry Ins., Sunstrand Corp. Trustee Millikin U.; mem. Grad. Dirs. Council Decatur Meml. Hosp. Served to 1st lt. AUS, 1943-46, 51-52. Mem. Am., Chgo., Decatur bar assns., Decatur Assn. Commerce, Phi Alpha Delta. Club: Legal (Chgo.). Home: 260 N Oakcrest Ave Decatur IL 62522 Office: AE Staley Mfg Co Decatur IL 62525

NORDMAN, CHRISTER ERIC, educator; b. Helsinki, Finland, Jan. 23, 1925; s. Eric Johan and Gertrud (Nordgren) N.; Dipl. Ing., Finnish Inst. Tech., Helsinki, 1949; Ph.D., U. Minn., 1953; m. Barbara Lorraine Neal, Nov. 28, 1952; children—Christina, Aleta, Eric, Carl. Came to U.S., 1948, naturalized, 1960. Research asso. Inst. Cancer Research, Phila., 1953-55; mem. faculty U. Mich., Ann Arbor, 1955—, prof. chemistry, 1964—. Mem. U.S. Nat. Com. Crystallography, 1970-72. Served with Finnish Army, 1943-44. NIH spl. fellow, 1971-72. Mem. AAAS, Am. Chem. Soc., Am. Phys. Soc., Am. Crystallographic Assn. Home: 1109 Heatherway Ann Arbor MI 48104

NORDQUEST, RICHARD EDWARD, mfg. co. exec.; b. Ashtabula, Ohio, Mar. 18, 1918; s. Harmon Richard and Clara (Lorentzen) N.; B.B.A., Cleve. State U., 1949; m. Eunice Miriam Stanton, May 26, 1951. Methods analyst Allied Stores Corp., 1949-51; supr. accounting Precision Castings Co., Syracuse, N.Y., 1951-56; internal auditor Harsco Corp., Harrisburg, Pa., 1956-65, treas., 1965-72, v.p. finance, 1972-78. Sec. Harsco Corp. Fund, 1964—. Served with USNR, 1942-46. Mem. Nat. Assn. Accountants. Rotarian. Address: Harsco Corp Camp Hill PA 17011

NORDSTRAND, RAYMOND WILLIAM, broadcasting co. exec., publisher; b. Evanston, Ill., Sept. 13, 1932; s. Nels Eric and Frida Elise (Kuehl) N.; B.A., Northwestern U., 1953, M.S., 1956; m. Susan Diane Ports, June 15, 1963; 1 dau., Susan Erika. Instr. econs. Northwestern U., 1953-55; announcer WFMT Radio, Chgo., 1953-57, asst. mgr., 1957-63, comml. mgr., 1963-68, sta. mgr., 1968-70, gen. mgr., 1970—; pres. WFMT, Inc., 1970—; pub. Chgo. mag., 1970—. Co-producer nationally syndicated radio program Midnight Special; syndicator radio series Chgo. Symphony, Chgo. Lyric Opera. Treas., trustee Broadcasting Found. Am.; chmn., trustee Cinema/Chgo.; mem. Joseph Jefferson Com.; v.p., trustee Old Town Sch. Folk Music. Recipient Maj. Armstrong award for Midnight Spl. program, 1971; named Outstanding Citizen by resolution of mayor and City Council Chgo., 1973. Mem. Concert Music Broadcasters Assn. (exec. com., chmn. 1975-76), City and Regional Mag. Assn., Nat. Radio Broadcasters Assn., Phi Beta Kappa. Club: Chgo. Advt. (dir.) Contbr. articles to profl. publs. Home: 518 W Roscoe St Chicago IL 60657 Office: 500 N Michigan Ave Chicago IL 60611

NORDSTROM, CARL CLIFFORD, assn. exec.; b. Topeka, Mar. 5, 1916; s. Edward and Betty (Holcomb) N.; A.B., Washburn U., Topeka, 1938; m. Virginia Hamm, Apr. 2, 1943; children—Carla (Mrs. Randy Hearrell), Mary (Mrs. Fred Foster), Mark. Mem. staff research dept. Kan. Legis. Council, 1938-42, 45-46; research dir. Kans. C. of C., 1946-70, asst. mgr., 1954-70; exec. v.p., gen. mgr. Kans. Assn. Commerce and Industry, Topeka, 1970—. Served from ensign to lt., USNR, 1942-46. Mem. Am., Kans. socs. assn. execs., Kans. C. of C. Execs. (past pres.), Washburn U. Alumni Assn. (pres. 1976-77). Home: 813 Oakley St Topeka KS 66606 Office: 500 First Nat Tower Topeka KS 66603

NORDSTROM, CLIFFORD LEO, hosp. adminstr.; b. Randolph, Kans., Sept. 5, 1914; s. Elmer Abraham and Hattie Winfred (Larson) N.; B.A. in Edn., U. Kans., 1942; m. Harriet Louise Brown, Sept. 1, 1944; children—Jon Robert, Mary Kathryn. Asst. dir. hosps. in Beckley, W.Va., 1963-66, Marlin, Tex., 1966-67, Marion, Ind., 1967-69; hosp. adminstrn. specialist VA Central Office, Washington, 1969-72; asst. hosp. dir. Milw. VA Hosp., Wood, Wis., 1972-73; dir. VA Hosp., Allen Park, Mich., 1973-75, Marion, 1975—. Served with USN, 1942-45. Mem. Am. Coll. Hosp. Adminstrs., AmVets, Am. Legion. Clubs: Elks, Moose, Lions, Rotary. Home: 1105 Sherwood Dr Marion IN 46952 Office: VA Hosp Marion IN 46952

NORDSTROM, ROBERT JOHN, educator; b. Cadillac, Mich., May 14, 1924; s. Ernest Conrad and Bernice Mildred (Sutherland) N.; A.B. summa cum laude, Western Mich. U., 1948; J.D., U. Mich., 1949; m. Avis Kathryn VanderWeele, Feb. 25, 1945; children—Robert James, Kathryn Sue, Janet Ellen. Admitted to R.I. bar, 1949, Ohio bar, 1956; with firm Hinckley, Allen, Salisbury & Parsons, Providence, 1949-51; faculty Ohio State U., Columbus, 1951-78, prof. law, 1957-78, asso. dean Coll. Law, 1951-64, chmn. Mershon Center Edn. in Nat. Security, 1959-65; vis. prof. Duke, 1968-69; of counsel Porter, Stanley, Platt & Arthur, Columbus, 1970-73; partner Porter, Wright, Morris & Arthur, Columbus, 1973—. Bd. trustees Ohio Legal Center, chmn., 1972-73; trustee Wesley Found. Ohio. Named Outstanding Young Man Columbus, 1958, 1 of 5 in Ohio, 1958. Mem. League Ohio Law Schs. (past sec.-treas. and past pres.), Ohio Bar Assn. Author: Introduction to Study of Law, 1958; Handbook on the Law of Sales, 1970; co-author Sales and Secured Transactions, 1968; Commercial Paper, 1972, also articles, chpts. in legal encys. Home: 454 Village Dr Columbus OH 43214

NORFLEET, MORRIS LEE, univ. pres.; b. Nancy, Ky., Dec. 15, 1930; s. Hewey and Edna (McFall) N.; B.S., U. Ky., 1952; M.S. in Edn., Purdue U., 1957, Ph.D. in Edn., 1962; m. Loistene Tarter, Dec. 27, 1952; 1 son, Douglas Lee. Tchr., Spiceland (Ind.) Public Schs., 1952-58; public relations asst. Ind. Farm Bur. Coop. Assn., Indpls., 1958-60, market research analyst, 1960; instr. edn. Purdue U., Lafayette, Ind., 1960-62; asso. prof. edn. and dir. student teaching Morehead (KY.) State U.. 1962-65, prof. edn. and dir. research and program devel., 1965-68, v.p. research and devel., 1968-76, acting pres., 1976, pres., 1977—; mem. fed. relations com. Am. Assn. State Colls. and Univs., 1977; mem. bd. dirs. Area Health Edn. System, 1974—; mem. Ky. Council Higher Edn., 1977—, chmn. comprehensive planning task force, 1974-75; asso. project dir. Commn. on Future of State Colls. and Univs. of Am. Assn. State Colls. and Univs. and Morehead State U., 1971-72; cons. U.S. Office of Edn., U.S. OEO, NSF, Danforth Found.; interim dir. Appalachian Adult Basic Edn. Research and Demonstration Center, 1967. Trustee, Campbellsville (KY.) Coll., 1973-78; bd. dirs. Gateway Area Devel. Dist., 1977-79; chmn. Gateway Comprehensive Health Planning Council, 1973; bd. dirs. Cave Run Comprehensive Mental Health Assn., 1969-70; mem. Ky. Sci. and Tech. Commn., 1968-70, N.E. Ky. Crime Commn., 1969-71; mem. steering com. Gov's Efficiency Task Force, 1966; mem. Morehead Indsl. Com., 1968-72; ch. conf. moderator Morehead Baptist Ch., 1968-72, chmn. deacons, 1966-72, supt. young people's dept., 1963-66, tchr., 1963-66. Recipient award Morehead Optimist Club, 1975, Ky. Dept. Human Resources, 1974. Mem. Am. Assn. Tchr. Edn., Ky. Edn. Assn., Am. Assn. Higher Edn., Am. Ednl. Research Assn., Council Advancement and Support of Edn., Nat. Coll. and Univ. Research Adminstrs., Soc. Coll. and Univ. Planning, Phi Kappa Phi, Phi Delta Kappa. Clubs: Lions, Kiwanis, Optimists, Gideons. Home: 328 University Blvd Morehead KY 40351 Office: 201 Howell-McDowell Adminstrn Bldg Morehead State U Morehead KY 40351

NORGREN, C. NEIL, mfg. exec.; b. Silt, Colo., Aug. 23, 1923; s. Carl August and Juliet (Lien) N.; student U. Colo., 1941-43; m. 2d, Lillian M. Simmons, June 7, 1963; children by previous marriage—Jeraldine Leigh, Carol Ann, John Carl, David Laurence. With C.A. Norgren Co., mfrs. pneumatic products, Englewood, Colo., 1938—, purchasing agt., office mgr., 1947-49, asst. gen. mgr., 1949-53, v.p., 1953-55, exec. v.p., 1955-62, pres., 1962—, also dir.; chmn. bd., dir. C.W. Morris Co.; v.p., dir. Tokyo Automatic Control Co. Ltd.; dir. Pneumatic-Norgren S.A. (Argentina), Shavo Norgren (India) Pvt. Ltd. Fabricacion de Equipos Neumaticos S.A. (Mexico), Norgren Shipston Ltd. (Eng.), Unitog Co., United Bank of Denver (mem. exec. com.), Line Investment Co. Dir. Bus.-Industry Polit. Action Com., 1967—. Past pres. Met. Denver chpt. Jr. Achievement; dir. Mile High United Way. Bd. dirs. Denver Mus. Natural History, Carl A. Norgren Found., Nat. Jewish Hosp. and Research Center; past dir. U. Colo. Devel. Found. Served as staff sgt. USAAF, 1942-46. Mem. N.A.M. (dir., regional v.p. 1966-70, exec. com. 1968—, divisional v.p. 1973-78), Nat. Fluid Power Assn., Nat. Council Profit Sharing Industries (past chmn. exec. com.), Colo., Denver chambers commerce, Colo. Assn. Commerce and Industry (dir.), Western Stock Show Assn. (dir.), Gyro Internat., Inst. Dirs., Beta Theta Pi. Clubs: Denver Executives (co-founder, past pres.), Athletic, Cherry Hills Country, Pinehurst Country; Eldorado Country (Calif.); Curzon (London); Garden of the Gods, Air Force Acad. Golf (Colorado Springs, Colo.); Flatirons (dir. 1966—). Home: 17 Sedgwick Dr Englewood CO 80110 Office: 5400 S Delaware St Littleton CO 80120

NORLAND, DONALD RICHARD, fgn. service officer; b. Laurens, Iowa, June 14, 1924; s. Norman and Aletta (Brunsvold) N.; student Iowa State Tchrs. Coll., 1941-43, N.W. Mo. State Tchrs. Coll., 1943-44; B.A., U. Minn., 1948, M.A., 1950; postgrad. U. Mich., 1951-52, Grenoble (France) U., 1948-49; m. Patricia Bamman, Dec. 13, 1952; children—Richard Boyce, David, Patricia D. Instr. history and polit. sci. U. No. Iowa, 1949-51; teaching fellow U. Mich., 1951-52; joined U.S. Fgn. Service, 1952; posts include Rabat, Morocco, 1952-56, Washington, 1956-58, Abidjan, Ivory Coast, 1958-60; mem. NATO delegation, Paris, France, 1961-63, The Hague, The Netherlands, 1964-69; dep. chief mission, Conakry, Guinea, 1970-72; dep. dir. Office Mil. Assistance and Sales, Bur. Politico-Mil. Affairs, Dept. State, Washington, 1972-73, chief polit. officers counseling br. Office Personnel, 1973-75; dep. dir. Office Mgmt. Ops., 1975-76; ambassador to Botswana and Lesotho and Swaziland with principal residence in Gaborone, Botswana, 1976—. Served to lt. (j.g.) USNR, 1943-46. State Dept. fellow Stanford, 1969-70. Mem. Am. Fgn. Service Assn. Contbr. articles to profl. jours. Home: care Am Embassy Gaborone Botswana also 1113 3d St Mason City IA 50401 Office: PO Box 90 Am Embassy Gaborone Botswana

NORMAN, ALBERT GEORGE, JR., lawyer; b. Birmingham, Ala., May 29, 1929; s. Albert G. and Ila Mae (Carroll) N.; B.A., Auburn U., 1953; LL.B., Emory U., 1958; M.A., U. N.C., 1960; m. Catherine Marshall DeShazo, Sept. 3, 1955; children—Catherine Marshall, Albert George III. Admitted to Ga. bar, 1957; asso. firm Moise, Post & Gardner, Atlanta, 1958-60, partner, 1960-62; partner firm Hansell, Post, Brandon & Dorsey, Atlanta, 1962—; dir. Atlanta Gas Light Co. Served with USAF, 1946-49. Mem. Am., Ga., Atlanta bar assns., Lawyers Club Atlanta (pres. 1973-74), Am. Law Inst., Am. Judicature Soc. (dir. 1975-78). Club: Cherokee Town and Country. Home: 3381 Valley Circle NW Atlanta GA 30305 Office: 3300 First National Bank Tower Atlanta GA 30303

NORMAN, ANDREW EDWARD, publisher; b. N.Y.C., Sept. 22, 1930; s. Edward Albert and Dorothy (Stecker) N.; B.A., Harvard, 1951, LL.B., 1954; m. Helen Dwelle Davis, Dec. 29, 1954; children—Abigail, Sarah Elizabeth, Margaret, Rebecca Dorothy. Reporter, Newark Evening News, 1956-58; law and psychiatry project developer Washington Sch. Psychiatry, 1958-59; asso. editor Current mag., 1960-65; community action program supr. OEO, 1966-67; v.p. Chelsea House Ednl. Communications, Inc., N.Y.C., 1968-70, pres., 1970—. Mem. Rockland County (N.Y.) Democratic Com., 1961-66, 68—; sec. Orangetown (N.Y.) Dem. Com., 1968-72, co-chmn., 1972-74, chmn., 1974-76; Dem. candidate for supr. Orangetown, 1965. Bd. dirs. Scholarship, Edn. and Def. Fund for Racial Equality, 1962—, pres., 1962-70, chmn. exec. com., 1970—; bd. dirs. Norman Found., 1955—, chmn., 1966—; trustee Palisades (N.Y.) Free Library, 1962-66, 68-72, pres., 1964-65, treas., 1969-72; bd. dirs. N.Y. Civil Liberties Union, 1969-72, Potomac Inst., 1964—, Am. Com. on Africa, 1960-77, Palisades Community Center, 1969-72; bd. dirs., treas. Africa Fund, 1966-77; trustee Rockland Community Coll., 1977—. Served with AUS, 1954-56. Home: Ludlow Ln Palisades NY 10964 Office: 70 W 40th St New York NY 10018

NORMAN, ARTHUR GEOFFREY, biochemist, univ. adminstr.; b. Birmingham, Eng., Nov. 26, 1905; s. Arthur and Charlotte (Mant) N.; B.Sc., U. Birmingham, 1925, Ph.D., 1928; M.S. (Rockefeller fellow), U. Wis., 1932; D.Sc., U. London, 1933; m. Marian Foote, Sept. 5, 1933; children—Anthony Westcott, Stephen Trevor. Came to U.S., 1930, naturalized, 1946. Research asso. U. Wis., 1932; biochemist Rothamsted Exptl. Sta., Harpenden, Eng., 1933-37; prof. soils Iowa State U., research prof. Iowa Agrl. Exptl. Sta., 1937-46; biochemist and div. chief Chem. Corps. Biol. Labs., Frederick, Md., 1946-52; prof. botany U. Mich., Ann Arbor, 1952—, v.p. for research, 1964-72, dir. Bot. Gardens, 1955-66, dir. Inst. for Environ. Quality, 1972-76. Adviser to pres. Nat. Acad. Scis., 1963-64; chmn. div. biology and agr. NRC 1965-69; trustee Inst. Def. Analysis, 1968-77; trustee Univ. Research Assos., 1969-74, chmn., 1973-74; trustee Biol. Sci. Info. Service, 1972-77, pres., 1976-77. Fellow Am. Soc. Agronomy (pres. 1956-57), Royal Inst. Chemistry, Am. Acad. Microbiology, AAAS; mem. Biochem. Soc., Soil Sci. Soc. Am., Am. Soc. Microbiology, Am. Soc. Plant Physiologists, Sigma Xi, Phi Kappa Phi. Author: The Biochemistry of Cellulose, 1937. Editor: Advances in Agronomy (vols. 1 to XX), 1949-68; Agronomy Monographs (Vols. I to VI), 1948-56. Contbr. profl. papers to tech. jours. Home: 9 Haverhill Ct Ann Arbor MI 48105. *One cannot improve on Francis Bacon: "I hold every man a debtor to his profession, from which as men of course do seek to receive countenance and profit, so ought they of duty to endeavor themselves by way of amends to be a help and ornament thereunto."*

NORMAN, GEORGE E., graphic historian; b. Detroit, Dec. 26, 1923; s. Alex and Elizabeth (Cunningham) N.; student Prairie View Coll., 1941. One man shows include Mich. State U., 1969, U.S.S. Independence, 1971, Norfolk Jewish Center, 1971, Ford Motor Co., 1970, 72, N.E.A., Cobo Hall, Detroit, 1971, Assn. for Study Curriculum Devel., Phila., 1972, John Kennedy Center, Atlanta, 1972, S.C. State Coll., 1973, others. Served with USNR, 1943-46. Recipient Prior Foster award Research Assn. for Mich. Negro History, 1969, Carter G. Woodson award NEA, 1970. Black Odyssey history and art exhbns. have been cited by historians and educators as innovative tool for teaching black history. Home: 17525 Midland St Detroit MI 48227 Office: Box 143 Detroit MI 48232

NORMAN, GEORGE EMERSON, JR., textile cons.; b. Charlotte, N.C., June 14, 1914; s. George Emerson and Lucy Bowden (Smith) N.; B.S., N.C. State Coll., 1938; m. Jane Webb, June 29, 1943 (dec. 1950); children—Lane Smith, George Emerson III; m. 2d, Hilda Graham Roberts, Sept. 25, 1952; children—Vernon Roberts, Dean Graham. With Burlington Industries, 1938—, beginning in quality control and devel. depts., successively exec. hosiery div., decorative fabrics div., asst. to pres., charge subsidiary Goodall Sanford, Inc., 1954-56, exec. v.p. Goodall Sanford, Inc., 1956-59, pres. 1959-63, v.p. Burlington Industries, 1959-63, v.p. charge corp. research and devel., 1963-69, v.p. new ventures, 1969-75, v.p. energy planning and conservation, 1975-77, v.p. public affairs, 1977-79, cons., 1979—; dir., exec. com. Jewel Box Stores Corp., 1969—; mem. exec. com., trustee Textile Research Inst., Princeton U., 1965-73. Mem. Greensboro Sports Council, 1972. Mem. Greensboro (N.C.) Bd. Edn., 1959-72, chmn., 1970-72; chmn. rev. bd. Gateways, Inc., 1974-76; mem. bd. Engring. Found. N.C. State U., 1968—, pres., 1975-77; mem. exec. com. Met. bd. YMCA, 1969—, pres., 1978; bd. dirs. Blue Ridge Assembly SE Region YMCA, 1976. bd. dirs. United Arts Council, 1970—, pres., 1971-72; exec. com., bd. dirs. United Way of Greater Greensboro, 1971—, compaign chmn., 1972, exec. v.p., 1973, pres., 1974-75; exec. com., bd. dirs. N.C. Symphony Soc., 1970—, sec.-treas., 1972-77, vice chmn., 1977, chmn., 1978; exec. com., bd. dirs. Greensboro Coll., 1971—, vice-chmn., 1974—; bd. dirs. Oak Ridge Acad., 1969—; bd. dirs. Goodwill Industries, 1974—, pres., 1978; bd. dirs. Greensboro Cerebral Palsy and Orthopedic Sch., 1975—; bd. dirs. Research Triangle Inst., 1973—, exec. com., 1974; bd. visitors Appalachian State U., Boone, N.C., 1975—, Guilford Coll., Greensboro, 1975—; bd. dirs. Eastern Music Festival, 1973—, exec. com., 1974; bd. dirs. N.C. State U. Found., 1977—; mem. N.C. Energy Policy Council, 1977—; bd. dirs. Nat. Metric Council, 1975—, exec. com., 1978; pres. Musical Arts Guild, U. N.C., Greensboro, 1978. Served as capt. AUS, 1942-46. Recipient Community Arts award Greensboro Altrusa Club, 1979; Service to Mankind award Sertoma Club, 1979; Disting. Service award Mayor's Com. on Handicapped, 1979; named Civic Leader Year, 1973. Mem. N.C. State U. Alumni Assn. (dir. 1968-74, exec. com. 1968, pres. 1972, chmn. 1973), Greensboro C. of C. (dir. 1972-73, Disting. Citizen award 1979), Scabbard and Blade, Pi Kappa Phi, Phi Psi. Club: Civitan (pres.). Home: 1901 Pembroke Rd Greensboro NC 27408 Office: 3330 W Friendly Ave Greensboro NC 27410

NORMAN, JESSYE, soprano; b. Augusta, Ga., Sept. 15, 1945; d. Silas and Janie (King) N.; B.M. cum laude, Howard U., 1967; postgrad. Peabody Conservatory Music, 1967, U. Mich., 1967-68. Debut Deutsche Oper Berlin, 1969, Italy, 1970; appeared in operas Idomeneo, L'Africaine, Marriage of Figaro, Aida, Don Giovanni, Tannhauser, Götterdämmerung, Ariadne auf Naxos; debut La Scala, Milan, Italy, 1972, Salzburg Festival, 1977; U.S. debut Hollywood Bowl, 1972; appeared with Tanglewood Festival, Mass.; also Edinburgh (Scotland) Festival; debut Covent Garden, 1972; appeared in Great Performers recital Lincoln Center, N.Y.C., 1973—; other guest performances include Los Angeles Philharmonic Orch., Boston Symphony Orch., Am. Symphony Orch., Chgo. Symphony Orch., San Francisco Symphony Orch., Cleve. Orch., Detroit Symphony, N.Y. Philharmonic Orch., London Symphony Orch., London Philharmonic Orch., BBC Orch., Israel Philharmonic Orch., Orchestre de Paris, Nat. Symphony Orch., English Chamber Orch., numerous other recitals and guest appearances, tours Europe, S. Am., Australia; numerous recs. Columbia, EMI, Philips Records. Recipient 1st prize Bavarian Radio Corp. Internat. Music Competition, 1968, Grand Prix du Disque, Deutsche Schallplatten; presented Key to City of Augusta (Ga.), 1970; numerous other awards. Mem. Gamma Sigma Sigma, Sigma Alpha Iota, Pi Kappa Lambda. Club: Friday Morning Music (Washington). Address: care Harry Beall Mgmt 119 W 57 St New York NY 10019

NORMAN, LALANDER STADIG, ins. co. exec.; b. Binford, N.D., Apr. 10, 1912; s. John and Corinne (Stadig) N.; A.B., U. Mich., 1935, M.B.A., 1937; m. Garnet Johnston, Nov. 8, 1941; children—Eric John, Martha Mary (Mrs. James Neely), Carol Jean McBroom, Shirley Ann (Mrs. George Richard Cook, Jr.). Actuarial asst. Central Life Ins. Co. of Ill., Chgo., 1937-40, mgr. Eastern dept., 1940-41; actuary Mich. Life Ins. Co., Detroit, 1941-43; asst. actuary Guarantee Mut. Life Co., Omaha, 1946-49; asso. actuary Am. United Life Ins. Co., Indpls., 1949, actuary, 1950-77, dir., 1959-77, v.p., 1962-69, sr. v.p., 1969-77; ret., 1977; bd. mgrs. AUL Fund B, 1969—, chmn., 1973—; actuary Ind. Dept. Ins. Served with USNR, 1943-46. Recipient Theta Xi Distinguished Service award, 1958. Fellow Soc. Actuaries; mem. Am. Acad. Actuaries, Canadian Inst. Actuaries, Indpls. Actuarial Club (past pres.), Phi Beta Kappa, Theta Xi (regional dir. 1953-59), Phi Kappa Phi, Beta Gamma Sigma. Republican. Clubs: Woodland Country (Carmel); Sugarmill Woods Golf and Racquet. Home: Route 2 Box 127-B SMW Hamosassa FL 32646 Office: 1 W 26th St Indianapolis IN 46206

NORMAN, LEWIS SHEPPARD, JR., bus. exec., ret. air force officer; b. Vancouver, Wash., May 9, 1923; s. Lewis Sheppard and Bertha Frances (Zaleska) N.; B.S., U.S. Mil. Acad., 1944; M.S., U. Mich., 1950; m. Joan Jay Asensio, Nov. 28, 1952; children—Joan Jay, Kerry Lynn, Christine West. Commd. 2d lt. USAAF, 1944, advanced through grades to brig. gen. USAF, 1971; comdr. missile research and devel., 1957-59; mil. space project engr., 1959-62; manned space flight research and devel., 1962-69; comdr. Worldwide Spacecraft Tracking and Control Network, 1969-71; dir. advanced planning and current projects Def. Communications Agy., 1971-74; dir. plans and programs Communications Satellite Corp., 1974-78, gen. mgr. communications products div., 1978—; exec. v.p., gen. mgr. Comsat Gen. Telesystems, Inc., 1979—. Decorated Legion of Merit with oak leaf cluster, Air Force Commendation medal with oak leaf cluster, D.S.M., Army Commendation medal, Air medal. Mem. IEEE (sr.), Am. Radio Relay League, Nat. Rifle Assn., Sigma Xi. Club: Army Navy Country. Home: 3211 Chichester Ln Fairfax VA 22031

NORMAN, PHILIP SIDNEY, physician; b. Pittsburg, Kans., Aug. 4, 1924; s. P. Sidney and Mildred A. (Lawyer) N.; A.B., Kans. State Coll., 1947; M.D. cum laude, Washington U., St. Louis, 1951; m. Marion Birmingham, Apr. 15, 1955; children—Margaret Reynolds, Meredith Andrew, Helen Elizabeth. Intern, Barnes Hosp., St. Louis, 1951-52; resident Vanderbilt U. Hosp., Nashville, 1952-54; fellow Rockefeller Inst., 1954-56; instr. medicine Johns Hopkins U. Sch. Medicine, Balt., 1956-59, asst. prof., 1959-64, asso. prof., 1964-75, prof., 1975—, chief allergy and immunology div., 1971—. Served with USAAF, 1943-46, USPHS, 1954-56. Fellow Am. Acad. Allergy (pres. 1975); mem. Am. Fedn. Clin. Research, Am. Assn. Immunologists, Am. Soc. Clin. Investigation, N.Y. Acad. Scis., Soc. Exptl. Biology and Medicine, Am. Thoracic Soc., Am. Clin. and Climatol. Assn., Johns Hopkins Med. Soc., Alpha Omega Alpha. Episcopalian. Contbr. chpt. to books, articles to profl. jours. Home: 13500 Manor Rd Baldwin MD 21013 Office: Johns Hopkins U Sch Medicine at Good Samaritan Hosp 5601 Loch Raven Blvd Baltimore MD 21239*

NORMAN, RALPH DAVID, univ. adminstr.; b. N.Y.C., June 2, 1915; s. Selig J. and Rose (Bernstein) N.; B.S., CCNY, 1934; M.A., Columbia U., 1936; Ph.D., Ohio State U., 1946; m. Rose Libovsky, Aug. 23, 1942; children—Robert, Patricia. Psychologist, Juvenile Ct., N.Y.C., 1936-37, N.Y. State Prison, Dannemora, N.Y., 1937-38, Miss. State Hosp., Whitfield, 1938-39, U.S. Reformatory, Chillicothe, Ohio, 1939-40; personnel technician U.S. Army Air Force, Chanute Field, Ill., 1941-42; asst. prof. psychology Princeton U., 1947-48, U. Mich., 1948-49; faculty U. N.Mex., Albuquerque, 1949—, prof., 1957—, asso. dean Arts and Scis. Coll., 1970—; mem. N.Mex. State

Bd. Psychol. Examiners, chmn. 1963-66; cons. in field. Served with USNR, 1942-46. Diplomate Am. Bd. Profl. Psychology. Fellow Am. Psychol. Assn.; mem. AAUP, Rocky Mountain Psychol. Assn. (pres. 1952-53), Sigma Xi, Phi Delta Kappa. Contbr. articles to profl. publs. Home: 5012 Sunningdale Ave NE Albuquerque NM 87110 Office: 203B Ortega Hall U NMex Albuquerque NM 87106

NORMAN, RALPH LOUIS, physicist; b. Kingston, Tenn., Mar. 25, 1933; s. Walter Hugh and Helen Irene (Smith) N.; B.S., U. Tenn., 1959; LL.B., Blackstone Sch. Law, 1967, J.D., 1971; certificate Indsl. Coll. Armed Forces, 1969; M.A. in Pub. Adminstrn., U. Okla., 1971; m. Agnes Irene Pickel, Sept. 5, 1964; children—Mark Alan, Max Alvin. Engr., Chrysler Corp. Missile Div., Huntsville, Ala., 1959-60; physicist Army Rocket & Guided Missile Agy., Redstone Arsenal, Ala., 1960-61; asst. project mgr. Army Missile Command, Redstone Arsenal, 1961-62, project mgr., 1962—; faculty, Athens (Ala.) Coll., 1970-71, Calhoun Jr. Coll., Decatur, Ala., 1971-74, U. Montevallo (Ala.), 1973-74, U. Ala. at Huntsville, 1976-77, Columbia (Mo.) Coll., 1977—; cons. firm Bishop and Sexton; 1973—, Athens (Ala.) State Coll. reviewer NSF, 1974-76. Served with USN, 1951-55. Recipient Dept. Def. commendations, 1961, 65, Dept. Army commendation, 1972. Mem. N.Y. Acad. Scis., Internat. Soc. Supramolecular Biology, Assn. U.S. Army. Contbr. articles profl. jours. Home: Route 1 Box 726 Harvest AL 35749 Office: Hdqrs US Army Missile Command Redstone Arsenal AL 35809. *I strive to make the knowledge gained through my research benefit all mankind.*

NORMAN, RALPH VERNON, JR., ednl. adminstr.; b. Johnson City, Tenn., Feb. 5, 1933; s. Ralph Vernon and Anna (Crisp) N.; B.A., U. Tenn., 1954, M.A., 1956; student Eberhardt-Karls U., Tuebingen, Germany, 1955-56; B.D., Yale, 1958, M.A., 1960, Ph.D., 1961; m. Cornelia June Shirley, July 16, 1955; children—Emily Celeste, Stephen Christopher. Asst. prof. philosophy and religion Miami U., Oxford, Ohio, 1961-66; prof. religious studies, head dept. U. Tenn., 1966-71, asso. dean Coll. Liberal Arts, 1971-73, asso. vice chancellor for acad. affairs, 1973—. Chmn. Tenn. Com. for Humanities, 1974-76; v.p. Knoxville Arts Council; bd. dirs. Knox County Planned Parenthood Assn. Fulbright fellow, 1955-56; Rockefeller doctoral fellow theology, 1960-61. Mem. Am. Acad. Religion, Am. Comparative Lit. Assn., Am. Philos. Assn., So. Soc. Philosophy and Psychology, Soc. Values in Higher Edn., Phi Kappa Phi, Sigma Phi Epsilon. Episcopalian. Author articles in field. Home: 6900 Stone Mill Rd Knoxville TN 37919

NORMAN, RICHARD ARTHUR, educator; b. Columbus, Ohio, July 11, 1915; s. Norman Oscar and Marie (Falter) Kuhnheim; B.A., George Washington U., 1951; M.A., Columbia, 1952, Ph.D., 1957. Radio announcer, producer, actor, 1934-50; commentator for chamber music concert, broadcast from Library of Congress, Washington, 1948-50; instr. Columbia, N.Y.C., 1952-57, asst. prof. English, Barnard Coll., 1957-64, asso. prof., 1964-72, prof., 1972—, chmn. dept. English, 1971-74; instr. grad. div. Hunter Coll., 1960-62. Speech cons. CBS News, 1971—; reader Talking Books, Am. Found. for Blind, 1973—. Vice pres. Axe-Houghton Found. Served to capt. USAAF, 1942-45. Author: (with George W. Hibbitt) A Guide to Speech Training, 1964; (radio series) The Wonder of Words, 1962. Home: 560 Riverside Dr New York NY 10027

NORMANDEAU, ANDRE GABRIEL, educator; b. Montreal, Que., Can., May 4, 1942; s. Gabriel E. and Laurette D. (Sauve) N.; M.A. in Criminology, U. Pa., 1965, Ph.D. in Sociology, 1968; m. Pierrette Normandeau, Aug. 14, 1965; children—Alain, Louis, Jean. Asst. prof. criminology U. Montreal, 1968-71, asso. prof., 1971-76, prof., 1976—, chmn. dept. criminology, 1970—. Dir. program Parti Quebecois, Province of Que., 1976—. Woodrow Wilson fellow, 1964-68. Mem. Internat. Soc. Criminology, Am. Soc. Criminology, Am. Sociol. Assn. Roman Catholic. Author: Public Attitudes and Crime, 1970; The Measurement of Crime, 1975. Home: 3150 Ave Kent Montreal PQ H3S 1N1 Canada Office: Dept Criminology U Montreal Montreal PQ H3C 3J7 Canada. *Happiness is achieved by working for it, not by waiting for it to come to you.*

NORRIS, ARTHUR HUGHES, gerontologist; b. Indpls., Apr. 25, 1925; s. Arthur Grove and Della Rice (Hughes) N.; B.A., Westminster Coll., 1947; M.S., George Washington U., 1969; m. Jean Kelley, Dec. 22, 1952; 1 son, Arthur Thomas. Biologist gerontology br. Nat. Heart Inst., NIH, 1947-65, coordinator Balt. longitudinal study, gerontology research center Nat. Inst. Child Health and Human Devel., 1958-71, chief human performance sect., clin. physiology br., gerontology research center Nat. Inst. on Aging, 1967-71, 73—; commd. USPHS, 1951, advanced through grades to health services dir., 1965, ret., 1971; pvt. practice gerontology cons., 1971-73. Served in USNR, 1943-46. Recipient award merit NIH, 1978. Fellow Gerontol. Soc.; mem. AAAS, Assn. Mil. Surgeons U.S., Commd. Officer Assn. USPHS, N.Y. Acad. Scis. Republican. Contbr. papers in field of gerontology. Home: 913 Oakdale Circle Millersville MD 21108 Office: Gerontology Research Center Balt City Hosps Baltimore MD 21224

NORRIS, CHARLES MORGAN, laryngologist, educator; b. New Milford, Pa., Aug. 17, 1915; s. Ben Clark and Emma (Morgan) N.; B.S., Pa. State Coll., 1935; M.D., Temple U., 1939; M.S., 1944; m. Sarah Wistar Harwood, Nov. 6, 1948; children—Charles Morgan, Stephen Harwood. Intern, Temple U. Hosp, 1939-41, resident otolaryngology and broncho-esophagology, 1941-44, mem. faculty Med. Sch., 1944—, prof., chmn. dept. laryngology and broncho-esophagology, 1961—; cons. Lankenau Hosp., Phila., Pa. Hosp. Recipient Alumni award Temple U., 1954. Mem. Am. Broncho-Esophagological Assn. (pres. 1964-65), Pan. Am. Assn. Oto-Rhino-Laryngology and Broncho-Esophagology (sec. 1961-66), Internat. Bronchoesophagological Soc. (sec. 1961—), Am. Laryngol. Assn. (pres. 1976-77), A.C.S., Am. Acad. Opthalomology and Otolaryngology, Am. Soc. Head and Neck Surgery (pres. 1973-74), Am. Larygol., Rhinol. and Otol. Soc. (v.p. 1973-74), Am. Coll. Chest Physicians. Clubs: Union League, Cricket (Phila.) Home: 8007 Navajo St Philadelphia PA 19118

NORRIS, JOHN WINDSOR, JR., mfg. co. exec.; b. Marshalltown, Iowa, Feb. 10, 1936; s. John Windsor Norris and Mary Merrill Margerin; B.S. in Bus. Adminstrn., M.I.T., 1960; m. Terry Reibsamen, Dec. 26, 1956; children—John Windsor III, Julie, Jeffrey. With Lennox Industries Inc., 1960—, sr. v.p., Dallas, 1975-77, pres., 1977-80, pres., chief exec. officer, 1980—; dir. Central Life Assurance Co., Des Moines. Chmn. parents div., mem. ann. gifts council Tex. Christian U. Mem. ARI (dir. at large, vice chmn. cert. programs and policy com., vice chmn. communications com.), GAMA (chmn. furnace div. 1978-79, chmn. bd. 1980). Club: Bent Tree Country (Dallas). Home: 6321 Duffield Dr Dallas TX 75248 Office: Lennox Industries Inc Promenade Tower PO Box 400450 Dallas TX 75240

NORRIS, LESTER J., bus. exec.; b. Elgin, Ill., Nov. 26, 1900; s. Carroll William and Gertrude (Flinn) N.; grad. St. Charles High Sch., Chgo. Acad. Fine Arts; m. Dellora F. Angell, Mar. 28, 1923; children—Lavern G. (Mrs. George Gaynor), Lester J. (dec.), Joann D. (Mrs. James Collins), Robert, John (dec.). Comml. artist, cartoonist, 1921-25; chmn. bd. dirs. State Bank of St. Charles; dir., mem. exec. com. Texaco, Inc., 1933-73. Pres. Norbak Corp., Naples, Fla.; v.p. Collier County Cons. Bd. dirs. St. Charles Charities; life trustee Northwestern U.; trustee Delnor Hosp., Henry Rockwell Baker Community Center; exec. pres. Key Island, Inc.; bd. dirs. Miami Heart Inst., Inc.; chmn. Nat. Victory Garden Inst., 1942-47. Mem. Nat. Audubon Soc., Ill. Wildlife Fedn. Methodist. Clubs: The Union League, The Dunham Woods Riding, St. Charles Country, National Press; Hole-in-the-Wall Golf, Naples Yacht (Naples, Fla.) Home: 808 N 5th Ave Saint Charles IL 60174 Office: 1 E Main St Saint Charles IL 60174

NORRIS, MARTIN JOSEPH, lawyer; b. N.Y.C., Mar. 23, 1907; s. Louis and Esther (Wohlgemuth) Knaris; LL.B., Bklyn. Law Sch., 1930; m. Helen Stella Hecht, June 5, 1930; 1 dau., Barbara. Admitted to N.Y. bar, 1932; individual practice law, N.Y.C., 1932-35; atty. U.S. Shipping Bd. Bur., Dept. Commerce, Washington, 1935-36, U.S. Maritime Commn., Washington and N.Y.C., 1936-42, War Shipping Adminstrn., N.Y.C., 1945-50; admiralty trial atty. admiralty and shipping sect. Dept. Justice, N.Y.C., 1950-56; adminstrv. law judge U.S. Coast Guard, N.Y.C., 1956-70; lectr. Sch. for World Trade, N.Y.C., Practicing Law Inst., N.Y.C., Lawyers Sq. Club, N.Y.C., U.S. Merchant Marine Acad., N.Y. State Maritime Coll.; cons. maritime law, shipping. Bd. dirs. Philharmonic Symphony of Westchester, Mt. Vernon, N.Y., 1976—. Served to capt. U.S. Army, 1942-45. Mem. Noah Benevolent Soc. Jewish. Author: The Law of Salvage, 1958; Your Boat and the Law, 1965; The Law of Seamen, 3 vols., 3rd edit., 1970; The Law of Maritime Personal Injuries, 2 vols., 3rd edit., 1975; contbr. articles in field to legal jours. Home and Office: Eastchester NY 10709

NORRIS, ROBERT BAYLESS, educator; b. Montrose, Pa., Mar. 12, 1918; s. Kenneth I. and Helen (Bayless) N.; B.S. in Edn., Mansfield (Pa.) State Tchrs. Coll., 1939; M.Ed., Harvard, 1946; Ed.D., Columbia, 1951; m. Mary Elizabeth Holloway, Sept. 15, 1945; children—Thomas J., Helen Holloway, Susan A., Mary Elizabeth. Tchr., coach, Great Bend, Pa., 1939-41; supr. prin., LeRaysville, Pa., 1946-47; instr. Cortland (N.Y.) State Tchrs. Coll., 1947-49; asst., then asso. prof. edn. Lehigh U., 1950-55; dir. secondary edn., Doylestown, Pa., 1955-58; supt. schs., Freehold, N.J., 1958-60; prof. edn. U. Conn., 1960—, dean continuing edn. services, 1960-72. Mem. bd. Windham Area Community Action Program, 1966-68; justice of peace, 1962—. Served to maj. USAAF, 1941-45. Mem. Conn. Assn. Continuing Edn. (pres. 1966-67), Soc. Conn. Craftsmen (dir. 1966—), Am. Crafts Council (New Eng. rep. 1967), Am. Assn. Sch. Adminstrs., Guild Conn. Craftsmen (exec. dir. 1970-76), Phi Delta Kappa. Democrat. Rotarian (pres. Willimantic 1967-68, dist. gov. 1969-70, youth exchange officer 1971-74). Author: (with others) Foundations for Elementary School Teaching, 1963. Home: 52 Willowbrook Rd Storrs CT 06268

NORRIS, ROBERT FOGG, physician; b. Wilmington, Del., Dec. 23, 1905; s. Herschel Augustus and Elizabeth Lippincott (Fogg) N.; grad. Phillips Exeter Acad., 1922-24; A.B., Princeton, 1928; M.D., U. Pa., 1932; m. Mary Scattergood, June 13, 1931; children—Anne (Mrs. Baldwin), Victoria (Mrs. Dean). Intern Pa. Hosp., Phila., 1932-34, asst. dir. Ayer Clin. Lab., 1935-41; asst. in pathology Johns Hopkins Med. Sch., 1934-35; asso. William Pepper Lab. of Clin. Medicine, U. Pa., 1946-50, asso. in medicine, 1946-47, asst. prof. clin. medicine, 1947-48, asso. prof., 1948-53, dir. Wm. Pepper Lab., 1950-68, prof. clin. pathology, 1953-68, prof. pathology, 1968-74, prof. emeritus, 1974—; dir. Penndel Labs., Inc., Ardmore, Pa., 1974—; cons. in pathology U.S. Naval Hosp., Phila., 1946-68, Princeton (N.J.) Hosp., 1952-68, VA Hosp., Phila., 1965-70. Treas. 6th Congress Internat. Soc. Blood Transfusions, 1956; chmn. Biol. Warfare Def. Com. Phila., 1950-52; asst. dir. div. 5, Phila. Civil Def. Council, 1952-53; mem. Pa. Disaster Med. Council, 1959-65; mem. commn. disaster med. services Pa. Med. Soc., 1959-67. Served from lt. to comdr., USNR, 1941-46; capt. Res. (ret.). Diplomate Am. Bd. Pathology. Mem. AMA, Coll. Am. Pathologists, Am. Soc. Clin. Pathologists, Am. Assn. Pathologists and Bacteriologists, Am. Soc. Microbiologists, AAAS, Coll. Phys. of Phila., Pa. Assn. Clin. Pathologists (pres. 1969), Pathol. Soc. Phila. (v.p. 1956-57, pres. 1958-59), Pa. Assn. Blood Banks (pres. 1958-59), Internat. Soc. Blood Transfusions (v.p. 1958-64), Pa. Med. Soc. (chmn. commn. blood banks, 1947-59), Physiol. Soc. Phila., Phila. County Med. Soc. (chmn. sect. clin. pathology 1953), Sigma Xi, Nu Sigma Nu, Alpha Omega Alpha. Home: 430 Colebrook Ln Bryn Mawr PA 19010 Office: Gates Bldg Hosp of U of Pa Philadelphia PA 19104

NORRIS, ROBERT FRANK, wholesale goods distbg. co. exec.; b. Apr. 26, 1922; s. Frank L. and Frances T. (Brown) N.; student U. Pa., 1943, Columbia U., 1944; B.S., U. Kans., 1946; m. Margaret Elizabeth Culley, Apr. 15, 1944; children—Sue, Scott. With Fleming Co., Topeka, 1946-72, dir. sales, 1963-65, exec. v.p., 1965-72, also dir.; pres., chief operating officer, dir. M. Loeb Ltd., Ottawa, Ont., Can., 1972-73; pres., chief operating officer S.M. Flickinger Co., Inc., Buffalo, 1973-74, pres., 1974-77, chief exec. officer, 1974—, chmn. bd., 1977—, chmn. exec. com., 1977—, also dir. Served to lt. (j.g.) USNR, World War II. Office: 45 Azalea Dr Buffalo NY 14240

NORRIS, ROBERT JAMES, airline co. exec.; b. Burlington, Wash., Apr. 18, 1925; s. Ross H. and Verna (Adam) N.; B.A., U. Wash., 1948; m. Thelma Louise Paulsen, July 10, 1948; children—Stephen, Janet, Robert, Shirley. Sr. credit analyst Seattle First Nat. Bank, 1948-52; sec.-treas. Alaska Airlines, Inc., 1952-57; asst. to v.p. maintenance and engring. Pacific No. Airlines, Inc., 1957-60; operations analyst transp. div. Boeing Co., 1960-61; v.p. finance Aloha Airlines, 1961-64; asst. controller Martin Marietta Corp., 1964-66, controller, 1966-70, v.p., controller, 1970-74, treas., 1971-74, v.p. finance, 1974; sr. v.p. finance Am. Airlines, Inc., N.Y.C., 1974-76; dir. adminstrn. Fin. Execs. Inst., 1977-79; exec. v.p. Air New Eng. Inc., 1979—. Served as pilot USAAF, World War II. Mem. Tau Kappa Epsilon. Home: PO Box 4122 Wildemere Beach Sta Milford CT 06460

NORRIS, ROBERT MANNING, orgn. exec.; b. Haddon Heights, N.J., Mar. 9, 1910; s. Z. John and Adele M. (Manning) N.; LL.B., Rutgers U., 1933; m. Rita Custer Wilkes, June 6, 1942; children—Rita Wilkes, Robert Manning, John Wilkes. Admitted to N.J. bar, 1934; practice in N.J., 1934-41; trust officer Camden Trust Co. (N.J.), 1940-46; tchr. constl. law Rutgers U. Law Sch. 1939-42; with Lederle Labs. div. Am. Cyanamid Co., 1946-54; dir. licensing and Latin Am. operations Avco Corp., 1954-57; mgr. corp. services Philco Internat. Corp., v.p. Bucyrus-Erie Co., 1959; mng. dir. Philco Corp., S.A., Switzerland, 1959-61; v.p. RCA Internat. Ltd., Rome, 1961-63; pres., dir. Nat. Fgn. Trade Council N.Y.C., 1963-79, dir., cons., 1979—; dir. Daiwa Bank Trust Co., N.Y.C. Mem. adv. com. on transnat. enterprises Dept. State. Asso. trustee Council of Ams. Served to maj. with AUS, 1941-46. Mem. Pan Am. Soc. U.S., Am. Acad. Polit. and Social Sci. Clubs: Metropolitan, Economic (N.Y.C.); Pine Valley (N.J.) Golf. Author numerous articles on world trade and investment. Home: Sneden's Landing Palisades NY 10964 Office: 10 Rockefeller Plaza New York NY 10020

NORRIS, WILLIAM C., corp. exec.; b. Inavale, Nebr., July 14, 1911; s. William H. and Mildred A. (McCall) N.; B.S., U. Nebr., 1932; m. Jane Malley, Sept. 15, 1943; children—W. Charles, George, Daniel, Brian, Constance, Roger, Mary N., David. Sales engr. Westinghouse Electric Mfg. Co., Chgo., 1935-41; v.p., gen. mgr. Engring. Research Assos., 1946-55; v.p., gen. mgr. Univac div. Sperry Rand Corp., 1955-57; pres. Control Data Corp., 1957—, now also chmn.; bd. dirs. N.W. Bank Corp., N.W. Growth Fund, Tronchemics, Inc. Trustee Hill Reference Library; adv. com. White House Conf. on Balanced Nat. Growth and Econ. Devel., 1978—. Served to comdr. USNR, 1941-46. Office: Control Data Corp 8100 34th Ave S Minneapolis MN 55415*

NORRIS, WILLIAM CLARK, air force officer; b. Port Jervis, N.Y., Sept. 20, 1926; s. William and Iva Mary (Weber) N.; student Calif.-Aero. Tech. Sch., 1947, Roosevelt Sch. Aviation, Mineola, N.Y., 1947-48, U. Alaska, 1959-60, U. Colo., 1962-65; m. Marcie Lee Myhra, Sept. 27, 1952; children—Kathleen Theresa, Matthew Clark. Served with USAAF, 1945-46; enlisted USAF, 1948, commd. 2d lt., 1949, advanced through grades to maj. gen.; chief ops. br. 355th Tactical Fighter Wing, Takhli Royal Thai AFB, 1966-67, comdr. 333d Tactical Fighter Squadron, 1966-67, asst. exec. officer Chief of N.G. Bur., Pentagon, 1967-68, dir. operational readiness inspection Aerospace Def. Command, 1968-70, comdr. 50th Tactical Fighter Wing, USAF-Europe, Hahn Air Base, Germany, 1971-73, 20th Tactical Fighter Wing, RAF, Upper Heyford, Eng., 1973, dept. chief of staff, plans USAF-Europe, Ramstein Air Base, Germany, 1973-74, insp. gen., 1974-75, comdr. Hdqrs. Command USAF, Bolling AFB, Washington, 1975-76, 76th Airlift Div., Andrews AFB, Md., 1976-77, 3d Air Force, RAF Mildenhall, Bury St. Edmunds, Eng., 1977—. Decorated Air Force Cross, D.S.M., Silver Star, Legion of Merit, D.F.C. with oak leaf cluster, Bronze Star, Air medal with 12 oak leaf clusters, many others. Roman Catholic. Home: 63 Canal St Port Jervis NY 12771 Office: Hdqrs 3d Air Face USAFE RAF Mildenhall Bury St Edmunds Eng APO New York NY 09127*

NORRIS, WILLIAM ELMORE, JR., educator, scientist; b. Nixon, Tex., Feb. 23, 1921; s. William Elmore and Persia (Kiser) N.; B.S., S.W. Tex. State Coll., 1940; Ph.D., U. Tex., 1948; m. Theresa R. Margerum, Oct. 7, 1944; children—Thomas Elmore, Susan Elizabeth, Robert William. Tutor, instr. physiology U. Tex., Austin, 1940-42, 1946-47; instr., asst. prof. biology Bryn Mawr Coll., 1947-49, asso. prof., 1949-52, prof. biology, chmn. biology, 1952-65, prof., chmn. and dean Sch. Sci., 1965-67; prof. biology, dean Sch. Sci. S.W. Tex. State U., San Marcos, 1967-70, prof. biology, dean Coll. Arts and Scis., 1970-74, v.p. for acad. affairs, 1974—. Active Boy Scouts Am. Served with USNR, 1942-46. Fellow AAAS; mem. Am. Soc. Plant Physiologists (chmn. so. sect. 1968), Scandinavian Soc. Plant Physiology, Am. Inst. Biol. Sci., Tex. Acad. Sci. (pres. 1969), AAUP, Tex. Assn. Coll. Tchrs., Sigma Xi, Alpha Chi, Beta Beta Beta, Phi Sigma. Contbr. articles to profl. jours. Home: 808 Bluebonnet Dr San Marcos TX 78666

NORSTAD, LAURIS, business exec.; b. Mpls., Mar. 24, 1907; s. Martin and Marie (Johnson) N.; B.S., U.S. Mil. Acad., 1930; grad. A.C. Sch., 1931; A.C. Tactical Sch., 1939; m. Isabelle Helen Jenkins, Apr. 27, 1935; 1 dau., Kristin. Commd. 2d lt. cav., 1930; advanced through grades to gen., 1952; duty with Gen. Hdqrs. Air Force, 1940-42, 12th Air Force, 1943; with N.W. African Air Force; dept. chief staff operations Hdqrs. USAF, acting vice chief staff. Air Forces, 1950; comdr. in chief U.S. and Allied Air Forces in Central Europe, 1951; air dep. SHAPE, 1953-56; supreme allied comdr. Europe, SHAPE, 1956-63; pres. Owens-Corning Fiberglas Corp., 1964-67, chmn., 1967-72, ret., 1972, now chmn. emeritus; dir. emeritus United Air Lines. Hon. trustee Eisenhower Coll. Decorated D.S.M., Silver Star, Legion Merit, Air medal; hon. comdr. Order Brit. Empire; comdr. Legion Honor, Croix de Guerre avec Palme (French); grand officer l'Ordre Ouissam quissam Alaouite Cherifien (Morocco); grand cross Aviz (Portugal); grand cross Order of Merit (Germany); grand cross Royal Order of George I (Greece); knight grand cross Order on Merit of Italian Republic; grand cordon Order of Leopold (Belgium); grand cross Royal Norwegian Order of St. Olaf; grand cross Order of Orange-Nassau (Netherlands); grand cross Order Crown of Chene (Luxembourg). Mem. English-Speaking Union U.S. (dir.). Clubs: Army and Navy (Washington); Links, Belmont Country (Toledo). Home: Dublin NH 03444

NORTH, ALEX, composer; b. Chester, Pa., Dec. 4, 1910; student Juilliard Sch. Music, Moscow Conservatory. Composer: (opera) Hither and Thither of Danny Dither; (ballet) Streetcar Named Desire, American Lyric, 1937, Daddy Long Legs, Mal de siècle, Wall Street Ballet; (musicals) 'Tis of Thee, Queen of Sheba, The Great Campaign; Rhapsody for piano and orch., 1941; Revue for clarinet and orch., performed by Benny Goodman, 1946; 3 symphonies, 1947, 68, 71; 3 symphonic suites from film scores; Holiday set, 1948; (cantatas for chorus and orch.) Morning Star, 1947, Negro Mother, 1948; (film scores) Streetcar Named Desire, 1951, Death of a Salesman, Viva Zapata, 1952, Member of the Wedding, The Rose Tattoo, 1955, song Unchained Melody, The Bad Seed, The Rainmaker, Spartacus, 1960, Cleopatra, 1963, The Agony and the Ecstasy, Who's Afraid of Virginia Woolf?, 1966, 2001: A Space Odyssey, Once Upon a Scoundrel, Bite the Bullet, Shanks, Wise Blood, many others; (TV scores) Billy Rose Show, Playhouse 90, Nero Wolfe, I'm a Lawyer, others. Guggenheim fellow; recipient Composers and Lyricists Guild award, 1963; Laurel award, 1956, 57, 66, 67, 69; Golden Globe award, 1969; Emmy for series Rich Man, Poor Man, 1976; 14 Acad. award nominations. Address: 630 Resolano Dr Pacific Palisades CA 90272

NORTH, ANDREW STEWART, golfer; b. Stanley, Wis., Mar. 9, 1950; s. Stewart Donovan and Mary Gloria (Engebretson) N.; B.S., U. Fla., 1972; m. Susan Sullivan, July 1, 1972; children—Nichole Susan, Andrea Lee. Profl. golfer; winner Westchester Classic, 1977, U.S. Open, 1978. Hon. Wis. state chmn. Am. Cancer Soc., 1978. Named Wis. Co-Sportsman of Year, 1978. Mem. Profl. Golfers Am.

NORTH, CECIL JACKSON, ins. exec.; b. Kansas City, Mo., Nov. 15, 1894; s. Cecil Barber and Elizabeth (Keating) N.; B.S., Harvard U., 1917, M.B.A., 1921; m. Adelaide E. Marler, Apr. 9, 1928; children—Cecil J., Mary A. (Mrs. Alan F. French), Sarah (Mrs. Peter N. Hillyer). With Met. Life Ins. Co., N.Y.C., 1920—, v.p., 1937-58, exec. v.p., dir., 1958-59, pres., dir., 1959-67. Dir. and mem. exec. com. Life Ins. Sales Agy. Mgmt. Assn., Hartford, Conn. (pres. 1946), Am. Coll. Life Underwriters. Served as capt. F.A., 4th Div., U.S. Army, World War I. Republican. Presbyterian. Clubs: Seminole; Tequesta Country; Harvard of City N.Y. Home: 82 Lighthouse Dr Jupiter FL 33458 Office: 1 Madison Ave New York NY 10010

NORTH, DOUGLASS CECIL, economist, educator; b. Cambridge, Mass., Nov. 5, 1920; s. Henry Emerson and Edith (Saitta) N.; B.A., U. Calif., Berkeley, 1942, Ph.D., 1952; m. Elisabeth Willard Case, Sept. 28, 1972; children by previous marriage—Douglass Alan, Christopher, Malcolm Peter. Asst. prof. econs. U. Wash., 1950-56, asso. prof., 1957-60, prof., 1960—, chmn. dept., 1967—, dir. Inst. Econ. Research, 1960-66; dir. Nat. Bur. Econ. Research. Guggenheim fellow, 1972-73; Social Sci. Research Council grantee, 1962; Rockefeller Found. grantee, 1960-63; Ford Found. grantee, 1961, 66, NSF grantee, 1967-73. Mem. Am. Econ. Assn., Econ. History Assn., Am. History Assn. Author: The Economic Growth of the U.S. 1790-1860, 1961; Growth and Welfare in the American Past, 1966; (with L. Davis) Institutional Change and American Economic Growth, 1971; (with R. Miller) The Economics of Public Issues, 1971, 74, 76, 78; (with R. Thomas) The Rise of the Western World, 1973.

Home: 3413 E Laurelhurst Dr NE Seattle WA 98105 Office: 301 Savery Hall Department of Economics University of Washington Seattle WA 98195

NORTH, EDMUND HALL, screenwriter; b. N.Y.C., Mar. 12, 1911; s. Robert and Eleanor (Hall) N.; student Stanford U., 1928-30; m. Collette Ford, Oct. 11, 1947; children—Susan, Bobbie. Free-lance screenwriter, 1934—; films include: One Night of Love, 1934, I Dream Too Much, 1935, Young Man With A Horn, 1950, The Day The Earth Stood Still, 1951, Cowboy, 1958, Sink the Bismarck, 1960, Patton (Acad. award for story and screenplay, Writers Guild award for story and screenplay), 1970, Meteor, 1979; chmn. bd. Producer-Writers Guild Pension Plan, 1963-64. Served with Signal Corps, U.S. Army, 1941-45. Mem. Writers Guild Am. (Valentine Davies award 1967, Morgan Cox award 1975, pres. Screen br. 1956-57), Acad. Motion Picture Arts and Scis.

NORTH, ELEANOR BERYL, educator, author; b. Mercer, Pa., July 6, 1898; d. Jacob Z. and Lois (Caldwell) North; B.A., Pa. State U., 1923, M.A., 1925; postgrad. Cambridge (Eng.) U., 1929, 30-32, Oxford (Eng.) U., 1934-36, Brit. Mus., 1936, 39, 49, (Philosophy scholar) Harvard, 1942-43. Asst. prof. English lit. Juniata Coll., 1925-28; prof. Youngstown (Ohio) U., 1929-37, Md. State Coll., 1941-49; prof. Shakespeare and world lit. Berry Coll., Mt. Berry, Ga., 1951-63. Lectr. to lit., ednl., ch. orgns.; judge poetry contests, London, Eng., Sidney, Australia, 1971-72; lit. cons. Internat. Poetry Soc., 1974. Lit. research grant, 1963-67, 70-71, 72, 73, 75; medal Academia Internat. Rome, 1968. Fellow Internat. Poets Acad. (founder), Internat. Biog. Assn.; mem. Royal Order Bookfellows, Modern Lang. Assn., Poetry League Am. (adv. council), Shakespeare Found., AAUP, Poetry Guild, Internat. Poetry Soc. (lit. cons.), Am. Classical Assn., Wagner Music Assn., Art League, Am. Philos. Assn., Nat. Council Tchrs. English, Authors' League, Internat. Acad. Poets, Centro Studi e Scambi Accademia Internat. (hon. v.p. 1973), Am. Poets Fellowship Soc., Writers Guild Gt. Britain, AAUW, Delta Kappa Gamma, Sigma Tau Delta (founder poetry contest 1972). Author: Reading and Personnel Guidance, 1942; (poetry) Star Dust, 1930; Fall 'o Dew, 1936; Grace Notes, 1952 (included in internat. poetry archive Manchester (Eng.) Library; My Heart Sings, 1969; High Tide, 1973; Bright Star, 1975; (poetry) Sunrise, 1979; also articles. Address: 204 E Hamilton Ave State College PA 16801

NORTH, HARPER QUA, physicist, govt. exec.; b. Los Angeles, Jan. 24, 1917; s. Richard L. and Mary Elizabeth (Qua) N.; B.S., Calif. Inst. Tech., 1938; M.A., U. Calif. at Los Angeles, 1940, Ph.D., 1947; m. Frances Norris, June 14, 1969; children—Anita M., James S. Research asso. Gen. Electric Co., 1940-49; dir. semiconductor div. Hughes Aircraft Co., Culver City, Calif., 1949-54; pres. Pacific Semiconductors, Inc., Lawndale, Calif., 1954-61, chmn. bd., 1961-62; chmn. bd. TRW Electronics, Lawndale, 1962; v.p. research and devel. TRW Inc., Los Angeles, 1962-69; mgr. electro-optical dept. Northrop Corp., Palos Verdes Peninsula, Calif., 1969-73; asso. dir. research (electronics), Naval Research Lab., Washington, 1975—. cons. Dept. Def., 1951-75, chmn. adv. group electron devices, 1968-75; pioneer research germanium for semiconductor devices; discoverer semicondr. varactor amplifier. Mem. Nat. Export Expansion Council, 1962-64. Pres. Schenectady Light Opera Co., 1948-49. Bd. dirs. So. Calif. Industry Edn. Council, 1963-65, Calif. Inst. Cancer Research, 1964-69. Fellow Am. Phys. Soc., IEEE; mem. Electronic Industries Assn. (chmn. 1964-66, hon. bd. mem.; recipient medal of honor 1966), Sigma Xi. Home: 12440 Surrey Circle Fort Washington MD 20022 Office: Code 5000 Naval Research Lab Washington DC 20375

NORTH, HELEN FLORENCE, educator; b. Utica, N.Y.; d. James H. and Catherine (Debbold) North; A.B., Cornell U., 1942, M.A., 1943, Ph.D., 1945. Instr. classical lang. Rosary Coll., River Forest, Ill., 1946-48; mem. faculty Swarthmore Coll., 1948—, prof. classics, 1961—, chmn. dept., 1959—, Centennial prof. classics, 1966-73, Kenan prof., 1973—; vis. asst. prof. Cornell U., 1952—; vis. asso. prof. Barnard Coll., 1954-55; vis. prof. LaSalle Coll., Phila., 1965, Am. Sch. Classical Studies, Athens, 1975; Blegen disting. vis. research prof. Vassar Coll., 1979. Bd. dirs. Am. Council Learned Socs., 1977—, King's Coll., LaSalle Coll., Am. Acad. in Rome. Recipient Harbison prize Danforth Found., 1969; grantee Am. Council Learned Socs., 1943-45, 73, fellow, 1971-72; Mary Isabel Sibley fellow Phi Beta Kappa Found., 1945-46; Ford Fund Advancement Edn. fellow, also Fulbright fellow, Rome, 1953-54, Guggenheim fellow, 1958-59; grantee Danforth Found., 1962, Lindbach Found., 1966; fellow AAUW, 1963-64; sr. fellow Nat. Endowment for Humanities, 1967-68; Martin classical lectr. Oberlin Coll., 1972; Guggenheim fellow, 1975-76. Mem. Am. Philol. Assn. (dir. 1968—, pres. 1976—, Charles J. Goodwin award of merit 1969), Classical Assn. Atlantic States, Catholic Commn. Intellectual and Cultural Affairs (chmn. 1968-69), Am. Acad. Arts and Scis., Soc. Religion Higher Edn., Phi Beta Kappa (mem. bd. vis. scholars 1975-76), Phi Kappa Phi. Author: Sophrosyne: Self-Knowledge and Self-Restraint in Greek Literature, 1966; From Myth to Icon: Reflections of Greek Ethical Doctrine in Literature and Art, 1979. Translator: John Milton's Second Defense of the English People, 1966. Editor: Interpretations of Plato: A Swarthmore Symposium, 1977; co-editor: Of Eloquence, 1970; editor Jour. History of Ideas; mem. editorial bd. Catalogues Translationum et Commentariorum, 1979—. Home: 604 Ogden Ave Swarthmore PA 19081

NORTH, JAMES DENNIS, business exec.; b. Columbus, Ohio, Jan. 12, 1911; s. William A. and Burnettie (Dennis) N.; A.B., Dartmouth, 1932; grad. Advanced Mgmt. Program, Harvard, 1955; m. Margaret Peters, Aug. 17, 1935; 1 son, Daniel Warner. With U.S. Rubber Co., 1932-37, Gen. Foods Corp., 1937-47; v.p. Foote, Cone & Belding, 1947-49; gen. mgr. Western Beet Sugar Producers Inc., 1949-53; v.p. Market Research Corp. Am., 1952-54; mktg. exec. Gen. Foods Corp., 1954-61, v.p. mktg. services, 1961-67, v.p. sales and customer services, 1967-69; exec. v.p. Communication and Edn. for Industry, Inc., Greenwich, Conn., 1969-73; v.p. Coquina Oil Corp., Midland, Tex., 1973-78; pres., dir. Pacific Inst. for Public Policy Research, Inc., San Francisco, 1978—; dir. Gt. Western Fin. Corp. Served to maj. USAAF, 1942-45. Clubs: Bohemian (San Francisco). Home: 1715 Taylor St San Francisco CA 94133

NORTH, JAMES WEIR, lawyer; b. Bklyn., Nov. 16, 1923; s. Nelson Luther and Sarah Evelyn (Weir) N.; student Princeton, 1941-43; A.B., Columbia, 1947, LL.B., 1949; m. Lois Emily Gunthel, Aug. 23, 1947; children—James Weir, Nancy Anne, Cynthia Lois. Admitted to N.Y. bar, 1950; with Home Title Guaranty Co., Garden City, N.Y., 1949-51; with trust dept. Chase Manhattan Bank, N.Y.C., 1951-77, exec. v.p. trust dept., 1971-77; mem. firm Payne, Wood & Littlejohn, Glen Cove, N.Y., 1977—; mem. Nat. Market Adv. Bd., 1975—; dir. Marginic Head Inc., MCP Facilities Corp. Mem. Glen Cove (N.Y.) Bd. Edn., 1957-61, pres., 1961; mem. bd. edn. North Shore Central Sch. Dist. 1, 1965-68, pres., 1968; trustee N.Y. State Tchrs. Retirement System, 1974—; bd. dirs. Community Hosp. at Glen Cove, 1978—, St. Christopher's Home. Served with AUS, 1943-45. Mem. Am. Bankers Assn. (pres. trust div. 1976-77). Clubs: Princeton (N.Y.C.); Sea Cliff Yacht. Home: Tanglewood Ln Sea Cliff NY 11579 Office: 139 Glen St Glen Cove NY 11542

NORTH, JOHN RINGLING, circus dir.; b. Baraboo, Wis., Aug. 14, 1903; s. Henry Whitestone and Ida Lorraine Wilhelmina (Ringling) N.; student U. Wis., 1921-22, Yale, 1922-24; m. Jane Donnelley, Sept. 2, 1924 (div. 1930); m. 2d, Germaine Aussey, May 11, 1940 (div. 1945). Concession vender with Ringling Bros. Circus, summer 1916; with Solomon Bros. & Hutzler, brokers, N.Y.C., 1924; mem. sales force John Ringling's real estate cos., Sarasota, Fla., winters, 1926-28; cashier of concessions, handling banking of money with Ringling Bros. Circus, summers 1926-28; customer's man. J.R. Schmeltzer & Co., then Parrish & Co., N.Y.C., 1929-36; from 1932 until John Ringling's death in 1936, assisted him in all affairs of circus, real estate and other interests; pres., dir. Ringling Bros. and Barnum & Bailey Combined Shows, Inc., 1937-43; pres. majority stockholder Ringling Bros., Barnum & Bailey Combined Shows, Inc., 1947-67, chmn. bd., 1955-67, spl. adviser, 1967—; pres., dir. White Sulphur Springs and Yellowstone Park R.R., Rockland Oil Co., Sarasota Oil Co. Appointed col. aide-de-camp, Wis. N.G. by Governor Heil, 1940; lt. col., Tex., 1941. Mem. Catholic Actors Guild, A.S.C.A.P., Psi Upsilon. Episcopalian. Clubs: Yale, Players (N.Y.C.); Sarasota (Fla.) Yacht. Office: Ringling Bros-Barnum & Bailey Circus Venice FL 33578

NORTH, JOHN S(ARGENT), utility co. exec.; b. Woodsville, N.H., Aug. 25, 1930; s. Ernest D. and Muriel S. N.; B.A., Dartmouth Coll., 1952, M.B.A., 1953; m. Judith L. Hyde, Aug. 18, 1956; children—Jeffrey S., David R., Deborah D., Susan H. With Mich. Bell Telephone Co., 1955-73; asst. v.p. network ops. AT&T, N.Y.C., 1973-75; exec. v.p. New Eng. Tel.&Tel., Boston, 1975—. Served to lt. (j.g.) USNR, 1953-55. Office: 185 Franklin St Boston MA 02107

NORTH, NELSON LUTHER, banker; b. N.Y.C.; Feb. 28, 1918; s. Nelson Luther and S. Evelyn (Weir) N.; B.A., Wesleyan U., Middletown, Conn., 1940; grad. student Columbia Sch. Law, 1941, Am. Inst. Banking, N.Y.U., Rutgers U. Grad. Sch. Banking, 1957; m. Carolyn Ruth Willis, Jan. 3, 1942; children—Nelson Luther, Bruce Willis. Exec. trainee, account mgr. Chase Nat. Bank, 1946-52; with City Trust Co., Bridgeport, Conn., 1952-71, exec. v.p., 1961-65, pres., 1965-71, also mem. exec. com.; chmn. bd., chief exec. officer, dir. City Nat. Bank, Bridgeport, 1971-76; pres., dir. Conn. Fin. Services Corp.; partner Knowles Assos.; dir. So. Conn. Gas Co., Bass Harbor Marine. Selectman, Town of Tremont (Maine). Bd. dirs. Bridgeport Hosp., YMCA Greater Bridgeport, Conn.; trustee Mt. Desert Island Hosp., Tremont Elementary Sch. Dist. Served with AUS, World War II; maj. Res. Decorated Croix de Guerre; Bronze Star. Mem. Am. Radio Relay League, Beta Theta Pi. Clubs: N.Y. Yacht; NE Harbor Fleet. Home: Bass Harbor ME 04653

NORTH, PHIL RECORD, business exec.; b. Fort Worth, July 6, 1918; s. James M. and Lottie R. N.; A.B., U. Notre Dame, 1939; m. Janis Harris, July 28, 1944; children—Phillip Kevin, Kerry Lawrence, Mairin Kathleen, Deirdre Aine. With Fort Worth Star Telegram, 1937-62, exec. editor, 1956-62, asst. gen. mgr., 1959-62; v.p. Carter Publs., Inc., 1949-62; with Tandy Corp., Fort Worth, 1966—, chief exec. officer, 1978—, pres., 1978—, chmn. bd., 1978—; dir. Continental Nat. Bank. Served to maj. AUS, 1940-46. Decorated Bronze Star. Roman Catholic. Clubs: Fort Worth, River Crest, Shady Oaks, Little Bay, Live Oak. Office: 1800 1 Tandy Center Fort Worth TX 76102

NORTH, ROBERT HUGH, trade assn. exec.; b. Honeycreek, Wis., Dec. 22, 1911; s. Robert H. and Mable S. (Grant) N.; A.A., Southeastern U., 1941, B.S., 1942, LL.B., 1945; m. June V. Langerude, Mar. 9, 1946; 1 son, Christopher E. Commr., Wis. Grain and Warehouse Commn., 1936-39; congl. sec. to B.J. Gehrmann, U.S. rep. from Wis., 1939-42; information specialist Dept. Agr., 1942-45; admitted to Wis., D.C., FCC bar assns.; with Internat. Assn. Ice Cream Mfrs., Washington, 1945-76, exec. sec., 1957-62, exec. v.p., 1962—; exec. v.p. Milk Industry Found., 1964-76, Am. Cultured Dairy Products Assn., 1971-76; adv. dir. Madison Nat. Bank, Washington. Treas., sec. Dairy Products Improvement Inst.; bd. dirs. Pvt. Truck Council Am., 1976; adminstrv. com. Nat. Hwy. Users Conf.; sec., treas. Dairy Industry Com., 1976; former exec. v.p. Dairy Tng. and Merchandising Inst.; past vice chmn. bus. adv. council on Fed. Report; trade assn. cons. Mem. Am. Soc. Assn. Execs. (sr. v.p. 1962, pres. 1963, dir., exec. com.; chmn. Fund Q 1971-76), Washington Trade Assn. Execs. (past pres.), U.S. C. of C. (past chmn. bd. regents insts. for trade assn. mgmt.). Methodist. Home and Office: 5905 Tanglewood Dr Bethesda MD 20034

NORTH, WARREN JAMES, govt. ofcl.; b. Winchester, Ill., Apr. 28, 1922; s. Clyde James and Lucille Adele (Bishop) N.; B.S. in Engring., Purdue U., 1947; M.S., Case Inst. Tech., 1954; M.S., Princeton, 1956; m. Carolyn Renfrow; children—James Warren, Mary Kay, Susan Lee, Diane. Engr. and test pilot NACA, Cleve., 1947-55, asst. chief aerodynamics br., 1955-59; chief manned satellites NASA, Washington, 1959-62, chief flight crew support div. Manned Spacecraft Center, Houston, 1972, asst. dir. space shuttle Flight Ops. Directorate, 1971—. Served with USAAF, 1943-45. Recipient DeFlorez tng. award, 1966; NASA award for exceptional service, 1968, 69. Mem. Am. Inst. Aero. and Astronautics (asso. fellow 1955), Tau Beta Pi, Pi Tau Sigma. Mason. Contbr. articles to profl. jours. Home: 221 Palm Aire Dr Friendswood TX 77546 Office: NASA-MSC Houston TX 77058

NORTH, WHEELER JAMES, educator, marine ecologist; b. San Francisco, Jan. 2, 1922; s. Wheeler Orrin and Florence Julia (Ross) N.; B.S. in Engring., Calif. Inst. Tech., 1944; M.S. in Oceanography, U. Calif. at San Diego, 1953, Ph.D. (Rockefeller postdoctoral fellow), 1953; NSF postdoctoral fellow Cambridge (Eng.) U.; m. Barbara Alice Best, Apr. 25, 1964; children—Hannah Catherine, Wheeler Orrin. Electronics engr. U.S. Navy Electronics Lab., Point Loma, Calif., 1947-48; asst. research biologist Scripps Inst. Oceanography, U. Calif. at San Diego, 1953, Inst. Marine Resources, 1956-63; asso. prof. Calif. Inst. Tech., Pasadena, 1963-70, prof., 1970—. Cons. marine biology U.S. Govt., State of Calif., San Francisco, Los Angeles, San Diego, numerous industries, 1957—; Phi Beta Kappa vis. scholar, 1973-74; mem. Calif. Adv. Commn., 1972-73, Nav. and Ocean Devel. Commn., 1973-76; dir. Marine Biol. Cons. Recipient NOGI award Underwater Soc. Am., 1975. Mem. Am. Littoral Soc. (James Duggan award), AAAS, Am. Soc. Limnology and Oceanography, Am. Soc. Zoology, Soc. Gen. Physiology, Calif. Acad. Sci., Fish Protective Assn. (dir.), N.Y. Acad. Sci., Am. Geophys. Union, Smithsonian Instn., Am. San Diego museums, Marine Tech. Soc., Western Soc. Naturalists, Calif. Soc. Profl. Engrs., Am. Zoomalac Soc., Internat. Oceanographic Found., Sigma Xi. Contbr. articles to profl. jours. Home: 205 Carnation Corona Del Mar CA 92625 Office: Calif Inst Tech Div Engring and Applied Sci Pasadena CA 91125

NORTH, WILLIAM HAVEN, fgn. service officer; b. Summit, N.J., Aug. 17, 1926; s. Eric M. and Gladys (Haven) N.; B.A. with high distinction and honors in History, Wesleyan U., Middletown, Conn., 1949; M.A. In History, Columbia, 1951; m. Jeanne Foote, Sept. 2, 1950; children—Jeannette, William Ashby, Charles Eric. Program officer ICA, Ethiopia, 1953-57, then dep. chief program div. African-European Regional Office, Washington; asst. dir. for program Lagos, Nigeria, AID, until 1966; dir. central and W. African affairs AID, Washington, 1966-70; dir. U.S. AID mission to Ghana, 1970-76; dep. asst. adminstr. Africa Bur., AID, 1976—. Fellow Center for Internat. Affairs, Harvard, 1965-66. Served with AUS, 1944-46. Recipient Meritorious Service award for exemplary achievement in pub. adminstrn., W.A. Jump Honor certificate, Superior Honor award for Nigerian Relief Adminstrn., Equal Employment Opportunity award, Disting. Honor award AID Mem. Am. Hist. Assn., Soc. for Internat. Devel. Socratic Lit. Soc. Methodist. Club: Appalachian Mountain. Home: 6500 Bannockburn Dr Bethesda MD 20034 Office: Africa Bureau AID Dept of State Washington DC 20523

NORTHART, LEO JOSEPH, editor; b. Pitts., Aug. 23, 1929; s. Leo Joseph and Mozelt Larue (Ellington) N.; A.B., U. N.C., 1952, M.A., 1953; m. Thelma Irene Harvey, Dec. 20, 1948; children—Leo Joseph III, Pamela Leigh. Advt. and sales promotion copywriter Gen. Electric Co., Schenectady, 1953-56; dept. editor Chem. Week mag., N.Y.C., 1956-60; internat. div. mgr. Am. Mgmt. Assn., N.Y.C., 1960-63; dir. publs. Copley Internat. Corp., N.Y.C., 1963-68; editorial dir. Johnston Internat. Pub. Corp., N.Y.C., 1968-74; editor Pub. Relations Jour., Pub. Relations Soc. Am., N.Y.C., 1974—. Cons., Westinghouse Internat., UN; lectr. Internat. Execs. Inst., Internat. Study and Research Inst.; mem. adv. bd. Rutger U. Inst. Internat. Bus.; mem. Select Businessmens Com. on Fgn. Trade, N.Y.C. Scoutmaster, Boy Scouts Am., 1961-63. Served with USMC, 1946-48. Mem. World Trade Writers New York (pres. 1965), N.Y. Bus. Press Editors, Am. Soc. Mag. Editors. Mem. Reformed Ch. Am. (elder). Lion. Author: (with William H. Baumer) Buy, Sell, Merge: How to Do It, 1971. Home: 25 Meadow Pl Freehold NJ 07728 Office: 845 3d Ave New York City NY 10022

NORTHCUTT, CLARENCE DEWEY, lawyer; b. Guin, Ala., July 7, 1916; s. Walter G. and Nancy E. (Homer) N.; A.B., U. Okla., 1939, LL.B., 1938; m. Ruth Eleanor Storms, May 25, 1941; children—Gayle Marie (Mrs. John J. Young), John E. Admitted to Okla. bar, 1938, since practiced in Ponca City; gen. counsel Frontier Fed. Savs. and Loan Assn. Mem. bd. visitors U. Okla. Served with AUS, 1941-46. Decorated Bronze Star, Air medal with oak leaf cluster. Fellow Am. Coll. Trial Lawyers, Am. Coll. Probate Counsel, Am. Bar Found.; mem. Acad. Univ. Fellows, Internat. Soc. Barristers, Internat. Acad. Trial Lawyers, Okla. Bar Assn. (pres. 1975, bd. govs.), Ponca City C. of C. (past pres.). Democrat. Baptist. Mason, Kiwanian. Home: 132 Whitworth St Ponca City OK 74601 Office: P O Box 1669 Ponca City OK 74601

NORTHCUTT, JESSE JAMES, seminary ofcl.; b. Haskell, Tex., June 11, 1914; s. Elijah Lecil and Mittie Pearl (Lamkin) N.; A.B., Okla. Baptist U., 1936; Th.M., Southwestern Bapt. Theol. Sem., 1939, Th.D., 1947; m. Fannie Sophie Yaeger, Dec. 24, 1933; children—Shirley Ruth (Mrs. James Flamming), Jessie Ann (Mrs. Robert Cook). Ordained to ministry Baptist Ch., 1932; served as pastor in Rio Vista, Tex., 1940-48, Abilene, Tex., 1948-50; prof. preaching Southwestern Bapt. Theol. Sem., 1939-48, 50-73, dean Sch. Theology, 1953-73, v.p. acad. affairs, 1973—. Mem. Am. Acad. Religion, Southwestern Assn. Bapt. Tchrs. Religion. Rotarian. Home: 3805 Curry Rd Arlington TX 76017

NORTHCUTT, RICHARD GLENN, neurobiologist; b. Mt. Vernon, Ill., Aug. 7, 1941; s. Glenn Donald and Effie Jane (Dodson) N.; B.A. cum laude, Millikin U., 1963; M.S., U. Ill., 1966, Ph.D., 1968; m. Mary Sue Caudle, June 26, 1965. Asst. prof. anatomy Case Western Res. U., Cleve., 1968-72; asso. prof. zoology U. Mich., Ann Arbor, 1972-77, prof. biol. scis., 1977—; vis. prof. dept. neuroscis. U. Calif., San Diego, 1979. Guggenheim fellow, 1979; recipient numerous grants NSF, NIH. Mem. AAAS, Am. Assn. Anatomists, Am. Soc. Ichthyologists and Herpetologists, Am. Soc. Zoologists, Soc. Animal Behavior, Internat. Brain Research Orgn., Soc. Neurosci. Author: (with K.L. Williams, R.P. Barber) Atlas of the Sheep Brain, 1966. Home: 3777 Greenook Rt 1 Ann Arbor MI 48103 Office: Div Biol Scis U Mich Ann Arbor MI 48109

NORTHCUTT, TRAVIS J., JR., behavioral scientist; b. McFarlan, N.C., Feb. 18, 1929; s. Travis J. and Eva Beatrice (Stubbs) N.; student Jacksonville U., 1949-52; B.S., Fla. State U., 1954, M.S., 1955, Ph.D. (Grad. fellow), 1959; M.P.H. (USPHS fellow), U. N.C., 1959; m. Rebecca L. Purvis, Nov. 17, 1969; children—Stevan Travis, Jeffrey Hugh, Holly Rebecca. Chief social scientist Fla. Bd. Health, 1959-62; state dir. Fla. Community Mental Health Research, 1963-64; research asso. Inst. Social Research, Fla. State U., 1965-69, asst. prof., 1965-67, asso. prof. dept. sociology, 1967-69; dir. Social Scis. and Law, State U. System of Fla. Bd. Regents, Tallahassee, 1969-70, dir. acad. planning and community services, 1970-72; prof., dir. planning and devel. Coll. Social and Behavioral Scis., U. S.Fla., Tampa, 1972-73, prof., dean Coll., 1973—, acting dir. Human Resources Inst., 1975-77; mem. So. Regional Edn. Bd., 1962-64; mem. Gov.'s Commn. on Criminal Justice Standards and Goals, 1970-78; advisor Fla. Children's Commn., 1959-61; cons. nat. study health needs of agrl. migrants Am. Public Health Assn., 1963-64; dir. research, planning Gov.'s Commn. on Comprehensive Mental Health Planning in Fla., 1962-63; mem. research adv. com. Fla. Alcoholic Rehab. Program, 1962-67; mem. Fla. Commn. for 1960 White House Conf. on Children and Youth; mem. adv. council Fla. Mental Health Inst., 1978—; cons., lectr. Planned Parenthood/World Population, 1960-70; cons. Research Group, Inc., Atlanta, 1968-72; guest lectr., cons. numerous univs., 1959—. Bd. dirs. Northside Comprehensive Community Mental Health Center, Tampa, 1975—, S.W. Fla. Blood Bank, 1976—; mem. Tampa Fine Arts Council, 1977—. Recipient numerous grants for study including Arthur Vining Davis Found., James Davis Found., NIH, USPHS, NIMH, Law Enforcement Assistance Adminstrn., U.S. Office Edn. Fellow Am. Sociol. Assn. (charter mem. med. sociology sect.), Am. Public Health Assn., So. Sociol. Assn.; mem. Fla. Public Health Assn., Greater Tampa C. of C. (planning and devel. com. 1978—), Sun Belt Athletic Conf. (pres. 1977-78). Democrat. Methodist. Co-author 4 monographs; contbr. chpts. to books, articles, papers to profl. lit. Editorial bd. Community Psychology, 1973-77. Home: 3007 Peacock Ln Tampa FL 33618 Office: Coll of Social and Behavioral Scis U South Fla Tampa FL 33620. *Growing up in the foothills of North Carolina, I was taught by my parents that by birth I was as good as—but no better than—anyone else. As a young athlete I learned to respect and enjoy competing with worthy opponents. These very simple, but basic, principles have influenced and characterized both my personal and professional life.*

NORTHFELT, MERLYN WINFIELD, sem. pres.; b. Mpls., Dec. 16, 1915; s. Frank Ivar and Esther (Eckgren) N.; B.A., Seattle Pacific Coll., 1942; M.Div., Garrett Theol. Sem., 1946; D.D., Morningside Coll., 1966; L.H.D., Iowa Wesleyan Coll., 1975, North Central Coll., 1975; D.D., Seabury/Western Theol. Sem., 1976; m. Dorothy May Underwood, Oct. 11, 1938; children—Marilyn Ann (Mrs. Thomas Coffey), Sandra Lou (Mrs. Thomas Landon). Ordained to ministry Meth. Ch., 1945; minister in Yorkville, Ill., 1943-51, Lake Bluff, Ill., 1951-61; dist. supt. Rockford (Ill.) Dist., 1961-65, No. Dist., 1965-66; program coordinator No. Ill. Ann. Conf., 1966-70; pres. Garrett Theol. Sem., 1970-74, Garrett-Evang. Theol. Sem., 1974—. Del. gen. conf. Meth. Ch., 1964, 66, 68, 70, 72, 76, chmn. legis. com. on local ch., 1964-68, mem. quadrennial com. on local ch., 1964-68, mem. bd. global ministries, chmn. gen. conf. commn. to study offices of episcopacy and dist. superintendency; del. World Meth. Conf., London, 1966, 76; mem. gen. assembly Nat. Council Chs., 1966-69, mem. gen. bd., 1969—. Mem. exec. com. Lake Forest-Highland Park Family Service, 1957-61, Wesley Willows Retirement Home, Rockford, 1963-65; pres. bd. Rosecrance Meml. Home Boys, 1961-65; pres. Assn. Chgo. Theol. Schs., 1971-73. Home: 2426 Lincolnwood Dr Evanston IL 60201

NORTHRIP, RICHARD ARTHUR, labor union exec.; b. Daytona Beach, Fla., Jan. 27, 1929; s. Norman A. and W. Lee (Fretwell) N.; student pub. schs., Fla.; m. Mildred Elizabeth Shiles, Sept. 5, 1948; children—Richard Michael, Janet Lee, Deborah Ann, Robert Arthur. With Lehigh Portland Cement Co., Flagler Beach, Fla., 1953-57; pres. local union United Cement, Lime & Gypsum Workers Internat. Union, Chgo., 1956-57, dist. rep., 1957-58, sec.-treas. dist., 1958-74, dist. policy chmn., 1968-74, sec.-treas. internat. union, 1974—. Served with USAF, 1948-52. Address: United Cement Lime & Gypsum Workers Internat Union 7830 W Lawrence Ave Chicago IL 60656

NORTHROP, CHARLES ARTHUR, data processing co. exec.; b. Irvington, N.Y., June 23, 1923; s. Clyde McCall and Elizabeth Josephine (Oubre) N.; B.S., Columbia U.; m. Ellen M. Murray, Feb. 9, 1941; children—Ellen Joan, Carol Ann, Peggy Jean. With IBM Corp., 1942—, mgr. gen. acctg., 1956-59, mgr. acctg. services gen. products div., 1959-61, controller fed. systems div., 1961-64, chief acct., 1964-67, asst. controller IBM World Trade Corp., 1967-69, asst. controller IBM Corp., 1969-74, controller, 1974-78, treas., 1978—; mem. Greater Westchester adv. bd. Mfrs. Hanover Trust Co. Bd. dirs. Westchester-Putnam Council Boy Scouts Am. Served with USNR, 1944-46. Mem. Fin. Execs. Inst., Nat. Assn. Accts., Treas.'s Club, Soc. Internat. Treas. Home: 11 Hayrake Ln Chappaqua NY 10514 Office: Old Orchard Rd Armonk NY 10504

NORTHROP, CHARLES PORTER, lawyer; b. Rochester, N.Y., Aug. 6, 1941; s. William Watson and Julia Allen (Stebbins) N.; B.A., Amherst Coll., 1963; J.D., U. Pa., 1966; m. Jacquelyn Kay Sheetz, Nov. 29, 1969; 1 dau., Kimberly Carrington. Admitted to N.Y. State bar, 1966; asso. firm Nixon, Hargrave, Devans & Doyle, Rochester, N.Y., 1966-71; with Stirling Homex Corp., Avon, N.Y., 1971-78, gen. counsel, 1972-73, pres., 1973-78; v.p. law Consol. Rail Corp. (Conrail), Phila., 1979—. Mem. Am. Bar Assn., N.Y. State Bar Assn. Clubs: Racquet (Phila.); Genesee Valley (Rochester, N.Y.). Home: Harvest Ln Haverford PA 19041 Office: 1838 Six Penn Center Philadelphia PA 19104

NORTHROP, EDWARD SKOTTOWE, U.S. judge; b. Chevy Chase, Md., June 12, 1911; s. Claudian Bellinger and Eleanor Smythe (Grimke) N.; LL.B., George Washington U., 1937; m. Barbara Middleton Burdette, Apr. 22, 1939; children—Edward M., St. Julien (Mrs. Kevin Butler), Peter. Village mgr., Chevy Chase, Md., 1934-41; admitted Md. bar, 1937; practiced in Rockville, Md., Washington, D.C., 1937-61; judge U.S. Dist. Ct. of Md., Balt., 1961—, chief judge, 1970—; mem. Met. Chief Judges Conf., 1970—. Mem. Md. Senate, 1954-61, chmn. finance com.; majority leader, 1959-61; mem. Jud. Conf. Com. on Adminstrn. of Probation System, 1973-79; mem. Adv. Corrections Council U.S., 1976—; mem. Jud. Panel on Multidist. Legislation, 1979—. Trustee Woodberry Forest Sch. Served to comdr. USNR, 1941-45. Mem. Am., Md., D.C., Montgomery County bar assns., Barristers, Washington Center Met. Studies, Gate and Key, St. Cecilia Soc., Georgetown Assembly, S.R., Sigma Alpha Epsilon. Democrat. Episcopalian; Rotarian. Club: Chevy Chase (Md.). Home: 4309 Wendover Rd Baltimore MD 21218 Office: U S Court House Baltimore MD 21201

NORTHROP, EUGENE STANLEY, banker; b. Kansas City, Mo., May 21, 1905; s. Eugene H. and Josephine (Cooper) N.; A.B., U. Pa., 1927; grad. Grad. Sch. Banking Rutgers U., 1948; m. Elizabeth Lee Latimer, Apr. 11, 1931. With Equitable Trust Co., N.Y.C., 1927-31, Mfrs. Hanover Trust Co. (formerly Mfrs. Trust Co.), N.Y.C., 1931—, v.p., 1948-57, sr. v.p., 1957-61, exec. v.p., 1961—, vice chmn. bd., 1962-70, dir., until 1971; dir. Allied Stores Corp. Bd. dirs. Vis. Nurse Service N.Y. Served to comdr. USNR, 1942-45; in Pacific on USS Enterprise and USS Boxer. Mem. Phi Gamma Delta (past pres., bd. govs. N.Y. Club). Republican. Clubs: University, Blind Brook (N.Y.C.); Pine Valley Golf; Woodway Country; Royal Poincian Golf (Naples, Fla.). Author: Mathematical Odds in Contract Bridge (with Arthur Stein), 1933. Home: 51 Bank St New Canaan CT 06840 also 2200 Gulf Shore Blvd Naples FL 33940 Office: 350 Park Ave New York NY 10022

NORTHROP, FILMER STUART CUCKOW, educator; b. Janesville, Wis., Nov. 27, 1893; s. Marshall Ellsworth and Ruth (Cuckow) N.; A.B., Beloit Coll., 1915; A.M. in Econs., Yale, 1919; A.M. in Philosophy, Harvard, 1922, Ph.D. in Philosophy of Sci., 1924; postgrad. Freiburg, Germany, 1922, Imperial Coll. Sci. and Tech., U. London, and Trinity Coll., Cambridge, 1922-23, LL.D., U. Hawaii, 1949, Rollins Coll., 1955; Litt.D., Beloit Coll., 1946; H.H.D., Pratt Inst., 1961; m. Christine Johnston, Aug. 6, 1919 (dec. 1969); children—Filmer Johnston, Stuart Johnston; m. 2d, Marjorie Carey, 1969. Social work, N.Y.C., 1915-16; ednl. sec. Internat. Com. YMCA, Hong Kong, 1919-20; instr. philosophy, Yale, 1923-26, asst. prof., 1926-29, asso. prof., 1929-32, prof. philosophy, 1932-47, master Silliman Coll., 1940-47, Sterling prof. philosophy and law, 1947-62, Sterling prof. philosophy and law emeritus, 1962—; vis. prof. univs. of Iowa, Mich., Va., Hawaii, Rollins Coll., Nat. U. Mexico, 1949; prof. extraordinaire Nat. Autonomous U. Mexico, 1949—; vis. prof. Boston Coll., 1976. Bd. dirs. Sch. for Asiatic Studies; 1st v.p., bd. dirs., mem. corp. Werner-Gren Found. for Anthrop. Research, 1955-63, life research asso., 1964—; founding fellow Nat. Conf. Sci. Philosophy and Religion, E.-W. Philosophy Confs. Honolulu, Found. for Integrative Edn., Am. Soc. for Cybernetics. Served to 2d lt. Tank Corps, U.S. Army, 1917-19. Decorated Order Aztec Eagle, Govt. Mexico; recipient William Clyde De Vane Phi Beta Kappa award, 1968; Am. Council Learned Socs. prize, 1962; Wilbur L. Cross Yale Grad. Sch. award, 1968. Guggenheim fellow, 1932-33. Fellow AAAS, Assn. History and Philosophy (pres. 1947), Am. Acad. Polit. and Social Sci., Am. Acad. Arts and Sci.; mem. Assn. Am. Law Schs., Am. Philos. Assn. (pres. 1952), N.Y. Philosophy Club, Am. Oriental Soc., Century Assn., Phi Beta Kappa, Delta Sigma Rho, Sigma Xi. Conglist. and Buddhist. Clubs: Lawn, Graduate, Beaumont. Mory's, Elizabethan, Aurelian, Berzelius (New Haven). Author: Science and First Principles, 1931; The Meeting of East and West, 1946; The Logic of the Sciences and the Humanities, 1947; The Taming of the Nations, 1952 (Freedom House award); (with Mason Gross) Alfred North Whitehead: An Anthology, 1953; European Union and United States Foreign Policy, 1954; The Complexity of Legal and Ethical Experience, 1959; Philosophical Anthropology and Practical Politics, 1960; Man, Nature and God, 1962. Editor, contbr. Ideological Differences and World Order, 1949; (with H.H. Livingston) Cross-Cultural Understanding; Epistemology in Anthropology, 1964; contbg. author Contemporary American Philosophy, 2d series, 1970. Contbr. numerous articles to sci., philos., legal and anthrop. jours. Home: Suite 169 Red Jacket Mountain View Inn North Conway NH 03860

NORTHROP, JOHN HOWARD, scientist; b. Yonkers, N.Y., July 5, 1891; s. John I. and Alice Belle (Rich) N.; B.S., Columbia U., 1912, M.A., 1913, Ph.D., 1915, D.Sc., 1937; D.Sc., Harvard U., 1936, Yale U., 1937, Princeton U., 1940, Rutgers U. 1941; LL.D., U. Calif., 1939; m. Louise Walker, June 1918; children—Alice Havemeyer, John. W.B. Cutting traveling fellow Columbia U., 1915; apptd. asst. Rockefeller Inst. for Med. Research, 1916, asso. mem., 1922, member of Inst., 1924-62, prof. of Inst. emeritus, 1962—; Hitchcock prof. U. Calif., 1939; Thayer lectr. Johns Hopkins U., 1940, De Lamar lectr., 1937; Jesup lectr. Columbia, 1938; prof. bacteriology, biophysics, research biophysicist Donner Lab., U. Calif., 1958-59, prof. emeritus, 1959—; mem. com. on proteins NRC cons. and official investigator to NDRC, 1942. Capt. C.W.S., U.S. Army, 1918-19. Trustee Marine Biol. Lab., Woods Hole, Mass. Recipient Stevens prize Coll. Phys. and Surg., Columbia, 1930; Chandler medal, Columbia, 1937; Giraud medal, Nat. Acad. Sci., 1944: shared Nobel prize in chemistry, 1946; certificate of merit, 1948; Columbia Lion Award, Alumni Club of Essex County, 1949. Alexander Hamilton medal Columbia U., 1961. Hon. fellow Chem. Soc., London. Mem. Nat. Acad. Sci., S.A.R., Am. Soc. Biol. Chemistry, Soc. Gen. Physiologists, Soc. Philomathique (Paris), Am. Philos. Soc., Sigma Xi (research fellowship com.), Phi Lambda Upsilon, Kais. Deutch. Akad. der Naturforscher, Delta Kappa Epsilon. Clubs: Century Assn. Author: Crystalline Enzymes. Hon. editor, contbr. Jour. Gen. Physiology; contbg. editor Funk & Wagnalls Ency. Home: PO Box 1387 Wickenberg AZ 85358

NORTHROP, MONROE, lawyer; b. Houston, Jan. 1, 1931; s. Joseph Walter and Mary (Harris) N.; B.B.A., U. Tex., 1953, LL.B., 1954; m. Jane Ann Palmer, Dec. 4, 1970; 1 son, Ronald Viator. Admitted to Tex. bar, 1954; practiced in Houston, 1957—; asst. dist. atty. Harris County, Houston, 1957-59; asst. U.S. atty. So. Dist. Tex., Houston, 1959-61; mem. firm Austin, Dabney, Northrop & Garwood, 1968-75, Austin & Arnett, 1975—. Served with C.I.C., AUS, 1955-57. Fellow Tex. Bar Found.; mem. Am., Tex., Houston bar assns., Am. Judicature Soc., Tex., Houston trial lawyers assns., Lawyer Soc. Houston, Sigma Chi. Republican. Episcopalian. Home: 4722 Waring St Houston TX 77027 Office: 1938 Bank of SW Bldg Houston TX 77002

NORTHROP, STUART JOHNSTON, mfg. co. exec.; b. New Haven, Oct. 22, 1925; s. Filmer Stuart Cuckow and Christine (Johnston) N.; B.A., Yale, 1948; m. Cynthia Stafford Daniell, Feb. 23, 1946; children—Christine Daniell, Richard Rockwell Stafford. Indsl. engr. U.S. Rubber Co., Naugatuck, Conn., 1948-51; head indsl. engring. dept. Am. Cyanamid Co., Wallingford, Conn., 1951-54; mfg. mgr. Linear, Inc., Phila., 1954-57; mgr. quality control and mfg. Westinghouse Electric Co., Pitts., 1957-58; mfg. supt. SKF Industries, Phila., 1958-61; v.p. mfg. Am. Meter Co., Phila., 1961-69; founder, v.p., gen. mgr. water resources div. Singer Co., Phila.; pres., dir. Buffalo Meter Co., Four Layne Cos.; dir. Gen. Filter Co., 1969-72; chmn., chief exec. officer, dir. Huffy Corp., Dayton, Ohio; dir. Danis Industries, Inc., Dayton, Dariron Co., Dayton. Bd. dirs. Wynnewood (Pa.) Civic Assn.; trustee Dayton Art Inst., Center City Sch., Dayton, Dayton Mus. Natural History. Served with USAAF, 1944-45. Mem. Delaware Valley Investors (past pres.), Interlocutors, Elihu, Delta Kappa Epsilon, KOA Soc. Clubs: Moraine Country, Dayton Racquet (Dayton). Home: 3732 Blossom Heath Dayton OH 45419 Office: 7701 Byers Rd Dayton OH 45401

NORTHRUP, HERBERT ROOF, economist, business exec.; b. Irvington, N.J., Mar. 6, 1918; A.B., Duke U., 1939; A.M., Harvard U., 1941, Ph.D., 1942; m. Eleanor Pearson, June 3, 1944; children—James Pearson, Nancy Warren, Jonathan Peter, David, Philip. Instr. econs. Cornell U., 1942-43; sr. hearing officer Nat. War Labor Bd., 1943-45; asst. prof. econs. Columbia, 1945-49; labor economist Nat. Indsl. Conf. Bd., 1949-52; indsl. relations cons. Ebasco Services, 1952-55; v.p. indsl. relations Penn-Texas Corp., N.Y.C., 1955-58; employee relations cons. Gen. Electric Co., 1958-61; prof. industry Wharton Sch., U. Pa., Phila., 1961—, chmn. dept. industry, 1964-69, dir. indsl. research unit, 1964—, chmn. Labor Relations Council, 1968—; cons. on manpower, personnel and labor relations problems to many companies; arbitrator in labor relations disputes. Mem. Am. Econ. Assn., Indsl. Relations Research Assn., Am. Arbitration Assn., Phi Beta Kappa. Clubs: Harvard (N.Y.C.); Peale (Phila.); University (Washington); La Coquille (Palm Beach, Fla.). Author: Organized Labor and the Negro, 1944; Unionization of Professional Engineers and Chemists, 1946; Economics of Labor Relations, 1950, 8th edit., 1977; Government and Labor, 1963; Readings in Labor Economics, 1963; Boulwarism: Labor Policies of General Electric Company, 1964; Negro and Employment Opportunity, 1965; Hours of Labor, 1965; Compulsory Arbitration and Government Intervention in Labor Disputes, 1966; Restrictive Labor Practices in Supermarket Industry, 1967; Negro in the Automobile Industry, 1968; Negro in the Aerospace Industry, 1968; Negro in the Rubber Tire Industry, 1969; Negro in Paper Industry, 1969; Negro in the Tobacco Industry, 1970; Negro Employment in Basic Industry, 1970; Negro Employment in Southern Industry, 1970; Negro Employment in Land and Air Transport, 1971; Impact of Government Manpower Programs, 1975; Open Shop Construction, 1975; The Impact of OSHA, 1978; Objective Selection of Supervisors, 1978; Black and Other Minority Participation in the All-Volunteer Navy and Marine Corps, 1979; Manpower in the Retail Pharmacy Industry, 1979; The Impact of the ATT-EEO Consent Decree, 1979; Multinational Collective Bargaining Attempts, 1979; also articles in field. Home: 517 Thornbury Rd Haverford PA 19041 Office: Wharton Sch U Pa Philadelphia PA 19104

NORTHRUP, LANESS DONALD, state senator Wyo.; b. Braymer, Mo., June 8, 1904; s. Joseph R. and Mary (Creswell) N.; student Iowa U., 1925-27; m. Ermine Marcelle Davidson, Aug. 17, 1928 (dec.); m. 2d, Jane Dart Clark, Dec. 22, 1966; children—Laness D., M. Juletta Northrup Corbin. Farmer, cattle feeder, Powell, Wyo., 1929—; mem. Wyo. Ho. of Reps., 1956-66; mem. Wyo. State Senate, 1967—, pres., 1977-78. Mem. Sch. Bd., Powell, 1944-59, pres., 1950-55; pres. Big Horn Basin Sch. Trustees Assn., 1948-55; mem. adv. council Big Horn Nat. Forest, 1948-51; mem. Park County Bd. Pub. Assistance and Social Services. Mem. Wyo. Farm Bur., Park County Stock Growers Assn. (past pres.). Republican. Methodist. Clubs: Rotary, Masons, Shriners, Eastern Star, Elks. Home: Star Route Box 56 Powell WY 82435

NORTHUP, GEORGE WARREN, osteopathic physician; b. Syracuse, N.Y., Oct. 9, 1915; s. Thomas Larkham and Anna Laura (Carleton) N.; student Brothers Coll., Drew U., 1933-35; D.O., Phila. Coll. Osteopathy, 1939, postgrad., 1939-41; postgrad. Seton Hall Coll., 1949-50; m. Elsie May Webster, Sept. 3, 1941; 1 son, Jeffrey Carleton. Mem. founding staff West Essex Gen. Hosp., chmn. exec. com., 1960-72, trustee, 1969-72, chmn. dept. phys. medicine, 1960-72; dir. med. edn., dir. dept. rehab. medicine Mesa (Ariz.) Gen. Hosp., 1973—, adminstr., 1973-74, chief staff, 1975, med. dir., 1975—, pres. bd. trustees, 1976—. Mem. 4-man com. rep. osteopathic profession to NRC; del. Am. Council on Edn., 1953, 54, 59; del. Nat. Health Council, 1959, also mem. bd. dirs.; del. White House Conf. Children and Youth, 1960. Pres. Livingston Profl. Labs., 1951-59; cons. Surgeon Gen.'s Conf. on Asian Flu, 1957; cons. sec. health, edn. and welfare conf. on food additives, 1958; mem. exec. com., treas. Nat. Coordinating Com. on Drug Abuse, 1967—; vice chmn. commn. on med. malpractice HEW, 1971-72, del. Conf. on Manipulation. Named physician of year N.J. Assn. Osteo. Physicians and Surgeons, 1958, hon. citizen Tex., 1959, hon. chief Acoma Indian Tribe, Okla., 1959; recipient Phi Sigma Alpha award, 1962, Drew Alumni Achievement award in Scis., 1962; hon. citizen of Kansas City, 1962; alumni award Phila. Coll. Osteo. Medicine, 1971, O.J. Snyder Meml. medal, 1972, 1st Northup Disting. Service award Nat. Student Osteo. Med. Assn.; lic. osteopath, N.J., Pa., 1939, lic. to practice medicine and surgery, N.J., 1941, Ariz., 1963. Diplomate Am. Osteo. Bd. Phys. Medicine and Rehab. Fellow N.Y. Acad. Osteopathy, Am. Coll. Osteopathy Internists (hon.), Am. Acad. Osteopathy, Am. Coll. Osteo. Surgeons; mem. Am. Osteo. Assn. (gen. program chmn. conv. Boston, 1948; mem. ho. of dels. 1951, 53, 54, 55, 56, trustee 1954-59, pres. 1958-59, editor 1961—), Acad. Applied Osteopathy (pres. 1950-51), Am. Council Edn., N.J. (pres. 1956-57; speaker ho. dels. 1964), Essex County assns. osteo. physicians and surgeons, Nat. Health Council (treas. 1964-73), Ariz. Osteo. Med. Assn. (speaker ho. dels.), Am. Osteo. Acad. Orthopedics (hon.), AAAS, Am. Pub. Health Assn., Am. Coll. Osteo. Surgeons (hon.), N.Y. Acad. Scis., Phi Sigma Alpha, Sigma Sigma Phi, Theta Psi. Republican. Baptist. Mason. Author books, sci. and med. articles on osteo. medicine. Home: 6310 Double Tree Ranch Rd Paradise Valley AZ 85253 Office: Mesa Gen Hosp 515 N Mesa Dr Mesa AZ 85201. *Life has rarely been so bad as my fears nor quite as good as my hopes. The bad has helped me appreciate the good; the good helps to understand the bad.*

NORTHUP, JOHN DAVID, inventor; b. Toledo, Sept. 8, 1910; s. Charles S. and Alice Delia (Bachelder) N.; B.S., Mass. Inst. Tech., 1932; m. Ruth Bender, Jan. 15, 1937; children—John David, Mary Elizabeth, Nancy Ross (Mrs. H.T. Lehrkind). With Owens-Ill. Glass Co., 1933-74, mgr. Clarion, Pa., 1943-46, Charleston, W.Va., 1946-47, gen. purchasing agt. glass container div., 1947-49, gen. mgr. corrugated package ops., 1949-53, dir. engring., 1953-55, v.p. administrv. div., 1956-61, v.p., gen. mgr. Closure div., 1961-72, v.p. charge glass container mfg., 1972-74; ind. inventor, 1974—; sec.-treas. Daelrod, Inc., 1978—. Chmn. closure com. Glass Container Mfrs. Inst., 1966-69; tech. adviser on poison prevention packaging FDA, 1971-72. Mem. Beta Theta Pi. Republican. Unitarian. Club: Inverness (Toledo). Home: 2460 Underhill Rd Toledo OH 43615

NORTHUP, ROBERT EDGAR, railroad exec., lawyer; b. Malone, N.Y., Mar. 20, 1915; s. Robert Miles and Laura Margaret (McCall) N.; A.B., Colgate U., 1935; J.D. cum laude, DePaul U., 1940; m. June Margaret Sheasby, June 3, 1944; children—Stephen A., Robert W., Katherine J. (Mrs. Frank V. Doria), Richard M. Admitted to Ill. and Va. bars; legal stenographer C. & W.I. R.R., Chgo., 1937-42; legal coordinator Chgo. Ordnance Dist., 1942-44; asst. gen. atty. Rheem Mfg. Co., N.Y.C., 1944-48; gen. atty. Seaboard Coast Line R.R. Co., Richmond, Va., 1948-56, sr. gen. atty, 1956-61, gen. solicitor, 1961-73, sec., 1971—, v.p., 1973—, dir., 1972—. Mem. Am., Va., Richmond bar assns., Delta Upsilon. Methodist (adminstrv. bd. 1971—). Club: Willow Oaks Country. Home: 6314 Ridgeway Rd Richmond VA 23226 Office: 3600 W Broad St Richmond VA 23230

NORTON, ADELBERT JAMES, coll. dean; b. Bklyn., Mar. 11, 1918; s. Francis Edward and Catherine (Jost) N.; B.A., Manhattan Coll., 1940; M.A., Catholic U., 1943; Ph.D., St. John's U., 1955. Joined Bros. Christian Schs., 1940; tchr. De La Salle Coll., Washington, 1942-43; tchrs., head English dept. Bishop Loughlin High Sch., Bklyn., 1943-52; prof. edn., head dept. Manhattan Coll., 1952-64, dean Sch. Tchr. Preparation, 1964—; adj. prof. Maryknoll (N.Y.) Sem., 1956-71; vis. lectr. St. Mary's (Cal.) Coll., summer 1960. Del. regional chpt. Bros. Christian Schs., 1966, del. dist. chpt., 1967, 74-75, 77-78; founder, past pres. Catholic Coll. Council on Tchr. Preparation; mem. adv. com. Notre Dame Study Cath. Edn., 1962-64; mem. N.Y. State Regents Bd. on Tchr. Edn., Cert. and Practice, 1979—. Bd. mgrs. Lincoln Hall, Lincolndale, N.Y., 1966—; trustee Sgt. Robert O'Malley Fund, 1967-77. Recipient Distinguished Alumnus award in edn. Manhattan Coll., 1971, also Bonus et Fidelis medal, 1977. Mem. Am. Personnel and Guidance Assn., Assn. Higher Edn., Nat. Soc. Study Edn., Assn. Counselor Edn. and Supervision, Kappa Delta Pi, Phi Epsilon Kappa. Contbr. profl. jour. Asso. editor La Sallian Digest, 1960-71; asso. editor, mem. editorial bd. Jour. Nat. Cath. Guidance Council, 1958-65. Address: Manhattan Coll Bronx NY 10471. *St. John Baptist De La Salle, founder of the Brothers of the Christian Schools and founder of the first Training School for lay teachers, insisted that all teachers needed the virtues of faith and zeal. Faith, even on the human level, enables me to see my labor as worthwhile even when tangible evidence in students is not apparent. Zeal drives me that extra step to go beyond the clock in my efforts to help others or to carry extra work.*

NORTON, ANDRE ALICE, author; b. Cleve.; d. Adalbert and Bertha Stemm N. Librarian, Cleve. Public Library, until 1951; author 89 books. Mem. Authors League, Penwomen, Women in Communication, Sci. Fiction Writers Am. Address: 682 S Lakemont Winter Park FL 32789

NORTON, CLARENCE CLIFFORD, educator; b. Benton, Miss., July 2, 1896; s. Rev. Henry L. and May (Bogan) N.; B.S., Millsaps Coll., Jackson, Miss., 1919; M.A., Emory U., 1920; Ph.D., U.N.C., 1927; LL.D., Wofford Coll., 1953; m. Mable Binning, Aug. 22, 1922; children—Dorothy Alice, Howard Binning. Dean, prof. social sci. Lon Morris Coll., 1920-23; teaching fellow and instr. history, U. N.C., 1923-25; prof. polit. sci. and sociology Wofford Coll., 1925-47, 53-58, John M. Reeves prof. sociology, 1958-62, emeritus, 1962—, chmn. dept., 1958-62, prof. sociology, 1947-53, dean coll., 1942-49, 52-53, dir. Summer Sch., 1942-53, dean adminstrn., 1949-52, acting pres., 1951-52; vis. prof. Am. govt. Wake Forest Coll., 1927. Del. World Meth. Conf., London, Eng., 1966. Mem. S.C. State Planning Bd. 1939-45, S.C. Council Tchr. Edn.; trustee Lake Junaluska Assembly, 1940-48, 52-56; past pres. Spartanburg Community Chest. Pres. Spartanburg Council Social Workers, 1936. Mem. Phi Beta Kappa, Sigma Upsilon, Alpha Psi Delta, Pi Kappa Alpha, Blue Key. Mason, Rotarian (gov. internat. 1958-59). Author: The Democratic Party in Ante-Bellum North Carolina; 1930; Enriching Family Life, 1945, rev. edit., 1962; The Art of Caricature, 1951; A Cartoon Commentary on Church Folks, 1967; Little Church Folks in Cartoons, 1969. Contbr. to various periodicals. Creator of Church Folks, syndicated cartoon. Home: 1511 Mizell Ave Winter Park FL 32789. *Early in my preparation for a career I was guided by the ideals of a constructive and creative contribution to society. I deliberately chose the field of higher education as a medium for my life's work. I definitely desired to relate myself to youth in their most formative period of life. Allied with a scholarly quest for truth has been an emphasis on character. I am grateful for the privilege of having a share in the development of young men and women toward meaningful and constructive goals in life.*

NORTON, DELMAR LYNN, candy co. exec.; b. Vernal, Utah, Sept. 6, 1944; s. La Mar and Velma (Hullinger) N.; student U. Utah, 1962-63, Famous Artists Sch., 1966-69; m. Connie Jean Bryan, Mar. 10, 1966; children—Bryan Lynn, Christopher Max, Wendy. Nat. sales mgr. Maxfield Candy Co., Salt Lake City, 1965-72; sec.-treas. Ice Cream & Candy Shops, Salt Lake City, 1972-73; pres., gen. mgr. Ostlers' Candy Co., Salt Lake City, 1973—; chmn. bd. Nat. Mktg. Co., Salt Lake City, 1974—. Mem. Ch. of Jesus Christ of Latter-Day Saints (missionary). Home: 4240 S 1650 E Salt Lake City UT 84107 Office: 3331 South 900 East Suite 200 Salt Lake City UT 84117

NORTON, ELEANOR HOLMES, govt. ofcl.; b. Washington, June 13, 1937; B.A., Antioch Coll., 1960; M.A. in Am. Studies, Yale U., 1963, LL.B., 1964. Law clk. to Fed. Dist. Ct. Judge A. Leon Higginbotham, 1964-65; asst. legal dir. ACLU, 1965-70; exec. asst. to mayor N.Y.C., 1971-74; chmn., mem. Equal Employment Opportunity Commn., 1977—. Recipient Louise Waterman Wise award. Democrat. Author: Sex Discrimination and the Law; also articles in jours.*

NORTON, (WILLIAM) ELLIOT, drama critic; b. Boston, May 17, 1903; s. William L. and Mary E. (Fitzgerald) N.; A.B., Harvard, 1926; M.A. (hon.) Emerson Coll. 1955, Litt.D., 1963; D. Journalism (hon.), Suffolk U., 1956; L.H.D., Fairfield (Conn.) U., 1964, Boston Coll., 1970, St. Francis Coll., 1970, St. Joseph's Coll., 1976, Assumption Coll., 1979; D.Litt., Northeastern U., 1966, Merrimack Coll., 1977; m. Florence E. Stelmach, Sept. 9, 1934; children—Elizabeth Noel, Jane Florence, David Andrew. Reporter, 1926-34; drama critic Boston Post, 1934-56, Boston Daily Record and Boston Sunday Advertiser, 1956-62, Boston Record Am. and Sunday Advertiser, 1962-73, Boston Herald Am., 1973—; part time mem. faculty Emerson Coll., 1935-62, Boston Coll., 1948-62; lectr. dramatic lit. Boston U. Sch. Fine and Applied Arts, 1954-67, adj. prof. dramatic lit., 1967—; Phi Beta Kappa orator Tufts U., 1967; lectr. Drama Workshop Fgn. Studies League London, Nottingham, 1967, Reading (Eng.), 1968; star TV program Elliot Norton Revs., 1958—. Pres. New Eng. Theatre Conf., 1951-53; vice chmn. Mass. Council Arts and Humanities, 1966-71; mem. pres.'s council Fairfield U. 1967-69; exec. com. Am. Theatre Critics Assn., 1974-79; mem. Pulitzer Prize Play Jury, 1964-68, 72-73. Recipient First Ann. Citation Merit, Boston Coll., 1947; Connor Meml. award Emerson Coll., 1956; Rodgers and Hammerstein Coll. President's award, 1962; Peabody award for Elliot Norton Revs., 1962; George Jean Nathan award, 1963-64; Spl. Antoinette Perry award, 1971; citation Nat. Council Tchrs. English, 1971; gold medal Am. Coll. Theater Festival, 1973; Nat. award New Eng. Theatre Conf., 1974; Yankee Quill award Acad. NE Journalists, 1976; award for outstanding achievement in arts Mass. chpt. Nat. Multiple Sclerosis Soc., 1977; named Grand Bostonian, City of Boston, 1977; theater park named in his honor, Boston, 1977. Fellow Am. Acad. Arts and Scis.; mem. Nat. Theatre Conf. (hon.) Clubs: Boston Press (pres. 1950-52), Harvard; Players (N.Y.C.). Author: Broadway Down East, 1978. Home: 126 Church St Watertown MA 02172 Office: 300 Harrison Ave Boston MA 02106

NORTON, EUNICE, pianist; b. Mpls., June 30, 1908; d. Willis I. and Charlotte (O'Brien) Norton; student U. Minn., 1922-24, Tobias Matthay Pianoforte Sch., London, 1924-31, Artur Schabel Master Piano Classes, Berlin, 1931-33, Italy, 1933; Mus. D. (hon.), Wooster Coll., 1977; m. Bernard Lewis, May 4, 1934; 1 son, Norton Lewis. Concert pianist, U.S., Europe, 1927—; soloist with numerous symphony orchs., including N.Y. Philharmonic, Boston Symphony Orch., Phila. Symphony Orch., Pitts. Symphony Orch., Mpls. Symphony Orch., London Symphony Orch., Berlin Symphony Orch., also orchs. in Leipzig, Germany, Vienna, Austria, Birmingham, Eng., Manchester, Eng.; chamber musician with Budapest, Julliard and Griller string quartets, and Am. Chamber Orch.; vis. prof. piano Carnegie Mellon U.; lectr., condr. master piano classes univs.; condr. pvt. master classes, Pitts., N.Y.C., Vt.; dir. Peacham (Vt.) Piano Festivals; founder, musical dir. Pitts. New Friends of Music, Pitts. Concert Artists. Recipient Bach prize, 1927, Chappell Gold medal Chappell Piano Co., London, 1928. Mem. Am. Matthay Piano Assn. (founder mem.), Sigma Alpha Iota (hon.). Home: 5863 Marlborough Ave Pittsburgh PA 15217. *I am convinced that music is not an ornament but an essential part of life. It is a serious activity. I live with the principle of uncompromising adherence to musical values without regard for popular approval and economic gain.*

NORTON, HOWARD MELVIN, journalist; b. Haverhill, Mass., May 30, 1911; s. Clarence Alfred and Grace Frances (Eckel) N.; B.S.J., U. Fla., 1933; m. Marjorie Anderson, July 7, 1940; children—Howard Melvin, Martha (Mrs. Charles P. Izzo, Jr.), Mary, Deborah. Fgn. corr. in Far East (hdqrs. in Tokyo) for Whaley-Eaton Service, Los Angeles Times, San Francisco Chronicle, Kansas City Star, Phila. Inquirer, 1933-40; Behind-the-News editor, Balt. Evening Sun, 1940, 41; fgn. editor, Balt. Sun (morning), 1942, war corr. 1943, 44, Washington corr. 1945-50, chief of London bur., 1950-51; chief Moscow bur., 1956-59, Washington bur., 1959-64; mem. nat. staff of U.S. News and World Report, 1964-65, asso. editor, 1965-70, White House corr., 1970-76; chief Washington bur. Nat. Courier, 1976-77; dir. publs. Nat. Assn. Community Action Dirs., Washington, 1978—; freelance author and Washington corr., 1978—. Author series of articles on Unemployment Compensation which won Pulitzer Prize for the Balt. Sun, 1947. Author series of articles exposing deficiencies of Md.'s mental hosps. which resulted in revision of mental health law and legislation appropriation of $28,000,000 to rebuild hosps., 1949. Recipient Centennial award in Journalism, U. Fla., 1953; Pacific-Asiatic Service medal, 1945; commendations Army and Navy, 1946; named Disting. Alumni, U. Fla. Coll. Journalism and Communications, 1978. Mem. White House Corrs. Assn., Sigma Delta Chi. Presbyterian. Clubs: Lakewood Country; Nat. Press (Washington). Author: Only in Russia, 1961; The Miracle of Jimmy Carter, 1976; Rosalynn—A Portrait, 1977; When the Angels Laughed, 1977; Good News About Trouble, 1978. Home: 4007 Laird Pl Chevy Chase MD 20015 Office: NCAAEDA 815 15th St NW Washington DC 20005

NORTON, HUGH STANTON, educator, economist; b. Delta, Colo., Sept. 18, 1921; s. Cecil A. and Olive S. (Stanton) N.; A.B., George Washington U., 1947, Ph.D., 1956; m. Miriam Jarmon, Dec. 19, 1949; children—Pamela, John. Instr. econs. U. Md., 1949-54; economist U.S. Govt., 1954-57; asso. prof., prof. U. Tenn., 1957-66; Johnson prof. econs. U. S.C., Columbia, 1968—, chmn. dept. econs., 1970-74; cons. anti-trust and transp. econs. to indsl. firms. Served with Signal Corps, AUS, 1942-45. Recipient Russell award for creative research, 1969. Mem. Am., So. econ. assns., Nat. Assn. Bus. Economists. Club: Cosmos (Washington). Author: Modern Transportation Economics, 1963, 2d edit., 1971; Economic Policy: Business and Government, 1963; National Transportation Policy: Formation and Implementation, 1968; The Role of the Economist in Government Policy Making, 1969; The World of the Economist, 1973, 2d edit., 1977; The Employment Act and the Council of Economic Advisers 1946-76, 1977. Home: 3335 Overcreek Rd Columbia SC 29206

NORTON, JAMES ADOLPHUS, ednl. adminstr.; b. Haynesville, La., May 28, 1922; s. George Thurman and Sue Annie (Tinsley) N.; student La. Poly. Inst., 1939-42; B.A., La. State U., 1945, M.A., 1946; M.A., Harvard U., 1949, Ph.D., 1950; LL.D. (hon.), Cleve. Marshall Law Sch.; L.H.D. (hon.), Kent State U., 1973, Urbana Coll., 1977; D.Public Service, Bowling Green State U., 1973; Litt.D. (hon.), Baldwin Wallace Coll., 1978; m. Fay-Tyler Murray, Mar. 4, 1945; 1 dau., Diana Maurine Norton Haptonstahl. Instr., U. Tex., 1946-47; vis. asst. prof. La. State U., 1949; asst. prof. Fla. State U., 1949-52, asso. prof., 1952-56, prof., 1956; lectr. Sch. Pub. Health, Harvard U., 1954-55; vis. prof. Western Res. U., 1959-60; prof. area devel. Case Inst. Tech., 1960-62; exec. dir. Cleve. Met. Services Commn., 1956-59; pres. Greater Cleve. Asso. Found., 1962-73; exec. dir. Cleve. Found., 1968-73; chancellor Ohio Bd. Regents, 1973-78; vis. chancellor Case Western Res. U., 1978-79; Fla. corr. Pub. Mgmt. and Municipal Yearbook, 1952-56; lectr. Murray Seasongood Good Govt. Fund, 1957-65; radio announcer, 1945-46; TV moderator, 1961-62. Spl. projects officer Fla. Civil Def. Council, 1956; chmn. housing com., trustee Urban League, 1959-62; mem. Mayor's Com. on Met. Charter, 1957-61; chmn. research com. Greater Cleve. Growth Bd., 1962-68; chmn. econ. research com. Ohio Dept. Devel., 1965-69; adv. com. Urban poverty, met. govt. Council for Econ. Opportunity, 1968-69; trustee Cleve. Baptist Assn., 1959-63, Hiram Coll., 1979—, St. Mary's Sem., 1970-73. Served with USAAF, 1942-43. Recipient Fruin-Colnon award Nat. Municipal League, 1959, Distinguished Service award United Appeal, 1964, Exec. Order Ohio Commodores, 1966; Distinguished Service award Kent State U., 1969, Distinguished Service award Fedn. Community Planning, 1973. Mem. Am. Polit. Sci. Assn., Nat. Municipal League (trustee 1975—), State Higher Edn. Exec. Officers Orgn. (chmn. fed. relations com. 1977-78), Internat. City Mgrs. Assn., Am. Soc. Pub. Adminstrn. (past pres.), Nat. Acad. Pub. Adminstrn., James A. Garfield Soc. of Hiram Coll., Pi Sigma Alpha, Phi Alpha Sigma, Kappa Sigma. Democrat. Baptist. Author: The Metro Experience, 1963; contbr. articles to profl. jours. Home: 1801 E 12th St Cleveland OH 44114 Office: Case Western Reserve U Cleveland OH 44106

NORTON, JOHN C., mfg. co. cons.; b. July 9, 1916; s. John A. and Harriette (Stinson) N.; B.A., U. Minn., 1938; m. Margaret E. Jeffrey, Feb. 14, 1941; children—Sharon, John, Nancy. With Toro Co., Bloomington, Minn., 1947—, v.p., 1966-76, exec. v.p., 1976-79, cons. to sr. mgmt., 1979—; dir. Minn. Toro, Inc., Erickson Corp., S.W. Toro, Turf Care Products Ltd.-Ont., Irrigation & Power Equipment (Colo.); pres. Toros Sales Co., Toro Internat. Sales Co., Toro Irrigation Ltd. (U.K.), Toro Australia Pty. Ltd. Served with U.S. Army, 1942-46. Roman Catholic. Clubs: Town and Country, Pool and Yacht, Decathlon. Office: One Appletree Sq Suite 1281 Bloomington MN 55420

NORTON, JOSEPH RANDOLPH, cons.; b. Lisbon, Ark., Dec. 23, 1915; s. James Magnus and Mary Anna (Caldwell) N.; B.S., Okla. State U., 1939, M.S., 1952; Ph.D., U. Tex., 1963; m. Jewell Mildred Krueger, Apr. 2, 1939 (dec. Oct. 1971); children—Donna Jo (Mrs. Gary Paul Going), James Harry; m. 2d, Virginia Lee Davis. June 18, 1973. Design engr. W.C. Norris, Inc., Tulsa, 1939-43, research engr., 1943-46; asso. dir. engring. research Okla. State U., Stillwater, 1946-63, head Sch. Gen. Engring., 1963-78, ret., 1978; cons. Fenix & Scisson, Inc., Gen. Electric Co., Schenectady, N.Y., Tulsa and Las Vegas, Nev., also Grand River Dam Authority, Vinita, Okla. Mem. Nat., Okla. socs. profl. engrs., Am. Soc. Engring. Edn., Sigma Xi, Phi Kappa Phi, Sigma Tau. Home: 724 Skyline Pl Stillwater OK 74074

NORTON, KEN, profl. boxer; b. Jacksonville, Ill., Aug. 9, 1945; s. John and Ruth N.; student N.E. Mo. State Coll., 1960-63; m. Jackie Halton; children—Kenneth, Brandon, Kenisha Eronda. Profl. boxer, 1967—; winner bout with Muhammad Ali, 1973; world heavyweight contender, 1976; winner bout with Duane Bobick, 1977, with Jimmy Young, 1977; sports commentator with major networks; appeared in motion pictures Mandingo, 1974, Drum, 1975. Hon. chmn. Ken Norton Golf Tournament for Cystic Fibrosis. Served with USMC, 1963-67. Recipient Napoleon Hill Found. award, 1973. Address: 500 Shatto Pl Los Angeles CA 90020

NORTON, PAUL ALLEN, ins. exec.; b. Ardmore, S.D., Sept. 10, 1913; s. Albert James and Leota (Clute) N.; A.B. magna cum laude, Chadron State Coll., 1935; M.B.A. with distinction, Harvard, 1937; LL.D., Bethany Coll., 1973; m. Ruth Stephens Richards, July 4, 1941; children—Richard Allen, Carolyn Ruth (Mrs. Robert Padgette). Mgr., N.Y. Life Ins. Co., Worcester, Mass., 1938-41, Boston. 1941-43, mgr., Phila., 1944-47, asst. supt. agencies, 1947, mgr., Houston, 1948-49, supt. agys., N.Y., 1947, mgr., Houston, 1948-49, supt. agencies, N.Y.C., 1950, v.p. charge group sales, 1951, agy. v.p., 1952, field v.p., 1952, regional v.p., 1953, v.p., 1954-59, v.p. in charge sales mgmt., 1959-62, v.p. in charge mktg., 1962-64, sr. v.p. in charge mktg., 1964-69, exec. v.p., 1969-73; vice chmn. Calif. Life, 1973—; dir. Am. Gen. Funds, CLF Inc., Viacom Internat., Inc., Calif. Life Ins. Co., Grolier Internat. Hon. chmn. Greater N.Y. council Boy Scouts Am.; bd. dirs. Insts. Religion and Health. Mem. Life Ins. Agy. Mgmt. Assn. (past pres.), Nat. Assn. Life Underwriters (v.p. Worcester chpt. 1940-41), Exec. Assn. (pres. Worcester chpt. 1939-41), Am. Soc. C.L.U.'s (dir.). Clubs: Harvard School Business, Optimist (Houston); Church; Harvard, Economic (N.Y.C.); Shrine (San Francisco); Am. Yacht (Rye, N.Y.). Contbr. articles to profl. publs. Home: 20 Church St Greenwich CT 06830 Office: 800 2d Ave New York NY 10017

NORTON, PAUL FOOTE, educator; b. Newton, Mass., Jan. 23, 1917; s. John Foote and Margaret (Goodrich) N.; A.B., Oberlin Coll., 1938; M.F.A., Princeton, 1947, Ph.D., 1952; m. Alison Edmunds Stuart, May 7, 1942; children—John Douglas, Mary Reed, Hilary Stuart. Asst. prof. art, then asso. prof. Pa. State U., 1947-58; chmn. dept. art U. Mass., 1958-71, prof. art, 1959—; vis. asso. prof. Amherst Coll., 1959-60, coach squash and tennis teams, 1979-80. Chmn. Amherst Hist. Commn., 1973-76. Served with USNR, 1942-46. Am. Council Learned Socs. fellow, 1951-52; Fulbright fellow, 1953-54; Ford Found. grantee, 1965; Nat. Endowment for Humanities sr. fellow, 1971-72. Fellow Royal Soc. Arts; mem. Coll. Art Assn., Soc. Archtl. Historians (editor book revs. for jour. 1955-58, editor jour. 1959-64; bd. dirs. 1952, 57-64, 66-69), Soc. Francais d'Archeologie, Nat. Trust (Eng.), Nat. Trust (U.S.), Archaeol. Inst. Am., Soc. Archtl. Bibliographers, Soc. Archtl. Historians Gt. Britain, Soc. Preservation New Eng. Antiquities, Pioneer Am. Soc., Norsk Arkeologisk Selskap, U.S. Capitol Hist. Soc., U.S. Lawn Tennis Assn., U.S. Squash Assn., Appalachian Mountain Club. Author: (with others) The Arts in America: The Nineteenth Century, 1969; Amherst: A Guide to its Architecture, 1975; Latrobe, Jefferson and the National Capitol, 1977; editor: The Papers of Samuel McIntire, architect, 1978—; also numerous articles. Home: 57 Woodside Ave Amherst MA 01002

NORTON, PETER BOWES, pub. co. exec.; b. London, Eng., May 4, 1929; s. James Peter and Margaret (Bowes) N.; came to U.S., 1974; student S.E. Essex Tech. Coll., 1942-45, Royal Naval Colls., Dartmouth and Greenwich, 1949-54; m. Heather Pearch, Jan. 16, 1954; children—Jan Heather, Fiona Mary. Commd. officer Royal Navy, 1945, advanced through grades to lt., 1954; ret., 1960; personnel officer United Dominions Trust, London, 1960-63; jr. exec. to mng. dir. Ency. Brit., London, 1963-68, mng. dir., 1968-69, v.p. internat. div., Chgo., 1969-70, pres. Ency. Brit. Can., 1970-73, pres. Ency. Brit. U.S.A., Chgo., 1974—; chmn. Club Vacations Internat., Inc., 1978—. Fellow Chartered Inst. Secs. (Eng.), Inst. Dirs. (Eng.). Mem. Ch. of Eng. Club: Royal Automobile (London). Home: 333 W Belden St Chicago IL 60614 Office: 425 N Michigan Ave Chicago IL 60611

NORTON, VICTOR THANE, mfg. exec.; b. Ridgway, Pa., Jan. 15, 1904; s. Homer Burdette and Gertrude (Callula) N.; B.S. in Civil Engring., Northwestern U., 1926; m. Elizabeth Smith, July 2, 1932; children—Victor Thane, Nina R., Elizabeth R. Asst. to pres. Jewel Tea Co., Inc., 1927-39; v.p. Cudahy Packing Co., 1939-44; v.p. Kenyon & Eckhardt, 1944-46; pres. Am. Home Foods, Inc. 1946-50; v.p. NBC, 1950-53; pres. Am. Hard Rubber Co., N.Y.C., 1953-57, Pequanoc Rubber Co., Butler, N.J., 1953-58, also dir.; pres., dir., chmn. exec. com. Amerace Corp., N.Y.C., 1957-62, chmn., dir. 1962-68; chmn., dir. exec. com. Amerace Corp., 1968—, also mem. finance com.; past chmn. bd., dir., chmn. exec. com. Knox Glass Bottle Co. Mem. Beta Theta Pi, Delta Sigma Rho. Clubs: University (N.Y.C.); Beaverkill (Livingston Manor, N.Y.); Riverside Yacht (past gov.). Office: Amerace Corp 555 Fifth Ave New York NY 10017*

NORTRUP, LAWRENCE WEIR, banker; b. Jacksonville, Ill., Aug. 20, 1926; s. Ernest F. and Velma L. (Lawrence) N.; B.S., U. Ill., 1949; m. Doreen Embs, Sept. 2, 1950; children—James, Thomas, Jane. Asst. nat. bank examiner, 1949-52; pres., chief exec. officer Bank of Park Forest (Ill.), 1952-63, Hartford Plaza Bank, Chgo., 1963-77, Mich. Ave. Nat. Bank, Chgo., 1977—. Served with U.S. Army, 1946-47. Mem. Am. Bankers Assn., Robert Morris Assos. Republican. Presbyterian. Clubs: Westmoreland Country; Chgo. Athletic Assn., Bankers, Economic (Chgo). Home: 550 Earlston Rd Kenilworth IL 60043 Office: 30 N Michigan Ave Chicago IL 60602

NORWOOD, BERNARD, economist; b. Boston, Nov. 21, 1922; s. Hyman and Rose (Fink) N.; B.A., Boston U., 1947; M.A., Fletcher Sch. Law and Diplomacy, 1948, Ph.D., 1957; m. Janet Lippe, June 25, 1943; children—Stephen Harlan, Peter Carlton. Internat. economist State Dept., 1949-58; joined U.S. Fgn. Service, 1955; 1st. sec. U.S. mission to European Communities, Brussels, Belgium, 1958-62; asst. chief comml. policy and treaties div. Dept. State, 1962; chmn. trade staff com. Office Spl. Rep. for Trade Negotiations, Exec. Office Pres., 1963-67; assigned The Nat. War Coll., 1967-68; adviser div. internat finance bd. govs. Fed. Res. System, 1968-75; prin. asso. Robert R. Nathan Assos., Inc., 1975—. Mem. U.S. delegation to negotiations and confs. GATT, Geneva, Switzerland, 1953-67. Served with AUS, 1943-46. Home: 6409 Marjory Ln Bethesda MD 20034 Office: Robert R Nathan Assos Inc 1200 18th St NW Washington DC 20036

NORWOOD, DAVID, lawyer, ins. co. exec.; b. Glasgow, Scotland, Apr. 9, 1933; s. George and Mary Elizabeth (Harbinson) N.; immigrated to Can., 1957; M.A., U. Glasgow, 1953, LL.B., 1957; m. Marion Murdoch Mitchell, Apr. 11, 1957; 1 dau., Ailsa Mari. With firm McRobert, Son & Hutchinson, solicitors, Glasgow, 1953-57; with Can. Life Assurance Co., Toronto, 1957—, joint sec. corp. and legal, 1973-75, legal v.p. gen. counsel, 1975—; sec. Can. Life Ins. Co. N.Y.; dir. various subsidiaries, also Sherway Centre Ltd.; profl. writer and speaker. Mem. Law Soc. Upper Can., Can. Bar Assn., Law. Soc. Scotland, Can. Life Ins. Assn., Internat. Claim Assn., Am. Council Life Ins., Assn. Life Ins. Counsel. Conservative. Club: University (Toronto). Author: The Uniform Life Insurance Law of Canada, 1974; Life Insurance Law in Canada, 1977. Home: 1352 Aldo Dr Mississauga ON L5H 3E9 Canada Office: 330 University Ave Toronto ON M5G 1R8 Canada

NORWOOD, FRED WAYLAND, accountant; b. Oxford, Miss., June 21, 1920; s. Frank and Beady (Branch) N.; student U. Durham (Eng.), 1945; B.B.A., U. Miss., 1947, M.B.A., 1948; Ph.D., U. Tex., 1951; m. Patricia Chalmers, Jan. 21, 1947; children—Patricia Isabel (Mrs. Eugene Phillips), Lillian Beady (Mrs. Jon Brinkley), Fred Wayland. Instr., U. Miss., 1947-48, U. Tex., 1948-51; prof. accounting Tex. Tech. U., 1951-56, 58-68; mgmt. cons. Peat, Marwick & Co., C.P.A.'s, Dallas, 1956-58; prof. accounting, chmn. dept. Colo. State U., 1968—. Served with AUS, 1942-45. C.P.A., Tex., Colo. Mem. Am. Inst. C.P.A.'s, Colo., Tex. socs. C.P.A.'s, Am. Accounting Assn., S.W. Social Sci. Assn., Phi Kappa Phi, Delta Sigma Pi, Beta Alpha Psi, Beta Gamma Sigma. Author: (with Sam W. Chisholm) Federal Income Taxes: Research and Planning, 1962; (with P.W. Ljungdahl, S.W. Chisholm) Accounting for Agricultural Enterprises, 1968; (with S.W. Chisholm, Marilynn G. Phelan) Principles in Federal Income Tax Law and Their Surrounding Forces, 1968; (with S.W. Chisholm) Management of Income Taxes for Agricultural Enterprises, 1968; The Nature of Accounting Principles, 1969; (with others) Federal Taxation: Research, Planning and Procedures, 1979. Home: 1830 Dayton Dr Fort Collins CO 80521

NORWOOD, GEORGE MCINTOSH, JR., ret. univ. adminstr.; b. Goldsboro, N.C., July 15, 1921; s. George McIntosh and Helen Mary (Allen) N.; B.A., U. N.C., 1942; m. Zabelle Corwin, June 3, 1944 (dec. 1978); children—Allen Corwin, Martha Pryor Norwood Shope, Geoffrey Alexander, Anthony Wray; m. 2d, Bernice C. Harris, Aug. 5, 1978. Technician U.S. Rubber Co., Charlotte, N.C., 1942-45; officer Norwood Brick Co., Lillington, N.C., 1947-54; fiscal officer N.C. Meml. Hosp., U. N.C., Chapel Hill, 1954-57; bus. officer U. N.C., 1957-65; v.p. for bus. and fin. Jefferson Med. Coll., Phila., 1965-70; v.p. for planning Thomas Jefferson U., Phila., 1970-76, 77-79, interim pres., 1976-77. Trustee St. Peter's Sch., Phila., 1966-74; trustee Magee Meml. Hosp., Phila., 1965-79; dir. Federated Med. Resources, Phila., 1966-79. Served with U.S. Army, 1945-46. Mem. Nat. Assn. Coll. and Univ. Bus. Officers, Assn. Am. Med. Colls. Democrat. Episcopalian. Home: Route 2 Fox Hill Rd Louisville TN 37777

NORWOOD, JANET LIPPE, govt. ofcl.; b. Newark, Dec. 11, 1923; d. M. Turner and Thelma (Levinson) Lippe; B.A., N.J. Coll. Women, 1945; M.A., Fletcher Sch. Law and Diplomacy, 1946, Ph.D., 1949; LL.D., Fla. Internat. U., 1979; m. Bernard Norwood, June 25, 1943; children—Stephen Harlan, Peter Carlton. Instr., Wellesley Coll., 1948-49; economist William L. Clayton Center, Fletcher Sch. Law and Diplomacy, 1953-58; with Bur. Labor Statistics, Dept. Labor, Washington, 1963—, dep. commr., then acting commr., 1975-79, commr. labor stats., 1979—; visitors com. Harvard U.; exec. adv. com. U. Md. Recipient Disting. Achievement award Dept. Labor, 1972, Spl. Commendation award, 1977, Philip Arnow award, 1979. Fellow Am. Statis. Assn.; mem. Am. Econ. Assn., Nat. Economists Club, Indsl. Relations Research Assn., Nat. Assn. Bus. Economists, Women's Caucus in Stats., Com. Status Women Econs. Profession, Exec. Women in Govt., Douglass Soc. Disting. Achievement. Author papers, reports in field. Home: 6409 Marjory Ln Bethesda MD 20034 Office: 441 G St NW Washington DC 20212

NOSENZO, LOUIS VINCENT, govt. ofcl.; b. Kingston, N.Y., Dec. 8, 1933; s. Frank Joseph and Jennie (Castellucci) N.; B.E.E., Cornell U., 1956; M.S., M.I.T., 1960; m. Helen Ann Dittmar, Aug. 16, 1956; children—Louis Vincent, Angela, Christopher. Research asst. Willow Run Research Labs., U. Mich., 1957; dir. missiles and space systems planning United Aircraft Corp., Redondo Beach, Calif., 1963-69; v.p., dir. systems planning Lulejian & Assos., Inc., Redondo Beach, Calif., 1969-71; v.p., gen. mgr. Los Angeles operations, Torrance, Calif., 1972-73; spl. asst. Bur. of Politico-Military affairs Dept. State, Washington, 1973-74, office dir., 1974-76, dep. asst. sec. for nuclear energy and energy tech. affairs, Bur. Oceans and Internat. Environ. and Sci. Affairs, Dept. State, Washington, 1977—. Served with USAF, 1957-63. Roman Catholic. Home: 5906 Calla Dr McLean VA 22101 Office: Dept State 22d and C Sts NW Washington DC 20520

NOSS, JOHN BOYER, educator; b. Sendal, Japan, Oct. 5, 1896; s. Christopher and Lura (Boyer) N. (parents Am. missionaries); came to U.S., 1912; A.B., Franklin and Marshall Coll., 1916, D.D., 1964; B.D., Theol. Sem. Ref. Ch. in U.S., Lancaster, 1922; Ph.D., U. of Edinburgh, Scotland, 1928; m. Mary Williamson Bell, June 14, 1922 (dec. 1968); m. 2d, Flora B. Rudisill, Apr. 14, 1976. Ordained to ministry United Ch. Christ, 1922, and served Ephrata, Pa., 1922-26; mem. faculty Franklin and Marshall Coll., 1928-63, prof. religion, 1931-45, head dept. philosophy, 1945-63; lectr. history of religions Union Theol. Sem., N.Y., 1952-65; adj. prof. Christianity and history of religions Lancaster Theol. Sem., 1958—. Mem. Am. Philos. Assn., Phi Beta Kappa. Clubs: Torch, Sphinx (Lancaster). Author: Man's Religions, 6th edit. Past editor research abstracts in History of Religions, Jour. of Bible and Religion. Contbr. encys., dictionaries. Home: 509 N President Ave Lancaster PA 17603

NOSSEN, ROBERT JOSEPH, coll. adminstr.; b. San Francisco, Sept. 4, 1920; s. William I. and Miriam Mae (Levey) N.; A.B., U. Calif. at Berkeley, 1944; M.A., Northwestern U., 1948; Ph.D., 1951; m. Evon Holland, Nov. 17, 1945. Asst. prof. English, Creighton U., 1950-54, chmn. dept., 1951-54; prof., chmn. dept. English, Lamar State U., 1954-60; prof. N.Y. State U. Coll. at Fredonia, 1960-69, chmn. dept. English, 1960-62, dean arts and scis., 1962-65, coll. dean, 1965-66, v.p. acad. affairs, 1966-69; pres. Bloomsburg State Coll., 1969-72; asso. provost, prof. higher edn. U. Pitts., 1972—; cons. in instl. evaluation, collective bargaining in higher edn.; pres., mem. exec. council Southwest Pa. Council Higher Edn. Pres. Monsour Med. Found., 1973-78; bd. dirs. Geisinger Med. Center, Geisinger Inst. for Med. Edn. and Research; bd. edn. Episcopal Diocese Central Pa. Church Soc. Coll. Work fellow, 1958. Mem. Am. Assn. for Higher Edn. Episcopalian. Mason (Shriner), Kiwanian. Clubs: Greensburg Country. Author: Collective Bargaining in Higher Education, 1978. Contbr. articles to profl. jours. Home: 274 Shasta Dr Pittsburgh PA 15239

NOSSITER, BERNARD DANIEL, journalist; b. N.Y.C., Apr. 10, 1926; s. Murry Paul and Rose (Weingarten) N.; A.B. magna cum laude, Dartmouth, 1947; M.A., Harvard, 1948; m. Jacqueline Sarah Robinson, Dec. 3, 1950; children—Daniel, Joshua, Adam, Jonathan. Reporter, World Telegram and Sun, N.Y.C., 1952-55; nat. econs. reporter Washington Post, 1955-64, European econs. corr., Paris, France, 1964-67, S. Asia corr., 1967-68, London corr., 1971-79; UN bur. chief N.Y. Times, 1979—. Served with AUS, 1944-46, to 2d lt. inf., 1950-51. Recipient medal for distinguished Washington corr. Sigma Delta Chi, 1961; Hillman Found. award for book, 1965; Fairchild award Overseas Press Club, 1966; George Polk award, 1969; Nieman fellow, 1962-63. Mem. Phi Beta Kappa. Author: The Mythmakers: An Essay on Power and Wealth, 1964; Soft State: A Newspaperman's Chronicle of India, 1970; Britain—A Future That Works, 1978; contbr. articles to nat. mags. Office: NY Times Room 453 UN Bur New York NY 10017

NOSTRAND, HOWARD LEE, educator; b. N.Y.C., Nov. 16, 1910; s. Elijah H. and Ida J. (Maeder) N.; A.B., Amherst Coll., 1932; A.M., Harvard U., 1933; Docteur de l'Univ. de Paris, 1934: m. Frances Anne Levering, June 23, 1933; children—David, Richard, Robert; m. 2d, Frances Brewer Creore, Aug. 9, 1967. Instr. U. Buffalo, 1934-36, U.S. Naval Acad., 1936-38; asst. prof. French, Brown U., 1938-39; prof. Romance langs. and lit. U. Wash., 1939—, chmn. dept., 1939-64; vis. prof. Collège de France, autumn 1975; cultural relations attaché Am. embassy, Lima, Peru, 1944-47; temp. staff asso. Am. Council Edn., for nat. conf. on role of colls. and univs. in internat. understanding, 1949; dir. U. Wash. Inst. Modern Lang. Tchrs., 1959, co-dir. French Culture Inst.-Workshop, summer 1978; vis. prof. Coll. de France, 1975. Mem. Adv. Com. on New Ednl. Media 1958-61; mem. Nat. Commn. Tchr. Edn. and Profl. Standards, 1963-67, chmn., 1966-67; adv. bd. Modern Lang. Assn. Ednl. Research Info. Center, 1966-71; mem. advanced French com. Grad. Record Exam., 1969-74; mem. coordinating bd. Nat. Council Accreditation Tchr. Edn., 1968-73. Mem. humanities com. World Book Ency., 1964-76. Recipient Pro lingua award Wash. Assn. Fgn. Lang. Tchrs., 1977, Leadership award NE Conf. on Teaching Fgn. Langs., 1978; Guggenheim Found. fellow, 1953-54. Decorated Order of Sun (Peru), Palmes academiques, Legion d'Honneur, officier l'Ordre des Arts et des Lettres (France). Mem. Modern Lang. Assn., Am. Assn. Tchrs. French (hon. mem.; pres. 1960-62, chmn. nat. com. on ethnography 1974—), NEA (bd. dept. fgn. lang. 1960-66). Author: Le Théâtre antique, 1934; Ortega y Gasset's Mission of the University, 1944; Dos Problemas de educación cultural, 1946; The Cultural Attaché, 1947; Research on Language Teaching, 1962, 65; La France en mutation, 1979. Address: Padelford Hall GN-60 University of Washington Seattle WA 98195

NOSWORTHY, JOHN MARSHALL, banker; b. Bronxville, N.Y. Apr. 5, 1921; s. Thomas Arthur and Harriet (Fischer) N.; student Taft Sch., 1936-40, Wesleyan U., Middletown, Conn., 1941-42; B.S., Rutgers U., 1952; m. Suzanne Lee Christensen, July 28, 1962; children—John Scott, Paul Marshall, Alan Trube, Suzanne Lee Christensen, Anne Carter Christensen. Account mgr. Bankers Trust Co., N.Y.C., 1946-50; asst. to pres., trustee Bronx Savs. Bank (name now Eastern Savs. Bank), N.Y.C., 1951-56, exec. v.p., 1956-61, pres., chief exec. officer, 1961-74, chmn. bd., chief exec. officer, 1974—; v.p., dir. CBC Corp.; mem. adv. bd. Chase Manhattan Bank, 1956-78. Chmn., Bronx Salvation Army Bd., 1958-62. Served with AUS, 1942-46. Mem. Investment Officers Assn. Savs. Banks N.Y. State (pres.), Bronx C. of C. (dir.), Chi Psi. Club: Union League (N.Y.C.). Home: Brookridge Dr Greenwich CT 06830 Office: Eastern Savings Bank Park and Tremont Aves Bronx NY 10457

NOTARI, PAUL CELESTIN, assn. exec.; b. Chgo., Sept. 8, 1926; s. Peter and Mae Rose (Luvisi) N.; B.S. in Physics, DePaul U., 1952; M.S. in Comml. Sci., Rollins Coll., 1968; m. Marlene Fineman, Feb. 21, 1969; children—Cathy Notari Davidson, Kenneth, Sharon, Mindy, Debbie. Mgr. publs. and tng. Motorola Inc., Chgo., 1952-65; supr., publs. engr. Martin Co., Orlando, Fla., 1966-67; dir. communications Bus. Equipment Mfrs. Assn., N.Y.C., 1967-70; dir. publs., pub. jour. Am. Water Works Assn., Denver, 1971-79; chief info. dissemination systems Solar Energy Research Inst., Denver, 1979—; lectr. bus. communications Northwestern U., 1964-66. Active Boy Scouts Am. Served with USNR, 1944-46. Mem. Assn. Computer Programmers and Analysts (founding pres. 1970-73), Soc. Tech. Writers and Pubs. (chmn. chpt. 1965-66). Home: 1000 S Monaco St Denver CO 80224 Office: 6666 W Quincy St Denver CO 80235

NOTARO, JAMES F., polit. party ofcl.; b. Buffalo, Feb. 24, 1936; s. Philip and Mary (Alessi) N.; student U. Buffalo, 1954-57, Millard Fillmore Coll., 1958-59; m. Shirley A. Jannotte, Apr. 28, 1956; children—Paulette, James F., Anthony, Cynthia, Charles, Maria, Donald, Daniel. Employed in mgmt. position in ins. field, 1958-64; regional dir. Liberal Party N.Y. State, 1964-65, upstate dir., 1965-77, state exec. dir., 1977—; sec. Erie County Liberal Party; bus. agt. United Hatters Internat. Workers Union. Roman Catholic. Home: 16 Russell St Buffalo NY 14214 Office: Liberal Party of NY State 165 W 46th St New York NY 10036

NOTARO, MICHAEL R., data processing and computer service exec.; b. Chgo., Nov. 1, 1912; s. Anthony and Felicia Franzese) N.; student Northwestern U. Sch. Commerce, 1930-36, Chgo. Law Sch., 1930-32; LL.D., DePaul U.; m. Irene Hapsude, May 5, 1936 (dec.); children—Michael R., Phyllis Ann. Founder, 1936, since chmn. bd., pres., chief exec. officer Statis. Tabulating Corp., Chgo. (divs. StatiTab, StatiCom, CAM); dir. St. Paul Federal Savs. and Loan. Bd. dirs. Catholic Charities of Archdiocese of Chgo.; chmn. DePaul U. Corp.; bd. dirs. Better Bus. Bur., Lawson YMCA, Chgo., Boys Clubs Chgo.; mem. citizens' bd. Ill. Masonic Hosp., Loyola U. Decorated knight Malta, knight St. Gregory, Knight comdr. Order Merit (Italy). Roman Catholic (lay trustee). Clubs: Executives, Ill. Athletic, Union League, Mid-Am., Tavern, Chgo. Athletic Assn. (Chgo.); Butterfield Country (Hinsdale, Ill.). Home: 500 Linden Ave Oak Park IL 60302 Office: 2 N Riverside Plaza Chicago IL 60606

NOTESTEIN, FRANK WALLACE, demographer; b. Alma. Mich., Aug. 16, 1902; s. Frank Newton and Mary Elizabeth (Wallace) N.: student Alma (Mich.) Coll., 1919-20, LL.D., 1964; B.S. Wooster, Coll., 1923, LL.D., 1946; Ph.D., Cornell, 1927; D.Sc., Northwestern U., Evanston, Ill., 1953, Princeton, 1963; D.Sc., U. Mich., 1967; m. Daphne Limbach, Oct. 8, 1927. Instr. econs. Cornell U., 1926-27; fellow Social Science Research Council, 1927-28; research asso. Milbank Meml. Fund, 1928-29, mem. tech. staff, 1929-36; lectr. charge Office Population Research, Princeton, 1936-41, dir., 1941-59, prof. demography, 1945-59, vis. sr. research demographer, 1959—, vis. lectr. Woodrow Wilson Sch., 1969-71; pres. Population Council, N.Y.C., 1959-68, now pres. emeritus; cons.-dir. population div. dept. social affairs, UN, 1946-48; mem. UN adv. com. Experts on World Population Plan of Action; mem. Nat. Commn. Obervance World Population Year, 1974. Fellow Am. Acad. Arts and Scis.; mem. Council on Fgn. Relations, AAAS, Am. Philos. Soc., Am. Sociol. Soc., Am. Statis. Assn., Population Assn. Am., Internat. Statis. Inst., Internat. Union for Sci. Studies Population, Phi Beta Kappa, Sigma Xi. Clubs: Princeton (N.Y.); Nassau (Princeton). Co-author: Controlled Fertility, 1940: The Future Population of Europe and the Soviet Union, 1944. Co-editor, Population Index, 1936-57, cons. editor, 1958-63. Home: 24 Roper Rd Princeton NJ 08540 Office: Office Population Research 21 Prospect Ave Princeton NJ 08540

NOTHMANN, GERHARD ADOLF, research engr.; b. Berlin, Germany, Dec. 9, 1921; s. Rudolf and Margarete (Caro) N.; came to U.S., 1939, naturalized, 1944; B.S. in Mech. Engring., Purdue U., 1942, M.S. in Mech. Engring., 1942; Ph.D., Cornell U., 1948; m. Charlotte Braude, June 21, 1943; children—Joyce Anne, Ruth Ellen, Barbara Fay. Tchr. machine design and kinematics Cornell U., 1942-44, 46-48, instr., 1942-44, 46-48, asst. prof., 1948; engr. for design spl. bindery R. R. Donnelley & Sons, 1946-47; research engr. Armour Research Found., Ill. Inst. Tech., Chgo., 1948-59, successively asst. supr., asst. chmn., chmn., mgr. dept. mech. engring. research, 1952-59; dir. creative and devel. engring. Miehle div. Miehle-Goss-Dexter, Inc., 1959-62, dir. research and devel., 1962-64, dir. engring., 1964-67, dir. tech. research, 1967-68; dir. engring. Robertson Photo-Mechanix, Inc., 1968-69, v.p. engring., 1969-71; chief engr. duplicators Addressograph Multigraph Corp., 1971-77; dir. engring. Visual Graphics Corp., Tamarac, Fla., 1977-79; prin. engr. Xerox Corp., Pasadena, Calif., 1979—; chmn. mechanics colloquim Ill. Inst. Tech., 1953-54; mem. adv. com. Graphic Arts Tech. Found. Pres. bd. dirs. Wilmette United Fund, 1963. Mem. Wilmette Sch. Bd., 1968-74. Served with USNR, 1944-46. Named one of six outstanding young men in Chgo. area. Chgo. Jr. Assn. Commerce and Industry, 1954. Mem. Am. Soc. M.E., Am. Soc. Engring. Edn., Tech. Assn. for Graphic Arts, Sigma Xi, Tau Beta Pi, Pi Tau Sigma. Home: 3760 Edgeview Dr Pasadena CA 91107 Office: 300 N Halstead St Pasadena CA 91107

NOTKIN, LEONARD SHELDON, architect; b. N.Y.C., Apr. 1, 1931; s. Murry and Evelyn (Mofshatz) N.; B.Arch., U. Pa., 1954; m. Ann Mathilda Stefanko, Nov. 24, 1956; children—Jennifer, Mead. Architect, Percival Goodman, Architect, N.Y.C., 1956-58, Bloch and Hesse, Architects, N.Y.C., 1958-59, Resnick and Green, Architects, N.Y.C., 1959-60; architect, prin., v.p. The Architects Collaborative, Inc., Cambridge, Mass., 1960—; chief design critic Boston Archtl. Center, 1964-69; mem. Lexington (Mass.) Design Adv. Com., 1970-73, chmn., 1972; profl. studio critic Harvard Grad. Sch. Design, 1974-76. Served with U.S. Army, 1954-56. Recipient Design award for IBM Hdqrs., Gaithersburg, Md., Progressive Architecture mag., 1964; 1st pl. award for Worcester (Mass.) Community Center, AIA, 1966; Design award for Worcester Found. Exptl. Biology bldg. Mass. chpt. AIA, 1968; Design award NIH Research Lab., Bethesda, Md., GSA, 1972; Best Bldg. of Yr. award for Norwalk (Conn.) High Sch., Assn. for Better Community Design, 1972; Honor award Conn. Soc. Architects AIA, 1974. Registered architect N.Y., State, Mass., Ohio, Pa., Nat. Council Archtl. Registration Bds. Mem. AIA, Boston Soc. Architects (bd. dirs. 1976-79), Mass. State Assn. Architects. Maj. recent works include Intermediate Sch. 137, Bronx, N.Y., 1976, Visual Arts Instructional Facility, SUNY Coll. at Purchase, 1976, Lahey Clinic Med. Center, Burlington, Mass., 1976—, W. Penn Hosp., Pitts., 1977, St. Francis/St. George Hosp., Cin., 1978. Home: 1 Field Rd Lexington MA 02173 Office: 46 Brattle St Cambridge MA 02138

NOTMAN, DONALD DOUGLAS, ret. banker; b. Buffalo, July 11, 1924; s. Walter John and Ernestine (Spaulding) N.; B.A., Yale U., 1949; m. Gertrude L. M. Raynor-Smith, Apr. 26, 1950; children—Gaier L., Andrea T., Donald Douglas. With Marine Midland Bank, Western, Buffalo, 1949-73, sr. v.p., 1969-73; chmn. Nat. Bank Washington, 1973-78. Bd. dirs. United Way, Washington, chmn., 1976; bd. dirs. Washington council Boy Scouts Am., Fed. City council Rec. for Blind. Served with U.S. Army, 1943-46. Decorated Purple Heart. Mem. Am., D.C. bankers assns., D.C. Clearing House Assn. (dir.). Episcopalian. Home: 1633 31st St NW Washington DC 20007

NOTTER, GEORGE MADISON, JR., architect; b. Jacksonville, Fla., Aug. 7, 1933; s. George Madison and Ione (Nichols) N.; A.B. summa cum laude, Harvard U., 1955, M.Arch., 1958; m. Sarah McIntyre Wolfe, June 13, 1959; children—David McIntyre, James Alexander. Designer, project architect Minoru Yamasaki & Assos., architects, Birmingham, Mich., 1960-65; prin. J. Timothy Anderson & Assos., Inc., architects, Boston, 1965-70; prin. Anderson Notter Finegold Inc., architects and preservation planners, Boston, 1970—. Served to 1st lt. USAAF, 1958-60. Fellow AIA (ins. com. 1973-75; vice chmn. 1975, chmn. architects liability bd. 1976-78, com. historic resources 1976-78); mem. Boston Soc. Architects (chmn. Blue Book com. 1968-70, dir. and commr. profl. practice 1971-75, v.p. and commr. profl. soc. 1975, pres. 1976), Soc. Indsl. Archaeology (dir. 1975—), Nat. Trust Historic Preservation, Soc. Preservation New Eng. Antiquities, Soc. Archtl. Historians, Phi Beta Kappa. Clubs: Harvard Varsity, Harvard (Boston). Editor: Housing Study, 1958; Economic Benefits of Preserving Old Buildings, 1976. Archtl. works: Brockton (Mass.) Arts Center, 1969; Sunoco Service Center, Boston, 1970; Old City Hall Renovation, Boston, 1971 (AIA honor award 1976); Capital Bank & Trust Office Bldg., Boston, 1973; Customs House and Chart House Restaurant Renovation, Long Wharf, Boston, 1974; The Tannery, conversion to housing, Peabody, Mass., 1975; Central Grammar, conversion to housing, Gloucester, Mass., 1975; Union Railroad Station Renovation, New London, Conn., 1976. Home: One Longfellow Pl #2321 Boston MA 02114 Office: 77 Washington St N Boston MA 02114

NOVA, SAUL HARRY, apparel co. exec.; b. Boston, May 24, 1924; s. Meyer and Sonia (Schwartzberg) N.; student Syracuse (N.Y.) U., 1941-42; m. Pansy Mae Adair, Jan. 8, 1945; children—Melvin, Ilene, Jeffrey. With Henry I. Siegel Co., N.Y.C., 1951—, nat. sales mgr., 1963-65, gen. mdse. mgr., v.p. marketing, 1966-69, exec. v.p., 1970—. Served with USAAF, 1942-46. Mem. Am. Arbitration Assn. (panelist). Home: 26 Leatherstocking Ln Scarsdale NY 10583 Office: 16 E 34th St New York City NY 10016. *There are the few that make things happen. There are the many that watch things happen. And there are the rest who never know what's happening. I've always strived to be one of the few.*

NOVACK, GEORGE, author; b. Boston, Aug. 5, 1905; s. Israel and Ada (Marcus) N.; student Harvard, 1926; m. Evelyn Andreas, June 22, 1942. Editor, Internat. Socialist Rev., 1965—. Treas. nat. campaign com. Socialist Workers Party, 1968, sec., 1972, treas., 1980. Author: The Logic of Marxism, 1942; The Law of Uneven and Combined Development, 1958; The Long View of History, 1960; Moscow versus Peking, 1963; The Age of Permanent Revolution, 1964; The Origins of Materialism, 1965; Existentialism versus Marxism, 1966; Empiricism and Its Evolution, 1969; Democracy and Revolution, 1971; Understanding History, 1972; Humanism and Socialism, 1973; The First Three Internationals, 1974; Pragmatism Versus Marxism, 1975; America's Revolutionary Heritage, 1976; Polemics in Marxist Philosophy, 1978. Address: 326 W 19th St New York NY 10011

NOVACK, KENNETH JOSEPH, lawyer; b. Boston, Aug. 25, 1941; s. Hyman and Dorothy Ruth N.; B.A. (Rufus Choate scholar), Dartmouth Coll., 1963; LL.B., Harvard U., 1966; m. Mary Lou Baron, Aug. 30, 1961; children—Laura Ann, Sarah Elizabeth, Emily Kate. Admitted to Mass. bar, 1966; partner firm Mintz, Levin, Cohn, Glovsky and Popeo, Boston, 1966—, mng. partner, 1972—; dir. Charles River Breeding Labs., Inc. Mem. Am. Bar Assn., Boston Bar Assn. (co-chmn. securities law com. 1970—), Am. Law Inst. Clubs: Union of Boston, St. Botolph, Harvard of Boston. Office: 1 Center Plaza Boston MA 02108

NOVAK, ALFRED, educator; b. Chgo., Jan. 28, 1915; s. Phillip and Celia (Kaplan) N.; A.A., U. Chgo., 1934, B.S., 1936, M.S., 1941; M.Ed., Chgo. Tchrs. Coll., 1940; Ph.D., Mich. State U., 1950; m. Helen Ascher, Feb. 19, 1944; children—Paul, Gregory, David. Mem. faculty Mich. State U., 1945-61, asso. prof. biology, 1951-55, prof., 1955-61; sci. coordinator, prof. biology Stephens Coll., Columbia, Mo., 1961—, also dir. allied health programs; cons., writer Biol. Sci. Curriculum Study, Boulder, Colo., 1960-61; cons. sci. curriculum, facilities planning for colls. and univs., 1955—; heart damage research U. Bologna (Italy) Med. Sch., 1972. Bd. dirs. Allied Health Programs. Served with USAAF, 1941-44. Recipient Favilli medal Istituto di Patologia Generale, Bologna, 1972. Guggenheim fellow Cambridge (Eng.) U., 1957-58; NIH fellow Cal. Inst. Tech., 1950. Mem. Am. Assn. Gen. Liberal Edn. (past pres.), Nat. Assn. Biology Tchrs., AAAS. Adv. biology editor, writer Ency. Americana, 1959-69. Discovered cold pack treatment for mumps orchitis, 1945. Home: 101 E Green Meadows Rd Apt 35 Columbia MO 65201. *I have lived through two major wars, one depression, the turbulent 60's, and now the distressing inflation of the 70's. As an idealist I am dismayed with bureaucratic waste, with the decay in character and morality. Democracy, however, must survive.*

NOVAK, ANTHONY, ret. fgn. service officer; b. Ill., June 9, 1915; s. Anton and Victoria (Kurek) N.; A.A., George Washington U., 1942; B.C.S., Columbus, 1944, M.F.A., 1947; m. Loretta Mroczko, Apr. 17, 1937; children—Loreen, Anthony, Vicki Ann. Bookkeeper, Dept. Treasury, 1936-43; accountant GAO, 1944-47; fiscal insp. Dept. Agr., 1947-49, budget examiner, 1949-50; examiner Dept. Navy, 1950-51; budget examiner Dept. State, 1951-53; chief accountant Mut. Security Agy., ICA, 1953-56; dir. accounts div. AID, 1956-62; dir. Office Fin., State Dept., 1962-66, dir. fin. systems devel. staff, 1966-70; cons. to govt., 1970—. Recipient Superior Honor award State Dept., 1966. Served with AUS, 1945-46. Address: 5511 24th St N Arlington VA 22205

NOVAK, ARTHUR FRANCIS, educator; b. Balt., Oct. 25, 1916; s. Frank C. and Anna Barbara (Hulka) N.; B.S., U. Md., 1937; M.S., U. Ala., 1939; Ph.D., Purdue U., 1947; postgrad. Johns Hopkins U., 1939-40, U. Louisville, 1941-42, U. So. Calif., 1951-53; m. Mary Frances Miller, May 15, 1947; children—Martha Neal, Katrina Marie, Stephen Francis. Supr. fermentation Seagram-Calvert, Louisville, 1940-47; prof. bacteriology and chemistry U. Fla., Gainesville, 1947-51; dir. research Nutrilite Products, Inc., Buena Park, Calif., 1951-54; prof., head dept. food sci. and tech., prof. marine sci. La. State U., Baton Rouge, 1954—; pres. Internat. Tech. Consultants, 1978—; v.p. for sci. and tech. Singleton Packing Corp., Tampa, Fla., 1979—; cons. foods and drugs, 1947—; cons. to state and fed. agys., 1949—; Ford Found. adviser oceanography, food sci. to Brazil, 1968-69; prof. physiology U. Sao Paulo (Brazil) Faculty Medicine; adviser to India food programs, 1976; adviser to Venezuela, 1977; tech. dir. Internat. Shrimp Council, 1967—. Mem. Internat. Tech. Assistance Com., 1960—. Bd. dirs. Boys Clubs So. Calif., pres., 1952-54. Fellow Am. Inst. Chemists; mem. AAAS, Gulf Coast Inst. Food Technologists (pres. 1964-65, Man of Year award 1976), Am. Pharm. Assn., Am. Nuclear Soc., Oyster Inst. N.Am., Nat. Fisheries Inst., Nat. Shell Fisheries Assn., Am. Soc. Microbiology, Am. Chem. Soc., Marine Tech. Soc., Shrimp Assn. Ams., Shrimp Breeders and Processors Am. (tech. dir.), So. Assn. Food and Drug Ofcls., Council Am. Bioanalysts, ASHRAE, Inst. Food Technologists (chmn. constn. and by-laws, food quality control coms.), Rho Chi, Gamma Sigma Epsilon, Phi Kappa Phi, Gamma Sigma Delta, Pi Tau Sigma, Lambda Tau, Phi Kappa, Omicron Delta Kappa. Author: Microbiology of Shellfish, 1962, Fundamentals of Food Science, Fish Proteins, 1977. Contbr. articles to profl. jours. Patentee in field. Home: 656 College Hill Dr Baton Rouge LA 70808. *Success is a combination of knowledge, honesty, integrity, respect, responsibility, dependability and good manners. Without these traits you may become wealthy, but not necessarily intelligent or successful.*

NOVAK, DENNIS WAYNE, accountant, investment co. exec.; b. Milw., Sept. 12, 1941; s. Elmer Joseph and Regina Mary Ann (Puza) N.; B.B.A., U. Wis., Milw., 1969; m. Mary Hachey, June 15, 1968; children—Lorine, Jennifer, Scott. Auditor, Arthur Young & Co., Milw., 1969-72; controller-treas. Mortgage Guaranty Ins. Corp., Milw., 1972-77; controller ins. ops. MGIC Investment Corp., Milw., 1977—. Mem. speakers bur. United Way of Greater Milw. Served with U.S. N.G., 1963-69. C.P.A., Wis. Mem. Am. Inst. C.P.A.'s, Wis. Soc. C.P.A.'s, Ins. Accountants and Statis. Assn. Office: MGIC Investment Corp MGIC Plaza Milwaukee WI 53201

NOVAK, EUGENE FRANCIS, advt. exec.; b. Johnstown, Pa., May 4, 1925; s. John F. and Amelia (Havel) N.; B.A., U. Pitts., 1948; m. Joan Tross, Apr. 12, 1947; children—Gregory, Mark. With radio sta. WKBW, Buffalo, 1950-52; mgr. continuity dept. sta. WBEN-TV, Buffalo, 1952-54; TV writer, dir. Comstock Advt., Buffalo, 1954-58; radio-TV dir Rumrill-Hoyt, advt., N.Y.C., 1959-69, pres., creative dir., 1969—; Bd. dirs. Fair Campaign Practices Com., Washington, Nat. Advt. Rev. Bd., Advt. Council. Served with AUS, 1943-46; ETO. Mem. Pi Delta Epsilon. Author articles. Home: 303 E 57th St New York City NY 10022 Office: 635 Madison Ave New York NY 10022

NOVAK, KIM (MARILYN NOVAK), actress; b. Chgo., Feb. 18, 1933; d. Joseph A. and Blanche (Kral) Novak; student Wright Jr. College, Chgo.; A.A., Los Angeles City College 1958; m. Richard Johnson, April 1965 (div.). Motion picture debut, 1954; appeared in motion pictures including Man With Golden Arm, Eddy Duchin Story, Picnic, Pal Joey, Jeanne Eagels Story, Bell, Book and Candle, Middle of the Night, Strangers When We Meet, Boys Night Out, Notorious Landlady, Amorous Adventures of Moll Flanders, Kiss Me Stupid, The Legend of Lylah Clare, 1967, The Great Bank Robbery, 1969, Tales That Witness Madness, 1973, The White Buffalo, 1977; TV movies Third Girl from the Left, 1974, Satan's Triangle, 1975. Named one of 10 most popular movie stars by Box-Office mag., 1956, All-Am. Favorite, 1961; Brussels World Fair poll as favorite all-time actress in world, 1958. Office: care Agy for Performing Arts 9000 Sunset Blvd Suite 315 Los Angeles CA 90069

NOVAK, MAXIMILLIAN ERWIN, educator; b. N.Y.C., Mar. 26, 1930; s. George and Elsie (Loewy) N.; Ph.D., U. Calif. at Los Angeles, 1958; D.Phil., St. John's Coll., Oxford (Eng.) U., 1961; m. Estelle Gershgoren, Aug. 21, 1966; children—Ralph, Daniel, Rachel. Asst. prof. English, U. Mich., Ann Arbor, 1958-62; prof. English, U. Calif. at Los Angeles, 1962—, Clark Library prof., 1973-74. Fulbright fellow, 1955-57, Guggenheim fellow, 1965-66, Am. Philos. Soc. fellow, 1979. Mem. Modern Lang. Assn. Democrat. Jewish. Author: Economics and the Fiction of Daniel Defoe, 1962; Defoe and the Nature of Man, 1963; Congreve, 1971; The Wild Man Within, 1972; English Literature in the Age of Disguise, 1977; editor: Augustan Reprint Soc. Dryden: Works, vol. 10, 1970; Southerne, Oroonoko, 1976; Collected Writings of Daniel Defoe. Home: 10380 Dunleer Dr Los Angeles CA 90064

NOVAK, MICHAEL (JOHN), (JR.), educator; b. Johnstown, Pa., Sept. 9, 1933; s. Michael John and Irene (Sakmar) N.; A.B. summa cum laude, Stonehill Coll., N. Easton, Mass., 1956; B.T. cum laude, Gregorian U., Rome, 1958; M.A., Harvard U., 1965; LL.D., Keuka (N.Y.) Coll., 1970, Stonehill Coll., Mass., 1977; L.H.D., Davis and Elkins (W.Va.) Coll., 1971, LeMoyne (N.Y.) Coll., 1976, Sacred Heart U., 1977, Muhlenberg Coll., 1979; m. Karen Ruth Laub, June 29, 1963; children—Richard, Tanya, Jana. Teaching fellow Harvard U., 1961-63; asst. prof. Stanford U., 1965-68; asso. prof. philosophy and religious studies State U. N.Y., Old Westbury, 1968-71; asso. dir. humanities Rockefeller Found., N.Y.C., 1973-75; provost Disciplines Coll., State U. N.Y., Old Westbury, 1969-71; vis. prof. Jan. sessions Carleton Coll., Northfield, Minn., 1970, Immaculate Heart Coll., Hollywood, Calif., 1971, U. Calif., Santa Barbara, 1972, U. Calif., Riverside, 1975; Ledden-Watson disting. prof. religion, 1977-79; journalist nat. elections Newsday, 1972; writer in residence The Washington Star, 1976, syndicated columnist, 1976—; resident scholar in religion and public policy Am. Enterprise Inst., Washington, 1978—; asso. editor Commonweal mag., 1966-69; contbg. editor Christian Century, 1967—, Christianity and Crisis, 1968-76, Jour. Ecumenical Studies, 1967—; judge Nat. Book awards, 1971, DuPont Broadcast Journalism awards, 1971—; speechwriter nat. polit. campaigns, 1970, 72. Kent fellow, 1961; fellow Hastings Inst., 1970-76; named Most Influential Prof., Sr. Class Stanford U., 1967, 68; Man of Yr., Johnstown, Pa., 1978; recipient Faith and Freedom award Religious Heritage Am., 1978. Mem. Soc. Religion in Higher Edn. (central com. 1970-73), Am. Acad. Religion (program dir. 1968-72), Council Fgn. Relations, Council Religion and Internat. Affairs. Author: The Tiber was Silver (novel), 1961; Naked I Leave (novel), 1970; Belief and Unbelief, 1965; The Experience of Nothingness, 1970; The Rise of the Unmeltable Ethnics, 1972; Choosing Our King, 1974; The Joy of Sports, 1976; The Guns of Lattimer, 1978; The American Vision, 1978. Address: American Enterprise Inst 1150 17th St Washington DC 20036. *Many persons have found a certain emptiness at the heart of human life — an experience of nothingness. Hidden in it, implicit in it, are prior commitments to honesty, courage, freedom, community. To increase the frequency of such acts in our lives is to grow, and to feel them diminish is to wither.*

NOVAK, MILAN VACLAV, educator; b. Cobb, Wis., Dec. 24, 1907; s. Philip and Barbara (Vavrina) N; B.A., Macalester Coll., 1929, D.Sc., 1947; M.S., U. Minn., 1930, Ph.D., 1932, B.S., 1936, M.B., 1938, M.D., 1938; m. Dorothy Flint, July 28, 1934; children—Mary Dayle, John Lotus, Raymond William. Asst. prof. bacteriology U. Tenn., 1932-33; pharmacology research fellow U. Minn., 1933-34, part-time instr. bacteriology, 1934-38, chief bacteriologist, dir. blood bank U. Minn. Hosps., 1938-40, instr. in med. bacteriology, 1938-40; asso. prof. bacteriology and pub. health, U. Ill., 1940-43, prof., head dept. bacteriology and pub. health, 1943-64, asso. dean Grad. Coll., 1950-68, acting dean Grad. Coll., 1968-69, dir. blood bank, 1942-54; asso. internal medicine U. Ariz. Coll. Medicine, 1970—, coordinator Ariz. Regional Med. Program in Pulmonary Diseases, 1970—; dir. State Bank of Lombard (Ill.). Pres., Tb Inst. Chgo. and Cook County, 1960, Midwest Conf. Grad. Study, 1960, grad. div. Land Grant Colls. and State Univs., 1965. Bd. dirs. Am. Lung Assn., 1956-70, Ariz. Lung Assn., 1970—. Fellow AAAS; mem. Am. Thoracic Soc., AMA, Soc. Exptl. Biology and Medicine, Soc. Am. Bacteriologists, Macalester Coll. Allumni Assn. (dir. 1960-65), Phi Beta Pi, Gamma Alpha, Sigma Xi. Presbyn. Author: Bacteriology Lab. Directions for Students of the Med. Scis. Editor Nat. Ofcl. Handbook for Speedskating, 1960-75. Work on improved methods for safe storage and adminstrn. of blood and plasma, also work on antibiotics. Home: 1231 Sobre Lomas Tucson AZ 85718 Office: Ariz Med Center Tucson AZ 85724

NOVAK, ROBERT DAVID SANDERS, journalist; b. Joliet, Ill., Feb. 26, 1931; s. Maurice Pall and Jane Anne (Sanders) N.; student U. Ill., 1948-52; m. Geraldine Williams, Nov. 10, 1962; children—Zelda, Alexander Augustus Williams. Reporter, Joliet Herald-News, 1948-50, Champaign-Urbana (Ill.) Courier, 1951-52, A.P., 1954-58; Congl. and polit. corr. Wall St. Jour., 1958-63; polit. columnist N.Y. Herald-Tribune Syndicate, 1963-66, Publishers Hall Syndicate, 1966-78, Field Newspaper Syndicate, 1978—. Served to 1st lt. AUS, 1952-54. Mem. Authors Guild, Sigma Delta Chi. Club: Nat. Press (Washington). Author: The Agony of the GOP 1964, 1965; (with Rowland Evans, Jr.) Lyndon B. Johnson: The Exercise of Power, 1966; (with Rowland Evans, Jr.) Nixon in the White House: The Frustration of Power, 1971. Office: 1750 Pennsylvania Ave NW Washington DC 20006*

NOVAK, TERRY LEE, city adminstr.; b. Chamberlain, S.D., Sept. 1, 1940; s. Warren F. and Elaine M. N.; B.Sc., S.D. State U., 1962; postgrad. (Rotary fellow) U. Paris, 1962-63; M.P.A., Colo. U., 1965, Ph.D., 1970; m. Pamela Cline, July 31, 1965 (div.); children—Stephen, David. Asst. city mgr. City of Anchorage, 1966-68; city mgr. City of Hopkins (Minn.), 1968-74, City of Columbia (Mo.), 1974-78, City of Spokane, 1978—; asst. adj. prof. U. Mo., 1975, 77. Mem. Internat. City Mgrs.' Assn. (Acad. Profl. Devel.), Am. Soc. Public Adminstrn. Unitarian. Club: Rotary. Author: Special Assessment Financing in American Cities, 1970; contbr. articles to profl. jours. Office: 221 N Wall St Spokane WA 99201

NOVAK, WILLIAM JOSEPH, editor; b. Chgo., June 12, 1921; s. Joseph and Rose (Krivanek) N.; B.S. in Elec. Engring., Ill. Inst. Tech., 1950; m. Mildred Bastl, Sept. 11, 1943; children—Michael, Patricia. Elec. engr. Internat. Harvester Co., Chgo., 1941-50; asst. editor Elec. Constrn. and Maintenance mag. McGraw-Hill Publs. Co., N.Y.C., 1953-62, asso. editor, 1962-69, mng. editor, 1969-76, exec. editor, 1976-77, chief editor, 1977—. Served to 1st lt., Signal Corps, U.S. Army, 1943-46, 50-53; Korea. Decorated Bronze Star. Mem. IEEE, Nat. Fire Protection Assn., Internat. Assn. Elec. Insps. Author: (with J.F. McPartland) Electrical Design Details, 1960; Practical Electricity, 1964; Electrical Equipment Manual, 1965; contbr. numerous articles to tech. publs. Home: 12 Bayley Pl Huntington Station NY 11746 Office: 1221 Ave Americas New York City NY 10020

NOVALES, RONALD RICHARDS, zoologist, educator; b. San Francisco, Apr. 24, 1928; s. William Henry and Dorothy (Richards) N.; B.A., U. Calif., Berkeley, 1950, M.A., 1953, Ph.D., 1958; postgrad. U. Calif. Los Angeles, 1951-52; m. Barbara Jean Martin, Dec. 19, 1953; children—Nancy Ann, Mary Elizabeth. Asst. prof. biol. scis. Northwestern U., Evanston, Ill., 1958-64, asso. prof., 1964-70, prof., 1970—; cons. A.J. Nystrom Co., 1969. Served with U.S. Army, 1953-55. NSF research grantee, 1959-73, 75-78. Fellow AAAS; mem. Am. Soc. Zoologists (sec. 1966-67, chmn. div. comparative endocrinology 1974-75), Endocrine Soc., Internat. Endocrine Soc., Am. Soc. Cell Biology, Internat. Pigment Cell Soc., Phi Beta Kappa, Sigma Xi. Unitarian. Mem. editorial bd. The American Zoologist, 1969-73. Contbr. articles to profl. jours., Handbook of Physiology, Ency. Brit. Book of Year. Home: 2008 McDaniel Ave Evanston IL 60201 Office: Dept Biol Scis Northwestern U Evanston IL 60201

NOVARR, DAVID, educator; b. Hartford, Conn., June 29, 1917; s. Bennie and Minnie (Katz) N.; B.A., Yale, 1939, M.A., 1942, Ph.D., 1949; m. Ruth Victoria Gordon, Feb. 4, 1942; children—John Gordon, Frances (Mrs. David Sheldon Strayer). Instr. English, Cornell U., 1946-51, asst. prof. 1951-56, asso. prof., 1956-63, prof. English, 1963—, asst. chmn. dept., 1966-68, acting chmn., 1968-69. Served with USNR, 1942-45. Fund for Advancement Edn. fellow, 1951-52; Huntington Library fellow, 1978. Mem. AAUP, Modern Lang. Assn. Am., Phi Beta Kappa. Author: The Making of Walton's Lives, 1958. Editor: Seventeenth-Century English Prose, 1967. Contbr. articles to profl. jours. Home: 226 Valley Rd Ithaca NY 14850

NOVELLO, FREDERICK CHARLES, chemist; b. Somerville, Mass., July 27, 1916; s. Charles and Elena (Capodanno) N.; S.B. cum laude, Harvard U., 1938, M.A., 1939, Ph.D., 1941; m. Sally Catherine Mickey, June 26, 1948; children—Frederick Charles, Barbara Anne, Carol Susan. Research chemist Nat. Def. Research Council, Harvard U., 1941-43; research chemist Sharp and Dohme, Glenolden, Pa., 1943—, sr. investigator Merck Sharp and Dohme Research Labs., West Point, Pa., 1973—. Bd. dirs. Inter-County Hospitalization Plan, Inc. Recipient Albert Lasker spl. award Albert and Mary Lasker Found., 1975. Mem. Am. Chem. Soc. Republican. Roman Catholic. Club: Harvard (Phila.). Contbr. articles to profl. jours. Patentee in field. Home: 786 Bair Rd Berwyn PA 19312 Office: Merck Sharp and Dohme West Point PA 19486

NOVER, NAOMI (GOLL), journalist, editor, author; b. Buffalo; d. B.B. and Rebecca (Shane) Goll; student U. Buffalo; B.S., Buffalo State Tchrs. Coll., 1934; M.A., George Washington U., 1951; m. Barnet Nover (dec. 1973). News, features, editorial asst. Buffalo Times; tchr. pub., pvt. schs. Buffalo Park Sch. of U. Buffalo, Snyder, N.Y.; music critic Denver Post at Goethe Music Festival, Aspen, Colo., 1949; news corr., columnist Washington bur. Denver Post, 1952-72; editor Nover News Bur., Washington, 1972—. Corr. on mission to Europe, Portland Oregonian; White House corr. Pres. Ford European tour, 1975, Pres. Ford China and trip to Indonesia, Japan, Philippines, Hawaii, 1975; writer, dir. plays produced in Buffalo; participated radio and television plays; producer nationally syndicated radio program Views and Interviews; author nationally syndicated feature stories and column Washington Deadline, 1952—. Formerly active ARC, U.S. Treasury War Bonds; chmn. Kalorama area Community Chest, 1947-49; originator embassy participation groups, jr. hostess, chmn., originator embassy tour Goodwill Industries; chmn., producer program with 1,000 Girl Scouts at Pan Am. Union; past mem. council Girl Scouts U.S.A.; chmn. program com. Columbian Women of George Washington U., 1953-56; nat. chmn. War Nurses Meml. Com. Mem. women's bd. George Washington U. Hosp. Recipient award pin U.S. Treasury Dept.; Silver Eagle award Girl Scouts U.S.A. Mem. White House Corrs. Assn., State Dept. Corrs. Assn., Congl. Press Galleries Corrs. Assn., AAUW, Nat. League Am. Pen Women, Sigma Delta Chi, Welcome to Washington, Ikebana, Pi Lambda Theta (past corr. ofcl. publ.). Clubs: National Press, Washington Press, Am. Newspaper Women's, Overseas Writers (Washington); Wychmere Harbor (Chatham, Mass.). Contbr. articles to mags. Home: 3001 Veazey Terr NW Washington DC 20008 Office: Nat Press Bldg Washington DC 20045

NOVICK, AARON, molecular biologist; b. Toledo, June 24, 1919; s. Sam and Rose N.; B.S., U. Chgo., 1940, Ph.D., 1943; m. Jane Graham, Jan. 25, 1948; children—David G., Adam P. Research scientist Manhattan Project, 1943-47; asst. prof. biophysics, microbiology U. Chgo., 1948-54, asso. prof., 1955-58; prof. biology U. Oreg., Eugene, 1959—, dir. Inst. Molecular Biology, 1959-71, dean Grad. Sch., 1971—. Home: 3960 Blanton Rd Eugene OR 97405 Office: Grad Sch U Oreg Eugene OR 97403

NOVICK, DAVID, civil engr., educator; b. N.Y.C., May 14, 1926; s. Harry and Charlotte (Menzin) N.; B.C.E., Columbia U., 1948; M.S., 1954; m. Minna Sommer, Aug. 28, 1953; children—Martha, Linda, Emily. Founds. and soils engr. Tippetts-Abbett-McCarthy-Stratton, N.Y.C., 1948-54; found., structural engr., exec. v.p. Goodkind & O'Dea, Inc., Hamden, Conn., 1954-56, Chgo., 1956-60; pres. Westenhoff & Novick, Inc., Chgo., 1960-77; exec. v.p. Lester B. Knight & Assos., Chgo., 1977—; vis. prof., asso. dir. Urban Systems Lab., U. Ill., Chgo., 1977, adj. prof. systems engring., 1977—; lectr. civil engring. Ill. Inst. Tech., 1970-76; mem., sec. Ill. Structural Engr. Exam. Com., 1970-75. Mem. Chgo. exec. com. Anti-Defamation League; trustee North Suburban Mass Transit Dist., 1970-74. Served with AUS, 1944-46. Registered profl. engr., N.Y., Ill., Conn., Ky., Iowa, Ind., Mo., Wis., Wash., La., Md., Fla., Kans., D.C., Minn., Pa., Va. Fellow ASCE (nat. dir. 1977-80; pres. Ill. sect. nat. com. pub. affairs 1969-74, co-chmn. task com. nat. civil engring. edn. conf. 1979, Washington award commn. 1972-78, chmn. publs. com. 1979-80), Am. Cons. Engrs. Council; mem. Am. Ry. Engring. Assn., ASTM, Nat., Ill. (v.p. 1963-64), socs. profl. engrs., Nat. (trustee 1972-78), Western socs. engrs., Internat. Soc. Bridge and Structural Engrs., Internat. Soc. Soil Mechanics and Found. Engrs., Am. Arbitration Assn. (panel arbitrators, regional bd.), Chi Epsilon (hon.). Clubs: Univ. (Chgo.); Princeton (N.Y.C.). Contbr. articles to profl. jours. Home: 2275 Sheridan Rd Highland Park IL 60035 Office: 549 W Randolph St Chicago IL 60606

NOVICK, DAVID MICHAEL, journalist; b. Chgo., May 27, 1942; s. Bernard R. and Alice (Chaffee) N.; student U. Wis.-Milw., 1960-62; 1 son, Jason. Mng. editor Milw. Star, 1965-67, 70, Milw. Courier, 1967-70, entertainment editor, 1970-72; staff writer, asso. editor Investor Mag., 1973-75; mng. editor Steppin' Out Mag., 1977-79; news reporter sta. WAWA, 1970; folk music producer, co-host sta. WUWM, 1971-72; writer, cons. Harambee Shopper, monthly supportive publ. of Harambee Community Sch., Milw.; organizer Met. Milw. Fair Housing Council. Bd. dirs. Pulsar Communications Found.; co-coordinator Protect Political Rights. Editorial contbr. Project Uplift of Nat. Jaycees, 1973. Writer Kaleidoscope, 1970-72; contbr. articles to Milw. Impressions mag. Home: 3059 N Humboldt Milwaukee WI 53212

NOVICK, LLOYD F., state ofcl., physician; b. Bklyn., Apr. 23, 1941; s. Edward and Gertrude (Folson) N.; B.A., Colgate U., 1961; M.D., N.Y. U., 1965; M.P.H., Yale U., 1971; m. Carole Leutner, Feb. 4, 1971; children—Sarah, Ethan. Asst. prof. public health and pediatrics Columbia U., 1972-74; asso. commr. N.Y.C. Dept. Health, 1975-77, dep. commr., profl. standards and rev., 1977-78; commr. Vt. Dept. Health, Burlington, 1978—; clin. asso. prof. medicine U. Vt.; adj. asso. prof. public health Columbia U. Served with USPHS, 1966-68. Mem. Am. Public Health Assn., Public Health Assn. N.Y.C. (pres. 1975). Jewish. Contbr. articles to profl. publs. Home: Guinea Rd Charlotte VT 05445 Office: 60 Main St Burlington VT 05401*

NOVICK, ROBERT, educator, physicist; b. N.Y.C., May 3, 1923; s. Abraham and Carolyn (Weisberg) N.; M.E., Stevens Inst. Tech., 1944, M.S., 1949; Ph.D., Columbia, 1955; m. Bernice Lehrman, July 2, 1947; children—Beth, Amy, Peter. Microwave engr. Wheeler Lab., Inc., 1946-47; faculty Columbia, 1952-54, 57, 60—, prof. physics, 1962—, research asso., 1954-57, dir. Radiation Lab., 1960-68, co-dir. Astrophysics Lab., 1968—; asst. prof. U. Ill., Urbana, 1957-59, asso. prof., 1959-60. Cons to labs., research insts.; chmn. subpanel on atomic and molecular physics Nat. Acad. Sci., 1964-65. A.P. Sloan fellow, 1958-70. Fellow Am. Phys. Soc., IEEE; mem. Am. Astron. Soc. (sec.-treas. high energy astrophysics sect. 1975-78), Internat. Astron. Union. Research, publs. on atomic physics, atomic collisions, quantum electronics, atomic frequency standards, nuclear spins and moments, X-ray astronomy. Home: 366 W 245th St Riverdale NY 10471 Office: Columbia Astrophysics Lab 538 W 120th St New York NY 10027

NOVICK, SHELDON MARK, author, lawyer; b. N.Y.C., June 19, 1941; s. Irving and Ruth (Rosenblatt) N.; B.A., Antioch Coll., 1963; J.D., Washington U. Sch. Law, 1977; m. Sherwood Mitchell, May 3, 1968; 1 dau. by previous marriage, Melia Bensussen. Adminstr., Center for Biology of Natural Systems, Washington U., St. Louis, 1966-69; asso. editor Environment mag., St. Louis, 1964-69, editor, 1969-77, pub., 1972-74; asso. firm Milgrim Thomajan & Jacobs, N.Y.C., 1977-78; regional counsel U.S. EPA, Phila., 1978—. Democrat. Author: The Careless Atom, 1969; The Electric War, 1976. Editor: (with Dorothy Cottrell) Our World in Peril, 1971. Home: 409 Sycamore Ave Merion PA 19066 Office: EPA 6th and Walnut Sts Philadelphia PA 19106

NOVIK, YLDA FARKAS (MRS. DAVID NOVIK), pianist; b. Szatmar, Hungary, Aug. 10, 1922; d. Jack and Yolan (Zipser) Farkas; came to U.S., 1927, naturalized, 1944; B.Mus., Cleve. Inst. Music, 1943; postgrad. Juilliard Sch. Music, 1943-44; m. David Novik, June 15, 1944; children—Lewis Gregory, Jill Susan. Concert pianist, 1957—; toured U.S., Japan, Europe, Latin Am.; adj. prof. Montgomery Coll., 1968; lectr. George Washington U., 1970; contbg. critic Washington Star-News, 1967-73; U.S. corr. Inter-Am. Music Bull., 1970-74; editor, performer series Young Pianists Guide. Hon. bd. dirs. D.C. Community Orch., Nat. Choral Found.; adv. council Washington Chamber Orch. Mem. Music Tchrs. Nat. Assn., Am. Liszt Soc., Mu Phi Epsilon. Recs. of Bartok music for Toshiba, 1972; piano editor Am. Music Tchr., 1968-72; contbg. editor Piano Quar. Address: 4805 Grantham Ave Chevy Chase MD 20015

NOVIKOFF, ALEX BENJAMIN, cell biologist; b. Russia, Feb. 28, 1913; s. Jack and Anna (Tretyakoff) N.; came to U.S., 1913, naturalized, 1918; B.S., Columbia U., 1931, M.A., 1933, Ph.D., 1938; m. Phyllis M. Iaciofano, Dec. 1, 1968; children—Kenneth, Lawrence. Fellow biology dept. Bklyn. Coll., 1931-35, instr., 1936-47, asst. prof. biology, 1947-48; Am. Cancer Soc. research fellow U. Wis. Med. Sch., 1946-47; prof. exptl. pathology, asso. prof. bio-chemistry U. Vt. Coll. Medicine, 1948-53; sr. investigator Waldemar Med. Research Found., Port Washington, N.Y., 1954-55; asso. research prof. biochem. cytology Albert Einstein Coll. Medicine, 1955-57, prof. pathology, 1958—. Recipient Distinguished Service award Columbia U., 1960, 74; Nat. Cancer Inst. Research Career award, 1962—. Mem. Nat. Acad. Scis., Japanese Soc. Cell Biology (hon.), Societe Francaise de Microscopie Electronique (hon.), Japanese Histochem. Soc. (hon.). Author: (with Eric Holtzman) Cells and Organelles, 1970, 2d edit., 1976; author books on sci. for children, films on enzymes and carbohydrate metabolism for U.S. Army; contbr. numerous articles to profl. publs. Office: Albert Einstein Coll Medicine Dept Pathology 1300 Morris Park Ave Bronx NY 10461

NOVOSAL, PAUL PETER, archivist; b. St. Louis, Oct. 5, 1918; s. Paul Michael and Eva Pavlacich) N.; B.S., U. Dayton, 1940; B.L.S., Our Lady of the Lake Coll., San Antonio, Tex., 1941; M.A., St. Mary's U., 1965. Entered Soc. of Mary, 1936; tchr., librarian Central Cath. High Sch., San Antonio, 1941-45, McBride High Sch., St. Louis, 1945-46, Central Cath. Sch., San Antonio, 1946, St. Joseph High Sch., Victoria, Tex., 1946-47; librarian, instr. English, St. Mary's U., San Antonio, 1947-58, dir. libraries, asst. prof. English, 1958-67, prof. English, 1967—; archivist Soc. of Mary, 1973—. Mem. Soc. Am. Archivists, Nat. Trust Historic Preservation. Home: St Mary's U San Antonio TX 78284

NOVOTNY, DONALD WAYNE, elec. engr.; b. Chgo., Dec. 15, 1934; s. Adolph and Margaret Novotny; B.E.E., Ill. Inst. Tech., 1956, M.S., 1957; Ph.D., U. Wis., 1961; m. Louise J. Eenigenburg, June 26, 1954; children—Donna Jo, Cynthia Jean. Instr., Ill. Inst. Tech., 1957-58; mem. faculty U. Wis., Madison, 1958—, prof. elec. engring., 1969—, chmn. dept. elec. and computer engring., 1976—; vis. prof. Mont. State U., 1966, Eindhoven Tech. U., Netherlands, 1974; cons. to industry. Fellow Gen. Electric Co., 1956, Ford Found., 1960; recipient Kiekhofer Teaching award U. Wis., 1964; Outstanding Paper award Engring. Inst. Can., 1966; grantee numerous industries and govt. agencies. Registered profl. engr., Wis. Mem. IEEE, Am. Soc. Engring. Edn., Sigma Xi, Tau Beta Pi, Eta Kappa Nu. Congregationalist. Author: Introductory Electromechanics, 1965; also research papers; asso. editor Electric Machines and Electromechanics, 1976—. Home: 1421 E Skyline Dr Madison WI 53705 Office: Dept Elec and Computer Engring 1415 Johnson Dr U Wis Madison WI 53706

NOVOTNY, RUDOLPH FRANCIS, banker; b. N.Y.C., Sept. 17, 1923; s. Rudulph E. and Catherine V. (McAndrews) N.; grad. Pace Coll., 1957; m. Louanna M. Killackey, Apr. 18, 1953; children—Rudolph, Wayne, Nancy, Cathy, Maureen, Richard. With Bowery Savs. Bank, N.Y.C., 1946-58; asst. v.p. Instl. Securities Corp., N.Y.C., 1958-60; v.p. Allied Bldg. Credits Corp., N.Y.C., 1960-62, Instl.-Wallace, Inc., 1962-65; v.p. U.S. Savs. Bank, Newark, 1965-73, pres., chief exec. officer, 1973—; trustee Monmouth Real Estate Investment Trust Co.; mem. N.J. Mortgage Study Commn., 1971—, Task Force Bus. Efficiency in Pub. Schs., 1976-78. Served with USNR, 1944-46, 50-51. Mem. Greater Newark C. of C. (vice chmn., chmn. municipal govt. com.), Greater Newark Urban Coalition (dir.), Nat. Assn. Mut. Savs. Banks (edn. com.), Mortgage Bankers Assn. N.J. (2d v.p.). Office: 772 Broad St Newark NJ 07102

NOWACZYNSKI, WOJCIECH JERZY, endocrinologist, educator; b. Nisko, Poland, Mar. 27, 1925; s. Jan and Irena (Listowska) N.; came to Can., 1953, naturalized, 1959; B.Sc., Cyprian Norvid Polish Coll., Paris, France, 1942, Polish Coll., Zurich, Switzerland, 1944; Doctorandum, U. Fribourg (Switzerland), 1950, D.Sc. magna cum laude, 1952; m. Beverly Kathleen Cooke, Oct. 31, 1953; children—Maria, Barbara, Mark, Francis, Paula, Peter. With dept. clin. research Hotel-Dieu Hosp., Montreal, Que., Can., 1953; asst. prof. medicine U. Montreal, 1962-65, asso. prof., 1965-70, prof., 1970-79; lectr. McGill U., Montreal, 1964-65, asst. prof. exptl. medicine, 1965, asso. prof., 1966-70, prof., 1970-79; prof. medicine U. B.C., Vancouver, 1979—; mem. div. endocrinology and metabolism, dept. medicine St. Paul's Hosp., Vancouver, 1979—. Research asso. Med. Research Council Can., 1962-65, permanent research asso., 1965—, prin. investigator research group on hypertension, 1972-79; dir. dept. steroid research Clin. Research Inst. of Montreal, 1967-79; career investigator Med. Research Council Can., 1979—; mem. med. adv. bd. council for high blood pressure research Am. Heart Assn., 1968—. Recipient Marcel Piché award for discovery of aldosterone-binding specific plasma globulin and its relationship to human hypertension. Mem. Internat. Soc. Hypertension, Inter-Am. Soc. Hypertension (mem. council 1978—), Am. Endocrine Soc., Can. Soc. Clin. Investigation. Contbr. articles to profl. jours. Research on role of adrenal cortex in pathogenesis of arterial hypertension; demonstration of an altered hepatic metabolism of aldosterone in primary hypertension. Home: 4356 Quinton Pl North Vancouver BC V7R 4A7 Canada Office: Dept Medicine St Paul's Hosp Vancouver BC V6Z 1Y6 Canada

NOWAK, HENRY JAMES, congressman; b. Buffalo, Feb. 21, 1935; s. Joseph Jacob and Helen (Batkiewcz) N.; B.B.A., Canisius Coll., 1957; J.D., State U. N.Y. at Buffalo, 1961; m. Rose Santa Lucia, Nov. 27, 1965; children—Diane, Henry Joseph. Admitted to N.Y. bar, 1962; atty., asst. dist. atty. State of N.Y., Buffalo, 1964-65; asst. dist. atty. Erie County, N.Y., Buffalo, 1965-66; confidential sec. Supreme Ct. Justice Arthur Cosgrove, Buffalo, 1965-66; comptroller Erie County, 1966-74; mem. 94th-96th Congresses from 37th N.Y. Dist., chmn. small bus. subcom. on access to equity capital and bus. opportunities. Served with AUS, 1957-58, 61-62. Named An Outstanding Citizen, Buffalo Eve. News, 1976; recipient Am-Pol Eagle Citizen of Year award, 1976. Mem. N.Y. State, Erie County bar assns., Jr. C. of C., Council Polish-Am. Affairs. Office: 1514 Longworth House Office Bldg Washington DC 20515

NOWELL, PETER CAREY, educator, pathologist; b. Phila., Feb. 8, 1928; s. Foster and Margaret (Matlack) N.; B.A., Wesleyan U., Middletown, Conn., 1948; M.D., U. Pa., 1952; m. Helen Worst, Sept. 9, 1950; children—Sharon, Timothy, Karen, Kristin, Michael. Intern Phila. Gen. Hosp., 1952-53; resident pathology Presbyn. Hosp., Phila., 1953-54; med.-teaching, research specializing in exptl. pathology, Phila., 1956—; from instr. to prof. pathology Sch. Medicine U. Pa., 1956—, chmn. dept. pathology, 1967-73; dir. Cancer Center, 1973-75. Served to lt., M.C., USNR, 1954-56. Recipient Research Career award USPHS, 1964-67, Parke-Davis award, 1965, Lindback Distinguished Teaching award, 1967. Mem. Am. Soc. Exptl. Pathology (pres. 1970), Am. Assn. Cancer Research, Path. Soc. Phila., Radiation Research Soc., Nat. Acad. Sci., Transplantation Soc., Am. Assn. Immunologists. Home: 345 Mt Alverno Rd Media PA 19063 Office: Dept Pathology Sch Medicine Univ of Pennsylvania Philadelphia PA 19104

NOWELS, RICHARD WRIGHT, newspaper publisher; b. Colorado Springs, Colo., Dec. 15, 1917; s. T. Ernest and Bertie May (Wright) N.; B.A., U. Colo., 1938; m. Kathryn L. Colfer, Aug. 17, 1951; children—Carol, Nancy, Melinda, Richard Wright, Mary K. Editor, Colorado Springs Gazette-Telegraph, 1939; editor, editorial writer Havana (Cuba) Post, 1940; rewrite man AP, Denver, 1941; advt. mgr. newspapers Colorado Springs, 1942; owner, pub. Mountain View (Calif.) Daily Register, 1951-55, Buena Park (Calif.) News, 1955-64, La Mirada (Calif.) Lamplighter, 1957-64; owner, pub., gen. mgr. Nowels Publs. Internat., Menlo Park, Calif., 1965—, publs. include Menlo-Atherton Recorder, Sequoia Sempervirens, San Carlos Enquirer, Belmont Courier-Bull., Ravenswood Post, others; also printer Stanford Daily, Taiwan Sun Times. Chmn. San Mateo County Muscular Dystrophy Fund, 1967—; bd. dirs. Buena Park and Herbert Hoover Boys Clubs, 1955-68. Served to 1st lt., flying instr. B-17's, B-29's, USAAC, 1942-45; mem. USAF hon. res., 1951—. Mem. Mountain View (bd. dirs.), Buena Park (bd. dirs.), La Mirada (bd. dirs.), Menlo Park (bd. dirs.) chambers of commerce, San Francisco Press Club, San Francisco, Peninsula advt. clubs, Calif. Newspaper Pubs. Assn., San Mateo County Pubs. Assn. (pres. 1967—), Chi Psi. Clubs: Elks, Atherton, Menlo Town. Patentee automatic electric bed-making device. Home: 14465 Manuella Rd Los Altos Hills CA 94022 Office: 640 Roble Ave Menlo Park CA 94025

NOWLAN, ALDEN, author; b. near Windsor, N.S., Can., Jan. 25, 1933; s. Freeman and Grace (Reese) N.; Litt.D. (hon.), U. N.B., 1971; LL.D., Dalhousie U., 1976; m. Claudine Orser, Aug. 27, 1963; 1 son, John. News editor Telegraph-Jour., St. John, N.B., Can., 1963-68; writer in residence U. N.B., Fredericton, 1968—. Recipient Gov. Gen.'s award for poetry, 1968, medal for poetry Can. Authors Assn., 1978, Queen's Silver Jubilee medal, 1978; Can. Council fellow, 1961, 67, Guggenheim fellow, 1968. Mem. Writers Union of Can. Author: The Rose and the Puritan, 1958; A Darkness in the Earth, 1959; Under the Ice, 1961; Wind in a Rocky Country, 1961; The Things Which Are, 1962; Bread, Wine and Salt, 1967; Miracle at Indian River, 1968; The Mysterious Naked Man, 1969; Playing the Jesus Game, 1970; Between Tears and Laughter, 1971; Various Persons Named Kevin O'Brien, 1973; I'm A Stranger Here Myself, 1974; Campobello: The Outer Island, 1975; Smoked Glass, 1977; Double Exposure, 1978; (plays, with Walter Learning) Frankenstein, The Man Who Became God, 1974, The Dollar Woman, 1977, The Incredible Murder of Cardinal Tosca, 1978. Home: 676 Windsor St Fredericton NB Canada

NOWLAN, HIRAM MERRILL, JR., corp. exec., lawyer; b. Janesville, Wis., Apr. 5, 1929; s. Hiram Merrill and Mildred (Biemiller) N.; B.A., Yale, 1951; J.D., Harvard, 1954; m. Patricia J. Miller, June 17, 1957; children—Katherine, Jean, Andrew. Admitted to Wis. bar, 1954, Ga. bar, 1968; partner Nowlan, Mouat, Lovejoy, McGuire & Wood, Janesville, 1956-68; corporate sec. Fuqua Industries, Inc., Atlanta, 1968—. Served with AUS, 1954-56. Mem. Am. Soc. Corp. Secs. (dir. 1973-77), Southeastern Regional Group (pres. 1977-78). Home: 2310 Bohler Rd NW Atlanta GA 30327 Office: 3800 First Nat Bank Tower Atlanta GA 30303

NOWOTNY, HANS, metallurgist, educator; b. Linz, Austria, Sept. 27, 1911; s. Leopold and Anna (Priesner) N.; came to U.S., 1977; diploma engring. Inst. Tech., Vienna, Austria, 1933, Dr. Tech., 1934; Dr. Mont. h.c., Sch. Mines, Leoben, 1965; m. Hildegard Hamma, Feb. 11, 1944; 1 son, Axel. Research asst. Inst. Tech., Vienna, 1934-41, prof., 1952-58; research asst. Inst. Tech., Karlsruhe, 1938-41, Max Planck Inst., Stuttgart, 1941-45; sci. dir. Inst. Metallurgy, Tettnang, Germany, 1945-47; asso. prof. phys. chemistry U. Vienna, 1947-52, prof., 1958-77, also head Chem. Inst., prof. emeritus, 1977—; prof. metallurgy U. Conn., 1977—; vis. prof. in field. Recipient Lavoisier medal (France), 1960; Lebeau medal, 1967; Wilhelm Exner medal, 1968; Loschmidt medal, 1973; medal for Sci. and Art, Austria, 1978; Schrödinger prize, 1968. Mem. Austrian Acad. Sci., Acad. Sci. Göttingen, Acad. Sci Leopoldina, Hungarian Acad. Sci., Conn. Acad. Sci. and Engring., Inst. Metals, Soc. Francaise Metall., Soc. German Chemists. Contbr. numerous articles to profl. jours. Home: 38 Mansfield Apts Storrs CT 06268 Office: Inst Material Sci U Conn Storrs CT 06268

NOYCE, DONALD STERLING, educator; b. Burlington, Iowa, May 26, 1923; s. Ralph B. and Harriet (Norton) N.; A.B., Grinnell Coll., 1944; M.A., Columbia, 1945, Ph.D., 1947; m. Bettie Grace Neville, June 18, 1946; children—Robert D., Donald B., Nancy Anne. Mem. faculty U. Calif. at Berkeley, 1948—, prof. chemistry, 1960—, asst. dean Coll. Chemistry, 1952-60, 66-68, 74—. Mem. adv. com. chemistry Air Force Office Sci. Research, 1963-71. NIH fellow, 1947-48; Guggenheim fellow, 1957; NSF sr. fellow, 1964. Fellow Am. Chem. Soc. (chmn. Calif. sect. 1967), Chem. Soc. London (Eng.). Home: 1504 Olympus Ave Berkeley CA 94720

NOYCE, ROBERT NORTON, mfg. co. exec.; b. Burlington, Iowa, Dec. 12, 1927; s. Ralph B. and Harriet (Norton) N.; B.A., Grinnell Coll., 1949; Ph.D., Mass. Inst. Tech., 1953; m. Ann S. Bowers, Nov. 27, 1975; children—William B., Pendred, Priscilla, Margaret. Research engr. Philco Corp., Phila., 1953-56; research engr. Shockley Semicondr. Lab., Mountain View, Calif., 1956-57; founder, dir. research Fairchild Semicondr., Mountain View, 1957-59, v.p., gen. mgr., 1959-65; group v.p. Fairchild Camera & Instrument, Mountain View, 1965-68; founder, pres. Intel Corp., Santa Clara, Calif., 1968—, vice chmn., 1979—; dir. Coherent Radiation, Palo Alto, Calif. Trustee Grinnell Coll., 1962—. Recipient Stuart Ballentine award Franklin Inst., 1967, Harry Goode award AFIPS, 1978. Fellow IEEE (Cledo Brunetti award 1978, medal of honor 1978, Faraday medal 1979); mem. Nat. Acad. Engring. Patentee in field. Home: 690 Loyola Dr Los Altos CA 94022 Office: 3065 Bowers Ave Santa Clara CA 90951

NOYES, DONALD PARTELOW, banker; b. Lynn, Mass., Jan. 19, 1924; s. Leon A. and Georgia (Bain) N.; B.S., Boston U., 1949; m. Edith J. Colegrove, June 1, 1947; children—John Philip, Nancy Elizabeth. Asst. treas. Harvard Trust Co., Cambridge, Mass., 1960-64, treas., 1964-67; pres. North Ave Savs. Bank, Cambridge, 1967-71; pres. Cambridge Savs. Bank, 1971—; vice chmn. Savs. Bank Life Ins. Council. Trustee Mt. Auburn Hosp., Cambridge, 1964-69, 74—. Served with USAAF, 1943-46. Mem. Cambridge C. of C. (pres. 1973-76). Office: 1374 Massachusetts Ave Cambridge MA 02138

NOYES, EDWARD ROLAND, JR., ins. co. exec.; b. Marlboro, Mass., July 21, 1927; s. Edward Roland and Gretchen (Billings) N.; A.B., Bowdoin Coll., 1948; m. Barbara B. Caldwell, Sept. 15, 1963; 1 dau., Dara Lee. With Mass. Indemnity & Life Ins. Co., Boston, 1949—, pres., 1969—, chmn. bd., 1975—. Served with USAF, 1951-53. Congregationalist. Office: Mass Indemnity & Life Ins Co 225 Franklin St Boston MA

NOYES, GUY EMERSON, economist, banker; b. Columbia, Mo., Dec. 27, 1913; s. Guy L. and Lucia (Weigand) N.; A.B., U. Mo., 1934; grad. study Yale, 1935-39; m. Patricia Hartnett, July 9, 1943 (dec. Dec. 18, 1972); children—Guy Lincoln, Pamela Ann; m. 2d, Irene Starke Lane, Aug. 28, 1976. Instr. econs. Yale, 1938-41; sr. economist OPA, 1941-42; dir. research and statistics Dept. of State, 1946-48; asst. dir. research and statistics Fed. Res. Bd., 1948-56, dir. selective credit regulation, 1951-52, adviser, 1956-60, 64-65, dir. research and statistics, 1960-63; economist Fed. Open Market Com., 1962-65; sr. v.p., economist Morgan Guaranty Trust Co., N.Y.C., 1965-78; dir. Am. Re-Ins. Co., Central La. Energy Co.; asst. White House staff, 1954. Served as lt. col., AUS, World War II. Eisenhower Exchange fellow. Mem. Phi Gamma Delta. Club: Cosmos (Washington). Home: 2600 N Gulf Shore Blvd Naples FL 33940

NOYES, H(ENRY) PIERRE, physicist; b. Paris, Dec. 10, 1923 (parents Am. citizens); s. William Albert and Katharine Haworth (Macy) N.; B.A., Harvard U., 1943; Ph.D., U. Calif., Berkeley, 1950; m. Mary Wilson, Dec. 20, 1947; children—David Brian, Alan Guinn, Katharine Hope. Physicist, MIT, 1943-44, U. Calif., Berkeley, 1949-50; Fulbright fellow U. Birmingham (Eng.), 1950-51; asst. prof. U. Rochester (N.Y.), 1951-55; group leader Lawrence Livermoore Lab., 1955-62; Leverhulme lectr. U. Liverpool (Eng.), 1957-58; adminstrv. head theory sect. Stanford Linear Accelerator Center, 1962-69, asso. prof. Stanford U., 1962-67, prof., 1967—; vis. scholar Center Advanced Study Behavioral Scis., Stanford, 1968-69; cons. in field. Chmn. Com. for Direct Attack on Legality of Vietnam War, 1969-72; mem. steering com. Faculty Political Action Group, Stanford U., 1970-72; mem. policy com. U.S. People's Com. on Iran, 1977-79. Served with USNR, 1944-46. Fellow NSF, 1962, Nat. Humanities Faculty, 1970; recipient Alexander von Humboldt U.S. Sr. Scientist award, 1979. Mem. Alternative Natural Philosophy Assn. (pres. 1979—), Am. Phys. Soc., AAAS, Philosophy Sci. Assn., Sigma Xi. Author papers in field. Home: 823 Lathrop Dr Stanford CA 94305 Office: SLAC Bin 81 PO Box 4349 Stanford CA 94305

NOYES, JANSEN, JR., investment banker; b. Montclair, N.J., Apr. 7, 1917; s. Jansen and Agnes (Blancke) N.; grad. Lawrenceville (N.J.) Sch., 1935; M.E., Cornell U., 1939; student Harvard, 1941; m. Dorothy O'Day, Mar. 20, 1942; children—Jansen III, Mildred Dorothy, Michael O'Day, Karen. With Hemphill Noyes & Co., N.Y.C. 1939-64, gen. partner, 1946-64; gen. partner Hornblower, Weeks, Noyes & Trask, Inc. (formerly Hornblower & Weeks-Hemphill, Noyes, Inc.), 1965-72, pres., chief exec. officer, 1972-75, chmn. bd., 1975—. Trustee Cornell U., 1961—, vice chmn., 1969-78, chmn., 1978—, also mem. exec. com., past chmn. investment com., past chmn. devel. adv. com., gen. chmn. centennial campaign, 1961-65; mem. com. purchases Blind-Made Products, 1959-71; pres. Am. Found. Blind, 1958-70, chmn., 1970—; mem. Com. for Purchase from Blind and Other Severely Handicapped, 1971—; bd. dirs. Nat. Industries Blind, pres., 1958-63, chmn., 1963-70; bd. dirs. Nat. Soc. Prevention Blindness; pres. Am. Found. for Overseas Blind (name now Helen Keller Internat.), 1958-70, chmn., 1970—. Served to lt. comdr. USNR, 1941-45. Mem. Psi Upsilon. Episcopalian. Clubs: Links, Down Town Assn., Bond, Broad St., (bd. govs., past pres.), Cornell (N.Y.C.); Fishers Island (N.Y.) Country; Wee Burn Country (Darien). Home: 299 Hollow Tree Ridge Rd Darien CT 06820 Office: 14 Wall St New York NY 10005

NOYES, PIERREPONT T., mfg. exec.; b. Oneida, N.Y., 1914; grad. Colgate U., 1936. Chmn. bd., chief exec. officer Oneida Ltd.; vice chmn. bd. Camden Wire Co.; mem. adv. bd. Liberty Mut. Ins. Co.; dir. Lincoln Nat. Bank & Trust Co. of Central N.Y., Lincoln First Group, Inc., Rena Ware Distbrs., Inc. Mem. Saratoga Springs Commn. Bd. dirs. N.Y. State Council Econ. Edn., Asso. Industries N.Y. State, Indsl. Assn. Mohawk Valley; bd. dirs., mem. exec. com. Saratoga Performing Arts Center. bd. visitors Marcy State Hosp.; trustee Oneida Improvement Assn., Colgate U. Mem. Sterling Silversmiths Guild (past pres.), Silver Users Assn. (adv. com.). Home: 138 Kenwood Ave Oneida NY 13421 Office: Oneida Ltd Oneida NY 13421

NOYES, RICHARD HALL, bookseller; b. Evanston, Ill., Feb. 12, 1930; s. George Frederick and Dorothy (Hall) N.; B.A., Wesleyan U., 1952; m. Judith Claire Mitchell, Oct. 10, 1953; children—Catherine, Stephanie, Matthew. Tng. program, elementary-high sch. salesman Rand McNally & Co., Colo., Utah, Idaho, Wyo., 1955-59; founder, owner, mgr. Chinook Bookshop, Colorado Springs, Colo., 1959—. Co-chmn. Colo. Media Coalition, 1974—; bd. dirs. Colorado Springs Fine Arts Center, 1977—, Citizens Goals for Colorado Springs, 1976—; trustee Fountain Valley Sch., 1979—. Served with AUS, 1952-54. Recipient Intellectual Freedom award Mountain Plains Librarians Assn., 1977. Mem. Am. Booksellers Assn. (pres., dir.). Contbr. to A Manual on Bookselling, 1974. Contbr. articles to newspapers and trade jours. Home: 1601 Constellation Dr Colorado Springs CO 80906 Office: 210 N Tejon St Colorado Springs CO 80903

NOYES, RICHARD MACY, educator, phys. chemist; b. Champaign, Ill., Apr. 6, 1919; s. William Albert and Katharine Haworth (Macy) N.; A.B. summa cum laude, Harvard U., 1939; Ph.D., Calif. Inst. Tech., 1942; m. Winninette Arnold, July 12, 1946 (dec. Mar. 1972); m. 2d, Patricia Jean Harris, Jan. 26, 1973. Research asso. rocket propellants Calif. Inst. Tech., 1942-46; mem. faculty Columbia U., 1946-58, asso. prof., 1954-58; Guggenheim fellow, vis. prof. U. Leeds (Eng.) 1955-56; prof. chemistry U. Oreg., 1958—, head dept., 1963-68, 75-78. Fulbright fellow Victoria U., Wellington, New Zealand, 1964; NSF sr. postdoctoral fellow Max Planck Inst. für Physikalische Chemie, Göttingen, Germany, 1965; sr. Am. scientist awardee Alexander von Humboldt Found., 1978-79. Fellow Am. Phys. Soc.; mem. Nat. Acad. Scis., Am. Chem. Soc. (chmn. div. phys. chemistry 1961-62, exec. com. div. 1960-75, mem. council 1960-75, chmn. Oreg. sect. 1967-68; com. on nominations and elections 1962-68, com. on publs. 1969-72), Chem. Soc. (London), Wilderness Soc., ACLU, Soc. Social Responsibility in Sci., Phi Beta Kappa, Sigma Xi. Club: Sierra (past chmn. Atlantic and Pacific N.W. chpts., N.W. regional v.p. 1973-74). Asso. editor Chem. Revs., 1967-69, Jour. Phys. Chemistry, 1973—, Internat. Jour. Chem. Kinetics, 1972—. Contbr. to profl. jours. Research mechanisms chem. reactions, developing gen. theories, intrepretation phys. properties chemicals. Home: 2014 Elk Dr Eugene OR 97403. *When I was young, I wanted to be an "explorer." I am fortunate to have a job in which I can make discoveries as exciting as those of the explorers who first sailed uncharted seas. Then I can try to convey the excitement to another generation. As an avocation, I try to influence government policies toward our least developed lands. It is a gratifying mix of satisfying curiousity and serving society.*

NOYES, ROBERT EDWIN, publisher, author; b. N.Y.C., June 22, 1925; s. Clarence A. and Edith (LaDomus) N.; B.S. in Chem. Engring., Northwestern U., 1945; m. Janet Brown, Mar. 24, 1952 (div. June 1963); children—Keith, Steven, Mark, Geoffrey; m. 2d, Mariel Jones, July 24, 1964; children—Rebecca, Robert. Chem. engr. Am. Cyanamid Co., Pearl River, N.Y., 1947; sales exec. Titanium Pigment Corp., N.Y.C., 1948-55; market research mgr. U.S. Indsl. Chem. Co., N.Y.C., 1956-58; sales mgr. atomic energy Curtiss Wright Export, N.Y.C., 1958-60; founder, pres., chmn. bd. Noyes Data Corp., Park Ridge, N.J., 1960—; pub. Noyes Press, Park Ridge, 1961—. 1961—. Served to lt. (j.g.) USNR, 1945-47. Mem. Am. Chem. Soc., Am. Inst. Chem. Engrs., Chemists Club, Archaeol. Inst. Am., Pi Mu Alpha. Episcopalian. Author numerous books in fields of internat. fin., devel., tech. Home: 224 W Saddle River Rd Saddle River NJ 07458 Office: Noyes Bldg Park Ridge NJ 07656

NOYES, ROBERT WALLACE, physician, educator; b. Berkeley, Calif., June 3, 1919; s. Chester Bromley and Mary (Schmidt) N.; A.B., U. Calif. at Berkeley, 1941, M.D., 1944; m. Mary Holley, May 30, 1941; children—Martha Holley, Paul David. Intern obstetrics and gynecology Johns Hopkins Hosp., 1944-45; resident U. Calif. Hosp., San Francisco, 1945-46; research fellow Free Hosp. for Women, Harvard Med. Sch., Boston, 1948-49; asst. resident Stanford Hosp., 1949-50, mem. faculty. Med. Sch., 1951-61, asso. prof. obstetrics and gynecology, 1960-61; research prof. Agr. Research Council, U. Cambridge (Eng.), 1957-58, Inst. Research Agronomique Station de Recherches de Physiologie Animale Jouy-en-Josas, France, 1961; prof. obstetrics and gynecology, chmn. dept. Vanderbilt U. Sch. Medicine, 1961-65; prof., chmn. dept. anatomy, asso. dean profl. affairs U. Hawaii Sch. Medicine, Honolulu, 1965-70, chief sect. obstetrics and gynecology, 1967-70; prof. maternal and child health Sch. Pub. Health, also prof. obstetrics and gynecology Sch. Medicine, U. N.C., Chapel Hill, 1970-72; dir. med. research reproduction Ortho Research Found., Raritan, N.J., 1973-75; dir. clin. services and research Planned Parenthood Assn. Santa Clara County, San Jose, Calif., 1975-76; asso. med. dir. Syntex Labs., Palo Alto, Calif., 1976-77; staff physician Family Planning Alternatives, Sunnyvale, Calif., 1977-78; med. dir. family planning program Santa Clara County Health Dept., San Jose, Calif., 1978—. Served to capt. M.C., AUS, 1946-48. John and Mary R. Markle scholar med. sci.; recipient Ortho Found. award, 1955, Squibb prize, 1959, Rubin award, 1959, 61, 62. Mem. Am. Coll. Obstetricians and Gynecologists, Soc. Profs. Obstetrics and Gynecology. Office: 2220 Moorpark Ave San Jose CA 95128

NOYES, WARD DAVID, physician, educator; b. Schenectady, Aug. 25, 1927; s. Ward and Marion (French) N.; B.A., U. Rochester, 1949, M.D., 1953; m. Nancy Adair, Aug. 10, 1973; children—Patricia, Ward David, Jeffrey, Katherine, John, Elizabeth, Layne. Intern King County Hosp., Seattle, 1953-54, resident, 1954-56; practice medicine specializing in internal medicine; instr. medicine U. Wash., Seattle, 1959-61, asst. prof., 1961-65, asso. prof., 1965-68; asso. prof., head hematology Sch. Medicine U. Fla., Gainesville, 1968-70, prof., 1970—, chief hematology, 1968—. Cons. in hematology WHO, 1974-75, 78. Served with USAAF, 1946-47. USPHS fellow, 1956-69. Mem. Fla. Med. Assn., Alachua County Med. Soc., Am. Fedn. Clin. Research, Am. Soc. Hematology, Internat. Soc. Hematology, So. Soc. Clin. Investigation, Alpha Omega Alpha. Research in iron metabolism. Contbr. to profl. jours. Home: 538 NE 7th Ave Gainesville FL 32601

NOYES, WILLIAM ALBERT, JR., chemist, educator; b. Terre Haute, Ind., Apr. 18, 1898; s. William Albert and Flora (Collier) N.; student U. Ill., 1916-17, D.Sc., 1964; A.B., Grinnell (Iowa) Coll., 1919, D.Sc., 1946; D.-ès-Sc., U. of Paris, France, 1920, Dr.h.c.; postgrad. U. Geneva, Switzerland, 1920, U. Cal., 1920-21; D.Sc., Grinnell Coll., U. R.I., Ind. U., U. Ottawa, U. Ill., U. Montreal, U. Rochester, Carleton U., Laval U.; m. Sabine Onillon, June 10, 1921; 1 son, Claude Charles. Instr., U. Calif., 1921-22; instr. U. Chgo., 1922-23, asst. prof., 1923-29; asso. prof., Brown U., 1929-35, prof., 1935-38; prof. U. Rochester, 1938-63, emeritus distinguished prof. chemistry, 1963, chmn. dept. chemistry, 1939-55, dean Grad. Sch., 1952-56, acting dean, then dean Coll. Arts and Sci., 1956-58; vis. lectr. U. Tex. at Austin, 1958, Ashbel Smith prof. chemistry, 1963-73, Ashbel Smith prof. emeritus, 1973—; chmn. div. Chemistry and Chemical Tech., NRC, 1947-53; chmn. com. on chem. warfare Research and Devel. Bd., 1948-50; v.p. Internat. Union of Chemistry, 1947-51; treas. Internat. Council Sci. Unions, 1952-55; exec. com. Internat. Union Pure and Applied Chemistry, 1955-59, pres., 1959-63; Montgomery lectr., U. Neb., 1956; Westman Meml. lectr., Chem. Inst. Can., 1955; Harkins lectr., U. Chgo., 1956. Trustee Sloan-Kettering Inst. Cancer Research, 1950-62. Served from sgt. to

2d lt. Signal Corps, U.S. Army, 1917-19; sect. chmn. Nat. Def. Research Com., 1940-42; div. chmn., 1942-46. On staff of chief Tech. Div., Chem. Warfare Service, U.S. Army, 1942-46; adviser U.S. delegation 1st conf. UNESCO, 1946, alt. del., 3rd conf., 1948, alternate delegate to 10th conf., 1958; mem. Naval Research Adv. Com., 1947-52; Officer Legion of Honor, France. Received Kings Medal for Service in Cause of Freedom, Medal for Merit, Am. Philos. Soc., 1948; Priestley medal Am. Chem. Soc., 1954; Willard Gibbs medal, 1957. Mem. Société Chimique de France (hon.), Chem. Soc. London (hon.), Nat. Acad. Scis. (mem. council 1947-50), Am. Chem. Soc. (chmn. com. profl. tng. of chemists, pres. 1947, Austin M. Patterson award Dayton sect. 1963), Am. Acad. Arts and Scis., Am. Phys. Soc., N.Y. Acad. Scis., Ill. Acad. Scis., Royal Soc. Physics and Chemistry (Spain), Société Chimique de Belgique, Acad. Scis. Lisbon, Portugal (corr.), Acad. Scis. France (corr.), Am. Inst. Chemistry, Phi Beta Kappa, Sigma Xi, Sigma Alpha Epsilon, Alpha Chi Sigma, Phi Lambda Upsilon, Phi Kappa Phi. Conglist. Author: Modern Alchemy (with W. A. Noyes, Sr.), 1932; Photochimie et Spectroscopie, 1937; Photochemistry of Gases (with P.A. Leighton), 1941; Traité de Chimie Physique (with H. Weiss) (translation into French of text by E. W. Washburn), 1925; Spectroscopie et les Réactions Initiées par la Lumieré, 1938; Chemistry in World War II. Editor: (with J. N. Pitts, George Hammond) Advances in Photochemistry, vols 1-7, Editor: Chem. Revs., 1939-49, Jour. Am. Chem. Soc., 1950-62, Jour. Phys. Chemistry, 1952-64. Home: 5102 Fairview Dr Austin TX 78731. *No single person, no matter how gifted can make great accomplishments in science or any other field. Ultimately his imprint will only be great if through relatives, friends and colleagues, he obtains not only stimulation but sincere cooperation from them.*

NOZICK, MARTIN, educator; b. N.Y.C., June 28, 1917; s. Solomon and Mary (Seidman) N.; B.A., Bklyn. Coll., 1936; M.A., Columbia, 1943, Ph.D., 1953. Instr., Colgate U., 1946-47, Oberlin (Ohio) Coll., 1947-49; mem. faculty Queens Coll., Flushing, N.Y., 1949—, prof. Romance langs., 1965—, also chmn. dept.; exec. officer Ph.D. program in Spanish, Grad. Center, City U. N.Y., 1974—. Author: Generation of 1898 and After, 1960; Spanish Literature 1700-1900, 1964; Miguel de Unamuno, 1971; Spanish Literature After the Civil War, 1973. Editor: Bollingen Selected Works of Unamuno, 9 vols. Contbr. articles to profl. jours. Home: 420 E 55th St New York City NY 10022 Office: 33 W 42d St New York City NY 10036

NOZICK, ROBERT, educator; b. Bklyn., Nov. 16, 1938; s. Max and Sophie (Cohen) N.; A.B., Columbia, 1959; A.M., Princeton, 1961, Ph.D., 1963; A.M. (hon.), Harvard, 1969; m. Barbara Claire Fierer, Aug. 15, 1959; children—Emily, David. Asst. dir. Social Sci. Research Council Summer Inst., 1962; instr. philosophy Princeton, 1962-63, asst. prof., 1964-65; Fulbright scholar Oxford (Eng.) U., 1963-64; asst. prof. philosophy Harvard, Cambridge, Mass., 1965-67, prof., 1969—; asso. prof. Rockefeller U., 1967-69. Fellow Center Advanced Study Behavorial Scis., 1971-72. Mem. Am. Philos. Assn., Soc. Ethical and Legal Philosophy, Philosophy of Sci. Assn., AAUP, Jewish Vegetarian Soc., Phi Beta Kappa. Author: Anarchy, State, and Utopia, 1974 (Nat. Book award 1975). Bd. editors Philosophy and Pub. Affairs. Contbr. articles to profl. jours. Home: 26 Hillside Terr Belmont MA 02178 Office: Emerson Hall Harvard Univ Cambridge MA 02138

NOZNESKY, HARRY JOSEPH, battery mfg. co. exec.; b. Kennett Sq., Pa., Dec. 21, 1909; s. Jacob and Anna J. (Gralitzer) N.; B.Fgn. Service, Georgetown U., 1933, LL.D.; m. Serena Graul, May 5, 1932; children—Peter H., Serena V., Philip A. Clk., Pa. Co. Banking and Trust, Phila., 1933-35; dist. sales mgr. U.S. Rubber Co., 1935-49; v.p. sales Fox Products Co., 1949-50; pres., dir. Gen. Battery Corp., Reading, Pa., 1950-78, chmn. emeritus, 1978—; dir. Reading Phillies Baseball Club. Bd. dirs. Hawk Mountain council Boy Scouts Am., Chit-Chat Found., Wernersville, Pa.; bd. govs. Georgetown U., Washington, bd. visitors and v.p. Sch. Fgn. Service; trustee Albright Coll., Reading, Pa. Mem. Soc. Automotive Engrs., C. of C. Reading and Berks County (dir. 1964), Mfrs. Assn. Berks County, Battery Council Internat. (bd. dirs., pres. 1973-74). Home: 1198 Reading Blvd Wyomissing PA 19610 Office: Gen Battery Corp PO Box 1262 Reading PA 19603

NUCKOLLS, LEONARD ARNOLD, hosp. adminstr.; b. Park City, Utah, Feb. 22, 1917; s. Harry Leonard and Mabel Hill (Ganson) N.; A.B., Pueblo Jr. Coll., 1938; B.A., U. Colo., 1940; m. Rachel A. Beckner, Apr. 18, 1942; children—Rachel (Mrs. Michael Dale Conine), Peter Leonard. Joined U.S. Army, 1942, advanced through grades to lt. col. 1962; adj. gen. 2d Army Div., Ft. Hood, Tex., 1960-62; ret., 1962; accountant Colo. State Hosp., Pueblo, 1963-64; caseworker N.Mex. Dept. Pub. Welfare, Clovis, 1964-66; unit coordinator N.Mex. Dept. Hosps. and Instns., Las Vegas State Hosp., 1966-69; hosp. adminstr. Las Vegas Med. Center, 1969-76; vol. Internat. Exec. Service Corps; exec. dir. N.Mex. Mental Health Assn. Mem. Am. Hosp. Adminstrs., C. of C., Nursing Home Adminstrs., Ret. Officers Assn., Mensa. Rotarian. Home: 810 Faldas de la Sierra Santa Fe NM 87501

NUCKOLLS, ROBERT THEODORE, cemetery exec.; b. Welch, W.Va., Jan. 30, 1933; s. John Samuel and Maude (Bartee) N.; children—Robert Lance, Mark Theodore. Vice pres. Ft. Lincoln Cemetery, Washington, 1953-63; founder, pres. Eastern Meml. Inc., Wilmington, Del., 1963-69; pres. Cross Mausoleums Funeral Homes Corp., Nashville, 1969-72; exec. v.p. Loudon Park and Druid Ridge Cemeteries, Balt., 1972—; chmn. Md.-D.C. Cemetery Assn. Legis. Com., 1976—. Recipient medallion Am. Inst. Comemorative Art, 1978. Mem. Am., Nat. (mem. faculty schs. and seminars; pres. 1977-78) cemetery assns., Execs. Assn. of Balt. (dir. 1975—). Contbr. numerous articles on cemetery mgmt. and mktg. to trade jours. Home: 6306 N Charles St Baltimore MD 21212 Office: PO Box 2926 Baltimore MD 21229

NUESSE, CELESTINE JOSEPH, ednl. adminstr.; b. Sevastopol, Wis., Nov. 25, 1913; s. George and Salome Helen (Martens) N.; B.E., Central State Tchrs. Coll., Stevens Point, Wis., 1934; M.A., Northwestern U., 1937; Ph.D., Cath. U. Am., 1944; LL.D., Merrimack Coll., 1960; m. Margaret O'Donoghue, 1969. Tchr. social studies Pub. High Sch., Antigo, Wis., 1934-40; instr. sociology Coll. St. Catherine, St. Paul, 1943, Marquette U., 1943-45; instr. Cath. U. Am., Washington, 1945-48, asst. prof., 1948-52, asso. prof. sociology, 1952-64, prof., 1964—, dean Sch. Social Sci., 1952-61, exec. v.p., 1967—, provost, 1967-79. Spl. rep. in Germany, Nat. Cath. Welfare Conf., 1950-51; mem. U.S. Nat. Commn. for UNESCO, 1950-56, 63-69, exec. com., 1954-56, mem. gov. bd. UNESCO Youth Inst., Munich, Germany, 1955-59; mem. U.S. Bd. Fgn. Scholarships, 1954-58, chmn., 1956-58; mem. D.C. Commr.'s Council Human Relations, 1958-64, D.C. Commn. on Postsecondary Edn., 1975—. Mem. Am. Cath. Hist. Assn., Am. Cath. Sociol. Soc. (pres. 1954), Am. Sociol. Assn., Cath. Assn. Internat. Peace (pres. 1954-56), Cath. Commn. Intellectual and Cultural Affairs, Inst. Internat. Sociologie, Internat. Conf. on Sociology of Religion (past v.p.), Nat. Cath. Ednl. Assn., Cath. Interracial Council Washington (pres. 1962-66), Phi Beta Kappa (hon.), Alpha Kappa Delta, Pi Gamma Mu, Sigma Tau Delta, Phi Sigma Epsilon. K.C. Club: Cosmos (Washington). Author: The Social Thought of American Catholics, 1634-1829, 1945. Co-author, co-editor: The Sociology of the Parish, 1951. Staff editor New Cath. Ency., 1963-66, chmn. editorial bd. supplements, 1973-79. Contbr. articles to profl. jours. Home: 3016 Edgewater Dr Edgewater MD 21037

NUGENT, BILL ALLEN, univ. ofcl.; b. Courtland, Ala., Sept. 26, 1934; s. M.A. and Velma Gertrude (Randolph) N.; Mus.B., So. Meth. U., 1956, Mus.M., 1957; Ph.D. in Musicology, No. Tex. State U., 1970; m. Dorothy Campbell, July 22, 1957. Faculty, So. Meth. U., 1956-57, Samford U., Birmingham, Ala., 1957-59, N.Tex. State U., Denton, 1959-61; head dept. music Emporia (Kans.) State U., 1961-71; dir. Sch. Music, U. Okla., 1971-74, also chmn. projects to establish Guy Fraser Harrison Endowed Chair and Ritter Research Lab.; dean Coll. Scis. and Arts, Wash. State U., Pullman, 1974-79; v.p. for acad. affairs W.Va. U., Morgantown, 1980—. HEW grantee, 1964-71; Ind. U. Hist. Insts. lectr. throughout Europe and Mediterranean, 1969-71. Active, Nat. Council on Philanthropy, N.Central Assn.; advisory council Edward R. Murrow Symposia on World Freedoms; cons. Nat. Endowment for Humanities, Ministry of Edn. Republic of China; pres., bd. dirs. Wash.-Idaho Symphony Assn.; bd. dirs. Oklahoma City Symphony Soc., Mus. Makah Indian Nation; trustee Wash. Commn. for Humanities. Mem. Pi Kappa Lambda, Kappa Kappa Psi, Tau Beta Sigma, Phi Mu Alpha. Methodist. Club: Rotary Internat. Author: Music and the Arts, An Odyssey, 1971. Editor: Oklahoma Tenor, 1973; The Collected Works of Antonius Divitis, 1980. Office: Adminstrn Bldg WVa U Morgantown WV 26506

NUGENT, D. EUGENE, paper co. exec.; b. Chgo., Dec. 18, 1927; s. Daniel Edward and Pearl A. (Trieger) N.; B.S. in Mech. Engring., Northwestern U., 1951; m. Bonnie Lynn Weidman, July 1, 1950; children—Cynthia Lynn, Mark Alan, Dale Alan. With U.S. Gypsum Co., Chgo., 1951-70, dir. corp. devel., to 1970; pres. Am. Louver Co., Chgo., 1970-73; v.p. ops. ITT Corp., Cleve., 1973-75, exec. v.p., St. Paul; pres., chief exec. officer Pentair, Inc., St. Paul, 1975—, also dir.; dir. Niagara of Wis. Paper Corp., Flembeau Paper Corp., Mariners Cove, Inc. Vice chmn. local planning commn., 1968-72; vice chmn., trustee Harper Coll., Chgo., 1970-74. Served with AUS, 1946-47. Mem. ASME, Am. Mgmt. Assn. Republican. Presbyterian. Club: N. Oaks Golf. Office: 1700 W Hwy 36 Saint Paul MN 55113

NUGENT, DANIEL PAUL, valve and pipe co. exec.; b. Harrison, N.J., Oct. 7, 1925; s. James Edward and Helen Marie (McDonald) N.; Alfred Barnes Palmer scholar, Yale U., 1946-49; m. Margorie Magnier, June 18, 1949; children—Mary, James, Daniel Paul, Anthony, Catherine, Sheila, Christopher. Pres., chief exec. officer, dir. ITT Grinnell Corp., Providence, 1974—; pres. Phelps Dodge Brass Co., N.Y.C.; v.p., gen. mgr. Crane U.S.A., N.Y.C.; corporate v.p., gen. mgr. L.A. Darling Co., Bronson, Mich.; dir. ITT Industries, ITT Ltd. of Can., NTCC Co., Peninsular Supply Co., Kennedy Valve Co., M & M Supply Co., Jones-Newby Co., No. Power Co., ITT Rayonier B.C., Grinnell de Mex. Pres., Convent Assn., 1959-62; vice chmn. United Way, 1974; mem. Com. for Yale U., 1977; trustee Morristown Mus., N.Y. U. Grad. Sch. Retailing, 1965-69, Oak Knoll Sch.; mem. council Providence Coll. Served with inf., AUS, 1943-46. Decorated Bronze Star medal. Mem. Copper Devel. Assn., Copper and Brass Inst., Valve Mfrs. Assn., Am. Supply Assn. Roman Catholic. Clubs: Yale (N.Y.C.), Mory's Assn., Morris County Golf, Watch Hill Yacht, Misquamicut Golf, Serra (pres. 1953-56), Yale of N.J. (dir.). Home: Spring Valley Rd Morristown NJ 07960 Office: 260 W Exchange St Providence RI 02901

NUGENT, BROTHER GREGORY, educator; b. Troy, N.Y., Oct. 17, 1911; s. Harry Bartholomew and Margaret (Woods) Nugent; student Manhattan Coll., N.Y.C., 1929-30; A.B., Cath. U. Am., 1934; A.M., N.Y.U., 1939, Ph.D., 1945; LL.D., Manhattanville Coll., 1963, Iona Coll., 1963; D.R.E., Providence Coll., 1971; L.H.D., Pace U., 1973; Litt. D., Coll. of Mt. St. Vincent, 1975. Entered Inst. of Bros. Christian Schs., 1930; instr. langs. De La Salle Inst., N.Y.C., 1934-46; asst. prof. German, Manhattan (N.Y.) Coll., 1946-50, asso. prof., 1950-51, prof. 1951-75, asst. dean liberal arts program, 1951-52, dean sch. arts and sci., 1952-59, acad. v.p., 1959-62, pres., 1962-75; spl. asst. to pres. Cath. U. Am., 1975—. Trustee Coll. Entrance Exam. Bd., 1962-65; mem. N.Y. State Adv. Council on Higher Edn., 1963-67; mem. Regents Regional Coordinating Council for Postsecondary Edn., N.Y.C., 1973. Bd. govs. Coll. of Mt. St. Vincent, 1965-68, trustee, 1968—; trustee Cath. U. Am., 1968-75, Manhattan Coll., 1959-75, La Salle Coll., 1969—. Recipient Mother Scholastica Meml. award Medaille Coll., 1966. Mem. Middle States Assn. (com. instns. higher edn., trustee), Am. Council Edn. (com. Fed. Relations), Assn. Am. Colls. (com. religion higher edn.), Council Higher Ednl. Instns. N.Y.C. (dir. 1962-64, 67-75), Assn. Colls. and Univs. State N.Y. (mem. exec. com.), Religious Edn. Assn. (dir. 1959-77), Modern Lang. Assn., Am. Assn. Tchrs. German, Cath. Renascence Soc. (asst. treas., bd. dirs. 1952-54), Nat. Cath. Edn. Assn. (vice pres. coll. and univ. dept. 1962-64, pres. 1964-66, mem. gen. exec. bd. 1966-73), Internat. Assn. U. Profs., N.Y. Acad. of Pub. Edn., Am. Assn. for Higher Edn., Assn. Modern Lang. Tchrs. Middle States (pres. 1949), Am. Conf. Acad. Deans, Christian Bros. Edn. Assn., Eastern Assn. Coll. Deans. Author: Catholicism in Schiller's Dramas, 1949. Office: Catholic Univ Am Washington DC 20064

NUGENT, JAMES MILFORD, engring. and constrn. co. exec.; b. Audubon, N.J., May 9, 1926; s. Harry Roden and Mary Ellen (McDowell) N.; B.S.C.E., Drexel U., 1957; m. Jane Alice Maconaghy, June 12, 1948; children—Gary, Margaret, John. Structural engr. United Engrs. and Constructors, 1950-53; project mgr. Catalytic, Inc., 1953-60; v.p. engring. Day and Zimmermann, Inc., 1960-70; group v.p. Jacobs Engring. Co., 1970-74; pres., chief exec. officer Barnard and Burk, Inc., Pasadena, Calif., 1974—. Served with USMC, 1943-46. Mem. Nat. Soc. Profl. Engrs., Am. Inst. Chem. Engrs., ASCE, Pasadena C. of C. Republican. Club: San Gabriel Country, Jonathan, Town Hall. Home: 1223 Sherwood Rd San Marino CA 91108 Office: 150 S Los Robles Ave Pasadena CA 91101

NUGENT, JOSEPH C., stock broker; b. N.Y.C., Sept. 25, 1903; s. Henry J. and Mary Henrietta (Clark) N.; A.B. in Econs., Columbia, 1925; L.H.D., Marymount Manhattan Coll., 1970; m. Kathleen M. Dolan, Nov. 19, 1927 (dec.); children—Barbara (Mrs. Donald P. Bovers), Constance (Mrs. James R. McQuade), Joseph C. With Whitney & Co., stocks and bonds, 1925-38; with Mabon & Co. (firm name changed to Mabon, Nugent & Co. 1965), N.Y.C., 1938—, partner, 1941, now ltd. partner; former mem. N.Y. State Banking Bd. Vice pres. Cardinal's Com. of Laity; chmn. bd. trustees Marymount Manhattan Coll.; pres. Cath. Youth Orgn., N.Y.; trustee Cath. Charities; treas. Roman Cath. Orphan Asylum. Decorated knight comdr. Order of Holy Sepulchre of Jerusalem, Knight of Malta. Mem. Friendly Sons of St. Patrick (past pres.), John Jay Assos. of Columbia. Clubs: Bond, World Trade Center (N.Y.C.); Spring Lake Golf; Spring Lake Bath and Tennis. Home: 16 Sutton Pl New York NY 10022 Office: 115 Broadway New York NY 10006

NUGENT, RICHARD JOSEPH, JR., photojournalist; b. Louisville, Apr. 21, 1949; s. Richard Joseph and Virginia Ewing (Cronan) N.; B.S. in Bus. Adminstrn., Babson Coll., Wellesley, Mass., 1971. Photojournalist, Courier Jour. and Louisville Times, 1971-73, Courier Jour. and Times Sunday mag., 1973—. Pres. bd. dirs. Westport (Ky.) Fire Dept., 1973—. Co-recipient Pulitzer prize, 1975; named Coll. Photographer of Year, Nat. Press Photographers Assn., 1971, recipient Picture of Year award, 1972-75. Home: 7200 Hwy 524 Westport KY 40077 Office: 525 W Broadway Louisville KY 40202

NUGENT, VINCENT JOSEPH, clergyman; b. Phila., July 30, 1913; s. Frank J. and Mary (McCullagh) N.; B.A., St. Joseph's Coll., Princeton, N.J., 1937; student St. Vincent's Sem., Germantown, Phila., 1937-39, Mary Immaculate Sem., Northampton, Pa., 1939-42; S.T.D., Cath. U. Am. Ordained priest Roman Cath. Ch., 1942; mem. faculty Mary Immaculate Sem., 1944-45, prof. spl. dogmatic theology, 1945-53; established dept. sacred sci. St. John's U., 1953, chmn. grad., undergrad. dept. theology, 1957-65, lectr., dir. Mariological Inst., 1958-65; asst. to Most Rev. Fulton J. Sheen, Soc. for Propagation of the Faith, N.Y.C., 1965—; theol. cons. to U.S. del. World Synod of Bishops, Rome, 1974. Mem. Cath. Theol. Soc. Am. (dir., v.p., sec.), Cath. Mariological Soc. Am. (dir.), Soc. Cath. Coll. Tchrs. Sacred Doctrine (regional dir. N.Y.). Author: Concept of Charity in the Writings of St. Gregory the Great, 1949; Modernism, 1955. Contbr. articles to theol., ecclesiastical jours. Compiler: Directory Am. Cath. Theologians, 1963, 2d edit., 1965. Home: 109 E 38th St New York NY Office: 366 Fifth Ave New York NY 10001

NUGENT, WALTER TERRY KING, educator; b. Watertown, N.Y., Jan. 11, 1935; s. Clarence A. and Florence (King) N.; A.B. cum laude, St. Benedict's Coll., 1954, D.Litt., 1968; M.A., Georgetown U., 1956; Ph.D., U. Chgo., 1961; m. Katherine A. Cleary, Aug. 20, 1955; children—Katherine, Rachel, David, Douglas, Walter Terry King, Mary Sourire. Instr. history Washburn U., 1957-58; asst. prof. Am. history Kans. State U., 1961-63; asst. prof. history Ind. U., 1963-64, asso. prof., 1964-68, prof., 1968—, asso. dean Coll. Arts and Scis., 1967-71, asso. dean overseas study, 1972-76, acting chmn. dept. Near Eastern langs. and lit., 1968-69, chmn. history dept., 1974-77; editorial cons. publishers, also jours., 1963—. Newberry Library fellow, 1962; Guggenheim fellow, 1964-65; Fulbright vis. prof. Hebrew U. Jerusalem, 1978-79; Nat. Endowment for Humanities grantee, 1979; Nat. Endowment for Humanities-Huntington Library fellow, 1979. Mem. Am. Hist. Assn., Orgn. Am. Historians, Authors Guild Am., Authors League Am. Roman Catholic. Author: The Tolerant Populists, 1963; Creative History, 1967, 2d edit., 1973; The Money Question During Reconstruction, 1967; Money and American Society 1865-1880, 1968; Modern America, 1973; From Centennial to World War: American Society 1876-1917, 1977. Home: 219 E 8th St Bloomington IN 47401

NULAND, JAMES GREENBURY, corp. exec.; b. Tientsin, China, Mar. 19, 1925; s. Lester Hall and Robbie (Stewart) N.; B.A., Harvard, 1945, M.B.A., 1948; m. Kathleen FitzGibbon, June 30, 1951; children—Patricia, James Greenbury, Timothy, Christopher. With Loeb Rhoades Co., N.Y.C., 1948-56; partner Treves Co., also pres. Petrol Oil and Gas Co., 1956-61; partner F.S. Smithers & Co., N.Y.C., 1961-70; sr. v.p. Stone & Webster Securities, 1970-73; v.p. Burmah Oil Inc., N.Y.C., 1973—, Burmah Oil Tankers Ltd., 1975—; v.p., treas. Wylain, Dallas, 1976-78; v.p. Halliburton Co., 1978—. Served to lt. (j.g.) USNR, 1941-46. Clubs: Bent Tree, Petroleum (Dallas); Harvard (N.Y.C.). Home: 7020 Teakwood Dr Dallas TX 75240 Office: 2600 Southland Center Dallas TX 75201

NULTY, LAWRENCE FREDERICK, architect; b. Chgo., Aug. 26, 1921; s. Francis Edward and Hazel (Tuch) N.; student Sch. Art Inst. Chgo., 1946-47; M.Arch., Yale, 1952; m. Helena Gray Smith, Feb. 12, 1945; children—Christopher Tuch, Nicholas Richard. Archtl. draftsman Friedman, Alschular & Sincere, Chgo., 1945-46, Haarstick Lundgren Assos., St. Paul, 1952-54, Samuel Glaser Assos., Boston, 1955; architect, mng. partner Campbell, Aldrich & Nulty, Boston, 1955-74; partner Nulty Merithew Palk & Sterling Partnership, Boston. 1974—; lectr. archtl. design U. Minn., 1952-54; prin. works include Dartmouth Coll. bldgs., Derby Acad. bldgs., Grad. Research Center for U. Mass., Army Precision Photogrammetric Bldg., Washington, transit stas. for Mass. Bay Transit Authority, First Nat. Bank Boston office bldg. Mem. Nat. Council Archtl. Registration Bds. Area chmn. United Fund, Wellesley, Mass., 1957. Served with USAAF, 1942-45; ETO, MTO. Decorated Bronze Star medal. Fellow Royal Soc. Arts (London); mem. A.I.A., Boston Soc. Architects. Home: 15 Whittier Rd Wellesley MA 02181 Office: 177 Custom House Plaza Boston MA 02109

NUNES, GORDON MAXWELL, educator, painter; b. Porterville, Calif., Aug. 1, 1914; s. John J. and Minnie (Witt) N. With Douglas Aircraft Engring Co., 1941-45; creator animated cartoons, 1937-41; mem. faculty U. Calif. at Los Angeles, 1948—, now prof. painting. Paintings exhbt. throughout U.S., 1950—. Mem. Inst. Creative Art, 1963, 67. Home: 150 S Burlingame Ave Los Angeles CA 90049

NUNIS, DOYCE BLACKMAN, JR., historian; b. Cedartown, Ga., May 30, 1924; s. Doyce Blackman and Winnie Ethel (Morris) N.; B.A., U. Calif., Los Angeles, 1947; M.S., U. So. Calif., 1950, M.Ed., 1952, Ph.D., 1958. Lectr. U. So. Calif., 1951-56, asso. prof. history, 1965-68, profl., 1968—; instr. El Camino Coll., 1956-59; asst. research historian U. Calif., Los Angeles, 1959-63, asso., 1963-65, lectr., 1960-61, asst. prof. edn. and history, 1961-64, asso. prof. 1964-65. Mem. Los Angeles Mayor's Com. to Preserve History of Los Angeles, 1961-63; bd. dirs. Mission Santa Barbara Archive-Library, 1970—. Del Amo Found. grantee, 1956; Henry E. Huntington Library grantee-in-aid, 1960; Guggenheim fellow, 1963-64; Am. Philos. Soc. grantee, 1969. Mem. Hist. Soc. So. Calif. (dir. 1962-65), Am. Hist. Assn., Orgn. Am. Historians, Calif. Hist. Soc., Am. Soc. Legal History, AAUP, Phi Alpha Theta, Pi Sigma Alpha. Author: Andrew Sublette, Rocky Mountain Prince, 1960; Josiah Belden, 1841 California Overland Pioneer, 1962; The Golden Frontier; The Recollections of Herman Francis Rinehart, 1851-69, 1962; The California Diary of Faxon Dean Atherton, 1936-39, 1964; Letters of a Young Miner, 1964; The Journal of James H. Bull, 1965; The Trials of Isaac Graham, 1967; The Medical Journey of Pierre Garnier in California, 1851, 1967; Past is Prologue, 1968; Hudson's Bay Company's First Fur Brigade to the Sacramento Valley, 1968; Sketches of a Journey on Two Oceans by H.J.A.Alric, 1850-1867, 1971; San Francisco 1856 Vigilance Committee: Three Views, 1971; A Jesuit Artist in Baja California, 1972; Los Angeles and Its Environs in the 20th Century, A Bibliography, 1973; A History of American Political Thought, 2 vols., 1975; The Mexican War in Baja California, 1977; editor So. Calif. Quar., 1962—; contbr. articles to profl. jours. Home: 4426 Cromwell Ave Los Angeles CA 90027

NUNIS, RICHARD ARLEN, amusement parks exec.; b. Cedartown, Ga., May 30, 1932; s. Doyce Blackman and Winnie E. (Morris) N.; B.S. in Edn., U. So. Calif., 1955; m. June Elaine Kirk, June 13, 1954; children—Lisa Lea (dec.), Richard Dean. With Walt Disney Prodns., 1955—, mem. supervisory and mgmt. staff Disneyland, Calif., 1955-61, dir. ops., 1961-68, chmn. park ops. com., 1968-74, corporate v.p. Disneyland ops., 1968—, Walt Disney World, Orlando, Fla., 1971—, exec. v.p. Disneyland and Walt Disney World, 1972—; mem. adv. bd. Anaheim (Calif.) br. Bank of Am. Mem. bus. and industry adv. bd. Pres.'s Council on Phys. Fitness and Sports; bd. dirs. Jr. Achievement, Jr. Achievement So. Calif. Mem. Nat. Alliance Businessmen, Orange County Metro (adv. bd.). Republican. Methodist. First academic All-American, U. So. Calif., 1952. Office: 1313 Harbor Blvd Anaheim CA 92803. *Do the best job you can with* *the job you are given to do. Those who look over the hill never climb the mountain.*

NUNN, GRADY HARRISON, educator; b. Arlington, Tex., Apr. 12, 1918; s. William Roy and Floy Brooke (Dugan) N.; B.A., U. Okla., 1939, M.A., 1941; Ph.D. (Penfield fellow), N.Y.U., 1961; m. Ann Torrey Welsh, June 15, 1951; 1 dau., Therese von Hohoff. Instr., N.Y.U., 1946-49; from instr. to asso. prof. U. Ala., Tuscaloosa, 1949-65; prof., chmn. dept. polit. sci. U. Ala., Birmingham, 1969—; vis. asst. prof. Ind. U., 1960-61; asst. prof., asso. prof. U. Pitts. at Ahmadu Bello U., Nigeria, 1964-68; asso. prof. U. Pitts., 1968; asso. prof. Auburn U., 1968-69. Fellow Inter-Univ. Seminar Armed Forces and Soc.; bd. dirs. Unitarian Universalist Service Com., 1978—. Served to capt., F.A., AUS, 1942-46. Ford Found. Fgn. Area fellow, 1956-57. Fellow African Studies Assn.; mem. Africa Bur., Internat., Am., So. (exec. council 1974-77) polit. sci. assns., Am. Soc. Internat. Law, Internat. Studies Assn., Royal African Soc., AAUP (pres. Ala. conf.), Phi Beta Kappa, Pi Sigma Alpha, Phi Eta Sigma, Alpha Tau Omega, Omicron Delta Kappa. Unitarian. Asso. editor Background on World Politics, 1957-62. Contbr. to Readings in Government in American Society, 1949; Federalism in the Commonwealth, 1963; The Politics and Administration of Nigerian Government, 1965; editorial bd. Jour. of Politics, 1971-74. Home: 740 Linwood Rd Birmingham AL 35222

NUNN, LOUIE B., lawyer, former gov. of Ky.; b. Mar. 8, 1924; ed. Bowling Green Bus. U., U. Cin.; LL.B., U. Louisville; m. Buela Cornelius Aspley; 2 children. Elected judge Barren County (Ky.), 1953; mgr. Eisenhower-Cooper-Morton campaign, 1956, Cooper, Nixon, and Morton campaigns, 1960, 62; gov. State of Ky., 1967-71; mem. firm Nunn, Odear & Arnold, Lexington, Ky. Past pres. Glasgow (Ky.) PTA; past dist. pres. Ky. Welfare Assn. Del. Republican Nat. Conv., 1968, 72, 76. Served with AUS, World War II. Named One of 3 Outstanding Young Men of Ky., 1956. Mem. Am. Legion (past comdr.), C. of C. (past v.p.). Mason (33 deg.), Rotarian (past v.p.). Mem. Christian Ch. (chmn. bd. elders). Office: Nunn Odear & Arnold 1300 First Nat Bldg Lexington KY 40507 & Arnold 1300 First Nat Bldg Lexington KY 40507*

NUNN, SAM, U.S. senator; b. Perry, Ga., Sept. 8, 1938; s. Samuel Augustus and Elizabeth (Cannon) N.; student Ga. Tech. Coll., 1956-59; LL.B., Emory U., 1962; m. Colleen O'Brien, Sept. 25, 1965; children—Michelle, Brian. Admitted to Ga. bar, 1962; legal counsel armed services com. U.S. Ho. Reps., 1963; mem. firm Nunn, Geiger & Rampey, Perry, Ga., 1964-73; mem. Ga. Ho. Reps., 1968-72; U.S. senator from Ga., 1973—, mem. Armed Services Com., Govtl. Affairs Com., Select Com. Small Bus.; farmer, Perry, 1964—. Named One of Five Outstanding Young Men in Ga. by Ga. Jaycees, 1971; recipient Most Effective Legislator award Dist. Attys. Assn., 1972. Mem. Perry C. of C. (pres. 1964), Ga. Planning Assn. (dir. 1966, pres. 1971). Office: 3241 Dirksen Senate Office Bldg Washington DC 20510

NUNNELEY, EMORY TRUFANT, lawyer; b. Mt. Clemens, Mich., Sept. 16, 1908; s. Emory Trufant and Anna M. (Dalby) N.; A.B., U. Mich., 1930; LL.B., Harvard, 1933; m. Faithe D. Shaw, Jan. 13, 1935; 1 dau., Sarah Ann. Admitted to N.Y. bar, 1934, Minn. and D.C. bars, 1955; mem. firm Root, Clark, Buckner and Ballantine, N.Y.C., 1933-39; atty. CAB, 1939-42, asst. gen. counsel, 1942-46, gen. counsel, 1946-55; gen. counsel Investors Diversified Services, Inc., Mpls., 1955-60; v.p., gen. counsel Northwest Air Lines, St. Paul, 1960-69; counsel firm Kaler, Worsley, Daniel and Hollman, Washington, 1970—. Chmn. legal com. Internat. Civil Aviation Orgn., 1950, U.S. del. annual assemblies, 1947-48, 50; chmn. U.S. del. Internat. Conf. on Rome Conv., 1952. Served in Naval Air Trans. Service, USN, 1944-45. Mem. Am., D.C. bar assns., Phi Beta Kappa. Clubs: Belle Haven Courtry; Internat. Aviation (Washington). Home: 1952 Marthas Rd Alexandria VA 22307 Office: Ring Bldg Washington DC 20036

NUNNEMACHER, RUDOLPH FINK, educator, zoologist; b. Milw., Mar. 21, 1912; s. Henry Jacob and Gertrude Anita (Fink) N.; B.Sc., Kenyon Coll., 1934; M.A., Harvard, 1936, Ph.D., 1938; m. Sylvia Acken Hendricks, Dec. 29, 1938 (dec. Feb. 3, 1975); children—Robert, Sallie, Gretl, Dorothea; m. 2d, Doris C. Adams, Aug. 9, 1975. Instr. in histology Okla. U. Med. Sch., 1938-39; mem. faculty Clark U., Worcester, Mass., 1939—, prof. zoology, 1956—, chmn. dept. biology, 1958-76, dir. Evening Coll., 1953-54, dir. Summer Sch., 1954-56. spl. research comparative study electron microscopy nerves. Mem. Sutton Sch. Com., 1966-69, chmn., 1972-75. Trustee Bermuda Biol. Sta. Mem. Am. Soc. Zoology, Electron Microscopy Soc. Am., Sigma Xi. Home: Putnam Hill Rd Sutton MA 01527 Office: Clark Univ Worcester MA 01610

NUREYEV, RUDOLF HAMETOVICH, dancer; b. Russia, Mar. 17, 1938; ballet tng. Lenigrad Ballet Sch. Joined Kirov Ballet, Leningrad, 1955, soloist, 1958, danced leading classical roles; defected May 1961; joined Ballet of Marquis de Cuevas, 1961; London debuts, charity gala, Giselle with Margot Fonteyn and Royal Ballet, 1962; Am. debut on Bell Telephone Hour TV with Maria Tallchief, with Ruth Page and Chgo. Opera Ballet, 1962; has appeared as guest artist with 25 companies including Am. Ballet Theatre, Australian Ballet, Colon Theatre Ballet, Deutsche Opera Ballet, Berlin, Dutch Nat. Ballet, Nat. Ballet Canada, Paris Opera Ballet, Royal Danish Ballet, others; choreographic prodns. include La Bayadere, Raymonda, Swan Lake, Tancredi, Sleeping Beauty, Nutcracker, Don Quixote, Don Juan, Giselle, Romeo and Juliet; films include Evening with Royal Ballet, Romeo and Juliet, I Am a Dancer, Don Quixote, Valentino. Address: care SA Gorlinsky Ltd 35 Dover St London W1 England

NURICK, GILBERT, lawyer; b. Hickory Corners, Pa., Nov. 23, 1906; s. Charles and Anna (Katz) N.; A.B., Pa. State U., 1928; LL.B., Dickinson Sch. Law, 1931, LL.D., 1967; m. Sylvia Krauss, Oct. 14, 1932 (dec. Jan. 1965); children—Carl J., Herbert R. Admitted to Pa. bar, 1931, since practiced in Harrisburg; partner firm McNees, Wallace & Nurick, and predecessors, 1931-59, sr. partner, 1959-78, of counsel, 1978—; adv. bd. Commonwealth Nat. Bank; dir. Hershey Foods Corp., 1965-71; adj. prof. law Dickinson Sch. Law, 1975—. Chmn. Disciplinary Bd. Supreme Ct. Pa., 1972-75. Pres. Tri-county United Fund, 1957, United Jewish Community, Harrisburg, 1947-48. Bd. dirs. Polyclinic Med. Center, 1954—, Family and Children's Service Bur., Harrisburg, 1961-64; trustee The Hershey Fund, 1965-71. Served with USNR, 1943-45. Decorated Commendation ribbon and citation; recipient Distinguished Alumni award Pa. State U. 1968; Outstanding Alumnus award Dickinson Sch. Law, 1975. Fellow Am. Bar Found.; mem. Am. (ho. of dels. 1966-67), Pa. (chmn. sect. jud. adminstrn. 1963-64, bd. govs. 1964-68, pres. 1967, Disting. Service medal 1978), Dauphin County (pres. 1949-50) bar assns., Am. Law Inst., Harrisburg Area C. of C. (dir. 1958), Pa. C. of C. (dir. 1972—). Author articles. Home: Park-Scottsdale Apts Harrisburg PA 17111 Office: 100 Pine St Harrisburg PA

NURMI, MARTIN KARL, educator; b. Duluth, Minn., Sept. 4, 1920; s. Kalle Alexander and Maiju (Onkka) N.; student Superior (Wis.) State U., 1939-40, 41-42; M.A., U. Chgo., 1948; Ph.D., U. Minn., 1954; postgrad. Princeton U., 1954-55; m. Ruth Elizabeth Swanson, June 14, 1944 (div. June 1979); children—Michael, Katherine, Susan; m. 2d, Mary Ellen Gilpatric, June 1979. Electronics engr. Belmont Radio Corp., 1944-45; instr. English, Florence (Ala.) State Coll., 1948-49, U. N.D., 1952-54; mem. faculty Kent (Ohio) State U., 1955—, prof. English, 1963—, dean Grad. Sch., 1964-68, chmn. dept. English, 1971-75; vis. asso. prof. U. Wash., summer 1962, U. Minn., 1962-63; vis. prof. Mich. State U., summer 1966, U. B.C., summer 1967. Recipient Faculty fellow award Fund Advancement Edn., 1954-55, Pres.'s medal Kent State U., 1977. Mem. AAUP, Modern Lang. Assn. Author: Blake's Marriage of Heaven and Hell; A Critical Study, 1957; (with G.E. Bentley, Jr.) A Blake Bibliography, 1964; (with C.S. Felver) Poetry; An Introduction and Anthology, 1967; William Blake, 1975; also articles. Home: 1400 Ridgecrest Dr Kent OH 44240

NURNBERGER, JOHN IGNATIUS, physician; b. Chgo., Apr. 9, 1916; s. L.L. and Anna M. (Burke) N.; B.S., Loyola U., 1938; M.S. (Frederick Robert Zeit fellow), Northwestern U., 1942; B.M., 1942, M.D., 1943; D.Sc. (hon.), Marion Coll., 1958; m. Mary Cornelia McNulty, Aug. 21, 1943; children—John, Joanna, Raul, David, Cornelia. Research fellow cytochemistry of nervous system Med. Nobel Inst. Cell Research and Genetics, Stockholm, Sweden, 1949-50; resident in neurology and neuropathology N.Y. Neurol. Inst., 1946-48; dir. labs., chief cyto-chemistry lab. Inst. Living, Hartford, Conn., later ednl. dir.; former asst. clin prof. medicine (neurology) and psychiatry Yale Sch. Medicine; prof., chmn. dept. psychiatry, former acting dean Ind. U. Med. Sch., Indpls., Distinguished Univ. prof., 1972—, also dir. Inst. Psychiat. Research, Ind. U. Med. Center. Former mem. tng. com. basic biol. scis. Nat. Inst. Mental Health. Chmn. bd. dirs. St. Meinrad Coll. and Sch. Theology; bd. dirs. Found. Fund For Research in Psychiatry. Served from capt. to maj. M.C., AUS, 1943-46. Fellow Am. Psychiat. Assn.; mem. Central Neuropsychiat. Assn., Soc. for Biol. Psychiatry, Assn. for Research Nervous and Mental Diseases, Am. Neurol. Assn., Alpha Kappa Kappa, Alpha Omega Alpha. Mem. editorial bd. Jour. Nervous and Mental Diseases, Biological Psychiatry. Home: 5215 Washington Blvd Indianapolis IN 46220 Office: 1100 W Michigan St Indianapolis IN 46202

NUSS, ELDON PAUL, metal component parts mfr.; b. Sumner, Iowa, Apr. 24, 1933; s. Paul John and Helen (Nolting) N.; student Grinnell Coll., 1950; B.S. with highest honors, U. Iowa, 1954; student Harvard, 1971; m. Carolyn Ann Krug, June 6, 1959; children—Susan Elizabeth, Laurie Ann. With Arthur Young & Co., C.P.A.'s, 1957-68, prin., Houston, 1967-68; v.p. Marathon Mfg. Co., Houston, 1969-71, exec. v.p., dir., 1972-75; pres., chief exec. officer PMI Industries, Houston, 1975—. Served with USNR, 1955-57. Mem. Assn. for Corporate Growth (dir. Houston chpt.). Am. Inst. C.P.A.'s. Lutheran (council 1966-67). Club: Lakeside Country. Home: 327 Knipp Forest Houston TX 77024 Office: 1770 St James Pl Houston TX 77056

NUSSBAUM, MURRAY, physician; b. Bklyn., May 19, 1927; s. Jacob and Ida (Witkoff) N.; B.S., U. Vt., 1949, M.D., 1952; m. Sue-Carol Ludacer, Apr. 3, 1954; children—Jonathan David, Robert Alan. Intern, New Eng. Med. Center, Boston, 1952-53; resident Boston City Hosp., 1953-54; asst. in medicine Tufts U. Med. Sch., Boston, 1955-56; instr. in medicine Seton Hall Coll. Medicine, Jersey City, 1957-59; asst. prof. medicine Coll. Medicine and Dentistry, N.J. Med. Sch., Newark, 1959-66, asso. prof., 1966-70, prof. medicine, 1970—; dir. hematology div. N.J. Med. Sch. Served with AUS, 1945-47, USPHS research fellow in hematology, 1954-55. Diplomate Am. Bd. Internal Medicine. Fellow A.C.P., Internat. Soc. Hematology; mem. Am. Soc. Hematology, Am. Heart Assn. (council on Thrombosis). Democrat. Jewish. Author: Understanding Hematology, 1973; contbr. research articles to jours. Home: 397 Terhune Dr Wayne NJ 07470 Office: 174 Union St Ridgewood NJ 07450

NUTT, THOMAS JOSEPH, chem. co. exec.; b. River Rouge, Mich., Oct. 22, 1933; s. Frank George and Mary Louise (Hodges) N.; B.S., Eastern Mich. U., 1955; M.B.A., U. Detroit, 1958; postgrad. in corp. fin. mgmt. Harvard U., 1978; m. Kathleen M. Perlich, Jan. 26, 1974; children by previous marriage—Thomas, Mark, Julie, Jeff, Lisa. With Ford Motor Co., 1955-67; dir. accounting and fin. Cleve. Pneumatic Tool Co., 1967-68; controller auto products Rockwell Internat., 1968-71; v.p. fin., pres. J & H Internat., Niles, Ill., 1971-73; treas. Richardson Co., Des Plaines, Ill., 1973-76, v.p., treas., 1976, v.p. fin. treas., chief fin. officer, 1977—. Mem. Fin. Execs. Inst., Nat. Assn. Accountants, Assn. for Corp. Growth. Roman Catholic. Home: 723 E High Ridge Rd Roselle IL 60172 Office: 2400 E Devon Ave Des Plaines IL 60018

NUTTER, CHARLES ARMEL, Realtor; b. Milford, Del., Nov. 13, 1900; s. Charles and Mary (Polk) N.; B.S., U. Del., 1923; postgrad. Temple U., South Jersey law schs., 1926-27; m. Helen Wertsner, Oct. 27, 1927; children—Charles Armel, Patricia Ann (Mrs. Edgar B. Cutter), Helen N. (Mrs. Leo McChesney), Nancy V. (Mrs. William M.E. Powers, Jr.), Joan E. (Mrs. Samuel P. Collins, Jr.). Pres. Nutter Mortgage Service, Phila. and Camden, N.J., 1931-74. Pres. Camden County Real Estate Bd., 1936, chmn., mem. numerous coms., 1945-59; mem. Pa. Bd. Realtors; vice-chmn. Nat. Assn. Com. Phila. Bd. Realtors, 1952, 56, 57, mem. Nat. Assn. Com., 1947-48, 54-55, 66-70; mem. U.S. Vol. Home Mortgage Credit Program 1954-59, 61-63; mem. FHA Industry Adv. Com. on Coops., 1955. Chmn. Ann. Drive Cooper Hosp., 1953; mem. Industry Adv. Com. Moorestown, N.J., 1968-73. Recipient Morton Bodfish award Soc. Residential Appraisers, 1959, award N.Y. U. Grad. Sch. Bus. Adminstrn., 1968, service appreciation award Can. Real Estate Assn., 1975. Mem. Nat. Assn. Real Estate Bds. (regional v.p. 1947, nat. membership chmn. 1947-48, mem. exec. com. 1951-60, treas., chmn. finance com. 1956-59, pres. 1960, dir. 1947-79, mem. operational survey com. 1969-70, 78—, mem. Realtors' Washington com. 1952, 54-66, 68-72, exchange dir. for Can. 1963, 64, 68), Internat. Real Estate Fedn. (treas. Am. chpt. 1956-59, v.p. Am. chpt. 1969, pres. Am. chpt. 1970, bd. govs., medal of honor 1971, 74), Féderation Internationale des Professions Immobilieres (dir. 1965-79, mem. exec. com. 1941-53, gov. 1941-53, recipient Honor award 1970), mortgage bankers assns., Am. (gov., mem. exec. com. 1941-53, regional v.p. 1947-48, mem. mortgage bankers legion 1945-79), N.J. (mem. pub. relations com., FHA loan com. 1958), Phila. (pres. 1949, mem. legis. com. 1965-69) mortgage bankers assns., N.J. Assn. Realtor Bds. (pres. 1941, mem. lawyer-realtor com. 1947-70, 71-73), Soc. Real Estate Appraisers (pres. South Jersey chpt. 1940, v.p. 1956, internat. pres. 1959), Kappa Alpha. Methodist (past pres. trustees). Mason (Shriner, 32 deg.). Clubs: Union League (Phila.), City (Camden). Home and Office: 508 Chester Ave Moorestown NJ 08057

NUTTER, HAROLD LEE, bishop; b. Welsford, N.B., Can., Dec, 29, 1923; s. William Lawton and Lillian Agnes (Joyce) N.; B.A., Mt. Allison U., Sackville, N.B., 1944, LL.D. (hon.), 1972; B.S.Litt., King's Coll., Halifax, N.S., 1947, D.D., 1960; M.A., Dalhousie U., Halifax, 1947; m. Edith Maud Carew, Sept. 21, 1946; children—Particia Nutter Hunsley, Bruce. Ordained priest Anglican Ch. of Can., 1947, consecrated bishop, 1971; rector Parish of Simond sand Upham, N.B., 1947-51, Parish of Woodstock, N.B., 1951-57, Parish of St. Mark, St. John, N.B., 1957-60; dean of Fredericton (N.B.), 1960-71, bishop, 1971—. Co-chmn. N.B. Task Force on Social Devel., 1970-71; mem. Com. on Multiculturalism of Can., 1973—. Home: 791 Brunswick St Fredericton NB E3B 1H8 Canada*

NUTTING, CHARLES BERNARD, educator, lawyer, b. Iowa City, Dec. 8, 1906; s. Charles C. and Eloise (Willis) N.; B.A., State U. Iowa, 1927, J.D., 1930; LL.M., Harvard, 1932, S.J.D., 1933; LL.D., U. Pitts., 1957, Dickinson Coll. Law, 1960; Litt. D., Geneva Coll., 1957; L.H.D., Seton Hill Coll., 1957; m. Mary A. Flannagan, Aug. 17, 1933; children—Catherine (Mrs. Elmer L. Lampe), Elizabeth (Mrs. John D. Verhoeven), Margaret (Mrs. Donald Ralph). Admitted to Iowa bar, 1930, Kans. bar, 1930, U.S. Supreme Ct. bar, 1943, Pa. bar, 1956, D.C. bar, 1964; practiced with Holmes and Adams, Wichita, Kans., 1930-31; asst. prof. law U. Nebr., Lincoln, 1933-35, asso. prof., 1936-38, prof., 1938-46; asso. prof. law. U. Tex., Austin, 1935-36; asso. solicitor Dept. Agr., Washington, 1942-46; prof. law, vice dean U. Pitts. Law Sch., 1946-49, dean, 1949-52, vice chancellor, 1952-56; vis. prof. law U. Mich., summer 1948; dir. Buhl Found., Pitts., 1956-60; pres. Action-Housing, Inc., 1957-60; dean Nat. Law Center, George Washington U., 1960-66, prof. 1966-72, emeritus, 1972; prof. Hastings Coll. Law U. Calif., San Francisco, 1972-76. Mem. Fed. City Council, 1960-72, Gov.'s Citizen's Com. Housing, 1956, Pres.'s Conf. Adminstrv. Procedure, Washington Channel Waterfront, Inc., 1961—. Mem. Am. (vice chmn. adminstrn. law sect 1950-51, chmn. 1951-52), Fed. bar assns., Assn. Am. Law Sch. (pres. 1953), Am. Law Inst., Phi Beta Kappa, Order of Coif, Delta Sigma Rho, Phi Delta Phi, Omicron Delta Kappa. Presbyterian. Clubs: Nat. Lawyers, Cosmos (Washington). Editor (with F. Reed Dickerson): Cases and Materials on Legislation. Contbr. articles to legal publs. Home: 101 S Hanover Ave Lexington KY 40502

NUTTLI, OTTO WILLIAM, geophysicist; b. St. Louis, Dec. 11, 1926; s. Otto Peter and Marie Bertha (Wehinger) N.; B.S., St. Louis U., 1948, M.S., 1950, Ph.D., 1953. Instr. geophysics St. Louis U., 1952-56, asst. prof., 1956-59, asso. prof., 1959-62, prof., 1962—; vis. research scientist U. Mich., summer 1962, U. Calif., Berkeley, summers 1964, 67; mem. adv. panel NSF and C.E.; cons. to fed. govt. and industry; mem. U.S. Nat. Com. on Geology, 1975-79, Com. on Seismology, 1976-79. Fellow Am. Geophys. Union (asso. editor Jour. Geophys. Research 1978—), Royal Astron. Soc.; mem. Seismol. Soc. Am. (pres. 1976-77, editor Bull, 1971-75), Soc. Exploration Geophysicists, Earthquake Engring. Research Inst. Home: 5422 Finkman St Saint Louis MO 63109 Office: 221 N Grand Blvd Saint Louis MO 63103

NUTZLE, FUTZIE (BRUCE JOHN KLEINSMITH), artist, cartoonist; b. Lakewood, Ohio, Feb. 21, 1942; s. Adrian Ralph and Naomi Irene (Rupert) Kleinsmith; m. Laura Warner; 1 son, Adrian David. Exhbns. include: San Francisco Mus. Art, 1972, Indpls. Mus. Art, 1975, Leica, Los Angeles, 1978, Contemporary Graphic Exhbn., Santa Barbara, Calif., 1978; represented in permanent collections: Mus. Modern Art, N.Y.C., San Francisco Mus. Art, Oakland Mus., Whitney Mus. Am. Art, N.Y.C.; work appearing in Balloon Newspaper, The Real Paper, Boston, Rolling Stone; illustrator The Armies Encamped in the Fields Beyond the Unfinished Avenues (Morton Marcus), 1977; contbr. illustrations to various mags. Address: PO Box 325 Aromas CA 95004

NUZZO, SALVATORE JOSEPH, electronics co. exec.; b. Norwalk, Conn., Aug. 6, 1931; s. Rocco and Angelina (Ranzulli) N.; B.S. in Elec. Engring., Yale U., 1953; M.S. in Bus., Columbia U., 1974; m. Lucille Cocco, Oct. 3, 1953; children—James, David, Thomas, Dana. With Hazeltine Corp., Greenlawn, N.Y., 1953—, v.p. govt. products and mktg., 1969-73, v.p. govt. products div., 1973-74, sr. v.p. ops., 1974-76, exec. v.p., chief operating officer, 1976, pres., chief operating officer, 1977—. Mem. Armed Forces Communications and Electronics Assn., Am. Def. Preparedness Assn., Assn. U.S. Army, Electronic Industries Assn., Nat. Security Indsl. Assn., Am. Mgmt. Assn., NAM, Yale Sci. and Engring. Assn., Assn. Yale Alumni, Columbia Sch. Bus. Alumni Assn. (bd. dirs.). Home: 94 Holst Dr W Huntington NY 11743 Office: Hazeltine Corp Greenlawn NY 11740

NYBORG, WESLEY LEMARS, educator; b. Ruthven, Iowa, May 15, 1917; s. Isaac and Leva (Larson) N.; B.A., Luther Coll., 1941; M.S., Pa. State U., 1944, Ph.D., 1947; m. Beth Woolsey, Sept. 8, 1945; 1 dau., Elsa Beth. Asst. prof. physics Pa. State U., Univ. Park, 1948-50; asst. prof. Brown U., Providence, 1950-54, asso. prof., 1954-60; prof. U. Vt., Burlington, 1960—, acting chmn. physics dept., 1978-79; vis. scientist Oxford (Eng.) U., 1960-61, Univ. Coll., Cardiff, Wales, 1969. Exec. council Am. Inst. Ultrasound in Medicine, 1972-74, 76-78, chmn. bioeffects com., 1976-78; adv. bd. Bur. Radiol. Health, 1972-75; cons. FDA, 1976—. Recipient Presdl. recognition award Am. Inst. Ultrasound in Medicine, 1977. USPHS fellow Mass. Inst. Tech., 1956-57; research grantee, NIH, 1955—. Fellow Acoustical Soc. Am. (exec. council 1965-68), AAAS, Am. Inst. for Ultrasound in Medicine; mem. Am. Phys. Soc., Biophys. Soc., Am. Assn. Physics Tchrs., Sigma Xi, Sigma Pi Sigma. Author: Intermediate Biophysical Mechanics, 1975. Editorial bd. Jour. Biol. Physics, Ultrasound in Medicine and Biology; internat. adv. editor Ultrasonics; contbr. to profl. jours. Home: 2 Stirling Pl Burlington VT 05401

NYE, EDWIN PACKARD, coll. dean; b. Atkinson, N.H., Jan. 29, 1920; s. Eben W. and Gertrude Florence (Dunn) N.; B.S. with high honor, U. N.H., 1941; Sc.M., Harvard, 1947; m. Persephone Fern Drumheller, Aug. 12, 1944; children—David Edwin, Sarah Leone, Benjamin Alfred. Service engr. Bailey Meter Co., Cleve., 1941-42; instr. mech. engring. U. N.H., 1942-44; project engr. NACA, 1944-46; from instr. to asso. prof. mech. engring. Pa. State U., 1947-59; Hallden prof. Trinity Coll., Hartford, Conn., 1959—, chmn. dept. engring., 1960-70, dean of faculty, 1970-79. Sec., Univ. Research Inst. Conn., 1964-68, pres., 1968-71, chmn., 1971-74; dir. Hallden Machine Co.; chmn. coll. work Episcopal Diocese Conn., 1960-64. Mem. bd. edn., Bloomfield, Conn., 1961-65; mem. State Bd. Acad. Awards, 1974—, dean faculty, 1979—; corporator Hartford Public Library, 1978—. Registered profl. engr., Pa., Conn. Mem. ASME, Am. Soc. Engring. Edn., Conn. Acad. Sci. and Engring., Phi Kappa Phi, Pi Tau Sigma. Co-author: Steam Power Plants, 1952; Power Plants, 1956; Thermal Engineering, 1959. Home: 125 Vernon St Hartford CT 06106

NYE, RUSSEL BLAINE, educator; b. Viola, Wis., Feb. 17, 1913; s. Charles Henry and Zelma (Shimmeyer) N.; A.B., Oberlin Coll., 1934; A.M., U. Wis., 1935, Ph.D., 1939; L.H.D., No. Mich. U., 1968; m. Mary Kathryn Chaney, Aug. 6, 1938; 1 son, Peter William, Instr. of English, Jordan Coll., 1935-36, U. Wis., Madison, 1936-39, Adelphi Coll., 1939-40; faculty Mich. State U., East Lansing, 1940—, distinguished prof., 1963—. Mem. bd. control Ferris Inst., 1950-67. Knopf fellow in biography, 1942-43; Rockefeller fellow, 1944-45, Newberry fellow in Midwestern studies, 1947-48. Mem. Modern Lang. Assn., Popular Culture Assn. (pres. 1969—), Canadian Hist. Assn., Am. Studies Assn. (v.p. 1962-65, pres. 1965-67), Am. Hist. Soc., Delta Chi. Author: George Bancroft, Brahmin Rebel (Pulitzer prize, biography), 1944; Civil Liberty and Slavery, 1948; Midwestern Progressive Politics, 1951; (with J.E. Morpurgo) The History of the United States, 1955, rev. edit., 1970; A Baker's Dozen, 1956; Cultural Life of the New Nation, 1960; This Almost Chosen People, 1966; The Unembarrassed Muse, 1970; Society and Culture in America, 1974. Contbr. to hist. mags. Home: 301 Oxford Rd East Lansing MI 48823

NYE, THOMAS RUSSELL, drafting, reprodn. and surveying co. exec.; b. Arlington, Mass., July 16, 1928; s. Russell Van Buren and Sibyl (Partridge) N.; A.B., Brown U., 1950; M.B.A., Harvard U., 1952;

m. Patricia Bentley, Dec. 14, 1951; children—Bradford V.B., Debra B. Salesman, Russell Nye Co., Inc., Boston, 1951-52; assignment dir., sr. asso. Bruce Payne & Assos., N.Y.C., 1953-59; with Keuffel & Esser Co., Morristown, N.J., 1959—, exec. v.p., 1970, pres., 1970—, chief exec. officer, 1971—; dir. Summit & Elizabeth Trust Co., Adamas Carbide Corp., J.K. Adams Co. Inc., Barker Graphics. Bd. dirs. United Way, Madison, N.J., 1968-73, Madison YMCA, 1970-72; mem. corp. United Way Morris County, 1973—; mem. local council Boy Scouts Am., 1971-75; trustee N.J. Shakespeare Festival. Served as officer USAF, 1952-53. Mem. Assn. Reprodn. Materials Mfrs. (pres., dir.), Am. Mgmt. Assn., NAM, Internat. Assn. Blueprinters and Allied Industries, Am. Congress Mapping and Surveying, Newcomen Soc., Soc. Advancement Mgmt. Presbyterian. Club: Morris County Golf (Convent, N.J.). Author articles. Home: 46 East Ln Madison NJ 07940 Office: 20 Whippany Rd Morristown NJ 07960

NYE, WILLIAM ALLEN, educator; b. Middletown, N.Y., Feb. 6, 1937; s. William Earl and Marion (Allen) N.; student Syracuse U., 1954-56; B.S. in Econs., U. Pa., 1958, Ph.D., 1962; m. Barbara Randall, Apr. 15, 1961; children—Linda Marie, Jeffrey Dale, James Brandon. Instr., Temple U., 1962; asst. prof. San Diego State Coll., 1962-65, asso. prof., 1965-69, prof., 1969—, chmn. dept. finance Sch. Bus., 1969-71. Pres. Estate Planning Council San Diego, 1971; investment rep., life ins. agt., 1967—. Named Outstanding Prof., Sch. Bus. Adminstrn. San Diego State Coll., 1966, 70, 71. Home: 4696 Normandie Pl La Mesa CA 92041 Office: 5402 College Ave San Diego CA 92115

NYEMASTER, RAY, lawyer; b. Davenport, Iowa, Mar. 23, 1914; s. Jesse Ray and Clara Elva (Stucker) N.; student Cornell Coll., Mt. Vernon, Iowa, 1931-32; B.A., State U. Iowa, 1936, J.D., 1938; children by previous marriage—Thomas Lee, Martha Merry; m. Martha Jane Backman Jaeger, Dec. 27, 1968; stepchildren—William John Jaeger, Judith Ann Jaeger Hand. Admitted to Iowa bar, 1938, since practiced in Des Moines; asso. partner firm Parrish, Guthrie, Colflesh & O'Brien, 1938-68, partner Nyemaster, Goode, McLaughlin, Emery & O'Brien, 1968—; dir. Vernon Co., Newton, Iowa, Central Life Ins. Co., Des Moines. Chmn., Iowa Aero. Commn., 1961-73. Bd. dirs. Des Moines Center Sci. and Industry; trustee Cornell Coll., Mt. Vernon, Iowa. Mem. Am., Iowa, Polk County bar assns., Des Moines C. of C. Mason (Shriner, 32 deg., Jester, royal impresario), Rotarian. Clubs: Des Moines, Embassy, Wakonda (Des Moines). Home: 694 61st St Des Moines IA 50312 Office: Hubbell Bldg Des Moines IA 50309

NYERE, ROBERT ALAN, banker; b. Aberdeen, Wash., July 19, 1917; s. George Louis and Augusta (Draheim) N.; B.A., U. Wash., 1939; M.B.A., Harvard U., 1941; grad. Stonier Sch. Banking, Rutgers U., 1951; m. Jeanne Fortier, Nov. 8, 1941; children—Sharon L. Nyere Olson, Barbara J. Nyere Slevin. With First Nat. Bank of Boston, 1941—, asst. mgr., mgr., asst. v.p., 1948-58, v.p., 1958-69, sr. v.p., 1969-79; dir. Interbank Card Assn., FNBC Acceptance Corp., 1st La. Acceptance Corp., Boston Trust & Savs., Ltd. Served from ensign to lt. USNR, 1942-46. Mem. Alpha Kappa Psi. Episcopalian. Clubs: Masons (32 deg.), Shriners; Algonquin, Harvard Bus., Winchester Country. Home: 92 Riverview Dr Chatham MA 02633

NYGAARD, HENRY SIGURD, lawyer; b. Salt Lake City, Jan. 14, 1929; s. Sigurd Olaf and Dagmar (Andersen) N.; B.S., U. Utah, 1951, LL.D., J.D., 1955; m. Grace Ann Lawrence, June 12, 1958; children—Jane, Ann, Gretchen, Julie. Admitted to Utah bar, 1955; partner Simmons, Beaslin & Nygaard, Salt Lake City, 1955-58, Beaslin, Mygaard, Coke & Vincent, Salt Lake City, 1958—; chief clk. Utah Ho. of Reps., 1957, 61. State fin. chmn. Republican Central Com., 1965-69; mem. Utah State Judicial Selection Commn., Salt Lake County Bd. Adjustment; sec. Utah Arthritis Found., 1966—. Served with AUS, 1951-53. Mem. Skull and Bones, Owland Key, Phi Kappa Phi, Phi Eta Sigma, Phi Delta Phi. Mem. Ch. Jesus Christ of Latter-day Saints. Lion (dep. dist. gov. 1960-61). Home: 1792 Mountain View Dr Salt Lake City UT 84106 Office: Boston Bldg Salt Lake City UT 84111

NYGREN, MAIE ANABEL, home economist; b. Fallon, Nev., Oct. 9, 1924; d. Walter Leander and Anabel (Hunter) N.; B.S., U. Nev., 1946; M.S., Oreg. State U., 1954; Ed.D., Okla. State U., 1960. Tchr. vocat. home econs. Douglas County (Nev.) High Sch., 1946-49, Churchill County (Nev.) High Sch., 1949-53; asst. prof. home econs. San Jose (Calif.) State U., 1953-57; prof., head dept. housing and interior design Okla. State U., 1960-66; prof. home econs., chmn. dept. San Francisco State U., 1966—; vis. lectr. U. Nev., 1964, U. Ariz., 1968, Oreg. State U., 1970; adv. com. home mgmt. for home ownership by low income families Calif. Dept. Housing and Community Devel.; condr. workshops. Mem. Am., Calif. (pres. 1975-77) home econs. assns., Nev. Vocat. Edn. Assn. (past pres.), Am. Assn. Housing Educators (past pres.), Am. Sociol. Assn., Kappa Delta Pi, Omicron Nu, Phi Upsilon Omicron, Phi Kappa Phi. Co-author: Rural Housing in Garfield County Oklahoma: A Study of Processes, Images and Values, 1959; contbr. articles to profl. jours. Home: 44 Garden Side Dr San Francisco CA 94131 Office: Home Econs Dept San Francisco State U 1600 Holloway St San Francisco CA 94132

NYHAN, WILLIAM LEO, pediatrician, educator; b. Boston, Mar. 13, 1926; s. W. Leo and Mary (Cleary) N.; student Harvard U., 1943-45; M.D., Columbia U., 1949; M.S., U. Ill., 1956, Ph.D., 1958; m. Christine Murphy, Nov. 20, 1948; children—Christopher, Abigail. Intern Yale U.-Grace-New Haven Hosp., 1949-50, resident, 1950-51, 53-55; asst. prof. pediatrics Johns Hopkins U., 1958-61, asso. prof., 1961-63; prof. pediatrics, biochemistry U. Miami, 1963-69, chmn. dept. pediatrics, 1963-69; prof. U. Calif., San Diego, 1969—, chmn. dept. pediatrics, 1969—; mem. FDA adv. com. on Teratogenic Effect on Certain Drugs, 1964-70; mem. pediatric panel AMA Council on Drugs, 1964-70; mem. Nat. Adv. Child Health and Human Devel. Council, 1967-71; mem. research adv. com. Calif. Dept. Mental Hygiene, 1969-72; mem. med. and sci. adv. com. Leukemia Soc. Am., Inc., 1968-72; mem. basic adv. com. Nat. Found. March of Dimes, 1973, mem. Basil O'Connor Starter grants com., 1973—; mem. clin. cancer program project rev. com. Nat. Cancer Inst., 1977—. Served with U.S. Navy, 1944-46, U.S. Army, 1951-53. Nat. Found. Infantile Paralysis fellow, 1955-58; recipient Commemorative medallion Columbia U. Coll. Physicians and Surgeons, 1967. Mem. AAAS, Am. Fedn. Clin. Research, Am. Chem. Soc., Soc. Pediatric Research, Am. Assn. Cancer Research, Am. Soc. Pharmacology and Exptl. Therapeutics, Western Soc. Pediatric Research (pres. 1976-77), N.Y. Acad. Sci., Am. Acad. Pediatrics, Am. Pediatric Soc., Am. Inst. Biol. Scis., Soc. Exptl. Biology and Medicine, Am. Soc. Clin. Investigation, Am. Soc. Human Genetics (dir. 1978—), Biochem. Soc., Sigma Xi, Alpha Omega Alpha. Author: (with E. Edelson) The Heredity Factor, Genes, Chromosomes and You, 1976; (with N.O. Sakati) Genetic & Malformation Syndromes in Clinical Medicine, 1976; editor: Amino Acid Metabolism and Genetic Variation, 1967; Heritable Disorders of Amino Acid Metabolism, 1974; editorial bd. Jour. Pediatrics, 1964-78, Western Jour. Medicine, 1974—; editorial staff Med. and Pediatric Oncology, 1975—. Office: Dept Pediatrics U Calif San Diego CA La Jolla CA 92093

NYHUS, LLOYD MILTON, surgeon, educator; b. Mt. Vernon, Wash., June 24, 1923; s. Lewis Guttorm and Mary (Shervem) N.; B.S., Pacific Luth. Coll., 1945; M.D., Med. Coll. Ala., 1947; Honoris Doctoris Causa, Aristotelian U., Thessalonika, Greece, 1968, Uppsala U. (Sweden), 1974, U. Chihuahua (Mex.), 1975; m. Margaret Goldie Sheldon, Nov. 25, 1949; children—Sheila Margaret, Leif Torger. Intern, King County Hosp., Seattle, 1947-48, resident in surgery, 1948-55; practice medicine specializing in surgery, Seattle, 1956-67, Chgo., 1967—; instr. surgery U. Wash., Seattle, 1954-56, asst. prof., 1956-59, asso. prof., 1959-64, prof., 1964-67; Warren H. Cole prof., head dept. surgery U. Ill. Coll. Medicine, 1967—; postdoctoral fellow USPHS, 1952-53; John Simon Guggenheim fellow, 1955-56; surgeon-in-chief U. Ill. Hosp.; sr. cons. surgeon Cook County, West Side VA, Hines (Ill.) VA hosps. Cons. to Surgeon Gen. NIH, 1965-69; 1st vis. prof. Honolulu, 1961; spl. invited lectr. 65th Japanese Surg. Soc., Tokyo, 1965, 77th, 1977; Vogt lectr. St. Louis U., 1966; Richardson lectr. Harvard, 1970; Edwards lectr. Vanderbilt U., 1976; Hodgen lectr. St. Louis Surg. Soc., 1976; spl. invited lectr. Bavarian Surg. Congress, Munich, Germany, 1968; spl. invited lectr. 4th World Congress Gastroenterology, Copenhagen, Denmark, 1970, 5th World Congress Gastroenterology, Mexico City, 1974; 1st R.H. Nimmo vis. prof. Royal Adelaide Hosp., Australia, 1970, vis. prof. U. Witswatersrand, Johannesburg, South Africa, 1972, U. Auckland, New Zealand, 1973, XIII Congress Pan Am. Gastroenterology, Buenos Aires, 1973, XV Congress Pan Am. Gastroenterology, Rio de Janiero, 1977, XIII Congress Venezuelean Soc. Surg., 1975. Served to lt. M.C., USNR, 1943-46, 50-52. Recipient M. Shipley award So. Surg. Assn., 1967, Rovsing medal Danish Surg. Soc., 1973. Diplomate Am. Bd. Surgery (chmn. 1974-76). Fellow A.C.S., Royal Soc. Medicine, Assn. Surgeons Gt. Brit. and Ireland (corr.); mem. Am. Gastroent. Assn., A.M.A., Am. Physiol. Soc., Pacific Coast, Am. Surg. Assn. (recorder 1976—), Western Surg. Assn., Central Soc. Clin. Research, Chgo. (pres. 1974), Seattle, St. Paul (hon.), Kansas City (hon.) surg. socs., Illingworth Surg. Club, Inst. Medicine Chgo., Internat. Soc. Surgery, Collegium Internat. Chirurgiae Digestivae (pres. III world congress Chgo. 1974, internat. pres. 1978—), Soc. for Surgery Alimentary Tract (sec. 1969-73, pres. 1974), Soc. Clin. Surgery, Soc. Surg. Chairmen, Soc. U. Surgeons (past pres.), Deutschen Gesselschaft für Chirurgie (corr.), L'Academie de Chirurgie (France; corr.), Brazilian Coll. Surgeons (corr.), Surg. Biology Club, Warren H. Cole Soc., Sigma Xi, Alpha Omega Alpha, Phi Beta Pi. Author: Surgery of the Stomach and Duodenum, 1962, 3d edit., 1977; Hernia, 1964, 2d edit., 1978; Abdominal Pain: A Guide to Rapid Diagnosis, 1969; Manual of Surgical Therapeutics, 1969, rev. 1972, 75, 78; Surgery Annual, 1970-79; Treatment of Shock, 1970, 74. Editor-in-chief Rev. of Surgery, 1967-77, Current Surgery, 1978; asso. editor: Quar. Rev. Surgery, 1958-61; editorial bd.: Am. Jour. Digestive Diseases, 1961-67, Scandinavian Jour. Gastroenterology, 1966—, Am. Surgeon, 1967, Jour. Surg. Oncology, 1969, Archives of Surgery, 1977—, World Jour. Surgery. Contbr. articles to profl. jours. Home: 310 Maple Row Northbrook IL 60062 Office: 840 S Wood St Chicago IL 60612

NYHUS, PAUL LUTHER, coll. dean; b. Williston, N.D., Aug. 6, 1935; s. Horace E. and Ida J. (Vigoren) N.; A.B., Augsburg Coll., Mpls., 1957; exchange student U. Heidelberg (Ger.), 1957-58; S.T.B., Harvard U., 1961, Ph.D., 1967; m. Ellen Jane Lundblad, Aug. 27, 1960; children—Kristina, Karen, Katharine. Sr. resident Radcliffe Coll., 1962-66; teaching fellow gen. edn. Harvard U., 1964-66; mem. faculty Bowdoin Coll., Brunswick, Maine, 1966—, asso. prof. history, 1967—, dean students, 1969-75, dean coll., 1975—. Trustee Roxbury Latin Sch., 1973-76. Author articles, revs. Address: Office Dean Coll Bowdoin Coll Brunswick ME 04011

NYIRJESY, ISTVAN, obstetrician, gynecologist; b. Budapest, Hungary, Nov. 14, 1929; s. Sandor D. and Margit (Bertalan) N.; came to U.S., 1954, naturalized, 1960; M.D., Catholic U. Louvain (Belgium), 1955; m. Michelle Shoepp, June 16, 1956; children—Francis, Paul, Christine. Intern, Cath. U. Louvain and Little Co. Mary Hosp., Evergeen Park, Ill., 1954-55; officer M.C., U.S. Navy, 1956-68, advanced through grades to comdr.; resident in gynecology obstetrics, 1960-63; chief obstetrical research Nat. Naval Med. Center, Bethesda, Md., 1966-68; ret., 1968; practice medicine specializing in Ob-Gyn, Bethesda, 1968—; clin. prof. Ob-Gyn, Georgetown U., 1968—; cons. NIH, 1974—, FDA, 1977—. Recipient Sword of Hope pin Am. Cancer Soc., 1973; diplomate Am. Bd. Ob-Gyn. Fellow Am. Coll. Obstetricians Gynecologists (Host award 1964); mem. Montgomery County (Md.) Med. Soc. (chmn. profl. edn. com. 1971-72), Gynecol. Soc. Study of Breast Disease (pres.), Am. Fertility Soc. Contbr. articles to med. jours. Office: 5272 River Rd Bethesda MD 20016

NYKIEL, FRANK PETER, diversified co. exec.; b. Chgo., Dec. 30, 1917; s. Joseph and Ann (Jerz) N.; B.S. in Accounting, U. Ill., 1941; m. Marie Papa, Mar. 1, 1942; children—Carol Ann (Mrs. Thomas J. Barta), Frank Peter II. With Arthur Andersen & Co., C.P.A., Chgo., 1947-52, sr. accountant, 1951-52; with Consumers Co., Chgo., 1952-60, exec. v.p., 1959-60; v.p., treas. Miss. Valley Barge Line Co., St. Louis, 1960-62, exec. v.p., dir., 1962—, (merger Miss. Valley Barge Line Co. and Chromalloy Am. Corp. to Valley Line Co., 1968), v.p. marine-finance, dir. Chromalloy Am. Corp., 1968-70, vice chmn. bd. finance, dir., 1970—; chmn. bd., chief exec. officer, dir. Water Treatment Corp., 1968-71. Served with USAAF, World War II. C.P.A. Clubs: Mo. Athletic; Sunset Country. Home: 6 Chapel Hill Town and Country Saint Louis MO 63131 Office: 120 S Central Ave Saint Louis MO 63105

NYMAN, CARL JOHN, JR., univ. dean; b. New Orleans, Oct. 21, 1924; s. Carl John and Dorothy (Kraft) N.; B.S., Tulane U., 1944, M.S., 1945; Ph.D., U. Ill., 1948; m. Betty Spiegelberg, July 15, 1950; children—Gail Katherine, John Victor, Nancy Kraft. Jr. technologist Shell Oil Co., Wilmington, Cal., 1944; instr. chemistry U. Ill., 1948; instr. chemistry Wash. State U., Pullman, 1948-50, asst. prof., 1950-55, asso. prof., 1955-61, prof., 1961—, acting dean grad. sch., 1968-70, dean, 1970—; vis. asst. prof. Tulane U., summer 1950; vis. fellow Cornell U., 1959-60, Imperial Coll. Sci. and Tech., 1966-67. Chmn. acad. council Center Grad. Study, Richland, Wash., 1968-70, N.W. Assn. Colls. and Univs. for Sci., 1969; mem. Gov.'s Adv. Council on Nuclear Energy. Mem. Am. Chem. Soc. (chmn. Wash.-Idaho border sect. 1961-62), AAAS, Sigma Xi, Phi Lambda Upsilon, Alpha Chi Sigma, Omicron Delta Kappa. Author: (with G.B. King) Problems for General Chemistry and Qualitative Analysis, 3d edit., 1975; (with R.E. Homm) Chemical Equilibrium, 1967; (with W.E. Newton) Procs. of the 1st Internat. Conf. Nitrogen Fixation. Contbr. articles to profl. jours. Home: NW 1320 Orion Dr Pullman WA 99163

NYQUIST, JOHN DAVIS, former radio mfg. co. exec.; b. Peoria, Ill., May 28, 1918; s. Eliud and Linnea (Widen) N.; B.S. in Mech. Engring., U. Ill., 1941; m. Alice Schmidt, June 5, 1942; 1 dau., Sarah Lynn. With Collins Radio Co., Cedar Rapids, Iowa, 1941—, v.p., gen. mgr., Cedar Rapids (Iowa) region, 1965-69, v.p. operations, 1969-70, sr. v.p., 1970—, also dir.; dir. Peoples Bank & Trust Co., Cedar Rapids. Bd. dirs. Am. Cancer Soc., YMCA, St. Lukes Hosp. Recipient award for outstanding achievement Am. Inst. Indsl. Engrs., 1966, Indsl. Engring. award, 1969, Coll. Engring. Alumni Honor award, 1977 (both U. Ill.). Mem. Iowa Mfrs. Assn., Am. Mgmt. Assn., Am. Inst. Indsl. Engrs., IEEE, Cedar Rapids C. of C. (dir.). Club: Cedar Rapids Country. Home: Rt 2 Springville IA 52336 Office: 5225 C Ave NE Cedar Rapids IA 52406

NYRO, LAURA, composer, singer; b. Bronx, N.Y., Oct. 18, 1947. Compositions include Stone Soul Picnic and Sweet Blindness, Wedding Bell Blues, Eli's Comin', And When I Die; records include Eli and the Thirteenth Confession, New York Tendaberry, Christmas and the Beads of Sweat, The First Songs, It's Gonna Take A Miracle, Smile, Season of Lights. Address: care Rosco Harding PO Box 186 Shoreham NY 11786*

NYROP, DONALD WILLIAM, airlines exec.; b. Elgin, Nebr., Apr. 1, 1912; s. William A. and Nellie (Wylie) N.; A.B., Doane Coll., 1934; LL.B., George Washington U., 1939; m. Grace Cary, Apr. 19, 1941; children—Nancy, William, Karen, Kathryn. Admitted to the D.C. bar, 1938; atty. Gen. Counsel's Office, CAA and CAB, Washington, 1939-41, exec. officer to chmn. CAB, 1942, chmn., 1952; rep. U.S. airlines, mem. ofcl. U.S. delegations Internat. Civil Aviation Orgn. Assemblies, 1946, 47; dep. adminstr. for ops. CAA, 1948-50, adminstr., 1950-51; pres. Northwest Airlines, Inc., 1954-78; dir. Northwest Airlines, First Bank System, Inc., Gould, Inc., Minn. Mut. Life Ins. Co., Northwestern Bell Telephone Co. Served with Air Transport Command, USAAF, 1942-46. Recipient Legion of Merit. Clubs: Minneapolis, Minnesota. Home: 4505 Golf Terr Minneapolis MN 55424 Office: Mpls/St Paul Internat Airport Saint Paul MN 55111

NYSTROM, HAROLD CHARLES, lawyer, labor cons.; b. White, S.D., Apr. 6, 1906; s. Charles Alfred and Augusta Cornelia (Olson) N.; student S.D. State Sch. Mines and Tech., 1922-23; A.B. cum laude, U. S.D., 1926; J.D. with honors, George Washington U., 1931; m. Ruth Greenwood, Sept. 30, 1931; children—Nancy Ann (Mrs. William Scott Railton), Erik Linfred. Admitted to S.D. bar, 1931, practiced in Rapid City, 1931-35; cons. Bethesda, Md., 1975-78, Rockville, Md., 1978—; editorial staff Lawyers Coop. Pub. Co., Rochester, N.Y., 1935-41; staff Office of Solicitor, U.S. Dept. Labor, 1941-74, chief codification unit, chief interpretations sect., chief wage-hour hdqrs. sect., N.Y.C., chief interpretations br., Washington, acting asst. solicitor for legislation and gen. legal services, asst. solicitor, 1941-58, dep. solicitor, 1958-59, acting solicitor, 1959-61, dep. solicitor, 1961-62, asso. solicitor, 1962-74; cons. fed. labor standards, 1975—. Lectr., Labor Law Inst. Southwestern Legal Found., Dallas, 1960; lectr. Banking Law Inst., N.Y., 1967; speaker labor law sect. Assn. Bar City N.Y., 1967, Labor Relations Inst., Atlanta Lawyers Found., 1969, 73. Sec.-treas. Oakmont (Md.) Citizens Com., 1950-59. Recipient award for meritorious service Dept. Labor, 1957, award for distinguished service, 1961, award for distinguished career service, 1973; certificate of appreciation Employment Standards Adminstrn., 1975. Mem. Am. (vice chmn. agy. liaison com. adminstrv. law sect. 1960-73), Fed. (speaker BNA Labor Law briefing conf. 1967), Tenn. (hon. life mem. labor law sect.) bar assns., S.D. State Bar, Old Georgetown Road Citizens Assn. (exec. bd. 1958-60), Phi Beta Kappa, Phi Alpha Delta. Presbyn. (deacon). Club: National Lawyers. Contbr. articles to legal publs. Home and Office: 11425 Luxmanor Rd Rockville MD 20852

NYSTROM, JOHN WARREN, geographer, educator; b. Worcester, Mass., Nov. 22, 1913; s. John Walfred and Hulda Alfreda (Sundstrom) N.; A.B., Clark U., 1936, A.M., 1937, Ph.D., 1942; m. Anne Hildegarde Carlson, Aug. 6, 1938; children—Jon Alfred, David Alan, Karen Elizabeth. Instr., R.I. Coll. Edn., 1937-40, asst. prof. geography, 1940-43; asst. prof. U. Pitts., 1943-45, asso. prof., 1945, prof., dept. head, 1947-53; head fgn. policy dept. U.S. C. of C., 1953-62, adminstrv. coordinator, 1956-62; partner firm Allen, Murden & Nystrom, internat. relations, Washington, 1962-64; mem. sr. staff Brookings Instn., 1964-66; exec. dir. Assn. Am. Geographers, Washington, 1966-79; prof. George Washington U., 1973-79; prof. geography U. Miami, 1980—; exec. dir. Pitts. regional Inter-Am. Center, 1943-45, Fgn. Policy Assn. Pitts., 1945-53; cons. Dept. State, 1976—. Chmn. U.S. Nat. Com. Internat. Geog. Union; chmn. U.S. delegation Internat. Geographic Congress, Stockholm, Sweden, 1960, London, 1964, New Delhi, 1968, Budapest, 1971, Montreal, 1972, Moscow, 1976; mem. geography commn. NRC; chmn. Conf. of Secs., Am. Council Learned Socs., 1973-75; U.S. rep. Pan Am. Inst. Geography and History, 1973-77, ofcl. del., Panama, 1973, Quito, Ecuador, 1977; mem. U.S. Nat. Commn. for UNESCO, 1979—. Trustee Clark U. Mem. Nat. Council Geog. Edn., Assn. Am. Geographers, Am. Geog. Soc., AAUP, Sigma Xi. Club: Cosmos. Author: Surinam, A Geographic Study-Netherlands Information, 1942; Beyond Our Borders, 1954; Within Our Borders, 1957; Within The Americas, 1957; The Common Market, 1962; Alliance for Progress, 1966; The Common Market, 1976. Home: 783 SW 3d St Boca Raton FL 33432 Office: Dept Geography U Miami PO Box 248152 Coral Gables FL 33124

NYSTROM, ROBERT FORREST, educator, chemist; b. Chgo., May 30, 1920; s. Carl Forrest and Frances (Rulau) N.; B.S., U. Chgo., 1942, Ph.D., 1947; m. Mary Jane Thomas, Oct. 21, 1944; children—Frederick Forrest, Laurelyn Frances, Sandra Louise. Chemist, U. Chgo., 1943-45, Oak Ridge Nat. Lab., 1947-48; mem. faculty U. Ill. at Urbana, 1948—, prof. chemistry, dir. Radioisotope Lab., 1961—. Fellow Am. Inst. Chemists; mem. Am. Chem. Soc., AAAS, Am. Nuclear Soc. (Radiation Industry award 1968), Sigma Xi, Alpha Chi Sigma. Author research publns. Home: Rural Route 3 Urbana IL 61801

OAKAR, MARY ROSE, congresswoman; b. Cleve., Mar. 5, 1940; d. Joseph M. and Margaret Mary (Ellison) Oakar; B.A. in English, Speech and Drama, Ursuline Coll., Cleve., 1962; M.A. in Fine Arts, John Carroll U., Cleve., 1966. Instr., English and drama Lourdes Acad., Cleve., 1963-70; asst. prof. English, speech and drama Cuyahoga Community Coll., Cleve., 1968-75; mem. Cleve. City Council from 8th Ward, 1973-76; mem. 95th Congress, 20th Dist. Ohio, Founder, vol.-dir. Near West Side Civic Arts Center, Cleve., 1970; ward leader Cuyahoga County Democratic Party, 1972-76; mem. Ohio Dem. Central Com. from 20th Dist., 1974; trustee Fedn. Community Planning, Cleve., Health and Planning Commn. Cleve., Community Info. Service Cleve., Cleve. Soc. Crippled Children, Nationalities Services Center, Cleve., Cleve. YWCA. Recipient Outstanding Service awards OEO, 1973-78, Community Service award Am. Indian Center, Cleve., 1973, Nationalities Service Center, 1974, Club San Lorenzo, Cleve., 1976, Cuyahoga County Dem. Woman of Yr., 1977, Ursuline Coll. Alumna of Yr. award, 1977. Address: Room 107 Cannon House Office Bldg Washington DC 20515 also 523 Federal Courthouse 215 Superior St Cleveland OH 44114

OAKES, HERBERT LEE, stone, clay and glass co. exec.; b. Chattanooga, May 21, 1914; s. Thomas Fisher and Velma (Wooden) O.; B.B.A., U. Chattanooga, 1936; m. Mary Alice Hedges, June 23, 1974; children—Herbert Lee, Evelyn Anderson. With firm Battle & Battle, C.P.A.'s, Chattanooga, 1938-51; pvt. practice accounting, Chattanooga, 1951-53; with Chattanooga Glass Co., 1953—, pres., dir., 1963-70, 74—, chmn. bd., 1970-77; pres., dir. Dorsey Corp., Chattanooga, 1969-77, chmn. bd., 1977—; dir. Coca-Cola Bottling Co. Consol., Wayne Gossard Corp., Commerce Union Bank

Chattanooga. Served to lt. USNR, 1942-46. Mem. Glass Container Mfrs. Inst. (chmn. 1971-72). Office: Dorsey Corp 400 W 45th St Chattanooga TN 37410*

OAKES, HOWARD EDWARD, financial cons.; b. Concord, N.H., Apr. 9, 1914; s. Winfield Edward and Elizabeth G. (MacLeod) O.; m. Barbara Ann Boyce, June 23, 1938; 1 dau., Deborah A. Oakes (Mrs. Richard M. Whitney Jr.). Store mgr. Firestone Tire & Rubber Co., 1935-41; with Montgomery Ward & Co., 1941-51; retail mdse. mgr. Spiegel, Inc., Chgo., 1951-53; gen. sales mgr. Westinghouse Electric Supply Co., 1953-56; mgr. label appliance sales Westinghouse Electric Corp., 1956-58; pres., gen. mgr., dir. Cool-Ray, Inc., Boston, 1958-67, chmn. bd., 1968-73; with Am. Optical Co., Southbridge, Mass., 1958-73, exec. v.p., 1967-72, vice chmn., 1972-73; corp. financial cons., Weston, Mass., 1973—. Republican. Roman Catholic. Clubs: Algonquin (Boston); Canadian (N.Y.C.); Weston Golf. Home: 7 Buttonwood Ln Weston MA 02193

OAKES, JAMES L., U.S. judge; b. Springfield, Ill., Feb. 21, 1924; A.B., Harvard 1945, LL.B., 1947; LL.D. (hon.), New Eng. Coll., 1976; m. Evelena S. Kenworthy, Dec. 29, 1973; one son, two daus. by previous marriage. Admitted to Vt. bar; practiced in Brattleboro, Vt.; spl. counsel Vt. Pub. Service Commn., 1959-60; counsel Vt. Statutory Revision Commn., 1957-60; mem. Vt. Senate, 1961, 63; atty. gen. Vt., 1967-69; U.S. dist. judge, 1970-71; U.S. circuit judge 2d Circuit Ct. Appeals, 1971—. Address: Box 696 Brattleboro VT 05301

OAKES, JOHN BERTRAM, editor; b. Elkins Park, Pa., Apr. 23, 1913; s. George Washington and Bertie (Gans) Ochs-Oakes; A.B. magna cum laude, Princeton, 1934; A.B., A.M. (Rhodes scholar), Queen's Coll., Oxford, 1936; LL.D., U. Hartford, 1960; L.H.D., Chatham Coll., 1969; Litt.D., City U. N.Y., 1976; m. Margery Caroline Hartman, Oct. 24, 1945; children—Andra N., Alison H., Cynthia J., John G. H. Reporter Trenton (N.J.) State Gazette, Trenton Times, 1936-37; polit. reporter, spl. feature writer Washington Post, 1937-41; editor Rev. of the Week, Sunday N.Y. Times, 1946-49, mem. editorial bd. N.Y. Times, also contbr. Sunday mag., Book Rev., spl. articles, 1949-61, editor of editorial page, 1961-77, sr. editor, 1977-78; vis. prof. S.I. Newhouse Sch. Communications, Syracuse (N.Y.) U., 1977-78. Mem. adv. bd. Nat. Parks, Hist. Sites, Bldgs. and Monuments Dept. Interior, 1955-62. Mem. Pres.'s Commn. White House Fellowships, 1964-69; trustee Washington Journalism Center, Chatham Coll., Natural Resources Def. Council; bd. govs. Nature Conservancy; mem. adv. council Friends of Earth, Sierra Club Found., ACLU; bd. dirs. French-Am. Found. Served from pvt. to maj. AUS, 1941-45; lt. col. USAR. Decorated Bronze Star medal (U.S.), Order Brit. Empire; Croix de Guerre, Medaille de Reconnaissance (France); recipient Carnegie travelling fellowship, 1959; Columbia-Catherwood award for distinguished journalism, 1961; Collegiate Sch. Alumni award, 1963; Dept. Interior Conservation service award 1963; Princeton Class 1934 Distinguished Service award, 1964; George Polk Meml. award for editorial comment, 1965; Jefferson award Unitarians, 1968; Silurian Soc. award for editorial writing, 1969; Francis K. Hutchinson award Garden Club of Am., 1969; Woodrow Wilson award Princeton, 1970; Appalachian Highlands Assn. award, 1970; John Muir award Sierra Club, 1974; Audubon medal Nat. Audubon Soc., 1976; Environment award Natural Resources Def. Council, 1977. Mem. Am. Assn. Rhodes Scholars (dir.), Am. Soc. Newspaper Editors, Council Fgn. Relations, Sierra Club, Phi Beta Kappa. Jewish (trustee temple). Clubs: Century Assn., Coffee House (N.Y.C.); Nassau (Princeton); Cosmos (Washington). Author: The Edge of Freedom, 1961. Home: 1120 Fifth Ave New York NY 10028 Office: 229 W 43d St New York NY 10036

OAKES, JOHN COGSWELL, ret. army officer; b. Galveston, Tex., Oct. 16, 1906; s. John Calvin and Sue Murray (Hawley) O.; student Yale, 1923-24; B.S., U.S. Mill. Acad., 1928; m. Margaret McKinley, July 28, 1933; children—John Hawley, Sue Allison, Margaret, James McKinley. Commd. 2d lt. U.S. Army, 1928, advanced through grades to lt. gen., 1959; exec. officer XIII Corps Arty., Work War II; mem. Van Fleet Mission to Greece, Greek Civil War, 1948-50; comdg. gen. 25th Div. Arty., also 25th Inf. Div., Korea, 1953-54; chief staff 7th U.S. Army, Germany, 1956-57, dep. comdg. gen., 1957-59; dep. chief of staff for mil. operations Dept. Army, 1959-61; condg. gen. VII Corps, Germany, 1961-62, 7th Army, 1962-63; ret. 1963. Pres. Army Distaff Found., 1967—; v.p. Assn. Grads. USMA, 1968—. Decorated Legion of Merit with cluster, Bronze Star medal, D.S.M.; Order of Leopold with Palm, Croix de Guerre with palm (Belgium); Order of Phoenix (Greece); Order Taeguk (Korea). Home: 4301 Massachusetts Ave NW Washington DC 20016

OAKES, KEITH RONALD, ednl. adminstr.; b. Hyrum, Utah, Jan. 7, 1914; s. Harry W. and Lottie (Anderson) O.; B.S. in History and Edn., Utah State U., 1940; M.S. in Ednl. Adminstrn., U. Utah, 1948; Ed.D. in Ednl. Adminstrn., U. So. Calif., 1954; m. Carol O'Driscoll, July 21, 1947; children—Christine, Cynthia, Marcie, Gregory. Tchr. history Salt Lake City pub. schs., 1940-42, 46-47; supr., adminstr. Contra Costa County Calif.) schs., 1950-52; asst. prof. ednl. adminstrn. Utah State U., Salt Lake City, 1949-50, 52-54; counselor-trainer Utah Dept. Edn., 1952-53; asso. prof. edn. U. So. Calif., Los Angeles, 1954-57; prof. edn. Brigham Young U., Salt Lake City, 1957—, dir. Summer Sch., 1963—, asst. adminstr. ch. schs., 1966-70, adminstr., 1970—, dir. internat. programs Coll. Edn., 1974—; cons. on higher and pub. sch. edn. Dir. sch. surveys; mem. accreditation teams higher edn. Served with USAAF, 1943-46; PTO. Decorated Bronze Star. Mem. Am. Assn. Sch. Adminstrs., Nat., Utah edn. assns., Nat. Conf. Profs. Sch. Adminstrn., Nat. Orgn. on Legal Problems In Edn. Home: 2511 North 820 East Provo UT 84601

OAKES, ROBERT JAMES, educator; b. Mpls., Jan. 21, 1936; s. Sherman E. and Josephine J. (Olson) O.; B.S., U. Minn., 1957, M.S., 1959, Ph.D., 1962; m. Diane M. Swenson, June 11, 1955; children—Cindy L., Lisa A. NSF fellow Stanford U., 1962-64; asst. prof. physics, 1964-68; asso. prof. physics Northwestern U., 1968-70, prof. physics, 1970-76, prof. physics and astronomy, 1976—; vis. staff mem. Los Alamos Sci. Lab., 1971—; vis. scientist Fermi Nat. Accelerator Lab., 1975—; Fulbright-Hays Disting. prof. U. Sarajevo (Yugoslavia), 1979. A.P. Sloan fellow, 1965-68; Air Force Office Sci. Research grantee, 1969-71; NSF grantee, 1971—. Fellow Am. Phys. Soc.; mem. AAAS, N.Y. Acad. Sci., Ill. Acad. Sci., Sigma Xi, Tau Beta Pi. Club: Physics (Chgo.). Office: Dept Physics and Astronomy Northwestern U Evanston IL 60201

OAKLAND, RALPH EDWARD, automotive co. exec.; b. Chgo., Jan. 12, 1899; s. Edward T. and Fannie (Darrow) O.; student Northwestern U.; C.P.A., U. Ill., 1922; m. Ruth Turnquist, Oct. 20, 1922; children—David D., Barbara. Bookkeeper, Livestock Exchange Bank, 1915-16, Safe-Guard Account Co., 1916-17; controller Commonwealth Motors Co., 1919-20; accountant Price, Waterhouse & Co., 1920-21, 22-23, Nat. Tea Co., 1921-22, S.W. Straus and Co., 1923-24; with Checker Cab Mfg. Corp. (name later changed to Checker Motors Corp.) Kalamazoo, 1924—, now v.p. Served with U.S. Army, 1917-19. Mem. Am. Inst. C.P.A.'s. Mason, Elk. Clubs: Kalamazoo Country, Park. Home: 5132 Woodmont Dr Kalamazoo MI 49001 Office: Checker Motors Corp Kalamazoo MI 49007

OAKLAND, SIMON, actor; b. N.Y.C., 1922; student Am. Theatre Wing. Former profl. violinist; 1st Broadway appearance in Skipper Next to God; motion pictures include: The Brothers Karamazov, I Want to Live, 1958, Who Was That Lady?, 1960, The Rise and Fall of Legs Diamond, 1960, Psycho, 1960, Murder, Inc., 1960, West Side Story, 1961, Follow That Dream, 1962, Third of a Man, Wall of Noise, 1963, The Satan Bug, 1965, The Plainsman, 1966, The Sand Pebbles, 1966, Tony Rome, 1967, Chubasco, 1968, Scandalous John, 1971, Chato's Land, 1972, Emperor of the North, 1973, Happy Mother's Day...Love, George, 1973; appeared in TV series Toma, 1973-74, The Night Stalker, 1974-75, Baa Baa Black Sheep, 1976-77, Black Sheep Squadron, 1977-78. Served in mil., World War II.*

OAKLEY, OWEN HORACE, naval architect; b. N.Y.C., Apr. 16, 1915; s. Owen Horace and Anna Truxtun (Craven) O.; B.Sc., Webb Inst. Naval Architecture and Marine Engring., 1937; M.Sc., Cath. U. Am., 1951; m. Kathleen Wigton, Oct. 4, 1940; children—Owen Horace, Nadine. With U.S. Navy, 1937—, chief naval architect, hull design br., 1957-59, tech. dir. ship concept design div., 1959-70; ret., 1970; chmn. ship research com. Nat. Acad. Scis., 1977—; mem. Maritime Transp. Research Bd., 1977-80. Registered profl. engr. D.C., Va. Recipient Superior Performance award, 1957, Superior Civilian Service award, 1967, Meritorious Civilian Service award, 1946 (all Navy); W.S. Owen award Webb Inst. Naval Architecture, 1973. Fellow Soc. Naval Architects and Marine Engrs. (tech. and research orgn. steering com. 1961-71), Am. Soc. Naval Engrs. (council 1965-67, hon. 1967—, Gold medal award 1967), Assn. Sr. Engrs. NAVSEC, NAVSHIPS (profl. achievement award 1954). Contbr. articles to profl. jours. Home: 6510 Brawner St McLean VA 22101

OAKLEY, RICHARD PUTNEY, investment banker; b. White Plains, N.Y., Apr. 8, 1920; A.B., N.Y. U., 1941. Partner Lehman Bros., N.Y.C., 1958-65; v.p., dir. One William St. Fund, N.Y.C., 1962-65; mgr. investment adv. Goldman, Sachs, 1965-66, partner, 1967-72; chmn. bd. Siff, Oakley & Marks, N.Y.C., 1973-77. Trustee No. Westchester Hosp. Center, 1977—. Fellow Fin. Analysts Fedn.; mem. Nat. Assn. Bus. Economists, N.Y. Soc. Security Analysts, N.Y. State Recreation Soc. Home: 7 Hays Hill Rd Pleasantville NY 10570 Office: 325 Manville Rd Pleasantville NY 10570

OAKLEY, ROBERT BIGGER, fgn. service officer; b. Dallas, Mar. 12, 1934; s. Robert Newell and Josephine (Bigger) O.; A.B., Princeton U., 1948-52; postgrad. Tulane U., 1955-56; m. Phyllis Elliott, June 8, 1958; children—Mary Bigger, Thomas Elliott. Commd. Fgn. Service officer Dept. State, 1957; with embassy, Khartoum, Sudan, 1958-60; internat. relations officer Dept. State, 1960-63; econ. and polit. officer, Abidjan, Ivory Coast, 1963-65; polit. officer, Saigon, 1965-67, Paris, 1967-69, UN, 1969-71; polit. counselor, Beirut, 1971-74, NSC, 1974-77; dep. asst. sec. of state for East Asia, Dept. State, Washington, 1977—. Served with USN, 1952-55. Recipient Meritorious Honor award Dept. State, 1963. Episcopalian. Home: 4512 Cathedral Ave Washington DC 20016 Office: Dept of State Washington DC 20520

OAKS, DALLIN HARRIS, univ. pres., lawyer; b. Provo, Utah, Aug. 12, 1932; s. Lloyd E. and Stella (Harris) O.; B.A. high honors, Brigham Young U., 1954; J.D. cum laude, U. Chgo., 1957; m. June Dixon, June 24, 1952; children—Sharmon, Cheri Lyn, Lloyd D., Dallin D., TruAnn, Jenny June. Admitted to Ill. bar, 1957, Utah bar, 1971; law clk. to Supreme Ct. chief justice Earl Warren, 1957-58; with firm Kirkland, Ellis, Hodson, Chaffetz & Masters, Chgo., 1958-61; mem. faculty U. Chgo. Law Sch., 1961-71, asso. dean and acting dean, 1962, prof., 1964-71, mem. vis. com., 1971-74; pres. Brigham Young U., Provo, Utah, 1971—, also prof. law J. Reuben Clark Law Sch., 1974—; asst. states atty. Cook County, Ill., summer 1964; legal counsel Bill of Rights com. Ill. Constl. Conv., 1970; dir. Deseret News Pub. Co., Union Pacific Corp. Mem. Wilson council Woodrow Wilson Internat. Center for Scholars 1973—; trustee Intermountain Health Care Inc., 1975—; mem. adv. com. Nat. Inst. Law Enforcement and Criminal Justice, 1974-76; mem., chmn. pro tem bd. dirs. Pub. Broadcasting Service, 1977—. Fellow Am. Bar Found. (exec. dir. 1970-71); mem. Am. Law Inst., Am. Bar Assn. (mem. com. to survey legal needs 1971—, mem. cons. panel on advanced legal and jud. edn. 1978—), Am. Assn. Presidents Ind. Colls. and Univs. (pres. 1975-78, dir. 1971-78), Nat. Assn. Ind. Colls. and Univs. (dir. 1977-79), Order Coif. Mem. Ch. of Jesus Christ of Latter-day Saints (regional rep. 1974—; past 1st counselor Chgo. South Stake). Author: (with G.G. Bogert) Cases on Trusts, 1967, 78; (with W. Lehman) A Criminal Justice System and The Indigent, 1968; The Criminal Justice Act in the Federal District Courts, 1969; (with M. Hill) Carthage Conspiracy, 1975. Editor: The Wall Between Church and State, 1963. Home: President's House Brigham Young U Provo UT 84602

OAKS, JAMES HOWARD, dentist, educator; b. Camden, N.J., Mar. 3, 1930; s. Alexander M. and Mildred (Rucker) O.; A.B., Wesleyan U., Middletown, Conn., 1952; D.M.D. cum laude, Harvard, 1956; m. Anne Mireille Hart, Feb. 16, 1957; children—James, Martha, William, Amy, Lawrence. Asst. dean for student affairs, asso. dean, dir. Dental Health Service, Harvard, 1956-67, acting dean Harvard Sch. Dental Medicine, 1967-68; prof., dean State U. N.Y. Sch. Dental Medicine, Stony Brook, 1968-74, v.p. for health scis., 1974—. Mem. dental edn. rev. com. USPHS div. dental health, 1967-70. Cons. div. edn. and research facilities NIH, 1970-73. Recipient Gold medal Harvard Dental Alumni Assn., 1956. Fellow Am. Coll. Dentists; mem. Omicron Kappa Upsilon. Home: Box 86 Port Jefferson NY 11777 Office: Health Scis Center State U NY Stony Brook NY 11794

OAKS, WILBUR WILSON, JR., physician; b. Phila., Oct. 12, 1928; s. Wilbur Wilson and Marion (Johnston) O.; B.A., Lafayette Coll., Easton, Pa., 1951; M.D., Hahnemann Med. Coll., Phila., 1955; m. Mary Ann Skelton, June 26, 1954; children—Susan, Cynthia, Sally Lou. Intern, then resident in internal medicine Hahnemann Hosp., 1958-61; mem. faculty Hahnemann Med. Coll., 1962—, prof. medicine, 1968—, chmn. dept., 1972—. Served as officer AUS, 1956-58. Recipient Lindback award, 1969; Golden Apple award Student AMA, 1963, 71. Diplomate Am. Bd. Internal Medicine. Mem. Am. Fedn. Clin. Research, AMA, Assn. Profs. Medicine, A.C.P., Am. Coll. Chest Physicians, Pan Am. Med. Assn., Assn. Am. Med. Colls., Pa. Med. Soc., Phila. County Med. Soc., Phila. Coll. Physicians, Alpha Omega Alpha. Republican. Methodist. Club: Variety. Contbr. articles to med. jours. 914 Stony Ln Gladwyne PA 19035 Office: 230 N Broad St Philadelphia PA 19102

OATES, GORDON CEDRIC, aero. engr., educator; b. Vancouver, B.C., Can., Feb. 28, 1932; s. Arthur James Lawson and Kathleen Maude Alix (Binns) O.; came to U.S., 1959, naturalized, 1967; B.A.Sc., U. B.C., 1954; M.Sc., U. Birmingham, Eng., 1956; Ph.D., Calif. Inst. Tech., 1959; m. Joan Buker, Aug. 23, 1961; children—Kenneth Marshall, Brian Cedric, Donald Lawson, Janine. Grad. apprentice Rolls Royce Co., Derby, Eng., 1954-55; asst. prof. dept. aeros. and astronautics M.I.T., 1959-64, asso. prof., 1964-67; asso. prof., U. Wash., 1967-70, prof., 1970—; cons. Pratt & Whitney, United Technologies Chem. Systems Div., Volvo Flygmotor. Athlone fellow, 1954-56. Asso. fellow AIAA; mem. ASME, Sigma Xi. Contbr. articles in field; patentee hydrodynamic focusing method and apparatus. Home: 4943 Stanford Ave NE Seattle WA 98105 Office: University of Washington Seattle WA 98195

OATES, JAMES FRANKLIN, JR., lawyer; b. Evanston, Ill., Nov. 11, 1899; s. James Franklin and Henrietta (Jennings) O.; grad. Phillips Exeter Acad., 1917; B.A., Princeton, 1921; J.D., Northwestern U., 1924; LL.D., Ill. Coll., 1952, Lake Forest Coll., 1958, George Williams Coll., 1959, Hampden-Sydney Coll., 1962, Centre Coll., 1967, Butler U., 1968, Willamette U., 1966, Hamline U., 1966; L.H.D., Neb. Wesleyan U., 1965; D.C.S., Pace Coll., 1965; Litt.D., Presbyn. Coll., 1968; m. Rosalind Wright, June 19, 1925; children—Rosalind (Mrs. Cabell Arnold Pearse), James Franklin III. Admitted to Ill. bar, 1924; asso. firm Cutting, Moore & Sidley, Chgo., and successor, Sidley, Austin, Burgess & Harper, Chgo., 1924-48, partner, 1931-48; counsel Sidley & Austin, 1970—. Legal adviser Chgo. Ordnance Dist., 1942; chief purchase policy Office Chief of Ordnance, Washington, 1942-44; chmn. chief exec. officer, dir. Peoples Gas Light & Coke Co., Chgo., 1948-57; chmn. bd., chief exec. officer, dir. Equitable Life Assurance Soc. U.S., N.Y.C., 1957-69. Mem. N.Y. State Commn. on Quality, Cost and Financing Elementary and Secondary Edn.; nat. chmn. Jobs for Vets. Charter emeritus trustee, former chmn. exec. com. bd. trustees Princeton; trustee Northwestern U. (life), George Williams Coll. (hon.), Chgo. Mus. Sci. and Industry (hon.), Chgo. Northwestern Meml. Hosp. Served as 2d lt., inf. U.S. Army, 1918-19. Recipient, Key Man award, Ave. of Ams. Assn., 1962, Gold Medal award, Gen. Insurance Brokers Assn., 1964, Gold Medal of Merit award, Wharton Sch. alumni assn., 1965, John Phillips award, Phillips Exeter Acad., 1966. Mem. Am., Chgo. (past pres.) bar assns. Republican. Presbyterian (past elder). Clubs: Links, Anglers, Princeton (N.Y.C.); Chicago, Law, Commercial (past pres.), Mid-Day (Chgo); Onwentsia, Old Elm (Lake Forest); University Cottage, Nassau (Princeton, N.J.). Home: 1201 N Elm Tree Rd Lake Forest IL 60045 Office: 401 N Michigan Ave Room 725 Chicago IL 60611

OATES, JOHN ALEXANDER, III, medical educator; b. Fayetteville, N.C., Apr. 23, 1932; s. John Alexander, Jr. and Isabelle (Crowder) O.; B.S. magna cum laudem Wake Forest Coll., 1953; M.D., Bowman Gray Sch. Medicine, 1956; m. Meredith Stringfield, June 12, 1956; children—David Alexander, Christine Larkin, James Caldwell. Intern, then asst. resident medicine N.Y. Hosp.-Cornell U. Med. Center, N.Y.C., 1956-58, 61-62; clin. asso., then sr. investigator Nat. Heart Inst., 1958-63; mem. faculty Vanderbilt U. Sch. Medicine, 1963—, prof. medicine and pharmacology, 1969—, Werthan prof. investigative medicine, 1974—. Mem. drug research bd. Nat. Acad. Scis.-NRC, 1967-71; chmn. pharmacology and toxicology tng. com. Nat. Inst. Gen. Med. Scis., 1969-70. Fellow A.C.P.; mem. Am. Fedn. Clin. Research (pres. 1970-71). Assn. Am. Physicians (sec. 1970-75, councillor 1975—), Am. Soc. Pharmacology and Exptl. Therapeutics (chmn. exec. com. div. clin. pharmacology 1967-69). Participated in discovery antihypertensive effect of methyldopa, elucidation of a number of interactions between drugs in man; research on the prostoglandin system. Home: 6440 Brownlee Dr Nashville TN 37205

OATES, JOHN FRANCIS, educator; b. Holyoke, Mass., Aug. 7, 1934; s. William Adrian and Lilian (Woods) O.; B.A., Yale U., 1956, M.A., 1958, Ph.D., 1960; postgrad. (Fulbright fellow) Am. Sch. Classical Studies in Athens (Greece), 1956-57; m. Rosemary Walsh, June 27, 1957; children—Elizabeth, Emily, John Francis, Sarah. Instr. classics Yale U., 1960-63, asst. prof., 1963-67; asso. prof. ancient history Duke U., 1967-71, prof., chmn. dept. classical studies, 1971—, chmn. Humanities Council, 1975—. Hon. research asst., Morse fellow Univ. Coll. London (Eng.), 1965-66; vis. prof. Smith Coll., Northampton, Mass., 1967, 68; mem. mng. com. Intercollegiate Center Classical Studies in Rome (Italy), 1972-77; mem. mng. com. Am. Sch. Classical Studies in Athens, 1973—, mem. com. on coms., 1975-77; mem. Council for Internat. Exchange of Scholars, 1974-77; v.p. Triangle Univs. Center for Advanced Study, Inc., 1975—; trustee Nat. Humanities Center, 1977—; adv. council Sch. Classical Studies, Am. Acad. in Rome, 1976—. Am. Council Learned Socs. fellow, 1973-74. Mem. Am. Philol. Assn. (chmn. com. computer activities 1974-75, dir. 1975-78, mem. N.C. humanities com. 1977—), Archaeol. Inst. Am., Am. Hist. Assn., Am. Soc. Papyrologists (v.p. 1971-73, pres. 1976—, dir.), Assn. Internationale de Papyrologues, Classical Assn. Middle West and South (v.p. 1972-74, pres. So. sect. 1974-76). Author: The Status Designation, 1963; (with A.E. Samuel, C.B. Welles) Yale Papyri in the Beinecke Library, 1967; (with W.H. Willis, R.S. Bagnall) A Checklist of Papyrological Editions, 2d edit., 1978; mem. adv. bd. Greek, Roman and Byzantine Studies, 1977—. Home: 2416 Alpine Rd Durham NC 27707 Office: Dept of Classical Studies Duke U Durham NC 27706

OATES, JOHN WILLIAM, writer, singer; b. N.Y.C., Apr. 7, 1948; s. Alfred William and Anna Jane (De Palma) O.; B.S. in Communications, Temple U., 1970. Rec. artist, 1972—; albums include: Abandoned, 1960; Luncheonette, 1973; Daryl Hall and John Oates, 1975; Bigger than Both of Us, 1976; Along the Red Ledge, 1978; Beauty on a Back Street, 1977 (all Gold Records); singles include: Sara Smile, 1975; Rich Girl, 1976. Recipient Best Song award Nat. Assn. TV and Rec. Artists, 1975. Mem. Am. Fedn. Musicians, ASCAP, AFTRA, Internat. Karting Fedn., World Karting Assn., L.I. Karting Assn. Office: care Champion Entertainment 130 W 57th St Suite 12B New York NY 10019

OATES, JOYCE CAROL, author; b. Lockport, N.Y., June 16, 1938; d. Frederic James and Caroline (Bush) Oates; B.A., Syracuse U., 1960; M.A., U. Wis., 1961; m. Raymond Joseph Smith, Jan. 23, 1961. Prof. English, U. Detroit, 1961-67, U. Windsor, Ont., Can., 1967—; writer-in-residence Princeton U., 1978—. Mem. Am. Acad. and Inst. Arts and Letters. Recipient O. Henry Prize Story award, 1967-68. Guggenheim fellow, 1967-68. Author: (stories) By The North Gate, 1963; (play) The Sweet Enemy, 1965; (novel) With Shuddering Fall, 1965; (stories) Upon the Sweeping Flood, 1966; (novel) A Garden of Earthly Delights, 1967; (poems) Women in Love, 1968; Expensive People, 1968; Them (Nat. Book award 1970), 1969; (poems) Anonymous Sins, 1969; (stories) The Wheel of Love, 1970; (poems) Love and its Derangements, 1970; (novel) Wonderland, 1971; (essays) The Edge of Impossibility, 1971; (stories) Marriages and Infidelities, 1972; (poems) Angel Fire, 1973; (novel) Do With Me What You Will, 1973; (play) Sunday Dinner, produced at Am. Place Theatre, 1970; (essays) The Hostile Sun; The Poetry of D.H. Lawrence, 1973; (poems) Dreaming America, 1973; (stories) The Hungry Ghosts, 1974; (stories) The Goddess and other Women, 1974; (essays) New Heaven, New Earth, 1974; (play) Miracle Play, 1974; (stories) Where Are You Going, Where Have You Been, 1974; (stories) The Poisoned Kiss and Other Portuguese Stories, 1975; (stories) The Seduction and Other Stories, 1975; (novel) The Assassins, 1975; (stories) Crossing the Border, 1976; (novels) Childwold, 1976, The Triumph of the Spider Monkey, 1977; (stories) Night-Side, 1977; (poems) Women Whose Lives Are Food, Men Whose Lives Are Money, 1978; (novels) Son of the Morning, 1978, Unholy Loves, 1979, Cybele, 1979; (stories) All the Good People I've Left Behind, 1979; (play) Daisy (prod. at Cubioulo Theatre, N.Y.C.), 1980; editor: Scenes from American Life, 1973, Ont. Rev.; The Best American Short Stories, 1979, also fiction in nat. mags. Office: Princeton U Creative Writing Program 185 Nassau St Princeton NJ 08540

OATES, STEPHEN BAERY, educator; b. Pampa, Tex., Jan. 5, 1936; s. Steve Theodore and Florence (Baer) O.; B.A. magna cum laude, U. Tex., 1958, M.A., 1960, Ph.D., 1968; div.; children—Gregory Allen, Stephanie. Prof. history U. Mass., Amherst, 1971—. Recipient Chancellor's medal for outstanding scholarship U. Mass., 1976. Guggenheim fellow, 1972; sr. summer fellow Nat. Endowment for Humanities, 1978. Fellow Tex. State Hist. Assn.; mem. Tex. Inst. Letters, So. Hist. Assn., Orgn. Am. Historians, Phi Beta Kappa. Author: Confederate Cavalry West of the River, 1961; Rip Ford's Texas, 1963; Republic of Texas, 1968; Visions of Glory, 1970; To Purge This Land With Blood: A Biography of John Brown, 1970; Portrait of America, 2 vols., 1973, rev. edit., 1976; The Fires of Jubilee: Nat Turner's Fierce Rebellion, 1975; With Malice Toward None: The Life of Abraham Lincoln (Christopher award for outstanding lit., Barondess/Lincoln award N.Y. Civil War Round Table), 1977, Brit. and Spanish edits., 1978; Our Fiery Trial: Abraham Lincoln, John Brown, and the Civil War Era, 1979. Contbr. articles and essays to periodicals; lectr. Home: 259 Grantwood Dr Amherst MA 01002 Office: Dept History U Mass Amherst MA 01002

OATIS, WILLIAM NATHAN, journalist; b. Marion, Ind., Jan. 7, 1914; s. John Ross and Cora Blanche (Eddy) O.; student DePauw U., Greencastle, Ind., 1932-33, U. Minn., 1943-44, U. Mich., 1945; m. Laurabelle Zack, Mar. 31, 1950; children—Jonathan, Jeremy. Reporter, Marion (Ind.) Leader-Tribune, 1933-37; rewrite man, reporter, Indpls. Bur. of A.P., 1937-42, rewrite man, New York Bur., 1946-48, rewrite man, reporter London Bur., 1948-50, bur. chief, Prague, 1950-51; detained by Czechoslovakian govt., 1951, tried and sentenced in Prague, 1951 and imprisoned, released to U.S. govt. and returned to U.S. 1953, exonerated in jud. rev., 1969; reporter, U.N. Bur., A.P., 1953. Served with AUS, 1942-46. Recipient Overseas Press Club's George Polk Meml. award, 1952, William the Silent Journalism Award, 1954. Mem. UN Corrs. Assn. (pres. 1970). Clubs: Press (Indpls. and London). Home: 524 E 20th St New York NY 10009 Office: 50 Rockefeller Plaza New York NY 10020

O'BAR, JACK, librarian; b. Cowlington, Okla., Dec. 15, 1926; s. Albert Idus and Eulalia Agusta (Holeman) O'B.; B.A., U. Okla., 1954, M.L.S., 1955; Ph.D., Ind. U., 1975; m. Anne Margaret Chrystal, Aug. 8, 1959; children—Moira, Barry. Asst. documents librarian Okla. State U., Stillwater, 1955-57; head librarian Southwestern State Coll., Weatherford, Okla., 1957-62, Mankato (Minn.) State Coll., 1962-69; teaching fellow Ind. U., Bloomington, 1969-72; dir. higher edn. Consortium Library U. Alaska, Anchorage, also Alaska Meth. U., 1972—. Chmn., Okla. State Council Coll. and Univ. Librarians, 1957-58; mem. ad hoc adv. com. Alaska Gov's. Council on Libraries, 1972—. Served with U.S. Army, 1944-46. Mem. Am., Alaska library assns., Phi Beta Kappa, Delta Phi Alpha, Kappa Gamma Epsilon. Democrat. Home: SRA Box 191A Shore Dr Anchorage AK 99502

OBEL, ARNE, chem. co. exec.; b. Copenhagen, Apr. 14, 1926; s. Holger and Irma (Lindahl) O.; B.S., U. Denver, 1951; student advanced mgmt. Cornell U., 1968, Stanford U., 1973; m. Nina Jean Wallis, May 31, 1952; children—Michael, Christopher. Dir. mktg. Goodyear Tire & Rubber Co., Akron, Ohio, in Scandinavia, 1952-63; pres. Downtown Valet, Inc., Phoenix, 1963-65; gen. mgr. rubber chems. div. Monsanto Co., St. Louis, 1965-75; group v.p. Diamond Shamrock Chem. Co., Cleve., 1975—; exec. v.p. corp. staff Diamond Shamrock Corp., Cleve., 1976—; dir. Centran Corp., Cleve. Nat. bd. dirs. Jr. Achievement, 1977. Lutheran. Clubs: Rolling Rock (Ligonier, Pa.); Northwood Country, Dallas (Dallas). Home: 7 Rue du Lac Dallas TX 75230 Office: 2300 Southland Center Dallas TX 75201

OBENCHAIN, IRVING ROCK, JR., electronics co. exec.; b. Birmingham, Ala., May 23, 1921; s. Irving Rock and Louise (Feminear) O.; B.S., U.S. Mil. Acad., 1942; S.M. in Elec. Engring., Mass. Inst. Tech., 1951; grad. Army Command and Gen. Staff Coll., 1954, Indsl. Coll. Armed Services, 1958; m. Mary Williamson, May 30, 1942 (div. July 1960); children—Kathleen Obenchain Glass, Irving Rock III, Mary Jane Obenchain Brooks; m. 2d, Yun Suk Lew, July 25, 1962; 1 stepdau., Jung Yun Kim (Mrs. Joseph Ma). Commd. 2d lt. U.S. Army, 1942, advanced through grades to brig. gen., 1967; dir. electronics testing Army Test and Evaluation Command, 1962-64; comdr. U.S. Army Strategic Communications Command, Europe, 1964-65; asst. mgr. operations, then dep. mgr. Nat. Communications System, Washington, 1966-67; dep. dir. Nat. Mil. Command System, Def. Communications Agy., Washington, 1968-69; comdg. gen. SAFEGUARD Communications Agy., Fort Huachuca, Ariz., 1969-72, ret. 1972; v.p. Tech. Service Corp., Santa Monica, Calif., 1972-77; chief engr. WWMCCS/NMCS engring. TRW, Redondo Beach, Calif., 1977—. Decorated D.S.M., Bronze Star, Legion Merit with oak leaf cluster. Mem. IEEE (sr.), Sigma Xi. Methodist. Co-inventor digital telephone switching system. Home: 1099 Vista Grande Pacific Palisades CA 90272 Office: One Space Park Redondo Beach CA 90278. *Solve problems, don't make them.*

OBENHAUS, VICTOR, educator, clergyman; b. Superior, Wis., Sept. 26, 1903; s. Herman and Grace (Dexter) O.; A.B., Oberlin Coll., 1925; B.D., Union Theol. Sem., N.Y.C., 1929; Ed.D., Columbia 1940; D.D., Chgo. Theol. Sem., 1973; m. Marion Pendleton, July 30, 1938; children—Constance, Helen, Mark. Ordained to ministry Congl. Christian Ch., 1929; asst. Ch. of Covenant, Cleve., 1929-36; mem. ministerial staff Riverside Ch., N.Y.C., 1936-38; prin. Pleasant Hill Acad., Tenn., 1938-44; mem. federated theol. faculty Chgo. Theol. Sem., U. Chgo., 1944—, asso. prof. ch. in agrl. and indsl. life, 1948-61; prof. Christian ethics Chgo. Theol. Sem., 1961—, acting pres., 1973—. Cons. com. on theol. edn. United Ch. Christ, exec. Mid Am. sems., 1974—. Vice chmn. bd. dirs. Kobe Coll. Corp., Japan; bd. dirs., co-founder Agropolitan Ministries; chmn. Ill. Prisons and Jails Project. Mem. Am., Rural sociol. socs., Religious Research Assn., Soc. for Sci. Study Religion, Ams. for Moral Integrity (chmn.), Chg. Com. To Defend Bill of Rights (co-chmn., Civil Libertarian of Yr. 1979), Am. Soc. Christian Ethics (pres. 1966-67). Author: Hebrew Prophets and America's Conscience, 1948; The Responsible Christian, 1957; Church and Faith in Mid-America, 1963. Co-author: Religion in American Culture, 1964; Ethics for An Industrial Age, 1965. Editor: The Church in Our World, 1965; And See The People, 1968; (with others) Suburban Religion, 1974. Home: 5549 Woodlawn Ave Chicago IL 60637

OBER, FRANK BENEDICT, lawyer; b. Balt., Sept. 25, 1889; s. Albert G. and Rebecca G. (Hambleton) O.; grad. Gilman Sch., Balt., 1906; A.B., Princeton, 1910; LL.B., Harvard, 1913; m. Margaret De Lancey Rochester, Apr. 16, 1914; children—Richard F., DeLancey R., Frank Benedict; m. 2d, Helen Montgomery, May 25, 1964. Admitted to Md. bar, 1912; since practiced in Balt.; mem. firm Ober, Grimes & Shriver, 1916—. Mem. State Commn. on Interracial Relations, 1942-45, War Emergency Legislation, 1942-43. Chmn. Md. Democrats for Dewey, 1944, Md. Commn. on Subversive Activities, 1948-49. Served to maj. F.A., U.S. Army, 1917-19, with AEF in France. Decorated Silver Star. Mem. Law Assn., Am. (mem. adv. bd. Jour. 1955-58), Md. (pres. 1950), Balt. bar assns. Clubs: Maryland, Merchants, Elkridge. Author: Communism and the Supreme Court (Lawyer's Treasury), 1956. Contbr. articles to law jours. Home: 908 St George's Rd Baltimore MD 21210

OBER, STUART ALAN, book publisher, investment cons.; b. N.Y.C., Oct. 2, 1946; s. Paul and Gertrude E. (Stollerman) O.; B.A., Wesleyan U., Middletown, Conn., 1968; postgrad. U. Sorbonne, Paris, 1970, Baruch Coll., City U. N.Y., 1976. Pres., editor-in-chief, chmn. bd., Beekman Pubs. Inc., N.Y.C., 1973—; investment cons., 1972—; tax shelter specialist Loeb, Rhoades & Co., 1976-77; div. dir. tax investment dept. Josephthal & Co., Inc., 1977; mgr. tax-shelter dept. Bruns, Nordeman, Rea & Co., 1978—. Home: 38 Hicks St Brooklyn Heights NY 11201 Office: 53 Park Pl New York NY 10007

OBER, WILLIAM B., pathologist, educator; b. Boston, May 15, 1920; s. Harry and Rebecca (Cohen) O.; A.B., Harvard, 1941; M.D., Boston U., 1946; m. Rhoda Schott, Sept. 2, 1952; children—Elaine Margaret, Stephen Frederick. Intern Beth Israel Hosp., Boston, 1946-48; resident Boston Lying-in Hosp., 1948; dir. labs. Knickerbocker Hosp., N.Y.C., 1956-70, Hackensack (N.J.) Hosp., 1977—; attending pathologist Beth Israel Hosp., N.Y.C., 1970—; clin. prof. pathology N.Y. Med. Coll., 1967-72; prof. pathology Mount Sinai Sch. Medicine, N.Y.C., 1973—; vis. prof. pathology N.J. Coll. Medicine, Newark, 1975—. Served with AUS, 1943-45. Nat. Cancer Inst. Research fellow, 1948-50. Mem. N.Y. Acad. Medicine, Royal Soc. Medicine. Author: Boswell's Clap and Other Essays, 1979. Contbr. articles to profl. jours. Home: 44 Woodland Park Dr Tenafly NJ 07670 Office: Hospital Pl Hackensack NJ 07601. *I am a failed pagan hedonist who has taken refuge in the work ethic.*

OBERBECK, ARTHUR WILLIAM, cons., ret. army officer; b. Chgo., Jan. 13, 1912; s. Arthur Walter and Edna (Trinkaus) O.; B.S., U.S. Mil. Acad., 1937; M.S. in Civil Engring., U. Calif. at Berkeley, 1940; grad. Army War Coll., 1955; J.D., U. Tex. Law Sch., 1975; m. Margaret Lanigan, Sept. 7, 1938, (dec. Nov. 1970); children—Donald D., Michael M.; m. 2d, Carole Kivela, June 23, 1972; children—Tracy Janine, Scott Ryan. Commd. 2d lt. C.E., 1937, advanced through grades to lt. gen., 1969; assigned 5th Engrs., Ft. Belvoir, Va., 1937-39, 3d Engrs., Hawaii and Pacific areas, 1940-44; div. engr. 24th Inf. Div., 1942-44, Hdgrs. S.W. Pacific, 1944-45, World War II; assigned Manhattan Engring. Dist and AEC, 1945-47; asst. prof. math. U.S. Mil. Acad., 1947-51; assigned Armed Forces Spl. Weapons Project, 1951-54; mem. strategic plans group, joint staff Joint Chiefs Staff, 1955-56; dir. spl. weapons devel. USCONARC, 1956-60; dir. coordination and analysis Office Army Chief Staff, 1960-62; comdg. gen. 1st Inf. Div., Ft. Riley, Kans., 1963-64; dir. J-3 div. U.S. European Command, Paris, France, 1964-66; comdr. Joint Task Force Eight and comdr. Test Command, DASA, Sandia Base, N.Mex., 1966-68; comdg. gen. U.S. Army Engr. Center, also comdt. U.S. Army Engr. Sch., Ft. Belvoir, Va., 1968; sr. army mem. Weapons Systems Evaluation group, Washington, 1968-69, dir., 1969-72; ret. 1972; legal cons. Center for Energy Studies, U. Tex., 1976—. Decorated D.S.M., Legion of Merit with two oak leaf clusters. Mem. State Bar Tex., Am. Bar Assn. Club: Balcones Country. Home: 3605 Steck Ave Apt 2131 Austin TX 78759 Office: CES ENS Bldg U Tex Austin TX

OBERDORFER, LOUIS F., fed. judge; b. Birmingham, Ala., Feb. 21, 1919; s. A. Leo and Stella Maud (Falk) O.; A.B., Dartmouth, 1939; LL.B., Yale, 1946; m. Elizabeth Weil, July 31, 1941; children—John Louis, Kathryn Lee, Thomas Lee, William L. Admitted to Ala. bar, 1946, D.C. bar, 1949; law clk. to Justice Hugo L. Black, 1946-47; practiced in Washington, 1947-77; pvt. practice, 1947-51; mem. firm Wilmer, Cutler, & Pickering and predecessors, 1951-61, 65-77; asst. atty. gen. tax div. Dept. of Justice, 1961-65; U.S. dist. judge for D.C., 1977—; Vis. lectr. Yale Law Sch., 1966, 71. Adv. com. Fed. Rules Civil Procedure, 1962—; co-chmn. lawyers com. Civil Rights Under Law, 1967-69. Served to capt. AUS, 1941-46. Mem. Am., D.C. (bd. govs. 1972-77, pres. 1977), Ala. bar assns., Yale Law Sch. Assn. (pres. 1971-73). Home: 1423 Kirby Rd McLean VA 22101 Office: US Courthouse John Marshall Pl and Constitution Ave NW Washington DC 20001

OBERG, ALBIN HAROLD, hosp. adminstr.; b. Stamford, Conn., Jan. 12, 1924; s. Gustaf Adolf and Carolina (Hayrinen) O.; B.B.A., Upsala Coll., 1949, LL.D., 1972; M. Hosp. Adminstrn., Northwestern U., 1951; m. Phyllis Iverson, Apr. 19, 1952; children—Karin Lisa, Carl Iver. Asst. dir. Malden (Mass.) Hosp., 1951-52; pres. Clara Maass Meml. Hosp., Belleville, N.J., 1952—. Mem. Belleville Found. Served with AUS, 1943-45; ETO. Decorated Purple Heart. Recipient Mary McGraw award Northwestern U., 1951; named Alumnus of Year, Upsala Coll., 1961. Fellow Am. Coll. Hosp. Adminstrs.; mem. N.J. (past pres.), Am. hosp. assns., Am. Pub. Health Assn., Swedish Pioneer Soc., Scandinavian Frat. Am., Scandanavian Found., Adminstrs. Forum of N.J. Club: Essex Fells Country. Home: 12 Hamilton Dr W North Caldwell NJ Office: 1-A Franklin Ave Belleville NJ 07109

OBERG, JAMES L., co. exec.; b. Caledonia, N.Y., 1917; ed. Lehigh U., 1940. Vice pres. Bangor Punta Corp., Greenwich, Conn., now pres. subsidiary Smith & Wesson, Springfield, Mass. Home: Suffield CT 06078 Office: Smith & Wesson Springfield MA

OBERG, ROGER WINSTON, educator; b. Mpls., Oct. 5, 1919; s. Ezra Nathaniel and Adele Erika Wilhelmina (Boquist) O.; student North Park Coll., 1937-38; B.B.A. with distinction, U. Minn., 1941; M.B.A., Ohio State U., 1947; Ph.D., M.I.T., 1955; m. Pansy Jane Sherrill, June 29, 1957; children—Sherrill Katherine, Roger Winston, Keith Eric, Elizabeth Jane. Mgmt. trainee Sears Roebuck & Co., 1941-43; grad. asst. Ohio State U., 1946-47, M.I.T., 1947-50; human relations research analyst Prudential Ins. Co., Newark, 1950-51; personnel specialist Esso Research & Engring. Co., Linden, N.J., 1952-57; prof. mgmt. Mich. State U., 1957—; vis. prof. Leeds U. (Eng.), 1959, U. Rio Grande do Sul (Brazil), 1959-61, Stanford U., 1964, North European Mgmt. Inst. (Norway), 1974-76. Vice chmn. Met. Lansing Transit Authority, 1971-72; chmn. Meridian Twp. Republican Com., 1966-72. Served to 2d lt. USAAF, 1943-46; PTO. Decorated Bronze Star medal; recipient Forensic medal U. Minn., 1941, Lit. Rev. prize, 1941. Mem. Am. Psychol. Assn., Acad. Mgmt., Internat. Registry of OD Profls., AAAS, Beta Gamma Sigma, Delta Sigma Rho. Mem. Evangelical Covenant Ch. Clubs: Univ. (Mich. State U.); Lansing Ski; Scandinavian Am. Mem. editorial bd. Mich. State U. Bus. Topics, Orgn. and Adminstrn., 1970-74, Quar. Jour. of Mgmt. Devel., 1968-74. Contbr. articles to profl. jours. Home: 1585 Hillside Dr Okemos MI 48864 Office: 243 Eppley Center Mich State U East Lansing MI 48823

OBERHELMAN, HARLEY DEAN, educator; b. Clay Center, Kans., June 30, 1928; s. Gideon Alfred and Anna (Vittetoe) O.; B.S., U. Kans., 1950, M.A., 1952, Ph.D., 1958; m. Hope Constance Nansen, Sept. 9, 1954; children—Richard Alfred, David Dean. Instr. in Spanish, Lawrence (Kans.) Pub. Schs., 1950-55, dir. fgn. langs., 1956-58; instr. U. Kans., Lawrence, 1955-56; mem. faculty Tex. Tech. U., Lubbock, 1958—, prof., 1963—, chmn. dept. classical and Romance langs., 1963-70; chmn. Latin Am. area studies, 1969-76. Fulbright lectr. English as fgn. lang. Nat. U. Tucuman (Argentina), 1961; lectr. in Argentina for NDEA, 1962, 63, 64; leader Rotary Internat. Study Team, Chile, 1970, Finland, 1973. Tex. Research grantee in Uruguay, 1962, Colombia, 1977. Mem. Am. Assn. Tchrs. Spanish and Portuguese, S.W. Council Latin Am. Studies. Author: (with Agnes M. Brady) Espanol Moderno, I and II, 1964, 65; Ernesto Sabato, 1970; asso. editor Hispania, 1953-65. Home: 6215 Louisville Dr Lubbock TX 79413

OBERHELMAN, HARRY ALVIN, JR., educator, surgeon; b. Chgo., Nov. 15, 1923; s. Harry Alvin and Beatrice (Babel) O.; student Yale, 1942-43; B.S., U. Chgo., 1946, M.D., 1947; m. Betty Jane Porter, June 12, 1946; children—Harry Alvin III, James I., Robert P., Thomas L., Nancy L. Intern, U. Chgo. Clinics, 1947-48, resident in surgery, 1948-51, 52-57; asst. prof., then asso. prof. surgery U. Chgo. Sch. Medicine, 1957-60; mem. faculty Stanford (Calif.) Sch. Medicine, 1960—, prof. surgery, 1964—. Bd. dirs. Inst. Med. Research, Santa Clara County, Calif., 1966—; mem. Calif. Bd. Med. Quality Assurance, 1970—. Served with USAF, 1951-53. Diplomate Am. Bd. Surgery. Mem. AMA, Calif. Med. Assn., Soc. Univ. Surgeons, Am., Western, Pacific Coast surg. assns., Soc. Alimentary Tract, Halsted Soc., Am. Gastroenterol. Assn., Fedn. State Med. Bds. U.S. (dir. 1979—). Author papers in field. Home: 668 Cabrillo St Stanford CA 94305

OBERHUBER, KONRAD JOHANNES, art museum curator, educator; b. Linz/Donau, Austria, Mar. 31, 1935; Ph.D., U. Vienna (Austria), 1959, Dozent, 1971; m. Marianne Liebknecht, 1964; children—Lukas, Nikolaus, Wanako, Mariella. Asst., U. Vienna delegated as research fellow to Austrian Inst. in Rome, 1959-61; asst., then curator Albertina, Vienna, 1961-71; research curator Nat. Gallery Art, Washington, 1971-74; guest lectr. Fogg Art Mus., Harvard U., Cambridge, Mass., spring 1974, curator of drawings, prof. fine arts, 1974—; Italian Ministry of Culture scholar, Rome, winter 1958; asst. prof. Smith Coll., 1964-65; Kress fellow Harvard Center for Renaissance Studies, Florence, Italy, 1965-66; guest prof. Cambridge (Eng.) U., 1968; fellow Inst. for Advanced Study, Princeton, N.J., 1974-75. Nat. Endowment for Humanities grantee, 1979-80. Mem. Print Council Am. Author books, the most recent being: (with others) Early Italian Engravings in the National Gallery of Art, 1973; (with S. Ferina) Maestri Umbri del Quattro e Cinquecento, 1977; contbr. articles to profl. publs. Office: Fogg Art Mus Harvard U Cambridge MA 02138

OBERLIN, DAVID WRIGHT, govt. ofcl.; b. Atchison, Kans., Jan. 6, 1920; s. William C. and Dorothy (Wright) O.; B.S. in Engring., U. Mich., 1948; m. A. Elinor Houston, Feb. 26, 1944; children—Diane, David Alan, Alida, Robert. Plant supt. Allied Chem. Co., 1947-57; asst. sec., fiscal officer Toledo-Lucas County Port Authority, 1957-67; port dir. Seaway Port Authority Duluth, 1967-69; adminstr. St. Lawrence Seaway Devel. Corp., 1969—, acting dir. Office Deepwater Ports Office Sec. Transp., 1975-76. Vice-pres., dir. Seaway Internat. Bridge Corp. Mem. Permanent Internat. Assn. Nav. Congresses; bd. dirs. Gt. Lakes Basin Commn. Served with USNR, 1940-46, 50-52. Decorated Silver Star, Personal Commendation ribbon; recipient Dept. Transp., Gold medal, 1973. Mem. Am. Assn. Port Authorities (dir.), Tau Beta Pi, Phi Kappa Phi. Home: 6401 Cavalier Corridor Falls Church VA 22044 Office: Adminstr St Lawrence Seaway Devel Corp 800 Independence Ave SW Washington DC 20591

OBERLY, JAMES RICHARD, lawyer, internat. consultant; b. Milw., Nov. 27, 1921; s. William Edward and Mae (Nichols) O.; B.A., U. Wis., 1943; J.D., Yale, 1948; m. Lucille Mary Kraus, Dec. 17, 1947 (dec. 1961); children—Kathryn, James. Admitted to Ill. bar, 1949, Wis. bar, 1971, U.S. Supreme Ct. bar, U.S. Tax Ct. bar; with firm Pope & Ballard, Chgo., 1948-50; asst. gen. counsel, asst. sec. Admiral Corp., Chgo., 1950-53, v.p., 1955-60; pres., dir. Admiral Internat. Corp., 1953-60, Admiral Corp. Interamericana, 1953-60; pres. Sunbeam Internat. A.G. Chgo., 1961-68, Sunbeam-Oster S.A., Nassau, 1961-68; cons. internat. bus., law with Schwartz & Oberly, Ltd., Manitowac, Wis., 1971-75; dir. Rowenta GmbH (West Germany), Corrada & Fenske, S.p.A. (Italy), Sunbeam Italiana, S.p.A. (Italy). Chmn. Manitowoc Indsl. Devel. Commn., 1973—. Mem. Nat. Fgn. Trade Council, Mexican C. of C. of U.S., Am. Arbitration Assn. (nat. panel), Am., Wis., Manitowoc County, Chgo. bar assns., State Bar Wis., Phi Delta Theta, Phi Eta Sigma, Phi Kappa Phi, Beta Gamma Sigma. Office: 926 S 8th St Manitowoc WI 54220

OBERMANN, C. ESCO, psychologist, rehab. cons.; b. Yarmouth, Iowa, July 31, 1904; s. Albert B. and Evalyne (Calloway) O.; A.B., U. Iowa, 1927, M.A., 1931, Ph.D., 1938; m. Avalon F. Law, June 3, 1929. Chief vocational edn. Rochester (Minn.) Schs., 1928-36; research fellow U. Iowa, Iowa City, 1938-40, asso. prof. psychology, 1966-70; asso. prof. psychology U. Tex., Austin, 1946; dir. vocational rehab. VA, 1946-60; dir. St. Paul Rehab. Center, 1960-63; research fellow Vocational Rehab. Adminstrn., 1963-65; asso. prof. psychology Iowa Wesleyan Coll., Mt. Pleasant, 1965-66; rehab. cons., Hudson, Wis., 1970—; adj. prof. Mankato (Minn.) State U., 1977—. Chmn. adv. council Rehab. Research Center, U. Minn. Med. Sch., 1978—; mem. adv. com. Univ. House, U. Iowa, 1979—; mem. com. handicapped People-to-People Program; mem. President's Com. on Employment Handicapped. Served to col. USAAF, 1940-46. Diplomate Am. Bd. Profl. Psychologists. Fellow Am. Psychol. Assn., AAAS; mem. Nat. Rehab. Counseling Assn. (chmn. ethics com.), Nat. Rehab. Assn. (pres. 1961-62, exec. bd., chmn. com. on sci. and practice), Minn. Rehab. Assn. (pres. 1954), Iowa Rehab. Assn. (pres. 1967), Am. Personnel and Guidance Assn., Am. Speech and Hearing Assn., Assn. Advancement of Psychology, Mil. Order World Wars, Sigma Xi, Delta Upsilon. Episcopalian. Mason. Author: A History of Vocational Rehabilitation in America, 1965; Coordination of Services for Handicapped Children and Youth, 1963; (with others) Continuing Education for Rehabilitation Counselors, 1969. Editor: Basic Issues In Rehabilitation, 1972. Home: Afton MN 55001 Office: Box 241 Hudson WI 54016

OBERMAYER, LEON JACOB, lawyer; b. Sciota, Ill., Sept. 24, 1886; s. Hermann and Veronika (Lehmann) O.; A.B., Central High Sch., Phila., Pa., 1904; J.D., U. Pa., 1908, certificate of merit, 1961; D.H.L. Hebrew Union Coll., Jewish Inst. Religion, 1954; LL.D. (hon.), Temple U., 1956, Drexel U., 1978; m. Julia L. Sinsheimer, May 24, 1923; children—Herman Joseph, Helen Adele (Mrs. Alfred M. Sellers), Arthur S. Admitted to Pa. bar, 1908; counsel firm Obermayer, Rebmann, Maxwell & Hippel, Phila. Chmn. Selective Service Bd., World Wars I and II; mem. appeal bd. East dist. Pa. Selective Service, 1966-70, exec. com. Am. Heart Assn., 1963-66, chmn. bd. S.E. Pa., 1962-64; former mem. Recreational Commn. Pa.; vice chmn. Hebrew Union Coll.-Jewish Inst. Religion, Cin., 1954; pres. YM-YWHA, Phila., 1915-26, Girls' Aid, 1921-28; mem. exec. com. Nat. Council Jewish Welfare Bd.; mem. exec. council, solicitor, hon. pres. Phila. council Boy Scouts Am., (Silver Beaver award 1941, spl. service medal, 1948); mem. Bd. Public Edn., Phila., 1938-61, pres., 1955-61; mem. U.S. nat. commn. UNESCO, 1954-60; bd. dirs. Albert Einstein Med. Center, 1917-54, Gov. Moss Rehab. Hosp., 1917—, United Fund Phila.; v.p. Jewish Hosp. Phila., 1917-54; hon. bd. dirs. Gratz Coll., Phila., 1950—; chmn., v.p. Woods Schs., Langhorne, Pa. Recipient First Isaac Mayer Wise award Phila., 1979. Brandeis U. fellow, 1968. Mem. Pa. Prison Soc. (gov.), Hebrew S.S. Soc. (gov.), Assn. Alumni Central High Sch. Phila. (hon. pres.), Pa. (past v.p.), Phila. (chmn. bd. govs. 1938, chmn. com. profl. guidance 1938-57, Fidelity Bank award 1972) bar assns., Am. Law Inst. (life), Acad. Natural Scis. Phila. (trustee), Area Council Econ. Edn. (v.p.), Am. Jewish Hist. Soc. (pres. 1965-68; chmn. bd. govs. 1968-71), Indian Rights Assn., Phila. World Affairs Council, Franklin Inst., U.

Pa. Law Alumni Assn. (pres. 1956-59), Zeta Beta Tau. Republican. Jewish (trustee synagogue). Mason, mem. B'nai B'rith. Clubs: Locust (gov.), Union League, Lawyers, Midday, Socialegal, Philmont Country (gov.), Sunday Breakfast, Peale, Right Angle. Home: 135 S 19th St Apt 1210 Philadelphia PA 19103 Office: Packard Bldg Philadelphia PA 19102

OBERMESSER, CLOVIS FERNAND, elec. mfg. co. exec.; b. Belgium, Apr. 7, 1925; s. Alfred Philip and Laure (Seutin) O.; Elec. Engr., U. Paul Pastur, Belgium, 1951; M.Sc. in Elec. Engring., U. Pitts., 1955; m. Madeleine Wilme, May 18, 1946; children—Myriam, Chantal, Christine. With Westinghouse Electric Corp., Pitts., 1955—, corp. v.p., 1979—, pres. Far East group, 1979—. Mem. IEEE. Republican. Roman Catholic. Clubs: Pitts. Field, Sky. Home: 109 Pheasant Dr Pittsburgh PA 15238 Office: Gateway Center Westinghouse Bldg Pittsburgh PA 15222

OBERMEYER, ERNEST DAVID, pub. co. exec.; b. N.Y.C., Nov. 6, 1924; s. David Harris and Marguerite (Floersheimer) O.; grad. Phillips Acad., Andover, Mass., 1942; B.A., Yale, 1948; m. Phyllis Horton, Oct. 12, 1951 (div. Nov. 1972); 1 son, David.; m. 2d, Shirley Weber, Nov. 18, 1972. Salesman, Gen. Foods Co., N.Y.C., 1948-50, Am. Molasses Co., N.Y.C., 1950-52; salesman Supermarket News, Fairchild Publs., N.Y.C., 1952-71, advt. dir., 1971-72, advt. dir., pub., 1972—, v.p. Fairchild Publs., 1974—. Served to 1st. lt. USAAF, 1943-46; PTO. Republican. Club: Yale (N.Y.C.). Home: 1095 Park Av New York NY 10028 Office: 7 E 12th St New York NY 10003

OBERMEYER, JACK ARTHUR, petroleum co. exec., ret. naval officer; b. Jacksonville, Ill., Mar. 19, 1915; s. Harry and Gertrude (Newman) O.; B.S., U.S. Naval Acad., 1937; M.S., Mass. Inst. Tech., 1941; M.A., George Washington U., 1962; m. Joan G. Dotson, Sept. 15, 1945; children—Jo Ann, Helen E. Commnd. ensign U.S. Navy, 1937, advanced through grades to capt., 1955; assigned USS Louisville, 1937-39, Naval Shipyard, Pearl Harbor, 1941-45, Boston, 1945-46; mem. Naval Mission to Brazil, 1946-49; assigned design br. Bur. Ships, Navy Dept., 1949-52, Naval Shipyard, Puget Sound, 1952-54; prof. naval architecture Mass. Inst. Tech., 1954-58; head, preliminary design br. Bur. of Ships, Navy Dept., Washington, 1958-59; dir. ship design, 1959-60; comdg. officer and dir. David Taylor Model Basin, Carderock, Md., 1960-63; comdg. officer U.S. Naval Ship Repair Facility, Yokosuka, Japan, 1963-67, Naval Ship Systems Command, Washington, 1967-68, ret., 1968; mgr. constrn. and tech. devel., marine dept. Texaco, Inc., N.Y.C., 1968—. Mem. nat. council Boy Scouts Am., 1954—. Mem. nat. com. Order of Arrow, 1954—. Recipient Silver Antelope, 1956; Silver Beaver, 1960. Mem. Soc. Naval Architects and Marine Engrs., Am. Soc. Naval Engrs., U.S. Naval Inst., Sigma Xi, Tau Beta Pi, Phi Delta Kappa. Mason (Shriner). Home: 27 La Forge Rd Darien CT 06820 Office: Texaco Inc 2000 Westchester Ave Harrison NY 10650

OBERNAUER, MARNE, corp. exec.; b. Pitts., Mar. 6, 1919; s. Arthur H. and Anna (Somerman) O.; grad. Cornell U., 1941; m. Joan Strassburger, Aug. 1, 1941; children—Marne, Wendy (Mrs. William VanBuren Damon). Chmn. bd., chief exec. officer Devon Group, Inc., Los Angeles, 1972—; chmn. Beverage Distbrs. Corp., Denver, 1974—; pres., chmn. exec. com., dir. Cramer Electronics, Inc., Newton, Mass., 1977—; dir., mem. exec. com. APCO Oil Corp., 1975—; dir. NW Energy Co., Simplicity Pattern Co., Inc.; bus. cons., pvt. investor. Pres., bd. dirs. Marne and Joan Obernauer Found. Served to lt. USNR, 1942-45. Clubs: Hillcrest Country (Los Angeles); Westmoreland Country, Concordia (Pitts.). Office: Devon Group Inc 1880 Century Park E Los Angeles CA 90067*

OBERNAUER, MARNE, business exec.; b. Lakehurst, N.J., July 1, 1943; s. Marne and Joan Carolyn (Strassburger) O.; B.A., Yale U., 1965; M.B.A., Harvard U., 1972; m. Marion Fleck Gislason, Aug. 22, 1976; 1 son, Matthew Gene. With First Nat. City Bank, N.Y.C., 1965-70, Donaldson, Lufkin & Jenrette, N.Y.C., 1972-74; with Devon Group, Inc., Los Angeles, 1974—, pres., chief operating officer, 1978—. Clubs: Yale of N.Y.C., The Board Room. Office: Devon Group Inc 450 Park Ave New York NY 10022

OBERON, MERLE, actress; b. Tasmania, Feb. 19, 1911; ed. India; m. Alexander Korda, 1939 (div. 1945); m. 2d, Lucien Ballard (div. 1949); m. 3d, Bruno Pagliai, 1957 (div. 1973); adopted children—Bruno, Francesca. Film debut Service for Ladies, 1931; other appearances include The Private Lives of Henry VIII, 1932, The Private Life of Don Juan, 1934, The Scarlet Pimpernel, 1935, The Dark Angel, 1935, These Three, 1936, Beloved Enemy, 1936, The Divorce of Lady X, 1938, Over the Moon, 1939, Wuthering Heights, 1939, The Lion Has Wings, 1939, Affectionately Yours, 1941, The Lodger, 1944, A Song to Remember, 1944, This Love of Ours, 1945, Berlin Express, 1946, Temptation, 1946, Night Song, 1948, The Lady from Boston, 1951, Twenty Four Hours of a Woman's Life, 1952, Deep in My Heart, 1954, Désirée, 1954, The Price of Fear, 1956, Of Love and Desire, 1963, Hotel, 1967, others; editor, co-producer, Star Interval, 1973, also TV series Assignment-Foreign Legion, 1956, and guest appearances. Address: care Allan & Ingersoll 1901 Ave of Stars Los Angeles CA 90067*

O'BERRY, PHILLIP AARON, veterinarian; b. Tampa, Fla., Feb. 1, 1933; s. Luther Lee and Marjorie Mae (Mahlum) O'B.; B.S. in Agr., U. Fla., 1955; D.V.M., Auburn (Ala.) U., 1960; Ph.D., Iowa State U., 1967; m. Terri Martin, July 31, 1960; children—Kelly, Eric, Holly, Danny, Andy, Toby. With Sci. and Edn. Adminstrn., Dept. Agr., 1960—, asst. to dir. vet. scis. research div., Beltsville, Md., 1967-72, asst. dir. Nat. Animal Disease Center, Ames, Iowa, 1972-73, dir., 1973—; mem. expert panel livestock infertility FAO; sci. adv. com. Pan Am. Zoonosis Center, Buenos Aires; com. fed. labs. Fed. Council Sci. and Tech.; com. animal health, world food and nutrition study NRC. Recipient certificate of merit Agrl. Research Service, 1972; Alumni Achievement award Gamma Sigma Delta, 1976. Mem. Am., Iowa vet. med. assns., N.Y. Acad. Scis., Conf. Research Workers Animal Diseases, Am. Soc. Microbiology, AAAS, U.S. Animal Health Assn., Phi Zeta. Democrat. Author research publns. Home: 3319 Woodland Ave Ames IA 50010 Office: Nat Animal Disease Center PO Box 70 Ames IA 50010

OBERST, PAUL, educator; b. Owensboro, Ky., Apr. 22, 1914; A.B., U. Evansville, 1936; J.D., U. Ky., 1939; LL.M., U. Mich., 1941. Admitted to Ky. bar, 1938, Mo. bar, 1942; asso. firm Ryland, Stinson, Mag & Thomson, Kansas City, Mo., 1941-42; asst. prof. law Coll. of Law, U. Ky., Lexington, 1946-47, prof., 1947—; vis. prof. U. Chgo., 1954-55; prof., dir. civil liberties program N.Y. U., 1959-61; mem. Nat. Commn. on Acad. Tenure, 1971-73. Mem. Ky. Commn. on Corrections, 1961-65; mem. Ky. Commn. on Human Rights, 1962-66, chmn., 1966-70, 73-76; trustee U. Ky., Lexington, 1963-69, 72-75. Mem. Am., Ky. bar assns., Am. Law Inst., Am. Assn. Law Schs., Am. Judicature Soc., Order of Coif, Phi Delta Phi. Contbr. articles to legal jours. Home: 829 Sherwood Dr Lexington KY 40502 Office: U Ky Coll of Law Lexington KY 40506

OBERSTAR, JAMES L., congressman; b. Chisholm, Minn., Sept. 10, 1934; s. Louis and Mary (Grillo) C.; B.A. summa cum laude, St. Thomas Coll.; postgrad. in French, Laval U., Que., Can.; M.S. in Govt. (scholar), Coll. Europe, Bruges, Belgium; postgrad. in govt. Georgetown U.; m. Marilynn Jo Garlick, Oct. 12, 1963; children—Thomas Edward, Katherine Noelle, Anne-Therese, Monica Rose. Adminstrv. asst. to Congressman John A. Blatnik, 1963-74; adminstr. Pub. Works Com., U.S. Ho. of Reps., 1971-74; mem. 94th-96th Congresses from 8th Minn. Dist. Mem. Am. Polit. Sci. Assn. Home: 317 NW 9th St Chisholm MN 55719 Office: 323 Cannon House Office Bldg Washington DC 20515

OBERT, EDWARD FREDRIC, educator; b. Detroit, Jan. 18, 1910; s. Edward and Jessie (Funderburg) O.; B.S., Northwestern U., 1933, M.E., 1934; M.S., U. Mich., 1940; m. Helen Florence Boyce, Sept. 14, 1935. Engr. mfg. Western Electric Co., Chgo., 1929-30; staff Office Naval Inspection, Chgo., 1934-37; prof. mech. engring. Northwestern U., 1937-58; prof. mech. engring. U. Wis., 1958—, chmn. dept., 1963-67. Propr., Profl. Engring. Consultants; cons. Nat. Acad. Scis., USAF Acad., Denver, Aeromed. Lab. Alaska. Committeeman, NRC-Nat. Acad. Scis. Recipient George Westinghouse award Am. Soc. Engring. Edn., 1953, G. Edwin Burks award, 1971; U.S. Army certificate of appreciation for patriotic civilian service, 1970; Benjamin Smith Reynolds award U. Wis., 1973. Fellow ASME; mem. Soc. Automotive Engrs., Sigma Xi, Pi Tau Sigma, Tau Beta Pi, Triangle Frat. Author: Thermodynamics, 1948, rev. edit., 1963; Elements of Thermodynamics and Heat Transfer, 1949, rev. edit., 1962; Internal Conbustion Engines, 1950, rev. edit., 1968, 73; Concepts of Thermodynamics, 1960. Cons. editor mech. engr. series of Internat. Textbook Co. Contbr. articles tech. jours. Holder patent on process for Arctic disposal of wastes. Home: 3534 Lake Mendota Dr Madison WI 53705

OBERT, PAUL RICHARD, merchandising co. exec., lawyer; b. Pitts., Aug. 24, 1928; s. Edgar F. and Elizabeth T. (Buchele) O.; B.S., Georgetown U., 1950; J.D., U. Pitts., 1953; m. Dawna Mary Groom, June 18, 1966. Admitted to Pa. bar, 1954, D.C. bar, 1956, Ohio bar, 1972, Ill. bar, 1974, U.S. Supreme Ct., 1970; pvt. practice, Pitts., 1954-60; asst. counsel H.K. Porter Co., Inc., Pitts., 1960-62, sec., gen. counsel, 1962-71; sec., gen. counsel Addressograph-Multigraph Corp., Cleve., 1972-74; v.p. law Marshall Field & Co., Chgo., 1974—, sec., 1976—, officer, dir. various subs. Served to lt. col. USAF. Mem. Am., Pa., Allegheny County, Ill., Chgo. bar assns., Am. Soc. Corp. Secs., Am. Retail Fedn. (dir. 1977—), Georgetown U. Alumni Assn. (bd. govs.), Delta Theta Phi. Clubs: Pitts. Athletic Assn.; Univ. (Chgo.). Home: 1035 Seminole Rd Wilmette IL 60091 Office: 25 E Washington St Chicago IL 60690

OBEY, DAVID ROSS, congressman; b. Okmulgee, Okla., Oct. 3, 1938; s. Orville John and Mary Jane (Chellis) O.; B.S. in Polit. Sci., U. Wis., 1960, M.A., 1962; m. Joan Therese Lepinski, June 9, 1962; children—Craig David, Douglas David. Mem. Wis. Gen. Assembly from Marathon County, 1963-69, asst. minority leader, 1967-69; mem. 91st-96th Congresses 7th Dist. Wis., chmn. Democratic study group, 1979—. Mem. adminstrv. com. Wis. Dem. Com., 1960-62. Named Edn. Legislator of Year rural div. N.E.A., 1968; recipient Legislative Leadership award Eagelton Inst. Politics, 1964; award of merit Nat. Council Sr. Citizens, 1976; citation for legis. statesmanship Council Exceptional Children, 1976. Office: 2230 Rayburn House Office Bldg Washington DC 20515*

OBLAD, ALEXANDER GOLDEN, chemist, chem. engr., educator; b. Salt Lake City, Nov. 26, 1909; s. Alexander H. and Louie May (Brewster) O.; B.A. in Chemistry, U. Utah, 1933, M.A. in Phys. Chemistry, 1934; Ph.D. in Phys. Chemistry, Purdue U., 1937, D.Sc. (hon.), 1959; m. Bessie Elizabeth Baker, Feb. 23, 1933; children—Alex Edward, Elizabeth (Mrs. D. Sonne), Virginia (Mrs. W. Barker), John R.B., Hayward B., Jean Rio B. Research chemist Standard Oil Co., Whiting, Ind., 1937-42, Magnolia Petroleum Co., Dallas, 1942-43, sect. leader, 1943-46, chief chem. research, 1946; head indsl. research Tex. Research Found., Dallas, 1947; dir. chem. research Houdry Process Corp., Marcus Hook, Pa., 1947-52, asso. mgr. research and devel., 1952-55, mgr., 1955, v.p., dir., 1955-57; v.p. research and devel. M.W. Kellogg Co., N.Y.C., 1957-66, v.p. research and engring. devel., N.Y.C., 1966-69; v.p. IRECO Chems., Salt Lake City, 1969-70; prof. metallurgy and fuels engring., U. Utah, 1969-75, distinguished prof. metallurgy and fuels engring., 1975—, prof. chemistry, 1975—, asso. dean Coll. of Mines, 1970-72, acting dean, 1972-75. Dir. Ireco Chem. Co., 1974—. Mem. Sec. of Interior's Saline Water Conversion Adv. Com., Office of Saline Water, Washington, 1959-61. Mem. alumni research council Purdue Research Found., Lafayette, Ind., 1960-63; chmn. sustaining membership campaign Orange Mountain council Boy Scouts Am., 1966-67; mem. adv. council Brigham Young U., Provo, Utah, 1967—. Bd. dirs. Internat. Congress on Catalysis, 1956-65, Energy Inst. Recipient First Purdue Chemist's award, 1959, Distinguished Alumni award U. Utah, 1962. Mem. Am. Chem. Soc. (mng. editor publs. div. petroleum chemistry 1857-69, sec. treas. div. petroleum chemistry 1952-54, E.V. Murphree award 1969), Am. Inst. Chem. Engrs., AAAS, Calif. Catalysis Soc., Nat. Acad. Engring., Am. Inst. Chemists (award 1972), Soc. Mining Engrs., Sigma Xi, Phi Lambda Upsilon, Sigma Pi Sigma, Phi Kappa Phi, Tau Beta Pi. Rotarian. Mem. Ch. of Jesus Christ of Latter-Day Saints. Mem. editorial bd. Catalysis Revs., Fuel Processing Tech., 1976; mem. internat. adv. bd. Ency. of Chem. Processing and Design, 1973—. Contbr. numerous articles on phys. chemistry, catalysis, petroleum chemistry and chem. engring. to tech. and sci. jours.; patentee in field. Home: 1415 Roxbury Rd Salt Lake City UT 84108 Office: 302 Browning Mineral Science Bldg Univ of Utah Salt Lake City UT

OBOLENSKY, MARILYN WALL, metals co. exec.; b. Detroit, Aug. 13, 1929; d. Albert Fraser and Christine (Frischkorn) Wall; student Duschesne Jr. Coll., 1947; m. William Zeder Breer, 1947; children—Albert F. Wall and Carl Breer (twins); m. 2d, Serge Obolensky, June 3, 1971. Chmn. bd. Wall-Colmondy Corp., Detroit, 1959-61, exec. sec., 1961—; chmn. bd. Wall-Gases Inc., Morrisville, Pa., 1959-61; cons. Serge Obolensky Assos. Bd. dirs. Heart and Lung Assn. N.Y.C., 1963—. Republican. Roman Catholic. Clubs: Bathing Corp., Southampton (Southampton, N.Y.). Home: 465 Park Ave New York NY 10022 also 45 Preston Pl Grosse Pointe Farms MI 48236 Office: 19345 John R St Detroit MI 48203

OBOLER, ELI MARTIN, librarian; b. Chgo., Sept. 26, 1915; s. Leo and Clara (Obeler) O.; B.A., U. Chgo., 1941, postgrad. Sch. Library Sci., 1946-49; B.S., Columbia, 1942; m. Marcia Lois Wolf, Dec. 25, 1938; children—Leon David, Carol Judy. Asst. chief Lend-Lease Expediting Bur., WPB, 1942-43; head reserved book room U. Chgo., 1946-49, librarian Univ. Coll., 1947-49; lectr. great books program U. Chgo., 1948-49; librarian Idaho State Coll., 1949-63; univ. librarian Idaho State U., 1963—. Summer sch. faculty Utah State U., 1960, 66, U. Wash., 1975; condr. weekly radio program Books and You, 1949-76; mem. panel weekly TV program Idaho Looks at the World, 1973-76; columnist Intermountain and Alameda Enterprise, 1952-60, Idaho State Jour., 1960-65; reviewer Library Jour., 1953—, Choice, 1964—, Intermountain Observer, 1967-73, Western Critic, 1973-75. Mem. Nat. Adv. Com. Library Research and Tng. Projects, 1966-69, chmn., 1968-69. Bd. dirs. Pocatello United Campaign Fund, 1961-66; mem. adv. council Pacific N.W. Regional Health Scis. Library, U. Wash., 1968-77; dir. for Idaho, Pacific N.W. Bibliog. Center, 1970-71. Trustee, exec. com. Freedom to Read Found., 1971-75, 76—, v.p., 1979-80. Served with U.S. Army, 1943-46. Recipient Robert Downs Intellectual Freedom award, 1976. Mem. ALA (councilor representing Idaho 1950-58, chmn. library periodicals roundtable 1953, Idaho chmn. membership com. 1954-59, intellectual freedom com. 1964-70, councilor-at-large 1977—, vice chmn. intellectual freedom round table 1979-80, H.W. Wilson periodical award 1964), Pacific N.W. (chmn. legis. com. 1951-53, pres. 1955-56, chmn. publs. com. 1958-67), Idaho (pres. 1950-53, chmn. publ. com. 1950-54, chmn. library edn. com. 1961-63, chmn. intellectual freedom com. 1967-79, named Idaho Librarian of Year 1974) library assns., Assn. Coll. and Research Libraries (mem. editorial bd. 1962-63, chmn. coll. sect. 1963-64). Jewish. Mem. B'nai B'rith (local pres. 1951-53). Author: The Fear of the Word, 1974; Ideas and the University Library, 1977; Defending Intellectual Freedom, 1980. Editor: Idaho Librarian, 1950-54, 57-58; asst. editor Library Periodicals Round Table Newsletter, 1953-54, editor, 1961-62. Editor: College and University Library Accreditation Standards, 1957, Pacific N.W. Library Assn. Quar., 1958-67. Contbr. articles to profl. jours. Home: 1397 Jane St Pocatello ID 83201 Office: Idaho State U Library Pocatello ID 83209. *Truth crushed to earth may rise again, but buried truth cannot. The Censor is the enemy of Truth; whoever opens the eyes of mankind to what is, whoever favors light against darkness—he is the vehicle for progress toward universal peace and freedom. Man's stumbling climb from savagery to civilization is only impeded, not stopped, by the Censor.*

O'BOYLE, JAMES BERNARD, utility co. exec.; b. Denver, June 11, 1928; s. James Aloysius and Helen Cecelia (Ryan) O'B.; A.S., Regis Coll., 1956; student Dartmouth Coll., 1970, Columbia U., 1973, Wharton Sch., U Pa., 1975; m. Mary Louise Swartz, May 21, 1949 (div. 1969); 1 son, Brian Dennis. With Mountain States Tel. & Tel. Co., 1947-60, 67-69, 72—, asst. v.p. rates, Denver, 1967-69, asst. v.p. costs., rates and regulatory matters, asst. v.p. corp. planning, 1972-77, treas., 1977—; engr. AT&T, N.Y.C., 1960-62, pvt. line rate engr., 1962-67, mktg. dir., 1969-72. Mem. adv. bd. Salvation Army, Denver; v.p., bd. dirs. Highlanders, Denver. Served with Air N.G., 1948-51, USAF, 1951-52. Mem. Fin. Execs. Inst., Stock Transfer Assn., Denver C. of C. Republican. Clubs: Pinehurst Country, Denver Athletic. Home: 62 S Vance Ct Lakewood CO 80226 Office: 931 14th St Denver CO 80202

O'BOYLE, PATRICK ALOYSIUS, Cardinal; b. Scranton, Pa., July 18, 1896; s. Michael and Mary (Muldoon) O'B.; student St. Thomas Coll. (now Scranton U.); grad. St. Joseph's Sem., Yonkers, N.Y., 1921, N.Y. Sch. Social Work, 1931. Ordained priest Roman Cath. Ch., 1921; Served St. Columba's Ch., 1921-26, tchr.; Fordham U. Sch. Social Services; exec. dir. Nat. Cath. War Relief Services; became exec. dir. Cath. Charities N.Y., 1947; consecrated archbishop Diocese Washington, Jan. 14, 1948, ret., 1973; elevated to cardinal, June 26, 1967. *

O'BOYLE, THOMAS PATRICK, mfg. co. exec.; b. Milw., Sept. 1, 1920; s. Oliver L. and Elizabeth (Forrestal) O'B.; A.B., Holy Cross Coll., 1942; J.D., Harvard U., 1948; m. Ann Dean, Nov. 29, 1944; children—Thomas D., Ann L., Barbara A., John D., Mary F., Elizabeth D. Treas. Union Tank Car Co. (now Trans Union Corp.), Lincolnshire, Ill., 1959-68, v.p., 1965-72, sr. v.p., 1972—, also dir.; pres., dir. Ecodyne Corp., Lincolnshire affiliate of Trans Union, 1970—. Served to lt. USNR, 1942-45. Clubs: Chicago, Economic, Mid-America. Home: 78 Robsart Rd Kenilworth IL 60043 Office: 90 Half Day Rd Lincolnshire IL 60015

O'BRIAN, HUGH, actor; b. Rochester, N.Y., Apr. 19, 1930; student U. Calif. at Los Angeles, U. Cin. Pres., owner H. OB., Inc., Beverly Hills, Calif., 1956—; pres. Hugh O'Brian TV Prodns.; pres., founder Hugh O'Brian Youth Found.; motion pictures include Young Lovers, Man from the Alamo, Saskatchewan, Meet Me at the Fair, White Feather, Broken Lance, There's No Business Like Show Business, The Fiend Who Walked the West, Come Fly With Me, 1963, Love Has Many Faces, 1964, Ten Little Indians, 1965, Cowboy in Africa, 1966, Ambush Bay, 1966, Killer Force, 1976, The Shootist, 1977, Game of Death, 1978; starred in Broadway play Destry Rides Again, 1959, First Love, 1963; star nat. co. Cactus Flower, 1967-68, Guys and Dolls, 1979; star Life and Legend of Wyatt Earp, ABC-TV, 1955-61; star Search, NBC-TV, 1972-73. Founder, 1st and 2d pres. founder Thalians, actor's group sponsoring clinic for mentally retarded children, 1956-58; chmn. Cal. div. Am. Cancer Soc. Crusade, 1966; nat. campaign chmn. Cystic Fibrosis Found., 1969-74. Served with USMC, 4 yrs. Recipient Golden Plate award Am. Acad. Achievement, 1973; Freedom through Knowledge award NASA, 1971; George Washington Honor medal Freedoms Found. at Valley Forge, 1974, Leadership award, 1975; Globe and Anchor award Nat. Marine Corp. Scholarship Found., 1974; Am. Patriot award VFW, 1976; Silver Helmet award AMVETS, 1979. Office: 132 S Rodeo Dr Beverly Hills CA 90212. *I do not believe all men are created equal. Physical and emotional differences, parental guidance, varying environments, being in the right place at the right time-all play a role in enhancing or limiting individual development. But I do believe every man or woman, if given the opportunity and encouragement to recognize his potential, regardless of background, has the freedom to choose for himself in our world. Will he or she be a taker or giver in life? Will he or she be satisfied merely to exist or will he or she seek a meaningful purpose? Will he or she dare to dream the impossible dream? I believe every person is created as the steward of his own destiny with great power for a specific purpose; to share with his fellowman, through service, a reverence for life in a spirit of love.*

O'BRIAN, JACK, journalist; b. Buffalo, Aug. 16, 1921; s. Charles Joseph and Josephine Loretto (Kelleher) O'B.; D.Litt. (hon.), Niagara U., Niagara Falls, N.Y., 1966, St. Josephs Coll., Wyndham, Maine, 1975, St. John's U., N.Y.C., 1978, Canisius Coll., Buffalo, 1979; m. Yvonne Johnston, Jan. 15, 1947; children—Bridget Mary, Kate Mary. With Buffalo Times, 1939, N.Y. World-Telegram, 1939-40, Buffalo News, 1940, Buffalo Courier-Express, 1940-43; drama critic, daily N.Y. columnist, movie and music critic Broadway columnist A.P., 1943-49; columnist N.Y. Jour.-Am., 1949-67; columnist Voice of Broadway, King Features Syndicate, N.Y.C., 1967—; host daily radio show Critics Circle, WOR, N.Y.C. Bd. dirs. Damon Runyon-Walter Winchell Fund for Cancer Research. Recipient Christophers award, 1955, Deems Taylor award ASCAP, 1974, 76, 79, United Jewish Appeal award, 1955, Am. Legion award, 1958, Nat. Catholic War Vets. award, 1972, Morality in Media award, 1971, 73, George M. Cohan award Cath. Actors Guild, 1977; nominated for Pulitzer prize, 1942, 61-62. Mem. Cath. Actors Guild (nat. pres. 1978—). Author: The Great Godfrey, 1953. Contbr. articles to popular mags. Home: 225 E 73d St New York NY 10021 Office: Sta WOR 1440 Broadway New York NY 10017 also King Features Syndicate 235 E 45th St New York NY 10018

O'BRIEN, ALBERT JAMES, mgmt. cons.; b. St. Louis, Oct. 30, 1914; s. James Daniel and Lydia Helena (Dreher) O'B.; A.B., Washington U., St. Louis, 1935, A.M., 1940; LL.B., Mo. Inst. Law and Accountancy, 1944; m. Ruth Virginia Foster, Mar. 26, 1938; children—Denis James, James Douglas, Douglas Alan. Banking trainee, asst. mgr. indsl. service dept. First Nat. Bank, St. Louis, 1935-42; spl. asst. to gen. mgr. Atlas Powder Co., Weldon Springs, Mo., 1942-44; personnel mgr. prodn., mgr. prodn. staff dept. Ralston Purina Co., 1944-57, sec., 1957-59, v.p. finance, sec., 1959-61, exec.

v.p., 1961-68, pres. 1968-69, vice chmn. bd., 1969-71; chmn. exec. com. R. Rowland & Co., St. Louis, 1972-74; bus. mgmt. cons., 1974—; chmn. bd. Union Bank of East St. Louis (Ill.), Mo. State Bank, St. Louis; vice chmn. bd. Simon Johnson Industries, Kansas City, Mo.; dir. Am. Investment Co. Mem. adv. bd. Salvation Army; bd. dirs. Met. YMCA, Boy Scouts Am., United Way Greater St. Louis; investment trustee St. Louis Pub. Sch. Retirement System. Presbyn. Clubs: Mo. Athletic, Washington U. (St. Louis); Algonquin Golf (Webster Groves, Mo.). Home: 30 Rolling Rock Ct Saint Louis MO 63124

O'BRIEN, (HAROLD) DALE, pub. relations, affairs cons.; b. Chgo., Nov. 12, 1916; s. Harold Dale and Charlotte (Klapper) O'B.; A.B., U. Kans., 1937; m. Helen Lundgren, June 7, 1941; children—Katherine, Harold Dale, John David. Dir. pub. relations and advt., bd. editors Ency. Brit., Inc., 1945-49; partner Mayer & O'Brien, Chgo., 1950-52, pres., 1952-61; pres. Dale O'Brien & Co., Chgo., 1961—; exec. v.p., dir. Wis. Week-End, Inc., 1972—. Pres. Wis. Acad. Scis., Arts and Letters, 1978. Address: PO Box 278 Spring Green WI 53588

O'BRIEN, DANIEL WILLIAM, lawyer, corp. exec.; b. St. Paul, Jan. 6, 1926; s. Daniel W. and Kathryn (Zenk) O'B.; student U. Dubuque, 1943, Ill. State U., 1944; B.S.L., U. Minn., 1948, LL.B., 1949; m. Sarah Ward Stoltze, June 20, 1952; children—Bridget Ann, Daniel William, Kevin Charles, Timothy John. Admitted to Minn. bar, 1949; practice in St. Paul, 1950—; partner Randall, Smith & Blomquist, 1955-65; of counsel Doherty, Rumble & Butler, 1965—; pres. F.H. Stoltze Land & Lumber Co., 1964—, Maple Island, Inc., 1968—; dir. Durex Products, Inc., Villaume Industries, Inc. Bd. dirs., treas. St. Paul Chamber Orch. Soc. Served to ensign USNR, 1943-46. Mem. Minn., Ramsey County bar assns., World Bus. Council, Chief Execs. Forum. Home: 685 Linwood Ave Saint Paul MN 55105 Office: 2815 Blaisdell Ave Minneapolis MN 55408

O'BRIEN, DARCY, writer, educator; b. Los Angeles, July 16, 1939; s. George and Marguerite (Churchill) O'B.; A.B., Princeton U., 1961; postgrad Cambridge (Eng.) U., 1963-64; M.A., U. Calif., Berkeley, 1963, Ph.D., 1965; m. Thelma Adelman, Apr. 21, 1970; 1 dau., Molly; 1 stepdau., Emily. Prof. English, Pomona Coll., 1965-77; prof. modern letters U. Tulsa, 1978—; author: The Conscience of James Joyce, 1968; W.R. Rodgers, 1971; Patrick Kavanagh, 1975; A Way of Life, Like Any Other (Ernest Hemingway Found. award 1978), Moment By Moment, 1978. U. Ill. Center for Advanced Study fellow, 1969-70; Mellon Found. fellow, 1973-74; Guggenheim fellow, 1978-79. Mem. James Joyce Soc. Office: Graduate Faculty of Modern Letters University of Tulsa Tulsa OK 74104. *The most important attributes an American writer needs are the ability to withstand rejection, faith in his abilities, and the knowledge that his country is made up of people, not ideas or aesthetic theories.*

O'BRIEN, DONALD EUGENE, dist. judge; b. Marcus, Iowa, Sept. 30, 1923; s. Michael John and Myrtle A. (Toomey) O'B.; LL.B., Creighton U., 1948; m. Ruth Mahon, Apr. 15, 1950; children—Teresa, Brien, John, Shuivaun. Admitted to Iowa bar, 1948, U.S. Supreme Ct. bar, 1963; asst. city atty., Sioux City, Iowa, 1949-53; county atty., Woodbury County, Iowa, 1955-58; mcple. judge, Sioux City, Iowa, 1959-60; U.S. atty., No. Iowa, 1961-67; individual practice law, Sioux City, 1967-78; U.S. Dist. judge, Sioux City, 1978—. Served with USAAF, 1943-45. Decorated D.F.C., air medals. Mem. Woodbury County Bar Assn., Iowa State Bar Assn. Roman Catholic. Office: PO Box 3141 Sioux City IA 51101

O'BRIEN, EDMOND, actor; b. N.Y.C., Sept. 10, 1915; s. James Alfred and Agnes (Baldwin) O'B.; student pub. schs., N.Y.C.; student Neighborhood Play House, Studio of the Theatre; m. Olga San Juan, Sept. 26, 1948; children—Bridget, Maria. Appeared numerous Broadway prodns., including the John Gielgud Hamlet, as Prince Hal in Henry IV, as Mercutio in Romeo and Juliet, also Moss Hart prodn. Winged Victory; motion pictures include Barefoot Contessa, Julius Caesar, 711 Ocean Drive, White Heat, D.O.A., Up Periscope, The Rack, The Last Voyage, Third Voice, The Longest Day, Sylvia, Seven Days in May, The Great Impostor, The Man Who Shot Liberty Valance, Birdman of Alcatraz, Fantastic Voyage, 1966, The Viscount, 1967, The Love God?, 1969, The Wild Bunch, To Commit a Murder, 1970, They Only Kill Their Masters, 99 and 44/100ths % Dead, 1974; star weekly TV series Sam Benedict, 1962. Served with USAAF, World War II. Recipient Look mag. award, 1955; Fgn. Correspondents award, 1955; Acad. award for Barefoot Contessa, 1954; Exhibitor Laurel awards, 1956, 57. Mem. Screen Actors Guild, Screen Dirs. Guild, A.F.R.T.A. Office: Mishkin Agy 9255 Sunset Blvd Los Angeles CA 90069*

O'BRIEN, EDMUND JOSEPH, ins. lawyer; b. Boston, Mar. 3, 1914; s. John Bernard and Catherine Marie (Barry) O'B.; LL.B., Northeastern U., 1941; m. Margaret Helen Smiddy, Nov. 11, 1940; children—Kevin B., Kathleen (Mrs. Walter James Pagel), Maureen C., Margaret A. Claims adjuster Aetna Casualty & Surety Co., Boston, 1939-44; admitted to Mass. bar, 1941, Ill. bar, 1964; atty. Mass. Dept. Ins., Boston, 1946-47; pvt. practice law, Boston, 1947-48; trial atty. Lumbermans Mut. Casualty Co., Boston, 1947-49; atty. Kemper Ins. Group, Chgo., 1949-79, gen. counsel, 1964, sr. v.p., 1976-79; mem. firm Burns and Levinson, Boston, 1979—; dir. Kemper Security Ins. Co., Am. Protection Ins. Co., Ill. Ins. Guaranty Fund, Chgo. Chmn. bd. govs. Ins. Inst. Hwy. Safety, Washington, 1962-63; chmn. Nat. Com. Ins. Guaranty Funds, 1976; pres. Ill. Ins. Info. Service, 1976—. Mem. Arlington Heights (Ill.) Citizens Bldg. Com., 1960, Arlington Heights Govt. Mgmt. Com., 1959. Chmn. Planning Commn. Arlington Heights, 1954-56, Northwest Suburban Planning Bd., 1954; mem. Bd. Local Improvements, 1957-58. Served with USMCR, 1944-46; PTO. Mem. Am., Ill., Chgo. Minn. (hon.) bar assns., Fedn. Ins. Counsel (v.p. 1960-63, gov. 1960-62), Assn. Life Ins. Counsel. Clubs: Execs. (Chgo.); Univ. (Washington). Home: 8 Capt Nickerson Ln PO Drawer O South Dennis MA 02260 Office: Burns and Levinson 45 School St Boston MA 02108

O'BRIEN, EDWARD IGNATIUS, assn. exec., lawyer; b. N.Y.C., Sept. 15, 1928; s. Edward I. and Marguerite (Malone) O'B.; A.B., Fordham U., 1950; LL.B., St. John's U., 1954; grad. Advanced Mgmt. Program, Cornell U., 1965; m. Margaret M. Feeney, June 29, 1957; children—Edward Ignatius III, Margaret Mary, Thomas Gerard, John Joseph. Admitted to N.Y. bar, 1954; with firm Hale, Kay & Brennan, N.Y.C., 1954-55; with Bache & Co., Inc., N.Y.C., 1955-74, gen. counsel, 1960, gen. partner, 1964, sec., 1968, v.p., 1965-68, sr. v.p., exec. com., 1969, exec. v.p., 1969, chmn. exec. com., 1971-74; pres. Securities Industry Assn., 1974—. Lectr., Am. Law Inst., Practicing Law Inst., Am. Mgmt. Assn. Exchange ofcl. Am. Stock Exchange, 1972; mem. adv. bd., exec. com. Securities Regulation Inst., U. Cal., 1975—. Mem. cardinal's com. Laity Cath. Archdiocese N.Y., mem. Cardinal's com. for edn.; chmn. Fordham U. Council, 1971-73; chmn. corp. devel. com. Fordham U. Trustee, chmn. bd. trustees Fordham Prep. Sch., 1975-77. Served to capt. AUS. Mem. Assn. Bar City N.Y., Am., N.Y. State bar assns., Am. Arbitration Assn., Am. Soc. Internat. Law, Guild Cath. Lawyers, Securities Industry Assn. (chmn. publicly owned firms com. 1972), Nat. Assn. Securities Dealers (dist. com. 1973-74). Democrat. Clubs: City Midday (N.Y.C.); Shenorock Shore (Rye, N.Y.); Town, Fox Meadow Tennis (Scarsdale). Home: 12 Woods Ln Scarsdale NY 10583 also Watergate S 700 New Hampshire Ave NW Washington DC 20037 Office: 20 Broad St New York NY 10005 also 490 L'Enfant Plaza East SW Washington DC 20024

O'BRIEN, EDWARD WILLIAM, journalist; b. Palisades, N.Y., Oct. 29, 1916; s. Dennis and Julia (Scanlan) O'B.; B.B.A., Manhattan Coll., 1937; M. B.A., N.Y.U., 1942; m. Marian Louise Johnson, Sept. 17, 1949; children—Julia Louise, Theodore William. With Equitable Life Assurance Soc. U.S., 1937-44; asst. editor Newsweek mag., 1944-45, bur. chief, Detroit, 1946-47, bur. chief, Chgo., 1948-49; mem. Republican Congl. Com., 1949-52, asst. dir. pub. relations, 1953-54; chief Washington bur. St. Louis Globe-Democrat, 1954—. Mem. White House Corrs. Assn. Clubs: Federal City, Nat. Press (Washington); Gridiron. Home: 940 Peacock Station Rd McLean VA 22102 Office: 1750 Pennsylvania Ave NW Washington DC 20006

O'BRIEN, ELMER JOHN, educator, librarian; b. Kemmerer, Wyo., Apr. 8, 1932; s. Ernest and Emily Catherine (Reinhart) O'B.; A.B., Birmingham So. Coll., 1954; Th.M., Iliff Sch. Theology, 1957; M.A., U. Denver, 1961; m. Betty Alice Peterson, July 2, 1966. Ordained to ministry Methodist Ch., 1957; pastor Meth. Ch., Pagosa Springs, Colo., 1957-60; circulation-reference librarian Boston U. Sch. Theology, Boston, 1961-65; asst. librarian Garrett-Evang. Theol. Sem., Evanston, Ill., 1965-69; librarian, prof. United Theol. Sem., Dayton, Ohio, 1969—. Abstractor, Am. Bibliog. Center, 1969-73. Mem. Am. Theol. Library Assn. (head bur. personnel and placement 1969-73, dir. 1973-76, v.p. 1977-78, pres. 1978-79), AAUP, Delta Sigma Phi, Omicron Delta Kappa, Eta Sigma Phi, Kappa Phi Kappa. Club: Torch International. Author: Bibliography of Festschriften in Religion Published Since 1960, 1972. Home: 7818 Lockport Blvd Centerville OH 45459

O'BRIEN, EUGENE LOUIS, paint mfr.; b. N.Y.C., Apr. 29, 1913; s. George Louis and Helen (Knott) O'B.; grad. Lake Forest Acad., 1931; A.B., U. Notre Dame, 1935; m. Mary Ellen Chrisman, Sept. 24, 1938 (div. 1956); children—George Dennis, Michael Francis, Eugene Louis, Frederick Joseph II, Christopher John, Mary Ellen, Ann Hilary; m. 2d, Laura Graflin Lee, Mar. 28, 1961. With O'Brien Paint Co., South Bend, Ind., 1935-63, exec. v.p., dir., 1950-63; pres., dir. Balt. Paint & Chem. Corp., 1963-69; v.p., dir. Thomas Mfg. Co., Parkton, Md., 1964—. Vice pres. Balt. Opera Co., Inc., 1965-72. Bd. dirs. South Bend chpt. Boy Scouts Am., 1946, South Bend YMCA, 1946, Tucson Opera Co., 1973-75; mem. Tucson Council for Arts and Culture, 1974-77. Named Outstanding Young Businessman South Bend, South Bend Jr. C. of C., 1948. Mem. Greater Balt. Com., Nat. Paint and Lacquer Assn., U. Notre Dame Alumni Assn. (pres. St. Joseph's Valley chpt. 1942). Clubs: Tucson Country, Charles Center (Balt.); Skyline Country, Old Pueblo, Pima County Polo (Tucson). Home: 5172 Gleneagles Dr Tucson AZ 85718 Office: 100 Dairy Rd Parkton MD 21120

O'BRIEN, FRANCIS JOSEPH, ins. exec.; b. Wheeling, W.Va., Aug. 29, 1903; s. Charles A. and Katherine A. (Hasenauer) O'B.; A.B., St. Vincent Coll., 1931, LL.D., 1962; postgrad. N.Y. U. Sch. Commerce; m. Mary Margaret Ziegler, Aug. 21, 1935; children—Charles Francis, Thomas Joseph, Margaret Louise. Dir. sales promotion Fidelity Investment Assn., Wheeling, 1935-40; dir. sales promotion Franklin Life Ins. Co., Springfield, Ill., 1940—, v.p., 1947—, dir., 1950—. Publicity chmn. Springfield Community Fund drive, 1955, A.R.C., 1955-56; mem. pub. relations com. Sangamon County Community Chest, 1950-56; chmn. Christmas Seal drive Sangamon County Tb Assn., 1955; pres. Sangamon County Tb Assn., 1959. Dir. Springfield Municipal Opera, 1955-56; dir. Springfield Pub. Libraries, 1949-56, pres. bd., 1954-64; dir. bd. lay trustees Springfield Jr. Coll., 1959. Mem. Life Ins. Advertisers Assn. (dir.), Ill., Springfield (dir.) chambers commerce, Springfield, Advt. Club (past pres.), Springfield Assn. Life Underwriters. K.C. (4 deg.), Rotarian (pres. 1975-76). Clubs: Island Bay Yacht; Sangamo. Author: Distinguished Service since 1884; Europe As We Saw It; The Fabulous Franklin Story; Six Months in the Orient. Contbr. articles periodicals. Home: 2040 S Glenwood St Springfield IL 62704 Office: 800 S 6th St Springfield IL 62705

O'BRIEN, G. ROBERT, ins. co. exec.; b. Hartford, Conn., Nov. 4, 1936; s. George J. and Gertrude O'B.; B.A., U. Conn., 1960; M.B.A., U. Hartford, 1964; m. Mary Murray, Oct. 18, 1958; children—Robert, Thomas, James, Michael. With Conn. Gen. Life Ins. Co., 1960—, sr. analyst orgn. and systems dept., 1967-70, 2d v.p. field ops. Aetna Ins. Co., 1970-75, v.p. group pension ops., 1975-78, sr. v.p. group pension ops., 1978-79, sr. v.p. group ins. ops., 1979—; dir. One Thousand Corp. Corporator Hartford Hosp., St. Francis Hosp.; treas. bd. trustees Boys Clubs of Hartford, 1977—; mem. Windsor Locks Zoning Bd. Appeals. Served with U.S. Army, 1956-58. Mem. Health Ins. Assn. Am., Chartered Life Underwriters, Charters Property and Casualty Underwriters, Windsor Locks Jr. C. of C. (sec.). Home: 65 Nook Farms Rd Windsor CT 06095 Office: Conn Gen Life Ins Co Hartford CT 06152

O'BRIEN, GEORGE DENNIS, coll. pres.; b. Chgo., Feb. 21, 1931; s. George Francis and Helen (Fehlandt) O'B.; A.B. in English, Yale, 1952; Carnegie research fellow U. Chgo., 1956-57, Ph.D. in Philosophy, 1961; m. Judith Alyce Johnson, June 21, 1958; children—Elizabeth Belle, Juliana Helen, Victoria Alyce. Tchr. humanities U. Chgo., 1957-58; successively instr., asst. prof., asst. dean coll. Princeton, 1958-65; on leave in Athens, Greece, 1963-64; spl. honors seminars LaSalle Coll., spring 1963, fall 1964, spring 1965; asso. prof. philosophy Middlebury Coll., 1965-69, prof., 1969, chmn. dept. philosophy, 1970-71, dean of men, 1965-67, dean of coll., 1967-75, dean faculty, 1975-76; pres. Bucknell U., 1976—. Fellow Am. Council Learned Socs., London, Eng., 1971-72. Trustee, LaSalle Coll., Phila., 1969—, St. Michael's Coll., Winooski, Vt., 1975-76. Mem. Am. Philos. Assn., Phi Beta Kappa. Author: Hegel on Reason and History, 1975. Contbr. articles to profl. jours. Home: 103 University Ave Lewisburg PA 17837

O'BRIEN, GEORGE MILLER, congressman; b. Chgo., June 17, 1917; s. Matthew J. and Isabel (Hyde) O'B.; A.B., Northwestern U., 1939; J.D., Yale, 1947; m. Mary Lou Peyla, Sept. 6, 1947; children—Caryl Isabel (Mrs. Timothy Bloch), Mary Deborah (Mrs. Richard L. Pershey). Admitted to Ill. bar, 1947; sr. partner O'Brien & Garrison, Joliet, 1966—; mem. 93d-96th Congresses from 17th Dist. Ill., mem. appropriations com. Chmn. Will County chpt. A.R.C., 1957-58; pres. Joliet-Will County Community Chest Program. Mem. Will County Bd. Suprs., 1956-64; mem. Legislative Adv. Com. to Northeastern Ill. Planning Commn., 1971-72; mem. Ill. Ho. Reps., 1970-72, mem. exec. and judiciary II coms. Served to lt. col. USAAF, 1941-45. Recipient Distinguished Service award Joliet Boys Club. Mem. Am., Ill., Chgo., Will County bar assns., Trial Lawyers Assn. Ill., Am. Legion, V.F.W., Phi Beta Kappa. Roman Catholic. Elk, Rotarian. Club: Union League (Chgo.). Office: 2439 Rayburn House Office Bldg Washington DC 20515

O'BRIEN, GERALD HARVEY, assn. exec.; b. Kansas City, Mo., Jan. 30, 1921; s. Frank B. and Kathryn Rose (Robbins) O'B.; B.A. in Polit. Sci., UCLA, 1942; m. Mary B. Burchell, June 29, 1947; children—Roger Denis, Laurel Virginia. Field dep. chmn. bd. suprs. County of Los Angeles, 1953-55; Washington rep. Los Angeles C. of C., 1955-56; exec. sec. Pepsi Cola Bottlers Assn., Chgo. and N.Y.C., 1956-65; exec. v.p. Am. Importers Assn., N.Y.C., 1965—. Served with USNR, 1942-46. Mem. Am. Soc. Assn. Execs., Internat. C. of C. (commn. on regulations and procedures in internat. trade). Contbr. articles to internat. trade jours. Office: 11 W 42d St New York NY 10036

O'BRIEN, HENRY XAVIER, state justice; b. Pitts., Nov. 29, 1903; s. Patrick Joseph and Delia Gertrude (Clougherty) O'B.; B.S. in Econs., Duquesne U., 1925, LL.B., 1928, LL.D., 1956; LL.D. honoris causa, St. Francis Coll., 1967; m. Caroline Nuttall, July 5, 1928 (dec. 1953); children—Henry Xavier, Carolyn Ann (Mrs. Thomas F. Staley); m. 2d, Rosemary Hager, Aug. 25, 1956. Admitted to Pa. bar, 1929; gen. practice, Pitts., 1929-47; asst. dist. atty., 1942-47; mem. faculty Duquesne U. Sch. Law, 1945-60; judge ct. common pleas 5th Jud. Dist. Pa., 1947-62; justice Supreme Ct. Pa., 1962—. Trustee Duquesne U. Home: 1400 Browning Rd Pittsburgh PA 15206 Office: City-County Bldg Pittsburgh PA 15219

O'BRIEN, HUBERT FRANCIS, mfg. exec.; b. East Orange, N.J., Jan. 9, 1910; s. Denis Francis and Ellen M. (Bourke) O'B.; B.S., Princeton, 1931; m. Virginia Maddock, Apr. 19, 1939; children—William Brian, Hubert Francis, Kerry Ann, Wendy Ellen. With maintenance shops, engring. dept. Transcontinental & Western Air, 1932-36; with A.P. Smith Mfg. Co., East Orange, 1936-66, dir., 1936, pres., 1941-66; v.p., dir. U.S. Pipe & Foundry Co., 1966-71; chmn. bd. Pirelli Cable Corp.; dir. Colonial Life Ins. Co., Howard Savs. Instn., N.J. Bell Telephone Co., Maytag Co., LFE Corp., Peerless Tube Co., Pennwalt Corp. Mem. N.J. Bd. Higher Edn.; mem. adv. com. on jud. conduct Supreme Ct. of N.J. Vice chmn. bd. trustees Newark Coll. Engring. Mem. Am. Water Works Assn., Am. Judicature Soc. (dir.). Clubs: Baltusrol Golf (Springfield, N.J.); Coral Beach (Paget, Bermuda); The Circumnavigators; Short Hills. Home: 62 Stewart Road Short Hills NJ 07078 Office: 1640 Vauxhall Rd Union NJ 07083

O'BRIEN, J. WILLARD, lawyer, educator; b. N.Y.C., Oct. 19, 1930; s. J. Willard and Anna C. (Carroll) O.'B.; B.S., Fordham U., 1952, J.D., 1957. Admitted to N.Y. bar, 1957; mem. firm Cahill, Gordon, Reindel & Ohl, N.Y.C., 1957-62; asst. prof. law Syracuse U. Coll. Law, 1962-65; prof. law Villanova (Pa.) U. Sch. Law, 1965—, dean, 1972—. Mem. Pa. Fed. Jud. Nominating Commn., 1977—, vice chmn., 1978—; mem. Pa. Law and Justice Inst., 1972-73, chmn. exec. com., 1973-75, pres., 1975-77. Served with USAF, 1952-54, N.Y. Air N.G., 1954-58. Mem. Am. Bar Assn., N.Y. State Bar Assn., Pa. Bar Assn., Canon Law Soc. Am. Roman Catholic. Editor-in-chief Fordham Law Rev., 1956-57. Home: 1062 Lancaster Ave Rosemont PA 19010 Office: Villanova Law Sch Villanova PA 19085

O'BRIEN, JAMES EDWARD, oil co. exec.; b. Trinidad, Colo., Mar. 22, 1912; s. George A. and Alice A. (Lapsley) O'B.; A.B., U. Calif. at Berkeley, 1932, J.D., 1935; m. Mary Louise James, Jan. 2, 1936 (dec. 1978); m. 2d, Jeanne Gilmore LaClair, 1979. Admitted to Calif. bar, 1935; practice in San Francisco, 1935-66; asso., partner Pillsbury, Madison & Sutro, 1935-66; v.p., dir. Standard Oil Co. Calif., San Francisco, 1966-77; of counsel firm Pillsbury, Madison & Sutro, 1977—; dir. W.P. Fuller & Co., El Portal Mining Co., Abercrombie & Fitch Co. Pres. bd. dirs. Stanford Hosp.; bd. dirs. Acad. for Ednl. Devel. N.Y., Nat. Fund for Med. Edn., Am. Enterprise Inst.; trustee Internat. and Comparative Law Center, Dallas, Southwestern Legal Found., Mills Coll., San Francisco Asian Art Commn. Served as lt. col. USAAF, 1942-46. Decorated Legion of Merit, Bronze Star; Croix de Guerre with Silver Star. Mem. San Francisco (past v.p., dir.), Internat. chambers commerce, Am. Bar Assn., Am. Soc. Internat. Law, Internat. Law Assn., Am. Law Inst. Clubs: Pacific-Union, Bohemian (San Francisco); Stock Exchange. Home: 1530 Waverley St Palo Alto CA 94301 Office: 225 Bush St San Francisco CA 94104

O'BRIEN, JAMES JEROME, constrn. mgmt. cons.; b. Phila., Oct. 20, 1929; s. Sylvester Jerome and Emma Belle Filer (Fulforth) O'B.; B.C.E., Cornell U., 1952; postgrad. U. Houston, 1957-58, D.Eng., World Open U., 1975; m. Carmen Hiester, June 10, 1952; children—Jessica Susan, Michael, David. Project engr. Rohm & Haas, Phila. and Tex., 1955-59; project engr. RCA Corp., Moorestown, N.J., Greenland and Alaska, 1959-62; cons. Mauchly Assos., Fort Washington, Pa., 1962-65; founding partner, exec. v.p. Meridian Engring. Co., Phila., 1965-68; partner James J. O'Brien, P.E., Cherry Hill, 1972-77; pres. O'Brien-Kreitzberg & Assos., N.Y.C., Cherry Hill, San Francisco, 1977—. Mem. ofcl. bd. Methodist Ch., 1964-68; commr. hist. com. Upper Makefield Hist. Commn., Bucks, Pa., 1972-74. Served to lt. USN, 1952-55. Recipient Profl. Mgr. award N.Y. chpt. Soc. Advancement Mgmt., 1969. Registered profl. engr., N.Y., N.J., Pa., Ga. Fellow ASCE (Constrn. Mgmt. award 1976); mem. Am. Inst. Indsl. Engrs., Am. Assn. Cost Engring., Soc. Am. Value Engring. (cert. value specialist), Soc. Advancement Mgmt. (v.p. CPM div. 1970), Project Mgmt. Inst. (sec. 1971, v.p. 1972, pres. 1973, chmn. bd. 1974-75), Am. Nat. Standards Inst., Tau Beta Pi, Chi Epsilon. Author: CPM in Construction Management-Scheduling by the Critical Path Method, 1965; CPM in Construction Management-Project Management with CPM, 2d edit., 1971; Management Information Systems-Concepts, Techniques and Applications, 1970; Management With Computers, 1972; Construction Inspection Handbook, 1974; Value Analysis in Design and Construction, 1976; Construction Delay-Risks, Responsibilities and Litigation, 1976; author, editor: Scheduling Handbook, 1969; contbg. author, editor, Contractor's Management Handbook, 1971; contbr. chpts. to Critical Control of Building Costs, 1967, Current Techniques in Architectural Practice, 1976; Contbr. numerous articles to profl. jours. Home: Eagle Rd RD 2 New Hope PA 18938 Office: 1502 Route 38 Cherry Hill NJ 08002 also 8 W 40th St New York NY 10007

O'BRIEN, JAMES JOSEPH, educator; b. N.Y.C., Aug. 10, 1935; s. Maurice J. and Beatrice (Cudihy) O'B.; B.S. in Chemistry, Rutgers U., 1957; M.S. in Meteorology (NASA fellow), Tex. A&M U., 1964, Ph.D. (NASA fellow), 1966; m. Sheila O'Keefe, Nov. 28, 1958; children—Karen, Kevin, Sean, Dealyn, Denis. Chemist, E.I. duPont de Nemours & Co., Inc., Wilmington, Del., 1960-62; research scientist Nat. Center for Atmospheric Research, Boulder, Colo., 1966-69; mem. faculty Fla. State U., Tallahassee, 1969—, prof. meteorology, oceanography, 1972—. Served with USAF, 1958-60. Recipient medal Honor Liege U., Belgium, 1978. Nat. Center for Atmospheric Research fellow, 1966. Mem. Am. Meteorol. Soc., Am. Geophys. Union (pres. elect oceanography sect. 1978-79); Meteorol. Soc. Japan, Oceanographical Soc. Japan, Royal Meteorol. Soc., Sigma Xi, Chi Epsilon Pi, Pi Mu Epsilon, Pi Kappa Phi, Alpha Chi Rho. Asso. editor: Jour. Phys. Oceanography, 1970—; editor: Progress in Oceanography, 1976—. Contbr. articles to profl. jours. Home: 3210 E Lakeshore Dr Tallahassee FL 32312

O'BRIEN, JEANNE DUFOUR, book publisher; b. Princess Anne, Md., Feb. 18, 1929; d. James Blair and Helen L. (Beahler) Hankins; B.A., Gettysburg (Pa.) Coll., 1950; m. Robert V. O'Brien, July 28, 1973; children by previous marriage—Louise, Kristin, David, Jonathan, Anthony. Advt. copy writer for agencies and retail companies, 1950-53; sec., publicity dir. Dufour Editions, Inc., Chester Springs, Pa., 1954-70, pres., 1970—. Democrat. Roman Catholic. Address: Dufour Editions Inc Chester Springs PA 19425

O'BRIEN, JOHN HARRINGTON, writer, ret. newspaperman; b. Laurium, Mich., Aug. 6, 1908; s. Michael E. and Nellie (Harrington) O'B.; A.B., U. Mich., 1935; m. Eleanor I. Johnson, Nov. 14, 1936; children—Ellen L. (Mrs. David A. Saunders), Anne E. (Mrs. Frank J. Carelli Jr.), Kathleen S. Reporter, writer Detroit Times, 1929-35, writer, 1938-48; free-lance writer, pub. relations, 1935-38; pub. relations Batten, Barton, Durstine & Osborn, Inc., 1948-52; exec. dir. campaign for better roads Hearst Newspapers, 1952-56; exec. editor Pitts. Sun-Telegraph, 1957-59; asso. editor, book critic Detroit News, 1959-65, mng. editor, 1965-69, asso. editor, 1969-73, editorial page columnist, 1969-76; free-lance writer, editorial cons., 1976—. Served to 2d lt. U.S. Army, 1942-45, ETO. Recipient medal Cranbrook Writers' Guild, 1976. Home: 409 Arbana Dr Ann Arbor MI 48103

O'BRIEN, JOHN ROBERT, lawyer, diversified co. exec.; b. Gallipolis, Ohio, May 25, 1934; s. Paul Raymond and Kathryn Mae (Williams) O'B.; B.A., Yale U., 1955; LL.B., Harvard U., 1958; m. Astra Linnea Carlson, Sept. 7, 1957; children—Robert Viking, Stephen Kent. Admitted to Ohio bar, 1958, Mich. bar, 1965, U.S. Supreme Ct. bar, 1970; asso. firm Thompson, Hine and Flory, Cleve., 1958-65; atty. Kellogg Co., Battle Creek, Mich., 1965-67, asst. gen. counsel, 1967-72, v.p., corporate counsel, 1972-78; v.p., gen. counsel, sec. Congoleum Corp., Milw., 1979—. Trustee Battle Creek Symphony Orch. Assn., 1973-77. Mem. Am. Bar Assn., Am. Soc. Corporate Secs., State Bar Mich., Mich. C. of C. (dir. 1974-78). Home: 9623 N Courtland Dr Mequon WI 53092 Office: Congoleum Corp 777 E Wisconsin Ave Milwaukee WI 53202

O'BRIEN, JOHN SMITH, physician; b. Rochester, N.Y., July 14, 1934; s. Esther (Lafferty) O'B.; student Loyola U., 1952-55; M.S., Creighton U., 1958, M.D., 1960; m. Joanne Dozier, Aug. 25, 1956; children—John, Bridget, Kathleen, Michael, Marguerite, Patrick, Mark. Instr. dept. pathology and medicine U. So. Calif. Sch. Medicine, Los Angeles, 1962-64, asst. prof., 1964-67, asso. prof., 1967-68, chief sect. of molecular pathology, 1964-68; asso. prof. dept. neuroscis. U. Calif., La Jolla, 1968-70, prof., chmn. dept., 1970-78, prof., dir. div. metabolic disorders, 1978—; cons. Children's Hosp. Los Angeles, Pacific State Hosp., Pomono, Calif., VA Hosp., San Diego, Fairview State Hosp., Costa Mesa, Calif., Children's Hosp., San Diego. Mem. nat. research adv. com. United Cerebral Palsy Found., 1966-69; mem. med. adv. com. So. Calif. chpt. Multiple Sclerosis Soc., 1967-68; mem. med. adv. com. Nat. Tay-Sachs Found., 1970-75; mem. mental retardation research and tng. com. NICHD, 1971-74. Recipient numerous grants USPHS, March of Dimes Found., HEW. Mem. Soc. Neuroscience, Am. Fedn. Clin. Research, Am. Soc. Exptl. Pathology, Am. Soc. Human Genetics, Am. Soc. Neurochemistry, AAAS, Western Soc. Pediatric Research, Soc. Inherited Metabolic Disorders, Fedn. Western Socs. Neurol. Scis., Internat. Soc. Neurochemistry, Internat. Brain Research Orgn., Can. Neurol. Soc., Alpha Omega Alpha. Alpha Sigma Nu. Contbr. articles to med. jours. Office: Dept Neuroscience Univ of Calif at San Diego La Jolla CA 92093*

O'BRIEN, JOHN WILFRID, univ. pres.; b. Toronto, Ont., Can., Aug. 4, 1931; s. Wilfred Edmond and Audrey (Swain) O'B.; B.A., McGill U., 1953, M.A., 1955, Ph.D., 1962, LL.D., 1976; postgrad. Inst. Polit. Studies, Paris, France, 1954; D.C.L., Bishop's U., 1976; m. Joyce Helen Bennett, Aug. 4, 1956; children—Margaret Anne, Catherine Audrey. Lectr. econs. Sir George Williams U., Montreal, 1954-57, asst. prof., 1957-61, asso. prof., 1961-63, asst. dean U., 1961-63, dean arts, 1963-68, vice prin. acad., 1968-69, prof., 1965—, prin., vice chancellor, pres., 1969-74; rector, vice chancellor, pres. Concordia U., Montreal, 1974—. Mem. Provincial Ednl. TV Com., Dept. Edn. Que., 1962-66, dep. chmn., 1965-66, mem. tchr. tng. planning com., 1964-66; mem. Gauthier Ad Hoc Com., Univ. Operating Budgets, 1965-68; mem. Council Univs., 1969-76; pres. Conf. Rectors and Prins. Que. Univs., 1974-77; mem. council Assn. Commonwealth Univs., 1975-78; bd. dirs. Assn. Univs. and Colls., Can., 1977-79; mem. Conseil Consultatif sur l'Immigration, Que. Gov., 1977-79; bd. govs. YMCA, 1969—, Vanier Coll., 1975-79, Fraser-Hickson Inst., 1975—, Que. div. Can. Mental Health Assn., 1977-79; hon. v.p. Que. Provincial council Boy Scouts Can., 1974—; hon. councillor Montreal Mus. Fine Arts, 1969—. Mem. Canadian, Am. econ. assns., Am. Assn. Higher Edn. Author: Canadian Money and Banking, 1964 (2d edit. with G. Lermer 1969). Home: 38 Holton Ave Montreal PQ H3Y 2E8 Canada Office: 1455 de Maisonneuve Blvd Montreal PQ H3G 1M8 Canada

O'BRIEN, JOHN WILLIAM VINCENT, internat. mgmt. cons.; b. N.Y.C., Apr. 9, 1922; s. Patrick Joseph and Anne (Gibbons) O'B.; B.S. in Econs., Wharton Sch., U. Pa., 1948; m. Mary Anna Kelly, Nov. 19, 1955; children—Padric Kelly, Catherine Mary, Colleen Anne, John Michael. Asst. in comptroller's dept. Am. Can Co., 1948-56; gen. mgr. finance div. Am. Mgmt. Assn., 1956-58; v.p. finance Hudson Pulp & Paper Corp., 1965-66, consumer and comml. sales mgr., 1958-66; sr. v.p., chief financial officer Brown Co., N.Y.C., 1966-69; v.p., chief financial officer Susquehanna Corp., 1969-70; exec. v.p. Statler Industries Inc., Medford, Mass., 1970-73; mgmt. cons., 1973—. Served to lt. (j.g.) USNR, 1942-46. Mem. Beta Gamma Sigma. Home: Deerwood Jacksonville FL Office: 1605 Timber Ct Elgin IL 60250 also 8014 Hollyridge Rd Jacksonville FL 32216

O'BRIEN, KENNETH ROBERT, life ins. co. exec.; b. Bklyn., June 18, 1937; s. Emmett Robert and Anna (Kelly) O'B.; B.S. in Bus. Adminstrn., Coll. Holy Cross, Worcester, Mass., 1959; m. Eileen M. Halligan, July 1, 1961; children—Joan Marie, Margaret Mary, Kathy Ann. With N.Y. Life Ins. Co., N.Y.C., 1962—, 2d v.p., 1973-77, v.p. investments, 1977—. Active Cath. Youth Orgn. Served to 1st lt. USAF, 1959-62. Mem. Nat. Consumer Fin. Assn., Fin. Forum, N.Y. Social Security Analysts. Home: 165 E Loines Ave Merrick NY 11566 Office: 51 Madison Ave New York NY 10010

O'BRIEN, LAWRENCE FRANCIS, basketball commr., former chmn. Democratic Nat. Com.; b. Springfield, Mass., July 7, 1917; s. Lawrence Francis and Myra Theresa (Sweeney) O'B.; LL.B., Northeastern U., 1942; LL.D., Western New Eng. Coll., 1962, Villanova U., 1966, Loyola U., 1967, Xavier U., 1971; L.H.D., Am. Internat. Coll., 1971, Wheeling Coll., 1971, St. Anselms Coll., 1966; D.Pub. Adminstrn., Northeastern U., 1965, Seton Hall U., 1967; D.S. in Bus. Adminstrn. (hon.), Bryant Coll., 1978; m. Elva Brassard, May 30, 1944; 1 son, Lawrence Francis III. Engaged in real estate and pub. relations, Springfield, 1943-60; active organizing polit. campaigns, 1938—; dir. orgn. Dem. Congl. campaigns 2d Dist. Mass., 1946, 48, 50; adminstrv. asst. to U.S. Rep. Furcolo, 1948-50; dir. orgn. Sen. John Kennedy's campaign, 1952, Mass. Dem. Com., 1956-57, Sen. Kennedy's re-election campaign, 1958; nat. dir. orgn. Kennedy for Pres. campaign, 1959-60, Dem. Nat. Com., 1960, Presdl. campaigns 1960, 64, 68, 72; spl. asst. to President Kennedy for Congl. relations, 1961-63; spl. asst. for Congl. relations to Pres. Johnson, 1963-65; postmaster gen. of U.S., 1965-68; chmn. Dem. Nat. Com., 1968-69, 70-72, Dem. Nat. Conv., 1972; pres. McDonnell & Co. Inc., investment bankers, N.Y.C., 1969; pres. O'Brien Assos., mgmt. cons., 1969, 73-75; commr. Nat. Basketball Assn., 1975—. Served with AUS, World War II. Author: The O'Brien Manual, 1960, 64, 68, 72; No Final Victories: A Life in Politics from John F. Kennedy to Watergate, 1974. Address: 860 UN Plaza New York NY 10017

O'BRIEN, MARGARET (ANGELA MAXINE O'BRIEN), actress; b. San Diego, Jan. 15, 1937; d. Lawrence and Gladys O'Brien; m. Harold Allen, Jr., Aug. 8, 1959. Appeared in motion picture Babes in Arms, 1941; later pictures include Journey for Margaret, Lost Angel, Jane Eyre, The Canterville Ghost, Dr. Gillespie's Criminal Case, Meet Me In St. Louis, Music for Millions, Our Vines Have Tender Grapes, Three Wise Fools, Unfinished Dance, Tenth Avenue Angel, Big City, Secret Garden, Little Women, Her First Romance, Anabelle Lee, Glory, Heller in Pink Tights, Diabolic Wedding; TV guest appearances, 1950—, including Perry Mason, 1963, Bob Hope Chrysler Theatre, 1964, Combat, 1967, Ironside, 1968, Love American Style, 1968, Adam-12, 1971, Marcus Welby M.D., 1972, also summer stock, plays. Received Acad. of Motion Picture Arts and Scis. award for best child actress, 1944. Address: care Metro-Goldwyn-Mayer Studios Culver City CA 90230*

O'BRIEN, MARY ELIZABETH, editor; b. N.Y.C., Aug. 11, 1917; d. Patrick James and Elizabeth (Donovan) O'Brien. Asst. to editor Flower Grower mag., to 1950; co-founder Popular Gardening and Living Outdoors (formerly Popular Gardening), mng. editor, 1950-58, editor, 1958-69; editor The Garden Jour., N.Y. Bot. Garden, 1969-77; editorial adv. bd. Garden mag., 1977—; co-editor Rhododendrons, N.Y. Bot. Garden, 1978—. Mem. Am. Hort. Soc., Hort. Soc. N.Y., Garden Writers Am. (dir. 1970—), Bklyn. Bot. Garden, N.Y. Bot. Garden, Am. Soc. Mag. Editors, Am. Assn. Bot. Gardens and Arboreta, Internat. Platform Assn. Roman Catholic. Club: Quota (N.Y.C.). Home: 314 W 22d St New York NY 10011 Office: NY Bot Garden New York NY 10458

O'BRIEN, MICHAEL, photojournalist; b. Memphis, June 27, 1950; s. Thomas John and Gere Belle (King) O'B., B.A., U. Tenn., Knoxville, 1972; m. Elizabeth Storer Owen, Feb. 10, 1975. Photographer, U. Tenn. Daily Beacon, 1969-72, Miami (Fla.) News, 1973—. Speaker, 19th Ann. Wilson Hicks Internat. Conf. on Visual Communications. Recipient So. Short Course award, 1973, Sigma Delta Chi Mark of Excellence award in feature photography, 1973, 1st in gen. news category and Best of Show award So. Photographer of Year Competition, 1974, 1st place in gen. news 32d Ann. Pictures of Year contest, 1974, 1st in black and white photography U. Fla. Newspaper Photography Contest, 1974, 1st in gen. news So. Photographer of Year Competition, 1975, Robert F. Kennedy award in photojournalism, 1975, 77. Mem. Nat. Press Photographers Assn. (Region 6 Photographer of Year award 1975-77). Home: 511 NE 110th Terr Miami FL 33161 Office: 1 Herald Plaza Miami FL 33132

O'BRIEN, MICHAEL JOHN, educator; b. N.Y.C., Apr. 27, 1930; s. Michael John and Mary (Collins) O'B.; B.A., Fordham U., 1951; M.A., Princeton, 1953, Ph.D., 1956; m. Anne Jordan Webb, July 25, 1959; children—David, Emily. Came to Can., 1966. Instr. classics Wesleyan U., Middletown, Conn., 1955-56; from instr. to asso. prof. dept. classics Yale, 1956-66; from asso. prof. to prof. classics Univ. Coll., U. Toronto (Ont., Can.), 1966—, chmn. dept., 1973—. Morse fellow Yale, Rome, Italy, 1963-64; Guggenheim fellow, 1972-73. Mem. Canadian Assn. U. Tchrs., Am. Philol. Assn., Classical Assn., Classical Assn. Can., Soc. Ancient Greek Philosophy, Classical Soc. of the Am. Acad. (Rome). Roman Catholic. Author: The Socratic Paradoxes and the Greek Mind, 1967. Editor: Twentieth-Century Interpretations of Oedipus Rex, 1968. Home: 67 Paperbirch Dr Don Mills ON Canada Office: Dept Classics Univ Toronto Toronto ON Canada

O'BRIEN, MORROUGH PARKER, educator, cons. engr.; b. Hammond Ind., Sept. 21, 1902; s. Morrough and Lulu (Parker) O'B.; B.S., Mass. Inst. Tech., 1925; D.Sc., Northwestern U., 1959; Dr. Engring., Purdue U., 1961; LL.D., U. Cal., 1968; m. Roberta Libbey, May 16, 1931 (div.); children—Sheila, Morrough; m. 2d, Mary Wallner Kremers, 1963. Engr., Hudson River Regulating Dist., 1925-27; research asst., Purdue U., 1925-27; Freeman scholar Am. Soc. C.E., 1927-28; asst. Royal Coll. Engring., Stockholm, Sweden, 1927-28; successively asst. prof., asso. prof., prof. U. Cal., 1928-59, prof. emeritus, 1959—, chmn. dept. mech. engring., 1937-43, dean Coll. Engring., 1943-59, dean emeritus, 1959—. Dir. research and engring. Air Reduction, Inc., 1947-49; cons. engr. aerospace and def. group Gen. Electric Co., 1949—. Mem. U.S. Coastal Engring. Research Bd., Def. Sci. Bd., 1961-65, Army Sci. Adv. Panel, 1955-74; mem. nat. sci. bd. NSF, 1958-60. Registered profl. engr., N.Y., Calif. Mem. ASCE (hon.), ASME, Am. Soc. Engring. Edn. (Lamme medal), Am. Shore and Beach Preservation Assn. (pres.), Nat. Acad. Engring., Sigma Xi, Tau Beta Pi, Delta Tau Delta. Clubs: Bohemian (San Francisco); Cosmos (Washington); Athenian-Nile (Oakland, Calif.); Faculty (Berkeley); Sleepy Hollow Country (Scarborough-on-Hudson, N.Y.); University (Mexico City). Author: Applied Fluid Mechanics, 1937. Home: PO Box 265 Cuernavaca Mexico

O'BRIEN, NEAL RAY, educator; b. Newark, Ohio, May 25, 1937; s. Raymond and Eleanor (Pryor) O'B.; B.A., DePauw U., 1959; Ph.D., U. Ill., 1963; m. Kathryn Louise Gronberg, Sept. 9, 1962; children—Tyler, Rebecca, Amber. Prof. geology State U. N.Y. at Potsdam, 1963—, chmn. dept., 1970—. Postdoctoral research fellow Kyoto U., Japan, 1969-70, 77-78. Mem. Geol. Soc. Am., Soc. Econ. Paleontology and Mineralogy. Contbr. articles to profl. jours. Research on clay sedimentology, electron microscope study of clay sediment, clays in Alaska glacial areas. Home: Box 123 West Stockholm NY 13696 Office: State Univ New York Potsdam NY 13676

O'BRIEN, RAYMOND FRANCIS, transp. and mfg. co. exec.; b. Atchison, Kans., May 31, 1922; s. James C. and Anna M. (Wagner) O'B.; B.S. in Bus. Adminstrn., U. Mo., 1948; grad. Advanced Mgmt. Program, Harvard, 1966; m. Mary Ann Baugher, Sept. 3, 1947; children—James B., William T., Kathleen A., Christopher R. Accountant-auditor Peat, Marwick, Mitchell & Co., Kansas City, Mo., 1948-52; controller-treas. Riss & Co., Kansas City, Mo., 1952-58; regional controller Consol. Freightways Corp. of Del., Indpls., also Akron, Ohio, 1958-61; with Consol. Freightways, Inc., San Francisco, 1961—, controller-treas., 1962-63, v.p., treas., 1963-67, v.p. finance, 1967-69, exec. v.p., 1969-75, pres., 1975—, chief exec., 1977, also dir.; dir. Consol. Freightways Corp. of Del., Freightliner Corp., Consol. Metco. Inc., Canadian Freightways Ltd., Canadian Freightways Eastern Ltd., CF Air Freight Inc.; treas. Western Hwy. Inst. Mem. bus. adv. bd. Northwestern U., U. Calif. at Berkeley. Served to 1st lt. USAAF, 1942-45. Mem. Am. Trucking Assn. (exec. com., dir.), Calif. C. of C. Clubs: World Trade, Commonwealth (San Francisco); Palo Alto Hills Golf and Country. Home: 26347 Esperanza Dr Los Altos Hills CA 94022 Office: 601 California St San Francisco CA 94108

O'BRIEN, RAYMOND VINCENT, JR., banker; b. Bronx, N.Y., Sept. 23, 1927; s. Raymond Vincent and Blanche (Harper) O'B.; A.B., Fordham U., 1951, J.D., 1958; postgrad. Advanced Mgmt. Program, Harvard, 1969; m. Theresa Sweeney, Mar. 29, 1952; children—Susan, Raymond, Christopher, Sean, Carol, Nancy. With Chase Manhattan Bank, N.A., N.Y.C., 1953-74; chmn., chief exec. officer Emigrant Savs. Bank, N.Y.C.; dir. Todd Shipyards Corp., Internat. Shipholding Corp. Trustee Christian Bros. Acad., Lincroft, N.J., Fordham U. Served with AUS, 1946-47, 51-53. Mem. Am., N.Y. bar assns., Savs. Bank Assn. N.Y. State, Nat. Assn. Mut. Savs. Banks, Guild Catholic Lawyers. Republican. Roman Catholic. Clubs: Knights of Malta, Sky, Econ., Madison Square Garden (N.Y.C.); Navesink Country (Middletown, N.J.). Home: 4 Mt Vernon Ct Colts Neck NJ 07722 Office: 5 E 42d St New York NY 10017

O'BRIEN, RICHARD DESMOND, univ. adminstr., neurobiologist; b. Sydenham, Eng., May 29, 1929; s. Joseph Andrew and Louise (Stevens) O'B.; B.Sc., Reading (Eng.) U., 1950; Ph.D. in Chemistry, U. Western Ont. (Can.), 1954, B.A. in Arts, 1956; m. Ann Margaret Thom, Mar. 16, 1961; 1 son, Ian Richard. Came to U.S., 1960, naturalized, 1967. Soil specialist Ont. Agrl. Coll., Guelph, 1950-51; chemist Pesticide Research Inst., London, Can., 1954-60; faculty Cornell U., 1960-78, prof. entomology, 1964-78, prof. neurobiology, 1965-78, chmn. dept. biochemistry, 1964-65, chmn. sect. neurobiology and behavior, 1965-70, dir. div. biol. scis., 1970-78; provost U. Rochester (N.Y.), 1978—; dir. First Nat. Bank Rochester; NRC fellow Babraham, Cambridge, Eng., 1956-57; vis. asso. prof. U. Wis., 1958-59; cons. Melpar Inc., 1960-65, Am. Cyanamid Co., 1960-69, USPHS, 1964-69. Trustee Center for Govtl. Research, 1979—, Rochester Museum and Sci. Center, 1979—. Guggenheim fellow, Naples, Italy, 1967-68. Fellow AAAS; mem. Am. Chem. Soc. (Internat. award pesticide chemistry 1970), Am. Soc. Biol. Chemists, Sigma Xi. Author: Toxic Phosphorus Esters, 1960; Radiation, Radioactivity and Insects (with L.S. Wolfe), 1964; Insecticides, Action and Metabolism, 1967; (with I. Yamamoto) Biochemical Toxicology of Insecticides, 1970; (with E.O. Wilson, others) Life on Earth, 1973; The Receptors, A Comprehensive Treatise, vol. I, 1979; also articles. Office: Office of Provost U Rochester Wilson Blvd Rochester NY 14627

O'BRIEN, RICHARD FRANK, coll. pres.; b. Ogden, Utah, Oct. 20, 1921; s. James William and Mary Eleanor (Hinley) O'B.; B.A. in History, U. Calif. at Santa Barbara, 1943; M.A. in Higher Edn., Stanford, 1947, Ed.D., 1950; m. Doris May Kirsten, Aug. 25, 1943; children—Susan Linda (Mrs. Cretarolo), Cynthia Ann (Mrs. Ford), Sally Jane. Mem. staff Stanford, 1947-64, dir. devel., 1959-64; v.p. planning and devel. U. Chgo., 1964-67; asst. to the pres. Stanford, 1967-69, sec. Stanford Med. Center, 1969-70; pres. Menlo Sch. and Coll., 1970—. Pres., Las Lomitas Sch. Bd., Atherton, Calif., 1955-58; campaign dir. Stanford PACE Program, 1959-64. Trustee Palo Alto Med. Research Found., No. Calif. Transplant Bank, Assn. Ind. Calif. Colls. and Univs. Served to lt. (j.g.) USNR, 1943-46; comdr. Res. Clubs: Palo Alto; Bohemian; Menlo Country; California. Author: The University Development Program, 1958. Home: 98 Leon Way Atherton CA 94025 Office: Menlo Sch and Coll Menlo Park CA 94025

O'BRIEN, ROBERT BROWNELL, JR., banker, savs. and loan exec.; b. N.Y.C., Sept. 6, 1934; s. Robert Brownell and Eloise (Boles) O'B.; B.A., Lehigh U., 1957; postgrad. N.Y. U. Grad. Sch. Bus. Adminstrn., 1959, Am. Inst. Banking, 1959; m. Sarah Lager, Nov. 28, 1958; children—Robert Brownell, III, William Stuart, Jennifer. Asst. treas., credit officer, br. locations officer Bankers Trust Co., N.Y.C., 1957-63; with George A. Murray Co., Gen. Contractors, N.Y.C., 1964; v.p., treas., dir. Mut. Savs. Bank Devel. Corp., N.Y.C., also v.p. Bowery Savs. Bank, 1964-69; dir., chief exec. and adminstrv. officer Fed. Savs. & Loan Ins. Corp., Washington, 1969-71; chmn. exec. com. Fed. Home Loan Bank Bd., 1969-71; v.p., Bowery Savs. Bank, N.Y.C., 1972; exec. v.p. First Fed. Savs. & Loan Assn., N.Y.C., 1973-75; pres., chief exec. officer, dir. Carteret Savs. & Loan Assn., Newark, 1975—; dir. Acron Corp., Remote Computing Corp., Central Corp. Savs. & Loan. Chmn. fin. com. Ocean County council Boy Scouts Am., 1967-68; bd. govs. N.J. State Opera; bd. dirs. N.J. Coll. Fund Assn., Childrens Specialized Hosp., United Way, Coalition for Fair Broadcasting, Neighborhood Housing Services N.J.; mem. adv. bd. Fairleigh Dickinson Coll. Bus. Adminstrn.; trustee Trinity Pawling Sch., St. Benedict's Prep. Sch., Gill-St. Bernards Sch., Drew U., Neighborhood Housing Services Am.; chmn. bd. Ind. Coll. Fund N.J.; mem. adv. council Credit Research Center, Krannert Grad. Sch., Purdue U.; mem. exec. com. Newark Preservation and Landmarks Com.; mem. Nat. Commn. on Neighborhoods. Mem. Nat. League Savs. Assns. (vice chmn. legis. com.), Essex County Savs. and Loan League (pres.), N.J. Hist. Soc. (v.p.), Greater Newark C. of C. (dir.). Republican. Episcopalian. Clubs: Union League; Baltusrol Golf; New York Yacht; Bay Head Yacht; Manasquan River Yacht; Beacon Hill. Contbr. articles to trade mags. Home: 61 Overleigh Rd Bernardsville NJ 07924 Office: 866 Broad St Newark NJ 07102

O'BRIEN, ROBERT NEVILLE, chemist, educator; b. Nanaimo, B.S., Can., June 14, 1921; s. Robert Emmette and Mary Ann (Crossan) O'B.; Chem. Engr., B.A., U. B.C., 1951, M.A. in Metall. Engring., 1952; Ph.D., U. Manchester (Eng.), 1955; m. Helen Treva Bryan, June 28, 1952; children—Daniel, Martha, Douglas, Timothy, Patrick. Nat. Research Council Can. postdoctoral fellow, 1955-57; asst. prof. chemistry U. Alta., Edmonton, Can., 1957-62, asso. prof., 1962-67; asso. prof. chemistry U. Victoria (B.C.), 1966-68, prof., 1968—; vis. scholar U. Calif. at Berkeley, 1964-65; chief metallurgist Western Can. Steel Co., Vancouver, B.C., 1952-53; cons. in field. Served with Royal Can. Arty., 1942-43, RCAF, 1943-46. Fellow Royal Soc. Arts, Can. Inst. Chemistry; mem. Am. Chem. Soc., Electrochem. Soc., AAAS. Author: (with G.M. Schmid) A Laboratory Manual of Modern Chemistry, 1966. Contbg. author Weissberger's Technique of Chemistry, Physical Methods, 1973. Contbr. articles to profl. jours. Home: 2614 Queenswood Dr Victoria BC V8N 1X5 Canada

O'BRIEN, ROBERT S., state ofcl.; b. Seattle, Sept. 14, 1918; s. Edward R. and Maude (Ransom) O'B.; student public schs.; m. Kathryn E. Arvan, Oct. 18, 1941. With Kaiser Co., 1938-46; restaurant owner, 1946-50; treas. Grant County, Wash., 1950-65, State of Wash., 1965—; chmn. Wash. Fin. Com., 1965—, Wash. Public Employees Retirement Bd., 1969-77, Law Enforcement Officers and Firefighters Retirement System, 1971-77; mem. Wash. Data Processing Adv. Bd., 1967-73; trustee Wash. Tchr.'s Retirement System, 1965—. Recipient Leadership award Joint Council County and City Employees-Fedn. State Employees, 1970, Eagles Leadership award, 1967. Mem. Nat. Assn. State Auditors, Comptrollers and Treasurers (pres. 1977), Nat. Assn. Mcpl. Fin. Officers, Nat. Assn. State Treasurers, Western State Treasurers Assn. (past pres.), Wash. County Treas. Assn. (pres. 1955-56), Wash. Assn. Elected County Ofcls. (pres. 1955-58), Olympia Area C. of C., Soap Lake C. of C. (pres. 1948). Democrat. Clubs: Elks (hon. life), Moose, Eagles, Lions, Omympia Yacht, Wash. Athletic, Olympia Country and Golf; Empire (Spokane). Address: Legislative Bldg Olympia WA 98504

O'BRIEN, ROBERT STEPHEN COX, lawyer; b. Westmount, Que., Can., Oct. 21, 1929; B.A., McGill U., 1951, B.C.L., 1953. Admitted to Que. bar, 1954; named Queen's Counsel; partner firm Lavery, O'Brien, Montreal. Mem. Montreal (treas. 1976-77), Que. bars, Canadian Bar Assn., Fedn. Ins. Counsel. Office: 3100 2 Complexe Desjardins Montreal PQ H5B 1G4 Canada

O'BRIEN, ROSANNE P., transp. co. exec.; b. Phila., May 27, 1943; d. James Miles and Rosalie Theresa (Wagner) O'B.; student St. Joseph Coll., Emmitsburg, Mass., 1960-62; B.S. in Bus. Adminstrn., U. Redlands, 1978. Asst. corp. sec. Flying Tiger Line Inc., Los Angeles,

1972-73, corporate sec., 1973—; asst. corporate sec. Tiger Internat., Inc., Los Angeles, 1972-73, corp. sec., 1973—, dir. public relations, 1979—. Mem. Am. Soc. Corp. Secs., Los Angeles County Mus. Art, Publicity Club Los Angeles, Greater Los Angeles Press Club. Republican. Roman Catholic. Home: 7801 Anise Ave Los Angeles CA 90045 Office: 1888 Century Park E Los Angeles CA 90067

O'BRIEN, SAMUEL GREENOUGH, lawyer; b. Oskaloosa, Iowa, July 11, 1920; s. Maxwell A. and Virginia (Slade) O'B.; B.A., U. Iowa, 1943, J.D., 1947; m. Carolyn R. Brenton, June 30, 1951; children—Samuel B., Carolyn J., Cynthia A. Admitted to Iowa bar, 1947, since practiced in Des Moines; partner firm Nyemaster, Goode, McLaughlin, Emery & O'Brien, 1947—. Dir. South Des Moines Nat. Bank, Inter-State Assurance Co. Served to capt., inf. AUS, 1943-46; ETO. Decorated Bronze Star. Mem. Am., Iowa, Polk County bar assns. Club: Des Moines. Home: 301 Tonawanda Dr Des Moines IA 50312 Office: Hubbell Bldg Des Moines IA 50309

O'BRIEN, TERRENCE PATRICK, utility exec.; b. St. Paul, Mar. 29, 1927; s. Thomas D. and Marie (Schorn) O'B.; B.S. in Bus. Adminstrn., Northwestern U., 1952; m. Helga M. Langhammer, Nov. 23, 1946; children—Claudia K., Patricia M., Ann M. Mem. staff Haskins & Sells, C.P.A.'s, Mpls., 1952-56; with Minn. Gas Co., 1952—, asst. treas., 1961-62, treas., 1962—. Served with AUS, 1945-47. C.P.A., Minn. Mem. Minn. Soc. C.P.A.'s, Am. Inst. C.P.A.'s, Am. Gas Assn. Club: Minneapolis Optimist, Mpls. Aquatennial Assn. Home: 5809 W 68th St Minneapolis MN 55435 Office: 733 Marquette Ave Minneapolis MN 55402

O'BRIEN, THOMAS FRANCIS, mfg. co. exec.; b. Cambridge, Mass., Mar. 28, 1938; s. Thomas Francis and Elizabeth Ann (Deneen) O'B.; B.S., Boston Coll., 1960; M.B.A., Boston U., 1965; m. Elizabeth A. Coppinger, Sept. 3, 1960; children—Nancy Ann, Thomas F., Lisa Jean. Analyst, Nat. Shawmut Bank Boston, 1964; fin. analyst Gen. Foods Corp., N.Y.C., 1965-66; asst. controller Hewitt Robins (Litton) Conn., Stamford, 1966-67; sec.-treas. controller Electra Motors (Litton) Calif., Anaheim, 1967-69; v.p., controller Power Transmission div. (Litton) Conn., Hartford, 1969-71; v.p., controller A-T-O, Inc., Willoughby, Ohio, 1971-74, v.p. Recreation Group, 1974—; pres. Rawlings Sporting Goods, 1974—; mem. faculty Westchester Community Coll., 1966-67. Bd. dirs. Central St. Louis County chpt. Am. Cancer Soc., St. Louis Amateur Sports Council. Served with AUS, 1960-63. Fellow Boston U., 1965. Home: 2821 Stonington Dr Frontenac MO 63131 Office: 2300 Delmar Blvd Saint Louis MO 63166

O'BRIEN, THOMAS JOSEPH, hotel exec.; b. Bklyn., Nov. 14, 1940; s. John Joseph and Ella (Hughes) O'B.; grad. N.Y. Hotel/Motel Law Course; m. Karen Ann Savoldy, Jan. 31, 1963; children—Margaret, John, Daniel, Patricia. Asst. mgr. Sheraton Inn, N.Y.C., 1963-68, sales rep., 1968-69, front office mgr., 1969-71, resident mgr. Sheraton Laguardia, 1971-72; resident mgr. Gramcery Park Hotel, N.Y.C., 1976-77, gen. mgr., 1977—. Served with USAF, 1961-63, Air N.G., 1963-67. Recipient Psychol. Tng. award Sheraton Hotels, 1972. Mem. N.Y. State Hotel-Motel Assn. (Law award 1968), Am. Hotel-Motel Assn. Republican. Roman Catholic. Home: 92-34 77th St Woodhaven NY 11421 Office: 2 Lexington Ave New York NY 10010

O'BRIEN, THOMAS STANLEY, III, lawyer; b. Albany, N.Y., May 28, 1916; s. Thomas Stanley and Marguerite Mary (Boyle) O'B.; A.B., Holy Cross Coll., 1937; LL.B., Harvard, 1942; m. Constance Ann Cole, Sept. 29, 1951; 1 dau., Ann Cole. Trust clk. First Trust Co., Albany, N.Y., 1937-38; admitted to N.Y. State bar, 1942, S.C. bar, 1978; asso. atty. Cravath Swaine & Moore, N.Y.C., 1942-48; atty., asst. sec. Air Reduction Co., Inc., 1948-51, sec., 1951-65, also sec. subs.; gen. counsel Union Camp Corp., 1965-76; mem. firm Roberts Vaux, Hilton Head Island, S.C., 1979—. Mem. Internat., Am., N.Y. State, S.C., Hilton Head bar assns., Am. Soc. Corp. Secs. Roman Catholic. Home and Office: 391 Briarwood Villa 15 Calibogue Cay Rd Hilton Head Island SC 29928

O'BRIEN, TIM ANDREW, journalist, lawyer; b. N.Y.C., July 11, 1943; s. Timothy Andrew and Hildegarde J. (Schenkel) O'B.; B.A. in Communications, Mich. State U., 1967; M.A. in Polit. Sci., U. Md., 1972; postgrad. Tulane U. Law Sch., 1974-75; J.D., Loyola U., New Orleans, 1976; m. Maria de Guadalupe Margarita Moreno, Jan. 15, 1971; children—Theresa Marie, Tim A. News writer, reporter, anchorman WKBD-TV, Detroit, 1968-69, WTOP-TV, Washington, 1969-72, WDSU-TV, New Orleans, 1972-74, WVUE-TV, New Orleans, 1974-77; Supreme Ct. corr. ABC News, Washington, 1977—; admitted to La. bar, 1976, D.C. bar, 1977. Recipient AP award for outstanding reporting of extraordinary event, 1976, New Orleans Press Club award for non-spot news reporting, 1976, Emmy award for documentary on D.C.'s troubled schs., 1969, Am. Bar Assn. awards merit, 1979. Mem. Radio-Television Corrs. Assn. Washington, Sigma Delta Chi, Pi Sigma Alpha, Phi Kappa Phi. Office: ABC News 1124 Connecticut Ave NW Washington DC 20036

O'BRIEN, WILLIAM CHRISTOPHER, magazine publisher; b. Watertown, N.Y., Apr. 4, 1941; s. Robert F. and Ernestine L. (Markham) O'B.; B.S. in Chem. Engring., Clarkson Coll., Potsdam, N.Y., 1963; M.B.A., Columbia U., 1969; m. Lois C. Wiltse, June 12, 1965; children—Cara Kathleen, Liam Christopher. Tech. sales rep., then mktg. research mgr. Union Carbide Corp., 1963-69; v.p., advt. M.B.A. Communications, N.Y.C., pubs. MBA mag., Juris Doctor mag., New Engr. mag. and Med. Dimensions mag., 1969-77, exec. v.p., pub., 1977—; lectr. in field. Mem. Essex County (N.J.) County Com., 1968-69. Served with USAR, 1964. Mem. Mag. Pubs. Assn. Republican. Home: 749 Boulevard E Weehawken NJ 07087 Office: 730 3d Ave New York NY 10017

O'BRIEN, WILLIAM HOWARD, mfg. co. exec.; b. White Plains, N.Y., July 6, 1918; s. George E. and Anna M. (Burns) O'B.; B.C.S., U. Notre Dame, 1940; m. Delores Smith, May 11, 1946; children—Maureen Joan, Richard William. With Shulton, Inc., N.Y.C., 1953-71, exec. v.p., 1963-69, pres., 1969-71, also dir.; pres. Mgmt. Techniques, Inc., 1971—; vice chmn. Meyer Labs., Inc., Fort Lauderdale, Fla., 1972—; dir. MEM Co., Inc. Served with USAAF, 1941-45; ETO. Mem. Fin. Execs. Inst. (dir. Newark), Am. Mgmt. Assn., Toilet Goods Assn. N.Y.C. (dir.). Clubs: University (N.Y.C.); Indian Trail (Franklin Lakes, N.J.); Hackensack Golf (Oradell, N.J.). Home: 600 S Ocean Blvd Boca Raton FL 33432 Office: 1900 W Commercial Blvd Fort Lauderdale FL 33309

O'BRIEN, WILLIAM JOHN, ins. co. exec.; b. Yonkers, N.Y., Nov. 18, 1932; s. Vincent J. and Margaret L. (Schaefer) O'B.; B.S., Fordham U., 1954; grad. student Seton Hall U., 1957-59; m. Catherine Kelaher, July 27, 1963; children—Kathleen, William, Christopher. Underwriter, then spl. agt. Gen. Ins. Co. Am., N.Y.C., 1956-60; with Security Ins. Group, New Haven, 1960-67, v.p., 1963-67; v.p. Glens Falls Ins. Co. (N.Y.), 1967-71, v.p. Hanover Ins. Co., Worcester, Mass., 1971-79, pres., 1979—. Club: Fayville Athletic Assn. Home: 22 Red Gate Ln Southboro MA 01772 Office: Hanover Ins Co Worcester MA 01605

O'BRIEN, WILLIAM MAHONY, automobile mfg. co. exec.; b. Chgo., Nov. 13, 1917; s. Charles Loren and Eleanor (Mahony) O'B.; A.B., Loyola U., Chgo., 1939, J.D., 1949; m. Mary Jane Bryar, June 3, 1944; children—Maureen J. O'Brien Doyle, Kathleen M. O'Brien Fox, Margaret M. With FBI, 1941-51; admitted to Ill. bar, 1949; indsl. relations mgr. Ford Motor Co., 1951-58; with Chrysler Corp., 1958—, v.p., dir. indsl. relations, 1962-63, v.p. personnel, 1963—. Mem. Ill. Bar Assn., Blue Key, Alpha Sigma Nu, Pi Gamma Mu. Roman Catholic. Clubs: Boat, Athletic, Press, Hundred (Detroit). Home: 65 Lake Shore Rd Grosse Pointe Farms MI 48236 Office: PO Box 1919 Detroit MI 48231

O'BRIEN, WILLIAM MARTIN, psychiatrist, hosp. adminstr.; b. St. Paul, May 11, 1909; s. William J. and Mary E. (Hogan) O'B.; student U. Minn., 1928-29; B.S., St. Louis U., 1931, M.D., 1933; m. Irma Helen Paulsen, Nov. 30, 1940; children—Tamra Diane (Mrs. David E. Kessler), Mieke Lynne (Mrs. Jackson E. Bray), Holly Noel (Mrs. Andrew Meyers), William Martin. Intern St. Mary's Hosp., East St. Louis, Ill., 1933-34; resident St. John's Hosp., St. Louis, 1936-37; practice medicine, specializing in psychiatry, St. Paul, 1937-41, 46-49; sr. psychiatrist Patton (Calif.) State Hosp., 1949-54; asst. supt., clin. dir. Mendocino (Calif.) State Hosp., 1954-57; supt., med. dir. Modesto (Calif.) State Hosp., 1957-69; supt., med. dir. DeWitt State Hosp., 1970-71; med. dir. Atascadero (Calif.) State Hosp., 1971-72; med. dir. Patton State Hosp., 1973—; preceptor Sch. Hosp. Adminstrn. Washington U., St. Louis; clin. instr. psychiatry Med. Sch., Coll. Med. Evangelist. Pres. San Bernardino Mental Health Soc. Bd. dirs. United Crusade. Served as col. M.C., AUS, 1941-46; ETO. Diplomate Am. Bd. Psychiatry and Neurology, Am. Bd. Mental Hosp. Adminstrs. Fellow Am. Psychiat. Assn.; mem. Central Calif. Psychiat. Soc. Address: 23332 Pebble Beach Ripon CA 95366

O'BRIEN, WILLIAM PATRICK, mfg. co. exec.; b. Chgo., Nov. 19, 1933; s. Leonard P. and Helen M. (Condon) O.; B.S.C., De Paul U., 1962; m. Donna Lee Collignon, June 24, 1972; children by previous marriage—Thomas, David, Tracy, Gary. Casualty claim adjuster Fidelity and Casualty Co. N.Y. (N.Y.), 1956-59, Am. Ins. Co. Newark, 1959-61; jr. staff auditor Alexander Grant and Co., Chgo., 1961-63; sr. staff auditor Leonard D. O'Brien and Co., Chgo., 1963-65; asst. mgr. fed. taxes Inland Steel, Chgo., 1965-71; exec. v.p. fin., dir. XCOR Internat. (formerly Seeburg Industries, Inc.), Oakbrook, Ill., 1971—. Served with AUS, 1954-56. Mem. Am. Inst. C.P.A.'s, Ill. Soc. C.P.A.'s, Am. Mgmt. Assn. Clubs: Econs. of Chgo.; N.Y. Athletic. Home: 12120 S 87th Ave Palos Park IL 60464 Office: 2001 Spring Rd Oakbrook IL 60521

O'BRYAN, JAMES WILLIAM, mag. exec.; b. Guantanamo, Cuba, Dec. 9, 1917 (parents Am. citizens); s. Walter E. and Adela Syria (Trujillo) O.; student Met. Mus. Art, 1930, Nat. Acad. Design, 1934-36, Art Students League, 1946-48; m. Sophie Kondos, Dec. 27, 1945; children—Mary Margaret, Michael James. Artist, N.Y. Evening Jour., N.Y.C., 1934, N.Y. Am., N.Y.C., 1935; promotion art dir. N.Y. Mirror, N.Y.C., 1937-61; art dir. Nat. Review Mag., N.Y.C., 1961—. Pres., Ultra Arts, Inc., N.Y.C., 1961—. Bd. dirs. Am.-Children Cultural Exchange. Served with USNR, 1942-45. Mem. Art Students League N.Y., N.Y. Art Center. Republican. Roman Catholic. Home: 445 Highbrook Ave Pelham Manor NY 10803 Office: 150 E 35th St New York NY 10016

O'BRYAN, JOHN RAYMOND, restaurant chain exec.; b. Louisville, Oct. 21, 1938; s. Richard M. and Mary Edna O'Bryan; B.A. in Acctg., U. Toledo, 1961; m. Shirley Marie Ehle, Jan. 17, 1959; children—Catherine Ann, John Raymond. Accountant, Arthur Young & Co., Toledo, 1961-64; asst. controller Haughton Elevator Co., Toledo, 1964-66; controller metals div. Fansteel, Inc., North Chicago, Ill., 1966-68; corp. v.p. Marriott Corp., Washington, 1968-77; exec. v.p. fin. and unit devel. Ponderosa System, Inc., Dayton, Ohio, 1977—. Fin. chmn. St. Albert the Gt. Roman Catholic Parish Council, Kettering, Ohio. Recipient Gordon Strong award U. Toledo, 1959; C.P.A., Ohio, Ill. Mem. Dayton Art Inst., PTA, U. Dayton Phys. Athletic Center, Citizens Choice, Fin. Exec. Inst., Ohio Soc. C.P.A.'s, Am. Mgmt. Assn., Nat. Restaurant Assn., Beta Gamma Sigma. Club: Sycamore Creek Country. Home: 729 Murrell Dr Kettering OH 45429 Office: PO Box 578 Dayton OH 45401

O'BRYAN, SAMUEL OLIVER, JR., lawyer; b. Manning, S.C., Dec. 10, 1916; s. Samuel Oliver and Frances (Davis) O'B.; B.A., U. Fla., 1938, LL.B., 1940; m. Patricia May Staudt, Mar. 25, 1948; children—Kathleen, Jennifer, Susan, Peter Davis. Admitted to Fla. bar, 1940, since practiced in Ft. Lauderdale; partner firm English, McCaughan & O'Bryan, and predecessor, 1952—. Chmn. First Fed. Savs. & Loan Assn. Broward County. Pres. Ft. Lauderdale Jr. C. of C., 1948-49. Served to capt. AUS, 1941-45. Mem. Am., Fla., Broward County bar assns. Democrat. Presbyterian. Clubs: Rotary (pres. Ft. Lauderdale 1963-64), One Hundred of Broward County (pres. 164-65). Home: 2616 NE 24th St Fort Lauderdale FL 33305 Office: First Fed Bldg Fort Lauderdale FL 33301

O'BRYAN, WILLIAM HALL, ins. co. exec.; b. Tulia, Tex., June 15, 1919; s. Barnett and Goldie (Hall) O'B.; student Internat. Bus. Coll., El Paso, Tex., 1936-37, Hills Bus. U., Oklahoma City, 1937, Tulsa Law Sch., 1939; m. Marjorie Mae Lewis, Apr. 14, 1962; children—Richard L., Clelie S. With Okla. Compensation Rating Bur., Oklahoma City, 1937; underwriter, v.p. Tri State Ins. Co., Tulsa, 1937-61; pres. Occidental Fire & Casualty Co., Denver, 1961-72; founder, owner Am. Underwriters, Denver, 1972-74; pres., chmn. bd. Prime Ins. Corp., 1973-74, exec. v.p., 1976-77; v.p. Asso. Internat. Mgmt., 1974-75; conservator Equity Educators Assurance Co., Denver, 1974-75, spl. dep. Colo. ins. commr. acting as receiver, 1975-77; receiver Mfrs. & Whosealers Indemnity Exchange, 1975-77; pres. Mo. Profl. Liability Ins. Assn., Jefferson City, Mo., 1977—; dir. Occidental Life Ins. Co. N.C., 1973-76. Served to capt. AUS, 1942-46. Episcopalian. Home: 2623 Schellridge Rd Jefferson City MO 65101 Office: PO Box 1498 Jefferson City MO 65102

O'BRYAN, WILLIAM MONTEITH, lawyer; b. Manning, S.C., Apr. 27, 1912; s. Samuel Oliver and Frances (Davis) O'B.; student U. Miami (Fla.), 1931-32; LL.B., U. Fla., 1937; m. Jeane Barrett, Nov. 22, 1942; 1 dau., Donna. Admitted to Fla. bar, 1937; practice in Miami, 1937-50, in Ft. Lauderdale, 1950—; partner firm Fleming, O'Bryan & Fleming, and predecessor, 1950—. Regional v.p. Def. Research Inst., 1963-65. Served to lt. USNR, 1942-45. Fellow Am. Coll. Trial Lawyers, Internat. Acad. Trial Lawyers; mem. Internat. Assn. Ins. Counsel (exec. com. 1964-67), Sigma Chi. Presbyn. Mason (Shriner), Rotarian (pres. Ft. Lauderdale 1954-55). Home: 707 NE 26th Ave Fort Lauderdale FL 33304 Office: 1415 E Sunrise Blvd Fort Lauderdale FL 33304

O'BYRNE, JOHN COATES, legal educator; b. Albany, N.Y., May 13, 1920; s. John C. and Katherine (Riley) O'B.; A.B., Syracuse U., 1941, M.S. in Pub. Adminstrn., 1943; LL.B., Harvard, 1948; m. Marjorie Ann Hinners, Apr. 28, 1945; children—Kathleen, Stephen, Margret, Mary. Admitted to N.Y. bar, 1948, Iowa bar, 1950, also U.S. Supreme Ct.; practice in Iowa City, 1950-66; prof. law Northwestern U. Sch. Law, 1966-72, dir. Corp. Counsel Inst., 1966-69; dean Sch. Law, Northeastern U., Boston, 1972-77; Shackelford prof. law U. Ga. Law Sch., Athens, 1977—; vis. prof. Boston Coll. Law Sch., 1965-66, Northwestern U. Sch. Law, 1956-57, Chgo.-Kent Law Sch., summers 1971, 74; mem. faculty U. Iowa Coll. Law, 1948-66; vis. prof. U. Tex. Sch. Law, 1953; cons. land reform AID, 1961-67; cons. IRS, 1972-76. Dir. Agrl. Law Center, U. Iowa, 1953-62; reporter Uniform Mgmt. Instl. Funds Act, 1970-72. Lt. comdr. (ret.) USNR. Mem. Am. Law Inst., Phi Beta Kappa. Author or co-author: Iowa's Water Resources, 1956; Legal Economic Research, 1959; Farm Income Tax Manual, 5th edit., 1977; (with Davenport) Farmers Tax Guide, 10th edit., 1979; (with Phelan, Wulf) Workbook for Iowa Estate Planners, 1966; (with McCord) Deskbook for Illinois Estate Planners, 1969; (with Pennell) Federal Taxation of Partners and Partnerships, 1971; (with Kahn) Sum and Substance of Federal Income Tax, 2d edit., 1973; also articles. Home: 550 Westview Dr Athens GA 30606 Office: Sch of Law Univ of Ga Athens GA 30602

O'BYRNE, PAUL J., bishop; b. Calgary, Alta., Can., Dec. 21, 1922. Ordained priest Roman Catholic Ch., 1948; bishop of Calgary, 1968—. Office: PO Box 4130 Station C Calgary AB T2T 5M9 Canada*

O'CALLAGHAN, J. PATRICK, publisher; b. Mallow, Ireland, Oct. 8, 1925; s. Michael Joseph and Marguerita (Hayes) O'C.; imigrated to Can., 1959, naturalized, 1964; student Christian Brothers Sch., Limerick, Ireland, 1931-32, Cotton Coll., Eng.; m. Lorna E. Nattriss, June 28, 1947; children—Patrick, Michael, Sean, Brendan, Fiona. Reporter, deskman English newspapers, 1947-53; asst. editor Liverpool (Eng.) Echo, 1953-59; mng. editor, asst. pub. Red Deer Advocate, Alta., 1959-68; asst. to pub. Edmonton (Alta.) Jour., 1968, pub., 1976—; exec. editor Southam News Services, Ottawa, Ont., Can., 1969-71, exec. asst. to mng. dir. Southam Press Ltd., 1971-72; v.p., pub. Windsor (Ont.) Star, 1972-76. Served with RAF, 1943-47. Mem. Canadian Daily Newspaper Pubs. Assn. (dir.), Canadian Press, Am. Press Inst. (dir.), Commonwealth Press Union, Internat. Press Inst. Roman Catholic. Home: 11 Riverside Crescent Edmonton AB Canada Office: Edmonton Jour 100 101st Ave Edmonton AB T5J 2S6 Canada

O'CALLAGHAN, JERRY ALEXANDER, govt. ofcl.; b. Klamath Falls, Oreg., Feb. 23, 1922; s. Jeremiah Patrick and Marie Jane (Alexander) O'C.; B.S. with honors, U. Oreg., 1943, M.A. with honors, 1947; Ph.D., Stanford, 1951; m. Florence Marie Sheehan, Aug. 6, 1949; children—Jane Mary, Susan Margaret. Acting instr. history Stanford, 1951-52, U. Wyo., 1952-53; oil editor Tribune-Herald, Casper, Wyo., 1953-55; acting asst. prof. U. Wyo., 1955-56; legislative asst. to Senator O'Mahoney, 1956-60; exec. asst. to Senator Hickey, 1961, asst. dir. lands and minerals mgmt. Bur. Land Mgmt., Dept. Interior, 1961-62, asst. dir. plans and legislation, 1962-64, chief legislation and office coop. relations, 1964-69, chief div. coop. relations, 1969—. Bd. govs. St. Columba's Episc. Nursery Sch., Washington, 1959-71. Served with AUS, 1943-46. Mem. Soc. of Forest History, Fed. Profl. Assn. (pres. 1972), Phi Kappa Psi. Episcopalian (vestryman 1964-68). Author: Disposition of the Public Domain in Oregon, 1960; America 200—The Legacy of Our Lands, 1976. Home: 5607 Chesterbrook Rd Bethesda MD 20016 Office: Bur Land Mgmt Dept of Interior Washington DC 20240

OCASEK, OLIVER ROBERT, state senator; b. Bedford, Ohio, Nov. 2, 1925; s. Jack Barney and Olive (Drabeck) O.; B.S., Kent (Ohio) State U., 1946, M.A., 1951, Ph.D. (hon.), 1975; Ph.D. (hon.), U. Akron, 1978, Rio Grande (Ohio) Coll., 1979; m. Virginia Hedjuk, June 18, 1955. High sch. tchr., adminstr., coll. prof. in Summit County, Ohio, 1946-78; now prof. emeritus U. Akron (Ohio); mem. Ohio Senate, 1959—, now pres., majority leader, chmn. Rules Com.; past mem. Ohio Constn. Revision Commn.; nat. chmn., mem. exec. com. Council State Govts. Chmn., Youth in Govt. in Ohio; past pres. bd. trustees Akron YMCA. Recipient Distinguished Service awards NEA, Outstanding Legislator awards Ohio Edn. Assn.; named One of Ten Outstanding Legislators, Assembly of Govt. Employees, 1977. Democrat. Presbyterian. Clubs: Masons (32 deg.), Valley of Akron. Office: Statehouse Columbus OH 43215

OCHELTREE, RICHARD LAWRENCE, forest products co. exec.; b. Springfield, Ill., Oct. 9, 1931; s. Chalmer Myerly and Helen Margaret (Camm) O.; A.B., Harvard U., 1953, LL.B., 1958; m. Ann Maureen Washburn, Apr. 11, 1958; children—Kirstin Ann, Lorraine Page, Tracy Lynn. Admitted to Calif. bar, 1959; sec., corp. counsel Bendix Forest Products Corp., San Francisco, 1961—. Served with USAF, 1953-55. Mem. Am., San Francisco bar assns. Republican. Congregationalist. Home: 17 Mount Burney Ct San Rafael CA 94903 Office: 2740 Hyde St San Francisco CA 94109

OCHILTREE, NED A., JR., metals mfg. co. exec.; b. Omaha, Dec. 23, 1919; s. Ned A. and Garnett (Briggs) O.; B.S., Purdue U., 1942; m. Isabel Hayden, Oct. 25, 1946; 1 dau., Judith Ann Ochiltree Herseth. Research engr. Gen. Motors Research Labs., 1942-47; with Ceco Corp., Cicero, Ill., 1947—, exec. v.p. mfg., 1964-70, exec. v.p. sales and prodn., 1970-71, pres., 1971—, chief exec. officer, 1976—, chmn., 1979—, also dir.; dir. Oak Park Trust & Savs. Bank (Ill.). Mem. Chgo. Crime Commn., 1966—. Presbyn. Clubs: River Forest Tennis; Oak Park Country; University, Economic (Chgo.). Home: 1043 Keystone Ave River Forest IL 60305 Office: 5601 W 26th St Cicero IL 60650

OCHOA, SEVERO, biochemist; b. Luarca, Spain, Sept. 24, 1905; s. Severo and Carmen (Albornoz) O.; A.B., Malaga (Spain) Coll., 1921; M.D., U. Madrid (Spain), 1929; D.Sc., Washington U., U. Brazil, 1957, U. Guadalajara (Mexico), 1959, Wesleyan U., U. Oxford, Eng., U. Salamanca, Spain, 1961, Gustavus Adolphus Coll., 1963, U. Pa., 1964, Brandeis U., 1965, U. Granada, Spain, U. Oviedo, Spain, 1967, U. Perugia, Italy, 1968; Dr. Med. Sci. (hon.), U. Santo Tomas, Manila, Philippines, 1963, U. Mich., U. Buenos Aires, 1968, U. Tucuman (Argentina), 1968; L.H.D., Yeshiva Univ., 1966; LL.D., U. Glasgow (Scotland), 1959; m. Carmen G. Cobian, July 8, 1931. Came to U.S., 1940, naturalized, 1956. Lectr. physiology U. Madrid Med. Sch., 1931-35, head physiol. div. Inst. for Med. Research, 1935-36; guest research asst. in physiology Kaiser-Wilhelm Inst. for Med. Research, Heidelberg, Germany, 1936-37; Ray Lankester investigator Marine Biol. Lab., Plymouth, Eng., 1937; demonstrator, Nuffield research asst. biochemistry Oxford (Eng.) U. Med. Sch., 1938-41; instr., research asso. pharmacology Washington U. Sch. of Medicine, St. Louis, 1941-42; research asso. medicine N.Y. U. Sch. Medicine, 1942-45, asst. prof. biochemistry, 1945-46, prof. pharmacology, chmn. dept., 1946-54, prof., chmn. dept. biochemistry, 1954—; distinguished mem. Roche Inst. Molecular Biology. Decorated Order Rising Sun (Japan); recipient (with Arthur Kornberg) 1959 Nobel prize in medicine, Albert Gallatin medal N.Y. U., 1970. Fellow N.Y. Acad. Scis., N.Y. Acad. Medicine, Am. Acad. of Arts and Sci., A.A.A.S.; mem. Nat. Acad. Sci., Am. Philos. Soc., Soc. for Exptl. Biology and Medicine, Soc. of Biol. Chemists (pres. 1958, editor jour. 1950-60), Internat. Union Biochemistry (pres. 1961-67), Biochem. Soc. (Eng.), Harvey Soc. (pres. 1953-54), Alpha Omega Alpha (hon.); fgn. mem. German Acad. Nat. Scis., Royal Spanish, USSR, Polish, Pullian, Italian, Argentinian, Barcelona (Spain), Brazilian acads. sci., Royal Soc. (Eng.), Argentinian Nat. Acad. Medicine. Author: publs. on biochem. of muscles, glycolysis in heart and brain, transphosphorylations in yeast fermentation, pyruvic acid oxidation in brain and role of vitamin B1; enzymatic mechanisms of carbon dioxide assimilation; RNA and Protein biosynthesis; genetic code. Home: 530 E 72d St New York NY 10021 Office: Roche Inst Molecular Biology Nutley NJ 07110

OCHS, ELMER RAYMOND, ret. army officer; b. Newton, Ill., Apr. 11, 1925; s. Aloyisous Raymond and Lela Arwilder (Miller) O.; B.S., U.S. Mil. Acad., 1946; postgrad. Command and Gen. Staff Coll., Ft. Leavenworth, Kans., 1958-59, U.S. Army War Coll., Carlisle Barracks, Pa., 1965-66; M.S. in Internat. Relations, George Washington U., 1966; m. Inez Donoho, Feb. 5, 1971; children—Richard G., Edward L., Patricia Ochs Cook. Commd. 2d lt. U.S. Army, 1946, advanced through grades to maj. gen., 1973; tactical officer 1st Regt., U.S. Mil. Acad., 1959-62, adj., 1962-63; comdr. 2d Bn., 8th Cav. Regt., 1st Cav. Div., U.S. Army Pacific, Korea, 1963-64; chief Plans, Programs and Rev. Div., Army Aviation, Office Asst. Chief of Staff for Force Devel., Washington, 1964-65; chief Policy and Plans br. Office Dir. Instrn., U.S. Army Inf. Sch., Ft. Benning, Ga., 1966-67, sec., 1967-68; chief Doctrine, Systems and Tng. Div., Hdqrs. U.S. Army, Vietnam, 1968; sr. mil. adviser civil ops. and rural devel. support III Corps, Mil. Assistance Command, Vietnam, 1968-69; dep. brigade comdr. 173d Airborne Brigade, Republic of Vietnam, 1969-70, comdr., 1970-71; comdr. U.S. Army Combat Devels. Experimentation Command, Ft. Ord, Calif., 1971-73; comdr. U.S. Army Operational Test and Evaluation Agy., Ft. Belvoir, Va., 1973-76; comdr. U.S. Army M.P. Sch./Tng. Center and Ft. McClellan, Ala., 1976-78; dep. comdr. XVIII Airborne Corps, Ft. Bragg, N.C., 1978-79, ret., 1979. Decorated Disting. Service medal with oak leaf cluster, Legion of Merit with oak leaf cluster, Bronze Star medal with V, Air medal with 9 oak leaf clusters, Army Commendation medal, Purple Heart, Vietnamese Cross of Gallantry with gold star, Combat Inf. badge, Parchute badge. Mem. Assn. U.S. Army. Roman Catholic. Address: 980 Bryn Mawr Blvd Mary Esther FL 32569

OCHS, MARTIN SHELBY, editor; b. Chattanooga, Aug. 18, 1923; s. Adolph Shelby and Rose Kirkpatrick (Martin) O.; A.B., Princeton, 1947; M.A. in Govt. U. Va., 1976; m. Celia Stratford Latimer, June 14, 1952; children—Patricia Stratford, Celia Martin, Shelby Latimer. Sports writer Chattanooga Times, 1947, courthouse reporter, copy editor, asst. city editor, 1948-50, asst. mng. editor, 1953, asso. editor and columnist, 1954, editor, 1958-71; univ. editor U. Va., Charlottesville, 1971-75, dir. info. services Med. Center, 1975-79; prof. mass communications Am. U. in Cairo, 1979—; N.Y. Times fgn. corr., London, Paris, Berlin, 1950-52; pres. Chattanooga Automobile Club, 1961-62. Vice chmn. bd. Bonny Oaks Sch., Hamilton County, Tenn.; pres. Chattanooga Goodwill Industries, 1953-55; mem. nat. com. Whitney Mus.; mem. exec. bd. Boy Scouts Am. Dir. Audubon Soc., Nat. Citizens Com. on Community Relations. Served as 1st lt. AUS, World War II. Mem. Am. Coll. Pub. Relations Assn., Newcomen Soc. N.Am. (Tenn., Va. coms.). Episcopalian. Office: 113 Sharia Kasr el Aini Cairo Egypt

OCHS, ROBERT DAVID, educator; b. Bloomington, Ill., Mar. 27, 1915; s. Herman Solomon and Fannie Leah (Livingston) O.; A.B., Ill. Wesleyan U., 1936; M.A., U. Ill., 1937, Ph.D., 1939; M.A., Oxford U., Eng., 1964. Research dir. Anti-Defamation League, 1939-41; mem. faculty U. S.C., 1946—, prof. history, 1957-76, Distinguished prof. emeritus, 1976—, chmn. dept., 1960-74, acting dean Coll. Arts and Sci., 1970-71; asso. editor U. S.C. Press, 1950-53. Vis. prof. Merton Coll., Oxford U., 1964. Mem. S.C. Archives Commn., 1960-74. Bd. dirs. Columbia Music Festival Assn., 1957-64, 77—, v.p. 1961-62, pres., 1962-63; dir. Columbia Festival Orch., Columbia Mus. Art, 1966-69, 74-77. Served to maj. AUS, 1941-46; lt. col. Res. Mem. Am., So. (exec. council 1973-76), S.C. (editor 1947-55, pres. 1956-57) hist. assns., Am. Studies Assn., Orgn. Am. Historians, Southeastern Am. Studies Assn. (pres. 1960-61), Omicron Delta Kappa. U.S. cons. History of The 20th Century, 1967. Home: Cornell Arms Columbia SC 29201

OCHS, SIDNEY, educator, neurophysiologist; b. Fall River, Mass., June 30, 1924; s. Nathan and Rose (Kniaz) O.; Ph.D., U. Chgo., 1952; m. Bess R. Ratner, Jan. 9, 1949; children—Rachel, Raymond, Susan. Research fellow Cal. Inst. Tech., 1954-56; NSF sr. postdoctoral fellow biophysics Univ. Coll., London, Eng., 1963-64; prof. physiology Ind. U. Med. Sch., 1961—, chmn. biophysics program, 1968—; vis. prof. Cento de Investigacion y de Estudios Avanzados del Instituto Politechnico Nacional de Mex., 1976. Served with AUS, 1943-45. Grantee NSF, 1978, NIH, 1978, Muscular Dystrophy Assn., 1978, John A. Lilly Found., 1977-79. Mem. Am. Physiol. Soc., Biophys. Soc., Am. Neurochem. Soc., Internat. Neurochem. Soc., Internat. Brain Research Orgn., Soc. Neurosci. (councillor 1971-74), Sigma Xi. Author: Elements of Neurophysiology, 1965; also articles, chpts. in books. Editor Jour. Neurobiology, 1969-77, asso. editor, 1977—. Home: 912 Forest Blvd N Dr Indianapolis IN 46240

OCHSNER, ALTON, surgeon; b. Kimball, S.D., May 4, 1896; s. Edward Phillip and Clara (Shontz) O.; A.B., U. S.D., 1918, D.Sc., 1936; M.D., Washington U., 1920; LL.D., Tulane U., 1966; Dr. h.c., U. Athens, Greece; m. Isabel Kathryn Lockwood, Sept. 13, 1923 (dec.); children—Alton, John Lockwood, Mims Gage, Isabel; m. 2d, Jane Kellogg Sturdy, Feb. 12, 1970. Intern, Barnes Hosp., St. Louis, 1920-21, Augustana Hosp., Chgo., 1921-22; exchange surg. asst. Kantons Hosp., Zurich, Switzerland, 1922-23, Staedtisches Krankenhaus, Frankfurt am Main, 1923-24; visited European and Am. clinics, 1924-25; instr. surgery Northwestern U. Med. Sch., 1925-26; asst. prof. surgery U. Wis. Med. Sch., 1926-27; prof. surgery, chmn. dept. Tulane U. Med. Sch., 1927-56, William Henderson prof. surgery, 1938-56, prof. clin. surgery, 1956-61, prof. emeritus, 1961—, cons. in gen. surgery Ochsner Clinic, Found. Hosp.; hon. staff Touro Infirmary; cons. surgeon Charity Hosp.; cons. thoracic surgery USPHS Hosp., VA Hosp., New Orleans. Dir. Fawley Enterprises Inc., Nat. Airlines, Inc., Fla. Nat. Banks Fla. Pres., Alton Ochsner Med. Found., 1942-70. Decorated Order Vasco Nunez de Balboa (Panama); Orden al Merito (Ecuador); Cruz El Roy Alfaro de Fundacion Internacional El Roy Alfaro (Panama); Orden Rodolfo Robles (Guatemala), Ordenal Merito (Spain); recipient Times-Picayune Loving Cup as New Orleans' outstanding citizen; Distinguished Service award A.M.A.; named Distinguished Salesman-at-Large of New Orleans; Thomas F. Cunningham award Internat. House New Orleans. Fellow A.C.S. (regent, past pres.), Am., So. (past pres.) surg. assns., Royal Coll. Surgeons Ireland (hon.), Royal Coll. Surgeons Eng. (hon.); mem. Internat. Soc. Surgery (past pres.), AMA, Am. Assn. Thoracic Surgery (past pres., hon.), Soc. Vascular Surgery (past pres.), Internat. Surg. Soc. Clin. Surgery, Southeastern (past pres.), So. (past pres.) surg. assns., Orleans Parish Med. Soc., Am. Cancer Soc. (dir.), Pan-Pacific Surg. Assn. (pres. 1963), So., La. med. assns., Am. Acad. Orthopedic Surgeons (hon.), Academie Royale de Medecine de Belgique (fgn. hon.), numerous fgn. sci. assns. (hon.), Phi Beta Kappa, Sigma Xi, Nu Sigma Nu, Alpha Omega Alpha, Omicron Delta Kappa, Phi Delta Theta. Clubs: Boston, New Orleans Country. Author: Smoking and Cancer, 1954; Smoking and Health, 1959; Smoking and Your Life, 1964; Smoking: Your Choice Between Life and Death, 1970. Writer: sect. on intestines Nelson's Loose Leaf Surgery, 1928; sect. on diseases of veins Lewis' System of Surgery; sect. on thoracic surgery and mediastinum Brennemann's Pediatrics; Monograph on Varicose Veins. Past chief editor Internat. Surg. Digest; past editor surg. sect. Cyclopedia of Medicine, Surgery and Specialties; past asst. editor Surgery of the Emergency; editor emeritus Surgery; past asso. editor Lewis Practice of Surgery. Home: 1347 Exposition Blvd New Orleans LA 70118 Office: Ochsner Clinic New Orleans LA 70121

OCKENGA, HAROLD JOHN, clergyman, theol. sem. pres. ex-officio; b. Chgo., July 6, 1905; s. Herman and Angie (Tetzlaff) O.; A.B., Taylor U., 1927, D.D., 1937; student Princeton Sem., 1927-29; Th.B., Westminister Sem., Phila., 1930; A.M., U. Pitts., 1934, Ph.D., 1939; Litt.D., Suffolk U., 1939; Hum. D., Bob Jones Coll., 1944; LL.D., Houghton Coll., 1946; D.D., Wheaton Coll., 1960, Fuller Theol. Sem., 1963; Litt.D., Norwich U. (Vt.), 1962, Seattle Pacific Coll., 1963, Chungang U., Seoul, Korea, 1975; D.D., Gordon Coll., 1968; m. Audrey L. Williamson, Aug. 6, 1935; children—Audrey Starr, Aldryth Sabra, Harold John. Ordained ministry Presbyn. Ch., 1931; asst. minister First Ch., Pitts., 1930-31; minister Point Breeze Ch., Pitts., 1931-36, Park St. Ch., Boston, 1936-69; pres. Fuller Theol. Sem., Pasadena, Cal., 1947-54, 59-63, chmn. bd., 1961-69; pres. Gordon Coll. and Gordon-Conwell Theol. Sem., 1969-79. Mem. Pres. Truman's Clergymen's Mission to Europe, 1947; vis. lectr. to missionary confs. and colls. on two world tours to 35 countries; summer supply preacher Westminster Chapel, London, 1946, 48, 51, 53, 57, 64. Travelled in Europe, Asia and Africa, S.Am., Australia. Pres. Nat. Assn. Evangs. for United Action, 1942-44; v.p. World Evang. Fellowship, 1951-61. Trustee Gordon Coll., Boston; trustee Suffolk U., Boston, 1939-49. Mem. Am. Acad. Polit. Sci. Rotarian. Club: Laconia Country. Author: These Religious Affections, 1937; Our Protestant Heritage, 1938; Have You Met These Women? 1940; Everyone That Believeth, 1942; The Comfort of God, 1944; Our Evangelical Faith, 1946; The Spirit of the Living God, 1947; Faithful in Christ Jesus, 1948; The Church in God, 1955; Protestant Preaching in Lent, 1956; Power Through Pentecost, 1959; Women Who Made Bible History, 1961; Preaching in Thessalonians, 1963; Faith in a Troubled World, 1972. Chmn. bd. Christianity Today, 1956—. Contbr. to religious jours. Home: 624 Bay Rd Hamilton MA 01936

OCKERSE, THOMAS, educator; b. Bandung, Java, Apr. 12, 1940 (parents Dutch citizens); s. Willem Fedor Pieter and Louise Johanna (Tideman) O.; came to U.S., 1957, naturalized, 1964; B.F.A., Ohio State U., 1963; M.F.A., Yale U., 1965; m. Susan Carol Florence, Aug. 31, 1963; children—Kirsten Ingred, Eerin Irene, Tara Manisses. Sr. designer Fogleman Assos., Morristown, N.J., 1965-67; asst. prof. Ind. U., Bloomington, 1967-71; asso. prof. graphic design R.I. Sch. Design, Providence, 1971—, head graphic design dept., 1973—, chmn. div. design, 1978—; artist, poet, free-lance graphic designer, Providence, 1965—; editor, pub. Tom Ockerse Edits., Providence, 1972—. Faculty Research grantee Ind. U., 1969; Scottish Internat. Trust grantee for edn. and art, 1972. Mem. AAUP, Sigma Chi. Author: SP-VII, 1968; Stamps-To, 1968; The A-Z Book, 1969; T.O.P., 1970; TV Documentracing, 1974; Son of Fury, 1974; Time, 1974; 26 Poems 1, 1975; Word and Image Equations, 1975; Fact or Fiction, 1976; Stamps-USA, 1975; Graphic Design Education: An Exposition, 1977; Space Window, 1977. Home: 37 Woodbury St Providence RI 02906 Office: RI Sch Design Providence RI 02903*

O'CONNELL, ARTHUR, actor; b. N.Y.C., Mar. 29, 1908; s. Michael and Julia (Byrne) O'C.; student St. John's High Sch. and Coll., Bklyn., 1922-28; m. Anne Hall Dunlop, June 23, 1962. Appeared in numerous motion pictures, including Citizen Kane, 1941, Naked City, 1948, Picnic (Acad. award nomination), 1955, Solid Gold Cadillac, 1956, The Man in the Gray Flannel Suit, 1956, The Proud Ones, 1956, Bus Stop, 1956, The Anatomy of a Murder (Acad. award nomination), 1959, Gidget, 1958, A Thunder of Drums, 1961, The Great Imposter, 1960, Man of the West, 1958, Seven Faces of Dr. Lao, 1963, Kissin' Cousins, 1963, The Monkey's Uncle, 1964, Fantastic Voyage, 1965, The Birds Do It, 1966, The Silencers, 1965, The Power, 1967, The Reluctant Astronaut, 1966, Suppose They Gave A War and Nobody Came, 1969, There Was A Crooked Man, 1969, The Last Valley, 1969, numerous others; stage debut in The Patsy, Dorchester, Mass., 1929; appeared in plays Remote Asylum, Los Angeles, 1970-71, Child's Play, Ft. Lauderdale and Miami, Fla., 1971; appeared on ABC-TV series The Second Hundred Years, 1967-68, Seven in Darkness, 1969; dir., actor The Army Play by Play, 1943; command performances Hyde Park for F.D.R., cabinet mems., Wilhelmina of Netherlands; actor in Army tng. films; dir. Broadway prodn. Brighten The Corner, 1945-46; toured Margaret Webster's Shakespeare Co.; studied with Mme. Ouspenskaya. Served with Signal Corps, AUS, 1940-45. Recipient certificate for profl. excellence in the theatre West Valley Coll., 1967, certificate of appreciation for efforts during Tet offensive in Viet Nam and Thailand, Dept. Def., 1968; hon. citizen N.Mex., Ky., Ala., Tenn. Mem. Screen Actors Guild, Actors Equity Assn., A.F.T.R.A., Acad. Motion Picture Arts and Scis., Nat. Acad. TV Arts and Scis., Players Club, Am. Coll. Theatre Festival (regional dir. 1968), ANTA (pres. Los Angeles chpt. 1966). Office: care Guild Mgmt Corp 9911 W Pico Blvd Los Angeles CA 90035

O'CONNELL, BRIAN, community organizer; b. Worcester, Mass., Jan. 23, 1930; s. Thomas J. and Mary (Carroll) O'C.; B.A., Tufts Coll., 1953; postgrad. Maxwell Sch. Citizenship and Pub. Adminstrn., 1953-54; m. Ann C. Brown, July 11, 1953; children—Todd, Tracey, Matthew. Field rep. Am. Heart Assn., Pa., 1954-56, exec. dir., Md., 1956-61, Calif., 1961-66; exec. dir. Nat. Assn. Mental Health, 1966-78, dir. emeritus, 1978—; pres. Nat. Council on Philanthropy, 1978—; exec. dir. Coalition of Nat. Vol. Orgns., 1978—; mem. U.S. Pres.'s Com. Employment of Handicapped, 1966-68; chmn. Liaison Group Mental Health, 1969-72. Head class agt. Tufts U., 1956-70; also mem. alumni council. Recipient Outstanding Agy. Profl. award United Way Am., 1979. Served with AUS, 1947-49. Fellow Am. Pub. Health Assn., Am. Orthopsychiat. Assn., Nat. Com. Patients' Rights (chmn. 1975-77); mem. Nat. Rehab. Assn., N.A.A.C.P., Nat. Assembly Health and Welfare (v.p.), Am. Soc. Pub. Adminstrn., Nat. Acad. Voluntarism, Joint Info. Service (exec. com.), Nat. Congress on Citizenship (health advisor). Author: Effective Leadership in Voluntary Organizations, 1976; Finding Values that Work: The Search for Fulfillment, 1977. Home: 1341 Woodside Dr McLean VA 22101 Office: 1828 L St NW Washington DC 20037

O'CONNELL, DANIEL CRAIG, educator; b. Sand Springs, Okla., May 20, 1928; s. John Albert and Letitia Rutherford (McGinnis) O'C.; B.A., St. Louis U., 1951, Ph.L., 1952, M.A., 1953, S.T.L., 1960; Ph.D., U. Ill., 1963. Joined Soc. of Jesus, 1945; asst. prof. psychology St. Louis U., 1964-66, asso. prof., 1966-72, prof., 1972—, trustee, 1973—, pres., 1974-78; vis. prof. U. Melbourne (Australia), 1972, U. Kans., 1978-79; Humboldt fellow Psychol. Inst., Free U. Berlin, 1968; sr. Fulbright lectr. Kassel U., W. Ger., 1979-80. Recipient Nancy McNeir Ring award for outstanding teaching St. Louis U., 1969. NSF fellow, 1961, 63, 65, 68, Humboldt Found. grantee, 1973. Fellow Am., Mo. psychol. assns.; mem. Midwestern, Southwestern, Eastern psychol. assns., Psychologists Interested in Religious Issues, Psychonomic Soc., Soc. for Scientific Study of Religion, N.Y., Mo. acads. sci., AAUP, AAAS, Phi Beta Kappa. Contbr. articles to profl. jours. Home: 3601 Lindell Blvd Saint Louis MO 63108 Office: 221 N Grand St Saint Louis MO 63103

O'CONNELL, DANIEL KEVIN, leasing co. exec.; b. Chgo., Mar. 8, 1929; s. Michael James and Mary Bridget (Enright) O'C.; B.A., So. Ill. U., 1953; LL.B., Georgetown U., 1957; m. Dolores Ann Naimo, Aug. 25, 1956; children—James, Thomas, Mary Bridget. Admitted to D.C. bar, 1957, Fla. bar, 1967; law clk. Circuit Judge Wilbur K. Miller, U.S. Ct. of Appeals for D.C., 1957-59; atty. Tex. Gas Transmission Corp., Owensboro, Ky., 1959-64; atty. Ryder System, Inc., Miami, Fla., 1964-67, gen. counsel, 1967-70, sec., 1968-70, v.p. finance, treas., 1970-73, group v.p., 1973-74, exec. v.p., 1974—. Served with USAF, 1946-49, 51. Mem. Fla. Bar Assn. Club: Royal Palm Tennis (Miami). Home: 7300 SW 108th Terr Miami FL 33156 Office: 3600 NW 82d Ave Miami FL 33166

O'CONNELL, DENIS JOSEPH, ednl. publisher; b. Bklyn., Nov. 2, 1947; s. John Joseph and Anne (Moore) O'C.; B.A. cum laude, Adelphi U., Garden City, N.Y., 1969. With Barnell Loft & Dexter Westbrook, Ltd., ednl. publs., Baldwin, N.Y., 1969—, v.p., nat. sales mgr., 1974-75, pres., chief exec. officer, 1976—; pres. Lowell & Lynwood, Ltd., Connaught E.A.B. Corp. Chmn. Skodak dist. drive, Nassau County council Boy Scouts Am., 1977-79. N.Y. State Regents scholar, 1965; named Young Republican Man of Year, 1979. Roman Catholic. Home: 147 S Forest Ave Rockville Centre NY 11570 Office: 958 Church St Baldwin NY 11510

O'CONNELL, DONALD WILLIAM, coll. adminstr.; b. N.Y.C., Mar. 22, 1916; s. William Patrick and May Josephine (McHugh) O'C.; A.B., Columbia, 1937, A.M. (Mitchell fellow 1937-38), 1938, Ph.D., 1953; student Cambridge (Eng.) U., 1938-39; m. Jeanne Marie Austin, Sept. 5, 1953; children—Ellen Coombs, Stephen Austin, Lauren Marie, Marcia Lidell. Mem. faculty Columbia, 1940-59, asso. prof. banking, 1957-59, asst. dean Grad. Sch. Bus., 1954-57; economist WPB, 1942; econ. editorial writer N.Y. Herald Tribune, 1949-56; program asso. econ. devel. and administrn. Ford Found., 1959-62; prof. econs. U. Md., 1962—, dean Coll. Bus. and Pub. Adminstrn., 1962-73, v.p. for gen. adminstrn., 1973-79. Served to lt. USNR, 1942-46. Mem. Am. Econ. Assn., Phi Beta Kappa, Beta Gamma Sigma, Alpha Kappa Psi, Beta Alpha Psi, Phi Chi Theta, Pi Sigma Alpha. Contbg. author: Chapters in Western Civilization, 1948; The American Economy in Operation, 1949; Business Loans of American Commercial Banks, 1959. Editor: Public Sector Labor Relations in Maryland: Issues and Prospects, 1972. Home: 3401 Rosemary Ln Hyattsville MD 20782 Office: Center of Adult Edn U Md College Park MD 20742

O'CONNELL, DORIS, assn. exec.; b. N.Y.C., Apr. 30, 1929; d. William and Lillian (Rentz) Wisneski; student Columbia U., N.Y. U.; m. May 24, 1952; children—William, Joanne, Paul, Timothy, Tina. Exec. sec. Nat. Music Council, N.Y.C.; pres. Port Singers. Recipient hon. awards Girl Scouts U.S.A., local schs. Office: 250 W 57th St New York NY 10019

O'CONNELL, GEORGE DANTHINE, artist; b. Madison, Wis., Oct. 16, 1926; s. George and Amelia (Danthine) O'C.; B.S., U. Wis., 1950, M.S., 1951; postgrad. Ohio State U., 1952-53, Rijksakademie Van Beeldende Kunsten, Amsterdam, Netherlands, 1959-60; m. Marilyn Winkler, July 12, 1947; 1 son, Timothy. Instr. painting and printmaking Calif. Coll. Arts and Crafts, Oakland, 1953-54; asst. prof. State U. Coll., Buffalo, 1954-61; asso. prof. U. Md., 1961-68; mus. technician Smithsonian Instn., Washington, summers 1962, 64; prof. State U. Coll., Oswego, N.Y., 1968—, chmn. dept., 1971-73; participant Art In Embassies program Dept. State, 1966, Vol. Artist Program, U.S. Army, summer 1971; project dir. Nat. Endowment Fine Arts, 1973-74; one-man shows include: State U. Coll., Fredonia, N.Y., 1956, Smithsonian Instn., 1962, Balt. Mus. Art, 1963, U. Md., 1968, Franz Bader Gallery, Washington, 1973, Everson Mus., Syracuse, N.Y., 1977; group shows throughout U.S. including: Butler Inst. Am. Art, 1955, 57, Albright-Knox Gallery, Buffalo, 1961, Bklyn. Mus., 1964, 66, U. Miami (Fla.), 1967, No. Ill. U., DeKalb, 1970, Davidson (N.C.) Coll., 1974, Oxford Gallery, Rochester, N.Y., 1976; represented in over 40 pub. collections including: Library of Congress, Washington, Nat. Collection Fine Arts, Washington, Phila. Mus. Fine Art, Gemeentemuseum Van Schone Kunsten, The Hague, Netherlands, Smithsonian Instn., Balt. Mus. Art, U.S. Embassy, Singapore and Dublin, N.Y. Pub. Library, Brit. Mus., London, Cleve. Mus. Art, and others. Address: 39 Baylis St Oswego NY 13126

O'CONNELL, HUGH MELLEN, JR., architect; b. Oak Park, Ill., Nov. 29, 1929; s. Hugh M. and Helen Mae (Evans) O'C.; student mech. engring. Purdue U., 1948-50; B.S. in Archtl. Engring., U. Ill., 1953; m. Frances Ann Small, Apr. 13, 1957; children—Patricia Lynn, Susan Marie, Jeanette Maureen. Designer, John Mackel, structural engr., Los Angeles, 1955-57; architect Harnish & Morgan & Causey, Ontario, Calif., 1957-63; self-employed architect, Ventura, Calif., 1963-69; architect Andrews/O'Connell, Ventura, 1970-78, Naval Constrn. Bn. Center, Port Hueneme, Calif., 1978—. Mem. tech. adv. com. Ventura Coll., 1965—; sec. Oxnard Citizens' Adv. Com., 1969—, v.p., 1970-72, pres., 1972—; chmn. Oxnard Beautification Com., 1969, 74; chmn. Oxnard Community Block Grant adv. com., 1975-76; mem. Oxnard Planning Commn., 1976—, vice chmn., 1978. Served with AUS, 1953-55. Registered architect, Ariz., Calif., La., Nev., Nat. Council Archtl. Registration Bds. Mem. AIA (pres. Ventura chpt. 1973), Am. Concrete Inst., Soc. Am. Registered Architects (Design award 1968, dir. 1970), Am. Legion, Alpha Rho Chi. Presbyterian (elder 1963, deacon 1967). Kiwanian (pres. 1969, div. sec. 1974-75), Elk. Home: 520 Ivywood Dr Oxnard CA 93030 Office: Bldg 850 Code 841 NCBC Port Hueneme CA 93042

O'CONNELL, JEFFREY, educator, lawyer; b. Worcester, Mass., Sept. 28, 1928; s. Thomas Joseph and Mary (Carroll) O'C.; grad. cum laude, Phillips Exeter Acad., 1947; A.B. cum laude, Dartmouth, 1951; J.D., Harvard, 1954; m. Virginia Kearns, Nov. 26, 1960; children—Mara, Devin. Instr. speech Tufts U., 1953-54; admitted to Mass. and Conn. bars, 1954, hon. admittance to Ark. and Minn. bars; with firm Sherburne, Powers & Needham, 1954-57, Hale & Dorr, Boston, 1958-59; asst. prof., then asso. prof. law U. Iowa Coll. Law, 1959-62; asso. dir. automobile claims study Harvard Law Sch., 1963-64; asso. prof. law U. Ill. Coll. Law., 1964-65, prof., 1965-79; prof. law U. Va. Law Sch., 1979—; summer vis. prof. Northwestern U., 1963, U. Mich., 1966, 75, So. Meth. U., 1972, U. Tex., 1977, U. Wash., 1979; vis. fellow Centre for Socio-Legal Studies, Wolfson Coll., Oxford (Eng.) U., 1973. Mem. Nat. Hwy. Safety Adv. Com., 1967-70; ednl. adv. bd. John Simon Guggenheim Found. Bd. dirs. Consumers Union, 1970-76. Guggenheim fellow, 1972-73, 79-80. Served as 1st lt. USAF, 1954-57. Mem. Am. Bar Assn., Minn., Ark. bars (hon.), Casque and Gauntlet, Phi Beta Kappa, Psi Upsilon. Democrat. Roman Catholic. Author: (with R.E. Keeton) Basic Protection for the Traffic Victim, 1965; After Cars Crash: The Need for Legal and Insurance Reform, 1967; (with Arthur Myers) Safety Last: An Indictment of the Auto Industry, 1966; (with R.E. Keeton, John McCord) Crisis in Car Insurance, 1968; (with Wallace Wilson) Car Insurance and Consumer Desires, 1969; The Injury Industry, 1971; (with Rita James Simon) Payment for Pain and Suffering, 1972; Ending Insult to Injury: No-Fault Insurance for Products and Services, 1975; (with Roger Henderson) Tort Law, No-Fault and Beyond, 1975; The Lawsuit Lottery: Only the Lawyers Win, 1979; also chpts. in books. Office: Univ Va Law Sch Charlottesville VA 22901

O'CONNELL, JOHN JAMES, III, publishing co. exec.; b. Bklyn., Feb. 17, 1921; s. John James and Hazel (Hines) O'C.; A.B., Manhattan Coll., 1941; m. Carmel K. O'Reilly, May 15, 1944;

children—Christine, John J. IV, Carmel, William Egan. With Office of Prodn., Washington, 1941; staff Cosmopolitan Mag., N.Y.C., 1946-59, editor-in-chief, 1951-59; editor-in-chief American Weekly, 1959-63; dir. editorial enterprises N.Y. Jour.-Am., 1963; exec. editor This Week mag., 1963-65, editor, 1965-68; dir. publs. Famous Schs., Inc., Westport, 1968-72; exec. asst. to William Randolph Hearst, Jr., Hearst Corp., N.Y.C., 1972-73; exec. editor Hearst Newspapers, 1973—; dir. Hearst Headline Service, 1973—. Served as lt. USNR, 1942-46; PTO. Decorated Bronze Star. Clubs: Dutch Treat (N.Y.C.); National Press, Overseas Press. Home: 30 Butternut Pl Stamford CT 06903 Office: 959 8th Av New York NY 10019

O'CONNELL, JOSEPH CLEOPHAS, univ. adminstr.; b. Dover, N.H., Sept. 25, 1918; s. Joseph C. and Mary C. (Lowey) O'C.; B.S.C., U. Notre Dame, 1940; m. Charlotte Rohonczy, Jan. 7, 1947; children—Sherry (Mrs. Howard Nenner), Joseph (dec.), Mary (Mrs. Mary Doyle), Thomas. With Studebaker Aviation, 1940-42; chief fiscal and accounting officer U.S. Govt. and Dept. of State, Bavaria, Germany, 1945-54; bus. mgr. Hunter Coll., 1954-61, N.Y. U., 1961-66; sec., bus. officer Cooper Union, N.Y.C., 1966-68; v.p. for bus. affairs, treas. U. R.I., Kingston, 1968-74; sr. v.p., treas. Rutgers, The State U., New Brunswick, N.J., 1974—; lectr. accounting Hunter Coll., 1955-67; dir. Colonial First Nat. Bank, Red Bank, N.J. Mem. N.Y.C. Community Planning Bd., 1966-68; pres. Washington Sq. Southeast Apts., N.Y.C., 1964; chmn. referral service Higher Edn. Adminstrn., 1975-77. Trustee Research and Design Inst., Providence, 1969-74; bd. dirs., treas. N.J. Soc. for Prevention Blindess, 1978—. Served to 1st lt. AUS, 1942-45; MTO. Decorated Bronze Star, Combat Inf. badge; recipient Humane Action medal Dept. Def., 1949; cited by Dept. Housing and Urban Devel., 1971. Mem. Eastern Assn. Coll. and Univ. Bus. Officers (exec. com. 1971-77), Soc. Coll. and Univ. Planning (treas. 1972-73), Nat. Assn. Coll. and Univ. Bus. Officers (dir. 1978-79). Contbr. articles to profl. jours. Home: Dana Ln Colts Neck NJ 07722

O'CONNELL, JOSEPH JAMES, JR., lawyer; b. Saranac Lake, N.Y., Nov. 8, 1905; s. Joseph James and Margaret (Cogan) O'C.; B.S., U. Vt., 1926; LL.B., Fordham U., 1930; LL.D., Rider Coll., 1950; m. Hazel Ashmore, Dec. 21, 1941; children—Shella Jo, Margaret. Admitted to N.Y. bar, 1930, D.C. bar, 1947; practice in N.Y.C., 1930-33; with PWA, 1933-38; with Treasury Dept., 1938-47, asst. gen. counsel, 1941-44, gen. counsel 1944-47; with firm Gardner, Morrison & Rogers, Washington, 1947-48; chmn. CAB, 1948-50; mem. firm Chapman, Walsh & O'Connell, 1950-58, Hawkins, Delafield & Wood, N.Y.C., 1958-64, Chapman & O'Connell, Washington, 1964-67; chmn. Nat. Transp. Safety Bd., 1967-69; mem. firm Lucas, O'Connell, Friedman & Man, Washington, 1969—. Mem. Alpha Tau Omega. Democrat. Home: 3031 Sherwood Blvd Delray Beach FL 33444

O'CONNELL, KENNETH JOHN, state justice; b. Bayfield, Wis., Dec. 8, 1909; s. Daniel W. and Kathryn B. (Smith) O'C.; LL.B., U. Wis., 1933, S.J.D., 1934; m. Evelyn L. Wachsmuth, June 2, 1938; children—Daniel, Thomas; m. 2d, Esther Erickson, July 3, 1964. Admitted to Wis. bar, 1933, Oreg. bar, 1944; assisted preparation Restatement of Law of Property, Am. Law Inst.; asst. atty. Wis. Tax Commn., 1934; pvt. practice law, Eugene, Oreg., 1944-47; mem. Oreg. Supreme Ct., 1958—, chief justice, 1970—; asst. prof. law U. Oreg. Law Sch., 1935-40, asso. prof., 1940-44, prof., 1947-58. Mem. faculty N.Y. U. Law Sch. Appellate Judges Seminar, 1966, 67; Distinguished vis. prof. law U. Oreg., 1977, Willamette U. Sch. Law, 1977. Chmn. Oreg. Statute Revision Council, 1950-54; mem. 2d Triennial Coif Award Com., 1965; mem. Oreg. Jud. Reform Commn., 1971—; vice chmn. Constl. Revision Com., Oreg., 1961-63; mem. exec. com. Conf. Chief Justices. Chmn. Oreg. Rhodes Scholarship Selection Com., 1969—; elector N.Y.U. Hall of Fame for Great Ams. Recipient Oreg. State Bar award of merit, 1953, Distinguished Service award U. Oreg., 1967; Herbert Harley award Am. Judicature Soc., 1976. Fellow Center Advanced Study Behavioral Scis., 1965-66. Mem. Oreg. Jud. Council, Oreg. State Bar, Order of Coif, Omicron Delta Tau, Phi Delta Phi. Author article, monographs legal topics. Home: 3393 Country Club Dr S Salem OR 97302

O'CONNELL, KEVIN, lawyer; b. Boston, Sept. 4, 1933; s. Michael Frederick and Kathryn Agnes (Kelley) O'C.; A.B., Harvard, 1955, J.D., 1960; m. Sarah Miller, Oct. 7, 1978; children—Tiffany W., Elizabeth H. Admitted to Calif. bar, 1961; asso. firm O'Melveny & Myers, Los Angeles, 1960-63; asst. U.S. atty. criminal div. Central Dist. Calif. Los Angeles, 1963-65; staff counsel Gov. Calif. Commn. to Investigate Watts Riot, Los Angeles, 1965-66; partner firm Tuttle & Taylor, Los Angeles, 1966-70; partner firm Coleman & O'Connell, Los Angeles, 1971-75; individual practice law, Los Angeles, 1975-78; of counsel firm Simon & Sheridan, Los Angeles, 1978—. Mem. Los Angeles County (Calif.) Democratic Central Com., 1973-74. Served to lt., USMCR, 1955-57. Bd. editors Harvard Law Rev., 1958-60. Home: 1883 Westridge Rd Los Angeles CA 90049 Office: 2404 Wilshire Blvd Los Angeles CA 90057

O'CONNELL, LENAHAN, lawyer; b. Wilkes-Barre, Pa., June 6, 1913; s. Joseph F. and Marisita R. (Lenahan) O'C.; A.B., Boston Coll., 1934; J.D., Boston U., 1938; m. Priscilla Halloran, Sept. 6, 1942; children—Lenahan L., Donn, Brendan H. Admitted to Mass. bar, 1938, since practiced in Boston; mem. firm O'Connell & O'Connell, 1938—; asst. atty. gen. Mass., 1949-53. Trustee Hibernia Savs. Bank, Boston. Mem. recess commn. re-disposition Benjamin Franklin Fund, 1957—; pres. Mass. Civic League, 1968—; sec. Mass. Civil War Centennial Com., 1959-66. Vice chmn. Boston Democratic Com., 1940-44. Bd. dirs. Boston Center Adult Edn.; trustee Boston Pub. Library, 1963-73, pres., 1966-68; trustee Boston Mus. Fine Arts, 1966- 68. Served to lt. col. AUS, 1942-46. Mem. Internat., Am., Mass., Boston bar assns., Eire Soc. Boston (pres., dir. 1953-54), Mil. Order Loyal Legion U.S. (comdr. in chief 1967-71), Judge Adv. Gens. Assn. (bd. dirs.), Ancient and Hon. Arty. Company Boston, Am. Legion (past post comdr.) Home: 5 Moss Hill Rd Boston MA 02130 Office: 31 Milk St Boston MA 02109

O'CONNELL, MAURICE DANIEL, lawyer; b. Ticonderoga, N.Y., Nov. 9, 1929; s. Maurice Daniel and Leila (Geraghty) O'C.; grad. Phillips Exeter Acad., 1946; A.B., Williams Coll., 1950; LL.B., Cornell U., 1956; m. Joan MacLure Landers, Aug. 2, 1952; children—Mark M., David L., Ann M., Leila K., Ellen A. Admitted to Ohio bar, 1956, since praticed in Toledo; asso. Williams, Eversman & Black, 1956-60; partner Robison, Curphey & O'Connell, 1961—; spl. hearing officer in conscientious objector cases U.S. Dept. Justice, 1966-68. Mem. Ottawa Hills Bd. Edn., 1963-66, pres., 1967-69; trustee Toledo Soc. for Handicapped, 1959—, sec., 1975—; trustee Woodlawn Cemetery, 1973—, v.p., 1976—; past trustee Toledo Hearing and Speech Center, Easter Seal Soc.; mem. alumni council Phillips Exeter Acad. Served to 1st lt. USMCR, 1950-53. Mem. NW Ohio Alumni Assn. of Williams Coll. (past pres.), Am., Ohio, Toledo (chmn. grievance com. 1971-74) bar assns., Kappa Alpha, Phi Delta Phi. Club: Toledo. Home: 3922 W Bancroft St Toledo OH 43606 Office: L O F Bldg Toledo OH 43624

O'CONNELL, PAUL EDMUND, publisher; b. Cambridge, Mass., Dec. 15, 1924; s. William Henry and Catherine O'C.; A.B., Harvard U., 1949; m. Phyllis B. Borgeson, July 20, 1970; children—Eileen Lucy, Brian Paul, Philip Bartlett, Douglas John, Donald Paul, Lori Ann, Stephanie Elizabeth, Kirsten Lynn. Salesman, Am. Tobacco Co., 1949-50; sales rep. dept. coll. texts Prentice-Hall Co., 1950-58, editor, 1958-62, exec. editor, asst. v.p., 1963-68; chmn. Winthrop Pubs. Inc. subs. Prentice Hall Co., Cambridge, Mass., 1969—. Served with AC, U.S. Army, 1943-47. Decorated Purple Heart. Mem. Nat. Council Tchrs. English, Am. Sociol. Assn. Home: 9 High Rock Rd Wayland MA 01778 Office: 17 Dunster St Cambridge MA 02138. *The days-and nights-have increasingly become more enjoyable with time and age. It would be nice if time slowed a bit, but it won't.*

O'CONNELL, PHILIP RAYMOND, forest products co. exec.; b. Woodside, N.Y., June 2, 1928; s. Michael Joseph and Ann (Blaney) O'C.; A.B., Manhattan Coll., 1949; LL.B., Columbia, 1956; grad. Advanced Mgmt. Program, Harvard, 1967; m. Joyce McCabe, July 6, 1957; children—Michael, Kathleen, Jennifer, David. Admitted to N.Y. State bar, 1956, also U.S. Supreme Ct. bar; asso. firm Dewey, Ballantine, Bushby, Palmer & Wood, N.Y.C., 1956-61, 62-64; gen. counsel, sec. Laurentide Finance Corp. Calif., San Francisco, 1961-62; gen. counsel Wallace-Murray Corp., and predecessor, 1964-66, divisional mgr., 1966-70; pres., chief exec. officer, dir., Universal Papertech Corp., Hatfield, Pa., 1970-71; sec. Champion Internat. Corp., Stamford, Conn., 1972—, v.p., 1979—. Served with USNR, 1951-54. Office: Champion International Corp 1 Landmark Square Stamford CT 06921

O'CONNELL, QUINN, lawyer; b. Redfield, S.D., May 5, 1924; s. John Ignatius and Ann (Quinn) O'C.; A.B., Georgetown U., 1946, J.D., 1955; M.F.A., Catholic U., 1950; m. Jane F. Salkeld, May 19, 1951; children—Quinn Jr., Jerome C., James S., John P., Maureen, Sharon Ann. Instr. U. Md., 1948-50; asst. procurator Catholic U., Washington, 1952-55; admitted to D.C. bar, 1955; asso. firm Weaver & Glassie, Washington, 1957-64, partner, 1964-68; partner firm Molloy & O'Connell, Washington, 1969-70, Connole and O'Connell, Washington, 1971—; v.p. Kelsea Internat., Inc. Served with USNR, 1943-46. Mem. Am., Fed., D.C. bar assns. Roman Catholic. Clubs: Metropolitan, Bethesda Country, International, National Lawyers (Washington). Home: 6704 Bradley Blvd Bethesda MD 20034 Office: 1 Farragut Sq S Washington DC 20006

O'CONNELL, RAYMOND GRIFFIN, mfg. co. exec.; b. Mamaroneck, N.Y., Mar. 21, 1920; s. Raymond T. and Josephine (Keating) O'C.; B.S. in Mech. Engring., Mass. Inst. Tech., 1941; postgrad. U.S. Naval Acad., 1941-42, Sloan Mgmt. Sch., 1967; m. Carolyn Lee Healy, Mar. 23, 1943; children—Raymond Griffin, James Garland. Trainee, Torrington Co. (Conn.), 1945-46, dist. engr., Chgo., 1946-47, dist. mgr., Detroit, 1948-55, asst. sales mgr., 1955-57, sales mgr., 1957-66, dir. marketing, 1966-67, exec. v.p., 1967-74, pres., 1974—; dir. Turner & Seymoor Co., Torrington. Mem. bd. edn., Elmhurst, Ill., 1948-52, Litchfield, Conn., 1957-69. Served to lt. comdr. USNR, 1941-45. Mem. Soc. Automotive Engrs., Sigma Xi, Tau Beta Pi. Home: Sheldon Ln Litchfield CT 06759 Office: Torrington Co Torrington CT 06790

O'CONNELL, RICHARD HENRY, profl. baseball exec.; b. Winthrop, Mass., Sept. 19, 1914; s. Henry Francis and Anne Frances (Cunning) O'C.; Ph.B., Boston Coll., 1937, A.M., 1938; m. Ethel W. Sears, Apr. 6, 1947; children—Kevin R., Stephen F., Kathleen M. Tchr., athletic dir. secondary schs., 1938-42; with Boston Red Sox, mems. Am. League Profl. Baseball Clubs, 1946—, exec. v.p., 1960-65, exec. v.p., gen. mgr., 1965-78; pres. R.H.O. Consultants, Boston, 1978—; corporator Charlestown Savs. Bank; dir. Barnett Bank, Winter Haven, Fla. Mem. pres.'s council Boston Coll.; dir. Boston council Boy Scouts Am. Trustee Sidney Farber Cancer Inst., New Eng. Bapt. Hosp.; bd. overseers athletics Brandeis U. Served with USNR, 1942-46. Decorated Bronze Star. Home: 49 Cedar Rd Belmont MA 02178 Office: PO Box 341 Boston MA 02178

O'CONNOR, CARROLL, actor, writer, producer; b. N.Y.C., Aug. 2, 1924; s. Edward Joseph and Elise Patricia (O'Connor) O'C.; B.A., Nat. U. Ireland, 1952; M.A., U. Mont., 1956; m. Nancy Fields, July 27, 1951; 1 son, Hugh. Actor, Dublin, Cork, Limerick, Galway, London, Paris, Edinburgh, 1950-54; appeared in N.Y. in Ulysses in Nightown, 1958, The Big Knife, 1959; TV appearances include The Sacco and Vanzetti Story, 1960, guest appearances U.S. Steel Hour, Kraft Theatre, Armstrong Circle Theater; films include Fever in the Blood, 1961, By Love Possessed, 1961, Lad a Dog, 1961, Lonely Are the Brave, 1962, Cleopatra, 1963, Not With My Wife, You Don't, 1966, Warning Shot, 1967, Marlowe, 1969, Death of a Gunfighter, 1969, Kelly's Heroes, 1970, Doctors' Wives, 1971, Law and Disorder; star TV series All in the Family, 1971—; also TV spls. including The Funny Papers, 1972, Of Thee I Sing, 1972, The Carroll O'Connor Special, 1973, spl. The Last Hurrah, 1973; night club appearances, Reno, Las Vegas. Recipient Emmy award for best actor, 1973, 77, 78, 79. Mem. The Players, Sigma Phi Epsilon. Address: PO Box 49514 Los Angeles CA 90049. *Everyone should rid himself of the illusion that his fulfillments are of much interest to anyone else.*

O'CONNOR, DENNIS MICHAEL, psychiatrist, hosp. adminstr.; b. Sioux City, Iowa, Apr. 18, 1942; s. A.M. and Edna M. O'C.; M.D., Creighton U., 1971; m. June 12, 1965; children—Patrick, Dennis. Intern, Herrick Meml. Hosp., Berkeley, Calif., 1971-72; resident in psychiatry Napa (Calif.) State Hosp., 1972-74, exec. dir., 1977—; practice medicine specializing in psychiatry, Napa, 1974-77. Served with USNR, 1961-64. Mem. Am. Psychiat. Assn., Calif. Med. Assn., No. Calif. Psychiat. Soc. Home: 3701 Jomar Dr Napa CA 94558 Office: Napa State Hosp Napa CA 94558

O'CONNOR, DONALD, actor; b. Chgo., Aug. 28, 1925; m. 2d, Gloria Noble, Nov. 1956. Began in vaudeville with family; actor Sons O'Fun, Syracuse, N.Y.; screen debut Sing You Sinners, 1938; other pictures include Sons of the Legion, Tom Sawyer Detective, Beau Geste, On Your Toes; vaudeville, 1940-41; motion picture roles include What's Cooking, 1942, Private Buckaroo, Give Out Sisters, When Johnny Comes Marching Home, Follow the Boys, Merry Monahans, Bowery to Broadway, Singing in the Rain, Call Me Madam, Walking My Baby Back Home, Cry for Happy, 1961, There's No Business Like Show Business, Anything Goes, 1956, That Funny Feeling, 1965, That's Entertainment, 1974, That's Entertainment, Part II, 1976, The Big Fix, 1978; actor Stars of Tomorrow, 1943; master ceremonies Acad. Awards, 1953; on Colgate TV comedy hour, 1953-54, Anything Goes, 1956, guest season premiere Judy Garland Show, 1963, and other TV programs, also star touring show. Voted best TV performance Motion Picture Daily Poll, 1953. Office: care Internat Creative Mgmt 8899 Beverly Blvd Los Angeles CA 90048*

O'CONNOR, DONALD J(OSEPH), environ. engr.; b. N.Y.C., Nov. 7, 1922; s. William John and Helen Gertrude (Ryan) O'C.; B.C.E. in San. Engring., Manhattan Coll., 1944; M.C.E., Poly. Inst. Bkly., 1947; Eng. Sc.D., N.Y. U., 1956; m. Anita Lordi, Oct. 31, 1948; children—Dennis, Arlene, Jeanette. Asst. prof. civil engring. Manhattan Coll., 1952-56, asso. prof., 1956-65, prof., 1965—; co-founder, cons. Hydrosci., Inc., cons. engrs., Westwood, N.J., 1953-73; dir./cons. numerous projects on water quality, water resource mgmt. for govtl. agys., industry; mem. adv. coms. on water quality mgmt. Nat. Acad. Scis., EPA, states of Calif., Tex., Va.; mem. U.S.-Can. Joint Internat. Commn. on Water Quality Mgmt. Served with U.S. Army, 1944-45. Recipient Most Significant Contbn. in Environ. Engring. award ASCE, 1958, 63. Mem. Nat. Acad. Engring., ASCE (hon.), Am. Geophys. Union, Am. Soc. Engring. Edn., Am. Assn. Profs. San. Engring., N.Y. State Water Pollution Control Assn., AAUP, Am. Soc. Limnology and Oceanography. Author: (with W. Ecrenfelder) Biological Waste Treatment, 1959; contbr. numerous articles to profl. jours. Home: 307 Dunham Pl Glen Rock NJ 07452 Office: Manhattan Coll Environ Engring and Sci Program Bronx NY 10471

O'CONNOR, EARL EUGENE, judge; b. Paola, Kans., Oct. 6, 1922; s. Nelson and Mayme (Scheetz) O.; B.S., U. Kans., 1947, LL.B., 1950; m. Florence M. Landis, Nov. 3, 1951 (dec. May 1962); children—Nelson, Clayton; m. 2d, Jean A. Timmons, May 24, 1963; 1 dau., Gayle. Admitted to Kans. bar, 1950; practiced in Mission, Kans., 1950-51; asst. atty. Johnson County, Kans., 1951-53; probate and juvenile judge, 1953-55; dist. judge 10th Jud. Dist., Olathe, Kans., 1955-65; justice Kans. Supreme Ct., 1965-71; judge U.S. Dist. Ct., Dist. of Kans., Kansas City, 1971—. Served with AUS, World War II; ETO. Mem. Am., Kans. bar assns., Nat. Conf. Fed. Trial Judges, Nat. Conf. State Trial Judges, Phi Alpha Delta. Mason, Rotarian. Home: 6654 Outlook Mission KS 66202 Office: US Courthouse Kansas City KS 66101

O'CONNOR, EDWARD DENNIS, educator; b. Denver, Oct. 28, 1922; s. Edward James and Mary Alethaire (Spalding) O'C.; A.B., Notre Dame U., 1944; sem. student Holy Cross Coll., 1944-48; S.T.L., Institut catholique de Paris, 1950; S.T.D., Angelicum, Rome, 1959. Ordained priest Roman Catholic Ch., 1948; with faculty U. Notre Dame, 1952—, now asso. prof. theology. Author: The Dogma of the Immaculate Conception, 1958; Faith in the Synoptic Gospels, 1961; The Pentecostal Movement in the Catholic Church, 1971; The Gifts of the Spirit, 1973; Perspectives on Charismatic Renewal, 1975; Pope Paul and the Spirit, 1978; others. Address: Box 353 Notre Dame IN 46556

O'CONNOR, ELIZABETH, librarian, archivist; B.A., Trinity Coll.; B.S. in L.S., Columbia U.; M.A., Manhattanville Coll. Librarian, prof. L.S., Manhattanville Coll., Purchase, N.Y.; mem. Religious of Sacred Heart Jesus. Office: Manhattanville Coll Purchase NY 10577

O'CONNOR, FRANCIS EDWARD, title ins. and trust co. exec.; b. Chgo., Feb. 8, 1918; s. Andrew Michael and Hannah Bridget (Bresnahan) O'C.; J.D. cum laude, DePaul U., 1940; M.B.A., U. Chgo., 1956; m. Esther M. Kruk, June 20, 1940; children—Janice, Maureen F. Admitted to Ill. bar, 1940; with Chgo. Title and Trust Co., 1941—, sr. v.p. personnel, public relations and mktg. div., 1966-77, exec. v.p., 1977—; pres. Chgo. Title and Trust Co. Found., 1966—, Chgo. Title and Trust Bldg. Corp., 1974—. Trustee, Catholic Charities, Chgo., Goodwill Industries, Chgo. Mem. Chgo. Bar Assn., Ill. Bar Assn., Am. Bar Assn., Ill. Land Title Assn., Am. Land Title Assn., Chgo. Council Fgn. Relations, Chgo. C. of C., Ill. C. of C., U.S. C. of C., Lambda Alpha, Beta Gamma Sigma. Roman Catholic. Clubs: Chgo. Athletic Assn., Mid-Am. Office: 111 N Washington St Chicago IL 60602

O'CONNOR, FRANCIS JOHN, lawyer; b. New Hampton, Iowa, Mar. 29, 1916; s. Frank A. and Mae (McNevin) O'C.; A.B., U. Iowa, 1937; J.D., Harvard U., 1940; LL.D. (hon.), Loras Coll., 1967, Clarke Coll., 1975; m. Marion Rhomberg, June 9, 1941; children—Frank R., Gerald R., Karen A., John C., Kevin T. Admitted to Iowa bar, 1940, since practiced in Dubuque; mem. firm O'Connor, Thomas, Hammer, Bertsch & Norby, 1946—. Lectr., Tax Sch., Iowa Bar Assn., 1944; chmn. Grievence Commn. Supreme Ct. Iowa, 1965-75; asst. county atty., 1942-43; dir. Dubuque Securities Co., A.Y. McDonald Mfg. Co., Jacobson Steel Co., E.J. Voggenthaler Co. Mem. exec. com. Dubuque Indsl. Bur., 1962-66; mem. Iowa Coordinating Council for Post High Sch. Edn., 1965-75; trustee U. Iowa Sch. Religion, 1954—, pres., 1961-63, v.p., 1967-68; bd. dirs. Archdiocese Dubuque, 1965—, St. Joseph Ch., 1967—, Mt. Olivet Cemetery Assn., 1962—; adv. bd. Xavier Hosp., 1965—; corporator, bd. dirs. Clarke Coll., 1967—; trustee Dubuque Post-War Indsl. Fund, 1946-66, Dubuque Boys Club, 1964—. Mem. Am. Bar Assn., Am. Judicature Soc., Am. Coll. Probate Coun., Am. Bar Found., Cath. Order Foresters, Phi Beta Kappa, Beta Theta Pi. Roman Catholic. K.C., Elk. Club: Dubuque Golf and Country (dir. 1945-50, pres. 1945). Home: 690 Sunset Ridge Dubuque IA 52001 Office: One Dubuque Plaza Suite 200 Dubuque IA 52001

O'CONNOR, FRANCIS X., business exec.; b. Bklyn., May 7, 1929; s. Richard B. and Mary (McCafferty) O'C.; B.S., St. Peter's Coll., 1951; m. Leona A. Windorf, June 30, 1951; children—Francis X., Edward K., Brendan T., Richard B. III, A. Bruce, Marianne, Margaret, Leona. Audit mgr. Lybrand, Ross Bros. & Montgomery, N.Y.C., 1951-65; controller Ward Foods, Inc., N.Y.C., 1965-66, v.p. fin., 1966-72, dir., 1968-73; v.p. fin. UMC Industries, Inc., N.Y.C., 1973-76; v.p. fin. and corp. devel. SKF Industries, Inc., King of Prussia, Pa., 1976—; dir. McQuay-Norris, Inc., St. Louis. C.P.A., N.Y., N.J. Mem. Am. Inst. C.P.A.'s, AIM, N.Y. State Soc. C.P.A.'s Nat. Assn. Accountants, Fin. Execs. Inst., Nat. Conf. on Power Transmission (trustee), St. Peter's Coll. Alumni Assn. (trustee, past pres. Monmouth chpt.), Navy League U.S. Clubs: Spring Lake Golf and Country (trustee); Seaview Country (Absecon, N.J.); Green Gables. Home: 16 St Clair Ave Spring Lake NJ 07762 Office: SKF Industries King of Prussia PA

O'CONNOR, SISTER GEORGE AQUIN (MARGARET M.), coll. pres.; b. Astoria, N.Y., Mar. 5, 1921; d. George M. and Joana T. (Loughlin) O'C.; B.A., Hunter Coll., 1943; M.A., Catholic U. Am., 1947; Ph.D. (NIMH fellow), N.Y. U., 1964. Tchr., St. Joseph's High Sch., Bklyn., 1944-45; mem. faculty St. Joseph's Coll., Bklyn., 1946—, prof. sociology and anthropology, 1966—, chmn. social sci. dept., 1966-69, pres., 1969—; mem. Regents Regional Coordinating Council Postsecondary Edn., 1973-76. Trustee Commn. on Ind. Colls. and Univs. of N.Y., 1979—. Fellow African Studies Assn., N.Y. Acad. Scis.; mem. Council Higher Ednl. Inst. N.Y.C. (dir. 1973—), Bklyn. Ednl. and Cultural Alliance (trustee 1972—), Bklyn. C. of C. (dir. 1973-82), Alpha Kappa Delta. Author: The Status and Role of West African Women: A Study in Cultural Change, 1964. Address: 245 Clinton Ave Brooklyn NY 11205

O'CONNOR, GEORGE E., life ins. co. exec.; b. Bklyn., Sept. 25, 1916; s. Charles M. and Margaret J. (Deering) O'C.; student Syracuse U. Grad. Sch. Sales Mgmt. and Mktg., 1960, Advanced Mgmt. Program Harvard U., 1962; m. Dorothy Reguci, Oct. 20, 1945; children—Gail O'Connor Bushey, Jane, Christopher. With N.Y. Life Ins. Co., N.Y.C., 1946—, v.p., 1969-74, sr. v.p., 1974—. Served to lt. col. inf., AUS, World War II. Decorated Silver Star, Bronze Star, Purple Heart, Croix de Guerre (France). Home: 132 E 72d St New York City NY 10021 Office: 51 Madison Ave New York City NY 10010

O'CONNOR, HARRY THOMAS, real estate exec.; b. Milw., Nov. 25, 1908; s. Harry F. and Anna (Kenney) O'C.; A.B., Marquette U., 1929, LL.B., 1932; m. Catherine Harrigan, Apr. 8, 1938; children—Barbara (Mrs. Gerald F. Meier), Thomas, Margaret (Mrs. Donald E. Delozier Jr.), Mary Kate (Mrs. Richard Stevenson). Admitted to Wis. bar, 1932; investigator atty. Milw. County, 1933-38;

spl. agt. FBI, Washington, 1938-52; asst. to pres. Holley Carburetor Co., Warren, Mich., 1952-59, v.p., gen. mgr. automotive div., 1959-62, exec. v.p., 1962, pres., until 1967, also dir.; dir. Holley Internat. Co., 1962-67; gen. mgr., dir. Howard T. Keating Assos. dir., asst. sec. Keating Internat. Corp.; exec. dir. Howard T. Keating Co.; now ret. Address: 1515 S Flagler Dr West Palm Beach FL 33401

O'CONNOR, HARVEY, writer; b. Mpls., Mar. 29, 1897; s. James and Jessie (Kenney) O'C.; ed. pub. schs.; m. Jessie Bross Lloyd, June 16, 1930; children—Stephen Lloyd, Kathleen Maverick. Labor editor Seattle Daily Union Record, 1919-24; asst. editor Locomotive Engrs. Jour., 1924-27; mgr. N.Y. bur. Federated Press, 1927-30; editor, publicity dir. Oil Workers Internat. Union, 1945-48. Chmn., Nat. Com. Against Repressive Legislation, 1964-76, chmn. emeritus, 1976—; mem. Pitts. Civil Liberties Com. (exec. com. 1934-36), Chgo. Civil Liberties Com. (exec. com. 1937-44), Emergency Civil Liberties Com. (chmn. 1955-63, nat. council 1966—). Unitarian. Club: Sakonnet (R.I.) Yacht. Author: Mellon's Millions, 1933; Steel-Dictator, 1935; The Guggenheims, 1937; The Astors, 1941; History of the Oil Workers International Union, 1950; The Empire of Oil, 1955; World Crisis in Oil, 1962; Revolution in Seattle, 1964. Home: Little Compton RI 02837

O'CONNOR, HUBERT PATRICK, bishop; b. Huntingdon, Que., Can., Feb. 17, 1928; s. Patrick Joseph and Mary Stella (Walsh) O'C.; B.A., St. Patrick's Coll., Ottawa, 1952; L.S.T., Holy Rosary Scholasticate, Ottawa, 1956. Joined Congregation Missionary Oblates Mary Immaculate, 1948, ordained priest Roman Cath. Ch., 1955; mem. staff Holy Rosary Scholasticate, 1956-61; pastor St. John's Parish, Lillooet, B.C., 1967-68; prin. Cariboo Indian Residential Sch., Williams Lake, B.C., 1961-67; sec.-treas. Order Oblates Mary Immaculate in B.C., Vancouver, 1968-71; dir. St. Paul's Provincial House, 1968-71, dir. Western region Oblate Fathers Indian-Eskimo Commn., 1968-71; bishop Diocese of Whitehouse, 1971—; nat. dir. Cath. Women's League Can., 1973-78. Club: K.C. Address: 5119 5th Ave Whitehorse YT Y1A 1L5 Canada

O'CONNOR, JAMES HARVEY, lawyer; b. Missoula, Mont., Apr. 24, 1922; s. Miles J. and Eleanor H. (Harvey) O'C.; student Pasadena Jr. Coll., 1940-41; B.S., U.S. Mil. Acad., 1944; postgrad. U. Mont., 1947-48, Loyola U., Los Angeles, 1948-49; LL.B., U. So. Calif., 1951; m. Deborah Ann Giles, Feb. 21, 1977; children—Sharon Michele, James Harvey, Ryan James. Admitted to Calif. bar, 1952, Ariz. bar, 1954; practice in Los Angeles, 1952-54, Phoenix, 1954-78; partner firm O'Connor, Cavanagh, Anderson, Westover, Killingsworth & Beshears, 1959-78; dir. Systems Capital Corp., Surety Savs. and Loan Assn. Bd. visitors Coll. Law, Ariz. State U. Served to capt. USAAF, 1944-46. Mem. Am. Coll. Trial Lawyers, Internat. Soc. Barristers, Internat. Assn. Ins. Counsel, Am., Ariz., Maricopa County (past pres.) bar assns. Clubs: Paradise Valley Country; Phoenix Country, Phoenix Lawyers (co-founder); Balboa (Mazatlan, Mexico). Home: 7242 Black Rock Trail Scottsdale AZ 85253 Office: 3003 N Central Ave Phoenix AZ 85012. *Died Oct. 18, 1978.*

O'CONNOR, JAMES JOHN, utility co. exec.; b. Chgo., Mar. 15, 1937; s. Fred James and Helen Elizabeth (Reilly) O'C.; B.S., Holy Cross Coll., 1958; M.B.A., Harvard, 1960; J.D., Georgetown U., 1963; m. Ellen Louise Lawlor, Nov. 24, 1960; children—Fred, John, James, Helen Elizabeth. Admitted to Ill. bar, 1963; with Commonwealth Edison Co., Chgo., 1963—, asst. to chmn. exec. com., 1964-65, comml. mgr., 1966, asst. v.p., 1967-70, v.p., 1970-73, exec. v.p., 1973-77, pres., 1977—, also dir.; dir. Talman Fed. Savs. & Loan Assn., Borg-Warner Corp., Esmark. Bd. dirs. Chgo. unit Am. Cancer Soc., chmn. bd., 1971-73; bd. dirs. Chgo. Boys Clubs, v.p., 1970—; bd. dirs. Assos. Harvard U. Grad. Sch. Bus. Adminstrn., Leadership Council for Met. Open Communities, Lyric Opera, Spl. Childrens Charities, Chgo. Conv. and Tourism Bur., Mus. Sci. and Industry, Sprague Meml. Inst., St. Xavier Coll., Arthritis Found., Cath. Charities Chgo., St. Joseph Carondolet Center, Reading Is Fundamental; bd. dirs. Citizenship Council of Met. Chgo., chmn., 1976—; trustee Adler Planetarium, Field Mus., Michael Reese Med. Center, Northwestern U., Children's Home and Aid Soc. Ill.; bd. dirs., chmn. Chgo. Urban League; bd. advs. Mercy Hosp. and Med. Center; mem. exec. bd. Chgo. Area Council Boy Scouts Am.; v.p. The Hundred Club Cook County; mem. adv. bd. Jesuit Retreat League; mem. businessmen's adv. com. Little Sisters of Poor; mem. citizens bd. U. Chgo. Served with USAF, 1960-63; civilian aide to Sec. Army. Mem. Am., Ill., Chgo. bar assns., Chgo. Assn. Commerce and Industry (dir.). Roman Catholic. Clubs: Commercial, Economic, Chgo. Chgo. Commonwealth, Metropolitan (Chgo.). Home: 9549 Monticello Ave Evanston IL 60203 Office: PO Box 767 One First National Plaza Chicago IL 60690

O'CONNOR, JAMES JOSEPH, lawyer, engring.-constrn. firm exec.; b. N.Y.C., Sept. 4, 1930; s. James Joseph and Viola G. (La Mothe) O'C.; B.S. in Engring., U.S. Coast Guard Acad., 1952; J.D., Fordham U., 1959; m. Jane I. Wagner, Dec. 26, 1955; children—Deborah J., David W., Daniel J. With Lummus Co., Bloomfield, N.J., 1960—, sec., 1964-70, v.p., gen. counsel, dir. 1970—; admitted to N.Y. State bar, 1960. Served with USCG, 1952-55. Mem. Am., N.Y. State bar assns. Republican. Roman Catholic. Clubs: Echo Lake Country, Mindowskin. Home: 25 Gallowae Westfield NJ 07090 Office: 1515 Broad St Bloomfield NJ 07003

O'CONNOR, JAMES JOSEPH, magazine editor; b. N.Y.C., Aug. 3, 1917; s. James John and Ellen M. (Lane) O'C.; B.E.E., N.Y. U., 1948; m. Mary E. O'Brien, June 16, 1940; children—Maureen, Carol, Colleen, Brian. Test engr. N.Y.C. Transit Authority, 1940-48; with Power mag., N.Y.C., 1948—, exec. engring. editor, 1963-68, chief engring. editor, 1968—; cons. engr. Fed. Energy Adminstrn.; engring. adviser Twp. Dumont (N.J.), 1952-56. Registered profl. engr., N.Y., N.J. Fellow IEEE; mem. Central Engring. Soc. (pres.), ASME, Am. Soc. Lubrication Engrs. Club: Engineers (N.Y.C.). Author: Standard Handbook of Lubrication Engineering, 1968. Home: 631 Birch Ave River Vale NJ 07675 Office: 1221 Ave of Americas New York NY 10020

O'CONNOR, JAMES PATRICK, univ. provost; b. Balt., Oct. 13, 1919; s. Thomas Francis and Laura Virginia (Hopkins), O'C.; M.A., Catholic U. Am., 1949, Ph.D., 1951; m. Helen Louise Klauenberg, June 24, 1944; children—Michael, Thomas, Patricia James. Mem. faculty Cath. U. Am., 1951—, prof. psychology, 1960—, head dept., 1959-60, dean Grad. Sch. Arts and Scis., 1960-68, vice provost, 1968-73, dir. Boys Town Youth Research Center, 1973—. Home: Ashton MD 20702

O'CONNOR, JEROME WILLIAM, broadcasting co. exec.; b. Pitts., Aug. 23, 1923; s. Thomas Lee and Bertha Marie (Bortell) O'C; student U. Ala., 1941, 42, U. Miami (Fla.), 1943, 44, Northwestern U., 1946; m. Dorothy June Conover, Dec. 22, 1944; children—Kerby William, Maureen Dee, Kathleen Dawn, Valerie Dodds, Clinton Anthony. With WGN Radio and Television, Chgo., 1946-50, Storer Broadcasting Co., Miami, Fla., 1950; ind. producer, announcer WCFL, WIND, WBKB-TV, WGN-TV, WMAQ, WENR, Chgo., 1951-65; pres. WCVS, Springfield, Ill., 1958-66, WBOW, Terre Haute, Ind., WHUT, Anderson, Ind., 1958-70; chmn. bd. WCIU-TV, Chgo., 1965—; dir. Weigel Broadcasting Co., Chgo., WRAC Broadcasting Co., Racine, Wis. Served with USNR, 1942-46. Mem. Broadcast Pioneers, Nat. Assn. Television Arts and Scis., Phi Gamma Delta. Clubs: Key Biscayne Yacht (Fla.); Metropolitan (Chgo.); Nat. Press (Washington). Home: Rural Route 1 Box 69 Bristol WI 53104 Office: Bd Trade Bldg 141 W Jackson Blvd Chicago IL 60604

O'CONNOR, JOHN ALBERT, JR., lawyer, corp. exec.; b. New Orleans, Apr. 10, 1913; s. John A. and Stella (Toledano) O'C.; A.B., Tulane, 1934, LL.B., 1936; m. Paula McKinney, Nov. 24, 1936; children—John A., Peter M., Paula T. (Mrs. Ben Smith III), Patricia M. (Mrs. Jon T. Ledlie). Admitted to La. bar, 1936, Ark. bar, 1937; atty. Lion Oil Co., El Dorado, Ark., 1936-41; partner Knox, Keith & O'Connor, 1941-45, Crumpler, O'Connor & Wynne (formerly Crumpler & O'Connor), 1945—; sec., dir. Radio Enterprises, Inc., (radio sta. KELD), 1946-73; sec. Ocean Drilling & Exploration Co., 1955-66, dir., 1955—, pres., dir. Brook Tarpaulin Co., Inc. (name changed to Brook Holding Co.), New Orleans, 1950—; sec. Murphy Oil Corp., 1954-66, v.p. gen. counsel, 1958-66, chmn. bd., 1966-72, chmn. exec. com., 1972-73, also dir. Pres. bd. dirs. El Dorado Sch. Dist. 15, 1949-50; pres. Community Chest, 1948-50. Served to lt. comdr. USNR, World War II. Mem. Am., La., Ark. bar assns., El Dorado C. of C. (dir., pres. 1950). Clubs: Eldorado Golf and Country; Boston, Internat. House, Plimsoll (New Orleans); Nat. Lawyers (Washington). Home: 510 E Faulkner St El Dorado AR 71730 Office: 308 NBC Plaza El Dorado AR 71730

O'CONNOR, JOHN JAY, III, lawyer; b. San Francisco, Jan. 10, 1930; s. John Jay and Sally (Flynn) O'C.; A.B., Stanford, 1951, LL.B., 1953; m. Sandra Day, Dec. 20, 1952; children—Scott, Brian, Jay. Admitted to Calif. bar, 1953, Ariz. bar, 1957, since practiced in Phoenix; asso., then partner, officer firm Fennemore, Craig, von Ammon & Udall, 1957—. Chmn. Ariz. Crippled Children's Services, 1968. Chmn. planning and zoning commn., Town of Paradise Valley, 1967. Chmn. Maricopa County Young Republicans, 1960, Ariz. Young Republican League, 1962. Chmn. bd. dirs. Maricopa County Gen. Hosp., 1967-70; exec. com. bd. visitors Stanford Law Sch., 1976—; mem. nat. council Salk Inst. for Biol. Studies, 1977—; pres. Phoenix-Scottsdale United Way, 1977-79; bd. dirs. World Affairs Council of Phoenix, 1973—, Legal Aid Soc. of Phoenix, Maricopa County Mental Health Assn.; mem. policy devel. com. Phoenix Community Service Fund, 1978; mem. exec. com. Valley Leadership, 1979—; bd. dirs. Trusteeship for St. Luke's Hosp., 1979—. Served to 1st lt. AUS, 1954-57. Mem. Am. Bar Assns., state bars Ariz., Calif., Am. Judicature Soc., Ariz. Tax Research Assn. (dir. 1972—), Stanford Assos., Ariz. Acad., Phoenix Wine and Food Soc., Delta Upsilon, Phi Delta Phi. Clubs: Paradise Valley Country (Scottsdale, Ariz.); Phoenix Rotary (pres. 1977-78); Ariz. (pres. 1979—); Valley Field Riding and Polo; Stanford of Phoenix (pres.); Iron Springs (pres. 1974-76). Home: 3651 E Denton Paradise Valley AZ 85253 Office: 100 W Washington St Phoenix AZ 85003

O'CONNOR, JOHN JOSEPH, naval officer, bishop; b. Phila., Jan. 15, 1920; s. Thomas Joseph and Dorothy Magdalene (Gomple) O'C.; M.A., St. Charles Coll., 1949, Catholic U. Am., 1954; Ph.D., Georgetown U., 1970; D.R.E., Villanova (Pa.) U., 1976. Ordained priest Roman Catholic Ch., 1945, elevated to monsignor, 1966, consecrated bishop, 1979; commd. officer Chaplain Corps, U.S. Navy, 1952, advanced through grades to rear adm.; service with Atlantic and Pacific fleets, also in Okinawa and Vietnam; sr. chaplain U.S. Naval Acad.; chief chaplains Bur. Naval Personnel, Washington; aux. bishop, mil. vicar Archdiocese of N.Y., 1979—. Mem. exec. council Nat. Cath. Com. Scouting; mem. Mil. Ordinariate Adv. Council. Decorated Legion of Merit (3), Meritorious Service medal. Mem. Am. Polit. Sci. Assn. Author: Principles and Problems of Naval Leadership, 1958; A Chaplain Looks at Vietnam, 1969. Office: Mil Ordinariate 1011 1st Ave New York NY 10022*

O'CONNOR, JOHN JOSEPH, journalist, critic; b. N.Y.C., July 10, 1934; s. James and Anna (Foley) O'C.; B.A., Coll. City N.Y., 1957; postgrad. Yale U., 1957-58. Instr. English, Coll. City N.Y., 1958-59; book editor Prentice Hall Book Co., N.Y.C., 1959-60; arts editor Wall St. Jour., 1960-71; TV/radio critic N.Y. Times, 1971—. Club: Century Assn. (N.Y.C.). Home: 301 E 66th St New York NY 10021 Office: 229 W 43d St New York NY 10036

O'CONNOR, JOHN JOSEPH, JR., lawyer; b. Balt., Mar. 11, 1913; s. J.J. and Ann E. (Connelly) O'C.; grad. summa cum laude, St. Charles Coll., 1931; LL.B., U. Balt., 1938; m. Jane S. Hale, Oct. 13, 1946; children—Craig C., Corinne J. Admitted to Md. bar, 1939, U.S. Ct. of Appeals bar, 1939, U.S. Supreme Ct. bar, 1954; practiced in Annapolis, Chestertown, Rockville, Towson, and Balt., Md., 1939—; partner firm O'Connor, Boyd, Ewell and Moran, 1939-41; trial atty. Office Price Adminstrn., Balt., 1947; asso. firm C.P. Mundy and E.A. Smith, Balt., 1948-52, Fisher, Krieger and Sweeten, Balt., 1953-57; sr. partner firm O'Connor, Preston, Glenn and Smith, P.A., Balt., 1958—. Mem. Cancer Control Soc., Com. for Freedom of Choice in Cancer Therapy, Inc., Citizens for Decency through Law; mem. Md. Crime Investigating Com., 1971—; trustee Dr. T.M. Schippell Naturopathic Found., Inc. Served with USCG, 1942-46; ETO. Decorated Purple Heart. Fellow Internat. Acad. Trial Lawyers, Am. Coll. Trial Lawyers; mem. Am. (mem. workman's compensation and employers liability ins. law com. 1957-70, com. on labor relations law 1966-70), Fed. (mem. com. on admiralty and maritime law 1958), Md. State (mem. com. on medico-legal problems 1967-68, 1972-77) bar assns., Bar Assn. of Balt. (chmn. jury com. 1965-66, mem. supreme bench-law cts. com. 1960-61), Maritime Law Assn. U.S., Am. (sustaining mem.), Md. (founder, pres. 1957, chmn. bd. govs. 1958, founder Counsel for the Plaintiff periodical 1958, editor 1958-67) trial lawyers assns., Nat. Police Res. Officers Assn., Heuisler Honor Soc., Mil. Order Purple Heart (past chmn. nat. Americanism commn.), Catholic War Vets. (past nat. Americanism officer), St. Thomas Moore Soc. of Md., Am. Legion, VFW, John Birch Soc., The Scribes, The Spirit of 76 Soc., Nat. Health Fedn., Nat. Wildlife Fedn. Democrat. Roman Catholic. Asso. editor Am. Trial Lawyers Assn. Jour., 1953-69. Contbr. articles on gen. and admiralty law to profl. jours. Office: The Law Bldg St Paul Pl at Franklin Baltimore MD 21202. *To avoid taking a myopic approach to life, very early I adopted as my personal slogan: "the horizon is my frontier."*

O'CONNOR, JOHN MARTIN, ins. co. exec.; b. Peckville, Pa., Sept. 17, 1929; s. Frank Michael and Sarah Pauline (Furey) O'C.; B.S., U. Scranton (Pa.), 1951; LL.B., Georgetown U., 1954; m. Grace Anne Donahoe, Aug. 22, 1953; children—Sally, Aline, Matthew, Brigid, Catherine, Patricia, Timothy, Michael. Admitted to D.C. bar, 1960; with Govt. Employees Ins. Co., Washington, 1958—, claims atty., then asst. sec., 1969-70, sec., 1970—; sec. Govt. Employees Life Ins. Co., Criterion Ins. Co., Govt. Employees Fin. Corp., 1970—, GEICO Corp., 1978—. Served to 1st lt. USMCR, 1954-58. Mem. D.C. Bar, Am. Soc. Corporate Secs. (chpt. v.p. 1973-74, 77-79). Roman Catholic. Club: Cleveland Park. Home: 3422 Quebec St NW Washington DC 20016 Office: 5260 Western Ave Chevy Chase MD 20076

O'CONNOR, JOHN MORRIS, III, assn. exec.; b. Evanston, Ill., Sept. 21, 1937; s. John Morris and Clare Evelyn (Merrick) O'C.; student Georgetown U., 1955-56; B.A., Cornell U., 1959; M.A., Harvard U., 1962, Ph.D., 1965; m. Mary Bittner, Dec. 31, 1960; 1 dau., Emily; m. 2d, Miranda E. P. Ind, Aug. 14, 1971; 1 dau., Amanda. Instr., Vassar Coll., 1964-66, asst. prof. philosophy, 1966-68; asst. prof. Case Western Res. U., 1968-70, asso. prof., 1970-77; exec. sec. Am. Philos. Assn. at U. Del., Newark, 1977—; asso. prof. U. Del., 1977—. Woodrow Wilson nat. fellow, 1959-60. Mem. AAUP. Contbr. articles to profl. jours.; editor: (with others) Introductory Philosophy, 1967; Modern Materialism, 1969; (with others) Moral Problems in Medicine, 1976. Office: Am Philos Assn U Del Newark DE 19711

O'CONNOR, KARL WILLIAM, lawyer, former judge; b. Washington, Aug. 1, 1931; s. Hector and Lucile (Johnson) O'C.; B.A., U. Va., 1952, LL.B., 1958; m. Judith Ann Byers, July 22, 1972; children—Blair, Frances, Brian, Brendan. Admitted to Va. bar, 1958, D.C. bar, 1959, Am. Samoa bar, 1976, Calif. bar, 1977; law clk. U.S. Dist. Ct. Va., Abingdon, 1958-59; practiced in Washington, 1959-61; trial atty. U.S. Dept. Justice, Washington, 1961-65; dep. dir. Men's Job Corps OEO, Washington, 1965-67; mem. civil rights div. Dept. of Justice, chief criminal sect., prin. dep. asst. atty. gen., 1967-75; spl. counsel for intelligence coordination, 1975; v.p., counsel Assn. of Motion Picture and Television Producers, Hollywood, Calif., 1975-76; asso. justice Am. Samoa, 1976, chief justice, 1977-78. Served with USMC, 1952-55. Mem. Am., D.C., Va., Calif., Am. Samoa bar assns., Phi Alpha Delta, Sigma Nu. Home: 3121 Sleepy Hollow Rd Falls Church VA 22042

O'CONNOR, LAWRENCE JOSEPH, JR., energy cons.; b. Tulsa, Dec. 29, 1914; s. Lawrence Joseph and Bess (Yarbrough) O'C.; student Tulsa U., 1932-33; A.B., Rice U., 1936; M.B.A., Harvard U., 1938. With Haskins & Sells, C.P.A.'s Houston, 1938-45; v.p., treas. Goldston Oil Corp., Houston, 1945-58; oil and gas cons., Houston, 1958-59; asst. dir. Office Oil and Gas, Dept. Interior, 1959-60, adminstr. oil import adminstrn., 1960-61; commr. Fed. Power Commn., 1961-71; v.p. Standard Oil Co. (Ohio), Washington, 1971-74; energy cons., Houston, 1975—. Roman Catholic. Clubs: Congressional Country, Houston Country. Home: 846 Augusta Dr Houston TX 77057 Office: PO Box 13014 Houston TX 77019

O'CONNOR, LEONARD ALBERT, utilities exec.; b. Springfield, Mass., Nov. 19, 1926; s. James W. and Eva (Tatro) O'C.; B.A., U. Mass., 1950; M.A., U. N.C., 1951; J.D., U. Conn. Law Sch., 1973; m. Mary Louise Mullen, June 6, 1952; children—Anita M., Charles F., Stephen J., Thomas J. Utilities analyst SEC, Washington, 1951-52; various exec. positions to tax accountant Conn. Light & Power Co., 1952-66; tax mgr. N.E. Utilities, Hartford, Conn., 1966-70, treas., 1970—, v.p., 1975—. Served with USNR, World War II. Mem. Am., Conn., County bar assns., Am. Econ. Assn., Edison Electric Inst., Tax Execs. Inst. Home: 8 Centerwood Dr Cromwell CT 06416 Office: PO Box 270 Hartford CT 06101

O'CONNOR, MARTIN JOHN, clergyman; b. Scranton, Pa., May 18, 1900; s. Martin J. and Belinda Catherine (Caffrey) O'C.; A.B., St. Thomas' Coll. (now U. Scranton), 1918; postgrad. N.Am. Coll., Rome, Italy, 1919-24; S.T.D., U. Propaganda, Rome, 1925; J.C.D., Lateran U., Rome, 1929; LL.D., Georgetown U., 1958, U. Notre Dame, 1960, Seton Hall U., 1964; L.H.D., Misericordia Coll., 1964. Ordained priest Roman Cath. Ch., 1924; asst. pastor St. Peter's Cathedral, Scranton, Pa., 1925-27; sec. to bishop, chancellor diocese, 1929-35; diocesan consultor, 1932-46; episcopal rep. for religious, 1936-46; vice officialis, 1935- 37, officialis, 1937-46, vicar gen., 1938-46, pastor St. Peter's Cathedral, 1934-43; elected titular bishop Thespiae, aux. bishop Scranton, 1942, consecrated, 1943; became pastor St. Mary's Ch., Wilkes-Barre, Pa., 1943; rector N.Am. Coll., Rome, 1946-64; pres. Pontifical Commn. Motion Pictures, 1947; mem. Central Com. Holy Year, 1950; asst. at Pontifical Throne, 1953—; consultor Sacred Congregation Sems. and Univs., 1954, Propaganda Fide, 1962; apptd. Apostolic Nuncio to Malta, 1965; v.p. Conciliar Commn. II Ecumenical Vatican Council for Apostolate of Laity and Mass Media, 1962-65; pres. Pontifical Commn. for Motion Pictures, Radio and Television, 1952-64, Pontifical Commn. for Social Communications, 1964-71; titular archbishop Laodicea in Syria, 1959—. Mem. Bishop's Synod, Rome, 1967-71. Trustee U. Scranton, 1932-42. Served with U.S. Army, 1918. Decorated grand officer Order of Merit (Italy), knight Holy Sepulchre, Sovereign Mil. Order Malta. Asso. editor: The Cath. Light, 1929-32. Pvt. chamberlain to Pope Pius XI. Dec. 8, 1931; Domestic Prelate, Jan. 27, 1936. Address: Palazzo San Carlo Vatican City 00120

O'CONNOR, MARY CONSOLATA, coll. pres.; b. Waterbury, Conn.; d. John Joseph and Nora (Perkinson) O'Connor; B.A., St. Joseph Coll., W. Hartford, Conn., 1939; M.A., Catholic U. Am., 1951, Ph.D., 1955. Joined Sisters of Mercy, Roman Cath. Ch., 1939; tchr. St. Peter's Sch., Hartford, Conn., 1942-46, Cathedral High Sch., Hartford, 1946-50; prof. history St. Joseph Coll., 1954-67, dean students, 1954-58, academic dean, 1958-69, pres., 1969—; mem. Conn. Council Higher Edn., 1971—, v.p., 1973-74, pres., 1974-75; sec.-treas. Conn. Conf. Ind. Colls., 1975-76, mem. exec. com., 1979—; sec. Greater Hartford Consortium Higher Edn., 1972-76, v.p., 1976—; trustee Soc. for Savs., Hartford, 1972—. Mem. Am., New Eng. hist. assns. Address: St Joseph Coll 1678 Asylum Ave West Hartford CT 06117

O'CONNOR, NEAL WILLIAM, advt. exec.; b. Milw., Aug. 25, 1925; s. Arthur J. and Helen (Radell) O'C.; B.S. cum laude, Syracuse U., 1949; m. Nancy K. Turner, July 8, 1950; children—Robert W., Thomas N., David J. With N.W. Ayer ABH Internat., Inc., N.Y.C., 1949—, v.p., mgr. N.Y. service, 1962-65, pres. 1965-73, chmn. bd., 1973—, chief exec. officer, 1966—, chmn. exec. com., 1976—. Past dir. Advt. Council; past. chmn. Am. Assn. Advt. Agys.; pres. Consumer Research Inst. Served with inf. AUS, 1943-45; ETO. Decorated Bronze Star, Combat Inf. badge. Mem. Beta Theta Pi, Alpha Delta Sigma. Clubs: Pretty Brook Tennis (Princeton, N.J.); Links (N.Y.C.); Chicago (Chgo.). Home: 539 Princeton-Kingston Rd Princeton NJ 08540 Office: NW Ayer ABH Internat Inc 1345 Ave of Americas New York NY 10019

O'CONNOR, NORMAN, jazz critic, clergyman; b. Detroit, 1922; student Cath. U., Paulist House of Studies. Ordained priest Roman Cath. Ch., 1947. Piano player with bands; radio series WRUR-FM; weekly TV show Father O'Connor's Jazz, WGBH-TV, ednl. channel; with George Shearing, orignated series half-hour shows Jazz Meets the Classics, for kinescoped use on ednl. channels, 1957; dir. radio and TV films Paulist Communications; host Dial M for Music, WCBS, N.Y.; now exec. dir. Share (Cath. Charities) Diocese Paterson, N.J. Chaplain Boston U. Mem. bd. Newport Jazz Festival. Mem. Nat. Acad. Rec. Arts and Scis. (pres., trustee N.Y. chpt.). Author: Death is all Metaphons, 1967. Address: Paulist Fathers Ridge Rd Oak Ridge NJ 07438

O'CONNOR, (ROBERT) PATRICK, editor; b. Braddock, Pa., Aug. 26, 1925; s. Patrick Francis and Mary Elizabeth (Meehan) O'C.; student U. Pitts., 1943, Cath. U. Am., 1946-50. Dir., co-founder Rochester (N.Y.) Arena Theater, 1950-52; sec. M.C.A. Talent Agy., N.Y.C., 1953-54; salesman Ofcl. Films, N.Y.C., 1954; pres. O'Connor Prodns., TV films, 1954-55; sec. Ivan Obolensky, Book Pub., N.Y.C., 1960; sr. editor Popular Library Pubs., Inc., 1962-67, editor-in-chief, 1973—; editor-in-chief Silver Screen mag., N.Y.C., 1965-67; sr. editor

New Am. Library, N.Y.C., 1967-71; editor-in-chief Curtis Books, N.Y.C., 1971-73; dance, theater critic sta. WNET-TV. Treas. Nat. Tap Dance Found. Served with AUS. Mem. Dance Critics Assn. (pres.). Editor: The Prayers of Man, 1962; No Poem for Fritz, Colo. Quar. issue, 1978. Contbr. articles, dance and theater revs. to mags. Office: 600 3d Ave New York NY 10016

O'CONNOR, RALPH STURGES, oil co. exec.; b. Pasadena, Calif., Aug. 27, 1926; s. Thomas Ireland and Edith Masury (Sturges) O'C.; B.A., Johns Hopkins, 1951; m. Alice Maconda Brown, Apr. 28, 1950; children—George Rufus, Thomas Ireland III, Nancy Isabel, John Herman. With Highland Resources, Inc., Houston, 1951—, exec. v.p., 1961-64, pres., 1964—; dir. Tex. Eastern Transmission Corp., Houston, Wilson Industries, Inc., Houston, First City Nat. Bank, Houston, E. Camden and Highland R.R., Westheimer Transfer & Storage, Houston. Ch. bd. dirs. Oldfields Sch., Glencoe, Md.; bd. govs. Rice U., Houston; mem. vis. com. Harvard Bus. Sch. Served with USAAF, 1943-46. Mem. Am. Assn. Petroleum Landmen. Clubs: Bayou, Ramada, River Oaks County (Houston). Home: 3335 Chevy Chase Houston TX 77019 Office: San Jacinto Bldg Houston TX 77002

O'CONNOR, RICHARD DONALD, advt. co. exec.; b. Nyack, N.Y., Dec. 29, 1931; s. James Patrick and Sophie Kathryn (Hensel) O'C.; B.A., U. Mich., 1954; m. Lucille Hartigan, Jan. 25, 1958; children—Richard D., Kathryn Helen, Timothy Joseph, Meghan Mary, John Patrick. With Campbell-Ewald Co., Detroit, 1956—, exec. v.p., chief operating officer, 1975-76, pres., 1976-79, vice chmn., chief exec. officer, 1979—; dir. Campbell-Ewald Worldwide; vice chmn. Clinton E. Frank, Inc.; chmn. Ceco Pub. Co. Mem. acad. adv. council Walsh Coll., Troy, Mich., 1976-77; promotion chmn. United Found. Torch Drive, 1976; mem. adv. com. Mich. Cancer Found., 1976-77; bd. dirs. Detroit Better Bus. Bur., 1977—; trustee Detroit Country Day Sch., Bloomfield Hills Acad., Bus./Edn. Alliance Southeastern Mich.; sec. Boys Clubs Metro Detroit. Served with U.S. Army, 1954-56. Recipient Robert E. Healy award Interpub. Group Cos., 1974. Mem. Adcraft Club Detroit (past pres.), Detroit Advt. Assn., Am. Assn. Advt. Agys. (dir.). Republican. Roman Catholic. Clubs: Recess, Bloomfield Hills, Detroit Athletic, Duquesne, Hundred. Office: Campbell-Ewald Co 30400 Van Dyke Warren MI 48093

O'CONNOR, ROBERT BARNARD, architect; b. Manhasset, N.Y., Nov. 21, 1895; s. Bernard F. and Anna McH. (Barnard) O'C.; A.B., Trinity Coll., 1916, Litt.D., 1976; M.F.A., Princeton U., 1920; D.F.A., Colgate U., 1959; m. Mary Wistar Morris, 1924; children—Robert Barnard, Anthony Morris, Fenwick (dec.). Archtl. practice, N.Y.C., 1921—; with Trowbridge & Livingston, Hyde & Shepherd, and Benjamin W. Morris, 1924-29; partner, Morris & O'Connor, 1930-42, R.B. O'Connor & W.H. Kilham, Jr., 1943-59; partner firm O'Connor & Kilham, N.Y.C., 1960-68; cons. Kilham, Beder & Chu, 1968-76; prin. archtl. works include: Brearley Sch., Union League Club, Continental Bank & Trust Co., N.Y.C., County Home for Aged, County Office Bldg., Westchester County, N.Y.; Avery Mus., Conn. Mut. Life Ins. Bldg., State Savs. Bank, Hartford, Conn.; N. Westchester Hosp., Mt. Kisco, N.Y.; Firestone Library, Moffett Biol. Research Labs., Chemistry Research Labs., Princeton U.; Crane Meml. at Berkshire Mus., Pittsfield, Mass.; alterations and additions to Met. Mus. Art, N.Y.C. (A. Embury II, asso. 1940-55); Phoenix Ins. Bldg., Hartford; Old Kenyon Dormitory, Gambier, Ohio; New Library, Math.-Physics Bldg., Arts Center, various dormitories, also Mather Student Center, Trinity Coll., Hartford, Conn.; Library, U. Louisville; Colgate U. Library; Helen Reid Hall, Barnard Coll., N.Y.C.; library and adminstrn. bldg. Gen. Theol. Sem., N.Y.C. Cons. architect N.Y. Stock Exchange, 1953-65; supervising architect, Princeton, 1949-54; cons. architect, library Internat. Christian U., Tokyo. Architect mem. N.Y.C. Art Commn., 1965-70. Trustee Trinity Coll., 1934-64, emeritus, 1964—; trustee St. Anthony Ednl. Found., 1956-71, Oaklands Fund, 1961—; trustee Art Commn. Assos., N.Y.C., 1971—, pres., 1976-78; fellow Pierpont Morgan Library, 1976—. Served as capt. F.A., AEF, during World War I; chief engr. (archtl.) Zone Constructing Q.M. Office, Zone II, AUS, 1941, in charge all War Dept. constrn. (except fortifications) in N.Y., N.J., Del. Fellow AIA (pres. N.Y. chpt. 1943-44, medal of honor N.Y. chpt. 1946); mem. Nat. Inst. Archtl. Edn., NAD (asso.), Archtl. League N.Y. (pres. 1956-57), Phi Beta Kappa, Delta Psi. Episcopalian. Clubs: Century Assn., St. Anthony (pres. 1966-68) (N.Y.C.). Contbr. sect. on museums to Forms and Functions of XXth Century Architecture, 1953; also articles to profl. publs. Home: Box 251 RD 2 Baldwin Rd Mt Kisco NY 10549

O'CONNOR, ROBERT BRENDAN, physician; b. Boston, Sept. 27, 1914; s. Joseph Francis and Elizabeth Frances (McDermott) O'C.; A.B., Boston Coll., 1935; M.D., Harvard U., 1939; m. Marie Therese Kerwin, June 27, 1952 (dec. July 8, 1974); m. 2d, Phyllis Reed Dinsmore, Nov. 29, 1975. Intern, Boston City Hosp., 1940-41; resident Millard Fillmore Hosp., Buffalo, 1941-42, surg. staff, 1943-44; asst. med. dir. Curtiss-Wright Corp., Buffalo, 1943-44; med. dir. Wright Aero. Corp., Paterson, N.J., 1944-47; surgeon, orthopedic staff St. Joseph's Hosp., Paterson, 1945-47; med. dir. loss prevention dept. Liberty Mut. Ins. Co., Boston, 1947-55; asst. prof. indsl. medicine Harvard Sch. Pub. Health, 1950-55; med. dir. U.S. Steel Corp., Pitts., 1956-61, v.p. health services, 1961-69, v.p. personnel and health service, 1969-72; cons. occupational medicine, 1973—; adj. prof. U. Pitts. Grad. Sch. Pub. Health, 1960-72; lectr. in occupational medicine Harvard Sch. Pub. Health; cons. occupational health Nat. Inst. Occupational Safety and Health, Am. Mut. Ins. Alliance, Indsl. Health Found. Mem. AMA, Am. Occupational Med. Assn., Am. Pub. Health Assn., Am. Indsl. Hygiene Assn., Am. Acad. Occupational Medicine, Pitts. Indsl. Med. Assn. Editor-in-chief Jour. Occupational Medicine, 1963-67, editor editorial sect., 1967-78. Address: Dyer Ln Castine ME 04421

O'CONNOR, ROBERT EMMET, paper co. exec.; b. N.Y.C., Mar. 27, 1919; A.B., Queen's Coll., Flushing, N.Y., 1941; LL.B., Columbia, 1948. Exec. v.p. Am. Paper Assn., 1957-64; pres. Am. Paper Inst., 1964-67; chmn., gen. mgr. Rising Paper Co, Housatonic, Mass., 1967—. Bd. dirs. Am. Viewpoint, Inc. Home: Amenia NY 12501 Office: Rising Paper Co Park St Housatonic MA 01236

O'CONNOR, ROD, chemist, educator; b. Cape Girardeau, Mo., July 4, 1934; s. Jay H. and Flora (Winters) O'C.; B.S., S.E. Mo. State Coll., 1955; Ph.D., U. Calif. at Berkeley, 1958; m. Shirley Ann Sander, Aug. 7, 1955; children—Mark Alan, Kara Ann, Shanna Suzanne, Timothy Patrick. Asst. prof. chemistry U. Omaha, 1958-60, Mont. State Coll., 1960-63; asso. prof. chemistry Mont. State U., 1963-66; asso. prof., coordinator gen. chemistry Kent (Ohio) State U., 1966-67; prof., dir. 1st year chemistry U. Ariz., Tucson, 1968-72; staff asso. Adv. Council on Coll. Chemistry, Stanford, 1967-68; vis. prof. Wash. State U., 1972-73; prof. chemistry Tex. A. and M. U., 1973—; cons. insect venoms Hollister-Stier Labs., Spokane, Wash., 1963-67; lab. separates editor W.H. Freeman Co., 1968-78; ednl. cons. TUCARA-4 Media Resources, Inc., 1971-74; mem. Coll. Chemistry Cons. Service, vis. scientist, tour lectr. Am. Chem. Soc., 1970—. Recipient nat. teaching award Mfg. Chemists Assn., 1978; 4 regional teaching awards. Fellow AAAS, Am. Inst. Chemists; mem. Internat. Soc. Toxinology, Am. Chem. Soc., Sigma Xi. Author: (with T. Moeller) Ions in Aqueous Systems, 1972; Fundamentals of Chemistry, 1977; (with C. Mickey and A. Hassell) Solving Problems in Chemistry, 1978; (with L. Peck and K. Irgolic) Fundamentals of Chemistry in The Laboratory, 1977; (films) Fundamental Techniques of Chemistry, Fundamentals of Chemistry, Laboratory Safety, 1971. Contbr. articles profl. jours. Office: Dept Chemistry Texas A and M U College Station TX 77843. *A teacher has a magnificent opportunity: when we impart knowledge to a student, we leave a fingerprint on a mind. If we impart that knowledge with obvious love for the student, we leave a fingerprint on a soul.*

O'CONNOR, STANLEY JAMES, educator; b. Des Moines, July 1, 1926; s. Stanley James and Marion (Stout) O'C.; B.A., Cornell U., 1951, Ph.D., 1964; M.A., U. Va., 1954; m. Janet Raleigh, Sept. 4, 1952; children—Stanley James, Janet, Cynthia. Sr. analyst U.S. Govt., Washington, 1952-60; fgn. area tng. fellow Cornell U., 1961-63, prof., 1964—, chmn. dept. Asian studies, 1966-69, chmn. dept. art history, 1970-76, dir. S.E. Asia program, 1979—; cons. Ford Found.; adv. bd. Andrew D. White Mus., Ithaca, 1969-73, Herbert F. Johnson Mus., 1974-76. Served with AUS, 1946-47. JDR 3d Found. fellow, 1966; Nat. Endowment Humanities sr. fellow, 1973-74; vis. fellow Inst. for Southeast Asian Studies, Singapore, 1973-74. Fellow Borneo Research Council, Explorers Club; mem. Assn. Asian Studies (SE Asia council 1978—), Royal Asiatic Soc. (Malaysian br.), Coll. Art Assn. Author: Hindu Gods of Peninsular Siam, 1972; (with T. Harrisson) Excavation of the Prehistoric Iron Industry in West Borneo, 1969; (with T. Harrisson) Gold and Megalithic Activity in Prehistoric and Recent West Borneo, 1970. Home: 617 Highland Rd Ithaca NY 14850

O'CONNOR, THOM JOSEPH, artist, educator; b. Detroit, June 26, 1937; s. Thomas Michael and Elmira Gladys (Reilich) O'C.; student U. Mich., 1955-56; B.A., Fla. State U., 1960; M.F.A., Cranbrook Acad. Art, 1962; m. Linda Howell, May 30, 1959; children—Sean, Ian. Mem. faculty dept. art SUNY, Albany; vis. artist Williams Coll., Vassar Coll., Clemson U., U. Mich., U. Wis., Swedish Acad. Fine Arts, U. London, Finnish Acad. Fine Arts; one-man exhbns. include: Hartley Gallery, N.Y.C., 1973, 74, 75, Taylor Gallery, Dallas, 1978; group exhbns. include Whitney Mus., N.Y.C., 1969, San Francisco Art Inst., 1977; represented in permanent collections Mus. Modern Art, N.Y.C., Brit. Mus., Puskin Mus., Moscow, Detroit Inst. Nat. Endowment Arts grantee, 1973. Home: Moss Rd Voorheesville NY 12186 Office: Art Dept SUNY Albany NY 12222

O'CONNOR, WILLIAM CHARLES, apparel co. exec.; b. Bowling Green, Ky., May 1, 1927; s. John S. and Mary (Schneider) O'C.; student Stevens Inst. Tech., 1945-46; B.S. in Accounting, Western Ky. U., 1949; LL.B., Nashville YMCA Evening Law Sch., 1958; m. Mary Margaret Campion, Apr. 7, 1951; children—Marianne, Margaret, Thomas. Staff accountant Osborn & Page, C.P.A.'s, Nashville, 1949-56; with Genesco, Inc., Nashville, 1956—, asst. v.p., after 1965, v.p., sec., 1975-78, sec., asst. gen. counsel, 1978—; admitted to Tenn. bar, 1958. Served with USNR, 1945-46. C.P.A., Tenn. Mem. Am., Tenn. bar assns., Serra Internat. K.C. Home: 117 Groome St Nashville TN 37205 Office: Genesco Park Nashville TN 37203

O'CONNOR, WILLIAM FRANCIS, educator, chemist; b. Yonkers, N.Y., Jan. 29, 1910; s. William Francis and Helen Veronica (Curley) O'C.; B.S. magna cum laude, Manhattan Coll., 1931, M.S., 1932; M.A., Columbia, 1933, Ph.D., 1935; postdoctoral student N.Y.U., 1935-37; m. May Josephine Cleary, Aug. 8, 1936; children—Mary Josephine, William Joseph, Maureen Josephine. From instr. to asso. prof. Manhattan Coll., 1930-35, prof., chmn. dept. chemistry, 1935-42; chem. engr. Koppers Co., Pitts., 1942-43; lectr. chem. engring. U. Pitts., 1942-44; asst. supt. Koppers Co., Kobuta, Pa., 1943-45; prof. Coll. Engring., N.Y.U., 1945-47; asso. prof. Fordham U., 1947-60, prof., 1960-70, prof. emeritus, 1979—, chmn. dept. chemistry, 1952-60; cons. chemist Recipient Radford medal for natural scis. Manhattan Coll., 1931. Mem. Am. Chem. Soc. (dir. N.Y. sect. 1950-51, 56-57, sec. 1951- 53), Tech. Socs. Council N.Y. (dir. 1947-52, sec. 1949-50), ASME, Electrochem. Soc., Chem. Soc. London, N.Y. Acad. Scis., Sigma Xi, Phi Lambda Upsilon. Club: Davenport (New Rochelle, N.Y.). Author tech., sci. papers. Patentee prodn. diphenic acid. Home and Office: 37 T Roosevelt St Yonkers NY 10701

O'CONNOR, WILLIAM FRANCIS, electric co. exec.; b. Boston, July 3, 1939; s. Cornelius A. and Anne E. (Linehan) O'C.; B.S., U.S. Naval Acad., 1961; M.B.A., Boston Coll., 1974; m. Claire T. Lukash, June 10, 1961; children—Kimberly Ann, W. Christopher, Neil M., Alicia Beth. With Gillette Safety Razor Co., Boston, 1966; exec. asst. Stone & Webster Mgmt. Cons., Inc., Boston, 1967-70; sec. Eastern Utilities Assos., Boston, 1971—, v.p. of subs., 1976—. Served with USN, 1961-65. Mem. Am. Soc. Corporate Secs. Home: 48 Granite St Medfield MA 02052 Office: 99 High St 28th Floor Boston MA 02110

O'CONNOR, WILLIAM JOSEPH, engring. and constrn. co. exec.; b. Phila., Oct. 1, 1920; s. William Joseph and Anne (McGowan) O'C.; B.S. in Bus. Adminstrn., Mt. St. Mary's Coll., Emmitsburg, Md., 1942; m. Margaret Theresa Donahue, June 25, 1949; children—Margaret Anne, Kathleen, William P., Joseph K., Patricia, Anne. Estimator, Gen. Chem. div. Allied Chem. & Dye Corp., 1946-52; mgr. estimating and planning Catalytic Constrn. Co., Phila., 1952-66; mgr. cost engring. Parson-Jurden Corp., N.Y.C., 1966; v.p., comptroller Catalytic, Inc., Phila., 1967-77, sr. v.p., gen. mgr. adminstrv. div., 1977—. Served with AUS, 1942-45. Mem. Am. Assn. Cost Engrs. (founding mem.), Delta Epsilon Sigma. Republican. Roman Catholic. Clubs: Penn Athletic, Union League, Quartette (Phila.) Home: 13430 Kelvin Ave Philadelphia PA 19116 Office: Centre Square West 1500 Market St Philadelphia PA 19102

O'CONOR, VINCENT JOHN, JR., physician; b. Chgo., Jan. 10, 1927; s. Vincent John and Katharine (Carey) O'C.; A.B., Yale U., 1949; M.D. cum laude, Northwestern U., 1953; m. Joan Mundie, Nov. 15, 1952; children—Rory, Vincent John, Andrea Duncan, Peter Carey. Intern, Peter Bent Brigham Hosp., Boston, 1953-54, jr. asst. resident in surgery, 1954-55, sr. asst. resident in surgery, 1957, asst. resident in urology, 1957-58; chief resident in urology Chgo. Wesley Meml. Hosp., 1958-59, chmn. dept. urology, 1963—; practice medicine specializing in surgery, Chgo., 1959—; instr. Northwestern U. Med. Sch., 1959-61, asso. in urology, 1961-63, asst. prof. urology, 1963-66, asso. prof., 1966-70, prof., 1970—; attending urologist VA Research Hosp., Chgo., 1959—, Rehab. Inst. Chgo., 1959—; cons. Gt. Lakes Naval Hosp., 1965—; dir., v.p. Carey Cos., Oklahoma City; dir. Nat. Security Bank of Chgo. Served to ensign U.S. Mcht. Marine, 1944-47; to capt. USAF, 1955-57. William Quinby fellow Harvard 1957. Fellow A.C.S.; mem. AMA, Ill., Chgo. med. socs., Pan Pacific Surg. Assn., Chgo. Urol. Soc. (pres. 1978), Am. (exec. com N. Central sect.), Internat. (v.p. U.S. sect.) urol. assns., Am. Assn. G.U. Surgeons, Clin. Soc. G.U. Surgeons, Nu Sigma Nu, Alpha Omega Alpha. Clubs: Glen View; Shoreacres; Hundred of Cook County (dir.), Chgo. Commonwealth. Home: 1011 Woodland Dr Glenview IL 60025 Office: 251 E Chicago Ave Chicago IL 60611

O'CROWLEY, JAMES FRANCIS, JR., corporate exec.; b. Asheville, N.C., May 23, 1923; s. James Francis and Frances (Curry) O'C.; B.S. in Liberal Arts, Georgetown U., 1947; M.S., N.Y. U., 1949; M.B.A., Harvard, 1951; m. Ruth Faubion, June 26, 1948; children—Patrick Kevin, Brian Faubion, James Francis III, Timothy Curry, Christopher John. Sec.-treas. Wm. Frear Co., Troy, N.Y., 1947-50, 53-55, dir., 1953-55; mdsg. exec. R.H. Macy & Co., N.Y.C., 1951-53; advanced exec. trainee Kroger Co., 1957-58; sec.-treas., controller Munsingwear, Inc., Mpls., 1958-63, 64-67, dir., 1964-67; corp. controller Trans World Airlines, N.Y.C., 1963-64; corp. controller, asst. to chmn. Phila. & Reading Corp., N.Y.C., 1967-68; sr. v.p. Nationwide Industries, Inc., Chgo., 1969, dir., 1969; v.p., cons. Donald R. Booz & Assos., Chgo., 1969-71, also dir.; pres., chief exec. officer, dir. Gateway Sporting Goods Co., Kansas City, Mo., 1971-77; chmn. bd., chief exec. officer Coalter Investment, Kansas City, Mo., 1977—; dir. Rose Marie Reid, 1964-67. Served as lt. (j.g.) USNR, 1942-46. Clubs: Kansas City; Indian Hills Country; Minneapolis; N.Y. Athletic; Univ.; Lotos. Home: 4402 W 111th Terr Leawood KS 66211 Office: 9300 W 110th St Suite 440 Overland Park KS 66210

ODA, ROBERT COLIN, hotel exec.; b. Honolulu, Oct. 29, 1947; s. Warren Takeo and Annie Kim Lam (Gum) O.; B.A., U. Redlands, 1969; m. Tara K. Donahue, May 13, 1972; children—Kalen, Ryan. With Holiday Isle Hotel, Honolulu, 1969-70; exec. asst. mgr. Waikiki Beachcomber Hotel, Honolulu, 1970-74, gen. mgr., 1974—. Served with USAR, 1969-70. Mem. Hawaii Hotel Assn., Honolulu C. of C. Republican. Home: 357 Lunalilo Home Rd Honolulu HI 96825 Office: 2300 Kalakaua Ave Honolulu HI 96815

O'DANIEL, FINIS ARCH, food co. exec.; b. Rutherford, Tenn., Nov. 7, 1920; s. John Arch and Hallie (Hall) O'D.; student public schs., Rutherford; m. Maude Marie Whitworth, Feb. 23, 1942; children—Deborah Nell, Keith Allen. Farmer, Rutherford, 1941-45; owner, operator grain and seed bus., Rutherford, 1946-51, grain, seed and rice bus., DeWitt, Ark., 1951-68; pres., chief exec. officer Pioneer Food Industries, Inc. (became div. Pillsbury Co. 1979), DeWitt, 1968—; dir. DeWitt Bank & Trust Co. Bd. dirs. Ark. C. of C. Served with U.S. Army, 1937-40. Mem. Rice Millers Assn. (pres. 1966-67). Club: Masons. Office: 1000 W Second St DeWitt AR 72042

O'DAY, ROYAL LEWIS, former banker; b. Avon, N.Y., Apr. 28, 1913; s. Roy Lyday and Winifred (Heath) O'D.; B.S., Syracuse U., 1936; m. Elizabeth M. Fearon, Oct. 12, 1952; children—Margaret (Mrs. Thomas W. Wright), Patti (Mrs. Warner Blow), Timothy N. With Gen. Motors Acceptance Corp., 1936-42; sr. v.p. Mchts. Nat. Bank & Trust Co., Syracuse, N.Y., 1942-61; exec. v.p. Marine Midland Bank—Central, Syracuse, 1961-68, pres., 1968-71, chmn. bd., 1971-76, chief exec. officer, 1973-76, cons., 1976—; dir. Syracuse Rigging Co.; chmn. bd. Syracuse Chiefs Baseball Club. Chmn. Central N.Y. Transp. Authority; chmn. bd. Syracuse Research Corp.; past pres. Met. Devel. Assn. Syracuse; past pres. Syracuse Republican Citizens Com. Past chmn. bd. trustees, now trustee Syracuse U.; chmn. bd. trustees N.Y. State Council Chs.; past chmn. bd. N.Y. div. Am. Cancer Soc.; trustee, asst. treas. Crouse Irving Meml. Hosp., Syracuse. Served as lt. USNR, World War II. Named Outstanding Man in Syracuse Area in Bus. and Fin., Syracuse Herald Jour., 1963; recipient Torch of Liberty award Anti-Defamation League of B'nai B'rith, 1974. Mem. Nat. Alumni Assn. Syracuse U. (pres. 1965-69), Automobile Club Syracuse (dir.), Hosp. Services Assn. Central N.Y. (dir.), Greater Syracuse C. of C. (past pres.), Phi Gamma Delta. Mem. Dewitt Community Ch. (finance com.). Mason (33 deg., Shriner, Jester). Club: Onondaga Golf and Country (Fayetteville, N.Y.). Home: 714 Scott Ave Syracuse NY 13224 Office: 344 S Warren St Syracuse NY 13201

ODDIS, JOSEPH ANTHONY, assn. exec.; b. Greensburg, Pa., Nov. 5, 1928; s. Giacinto and Felicetta (D'Amico) O.; B.S., Duquesne U., 1950; D.Sc. (hon.), Mass. Coll. Pharmacy, 1975, Phila. Coll. Pharmacy and Sci., 1975, Albany Coll. Pharmacy, Union U., 1976; m. Jeanne Trevena, July 10, 1954; children—Joseph Michael, Theresa Marie. Staff pharmacist Mercy Hosp., Pitts., 1950-51, asst. chief pharmacist, 1953-54; chief pharmacist Western Pa. Hosp., Pitts., 1954-56; staff rep. hosp. pharmacy Am. Hosp. Assn., Chgo., 1956-60; dir. div. hosp. pharmacy Am. Pharm., Washington, 1960-62; exec. v.p. Am. Soc. Hosp. Pharmacists, Washington, 1960—. Active Boy Scouts Am., Camp Fire Girls. Exec. dir. Am. Soc. Hosp. Pharmacists Research and Edn. Found., 1970—. Served with AUS, 1951-53. Recipient 1st certificate of Honor award Duquesne U. Sch. Pharmacy, 1969, also named Outstanding Alumnus, 1978; recipient Harvey A.K. Whitney award Am. Soc. Hosp. Pharmacists, 1970, Julius Sturmer Meml. Lecture award Rho Chi soc. Phila., 1971, Howard C. Newton Lecture award, 1977, Samuel Melendy Lecture award, 1978. Fellow AAAS; mem. Am. Pharm. Assn., Am. Soc. Hosp. Pharmacists, Am. Inst. History Pharmacy, Internat. Pharm. Fedn. (pres. hosp. pharmacy sect. 1977-81), Drug Info. Assn., Am. Soc. Assn. Execs., Can. Soc. Hosp. Pharmacists (hon.), Soc. Hosp. Pharmacists Australia (hon.), Pharm Soc. Gt. Britain (hon.), Rho Chi, Kappa Psi (hon.). Club: Duquesne U. Century (charter). Home: 6509 Rockhurst Rd Bethesda MD 20034 Office: 4630 Montgomery Ave Washington DC 20014

O'DEA, PAUL WILLIAM, pub. exec.; b. Chgo., May 19, 1929; s. Paul William and Marie Ann (Schofield) O'D.; A.B., San Diego State U., 1951; M.A., U. Chgo., 1956; m. Pauline Anne Tabor, July 2, 1955; children—Brian, David, Christopher, Jane. Tchr., U. Chgo. High Sch., Mundelein Coll., Chgo., 1956-66; mng. editor English dept. Random House Ednl., N.Y.C., 1967-71; dir. publs. Nat. Council Tchrs. English, Urbana, Ill., 1972—. Trustee, William Rainey Harper Coll., Palatine, Ill., 1964-67. Served with U.S. Army, 1951-53. Author: Developing Ideas, 1966; Solving Writing Problems, 1969. Contbr. articles to profl. jours. Home: 1410 Cambridge St Champaign IL 61820 Office: 1111 Kenyon Rd Urbana IL 61801

O'DEA, THOMAS EMMETT, pub. utility exec.; b. Washington, Nov. 4, 1922; s. Patrick L. and Margaret (McGuire) O'D.; A.A., George Washington U., 1948, LL.B., 1950; m. Anita F. Fahey, Jan. 20, 1951; children—Margaret Frances, Kathleen Virginia, Dianne Elizabeth. Admitted to D.C. bar, 1950; practiced in Washington, 1950-52; with Potomac Electric Power Co., 1952—, sec., asst. treas., asso. gen. counsel, 1972—; treas., dir. Dominion Fed. Savs. & Loan Assn., McLean, Va. Mem. Met. Washington Bd. Trade. Served with AUS, 1943-46. Mem. Am. Bar Assn., Bar Assn. D.C., Alexandria C. of C., Nat. Lawyers Club. Home: 4906 Terrell St Annandale VA 22003 Office: 1900 Pennsylvania Ave NW Washington DC 20068

ODEGAARD, CHARLES EDWIN, educator; b. Chicago Heights, Ill.; s. Charles Alfred and Mary (Cord) O.; A.B., Dartmouth Coll., 1932, LL.D., 1959; M.A., Harvard U., 1933, Ph.D., 1937; L.H.D., Lawrence Coll., 1951; LL.D., Miami U., Oxford, Ohio, 1955, U. B.C. (Can.), 1959, Gonzaga U., 1962, U. Calif. at Los Angeles, 1962, Seattle U., 1965, U. Mich., 1969; Litt.D., U. Puget Sound, 1963; m. Elizabeth Jane Ketchum, Apr. 12, 1941; 1 dau., Mary Ann Kriewall. Asst. in history Radcliffe Coll., 1935-37; from instr. to prof. U. Ill., 1937-48; exec. dir. Am. Council Learned Socs., Washington, 1948-52; prof. history, dean Coll. Lit., Sci. and Arts, U. Mich., 1952-58; pres. U. Wash., 1958-73, pres. emeritus, prof. higher edn., 1974—, prof. biomedical history, 1975—. Mem. U.S. Nat. Commn. UNESCO, 1949-55, advisor U.S. del. 5th Gen. Conf., Florence, Italy, 1950; chmn. Commn. Human Resources and Advanced Tng., 1949-53, pres. Internat. Council of Philosophy and Humanistic Studies, 1959-65; mem. adv. com. cultural info. USIA, 1955-62, Western Interstate Com. on Higher Edn., 1959-70, Citizens Com. on Grad. Med. Edn.,

1963-66, Nat. Adv. Health Council USPHS, 1964-68, Nat. Adv. Health Manpower, 1965-67, Nat. Endowment for Humanities, 1966-72, Study Commn. Pharmacy, 1973-75; mem. Macy Study Commn. on Acad. Psychiatry, 1978-79. Bd. regents Uniformed U. Health Scis., 1973—; chmn. Wash. State Bd. Continuing Legal Edn., 1976-79. Served from lt. (j.g.) to lt. comdr. USNR, 1942-46. Mem. Am. Council on Edn. (dir., chmn. 1962-63), Am. Hist. Assn., Mediaeval Acad. Am., Tchrs. Ins. and Annuity Assn. (dir. 1963-69), Phi Beta Kappa, Phi Eta Sigma, Beta Theta Pi. Clubs: Rainier, Seattle Yacht, University (Seattle); Cosmos (Washington); Century (N.Y.C.); Bohemian (San Francisco); Rotary. Author: Fideles and Vassi in the Carolingian Empire, 1945; Minorities in Medicine, 1977. Contbr. articles on mediaeval history and higher edn. to profl. jours. Home: 6333 Sand Point Way NE Seattle WA 98115

ODELL, ARTHUR GOULD, JR., architect; b. Concord, N.C., Nov. 22, 1913; s. Arthur Gould and Grace (Patterson) O.; student Duke U., 1930-31; B.Arch., Cornell U., 1935; Atelier Debat-Ponsan, Ecole des Beaux Arts, Paris, France, 1935-36; m. Polly Robinson, Nov. 10, 1941 (div. 1950); children—William R., Alexandra; m. 2d, Mary Walker Ehringhaus, Oct. 30, 1951; 1 son Charles; stepchildren—Carroll Eringhaus Niles, Michael Ehringhaus. Chmn. Odell Assos. Inc., Charlotte, N.C., Greensboro, N.C., Richmond, Va., Greenville, S.C., 1940—; works include Charlotte Auditorium and Coliseum, NCNB, Charlotte Library, Belk Bros. Co., Charlotte Meml. Hosp., Coca-Cola Consol., Charlotte Civic Center, Wachovia Bank & Trust, Raleigh, Greensboro and Salisbury, Duke U. Nuclear Lab., Burlington Industries Corp. Hdqrs., Greensboro, St. Andrews Coll., Laurinburg, Spl. Warfare Center, Ft. Bragg; R.J. Reynolds World Hdqrs., Winston-Salem, N.C. Blue Cross Blue Shield, Chapel Hill, Ciba Geigy Hdqrs. and Labs., Greensboro, Springs Mills offices and computer center, Lancaster, S.C.; Meml. Hosp., Chattanooga, Balt. Civic Center, Hagerstown (Md.) Library, So. Ry. UPS System, Atlanta, Virginia Beach Conv. Center, Hampton (Va.) Coliseum, U.S. Army Logistic Center, Va., U.S. Army Arsenal Hdqrs., Va., Richmond Eye Hosp., schs., univ. bldgs. and health facilities in Md., Va., N.C., S.C., plans of devel. for Charlotte, Raleigh, N.C. State Govt. Center, Camp Lejeune, N.C., Camp Barrett, Quantico, Va.; vis. critic Cornell U. Coll. Architecture, 1955-56. Chmn. N.C. Bldg. Code Council, 1957-59; mem. various nat. archtl. award juries; chmn. Potomac planning task force U.S. Dept. of Interior, 1965-67; pres. Mint Mus. Art, Charlotte, 1959-63; mem. Cornell U. Council, 1960-62, 65. Bd. dirs. N.C. Art Soc.; trustee N.C. Symphony. Decorated grand ofcl. Orden del Sol de Peru; recipient N.C. award; Sch. Exec. design award; Progressive Architecture citation; Copper and Brass Research Assn. design award; Instns. Mag. award. Fellow AIA (nat. comm. sch. bldgs. 1955-58, pres. N.C. chpt. 1953-55, nat. dir. 1959-63, nat. pres. 1964-65, various design awards); Served to lt. col. C.E., U.S. Army, 1941-45. Mem. Soc. of Cincinnati, Alpha Tau Omega. Methodist. Clubs: Charlotte Country, Charlotte City, Charlotte Athletic, Quail Hollow Country (Charlotte), Green Boundary (Aiken, SC). Home: 2149 Sherwood Ave Charlotte NC 28207 Office: 222 S Church St Charlotte NC 28202

O'DELL, BOYD LEE, educator, biochemist; b. Hale, Mo., Oct. 14, 1916; s. Orvis I. and Flossie (Hoover) O'D.; A.B., U. Mo., 1940, A.M., 1940, Ph.D., 1943; m. Vera L. Stone, Dec. 2, 1944; children—Ann Louise, David Lee. With Parke, Davis & Co., Detroit, 1943-46; mem. faculty U. Mo. at Columbia, 1946—, prof. agrl. chemistry, 1954—, chmn. dept., 1971—, prof. biochemistry, 1971—. Cons. nutrition study sect. USPHS, 1963-67. Guggenheim fellow, 1964; NIH spl. fellow, 1972, Fulbright-Hays scholar, Australia, 1973. Mem. Am. Soc. Biol. Chemists, Am. Inst. Nutrition (pres. 1969), Am. Chem. Soc., Soc. Exptl. Biology and Medicine, Phi Beta Kappa. Editorial bd. Jour. Nutrition, 1965-69. Research, publs. isolation and characterization folic acid; role folic acid and vitamin B12 in prevention congenital abnormalities; role of zinc deficiency in animals; effect of phytic acid on zinc availability; elucidated role of copper in connective tissue metabolism and magnesium in metastatic calcification. Home: 709 Morningside Dr Columbia MO 65201

O'DELL, CHARLES ROBERT, astronomer; b. Hamilton County, Ill., Mar. 16, 1937; s. Herman and Madge (Allen) O'D.; student U. Ill., 1957; B.S. in Edn., Ill. State U., 1959; Ph.D., U. Wis., 1962; m. Elizabeth Ann Welty, Feb. 14, 1959; children—Cynthia Dianne, Nicholle Ann. Carnegie fellow Hale Observatories, Pasedena, Calif., 1962-63; asst. prof. U. Calif., at Berkeley, 1963-64; faculty U. Chgo., 1964-72, prof. astronomy, 1967-72, chmn. dept., 1967-72; dir. Yerkes Obs., Williams Bay, Wis., 1966-72; cons. Marshall Space Flight Center, Huntsville, Ala., 1968-70, project scientist space telescope, 1972—, asso. dir. sci., 1976—. Mem. astronomy missions bd. NASA, 1967-70, astronomy adv. panel NSF, 1968-71; U.S. scientist Copernicus Astron. Center, Warsaw, Poland, 1972-78; lectr. U. Coll., London, 1970, U. Moscow, 1971. Trustee Adler Planetarium, Chgo., 1967-75. Recipient Gold medal Order of Merit, Polish govt., 1977. Mem. Am. Astron. Soc., Internat. Astron. Union, Internat. Aerobatic Club, Astron. Soc. Pacific, AAAS. Home: 1010 Henderson Rd Huntsville AL 35805 Office: DS 30 Marshall Space Flight Center AL 35812

ODELL, FRANK HAROLD, banker; b. Hobart, N.Y., May 17, 1922; s. Harold E. and Naomi (Cole) O.; A.B., U. Ala., 1943; M.B.A., Harvard, 1949; postgrad. Stonier Grad. Sch. Banking, Rutgers U., 1958; m. Elizabeth J. Hetherington, Dec. 29, 1946; children—Thomas A., Nancy E., Susan. With State Bank of Albany (N.Y.), 1949-71, v.p., 1963-69, sr. v.p. in charge bank's loan portfolio, 1969-71; exec. v.p. United Bank Corp. N.Y., Albany, 1971-72, now vice chmn., dir.; pres., dir. State Bank of Albany, 1972—; dir. UBC Leasing of N.Y. Inc. Former bd. dirs., vice-chmn. Mohawk-Hudson Council on Ednl. TV, Inc.; chmn. trustees YMCA; bd. dirs. Albany Inst. History and Art, Saratoga Performing Arts Center, Albany chpt. ARC, Albany United Fund; trustee Russell Sage Coll.; gov. Albany Med. Center Hosp. Served to capt. C.E., AUS, 1943. Mem. Robert Morris Assos. (past dir.), Albany C. of C. Republican. Methodist. Mason. Clubs: Harvard of Eastern N.Y., Fort Orange (trustee), Albany Country (Albany). Home: 33 Darnley Green Delmar NY 12054 Office: 69 State St Albany NY 12201

ODELL, GERARD BERLAGE, physician, educator; b. London, Eng., Nov. 20, 1925 (parents Am. citizens); s. Lawrence Gleason and Alice (Berlage) O.; B.A., N.Y. U., 1947; M.D., Yale, 1951; m. Louise Mitchell, Feb. 27, 1948; children—Gerard Berlage, Timothy M., John L., Thomas A. Intern New Haven Hosp., 1951-52, resident pediatrics, 1952-53; Commonwealth Fund fellow, Cambridge, Eng., 1953-54; Polio Found. fellow Yale, 1954; mem. faculty pediatrics Johns Hopkins Med. Sch., Balt., 1956-76, prof., 1970-76; prof. pediatrics, dir. div. pediatric gastroenterology U. Wis.-Madison, 1976—. Mem. gen. medicine A study sect. NIH, 1972-76, chmn., 1974-76; mem. sci. adv. bd. Nat. Kidney Found., 1971-74. Served with M.C., USNR, 1954-56. Markle scholar in med. sci., 1959-65. Mem. Am. Fedn. Clin. Research, Soc. Pediatric Research, Am. Pediatric Soc., Perinatal Soc., A.A.A.S. Home: 1611 Gateway St Middleton WI 53562 Office: Children's Hosp 1300 University Ave Madison WI 53706

ODELL, HARRY IRVINE, assn. exec., former fgn. service officer; b. Cornwall-on-Hudson, N.Y., Feb. 25, 1921; s. Harry Green and Mary (Conner) O.; A.B., Brown U., 1949; M.A., Fletcher Sch. Law and Diplomacy, 1949; M.A., Harvard, 1958; m. Barbara Lohmann, June 2, 1946; children—Deborah, David. Joined U.S. Fgn. Service, 1950; served in Germany, Israel, Washington, Ceylon, Greece; Jordan, dep. chief mission Am. embassy, Bern, Switzerland, 1975-78; exec. dir. Am.-Swiss Assn., N.Y.C., 1978—. Served to 1st lt. USAAF, World War II. Mem. Caledonian Soc., St. Andrews Soc. Mason. Club: Caterpillar. Office: 60 E 42d St Suite 511 New York NY 10017

ODELL, PATRICK LOWRY, educator, mathematician; b. Watongo, Okla., Nov. 29, 1930; s. Max Vernon and Pamela (Massey) O.; B.S., U. Tex., 1952; M.S., Okla. State U., 1958, Ph.D., 1962; postgrad. U. Calif. at Los Angeles, 1953-54, U. N.Mex., 1958-60; m. Norma Lou Maddox, Aug. 16, 1958; children—James M., David L., Michael R.L., Julie K., Patricia L., Deborah L. Mathematician, White Sands (N.M.) Proving Grounds, 1952-53, Kaman Nuclear, Albuquerque, 1958-59, U.S. Naval Nuclear Ordnance Evaluation Unit, 1959-62, Ling-Temco Vought Aeros., 1962; asst. prof. math. U. Tex., Austin, 1962-66; asso dir. Tex. Center for Research, Austin, 1964-66; prof., past chmn. dept. math. Tex. Technol. U., Lubbock, 1966-71, coordinator insts., dir. research Coll. Arts and Sci., 1971-72; prof. math. scis. and environ. scis. U. Tex., Dallas, 1972—, exec. dean grad. studies and research, 1972-75; research scientist Def. Research Lab., 1963-65; cons. math. statistician, 1962—. Served to capt. USAF, 1953-57. Fellow Tex. Acad. Sci., Am. Statis. Assn.; mem. Soc. Indsl. and Applied Math., AAAS. Home: 3105 Canyon Creek Dr Richardson TX 75080

O'DELL, SCOTT, writer; b. Los Angeles, 1903; s. Bennett Mason and May Elizabeth (Gabriel) O'D.; student Occidental Coll., 1919, U. Wis., 1920, Stanford, 1920-21, U. Rome (Italy), 1925. Recipient Hans Christian Andersen Internat. medal, 1972, U. So. Miss. medallion, 1976, Regina medal, 1978. Mem. Authors Guild. Author: Woman of Spain, 1934; Hill of the Hawk, 1947; (with William Doyle) Man Alone, 1953; Country of the Sun, 1957; The Sea is Red, 1958; Island of the Blue Dolphins (Newbery medal 1961, Rupert Hughes award 1960, Hans Christian Andersen award of merit 1962, William Allen White award 1963, German Juvenile Internat. award 1963, Nene award 1964), 1960; The King's Fifth (Newbery honor book, 1967, German Juvenile Internat. award, 1969), 1966; The Black Pearl (Newbery honor book, 1968), 1967; The Dark Canoe, 1968; Journey to Jericho, 1969; Sing Down The Moon (Newbery honor book 1971), 1970; The Treasure of Topo-el-Bampo, 1972; The Cruise of the Arctic Star, 1973; Child of Fire, 1974; The Hawk That Dare Not Hunt By Day, 1975; Zia, 1976; The 290, 1976; Carlota, 1977; Kathleen, Please Come Home, 1978; The Captive, 1979; Sarah Bishop, 1980. Address: care McIntosh & Otis Inc 475 Fifth Ave New York NY 10017

O'DELL, WILLIAM FRANCIS, bus. exec.; b. Detroit, Jan. 24, 1909; s. Frank Trevor and Garnet (Aikman) O'D.; B.S., U. Ill., 1930; m. Bess Baer, June 10, 1933; children—Peggy O'Dell Pinckard, David. With Penton Pub. Co., 1933-37; v.p. Ross Fed. Research Corp., 1937-44; mng. dir. Statis Research Co., 1944-45; pres. Market Facts, Inc., 1945-64, chmn. 1964-74; pres. ROC Internat., 1961-64; mem. census adv. bd. Dept. Commerce, 1963-73. Prof. mktg. McIntire Sch. Commerce U. Va., 1965-74; vis. prof. Chinese U. of Hong Kong, 1969. Recipient Leader in Mktg. award, 1970. Mem. Am. Mktg. Assn. (pres. 1960-61), N.Y. Biog. Soc., SAR, Delta Upsilon, Alpha Kappa Psi, Beta Gamma Sigma. Rotarian. Clubs: Colonnade, Farmington Country (Charlottesville, Va.); Riomar Bay Yacht, Moorings Golf and Tennis. Author: Marketing Decision, 1968; Marketing Decision Making, 1976, 2d edit., 1979; How to Make Lifetime Friends—With Peers and Parents, 1978. Editorial rev. bd. Jour. Mktg., 1964-73. Home: 501 Spyglass Ln The Moorings Vero Beach FL 32960 Office: 100 S Wacker Dr Chicago IL 60606

ODENHEIMER, KURT JOHN SIGMUND, educator, pathologist, dentist; b. Regensburg, Germany, May 9, 1911; s. Berthold S. and Charlotte (Hahn) O.; student U. Munich, 1932-35; D.D.S., U. Pitts., 1940, M.Ed., 1954; D.M.D., U. Heidelberg, 1958; L.D.S., U. West Germany, 1959; Ph.D., Western Res. U., 1964; m. Beatrice Peller, Sept. 19, 1939; children—Charlotte Ann (Mrs. Tore Hartmann-Hansen), Burtram Jon, Germaine Louise, Reynard Charles. Came to U.S., 1937, naturalized, 1947. Asst. chief Pitts. Skin and Cancer Clinic, 1940-49; chmn. oncology and gen. pathology U. Pitts. Dental Sch., 1949-55; research fellow Western Res. U., 1959-61; asso. prof. clin. oral pathology U. Buffalo, 1961-66; chmn., prof. oral diagnosis and radiology Loyola U., 1966-71; prof. oral pathology La. State U., 1968—, prof. pathology Med. Center, 1972—, prof. otolaryngology, 1973—; research asso. Tulane Delta Primate Center; research asso. Gulf South Research Inst.; cons. Pitts. Presbyn., Meyer Meml., Touro hosps. Bd. dirs. YMCA, 1950-55, New Orleans Cancer Assn., 1969—. Served as lt. col., Dental Corps, AUS, 1955-59. Fellow Am. Coll. Dentists, Am. Acad. Oral Pathology; mem. AAAS, Am. Assn. Cancer Edn. (chmn.-elect), Am. Assn. Dental Editors, Am. Dental Assn., AMA, Fedn. Dentaire Internationale, Nat. Sojourners (pres. 1957-58), Am. Assn. Univ. Profs., Internat. Assn. Dental Research (pres. 1968-69), N.Y. Acad. Scis. Mason (Shriner, 32 deg.). Contbr. New Oral Pathology (Thoma), 1969. Research on cancer, polio and other enteric viruses on head and neck region, non-lethal viruses on offspring of rhesus monkeys, the Myotatic splint as treatment for TMJ Dysfunction Syndrome, psychosomatic aspect oral disease, application to mucosa of topical medication to treat cancer, radioactive gold as etiologic factor in facial and oral cancer. Home: 4123 Vixen St New Orleans LA 70114. *My setbacks and failures are numerous. Although unrecorded (and often bitter), they produced the impetus and stamina to forge ahead. When fate and circumstance would plunge me into a dark abyss, I had no choice but to swim for a new shore. Thanks to bad luck, I found the sun again and again.*

ODENKIRCHEN, CARL JOSEF, educator; b. Uerdingen, Germany, Jan. 28, 1921; s. Apollinaris and Paula (Orth) O.; came to U.S., 1929, naturalized, 1940; A.B., Coll. Charleston (S.C.), 1942; M.A., U. Chgo., 1947; Ph.D., U. N.C., 1951; postgrad. Sorbonne, Paris, France, 1953-54; m. Stella Esther Goldberg, Sept. 6, 1948; children—David Michael, Susan Elizabeth. Instr. Romance langs. U. N.C., 1947-49; instr. French and Spanish, State U. N.Y. for Tchrs. at Albany, 1950-53; asst. prof. modern langs. Lake Forest (Ill.) Coll., 1956-58; asso. prof. Romance langs. and humanities State U. N.Y. at Albany, 1958-61, prof. Romance langs. and comparative lit., 1961—, chmn. dept. comparative lit., 1962-71; cons. higher edn. N.Y. State Edn. Dept., 1969—; vis. prof. Boston U., 1966-68. Mem. Albany Symphony Orch., 1958-61. Served with AUS, 1942-45. Fulbright scholar U. Rome, 1950. Mem. Modern Lang. Assn. Am., Am. Comparative Lit. Assn., Am. Assn. Tchrs. French, Am. Assn. Tchrs. Italian, AAUP, Dante Soc. Am. Author: A Preliminary Chrestomathy of Old Catalan, 1949; The Play of Adam (Ordo Representacionis Ade), 1976; The Life of St. Alexius, 1978. Home: 47 Brookview Ave Delmar NY 12054 Office: Wallace Hall 228 State U New York Albany NY 12222

ODIORNE, GEORGE STANLEY, educator; b. Merrimac, Mass., Nov. 4, 1920; s. Charles Thomas and Katherine (Hosford) O.; B.S., Rutgers U., 1948; M.B.A., N.Y. U., 1951, Ph.D., 1957; m. Margaret J. Hanna, Apr. 3, 1943; 1 son, Robert Howard. Mgr., Am. Can Co., Jersey City, 1938-51; chmn. mgmt. services Rutgers U., 1951-53; div. mgr. Am. Mgmt. Assn., N.Y.C., 1954-58; personnel mgr. Gen. Mills, Inc., Mpls., 1958-59; prof. indsl. relations U. Mich., 1959-69; dean., prof. mgmt. U. Utah, Salt Lake City, 1969-74; dean U. Mass., Amherst, 1974-78, prof. mgmt., 1978—; dir. Masterco Press, Inc., George Odiorne Assos., Pioneer Nat. Bank. Twp. committeeman, Bridgewater, N.J., 1956-57. Served to capt. AUS, 1942-46. Recipient N.Y. U. Founders Day award, 1957; Distinguished Achievement award U. Wis., 1969. Mem. Am. Econ. Assn., Acad. Polit. Sci., Am. Soc. Personnel Adminstrn., Am. Arbitration Assn., Am. Soc. for Tng. and Devel. Author: Management by Objectives, 1965; Management Decisions by Objectives, 1969; Green Power, 1969; Training by Objectives, 1970; Personnel Administration, 1971; Management and the Activity Trap, 1973; MBO II-A System of Leadership, 1979; Personnel Effectiveness, 1979. Contbr. numerous articles to profl. jours. Home: 315 Lincoln Ave Amherst MA 01002

ODISHAW, HUGH, sci. adminstr.; b. N. Battleford, Can., Oct. 13, 1916; s. Abraham and Miriam (Davajan) O.; A.B., Northwestern U., 1939, M.A., 1941; student Princeton, 1939-40; B.S., Ill. Inst. Tech., 1944; Sc.D., Carleton Coll., 1958; m. Marian Lee Scates, 1958. Came to U.S., 1922, naturalized, 1941. Instr., Ill. Inst. Tech., 1941-44; with Westinghouse Electric Corp. 1944-45, 45-46; staff OSRD, 1945; asst. to dir. Nat. Bur. Standards, 1946-54; exec. dir. U.S. nat. com. IGY, 1954-65; dir. IGY World Data Center A., 1954-72; exec. sec., div. phys. scis. Nat. Acad. Scis., 1966-72; dean Coll. Earth Scis., U. Ariz., Tucson, 1972—. Fellow Am. Geophys. Union; mem. Am. Phys. Soc., AAAS, Phi Beta Kappa. Presbyn. Author, editor: (with L. V. Berkner) Science in Space, 1961. Editor: (with E.U. Condon) The Handbook of Physics, 1958. Author sci articles. Home: 1531 Entrada Sexta Tucson AZ 85718 Office: U Ariz Tucson AZ 85721

ODLAND, GEORGE FISHER, dermatologist; b. Mpls., Aug. 27, 1922; s. Henry O. and Alice Chipman (Fisher) O.; student Princeton U., 1940-42; M.D., Harvard U., 1946; m. Elisabeth Ann Brierley, Sept. 25, 1945; children—Henry II, Peter B., John C. Intern, Mass. Gen. Hosp., Boston, 1946-47, asst. resident dermatology, 1953-54, chief resident, 1954, clin. and research fellow, 1952-53; research fellow anatomy Harvard U., 1949-51, research fellow dermatology, 1951-52, asst. in dermatology, 1952-54; clin. instr. anatomy U. Wash., Seattle, 1955-60, clin. instr. medicine, 1956-60, clin. asst. prof. depts. anatomy and medicine, 1960-62, asst. prof. biol. structure and medicine, 1962-64, asso. prof., 1964-69, prof., 1969—, head div. dermatology, 1962—; chmn. NIH tng. grants com., 1966-69, chmn. liaison com., 1976—, prin. investigator spl. com. analysis of priorities and needs for research in dermatology, 1977—; adv. council Nat. Insts. Arthritis, Metabolic and Digestive Diseases, 1973-76; mem. med. and sci. com. Dermatology Found., 1968-71; mem. med. adv. bd., trustee Nat. Psoriasis Found., 1972—. Active, United Way of King County, 1971—. Diplomate Am. Bd. Dermatology. Fellow Am. Acad. Dermatology (dir. seminars 1973-75); mem. Am., Pacific dermatol. assns., Pacific N.W., Seattle dermatol. socs., Soc. for Investigative Dermatology (dir. 1966-70, chmn. hon. membership com. 1976-77, pres. 1978—), Western Soc. Clin. Research, Seattle Acad. Internal Medicine, Western Assn. Physicians, N.Y. Acad. Scis., King County Med. Soc. (sec.-treas. 1971-72, jud. council 1972-75), Assn. Profs. Dermatology (dir. 1976—, pres. elect 1978), Sigma Xi. Clubs: Seattle Tennis; University. Contbr. articles to med. jours. Home: 1038 34th Ave E Seattle WA 98112 Office: Div Dermatology RM 14 Dept Medicine U Wash Sch Medicine Seattle WA 98195

O'DOHERTY, DESMOND SYLVESTER, physician; b. Dublin, Ireland, July 27, 1920; s. Sean and Mary Anne (Doherty) O'D.; came to U.S., 1923, naturalized, 1934; A.B., La Salle Coll., 1942; M.D., Jefferson Med. Coll., 1945; m. Marcella Duboce, Sept. 1, 1952; children—Marianne, Patrick. Intern, Fitzgerald-Mercy Hosp., Phila., 1945-46; resident psychiatry VA Hosp., Coatsville, Pa., 1948-49, Inst. Pa. Hosp., Phila., 1949; resident neurology Jefferson U. Hosp., 1949-50; chief resident neurology Georgetown U. Hosp., Washington, 1950-51, fellow neurophysiology, 1951-52; fellow neuropathology Med. Coll. Va., 1961; practice medicine, specializing in neurology, Washington, 1950—; from instr. to prof. Georgetown U. Med. Coll., 1952-63, prof., chmn. dept. neurology, 1958—; cons. VA, Surg. Gen. U.S. Navy. Served with AUS, 1943-45, U.S. Army, 1946-48. Diplomate Am. Bd. Psychiatry and Neurology. Fellow Am. Heart Assn., Am. Acad. Neurology; mem. AMA (council med. edn.), Assn. Research Nervous and Mental Diseases, Am. Neurol. Assn., Alpha Omega Alpha, Alpha Epsilon Delta. Roman Catholic. Club: Cosmos. Author: (with Y. Ramey) Electrical Studies on Unanesthetized Brain, 1960; (with J. Fermaglich) Handbook of Neurologic Emergencies, 1977. Contbr. sci. articles to profl. jours. Home: 3540 N Valley St Arlington VA 22207 Office: Dept Neurology Georgetown U Hosp 3800 Reservoir Rd Washington DC 20007

ODOM, ALFRED DARGAN, JR., financial services co. exec.; b. Atlanta, Mar. 6, 1926; s. Alfred Dargan and Alberta Theresa (Honour) O.; B.S. in Indsl. Mgmt., Ga. Inst. Tech., 1950; m. Joyce Ann Suttles, June 17, 1950; children—Lynn Marie, Steven A., Jennifer A. Sec.-treas. Trusco Finance Co., Atlanta, 1949-59; v.p., sec., treas. Motor Contract Co., Atlanta, 1959-68; sr. v.p., treas., then pres., chief operating officer Ga. Internat. Finance Co., Atlanta, 1968-73, pres., chief exec. officer, 1973—; dir. Ga. Internat. Life Ins. Co., Stone Mountain Ins. Co., MCC Financial Services Co. Served with AUS, 1944-46. Mem. Nat. Consumer Finance Assn. Methodist. Club: Terminus Internat. Tennis. Home: 115 Blackland Rd NW Atlanta GA 30342 Office: 300 Interstate N Atlanta GA 30339

ODOM, JOHN PERSHING, constrn. co. exec.; b. Rockingham, N.C., Jan. 7, 1918; s. Luther L. and Minnie (Allred) O.; student Brevard Coll., 1936-37; B.A., Furman U., 1947; m. Aileen Alewine, Mar. 30, 1941; 1 son, Taylor. Jr. accountant, then sr. accountant S.D. Leidesdorf & Co., Greenville, S.C. 1947-53; chief accountant S.C. div. Daniel Constrn. Co., Greenville, 1953-64, asst. sec., controller 1964-67, v.p. taxes, 1965-72; v.p., asst. treas. Daniel Internat. Corp., also subsidiaries, 1972—. Trustee Brevard Coll.; sec.-treas. Daniel Found. S.C. Served with USNR, 1943-45. Baptist. Mason (32 deg., Shriner), Lion. Home: 203 Rosemary Ln Greenville SC 29615 Office: Daniel Bldg Greenville SC 29602

O'DONNELL, ALICE LOUISE, govt. ofcl.; b. Stanwood, Wash., Oct. 7, 1914; d. John James and Jeannette May (Anderson) O'Donnell; student U. Wash., 1932, U. So. Calif., 1943-44; student George Washington U, 1940-42, J.D., 1954. Admitted to U.S. Dist. Ct., Supreme Ct., U.S. Ct. of Appeals bars; with staff Atty. Gen. U.S., 1945-49; mem. staff Justice Clark, Supreme Ct. of U.S., Washington, 1949-67; lawyer Fed. Jud. Center, Washington, 1968—, dir. div. inter-jud. affairs and info. services, 1971—; sec.-treas. Nat. Center for State Cts. Vice-chmn. bd. dirs. Potomac Law Sch., Washington. Fellow Judicature Soc. (program com.), Inst. Judicial Adminstrn.; mem. Am. (mem. div. judicial adminstrn., chmn. 1973-74), Fed. (mem. nat. council, mem. bd. dirs. D.C. chpt.) bar assns., Nat. Assn. Women Lawyers, Nat. Lawyers Club, Washington (bd. govs.), Supreme Ct. Hist. Soc. (trustee), Phi Alpha Delta. Roman Catholic. Home: 4201 Cathedral Ave NW Washington DC 20016 Office: Dolley Madison House 1520 H St NW Washington DC 20005

O'DONNELL, BERNARD JOSEPH, govt. ofcl.; b. Quincy, Mass., Sept. 27, 1923; s. Bernard Joseph and Mary Madeline (Ballard) O'D.; B.S. in Bus. Adminstrn., Boston U., 1949; M.B.A., Xavier U., 1966; m. Cecile Patricia Kelley, Nov. 9, 1949; children—Brian Patrick, Maureen Ellen, Michael William, Eileen Margaret. Advt. writer

Enterprise Stores, Boston, 1949-50; spl. agt. FBI, 1950-54; chief espionage investigations Office of Spl. Investigations, U.S. Air Force, 1954-56, asst. to dir. Office of Spl. Investigations in Europe, 1956-60; chief criminal investigations Office of Spl. Investigations, Wright-Patterson AFB, Ohio, 1960-69, dir. fraud investigations Office of Spl. Investigations, Washington, 1969, dir. personnel investigations, 1970-72; asst. dir. for ops. Def. Investigative Service, Dept. of Def., Washington, 1972-75, acting dir., 1975, dir., 1976—. Served with USAAF, 1942-45; ETO, MTO. Mem. Soc. Former Spl. Agts. FBI, Internat. Assn. Chiefs Police, Am. Soc. for Indsl. Security. Home: 14147 Flintrock Rd Rockville MD 20853 Office: Def Investigative Service 1000 Independence Ave SW Washington DC 20314

O'DONNELL, CLETUS FRANCIS, bishop; b. Waukun, Iowa, Aug. 22, 1917; s. Patrick E. and Isabelle A. (Duffy) O'D.; M.A., St. Mary of Lake Sem. (Ill.), 1941; J.C.D., Catholic U. Am., 1945. Ordained priest Roman Catholic Ch., 1941; asst. pastor Our Lady of Lourdes Ch., Chgo., 1941-42; vice chancellor Archdiocese of Chgo., 1947-60, vicar, gen. counsel, 1961; apptd. titular bishop Abrittum, aux. bishop Chgo., 1960; consecrated bishop, 1960; pastor Holy Name Cathedral, Chgo., 1966; bishop Diocese of Madison (Wis.), 1967—. Chmn. Am. Bd. Cath. Missions, 1966—, Nat. Catholic Edn. Assn., 1975—. Recipient C. Albert Koob award Nat. Cath. Edn. Assn., 1978. Address: 15 E Wilson St Madison WI 53711*

O'DONNELL, HUGH, banker; b. San Francisco, May 13, 1920; s. John and Joan (Baldwin) O'D.; B.A., Stanford U., 1941; student U. Chile, Santiago, Sorbonne, Paris; m. Anne Brown, Sept. 17, 1955; children—Michael, Peter. Various internat. banking positions through 1960's; with Crocker Nat. Bank, San Francisco, 1959—, v.p. internat., 1974—, now sr. v.p. Bd. regents St. Ignatius Coll. Prep. Sch. Served to comdr. USN, World War II; PTO. Mem. Knights of Malta, Brit./Am., Chile-No. Calif. (pres.) chambers commerce. Clubs: World Trade, Univ., Olympia (San Francisco); Menlo Circus (Atherton, Calif.). Home: 84 Spencer Ln Atherton CA 94025 Office: Crocker Nat Bank 1 Montgomery St San Francisco CA 94104

O'DONNELL, JAMES FRANCIS, health sci. adminstr.; b. Cleve., July 22, 1928; s. John Michael and Mary Louise (Hayes) O'D.; B.S. in Biology, St. Louis U., 1949; Ph.D. in Biochemistry, U. Chgo., 1957; m. Winifred Locke, Sept. 10, 1955; children—Anne Catherine, Patrick John, Mary Elizabeth. Asst., then asso. prof. biol. chemistry and exptl. medicine U. Cin. Coll. Medicine, 1957-68; grants asso. div. research grants NIH, Bethesda, Md., 1968-69, program dir. population and reprodn. grants br. Center for Population Research, Nat. Inst. Child Health and Human Devel., NIH, 1969-71, asst. dir. div. research resources NIH, 1971-76, dep. dir., 1976—, mem. grants assos. bd., 1973-77. Served with U.S. Army, 1950-52. Mem. N.Y. Acad. Scis. Home: 11601 Bunnell Ct Potomac MD 20854 Office: Room 5B03 Bldg 31 Nat Insts Health Bethesda MD 20014

O'DONNELL, JOHN DANIEL, bible inst. exec.; b. Steele, Ala., Apr. 5, 1929; s. Henry Alfred and Rhondor (Bowlin) O'D.; B.A., Bob Jones U. (S.C.), 1949; B.D., New Orleans Bapt. Theol. Sem., 1958, Th.D., 1961; m. Audy Willodean Gipson, Feb. 19, 1949; children—John Daniel, Joel David, Jeffrey Darryl. Ordained to ministry Bapt. Ch., 1946; prof. Free Will Bapt. Bible Coll., Nashville, 1961-65; pres. Hillsdale Coll., Moore, Okla., 1965-71; pastor Grant Ave. Free Will Bapt. Ch., Springfield, Mo., 1971-73; editorial mgr. Free Will Bapt. Sunday Sch. Dept., Nashville, 1973-78; pres. Bethel Bible Inst., Paintsville, Ky., 1978—. Asst. moderator Nat. Assn. Free Will Baptists, 1971-72, moderator, 1973-77. Republican. Author: Faith For Today, 1965; A Survey of Church History, 1973; Handbook For Deacons, 1973; The Preacher and His Preaching, 1974; Free Will Baptist Doctrines, 1974. Home: Hwy 40 E Paintsville KY 41240 Office: Box 1226 Paintsville KY 41240

O'DONNELL, JOHN LEONARD, educator; b. England, May 5, 1926; s. Leonard and Dorothy (Gascoigne-Parkin) O'D.; came to U.S., 1951, naturalized, 1959; B.A. with honours, Cambridge (Eng.) U., 1951, M.A., 1954; M.B.A., Ind. U., 1952, D.B.A., 1954; m. Lucinda J. Fall, June 12, 1953; children—George, John Leonard, David, Paul. Mem. faculty Notre Dame U., 1954-56; mem. faculty Mich. State U., East Lansing, 1956—, prof. fin., 1956—, dir. Bur. Bus. and Econ. Research, 1957-59, asst. dir., 1959-64, chief-of-party univ. group in Turkey, 1969-70; editor Mich. Econ. Record, 1959-64, adviser AID, Turkey, 1964-67; chmn. bd. State News, 1976—; cons. to industry. Served with Indian Army, 1944-48. Further Edn. scholar Cambridge U., 1948; Fulbright travel scholar, 1951; Eli Lily scholar, 1951; Edwards fellow, 1952. Mem. Fin. Mgmt. Assn., Am. Fin. Assn., Am. Econ. Assn., Midwest Econ. Assn. Episcopalian. Co-author: Elements of Financial Adminstration, 1962; contbr. to profl. jours. Address: 1051 Walbridge Dr East Lansing MI 48823

O'DONNELL, JOHN LOGAN, lawyer; b. Chgo., Mar. 6, 1914; s. William Joseph and Elizabeth (McLogan) O'D.; B.A., Williams Coll., 1934; J.D., Northwestern U., 1937; m. Mary Ellen Sipe, Sept. 2, 1939; 1 son, John Logan. Admitted to Ill. bar, 1937, N.Y. bar, 1943, D.C. bar, 1977; asso. firm Defrees, Buckingham, Jones and Hoffman, Chgo., 1937-38; staff atty. Office Gen. Counsel, SEC, 1938-41; instr. Cath. U. Law Sch., 1938-41; asso. firm Cravath, Swaine & Moore, N.Y.C., 1941-52; partner firm Olwine, Connelly, Chase, O'Donnell & Weyher, N.Y.C., 1952—. Bd. dirs. Near East Found. Fellow Am. Coll. Trial Lawyers; mem. Assn. Bar City N.Y., Am., Fed., N.Y. State, N.Y. County bar assns., Beta Theta Pi, Phi Delta Phi. Roman Catholic. Clubs: Univ., Williams, Sky (N.Y.C.). Home: 181 E 73d St New York City NY 10021 Office: 299 Park Ave New York City NY 10017

O'DONNELL, JOSEPH EDWARD, banker; b. Chgo., Dec. 12, 1932; s. Anthony Joseph and Loretta Evelyn (Oakes) O.; B.S. in Commerce, De Paul U., 1954; M.B.A., Northwestern U., 1968; m. Mary Elizabeth Saigh, June 16, 1962; children—Mary Joan, Anne Marie, Joseph Edward. Nat. bank examiner Comptroller Currency, U.S. Treasury Dept., Chgo., 1962-70; sr. v.p., dir. N.W. Nat. Bank Chgo., 1970-78; sr. v.p. First Nat. Bank Morton Grove (Ill.), 1979—; mem. adv. bd. Center for Sports Medicine. Served as officer USNR, 1954-59; comdr. Res. ret. Clubs: Tennaqua (Deerfield); Exmoor Country (Highland Park, Ill.). Office: 3985 Milwaukee Ave Chicago IL 60641

O'DONNELL, JOSEPH VINCENT, accountant; b. Wilkes-Barre, Pa., Apr. 6, 1929; s. James Vincent and Beatrice (Breslin) O'D.; B.S., King's Coll., 1957; married; children—Kevin Joseph, James Vincent, Jeffrey Alan. Staff accountant, mgmt. cons. Coopers & Lybrand, Phila., 1957-71, western regional partner Cons. Service, Los Angeles, 1971-77, mng. partner of S.W., U.S. Group, 1977—. Chmn. Am. Heart Assn., 1979; bd. dirs. Estelle Doheny Eye Found., Orthopaedic Hosp. Served with USAF; Korea. Mem. Calif. Soc. C.P.A.'s, Am. Inst. C.P.A.'s, Inst. Mgmt. Los Angeles C. of C. (dir.). Clubs: Calif., Jonathan, Los Angeles Country. Office: 1000 W 6th St Los Angeles CA 90017

O'DONNELL, JOSEPH WILLIAM, advt. agy. exec.; b. Boston, May 11, 1942; s. John Joseph and Alice Gertrude O'D.; B.A., Columbia U., 1964, postgrad., 1964-67; m. Barbara Stamler Isaac, Sept. 2, 1967; children—Mark Christopher, Kerry Stamler, Scott Tylor, Vice pres., mgmt. supr. Doyle Dane Bernbach, Inc., N.Y.C., 1967-74; exec. v.p., partner Cox & Co., Advt., N.Y.C., 1974-76; v.p. mgmt. supr. J. Walter Thompson Co., N.Y.C., 1976-78, exec. v.p., office mgr., Dearborn, Mich., 1978—. Served with USMC, 1965. Republican. Episcopalian. Clubs: Oakland Hills Country, Fairlane, Renaissance. Home: 32080 Waltham Beverly Hills MI 48009 Office: 17000 Executive Plaza Dr Dearborn MI 48126

O'DONNELL, SISTER MIRIAM TERESA, educator; b. N.Y.C., Nov. 9, 1916; d. Jeremiah P. and Ita (Ryan) O'Donnell; B.A., Hunter Coll., 1937; M.A., Columbia, 1956; L.H.D., Loyola Coll., Balt., 1973; H.D., King's Coll., 1975; LL.D., Coll. Misericordia, 1975. Statis. clk. Western Electric Co., N.Y.C., 1937-42; entered Sisters of Mercy, Dallas, Pa., 1942; tchr. St. Mary High Sch., Wilkes Barre, Pa., 1944-55; faculty Coll. Misericordia, Dallas, Pa., 1955-64, prof., 1976—, chmn. dept. math. and physics, 1978—, pres., 1964-66, 67-75; provincial councilor Sisters of Mercy, Scranton Province, 1963-66, asst. provincial, 1966-70. Chmn., Northeastern Pa. Ind. Colls., 1969-70; mem. exec. com. Commn. for Ind. Colls. of Pa. Assn. Colls. and Univs., 1971-74; mem. Liaison Com. for Ind. Higher Edn., Pa., 1971-74. Mem. Am. Assn. Physics Tchrs., Math. Assn. Am. Address: College Misericordia Dallas PA 18612

O'DONNELL, PATRICK JOSEPH, physicist; b. Port Glasgow, Scotland, Oct. 16, 1938; came to Can., 1965, naturalized, 1972; s. Daniel and Mary (Blaney) O'D.; B.S., Glasgow U., 1960, Ph.D., 1963; m. Mary Agnes Reynolds, Aug. 1, 1964; children—Daniel Paul, George Ciaran, Quentin Patrick. Research asst. Durham U. (Eng.), 1963-65; lectr. physics U. Toronto (Ont., Can.), 1965-66, asst. prof., 1966-70, asso. prof., 1970-77, prof., 1977—, acting chmn. div. sci. Scarborough Coll., 1971-72; council mem. Inst. Particle Physics Can., 1974-77; Sci. Research Council sr. vis. research fellow U. Southampton, Eng., 1976; sr. research fellow Glasgow U., 1979. Nat. Research Council Can. grantee, 1967—. Mem. Am. Phys. Soc., Can. Assn. Physicists. Contbr. articles to profl. publs. Home: 36 Sandrift Sq West Hill ON M1E 4N6 Canada Office: Physics Dept U Toronto Toronto ON M5S 1A7 Canada

O'DONNELL, RICHARD FRANCIS, direct sales co. exec.; b. Buffalo, Mar. 1, 1932; s. William Weber; s. Frank A. (stepfather) and Margaret Teresa (Ernst) O'D.; student public schs., Buffalo; m. Christine Joan Savasta, Sept. 29, 1956; children—Linda Susan, David Michael, Christopher Michael. Tabulating operator Iroquois Gas Corp., Buffalo, 1950-58; office mgr. br. office George H. Hees Co., Buffalo, 1958-59; with Sarah Coventry Inc., Newark, N.Y., 1959—, sr. v.p. sales, 1976-78, pres., 1978—; dir. C. H. Stuart Inc., Newark, N.Y. Served with Ordnance Corps., U.S. Army, 1952-54; Korea. Democrat. Roman Catholic. Office: Sarah Coventry Inc Stuart Park Newark NY 14593

O'DONNELL, WILLIAM CHARLES, broadcasting exec.; b. St. Louis, June 30, 1922; s. John Joseph and Sarah Regina (McCabe) O'D.; B.S., St. Louis U., 1944; m. Julia von Brecht, Dec. 27, 1958; children—Julie, Sally, Libby, Bill, John, Angela, Christopher. Salesman, gen. sales mgr., dir. Radio Sta. KXOK, St. Louis, 1950-61; mgr. St. Louis office CBS Radio Spot Sales, 1962-67; v.p. CBS TV Stas. Div., gen. mgr. KNXT, Los Angeles, 1971-73; v.p. CBS Radio Div., gen. mgr. WBBM Newsradio 78, Chgo., 1967-71, 73—; chmn. first Radio Comml. Workshop, St. Louis, Chgo. Broadcast Skills Bank, Creative Screening Panel for Internat. Broadcasting Awards; co-chmn. Chgo. chpt. VA Hosp. Bedside Network. Chmn. communications div. Girl Scouts of Chgo. Fund Drive; bd. dirs. Goodwill Industries; bd. dirs. Better Bus. Bur. of Chgo., Lawson YMCA, United Charities, Jr. Achivement of Chgo.; pres. Safer Found.; mem. Catholic TV Adv. Com.; mem. exec. com. Ill. div. Am. Cancer Soc.; mem. citizens com. Loyola U., Chgo.; asso. Berea Coll., Northwestern U. Recipient 1st Place awards Ill. A.P. and U.P.I. radio editorial competitions, 1973-76, Radio-Television News Dirs. Assn., 1975, Abe Lincoln award for outstanding contbns. to broadcasting and community, 1975, 78; editorial award Broadcast Industry Conf., 1977; Valley Forge honor award Freedoms Found., 1976-77. Address: WBBM 630 N McClurg Ct Chicago IL 60611

O'DONNELL, WILLIAM JAMES, engring. co. exec.; b. Pitts., June 19, 1935; s. William James and Elizabeth (Rau) O'D.; B.S.M.E., Carnegie Inst. Tech., 1957; M.S.M.E., U. Pitts., 1962, Ph.D., 1962; m. Joanne Mary Kusen, Jan. 31, 1959; children—Suzanne, Janice, William, Thomas, Kerry, Amy. Jr. engr. Westinghouse Research Lab., 1957-58, asso. engr., 1958; with Westinghouse Bettis Atomic Power Lab., West Mifflin, Pa., 1961-70, fellow engr., 1966-68, advanced engr., 1968; pres., chmn. bd. O'Donnell & Assos., Inc., Pitts., 1970—. Served with C.E., AUS, 1963-64. Recipient Machinery's Achievement award as outstanding mech. designer, 1957, Pi Tau Sigma Gold medal for achievements in engring., 1967. Fellow ASME (Nat. award for outstanding contbn. to engring. profession 1973); mem. Soc. Exptl. Stress Analysis, AAAS, Am. Soc. Metals, Am. Nuclear Soc., Nat. Soc. Profl. Engrs., ASTM, Sigma Xi, Tau Beta Pi, Pi Tau Sigma. Contbr. numerous articles on engring. and mechanics to profl. jours. Home: 3611 Maplevue Dr Bethel Park PA 15102 Office: O'Donnell & Assos 241 Curry Hollow Rd Pittsburgh PA 15236

O'DONNELL, WILLIAM THOMAS, labor union ofcl.; b. Phila., Dec. 19, 1931; s. Thomas William and Edith O'D.; student Antonellie Sch. Photography, St. Joseph Labor Sch. With Nannettes Mfg. Co., 1951-69; with United Garment Workers of Am., 1969—, asst. sec.-treas., N.Y.C., 1976-77, gen. pres., 1977—. Roman Catholic. Office: United Garment Workers of America 200 Park Ave S Suite 1610-1614 New York NY 10003

O'DOWD, DONALD DAVY, univ. ofcl.; b. Manchester, N.H., Jan. 23, 1927; s. Hugh Davy and Laura (Morin) O'D.; B.A. summa cum laude, Dartmouth Coll., 1951; postgrad. (Fulbright fellow), U. Edinburgh (Scotland), 1951-52; M.A., Harvard U., 1955, Ph.D., 1957; m. Janet Louise Fithian, Aug. 23, 1953; children—Daniel D., Diane K., James E., John M. Instr., asst. prof. psychology, dean freshmen Wesleyan U., Middletown, Conn., 1955-60, asso. prof., prof., 1960, dean Univ., 1960-65, provost, 1965-70; pres. Oakland U., Rochester, Mich., 1970-79; exec. vice chancellor SUNY, Albany, 1979—. Bd. dirs. Clinton Valley council Boy Scouts Am., Cranbrook Schs., Crittenton Hosp., Detroit Edn. TV Found., Detroit Symphony Orch., Met. Fund, Roeper City and Country Sch. Served with AUS, 1945-47. Carnegie Corp. fellow, 1965-66. Mem. Am., Mich. psychol. assns., AAAS, AAUP, Am. Assn. Univ. Adminstrs., Phi Beta Kappa, Sigma Xi. Clubs: Pine Lake Country; Renaissance, Economic (dir.) (Detroit). Office: SUNY Office of Exec Vice Chancellor Univ Plaza Albany NY 12246

O'DWYER, JOHN JOSEPH, educator; b. Grafton, New South Wales, Australia, Nov. 9, 1925; s. Joseph Daniel and Mary (Feehan) O'D.; B.Sc.B.E., Sydney U. (Australia), 1947; Ph.D., U. Liverpool (Eng.), 1951; m. Anneita Cawa, May 7, 1955; children—John, Mary, Anne, Luke, Helen. Came to U.S., 1964 Sr. research scientist Commonwealth Sci. and Indsl. Research Orgn., Sydney, 1951-58; asso. prof. U. New South Wales, 1958-66; prof. So. Ill. U., Carbondale, 1966-70; prof. physics, chmn. dept. State U. N.Y. at Oswego, 1970—. Fellow Inst. Physics (London); mem. Am. Phys. Soc., Dielectrics Conf. (chmn. 1974-75). Author: The Theory of Dielectric Breakdown of Solids, 1964; The Theory of Electrical Conduction and Breakdown in Dielectric Solids, 1973—. Home: RD 3 Oswego NY 13126

ODYNIEC, FRANCIS ANTHONY, JR., public relations ofcl.; b. Phila., Oct. 4, 1948; s. Francis Anthony and Mary Magdeline (Romaszka) O.; student Temple U., 1966-68; B.A. in Bus., Hiram Scott Coll., 1970. Contest mgr., with circulation sales promotion dept. Phila. Inquirer, 1971; sr. accounting clk. Phila. Electric Co., 1971-74; account, exec., copywriter, announcer Sta. WVPO, Stroudsburg, Pa., 1975; free-lance copywriter Shender, Eaby, Inc., Phila., 1975-76; sr. editor Indsl. Maintenance Plant Ops. Mgr., Phila., 1976, mng. editor Safety Product News mag., 1976-77; pub. relations writer chem. div. Thiokol Corp., Trenton, 1977—. Mem. Alpha Epsilon Pi. Home: 634 Hummingbird Ln Cornwells Heights PA 19020

OECHSLE, PIETER FERNANDO, retail toy chain co. exec.; s. Hans Christian and Ruth O.; B.Commerce, McGill U., 1957; m. Anita Graham, Jan. 10, 1963; children—Alexandra, Phillip, John. Mgr., dir. Oechsle CIA Comml. S.A., 1957-75; mgr., dir. Juguetis y Envases Nationales S.A., 1968-75; pres. F.A.O. Schwarz, Inc., N.Y.C., 1976—. Clubs: Gibson Island (Md.) Golf and Tennis. Office: FAO Schwarz 745 Fifth Ave New York NY 10022

OECHSLI, LEONARD PAUL, govt. ofcl.; b. Medan, Sumatra, Jan. 3, 1922 (parents Am. citizens); s. Leonard and Loula (Boicourt) O.; B.S., U. Cal. at Berkeley, 1947, M.S., 1948; postgrad. Inter-Am. Inst. Agrl. Scis., 1948-49, Cornell U., 1951-52; m. Helen Camelia George, Nov. 17, 1951; children—Camille, Christopher George, Mark Boicourt. With Am. Consulate, Sao Paulo, Brazil, 1942-43, Inst. Inter-Am. Affairs, Brazil, 1943-44; dir. research Am. Cocoa Research Inst., 1950-57; program officer AID, Chile, 1957-62; asst. dir. Office Devel. Planning and Programming, AID, 1962-66; mission dir. U.S. AID, Ecuador 1966-68, El Salvador, 1968-70, dep. dir., India, 1970-72, dir. East Asian affairs, Washington, 1972-74, dir. Middle East affairs, 1974-75; asst. program advisor Inter-Am. Devel. Bank, Washington, 1975-76, chief sectorial policies div., 1976—, assigned Nat. War Coll., 1965-66. Pres. Franklin Civic Assn., McLean, Va., 1964-66. Rotary Club overseas fellow, 1941-42. Methodist. Home: 1926 Rhode Island Ave McLean VA 22101 Office: Inter-Am Devel Bank Washington DC 20577

OEHLER, IRVING ARTHUR, mfg. co. exec.; b. Buffalo, July 11, 1911; s. Arthur O. and Louise (Hoffman) O.; E.E., Rensselaer Polytech. Inst., 1932, M.E.E., 1933, Ph.D., 1935; m. Hazel H. Burritt, May 1, 1937 (dec. Mar. 1976); children—Marion L. (Mrs. J. Scott Weaver), Gordon C., Robert B.; m. 2d, Anna Olivant, June 12, 1979. Asst chief metallurgist Republic Steel Corp., Buffalo, 1935-42; chief metallurgist Am. Welding & Mfg. Co., Warren, Ohio, 1942-44, dir. research, 1945-52, adminstrv. asst. to pres., gen. mgr., 1952-55, v.p., 1957-58, exec. v.p., 1958-60, pres., chief exec. officer, 1960—, chmn. bd., 1973-75, dir., 1957—; dir. Union Savings & Trust Co., Warren. U.S. del. to Internat. Orgn. for Standardization, 1964—, Am. Assembly, 1967-69. Bd. dirs. Warren YMCA; bd. dirs. Warren Area United Appeal Bd., pres., 1961-62; trustee Trumbull Meml. Hosp., 1962—. Recipient Meritorious Certificate award Am. Welding Soc., 1966, Outstanding Person award Mahoning Valley Tech. Socs. Council, 1963. Mem. Internat. Inst. Welding (gov. 1965—, chmn. Am. council 1965—, treas. 1972—), Am. Welding Soc. (v.p., pres. 1971-72, R.D. Thomas Meml. award 1971, Samuel Wylie Miller medal 1975), Sigma Xi, Tau Beta Pi. Contbr. articles to engring., tech. jours. Pioneer welds in titanium, 1948. Home: 4848 Mahoning St NW Warren OH 44483 Office: American Welding & Manufacturing Co Dietz Rd Warren OH 44482

OEHLERT, BENJAMIN HILBORN, JR., bus. cons., author; b. Phila. Sept. 13, 1909; s. Benjamin H. and Sarah (Landis) O.; B.S., U. Pa., 1930, J.D., 1933; m. Alice Greene, Mar. 27, 1937; children—Benjamin Hilborn, Alice Ann. Admitted to Pa. bar, 1933, gen. law practice, Phila., 1933-35; atty. Mexican claims div., State Dept., Washington, 1935-38; asst. counsel, Coca Cola Co., 1938-42, asst. to pres., v.p., 1942-48, v.p., 1953-65, sr. v.p., dir., 1965-67; U.S. ambassador to Pakistan, 1967-69; pres. Minute Maid Co., 1961-65; v.p., dir. W.R. Grace & Co., N.Y.C., 1948-53. Mem. Fed., Am., Pa., Phila. bar assns., Order of Coif, Phi Delta Phi, Theta Xi. Clubs: Capital City, Piedmont Driving (Atlanta); University (N.Y.C.); Everglades, Bath and Tennis, Four Arts (Palm Beach). Author: The Restatement in the Courts; Eminent Domain in Pennsylvania. Home: Everglades Club 356 Worth Ave Palm Beach FL 33480

OEHLERTS, DONALD ERVIN, librarian; b. Waterloo, Iowa, Aug. 3, 1927; s. Ervin L. and Mabel L. (Buehner) O.; B.A., U. Wis., 1953, M.L.S., 1958; Ph.D., Ind. U., 1975; m. Alberna Herrick, June 18, 1952; children—Steven, Susan, Paula, John, Ann. Newspaper librarian State Hist. Soc. Wis., Madison, 1953-58; periodicals librarian S.D. State Coll., Brookings, 1958-60; life scis. and social scis. librarian Colo. State U., Fort Collins, 1960-67; asst. dir. libraries U. Houston, 1970-72; dir. libraries Miami U., Oxford, Ohio, 1972—. Served with AUS, 1945-48. Mem. Ohio, Am. library assns. Editor: Guide to Wisconsin Newspapers, 1958; Guide to Colorado Newspapers, 1964. Home: 1114 Tollgate Dr Oxford OH 45056 Office: Miami U Oxford OH 45056

OEHME, REINHARD, physicist, educator; b. Wiesbaden, Germany, Jan. 26, 1928; s. Reinhold and Katharina (Kraus) O.; Dr. rer. nat., U. Goettingen (Germany), 1951; Diplom Physiker, U. Frankfurt am Main (Germany), 1948; m. Mafalda Pisani, Nov. 5, 1952. Came to U.S., 1956. Asst., Max Planck Inst. Physics, Goettingen, 1949-53; research asso. Fermi Inst. Nuclear Studies, U. Chgo., 1954-56, mem. faculty dept. physics and Fermi Inst., 1958—, prof. physics, 1964—; mem. Inst. Advanced Studies, Princeton, 1956-58; vis. prof. Inst. de Física Teórica, São Paulo, Brazil, 1952-53, U. Md., 1957, U. Vienna (Austria), 1961, Imperial Coll., London, Eng., 1963-64, U. Karlsruhe (Germany), 1974, 75, 77; Japan Soc. vis. prof. U. Tokyo, 1976; frequently vis. scientist Internat. Centre Theoretical Physics, Miramare-Trieste, Italy, Brookhaven Nat. Lab., Lawrence Radiation Lab., U. Calif. at Berkeley, CERN, Geneva, Switzerland; Guggenheim fellow, 1963-64; Humboldt award, 1974. Fellow Am. Phys. Soc. Author articles in field, chpts. in books. Office: Fermi Inst U Chgo Chicago IL 60637

OEHMKE, ROBERT HARVEY, educator, mathematician; b. Detroit, Aug. 6, 1927; s. Edwin Henry and Theresa (Ulaga) O.; B.S., U. Mich., 1948; M.S., U. Detroit, 1950; Ph.D., U. Chgo., 1954; m. Theresa Maria Chiaverini, Dec. 30, 1950; 1 son, James. Instr., Ill. Inst. Tech., 1953-54; asst. prof. Butler U., 1954-56, Mich. State U., 1956-62; mathematician Inst. Def. Analysis, 1962-64; prof. math., chmn. dept. U. Iowa, Iowa City, 1964—. Cons. in field. Served with USNR, 1945-46. Mem. Am. Math. Soc., Math. Assn. Am. Author: Fundamentals of College Algebra, 1963. Contbr. articles to profl. jours. Home: Rural Route 6 Iowa City IA 52240

OEHSER, PAUL HENRY, editor, writer, conservationist; b. Cherry Creek, N.Y., Mar. 27, 1904; s. Henry Christian and Agnes Theodosia (Abbey) O.; grad. Forestville (N.Y.) Free Acad., 1921; student U. Iowa, 1924; A.B., Greenville (Ill.) Coll., 1925; postgrad. Am. U., 1926-30; m. Grace M. Edgbert, Oct. 4, 1927; children—Gordon

Vincent, Richard Edgbert. Asst. editor Bur. Biol. Survey, Dept. Agr., 1925-31; editor U.S. Nat. Mus., Smithsonian Instn., 1931-50, chief editorial and publs. div., pub. relations officer Smithsonian Instn., 1950-66, research asso., 1966—; editor sci. publs. Nat. Geographic Soc., 1966-78; mng. editor Jour. Washington Acad. Scis., 1939-59; editor Proc. 8th Am. Sci. Congress, Dept. State, 1941-43. Bd. dirs. Greater Washington Ednl. TV Assn., Inc., 1958-64; trustee Westminster Sch., Annandale, Va. Fellow Washington Acad. Scis.; mem. Arlington County Hist. Soc. (editor mag. 1959-62), Philos. Soc. Washington, Am. Ornithol. Union, Biol. Soc. Washington, Wilderness Soc. (mem. governing council 1964-77, hon. council 1977—, asst. treas. 1965-70, 72-76, v.p. 1976-77), History of Sci. Club (Washington), Thoreau Soc. Am. (pres. 1961), Washington Biologists' Field Club (v.p. 1962-64, pres. 1964-67), Columbia Hist. Soc., Literary Soc. of Washington (corr. sec. and treas. 1972—). Clubs: Cosmos (sec. 1950-69, editor Bull. 1951-69, v.p. 1973, pres. 1974), Palaver (Washington). Author: Sons of Science, the Story of the Smithsonian Institution and Its Leaders, 1949; Fifty Poems, 1954; The Smithsonian Institution, 1970. Contbr. articles, reviews and verse to mags., jours., encys., news publs. Gen. editor United States Encyclopedia of History, 1967-68. Home: 9012 Old Dominion Dr McLean VA 22102. *Touchstones: Keep out of people's hair; don't talk too much; pay folks what you owe 'em (if you have the money); don't set your heart too much on the future; try to keep a sense of humor, and if you don't have one get one quick; there's no such thing as a bad pun . . .*

OELBAUM, HAROLD, lawyer, corp. exec.; b. Bklyn., Jan. 9, 1931; s. Max and Betty (Molomet) O.; A.B., Franklin and Marshall Coll., 1952; J.D., Harvard, 1955; LL.M., N.Y. U., 1959; m. Nancy Rothkopf, June 28, 1968; children—Louise, Andrew, Jennifer. Admitted to N.Y. bar, 1955, Mass. bar, 1960; atty. Hellerstein & Rosier, Esqs., N.Y.C., 1955-59; gen. atty. Raytheon Co., Lexington, Mass., 1959-68; sr. atty. Revlon, Inc., N.Y.C., 1968-72; exec. v.p., dir., mem. exec. com. Kane-Miller Corp., Tarrytown, N.Y., 1972—. Mem. Am. Meat Inst. (bd. dirs.). Dept. Editor Jour. of Taxation, 1959-72. Home: 410 E 57th St New York NY 10022 Office: 555 White Plains Rd Tarrytown NY 10591

OELGESCHLAGER, GUENTHER KARL, publisher; b. Jersey City, Apr. 19, 1934; s. Herman Wilhelm and Frieda Johanna (Onken) O.; B.A. cum laude, Princeton U., 1958; postgrad. Columbia U., 1959; m. Jacqueline L. Braley, July 16, 1962; children—Stacey, Lauren, Amy. Nat. sales mgr. Harper & Row Pubs., N.Y.C., 1959-67; dir. coll. div. F.A. Praeger Co., N.Y.C., 1968; v.p., gen. mgr. D.C. Heath & Co., Lexington, Mass., 1969-72; pres., dir. Ballinger Pub. Co., Cambridge, Mass., 1973-78; v.p., dir. J.B. Lippincott Co., Phila., 1973-78; pres. Oelgeschlager, Gunn & Hain, Pubs., Inc., Cambridge, 1979—. Served with U.S. Army, 1954-56. Mem. Am. Assn. Pubs. Democrat. Episcopalian. Office: 1278 Massachusetts Ave Cambridge MA 02138

OELMAN, ROBERT SCHANTZ, bus. exec.; b. Dayton, Ohio, June 9, 1909; s. William Walter and Edith (Schantz) O.; A.B., Dartmouth Coll., 1931; postgrad. U. Vienna, 1931-32; m. Mary Coolidge, Oct. 17, 1936; children—Bradford Coolidge, Robert Schantz, Jr., Kathryn Peirce, Martha Forrer. With NCR Corp., Dayton, 1933—, asst. to pres., 1942-45, asst. v.p. 1945-46, v.p., 1946-50, exec. v.p., 1950-57, pres., 1957-62, chmn., pres., 1962-64, chmn., 1962-74, chmn. exec. com., 1974—, dir., 1948—; dir. Ohio Bell Telephone Co., Koppers Co., Inc., Pitts., Winters Nat. Bank & Trust Co., Dayton, Ford Motor Co., Detroit. Mem. Dayton Area Progress Council, Bus. Council. Trustee C.F. Kettering Med. Center, Dayton; chmn. Air Force Mus., Dayton. Mem. Phi Beta Kappa, Delta Kappa Epsilon. Clubs: Moraine Country (Dayton); Country of Fla., Ocean (Delray Beach); Augusta (Ga.) Nat. Golf. Home: 2846 Upper Bellbrook Rd Bellbrook OH 45305 Office: 2485 Winters Bank Tower Dayton OH 45423

OESTREICH, CHARLES HENRY, coll. adminstr.; b. Columbus, Ohio, June 8, 1932; s. Henry F. and Martha (Schwartz) O.; B.S., Capital U., 1954; M.S., Ohio U., 1956, Ph.D., 1961; m. Rhoda J. Haseley, Aug. 26, 1957; children—Martha, Mary, David. Instr. chemistry Va. Military Inst., 1956-57; instr. Capital U., Columbus, 1962-64, asso. prof. chemistry, 1965-69; acad. dean Tex. Luth. Coll., Seguin, 1969-76, interim pres., 1976-77, pres., 1977—; postdoctoral research fellow Vanderbilt U., 1965-66. Bd. dirs. Mid-Tex. Symphony. Mem. Am. Chem. Soc., Council Advancement Small Colls. (dir.), Sigma Xi. Lutheran. Home: 605 Fleming Seguin TX 78155 Office: 1000 Court Seguin TX 78155

OETJEN, ROBERT ADRIAN, coll. adminstr.; b. Detroit, Mar. 31, 1912; s. Frederick Tobias and Vida Pearle (Au) O.; B.A., Asbury Coll., Wilmore, Ky., 1936; M.S., U. Mich., 1938, Ph.D., 1942; m. Dorothy Mae Myers, June 3, 1936; children—Barbara Oetjen Miller, Charlene Oetjen Gordon, Margaret Oetjen Williams, Charles, Marilyn Ruth Oetjen Philipp. Chemist, Mellon Inst. Indsl. Research, 1936-37; physicist Texaco Research Labs., Beacon, N.Y., 1941-46; mem. faculty Ohio State U., 1946-70, prof. physics, 1957-70, asso. dean Coll. Arts and Scis., 1960-62, 64-67, 69-70, acting dean, 1967-69; prof. physics U. Akron, 1970-77, dean Buchtel Coll. Arts and Scis., 1970-77; acting v.p. acad. affairs Malone Coll., Canton, Ohio, 1977-78, v.p. acad. affairs, 1978—, dean advance programs, 1977-78; asst. to dir. Ohio State U. Research Found., 1953-55; chief scientist Tokyo office NSF, 1962-64; mem. U.S. del. Internat. Comm. Optics, 1965-70. Fulbright grantee, 1955-57. Bd. dirs. Japan Internat. Christian U. Found.; trustee Malone Coll. Fellow Optical Soc. Am.; mem. Am. Conf. Acad. Deans (dir.), Am. Phys. Soc., Am. Assn. Physics Tchrs., Phys. Soc. Japan, Applied Physics Soc. Japan, Korean Phys. Soc., Japan Soc., Asia Soc. Home: 1231 Carol St NE North Canton OH 44720 Office: Malone Coll Canton OH 44709

OETTING, ROBERT BENFIELD, educator; b. Lee's Summit, Mo., Aug. 5, 1933; s. Albert Diederich and Ruth Inez (Benfield) O.; B.S. in Mech. Engring., Mo. Sch. Mines and Metallurgy, 1955; M.S. in Aero. Engring., Purdue U., 1957; Ph.D. in Mech. Engring., U. Md., 1965; m. Tommie Ruth Yost, Apr. 15, 1960; children—Anne Marie, John Robert. Turboprop engine test engr. Allison div. Gen. Motors Corp., Indpls., 1955-56; aerothermodynamist N.Am. Aviation, Downey, Calif., 1956; mech. engr. U.S. Naval Test Sta., China Lake, Calif., 1958; aerospace engr. U.S. Naval Ordnance Lab., Silver Spring, Md., summers, 1959-63; instr. mech. engring. Mo. Sch. Mines and Metallurgy, Rolla, 1958-59, U. Md., College Park, 1959-64; prof. mech. and aerospace engring. U. Mo.-Rolla, 1964—; cons. U.S. Army Aviation System Command, St. Louis, 1969; NATO postdoctoral fellow, von Karman Inst. for Fluid Dynamics, Belgium, 1972-73. Active Boy Scouts Am., 1969—. Served as ensign USNR, 1957. Am. Soc. for Engring. Edn.-NASA Summer Faculty fellow, 1966; NSF Faculty Research award, 1964. Mem. Am. Soc. for Engring. Edn. (space engring. com. 1971-76), Am. Inst. Aeros. and Astronautics (mem. student activities com. 1970-76, gen. aviation systems com. 1976, ednl. activities com. 1976—), Soc. Automotive Engrs. (Teeter award 1977) Am. Soc. Aerospace Edn., Aircraft Owners and Pilots Assn., Sigma Xi, Blue Key, Alpha Phi Omega, Tau Beta Pi, Sigma Gamma Tau (regional coordinator 1974—), Pi Tau Sigma. Contbr. articles to profl. jours. Home: 22 Burgher Dr Rolla MO 65401

OETTINGER, ANTHONY GERVIN, educator, mathematician; b. Nuremberg, Germany, Mar. 29, 1929; s. Albert and Marguerite (Bing) O.; came to U.S., 1941, naturalized, 1947; A.B., Harvard, 1951, Ph.D., 1954; Henry fellow, U. Cambridge (Eng.), 1951-52; m. Marilyn Tanner, June 20, 1954; children—Douglas, Marjorie. Mem. faculty Harvard, 1955—, asso. prof. applied math., 1960-63, prof. linguistics, 1963-75, Gordon McKay prof. applied math., 1963—, chmn. program on info. resources policy, 1972—, mem. faculty of govt., 1973—, prof. info. resources policy, 1975—; mem. communications command control and intelligence bd. Dept. Navy, 1978—; cons. Arthur D. Little, Inc., 1956—, Office Sci. and Tech., Exec. Office of Pres., 1960-73, Bellcomm, Inc., 1963-68, Systems Devel. Corp., 1965-68, Nat. Security Council, Exec. Office of Pres., 1975-77; chmn. Computer Sci. and Engring. Bd., Nat. Acad. Scis., 1968-73; commr. Mass. Community Antenna TV Commn., 1972—, chmn., 1975—; mem. research adv. bd. Com. for Econ. Devel., 1975-79. Fellow Am. Acad. Arts and Scis., AAAS, IEEE; mem. Assn. Computing Machinery (mem. council 1961-68, chmn. com. U.S. Govt. relations, 1964-66, editor computational linguisitics sect. Communications 1964-66, pres. 1966-68), Soc. Indsl. and Applied Math. (mem. council 1963-67), Council on Fgn. Relations, Phi Beta Kappa, Sigma Xi. Clubs: Cosmos (Washington); Harvard (N.Y.C.). Author: A Study for the Design of an Automatic Dictionary, 1954; Automatic Language Translation: Lexical and Technical Aspects, 1960; Run Computer Run: The Mythology of Educational Innovation, 1969; High and Low Politics: Information Resources for the 80s, 1977. Editor Proc. of a Symposium on Digital Computers and Their Applications, 1962. Home: 65 Elizabeth Rd Belmont MA 02178 Office: 33 Oxford St Cambridge MA 02138

OETTINGER, KATHERINE BROWNELL, social worker; b. Nyack, N.Y., Sept. 24, 1903; d. Charles Leonard and Eunice (Bennet) Brownell; A.B., Smith Coll., 1925, M.S. in Social Work, 1925, LL.D., 1957; postgrad. Marywood Coll., Pa. State U., Columbia, U. Pitts.; L.H.D. (hon.), Dickinson Coll., 1966; m. Malcolm H. Oettinger, July 1, 1931; children—Malcolm H., John Brownell. Social case-worker, N.Y.C., 1926-30; mental health cons., Scranton, Pa., 1930-50; chief div. community services Bur. Mental Health, Pa. Dept. Welfare, 1950-54; dean Sch. Social Work, Boston U., 1954-57; chief Children's Bur., HEW, 1957-68, dep. asst. sec. for population and family planning, 1968-70; lectr., cons. population and family planning, 1970—; cons. Internat. Assn. Schs. for Social Work Edn., 1971-76; dir. adolescent studies Inter-Am. Dialogue Center, Airlie, Va., 1976-77. Sec. 1960 White House Conf. on Children and Youth; U.S. rep. to UNICEF, 1957—; vice chmn. Nat. Com. Children and Youth, 1960—; coordinator 1st Inter-Hemisphere Conf. on Adolescent Fertility, 1977. Trustee, Boston U.; mem. nat. bd. Med. Coll. Pa., 1977—. Fellow Am. Orthopsychiat. Assn.; mem. Nat. Assn. Social Workers, Nat. Conf. Social Welfare, Am. Pub. Welfare Assn., Soc. Projective Techniques, Rorschach Inst., Inc., Council Social Work Edn., Phi Beta Kappa. Author: Readers Guide: Population and Family Planning: Analytical Abstracts for Social Work Educators and Related Disciplines, 1972; An Asian Prospective, 1975; Not My Daughter: Facing Up to Adolescent Pregnancy, 1979. Contbr. articles to profl. jours. Home: Canterbury Farm Washington VA 22747

OFFENBACHER, ELMER LAZARD, educator; b. Frankfurt am Main, Germany, Sept. 29, 1923; (parents Am. citizens); s. Emile and Beatrice Maud (Bondi) O.; B.A., Bklyn. Coll., 1943; postgrad. Amherst Coll., 1943-44; M.A., U. Pa., 1949, Ph.D., 1951; m. Esther Gladstone, June 29, 1952; children—Nathan Ezra, Beatrice Miriam, Joseph Eliyohu. Asst. instr. Amherst Coll., 1943-44; physicist NACA, Langley Field, Va., 1944; asst. instr. physics U. Pa., 1947-51; asst. prof. physics Temple U., Phila., 1951-56, asso. prof., 1956-65, prof. physics, 1965—. Vis. prof. Hebrew U., 1962, Cambridge U., 1971. Sec.-gen. World Council Orthodox Jewish Scientists, 1977—. Served with USNR, 1944-46. Mem. Am. Assn. U. Profs., Am. Assn. Physics Tchrs., Am. Phys. Soc., Assn. Orthodox Jewish Scientists (past pres., sec. 1976—). Home: New York City NY 10024 Office: Physics Dept Temple U Philadelphia PA 19122

OFFER, DANIEL, psychiatrist; b. Berlin, Germany, Dec. 24, 1929; grad. U. Chgo., 1957; married; 3 children. Intern Ill. Research and Ednl. Hosps., Chgo., 1957-58; resident Inst. Psychosomatics and Psychiat. Research and Tng. Michael Reese Hosp., Chgo., 1958-61; psychiatrist Chgo. Inst. Psychoanalysis, 1963-68; career investigator Nat. Inst. Mental Health, Psychosomatic and Psychiat. Inst., Michael Reese Hosp., 1961-64; asst. dir. Inst. Psychosomatics and Psychiat. Research and Tng., Chgo., 1961-64, asso. dir., 1965-74, co-dir., 1974-76, acting chmn., 1976-77, chmn., 1977—; asso. prof. psychiatry U. Chgo., 1969-73, prof., 1973—; fellow Center for Advanced Studies in Behavioral Scis., Stanford, 1973-74; cons. Ill. Dept. Mental Health. Served with Israeli Army. Fellow Chgo. Inst. Medicine; mem. AAAS, Am. Soc. Adolescent Psychiatry (pres. 1972-73), Internat. Assn. Child Psychiatry, Soc. Adolescent Psychiatry. Author: Normality: Theoretical and Clinical Concepts of Mental Health, 1966, rev. edit., 1973; The Psychological World of the Teen-ager, 1969; From Teenage to Young Manhood: A Psychological Study, 1975; Psychological World of the Juvenile Delinquent, 1979; also numerous articles. Editor-in-chief Jour. Youth and Adolescence; editorial bd. for psychiatry Internat. Profl. Communication, Inc., 1972—. Address: 2959 S Ellis Ave Chicago IL 60616

OFFICE, GERALD SIMMS, JR., fast food restaurant chain exec.; b. Dayton, Ohio, Oct. 22, 1941; s. Gerald Simms and Sarah (Lieberman) O.; B.B.A. with distinction, U. Mich., 1963; J.D. summa cum laude, Ohio State U., 1967; m. Lynn Elise Isaacson, Aug. 26, 1972; 1 son, Jeremy Simms. Admitted to Ohio bar, 1967; partner firm Office & Office, Dayton 1967-69; pres., chmn. bd. Ponderosa Systems, Inc., Dayton, 1969—; dir. MAPI, Inc., Dayton. Trustee Dayton Devel. Council, Dayton Art Inst., Cin. Contemporary Art Center; co-chmn. Spl. Olympics Dayton and Montgomery County, Ohio. Mem. Nat. Restaurant Assn. (dir.). Address: PO Box 578 Dayton OH 45401*

OFFIT, SIDNEY, writer, educator; b. Balt., Oct. 13, 1928; s. Barney and Lillian (Cohen) O.; B.A., Johns Hopkins, 1950; m. Avodah Crindell Komito, Aug. 8, 1952; children—Kenneth, Michael Robert. Editorial staff Mercury Publs., N.Y.C., 1952-53, Macfadden Publs., N.Y.C., 1953-54; contbg. editor Baseball mag., Washington, 1955-58; mem. faculty N.Y. U., 1964—, adj. prof. creative writing, 1977—; asso. editor Intellectual Digest, 1970-72, sr. editor, 1972-74; lectr. creative writing New Sch. Social Research, 1965—; curator George Polk Awards for Journalism, 1977—; mem. editorial bd. Remington Rev., 1974-78; mem. nat. bd. Nat. Book Com., 1973-75; commentator Channel 5 TV, N.Y.C., 1975—. Mem. selection com. Dist. Sch. Bd., N.Y.C., 1968. Mem. exec. bd. Lexington Democratic Club, N.Y.C., 1957-60, N.Y. Dem. County Com., 1966—; chmn. 19th Precinct Community Council of N.Y.C., 1964—. Recipient Distinguished Alumni award Valley Forge Mil. Acad., 1961, Otty Community Service award, 1975. Mem. Tudor and Stuart Club, Authors Guild (council 1970-77, 79—), Authors League (nat. council 1976-79), Am. Center of P.E.N. (exec. com. 1969—, v.p. 1970-74; internat. del. 1971, 72, 74). Clubs: Century Assn., Coffee House (N.Y.C.). Author: He Had it Made, 1959; The Other Side of the Street, 1962; Soupbone, 1963; Topsy Turvey, 1965; The Adventure of Homer Fink, 1966; The Boy Who Made a Million, 1968; Not All the Girls Have Million Dollar Smiles (short stories), 1971; Only a Girl Like You, 1972; What Kind of Guy Do You Think I Am?, 1977; series sports books for boys, 1961-65; also essays, revs., short stories; book editor Politics Today, 1978—. Home: 23 E 69th St New York NY 10021 Office: 315 E 65th St New York NY 10022. *I have been guided by a strong devotion to my family and friends and moderate ambition. In both these priorities I have been influenced by my parents. With my writing I have tried to fulfill my own needs, and for the most I have been satisfied by the reception. I do not aspire to fame or great fortune, and this leaves me free to enjoy the sharing of experiences with my friends and family. I consider myself a lucky man and this keeps me grateful to whatever forces there are that contrive man's fortune.*

OFFNER, ELLIOT MELVILLE, artist, educator; b. Bklyn., July 12, 1931; s. Samuel and Helen (Wolowitz) O.; certificate Cooper Union, 1952; B.F.A., Yale, 1953, M.F.A., 1959; m. Rosemary O'Connell, Apr. 14, 1957; children—Helen, Daniel, Emily. Numerous one-man exhbns. of sculpture, N.Y. and elsewhere, 1964—; represented in numerous group shows, U.S., Europe; sculpture and graphic work in permanent collections Bklyn. Mus., Allen Art Mus. Oberlin Coll., Library Congress, Met. Mus. Art (print collection), Victoria and Albert Mus., Harvard, Bodleian Library, De Cordova Mus., Hirschhorn Mus. and Sculpture Garden, Lowe Mus., Syracuse U., Mus. Religious Art, Cathedral St. John The Divine, Bryn Mawr Coll., Cooper Hewitt Mus., Slater Meml. Mus., Smith Coll., others; designer Steuben glass, 1955-57; mem. faculty Smith Coll., 1960—, prof. art, 1970—, chmn. dept. art, 1973-76, Andrew W. Mellon prof. humanities, 1974—, printer to coll., 1975—, dir. Student Printing Office: artist-in-residence Winsor Sch., 1977; vis. lectr. Royal Coll. Art, London, 1978; dir. Rosemary Press, Northampton, Mass. Served with AUS, 1953-55. Recipient various prizes and grants including Nat. Found. on Arts and Humanities, Nat. Inst. Arts and Letters, Tiffany Found. (2), Ford Found., Am. Philos. Soc., Ingram Merril Found., Pa. Acad. Fine Arts, others. Mem. Am. Printing Hist. Assn., Wynkyn De Worde Soc., William Morris Soc., Printing Hist. Soc., Bibliog. Soc., Soc. Italic Handwriting. Author: The Granjon Arabesque, 1969. Commns. include 10 Commandments, B'nai Israel, Northampton, Mass., 1964; permanent holocaust meml. Cathedral St. John the Divine; sculpture Kehileth Israel, Brookline, Mass., 1960, St. Francis of Assisi, Phila., 1976, St. Charles Sem., 1976. Home: 74 Washington Ave Northampton MA 01060

OFFNER, ERIC DELMONTE, lawyer; b. Vienna, Austria, June 23, 1928; s. Sigmund J. and Kathe (Delmonte) O.; came to U.S., 1941, naturalized, 1949; B.B.A., Coll. City N.Y., 1949; LL.B. in Internat. Affairs, Cornell U., 1952; m. Julie Cousins, 1955 (dec. 1959); m. 2d, Barbara Ann Shotton, July 2, 1961; 1 son, Gary Douglas. Admitted to N.Y. bar, 1952; asso. firm Langner, Parry, Card & Langner, N.Y.C., 1952-57; partner firm Haseltine, Lake, Waters & Offner, N.Y.C., 1957-77; sr. partner firm Offner & Kuhn, 1978—; instr. George Washington U. Law Sch., Cornell U. Law Sch.; spl. prof. law Hofstra Law Sch., Cornell Law Sch., 1979. Vice pres. Riverdale Mental Health Clinic, N.Y.C., 1966-67; pres. Riverdale Mental Health Assn., 1967-69; pres. Ethical Culture Soc., Riverdale-Yonkers, 1964-67; trustee Am. Ethical Union, 1967-73. Mem. N.Y. Patent Law Assn. (asso. editor Bull. 1961-66, gov. 1973-76), Am., City N.Y. (sec. 1962-64) bar assns., U.S. Trademark Assn., World Peace Through Law (charter), Trademark Soc. Washington (charter), Inst. Trade Mark Agts. (London), Australian Patent Inst., Internat. Assn. Protection Indsl. Property, Nat. Council Patent Law Assn., Internat. Patent, Trademark Assn., Phi Alpha Delta. Author: International Trademark Protection, 1964, Japanese edit., 1977; International Trademark Service, vols. I-III, 1970, vol. IV, 1972, vol. V., 1973, vol. VI, 1976; contbr. articles to profl. jours.; editor-in-chief Cornell Law Forum, 1950-51; editorial bd. Trademark Reporter, 1961-64, 69-72. Home: 5221 Arlington Ave New York NY 10471 Office: 1450 Broadway New York NY 10018. *Do unto others so as to elicit the best in them and thereby the best in yourself.*

OFFNER, FRANKLIN FALLER, educator; b. Chgo., Apr. 8, 1911; s. I.H. and Jennie (Faller) O.; B.Chemistry, Cornell U., 1933; M.S., Cal. Inst. Tech., 1934; Ph.D., U. Chgo., 1938; m. Janine Y. Zurcher, Sept. 22, 1956; children—Laurens, Alexandra, Sylvia, Robin. Pres. Offner Electronics Inc., Chgo., 1939-63; prof. biophysics Northwestern U., 1963—. Laureate in tech. Lincoln Acad. Ill., Fellow IEEE; mem. Am. Electroencephalographic Soc., Am. Phys. Soc., Biophys. Soc., Sigma Xi. Author research papers biophysics, electronics. Patentee electronics, control, hydraulics. Home: 1890 Telegraph Rd Bannockburn Deerfield IL 60015 Office: Technological Institute Northwestern U Evanston IL 60201

OFFNER, WALTER WORTHINGTON, cons. engr.; b. Munich, Germany, Feb. 15, 1906; s. Maximiliam F. and Maria (Bentey) O.; grad. Tech. U., Augsburg, Germany, 1927; postgrad. U. Chgo., 1930-31, U. Wash., 1939-40; m. Estelle Kerr Hadden, June 26, 1948. Engr. tube and test dept. Gen. Electric X-Ray Corp., Chgo., 1930-37; founder Indsl. X-Ray Labs., Seattle, 1938, pres., 1940-46, partner, 1943-46; pres. Standard X-Ray Sales Co., Seattle, 1940, v.p., 1941; founder, pres., tech. dir. X-Ray Engring. Co., Mill Valley, Cal., also San Francisco, 1946-56; founder, pres. X-Ray Engring. Internat., 1956—; dir. X-Ray Engring. Australia Pty., Ltd.; v.p. Radiografias Industriales, S.A., Mexico; v.p. X-Ray Engring. Hawaii, Ltd.; v.p., dir. X-Ray Engring. India, Ltd., Bombay; chmn. bd. X-Ray Engring., Japan; dir. X-Ray Engring., Kuwait; officer, dir. affiliated cos. Radiographic weld control first high-pressure oil pipeline in U.S., 1946, 30-inch gas pipeline, 1947: supervising, cons. engr. radiographic weld inspection Trans-Arabian Oil Pipe Line, 1947-50, Iraq Petroleum 30 inch pipeline, 1950, Tacagua Oil Pipe Line, Venezuela, 1950, Arabian Am. Oil Co. projects, Saudi Arabia, 1960—; weld quality control and constrn. supervision of super-tankers built in Japan, Sweden and Holland, 1967, constrn., supervision copper slurry pipeline in Turkey, 1969, quality control Abu Dhabi and Iraq pipelines, Bahrain, 1972—, supervision and quality control Chevron supertankers in Japan, Sweden and Denmark, 1972—; U.S. del. Internat. Inst. Welding; mem. ship research council NRC, 1970—. Mem. Am. Soc. M.E., Nat. Soc. Profl. Engrs., Am. Ordnance Assn., Soc. Non-Destructive Testing, Engrs. Club San Francisco, Am. Soc. Metals, Am. Welding Soc., San Francisco Port Engrs., Am. Soc. Testing Materials, Nat. Acad. Scis. (ship research com. 1969—), A.A.A.S., Am. Security Council (nat. adv. bd.). Author numerous articles on profl. subjects. Home: Route 1 Box 259D Kapaa Kauai HI 96746

OFFUTT, GEORGE QUENTIN, wooden pallet mfg. co. exec.; b. Knox City, Tex., May 2, 1940; s. Lonnie D. and Sara L. O.; B.S. in Acctg., Abilene Christian U., 1961; m. Linda Nell Guinn, May 27, 1960; children—Bradley, Brian. Staff acct. Ben M. Davis and Co., Abilene, Tex., 1961-66; chief fin. officer for various corps., Abilene, 1966-79, including North Am. Petroleum Corp., E-Z Serve, Inc. and Mulberry Lumber Co.; chmn. bd. Mulberry Lumber Co., Abilene, 1979—. Mem. adv. bd. Abilene Christian U.; pres. PTA, Bowie Elem. Sch., Abilene, 1978-79. Served with Army N.G., 1962. C.P.A., Tex. Mem. Fin. Execs. Inst., Am. Inst. C.P.A.'s, Tex. Soc. C.P.A.'s, Abilene Estate Planners, Abilene C. of C. Mem. Chs. of Christ. Clubs: Petroleum of Abilene, Fairway Oaks Country, Abilene Country, Lions (treas. club). Office: PO Box 3658 Abilene TX 79604

O'FLAHERTY, TERRENCE, journalist; b. What Cheer, Iowa, July 15, 1917; s. Leo J. and Lelia (Thomas) O'F.; B.A., U. Calif. at Berkeley, 1939. Hist. researcher Metro-Goldwyn-Mayer Studios, 1940-42; columnist San Francisco Chronicle, 1949—; writer nationally syndicated TV column, 1960—. Mem. bd. Peabody Awards for Radio and TV, 1952—; host TV program PM West, San Francisco, 1961-62. Served as lt., USNR, 1942-46. Mem. Beta Theta Pi. Contbr. articles to TV Guide, Readers Digest, McCalls. Office: San Francisco Chronicle San Francisco CA 94119

O'FLYNN, JAMES MAGUIRE, assn. exec.; b. St. Louis, Mar. 4, 1933; s. John Stanley and Katherine Butler (Maguire) O'F.; student St. Louis U., 1951-55; m. Barbara Jeanne Wingbermuehle, Sept. 19, 1959; children—Bridget, Mary Margaret, Kathryn, James Maguire. Vice pres. Bank of St. Louis, 1966-72, exec. v.p., 1974-76; sr. v.p. Gen. Bancshares, St. Louis, 1972-74; chmn. bd., chief exec. officer Traders Nat. Bank, Kansas City, Mo., 1976-78; pres. St. Louis Regional Commerce and Growth Assn., St. Louis, 1978—; bd. dirs. Downtown St. Louis, Inc., Laclede's Landing Devel. Corp.; chmn. Port of Met. St. Louis Promotion Com. Bd. dirs. Boys Club, St. Louis; mem. athletic adv. council St. Louis U. Served with U.S. Army, 1955-57. Mem. Mortgage Bankers Assn. St. Louis (past pres.), Home Builders Assn. Greater St. Louis (past chmn. com. mortgage fin.), Backstoppers (sec.). Roman Catholic. Clubs: Rotary, Mo. Athletic, Media. Home: 36 Frederick Ln Saint Louis MO 63122 Office: 10 Broadway Saint Louis MO 63102*

OGAN, RUSSELL GRIFFITH, air force officer; b. Reading, Pa., Nov. 20, 1923; s. Russell John and Edna Gwendlyn (Griffith) O.; student Wyomissing Polytech. Inst., 1942, Air Command Staff Coll., 1948, Nat. War Coll., 1963; m. Gloria Mae Withers, Oct. 30, 1943; children—Susan Ann (Mrs. Lee Harkins), Russell Lee. Enlisted as pvt. U.S. Army, 1942, advanced through grades to brig. gen. USAF, 1970; fighter squadron comdr. Dover AFB, Del., 1951; dir. combat operations 11th Air Div., Ladd AFB, Alaska, 1951-53; dir. Combat Operations Center, Hamilton AFB, Calif., 1953-56; with Hdqrs. Air Def. Command, Ent AFB, Colo., 1956-60; dir. Aerospace Def. Systems Office, Air Force Ballistic Missile Div., 1960-62; served in Germany, 1963-66; dep. dir. personnel data and records, USAF Mil. Personnel Center, Randolph AFB, Tex., 1966-68; comdr. 71st Missile Warning Wing, then vice comdr. 14th Aerospace Force, Ent AFB, Colo., 1968-71; dep. dir. personnel programs Hdqrs. USAF, Washington, 1971-72; dir. Prisoner of War and Missing in Action Affairs, Office Sec. Def., Washington, 1972—. Decorated D.S.M., Legion of Merit with bronze oak leaf cluster, Air medal with 1 silver, 1 bronze oak leaf cluster. Mem. Daedallions. Lutheran. Clubs: Kingsway Country; Army Navy Country (Arlington, Va.). Home: 1500 Appian Dr Punta Gorda Isle FL 33950 Office: Live Oak/SHAPE DCOS US APO New York NY 09055

OGANESOFF, IGOR MICHAEL, producer; b. N.Y.C., Sept. 29, 1924; s. Michael Minaitch and Olga Borisovna (Hoppe) O.; B.S., Columbia U., 1951, M.S., 1951; children by previous marriages—Eric, Risa, Tina. Free lance journalist, 1952-57; chief Far East bur. Wall St. Jour., Tokyo, 1957-64, chief Paris bur., 1964-65; chief Tokyo bur. CBS News, 1966-68; CBS corr. in Vietnam, N.E. Asia, 1966-68, wounded in Vietnam, 1968; producer documentaries CBS News, TV, N.Y.C., 1968-71, producer Sixty Minutes, 1971—; producer documentaries: The Japanese, (Nat. Acad. TV Arts and Scis. Emmy award, George Foster Peabody award for broadcasting, Christopher award, 1969, The Catholic Dilemma, 1970, Inflation, 1969, Reischauer on Asia, 1971. Served with U.S. Army, 1943-46. Mem. Dirs. Guild Am., Writers Guild Am., Am. Film Inst. Home: 140 West End Ave New York City NY 10023 Office: CBS News 524 W 57th St New York City NY 10019. *The hardest thing in life is to find not only what you can do well, but do well and thoroughly enjoy. Finding it requires the flexibility to experiment, to discover the most appropriate means of expressing your aptitudes. But once found, it is the surest way to become true to yourself.*

OGANOVIC, NICHOLAS JOSEPH, educator, former govt. ofcl.; b. Chisholm, Minn., Dec. 22, 1912; s. Dan and Angeline (Danculovic) O.; B.E., State Tchrs. Coll., St. Cloud, Minn., 1934; M.A., U. Minn., 1940; m. Helen Sperl, Oct. 14, 1948; 1 son, Robert Nicholas. Coordinator-tchr., also asst. prin.-tchr. pub. sch. systems, Brainerd and Lakefield, Minn., 1934-40; personnel officer, regional adminstr. Nat. Youth Adminstrn., St. Paul, 1940-43; with U.S. Civil Service Commn., 1943-71, dir. bur. deptl. operations, 1958-60, dep. exec. dir. commn., 1960-65, exec. dir., 1966-71; prof. adminstrn. Minn. Met. State U., St. Paul, 1971—. Recipient Pub. Personnel award President's Com. Employment Handicapped, 1962, Gold medal commr.'s award Civil Service Commn., 1962, Career Service award Nat. Civil Service League, 1963. Mem. Am. Soc. Pub. Adminstrn., Pub. Personnel Assn., Govt. Coll. Council, Am. Psychol. Assn., Soc. for Advancement Mgmt. Home: 2215 Mitchell Ave St Paul MN 55119

OGATA, KATSUHIKO, engr., educator; b. Tokyo, Jan. 6, 1925; s. Fukuhei and Teruko (Yasaki) O.; came to U.S., 1952; B.S., U. Tokyo, 1947; M.S., U. Ill., 1953; Ph.D., U. Calif., Berkeley, 1956; m. Asako Nakamura, Sept. 6, 1961; 1 son, Takahiko. Research asst. Sci. Research Inst., Tokyo, 1948-51; fuel engr. Nippon Steel Tube Co., Tokyo, 1951-52; mem. faculty U. Minn., 1956—, prof. mech. engring., 1961—; prof. elec. engring. Yokohama Nat. U., 1960-61, 64-65, 68-69. Mem. ASME, Sigma Xi, Pi Tau Sigma. Author: State Space Analysis of Control Systems, 1967; Modern Control Engineering, 1970; Dynamic Programming, 1973; Ingenieria de Control Moderna, 1974; Metody Przestrzeni Stanow w Teorii Sterowania, 1974; System Dynamics, 1978. Address: Dept Mech Engring U Minn Minneapolis MN 55455

OGATA, THOMAS SHOICHI, state justice; b. Waiakoa, Maui, Hawaii, Jan. 8, 1917; s. Seisuke and Kiyo (Sato) O.; B.A., U. Hawaii, 1938; LL.B., U. Mich., 1941; m. Dagmar Yaeko Morimoto, June 1971; children—Thomas Shoichi, Dennis K. Admitted to Hawaii bar, 1945; law clk., then dep. atty. City and County Honolulu, 1945-49; dep. county atty. Maui County, 1949-57, spl. counsel for bd. suprs., 1957-58; mem. Hawaii Territorial Senate, 1958-59; mem. Hawaii Senate from 3d Dist., 1959-64; judge 1st Circuit Ct. Hawaii, 1966; justice Hawaii Supreme Ct., 1974—. Mem. Maui County Democratic Com., 1955-57. Mem. Am., Hawaii bar assns. Democrat. Buddhist. Home: 5361 Kilauea Ave Honolulu HI 96816 Office: PO Box 2560 Supreme Ct Honolulu HI 96804

OGBURN, CHARLTON, writer; b. Atlanta, Mar. 15, 1911; s. Charlton and Dorothy (Stevens) O.; S.B. cum laude, Harvard, 1932; grad. Nat. War Coll., 1952; m. Mary C. Aldis, June 6, 1945 (div. 1951); 1 son, Charlton III; m. 2d, Vera Weidman, Feb. 24, 1951; children—Nyssa, Holly. Writer Alfred P. Sloan Found., 1937-39; book reviewer Book-of-the-Month Club, 1940-41; with Div. Southeast Asian Affairs, Dept. of State, 1946-50, polit. adviser, acting U.S. rep. com. good offices on Indonesia, UN Security Council, 1947-48, policy planning adviser Bur. Far Eastern Affairs, 1952-54, chief div. research Near East, S. Asia and Africa, 1954-57. Served to capt. AUS, 1941-46; India-Burma. Recipient John Burroughs medal 1967. Author: The White Falcon, 1955; The Bridge, 1957; Big Caesar, 1958; The Marauders, 1959; U.S. Army, 1960; The Gold of the River Sea, 1965; The Winter Beach, 1966; The Forging of Our Continent, 1968; The Continent in Our Hands, 1971; Winespring Mountain, 1973; The Southern Appalachians: A Wilderness Quest, 1975; The Adventures of Birds, 1976; Railroads: The Great American Adventure, 1977; co-author Shakespeare: The Man Behind the Name, 1962. Contbr. mags. Home: 10710 Vale Rd Oakton VA 22124

OGDEN, ALFRED, lawyer; b. Bklyn., Oct. 14, 1909; s. Alfred Trecartin and Sophronia (Wisner) O.; grad. Phillips Acad., 1928; B.A., Yale, 1932; LL.B., Harvard, 1935; m. Mary Fell Jordan, June 25, 1938; 1 son, Alfred Trecartin II. Admitted to N.Y. bar, 1936, since practiced in N.Y.C.; partner firm Alexander & Green, 1955-75; of counsel firm Morgan, Lewis & Bockius, 1979—. Pres., dir. C. Tennant, Sons & Co., N.Y.C., 1952-54. Trustee Fay Sch., Southborough, Mass., 1950-70, Population Reference Bur., 1963-68, Daniel and Florence Guggenheim Found., 1972—; trustee, v.p., bd. overseers Marine Hist. Assn., Mystic, Conn., 1959—; bd. mgrs., mem. exec. com. Meml. Hosp. Cancer and Allied Diseases, 1959—; trustee, exec. com. Robert Coll., Istanbul, Turkey, 1952-73, chmn., 1955-63; bd. dirs., v.p. English Speaking Union U.S., 1950—; bd. dirs., mem. exec. com. Winston Churchill Meml. Fund., 1966—; trustee Planned Parenthood N.Y.C., 1977—. Served to lt. col. Gen. Staff Corps, AUS, 1942-46. Decorated Legion of Merit. Mem. Am. Bar Assn., Internat. Law Assn., Soc. Colonial Wars, Pilgrims of U.S., Council Fgn. Relations. Clubs: Century Assn., Yale (N.Y.C.); Wadawanuck (Stonington, Conn.). Home: 150 E 73d St New York NY 10021 Office: 9 W 57th St New York NY 10038

OGDEN, DANIEL MILLER, JR., former univ. dean, educator; b. Clarksburg, W.Va., Apr. 28, 1922; s. Daniel Miller and Mary (Maphis) O.; B.A. in Polit. Sci., Wash. State U., 1944; M.A., U. Chgo., 1947, Ph.D., 1949; m. Valeria Juan Munson, Dec. 28, 1946; children—Janeth Lee (Mrs. K. Jefferson Martin), Patricia Jo (Mrs. Brad R. Hunter), Daniel Munson. From instr. to asso. prof. Wash. State U., 1949-61; staff asst. resources program staff Office Sec., Dept. Interior, 1961-64, asst. dir. Bur. Outdoor Recreation, 1964-67, dir. of budget. Dept. Interior 1967-68; dean Colo. State U. Coll. Humanities and Social Scis., Fort Collins, 1968-76, prof., 1976—. Mem. profl. staff Com. Interstate and Fgn. Commerce, U.S. Senate, 1956-57; spl. asst. to chmn. Democratic Nat. Com., 1960-61; lectr. Exec. Seminar Center, U.S. Civil Service Commn., 1966—. Committeeman, Wash. Dem. Central Com., 1952-56; chmn. Whitman County Dem. Central Com., 1958-60. Served with AUS, 1943-46. Mem. Am., Western, Pacific N.W. polit sci. assns., Western Social Sci. Assn., Phi Beta Kappa, Phi Kappa Phi, Pi Sigma Alpha, Sigma Delta Chi. Unitarian. Co-author: Electing the President, rev. edit., 1968; American National Government, 7th edit., 1970; American State and Local Government, 5th edit., 1972; Washington Politics, 1960. Home: 1812 Seminole Dr Fort Collins CO 80521. *Principles which have guided my career are: willingness to accept conclusions of fact determined by the scientific method; uncompromising advocacy of the freedom of individual inquiry and of individual expression of belief; respect for the dignity and worth of each individual; insistence upon democratic procedures at all levels in reaching human decisions based upon value judgments; the conviction that man is infinitely capable of improving himself and his level of life by deliberate efforts; and appreciation of beauty in nature and the works of man.*

OGDEN, FREDERIC DORRANCE, coll. adminstr.; b. Orange County, N.Y., Oct. 11, 1915; s. Fred Dorrance and Florence Caroline (Young) O.; A.B., Tusculum Coll., Greeneville, Tenn., 1938; Ph.D., Johns Hopkins, 1951; m. Jessie Cupitt, June 10, 1943; children—Elisabeth (Mrs. C. Lance Churchill), Katharine (Mrs. Carlyle B. Cornell). Clk., Edgewood Arsenal, Md., 1940-41; asst. mgr. Civilian Personnel Field Office, OSW Wright-Patterson Field, Ohio, 1941-42; from instr. to asso. prof. polit. sci. U. Ala., 1946-61; prof. polit. sci., chmn. dept. Eastern Ky. U., Richmond, 1961-65, dean Coll. Arts and Scis., 1965-79, asso. v.p. planning, 1977—; Fulbright lectr. Indian Sch. Internat. Studies, New Delhi, 1957-58; dir. internat. relations workshop Appalachian State U., N.C., summers 1960-61. Mem. Com. to Select City Mgr., Richmond, 1971, Ky. Sci. and Tech. Adv. Council, 1967-71, Citizens Adv. Subcom. Ky. Legis. Compensation, 1974; moderator seminars on constnl. conv. Ky. Legis. Research Com., 1977; mem. Spl. Adv. Com. on Constn. (Ky.), 1978; council visitors Tusculum Coll., 1978—. Served with USAAF, 1942-45. Commonwealth fellow Commonwealth Studies Center, Duke, summer 1959. Mem. Am., So., Ky. (pres. 1964-65) polit. sci. assns., AAUP (chpt. pres. 1964-65), Am. Conf. Acad. Deans (dir. 1974-77, editor, sec. 1975-77), Council Colls. Arts and Scis., Inst. Internat. Edn. (chmn. selection com. scholarships to South Asia 1975-76), UN Assn. (v.p. Ky. 1963-65), Order Ky. Cols., Pi Sigma Alpha, Phi Kappa Phi. Democrat. Episcopalian. Author: The Poll Tax in the South, 1959; The Public Papers of Governor Keen Johnson; contbg. author Analysis of Social Problems. Editorial bd. Univ. Press Ky., 1969-79. Home: 212 College View Dr Richmond KY 40475

OGDEN, SCHUBERT MILES, theologian; b. Cin., Mar. 2, 1928; s. Edgar Carson and Neva Louetta (Glancy) O.; A.B., Ohio Wesleyan U., 1950, awarded Litt.D. (hon.), 1965; fellow Am. Council Learned Socs., Johns Hopkins, 1950-51; D.B., U. Chgo., 1954, Ph.D., 1958; m. Joyce Ellen Schwettman, Aug. 26, 1950; children—Alan Scott, Andrew Merrick. Ordained to ministry United Methodist Ch., 1958; mem. faculty Perkins Sch. Theology, So. Meth. U., 1956-69, asso. prof. theology, 1961-64, prof., 1964-69; univ. prof. theology Div. Sch., U. Chgo., 1969-72; prof. theology Perkins Sch. Theology, So. Meth. U., Dallas, 1972—, dir. grad. program in religious studies, 1974—; Merrick lectr. Ohio Wesleyan U., 1965; vis. fellow Council of Humanities, Princeton U., 1977-78. Fulbright research prof., also Guggenheim fellow Marburg (Germany) U., 1962-63. Mem. Am. Acad. Religion (pres. 1976-77), Soc. Values in Higher Edn., Am. Philos. Assn., Am. Theol. Soc., Phi Beta Kappa, Omicron Delta Kappa, Phi Mu Alpha. Author: Christ Without Myth, 1961, 2d edit., 1979; The Reality of God, 1966, 2d edit., 1977; Faith and Freedom, 1979. Editor, translator: Existence and Faith; Shorter Writings of Rudolf Bultmann, 1960. Editorial bd. Jour. Religion, 1972—, Jour. of Am. Acad. Religion, 1977—. Office: Perkins School of Theology Southern Methodist U Dallas TX 75275. *Of greater help to me than anything else in keeping my work and career in proper perspective are these questions of the Apostle Paul: "What have you that you did not receive? If then you received it, why do you boast as if it were not a gift?" (1 Cor. 4:7).*

OGDEN, SQUIRE REDMON, lawyer; b. Winchester, Ky., Sept. 9, 1898; s. William Baldwin and Margaret (Redmon) O.; A.B., Georgetown (Ky.) Coll., 1920, LL.D., 1957; LL.B., Harvard, 1923; m. Jean Hollingsworth Stewart, June 2, 1934; children—Stewart, William Baldwin, John Carter. Admitted to Ky. bar, 1922; practiced law as asso. Bruce, Bullitt, Gordon & Laurent, 1923-26; partner firm Gordon, Laurent & Ogden, 1926-30, Gordon, Laurent, Ogden & Galphin, 1930-40, Ogden Galphin, Tarrant & Street, Louisville, 1940-1948, Ogden, Galphin & Abell, 1948-58, Ogden, Robertson & Marshall, 1958—; gen. counsel Ky. Utilities Co., dir., mem. exec. com., 1952-77; gen. counsel Commonwealth Life Ins. Co., 1953-78, also dir., mem. exec. com., 1952-71. Tchr., Jefferson Sch. of Law, 1928-30. Former mem. exec. com. Louisville ARC, 1950-68; former trustee Georgetown (Ky.) Coll., 1940-43; bd. govs. J.B. Speed Art Mus.; trustee Louisville Country Day Sch., 1950-57; nat. chmn. Harvard Law Sch. Fund, 1963-65; mem. vis. com. Harvard Law Sch., 1963-70. Served as 2d lt., U.S. Army, 1918. Fellow Am. Bar Found.; mem. Assn. Life Ins. Counsel, Harvard Alumni Assn. (bd. dirs. 1954-55), English Speaking Union (pres. Ky. br. 1958), Newcomen Soc., Am., Ky., Louisville (pres. 1953) bar assns., Am. Law Inst., Harvard Law Sch. Assn. (exec. com. 1961-64), Filson Club, Kappa Alpha. So. Baptist. Clubs: Pendennis, River Valley, Louisville Country, Wynn-Stay (Louisville). Home: Mockingbird Valley Louisville KY 40207 Office: 1200 One Riverfront Plaza Louisville KY 40270

OGDON, THOMAS HAMMER, advt. exec.; b. Alexandria, Va., Apr. 16, 1935; s. William Duley and Juanita L. (Hammer) O.; B.A., Amherst Coll., 1957; m. Michele Scharf, Oct. 30, 1976; children—David Hekma, William Barry, Kristin Angela. Copy trainee Ted Bates Advt., 1957-58; copywriter Grey Advt., 1958-61; with Benton & Bowles Advt., N.Y.C., 1961-75, sr. v.p., mgmt. supr., 1971-75; sr. v.p., dir. and dir. client service Needham, Harper & Steers Advt. Inc., N.Y.C., 1975-78; v.p., exec. recruiter Russell Reynolds Assos., N.Y.C., 1979—. Trustee Norwich Devel. Corp., 1967. Bd. dirs. counseling and testing br. Greater N.Y. YMCA. Mem. Psi Upsilon. Republican. Clubs: University (N.Y.C.); Indian Harbor Yacht, Stanwich (founder) (Greenwich); Gipsy Trail. Home: New York NY 10016 Office: Russell Reynolds Assos Inc 245 Park Ave New York NY 10017

OGDON, WILBUR, educator; b. Redlands, Calif., Apr. 19, 1921; s. Alfred Benjamin and Ethel (Brooks) O.; B. Mus., U. Wis., 1942; M.A., Hamline U., 1947; postgrad. U. Calif. at Berkeley, 1949-50, Ecole Normale de Musique, Paris, 1952-53; Ph.D., Ind. U., 1955; m. Beverly Jean Porter, Aug. 22, 1958; children—Bethany, Benjamin, Erica. Asst. prof. U. Tex., 1947-50, Coll. St. Catherine, St. Paul, 1955-56; asso. prof. Ill. Wesleyan U., 1956-65; dir. music Pacifica Found., KPFA, Berkeley, Calif., 1962-64; coordinator music programming U. Ill., 1965-66; prof. music U. Cal. at San Diego, 1966—, chmn. dept. music, 1966-71, research fellow Project for Music Expt., 1973—. Bd. dirs. San Diego Opera Inc., 1967-70, La Jolla Civic Orch. and Chorus Assn., 1967-72; hon. dir. N.C. Gov.'s Bd. Music, 1964—. Served with AUS, 1942-46. Nat. Endowment of Arts fellow, 1975. Mem. Anton Webern Soc. (charter), Music Execs. Calif., Cal. Profl. Music Tchrs. Assn. (hon.). Author: Three Sea Choruses, 1960-62; String Quartet, 1960; Diversions for Concert Wind Ensemble, 1961; By the Isar, 1969; Un Tombeau de Cocteau, 1964, theater version, 1972; (with others) Horizons Circled, 1974; Two Confessions (opera scene), 1976. Home: 482 15th St Del Mar CA 92014 Office: Dept Music U Calif at San Diego La Jolla CA 92037. *As years pass, one becomes increasingly aware of an indebtedness to others: to those who taught, encouraged, tolerated and even sacrificed. That increasing sense of indebtedness serves to sustain one's own efforts to teach and encourage.*

OGG, JAMES ELVIS, microbiologist, educator; b. Centralia, Ill., Dec. 24, 1924; s. James and Amelia (Glammeyer) O.; B.S., U. Ill., 1949; Ph.D., Cornell U., 1956; m. Betty Jane Ackerson, Dec. 27, 1948; children—James George, Susan Kay. Bacteriologist, Biol. Labs., Ft. Detrick, Md., 1950-53, cons., 1953-56, med. bacteriologist, 1956-58; prof. microbiology, Colo. State U., Ft. Collins, 1958—, asst. dean Grad. Sch., 1965-66, head dept. microbiology, 1967-77; dir. Advanced Sci. Edn. Program div. grad. edn. in sci. NSF, Washington, 1966-67; Fulbright-Hays sr. lectr. in microbiology, Nepal, 1976-77. Cons. NASA, 1968-69, NSF, 1968-73, Martin Marietta Corp., 1970—; cons.-evaluator North Central Assn. Colls. and Secondary Schs., 1974—. Served with AUS, 1943-46, 50-51. Fellow AAAS, Am. Acad. Microbiology; mem. Am. Soc. Microbiology (chmn. pub. service and adult edn. com. 1975—), Soc. Indsl. Microbiology, Colo.-Wyo. Acad. Sci., Fulbright Alumni Assn., Sigma Xi, Gamma Sigma Delta. Contbr. articles to profl. jours. Home: 768 Eastdale Dr Fort Collins CO 80524

OGIER, WALTER THOMAS, educator; b. Pasadena, Calif., June 18, 1925; s. Walter Williams and Aileen Vera (Polhamus) O.; B.S., Calif. Inst. Tech., 1947, Ph.D. in Physics, 1953; m. Mayrene Miriam Gorton, June 27, 1954; children—Walter Charles, Margaret Miriam, Thomas Earl, Kathryn Aileen. Research fellow Calif. Inst. Tech., 1953; instr. U. Calif. at Riverside, 1954-55, asst. prof. physics, 1955-60, asst. prof. physics Pomona Coll., Claremont, Calif., 1960-62, asso. prof., 1962-67, prof. physics, 1967—, chmn. dept., 1972—. Served with USNR, 1944-46. NSF Sci. Faculty fellow, 1966-67. Mem. AAAS, N.Y. Acad. Scis., Am. Phys. Soc., Am. Assn. Physics Tchrs. (pres. So. Calif. sect. 1967-69), Tau Beta Pi. Contbr. articles on metals, X-rays and proton produced X-rays to profl. jours. Home: 717 W 8th St Claremont CA 91711

OGILBY, LYMAN CUNNINGHAM, bishop; b. Hartford, Conn., Jan. 25, 1922; s. Remsen B. and Lois M. (Cunningham) O.; B.S., Hamilton Coll., 1943, D.D., 1963; B.D., Episcopal Theol. Sch., 1949; D.D., Trinity Coll., 1954; Ruth Dale, Nov. 4, 1953; children—Peter R., Lois E., Henry A. Ordained deacon Episcopal Ch., 1949, priest, 1950; chaplain, tchr. Brent Sch., Baguio, Philippines, 1949-53, asst. priest Epiphany Mission, 1950-53; suffragan bishop Philippines, 1953-57, bishop of Philippines, 1957-67; bishop coadjutor S.D., Sioux Falls, 1967-70; Procter fellow, lectr. Christian mission Episcopal Theol. Sch., Cambridge, Mass., 1970-71; asst. bishop of Pa., 1971-73, bishop-coadjutor of Pa., 1973, bishop, 1974—. Sec. Council Ch. of S.E. Asia, 1960-67; chmn. conv. Nat. Council Chs., Philippines, 1962-63; vice chmn. Nat. Council Chs. Philippines, 1963-65; sec. S.D. Council Chs., 1968-70. Chmn. bd. govs. St. Luke's Hosp., Quezon City, Philippines; chmn. trustees Brent Sch., Baguio, 1957-67; trustee Am. Assn. Philippines, 1960-62; chmn. bd. council Epis. Community Services, Diocese of Pa., 1974—; alumni trustee Hamilton Coll., Clinton, N.Y., 1975-79; bd. dirs. Met. Christian Council Phila., 1971—; trustee Gen. Theol. Sem., N.Y.C., 1973-79. Served as lt. USNR, 1943-46. Author articles, essays. Home: 316 N Princeton Ave Swarthmore PA 19081

OGILVIE, LLOYD JOHN, clergyman; b. Kenosha, Wis., Sept. 2, 1930; s. Vard Spencer and Katherine (Jacobson) O.; B.A., Lake Forest Coll., 1952, Garrett Theol. Sem., 1956; postgrad. New Coll., U. Edinburgh (Scotland), 1955-56; D.D., Whitworth Coll., 1973; L.H.D., U. Redlands, 1974; D.Humanities, Moravian Coll., 1975; m. Mary Jane Jenkins, Mar. 25, 1951; children—Heather Anne Ogilvie Sholl, Scott Varde, Andrew Ghiee. Ordained to ministry Presbyn. Ch., 1956; student pastor, Gurnee, Ill., 1952-56; first pastor Winnetka (Ill.) Presbyn. Ch., 1956-62; pastor 1st Presbyn. Ch., Bethlehem, Pa., 1962-72, 1st Presbyn. Ch., Hollywood, Calif., 1972—; preacher Chgo. Sunday Evening Club, 1962—, also frequent radio and TV host weekly syndicated TV program Let God Love You. Bd. dirs. Hollywood Presbyn. Hosp. Author: A Life Full of Surprises, 1969; Let God Love You, 1974; If I Should Wake Before I Die, 1973; Lord of the Ups and Downs, 1974; You've Got Charisma, 1975; Cup of Wonder, 1976; Life Without Limits, 1976; Drumbeat of Love, 1977; When God First Thought of You, 1978; The Autobiography of God, 1979; The Bush Is Still Burning, 1979. Office: 1760 N Gower St Hollywood CA 90028

OGILVIE, RICHARD BUELL, lawyer; b. Kansas City, Mo., Feb. 22, 1923; s. Kenneth S. and Edna Mae (Buell) O.; B.A., Yale, 1947; J.D., LL.D. (hon.), Chgo.-Kent Coll. Law, 1949; LL.D. (hon.), Lincoln Coll., Millikin U., Ill. Wesleyan U., Lake Forest Coll.,

MacMurray Coll., Greenville Coll.; m. Dorothy Louise Shriver, Feb. 11, 1950; 1 dau., Elizabeth. Admitted to Ill. bar, 1950; practiced in Chgo., 1950-54, 55-58, 61-62, 73—; asst. U.S. atty., Chgo., 1954-55; spl. asst. to U.S. Atty. Gen., Chgo., 1958-61; sheriff Cook County, Ill., 1962-66; pres. Bd. Commrs. Cook County, 1966-68; gov. of Ill., 1968-73; partner firm Isham, Lincoln & Beale, 1973—; trustee Chgo., Milw. & St. Paul Railroad Co.; dir. Jewel Cos., CNA Fin. Corp., Fansteel Corp., LaSalle St. Fund, Chgo. Bd. Options Exchange. Chmn. Young Republican Orgn. Cook County, 1953-54. Served with AUS, 1942-45. Mem. Am., Ill., Chgo., Fed. bar assns., Phi Alpha Delta, Beta Theta Pi. Republican. Presbyn. Mason. Clubs: Chicago, Glen View, Tavern, Old Elm, Casino; Sangamo. Home: 1500 N Lake Shore Dr Chicago IL 60610 Office: 1 First Nat Plaza Chicago IL 60670

OGILVIE, RICHARD IAN, clin. pharmacologist; b. Sudbury, Ont., Can., Oct. 9, 1936; s. Patrick Ian and Gena Hilda (Olson) O.; M.D., U. Toronto, 1960; m. Ernestine Tahedl, Oct. 9, 1965; children—Degen Elisabeth, Lars Ian. Intern, Toronto (Ont.) Gen. Hosp., 1960-61; resident Montreal Gen. and Univ. Alta. hosps., 1962-66; fellow in clin. pharmacology McGill U., Montreal, 1966-68, asst. prof. medicine, pharmacology and therapeutics, 1968-73, asso. prof., 1973-78, prof., 1978—, chmn. dept. pharmacology and therapeutics, 1978—; clin. pharmacologist Montreal Gen. Hosp., 1968—, dir. div. clin. pharmacology, 1976—. Grantee Med. Research Council Can., Quebec Heart Found., Can. Kidney Found., J.C. Edwards Found., Can. Found. Advancement Therapeutics, Conseil de la recherche en santé du Québec. Mem. Can. Soc. Clin. Investigation (council 1977—), Can. Hypertension Soc. (dir. 1979—), Can. Found. Advancement Clin. Pharmacology (dir. 1978—), Can Clin. Pharm. Soc. (pres. 1979—), Que. Heart Found. (pres. med. adv. com. 1976—), Pharm. Soc. Can., Can. Cardiovascular Soc., Am. Soc. Pharmacology and Exptl. Therapeutics, Am. Soc. Clin. Pharm., Am. Fedn. Clin. Research. Home: 1066 Rue Béique Mont Saint Hilaire PQ J3G 4S6 Canada Office: 3655 Drummond St Montreal PQ H3G 1Y6 Canada

OGILVIE, ROBERT EDWARD, educator; b. Wallace, Idaho, Sept. 25, 1923; s. Robert Leslie and Mary Ann (Nelson) O.; student Gonzaga U., 1946-47; B.S., U. Wash., 1950; S.M., Mass. Inst. Tech., 1952, Metall. Engr., 1954, ScD., 1955; children—Claudia Jean, Mary Lee, Robert Scott. Mem. faculty Mass. Inst. Tech., 1950—, prof. metallurgy, 1966—; dir. research Advanced Metals Research, Burlington, Mass., 1958—; visitor research lab. Boston Mus. Fine Arts, 1968. Served with USNR, 1943-45. Mem. Am. Soc. Metals, Am. Inst. M.E., ASTM, Electron Probe Analysis Soc. Am., Sigma Xi. Club: New Bedford Yacht. Patentee in field. Home: 2 Locke Ln Lexington MA 02173 Office: 77 Massachusetts Ave Cambridge MA 02139

OGILVIE, WILLIAM KAY, educator; b. Appleton, Wis., Nov. 1, 1916; s. Alexander and Dorothy (Grimmond) O.; B.S., LaCrosse State Coll., 1938; M.A., State U. Iowa, 1939; M.S. in Edn., U. Calif. at Los Angeles, 1951; Ed.D., Ind. U., 1955; m. Janis Carson, 1943; children—Judith Kay, Deborah Ann, Stewart Carson. Tchr. pub. schs., Appleton, 1940-41, San Luis Obispo, Calif., 1952-53; instr. Ind. U., 1954-55; asst. prof. to prof. No. Ill. U., DeKalb, 1955—, chmn. secondary edn., 1960-63, coordinator Community Coll. Service Center, 1964-66, dir. Community Coll. Services, 1966-72; Distinguished vis. lectr. Utah State U., summer 1972; vis. prof. Scottish Further Edn. Authority, 1974. Mem. Inter-Univ. Bur. for Jr. Colls., 1960-65; participant Berkeley Research Conf., Center for Research and Devel. in Higher Edn., U. Calif., 1969; vice chmn. Ill. Joint Council Com. on Articulation, 1969-72; chmn. Ill. Bd. Higher Edn. articulation study com., 1970-71. Served to maj. AUS, 1941-46, 51-52. Mem. N.E.A. (vice-chmn. adv. com. higher edn. 1969-70), Nat. Assn. Coll. and Univ. Adminstrs. (pres. 1969-71), Wis. Hist. Soc. Author: (with Max Raines) Perspectives on the Community-Junior College, 1970. Editor: Abstracts of Graduate Studies: Community (Junior) College, 1965-72. Mem. editorial bd. Community/Jr. Coll. Research Quar., 1976—. Contbr. articles to profl. jours. Home: 309 Knollwood Dr DeKalb IL 60115

OGILVY, DAVID MACKENZIE, advt. agy. exec.; b. West Horsley, Eng., June 23, 1911; s. Francis John Longley and Dorothy (Fairfield) O.; came to U.S., 1938; ed. Fettes Coll., Edinburgh, 1924-29, Christ Church, Oxford, 1929-31; Litt.D. (hon.), Adelphi U., 1977; m. Herta Lans, July 6, 1973; 1 son, David Fairfield. Asso. dir. Audience Research Inst., Princeton, 1939-42; with Brit. Security Coordination, 1942-44; 2d sec. Brit. embassy, Washington, 1944-45; founder, later chmn. Ogilvy & Mather, advt. agy., N.Y.C., 1948-73, chmn. bd., 1961-75, creative dir., 1973—. Chmn. pub. participation com. Lincoln Center, 1959; trustee Colby Coll., 1963-69; bd. dirs. N.Y. Philharmonic, 1957-67; chmn. United Negro Coll. Fund, 1968; trustee, mem. exec. council World Wildlife Fund Internat., 1975—. Decorated comdr. Order Brit. Empire; recipient Parlin award Am. Mktg. Assn., 1972; elected to Advt. Hall of Fame, 1977. Mem. Am. Assn. Advt. Agys. (gov. Eastern region 1959-61). Club: Brook (N.Y.C.). Author: Confessions of an Advertising Man, 1963; Blood, Brains and Beer, 1978. Home: Château de Touffou 86300 Bonnes France Office: 2 E 48th St New York City NY 10017

OGILVY, STEWART MARKS, editorial cons.; b. Winnipeg, Man., Can., Apr. 22, 1914; s. Ralph Wardlaw and May (Marks) O.; came to U.S., 1923, naturalized, 1943; grad. Kent Sch., 1932; B.S., Trinity Coll., Hartford, Conn., 1936; m. Barbara C. Swift, Feb. 4, 1961 (div. 1964); m. 2d, Avis Bigelow Reynick, Nov. 14, 1964. Instrn. asst. in English and fine arts Trinity Coll., 1936-37; promotion writer N.Y. Times, 1937-42; asso. copy dir. Muir & Co., advt., 1942-44; copywriter McCann-Erickson, Inc., 1944-46; mng. editor World Govt. News, N.Y.C., 1946-52; promotion writer Fortune mag., N.Y.C., 1952-57, writer editorial dept., 1957-61, asso. editor, 1961-69; exec. dir. Hugh Moore Fund, N.Y.C., 1969-71; editor-exec. Population Inst., N.Y.C., 1972-79; editorial cons., 1979—. Mem. N.Y. exec. bd. Fed. Union, Inc., 1939-41; editor N.Y. Corr., 1939-41; bd. dirs., sec., treas., publs. chmn. World Federalists, 1941-47; rep. World Federalists U.S.A. on U.S. Council Movement World Fed. Govt., 1946-47; chmn. nat. publs. com. United World Federalists, acting exec. dir., 1947; v.p. Friends of the Earth, 1969-76, bd. dirs., 1969-78, hon. pres., 1978—; v.p. Friends of Earth Found., 1972-78, dir. emeritus, 1978—; mem. adv. bd. Scenic Hudson Preservation Conf., 1970—; v.p. Negative Population Growth, Inc., 1972-73; adv. council Zero Population Growth, N.Y.C., 1973—. Bd. dirs. Am. Movement for World Govt., 1970—. Recipient Alumni medal for excellence Trinity Coll., 1963, Spl. Achievement award Sierra Club, 1966. Fellow Trinity Coll., 1957-63. Mem. Alpha Delta Phi. Democrat. Episcopalian. Club: Sierra (editor Argonaut 1957-59, chmn. Atlantic chpt. 1960-61). Editorial bd. World Peace News, 1974—. Contbr. articles, brochures, books and mags. Home: 7933 Willow St New Orleans LA 70118

OGLE, JANE HUTCHINSON, editor; b. N.Y.C.; d. George E. and Alma A. (Hodgson) Hutchinson; B.A., Smith Coll., 1944; m. Laird Ogle, Oct. 1, 1949. Fashion editor Vogue, 1944-49, sr. writer, 1964-72, beauty and health editor, 1977—; fashion editor Flair, 1949-51; fashion copywriter Harper's Bazaar, 1951-58, articles and health editor, 1972-77; advt. Elizabeth Arden account Hockaday Co., 1958-60; advt. mgr. Elizabeth Arden, 1960-64. Office: 350 Madison Ave New York City NY 10017

OGLESBY, DANIEL KIRKLAND, JR., hosp. adminstr.; b. Gastonia, N.C., Sept. 15, 1930; s. Daniel K. and Bettie Amelia (Smith) O.; B.S., Davidson Coll., 1952; certificate in hosp. adminstrn. Duke U., 1954; m. Bobbie Jean Owen, Apr. 4, 1953; children—Debra Lynn, Kathie Owen, Bettie Lee. Asst. adminstr. Blount Meml. Hosp., Maryville, Tenn., 1954-55; adminstr. Union Meml. Hosp., Monroe, N.C., 1955-59, Scotland Meml. Hosp., Laurinburg, N.C., 1959-67; adminstr. Anderson (S.C.) Meml. Hosp., 1967-77, pres., 1977—; dir. Anderson County Health Planning Council. Bd. dirs. Anderson County United Fund. Recipient Community Achievement certificate Laurinburg C. of C. Fellow Am. Coll. Hosp. Adminstrs. (council regents 1971-77); mem. Am. (del.), S.C. (dir., past pres.) hosp. assns., Southeastern Hosp. Conf. (dir., chmn.), Carolinas Hosp. and Health Services Inc. (dir., past pres.), Hosp. Data Center S.C. (dir.), Anderson Area C. of C. (v.p. 1976-77). Methodist. Club: Rotary (past chpts. pres.). Home: 1202 Melbourne Dr Anderson SC 29621 Office: 800 N Fant St Anderson SC 29621

OGNIBENE, ANDRE J(OHN), physician, army officer; b. N.Y.C., Nov. 18, 1931; s. Morris S. and Josephine C. (Macaluso) O.; B.A. cum laude, Columbia U., 1952; M.D., N.Y. U., 1956; m. Margaret A. Haug, Apr. 21, 1957; children— Judy, Andrea, Adrienne, Marc, Eric. Intern in medicine Bellevue Hosp., N.Y.C., 1956-57, resident in medicine, 1957-59; commd. capt. U.S. Army M.C., 1957, advanced through grades to brig. gen., 1978; resident in medicine Manhattan VA Hosp., N.Y.C. and chief resident in medicine, 1959-60; chief med. service U.S. Army Hosp., Nurnburg, Germany, 1961-62, chief dept. medicine, 1962-64; fellow in cardiology Walter Reed Gen. Hosp., Washington, 1964-65, asst. in cardiology, 1965-66, asst. chief dept. medicine, 1969-72; chief dept. medicine, chief profl. services U.S. Army Hosp., Ft. Meade, Md., 1966-68; cons. in medicine Hdqrs., U.S. Army, Vietnam, 1969; chief dept. medicine Brooke Army Med. Center, Ft. Sam Houston, Tex., 1972-76, dir. med. edn., 1976-78, dep. commdr. and chief profl. services, 1976-78, comdr., 1978—; instr. in medicine N.Y. Coll. Medicine, 1960; asso. clin. prof. Georgetown U., 1970-72; clin. prof. U. Tex. Health Sci. Center, San Antonio, 1973—, mem. postgrad. adv. com., 1977-78; bd. dirs., chmn. com. employee health edn. Bexar County (Tex.) unit Am. Cancer Soc. Bd. govs. S.W. Cancer Therapy Inst. Decorated Legion of Merit, Meritorious Service medal, Army Commendation medal. Diplomate Am. Bd. Internal Medicine. Fellow A.C.P.; mem. AMA, N.Y. Acad. Scis., Fedn. Clin. Research, Bexar County Med. Soc., Greater San Antonio C. of C. Contbr. articles to med. publs.; editor-in-chief: Internal Medicine in Vietnam, vol. I, 1977. Home: 6035 Winding Ridge San Antonio TX 78239 Office: Brooke Army Med Center Fort Sam Houston TX 78234

O'GORMAN, HELEN FOWLER, sculptor, painter, author; b. Superior, Wis., Aug. 29, 1904; d. Homer T. and Fannie Elizabeth (Alger) Fowler; student Bradford Jr. Coll., 1922; B.F.A., U. Wash., 1925; postgrad. Chouinard Sch. Art, 1930-31, student of Alexander Archipenko, 1931-37; m. Henry Coe Lanpher, Dec. 13, 1926 (div. 1939); 1 dau., Florence May (Mrs. Peter D. Ellis); m. 2d, Juan O'Gorman, Aug. 7, 1940; 1 dau., Maria Elena. Exhibited sculpture in group shows Los Angeles Mus., 1935, 36, 47th Annual Exhbn. Am. Painting and Sculpture, Art Inst. Chgo., 1936, 37, 38, N.Y. World's Fair, 1939, 40; exhibited paintings Salon de Pintura, Mexico City, 1943; one-man show Museo Nacional de Artes Plasticas, Palacio de Bellas Artes, Mexico, 1953. Bd. dirs. Botanical Gardens Universidad Nacional Autonoma de Mexico; mem. bd. examiners, lectrs., jurors and critics Inst. Allende, Guanajuato, Mexico. Recipient Order of the Delta Gamma Rose, 1975. Mem. Sociedad Botanica de Mexico, Sociedad Mexicana de Cactologia, Asociacion Mexicana de Orquidelogia, Mexico City Garden Club (hon.). Author, illustrator Mexican Flowering Trees and Plants, 1961; Plantas y Flores de Mexico, 1963. Columnist The News, Mexico City, 1953-56. Address: Calle Jardin 88 San Angel Inn Mexico 20 DF Mexico

O'GORMAN, JUAN, architect, artist; b. Coyoacan, D.F., Mexico, July 6, 1905; s. Cecil Crawford and Encarnacion (O'Gorman) O'G.; Architect deg., Nat. U. Mexico, 1926; m. Helen Fowler, Aug. 7, 1940; 1 dau., Maria Elena O'Gorman, Aug. 31, 1956. With C. Obregon Santacillia and J. Villagran, architects, 1926-29; pvt. practice architecture, 1929-32; prof. sch. engring. Politechnical Inst., Mexico City, 1932—; head dept. architecture Secretariat of Pub. Edn., 1932-35. Works include murals for Mexico City Air Port, Patzcuaro (Mich.) Library, (frescoes) Castle Chapultepec, (fresco) Banco Internacional S.A., (fresco) Center Social Studies Unidad Independencia (all Mexico City), (mosaic) Hotel Pasada de la Mision, Taxco, Guerrero, Mexico, (mosaic) Santiago, Chile; mosaics for the Library of the U. City of Mexico, Secretariat Pub. Works and Communications bldgs.; mosaics for Conv. Center Bldg., Hemisfair, San Antonio; one-man show easel paintings Palace of Fine Arts, Mexico City, 1950; paintings in permanent exhbn. Modern Mus. Art, N.Y.C., Palace of Fine Arts, Mexico City. Recipient Elias Sourasky prize, 1967; Nat. Prize for Arts, 1972. Mem. Acad. Arts Mexico, Council of Superior Edn. and Sci. Investigation, Mexican Soc. Architects. Author booklets and mag. articles on art and architecutre. Address: Calle Jardin 88 San Angel Inn Mexico 20 DF Mexico

O'GORMAN, NED, poet; b. 1931; A.B., St. Michael's Coll.; A.M., Columbia; 1 son, Richard. Author: The Night of the Hammer, 1961; Adam Before His Mirror, 1963; The Buzzard and the Peacock, 1965; The Harvesters' Vase, 1968; The Storefront: A Community of Children on Madison Avenue and 129th Street, 1970; (children's book) The Blue Butterfly, 1971; (poetry) The Flag the Hawk Flies, 1972; The Wilderness and the Laurel Tree: A Guide for Parents and Teachers on the Observation of Children, 1972; The Children Are Dying, 1978. Tchr. Bklyn. Coll., New Sch. Social Research, Manhattan Coll.; Am. studies specialist State Dept. in toured Chile, Argentina and Brazil, 1966. Bd. dirs. Fifth Ave Center of Harlem, The Childrens' Storefront Sch. Guggenheim fellow, 1956, 62; Rockefeller Found. Centre for Study fellow, Eng., 1972, Bellagio, Italy, 1977. Club: Metropolitan Opera. Sr. editor Jubilee mag., 1962-65; editor Prophetic Voices: Ideas and Words on Revolution, 1969. Address: 60 W 66th St New York City NY 10023

OGRA, PEARAY L., physician, educator; b. Srinagar, Kashmir, India, Mar. 19, 1939; s. Govinda Kaul and Gunvati (Daftari) O.; came to U.S., 1961, naturalized, 1969; M.B. B.S., Christian Med. Coll., Ludhiana, India, 1961; m. Swatantarta Seekree, Feb. 18, 1967; children—Sanjay, Monica. Intern, Binghamton (N.Y.) Gen. Hosp., 1962; resident U. Chgo., 1964, N.Y. U.-Bellevue Med Center, 1965; asst. prof. pediatrics SUNY, Buffalo, 1968-71, asso. prof. pediatrics and microbiology, 1972-74, prof., 1974—; dir. div. virology Children's Hosp. Buffalo, 1969—; cons. Erie County Virus Lab., West Seneca (N.Y.) Devel. Center. Buswell fellow, 1968-71; recipient E. Mead Johnson award for Pediatric Research, 1978. Fellow Royal Soc. Medicine, A.C.P., Am. Acad. Pediatrics, Am. Acad. Microbiology; mem. Am. Soc. Clin. Investigation, Soc. Pediatric Research, Infectious Disease Soc. Am., Soc. Exptl. Biology and Medicine, Am. Assn. Immunologists, Am. Soc. Microbiology, AAAS, Am. Fedn. Clin. Research, Reticuloendothelial Soc. Home: 79 Shadow Wood Dr East Amherst NY 14051 Office: 219 Bryant St Buffalo NY 14222

O'GRADY, GERALD PATRICK, former airline exec.; b. St. Albans, Vt., Jan. 9, 1914; s. James E. and Harriet M. (Coleman) O'G.; A.B. magna cum laude, Tufts Coll., 1935; LL.B., Georgetown U., 1939; m. Mary McDuffie, Nov. 10, 1942; children—Gerald Patrick, Kevin E. Admitted to D.C. bar, 1938, Calif. bar, 1971, U.S. Supreme Ct. bar, 1972; atty. CAB, Washington, 1939-41; asso. Whiteford, Hart, Carmody & Wilson, Washington, 1941-46; practice law, Washington, 1947-67; v.p. Western Air Lines, Inc., Los Angeles, 1967-72, sr. v.p., 1972-79; ret., 1979; dir. Pacific No. Airlines, Inc., 1947-67. Mem. Am., Fed., Los Angeles County bar assns., State Bar Calif., Am. Judicature Soc., Phi Beta Kappa, Alpha Sigma Phi. Clubs: Congl. Country (Washington); North Ranch Country. Home: 1716 Royal St George Dr Westlake Village CA 91361

O'GRADY, JAMES EDWARD, city ofcl.; b. Chgo., Jan. 21, 1929; s. Thomas Francis and Nora C. (Kearns) O'G.; grad. So. Police Inst. U. Louisville, 1962; B.A., DePaul U., 1978; m. Joan B. Koziol, July 30, 1955; children—Margaret, James T., Michael J., John P., Joanne. With Chgo. Police Dept., 1952—, lt., 1965-69, capt., 1969-71, dist. commdr., 1971-74, dep. chief detectives, 1974-76, chief detectives, 1976-78, supt. police, 1978-79. Recipient Chgo. Police Dept. Blue Star award. Mem. Am. Assn. Profl. Law Enforcement, Internat. Assn. Chiefs Police, Ill. Assn. Chiefs of Police, Ill. Police Assn., Fraternal Order Police. Roman Catholic. Clubs: Ill. Athletic, K. of C. Office: 1121 S State St Chicago IL 60605

O'GRADY, JOHN FERGUS, bishop; b. Macton, Ont., Can., July 27, 1908; s. Edward and Helen (Frith) O'G.; student St. John's Coll., Edmonton, Alta., Can., 1922-27, Oblate Sem., Ottawa, Ont., 1931-35. Ordained priest Roman Catholic Ch., 1934; asst. pastor St. Augustine's Parish, Vancouver, B.C., Can., 1935-36; superior, prin. St. Mary's Indian Reservation Sch., Mission, B.C., 1936-39, Kamloops (B.C.) Indian Reservation Sch., 1939-52, Cariboo Indian Reservation Sch., Williams Laake, B.C., 1952-53; provincial English oblates Can., 1953-56; bishop of Prince George, B.C., Can., 1956—. A founder integrated Indian schs.; founder Prince George Coll., 1962, Frontier apostolate, 1958. Address: College Rd Prince George BC V2N 2K6 Canada*

O'GRADY, JOSEPH GABRIEL, research and testing lab. exec.; b. North Bergen, N.J., Mar. 21, 1927; s. Michael J. and Anne (Kenny) O'G.; B.E.E., N.Y. U., 1954; m. Muriel Catherine Cotter, May 11, 1957; children—John, Brian, Peter. Mgr. energy lab. Public Service Electric and Gas Co., Maplewood, N.J., 1968-78; dir. research and testing lab. PSE&G Research Corp. subs. Public Service Electric and Gas Co., Maplewood, 1978—, v.p., 1978—. Served with USN, 1945-46, 51. Registered profl. engr., N.J. Mem. IEEE, ASTM (dir. 1974—, pres. 1978-79), Am. Assn. Lab. Accreditation (dir. 1978—), Edison Electric Inst. (chmn. standards com. 1979—). Roman Catholic. Home: 11 Bowling Dr Livingston NJ 07039 Office: 200 Boyden Ave Maplewood NJ 07040

OGRAM, GORDON FERN, physician, state govt. ofcl.; b. Youngstown, Ohio, Mar. 14, 1921; s. Jay Melvin and Florence (McFetrich) O.; A.B., Wittenberg U., 1943; M.D., Ohio State U., 1950; m. Doris Louise Keim, June 24, 1944; children—Beverly Ruth, Jeffrey Martin, Carolyn Kay, Hallie Gail. Intern USPHS Hosp., Detroit, 1951; resident Columbus (Ohio) State Hosp., 1951-53, Univ. hosps., Cleve., 1955-56; teaching fellow child psychiatry Western Res. U., 1956-57; med. dir. Erie (Ohio) County Guidance Center, Sandusky, 1957-64; supt. Athens (Ohio) State Hosp., 1964-67; asst. commr. mental health State of Ohio, 1967-72, chief Bur. Hosps., 1969-72, chief Bur. Community Services, 1969-72, dep. commr. mental health, 1972, commr., 1972-76; med. dir. Tiffin (Ohio) Mental Health and Mental Retardation Center, 1976—. Served with USNR, 1943-46; col. U.S. Army Res. Diplomate Am. Bd. Psychiatry and Neurology; certified Am. Bd. Psychiat. Adminstrn. Fellow Am. Psychiat. Assn. Home and office: PO Box 8 Tiffin OH 44883

O'GREEN, FREDERICK W., multi-industry co. exec.; b. Mason City, Iowa, Mar. 25, 1921; s. Oscar A. and Anna (Heikkinen) O'G.; student Mason City Jr. Coll., 1939-40; B.S. in Elec. Engring., Iowa State U., 1943; M.S. in Elec. Engring., U. Md., 1949; LL.D. (hon.), Pepperdine U., 1977; m. Mildred G. Ludlow, Mar. 21, 1943; children—Susan Renee, Jane Lynn O'Green Koenig, John Frederick, Eric Stephen. Project engr. Naval Ordnance Lab., White Oak, Md., 1943-55; dir. Agena D project Lockheed Aircraft Co., Sunnyvale, Calif., 1955-62; v.p. Litton Industries, Inc., Beverly Hills, Calif., 1962-66, sr. v.p., 1966-68, exec. v.p., 1968-74, pres., 1974—. Served with USNR, 1945. Recipient Meritorious Civilian Service award U.S. Navy, 1954; Outstanding Achievement award Air Force Systems Command, 1964; Distinguished Achievement citation Iowa State U., 1973. Mem. AIM, AIAA, U.S. C. of C., Assn. U.S. Army, Phi Kappa Psi, Phi Mu Alpha. Republican. Lutheran. Office: Litton Industries Inc 360 N Crescent Dr Beverly Hills CA 90210

OGREN, CARROLL WOODROW, hosp. adminstr.; b. Mpls., Mar. 22, 1927; s. Peter L. and Mabel (Wohleen) O.; B.A., U. Minn., 1952; M.Hosp. Adminstrn., Washington U., St. Louis, 1958. Asst. adminstr. Washoe Med. Center, Reno, 1958-64, adminstr., 1964—. Served with USNR, 1944-46, 50-54; PTO. Mem. Am. Coll. Hosp. Adminstrs., Am. (nat. com. state hosp. assns. 1967—), Nev. (pres. 1961-62, sec. 1961-66) hosp. assns. Club: Gourmet Toastmasters (pres. 1960) (Reno). Home: 2085 Dant Blvd Reno NV 89509 Office: 77 Pringle Way Reno NV 89502

OGREN, WILLIAM W., steel co. exec.; b. 1922; B.S. in Engring., Iowa State U., 1949; m. Betty Rayburn; children—Nancy, Jeffrey. With Alan Wood Steel Co., Conshohocken, Pa., 1955-76, v.p., gen. mgr. subsidiary Penco Products, Inc., 1963-66, pres., 1966-72, pres., chief operating officer parent co., 1972-76, also dir.; v.p. Victor Henry Assos., Cherry Hill, N.J., 1976-79; gen. mgr. indsl. products div. Republic Steel Corp., Canton, Ohio, 1979—.

OGRYZLO, ELMER ALEXANDER, chemist, educator; b. Dauphin, Man., Canada, Aug. 18, 1933; s. Alexander Edward and Pearl (Solomon) O.; B.Sc., U. Man., 1955, M.Sc., 1956; Ph.D., McGill U., 1959; m. Marie Trofimiak, Aug. 22, 1959; children—Janet R., Michael M., Mark A., Karen L. Postdoctoral fellow U. Sheffield, Eng., 1958-59; instr. chemistry U. B.C., 1959-62, asst. prof., 1962-66, asso. prof., 1966-72, prof., 1972—; vis. prof. U. Amsterdam, 1966-67, Cambridge (Eng.) U., 1972-73, UCLA, 1979—. Nat. Research Council Can. fellow, 1955-58, 66-67; Exhibition of 1851 Overseas scholar, 1958-59. Mem. Chem. Inst. Canada, Am. Chem. Soc. Mem. editorial bd. Jour. of Photochemistry, 1972—; contbr. articles in field to profl. jours. Home: 2810 W 31st Ave Vancouver BC V6L 2A2 Canada Office: 2075 Wesbrook Mall Vancouver BC V6T 1W5 Canada

OGURA, JOSEPH H., educator; b. San Francisco, May 25, 1915; s. Kikuji and Agnes (Akita) O.; B.A., U. Calif. at Berkeley, 1937; M.D., U. Calif. at San Francisco, 1941; m. Ruth Miyamoto, July 15, 1942; children—Susan, John, Peter. Instr., U. Calif. at San Francisco Med. Sch., 1942, U. Cin. Med. Sch., 1942-45; resident otolaryngology Washington U. Sch. Medicine, St. Louis, 1945-48, mem. faculty, 1948—, prof. otolaryngology, 1960—, Lindburg prof., head dept., 1966—. Mem. council Nat. Inst. Neurol. Diseases and Stroke, 1968—; mem. nat. cancer adv. bd. Nat. Cancer Inst. Recipient Semon award, 1977. Diplomate Am. Bd. Otolaryngology (bd. dirs.). Fellow A.C.S. (mem. coll. program com., adv. council for otorhinolaryngology); mem. Triological Soc. (editor jour. 1968—, v.p. middle sect. 1970, pres. 1976—), Am. Laryngol. Assn. (Newcomb award 1967, Casselberry award 1968, Modern Medicine award 1971, pres. 1974, de Roaldes award 1979), Am. Soc. Head and Neck Surgery (pres. 1963-65), Soc. Head and Neck Surgeons, James Ewing Soc., Am. Acad. Ophthalmology and Otolaryngology, (v.p.), Am. Coll. Chest Physicians, AMA, Am. Soc. U. Otolaryngologists, Am. Otolaryngol. Assn. (pres. 1975), Am. Acad. Facial Plastic and Reconstructive Surgery, Collegium Oto-Rhino-Larynologicum Amicitiae Sacrum, Am. Broncho-Esophologic Assn., AAUP, Am. Soc. Ophthal. and Otolargy Allergists, Soc. Acad. Chmn. in Otolaryngology (pres.). Contbr. articles to profl. jours.; author chpts. in books. Home: 1038 Winwood Dr Saint Louis MO 63124

O'HAIR, MADALYN MAYS (MRS. RICHARD FRANKLIN O'HAIR), lawyer; b. Pitts., Apr. 13, 1919; d. John Irvin and Lena (Scholle) Mays; student U. Toledo, 1936-37, U. Pitts., 1938-39; B.A., Ashland Coll., 1948; postgrad. Western Res. U., 1948-49, Ohio No. U., 1949-51; LL.B., South Tex. Coll. Law, 1953, J.D., 1975; postgrad. Howard U., 1952-54; Ph.D., Minn. Inst. Philosophy, 1971; m. Richard Franklin O'Hair, Oct. 18, 1965; children—William J. Murray III, Jon Garth Murray, Robin Eileen Murray O'Hair. Psychiat. social worker, supr. family and children's agys., probation dept., psychiat. insts., welfare depts., 1948-56, 59-64; atty. HEW, Washington, 1956-59; founder Soc. Separationists, Inc., Am. Atheist Library and Archives, Inc., Austin, Tex., 1970; founder United World Atheists, 1976, Am. Atheist Women, 1976, Am. Atheist U., 1979; dir. Am. Atheist Center, 1965-77; dir. Am. Atheist Radio Series, 1968-77; originated Am. Atheist mag., 1965, now editor-in-chief. Served to 2d lt. WAAC, WAC, World War II. Author: Why I am an Atheist, 1965; What on Earth Is an Atheist, 1966; The American Atheist, 1967; An Atheist Epic, 1968; The Atheist World, 1969; An Atheist Speaks, 1970; Atheist Heroes, 1971; Let Us Prey, an Atheist Looks at Church Wealth, 1970; Freedom from Religion: the Atheist Plea, 1973; An Atheist Believes, 1973; Atheism, Its Viewpoint, 1973; Freedom Under Siege, 1974; Atheism in the United States, 1976; The Religious Factors in the War in Vietnam, 1976; An Original Theory in Respect to the Origin of Religion, 1977; Women and Atheism, 1978; (juvenile) An Atheist Primer, 1979; An Atheist Views: Jesus Christ, Super Fraud, 1979; adv. editor The Atheist Viewpoint, 25 vols., 1972. Prin. U.S. Supreme Ct. case which removed Bible reading and prayer recitation in pub. schs., 1963. Home: 4203 Shoal Creek Blvd Austin TX 78756 Office: 2210 Hancock Dr Austin TX 78756. *Life is for living — not be used to prepare to die. Therefore, any Atheist seeks involvement, fulfillment, achievement. We honor individualism, self-sufficiency, education, outreach and commitment . . . in all of which I am involved.*

O'HALLORAN, CHARLES, librarian; b. Denver, Dec. 7, 1926; s. Charles and Jane (Parry) O'H.; B.A., U. Colo., 1950; student Western State Coll. Colo., 1953; M.A., U. Denver, 1954; m. Genevieve Miller, July 14, 1952; children—Paul M., Joan C., Hugh J. Tchr., Ft. Morgan, Colo., 1950-52, Denver, 1952-53; asst. reference librarian Kansas City (Mo.) Pub. Library, 1954-56, readers adviser, 1956-59; dir. Rosenberg Pub. Library, Galveston, Tex., 1959-64; state librarian Mo. State Library, Jefferson City, 1964—; interim commr. higher edn. State of Mo., 1976-77. Served with AUS, 1946-47. Mem. Am., Mo. library assns., Rocky Mountain Ry. Club. Contbr. profl. jours. Home: 119 Douglas Dr Jefferson City MO 65101 Office: 308 E High St Jefferson City MO 65101

O'HALLORAN, THOMAS ALPHONSUS, JR., physicist; b. Bklyn., Apr. 13, 1931; s. Thomas Alphonsus and Nora (Sheehan) O'H.; student San Jose State Coll., 1948-50; B.S., Oreg. State U., 1953, M.S., 1954; Ph.D., U. Calif., Berkeley, 1963; m. Barbara Joyce Hug, June 9, 1954; children—Theresa Joyce, Maureen Ann, Kevin Thomas, Patrick Joseph. Research asst. Lawrence Berkeley Lab., U. Calif., 1963-64; research fellow Harvard U., 1964-66; asst. prof. physics U. Ill., Urbana-Champaign, 1966-68, asso. prof., 1968-70, prof., 1970—. Served with USN, 1954-58. Guggenheim fellow, 1979-80. Fellow Am. Phys. Soc. Contbr. numerous articles on elem. particle physics to profl. jours. Home: 706 W Iowa St Urbana IL 61801 Office: Loomis Lab Physics U Ill Urbana IL 61801

OHANIAN, MIHRAN JACOB (JACK), educator; b. Istanbul, Turkey, Aug. 7, 1933; s. Mark and Mary Catherine (Sayabalian) O.; B.S.E.E. with high honors, Robert Coll. Engring. Sch., Istanbul, 1956; M.E.E., Rensselaer Poly. Inst., 1960, Ph.D. in Nuclear Engring. and Sci., 1963; m. Sandra Jean Blair, Apr. 22, 1962; children—Heather Jean, Holly Lynn. Came to U.S., 1956, naturalized, 1967. Lectr. nuclear engring. Rensselaer Poly. Inst., 1963, instr., 1958-62; asst. prof. nuclear engring. U. Fla., 1964-67, asso. prof., 1967-70, chmn. dept., 1969-79, prof., 1970—, asso. dir. Engring. and Indsl. Expt. Sta., 1977—, asso. dean for research Coll. Engring., 1979—; Sabbatical leave Inst. Energy Analysis, Oak Ridge, 1976-77, on assignment, 1977-78. Cons. Fla. Power Corp., Fla. Nuclear Assos., Inst. for Energy Analysis; U. Fla. rep. to Atomic Indsl. Forum, 1972—, mem. adv. council, 1972—; U. Fla. rep. to Oak Ridge Asso. Univs., 1972-76; mem. adv. com. Am. Soc. Engring. Edn./Ford Found. Resident Fellow Program, 1971-74. Trustee Fla. Defenders of the Environment, 1969-71, treas., 1969-70. Recipient valor medal, Am. Legion, 1966. Mem. Am Nuclear Soc. (bd. dirs. 1974-77, vice chmn., chmn. edn. div. 1975-76, chmn. nat. program com. 1975-77, chmn. nuclear engring. dept. heads' com. 1973-75, exec. com. nuclear fuel cycle div. 1978—), mem. edn. and engring. accreditation com. 1977—, chmn. tech. program), AAAS, Engrs.'s Council Profl. Devel. (dir. 1976-78), Am. Soc. Engring. Edn. (exec. com. nuclear engring. div. 1979—), Nat., Fla., Alachua (pres. 1965-66) Audubon socs. Sigma Xi, Tau Beta Pi (eminent engr.), Eta Kappa Nu. Presbyn. Rotarian. Contbr. articles to profl. jours. Home: 315 NW 28th St Gainesville FL 32607

O'HANLON, RICHARD E., sculptor; b. Long Beach, Calif., Oct. 7, 1906; s. Richard J. and Grace D. (Heales) O'H.; student Calif. Coll. Arts and Crafts, 1926-28, Calif. Sch. Fine Arts, 1930-33; m. Ann Rice O'Hanlon, Dec., 1932. Exhibitions include: Whitney Mus. Am. Art Annual, N.Y.C., 1948, San Francisco Art Assn. Annual, 1950-71, Sao Paulo Biennial, Brazil, 1955; one man exhbns. include: San Francisco Mus. Modern Art, 1961, Carnegie Inst., Pitts., 1967, Santa Barbara Mus. Art, 1969; prof. sculpture U. Calif., Berkeley, 1948-74, prof. emeritus, 1974—; represented in permanent collections: Worcester (Mass.) Mus. Art, Walker Art Center, Mpls., San Francisco Mus. Modern Art, Smith Coll. Collection, Chgo. Art Inst., Oakland Mus. Art; commd. works include: black granite sculpture Mill Valley Public Library, 1966, San Rafael, Calif., 1973, Oakland Mus. Art, 1974, Lawrence Hall Sci., U. Calif., Berkeley, 1977, and others. Recipient 1st prize for sculpture San Francisco Art Assn., 1958. Bd. dirs. San Francisco Art Inst., 1950-62. Mem. Internat. House of Japan, 1958—. Address: 616 Throckmorton Ave Mill Valley CA 94941

O'HARA, ALFRED PECK, lawyer; b. Patterson, N.Y., Apr. 27, 1919; s. Peter and Anna L. (Peck) O'H.; B.A., Syracuse U., 1940; LL.B., Fordham U., 1942; m. Muriel A. Sandberg, Aug. 30, 1940 (dec.); children—Jane Ann O'Hara Toth, Margaret Kathleen O'Hara Duff, Peter James, John Edward. Admitted to N.Y. bar, 1942, U.S. Supreme Ct., 1956; sec. to U.S. Dist. Ct., 1942-43; partner firm McLaughlin & Stiekles, 1946-52; asst. U.S. atty., chief civil div. So. Dist. N.Y., 1953-56; cons. to atty. gen. N.Y. State, 1956; partner firm Rogers Hoge & Hills, N.Y.C., 1958—; counsel U.S. Trademark Assn., 1967-70; pres., chief exec. officer, dir. Bacardi Corp., 1976—; dir. NAM, 1978—. Mem. Assn. Bar City N.Y., N.Y. State Bar Assn., Am. Bar Assn., Fed. Bar Council, Am. Law Inst., Internat. Patent and Trademark Assn. Clubs: Williams, Pinnacle, Bankers of P.R., Quaker Hill. Home: Birch Hill Rd Patterson NY 12563 Office: Rogers Hoge & Hills 90 Park Ave New York NY 10016 and Bacardi Corp PO Box G3549 San Juan PR 00936

O'HARA, JACK FRANKLIN, naval officer; b. Santa Fe, Apr. 11, 1930; s. John Sterling and Helen Jane (Espy) O'H.; B.S., U. N.Mex., 1951, U.S. Naval Postgrad. Sch., 1959; M.S. in Aero. Engring., Princeton U., 1960; postgrad. Armed Forces Staff Coll., 1964; m. Arlie Jo McGillivray, Dec. 22, 1950; children—John Michael, Steven Patrick. Commd. ensign U.S. Navy, 1951, advanced through grades to rear adm., 1977; served with U.S.S. Cabildo, Korea, 1951-53; naval aviator, carrier based air anti-submarine squadron, 1954-57; maintenance officer, jet attack squadron, 1960-63; comdr. attack squadron, mem. staff Task Force 77, comdr. attack carrier air wing, Vietnam, 1967-71, Naval Air Sta., Lemoore, Calif., 1973-75; mem. staff Chief Naval Ops., Washington, 1975-77; dir. div. tactical air, surface and electronic warfare devel. Office Chief Naval Ops., Washington, U.S. rep. NATO Naval Armaments Group, 1977-79; comdr. Fleet Air Western Pacific, 1979—; cons. in aviation NRC. Decorated Bronze Star, Meritorious Commendation medal, Air medal, Naval Commendation medal. Mem. Tailhook Assn. (life), Sigma Xi. Home and Office: COMFAIRWESTPAC Naval Air Facility Atsugi Japan FPO Seattle WA 98767

O'HARA, JAMES GRANT, lawyer, former congressman; b. Washington, Nov. 8, 1925; s. Raphael M. and Neta L. (Hemphill) O'H.; A.B., U. Mich., 1954, J.D., 1955; m. Susan Puskas, Feb. 14, 1953; children—Raphael M., Thomas A., Patrick J., Brendan P., Mary K., Brigid, Neal. Admitted to Mich. bar, 1955; practiced in Detroit and Macomb County, Mich.; mem. 86th-88th congresses from 7th Dist. Mich., 89th-94th congresses from 12th Dist. Mich.; mem. firm Patton, Boggs & Blow, Washington, 1977—. Chmn., Fed. Minimum Wage Study Commn.; chmn. jud. council Nat. Democratic Com., 1977—. Served with AUS, World War II; PTO. Mem. State Bar Mich., Macomb County, D.C. bar assns. Democrat. Office: Patton Boggs & Blow 2550 M St NW Washington DC 20037

O'HARA, JOHN BRANGS, accountant; b. Newark, Jan. 9, 1921; s. Ralph Leslie and Edna (Brangs) O'H.; B.S., Lehigh U., 1942; M.B.A., Harvard, 1946; m. Ruth Barbara McCabe, May 23, 1942; children—Ralph Leslie, Cynthia Senner. With Price Waterhouse & Co., C.P.A.'s, Phila., 1946—, partner, 1958—, partner in charge Phila. Office, 1963—. Past chmn., past mem. council, Harvard Bus. Sch. Fund; past mem. Com. of Seventy; bd. govs. Eastern div. Economy League; Independence Hall Assn. rep. on Independence Nat. Hist. Park Adv. Commn. Past mem. bd. commrs., Haverford Twp.; bd. dirs. Afro-Am. Hist. and Cultural Mus., Phila.; past bd. govs. Heart Assn. Southeastern Pa.; past trustee, past treas. Internat. House of Phila.; mem. vis. com. Bus. Coll., trustees bequests and trusts com. Lehigh U.; bd. dirs. Phila. Drama Guild. Served to capt. AUS, 1942-45; ETO. C.P.A., Pa. Mem. Am. (mem. council, ethics com.), Pa. (past mem. exec. com.) insts. C.P.A.'s, Pa. Soc., Greater Phila. C. of C. (past dir.). Presbyn. Clubs: Phila. Country, Union League (Phila.); Seaview Country (N.J.); Sky (N.Y.C.); Capitol Hill (Washington). Author (with Dr. Richard C. Clelland) Effective Use of Statistics in Accounting and Business, 1964. Home: 209 Glenn Rd Ardmore PA 19003 Office: 30 S 17th St Philadelphia PA 19103

O'HARA, JOHN FRANCIS, lawyer; b. Oakland, Calif., Nov. 29, 1917; s. Hugh and Beatrice M. (McIntyre) O'H.; Ph.B., U. Santa Clara (Calif.), 1939; J.D., Hastings Coll. Law, San Francisco, 1946; m. Elaine C. Seibel, Apr. 11, 1942; children—Jack, Catherine, Margaret, Dennis, Thomas. Admitted to Calif. bar, 1946, since practiced in Los Angeles; partner firm Parker, Milliken, Clark & O'Hara, 1963—; instr. law Law Sch., U. So. Calif., 1951-52; guest lectr. Inst. Indsl. Relations, U. Calif. at Los Angeles, 1960-73; bd. overseers Hastings Coll. Law, 1974—; dir. Western Gear Corp., Del E. Webb Corp. Bd. dirs. Little Company Mary Hosp., Los Angeles, 1975-78; bd. regents U. Santa Clara, 1959-71, trustee, 1971-77. Served to lt. comdr. USNR, 1941-45. Fellow Am. Bar Found.; mem. Am. (labor law com. 1969—), Los Angeles County (chmn. labor law com. 1973-74, chmn. fair polit. practices com. 1975-76) bar assns., Calif. State Bar (chmn. com. bar examiners 1977-78), Nat. Conf. Bar Examiners (bd. mgrs. 1976—). Clubs: Town Hall (life), Chancery, Calif. (Los Angeles). Home: 164 Aspen Way Rolling Hills Estates CA 90274 Office: 333 S Hope St 27th Floor Los Angeles CA 90071

O'HARA, MARY, (Mary O'Hara Alsop), author, composer; b. Cape May Point, N.J., July 10, 1885; d. Reese Fell and Mary Lee (Spring) Alsop; student Packer Inst., Brooklyn Heights; student langs., music in Europe; m. Kent K. Parrot, Oct. 1905; children—Mary O'Hara, Kent Kane, Jr.; m. 2d. Helge Sture-Vasa, Aug. 1922 (div. 1947). Author: My Friend Flicka, 1941; Thunderhead, 1943; Green Grass of Wyoming, 1946; The Son of Adam Wyngate, 1952; Novel-in-the-Making, 1954; Wyoming Summer, 1963; (mus. play) The Catch Colt, 1961, also novella, 1979; A Musical in the Making, 1966. Composer songs and piano studies. Roman Catholic. Home: 5507 Grove St Chevy Chase MD 20015

O'HARA, PAUL FRANKLIN, JR., engring. and mfg. co. exec.; b. East Liverpool, Ohio, Sept. 13, 1934; s. Paul Franklin and June (Boughner) O'H.; student Ohio U., 1953-55; B.B.A., Youngstown U., 1957; student Tex. A. and I. Coll., 1964-65; m. Carolyn A. Reynolds, Jan. 15, 1954; children—Barbara June, James Kevin, David William, Paul Stephen. Controller Mobil Coatings Co., Cleve., 1967-69; controller Raymond Internat. Inc., N.Y.C., 1969-72, v.p., controller, Houston, 1972-73, v.p. finance, controller, 1973-74, sr. group v.p., 1974-75; v.p. finance Research-Cottrell Co., Bedminster, N.J., 1975-79; pres. Research-Cottrell Energy Cos., 1979—. also dir. Mem. Nat. Accountants Assn., Financial Execs. Inst. Presbyn. Clubs: Roxiticus Golf, Fiddlers Elbow Country, Fripp Island Beach and Golf. Home: 38 Manor Dr Basking Ridge NJ 07920 Office: Box 750 Bound Brook NJ 08805

O'HARA, THOMAS EDWIN, assn. exec.; b. Springfield, Mo., July 28, 1915; s. Robert John and Olga Florence (Lindberg) O'H.; A.B., Wayne State U., 1938; m. Eleanor McLennan Urquhart, May 6, 1950; children—Thomas Edwin, Robert Andrew, Shelley Janette. Accountant, Nash-Kelvinator Corp., 1938-39, Gen. Electric Co., 1938-41, Ernst & Ernst, 1941-42; dir. payrolls Detroit Bd. Edn., 1942-58; chmn. bd. trustees Nat. Assn. Investment Clubs, Royal Oak, Mich., 1951—; treas. Sunshine Fifty, Inc., 1969—; vice chmn. H.W. Rickel & Co., 1971-76. Dir. N.Y. Stock Exchange, 1973-75, Investment Edn. Inst., 1962—. Bd. dirs. Detroit Bible Coll. Served with USAAF, 1942-45. Recipient Distinguished Service award in investment edn., 1969. Mem. World Fedn. Investment Clubs (dir.), Arab Frat., Gamma Beta Phi. Presbyn. Home: 755 Kennebec Ct Bloomfield Hills MI 48013 Office: 1515 E Eleven Mile Rd Royal Oak MI 48068

O'HARA, WILLIAM JAMES, drug co. exec.; b. Bklyn., Dec. 2, 1930; s. John Joseph and Mary (Quinn) O'H.; B.S., Fordham U., 1952; M.B.A., N.Y. U., 1956; m. Marilyn Mulcahy, July 7, 1956; children—Lynn Patricia, Kevin Joseph, Eileen, Gail Elizabeth, Nancy (dec.). With Equitable Life Assurance Soc. U.S., N.Y.C., 1954-55; with Continental Can Co., N.Y.C., 1955-56; several fin. positions with Gen. Foods Corp., White Plains, N.Y., 1956-69, controller Maxwell House div. 1966-69; corporate controller Schering Corp., Bloomfield, N.J., 1969-72, Schering-Plough Corp., 1972-73; v.p. finance Schering Corp., 1973-74, v.p. adminstrn. Schering div., 1975—. Served with AUS, 1952- 54. Mem. Financial Execs. Inst., Planning Execs. Inst., Nat. Assn. Accountants. Home: 14 Crestwood Dr Suffern NY 10901 Office: Galloping Hill Rd Kenilworth NJ 07033

O'HARE, JAMES RAYMOND, mfg. co. exec.; b. Evergreen Park, Ill., July 20, 1938; s. Raymond Clarence and Helen (Nickel) O.; B.S., Marquette U., 1960; M.B.A., U. Calif. at Los Angeles, 1961; m. Nan Jane Raleigh, Sept. 18, 1965; children—Joan, Daniel, Colleen, Patrick. With Peat, Marwick, Mitchell & Co., Chgo., 1961-68, mgr., South Bend, Ind., 1968-69; controller Essex Internat., Inc., Fort Wayne, Ind., 1969-76, Am. Air Filter Co., Inc., Louisville, 1976—. Bd. dirs. Stes. Mary and Elizabeth Hosp. Served with USNR, 1961. C.P.A., Ind., Ill. Mem. Evans Scholars, Am. Inst. C.P.A.'s, Fin. Execs. Inst., Beta Gamma Sigma. Club: Hunting Creek Country. Home: 7403 Shadwell Ln Prospect KY 40059 Office: 215 Central Ave Louisville KY 40277

O'HARE, SISTER JEANNE D'ARC, educator, former coll. pres.; b. Boston, Oct. 22, 1917; d. Michael J. and Theresa B. O'Hare; A.B., Regis Coll., Weston, Mass., 1939; A.M., Boston Coll., 1949, Ph.D., 1959; postgrad. U. Nigeria, 1964. Joined Order of Congregation of St. Joseph, 1944; tchr. Cathedral High Sch., Boston, 1946-50, Mt. St. Joseph Acad., Brighton, Mass., 1950-58; asst. prof. govt. Regis Coll., 1958-64, pres., 1964-74, prof. polit. sci., dir. continuing edn., 1975—. Trustee Cardinal Spellman Philatelic Mus., Weston, Mass. Mem. Assn. Am. Continuing Higher Edn. Home: 235 Wellesley St Weston MA 02193

O'HARE, STEPHEN THOMAS, ins. co. exec.; b. N.Y.C., Dec. 21, 1928; s. Stephen and Gertrude A. (Lawler) O'H.; B.A., St. Johns U., 1956; M.A., Stanford U., 1957; m. Phyllis Bernadette D'Angelo, June 6, 1953; children—Elizabeth, Allycyn. With Pacific Mut. Life Ins. Co., Newport Beach, Calif., 1957—, asst. mgr. policyowner service dept., 1965-68, asst. to pres., 1968-69, v.p., sec., 1969—. Bd. dirs. ARC. Served with U.S. Army, 1951-52. Republican. Roman Catholic. Club: Jack Kramer. Home: 2831 Via El Miro Rancho Palos Verdes CA 90274 Office: 700 Newport Center Dr Newport Beach CA 92660

O'HAREN, JAMES FRANCIS, metal products mfg. co. exec.; b. Shenandoah, Pa., July 21, 1930; s. James Francis and Elizabeth Margaret (Sauer) O'H.; B.S. cum laude, Mt. St. Mary's Coll., 1956; postgrad. U. Houston Law Sch., 1962-63, postgrad. LaSalle Extension U. Law Sch., 1971—; m. Florence V. Civiletto, May 17, 1958; 1 dau., Noel. Asst. sec., asst. treas. Tex. Butadiene & Chem. Internat., Ltd., Houston, 1956-59, N.Y.C., 1959-60, European comml. mgr., Lausanne, Switzerland, 1960-62; controller Maurice Pincoffs Co., Houston, 1963-65; controller Marathon Mfg. Co., Houston, 1965-68, asst. sec., 1966-71, treas., 1966-71, v.p., 1968-71, sec., 1971—; sec., dir. Marathon LeTourneau Co., 1970—, Marathon LeTourneau Leasing Co., 1978—, Marathon Internat. Co., 1972—, Marathon LeTourneau Offshore Co., 1970—, R.G. LeTourneau, Inc., 1971—, LeTourneau Offshore, Inc., 1971—; sec., dir. Marathon Shipbldg. Co., Marathon LeTourneau Sales & Service Co., Marathon RGL Co., 1970—, Shadywood Leasehold Co.; sec. Marathon Marine Engring. Co., 1974—, Marathon Marine Ventures, Inc., 1975—, Marathon Steel Co., George Franke Sons Co., 1971—, Marathon Shipbldg. Co. (U.K.) Ltd., Marathon Carey-McFall Co., Handy Window Creations Inc., 1969—, Southmost Supply Co., 1973—, Marathon LeTourneau Offshore Pty. Ltd., 1974—, Marathon Paving and Utility Constructors, Inc., 1972—; v.p., sec. Marathon Battery Co., Marathon Franke Co., Bus. Funds, Inc. (Del.), 1969—, Marathon Leasing Co., Marathon Metallic Bldg. Co., 1970—, Marathon Warehouse Co., 1968—; v.p., asst. sec. Marathon Morco Co., 1968—; v.p., sec., dir. Bus. Funds, Inc. (Tex.), Kelven, Inc., 1975—, Pearl River Devel. Corp., 1975—, Mgmt. Adv. Services, Inc., 1968—; pres. Tulsa So. Tennis Club. Served with AUS, 1949-50, 50-52; Korea. Mem. Fin. Execs. Inst., Am. Soc. Corporate Secs., U.S. Lawn Tennis Assn. Republican. Roman Catholic. Clubs: Houston, Houston Racquet, Houston Met. Racquet, Admirals (N.Y.C.). Home: 59 Williamsburg Ln Houston TX 77024 Office: Marathon Bldg 600 Jefferson St Houston TX 77002 also 3030 E 91st St Tulsa OK 74136

O'HEARN, ROBERT RAYMOND, stage designer; b. Elkhart, Ind., July 19, 1921; s. Robert Raymond, Sr., and Ella May (Stoldt) O'H.; B.A., Ind. U., 1939-43; student Art Students League, 1943-45. Designer, Brattle Theatre, Cambridge, Mass., 1948-52; stage designer Broadway shows The Relapse, 1950, Loves Labor's Lost, 1953, Othello, Festival, 1955, The Apple Cart, Child of Fortune, 1956; asst. designer Kismet, 1953, Pajama Game, 1955, My Fair Lady, 1956, West Side Story, 1958; designer for film A Clerical Error, 1955; designer prodns. Central City Opera House, 1959-63, Opera Soc. Washington, 1958-61, L'Elisir D'Amore at Met. Opera House, 1960, Die Meistersinger, 1962, Aida, 1963; stage designer plays As You Like It, Macbeth, Troilus and Cressida, Stratford, Conn., 1961; Kiss Me Kate, Los Angles Civic Light Opera, 1964, N.Y.C. Center, 1965; Samson and Delila, Met. Opera, 1964; La Sylphide, Am. Ballet Theatre, 1964; Italian Symphony, 1971; Adam Cochrane, Broadway, 1964; Pique Dame, Met. Opera, 1965; La Ventana, 1966; Die Frau Ohne Schatten, 1966; Porgy and Bess, Vienna Volksoper, 1965; Bregenzer Festspiele, 1971; Otello, Boston Opera, also Hamburg State Opera, 1967; Hansel and Gretel, Met. Opera, 1967; Nutcracker Ballet, San Francisco Ballet, 1967, 69; Die Fledermaus, Miami Opera, 1980; La Traviata, Santa Fe Opera, 1968, Rosalinda, Los Angeles Civic Light Opera, 1968; Der Rosenkavalier, Met. Opera, 1969; Tallis Fantasia, N.Y.C. Ballet, 1969; Boris Godunov (unproduced), Met. Opera, 1970; Parsifal, Met. Opera, 1970; Porgy and Bess, Bregenz Festspiel, Austria, 1971; Falstaff, Marriage of Figaro, Gianni Schicci, Central City Opera House, 1972; Barber of Seville, 1973; The Enchanted, Kennedy Center, 1973; The Mind with the Dirty Man, Los Angeles, 1973; Midsummer Night's Dream, Central City Opera, 1974; Coppelia, Ballet West, 1974; Carmen, Strasbourg, 1974; The Pearl Fishers, Miami Opera, 1974; Don Pasquale, 1976; Scipio Africanus, Central City Opera, 1975; Swan Lake, Strasbourg, 1975; Marriage of Figaro, Met. Opera, 1975; Die Meistersinger, Karlsruhe, Germany, 1975; Girl of the Golden West, Houston Opera, 1976; Vienna Staatsoper, 1976; Boris Godunov, Strasbourg, 1976; Der Rosenkavalier, Karlsruhe, 1976; Don Quixote, Ballet West, 1977; Girl of the Golden West, N.Y.C. Opera, 1977; Die Meistersinger, Chgo. Lyric Opera, 1977; Adriana Lecouvreur, Miami Opera, 1978, La Boheme, 1978; Coppelia, Pacific N.W. Dance, Seattle, 1978; Andrea Chenier, N.Y.C. Opera, 1978; Der Rosenkavalier, Can. Opera Co., Toronto, 1978; instr. Studio and Forum Scenic Design, 1968—. Mem. vis. com. Costume Inst., Met. Museum. Mem. United Scenic Artists. Address: 59 Fifth Ave New York City NY 10003

O'HEARNE, JOHN JOSEPH, psychiatrist; b. Memphis, Feb. 5, 1922; s. John Joseph and Norma Rose (Ford) O.; B.S., Southwestern U. at Memphis, 1944; M.D., U. Tenn., 1945; M.S. in Psychiatry, U. Colo., 1951; m. Janet E. Mules, May 16, 1979; children by previous marriage—Patricia Ann, Marilyn Eileen, John Stephen, Brian Donal. Intern, Denver Gen. Hosp., Denver, 1945-46; fellow U. Colo., Denver, 1948-51; instr., 1949-52, Denver U., 1951—; clin. dir. psychiatry Kan. City Gen. Hosp. and Psychiat. Receiving Center, Kansas City, Mo., 1952-56; pvt. practice psychiatry, Kansas City, Mo., 1956—; mem. staffs St. Luke's Hosp., Gen. Hosp., Menorah Hosp. Cons., Western Mo. Mental Health Center, 1964—; clin. prof. U. Kans., 1972—, U. Mo. Kansas City, 1974—; pres. Transactional Analysis Inst. Kansas City, 1971—. Served to capt. AUS, 1942-45, 46-48. Diplomate Am. Bd. Psychiatry and Neurology. Fellow Am. Psychiat. Assn., Am. Group Psychotherapy Assn. (dir. 1970-78, pres. 1974-76), Am. Orthopsychiat. Assn. (life); mem. Am. Psychiat. Assn. (pres. Western Mo. dist. br. 1964-65, 60-61), Mo. State Med. Assn. (chmn. mental health com. 1960-62), Jackson County Med. Soc. (chmn. mental health com. 1959-66), Internat. Transactional Analysis Assn. (trustee 1972—), MidContinent Psychiat. Assn., Am. Acad. Psychotherapists, Carriage Club. Republican. Lutheran. Contbr. articles to profl. jours. Office: 4706 Broadway Kansas City MO 64112

O'HERN, JANE SUSAN, psychologist, educator; b. Winthrop, Mass., Mar. 21, 1933; d. Joseph Francis and Mona (Garvey) O'H.; B.S., Boston U., 1954; M.A., Mich. State U., 1956; Ed.D., Boston U., 1962. Instr., Mercyhurst Coll., 1954-55, Hofstra Coll., 1956-57, State Coll. Salem and Boston, 1957-60; asst. prof. Boston U., 1962-67, asso. prof., 1967-75, chmn. dept. counselor edn., 1972-75, prof. edn. and psychiatry, 1975—, dir. mental health edn. program, 1975—, dir. internat. continuing edn. 1978—; mem. adv. bd. Aquinas Jr. Coll. Recipient grants U.S. Office Edn., NIMH. Mem. Am. Personnel and Guidance Assn., Assn. Counselor Educators and Suprs., N. Atlantic Assn. Counselor Edn. and Supervision (past pres.), Mass. Psychol. Assn., Pi Lambda Theta, Sigma Kappa, Mortar Bd. Democrat. Roman Catholic. Contbr. articles to profl. jours. Home: 111 Perkins St Apt 172 Boston MA 02130 Office: Boston U 745 Commonwealth Ave Boston MA 02215

O'HERRON, JONATHAN, investment banker; b. Pittsfield, Mass., Oct. 28, 1929; s. S. John and Helena (Coughlin) O'H.; B.A., Williams Coll., 1951; M.B.A., Harvard, 1957; m. Shirley O'Connell, Sept. 10, 1955; children—Jonathan, Anne, Sarah. Investment mgr. Gen. Electric Co., 1954-61; exec. v.p., treas. Buckeye Pipe Line Co., N.Y.C., 1962-69, also dir.; exec. v.p. finance Penn Central Co., 1969-70; gen. partner Lazard Freres & Co., N.Y.C., 1971—. Served to lt. (j.g.) USNR, 1951-54. Home: 42 Hamilton Ln Darien CT 06820 Office: One Rockefeller Plaza New York City NY 10020

OHL, DONALD CHARLES, news service exec.; b. Grand Junction, Iowa, Dec. 19, 1924; s. August and Agnes (Thornburg) O.; B.A., U. Iowa, 1950; m. Evelyn Marie Broadway, Jan. 21, 1955; 1 son, Gary Martin. Formerly mng. editor Guthrie Center (Iowa) Times-Guthrian, Sunday editor Galveston (Tex.) News-Tribune; asst. bur. mgr. UPI, N.Y.C., 1960-64; fgn. editor Copley News Service, San Diego, 1964-69, exec. news editor, 1969—, also gen. mgr. Home: 6815 Murray Park Dr San Diego CA 92119 Office: Copley News Service PO Box 190 San Diego CA 92112*

OHLIN, LLOYD EDGAR, educator, sociologist; b. Belmont, Mass., Aug. 27, 1918; s. Emil and Elise (Nelson) O.; A.B., Brown U., 1940; M.A., Ind. U., 1942; Ph.D., U. Chgo., 1954; m. Helen Barbara Hunter, Jan. 27, 1946; children—Janet, George, Robert, Nancy. Sociologist, actuary Ill. Parole and Pardon Bd., Joliet Penitentiary, 1947-50, supervising research sociologist Chgo. Parole Office, 1950-53; dir. Center for Edn. and Research in Corrections, U. Chgo., 1953-56; prof. sociology Columbia U. Sch. Social Work, 1956-67, dir. Research Center, 1962-66; asso. dir. Pres.' Commn. Law Enforcement and Adminstrn. Justice, 1966-67, Roscoe Pound prof. criminology Harvard U. Law Sch., Cambridge, Mass., 1967—; spl. asst. to sec. for juvenile delinquency Office of Sec., Dept. Health, Edn. and Welfare, Washington 1961-62. Past cons. youth, pub. affairs div. Ford Found.; cons. mem. ad hoc com. on delinquency Nat. Inst. Mental Heaalth 1957-65; mem. tng. review panel President's Com. on Juvenile Delinquency and Youth Crime, 1962-65; mem. research council Nat. Council Crime and Delinquency, 1962-75, div. youth State N.Y., 1963-65; chmn. adv. bd. Mass. Dept. Youth Services, 1970-72; chmn. adv. bd. Nat. Inst. Law Enforcement and Criminal Justice, Dept. Justice, 1978—. Served with CIC, AUS, 1942-45. Mem. Am. Sociol. Assn. (chmn. criminology sect. 1962-63), Phi Beta Kappa. Democrat. Author: Selection for Parole, 1951; Sociology and the Field of Corrections, 1956; (with Richard A. Cloward) Delinquency and Opportunity: A Theory of Delinquent Gangs, 1960; Prisoners in America, 1973; (with Alden D. Miller and Robert B. Coates) A Theory of Social Reform, 1977, Diversity in a Youth Correctional System, 1978. Home: 9 Red Coat Lane Lexington MA 02173 Office: Harvard U Law Sch Cambridge MA 02138

OHLKE, CLARENCE CARL, cons.; b. Kansas City, Mo., Feb. 16, 1916; s. William Erdman and Amanda (Rubin) O.; A.A., Kansas City Jr. Coll., 1935; B.S., U. Mo., 1940; m. Frances Woodley Nicholson, Oct. 9, 1954; children—Daniel N., Carl E., Amanda A. Personnel examiner Municipal Govt., Kansas City, 1940-41; personnel specialist WPB, Washington, 1942; dir. civilian personnel Chief Naval Operations, Washington, 1946-47; with AEC, Washington, 1947-66, asst. dir. operations div. contracts, 1961, asst. to asst. gen. mgr. operations, 1962-63, dir. Office Econ. Impact and Conversion, 1964-66; spl. asst. to dir., head congl. and pub. affairs, govt. and pub. programs dir. NSF, Washington, 1966-73; cons., dir. Center Urban Research and Environ. Studies, Drexel U., 1973-75; cons. pub. affairs, 1976—. Served to lt. USNR, 1942-46. Recipient Distinguished Service award NSF, 1973. Mem. Am. Polit. Sci. Assn., AAAS. Home: Bear Branch Farms Route 1 Adamstown MD 21710

OHLMEYER, DONALD WINFRED, JR., producer, prodn. co. exec.; b. New Orleans, Feb. 3, 1945; s. Donald W. and Eva Claire (Bivens) O.; B.A. in Communications, U. Notre Dame, 1967; m. Adrian Perry, Feb. 11, 1978; children by previous marriage—Justin Drew, Christopher Brett, Todd Bivens. Asso. dir. ABC Sports, N.Y.C., 1967-70, dir., 1971-72, producer, 1972-77, dir. Olympic Games, 1972, producer, dir. Summer and Winter Olympics, 1976, producer Monday Night Football, 1972-76; exec. producer NBC Sports, N.Y.C., 1977—, exec. producer 1980 Olympic Games; pres. Roadblock Prodns., 1977—. Recipient 7 Emmy awards, 1975-77, Cine Golden Eagle award, 1979, Miami Film Festival award, 1979. Mem. Dirs. Guild Am., Acad. TV Arts and Scis. Clubs: Outrigger Canoe, Waialae Country (Honolulu); Doubles (N.Y.C.).

OHLROGGE, ALVIN JOHN, agronomist; b. Chilton, Wis., Sept. 19, 1915; s. John Gustav and Anna Marie (Peters) O.; B.S., U. Wis., 1937; Ph.D., Purdue U., 1943; m. Harriet Lorraine Beyer, Sept. 9, 1944; children—Ann, John. Asst. agronomist Purdue U., 1942—, mem. faculty, 1945—, prof. agronomy, 1959—; FAO cons. to Govt. Pakistan, 1952; cons. to industry. NSF fellow, 1959; hon. life mem. Am. Soybean Assn., 1964—. Fellow Am. Soc. Agronomy (Soil Sci. award 1962, Agronomic Research award 1975), AAAS, Ind. Acad. Sci; mem. Council Agrl. and Sci. Tech., Internat. Soil Sci. Soc., Crop Sci. Soc. Am., Soil Sci. Soc. Am., Sigma Xi, Gamma Sigma Delta. Republican. Presbyterian. Author articles; contbr. chpts. to books. Home: 112 W Stadium West Lafayette IN 47906 Office: Agronomy Dept Life Sci Bldg Purdue U West Lafayette IN 47907

OHLSON, DOUGLAS DEAN, artist; b. Cherokee, Iowa, Nov, 18, 1936; s. Lloyd E. and Effie O. (Johnson) O.; B.A., U. Minn., 1961. One man shows: Fischbach Gallery, N.Y.C., 1964, 66-70, 72, Susan Caldwell Gallery, N.Y.C., 1974, 76, 77, 79, Portland (Oreg.) Center for the Visual Arts, 1977; group shows include: Mus. Modern Art, N.Y.C., 1968, Tate Gallery, London, 1969, Whitney Mus., N.Y.C., 1969, 71, Corcoran Gallery, Washington, 1972, 73, U. Calif., Los Angeles, 1975; represented in permanent collections: Am. Fedn. Art, circulating exhbn., Corcoran Gallery, Mpls. Inst. Art, Bklyn. Mus.; asso. prof. art Hunter Coll., N.Y.C., 1964—. Served with USMC, 1955-58. Guggenheim fellow, 1968; Creative Artists Pub. Service grantee, 1974; Nat. Endowment for Arts grantee, 1976. Home and studio: 35 Bond St New York NY 10012

OHLSSON, GARRICK OLOF, concert pianist; b. Bronxville, N.Y., Apr. 3, 1948; s. Alvar Oscar and Paulyne R. (Rosta) O.; B.Mus., Julliard Sch., 1971. Performances with major orchs. including N.Y. Philharmonic, Phila. Symphony Orch., New Philharmonia, London Symphony Orch., others; also performances radio, television, concert recitals. Winner, Montreal Internat. Piano Competition, 1968, Chopin Competition, Poland, 1970. Office: care Shaw Concerts Inc 1995 Broadway New York NY 10023*

OHMANN, RICHARD MALIN, educator; b. Cleve., July 11, 1931; s. Oliver Arthur and Grace (Malin) O.; B.A., Oberlin Coll., 1952; M.A., Harvard, 1954, Ph.D., 1960; m. Carol Alice Burke, June 25, 1955; children—Sarah Malin, William Burke. Teaching fellow Harvard, 1954-58, jr. fellow Soc. Fellows, 1958-61; mem. faculty Wesleyan U., Middletown, Conn., 1961—, prof. English, 1966—, asso. provost, 1966-69, chancellor protem, 1969-70; mem. supervising Com. English Inst., 1972-75. Mem. steering com. RESIST, 1967—. Guggenheim fellow, 1964-65. Mem. Modern Lang. Assn., Nat. Council Tchrs. English. Author: Shaw: The Style and the Man, 1962; (with others) The Logic and Rhetoric of Exposition, 3d edit., 1969; English in America: A Radical Critique of the Profession, 1976. Editor Coll. English, 1966-78. Home: 85 High St Middletown CT 06457 Office: Wesleyan U Middletown CT 06457

O'HORGAN, TOM, composer, dir.; b. Chgo., May 3, 1926; B.A. and M.A., DePaul U., Chgo. Debut performance in Fallout (off-Broadway revue), 1959; directing debut with prodn. The Maids, 1964; dir. Hair (nomination for Tony award 1968), Lenny (Drama Desk award 1971), Jesus Christ Super Star, Inner City, Six from La Mama, The Hessian Corporal, Futz (Obie award 1967), Tom Paine (Drama Desk award 1968), Massachusetts Trust, Dude, The Leaf People, Seargent Peppers Lonely Hearts Club Band on the Road, The Architect and The Emperor of Abyssinia; composer music for numerous prodns. including: The Tempest, Futz, Tom Paine, Massachusetts Trust, Lenny, Open Season at Second City; composer music for films including Alex in Wonderland, 1970, Rhinocerous, 1974; performer in film All Men Are Apes, 1965. Recipient Creative Arts award Brandeis U., 1968. Address: care William Morris Agency 151 El Camine Dr Beverly Hills CA 90212*

OHSOL, ERNEST OSBORNE, chem. engr.; b. Washington, May 28, 1916; s. Johann Gottfried and Klara Elizabeth (Karpowitz) O.; student Fed. Polytech. Inst., Zurich, Switzerland, 1934-35; B.S., Coll. City N.Y., 1936; Sc.D., Mass. Inst. Tech., 1939; m. Mary Rosamond Montgomery, June 15, 1940 (div. Jan. 4, 1977); children—Frederick M., Richard B., Barbara Alison (Mrs. Layton S. Allen, Jr.), Elizabeth Anne; m. 2d, Barbara I. Handy, Mar. 1977. Devel. engr. Standard Oil Devel. Co., Linden, N.J., 1939-50; mgr. process devel. chem. div. Gen. Elec. Co., Pittsfield, Mass., 1950-52; dir. research and devel. Pitts. Coke and Chem. Co., 1953-60; v.p. Haveg Industries, Inc., plastics, Wilmington, Del., 1960-65; v.p. Chem. Constrn. Corp., N.Y.C., 1965-67, Escambia Chem. Co., N.Y.C., 1967; dir. chem. engring. dept. Am. Cyanamid Co., central research div., Stamford, Conn., 1967-72; cons. chem. engr., Plainfield, N.J., 1973; chief process engr. Eastern group Jacobs Engring. Co., Mountainside, N.J., 1973-75; corp. mgr. European fluid processing Selas Corp. Am., Munich, W. Ger., 1975-78; coordinator C.H. Dexter div. Dexter Corp., Windsor Locks, Conn.; adj. prof. Grad. Sch., Stevens Inst. Tech., 1946-50. Naumburg fellow Coll. City N.Y., 1934-35; Arthur D. Little fellow Mass. Inst. Tech., 1937-38. Registered profl. engr., N.J. Fellow Am. Inst. Chem. Engrs. (dir. 1973); mem. Am. Chem. Soc., Chemists Club N.Y.C., Sigma Xi. Episcopalian (vestryman 1963-65). Patentee in field. Home: 278 Mountain View Rd Somers CT 06071 Office: One Elm St Windsor Locks CT 06096

OI, WALTER YASUO, economist; b. Los Angeles, July 1, 1929; s. Matsunosuke and Toshiko (Kawada) O.; B.S., UCLA, 1952, M.A., 1954; Ph.D. (Social Sci. Research Council fellow), U. Chgo., 1961; m. Marjorie Louise Robbins, Jan. 25, 1969; children—Jessica Sumiye, Eleanor Haruko. Instr. dept. econs. Iowa State U., 1957-58; research economist Transp. Center, Northwestern U., 1958-62; asso. prof. econs. U. Wash., 1962-65, prof., 1965-67; prof. Grad. Sch. Mgmt., U. Rochester, 1967-75, prof. econs., 1975-78, chmn. dept. econs., 1976—, Elmer B. Milliman prof. econs., 1978—; dir. econ. analyses sect. Mil. Manpower Policy Study, Dept. Def., 1964-65; research economist Inst. for Def. Analysis, Arlington, Va., 1966; staff economist Pres.'s Commn. on All-Vol. Armed Force, 1969-70; cons. Rand Corp., Santa Monica, Calif., 1970—; sr. research economist, indsl. relations sect. Princeton U., 1973-74. Adult co-chmn. for draft and nat. service White House Conf. on Youth, 1970-71; bd. dirs. Assn. for Blind of Rochester and Monroe County. Emma and Carol Rousch Disting. Vis. scholar Hoover Instn., Stanford U., 1970-71. Fellow Econometrics Soc. Contbr. articles to profl. jours. Home: 690 Winton Rd S Rochester NY 14618 Office: Dept Econs U Rochester Rochester NY 14627

OIKONOMIDES, NICOLAS CONSTANTINE, historian, educator; b. Athens, Greece, Feb. 17, 1934; s. Anthony and Iphigeneia (Peppas) O.; came to Can., 1969; B.A., U. Athens, 1956; Ph.D., U. Paris, 1961; m. Elizabeth Zachariadou, Oct. 29, 1966; children—Catherine, Theodora. Research asso. Center for Byzantine Research, Athens, 1961-69; prof. history U. Montreal, 1969—, chmn. dept. history, 1976—; advisor in Byzantine Sigillography, Dumbarton Oaks, Washington. Served with Greek Navy, 1956-58. Mem. Assn. Internationale des Etudes Byzantines (treas. 1963-76). Author: Actes de Dionysiou, 1968; Les Listes de preseance byzantines des ixe et xe siécles, 1972; Documents et etudes sur les institutions de Byzance, 1976; Actes de Kastamonitou, 1978. Home: 4801 Dornal St Montreal PQ H3W 1V9 Canada Office: Department of History University of Montreal Montreal PQ Canada

OINAS, FELIX JOHANNES, educator; b. Tartu, Estonia, Mar. 6, 1911; s. Ernst and Marie (Saarik) O.; came to U.S., 1949, naturalized, 1955; M.A., Tartu U., Estonia, 1937; postgrad. Budapest U., 1935-36, Heidelberg U., 1946-48; Ph.D., Ind. U., 1952; m. Lisbet Kove, July 10, 1935; children—Helina Oinas Piano, Valdar. Lectr., Budapest U., 1938-40; vis. lectr. Estonian Baltic U., Hamburg, 1946-49; lectr. Slavic langs. Ind. U., 1952-53, instr., 1953-55, asst. prof., 1955-61, asso. prof., 1961-65, prof. Slavic langs. and Uralic and Altaic studies, 1965—, fellow Folklore Inst., 1965—. Guggenheim fellow, 1961, 66; Fulbright grantee, 1961; Fulbright-Hays grantee, 1964; Nat. Endowment for Humanities grantee, 1974. Fellow Am. Folklore Soc., Finnish Literary Soc., Finno-Ugric Soc., Finnish Folklore Soc.; mem. Finnish Acad. Scis. Lutheran. Author, editor books in field. Contbr. articles to profl. jours. Home: 2513 E 8th St Bloomington IN 47401 Office: Slavic Dept Indiana Univ Bloomington IN 47405

OISHI, SATOSHI, engr., architect; b. Japan, Jan. 19, 1927; s. Mitsuhei and Yei Oishi; came to U.S., 1932, naturalized, 1954; B.S. in Civil Engring. with high honors, U. Conn., 1949; m. Jeanette Corrine Allard, July 2, 1960; 1 dau., Michelle Yuki. With Edwards & Kelcey, Newark, 1949—, chief structural engr., asso., 1958-65, partner in charge N.Y. and Mpls. offices, also sr. v.p. charge transit design, structural, planning and archtl. and recreation planning and park designs divs., 1965—; Spencer Miller lectr. Rutgers U., 1971; prin. works include Round Valley Recreation Area, Hunterdon County, N.J., 1973-75, also transit tunnels and sta. designs, Washington, Atlanta, Balt., and bridges, structures and r.r. projects; mem. transp. com. N.Y. C. of C. Chmn. Berkeley Heights (N.J.) Planning and Zoning Bd., 1974; adviser Berkeley Heights League Women Voters. Fellow ASCE, Am. Cons. Engrs. Council; mem. AIA, Internat. Assn. Bridge and Structural Engring., Am. Concrete Inst., Am. Pub. Transit Assn., Transp. Research Bd., Japan Soc., Sigma Xi, Chi Epsilon, Tau Beta Pi. Unitarian. Home: 67 Riverbend Rd Berkeley Heights NJ 07922 Office: 70 S Orange Ave Livingston NJ 07039

OJEDA, PEDRO, lawyer, Mexican govt. ofcl.; b. Mexico City, Jan. 19, 1934; s. Manuel and Adela (Paullada) O.; grad. in law, U. Mexico, Mexico City, 1954; m. Olga Cardenas, Dec. 26, 1959; children—Pedro Manuel, Olga Mónica, Elsa Carolina, Lucía Regina, Pablo Hector. Dep. dir. gen. of material improvements Mexican Ministry of Nat. Patrimony, Mexico City, 1959-65, dir. gen. legal affairs Ministry of Transport and Communications, 1966-70, chief clk. Ministry of Presidency, 1970-71, atty. gen. of republic, 1971-76, minister of labor and social welfare, 1976—. Pres., World Conf. Internat. Women's Year, 1975; pres. Conf. on Narcotics and Dangerous Drugs, UN Econ. and Social Council, Geneva, 1976; pres. LXIV Internat. Labor Conf., ILO, Geneva, 1978. Decorated Al Merito della Repubblica Italiana, Gt. Cross Italian Republic; Gt. Cross of Isabel la Catolica (Spain). Mem. Platform Mexican Profls. (founding mem.; pres. 1965-69), Mexican Fedn. Planning and Housing (sec. gen. 1964), Mexican U.S. Health Assn. Mem. Partido Revolucionario Institucional. Author tech. studies on public adminstrn., regional planning, transformation industries, electric industry, mining, housing, planning and environment. Office: Dr Rio de la Loza y Vertiz Mexico DF 7 Mexico

OKA, TAKESHI, physicist; b. Tokyo, June 10, 1932; s. Shumpei and Chiyoko O.; came to Can., 1963, naturalized, 1973; B.Sc., U. Tokyo, 1955, Ph.D., 1960; m. Keiko Nukui, Oct. 24, 1960; children—Ritsuko, Noriko, Kentaro, Yujiro. Research asso. U. Tokyo, 1960-63; fellow Nat. Research Council Canada, Ottawa, Ont., 1963-65, asst., 1965-68, asso., 1968-71, sr. research physicist, 1971—. Recipient Steacie prize, 1972. Fellow Royal Soc. Canada; mem. Canadian Assn. Physicists, Am. Phys. Soc., Am. Astron. Soc. Mem. editorial bd. Chem. Physics, 1972—, Jour. Molecular Spectroscopy, 1973—, Jour. Chem. Physics, 1975-77. Home: 28 Highburn Crescent Ottawa ON K1B 3H8 Canada Office: 100 Sussex Dr Ottawa ON K1A 0R6 Canada

OKADA, KENZO, painter; b. Sept. 28, 1902; came to U.S., 1950, naturalized, 1952; s. Kazo and Yasu O.; m. Kimi Kasono, May 10, 1931. Exhibited in one-man shows including: Betty Parsons Gallery, 12 shows, 1953-78, Corcoran Gallery, Washington, 1955, Sao Paolo (Brazil) Biennial, 1955, Venice (Italy) Biennial (award), 1958, Albright-Knox Art Gallery, Buffalo, 1965, Phillip Collection, Washington, 1979; represented in permanent collections including: Met. Mus. Art, N.Y.C., Mus. Modern Art, N.Y.C., Art Inst. Chgo., Guggenheim Mus., N.Y.C., Whitney Mus. Am. Art, N.Y.C., Albright-Knox Art Gallery, Phillips Gallery, Washington, Internat. Mus. Modern Art, Tokyo and Kyoto, Japan; works include: Mural for Hilton Hotel, Tokyo, Award Poster, N.Y. Council of the Arts, 1969. Recipient 1st prize Columbia (S.C.) Biennial, 1957, Mainichi Art award, 1966, Marjorie Peabody Waite award AAAL, 1977; recipient other awards and grants from: Nikakai, 1936, Showa Shorie, 1938, Yomiuri Press, 1947, Art Inst. Chgo., 1954, 57, Carnegie Internat., 1955, UNESCO, 1958, Ford Found., 1960, Dunn Internat., 1963. Subject of profl. articles. Office: care Betty Parsons Gallery 24 W 57th St New York NY

OKAMURA, ARTHUR, artist; b. Long Beach, Calif., Feb. 24, 1932; s. Frank Akira and Yuki Okamura; student Art Inst. of Chgo., 1950-54, U. Chgo., 1951, 52, 57; art seminar Yale, 1954; m. Elizabeth Tuomi, Aug. 7, 1953 (div.); children—Beth, Jonathan, Jane, Ethan. Faculty Central YMCA Coll., Chgo., 1956, 57, Evanston Art Center, 1956-57, Art Inst. Chgo., North Shore Art League, Winnetka, Ill., Acad. Art, San Francisco, 1957, Calif. Sch. Fine Arts, 1958, Ox Bow Summer Art Sch., Saugatuck, Mich.; faculty Calif. Coll. Arts and Crafts, 1958-59, asso. prof. arts, 1966—; dir. San Francisco Studio Art, 1958; one-man shows Charles Feingarten Galleries, Chgo., 1956, 58, 59, San Francisco, 1957, Santa Barbara Mus. Art, 1958, Oakland Mus. Art, 1959, Legion Honor, San Francisco, 1961, Dallas, 1962, LaJolla (Calif.) Mus., 1963, U. Utah, 1964, San Francisco Mus. Art, 1968, Hanssen Gallery, 1968; works exhibited in group shows Pa. Acad. Fine Art, U. Chgo., U. Wash., U. Ill., Art Inst. Chgo., Los Angeles County Mus., Am. Fedn. Art, Denver Mus., NAD, De Young Mus., San Francisco, Knoedler Gallery, N.Y.C., Feingarten Galleries, Whitney Mus. Art, others; represented in permanent collections Art Inst. Chgo., Borg-Warner Collection, Chgo., Whitney Mus. Art., N.Y.C., Santa Barbara Mus. Art, San Francisco Mus. Art, Ill. State Normal, Corcoran Mus., Nat. Collection Fine Arts, Smithsonian Instn., 1968, many others. Served as pvt. AUS, 1955-56. Recipient 1st prize religious art U. Chgo., 1953; Ryerson travelling fellow, 1954; Martin Cahn award contemporary Am. paintings Art Inst. Chgo., 1957; purchase award U. Ill., 1959, Nat. Soc. Arts and Letters, N.Y.C., 1960; Neysa McMein purchase award Whitney Mus. Art, 1960; Schwabacher-Frey award 79th Ann. of San Francisco Mus. Art, 1960. Mem. Am. Fedn. Arts. Lectr. in field. Author: (with Robert Creeley) 1, 2, 3, 4, 5, 6, 7, 8, 9, 0, 1971; (with Joel Weishaus) Ox-Herding, 1971; (with Robert Bly) Basho, 1972. Home: 155 Horseshoe Hill Rd Bolinas CA 94924 Office: Calif Coll Arts and Crafts 5212 Broadway Oakland CA 94618*

O'KANE, ROBERT MAXWELL, educator; b. Dover, N.H., Sept. 13, 1920; s. Bernard D. and Evelyn (Marcotte) O'K.; B.A., U. N.H., 1947; M.Ed., U. Vt., 1952; Ed.D., Harvard, 1958; m. Alice Katherine Dinneen, June 25, 1949; children—Robert Sean, Kevin Michael, Richard Casey, Timothy Brooks. Tchr., Dover Pub. Schs., 1948-51, prin., 1952-55; supt. schs., Ipswich, Mass., 1956-59, Glen Cove, N.Y., 1959-63; dir. U.S. Dependents Schs., Europe, Africa, Middle East, 1963-65; prof. edn. Rutgers U., 1965-67; dean Sch. Edn., U. N.C., Greensboro, 1967-74, prof. edn., 1974—. Cons. Ford Found., 1968, Center for Study Instrn., N.E.A., 1965-71, Gov.'s Conf. on Edn., N.J., 1966, N.C., 1968, U.S. Office Edn., 1965-67, sch. dists. in N.Y., N.J., N.C., Conn., 1965-73, Bur. Indian Affairs, 1969; spl. lectr. Nova U., 1974; mem. exec. com. N.C. Adv. Commn. Tchr. Edn., 1968-74. Mem. Transatlantic council Boy Scouts Am., 1963-65. Bd. dirs. Center for Study Human Values, Clemmons, N.C. Served with AUS, World War II. Decorated Purple Heart with oak leaf cluster, Bronze Star, Silver Star with 1 oak leaf cluster (U.S.); Croix de Guerre; recipient Sch. Bell award Overseas Edn. Assn., 1964. Mem. N.E.A., Nat. Soc. for Study Edn., Am. Assn. Higher Edn., European Congress P.T.A. (hon. life), Phi Delta Kappa, Kappa Phi Kappa. Research in area of moral dilemmas-decision making. Home: 306 Nut Wood Circle Jamestown NC 27282 Office: Sch Edn U NC Greensboro NC 27282

OKE, JOHN BEVERLEY, educator; b. Sault Ste. Marie, Ont., Can., Mar. 23, 1928; s. Charles Clare and Lyla Jane (Partushek) O.; B.A., U. Toronto, 1949, M.A., 1950; Ph.D., Princeton U., 1953; m. Nancy Sparling, Aug. 20, 1955; children—Christopher, Kevin, Jennifer, Valerie. Lectr. U. Toronto, 1953-55, asst. prof., 1955-58; asst. prof. Calif. Inst. Tech., Pasadena, 1958-61, asso. prof., 1961-64, prof., 1964—, asso. dir. Hale Observatories, 1970-78. Mem. Astron. Soc. of the Pacific, Am. Astronomical Soc. (councillor 1969-72), Internat. Astronomical Union. Office: Hale Observatories Calif Inst Tech Pasadena CA 91125

O'KEEFE, BERNARD JOSEPH, electronics co. exec.; b. Providence, Dec. 17, 1919; s. John B. and Christina (McNee) O'K.; student George Washington U., 1937-38; B.E.E., Cath. U. Am., 1941; m. Madeline M. Healey, Nov. 21, 1942; children—Geraldine M., Thomas J., Kathleen J., Carol J. Engr., Gen. Electric Co., 1941-43; with elec. engring. dept. Mass. Inst. Tech., 1946-47; with E G & G Inc., Wellesley, Mass., 1947—, exec. v.p., 1960-65, pres., 1965—, chmn. bd., 1972—, dir. New Eng. Mchts. Bank, John Hancock Life Ins. Co., Boston Edison Co., Bird Johnson Co., Health Advancement Inc., LFE Corp. Chmn. Gov.'s Mgmt. Task Force; trustee Lahey Clinic Found.; bd. dirs. Asso. Industries Mass., Family Counseling and Guidance Centers, Ams. for Energy Independence, Mass. Taxpayers Found. Served to lt. (j.g.) USNR, 1943-46. Mem. NAM (dir.), Greater Boston C. of C. (dir., past pres.). Home: 19 Forest Hill Rd Wayland MA 01778 Office: 45 William St Wellesley MA 02181

O'KEEFE, EDWARD FRANKLIN, lawyer; b. S.I., N.Y., June 9, 1937; s. Francis Franklin and Bertha (Hall) O'K.; A.B., U. N.C., 1959; J.D., U. Denver, 1961; m. Kirstin Lou Jensen, Sept. 9, 1961; children—Kira Kathleen, Douglas Franklin, Andrew Franklin, Alison Elizabeth. Admitted to Colo. bar, 1962; law clk. Colo. Supreme Ct., Denver, 1962-63; asso. gen. counsel Hamilton Mgmt. Corp., Denver, 1966-69, sec., 1968-76, v.p. legal, gen. counsel, 1969-76; asso. gen. counsel, sec. ITT Variable Annuity Ins. Co., Denver, 1969, v.p. legal, gen. counsel, 1969-70; sec. Hamilton Funds Inc., Denver, 1968-76. Served with USNR, 1963-66. Mem. Nat. Assn. Security Dealers (dist. conduct com., chmn. 1976), Colo. Assn. Corporate Counsel (pres. 1974-75). Home: 60 S Eudora St Denver CO 80222 Office: 1420 Lincoln Center Denver CO 80264

O'KEEFE, GERALD, clergyman; b. St. Paul, Mar. 30, 1918; s. Frank and Lucille (McDonald) O'K.; student St. Paul Sem., 1938-44; B.A., Coll. St. Thomas, 1945. Ordained priest Roman Catholic Ch., 1944; chancellor Archdiocese of St. Paul, 1945-61, aux. bishop, 1961-67, vicar gen., 1962-67; rector Cathedral of St. Paul, 1961-67; bishop, Davenport, Iowa, 1967—. Address: 2706 Gaines Davenport IA 52804

O'KEEFE, JAMES L., lawyer; b. Chgo., Jan. 8, 1910; s. Raymond T. and Sadie (Monahan) O'K.; student Northwestern U., 1927-31; J.D., Chgo.-Kent Coll., 1936; m. Josephine Killian, June 19, 1933; children—James L., William J., Dennis M. Asst. state's atty. Cook County, 1933-37; partner firm O'Keefe, Ashenden & Lyons, 1937—; master in chancery Circuit Ct. Cook County, 1942-62; pub. adminstr. Cook County, 1961-70; dir. Nat. Boulevard Bank Chgo., Daniel Woodhead Co., Chessie System, Inc., C.&O. Ry., B. & O. Ry., Brink's, Inc., White Sulphur Springs Corp., Peterson, Howell & Heather, Inc. Chmn. host. com. Democratic Nat. Convs., 1952, 56, del.-at-large, 1952, 56, 60, 64, exec. mem. fin. com., 1960; vice chmn. Chgo. Non-Partisan com. Republican Nat. Conv., 1960; trustee Chgo.-Kent Coll. Law, Evans Scholars Found.; mem. Am. Bar Commn. for Nat. Inst. Justice. Named Chicagoan of Year, Jr. C. of C., 1971. Mem. Ill. C. of C., Am., Ill., Chgo. bar assns., Chgo. Assn. Commerce and Industry (Man of Year for Sports 1973), Chgo. Conv. Bur., Chgo. Dist. (pres. 1966-67), Western (pres. 1955-56), U.S. (exec. com. 1968-69) golf assns., Law Club, Newcomen Soc. Clubs: Chicago, Mid-day (trustee), Metropolitan, Northwestern U. (past pres.) (Chgo.); Captains; Muirfield Village (Columbus, Ohio); Gulfstream Golf (Fla.); Evanston (Ill.) Golf; Ocean, Delray (Fla.) Yacht, Country of Fla. Home: 1420 Sheridan Rd Wilmette IL 60091 Office: 1 First National Plaza Suite 5100 Chicago IL 60670

O'KEEFE, MICHAEL HANLEY, lawyer, state senator; b. New Orleans, Dec. 1, 1931; s. Arthur J. and Eleonora (Gordon) O'K.; LL.B., Loyola U., 1955; m. Jean Ann VanGeffen, June 18, 1955; children—Michael H., Erin Elizabeth. Admitted to La. bar, 1955; partner firm O'Keefe, O'Keefe & Berrigan, 1955—; mem. La. Senate, 1959—, Senate floor leader, 1963-67, pres. pro tem, 1971-76, pres., 1976—. Chmn. La. Commn. on Intergovtl. Relations; mem. Council State Govts. Chmn. Goals for La.; v.p. Council for Music and Performing Arts, Archdiocesan Commn. on Housing and Community Life; mem. La. Commn. Status of Women; chmn. Gov.'s Com. Correctional Treatment and Rehab.; chmn. adv. com. La. Planning Office. Served to 1st lt. AUS, 1955-57. Mem. C. of C., Am., La., New Orleans bar assns., Res. Officers Assn., Blue Key (hon.). Roman Catholic. Clubs: Kiwanis, K.C. Home: 4 Gull St New Orleans LA 70124 Office: PO Box 19103 New Orleans LA 70179

O'KEEFE, MICHAEL THOMAS, govt. exec.; b. St. Cloud, Minn., Mar. 25, 1940; s. Thomas William and Genevieve B. (McCormick) O'K.; student (Nat. Merit scholar) Marquette U., 1961-65; B.S., Marquette U., 1965; M.S. in Nuclear Physics (Woodrow Wilson fellow 1965, alt. Danforth fellow 1965), U. Pitts., 1968; m. Kathleen Marie Gnifkowski, Aug. 20, 1966; children—Steven Michael, Ann Catherine. Dir. edn. planning HEW, Washington, 1969-70, dep. asst. sec., 1977—; dir. Washington internships in edn. George Washington U., 1970-73; dir. policy analysis and evaluation U. Ill., Chgo., 1973-74, asso. v.p. acad. affairs, 1974-77; mem. corp. bd. St. Mary Center for Learning, Chgo., 1974-76, chmn., 1976; bd. dirs. Center New Schs., Chgo., 1974-77, Carole Robertson Center for Learning, 1975-77; head U.S. del. to Orgn. Econ. Coop. and Devel., 1979; cons. in field. Mem. Am. Assn. Higher Edn., Am. Ednl. Research Assn. Democrat. Research in fed. edn. programs, acad. policies, internships, nuclear physics. Office: Room 404E 200 Independence Ave SW Washington DC 20201

O'KEEFE, RAYMOND THOMAS, JR., banker; b. Chgo., Sept. 8, 1911; s. Raymond Thomas and Sadie (Monahan) O'K.; grad. Mercersburg Acad., 1933, DePaul U., 1937; m. Florence Griffin, Apr. 1939; children—Raymond Thomas III, John G. Pub. relations counsel, 1938-41; investigation enemy aliens Dept. Justice, 1941-42; personnel dir. Kropp Forge Co., Chgo., 1942, dir. indsl. relations, 1943-44, v.p., 1944-55, dir., 1946-67, exec. v.p., treas., 1955-61, chmn., 1959-67, pres., chief exec. officer, 1961-67; v.p. Michigan Av. Nat. Bank, Chgo., 1967-73, also dir., mem. exec. com.; chmn. exec. com. 1st Bank of Oak Park (Ill.), 1973—; past trustee, pres., chmn., chief exec. officer Chgo. and West Towns Ry., Inc. Chmn. heavy mfg. group Community Fund drive, 1946; co-chmn. city div. A.R.C. fund drive, 1957, also active YMCA, March of Dimes, Chgo. Named outstanding young man of Chgo., Chgo. Jr. Assn. Commerce, 1947, outstanding young man of Ill., Ill. Jr. C. of C., 1947. Home: 533 Meadow Rd Winnetka IL 60093 Office: 11 Madison St Oak Park IL 60302

O'KEEFE, ROBERT JAMES, banker; b. Boston, Dec. 30, 1926; s. James J. and Irene (Egan) O'K.; A.B., Boston Coll., 1951; grad. Advanced Mgmt. Program, Harvard, 1968; m. Mary U. Hughes, Oct. 12, 1951 (dec.); children—Mary F., Robert James; m. Simone A. Charbonneau, Apr. 3, 1976. Mem. staff Mass. Inst. Tech., Cambridge, 1951-55; cons. Arthur D. Little, Inc., Cambridge, 1955-58; with Chase Manhattan Bank, N.Y.C., 1958-79, v.p., 1964-69, sr. v.p., 1969-79; sr. v.p. Am. Security Bank, Washington, 1979—. Trustee Boston Coll., 1974—; mem. computer sci. and engring. bd. Nat. Acad. Sci., 1971-73. Served with AUS, 1945-46. Recipient Alumni medal Boston Coll., 1970. Mem. Assn. for Computing Machinery, Boston Coll. Alumni Assn. (pres. 1973-74), Ops. Research Soc. Am., Bank Adminstrn. Inst. Club: City Tavern. Home: 1586 Forest Villa Ln McLean VA 22101 Office: 1501 Pennsylvania Ave NW Washington DC 20013

O'KEEFE, VINCENT THOMAS, clergyman; b. Jersey City, Jan. 10, 1920; s. James and Sarah (Allen) O'K.; A.B., Georgetown U., 1943; M.A., Woodstock Coll., 1945, Ph.L., 1944; Th.L., St. Albert de Louvain (Belgium), 1951; student Muenster (Germany) U., 1951-52; S.T.D., Gregorian U., Rome, 1954. Ordained priest Roman Catholic Ch., 1950; instr. Latin and math. Regis High Sch., N.Y.C., 1944-47; asso. prof. fundamental theology Woodstock Coll., 1954-60; acad. v.p. Fordham U., 1960-62, exec. v.p., 1962-63, pres., 1963-65; gen. asst. to superior gen. Soc. of Jesus, Rome, 1965—. Mem. regents exams. and scholarship center N.Y. State Dept. Edn.; pres., dir., mem. exec. com. Council Higher Ednl. Instns. of N.Y.C. Dir. N.Y. World's Fair 1964-65 Corp. Bd. mgrs. New York Bot. Garden; dir., mem. bd. Center Intercultural Formation, Cuernavaca, Mexico; trustee Fordham U. Fellow Royal Soc. Encouragement Arts Mfrs. and Commerce (London); mem. Council Higher Edn. City N.Y., Religion Council Cath. Secondary Schs. Archdiocese of N.Y., Cath. Bibl. Assn., Cath. Theol. Assn. Am., Religion Ednl. Assn., N.E.A., Jesuit Ednl. Assn., Nat. Cath. Edn. Assn., Internat. Assn. Univs., Soc. Cath. Coll. Tchrs. Sacred Doctrine, Phi Beta Kappa. Author: The History and Meaning of Ex Attrito Fit Contritus, 1957. Contbr. articles to religious publs., also book reviews. Address: Borgo S Spirito 5 Casella Postale 6139 Rome 00100 Italy

O'KEEFFE, CHARLES B(ENJAMIN), JR., presdl. asst.; b. Richmond, Va., Nov. 12, 1939; s. Charles B. and Marie Ellen (McDonough) O'K.; student Med. Coll. Va. Sch. Pharmacy, 1957-59; student Belmont Abbey Coll., 1959-60; B.S., Eckels Coll., 1961; M.B.A., Loyola Coll., Balt., 1977; m. Ann Lee Bliley, Jan. 27, 1962; children—Charles B. III, Joan, Kathleen, Brian. Funeral dir. Joseph W. Bliley Co., Richmond, Va., 1956-64; rep. Ayerst Labs., N.Y.C., 1964-68; pres. Drug Abuse Rehab. Services, Richmond, 1969-71, Pharm. Services Inc., Richmond, 1968-71; v.p. Washington Reference Lab. div. Electro-Nucleonics Inc., 1971-72, chief exec. officer, Silver Spring Md., 1972-75; exec. dir. Found. Internat. Resources, Washington, 1975-76; adv. White House, 1977-78; spl. asst. to Pres. U.S., 1978—; lectr. in field; cons. to govt. agys., govts. Europe, Asia, Can., health orgns.; exec. dir. Strategy Council, 1977. Democrat. Roman Catholic. Home: 12310 Robious Rd Midlothian VA 23113 Office: White House Washington DC 20500

O'KEEFFE, GEORGIA, artist; b. Sun Prairie, Wis., Nov. 15, 1887; d. Francis and Ida (Totto) O'Keeffe; student Art Inst. Chgo., 1904-05, Art Students' League, N.Y.C., 1907-08, U. Va., summer 1912, Columbia, 1914-16; D.F.A. (hon.), William and Mary Coll., 1938, U. N.M., 1964, Brown U., 1971, Minn. Coll. Art and Design, 1972; Litt.D., U. Wis., 1942, Mills Coll., 1951, Mt. Holyoke Coll., 1971; D.H.L., Columbia, 1971; D.Arts, Harvard, 1973; m. Alfred Stieglitz, Dec. 11, 1924. Began as illustrator for advt. cos., 1929; supr. art pub. schs., Amarillo, Tex., 1912-14; instr. art U. Va., summers, 1913-16; head art dept. West Tex. State Normal Coll., Canyon, 1916-18; became one of group sponsored by Alfred Stieglitz; paintings first exhibited by him at 291, N.Y.C., 1916-17, Anderson Galleries, 1923, 24, 25; ann. one-man shows at Intimate Gallery, An American Place till 1946, N.Y.C.; retrospective exhbn. Art Inst. Chgo., 1943, Mus. Modern Art, N.Y.C., 1946, Worcester (Mass.) Art Mus., 1960, Amon Carter Mus., Ft. Worth, 1966, Mus. Fine Arts, Houston, 1966, U. N.Mex., 1966, Whitney Mus. Am. Art, 1970, Art Inst. Chgo., 1971, San Francisco Mus. Art, 1971; represented in major museums throughout U.S. Recipient Creative Arts award Brandeis U., 1963, Gold Medal for painting Nat. Inst. Arts and Letters, 1970, M. Carey Thomas award Bryn Mawr Coll., 1971, Edward MacDowell medal MacDowell Colony, 1973, award Skowhegan Sch. Painting and Sculpture, 1973; Presdl. Medal of Honor, 1977. Mem. Nat. Inst. Arts and Letters, Am. Acad. Arts and Letters, Am. Acad. Arts and Scis. Author: Georgia O'Keeffe Drawings, 1968; Georgia O'Keeffe, 1976. Home: Abiquiu NM 87510

O'KEEFFE, JOHN JOSEPH, JR., service co. exec., lawyer; b. Norwalk, Conn., Dec. 21, 1941; s. John Joseph and Mary Ellen (Snee) O'K.; B.A., Fairfield U., 1965; J.D., George Washington U., 1968; m. Valerie Anne Moore, Sept. 2, 1967; children—Anna Gould, John Moore. Admitted to N.Y. State bar, 1969; atty. Pan Am. World Airways, Inc., N.Y.C., 1968-72; atty. Trans World Airlines, N.Y.C., 1972-77, corp. sec., asst. gen. counsel, 1977—; corp. sec., asst. gen. counsel Trans World Corp., N.Y.C., 1979—; sec. Hilton Internat. Co., 1977—, Canteen Corp., 1977—, Spartan Food Systems, Inc., 1979—. Mem. N.Y. State Bar Assn. Republican. Roman Catholic. Home: 11 Dante St Larchmont NY 10538 Office: 605 Third Ave New York NY 10016

O'KELLEY, GROVER DAVIS, educator, chemist; b. Birmingham, Ala., Nov. 23, 1928; s. Grover C. and Ruth (Davis) O'K.; A.B., Howard Coll., 1948; Ph.D., U. Cal., Berkeley, 1951; m. Genie Rae Slocum, June 23, 1950; children—Joanne Ruth, Kevin Davis. Research asst. U. Cal. Radiation Lab., 1948-51; lead chemist Cal. Research & Devel. Co., 1951-54; sr. chemist Oak Ridge Nat. Lab., 1954-59, group leader, 1959-74, sr. research staff mem., 1974—; prof. chemistry U. Tenn., 1964—. Mem. Lunar Sample Preliminary Exam. Team, cons. NASA; mem. com. on nuclear sci., chmn. subcom. on radiochemistry Nat. Acad. Scis.-NRC, 1974-78. Fellow Am. Phys. Soc.; mem. Am. Chem. Soc. (alt. councillor div. nuclear chemistry and tech. 1966-68, 77-79, chmn. 1971), AAAS, Am. Geophys. Union, Research Soc. Am., Sigma Xi. Author: (with N.R. Johnson, E. Eichler) Nuclear Chemistry, 1963. Contbr. articles to profl. jours. Home: 8228 Corteland Dr Knoxville TN 37919 Office: PO Box X Oak Ridge TN 37830

O'KELLEY, JOSEPH CHARLES, educator; b. Unadilla, Ga., May 9, 1922; s. Thomas Landrum and Maude (Hall) O'K.; A.B., U. N.C., 1943, M.A., 1948; Ph.D., Iowa State U., 1950; m. Hallie LaVonne Held, June 16, 1951; children—Susan Elaine, Celia Anne, Thomas Burnell, Ellen Catherine. Mem. faculty dept. biology U. Ala., University 1951—, asso. prof., 1958-61, prof., 1961—, chmn. dept., 1969-74, research prof., 1977—. Served with USAAF, 1943-46. Decorated Air medal. NSF postdoctoral fellow U. Wis., 1953-54; NIH spl. fellow Johns Hopkins, 1965-66. Fellow AAAS; mem. Am. Inst. Biol. Scis., Phi Beta Kappa. Home: 2910 17th St E Tuscaloosa AL 35404 Office: PO Box 1927 University AL 35486

O'KELLEY, WILLIAM CLARK, judge; b. Atlanta, Jan. 2, 1930; s. Ezra Clark and Theo (Johnson) O'K.; A.B., Emory U., 1951, LL.B., 1953; m. Ernestine Allen, Mar. 28, 1953; children—Virginia Leigh, William Clark. Admitted to Ga. bar, 1952, practiced in Atlanta, 1957-59; asst. U.S. atty. No. Dist. Ga., 1959-61; partner law firm O'Kelley, Hopkins & Van Gerpen, Atlanta, 1961-70; U.S. dist. judge No. Dist. Ga., Atlanta, 1970—. Corporate sec., dir. Gwinnett Bank & Trust Co., Norcross, Ga., 1968-70. Mem. exec. com., gen. counsel Ga. Republican Com., 1968-70. Served as 1st lt. USAF, 1953-57; capt. Res. Mem. Am., Atlanta bar assns., Ga. State Bar, Am. Judicature Soc., Dist. Judges Assn. 5th Circuit (pres. 1979-80), Sigma Chi, Phi Delta Phi, Omicron Delta Kappa. Baptist. Kiwanian (past pres.). Clubs: Atlanta Athletic, Lawyers of Atlanta; Berkeley Hills Golf (Norcross, Ga.). Home: 550 Ridgecrest Dr Norcross GA 30071 Office: US District Court 214 US Courthouse Atlanta GA 30303

O'KELLY, ALAN P., lawyer; b. Butte, Mont., Mar. 29, 1917; B.S., Harvard, 1938; LL.B., U. Calif. at Berkeley, 1941. Admitted to Calif. bar, 1941, Wash. bar, 1946; partner firm Paine, Lowe, Coffin, Herman & O'Kelly, Spokane, Wash. Instr. law, Gonzaga U., 1948-52. Mem. Spokane County, Wash., Am. bar assns., State Bar Calif., Phi Delta Phi. Office: Wash Trust Bank Bldg Spokane WA 99204

O'KELLY, BERNARD, coll. dean; b. Winnipeg, Man., Can., Aug. 10, 1926; s. Bartholomew Bernard and Cora (Beadle) O'K.; student U. Man., 1942-44; B.A., Coll. de l'Immaculée Conception, Montreal, 1950, L.Ph., 1950; M.A., Harvard, 1955, Ph.D., 1960; m. Marcia Herz Levin, Feb. 2, 1957; children—Christopher D.B. (dec.), Elizabeth S., Peter B.J. Came to U.S., 1954, permanent resident, 1957. Lectr. classics St. Paul's Coll., U. Man., 1950-52; lectr. French and English, Loyola Coll., Montreal, 1952-54; instr., then asst. prof. Ohio State U., 1957-66; research asso. Yale, 1964-65; prof. English, dean Coll. Arts and Scis., U. N.D., 1966—; asso. mem. Center Study Democratic Instns. Vice pres. Council Colls. Arts and Scis., 1972-73, pres., 1973-74; bd. dirs. Am. Conf. Acad. Deans, 1975—, sec., editor jour., 1976—; pres., chmn. exec. com. Fedn. Pub. Programs in the Humanities, 1977—. Hart scholar classics U. Man., 1944; Dexter travelling fellow Harvard, 1956; research grantee Am. Philos. Soc. Mem. Modern Lang. Assn., AAUP, Archaeol. Inst. Am., Nat. Council Tchrs. English, Renaissance Soc. Am., United World Federalists. Editor: The Renaissance Image of Man and the World, 1966. Home: 515 Campbell Dr Grand Forks ND 58201

O'KELLY, LAWRENCE IVAN, psychologist, educator; b. Marion, Iowa, June 3, 1913; s. Percy V. and Bertha (Domer) O.; B.A., U. Wyoming, 1934; M.A., Ohio State U., 1936, Ph.D., 1939; m. Barbara Ann Jones, June 3, 1965; 1 dau. by previous marriage, Leora S. Perkins. Instr. U. Colo. at Boulder, 1939-40, asst. prof., 1940-45, asso. prof., 1945-49; prof. U. Ill. at Urbana, 1949-68; prof. psychology Mich. State U. at East Lansing, 1968—, chmn. dept., 1968-73; cons. VA, Martin Aircraft, Hughes Aircraft. Served with AUS, 1942-46. Diplomate Am. Bd. Examiners in Psychology. Fellow Am. Psychol. Assn., AAAS; mem. Psychonomic Soc., Am. Assn. U. Profs., Animal Behavior Soc., Soc. for Neuroscience, Midwestern Psychol. Assn., Sigma Xi. Author: Introduction to Psychopatholgy, rev. edit., 1952. Home: 575 Dansville Rd Dansville MI 48819

O'KEY, CLIFFORD WILLIAM, city ofcl.; b. Chgo., Nov. 15, 1922; s. Floyd M. and Grace (Poore) O'K.; B.A., Westminster Coll., Pa., 1949; M.A. (Samuel Fels scholar), U. Pa., 1951; postgrad. U. Chgo., 1964; m. Ruth E. Gilliland, Sept. 26, 1945; children—Jeffrey, Allisyn, Susan, Clifford, Christopher. Asst. dir. research Pa. Tax Equalization Bd., 1950-52; dir. finance, asst. mgr., Milford, Conn., 1952-55; city adminstr., Rahway, N.J., 1955-57; city mgr., Clayton, Mo., 1957-65, Norman, Okla., 1965-67, Little Rock, 1967-68, Miami Beach, Fla., 1969-72, Tucson, 1972—; adviser to Turkey, AID, Dept. State, 1965. Recipient Time mag. awards, 1958, 60, first place award competition for civic improvement Okla. C. of C., 1965. Mem. Internat., Ariz. city mgrs. assns., Am. Soc. Pub. Adminstrn., Am. Soc. Planning Ofcls., Am. Pub. Works Assn., Nat. Municipal League, Municipal Finance Officers Assn., Nat. Assn. Cost Accountants. Kiwanian. Home: 5631 Towner Ave Tucson AZ 85712 Office: Office of City Manager Tucson AZ

OKIN, FRANKLIN JAY, ins. co. exec.; b. N.Y.C., May 8, 1932; s. Steven Irving and Helen Margaret (Johantgen) O.; A.B., Princeton U., 1957; LL.B. cum laude, Yale U., 1962; m. Janet L. Atkinson, Jan. 8, 1966; children—Steven, Laura. Admitted to D.C. bar, 1962, Conn. bar, 1967; with firm Covington & Burling, Washington, 1962-66; with Travelers Corp., Hartford, Conn., 1966—, sec., 1974—, asso. gen. counsel, 1975—; dir. Travelers Corp. Asia Ltd.; lectr. bus. adminstrn. U. Conn., Sec. 1969. Condr.'s council Hartford Symphony, 1972-74. Served with USAAF, 1951-55. Mem. Am. Soc. Corporate Secs. (dir.), Am., Conn., Fed., Hartford County bar assns., Assn. Life Ins. Counsel, Am. Council Life Ins., Order of Coif. Clubs: Hartford; Princeton (N.Y.C.). Home: 40 Pheasant Hill Dr West Hartford CT 06107 Office: 1 Tower Sq Hartford CT 06115

OKIN, ROBERT LAURENCE, state ofcl., psychiatrist; b. N.Y.C., July 22, 1942; s. Milton and Rose (Balton) O.; A.B., U. Chgo., 1964, M.D., 1967; m. Susan Moller, July 29, 1972; 1 dau., Laura. Intern, Albert Einstein Coll. Medicine, N.Y.C., resident in psychiatry, 1968-71; Mass. cons. NIMH, Boston, 1971-73; commr. Vt. Dept. Mental Health, Montpelier, 1973—, Mass. Dept. Mental Health, Boston, 1975—. Diplomate Am. Bd. Psychiatry and Neurology. Mem. Mass. Pub. Health Assn., Alpha Omega Alpha. Home: RFD 2 Bedford Rd Lincoln MA 01773 Office: 160 N Washington St Boston MA 02114

OKITA, GEORGE T., educator, pharmacologist; b. Seattle, Jan. 18, 1922; s. Kazuo and Fusao (Muguruma) O.; student U. Cin., 1943-44; B.A., Ohio State U., 1948; Ph.D., U. Chgo., 1951; m. Fujiko Shimizu, Nov. 29, 1958; children—Ronald Hajime, Sharon Mariko, Glenn

Torao. Research asst., research asso., instr., asst. prof. U. Chgo., 1949-63; asso. prof. Northwestern U., 1963-66, prof. pharmacology, 1966—, acting chmn. dept., 1968-70, 76-77. Served with AUS, 1944-46. NIH Postdoctoral fellow, 1952. Mem. A.A.A.S., Am. Assn. U. Profs., Am. Soc. Pharmacology and Exptl. Therapeutics, Internat. Soc. Biochem. Pharmacology, Am. Heart Assn., U.S. Pharmacopeidal Conv., Cardiac Muscle Soc., Sigma Xi. Contbr. articles to profl. jours. Research in med. field. Asst. editor Jour. Pharmacology and Exptl. Therapeutics, 1965-68. Home: 128 Heather Ln Wilmette IL 60091 Office: Searle Bldg Northwestern U Chicago IL 60611

O'KONSKI, A.E., former congressman; b. Kewaunee, Wis., May 26, 1904; s. Frank and Antonia (Paska) O'K.; B.S., State Teachers Coll., 1926; grad. student U. Ia., 1927-28, U. Wis., 1932; m. Veronica Hemming, Aug. 26, 1935. Instr. high schs., 1926-29; instr. speech Ore. State Coll., 1928-31; supt. schs., Pulaski, Wis., 1932-35; instr. Jr. Coll., Coleraine, Minn., 1935-36; head speech dept. U. Detroit, 1936-38; pub. relations counsel state Republican orgns., 1938-40; mem. 78th-92d Congresses, 10th Wis. Dist., mem. armed services com.; pres. Alvin E. O'Konski Enterprises, Inc., engaged in television ownership and mgmt.; pres. Northland Television, Inc. Pres., Am. Anti-Communist Orgn., Inc., 1947; mem. Katyn Forest Massacre Com.; past dir. World League to Stop Communism. Decorated Polonia Restituta medal (Polish govt. in Exile), 1953. Mem. Pi Kappa Delta. Republican. Author: Speech Practice, 1937. Home: 11 S Flag Dr Kissemme FL 32741

O'KONSKI, CHESTER THOMAS, scientist, educator; b. Kewaunee, Wis., May 12, 1921; s. Thomas Michael and Stella (Ratajczak) O'K.; B.S., U. Wis., 1942; M.S., Northwestern U., 1946, Ph.D., 1949; m. Annabelle Hollingsworth, Aug. 21, 1948; children—Holly Ann, Timothy Chester, Mark Steven, Brian Nelson. Research chemist Northwestern U., 1942-47, Ind. U., 1947-48; mem. faculty chemistry U. Calif. at Berkeley, 1948—, asso. prof., 1956-60, prof., 1960—; Knapp Meml. lectr. U. Wis., 1958; Miller Sci. Found. research prof. U. Calif., 1960; NIH fellow Princeton and Harvard, 1962-63; Nobel guest prof. Uppsala U., Sweden, 1970. Guggenheim fellow, 1955. Mem. A.A.A.S., Am. Chem. Soc., Am. Phys. Soc., Biophys. Soc., Soc. Neurosci., Phi Beta Kappa, Sigma Xi. Co-author, editor: Molecular Electro-optics, Part 1 Theory and Methods, 1976, Part 2, Applications to Biopolymers, 1978. Office: Dept Chemistry Univ California Berkeley CA 94720

OKRENT, DAVID, educator; b. Passaic, N.J., Apr. 19, 1922; s. Abram and Gussie (Pearlman) O.; M.E., Stevens Inst. Tech., 1943; M.A., Harvard, 1948, Ph.D., in Physics, 1951; m. Rita Gilda Holtzman, Feb. 1, 1948; children—Neil, Nina, Jocelyne. Mech. engr. NACA, Cleve., 1943-46; sr. physicist Argonne (Ill.) Nat. Lab., 1951-71; regents lectr. U. Calif. at Los Angeles, 1968, prof. engring., 1971—; vis. prof. U. Wash., Seattle, 1963, U. Ariz., Tucson, 1970-71; Isaac Taylor chair Technion, 1977-78. Mem. adv. com. on reactor safeguards AEC, 1963—, also chmn., 1966; sci. sec. to sec. gen. of Geneva Conf., 1958; mem. U.S. del. to all Geneva Atoms for Peace Confs. Guggenheim fellow, 1961-62, 77-78. recipient Distinguished Appointment award Argonne Univs. Assn., 1970. Fellow Am. Phys. Soc., Am. Nuclear Soc., Nat. Acad. Engring. Author: Fast Reactor Cross Sections, 1960; Computing Methods in Reactor Physics, 1968; Reactivity Coefficients in Large Fast Power Reactors, 1970. Contbr. articles to profl. jours. Home: 439 Veteran Ave Los Angeles CA 90024

OKRESS, ERNEST CARL, physicist-engr.; b. Hamtramck, Mich., Mar. 9, 1910; s. Ernest Steven and Emille (Schvanner) O.; B.E.E., U. Detroit, 1935; M.Sc., U. Mich., 1940; postgrad. N.Y. U., 1946-48, Poly. Inst. N.Y., 1951-53; D.Sc., Sussex (Eng.) Coll. Tech., 1974. Adv. engr., mgr. Microwave Center, Westinghouse Electric Corp., Bloomfield, N.J. and Elmira, N.Y., 1940-59; sr. research engr. Sperry Gyroscope Co., Great Neck, N.Y., 1959-62; mgr. plasma physics, research div. Am. Standard, Inc., Piscataway, N.J., 1962-68; sr. engr. cons. SFD Labs., Inc. subsidiary Varian Assos., Union, N.J., 1968; sr. physicist, mem. sci. staff Brookhaven Nat. Lab., Upton, N.Y., 1968-70; sr. research scientist Cons. Seversky Electron-Atom Corp., Garden City, N.Y., 1970; sr. research physicist EMR div. Schlumberger, Ltd., Princeton, N.J., 1970-72, cons. engr., 1972-74; cons. engr. Westinghouse Electric Corp., 1972, Princeton Electron Products, 1972-74, U.S. Dept. Agr., 1968-74; sr. physicist-engr. Gen. Electric Co., Space Scis. Lab., Valley Forge Space Center, 1974—; cons. physicist Gen. Electric Co., 1975-77, Univ. City Sci. Center, 1977-78; cons., prin. scientist Franklin Research Center div. Franklin Inst., Phila., 1978—; tchr. U.S. Office Edn., 1943. Recipient Westinghouse spl. patents awards for outstanding inventions, 1945, 50, certificate commendation U.S. Office Sci. Research and Devel., 1945. Certificate, Nat. Council Engring. Examiners; registered profl. engr., N.J. Fellow IEEE, Am. Phys. Soc.; mem. Sigma Xi. Author, editor: Crossed Field Microwave Devices, 1961; Microwave Power Engineering, 1968. Papers examiner, book reviewer Jour. Applied Physics, 1947, 49, 52, IEEE, 1953, 56; contbr. articles to profl. jours. Patentee in field. Pioneer superpower magnetrons, electromagnetic levitation and confinement of solid and liquid metals including tungsten, microwave power engring. non-equilibrium suppressed electric gas discharge ionization for closed cycle magnetohydrodynamic power generation and gas excitation of dynamic gas laser and elec. propulsion, high energy and high power nanosecond pulse generation, spacecraft charging technology, laser-matter interaction physics. Home: The Plaza Apt 6H Parkway at 18th St Philadelphia PA 19103

OKSENBERG, MICHEL CHARLES, polit. scientist; b. Antwerp, Belgium, Oct. 12, 1938; s. Israel Aron and Klara (Safier) O.; came to U.S., 1939, naturalized, 1945; B.A., Swarthmore Coll., 1960; M.A., Columbia, 1963, Ph.D., 1969; m. Lois Elinor Clarenbach, June 16, 1962; children—David Aron, Deborah Ann. Asst. prof. polit. sci. Stanford (Calif.) U., 1966-68; asst. prof. polit. sci. Columbia U., N.Y.C., 1968-71, asso. prof., 1972-74; asso. prof. polit. sci. U. Mich., Ann Arbor, 1973-76, prof., 1977—; mem. staff Nat. Security Council, Washington, 1977—; mem. East Asia adv. panel Dept. State, 1975-77. Mem. bd. mgrs. Swarthmore Coll., 1970-74. Fgn. Area Tng. fellow, 1964-66. Mem. Am. Polit. Sci. Assn., Assn. Asian Studies (dir. 1970-74), Council on Fgn. Relations, Asia Soc. (dir. China Council 1975-77). Author: China: The Convulsive Soc., 1971; (with Robert Oxnam) China and America, 1977; editor: China's Developmental Experience, 1973; The Dragon and the Eagle, 1978; mem. editorial bd. China Quar., 1970—, Chinese Law and Govt., 1972—, Contemporary China, 1976—. Office: Old Exec Office Bldg Washington DC

OKUMA, THOMAS MASAJL, clergyman, educator; b. Kauai, Hawaii, Nov. 20, 1919; s. Seichi and Uto (Kiyomura) O.; student U. Hawaii, 1938-40; B.A., Berea Coll., 1943; student Andover Newton Theol. Sch., 1943-44; B.D., Yale, 1946; Ph.D., Boston U., 1964; m. Naomi Chafin, June 7, 1945; children—Margaret Y., Kathryn H., David M. Ordained to ministry United Ch. Christ, 1946; minister in Hawaii conf., 1946-49; treas. Angola Mission, United Ch. Bd. World Ministries, 1950-60; sec., secretariat on racial and ethnic relations World Council Chs., 1964-66; asso. prof. religion and philosophy Hawaii Loa Coll., 1966—, prof., 1971—, dean of faculty, 1976—, dir. Inst. for Religion and Social Change, 1969-74; lectr. on Angola, African studies program, Boston, U., 1962. Mem. planning com. World Conf. on Ch. and Soc., Geneva, Switzerland, 1966. Author: Angola in Ferment, 1962. Editor: Race Relations in Ecumenical Perspective, 1964-66. Contbr. articles to profl. jours., encys. Home: 1947 Alaeloa St Honolulu HI 96821

OKUN, ARTHUR M., economist, econ. cons.; b. Jersey City, Nov. 28, 1928; s. Louis and Rose (Cantor) O.; A.B., Columbia, 1949, Ph.D., 1956; M.A. (hon.), Yale, 1963; m. Suzanne Grossman, July 1, 1951; children—Lewis Edward, Matthew James, Steven John. Instr. econs. Yale, New Haven, 1952-56, asst. prof., 1956-60, asso. prof., 1960-63, prof., 1963-67; staff mem. Cowles Found. for Research in Econs., Yale, 1956-67; staff economist Council Econ. Advisers, Washington, 1961-62, mem. council, 1964-68, chmn., 1968-69; econ. cons. Donaldson, Lufkin & Jenrette, N.Y.C., 1969—; cons. Am. Security & Trust Co., Washington, 1970—; dir. Intercapital Funds; sr. fellow Brookings Instn., Washington, 1969—; Godkin lectr. Harvard, 1974. Recipient medal for excellence Columbia, 1968, Frank E. Seidman Disting. award for polit. economy, 1979. Fellow Am. Statis. Assn., Am. Acad. Arts and Scis., Econometric Soc.; mem. Am. Econ. Assn. (v.p. 1972), Phi Beta Kappa. Author: The Political Economy of Prosperity, 1970 (McKinsey Found. Book award); Equality and Efficiency: The Big Tradeoff, 1975. Editor: Yale Economic Essays, 1963-64; The Battle Against Unemployment, 1964, rev. edit., 1972; co-editor Brookings Papers on Economic Activity, 1970—. Contbr. articles on econ. forecasting, potential output, fiscal and monetary policy profl. publs. Home: 2809 Ellicott St NW Washington DC 20008 Office: Brookings Instn 1775 Massachusetts Ave Washington DC 20036

OKUN, DANIEL ALEXANDER, educator; b. N.Y.C., June 19, 1917; s. William Howard and Leah (Seligman) O.; B.S., Cooper Union, 1937; M.S., Calif. Inst. Tech., 1938; D.Sc., Harvard, 1948; m. Elizabeth Griffin, Jan. 14, 1946; children—Michael Griffin, Tema Jon. With USPHS, 1940-42; teaching fellow Harvard, 1946-48; with Malcolm Pirnie, cons. environ. engrs., N.Y.C., 1948-52; asso. prof. dept. environ. scis. and engring. U. N.C. at Chapel Hill, 1952-55, prof., 1955-73, Kenan prof., 1973—, head dept. environ. scis. and engring., 1955-73, dir. Water Resources Research Inst., 1965—, chmn. faculty, 1970-73. Dir. Wapora, Inc. Vis. prof. Technol. U. Delft, 1960-61, Univ. Coll. London, 1966-67, 73-75; editor environ. scis. series Acad. Press, 1968-75; cons. to industry, cons. engrs., govtl. agys., World Bank, WHO. Adv. bd. Ackland Meml. Art Mus., 1973-78; bd. dirs. Warren Regional Planning Corp., 1971-77, Inter-Ch. Council Housing Corp., 1975—, N.C. Water Quality Council, 1975-77; adv. com. for med. research Pan Am. Health Orgn.; chmn. Washington Met. Area Water Supply Study Com., Nat. Acad Scis.-NRC; bd. sci. and tech. for internat. devel. NRC. Served from lt. to maj. AUS, 1942-46. Recipient Harrison Prescott Eddy medal for research Water Pollution Control Fedn., 1950, Catedratico Honorario, Univ. Nacional de Ingenieria, Lima, Peru, 1957, Gordon Maskew Fair award Am. Acad. Environ. Engrs., 1973, Thomas Jefferson award U. N.C. at Chapel Hill, 1973, Gordon Y. Billard award N.Y. Acad. Scis., 1975; Gordon Maskew Fair medal Water Pollution Control Fedn., 1978. NSF fellow, 1960-61, Fed. Water Pollution Control Adminstrn. fellow, 1966-67, Fulbright-Hayes lectr., 1973-74. Diplomate Am. Acad. Environ. Engrs. (pres. 1969-70); registered profl. engr., N.C., N.Y. Fellow ASCE (chmn. environ. engring. div. 1967-68, Simon W. Freese award 1977), Inst. Water Pollution Control (Eng.); mem. Nat. Acad. Engring., AAUP (chpt. pres. 1963-64), Water Pollution Control Fedn. (chmn. research com. 1961-66, dir.-at-large 1969-72), Sigma Xi (pres. chpt. 1968-69). Author: (with Gordon M. Fair and John C. Geyer) Water and Wastewater Engineering, 2 vols., 1966, 68; Elements of Water Supply and Wastewater Disposal, 1971; (with George Ponghis) Community Wastewater Collection and Disposal, 1975; Regionalization of Water Management—A Revolution in England and Wales, 1977. Editor: (with M.B. Pescod) Water Supply and Wastewater Disposal in Developing Countries, 1971. Contbr. to publs. in field. Home: Linden Rd Route 7 Chapel Hill NC 27514

OKUN, HERBERT STUART, fgn. service officer; b. N.Y.C., Nov. 27, 1930; s. Irving and Ida Muriel (Levine) O.; A.B., Stanford, 1951; postgrad. Syracuse U., 1951-52, Princeton U., 1952; M.P.A., Harvard U., 1959; m. Lorraine Joan Price, Dec. 5, 1954; children—Jennifer, Elizabeth, Alexandra. Joined U.S. Fgn. Service, 1955; vice consul, Munich, Germany, 1955-57; 2d sec. embassy, Moscow, USSR, 1961-63; consul, prin. officer Belo Horizonte, Brazil, 1964-65; 1st sec., prin. officer embassy, Brasilia, Brazil, 1965-66, counsellor embassy, prin. officer, 1967-68; assigned Naval War Coll., 1968-69; spl. asst. to sec. of state, 1969-71; alternate dir. Office Soviet Affairs, Dept. State, 1971-73; spl. asst. for internat. affairs to comdr.-in-chief NATO So. Command, Naples, Italy, 1973-74; minister-counsellor, dep. chief mission, Lisbon, Portugal, 1975-78; dep. chmn. SALT, Geneva, 1978—; dep. chmn. U.S. del. to U.S.-USSR Talks on Prevention Incidents at Sea, 1971-72. Served with AUS, 1952-54. Mem. Am. Fgn. Service Assn., Phi Beta Kappa. Home: 3907 Rosemary St Chevy Chase MD 20015 Office: Ave de la Paix 1-3 1202 Geneva Switzerland

OKUN, MILTON THEODORE, musical dir., producer, music co. exec.; b. Bklyn., Dec. 23, 1923; s. William H. and Leah (Seligman) O.; B.Music Edn., N.Y. U., 1949; M.Music Edn., Oberlin Conservatory Music, 1951; m. Rosemary Primont, May 12, 1958; children—Jennifer, Andrew. Singer-guitarist for record cos., 1958-62; arranger, producer various advt. agys., 1960—; arranger, record producer Chad Mitchell Trio, 1959-68, Peter, Paul and Mary, 1960-70; mus. dir. Brothers Four, 1962-64, John Denver, 1969—, Mary Travers, 1970-73, Peter Yarrow, 1971-72, Starland Vocal Band, 1975; singer with Harry Belafonte, 1958, asst. condr., arranger, 1959-61, condr., 1960-62; pres. Cherry Lane Music Co., Greenwich, Conn., 1960—. Mem. Nat. Acad. Rec. Arts and Scis. (gov. 1967-69, pres. N.Y. chpt. 1969-70). Author: Something to Sing About, 1968. Editor: New York Times Great Songs of the Sixties, 1970, Vol. 2, 1974; New York Times Great Songs of Lennon and McCartney, 1973; New York Times County Music's Greatest Songs, 1978; New York Times Great Songs of the 70's, 1978; arranger: Folksongs and Footnotes, 1961. Office: 50 Holly Hill Ln Greenwich CT 06830

OLAFSON, FREDERICK ARLAN, educator; b. Winnipeg, Man., Can., Sept. 1, 1924; (parents U.S. citizens); s. Kristinn K. and Fredericka (Björnson) O.; A.B., Harvard, 1947, M.A., 1948, Ph.D., 1951; m. Allie Lewis, June 20, 1952; children—Peter Niel, Christopher Arlan, Thomas Andrew. Instr. philosophy and gen. edn. Harvard, 1952-54; asst. prof. philosophy, then asso. prof. Vassar Coll., 1954-60; asso. prof. Johns Hopkins, 1960-64; prof. edn. and philosophy Harvard Grad. Sch. Edn., 1964-71; prof. philosophy U. Calif. at San Diego, 1971—, chmn. dept., 1973-76. Served to lt. (j.g.) USNR, 1943-46. Mem. Am. Philos. Assn. Author: Principles and Persons, 1967; Ethics and Twentieth Century Thought, 1973; The Dialectic of Action, 1979. Home: 6081 Ave Chamnez La Jolla CA 92037

OLAH, GEORGE ANDREW, educator, chemist; b. Budapest, Hungary, May 22, 1927; s. Julius and Magda (Krasznai) O.; Ph.D., Tech. U. Budapest, 1949; m. Judith Agnes Lengyel, July 9, 1949; children—George John, Ronald Peter. Came to U.S., 1964, naturalized, 1970. Mem. faculty Tech. U. Budapest, 1949-54; asso. dir. Central Chem. Research Inst., Hungarian Acad. Scis., 1954-56; research scientist Dow Chem. Can. Ltd., 1957-64, Dow Chem. Co., Framingham, Mass., 1964-65; prof. chemistry Case-Western Res. U., Cleve., 1965-69, C.F. Mabery prof. research, 1969-77; prof. chemistry, dir. Hydrocarbon Research Inst., U. So. Calif., Los Angeles, 1977—; vis. prof. chemistry Ohio State U., 1963, U. Heidelberg (Germany), 1965, U. Colo., 1969, Swiss Fed. Inst. Tech., 1972, U. Munich, 1973, U. London, 1973-79, L. Pasteur U., Strasbourg, 1974; cons. to industry. Recipient Leo Hendrik Baekeland award N.J. sect. Am. Chem. Soc., 1966, Morley medal Cleve. sect., 1970; Alexander von Humboldt sr. U.S. scientist award, 1979; Guggenheim fellow, 1972. Fellow Chem. Inst. Can., AAAS; mem. Nat. Acad. Scis., Am. (award petroleum chemistry 1964, award synthetic organic chemistry 1979), German, Brit. (Centenary lectr. 1978), Swiss chem. socs., Sigma Xi. Author: Friedel-Crafts Reactions, Vols. I-IV, 1963-64; (with P. Schleyer) Carbonium Ions, Vols. I-V, 1969-76; Friedel-Crafts Chemistry, 1973; Carbocations and Electrophilic Reactions, 1973; Halonium Ions, 1975; also chpts. in books, numerous papers in field. Patentee in field. Home: 2252 Gloaming Way Beverly Hills CA 90210 Office: Univ So Calif Los Angeles CA 90007. *America still is offering a new home and nearly unlimited possibilities to the newcomer who is willing to work hard for it. It is also where the "main action" in science and technology remains.*

OLAN, LEVI ARTHUR, clergyman, univ. regent; b. Cherkassy, Russia, Mar. 22, 1903; s. Max and Bessie (Leshinsky) O.; came to U.S., 1906, naturalized, 1912; student U. Rochester, 1921-23; B.A., U. Cin., 1925; Rabbi, Hebrew Union Coll., 1929, D.D., 1953; L.H.D., (hon.), Austin Coll., 1967, So. Methodist U., Dallas; m. Sarita Messer, June 9, 1931; children—Elizabeth (Mrs. James Hirsch), Frances, David. Rabbi, 1929; rabbi Temple Emanuel, Worcester, Mass., 1929-49, Dallas, 1949—. Lectr. Perkins Sch. Theology, So. Meth. U., Dallas, 1952—, Leo Baeck Coll., London, Eng.; adj. prof. U. Tex., Arlington, 1971—; vis. lectr. Tex. Christian U., 1976—. Pres. Jewish Family Service, 1932-40; v.p. Worcester chpt. ARC, 1939-45. Mem. bd. regents U. Tex. Mem. Central Conf. Am. Rabbis (pres. 1967-69), Dallas UN Assn. (pres. 1960). Home: 3131 Maple Ave Dallas TX 75201 Office: 8500 Hillcrest St Dallas TX 75225

OLANDER, LINDA MARIE PISKORSKI, mktg. analyst; b. Oceanside, Calif., July 19, 1950; d. Ernest Frank and Phyliss Rosemary (Staples) Piskorski; B.A., San Diego State U., 1973, postgrad., 1973—; m. Eric A. Olander, Nov. 15, 1975. Asso. editor Pvt. Pilot, Western Aviation, Carlsbad, Calif., 1974, asso. editor Emergency Product News, 1974, co-editor, 1974-75, sr. editor, 1975-76, mng. editor, 1976-78; free lance advt. and pub. relations cons., San Diego, 1978-79; mktg. analyst Markson Sci., Inc., Del Mar, Calif., 1979—. Mem. Am. Med. Writers Assn., Am. Soc. Bus. Press Editors. Democrat. Roman Catholic. Home: PO Box 99385 San Diego CA 92109 Office: PO Box 767 Del Mar CA 92014

OLCOTT, WILLIAM ALFRED, mag. editor; b. Bklyn., June 29, 1931; s. W. Alfred and Margaret Mary (Carr) O.; B.A. in Philosophy, Mary Immaculate Sem. and Coll., Northampton, Pa., 1957; postgrad. Columbia U.; m. Anne Maria Gorman, Sept. 7, 1963; children—Christopher, James, Katharine, William, Terence. Reporter, writer AP, 1960-66; with McGraw-Hill Publs. Co., 1966—, editor-in-chief 26 Plus mag., 1973—, Nat. Petroleum News mag., 1977—, chmn. corp. editorial bd., 1976-77. Mem. adv. com. Garden City (N.Y.) Bd. Edn., 1976—; prin. religious edn. home program St. Joseph's Roman Catholic Ch., Garden City, 1976—. Recipient Jesse H. Neal Editorial Achievement award Am. Bus. Press, 1974. Home: 108 Roxbury Rd Garden City NY 11530 Office: 1221 Ave of Americas New York City NY 10020

OLD, JONATHAN WHITEHEAD, JR., corp. exec.; b. Norfolk, Va., July 7, 1924; s. Jonathan Whitehead and Flora Stuart (Waller) O.; B.S. in Mech. Engring., U. Va., 1947; m. Mary Graham Hull, Oct. 18, 1958; children—Jonathan Whitehead III, Elizabeth Adams. With Liggett Group, 1947—, asst. to v.p. mfg., 1959-64, v.p., 1964-65, exec. v.p., 1965—, also dir. Served with USNR, 1943-46. Mem. Delta Kappa Epsilon. Clubs: Hope Valley Country (Durham, N.C.); Round Hill (Greenwich, Conn.). Address: care Liggett Group Inc 4100 Roxboro Rd Durham NC 27702

OLD, LLOYD JOHN, cancer biologist; b. San Francisco, Sept. 23, 1933; s. John H. and Edna A. (Marks) O.; B.A., U. Calif. at Berkeley, 1955, M.D. at San Francisco, 1958. Research fellow Sloan-Kettering Inst. Cancer Research, 1958-59, research asso., 1959-60, asso., 1960-64, asso. mem., 1964-67, mem., 1967—, chief div. immunology, 1967-72; research asso. biology Sloan-Kettering div. Grad. Sch. Med. Scis., Cornell U. Med. Coll., 1960-62, asst. prof. biology, 1962-66, asso. prof. biology, 1966-69, prof. biology, 1969—, acting asso. dir. research planning Sloan-Kettering Inst. Cancer Research, 1972, v.p., asso. dir., 1973-76, v.p., asso. dir. for sci. devel., 1976—, asso. dir. for research Meml. Sloan-Kettering Cancer Center and Meml. Hosp., 1973—; cons. Nat. Cancer Inst., 1967-70, mem. developmental research working group, 1969, spl. virus cancer program, 1970, mem. virus cancer program adv. com., 1975-78, mem. bd. sci. counselors div. cancer cause and prevention, 1978—; asso. med. dir. N.Y. Cancer Research Inst., Inc., 1970, med. dir., 1971—; mem. med. and sci. adv. bd. Leukemia Soc. Am., Inc., 1970-73, trustee, 1970-73; mem. sci. adv. com. Ludwig Inst. Cancer Research, 1974—; mem. sci. adv. bd. Jane Coffin Childs Meml. Fund for Med. Research, 1970-75; mem. research council Public Health Research Inst. City N.Y., 1977—. Recipient Roche ward, 1957, Alfred P. Sloan award cancer research, 1962, Lucy Wortham James award James Ewing Soc., 1970, Louis Gross award, 1972, Cancer Research Inst. award for immunology research, 1975, Rabbi Shai Shacknai Meml. award, 1976; Research Recognition award Noble Found., 1978. Mem. Am. Assn. Cancer Research, N.Y. Acad. Scis., Reticuloendothelial Soc., Soc. Exptl. Biology and Medicine, Harvey Soc., Am. Acad. Arts and Scis., AAAS, Am. Assn. Immunologists, Inst. Medicine of Nat. Acad. Scis., Phi Beta Kappa, Sigma Xi, Alpha Omega Alpha. Adv. editor Jour. Exptl. Medicine, 1971-75; Progress in Surface and Membrane Science, 1972-74; asso. editor Virology, 1972-74. Editorial adv. bd. Cancer Research, 1967-70, Cancer, 1968—, Recent Results in Cancer Research, 1972—. Contbr. articles to profl. jours. Office: Sloan-Kettering Inst Cancer Research 410 E 68th St New York NY 10021

OLDAM, PAUL BERNARD, corp. exec.; b. Newark, Aug. 20, 1934; s. Paul A. and Katherine A. (Kraft) O.; B.S. in Econs., Georgetown U., 1956; m. Margaret Henne, Oct. 6, 1956; children—Katherine A., Christine L., Mary M. Fin. mgmt. trainee Gen. Electric Co., 1956-57; asst. v.p. Pitts. Nat. Bank, 1961-67; v.p., treas. Allis-Chalmers Corp., Milw., 1967—; dir. Milw. County Bank. Bd. dirs. St. Coletta's Sch., St. Luke's Hosp.; mem. fin. com. Milw. Children's Hosp. Served with USAF, 1957-61. Mem. Nat. Investor Relations Inst., Fin. Execs. Inst. Home: 7837 Mary Ellen Pl Wauwatosa WI 53213 Office: PO Box 512 Milwaukee WI 53201

OLDBERG, ERIC, surgeon; b. Evanston, Ill., Nov. 7, 1901; s. Arne and Mary Georgiana (Sloan) O.; B.S., Northwestern U., 1923, M.S., 1926, M.D., 1927, Ph.D., 1928, LL.D. (hon.), 1961; LL.D., Ill. Inst. Tech., 1968; D.Sc. (hon.), Chgo. Coll. Osteo. Medicine, 1970; m. Hilda Edwards, June 3, 1929 (dec.); 1 son, George Sloan (dec.); m. 2d, Mary Swissler, Jan. 2, 1971. Instr. in physiology Northwestern U.

Med. Sch., 1925-28; Eliz. J. Ward fellowship in physiology, 1927-28; surg. house officer Peter Bent Brigham Hosp., Boston, 1928, asst. resident surgeon, 1929, resident neurol. surgeon to Dr. Harvey Cushing, 1930; Guggenheim traveling fellow, 1930 (resigned); George Gorham Peters traveling fellow Kaiser Wilhelm Inst., Berlin, Germany and Oxford (Eng.) U., 1930-31; asst. prof. surgery U. Ill. Coll. Medicine, 1931-34, asso. prof. surgery, acting head dept., 1934-36, prof., head dept. neurology and neurol. surgery, 1936-71; dir. neurol. div. and neurol. surgeon Neuropsychiat. Inst., U. Ill.; sr. attending neurol. surgeon, chmn. dept. Presbyn.-St. Luke's Hosp., Chgo., until 1970; sr. attending neurol. surgeon U. Ill. Hosps., Chgo., until 1972; sr. neurol. surgeon Hines VA Hosp., until 1972; pres. Chgo. Bd. Health, 1960-79; chmn. Mayor's commn. Bd. Edn., 1953-68; pres. Chgo. Health Research Found.; chmn. Chgo. Regional Commn. Heart Disease, Cancer and Stroke. Trustee Lake Forest Coll.; bd. dirs. Ednl. TV Channel 11, 1953-62, John Crerar Library; bd. dirs. Nat. Med. Fellowships, pres., 1964-65; gov., life mem. Art Inst. Chgo.; mem. Citizens Bd., U. Chgo.; life mem. Chgo. Natural History Mus.; dir. Chgo. Zool. Soc. hon. chmn. Chgo. Hort. Soc., recipient Hutchinson medal, 1975; advisory bd. YMCA Met. Chgo.; pres. Protestant Found. Greater Chgo. Recipient Northwestern U. Alumni medal, 1953, Chgo. medal of merit, 1961, Loyola U. citation for civic leadership, 1966. Diplomate Am. Bd. Neurol. Surgeons. Fellow A.C.S.; mem. AAAS, Am. Assn. Ry. Surgeons, Chgo. Surg. Soc., AMA, Am. Neurol. Assn., Am. Surg. Assn., Assn. Research in Nervous and Mental Diseases, Central Neuro-Psychol. Assn., Chgo. Inst. Traumatic Surgery, Chgo. Med. Soc., Chgo. Neurol. Soc. (pres. 1948), Chgo. Path. Soc., Harvey Cushing Soc. (pres. 1943), Ill. Med. Soc., Inst. Medicine Chgo. (pres. 1957, George H. Coleman award 1966), Soc. Exptl. Biology and Medicine, Soc. Neurol. Surgeons, Western Surg. Assn., Chgo. Orch. Assn. (pres. 1952-63), Sigma Xi, Alpha Chi Sigma, Alpha Omega Alpha, Phi Rho Sigma (Irving Cutter award 1956). Episcopalian. Clubs: University, Cliff Dwellers, Chicago, Commercial (pres. 1962-63), Lyric Opera (dir.), Chaos, Casino, Literary, Wayfarers (Chgo.); Onwentsia (Lake Forest). Asso. editor Jour. Neuropathology. Author articles and revs. Home: 901 Hawthorne Pl Lake Forest IL 60045

OLDENBURG, CLAES THURE, artist; b. Stockholm, Sweden, Jan. 28, 1929; s. Gosta and Sigrid Elisabeth (Lindforss) O.; B.A., Yale, 1950; student Art Inst., Chgo., 1952-54; m. Patricia Joan Muschinski, Apr. 13, 1960 (div. Apr. 1970). One-man shows Reuben Gallery, N.Y.C., 1960, Green Gallery, N.Y.C., 1962, Sidney Janis Gallery, N.Y.C., 1964-70, Pace Gallery, Boston, 1964, Galerie Ileana Sonnabend, Paris, 1964, Robert Fraser Gallery, London, 1966, Moderna Museet, Stockholm, 1966, Mus. Contemporary Art, Chgo., 1967, Irving Blum Gallery, Los Angeles, 1968, U. Calif. at Los Angeles Art Gallery, 1970, Nelson-Atkins Mus., Kansas City, 1972, Art Inst. Chgo., 1973, numerous others; exhibited in group shows at Martha Jackson Gallery, N.Y.C., 1960, 61, Dallas Mus. Contemporary Art, 1961, 62, Sidney Janis Gallery, 1962, 64, Arts Council YM/YWHA, 1962, 63, Inst. Contemporary Arts, London, 1963, Art Inst. Chgo., 1962, 63, Allen Art Mus. Oberlin (Ohio) Coll., 1963, Mus. Modern Art, N.Y.C., 1963, Washington Gallery Modern Art, 1963, Am. Pavilion, Venice, 1964, Moderna Museet, Stockholm, 1964, Gulbenkian Found. Tate Gallery, London, 1964, Rochester (N.Y.) Meml. Mus., 1964-65, Worcester (Mass.) Mus., 1965, Met. Mus. Art, N.Y.C., 1969, Foundation Maeght, France, 1970, Nat. Mus. Ireland, 1971, Walker Art Center, 1975, Kunsthalle, Tübingen W. Ger., 1975, others; rep. permanent collections at Mus. Modern Art, Albright-Knox Art Gallery, Buffalo, Moderna Museet, Rose Art Mus. Brandeis U., Waltham, Mass., Oberlin Coll., Art Gallery Ont., Toronto, Art Inst. Chgo., Whitney Mus. Modern Art, N.Y.C., numerous others. Recipient Creative Arts citation Brandeis U., 1971, medal AIA, 1977. Address: 556 Broome St New York NY 10013*

OLDENBURG, RICHARD ERIK, museum exec.; b. Stockholm, Sweden, Sept. 21, 1933; s. Gösta and Sigrid Elisabeth (Lindforss) O.; came to U.S., 1936, naturalized, 1959; A.B., Harvard, 1954; m. Harriet Lisa Turnure, Dec. 17, 1960. Mgr. design dept. Doubleday & Co., Inc., N.Y.C., 1958-61; mng. editor trade div. Macmillan Co., Inc., N.Y.C., 1961-69; dir. publs. Museum Modern Art, N.Y.C., 1969-72, dir. mus., 1972—. Mem. mus. aid panel N.Y. State Council on Arts, 1975-79; mem. mus. policy panel Nat. Endowment for Arts, 1976-78, chmn. mus. policy panel, 1979—. Served with AUS, 1956-58. Mem. Assn. Art Museum Dirs. Home: 447 E 57th St New York NY 10022 Office: 11 W 53d St New York NY 10019

OLDENQUIST, ANDREW G., educator; b. Evanston, Ill., Mar. 22, 1932; s. Andrew G. and Louise (Drouin) O.; B.S., Northwestern U., 1953; M.A., Brown U., 1955; Ph.D., Ohio State U., 1962; m. Riek Asikin Natanegara, Sept. 9, 1961; children—Nina, Mark. Fulbright fellow, Germany, 1957-58; instr. philosophy U. Conn., 1960-62; prof. Ohio State U., 1962—. Democrat. Club: Wheaton. Editor: Readings in Moral Philosophy, 1965; author editor: Moral Philosophy, 1978. Contbr. articles to profl. jours. Amateur entomologist and naturalist. Home: 176 Walhalla Dr Columbus OH 43210

OLDER, JACK STANLEY, banker; b. Phila., Feb. 20, 1934; s. Morris and Lee (Goldstein) O.; B.S. in Econs., U. Pa., 1955, LL.B., 1958; m. Sondra Chait, June 21, 1959; children—Michael, Stephen, Elizabeth, Carolyn. Admitted to N.Y. bar, 1959; atty. Office of Chief Counsel, IRS, 1960-66; editor Tax Research Inst. Am., 1966-68; asso. gen. counsel Nat. Assn. Mut. Savs. Banks, 1968-70; tax counsel Atlantic Richfield Co., 1970-72; v.p., sec., dep. office counsel Bowery Savs. Bank, N.Y.C., 1972, sec., office counsel, 1973-76, sr. v.p., sec., office counsel, 1976—; adj. asso. prof. taxation N.Y. U. Inst. Fed. Taxation; cons. Tax Research Inst. Am., Inc. Treas. Bowery Ofcls. Nonpartisan Polit. Com., 1974—. Served with U.S. Army, 1958-59. Mem. Am., N.Y. State bar assns., Beta Gamma Sigma, Beta Alpha Psi. Jewish. Club: N.Y. U. Author: Practicing Law Inst. Handbook on 1969 Tax Reform Act, 1970; Employee Retirement Income Security Act of 1974, 1975; ALI-ABA Handbook-Individual Retirement Accounts. Home: 7 Stratton Rd Scarsdale NY 10583 Office: 110 E 42d St New York NY 11017

OLDERSHAW, LOUIS FREDERICK, mfg. co. exec.; b. New Britain, Conn., Aug. 30, 1917; s. Louis A. and Annie Louise (Bold) O.; A.B., Dartmouth, 1939; LL.B., Yale 1942; m. Virginia Wakelin, Nov. 30, 1940; children—Peter W., Robert J., David L. Admitted to Mass. bar, 1946, Fed. bar, 1947; mem. legal staff Army Ordnance Dist., Springfield, Mass., 1942-43; with firm Lyon, Green, Whitmore, Doran & Brooks, Holyoke, Mass., 1947-49; partner firm Davenport, Millane & Oldershaw, Holyoke, 1949-64; treas. Nat. Blank Book Co., Inc., Holyoke, 1964-65, pres., 1965-78, chmn. bd., 1978—; group v.p., dir. Dennison Mfg. Co., Framingham, Mass., 1967—; dir. Old Colony Bank of Hampden County. Mem. adv. bd. U. Mass. Sch. Bus.; trustee Mt. Holyoke Coll., 1966-76. Served to lt. USNR, 1943-47. Republican. Mem. United Ch. Christ. Rotarian. Clubs: Yale (N.Y.C.); Longmeadow (Mass.) Country. Mem. editorial bd. Yale Law Jour., 1941-42. Home: Old County Rd Holyoke MA 01040 Office: Dennison Mfg Co 275 Wyman St Waltham MA 02154

OLDFATHER, CHARLES EUGENE, lawyer; b. Brady, Nebr., Oct. 7, 1927; s. Harold and Marcia (Hazlett) O.; student U. Colo., 1945, Kearney (Nebr.) State Tchrs. Coll., 1946-48, U. Cal. at Berkeley, 1949; A.B., U. Nebr., 1950; J.D. with distinction, U. Mich., 1953; m. Diane C. Harris, June 15, 1957; children—David H., Jane S. Admitted to Nebr. bar, 1953, since practiced in Lincoln; asso. Cline, Williams, Wright & Johnson, 1953-58; partner Cline, Williams, Wright, Johnson & Oldfather, 1958—. Sec., dir. NTV Enterprises, Inc. Past pres. Family Service Assn. Lincoln; past v.p., bd. dirs. Nebr. Soc. for Prevention Blindness. Served with Adj. Gen. Div., AUS, 1946-48. Mem. Am., Nebr., Lincoln bar assns., Lincoln C. of C. (past dir.), Phi Kappa Psi, Phi Delta Phi. Republican. Presbyn. Club: Lincoln Country. Bd. editors U. Mich Law Rev. 1952-53. Home: 6719 Old Cheney Rd Lincoln NE 68516 Office: 1900 First Nat Bank Bldg Lincoln NE 68508

OLDMAN, OLIVER, educator; b. N.Y.C., July 19, 1920; s. Max and Rose (Meyers) O.; grad. Mercersburg Acad., 1938; S.B., Harvard, 1942, LL.B., 1953; m. Barbara Lublin, May 2, 1943; children—Andrew, Margaret Erman, Michele. Jr. economist OPA, 1942; instr. econs. U. Buffalo, 1946-50; v.p. Lublin Constrn. Co., 1946-50; admitted to N.Y. bar, 1953; asso. firm Hodgson, Russ, Andrews, Woods & Goodyear, Buffalo, 1953-55; dir. tng. internat. tax program Harvard Law Sch., 1955-65, dir. internat. tax program, 1965—, prof. law, 1961-76, Learned Hand prof. law, 1976—; cons. on taxation Govts. of Argentina, Bolivia, Chile, Colombia, Egypt, El Salvador, Ethiopia, Indonesia, U.S., Venezuela, Mass., N.H., N.Y.C., R.I. and UN Secretariat. Served to 1st lt. AUS, 1943-46. Mem. Nat. Tax Assn., Am. Econ. Assn., Am. Bar Assn. Author: (with others) The Fiscal System of Venezuela, 1959; Financing Urban Development in Mexico City, 1967. Editor: (with R. Bird) Readings on Taxation in Developing Countries, 1964, rev. edit., 1967, 3d edit., 1975; (with P. Kelley) Readings on Income Tax Administration, 1973; (with F.P. Schoettle) State and Local Taxes and Finance, 1974. Home: 15 Buckingham St Cambridge MA 02138

OLDS, ELIZABETH, artist; b. Mpls., Dec. 10, 1896; d. Fred Allen and Harriet (Trussell) O.; student U. Minn., 1915-17, Mpls. Sch. Art, 1918-21, Art Students League, N.Y.C., 1921-22. One-woman exhbns. include: ACA Gallery, 1937, 41, 50, 52, 55, 60, 63, S.I. Inst. Arts and Scis., 1969; represented in permanent collections: Met. Mus., N.Y.C., Mus. Modern Art, N.Y.C., Bklyn. Mus., Phila. Mus.; author, illustrator 6 books for children including: The Big Fire, 1945; Riding the Rails, 1948; Feather Mountain, 1951; Deep Treasure, 1958; Plop, Plop Ploppie; Little Una. Guggenheim fellow, 1926. Address: 2221 Alvarado Ln Sarasota FL 33581

OLDS, GLENN ALVERO, univ. pres., former UN ambassador; b. Sherwood, Oreg., Feb. 28, 1921; s. Glenn Alvero and Hazel (Ross) O.; A.B. magna cum laude, Willamette U., 1942, D.D. (hon.), 1955; B.D. with highest distinction, Garrett Theol. Sem., 1945; M.A. in Philosophy with honors (Swift Travelling fellow), Northwestern U., 1945; Ph.D. in Philosophy (Robinson fellow), Yale U., 1948; D.Humanics (hon.), Springfield (Mass.) Coll., 1965; L.H.D., Inter-Am. U. P.R., 1968, Lakeland Coll., 1971, Muhlenberg Coll., 1972; LL.D., Akron U., 1971, Central Mich. U., 1976, St. Lawrence U., 1975; D.Litt., Redlands U., 1974; Hon. Academian, China Acad., Taiwan, 1967; Academico Honoris Causa, Mexican Acad. Internat. Law, 1967; D.Sc. (hon.), Chung-Ang U., Korea; m. Eva Belle Spelts, June 20, 1944; children—Linda Olds, Glenn Richard. Asst. in instruction Yale U., 1947-48; asst. prof. philosophy DePauw U., Greencastle, Ind., 1948; asso. prof. philosophy and ethics Garrett Theol. Sem., 1948-51; univ. chaplain, prof. U. Denver, 1951-54; dir. united religious work Cornell U., 1954-58; pres. Springfield Coll., 1958-65; exec. dean for internat. studies and world affairs State U. N.Y. System, 1965-68; spl. asst. to Pres. for policy and manpower devel., Washington, 1968-69; ambassador to UN, ECOSOC, 1969-71; pres. Kent (Ohio) State U., 1971-77, Alaska Pacific U., Anchorage, 1977—; mem. council Center for Integrative Edn., 1958—; vis. prof. philosophy Northwestern U., 1948-51; cons. in field; mem. exec. com. internat. edn. Nat. Assn. State Univs., Land-Grant Colls., 1966-68, mem. com. ednl. opportunities for minority groups, 1971—; trustee Interfaith Campus Ministry, 1973—, Dag Hammarskjold Coll., 1968—, N.E. Ohio Coll. Medicine, 1974—; bd. dirs. Ednl. Futures Internat., 1975—, Inst. Noetic Scis., 1974—, Commonwealth North, 1979; founding mem. U.S. Com. for UN Univ., 1972—; chmn. Consortium for Internat. Energy Research; mem. Commn. Honest Elections Alaska, 1978. Mem. Ohio Gov's. Adv. Council on Malabar, 1972—; mem. Met. Akron (Ohio) Jobs Council; bd. dirs. Council Study Mankind, 1971—; gov. Blossom Festival Soc. (Ohio), 1972—; pres. bd. Design Sci. Inst., 1972—; ex-officio trustee Akron Art Inst., 1974—. Recipient Outstanding Citizen award City of Springfield, 1965; Outstanding Tchr. award U. Denver, 1953; Nat. Council on Religion in Higher Edn. Nat. fellow, 1946. Mem. Oceanic Soc. (charter), Blue Key, Omicron Delta Kappa, Tau Kappa Alpha, Omicron Delta Sigma, Eta Sigma Gamma (hon.). Author: The Christian Corrective: Christ Transforming Culture: Study Guide for the Conscience of Culture, 1953; contbr. articles to profl. publs. Office: Office of Pres Alaska Pacific U Anchorage AK 99504

O'LEARY, BRIAN TODD, physicist, author, lectr.; b. Boston, Jan. 27, 1940; s. Frederick A. and Mary Mabel (Todd) O'L.; A.B., Williams Coll., 1961; M.A., Georgetown U., 1964; Ph.D., U. Calif. at Berkeley, 1967. Scientist-astronaut NASA Manned Spacecraft Center, Houston, also asst. prof. astronomy U. Tex., Austin, 1967-68; research asso. Cornell U., 1968-69, asst. prof. astronomy, 1969-71; vis. asso. Calif. Inst. Tech., 1971; asso. prof. interdisciplinary scis. San Francisco State Coll., 1971-72; vis. asso. prof. Sch. Law, U. Calif. at Berkeley, 1971-72; asst. prof. astronomy and sci. policy assessment Hampshire Coll., Amherst, Mass., 1972-75; spl. cons. on energy subcom. on energy and environment U.S. Ho. of Reps. Interior Com., Washington, 1975; research staff, lectr. physics Princeton, 1975-80. Fellow AAAS; mem. Am. Geophys. Union (sec. planetology), Am. Astron. Soc., Am. Fedn. Scientists. Author: The Making of an Ex-Astronaut, 1970 (Best Young Adult book ALA 1970); The Fertile Stars, 1980; contbr. articles to profl. jours., mags. Home: 51 Mitchell Rd Concord MA 01742. *Planning for the future has been limited to the terms of political office and short term corporate interest. Although the speculations of the futurists about the twenty-first century are inaccurate, it is essential to evolve a policy which will guide us through the next ten, twenty and thirty years. The limits to exploitation of energy, resources and food require that we implement conservation while seeking renewable sources compatable with the human environment. The use of energy and materials in outer space provides the most hope, a concept I am dedicated to. The challenge is a persistence in communicating these goals, in a world with vested interests, and to assure that their implementation is consistent with basic human values.*

O'LEARY, DANIEL HUGH, ret. univ. adminstr.; b. Boston, Feb. 6, 1907; s. James Joseph and Bridget Josephine (McVann) O'L.; A.B., Boston Coll., 1927, M.A., 1928, Ph.D., 1936; postgrad. Harvard, summers 1930, 32, 33, U. Cambridge, summer 1931, U. Rome, 1938-39; m. Marguerite F. Moriarty, Sept. 17, 1938; children—Nancy (Mrs. William Melia), James, Daniel, Ellen (Mrs. William Coughlin), Robert, Deborah (Mrs. William Chauncey Bryant). Tchr., Ashland (Mass.) High Sch., 1928-31, South Boston High Sch., Boston, 1931-46; instr. Boston Coll. Grad. Sch., 1936-37, Hyannis (Mass.) State Tchrs. Coll., summers 1937-50; head dept. Roxbury Girls High Sch., Boston, 1946-50; prin. Roxbury Evening Schs., Boston, 1946-50; head history dept. Boston Tchrs. Coll., 1949-50; pres. Lowell (Mass.) State Coll., 1950-74; chancellor U. Lowell (Mass.), 1975-77, chancellor emeritus, 1977—. Chmn. Mass. Bd. Ednl. Assistance, 1956-65; ednl. cons. to Venezuela, U.S. State Dept., 1963; ednl. cons. to Israel, Am. Assn. Colls. Tchr. Edn., 1965. Trustee Moses Parker Greeley Fund, 1951-72, Lowell City Library, 1962-74, Mass. Community Colls., 1968-72, New Eng. Coll. Optometry, 1977—. Recipient Honors award Internat. Assn. Univ. Pres., 1975. O'Leary Library at Lowell State Coll. named in his honor, 1974. Home: 213 Parkview Ave Lowell MA 01850 Office: Rolfe St Lowell MA 01854

O'LEARY, DENIS JOSEPH, physician, ins. co. exec.; b. Ireland, Feb. 5, 1924; s. Joseph and Mary Christine (Dennis) O'L.; came to U.S., 1949, naturalized, 1954; M.D., Nat. U. Ireland, Cork, 1947; m. Audrey Mary Ryan, Nov. 26, 1952; children—Michael, Brian, Denis, Kevin. Intern, St. Michael's Hosp., Toronto, Ont., Can., 1947-48, resident, 1948-49; resident St. Vincent's Hosp., N.Y.C., 1949-50, Triboro Hosp., Jamaica, N.Y., 1950-51; with N.Y. Life Ins. Co., N.Y.C., 1952—, med. dir. employees' health, 1961-70, v.p., 1970—; asst. attending physician Bellevue Hosp., N.Y.C., 1955-69, asso. attending physician, 1969-77, attending physician, 1977—; instr. in medicine Columbia U., 1958-63, asso. in medicine, 1963-68; asst. prof. clin. medicine N.Y. U., 1968—; sec. N.Y. Lung Assn., 1962-67, 69-71, v.p., 1967-69, dir., 1961—. Bd. dirs. Nat. Council on Alcoholism, N.Y.C., 1979—. Served as capt. M.C., AUS, 1953-55. Fellow Am. Coll. Chest Physicians, Am. Occupational Med. Assn., Am. Pub. Health Assn.; mem. AMA, N.Y. State, New York County med. socs., Am. Thoracic Assn., N.Y. Heart Assn., Chamber of Commerce and Industry Inc., Soc. Alumni Bellevue Hosp., N.Y. Occupational Med. Assn. (exec. com. 1967—, pres. 1973-74). Club: Scarsdale (N.Y.) Golf. Office: 51 Madison Ave New York NY 10010

O'LEARY, EDWARD CORNELIUS, bishop; b. Bangor, Maine, Aug. 21, 1920; s. Cornelius J. and Annabel (McManus) O'L.; B.A., Holy Cross Coll., Worcester, Mass., 1942; S.T.L., St. Paul's U. Sem., Ottawa, Can., 1946. Ordained priest Roman Cath. Ch., 1946, named monsignor, 1954, consecrated bishop, 1971; vice-chancellor, then chancellor of Diocese of Portland, Maine; diocesan consultor, pro-synodal judge of diocese, pres. priests senate, mem. finance com. of diocese, also dir. Commodity Service Corp., 1969-75; titular bishop of Moglaena, aux. bishop, Portland, Maine, 1971-74; adminstr. Roman Cath. Diocese Portland, bishop of Portland, 1974—; mem. Maine Office Religious Coop., 1973—. Mem. Nat. Conf. Catholic Bishops. Address: 510 Ocean Ave Portland ME 04103

O'LEARY, GEORGE FRANCIS, ins. co. exec.; b. Rosemount, Minn., Dec. 20, 1917; s. George Patrick and Helen (Wagner) O.; B.S. cum laude, St. Thomas Coll., 1941; postgrad. U. Iowa, 1941-42, U.S. Naval Acad., 1944-45; m. Maria Schultz, Oct. 25, 1941; children—George Patrick, James Joseph, John Francis. Actuarial asst. actuarial dept. Northwestern Nat. Life Ins. Co., Mpls., 1945-47, supr. night shift, 1947-48; statis. analyst, 1948-52, auditor, 1952-58, 2d v.p. planning, 1962-64, v.p., controller, 1964-69, sr. v.p. ops., 1969-76, exec. v.p. ops., 1976—; dir. North Atlantic Life Ins. Co., No. Life Ins. Co. Active Hennepin County United Fund; trustee Marycrest Coll. Served from ensign to lt. comdr. USNR, 1942-46. Decorated Bronze Star. Mem. Life Office Mgmt. Assn. (sr. adminstrv. office com.), Nat. Investor Relations Inst., Am. Life Ins. Assn. (joint com. fin. reporting principles, sub. com. participating ins.), Mpls. C. of C. (aviation com.). Home: 12822 Excellsior Blvd Minnetonka MN 55343 Office: 20 Washington Ave S Minneapolis MN 55440

O'LEARY, JAMES JOHN, economist; b. Manchester, Conn., May 7, 1914; s. James Henry and Helen Agnes (Hogan) O'L.; B.A., Wesleyan U., 1936, M.A., 1937; Ph.D., Duke, 1941; m. Rita Marie Phelps, May 31, 1941; children—James Phelps, Martha Ellen, Paul Howard, Mark Evans. Instr. econs. Wesleyan U., 1939-42, asst. prof., 1943-46; cons. Conn. Gen. Life Ins. Co., 1945-46; asso. prof. econs. Duke, 1946-47; dir. investment research, economist Life Ins. Assn. Am., 1947-59, v.p., dir. econ. research, economist, 1959-67; chmn., chief economist Lionel D. Edie & Co., 1967-69; exec. v.p., economist U.S. Trust Co. of N.Y. 1969-70, vice chmn., 1970—; dir. Kennecott Copper Corp., Bowery Savs. Bank, Guardian Life Ins. Co. Am., GAF Corp., Atlantic Mut. Ins. Co. Dir. research Com. on Pub. Debt Policy, 1946-47; mem. com. on research in finance Nat. Bur. Econ. Research; alternate mem. nat. com. vol. credit restraint program Fed. Res. Bd., 1951-52. Bd. dirs. Student Loan Marketing Assn., Fed. Nat. Mortgage Assn.; mem. adv. com. Grad. Sch. Bus. N.Y. U. Trustee Wesleyan U.; bd. dirs. Nat. Bur. Econ. Research, chmn., 1976; trustee St. Joseph Coll. Recipient of Distinguished Alumnus award Wesleyan U., 1965. Mem. Am., So. econ. assns., Am. Finance Assn., Am. Statis. Assn., Phi Beta Kappa, Pi Gamma Mu, Alpha Chi Rho. Club: University (N.Y.C.). Contbr. articles profl. publs. Home: 8 Crooked Mile Rd Westport CT 06880 Office: 45 Wall St New York NY 10005

O'LEARY, K(EITH) DANIEL, educator, clin. psychologist; b. West Chester, Pa., Oct. 3, 1940; s. Daniel Keith and Alma Rose (Boyer) O'L.; B.A., Pa. State U., 1962; M.A. (USPHS fellow), U. Ill., 1965, Ph.D., 1967; m. Susan Gilbert, Aug. 7, 1964; children—Michael Boyer, Kathryn Searls. Asst. prof. SUNY, Stony Brook, 1967-70, asso. prof., 1970-73, prof. clin. psychology, 1973—, chmn. dept. psychology, 1978—; cons. NIMH, 1972-75; dir. Point of Woods Lab. Sch., Stony Brook, 1969-73. U.S. Office Edn. grantee, 1969; NIMH grantee, 1971. Fellow Am. Psychol. Assn.; mem. Soc. for Research in Child devel., Phi Beta Kappa, Phi Kappa Phi. Author: (with O'Leary) Classroom Management: The Successful Use of Behavior Modification, 1972; (with G. T. Wilson) Behavior therapy: Application and Outcome, 1975; editor Jour. Applied Behavior Analysis, 1977-80; asso. editor Jour. Abnormal Child Psychology, 1973—; mem. editorial bd. Jour. Cons. and Clin. Psychology and Behavior Therapy; contbr. articles to profl. jours. Home: 236 Christian Ave Stony Brook NY 11790

O'LEARY, MAURICE GRATTAN, aluminium co. exec.; b. Ottawa, Ont., Can., Apr. 23, 1915; s. Michael Grattan and Mary H. (McKenna) O'L.; B.S., U. Toronto, 1938; m. Margaret Marie Campbell, Aug. 31, 1940; children—Patrick, Brian, Mary, Catherine. With Aluminium Co. Can., Shawinigan and Toronto, 1938-50, asst. works mgr. Kingston works, 1950-55; mng. dir. Aluminium Co. South Africa, 1955-59; works dir. Alcan Industries Ltd., London, 1960-64; v.p. Alcan Fiduciaries Ltd., 1964-68, Alcan Internat. Ltd., 1968-78; v.p. engring. and tech. Alcan Aluminium Ltd., Montreal, Que., Can., 1978—. Mem. Am. Soc. Metals. Roman Catholic. Clubs: Mt. Stephen, Beaconsfield Golf. Office: Alcan Aluminium Ltd 1 Pl Villa Marie Montreal PQ H3C 3H2 Canada

O'LEARY, RICHARD A., broadcasting exec.; b. San Francisco; grad. U. So. Calif.; m. Jeanette O'Leary; 4 children. With ABC, 1955—, v.p., gen. mgr. WLS-TV, Chgo., 1966-70, pres. ABC owned TV stas. div., N.Y.C., 1970—, ABC Internat. div. Served with USNR, World War II; ETO, PTO. Mem. Nat. Acad. TV Arts and Scis. (pres. internat. council), Internat. Radio and TV Soc. (1st v.p.), TV Bur. Advt. (dir.), Cath. Assn. Radio, TV and Advt. (dir.). Office: ABC 1330 Ave of Americas New York NY 10019*

O'LEARY, RICHARD EDWIN, electro-mech. mfg. co. exec.; b. Pittsburg, Kans., Apr. 23, 1934; s. Edwin John and Hazel Bernice (Wheeler) O'L.; A.B., U. Ill., 1955, J.D., 1963; m. Ann Hart

Matthews, Feb. 6, 1955; children—Lynn, Richard Douglas. Asst. dean men U. Ill., 1959-62; admitted to Mo. bar, 1964, N.Y. bar, 1967, Minn. bar, 1971; sr. atty. Monsanto Co., St. Louis, 1963-71; group exec. Studebaker-Worthington, Inc., 1971-76; v.p. corp. devel., sec., gen. counsel Onan Corp., Mpls., 1976—; dir. Contech, Inc. Served as officer U.S. Navy, 1955-59. Recipient William Jennings Bryan award U. Ill., 1954. Mem. Am. Bar Assn., Mo. Bar Assn., Bar Assn. City N.Y., Order of Coif, Phi Delta Phi. Clubs: Mpls. Athletic, Edina Country. Contbr. articles to legal jours. Home: 4403 Country Club Rd Edina MN 55424 Office: 1400 73d Ave NE Minneapolis MN 55432

O'LEARY, ROBERT THOMAS, lawyer; b. Butte, Mont., Jan. 17, 1932; s. Barry and Hanora O'L.; B.A., U. Notre Dame, 1954; J.D., Creighton U., 1957; m. Gay Loggins, Aug. 25, 1956; children—Mary I., Robert T. Admitted to Nebr. bar, 1957, Mont. bar, 1957; mem. firm Walsh & O'Leary, Anaconda, Mont., 1958-61; asst. U.S. atty., Butte, Mont., 1961-69; partner firm Burgess, Joyce, Prothero, Whelan & O'Leary, Butte, 1968-77; U.S. atty., Dist. of Mont., Butte, 1977—; chmn. Mont. Bd. Pardons, 1973-77. Mem. Mont. Bar Assn. Democrat. Roman Catholic. Clubs: Notre Dame of Mont. (pres. 1965-76), Butte Country, Elks. Office: PO Box 1478 Butte MT 59103

O'LEARY, THOMAS HOWARD, railroad exec.; b. N.Y.C., Mar. 19, 1934; s. Arthur J. and Eleanor (Howard) O'L.; A.B., Holy Cross Coll., 1954; postgrad. U. Pa., 1959-61; m. Barbara A. Mc Donough, 1977; children—Mark, Timothy, Thomas, Denis, Daniel, Mary Frances. Asst. cashier First Nat. City Bank, N.Y.C., 1961-65; asst. to chmn. finance com. Mo. Pacific R.R. Co., 1966-70, v.p. finance, 1971-76, dir., 1972—, chmn. finance com., 1976—; treas. Mo. Pacific Corp., St. Louis, 1968—, v.p. finance, 1971-72, exec. v.p., 1972-74, dir., 1972—, pres., 1974—; chmn. bd., chief exec. officer Mississippi River Transmission Corp., 1974—, dir. Merc. Trust Co., Merc. Bancorp., Interco, Inc., Kroger Co. Trustee St. Louis U., 1974—. Served to capt. USMC, 1954-58. Clubs: Blind Brook, Wall Street (N.Y.C.); Chicago. Office: 9900 Clayton Rd St Louis MO 63124

O'LEARY, VINCENT IGNATIUS, univ. adminstr.; b. San Francisco, July 31, 1924; s. Edward James and Elizabeth Mary (Bluitt) O'L.; B.A., San Francisco State U., 1948; M.A., U. Wash., 1956; m. Adele Daubenberg, Aug. 2, 1952; children—Elizabeth Adele, Catherine Marie. Intern, Nat. Tng. Labs., Bethel, Maine, 1965-66; chief probation and parole officer State of Wash., 1951-57; dir. parole State of Tex., 1957-62; dir. Nat. Parole Insts., Austin, Tex., 1962-64; exec. asst. to dir. Nat. Council on Crime and Delinquency, N.Y.C., 1964-65, dir. div. research, info. and tng., 1965-68; prof. criminal justice SUNY, Albany, 1968-77, acting dean, 1973-74, dean Sch. Criminal Justice, 1976-77, acting pres., 1977-78, pres., 1978—; asst. dir. Pres.'s Commn. on Law Enforcement and Adminstrn. of Justice, Washington, 1965-67; lectr. and cons. in field. Mem. Western Probation and Parole Assn. (v.p. 1956), Wash. Probation and Parole Assn. (dir. 1954), Adminstrs. of Inter-State Parole and Probation Compact (mem. exec. bd. 1969), Assn. Paroling Authorities, So. Council on Tng. for Prevention and Control of Crime and Delinquency (sec. 1962), Am. Correctional Assn., Tex. Probation and Parole Assn. (dir. 1959), So. States Probation and Parole Conf. (sec. 1969, v.p. 1961, pres. 1962), Assn. for Correctional Research and Statistics (treas. 1972-73). Clubs: Univ. N.Y.C.; Univ. (Albany, N.Y.). Author: (with K. Hanrahan) Parole Systems in the United States, 1977. Editor: Journal of Research in Crime and Delinquency, 1977-79. Contbr. monographs and articles in field. Office: State University of New York at Albany 1400 Washington Ave Albany NY 12222

O'LEARY, WILFRED LEO, educator; b. Boston, July 3, 1906; s. Daniel Joseph and Frances Marie (O'Hara) O'L.; grad. Boston Latin Sch., 1925; A.B., Boston Coll., 1929, A.M., 1930; Ed.M., State Coll. at Boston, 1938; Ed.D., Calvin Coolidge Coll., 1954; m. Gertrude Margaret Cashman, June 26, 1938; 1 dau., Ann Marie (Mrs. James S. Gessner). Master, Boston Latin Sch., 1934-42, 46-48, head master, 1964-76; head history dept. Jeremiah E. Burke High Sch., Dorchester, Mass., 1948-57; asst. prof. edn. Calvin Coolidge Coll., 1952-57; head master Roslindale High Sch., Mass., 1957-64. Vice pres., dir. Roslindale Coop. Bank. Mem. Mass. Adv. Council on Edn.; public mem. Mass. Bd. Dental Examiners, 1979; mem. adv. bd. Scholastic mag., 1960-64. Bd. dirs. Boston chpt. ARC; mem. ho. of dels. Mass. Easter Seal Soc., 1976—; chmn. founds. com. Pkwy. Boys Club, Boston, 1978. Served with USAF, 1942-46; col. Res. (ret.). Mem. Boston Headmasters Assn. (pres. 1963-65), Boston Latin Sch. Alumni Assn. (sec., librarian, Man of Year award 1975) Am. Hist. Assn., Boston Athenaeum, Nat. Council Social Studies Tchrs., Nat. (citation for outstanding contbns. to pub. edn. 1975), Mass. assns. secondary sch. prins., Bostonian Soc., Mil. Order Fgn. Wars U.S., Boston Head Masters' and Prins. Assn. (pres. 1966-69), Mass. Schoolmasters' Club (pres. 1964-65), The Headmasters Assn. (v.p. 1972-73, pres. 1976-77). Author: (With others) Communism vs. Democracy, 1955; Philosophy of the Mass. Secondary School Principals Assn., 1960. Home: 4 Calvin Rd Jamaica Plain MA 02130 Office: 78 Ave Louis Pasteur Boston MA 02115

OLECK, HOWARD L., legal educator, writer; b. N.Y.C., Jan. 6, 1911; s. Richard and Yvette (Leoner) O.; grad. Townsend Harris Hall Prep. Sch., 1928; A.B., U. Iowa, 1933; J.D., N.Y. Law Sch., 1938; LL.D., Baldwin Wallace Coll., 1964; Litt.D., J. Marshall U., 1967; m. Helen Eugenie Gemeiner, 1941; children—Mrs. Anabel Timte, Joan Valerie. Admitted to N.Y. bar, 1938, Ohio bar, 1957, also Fed. bar; asso. prof. N.Y. Law Sch., 1947-56; prof. law, asso. dean Cleve. State U., 1956-67, dean, 1967-68, 71, distinguished prof. law, 1968-74; prof. law Wake Forest U., Winston-Salem, N.C., 1974-78, Stetson U., St. Petersburg, Fla., 1978—; asst. to editor N.Y. Law Jour., 1946-52; law columnist Cleve. Plain Dealer, 1959-75, Winston-Salem Suburbanite and 40 N.C. newspapers, 1975-78. Cons. to congl. coms. and Presdl. commns., Am. Law Inst., Calif. Law Revision Commn., pub. service groups, others. Served to maj., tanks AUS, 1942-45; ETO; War Dept. historian. Decorated U.S. and fgn. medals; recipient various bar assn. honors. Mem. Am., N.C. bar assns., Am. Trial Lawyers Assn., League Ohio Law Schs. (pres. 1963-64), Scribes (pres. 1972-73), Phi Alpha Delta. Unitarian. Author: Creditors' Rights, 1947; Creditors' Rights and Remedies, 1949; History of Allied Planning of Operations, E.T.O., 1939-45, 1945; Debtor-Creditor Law, 1953; Negligence Investigation Manual, 1953; Negligence Forms of Pleading, 1954; New York Corporations, 1954; Damages to Persons and Property, 1955; Non-Profit Corporations and Associations, 1956; Encyclopedia of Negligence, 2 vols., 1960; Modern Corporation Law, 6 vols., 1960, supplement, 1978; Cases on Damages, 1962; Eye Witness World War II Battles, 1963; Heroic Battles of World War II, 1963; Law for Living, 1967; A Singular Fury, 1968; Law for Everyone, 1971; Nonprofit Corporations, Organization and Associations, 4th edit., 1980; Primer on Legal Writing, 1974, 4th edit., 1978; National Index to Insurance Laws, 1976; The Lion of Islam, 1977; Nonprofit Organizations Trends, 1977; Parliamentary Law for Non-Profit Organizations, 1978; Odin's Men, 1980; also War Dept. histories, 1945-46. Editor: Directors and Officers Ency. Manual, 1955; Negligence and Compensation Service, 1955-66; National Ins. Law Service, 1962—; also various jours., 1956—. Author over 300 mag. articles, poems under own and various pen names. Home: 1440 Sea Gull Dr S Saint Petersburg FL 33707 Office: Stetson U Coll Law Saint Petersburg FL 33707. *Pain and fear are preservers of human life, the endurance and conquest of them are preservers of human spirit, and moral courage and striving for excellence despite them, are ennoblers of human existence.*

OLEJNICZAK, DOMINIC, realtor, football exec.; b. Green Bay, Wis., Aug. 18, 1908; s. John A.B. and Victoria (Marshall) O.; ed. U. Wis., U. Chgo.; m. Regina Bettine, Nov. 24, 1938; children—Thomas, Mark. Owner realty firm, Green Bay, 1955—; pres. Green Bay Packer Football Corp., 1958—. Mem. Gov.'s Commn. on Mass Urban Transp., 1953-54; mem. City Council, Green Bay, 1936-44, mayor, 1945-55. Mem. Land Bank Assn. (past sec.), Wis. League Municipalities (past pres.). Roman Catholic (treas. congregation 1944—). Elk. Home: 1736 Carriage Ct Green Bay WI 54304 Office: 1265 Lombardi Ave Green Bay WI 54305*

OLEKSIW, DANIEL PHILIP, educator; b. Wilkes Barre, Pa., Feb. 5, 1921; s. Rev. Michael Nicholas and Maria Helena (von Kotzko) O.; B.A., Pa. State U., 1940; student Duke; postgrad. U. Mo., Princeton; grad. Nat. War Coll., 1962; m. Elizabeth Louise Hyatt, Aug. 21, 1948; children—Barbara Anne, Daniel Hyatt. Reporter, editor small newspapers Mo. and Mich.; advt. copywriter, Cleve.; information specialist Civilian Prodn. Adminstrn., Washington, 1946; dep. chief press br. USAF Hdqrs. pub. relations, Washington, 1947, 48; pub. advt. newspapers, Arlington and Alexandria, Va., 1948, 49; pub. relations officer U.S. Mission for Aid to Turkey, 1949-50; attache Am. embassy, information officer USIS, Ankara, 1951; attache Am. embassy, chief information officer, Cairo, 1952-55; 1st sec. Am. embassy, dep. pub. affairs officer USIS, Tehran, 1956-58; consul, pub. affairs officer consulate gen., Bombay, 1958-61; assigned Nat. War Coll., 1961-62; program coordinator for Africa, USIA, 1962-63; dep. area dir. for Africa, 1963-64; dir. media content USIA, 1964-65; spl. asst. to permanent rep. U.S. mission to UN, 1966; area dir. for East Asia and Pacific, USIA, 1966-70; minister-counselor pub. affairs Am. embassy, New Delhi, India, 1970-73, also dir. USIS, India; sr. faculty adviser Nat. War Coll., 1973; chief insp. USIA, Washington, 1973-78; dir. ednl. programming Middle East Services, Washington, 1979—. Served to 2d lt. inf. AUS, 1942-45. Recipient Distinguished Service award USIA, 1966. Roman Catholic. Home: 2821 38th St NW Washington DC 20007 Office: 1321 1/2 Wisconsin Ave NW Washington DC 20006

OLER, WESLEY MARION, III, physician; b. N.Y.C., Mar. 8, 1918; s. Wesley Marion and Imogene (Rubel) O.; grad. Phillips Andover Acad., 1936; A.B., Yale U., 1940; M.D., Columbia U., 1943; m. Virginia Carolyn Craemer, Dec. 8, 1951; children—Helen Louise (dec.), Wesley Marion IV, Stephen Scott. Intern, Bellevue Hosp., N.Y.C., 1944, resident, 1948-50; fellow Hosp. U. Pa., 1951; practice medicine specializing in internal medicine, Washington, 1952—; sr. adv. staff vice chmn. dept. medicine Washington Hosp. Center, 1962-64, v.p. med. bd., 1971-72, trustee, 1973—; clin. prof. medicine Med. Sch., Georgetown U. Founder, past pres. Washington Recorder Soc.; bd. dirs. Am. Recorder Soc. Served to maj. M.C., U.S. Army, 1944-47. Fellow A.C.P. (gov. 1980-84); mem. Mensa, Osler Soc. Washington (past pres.). Republican. Episcopalian. Clubs: Met., Cosmos, Chevy Chase. Contbr. articles on old musical instruments to jours. Home: 4800 Van Ness St NW Washington DC 20016 Office: 3301 New Mexico Ave NW Washington DC 20016

OLESEN, J.M., metal products co. exec.; b. Chgo., 1904; grad. U. Ill., 1925. Chmn. bd. Lyon Metal Products, Inc., Aurora, Ill.; dir. Mchts. Nat. Bank, First Am. Bank. Bd. govs. Copley Hosp.; bd. dirs. Aurora Coll. Clubs: Union League, Elks, Moose. Home: 1730 W Galena Blvd Aurora IL 60506

OLESEN, VIRGINIA LEE, sociologist; b. Lovelock, Nev., July 21, 1925; d. Ole H. and Leora (Noel) Olesen; B.A., U. Nev., 1947; M.A., U. Chgo., 1954; Ph.D., Stanford U., 1961. Asst. research sociologist U. Calif. Sch. Nursing, San Francisco, 1960-66, asst. prof., then asso. prof. sociology, 1966-73; prof. sociology U. Calif., San Francisco, 1973—, chmn. dept. social and behavioral scis., 1972-75; distinguished vis. prof. Am. U., Cairo, 1976. Grantee Population Council N.Y., 1971, NIMH, 1972-74. Mem. Am., Pacific sociol. assns., Soc. Study Social Problems, Cheiron Soc., AAUP, ACLU, Americans Democratic Action, Faculty Assn. U. Calif., Soc. Applied Anthropology, Med. Anthropology Soc. Co-author: The Silent Dialogue, 1968. Contbr. profl. jours. Home: 158 Funston Ave San Francisco CA 94118 Office: Room 631-N Sch Nursing Univ Calif San Francisco CA 94143

OLEVSKY, JULIAN, concert violinist; b. Berlin, Germany, May 7, 1926; s. Seigmund and Augustina (Schachmeister) O.; pupil of Alexander Petschnikoff; m. Estela Kersenbaum, Jan. 29, 1966; 1 dau., Diane; children by previous marriage—Roxane, Ronald. Came to U.S., 1947, naturalized, 1951. World Wide concert violin tours, 1936—; resident artist U. Mass., 1967-74; rec. artist for Westminster Records. Home: 68 Blue Hills Rd Amherst MA 01002

OLFE, DANIEL BURRHUS, educator; b. St. Louis, Feb. 4, 1935; s. Virgil Milton and Marjorie Mary (Burrhus) O.; B.S. in Engring., Princeton, 1957; Ph.D., Calif. Inst. Tech., 1960; m. Julie Ellen Thieme, June 13, 1964; children—Brian Christopher, Corey Benjamin. Research fellow Calif. Inst. Tech., 1960; asso. prof. N.Y.U., 1960-64; mem. faculty U. Calif. at San Diego, 1964—, prof. engring. sci., 1969—; vis. prof. U. Chgo., 1972. Guggenheim fellow jet propulsion, 1957-59; NSF fellow, 1959-60. Asso. fellow Am. Inst. Aero. and Astronautics; mem. Heat Transfer and Fluid Mechanics Inst. (gen. chmn. 1967), Phi Beta Kappa, Sigma Xi. Author: (with S.S. Penner) Radiation and Reentry, 1968. Editor: (with V. Zakkay) Supersonic Flow, Chemical Processes and Radiative Transfer, 1964; (with P.A. Libby and C.W. Van Atta) proc. Heat Transfer and Fluid Mechanics Inst., 1967; asso. editor Jour. Quantitative Spectroscopy and Radiative Transfer, 1967-69, Jour. Am. Inst. Aero. and Astronautics, 1969-71. Home: 8220 Paseo del Ocaso La Jolla CA 92037 Office: Univ Calif San Diego La Jolla CA 92093

OLIANSKY, JOEL, author, dir.; b. N.Y.C., Oct. 11, 1935; s. Albert and Florence (Shaw) O.; M.F.A., Yale, 1962; B.A., Hofstra U., Hempstead, N.Y., 1959. Playwright-in-residence Yale, 1962-64; co-founder Hartford Stage Co., 1963; writer Universal Studios, 1974—. Recipient Emmy award, 1971; Humanities prize, 1975; Writers Guild award, 1975. Author: Shame, Shame on the Johnson Boys!, 1966. *I have, I think, used less than 1 percent of my talent. If I have achieved anything, it is because others have used even less of theirs.*

OLICK, ARTHUR SEYMOUR, lawyer; b. N.Y.C., June 15, 1931; s. Jack and Anita (Babsky) O.; B.A., Yale, 1952, LL.B., J.D., 1955; m. Selma Ada Kaufman, June 27, 1954; children—Robert Scott, Karen Leslie. Admitted to N.Y. bar, 1956; asso. atty. Casey, Lane & Mittendorf, N.Y.C., 1957-62; asst. U.S. atty. So. Dist. N.Y., 1962-68, chief civil div., 1965-68; partner Otterbourg, Steindler, Houston & Rosen, N.Y.C., 1968-71; partner Kreindler, Relkin, Olick & Goldberg, N.Y.C., 1971-74; officer, dir. Anderson, Russell, Kill & Olick, P.C., N.Y.C., 1974—. Asst. in instrn. polit. sci. Yale, 1953-55; instr. polit. sci.-bus. law U. Ga., 1955-57; lectr. Practicing Law Inst., N.Y.C., 1965-71; candidate N.Y. State Supreme Ct., 1971; counsel Tarrytown (N.Y.) Urban Renewal Agy., 1968-73, 75-77; town atty., Greenburgh, N.Y., 1974; spl. counsel Town of New Castle, N.Y., 1979; village atty., Tarrytown, 1968-73, 75-77, Dobbs Ferry, N.Y., 1975-77; dir. Westchester County (N.Y.) Legal Aid Soc., 1976-79. Pres., Hartsdale (N.Y.) Bd. Edn., 1968-72; bd. dirs. Westchester County Municipal Planning Fedn., 1976-78, Circle in the Sq. Theater, 1978—; trustee, Calhoun Sch., N.Y.C., 1973—. Served with U.S. Army, 1955-57. Mem. Am., N.Y. State, Westchester County bar assns., Assn. Bar City New York, Fed. Bar Council, Am. Arbitration Assn. (nat. panel arbitrators), Phi Beta Kappa. Clubs: Yale, Merchants (N.Y.C.); Nat. Lawyers (Washington). Home: 98 Harvard Dr Hartsdale NY 10530 also Lake Oscawana Putnam Valley NY 10579 Office: 630 Fifth Ave New York NY 10020

OLICK, PHILIP STEWART, lawyer; b. N.Y.C., Oct. 2, 1936; s. Jack and Anita (Babsky) O.; B.A., Columbia, 1957; LL.B., N.Y. U., 1960; m. Alice D. Chait, Mar. 25, 1961; children—Jonathan A., Jeffrey K., Diana M. Admitted to N.Y. bar, 1961, Mo. bar, 1966; partner firm Benjamin, Galton, Robbins & Flato, N.Y.C., 1961-65; gen. counsel, v.p., sec. Nat. Bellas Hess, Inc., Kansas City, Mo., 1965-69, dir., 1970-76; mem. firm Burke & Burke, N.Y.C., 1970-73, Townley & Updike, 1973—; gen. counsel Combustion Equipment Assos., Inc., N.Y.C., 1975—. Bd. dirs. U. Glee Club N.Y.C.; bd. dirs., v.p. Wildwood Knolls Community Assn., Putnam Valley, N.Y. Served with AUS, 1960-61. Mem. Am., N.Y. bar assns., Assn. Bar City N.Y., N.Y.C. Lawyers Club. Home: 941 Park Ave New York City NY 10028 also Lake Front Rd Putnam Valley NY 10579 Office: 405 Lexington Ave New York City NY 10028

OLIN, JOHN MERRILL, chem. corp. exec.; b. Alton, Ill., Nov. 10, 1892; s. Franklin W. and Mary M. (Moulton) O.; grad. Cascadilla Sch., Ithaca, N.Y., 1909; B.S. in Chemistry, Cornell U., 1913; m. Evelyn B. Niedringhaus, May 11, 1940. With Olin Corp. and predecessor cos., 1913—, now hon. chmn., dir. Trustee emeritus Cornell U.; fellow of the bd. Johns Hopkins U.; life trustee Washington U. Corp.; hon. trustee Am. Mus. Natural History. Home: 21 St Andrews Dr St Louis MO 63124 Office: 7701 Forsyth Blvd St Louis MO 63105

OLIN, SPENCER TRUMAN, mfg. exec.; b. Alton, Ill., Aug. 20, 1900; s. Franklin W. and Mary (Moulton) O.; M.E., Cornell U., 1921; D.Sc., So. Ill. U., 1958; LL.D., Washington U., St. Louis, 1969; m. Ann Whitney, Jan. 12, 1928 (dec. Nov. 11, 1976); children—Mary Dell Olin Pritzlaff, Spencer Truman, Barbara Olin Taylor, Eunice Whitney Olin Higgins. Chief insp. Western Cartridge Co., East Alton, Ill., 1921-24, works mgr., 1924-43, sec., 1928-42, sales mgr., 1933-41, treas., 1935-43, v.p., 1942-45, 1st v.p. Olin Industries, Inc. (consolidation Western Cartridge Co., Winchester Repeating Arms Co., Olin Corp., others), 1945-54; dir. Olin Corp. (consolidation of Olin Industries Inc. and Mathieson Chem. Corp.), 1925-72; dir. St. Louis Union Trust Co.; hon. dir. First Nat. Bank & Trust Co., Alton. Chmn. Republican Nat. Fin. Com., 1958-60; treas. Rep. Nat. Com., 1960-62; trustee emeritus Washington U., St. Louis, Cornell U.; emeritus dir. Barnes Hosp. Recipient Civic award Alton Order DeMolay, 1950; Man of Year award St. Louis chpt. Kappa Sigma, 1953; Distinguished Citizen award Greater Alton Assn. Commerce, 1956. Mem. Kappa Sigma. Clubs: Elks; Log Cabin, Noonday, St. Louis Country, St. Louis (St. Louis); Seminole Golf (Palm Beach, Fla.); Links (N.Y.C.) Home: 801 S Skinker Blvd Saint Louis MO 63105 Office: 7701 Forsyth Blvd Saint Louis MO 63105

OLINER, ARTHUR AARON, physicist, educator; b. Shanghai, China, Mar. 5, 1921, (parents Am. citizens); s. Saul and Sarah (Schulsohn) O.; B.A., Bklyn. Coll., 1941; Ph.D., Cornell U., 1945; m. Frieda Ginsberg, June 16, 1946; children—Marian A., Eric J. Research asso. Microwave Research Inst., Poly. Inst. Bklyn., 1946-53, mem. faculty, 1953—, prof. electrophysics, 1957—, head dept., 1966-71, dir. Microwave Research Inst., 1967—, head dept. elec. engring. and electrophysics, 1971-74; Walker-Ames vis. prof. U. Wash., summer 1964; vis. prof. Cath. U. Rio de Janeiro (Brazil), summer 1973; vis. research scholar Tokyo Inst. Tech., spring 1978; tech. cons. to industry. Dir. Merrimac Industries, West Caldwell, N.J. Chmn. adv. panel Nat. Bur. Standards, 1960-64. Guggenheim fellow Ecole Normale Superieure, Paris, 1965-66; recipient Instn. premium Instn. Elec. Engrs., London, 1963; Microwave prize IEEE, 1967; citation for distinguished research Sigma Xi, 1974. Fellow AAAS, IEEE (hon. life, nat. chmn. Microwave Theory and Techniques Soc. 1959-60, nat. lectr. 1967, mem. publs. bd. 1971-74); mem. Internat. Union Radio Sci. (chmn. U.S. commn. I 1959-62), Am. Phys. Soc., Optical Soc. Am. Contbg. author Microwave Scanning Antennas, 1966. Contbr. numerous articles to profl. jours. Editorial bd. Advances in Microwaves, 1966—, Electronics Letters, London, 1969-75; co-editor Phased Array Antennas, 1972; editor, contbg. author Acoustic Surface Waves, 1978. Home: 545 Westminster Rd Brooklyn NY 11230 Office: Poly Inst NY 333 Jay St Brooklyn NY 11201

OLINS, ROBERT ABBOT, communications research exec.; b. Cambridge, Mass., Sept. 25, 1942; s. Harry and Janice Ray (Porosky) O.; student Hobart Coll., 1961-62, San Francisco Art Inst., 1962; B.A., U. Mass., 1967; postgrad. U. Tampa, 1968; M.A., U. Mo., 1969, Ph.D., 1972; m. Irma Westrich, June 16, 1976; 1 son, Matthew Abbott. With Marsteller, 1972, N.W. Ayer, 1972, Post, Keys & Gardner, Chgo., 1973; with Young & Rubicam, Chgo., 1973—, mng. dir. communications research div., 1976-77, pres., 1977, dir. Young & Rubicam Nat., 1976-78; pres., chief exec. officer, subs. Communications Research Inc., 1978-79. Recipient Chgo./4 award for creative excellence, 1974; Am. Assn. Advt. Agys. grantee 1968-71. Mem. Am. Mktg. Assn., Lake Michigan Yachting Assn. U.S. Yacht Racing Union. Clubs: Chicago Yacht, Skyline. Contbr. articles to profl. jours. Home: 2133 N Sedgwick Ave Chicago IL 60614 Office: Communications Research Inc 1 E Wacker Dr Chicago IL 60601

OLINSKY, TOSCA (MRS. CHARLES F. BARTEAU), painter; b. Florence, Italy, (parents U.S. citizens); d. Ivan G. and Genevieve (Karfunckel) Olinsky; student pub. schs., Nat. Acad. Design, Art Students League; m. Charles F. Barteau, Mar. 20, 1950. One man shows Grand Central Galleries, 1945, Lyman Allyn Museum, New London, Conn., 1958; exhibited at Nat. Acad. Design, Allied Artists, Audubon Artists, Am. Water Color Soc. Awarded Nat. Arts Club prize, 1936, 37, 39, 41; 3d Hallgarten prize Nat. Acad. Design, 1938-43; Allied Artist prize, 1940; Mencion Honorifica Instituto de Allende, Mexico, 1950; Gloria Layton prize Allied Artists Am., 1960, Jane Peterson prize, 1957, Lamont prize Audubon Artist Annual, 1959, Salmagundi Club prize for oil Allied Artists Show, 1972. Elected Nat. Academician, 1969. Mem. Audubon Artists, Am. Water Color Soc., Allied Artists, Lyme Art Assn. Address: Beckwith Lane Old Lyme CT 06371

OLIPHANT, BETTY, performing arts adminstr.; b. London, Eng., Aug. 5, 1918; d. Stuart and Yvonne (Mansfield) O.; student Queen's and St. Mary's Colls.; LL.D. (hon.), Queen's U., 1978, Brock U., 1978; children—Gail Marion Sadava, Carol Ann Roach. Prin. dancer and arranger Prince & Emile Littler Prodns., London, 1936-46; dance arranger Howard & Wyndham, London, 1936-46; tchr. ballet, London, 1936-40; dancer, dance arranger and ballet mistress Blue Pencils Concert Party, Eng., 1944-46; tchr. ballet Oliphant Sch., Toronto, Can., 1948-59; ballet mistress Nat. Ballet of Can., Toronto, 1951-62, prin. and dir., 1959, asso. artistic dir., 1962-75, artistic dir.,

1975—. Decorated Officer Order of Can.; recipient Can. Council Molson prize, 1978. Mem. Can. Dance Tchrs. Assn. (a founder, past pres.), Internat. Soc. of Tchrs. of Dancing. Contbr. articles on dance and teaching to profl. publs. Office: Nat Ballet School 111 Maitland St Toronto ON M4Y 1E4 Canada

OLIPHANT, PATRICK, editorial cartoonist; b. Adelaide, Australa, July 24, 1935; s. Donald Knox and Grace Lillian (Price) O.; m. Hendrika De Vries, Jan. 11, 1958; children—Laura Maria, Grant, Susan. Came to U.S., 1964. Copyboy, press artist Adelaide Advertiser, 1953-55, editorial cartoonist, 1955-64; world tour to study cartooning techniques, 1959; editorial cartoonist Denver Post, 1964-75, Washington Star, 1975—; syndicated by Los Angeles Times Syndicate, 1965—. Chmn. Internat. Salon Cartoons Jury. Recipient 2d place award as funniest cartoonist Internat. Fedn. Free Journalists in Fleet Street, London, 1958; 2d place award internat. cartoon competition Calif. Newspapers Pubs. Assn., 1960; Profl. Journalism award Sigma Delta Chi, 1966; Pulitzer prize for editorial cartooning, 1967. Author: The Oliphant Book, 1969; Four More Years, 1973; An Informal Gathering, 1978. Office: Washington Star 225 Virginia Ave SE Washington DC 20003

OLITSKI, JULES, artist; b. Snovsk, Russia, Mar. 27, 1922; s. Jevel and Anna (Zarnitsky) Demikovsky; student Academie de la Grande Chaumiere, Paris, 1950-51; B.S., N.Y.U., 1952, M.A., 1954; postgrad. Beaux Arts Inst., N.Y.C., 1940-42, Nat. Acad. Design, N.Y.C., 1940-42, Ednl. Alliance, 1947, Zadkine Sch. Sculpture, Paris, 1949; m. Gladys Katz, 1944 (div. 1951); 1 dau., Eve; m. 2d, Andrea Hill Pearce, Jan. 21, 1956 (div. 1974); 1 dau., Lauren. Came to U.S., 1923, naturalized, 1943. Exhibited in many one man shows, including Galerie Huit, Paris, 1951, Iolas Gallery, N.Y.C., 1958, French & Co., N.Y.C., 1959-61, Poindexter Gallery, N.Y.C., 1961-68, Bennington (Vt.) Coll., 1962, Kasmin, Ltd., London, 1964-75, Galerie Lawrence, Paris, 1964, David Mirvish Gallery, Toronto, Ont., 1964-78, Corcoran Gallery, Washington, 1967, 74, Am. Pavillion, Venice Biennale Art Exhbn., 1966, Andre Emmerich Gallery, N.Y.C., 1966-78, (Zurich, Switzerland 1973-78), Met. Mus. Art, N.Y.C., 1969, Laurence Rubin Gallery, N.Y.C., 1969-73, Knoedler Contemporary Art, N.Y.C., 1973-78, Mus. Fine Arts, Boston, 1973, 77, Whitney Mus. Am. Art, 1973, Galleria Dell'Ariete, Italy, 1974. Corcoran Gallery Art, 1974-76, Waddington Gallery, London, 1975, Galeria Wentzel, Germany, 1975, 77, Hirshhorn Mus., Washington, 1977, Edmonton (Alta., Can.) Art Gallery, 1979; exhibited in many group shows, including Carnegie Internat., Pitts., 1961, 1965, Washington Gallery Modern Art, 1963, Los Angeles County Mus., 1964, Fogg Art Mus. Harvard, 1965, Pasadena Art Mus., 1965, Mus. Basel (Switzerland), 1965, 74, Whitney Mus. Am. Art, 1972, 73; Musée d'Art Contemporain, Montreal, 1973, Hirshhorn Mus., 1974, Corcoran Gallery Art, 1975, Everson Mus. Art, Syracuse, 1976; represented in permanent collections including Mus. Modern Art, Art Inst. Chgo., Whitney Mus., Corcoran Art Gallery, Nat. Gallery Can., Met. Mus. Art, N.Y.C., Bklyn. Mus., Hirshhorn Mus., Washington, Everson Mus. Art, Syracuse, N.Y., Mus. Fine Arts, Boston, Norman MacKensie Art Gallery, Regina, Can., also pvt. collections; asso. prof. art State U. Coll. at New Paltz (N.Y.), 1954-55; curator Art Edn. Gallery, N.Y. U., 1955-56; chmn. fine arts div. C.W. Post Coll. L.I. U., Greenvale, N.Y., 1956-63; tchr. Bennington Coll., 1963-67. Recipient 2d prize Carnegie Internat., 1961; 1st prize Corcoran Biennial, Washington, 1967. Home: New Hampshire Office: New York NY 10003

OLITT, ARNOLD, marketing cons.; b. Portland, Oreg., Oct. 13, 1913; s. Israel Benjamin and Ethel (Kelman) O.; student U. Calif., Los Angeles, 1931-33; B.S. in Civil Engring., U. Calif., Berkeley, 1943, postgrad., 1943-44; m. Suzanne Hopusch, Oct. 13, 1938; children—Kenneth, Richard and Raymond (twins). Faculty civil engring. dept. U. Calif., Berkeley, 1943-50; founder, dir. Woodward-Clyde & Assos. (now Woodward-Clyde Cons.), San Francisco, 1950-73; chmn. bd. Woodward-Moorhouse & Assos., 1972; cons. mktg. of profl. services, Incline Village, Nev., 1973—; dir. Woodward-Envicon, 1968-70, Materials Research & Devel., Inc., 1967-70. Mem. Mayor's Adv. Com. for Capital Improvements, Berkeley, 1965; mem. Alameda County Democratic Central Com., 1963-68; trustee Voters Organized in Community Edn., Berkeley; treas., dir. North Tahoe Fine Arts Council; past pres. North Lake Tahoe Symphony Assn.; sustaining mem. Nev. Opera Guild. Registered profl. engr., N.Y. Fellow ASCE (pres. San Francisco sect. 1968, certificates of appreciation 1968, 73), Am. Cons. Engrs. Council; mem. U.S. Com. on Large Dams, Nat. Soc. Profl. Engrs., Soc. Am. Mil. Engrs., Structural Engrs. Assn. No. Calif., Soc. for Mktg. Profl. Services, Incline Village-Crystal Bay C. of C. Clubs: Engineers (San Francisco); Incline Village Golf, Incline Ski. Contbr. articles to profl. jours. Home and office: PO Box 4395 Incline Village NV 89450

OLIVAREZ, GRACIELA, govt. ofcl.; b. Phoenix, Mar. 9, 1928; J.D., Notre Dame U., 1970; L.H.D. (hon.), Amherst Coll., 1973. Dir. women's program Sta. KIFN, Phoenix, 1952-62; staff specialist Chaote Found., Phoenix, 1962-66, also exec. sec. Nat. Conf. on Poverty in S.W.; dir Ariz. office OEO, 1966-67, OEO project rep. with Dept. Labor and HEW, Los Angeles, 1967; mem. task force on problems of chronically unemployed Dept. Labor, 1967; field suveyor U.S. Civil Rights Commn., 1968; with Bur. Consus, 1969; mgr. OEO-funded program to improve fed. food programs, 1970-72; prof. law, dir. Inst. for Social Research and Devel., U. N.Mex., 1972-75; dir. N.Mex. Planning Office, Albuquerque, 1975-77; dir. Community Services Adminstrn., Washington, 1977—; cons. on municipal law Urban Devel. Inst., Purdue U., 1968-69, cons. on Mexican-Am. affairs Nat. Urban Coalition, 1970; cons. Nat. Commn. on Rural Poverty; lectr. on Mexican-Am. culture numerous Univs.; mem. Nat. Adv. Council on Econ. Opportunity; panel mem. White House Conf. on Food, Nutrition and Health, 1969. Bd. dirs. ACLU, Common Cause. Recipient nat. award Am. Cancer Soc., award Mexican C. of C. of Phoenix. Office: Community Services Adminstrn 1200 19th St NW Washington DC 20506

OLIVE, LINDSAY SHEPHERD, biologist; b. Florence, S.C., Apr. 30, 1917; s. Lindsay Shepherd and Sarah Carolyn (Williamson) O.; A.B., U. N.C., 1938, M.A., 1940, Ph.D., 1942; m. Anna Jean Grant, Aug. 28, 1942. Instr. botany U. N.C., 1942-44; mycologist, plant disease diagnostician Dept. Agr., 1944-45; asst. prof. botany U. Ga., 1945-46; asso. prof. botany La. State U., 1946-49; asso. prof. botany Columbia, 1949-57, prof., 1957-67; prof. dept. botany U. N.C., Chapel Hill, 1968-69, distinguished univ. prof., 1970—. Guggenheim fellow, 1956. Fellow AAAS; mem. Nature Conservancy (former project com. chmn.), Am. Bot. Soc., Mycological Soc. Am. (pres. 1966), Soc. Protozoologists, Torrey Bot. Club (pres. 1962), Brit. Mycological Soc. (hon.), Phi Beta Kappa, Sigma Xi. Contbr. Ency. Americana. Author The Mycetozoans, 1975; also numerous articles on classification, life histories, cytology genetics, evolution of fungi and mycetozoans. Home: 501 Laurel Hill Rd Chapel Hill NC 27514

OLIVEIRA, ELMAR, violinist; b. Conn., 1950; student Hartt Coll. Music, Hartford, Conn., Manhattan Sch. Music; studied with Raphael Bronstein, Ariana Bronne. Debut with Hartford Symphony Orch.; appeared on nat. TV as soloist with Young People's Concert series of N.Y. Philharmonic; N.Y.C. debut in Town Hall, 1973; appeared in recitals at Alice Tully Hall, 1976, 77; violinist Houston Symphony; vis. prof. Harper Coll., Binghamton, N.Y.; appeared with Chgo. Symphony, Cleve. Orch., Los Angeles Chamber Orch., Phila. Orch., Casals Festival Orch. Winner gold medal in violin category Tchaikovsky Internat. Competition, 1978; winner 1st prize Naumberg String Competition, 1975; winner 1st prize G.B. Dealey-Dallas News award. Office: care Robert N Levin 180 West End Ave New York NY 10023*

OLIVER, ALEXANDER ROGER, mgmt. cons.; b. Liverpool, Eng., Jan. 25, 1944; s. Cecil Brisbane and Eileen Frances (Brand) O.; B.A., Queens' Coll. Cambridge (Eng.) U., 1965, M.A., 1968; M.B.A., Stanford, 1970; m. Theodora Mary Hodges, Mar. 25, 1968; 1 son, Marcus Boston. Mktg. exec. J. Walter Thompson Co. Ltd., London, Eng., 1965-68; mgr. Boston Cons. Group Inc., 1970-74; sr. v.p. M. Lowenstein & Sons Inc., N.Y.C., 1975-78; pres. Lucrum Group, Inc., N.Y.C., 1979—. Harkness fellow Commonwealth Fund N.Y., 1968-70. Home and office: 60 E 8th St New York NY 10003

OLIVER, ALLEN LAWS, JR., investment co. exec.; b. Cape Girardeau, Mo., May 23, 1915; s. Allen Laws and Olivia (Leachman) O.; B.A., U. Mo., 1936; M.B.A., Harvard, 1938; m. Margaret Smith, Sept. 27, 1940; children—Allen Laws III, Margaret S. (Mrs. Don Garretson), Olivia Leachman (Mrs. George W. Bramblett, Jr.). Asst. trader Merrill, Lynch, Pierce, Fenner & Bean, 1945-47; account exec. E.F. Hutton & Co., Dallas, 1947-55; partner Sanders & Co., 1955-64; chmn. bd., sec. Sanders & Co., Inc., 1964-70; with W.E. Hutton & Co., Dallas, 1970-73, Republic Nat. Life Ins. Co., 1974—; v.p. Stonegate Securities Co., 1975-78; pres. Oliver Investments, Inc., 1978—. Mem. N.Y. Stock Exchange, 1963-70; asso. mem. Am. Stock Exchange, 1963-70. Chmn. exec. com. Highland Park Community League; chmn. Highland Park Bd. Adjustment. Bd. dirs. YMCA Camp Grady Spruce, chmn., 1970-71. Mem. Dallas Security Dealers Assn. (pres. 1961), Nat. Security Traders Assn. (exec. council 1961-67, pres. 1965), S.A.R. Presbyn. Clubs: Northwood, Idlewild, Terpsichorean, Petroleum (Dallas). Home: 3709 Lexington Dallas TX 75205

OLIVER, ALVIN E., trade assn. exec.; b. Sterling, Mich., Nov. 4, 1918; s. Hugh and Blanche (Knight) O.; B.S., M.S. in Agr., Mich. State U.; m. Jean Stanton, Aug. 6, 1943; children—Dale, Donald, Richard, James. Tchr. pub. schs., 1936- 39; asst. prof. Mich. State U., 1946-54, coordinator elevator tng. program; asst. exec. v.p. Nat. Grain and Feed Assn., 1954-55, exec. mgr., 1955-56, exec. v.p., Washington, 1956—. Mem. President's Food for Peace Council, 1961-64; adv. com. wheat and feed grain Dept. Agr., 1961-63; U.S. del. European-Am. Trade Symposium, 1963; participant World Food Congress UN; mem. Agrl. Assn. Exec. Council; del. Pres.'s Conf. on Inflation, 1974; mem. adv. com. on regulation commodity futures trading profls. Commodity Futures Trading Commn., 1975-76. Sec.-treas. Grain and Feed Dealers Nat. Found., 1966—; mem. feed industry adv. com. Kans. State U. Active Boy Scouts Am., 4-H Service Club Mich. Served with AUS, 1943-45. Decorated Bronze Star medal with cluster; recipient Nat. Distinguished Service award Future Farmers Am.; Hon. Am. Farm award Future Farmers Am., 1974. Mem. Am. Soc. of Assn. Execs., Food Group (chmn. 1960-61), Washington Trade Assn. Execs., Mt. Vernon Citizens Assn., C. of C. of U.S. (com. on agr. 1974-76), Alpha Zeta, Kappa Delta Pi, The Farm House Frat. (hon.). Methodist. Club: University (Washington). Home: 1700 River Farm Dr Alexandria VA 22308 Office: 725 15th St NW Washington DC 20005. *Integrity and honesty are too precious to squander.*

OLIVER, COVEY THOMAS, lawyer, educator; b. Laredo, Tex., Apr. 21, 1913; s. Pheneas Roan and Jane Covey (Thomas) O.; B.A. summa cum laude, U. Tex., 1933, LL.B., summa cum laude, 1936; LL.M., Columbia, 1953, J.S.D., 1954; m. Barbara Frances Hauer, Dec. 28, 1946; children—Jane Covey, Lucy Oliver Sampson, Woodlief Hauer, Scotti Longan, Jefferson Thomas. Admitted to Tex. bar, 1936; mem. law faculty U. Tex., 1936-48; sr. atty. Bd. Econ. Warfare, 1942; joined U.S. Fgn. Service Res., 1942; chief econ. controls sect. embassy, Madrid, Spain, 1942-44; head various divs. State Dept., 1944-49; mem. U.S. delegation Paris Peace Conf., also other dels., 1946-49; prof. law U. Calif. at Berkeley, 1949-56; prof law U. Pa., 1956-66, Hubbell prof. internat. law., 1966-78, Hubbell prof. emeritus, 1978—; acting dean, 1978—; Tsanoff prof. public affairs Rice U., Houston, 1979—; ambassador to Colombia, 1964-66; asst. sec. state for inter-Am. affairs; U.S. coordinator Alliance for Progress, 1967-69; U.S. exec. dir. Internat. Bank for Reconstruction and Devel. and affiliates, 1969; Fulbright scholar and lectr. U. de Sao Paulo (Brazil), 1963; Am. mem. Inter-Am. Jud. Com. of OAS, 1963-65. Mem. Am. Soc. Internat. Law (v.p., bd. editors Jour.), Council on Fgn. Relations, Internat. Law Assn., Fgn. Service Assn., Phi Beta Kappa, Order of Coif, Chancellors, Phi Delta Phi. Democrat. Author: The Inter-American Security System and the Cuban Crisis, 1964; numerous articles. Co-author: Restatement of the Foreign Relations Law of the United States, 1963; The International Legal System (and supplement), 1973; Home: Ingleton-on-Miles RFD 1 Box 194 Easton MD 21601 Office: Law Sch U Pa Philadelphia PA 19104 also Jones Grad Sch Adminstrn Box 1892 Rice U Houston TX 77001

OLIVER, DONALD LYNN, television news corr.; b. Billings, Mont., July 14, 1936; s. Foster Loveland and Lucille Oma (Miles) O.; B.A. in Journalism, U. Mont., 1958; M.A. (Earl Godwin Meml. fellow), Columbia U., 1962; m. Sharon Lynne Nelson, June 14, 1958 (div. 1974); children—Catholeen, Christina, Cheri. Reporter, UPI, Helena, Mont., 1958; announcer KFBB Radio and TV, Great Falls, Mont., 1959; newsman KHQ Radio and TV, Spokane, Wash., 1960; reporter, polit. corr. KCRA-TV, Sacramento, 1962-65; news dir. KREM-TV, Spokane, 1965; anchorman, network corr. NBC News, Cleve. Bur., 1966-69, corr., Los Angeles Bur., 1969-73, 76—, Tokyo Bur., 1974-76; vis. lectr U. Mont., 1969. Mem. Fgn. Corr. Assn. Japan, Sigma Delta Chi, Sigma Chi. Club: Internat. of Haiphong. Office: 3000 W Alameda St Burbank CA 91523

OLIVER, EDITH, theatrical reviewer; b. N.Y.C., Aug. 11, 1913; d. Samuel and Maude (Biow) Goldsmith; grad. Horace Mann Sch., N.Y.C., 1931; student Smith Coll., 1931-33. Author radio program Take It Or Leave It, 1940-52; mem. editorial staff New Yorker mag., 1947—; off-Broadway reviewer, 1961—; dramaturg Eugene O'Neill Theatre Center, 1971-79. Office: New Yorker Magazine 25 W 43d St New York City NY 10036

OLIVER, GERALD WINES, constrn. co. exec.; b. Jackson, Mich., Oct. 11, 1925; s. Harry Edwin and Elizabeth Clark (Wines) O.; B.S., Alma (Mich.) Coll., 1949; m. Jane Ann Zimmerman, Dec. 9, 1950; children—Craig W., Kurt H., Jeffrey L. With No. Builders Co., Traverse City, Mich., 1949-58; with Zimmerman Constrn. Co., Traverse City, 1958—, constrn. coordinator, 1959—. Served with USAAF, 1943-46. Mem. Asso. Builders and Contractors (pres. 1977), Mich. Contractors and Suppliers Assn. Republican. Conglist. Home: 1741 Apache Pass Traverse City MI 49684 Office: 1214 Garfield Ave Traverse City MI 49684

OLIVER, HAROLD, newspaper exec.; b. Ulverston, Lancs, Eng., Dec. 23, 1921; s. Isaac and Amelia (Howarth) T.; diploma in personnel mgmt. McMaster U., 1959; grad. Exec. Summer Sch., Queen's U., Kingston, Ont., Can., 1965; m. Dorothy L. Parke, Aug. 28, 1945; children—Robert, James. With Hamilton Spectator, 1946-70, personnel relations mgr., asst. bus. mgr.; bus. mgr. Calgary (Alta., Can.) Herald, 1970-77, gen. mgr., 1977—. Served with RAF, 1940-46. Mem. Newspaper Personnel Relations Assn. (past pres.), Inst. Newspaper Controllers and Fin. Officers, Can. Daily Newspaper Pubs. Assn., Calgary C. of C., Calgary Downtown Bus. Assn., Calgary Tourist and Conv. Assn., Confrerie de la Chaine des Rotisseurs. Clubs: Rotary, Ranchmen's, Calgary Petroleum, Men's Can. Office: 206 7th Ave SW Calgary AB T2P 0W9 Canada*

OLIVER, HARRY MAYNARD, JR., ins. brokerage exec.; b. Kansas City, Mo., Jan. 21, 1921; s. Harry Maynard and Marie (Curtin) O.; B.A., Williams Coll., 1943. Pres., M.A. Gesner & Co., Marsh & McLennan Co., Chgo., 1947—. Chmn. Chgo. Commn. for Sr. Citizens, 1960-69; mem. Chgo. Bd. Edn., 1966-69; pres. Vol. Agys. Chgo.; mem. vis. com. Sch. Edn. and div. of social scis., U. Chgo. Pres., bd. dirs. Benton House Settlement, 1953-58; bd. dirs. Adult Edn. Council Greater Chgo., Nat. Fedn. Settlements and Community Centers, 1961-67; trustee Old Peoples Home Chgo., Pub. Sch. Tchrs. Pension and Retirement Fund Chgo., 1966-69, George M. Pullman Ednl. Found., Field Mus. Natural History, 1971-75. Served to lt. (j.g.) USNR, World War II. Mem. Chi Psi. Clubs: Chicago, Racquet, Commonwealth, Metropolitan (Chgo.); Onwentsia (Lake Forest, Ill.). Home: 1948 N Lincoln Ave Chicago IL 60614 also New Richmond MI 49447 Office: 222 S Riverside Chicago IL 60606

OLIVER, HERBERT ARNOLD DIMITRI, lawyer; b. June 11, 1921; came to Can., 1952; s. David and Edith O.; B.Sc., London U., 1948; student Law Soc.'s Sch. Law, 1949; m. Jeanne Hilda King, Jan. 3, 1959; children—David Richard Benedict, Mark Justin Dominic, Alexandra Edith Amelia. Called to B.C. bar, 1952, Alta. bar, 1973; solicitor Supreme Ct. Eng., 1949; asso. Rowley Ashworth & Co., London, 1949-52; sr. partner firm Oliver, Waldock & Richardson and predecessors, Vancouver, B.C., Can., 1952—; consul-gen. of Liberia for Western Can., from 1954; sec.-gen. Consular Corps in B.C., from 1956; pres. Assn. Hon. Consuls Accredited to Govt. Can., 1980—; mem. Jud. Council B.C.; dir. Williams Hudson (Can.) Ltd. Freeman, City of London; mem. Control Commn. for Germany, 1945-46. Served with Brit. Army, 1939-45. Decorated knight Gt. Band. Order African Redemption (Liberia); officer Fed. Order Merit (W. Ger.); knight Order St. John of Jerusalem (Denmark); croix-de-guerre (France). Fellow Inst. Arbitrators, Royal Econ. Soc.; mem. Law Soc. Eng., Law Soc. B.C., Law Soc. Alta. (Can.), Can. Bar Assn., Internat. Bar Assn., Internat. Commn. Jurists, Consular Law Soc., Assn. Trial Lawyers Am. (gov. 1973—), Brit. Acad. Forensic Scis., Western Can. Forensic Soc., Found. Legal Research Can., Royal African Soc., Royal Commonwealth Soc., Alliance Francaise, Internat. Wine and Food Soc. Anglican. Clubs: Royal Vancouver Yacht; Law Soc. Yacht (Eng.); East India (London); Union (Victoria, B.C.). Office: 1030 W Georgia St Vancouver BC V6E 3B5 Canada

OLIVER, JACK ERTLE, geophysicist; b. Massillon, Ohio, Sept. 26, 1923; s. Chester L. and Marie (Ertle) O.; A.B., Columbia U., 1947, M.A., 1950, Ph.D., 1953; m. Gertrude van der Hoeven, Apr. 16, 1964; children—Cornelia Oliver, Amy Oliver. Research asst., then research asso. Columbia, 1947-55, mem. faculty, 1955-73, prof. geology, 1961-71, chmn. dept., 1969-71, adj. prof., 1971-73; Irving Porter Church prof. engring., chmn. dept. geol. scis. Cornell U., 1971—. Terrestrial physicist USAF Cambridge (Mass.) Research Labs., 1951; cons. AEC, 1969-72, ACDA, 1962-74, USAF Tech. Applications Center, 1959-65; mem. Polar Research Com., also nat. commn. uppermantle program, 1963-71; mem. panel solid earth problems Nat. Acad. Sci.; mem. adv. com. U.S. Coast and Geodetic Survey, 1962-66, on seismology, 1960-72, chmn., 1966-70; mem. Geophysics Research Bd., 1969-70; U.S. coordinator 2d U.S.-Japan Earthquake Prediction Conf., Palisades, 1966; earth sci. panel NSF, 1962-65; mem. USAF Sci. Adv. Bd., 1960-63, 64-69; mem. geophysics adv. panel Office Sci. Research, USAF, 1961-74, chmn., 1966-68; U.S. del. Test Ban Conf., Geneva, Switzerland, 1958-59, intergovtl. meeting seismology and earthquake engring., mem. exec. com. IASPEI, 1968-71, mem. governing com. Internat. Seismol. Summary Commn., 1963-67, 75-76; mem. exec. com. UNESCO, Paris, France, 1964, U.S.-Japan Earthquake Prediction Conf., Tokyo, 1964; mem. UNESCO Joint Com. on Seismology and Earthquake Engring., 1965—; chmn. exec. com. Office Earth Scis., NRC, 1976-79; chmn. exec. com. Internat. Seismol. Centre, 1976-78. Served with USNR, 1943-46. Fellow Am. Geophys. Union (pres. seismology sect. 1964-68), Geol. Soc. Am. (council 1970-73); mem. Seismol. Soc. Am. (pres. 1964-65, bd. dirs. 1961-70, 73—), Acoustical Soc. Am. (1954-69), Am. Phys. Soc. (1950-66), Soc. Exploration Geophysicists, A.A.A.S., Sigma Xi. Home: 125 Cayuga Park Rd Ithaca NY 14850

OLIVER, JAMES ARTHUR, zoologist; b. Caruthersville, Mo., Jan. 1, 1914; s. Arthur L. and Mary E. (Roberts) O.; student U. Tex., 1932-34; A.B., U. Mich., 1936, A.M., 1937, Ph.D. (Univ. fellow 1938-40, Hinsdale scholar 1940-41), 1941; Sc.D., Southampton Coll., L.I. U., 1975; m. Elizabeth Kimball, May 3, 1941; children—Patricia A., Dexter K.; m. 2d, Ruth H. Norton, Dec. 22, 1967. Instr. No. Mich. Coll. Edn., 1941-42; asst. curator Am. Museum Natural History, N.Y.C., 1942-47, asso. curator, 1947-48; asst. prof. zoology U. Fla., 1948-51; curator reptiles N.Y. Zool. Soc., 1951-59, asst. dir. Zool. Park, 1958, dir., 1958-59, dir. emeritus, 1977—; research asso. Am. Mus. Natural History, 1948-59, dir., 1959-69, coordinator sci. and environment programs, 1969-70, dir. emeritus, 1973—; dir. N.Y. Aquarium, 1970-76. Adv. com. Mianus River Gorge Conservation Commn.; bd. dirs. Caribbean Conservation Corp.; steering com. Biol. Sci. Curriculum Study, 1962-66, exec. com., 1964-66; com. mus. resources N.Y. Commr. Edn., 1961- 64; organizing com. 16th Internat. Congress Zoologists, 1963; mem. Am. Commn. Internat. Wildlife Protection; trustee, treas., pres. Biol. Scis. Information Services, 1964-72. Served with USNR, 1943-46. Recipient Outstanding Achievement award U. Mich., 1963. Fellow Royal Soc. Arts (London), N.Y. Zool. Soc., Rochester Mus. Assn.; mem. Am. Soc. Ichthyologists and Herpetologists (bd. govs., editorial bd.), Herpetologists League, AAAS, Am. Assn. Museums (chmn. environment com. 1969-70, mem. council 1967-75, mem. accreditation commn. 1971-76), Mus. Council N.Y.C., Palisades Nature Assn. (dir.), N.Y. State Assn. Museums (council, v.p. 1964), Internat. Council Museums (exec. com.), Assn. Dirs. Systematic Collections, Dirs. Sci. Museums and Cultural Instns. N.Y.C., N.Y. Hist. Soc. (asso., Pintard fellow), Bklyn. Arts and Culture Council (trustee). Clubs: Century Assn. Author: The Natural History of North American Amphibians and Reptiles, 1955; Snakes in Fact and Fiction, 1958; Prevention and Treatment of Snake Bite, 1952; also sci. papers. Address: NY Zool Park Bronx NY 10460

OLIVER, JAMES HENRY, historian; b. N.Y.C., Apr. 26, 1905; s. James Henry and Louise (McGratty) O.; A.B., Yale, 1926, Ph.D. (fellow Soldiers and Sailors Meml. 1926-28), 1931; student U. Bonn, 1927-28; Jesse B. Carter fellow Am. Acad. in Rome, 1928-30; m. Janet Carnochan, June 26, 1936. Instr. Latin, Yale, 1930-32; excavator, epigraphist Agora Excavations, Athens, Greece, 1932-36; asst. prof. ancient history Barnard Coll., 1936-42; prof. classics Johns Hopkins, 1946-70, Francis White prof. Greek, 1957-70. Guest 10th ann. congress Société des Droits de l'Antiquité, Brussels, 1955, 1st Spanish Congress Classical Studies, Madrid, 1956; organizing com. 3d Internat. Congress Epigraphy, 1956-57; sr. fellow Center for Hellenic Studies, 1962-71. Served from capt. to maj., AUS, 1943-45.

Guggenheim fellow, 1946, 55-56; Fulbright grantee, Italy, 1963-64; research scholar, Athens, 1939-40, 70-71; sr. fellow Nat. Endowment for Humanities, 1973-74.) Mem. Am. Philol. Assn. (dir. 1965-70, v.p. 1972-74, pres. 1974-75), Archael. Inst. Am. (chmn. monograph com. 1957-68), Am. Soc. Papyrologists, Soc. Promotion Roman Studies, Austrian Archaeol. Inst. (hon.), Ovidianum (Bucharest). Author: (with H.G. Evelyn White) Greek Inscriptions of Hibis, 1938; The Sacred Gerusia, 1941; The Athenian Expounders of the Sacred and Ancestral Law, 1950; The Ruling Power, 1953; Demokratia, the Gods, and The Free World, 1960; The Civilizing Power, 1968; Marcus Aurelius, 1970. Hon. editor Am. Jour. Philology; adviser to Greek, Roman and Byzantine Studies, 1958—; publs. com. Am. Sch. Classical Studies at Athens, 1952-69, exec. com., 1961-65. Contbr. articles to profl. jours. Home: 322 St Dunstans Rd Baltimore MD 21212

OLIVER, JAMES WILLARD, educator; b. Webb City, Mo., Aug. 3, 1912; s. James Walter and Emma (Thurtell) O.; B.A., U. Fla., 1935; M.A., Harvard, 1949, Ph.D., 1949; m. Marjorie Elinor Burrill, Nov. 10, 1961; 1 son, Walter Frederick. Asst. prof. philosophy U. Fla., 1949-53, asso. prof., 1953-59; sr. scientist Litton Industries, Canoga Park, Cal., 1959-60; asso. prof. U. So. Calif., 1960-64; prof. philosophy U. S.C., Columbia, 1964—, chmn. dept., 1964-72. Served with AUS, 1942-46. Mem. Am. Philos. Assn., Assn. for Symbolic Logic, Royal Inst. Philosophy, So. Soc. for Philosophy and Psychology, S.C. Soc. Philosophy (pres. 1967-68), AAUP, Soc. Advancement Am. Philosophy, S.C. Com. for Humanities. Contbr. articles to profl. jours. Home: 1010 Rickenbaker Rd Columbia SC 29205

OLIVER, JOHN SANFORD, condr.; b. Teaneck, N.J., June 4, 1939; s. Frank Edward and Marie Katherine (Krenzer) O.; B.Music, U. Notre Dame, 1961; M.Music, New Eng. Conservatory Music, 1967. Asst. to music dir. for choral and vocal activities Berkshire Music Center, Tanglewood, Mass., 1968-69; mem. music faculty, condr. glee club Newton Coll. of the Sacred Heart, 1966-71; instr. advanced choral conducting, conductor chorus Boston U., 1971-72; condr. Framingham Choral Soc., 1966-72; asst. condr. M.I.T. Glee Club and Choral Soc., 1965-72; condr. Tanglewood Festival Chorus, dir. vocal and choral activities Berkshire Music Center at Tanglewood, Boston Symphony Orch., 1970—; lectr. music, condr. M.I.T. Choral Soc., M.I.T. 1972—; founder, condr. John Oliver Chorale. Grammy nominee, 1975. Numerous recordings with New World Records, Deutsche Grammophon Records, RCA, Phillips Records. Office: Boston Symphony Orch Symphony Hall Boston MA 02115

OLIVER, JOHN WATKINS, judge; b. Cape Girardeau, Mo., Dec. 17, 1914; s. Robert Burett and Jessie (McCreery) O.; A.B., U. Mo., 1934, LL.B., 1936; m. Gertrude Field, Jan. 24, 1940; children—John Watkins II, Gertrude, Jane, David. Admitted to Mo. bar, 1936; practiced in Kansas City, 1936-62; U.S. judge, Western Dist. Mo., 1962—, now chief judge; mem. Jud. Conf. U.S. Standing Com. on Adminstrn. Probation, 1963—. Chmn. bd. of election commrs., Kansas City, 1950-54; mem. Mo. Bd. Law Examiners, 1952-62. Bd. dirs. Mo. Law Sch. Found., Am. Law Inst. Mem. Am., Kansas City bar assns., Mo. State Bar (gov. 1945-46), Lawyers Assn. Kansas City (dir. 1942), Am. Judicature Soc., Mo. Hist. Soc. Mem. Soc. of Friends. Home: 848 W 57 St Kansas City MO 64113 Office: Room 404 US Court House 811 Grand Ave Kansas City MO 64106*

OLIVER, MARY, poet; b. Maple Heights, Ohio, Sept. 10, 1935; d. Edward William and Helen Marie (Vlasak) Oliver; student Ohio State U., 1955-56, Vassar Coll., 1956-57. Author: No Voyage and Other Poems, 1963, enlarged edit., 1965; The River Styx, Ohio, 1972; The Night Traveler, 1978; Twelve Moons, 1979; contbr. Am. Scholar, Atlantic Monthly, Harpers, New Republic, New Yorker, Ohio Rev., Yale Rev., others. Chmn. writing dept. Fine Arts Work Center, Provincetown, 1972, 73. Recipient Shelley Meml. award, 1970, Alice Fay di Castagnola award, 1973; Cleve. Arts prize for lit., 1979; Nat. Endowment fellow, 1972-73. Mem. Poetry Soc. Am., PEN. Home: care Molly Malone Cook Lit Agy Box 338 Provincetown MA 02657

OLIVER, MARY WILHELMINA, law librarian, educator; b. Cumberland, Md., May 4, 1919; d. John Arlington and Sophia (Lear) Oliver; A.B., Western Md. Coll., 1940; B.S. in Library Sci., Drexel Inst. Tech., 1943; J.D., U. N.C., 1951. Asst. circulation librarian N.J. Coll. Women, 1943-45; asst. in law library U. Va., 1945-47; asst. reference, social sci. librarian Drake U., 1947-49; research asst. Inst. Govt., U. N.C., 1951-52, asst. law librarian, 1952-55, asst. prof. law, law librarian, 1955-59, asso. prof. law, law librarian, 1959-69, prof. law, law librarian, 1969—; admitted to N.C. bar, 1951. Mem. Internat., Am. (pres.) assns. law libraries, Spl. Libraries Assn., Am., N.C. bar assns., Assn. Am. Law Schs. (exec. com. 1979—), Am. Soc. Legal History, Law Alumni Assn. U. N.C., Seldon Soc., Order of Coif. Home: Box 733 Chapel Hill NC 27514 Office: U NC Law Library Chapel Hill NC 27514

OLIVER, MICHAEL KELWAY, assn. exec.; b. North Bay, Ont., Can., Feb. 2, 1925; s. Gilbert Salt and Winifred Maud (Kelway) O.; B.A., McGill U. (Can.), 1948, M.A., 1950, Ph.D., 1956, LL.D., 1972; D.U., U. Laval, 1977; postgrad. Institut d'Etudes Politiques, Paris, France, 1949; m. Joan Alexander Nelson, Dec. 18, 1948; children—David, James, Victoria, Geoffrey, Cynthia. Asst. prof. U. N.B. (Can.), 1950-51; asso. prof. United Coll., Winnipeg, Man., Can., 1952-57; vis. prof. Laval U., 1958; asso. prof. McGill U., Montreal, Que., 1958-67, prof., 1967—, vice prin. acad., 1967-72; pres. Carleton U., Ottawa, Ont., 1972-78; dir. internat. devel. office Assn. Univs. and Colls. Can., 1979—. Mem. Superior Labour Council Que., 1960-61; dir. research Royal Commn. on Bilingualism and Biculturalism, 1964; chmn. Man. Task Force on Post-Secondary Edn., 1972-73. Fed. pres. New Democratic Party, 1961-63. Served with Royal Canadian Arty., 1943-45. Mem. Internat. (past mem. council), Canadian (past mem. exec. council), Am. polit. sci. assns., Soc. Canadienne des scis. politiques, Assn. canadienne-francaise pour l'avancement des scis. Club: Cercle Universitaire (Ottawa). Editor: Social Purpose for Canada, 1961; (with F.R. Scott) Quebec States her Case, 1964. Home: 116 Buell St Ottawa ON K1Z 7E8 Canada

OLIVER, ROBERT BRUCE, investment co. exec.; b. Brockton, Mass., Aug. 1, 1931; s. Stanley Thomas and Helen (Sabine) O.; A.B., Harvard U., 1953, postgrad. Bus. Sch., 1971; postgrad. Boston U. Law Sch., 1955-57; M.A., Mich. State U., 1958; m. Sylvia E. Bell, Feb. 17, 1954; children—Susan Pamela, Robert Bruce. Pres., dir. John Hancock Income Securities Corp., Boston, 1973—; pres., dir. John Hancock Investors, Inc., John Hancock Bond Fund, Inc., John Hancock Growth Fund, Inc., John Hancock Balanced Fund, Inc., John Hancock Advisers, Inc.; pres., trustee John Hancock Tax Exempt Income Trust, John Hancock Cash Mgmt. Trust; dir. John Hancock Distbrs., Inc.; mem. investment adv. div. com. Investment Co. Inst., 1977—. Served to 1st lt. USMCR, 1953-55. Mem. Investment Co. Inst. (gov.), Harvard Bus. Sch. Assn. Boston. Clubs: St. Botolph, Old Colony Harvard; Blue Hill Tennis. Home: 378 Adams St Milton MA 02816 Office: John Hancock Pl Boston MA 02117

OLIVER, ROBERT CLIFTON, cons. engr.; b. Kansas City, Mo., Mar. 9, 1912; s. Robert C. and Katherine (Kirk) O.; B.S., U. Kans., 1934; m. Rosamond Augusta Hadley, Feb. 12, 1937; children—Robert, Daniel, John. Asso., Geophys. Services, Inc., 1934-35; exec. partner Black & Veatch Engrs., Kansas City, 1935—. Mem. local sch. bd., 1963-67; active Kansas City Friends of Art, Am. Cancer Soc. Served with USN, World War II. Registered profl. engr., Ill., Iowa, Ind., Kans., Ky., Mich., Minn., Mo., Nebr., Tenn., Wis., S.C., Calif., Ark., Colo. Fellow Am. Cons. Engrs. Council; mem. Nat., Mo. socs. profl. engrs., Profl. Engrs. in Pvt. Practice, IEEE, ASME, Engrs. Club Kansas City. Contbr. engring. articles to profl. jours. Home: 2520 Red Bridge Terr Kansas City MO 64131 Office: PO Box 8405 Kansas City MO 64114

OLIVER, THOMAS KEYSER, JR., physician, educator; b. Hobart Mills, Calif., Dec. 21, 1925; s. Thomas Keyser and Minora E. (McCabe) O.; student U. Calif. at Berkeley, 1943-45; M.D., Harvard, 1949; m. Lois A. Pounds; children—Katherine, Thomas D. Intern, N.Y. Hosp.-Cornell Med. Center, 1949-50, resident, 1950-51, 53-55; from asst. prof. to asso. prof. Ohio State U., 1955-63; dir. Newborn Nurseries and Premature Center U. Hosp., also head div. neonatal biology dept. pediatrics U. Wash., Seattle, 1963-70, asso. dir. Child Devel. and Mental Retardation Center, 1968-70; prof., chmn. dept. pediatrics U. Pitts., 1970—; med. dir. Children's Hosp. Pitts., 1970-78. Served with M.C., AUS, 1951-53. Diplomate Am. Bd. Pediatrics (examiner 1971—, chmn. sub-bd. neonatal-perinatal pediatrics 1976-77, mem. 1980—), Nat. Bd. Med. Examiners. Fellow Am. Acad. Pediatrics; mem. Am. Pediatric Soc. (council 1976—), Soc. for Pediatrics Research (council 1964-66), Assn. Am. Med. Colls. (adminstrv. bd. Council Acad. Socs. 1974—, chmn. 1978), Pa., Allegheny County med. socs. Editorial bd. Pediatrics, 1969-74; co-editor Seminars in Perinatology; cons. editor Monographs in Neonatology. Home: 6313 Kentucky Ave Pittsburgh PA 15206 Office: 125 DeSoto St Pittsburgh PA 15213

OLIVER, WILLIAM ALBERT, JR., paleontologist; b. Columbus, Ohio, June 26, 1926; s. William Albert and Mary-Maud (Thompson) O.; B.S., U. Ill., 1948; M.A., Cornell U., 1950; Ph.D., 1952; m. Johanna L. Kramer, Sept. 1, 1948; children—Robert A., James A. Instr., then asst. prof. geology Brown U., Providence, 1952-57; research geologist-paleontology U.S. Geol. Survey, Washington, 1957—; mem. U.S. Nat. Com. on Geology, 1975-79, chmn., 1978-79. Fellow Geol. Soc. Am.; mem. Paleontol. Soc. (councilor 1964-69, 73-76, editor Jour. 1964-69, pres. 1974-75), Paleontol. Assn. (London), AAAS (council 1971-73), Paleontol. Research Inst. (trustee 1976—), Am. Geol. Inst. (dir. 1974-77, v.p. 1975-76, pres. 1976-77). Contbr. articles to profl. jours. Home: 4203 McCain Ct Kensington MD 20795 Office: E-305 Nat Mus Bldg Washington DC 20560

OLIVER, WILLIAM JOHN, pediatrician, educator; b. Blackshear, Ga., Mar. 30, 1925; s. John Wesley and Katherine (Schalwig) O.; student Ga. Southwestern Coll., 1942-43, Mercer U., 1943-44; M.D. cum laude, U. Mich., 1948; m. Marguerite Bertoni, May 28, 1949; children—Ralph Scott, Catherine, Susan. Intern, resident U. Mich. Med. Center, 1948-53, dir. pediatric labs., 1959-67; practice medicine specializing in pediatrics, Ann Arbor, Mich., 1953—; instr. dept. pediatrics U. Mich., 1953-56, asst. prof., 1956-61, asso. prof., 1961-65, prof., 1965, chmn. dept. pediatrics, 1967-79; chief pediatric service Wayne County Hosp., 1958-61; co-chmn. task force on recent advances of coordinating com. on continuing edn. and recertification Am. Bd. Pediatrics and Am. Acad. Pediatrics, 1977-80; cons. U. Riyad (Saudi Arabia). Pres., Mich. Kidney Disease Found., 1969, Washtenaw County br. Mich. Childrens Aid Soc., 1964. Served with USNR, 1950-52. Diplomate Am. Bd. Pediatrics (examiner), subsplty. bd. pediatric nephrology. Fellow Am. Acad. Pediatrics (chmn. com. med. edn. 1974-80, chmn. council on pediatric edn. 1975-80, Clifford G. Grulee award 1979); mem. Soc. Pediatric Research, Midwest Soc. Pediatric Research (pres. 1968), Am. Soc. Nephrology, Assn. Med. Sch. Pediatric Dept. Chairmen (mem. council 1977-79), Soc. for Exptl. Biology and Medicine, Am. Pediatric Soc., Alpha Omega Alpha, Gamma Sigma Epsilon. Home: 2892 Bay Ridge St Ann Arbor MI 48103 Office: Mott Bldg U Mich Med Center Ann Arbor MI 48109

OLIVERO, MAGDA, opera singer; b. Saluzzo, Italy, Mar. 25; student Turin (Italy) Conservatory; m. Alfo Busch, 1941. Operatic debut as Lauretta in Gianni Schicchi, Teatro Emanuele, Turin, 1933; appeared subsequently in opera houses throughout Italy; during World War II sang in hosps. and at Red Cross benefits; Am. debut as Medea with Dallas Civic Opera, 1967; East Coast debut in Adriana Lecouvreur, Conn. Opera Assn., 1969; N.Y. debut as soloist with Little Orch. Soc. in La Voix Humaine, 1971; Met. Opera debut in Tosca, 1975; performs with opera cos. throughout Europe, U.S.; recitalist; voice tchr.; repertoire coach; recs. for Decca, Cetra, London. Office: care Matthews/Napal Ltd 270 West End Ave New York NY 10023*

OLIVEROS, PAULINE, composer; b. Houston, 1932; studied composition with Erickson and Nee. Mem. San Francisco Tape Music, Center, Mills Coll., 1961-67; dir. Tape Music Center, Mills Coll., 1966; prof. music. U. Calif. at San Diego; dir. Center for Music Experiment, U. San Diego. Recipient Beethoven prize City of Bonn, 1977; Guggenheim fellow, 1972-73. Composer: I of IV, 1966; Sonic Meditations. Home: 1602 Burgundy Leucadia CA 92024 Address: Dept Music Univ Calif La Jolla CA 92037. *I kept doing what I wanted to do until I was paid for it.*

OLIVIER, LAURENCE KERR, actor; b. Dorking, Surrey, Eng., May 22, 1907; s. Gerard Kerr and Agnes Louise (Crookenden) O.; student St. Edward's Sch., Oxford, Eng.; M.A. (hon.), Tufts Coll., 1946; D. Litt. (hon.), Oxford U.; LL.D. (hon.), Edinburgh U.; m. Jill Esmond, 1930 (div. 1940); 1 son, Simon Tarquin; m. 2d, Vivien Leigh, Aug. 30, 1940 (div. 1960); m. 3d, Joan Plowright, Mar. 17, 1960; children—Richard Kerr, Tamsin Agnes Margaret, Julie Kate. Actor, Birmingham Repertory Co., 1925-28, Old Vic Theatre Co., 1937-38; founder new Old Vic Theatre Co., 1944, actor, 1944-46, 49; toured Australia and N. Z., 1948; mgr., actor St. James' Theatre, 1950-51; producer, actor Festival of Britain, 1951-54; actor Shakespeare Meml. Theatre, 1955; 1st dir. Chichester Festival Theatre, Nat. Theatre Gt. Brit., 1963-73; stage appearances include: Byron, Henry IV (parts I, II), Henry VIII, The Marvellous History of St. Bernard, The Farmer's Wife, The Adding Machines, Macbeth, Harold, Back to Methuselah, Taming of the Shrew, Bird in Hand, Stranger Within, The Last Enemy, Private Lives, Biography, Queen of Scots, The Ringmaster, Golden Arrow, Romeo and Juliet, Bees on the Boat Deck, Hamlet, Henry V, Othello, King of Nowhere, Coriolanus, Peer Gynt, Arms and the Man, Richard III, Uncle Vanya, Antigone, Oedipus, School for Scandal, Skin of Our Teeth, The Critic, Titus Andronieus, Twelfth Night, Rhinoceros, Becket, Murder on the Second Floor; dir., actor King Lear, 1946; dir. Skin of Our Teeth, 1946; producer and dir. Born Yesterday, 1946; motion picture debut, 1930; has appeared in Too Many Crooks, Potiphar's Wife, Friends and Lovers, The Yellow Ticket, Westward Passage, The Temporary Widow, As You Like It, Fire Over England, Twenty-one Days, The Divorce of Lady X, Q Planes, Wuthering Heights, Rebecca, Pride and Prejudice, 49th Parallel, Lady Hamilton, Demi Paradise, Henry V, The Devil's Disciple, The Entertainer, Spartacus, Carrie, Beggars' Opera, Term of Trial, Bunny Lake is Missing, Khartoum, Othello, Dance of Death, Sleuth, The Shoes of the Fisherman, Battle of Britain, Oh What a Lovely War, Three Sisters, Marathon Man, The Seven Percent Solution, A Bridge Too Far, The Betsy, The Boys from Brazil, A Little Romance, Dracula; dir., producer and actor Hamlet, 1947, Venus Observed, 1950; dir., actor Richard III, 1954; The Prince and the Showgirl, 1956, John Gabriel Borkman, 1958; TV appearances include: The Power and the Glory, John Gabriel Borkman, The Moon and Sixpence, Long Day's Journey Into Night, Love Among the Ruins, Jesus of Nazareth, Cat on a Hot Tin Roof, The Collection (Emmy award), Come Back Little Sheba, Daphne Laureola, Saturday Sunday Monday; appearances with Nat. Theatre include: Uncle Vanya, The Recruiting Officer, 1963, The Master Builder, 1964, Love for Love, 1966, Dance of Death, 1966, Othello, 1963, 66, Flea in Her Ear, 1967, Home and Beauty, 1969, Merchant of Venice, 1969. Served with Brit. Fleet Air Arm, 1940-43. Created knight by King George VI, lord by Queen Elizabeth; decorated comdr. Order Dannebrog (Denmark), officer Legion of Honour, grand officer Ordine al Merito della Repubblica (Italy), Order of Yugoslav Flag with Gold Wreath, 1971; recipient Oscar award for best actor Motion Picture Acad., 1948, award for directing, producing and acting in Hamlet, Brit. film industry, Emmy award for The Moon and Sixpence, Acad. TV Arts and Scis., 1960, for Long Day's Journey Into Night, 1973; Danish Sonning prize, 1966; Gold medallion Swedish Acad. Lit., Hon. Oscar for lifelong contbn. to art of film, 1979. Club: Garrick. Address: care LOP Ltd-33-34 Chancery Ln London WC2 A 11 N England*

OLKOWSKA, KRYSTYNA MARIA NARDELLI, educator, physician; b. Myslowice, Poland, June 23, 1939; d. Walerian and Stefania (Jasinska) Nardelli; M.D., Silesian U. Med. Sch., 1964; m. Zbigniew L. Olkowski, Apr. 15, 1963. Intern, resident ophthalmology Teaching Hosp., Silesian Acad. Medicine, Katowice, Poland, 1965-66; resident ophthalmology Central Hosp. for workers of coal mines, Bytom, Poland, 1967-69, asst. prof. ophthalmology, 1969-71; asst. prof. dept. ophthalmology Emory U. Med. Sch., Atlanta, 1972—. Postdoctoral fellow Fight for Sight, 1974—. Mem. Am. Soc. Research in Ophthalmology. Home: Villa Sadyba 1018 McConnell Dr Decatur GA 30033 Office: 1365 Clifton Rd Atlanta GA 30322

OLLEMAN, ROGER DEAN, cons., educator; b. Cornelia, Ga., Nov. 25, 1923; s. Faye Erlando and Esther (Perkins) O.; B.S. in Mech. Engring., U. Wash., 1948; M.S. in Metall. Engring., Carnegie Inst. Tech., 1950; Ph.D., U. Pitts., 1955; m. Elizabeth Ann Deutsch, May 24, 1947; children—Esther Jean, Ruth Ellen, Mark Charles. Group leader Westinghouse Research Labs., Pitts., 1950-55; asst. br. head, dept. metall. research Kaiser Aluminum & Chem. Corp., Spokane, Wash., 1955-59; mem. faculty dept. mech. and metall. engring. Oreg. State U., Corvallis, 1959-76, now courtesy prof.; pres. Accident and Failure Investigations, Inc., 1974—. Cons. to industry, also Lawrence Radiation Lab., 1965-66, U.S. Bur. Mines Metallurgy Research Center, Albany, 1962-72. Bd. dirs. Benton Assn. Retarded Children. Served with AUS, 1944-46. Recipient Lloyd Carter award outstanding teaching Sch. Engring., Oreg. State U., 1962. Mem. Am. Soc. Testing and Materials (Templin award 1953), Am. Soc. M.E. (past sec., mem. nonferrous subcom. boiler and pressure vessel code), Am. Soc. Engring. Edn., Am. Soc. Metals, Am. Inst. Mining, Metall. and Petroleum Engrs., Sigma Xi, Tau Beta Pi, Pi Tau Sigma. Home: 1005 NW 30th St Corvallis OR 97330

OLLER, ANNA KATHRYN, educator; b. Waynesboro, Pa., July 1, 1916; d. Daniel G. and Blanche (Ruthrauff) Oller; A.B., Juniata Coll., 1938; B.S., Drexel Inst. Tech., 1939; M.S., U. Ill., 1951; Ph.D., U. Mich., 1963. Researcher, U. Ill., 1949-50, teaching fellow, 1950-51; instr. Fla. State U., 1951-52; asst. prof. Grad. Sch. Library Sci., Drexel Inst. Tech., Phila., 1952-54, asso. prof., 1955-67, acting dean, 1967-68; prof. library sci., asso. dean Sch. Library and Info. Sci., Drexel U., Phila., 1969—; vis. prof. Pa. State U., summers 1947-49, 51, Emory U., summer 1953, U. Mich., summer 1954. Asst. librarian Huntingdon County Library, 1939-40, librarian, 1942-45; cataloger Juniata Coll. Library, 1940-42; librarian Adams County (Pa.) Library, 1945-47; asst. extension librarian Pa. State Library, 1947-49. Mem. ALA (chmn. Isadore Mudge Citation Jury 1967-68), Pa. Library Assn., Am. Assn. Library Schs., Germantown Hist. Soc., Hist. Soc. Pa., AAUP, Am. Soc. Information Sci., Beta Phi Mu. Contbr. articles to profl. jours. Home: 706C Alden Park Manor Philadelphia PA 19144

OLLER, WILLIAM MAXWELL, petroleum co. exec.; b. Lancaster, Pa., Apr. 7, 1924; s. John Secrist and Mabel Margaret (Coffman) O.; B.S., U.S. Naval Acad., 1946; M.B.A., George Washington U., 1960; m. Doris Seitz Greenleaf, June 15, 1946; children—Arthur G., J. Richard. Commd. ensign U.S. Navy, 1946, advanced through grades to rear adm., 1972; service in Samoa, Philippines and Italy; exec. officer Naval Supply Center, Newport, R.I., 1966-67, Ships Parts Control Center, Mechanicsberg, Pa., 1970-72; comdr. Def. Fuel Supply Center, Alexandria, Va., 1972-76; comdg. officer Naval Supply Center, Norfolk, Va., 1976-77; mgr. corporate supply and distbn. Champlin Petroleum Co., Houston, 1977-79, Ft. Worth, 1979—. Decorated Legion of Merit with gold star, Meritorious Service medal with gold star, Joint Service Commendation medal. Mem. U.S. Naval Inst. Presbyterian. Clubs: Army-Navy Country (Arlington, Va.); Ridglea Country, Petroleum (Ft. Worth); Petroleum Houston). Home: 6651 Make Lane Ct Fort Worth TX 76116 Office: 5301 Camp Bowie Blvd Fort Worth TX 76107

OLLERICH, DWAYNE ADOLPH, anatomist; b. Sioux Falls, S.D., June 30, 1934; s. August and Minnie Ida Ollerich; B.A., Augustana Coll., Sioux Falls, 1960; M.S. (NDEA fellow 1960-64), U. N.D., Grand Forks, 1962, Ph.D., 1964; m. Veronica K. Nielson, Dec. 17, 1977; children—Daniel Lee, Mary Sue, Jeffrey Scott, David Christian. NIH postdoctoral fellow, then asst. prof. anatomy U. Alta. (Can.), 1964-66; mem. faculty U. N.D. Med. Sch., 1966—, prof. anatomy, 1976—, chmn. dept., 1976-79, asso. dean acad. affairs, 1979—. Mem. Am. Assn. Anatomists, Am. Assn. Anatomy Chmn., Am. Soc. Cell Biology, N.D. Acad. Sci., Sigma Xi. Mem. Assembly of God Ch. Author papers in field. Home: 407 Hamline St Grand Forks ND 58201 Office: Sch Medicine Univ ND Grand Forks ND 58201

OLLING, EDWARD HENRY, aerospace engr., cons. firm exec.; b. Zion, Ill., Feb. 18, 1922; s. Edward and Lydia Ester (Amstudz) O.; B.S.M.E., Purdue U., 1949; postgrad. U. Calif. at Los Angeles, 1952-54, U. Houston, 1963-66; m. Alice L. Van Der Werken, May 5, 1978; children—Linda Cottrell, Charles R., Carole (Mrs. Robert Forrest). Sr. thermodynamics engr. Lockheed Aircraft Corp., Burbank, Calif., 1954-56; project mgr. NASA Project Mercury, Garret Airesearch Corp., Los Angeles, 1956-60; chief advanced earth orbital missions office and space sta. office NASA, Houston, 1960-70; dir. Galaxy Engring. Inc., Captiva Island, Fla., 1971—. Cons. in oceanography, energy, environment, conservation. Mem. Sanibel Island Home Rule Com. Bd. dirs. Captiva Island Wildlife Sci. Research Found., Captiva Seaside Flora Research Center, Concerned Captiva Citizens. Served with USAAC, 1942-46. Recipient Sustained Superior Performance award NASA, Inventions and Contbns. award. Registered profl. engr., Tex. Mem. Nat. Space Inst., Nat. Energy Inst., Nat. Audubon Soc., Sanibel Captiva Conservation Assn., Captiva Civic Assn., Am., Fla. stamp dealers assns., Am. Topical Assn., Rocket Mail Soc., Tex. Profl. Engring. Soc., Am. Legion, LBJ Space Center Stamp Club, Jack Knight Aerospace Philatelic Assn. Contbg. author: Enciclopedia Mondadori (Italy). Contbr. articles to profl. jours. Inventor in field; concept originator Sky Lab, Space Shuttle, others. Address: PO Box 78 Captiva Island FL 33924

OLLOM, JOHN FREDERICK, educator, physicist; b. Ward, W.Va., Dec. 28, 1922; s. Fred James and Geraldine (King) O.; B.S., U. N.H., 1947; M.S., W.Va. U., 1947; M.A., Harvard, 1948, Ph.D., 1952; m. Carolyn Christine Cline, Sept. 18, 1954; children—Randolph, Barbara, Catherine, William. Asst. prof. physics W.Va. U., 1951-56; prof. physics Drew U., 1956—, Robert Fisher Oxham prof. sci. and society, 1977—; mem. staff Bell Telephone Labs., Whippany, N.J., 1958—. Served with AUS, 1943-46. Fellow Soc. for Study Religion in Higher Edn.; mem. A.A.A.S., Am. Assn. U. Profs., Am. Phys. Soc., Am. Assn. Physics Tchrs., Civil War Round Table of N.J., Sigma Xi, Phi Kappa Phi, Pi Kappa Alpha. Democrat. Presbyn. Home: 17 Albright Circle Madison NJ 07940

OLMSTEAD, CECIL JAY, petroleum co. exec.; b. Jacksonville, Fla., Oct. 15, 1920; s. Cecil Jay and Bessie (Irby) O.; B.A., U. Ga., 1950, LL.B., 1951; Sterling Grad. fellow, Yale Law Sch., 1951-52; LL.D. (hon.), U. Hull (Eng.), 1978; m. Frances Hughes; children—Cecil Jay, Frank Hughes, Jane Olmstead Murphy, Amy Louise. Admitted to Ga. bar, 1950, U.S. Supreme Ct., 1964, D.C. bar, 1978; asst. to legal adviser Dept. State, counsel Mut. Security Agy., counsel Hoover Commn. on Orgn. Exec. Br. of Govt., 1952-55; prof. N.Y. U. Sch. Law, 1953-61, dir. Inter-Am. Law Inst., 1958-61, adj. prof. law, 1961—; atty. Texaco, Inc., N.Y.C., 1961-62, asst. to chmn. bd., 1962-70, v.p., asst. to chmn. bd., 1970, v.p., asst. to pres., 1970-71, v.p., asst. to chief exec. officer, 1971-73, exec. dept., v.p., 1973—. Mem. adv. panel on internat. law to sec. state; adv. com. law of sea State Dept., also adv. com. transnat. enterprise; U.S. del. UN Com. on Law of Sea, 1972-73; U.S. del. UN Conf. on Law of Sea, 1974-76; Eisenhower lectr. Nat. War Coll., 1973. Mem. Internat. Law Assn. (pres. Am. br. 1966-73), Internat. Law Assn. (pres. 1972-75, vice chmn. exec. council 1975—), Am. Law Inst. (asso. reporter Restatement of the Fgn. Relations Law of the U.S.), Council on Fgn. Relations, Am. Soc. Internat. Law, Nat. Petroleum Council, Nat. Fgn. Trade Council (dir.), Am. Council on Germany (dir). Episcopalian. Clubs: Knickerbocker, Yale (N.Y.C.); Fairfield County Hunt (Westport); 1925 F Street (Washington); Fla. Yacht (Jacksonville). Home: 4 Sprucewood Ln Westport CT 06880 Office: 2000 Westchester Ave White Plains NY 10650

OLMSTEAD, RALPH W., business exec.; b. Milner, Idaho, June 2, 1911; s. Fred Loomis and Lulu (Bates) O.; A.B., U. Idaho, 1932; LL.B., J.D., George Washington U., 1935; m. Jeanne Charrier, Aug. 29, 1937; children—Frederick Law, Carol Emilie. Sec. to U.S. senator, 1933-39; with Office Sec. Agr., 1939, Office Personnel, 1940, asst. to sec. agr., 1941; asst. to adminstr. Surplus Marketing Adminstrn., and its successors, Agrl. Marketing Adminstrn., Food Distbn. Adminstrn. and Office Distbn., 1941-45; dir. supply CCC War Food Adminstrn. 1945, v.p., dir.; pres. Fed. Surplus Commodities Corp. UNRRA, 1945; dir. Henningsen Produce Co., Shanghai, China, 1946, gen. mgr., 1947—, also gen. counsel; gen. counsel Fed., Inc., Harkson Motors; pres., chmn. bd. H.K. Ferguson Co., Cleve., until 1971; v.p., dir. Morrison Knudson Co., Mc., Boise, Ida. Mem. Nat. Public Adv. Com. Regional Econ. Devel., Washington; adviser to Premier of China; founding mayor Foxfire Village (N.C.). Commd. 2d lt. O.R.C., AUS, 1932, served to lt. col., 1942-46. Decorated Legion of Merit. Mem. Am. Soc. Pub. Adminstrn., D.C. Bar, Blue Key, Scabbard and Blade, Delta Sigma Rho, Kappa Sigma. Democrat. Mason, Elk. Clubs: Shaker Heights Country (Cleve.); Fox Fire Country (Pinehurst, N.C.); Georgetown (Washington). Home: Route 1 Box 41 Jackson Springs NC 27281

OLMSTEAD, STEPHEN GOODWIN, marine officer; b. Albany, N.Y., Nov. 10, 1929; s. Leo Henry and Charlotte Hastings (Boody) O.; student Champlain Coll., 1947-50; B.S., U. Md., 1963; M.S., George Washington U., 1970; student Inf. Sch., 1960, U.S. Naval War Coll., 1970, U.S. Naval Sch. Justice, 1970; m. Vera Lucille Mead, May 10, 1952; children—Barbara J. Olmstead Schneble, Elizabeth A., Stephen Goodwin. Served as enlisted man U.S. Marine Corps, 1948-51, commd. 2d lt., 1951, advanced through grades to maj. gen., 1978; comdr. 9th Marine Regt., 1973-74; various staff positions in intelligence, tng., logistics and research and devel., to 1976; dir. Marine Corps Devel. Center, Quantico, Va., 1976-78; comdg. gen. Marine Corps Base, Camp Pendleton, Calif., 1978—; pres. Camp Pendleton Aux., Navy Relief Soc. Bd. dirs. North County dist. United Way San Diego; hon. chmn. North County bd. dirs. Armed Services YMCA. Decorated Bronze Star, Army Commendation medal, Navy Commendation medal, Joint Service Commendation medal. Episcopalian. Home: Ranch House Marine Corps Base Camp Pendleton CA 92055 Office: Comdg Gen Marine Corps Base Camp Pendleton CA 92055

OLMSTEAD, WALTER ROGERS, food co. exec.; b. Jersey City, Feb. 5, 1915; s. Walter and Florence Rogers (Adler) O.; student Va. Poly. Inst., 1934-36, Lehigh U., 1937; m. Lillian Wylie Jaimeson, Feb. 5, 1945; children—Francis, Joan. With Borden Inc., 1937—, sales mgr. Western Hemisphere, N.Y.C., 1953-58, asst. v.p. internat. div., 1958-60, charge overseas acquisition program, 1960-61, v.p., 1961-62, exec. v.p., internat. div., 1962-64, corporate v.p., pres. foods div., 1964-67, exec. v.p. Borden, Inc., 1967-73, vice chmn. bd., 1973-77, now dir. Served to 1st lt. USMCR, 1943-46. Home: 17292 Prado Rd San Diego CA 92128 Office: 277 Park Ave New York NY 10017

OLMSTEAD, WILLIAM EDWARD, educator; b. San Antonio, June 2, 1936; s. William Harold and Gwendolyn (Littlefield) O.; B.S., Rice U., 1959; M.S., Northwestern U., 1962, Ph.D., 1963; m. Adele Cross, Aug. 14, 1957 (div. 1967); children—William Harold, Randell Edward; m. 2d, Jo-Ann Irene Hopkins, June 7, 1971. Mem. research staff S.W. Research Inst., San Antonio, 1959-60; Sloan Found. postdoctoral fellow Johns Hopkins, 1963-64; prof. applied math. Northwestern U., Evanston, Ill., 1964—. Vis. mem. Courant Inst. Math. Scis. N.Y. U., 1967-68; faculty visitor Univ. Coll. London (Eng.), 1973. Mem. Am. Math. Soc., Am. Phys. Soc., Soc. Indsl. and Applied Math., Am. Contract Bridge League (life master), Sigma Xi, Tau Beta Pi, Sigma Tau. Episcopalian. Contbr. articles to profl. jours. Home: 141 Lockerbie Ln Wilmette IL 60091 Office: Tech Inst Northwestern U Evanston IL 60201

OLMSTED, DAVID LOCKWOOD, educator, linguist, anthropologist; b. Jamestown, N.Y., Mar. 11, 1926; s. George La Prake and Marjorie (Lockwood) O.; A.B., Cornell U., 1947, M.A., 1948, Ph.D., 1950; m. Flora Julia Sanchez, 1946 (div. 1972); children—Elaine M., Frederick J.S.; m. 2d, Lenora A. Timm, 1973. Instr. anthropology Northwestern U., 1950-51; fellow behavior sci. Yale, 1951-54, asst. prof. linguistics, 1952-54; mem. faculty U. Calif. at Davis, 1954—, prof. anthropology, 1961—, chmn. dept., 1959-64, mem. panel editors univ. publs. in linguistics, 1960—; exchange prof. linguistics univs. Moscow and Leningrad (USSR), spring 1963. Social Sci. Faculty Research fellow, 1956-58; Guggenheim fellow, 1961; fellow Center Advanced Study Behavioral Scis., 1966-67. Served with AUS, 1944-46. Life mem. Linguistic Soc. Am. (com. publs.); fellow Am. Anthrop. Assn. (exec. bd. 1973-76); mem. Sigma Xi. Author: Ethnolinguistics So Far, 1950; (with others) Behavior Theory and Social Science, 1955; Korean Folklore Reader, 1963; A History of Palaihnihan Phonology, 1964; Achumawi Dictionary, 1965; Out of the Mouth of Babes, 1971; also numerous articles. Editor-in-chief American Anthropologist, 1978—. Home: Route 1 Box 776 Woodland CA 95695

OLMSTED, DONALD WARREN, educator; b. Duluth, Minn., May 28, 1921; s. C. Howard and Rosella (Wais) O.; B.A., U. Wis., 1942, M.A., 1948; Ph.D., U. Minn., 1955; m. W. Ann Garver, Sept. 9, 1950; 1 dau., Caroline. Instr. sociology W.Va. U., 1948-50; research fellow U. Minn., 1953-55; instr. sociology U. Wis., 1955-57; asst. prof. to prof. Mich. State U., East Lansing, 1957—, asst. dean, 1962-66, dir. Social Sci. Research Bur., 1964-66. Served with USAAF, 1942-46. Fulbright prof. U. Belgrade, Yugoslavia, 1972-73. Fellow Am. Sociol. Assn.; mem. Am. Psychol. Assn. Contbr. articles profl. jours. Home: 660 Pebblebrook Ln East Lansing MI 48823

OLMSTED, GEORGE HAMDEN, banking and ins. exec.; b. Des Moines, Mar. 18, 1901; s. Ernest Sargent and Alice (Lockwood) O.; matriculated in Iowa State Coll., 1918; grad. U.S. Mil. Acad. (distinguished cadet), 1922; LL.D., Drake U.; D.Bus. Adminstrn. (hon.), Iowa Wesleyan Coll.; D.Internat. Relations (hon.), Southeastern U., Washington; m. Virginia Camp, Sept. 13, 1924 (dec. 1944); children—Alice Louise (Mrs. Wallace J. Burt, Jr.), George Hamden, Jerauld Lockwood; m. 2d, Carol S. Hoy, Jan. 15, 1949. Commd. 2d lt. F.A., 1922; resigned from Army, 1923; capt. cav., Ia. N.G., 1923-32; lt. col., 1932; returned to active duty as maj., U.S. Army, Mar. 1942, brig. gen., Gen. Staff Corps, G-5, U.S. Forces China Theater, 1944-45; recalled to active duty, 1950; dir. mil. assistance Office Sec. of Def., 1951-53; maj. gen., 1951; maj. gen. Commanding 103 Inf. Div., 1951-59; now maj. gen. USAR (Ret.). Organized Olmsted Inc. Agy., gen. ins., Des Moines, 1923; purchased Travelers Mut. Casualty Co., 1927; organizer, chmn. First Ins. Finance Co.; chmn. United Security Ins. Co., Northeastern Ins. Co., Hawkeye-Security Ins. Co., United Service Life Ins. Co., Internat. Bank, Internat. Gen. Industries, Inc. (Washington), Internat. Trust Co. Liberia (Monrovia), Credit European (Luxembourg); chmn. Gen. Services Life Co., Bankers Security Life Soc. N.Y.; founder United Fed. Savs. & Loan Assn., Des Moines; dir. Transorient Bank, Beirut, Lebanon; chmn. I.B. Credit Corp., Washington, Avis Indsl. Corp., Upland, Ind., Woodman Co., Decatur, Ga., Europa Bank NV, Ghent, Belgium, Internat. Bank Washington (Bahamas) Ltd., Kliklok Corp., N.Y.C.; dir. Foster Wheeler Corp. Pres., U.S. Jr. C. of C., 1931-32; elected 1st chmn. Young Rep. Nat. Com., 1934; mem. Iowa Rep. State Central Com., 1938-40. Trustee Drake U., West Point Alumni Found., Am. U.; bd. visitors U.S. Mil. Acad., 1973-78; bd. dirs. Washington Fin. Center; founder George Olmsted Found., Olmsted Scholar Program. Decorated D.S.M. Legion Merit, Bronze Star (U.S.); comdr. Brit. Empire, French Legion of Honor, Chinese Order of Sacred Tripod. Mem. N.Y. Soc. of Cincinnati, Am. Legion. Republican. Episcopalian. Mason (32, Shriner). Clubs: Des Moines; Metropolitan, Army-Navy (Washington): Washington Golf and Country (Arlington). Home: 2775 N Quebec St Arlington VA 22207 Office: 1701 Pennsylvania Ave NW Washington DC 20006

OLMSTED, MARY SEYMOUR, ambassador; b. Sept. 28, 1919; B.A., Mt. Holyoke Coll., 1941; M.A., Columbia U., 1945. Research asst. Nat. Bur. Econ. Research, 1943-45; jr. econ. analyst Dept. State, 1945-46; consular officer, Amsterdam, the Netherlands, 1946-48; polit. officer, Reykjavik, Iceland, 1949-51; econ. officer, Vienna, 1951-55; intelligence research specialist Dept. State, 1956; assigned Dept. Commerce, 1957-60; econ. officer, New Delhi, India, 1960-66; supervising econ. officer Fgn. Service Inst., 1966-71; dep. dir. personnel mgmt. and services Dept. State, 1971-72, dep. dir. personnel for policy, classification and evaluation, 1972-73, acting dir. personnel, acting dep. dir. gen., 1973-74; Am. consul, Port Moresby, New Guinea, 1974-75, ambassador, 1975—. Recipient Christian A. Herter award, 1972. Office: American Embassy Armitt St PO Box 3492 Port Moresby New Guinea

OLMSTED, MILDRED SCOTT (MRS. ALLEN SEYMOUR OLMSTED, II), social worker; b. Glenolden, Pa.; d. Henry J. and Adele Brebant (Hamrick) Scott; B.A., Smith Coll., 1912, L.H.D., 1974; certificate (Coll. Settlements' Assn. fellow), U. Pa. Sch. Social Work, 1913; m. Allen Seymour Olmsted II, Oct. 30, 1921 (dec. 1977); children—Peter Scott (dec.), Enid Scott Olmsted Burke, Anthony Scott. Sec., Main Line Fedn. Chs., internat. relief work Am. Friends' Service Com., France and Germany, World War I; asst. dir. White Williams Found., 1920-22; leader European and Russian Good-will Tour, 1932; nat. exec. dir. U.S. sect. Women's Internat. League for Peace and Freedom, mem. internat. exec. com., 1935-49, exec. dir. emeritus, 1966—. Mem. U.S. del. to internat. congresses at Prague, Grenoble, Zurich, Luhacovice, Luxembourg, Paris, Copenhagen, Birmingham (Eng.), Stockholm, Asilomar (U.S.), The Hague, Nyborg, Denmark, Japan, New Delhi, Tokyo, rep. to UN Council Non-Governmental Orgns., 1949, to Confs. Church and War, 1950, to Conf. Church and Peace, 1953, Soviet-Am. Women's Conf., Bryn Mawr, Pa., Moscow, Internat. Women's Congress, New Delhi, 1970, Women, SALT and Arms Control, Washington, 1978; rep. World Conf. Religion for Peace, 1971—. Organized social service dept. Bryn Mawr Hosp., became head worker; co-founder Sch. in Rose Valley, 1929; mem. state and local bds. Nat. Youth Adminstrn., 1938-40; dir. Nat. Women's Com. to Oppose Conscription, 1942-47; mem. Consultative Peace Council, vice chmn. Nat. Peace Conf., 1940-51; vice chmn. Joint Friends' Peace Com.; mem. governing bd. Post War World Council, 1944; governing council Upland Inst. Social Conflict Mgmt.; bd. Phila. Birth Control League; mem. bd. Promoting Enduring Peace; mem. exec. com. peace edn. Am. Friends Service Com.; clk. Providence Friends Meeting, 1970—; mem. Phila. yearly meeting Friends Commn. on Projects and Concerns, 1974—; co-chairperson Bane Peace Award Dinner, Oct. 1978. Recipient Sane Phila. Peace award, 1972; Disting. Alumna award Friends Central Sch., 1974. Mem. A.A.U.W., Am. Acad. Certified Social Workers, World Affairs Council, Fgn. Policy Assn., Women's Overseas Service League (mem. council and exec. com. Turn Toward Peace Movement 1961—), Morris, Tyler arboreteums, Nat. Assn. Social Workers, S.E. Pa. (vice chmn.), Am. (Pa. dir.) civil liberties unions, The Welfare Conservancy, Internat. Planned Parenthood, Nat. Wildlife Fedn., Internat. Wildlife Fedn., Audubon Soc., Nat. Trust Historic Preservation. Home: Rose Valley Moylan PA 19065 Office: 1213 Rece St Philadelphia PA 19107. *When one has lived long enough one can see that the world moves forward. In my generation it has become obvious that all peoples are interdependent. No nation is really able to defend itself or to isolate itself— we are responsible for the welfare of all at home and abroad. Military wars are becoming anachronistic, like armored knights after the development of gun powder. Population control is essential and the equality of women must be recognized.*

OLMSTED, RICHARD WILLIAMS, physician, educator; b. Darien, Conn., June 27, 1920; s. Horace B. and Julia (Williams) O.; B.A., Dartmouth, 1941; M.D., Harvard, 1944; m. Barbara Andrews, May 22, 1943; children—Gail Alden, Richard Williams, Jonathan Leete, Timothy Fuller. Resident pediatrics Yale, 1944-49; practice medicine specializing in pediatrics, Stratford, Conn., 1949-53; asso. prof. pediatrics Temple U. Med. Sch., 1955-62; prof. pediatrics, chmn. dept. U. Oreg. Med. Sch., 1962-73; asso. exec. dir. Am. Acad. Pediatrics, 1973-77; med. dir. Children's Hosp., Denver, 1978—; prof. pediatrics U. Colo. Sch. Medicine, 1978—. Served with USNR, 1944-45, 53-55. Mem. Am. Pediatric Soc., Am. Acad. Pediatrics. Home: 2900 S University Blvd Denver CO 80710

OLMSTED, ROBERT GROVES, investment exec.; b. Buffalo, Nov. 19, 1908; s. George W. and Iva C. (Groves) O.; grad. Phillips Exeter Acad., 1927; A.B., Yale, 1931; M.B.A., Harvard, 1933; LL.D., Adelphi U., 1969; L.H.D., Dowling Coll., 1973; m. Louise MacCracken. Treas., L.I. Lighting Co., Mineola, 1938-42, v.p., 1946-57, vice chmn. bd., 1957-60, dir., 1951-78; v.p. for bus. and finance Columbia U., 1960-65; pres. Adelphi U., Garden City, N.Y., 1967-69; dir. Broad St. Investing Corp., Nat. Investors Corp., Union Capital Fund, Union Cash Mgmt. Fund, Union Income Fund. Home: 680 Steamboat Rd Greenwich CT 06830

OLMSTED, STERLING PITKIN, coll. adminstr.; b. Hartford, Conn., Feb. 16, 1915; s. Harry Dwight and Luella Grace (Recor) O.; A.B., Rollins Coll., 1936; M.A., Yale, 1938, Ph.D., 1940; m. Barbara Starr, Apr. 26, 1942; 1 dau., Ruth. Faculty, Rensselaer Poly. Inst., 1939-68, prof. English, head dept., 1953-56, prof., head dept. lang. and lit., 1956-68; dean of faculty Wilmington (Ohio) Coll., 1968-70, provost, 1970-76, planning dir., 1976—. Mem. Am. Soc. Engring. Edn. (chmn. div. humanities and social scis. 1953-54, nat. council 1957-59), Conf. Coll. Communication and Composition (nat. edn. com. 1959—), Nat. Council Tchrs. English, Modern Lang. Assn. Am., Soc. Tech. Writers and Editors, Coll. English Assn. Author: (with Jay R. Gould) Exposition: Technical and Popular, 1948. Editor: (with J. Shirley and G. Gullette) General Education in Engineering, 1956; (with W.K. Brown) Three Uses of Language, 1960, Language and Literature, 1962; (with others) Ethical Problems in Engineering, 1965; Liberal Learning for The Engineer, 1968. Home: 490 W Locust St Wilmington OH 45177

OLNEY, DANIEL CLANTON, lawyer; b. Tucson, Feb. 26, 1924; s. Daniel Clinton and Mathilda (Clifford) O.; student Magdalen Coll. Oxford (Eng.) U., 1945; B.S. in Bus., U. So. Calif., 1950, LL.D., 1951; m. Norma Med Callaway, Mar. 11, 1949; children—Dan C., Susan (Mrs. Dana Denton), John D., Norma. Admitted to Ariz. bar, 1951, Calif. bar, 1952; mem. firm Magana & Olney, Los Angeles, 1955-70, Olney, Levy, Kaplan & Tenner, Los Angeles, 1970—. Served as paratrooper AUS, World War II; ETO. Decorated Purple Heart with one oak leaf cluster, Bronze Star (U.S.); Croix de Guerre (Belgium). Mem. Am., Calif., Ariz., Los Angeles bar assns., Am. Bd. Trial Advocates, Am. Trial Lawyers Assn. Home: 10062 Hillgrove Dr Beverly Hills CA 90210 Office: 3435 Wilshire Blvd Los Angeles CA 90010

O'LOUGHLIN, JOHN KIRBY, ins. co. exec.; b. Bklyn., Mar. 31, 1929; s. John Francis and Anne (Kirby) O'L.; B.A. in Econs., St. Lawrence U., Canton, N.Y., 1951; m. Janet R. Tag, July 5, 1952; children—Robert K., Steven M., Patricia A., John A. State agt. Royal Globe Ins. Group, 1953-58; with Allstate Ins. Co., 1958—, mktg. v.p., group v.p., then exec. v.p., 1972—, pres. Allstate Life Ins. Co., 1977—; chmn. bd. Allstate Ins. Co. and Life Co. Can., 1976—; dir. Allstate Ins. Co., Allstate Life Ins. Co., Allstate Ins. Co. Can., Northbrook P&C Co., Northbrook E&S Co., Northbrook Life Ins. Co., Allstate ENTR, Inc. Trustee St. Lawrence U., Grad. Sch. Sales Mgmt., Syracuse, N.Y.; elder First United Presbyn. Ch., Lake Forest, Ill. Served to capt. USMCR, 1951-53. Mem. Sales and Mktg. Execs. Internat. (dir.), Alpha Tau Omega. Clubs: Met. (Chgo.); Knollwood, Racquet (Lake Forest). Home: 752 N Waukegan Rd Lake Forest IL 60045 Office: Allstate Plaza Bldg G-6 Northbrook IL 60062

O'LOUGHLIN, ROBERT FRANCIS, hotel exec.; b. Hartford, Conn., Mar. 30, 1944; s. Francis Thomas and Dolores Grace (Hunnting) O'L.; B.S. in Acctg., U. Hartford; m. Kathleen Guertin, June 26, 1964; children—Erin, Sean, Stephen. Resident mgr. Netherland Hilton, 1970-73; gen. mgr. Oakland (Calif.) Hilton, 1973-76, San Francisco Hilton, 1976; gen. mgr. Stouffers Riverfront Towers, St. Louis, 1976—. Bd. dirs. Downtown St. Louis Inc. Named Gen. Mgr. of Yr., 1978. Mem. Mo. Hotel Assn. (v.p.), St. Louis Hotel Assn. (v.p.). Democrat. Roman Catholic. Clubs: Rotary, Mo. Athletic. Office: Stouffers Riverfront Towers 200 S 4th St Saint Louis MO 63102*

OLSCAMP, PAUL JAMES, univ. pres.; b. Montreal, Que., Can., Aug. 29, 1937; s. James J. and Luella M. (Brush) O.; B.A., U. Western Ont., 1958, M.A., 1960; Ph.D., U. Rochester, 1962; m. Ruth I. Pratt, Dec. 2, 1978; children by previous marriage—Rebecca Ann, Adam James. Instr. Ohio State U., 1962, asst. prof., 1963-66, asso. prof., 1966-69, asso. dean humanities, 1969; dean faculties, prof. philosophy Roosevelt U., Chgo., 1970-71, v.p. acad. affairs, 1971-72; prof. philosophy Syracuse U., 1972-75, exec. asst. to chancellor, 1972, vice chancellor student programs, 1972-75; pres. Western Wash. U., Bellingham, 1975—. Grad. fellow in humanities U. Western Ont., 1959; Mackintosh Pub. Speaking and Lecturing award U. Western Ont., 1959, 60; Grad. Studies fellow U. Rochester, 1960, 61-62; Danforth Found. asso., 1966—; Alfred J. Wright award Ohio State U., 1970. Mem. Am. Philos Assn. Author: Descartes: The Discourse, Optics, Geometry and Meteorology, 1965; The Moral Philosophy of George Berkeley, 1970; An Inroduction to Philosophy, 1971. Contbr. articles to profl. jours. Office: Western Wash Univ Bellingham WA 98225

OLSEN, ALFRED JON, lawyer; b. Phoenix, Oct. 5, 1940; s. William Hans and Vera (Bearden) O.; B.A. in History, U. Ariz., 1962; M.S. in Acctg., Ariz. State U., 1964; J.D., Northwestern U., 1966; m. Susan K. Smith, Apr. 15, 1979. Admitted to Ariz. bar; acct. Arthur Young & Co., C.P.A.'s, Chgo., 1966-68; asso. firm Streich, Lang, Weeks, Gardon & French, Phoenix, 1968; now partner firm Olsen-Smith, Ltd., Phoenix. Mem. Phoenix adv. bd. Salvation Army. C.P.A., Ill. Mem. Central Ariz. Estate Planning Council (pres. 1972-73), State Bar Ariz. (chmn. tax sect. 1977-78), Am. Bar Assn. (chmn. com. on agr., sect. taxation 1976-78), Am. Law Inst. (chmn. tax planning for agr. 1973—), Nat. Cattlemen's Assn. (tax com. 1979—). Bd. editors Agrl. Law Jour., 1978—. Office: 2900 Ariz Bank Bldg 101 N First Ave Phoenix AZ 85003

OLSEN, ALVIN GORDON, lawyer; b. Pitts., July 5, 1927; s. Alvin Gordon and Alma (Wollbrandt) O.; student Duquesne U., 1947-48; B.A., Pa. State U., 1951; LL.B., Fordham U., 1957; m. Nancy Smith, Dec. 26, 1955; children—Lars Andrew, Lisa Wells. Sr. asst. furniture buyer Macy's, N.Y.C., 1953-54; admitted to Ariz. bar, 1958, since practiced in Phoenix; law clk. to justice Ariz. Supreme Ct., 1957-58; asso. Lewis & Roca, 1958-63, partner, 1963—. Bd. dirs. Family Service Phoenix, 1962-68, pres., 1966-67; bd. dirs. Ariz. Assn. for Health and Welfare, 1967-70, 1st v.p., 1967-68; bd. dirs. Community Council, 1969-75; commr. LEAP Commn., Phoenix Community Action Agy., 1971-75, chmn., 1972-73; mem. plan steering com. Comprehensive Health Planning Council, 1973-75; mem. CETA Manpower Adv. Council, 1974-76, chmn., 1974-75, vice chmn., 1975-76; bd. dirs. Planned Parenthood Central and No. Ariz., 1975—, pres., 1977-78. Served with USNR, 1945-46; as 1st lt. USAF, 1951-53. Mem. Am. Bar Assn. Home: 232 W Frier Dr Phoenix AZ 85021 Office: 100 W Washington St Phoenix AZ 85003

OLSEN, ARNOLD, lawyer, former congressman; b. Butte, Mont., Dec. 17, 1916; s. Albert and Anna G. (Vennes) O.; student Mont. Sch. Mines, 1935-37; LL.B., U. Mont., 1940; m. Margaret M. Williams, Aug. 12, 1942; children—Margaret Rae, Anna Kristine, Karin Synneve. Admitted to Mont. bar, 1940; pvt. practice, Butte, 1940-42,

46-48, Helena, 1956-60, 71-75, 75—; atty. gen. Mont., 1948-56; mem. 87th-91st Congresses 1st Dist. Mont.; dist. judge Mont., 1975. Mem. Mont. Bd. Edn., 1948-56. Served as officer USNR, World War II. Mem. Am. Judicature Soc., Am. Region, V.F.W., Am. Vets. World War II, Scandinavian Frat. Am., Phi Delta Phi. Mason (Shriner), Elk, Eagle. Office: Country Club Manor Butte MT 59701

OLSEN, ARTHUR MARTIN, physician; b. Chgo., Aug. 29, 1909; s. Martin I. and Aagot (Rovelstad) O.; A.B., Dartmouth, 1930; M.D., Rush Med. Coll., U. Chgo., 1935; M.S., U. Minn., 1938; m. Yelena Pavlinova, Sept. 16, 1936; children—Margaret Ann (Mrs. Frank A. Jost), David Martin, Karen Yelena (Mrs. Dori Kanellos), Mary Elizabeth. Intern, Cook County Hosp., Chgo., 1935-36; fellow medicine Mayo Found., U. Minn., 1936-40, instr. to asso. prof. medicine, 1950-57, prof. medicine, 1957—, cons. medicine Mayo Clinic, 1940-76, chmn. div. thoracic diseases, 1968-71; dir. internat. activities Am. Coll. Chest Physicians, 1976—. Mem. nat. heart and lung adv. council NIH, 1970-71; trustee Mayo Found., 1961-68. Recipient Billings gold medal for exhibit on esophagitis A.M.A., 1955; Alexander B. Vishnevski medal Inst. Surgery, Moscow, 1966. Diplomate Am. Bd. Internal Medicine, mem. subspecialty bd. pulmonary diseases, 1958—, chmn., 1961-63. Fellow A.C.P., Am. Coll. Chest Physicians (regent 1955—, chmn. 1959-66, pres. 1970); mem. Am. Soc. Gastrointestinal Endoscopy (pres. 1962-63), Minn. Respiratory Health Assn. (pres. 1964-68), Am., Minn. med. assns., Am. Assn. Thoracic Sur., Am., Minn. (pres. 1952) thoracic soc., Am. Bronchoesophagol. Assn. (pres. 1969-70, Chevalier Jackson award 1973), Minn. Soc. Internal Medicine, Sigma Xi, Alpha Omega Alpha. Episcopalian. Author numerous publs. on diseases lungs and esophagus. Home: Box 87 Oronoco MN 55960 Office: Mayo Clinic Rochester MN 55901

OLSEN, CHARLES NICHOLAS, corp. exec.; b. Omaha, Feb. 23, 1925; s. Charles H. and Minnie Anna (Arndt) O.; student U. Omaha, 1946-48; grad. program mgmt. devel. Harvard U., 1969; m. Helen Savich, May 22, 1949; children—Christopher Leigh, Scott Nicholas. With U.P. R.R., 1942—, sec. to pres., Omaha, 1958-64, asst. to sec., N.Y.C., 1965, asst. sec., 1966-70; sec. U.P. Corp., N.Y.C., 1970—; dir. St. Joseph and Grand Island R.R., Spokane Internat. R.R., Los Angeles & Salt Lake R.R. Co., Oreg. Short Line R.R. Co., Oreg.-Wash. R.R. & Nav. Co. Served with USNR, 1943-46. Mem. Am. Soc. Corp. Secs. Lutheran. Clubs: Harvard Bus. Sch., Manhattan (N.Y.C.). Home: 11 E Glen Ave Ridgewood NJ 07450 Office: 345 Park Ave New York NY 10022

OLSEN, DONAL ALAN, architect; b. Chgo., Mar. 27, 1922; s. Leif Ericson and Goldie A. (Anderson) O.; B.S., U. Ill., 1948; m. Evelyn Martha Harsch, June 18, 1946; children—Donal Alan, Bret George, Diane Elizabeth, Jon Kurt. Apprentice, Olsen & Urbain, architects, Chgo., 1948-56, partner, 1957-68; pres. Donal A. Olsen. architects, Inc., 1969—, Environ. Tectonics, Inc., 1970-75; indsl. architect, designer and cons. for aquariums; dir. Petroleum Energy Producing Corp., 1968-74, Omnibyte Corp., 1977—. Exec. Internat. Exec. Service Corp., Singapore, 1970. Mem. Glen Ellyn (Ill.) Zoning Bd., 1963-69, Dist. 87 Sch. Bd., 1969-72, Glen Ellyn Planning Commn., 1969-70. Bd. dirs. Glen Ellyn Pub. Library; trustee John G. Shedd Aquarium, Chgo. Served with USNR, 1942-43, USAAF, 1944-45. Recipient Honor award AIA, 1962. Mem. AIA, Soc. Am. Registered Architects, Chgo. Assn. Commerce, Alpha Tau Omega. Rotarian. Club: Glen Oak Country (Glen Ellyn). Important works include Seven Seas Panorama, Brookfield, Ill., Reef Display Aquarium Tank, Shedd Aquarium. Home: 256 Merton Ave Glen Ellyn IL 60137 Office: 799 Roosevelt Rd Glen Ellyn IL 60137

OLSEN, DONALD JAMES, educator; b. Seattle, Jan. 8, 1929; s. Iver John and Anna Marie (Lungdahl) O.; B.A., Yale, 1949, M.A., 1951, Ph.D., 1954; postgrad. (Fulbright scholar), Univ. Coll., London, 1951-52. Acting lectr. history Univ. Coll. Hull (Eng.), 1952-53; instr. history U. Mass., 1954-55; instr. history Vassar Coll., Poughkeepsie, N.Y., 1955-58, asst. prof., 1958-65, asso. prof., 1965-70, prof., 1970-72, Eloise Ellery prof., 1972—. Vis. prof. Victorian Studies Centre, U. Leicester (Eng.), 1970. Guggenheim fellow, 1967-68, 79-80. Mem. Am. Hist. Assn., Conf. on Brit. Studies, Am. Soc. 18th Century Studies, London Topographical Soc., Soc. Archtl. Historians, Phi Beta Kappa. Club: Yale (N.Y.C.). Author: Town Planning in London: The Eighteenth and Nineteenth Centuries, 1964; The Growth of Victorian London, 1976. Address: History Dept Vassar College Poughkeepsie NY 12601

OLSEN, EDWARD GUSTAVE, educator; b. Portland, Oreg., Mar. 26, 1908; s. Gustav Adolph and Emma Maria (Bush) O.; A.B., Pacific U., Forest Grove, Oreg., 1930; B.D. (Fayerweather prize scholar, fellow), Union Theol. Sem., N.Y.C., 1933; A.M., Columbia, 1932, Ed.D., 1937; m. Faith Theresa Elliott, June 25, 1931 (died 1947); children—Marvin Elliott, Marcia Evelyn; m. 2d, Pauline Marie Walsh, Sept. 11, 1948; 1 son, Douglas Walsh. Instr., acting chmn. dept. edn., Colgate U., 1935- 41; asso. prof., dir. sch. edn., Russell Sage Coll., 1941-45; dir. sch. and community relations Wash. State Office of Pub. Instrn., 1945-50; asso. prof. ednl. adminstrn. U. Tex., 1950-51; edn. dir. NCCJ, Chgo. region, 1951-66; prof. edn., Calif. State U. at Hayward, 1966-73, emeritus, 1973—; formerly vis. prof. Ga. Tchrs. Coll., U. Wash., William and Mary, Western Wash. Coll. Edn., U. Maine, Wash. State U., Stanford; cons. Phila. Teachers Workshop; dir. Kitsap County Teachers' Workshop; dir. workshop on community resources U. Tex., Mont. State U.; dir. workshop on human relations, Northwestern U., Nat. Coll. Edn., U. Oreg., Roosevelt U., U. Chgo., Pacific U., Pacific Lutheran U. Recipient Thomas H. Wright award City of Chgo., 1957; Distinguished Service award Nat. Community Edn. Assn., 1969. Fulbright scholar U. Coll. Rhodesia and Nyasaland, 1958. Exec. sec. Wash. State Coordinating Council for UNESCO; pres. Park Ridge Council Human Relations. Mem. NEA (life), Nat. Community Edn. Assn. (life mem. award 1977), Blue Key, Kappa Delta Pi, Phi Delta Kappa. Rotarian. Co-author: Life Centering Education. Compiler: School and Community Programs; compiler, editor: The School and Community Reader; editor The Modern Community School; editor, chief author: School and Community; Then Till Now: A Social History of the Brookings-Harbor Community, 1979; contbr. numerous articles to profl. jours. Home: 317 Memory Ln Brookings OR 97415. *The goal of education should be to improve the quality of human living, both as individuals and in group life on this planet. The school curriculum must be centered in the enduring life concerns of human kind, oriented to the future yet ever aware of the relevant past in relation to present human needs.*

OLSEN, EDWARD JOHN, geologist, museum curator; b. Chgo., Nov. 23, 1927; s. Edward John and Elizabeth (Bornemann) O.; A.B., U. Chgo., 1951, M.S., 1955, Ph.D., 1959; children—Andrea, Ericka. Geologist, Geol. Survey Can., 1953, U.S. Geol. Survey, 1954—, Canadian Johns-Manville Co., Ltd., 1956, 57, 59; asst. prof. Case Inst. Tech., also Western Res. U., 1959-60; curator mineralogy Field Mus. Natural History, 1960—, chmn. dept. geology, 1974-78; research asso. prof. dept. geophysical scis. U. Chgo., 1977—; adj. prof. U. Ill., Chgo. Circle, 1970—; spl. research stability relations of minerals in earth's mantle and meteorites, acquisition gem. stones and minerals. Fellow Mineral. Soc. Am.; mem. Mineral. Assn. Can., Geochem. Soc., Meteoritical Soc. Home: 1110 Grove St 2J Downers Grove IL 60515 Office: Field Mus Natural History Roosevelt Rd at Lake Shore Dr Chicago IL 60605

OLSEN, EINAR ARTHUR, coll. pres.; b. Gloucester, Mass., Apr. 14, 1917; s. Carl Johann and Aina Elena (Kaupilla) O.; B.S., U. Maine, Orono, 1946, M.Ed., 1947; Ed.D., Boston U., 1952; m. Vera A. Seppala, Aug. 24, 1947; children—Donald, Stephen. Pub. sch. tchr., Jonesport, Me., 1947-49; health dir. Essex County, Mass., 1952-55; asso. prof. health Tex. Western Coll., El Paso, 1955-57; asso. prof., then prof. health Mankato (Minn.) State Coll., 1957-67, chmn. dept., 1960-67; dean instr. Farmington (Maine) State Coll., 1967-68, acting pres., 1968-69; pres. U. Maine Farmington, 1969—; vis. prof. U. N.Mex., Albuquerque, 1957; mem. faculty N.D. Internat. Sch. Alcohol Studies, 1965. Mem. Maine Gov.'s Adv. Council Alcohol and Drug Abuse, 1971-76, chmn., 1971-73; mem. Maine Gov.'s Adv. Council Pub. Broadcasting, 1974-76. Bd. dirs. Me. Lung Assn., Rural Health Assn. Franklin County, Maine; trustee Bancroft Sch.; mem. com. research and planning Maine Hosp. Assn. Teaching fellow, Boston U., 1950-52; grantee Hill Found., 1965, 67, Maine Regional Med. Program, 1973. Served with USN, 1942-45. Mem. Am. Assn. State Colls. and Univs. (rep. Maine 1971—, chmn. allied health professions com. 1974-76), Am. Assn. Colls. Tchr. Edn. (Maine rep. 1971-74), Am. Assn. Higher Edn., AAHPER, Phi Delta Kappa. Mason, Kiwanian. Author: (juveniles) Killer in the Trap; The Lobster King; Adrift on a Raft; Mystery at Salvage Rock; co-author: Golf, Swimming, Tennis, 1961; The Foundations of Health, 1967, 2d edit., 1976; Programmed Instruction in Health Education and Physical Education, 1970. Mem. adv. coms. drug abuse and alcohol edn. books. Home: 88 Main St Farmington ME 04938 Office: U Maine-Farmington 86 Main St Farmington ME 04938*

OLSEN, HAROLD FREMONT, lawyer; b. Davenport, Wash., Oct. 17, 1920; s. Oscar E. and Dorothy (Sprowls) O.; B.A., Wash. State U., 1942; LL.B., Harvard, 1948; m. Jeanne L. Rounds, Aug. 30, 1942; children—Eric O., Ronald R., Margaret Ruth. Instr., Oxford Bus. Sch., Cambridge, Mass., 1946-47; admitted to Wash. bar, 1948; examiner Wash. State Dept. Pub. Utilities, 1948; with firm Perkins, Coie, Stone, Olsen & Williams, and predecessors, Seattle, 1949—, partner, 1954—. Served to maj. USAAF, 1942-45. Decorated Silver Star. Mem. Am., Wash., Seattle bar assns., Aircraft Industry Assn. (chmn. legal com. 1957), Nat. Contract Mgmt. Assn., Alumni Assn. Wash. State U. (pres. 1956), Municipal League Seattle and King County, Seattle C. of C., Internat. Law Soc., Am. Judicature Assn., Phi Beta Kappa, Phi Kappa Phi, Tau Kappa Epsilon. Conglist. Clubs: Rainier, Seattle Golf (Seattle). Home: 8875 Overlake Dr W Bellevue WA 98004 Office: Washington Bldg Seattle WA 98101

OLSEN, HERLUF VAGN, JR., hosp. exec.; b. Wilmington, Del., Mar. 9, 1927; s. Herluf Vagn and Elspeth (Duncan) O.; A.B., Dartmouth, 1950; M.H.A., U. Minn., 1952; m. Beverly Ann Bartlett, June 21, 1952; children—Robert D., Deborah A., Theodore A., Cynthia, Thomas C. Asst. dir. R.I. Hosp., Providence, 1952-65; dir. Shands Teaching Hosp. and Clinic, also asso. chmn. Grad. Program in Hosp. Adminstrn., U. Fla., 1965-67; exec. dir. Med. Center Hosp. Vt., Burlington, 1967-71, pres., 1971—; asso. prof. U. Fla., 1965-67; prof. U. Vt., 1967—; cons. USPHS. Served with inf. AUS, 1945-46. Mem. Am. Coll. Hosp. Adminstrs., Am., Vt. (pres. 1971-74) hosp. assns., New Eng. Hosp. Assembly (pres. 1977). Kiwanian, Rotarian. Home: Mt Philo Rd Charlotte VT 05445 Office: Colchester Ave Burlington VT 05401

OLSEN, JACK, author; b. Indpls., June 7, 1925; s. Rudolph O. and Florence (Drecksage) O.; student U. Pa., 1946-47; m. Su Peterson, 1966; children—John Robert, Susan Joyce, Jonathan Rhoades, Julia Crispin, Evan Pierce, Barrie Elizabeth, Emily Sara Peterson. Newspaper reporter San Diego Union Tribune, 1947-48, San Diego Jour., 1949-50, Washington Daily News, 1950- 51; TV news editor and broadcaster sta. WMAL-TV, Washington, 1950-51; newspaper reporter New Orleans Item, 1952-53, Chgo. Sun-Times, 1954-55; corr. Time mag., 1956-58, Midwest chief, 1959-59; sr. editor Sports Illus. mag., 1960-70. Served with OSS, AUS, 1943-44. Recipient Page One award Chgo. Newspaper Guild; Nat. Headliners award; citations U. Ind., Columbia U. Author: The Mad World of Bridge, 1960; (pseudonym Jonathan Rhoades) Over the Fence is Out, 1961; The Climb up to Hell, 1962; (with Charles Goren) Bridge Is My Game, 1965; Black is Best: The Riddle of Cassius Clay, 1967; The Black Athlete: A Shameful Story, 1968; Silence on Monte Sole, 1968; Night of the Grizzlies, 1969; The Bridge at Chappaquiddick, 1970; Aphrodite: Desperate Mission, 1970; Slaughter the Animals, Poison the Earth, 1971; The Girls in the Office, 1971; The Girls on the Campus, 1972; Sweet Street, 1973; The Man with the Candy, 1974; Alphabet Jackson, 1974; Massy's Game, 1976; The Secret of Fire Five, 1977; Night Watch, 1979; work included in numerous anthologies. Home: 7954 NE Baker Hill Rd Bainbridge Island WA 98110

OLSEN, KENNETH HARRY, mfg. co. exec.; b. Bridgeport Conn., Feb. 20, 1926; s. Oswald and Svea (Nordling) O.; B.S. in Elec. Engring., Mass. Inst. Tech., 1950, M.S., 1952; m. Eeva-Liisa Aulikki Valve, Dec. 12, 1950; children—Ava-Lisa Eleanor, Glenn Charles, James Jonathan. Elec. engr. Lincoln Lab., Mass. Inst. Tech., 1950-57; founder, 1957, since pres. Digital Equipment Corp., Maynard, Mass.; dir. Polaroid Corp., Shawmut Assn., Ford Motor Co. Mem. Pres.'s Sci. Adv. Com., 1971-73. Mem. corp., v.p. Joslin Diabetes Found., Wentworth Inst., Boston, M.I.T., Cambridge; trustee Gordon Coll., Wenham, Mass. Served with USNR, 1944-46. Named Young Elec. Engr. of Year, Eta Kappa Nu, 1960. Patentee magnetic devices. Home: Weston Rd Lincoln MA 01773 Office: Digital Equipment Corp Maynard MA 01754

OLSEN, KURT H., investment adviser; b. Astoria, Oreg., Nov. 2, 1924; s. Matt J. and Irene (Lindholm) O.; B.S., U. Oreg., 1949; m. Lois Helen Giberson, Mar. 23, 1947; children—Kurt F., Eric J., Mark C. Registered rep., resident mgr., resident partner Foster & Marshall, Eugene, Oreg., 1948-61; resident mgr., v.p., dir. Harris, Upham & Co., Portland, Oreg., 1961-70; v.p., dir. Foster & Marshall Inc., Portland, 1971-76; investment adviser, 1976—; pres. Alpen Securities, Inc., Portland, 1977—. Mem. adv. bd. Columbia Pacific council Boy Scouts Am., mem. nat. council, 1966-73. Bd. dirs. United Way of Columbia Willamette, 1973-77. Served with USNR, 1944-46. Mem. Nat. Assn. Securities Dealers (chmn. dist. 1 1967), Investment Bankers Assn. Am. (bd. govs. 1968-70), Sigma Alpha Epsilon. Rotarian. Home: 3707 SW 52d Pl Portland OR 97221 Office: 1225 Yeon Bldg Portland OR 97204

OLSEN, LEIF HENRY, banker, economist; b. Notteroy, Norway, Mar. 31, 1926 (father U.S. citizen); s. Olaf and Marie (Sorensen) O.; B.A., U. Okla., 1951; student U. Oslo (Norway), summer 1949; m. Gloria E. Snyder, Mar. 22, 1952; children—Erik L., Peter, Jennifer, Kirsten. Financial writer Wall St. Jour., 1952-55, N.Y. Times, 1955-56; chief pub. information div. Fed. Res. Bank N.Y., 1956-58; v.p. M.A. Schapiro & Co., Inc., 1958-62; with Citibank, N.Y.C., 1962—, v.p., 1962-65, sr. v.p., economist, 1965-77, chmn. econ. policy com., 1977—. Mem. Am. Bankers Assn. (dir.), Nat. Assn. Bus. Economists. Home: 409 Carter St New Canaan CT 06840

OLSEN, LYMAN JEAN, physician, state ofcl.; b. Pleasant Grove, Utah, Jan. 11, 1927; s. Albert John and Jenav (Smith) O.; B.A., U. Utah, 1951, M.D., 1954; M.P.H., U. Calif., Berkeley, 1969; m. Betty Jean Walser, Apr. 16, 1958; children—Cheryl Ann, Karen Jean, Kelly Denise, Kevin Neal. Intern, Salt Lake County (Utah) Gen. Hosp., Salt Lake City, 1954-55; resident U. Utah Affiliated Hosps., 1955-56, 57-58, Charity Hosp. La., New Orleans, 1956-57; practice medicine specializing in pediatrics, Provo, Utah, 1958-68; chief maternal and child health Utah Div. Health, Salt Lake City, 1969, dir. spl. health services, chief crippled children's service, 1969-70, dir. Utah Div. Health, 1970-79; chief bur. crippled children's services Ariz. State Dept. Health Services, Tempe, 1979—; asst. clin. prof. pediatrics U. Utah, 1967-79, asst. clin. prof. community and family medicine, 1970-79, adj. prof. health, 1974-79; pres. United Cerebral Palsy of Utah County, 1966-68; mem. Utah Adv. Com. for Handicapped Children, Utah Health Planning Council, 1976-79, Utah Pesticide Control Com., regional adv. group Intermountain Regional Med. Program; mem. nat. adv. council on health manpower shortage areas HEW, 1974-77; chmn. Utah Nursing Home Adv. Council, 1970-79, Med. Facilities Council, 1970-79. mem. Utah Air Conservation Com., Water Pollution Control Com. Served with Signal Corps, AUS, 1945-47, to maj. M.C., AUS, 1961-62. Recipient Beatty award Utah Pub. Health Assn., 1977. Diplomate Am. Bd. Pediatrics, Am. Bd. Preventive Medicine. Mem. Am. Acad. Pediatrics, Am. Acad. Cerebral Palsy, Am. Coll. Preventive Medicine, Assn. State and Territorial Health Ofcls. (pres. 1977), Am. Pub. Health Assn. (governing council 1975-76), Intermountain Pediatric Soc. (chmn. maternal and child health sect. 1978-80), Ariz. Pediatric Soc., Maricopa County Pediatric Soc. Home: 4301 E Sequoia Dr Phoenix AZ 85044 Office: Ariz Children's Hosp 200 N Curry Rd Tempe AZ 85281

OLSEN, MERRILL ELVIN, lawyer; b. Cooperstown, N.D., Dec. 18, 1906; s. Christian A. and A. Rodina (Runice) O.; A.B., U. Mich., 1930, LL.B., 1934; m. Catherine A. McColl, Nov. 13, 1937; children—Thomas M., Virginia C. Admitted to Mich. bar, 1934, Ill. bar, 1941; with Prescott, Coulter & Baxter, Detroit, 1934-41; with The Quaker Oats Co., Chgo., 1941-72, successively atty., counsel, gen. counsel, 1954-56, v.p. and gen. counsel, 1956-72, dir., 1957-74. Mem. Chgo. Bar Assn., Law Club Chgo., Sigma Pi. Clubs: Glen View; Country (Naples, Fla.). Home: 1121 Gulf Shore Blvd N Naples FL 33940 Office: Merchandise Mart Chicago IL 60654

OLSEN, NORMAN HARRY, dentist, educator; b. Omaha, June 9, 1926; s. Carl and Johanna (Jorgensen) O.; student U. Idaho, 1945-46; D.D.S., Creighton U., 1951; M.S.D., Northwestern U., 1953; m. Donna Roberts, Sept. 14, 1947; children—Karl Raymond, Heidi Roberts, Holly Roberts. Montgomery Ward fellow Northwestern U., 1951-53, prof. pedodontics, 1954—, chmn. dept., 1954-72, dean, 1972—; prof., chmn. dept. pedodontics U. Kansas City Sch. Dentistry, 1953-54; staff Meml. Mercy Hosp., Kansas City, 1953-54, Northwestern Meml. Hosp., 1974—; head dental service Childrens Meml. Hosp., Chgo., 1954—; courtesy staff Evanston Hosp., St. Francis Hosp., Evanston; mem. Cleft Palate Inst., Northwestern U. and Childrens Meml. Hosp.; cons. Throat Culturing Research Program, Stickney Twp. Health Dept.; chmn. Am. Bd. Pedodontic Examiners, 1973-74. Commr. Joint Commn. on Accreditation Dental Labs. Sec. faculty com. intercollegiate athletics Northwestern U., 1962-68; chmn. profl. div. Evanston United Fund, 1967-68. Pres., First Ward Non-Partisan Civic Assn., Evanston; former trustee Roycemorce Sch., Evanston; mem. exec. com. Dist. 65 Sch. Bd.; bd. dirs. Infant Welfare Soc., Chgo. Served with USNR, 1944-46. Recipient Service award Northwestern U., 1966; Merit award Am. Soc. Dentistry for Children, 1951; Alumni Merit award Creighton U., 1975; diplomate Am. Bd. Pedodontics (bd. examiners). Fellow Am. Coll. Dentistry (vice chmn. Ill. sect. 1979-80), Internat. Coll. Dentists, Chgo. Inst. Medicine; mem. ADA (pedodontic adv. com. Joint Commn. Accreditation, past sect. chmn.), Ill. (past program chmn.), Chgo. (past program chmn.) dental socs., Am. Acad. Pedodontics (pres. 1973-74), Am. Soc. Dentistry Children (past pres. Ill., award of Excellence 1974), Internat. Assn. for Dental Research, Am. Assn. for Cleft Palate Rehab., Am. Acad. Gold Foil Operators, Odontographic Soc. Chgo. (bd. govs., past program chmn.), Ill. Pedodontics (charter), Am. Dental Soc. of Europe (hon.), GV Black Soc. Northwestern U., (sec.), Northwestern U. Dental Alumni Assn. (past pres.), Am. Assn. Dental Schs. (past sect. chmn.), Sigma Alpha Epsilon, Delta Sigma Delta, Omicron Kappa Upsilon. Clubs: Evanston (dir.), Rotary (pres. elect Evanston chpt. 1979-80), John Evans (Northwestern U.) (dir.). Co-editor: 4th edit. Current Therapy in Dentistry, 1970, editor pedodontic sect., 5th edit., 1974. Contbr. chpt. Dental Clinics of N.Am., 1961. Contbr. articles profl. jours. Home: 221 Winnetka Ave Winnetka IL 60093 Office: 311 E Chicago Ave Chicago IL 60611

OLSEN, REX NORMAN, trade assn. exec.; b. Hazeltown, Idaho, Apr. 9, 1925; s. Adolph Lars and Pearl (Robbins) O.; B.J., B.A. in English, U. Mo., 1950. Editor, Clissold Pub. Co., Chgo., 1950-54; copy editor Am. Peoples Ency., Chgo., 1955; asst. editor Am. Hosp. Assn., Chgo., 1956-59, mng. editor, 1959-64, dir. jours. div., 1964-69, dir. publs. bur., 1969-75, exec. editor, asso. pub., 1975—. Served with USNR, 1943-46. Mem. Am. Pub. Health Assn., Am. Med. Writers Assn., Soc. Nat. Assn. Pubs. (sec. 1975-76, 2d v.p. 1976-77, 1st v.p. 1977-78, pres. 1978-79), Chgo. Bus. Publs. Assn. (dir. 1974-78, 4th v.p. 1978-79), Sigma Delta Chi. Home: 3845 Alta Vista Terr Chicago IL 60613 Office: 840 N Lake Shore Dr Chicago IL 60611

OLSEN, TILLIE, author; b. Nebr., Jan. 14, 1913; d. Samuel and Ida (Beber) Lerner; grad. high sch.; D.Arts and Letters (Hon.), U. Nebr., 1979; m. Jack Olsen; children—Karla, Julie, Kathie, Laurie. Author: Tell Me A Riddle (title story received O'Henry 1st Prize award, 1961), 1962; Yonnondio: From the Thirties, 1974; Rebecca Harding Davis: Life in the Iron Mills, 1973; Silences, 1978; short fiction published in 40 anthologies. Writer-in-residence or vis. faculty English, Amherst Coll., 1969-70, Stanford, 1972, Mass. Inst. Tech., 1973-74, U. Mass., Boston, 1974; cons. on lit.; reader and lectr. Recipient Nat. Endowment for Arts award, 1967; Am. Acad. Nat. Inst. award for distinguished contbn. to Am. letters, 1975; Ford Found. grantee, 1959, Stanford writing fellow, 1956, Radcliffe Inst. fellow, 1962-64, Guggenheim fellow, 1975-76; Copeland fellow Amherst Coll., 1977; Regents lectr. U. Calif. at San Diego, 1977. Mem. Authors Guild, PEN. Home: 1712 West Cliff Santa Cruz CA 95060

OLSHAN, KENNETH S., advt. agy. exec.; b. Evansville, Ind., July 15, 1932; s. Harry and Ethel (Hamburg) O.; A.B., Ind. U., 1954; postgrad. Grad. Sch. Bus. Washington U., 1955; m. Patricia E. Shane, Aug. 25, 1954; children—Margot E., Mathew S., John K. Trainee, television-radio buyer Batten Barton Durstine & Osborn, Advt., N.Y.C., 1958-60; v.p., account exec. Doherty, Clifford, Steers & Shenfield, N.Y.C., 1960-64; v.p., account mgmt. supr. McCaffrey & McCall, N.Y.C., 1964-67; pres. Olshan, Smith & Gould, N.Y.C., 1967-69, Doherty, Mann & Olshan, N.Y.C., 1969-76; exec. v.p. Wells, Rich, Greene, N.Y.C., 1976—, also dir.; dir. Hollandia Yacht. Chmn., Communication Arts Lunch-O-Ree, N.Y. council Boy Scouts Am., 1974; v.p., dir. Inter-Community Camp, 1974-78; mem. Democratic Town Com., Westport, Conn., 1973—; trustee Westport Pub. Library, 1976-80. Served with U.S. Army, 1954-56. Mem. Ind. U. Found., Blue Key, Sigma Alpha Mu. Home: Nash Ln Westport CT 06880 Office: 767 Fifth Ave New York NY 10022

OLSHAN, LARRY A., advt. agy. exec.; b. Evansville, Ind., July 15, 1938; s. Harry and Ethel (Hamburg) O.; B.S. in Bus., Ind. U., 1960; m. Sally Ann Berebitsky, May 23, 1942; children—Leslie, Joshua. Salesman, VARCO, Inc., 1961; media buyer Tatham-Larid Co., Chgo., 1961-63; media supr. Foote, Cone & Belding Co., Chgo., 1963-67; sr. v.p., media dir. J. Walter Thompson Co., Chgo., 1968-76, sr. v.p., gen. mgr., Los Angeles, 1976—. Served with U.S. Army, 1960. Mem. Am. Assn. Advt. Agys., Advt. Club Los Angeles. Office: 10100 Santa Monica Blvd Los Angeles CA 90067*

OLSON, ALLEN INGVAR, state ofcl.; b. Rolla, N.D., Nov. 5, 1938; s. Elmer Martin and Olga (Sundin) O.; B.S.B.A., U. N.D., 1960, J.D., 1963; m. Barbara Starr Benner, Aug. 29, 1964; children—Kristin, Robin, Craig. Admitted to N.D. bar, 1963; U.S. Supreme Ct. bar, 1967; asst. dir. N.D. Legis. Council, 1967-69; partner firm Conmy, Rosenberg, Lucas and Olson, Bismarck, N.D., 1969-72; atty. gen. State of N.D., Bismarck, 1972—; dir. Bank of N.D., N.D. Mill and Elevator. Pres. Dakota Zool. Soc., 1977; bd. dirs. Missouri Valley YMCA. Served with Judge Adv. Gen. Corps, U.S. Army, 1963-67. Named Am. of Year, Am. Religious Town Hall Found., 1977. Mem. N.D., Burleigh County bar assns. Republican. Presbyterian. Clubs: Exchange, Masons, Elks. Office: Office of Atty Gen State Capitol Bismarck ND 58501*

OLSON, CAL, newspaperman; b. Vining, Minn., Nov. 13, 1924; s. J. Alvin and Ellen (Dahl) O.; student Moorhead (Minn.) State U., 1942; B.A., U. Minn., 1948; m. Joanne L. Salomonson, Apr. 16, 1950; children—Catherine, Charles. City editor Moorhead Daily News, 1948-50; mem. staff The Forum, Fargo, N.D., 1950—, spl. projects editor, 1967-68, city editor, 1968-72, mng. editor, 1972-74; editor-in-residence Moorhead State U., 1974-75; dir. pub. affairs KFME-TV, 1976-78; editor Sioux City (Iowa) Jour., 1978—. Served with USNR, 1943-45. Recipient George Polk Meml. award for local reporting, 1967, Paul Tobenkin award racial reporting, 1967. Mem. Nat. Press Photographers Assn. (pres. 1965-66, editor mag. 1967-71; Mellor award 1962, Costa award 1965, Sprague award 1973). Lutheran. Home: 3107 Summit Sioux City IA 51104

OLSON, CLARENCE ELMER, JR., editor; b. Edgerton, Wis., July 1, 1927; s. C. Elmer and Helen (Turnbull) O.; B.S., U. Wis., 1950; m. Arielle North, Sept. 4, 1954; children—Randall Jack, Christina North, Jens Sterling Elmer. News editor Edgerton Reporter, 1953; photographer, writer Madison (Wis.) Capitol Times, 1953-59; writer St. Louis Post-Dispatch Pictures mag., 1959-65, asst. editor, 1965-68; asst. mng. editor Careers Today mag., Delmar, Calif., 1968-69; book editor St. Louis Post-Dispatch, 1969—. Served with USNR, 1945-46. Mem. Nat. Book Critics Circle (v.p.). Home: 236 N Elm Ave Webster Groves MO 63119 Office: 900 N 12th St St Louis MO 63101

OLSON, CLINTON LOUIS, fgn. service officer, former ambassador; b. S.D., Mar. 31, 1916; s. William H. and Allie (Sparling) O.; B.S., Stanford, 1939, M.B.A., 1941; m. Ethel Hoover, June 14, 1943; children—Merilee, Peter, David, Steven. Petroleum engr. with Robert S. Lytle, 1939-40; partner Chino Homes, Inc., realtors, 1946-47; pres. EXIM of Calif., 1946-48; with U.S. Fgn. Service, 1948-75, 2d sec. U.S. legation, Vienna, Austria, 1948-52; consul. French West Indies, 1953-55; budget examiner State Dept., 1956, exec. dir. bur. Inter-Am. Affairs, 1957-59; assigned Nat. War Coll., 1959-60; counselor of embassy, London, Eng., 1960-62; counselor econ. affairs Am. embassy, Vienna, 1962-66; charge d'affaires, minister-counselor Am. embassy, Lagos, Nigeria, 1966-70; sr. fgn. service insp., 1970-72; U.S. ambassador to Sierra Leone, 1972-75; internat. cons., 1975—. Served to lt. col., ordnance, AUS, 1941-46; Russia, Iran. Fellow Explorers Club; mem. Fgn. Service Assn., Theta Xi. Clubs: American, Hampstead Golf (London); Rolling Rock (Ligonier, Pa.); Ross Mountain (Pa.). Home: Ross Mountain Club New Florence PA 15944

OLSON, DAVID C., constrn. co. exec.; b. Lincoln, Nebr., June 25, 1933; s. Carl W. and Charlotte J. O.; B.Sc., U. Nebr., 1956; m. Agnes A. Anderson, Feb. 4, 1956; children—Charles J., Christopher O., Emily E. With Olson Constrn. Co., Lincoln, 1959—, now pres., chief exec. officer; dir. First Nat. Lincoln Corp., Woodmen Accident and Life Co. Trustee, U. Nebr. Found. Served with USN, 1956-59. Republican. Office: 410 W 7th St Lincoln NE 68501

OLSON, DAVID HENRY, aircraft mfg. co. exec.; b. Milw., Sept. 19, 1933; s. Henry John and Evelyn Bertha (Bergstrom) O.; A.B., U. Calif. at Los Angeles, 1955, LL.B., at Berkeley, 1958; m. Kathryn Townsend Snow, Sept. 4, 1965; children—Henry David, Andrew Alan, Kathryn Perry, David Charles. Admitted to Cal. bar, 1959; trial atty. Transit Casualty Co., Los Angeles, 1961-64, Republic Indemnity Co., Los Angeles, 1964-65, Veatch, Carlson, Dorsey & Quimby, Los Angeles, 1965-67; asst. sec. Northrop Corp., Los Angeles, 1967-72, sec., 1973-76, div. gen. counsel, 1976—. Served with USAF, 1959-61. Mem. Los Angeles Bar Assn., Los Angeles Lawyers Club, Am. Soc. Corporate Secs., Am. Bd. Trial Advocates, Phi Delta Phi. Unitarian. Home: 415 Avondale Ave Los Angeles CA 90049 Office: 1800 Century Park East Los Angeles CA 90067

OLSON, DONALD ERNEST, physician; b. Portland, Oreg., June 22, 1921; s. Ernest S. and Edith (Swanman) O.; B.A., Reed Coll., 1943; M.S., U. Oreg., 1947, M.D., 1947, Ph.D., 1948; m. Alice Curtis Bergh, July 7, 1951; children—Julie Rene, Reid Martin, Kathy Ruth, Marc Ernest. Intern, U. Hosps., Madison, Wis., 1948-49, resident, 1949-51; research fellow dept. medicine U. Wis., 1952-53; staff physician VA Hosp., Madison, 1952-53; staff physician Portland Clinic, 1955—; mem. staff VA Hosp., Portland; asso. clin. prof. medicine U. Oreg. Served with M.C., AUS, 1953-55. Diplomate Am. Bd. Internal Medicine (chmn. subsplty. pulmonary disease 1968-70; mem. bd. 1972-79). Fellow A.C.P.; mem. Am., Oreg. thoracic socs., Am. Coll. Chest Physicians, North Pacific Soc. Internal Medicine, Am., Ore. med. assns., Am. Clin. and Climatol. Assn., Multnomah County Med. Soc., Phi Beta Kappa, Alpha Omega Alpha. Home: 8375 SW Crestwood Ln Portland OR 97225 Office: Portland Clinic 800 SW 13th Ave Portland OR 97205

OLSON, EARL EIDSWOLD, ch. ofcl.; b. Salt Lake City, May 17, 1916; s. Alvin E. and Eva (Jenson) O.; student Latter-day Saints Bus. Coll., 1940-42; m. Verene Stott, Mar. 24, 1944; children—Earlene, Janalyn, Craig. Hist. compiler, historian's office Ch. of Jesus Christ of Latter-day Saints, 1933-37, ch. missionary, Denmark, 1937-39, asst. ch. historian, 1965-72, chmn. ch. library coordinating com., 1968-72, ch. archivist, 1972-74, asst. mng. dir. hist. dept., 1974—; supr. Geneal. Soc. Archives, 1946-47, asst. librarian, 1947-48, librarian-archivist, 1948-68. Mem. adv. council Regional Archives Gen. Services Adminstrn., region 8, 1971-74; mem. Utah State Geog. Names Com., 1975—, Utah State Hist. Records Adv. Bd., 1979—. Served with AUS, 1942-46. Mem. Am. Assn. State and Local History, Soc. Am. Archivists, Western, Mormon (spl. citation), Utah (service award), hist. assns., Utah Acad. Arts and Scis., Utah Westerners. Home: 44 S Moss Hill Dr Circle Bountiful UT 84010 Office: 50 East North Temple St Salt Lake City UT 84150

OLSON, ELDER JAMES, educator, poet; b. Chgo., Mar. 9, 1909; s. Elder James and Hilda (Schroeder) O.; B.A., U. Chgo., 1934, M.A., 1935, Ph.D., 1938; m. Ann E. Jones, Feb. 13, 1937 (div. 1948); children—Ann (Mrs. David Burr), Elder; m. 2d, Geraldine Hays, Sept. 17, 1948; children—Inez Olivia (Mrs. Alexander Besher), Shelley (Mrs. Joao deAbreu). Instr. Armour Inst. Tech., Chgo., 1935-42; mem. faculty U. Chgo., 1942—, prof. English, 1954—, Distinguished Service prof., 1971-77, Distinguished Service prof. emeritus, 1977—; M.D. Anderson Distinguished prof. U. Houston, 1978-79; Rockefeller prof. U. Frankfurt (Germany), 1948, U. Philippines, 1966-67; vis. prof. U. P.R., 1952-53; Mahlon Powell prof. philosophy Ind. U., 1955, vis. prof. lit. criticism, 1958-59, fellow Sch. Letters, 1961, Patten lectr., 1964. Recipient Witter Bynner award, 1927; Guarantor's award Poetry mag., 1931, Tietjens award, 1953; Emily Clark Balch award Va. Quar. Rev., 1965; Quantrell award U. Chgo., 1966; Distinguished Service award U. Philippines, 1967; grantee Longview Found., 1958; award Poetry Soc. Am., 1955, Acad. Am. Poets, 1956, Soc. Midland Authors, 1976. Mem. Modern Lang Assn., P.E.N. Internat., Soc. européenne de culture. Phi Beta Kappa. Author: Thing of Sorrow, 1934; The Cock of Heaven. 1940; (with others) Critics and Criticism. 1952; The Poetry of Dylan Thomas, 1954; The Scarecrow Christ, 1954; Plays and Poems, 1958; Tragedy and The Theory of Drama, 1961; American Lyric Poems, 1963; Collected Poems, 1963; Aristotle's Poetics and English Literature, 1965; The Theory of Comedy, 1968; (poems) Olson's Penny Arcade, 1975; On Value Judgments in the Arts & Other Essays, 1976. Editor: Major Voices, 1973. Home: 1501 Los Alamos Ave Albuquerque NM 87104

OLSON, ELDON, lawyer; b. Kingsley, Mich., Aug. 3, 1935; s. Andrew L. and Margaret T. (Hall) O.; B.B.A. with distinction, U. Mich., 1958, J.D., 1961, M.B.A. with high distinction in Acctg., 1961; m. Mary L. Maxwell, June 10, 1961; children—Eric, Ann, Evan. Admitted to Mich. bar, 1961, N.Y. bar, 1962, U.S. Supreme Ct. bar, 1967; clk. to Judge Moore, U.S. Ct. Appeals, 2d Circuit, 1961-62; asso. firm Cravath, Swaine & Moore, N.Y.C., 1962-70; gen. counsel Price Waterhouse & Co., N.Y.C., 1970—; lectr. in field. Republican. Baptist. Clubs: Lawrence Beach, Rockaway Hunting. Home: 1075 Park Ave New York NY 10028 Office: 1251 Ave of Americas New York NY 10020

OLSON, ERNEST LEROY, educator; b. Salt Lake City, June 24, 1916; s. Ernest Herman and Hannah Augusta (Johnson) O.; B.A., U. Utah, 1948, M.A., 1949, postgrad., 1949-53; postgrad. U. Calif. at Los Angeles, 1949-50; m. Mary Harris, Mar. 11, 1944; children—Suzanne (dec.), Miken, Bruce, Wendy, Scott. Gen. office worker Beneficial Life Ins. Co., Salt Lake City, 1933-37, 39-40; missionary to Sweden, Ch. Jesus Christ of Latter-day Saints, 1937-39; grad. asst. English dept. U. Utah, Salt Lake City, 1949-50, 51-53; faculty English dept. Brigham Young U., Provo, Utah, 1953—, asst. prof., 1960-72, asso. prof., 1972—, univ. editor, 1956-66, dir. Univ. Press, 1967—; chmn. Western Univ. Presses Ann. Meeting, 1973, 75; chmn. program com. Assn. Am. Univ. Presses Ann. Meeting, 1979. Chmn. Republican Dist. Com., 1968; del. County Rep. Conv., 1968, Utah Rep. Conv., 1969, 74. Served with AUS, 1942-46. Mem. Mil. Chaplains Assn. Mem. Ch. Jesus Christ of Latter-day Saints (stake pres. 1971—). Home: 101 East 2120 N Provo UT 84601. *The basis of true success in life is integrity, including total honesty with oneself and all others, love and respect for others and for oneself as a divinely created son or daughter of a loving father in heaven, and a conviction that each of us has a mission on earth and an eternal destiny.*

OLSON, EUGENE RUDOLPH, printing co. exec.; b. St. Paul, Apr. 9, 1926; s. Rudolph and Martha E. (Karlson) O.; m. Leona F. Solie, June 28, 1952; children—Kathleen, Wayne, Brian. With Deluxe Check Printers Inc., St. Paul, 1944—, mgr. related products div., 1964-70, nat. dir. market research, 1970-72, v.p., 1972-76, pres., 1976—, chief exec. officer, 1977—, also dir.; dir. Data Card Corp. Mem. Bank Stationers Assn. Baptist. Club: Midland Hills Country. Home: 2024 Evergreen Ct Saint Paul MN 55113 Office: 1080 W County Rd F Saint Paul MN 55112

OLSON, EVERETT CLAIRE, vertebrate paleontologist, educator; b. Waupaca, Wis., Nov. 6, 1910; s. Claire Myron and Aimee Louise (Hicks) O.; S.B., U. Chgo., 1932, M.S., 1933, Ph.D., 1935; m. Lila Baker, July 15, 1939; children—Claire, George Everett, Mary Ellen. Instr. geology U. Chgo., 1935-43, asst. prof., 1943-47, asso. prof., 1947—, asso. dean phys. scis., 1948-59, chmn. com. paleozoology, 1948—, prof. geology, 1953-69, chmn. dept. geology, 1957-61; prof. zoology U. Calif. at Los Angeles, 1969-78, prof. emeritus, 1978—, chmn. dept., 1970-72. Dir. Am. Geol. Inst., 1948-49. Mem. Ecol. Soc. Am., AAAS, Am. Soc. for Systematic Zoology (pres. 1979), Geol. Soc. Am., Soc. Vertebrate Paleontology (pres. 1949-50), Soc. for Study Evolution (pres. 1964), Am. Soc. Zoologists, Phi Beta Kappa, Sigma Xi, Phi Kappa Psi. Author: (with Agnes Whitmarsh) Foreign Maps, 1944; (with R.L. Miller) Morphological Integration Book, 1958; The Evolution of Life, 1965; Vertebrate Paleozoology, 1971; (with J.A. Robinson) Concepts of Evolution, 1975. Editor: Evolution, 1953-58, Jour. Geology, 1962-67. Contbr. articles to sci. jours. Home: 13760 Bayliss Los Angeles CA 90049

OLSON, FRANK ALBERT, car rental co. exec.; b. San Francisco, July 19, 1932; s. Alfred and Edith Mary (Hazeldine) O.; A.A., City Coll. San Francisco; m. Sarah Jean Blakely, Oct. 19, 1957; children—Kimberly, Blake, Christopher. Gen. mgr. Barren Transp. Co., San Francisco, 1964, Valcar Co. subs. Hertz Corp., San Francisco, 1964-68; with Hertz Corp., N.Y.C., 1969—, v.p., gen. mgr. Rent-a-Car div., 1970-73, exec. v.p. corp., 1973-77, pres., 1977—; dir. Transp. Co. Am., 1977—. Pres. San Francisco Jr. C. of C., 1960. Served with AUS, 1957. Mem. Sales Execs. Club N.Y.C. Republican. Roman Catholic. Clubs: Arcola Country (Paramus, N.J.); Prouts Neck Country (Scarburgh, Maine); N.Y. Athletic (N.Y.C.). Office: Hertz Corp 660 Madison Ave New York NY 10021*

OLSON, FREDERICK IRVING, educator; b. Milw., May 30, 1916; s. Frank and Clara (Hansen) O.; B.A. magna cum laude, Harvard U., 1938, M.A. (George W. Dillaway fellow 1938- 39), 1939, Ph.D. in History, 1952; m. Jane Marian Correll, June 8, 1946; children—David Frederick, Donald Frank, Roger Alan. Mem. faculty U. Wis.-Milw., 1946—, prof. history, 1956—, chmn. com. on future, 1959-60, chmn. dept. history, 1960-62, 67-70, asso. dean Coll. Letters and Sci., 1971-76, acting dean Sch. Library Sci., 1977-79; exec. dir. Milw. Humanities Program, 1979—; vis. prof. history U. Wis.-Madison, summer 1957; asso. dean U. Wis. extension-Milw., 1960-68. Dir. Wauwatosa State Bank. Mem. Milw. Landmarks Commn., 1964-71. Trustee Milw. Pub. Museum, 1951-52; bd. dirs. Milw. County Hist. Soc., 1947—, pres., 1953-57, 72-75; bd. curators State Hist. Soc. Wis., 1961—; chmn. Milwaukee County Landmarks Com., 1976—; mem. Wis. Historic Preservation Rev. Bd., 1978—. Served with AUS, 1942-45. Mem. Am. Hist. Assn., Orgn. Am. Historians, Wis. Acad. Scis., Arts and Letters, AAUP, Lincoln Group (Boston), Phi Beta Kappa, Phi Alpha Theta, Phi Kappa Phi. Lutheran. Club: North Hills Country (Waukesha). Contbr. articles to profl. jours. Home: 2437 N 90th St Wauwatosa WI 53226 Office: Univ Wis Milwaukee WI 53201

OLSON, GORDON BENNIE, coll. pres.; b. Almont, N.D., Oct. 19, 1924; s. Bernard T. and Huldah Mae (Monson) O.; B.S., Dickinson Coll., 1948; M.A., U. N.D., 1952, Ph.D., 1953; m. Carley Yates, Jan. 20, 1945; children—Linda Olson Bittay, Corliss Olson Clark, Wendy Olson Sletto. Supt. schs., Bucyrus, N.D., 1948-51; v.p. acad. affairs Dickinson (N.D.) State Coll., 1953-67; pres. Minot (N.D.) State Coll., 1967—. Bd. dirs. Salvation Army, St. Joseph's Hosp., Minot. Served with AUS, 1943-46. Recipient Alumni Chief award Dickinson State Coll., 1973. Mem. Am. Assn. State Colls. and Univs. (nat. service com.), Am. Assn. Colls. Tchr. Edn. (state liaison rep.), Minot C. of C. (dir.). Lutheran. (bd. dirs.). Club: Elks. Home: 9th Ave NW Minot ND 58701 Office: Minot State Coll Minot ND 58701

OLSON, HARRY ANDREW, JR., financial and travel services co. exec.; b. Nashwauk, Minn., Jan. 8, 1923; s. Harry Arnold and Elizabeth C. (Wigen) O.; B.S., U. Minn., 1948; LL.B., St. Paul Coll. Law, 1950. Admitted to Minn. bar, 1950; investment analyst Investors Diversified, Mpls., 1954-57, dir. investment div., 1958-61; pres., dir. Am. Plan, Mpls., 1961-66; v.p. investments Fireman's Fund, San Francisco, 1966-67, Fund Am., 1967-69; v.p. corp. devel. Am. Express Co., N.Y.C., 1969-72, sr. v.p. corp. personnel, 1974-78, sr. v.p. investment planning and adminstrn., 1978—; pres., dir. Am. Express Investment Mgmt. Co., 1972-74. Unitarian. Office: Am Express Co 125 Broad St New York NY 10004

OLSON, HARRY F., research dir.; b. Mt. Pleasant, Iowa, Dec. 28, 1902; s. Frans O. and Nelly (Benson) O.; B.E., U. Iowa, 1924, M.S., 1925, Ph.D., 1928, E.E., 1932; D.Sc., Iowa Wesleyan U., 1959; m. Lorene E. Johnson, June 11, 1935. Acoustical research Radio Corp. Am., Princeton, 1928—, dir. Acoustical Lab., RCA Labs., 1945—, also staff v.p. acoustical and electromech. research, 1966—, pioneered in research and devel. of various types of directional microphones; lectr. acoustical engring. Columbia, 1939-42. Recipient John H. Potts medal Audio Engring. Soc., 1949; Warner medal Soc. Motion Picture and Television Engrs., Scott award Engrs. Club, Phila. 1956; John Ericsson medal Am. Soc. Swedish Engrs.; Mervin Kelly medal and Lamme medal IEEE, 1967, 69. Fellow IEEE (chmn. profl. group audio 1957-58), Acoustical Soc. Am. (pres. 1952, First Silver medal 1974), Am. Phys. Soc., Soc. Motion Picture and TV Engrs., Audio Engring. Soc. (pres. 1960); mem. of Nat. Acad. Scis., Sigma Xi, Tau Beta Pi. Author: Dynamical Analogies, 1943; Elements of Acoustical Engring., 1947; Musical Engineering, 1952; Acoustical Engineering, 1958; Music, Physics and Engineering, 1966; Modern Sound Reproduction, 1972. Contbr. articles to sci. jours. Patentee in field. Home: 71 Palmer Sq W Princeton NJ 08540 Office: RCA Laboratories Princeton NJ 08540

OLSON, HARVEY S., travel agy. exec.; b. Chgo., Feb. 28, 1908; s. Nils and Hildur (Lind) O.; B.S., Purdue U., 1929; m. Paula C. Jonas, July 23, 1966. Founder, past pres. Campus Tours, Inc., Chgo., 1930—, Olson Travel Orgn., Chgo., 1946—, Olson's Royal Coach Tours, Inc., Chgo., 1968—; founder cons. Olson-Travelworld Orgn.; speaker on travel on radio and TV. Served to lt. comdr. USNR, 1942-45. Decorated officer Tourist Order Merit (France); recipient Shalom award Israel Tourist Office, 1973. Mem. Conf. Tour Operators (past chmn.), Am. Soc. Travel Agts., Soc. Midland Authors, Western Golf Assn. (dir. 1964-67). Clubs: Executives (pres. 1964-65), Internat. (Chgo.); Oak Hills Country (San Antonio). Author: Aboard and Abroad, 13th edit., 1968; Olson's Orient Guide, 1962; Olson's Hotel, Restaurant and Shopping Guide to Europe, 1963; Olson's Complete Motoring Guide to the British Isles, 1967; Olson's Complete Motoring Guide to France, Switzerland and Italy, 1967; Olson's Complete Motoring Guide to Germany, Austria and The Benelux Countries, 1968. Home: 2707 Marlborough Dr San Antonio TX 78230 Office: 8848 Tradeway San Antonio TX 78217

OLSON, JACK B., former lt. gov. Wis., ambassador; b. Kilbourn, Wis., Aug. 29, 1920; s. Grover and Jane (Zimmerman) O.; student U. Wis., 1938-39; B.S., Western Mich. U., Kalamazoo, 1942; m. Eleanor Lang; children—Jill (Mrs. William Gaffney), Sally (Mrs. Alexander Bracken). Pres., Olson Boat Co., Wis. Dells; dir. Bank Wis. Dells; dir. Bur. Bus. Research, U. Hawaii, 1961; mem. President's Air Quality Control Adv. Bd., 1970—; U.S. ambassador to Bahamas, 1976-77. Pres. Wis. Vacationland Council, 1952-57; dir. Wis. Trade Mission Europe, 1964, ofcl. rep., 1965; exec. chmn. Wis. World's Fair Participation Corp., 1964-65; pres. No. Gt. Lakes Area Council, 1958; pres. Greater Wis. Found., 1969; mem. Pres.'s Citizens Adv. Com. on Environ. Quality. Chmn. Wis. March of Dimes, 1965-66. Chmn. Wis. Volunteers for Nixon, 1963-64; lt. gov. Wis., 1963-64, 67-70; candidate for gov. Wis., 1970; Bd. dirs. Wis. Good Roads Assn. Served to lt. (j.g.) USNR, 1942-46; ETO. Recipient Distinguished Alumnus award Western Mich. U., 1964; Sports Illus. Silver Anniversary All Am. Football award, 1966. Mem. Am. Legion, VFW, Wis. Dells C. of C. (dir.), Western Mich. U. Alumni Assn. (dir.). Presbyn. Rotarian. Address: 834 Meadow Ln Wisconsin Dells WI 53965

OLSON, JAMES CHESTER, mgmt. cons.; b. Elkhart, Ind., Jan. 11, 1907; s. Julius Axel and Chalmers Berdice (Hess) O.; A.B., Wittenberg Coll., 1930, LL.D., 1955; M.B.A., Harvard, 1933; m. Jean Lorraine Stewart, Apr. 7, 1945; children—James Stewart, Julia Jean (Mrs. F. Graham Luckenbill II), David Chalmers. Instr. econs. and bus. adminstrn., asst. dir. admissions Wittenberg Coll., 1933-36; cons. Booz, Allen & Hamilton, 1936-40, jr. partner, 1940-42, partner, 1942-62, mem. exec. com., 1948-62, vice chmn., exec. com., 1960-62; dir. Booz Allen Method Systems Inc., Booz Allen & Hamilton Internat., Ltd., Booz Allen Applied Research, Inc.; v.p., dir. Booz, Allen & Hamilton, Inc., 1962-64; dir. Bancroft Racket Co. Inc. and affiliates, 1945-74, chmn. bd., 1966-74; dir. Colonial Trust Co., 1954-56, Church & Dwight Co. Inc., 1969-74, 1158 Fifth Av. Corp., 1950-52, 1115 Fifth Ave. Corp., N.Y.C., 1977—; bd. mgrs. Candlewood Lake Club Owners Corp., 1962-65, pres., chmn. bd., 1970-71. Mem. U.S. Mut. Security Adminstrn. (now AID) program evaluation project Greece, 1953. Trustee Wittenberg U., 1969—, chmn. audit com., 1971-72. Mem. Nat. Sales Execs. Inc., Phi Kappa Psi. Lutheran. Clubs: Union League (Chgo.); Harvard, Sales Executives (dir. 1951-52) (N.Y.C.). Home: Candlewood Lake Club Brookfield CT 06804 also 1115 Fifth Ave New York NY 10028 Office: 245 Park Ave New York NY 10017

OLSON, JAMES CLIFTON, historian, educator; b. Bradgate, Iowa, Jan. 23, 1917; s. Arthur Edwin and Abbie (Anderson) O.; A.B., Morningside Coll., 1938, LL.D., 1968; M.A., U. Nebr., 1939, PhD., 1942; m. Vera Blanche Farrington, June 6, 1941; children—Elizabeth, Sarah Margaret. Instr., N.W. Mo. State Tchrs. Coll., summers 1940, 42; dir. Nebr. Hist. Soc., 1946-56; lectr. U. Omaha, 1947-50; part-time lectr. U. Nebr., 1946-54, part-time asso. prof., 1954-56, prof., chmn. dept. history, 1956-65, Bennett S. and Dorothy Martin prof. history, chmn. dept., 1962-65, dean Grad. Coll., univ. research adminstr., 1966-68, vice chancellor, 1968; chancellor U. Mo., Kansas City, 1968-76; interim pres. U. Mo. System, 1976-77, pres., 1977—; OAS prof. Am. history El Colegio de Mexico, Mexico City, 1962. Dir. Standard Milling Co., Kansas City, Mo., United Telecommunications, Inc., Westwood, Kans., 1977—. Commr., North Central Assn. Colls. and Schs. Bd. dirs., v.p., chmn. com. on grants in aid Harry S. Truman Library Inst.; bd. dirs. Mid-Am. Arts Alliance, chmn., 1976—; bd. dirs. Council on Post Secondary Accreditation 1974-77; trustee Morningside Coll., Sioux City, Iowa, Midwest Research Inst., Kansas City. Served to 1st lt. USAAF, 1942-46. Mem. Agrl. History Soc. (v.p. 1961-62), Am. Assn. State and Local History (mem. council 1948-56, regional v.p. 1956-62, pres. 1962-64, chmn. research and publs. com.), AAUP (v.p. U. Nebr. chpt. 1958-59), Assn. Urban Univs. (v.p. 1972-73 pres. 1973-75), Council Basic Edn., Am., Mo. (trustee), Nebr. (dir. 1946-56), Miss. Valley sec.-treas. 1953-56, mem. bd.

editors, 1960-63, exec. com., 1963-66) hist. assns., Nebr. History and Social Studies Tchrs. Assn. (pres. 1957-58), Nebr. Writers Guild (pres. 1951-53), Rotary Club of Columbia, Mo., Nelson Gallery Found. & William R. Nelson Trust (trustee), Phi Beta Kappa, Omicron Delta Kappa, Phi Kappa Phi, Pi Gamma Mu. Club: Cosmos (Washington). Author: J. Sterling Morton, 1942, The Nebraska Story, 1951, History of Nebraska, 1955, (with Vera Farrington Olson) Nebraska is My Home, 1956, This is Nebraska, 1960, Red Cloud and the Sioux Problem, 1965. Contbg. author: The Army Air Force in World War II, 1951, 55. Editor: Nebraska History, 1946-56. Contbr. articles to profl. jours., encys. Home: 1900 S Providence Rd Columbia MO 65201

OLSON, JAMES ELIAS, telephone co. exec.; b. Devils Lake, N.D., Dec. 3, 1925; s. Olaf John and Laura Olive (Larson) O.; B.S. and Commerce, U. N.D., 1950; postgrad. U. Pa. Inst. Humanistic Studies, 1957-58; D.B.A. (hon.), Marian Coll., Indpls., 1975; m. Wilma Jean Wolfe, Apr. 2, 1955; children—James, Julia. With Northwestern Bell Telephone Co., 1943-58, 60-70, gen. comml. mgr., Mpls., 1961-64, v.p., gen. mgr. Neb. area, Omaha, 1964-66, Ia. area, Des Moines, 1966-70; with traffic div. Am. Tel. and Tel. Co., N.Y.C., 1958-60; v.p. operations Ind. Bell Telephone Co., Inc., Indpls., 1970-72, pres., 1972-74, dir., 1970-74; pres. dir. Ill. Bell Telephone Co., Chgo., 1974-77; exec. v.p. AT&T, N.Y.C., 1977-79, vice chmn., 1979—, also dir.; dir. Borg-Warner Corp., N.Y. Telephone Co., Chase Manhattan Bank, N.A., Chase Manhattan Corp., Jewel Cos. Inc., AT&T Long Lines Dept. Mem. bus.-higher edn. forum Am. Council on Edn.; mem. council Grad. Sch. Bus., U. Chgo.; mem. steering com. Nat. Urban Coalition. Served with USAAF, 1943-46. Recipient Outstanding Service award Des Moines Human Rights Commn., 1969; Disting. Service award NCCJ, Des Moines, 1970. Clubs: Baltusrol Golf (N.J.); Internat. (Washington); Royal Poinciana (Fla.). Office: AT&T 195 Broadway New York NY 10007

OLSON, JAMES RICHARD, food co. exec.; b. Alexandria, Minn., Mar. 11, 1941; s. Orie D. and Theresa Marie (Erickson) O.; B.S., N.D. State U., 1963; LL.B., U. Minn., 1966; M.B.A., Harvard U., 1968; m. Ronna Lee, Feb. 1, 1969 (dec.); 1 son, Trevor James. Asst. to v.p. finance Cargill Inc., Mpls., 1968-69; with Graco Inc., Mpls., 1969-75, v.p. finance, 1972-75; exec. v.p. finance Ponderosa System, Inc., Dayton, Ohio, 1975-77; v.p. planning Pillsbury Co., Mpls., 1977-79, v.p. restaurant group, 1979—. Mem. Financial Execs. Inst., Citizens League Mpls.-St. Paul, Harvard Bus. Sch. Club Minn. (past pres.). Lutheran. Home: 1788 Fremont Ave S Minneapolis MN 55403 Office: 608 2d Ave S Minneapolis MN 55402

OLSON, JANE VIRGINIA, editor; b. Chgo., Dec. 14, 1916; d. Oscar Wilford and Mary (Bowles) Olson; B.A., U. N.Mex., 1939; m. William M. Gooden, Feb. 16, 1955 (div. 1957). Copy editor Atlantic Monthly mag., Boston, 1942-46; copy editor Vogue mag., N.Y.C., 1946-49; tech. editor Ill. Geol. Survey, Urbana, 1949-55; sci. and social sci. editor Yale U. Press, New Haven, 1958-69; editor Am. Scientist mag., New Haven, 1969—. Bd. dirs. Peabody Mus. Assos. Fellow Saybrook Coll., Yale U. Mem. League Women Voters, Sigma Xi. Home: 60 Ardmore St Hamden CT 06517 Office: 345 Whitney Ave New Haven CT 06511

OLSON, JAY RAYMOND, JR., mfg. co. exec.; b. Bemidji, Minn., July 3, 1933; s. Jay Raymond and Jonnie (MacMaster) O.; B.A. in Econs., Dartmouth Coll., 1955; m. Kathlyn Lyon, Sept. 4, 1954; children—Nancy, Jay, Charles. Asst. treas. Continental Can Co., 1955-69; v.p., treas. Diversa-Graphics Co., N.Y.C., 1969-70; with GAF Corp., N.Y.C., 1970—, treas., 1973-76, v.p., asst. to pres., 1976-77, sr. v.p. finance, 1977-78, exec. v.p. fin. and adminstrv. systems, 1978—; fin. cons. CONSCO Inc., N.Y.C. Mem. Fin. Execs. Inst., Phi Delta Theta. Republican. Mem. Christian Missionary Alliance. Clubs: Univ.; Whippoorwill Country, Point O'Woods Assn. Home: 11 Rock Ledge Rd Pleasantville NY 10570 Office: 140 W 51st St New York NY 10020

OLSON, JERRY CARL, supt. schs.; b. Brookville, Pa., Aug. 16, 1932; s. Carl and Charlotte (Knappenberger) O.; B.S., California (Pa.) State Coll., 1957; M.Ed., U. Pitts., 1960; Ph.D., Ohio State U., 1964; m. Virginia Haogh, Nov. 10, 1955; children—Phillip, Elizabeth Ann. Asst. supt. occupational vocat.-tech. edn. Pitts. Pub. Schs., 1968-70, asst. supt. system-wide programs and services, 1970-73, acting supt., 1973, supt., 1973—; vis. prof. Oreg. State U., Corvallis, summers 1968-70, U. Minn., Mpls. summer 1971; adj. prof. U. Pitts., 1974-76; mem. edn. steering com. Graphic Arts Tech. Found., 1965-72. Bd. dirs. Jr. Achievement S.W. Pa., 1971—, Psychol. Service of Pitts., 1971—. Served with U.S. Army, 1953-54. Recipient spl. citation for leadership Wayne State U., 1968, cert. of recognition indsl. arts curriculum project Ohio State U., 1971, cert. of leadership recognition Am. Soc. Tng. and Devel., 1971; Ohio State U. Disting. Alumni award, 1979. Mem. Epsilon Pi Tau, Phi Delta Kappa. Club: Pitts. Press. Author: Plastics Technology: A Curriculum Resource Study, 1962; Graphic Communication Series, 8 Textbooks, 1970. Med. editorial bd. Sch. Shop, 1970-72. Home: 5449 Fair Oaks St Pittsburgh PA 15217 Office: Pitts Pub Schs 341 S Bellefield Ave Pittsburgh PA 15213

OLSON, JOHN LAWRENCE, mfg. co. exec.; b. LaCrosse, Wis., June 21, 1941; s. William H. and Ethel M. (Bagnewski) O.; B.C.S., Seattle U., 1964; m. Cherri Derosier, June 6, 1963; children—Michael, Tami, Tina. Sr. accountant Main, LaFrentz & Co., C.P.A.'s; div. controller Nat. Industries, Inc., Century City, Calif.; now v.p., controller Republic Corp. Home: 10478 Salinas River Circle Fountain Valley CA 92708 Office: 1900 Ave of the Stars Century City CA 90067

OLSON, JOHN VICTOR, educator; b. Kibbie, Mich., June 24, 1913; s. John Leonard and Elizabeth Johanna (Ytterberg) O.; D.D.S., U. Mich., 1936, M.S., 1938; m. Margaret Pray; 1 dau., Nancy. Pvt. practice dentistry, South Haven, Mich., 1938-42; asst. prof. prosthetics St. Louis U. Sch. Dentistry, 1947-49, asso. prof., 1949-50, dir. postgrad. dental edn., 1948-50; prof. restorative dentistry, dental br. U. Tex., 1950—, dean, 1952—, dean-elect Dental Sch., San Antonio, 1969-72, acting pres. Health Sci. Center, Houston, 1972-74; mem. med. bd. Ben Taub Hosp., Houston; cons. in prosthodontia VA Hosp., Houston, 1952—. Served from 1st lt. to maj. Dental Corps, U.S. Army, 1942-46. Fellow Am. Coll. Dentists, Internat. Coll. Dentists; mem. Am., Tex., dental assns., Houston Dist. Dental Soc., AAAS, Phi Kappa Phi, Omicron Kappa Upsilon, Xi Psi Phi. Home: 2725 Pemberton St Houston TX 77005 Office: PO Box 20068 Houston TX 77025

OLSON, LAWRENCE, educator; b. Memphis, May 7, 1918; s. Lawrence A. and Wanda (Liddell) O.; B.A., U. Miss., 1938; M.A., Harvard, 1939, Ph.D., 1955; M.A. (hon.), Wesleyan U., Middletown, Conn., 1969; m. Jeane E. Noordhoff, Dec. 19, 1941; children—Alexandra Lyman, Sarah Liddell. Cultural attache Am. embassy, Manila, Philippines, 1951-52; staff asso. Am. Univs. Field Staff, 1955-66, sr. staff asso., 1962-66; vis. prof. Dartmouth, 1964-65; prof. history Wesleyan U., 1966—. Served to lt. (j.g.) USNR, 1942-46. Ford fellow, 1952-54; Rockefeller fellow, 1963; Fulbright research fellow, Japan, 1973-74; Woodrow Wilson Internat. Center for Scholars fellow, 1979-80. Mem. Council Fgn. Relations (vis. fellow 1968-69), Japan Soc., Arctic Inst. N.Am., Assn. Asian Studies. Author: The Cranes on Dying River and Other Poems, 1947; Dimensions of Japan, 1963; Japan in Postwar Asia, 1970. Home: PO Box O Middle Haddam CT 06456 Office: Dept History Wesleyan Univ Middletown CT 06457

OLSON, LOREN KEITH, lawyer, ex-govt. ofcl.; b. Wheeler, Wis., Feb. 28, 1914; s. Alfred J. and Zella H. (McPherson) O.; B.S., Eau Claire State Coll., 1938; J.S.D., U. Wis., 1940; m. Lilly C. Johnson, July 31, 1937; children—Douglas Keith, Loren Keith. Admitted to Wis. bar, 1940; atty. Wis. Indsl. Commn., 1936-42; counsel to asst. sec. navy (comptroller), 1946-50; partner firm Dudley, Lax, Olson & Shook, Washington, 1950-57; gen. counsel AEC, 1958-60, commr., 1960-62; partner Blum, Olson & Oulahan, 1963-66, King & King, 1967-69, Morgan, Lewis & Bockius, 1970—. Dir. Fluor Corp., Ladish Co. Served with USNR, 1943-45, Mem. Wis., D.C., Am. bar assns. Conglist. Clubs: Nat. Lawyers, Cosmos, Capitol Hill, Army and Navy (Washington). Home: 5335 Falmouth Rd Washington DC 20016 Office: 1800 M St NW Washington DC 20036

OLSON, MERLIN IVER, hosp. adminstr.; b. Eau Claire, Wis., Aug. 22, 1941; s. Iver Berton and Myrtle Alice (Langness) O.; B.A., Nat. Office Mgmt. Assn. scholar), Augsburg Coll., 1964; M.H.A. (USPHS trainee), U. Minn., 1966; m. Carol Joyce Slater, Apr. 25, 1975; children—Mark, Michael, Bradford, Matthew, Martin, Catherine, Mitchell. Asst. to bus. mgr. Mt. Sinai Hosp., Mpls., 1963-64; adminstrv. asst. Miller Hosp., St. Paul, 1965-67; asso. dir. Variety Children's Hosp., Miami, Fla., 1967-70; adminstr. U. Kans. Med. Center, 1970-76; exec. dir. hosps. U. Colo. Med. Center, 1976-79; sr. v.p. Robert Douglass Assos., 1979—; clin. preceptor program in hosp. and health care adminstrn., mem. resident faculty summer sessions U. Minn.; instr. program in health adminstrn. U.Colo. Sch. Medicine; br.-site vis., mem. adv. com. HEW Gen. Clin. Research Center; mem. task force on asso. degree in nursing Kellogg Found.; dir. Blue Cross Blue Shield of Colo.; chmn. bd. Minn. M.H.A. Alumni Found.; seminar and inst. speaker. Mem. Am. Coll. Hosp. Adminstrs., Am. Hosp. Assn., Assn. Am. Med. Colls. (gen. assembly, task force on grad. med. edn.), Western Univ. Hosp. Council, Council Univ. Teaching Hosps., Colo. Hosp. Assn. (council legis. affairs, pres. bd. assn. trust). Republican. Lutheran. Author: The Role of the Chief Executive, 1974; Problem Solving and Decision Making, 1974; Administration of Supportive Services, 1975; contbr. articles to profl. jours. Home: Parkdale Dr Kingwood TX 77339 Office: 1020 Holcombe Suite 1600 Houston TX 77030

OLSON, OSCAR DONALD, banker; b. Pueblo, Colo., Feb. 9, 1917; s. Oscar and Iva (Ackerman) O.; B.A., U. Chgo., 1941, M.B.A., 1948; m. Bonnie B. Waggoner-Breternitz, May 17, 1944; children—Pamela, Douglas. Asst. personnel dir. No. Trust Co., Chgo., 1941-54; pres. Exchange Nat. Bank, Colorado Springs, Colo., 1954-72, Citizens Nat. Bank, Colorado Springs, 1975-77; pres. Air Acad. Nat. Bank, 1966-71; pres. Warehouses, Inc. Served with USAAF, 1942-45; now maj. gen. Res. ret. Decorated Silver Star medal, Legion of Merit, D.F.C., Air medal; recipient Alumni citation U. Chgo., 1961. Mem. Am. Bankers Assn., C. of C. (past pres.), Air Force Assn. (past dir.), Sigma Chi. Home: 1211 Culebra Ave Colorado Springs CO 80903 Office: PO Box 700 Colorado Springs CO 80901

OLSON, RAYMOND MARION, coll. pres., clergyman; b. Eagle Grove, Iowa, June 15, 1910; s. Lester O. and Severina (Roseland) O.; B.A. Augustana Coll., 1934, D.D., 1954; B.Th., Luther Theol. Sem., 1939, M.Th., 1943; LL.D., Calif. Luth. Coll., 1971; m. Helen A. Hilleson, June 26, 1937; children—Signe M., Rolf T., Eloise N. Tchr. Christianity and speech Waldorf Coll., Forest City, Ia., 1936-38; ordained to ministry Evang. Luth. Ch., 1939; pastor, Armstrong, Iowa, 1939-41. Caliender, Iowa, 1941-43, Portland, Oreg., 1943-48, Mpls., 1948-52; news editor Luth. Herald, 1949-56; dir. stewardship Evang. Luth. Ch., 1952-61, Am. Luth. Ch., Mpls., 1961-63; pres. Calif. Luth. Coll., Thousand Oaks, 1963-71; pastor Shepherd of the Valley Luth. Ch., Canoga Park, Calif., 1971-77. Pres. Conejo Future Found., 1971—. Trustee Evang. Luth. Ch., 1948-52; councilor Nat. Luth. Council, 1954-66, sec., 1956-59, v.p., 1959-61, pres., 1961-65; chmn. Commn. Stewardship and Congl. Life, Luth. World Fedn., 1957-63. Trustee Fairview Hosp., Mpls., 1952- 63. Rotarian. Author: The Child in Your Midst, 1948; Stewards Appointed, 1958. Home: 3078 N Saddleback Ct Thousand Oaks CA 91360

OLSON, RAYMOND VERLIN, agronomist, educator; b. Cavalier, N.D., Oct. 4, 1919; s. Henry L. and Lean B. (Bobert) O.; student N.D. Sch. Forestry, 1937-39; B.S., N.D. State Agrl. Coll., 1941; M.S., U. Wis., 1942, Ph.D., 1947; m. Jean Schumacher, May 25, 1943; children—Nancy, Peter, Susan. Chemist, Hercules Powder Co., Wilmington. Del., 1942-45; asso. prof. soils Kans. State U., 1947-50, prof., 1950—, head dept. agronomy, 1952-70; dir. Internat. Agrl. Programs, 1970-72; chief Kans. State U. project Ahmadu Bello U., Zaria, Nigeria, 1964-66, 72-74, dean faculty agr., 1964-66, provost for agr. and vet. medicine, 1972-74. Internat. Exec. Service Corps vol. to ministry agr. Iran, 1968; agrl. cons. I.R.I. Inst., New York in Brazil, 1969; cons. AID, West Africa, 1976; cons. USDA, Govt. Philippines, 1977. Chmn. Nat. Soil Research Com., 1957-58. Fellow Am. Soc. Agronomy; mem. Soil Sci. Soc. Am. (chmn. com. chem. analysis; asso. editor proc. 1954-56), AAAS, Sigma Xi, Phi Kappa Phi, Gamma Sigma Delta (recipient Internat. Service to Agr. award 1968), Alpha Zeta. Contbr. articles to profl. jours. Home: 2007 Anderson Ave Manhattan KS 66502

OLSON, RICHARD E., mayor Des Moines; b. Aurora, Ill., Aug. 3, 1929; student U. Ill., 1948; grad. Drake U., 1951; m. Cleojean Meredith, Mar. 28, 1951; children—Meredith, Dave, Dana, Brad. Former salesman Minn. Mining Corp.; with Bankers Life Co., 1954-68, salesman, then asst. supr. home office, asst. mgr., Des Moines, agency mgr., 1960-68; councilman, Des Moines, 1968-71, mayor, 1972—. Mem. Alpha Tau Omega. Office: Office of Mayor City Hall E 1st and Locust Sts Des Moines IA 50307 also 610 Liberty Bldg Des Moines IA 50309*

OLSON, ROBERT EUGENE, physician, biochemist; b. Minn., Jan. 23, 1919; s. Ralph William and Minnie (Holtin) O.; A.B., Gustavus Adolphus Coll., 1938; Ph.D., St. Louis U., 1944; M.D., Harvard, 1951; m. Catherine Silvoso, Oct. 21, 1944; children—Barbara Lynn, Robert E., Mark Alan, Mary Ellen, Carol Louise. Postgrad. research asst. biochemistry St. Louis U. Sch. Medicine, 1938-43, asst. biochemistry, 1943-44, Alice A. Doisy prof. biochemistry, chmn. dept. biochemistry, 1965—, asso. prof. medicine, 1966-72, prof. medicine, 1972—; vis. prof. (sabbatical) dept. biochemistry U. Freiburg, Breisgau, West Germany, 1970-71, also Hoffman-La Roche Co., Basel, Switzerland, 1970-71; instr. biochemistry and nutrition Harvard Sch. Pub. Health, 1946-47; research fellow Nutrition Found., 1947-49; research fellow Am. Heart Assn., 1949-51, established investigator, 1951-52; house officer Peter Bent Brigham Hosp., Boston, 1951-52; prof., head dept. biochemistry and nutrition Grad. Sch. Pub. Health U. Pitts., lectr. medicine Sch. Medicine, 1952-65; mem. panel malnutrition Japan-U.S. Med. Scis. Program, 1965-69; dir. Nutrition Clinic, Falk Clinic, 1953-65; mem. sr. staff Presbyn. Hosp., dir. metabolic unit, 1960-65; mem. staff St. Louis U. Hosp., 1965—; cons. Mercy Hosp., U. Pitts. Med. Center; asso. medicine St. Margaret's Meml. Hosp., Pitts., dir. metabolic unit, 1954-60; cons. div. research grants USPHS, 1954-69, 73—; dir. Anemia and Malnutrition Center, Chiang Mai, Thailand, 1967-77; vis. scholar dept. biochemistry Oxford (Eng.) U., 1961-62; vis. prof. dept. biochemistry U. Freiburg (West Germany), 1970-71. Mem. food and nutrition bd. Nat. Research Council, 1977—; bd. dirs. Nat. Nutrition Consortium, 1977—. Served as lt. (j.g.) USNR, 1944-46. Recipient Fulbright award 1961-62; Guggenheim Found. award, 1961-62, 70-71; McCollum award, 1965; Joseph Goldberger award, 1974; Atwater Meml. lectr., 1978; Geiger Meml. lectr., 1979. Diplomate Nat. Bd. Med. Examiners, Am. Bd. Nutrition (pres. 1962-63). Fellow Am. Pub. Health Assn. (chmn. food and nutrition sect. 1960-61), A.C.P., Assn. Am. Physicians; mem. Am. Assn. Cancer Research, Am. Heart Assn., AMA (mem. council food and nutrition 1959-67; vice chmn. 1962-67), Royal Soc. Health (London), N.Y. Acad. Scis., Am. Fedn. Clin. Research, Am. Soc. Clin. Investigation, Boyleston Med. Soc., Am. Chem. Soc. (pres. biochemistry group Pitts. sect. 1960-61), Am. Soc. Biol. Chemists, Am. Inst. Nutrition, AAAS (sec. med. scis. N sect. 1965-67), Soc. Exptl. Biology and Medicine, Am. Soc. Clin. Nutrition (pres. 1961-62; McCollum award 1965), Assn. Med. Sch. Depts. Biochemistry (pres. 1979—), Pa., St. Louis, Allegheny County med. socs., Am. Soc. Study Liver Diseases, Phi Beta Kappa, Sigma Xi, Phi Lambda Upsilon, Alpha Omega Alpha, Alpha Sigma Nu. Clubs: Norwood Hills Country (St. Louis); Cosmos (Washington). Asso. editor Nutrition Reviews, 1954-56, editor, 1978—; asso. editor Am. Jour. Medicine, 1956-65, Circulation Research, 1956-67, Am. Heart Jour., 1958-65, Am. Jour. Clin. Nutrition, 1960-66, Methods in Med. Research, 1963-70, Biochem. Medicine, 1967, Molecular and Cellular Cardiology, 1969; co-editor Vitamins and Hormones, 1975—. Home: 9060 Clayton Rd Saint Louis MO 63117 Office: 1402 S Grand Ave Saint Louis MO 63104

OLSON, ROBERT GOODWIN, educator; b. Mpls., May 8, 1924; s. Goodwin Carl and Mary Helen (Hutchins) O.; B.A., U. Minn., 1943; Docteur (French Govt. scholar 1951), U. Paris, 1953; Ph.D., U. Mich., 1957. Staff editor Grolier Soc., N.Y.C., 1946-48; historian Office Mil. Govt., Berlin, Germany, 1948-49; asst. prof. philosophy Ripon (Wis.) Coll., 1953-56; instr. philosophy U. Mich., 1956-58; asst. prof. Columbia U., 1958-61; asso. prof., chmn. dept. philosophy Rutgers U., 1961-65, prof., chmn. dept. philosophy, 1965-69; prof., chmn. dept. philosophy L.I. U., Bklyn., 1969—. Served with USAAF, 1943-46. Mem. Am., L.I. philos. assns., AAUP, United Fedn. Coll. Tchrs. Author: An Introduction to Existentialism, 1962; The Morality of Self-Interest, 1965; A Short Introduction to Philosophy, 1967; Meaning and Argument, 1969; Ethics: A Short Introduction, 1977. Contbr. articles to profl. jours. Home: 123 E 61st St New York City NY 10021 Office: Long Island U Brooklyn Center Brooklyn NY 11201

OLSON, ROBERT LESLIE, electronics co. exec.; b. Oakland, Calif., Aug. 31, 1922; s. Wilbert Harold and Charlotte May (Hunter) O.; B.A.S., U. Calif. at Berkeley, 1943, postgrad., 1947-48; postgrad. U. Calif. at Los Angeles, 1961-62; m. Thelma Jane Nairne, June 6, 1942; children—Janet Kay (Mrs. Thomas Albert Howard), David Stuart. Design engr. Radiation Lab., Berkeley and Livermore, Calif., 1946-51; research engr., engring. mgr. Atomics Internat., Canoga Park, Calif., 1951-58; mgr. N.Am. Aviation, Inc., Los Angeles, 1959-66, 67-68; v.p. M.W. Kellogg Co., N.Y.C., 1966-67; v.p. Internat. Tel. & Tel. Corp., Nutley, N.J., 1968—. Treas., dir., mgr. West Sepulveda (Calif.) Little League, 1956-60. Bd. dirs. Pleasant Hills (Calif.) County Water Dist., 1949-51, Big Bros., Orange County, Calif., 1964-65. Served with C.E., AUS, 1943-46. Registered profl. engr., Calif. Mem. Am. Soc. M.E., Am. Nuclear Soc., Am. Inst. Aeros. and Astronautics, Navy League, Electronic Industries Assn., Aerospace Industries Assn., Nat. Security Indsl. Assn., U. Calif. Los Angeles Exec. Program Alumni Assn., Tau Beta Pi. Republican. Methodist. Clubs: University of California, Crew (Berkeley). Home: 421 Carriage Ln Wyckoff NJ 07481 Office: 500 Washington Ave Nutley NJ 07110

OLSON, ROBERT LUTHER, basketball coach; b. Mayville, N.D., Sept. 22, 1934; s. Albert A. and Alinda A. (Halvorson) O.; B.A., Augsburg Coll., Mpls., 1956; M.A., Chapman Coll., 1968; m. Roberta Rae Russell, Nov. 27, 1953; children—Vicki Wulfsberg, Jodi Brase, Gregory, Christi, Steven. Basketball coach Mahnomen (Minn.) High Sch., 1957, Two Harbors (Minn.) High Sch., 1958-61, Marina High Sch., Huntington Beach, Calif., 1965-69, Loara High Sch., Anaheim, Calif., 1964, Long Beach City Coll., 1969-73, Long Beach State U., 1973-74; basketball Coach U. Iowa, Iowa City, 1974—. Named Coach of Year, Big Ten, 1979. Mem. Nat. Assn. Basketball Coaches. Lutheran. Contbr. articles to sports mags. Home: 1425 Bristol Dr Iowa City IA 52240 Office: Athletic Office Bldg Univ of Iowa Iowa City IA 52242

OLSON, RONALD WAYNE, lawyer; b. Chgo., Oct. 29, 1931; s. Philip John and Adeline (Hoffmann) O.; student U. Ill., 1949-52; B.S., Northwestern U., 1953, J.D., 1955; LL.M., Georgetown U., 1958; m. Sandra Jane Forbes, Sept. 2, 1967; children—Ronald Wayne, Kirsten Ann. Admitted to Ill. bar, 1956; practice in Chgo., 1959—; atty. Spencer & Crowe, 1959-62; asst. states atty. Cook County, Ill., 1961-62; atty., mem. firm Rhyne & Rhyne, Washington, 1962-63; atty. Bergstrom, Rohde, Dahlgren & Olson, 1963-73; counsel Bergstrom, Davis & Teeple, 1973—; lectr. pension-profit sharing plans U. Chgo., 1960; faculty John Marshall Sch. Law, Chgo., 1965—, now asso. prof., asst. dean, dir. gen. practice grad. sch. Conducted study def. of indigent accused in Cook County under auspices of Ill. Pub. Defenders Assn., 1969. Candidate Ill. Constl. Conv., 1969. Served to ensign USNR, 1955-59; capt. JAG Corps Res. ret. Mem. Chgo. and Ill. Assn. Commerce and Industry, Am. Arbitration Assn. (arbitrator, chmn. lawyers in armed services standing com.), U. Ill. Civil Service Bd., Navy League (judge adv. gen. Chgo. chpt.), Theta Xi, Phi Delta Phi. Home: 220 E Walton Pl Chicago IL 60611 Office: 315 S Plymouth Ct Chicago IL 60604

OLSON, ROY EDWIN, civil engr.; b. Richmond, Ind., Sept. 13, 1931; s. Roy Edwin and Hester Elizabeth (Nelson) O.; B.S., U. Minn., 1953, M.C.E. (1st Minn. Surveyors and Engr. Soc. scholar), 1955; Ph.D. (1st ASTM fellow), U. Ill., 1960; m. Corrine Hoisington, Aug. 5, 1967; children—Sandra Lee, Cheryl Ann, Chresten Edwin. Asst. prof. U. Ill., Urbana, 1960-62, asso. prof., 1962-66, prof. civil engring., 1966-70; prof. civil engring. U. Tex., Austin, 1970—; cons. to industry, U.S. Govt. Mem. ASCE (Walter L. Huber Research prize 1972, Norman medal 1975), ASTM (Hogentogler award 1973), Transp. Research Bd., Clay Minerals Soc. Home: 4302 Far West Blvd Austin TX 78731

OLSON, RUSSEL EINAR, utility co. fin. exec.; b. Seattle, Apr. 20, 1931; s. Olaf Einar and Margot Marie O.; B.A. in Acctg., U. Wash. 1959, grad. exec. devel. program, 1968; postgrad. in fin. Pacific Luth. U., 1974-79; m. Betty Virginia Rygg, Apr. 21, 1951; children—Charlene, David, Steven. With Puget Sound Power & Light Co., Bellevue, Wash., 1959-61, 62-65, 69—, budget supr., 1969-70, fin. planning supr., 1970-72, mgr. fin. planning, 1972-74, asst. treas., 1974-77, treas., 1977—; auditor Coopers & Lybrand, Seattle, 1961-62; spl. acct. Puget Western, Inc., Renton, Wash., 1965-68, asst. v.p., 1968-69; tchr. acctg. adult edn., 1963-65. Served with USCG, 1950-53. Mem. Nat. Assn. Accts. (sec. Seattle-Tacoma chpt. 1971-72, dir. chpt. 1969-72), Planning Execs. Inst. (dir. Puget Sound chpt.

1975-77), Fin. Execs. Inst., Electric League Puget Sound, N.W. Electric Light and Power Assn. Clubs: Washington Athletic, Elks. Office: 10608 NE 4th St Bellevue WA 98004

OLSON, RUSSELL A., lt. gov. Wis.; b. Chgo., Feb. 19, 1924; ed. U. Ill., Champaign; married; 4 children. Owner, operator Rolling Hills Farms, Bassett, Wis.; mem. Wis. Assembly; lt. gov. State of Wis., 1979—. Treas., Kenosha County (Wis.) Fair Assn. Served with USMC, 1942-46. Mem. Farm Bur., Wis. Cattlemen's Assn., Twin Lakes Businessmen's Assn. Republican. Clubs: Am. Legion, VFW, Eagles. Office: Office Lt Gov 22 E State Capitol Madison WI 53702*

OLSON, STANLEY GRANVILLE, petroleum co. exec.; b. Watford City, N.D., Oct. 10, 1918; s. Thor Oscar and Hilda (Swanson) O.; B.S. in Geol. Engring., Mont. Coll. Minerals Sci. and Tech., 1948, petroleum Engr. (hon.), 1968; m. Lillian June Ralph, Mar. 6, 1944; children—Michael Eric, Thora Lynn. Geol. engr., econs. analyst Continental Oil Co., Ponca City, Okla. and Houston, 1948-52; with Hudson's Bay Oil & Gas Co. Ltd., Calgary, Alta., Can., 1952—, v.p. prodn., 1966-70, exec. v.p., 1970-77, pres., chief exec. officer, 1977—, also dir. Served with USAAF, World War II; ETO. Decorated Air medal with 5 clusters, D.F.C. Mem. Am. Inst. Mining, Metall. and Petroleum Engrs., Canadian Inst. Mining and Metallurgy, Assn. Profl. Engrs., Geologists and Geophysicists Alta. Home: 1002 330 26th Ave SW Calgary AB T2S 2T3 Canada Office: 700 2d St W Calgary AB T2P 0X5 Canada

OLSON, STANLEY WILLIAM, physician, educator; b. Chgo., Feb. 10, 1914; s. David William and Agnes (Nelson) O.; B.S., Wheaton Coll., 1934; M.D., U. Ill., 1938; M.S. in Medicine (fellow), U. Minn., Mayo Found., 1943; m. Lorraine Caroline Lofdahl, June 26, 1936; children—Patricia Ann, Richard David, Robert Dean. Intern Cook County Hosp., Chgo., 1938-40; asst. dir. Mayo Found.; cons. medicine Mayo Clinic; instr. medicine grad. sch. U. Minn., 1947-50; dean coll. medicine, med. dir. Research and Ednl. Hosp., U. Ill., 1950-53; dean coll. medicine Baylor U., Tex. Med. Center, Houston, 1953-66; prof. medicine Vanderbilt U., clin. prof. medicine Meharry Med. Coll., 1966-68; dir. Tenn. Mid-South Regional Med. Program, 1967-68; dir. Div. Regional Med. Programs Service, USPHS, 1968-70; pres. S.W. Found. for Research and Edn., San Antonio, 1970-73; provost N.E. Ohio Univs. Coll. Medicine, 1973-79, cons. med. edn., 1980—; past chmn. med. bd., chief staff Ben Taub Hosp., Jefferson Davis Hosp., Houston; nat. adv. council for health research facilities, NIH, 1963-68; rev. panel constrn. med. schs. USPHS, 1964-65. spl. cons. div. Regional Med. Programs NIH, 1966-68; med. cons. bd. trustees. State U., N.Y., 1949; cons. to Hoover Commn., 1954; mem. bd. trustees. Wheaton Coll. (Ill.), 1953-68. Served as capt., M.C., AUS, 1943-46. Diplomate Am. Bd. Internal Medicine. Mem. Houston Philos. Soc. (pres. 1962-63), Tex. Philos. Soc., Assn. Am. Med. Colls., AMA, Alumni Assn. Mayo Found., Sigma Xi, Alpha Kappa Kappa, Alpha Omega Alpha. Baptist. Contbr. articles to profl. jours. Home: 226 Frances Dr Kent OH 44240 Office: Rootstown OH 44272

OLSON, SYLVESTER IRWIN, govt. ofcl.; b. Herman, Minn., Apr. 2, 1907; s. Jacob John and Theresia Mary (Kremer) O.; student Marquette U., 1925-26; B.A., U. Minn., 1929, J.D., 1931; m. Virginia Varney Colbert, Aug. 19, 1948; children—Karen Therese, Eric Sylvester. Admitted to Minn. bar, 1931, Wash. bar, 1949, Republic of Korea bar, 1954, D.C. bar, 1962; asso. Ewing & Lehmann, St. Paul, 1931-33, Harold E. Stassen, Elmer J. Ryan, Farmington, Minn., 1933-34, mem. firm Stassen, Olson, Kelly & LeVander, South St. Paul, Minn., 1935-39; asst. county atty., Dakota County, Minn., 1933-39; dep. chief counsel Dept. Rural Credit Minn., 1939-42; chief counsel div. adminstrv. mgmt., Minn., 1942-43, atty. and pub. relations counsel Minn., 1944-48; mem. firm Brown, Olson & Clarke, Yakima, Wash.; asso. counsel Graves, Kizer & Graves, Spokane, 1949-54; legal cons. UN Econ. Coordinator, Korea, 1954; minister embassy, dir. U.S. Operations Mission to Portugal, FOA, 1954-55; dep. dir. U.S. Operations Mission, ICA, also attached Am. Embassy, Tokyo, Japan, 1956-58; asst. dir. office Territories, Dept. Interior, 1959-61; practiced in Washington, 1962-66; program adviser Fed. Water Pollution Control Adminstrn., 1967-68; dir. enforcement div. EPA, 1969-76, spl. asst. dir. water enforcement, 1976-77. Pres. Wells Olson Co., Herman, 1946-78; dir. Pacific N.W., Trans-N.W. Gas, Inc., 1951-55. Chmn. Citation Crusade for Freedom, Central Wash., 1951. Mem. Yakima C. of C. (dir. 1951-53). Fed., Wash., Minn., D.C. bar assns., Tau Kappa Epsilon, Phi Alpha Delta. Home: Route 6 Box 679-M Fairview NC 28730

OLSON, THEODORE ALEXANDER, educator; b. Oakes, N.D., Sept. 12, 1904; s. Henry Martin and Anna R. (Anderson) O.; B.S., U. Minn., 1926; M.A., Harvard, 1938, Ph.D., 1958; m. Grace Myrtle Lundberg, Jan. 5, 1929; children—Theodore A., R. Thomas, Robert C. Econ. entomologist U. Wis., 1926; instr. entomology U. Minn., 1926-28, prof. environmental biology Sch. Pub. Health, 1938—; biologist Minn. Dept. Health, 1928-38. Cons. health depts. Minn., N.Y., Wash., Ohio River Valley Sanitation Commn., WHO, Norwegian Inst. Water Research, NIH; participant internat. study rodent control, Europe, Mid East, Pacific WHO, 1965, Internat. Conf., Munich, 1966. Served from 1st lt to lt. col. San. Corps, AUS, 1942-46. Rockefeller fellow, 1947, WHO fellow, Caribbean, 1955, USPHS fellow, N. Europe, 1962. Mem. AAAS, Am. Pub. Health Assn. (sect. vice chmn., chmn. lab. sect., governing council 1960-70), Am. Soc. Limnology and Oceanography, Am. Micros. Soc., Entomol. Soc. Am., State and Territorial Lab. Dirs. Assn., Sigma Xi, Internat. Assn. Great Lakes Research (dir., pres. 1968—). Clubs: University Minnesota, Harvard. Author 1 book and over 100 profl. publs.; research on basic limnology of Lake Superior. Home: 4752 16th Ave S Minneapolis MN 55407

OLSON, WALLACE EARL, assn. exec.; b. LaCrosse, Wis., May 14, 1921; s. Emil Gustav and Anna Dagne (Sather) O.; Ph.B., U. Wis., 1943; m. Kathryn Louise Schenck, Jan. 2, 1942; children—Steven Paul, Richard Alan, Jane Ellen Olson Affeldt, Ellen Ann. With Alexander Grant & Co., C.P.A.'s., 1946-72, mng. partner, Chgo., 1961-66, exec. partner, 1967-72; exec. v.p. Am. Inst. C.P.A.'s., N.Y.C., 1972-73, pres., 1974—, chmn. div. profl. ethics, 1970-72. Served with U.S. Mcht. Marine, 1943-44, to lt. j.g. USNR, 1944-46. Mem. Am. Acctg. Assn. Clubs: University, Board Room (N.Y.C.). Office: Am Inst CPA's 1211 Ave of Americas New York NY 10036*

OLSON, WALTER, coll. pres. b. Yakima, Wash., May 16, 1924; s. Alvin Walter and Lillian (Johnson) O.; B.A., U. Wash., 1947, postgrad., 1949-50; M.A., Coll. Puget Sound, 1949; postgrad. Stanford, 1950-51; Ph.D., Syracuse U., 1956; m. Jean McCrea, Feb. 2, 1957; children—Karen Anne, Marc William, Linda Kristine. Vis. prof., acad. intern Ellis L. Phillips Found., U. Wis.-Madison, 1962-63; asst. to pres. Mills Coll., Oakland, Calif., 1964-66; prof. geography San Francisco State Coll., 1955-70, asst. div. chmn. social sci., 1959-60, chmn. dept., 1966-70; dean of arts and scis. Western Ill. U. at Macomb, 1970-75 pres. Calif. State Coll., Stanislaus, 1975—. Dir., grantee NDEA Inst. in Geography, Fresno State Coll. Center, Bakersfield, Cal., summer 1966, 67. Served with USNR, 1943-46. Mem. Assn. Am. Geographers, Calif. Council of Geographers, Phi Kappa Phi, Phi Delta Kappa, Pi Gamma Mu, Beta Theta Pi. Clubs: Tiburon Peninsula (dir. 1968-70, pres. 1970). Contbr. articles to profl. jours. Office: Calif State College Stanislaus Turlock CA 95380

OLSON, WALTER THEODORE, govt. ofcl.; b. Royal Oak, Mich., July 4, 1917; s. Oscar Thomas and Edith Margaret (Ketcham) O.; A.B., DePauw U., 1939; M.S., Case Inst. Tech., 1940, Ph.D., 1942; m. Ruth Elisabeth Barker, Oct. 28, 1943; 1 son, David Paul. Instr., Case Inst. Tech., 1941-42; research scientist Lewis Research Center, NASA, Cleve.,1942-45, chief combustion br., 1945-50, chief chemistry and energy conversion research div., 1950-63, asst. dir. Lewis Research Center, 1963-72, dir. tech. utilization and public affairs, 1972—; mem. numerous govt. adv. coms. Vice chmn. United Appeal Greater Cleve., 1965-73; chmn. legis. affairs Ohio Assn. Gifted Children, 1969-76; trustee Blue Cross N.E. Ohio, 1972—; chmn. industry adv. com. Coll. Engrs., Cleve. State U., 1975-76. Recipient Career Service award Greater Cleve. Growth Assn., 1972. Fellow AIAA (dir. 1969-75, Disting. Service award Cleve.-Akron sect. 1966, 75); mem. Combustion Inst. (dir. 1954—), Am. Chem. Soc., Sigma Xi, Phi Gamma Delta. Methodist. Clubs: Cosmos (Washington). Editor: (with W.R. Hawthorne) Design and Performance of Gas Turbine Power Plants, 1960; editorial bd. Combustion and Flame, 1955-65; contbr. articles to profl. jours.; patentee in field. Home: 18960 Coffinberry Blvd Fairview Park OH 44126 Office: 21000 Brookpark Rd Cleveland OH 44135

OLSON, WILLIAM CLINTON, univ. adminstr.; b. Denver, Aug. 19, 1920; s. Albert Merrill and Frances (Murray) O.; A.B. (Outstanding Sr. award), U. Denver, 1942; M.A., Yale U., 1951, Ph.D., 1953, m. Mary Elizabeth Matthews, Aug. 16, 1943; children—Jon Eric, Peter Murray, Elizabeth Ann. Staff officer Social Sci. Found., Denver, 1947-49; asst. prof., then asso. prof. govt. Pomona Coll. and Claremont Grad. Sch., 1953-61; sr. mem. St. Antonys Coll., Oxford (Eng.) U., 1959-60; chief fgn. affairs div., legis. reference service Library of Congress, 1961-65; vis. prof. Columbia U., 1964-65, 69-70, asso. dean Sch. Internat. Affairs, also research asso. Inst. War and Peace Studies, 1965-67; asso. dir. for social scis. Rockefeller Found., N.Y.C., 1967-79, prof., dean Sch. Internat. Service, Am. U., Washington, 1979—; lectr.-in-residence U. Redlands, 1968; dir. Bellagio Study and Conf. Center, The Villa Serbelloni, Italy, 1970-79; mem. adv. group Center for Congress and Presdl. Studies; lectr. internat. politics Sch. Advanced Internat. Studies, Johns Hopkins U., 1962-64; vis. prof. Bologna (Italy) Center, 1973-75; disting. vis. prof. Am. U. of Cairo, 1971; prof. Grad. Inst. Internat. Studies, Geneva, Switzerland, part-time 1976-78; Faculty lectr. NATO Def. Coll., Rome, 1977-79; vis. fellow Clare Hall, Cambridge, 1979; mem. U.S. del. Conf. Univ. Teaching Internat. Relations, Paris, France, 1960. Trustee Expt. in Internat. Living, 1959-65, chmn. advisory council, 1965-70; trustee Social Sci. Found. and Grad. Sch. Internat. Studies, U. Denver, 1968-76. Signer Declaration of Atlantic Unity, 1968. Pres. Am. Friends Wilton Park, Inc., 1967-68, chmn. bd. trustees, 1968-69. Served to capt. U.S. Army, 1942-47; ETO. Mem. Council Fgn. Relations, Washington Inst. Fgn. Affairs, Royal Inst. Internat. Affairs (fgn. asso. London), Internat. Inst. Strategic Studies, Istituto Affari Internazionale (Rome), Internat. Studies Assn. (nat. pres. 1968-69), Phi Beta Kappa (pres. Gamma of Calif. 1957-58). Clubs: Cosmos (Washington); Century Assn. (N.Y.C.); Chanctonbury Ring (Steyning). Co-author, editor: The Theory and Practice of International Relations, 4th edit., 1974; contbr.: The Aberystwyth Papers, 1972. Lectr. on Congress and fgn. policy, 14 countries. Office: Am U Massachusetts and Nebraska Aves NW Washington DC 20016

OLSSON, CARL ALFRED, urologist; b. Boston, Nov. 29, 1938; s. Charles Rudolph and Ruth Marion (Bostrom) O.; grad. Bowdoin Coll., 1959; M.D., Boston U., 1963; m. Mary DeVore, Nov. 4, 1962; children—Ingrid, Leif Eric. Asst. prof. urology Boston U. Sch. Medicine, 1971-72, asso. prof., 1972-74, prof., chmn. dept., 1974—; dir. urology dept. Boston City Hosp., 1974-77; chief urology dept. Boston VA Med. Center, 1971-75; urologist-in-chief Univ. Hosp., Boston, 1971—; lectr. surgery Tufts U. Sch. Medicine. Diplomate Am. Bd. Urology. Fellow A.C.S.; mem. Am. Urol. Assn. (coordinator continuing med. edn. New Eng. sect. 1977—), Boston Surg. Soc. (exec. com. 1976—), Am. Assn. Clin. Urologists, Am. Assn. Genitourinary Surgeons, Am. Fertility Soc., AMA, Assn. Acad. Surgery, Am. Soc. Artificial Internal Organs, Am. Soc. Transplant Surgeons, Assn. Med. Colls., Internat. Urodynamics Soc., Mass. Med. Soc., Soc. Govt. Urologists, Soc. Univ. Urologists, Alpha Omega Alpha. Episcopalian. Clubs: U.S. Yacht Racing Union, Yacht Racing Union Massachusetts Bay, Cottage Park Yacht. Contbr. chpts. to books, articles to med. jours. Home: 240 Highland Ave Newton MA 02165 Office: 75 E Newton St Boston MA 02118

OLSSON, HARRY ENOCH, mgmt. cons.; b. Camden, N.J., Nov. 19, 1919; s. Harry Enoch and Margaret (Fleming) O.; student Drexel Inst. Tech., 1944-45; m. Linda Eppinger, Jan. 6, 1945; children—Carl Alan, Maralyn Jean, Eric David. With Dennison's Foods, 1946-54, gen. mgr., 1951-54; asst. to exec. v.p. Pacific Can Co., 1954-55; prodn. mgr. Leslie Salt Co., 1955-58, v.p. prodn., 1958-59, exec. v.p., 1959-67; mgmt. cons., 1967-69; exec. v.p. Allied Properties, San Francisco, 1969-77; mgmt. cons., 1977-78; v.p. property adminstrn. San Francisco Real Estate Investors, 1978—. Home: 2422 Abaca Way Fremont CA 94538

OLSSON, NILS WILLIAM, assn. exec.; b. Seattle, June 11, 1909; s. Nils A. and Mathilda (Lejkell) O.; student North Park Coll., Chgo., Northwestern U., U. Minn., 1929-34; A.M., U. Chgo., 1938, Ph.D., 1949; Ph.D., U. Uppsala (Sweden), 1968; m. Dagmar T. Gavert, June 15, 1940; children—Karna B. (Mrs. Paul Carlson), Nils G. and Pehr C. (twins). Admissions counselor, instr. Swedish, North Park Coll., 1937-39; asst. Scandinavian U. Chgo., 1939-42, instr., 1945-50, asst. prof., 1950; exec. sec. Swedish Pioneer Centennial Assn., 1947-48; mem. U.S. diplomatic service, 1950-67; 2d sec., pub. affairs officer Am. legation, Reykjavik, Iceland, 1950-52; attache, pub. affairs officer Am. embassy, Stockholm, Sweden, 1952-55, 1st. sec., consul, 1955-57; pub. affairs adviser Dept. State, 1957-59, chief Am. sponsored schs. abroad, 1959-62; 1st sec. Am. embassy, Oslo, Norway, 1962-64, counselor for polit. affairs, 1964-66; diplomat in residence Ind. U., 1966-67; dir. Am. Swedish Inst., Mpls., 1967-73; exec. dir. Swedish Council of Am., 1973—. Mem. bd. Evang. Covenant Hist. Commn., Chgo., 1958. Served from lt. (j.g.) to lt. comdr., USNR, 1942-45; asst. naval attache Am. legation, Stockholm, 1943-45. Decorated knight Order Vasa 1st class, knight comdr. Order North Star (Sweden); recipient Swedish Pioneer Centennial medal, 1948; King Carl XVI Gustaf Bicentennial Gold medal; named Swedish Am. of Year, Stockholm, 1969. Fellow Geneal. Soc. (Finland), Geneal. Soc. (Sweden), Am. Soc. Genealogists; mem. Nat. Geneal. Soc., Swedish Pioneer Hist. Soc. (exec. sec. 1949-50, 57-68); fgn. corr. mem. Royal Acad. Belles Lettres, History and Antiquities (Sweden); hon. mem. Pro Fide et Christianismo (Sweden); fgn. mem. Royal Soc. Pub. Manuscripts Dealing with Scandinavian History (Sweden). Clubs: Skylight (Mpls.); Grolier (N.Y.C.); Cosmos (Washington); Explorers (Central Fla.). Author: Swedish Passenger Arrivals in New York 1820-1850, 1967; Swedish Passenger Arrivals in U.S. Ports (except New York) 1820-1850, 1979; Tracing Your Swedish Ancestry, 1974. Editor: A Pioneer in Northwest America, 1841-1858, vol. I, 1950, vol. II, 1959. Contbr. hist. and ednl. jours. Home: 662 Granville Dr Winter Park FL 32789 Office 2600 Park Ave Minneapolis MN 55407

OLSSON, STURE GORDON, mfg. exec.; b. Richmond, Va., July 1, 1920; s. Elis and Signe (Granberg) O.; B.S., U. Va., 1942; m. Anne Shirley Carter, June 8, 1957; children—Lisa Maria, Anne Carter, Inga Maja, Charles Elis. Service engr. Sperry Gyroscope Co., Inc., 1943-44; plant engr. Chesapeake Corp. Va., 1946-51, v.p. charge mfg., 1952, exec. v.p., gen. mgr., 1952, pres., dir., 1952-68, chmn. bd., 1968—; dir. Greenlife Products Co., United Va. Bankshares, Citizens & Farmers Bank, Chesapeake Bay Plywood. Mem. Business-Industry Polit. Action Com.; dir. Am. Paper Inst. Bd. dirs. Va. Forests Ednl. Fund; trustee West Point Armory and Recreation Center, St. Margaret's Sch.; sponsor Ducks Unlimited. Served as lt. (j.g.), USNR, 1944-46. Decorated Swedish Royal Order North Star. Mem. Va. Mfrs. Assn. (exec. com., past pres.), Am. Legion, Am. Horse Council, Raven Soc. of U. Va. Clubs: Capitol Hill (Washington); West Point Country. Country of Virginia, Commonwealth. Home: Romancoke West Point VA 23181 Office: Chesapeake Corp of Va West Point VA 23181

OLSTAD, ROGER GALE, coll. dean; b. Mpls., Jan. 16, 1934; s. Arnold William and Myra (Stroschein) O.; B.S., U. Minn., 1955, M.A., 1959, Ph.D., 1963; m. Constance Elizabeth Jackson, Aug. 20, 1955; children—Karen Louise, Kenneth Bradley. Instr., U. Minn., Mpls., 1956-63; asst. prof. U. Ill., Urbana, 1963-64; mem. faculty U. Wash., Seattle, 1964—, asso. prof. sci. edn., 1967-71, prof., 1971—, asso. dean grad. studies Coll. of Edn., 1969—. Fellow AAAS; mem. Nat. (dir.), Wash. (pres. 1973-74) sci. tchrs. assns., Nat. Assn. Research Sci. Teaching (pres. 1977-78, dir.), N.W. Sci. Assn. (chmn. 1966-68), Assn. Edn. Tchrs. in Sci. (regional pres. 1966-68), Nat. Assn. Biology Tchrs., Phi Delta Kappa. Club: U. Wash. Faculty. Home: 20143 53d Ave NE Seattle WA 98155 Office: U Wash Coll of Edn Seattle WA 98195

OLTON, ROY, educator; b. Richmond Hill, N.Y., Aug. 4, 1922; s. Bertrand Fitzroy and Miriam (Knies) O.; B.A., Ohio Wesleyan U., 1947; M.A., Fletcher Sch. Law and Diplomacy, 1948, Ph.D., 1954; m. Priscilla June Smith, Sept. 17, 1946; children—Bertrand Lee, Leslie Miriam. Instr. Mass. Inst. Tech., 1951-54, asst. prof., 1954-57; asst. prof. Western Mich. U., 1957-61, asso. prof., 1961-65, prof., 1965—, chmn. dept. polit. sci., 1969-79. Served with AUS, 1943-46. Mem. Am., Midwest, Mich. polit. sci. assns., Internat. Studies Assn. Author (with Jack C. Plano) The International Relations Dictionary, 1969, 2d rev. edit., 1979; Diccionario de los Relationes Internales, 1971; (with Jack C. Plano, Milton Greenberg, Robert Riggs) Political Science Dictionary, 1973. Office: Dept Polit Sci Western Mich U Kalamazoo MI 49008

OLUM, PAUL, mathematician, univ. adminstr.; b. Binghamton, N.Y., Aug. 16, 1918; s. Jacob and Rose (Citlen) O.; A.B. summa cum laude, Harvard, 1940, Ph.D. (NRC predoctoral fellow 1946-47), 1947; M.A., Princeton, 1942; m. Vivian Goldstein, June 8, 1942; children—Judith Ann, Joyce Margaret, Kenneth Daniel. Theoretical physicist Manhattan Project, Princeton, 1941-42, Los Alamos Sci. Lab., 1943-45; Frank B. Jewett postdoctoral fellow Harvard, 1947-48, Inst. Advanced Study, 1948-49; mem. faculty Cornell U., Ithaca, N.Y., 1949-74, prof. math., 1957-74, chmn. dept. 1963-66, trustee, 1971-75; prof. math., dean Coll. Natural Scis. U. Tex. at Austin, 1974-76; prof. math., v.p. for acad. affairs, provost U. Oreg., Eugene, 1976—; mem. Inst. Advanced Study, 1955-56; on leave at U. Paris (France) and Hebrew U., Jerusalem, 1962-63. NSF fellow Stanford, 1966-67; vis. prof. U. Wash., 1970-71. Mem. adv. com. Office Ordnance Research, NRC, 1958-61. Mem. Am. Math. Soc., AAUP, Math Assn. Am., Phi Beta Kappa, Sigma Xi. Author monograph, research articles on algebraic topology. Office: Office of Provost U Oreg Eugene OR 97403

OLWIN, JOHN HURST, surgeon; b. Robinson, Ill., May 28, 1907; s. Charles Hurst and Etta (Campbell) O.; B.A., U. Ill., 1929; M.D., U. Chgo., 1934; m. Betty Smothers, Apr. 17, 1943; children—Holly Corinne, Barbara Hurst. Intern Presbyn. Hosp., Chgo., 1935-36, surg. resident, 1937-39; practice in Chgo., 1938—; attending surgeon Presbyn.-St. Luke's Hosp., Chgo., Skokie Valley Community Hosp.; clin. prof. surgery U. Ill. Coll. Medicine, 1959-71, Rush Med. Coll., 1970—. Dir. Growth Industry Shares, Inc. Bd. dirs. Vascular Disease Research Found., 1963—. Served to lt. col., M.C., AUS, 1940-46. Decorated Bronze Star. Diplomate Am. Bd. Surgery. Mem. AMA, Chgo., Western, Central surg. assns., Soc. Vascular Surgery (recorder 1960-66), Internat. Cardiovascular Soc., Internat. Surg. Soc. Episcopalian (warden). Contbr. numerous articles to profl. jours. Home: 1513 Forest Ave Evanston IL 60201 Office: One Concourse Plaza 4711 Golf Rd Skokie IL 60076

OLZMAN, SAUL, paper co. exec.; b. N.Y.C., Oct. 17, 1920; s. Samuel and Anna (Wagonstein) O.; B.B.A., Coll. City N.Y., 1941; m. Hazel Schwartz, July 4, 1971; children—Rona Olzman, William. With Uptown Paper Envelope Corp., N.Y.C., 1946-54, pres., 1955-61; founder Williamhouse-Regency Inc., N.Y.C., 1961, chmn. bd., 1961—, also chmn. exec. com., dir.; pres. Home Adv. Council, N.Y., 1970-71. Pres., N.Y. Friends for Hartke, 1970. Trustee Coll. City N.Y. Alumni Fund. Served to 1st lt. USAAF, 1941-46. Club: Paper (N.Y.C.). Home: 51 Bowers Ln Closter NJ 07624 Office: 28 W 23d St New York City NY 10010

O'MAHONEY, ROBERT M., govt. ofcl.; b. Indpls., Jan. 4, 1925; s. Joseph Francis and Evelyn (O'Connor) O'M.; B.S., Purdue U., 1948; J.D., Georgetown U., 1954; m. Mary C. Mitchell, Sept. 12, 1953; children-Terrance M., Patrick J., Mary E., Susan M., Sharon A. Admitted to D.C. and Ind. bar, 1954; asso. firm Ross McCord, Ice and Miller, Indpls., 1954-55; dep. atty. gen. Ind., 1954-59; gen. counsel Def. Air Transp. Adminstrn., 1959; dep. asst. gen. counsel for transp. Dept. Commerce 1959-66; adviser to dep. asst. sec. state for transp. and communications 1966-67; asst. gen. counsel Fed. Hwy. Adminstrn., 1968-69; commr. transp. and telecommunications service Gen. Service Adminstrn., 1969-73; transp. cons. EPA, 1973; atty. Fed. Power Commn., Washington, 1973-77, Fed. Energy Regulatory Commn., Washington, 1977—. Served with USAAF, 1943-45, USAF, 1950-52. Decorated Air medal with oak leaf cluster. Mem. Phi Alpha Delta. Republican. Roman Catholic. Co-author Great Lakes Pilotage Act, 1960. Home: 9108 Cherbourg Dr Potomac MD 20854 Office: Fed Energy Regulatory Commn 825 N Capitol St Washington DC 20426

O'MALLEY, BERT WILLIAM, physician, educator; b. Pitts., Dec. 19, 1936; s. Bert Aloysius and Rebecca Evelyn (Kennelly) O'M.; B.S., U. Pitts., 1959, M.D. summa cum laude, 1963; m. Sally Johnson, Aug. 20, 1960; children—Bert W., Sally, Rebecca, Erin K. Intern, resident Duke, 1963-65; clin. asso. Nat. Cancer Inst., NIH, 1965-67, head molecular biology sect. endocrine br., 1967-69; prof., occupant Lucius Birch chair of reproductive biology, dir. population center Vanderbilt Sch. Medicine, 1969-73; prof., chmn. dept. cell biology, dir. Baylor Center for Population Research and Reproductive Biology, Baylor Coll. Medicine, Houston, 1973—. Served with USPHS, 1965-68. Recipient Oppenheimer, Pincus, Gruber, Borden, Dickson prizes in medicine, others. Mem. Am. Soc. Biol. Chemists, Endocrine Soc., Am. Soc. Clin. Investigation, Am. Inst. Chemists, Am. Fedn. Clin. Research, AAAS. Mem. editorial bds. numerous med. jours. Contbr. numerous articles to med. jours. Research in molecular endocrinology, hormone action, regulatory and molecular biology.

Home: 639 Ramblewood Houston TX 77079 Office: 1200 Moursund Ave Houston TX 77030

O'MALLEY, CARLON MARTIN, JR., lawyer; b. Phila., Sept. 7, 1929; s. Carlon Martin and Lucy (Boland) O'M.; B.A., Pa. State U., 1951; LL.B., Temple U., 1954; m. Mary Catherine Lyons, Aug. 17, 1957; children—Carlon Martin III, Kathleen B., Harry Tighe, John Todd, Cara M. Admitted to Pa. Supreme Ct. bar, 1955, Fla. Supreme Ct. bar, 1973, U.S. Supreme Ct. bar, 1973; practiced law, 1957-61; asst. U.S. atty. for Middle Dist. Pa., Dept. Justice, 1961-69, U.S. atty., 1979—; mem. firm O'Malley, Jordan & Nullaney and predecessor firms, 1970-79. Pres. Lackawanna County (Pa.) unit Am. Cancer Soc., 1966-67; bd. dirs. Pa. Cancer Soc., 1967-68, Lackawanna County chpt. ARC, 1967-69; mem. solicitation team, govtl. div. Lackawanna United Fund, 1963-68; chmn. profl. div. Greater Scranton (Pa.) YMCA Membership Drives. Served with USAF, 1955-57. Lic. real estate broker, Pa. Mem. Am. Bar Assn., Pa. Bar Assn., Lackawanna County Bar Assn., Fla. Bar Assn., Phi Kappa, Phi Delta Phi. Democrat. Roman Catholic. Clubs: Country of Scranton, Elks (pres. Pa. Elks State Assn. 1978-79), K.C. Editorial bd. Temple Law Rev., 1952-53. Office: US Atty's Office PO Bldg Scranton PA 18501

O'MALLEY, JAMES, JR., lawyer; b. N.Y.C., Aug. 13, 1910; s. James and Charlotte (Bigelow) O'M.; A.B., Princeton, 1932; LL.B., Harvard, 1935; m. Marcella Butler, Feb. 14, 1942; children—Malcolm Butler, Marcella Anne Bigelow. Admitted to N.Y. bar, 1936; asso. firm Root, Clark, Buckner and Ballantine, N.Y.C., 1935-38; dep. asst. dist. atty. N.Y. County under Thomas E. Dewey, 1938-42; asso. firm LeBoeuf, Lamb, Leiby & MacRae, N.Y.C., 1945-46, partner, 1947-65, sr. partner, 1965—; spl. asst. to U.S. atty. gen. for SSS hearings, 1953-55; counsel Gov. N.Y. Adv. Com. Atomic Energy, 1956-58. Dir. AGIP-USA, Inc., Pignone, Inc., Snam Progetti-USA, Inc., 1968-72; pres. 943 Lexington Ave. Corp., 1975—. Mem. N.Y. Waterfront Commn., N.Y. Harbor, 1959-61. Mem. Greater N.Y. council Boy Scouts Am., 1956—. Served to lt. comdr. USNR, 1941-45. Mem. Fed. Power (pres. 1957-58), N.Y. State (chmn. atomic energy law com. 1956-63), Am. (chmn. gas and electric law com. 1955-56) bar assns., N.Y. Law Inst. (3d v.p. 1976—), Assn. Bar City N.Y. (exec. com. 1953-56, vice chmn. grievance com. 1964-67), ICC Practitioners Assn., Dewey Assos. (sec. 1977—), Phi Beta Kappa. Republican. Roman Cath. Clubs: Cloister Inn (Princeton, N.J.); Lincoln's Inn Soc. (Cambridge, Mass.); Down Town Assn., Princeton (N.Y.C.). Home: 131 E 69th St New York NY 10021 Office: 140 Broadway New York NY 10005

O'MALLEY, JEROME FRANCIS, air force officer; b. Carbondale, Pa., Feb. 25, 1932; s. James Francis and Mabel (McNulty) O'M.; B.S., U.S. Mil. Acad.; M.B.A., George Washington U., 1965; postgrad. Air Command and Staff Coll., 1965, Naval War Coll., 1970; m. Diane Muennink, Apr. 16, 1955; children—Margaret Anne O'Malley Neal, Sharon Kay, James Francis, John Thomas. Commd. in U.S. Air Force, advanced through grades to maj. gen., 1977; comdr. 9th Strategic Wing, Beale AFB, Calif., 1972-73; comdr. 22d Bomb Wing, March AFB, Calif., 1973-74; asst. dep. chief of staff plans, dep. chief of staff ops. plans, Hdqrs. SAC, 1974-77; vice dir. ops. office Joint Chiefs of Staff, Washington, 1977-79; asst. dep. chief of staff ops. plans and readiness U.S. Air Force, Washington, 1977—. Decorated D.S.M., Legion of Merit, D.F.S. with 1 oak leaf cluster, Air medal with 9 oak leaf clusters, others. Home: 65 Westover Ave Bolling AFB Washington DC 20336 Office: HQ USAF AF/XO Pentagon Washington DC 20330

O'MALLEY, JOHN DANIEL, educator; b. Chgo., Dec. 18, 1926; s. William D. and Paula A. (Skaugh) O'M.; grad. St. Thomas Mil. Acad., 1945; B.S., Loyola U., Chgo., 1950, M.A., 1952, J.D., 1953; grad. U.S. Army Intelligence Sch., 1962, Command & Gen. Staff Coll., 1965; m. Caroline Tyler Taylor, July 12, 1958; children—John Daniel, Taylor John. Admitted to Ill. bar, 1953, Mich. bar, 1954; U.S. Supreme Ct., 1962. Asst. prof. law Loyola U., 1953-59, asso. prof., 1959-65; formerly spl. counsel and bond claims mgr. Fed. Ins. Co.; prof. law Loyola U. Grad. Sch. Bus., 1965—, chmn. dept. law, 1968—; trust officer, v.p. First Nat. Bank Highland Park (Ill.), Marina City Bank, Chgo., Hyde Park Bank & Trust Co., 1970-75; sr. v.p. 1st Nat. Bank of Winnetka (Ill.), 1975—; pres. Manor House Antiques, Inc., Kenilworth, Ill., 1975—. Chmn. athletic bd. Loyola U. Served to maj. AUS, 1945-47, 61-62. Mem. Am., Chgo., Ill., Mich. bar assns., French Nat. Hon. Soc., Am., Chgo. bus. law assns., Chgo. Surety Assn., Mil. Govt. Assn., Alpha Kappa Psi, Phi Alpha Delta. Author: Subrogation Against Banks on Forged Checks, 1967; Common Check Frauds and the Uniform Commercial Code, 1969. Contbr. articles to profl. jours. and law revs. Home 1040 Chestnut St Wilmette IL 60091 Office: 820 N Michigan Ave Chicago IL 60611

O'MALLEY, JOHN G., JR., lumber co. exec.; b. Phoenix, Apr. 30, 1914; s. John G. and Mary (Corrigan) O'M.; B.C.S. cum laude, U. Notre Dame, 1936; m. Geraldine Dickmann, Oct. 24, 1946; children—Mark Edward, Susan Louise. Engaged in retail lumber bus., 1936-42; a founder Mallco Distbrs., 1946, mgr., 1946-67, dir.; pres. O'Malley Lumber Co., Phoenix, 1967—, also dir.; dir. O'Malley Investment Co., Standard Credit Corp., O'Malley Investment & Realty Co. Past chmn. Phoenix U.S.O., mem. nat. council, 1962-64. Past bd. dirs. Heard Mus. Phoenix; mem. exec. com. Maricopa County Gen. Hosp., 1967-73; past mem. Newman Found., Ariz. State U.; mem. adv. Council Nat. Multiple Sclerosis Soc.; bd. regents Phoenix Catholic High Sch., 1969-71; bd. dirs. Brophy Prep. Sch., 1972—; mem. Phoenix adv. bd. Salvation Army, 1977—; mem. Goodwill Industries, Ariz. Acad. Town Hall. Served with AUS, 1942-45. Mem. Phoenix C. of C., Assn. U.S. Army (bd. govs.), Am. Legion, Phoenix Execs. Club, Am. Mgmt. Assn. (pres.'s assn.). Roman Catholic. K.C., Kiwanian. Clubs: Phoenix Country, Kiva (Phoenix). Home: 41 E Country Club Dr Phoenix AZ 85014 Office: PO Box 3558 Phoenix AZ 85030

O'MALLEY, PATRICK LAWRENCE, corp. exec.; b. Boston, Jan. 2, 1911; s. Matthias and Bridget (Sweeney) O'M; student Harvard, 1930-31; hon. degrees St. Joseph Coll., Mundelein Coll., St. Procopius Coll., Bryant Coll.; m. Helen Lee, Oct. 29, 1933; 1 son, Patrick Lawrence. With Employers Liability Assurance Co., 1930, Western Electric Co., 1931; salesman Coca-Cola Bottling Co., Boston, 1932-35, mgr., 1935-42; tech. observer Coca-Cola Export Corp., 1942-45; with Coca-Cola Bottling Co., Stamford, Conn. 1946-48. Oshkosh, Wis., 1948-52, v.p., then pres. Chgo., 1952-60; v.p. nat. sales Coca Cola Co., Atlanta, 1960-62; chmn., dir., chief exec. officer Canteen Corp. (formerly Automatic Canteen Co. Am.), Chgo., 1962—; chmn., dir. Casualty Ins. Co., Michigan Ave. Nat. Bank; dir. Transworld Airlines, Stone Container Corp., Del Webb Corp. Bd. dirs. Better Bus. Bur. Chgo., Chgo. Conv. and Tourism Bur., Regional Transp. Authority; trustee Roosevelt U., Mundelein Coll., Chgo.; mem. adv. council Coll. Bus. Adminstrn. U. Notre Dame; chmn. exec. adv. bd. St. Joseph Hosp., Chgo.; pres. Chgo. Park Dist. Recipient outstanding bus. award Oshkosh Jr. C. of C., 1950; Horatio Alger award; Great Am. award B'nai B'rith; Golden Plate award Am. Acad. Achievement, others. Mem. Nat. Inst. Food Service Industry (past pres.), Nat. Restaurant Assn. (past pres.), Ill. Coca Cola Bottlers Assn. (pres.), Chgo. Sales Marketing Execs. (pres. 1960), Quincy (Mass.) C. of C. (v.p.), Atlantic Council of U.S. (dir.). Elk, K.C. Clubs: Beverly Country (Chgo); Oshkosh Rotary (pres. 1952). Home: 229 E Lake Shore Dr Chicago IL 60611 Office: 1430 Merchandise Mart Chicago IL 60654

O'MALLEY, PAUL W., wire co. exec.; b. Susquehanna, Pa., Aug. 29, 1929; B.S., Pa. State U., 1942: LL.B., U. Mich., 1952; m. Marcella S. Mauer, Feb. 1, 1947; children—Ann J. (Mrs. Jack Craig), Jane F. (Mrs. A. Kluczkowski), Paul W., Kevin J. Various engring. positions, Pa., to 1952; admitted to Mich. bar, 1952, Ind. bar; atty. Essex Internat. Inc. (formerly Wire Corp.), Detroit, dir. engring., Ft. Wayne, Ind., 1952-58, head wire and cable div., 1958-62, dir., 1962-74, pres., 1966-74, chmn. bd., chief exec. officer, pres. Essex subsidiary United Aircraft Corp., 1975—, group v.p. United Techs., mem. operational and policy com., dir. parent co., 1974—; dir. Tecumseh Products Co. (Mich.), Detroit Bank Corp., Detroit Bank & Trust Co., Lincoln Fin. Corp., Ft. Wayne, Lincoln Nat. Bank & Trust Co., Ft. Wayne. Regional dir. Nat. Alliance of Businessmen, Ft. Wayne, 1975. Served with U.S. Army, World War II. Office: Essex Internat Inc 1601 Wall St Fort Wayne IN 46804*

O'MALLEY, PETER, profl. baseball club exec.; b. N.Y.C., Dec. 12, 1937; s. Walter F. and Kay (Hanson) O'M.; B.S. in Econs., U. Pa., 1960; m. Annette Zacho, July 10, 1971; children—Katherine, Kevin, Brian. Dir. Dodgertown, Vero Beach, Fla., 1962-64; pres., gen. mgr. Spokane Baseball Club, 1965-66; v.p. Los Angeles Dodgers Baseball Club, 1967-68, exec. v.p., 1968—; pres. Los Angeles Dodgers, Inc., 1970—; dir. Union Oil Co.; dir. Bank of Am. Bd. dirs. Los Angeles Central City, Los Angeles Police Meml. Found.; bd. govs. Los Angeles Music Center Performing Arts Council. Home: 1000 Elysian Park Ave Los Angeles CA 90012 Office: Dodger Stadium 1000 Elysian Park Ave Los Angeles CA 90012

O'MALLEY, THOMAS PATRICK, coll. pres.; b. Milton, Mass., Mar. 1, 1930; s. Austin and Ann Marie (Feeney) O'M.; B.A., Boston Coll., 1951; M.A., Fordham U., 1953; S.T.L., Coll. St.-Albert de Louvain, 1962; D.Litt., U. Nijmegen, 1967. Instr. classics Coll. of Holy Cross, Worcester, Mass., 1956-58; asst. prof., chmn. dept. classics Boston Coll., 1967-69, asso. prof., chmn. dept. theology, 1969-73, dean Coll. Arts and Scis., 1973-80; pres. John Carroll U., Cleve., 1980—. Trustee, Boston Theol. Inst., 1969-73, Fairfield U., 1971—, John Carroll U., 1974—. Mem. A.A.U.P., Soc. Bibl. Lit., N.Am. Patristic Soc. Author: Tertullian and the Bible, 1967. Office: John Carroll U University Hts Cleveland OH 44118

OMAN, CLIFFORD EDWARD, chem. co. exec.; b. Chisholm, Minn., Dec. 23, 1918; s. Clifford Leonard and Myrtle Agnes (Anderson) O.; B.Chem. Engring., U. Minn., 1940; postgrad. sr. exec. program Mass. Inst. Tech., 1959; m. Phyllis Jocelyn Swanson, Sept. 18, 1942; children—Judith Oman Sneed, Bruce Edward. With Elgin Softener Corp., 1940, Atlas Powder Co., Tamaqua, Pa., 1940-43, Shell Oil Co., Wood River, Ill., 1943-51; with Nat. Distillers & Chem. Corp., N.Y.C., 1951—, gen. mgr. chem. div., 1972—, also dir.; pres. Emery Industries, 1978—; dir. Nat. Helium Corp., Nat. PetroChemicals Corp., USI Far East Corp., United Polymers Corp. Mem. Am. Inst. Chem. Engrs., Soc. Plastics Industries, Mfg. Chemists Assn. (co. rep.), Nat. Petroleum Refiners Assn. (co. rep.). Home: 1008 Sturges Hwy Westport CT 06880 Office: 99 Park Ave New York NY 10016

OMAN, LAFEL EARL, former chief justice N.Mex. Supreme Ct.; b. Price, Utah, May 7, 1912; s. Earl Andrew and Mabel (Larsen) O.; J.D., U. Utah, 1936; m. Arlie Edna Giles, June 3, 1936; children—Sharon O. Beck, Phyllis O. Bowman, Conrad LaFel, Kester LaFel. Admitted to Utah bar, 1936, N.Mex. bar, 1947; practiced law in Salt Lake City and Helper, Utah, 1937-40, in Las Cruces, N.Mex., 1948-66; investigator, examiner CSC, Denver, 1941-43; with office chief atty. VA, Albuquerque, 1946-48; asst. city atty., Las Cruces, 1958-59; city atty. City of Truth or Consequences (N.Mex.), 1959-61; judge N.Mex. Ct. Appeals, Santa Fe, 1966-70; justice N.Mex. Supreme Ct., 1971-77, chief justice, 1976-77; mem. N.Mex. Jud. Standards Commn., 1968-70, 71-72; mem. N.Mex. Jud Council, 1972-77; mem. N.Mex. Bd. Bar Examiners; bd. dirs. N.Mex. Continuing Legal Edn., Inc. Bd. dirs. N.Mex. Soc. Crippled Children; active Boy Scouts Am., Girl Scouts U.S.A., Polio Found.; chmn. ofcl. bd. St. John's United Methodist Ch., Santa Fe. Served to lt. USNR, 1943-46. Mem. Am., Utah, N.Mex., Dona Ana County (N.Mex.) (pres. 1952-53), 1st Judicial Dist. bar assns., N.Mex., Santa Fe hist. socs., Santa Fe Opera Guild, Law-Sci. Acad., Def. Research Inst., Am. Trial Lawyers Assn., Inst. Jud. Adminstrn., Appellate Judges Conf., Nat. Legal Aid and Defender Assn., Am. Judicature Soc. (dir. 1970-74), Phi Alpha Delta. Club: Rotary (pres. Las Cruces club 1952-53, Santa Fe club 1976-77). Home: 510 Camino Pinones Santa Fe NM 87501. *Success depends upon the personal qualities of industry, initiative, integrity, intelligence, cooperativeness, compassion, loyalty and willingness to assume responsibility.*

OMAN, RICHARD HEER, lawyer; b. Columbus, Ohio, Jan. 4, 1926; s. B. R. Oman and Marguerite O. Andrews; B.A., Ohio State U., 1948, J.D., 1951; m. Jane Ellen Wert, Oct. 5, 1963; children—Sarah M., David W. Admitted to Ohio bar, 1951; atty. Ohio Nat. Bank, Columbus, 1951-55; partner firm Isaac, Postlewaite, O'Brien & Oman, Columbus, 1955-71; dir. Columbus Found., 1955-77; partner firm Porter, Wright, Morris and Arthur (and predecessor firm), Columbus, 1972—. Mem. Columbus Airport Commn., 1960-64; trustee Meml. Homes Found., Cin.; Grant Hosp., Harding Hosp., Columbus Symphony Orch., Franklin U., Fellow Ohio State Bar Found.; mem. Am. Bar Assn., Ohio State Bar Assn. (bd. govs. probate and trust law sect.), Columbus Bar Assn. Republican. Episcopalian. Clubs: Columbus, Rocky Fork Hunt and Country, Nantucket (Mass.) Yacht. Home: 195 S Parkview Ave Columbus OH 43209 Office: 37 W Broad St Columbus OH 43215

OMAN, WILLIAM MORSE, publishing co. exec.; b. N.Y.C., Dec 30, 1911; s. Joseph Wallace and Virginia Center (Morse) O.; student Trinity Sch., N.Y.C., 1921-30; A.B., Princeton U., 1934; m. Janet Lyle McMaster, Mar. 21, 1942 (div. July 1966); children—Charles, William Morse, Virginia; m. 2d, Janet Waters Weisman, June 14, 1968. Coll. rep. Oxford U. Press, N.Y.C., 1934-37, asst. mgr. coll. dept., 1937-41, mgr., editor coll. dept., 1941-48, v.p., 1948, v.p., editor in chief, 1949-55, v.p. charge ednl. depts., 1955-57; v.p., dir. Dodd, Mead, 1957-75; mem. adv. council dept. English, Princeton U., 1948-60; dir. Franklin Book Programs, Inc., 1962-67, treas., 1963-64. Chmn. Coll. Pubs. Group, 1947-48. Served as 2d lt. F.A., O.R.C., 1934-42; commd. lt. (j.g.), USNR, 1942, advanced through grades to lt. comdr.; asst. convoy officer, N.Y. Port Dir., 1942-44; convoy and routing officer Okinawa Invasion, 1945, Adm. Nimitz staff, 1945. Decorated Commendation ribbon with combat V. Clubs: Dutch Treat (N.Y.C.); Woodstock Country (Vt.) Home: Box 17 North Pomfret VT 05053

OMANG, JOANNE BRENDA, journalist; b. Seattle, Jan. 7, 1943; s. Boyd Ansel and Viola May (Streimikes) Omang; B.A., Sophie Newcomb Coll., Tulane U., 1964; student London Sch. Econs., 1962-63. Vol., Peace Corps, Gaziantep, Turkey, 1964-66; with U.P.I., Sioux Falls, S.D., 1967, reporter, Springfield, Mass., 1968, Boston, 1969-71; Congl. fellow Am. Polit. Sci. Assn., 1972; reporter Washington Post, 1973—, fgn. corr., Buenos Aires, Argentina, 1975-77. Urban Journalism fellow U. Chgo., 1971. Office: 1150 15th St NW Washington DC 20071

O'MARA, JOHN ALOYSIUS, bishop; b. Buffalo, Nov. 17, 1924; s. John Aloysius and Anna Theresa (Schenck) O'M.; student St. Augustine's Sem., Toronto, Ont., Can., 1944-51; J.C.L., St. Thomas U., Rome, 1953. Ordained priest Roman Cath. Ch., 1951; mem. chancery Archdiocese of Toronto, 1953-69; pres., rector St. Augustine's Sem., Toronto, 1969-75; pastor St. Lawrence Parish, Scorboro, Ont., 1975-76; bishop of Thunder Bay, Ont., 1976—; named hon. prelate of Papal Household with title monsignor, 1954. Bd. dirs. Ont. Hosp. Assn., 1961-65; mem. Ont. Hosp. Services Commn., 1964-69. Address: PO Box 113 Thunder Bay ON P7C 4V5 Canada

O'MARA, JOHN MOWBRAY, investment co. exec.; b. Cin., Aug. 8, 1927; s. John Thomas and Juanita Catherine (Mowbray) O'M.; grad. Hill Sch., 1945; A.B., Princeton, 1950; LL.B., U. Va., 1953; m. Margot Murray, June 15, 1962; children—Margot Courtney, Monique, Deirdre Mowbray. Asso., Waite, Schindel, Bayless & Schneider, Cin., 1954-57, partner, 1958-63; asso. W.E. Hutton & Co., N.Y.C., 1963-65, partner, 1965-74; 1st v.p. Merrill Lynch White Weld Capital Markets Group div. Merrill Lynch Pierce Fenner & Smith, Inc., N.Y.C., 1974—; dir. Fed. Nat. Mortgage Assn., Ariz.-Colo. Land & Cattle Co. Served with AUS, 1946-47; ETO. Clubs: Brook, Down Town Assn., Round Hill, Meadow, Bathing Corp. of Southampton. Home: 623 Lake Ave Greenwich CT 06830 Office: 1 Liberty Plaza New York City NY 10006

O'MARA, ROBERT EDMUND GEORGE, physician; b. Flushing, N.Y., Dec. 8, 1933; s. George Harold and Leonora (Potter) O'M.; B.S., U. Rochester, 1955; M.D., Albany Coll. Medicine, 1959; m. Brenda Mae Millard, Feb. 15, 1964; children—Robert, Susan, Bridget. Resident in radiology St. Vincent's Hosp., N.Y.C., 1963-66; fellow in nuclear medicine Upstate Med. Center SUNY, Syracuse, 1966-67, instr. radiology, 1967-68, asst. prof. radiology, 1968-71; asso. prof. radiology, dir. nuclear medicine U. Ariz., Tucson, 1971-74, prof., dir. nuclear medicine, 1974-75; prof. radiology, chief div. nuclear medicine U. Rochester Sch. Medicine and Dentistry, 1975—; med. dir. nuclear medicine tech. program Rochester Inst. Tech., 1976—. Pres., Clover Hills Assn., Rochester, N.Y., 1978-79; pres. Fruchtendler Parent Tchr. Assn., Tucson, 1974-75. Served with M.C., USAF, 1960-62. Diplomate Am. Bd. Radiology, Am. Bd. Nuclear Medicine. Mem. A.C.P. (pres. 1980), Am. Coll. Nuclear Physicians, Soc. Nuclear Medicine (Gold medal for sci. exhibit 1977) Am. Coll. Radiology, Radiol. Soc. N.Am., Assn. Univ. Radiologists. Contbr. articles to med. jours. Home: 611 Clover Hills Dr Rochester NY 14618

OMATA, ROBERT ROKURO, ofcl. NIH; b. Hanford, Calif., Nov. 3, 1920; s. George Jitsuzo and Kane (Okazaki) O.; A.B., U. Calif., Berkeley, 1944; M.S., U. Minn., 1946, Ph.D., 1949; m. Hiroko Kamikawa, Nov. 25, 1948; children—Douglas M., Roberta K., Donna R. Research asso. Nat. Inst. Dental Research, NIH, Bethesda, Md., 1949-53, research bacteriologist, 1953-60, exec. sec. career devel. rev. br., div. research grants, 1960-63, exec. sec. Office Internat. Research, 1963-64, asst. chief NIH Pacific office, Tokyo, 1964-67, head internat. fellowships sect., scholars and fellowships program br. Fogarty Internat. Center, Bethesda, 1967-74; internat. programs specialist Office Internat. Affairs Nat. Cancer Inst., Bethesda, 1974—; scientist USPHS, 1953, advanced through grades to scientist dir., 1963—. NIH research fellow, 1947-48; ADA postdoctoral fellow, 1949-53. Mem. Sigma Xi. Research in oral microbiology. Office: Nat Cancer Inst NIH Bethesda MD 20205

OMBERG, ARTHUR CHALMERS, telecommunications, electronic cons.; b. Memphis, Nov. 4, 1909; s. William and Katharin (Rogers) O.; B. Engring., Vanderbilt U., 1932, M.A. in Math., 1934, E.E., 1935; m. Helen Philips, Nov. 20, 1934; children—William F., A. Chalmers, Helen K. Ship operator Radio Marine Corp., 1928-29; transmitter supr. radio sta. WSM, 1932-42; cons. physicist Vanderbilt Hosp., Nashville, 1934-42; asst. dir. operations research group Signal Corps, U.S. Army, 1942-44; with Bendix Corp., 1944-65, gen. mgr. Bendix Products div., 1954-58, v.p., group exec. corp., 1961-65; v.p. McDonnell Aircraft Corp., 1965-67; dir. Office Telecommunications, Dept. Commerce, 1968-69. Mem. adv. bd. Vanderbilt U. Sch. Engring.; profl. asso. Nat. Acad. Engring., 1969-70. Registered profl. engr., Mo. Mem. Soc. of Cincinnati, Kappa Alpha. Home: 698 Timber Ln Nashville TN 37215

O'MEARA, EDWARD THOMAS, bishop; b. St. Louis, Aug. 3, 1921; s. John and Mary (Fogarty) O'M.; student Kenrick Sem., 1943-46; S.T.D., Angelicum U., Rome, 1953. Ordained priest Roman Catholic Ch., then became monseignor, ordained bishop, 1972; asst. pastor St. Louis Cathedral, 1952-55; asst. nat. dir. Soc. for Propagation of the Faith, 1956-60, dir. St. Louis area, 1960-67, nat. dir., N.Y.C., 1967-79; archbishop of Indpls., 1979—. Editor Mission mag., World mission mag. Home: Chancery Office 1350 N Pennsylvania St Indianapolis IN 46202*

O'MEARA, ONORATO TIMOTHY, mathematician; b. Cape Town, S. Africa, Jan. 29, 1928; s. Daniel and Fiorina (Allorto) O'M.; B. Sc., U. Cape Town, 1947, M.Sc., 1948; Ph.D., Princeton, 1953; m. Jean T. Fadden, Sept. 12, 1953; children—Maria, Timothy, Jean, Kathleen, Eileen. Came to U.S., 1957. Lectr., U. Otago, New Zealand, 1953-56; mem. Inst. for Advanced Study, Princeton, N.J., 1957-58, 62; asst. prof. Princeton, 1958-62; prof. math. U. Notre Dame, Ind., 1962-76, chmn. dept., 1965-66, 68-72, Kenna prof. math., 1976—, provost, 1978—; vis. prof. Calif. Inst. Tech., 1968; Gauss prof. Göttingen Acad. Sci., 1978; mem. adv. panel math. scis. NSF, 1974-77. Mem. Cath. Commn. Intellectual and Cultural Affairs, 1962—. Alfred P. Sloan fellow, 1960-63. Mem. Am. Math. Soc. Roman Catholic. Author: Introduction to Quadratic Forms, 1963, 71, 73; Lectures on Linear Groups, 1974, 2d edit., 1977, Russian transl., 1976; Symplectic Groups, 1978. Contbr. articles on arithmetic theory of quadratic forms and isomorphism theory of linear groups to Am. and European profl. jours. Home: 1227 E Irvington Ave South Bend IN 46614 Office: Dept Math Univ Notre Dame Notre Dame IN 46556

O'MELIA, DONALD C., lawyer; b. Rhinelander, Wis., May 24, 1917; s. Albert James and Eva (Hildebrand) O'M.; U. Notre Dame, 1939; LL.B., Marquette U., 1941; m. Margaret L. McDonald, June 7, 1937; children—Nora Ann (Mrs. Donald Bluhm), Michael John, Mary (Mrs. David Peterson), Patricia (Mrs. Louis E. Widule), Susan (Mrs. James Jankowski), Christine (Mrs. James Kasson), Donald C., Margaret (Mrs. David Gillis), Brian, David, Dennis. Admitted to Wis. bar; pvt. practice, 1941-43; dist. atty. Oneida County, 1943-49; now partner firm O'Melia Law Offices, Rhinelander, Dir., Martin Ins. Co., Heart of Lakes Savs. & Loan, Rhinelander Telephone Co. Mem. Gov.'s 1st Conf. Home and Family, Milw., 1966, Gov.'s Council Phys. Activity and Sports, 1965—; mem. Rhinelander High Sch. Bd. Edn., 1955-78, Oneida County Safety Com., Wis. Gov.'s Council on Phys. Fitness, 1968—; dist. chmn. Boy Scouts Am. Del. Republican Nat. Conv., 1960, Wis. Rep. Conv., 1944-73; chmn. Oneida Rep. Com.; state chmn. Lawyers for Nixon-Agnew, 1968; bd. dirs. St. Mary's Hosp., Wis. Judicare, Inc. Served with USMCR, 1937-41, AUS, 1944-45. Mem. Am. Judicature Soc., Wis. Bar Found., State Bar Wis.

(gov. 1960-64, exec. com. 1964-65, 66-67, pres. 1965-66; Spl. Merit award), Milw., Oneida County (past pres.) bar assns., Wis. Dist. Attys. Assn. (pres. 1946-47, sec.-treas. 1944-45), Wis. Acad. Trial Lawyers, Bar Assn. of 7th Fed. Circuit, Rhinelander C. of C. (dir.), Wis. Cancer Soc. (chmn. state legacy com. 1965-71), Am. Legion, Delta Theta Pi. K.C. (advocate), Eagle (trustee 1944-45), Lion. Clubs: Rhinelander Country (dir. 1956-57), Dilemma. Home: 203 Pleasant St Rhinelander WI 54501 Office: 4 S Stevens St Rhinelander WI 54501

O'MELVENY, JOHN, lawyer; b. Los Angeles, Dec. 1, 1894; s. Henry William and Marie Antoinette (Schilling) O'M.; A.B., U. Calif., 1918; J.D., Harvard, 1922; m. Alice Nilson, Sept. 16, 1967; children—Joan (Mrs. Mills), Patrick. Admitted to Calif. bar, 1922; asso. atty. firm O'Melveny, Millikin, Tuller & Macneil, 1922-23, partner, 1923-36; sr. partner successor firm O'Melveny & Myers, Los Angeles, 1939-75, of counsel, 1976—. Exec. v.p., dir. Crosby Investment Corp., Greenwich Corp.; dir. Security-Pacific Nat. Bank of Los Angeles, 1940-72. Life mem. adv. bd. Salvation Army; trustee, mem. exec. com. Calif. Inst. Tech., 1940-68, hon. life trustee, 1968—; chmn. budget and rev. com., dir., mem. exec. com. Los Angeles War Chest, 1942-46; dir. Legal Aid Found., Metabolic Found., Barlow Hosp. Guild. Los Angeles. Served as ensign, USNRF, 1918-19. Mem. Am., Calif., Los Angeles bar assns., Phi Beta Kappa, Psi Upsilon. Republican. Clubs: Century (N.Y.C.); California, Sunset (Los Angeles); Bohemian (San Francisco). Home: 2535 N Vermont Ave Los Angeles CA 90027 Office: 611 W 6th St Los Angeles CA 90017

OMENN, GILBERT STANLEY, physician, govt. sci. adminstr.; b. Chester, Pa., Aug. 30, 1941; s. Leonard and Leah (Miller) O.; A.B., Princeton U., 1961; M.D., Harvard U., 1965; Ph.D. in Genetics, U. Wash., 1972; children by previous marriage—Rachel Andrea, Jason Montgomery. Intern, Mass. Gen. Hosp., Boston, 1965-66, asst. resident in medicine, 1966-67; research asso NIH, Bethesda, Md., 1967-69; fellow U. Wash., 1969-71, asst. prof. medicine, 1971-74, asso. prof., 1974-79, prof., 1979—; asso. dir. Office Sci. and Tech. Policy, The White House, 1977—; cons. to govt. agys.; Howard Hughes Med. Inst. investigator, 1976-77. Mem. Wash. State Gov.'s Commn. on Social and Health Services; mem. Nat. Cancer Adv. Bd.; mem. adv. com. Woodrow Wilson Sch., Princeton U. Trustee, Pacific Sci. Center, Seattle Symphony Orch., Seattle Youth Symphony Orch.; chmn. rules com. Democratic Conv., King County, Wash., 1972. Served with USPHS, 1967-69. Recipient Research Career Devel. award USPHS, 1972; White House fellow, 1973-74. Fellow A.C.P.; mem. White House Fellows Assn. (dir.), Am. Soc. Neurochemistry, Am. Soc. Human Genetics, Behavior Genetics Assn., Western Soc. Clin. Research, Soc. Study Social Biology (dir.), Nat. Acad. Scis., Inst. Medicine. Jewish. Contbr. articles on human biochem. genetics, prenatal diagnosis of inherited disorders, susceptibility to environ. agts., clin. medicine and health policy to profl. publs.; editor: (with others) Genetics, Environment and Behavior: Implications for Educational Policy, 1972; editorial bd. Am. Jour. Human Genetics, Am. Jour. Med. Genetics, Behavior Genetics, Forum in Medicine. Home: 2828 Wisconsin Ave NW Apt 312 Washington DC 20007 Office: Office Sci and Tech Policy Exec Office of Pres Washington DC 20500

OMER, DANIEL OLIVER, lawyer; b. Quincy, Ill., Sept. 11, 1900; s. Oscar Ellsworth and Sarah Margaret (Lawless) O.; student Knox Coll., 1917-18; J.D., U.S.D., 1925; m. Doris Viola Olson, June 10, 1925 (dec. Jan. 1974); m. 2d, Helen F. King, Jan. 9, 1975. Admitted to S.D. bar, 1925, Va. bar, 1945, U.S. Supreme Ct., U.S. Ct. Mil. Appeals, 1953; law writer West Publishing Co., St. Paul, 1925-38; editor unemployment compensation interpretation service Social Security Bd., 1938-40; staff SSS, Washington, 1940-70, gen. counsel, 1946-70, dep. dir., 1959-70, dep. dir., legal adviser, 1970, spl. asst. to dir., 1970. Adv. com. Nat. Juvenile Ct. Found., 1952. Del. Nat. council Boy Scouts Am., 1962—. Served as pvt. U.S. Army, 1918; cpl. S.D.N.G., 1924; from 2d lt. to col., AUS, 1924-45, active duty, 1940-46, 50-60. Decorated Legion of Merit with oak leaf cluster, Army Commendation medal; recipient Selective Service medal Selective Service Distinguished Service award; Ala. Distinguished Service medal. Mem. Inst. Mil. Law, Delta Theta Phi, Lambda Chi Alpha, Scabbard and Blade. Mason (Shriner). Club: Army-Navy Country (Arlington, Va.). Contbg. editor Corpus Juris, 1935-38; editor: Legal Aspects of Selective Service, 1953. Home: 3616 Oval Dr Alexandria VA 22305 Office: 106 Little Falls St Falls Church VA 22046

OMER, GEORGE ELBERT, JR., physician, educator; b. Kansas City, Kans., Dec. 23, 1922; s. George Elbert and Edith May (Peck) O.; B.A., Ft. Hays State U., 1944; M.D., Kans. U., 1950; M.Sc. in Orthopaedic Surgery, Baylor U., 1955; m. Wendie Vilven, Nov. 6, 1949; children—George Eric, Michael Lee. Commd. 1st lt. M.C., U.S. Army, 1949, advanced through grades to col., 1967; rotating intern Bethany Hosp., Kansas City, 1950-51; resident in orthopaedic surgery Brooke Gen. Hosp., San Antonio, 1952-55, William Beaumont Gen. Hosp., El Paso, Tex., 1955-56; chief surgery Irwin Army Hosp., Ft. Riley, Kans., 1957-59; cons. in orthopaedic surgery 8th Army, Korea, 1959-60; asst. chief orthopaedic surgeon, chief hand surgeon Fitzsimons Army Med. Center, Denver, 1960-63; dir. orthopaedic residency tng. Armed Forces Inst. Pathology, Washington, 1963-65; chief orthopaedic surgery and chief Army Hand Surg. Center, Brooke Army Med. Center, 1965-70; cons. in orthopaedic surgery to Surgeon Gen. Army, 1967-70, ret., 1970; prof. orthopaedics, chmn. dept. orthopaedic surgery, prof. hand surgery, prof. anatomy, U. N.Mex., 1970—, med. dir. phys. therapy, 1972—; mem. active staff Bernalillo County Med. Center, Albuquerque; cons. staff other Albuquerque hosps.; cons. orthopaedic surgery USPHS, 1966—, U.S. Army, 1970—, U.S. Air Force, 1970—, VA, 1970—, Carrie Tingley Hosp. for Crippled Children, 1970—. Decorated Legion of Merit, Army Commendation medal with 2 oak leaf clusters; recipient Alumni Achievement award Ft. Hays State U., 1973; diplomate Am. Bd. Orthopaedic Surgery. Fellow A.C.S., Am. Orthopaedic Assn., Am. Acad. Orthopaedic Surgeons, N.Mex. Orthopaedic Assn. (pres. 1979-80), La. Orthopaedic Assn. (hon.), Korean Orthopaedic Assn. (hon.), Caribbean Hand Soc., Am. Soc. Surgery Hand (pres. 1978-79), Am. Assn. Surgery of Trauma, Assn. Bone, Joint Surgeons, Assn. Mil. Surgeons U.S., Riordan Hand Soc., Soc. Mil. Orthopaedic Surgeons, Brazilian Hand Soc., S.Am. Hand Soc. (hon.), Western Orthopaedic Assn., Assn. Orthopaedic Chmn., AAAS, Russell A. Hibbs Soc. (pres. 1977-78), 38th Parallel Med. Soc. (Korea); mem. AMA, Phi Kappa Phi, Phi Sigma, Phi Beta Pi. Bd. editors Clin. Orthopaedics Research, 1973—, Jour. AMA, 1973-74, Jour. Hand Surgery, 1976—; contbr. over 80 articles to profl. jours. and books, chpts. to books. Home: 3419 La Sala Del Oeste NE Albuquerque NM 87111

OMER, GUY CLIFTON, JR., educator; b. Mankato, Kans., Mar. 20, 1912; s. Guy Clifton and Margaret (Callahan) O.; B.S. in Elec. Engring., U. Kans., 1936, M.S. in Physics, 1937; Ph.D. cum laude in Physics, Calif. Inst. Tech., 1947; m. Martha Grace Steer, Sept. 13, 1942; children—Guy Clifton III, Richard William. Instr. physics U. Hawaii, 1941-43; asst. prof. physics and astronomy Occidental Coll., 1947-48; research asso. astrophysics Calif. Inst. Tech., 1947-48; asst. prof. U. Oreg., 1948-49, U. Chgo., 1949-55; prof. phys. scis., physics and astronomy U. Fla., 1955-72, chmn. dept. phys. sci., 1967-72, prof. physics and astronomy, 1972—; vis. prof. astronomy U. Calif. at Los Angeles, 1964-65. Fellow Royal Astron. Soc.; mem. Am. Phys. Soc., Am. Astron. Soc., Am. Assn. Physics Tchrs., Internat. Astron. Union, Seismological Soc. Am. Co-author: Physical Science; Men and Concepts, 1962; also articles. Home: 1080 SW 11th Terr Gainesville FL 32601

OMLOR, JOHN JOSEPH, steel co. exec.; b. Ashland, Pa., Mar. 15, 1935; s. Victor S. and Mary C. (Keller) O.; B.S., Pa. State U., 1960; M.B.A., Drexel Inst., 1971; m. Shirley A. Sich, Aug. 30, 1958; children—John V., David J. Jr. accountant Peat, Marwick, Mitchell & Co., Phoenix, 1960; chief accountant Honeywell Corp., Ft. Washington, Pa., 1961-63; chief accountant, div. controller, corporate controller Standard Pressed Steel Co., Jenkintown, Pa., 1963—; group v.p. material handling div. SPS Techs.; pres. Hallowell div. SPS Techs.; tchr. Evening Faculty, Pa. State U. Served with AUS, 1954-56. C.P.A. Mem. Financial Exec. Inst., Am., Pa. insts. C.P.A.'s. Contbr. articles to mags. Home: 1260 Millcreek Rd Southampton PA 18966 Office: Benson E Jenkintown PA 19046

OMRAN, ABDEL RAHIM, educator, epidemiologist; b. Cairo, Egypt, Mar. 29, 1925; s. Omran and Khadiga O. (Saad) O.; M.D., Cairo U., 1952, D.P.H., 1954; M.P.H., Columbia U., 1956, D.P.H., 1959; postgrad. Trudeau Sch. Tb, Saranac Lake, N.Y., 1959; m. Khairia Y. Fawzy, Sept. 13, 1952; children—Mohamed, Eman, Hanan. Came to U.S., 1963. Lectr., Cairo U., 1959-63; research scientist, clin. asso. prof. N.Y. U., 1963-66; asso. prof. U. N.C., Chapel Hill, 1966-71, prof. epidemiology, dir. WHO Internat. Reference Center for Human Reprodn., 1971—; asso. dir. Carolina Population Center, 1969—; coordinator WHO Health and Fertility Studies, 1969—; cons. Ford Found., UNFPA, World Bank, 1969—; mem. WHO Expert Advisory Panel Human Reprodn., 1978—; sci. advisor Egyptian Ministry Health, 1978. Recipient Medal of Sci. Achievement, Govt. Egypt, 1955. Fellow Royal Soc. Health, Am. Pub. Health Assn. (life); mem. Am. Population Assn., Egyptian Med. Assn., Internat. Epidemiol. Assn., Delta Omega. Author: Theory of Epidemiologic Transition, 1971, The Health Theme in Family Planning, 1971; The Arab Populations, 1979. Editor: Egypt - Population Problems and Prospects, 1973, Community Medicine in Developing Countries, 1974, Liberalization of Abortion Laws, Implications, 1976, Family Formation Patterns and Health, 1976. Contbr. chpts. to books, articles to profl. jours. Home: 304 Granville Rd Chapel Hill NC 27514 Office: 407 Pittsboro St Chapel Hill NC 27514

ONAK, THOMAS PHILIP, educator; b. Omaha, July 30, 1932; s. Louis Albert and Louise Marie (Penner) O.; B.A., Calif. State U., San Diego, 1954; Ph.D., U. Cal. at Berkeley, 1957; m. Sharon Colleen Neal, June 18, 1954. Research chemist Olin Mathieson Chem. Corp., Pasadena, Calif., 1957-59; asst. prof. Calif. State U., Los Angeles, 1959-63, asso. prof., 1963-66, prof. chemistry, 1966—. Recipient Research Career award NIH, 1973-78; Fulbright research fellow U. Cambridge (Eng.), 1965-66. Author: Organoborane Chemistry, 1975. Contbr. articles to profl. jours., chpts. to books. Home: 632 Alta Vista Circle South Pasadena CA 91030 Office: Dept Chemistry Calif State U 5151 State U Dr Los Angeles CA 90032

ONASCH, DONALD CARL, bus. exec.; b. New Castle, Pa., July 5, 1927; B.A., Washington and Jefferson Coll., 1950; M.S. in Retailing, U. Pitts., 1952; m. Ruth Ellen Widman; children—Gregory W., Jay W., David R. Div. merchandise mgr. Higbee Co., Cleve., 1953-65; div. merchandise mgr. Sibley, Lindsay & Curr, Rochester, N.Y., 1965-70; v.p., gen. merchandise mgr. Liberty House of Hawaii, Honolulu, 1970-72, pres., 1973-77; v.p. Amfac, Inc., Honolulu, 1977-78, exec. v.p., 1978—; dir. Associated Merchandising Corp. Served with U.S. Coast Guard, 1945-46. Club: Oahu Country. Office: PO Box 3230 Honolulu HI 96801

ONASSIS, JACQUELINE BOUVIER KENNEDY (MRS. ARISTOTLE ONASSIS), widow of 35th Pres. of U.S., editor; b. Southampton, L.I., N.Y., July 28, 1929; d. John Vernou III and Janet (Lee) Bouvier; grad. Miss Porter's Sch., Farmington, Conn., 1947; student Vassar Coll., 1947-48, The Sorbonne, Paris, France, 1949; B.A., George Washington U., 1951; m. John Fitzgerald Kennedy, Sept. 12, 1953 (35th Pres. U.S.A.) (dec. Nov. 22, 1963); children—Caroline Bouvier, John Fitzgerald, Patrick Bouvier (dec.); m. 2d, Aristotle Onassis, Oct. 20, 1968 (dec. Mar. 1975). Inquiring photographer Washington Times-Herald (now Washington Post and Times Herald), 1952; planned and conducted restoration decor of White House, 1961-63; cons. editor Viking Press, 1975-77; asso. editor Doubleday & Co., 1978—. Trustee Whitney Mus. Am. Art. Recipient Prix de Paris, Vogue mag., 1951; TV Emmy award for public service 1962. Office: Doubleday & Co 245 Park Ave New York NY 10017*

ONDAATJE, CHRISTOPHER, publisher, investment dealer; b. Kandy, Ceylon, Feb. 22, 1933; came to Can., 1955, naturalized, 1960; s. Mervyn and Doris O.; student Blundell's Sch., Eng., 1947-51, London Sch. Econs., 1953-54; m. 1959; children—David, Sarah, Janet. Pres., Pagurian Corp., Ltd., Toronto, Ont., Can., 1955—; pres. Pagurian Press, Ltd.; v.p. Loewen, Ondaatje, McCutcheon & Co., Ltd. Mem. Can. Olympic Bob-Sled team, 1964; bd. govs. Lakefield Coll. Sch., Can. Mem. Inst. Bankers (Eng.) (asso.). Mem. Christian Ch. Club: Badminton and Racquet (Toronto). Author: The Prime Ministers of Canada, 1867-1976; Olympic Victory, 1964. Office: Pagurian Press Ltd 335 Bay St Suite 1106 Toronto ON M5H 2R3 Canada

ONDETTI, MIGUEL ANGEL, chemist; b. Buenos Aires, Argentina, May 14, 1930; s. Emilio Pablo and Sara Cecilia (Cerutti) O.; came to U.S., 1960, naturalized, 1971; Licensiate in Chemistry, U. Buenos Aires, 1956, D.Sc., 1957; m. Josephine Elizabeth Garcia, June 6, 1958; children—Giselle Christine, Gabriel Alexander. Prof. chemistry Inst. for Tchrs., Buenos Aires, 1957-60; instr. organic chemistry U. Buenos Aires, 1957-60; research scientist Squibb Inst. for Med. Research, Buenos Aires, 1957-60, research investigator, Princeton, N.J., 1960-67, research supr., 1967-73, sect. head, 1973-76, dir. biol. chemistry, 1977—; ad-hoc cons. NIH. Served with Argentine Army, 1950-51. Brit. Council scholar, 1960, Squibb scholar, 1956. Mem. Am., Swiss chem. socs., Am. Soc. Biol. Chemists, Sigma Xi. Roman Catholic. Author: (with M. Bodanszky) Peptide Synthesis, 2d edit., 1976. Contbr. sci. articles to profl. jours. Home: 79 Hemlock Circle Princeton NJ 08540 Office: PO Box 4000 Princeton NJ 08540

O'NEAL, ARTHUR DANIEL, JR., chmn. ICC; b. Bremerton, Wash., May 15, 1936; s. Arthur Daniel and Louise Ragna (Nordahl) O'N.; A.B., Whitman Coll., 1959; J.D., U. Wash., 1965; m. Diane Gay Reedy, Aug. 5, 1961; children—Daniel Stewart, Reed Kazis, David Christopher, Beth Marie. Admitted to Wash. bar, 1965, D.C. bar, 1976, U.S. Supreme Ct. bar, 1978; staff counsel Senate Commerce Com., Washington, 1965-67, surface transp. counsel, 1969-71, transp. counsel, 1971-73; legis. asst. to Senator Warren G. Magnuson, Washington, 1967-69; commr. ICC, Washington, 1973-77, chmn., 1977—. Overseer Whitman Coll. Served with USN, 1959-63. Mem. Wash. State, D.C. bar assns. Home: 1905 Torregrossa Ct McLean VA 22101 Office: ICC 12th St and Constitution Ave NW Washington DC 20423

O'NEAL, DAVID CORTLAND, lt. gov. Ill.; b. Belleville, Ill., Jan. 24, 1937; s. Floyd Cortland and Edna Ruth (Barrow) O'N.; student McKendree Coll., 1955-56; B.S., St. Louis Coll. Pharmacy, 1962; m. Sandra Finley, Dec. 26, 1958; children—Allison, Kelly. Pres., Westown Pharmacy, Inc., Belleville, 1962-70; sheriff St. Clair County (Ill.), 1970-76; lt. gov. Ill., 1977—; mem. adminstrn. justice task force E.-W. Gateway Council, 1971—; mem. Ill. Law Enforcement Commn., 1971-73. Mem. Young Republicans, Men's Rep. Club; bd. dirs. Okaw Valley council Boy Scouts Am., St. Clair County Health and Welfare Council, Metro-E. Health Council; trustee McKendree Coll., Lebanon, Ill. Served with USMC, 1956-59. Recipient Distinguished Service award Belleville Jaycees, 1971; named Outstanding Young Rep., 1971, Outstanding Young Rep. of Nation, 1975. Mem. Belleville C. of C., Madison-St. Clair Profl. Pharmacy Assn. Office: Office Lt Gov 214 State House Springfield IL 62706*

O'NEAL, FOREST HODGE, prof. law; b. Rayville, La., Sept. 17, 1917; s. Forest Hodge and Nancy (Wright) O'N.; Certificate, Northeast Jr. Coll., Monroe, La., 1936; A.B., La. State U., 1938; LL.B., 1940; J.S.D., Yale, 1949; S.J.D., Harvard, 1954; m. Marnay Martha Shepetis, Oct. 19, 1974; children by previous marriage-Forest Hodge III, Laurie, Mark N., Dee, Nancy, Karen. Admitted to La. bar, 1940, Ga. bar, 1955, Mo. bar, 1977; asso. firm Sullivan & Cromwell, N.Y.C., 1941; asso. prof. law U. Miss., 1945-46, prof. law, 1946-47; acting dean and prof. law Walter F. George Sch. of Law, Mercer U., 1947-48; dean, 1949-56; prof. law Vanderbilt U. Law Sch., 1956-59; prof. law Duke U. Sch. Law, 1959-76, dean, 1966-68, James B. Duke prof. law, 1972-76; George Alexander Madill prof. law Washington U. Sch. Law, St. Louis, 1976—, dean, 1980—; vis. prof. law N.Y. U., 1957-58, U. Minn., 1973. Chmn. Southern Law Rev. Conf., 1948; commr. Uniform State Laws for Ga., 1955; chmn. S. Eastern Regional Conf. Assn. Am. Law Schs., 1968-69. Served to lt. USNR, 1942-45; U.S. Naval Base, Saipan, 1945. Sterling fellow Yale, 1940. Mem. Am. Bar Assn. (bd. editors jour. 1971-77), Ga. Bar Assn. (bd. govs. 1948-49, 1951-52, 1954-55), Assn. Am. Law Schs. (mem. exec. com. 1968-70), Order of Coif, Omicron Delta Kappa, Gamma Eta Gamma, Phi Kappa Phi. Baptist. Author: (with Kurt F. Pantzer) The Drafting of Corporate Charters and By-Laws; Close Corporations: Law and Practice (2 vols.), 1958, 2d edit., 1971; (with Jordan Derwin) Expulsion or Oppression of Business Associates: Squeeze-Outs in Small Enterprises, 1961; (with Annie Laurie O'Neal) Humor, The Politician's Tool, 1964; Squeeze-Outs of Minority Shareholders: Expulsion or Oppression of Business Associates, 1975. Editor-in-chief La. Law Rev., 1939-40; faculty adviser Miss. Law Rev., 1940-47; editor Corporate Practice Commentator, 1959—. Contbr. articles to law and bus. revs. Home: 69 Lake Forest St Louis MO 63117

O'NEAL, FREDERICK, actor, director; b. Brooksville, Miss., Aug. 27 1905; s. Ransome James and Ninnie Bell (Thompson) O'N.; ed. New Theatre Sch., N.Y.C., Am. Theatre Wing, N.Y.C., also pvt. instrn.; A.F.D., Columbia Coll., Chgo., 1966; H.H.D., Lincoln U., 1976; D.F.A., Coll. of Wooster, 1976; m. Charlotte T. Hainey, Apr. 18, 1942. Numerous theatrical appearances U.S. and abroad, 1944-70; also motion picture, 1949—; numerous TV appearances; founder Aldridge Players, St. Louis, 1927, Am. Negro Theatre, N.Y.C., 1940, Brit. Negro Theatre, London, 1948; vis. prof. So. Ill. U., 1962, Clark Coll., Atlanta, 1963; v.p., chmn. civil rights com. AFL-CIO; sec.-treas. African-Am. Labor Center; dir. Schomburg Corp. Bd. dirs. Inst. for Advanced Studies in Theatre Arts, pres. emeritus, 1977—; bd. dirs. AFL-CIO Labor Studies Center, Am. Arbitration Assn., Muscular Distrophy Assn. Am., UN Devel. Corp., Nat. Com. U.S./China Relations, Internat. Theatre Inst.; mem. N.Y.C. Cultural Assistance Council, 1978—. Recipient Derwent award, 1945, first and 2d place N.Y. Critics poll, 1945, Donaldson award, 1945, Dutch Treat disc, 1944-45, spl. award New Eng. Theatre Conf., 1963, citation Ohio Community Theatre Assn., 1964, Hoey award Catholic Interracial Council, 1964, award Am. Jewish Congress, 1964, Canada Lee Found. Achievement award, 1954, Motion Pictures Critics award, 1957, Ira Aldridge citation Assn. Study Negro Life and History, 1963, N.Y.C. Central Labor Council award, 1967, City of St. Louis award, 1968, Nat. Urban League EOD award, 1966, Am. Vet.'s Com. George W. Norris Civil Rights award, 1970; League for Indsl. Democracy award, 1973; named to Black Filmmakers Hall of Fame, 1975. Served with inf. AUS, 1942-43. Mem. Actors Equity Assn. (pres. 1964-73, pres. emeritus 1973—, pres. Found. 1964-73), Acad. Television Arts and Scis., Asso. Actors and Artistes of Am. (internat. pres. 1970—), Actors Fund, Am. Screen Actors Guild, AFTRA, ANTA, Urban League, NAACP, Cath. Interracial Council (pres. 1979), Knights St. Peter Claver, Am. Vets. Com. Clubs: Players, Lambs. Author: The Negro in American Theatre, 1956. Office: 1500 Broadway New York NY 10036

O'NEAL, JOHN MILTON, JR., playwright, producer, dir.; b. Mound City, Ill., Sept. 25, 1940; s. John Milton and Geneva Rosetta (Crenshaw) O'N.; B.A., So. Ill. U., Carbondale, 1962; m. Marilyn Norton, June 10, 1972; children—Wendi Autumn, William Edward Burghardt. Field sec. Student Nonviolent Coordinating Com., 1962-64; producing dir. Free So. Theater, New Orleans, 1963—; child care worker Abbott House, 1965; trainer Haryou Act, Inc., 1965; dir. Council for a Better East New York, 1965-66; field program dir. Com. for Racial Justice, United Ch. of Christ, 1966-68. Cons. gen. conv. spl. program Episcopal Ch., 1968-70. Mem. Alpha Phi Alpha. Author several plays, essays and poems, 1964—.

O'NEAL, MICHAEL LEONARD, judge; b. Amarillo, Tex., June 28, 1937; s. James Hilliard and Anne Pauline (Whelchel) O'N.; B.Mus., So. Methodist U., 1959, M.Mus., 1961, J.D., 1969; m. Keith Newman, Sept. 24, 1966; children—Sean Michael, Terrence Patrick. With Graybar Electric Co., 1961-65, LTV Electro Systems Co., 1967-69, Data Systems Dept., 1968-69; admitted to Tex. bar, 1969, since practiced in Dallas; partner firm Rosenfield Mittenthal & O'Neal, 1973-77; asso. judge Dallas Mcpl. Cts., 1972-77, adminstrv. judge, 1977—. Minister music Central Congl. Ch., Dallas, 1971-76; bd. dirs. Dallas Council on Alcoholism. Named Boss of Year, Dallas Assn. Legal Secs., 1975. Mem. Dallas Bar Assn., State Bar Tex. (dir. mcpl. ct. sect.), Dallas Criminal Bar Assn., Soc. Preservation and Encouragement of Barbershop Quartet Singing in Am. (dir. Dallas chpt., Internat. Chorus champions 1979). Democrat. Episcopalian. Club: Metropolitan. Composer choral music. Home: 5830 Glendora St Dallas TX 75230 Office: Municipal Ct 106 S Harwood Dallas TX 75201. *A Successful life is built upon accepting the challenges that are available to everyone, not merely to succeed financially but to accomplish and excel. I further feel that it is far better to have accepted the challenge and fail than to avoid it. I have found that the more challenges one accepts, the fewer failures one must overcome.*

O'NEAL, ROBERT MUNGER, physician; b. Wiggins, Miss., Oct. 7, 1922; s. Charles Ernest and Myra Mae (Munger) O'N.; B.S., U. Miss., 1943; M.D., U. Tenn., 1945; m. Mildred Estell Morris, June 14, 1947; children—Julia Ann, Clarence Ernest, Margaret Alice, John Munger. Intern. Gorgas Hosp., C.Z., 1945-46; intern Baptist Hosp., Memphis, 1946-47, resident pathology, 1947-48; resident chest disease Miss. State Sanitarium, 1949-52; Am. Cancer Soc. fellow pathology Mass. Gen. Hosp., Boston, 1952-54; from instr. to asso. prof. pathology Washington U. Sch. Medicine, St. Louis, 1954-61; pathologist Greenwood (Miss.) Hosp., 1956-57; prof. pathology, chmn. dept. Baylor U. Coll. Medicine, 1961-69; prof. pathology Albany (N.Y.)

Med. Coll., 1969-72; dir. Bender Hygienic Lab., Albany, 1969-72; prof. pathology, chmn. dept. Coll. Medicine and Dentistry, U. Okla., 1973-78; prof. pathology, chmn. dept. Univ. Med. Center, U. Miss., 1978—; spl. research pulmonary and cardiovascular diseases; mem. pathology test com. Nat. Bd. Med. Examiners, 1963-68, heart tng. com. Nat. Heart Inst., 1963-68; mem. cardiovascular A. study sect. Nat. Heart and Lung Inst., 1968-73. Recipient Lederle Med. Faculty award, 1958-61. Mem. Am. Assn. Pathologists, Am. Coll. Chest Physicians, Internat. Acad. Pathology, Am. Heart Assn. (council arteriosclerosis), Am. Thoracic Soc., Sigma Xi. Asso. editor Exptl. Molecular Pathology, 1965—. Home: 2070 Cherokee Jackson MS 39211

O'NEAL, RYAN, actor; b. Los Angeles, Apr. 20, 1941; s. Charles and Patricia (Callaghan) O'N.; grad. high sch.; m. Joanna Moore, Apr. 1963 (div. Feb. 1967); children—Tatum Beatrice, Griffin Patrick; m. 2d, Leigh Taylor-Young, Feb. 1967; 1 son, Patrick. Appeared in several television series in early 1960s, including Dobie Gillis, Two Faces West, Perry Mason, G.E. Theatre, The Virginian, This Is the Life, The Untouchables, My Three Sons, Bachelor Father, June Allyson Show, Empire, Peyton Place, 1964-69; appeared in motion pictures The Big Bounce, 1969, The Games, 1970, Love Story, 1970 (David of Donatello award), The Wild Rovers, 1971, What's Up, Doc?, 1972, The Thief Who Came to Dinner, 1973, Paper Moon, 1973, Barry Lyndon, 1975, Nickelodeon, 1976, A Bridge Too Far, 1977, Oliver's Story, 1978; appeared in TV movie The Driver, 1978. Address: care Internat Creative Mgmt 40 W 57th St New York NY 10019*

O'NEAL, TATUM, actress; b. Nov. 5, 1963; d. Ryan and Joanna (Moore) O'Neal; ed. pvt. schs. and tutors. Appeared in films Paper Moon (Acad. award for best supporting actress), 1973, The Bad News Bears, 1976, Nickelodeon, 1976, Internat. Velvet, 1978.*

O'NEAL, WILLIAM BAINTER, educator; b. Zanesville, Ohio, Aug. 21, 1907; s. Eugene Ferdinand and Nora (Bainter) O'N.; B.Arch., Carnegie Mellon U., 1930; student Pa. Acad. Fine Arts, 1932-34. With U.S. Engrs. Dept., 1934-37; pvt. practice architecture, 1937-42; chmn. div. archtl. history U. Va., 1946-72; tchr. Ga. Inst. Tech., summers 1947-48; cons. Portsmouth (Va.) Old Town Assn. Bd. dirs. U. Press Va., 1962-66, Tuesday Evening Concert Assn., 1955-61, 66-69; pres. Va. Art Alliance, 1955-56; mem. Art Commn. Commonwealth Va., 1974-78. Served with C.E., AUS, 1942-45. Fellow AIA; mem. Soc. Archtl. Historians (dir. 1972-75), Am. Assn. Archtl. Biographers (gov., editor 1954), Royal Soc. Arts, Irish Georgian Soc. Author: Jefferson's Fine Arts Library for the University of Virginia, 1956; Charles Smith, Prints and Paintings, 1958; Primitive Into Painter, 1960; Jefferson's Buildings at the University of Virginia, 1960; Architecture in Virginia, 1968; Pictorial History of the University of Virginia, 1968; Architectural Drawing in Virginia, 1819-1969, 1969. Home: 1716 King Mountain Rd Charlottesville VA 22901

O'NEIL, BRUCE WILLIAM, artist, educator; b. Winnipeg, Man., Can., July 14, 1942; s. Bruce Johnston and Marjorie Ellen (Riggall) O'N.; painting diploma Alta. Coll. Art, 1964; postgrad. (scholar), Instituto Allende, 1965; m. Karen Gaye, Oct. 18, 1963; children—Sara, Courtenay. Exhibited in one man shows including Loyola Coll., Montreal, 1968, Edmonton Art Gallery, 1975, Mira Godard Gallery, Toronto, 1977, 78; exhibited in group shows including all maj. Can. museums, Hirshorn Mus. and Sculpture Garden, Smithsonian Instn., 1977; represented in permanent collections including Edmonton Art Gallery, Can. Council Art Bank, Ottawa, Meml. U., St. John's, Nfld.; mem. part-time faculty Allied Arts Center, 1966-68; instr. painting Alta. Coll. Art, Calgary, 1971—. Can. Council grantee, 1975, 78. Mem. Canadian Artists Reps., Alta. Soc. Artists. Home: 2206 30th Ave SW Calgary AB T2T 1R2 Canada Office: Alta Coll Art 1301 16th Ave NW Calgary AB Canada

O'NEIL, C. RODERICK, ins. co. exec.; b. N.Y.C., Jan. 26, 1931; s. Charles A. and Elizabeth (Whyte) O'N.; B.A., Princeton U., 1953; M.B.A., U. Chgo., 1957; m. Nancy Galante, Nov. 25, 1950; children—Brian, Sarah, Timothy, Kevin, John, Anne. Asst. mgr. investment dept. No. Trust Co., Chgo., 1953-59; v.p. H.M. Byllesby & Co., Chgo., 1959-62, A.G. Becker & Co., Chgo., 1962-64; with Mfrs. Hanover Trust, N.Y.C., 1964-77, exec. v.p., head trust div., 1970-77; chmn. fin. com., dir. Travelers Corp., Hartford, Conn., 1977—; mem. investment adv. com. N.Y. State Tchrs. Retirement System, 1976—, N.Y. State Employees Retirement Systems, 1979—; mem. investment policy panel Pension Benefit Guaranty Corp., 1975—. Trustee, Meml. Dr. Trust, 1974—, Calif. Inst. Arts, 1976—; bd. dirs. St. Francis Hosp., 1977—, Hartford Stage Co., 1977—; mem. Hartford Concerned Citizens for Effective Govt., 1978—. Chartered Fin. Analyst. Mem. Inst. Chartered Fin. Analysts (pres. 1978-79, trustee 1974—) Fin. Analysts Fedn., N.Y. Soc. Security Analysts, Hartford Soc. Security Analysts, Greater Hartford C. of C. (chmn. city wide living com. 1979—). Clubs: Princeton, Madison Sq. Garden (N.Y.C.); Univ. (Chgo.); Hartford Golf. Office: Travelers Corp 1 Tower Sq Hartford CT 06115

O'NEIL, JAMES FRANCIS, magazine pub.; b. Manchester, N.H., June 13, 1898; s. Joseph H. and Mary (Dalton) O'N.; M.A., U. N.H., 1948; LL.D., St. Anselm's Coll., 1948; m. Edythe Reid Graf, Sept. 7, 1925; children—Kenneth G., J. Russell. Chief police Manchester, 1937-50; dir. aero. N.H., 1938-40, dir. civil def., 1940-44; pub. Am. Legiom mag., N.Y.C., 1950-78, pub. emeritus, 1978—; dir. N.H. Pub. Service Co. Mem. President's Amnesty Bd., 1946-47; spl. asst. to sec. navy, 1945-46; mem. Golf Course & Stadium Authority, Manchester, 1929-37; mem. adv. com. MacArthur Meml. Found., 1967—; chmn. bd. dirs. Manchester Airport. Served to lt., inf., U.S. Army, 1916-19; AEF. Decorated Legion Honor, Croix de Guerre with palm (France); Navy Certificate Merit. Mem. Am. Legion (nat. comdr. 1947-48), Newcomen Soc., Army, Navy and Air Force Vets. Can. and U.S. (pres. U.S. chpt.), Ancient and Hon. Arty. Co. Boston, Internat. Platform Assn. Republican. Catholic. Club: Dutch Treat (N.Y.C.). Home: 10 Holder Pl Forest Hills NY 11375. *If I have been successful I can attribute it largely to an associate and friend, an elder statesman, if you will. He said, "Life is crowded with decision-makings. In trying to arrive at the correct ones, assemble all the facts possible; make up your mind; and don't change it unless someone can document error. Such a course will develop right instincts when time factors prevent study." I owe much to such counsel.*

O'NEIL, JOHN, painter; b. Kansas City, Mo., June 16, 1915; s. Michael and Emma (Harms) O'N.; B.F.A., U. Okla., 1936, M.F.A., 1939; student Taos Sch. Art, 1942, U. Florence (Italy), 1951. Dir. U. Okla. Sch. Art, 1951-65; chmn. dept. fine arts Rice U., Houston, 1965-70, dir. Sewall Art Gallery, 1972-77, Joseph and Joanna Nazro prof. art and art history, 1979—; vis. lectr. N.Y.U., U. Mich., U. Mass., l'Accademia di Belle Arti, Rome, Mus. Art, U. Okla., Sask. (Can.) Art Centers; Moana Olu Coll., Hawaii; exhibited one man shows Seattle Art Mus., M-59 Galleries, Copenhagen, Denmark, Los Robles Galleries, Calif., La. Gallery, Houston; works exhibited Carnegie Inst., Artists West of Mississippi at Colorado Springs, Denver Art Mus., San Francisco Mus., Art Inst. of Chgo., U. Ill., Dallas Mus., Cin. Mus., Sadeer Gallery, Kuwait; rep. collections Philbrook Art Center, U. Mich., Denver Art Mus., Dallas Mus., others. Recipient 30 painting and graphics awards. Painting fellowship Huntington Hartford Found., MacDowell Colony, Montalvo Assn. Mem. Coll. Art Assn., Southwestern, Mid-Am. art confs., Delta Phi Delta. Home: 2224 Wroxton Houston TX 77005

O'NEIL, JOHN JAMES, rubber co. exec.; b. Akron, Ohio, June 24, 1917; s. William and Grace (Savage) O'N.; A.B., Holy Cross Coll., 1938; LL.B., Harvard, 1941; S.T.L., Catholic U. Am., 1954; m. Helene Connellan, May 27, 1959; children—Helene, John, Ann, Jane. Dir. Gen. Tire & Rubber Co., 1949-50, 55—, chmn. finance com., 1960—, treas., 1948-50. Served as lt. USCG, 1942-46. K.C.

O'NEIL, KITTY LINN, stuntwoman, motor sport racer; b. Corpus Christi, Tex., Mar. 24, 1946; d. John II and Patsy (Compton) O'N.; attended Fullerton (Calif.) Jr. Coll., 1 semester; studied diving with Sammy Lee. Formerly diving and swimming competitor; now motor sports racer, especially off-road racing, including Mint 400, Mexican 1000, Baja 500, S.C.O.R.E. World Championship Off-Road Race; stuntwoman, 1976—; TV appearances include: Bionic Woman, Baretta, Motor Sports International, The Blues Brothers, Tomorrow Show, Nova, 240 Robert, Fantasy Islands, Family, Wonder Woman, others; former AAU Jr. Olympics Diving Champion; world records include: Land Speed for Women, Quarter Mile Acceleration From Standing Start, 500 Meter Acceleration From Standing Start. Recipient numerous awards including 17 first pl. trophies for swimming and diving, 31 gold medals for swimming and diving, Young Am. of Month award Am. Youth Mag., achievement awards from instns. for deaf and other handicapped, Volta award 1979. Mem. Stunts Unltd., Screen Actors Guild, Sports Car Club Am., Fedn. Internat. Motorcyclists, U.S. Automobile Club, Nat. Assn. Stock Cars, Fedn. Internat. Automobiles, So. Calif. Off-Road Enterprises, Am. Motorcycle Assn., Nat. Hot Rod Assn., Nat. Power Boat Assn., Am. Power Boat Assn. Has been totally deaf since infancy; subject of CBS Movie of the Week, Silent Victory, 1979. Office: care Kitty O'Neil Fan Club PO Box 604 Medina OH 44256

O'NEIL, LOUIS COUILLARD, univ. adminstr.; b. Sherbrooke, Que., Can., Jan. 20, 1930; s. Louis Couillard and Marthe (Belleau) O'N.; B.A., Seminaire St. Charles, 1950; B.Sc.A., U. Laval, 1954; M.Sc., N.Y. Coll. Forestry, Syracuse U., 1956, Ph.D., 1961; m. Huguette Tanguay, Sept. 3, 1955; children—Marie-Jose, Christine, Bernard, Anne, Lucie. Research officer Gov. Can. Dept. Agriculture, Que., 1955-62; lectr. U. Sherbrooke, 1962, asst. prof., 1963-66, asso. prof., 1966-70, prof., 1970—, sec. Faculté des Scis., 1967-70, chmn. dept. biology, 1970-72, dean, 1972-78, dir. personnel, 1978—; research asso. Yale Sch. Forestry, summers, 1965-67. Mem. Entomol. Soc. Can., Soc. des. Zoologistes Canadiens, Société Entomologique du Quebec, Société de Protection des Plantes du Quebec, Assn. Canadienne Francaise Pour L'Avancement des Sciences. Contbr. articles sci. jours. Home: 153 St Francis St Lennoxville PQ Canada Office: U de Sherbrooke Service des Personnels Shebrooke PQ Canada

O'NEIL, MICHAEL GERALD, bus. exec.; b. Akron, Ohio, Jan. 29, 1922; s. William Francis and Grace (Savage) O'N.; A.B., Coll. of Holy Cross, 1943; postgrad. Sch. Bus., Harvard, 1948; LL.D., U. Akron, 1962, Ashland, Coll., 1967; m. Juliet P. Rudolph, Jan. 7, 1950; children—Michael, Gregory, Jeffrey, Shawn, Julie, Nancy, Susan. With Gen. Tire Co., 1947—, staff inter-plant ops., Venezuela, 1947-48, dir., 1950—, exec. asst. to pres., 1951-60, pres., 1960—, mem. exec., finance coms.; dir., chmn. bd. Aerojet-Gen. Corp.; dir. 1st Nat. Bank of Akron. Served as lt. USAAF, 1944-45. Clubs: Portage Country, Akron City; Detroit Athletic, Sharon Golf. Office: One General St Akron OH 44329

O'NEIL, STEPHEN EDWARD, mfg. co. exec., lawyer; b. N.Y.C., Sept. 28, 1932; s. Edward Francis and Ethel (Cooney) O'N.; A.B. cum laude, Princeton, 1954; LL.B. cum laude, Harvard, 1957; m. Katharine Thomas, May 7, 1960; children—Margaret, Stephen, Charles. Admitted to N.Y. bar, 1958; asso. Cravath, Swaine & Moore, 1957-68; v.p., gen. counsel, dir. City Investing Co., N.Y.C., 1968-72, exec. v.p., 1972-75, pres. ins. and energy, 1975-78, pres., 1978—; dir. Fiduciary Growth Assos., Inc., First Union Bancorp., Brown-Forman Distillers Corp., Rheem Mfg. Co., World Color Press, Castle Convertible Fund. Mem. Am. Bar Assn., Assn. Bar City N.Y., Phi Beta Kappa. Home: 1220 Park Ave New York City NY 10028 Office: 767 Fifth Ave New York City NY 10022

O'NEIL, THOMAS FRANCIS, broadcasting and rubber co. exec.; b. Kansas City, Mo., Apr. 18, 1915; s. William and Grace Agnes (Savage) O'N.; A.B., Holy Cross Coll., 1937; m. Claire Miller McCahey, June 15, 1946; children—Shane, Eileen, Mark, Conn, Claire, Liam, Grace, Carol, Owen. With Gen. Tire & Rubber Co., Akron, Ohio, 1937-41, 46—, dir., 1948—, v.p., 1950-60, vice chmn. bd., 1960, chmn., 1961—; v.p., dir. The Yankee Network, Boston, 1948-51; pres., dir. RKO Gen., Inc., N.Y.C., 1955-66, chmn. bd., 1966-76, now chmn. exec. com.; dir. Frontier Airlines, Inc., Flintkote Co. Served to lt. USCG, World War II. Office: Gen Tire & Rubber Co One General St Akron OH 44329*

O'NEIL, WAYNE, linguist; b. Kenosha, Wis., Dec. 22, 1931; s. L.J. and Kathryn (Obermeyer) O'N.; A.B., U. Wis., 1955, A.M., 1956, Ph.D., 1960; A.M. (hon.), Harvard U., 1965; children—Scott Leslie, Patrick Sean, Elizabeth Erla. Asst. prof. linguistics and lit. U. Oreg., 1961-65; prof. linguistics and edn. Harvard U., 1965-68, lectr. edn., 1968-72, 78—, dir. NDEA Summer Inst. on Psycho and Socio-linguistics, 1968; prof. linguistics and humanities M.I.T., 1968—, chmn. lit. faculty, 1969-75, dir. Nat. Endowment Humanities Summer Inst. on Lang. Change, 1978. Mem. steering com. Resist, 1967—, Peoples Coalition for Peace and Justice, 1970-72. Served with U.S. Army, 1952-54. Fulbright fellow in Iceland, 1961, Am. Council Learned Socs. study fellow M.I.T., 1964-65. Mem. Linguistic Soc. Am., MLA, Nat. Council Tchrs. English, AAAS, Soc. for Advancement Scandinavian Study. Med. editorial group Radical Teacher, 1975—. Contbr. articles to profl. jours. Office: Mass Inst Tech Depts Linguistics and Philosophy Cambridge MA 02139

O'NEILL, ALBERT CLARENCE, JR., lawyer; b. Gainesville, Fla., Nov. 25, 1939; s. Albert Clarence and Sue Virginia (Henry) O'N.; B.A. with high honors, U. Fla., 1962; LL.B. magna cum laude, Harvard U., 1965; m. Vanda Marie Nigels, Apr. 26, 1969; 1 dau., Heather Marie. Admitted to Fla. bar, 1965; law clk. to judge U.S. Dist. Ct. Middle Dist. Fla., Jacksonville, 1965-66; asso. firm Fowler, White, Collins, Gillen, Humkey & Trenam, Tampa, Fla., 1966-69; partner firm Trenam, Simmons, Kemker, Scharf & Barkin, Tampa, 1970-77; mem. firm Trenam, Simmons, Kemker, Scharf, Barkin, Frye & O'Neill, P.A., Tampa, 1977—, also dir.; vis. lectr. law Stetson Law Sch., 1970-73. Bd. dirs. Fla. Gulf Coast Symphony, Inc., 1975—, U. Fla. Found., Inc., 1976—. Mem. Fla. Bar (chmn. tax sect. 1975-76), Am. Bar Assn., Am. Law Inst., Phi Beta Kappa. Exec. editor Harvard Law Rev., 1964-65; contbr. articles to profl. jours. Home: 10709 Carroll Lake Dr Tampa FL 33618 Office: 2600 1st Florida Tower 111 Madison St Tampa FL 33602

O'NEILL, ARTHUR J., bishop; b. East Dubuque, Ill., Dec. 14, 1917; student Loras Coll., Dubuque, Iowa, St. Mary's Sem., Balt. Ordained priest Roman Catholic Ch., 1943; bishop of Rockford (Ill.), 1968—. Office: 1245 N Court St Rockford IL 61101*

O'NEILL, BRIAN EDWARD, lawyer, oil and gas co. exec.; b. San Diego, Sept. 10, 1935; s. Edward J. and Susan (Ellis) O'N.; B.S., U.S. Naval Acad., 1957; LL.B., U. Tex., 1965; m. Kathryn T. Luongo, May 5, 1962; children—Kelley, Sean. Admitted to Tex. bar; partner firm Andrews, Kurth, Campbell & Jones, Houston, 1965-75; sr. v.p., gen. counsel Transco Co., Inc., Houston, 1975—. Served to lt. USNR, 1957-62. Mem. Am., Tex. State, Houston bar assns., Fed. Energy Bar Assn., Interstate Natural Gas Assn. Am., Southeastern Gas Assn., Tex. Law Sch. Assn. (bd. dirs.), Order of Coif, Phi Delta Phi. Roman Catholic. Clubs: Univ., Houston Country. Home: 6118 Riverview Way Houston TX 77057 Office: PO Box 1396 Houston TX 77001

O'NEILL, BRIAN FRANCIS, profl. hockey exec.; b. Montreal, Que., Can., Jan. 29, 1929; s. Stafford John and Jean (Ferry) O'N.; B.A., Loyola Coll., Montreal, 1949; B.Com., McGill U., Montreal, 1951; m. Jean Yates, Aug. 20, 1955; children—Sean, Darcy, Nancy, Patrick, Sandra. Publisher, Wallace Pub. Co., Montreal, 1953-62; bus. mgr. Fin. Times Can., Montreal, 1961-66; with Nat. Hockey League, Montreal, 1966—, exec. dir., 1970—. Adv. council Laurentian U., Sudbury, Ont.; bd. dirs., pres. St. Mary's Hosp., Montreal; bd. dirs. Que. Student Intra Exchange Program. Mem. Montreal Amateur Athletic Assn. Roman Catholic. Home: 212 Kenaston Ave Mount Royal PQ Canada Office: 920 Sun Life Bldg Montreal PQ H3B 2W2 Canada

O'NEILL, CHARLES KELLY, advt. co. exec.; b. Springfield, Mo., Apr. 2, 1933; s. Charles Chester and Frances (Kelly) O'N.; B.J., U. Mo., 1955; m. Barbara Lorene Maxwell, Nov. 21, 1964. With Galvin-Farris-Alvine, Kansas City, Mo., 1957-58, copy chief, 1958; with Potts-Woodbury, Inc., Kansas City, 1958-61, chief time buyer, 1960-61; with Gardner Advt. Co., St. Louis, 1962—, asso. media dir., 1964-65, media dir., 1965-69, v.p., 1966-76, corporate media dir., dir. co., 1969—, sr. v.p., 1976—, gen. mgr. Advanswers div., 1971-72, pres. Advanswers Media/Programming, Inc., 1973—; v.p. Wells, Rich, Greene, N.Y.C., 1974—, exec. v.p., 1979—, dir., 1978—; pres. Gardner Advt. Co., 1978—; dir. Westgate Research, Inc., Vangard Communications, Inc. Served to lt. (j.g.) USN, 1955-57. Mem. Sigma Chi, Alpha Delta Sigma. Clubs: St. Louis, St. Louis Racquet. Home: 6321 Rosebury St St Louis MO 63105 Office: 10 Broadway St Louis MO 63120 also 600 Madison Ave New York NY 10022

O'NEILL, DANIEL PATRICK, banker; b. St. Paul, June 8, 1919; s. Patrick Joseph and Florence (Millette) O'N.; ed. pub. schs.; grad. Sch. Mortgage Banking of Northwestern U., 1963; m. Elizabeth Lola Neahr, Feb. 8, 1945; children—Michael James, Linda Marie, Camille Lynn. Asst. cashier Bank Am., Long Beach, Calif., 1938-51, Long Beach Nat. Bank, 1951-52; asst. mgr. to asst. v.p. Security Pacific Nat. Bank, Los Angeles, 1952-69, v.p., br. mgr., Artesia, Calif., 1969-71, Cerritos, Calif., 1971-79. Served to 2d lt. USAAF, 1943-46. Mem. Am. Inst. Banking, Artesia C. of C. (pres., dir. 1970). Republican. Roman Catholic. Clubs: Artesia-Cerritos Rotary (treas., dir.). Address: 9949 Ledgeside Spring Valley CA 92078

O'NEILL, EDWARD ARTHUR, ins. co. exec.; b. Syracuse, N.Y., Feb. 28, 1914; s. Frank James and Grace (Northrup) O'N.; student George Sch. (Pa.), 1932-34; B.A., Williams Coll., 1937; m. Helen Florine Sampson, July 9, 1937 (dec. June 1971); 1 dau., Frances Armitage (Mrs. William Boardman Mosle, Jr.); m. 2d, Louise E. Henderson, Mar. 13, 1972. Claims adjuster Great Am. Ins. Co., N.Y.C., 1937-39, spl. agt., Newark, 1939-41, v.p., dir., N.Y.C., 1963-65, pres., dir., mem. exec. com., 1965-68; asst. prodn. mgr. Royal-Globe Ins. Co., 1941-45, regional mgr., Milw., 1945-57, Los Angeles, 1957-58; pres., dir. First Ins. Co. Hawaii, Ltd., Honolulu, 1958-65, vice chmn., 1965-68; v.p. ins. C.I.T. Fin. Corp., 1968-70; dir. Service Fire Ins. Co., N.Y.C., Service Casualty Co., N.Y.C., N.Am. Accident Ins. Co., N.Y.C., N.Am. Co. Health and Life Ins. (Ill.); pres., dir. Am. Nat. Fire Ins. Co., 1965-68; v.p. Gt. Am. Life Ins. Co., 1965-68; vice chmn., dir. Constellation Ins. Co., 1966-68; v.p. Continental Ins. Cos., 1970—; sr. v.p., dir. First Ins. Co. Hawaii, 1976—; pres., dir. Lydgate Calif. Inc., 1976—. Pres. Honolulu Community Chest, 1963-64. Mem. governing bd. Armed Services YMCA, Honolulu; bd. regents Chaminade Coll., Honolulu, 1972-74. Recipient Pub. Service citation Hawaii Legislature, 1965. Mem. Gen. Adjustment Bur. (dir.), Hawaii Ins. Rating Bur. (pres. 1972-73, exec. com. 1970—), Hawaii C. of C. (pres. 1965), Nat. Inst. Social Scis., Hawaii Insurers Council (chmn. 1977—), Navy League U.S. (nat. v.p. 1974-76, nat. exec. com., nat. dir., regional pres. 1978—), Ducks Unlimited, Delta Kappa Epsilon. Clubs: Pacific, Waialae Country (Honolulu). Home: 3965 Noela Pl Honolulu HI 96815 Office: 1100 Ward Ave Honolulu HI 96814

O'NEILL, EUGENE FRANCIS, communications engr.; b. N.Y.C., July 2, 1918; s. John J. and Agnes (Willmeyer) O'N.; B.S. in Elec. Engring., Columbia, 1940, M.S., 1941; D.Sc. (hon.), Bates Coll.; D.Engring. (hon.), Politecnico di Milano; D.Sc. (hon.), St. John's U., N.Y.C.; m. Kathryn M. Walls, Oct. 24, 1942; children—Kathryn Anne, Kevin, Jane A., Andrew Thomas. With Bell Telephone Labs., Holmdel, N.J., 1941—, engaged in radar devel., 1941-45, coaxial and submarine cable and microwave radio relay, 1945-56, headed devel. of speech interpolation terminals which doubled capacity submarine telephone cables, 1956-60, dir. Telstar satellite projects, 1960-66, exec. dir. network projects, 1966-78. Pulitzer prize scholar Columbia, 1936-40. Fellow IEEE; mem. Nat. Acad. Engring., Sigma Xi, Tau Beta Pi. Home: 17 Dellwood Ct Middletown NJ 07748 Office: Bell Telephone Labs Holmdel NJ 07733

O'NEILL, EUGENE MILTON, food wholesaler; b. Richmond, Calif., Nov. 4, 1925; s. John Milton and Vivian Elda (Vogel) O'N.; B.S. in Bus. and Pub. Adminstrn., Washington U., St. Louis, 1949; m. Jane Prigmore; children—Karen, Kay, Mary. Accountant, Jeff K. Stone & Co., St. Louis, 1948-52; controller Campbell Holton & Co. div. Gen. Grocer Co., Bloomington, Ill., 1953-54, pres., 1955-57; v.p. Gen. Grocer Co., St. Louis, 1957-60, pres., 1960-74, chmn. bd., pres., 1974—; dir. Boatman's Nat. Bank, St. Louis. Served with USAAF, 1943-45. Mem. Food Mktg. Inst. (dir.), Nat. Wholesale Am. Grocers Assn. (past chmn.). Home: 8 Deacon Dr Saint Louis MO 63131 Office: 8514 Eager Rd Brentwood MO 63144

O'NEILL, FRANCIS ALOYSIUS, JR., ret. govt. ofcl.; b. Bklyn., Apr. 3, 1908; s. Francis Aloysius and Elizabeth (Evans) O.; A.B., Fordham U., 1929, LL.B., 1932; m. Esther I. McNellen, Nov. 1, 1969. Admitted to N.Y. bar, 1933, practice law with father, 1933-39; atty. N.Y. State Labor Relations Bd., 1939-41, trial examiner, 1941-43, chief trial examiner, 1946-47; mem. Nat. Mediation Bd., 1947-71; past mem. R.R. Wage-Bd.; now labor cons. and arbitrator. Served with USNR 1943-45; labor relations officer, Cin., 1944-45. Mem. N.Y. County Lawyers Assn., Fordham U. Alumni Assn. Republican. Roman Catholic. K.C. Home: 2412 Riverside Terr Manasquan NJ 08736

O'NEILL, GERARD KITCHEN, physicist; b. Bklyn., Feb. 6, 1927; s. Edward G. and Dorothy (Kitchen) O'N.; B.A., Swarthmore Coll., 1950, also Sc.D. (hon.), 1978; Ph.D., Cornell U., 1954; m. 1950 (div. 1966); children—Janet, Roger, Eleanor; m. 2d, Renate Steffen, 1973.

Mem. faculty Princeton, 1954—, prof. physics, 1965—. Mem. vis. com. Nat. Air and Space Mus., 1976—; Hunsaker prof. aerospace Mass. Inst. Tech., 1976-77. Served with USNR, 1944-46. Recipient Glover medal, 1977, Sci. Book award Phi Beta Kappa, 1977. Instr. rated pilot. Fellow Am. Phys. Soc., Am. Inst. Aeros. and Astronautics; mem. Soaring Soc. Am., Exptl. Aircraft Assn. Research, publs. on exptl. elementary particle physics, particle storage rings, nuclear physics, space devel. techniques. Author: The High Frontier, 1977. Editor: Space Manufacturing from Non-Terrestrial Materials, 1977; Introduction to Elementary Particle Physics, 1979. Address: Physics Dept Box 708 Princeton NJ 08540. *To me the ideals of human freedom, of individual choice, and of concern for others have always been of the greatest importance. Much of my favorite reading is of authors who wrote in the early part of this century, when right and wrong seemed more clearcut than they do today, and when individual achievement was more highly regarded. I find my greatest personal satisfaction in a warm and intense family life embracing several generations, and in those achievements, modest though they may be, which I know to be my own. I hope that at the end of my life I can look back on work honestly done and on fair dealings with others.*

O'NEILL, GROVER, JR., business exec.; b. N.Y.C., Dec. 30, 1922; s. Grover and Catharine Gray (Porter) O'N.; grad. St. Marks Sch., 1940; B.A., Harvard, 1944; m. Kathryn Dunscombe, May 24, 1944; children—Carol Boker Wendell, Grover III. Security analyst Grover O'Neill & Co., N.Y.C., 1946-48; security analyst, registered rep. Fahnestock & Co., 1948-56, partner, 1957-67; mng. partner Wood, Walker & Co., N.Y.C., 1967-72; chmn. Piedmont Adv. Inc. 1972—. Vice chmn., trustee St. Barnabas Hosp., Bronx. Served to 1st lt. AUS, 1943-46. Episcopalian. Club: Piping Rock (Locust Valley, N.Y.). Home: 161 E 79th St New York NY 10021 Office: 111 Prospect St Stamford CT 06904

O'NEILL, HARRY WILLIAM, survey research co. exec.; b. Atlantic City, Jan. 30, 1929; s. Harry William and Marian Elizabeth (Kuhl) O'N.; B.A., Colgate U., 1950; M.S., Pa. State U., 1951; m. Carmel Gullo, Sept. 21, 1952; children—Sharon Ruth, Randal Bruce. Research analyst Prudential Ins. Co., Newark, 1957-62; with Opinion Research Corp., Princeton, N.J., 1962—, sr. v.p., 1970-73, exec. v.p., 1973—, also dir.; mem. coadj. faculty Rutgers U., 1959-64; trustee Nat. Council Public Polls. Mem. Highland Park (N.J.) Human Rights Commn., 1973-77; bd. dirs. Delaware-Raritan Lung Assn., 1974—, v.p., 1977—; fin. chmn. Highland Park Republican Orgn., 1977—. Served with USAF, 1951-54. Recipient Maroon citation Colgate U., 1975; lic. practicing psychologist, N.J. Mem. Am. Psychol. Assn., Eastern Psychol. Assn., Am. Assn. Public Opinion Research, Met. N.Y. Assn. Applied Psychology, Assn. Consumer Research. Presbyterian. Clubs: Highland Park Republican, Masons, Elks. Home: 2 Cleveland Ave Highland Park NJ 08904 Office: Opinion Research Corp N Harrison St Princeton NJ 08540

O'NEILL, JAMES EDWARD, banker; b. Washington, Jan. 3, 1923; s. James Edward and Della Rae (Crown) O'N.; B.C.S., Strayer Coll., 1948; grad. with honors Sch. Bank Adminstrn., U. Wis., 1963; grad. Nat. Automation Sch., Purdue U., 1969; m. Joyce Ann Stovall, May 4, 1945; children—James Richard, JoAnn. With Riggs Nat. Bank, Washington, 1941—, dep. comptroller, 1958-68, v.p., 1968—, comptroller, 1971—, sr. v.p., 1976—; mem. faculty Washington chpt. Am. Inst. Bank, 1954-56. Asst. treas. Inaugural Com., 1969. Served with USNR, 1943-45. Mem. Bank Adminstrn. Inst. (pres. Washington chpt. 1967-68, nat. dir. 1970-72, dir.-at-large 1974-76, Washington liaison rep. 1976—, nat. dir. 1977—). Baptist (deacon 1972—, treas. 1956-59). Home: 4512 Woodfield Rd Kensington MD 20795 Office: 1503 Pennsylvania Ave NW Washington DC 20013

O'NEILL, JAMES EUGENE, paper co. exec.; b. Marlboro, N.Y., May 18, 1923; s. James Joseph and Alice J. O'Neill; grad. St. Joseph's U., Phila.; m. Mary Jane Tague, Apr. 19, 1952; children—James Eugene, Michael J., Terence F., Brian S. With Scott Paper Co., Phila., div. v.p., gen. mgr. tissue div., v.p. consumer products mktg. and sales, now sr. v.p. indsl. relations. Served with AUS, 1943-46. Mem. Am. Paper Inst. Republican. Roman Catholic. Office: Scott Paper Co Scott Plaza Philadelphia PA 19113

O'NEILL, JAMES WARD, lawyer; b. N.Y.C., Aug. 20, 1903; s. Charles Joseph and Sarah T. (Ward) O'N.; A.B., Fordham U., 1924, LL.B., 1929; m. Helen M. Faller, Sept. 23, 1933; children—James Ward, Theodore George, Charles Kenneth. Admitted to N.Y. bar, 1930, U.S. Supreme Ct., 1953, numerous fed. cts.; practice in N.Y.C., 1930—; partner firm Haight, Gardner, Poor & Havens, 1947—; lectr. N.Y.U., 1953, Practicing Law Inst., N.Y.C., 1953—. Pres. Faller Devel. Corp., S.I., Moravian Holding Co., S.I. Chmn. Citizens Com. for Erection of Carle Place (N.Y.) High Sch. Bd. govs. Fordham U., 1955-59, Fordham U. Law Sch.; adv. com. Talbot Perkins Adoption Service, Bklyn., 1957—. Recipient Achievement award in law Fordham U., 1974. Fellow Am. Coll. Trial Lawyers (admissions com. Downstate N.Y.); mem. Am. Internat. bar assns., Maritime Law Assn. (exec. com.), N.Y. Law Inst., Average Adjusters Assn., Fed. Bar Council, Maritime Exchange Port N.Y., Guild Cath. Lawyers, Fordham Coll. Alumni Assn. (dir. 1953-58), Fordham Law School Alumni Assn. (dir.), Knights of Malta. Clubs: Harborview; Propeller (gov.); N.Y. Plaza; India House; Douglaston, Douglaston Yacht, Squadron, Circumnavigators, Friendly Sons of St. Patrick. Home: 304 Shore Rd Douglaston NY 11363 Office: 1 State St Plaza New York City NY 10004

O'NEILL, JOHN JOSEPH, educator; b. De Pere, Wis., Dec. 6, 1920; s. John Joseph and Elizabeth (Murray) O'N.; B.S., Ohio State U., 1947, Ph.D., 1951; m. Dorothy Jane Arnold, Dec. 28, 1943; children—Katherine, Thomas, John, Philip, From instr. to asso. prof. speech Ohio State U., 1949-59; prof. speech U. Ill. at Champaign, 1959—; prof. audiology U. Ill. Coll. Medicine, Chgo., 1965—, head speech and hearing sci. dept., 1973—; research asso. U.S. Naval Sch. Aviation Medicine, summers 1953, 54; cons. in field. Pres. Columbus Hearing Soc., 1956-58. Bd. dirs. Champaign County Assn. Crippled-United Cerebral Palsy, 1961-63. Served with inf. AUS, 1942-46. Decorated Purple Heart, Bronze Star with oak leaf cluster; recipient Distinguished Alumnus award Dept. Speech, Ohio State U., 1969. Fellow Am. Speech and Hearing Assn. (pres. 1969), Ohio Psychol. Assn.; mem. Am. Bd. Examiners Speech Pathology and Audiology (pres. 1967-68) Acad. Rehabilitative Audiology (pres. 1969). Co-author: Visual Communication, 1961; Hard of Hearing, 1964; Applied Audiometry, 1966. Home: 1113 W Church St Champaign IL 61820

O'NEILL, JOHN JOSEPH, JR., chem. co. exec.; b. N.Y.C., Sept. 13, 1919; s. John Joseph and Margaret (Patterson) O'N.; B.S. in Chem. Engring., Mo. Sch. Mines, 1940, Chem. Engr., 1951; m. Irene Ray, Apr. 18, 1940; children—Anne, Mary (Mrs. George Schuler). Research engr. Western Cartridge Co., 1940-49; with Olin Industries, Inc., 1949-60, dir. prodn. explosives operations, energy div., 1959-60; with Olin Mathieson Chem. Corp., 1960-71, asst. to pres., 1963-64, staff v.p. planning, 1964-65, v.p. comml. devel., chems. group, 1965-67, corporate v.p. plastics, 1967-70, corporate v.p. product diverification, 1970-71; cons., 1971-72; exec. v.p., chief operating officer Kleer-Vu Inc., N.Y.C., 1972-76; v.p. planning and devel. Vertac Consol., 1976-77; pres., chief exec. officer Vertac, Inc., 1977-78, cons., 1979—. Trustee, St. Mary-of-Woods Coll., Terre Haute, Ind. Fellow Am. Inst. Chemists; mem. Am. Inst. Chem. Engring. Club: Chemists (N.Y.C.). Author articles, patentee explosives, chemicals, ordnance items. Home: 2310 Penbrook Fairway Cordova TN 38018 Office: 5100 Poplar Ave Memphis TN 38137

O'NEILL, JOHN JOSEPH, JR., publishing co. exec., former fgn. service officer; b. New Haven, Aug. 16, 1922; s. John J. and Mary A. (Farren) O'Neill; B.S., U.S. Naval Acad., 1947; certificate Yale Sch. Eastern Langs., 1950; M.A., Columbia, 1955; m. Jessie R. Piccolo, Sept. 29, 1951; children—Mary, John, Barbara, Stephen. With U.S. Fgn. Service, 1960-78; comml. attache, Bangkok, 1960-64; assigned Dept. State, 1964-69; dep. chief mission, Singapore, 1971-73; diplomat-in-residence U. N.H., 1973; dir. Office Internat. Communications Policy, Dept. State, Washington, 1974-78; v.p. corp. devel. Horizon House, Dedham, Mass., 1978—; del. AEROSAT Council, 1974-78; U.S. rep. adminstrv. Council Internat. Telecommunications Union, 1974-77. Served with USN, 1943-46, USMCR, 1946-49, 51-53. Clubs: Army Navy Country (Arlington, Va.); Singapore Cricket, Tanglin (Singapore). Home: 145 Middlebeach Rd Madison CT 06443

O'NEILL, JOSEPH JAMES, publisher; b. St. Louis, Jan. 12, 1917; s. Joseph James and Dorothy (Frei) O'N.; B. Journalism, U. Mo., 1939; m. Anne Hill, Feb. 3, 1940; children—Julie M. (Mrs. Kevin P. Connelly), Lawrence H. Advt. rep., nat. advt. mgr. Aurora (Ill.) Beacon-News, 1939-42; advt. rep. Evansville (Ind.) Courier-Press, 1942-43; dir. pub. relations Pratt & Whitney Aircraft Co., 1943-44; with Maclean-Hunter Pub. Corp., Chgo., 1944—, pub., 1950—, pres., 1964—, also dir.; dir. Am. Bus. Press, Inc., N.Y.C. Mem. Tau Kappa Epsilon, Kappa Tau Alpha. Clubs: University, Executives (Chgo.); Medinah (Ill.) Country; Delray Dunes (Fla.) Country. Home: 23 W 060 Mulberry Ln Glen Ellyn IL 60137 Office: 300 W Adams St Chicago IL 60606

O'NEILL, MARK PATRICK, lawyer; b. Mpls., Dec. 6, 1925; s. Francis Lawrence and Gertrude Jane (Timmerman) O'N.; A.B., Harvard U., 1949, LL.B., 1952; m. Edna Drexler, Aug. 1, 1953; children—Kevin Francis, David William, Timothy Gareth. Admitted to Ohio bar, 1952, U.S. Supreme Ct. bar, 1974; asso. firm McConnell, Blackmore, Cory & Burke, Cleve., 1952-61; partner firm Weston, Hurd, Fallon, Paisley & Howley, Cleve., 1962—, mem. exec. com. Mem. Communications Commn., City of University Heights, Ohio, 1976-78; chmn. Charter Rev. Commn., University Heights, 1979. Served with USNR, 1943-44, USMC, 1944-46. Mem. Bar Assn. Greater Cleve. (bd. trustees 1971-73, chmn. judicial selection com. 1970), Ohio State Bar Assn., Am. Bar Assn., Internat. Assn. Ins. Counsel, Ohio Def. Assn., Def. Research Inst. (vice chmn. profl. liability com. 1977-78), Am. Law Inst., Am. Coll. Trial Lawyers. Club: Harvard (Cleve.). Home: 2349 S Belvoir Blvd University Heights OH 44118 Office: 2500 Terminal Tower Cleveland OH 44113

O'NEILL, MICHAEL JAMES, editor; b. Detroit, Nov. 19, 1922; s. Michael J. and Ellen Mary (Dacey) O'N.; B.A., U. Detroit, 1946, L.H.D. (hon.), 1977; grad. student Fordham U., 1946-47; m. Mary Jane Kilcoyne, May 31, 1948; children—Michael, Maureen, Kevin, John, Kathyrn. Pub. relations cons., 1945-46; radio commentator sta. WJBK, Detroit, 1946; writer Standard News Assn., N.Y.C., 1946-47; with U.P.I., 1947-56, Washington overnight editor, 1954-56; Washington corr. N.Y. Daily News, 1956-66, asst. mng. editor, 1966-68, mng. editor, 1968-74, exec. editor, 1974-75, editor, 1975—, v.p., dir., 1971—. Former mem. Nat. Adv. Council Health Professions Edn. Served with AUS, 1943-45; ETO. Decorated Bronze Star. Recipient Nat. Affairs Reporting award Nat. Headliner's, 1956. Mem. State Dept. Corr. Assn. (pres. 1964-65), Overseas Writers (pres. 1965), N.Y. Acad. Scis., Council on Fgn. Relations, China Council. Club: Century (N.Y.C.). Author: (with L. Tanzer) The Kennedy Circle, 1961; China Today, 1976. Office: N Y Daily News 220 E 42d St New York City NY 10017

O'NEILL, MICHAEL JOYCE, mag. pub.; b. Shreveport, La., Apr. 2, 1922; s. Michael Joyce and Anna (McCrea) O.; B.S., U. Pa., 1947; m. Marie Clark, Apr. 24, 1948; children—Michael, James, Kate, Clark; m. 2d, Betty Wright Landreth, Nov. 6, 1976. Dir. spl. events Phila. Inquirer, 1947-49, regional mgr. advt. dept., 1949-51, exec. dir. Phila. Inquirer Charities, 1951-53; advt. dir. TV Guide, Phila., 1953-62; pres. Liberty Bell Park, Phila., 1962-64; chmn. Phila. Eagles Football Club, 1962-64; v.p., dir. corp. relations Young & Rubicam, Inc., N.Y.C., 1964-66; v.p., advt. dir. Look Mag., N.Y.C., 1966-70; v.p., pub. Field & Stream, N.Y.C., 1970-72; v.p., pub. Epicure, 1972-74; v.p., group pub. CBS Publs., 1976—. Trustee Annenberg Sch. Communications U. Pa. Served with USNR, 1941-45. Mem. Mag. Pubs. Assn. (dir.), Advt. Council (mag. dir.), Hunting Hall of Fame (dir.), Am. League Anglers (dir.), Pa. Soc. Clubs: University, Racquet (Phila.); Sky, Dutch Treat, African Safari. Home: 1 W 54th St New York NY 10022 Office: 1515 Broadway New York NY 10036. *I believe that we are the architects of our own destinies, and that success is not a destination you arrive at, but a way of traveling.*

O'NEILL, PATRICK HENRY, mining engr.; b. Cordova, Alaska, Aug. 11, 1915; s. Harry I. and Florence (Leahy) O'N.; B.S., U. Alaska, 1941, E.M., 1953, D.Sc. (hon.), 1976; m. 2d, Sandra Dorris, Dec. 5, 1967; children—Kevin Reddy, Erin Dorris, Patrick Henry, Timothy Hazleton, Frederick Leahy. Assayer, engr. U.S. Smelting Refining & Mining Co., Fairbanks, Alaska, 1939, asst. exploration engr., 1940-41, exploration engr., 1946-50, dredge supt., 1950-53; chief engr. Compania Minera Choco Pacifico, Colombia, South Am., 1953-54; v.p. South Am. Gold & Platinum Co., N.Y.C., 1954-57, exec. v.p., 1957-63, merged into Internat. Mining Corp., 1963, exec. v.p. corp., 1963-70, pres., 1970-77; sr. v.p. Rosario Resources Corp., N.Y.C., 1977—; v.p. Pato Consol Gold Dredging, Ltd. (Bermuda); pres. Rosario Mining of Nicaragua; pres. Fresnillo Co., N.Y.C.; dir. Rosario Dominicana, Dominican Republic, Compania Fresnillo, S.A., Mexico, Minera Mexicana Sombrerete; Pacific Tin Consol. Corp., Internat. Mining Corp. Trustee, Joslin Diabetes Found. Served to maj. USAAF, 1941-46. Mem. Mining and Metall. Soc. Am., Am. Inst. Mining, Metall. and Petroleum Engrs., Canadian Inst. Mining and Metallurgy, Arctic Inst., NAM (gov., chmn. 1972-73), Pioneers of Alaska, Instn. Mining and Metallurgy London, Am. Geog. Soc. (councilor), Pan Am. Soc. (dir.), Colombian-Am. (dir.), Mexican of U.S. (dir.) chambers commerce, Bolivarian Soc. U.S. (dir.). Clubs: Board Room, Explorers, Mining, Wings (N.Y.C.); Darien Country; Woodway Country. Home: 42 Dunning Rd New Canaan CT 06840 Office: 375 Park Ave Suite 310 New York NY 10022

O'NEILL, PAUL HENRY, paper co. exec.; b. St. Louis, Dec. 4, 1935; s. John Paul and Gaynald Elsie (Irvin) O'N.; A.B., Fresno State Coll., 1960; Haynes Found. fellow, Claremont Grad. Sch., 1960-61; postgrad. George Washington U., 1962-65; M.P.A., Ind. U., 1966; m. Nancy Jo Wolfe, Sept. 4, 1955; children—Patricia, Margaret, Julie, Paul Henry. Site engr. Morrison-Knudsen, Inc., Anchorage, 1955-57; systems analyst VA, Washington, 1961-66; budget examiner Bur. of Budget, Washington, 1967-69; chief human resources program div. U.S. Govt. Office of Mgmt. and Budget, Washington, 1969-70, asst. dir., 1971-72, asso. dir., 1973-74, dep. dir., 1975-77; v.p. Internat. Paper Co., N.Y.C., 1977—. Chmn. health and welfare com. Fairfax Fedn. Civic Assns., 1967; mem. JFK bd. visitors Harvard U., 1977—. Recipient Nat. Inst. Pub. Affairs Career Edn. award, 1965, William A. Jump Meritorious award, 1971. Fellow Nat. Inst. Pub. Affairs, 1966. Methodist. Home: 23 Pond View Ln New Canaan CT 06840 Office: Internat Paper Co 220 E 42d St New York NY 10017

O'NEILL, REGINALD FINBARR, educator; b. Nfld., Sept. 25, 1915; s. Patrick and Esther (Brophy) O'N.; A.B., Boston Coll., 1940, M.A., 1941; S.T.L., Weston Coll., 1947; Ph.D., Fordham U., 1952. Joined Soc. of Jesus, 1934, ordained priest Roman Cath. Ch., 1946; prof. philosophy Boston Coll. Sch. Philosophy, 1951-69, dean, 1962-69; vis. prof. philosophy U. W.I., Kingston, Jamaica 1969-70; prof. philosophy Fitchburg (Mass.) State Coll., 1970—; vis. summer prof. Holy Cross Coll., 1957, Loyola U., Chgo., 1961, Fordham U., 1960. Mem. Am. Cath., Jesuit (sec. 1957-60, pres. 1963-64) philos. assns., Soc. Phenomenology and Existential Philosophy, Metaphysical Soc. Am. Author: Theories of Knowledge, 1960; Readings in Epistemology, 1962. Home: 34 Carriage Way Dr Fitchburg MA 01420 Office: Fitchburg State Coll Fitchburg MA 01420

O'NEILL, RICHARD WINSLOW, housing exec.; b. Madison, Wis., Sept. 5, 1925; s. James Milton and Edith (Winslow) O'N.; student Hotchkiss Sch., 1941-43; B.S., Yale, 1950; student Oxford (Eng.) U., 1949; m. Barbara Powell, Jan. 3, 1953 (div. Feb. 1966); children—Richard Winslow, Susan Powell, Jennifer Anne, Julia Kay; m. 2d, Patricia Betz, Nov. 21, 1969. Constrn. supt. Bing & Bing, N.Y.C., 1950-53; asst. editor Engring. News-Record, McGraw-Hill Pub. Co., N.Y.C., 1953-55, asso. editor House & Home, 1955-64, chief editor, 1964-70; pres. Housing Adv. Council, Ltd., 1971—. Mem. Citizens Housing and Planning Council N.Y., 1967-74, Nat. Commn. on Urban Problems, 1967-68. Served with inf. AUS, 1943-46; ETO, PTO. Independent. Author: High Steel, Hard Rock and Deep Water, 1965: The Unhandyman's Guide to Home Repair, 1966; The Dynamics of the New Housing Industry, 1970. Home: PO Box 384 Lakeville CT 06039

O'NEILL, ROBERT CHARLES, cons., inventor; b. Buffalo, Dec. 3, 1923; s. Albert T. and Helen (Lynch) O'N.; B.S. in Chemistry, Rensselaer Poly. Inst., 1945; Ph.D. in Organic Chemistry, Mass. Inst. Tech., 1950; m. Agnes Balischak; 1 dau., Eileen Anne. Sr. chemist Merck & Co., Inc., Rahway, N.J., 1950-56, marketing devel. specialist, 1956-58; v.p. Stauffer Pharms. div. Stauffer Chem. Co., N.Y.C., 1958-61; v.p., dir. research and devel. Cooper Labs., Inc., 1961-70, exec. v.p., 1970-76, gen. mgr., 1975-76, pres., 1976-77, also dir.; cons., inventor, 1977—. Served with USNR, 1943-46. Mem. Am. Chem. Soc., Chemists Club N.Y. Contbr. articles to profl. jours. Patentee in field. Home: 10 Whitlaw Close Chappaqua NY 10514

O'NEILL, ROBERT EDWARD, editor; b. N.Y.C., Aug. 30, 1925; s. Joseph Michael and Ethel Agnes (Seymour) O'N.; B.A. in Journalism, Syracuse (N.Y.) U., 1950; m. Phyllis Ann Schreck, Apr. 19, 1952; children—Keith, Kathy, Kim, Karen. Reporter Southeasterner, Long Island, N.Y., 1950-51; rep. Bklyn. Daily, 1952; asso. editor Progressive Grocer, N.Y.C., 1952-62, sr. editor, 1962-69, exec. editor, 1970—. Served with USN, 1944-47. Mem. Am. Bus. Press (editorial com. 1974-75 co-winner Jesse H. Neal award 1974), Glacier Hills Assn. (pres. 1964-66), Sigma Delta Chi. Contbg. author/editor: Foodtown Study, 1954, Super Valu Study, 1957, Dillon Study, 1959, Colonial Study, 1961, Outstanding New Super Markets, 1961, Consumer Dynamics, 1963, A & P Study, 1970, Merchandising in Action, 1972; Consumer Behavior Study, 1976; Brand Power Study, 1977. Home: 67 Moraine Rd Morris Plains NJ 07950 Office: Progressive Grocer 708 3d Ave New York NY 10017

O'NEILL, RUSSELL RICHARD, univ. dean; b. Chgo., June 6, 1916; s. Dennis Alysious and Florence Agnes (Mathurin) O'N.; B.S. in Mech. Engring., U. Calif. at Berkeley, M.S. in Mech. Engring., 1940; Ph.D., U. Calif. at Los Angeles, 1956; m. Margaret Bock, Dec. 15, 1939; children—Richard A., John R.; m. 2d, Sallie Boyd, June 30, 1967. Design engr. Dowell, Inc., Midland, Mich., 1940-41; design engr. Dow Chem. Co., Midland, 1941-44; design engr. Airesearch Mfg. Co., Los Angeles, 1944-46; lectr. engring. U. Calif. at Los Angeles, 1946-56, prof. engring., 1956, asst. dean engring., 1956-61, asso. dean., 1961-73, acting dean, 1965-66, 73—; staff engr. Nat. Acad. Sci.-NRC, 1954. Mem. engring. task force Space Era Edn. Study Fla. Bd. Control, 1963; mem. regional Export Expansion Council Dept. Commerce, 1960-66, Los Angeles Mayor's Space Adv. Com., 1964-69. Registered profl. engr., Calif. Mem. Nat. Acad. Engring., Am. Soc. Engring. Edn., Soc. Naval Architects and Marine Engrs., Triangle, Sigma Xi, Tau Beta Pi. Home: 15430 Longbow Dr Sherman Oaks CA 91403 Office: 405 Hilgard Ave Los Angeles CA 90024

O'NEILL, THOMAS NEWMAN, JR., lawyer; b. Hanover, Pa., July 6, 1928; s. Thomas Newman and Emma (Cornpropst) O'N.; A.B. magna cum laude, Catholic U. Am., 1950; LL.B. magna cum laude, U. Pa., 1953; postgrad. (Fulbright grantee) London Sch. Econs., 1955-56; m. Jeanne M. Corr. Feb. 4, 1961; children—Caroline Jeanne, Thomas Newman, Ellen Gitt. Admitted to Pa. bar, 1954, U.S. Supreme Ct. bar, 1959; law clk. to judge U.S. Ct. Appeals 3d Circuit, 1953-54, to Justice Harold H. Burton, U.S. Supreme Ct., 1954-55; asso. firm Montgomery, McCracken, Walker & Rhoads, Phila., 1956-63, partner, 1963-; counsel Pa. Legis. Reapportionment Commn., 1971-72; lectr. U. Pa. Law Sch., 1973. Fellow Am. Bar Found.; mem. Am. Law Inst., Phila. Bar Assn. (chancellor 1976), Pa. Bar Assn. (gov. 1978—), Am. Bar Assn. (del 1976), Jud. Conf. Third Circuit (permanent del.), U. Pa. Law Alumni Soc. (pres. 1976-77), Order of Coif (pres. U. Pa. chpt. 1971-73), Phi Beta Kappa. Clubs: Merion Cricket, Union League. Articles editor U. Pa. Law Rev., 1952-53. Home: 512 Conshohocken State Rd Gladwyne PA 19035 Office: 3 Parkway Philadelphia PA 19102

O'NEILL, THOMAS P., congressman; b. Dec. 9, 1912; s. Thomas P. and Rose Anne (Tolan) O'N.; ed. St. John's High Sch. and Boston Coll.; m. Mildred Anne Miller, June 17, 1941; children—Rosemary, Thomas III, Susan, Christopher, Michael Tolan. Engaged in ins. bus., Cambridge, Mass.; mem. Cambridge Sch. Com., 1946, 49; mem. Mass. Legislature, 1936-52, minority leader, 1947, 48, speaker of house, 1948-52; mem. 83d-87th Congresses 11th Mass. Dist., mem. 88th-96th Congresses from 8th Mass. Dist., majority whip, 1971-73, majority leader, 1973-77, speaker, 1977—. Democrat. Address: Room H-204 US Capitol Washington DC 20515

O'NEILL, THOMAS P., III, state ofcl.; b. Cambridge, Mass., Sept. 20, 1944; s. Thomas P., Jr. and Mildred Anne (Miller) O'N.; B.A., Boston Coll., 1968; postgrad. U. Finance, N.Y., 1969; m. Jacqueline Anne Demartino, 1969. Stockbroker, Harris Upham & Co., from 1968; mem. Mass. Legislature, 1972-75; lt. gov. Mass., Boston, 1975—. Vice chmn. Cambridge Democratic City Com., 1968-72; chmn. Ward 10 Dem. Com., 1968-72; mem. War 11 Dem. Com., from 1972; chmn. drive Cambridge United Fund, 1972; bd. dirs. New Eng. Home for Little Wanderers; v.p., bd. dirs. Paraplegic Research Fund. Served with U.S. Army Res., 1968-73. Named Outstanding Young Man of Year, Jr. C. of C., 1973. Mem. Cambridge Jr. C. of C. (dir.), Amvets. Roman Catholic. Club: K.C. Office: Office of Lt Gov State House Room 259 Boston MA 02133*

O'NEILL, WILLIAM A(TCHISON), lt. gov. Conn.; b. Hartford, Conn., Aug. 11, 1930; ed. New Brit. Tchr.'s Coll., U. Hartford; m. Natalie. Owner, O'Neill's Restaurant, East Hampton, Conn.; mem. Conn. Ho. of Reps., asst. house majority leader, 1971-72, asst. minority leader, 1973-74, house majority leader, 1975-76, 77-78, chmn. com. on exec. nominations; lt. gov. State of Conn., 1979—; mem. Conn. Gov.'s Fin. Adv. Com., 1968-74. Mem. East Hampton Democratic Town Com., 1954-78; mem. East Hampton Zoning Bd. Appeals; mem. East Hampton Bd. Fin.; mem. East Hampton Fire Dist. Commn.; state chmn. Ella Grasso For Gov. Com., 1974; chmn. Conn. Dem. Party, 1975-78. Served with USAF, 1950-53. Recipient Am. Legion Dept. Conn. award as outstanding legis. leader, 1974. Mem. C. of C. of East Hampton (pres.). Clubs: Elks, Am. Legion Moose, VFW. Office: Office Lt Gov State Capitol Room 304 Hartford CT 06115

O'NEILL, WILLIAM JAMES, leasing transp. co. exec; b. Cleve., Sept. 21, 1906; s. Hugh and Louise (Berchtold) O'N.; A.B., Notre Dame, 1928; m. Dorothy Kundtz, May 28, 1932; children—William, Dorothy (Mrs. John Donahey), Kathleen (Mrs. William France), Molly (Mrs. George Sweeney), Timothy. Operating mgr. Superior Transfer Co., CCC Hwy., Motor Express Inc., 1928-30; chief operating officer over-the-road carrier subs. U.S. Truck Lines, Inc., 1930-37; founder pres., chief exec. officer owner Niagara Motor Express, 1938-59; chmn. bd. Lease Plan Internat. Corp., N.Y.C., 1959-61; founder, chmn. bd., chief exec. officer pres. Transp. Finance Corp., 1954—; pres., chief exec. officer Leaseway, Ltd., Can., 1959-75; founder, pres., chmn. bd., chief exec. officer Leaseway Transp. Corp., 1961-75; chmn. bd. Leaseway Intercontinental (LEASECO) S.A., Zug, Switzerland, 1962-72; founder seven fin. leasing cos., Europe, Mex., Can.; partner N.Y. Yankees; dir. PORTEC. Pres., trustee O'Neill Bros. Found.; trustee, mem. distbn. com. Cleve. Found.; trustee W.J. and D.K. O'Neill Fund, Sherwick Fund; 1st lay pres. Gilmour Acad., Gates Mills, Ohio; hon. trustee Robinson Sch., West Hartford, Conn. Mem. Newcomen Soc. N.A. Clubs: Pepper Pike, Country (Pepper Pike, Ohio); Metropolitan (N.Y.C.); Chagrin Valley Hunt (Gates Mills, Ohio); Union (Cleve.). Home: Clandonderry Ct Daisy Hill RD 3 Chagrin Falls OH 44022 Office: 3733 Park East Dr Suite 101 Beachwood OH 44122

O'NEILL, WILLIAM JAMES, JR., transp. co. exec.; b. Cleve., Aug. 28, 1933; s. William James and Dorothy (Kundtz) O'N.; B.S. cum laude, Georgetown U., 1955; J.D., Harvard U., 1958; m. Deborah J. Baker, Oct. 22, 1966; children—Alec M., Sara L., Jessie A., Laura E. Admitted to Ohio bar, 1958; gen. counsel Leaseway Transp. Corp. and subs., 1961-67, East coast group head, Phila., 1967-68, v.p. East Coast group, 1968-69, sr. v.p., Cleve., 1969-74, pres., chief operating officer, 1974—, also dir.; dir. Trala, Washington. Trustee, Dyke Coll. Corp., Cleve., O'Neill Bros. Found., Cleve., Gilmour Acad., Cleve., Bluecoats, Cleve. Served to capt. USAF, 1958-61. Recipient Air Force Commendation medal with oak leaf clusters; named Man of Year, Gilmour Acad., 1974. Mem. Am. Bar Assn. Roman Catholic. Clubs: Hunting Valley Gun, Country, Cleve. Polo, Park East Racquet. Home: 2735 Cranlyn Rd Shaker Heights OH 44122 Office: 3700 Park East Dr Cleveland OH 44122

O'NEILL, WILLIAM LAWRENCE, historian; b. Big Rapids, Mich., Apr. 18, 1935; s. John Patrick and Helen Elizabeth (Marsh) O'N.; A.B., U. Mich., 1957; M.A., U. Calif., Berkeley, 1958, Ph.D., 1963; m. Elizabeth Carol Knollmueller, Aug. 20, 1960; children—Cassandra Leigh, Catherine Lorraine. Asst. prof. history U. Colo., 1964-66; asst. prof. U. Wis., 1966-69, asso. prof., 1969-71; prof. Rutgers U., New Brunswick, N.J., 1971—; vis. asst. prof. U. Pitts., 1963-64; vis. asso. prof. U. Pa., 1969-70. Nat. Endowment Humanities fellow, 1979-80. Mem. Am. Hist. Assn., Orgn. Am. Historians, Author's Guild. Author: Divorce in the Progressive Era, 1967; Everyone Was Brave: The Rise and Fall of Feminism in America, 1969; Coming Apart: An Informal History of America in the 1960's, 1971; The Last Romantic: A Life of Max Eastman, 1978. Home: 232 Harrison Ave Highland Park NJ 08904 Office: Dept History Rutgers U New Brunswick NJ 08903. *Apart from my electric typewriter, an author's best friend, I owe everything to luck.*

O'NEILL, WILLIAM T., shipyard exec.; b. N.Y.C., Sept. 4, 1920; s. William A. and Mary R. (Amberson) O'N.; B.Indsl. Engring., N.Y. U., 1953; postgrad. Stevens Inst. Tech., 1956-57; m. Cynthia Bereinguer, Sept. 25, 1948; children—William, Stephen, James, Kathleen, Laura, Randolph. Engring. supr. Western Union, 1953-54; with Colgate Palmolive, 1954-61, chief engr., 1961, chief engr., Colgate Palmolive Internat., London, 1962-66; corp. dir. spl. projects, dir. fin. controls ITT, 1966-74; with Newport News Shipbldg. (Va.), 1974—, now exec. v.p. tech.; dir. James River Oyster Co., Newport News Offshore Systems, Newport News Indsl., Greenville Metal Mfg. Inc., Newport News Indsl. of Ohio, 1st and Mchts. Bank of Peninsula. Bd. dirs., Peninsula Arts Assn., Peninsula United Fund, Coll. William and Mary Sch. of Bus. Served with USNR, 1942-46. Mem. Va. C. of C., Am. Banking Inst. Va. Mfg. Assn. Clubs: James River Country (dir.), Kingsmill Golf. Office: 4101 Washington Ave Newport News VA 23607

ONETO, GEORGE J., union exec.; b. May 20, 1910; m. Rose. Vice-pres., Distillery, Wine and Allied Workers Internat. Union, AFL-CIO, Englewood, N.J., 1940-57, gen. sec.-treas., 1957-74, gen. pres., 1974—, pres. Local 1, 1936—; mem. exec. com. Internat. Union Food and Allied Workers Assn., Geneva. Served with U.S. Army, World War II. Office: 66 Grand Ave PO Box 567 Englewood NJ 07631. *The prime requisite for a labor leader is the sincere desire to help people.*

ONG, JOHN DOYLE, rubber products co. exec.; b. Uhrichsville, Ohio, Sept. 29, 1933; s. Louis Brosee and Mary Ellen (Liggett) O.; B.A., Ohio State U., 1954, M.A., 1954; LL.B., Harvard, 1957; m. Mary Lee Schupp, July 20, 1957; children—John Francis Harlan, Richard Penn Blackburn, Mary Katherine Caine. Admitted to Ohio bar, 1958; asst. counsel B.F. Goodrich Co., Akron, 1961-66, group v.p., 1972-73, exec. v.p., 1973-74, vice chmn., 1974-75, pres., dir., 1975-77, pres., chief operating officer, dir., 1978-79, chmn. bd., pres., chief exec. officer, 1979—; asst. to pres. Internat. B.F. Goodrich Co., Akron, 1966-69, v.p., 1969-70, pres., 1970-72; dir. Cooper Industries, The Kroger Co. Vice-pres. exploring Great Trail council Boy Scouts Am., 1974-77; v.p. Akron Community Trusts. Trustee Akron Regional Devel. Bd., Mus. Arts Assn., Cleve., Bexley Hall Sem., 1974—; trustee Hudson (Ohio) Library and Hist. Soc., pres., 1971-72; trustee Western Res. Acad., Hudson, 1975—, pres. bd. trustees, 1977—; nat. trustee Nat. Symphony Orch., 1975—; mem. bus. adv. com. Transp. Center, Northwestern U., 1975-78, Carnegie-Mellon U., 1978—; mem. adv. bd. Blossom Music Center. Served with JAGC, AUS, 1957-61. Mem. Ohio Bar Assn. (bd. govs. corp. counsel sect. 1962-74, chmn. 1970), Rubber Mfrs. Assn. (dir. 1974—), Conf. Bd., Phi Beta Kappa, Phi Alpha Theta. Episcopalian. Clubs: Portage Country, Akron City; Union (Cleve.); Links, Union League (N.Y.C.); Country of Hudson (Ohio); Georgetown (Washington); Rolling Rock (Ligonier, Pa.); Castalia Trout. Home: 230 Aurora St Hudson OH 44236 Office: 500 S Main St Akron OH 44318

ONG, WALTER JACKSON, clergyman, educator, author: b. Kansas City, Mo., Nov. 30, 1912; s. Walter Jackson and Blanche Eugenia (Mense) O.; A.B., Rockhurst Coll., 1933; Ph.L., St. Louis U., 1940, A.M., 1941, S.T.L., 1948; Ph.D., Harvard U., 1955; various hon. degrees. Newspaper, comml. positions until 1935; entered Soc. of Jesus, 1935, ordained priest, Roman Catholic Ch., 1946; instr. English and French, Regis Coll., Denver, 1941-43; asst. English, St. Louis U., 1944-47, instr., 1953-54, asst. prof., 1954-57, asso. prof., 1957-59. prof., 1959—, prof. humanities in psychiatry Sch. Medicine, 1970—. Mem. Fulbright nat. selection com., France, 1957-58, chmn., 1958; regional asso. Am. Council Learned Socs. 1957-66; mem. White House Task Force on Edn., 1966-67; mem. Nat. Council on Humanities, 1968-74, vice chmn., 1971-74; co-chmn. adv. com. on sci., tech. and human values Nat. Endowment for Humanities, 1974-78; mem. Rockefeller Found. Commn. on Humanities, 1978—. Guggenheim fellow, 1949-50, 51-52; fellow Center Advanced Studies, Wesleyan U., Middletown, Conn., 1961-62, Sch. Letters, Ind. U., 1965—; fellow Center for Advanced Study in Behavioral Scis., Stanford, 1973-74; vis. prof. U. Calif., 1960; Terry lectr. Yale, 1963-64; vis. lectr. U. Poitiers, 1962; Berg prof. English, N.Y. U., 1966-67; McDonald lectr. McGill U., 1967-68; Willett vis. prof. humanities U. Chgo., 1968-69; nat. Phi Beta Kappa vis. scholar, 1969-70; Lincoln lectr. Central and West Africa, 1973-74; Messenger lectr. Cornell U., 1979-80. Adv. bd. John Simon Guggenheim Meml. Found.; trustee Nat. Humanities Faculty, 1968-76, chmn., 1974-76. Decorated chevalier l'Ordre des Palmes Académiques (France). Fellow Am. Acad. Arts and Scis.; mem. AAUP, Renaissance Soc. Am. (adv. council 1957-59), Modern Lang. Assn. (pres. 1978), Modern Humanities Research Assn., Nat. Council Tchrs. English, Cambridge Bibliog. Soc. (Eng.), Catholic Commn. Intellectual and Cultural Affairs (exec. com. 1962-63), Milton Soc. of Am. (pres. 1967), Phi Beta Kappa, Alpha Sigma Nu. Author: Frontiers in American Catholicism, 1957; Ramus, Method, and the Decay of Dialogue, 1958; Ramus and Talon Inventory, 1958; Am. Cath. Crossroads, 1959; The Barbarian Within, 1962; In the Human Grain, 1967; The Presence of the Word, 1967; Rhetoric, Romance and Technology, 1971; Why Talk?, 1973; Interfaces of the Word, 1977; co-author, editor: Darwin's Vision and Christian Perspectives, 1960; Knowledge and the Future of Man, 1968. Editor: Petrus Ramus and Audomarus Talaeus, Collectaneae praefationes epistolae, orationes, 1969; Petrus Ramus, Scholae in liberales artes, 1970. Editorial bd. Studies in English Literature, 1962—; editorial adv. bd. Philosophy and Rhetoric, 1967—. The English Literary Renaissance, 1969—, Manuscripta, 1957—, others. Contbr. articles, chpts. learned and popular publs. Address: St Louis University St Louis MO 63103

ONGLEY, PATRICK AUGUSTINE, med. found. exec.; b. Oamaru, N.Z., Apr. 17, 1919; s. Frederick William and Annie (Milne) O.; came to U.S., 1951, naturalized, 1959; M.B., Ch.B., Otago (N.Z.) U., 1944; m. Judith Ann Ashby, Feb. 17, 1947; children—James Patrick, Jennifer Susan. Rotating intern Dunedin (N.Z.) Pub. Hosp., 1945, sr. resident in medicine and surgery, 1947; lectr. anatomy Otago U. Med. Sch., 1946; practice medicine, Auckland, N.Z., 1947-51; grad. cardiovascular disease Harvard U. Med. Sch., 1951-52, teaching fellow pediatrics, 1954-55; clin. fellow medicine Mass. Gen. Hosp., Boston, 1952-54; clin. and research fellow rheumatic fever House of Good Samaritan, Boston, 1953-54; asst. cardiologist, acting dir. Congenital Heart Disease Clinic, Children's Med. Center, Boston, 1956-57; successively spl. fellow pediatrics, asst. to staff pediatrics, cons. pediatrics Mayo Found., Rochester, Minn., 1957-69, from asst. prof. to prof. pediatrics, 1959-69; clin. prof. Yale U. Med. Sch., 1976—; dir. China Med. Bd., N.Y.C., 1970-73, pres., 1973—; hon. lectr. 5th Congress Cardiology, Rosario, Argentina, 1963; Francis Hernandez lectr. U. Fla., 1971; chmn. Paul Dudley White Fund, 1975-76. Recipient Theodore and Susan Cummings Humanitarian award Am. Coll. Cardiology, 1964, 65. Diplomate Am. Bd. Pediatrics. Fellow Am. Coll. Cardiology, Am. Coll. Chest Physicians, Am. Acad. Pediatrics; mem. AMA (Billings Gold medal 1968), Am. Heart Assn. (chmn. com. internat. program 1975-76), Argentine, Venezuelan, Chilean socs. cardiology, Australia and N.Z. Cardiac Soc. Contbr. articles to med. jours. Home: 140 Fair Oak Dr Fairfield CT 06430 Office: 622 3d Ave New York City NY 10017

ONKEN, GEORGE MARCELLUS, cons., lawyer; b. Bklyn., Aug. 15, 1914; s. William Henry and Lillian Charlotte (Dawe) O.; A.B., Princeton, 1936; LL.B., Columbia, 1948; LL.M., N.Y.U., 1952; m. Mildred Ann Tausch, Dec. 13, 1958; children—Jane Elizabeth, Nancy Catherine. Admitted to N.Y. bar, 1949; asst. to pres. Welsbach Engring. and Mgmt. Corp., Phila., 1939-43; mem. legal staff L.I. R.R., 1949-78, gen. counsel, 1963-78, v.p., 1966-78, sec., 1968-78. Bd. dirs. Orphan Asylum Soc. Bklyn., 1958—; bd. mgrs. Pa. R.R. br. YMCA, N.Y.C., 1957—, chmn., 1967—; bd. dirs. YMCA Greater N.Y., 1963—; trustee Bklyn. YWCA, 1976—. Served to lt. (j.g.) USNR, 1943-46. Recipient Man of Year award YMCA, 1977. Mem. Newcomen Soc. N.Am. Republican. Episcopalian (vestry 1958-64, 76—). Clubs: Union League, Church (N.Y.C.); Rembrandt, Heights Casino, Ihpetonga, (Bklyn.). Home: 215 Adams St Brooklyn NY 11201

ONORATO, NICHOLAS LOUIS, educator; b. South Barre, Mass., Feb. 24, 1925; s. Charles and Amalia (Tartaglia) O.; B.S., in Pub. Relations, Boston U., 1951; M.A. in Econs., Clark U., 1952, Ph.D., 1959; m. Elizabeth Louise Settergren, July 19, 1947; children—Gary, Deborah, Nicholas, Jeffrey, Glenn, Charles, Lisa. Mem. faculty Becker Jr. Coll., Worcester, Mass., 1952-54; prof. econs. Worcester Poly. Inst., 1955-68, chmn. dept. econs., govt., bus., 1968-74, dir. Sch. Indsl. Mgmt., 1972—; vis. prof. Clark U., Worcester, 1964-66; financial cons. Coz Chem. Co., Northbridge, Mass., 1959—. Trustee Bay State Savs. Bank, Worcester. Served with USNR, 1943-46. Mem. Am. Finance Assn., Am. Econ. Assn., Am. Accounting Assn., Phi Kappa Theta. Club: Torch (pres. Worcester 1967). Contbr. to newspapers and mags. Home: 39 Knollwood Dr Shrewsbury MA 01545 Office: Institute Rd Worcester MA 01609

ONTHANK, JOHN BONTIES, candy and soft drink co. exec.; b. Greenwich, Conn., Apr. 12, 1936; s. Pierce and Nancy (Fuller) O.; B.A. in Econs., Yale U., 1957; m. Judy Howse, Nov. 2, 1957; children—Robert Pierce, Christopher Howse, John Bonties. Mktg. exec. Can. Dry Corp., N.Y.C., 1960-68, Coca-Cola U.S.A., Atlanta, 1968-71, mktg. exec. Schweppes U.S.A., Stamford, Conn., 1971-75, pres., 1976—; pres. Cadbury Schweppes U.S.A. Inc., Stamford, 1976-78, Schweppes N.Am., 1977—, Rondo Beverage Corp., 1978—. Served to lt. USN, 1957-60. Mem. Am. Mgmt. Assn., Young Presidents Orgn., Presidents Assn. Republican. Episcopalian. Club: Wilton Riding. Home: 18 Turner Ridge Ct Wilton CT 06897 Office: 1200 High Ridge Rd Stamford CT 06905

ONYSZCHUK, MARIO, educator; b. Wolkow, Poland, July 21, 1930; s. Andrew and Mary (Palewicz) O.; B.Sc. with honours in Chemistry, McGill U., 1951, Ph.D., 1954; M.Sc., U. Western Ont., 1952; Ph.D., Cambridge (Eng.) U., 1956; m. Anastasia Anna Kushnir, June 27, 1959; children—Ivan, Gregory, Timothy. Mem. faculty McGill U., 1956—, prof. chemistry, 1968—. Nat. Research Council Can. scholar, 1952-54, grantee, 1956—; Royal Commn. for Exhbn. of 1851 scholar, 1954-56. Fellow Chem. Inst. Can., Chem. Soc. London; mem. Am. Chem. Soc., Sigma Xi. Author articles in field. Home: 60 Balfour Ave Montreal PQ H3P 1L6 Canada

OOMS, VAN DOORN, economist; b. Chgo., Oct. 29, 1934; s. Casper William and Ruth P. (Miller) O.; B.A. summa cum laude, Amherst Coll., 1956; B.A. with first class honors (Rhodes scholar), Oxford (Eng.) U., 1958, M.A. (Rhodes scholar), 1962; M.A., Yale U., 1960, Ph.D. (Ford Found. dissertation fellow), 1965; m. Theodora J. Parfit, June 17, 1961; children—Katrina, Caspar, Tamara. Lectr., Yale U., 1962, asst. prof. econs., to 1968; asso. prof. Swarthmore Coll., 1968, prof., to 1978; chief economist U.S. Senate Budget Com., Washington, 1977-78; asst. dir. for econ. policy U.S. Office Mgmt. and Budget, 1978— Washington, 1978—. Mem. Am. Econ. Assn. Author: (with R. Keohane) The Multinational Firm and International Regulation, 1976; (with A. Packer) The International Economy and the Federal Budget, 1976. Home: 5111 Battery Ln Bethesda MD 20014 Office: Office Mgmt and Budget Room 256 Exec Office Bldg Washington DC 20503

OOST, STEWART IRVIN, educator; b. Grand Rapids, Mich., May 20, 1921; s. Jacob John and Bessie (Stewart) O.; A.B., U. Chgo., 1941, M.A., 1947, Ph.D. 1950; student Yale, 1943-44. Tchr., Starr Commonwealth for Boys, Albion, Mich., 1941-42; from instr. to asso. prof. history So. Methodist U., 1948-59; mem. faculty U. Chgo., 1959—, prof. ancient history, 1965—. Served with AUS, 1942-46. Ford fellow, Italy, 1955-56. Mem. Am. Hist. Assn., Am. Philol. Assn., Phi Beta Kappa (past pres. Gamma of Tex.). Republican. Methodist. Author: Roman Policy in Epirus and Acarnania in the Age of the Roman Conquest of Greece, 1954; Galla Placidia Augusta; A Biographical Essay, 1968; also articles. Mem. editorial bd. Classical philology, 1959—, editor in chief, 1978—. Home: 9652 S Seeley Ave Chicago IL 60643

OOSTHUIZEN, PIETER GERHARD KEYTER, banker; b. Pretoria, S. Africa, Jan. 7, 1932; s. Burgert Adriaan and Anna Petronella (Schoeman) O.; Diploma, Inst. of Bankers, Coll. of Commerce, Capetown, S. Africa, 1957; student U. South Africa, Pretoria, 1961; m. Jacqueline Johanna Cornelia Van de Wetering, Aug. 15, 1961. With Netherlands Bank of S. Africa Ltd., 1949-58; with First Nat. City Bank, N.Y., 1958-75, v.p. N.Y. Banking Group, 1973-75; sr. v.p., gen. mgr. internat. banking Bank of Montreal (Que., Can.), 1975, exec. v.p., gen. mgr. internat. banking, 1976—; dir. Arab Internat. Trust S.A., Luxembourg, Australian Internat. Fin. Corp. Ltd., Melbourne; chmn., dir. Bank of Montreal Trust Co., N.Y.; gov. Adela Investment Co. S.A., Luxembourg; chmn. supervisory bd. First Canadian Fin. Corp. BV, Amsterdam; dir. numerous other subsidiaries and firms. Clubs: Mt. Royal, St. James's, Montreal Badminton and Squash, Mt. Royal Tennis (Montreal); Wanderers (Transvaal); Nederlandsche (Capetown). Office: Bank of Montreal Head Office 3d Floor 129 St James St W Montreal PQ H2Y 1L6 Canada

OPALA, MARIAN P(ETER), justice Okla. Supreme Ct.; b. Lodz, Poland, Jan. 20, 1921; B.S. in Econs., Oklahoma City U., 1957, J.D., 1953; LL.M., N.Y. U., 1968. Admitted to Okla. bar, 1953, U.S. Supreme Ct. bar, 1970; asst. county atty. Oklahoma County, 1953-56; practiced law, Oklahoma City, 1956-60, 65-69; referee Okla. Supreme Ct., Oklahoma City, 1960-65; prof. law Oklahoma City U., 1967-68; asso. prof. U. Okla., 1969—; adminstrv. dir. Cts. Okla., 1968-77; presiding judge Okla. State Indsl. Ct., 1977-78; judge Workers Compensation Ct., 1978; justice Okla. Supreme Ct., 1978—; mem. permanent faculty Am. Acad. Jud. Edn., 1970—; mem. faculty Nat. Jud. Coll., U. Nev., 1975—; chmn. Nat. Conf. State Ct. Adminstrs., 1976-77. Recipient Herbert Harley award Am. Judicature Soc., 1977, Disting. Alumni award Oklahoma City U., 1979; named Outstanding Okla. Public Adminstr., Am. Soc. Public Adminstrn., 1979. Mem. Am. Soc. Legal History, Order of Coif, Phi Delta Phi (Oklahoma City U. Alumni award 1962). Office: Supreme Ct Okla 202 State Capitol Oklahoma City OK 73105*

OPEL, JOHN ROBERTS, data processing co. exec.; b. Kansas City, Mo., Jan. 5, 1925; s. Norman J. and Esther (Roberts) O.; A.B., Westminster Coll., 1948; M.B.A., U. Chgo., 1949; m. Julia Carole Stout, Dec. 28, 1953; children—Robert, Nancy, Julia, Mary, John. With IBM, Armonk, N.Y., 1949—, salesman, 1949-56, v.p. mktg. data processing div., 1964-65, v.p., 1966-68, mem. mgmt. com., 1967, v.p. corp. finance and planning, 1968-69, sr. v.p. finance and planning, 1969-72, group exec. data processing group, 1972-74, pres., mem. corp. office, 1974—; dir. Pfizer, Inc., Bank of N.Y., Bank N.Y. Co., Inc. Trustee Inst. Advanced Study, Westminster Coll., Joint Council on Econ. Edn.; bd. govs. United Way Am. Served with AUS, 1943-45. Office: IBM Corp Old Orchard Rd Armonk NY 10504

OPENSHAW, MAYNARD KARL, educator; b. Santaquin, Utah, June 13, 1925; s. Herbert N. and Ruby (Crook) O.; B.A., U. Utah, 1952, M.S., 1957; Ed.D., Columbia, 1963; m. Esther Jeanne Bailey, Feb. 8, 1951; children—Marci Ann, James Karl. Instr., U. Utah, 1953-58, Adelphi U., Garden City, N.Y., 1959-61; asso. sec. Nat. Assn. for Supervision and Curriculum Devel., 1961-63; asso. prof. Ohio State U., 1963-66, prof., 1967, asso. dir. Sch. Edn., 1965-67; dean Sch. Edn., Cal. State U., Sacramento, 1967-71; prof. U. Colo. Sch. Edn., Boulder, 1971—, dean, 1971-77. Cons. edn. and tng. IBM, White Plains, N.Y., 1963-65, Bur. Research, U.S. Office Edn. 1966-75. Bd. dirs. John Day Found., Inc., Sacramento. Served with USAAF, 1943-46. Mem. Phi Delta Kappa (pres. Utah chpt. 1957-58), Nat. Assn. for Supervision and Curriculum Devel., Council of Deans for Edn. Cal. State Coll. System (chmn. 1969-70), John Dewey Soc. (exec. bd. 1966-69). Research on teacher classroom behavior. Research editor Jour. Tchr. Edn., 1966-73; editorial bd. Ednl. Forum, 1978—. Contbr. articles to profl. jours. Office: Sch Edn Univ Colo Boulder CO 80309

OPENSHAW, RICHARD ALFRED, publisher; b. Cin., Oct. 7, 1930; s. Arthur Benson and Marguerite (Liselle) O.; ed. U. Ill.; m. Dorothy Ann Stone, Jan. 25, 1958; children—Richard Alfred, Kirk Andrew. With Hearst Corp., N.Y.C., 1956—, advt. dir. Sports Afield, 1970-74, pub. Motor Boating & Sailing, 1974—; nat. mktg. dir. Outdoor Empire Pub. Co., 1976—. Served with USN, 1951-55. Republican. Episcopalian. Clubs: Channel Yacht, Bamm Hollow Country. Home: 81 Ballantine Rd Middletown NJ 07748 Office: 224 W 57th St New York City NY 10019

OPHULS, MARCEL, film producer-dir.; b. Frankfurt, Germany, Nov. 1, 1927; s. Max and Hilda (Wall) Oppenheimer; came to U.S., 1947, naturalized, 1950; student Occidental Coll., Los Angeles, 1946-49; License e Letters, U. Paris, 1950; m. Regine Ackerman, Aug. 21, 1956; children—Catherine Julie, Danielle, Jeanne Dorothee. Asst. dir. for films in France, 1951-56; program dir. TV and radio plays, Sudwestfunk, Germany, 1956-60; dir. feature films, Paris, 1961-65; producer-dir. documentary firms, 1966—; prin. films include Banana Peel, 1963, Fire at Will, 1964, Munich, or Peace in Our Time, 1966, The Sorrow and The Pity, 1971, America Revisted, 1972, A Sense of Loss, 1972, The Memory of Justice, 1976, also sketch in Love at Twenty, 1961; tchr. film Princeton U., 1973-74, also sr. vis. fellow council humanities and mem. adv. council sociology dept. Served with AUS, 1946-47. Recipient numerous internat. film and TV awards. Mem. French Authors Guild. *I believe that individuals shape history, but are also shaped by it.*

OPIE, RUTH ROBERT, banker; b. Whitehall, Mont., Dec. 31, 1916; d. Alex W. and Rubie E. (Maxwell) Robert; A.A., U. Minn., 1936; postgrad. Butte Bus. Coll., 1936-37; m. Francis M. Opie, Aug. 5, 1937; children—Robert A. Opie Dapp, Everett T., Janice M. Opie Hunt, James A. Cashier, then asst. cashier Whitehall State Bank, 1934-62, dir., 1960—, v.p., then exec. v.p., 1962-72, pres., 1972—; bookkeeper, teller Western Mont. Bank, Missoula, 1951-55; asst. cashier Security Bank, Butte, 1955-59; pres., dir. Security Bank, Three Forks, Mont., 1965—; past pres. Bank of Sheridan (Mont.); agt. Robert Ins. Agy., Whitehall and Sheridan. Pres. Council Catholic Women, 1960-62; county chmn. Nat. Found. Infantile Paralysis, 1960-65. Mem. Whitehall C. of C. (past pres.). Address: Whitehall MT 59759

OPLER, MARVIN KAUFMANN, educator; b. Buffalo, June 13, 1914; s. Arthur and Fanny (Coleman-Haas) O.; student U. Buffalo, 1932-34; A.B., U. Mich., 1935; Ph.D., Columbia, 1938; m. Charlotte Fox, Dec. 30, 1935; children—Ruth Ellen, Lewis Alan; m. 2d, Ruth Hyman, Dec. 23, 1973. Head sociology, anthropology dept. Reed Coll., 1938-43; chief community analysis sect. War Relocation Authority, Dept. Interior, 1943-46; asso. prof. anthropology U. Cal. at Los Angeles, Occidental, 1946-48; asso. prof. anthropology Stanford, 1948-50; lectr. Los Angeles Inst. Psychoanalysis, 1946-48; Los Angeles Neuropsychiat. Vets. Hosp., 1948; lectr., asso. prof. dept. social relations Harvard, 1950-52; prof. anthropology, social psychiatry Cornell U. Med. Coll., Payne Whitney Psychiat. Clinic, 1952-58; prof. social psychiatry, sociology and anthropology State U. N.Y. at Buffalo, 1958—, chmn. anthropology, 1969-73; vis. prof. sociology, anthropology New Sch. Social Research, 1957-58; spl. lectr. grad. dept. psychology Clark U., 1950; vis. prof. William Alanson White Found., N.Y.C., 1957-59. Vice chmn. Portland Council Social Agys., 1938-53; chmn. social services Multnomah County chpt. ARC, 1938-43; chmn. statistics Welfare Council Greater Los Angeles, 1946-48; mem. nat. com. suicide study Nat. Inst. Mental Health. Social Sci. Research Council fellow, 1937-38, recipient award, 1946-47, grant-in-aid research, 1949. Mem. Internat. Assn. Social Psychiatry (v.p.), Am. Anthrop. Assn., Am. Sociol. Soc., Acad. Psychoanalysis, Soc. Study Social Problems, Western N.Y. Sociol. Soc., Am. Ethnol. Soc., N.E. Anthrop. Assn. (charter mem., 1st pres., 1965-66), Sigma Xi. Author: Culture, Psychiatry and Human Values, 1956; Culture and Social Psychiatry, 1967; Cultural Anthropology: Selected Themes, 1969; co-author Mental Health in the Metropolis: Midtown, 1962, rev. edit., 1977; Impounded People, 1970; North American Indians in Historical Perspective, 1971. Editor: Culture and Mental Health, 1959; asso. editor Internat. Jour. Social Psychiatry, 1957-58, editor, 1958—; asso. editor Am. Anthropologist, 1962—. Contbr. articles to profl. jours. Home: 61 Heritage Rd E Williamsville NY 14221 Office: Dept Anthropology State U N Y Buffalo NY 14261

OPOTOWSKY, MAURICE LEON, editor; b. New Orleans, Dec. 13, 1931; s. Sol and Fannie (Latter) O.; student Tulane U., 1949-51; B.A. cum laude, Williams Coll., 1953; m. Madeleine Duhamel, Feb. 28, 1959; children—Didier Sol Duhamel, Joelle Duhamel, Arielle Duhamel (dec.). Reporter, Berkshire Eagle, Pittsfield, Mass., 1951-53; pub. Sea Coast Echo, Bay St. Louis, Miss., 1953-54; reporter U.P.I., 1956-62; feature editor Newsday, Ronkonkoma, N.Y., 1962-64, Suffolk day editor, 1964-65, Nassau night editor, 1965-67, nat. editor, 1967-70, Suffolk editor, 1970-72; dir. L.I. Mag., 1972; day editor Riverside (Calif.) Press-Enterprise, 1973—. Chief N.Y. State Syndicate Service, 1961—; mem. Calif. Freedom of Info. Exec. Com. Trustee Harbor Country Day Sch., 1970-72; bd. dirs. Calif. Newspaper Pub. Editor Conf. Bd., 1978—; mem. Smithtown (N.Y.) Hunt, 1970-73, West Hills Hunt, 1976—. Served with AUS, 1954-56. Mem. AP News Execs. Calif. (chmn. freedom of info. com.). Home: 3512 14th Riverside CA 92502 Office: Press Enterprise Box 792 Riverside CA 92502

OPPEDAHL, JOHN FREDRICK, journalist; b. Duluth, Minn., Nov. 9, 1944; s. Walter H. and Lucille (Hole) O.; B.A., U. Calif., Berkeley, 1967; M.A., Columbia U., 1968; m. Alison Owen, Dec. 30, 1971. Reporter, San Francisco Examiner, 1967; reporter, editor Detroit Free Press, 1968-79, city editor, 1975—. Office: Detroit Free Press 321 W Lafayette Blvd Detroit MI 48231

OPPEN, GEORGE, author; b. New Rochelle, N.Y., Apr. 24, 1908; s. George A. and Elsie (Rothfeld) O.; ed. pub. schs., Calif.; m. Mary Colby, Aug. 11, 1928; 1 dau., Linda (Mrs. Alexander Mourelatos). Mem. Objectivist Press Coop., 1934-36; pub. To, Toulon, France, 1930-33. Served with inf. AUS, 1943-45. Decorated Purple Heart, Combat Inf. award. Author: Discret-Series, 1934; The Materials, 1962; This in Which, 1965; Of Being Numerous, 1968 (Pulitzer prize 1969); Seascape: Needle's Eye, 1973; Collected Poems 1929-1975, 1975; Collected Poems, 1976; Primitive, 1978. Home: 2811 Polk St San Francisco CA 94109

OPPENHEIM, ALFRED, wholesale grocery exec.; b. Brockton, Mass., June 15, 1915; s. Abraham M. and Leonora (Wiscotch) O.; student City U., Paris, France, 1945; m. Naomi Mezoff, Oct. 30, 1942; children—Betsy, Jeffrey. Sales mgr. Brockton Products Co., 1934; sales supr. New Eng. Grocers Supply Co., Worcester, Mass., 1935-39; sales mgr. Silver Bros., Manchester, N.H., 1939-41; pres. Cressey, Dockham & Co., Inc., Salem, Mass., 1946-51, 53-74, chmn. bd., chief exec. officer, 1975—. Served to capt. AUS, 1942-46, 51-53. Decorated Bronze Star, Bronze Star with oak leaf cluster; Chung Moo Distinguished Service medal (Korea). Mem. C. of C., Nat. Am., New Eng. (pres. 1963-64) wholesale grocers assns., Ind. Grocers Alliance (dir. 1974—). Jewish religion (dir. temple). Clubs: Dolphin Yacht (commodore 1960-61 Marblehead); Ferncroft Country (Danvers, Mass.). Home: Ferncroft Towers PH6 Danvers MA 01923 also 13702 Via Flora Villa del Rey Palm Greens Del Ray Beach FL Office: 1 IGA Way Andover MA 01810

OPPENHEIM, ANTONI KAZIMIERZ, mech. engr.; b. Warsaw, Poland, Aug. 11, 1915; s. Tadeusz and Zuzanna (Zuckerwar) O.; Dipl. Ing., Warsaw Inst. Tech., London, 1943; D.I.C., Ph.D. in Engring., City and Guilds Coll., Imperial Coll. Sci. and Tech., U. London, 1945, D.Sc., 1976; m. Lavinia Stephens, July 18, 1945; 1 dau., Terry Ann. Came to U.S., 1948, naturalized, 1954. Research asst. City and Guilds Coll., 1942-48, lectr., 1946-48; asst. prof. mech. engring. Stanford U., 1948-50; faculty U. Calif. at Berkeley, 1950—, prof. mech. engring. 1958—, Miller prof., 1961-62; vis. prof. Sorbonne, Paris, 1960-61, U. Poitiers (France), 1973; staff cons. Shell Devel. Co., 1952-60; chmn. Heat Transfer and Fluid Mechanics Inst., 1958, IAA Com. on Gasdynamics of Explosions, 1968—; organizer Internat. Colloquia on Gas Dynamics of Explosions and Reactive Systems, 1967, 69, 71, 73, 75, 77, 79; spl. research compressible fluid flow, gas turbines and internal combustion engines, heat transfer, combustion, detonation and blast waves; mem. NASA adv. com. fluid mechanics, 1963-69. Registered profl. engr., Calif. Fellow Am. Rocket Soc. (nat. dir. 1959-62, founder, pres. No. Calif. sect. 1957), ASME (chmn. profl. conf. 1958, program chmn. San Francisco 1959-60), Am. Inst. Aeros. and Astronautics (Pendray award 1966); elected mem. Internat. Acad. Astronautics, Nat. Acad. Engring.; mem. Inst. Mech. Engrs. (Water Arbitration prize 1948), Am. Phys. Soc., Am. Soc. Engring. Edn., Sigma Xi, Psi Tau Sigma, Tau Beta Psi. Editor-in-chief Acta Astronautica, 1974-79; contbr. articles to profl. jours., also monographs. Home: 54 Norwood Ave Berkeley CA 94707

OPPENHEIM, DENNIS ALLEN, artist; b. Mason City, Wash., Sept. 6, 1938; s. David Alfred and Katherine (Belknap) O.; B.F.A., Calif. Coll. Arts and Crafts, Oakland, 1964; M.F.A., Stanford, 1965; m. Karen Cackett, May 9, 1959; children—Kristin, Erik, Chandra. Exhibited in one man shows at Stedelijk Mus., Amsterdam, 1974, Palais de Beaux-Arts, Brussels, 1975, Art Gallery Ont., Toronto, 1978, Kunsthalle Basel (Switzerland), 1979, Israel Mus., Jerusalem, 1979; exhibited Earthworks, Dwan Gallery, N.Y.C., 1968, A Report-2 Ocean Projects, Mus. Modern Art, N.Y.C., 1969, Op Losse Schroeven, Stedelijk Mus., 1969, Information, Mus. Modern Art, 1970, Conceptual Art, Conceptual Aspects, New York Cultural Center, 1970, Sonsbeek Rijks Mus. Kroller-Muller, Oherlo, Holland, 1971, Persona 2, Incontri Internazionali D'Arte Roma, 1972, Art Now, Kennedy Center, Washington, 1974. Guest lectr., artist Yale, 1969, Chgo. Art Inst., 1969, N.Y. U., 1970, Boston Mus. Sch., 1970, U. Calif., Berkeley, 1971, U. Colo., 1972, U. Kans., U. Wis., 1970, Visual Arts, N.Y.C., 1970. Newhouse Found. grantee, 1966, Nat. Endowment for Arts grantee, 1974. Guggenheim fellow for sculpture, 1972. Author: Indentations, 1969; Dennis Oppenheim Proposals, 1967-73, 1973. Address: 54 Franklin St New York NY 10013

OPPENHEIM, IRWIN, educator, chem. physicist; b. Boston, June 30, 1929; s. James L. and Rose (Rosenberg) O.; A.B. summa cum laude, Harvard, 1949; postgrad. Cal. Inst. Tech., 1949-51; Ph.D., Yale, 1956; m. Bernice Buresh, May 18, 1974; 1 son, Joshua Buresh. Physicist, Nat. Bur. Standards, Washington, 1953-60; chief theoretical physics Gen. Dynamics/Convair, San Diego, 1960-61; asso. prof. chemistry Mass. Inst. Tech., Cambridge, 1961-65, prof., 1965—; lectr. physics U. Md., 1953-60; vis. asso. prof. physics U. Leiden, 1955-56; vis. prof. Weizmann Inst. Sci., 1958-59, U. Calif., San Diego, 1966-67; Van der Waals prof. U. Amsterdam, 1966-67; cons., dir. Phys. Dynamics. Trustee, cons. LaJolla Inst. Fellow Am. Phys. Soc., Am. Acad. Arts and Scis., Washington Acad. Sci.; mem. Phi Beta Kappa, Sigma Xi. Author: (with J.G. Kirkwood) Chemical Thermodynamics, 1961. Research in quantum statis. mechanics, statis. mechanics of transport processes, thermodynamics. Home: 140 Upland Rd Cambridge MA 02140

OPPENHEIM, JUSTIN SABLE, bus. exec.; b. N.Y.C., Aug. 17, 1923; s. Ferdinand S. and Esther D. (Hirsch) O.; B.S., N.Y. U., 1943; postgrad. Cambridge U., 1945, New Sch. for Social Research, 1963; m. Joyce Marrits, June 26, 1949; children—Janet, Judi, Jeffrey. Vice pres. Consol. Mercantile Industries, N.Y.C., 1946-52; adminstrn. and mgmt. Norden div. United Aircraft Co., 1952-60; pres., gen. mgr. Potentiometer div. Litton Industries, Floral Park, N.Y., 1960-68, pres. Office Products Centers div., 1968-70, v.p. Litton Industries, 1970—, also v.p. Litton Bus. Systems, Inc., Litton Bus. Equipment Ltd. (Can.), Standard Desk Ltd. (Can.); pres., dir. Streater Industries Ltd.; dir. Atal S.A. (France); lectr. on advt. N.Y. U., CCNY, 1954-57. Mem. adv. com. N. Hempstead Housing Authority, 1956-59; mem. Nassau County Republican Com., 1961-73; mem. adv. council Center for Econ. Research, L.I. U. Served with AUS, 1943-45. Hon. Adm. Tex. Navy, 1969. Mem. SAR, Actor's Fund (life), Alpha Epsilon Pi. Jewish. Clubs: Masons, Lambs (N.Y.). Contbr. articles to profl. jours. Home: 14 Sherwood Ln Roslyn Heights NY 11577 Office: 135 Community Dr Great Neck NY 11021

OPPENHEIM, LOUIS HERMAN, civil engr., indsl. exec.; b. Oklahoma City, Oct. 16, 1912; s. Herman J. and Aimee Oueilhe (Peterson) O.; student U. So. Calif., 1929-33; B.S. in Engring., U. Calif., 1938; m. Mildred Flanagan, Dec. 27, 1949; children—Susan Marie, David Louis, Stephen Louis, John Louis. Plant engr. Henry J. Kaiser Co., 1938-42; asst. chief engr. Kaiser Steel Corp., 1942-45; asst. chief engr., asst. gen. mgr. Kaiser Engrs. div. Henry J. Kaiser Co., 1945-58, v.p., 1953-77, gen. mgr., 1958-73; dir., chmn. exec. com. Nat. Steel & Shipbldg. Co., 1959-73; v.p. Kaiser Industries Corp., Oakland, Calif., 1960-69, exec. v.p., 1969-73, sr. v.p., 1973-77. Registered profl. engr. Fellow ASCE; mem. Soc. Am. Mil. Engrs., Am. Iron and Steel Inst., Assn. Iron and Steel Engrs., Sigma Xi, Tau Beta Pi, Chi Epsilon. Clubs: Orinda (Calif.) Country; Silverado Country (Napa, Cal.). Home: 117 Requa Rd Piedmont CA 94611

OPPENHEIM, SAUL CHESTERFIELD, educator; b. N.Y.C., Jan. 16, 1897; s. Jacob and Julia (Jaffe) O.; A.B. summa cum laude in econs. and history, Columbia, 1918, A.M., 1920; J.D., U. Mich., 1926, S.J.D., 1929; LL.D., George Washington U., 1973; m. Morgery H. Heiman, Sept. 22, 1922; 1 son, Daniel Payne; m. Carrington Shields, May 8, 1976. Instr. econs. U. Mich., 1921-26, teaching and research asst. to dean law sch., 1926-27, prof. law, 1952-65; admitted to Mich. bar, 1926, D.C. bar, Supreme Ct. bar, 1935; prof. law George Washington U., 1927-52, univ. adviser on research George Washington Patent, Trademark and Copyright Research Inst., 1952-72. Chmn. adv. council U.S. Marketing Laws Survey, 1938-40; co-chmn. Atty. Gen.'s Nat. Com. to Study Antitrust Laws, 1953-55. Served with U.S. Army, 1918-19. Recipient Jefferson medal N.J. Patent Law Assn., 1951; Charles F. Kettering award George Washington U. Patent, Trademark, Copyright Research Inst., 1957. Mem. Assn. Am. Law Schs. (chmn. com. on coop. with Am. Law Inst., 1950-53), Am. (chmn. FTC com. 1951-53, chmn. Clayton Act Com. sect. antitrust law 1955-56, del. to Ho. of Dels. antitrust sect. 1958-60, chmn. sect. antitrust law 1961-62), Fed. bar assns., Phi Beta Kappa, Order of Coif. Clubs: Nat. Lawyers, Cosmos (Washington). Author: Cases on Trade Regulation, 1936; Cases on Federal Antitrust Laws, 1948; Unfair Trade Practices Cases, Comments and Materials, 1950, 3d edit., 1974; National Transportation Policy and Inter-Carrier Competitive Rates, 1945; Antitrust law; Cases and Comment, 1959, 3d edit., 1970; Lawyer's Robinson-Patman Act Sourcebook, 4 vols., 1972. Editor-in-chief Trade Regulation Law Series. Contbr. articles to legal jours. Home: 3732 Chesapeake St NW Washington DC 20016

OPPENHEIMER, CARL HENRY, marine ecologist, microbiologist; b. Los Angeles, Nov. 13, 1921; s. Carl Henry and Marie Vivian (Hess) O.; B.A., U. So. Calif., 1947, M.A., 1949; Ph.D., Scripps Instn. Oceanography of U. Calif., 1951; Fulbright fellow U. Oslo, 1952-53; m. Dorothy Ann Paul, Mar. 1, 1971; children by previous marriage—Douglas Lee, John Carl, Donna (Mrs. Richard Green). Asst. marine biologist Scripps Instn. Oceanography, 1951-55; sr. research scientist Pan Am. Petroleum Corp. Research Center, 1955-57; research scientist, lectr. U. Tex., 1957-61; asso. prof. Inst. Marine Sci. of U. Miami, 1961-64; dir., prof. Oceanographic Inst. of Fla. State U., 1964-66, chmn. dept. oceanography, 1966-69, dir. Marine Lab., 1966-71; dir. U. Tex. Marine Sci. Inst., 1971-73, prof., 1971—; Fulbright fellow U. Naples, 1978. U.S. rep. eco-scis. panel NATO, 1971-73, chmn. panel, 1973; mem. Tex. Senate Interim Coastal Zone Study Com., 1971-72, environmental sci. panel NSF, 1969-72, Pres.'s Oil Pollution Panel, Santa Barbara, Calif., 1969-70, environ. quality com. Coastal Bend Council Govts., Corpus Christi, Tex., 1972—; environ. quality advisor So. States Energy Bd., 1972—North Sea oil expdn. NATO, 1975-76. Served with USNR, 1941-45. Recipient Gold medal Italian Biol. Assn., 1976. Mem. Am. Soc. Microbiologists, Soc. Limnology and Oceanography, Soc. Gen. Microbiology, Geochem. Soc., Sigma Xi. Symposium on Marine Microbiology, 1963; transl. Fundamentals Geomicrobiology, 1963; Marine Biology II, 1966; Marine Biology IV, 1968; Microflora of Lakes and Its Geochemical Activities, 1975; Environmental Data Management, 1976. Chmn., editor Conf. on Environ. Data Mgmt., 1976. Contbr. articles to profl. jours. Home: 300 White St Port Aransas TX 78373 Office: University of Texas Marine Science Inst Port Aransas Marine Lab Port Aransas TX 78373

OPPENHEIMER, FRANZ MARTIN, lawyer; b. Mainz, Germany, Sept. 7, 1919; s. Arnold and Johanna (Mayer) O.; B.S., U. Chgo., 1942; student Université de Grenoble, France, 1938-39; LL.B. cum laude (note editor Law Jour. 1945), Yale, 1945; m. Margaret Spencer Foote, June 17, 1944; children—Martin Foote, Roxana Foote, Edward Arnold. Research asst. com. human devel. U. Chgo., 1942-43; admitted to N.Y. bar, 1946, D.C. bar, 1955; law clk. to Judge Swan, U.S. Circuit Ct. of Appeals, N.Y., 1945-46; asso. atty. Chadbourne, Wallace, Parke & Whiteside, N.Y.C., 1946-47; atty. Internat. Bank for Reconstrn. and Devel., Washington, 1947-57; individual practice law, 1958—; partner Leva, Hawes, Symington, Martin & Oppenheimer, 1959—. Bd. dirs. Internat. Student House; founding mem. Company of Christian Jews; trustee Inst. Empirical Econ. Research, Berlin, West Germany, Com. 100 on Fed. City, Washington, Chatham (Va.) Hall. Mem. Am. Psychol. Assn., Am., Fed. bar assns., Am. Soc. Internat. Law (treas. 1964-76), Council Fgn. Relations. Episcopalian. Clubs: Yale, Chaos (N.Y.C.); Federal City, City Tavern, Metropolitan (Washington). Contbr. articles to profl. and other jours. Home: 3248 O St NW Washington DC 20007 Office: 815 Connecticut Ave NW Washington DC 20006

OPPENHEIMER, JANE MARION, educator, historian, biologist; b. Phila., Sept. 19, 1911; d. James Harry and Sylvia (Stern) Oppenheimer; B.A., Bryn Mawr Coll., 1932; Ph.D., Yale, 1935, postgrad. (Sterling fellow), 1935-36, (Am. Assn. U. Women fellow), 1936-37; Sc.D. (hon.), Brown U., 1976. Research fellow embryology U. Rochester, 1937-38; faculty Bryn Mawr (Pa.) Coll., 1938—, prof., 1953—, acting dean grad. sch., 2d semester, 1946-47. Vis. prof. biology Johns Hopkins, 1966-67; exchange prof. U. Paris, 1969. Mem. history life scis. study sect. NIH, 1966-70. Recipient Lucius Wilbur Cross medal Yale Grad. Alumni Assn., 1971. Guggenheim Meml. Found. fellow, 1942-43, 52-53; Rockefeller Found. fellow, 1950-51; NSF postdoctoral fellow, 1959-60. Fellow A.A.A.S. (sec. sect. L 1955-58, council del. sect. G 1980—), Phila. Coll. Physicians (hon.); mem. Am. Soc. Zoologists (treas. 1957-59, chmn. div. devel. biology 1967, pres. 1973), Am. Assn. Anatomists, History of Sci. Soc. (mem. council 1975-77), Am. Assn. History Medicine (mem. council 1971-74), Am. Soc. Naturalists, Soc. for Developmental Biology, Internat. Soc. for Developmental Biology, Am. Inst. Biol. Scis. (mem. at large governing bd. 1974-77), Internat. Soc. History Medicine, Internat. Acad. History of Sci. (Paris) (corr.), Internat. Acad. History Medicine (Paris), AAUW. Author: New Aspects of John and William Hunter, 1946; Essays in History of Embryology and Biology, 1967. Co-editor Founds. Exptl. Embryology, 1964, editor 2d edit., 1974; asso. editor Jour. Morphology, 1956-58, Quar. Rev. Biol., 1963-64; mem. editorial bd. Am. Zoologist, 1965-70, Jour. History Biology, 1967-75, Quar. Rev. Biology, 1968-75; sect. editor developmental biology Biol. Abstracts, 1970-73. Office: Biology Bldg Bryn Mawr Coll Bryn Mawr PA 19010

OPPENHEIMER, JESS, TV producer, dir., writer; b. San Francisco, Nov. 11, 1913; s. James and Stella C. (Jessurun) O.; student Stanford U., 1931-33; m. Estelle Weiss, Aug. 5, 1947; children—Joanne, Gregg. Writer Fred Astaire Packard program, 1936-38; head writer Screen Guild program, 1938-40; writer Rudy Vallee Sealtest program, 1940-41; writer, dir., producer, Fanny Brice in Baby Snooks program, 1942-47; producer, dir., head writer Lucille Ball in My Favorite Husband, 1948-51; producer, head writer I Love Lucy, 1951-56; NBC exec., producer Gen. Motors 50th Anniversary Show, 1956—; exec. producer creater Angel, 1960-61; creator exec. producer Glynis TV series, 1963-64; producer, writer, dir. Bob Hope Chrysler Theater, 1965-66; producer, writer Get Smart, 1967-68; pres. Rinkeed, Inc.; creator, exec. producer, writer Debbie Reynolds show, 1968-69. Dir. Vista del Mar Child Care Service; gov. TV Acad., 1966—. Served with USCGR, 1941-45. Recipient Sylvania award for I Love Lucy, 1952, Emmy award, 1952, 53, Michael award, 1953; nominee for Emmy award for I Love Lucy, 1954, 55, Gen. Motors 50th Anniversary Show, 1957, Wonderful World of Entertainment, 1959, Danny Kay Show, 1962. Bd. govs. City of Hope. Mem. Soc. Motion Picture and TV Engrs., Writers Guild, Dirs. Guild, TV Producers Guild. Home: 549 Moreno Ave W Los Angeles CA 90049 Office: 262 26th St Santa Monica CA 90402

OPPENHEIMER, JOEL LESTER, author; b. Yonkers, N.Y., Feb. 18, 1930; s. Leopold and Kate Blanche (Rosenwasser) O.; student Cornell U., 1947-48, U. Chgo., 1948-49, Black Mountain Coll., 1950-53; m. Rena Mary Margaret Julia Ann Furlong, June 5, 1952 (div. June 1959); children—Nicholas Patrick, Daniel Eben; m. 2d, Helen Joan Bukberg, June 5, 1966 (div. Nov. 1977); children—Nathaniel Ezra, Lemuel Shandy Davin. Various advt. and typography positions, 1953-66; free lance writer, 1966—; columnist Village Voice, N.Y.C., 1970—. Dir., Poetry Project, St. Mark's Ch. in the Bowery, 1966-68, Tchrs. and Writers Collaborative, 1969; poet-in-residence City Coll., City U. N.Y., 1969—; vis. poet St. Andrews Presbyn. Coll., 1977—. Creative Artists Pub. Service Program grantee N.Y. State Council on Arts, 1971. Mem. Norman Louis Newsom Soc. (asso. dir.), Authors Guild, P.E.N., Poetry Soc. Am., Soc. for Am. Baseball Research. Author: (poems) The Dutiful Son, 1956, The Love Bit, 1961, In Time, 1969, On Occasion, 1973, The Woman Poems, 1975, Names, Dates, and Places, 1979, Just Friends/Friends and Lovers, 1980; (play) The Great American Desert, 1961; (non-fiction) The Wrong Season, 1973; (stories) Pan's Eyes, 1974. Home: 463 West St New York NY 10014

OPPENHEIMER, MAX, JR., real estate broker, educator; b. N.Y.C., July 27, 1917; s. Max and Louise (Pourfurst) O.; Bachelier ès Lettres, U. Paris (France), 1935; B.A. cum laude, N.Y. U., 1941; M.A., U. Calif. at Los Angeles, 1942; Ph.D., U. So. Calif., 1947; m. Christine Backus, Oct. 14, 1942; children—Edmund Max, Carolyn Christine. Instr. fgn. langs. San Diego State Coll., 1947-49; asst. prof. Romance langs. Washington U., St. Louis, 1949-51; asso. prof. modern langs. Fla. State U., 1958-61; prof., chmn. dept. Russian, U. Iowa, 1961-67; prof. State U. N.Y., Fredonia, 1967-76, prof. emeritus, 1976—, chmn. fgn. langs. dept., 1967-73. Intelligence officer CIA, 1956-58. Served to lt. col., M.I., AUS, 1942-46, 51-56, lt. col. Res. ret. Decorated Bronze Star medal. Fla. State U. grantee, 1961; Office Naval Research grantee, 1965; State U. N.Y. grantee, 1973. Mem. Modern Lang. Assn., Am. Soc. Geolinguistics (pres. 1975-76), YMCA, Phi Beta Kappa, Sigma Delta Pi, Pi Delta Phi (nat. pres. 1946-51), Alpha Mu Gamma, Dobro Slovo. Elk. Author: Outline of Russian Grammar, 1962; translator Davydov, Theory of Molecular Excitons, 1962; Kostyukov, Theory of Ship Waves and Wave Resistance, 1968; The Fake Astrologer (Calderón de la Barca), 1976; The Lady Simpleton (Lope de Vega), 1976; Don Juan (Tirso de Molina), 1976. Contbr. articles to profl. lit. Home: Box 5529 Santa Fe NM 87502. *When you speak, always say what you think, not what you think you should say for the sake of expediency. Steadfastly, stubbornly, cling to your ideals, principles and beliefs, but be flexible enough to change whenever changing them reflects wisdom, not weakness or compromise. Avoid ego trips or being awed by your own alleged accomplishments.*

OPPENHEIMER, MICHAEL, physicist; b. Bklyn., Feb. 28, 1946; s. Harry and Shirley Meyer Oppenheimer; S.B., M.I.T., 1966; Ph.D., U. Chgo., 1970. Research fellow Harvard Coll., 1971-72, lectr. astronomy Harvard U., 1972—, physicist Harvard-Smithsonian Center for Astrophysics, Harvard U., 1973—; vis. astronomer Lick Obs., U. Calif., Santa Cruz, 1978-79. Union Carbide fellow, 1969-70; A.F. Morrison fellow, 1979; Guggenheim fellow, 1978-79. Mem. Am. Phys. Soc., Am. Geophys. Union, AAAS. Contbr. articles to profl. jours. Office: Center for Astrophysics 60 Garden St Cambridge MA 02138

OPPENHEIMER, REUBEN, ret. judge; b. Balt., Oct. 24, 1897; s. Leon H. and Flora (Oppenheimer) Schwab; A.B., Johns Hopkins, 1917; LL.B. cum laude, Harvard, 1920; m. Selma C. Levy, June 26, 1922; children—Martin J., Joan F. (Mrs. Stanley Weiss). Admitted to Md. bar, 1921; partner firm Emory, Beeuwkes, Skeen & Oppenheimer, and successors, Balt., 1922-55; asso. judge Supreme Bench Balt. City, 1955-65; asso. judge Ct. Appeals, Md., 1964-67; lectr. U. Md. Law Sch., 1947-55. Pub. mem., co-chmn. appeals and review coms. WLB, 1943-45; chief atty. Md. office OPA, 1942-43; chmn. com. reorgn. Peoples Ct. Balt. City, 1938; chmn. com. additional tax revenue, Balt., 1945; chmn. bd. Md. Dept. Correction, 1947-51; mem. U.S. delegation Internat. Penal and Penitentiary Congress, The Hague, 1950; mem. Com. Adminstrv. Orgn. Md., 1951-53, Com. Jud. Adminstrn., 1953-55; chmn. Com. Amendments Balt. City Charter, 1969-71; chmn. Md. Bd. Ethics, 1969-79. Mem. exec. bd. Am. Jewish Com., 1946—; pres. Balt. Jewish Council, 1940-41; Jewish Welfare Fund Balt., 1942. Trustee Sheppard and Enoch Pratt Hosp., 1963-75. Served with USNRF, World War I. Mem. Bar Assn. Balt. City (pres. 1952-53), Am., Md. (pres. 1955-56) bar assns., Harvard Law Sch. Assn. Md. (pres. 1955-56), Phi Beta Kappa, Order Coif, Omicron Delta Kappa. Contbr. articles to profl. jours. Home: 7121 Park Heights Ave Baltimore MD 21215 Office: 408 The Quadrangle Village of Cross Keys Baltimore MD 21210

OPPENLANDER, ROBERT, air line exec.; b. N.Y.C., May 20, 1923; s. Robert and Lillian (Ahrens) O.; B.S., Mass. Inst. Tech., 1944; M.B.A., Harvard, 1948; m. Jessie I. Major, Sept. 30, 1950; children—Kris (Mrs. John Paul Austin, Jr.), Robert Kirk, Tenley. With Metals & Controls Corp., Attleboro, Mass., 1948-53; prin. Cresap, McCormick & Paget, N.Y.C., 1953-58; comptroller, treas. Delta Air Lines, Inc., Atlanta, 1958—, v.p. fin., 1964-67, sr. v.p. fin., treas., 1967-78, sr. v.p. fin., 1978—, also dir. Served to lt. USNR, 1944-46. Club: Capital City. Home: 3944 Powers Ferry Rd NW Atlanta GA 30342 Office: Delta Air Lines Inc Hartsfield Atlanta Internat Airport Atlanta GA 30320

OPPER, FRANZ FREDERICK, lawyer; b. Fayetteville, Ark., July 4, 1939; s. Lincoln and Charlotte Henrietta (Jantzen) O.; B.A., Yale U., 1961; LL.B., U. Pa., 1964; m. Barbara Ann Negri, Dec. 2, 1967; children—Gretchen Elizabeth, Stephen Frederick. Admitted to D.C. bar, 1971, Conn. bar, 1965, U.S. Supreme Ct. bar, 1970; regional counsel U.S. Comptroller of Currency, Washington, 1965-68; spl. counsel SEC, Washington, 1968-72; gen. counsel Hartford Nat. Corp. (Conn.), 1972-76; counsel Interstate and Fgn. Commerce Com. U.S. Ho. of Reps., Washington, 1976—. Mem. Fed. Bar Assn. Democrat. Episcopalian. Home: 7004 Meadow Ln Chevy Chase MD 20015 Office: Interstate Fgn Commerce Com Rayburn House Office Bldg Washington DC 20515

OPPERTHAUSER, EARL CHARLES, lawyer; b. Detroit, Jan. 4, 1925; s. Alvin and Malvena Catherine (Fisher) O.; J.D., Wayne State U., 1949; m. Eugenia Ann Roshirt, Nov. 29, 1951; children—Denise, Kathy, Steve, Scott. Admitted to Mich. bar, 1949; individual practice law, 1949-51, 53-55; atty. Detroit Ordnance Dist., Dept. Army, 1951-53; with law dept. Grand Trunk Western R.R., Detroit, 1955—, gen. counsel, 1972—; dir. Detroit Terminal R.R. Co. Trustee Farmington Twp., (Mich.), 1962-73; councilman, Farmington Hills, Mich., 1973—, mayor, 1975-76, 78-79. Served with USAAF, 1943-45. Mem. Am., Fed., Mich., Oakland County, Detroit (dir.) bar assns., Nat. Assn. R.R. Trial Counsel, Am. Judicature Soc. Republican. Presbyterian. Club: Masons. Home: 32216 Baintree Rd Farmington Hills MI 48018 Office: 131 W Lafayette Blvd Detroit MI 48226

OPPOLD, WILLIAM ANDREW, chem. co. exec.; b. Fort Dodge, Iowa, Dec. 28, 1920; s. William J. and Bessie (Belt) O.; B.S. in Chem. Engring., Iowa State Coll., 1943; m. Ruth M. Scheerer, Apr. 4, 1943; children—Sara Jane, William Lindsay. With Mallinckrodt Chem. Corp., St. Louis, 1943-52; chief ops. AEC, Fernald, O., 1952-54; works mgr. Wyandotte Chem. Corp., 1954-60; v.p. ops. Jack's Cookie Corp., Charlotte, N.C., 1960-64; v.p. prodn. and engring. Olin Mathieson Chem. Corp., N.Y.C., 1964-70, v.p. mfg., chems. group, 1969-73, 76-79, v.p. mfg. and constrn., chems. group, 1979—, mng. dir. Marstolin Group, 1973-76; dir. Citizens Savs. Bank. Mem. Am. Inst. Chem. Engrs. Home: 50 Glenbrook Rd Stamford CT 06902 Office: 120 Long Ridge Rd Stamford CT 06904

OPRE, THOMAS EDWARD, editor; b. Evansville, Ind., Nov. 6, 1943; m. William Jennings and Ruth (Strouss) O.; A.B. in Journalism, Ind. U., 1965; m. Norlin Kay Hartley, June 20, 1965; children—Thomas Andrew, William Hartley. Sports and outdoor writer Decatur (Ill.) Herald & Rev., 1965-66; outdoor editor Detroit Free Press, 1966—; midwest field editor Field and Stream mag., 1971—; editorial dir. Gt. Lakes Sportsman mag., 1972-75; pres. Tom Opre Prodns., outdoor entertainment films, 1967—. Recipient James Henshall award Am. Fish Tackle Mfrs. Assn., 1969, Teddy award Nat. Outdoor Travel Film Festival, 1973, Environ. award EPA, 1977, Nat. Writer's award Safari Club Internat., 1977, Deep Woods Writing award OWAA, 1977, Conservation Service award Ducks Unltd., 1977; named to Internat. Fishing Hall of Fame, 1968. Mem. Outdoor Writers Assn. Am. (dir., pres.), Assn. Gt. Lakes Outdoor Writers (dir., past chmn. bd., pres., v.p.), Mich. Outdoor Writers Assn. (dir.), Sigma Delta Chi, Alpha Tau Omega. Author numerous articles in outdoor and travel fields. Home: 6193 Kinyon Dr Brighton MI 48116 Office: 321 W Lafayette Blvd Detroit MI 48231

O'QUINN, SILAS EDGAR, physician, med. center adminstr.; b. Brunswick, Ga., Feb. 24, 1924; s. Silas Edgar and Jewel Ella (Cook) O'Q.; student U. Ga., 1941-42, U. Ill., 1942-44; M.D., U. Mich., 1949. Intern, Charity Hosp., New Orleans, 1949-50, fellow div. dermatology Tulane Service, 1959, resident La. State U. Service, 1960-62, sr. vis. physician, 1966, dermatologist-in-chief, 1966-74, sec. vis. staff, 1970-71, v.p., 1971-72, pres., 1972-73; mem. regional adv. group La. Regional Med. Program, 1973—; chmn. bd. govs. La. Cancer Center, 1974-77; cons. dermatology, chmn. deans com. VA Hosp., New Orleans, 1975-77; instr. dermatology La. State U. Sch. Medicine, 1962-63, asst. prof., 1963-64, asso. prof., 1965-68, asso. prof., head dept. dermatology, 1966-68, prof., head dept. dermatology, 1968-74, asso. dean, 1971-73, dean, 1973—; vice chancellor for clin. affairs La. State U. Med. Center, 1977—. Served with AUS, 1941-43; to capt., M.C., USAF, 1951-53. Fellow Am. Acad. Dermatology (dir. sci. exhibits 1970-74, dir. 1970-73); mem. La. (del. 1973-74, 76—), Orleans Parish (bd. govs. 1973-74, 76—) med. socs., Am., La. (sec.-treas. 1963-64, pres. 1965-66) dermatol. socs., Am. Cancer Soc. (dir. Greater New Orleans Area unit 1973-77), Cancer Assn. Greater New Orleans (dir. 1970—). Home: 1009 Burgundy St New Orleans LA 70116 Office: 1440 Canal St Suite 1510 New Orleans LA 70112

ORAVA, RAIMO NORMAN, coll. adminstr.; b. Toronto, Ont., Can., Sept. 23, 1935; came to U.S., 1963, naturalized, 1978; s. Oscar and Annikki (Virsu) O.; B.A.Sc., U. Toronto, 1957; M.A.Sc., U. B.C., 1959; Ph.D., D.I.C., Imperial Coll., U. London, 1963; m. Louise Orava, Oct. 3, 1959; children—Robert Scott, Stephen James. Sci. officer Can. Dept. Mines and Tech. Survey, 1957; lectr. math. U. Waterloo, 1959, lectr. applied physics, 1959-60; sr. scientist non-ferrous metall. div. Battelle Meml. Inst., 1963-64; research metallurgist Franklin Inst., Phila., 1964-65, sr. research metallurgist, 1965-66; research metallurgist Denver Research Inst., U. Denver, 1966-74, lectr., 1970-74, sr. research metallurgist, 1974; prof. metall. engring. S.D. Sch. Mines and Tech., Rapid City, 1974—, acting v.p., dean engring., 1975-77, dean grad. div., dir. research, 1977—; dir. MASEC Corp., 1979—; bd. dirs. Consortium of Univs. for Research on Energy, 1978—; chief negotiator, agreement mgr. S.D. Higher Edn. System Collective Bargaining, 1979—. Sec., Black Hills Pony League, 1978-79. Ont. Research Found. fellow, 1960-63. Mem. Am. Soc. Engring. Edn., Am. Inst. Mining Engrs., Am. Soc. Metals, Nat. Council Univ. Research Adminstrs., Rapid City C. of C. (co-chmn. energy task force), Sigma Xi. Republican. Lutheran. Club: Rotary. Contbr. articles to profl. jours. Home: 3029 Tomahawk Dr Rapid City SD 57701 Office: SD Sch of Mines and Tech Rapid City SD 57701

ORB, JOHN ALEXANDER, investment banker; b. Chgo., Feb. 19, 1919; s. John A. and Rowena W. (Monahan) O.; B.A., Yale U., 1941; m. Elizabeth Nevins, Feb. 28, 1942 (dec.); children—John Alexander IV, Joan Orb Garrison, Linda Orb Drake; m. 2d, Jean G. Tennant, June 23, 1961. Exec. v.p., dir. Merrill Lynch, Pierce, Fenner & Smith Inc., N.Y.C., until 1975; exec. v.p. Smith Barney, Harris Upham & Co. Inc., N.Y.C., 1975-77, pres., chief operating officer, 1977—, also dir.; bd. dirs. Chgo. Bd. Trade, 1973; bd. govs. Midwest Stock Exchange, 1965-69. Served to lt. col. USAAF, 1941-46. Decorated D.F.C. Mem. Nat. Assn. Securities Dealers (dist. chmn. 1968), Investment Bankers Assn. (past vice chmn. Central states group). Clubs: Bond, Yale (N.Y.C.); Chicago, Tavern (Chgo.); Hyannisport (Mass.). Office: 1345 Ave Americas New York NY 10019

ORBACH, JERRY, actor, singer; b. N.Y.C., Oct. 20, 1935; s. Leon and Emily (Olexy) O.; student U. Ill., 1952-53, Northwestern U., 1953-55; studied acting with Herbert Berghof, Mira Rostova, Lee Strasberg, N.Y.C.; studied singing with Hazel Schweppe, N.Y.C.; m. Marta Curro, June 21, 1958; children—Anthony Nicholas, Christopher Ben. Made profl. debut on stage in Room Service, 1952; resident actor Show Case Theatre, Evanston, Ill., summers 1953-54; made N.Y.C. stage debut in 3 Penny Opera, 1955; stage appearances include 3 Penny Opera, The Fantasticks, Carnival, Scuba Duba, Promises Promises, The Rose Tattoo, 6 Rums Riv Vu, The King and I, Guys and Dolls, The Student Prince, Annie Get Your Gun, The Trouble With People . . . And Other Things, Chicago; appeared in films Please Come Home, 1964, The Gang That Couldn't Shoot Straight, 1971, A Fan's Notes, 1974, Sentinel, 1977; numerous TV appearances including Shari Lewis Show, Jack Paar Show, The Nurses, Bob Hope Presents, Love American Style. Recipient New March of Dimes Horizon award, 1961, award of merit Actors Fund, 1961, Tony award, 1968. Mem. AFTRA, Screen Actors Guild, Actors Equity Assn. Address: 232 W 23d St New York NY 10011*

ORBACH, RAYMOND LEE, physicist, educator; b. Los Angeles, July 12, 1934; s. Morris Albert and Mary Ruth (Miller) O.; B.S., Calif. Inst. Tech., 1956; Ph.D., U. Calif. at Berkeley, 1960; m. Eva Hannah Spiegler, Aug. 26, 1956; children—David Miller, Deborah Hedwig, Thomas Randolph. NSF postdoctoral fellow Oxford U., 1960-61; asst. prof. applied physics Harvard, 1961-63; prof. physics U. Calif. at Los Angeles, 1963—, asst. vice chancellor acad. change and curriculum devel., 1970-72, chmn. Los Angeles div. acad. senate, 1976-77. Cons. Aerospace Corp., 1965-70; mem. physics adv. panel NSF, 1970-73; mem. vis. com. Brookhaven Nat. Lab., 1970-74; mem. materials research lab. adv. panel NSF, 1974-77; mem. Nat. Commn. on Research, 1978—. Alfred P. Sloan Found. fellow, 1963-67; NSF sr. postdoctoral fellow Imperial Coll., 1967-68; Guggenheim fellow Tel Aviv U., 1973-74. Mem. Am. Phys. Soc., Phys. Soc. (London), Phi Beta Kappa, Sigma Xi, Tau Beta Pi. Author: (with A.A. Manenkov) SpinLattice Relaxation in Ionic Solids, 1966. Contbr. articles profl. jours. Home: 339 Arno Way Pacific Palisades CA 90272 Office: Knudsen Hall U Calif Los Angeles CA 90024

ORBAN, KURT, fgn. trade co. exec.; b. S.I., N.Y., Aug. 6, 1916; s. Kurt and Gertrude (Astfalck) Orbanowski; grad. steel fgn. trade course Stahlunion-Export GmbH, Duesseldorf, Germany, 1938; m. Katrina Tribble, Sept. 1966; children—Robert Arnold, Robin Ann, Kurt-Matthew, Jonathan. Fgn. trade corr. Stahlunion, Dusseldorf, 1938, rep., Bulgaria, 1939-40; steel export trader Steel Union Sheet Piling Co., N.Y.C., 1941; v.p. North River Steel Co., N.Y.C., 1941; chmn., pres. Kurt Orban Co., Inc., Wayne, N.J., 1946—; pres. Kurt Orban Can., Ltd., Toronto, Ont., Kurt Orban Co. Bruxelles, Brussels, Belgium, Kurt Orban (U.K.) Ltd., London, Kurt Orban Co., Japan, chmn. Northampton Mfg. Co. (Mass.), Orban Industries, Buffalo, N.Y. E.B. Giberson Co., North Brunswick, N.J.; dir. Atlantic Wire Co., Branford, Conn. Mem. field hockey games com. U.S. Olympic Com., 1948-61; playing mgr. U.S. Field Hockey Team. London, Eng., 1948, playing coach, Melbourne, Australia, 1956; U.S. rep. Bur. Internat. Hockey Fedn., Brussels, 1954-62. Served to 1st lt. USAAF, 1943-45. Mem. Am. Inst. Imported Steel (pres. 1966-68, 78-79, dir. N.Y.C.), Am. Importers Assn. (pres. 1972-73, dir.). Address: Orban Way Wayne NJ 07470

ORBEN, ROBERT ALLEN, engine co. exec.; b. Bklyn., Aug. 17, 1936; s. Stanley Souza and Helena Emily (Hall) O.; B.A., Lehigh U., 1958; M.B.A., Rutgers U., 1960; m. Mary West Foster, May 7, 1960; children—Christopher Riis, Janet Hyde, Virginia Hamilton, William Robert. Audit mgr. Price Waterhouse & Co., N.Y.C., 1960-73; asst. controller NCR Corp., Dayton, Ohio, 1973-74, controller, 1974-77; v.p., controller Cummins Engine Co., Inc., Columbus, Ind., 1977—. Trustee, Dayton Art Inst. Served to 1st lt. AUS, 1960-62. Decorated Army Commendation medal. C.P.A., N.Y., N.J. Mem. Financial Execs. Inst., Chi Phi. Republican. Presbyn. Home: 4390 N Riverside Dr Columbus IN 47201 Office: 1460 N National Rd Columbus IN 47201

ORBISON, JAMES LOWELL, pathologist, educator; b. Bronson, Kans., Mar. 8, 1915; s. Franklin Lloyd and Mary Edna (Ireland) O.; A.B., Ottawa (Kans.) U., 1937, D.Sc. (hon.), 1966; M.S., Mich. State U., 1939; M.D., Northwestern U., 1944; D.Sc. (hon.), Bucknell U., 1975; D.LL. (hon.), Nazareth Coll., N.Y., 1979; m. Olga Dianich, June 21, 1941; children—Margaret Chase, James Graham. Intern, St. Luke's Hosp., Chgo., 1944; asst. resident pathology Univ. Hosps., Cleve., 1944-45; resident pathology Cleve. City Hosp., 1947; from sr. instr. to asso. prof. pathology Western Res. U., 1947-55; George H. Whipple prof., chmn. dept. pathology U. Rochester, 1955-70, acting dean, acting dir. Med. Center, 1966-67, dean, dir., 1967-79, dean emeritus, 1979—; mem. pathology test com. Nat. Bd. Med. Examiners, 1956-62, chmn., 1961-62; sci. adv. bd. Armed Forces Inst. Pathology, 1957-62, 70-74; pathology tng. com. NIH, 1960-66, chmn., 1963-66; mem. pathology com. Nat. Acad. Scis., 1966-71; mem. Intersoc. Com. Research Potential Pathology, 1959-78, pres., 1961-78; mem. NIH Cancer Research Center Com., 1969-72, chmn., 1973-77. Served to capt. M.C., AUS, 1945-47. Diplomate Nat. Bd. Med. Examiners. Mem. Internat. Acad. Pathology (chmn. edn. com. 1959-65, pres. 1963-64), Am. Assn. Pathologists and Bacteriologists (council 1964-71, sec.-treas. 1965-68, pres. 1969-70), Am. Soc. Exptl. Pathology, Sigma Xi, Alpha Omega Alpha, Phi Chi. Editor: (with David Smith) Pathologic Physiology and Anatomy of Peripheral Vessels, 1962; mem. editorial bd. Circulation Research, 1955-66, Arthritis and Rheumatism, 1962-64, Procs. Soc. Exptl. Biology and Medicine. 1962-66, Lab. Investigations. 1967-74. Home: 105 Stoney Brook Dr Rochester NY 14618

ORCHIN, MILTON, educator, chemist; b. Barnesboro, Pa., June 4, 1914; s. Morris and Mary (Rifkin) O.; B.A., Ohio State U., 1936, M.A., 1937, Ph.D., 1939; m. Ruth Wilner, June 4, 1941; children—Morton Lewis, Michael David. Chemist, FDA, Cin., Chgo., 1939-42; chief organic chemistry sect. U.S. Bur. Mines, 1943-53; asso. prof. chemistry U. Cin., 1953-56, prof., head dept., 1956-62, prof. chemistry, dir. basic sci. lab., 1962-70, dir. Hoke S. Greene Lab. for Catalysis, 1970—. Bd. govs. Ben Gurion U. of Negev (Israel), 1974—. Guggenheim fellow, 1947-48. Mem. A.A.A.S. (chmn. chemistry sect. 1963), Am. Chem. Soc. (chmn. Cin. sect. 1962, Eminent Chemist award Cin. sect. 1957 E.V. Murphree award in indsl. and engring. chemistry 1979), Chem. Soc. London, Phi Beta Kappa, Sigma Xi. Co-author 6 books. Contbr. numerous articles research publs. Patentee in field. Home: 3763 Middleton Ave Cincinnati OH 45220

ORCUTT, GUY HENDERSON, economist; b. Wyandotte, Mich., July 5, 1917; B.S. with honors in Physics, U. Mich., 1939, M.A. in Econs., 1940, Ph.D. (Rackham fellow), 1944; m.; four children. Teaching fellow econs. U. Mich., 1940-41, lab. asst., statistician Univ. Hosp., 1944; instr. econs. Mass. Inst. Tech., 1944-46; sr. research worker, dept. applied econs. Cambridge (Eng.) U., 1946-48; economist IMF, 1949, cons., 1951-53; asst. prof. then asso. prof. econs. Harvard U., 1949-58, dir. Littauer Statis. Lab., 1952-56, vis. prof., 1965-66; Brittingham prof. econs. U. Wis., 1958-69, dir. Social Systems Research Inst., 1959-62, dir. research, 1962-64, chmn., 1964-65; sr. adviser IBRD, 1967-68; dir. Poverty and Inequality Project, Urban Inst., 1968-75; Irving Fisher vis. prof. Yale U., New Haven, 1969-70, prof. econs., A. Whitney Griswold prof. urban studies, 1970—, chmn. Center for Studies of City and Its Environment, 1970-73; Nuffield fellow, 1947; cons. Fed. Res. Bd., 1954, Office Statis. Standards, Bur. of Budget, 1961-62; mem. exec. com., div. behavioral scis. Nat. Acad. Scis.-NRC, 1968-70; bd. dirs. Social Sci. Research Com., 1975—, treas., 1976—. Fellow Am. Statis. Assn. (v.p. 1959-61), Econometric Soc. (council mem. 1961-62, 68-71); mem. Am. Econ. Assn. (exec. com. 1972-75). Contbr. articles on econs. to profl. jours. Address: Yale U Dept Econs New Haven CT 06520

ORDEN, ALEX, educator; b. Rochester, N.Y., Aug. 9, 1916; s. Abraham and Esther (Katz); O.B.S. in Optics, U. Rochester, 1937; M.S. in Physics, U. Mich., 1939; Ph.D. in Math., Mass. Inst. Tech., 1950; m. Susan Rabinowitz, Dec. 8, 1946; children—Ruth Diane, David Robert, Jeanne Madeline. Physicist, Nat. Bur. Standards, 1942-47; instr. Mass. Inst. Tech., 1947-50; mathematician Hdqrs. USAF, 1950-52; mgr. applied math. sect. Burroughs Corp., 1952-58; dir. operations analysis lab. U. Chgo., 1958-62, prof. mgmt. sci., 1958—. Vis. prof. London (Eng.) Sch. Econs., 1964; vis. Vasser Woolley prof. Ga. Inst. Tech., 1966, 67, 70. Mem. Ill. Sci. Adv. Council, 1965-67. Mem. Inst. Mgmt. Scis. (sec. 1953, chmn. nat. meeting 1969), Assn. Computing Machinery (nat. lectr. 1965, chmn. spl. interest group in math. programming 1969-71), Math Programming Soc. (chmn. organizing com. 1970-72), Phi Beta Kappa, Sigma Xi. Contbr. articles to profl. jours. Home: 5715 S Kenwood Ave Chicago IL 60637

ORDILE, JOSEPH ROBERT, podiatrist; b. Phila., Apr. 29, 1922; s. John Joseph and Teresa (Zurzolo) O.; D.Podiatric Medicine, Temple U., Phila., 1946; m. Wanda Helene Garland, Dec. 17, 1944; 1 dau., Margaret. Podiatrist, Ft. Worth, 1947—; pres. Tex. Bd. Examiners Podiatry, 1973-75; lectr., cons. in field; v.p. Med-Lease, Inc.; sec., mem. exec. com. Boulevard Hosp.; del. county and state Democratic convs.; pres. Tanglewood Sch. PTA, 1967. Served with M.C., AUS, 1943-45. Diplomate Am. Bd. Podiatric Surgery. Fellow Am. Coll. Foot Surgery; mem. Am. (pres. 1977-78), Tex. (pres. 1957, Merit award 1957, Distinguished Service award 1970), Tarrant County (pres. 1952) podiatry assns. Baptist. Clubs: Colonial Country, Ft. Worth Rotary. Co-author: Texas Chiropodical Formulary, 1950. Home: 3800 Trails Edge Rd Fort Worth TX 78109 Office: 909 8th Ave Fort Worth TX 78104 -

ORDIN, ANDREA SHERIDAN, U.S. atty.; A.B., U. Calif., Los Angeles, 1962, LL.B., 1965; m. Robert Ordin; 1 dau., Maria; stepchildren—Allison, Richard. Admitted to Calif. bar; dep. atty. gen. Calif., 1965-72; So. Calif. legal counsel Fair Employment Practices Commn., 1972-73; asst. dist. atty. Los Angeles County, 1975-77; U.S. atty. for Central Dist. Calif., Los Angeles, 1977—. Mem. Los Angeles County Bar Assn. (past dir.). Address: US Attys Office 312 N Spring St Los Angeles CA 90012

ORDING, JAMES HENRY, trade assn. exec.; b. Bklyn., Jan. 31, 1911; s. James Henry and Helena (Menne) O.; student Cooper Union Inst. Tech., 1928-29, N.Y. U., 1932-34; grad. Am. Inst. Banking, 1931; m. Elizabeth Van Zile, Sept. 15, 1933 (dec. 1958); m. 2d, Nancy Marie Burns, Dec. 20, 1958; 1 son, James Henry. With N.Y. Stock Exchange, 1929-50, mgr. div. conduct and finance, 1937-50; stockbroker Parrish & Co., N.Y.C., 1950-51; with Assn. Stock Exchange Firms, N.Y.C., 1951—, sec., 1956—, exec. dir., 1962—; trustee Assn. Stock Exchange Firms Inst. Trust, 1960; sec. Securities Industry Assn., 1972. Served with AUS, 1943-46. Mem. Am. Soc. Assn. Execs. Club: Bankers of Am. (N.Y.C.). Home: 3479 Surele Rd Wantagh NY 11793 Office: 20 Broad St New York City NY 10005

ORDUNG, PHILIP FRANKLIN, educator; b. Luverne, Minn., Aug. 12, 1919; s. Philip N. and Katherine (Franklin) O.; B.S., S.D. State Coll., 1940; M. Engring., Yale U., 1942, D. Engring., 1949; m. Betty Jane Soergel, Dec. 22, 1945; children—Christine Soergel, Katherine Louise. Grad. asst. dept. elec. engring. Yale, 1940- 42, instr. to asso. prof., 1942-57, prof. elec. engring., 1957-62; prof. elec. engring. U. Calif., Santa Barbara, 1962—, chmn. dept. elec. engring., 1962-68. Vis. prof. Tech. U. Norway, 1969-70. Dir. Optoelectronics, 1969—. Mem. bd. edn., Branford, Conn., 1955-61, chmn., 1959-61. Bd. dirs. Santa Barbara Sci. and Engring. Council, 1969-72; regent Calif. Luth. Coll. Served as ensign USNR, 1944-45. Fellow IEEE (regional sec.-treas. 1956-58, Royal W. Sorenson fellow 1962), AAAS; mem. N.Y. Acad. Scis., Yale Engring. Assn. (award for advancement basic and applied scis. 1953), Sigma Xi, Sigma Tau, Eta Kappa Nu. Home: 226 Northridge Rd Santa Barbara CA 93105

ORDWAY, FREDERICK IRA, III, educator, cons., researcher, author; b. N.Y.C., Apr. 4, 1927; s. Frederick Ira and Frances Antoinette (Wright) O.; S.B., Harvard, 1949; postgrad. U. Alger, 1950, U. Paris (France), 1950-51, 53-54, U. Barcelona (Spain), 1953, U. Innsbruck (Austria), 1954, Air U., 1952-63, Alexander Hamilton Bus. Inst., 1952-58, Indsl. Coll. Armed Forces, 1953, 63; m. Maria

Victoria Arenas, Apr. 13, 1950; children—Frederick Ira IV, Albert James, Aliette Marisol. Various geol., engring. positions Mene Grande Oil Co., San Tome, Venezuela, 1949-50, Orinoco Mining Co., Venezuela, 1950, Reaction Motors, Inc., Lake Denmark, N.J., 1951-53; with guided missiles div. Republic Aviation Corp., 1954-55; pres. Gen. Astronautics Research Corp., Huntsville, Ala., 1955-75; v.p. Nat. Research & Devel. Corp., Atlanta, 1957-59; asst. to dir. Saturn Systems Office, Army Ballistic Missile Agy., Huntsville, 1957-60; chief space information systems br. George C. Marshall Space Flight Center NASA, 1960-64; prof. sci. and tech. applications Sch. Grad. Studies and Research, U. Ala. Research Inst., 1967-73; cons. Sci. and Tech. Policy Office, NSF, 1974-76; cons. Ops. Analysis div. Gen. Research Corp., 1974-76; asst. to adminstr. ERDA, 1975-77; cons. Office of Asst. Sec. Policy and Evaluation, Dept. Energy, 1977—, also participant internat. energy devel. program. Cons. to industry, Ency. Brit., Am. Coll. Dictionary, Random House Unabridged Dictionary of English Lang., M.G.M. film 2001: A Space Odyssey, 1965-66; Paramount Pictures Corp., The Adventurers, 1968-69; internat. lectr. space flight and energy programs. Recipient (with W. von Braun) diplôme d'honneur French Commn. d'Histoire, Arts et Letters, Paris, 1969. Served with USNR, 1945. Fellow AAAS, Royal Astron. Soc., Brit., South African interplanetary socs., Canadian Inst. Aeros. and Astronautics, Am. Inst. Aeros. and Astronautics (asso.); dir. Ala. sect.; Pendray award 1974, Hermann Oberth award 1977); mem. Aerospace Med. Assn., Agrupación Astronáutica Espanola, Am. Astron. Soc., Am. Geophys. Union, Asociación Argentina Interplanetaria, Aviation Space Writers Assn., Internat. Acad. Astronautics, Sociedad Astronómica de Espana y America, Société Francaise d'Astronautique, Alliance Francaise (v.p. Huntsville chpt.), World Future Soc. (dir. Ala. sect.). Author: (with C.C. Adams) Space Flight, 1958; (with Ronald C. Wakeford) International Missile and Spacecraft Guide, 1960; Annotated Bibliography of Space Science and Technology, 1962; (with J.P. Gardner, M.R. Sharpe, Jr.) Basic Astronautics: An Introduction to Space Science, Engineering and Medicine, 1962; (with Adams, Wernher von Braun) Careers in Astronautics and Rocketry, 1962; (with Gardner, Sharpe, R.C. Wakeford) Applied Astronautics: An Introduction to Space Flight, 1963; (with Wakeford) Conquering the Sun's Empire, 1963; Life in Other Solar Systems, 1965; (with Roger A. MacGowan) Intelligence in the Universe, 1966; (with W. von Braun) History of Rocketry and Space Travel, 1966, 1969, 75, L'Histoire Mondial de l'Astronautique, 1968, 70, Rockets Red Glare, 1976; (with C.C. Adams, M.R. Sharpe) Dividends from Space, 1972; Pictorial Guide to Planet Earth, 1975; (with W. von Braun) New Worlds, 1979; (with M.R. Sharpe) The Rocket Team, 1979. Editor: Advances in Space Science and Technology, vols. I-XII, 2 supplements, 1959-72; (with R.M.L. Baker, N.W. Makemson) Introduction to Astrodynamics, 1960; (with others) From Peenemünde to Outer Space, 1962, Astronautical Engineering and Science, 1963; mem. editorial bd. IX Internat. Astronautical Congress procs., 2 vols., 1959, Xth Congress procs., 2 vols., 1960. Contbr. numerous articles to profl. jours., chpts. to books, sects. to Ency. Brit., Ency. Am., World Book, others. Home: 4118 Shelby Ave SE Huntsville AL 38501 also 2401 N Taylor St Arlington VA 22207 Office: Dept Energy Forrestal Bldg Washington DC 20585

OREAR, JAY, educator; b. Chgo., Nov. 6, 1925; s. Leslie and Edna (Tragnitz) O.; Ph.B., U. Chgo., 1944, Ph.D., 1953; m. Jeanne Bliven, Mar. 10, 1951; children—Scott, Robin, Wendy; m. 2d, Virginia Watts, Sept. 6, 1974. Research asso. U. Chgo., 1953-54; instr. to asst. prof. Columbia, 1954-58; asso. prof. Cornell U., 1958-64, prof. physics, nuclear studies, 1964—. Chmn. Fedn. Am. Scientists, 1967—. Served with USNR, 1944-46. Fellow Am. Phys. Soc. (editor Forum Newsletter 1972—); mem. Phi Beta Kappa, Sigma Xi. Author: Nuclear Physics, 1951; Fundamental Physics, 1961; Programmed Manual, 1963; Statistics for Physicists, 1958; Physics, 1979. Home: 1656 E Shore Dr Ithaca NY 14850

OREFFICE, PAUL FAUSTO, chem. co. exec.; b. Venice, Italy, Nov. 29, 1927; s. Max and Elena (Friedenberg) O.; came to U.S., 1945, naturalized, 1951; B.S. in Chem. Engring., Purdue U., 1949; m. Franca Giuseppina Ruffini, May 26, 1956; children—Laura Emma, Andrew T. With Dow Chem. Co., various internat. locations, 1955—, pres. Dow Chem. Inter-Am., Ltd., Sao Paulo, Brazil and Bilbao, Spain, 1967-69, v.p., dir. financial services Dow Chem. Internat., Inc., Coral Gables, Fla., 1969-70, v.p. finance Dow Chem. Co., Midland, Mich., 1970-74, v.p., treas., 1974-75, pres., 1978—, pres. Dow Chem. U.S.A., 1975-78, also dir.; dir. 1st Midland Bank & Trust Co., Midland, Conn. Gen. Ins. Co., Dow Corning, European-Am. Bank & Trust Co. Nat. bd. dirs. Jr. Achievement; chmn. Am. Indsl. Health Council, 1977—. Served with AUS, 1951-53. Decorated Encomienda del Merito Civil (Spain), 1966. Mem. Mfg. Chemists Assn. (dir. 1977—). Office: Dow Center Midland MI 48640

O'REGAN, RICHARD ARTHUR, fgn. corr.; b. Boston, July 15, 1919; s. Arthur R. and Amelia H. (Egbers) O'R.; student Temple U., 1940-41, Vienna U. (Austria), 1953-54; m. Elizabeth A. Hill, Mar. 23, 1946; children—John K., Michael L. With London Daily Mail and London Daily Sketch, 1938-39; reporter, night city editor Phila. Bull., 1939-43; writer Russian-German war specialist U.P.I., 1943-45; fgn. corr. A.P., 1945—, assigned London, Paris, Germany, 1945-50, chief bur., Vienna, 1950-55, Germany, 1956-66, London, 1966-77, dir. gen. for Europe, Africa and Middle East, 1977—; dir. A.P. Ltd. Mem. Assn. Am. Corrs. in London (pres. 1969). Clubs: Overseas Press (N.Y.C.); Press (past pres.) (Frankfurt, Germany); London Press, London Directors. Home: 33 Chemin de Grange Canal 1208 Geneva Switzerland Office: care Asso Press Palais des Nations 1211 Geneva Switzerland

O'REILLY, ANTHONY JOHN FRANCIS, food co. exec.; b. Dublin, Ireland, May 7, 1936; s. John Patrick and Aileen (O'Connor) O'R.; student Belvedere Coll., Dublin, Univ. Coll., Dublin, Wharton Bus. Sch. Overseas, 1965; B.C.L.; LL.D. (hon.), Wheeling Coll., Trinity Coll., Dublin, Rollins U.; m. Susan Cameron, May 5, 1962; children—Susan, Cameron, Justine, Gavin, Caroline, Tony. Indsl. cons. Weston Evans, 1958-60; personal asst. to chmn. Suttons Ltd., Cork, 1960-62; lectr. dept. applied psychology Univ. Coll., Cork, 1960-62; dir. Robert McCowen & Sons Ltd., Tralee, 1961-62; chief exec. An Bord Bainne/Irish Dairy Bd., 1962-66; dir. Agrl. Credit Corp. Ltd., 1965-66; dir. Nitrigin Eireann Teoranta, 1965-66; mng. dir., chief exec. officer Comhlucht Siuicre Eireann Teo. and Erin Foods Ltd., 1966-69; joint mng. dir. Heinz-Erin Ltd., 1967-70; dir. Allied Irish Investment Bank Ltd., 1968-71; mng. dir. H.J. Heinz Co. Ltd., U.K., 1969-71, dir. Thyssen-Bornemisza Co., Rotterdam, 1970-71; sr. v.p. N.Am. and Pacific, past sr. v.p. H.J. Heinz Co., 1971-72, now pres., chief operating officer, dir. World Hdqrs., Pitts., 1973—. Fellow Brit. Inst. Mgmt.; mem. Inst. Dirs., Inc. Law Soc. Ireland. Clubs: St. Stephens Green (Dublin); Annabels (London); Union League (N.Y.C.); Duquesne, Allegheny, Fox Chapel Golf, Pittsburgh Golf (Pitts.); Rolling Rock (Ligonier); Lyford Cay (Bahamas). Author: Prospect, 1962; Developing Creative Management, 1970; The Conservative Consumer, 1971; Food for Thought, 1972. Home: 835 Fox Chapel Rd Pittsburgh PA 15238 Office: PO Box 57 Pittsburgh PA 15230

O'REILLY, CHARLES TERRANCE, educator; b. Chgo., May 30, 1921; s. William Patrick and Ann Elizabeth (Madden) O'R.; B.A., Loyola U., Chgo., 1942, M.S.W., 1948; postgrad. Universita Cattolica, Milan, Italy, 1949-50; Ph.D., U. Notre Dame, 1954; m. Rosella Catherine Neilland, June 4, 1955; children—Terrance, Gregory, Kevin, Joan Bridget, Kathleen Ann. Instr. DePaul U., Chgo., 1948-49; asst. in psychology Univ. Cattolica, 1949-50; caseworker Cath. Charities, N.Y.C., 1953-54; exec. dir. Family Service, Long Branch, N.J., 1954-55; asst. prof. Loyola U., 1955-59; vis. lectr. Ensiss Sch. Social Work, Milan, 1959-60; asso. prof. U. Wis.-Milw., 1961-64; prof., asso. dir. U. Wis. Sch. Social Work Madison, 1965-68; dean social welfare, v.p. acad. affairs State U. N.Y. at Albany, 1968-76; dean social work Loyola U., Chgo., 1976—. Pres., Community Action Commn. Dane County, Wis., 1967-68. Bd. dirs. Council Community Services, Albany, Family and Children's Service, Albany. Served with AUS, 1942-46, 51-52. Fulbright scholar, 1949-50, fellow, 1959-60. Mem. Am. Assn. U. Profs., Nat. Assn. Social Workers. Roman Catholic. Author: OAA Profile, 1961; People of Inner Core North, 1965; Men in Jail, 1968. Contbr. articles to profl. jours. Home: 4073 Bunker Ln Wilmette IL 60091 Office: Sch Social Work Loyola Univ Chicago IL 60611

O'REILLY, DANIEL ELLIOTT, physician, educator; b. University City, Mo., Oct. 17, 1916; s. James Archer and Jane Elliott (Sever) O'R.; B.A., Harvard, 1938, M.D., 1942; M.Orthopedics, St. Louis U., 1949; m. Lucia King, May 21, 1948; children—Elliott H., Lucia Gregg, Marian King, Ann Warren. Surg. intern Barnes Hosp., St. Louis, 1942-43, asst. resident in surgery, 1946-47; resident in orthopedics St. Louis U. Group Hosps., 1947-49; fellow phys. medicine and rehab. N.Y. U., 1949-50; practice medicine specializing in orthopedic surgery, St. Louis, 1950—; chief orthopedist St. Louis U. Hosp.; chief orthopedics Cardinal Glennon Meml. Hosp. for Children, St. Mary's Hosp., St. John's Mercy Hosp.; instr. dept. orthopedic surgery St. Louis U. Sch. Medicine, 1949-53, sr. instr., 1953-58, asst. clin. prof., 1958-67, asso. clin. prof., 1967-70, asso. prof., 1970-71, prof., 1971—, chmn. dept., 1968—; med. dir. Vocational Counseling and Rehab. Services, Inc., 1955—; dir. Guaranty Trust Co. Mo. Bd. dirs., med. adv. com. St. Louis Soc. Crippled Children, 1957-59, chmn. ho. of dels., 1967-69; pres. Mo. Soc. Crippled Children, 1957-59; med. adv. com. United Cerebral Palsy Assn., 1954—; mem. Mo. Bd. Registration for the Healing Arts, 1959-65; trustee profl. adv. council Nat. Soc. Crippled Children, 1972—; bd. dirs. Vis. Nurses Assn., 1973—. Served to capt. M.C., AUS, 1943-45. Decorated Purple Heart. Fellow A.C.S.; mem. Am. Acad. Cerebral Palsy (treas. 1966-72, pres. 1974), AMA, Mo., So. med. assns., St. Louis Surg. Soc., St. Louis Med. Soc. (mem. council 1965-68), Clin., Mid-Central States, St. Louis (pres. 1967) orthopedic socs., St. Louis Rheumatism Soc. (pres. 1953-54), Am. Congress Rehab. Medicine. Clubs: St. Louis Country, University (St. Louis). Home: 9054 Clayton Rd Saint Louis MO 63117

O'REILLY, PHILLIP ANDREW, mfg. co. exec.; b. Chgo., Dec. 21, 1926; s. Martin and Phyllis (O'Donnell) O'R.; B.S. in Mech. Engring., Purdue U., 1949, B.Naval Sci. and Tactics, 1949; m. Patricia Ann Considine, June 28, 1952; children—M. Gordon, Phillip A., Ann, Robert S., S. Regan. Research and devel. engr. Am. Brake Shoe Co., Chgo., 1949-50, salesman, dist. sales mgr., Rochester, N.Y., 1951-60; with Houdaille Industries, Inc., various locations, 1960—, v.p. mfg. ops., Buffalo, 1972-76, exec. v.p., Buffalo, then Fort Lauderdale, Fla., 1976-79, pres., chief exec. officer, 1979—, also dir. Served with USN, 1945-46. Mem. Nat. Machine Tool Builders Assn. Office: Houdaille Industries Inc One Financial Plaza 12th Floor Fort Lauderdale FL 33394

O'REILLY, RICHARD THOMAS, advt. exec.; b. N.Y.C., Aug. 30, 1921; s. Edward John and Marie (Kiegler) O'R.; student Colo. Sch. Mines, 1943-44; m. Mary Lou Burrichter, Aug. 24, 1946; children—Richard Thomas, Brian Francis. Sr. v.p., dir. N.W. Ayer & Son, 1946-65; exec. v.p., dir. SSC & B, 1966-68; vice chmn. bd., dir. Wells, Rich, Greene, Inc., N.Y.C., 1969-76; pres. Richard T. O'Reilly, Inc., 1976—; dir. Tudor Hedge Fund, Am. Dual-Vest Fund, Centennial Capital Spl. Fund., Serino, Coyne & Nappi, Inc., Splty. Brands Inc.; trustee Centennial Capital Cash Mgmt. Trust. Bd. dirs., exec. com. Phoenix Theatre, N.Y.C. Served with AUS, 1942-46. Clubs: Stanwich (Greenwich); N.Y. Athletic (N.Y.C.). Author: Newspaper Advertising, 1949. Home: Rockwood Lane Spur Greenwich CT 06830 Office: Rockwood Ln Spur Greenwich CT

O'REILLY, TERRY JOSEPH, profl. hockey player; b. Niagara Falls, Ont., Can., June 7, 1951; s. James Patrick and Audrey (Willick) O'R.; came to U.S., 1971; student U. Toronto (Ont.), 1971; m. Lourdes Celeste Kamirez, June 12, 1977. Played amateur hockey, Oshawa, Ont., 1960-70; right wing, forward Boston Bruins Hockey Club, Nat. Hockey League, 1971—. Mem. Lenny Loogan Club N.Am. (v.p. New Eng. chpt.). Office: 150 Causeway St Boston MA 02114

ORELL, BERNARD LEO, forest products co. exec.; b. Portland, Oreg., Jan. 26, 1914; s. Leo J. and Lucy (LaMere) O.; B.S. in Forestry, Oreg. State Coll., 1939, M.F., B.S. in Edn., 1941; D.Bus. Adminstrn. (hon.), Dakota Wesleyan U.; m. Helen M. Kirchoff, June 24, 1941; children—Terrence M., Mary Kay. Recreation officer Mt. Hood Nat. Forest, 1935-40; tng. officer Oreg. Dept. Forestry, 1941-47; asst. prof. forestry U. Wash. Sch. Forestry, 1947-49; state forester div. forestry Wash., 1949-53; v.p. Weyerhaeuser Sales Co., 1953-58, Weyerhaeuser Co., 1958-79, spl. asst. to pres., 1979—; mem. adv. bd. Seattle-1st Nat. Bank, Tacoma; dir. Gt. Northwest Fed. Savs. & Loan Assn. Mem. natural resources com. Pres.'s Commn. on Intergovtl. Relations, 1955-56; mem. Pres.'s Outdoor Recreation Resources Rev. Commn., 1959-64; dir. forest products div. Dept. Commerce, 1954. Trustee Weyerhaeuser Co. Found., Am. Forest Inst.; bd. dirs. Tacoma Gen. Hosp. Served to 1st lt. AUS, 1942-46. Fellow Soc. Am. Foresters (v.p., pres.), Forest History Soc. (past pres., trustee, chmn. finance com.); mem. NAM (past dir., exec. com., regional v.p.), Forest Industries Council (past chmn.), Am. Pulpwood Assn. (past dir., past mem. exec. com.), Nat. Recreation Assn. (past dir.), Am. Forest Products Industries (pres. 1964-67), Am. Hort. Soc. (past dir.), Assn. Washington Bus. (past chmn.), Kappa Delta Rho, Xi Sigma Pi, Phi Sigma, Alpha Phi Omega. Clubs: Tacoma Country and Golf, Tacoma. Home: 12505 Gravelly Lake Dr Tacoma WA 98499 Office: PO Box 1645 Tacoma WA 98477

OREM, CHARLES REACE, financial services co. exec.; b. Nashville, Aug. 23, 1916; s. Charles Reace and Helen A. (Adcock) O.; student U. Ky., 1935-37; B.S., Columbia, 1937-39; LL.B., Fordham U., 1951; postgrad. N.Y. U., 1953; grad. Advanced Mgmt. Program, Harvard, 1957; m. Martha E. Haley, Oct. 24, 1945; 1 dau., Carol R. With Shell Oil Co., 1939-51; admitted to N.Y. bar, 1951; mgr. Peat, Marwick, Mitchell & Co., C.P.A.'s, N.Y.C., 1952-54; tax mgr., asst. treas. Sylvania Electric Products, Inc., N.Y.C., 1955-60; treas., v.p. finance Pickands Mather & Co., Cleve., 1961-64; v.p., controller Armour & Co., Chgo., 1964-65, v.p. finance, 1965-67, sr. v.p. adminstrn. and finance, 1967-68, pres., 1968-71; dir., pres., chief exec. officer Investors Diversified Services, Inc., Mpls., 1971—; chmn. bd. Investors Syndicate Am., IDS Life Ins. Co.; dir. IDS Mortgage, IDS Tax Emempt Bond Fund, IDS Cash Mgmt. Fund, IDS New Dimensions Fund, IDS Progressive Fund, IDS Growth Fund, Investors Mut. Fund, Investors Stock Fund, Investors Selective Fund, Investors Variable Payment Fund, IDS Adv. Corp., IDS Bond Fund, IDS Securities Corp. Bd. dirs. Minn. Orch. Assn. Mem. Mpls. C. of C. (dir. 1973—). Home: 4904 Merilane Ave Edina MN 55436 Office: Investors Diversified Services Inc 2900 IDS Tower Minneapolis MN 55402

OREN, JOHN BIRDSELL, coast guard officer; b. Madison, Wis., Dec. 27, 1909; s. Arthur Baker and Lucile Grace (Comfort) O.; B.S., USCG Acad., 1933; M.S. in Marine Engring., Mass. Inst. Tech., 1942; m. Harriet Virginia Prentis, Feb. 9, 1934; children—Virginia Joan (Mrs. Luther Warren Strickler II), John Edward. Commd. ensign USCG, 1933, advanced through grades to rear adm., 1964; chief engring. div. 11th Coast Guard Dist., 1957-59, 12th Coast Guard Dist., 1960-61; dep. chief Office Engring., Washington, 1962-63, chief, 1965—. Mem. Mcht. Marine Council, 1964—; chmn. ship structures com. Transp. Dept., 1964—; exec. dir. Maritime Transp. Research Bd., Nat. Acad. Scis., 1968—. Recipient Legion of Merit. Mem. Am. Soc. Mil. Engrs. (pres. 1966), Am. Soc. Naval Engrs. (pres. 1965), Internat. Inst. Welding (vice chmn. Am. council 1964), Soc. Naval Architects and Marine Engrs., Newcomen Soc., Ret. Officers Assn. (dir.), Pan Am. Inst. Naval Engring. Republican. Episcopalian. Mason. Home: 5539 Columbia Pike Arlington VA 22204

ORESKES, IRWIN, biochemist; b. Chgo., June 30, 1926; s. Herman and Clara (Rubenstein) O.; B.S. in Chemistry, CCNY, 1949; M.A. in Phys. Chemistry, Bklyn. Coll., 1956; Ph.D. in Biochemistry, City U. N.Y., 1969; m. Susan E. Nagin, June 18, 1949; children—Michael, Daniel, Naomi, Rebecca. Chemist, Tech. Tape Co., Bronx, N.Y., 1949; technician N.Y. U. Sch. Medicine, 1950-51; phys. chemist Kingsbrook Jewish Med. Center, 1951-56; research fellow Poly. Inst. N.Y., 1957-58; research asso. Mt. Sinai Hosp., N.Y., 1959-68; research asst. prof. Mt. Sinai Sch. Medicine, 1969-74, research asso. prof., 1974—; asso. prof. Hunter Coll. Sch. Health Scis., City U. N.Y., 1970-74, prof., 1974—, dean Sch. Health Scis., 1977—, mem. doctoral faculty in biochemistry Grad. Center, 1970—; vis. prof. Johns Hopkins U. Sch. Health Services, 1976-77; cons to diagnostic reagent and instrument mfrs., 1953—; mem. Internat. Sci. Council, Albert Einstein Research Inst., Buenos Aires, Argentina, 1969—, mem. bd. examiners for clin. labs. N.Y.C. Dept. Health, 1973-75. Served with U.S. Army, 1944-46. Nat. Inst. Arthritis and Metabolic Diseases grantee, 1961-69; Arthritis Found. grantee, 1961-65, 69, 72; Lupus Fedn. grantee, 1975-76; cert. clin. lab. dir. N.Y. State, N.Y.C. Mem. Am. Chem. Soc., Am. Rheumatism Assn., AAAS, N.Y. Acad. Scis., Am. Assn. Immunologists, Harvey Soc., Nat. Acad. Clin. Biochemistry, Nat. Acad. Clin. Lab. Physicians and Scientists, Sigma Xi, Phi Lambda Upsilon. Contbr. numerous articles to profl. jours. Home: 670 West End Ave New York NY 10025 Office: Hunter College Sch Health Sci 440 E 26th St New York NY 10010. *I have always tried to live and work by the ideas that strength is not harshness, caring is not sentimentality, and honesty is not vulnerability.*

ORFILA, ALEJANDRO, Argentine diplomat; b. Mendoza, Argentina, Mar. 9, 1925; s. Alejandro and Angelica (deBenito) O.; student law, U. Buenos Aires, polit. sci., Stanford U., fgn. trade, Tulane U.; LL.D. (hon.), U. Miami, U. Akron, Am. Grad. Sch. Internat. Mgmt., Central Mich. U., Calif. Western Sch. Law; children—Linda, Alejandro, Martin, Miguel. Sec. Embassy, Ministry Fgn. Affairs, Buenos Aires, Argentina, 1946; sec. Argentine Embassy, Moscow, 1946-47; Argentine consul, Warsaw, 1947-48, San Francisco, 1948-49; Argentine consul gen., New Orleans, 1949-50; sec. Argentine Embassy, Washington, 1951-52; mgr. Jose Orfila Ltds., Mendoza, 1952; dir. info. OAS, Washington, 1953-58; minister plenipotentiary Argentine Embassy, Washington, 1958-60; ambassador to Japan, 1960-62; pvt. cons. internat. fin. and econ. affairs, 1962-73; ambassador to U.S., 1973-75; sec.-gen. OAS, Washington, 1975—; hon. prof. U. Central del Este San Pedro de Macoris, Dominican Republic. Decorated by govts. Spain, Belgium, France, Germany, Netherlands, Italy, Vatican, Thailand, Japan, Greece; recipient Internat. Achievement award World Trade Council San Francisco, 1979. Author articles on internat. affairs. Office: Orgn Am States Hdqrs Orgn American States Bldg 17th St and Constitution Ave Washington DC 20006

ORGAIN, BENJAMIN DARBY, lawyer; b. Bastrop, Tex., Dec. 26, 1909; s. William Edmund and May (Bolinger) O.; student South Park Coll., Beaumont, Tex., 1926-27; B.A., LL.B., U. Tex., 1933; LL.M., Harvard, 1934; m. 2d, Martha Chastain Avery, Apr. 16, 1977; children—Lucy Allen Orgain Ellis, Benjamin Darby. Admitted to Tex. bar, 1933, since practiced in Beaumont; partner firm Orgain, Bell & Tucker, 1941—. Dir. Gulf States Utilities Co., 1963-75, adv. dir., 1975—; dir. Am. Nat. Bank, Beaumont. Chmn. Jefferson County Democratic Com., 1940-42. Vice chmn. devel. bd. U. Tex., 1966-68, mem. 1963—; trustee U. Tex. Law Sch. Found.; mem. Chancellor's Council U. Tex. Served to lt. comdr. USNR, 1942-46. Decorated Commendation ribbon. Fellow Am. Bar Found.; mem. Am., Tex., Jefferson County bar assns., Tex. Ornithol. Soc. (pres. 1979-80), Beaumont C. of C., Friar Soc., Phi Delta Phi, Kappa Sigma. Methodist. Rotarian. Clubs: Beaumont, Beaumont Country; Headliners (Austin). Home: 1970 Shady Lane Beaumont TX 77706 Office: Beaumont Savs Bldg Beaumont TX 77701

ORGAN, CLAUDE H., JR., physician, surgeon, educator; B.S. cum laude, Xavier U., 1948; M.D., Creighton U., 1952, M.S. in Surgery, 1957; L.H.D., U. Nebr. at Omaha, 1976. Intern, Creighton Meml. St. Joseph Hosp., 1952-53, now chief physician in surgery; resident surgery Creighton U. Hosps., 1953-57; practice medicine, specializing in surgery, Omaha; mem. staff VA Hosp., Omaha, Children's Meml. Hosp., Archbishop Bergan Mercy Hosp., Clarkson Hosp.; instr. dept. surgery Creighton U., 1960-63, asst. prof., 1963-66, asso. prof., 1966-71, prof., 1971—, chmn. dept. surgery, 1971—; dir. Creighton U. Surg. Service, Douglas County Hosp., 1963-71. Cons., USPHS, Winnebago, Nebr.; dir. Nat. Surg. Adjuvant Breast Project; mem. Emergency Med. Services Com. Nebr., 1972—; chmn. surgery sect. Omaha Mid-West Clin. Assembly, 1973-74; mem. sci. advisory com. Muzak, Inc.; mem. nat. profl. edn. com. Am. Cancer Soc.; mem. surgery exam. rev. com. Nat. Bd. Med. Examiners, 1978—; dir. Northwestern Bell Telephone Co., St. Paul Cos. Chmn. health com. Nat. Urban Coalition, 1970; mem. Trauma Com., State of Nebr. Pres., Urban Housing Found., 1971-74, Nebr. Urban League, 1964-66; bd. dirs. Boystown, Inc., Nat. Catholic Conf. for Human Justice, 1972-74; trustee Xavier U., 1972-77, Fontbonne Coll., 1970-72; chmn. exec. com. U.N.C.F. (Nebr.), 1973-75; trustee Ednl. Commn. Fgn. Med. Grads. Served to lt. comdr. M.C., USNR, 1957-59. Diplomate Am. Bd. Surgery (examiner, sr. mem. bd. dirs. 1977-79, dir. 1979—). Fellow A.C.S.; mem. Am., Nat. (chmn. council on med. edn. and hosps. 1969-73, chmn. surgery sect. 1973-74), Nebr. med. assns., Douglas County Med. Soc., Soc. Head and Neck Surgeons, S.W. Surg. Congress, Central Surg. Assn., Am. Burn Assn., Allen O. Whipple Surg. Soc., Soc. Univ. Chairmen, Assn. Mil. Surgeons U.S.A., Omaha Mid-West Clin. Soc., Soc. Surg. Oncology, Collegium Internationale Chirurgial Digestive, Internat. Soc. Surgery, Soc. Surgery Alimentary Tract, Western Surg. Assn., Pan Pacific Surg. Assn., Soc. Univ. Chmn., Internat. Surg. Soc., Alpha Omega Alpha, Alpha Sigma Nu. Contbr. articles to profl. jours. Office: Dept Surgery Sch Medicine Creighton U 601 N 30th St Omaha NE 68131

ORGANSKI, ABRAMO FIMO KENNETH, educator, polit. scientist; b. Rome, Italy, May 17, 1923; s. Menasce and Anna (Feinstein) O.; came to U.S., 1939, naturalized, 1944; B.A., N.Y.U., 1947, M.A., 1948, Ph.D., 1951; student Ginnasio Liceo Torquato Tasso, Rome 1933-38; m. Katherine Davis Fox, May 29, 1947; children—Eric Fox, Elizabeth Anna. From asst. prof. to prof. polit. sci. City U. N.Y., Bklyn. Coll., 1952-64; adj. prof. polit. sci. N.Y. U. Grad. Sch. Pub. Adminstrn., 1960; vis. asso. prof. pub. law and govt. Columbia, 1961-62; vis. prof. govt. Dartmouth, summers 1963, 64; vis. prof. Fletcher Sch. Law and Diplomacy, 1963-66; prof. polit. sci. U. Mich., 1965—, program dir. Center Polit. Sci., Inst. Social Research, 1969—; lectr. pvt., govtl. instns. U.S., abroad, 1960—; cons. pvt., govtl. instns., 1961—. Served with U.S. Army, 1943-45. Decorated cavaliere della Republica Italiana. Mem. Am. (council 1969), Internat. polit. scis. assns. Author: World Politics, 1958, 68; (with Katherine Organski) Population and World Power, 1961; Stages of Political Development, 1965; (with Jacek Kugler) The War Ledger, 1979. Bd. editors Jour. of Conflict Resolution, Comparative Political Studies, Comparative Politics, Affari Sociali Internazionali. Home: 460 Hillspur Rd Ann Arbor MI 48105

ORGEL, LESLIE ELEAZER, chemist; b. London, Jan. 12, 1927; s. Simon and Deborah (Gnivish) O.; came to U.S., 1964; B.A., Oxford (Eng.) U., 1948, D.Phil., 1951; m. Hassia Alice Levinson, July 30, 1950; children—Vivienne, Richard, Robert. Reader univ. chemistry lab. Cambridge (Eng.) U., 1963-64, fellow Peterhouse Coll., 1957-64; sr. fellow Salk Inst. Biol. Studies, La Jolla, Calif., 1964—; adj. prof. U. Calif., San Diego, 1964—. Recipient Harrison prize Chem. Soc. London, 1957. Fellow Royal Soc. Author: An Introduction to Transition-Metal Chemistry, Ligand-Field Theory, 1960; The Origins of Life: Molecules and Natural Selection, 1973; co-author: The Origins of Life on the Earth, 1974. Home: 6102 Terryhill Dr La Jolla CA 92037 Office: Salk Inst PO Box 85800 San Diego CA 92138

ORGEL, STEPHEN KITAY, educator; b. N.Y.C., Apr. 11, 1933; s. Samuel Zachary and Esther (Kitay) O.; A.B., Columbia, 1954; Ph.D. (Woodrow Wilson fellow), Harvard, 1959. Instr. in English, Harvard, Cambridge, Mass., 1959-60; asst. prof. U. Calif., Berkeley, 1960-66, asso. prof., 1966-72, prof., 1972-76; prof. Johns Hopkins U., Balt., 1976—; bd. suprs. English Inst., 1974-77, chmn., 1976-77. Am. Council Learned Socs. fellow 1968, 73. Mem. Modern Lang. Assn., Renaissance Soc. Am., Shakespeare Assn. Am. Author: The Jonsonian Masque, 1965; (with Roy Strong) Inigo Jones, 1973; The Illusion of Power, 1975. Editor: Ben Jonson's Masques, 1969; Marlowe's Poems and Translations, 1971. Office: Dept English Johns Hopkins U Baltimore MD 21218

ORISCAK, JOSEPH JOHN, banker; b. Cliffside Park, N.J., July 17, 1940; s. Joseph and Rosalie (Cangialosi) O.; student Am. Inst. Banking, 1958-64; B.S. in Mgmt., St. Peter's Coll., Jersey City, 1970; m. Celia Thiel, Oct. 2, 1966. With Mfrs. Trust Co., N.Y.C., 1958-60, United Nat. Bank Cliffside Park, 1960-64; auditor First Jersey Nat. Bank, Jersey City, 1964—, mgr. main office, asst. v.p., 1972—; v.p. First Nat. State Bank-County, Tenafly, N.J., 1974—. Served with USAF, 1969. Chartered bank auditor. Home: Closter Dock Rd Alpine NJ 07620 Office: 100 Park Ave Park Ridge NJ 07656

ORKIN, LAZARUS ALLERTON, physician; b. N.Y.C., Feb. 2, 1910; s. John and Anne (Davidow) O.; B.S., N.Y.U., 1930, M.S., 1931, M.D., 1935; m. Sylvia M. Hollard, May 30, 1941; children—Fredrick, Stuart. Intern Bellevue Hosp., N.Y.C., 1935-37, asst. resident obstetrics and gynecology, 1937-38, resident urology, 1940-42; resident urology Royal Victoria Hosp., Montreal, Que., Can., 1938-40; individual practice, N.Y.C., 1942-64; cons. urologist Beekman Downtown; dir. urology Beth Israel Hosp., 1964-78, dir. urology emeritus, cons. urologist, 1978—; clin. prof. urology Mt. Sinai Sch. Medicine, N.Y.C., 1970-78, emeritus, 1978—; cons. urologist Peninsula Gen. Hosp., Far Rockaway Hosp., N.Y., Gracie Sq. Hosp., Cath. Med. Center Bklyn. Diplomate Am. Bd. Urology. Fellow Internat. Fertility Assn., Am. Soc. Study Sterility, A.C.S., Am. Geriatrics Soc., Am. Trauma Soc. (founding), Am. Assn. Surgery Trauma, Acad. Medicine N.Y., Pan Pacific Surg. Assn.; mem. Am., Canadian urol. assns., N.Y. Urol. Soc., A.M.A., Pan Am. Med. Assn., Phi Beta Kappa, Sigma Xi, Alpha Omega Alpha. Club: Town (N.Y.C.). Author: Surgery of Trauma of the Ureter, 1962; Genito Urinary Trauma in Lawyer's Medical Cyclopedia, 1963; Trauma to the Ureter Its Pathogenesis and Management, Textbook, 1964; Urinary Tract Infections. Asso. editor Trauma; contbg. editor Trauma to Bladder, Ureter, and Kidney (Davis Obstetrics and Gynecology), Aggiornamenti in ostetricae ginecologia. Home: 235 E 57th St New York NY 10022 also 9240 W Bay Harbor Dr Bay Harbor Island Miami FL 33154

ORKIN, LOUIS RICHARD, physician, educator; b. N.Y.C., Dec. 23, 1915; s. Samuel David and Rebecca (Rish) O.; B.A., U. Wis., 1937; M.D., N.Y. U., 1941; m. Florence Fine, Mar. 5, 1938; 1 dau., Rita. Intern, Bellevue Hosp., N.Y.C., 1942, resident anesthesiology, 1946-48; practice medicine specializing in anesthesiology, Bronx, N.Y., 1946—; dir. anesthesiology Backus Hosp., Norwich, Conn., 1948-50; asst. prof. anesthesiology N.Y. U. Coll. Medicine 1950-55; prof., chmn. dept. anesthesiology Albert Einstein Coll. Medicine, 1955—; vis. prof. depts. bioengring., anesthesiology U. Calif., San Diego, 1971. Cons. VA, USPHS, USN; mem. com. anesthesiology Nat. Acad. Scis., 1964-69; mem. com. anesthetic drugs FDA, Dept. Health, Edn. and Welfare, 1970—. Vice pres., trustee Wood Library Mus. Served to capt. M.C., AUS, 1942-45. Decorated Bronze Star medal. Fellow Am. Coll. Chest Physicians, N.Y. Acad. Sci., N.Y. Acad. Medicine, Am. Coll. Anesthesiology (past chmn. bd. govs.); mem. N.Y. State Soc. Anethesiologists (past pres.). Author: Patient in Shock, 1965; Physiology of Obstetrical Anesthesia, 1969. Contbr. articles to profl. jours. Home: 11 Stuyvesant Oval New York City NY 10009 Office: Albert Einstein Coll Medicine Bronx NY 10461

ORKIN, SAUL, coll. exec.; b. N.Y.C., Sept. 4, 1923; s. Aaron and Minnie O.; B.A., Rutgers U., 1949; M.A., U. Mich., 1951; Ph.D., Columbia U., 1971; m. Maria Lydia Astorga, Nov. 21, 1953; children—Philip, Neil. Instr., Highland Manor Jr. Coll., 1949-50; teaching fellow U. Mich., 1951-53; instr. Union Coll., Cranford, N.J., 1955-58, asst. prof. polit. sci., 1959-64, asso. prof., 1965-67, chmn. dept. social scis., 1959-67, dir. admission, 1961-65, pres., 1974—; dean Somerset County Coll., 1967-74; chmn. N.J. Consortium on Community Coll., 1975—. Del., N.J. Constl. Conv. on Reapportionment, 1966; mem. Plainfield (N.J.) Charter Study Com., 1967. Served with AC, U.S. Army, 1943-46. Mem. Phi Beta Kappa. Home: 12 Wolfe Dr Somerville NJ 08876 Office: 1033 Springfield Ave Cranford NJ 07016

ORLAND, FRANK J., educator, historiographer, oral microbiologist; b. Little Falls, N.Y., Jan. 23, 1917; s. Michael and Rose (Dorner) O.; A.A., U. Chgo., 1937, S.M., 1945, Ph.D., 1949; B.S., U. Ill., 1939, D.D.S., 1941; m. Phyllis Therese Mrazek, May 8, 1943; children—Frank R., Carl P., June R., Ralph M. With U. Chgo., 1941—, intern Zoller Meml. Dental Clinic, 1941-42, Zoller fellow, asst. in dental surgery, 1942-49, instr., asst. prof., asso. prof., prof. dental surgery, 1949—, instr., asst. prof., asso. prof. microbiology, 1950-58; research asso. (prof.), 1958-64; attending dentist Country Home for Convalescent Children, 1942-45; dir. W.G. Zoller Meml. Dental Clinic of U. Chgo., 1954-66; spl. cons. Nat. Inst. Dental Research of NIH, Bethesda, Md. Mem. panel on dental drugs The Nat. Formulary. Past chmn. adv. council Forest Park (Ill.) Bd. Edn.; mem. Forest Park Citizens Com. for Better Schs.; past pres. Garfield Sch. P.T.A., 1953-55; chairperson heritage com. Bicentennial Commn. of Forest Park. Recipient Research Essay award Chgo. Dental Soc., 1955. Diplomate Am. Bd. Microbiology. Fellow Inst. Medicine Chgo. (chmn. com. publ. communications), Am. Acad. Microbiology, A.A.A.S.; mem. Internat. Assn. Dental Research (pres. 1971-72, past councilor Chgo. sect.; past chmn. program com., past chmn. com. on history), Am. Dental Assn. (past chmn. council dental therapeutics), A.A.U.P., Am. Assn. Dental Schs. (past chmn. conf. oral microbiology past chmn. com. on advanced edn.), Am. Assn. Dental Editors (hon. mention, William Gies Editorial award 1968), Ill. State Dental Soc. (chmn. com. on history), Fedn. Dentaire Internat., Am. Acad. History Dentistry (past pres.), Hist. Soc. Forest Park (pres.), Soc. Med. History Chgo. (pres.), Sigma Xi, Gamma Alpha. (pres. Chgo. chpt.). Club: Chgo. Literary. Author: The First Fifty-Year History of the International Association for Dental Research, 1974. Editor: Journal Dental Research, 1958-69; past chmn. dental adv. bd. Med. Heritage Soc.; editor, contbr. The Chronicles of Forest Park. Contbr. articles to profl. jours. Home: 521 Jackson Blvd Forest Park IL 60130 Office: U Chgo 950 E 59th St Chicago IL 60637

ORLANDO, GEORGE J(OSEPH), union exec.; b. N.Y.C., Nov. 27, 1944; s. Joseph and Anita O.; B.A. in Polit. Sci., St. John's U., Bklyn., 1966; m. Joan Perrotta, Nov. 5, 1967; children—Gregory, Valerie, Dana, Christopher. Adminstrv. asst. Distillery, Wine and Allied Workers Internat., Englewood, N.J., 1966-67, internat. v.p., 1968-74, gen. sec.-treas., 1974—; alt. mem. Internat. Union Food and Allied Assns., Switzerland, 1974; labor trustee Distillery, Wine and Allied Workers Internat.-Social Security Fund, 1974; mem. exec. bd. dept. food and beverage trades AFL-CIO, 1975. Office: 66 Grand Ave Englewood NJ 07631

ORLANDO, TONY (MICHAEL ANTHONY ORLANDO CASSAVITIS), singer; b. N.Y.C., Apr. 3, 1944; ed. pub. schs., N.Y.C.; m. Elaine, 1964; 1 son, Jon. Began singing professionally at age 16; record promoter; v.p. April-Blackwood div. CBS Records; formed vocal group Dawn with Telma Hopkins and Joyce Vincent Wilson, 1970 (name later Tony Orlando and Dawn); star variety show Tony Orlando & Dawn, CBS-TV; now solo performer; solo songs recorded: Halfway to Paradise, 1961, Bless You, 1961; (with Dawn) Candida, 1970, Knock Three Times, 1970, I Play and Sing, 1971, What Are You Doing Someday, 1971, Tie a Yellow Ribbon 'Round the Old Oak Tree, 1973, Say, Has Anybody Seen My Sweet Gypsy Rose, 1973; albums include: Candida, 1971, Dawn, 1972, Tuneweaving, 1973, Before Dawn, Greatest Hits, He Don't, To Be With, World of Tony Orlando & Dawn, Tony Orlando, 1978. Hon. chmn. Nat. Assn. Retarded Citizens. Roman Catholic. Office: care William Morris Agy 151 El Camino Dr Beverly Hills CA 90212

ORLIN, LOUIS LAWRENCE, educator; b. Bayonne, N.J., Nov. 7, 1925; B.A., U. Mich., 1949, M.A., 1950, Ph.D., 1960; children—Leslie, David, Hugh, Celia. Mem. faculty U. Mich., 1955—, prof. ancient Near Eastern history and lit., 1961—, dir. residential coll., 1973—. Active Ann Arbor Symphony Orch. Served with inf. U.S. Army, 1943-45. Decorated Bronze Star, Purple Heart; recipient E. Harris Harbison award Danforth Found., 1966; Disting. Service award U. Mich., 1961. Mem. Am. Hist. Assn., Am. Oriental Soc., Am. Inst. Archaeology, Assn. Ancient Historians, Phi Kappa Phi. Author: (TV series) The City of Time, 1964; Ancient Near Eastern Literature: A Bibliography, 1969; Assyrian Colonies in Cappadocia, 1970. Editor: (Janus) Essays in Ancient and Modern Studies, 1975; Michigan Oriental Studies in Honor of George G. Cameron, 1975. Home: 1331 Culver Rd Ann Arbor MI 48103 Office: 3084 Frieze Bldg Ann Arbor MI 48109

ORLISS, THEODORE EUGENE, lawyer; b. Mpls., Mar. 3, 1936; s. Morris and Mary (Nudell) O.; B.A. magna cum laude, U. Wash., 1957; LL.B., Harvard, 1961; m. Kristin Elizabeth Moore, Aug. 2, 1970; children—Micah James, Maret Rebecca. Admitted to Calif. bar, 1962, U.S. Dist. Cts. bar, 1962, U.S. Ct. Appeals bar, 1965, U.S. Supreme Ct. bar, 1971; practiced in Los Angeles, 1962—; asso. firm McKenna & Fitting, Los Angeles, 1962-65; asst. U.S. atty. Central and So. Dist. Calif., 1965-70; mem. firm Jaffe & Orliss, Los Angeles, 1970-74; pvt. practice, 1975-76; of counsel firm Berris & Seton, 1976-78; judge protem Municipal Ct., Los Angeles, 1973-76; of counsel firm Schroeder & Davis, Inc., Monterey, Calif., 1979—. Trustee Los Angeles Family Sch., 1975-76. Served to capt. J.A.G. Corps, AUS, 1957-65. Mem. Am., Calif., Los Angeles County (fed. cts. com. 1971—, mem. com. fed. indigent def. panel 1971-77, chmn. 1976-77) bar assns., State Bar Calif., Assn. Bus. Trial Lawyers, Phi Beta Kappa. Home: 4129 El Bosque Dr Pebble Beach CA 93953 Office: 215 W Franklin St Monterey CA 93940 also 1930 Century Park W Suite 400 Los Angeles CA 90036

ORLOFF, JACK, physician, research physiologist; b. Bklyn., Dec. 22, 1921; s. Samuel and Rebecca (Kaplan) O.; student Columbia U., 1937-38, Harvard U., 1938-40; M.D., N.Y. U., 1943; m. Martha Vaughan, Aug. 4, 1951; children—Jonathan Michael, David Geoffrey, Gregory Joshua; (by previous marriage) Lee Frances. Intern, Mt. Sinai Hosp., N.Y.C., 1944; resident medicine Montefiore Hosp., N.Y.C., 1944-46; research fellow Yale Med. Sch., 1948-50; mem. sr. research staff Nat. Heart Inst., Bethesda, Md., 1950-57, dep. chief lab. kidney and electrolyte metabolism, 1957-62, chief lab., 1962-75; dir. intramural research Nat. Heart, Lung and Blood Inst., 1974—; professorial lectr. physiology, med. Georgetown U. Med. Sch., 1962—. Del.-at- large exec. council Fedn. Am. Sci., 1962-64, exec. com., treas., 1963-64. Trustee Greenacres Sch., Rockville, Md., 1960-64, v.p. bd. trustees, 1962-63. Mem. sci. adv. bd. Nat. Kidney Found., 1962-71; mem. Inst. Medicine Nat. Acad. Scis. Served to capt. M.C., AUS, 1946-48. Recipient Homer Smith award N.Y. Heart Assn., 1973, Meritorious Service award USPHS, 1974, Distinguished Alumni Achievement award in basic sci. N.Y. U., 1976; Distinguished Service medal HEW, 1977. Mem. Am. So. Clin. Investigation, Am. Physiol. Soc., Fedn. Am. Scientists (vice-chmn. 1963-64), Assn. Am. Physicians, Am. Soc. Nephrology (sec.-treas. 1970-72, pres. 1973-74), Sigma Xi, Alpha Omega Alpha. Club: Cosmos. Contbg. author textbooks; Essays in Metabolism, 1957; Metabolic Disturbances in Clinical Medicine, 1958; The Metabolic Basis of Inherited Disease, 1972; Heart, Kidney and Electrolytes, 1962; Diseases of the Kidney, 1971; Cellular Function of Metabolic Transport, 1964; Hormones and the Kidney, 1964; Nobel Symposium on Prostaglandins, 1967; Physioli of Diuretic Agents, 1966; Ocytocin, Vasopressin and their Structural Analogues, 1964. Editorial bd. Am. Jour. Physiology; sect. editor Am. Jour. Physiology, 1964-68, Jour. Applied Physiology, 1964-68; Renal Physiology sect. 8, Handbook of Physiology, 1973; asso. editor Kidney Internat.; cons. editor Life Scis., 1973-78. Home: 11608 W Hill Dr Rockville MD 20855 Office: Nat Heart Lung and Blood Inst Bethesda MD 20205

ORLOFF, MONFORD ARTHUR, mfg. co. exec.; b. Omaha, Mar. 29, 1914; s. Samuel and Hannah (Masters) O.; A.B., Stanford, 1937; LL.B., Harvard, 1940; m. Janice Diamond, Feb. 2, 1941; children—Jonathan Harris, Carole Sue, Chester Lloyd. With Evans Products Co., Portland, Oreg., 1961—, pres., 1968—, chief exec. officer, chmn. bd., 1964—; dir. 1st State Bank Ore., Precision Cast Parts. Vice chmn. bd. trustees Reed Coll., Portland. Served to capt. AUS, 1941-46. Mem. Phi Beta Kappa. Home: 2670 SW Tichner Dr Portland OR 97201 Office: 1121 SW Salmon St Portland OR 97205

ORMAN, LEONARD ARNOLD, lawyer; b. Balt., June 15, 1930; s. Samuel and Bertie (Adler) O.; A.B. summa cum laude, U. Md., 1952, J.D., 1955; m. Barbara Gold, June 9, 1978; children—Richard Harold, Robert Barton. Admitted to Md. bar, 1955; law clk. Hon. Frederick W. Brune, Chief Judge Md. Ct. of Appeals, 1955-56; mem. dept. legis. reference Md. Legislature, 1957-58; mem. Gov.'s Commn. to Revise Criminal Code, 1958-59; pvt. practice law, Balt., 1956—. Pres., Young Democrats 2d Dist., Balt., 1960-63. Served with AUS, 1948-49; lt. col. USAF Res. ret. Mem. Am. Assn. Trial Lawyers (nat. committeeman 1976-79), Md. Trial Lawyers Assn. (bd. govs., parliamentarian), Md., Balt. City bar assns., Order of Coif (lectr. trial tactics). Club: Masons. Mem. editorial bd. Md. Law Rev., 1953-55. Contbr. articles to profl. jours. Home: 2 Celadon Rd Owings Mills MD 21117 Office: Suite 1605 1 S Calvert Bldg Baltimore MD 21202

ORMANDY, EUGENE, music dir.; b. Budapest, Hungary, Nov. 18, 1899; s. Benjamin and Rosalie Ormandy; boy music prodigy at age 3 1/2 yrs.; youngest pupil at Royal State Acad. of Music at 5 1/2, B.A. at 14 1/2, state diploma for art of violin playing, 2 yrs. later, state diploma as prof.; student U. of Budapest, 1917-20; Mus.D., Hamline U., St. Paul, 1934, U. Pa., 1937, Phila. Acad. Music, 1939, Curtis Inst. Music, 1946; LL.D., Temple U., 1949; L.H.D., Lehigh U., 1953, C.W. Post Coll., 1965, Hahnemann Med. Coll. and Hosp., 1979; Mus.D. (hon.), U. Mich., 1952; Dr. honoris causa, Clarke U., 1956, Miami U., Oxford, Ohio, 1959, Rutgers U., 1960, L.I. U., 1965; Litt.D., Lafayette Coll., 1966: Mus.D., Villanova U., Peabody Inst., Renssalaer Poly. Inst., 1968, U. Ill., 1969, Jefferson Coll., 1974, Moravian Coll., 1976; m. Steffy Goldner, 1922 (dec.); m. 2d, Margaret Frances Hitsch, May 15, 1950. Came to U.S., 1921, naturalized, 1927. Toured Hungary as child prodigy, later toured Central Europe; apptd. head of master classes State Conservatorium of Music, Budapest, at age 20; substituted for Toscanini as condr. Phila. Orch.; condr. Mpls. Symphony Orch., 1931-36; condr., music dir. Phila. Orch., 1936—. Decorated comdr. French Legion Honor, Order of Dannebrog (Denmark), Order of Lion (Finland); Order Merit Juan Pablo Duarte (Dominican Republic), knight Order of White Rose of Finland, commandatore of merit Italian Republic; hon. knight comdr. Order Brit. Empire; recipient citation Distinguished Service in music Boston U., 1957; Honor Cross for Arts and Sci., Austria, 1966; Golden medallion Vienna Philharmonic, 1967; Presdl. Medal Freedom, 1970; 1st award for excellence Pa. Council on Arts, 1970; Phila. award, 1970; Nat. Recognition award Freedoms Found., 1970; Gov.'s Com. 100,000 Pennsylvanians award for excellence in performing arts, 1968; Gallantry award Easter Seal Soc., 1971; Alice M. Ditson Condrs. award, 1977; Broadcast Pioneer award, 1979; Gold Baton award Am. Symphony Orch. League, 1979. Mem. Am. Philos. Soc., Musical Fund Soc. Phila. (hon. life). Address: care Phila Orch Assn 1420 Locust St Philadelphia PA 19102

ORME, KEITH MARTELL, mfg. co. exec.; b. St. Anthony, Idaho, Aug. 17, 1930; s. Martel and Annette (Walker) O.; B.S., Brigham Young U., 1952; M.B.A. with distinction (Baker scholar), Harvard U., 1954; m. Paula Tollefson, June 5, 1976; children by previous marriage—Gregory, Kathleen, Robert, Allyson, Sherry. Mem. staff Harvard Bus. Sch., 1954-55; controller Josten's Inc., Owatonna, Minn., 1955-59; asst. to gen. mgr. Amalgamated Sugar Co., Ogden, Utah, 1959-61, sec.-treas., 1961-64, v.p. finance, 1964-65, exec. v.p., 1965-68; exec. v.p., dir. Conroy, Inc., San Antonio, 1968-70, pres., chief exec. officer, 1970—; dir. Main Bank & Trust, San Antonio. Bd. dirs. YMCA. Mem. Conf. Bd., Phi Kappa Phi. Home: 11712 Caprock San Antonio TX 78230 Office: 3355 Cherry Ridge Dr PO Box 4GG San Antonio TX 78201. *These three thoughts have been prominent in my appoach to life. Change: Never hesitate to pay the price of stress or work nor to bear the risk of failure in order to change what ought to be changed. Tolerance: Reach out to people. Feel the life and philosophy of people of various ages and backgrounds. Marvel at the complexity and variety of the human mind and soul. And then remind yourself again that differences in attitude and behavior are the consequences of the unique set of experiences each has faced. Appreciation: A sincere expression of appreciation creates a constructive feeling in nearly every human being. By contrast, being thoughtless, complaining, or increasingly demanding develops a natural reaction of despair and animosity. An atmosphere of appreciation is a productive environment in which people can grow.*

ORMES, ROBERT VERNER, editor; b. N.Y.C., Sept. 10, 1921; s. Ferguson Reddie and Mabrie (Verner) O.; A.B., Wabash Coll., 1943; postgrad. Columbia; m. Mary Ann Otto, Sept. 2, 1950; children—Julia C., Carolyn V., Margaret F. Instr. English, math. and contemporary civilization Wabash Coll., Crawfordsville, Ind., 1947-49; tech. writer Cushing & Nevell, N.Y.C., 1954; editorial asst. Science, jour. A.A.A.S., Washington, 1954-57, asst. editor, 1957-60, mng. editor, 1961—. Served to lt. (j.g.), USNR, 1943-46. Mem. A.A.A.S., Council Biology Editors, Beta Theta Pi, Phi Beta Kappa. Democrat. Home: 2810 Central Ave Alexandria VA 22302 Office: 1515 Massachusetts Ave NW Washington DC 20005

ORMSBY, ANTHONY JOHN, mfg. co. exec.; b. Toronto, Ont., Can., Mar. 25, 1927; s. Gerald Yeadon and Helen Marion (Macdonell) O.; student Royal Canadian Naval Coll., 1944-45, Inst. Chartered Accountants, 1946-51; m. Margaret Joan Patton, Nov. 14, 1953; children—Anthony Robert, Timothy John. Partner, Ormsby & Ormsby, chartered accountants, Toronto, 1952-60; sec.-treas. Norris div. Dover Corp., Tulsa, 1961-63; v.p. Dover Corp., N.Y.C., 1963-68, exec. v.p., 1970-71, pres., 1971-72, now dir., mem. exec. com.; chmn. bd. Dover Corp. (Can.), Ltd., Toronto, 1968—, also dir.; partner MacGillivray & Co., Chartered Accountants; dir. Heintzman Ltd., Hamilton Porcelains Ltd., Municipal Savs. and Loan Corp., Clairborne Industries Ltd. Chmn., Toronto Harbour Commn.; mem. Toronto area Indsl. Devel.; mem. council Met. Toronto Bd. Trade. Bd. Chmn. bd. govs. Upper Can. Coll. Mem. Inst. Chartered Accountants. Clubs: Toronto, Badminton and Racquet (Toronto). Home: 118 Douglas Dr Toronto ON Canada Office: 390 Bay St Suite 2400 Toronto ON M5H 2R6 Canada

ORMSBY, CHARLES ALFRED, life ins. co. exec.; b. N. Collins, N.Y., Sept. 30, 1917; s. Edgar D. and Winifred (Wallace) O.; A.B. in Math. with honors, U. Mich., 1939, M.A., 1940; grad. program sr. exec. Mass. Inst. Tech., 1963; Exec. seminar Aspen Inst. for Humanistic Studies, 1972; m. Helen C. Brown, Aug. 20, 1937; children—Beverly, Charles, Ronald, Douglas. Tchr. math. Alden (N.Y.) High Sch., 1940-41, Amherst Central High Sch., Snyder, N.Y., 1941-43; aero. engr. Bell Aircraft Corp., 1943-45; with Conn. Gen. Life Ins. Co., Hartford, Conn., 1945-58, sec. reins. dept., 1956-58; with John Hancock Life Ins. Co., 1958—, sr. v.p., 1968—. Mem. exec. com. Med. Info. Bur., 1973-75, chmn., 1975. Campaign vice chmn. Mass. Bay United Fund, 1971-72. Fellow Soc. Actuaries (chmn. com. on mortality under ordinary ins. and annuities, 1971-77, chmn. com. to recommend new mortality tables for valuation 1976—, bd. govs. 1979—), Am. Acad. Actuaries; mem. Home Office Life Underwriters Assn. (pres. 1971-72), Phi Beta Kappa. Kiwanian (pres. Boston 1966).

Author papers, chpts. in field. Home: 6 Driftwood Ln Weston MA 02193 Office: John Hancock Pl PO Box 111 Boston MA 02117

ORMSBY, ROBERT BENZEIN, JR., aeronautics co. exec.; b. Winston Salem, N.C., Aug. 13, 1924; s. Robert Benzein and Ruth Olive (Hart) O.; B.S. in Aeros., Ga. Inst. Tech., 1945; postgrad. Stanford U., 1960; m. Margarett Williams, May 17, 1947; children—Marka Robin, Robin Patricia. Aerodynamicist, Glenn L. Martin Co., 1945-47; dep. div. head U.S. Navy Bur. Aeros., 1947-54; with Lockheed-Ga. Co., Marietta, 1954-74, 75—, v.p. maj. engring. and ops. programs, pres., 1975—; v.p., gen. mgr. research and devel. Lockheed Missiles & Space Co., Burbank, Calif., 1974-75, sr. v.p., 1975—; chmn. bd. Lockheed-Ga. Internat. Services, Inc.; mem. aeros. and space engring. bd. NRC. Bd. dirs. Ga. Motor Club. Recipient Silver Knight of Mgmt. award, 1976. Fellow AIAA (asso.); mem. Air Force Assn., Am. Def. Preparedness Assn., Assn. U.S. Army, Nat. Assn. Remotely Piloted Vehicles, Navy League, Soc. Automotive Engrs., Soc. Logistics Engrs., Soc. Material Processing Engrs. Club: Kiwanis. Office: 86 S Cobb Dr SE Marietta GA 30063*

ORN, CLAYTON LINCOLN, lawyer; b. Weatherford, Tex., June 20, 1902; s. Jacob J. and Etta (Hill) O.; student Baylor U., 1921-23; J.D., George Washington U., 1925; m. Zara Laura Sims, July 27, 1927; 1 dau., Camille (Mrs. W.R. Haynes). Admitted to Tex. bar, 1925, Ohio and D.C. bars, 1954; practice of law, Cisco, Tex., 1925-31; mem. firm Phillips, Trammel, Estes, Edwards & Orn, Ft. Worth, 1931-42; div. atty. Marathon Oil Co., Houston, 1942-54, gen. atty., Findlay, Ohio, 1954-61, dir., gen. counsel, 1961-67; sr. partner firm Anderson, Brown, Orn & Jones, 1967—. Mem. adv. bd. Southwestern Legal Found. Mem. Am. (ho. dels. 1959-60; chmn. mineral sect. 1956-57), Tex. (chmn. mineral sect. 1953-54) bar assns., Mid-Continent Oil and Gas Assn. (distinguished service award 1965), Am. Petroleum Inst., Am. Judicature Soc. Presbyterian. Contbr. articles to legal jours. Home: 2929 Buffalo Speedway Houston TX 77098 Office: Southwest Tower Houston TX 77002

ORNAUER, RICHARD LEWIS, county ofcl.; b. Bklyn., Oct. 19, 1922; s. Edwin L. and Emma (Handler) O.; B.J., U. Mo., 1947; m. Jane Robb, May 15, 1955 (div. Jan. 7, 1976); children—David S., Michael J., Sara Jo. Wire editor Coastal Georgian, Brunswick, Ga., 1947-48; reporter copyreader, night editor, city editor Nassau Daily Rev.-Star, Rockville Centre, N.Y., 1948-53; city editor L.I. Press, Jamaica, N.Y., 1953-71; asst. commr. Nassau County Dept. Social Services, Mineola, 1971-74; pub. health info. program officer Nassau County Dept. Health, Mineola, 1974—. Instr., Queens Coll., Flushing, N.Y., 1955-59; mem. exec. bd. Nassau County Sch. Forum, 1969—. Chmn., Merrick Planning Com., 1959-61; mem. publs. com. N.Y. State Sch. Bds. Assn., 1961-64, mem. BOCES com., 1971-74; vice chmn. State Sch. Bd. Leaders Com., 1975-79, bd. dirs., 1979—; del. L.I. Ednl. Conf. Bd., 1967—; trustee Merrick Bd. Edn., 1962—, pres., 1966-71; trustee Bd. Coop. Ednl. Services Nassau County, 1967—, v.p., 1967-71, pres., 1971—; v.p., mem. exec. com. Nassau-Suffolk Sch. Bds. Assn., 1962—, pres., 1977-79; mem. exec. com. Merrick Citizens Com. for Pub. Schs., 1959—; mem. fed. relations network 4th Congl. dist. Nat. Sch. Bds. Assn., 1973-79, study com. on career edn., 1976-78, also sub-chmn. for N.E. region presdl. task force on edn. of handicapped children, 1977-78, mem. presdl. task force on critical viewing of TV by children, 1979-80; mem. Instructional Service Television Com. WLIW-TV/Channel 21, pres., 1973—; mem. Com. for Better Schs. of Merrick, 1975—; mem. Hist. Soc. Merricks, 1976—. Served with AUS, 1942-45; PTO. Recipient citations N.Y. State Police Conf., 1949, Rockville Centre Police Benevolent Assn., 1953, Nassau Div. Am. Cancer Soc., 1961, Nassau Am. Legion, 1963, Nassau Library System, 1964, Firemen's Assn. of Nassau County, 1964, Nassau County Scholastic Press Assn., 1965, United Fund of L.I., 1970, Kiwanis Clubs Internat., 1971, Jewish War Vets., 1972; Educator of Year award Hofstra U. chpt. Phi Delta Kappa, 1973, assn. for the Help of Retarded Children, Nassau County chpt., 1977; Disting. Service award Nassau-Suffolk Sch. Bds. Assn., 1979; named Man of Yr., L.I. Spl. Edn. Adminstrs. Assn., 1979. Mem. Nat. Sch. Pub. Relations Assn., Edn. Writers Assn., Am. Newspaper Guild, N.Y. State Congress Parents and Tchrs. (life), N.Y. State Pub. Health Assn., Assn. Emotionally Handicapped Children, Assn. to Help Retarded Children, Assn. Children With Learning Abilities, N.Y. Citizens Com. Pub. Schs., ad hoc Planning Com. Mobilized Community Resources, L.I. Sch.-Community Relations Assn., N.Y. Civil Service Employees Assn., Sigma Delta Chi (life). Jewish religion (trustee congregation). Home: 2105 Washington St Merrick NY 11566 Office: Nassau County Office Bldg 240 Old Country Rd Mineola NY 11501

ORNDUFF, ROBERT, educator; b. Portland, Oreg., June 13, 1932; s. Robert and Kathryn (Davis) O.; B.A., Reed Coll., 1953; M.Sc., U. Wash., 1956; Ph.D., U. Calif., Berkeley, 1961. Asst. prof. Reed Coll., 1962, Duke U., 1963; asst. prof. botany U. Calif. Berkeley, 1963-66, asso. prof., 1966-69, prof., 1969—, dir. Univ. Bot. Garden, 1973—, Jepson Herbarium, 1968—, dir. U. Herbarium, 1975—. Fellow Calif. Acad. Scis.; mem. Calif. Native Plant Soc. (pres. 1972-73), Am. Soc. Plant Taxonomists (pres. 1975). Editor: Madrono, 1971-73. Home: 490 Arlington Ave Berkeley CA 94707 Office: Dept Botany U Calif Berkeley CA 94720

ORNE, MARTIN THEODORE, research psychiatrist, psychologist; b. Vienna, Austria, Oct. 16, 1927; s. Frank Edward and Martha (Brunner) O.; A.B., Harvard U., 1948, A.M., 1951, Ph.D., 1958; M.D., Tufts U., 1955; m. Emily Farrell Carota, Feb. 3, 1962. Pvt. practice psychiatry, Boston, 1959-64, Phila., 1964—; lectr. Grad. Sch. Arts and Scis., Harvard U., 1958-59, instr. Med. Sch., 1959-62, asso. in psychiatry, 1962-64; asso. prof. psychiatry U. Pa. Med. Sch., 1964-67, prof., 1967—; dir. studies in hypnosis project Mass. Mental Health Center, Boston, 1960-64; dir. unit for exptl. psychiatry Inst. of Pa. Hosp., Phila., 1964—; cons. VA Hosp., Phila., 1971—. Mem. NIMH study sect. Washington, 1966-74; exec. dir. Inst. Exptl. Psychiatry, Boston, 1961—. Served with AUS, 1945-47. Rantoul scholar, 1949-50; Fulbright scholar, 1960. Fellow AAAS, AMA, Am. Psychiat. Assn., Am. Psychol. Assn., Am. Soc. Clin. Hypnosis, N.Y. Acad. Sci., Soc. Clin. and Exptl. Hypnosis (pres. 1971-73); mem. Assn. Psychophysiol. Study Sleep, Biofeedback Research Soc., Am. Psychosomatic Soc., Internat. Soc. Hypnosis (pres. 1976-79), Psychiat. Research Soc., Soc. Psychophysiol. Research, Soc. Psychotherapy Research. Editor: Internat. Jour. of Clinical and Experimental Hypnosis, 1964—; (with R.E. Shor) The Nature of Hypnosis: Selected Basic Readings, 1965. Contbr. numerous articles, also chpts. to sci. books, publs. Home: 290 Sycamore Ave Merion Station PA 19066 Office: 111 N 49th St Philadelphia PA 19139

ORNER, FREDERICK JUDD, transp. cons.; b. Newark, Nov. 20, 1911; s. George Darmon and Harriet Frances (Judd) O.; A.B., Dartmouth, 1932; M.B.A., Harvard, 1934; m. Phyllis Kay, Sept. 11, 1935; children—Karen K. (Mrs. Harry R. Rudin Jr.), Keith S. With S.H. Kress & Co., N.Y.C., 1934-35, N.Y., N.H. & H. R.R. Co., 1935-68; sr. cons. New Eng. Penn Central, 1969-73; asso. GO Assos., 1973—; with Def. Transport Adminstrn., 1951-53. Mem. Assn. Am. R.R. Supts. Mem. United Ch. Christ. Home: RFD S Walden Hardwick VT 05843

ORNITZ, ARTHUR JACOB, dir.; b. N.Y.C., Nov. 28, 1916; s. Samuel B. and Sadie F. (Lesser) O.; student UCLA, 1934-36; m. Stephania F. Duncan, Aug. 13, 1976; children by previous marriage—Zev Andrew (dec.), Kim Harris. Dir. films Wanted A Master, Metro Goldwyn Mayer, 1936 (nominated academy award); The Godess Columbia Pictures, 1956; Requiem for a Heavyweight United Artists, 1958 (nominated for academy award); The Connection, United Artists, 1962; The World of Henry Orient, 1964; A Mid-Summer's Night's Dream, Columbia Pictures, 1965; Charly, Selmur, 1966; One Thousand Clowns, 1967; Boys In The Band, 1968; Anderson Tapes, 1969; Serpico, Di Laurentis, 1973; Next Stop Greenwich Village, 20th Fox, 1975, An Unmarried Woman, 1977; instr. N.Y. U.; lectr. Dartmouth U. Served with U.S. Army, 1942-46. Mem. Dir. Guild of Am., Internat. Alliance Theatrical and Stage Employees (pres. local 644 1964-66). Office: 465 W 23d St New York NY 10011

ORNSTEIN, FRANKLIN H., banker; b. Lido Beach, N.Y., Nov. 8, 1930; s. Theodore and Rose (Weisinger) O.; student U. Wis., N.Y. U. Law Sch.; m. Anita; children—Aimee, Emilie, Alec. Title reader, examiner, closer Intercounty Title Guarantee & Mortgage Co., N.Y.C., 1954-56; asso. firm Morris Permit, N.Y.C., 1956-57; partner firm Elman & Ornstein, N.Y.C., 1957-64; county clk. Nassau County (N.Y.), 1964-67; mng. partner in charge corp. div. firm Shayne, Dachs, Weiss, Kolbrener, Levy and Levine, Mineola, N.Y., 1968-70; with Central Fed. Savs. and Loan Assn. of Nassau County, Long Beach, 1970—, exec. v.p. in charge of ops., 1973-75, pres., chief exec. officer, dir., 1975—; dir. Fed. Home Loan Bank; adj. prof. banking Adelphi U.; exec. mem. bd. Center of Banking Adelphi U.; pres. L.I. Mid-Suffolk Businessmen's Assn. Chmn. NCCJ, L.I.; L.I. chmn. State of Israel Bonds; mem. exec. com. L.I. council Boy Scouts Am.; mem. exec. com. Long Beach Meml. Hosp., Assn. Retarded Children, L.I.; bd. dirs. N.Y. Higher Edn. Services Corp. Democratic candidate for N.Y. State Senate, 1970, for U.S. Ho. of Reps., 1974; 1st vice chmn. Nassau County Dem. Party, 1973; mem. Nassau County Legislature, 1975. Mem. Nat., U.S. savs. and loan leagues, Savs. and Loan League N.Y. (mem. exec. com.). Home: 177 Regent Dr Lido Beach NY 11561 Office: 249 E Park Ave Long Beach NY 11561

ORNSTEIN, ROBERT, educator; b. N.Y.C., Nov. 3, 1925; s. Max and Frances (Saphire) O.; B.A., N.Y.U., 1948; M.A., U. Wis., 1949, Ph.D., 1954; m. Doris L. Robbins, Aug. 19, 1951; children—Suzanne Ruth, Lisa, Adam Samuel. Instr. English, Oberlin Coll., 1952-54, U. Conn., 1954-58; from asst. prof. to prof. English, U. Ill., 1958-66; prof. English, 1966—, Oviatt prof. English, 1974—, chmn. dept. Case Western Res. U., 1966-68. Served C.E., AUS, 1944-46; ETO. Fulbright scholar, London, Eng., 1951-52; Guggenheim fellow, 1961-62; Nat. Endowment for Humanities fellow, 1976. Mem. Modern Lang. Assn. (sec.-treas. assn. depts. English 1966, English program adv. com. 1966-69), Shakespeare Assn. Am. (pres. 1977-78), Renaissance Soc., Phi Beta Kappa. Author: The Moral Vision of Jacobean Tragedy, 1960; A Kingdom for a Stage, 1972; also articles. Author films: A Poet's World, 1973, Sidewalks and Similes, 1973, Dead Ends and New Dreams, 1973, In the Last Days, 1973; author, producer, dir. ednl. films: Harpsichord Building in America, 1976, The Staging of Shakespeare, 1976, The Poetry of Robert Frost, 1976. Editor: Shakespeare's Problem Comedies, 1961; (with Hazelton Spencer) Elizabethan and Jacobean Comedy, 1964, Elizabethan and Jacobean Tragedy, 1964. Home: 3122 Woodbury Rd Shaker Heights OH 44120 Office: Dept English Case Western Res Univ Cleveland OH 44106

ORO, JUAN, biochemist, educator; b. Lerida, Spain, Oct. 26, 1923; s. Juan and Maria Florensa (Rue) Oro-Vallverdu; Licenciate in Chem. Scis., U. Barcelona, Spain, 1947; Ph.D., Baylor U., 1956; Dr. honoris causa, U. Granada (Spain), 1972; m. Francisca Forteza, May 19, 1948; children—Maria Elena, Juan, Jaime, David. Came to U.S., 1952. Mem. faculty, U. Houston, 1955—, asst. prof., 1956-58, asso. prof., 1958-63, prof., 1963—, chmn. dept. biophysical scis., 1967-69; research chemist Lawrence Radiation Lab., U. Cal. at Berkeley, summer 1962; Catedratico Universidad Autonoma de Barcelona, 1971; prin. investigator NASA Lunar Sample Analysis, 1967—; molecular analysis team mem. NASA Unmanned Mars Landing, 1970—; dir. Instituto de Biofisica y Neurobiologia, Barcelona, Spain, 1977. Founding mem., v.p. Spain and Tex. Soc., Inc., Houston, 1970—. Recipient medal and hon. councilor Consejo Superior de Investigaciones Cientificas, 1969; Gran Cruz de la Orden Civil de Alfonso X el Sabio, Madrid, 1974; Life Scientist award NASA, 1974-75; Gold medal City of Lerida, 1976; named Important Scientist of Year, Barcelona, 1970, Madrid, 1977. Mem. Am. Soc. Biol. Chemists, Am. Chem. Soc., Nat. Assn. Chemists Spain, Spanish Soc. Biochemists, Royal Acad. Arts and Scis. of Barcelona, Inst. Hispanic Culture (founding mem.), Internat. Soc. for Study Origin of Life (exec. council 1974), Spanish Soc. Biochemistry (hon.), Sigma Xi. Editor Biogenesis sect. Jour. Molecular Evolution, 1972; (with others) Prebiotic and Biochemical Evolution, 1971; Viral Replication and Cancer, 1973; Cosmochemical Evolution and the Origins of Life, 1974; Reflections on Biochemistry, 1976; Avances de la Bioquimica, 1977; The Viking Mission and the Question of Life on Mars, 1979. Contbr. articles to profl. publs. Home: 11306 Endicott Ln Houston TX 77035 Office: Dept Biophysical Scis U Houston Houston TX 77004

O'ROARK, SARAH ANN (MRS. THOMAS L. O'ROARK), banker; b. Bradford, Pa., Sept. 28, 1921; d. Francis H. and Louise M. (MacFarlane) Davitt; student U. Buffalo Grad. Sch. Savs. Banking, 1969; m. Thomas L. O'Roark, Sept. 3, 1942. With Erie County Savs. Bank, Buffalo, 1946—, asst. treas., 1963-68, treas., operations mgr., 1968-69, v.p., treas., 1969—. Mem. contbns. eval. com. Buffalo Clearing House. Treas. Jesse Ketchum Meml. Fund; chmn. planning and community services exec. com. United Way of Buffalo and Erie County, also bd. dirs.; mem. Buffalo Public Schs. Supts. Vocat. Edn. Adv. Council; mem. devel. com. Health Systems Agy. of Western N.Y. mem. adv. council on women Medaille Coll.; bd. dirs. Franciscan Sisters of Divine Child; pres. D'Youville Coll. Center for Women in Mgmt. Mem. Zonta Club of Buffalo, Zonta Internat. Office: 1 Main Pl Buffalo NY 14202

O'RORKE, EDWARD ARTHUR, ret. pub. co. exec.; b. N.Y.C., Jan. 7, 1907; s. Michael and Mary (O'Rorke) O'R.; A.B., Holy Cross Coll., 1929, D.Litt. (hon.), 1976; J.D., Yale, 1932; postgrad. Harvard, 1937; m. Louise McEwan, Nov. 9, 1937. Admitted to N.Y. bar, 1933; personnel mgr. R.H. Macy & Co., N.Y.C., 1932-41; prodn. mgr. Uarco, Inc., Chgo., 1941-48; v.p., gen. mgr. Manifold Bus. Forms, Chgo., 1948-51; operating v.p. R.H. Donnelley Corp., N.Y.C., 1951-62, sr. v.p., 1962-67, exec. v.p., 1967-72, also dir.; chmn. bd. Asso. Bus. Publs., N.Y.C.; pres. Brewster/Carver, Inc.; v.p. Econ. Devel. Council N.Y.C., 1972-78; counsel firm Bradey & Tarpey, N.Y.C., 1978—; dir. Lejacq Publs. Chmn. pres.'s council, asso. trustee, chmn. devel. com. Holy Cross Coll.; trustee Daytop Found., Regis High Sch., N.Y.C. Served to lt. comdr. USNR, 1943-46. Mem. N.Y. Bar Assn., N.Y. State C. of C. and Industry (pres. 1977-78). Clubs: University (N.Y.C.); Am. Yacht (Rye, N.Y.); Siwanoy Country (Bronxville, N.Y.). Home: 17 Alden Pl Bronxville NY 10708 Office: 130 John St New York NY 10038

O'ROURKE, ANDREW TERENCE, transit exec.; b. N.Y.C., May 7, 1918; s. Andrew and Ellen (Keane) O'R.; B.B.A., Manhattan Coll., 1940; M.B.A., N.Y. U., 1956; m. Anna Mary Mullen, Aug. 27, 1945; children—Terence, Patricia, Ellen, Kathryn, Amy, Andrew. Tchr. accounting Fordham U., 1946-47; fin. mgr. Sperry-Rand Corp., N.Y. and Fla., 1949-60; controller Eitel-McCullough, Inc., San Carlos, Calif., 1960-63; treas. Systron-Donner Corp., Concord, Calif., 1963-65; controller Evans Products Co., Portland, Oreg., 1965-67, v.p., 1967-68; controller Crane U.S.A., N.Y.C., 1968-69, 71-72; sr. v.p. finance and adminstrn. Nytronics, Inc., Pelham Manor, N.Y., 1969-70; exec. officer, controller N.Y.C. Transit Authority, 1972—; v.p., dir. South Bklyn. Ry. Co. C.P.A., N.Y. Mem. Nat. Assn. Accountants (pres. Peninsula-Palo Alto chpt. 1965-66), Fin. Execs. Inst., Am. Mgmt. Assn. Co-author bull. Home: 48 Rings End Rd Darien CT 06820

O'ROURKE, DENNIS, lawyer, mgmt. cons.; b. Whiteclay, Nebr., Oct. 31, 1914; s. Frank L. and Jerene (Rebbeck) O'R.; A.B. cum laude, Nebr. Tchrs. Coll., 1935; J.D. with distinction, George Washington U., 1939; m. Ruth Rouss, Jan. 21, 1940; children—Susan, Kathleen, Brian, Dennis, Ruth, Dolores. Admitted to D.C. bar, 1939, U.S. Supreme Ct., 1945, Colo. bar, 1946; typist, auditor Gen. Accounting Office, Washington, 1935-39; lawyer solicitor's office U.S. Dept. Agr., Washington, 1939-45, chief basic commodity div., 1945; gen. counsel Group Health Assn., Washington, 1943; gen. counsel Holly Sugar Corp., Colorado Springs, Colo., 1945, v.p., 1953-63, pres., 1963-67, chmn. bd., 1967-69, also dir.; v.p., gen. counsel Holly Oil Co., 1955-63; sr. partner firm Rouss & O'Rourke, Colorado Springs and Washington; U.S. counsel Union Nacional de Productores de Azucar, Mexico, 1970—; pres. Man Exec., Inc., Colorado Springs and Washington; dir. 1st Nat. Bank Colorado Springs. Bd. dirs. Colo. Pub. Expenditure Council, vice chmn., exec. com., 1968-76; dir. Nat. C. of C. of the U.S., 1968-70; trustee, pres. Colorado Springs Fine Arts Center, 1961-62, 68-71, 73. Mem. Bus. and Industry Adv. Com. OECD, Paris, France, 1969-71; adviser U.S. dels. Internat. Sugar Confs., Geneva, 1965, Mexico City, 1959; chmn. Colorado Springs-El Paso County Citizens' Task Force on Local Govt. Reorgn., 1976-77. Mem. Newcomen Soc., Am. Soc. Sugar Beet Technologists, Am., Fed., Colo., El Paso County bar assns., Mex.-U.S. Com. of Council of Ams., Order of Coif, Phi Delta Phi. Clubs: Cheyenne Mountain Country; El Paso; Rotary; Garden of Gods (Colorado Springs); Sugar (N.Y.C.); Metropolitan (Washington); Commonwealth of Calif. Contbr. articles financial and bus. jours. Home: 8 Heather Dr Broadmoor Colorado Springs CO 80906 Office: Box 572 Colorado Springs CO 80901 also 1614 20th St NW Washington DC 20009

O'ROURKE, EDWARD WILLIAM, bishop; b. Downs, Ill., Oct. 31, 1917; s. Martin and Mary (Hickey) O'R.; student St. Henry's Coll., Belleville, Ill., 1935-38; B.A., St. Mary of the Lake Sem., Mundelein, Ill., 1940, M.A., 1942, S.T.L., 1944; Licentiate of Philosophy, Aquinas Inst., River Forest, Ill., 1960. Ordained priest Roman Catholic Ch., 1944, bishop, 1971; asst. chaplain Newman Found., U. Ill., 1944-59; exec. dir. Nat. Cath. Rural Life Conf., Des Moines, 1960-71; bishop of Peoria, Ill., 1971—. Dir. refugee resettlement Diocese of Peoria, 1948-59; chmn. arbitration com. Nat. Conf. Cath. Bishops, 1973-76. Chmn. priorities com. Peoria United Fund, 1972-73. Bd. dirs. Internat. Vol. Services, 1960-71; trustee Cath. Relief Services; chmn. bd. Am. Coll. Louvain. Recipient John Henry Newman award, 1959, Nat. Cath. Rural Life Conf. Distinguished Service award, 1973. K.C. (4 deg.). Author: Marriage and Family Life, 1955; Fundamentals of Philosophy, 1956; Gift of Gifts, 1977; Self Help Works, 1978; Living Like a King, 1979. Editor: Catholic Rural Life Mag., 1960-71. Address: 607 NE Madison Ave Peoria IL 61603

O'ROURKE, LAWRENCE MICHAEL, journalist, lawyer; b. Phila., Mar. 12, 1938; s. Lawrence Michael and Margaret Mary (Higgins) O'R.; A.B., Villanova (Pa.) U., 1959; J.D., Georgetown U., 1970; m. Patricia Coe, Aug. 26, 1967; children—Christopher, Katherine, Jennifer, Timothy. With Phila. Bull., 1955—, reporter, 1957-70, chief bur., White House corr., Washington, 1970—; admitted to D.C. bar, 1970; practiced in Washington, 1970—; lectr. in field. Served with AUS, 1960-62. Recipient First Pl. award for news reporting Pa. Press Assn., 1963; named Man of Year North City Congress of Phila., 1965, United Vets. Council of Phila., 1973; LaSalle Collegian award, 1978. Mem. White House Corrs. Assn. (pres. 1976), D.C. Bar Assn., Sigma Delta Chi. Clubs: Nat. Press, Gridiron (Washington). Roman Catholic. Contbr. articles to profl. jours., popular mags. Home: 3904 Rosemary St Chevy Chase MD 20015 Office: 1296 Nat Press Bldg Washington DC 20045

O'ROURKE, LAWRENCE STEPHEN, metals co. exec.; Providence, Apr. 13, 1924; s. Lawrence Stephen and Genevieve Rose (Tracy) O'R.; B.S. in Physics, Canisius Coll., Buffalo, 1946; postgrad. Brown U., 1947; m. Dorothy Jean Rooney, Oct. 18, 1947; children—Thomas, Paul, Steven, Susan, Daniel, David. Various positions nuclear div. Union Carbide Corp., 1947-63, metals div., 1964-68, electronics div., 1968-71, Linde div., 1971-74; sr. v.p. N.J. Zinc Co. div. Gulf & Western Inc., Bethlehem, Pa., 1974-75, exec. v.p., 1975-76, pres., 1976-78; pres. Kawecki Berylco Industries Inc. subs. Cabot Corp., Reading, Pa., 1978—; v.p. Cabot Corp., 1978—; dir. Tanco Mining Co., Showa-KBI Ltd. Served with C.E., AUS, 1943-46. Mem. ASME, Am. Soc. Metals. Home: Riverbend Rd RD 2 Allentown PA 18103 Office: Box 211 Reading PA 19603

O'ROURKE, PATRICK JAKE, magazine editor; b. Toledo, Nov. 14, 1947; s. Clifford Bronson and Delphine (Loy) O'R.; B.A., Miami U., Oxford, Ohio, 1969; M.A., Johns Hopkins U., 1970. Editor, Harry, underground newspaper, Balt., 1970-71; feature editor The Herald, N.Y.C., 1971-72; exec. editor, then mng. editor Nat. Lampoon, N.Y.C., 1973-77, editor in chief, 1977—. Woodrow Wilson fellow, 1969-70. Author; Nancy Adler Poems, 1970; Our Friend the Vowel, 1976. Co-editor: National Lampoon 1964 High School Yearbook Parody, 1974; editor: National Lampoon Sunday Newspaper Parody, 1978. Home: 225 E 36th St New York City NY 10016 Office: 635 Madison Ave New York City NY 10022

O'ROURKE, PETER EDWARD, lawyer; b. Detroit, Nov. 14, 1933; s. Randall Michael and Alice Ellen (White) O'R.; B.A., Wayne State U., 1955; J.D., Detroit Coll. Law, 1958; m. Susan Ellen Gehrke, Sept. 30, 1968; children—Kathleen Ann, Peter Edward. Admitted to Mich. bar, 1958; practiced in Detroit, 1961—; partner firm Porritt, Hegarty & O'Rourke, 1964-75; sr. partner firm O'Rourke, Fitzgerald, Kazul & Rutledge, 1975—. Chmn. Mich. Employment Security Appeal Bd., 1969-72; mem. Regional Export Expansion Council, 1971-76, Gov.'s Spl. Commn. on Energy, 1972-76. Republican candidate for Mich. Senate, 1966, U.S. Congress, 1968. Served to comdr. USCGR, 1958-77. Mem. Mich., Detroit bar assns., Mich. C. of C., Am. Judicature Soc. Roman Catholic. Clubs: Mackinac Island (Mich.) Yacht (commodore); Grosse Pointe Yacht (dir.). Home: 241 Lewiston Rd Grosse Pointe Farms MI 48236 Office: 2000 1st Federal Bldg Detroit MI 48226

O'ROURKE, WILLIAM ANDREW, author, educator; b. Chgo., Dec. 4, 1945; s. William Andrew and Elizabeth (Kompare) O'R.; B.A., U. Mo. at Kansas City, 1968; M.F.A., Columbia U., 1970. Instr. journalism Kean Coll., Union, N.J., 1973; asst. prof. English, Rutgers U., 1975-78; asst. prof. English, Mount Holyoke Coll., 1978—. Fine

editor-at-large, 1963-71. Chmn. broadcasting and film commn. Nat. Council Chs., 1969-72, mem. gen. bd., 1966-72; producer-dir. nat. TV programs including series, Off to Adventure, 1956, Tangled World, 1965; producer motion pictures Tomorrow?, 1962, The Procession, 1961, The Pumpkin Coach, 1960; originator series Six American Families, PBS-TV, 1977. Recipient Human Relations award Am. Jewish Com., 1966, Faith and Freedom award Religious Heritage Found., 1966, 77, Alfred I. DuPont-Columbia U. award pub. service in broadcasting, 1969; Roman Cath. Broadcasters Gabriel award pub. service, 1970; Lincoln U. award significant contbn. human relations, 1971; Racial Justice award Com. for Racial Justice, United Ch. Christ, 1973; Ch. Leadership award Council for Christian Social Action, 1973; Public Service award Black Citizens for a Fair Media, 1979. Club: Yale (N.Y.C.). Author: Religious Radio, 1948; Film Use in the Church, 1953; The Television-Radio Audience and Religion, 1955; Religious Television 1961; (with others) Television, Radio, Film for Churchmen, 1969. Home: 11 Midland Ave White Plains NY 10606 Office: 105 Madison Ave New York NY 10016

PARKER, FRANCIS DUNBAR, educator, mathematician; b. Boston, July 27, 1918; s. Francis Alpheus and Irene (Plummer) P.; A.B., Middlebury Coll., 1939; A.M., Boston U., 1942; Ph.D., Case Inst. Tech., 1951; m. Marjorie Alice Gardner, May 23, 1942; children—Carolyn, John, Harold, Martha. Tchr., Cranbrook Sch., 1939-40, Staunton Mil. Acad., 1940-41, Montclair Acad., 1941-42; mem. staff radiation lab. Mass. Inst. Tech., 1942-45; instr. Case Inst. Tech., 1945-51; asst. prof. St. Lawrence U., 1951-53; asso. prof. Clarkson Coll., 1953-57; prof. math., head dept. U. Alaska, 1957-63, State U. N.Y. at Buffalo, 1963-66, 67-70, St. Lawrence U., 1966—; vis. prof. U. Aberdeen (Scotland), 1973, U. York (Eng.), 1974, Calif. State U., Los Angeles, 1975, 77-78, Plymouth (Eng.) Poly., 1978-79. Mem. Math. Assn. Am. (bd. govs. 1967-70), Am. Math. Soc., Soc. Indsl. and Applied Math., AAUP, Sigma Xi. Author: The Structure of Number Systems, 1966; also articles. Home: Star Route Canton NY 13617 Office: Dept Math St Lawrence Univ Canton NY 13617

PARKER, FRANCIS HOWARD, educator, philosopher; b. Kuala Lumpur, Malaysia, June 23, 1920 (parents Am. citizens); s. Walter Guy and Alma (Shell) P.; A.B., U. Evansville (Ind.), 1941; A.M., Ind. U., 1947; Ph.D., Harvard U., 1949; m. Audrey Janell Schriber, Dec. 15, 1945; children—Cynthia Ann, Brian Gareth, Valerie Gail, Diana Leigh. Teaching fellow Harvard U., 1948-49; mem. faculty Haverford Coll., 1949-66, prof. philosophy, 1961-66, chmn. dept., 1963-66; vis. asso. prof. Ind. U., 1961; vis. lectr. Bryn Mawr Coll., 1965-66; prof. philosophy, head dept. Purdue U., 1966-71; Charles A. Dana prof. philosophy and religion Colby Coll., 1971—, dept. chmn., 1971-77. Formerly lectr. adult edn. programs suburban Phila.; Aquinas lectr. Marquette U., 1971; Robert Simpson Charles lectr. ethics Earlham (Ind.) Coll., 1979. Served to capt. USAAF, 1942-46. Decorated Air medal. Am. Council Learned Socs. fellow, 1962-63; Fulbright research scholar, Athens, Greece, 1962-63; Soc. for Values in Higher Edn. postdoctoral fellow, 1971—. Mem. Metaphys. Soc. Am. (sec.-treas. 1959-62; pres. 1964-65), Internat. Soc. Metaphysics, Am. Philos. Assn. (exec. com. Eastern div. 1961-64), Assn. Realistic Philosophy (pres. 1959-61), Soc. Phenomenology and Existential Philosophy, Am. Assn. U. Profs. (pres. Haverford Coll. chpt. 1957-58), Fullerton Club (pres. 1958-59), Phi Beta Kappa (hon. Haverford Coll. chpt., charter mem. Purdue U. chpt., pres. Colby Coll. chpt. 1974-75), Pi Gamma Mu. Author: (with H.B. Veatch) Logic as a Human Instrument, 1959; The Story of Western Philosophy, 1967; Reason and Faith Revisited, 1971; also articles. Home: Rural Route 1 North Vassalboro ME 04962

PARKER, FRANKLIN, educator, writer; b. N.Y.C., June 2, 1921; B.A., Berea (Ky.) Coll., 1949; M.S., U. Ill., 1950; Ed.D., George Peabody Coll. Tchrs., 1956; research fellow Univ. Coll. Rhodesia (Africa), 1957-58, Rhodes-Livingstone Inst. Social Research (Africa), 1961-62; m. Betty June Parker, June 12, 1950. Librarian, speech tchr. Ferrum (Va.) Jr. Coll., 1950-52, Belmont Coll., Nashville, 1952-54, George Peabody Coll. Tchrs., 1955-56; asso. prof. edn. State U. Coll., New Paltz, N.Y., 1956-57, U. Tex., 1957-64; prof. edn. U. Okla., 1964-68; Benedum prof. edn. W.Va. U., Morgantown, 1968—; prof. edn. U. Calgary (Can.), summer 1969, U. Alta. (Can.), summer 1970, No. Ariz. U., summer 1971, U. Lethbridge (Can.), summers 1971-73, Meml. U. Nfld. (Can.), summer 1974. Mem. Internat. Conf. African Adminstrn., Cambridge (Eng.) U., 1957, European Bur. Adult Edn., Finland and W. Germany, 1966, nat. conf. White House Conf. on Edn., 1965, Nat. Fgn. Policy Conf. for Educators, State Dept., 1966; cons. Office Edn., HEW, 1970—. Served USAAF, 1942-46. Sr. Fulbright research scholar, 1961-62. Mem. African Studies Assn., S.W. Philosophy Edn. Soc. (pres. 1960), Am. Acad. Polit. and Social Sci., Am. Ednl. Research Assn., U.S.A. Comparative and Internat. Edn. Soc. (internat. sec. 1965-68; feature writer 1963-68, v.p. 1963-64), Canadian Comparative and Internat. Edn. Soc., Comparative Edn. Soc. Europe, History Edn. Soc. (pres. 1963-64), Kappa Delta Pi (Harold R. W. Benjamin fellow internat. edn. 1957-58, sec. commn. on internat. edn. 1968-70), Phi Delta Kappa (life mem.; research award chmn. commn. on internat. relations in edn. 1963-67), Pi Gamma Mu, Phi Kappa Phi. Author: African Development and Education in Southern Rhodesia, 1960, reprinted, 1974; Africa South of the Sahara, 1966; George Peabody, A Biography, 1971; The Battle of the Books: Kanawha County, 1975; What Can We Learn from the Schools of China?, 1977; British Schools and Ours, 1979; co-author: John Dewey: Master Educator, 2d edit., 1961; Government Policy and International Education, 1965; Church and State in Education, 1966; Strategies for Curriculum Change: Cases from 13 Nations, 1968; Dimensions of Physical Education, 1969; International Education: Understandings and Misunderstandings, 1969; Understanding the American Public High School, 1969; Education in Southern Africa, 1970; Curriculum for Man in an International World, 1971; Administrative Dimensions of Health and Physical Education Programs, Including Athletics, 1971; Education and the Many Faces of the Disadvantaged, 1972; The Saber-Tooth Curriculum, meml. edit., 1972; Accelerated Development in Southern Africa, 1974; Myth and Reality: A Reader in Education, 1975; Six Questions; Controversy and Conflict in Education, 1975; Crucial Issues in Education, 6th edit., 1977; also articles. Series editor American Dissertations on Foreign Education, A Bibliography with Abstracts, Vol. I, Canada, 1971, Vol. II, India, 1972, Vol. III, Japan, 1972, Vol. IV, Africa, 1973, Vol. V, Scandinavia, 1974, Vol. VI, China, 1975, Vol. VII, Korea, 1976, Vol. VIII, Mexico, 1976, Vol. IX, South America, 1977, Vol. X, Central America, 1978, Vol. XI, Pakistan and Bangladesh, 1979, Vol. XII, Iran and Iraq, 1980, Vol. XIII, Israel, 1980; (with Betty June Parker) Education in Puerto Rico and of Puerto Ricans in the U.S.A., 1978, Women's Education—A World View: Annotated Bibliography of Doctoral Dissertations, 1979, Higher Education in America: A Guide to Information Sources, 1980; cons. editor Jour. Thought, 1965—, Western Carolina U. Jour. Edn., 1969-76, W.Va. U. Mag., 1969-78, Ednl. Studies (Eng.), 1975-77, Rev. of Edn., 1977—, CORE (Collected Original Resources in Edn.), 1977—, Internat. Jour. African Hist. Studies, 1977—; contbr. to encys. Americana Annual, 1961—, Collier's Yearbook, 1965-72, Compton's Yearbook, 1965-66, Dictionary of Am. Biography, 1951-55, Dictionary of Scientific Biography, Ency. of Edn., 1971, McGraw-Hill Ency. of World Biography, 1973, Reader's Digest Almanac and Yearbook, 1968-73. Home: 750 Amherst Rd Morgantown WV 26505

PARKER, GARLAND GLENWOOD, educator, univ. adminstr.; b. Kennett, Mo., July 12, 1915; s. Clarence Allen and Onie Corrine (Stanley) P.; B.S. in Edn., S.E. Mo. State U., 1937; M. Philosophy, U. Wis., 1941, Ph.D., 1948; postgrad. Tulane U., 1944-45; m. Anna Elizabeth Smith, Nov. 14, 1937; children—Alice Hope (Mrs. William Ancil Brandenburgh, Jr.), Anne (Mrs. Edward John Colter). High sch. tchr. social studies, English and speech, Jackson, Mo., 1937-38, Sikeston, Mo., 1938-41, Newman Sch., New Orleans, 1941-46; asst. prof. U. Cin., 1948-54, asso. prof., 1954-67, prof. history and ednl. research, 1967—, asst. to dean Summer Sch., 1955-56, registrar, 1956, vice provost for admissions and records, 1967-76, exec. dir. enrollment policy and ednl. research, 1976—. Pres., Mt. Auburn Childrens Services Found.; state rep. for Ohio to Am. Coll. Testing Program Nat. Corp., 1968-78, trustee ACT, 1971-78, vice chmn., 1973-75; bd. dirs. Hamilton County (Ohio) YMCA, 1955-57, No. Bapt. Theol. Sem., 1970-73; mem. adv. com. Deaconess Hosp. Sch. Nursing, 1966—. Research and Travel grantee Am. Friends of Middle East and Am. Assn. Collegiate Registrars and Admissions Officers, 1964, citation as one of Eleven Great Alumni, S.E. Mo. State Signal, 1968; research grantee for Syrian edn. study Am. Assn. Collegiate Registrars and Admissions Officers, U.S. Dept. State, 1976-77. Mem. Am. (pres. 1975-76), Ohio (pres. 1965-66) assns. collegiate registrars and admissions officers, Am. Higher Edn. Assn., Conf. on Brit. Studies, S.E. Mo. State U. Alumni Assn. (Merit award 1963), YMCA, Alpha Kappa Psi, Delta Mu Delta, Kappa Delta Pi, Phi Alpha Theta, Pi Kappa Delta, Omicron Delta Kappa, Sigma Phi Epsilon (citation, Highest Career award 1975). Methodist. Author: The Enrollment Explosion: A Half Century of Attendance in U.S. Colleges and Universities (Outstanding Acad. Book of Year, Choice mag., Outstanding Edn. Book of Year, Sch. and Soc. mag.), 1971; Syrian Arab Republic: A Study of the Educational System of the Syrian Arab Republic, 1978. Contbr. articles to profl. jours. Home: 2657 Westwood-Northern Blvd Cincinnati OH 45211

PARKER, GEORGE, pen mfg. co. exec.; b. Janesville, Wis., Nov. 9, 1929; s. Russell C. and Eleanor (Jackson) P.; B.A., Brown U., 1951; M.A., U. Mich., 1952; LL.D., Milton Coll., 1974; m. Nancy E. Bauhan, Aug. 11, 1951; children—George Safford III, Elizabeth, Martha, Patricia. With Parker Pen Co., Janesville, 1952—, beginning as asst. to gen. mgr. subsidiary Gilman Engring. Co., successively asst. domestic advt. mgr., fgn. advt. mgr., dir. fgn. sales, dir. domestic sales, v.p., gen. mgr., 1958-60, exec. v.p., 1960-66, pres. Parker Pen Co., 1966-77, chief exec. officer, 1966—, chmn. bd., 1976—; chmn. bd. M & S Bancorp; dir. Mchts. & Savs. Bank, Marine Corp., NN Corp., Wis. Mfrs. & Commerce. Fin. chmn. Wis. Republican Com., 1971-73, state chmn., 1974-76. mem. Nat. Rep. Fin. Com., 1971-73, Rep. Nat. Com., 1974-76. Pres., trustee Janesville Found.; fellow Lake Forest Acad.; trustee emeritus Brown U., Beloit Coll. Mem. Archeol. Assn. Am., Psi Upsilon. Clubs: Milw., Univ. (Milw.). Home: 700 St Lawrence Ave Janesville WI 53545 Office: Parker Pen Co 219 E Court St Janesville WI 53545

PARKER, GEORGE CONRAD, oil co. exec.; b. George, N.C., Feb. 2, 1912; s. William Edgar and Ruth Eva (Peele) P.; B.S., Guilford Coll., 1935; m. Elizabeth Hunter Gilliam, Mar. 20, 1938; children—William Conrad, Elwood Gilliam, George Edgar, John Gurney, Elizabeth LeMay. With Northeastern Oil Co., Inc., Murfreesboro, N.C., 1935—, office mgr., petroleum jobber, 1935-43, exec. v.p., 1943-72, sec.-treas., 1972—, also dir.; sec.-treas., dir. East Coast Sales, Inc., 1969—; mem. Woodland City bd. N.C. Nat. Bank. Bd. dirs. Roanoke Chowan Mental Health Service, 1973—; mem. local sch. com., Northampton County, N.C., 1957-69. Bd. visitors Guilford Coll., 1970—; trustee Roanoke Chowan Hosp., Ahoskie, N.C., 1970—; bd. dirs. Pine Forest Rest, Potecasi, N.C., 1973—, pres., 1975; bd. dirs., pres. N.C. Friends Hist. Soc., 1976. Recipient (with wife) Distinguished Alumni award Guilford Coll., 1969, named to Athletic Hall of Fame, 1970. Democrat. Mem. Religious Soc. of Friends (pres. clk. N.C. Yearly Meeting 1961-77, recorded minister, treas. Rich Sq. Monthly Meeting). Club: Valley Pine Country (Lasker, N.C.). Home: Woodland NC 27897 Office: Northeastern Oil Co Murfreesboro NC 27855

PARKER, GEORGE EARL, lawyer; b. Laurel, Miss., Sept. 12, 1937; s. George Edward and Ruth Lee (Gardner) P.; B.B.A., U. Miss., 1960, LL.B., 1962; postgrad. N.Y. U. Grad. Sch. Law, 1969-70; m. Ruth Nora Holloway, Oct. 23, 1965; children—Marshall Lee, Allison Victoria, Jonathan Wesley. Admitted to Miss. bar, 1962; mem. firm Satterfield, Shell, Williams and Buford, Jackson, Miss., 1966-67; counsel, asst. sec. Schick Electric, Inc., Lancaster, Pa., 1967-68; atty., asst. sec. Johns-Manville Corp., Denver, 1969-71, counsel, asst. v.p., 1971-73, v.p., corp. counsel, 1973—, v.p., gen. counsel, 1976—. Bd. dirs. Center for Creative Living; trustee Partners Inc. Served with JAGC, AUS, 1963-66. Mem. Miss., N.Y. State, Colo., D.C. bar assns., Assn. Bar City N.Y., Assn. Corp. Secs., Omicron Delta Kappa, Sigma Nu. Republican. Episcopalian. Club: Denver Country (Denver). Office: Johns-Manville Corp Ken-Caryl Ranch Denver CO 80217

PARKER, GEORGE FREDERICK, educator; b. Chester, Mass., Nov. 7, 1918; s. Owen F. and Nettie (Twenty) P.; B.A., Boston U., 1940; B.D., Yale U., 1943, M.A., 1955; Ph.D., U. Pitts., 1959; postdoctoral scholar Harvard U., 1960; m. Ivol E. Godby, June 7, 1947; children—Owen DeWitt, Frederick Nathan. Asst. prof. philosophy and religion Evansville (Ind.) Coll., 1946-49; asst. prof. Fisk U., 1949-51; chaplain Chatham Coll., Pitts., 1952-60; asso. prof. ch. history, dean Crozer Theol. Sem., Chester, Pa., 1960-64; prof. philosophy, chmn. dept. Ky. So. Coll., 1964-69, Berea (Ky.) Coll., 1969—. Mem. Am. Philos. Assn., AAUP. Democrat. Author articles, revs. Home: 316 Pine Ave Berea KY 40403

PARKER, H. LAWRENCE, investment banker; b. Portchester, N.Y., June 16, 1926; s. Raeburn H. and Alice (Lawrence) P.; B.A., Yale, 1949; m. Eleanor Sage, Mar. 3, 1951; children—Katherine, Richard, Michael, Douglas (dec.); m. 2d, Joanne Louise Marston, Nov. 22, 1967. With Morgan Stanley & Co., N.Y.C., 1950—, partner, 1959—; pres. Morgan Stanley Can. Ltd., 1976-79, chmn., 1979—. Served with USMCR, 1944-46. Mem. Investment Bankers Assn. Am. (bd. govs. 1966-70, pres. 1969). Clubs: Nat. Golf Links Am.; Links, Bond (N.Y.C.); Augusta Nat. Golf; Blind Brook. Home: Bedford NY 10506 Office: 1251 Ave of Americas New York NY 10020

PARKER, HAMPTON BROOKS, r.r. exec.; b. Chattanooga, Oct. 5, 1918; s. E. H. and Anne (Herriford) P.; M.B.A., Harvard, 1955; m. Frances L. Thompson, Apr. 9, 1939; children—Penny, Richard H. With So. Ry. Co., 1937-47, chief clk., asst. v.p., 1945-47; with St. Louis-San Francisco Ry. Co., 1947—, v.p. finance, treas., Springfield, Mo., 1972—; dir. Bank of Springfield. Bd. dirs., v.p. YMCA. Club: Hickory Hills Country (dir., treas.). Home: Rural Route 2 Box 152-C Ozark MO 65721 Office: 3253 E Trafficway Springfield MO 65802

PARKER, HANS J., bank exec.; b. Ratibor, Germany, Oct. 18, 1926; came to U.S., 1953, naturalized, 1958; s. Richard and Olga (Hoffmann) Pajunk; B.A. in Econs. and Fin., Albion Coll., 1957; postgrad. Stonier Grad. Sch. Banking, Rutgers U., 1961-64; m. Patricia Misuraca, Oct. 30, 1964; 1 son, Brian Matthew. With City Nat. Bank of Detroit, 1957-66, asst. v.p., v.p. investments, 1957-66; European rep. govt. securities Merrill Lynch, Pierce, Fenner & Smith, 1966-71; v.p. investments Ann Arbor Bank & Trust (Mich.), 1971-76; v.p. investments, exec. v.p. Western N.Y. Savs. Bank, Buffalo, 1976—; instr. Am. Inst. Banking. Mem. Buffalo Bond Club, Nat. Fedn. Fin. Analysts. Club: Buffalo. Office: Western NY Savs Bank Main and Court Buffalo NY 14202*

PARKER, HAROLD TALBOT, educator; b. Cin., Dec. 26, 1907; s. Samuel Chester and Lucille (Jones) P.; Ph.B., U. Chgo., 1928, Ph.D., 1934; postgrad. Cornell U., 1929-30. Mem. faculty Duke U., Durham, N.C., 1939—, asso. prof., 1950-57, prof. history, 1957—. Served with USAAF, 1942-45. Mem. French Hist. Studies (pres. 1957), AAUP (pres. Duke U. chpt. 1960), Phi Beta Kappa (pres. Duke chpt. 1961). Episcopalian. Author: The Cult of Antiquity and the French Revolutionaries, 1937, Three Napoleonic Battles, 1943, (with Marvin Brown) Major Themes in Modern European History, 3 vols., 1974; Bureau of Commerce in 1780, 1979. Editor: (with Richard Herr) Ideas in History, 1965; Problems in European History, 1979. Home: 1005 Demerius St Durham NC 27701

PARKER, HAROLD WALDEMAR, JR., coast guard officer; b. Juneau, Alaska, Oct. 14, 1928; s. Harold Waldemar and Nona (Saylor) P.; B.S., U.S. Coast Guard Acad., 1950; m. Alice Dolores Mahoney, Apr. 19, 1952; children—Claudia, Steven, Alison, Michelle, Harold, Jacqueline, John. Stock boy Roos Bros. Dept. Store, San Francisco, 1943-44; driver Moffat Meat Packers, San Francisco, 1944-45; clk. So. Pacific R.R., San Francisco, 1945-46; commd. ensign U.S. Coast Guard, 1950, advanced through grades to rear adm., 1978; served aboard several coast guard cutters, Atlantic and Pacific coasts, 1950-72; comdr. Sta. Iwo Jima, 1954-55; served in U.S. Coast Guard Hdqrs., 1972-74; comdr. Coast Guard Sect., San Juan, P.R., 1974-76; comdr. 11th Coast Guard Dist., Long Beach, Calif., 1978—. Decorated Coast Guard Commendation medal with oak leaf cluster (U.S.); cavalier Order of Merit (Italy); named hon. Ky. col. Republican. Roman Catholic. Clubs: Rotary, Propeller, K.C. As search and rescue officer, coordinated rescue of survivors of Andrea Doria-Stockholm collision, 1956. Home: Quarters A US Coast Guard Base Terminal Island CA 90731 Office: 11th Coast Guard Dist 400 Oceangate Long Beach CA 90822

PARKER, HARRY LAMBERT, univ. rowing coach; b. Fitchburg, Mass., Oct. 28, 1935; s. Lambert Achilles and Ruth Margaret (Burnham) P.; A.B., U. Pa., 1957; m. Elinor Ruth Goodman, Apr. 4, 1959; children—George Franklin, David Lambert. Rowing coach Harvard, 1960—, U.S. Olympic team 1964, 68, 72; mem. U.S. Olympic Rowing com., 1964-68, 72—; head coach U.S. Women's Olympic rowing team, 1976. Mem. town meeting Winchester (Mass.), 1971-73. Served with USNR, 1957-60. Mem. Rowing Hall of Fame. Mem. Nat. Assn. Amateur Oarsmen (dir. 1966—). Coach U.S. eight-oared crew, silver medalist 1972 Olympics, several nat. intercollegiate championship crews. Home: 14 Quincy St Cambridge MA 02138 Office: Harvard 60 Boylston St Cambridge MA 02138

PARKER, HARRY S., III, museum dir.; b. St. Petersburg, Fla., Dec. 23, 1939; s. Harry S. and Catherine (Baillie) P.; B.A., Harvard, 1961; postgrad. U. Utrecht (Netherlands); M.A., N.Y. U., 1966; m. Ellen Margaret McCance, May 23, 1964; children—Elizabeth Day, Thomas Baillie, Samuel Ferguson, Catherine Allan. With Met. Mus. Art, N.Y.C., 1963-74, chmn. edn. dept., 1967-69, vice dir. edn., 1970-73; dir. Dallas Mus. Fine Arts, 1974—. Trustee Greenhill Sch., Dallas, Lamplighter Sch., Dallas. Fulbright fellow, 1961-62. Home: 9612 Rockbrook Dr Dallas TX 75220 Office: Dallas Museum Fine Arts Fair Park Dallas TX 75226

PARKER, ISRAEL FRANK, union ofcl.; b. Sylvania, Ga., Oct. 29, 1917; s. Cornelius Dean and Mary Eunice (Lewis) P.; student Ga. So. U., 1935-36, U. Ala., Birmingham, 1942-43, 49-50; m. Mary Alice, Dec. 26, 1938; 1 dau., Rebecca Gaye. Bus. mgr. United Bakery Workers Local 441, Birmingham, 1941-42; internat. rep. Retail, Wholesale and Dept. Store Union, AFL-CIO, Birmingham, 1942-52, asst. regional dir. So. area, Birmingham, 1957-60, regional dir. So. area, 1970-76, internat. sec.-treas., N.Y.C., 1976—; mem. bd. appeals Ala. Unemployment Compensation; trustee Retail, Wholesale and Dept. Store Internat. Union and Industry Health and Benefit Fund and Pension Fund; bd. dirs. Internat. Found. Employee Benefit Plans; chmn. Ala. Trade Union Council for Histadrut, 1970. Served with USN, 1944-46. Named Man of Year, Birmingham Frat. Order Police, 1972. Methodist. Club: Altadena Valley Golf and Country. Home: 745 Bentley Dr Birmingham AL 35213 Office: 101 W 31st St New York NY 10001

PARKER, JACK HORACE, linguist, educator; b. Parkersville, Ont., Can., Apr. 4, 1914; s. Ernest Frank and Jessie Blanche (Bain) P.; B.A., U. Toronto (Ont.), 1935, M.A., 1936, Ph.D., 1941; m. Marjorie Minnes, June 11, 1946; children—John Geoffrey, Ceciley Margaret. Instr. in Spanish, U. Toronto, 1936-41, asst. prof. Spanish and Portuguese, 1946-53, asso. prof., 1953-57, prof., 1957—, chmn. Toronto Dept., 1966-69, asso. dean Grad. Studies, 1969-73; instr. in Spanish, Columbia U., 1941-42, Ind. U., 1942-43; asst. prof. Spanish, U. B.C., 1945-46; vis. prof. U. San Carlos (Guatemala), summers 1947, 48, SUNY, Buffalo, fall 1965, U. Ill., spring 1962. Served with Can. Army, 1943-45. Decorated knight Order Civil Merit (Spain); Am. Council Learned Socs. fellow, 1942; Can. Council grantee, 1973-74. Fellow Royal Soc. Can.; mem. Am. Assn. Tchrs. Spanish and Portuguese (pres. 1975), Can. Assn. Hispanists (pres. 1968-70), MLA, Renaissance Soc. Am. Author: Gil Vicente, 1967; Juan Pérez de Montalvan, 1975; contbr. numerous articles to lang., linguistic jours., especially on Spanish and Portuguese lit. of 16th-17th centuries. Home: 100 Wychwood Park Toronto ON M6G 2V5 Canada Office: Dept Spanish and Portuguese U Toronto Toronto ON M5S 1A1 Canada

PARKER, JACK ROYAL, engring. co. exec.; b. N.Y.C., Apr. 25, 1919; s. Harry and Clara (Saxe) P.; student Bklyn. Poly. Inst., 1943; D.Sc. (hon.), Pacific Internat. U., 1956; m. Selma Blossom, Dec. 8, 1946; children—Leslie Janet, Andrew Charles. Instr., Indsl. Tng. Inst., 1938-39; engr. Brewster Aero Corp., 1939-40; pres. Am. Drafting Co., 1940; design engr., plan div. Navy Dept., 1941-44, also supr. instr. N.Y. Drafting Inst.; instr. Gasoline Handling Sch., also Inert Gas Sch., U.S.N.T.S., Newport, R.I., 1944-46; cons. Todd Shipyards Corp., 1947-54; tech. adviser to pres. Rollins Coll., 1949-50; v.p. Wattpar Corp., 1947-54; pres. Parco Co. Can. Ltd., 1951-55; pres., dir., chief project mgr. Royalpar Industries, Inc., N.Y.C., 1947-75; chmn. Med. Engrs. Ltd., Nassau, Bahamas, 1957-60; pres. Parco Chem. Systems, Inc., 1965-69; pres., dir. Parco Internat., Inc., 1965-69; pres. Guyana Oil Refining Ltd., S.A., 1966-69, Refineria Peruana del Sur S.A., 1965-68; v.p., dir., founder Refinadora Costarricense de Petreoleo, S.A., 1963—; pres. Oleoducto Trans Costa Rica, 1970-73, Trans Costa Rica Pipeline Operating Co., 1970-73; gen. mgr. Kellex power services Pullman Kellogg Co., 1975-77; past pres., sec., dir. Vernitron Corp., Amsterdam Fund, European securities Pub. Co. Cons. Dominican Republic, 1964, Republic Costa Rica, 1964-65, Malta Indsl. Devel. Study Co. Ltd., 1965-67, Hambros Bank Ltd., London, 1967-68, Stone & Webster Engring. Corp., Boston, 1957-75, Hambro Am. Bank & Trust Co., N.Y.C., 1968-70; pres. J. Royal Parker Assos., Inc., 1975—, Internat. Mfg. Centers, Inc., 1977—, Delaware Valley Fgn. Trade Zone, Inc., 1977—; lectr. One World Club, Cornell U., 1963. Mem. adv. bd. Drafting Ednl. Adv. Commn. N.Y.C. Bd. Edn., 1968; mem. museum adv. com. U.S. Mcht. Marine Acad., 1977. Trustee Coll. Adv. Sci., Canaan, N.H. Decorated knight Order St. John of Jersusalem. Recipient Humanitarian award Fairleigh Dickinson U., 1974. Fellow A.A.A.S.; mem. Inst. Engring. Designers (London), Am. Petroleum Inst., Soc. Am. Mil. Engrs., Presidents Assn., Am. Mgmt. Assn., Am. Inst. Chem. Engrs., Am. Inst. Dsgn. and Drafting. Republican. Clubs: Masons; Marco Polo (N.Y.C.); Royal Automobile (London). Author: Gasoline Systems, 1945; also articles. Patentee in field; inventor Lazy Golfer. Developer Operation Centraport (Limon Internat. Freezone Trade), Limon, Costa Rica. Home: 106 The Mews Haddonfield NJ 08033 Office: 900 Haddon Ave Collingswood NJ 08033. *I do not consider myself successful as measured by most yardsticks. Success will be mine when I can create a meaningful life for people in so-called underdeveloped countries. Only then can life be rewarding and satisfying.*

PARKER, JACK STEELE, ret. corp. exec.; b. Palo Alto, Calif., July 6, 1918; s. William L. and Mary I. (Steele) P.; student Menlo Jr. Coll., 1935-37, B.S., Leland Stanford Jr. U., 1939; LL.D., Clark U.; D.B.A., S.E. Mass. U.; m. Elaine Simons, 1946; 1 dau., Kaaren Lee. Mech. engr. Western Pipe & Steel Co. Calif., San Francisco, 1939-40; marine surveyor Am. Bur. Shipping, Seattle, 1940-42; asst. gen. supt. Todd Shipyards, Inc., Houston, 1942-44, gen. supt. outfitting, San Pedro, Calif., 1944-46; asst. chief engr. Am. Potash & Chem. Co., Trona, Calif., 1946-50; asst. mgr. design and constrn. Gen. Electric Co., Richland, Wash., 1950-52, operations mgr. aircraft nuclear propulsion project, Cin., 1952-53; gen. mgr. small aircraft engine dept., Lynn, Mass., 1953-54, gen. mgr. aircraft gas turbine div., Cin., 1955-57; v.p. Gen. Electric Co., 1956-68, v.p. relations services, exec. office, 1957-61; v.p., group exec. aerospace and def. group, 1961-68, exec. v.p., 1968, vice chmn. bd., exec. officer, 1968-80; dir. Utah Internat., The Continental Group. So. Pacific Co., J.G. Boswell Co., T.R.W. Inc.; pres. Bonnieview Ranch Inc. Trustee St. Louis U., 1967-69, Rensselaer Poly. Inst., Grand Central Art Galleries, Conf. Bd. (chmn. 1972-74), Am. Enterprise Inst., Council Fin. Aid to Edn., 1970-76; bd. overseers Hoover Instn., chmn., 1973-76; chmn. advisory council Stanford Grad. Sch. Bus., 1976-78; commr., pres. Exec. Exchange Program. Asso. fellow Royal Aero. Soc.; fellow Am. Inst. Aeros. and Astronautics (sr.), Inst. Jud. Adminstrn., ASME; mem. NAM (dir. 1958-62), Nat. Aviation Assn. (dir.), Aerospace Industries Assn. (chmn. bd. govs. 1966), Nat. Acad. Engring., Soc. Automotive Engrs., Air Force Assn., U.S. C. of C. (dir. 1976-79), Newcomen Soc., Conquistadores Del Cielo. Clubs: Augusta Nat. Golf; Burning Tree, George Towne (Washington); Commonwealth, Queen City, Commercial (Cin.); University, Links, SKY (N.Y.C.); Question; Blind Brook; Rolling Rock; Camp Fire of America; Round Hill; Clove Valley Rod and Gun; Desert Forest Golf; Bohemian (San Francisco); Boone and Crockett. Home: Round Hill Club Rd Greenwich CT 06830 Office: 3135 Easton Turnpike Fairfield CT 06431

PARKER, JAMES, curator; b. Boston, Jan. 22, 1924; s. Cortlandt and Elizabeth (Gray) P.; A.B., Harvard, 1946. Fellow in European decorative arts, 16th-19th centuries Met. Mus. Art, N.Y.C., 1951, asst., 1952-54, asst. curator, 1954-62, asso. curator, 1962-68, curator, 1968—; adj. prof. Inst. Fine Arts, N.Y. U., 1968-69, 71-72. Trustee, French Inst.-Alliance Francaise, N.Y.C. Served with F.A., AUS, 1944-45; PTO. Club: Union (N.Y.C.). Author: (with others) Decorative Art from the Samuel H. Kress Collection at the Metropolitan Museum of Art, 1964. Contbr. articles museum bulls. Home: 52 E 83d St New York City NY 10028 Office: Met Mus Art Fifth Ave and 82d St New York City NY 10028

PARKER, JOHN CRUMP, lawyer; b. Franklin, Va., June 28, 1895; s. John Crafford and Emily Virginia (Norfleet) P.; B.S., 6th distinguished, Va. Mil. Inst., 1914; legal edn. Washington and Lee U., 1915, U. Va., 1915-17, 19; m. Alice Saunders Dabney, Dec. 7, 1935; children—Alice Fleming (Mrs. R. E. Rutledge, Jr.), Elizabeth (Mrs. James C. McColl). Admitted to Va. bar, 1919, since practiced in Franklin; legal cons. Union Camp Corp. Pres. Va. Constl. Conv., 1956. Served as 1st lt., A.C., U.S. Army, 1918-19. Mem. Council Va. State Bar, 1938-45, 63-69, exec. com., 1943-45; chmn. com. on unauthorized practice of law, War Service Com.; com. on law lists. Va. State Bar, v.p., 1942, pres., 1943-44. Dir., sec. Camp Found.; dir. George C. Marshall Research Found.; dir. Lee-Jackson Meml., Inc., Historic Saint Luke's Restoration; pres. bd. visitors Va. Mil. Inst., 1956-58. Mem. Am., Southampton County (past pres.) bar assns., U. Va. Law Sch. Assn. (pres. 1950-51), English-Speaking Union, Am. Legion (charter mem. Southampton County, past post comdr.), Raven Soc., Soc. of Cin. of Va., Sigma Chi, Phi Delta Phi, Order of Coif (hon.). Democrat. Episcopalian. Clubs: Farmington Country (Charlottesville, Va.), Commonwealth (Richmond, Va.); Cypress Cove Country (dir. and past pres.), (Franklin). Home: 309 1st Ave Franklin VA 23851

PARKER, JOHN EGER, advt. agy. exec.; b. Burbank, Calif., Nov. 14, 1928; s. John Warren and Mary Neff (Eger) P.; B.S., U. Calif. at Los Angeles, 1950; m. Iris Landry, Dec. 31, 1955; children—Brian, Lia. Copy writer Batten Barton Durstin & Osborne, advt., Los Angeles, 1953-54; account exec. Larry Raymond Co., Los Angeles, 1954-59; pres., account exec. Parker Advt. Inc., Palos Verdes Peninsula, Calif., 1959-77; v.p. Easy Rest, Los Angeles, 1968—, Torrance (Calif.) Datsun, 1969—, United TV Programing Service, Los Angeles, 1973—, Pacific Gourmet, Los Angeles, 1973—; pres. Parker N.J., Los Angeles, 1968—, Parker Industries, Los Angeles, 1971—. Founder Palos Verdes Community Arts Assn., 1975, Los Angeles Music Center. Served to 1st lt., AUS, 1951-53; Korea. Mem. Palos Verdes C. of C. (dir. 1967), Am. Assn. Advt. Agys. (gov. Calif. council 1969-70), San Pedro Fine Arts Assn., Sigma Pi, Alpha Kappa Psi. Rotarian (v.p. Los Angeles 1958-65). Clubs: Old Men's, Lomas Santa Fe Country. Home: 172 Torrey Pines Terr Del Mar CA 92014 Office: Parker Industries Inc 2408 1st Ave San Diego CA 92101

PARKER, JOHN HAVELOCK, Can. provincial ofcl.; b. Didsbury, Alta., Can., Feb. 2, 1929; s. Bruce T. and Rose P. Parker; B.Sc. in Engring. Geology, U. Alta., Edmonton, 1951; m. Helen A. Panabaker, 1955; children—Sharon, Gordon. Mng. engr. Norman W. Byrne, Ltd., Uranium City and Yellowknife (N.W.T., Can.), 1951-63; pres. Precambrian Mining Services Ltd., 1964-67; councillor Town of Yellowknife, 1959-63, mayor, 1964-67; councillor N.W.T., 1967-74, dep. commr., 1967-79, commr., 1979—. Pres., N.W.T. council Boy Scouts Can. Fellow Arctic Inst. N.Am.; mem. Can. Inst. Mining and Metallurgy, Assn. Profl. Engrs. Alta.

PARKER, JOHN HENRY, mgmt. exec.; b. Balt., July 20, 1908; s. Roland and Edith (Bottomer) P.; M.E., Cornell U., 1933; m. Elizabeth V. Presher. Nov. 30, 1933; children—Henry Randall, Helen Elizabeth, Edith Leorah. Indsl. engr. Joseph Bancroft & Sons Co., Wilmington, Del., 1933-35, J. Edwards & Co., Phila., 1935-36; cons. engr. Rath & Strong, Boston, 1936-56, exec. v.p., dir., 1956-65; pres., dir. Scott & Williams Inc., Laconia, N.H., 1965-66, Claremont Airways, Inc. (N.H.), 1963-68, AMSL Corp., High Point, N.C., 1966-69; exec. v.p., dir. Rath & Strong, Inc., Boston, 1966-69, chmn. bd., 1969-74, chmn. emeritus, 1974—; dir. Scott & Williams S.A., Bruges, Belgium, 1965-66. Chmn. com. to establish new city govt., Claremont, 1947; councilman, Claremont, 1950-54. Registered profl. engr., Mass. Mem. Inst. Mgmt. Cons. (founding mem.), Cornell Soc. Engrs., Am. Mgmt. Assn., Wilderness Soc., Am. Bonanza Soc., Aircraft Owners and Pilots Assn. Mason. Club: Morgan Horse (Westmoreland, N.Y.). Home: Green Mountain Rd Claremont NH 03743 Office: 21 Worthen Rd Lexington MA 02173

PARKER, JOHN RICHARD, corp. exec.; b. Three Rivers, Mich., Sept. 9, 1917; s. Guy E. and Esther (Fulcher) P.; B.S. in Mech. Engring., U. Mich., 1939; m. Roberta Irene Chissus, Nov. 2, 1940; children—Robert A., Joan E., Ann B. Richard G. With A.O. Smith Corp., Milw., 1939—, successively detail draftsman, exec. engr. aircraft landing gears, chief product engr. auto div., dir. sales and engring. auto div., v.p. automotive and r.r. products, 1960-64, group v.p. contract products, 1964-75, pres., dir., 1975—, also dir. subsidiaries; dir. Briggs & Stratton Corp., Marine Nat. Exchange Bank. Bd. dirs. Luth. Hosp. Milw.; trustee Citizens Govtl. Research Bur., Milw. Boys' Club; mem. adv. council U. Wis.-Milw. Sch. Bus. Adminstrn. Mem. Machinery and Allied Products Inst. (exec. com.), Soc. Automotive Engrs. Clubs: Milw. Athletic, Milw. Yacht, Chenequa Country, University. Office: 3533 N 27th St Milwaukee WI 53216

PARKER, JOSEPH B., JR., physician, educator; b. Knox County, Tenn., July 8, 1916; s. Joseph B. and Sue (York) P.; B.S., U. Tenn., 1939, M.D., 1941; m. Phyllis Maxine Foster, May 25, 1946; children—Suzanna Margaret, Joseph B. III. Intern Knoxville Gen. Hosp., 1941-42; resident Duke Hosp., Durham, N.C., 1946-48; resident psychiatry St. Elizabeth Hosp., Washington, 1944-45; practice medicine, specializing psychiatry, Durham, 1948-49, 53-59, Memphis, 1949-53, Lexington, Ky., 1959-70; instr. psychiatry Duke, 1948-49, asso. prof., 1953-59; asso. prof. psychiatry, dir. Child Guidance Clinic U. Tenn. Coll. Medicine, 1949-53; chief psychiatry VA Hosp., Durham, 1953-59; prof., chmn. dept. psychiatry U. Ky. Med. Center, 1959-69; prof. psychiatry Duke Med. Center, 1970—; vis. faculty U. Pitts., 1967, Harvard, 1968-69; cons. USPHS Hosp., VA Hosp., Lexington; mem. prof. adv. com. Cerebral Palsy, Jr. League Opportunity Workshop; mem. Gov. Ky. Adv. Council Mental Health, 1962—, Gov. Ky. Manpower Commn., 1963—; exec. com., trustee Central Ky. Mental Health Bd. Served to lt. comdr., M.C., USNR, 1941-46. Diplomate Am. Bd. Psychiatry and Neurology. Fellow Am. Psychiat. Assn. (cons. continuing edn. project 1971—), Am. Coll. Psychiatrists, So. Psychiat. Assn. (regent, pres. 1972), Ky. Psychiat. Assn. (past pres.); mem. Am. Psychopath. Assn., Assn. Research Nervous, Mental Diseases, Soc. Biol. Psychiatry, Delta Tau Delta, Phi Chi, Delta Phi Alpha, Alpha Omega Alpha. Address: Dept Psychiatry Duke Med Center Durham NC 27710

PARKER, JOSEPH ORVILLE, govt. ofcl.; b. Pratt, Kans., Dec. 11, 1908; s. Jackson O. and Louise (Fritsche) P.; student Southwestern Coll., 1927-28; A.B., U. Kans., 1931; LL.B., Harvard U., 1934; m. Mary Louise Klose Parker, Apr. 1, 1936; 1 dau., Dorothy Louise Parker Johnson. Admitted to Kans. bar, 1935, U.S. Supreme Ct. bar, 1947; practice law, Pratt, 1935-36; atty. Office of Solicitor, Dept. Agr., Washington, 1936-44; dir. mktg. investigation and counsel Com. on Agr., U.S. Ho. of Reps., Washington, 1945-46, gen. counsel, 1947-51; asso. firm L. Alton Denslow Law Offices, Washington, 1951-71; mem. U.S. Internat. Trade Commn., Washington, 1971—, vice chmn., 1971-75, 76-78, chmn., 1978—; sr. cons. Select Com. on Fgn. Aid, U.S. Ho. Reps., 1947; adv. Presdl. Commn. on Indsl. Use of Agrl. Commodities, 1956-57, U.S. del FAO, Rome, 1955; chmn. internat. trade devel. bd. Inst. Am. Poultry Industries, 1956-71. Served with USN, 1944. Mem. Am. Bar Assn., Fed. Bar Assn., Harvard Law Sch. Assn., Nat. Grange, Bohlen Law Club, Delta Upsilon. Republican. Presbyterian. Clubs: Nat. Lawyers, Capitol Hill. Home: 4026 25th St N Arlington VA 22207 Office: US Internat Trade Commn Washington DC 20436

PARKER, KARR, elec. engr.; b. Sebree, Ky., July 3, 1892; s. Sanford Ruby and Victoria (Wilson) P.; student Carthage Coll.; B.S., U. Ill., 1913, M.S., 1914, D.Sc., 1929; m. Enid Marie Sympson, Dec. 30, 1915 (dec. Feb. 1968); children—Karr, Marjorie; m. 2d, Mary Gallagher, Nov. 1968. Radio engr. Marconi Wireless Telegraph Co. Am., Cleve. and Milw., 1913-15; elec. engr. McCarthy Bros. & Ford, elec. engrs., 1930—; chmn. Buffalo Electric Co.; mem. bd. dirs. Buffalo Savs. Bank. Exec. com. Buffalo War Council. Mem. council, chmn. bldgs. and grounds com. U. Buffalo. Fellow ASME; mem. Buffalo C. of C. (past pres.), Electric League Niagara Frontier (past pres.), Asso. Electric Contractors of Buffalo (past pres.), Engring. Soc. Buffalo (past pres.), Am. Inst. E.E., Illuminating Engring. Soc., Sigma Xi. Republican. Episcopalian. Clubs: Yacht (commodore), Buffalo, Country, Athletic, Twin Falls (pres.) (Buffalo); Engineers (N.Y.C.); Wianno (Cape Cod, Mass.). Home: 234 Depew Ave Buffalo NY 14214 (summer); Osterville MA 02655 (winter): 86 McFarlane Dr Delray Beach FL 33444 Office: 75 W Mohawk St Buffalo NY 14202

PARKER, KENNETH WHITTEN, public relations co. exec.; b. Conway, Ark., Feb. 20, 1929; s. Kelsey William and Daisy Henrietta (Saye) P.; B.A., Hendrix Coll., 1950; m. Charlene Lester, Jan. 16, 1953; children—Nancy, Mark, Mary Ruth. Reporter, Ark. Gazette, Little Rock, 1950-51, asst. state editor, 1951-53, state editor, 1953-60; dir. pub. relations Ark. Valley Industries, Inc., Dardanelle, 1960-64; mgr. pub. relations Crossett (Ark.) div. Ga.-Pacific Corp., 1964-66; dir. pub. relations Murphy Oil Corp., El Dorado, 1966-72; regional pub. relations mgr. Reynolds Metals Co., Little Rock, 1973-78; owner Ken Parker Public Relations, Little Rock, 1978—. Mem. El Dorado Municipal Auditorium Commn., 1970-72, chmn., 1972. Bd. dirs. El Dorado Sch. Dist., South Ark. Mental Health Center, El Dorado, Vis. Nurse Assn. of Pulaski County, Little Rock; exec. bd. De Soto Area council Boy Scouts Am. Mem. Pub. Relations Soc. Am. (dir. 1971-72, chpt. pres. 1966, assembly del. 1967-70, 74-76). Methodist. Rotarian (pres. 1963-64). Contbr. articles to Ency. Brit. Home: 2103 Old Forge Rd Little Rock AR 72207

PARKER, NORMAN FRANCIS, electronics co. exec.; b. Fremont, Nebr., May 14, 1923; s. Frank Huddleston and Rose Johanna (Launer) P.; student W.Va. U., 1943-44; B.S. in Elec. Engring. (George Westinghouse scholar), Carnegie-Mellon U., 1947, M.S. in Elec. Engring., 1947, D.Sc. in Engring. (Buhl fellow), 1948; m. Carol Hope Watt, June 12, 1949; children—Leslie Ann, Kerry Irene, Sandra Jean, Noel Louise. Engr., Westinghouse Electric Corp., East Pittsburgh, Pa., summer 1941, Bloomfield, N.J., summer 1942, U. Calif. Radiation Lab., Oak Ridge, 1944-45; with Autonetics div. N.Am. Aviation, Inc., Anaheim, Calif., 1948-67, asst. chief engr., 1956-59, v.p., gen. mgr. Data Systems div., 1959-62, exec. v.p., 1962-66, pres. autonetics div., 1966-67, v.p. N.Am. Aviation, Inc., 1966-67; exec. v.p., dir. Bendix Corp., 1967-68; pres., dir. Varian Assos., Inc., 1968—, chief exec. officer, 1972—. Life trustee Carnegie-Mellon U., mem. bus. adv. com. Grad. Sch. Indsl. Adminstrn. Served with AUS, 1943-46. Fellow IEEE; mem. Am. Inst. Aeros. and Astronautics, Nat. Acad. Engring., Sigma Xi, Tau Beta Pi, Eta Kappa Nu, Phi Kappa Phi, Pi Mu Epsilon. Patentee curve follower and gyroscopes. Office: 611 Hansen Way Palo Alto CA 94303

PARKER, PATRICK S., bus. exec.; b. Cleve., 1929; A.B., Williams Coll.; M.B.A., Harvard; married. With Parker-Hannifin Corp. and predecessor, Cleve., mgr. Fittings div., 1957-63, mgr. Aerospace Products div., 1963-65, v.p., 1967-69, pres., dir., 1969—, chief exec. officer, 1971—, chmn. bd., 1977—; dir. Soc. Nat. Bank, Cleve., Sherwin Williams Co., Cleve., Reliance Electric Co., Cleve., Acme-Cleve. Corp. Trustee, Salvation Army, Woodruff Hosp., Coll. of Wooster, Kolff Found. Served with USNR, 1954-57. Office: 17325 Euclid Ave Cleveland OH 44112

PARKER, PAUL LANGE, food co. exec.; b. Des Moines, Apr. 27, 1921; s. Addison Melvin and Ida Louise (Lange) P.; grad. Phillips Exeter Acad., 1939; B.A., Dartmouth, 1943; J.D., U. Iowa, 1948; m. Allegra Willis, Sept. 6, 1947; children—Hugh C., Melissa W., Paul W. Admitted to Iowa bar, 1948; practice in Des Moines, 1948-56; asst. atty. Polk County, 1949-50; exec. asst. to gov. of Iowa, 1955-56; gen. mgr. Canadian ops. Gen. Mills, Inc., Toronto, Ont., 1960-62, gen. mgr. internat. div., Mpls., 1962-64, v.p., dir. pub. relations, 1965-69, sr. v.p. employee and pub. relations, 1969-76, exec. v.p., chief adminstrv. officer, 1976—; trustee Farmers & Mechanics Savs. Bank Mpls.; dir. Charles Lindbergh Fund, Inc., Equitable of Iowa, Burlington No. Trustee Simpson Coll. Home: 785 N Ferndale Wayzata MN 55391 Office: 9200 Wayzata Blvd Minneapolis MN 55426

PARKER, PIERSON, clergyman, educator; b. Shanghai, China, May 27, 1905; s. Alvin Pierson and Susie Estelle (Williams) P.; A.B., U. Calif., 1927; student So. Meth. U., 1928-29; M.A., Pacific Sch. Religion, 1933, Th.D. magna cum laude, 1934; S.T.D., Ch. Div. Sch. of Pacific, 1964; m. Mildred Ruth Sorg, June 12, 1933; 1 son, Peter Pierson. Ordained to ministry, Congl. Ch., 1936, Episcopal, 1944; instr. Bibl. lang. and lit. Pacific Sch. Religion, 1934-36; pastor North Congl. Ch., Berkeley, Calif., 1936-44; pres. No. Calif. Congl. Conf., 1938-39; lectr. Bibl. lit. Ch. Div. Sch. Pacific, 1940-43, instr., 1943-44, asst. prof., 1944-47, asso. prof., 1947-49; Glorvina Rossell Hoffman prof. N.T. lit. and interpretation Gen. Theol. Sem., N.Y.C., 1949-74, sub-dean, 1972-74; chaplain to seminarians Diocese of Los Angeles, 1974—; distinguished prof. in residence Cathedral of St. John the Divine, N.Y.C., 1975; prof. N.T., Grad. Sch. Theology, U. of South, 1951-52, 54-55, 56-57, 58-60, 67-69, 71-74; research scholar Oxford U., 1957; lectr. N.T., St. Augustine's Coll., Canterbury, Eng., 1955; seminar asso. Columbia U.; vis. prof. Pacific Sch. of Religion, Ch. Divinity Sch. Pacific, 1965, 1966, U. of South, 1975, Bloy Episc. Sch. Theology, 1978-79; priest-in-charge Ch. of Holy Spirit, Nice, France, 1962, St. Helena's Ch., Istanbul, Turkey, 1969; canon Cathedral Ch. of St. Paul, Los Angeles, 1977—. Mem. Studiorum Novi Testamenti Societas, Soc. Bibl. Lit. and Exegesis (pres. Pacific Coast sect. 1946-48, mem. council 1944, v.p. Middle Atlantic sect. 1959-60, pres. 1960-61, archivist 1976—, nat. hon. pres. 1978), Pacific Theol. Group, Inst. Antiquity and Christianity, Pacific Sch. Religion Alumni Assn. (pres. 1943-46), Alpha Sigma Phi. Author: Interpreters' Bible (volume on Deuteronomy), 1951 (with H.H. Shires, G. E. Wright); The Gospel Before Mark, 1953; Inherit the Promise, 1957; Christ Our Hope, 1958; Meditations on the Life of Christ, 1959; Good News in Matthew, 1976. Mem. editorial bd. Anglican Theol. Rev., 1949, Jour. Bibl. Lit., 1960-74. Contbr. to religious publs., Interpreters Bible Dictionary, Grolier Ency., Ency. American. Home: 3916 Mural Dr Claremont CA 91711

PARKER, RALPH HALSTEAD, librarian; b. Bertram, Tex., Apr. 21, 1909; s. James Francis and Rosalthe Lee (Lawhon) P.; B.A., U. Tex., 1929, M.A., 1930, Ph.D., 1935; grad. student U. Chgo., 1936-37; m. Mary Kate Norman, June 23, 1935; 1 dau., Judith Kay. Loan librarian U. Tex., 1930-36; librarian Pomona Coll., Claremont, Calif., 1937-40; dir. libraries U. Ga., 1940- 47; librarian U. Mo., 1947-67, dean Sch. Library and Info. Sci., 1966-74, prof., 1974-78, prof. emeritus, 1978—. Mem. Mo. Library Commn., 1946-67, pres., 1959-66. Served with AUS, 1943-46. Mem. A.L.A. (chmn. library equipment com. 1942-43, financial adminstrn. sect. 1957-59), Mo. Library Assn. (pres. 1951-52), Am. Soc. for Information Sci., State Hist. Soc. Mo., Sigma Delta Chi. Author: Library Applications of Punched Cards, 1952. Contbr. articles to profl. jours. Democrat. Methodist. Home: 1104 S Glenwood Columbia MO 65201

PARKER, RAYMOND, artist, educator; b. Beresford, S.D., Aug. 22, 1922; s. Roscoe J. and Esther (Mork) P.; B.A., State U. Iowa, 1946, M.F.A., 1948; m. Denise Griffin, Mar. 30, 1954; children—Kate, Caroline. Mem. faculty Hunter Coll., 1955—, prof. art, 1962—; one-man exhbns. include Walker Art Center, Mpls., 1950, Paul Kantor Gallery, Los Angeles, 1953, 56, Memphis Acad. Art, 1953, Louisville Art Center, 1954, Union Coll., Schenectady, 1955, Martin Widdifield Gallery, N.Y.C., 1957, 59, U. So. Calif., 1959, Kootz Gallery, N.Y.C., 1960-64, 66, Galerie Neufville, Paris, France, 1960, Galleria Dell Ariete, Milan, Italy, 1961, Dwan Gallery, Los Angeles, 1960, 62, Guggenheim Mus., 1961, Bennington Coll., 1961, Des Moines Art Center, 1962, 63, Dayton (Ohio) Art Inst., 1965, Gertrude Kasle Gallery, Detroit, 1966, 70, Washington Gallery Modern Art, 1966, San Francisco Mus. Art, 1967, Quay Gallery, San Francisco, 1970, 72, 74, Chgo. Arts Club, 1971, Fischbach Gallery, N.Y.C., 1970, 71, 73, Sch. Visual Arts, N.Y.C., 1971, David Berger Gallery, Pitts., 1974, Portland Center for Visual Arts, 1974, Benson Gallery, Bridgehamton, N.Y., 1974, Berenson Gallery, Miami, Fla., 1974, Fischbach Gallery, N.Y.C., 1974, Am. U., Washington, 1975, Susan Caldwell Gallery, N.Y.C., 1976, U. Md., 1977, Caldwell Gallery, 1977, U. Tex., Austin, 1977, Billiard Room Gallery, Cambridge, Mass., 1978, Betty Cunningham Gallery, N.Y.C., 1979, The Phillips Collection, Washington, 1979; work represented in permanent collections Albright-Knox Art Gallery, Dayton Art Inst., Des Moines Art Center, Ft. Worth Mus., Guggenheim Mus., James A. Michener Found., Allentown, Pa., Los Angeles County Mus., Mpls. Inst. Art, Minn. Hist. Soc., Mus. Modern Art, Rose Art Mus. at Brandeis U., State U. Iowa, Tate Gallery, London, Eng., Walker Art Center, Whitney Mus., Miami (Fla.)-Dade Jr. Coll., Met. Mus., N.Y.C., Childe Hassim Found., Wadsworth Atheneum, Art Inst. Chgo., Mass. Inst. Tech., Internat. Minerals and Chems. Corp., Skokie, Ill., Larry Aldrich Old Hundred, Ridgefield, Conn., Portland (Maine) Mus., San Francisco Mus. Art., Cleve. Mus., U. Tex. Mus., Austin, U. N.Mex. Mus., Delgado Mus., New Orleans, Akron (Ohio) Mus., Phila. Mus., Am. U., Vassar Coll., Milw. Art Center, others. Mem. adv. com. Artists for CORE, 1964—; mem. Fulbright-Hays com. on awards Internat. Exchange Program. Recipient Ford Found. award Corcoran Biennial, 1963; award Nat. Council Arts, 1967; Guggenheim fellow, 1967. Home: 52 Carmine St New York NY 10014

PARKER, RICHARD ALAN, educator; b. Milw., May 20, 1931; s. Wayne Harvey and Romana (Bachhuber) P.; B.S., Utah State U., 1953; M.S., U. Wis., 1954, Ph.D., 1956; m. Theda Hull, Sept. 12, 1953; children—Katherine, Gina, Douglas, Steven, Sharon, Linda, Gregory. From instr. to prof. zoology Wash. State U., 1956—, asso. prof. to prof. computer sci., 1963—, chmn. dept. zoology, 1965-72, chmn. environ. sci. program, 1968-71, acting dir. computing center, 1964-65. NSF sr. postdoctoral fellow, Oxford U., 1968-69; Erskine fellow Canterbury U., 1976; Fulbright research scholar U. Liège (Belgium), 1980. Mem. Am. Soc. Naturalists, Am. Soc. Limnology and Oceanography, Internat. Assn. for Ecology, Societas Internationalis Limnologiae, Sigma Xi. Home: RFD 2 Box 277 Moscow ID 83843 Office: Washington State Univ Pullman WA 99164

PARKER, RICHARD ANTHONY, Egyptologist; b. Chgo., Dec. 10, 1905; s. Thomas Frank and Emma Ursula (Heldman) P.; A.B., Dartmouth Coll., 1930; Ph.D., U. Chgo., 1938; m. Gladys Anne Burns, Feb. 10, 1934; children—Michael (dec.), Beatrice Ann.

Research asst. Oriental Inst., U. Chgo., 1938-42, research asso., 1942-46, asst. prof. of Egyptology, 1946-48; Wilbour prof. Egyptology, Brown U., 1948-72, prof. emeritus, 1972—; epigrapher, epigraphic and archtl. survey, Luxor, Egypt, 1938-40; asst. field dir., epigraphic and archtl. survey, 1946-47, field dir., 1947-49. Trustee Am. Research Center Egypt; mem. vis. com. dept. Middle Eastern civilizations Harvard, 1950-61, dept. Egyptian art Boston Mus. Fine Arts, 1950—. Corr. fellow Brit. Acad.; mem. Oriental Soc., Egypt Exploration Soc., Société Française d'Egyptologie, Deutsches Archaologisches Institut, Phi Beta Kappa, Theta Chi. Roman Catholic. Author: Medinet Habu IV. Festival Scenes of Rameses III (with Harold H. Nelson and others), 1940; Baybylonian Chronology 626 B.C.-A.D. 45, 1942 (with Waldo H. Dubberstein), 1946, rev. edit. 626 B.C.-A.D. 75, 1956; The Calendars of Ancient Egypt, 1950; (with G. R. Hughes and others) Reliefs and Inscriptions at Karnak III; The Bubastite Portal, 1953, Medinet Habu V: The Temple Proper, Part I, 1957, Medinet Habu VI: The Temple Proper, Part 11, 1963; A Vienna Demotic Papyrus on Eclipse and Lunar-Omina, 1959; (with O. Neugebauer) Egyptian Astronomical Texts I: The Early Decans, 1960, Egyptian Astronomical Texts II: The Ramesside Star Clocks, 1964, Egyptian Astronomical Texts III: Decans, Planets, Constellations and Zodiacs, 1969; A Saite Oracle Papyrus from Thebes, 1962; Demotic Mathematical Papyri, 1972; (with J. Leclant and J.C. Goyon) The Edifice of Taharqa by the Sacred Lake of Karnak, 1979. Home: 93 Congdon St Providence RI 02906

PARKER, RICHARD BENNETT, educator; b. Ontario, Oreg., Sept. 19, 1925; s. William T. and May Belle (Bennett) P.; student Wis. State Coll., 1943-44, Boise Jr. Coll., 1947-48; M.S., Oreg. State Coll., 1952, Ph.D., 1956; postgrad. U. Wis., 1954-55, U. Calif. at Los Angeles, 1958-59; m. Jeanette Steege, June 27, 1946; children—Dawn Parker Forrest, Marsha Parker Sundquist, Barbara Parker Weaver, Heidi. Project asst. Oreg. State Coll., 1949-50, grad. research asst., 1950-52, instr., 1952-54; teaching asst. U. Wis., 1954-55; sr. scientist Carnation Research Center, Van Nuys, Calif., 1955-59; asst. prof. bacteriology U. Oreg. Dental Sch., Portland, 1959-61, asso. prof., 1961-64, prof. microbiology, 1964—, dir. div. oral biology, 1968—, asso. prof. bacteriology Med. Sch., 1968, chmn. dept. microbiology, 1969—; v.p. research and devel. NuLabs div. Pioneer Hi-Bred Internat., Portland. Bd. dirs. Oreg. Found. Dental Research, Portland, Cascade Coll., Portland. Served with USAAF, 1943-46. Mem. A.A.A.S., Am. Inst. Biol. Scis., Am. Soc. Microbiology, Internat. Assn. Dental Research, Soc. Exptl. Biology and Medicine, Sigma Xi, Omicron Kappa Upsilon, Alpha Zeta. Author four sci. texts. Contbg. author ORBANS Periodontics, 1968. Contbr. articles to profl. jours. Home: 296 S Birdshill Loop Portland OR 97219

PARKER, RICHARD BORDEAUX, fgn. service officer; b. Philippine Islands, July 3, 1923 (parents U.S. citizens); s. Roscoe Stuart and Marguerite (Blossom) P.; B.S., Kan. State U., 1947, M.S., 1948; m. Jeanne Jaccard, June 23, 1944; children—Alison, Jeffrey, Jill, Richard. Exec. sec. Kan. Commn. for UNESCO, 1948; joined U.S. Fgn. Service, 1949; assigned Sydney, Australia, 1949-51, Jerusalem, Palestine, 1951-53, Beirut, Lebanon, 1954, Amman, Jordan, 1955-56, State Dept., Washington, 1956-61; chief polit. sect. embassy, Beirut, 1961-64; polit. counselor embassy, Cairo, 1965-67; country dir. UAR, 1967-70; dep. chief mission embassy, Rabat, 1970-74; ambassador to Algeria, 1975-77, to Lebanon, 1977-78, to Morocco, 1978—. Served to 1st lt. U.S. Army, 1943-47. Mid-career fellow Woodrow Wilson Sch., Princeton, 1964-65. Mem. Royal Central Asia Soc., Middle East Studies Assn. Address: American Embassy Rabat Morocco

PARKER, ROBERT ALLAN RIDLEY, astronaut; b. N.Y.C., Dec. 14, 1936; s. Allan Elwood and Alice (Heywood) P.; A.B., Amherst Coll., 1958; Ph.D., Calif. Inst. Tech., 1962; m. Joan Audrey Capers, June 14, 1958; children—Kimberly Ellen, Brian David Capers. NSF postdoctoral fellow U. Wis., 1962-63, asst. prof., then asso. prof. astronomy, 1963-74; astronaut NASA, Johnson Space Center, 1967—, mem. support crew Apollo XV and XVII, mission scientist Apollo XVII, program scientist Skylab program, mission specialist for Spacelab I. Mem. Am. Astron. Soc., Phi Beta Kappa, Sigma Xi. Home: 311 Cedar Ln Seabrook TX 77586 Office: Code CB NASA-JSC Houston TX 77058

PARKER, ROBERT ANDREW, painter; b. Norfolk, Va., May 14, 1927; s. William Clay and Harriet (Cowdin) P.; B.A.E., Sch. Art Inst. Chgo., 1952; student Atelier 17, N.Y.C., 1952-53; m. Dorothy Lane Daniels, Nov. 20, 1948; children—Christopher, Anthony, Eric, Geoffrey, Nicholas. One-man shows include Roko Gallery, N.Y.C., 1954, 55, 56, 58, World House Gallery, N.Y.C., 1961, J.L. Hudson Gallery, Detroit, 1963, Terry Dintenfass Gallery, N.Y.C., 1966, 67, annually 1969-74; group exhbns. include Watercolors, Drawings and Prints, Met. Mus., 1952, Young Am. Print Makers, Mus. Modern Art, 1953, Young Am., Whitney Mus., 1957, Recent Acquisitions, Mus. Modern Art, 1957; rep. permanent collections Mus. Modern Art, Whitney Mus., Met. Mus., Bklyn. Mus., Am. Acad. Arts and Letters, Morgan Library, Dublin Mus., Los Angeles County Mus.; artist in residence Sch. Visual Arts, N.Y.C., 1968. Served with USAAF, 1945-46. Recipient Richard and Hinda Rosenthal award Nat. Inst. Arts and Letters, 1962; grantee Tamarand Lithography Workshop, Los Angeles, 1967; John Simon Guggenheim Found. fellow, 1969. Illustrated handcolored ltd. edits. Marianne Moore poems, 1962, Randall Jarrells' Death of the Ball Turret Gunner, 1971; illustrated poetry of Wilfred Owen for film The Days of Wilfred Owen, 1966, poetry of Keith Douglas for film How to Kill, 1970. Address: Parsonage Ln Washington CT 06793

PARKER, ROBERT BROWN, novelist; b. Springfield, Mass., Sept. 17, 1932; s. Carroll Snow and Mary Pauline (Murphy) P.; B.A., Colby Coll., 1954; M.A., Boston U., 1957, Ph.D., 1971; m. Joan Hall, Aug. 26, 1956; children—David, Daniel. In various bus. and advt. positions, N.Y.C. and Boston, 1956-62; mem. faculty Lowell State Coll., 1964-66, Bridgewater State Coll., 1966-68; asst. prof. English, Northeastern U., 1968-73, asso. prof., 1973-76, prof., 1976-78; author: The Personal Response to Literature, 1971, Order and Diversity, 1973, Training with Weights, 1973, Godwulf MS, 1974, God Save The Child, 1974, Mortal Stakes, 1975, Promised Land, 1976 (Edgar Allan Poe award for best novel 1976), Judas Goat, 1978, (with Joan Parker) Three Weeks in Spring, 1978; Wilderness, 1979. Served with U.S. Army, 1954-56. . *I have always known very clearly what my priorities are and I have always tried to remain unconfused about that. I have tried to avoid too much concern with the "tyrannical shoulds." And I have had the good fortune to marry Joan Parker.*

PARKER, ROBERT FREDERIC, univ. dean; b. St. Louis, Oct. 29, 1907; s. Charles T. and Lydia (Gronemeyer) P.; B.S., Washington U., St. Louis, 1925, M.D., 1929; m. Mary L. Warner, June 20, 1934; children—David Frederic, June Eleanor (Mrs. Howard H. Hush, Jr.). Asst. radiology Washington U. Med. Sch., 1929-30, instr. medicine, 1932-33; asst. Rockefeller Inst., 1933-36; mem. faculty Case Western Res. U., 1936—, prof. microbiology, 1954-77, prof. emeritus, 1977—, asso. dean, 1965-73, dean, 1973-76, dean emeritus, 1976—. Mem. Nat. Bd. Med. Examiners. Diplomate Am. Bd. Microbiology. Mem. Cleve. Acad. Medicine (past bd. dirs.), Am. Soc. Clin. Investigation, Central Soc. Clin. Research, Am. Acad. Microbiology, Sigma Xi, Alpha Omega Alpha. Spl. research virus immunology, quantitative aspects virus infection, tissue culture, action of antibiotics. Home: 2819 Coleridge Rd Cleveland Heights OH 44118 Office: 2046 Adelbert Rd Cleveland OH 44106

PARKER, ROBERT HUTSON, clergyman; b. Cumberland, Md., Mar. 17, 1912; s. Robert Reese and Lucretia (Hutson) P.; A.B., Am. U., 1934; B.D., Drew Theol. Sem., 1937; D.D., Western Md. Coll., 1953; L.H.D., Am. U., 1962; m. Meredith Snowden, Aug. 5, 1937; children—Sylvia (Mrs. William R. Bowles), Sharon Parker (Mrs. F. Daniel Mitchell). Ordained to ministry Methodist Ch., 1937; minister Methodist Ch., Cumberland, Methodist Ch., Balt., Methodist Ch., Parkton (all Md.), 1937-58, dist. supt., 1958-60; pres. Wesley Coll., Dover, Del., 1960-75; dir. devel. Asbury Meth. Village, Gaithersburg, Md., 1975—. Home: 401 Russell Ave Apt 612 Gaithersburg MD 20760

PARKER, ROBERT L., lawyer; b. El Paso, Tex., Jan 29, 1920; A.B. in Chemistry, Occidental Coll., 1941; J.D., Loyola U., 1949. Admitted to Calif. bar, 1949; now mem. firm Christie, Parker & Hale, Pasadena. Mem. Am., Pasadena, Los Angeles County bar assns., State Bar Calif., Am. Chem. Soc., Am. Patent Law Assn., Am. Soc. Internat. Law, Internat. Assn. for Protection of Indsl. Property, Licensing Execs. Soc., Los Angeles Council on Fgn. Relations, Phi Delta Phi. Office: Union Bank Plaza 201 S Lake Ave Pasadena CA 91101

PARKER, ROBERT ROY, ret. govt. ofcl.; b. Chgo., Oct. 6, 1926; s. Roy C. and Helen (Cavanaugh) P.; student Ohio State U., 1946-48; J.D., Cath. U., 1954; M.S. in Bus. Adminstrn., George Washington U., 1967; m. Connie Stafford, Aug. 23, 1950; children—Mary Elizabeth, Robert Roy, Susan Lee. Patrolman, Ohio State Patrol, 1948-50; investigator U.S. Govt., 1951-54; admitted to Md. bar, 1954, U.S. Supreme Ct. bar, 1959, Nev. bar, 1977; lawyer U.S. Govt. in Japan, 1954-56; legal counsel Office Econ. Coordinator UN Command, Seoul, Korea, 1956-58; regional legal adviser Office Near East and South Asia, Office Gen. Counsel, ICA, State Dept., 1958-59, Am. embassy AID, New Delhi, India, 1959-62; legal adviser AID, Am. embassy, Lagos, Nigeria, 1962-65; asst. gen. counsel AID, 1965-67; asso. dir. AID, Am. embassy. Saigon, Vietnam, 1967-69, attaché of embassy, 1967-69; regional legal counsel for C. Am., AID, 1970-72, asst. dir. operations for C. Am., 1972-73, dep. dir. Regional Office for C.Am. and Panama, Guatemala City, Guatemala, 1973-75; dir. Office Inspections and Investigations, Washington, 1975-77; pvt. practice law, 1977—. AID sr. officer tng. Indsl. Coll. Armed Forces, 1966, diploma, 1967. Served with AUS, 1944-46. Recipient Lawyers Coop. Book award for scholarship constl. law, 1953; Meritorious Service citation ICA, State Dept., 1961; Distinguished Career Service award AID, Dept. State, 1977. Mem. Am., Fed. bar assns., Internat. Assn. Chiefs Police, Internat. City Mgrs. Assn., Am. Soc. Internat. Law, Am. Judicature Soc., Phi Eta Sigma. Mason (Shriner), K.T. Club: Nat. Lawyers (a founder) (Washington). Home: 3336 Meadowland Dr Sparks NV 89431 Office: 413 Pyramid Way Sparks NV 89431

PARKER, RODGER DUANE, educator; b. St. Louis, July 2, 1934; s. Arch Newall and Ruth L. (White) P.; A.B., Drury Coll., 1956; M.A., Ind. U., 1960; Ph.D., Johns Hopkins, 1965; m. Betty Alice Weinstock, June 9, 1969; children—Laura L., Sarah S., Susan E., Michelle E. Cons., Booz, Allen Applied Research Co., Washington, 1962-68; mem. faculty Johns Hopkins U., 1965—, prof. ops. research, 1973—; cons. in field. Served with AUS, 1957-59. Contbr. articles to profl. jours. Home: 206 Hawthorn Rd Baltimore MD 21210 Office: 615 N Wolfe St Baltimore MD 21205

PARKER, ROY TURNAGE, educator, physician; b. Pinetops, N.C., Sept. 7, 1920; s. Samuel L. and Maude (Turnage) P.; A.B., U. N.C., 1941; M.D., Med. Coll. Va., 1944; m. Georgia James Sugg, Sept. 26, 1944; children—David Turnage, Nancy Payne. Intern U.S. Naval Hosp., Bethesda, Md., 1944-45; asst. resident obstetrics and gynecology Duke Hosp., 1946-50, resident instr., 1951; pvt. practice Kinston (N.C.) Clinic, 1952-53; mem. faculty Duke Med. Center, 1955—, prof. obstetrics and gynecology, 1963—; chmn. dept., 1964—; cons. VA Hosp., Durham County Hosp., Lenoir Meml. Hosp. Served to lt. (j.g.), M.C. USNR, 1943-46, to lt., 1953-54. Diplomate Am. Bd. Obstetrics and Gynecology (bd. dirs.). Mem. Am., So. med. assns., Med. Soc. N.C., N.C. Obstet. and Gynecol. Soc., So. Atlantic (pres.-elect 1979), Am. (pres. Found. 1978) assns. obstetricians and gynecologists, Am. Coll. Obstetricians and Gynecologists (pres. 1975-76), Am. Gynecol. Club, Soc. Pelvic Surgeons, Am. Fertility Soc., Am. Gynecol. Soc. (mem. council), Assn. Profs. Gynecology and Obstetrics (pres. 1968-69), F. Bayard Carter Soc. (pres. 1968-69), Alpha Omega Alpha. Mem. editorial bd. Obstetrics and Gynecology Jour., Am. Jour. Ob-Gyn.; contbr. articles to profl. jours. Home: 111 Pinecrest Rd Durham NC 27705

PARKER, ROYAL, glass co. exec.; b. Pitts., July 2, 1928; s. William and Mary E. (Heverly) P.; B.S. in Commerce, Grove City (Pa.) Coll., 1952; m. Miriam Jean Shellito, Oct. 11, 1952; children—David Alan, Judith Joanne, Cynthia Diane. Mgr., U.S. Steel Corp., Lorain, O., Chgo. and N.Y.C., 1952-67; sr. cons. Peat, Marwick, Mitchell, C.P.A.'s, N.Y.C., 1967-71; dir. finance Gulf & Western Corp., 1971-73; fin. dir. Anchor Hocking Corp., Lancaster, Ohio, 1973—. Active local Boy Scouts Am., Little League. Served with U.S. Army, 1946-47. Republican. Presbyterian (elder, deacon). Club: Lancaster Country. Home: 115 E Wheeling St Lancaster OH 43130 Office: 109 N Broad St Lancaster OH 43130

PARKER, SYDNEY RICHARD, elec. engr., educator, univ. dean; b. N.Y.C., Apr. 18, 1923; s. Morris and Rose (DuGoff) P.; B.S., Coll. City N.Y., 1944; M.S., Stevens Inst. Tech., 1948, Sc.D., 1964; m. Dorothy Begg, Jan. 25, 1947; children—Stephen Bruce, Susan Margaret. Lectr. Mass. Inst. Tech., 1948-51; project engr. RCA, 1951-56; asso. prof. elec. engring. Coll. City N.Y., 1956-65; prof. elec. engring. U. Houston, 1965-66; prof. elec. engring. Naval Postgrad. Sch., Monterey, Calif., 1966-75, chmn. dept., 1969-75; prof. elec. engring. and computer sci. Rutgers U., New Brunswick, N.J., 1975-76, dean Coll. Engring., 1975-76; prof. elec. engring. Naval Postgrad. Sch., Monterey, Calif., 1976—. Mem. engring. edn. accreditation com. Engrs. Council for Profl. Devel., 1975—; cons. to industry. Served to 1st lt. AUS, 1944-46. Recipient Sigma Xi research award Naval Postgrad. Sch., 1977; registered profl. engr., N.Y., N.J., Pa., Calif. Fellow IEEE (dir. Asilomar conf. circuits and systems 1966-74, v.p. circuits and systems soc. 1973, pres. soc. 1974, mem. tech. activities bd. 1974, ednl. activities bd. 1973-77); mem. Am. Assn. Engring. Edn. (dir. Pacific region 1974-75), AAAS, N.Y. Acad. Scis., Sigma Xi, Tau Beta Pi, Eta Kappa Nu (dir. 1977-78, v.p. 1979). Author: Principles of Control Systems Engineering, 1960. Asso. editor IEEE Trans. on Circuits and Systems, 1975-77; editor ASEE Trans. on Computers in Engring. Edn., 1975. Contbr. articles to tech. jours. Office: Dept Elec Engring Naval Postgrad Sch Monterey CA 93940

PARKER, VINCENT EVELAND, physicist; b. Kuala Lumpur, Federated Malay States, Sept. 18, 1914; (parents Am. citizens); s. Walter Guy and Alma Estelle (Shell) P.; A.B., Evansville (Ind.) Coll., 1936; Ph.D., Ind. U., 1940; m. Laverne Martin, June 18, 1938 (dec.); children—Don, Roger, Paul, David; m. 2d, Ruth Barber Boyer, Feb. 3, 1967; stepson, Charles. Came to U.S., 1924. Asso. prof., head, dept. phys. sci., Central Normal Coll. (now Canterbury Coll.), Danville, Ind., 1940-41; instr. chemistry (half-time) and asst. microchemist (half-time) U. Del. and Biochem. Research Found., Newark, Del., 1941-43; asst. prof. chemistry and physics U. Del., 1943-44; asst. prof., acting head dept. physics, 1944-46, asso. prof., chmn. dept. physics, 1946-48, prof., chmn. dept., 1948-50; prof., head dept. physics and astronomy La. State U., 1950-62, cooperating in instructing La. Radiol. Def. Sch., 1950-51; chief physicist Oak Ridge Nat. Lab., summers 1953, 55; dep. dir. Oak Ridge Asso. Univs., 1962-67; prof. physics, dean Sch. Sci., Calif. State Poly. U., 1967—. State dir. radiol. civil def. for Del., 1950. Rep. State Del. at radiol. course at Brookhaven Nat. Lab., chmn. So. Regional Accelerator Com., 1956-60; mem. Commn. Coll. Physics, 1960-64; trustee Coll. Oak Ridge, vice chmn., 1964-66; chmn. Interservice Com. on Tech. Facilities, Southeastern U.S.A., 1966; mem. U.S. nat. com. Internat. Union of Pure and Applied Physics, 1967-70. Exec. dir. La. State Sci. Fair, 1955-58; dir. Baton Rouge Community Services Council, 1956-59, pres., 1959-61, chmn. planning com., 1957-59. Recipient Distinguished Service citation Am. Assn. Physics Teachers, 1967. Fellow AAAS (exec. council), Am. Phys. Soc. (vice chmn. S.E. sect. 1956-57, chmn. 1958-59); mem. Am. Chem. Soc., Am. Assn. Physics Tchrs. (pres. 1963), AAUP (pres. U. Del. chpt. 1948-49), Am. Inst. Physics (governing bd.; exec. com. governing bd.), Sigma Xi, Sigma Pi Sigma (nat. pres. 1954-59), Phi Lambda Upsilon, Phi Beta Chi, Pi Epsilon Phi, Omicron Delta Kappa, Alpha Chi Sigma. Rotarian. Asso. editor Am. Jour. Physics, 1958-61; fgn. editor Nuclear Energy Engr.; editor La. State U. studies, phys. sci. sec. Home: 1679 N 1st Ave Upland CA 91786 Office: Calif State Poly U Pomona CA 91768

PARKER, WALTER BURR, safety engr.; b. Monteagle, Tenn., June 15, 1909; s. James Page and Gertrude Parker; B.S. in Mech. Engring., U. Tenn., 1933; m. M. Katherine Hockenjos, June 2, 1934; children—Mary Kay, William Page. With Combustion Engring., Inc., 1933-35; successively field insp., adjuster, asst. chief engr. Hartford Steam Boiler Insp. & Ins. Co. (Conn.), 1935-73; safety inspection engr. Uniform Boiler and Pressure Vessel Laws Soc., Hartford, 1963—, chmn., 1973—. Fellow ASME; mem. TAPPI. Republican. Baptist. Club: Hartford Exchange (past pres.). Home: Skylark Dr Spring Hill FL 33526 Office: 57 Pratt St Hartford CT 06103

PARKER, WILLIAM CODA, artist; b. Josephine, Tex., Mar. 2, 1924; s. William Coda and Ivah Merle (McBride) P.; student pub. schs., Corpus Christi, Tex.; m. Madeleine Bangos, July 11, 1959. With San Diego Sch. Fine Arts, 1947-49, San Francisco Sch. Fine Arts, 1949, Hans Hoffmans Studio, N.Y.C., 1950-51, Academie de la Grande Chaumiére, Paris, 1952; exhibits include: Stedelijk Mus., Amsterdam, the Netherlands, 1955, Salon de Mai, Paris, 1956, U. Ill., 1957, U. Maine, 1963, Chase Gallery, N.Y.C., 1963-70, M. Kagenovitch, Paris, 1979, others; represented in pub. collections: Mus. Modern Art, Paris, Stedelijk Mus., Amsterdam, Whitney Mus. Am. Art, N.Y.C., Moscow Mus., U. Maine, City U. N.Y., Mus. Beaux Arts, Bordeaux, France, Wichita (Kans.) Art Mus., others. Served with USAF, 1941-45. Recipient Burhle prize Gallery Kaganovitch, Paris, 1952. Address: 2 rue Gathelot Clamart France 92140

PARKER, WILLIAM KENT, baritone; b. Butler, Pa., Aug. 5, 1943; s. Harold M. and Louise (Cotter) P.; A.B. in Germanic Langs. and Lit., Princeton U., 1965. Baritone, Vienna (Austria) Volks Opera, 1971-73, also recital and concert appearances in Europe; singer with N.Y.C., San Francisco, Kansas City (Mo.) symphonies, Boston, San Francisco, Cin., Santa Fe, Washington, Balt., Chautauqua, Tulsa, Orlando (Fla.) operas, 1973—; rec. artist EMI, New World records. Served with chorus U.S. Army, 1966-70. Named Singer of Year, Nat. Assn. Tchrs. Singing, 1970; recipient Grand prize Internat. Singing competitions in Paris, Toulouse, France and Barcelona, Spain, also 1st prize Balt. Opera competition; winner Joy in Singing competition, N.Y.C., 1976; 1st Place prize Kennedy Center/Rockefeller Found. competition, 1979. Mem. Am. Guild Mus. Artists. Address: care Colbert 111 W 57th St New York City NY 10019*

PARKER, WILLIAM NELSON, educator; b. Columbus, Ohio, June 14, 1919; s. Murray Nelson and Evalyn Mae (Gares) P.; A.B. magna cum laude, Harvard, 1939, M.A., 1941, Ph.D., 1951; M.A., Yale, 1962; m. Josephine Yvonne Forbus, Sept. 20, 1948; children—Yvonne Victoria, Jarrett Nelson. Economist atomic energy com. U.S. Senate, 1946, Dept. State, 1947-48; cons. President's Materials Policy Commn., 1951; asst. prof. econs. Williams Coll., 1951-56; asso. prof., then prof. econs. U. N.C. at Chapel Hill, 1956-62; prof. econs. Yale, 1962—, dir. grad. studies in econs., 1968-72, 74-78. Del. to Am. Council Learned Socs., 1975-78. Served to maj. AUS, 1941-45. Nat. fellow, Harvard, 1935-41; Social Sci. Research Council fellow, 1948-51, 62-63; Ford Faculty fellow, 1958-59; Resources for Future research fellow, 1955-57; Guggenheim fellow, 1966-67. Mem. Econ. History Assn. (pres. (1969-70), Agrl. History Assn. (pres. 1979—). Author articles. Co-author: Coal and Steel in Western Europe, 1957. Contbr. 1st Internat. Conf. Econ. History, Stockholm, Sweden, 1960, 3d conf., Munich, Germany, 1965, 7th conf., Edinburgh, 1978; U.S./USSR Historians Conf., Moscow, 1978. Editor, contbr.: Trends in the American Economy in the Nineteenth Century, 1958; The Structure of the Cotton Economy of the Antebellum South, 1970; American Economic Growth, 1972; European Peasants and Their Markets, 1976; co-editor Jour. Econ. History, 1960-66. Home: 144 Edgehill Rd Hamden CT 06511

PARKER, WILLIAM RAYMOND, advt. exec.; b. New Castle, Pa., Apr. 28, 1913; s. Wayne D. and Elizabeth M. (Lee) P.; B.S., U. Pitts., 1935, M.A., 1938; postgrad. Duke U., 1937; m. Mildred Echko, Sept. 6, 1938 (div. Aug. 1966); children—Judith (Mrs. John S. Bernhard), Bonnie (Mrs. Stanley E. Porter), Robert Wayne; m. 2d, Doris Marsh, June 17, 1967. Head dept. bus. adminstrn. Lynchburg (Va.) Coll., 1941-42; sect. mgr. market devel. Westinghouse Electric Corp., 1942-47; with Ketchum MacLeod & Grove Inc., Pitts., 1947—, exec. v.p., 1970—, also dir.; chmn. bd., dir. Ketchum Internat., Inc., 1978—; sr. v.p., dir. Botsford Ketchum Inc., 1969—; chmn. bd. Botsford Ketchum Internat., Inc., 1972—; pres., chief exec. officer Ketchum Yellow Pages, Inc.; chmn., dir. Ketchum Internat. Ltd., London, 1972—; dir. David Williams & Ketchum Ltd., London, Durana Ketchum Werbeagentur, GmbH, Frankfurt, Germany, Roberts Ketchum Internat., Can. Treas., Pitts. PTA, 1970—; exec. com. assos. council U. Pitts.; chmn. troop com. Allegheny Trails council Boy Scouts Am., 1940-50; div. chmn. fund raising drives A.R.C., 1950-51, United Fund, 1960—. Bd. dirs., exec. com. Consumer Credit Counseling Service, Pitts. Conv. and Visitors' Bur.; bd. dirs. Better Bus. Bur.; v.p., bd. dirs. Jr. Achievement Southwest Pa.; trustee Ketchum, MacLeod & Grove Found. Mem. Am. Mktg. assn. (past pres.), Am. Mgmt. Assn., Fin. Execs. Inst., C. of C., Am. Assn. Advt. Agys. Rotarian (dir. 1968-69). Clubs: Duquesne, Highland Country (Pitts.). Contbr. to profl. jours. Home: 9909 Tomahawk Trail Wexford PA 15090 Office: 4 Gateway Center Pittsburgh PA 15222

PARKER, WYMAN WEST, librarian; b. Woburn, Mass., Oct. 31, 1912; s. Austin Wilbur and Elizabeth (West) P.; A.B., Middlebury Coll., 1934, A.M., 1939; B.L.S., Columbia, 1935; m. Jane Kingsley, Aug. 21, 1941; children—Christopher West, Kingsley Wyman, Andrew Duff. Stack supr., reference div. N.Y. Pub. Library, 1935-36; librarian Pynson Printers, 1936; acting librarian Middlebury Coll., 1936-37, librarian, 1938-41, librarian Bread Loaf Summer Sch. of English, 1933-37, Kenyon Coll., 1946-51, U. Cin., 1951-56, Wesleyan

U. Library, 1956-76; asst. prof. div. library sci. So. Conn. State Coll., 1976—; bd. dirs. Midwest Inter-Library Corp., 1951-56. Mem. adv. bd. W.P.A. Hist. Records Survey in Vt., 1941-42; adv. council Columbia Sch. Library Service, 1960-70. Served as lt. comdr. intelligence officer, U.S. Navy, Office Naval Intelligence, Cominch, Comsouwespac, 1941-45. Mem. A.L.A. (chmn. coll. libraries sect. 1949-50, chmn. awards com. 1957-59), Assn. Coll. and Reference Libraries (v.p. 1958-59, pres. 1959-60), Conn., Ohio library assns., Ohio Coll. Assn. (pres. library sect. 1948-49), Bibliog. Soc. Am., Bibliog. Soc. London, Am. Assn. U. Profs., Chi Psi. Conglist. Clubs: Grolier, Columbiad. Author: Henry Stevens of Vermont, 1963; Connecticut's Colonial and Continental Money, 1976; editorial bd. ACRL Book Selection Service, 1963-66, ACRL Choice mag., 1963-67. Contbr. articles library, bibliog., hist. mags. Home: 330 Pine St Middletown CT 06457

PARKES, ED, natural gas co. exec.; b. Bessemer, Ala., Nov. 22, 1904; s. William Jay and Myra (Huey) P.; B. Mech. Engring., U. Ark., 1925; m. Alice Washburn, Oct. 14, 1930; children—Ruth P. Bondurant, Myra P. Winder. Design engr. Ark. Power & Light Co., 1926-28; engr. United Gas Pipe Line Co. and predecessors, 1928-29, dist. supt., 1929-30, asst. gen. supt., 1930-37, gen. supt. field lines, 1937-47, v.p., dir., 1947-55, pres., 1956-67, also pres. Union Producing Co.; exec. v.p., dir. United Gas Corp., 1955-58, pres., dir., 1958-67, chmn. exec. com., 1967-68, dir., 1958-67; dir., chmn. exec. com. Pennzoil United, Inc., 1967-72; adv. dir. Pennzoil Co., 1972-76, dir. emeritus, 1976—. Chmn. Shreveport Downtown Devel. Commn., 1967-70; trustee Miss. Found. Ind. Coll., 1959-65, Inst. Gas Tech., 1959-65. Mem. Am. Petroleum Inst. (dir. 1956-68, exec. com. 1963-68), Am. Gas Assn. (pres. 1964, chmn. natural gas reserves com. 1957-69), Gulf South Research Inst. (trustee 1965-70), Ind. Natural Gas Assn. Am., Ind. Petroleum Assn. Am., Tau Beta Pi. Clubs: Rotary; Boston (New Orleans); Shreveport (La.). Home: 5815 Creswell Rd Shreveport LA 71106

PARKES, KENNETH CARROLL, ornithologist; b. Hackensack, N.J., Aug. 8, 1922; s. Walter Carroll and Lillian Carolyn (Capelle) P.; B.S., Cornell U., 1943, M.S., 1948, Ph.D., 1952; m. Ellen Pierce Stone, Sept. 6, 1953. Curator birds Cornell U., 1947-52; mem. staff Carnegie Mus., Pitts., 1953—, curator birds, 1962—, chief curator life scis., 1975—; research fellow epidemiology and microbiology U. Pitts., 1956, vis. lectr. Pymatuning Field Lab., 1957, adj. mem. grad. faculty, 1963—. Mem. adminstrv. bd. Lab. Ornithology, Cornell U., 1962-68, 70-75. Bd. dirs. Del. Mus. Natural History, 1976—. Served with AUS, 1943-46. Fellow Am. Ornithologists Union (2d v.p. 1975-76); mem. Wilson Ornithol. Soc. (pres. 1973-75). Democrat. Unitarian. Taxonomic editor: Avian Biology, 1971-75, co-editor, 1977—. Contbr. articles to profl. jours., encys. Office: Carnegie Museum Natural History Pittsburgh PA 15213

PARKES, ROSS LINDSAY MICHAEL, dancer, choreographer; b. Sydney, Australia, June 17, 1940; s. Edmund Hereward and Doris Lillian (Porter) P.; came to U.S., 1964; student Valrene Tweedie Studio, Sydney, 1960-61, Audrey de Vos, London, 1962-64, Martha Graham Studio, N.Y.C., 1964-66, Mary Anthony, N.Y.C., 1966—. Mem. Ballet Francais, Sydney, 1959, Ballet Australia, Sydney, 1961, Ethel Winter Co., N.Y.C., 1965; soloist Bertram Ross Co., N.Y.C., 1965-66, Helen McGehee Co., N.Y.C., 1965-73; mem. Martha Graham Co., N.Y.C., 1965, prin. dancer, 72-76, asso. artistic dir., 1975; soloist Sophie Maslow Co., N.Y.C., 1965-67, Carmen de Lavallade Co., N.Y.C., 1967, Glen Tetley Co., N.Y.C., 1966-67; prin. dancer Pa. Ballet Co., Phila., 1966-72, Mary Anthony Co., N.Y.C., 1966—; asst. dir. Mary Anthony Dance Theatre, 1970-79, co-dir., 1979—; guest artist Bat-Dor Co., Tel Aviv, 1969, Jeff Duncan Co., N.Y.C., 1970; appearances include: Yankee Doodle Comes to Town, Oxford, Liverpool, Bristol, and Glasgow, Eng., 1962-63, No Strings, London, 1963-64, The Five Senses, Nat. Ednl. TV, 1968; lectr., tchr. in field; choreography works: Inside of Him, 1971, 12345, 1971, Tides, 1973, Land of Make Believe, 1977; Quartet for the End of Time, 1978, Songs by Request, 1978. Nat. Endowment of Arts grantee, 1973. Home: 259 Bleecker St New York NY 10014 Office: 736 Broadway New York NY 10003

PARKHURST, CHARLES, museum ofcl.; b. Columbus, Ohio, Jan. 23, 1913; s. Charles Percy and Isabella Woodbridge P.; B.A., Williams Coll., 1935; A.M., Oberlin Coll., 1938; M.F.A., Princeton, 1941; m. Elizabeth Huntington Rusling, June 15, 1938 (div. 1962); children—Andrew Christopher, Bruce; m. 2d, Rima Zevin Julyan, Sept. 1, 1962 (div. 1974); 1 dau., Brooke; stepchildren—Candace, David, Mark. Research asst. Nat. Gallery of Art, Washington, 1941-42, asst. curator (registrar), 1942-43; dep. chief, monuments, fine arts and archives sect. Allied Mil. Govt. in both U.S. Zones, Germany, 1945-46; asst. curator, Albright Art Gallery, Buffalo, 1946-47; asst. prof. art and archaeology Princeton, also asst. dir. Princeton Art Mus., 1947-49; head dept. fine arts, dir. Art Mus., prof. history and appreciation of art Oberlin Coll., 1949-62; dir. Balt. Mus. Art, 1962-70; asst. dir. Nat. Gallery Art, Washington, 1971—; faculty fellow Fund for Advancement Edn., 1952-53; Fulbright research scholar U. Utrecht (Netherlands), 1956-57; vis. faculty U. Minn., 1953, UCLA, 1964, Johns Hopkins, 1971, U. Wis., 1979, Williams Coll., 1980; lectr. on art, color theory and museology. Chmn. Md. Arts Council, 1967-68; chmn. Md. Revolutionary War Bicentennial Commn., 1968-70; chmn. Gov.'s Council on Arts in Md., 1966-68. Served with USNR, 1943-62. Decorated chevalier Legion d'Honneur de la République Francaise, 1947. Recipient research grants Am. Council Learned Socs. and Am. Philos. Soc., 1961. Mem. Coll. Art Assn. (pres. 1958-60, dir.), Intermuseum Conservation Assn. (co-founder), Am. Assn. Mus. Dirs., Am. Assn. Museums (pres. 1966-68, accreditation com. 1970-76). Contbr. articles to profl. jours. Office: Nat Gallery of Art Washington DC 20565

PARKHURST, CHARLES CHANDLER, ret. educator, author, indsl. communications cons.; b. Somerville, Mass., Dec. 19, 1904; s. Charles Erwin and Helen Augusta (Chandler) P.; B.B.A., Boston U. Coll. of Bus. Adminstrn., 1926, A.M., 1930; D.Sc. in Bus Adminstrn., Piedmont Coll., 1964; Litt.D. (hon.), Olivet (Mich.) Coll., 1966; m. Lillian Andrews, June 1935. With Ford Motor Co., 1926, Chrysler Motor Car sales div., 1928; dir. English, Catherine Gibbs Sch., 1929-30; instr. English, Everett High Sch., 1930-37; chmn. All-University English Dept., 1949-51; instr. English, Boston U. Coll. of Bus. Adminstrn., 1931-35, asst. prof., 1935-42, asso. prof. 1943-69, prof., head English dept. Boston U. Coll. of Practical Arts and Letters, 1944, prof. English and Bus. Communications Coll. Bus. Adminstrn., 1956-69; indsl. communications cons., lectr., 1970—; lectr. Am. Inst. Banking; dir. English, Bentley Sch. of Accounting and Finance, 1937-48; lit. counsellor and corr. cons. for banks, ins. cos., bus. and indsl. plants; dir. edn. programs for bus. and indsl. orgns. Dir. Ware and Post-War Tng. Inst., Boston U. Coll. Bus. Adminstrn. Mem. Winchester Finance Com.; mem. Park Commn., Winchester, Mass.; pres. Hedding (N.H.) Chatauqua Assn.; trustee Hedding Camp Meeting Assn. Fellow Am. Bus. Writing Assn. (past pres.); mem. Nat. Office Mgr. Assn., AAUP, NEA, Nat. Council English Tchrs., Modern Lang. Assn., Eastern Comml. Tchrs. Assn., Newcomen Soc. of Eng., U.S. Power Squadron, USCG Aux., Francis Scott Key Meml. Assn., Lambda Chi Alpha. Methodist. Clubs: Internat. Rotary (hon.), Boston Authors, Boston University Faculty. Republican. Author: (with Grove) English Elements and Principles; (with Roy Davis) Business Writing Theory and Practice; Modern Business English; English for Business rev. 1964; Practical Problems in English for Business, rev. 1958; Using Words Effectively (vols A. and B.), rev. 1958; A Direct Approach to Writing; Business English for College, 1957; Modern Business Communication for Better Human Relations, 1942, rev. edits., 1949, 55, 61, 66, 76; Case Studies in Business Communication, 1960; Modern Executive's Guide to Effective Communication, 1962; also articles ednl., bus. mags. Editor: Say What You See. Home: 5 Everell Rd Winchester MA 01890 summer 33 Crosby St South Yarmouth Cape Cod MA 02664 Office: 5 Everell Rd Winchester MA 01890

PARKHURST, GEORGE LEIGH, oil and chem. exec.; b. Evanston, Ill., Jan. 10, 1907; s. George T. and Jessie (Furness) P.; B.S., Armour Inst. Tech., 1927; grad. study U. Chgo., 1927-30; J.D., De Paul U., 1934; m. Margaret Sarles, July 2, 1932; children—Peter, Perry, Paul. Chemist, chem. engr., sr. patent atty. Standard Oil Co. (Ind.), Whiting, Ind. and Chgo., 1927-41; asst. dir. refining, contract exec. Petroleum Adminstrn. for War, Washington, 1941-45; pres. Oronite Chem. Co., San Francisco, 1946-49, chmn. bd., 1949-55; chmn. bd. Chevron Research Corp., 1949-53, dirn., 1945-71; v.p. Standard Oil Co. Calif., 1949-71, dir., 1955-71; v.p., dir. Calif. Oil Co., 1960-68; pres. Chevron Chem. Co., 1956-58, dir., 1956—; chmn. Irving Oil Co., 1962-63; dir. Arabian-Am. Oil Co., 1955-71; dir. Trans-Arabian Pipe Line Co., 1955-71; cons., 1972—; dir. Fisher Berkeley Corp., Natomas Co. Bd. dirs. Coll. Prep. Sch., 1973-77. Fellow AAAS (v.p. 1954), Am. Inst. Chemists; mem. Am. Chem. Soc. (chmn. Chgo. sect. 1971, trustee Calif. sect. 1969—), San Francisco Com. on Fgn. Relations, Alpha Chi Sigma, Tau Beta Pi, Phi Lambda Upsilon, Delta Theta Phi. Clubs: World Trade, Bohemian (San Francisco); Chemists (Chgo.). Contbr. articles to tech. publs. Patentee in field. Home: 150 Val de Flores Dr Burlingame CA 94010

PARKHURST, JOHN DAVID, environ. engr.; b. Bridger, Mont., July 1, 1917; s. William Elisha and Cornelia May (Parks) P.; B.S.C.E., U. Calif., Berkeley, 1942; m. Grace Allee Covey, June 27, 1942; children—Ellen, David, Elizabeth. Chief engr., gen. mgr. Los Angeles County San. Dists., 1961-79, ret., 1979; cons. environ. engring. to various govt. agys. Served with USPHS, 1944-46. Named 1 of 10 Top Public Works Engrs., Am. Public Works Assn., 1970, Engr. of Yr., Inst. Advancement Engring., 1978. Mem. Water Pollution Control Fedn. (pres. 1974), Am. Acad. Environ. Engring. (pres. 1977), ASCE (Rudolph Hering medal 1973), Internat. Assn. Water Pollution Research. Contbr. numerous articles on research, design and operation engring. projects to profl. jours. Home: 154 W La Sierra Dr Arcadia CA 91006*

PARKHURST, STEPHEN RYDER, banker; b. Boston, Sept. 15, 1930; s. Richard and Katharine (Ryder) P.; A.B., Dartmouth, 1952; M.B.A., Babson Inst., Wellesley, Mass., 1957; m. Lorraine H. St. Croix, Sept. 15, 1956; children—John Lewis, Laura, Sarah, David Andrew, Susan. With First Nat. Bank Boston, 1953-55; with New Eng. Mchts. Nat. Bank, Boston, 1957—, v.p., comptroller, 1967-68, v.p. advanced computer systems planning and mgmt. sci., 1968-71, v.p., cashier, 1971—, asst. sec., 1971-73, sec., 1973—; sec. New Eng. Mchts. Co., Inc., 1971—; sec., dir. New Eng. Mchts. Bank Internat., 1971—, New Eng. Merchants Leasing Corp., 1971—, New Eng. Enterprise Capital Corp., 1971—, Savs. Mgmt. Computer Corp., 1968-73, New Eng. Investment Services Corp., 1974—; dir. Charlesbank Homes, 1977—. Instr., Am. Inst. Banking, 1965-68. Chmn. Winchester Sch. Com., 1971-76; mem. fin. com., Winchester, 1968-70, chmn. forest com., 1978—; trustee Lincoln Filene Center Citizenship and Pub. Affairs, Tufts U., 1968—. Mem. Am. Soc. Corp. Secs., Bank Adminstrn. Inst. (v.p. Boston chpt. 1979-80), Dartmouth Alumni Assn. Boston (sec. 1968-71). Unitarian (treas., mem. standing com. 1963- 70). Home: 21 Ridgefield Rd Winchester MA 01890 Office: New Eng Merchants Nat Bank 28 State St Boston MA 02109

PARKHURST, VIOLET KINNEY, artist; b. Derby Line, Vt., Apr. 26, 1926; d. Edson Frank and Rosa (Beauchene) Kinney; student Mus. Fine Arts, Boston, 1941-42, Baylor Coll., 1942-43; Calif. State U., Los Angeles, 1955-56; m. Donald W. Parkhurst, Apr. 10, 1948. Fgn. corr. Brazilian mags., 1944-51; tech. illustrator Douglas Aircraft, 1952-53; one man shows include: Biltmore Galleries, Los Angeles, 1975-76, Saddleback Gallery, Santa Ana, Calif., 1977: group exhbns. include: Cultural Exchange Tour of European Museums, 1962-67, Laguna Art Festival, 1964, Catalina Invitational, 1975-77; owner galleries Ports o Call, Los Angeles, Laguna Beach, Calif., Seaport, Long Beach, Calif., Queen Mary, Long Beach. Fellow Am. Inst. Fine Arts. Author: Parkhurst on Seascapes, 1973; Parkhurst Painting at the Seashore, Parkhurst on Sunsets. Home: 2300 Daladier Dr Rancho Palos Verdes CA 90274. *The mystery and fascination of the sea, a source of food, transportation and recreation, has always held a special place in my heart. I have tried to capture it on canvas in a traditional approach so that everyone can share its beauty. My spirit seems refreshed and revived when I am near the sea. The shimmering blue depths is my way of communing with the elements from whence life sprang.*

PARKINS, BARBARA, actress; b. 1942. Regular on TV series Peyton Place; movies: Valley of the Dolls, 1967, The Kremlin Letter, 1970, The Mephisto Waltz, 1971, Puppet on a Chain, 1972, Asylum, 1972, Shout at the Devil, 1976; appeared on novel-for-TV Captains and the Kings, 1976; ltd. dramatic series Testimony of Two Men, 1977, Jennie: Lady Randolph Churchill, 1975, TV movies The Law of the Land, 1976, Ziegfield: The Man and His Women, 1978. Office: care William Morris Agy 151 El Camino Beverly Hills CA 90212*

PARKINS, FREDERICK MILTON, educator; b. Princeton, N.J., Sept. 8, 1935; s. William Milton and Phyllis Virginia (Plyler) P.; student Carleton Coll., 1953-56; D.D.S., U. Pa., 1960; M.S.D. in Pedodontics, U. N.C., Chapel Hill, 1965; Ph.D. in Physiology, 1969; m. Carolyn R. Rude; children—Bradford, Christopher, Eric. Instr. pedodontics U. N.C., 1965-67; asst. prof. pedodontics U. Pa., 1967-69, dir. Dental Aux. Utilization program, chmn. pedodontics, 1968-69; asso. prof., head pedodontics U. Iowa, Iowa City, 1969-72, prof., head pedodontics, 1972-74, asst. dean acad. affairs Coll. Dentistry, 1974-75, asso. dean acad. affairs, 1975-79, dir. continuing edn., 1975-79; prof., dean Sch. Dentistry, U. Louisville, 1979—. Cons. Div. Dental Health USPHS, 1969-72; dental cons., med. staff Children's Hosp. Phila., 1968-71; cons., mem. pedodontic adv. com. Council Dental Edn., 1974—, chmn. pedodontic adv. com., 1978-79, cons. council on legislation, 1978—; dental cons. Aux. Utilization VA, 1968-69; cons. Bur. Health Resources Devel., 1974-76; Robert Wood Johnson Congl. fellow Inst. of Medicine, 1977-78. Served with USNR, 1960-63. USPHS postdoctoral fellow, 1963-67; NIH grantee, 1971-75. Recipient Earle Banks Hoyt Teaching award, 1969. Fellow Am. Acad. Pedodontics (chmn. research com. 1973, Ann. Research award 1968; chmn. advanced edn. com. 1974-75, chmn. dental care programs com. 1979—), AAAS; mem. Am. Soc. Dentistry for Children (exec. bd. Iowa unit 1969-75; award com. 1973-76, edn. com. 1974-77, chmn. research adv. com. 1973-77), Biophys. Soc., Internat. Assn. Dental Research, N.Y. Acad. Dentistry, Am. Dental Assn., Am. Assn. Dental Schs. (chmn. pedodontics sect. chmn. 1976, chmn. continuing edn. sect. 1979, legislation com. 1978—), Aircraft Owners and Pilots Assn., Sigma Xi, Omicron Kappa Upsilon. Unitarian. Asso. editor, mem. editorial bd. Jour. Preventive Dentistry, 1975-79; dental editorial reviewer Jour. Pediatrics, 1969—; editorial reviewer Jour. Dental Edn., 1978—. Contbr. to profl. publs. Office: Sch Dentistry Univ Louisville Louisville KY 40232

PARKINSON, CHARLES JAY, corp. exec., lawyer; b. Salt Lake City, Apr. 30, 1909; s. Fred L. and Lydia (Rich) P.; student Oxford (Eng.) U., 1929-30; B.S., U. Utah, 1931, J.D., 1934; m. Edith Williams, Jan. 1, 1936 (dec. 1977); children—Dennis J., Christine Parkinson Mitchell; m. 2d, Adele Williams Warden, 1978. Admitted to Utah bar, 1934, Nev. bar 1944, Calif. bar, 1945, N.Y. bar, 1959; mem. various law firms Salt Lake City, 1934-40; counsel, asst. sec. Basic Magnesium Inc., Henderson, Nev.; partner firm Lawson & Parkinson, Los Angeles, 1945; mem. firm Van Cott, Bagley, Cornwall & McCarthy, Salt Lake City, 1945-56; v.p., dir. Anaconda Aluminum Co., N.Y.C. 1955-57; with Anaconda Co., N.Y.C., 1957-71, pres., 1964-69, chmn. bd., chief exec. officer, 1969-71; former chmn., dir. Chile Copper Co., Chile Exploration Co., Andes Copper Mining Co.; dir. Stauffer Chem. Co., Westport, Conn., TRI Holdings, S.A., San Francisco. Former atty. for Morgan County, Utah. Vice pres. bd. dirs. Speech and Hearing Rehab. Inst., N.Y.C.; bd. dirs. United Cerebral Palsy Research and Edn., Inc., until 1979. Mem. Am. Bar Assn., bar assns. Calif., Utah, Nev., N.Y., Am. Arbitration Assn. (Sylvan Gotshal World Trade Arbitration medal 1969), Downtown Lower Manhattan Assn. (dir. 1965-70), Conf. Bd., Assn. Gen. Counsel, N.Y. State C. of C. (past v.p.), Am. Inst. Mining, Metall. and Petroleum Engrs. (asso.), Pi Kappa Alpha. Mem. Ch. of Jesus Christ of Latter-day Saints. Clubs: Alta (Salt Lake City); Owl and Key; Creek, Lawyers, University (N.Y.C.). Home: 2162 Arbor Ln PO Box 17556 Salt Lake City UT 84117 Office: PO Box 17556 Salt Lake City UT 84117 also 2164 Arbor Ln Salt Lake City UT 84117

PARKINSON, CYRIL NORTHCOTE, historian, author; b. Barnard Castle, Eng., July 30, 1909; s. William Edward and Rose Emily Mary (Curnow) P.; M.A., Emmanuel Coll., Cambridge U., 1932; Ph.D., Kings Coll., U. London, 1933-35; LL.D. (hon.), U. Md., 1974; D.Litt., Troy State U., 1977; m. Elizabeth Ann Fry, Sept. 23, 1952; children—Charles Nigel Kennedy, Antonia Patricia Jane, Jonathan Neville Trollope. Fellow Emmanuel Coll., 1935-37; sr. history master Blundell's Sch., Tiverton, Eng., 1937-39; lectr. naval and maritime history U. Liverpool, 1945-50; Raffles prof. history U. Malaya, 1950-58; vis. prof. Harvard, U. Ill., U. Calif. at Berkeley, 1958-60; prof. emeritus Troy State U., Ala.; chmn. Leviathan House Pub. Co., London and N.Y.C.; frequent TV appearances. Vice pres. Malayan Hist. Soc., 1955-58. Recipient Julian Corbett prize London U., 1935. Served to maj. Brit. Army, 1940-45. Fellow Royal Hist. Soc.; mem. Academie de Marine, Soc. Nautical Research (past council mem.). Author: Edward Pellew, Viscount Exmouth, 1934; Trade in the Eastern Seas, 1937; The Trade Winds, 1948; War in the Eastern Seas, 1954; Portsmouth Point (anthology), 1948; Always a Fusilier, 1949; British Intervention in Malaya, 1960; The Rise of Port Liverpool, 1952; (with Mrs. Parkinson) Heroes of Malaya, 1956; Parkinson's Law, 1957; The Evolution of Political Thought, 1959; The Law and the Profits, 1960; In-laws and Outlaws, 1962; East and West, 1963; Ponies Plot, 1965; A Law Unto Themselves, 1966; Left Luggage, 1967; Mrs. Parkinson's Law, 1968; The Law of Delay, 1970; The Life and Times of Horatio Hornblower, 1971; The Fur-Lined Mousetrap, 1972; Devil to Pay, 1973; Big Business, 1974; The Fireship, 1975; The Rise of Big Business, 1976; Gunpowder, Treason and Plot, 1977; Britannia Rules, 1978; Dean Reckoning, 1978; Jeeves, a gentleman's personal gentleman, 1979. Home: Anneville Manor Anneville Rd Vale Guernsey Channel Islands Great Britain. *We have to discard our idea of progress. Civilizations trace a curve of achievement. When we are on the upward slope we imagine that we shall rise indefinitely. But the curve levels off and then the descent begins. This has happened to western civilization in the 20th century and all who have been taught to believe in progress feel bewildered, cheated and lost. We should understand the situation better if we realized that it has all happened before, not once but many times, and that what follows summer must always be autumn. There is much we can do in autumn but not until we have admitted to ourselves that autumn has come and that winter lies ahead.*

PARKINSON, ELIZABETH BLISS, civic worker; b. N.Y.C., Sept. 25, 1907; d. Cornelius Newton and Zaidee Clark (Cobb) Bliss; grad. Chapin Sch., N.Y.C.; m. John Parkinson, Jr., Dec., 1932 (div. Dec. 1945); children—John III, Zaidee (Mrs. Richard John Dufallo). Asst. dir. vols. and home service vols. N.Y. chpt. A.R.C., 1942-45; mem. art com. Addison Gallery, Phillips Acad., Andover, Mass., 1953-72. Trustee, Archives Am. Art; trustee Mus. Modern Art, 1941—, pres., 1965-68, v.p., 1968-78, vice chmn., 1978—, pres. internat. council, 1957-65. Address: 215 E 72d St New York NY 10021

PARKINSON, ETHELYN MINERVA, author; b. nr. Oconto, Wis., Sept. 13, 1906; d. James Nelson and Ethel Mabelle (Bigelow) P.; teaching certificate County Normal Sch., Oconto Falls, Wis., 1923; R.N., Bellin Meml. Sch. Nursing, 1928; Recipient Wis. Dramatic Soc. 1st place for playwriting, 1933; 1st place children's fiction Scholastic Book Services, 1957; Abingdon award, 1970; award of merit Wis. Hist. Soc., 1971. Republican. Presbyn. Author: Double Trouble for Rupert, 1958; Triple Trouble for Rupert, 1960; Good Old Archibald, 1960; The Merry Mad Bachelors, 1961; The Terrible Troubles of Rupert Piper, 1963; The Operation that Happened to Rupert Piper, 1966; Today I Am a Ham, 1968; Higgins of the Railroad Museum, 1970; Elf King Joe, 1970; Never Go Anywhere with Digby, 1971; Rupert Piper and Megan, the Valuable Girl, 1972; Rupert Piper and the Dear, Dear Birds (Jr. Lit. Guild selection), 1976; Rupert Piper and the Boy Who Could Knit, 1979. Address: 1031 Anderson Dr Green Bay WI 54304. *I look at any success I may have had most humbly and most thankfully. I'm humble because I have a feeling that I haven't done things, but rather that things have happened to me. Perhaps that's because people have inspired and so helped me, all the way, children especially. I'm dedicated to giving as much happiness as I can to children, through my writing, and other ways. Childhood seems shorter now than ever, and when one of my stories makes children happy, makes them laugh, I am happy, too, and grateful.*

PARKINSON, GEORGE AMBROSE, educator; b. Columbus, Ohio, Jan. 22, 1899; s. Daniel Homer and Cynthia Catherine (English) P.; B.S., Ohio State U., 1922, M.A., 1923; Ph.D., U. Wis., 1929; m. Mildred Jane Smith, June 17, 1920 (dec.); children—Virginia Jane, George (dec.), Daniel Smith; m. 2d, Myrtle Ann Volger, June 20, 1975. Prin., Parkinson High Sch., Zanesville, Ohio, 1916-17, Ripley High Sch., Greenwich, Ohio, 1917-18; instr. math. Worthington (Ohio) High Sch., 1921-23; instr. engring. math. U. Wis., 1923-27 mem. faculty Milw. extension div., 1927- 56, div. dir., prof., 1945-56; vice provost, prof. U. Wis., 1956-58; dir. Milw. Tech. Coll., 1958-68, dir. emeritus, 1968—; dir. NROS, Milw., 1949-59; adv. com. USCG Acad., 1955-63, chmn., 1960-62. Mem. Res. Forces Policy Bd. Office Sec. Def., 1949-56; mem. Govs. adv. com. Civil Def., Wis., 1951-56; dep. dir. Milw. Civil Def. Adminstrn., 1948-62, dir., 1962-63. Chmn. Milw. Social Devel. Commn., 1962-65; chmn. program devel. com., dir. Milw. Met. YMCA, 1950-69; dir. Milw. Council Adult Learning; mem. Gov.'s Adv. Com. Title I, Higher Edn. Act of 1965, 1966—. Trustee, v.p. Midwestern Ednl. TV, Inc.; mem. policy bd. Gt. Plains Nat. Instrnl. TV Library, 1962—; cons. vocat. and tech. edn. HEW, 1969, GAO Evaluation Manpower Programs, 1969—. Served with USN, 1940-45, comdg. officer Escort Div. 48, Atlantic Fleet, 1944-45; now vice adm., ret. Decorated Legion Merit, D.S.M. with Gold Star,

Naval Res. medal, Armed Forces Res. medal; Engr. of the Yr., Milw. Soc. Engrs., 1955; Citizenship gold medal, S.A.R.; State award Merit, Wis. Restaurant Assn., 1967; Disting. Service award Milw. Council Adult Learning, 1967; Headliner award Milw. Press Club, 1968; Wisdom award of Honor, 1970. Mem. Am. Tech. Edn. Assn. (trustee 1962-75), Am. Math. Soc., Am. Math. Assn. (chmn. Wis. sect. 1935-36), Nat. Assn. Adult Edn., Assn. U. Evening Colls. (nat. pres. 1956), Wis. Vocat. Dirs. Assn. (pres. 1965-66), S.A.R. (pres. Wis. 1955; nat. v.p. gen. 1957), Res. Officers Assn. U.S. (nat. chmn. naval affairs com.; pres. Wis. Dept.), Navy League U.S. (chmn., dir. Milw. council), Alpha Kappa Psi, Sigma Xi, Phi Delta Kappa, Gamma Alpha, Pi Mu Epsilon, Phi Eta Sigma. Acacia. Presbyn. Mason. Clubs: University, Milwaukee Press (Milw.); Army and Navy (Washington); University (life) (Madison, Wis.). Author: Brief Introduction to Analytic Geometry, 1938; co-author: Mathematics and Society, 1939; also papers and articles on vocational, tech., adult edn. and civil def. Home: Rural Route 2 Box 662 Oostburg WI 53070 Office: 1015 N 6th St Milwaukee WI 53203. *Pay your debts; keep your word; and walk humbly with your God.*

PARKINSON, JOHN DAVID, elec. and electronic mfg. co. exec.; b. Phila., Nov. 26, 1929; s. Granville and Dorothy (Crooks) P.; B.S., Rutgers U., 1951; m. Sally Ann Brokaw, Nov. 10, 1956; children—David Gregory, Rex Granville, Leanne. With Thomas & Betts Corp., Elizabeth, N.J., 1954—, dist. sales mgr., Syracuse, 1960-62, Phila., 1962, asst. gen. sales mgr., 1963-66, gen. sales mgr., 1967, v.p. mktg., dir., 1968—, v.p., gen. mgr., 1969, pres. div., 1969—, v.p. corp., 1971, exec. v.p., 1971-74, pres., chief exec. officer, 1974—, chmn. bd., 1975—; dir. Perkin-Elmer Corp. Mem. Nat. Elec. Mfrs. Assn. (bd. govs.), Elec. Mfrs. Club. Clubs: Fiddler's Elbow Country (Bedminster, N.J.); Union League (N.Y.C.). Home: Spring Hollow Rd Far Hills NJ 07931 Office: 920 Route 202 Raritan NJ 08869

PARKINSON, THOMAS CARTER, food co. exec.; b. Washington, Feb. 29, 1920; s. Clinton Joseph and Lillian Estelle (Carter) P.; student U. Va., 1938-40; m. Joan Gorsuch, June 1, 1974; children—Thomas Carter, Elizabeth Lee. With McCormick & Co., Inc., Balt., 1946—, v.p., gen. mgr., 1964-68, v.p., mem. exec. com., 1968-69, exec. v.p., 1969—; chmn. bd. Club House Foods, Ltd.; dir. Tubed Products, Inc. Bd. govs. Acad. Food Mktg., St. Josephs U. Served to lt. col. USAAF, 1940-45. Decorated Silver Star, Legion of Merit, D.F.C., Air medal with 4 oak leaf clusters. Mem. Advt. Club Balt., Mchts. Club Balt., Food Merchandisers Edn. Council. Clubs: Shriners; Center; Balt. Country; Farmington Country; N.Y. Athletic. Office: 414 Light St Baltimore MD 21202

PARKINSON, THOMAS FRANCIS, educator, author; b. San Francisco, Feb. 24, 1920; s. T. F. and Catherine (Green) P.; A.B. summa cum laude, U. Calif. at Berkeley, 1945, M.A., 1946, Ph.D., 1948; m. Ariel Reynolds, Dec. 23, 1948; children—Katherine, Chrysa. Asst. prof. English, U. Calif. at Berkeley, 1948-53, asso. prof., 1953-60, prof. English, 1960—; vis. asst. prof. Wesleyan U., Conn., 1951-52; Fulbright prof. U. Bordeaux (France), 1953-54, U. Frankfurt, (Germany), 1954, Nice and Grenoble (France), 1965-66; vis. prof. U. Wash., Seattle, 1968; vis. lectr. Oxford (Eng.) U., 1969; vis. prof. U. York (Eng.), 1970; mem. lit. panel Nat. Endowment for Arts, 1971-74. Served with USAAF, 1943. Guggenheim fellow, 1957-58; Inst. Creative Art fellow, 1963-64; Am. Philos. Soc. Travel grantee, 1957, 68. Mem. AAUP (pres. Berkeley chpt. 1962-63), Modern Lang. Assn. Democrat. Roman Catholic. Author: Men, Women, Vines, 1959; Thanatos, 1965, rev. edit., 1975; Protect the Earth, 1970; Homage to Jack Spicer, 1970; W.B. Yeats, Self-Critic and the Later Poetry, 2 vols., 1971; (verse drama) What the Blind Man Saw, 1974; (verse) The Canters of Thomas Parkinson, 1977; Hart Crane and Yvor Winters: Their Literary Correspondence, 1978. Editor: A Casebook on the Beat, 1960; Masterworks of Prose, 1961, Robert Lowell, 1969. Home: 1001 Cragmont Berkeley CA 94708 Office: Dept English Univ Calif Berkeley CA 94720

PARKINSON, WILLIAM CHARLES, physicist; b. Jarvis, Ont., Can., Feb. 11, 1918; s. Charles Franklin and Euphemia Alice (Johnston) P.; came to U.S., 1925, naturalized, 1941; B.S.E., U. Mich., Ann Arbor, 1940, M.S., 1941, Ph.D., 1948; m. Martha Bennett Capron, Aug. 2, 1944; children—Martha Reed, William Reid. Physicist, Applied Physics Lab., Johns Hopkins U., 1942-46, OSRD, 1943-44; mem. faculty U. Mich., 1947—, prof. physics, 1958—, dir. cyclotron lab., 1962-77; mem. subcom. nuclear structure NRC, 1959-68; mem. nuclear physics sub panel mgmt. and costs nuclear program, 1969-70; adv. panel physics NSF, 1966-69, cons. grad. sci. facilities, 1968, chmn. postdoctoral fellowship evaluation panel, 1969; cons. to govt. and industry, 1955—; occasional mem. Trinity Coll., Cambridge, Eng. Recipient Ordnance Devel. award Navy Dept., 1946; Fulbright research scholar Cavendish Lab., Cambridge U., 1952-53. Fellow Am. Phys. Soc.; mem. N.Y. Acad. Scis., Sigma Xi, Phi Kappa Phi, Kappa Kappa Phi. Patentee in field. Home: 1600 Sheridan Dr Ann Arbor MI 48104 Office: Dept Physics Univ Mich Ann Arbor MI 48109

PARKMAN, PAUL DOUGLAS, FDA ofcl. HEW; b. Auburn, N.Y., May 29, 1932; B.S., St. Lawrence U., 1957, D.Sc. (hon.), 1970; M.D., SUNY, 1957; m. Elmerina Leonardi, July 2, 1955. Intern, Mary Imogene Bassett Hosp., Cooperstown, N.Y., 1957-58; resident pediatrics Upstate Med. Center Hosp., SUNY, Syracuse, 1958-60; med. officer Walter Reed Army Inst. Research, 1960-63; chief sect. gen. virology Lab. Viral Immunology NIH, HEW, 1963-72, dir. div. virology Bur. Biologics, FDA, Bethesda, Md., 1972-73, dep. dir. Bur. Biologics, 1973—. Recipient Superior Service award, 1966, Disting. Service award, 1969 (both HEW); Letter of Commendation, Pres. L.B. Johnson, 1966; E. Mead Johnson award Am. Acad. Pediatrics, 1967; Max Weinstein award U.S. Cerebral Palsy, 1967; award for disting. service to children Parents' Mag., 1969; Gold Plate award Am. Acad. Achievement, 1970; Internat. award J.P. Kennedy, Jr. Found., 1971; Centennial medallion, Upstate Med. Center, 1972; Commendable Service award, 1975, award of merit, 1977 (both FDA); named One of Ten Outstanding Young Men, U.S. Jaycees, 1967. Diplomate Am. Bd. Pediatrics. Mem. Assn. Immunology, Soc. Pediatric Research (emeritus), Am. Epidemiol. Soc., AAAS, Am. Soc. Microbiology, Am. Acad. Microbiology. Office: Bur Biologics NIH Bldg 29 8800 Rockville Pike Bethesda MD 20205

PARKS, ALBERT (FIELDING), ret. govt. ofcl.; b. Sulphur Rock, Ark., June 27, 1909; s. Hugh Woodsworth and Sarah (Runyan) P.; A.B., Ark. Coll., 1929; postgrad. U. Tenn., 1929-30, 35; M.S., N.Y.U., 1931; m. Agnes Murillo Braley, Nov. 12, 1933; 1 dau., Stephanie. Teaching fellow U. Tenn., 1929-30; teaching fellow N.Y.U., 1930-31; head chemistry dept. Ark. Coll., 1931-36; head Farm Mapping Program, Dept. Agr., Batesville, Ark., 1936; jr. seafood inspector FDA, HEW, New Orleans, 1937; asst. chief U.S. Customs Lab., New Orleans, 1937-49; asst. chief Tech. Service, Bur. Customs, 1949-59; asst. chief tech. service U.S. Tariff Commn., Washington, 1960-69, dir. Office Trade and Industry, 1969-75, chmn. interdepartmental com. for statis. annotation of tariff schedules; ret., 1975; ofcl. U.S. observer Customs Cooperation Council, Brussels, Belgium, 1965; adviser to House Com. on Ways and Means and Senate Com. on Fin. on Tariffs and Trade Matters; cons. for internat. trade, 1975—. Mem. exams. div. Ark. Bd. Edn., 1932-35; mem. Bd. Health, Batesville, 1931-35, N. Ridge Citizens Assn., Alexandria, Va.; bd. dirs. Ark. Inter-Collegiate Athletic Assn. Served to lt. comdr. USNR, 1943-46. Recipient letters of commendation Chmn. Ways and Means Com. and Chief Counsel Senate Fin. Com., 1969. Fellow Am. Inst. Chemists (past pres. Washington chpt.); mem. Am. Chem. Soc., Am. Soc. Quality Control, N.Y. Acad. Scis., Res. Officers Assn., Alpha Chi Sigma, Alpha Lambda Tau. Methodist. Home: 1500 Fairway Dr West Memphis AR 72301 Office: Suite 902A Crystal Mall I 911 Jefferson Davis Hwy Arlington VA 22202

PARKS, BERT, entertainer; b. Atlanta, Dec. 30, 1914; s. Aaron and Hattie (Spiegel) Jacobson; student Marist Coll., Atlanta, 1926-32; m. Annette Liebman, June 8, 1943; children—Jeffrey, Joel, Annette. Radio announcer radio sta. WGST, Atlanta, 1932; staff announcer CBS, N.Y.C., 1933-39; master of ceremonies Break the Bank, radio and TV, 1946-56, Stop the Music, radio and TV, 1947-55, Double or Nothing, TV, 1953-55; announcer Miss America Pageant, 1956-79; appeared in Music Man on Broadway, 1960-61, Yours for a Song on TV, 1961-63. Served with AUS, 1942-45; CBI. Decorated Bronze Star medal; recipient Poor Richard award, 1957, City of Hope award, 1958, TV Forecast award, 1950, March of Dimes Man of Year award, 1963. Address: care Dean Parker Abrams-Rubaloff 9012 Beverly Blvd Los Angeles CA 90048

PARKS, GEORGE ALBERT, geochemist; b. Calif., May 3, 1931; s. John Willis and Elsie Davis (Tebbe) P.; B.S., U. Calif., Berkeley, 1953, M.S., 1954; Ph.D., M.I.T., 1960; m. Anna Despella Scoufopoulos, May 20, 1956; children—Peter John, Louisa Ann. Mem. faculty Stanford U., 1959—, prof. applied earth scis., 1970—, asso. chmn. dept., 1975-79, prof. environ. civil engring., 1974—, Donald and Donald M. Steel prof. earth scis., 1978—, asso. dean research Sch. Earth Scis., 1979—; cons. in field. Mem. Geochem. Soc., AIME, Am. Chem. Soc., Soc. Environ. Geochemistry and Health, Phi Beta Kappa, Sigma Xi, Tau Beta Pi. Contbr. articles to profl. jours. Office: Sch Earth Scis Stanford Univ Stanford CA 94305

PARKS, GEORGE RICHARD, librarian; b. Boston, Apr. 11, 1935; A.B. summa cum laude, U. N.H., 1959; M.A.L.S., U. Mich., 1962; postgrad. Johns Hopkins, 1959-65; m. Carol A. Richmond; children—Elizabeth, Jennifer, Geoffrey. Preprofl. young adult librarian Enoch Pratt Free Library, Balt., 1960-61, br. librarian, 1964-65, asst. to asst. dir., 1965-66; asst. dir. libraries U. Rochester, 1966-69; dean of libraries U. R.I., 1969—; lectr. in field; cons. library bldg. Mem. New Eng. Library Bd. Recipient Margaret Mann award U. Mich., 1962; Phillips Exter Acad. scholar, 1952-54; U. N.H. scholar, 1955-59; Johns Hopkins U. scholar, 1959-60; Enoch Pratt Free Library scholar, 1961-62. Mem. Assn. Coll. Research Libraries (pres. New Eng. chpt. 1975, chmn. nat. conf. 1969-74), ALA, Consortium R.I. Acad. Research Libraries (chmn. 1972-73), New Eng. Library Assn., R.I. Library Assn., Phi Beta Kappa, Phi Kappa Phi, Beta Phi Mu. Home: 10 Oak Hill Rd Peace Dale RI 02879 Office: U of RI - Library Kingston RI 02881

PARKS, GORDON ALEXANDER BUCHANAN, film dir., author, photographer, composer; b. Ft. Scott, Kans., Nov. 30, 1912; s. Jackson and Sarah (Ross) P.; ed. pub. schs., St. Paul; A.F.D., Md. Inst.; Litt.D., Kans. State U., 1970; H.H.D., St. Olaf Coll., 1973; hon. degrees, Fairfield U., 1969, Boston U., 1969, Macalaster Coll., 1974, Colby Coll., 1974, Lincoln U., 1975; m. Genevieve Young, Aug. 26, 1973; children by previous marriage—Gordon Roger (dec.), Toni Parks Brouillaud, David, Leslie. Photographer, FSA, 1942-43, OWI, 1944, Standard Oil Co. (N.J.), 1945-48, Life mag., 1948-72; writer, producer, dir. The Learning Tree, 1969; dir. movie Shaft, 1972, Shaft's Big Score, 1972, The Super Cops, 1974, Leadbelly, 1976; color and black and white cons. motion picture prodns., U.S. and Europe, 1954—. Rosenwald fellow, 1942-43. Recipient awards Nat. Council Christians and Jews, 1964, Syracuse U. Sch. Journalism, 1963, Phila. Mus. Art, 1964, N.Y. Art Dirs. Club, 1964, 68, Frederic W. Brehm award, 1962, Carr Van Anda Journalism award Ohio U., 1970, U. Miami, 1964. Mem. Urban League N.Y., NAACP (Spingarn award 1972), Newspaper Guild, Assn. Composers and Dirs., Dirs. Guild (nat. dir.), Dirs. Guild N.Y., Am. Soc. Mag. Photographers (award 1963), Kappa Alpha Mu. Club: Players. Author: (novel) The Learning Tree, 1963; (autobiography) A Choice of Weapons, 1966; A Poet and His Camera, 1968; Whispers of Intimate Things, 1971; Born Black, 1971; In Love, 1971; Moments Without Proper Names, 1975; Flavio (Christopher award for outstanding biography), 1977; (autobiography) To Smile in Autumn, 1979; editorial dir. Essence mag., 1970-73. Composer: Piano Concerto, 1953; Tree Symphony, 1967; 3 piano sonatas, 1956, 58, 60; modern works for piano and wind instruments. Home: 860 United Nations Plaza New York NY 10017

PARKS, HAROLD FRANCIS, educator, anatomist; b. Anna, Ill., Sept. 28, 1920; s. Guy Clay and Margaret (McCumiskey) P.; B.Ed., So. Ill. U., 1942; Ph.D., Cornell U., 1950; m. Margaret Bryner, Sept. 11, 1948; children—Edwin Thomas, Margaret Caroline. Tchr. music Martinsville (Ill.) High Sch., 1942; asst. band dir. Cornell U., 1942-43, dir. bands, 1943-46, teaching asst. comparative anatomy and histology and embryology, 1945-50, prof. zoology, 1961-64; instr., then asst. prof. anatomy U. N.C. Med. Sch., 1950-54; asst. prof., then asso. prof. anatomy U. Rochester Sch. Medicine and Dentistry, 1954-61; prof. anatomy U. Ky. Med. Center, 1964—, chmn. dept., 1964-79; vis. scientist Karolinska Inst., 1956. Exec. com. Ky.-Mich.-Ohio Regional Med. Library Program. Mem. AAAS, Am. Inst. Biol. Scis., Am. Assn. Anatomists (com. on status of women in anatomy 1978), Am. Soc. Cell Biology, Electron Microscopy Soc. Am., Am. Soc. Zoologists, So. Soc. Anatomists (council 1968-69), Assn. Anatomy Chmn. (council 1971-72), Sigma Xi, Phi Kappa Phi. Home: 837 Cahaba Rd Lexington KY 40502

PARKS, HENRY EMSLIE, lawyer; b. Balt., Mar. 14, 1930; s. Z. Townsend and Harriet (Forrester) P.; B.S., Johns Hopkins, 1953; LL.B., U. Md., 1956; m. Arlene Marie Garverich, June 14, 1952; children—Douglas Wayne, Cinda Lee, Donna Lynn. Admitted to Md. bar, 1956; clk. Chief Judge Emory H. Niles, Balt., 1954-56; practice law, Balt. and Towson, Md., 1956—, mem. firm Wright and Parks. Mem. Baltimore County Bd. Edn., 1964-75, chmn. community coll. com., 1967-71, pres. bd., 1971-75. Mem. bd. advisers Towson Coop. Nursery for Retarded Children, 1964-68; trustee Md. State Colls., 1968-70; v.p. bd. trustees Baltimore County Gen. Hosp., 1964-67. Named Outstanding Young Man of Year, Md. Jaycees, 1965, Boss of Year, Towson chpt. Nat. Secs. Assn., 1973. Mem. Am., Md., Balt. (family law com.) bar assns., Sigma Phi Epsilon, Delta Theta Phi. Episcopalian. Home: Granite Rd Woodstock MD 21163 Office: 305 W Chesapeake Ave Towson MD 21204 also 6th Floor Sun Life Bldg Charles Center Baltimore MD 21201

PARKS, JOHN EMORY, lawyer; b. Bridgeport, Conn., Sept. 1, 1909; s. John E. and Minerva Alida (Smith) P.; J.D., U. Va., 1934; children—Deborah, John (dec.). Admitted to Va. bar, 1933; asso. with Judge P. L. Rice in practice of law, Hawaii, 1937-38; asst. U.S. atty. for Hawaii, Honolulu, 1939-41; asst. public prosecutor City and County of Honolulu, 1941-46; adminstr. Rent Control Commn., Honolulu, 1942-43; pvt. practice law, Honolulu, 1946-47; chmn. Public Utilities Commn. of Ter. Hawaii, 1946-47; judge First Circuit Ct. of Hawaii, 1947-52; pvt. practice law, 1952—. Mem. exec. bd. Honolulu council Boy Scouts Am., 1948—; dir. Civic Light Opera Assn. Honolulu. Mem. Am. Bar Assn., Bar Assn. Hawaii, Va. Bar, Acad. Arts of Honolulu, Honolulu C. of C. (past dir.), Hawaii Cancer Soc., Ltd., Nat. Soc. S.A.R. Episcopalian. Clubs: Masons, Shriners, Commercial, Propeller, Waikiki Yacht (Honolulu); Outrigger Canoe. Participant 1949 yacht race from Calif. to Hawaii on staysail schooner, Lady Jo. Home: 3617 Diamond Head Rd Honolulu HI 96816 Office: 1640 Pacific Trade Center 190 S King St Honolulu HI 96813

PARKS, MADELYN N., nurse, ret. army officer; b. Jordan, Okla.; diploma Corpus Christi (Tex.) Sch. Nursing, 1943; B.S.N., Incarnate Word Coll., San Antonio, 1961; M.H.A. in Health Care Adminstrn., Baylor U., 1965. Commd. 2d lt. Army Nurse Corps, 1943, advanced through grades to brig. gen., 1975; basic tng., Fort Meade, Md., 1944; staff nurse eye ward Valley Forge (Pa.) Gen. Hosp., 1944; served in India, Iran, Italy, 1944-45; gen. duty staff nurse, Fort Polk, La., 1951; nurse eye clinic Tripler Army Med. Center, Hawaii, 1951-54; staff nurse eye, ear, nose and throat ward Brooke Army Med. Center, San Antonio, 1954-57; ednl. coordinator, Fort Dix, N.J., 1957-58; instr., supr. enlisted med. tng. U.S. Army Med. Tng. Center, Fort Sam Houston, Tex., 1959-61; chief nurse surg. field hosp., sr. nurse coordinator 62d Med. Group, Germany, 1961-63; adminstrn. resident Letterman Gen. Hosp., San Francisco, 1964-65, dir. clin. specialist course, 1965-67; chief nurse 85th Evacuation Hosp., Qui Nhon, Vietnam, 1967-68; asst. chief nursing sci. div., asst. prof. Med. Field Service Sch., U.S. Army-Baylor U. Program in Health Care Adminstrn., 1968-72; chief nurse surgeons office Hdqrs. Continental Army Command, Fort Monroe, Va., 1972-73; chief dept. nursing Walter Reed Army Med. Center, Washington, 1973-75; chief Army Nurse Corps, Office of Surgeon Gen., Dept. Army, Washington, 1975-79, ret., 1979. Faculty asso. adminstr. U. Md., 1974—. Decorated Army Commendation medal with 2 oak leaf clusters, Legion of Merit, Meritorious Service medal. Mem. Am., Tex. nurses assns., Am. Hosp. Assn., Am. Coll. Hosp. Adminstrs. Address: 5211 Metcalf Dr San Antonio TX 78239

PARKS, OLIVER LAFAYETTE, aero. coll. adminstr.; b. Minonk, Ill., June 10, 1899; s. Alvah Harrison and Sarah Adeline (Melchart) P.; ed. in pub. schs.; D. Sc. (honoris causa) St. Louis U.; m. Margaret Struif, July 4, 1922; 1 son, Oliver Lafayette. Engaged in various bus. enterprises prior to organizing and becoming pres. Parks Air Coll. (now Parks Coll. of St. Louis U.), East St. Louis, 1927 (coll. a part of St. Louis U., 1946—), now mem. exec. com.; pres., dir. Oliver L. Parks Realty Co., Inc. Dir. devel. Archdiocese of St. Louis. Enlisted in U.S. Marines, 1917, served in W.I. and France, 2 yrs. Decorated Knight of Malta, Knight of Holy Sepulchre, King George VI medal; recipient certificate merit for pilot tng., World War II, Elder Statesman of Aviation award Nat. Aero. Assn., Fleur-de-Lis award St. Louis U. Mem. Am. Legion, Knight of St. Gregory. Clubs: Serra, Rotary, Quiet Birdmen, Missouri Athletic. Roman Catholic. Home: 7 McKnight Ln Saint Louis MO 63124

PARKS, PAUL FRANKLIN, univ. adminstr., nutritional biochemist; b. Opelika, Ala., Nov. 9, 1933; s. James William and Annie Ruth (Edwards) P.; B.S., Auburn U., 1956, M.S., 1959; Ph.D., Tex. A&M U., 1962; m. Martha Gaynell Bailey, July 17, 1953; children—Paul, Angelia, Amy, Carrie. Asst. prof. biochemistry, leader feed analysis lab. Dept. Agr. Analytical Services at Tex. A&M U., 1962-65; asso. prof. animal scis. Auburn U., 1965-68, prof., 1974—, asst. dean Grad. Sch., 1968-72, dean Grad. Sch., 1972—. Pres., Lee County (Ala.) Council for Neglected and Dependent Children; pres. bd. dirs. Lee County Youth Devel. Center. Cancer Inst. grantee, 1965-70; NIH Heart and Lung Inst. grantee, 1965-73. Mem. Am. Inst. Nutrition, AAAS, Oak Ridge Associated Univs. (council), So. Assn. Land Grant Colls. and State Univs. (sec.-treas.), Sigma Xi, Alpha Zeta, Gamma Sigma Delta, Phi Kappa Phi. Contbr. articles on nutritional biochemistry and analytical methods to profl. jours. Home: 209 Bibb Ave Auburn AL 36830 Office: Auburn U Grad Sch Auburn AL 36830

PARKS, ROBERT EMMETT, JR., educator, med. scientist; b. Glendale, N.Y., July 29, 1921; s. Robert Emmett and Carolyn M. (Heinemann) P.; A.B., Brown U., 1944; M.D., Harvard, 1945; Ph.D., U. Wis., 1954; m. Margaret Ellen Ward, June 15, 1945; children—Robert Emmett III, Walter Ward, Chrisopher Carr. Intern, Boston Children's Hosp., 1945-46; research asso. Amherst Coll., 1948-51; postdoctoral fellow Enzyme Inst., Madison, Wis., 1951-54; mem. faculty U. Wis. Med. Sch., 1954-63, prof. pharmacology, 1961-63; prof. med. sci., chmn. biochem. pharmacology Brown U., 1963—. Cons. NIH. Served with AUS, 1943-45, 46-48. Scholar acad. medicine John and Mary Markle Found., 1956-61. Mem. Am. Soc. Pharmacology and Exptl. Therapeutics, Am. Soc. Biol. Chemists, Am. Assn. Cancer Research, Sigma Xi. Author articles in field. Home: 62 Alumni Ave Providence RI 02906

PARKS, ROBERT MYERS, appliance mfg. co. exec.; b. Nevada, Mo., July 18, 1927; s. Cecil R. and Marcella (Myers) P.; B.S., U. Mo., 1949; M.B.A., Harvard, 1952; m. Audrey Lenora Jones, June 18, 1955; children—John Robert, Janet M. Asst. dept. mgr. Jewett & Sherman Co., Kansas City, Mo., 1949-50; staff cons. Harbridge House, Inc., Boston, 1952; v.p. Electronic Splty. Co., Inc., Los Angeles, 1952-57; pres. Parks Products, Inc., Hollywood, Calif., 1957—; pres. Generalist Industries, Inc., Hollywood, 1960-73; chmn. bd. Shaver Corp. Am., Los Angeles, 1965—; lectr. mktg. UCLA Extension div., 1960-61. Active YMCA; bd. dirs. Hollywood Presbyn. Med. Center Found. Served with USNR, 1944-45. Mem. Sales and Marketing Execs. Assn., C. of C., Navy League, Calif. Caballeros, Rangers, Vaqueros del Desierto, Los Caballeros, E Clampus Vitus, Delta Sigma Pi, Sigma Chi. Presbyn. Mason (Shriner). Clubs: Los Angeles Breakfast, Braemar Country, Saddle and Sirloin. Contbr. articles on mktg. and bus. mgmt. to profl. publs. Patentee in field. Home: 7421 Woodrow Wilson Dr Hollywood CA 90046 Office: 3611 Cahuenga Blvd Hollywood CA 90068

PARKS, RONALD DEE, educator; b. Kansas City, Mo., Feb. 9, 1935; s. Alfred Wesley and Martha Mae (Frazer) P.; B.S., Kans. State U., 1956; M.S., Stanford, 1958, Ph.D., 1961; m. Jean Ming Liu, Apr. 29, 1957; children—Bruce, Scott, Jill, Kelly. Research asso. physics dept. Stanford U., 1961-62; asst. prof. U. Rochester (N.Y.), 1962-65, asso. prof., 1965-68, prof. physics, 1968-79; prof. physics and chemistry Poly. Inst. N.Y., 1979—. NSF fellow, 1961-62; Alfred P. Sloan Research fellow, 1963-65, 65-67. Fellow Am. Phys. Soc. Home: 180 Garfield Pl Brooklyn NY 11215

PARKS, ROSA, civil rights leader; b. Tuskegee, Ala., Feb. 4, 1913; student Ala. State Coll.; hon. degree Shaw Coll., Detroit. Former clk., ins. saleswoman, tailor's asst.; former youth adv. Montgomery (Ala.) NAACP; active SCLC, Detroit, also Women's Public Affairs Com.; former receptionist Detroit office U.S. Rep. John Conyers, now staff asst. Honored by Women's Missionary Soc., A.M.E. Ch., 1971; recipient Martin Luther King, Jr. Nonviolent Peace Prize, 1980. Initiated the bus boycott in Montgomery, Ala. as beginning of concerted civil rights movement, 1955; known as Mother of Modern Civil Rights Movement; ann. Rosa Parks Freedom award sponsored by SCLC. Address: 305 Federal Bldg 231 W Lafayette Detroit MI 48226*

PARKS, SEIGLE WILSON, physician; b. Middlebourne, W.Va., Mar. 15, 1913; s. Charles Layman and Mona G. (Langfitt) P.; A.B., W.Va. U., 1935; M.D., U. Md., 1939; m. Eleanor Z. Hastings, June 7, 1941; children—Eleanor L. Parks Gaunder, Charles L., Margaret Ann. Resident in medicine St. Agnes Hosp., Balt., 1940-42; asst. resident in medicine U. Md. Hosp., 1947-48; plant physician Westinghouse Electric Co., Fairmont, W.Va., 1946-64; med. dir. Monongahela Power Co., Fairmont, 1953-64, Chesapeake & Potomac Telephone Co., Charleston, W.Va., 1964—; v.p. W.Va. Arthritis Found., 1969—; mem. Gov. W.Va. Task Force Health. Served with M.C., AUS, 1942-44. Fellow Am. Acad. Family Physicians (president's award 1976), Indsl. Med. Assn. (pres. Pitts.-Cleve. chpt. 1967); mem. Am., W.Va. (pres. 1965) med. assns., Am. Acad. Family Practice (pres. W.Va. 1959), Am. Acad. Occupational Medicine, Allied Artists W.Va. (pres. 1975-77). Republican. Methodist. Clubs: Charleston Rotary, Edgewood Country. Home: 710 Myrtle Rd Charleston WV 35214 Office: 1500 MacCorkle Ave Charleston WV 25314

PARKS, WILLIAM ROBERT, univ. adminstr.; b. Lincoln County, Tenn., Oct. 13, 1915; s. Benjamin N. and Minnie A. (Taylor) P.; B.A., Berea Coll., 1937, LL.D. (hon.), 1966; M.A., U. Ky., 1938, D.Sc. (hon.), 1973; Ph.D., U. Wis., 1948; LL.D., Drake U., 1968; L.H.D., Westmar Coll., 1968; m. Ellen R. Sorge, July 1, 1940; children—Andrea, Cynthia. Economist bur. agrl. econs. Dept. Agr., 1940-48; prof. govt. Iowa State Coll., 1948-56; prof. agrl. econs. U. Wis., 1956-58; dean of instrn. Iowa State U., 1958-61; v.p. academic affairs, 1961-65, pres., 1965—. Cons. TVA, part-time 1956-57, also Dept. Interior; dir. Northwestern Bell Telephone Co., Central Life Assurance Co. Trustee Coll. Retirement Equity Fund, U. of Mid-Am. Served to lt. (j.g.) USNR, 1943-46. Mem. Assn. Am. Univs. (pres. 1977, chmn. 1978), Mid-Am. State Univs. Assn. (pres. 1965), Nat. Assn. State Univs. and Land Grant Colls. (pres. 1973). Contbr. articles to profl. jours. Home: The Knoll Iowa State U Ames IA 50010

PARLETT, ROBERT CARLETON, educator; b. Albuquerque, May 7, 1925; s. Roger Vinton and Sophia Frances (Hessler) P.; B.A., U. Ariz., 1948, M.S., 1951; Ph.D., Northwestern U., 1956, M.S., 1958. Teaching fellow microbiology U. Ariz., 1950-51, research fellow to Dr. M.E. Caldwell, 1951-52; teaching fellow Northwestern U. Sch. Medicine, 1952- 56, instr. microbiology, 1956-58, asst. prof., 1958-62; jr. investigator Nat. Tb Assn., 1956-60; prof. microbiology, chmn. dept. George Washington U. Med. Sch., 1962-72; asso. dean med. scis. Sch. Medicine, So. Ill. U., Springfield, 1972-74; v.p. health scis., dean Sch. Medicine, Marshall U., Huntington, W.Va., 1974-76; dir. research Alfred I. duPont Inst., Wilmington, Del., 1976—; cons. in field, 1948—. Chmn. med. adv. bd. Leonard Wood Meml. Found., 1961—, trustee, 1969—; mem. med. adv. bd. Wilmington VA Hosp., 1966—; mem. expert panel TB, WHO, 1965—, chmn. com. Tb, 1963; U.S. del. Pan Am. Health Orgn. Conf. Epidemiology, Montevideo, Uruguay, 1968; participant Tb. Internat. Meeting, Rome, Italy, 1963, del. Am. Soc. Microbiology to NRC, 1966—. Served to lt. USNR, 1943-46. Recipient Med. Student Borden award for research, 1958. Discoverer gel-diffusion test for Tb, 1958. Home: 1901 Field Rd Wilmington DE 19806

PARLOFF, MICHAEL LEON, flutist; b. Balt., Oct. 14, 1952; s. Morris Bernard and Gloria June (Harnick) P.; Mus.B., Juilliard Sch., 1974. Prin. flutist Met. Opera Orch., N.Y.C., 1977—. Office: Met Opera Lincoln Center New York NY 10023

PARMELEE, ARTHUR HAWLEY, JR., medical educator; b. Chgo., Oct. 29, 1917; s. Arthur Hawley and Ruth Frances (Brown) P.; B.S., U. Chgo., 1940, M.D., 1943; m. Jean Kern Rheinfrank, Nov. 11, 1939; children—Arthur Hawley III, Ann (Mrs. John C. Minahan, Jr.), Timothy, Ruth Ellen. Intern U.S. Naval Hosp., Bethesda, Md., 1943-44; extern Yale Inst. Child Devel., 1947, New Haven Hosp., 1947-48, Los Angeles Children's Hosp., 1948-49; mem. faculty U. Calif. at Los Angeles Med. Sch., 1951—, prof. pediatrics, 1967—, dir. div. child devel., 1964—, mem. Brain Research Inst., 1966—, mem. Mental Retardation Center, 1970—; research prof. pediatrics U. Göttingen (Germany), 1967-68; mem. com. child devel. research and public policy NRC, 1977—. cons. Nat. Inst. Child Health and Human Devel., 1963-70, Holy Family Adoption Service, 1949—. Trustee, Los Angeles Children's Mus., 1979. Served with USN, 1943-47. Recipient C. Anderson Aldrich award in child devel., 1975. Commonwealth fellow Centre de Recherches Biologiques Neonatales, Clinique Obstetricale Baudelocque, Paris, 1959-60. Diplomate Am. Bd. Pediatrics (examiner 1966—). Mem. Am. Pediatric Soc., Soc. Pediatric Research, Western Soc. Pediatric Research, Am. Acad. Pediatrics (chmn. com. of sect. child devel. 1966), Assn. Ambulatory Pediatrics (council 1966-69), Research Soc. Child Devel., Assn. Psychophysiol. Study Sleep, A.M.A., Los Angeles County Med. Soc., Phi Beta Kappa. Author articles, chpts. in books. Home: 764 Iliff St Pacific Palisades CA 90272 Office: Dept Pediatrics Univ Calif Los Angeles CA 90024

PARMELEE, DAVID FREELAND, biologist; b. Oshkosh, Wis., June 20, 1924; s. Gale Freeland and Helen Dale (MacNaughton) P.; B.A., Lawrence U., Appleton, Wis., 1950; M.S., U. Mich., 1952; Ph.D., U. Okla., 1957; m. Jean Marie Peterson, Dec. 4, 1943; 1 dau., Helen Gale. Grad. instr., then instr. U. Okla., 1952-58; from asst. prof. to prof. biology Kans. State Coll., Emporia, 1958-70; prof. ecology and behavioral biology, chmn. field biology program U. Minn., Mpls., 1970—; dir. field ops. bird virus and parasite research studies U. Okla. Med. Center, 1963-65; program dir. U. Minn. Forestry and Biol. Sta., Lake Itasca, Cedar Creek Natural History Area, Anoka and Isanti counties, 1970—. Served with USMCR, 1943-46. Grantee NSF-U.S. Antaractic Research Program, 1972—, Canadian Arctic Research Programs-NSF-Arctic Inst. N.Am.-Nat. Museum Can., 1953-71; recipient Conservation Edn. award Kans. Wildlife Fedn., Sears-Roebuck Found., 1965. Mem. Orgn. Biol. Field Stas., Nature Conservancy, Cooper Ornithol. Soc., Wilson Ornithol. Club. Club: Explorers (fellow). Home: 1595 Northrop St St Paul MN 55108 Office: 349 James Ford Bell Museum Natural History Univ Minn Minneapolis MN 55455

PARMENTER, ROBERT HALEY, educator; b. Portland, Maine, Sept. 19, 1925; s. LeClare Fall and Esther (Haley) P.; B.S., U. Maine, 1947; Ph.D., Mass. Inst. Tech., 1952; m. Elizabeth Kinnecom, Oct. 27, 1951; children—David Alan, Douglas Ian. Mem. staff solid state and molecular theory group Mass. Inst. Tech., 1951-54; guest scientist Brookhaven Nat. Lab., 1951-52; mem. staff Lincoln Lab., 1952-54; mem. staff RCA Labs., 1954-66, vis. scientists, Zurich, Switzerland, 1958, acting head solid state research group, 1962-65; prof. physics U. Ariz., 1966—, chmn. dept., 1977—. Mem. NASA research adv. com. electrophysics, 1964-68, chmn., 1966-68; mem. NASA research and tech. adv. com. basic research, 1966-68. Served with USNR, 1944-46. Fellow AAAS, Am. Phys. Soc.; mem. Sigma Xi, Tau Beta Pi. Home; 1440 E Ina Rd Tucson AZ 85718

PARMER, HARRY WEBB, electronic cons.; b. Fort Deposit, Ala., Apr. 28, 1907; s. Claude Eugene and Edith Etole (Webb) P.; B.S. in Elec. Engring., Ala. Poly. Inst., 1929; m. Mary Eunice Sexton, July 21, 1931; 1 dau., Nancy Lou. With U.S. Army Signal Research and Devel. Lab., 1929-71, successively chief telegraph equipment sect., officer charge sound, light and heat br., officer charge wire communications br., chief advanced systems engring., 1929-56, dir. tech. plans, 1956-71, cons. in electronics and communications, 1971—. Chmn. mil. communication system tech. standards com.; mem. panel on communications Research and Devel. Bd.; cryptographic officer Signal Corps Engring. Lab. Served from maj. to lt. col., AUS, 1942-46. Decorated Legion of Merit. Sr. mem. IEEE; mem. Armed Forces Communications Assn. Club: Oakhurst Men's. Author mag. articles on research and devel. mgmt. and tech. subjects. Patentee teletype and gryptographic equipment, signaling devices and systems. Home: 239 Pinewood Ave Oakhurst NJ 07755

PARMER, JESS NORMAN, univ. ofcl.; b. Elkhart, Ind., Nov. 23, 1925; s. Jess Noah and Zayda Irene (Tressler) P.; B.A., Ind. U., 1949; M.A., U. Conn., 1951; Ph.D., Cornell U., 1957; m. Bessie Norma Peterson, September 12, 1948; children—Thomas Norman, Sarah Irene. Resident in Malaya, Southeast Asia program, Cornell U., 1952-55; instr., then asst. prof. history U. Md., 1956-59; mem. faculty No. Ill. U., 1959-67, prof. history, 1960-67, chmn. dept., 1959-63; asso. dean Coll. Arts and Scis., also dir. Center Internat. Studies, Ohio U., 1967-69, asst. dean faculties for internat. studies, 1969-75; v.p. acad. affairs Trinity U., San Antonio, 1975—. Peace Corps rep. in Malaya, 1961-63, Tanzania, summer 1965, Malawi, summer 1966, Korea, 1967; lectr. Fgn. Service Inst., 1958, 61, 65; cons. social scis. com. Ill. Curriculum Program, 1961. Served with inf. AUS, 1944-46; ETO. Mem. Assn. Asian Studies (chmn. S.E. Asia regional council 1968-72, dir. 1969-72), Midwest Conf. Asian Affairs (chmn. library com. 1960-61), Am. Hist. Assn., AAUP, ACLU, Royal Asiatic Soc. Great Britain and Ireland, Conf. Brit. Studies, Asia Soc. Author: Governments and Politics of Southeast Asia, 2d edit., 1964; Colonial Labor Policy and Adminstration, 1960; Southeast Asia: Documents of Political Development and Change, 1974; People and Progress: A Global History, 1977. Home: 151 Oakmount Ct San Antonio TX 78212. *I find my life full of opportunity, excitement and satisfaction. Satisfaction comes from seeing ideas find institutional or behavioral expression and influencing people in positive ways. Self-fulfillment, hard work, respect for others, and honesty have been guiding principles and I have found them compatible and rewarding.*

PARMLEY, WILLIAM WATTS, cardiologist; b. Salt Lake City, Jan. 22, 1936; s. Thomas Jennison and Martha Lavern (Watts) P.; A.B., Harvard U., 1957; M.D., Johns Hopkins U., 1963; m. Shanna Lee Nielsen, Aug. 17, 1961; children—Michael William, John Nielsen, Todd Jennison, Ann. Intern, Johns Hopkins Hosp., 1963-64, resident in medicine, 1964-65; clin. asso. Nat. Heart Inst. NIH, Bethesda, Md., 1965-67; fellow in cardiology Peter Bent Brigham Hosp., Boston, 1967-69; asso. dir. cardiology Cedars-Sinai Med. Center, Los Angeles, 1969-73; mem. faculty dept. medicine U. Calif., San Francisco, 1974—; chief cardiology Moffitt Hosp., San Francisco, 1974—; established investigator Am. Heart Assn., 1971-74. Bishop Mormon Ch., 1977—. Served with USPHS, 1967-69. Fellow Am. Coll. Cardiology, A.C.P.; mem. Am. Soc. Clin. Investigation, Western Assn. Physicians, Assn. Am. Physicians, Phi Beta Kappa, Alpha Omega Alpha. Republican. Contbr. numerous articles to med. jours. Home: 2574 Roundhill Dr Alamo CA 94507 Office: 1186 Moffitt Hosp 3d and Parnassus Ave San Francisco CA 94143

PARNASS, HENRY WAGNER, paper mfg. co. exec.; b. Bklyn., Oct. 9, 1925; s. Samuel and Ida (Wagner) P.; A.B., Amherst Coll., 1947; M.B.A., Harvard U., 1956; m. Barbara Johnson, Sept. 2, 1950; children—Geofrrey, Lawrence, John. With Hammermill Paper Co., 1956-71, v.p. sales, 1967-71; pres. Newton Falls Paper Mill, Inc. (N.Y.), 1971—, also dir.; dir. No. div. Marine Midland Bank; adj. prof. Clarkson Coll. Tech. Trustee Paul Smiths Coll., Saranac Lake (N.Y.) Library. Served with USN, 1943-46. Mem. TAPPI, Am. Paper Inst. (dir.). Home: PO Box 767 Saranac Lake NY 12983 Office: Newton Falls Paper Mill Inc Newton Falls NY 13666

PARNELL, FRANCIS WILLIAM, JR., physician; b. Woonsocket, R.I., May 22, 1940; s. Francis W. and Dorothy V. (Lalor) P.; student Coll. Holy Cross, 1957-58; A.B., Clark U., 1961; M.D., Georgetown U., 1965; m. Diana DeAngelis, Feb. 27, 1965; children—Cheryl Lynn, John Francis, Kathleen Diana, Alison Anne, Thomas William. Intern, Univ. Hosps., Madison, Wis., 1965-66, resident in gen. surgery, 1966-67, otolaryngology, 1967-70; practice medicine, specializing in otolaryngology, San Rafael, Calif., 1972-75, Greenbrae, Calif., 1972-75, 78—; cons. corp. med. affairs, 1978—; corp. med. dir. Becton, Dickinson & Co., Rutherford, N.J., 1976-78; clin. instr. U. Calif. at San Francisco, 1972-75, asst. clin. prof., 1975-76. Alt. del. U.S. Del. 27th World Health Assembly WHO, Geneva, Switzerland, 1974; cons. Bur. Health and Social Services, Madison, 1968-70, Bur. Crippled Children Services Calif. Dept. Pub. Health, 1972-75. Mem. Marin Republican Council, Marin County, Calif., 1972-75; mem. Dane County (Wis.) Rep. Com., 1967-70; chmn. Physicians Com. to Re-elect Pres., Marin County, 1972. Bd. dirs. Marin County Am. Cancer Soc., 1973-75. Served to maj. M.C., AUS, 1970-72. Diplomate Nat. Bd. Med. Examiners, Am. Bd. Otolaryngology. Fellow Am. Acad. Otolaryngology, A.C.S.; mem. AMA, Pacific Coast Oto-Ophthalmol. Soc. Contbr. articles to profl. jours. Home: PO Box 1383 Ross CA 94957 Office: 599 Sir Francis Drake Blvd Greenbrae CA 94904

PARNELL, JAMES QUINCY, JR., chem. fertilizer mfg. co. exec.; b. Parkton, N.C., May 20, 1921; s. J. Quincy and Clelia Mae (Britt) P.; student U. N.C.; m. Carol Galbraith Stiles, Jan. 16, 1942; children—Rebecca Parnell Standing, Patricia Parnell Rice, James Quincy, III, Don Stiles, Steve Britt. Self-employed, 1945-54; with Royster Co., Norfolk, Va., 1954—, v.p. mktg., 1967, exec. v.p., 1967-76, pres., chief exec. officer, 1977—, also dir.; dir. United Va./Seaboard Nat. Bank, New Bern Oil & Fertilizer Co., Inc. Bd. dirs. Greater Norfolk Corp., 1977—, Norfolk Planning Council, 1978—; bd. dirs., exec. com. Va. Orch. Group, 1978—. Served to 1st lt., inf., AUS, 1942-45. Mem. Fertilizer Inst. (dir.), Potash and Phosphate Inst. (dir.). Baptist. Clubs: Princess Anne Country (Virginia Beach); Virginia, Harbor (Norfolk). Home: 716 Cavalier Dr Virginia Beach VA 23451 Office: PO Drawer 1940 Norfolk VA 23501

PARNELL, THOMAS ALFRED, physicist; b. Lumberton, N.C., Nov. 24, 1931; s. Johnathan Alfred and Lula Beale (Lashley) P.; B.S. in Physics, U. N.C., 1954, M.S. in Physics, 1962, Ph.D. in Physics, 1965; m. Elizabeth G. Brite, June 4, 1955; children—Marc Thomas, Gina Ann. Research adj., dept. physics U. N.C., Chapel Hill, 1962-65; ops. analyst U.S. Air Force Europe, Wiesbaden, W. Ger., 1965-66; asst. prof. physics Marshall U., Huntington, W.Va., 1966-67; physicist NASA-Marshall Space Flight Center, Huntsville, Ala., 1967-69, chief astrophysics br., 1969—; mem. grad. faculty U. Ala., Huntsville. Served with USN, 1954-58. Recipient Exceptional Sci. Achievement medal NASA. Mem. Am. Phys. Soc., Sigma Xi. Club: Monte Sano (Huntsville). Contbr. articles to profl. jours. Home: 907 Corinth Circle Huntsville AL 35801 Office: E562 Marshall Space Flight Center AL 35812

PARNES, SIDMORE, editor; b. N.Y.C., Mar. 22, 1928; s. Jack and Rose (Platt) P.; B.A. cum laude, Coll. City N.Y., 1949. Editor-in-chief Cashbox Mag., N.Y.C., 1950-58; pres. Sidmore Pub. Co., music pub., N.Y.C., 1959-63; founder, editor-in-chief, sec./treas. Record World Mag., record industry trade pub., N.Y.C., 1964—. Contbr. numerous articles on music industry to trade papers. Pub. Acad. award-winning song Never on Sunday, 1961. Home: 208 E 62d St New York NY also Wilton CT 10022 Office: 1700 Broadway New York NY 10019

PARO, TOM EDWARD, broadcasting co. exec.; b. Belleville, Ill., July 7, 1923; s. Edward Westermann and Alice Jane (Price) P.; B.J., U. Mo., 1948; m. Aileen Nance, Oct. 1, 1955; children—Jeffrey, Daniel, Kathleen. With MBS, 1948-54; with sales dept. NBC, 1955-59; dir. sales WRC-TV, Washington, 1960-62, sta. mgr., 1962-65, gen. mgr., 1969-76; sta. mgr. WNBC-TV, N.Y.C., 1966-69; v.p. NBC, Washington, 1969-77; exec. v.p. Assn. Maximum Service Telecasters Inc., 1977-78, pres., 1978—; mem. adv. bd. Riggs Nat. Bank Bd. dirs. D.C. Crippled Children's Soc., Heart Assn., Boy Scouts Am., Meridian House. Served to lt. AUS, 1943-46; ETO; to capt., 1951-53. Kiwanian. Clubs: Burning Tree, Congressional Country; International; National Broadcasters. Home: 5913 Searl Terr Washington DC 20016 Office: 1735 De Sales St NW Washington DC 20036

PARR, FERDINAND VAN SICLEN, JR., lawyer; b. Bklyn., June 13, 1908; s. Ferdinand Van Siclen and Mabel Kendrick (Skidmore) P.; B.A., Wesleyan U., 1929; LL.B., St. Lawrence U., 1933; m. Helene Elizabeth Ham, Sept. 7, 1938; children—Elizabeth Ham, Grant Van Siclen, Sarah Leota. Admitted to N.Y. bar, 1934; with Bond & Mortgage Guarantee Co., N.Y.C., 1929-33; with Title Guarantee and Trust Co., 1933-37, asst. trust officer, 1935-37; with Lewis & Kelsey, 1937-41; with firm Parr, Doherty, Polk & Sargent, and predecessors, 1941-70, partner Whitman & Ransom, 1970—. Sec., dir. Benrus Corp.; dir. First Investors Life Ins. Co., Chromalloy Am. Corp., Transport of N.J. Trustee, Wesleyan U. Mem. Am., N.Y. bar assns., Bar Assn. City N.Y., Phi Beta Kappa, Chi Psi, Phi Delta Phi. Clubs: University, Down Town Assn., Sky, N.Y. Athletic (N.Y.C.); Morris County Golf. Home: 419 Mount Kemble Ave Morristown NJ 07960 Office: 522 Fifth Ave New York NY 10036

PARR, JAMES GORDON, ednl. broadcasting exec.; b. Peterborough, Eng. May 26, 1927; s. Reuben Scotney and Edith Grace (Rollings) P.; B.Sc., U. Leeds, 1947; Ph.D., U. Liverpool, 1953; children—Mark Anthony, Katharine Elizabeth, Daniel John. Came to Can., 1953. Lectr., U. Liverpool, 1948-53; research asso., lectr. U. B.C., Vancouver, 1953-55; asso. prof., then prof. U. Alta., Edmonton, 1955-64; dean applied sci. U. Windsor (Ont., Can.), 1964-72; chmn. com. univ. affairs Govt. Ont., Toronto, 1972; dep. minister Ministry Colls. and Univs., Govt. Ont., 1973-79; chmn., chief exec. officer Ont. Ednl. Communications Authority, Toronto, 1979—. Founding pres. Indsl. Research Inst., U. Windsor, 1967-72. Recipient Centennial medal Canada, 1967, Jubilee medal, 1977. Fellow Royal Soc. Can., Am. Soc. Metals, Royal Soc. Arts, Engring. Inst. Can. Author: Man, Metals and Modern Magic, 1958; (with A. Hanson) An Introduction to Stainless Steel, 1965, The Engineer's Guide to Steel, 1965; Any Other Business, 1977; Is There Anybody There? Collected Verse, 1979. Home: 100 Wellesley St E Apt 2413 Toronto ON M4Y 1H5 Canada Office: Ont Ednl Communications Authority Box 200 Sta Q Toronto ON M4T 2T1 Canada

PARR, JOHN FRANCIS, ret. coll. dean; b. Lafayette, Ind., Nov. 8, 1914; s. William Clarence and Mary Louise (de Marcus) P.; B.S., Georgetown U., 1939, M.A., 1948; Ph.D., U. Fribourg, Switzerland, 1951. Grad. asst. Georgetown U., 1939; asst. dir. internat. relations bur. Nat. Cath. Welfare Conf., 1945-49; asst. prof. U. Md. Overseas Program, 1951-53, U. Fribourg, Switzerland, 1953-56; asst. dean Edmund A. Walsh Sch. Fgn. Service, Georgetown U., 1956-58, dean, 1958-61; resident dean U. Md., Munich, Germany, 1961-69; v.p., dean Fleming Coll., Lugano, Switzerland, 1969-70; dean liberal arts Anne Arundel Community Coll., 1971-77, dean emeritus, 1977—. Mem. Am. com. UNESCO; organized Inter-Am. Cath. Social Action confs., Dominican Republic, Rio de Janeiro, Brazil. Served from ensign to lt. comdr., intelligence, USNR, 1941-45. Decorated Officer de l'Ordre des Palmes Académiques (France); bailiff Order St. John (Yugoslavia); recipient outstanding civilian service medal AUS, lifetime mem. 24th Inf. div. U.S. Army. Mem. Pi Gamma Mu. Roman Catholic. Clubs: Cornell (N.Y.C.); University (Washington). Author: (with Richard Pattee) Love Thy Neighbor, 1950; Theophile Delcasse, 1952. Home: Villa de la Grangette Lens-Lestang 26210 Saint-Sorlin-en-Valloire France also University Club 1135 16th St NW Washington DC 20036. *No amount of knowledge, technical skill, or professional formation can substitute for character.*

PARR, ROBERT GHORMLEY, educator; b. Chgo., Sept. 22, 1921; s. Leland Wilbur and Grace (Ghormley) P.; A.B. magna cum laude with high honors in Chemistry, Brown U., 1942; Ph.D. in Phys. Chemistry, U. Minn., 1947; m. Jane Bolstad, May 28, 1944; children—Steven Robert, Jeanne Karen, Carol Jane. Asst. prof. chemistry U. Minn., 1947-48; mem. faculty Carnegie Inst. Tech., 1948-62, prof. chemistry, 1957-62; prof. chemistry Johns Hopkins U., 1962-74, chmn. dept., 1969-72; William R. Kenan, Jr. prof. theoretical chemistry U. N.C., Chapel Hill, 1974—. Vis. prof. chemistry, mem. Center Advanced Study, U. Ill., 1962; distinguished vis. prof. State U. N.Y. at Buffalo, also Pa. State U., 1967; vis. prof. Japan Soc. Promotion Sci., 1968, U. Haifa, 1977, Free U. Berlin, 1977; Firth prof. U. Sheffield, 1976. Chmn. com. postdoctoral fellowships in chemistry Nat. Acad. Sci.-NRC, 1961-63; chmn. panel theoretical chemistry Westheimer com. survey chemistry Nat. Acad. Sci., 1964; mem. council Gordon Research Conf., 1974-76. Recipient Outstanding Achievement award U. Minn., 1968; fellow U. Chgo., 1949, research asso., 1957; Fulbright scholar U. Cambridge (Eng.), 1953-54; Guggenheim fellow, 1953-54; NSF sr. postdoctoral fellow U. Oxford (Eng.) and Commonwealth Sci. and Indsl. Research Orgn., Melbourne, Australia, 1967-68; Sloan fellow, 1956-60. Fellow Am. Phys. Soc. (chmn. div. chem. physics 1963-64), AAAS; mem. Am. Chem. Soc. (chmn. div. phys. chemistry 1978), AAUP, Nat. Acad. Scis., Internat. Acad. Quantum Molecular Sci. (v.p. 1973-79), Phi Beta Kappa, Sigma Xi, Phi Lambda Upsilon, Pi Mu Epsilon. Author: Quantum Theory of Molecular Electronic Structure, 1963; also numerous articles. Asso. editor Jour. Chem. Physics, 1956-58, Chem. Revs, 1961-63, Jour. Phys. Chemistry, 1963-67, 77-79, Am. Chem. Soc. Monographs, 1966-71, Theoretica Chimica Acta, 1966-69; bd. editors Jour. Am. Chem. Soc., 1969-77; adv. editorial bd. Internat. Jour. Quantum Chemistry, 1967—, Chem. Physics Letters, 1967-79. Home: 701 Kenmore Rd Chapel Hill NC 27514 Office: Dept Chemistry U North Carolina Chapel Hill NC 27514

PARR, ROYSE MILTON, lawyer; b. Elk City, Okla., Sept. 11, 1935; s. Clinton Riley and Ruth Caroline (Royse) P.; B.S., Okla. State U., 1958; J.D., U. Tulsa, 1964; m. Sheila Ann Harshaw, May 28, 1960; children—Clint Howard, Reagan Royse. Research scout Jersey Prodn. Research Co., Tulsa, 1960-64; admitted to Okla. bar, 1964; atty. Sun Oil Co., 1964-70, White Shield Corp., 1970-71; sec., atty., asst. gen. counsel MAPCO, Inc., Tulsa, 1971—. Vice chmn. Tulsa County Election Bd., 1974—. Served to 1st lt. U.S. Army, 1958-60. Mem. Am. Bar Assn., ASME, Soc. Petroleum Engrs., Okla. Bar Assn., Tulsa County Bar Assn. Republican. Methodist. Home: 2521 E 31st St Tulsa OK 74105 Office: 1800 S Baltimore Ave Tulsa OK 74119

PARRA, FRANCISCO JOSÉ, lawyer; b. Ponce, P.R., Nov. 18, 1904; s. Pedro Juan and Matilde (Toro) P.; LL.B., U. P.R., 1927; m. Maria Isabel Sanchez, Aug. 24, 1931; children—Margarita, Maria Isabel.

Admitted to P.R. bar, 1927, since practiced in Ponce; partner firm Parra, del Valle & Frau, 1968—; dir. Banco de Ponce, 1951-75, vice chmn., 1971-75; mem. cons. com. P.R. Law Rev., Catholic U. P.R., 1961-67; mem. Jud. Council P.R., 1939-41, P.R. Bar Examiners Bd., 1947-48, P.R. Commn. Reputation for Admission to Bar, 1974—. Municipal assembly-man, Ponce, 1932-36; mem. P.R. Municipal Complaints Commn., 1956-77; trustee U. P.R., 1934-41, Cath. U. P.R., 1958-61, Damas Hosp., 1946—. Served to col. AUS, 1940-46. Decorated Legion of Merit, Army Commendation medal; Knight Equestrian Order of St. Sylvester (Vatican). Mem. Am., P.R. (dir. 1932-33, chmn. Ponce 1954-56) bar assns. Roman Catholic. Clubs: Rotary (past pres.), Deportivo, Yacht and Fishing (Ponce). Home: 12 Granada St Ponce PR 00731 Office: Banco de Ponce Bldg 2d Floor Ponce PR 00731 Mailing Address: PO Box 331 Ponce PR 00731

PARRACK, EDWARD TAYLOR, advt. exec.; b. Atlanta, Mar. 7, 1914; s. Ernest E. and Mabel (Taylor) P.; A.B., U. Pitts., 1936; m. Elizabeth Rees Felix, Aug. 17, 1940; 1 son, Edward Taylor. With Ketchum, MacLeod & Grove, Inc. (name now KM&G Internat. Inc.), Pitts., 1936—, account asst., asst. to pres., v.p., 1936-55, exec. v.p. service, 1955-62, pres., chief exec. officer, 1962-70; chmn. bd., chief exec. officer, 1970-79, vice-chmn., 1979—, also chmn. exec. com. Lease officer for Middle East, 1942-43; asst. to sec. U.S. del. San Francisco Peace Conf., 1945. Trustee, mem. art com. Carnegie Inst., Pitts. Episcopalian. Clubs: Fox Chapel Golf; Duquesne (Pitts.); Rolling Rock, Laurel Valley Golf (Ligonier, Pa.); Pinnacle (N.Y.C.). Home: 5023 Frew Ave Pittsburgh PA 15213 Office: Four Gateway Center Pittsburgh PA 15222

PARRATT, LYMAN GEORGE, educator, physicist; b. Salt Lake City, May 17, 1908; s. Delbert William and Mary (Wardrop) P.; A.B., U. Utah, 1928; Ph.D., U. Chgo., 1932; m. Rhea Gibson, Feb. 11, 1944; children—Carolyn, Portia. NRC fellow Cornell U., 1933-35, mem. faculty, 1935-43, 46—, chmn. dept. physics, 1959-69, now prof. emeritus physics, prof. Lab. Nuclear Studies, prof. Lab. Atomic and Solid State Physics; with engring. div. research Naval Ordnance Lab., Washington, 1941-43; physicist, group leader Atomic Bomb Research, Los Alamos 1943-46. Mem. UN Assn., Fedn. Am. Scientists, Am. Phys. Soc., Am. Assn. Physics Tchrs., AAAS, Sigma Xi, Gamma Alpha, Sigma Pi Sigma. Author: Probability and Experimental Errors in Science, 1961; also articles on X-ray physics and electronics in scientific jours. Home: 513 Wyckoff Rd Ithaca NY 14850

PARRIOTT, JAMES DEFORIS, JR., oil co. exec.; b. Moundsville, W. Va., Aug. 21, 1923; s. James D. and Bessie (Sadler) P.; student Ohio Wesleyan U., 1941-43; LL.B., U. Colo., 1949; m. Marynette Sonneland, Aug. 3, 1946; children—James Deforis III, Sara. Admitted to Colo. bar, 1949; practice in Denver, 1949-53; asst. city atty., Denver, 1950-51; asst. atty. gen., Colo., 1952-53; chief counsel Bur. Land Mgmt., Dept. Interior, 1953, asso. solicitor lands and minerals, 1954-56; atty. Ohio Oil Co., Washington, 1956-60, Findlay, Ohio, 1960-62; mgr. employee relations Marathon Oil Co., 1962-69, dir. pub. affairs, 1969-74, dir. pub. and govt. affairs, 1974—. Council pres. Boy Scouts Am. Served as pilot, 2d lt., USAAF, 1943-46. Mem. Am., Fed. bar assns., Phi Alpha Delta, Phi Gamma Delta. Republican. Episcopalian. Clubs: University, Capitol Hill (Washington); Findlay Country. Home: 1932 Queenswood Dr Findlay OH 45840 Office: 539 S Main St Findlay OH 45840

PARRIS, JAMES LEONARD, lawyer, govt. ofcl.; b. Baltimore County, Md., Dec. 12, 1922; s. Russell J. and Ruth (Smith) P.; B.A., Washington Coll., Chestertown, Md., 1943; LL.B. (Harlan Fiske Stone Scholar), Columbia, 1948; m. Miriam Hucks, June 15, 1972; children by previous marriage—Barbara, Stephen. Admitted to N.Y. bar, 1948, Mich. bar, 1958; asso. firm Simpson, Thacher & Bartlett, N.Y.C, 1948-57; sr. atty. Office Gen. Counsel, Ford Motor Co., 1957-62; dep. adminstr. Small Bus. Adminstrn., 1962-65; asst. gen. counsel Dept. Commerce, 1965-69; partner firm Dykema, Gossett, Spencer, Goodnow & Trigg, Detroit, 1970-76; dir. Small Bus. Policy SEC, 1976; spl. counsel Pension Benefit Guaranty Corp., U.S. Govt., 1977—. Sec. Ford Motor Credit Co., 1959. Recipient Robert Toppan prize in constl. law Columbia U., 1947. Served to lt. (j.g.) USNR, 1943-45. Mem. Am. Bar Assn., Omicron Delta Kappa. Home: 13204 Tamarack Silver Spring MD 20904 Office: 2020 K St Washington DC 20006

PARRIS, PORTER P., hotel exec.; b. Gilliland, Tex., Aug. 7, 1917; s. Samuel B. and Gertrude (Collier) P.; student North Tex. State Coll., 1934; grad. Tex. Technol. Coll., 1938; m. Mary Ross Edwards, Nov. 5, 1938; children—Porter Ross, Thomas Baxter. Various positions Hilton Hotels, 1935—; including El Paso, Tex., Long Beach, Calif., Lubbock, Tex., 1935-43; asst. mgr. Roosevelt Hotel, N.Y.C., 1943-44, gen. mg. Dayton-Biltmore Hotel, Dayton, O., 1949-51, resident mgr. Conrad Hilton Hotel, Chgo., 1951-53, gen. mgr., 1962-68; gen. mgr. Hotel Plaza, N.Y.C., 1954-55; v.p., gen. mgr. Shamrock Hilton, Houston, 1952-62, mng. dir., 1970-74, gen. mgr. Statler Hilton, Washington, 1968-69; v.p., gen. mgr. Statler Hilton, Boston, 1969-70; v.p. Hilton Hotels Corp., 1962-74, v.p., div. dir. S.W. div. Hilton Hotels, 1970-74; v.p., mng. dir. Palmer House, Chgo., 1974—. Served as sgt. maj., inf., AUS, 1944-46. Mem. Am. (pres. 1979), Chgo. hotel-motel assns. Address: Palmer House Chicago IL 60690

PARRIS, ROBERT, composer; b. Phila., May 21, 1924; s. Louis and Rae (Oettinger) P.; B.S. in Music Edn., U. Pa., 1945, M.S., 1946; B.S., Juilliard Sch. Music, 1948; student Ecole Normale de Musique, Paris, Frnace, 1952-53. Mem. faculty Wash. State Coll., 1948-49, Juilliard Summer Sch., 1948; pvt. tchr., 1949-63; prof. music George Washington U., 1963—; solo recitals on harpsichord and piano, also in chamber music. Mem. Broadcast Music, Inc. Composer: Concerto for Five Kettledrums and Orchestra, 1961; Fantasy and Fugue for Solo Cello; Lamentations and Praises, 1966; Sonata for Solo Violin, 1967; The Messengers for orch. (commd. by Nat. Endowment for Arts), 1974. Home: 3307 Cummings Ln Chevy Chase MD 20015 Office: 2025 H St Washington DC 20006

PARRISH, ALVIN EDWARD, univ. dean, physician; b. Washington, Sept. 6, 1922; s. John Edward and Thyrza Carrie (Morse) P.; M.D., George Washington U., 1945; m. Mary Wharton Votaw, June 2, 1945; children—Karen Marie, Anne Elizabeth. Intern, D.C. Gen. Hosp., Washington, 1945-46; instr. physiology George Washington U., 1947-48: resident medicine Gallinger Municipal Hosp. and VA Hosp., Washington, 1948-50; chief resident medicine Gallinger Municipal Hosp., 1950-51; asst. chief med. service VA Hosp., Washington, 1951-57, chief metabolic lab., 1955-57; asso. dean Sch. Medicine, George Washington U., 1957-66, prof. medicine, 1964—; chief renal lab. George Washington div. D.C. Gen. Hosp., 1957-66, clin. coordinator, 1960-66; dir. div. renal diseases George Washington Univ. Medical Center, 1967-79; dir. office of human research George Washington U. Hosp. Served to capt., M.C. AUS, 1946-47; lt. col. Res. Mem. A.C.P., AMA, Am. Diabetes Assn., N.Y. Acad. Sci., AAAS, So. Soc. Clin. Investigation, Am. Soc. Nephrology, Am. Fedn. Clin. Research, Pi Kappa Alpha. Author book, articles. Home: 5908 Calla Dr McLean VA 22101 Office: George Washington Univ Hosp Washington DC 20037

PARRISH, CHARLES MILTON, III, polit. party adminstr.; b. Columbus, Ga., Feb. 13, 1947; s. Charles Milton Parrish and Rebecca Parrish Ferguson; B.S. in Indsl. Mgmt., Ga. Inst. Tech., 1969. Dir. office planning and research Ga. Dept. Natural Resources, 1972-76; exec. asst. to com. Ga., 1976; Tex. state coordinator Carter/Mondale Campaign, 1976; mem. Carter/Mondale Transition Team, 1976-77; exec. asst. to sec. Interior, Dept. Interior, Washington, 1977-79; nat. field dir. Carter/Mondale Presdl. Com., 1979; Okla. and Tex. coordinator Carter/Mondale Com., 1979—. Served with USAF, 1971. Mem. Beta Theta Pi. Episcopalian. Home: 4815 Reservoir Rd Washington DC 20007 Office: 500 NW 13th St Oklahoma City OK 73101

PARRISH, CHESTER WARNER, labor union exec.; b. Lakeland, Fla., Dec. 11, 1924; s. Clyde C. and Mary (Warner) P.; ed. U. Miami (Fla.); m. Mary Ruth Jernigan, May 18, 1947; children—Russell C., Gary Lee. With Civilian Conservation Corps, 1940; with U.S. Postal Service, Washington, 1945—; v.p. Nat. Fedn. Post Office Motor Vehicle Employees, AFL-CIO, 1954-58, treas., 1958-68, sec., 1964-68, pres., 1968-71; pres. Am. Postal Workers Union, AFL-CIO (merger Nat. Fedn. Post Office Motor Vehicle Employees and Am. Postal Workers Union), 1971-74, now gen. sec., treas.; bd. officers govt. employees council AFL-CIO; chmn. Council Am. Postal Employees; treas. Postal Co-ordinated Bargaining Council. Mem. Pres.'s Adv. Council for U.S. Postal Service. Served with USNR, 1941-45. Mem. Fla. State Soc. Washington, Nat. Fedn. Crafts, D.A.V. Mason. Office: Am Postal Workers Union 817 14th St NW Washington DC 20005

PARRISH, EUGENE MILTON, oil co. exec.; b. Searcy, Ark., June 15, 1929; s. John Wesley and Cleavie Genevia (Buckner) P.; B.S. in Acctg., Miss. State U., 1955; m. Sadie Hollingsworth, Nov. 24, 1955; children—Elisa, Genevieve, Patricia, Brenda. Accountant, Texaco, Inc., New Orleans, 1955-58; with La. Land & Exploration Co., New Orleans, 1959—, treas., 1974-75, v.p., treas., 1975—; dir. La. Land Offshore Exploration Co. Vice pres. Boys Clubs of Greater New Orleans, 1976-79, pres., 1979—. Served with U.S. Army, 1950-52. C.P.A., La. Mem. C.P.A.'s of La. Republican. Clubs: Petroleum of New Orleans, Chateau Country. Home: 4209 Ferran Dr Metairie LA 70002 Office: 225 Baronne St New Orleans LA 70112

PARRISH, FRANK JENNINGS, frozen foods co. exec.; b. Manassas, Va., Dec. 29, 1923; s. Edgar Goodloe and Alverda (Jennings) P.; student Va. Poly. Inst., 1942-43; m. Lorene Lomax, Feb. 11, 1944; children—Edgar Lee, Julia Lorene. Pres. Manassas Frozen Foods, Inc., 1946—; pres., mgr. Certified Food Buyers Service, Inc., 1953—; pres. First Nat. Acceptance Co., 1966—; v.p. Manassas Ice & Fuel Co. Mem. bus. adminstrn. adv. com. No. Va. Community Coll. Served to maj. USAAF, 1943-46; CBI; ret. brig. gen. Res.; comdr. 909th TAC Airlift Group, 1969-73, moblzn. asst. DCS plans and ops. Hdqrs. USAF, 1973—. Decorated Legion of Merit, Air medal. Mem. Nat. Inst. Locker and Freezer Provisioners Am. (past pres.; Industry Leadership award 1968), Va. Frozen Foods Assn. (past pres., dir.), Hump Pilots Assn. Methodist (chmn. bd. trustees 1958-66). Kiwanian, Moose. Home: 9107 Park Ave Manassas VA 22110 Office: 100 N Washington St Falls Church VA 22046 also 9414 Main St Manassas VA 22110 also 1500 E Little Creek Rd Norfolk VA 23518. *Do unto others as you would have them do unto you.*

PARRISH, HERBERT CHARLES, educator; b. Jacksboro, Tex., Oct. 8, 1919; s. Jake N. and Amy R. (Wilton) P.; B.S., N. Tex. State Coll., 1939, M.S., 1941; Ph.D., Ohio State U., 1955; m. Edrie M. Talley, Aug. 12, 1941; children—Byron N., Norman W., Roberta J. Instr. math. Ohio State U., 1948-49; asst. prof. math. N. Tex. State U., 1949-55, asso. prof., 1955-58, prof., 1958—, dir. dept., 1958-65. Served from ensign to lt. (j.g.), USNR, 1944-46; lt. comdr. Res. Mem. Nat. Council Tchrs. Math., Math. Assn. Am. (chmn. Tex. sect. 1963-64, sect. gov. 1962-65), Am. Math. Soc., Sigma Xi, Pi Mu Epsilon, Kappa Mu Epislon, Kappa Delta Pi. Baptist. Home: 1001 Ector St Denton TX 76201

PARRISH, JAMES MILTON, coll. dean; b. Phil Campbell, Ala., June 9, 1922; s. Felix N. and Martha (Wamsley) P.; B.S., U. Ala., 1943, M.S., 1948; Ph.D., U. N.C., 1954; m. Doris Todd, Mar. 21, 1942; children—James, Patricia, Todd, Michael, Stephen. Asst. dean Sch. Bus. Adminstrn., U. N.C., 1952-55; asso. prof. mktg. Washington U., 1955-56; dean Sch. Bus. and Industry, Miss. State Coll., 1956-62; dir. of edn. OPD, Dept. Army, 1962-64; dean Coll. Bus. Adminstrn., Drexel Inst. Tech., 1964-70, U.N. Fla., Jacksonville, 1970—; mktg. cons. various firms. Served to 1st lt., inf., AUS, World War II. Mem. Am. Mktg. Assn., Soc. Econs. Assn., Beta Gamma Sigma, Omicron Delta Kappa. Phi Kappa Phi. Alpha Kappa Psi, Blue Key. Rotarian. Home: 6229 Grayling Dr Jacksonville FL 32216

PARRISH, JOHN BISHOP, economist; b. Decatur, Ill., June 11, 1911; s. Roy C. and Frances Effie (Wayne) P.; B.A., U. Ill., Urbana-Champaign, 1934, Ph.D., 1939; m. Anne D'Nelle Bullock, Aug. 31, 1940; children—Adrianne Parrish Casey, John Gregory. Sr. economist War Manpower Commn., Washington, 1941-42; prin. economist Nat. War Labor Bd., 1942-44; regional dir. Bur. Labor Statistics, Chgo., 1944-47; mem. faculty U. Ill., 1947—, prof. econs., 1956—; mem. ednl. adv. com. NAM, Am. Mgmt. Assn. Bd. visitors Mary Baldwin Coll., Staunton, Va., 1974—. Recipient Disting. Service award in social scis. Phi Gamma Mu, Rodney D. Chip award Soc. Women Engrs., 1972. Mem. Am., Midwest econ. assns., Phi Beta Kappa, Phi Eta Sigma, Kappa Zeta Psi. Co-author: The Labor Problems of American Society, 1952. Home: 1801 Pleasant Circle Urbana IL 61801 Office: Dept Econs Univ Ill Urbana IL 61801

PARRISH, JUNE AUSTIN, reins. co. exec.; b. Kansas City, Mo., June 25, 1917; d. Harry Winthrop and Marguerite Georgia (McClune) Austin; A.A., Kansas City Jr. Coll., 1935; J.D., U. Mo., Kansas City, 1950; m. Tom Howell Parrish, June 25, 1956. Admitted to Mo. bar, 1950, U.S. Supreme Ct. bar, 1958; with Employers Reins. Corp., Kansas City, Mo., 1941—, asso. gen. counsel, 1968-73, gen. counsel, 1974—. Mem. Jackson County Bd. Visitors, 1958-60; bd. dirs. Kansas City Assn. Blind, 1950-56, Legal Aid Soc. Kansas City, 1969-73, Midwest council Girl Scouts U.S., 1972-79; bd. dirs. Rehab. Inst. Kansas City, 1960-69, pres., 1966-69. Mem. Am., Mo. (chmn. ins. law com. 1975-77), Kansas City, Kansas City Women's (pres. 1956) bar assns., Lawyers Assn., Kansas City Women's C. of C. (dir. 1953-56), U. Mo.-Kansas City Law Sch. Alumni Assn. (adv. bd. dirs.), Scribes, Kappa Beta Pi. Presbyterian. Clubs: Kansas City Soroptimist (pres. 1956), Woman's City (bd. dirs. 1955-58). Co-author: Liability Insurance Cases, 1957—. Home: 41 Compton Ct Shawnee Mission KS 66208 Office: 21 W 10th St Kansas City MO 64105

PARRISH, LEMAR, profl. football player; b. West Palm Beach, Fla., Dec. 9, 1947; s. Leroy and Christine P.; degree in psychology Lincoln U., 1971; m. Donna B., Dec. 25, 1975; children by previous marriage—Tracy Anne, Raymond. Mem. Cin. Bengals, 1970-78; cornerback Washington Redskins, 1977—. Active Urban League, West Palm Beach. Named All-Pro, Am. Football Conf., 1971, 72, 74, 75, 76, 77, Leading in Punt Return, 1974, Outstanding Rookie, 1970. Mem. Nat. Football Players Assn. Office: Washington Redskins Washington DC 20041

PARRISH, OVERTON BURGIN, JR., pharm. corp. exec.; b. Cin., May 26, 1933; s. Overton Burgin and Geneva Opal (Shinn) P.; B.S., Lawrence U., 1955; M.B.A., U. Chgo., 1959. With Pfizer Internat., 1959—, pharm. salesman, Chgo., 1959-62, asst. mktg. product mgr., N.Y.C., 1962-63, product mgr., 1964-66, group product mgr., 1966-67, mktg. mgr., 1967-68, v.p. mktg., 1969-70, v.p., dir. ops., 1970-71, exec. v.p. domestic pharm. div., 1971-72, exec. v.p., dir. Pfizer Internat., 1972-74; pres., chief operating officer G.D. Searle Internat., Skokie, Ill., 1974-75, pres., chief exec. officer, 1975-77; pres. Worldwide Pharm./Consumer Products Group, 1977—; v.p., mem. exec. com. G.D. Searle, 1975—. Trustee Mktg. Sci. Inst.; bd. dirs. Proprietary Assn., 1979—, Food and Drug Law Inst., 1979—. Served to 1st lt. USAF, 1955-57. Mem. Am. Mktg. Assn., Am. Mgmt. Assn., Beta Gamma Sigma, Phi Kappa Tau. Author: The Future Pharmaceutical Marketing; International Drug Pricing, 1971. Home: 505 N Lake Shore Dr Chicago IL 60611 Office: Golf Rd Skokie IL 60680

PARRISH, STEPHEN MAXFIELD, educator; b. Mpls., June 11, 1921; s. Wayland Maxfield and Blanche Greeta (Leigh) P.; A.B., U. Ill., 1942; M.A., Harvard U., 1947, Ph.D., 1954; m. Jean Jacob, Feb. 26, 1945 (div. Sept. 1969); children—Madeleine, Anne Leigh; m. 2d, Priscilla Alden Kiefer Baker-Carr, Dec. 1969. Teaching fellow Harvard U., 1948-50, 52-54; mem. faculty Cornell U., 1954—, prof. English, 1966—, asso. dean Coll. Arts and Scis., also dir. 6-year Ph.D. program, 1965-69; vis. prof. U.S. Mil. Acad., 1964. Chmn. region III, Woodrow Wilson Fellowship Found., 1962-70. Served to lt. comdr. USNR, 1942-46, 50-52; capt. Res. Guggenheim fellow, 1959. Mem. Modern Lang. Assn., Phi Beta Kappa. Democrat. Mem. Soc. Friends. Author: The Art of the Lyrical Ballads; (with Hyder Rollins) Keats and the Bostonians; Wordsworth's Prelude, 1798-99; Concordances to Arnold, 1959; Yeats, 1963; (with S. A. Guttman and Randall Jones) Freud, 1980; gen. editor: The Cornell Concordances; The Cornell Wordsworth. Home: 116 The Parkway Ithaca NY 14850

PARRISH, THOMAS EVERT, utilities co. exec., lawyer; b. Montgomery, W.Va., May 25, 1936; s. Merlin D. and Ruth (Stewart) P.; B.S., W.Va. U., 1958, LL.B., 1959; m. Mary Ellen Glisan, June 9, 1956; children—Diana Joy, Richard Russell, Kimberly Sue, Martha Ellen. Admitted to W.Va. bar, 1959, Ariz. bar, 1962; practiced in Phoenix, 1962—; mem. firm Snell & Wilmer, 1962-73, partner, 1968-73; mgr. legal dept. Ariz. Pub. Service Co., Phoenix, 1973—. Served to capt. Judge Adv. Gen. Corps, U.S. Army, 1959- 62. Mem. Am., Ariz., W.Va., Maricopa County bar assns., Am. Arbitration Assn. (comml. panel mem.), Ariz. State C. of C. (legal com.), Phi Alpha Delta, Sigma Phi Epsilon. Home: 3729 S Kenneth Pl Tempe AZ 85282 Office: Valley Center Phoenix AZ 85036

PARRISH, THOMAS KIRKPATRICK, III, advt. agy. exec.; b. Richmond, Va., May 18, 1930; s. Thomas Kirkpatrick and Sally Cary (Friend) P.; A.B., Princeton U., 1952; m. Linda Kirkland Riley, Oct. 27, 1979; children by previous marriage—Linn Cary, Wayne Elizabeth, Susan Scott. Product mgr. Vick Chem. Co. div. Richardson-Merrell Co., N.Y.C., 1955-58; v.p. Benton & Bowles Advt. Agy., N.Y.C., 1958-65; pres. Am. Chicle Co. div. Warner-Lambert Co., Morris Plains, N.J., 1965-70; pres. Life Savers Inc. div. Squibb Corp., N.Y.C., 1970-73; pres. Lanvin-Charles of Ritz Inc. subs. Squibb Corp., N.Y.C., 1974-76; group dir. new bus. devel. Gillette Co., Boston, 1977-78; exec. v.p. SSC & B, Inc., N.Y.C., 1978—. Mem. N.Y. State Republican Com., 1962-63; bd. dirs. YMCA Center for Internat. Mgmt. Studies, N.Y.C., 1970—. Served to lt., jr. grade, USN, 1952-55. Club: Knickerbocker (N.Y.C.). Home: 35 E 85th St New York NY 10028 Office: SSC&B Inc One Dag Hammarskjold Plaza New York NY 10017

PARROT, JEAN-CLAUDE, union ofcl.; b. Montreal, July 24, 1936; s. Gilles and Marie-Anne (Boucher) P.; m. Louisette Hamel, July 25, 1959; children—Manon, Johanne. Clk., Can. Nat. Bank, Montreal, 1952-54; postal clk. Can. Post Office, Montreal, 1954-68; v.p. Can. Union Postal Workers, Montreal, 1968-71, nat. chief steward, Ottawa, 1971-74, nat. v.p., 1974-77, nat. pres., 1977—, chief negotiator, 1975—. Roman Catholic. Home: 2026 Beaconwood Dr Ottawa ON Canada Office: 280 Metcalfe St Ottawa ON Canada

PARROTT, LESLIE, coll. pres.; b. Clarksville, Tenn., Apr. 2, 1922; s. Alonzo Leslie and Lucille (Elliot) P.; Th.B., Olivet Nazarene Coll., 1944; M.A., Willamette U., 1950; Ph.D., Mich. State U., 1958; m. Lora Lee Montgomery, July 7, 1943; children—Richard, Roger, Leslie III. Ordained to ministry Nazarene Ch.; pastor First Ch. of the Nazarene, Flint, Mich., 1953-61, First Ch. of the Nazarene, Portland, Oreg., 1962-70; pres. Eastern Nazarene Coll., Wollaston, Mass., 1970-75, Olivet Nazarene Coll., Kankakee, Ill., 1975—. Dir. research project on higher edn. for Ch. of the Nazarene, 1960-64. Rotarian. Club: Neighborhood. Author: The Art of Happy Christian Living; The Power of Your Attitudes; What is Sanctification?; Easy to Live With, 1970; Building Today's Church, 1971; Trying to Live Like a Christian in a World That Doesn't Understand, 1973; The New Spirit in "76", 1976; Renewing the Spirit of Revival, 1978; Sons of Africa, 1979. Home: 925 S Chicago St Kankakee IL 60901

PARROTT, RAYMOND CLEO, mgmt. cons.; b. Jaffrey, N.H., June 12, 1929; s. Raymond Charles and Doretta Mary (Lambert) P.; A.B., Trinity Coll., Hartford, Conn., 1953; M.A. (Clayton fellow 1953-54), Fletcher Sch. Law and Diplomacy, 1954; m. Athena Costopoulos; children—Jonathan G., Judith Maxwell, Suzanne Rebecca, Christopher Collins. Sr. staff cons. Arthur D. Little, Inc., Cambridge, Mass., 1954-59; on spl. assignment as econ. adviser to gov. W.Va., 1955-57; spl. asst. to pres. N&W Ry., 1959-60, economist, 1960-61; dep. dir. Peace Corps in Ghana, 1960-61, acting dir. in Nigeria, 1961-62, spl. asst. to dir., Washington, 1962-63, dir. div. nat. vol. service programs, Washington, 1963-69; regional dir. N.E. Peace Corps Center, 1968-69; mgr. spl. projects Bio-Dynamics, Inc., Cambridge, Mass., 1969-71; cons. internat. programs, ednl. and social problems, 1971-72. Econ. adviser, Fla., 1957-58; cons., Alaska, 1960; exec. dir. Advisory Council Vocat.-Tech. Edn. Mass., 1973-78; exec. dir. Nat. Advisory Council on Vocat. Edn., 1978—. Mem. exec. bd. Roanoka (Va.) council Boy Scouts Am., 1959-61; co-chmn. Burrell Meml. Hosp. drive, Roanoke, 1960; pres. Concord-Carlisle Youth Center Corp. Bd. dirs. Chevy Chase (Md.) Elementary Sch. P.T.A., 1963, Roanoke Fine Arts Center, 1959—. Served with USN, 1947-49. Recipient Meritorious award outstanding contbn. sports sec. of navy, 1948. Mem. N.A.M., Regional Sci. Assn. Phi Betta Kappa, Pi Gamma Mu, Alpha Delta Phi. Congregationalist. Home: 1805 T St NW Apt B Washington DC 20009 Office: Suite 412 425 13th St NW Washington DC 20004

PARROTT, ROBERT BELGROVE, agribus. cons., ret. grain mcht.; b. Fargo, N.D., Feb. 1, 1913; s. Alfred H. and Pearl (Canniff) P.; B.S., N.D. State U., 1935, LL.D. (hon.), 1960; m. Paula C. Verne, June 14, 1938; children—Michael, Christopher, Stephen. Asst. v.p. Northwest div. Cargill, Inc., Mpls., 1935-56; sr. exec. v.p. Central Soya Co., Inc., Ft. Wayne, Ind., 1956-78, also dir.; pres. Robert B. Parrott Inc., Agribus. Cons., 1978—; dir. Early and Daniel Industries Inc., Gen. Grain Co., Tidewater Grain Co., Phila., Varied Industry Plan Investment Fund. Adviser, Commodity Futures Trading Commn. Trustee N.D. State U.; bd. dirs. Chgo. Bd. Trade, Parkview Hosp., Ft. Wayne. Mem. Nat. Grain Trade Council (bd.), Grain and Feed

Dealers Nat. Assn. (bd.), Mpls. Grain Exchange, Chgo. Mercantile Exchange, Blue Key, Sigma Chi. Republican. Episcopalian. Mason (Shriner). Clubs: Quest, Fort Wayne Country: Union League (Chgo.). Home: 10333 Vermilyea Pass Fort Wayne IN 46804 Office: Fort Wayne Nat Bank Bldg Fort Wayne IN 46802

PARROTT, THOMAS CURTIS, govt. ofcl.; b. Filbert, S.C., Sept. 18, 1911; s. William Joseph and Minnie (Enloe) P.; A.B., Erskine Coll., 1931; LL.B., Southeastern U., 1940; m. Zoe Charlotte McFadden, May 8, 1943; children—Thomas Mc., Emily K. With Social Security Adminstrn., 1940—, now dir. Office of Internat. Policy. Mem. exec. commn. Permanent Interam. Com. on Social Security, 1971—. Pres. Dickeyville Assn., 1967; v.p. bd. trustees Kernan Hosp. for Children, 1978—; bd. dirs. Md. Health Care System, Inc. Recipient Commr.'s Citation Honor award, 1970, Distinguished Service award HEW, 1973. Mem. Am. Pub. Welfare Assn., Internat. Social Security Assn. (mem. bur. 1976). Presbyterian (elder). Home: 2326 Pickwick Rd Baltimore MD 21207 Office: 6401 Security Blvd Baltimore MD 21235

PARRY, ALBERT, educator, writer, lectr.; b. Rostov on-the-Don, Russia, Feb. 24, 1901; s. Joseph and Elizabeth (Blass) P.; came to U.S., 1921, naturalized, 1926; student Columbia U., 1925-26; A.B., U. Chgo., 1935, Ph.D., 1938; m. Louise Emily Goodman, Oct. 25, 1941 (div. 1971); children—James Donald, Thomas Hugh. Newspaper and mag. free-lance writer, 1921-37; editor Consol. Book Pubs., Inc., Chgo., 1937-41; asst. div. social scis. U. Chgo., 1939; research dir. radio broadcasts Chgo. Sun, 1941-42; information officer OSS, Washington, 1942-45; exec. bd. Chgo. Council Fgn. Relations, 1943-47; asso. prof. polit. sci. Northwestern U., 1946-47; prof. Russian civilization and lang., chmn. dept. Russian studies Colgate U., 1947-69, dir. Russian Area and Lang. Insts., 1961-66, prof. emeritus; prof. Russian civlization and lang., chmn. Slavic studies Case Western Res. U., 1969-71; program cons. Radio Free Europe, N.Y.C., 1950-52; vis. lectr., cons. U.S. Army War Coll., 1958-72; cons. Spl. Ops. Research Office, Dept. Army, 1960; vis. lectr. Inter-Am. Def. Coll., 1962-68; vis. scholar Radio Liberty, Munich, 1967-68. Exec. officer Com. to Defend Am. by Aiding Allies, 1940-41, Fight for Freedom Com., 1941. Grantee Am. Council Learned Socs., 1961, U.S. Office Edn., Modern Lang. Assn., 1965-66. Mem. Am. Assn. Tchrs. Slavic and East European Langs. (nat. pres. 1961), Am. Assn. Advancement Slavic Studies, Phi Beta Kappa. Author: Garrets and Pretenders, a history of bohemianism in America, 1933, rev. edit., 1960; Tattoo, 1933; Whistler's Father, 1939; Riddle of the Reich (with Wythe Williams), 1941; Russian Cavalcade, a military record, 1944; Korea, an annotated bibliography of Russian publications (with John T. Dorosh and Elizabeth G. Dorosh), 1950; Russia's Rockets and Missiles, 1960; The New Class Divided, Science and Technology Versus Communism, 1966; America Learns Russian, 1967; The Russian Scientist, 1973; Twentieth-Century Russian Literature (with Harry T. Moore), 1974; Terrorism: From Robespierre to Arafat, 1976; column Soviet Affairs in Missiles and Rockets mag., 1957-63. Contbr. Some Historians of Modern Europe, 1942. Translator, editor: Building Lenin's Russia (Liberman), 1945; Peter Kapitsa on Life and Science, 1968; The Moscow Puzzles (Kordemsky), 1972. Frequent contbr. profl. and popular jours. Address: 6919 Place de la Paix South Pasadena FL 33707

PARRY, ERNEST BRUCE, ednl. adminstr.; b. Syracuse, N.Y., Nov. 29, 1922; s. Marvin Emory and Ida Mae (Ayres) P.; B.S. in Indsl. Arts, Oswego (N.Y.) State Tchrs. Coll., 1951; M.Ed., U. Md., 1955; D.Ed. in Adminstrn. and Supervision, U. N.C., Chapel Hill, 1968; m. Edna Ogburn, Jan. 12, 1945; children—Ann Parry Malia, Marvin Bruce. Instr. schs. in N.Y. and Va., 1951-58; instr., supr. student tchrs. in off-campus schs. No. Ill. U., 1958-61; chief adminstrv. officer Forsyth County (N.C.) Indsl. Edn. Center, 1962-63, Forsyth Tech. Inst., Winston-Salem, N.C., 1963-71; pres. Wilson County Tech. Inst., Wilson, N.C., 1971—. Past pres. United Fund Wilson; bd. dirs. Wilson County chpt. ARC. Served with AUS, 1941-45. HEW grantee. Mem. Am. Vocat. Assn. (life), Motor Vehicles Mfrs. Assn. (industry planning council), N.C. Vocat. Assn., N.C. Assn. Pub. Community Coll. Presidents, Wilson C. of C., Wilson Arts Council. Democrat. Methodist. Club: Kiwanis. Home: 1120 Laurel Ln Wilson NC 27893 Office: 902 Herring Ave Wilson NC 27893

PARRY, HUGH JONES (JAMES CROSS), educator, social scientist, author; b. London, Eng., Mar. 10, 1916; s. John and Jane Myfanwy (Jones) Parry; brought to U.S., 1919, naturalized, 1924; A.B., Yale, 1937, postgrad. 1938; M.S., Columbia, 1939; Ph.D., U. So. Calif., 1949; m. Helen Mason Weston, May 30, 1941 (div. 1960); 1 son, John; m. 2d, Betty Brawer, Mar. 10, 1961; 1 son, Brian. Asso. dir. Opinion Research Center, U. Denver, 1947-49, also prof. sociology,; asst. dir. Troop Attitude Research br., U.S. Forces in Europe, 1950-52; project dir. evaluation staff U.S. High Commn. for Germany, 1952-53; research officer U.S. Embassy, Paris, 1956-58; chief Western European br., survey research div. USIA, 1958-61, survey dir. Office Research and Analysis, 1961-62, chief of survey research and Analysis, 1961-62, chief of survey research div., 1962-63, dir. research Western Europe, 1963-66; asso. dir. Social Research Group, prof. sociology George Washington U., Washington, 1966—. Served to lt. (s.g.) with USNR, 1942-46. Nat. Endowment for Lit. creative writing grantee, 1975. Mem. Am. Assn. Pub. Opinion Research, World Assn. Pub. Opinion Research (chmn. membership com. 1956-58), Am. Hist. Assn., Am. Sociol. Soc., Phi Beta Kappa, Phi Delta Theta. Club: Cosmos (Washington). Author: (with Leo P. Crespi) Public Opinion in Western Europe, 1953; Root of Evil, 1957; The Dark Road, 1959; The Grave of Heroes, 1961; To Hell for Half a Crown, 1967. Home: 4814 Falstone Ave Chevy Chase MD 20015 Office: 2401 Virginia Ave NW Washington DC 20037

PARRY, JOHN HORACE, historian, educatpr; b. Handsworth, Eng., Apr. 26, 1914; s. Walter Austin and Ethel (Piddock) P.; came to U.S., 1965; M.A., Ph.D., Clare Coll., Cambridge U., 1938; student Harvard U., 1936-37; m. Joyce Carter, Mar. 18, 1939; children—Michael, Joanna, Katherine, Elizabeth. Fellow, Clare Coll., 1938-49, univ. lectr. history, 1945-49; prof. modern history Univ. Coll. West Indies, 1949-55; vis. prof. history Harvard, 1955-56; prin. Univ. Coll., Ibadan, Nigeria, 1956-60, Univ. Coll., Swansea, Wales, 1960-65; vice-chancellor U. Wales, 1963-65; Gardiner prof. oceanic history and affairs Harvard U., 1965—. Served with Royal Brit. Navy, 1940-45. Decorated Order Brit. Empire, 1942; companion Order St. Michael and St. George, 1960; comdr. Order of Alfonso X (Spain). Fellow Royal Hist. Soc., Am. Acad. Arts and Scis.; mem. Am. Philos. Soc. Clubs: Oxford and Cambridge, Athenaeum (London); Harvard (N.Y.C.); Odd Volumes (Boston). Author: the Spanish Theory of Empire, 1940; The Audiencia of New Galicia, 1948; Europe and a Wider World, 1949; The Sale of Public Office in the Spanish Indies, 1953; A Short History of the West Indies, 1956; The Age of Reconnaissance, 1963; The Spanish Seaborne Empire, 1965; Trade and Dominion, 1971; The Discovery of the Sea, 1974; The Discovery of South America, 1979; also articles. Home: Pinnacle Rd Harvard MA 01451 Office: Widener 45 Cambridge MA 02138

PARRY, ROBERT WALTER, educator, chemist; b. Ogden, Utah, Oct. 1, 1917; s. Walter and Jeanette (Petterson) P.; B.S., Utah State Agr. Coll., 1940; M.S., Cornell U., 1942; Ph.D., U. Ill., 1946; m. Marjorie J. Nelson, July 6, 1945; children—Robert Bryce, Mark Nelson. Research asst. NDRC Munitions Devel. Lab., U. Ill. at Urbana, teaching fellow 1943-45; mem. faculty U. Mich., 1946-69, prof. chemistry, 1958-69; Distinguished prof. chemistry U. Utah, 1969—; indsl. cons., 1952—. Chmn. com. teaching chemistry Internat. Union Pure and Applied Chemistry 1969-74. Recipient Mfg. Chemists award for coll. teaching, 1972, Sr. U.S. Scientist award Alexander Von Humboldt-Stiftung (W. Ger.), 1980. Mem. Am. Chem. Soc. (Utah award Utah Sect. 1978, dir., past chmn. inorganic div. and div. chem. edn. award for distinguished service to inorganic chemistry 1965, for chem. edn., 1977, dir. 1973—, bd. editors jour. 1969—), Internat. Union Pure and Applied Chemistry (U.S. nat. com.), AAAS, Sigma Xi. Founding editor Inorganic Chemistry, 1961-63. Research, publs. on some structural problems of inorganic chemistry, and incorporation results into theoretical models chemistry, phosphorus, boron and fluorine chemistry. Office: U Utah Dept Chemistry Salt Lake City UT 84112

PARSEGHIAN, ARA RAOUL, former football coach, commentator; b. Akron, Ohio, May 21, 1923; s. Michael and Amelia (Bonneau) P.; B.A., Miami U., Oxford, Ohio, 1949, M.A., 1951; m. Kathleen Davis, Dec. 30, 1948; children—Karan, Kristan, Michael. Football coach Miami U., 1950-55, Northwestern U., 1956-63, U. Notre Dame, 1964-75; commentator ABC's NCAA Football; host TV series Ara's Sports World. Served with USNR, 1942-45. Named Coach of Year, 1964. Address: St Joseph Bank Bldg South Bend IN 46601*

PARSHALL, WALTER RAYMOND, corp. exec.; b. Phila., Nov. 4, 1905; s. George Baldwin and Rachel (Burton) P.; student Drexel Inst., 1923-26; C.P.A., Pa., 1931; m. Lillian Force, Apr. 6, 1926; children—George William, Richard Jay, Walter Raymond, Jean, Barbara. Bookkeeper, Commonwealth Title Ins. & Trust Co., Phila., 1923-26; accountant Hare, Schenck & Co., pub. accountants, 1926-35, Lybrand, Ross Bros. & Montgomery, pub. accountants, 1935-41; with Baldwin-Lima-Hamilton Corp., Eddystone, Pa., 1941-53, controller, 1946-53; treas., controller, dir. Fed. Pacific Electric Co., Newark, 1953-56; treas. Van Norman Industries, Inc., 1957- 62; treas., controller, sec. Transitron Electronic Corp., 1962-66; treas. Lapointe Machine Tool Co., Hudson, Mass., 1966-67; treas. Am. Safety Equipment Corp., Encino, Calif. 1967-76; v.p., treas. Perkins Industries, Los Angeles, 1977-79; controller Hartwell Devel. Inc., Los Angeles, 1978; v.p., treas., asst. tax dir. Healthco, Inc., Boston, 1979—. Mem. Fin. Execs. Inst., Am., Pa. insts. C.P.A.'s. Methodist. Home: 11 Woodchester Dr Acton MA 01720 Office: 25 Stuart St Boston MA 02116

PARSONS, ALBERT L., TV exec.; b. Wheeling, W.Va., June 5, 1939; s. Albert L. and Marie Damron (Balderson) P.; student public schs.; children—Scott, Jill, Grant. Store mgr. F.W. Woolworth Co., Phila., 1960-62, mdsg. mgr., Tom's River, N.J., 1962-65; promotion mgr. Montgomery Ward & Co., Oklahoma City, 1965-68; salesman, then v.p., gen. sales mgr. Sta. KOCO-TV, Oklahoma City, 1968-76, pres., gen. mgr., 1976—. Bd. dirs. Okla. Theatre Center, Cerebral Palsy Assn. Oklahoma City. Mem. Nat. Assn. TV Programming Execs., Nat. Assn. Broadcasters, Okla. Broadcasters Assn., Oklahoma City C. of C., Okla. Heritage Assn. Republican. Methodist. Clubs: Sirloin, Quail Creek Golf and Country, Oak Tree Golf and Country. Home: 9111 Autumn Rd Oklahoma City OK 73151 Office: PO Box 32325 Oklahoma City OK 73123

PARSONS, BETTY PIERSON, artist, art dealer; b. N.Y.C., Jan. 31, 1900; d. J. Fred and Suzanne (Miles) Pierson; pvt. study sculpture and painting; m. Schuyler Livingston Parsons, May 8, 1919. Dir. Cornelius Sullivan Gallery, 1936-39, Wakefield Gallery, 1939-43, Mortimer Brandt Contemporary Gallery, 1943-46, Betty Parsons Gallery, N.Y.C., 1946—; works exhibited in Paris, 1932, Calif., 1934, throughout U.S.; one-woman shows Midtown Galleries, Miami Mus. Art, New Arts Gallery, Atlanta, Bennington Coll., Gallery Seven, Boston, Grand Central Modern, N.Y.C., White Chapel Gallery, London, Eng., Studio Gallery, Washington, Sachs Gallery, N.Y.C., Drew U., Benson Gallery, Bridgehampton, L.I., N.Y., David Hendriks Gallery, Dublin, Ireland, Kornblee Gallery, N.Y.C., USIA Traveling Exhbn., 1977, Louise Himelfarb Gallery, Watermill, L.I., 1977, 79, R.I. Sch. Design Mus., Providence, 1977, Barnard Coll., N.Y.C., 1977, Heath Gallery, Atlanta, 1978, 79, Kornblee Gallery, N.Y.C., 1978, Truman Gallery, N.Y.C., 1978, Jeff Parsons Gallery, Shelter Island, N.Y., 1979, Hoshour Gallery, Albuquerque, 1979, Summit (N.J.) Art Center, 1979, Fairweather Hardin Gallery, Chgo., 1979; exhibited Finch Coll., Montclair Mus., Cranbrook Acad. Art, Mich., Brooks Meml. Art Gallery, Tenn. Home: 7 W 81st St New York NY 10024 Office: 24 W 57th St New York NY 10019

PARSONS, CHARLES DACRE, educator; b. Cambridge, Mass., Apr. 13, 1933; s. Talcott and Helen B. (Walker) P.; A.B., Harvard, 1954, A.M., 1956, Ph.D., 1961; postgrad. U. Cambridge, Eng., 1954-55; m. Marjorie Louise Wood, Sept. 6, 1968; children—Jotham Wood, Sylvia Anne. Jr. fellow Soc. Fellows, Harvard, 1958-61, asst. prof. philosophy, 1962-65; asst. prof. philosophy Cornell U., 1961-62; asso. prof. philosophy Columbia, N.Y.C., 1965-69, prof., 1969—, chmn. dept., 1976-79. George Santayana fellow in philosophy Harvard, 1964-65; Nat. Endowment Humanities fellow, 1979-80. Mem. Assn. Symbolic Logic (sec. 1971-76), Am. Math. Soc., Am. Philos. Assn., Soc. for Philosophy and Pub. Affairs. Author articles in field. Editor: Jour. of Philosophy, 1966—. Home: 15 Claremont Ave New York NY 10027

PARSONS, DONALD FREDERICK, biophysicist; b. Shoreham-by-sea, Sussex, Eng., Nov. 28, 1928; s. Reginald Alexander and Gladys (West) P.; B.Sc. in Chemistry, U. London, 1950, Ph.D., D.I.C. in Phys. Chemistry (Ministry of Supply Sci. scholar), 1953, M.B., B.S. (St. Bartholomew's Hosp. scholar), 1957, D.Sc., 1975; m. Julieta Perez-Medrano, Aug. 1, 1958; children—Clare Olivia, Raymond Anthony, Francis Robin, Catherine Leslie. Research asso. dept. exptl. surgery Duke, 1957-59; biophysicist biology div. Oak Ridge Nat. Lab., 1959-61; asst. prof. med. biophysics U. Toronto (Ont., Can.), 1961-66; prin. cancer research scientist Electron Optics Lab., Roswell Park Meml. Inst., Buffalo, research prof. biophysics State U. N.Y., Buffalo, 1966-76; research physician, div. labs. research Dept. Health N.Y. State, Albany, 1976—; dir. High Voltage Electron Microscopy Lab., research prof. biology Rensselaer Poly. Inst., Troy, N.Y., 1976—, SUNY, Albany, 1978—. Lic. practising physician, N.Y. State. Fellow Royal Micros. Soc.; mem. Biophys. Soc., Am. Crystallographic Assn., Am. Assn. Cancer Research, Am. Soc. Clin. Oncology, Electron Microscope Soc. Am., Internat. Soc. Cell Biologists. Editor: Biochimica Biophysica Acta, 1966—. Devel. methods for analysis of structure of cells and viruses; research in electron microscopy, x-ray diffraction, electron diffraction, high voltage electron microscopy, cancer cell cytology, oncology. Home: 150 Mosher Rd Delmar NY 12054 Office: Dept Health NY State Div Labs and Research Empire State Plaza Albany NY 12201

PARSONS, DONALD HOLCOMBE, investment co. exec., lawyer; b. Detroit, June 17, 1930; s. George Holcombe and Katharine (Babst) P.; grad. Phillips Acad., Andover, 1948; B.A., Yale, 1952; LL.B., U. Mich., 1955, M.B.A., 1956; m. Sarah Caswell Angell, Dec. 18, 1954; children—James Angell, Sarah Babst, Donald Holcombe; m. 2d, Louise Garner Price, Aug. 31, 1974; 1 son, Adam. Admitted to Mich. bar, 1956, since practiced in Detroit; asso. firm Miller, Canfield, Paddock & Stone, 1956-59; sr. partner Emery, Parsons, Bahr, Tennent & Hogan, 1963-65, Parsons, Tennent, Hammond, Hardig & Ziegelman, 1965-70; chmn. Resources Planning Corp., 1971—; past chmn. bd. Bank of the Commonwealth, Creative Capital Corp., Indsl. State Bank & Trust Co., Kalamazoo, Birmingham Bloomfield Bank, Bank of Lansing; incorporator, past dir. Huron Valley Nat. Bank, Ann Arbor. Mem. Am., Detroit, Oakland County bar assns., State Bar Mich. Clubs: Birmingham Athletic; Chicago (Charlevoix, Mich.); Beach, Bath and Tennis (Palm Beach, Fla.); River (N.Y.C.); Litchfield Country (S.C.). Home: 1205 Timberview Trail Bloomfield Hills MI 48013 also 246 Tangier Ave Palm Beach FL 33480 Office: 777 Bowers Birmingham MI 48008 also 319 Clematis St 10th Floor West Palm Beach FL 33401

PARSONS, DONALD JAMES, bishop; b. Phila., Mar. 28, 1922; s. Earl and Helen (Drabble) P.; B.A., Temple U., 1943; M.Div., Phila. Div. Sch., 1946, Th.D., 1951, D.D. (hon.), 1964; postgrad. U. Nottingham (Eng.), 1968; D.C.L., Nashotah (Wis.) House, 1973; m. Mary Russell, Sept. 17, 1955; children—Mary, Rebecca, Bradford. Ordained priest Episcopal Ch., 1946, consecrated bishop, 1973; curate Immanual Ch., Wilmington, Del., 1946-49; rector St. Peter's Ch., Smyrna, Del., 1949-50; prof. N.T., Nashotah House, 1950-73, pres., dean, 1963-73; bishop Diocese of Quincy (Ill.), 1973—. Author: A Life-time Road to God, 1966; In Time with Jesus, 1973; Holy Eucharist: Rite Two, 1976. Home: 308 W Edgevale Peoria IL 61604 Office: 3601 N North St Peoria IL 61604

PARSONS, EDWARD ERSKINE, JR., investment broker; b. Wilkinsburg, Pa., Dec. 3, 1905; s. Edward E. and Alice (Blake) P.; student Antioch Coll., 1923-24; m. Myrtle Stebner, Aug. 17, 1929; children—Edward Erskine III. Robert. Pres., dir. Parsons & Co., Inc., Cleve., 1951—, Forest City Industries, Inc., Cleve., 1950—; dir. Cleve. Mortgage Co. Mem. Nat. Security Traders Assn. (past pres.). Home: 13964 Edgewater Dr Lakewood OH 44107 Office: Superior Bldg Cleveland OH 44114

PARSONS, EDWIN SPENCER, educator, clergyman; b. Brockton, Mass., Feb. 16, 1919; s. Edwin Webber and Ethel Faunce (Marsh) P.; A.B., Denison U., 1941, D.D., 1967; B.D., Andover Newton Theol. Sch., 1945; D.D., Kalamazoo Coll., 1966; L.H.D., Chgo. Coll. Osteo. Medicine, 1978; m. Eleanor Millard, Nov. 3, 1944; children—William Spencer, Ellen, James Millard, Bradford Delano. Ordained to ministry Am. Baptist Ch., 1944; asst. minister First Bapt. Ch., Newton Centre, Mass., 1945-47; exec. dir. Bapt. Student Found., Inc., Cambridge, Mass., 1947-59; pastor Hyde Park Union Ch., Chgo., 1959-65; asso. prof. ethics U. Chgo. Div. Sch., 1965-78, prof., 1978-79; dir. ministerial field edn., 1977-79, dean Rockefeller Meml. Chapel, 1965-80; dir. New Eng. office Health Resources Ltd., Kansas City, Mo., 1979—. Pres., Council Hyde Park-Kenwood Chs. and Synagogues, 1963; chmn. Abortion Rights Assn. Ill., 1974-79; founder, chmn. Ill. Religious Coalition for Abortion Rights, 1975, Ill. Clergy Consultation Services on Problem Pregnancies, 1971-79; bd. dirs., chmn. clergy adv. com. Planned Parenthood Assn., Chgo., 1977-79. Bd. dirs. Hyde Park YMCA; bd. govs. Internat. House, Chgo.; trustee Packard Manse (Mass.), Bapt. Theol. Union, Chgo., 1960-70; pres., bd. mgrs. Ministers and Missionaries Benefit Bd., 1975—; mem. gen. bd., mem. exec. com., mem. commn. on Christian unity Am. Bapt. Chs., 1963-72, 74—. Democrat. Author: The Christian Yes or No, 1964. Home: 69 Fort Point Rd North Weymouth MA 02191

PARSONS, ELMER EARL, clergyman; b. Cloverland, Wash., Oct. 4, 1919; s. Claud Solomon and Bessie Lillian (Campbell) P.; B.A., Seattle Pacific U., 1942; S.T.B., N.Y. Theol. Sem., 1945; S.T.M., Asbury Theol. Sem., Wilmore, Ky., 1955; D.D. (hon.), Greenville (Ill.) Coll., 1958; m. Marjorie Emma Carlson, Aug. 29, 1942; children—Karl Elmer, James Myron, Helen Joy, Ann Elizabeth, Lois Marie, Louise Melba. Ordained to ministry Free Methodist Ch., 1944; acad. dean Washington Springs (S.D.) Coll., 1945-47; missionary to China, 1947-49; missionary to Japan, 1949-54, supt. Japan Free Meth. Mission, 1950-54; pres. Central Coll., McPherson, Kans., 1955-64, Osaka (Japan) Christian Coll., 1964-74; Asia area sec. Free Meth. Ch., 1964-74; bishop Free Meth. Ch. N.Am., 1974—. Named Alumnus of Year, Seattle Pacific U., 1976. Mem. Wesleyan Theol. Soc. Author: Witness to the Resurrection, 1967. Home: 1302 W Winona Ave Warsaw IN 46580 Office: 901 College Ave Winona Lake IN 46590

PARSONS, ERVIN IVY, JR., petroleum co. exec.; b. Moran, Tex., June 26, 1928; s. Ervin Ivy and Eva Lena (Childers) P.; B.B.A., U. Houston, 1957; m. LaVerne Good, Nov. 3, 1951; children—Robert Sherrell, Eva Louise. With Continental Oil Co., 1963-74, asst. treas., 1970-72, treas., 1972-74, fin. exec. various subsidiaries, 1963-70; sr. v.p. finance Tex. Oil & Gas Corp., Dallas, 1974-76, also dir.; pres. Holly Corp.; pres. Holly Energy Inc., 1976—, also dir. Served with USAF, 1951-53. Mem. Financial Execs. Inst., Dallas, Petroleum Club of Dallas, Inwood Racquet. Home: 5421 Pebblebrook Dr Dallas TX 75229 Office: 2001 Bryan Tower Dallas TX 75201

PARSONS, ESTELLE, actress; b. Lynn, Mass., Nov. 20, 1927; d. Eben and Elinor (Mattson) Parsons; B.A. in Polit. Sci., Conn. Coll. Women, 1949; student Boston U. Law Sch., 1949-50; m. Richard Gehman, Dec. 19, 1953 (div. Aug. 1958); children—Martha and Abbie (twins). Stage appearances include Happy Hunting, 1957; Whoop Up, 1958; Beg, Borrow or Steal, 1960; Threepenny Opera, 1960; Mrs. Dally Has a Lover, 1962; Ready When You Are C.B., 1964; Malcolm, 1965; Seven Descents of Myrtle, 1968; And Miss Reardon Drinks a Little, 1971; Mert and Phil, 1974; The Norman Conquests, 1975-76; Ladies of the Alamo, 1977; Miss Margarida's Way, 1977-78; film appearances include Bonnie and Clyde, 1966; Rachel, Rachel, 1967; I Never Sang for My Father, 1969. Recipient Theatre World award, 1962-63, Obie award, 1964, Motion Picture Acad. Arts and Scis. award, 1967, Conn. Coll. medal of honor, 1969. Home: 505 West End Ave New York City NY 10024. *It's in attempting all, that one succeeds.*

PARSONS, GEOFFREY, JR., ret. corp. exec.; b. N.Y.C., July 3, 1908; s. Geoffrey and Carle (Taylor) P.; student Ecole de Soisy-Sous-Etioles, France, 1922-23, Phillips Exeter Acad., 1923-26, Harvard, 1927-31; m. Brenda Tweed, Sept. 12, 1933 (div. 1939); 1 son, Geoffrey; m. 2d, Dorothy Blackman Tartiere, June 6, 1945. Reporter Boston Globe, 1931-36; midwestern corr. New York Herald Tribune (hdqrs. Chicago), 1937-41, war corr., London, 1941, chief of London Bur., 1943-44, editor European edit. New York Herald Tribune, 1944-50; became chief of press and pub. relations NATO 1950, dir. information, 1954-57; v.p. for Europe, Northrop Internat., 1957-65; v.p. and European rep., 1965; European rep., 1977-78. Decorated comdr. French Legion of Honor. Mem. Assn. U.S. Aerospace Industries in Europe (pres. 1962-63), Anglo-Am. Press Assn. (Paris). Clubs: American of Paris; Century (N.Y.C.). Contbr. articles to Saturday Evening Post, Reader's Digest, others. Home: 50 Ave Foch Paris 75116 France

PARSONS, GEORGE W., hosp. adminstr.; B.S. in Edn., U. Va.; grad. USN Res. Command Sch., Insdl. Coll. Armed Forces, Fed. Health Care Inst. With VA, 1962—, now dir. VA Med. Center, Bklyn. Fellow Am. Coll. Hosp. Adminstrs.; mem. Am. Hosp. Assn., Assn. Mil.

Surgeons, U.S., Fed. Hosp. Inst. Alumni Assn., Fed. Exec. Bd. Office: VA Med Center 800 Poly Pl Brooklyn NY 11209

PARSONS, GEORGE WILLIAMS, med. center adminstr., cattle rancher; b. Natural Bridge, Va., Jan. 21, 1918; s. George Washington and Mary Elizabeth (Williams) P.; student Washington and Lee U., 1935-37; B.S. in Edn., U. Va., 1941; grad. USNR Tng. Sch., 1942, USNR Officer Candidate Sch., 1944, USNR Command Sch., 1944, Ind. Coll. Armed Forces, 1963, Fed. Health Care Inst., 1966; m. Miriam Rebecca Boyer, May 2, 1942; children—Mary Locke Parsons Black, Ann Boyer Parsons Talkington, George Russell. Tchr., Winchester, Va., 1941-42; asst. phys. dir. VA Hosp., Roanoke, Va., 1946-47, asst. chmn. spl. services, 1947-51; chmn. spl. services VA Hosp., Lyons, N.J., 1951-58; spl. asst. to hosp. mgr. VA Hosp., Pitts., 1958-62; asst. dir. VA Hosp., Clarksburg, W.Va., 1962-67, VA Hosp., Erie, Pa., 1967-69, VA Hosp., Marion, Ind., 1969-72, VA Hosp., Bklyn., 1972-75; dir. VA Outpatient Clinic, Lubbock, Tex., 1975-76; dir. VA Med. Center, Bklyn., 1976—; cattle rancher, Natural Bridge; preceptor M.P.H./M.B.A. Program in Health Adminstrn., Columbia U.; mem. steering com. Fed. Exec. Bd., N.Y.C.; mem. dist. bd. Health Systems Agy., Bklyn.; mem. Rockbridge County (Va.) Farm Bur. Served with USNR, 1942-46; PTO. Recipient Outstanding Achievement award Am. Legion, 1975, Disting. Service award, 1975, Recognition award, 1978; Recognition award VFW, 1975, United Vets. Assn. award, Queens, N.Y., 1979, also numerous other awards and commendations from VA, vets. and civic orgns., 1946-74. Fellow Am. Coll. Hosp. Adminstrs. (oral examiner), Royal Soc. Health; mem. Assn. Mil. Surgeons U.S. (pres. N.Y. chpt. 1979-80), Am. Hosp. Assn., Sr. Exec. Service U.S. Govt., Fed. Hosp. Inst. Alumni Assn., N.Y. Acad. Scis., Res. Officers Assn. U.S.A. (pres. W.Va. chpt. 1967). Office: VA Med Center 800 Poly Pl Brooklyn NY 11209 also Route #1 Natural Bridge VA 24579

PARSONS, HARRIET OETTINGER, film producer, writer, realtor asso.; b. Burlington, Iowa; d. John Dement and Louella Rose (Oettinger) Parsons; grad. Horace Mann Sch. Girls, 1924; B.A., Wellesley Coll., 1928; m. King Kennedy, Sept. 28, 1939 (div. 1946). Mem. scenario staff Metro-Goldwyn-Mayer Studios, Hollywood, 1928; columnist, staff interviewer, asso. editor Photoplay mag., 1929, staff writer, 1930; free lance writer fan mags., 1930-33; condr. column Liberty mag.; columnist, feature writer Hearst's Universal Service (later merged with Internat. News Service), 1931-43; producer Screen Snapshots, Columbia Pictures, 1933-40; mem. motion picture staff Los Angeles Examiner, 1935-43; weekly radio program Hollywood Highlights, NBC, 1938; editor column Hollywood in Review, Woman's Day, 1938-40; producer Meet the Stars, Republic Studios, 1940-43, Joan of Ozark, 1942; writer, producer R-K-O Radio Pictures, 1943-55, including Enchanted Cottage, 1945, Night Song, 1947, I Remember Mama, 1948, Never a Dull Moment, 1950, Clash by Night, 1952, Susan Slept Here, 1954; co-producer Broadway play The Rape of the Belt, 1960; producer 20th Century Fox TV, 1956-57; lectr. U. So. Calif., 1952. Dir., mem. entertainment com. Hollywood Canteen; realtor-asso. Lawrence Block Co., 1964—. Mem. Acad. Motion Picture Arts and Sci., Wellesley Alumnae Assn., Producers Guild Am., Beverly Hills Realty Bd., Zeta Alpha. Republican. Club: Hollywood Women's Press. Home: 2253 Coldwater Canyon Dr Beverly Hills CA 90210

PARSONS, HENRY MCILVAINE, psychologist; b. Lenox, Mass., Aug. 31, 1911; s. Herbert and Elsie Worthington (Clews) P.; B.A., Yale U., 1933; M.A., Columbia U., 1947; Ph.D., U. Calif., Los Angeles, 1963; m. Renee Oakman, 1938 (div. 1945); children—Robert; m. 2d, Marina Svetlova, 1949 (div. 1957); m. 3d, Marjorie Thorson, 1957. Reporter, N.Y. Herald Tribune, 1935-42; organizer N.Y. Newspaper Guild, 1942; asst., then lectr. psychology Columbia U., 1947-52; research asso. N.Y. U., 1951-52; supr. Electronics Research Labs., Columbia U., 1952-58; mem. human factors staff Douglas Aircraft Co., Long Beach and Santa Monica, Calif., 1956-58; sr. human factors scientist, br. head System Devel. Corp., Santa Monica and Falls Church, Va., 1958-68; self-employed cons., 1968-69; 70-73; v.p. research Riverside Research Inst., N.Y.C., 1969-70; exec. dir. Inst. Behavioral Research Inc., Silver Spring, Md., 1974—; pres. Exptl. Coll. of Inst. Behavioral Research, Silver Spring, 1974—. Served with USNR, 1942-45. Fellow Am. Psychol. Assn. (pres. div. 21, 1975-76), Human Factors Soc. (pres. 1968-69), AAAS; mem. N.Y. Acad. Scis., Ergonomics Soc., Am. Ednl. Research Assn., Sigma Xi. Clubs: Century (N.Y.C.); Cosmos (Washington). Author: Man-Machine System Experiments, 1972; also articles. Home: 4701 Willard Ave Chevy Chase MD 20015 Office: 2429 Linden Ln Silver Spring MD 20910

PARSONS, IRENE, mgmt. cons.; b. North Wilkesboro, N.C.; d. Everett T. and Martha (Minton) Parsons; B.S. in Bus. Edn. and Adminstrn., U. N.C., 1941, LL.D. (hon.), 1967; M.S. in Pub. Adminstrn., George Washington U., 1965. Tchr., Roanoake Rapids (N.C.) High Sch., 1941-42; rep. U.S. Civil Service Commn., 1942-43; with VA, 1946-74, asst. adminstr. vets. affairs, dir. personnel, dir. equal employment opportunity, 1965-74; mgmt. cons., 1974—. Exec. com. Pres.'s Study Group Careers for Women. Served to lt. USCGR, 1943-46. Recipient Fed. Woman's Outstanding Achievement award, 1966, Silver Helmet award Amvets, 1971, Career Service award Nat. Civil Service League, 1972, Alumni Achievement award George Washington U., 1973. Mem. Assn. Fed. Woman's Award Recipients (chmn. 1972—). Office: 2522 I St NW Washington DC 20037

PARSONS, JAMES BENTON, U.S. dist. judge; b. Kansas City, Mo., Aug. 13, 1913; s. James B. and Maggie Virgia (Mason) P.; B.A., James Millikin U., 1934; student U. Wis., summers, 1935-39; M.A., U. Chgo., 1946, LL.D., 1949; m. Amy Margaret Maxwell, Dec. 24, 1952; 1 son, Hans-Dieter K. Successively field agt., asst. to dean men, instr. polit. sci. Lincoln U., Jefferson City, Mo., 1934-38, acting head music dept., 1938-40; tchr. pub. schs., Greensboro, N.C., 1940-42; admitted to Ill. bar, 1949; mem. firm Gassaway, Crosson, Turner & Parsons, Chgo., 1949-51; tchr. constl. govt. John Marshall Law Sch., Chgo., 1949-51; asst. corp. counsel City of Chgo., 1949-51; asst. U.S. dist. atty., 1951-60; judge superior court Cook County, Ill., 1960-61; judge U.S. Dist. Ct. No. Dist. Ill., 1961—, now chief judge. Co-chmn. Ill. Commn. N.Y. World's Fair; chmn. Chgo. Conf. Race and Religion; exec. bd. Chgo. Area council Boy Scouts Am. Bd. dirs. Trotting Charities, Inc., Chgo. Urban League; trustee Lincoln Acad. Ill., Chgo. Med. Podiatry Hosp.; hon. bd. dirs. Leukemia Research Found., Inc.; nat. bd. trustees Nat. Conf. Christians and Jews; citizens com. U. Ill. Served with USNR, 1942-46. Mem. Am., Chgo., Ill., Fed., Nat., Cook County bar assns., Ill. Acad. Criminology, N.A.A.C.P., Sigma Pi, Pi Beta Phi, Kappa Alpha Psi. Conglist. (asst. treas.). Clubs: Standard, Navy League, Covenant (Chgo.). Office: US Courthouse 219 S Dearborn Ave Chicago IL 60604*

PARSONS, JAMES JEROME, geographer, educator; b. Cortland, N.Y., Nov. 15, 1915; s. James Jerome and Edith (Gere) P.; A.B., U. Calif. at Berkeley, 1937, M.A., 1939, Ph.D., 1948; m. Betty Rupp, Oct. 30, 1942; children—David, John, Sally. Mem. faculty U. Calif. at Berkeley, 1946—, prof. geography, 1959—, chmn. dept. geography, 1960-66, 75—. Served to maj., USAAF, 1941-45. Guggenheim fellow in Spain, 1959-60. Mem. AAAS, Assn. Am. Geographers (pres. 1974-75), Assn. Pacific Coast Geographers (pres. 1952), Acad. Colombiana de Historia (hon.). Author: Antioqueño Colonization in Western Colombia, 1949; San Andres and Providencia, 1955; The Green Turtle and Man, 1962; Antioquia's Corridor to the Sea, 1967. Home: 670 Woodmont Ave Berkeley CA 94708

PARSONS, JAMES WILSON, JR., educator; b. Mansfield, La., Mar. 11, 1926; s. James Wilson and Irene (Shortal) P.; B.S., La. State U., 1948, M.B.A., 1949, Ph.D., 1955; m. Mary Joan Fidler, Sept. 7, 1948; children—James Gregg, Jack Wilson, Joe Fidler. Grad. asst. La. State U., 1948-49, instr. statistics, 1949-55; asso. prof. accounting Baylor U., 1955-59, prof., 1959—; pvt. practice accounting, 1959—. Treas., dir. Waco Pastoral Counseling Center, 1966-67. Served with USAAF, 1944-45. Named outstanding prof. Hankamer Sch. Bus., Baylor U., 1962, 67, 73. C.P.A., La., Tex. Mem. Am. Inst. C.P.A.'s, Am. Accounting Assn., Omicron Delta Kappa, Phi Eta Sigma, Beta Alpha Psi, Beta Gamma Sigma. Baptist (deacon). Home: 2224 Charboneau St Waco TX 76710

PARSONS, JEFFREY ROBINSON, anthropologist; b. Washington, Oct. 9, 1939; s. Merton Stanley and Elisabeth (Oldenburg) P.; B.S., Pa. State U., 1961; Ph.D., U. Mich., 1966; m. Mary Thomson Hrones, Apr. 27, 1968; 1 dau., Apphia Hrones. Asst. prof. anthropology U. Mich., Ann Arbor, 1966-71, asso. prof., 1971-76, prof., 1976—. NSF research grantee, 1967, 70, 72-73, 75-76. Mem. Am. Anthrop. Assn., Soc. for Am. Archaeology, AAAS, Inst. Andean Research, Inst. Andean Studies, Sociedad Mexicana de Antropologia. Author: Prehistoric Settlement Patterns in the Texcoco Region, Mexico, 1971; (with William T. Sanders and Robert Santley) The Basin of Mexico: The Cultural Ecology of a Civilization, 1979. Office: Museum of Anthropology U Mich Ann Arbor MI 48109

PARSONS, KEITH I., lawyer; b. Davenport, Iowa, Apr. 28, 1912; s. Alfred and Cora Pearl (McDowell) P.; Ph.B., U. Chgo., 1933, J.D., 1937; m. Lorraine Watson, June 28, 1939; children—Robert, Susan, James. Asst. to sec. U. Chgo., 1934-37; admitted to Ill. bar. 1938, since practiced in Chgo.; asst. chief, later chief legal div. Chgo. Ordnance Dist., 1942-46; partner firm Milliken, Vollers & Parsons, 1946-64; partner firm Ross, Hardies, O'Keefe, Babcock & Parsons, 1965—. Mem. Hinsdale (Ill.) Bd. Edn., 1957-63, pres., 1959-63; mem. Chgo. Crime Commn., 1960—; mem. citizens bd. U. Chgo., 1964—. Mem. bd. govs. Ill. State Colls. and Univs., 1970-73. Served to lt. col. AUS, 1942-46. Mem. Am., Ill., Chgo. (past chmn. corp. law com.; mem. bd. mgrs. 1967-69) bar assns., Econ. Club Chgo., Law Club, Legal Club (past pres.), Phi Beta Kappa, Psi Upsilon. Clubs: Chicago, University, Commonwealth (Chgo.); Hinsdale Golf; Chikaming Country (Lakeside, Mich.). Home: 744 Cleveland Rd Hinsdale IL 60521 Office: One IBM Plaza Chicago IL 60611

PARSONS, KERMIT CARLYLE, univ. dean; b. Cleve., July 15, 1927; s. Kermit Carlyle and Emma (Siebert) P.; B. Arch., Miami U., Oxford, Ohio, 1951; M.R.P., Cornell U., 1953; m. Janice Ingram Patten, June 30, 1951; children—John Everett, Stephen Carl, Katherine Ingram. Head community planning sect. Cleve. City Planning Commn., 1953-57; mem. faculty Cornell U., 1957—, chmn. dept. city and regional planning, 1964-71, prof., 1965—, dean Coll. Architecture, Art and Planning, 1971—; vis. prof. U. P.R., 1969-70; asso. cons. William Gould & Assos., 1970-72; cons. Ford Found., 1970-76; cons. Philippine Ministry Edn. and Culture, 1979—; coll and univ., also city planning cons. Served with USNR, 1945-46. Recipient Seipp prize Miami U., 1949, Dunbar award, 1951; Univ. fellow Cornell U., 1951-53; fellow Woodrow Wilson Internat. Center for Scholars, 1977. Mem. Soc. Coll. and Univ. Planning (pres. 1966-69), Am. Planning Assn. (pres. N.Y. upstate chpt. 1966-68), AIA, Am. Soc. Planning Ofcls., Soc. Archtl. Historians. Author: The Cornell Campus: A History of its Planning and Development, 1968; (with others) Public Land Acquisition for New Communities and the Control of Urban Growth, 1973; (with Pierre Clavel) National Growth Policy-An Institutional Prespective, 1976; also articles. Home: 1604 Dryden Rd RD 2 Freeville NY 13068 Office: Sibley Hall Cornell U Ithaca NY 14853

PARSONS, MALCOLM BARNINGHAM, polit. scientist, educator; b. Greenville, Mich., Oct. 29, 1919; s. St. Clare and Mary (Barningham) P.; B.A. magna cum laude, U. Ariz., 1946, M.A., 1947; Ph.D., U. Ill., 1950; m. Jeanne Elizabeth Cram, Dec. 3, 1950; 1 son, John Malcolm. Fellow polit. sci. U. Ariz., 1946-47; asst. polit. sci. U. Ill., 1947-49; instr. govt. U. Okla., 1949-50, asst. prof., 1950-51; asst. prof. pub. adminstrn. Fla. State U., Tallahassee, 1951-53, asso. prof., 1953-57, prof., 1957-59, chmn. div. instrn. pub. adminstrn., 1954-55, 56-58, prof. govt., 1959-76, chmn. dept. govt., 1963-69, vis. scholar univ. study center, Florence, Italy, 1973, acting dir. pub. adminstrn. program, 1974, prof. govt. and pub. adminstrn., 1976—; vis. prof., tech. asst. U. Mich. assigned to U. Philippines, 1955-56; vis. scholar U. Calif. at Berkeley, 1969, Univ. Study Center, London, 1978. Patron LeMoyne Art Found., Fla. State U. Theatre Found. Served with AUS, 1942-45. Recipient sr. scholarship award U. Ariz., 1946; Faculty devel. grantee Fla. State U., 1969. Mem. Am. Soc. Pub. Adminstrn., Am. Polit. Sci. Assn., So. Polit. Sci. Assn. (v.p., program chmn. 1971, mem. Chastain awards com.), Phi Beta Kappa, Omicron Delta Kappa, Phi Kappa Phi, Pi Sigma Alpha, Pi Alpha Alpha. Author: Use of the Licensing Power by the City of Chicago, 1952; (with others) Governmental Services in the Philippines, 1956. Editor, contbr. Perspectives in the Study of Politics, 1968; contbr. to Future of the American Presidency, 1975; also articles to profl. jours. Contbr. Political Behavior in America, 1966. Home: 1010 Lothian Dr Tallahassee FL 32312

PARSONS, ROBERT WADE, ret. investment banker; b. Elizabeth, N.J., June 11, 1900; s. Elias W. and Lily (Barnard) P.; B.S., Wesleyan U., Middletown, Conn., 1922; m. Irene Johnson, Nov 11, 1931; children—Robert W., Roger B., Stanley G. (dec.). With Bankers Trust Co., N.Y.C., 1922-60, successively sales mgr., asst. v.p., 1922-54, v.p., 1954-60; ret.; past chmn., dir. Charles E. Pettinos Graphite Corp.; former chmn. bd. dirs. Intercontinental Adv. Corp., Ltd.; former treas. Eurofund, Inc.; former cons. Continental Research Corp.; dir. Previews, Inc., Summit & Elizabeth Trust Co.; past dir. Seatrain Lines, Inc., Waddell & Reed, Inc. Past pres. Mantoloking (N.J.) Borough Council; mem. N.J. Am. Revolution Bicentennial Celebration Commn.; chmn. dir. John Jay and Eliza Jane Watson Found., Charles E. and Joy C. Pettinos Found.; chmn., trustee Lillia Babbitt Hyde Found.; trustee emeritus Wesleyan U.; former trustee N.Y. Skin and Cancer Hosp., Stuyvesant Square Hosp., N.Y.U. Med. Center; past trustee, treas. Inst. for Sci. and Tech., N.J.; chmn. bd. trustees Pingry Sch.; pres., trustee Historic Deerfield, Inc.; former pres., trustee Elizabethtown Hist. Found.; trustee Psi Upsilon Found., N.J. Coll. Medicine and Dentistry Found.; former trustee Overlook Hosp.; trustee N.J. Hist. Soc. Mem. Squadron A. Ex-mems. Assn., Skull and Serpent Soc., S.A.R., Psi Upsilon (exec. council). Episcopalian (former vestryman). Clubs: Bay Head (N.J.) Yacht; University (N.Y.C.); Baltusrol Golf (Springfield, N.J.); Spring Lake (N.J.) Golf; Nassau (Princeton, N.J.). Home: 44 Lenox Rd Summit NJ 07901 also 941 East Ave Mantoloking NJ 08738 Office: 507 Westminster Ave Elizabeth NJ 07208

PARSONS, RUSSELL JAMES, mfg. co. exec.; b. Davenport, Iowa, Dec. 16, 1918; s. Alfred and Cora Pearl (McDowell) P.; A.B., U. Chgo., 1940, J.D., 1942; m. Barbara Richlian Clancy, Apr. 30, 1949; children—Caro Lloyd, Donald Scott, Patricia. Admitted to Ill. and Iowa bar, 1942; with Borg-Warner Corp., Chgo., 1946—, asst. gen. counsel, 1956-68, asso. gen. counsel, 1968-72, sec., 1965—, v.p., gen. counsel, 1972-76, sr. v.p., 1976—. Served to capt. USMCR, 1942-46. Mem. Am., Ill., Chgo. bar assns. Mem. Union Ch. Clubs: University, Economic, Law, Legal (Chgo.); Hinsdale Golf. Home: 510 S Washington St Hinsdale IL 60521 Office: 200 S Michigan Ave Chicago IL 60604

PARSONS, THERAN DUANE, educator; b. St. Maries, Idaho, Dec. 26, 1922; s. Anthony Mason and Freda (Tucker) P.; student LaVerne Coll., 1941-43; B.S., U. Wash., 1949, Ph.D., 1953; m. Velma May Rankin, May 9, 1945; children—Heather Nance, Jeffrey Lee. Research asso. U. Chgo., 1953-55; mem. faculty, adminstrn. Oreg. State U., Corvallis, 1955—, prof. chemistry, 1968—, asso. dean Coll. Sci., 1970—. Served to capt. USAF, 1943-46. Decorated Air medal with 5 oak leaf clusters, Bronze Star; recipient Carter Teaching award, 1959, Mosser Teaching award, 1965, both Oreg. State U., 6 NSF grants, 10 Office Nav. Research grants; NSF predoctoral fellow, 1951-53. Mem. Am. Chem. Soc. (chmn. Oreg. 1970-71), Phi Beta Kappa, Sigma Xi, Phi Kappa Phi, Phi Lambda Upsilon. Episcopalian. Rotarian. Author: (with W.H. Slabaugh) General Chemistry, 3d edit., 1976. Contbr. articles to profl. jours. Home: 3960 Elizabeth Pl NW Corvallis OR 97330

PARSONS, VINSON ADAIR, chem. co. exec.; b. Frankfort, Ky., Oct. 22, 1932; s. Richard Adair and Nina (Mefford) P.; A.S., Mitchell Coll., 1959; B.S., U. Conn., 1960; m. Elizabeth Ann Peltier, June 2, 1956. Auditor, Price Waterhouse & Co., C.P.A.'s, Hartford, Conn., 1960-65; controller Pervel Industries Inc., Plainfield, Conn., 1965-70; v.p., controller Akzona Inc., Asheville, N.C., 1970—. Served with USN, 1953-57. Mem. Am. Mgmt. Assn., Financial Execs. Inst., Nat. Assn. Accountants (pres. local chpt. 1969-70). Clubs: Asheville Country, Asheville City; University (N.Y.C.). Home: 7 Highlander Rd Asheville NC 28804 Office: Box 2930 Asheville NC 28802

PARSONS, WILLIAM, lawyer; b. Kennebunk, Maine, July 23, 1909; s. Robert William and Alice (Read) P.; B.A., Yale U., 1931, LL.B., 1934; LL.D., Buena Vista Coll., Storm Lake, Iowa, 1964; m. Louise Bigelow, June 27, 1936; children—Llewellyn S. (Mrs. George P. Smith), Louise (Mrs. David L. Weld), William. Admitted to N.Y. bar, 1935, since practiced in N.Y.C.; partner firm Milbank, Tweed, Hadley & McCloy, 1951—. Chmn. bd. trustees Tchrs. Coll. Columbia, 1963—. Community Funds, Inc., 1971—; trustee N.Y. Cancer Research Inst., Environ. Def. Fund, R.I. Hist. Soc.; chmn. distbn. com. N.Y. Community Trust. Served to lt. USNR, 1944-46. Mem. Am., N.Y. State bar assns., Bar Assn. City N.Y. Club: Downtown Assn. (N.Y.C.). Author: (with Harrison Tweed) Lifetime and Testamentary Estate Planning, 1949. Home: 114 E 84th St New York NY 10028 also Cold Spring Harbor NY 11724 Office: 1 Chase Manhattan Plaza New York NY 10005

PARSONS, WILLIAM SIMEON, ret. electronic components mfr.; b. Litchfield, Minn., Dec. 12, 1904; s. Frederick William and Kittie (Patrick) P.; student U. Minn., Chgo. Tech. Coll.; m. Jeanne Barbara Marohn, Nov. 23, 1927; children—W. Stuart, Susan R., Douglas J. Devel. engr. Western Electric Co., Chgo., 1927-28; asst. to chief engr. Webster Electric Co., Racine, Wis. 1928—; asst. to v.p. charge radio Story & Clark Piano Co., Chgo., 1930-31; asst. sales mgr. Centralab div. Globe-Union, Inc., Milw., 1931-40, sales mgr., 1940—, v.p., 1946-52, pres., 1952-64, v.p. gen. mgr. internat. div., 1964-70, dir. corp., 1952-64; chmn. bd., pres. Centralab Can., Ltd., 1953-64; pres. Wilrite Products, Inc., 1961-64; dir. Globe-Union Overseas (Eng.), 1969-71, Centralab Ltd. (Eng.), 1969-71; past pres., dir. Electronic Show Corp.; cons. to electric and electronic industry. Mem. adv. com. electronic components WPB/OPA, 1942-46. Mem. Electronic Industries Assn. (past v.p. dir.; hon. life), Brotherhood St. Andrew. Republican. Episcopalian. Clubs: Chenequa Country; Milwaukee Athletic. Address: 1417 Seton Hall Dr Sun City Center FL 33570

PARSONS, WILLIAM WALTER, govt. ofcl.; b. Los Angeles, June 18, 1912; s. Hazen M. and Alice (LeSueur) P.; B.S. magna cum laude, U. So. Calif., 1935; M.S. (fellow), Syracuse U., 1938; postgrad. Am. U., 1941-42; LL.D., Southeastern U., 1957; m. Lois G. Shattuck, Sept. 14, 1935; children—Roger Paul, Richard Walter, Arthur Shattuck. Mem. field staff Regent's Edn. Inquiry, Albany, N.Y., 1936; field cons. Pub. Adminstrn. Service, Chgo., 1937-40; spl. asst. N.Y. State Dept. Edn., 1940-41; budget examiner Bur. Budget, 1941-44; dep. dir. mgmt. procurement div. Treasury Dept., 1944-45; tech. asst. Office Sec. Treasury, 1945-46, adminstrv. asst. to sec. treasury, 1946-50, adminstrv. asst. sec. treasury, 1950-59; v.p. System Devel. Corp., Santa Monica, 1959-63, sr. v.p., 1963-68, v.p. adminstrn., 1968-70; v.p. bus. affairs U. Hawaii, 1970-72; spl. cons. to comptroller gen. U.S., 1972-73; asst. regional mgr. U.S. GAO, San Francisco, 1973-74, Los Angeles, 1974-79; Disting. practitioner in residence Sch. Public Adminstrn., U. So. Calif., Los Angeles, 1979—; on loan as asst. adminstr. mgmt. Economic Stblzn. Agy., 1950. Trustee, mem. budget com. United Community Services, Washington, 1949-52; mem. exec. com., chmn. hdqrs. com. Community Chest Fedn., Washington, 1952-56; bd. dirs., mem. exec. com. United Givers Fund, Washington, 1956-58; dir. D.C. chpt. A.R.C., 1956-58; v.p. Health and Welfare Council Nat. Capital Area. 1958-59. Mem. Am. Soc. Pub. Adminstrn. (pres. 1954, council and exec. com. 1953-56), Nat. Acad. Pub. Adminstrn., Phi Beta Phi, Beta Gamma Sigma, Beta Alpha Psi. Editorial bd. Pub. Adminstrn. Rev., 1949-52. Home: 1150 Tellem Dr Pacific Palisades CA 90272 Office: U So Calif Sch Public Adminstrn Los Angeles CA 90007

PARTAIN, EDWARD ALLEN, army officer; b. Memphis, June 26, 1929; s. Eugene Gardner and Zoe Louise (Allen) P.; B.S., U.S. Mil. Acad., 1951; m. Mary Frances Johnson, June 5, 1951; children—Lisa, John David. Commd. 2d lt. U.S. Army, 1951, advanced through grades to maj. gen., 1978; inf. co. commdr. and regimental staff officer 27th Inf. Regiment, Korea, 1952-53; inf. co. commdr. 82nd Airborne Div., Fort Bragg, N.C., also div. staff officer, aide-de-camp, 1953-56; airborne unit leader Brit. Parachute Regiment, Aldershot, Eng., 1956-57; airborne unit leader and group staff officer 10th Spl. Forces, Bad Tolz, Germany, 1957-59; co. tactical officer U.S. Corps of Cadets, U.S. Mil. Acad., West Point, N.Y., 1960-63; student U.S. Army Command and Gen. Staff Coll., 1963-64; staff officer U.S. Mil. Assistance Command, Vietnam, Saigon, 1964-65; student Armed Forces Staff Coll., Norfolk, Va., 1965-66; staff officer Officer Personnel Directorate Dept. Army, Washington, 1966-67; comdr. 2d Bn., 173rd Airborne Brigade, Republic of Vietnam, 1967; personnel staff officer Hdqrs. U.S. Army Pacific, Honolulu, 1968; student U.S. Army War Coll., Carlisle Barracks, Pa., 1968-69; staff officer Office of Dep. Chief of Staff for plans and ops. Dept. Army, Washington, dep. dir. ops., 1969-70; support command comdr. 82nd Airborne Div., Fort Bragg, chief of staff and brigade comdr., 1970-73; chief Army Sect. ARMISH-MAAG, Tehran, Iran, 1974-76; asst. div. comdr. 1st Armored Div., Nürnberg, Germany, 1976-77; dir. logistics and security assistance Hdqrs. U.S. European Command, Stuttgart, Germany, 1977-79; dep. comdg. gen. XVIII Airborne Corps, Fort Bragg, N.C., 1979—. Decorated D.F.C., two Bronze Stars, Silver Star, three Purple Hearts, Legion of Merit. Mem. Assn. of U.S. Army, Nat. Def. Transp. Assn., Army Aviation Assn. of Am. Episcopalian. Home: 3 Hoyle Place Fort Bragg NC 28307 Office: Deputy CG XVIII Airborne Corps Fort Bragg NC 28307

PARTANEN, CARL RICHARD, educator; b. Portland, Oreg., Nov. 23, 1921; s. Emil and Ellen (Engstrom) P.; student Multnomah Jr. Coll., 1946-48; B.A., Lewis and Clark Coll., 1950; M.A., Harvard, 1951, Ph.D., 1954; m. Jane Nelson, June 24, 1961; children—Karen, Richard, Kirsten. Am. Cancer Soc. postdoctoral research fellow Columbia, 1954-55, Harvard, 1955-57; research asso. Childrens Cancer Research Found., Boston, 1957-61; asso. prof. biology U. Pitts., 1961-64, prof. biology, 1964—, chmn. biology, 1964-70. Research fellow U. Edinburgh (Scotland), 1971-72, U. Nottingham (Eng.), 1978-79. Served with AUS, 1942-45; ETO. Recipient Distinguished Achievement award Lewis and Clark Coll., 1968. Mem. Am. Genetic Assn., Am. Soc. for Cell. Biology, Bot. Soc. Am., Genetics Soc. Am., Soc. for Developmental Biology, Tissue Culture Assn., Am. Inst. Biol. Scis., AAAS, Sigma Xi. Contbr. articles to profl. jours. Home: 1112 Farragut St Pittsburgh PA 15206 Office: Dept Biol Scis Univ Pitts Pittsburgh PA 15260

PARTCH, KENNETH PAUL, editor, cons.; b. Mt. Vernon, N.Y., June 22, 1925; s. Edward Augustus and Grace Jane (Crabb) P.; A.B., Bklyn. Coll., 1949; m. Dorothy Sophia Iversen, July 16, 1953; children—Marjorie, Stephen, Jessica. Mng. editor Moore Publishing Co., 1955, Chain Store Age mag., 1955-59, Sales Mgmt. mag., 1961; editor Food Topics mag., 1961-68; dir. mktg. Grocery Mfrs. Am., 1969-70; editor Chain Store Age-Supermarket Group, N.Y.C., 1970-77; cons. to supermarket industry, 1977—. Served with USAAF, 1943-46. Decorated Air medal; recipient Jesse Neal award Asso. Bus. Press, 1968. Mem. Sigma Delta Chi. Contbr. Crowell-Collier Ency. Home: 20 Devils Garden Rd South Norwalk CT 06854

PARTCH, VIRGIL FRANKLIN, II, cartoonist; b. St. Paul Island, Alaska, Oct. 17, 1916; s. Paul C. and Anna (Pavaloff) P.; ed. U. Ariz., Chouinard Art Inst., Calif., Disney Extra Curr. Art; m. Helen Marie Aldridge, 1938; 2 sons, 1 dau. Contbr. cartoons to New Yorker, Sat. Eve. Post. This Week, True; creator newspaper comic strip, Big George. Author: New Faces on the Barroom Floor, 1961; VIP's Ouios, 1975. Office: care Field Newspaper Syndicate 401 N Wabash Chicago IL 60611*

PARTEE, CECIL A., city ofcl.; b. Blytheville, Ark., Apr. 10, 1921; s. Charles C. and Bessie (Dupree) P.; B.S., Tenn. State U., 1944; J.D., Northwestern U., 1946; m. Paris Bradley, Dec. 23, 1955; children—Paris Irene, Cecile. Partner law firm Partee & Green, Chgo.; asst. state's atty., Ill., 1948-56; mem. Ill. Ho. of Reps., 1957-66, Ill. Senate, 1967-77, pres. pro tem, also majority leader, 1975-77; commr. Dept. Human Services City of Chgo., 1977-79; city treas. City of Chgo., 1979—. Active various community drives. Mem. NAACP. Home: 6032 S Michigan Ave Chicago IL 60637 Office: City Treasurer's Office 206 City Hall Chicago IL 60602

PARTEE, JOHN CHARLES, economist; b. Defiance, Ohio, Oct. 21, 1927; s. Lauren W. and Florence (Paxton) P.; B.S., Ind. U., 1948, M.B.A., 1949; postgrad. U. Chgo., 1952-53; m. Gail Voegelin, June 17, 1946; children—Eric Douglas, Sharon Brooke, Pamela Erminie. Economist, Fed. Res. Bank Chgo., 1949-56; asso. economist, 2d v.p. No. Trust Co., Chgo., 1956-61; with Fed. Res. Bd., 1962—, adviser, 1964—, dir. research, 1969-73, mng. dir. for research and econ. policy, 1973-75, mem. bd. from Va., 1976—; dir. Neighborhood Reinvestment Corp.; Ind. U. Alumni fellow. Mem. Conf. Bus. Economists, Beta Gamma Sigma. Home: 931 Leigh Mill Rd Great Falls VA 22066 Office: Federal Reserve Board Washington DC 20551

PARTEN, JUBAL R., petroleum producer; b. Madisonville, Tex., Feb. 16, 1896; s. Wayne Lafayette and Ella Mae (Brooks) P.; student U. Tex., 1913-17; m. Patsy E. Puterbaugh, Oct. 31, 1947; 1 son, John Randolph. Entered oil industry, 1919; pres., gen. mgr. Woodley Petroleum Co., Houston, 1922-60; founder, pres. Pan Am. Sulphur Co., Houston, 1947-53, chmn. bd. dirs., 1953-60, also dir.; dir. Pure Oil, 1960-65, organizer, chmn. bd. dirs. Woodley Can. Oil Co., Great No. Oil Co., Minn. Pipe Line Co.; chmn., dir. Fed. Res. Bank of Dallas, 1944-54. Chmn. bd. regents U. Tex., 1935-41; organizing dir. Fund for the Republic, Inc., 1953-75; trustee, vice chmn. bd. St. Stephen's Episcopal Sch., Austin, Tex., 1961—. Served to maj. U.S. Army, World War I. Apptd. mem. Am. Del. to Allied Commn. on Reparations, Moscow, 1945. Mem. Mid-Continent Oil and Gas Assn., Am. Petroleum Inst., Tex. Ind. Producers and Royalty Owners Assn. Democrat. Episcopalian. Clubs: Ramada, Petroleum (Houston); Oakridge Country (Madisonville, Tex.); Twenty-Five Year. Home: PO Box 458 Madisonville TX 77864 Office: 1638 Bank of the Southwest Bldg Houston TX 77002

PARTER, SEYMOUR VICTOR, educator; b. Chgo., June 9, 1927; s. Peter and Tillie (Dekovetzky) P.; B.S., Ill. Inst. Tech., 1949, M.S., 1951; Ph.D., N.Y.U., 1958; m. Ruth Ghitman, Oct. 9, 1957; children—Paul Jeffry, David William. Staff mem. Los Alamos Sci. Lab., 1951-57; instr. math. Mass. Inst. Tech., 1957-58; asst. prof. math. Ind. U., 1958-60; asst. prof. math. Cornell U., 1960-62; vis. asst. prof. computer sci. Stanford, 1962-63; asso. prof. computer sci. and math. U. Wis., Madison, 1963-65, prof., 1965—, chmn. computer sci. dept., 1968-70. Mem. NRC adv. com. on math. to Office Naval Research, 1970-72; mem. adv. com. on computing to pres. Stanford, 1969-72. Mem. Am. Math. Soc., Math. Assn. Am., Soc. Indsl. and Applied Math. (vis. lectr. 1969-72, mem. council 1978—, editor Jour. on Numerical Analysis; mng. editor Jour. Numerical Analysis, 1977—, pres. elect 1980), Assn. for Computing Machinery, Sigma Xi. Contbr. articles to profl. jours. Home: 5 S Rock Rd Madison WI 53705

PARTHEMOS, GEORGE STEVEN, educator; b. Charleston, S.C., Dec. 4, 1921; s. Steven George and Katina (Arros) P.; A.B., Erskine Coll., 1947; M.A., U. S.C., 1949; Ph.D., U. N.C., 1953; m. Georgia Kachavos, July 10, 1947; children—Steven George, Pota Elaine. Instr. polit. sci. U. Ga., 1953-55, asst. prof., 1955-58, asso. prof., 1958-63, prof. polit. sci., 1963—, head dept. polit. sci., 1961-65, v.p. instrn., 1964-71, Alumni Found. Distinguished prof., 1971—. Mem. Ga. Sci. and Tech. Commn., 1969-73. Bd. dirs. St. Mary's Hosp., Athens, Ga., So. Consortium for Internat. Edn. Served with USNR, 1943-46. Recipient U. Ga. Alumni Distinguished Faculty Service award, 1974; Rockefeller Found. fellow, 1958-59. Fellow Royal Soc. Arts; mem. Am., So. (v.p. 1968) polit. sci. assns., Am. Acad. Social and Polit. Sci., U. Ga. Alumni Soc. (dir.), Phi Beta Kappa, Phi Kappa Phi, Kappa Delta Pi, Pi Sigma Alpha, Omicron Delta Kappa. Author: Political Perspectives, 1961; (with Thomas R. Dye and Lee S. Green) American Government: Theory, Structure and Process, 2d edit., 1972; American Government: Policies and Function, 1967; Governing the American Democracy, 1980; editor, contbr. Higher Education in a World of Conflict, 1962. Contbr. articles profl. jours. Home: 165 Lullwater Dr Athens GA 30606

PARTHEMOS, JAMES, banker; b. Abbeville, S.C., Mar. 15, 1920; s. Steven George and Katina (Arahovitis) P.; student Clemson U., 1937-38; A.B., Erskine Coll., 1942; M.A., U. S.C., 1950; postgrad. U. Athens (Fulbright scholar), 1950-51, Duke U. (Earhart fellow), 1954-57; m. Helen Evanthia Sterghos, June 28, 1945; children—Katina Maria (Mrs. John Raymond Walser), Nikolas Emmanuel, Stylian Paul. News reporter The State Co., Columbia, S.C., 1945-46; teaching asst. U. S.C. at Columbia, 1946-49, asst. prof. econs., 1953-54; asst. prof. Catawba Coll., Salisbury, N.C., 1949-50, Presbyn. Coll., 1952-53; instr. Duke, 1954-57, Tulane U., 1957-60; asso. economist Fed. Res. Bank Richmond, VA., 1960, economist, 1961, asst. v.p., 1962, sr. v.p., dir. research, 1969—. Dir. Va. Council on Econ. Edn. Mem. bus. adv. council Coll. Bus. Adminstrn., Va. Poly. Inst., State U. Served to lt. (s.g.) USNR, 1942-45. Mem. Am., So. econs. assns., Newcomen Soc. N. Am. Research mechanisms of monetary control. Home: 7717 Whittington Dr Richmond VA 23225 Office: Fed Res Bank 9th and Franklins Sts Richmond VA 23213

PARTNOY, RONALD ALLEN, lawyer; b. Norwalk, Conn., Dec. 23, 1933; s. Maurice and Ethel Marguerite (Roselle) P.; B.A., Yale U., 1956; LL.B., Harvard U., 1961; LL.M., Boston U., 1965; m. Diane Catherine Keenan, Sept. 18, 1965. Admitted to Mass. bar, 1962, Conn. bar, 1966; atty. Liberty Mut. Ins. Co., Boston, 1961-65; asso. counsel Remington Arms Co., Bridgeport, Conn., 1965-70, gen. counsel, 1970—. Served with USN, 1956-58, to capt. USNR, 1956—. Mem. Sporting Arms and Ammunition Mfrs. Inst. (chmn. legis. and legal affairs com. 1971—), Am. Bar Assn., Conn. Bar Assn., Bridgeport Bar Assn., Westchester-Fairfield Corp. Counsel Assn., Am. Judicature Soc., U.S. Navy League (pres. Bridgeport council 1975-77, nat. dir., Conn. pres 1977—). Clubs: Chancery, Harvard of Boston, Yale of N.Y.C. Home: 135 Parkwood Rd Fairfield CT 06430 Office: 939 Barnum Ave Bridgeport CT 06602

PARTON, DOLLY REBECCA, singer, composer; b. Sevier County, Tenn., Jan. 19, 1946; d. Robert Lee and Avie Lee (Owens) P.; m. Carl Dean, May 30, 1966. Country music singer, rec. artist, composer, radio and TV personality; radio appearances include Grand Ole Opry, WSM Radio, Nashville, Cass Walker program, Knoxville; TV appearances include Porter Wagoner Show, 1967—, Cass Walker program, Bill Anderson Show, Wilburn Bros. Show; rec. artist Mercury, Monument, RCA record cos. Recipient (with Porter Wagoner) Vocal Group of Yr. award, 1968, Vocal Duo of Yr. award, all Country Music Assn., 1970, 71; Nashville Metronome award, 1979; named Female Vocalist of Yr., 1975, 76; Country Star of Yr., Sullivan Prodns., 1977; Entertainer of Yr., Country Music Assn., 1978; Dolly Parton Day, Sevier County, Tenn., designated Oct. 7, 1967. Recordings include Dumb Blonde, Something Fishy, I Couldn't Wait Forever, Daddy Was an Old Time Preacher Man, Joshua, Jolena, Coat of Many Colors, I Will Always Love You, Love is Like a Butterfly, The Bargain Store, The Seeker, We Used To, All I Can Do. Composer: Dumb Blonde, Something Fishy; (with others) I'm in No Condition, Ol' Handy Man, Friends Tell Me, Put It Off Until Tomorrow, The Company You Keep, You Know How to Hurt A Guy, numerous others. Address: care Katz-Gallin-Morey 9255 Sunset Blvd Los Angeles CA 90069*

PARTON, JAMES, publisher; b. Newburyport, Mass., Dec. 10, 1912; s. Hugo and Agnes (Leach) Parton; A.B., Harvard, 1934; m. Jane Audra Bourne, Dec. 9, 1950 (dec. 1962); children—James III, Dana, Sara; m. 2d, Caroline M. Houser, July 8, 1966 (div. Sept. 1972); m. 3d, Jane T. Carlson, Aug. 8, 1976. Asst. E.L. Bernays, N.Y.C., 1934-35; aviation editor Time Mag., 1935-36, bus. and financial editor, 1937-39, asst. gen. mgr., 1940, bus. mgr. air express edit., 1941, promotion mgr. Time-Life Internat., 1945; editorial dir., Pacific Coast News Burs., Time, Inc., 1947; editor and pub. Los Angeles Ind., 1948-49; cons. U.S. Dept. of State, 1949; promotion dir. N.Y. Herald Tribune, 1950, asst. to the pres., chmn. Herald Tribune Forum and dir. N.Y. Herald Tribune, Inc., 1951-53; v.p., treas. Thorndike, Jensen & Parton, Inc., 1953-57; founder, pres. Am. Heritage Pub. Co., Inc., 1954-70; pres. Ency. Brit. Ednl. Corp., Chgo., 1970-72, chmn. exec. com., 1973; pres. James Parton & Co., N.Y.C., 1973—; dir. planning study Custom House Inst., N.Y.C., 1973; chmn. Nat. Advt. Rev. Bd., 1974-76; asst. librarian for pub. edn. Library of Congress, 1976-77; chmn. exec. com. Hist. Times, Inc., 1979—. Trustee Loomis Inst., 1952—, pres., 1964-66, chmn. 1967-70; trustee USAF Hist. Found.; bd. dirs. Hist. Times, Inc., 1978—; vice-chmn. Center Info. on Am.; hon. trustee Inst. Internat. Edn. Commd. 2d lt. in USAAF, 1942, and advanced through grades to lt. col., 1944. Decorated Legion of Merit, Bronze Star Medal, European Theater ribbon with 4 battle stars. Chmn. U.S. Army com. which produced ofcl. Eighth Air Force book; Target-Germany, 1943. Clubs: Harvard. Century, (N.Y.C.); Army and Navy (Washington). Home: 300 E 56th St New York NY 10022 Office: 15 E 48th St New York NY 10017

PARTRIDGE, DAVID MEL, savs. and loan exec.; b. Los Angeles, July 10, 1945; s. John M. and Barbara J. (Mel) P.; B.S., U.S. Mil. Acad., 1967; M.B.A., Harvard U., 1973; m. Rebecca E. Horne, June 17, 1967; children—Catherine, Elizabeth. Mgmt. cons. Peat, Marwick, Mitchell & Co., San Francisco, 1973; v.p. corp. devel. Fidelity Savs. and Loan Assn., Oakland, Calif., 1974-75, exec. v.p., 1975—; instr. bus. policy M.B.A. Program Golden Gate U., 1975—; mem. various Calif. savs. and loan coms. Campaign chmn. Bay Area chpt. March of Dimes, 1975; mem. Berkeley (Calif.) United Sch. Dist. Bd. Edn., 1978—. Served with U.S. Army, 1967-71. Decorated Bronze Star with oak leaf cluster, Army Commendation medal with oak leaf cluster. Club: Commonwealth. Office: 2000 Franklin St Oakland CA 94612

PARTRIDGE, ERNEST DEALTON, educator; b. Provo, Utah, Nov. 6, 1906; s. Ernest DeAlton and Elizabeth (Truman) P.; B.S., Brigham Young U., 1930; Ph.D., Columbia, 1934; LL.D., Montclair State Coll., 1976; m. Nell Clark, Jan., 28, 1931; children—Lyman Clark, Ernest DeAlton, Robert Truman. Statistician, Nat. council Boy Scouts Am., 1928-34, dir. research, 1934-37, mem. nat. personnel com., 1952-71; asst. prof. psychology Montclair State Coll., Upper Montclair, N.J., 1937-46, dean instrn., 1947-51, pres., 1951-66; pres. Near East Found., 1964-71; vis. disting. scholar Westminster Coll., Salt Lake City, 1971-79; cons. visual communications, 1946-47; ednl. cons. Coronet Films, 1953-65. Chmn. Com. Continental Classroom, first network TV course for coll. credit, sponsored by Am. Assn. Colls. Tchrs. Edn. and NBC, 1958; mem. TV com. Am. Council Edn., 1956-59; dir. Learning Resources Inst., 1959-70, Inst. Human Communications, 1954-70; chmn. Nat. Commn. on Econs. in Tchr. Edn., 1955-64. Life mem. Nat. council, mem. nat. bd., mem. exec. com. Campfire Girls Am.; bd. dirs. LDS Hosp.-Deseret Found., Salt Lake City, 1976-79. Served to lt. comdr. USNR, 1943-45. Mem. NEA, N.J. Edn. Assn., Outdoor Edn. Assn. (dir.), Soc. Mayflower Descs. Clubs: Rotary, Explorers, Lochinvar (N.Y.C.); Timpanogos (Utah); Cosmopolitan (Montclair). Author: Leadership Among Adolescent Boys, 1934; Social Psychology of Adolescence, 1938; (with Catherine Mooney) Time Out for Living, 1940. Home: 1710 Harvard Ave Salt Lake City UT 84108. *I have found that the most important trait for the growth of the individual, emotionally and in wisdom, is the ability to accept and utilize criticism. This includes self-criticism as well as the constructive suggestions of others. Often it will be your adversaries or even enemies who will help you to become a truly mature adult.*

PARTRIDGE, (ERNEST) JOHN, co. dir.; b. Bristol, Eng., July 18, 1908; s. William Henry and Alice Mary P.; ed. Queen Elizabeth's Hosp., Bristol; hon. LL.D., Bristol U., 1972; hon. D.Sc., Cranfield Inst. Tech., 1974; m. Madeline Fabian, 1934 (dec. 1944); 1 son, 1 dau.; m. 2d, Joan Johnson, 1949; 1 son, 1 dau. Joined Imperial Group, Ltd., 1923, asst. sec., 1944-46, sec., 1946-57, dir., 1949-75, dep. chmn., 1960-64, chmn., 1964-75; dir. Dunlop Holdings Ltd., Delta Metal Co. Ltd.; pres. Confedn. Brit. Industry, 1970-72, v.p., 1972-76; chmn. CBI Edn. Found., 1976—; mem. Tobacco Adv. Com., 1945-58, Cheque Endorsement Com., 1955-56, Nat. Econ. Devel. Council, 1967-75, Brit. Nat. Export Council, 1968-71; mem. Internat. Adv. Bd. Chem. Bank U.S.A., 1972-78. Pres., Found. for Mgmt. Edn., 1972—, Nat. Council Social Service, 1973—. Gov., Queen Elizabeth's Hosp., Clifton Coll., Badminton Sch., Nat. Inst. Econ. and Social Research; chmn. United World Coll. of Atlantic, 1979—. Decorated knight comdr. Order of Brit. Empire. Fellow Brit. Inst. Mgmt.; mem. Council of Industry for Mgmt. Edn. (chmn. 1967-71), Soc. Bus. Economists (v.p. 1976—). Address: Wildwood Haslemere Surrey England

PARTRIDGE, JOHN FRANCIS, lawyer, ret. corp. exec.; b. Chatham, Va., May 29, 1914; s. Horace E. and Mary (Johnson) P.; B.S. in Bus. Adminstrn., U. Fla., 1936; C.P.A., U. Ill., 1939; J.D., Chgo.-Kent Coll. Law, 1947; grad. Exec. Program Bus. Adminstrn., Columbia, 1956; m. Evelyn Weeks, Dec. 28, 1949; children—Lawrence Scott, Jacquelyn Mary. Accountant, Oldham & Gouwens, Chgo., summer 1936; investment analyst Welsh & Green, Inc., Chgo., 1937- 38; with Welsh, Davis & Co., Chgo., 1939-51, exec. v.p., 1948-51; admitted to Ill. bar, 1947; with AMSTED Industries Inc., Chgo., 1951—, sec., counsel, 1959-73; practice law, Chgo., 1973—. Instr. accounting U. Iowa, 1936-37; asst. prof. law Chgo.-Kent Coll. Law, 1947. Treas. local troop Boy Scouts Am., 1962- 65; mem. com. to investigate pub. transp. for handicapped Welfare Council Met. Chgo., 1966; chmn. caucus in Wilmette, Ill. for Cook County Sch. Dist., 39, 1962. Bd. dirs., sec. Rehab. Inst. Chgo., 1961—. Mem. Am., Ill. (mem. council corp. law dept. 1965—, sec. corp. law dept. 1967-68, vice chmn. 1968-69, chmn. 1969-70), Chgo. bar assns., Am. Soc. Corp. Secretaries (sec. Chgo. regional group 1965-67, v.p. 1967-68, pres. 1969-70, chmn. mem. relations com. 1965—, mem. adv. com. 1965-68, v.p., dir. nat. 1970—). Presbyn. (elder 1960-62, trustee sec. bd. 1966-67, pres. 1968). Home: 8641 Skokie Blvd Skokie IL 60079

PARTRIDGE, LLOYD DONALD, educator; b. Cortland, N.Y., Dec. 18, 1922; s. Bert James and Marian (Rice) P.; B.S., U. Mich., 1948, M.S., 1949, Ph.D., 1953; m. Jean Marie Rutledge, Aug. 6, 1944; children—Lloyd Donald, David Lee, Gayle Ann Partridge Kneller. Instr., U. Mich., Ann Arbor, 1953-56; asst. prof. Yale U., New Haven, 1956-62; asso. prof. neurophysiology U. Tenn., Memphis, 1962-70, prof., 1970—. Served with AUS, 1944-46. Asso. editor Trans Bio. Med. Engring., 1973—. Contbr. chpts. to books, articles to profl. jours. Home: 3061 Dumbarton St Memphis TN 38128

PARTRIDGE, ROI, etcher; b. Centralia, Ter. of Wash., Oct. 14, 1888; s. Archibald E. and Florence (George) P.; ed. N.A.D., N.Y.C., also in Europe; m. Imogen Cunningham, Feb. 11, 1915 (div. 1934, dec. June 1976); children—Gryffyd, Rondal and Padraic (twins); m. 2d, Marion Lyman, June 27, 1935 (dec. Aug. 1940); m. 3d, May Ellen Fisher, July 29, 1941. Instr. dept. art Mills Coll., 1920-22, prof., 1922-48, now ret.; academician in graphic arts N.A.D., 1949—; has exhibited widely; represented in permanent collections Art Inst. Chgo., Worcester (Mass.) Mus., Toronto Art Gallery, Library of Congress; Los Angeles Mus. Sci. and Art, Oakland, (Calif.) Mus., Walker Art Gallery, Liverpool, Eng.; Met. Mus.; Achenbach Collection at Palace of Legion of Honor, San Francisco; Acad. Arts, Honolulu, Wells Coll., Aurora, N.Y., Carnegie Inst.; Nat. Fine Arts Collection, Washington; Bklyn. Mus., Mus. Modern Art. Recipient Syndam silver medal N.A.D., 1910; Logan medal Art Inst. Chgo., 1921; Bijar prize Bklyn. Soc. Etchers, 1921; O'Melveney prize Print Makers Calif., 1922, BUMA prize, 1925; Los Angeles gold medal, 1928; Gold medal, San Diego, 1969. Pantheist. Home: 1601 Skycrest Dr Walnut Creek CA 94595

PARTRIDGE, WAYNE EARL, aviation co. exec.; b. Salt Lake City, Jan. 22, 1940; s. J. Leo and Margarette (Foster) P.; A.B. with honors, U. Calif. at Los Angeles, 1961; J.D., Harvard, 1964; m. Masako Gohda, Mar. 6, 1970. Admitted to Cal. bar, 1965, N.Y. bar, 1968; atty. firm Anderson, Mori & Rabinowitz, Tokyo, Japan, 1964-66, Anderson & Martin, N.Y.C., 1967-69; gen. atty. Flying Tiger Line Inc., Los Angeles, 1969-73, v.p. law, 1973—; gen. counsel Flying Tiger Corp., Los Angeles, 1970-74. Home: 3520 The Strand Manhattan Beach CA 90266 Office: 7401 World Way W Los Angeles CA 90009

PARTRIDGE, WILLIAM SCHAUBEL, univ. ofcl.; b. Ranchester, Wyo., Jan. 20, 1922; s. William Clayton and Elsie (Schaubel) P.; B.A., U. Wyo., 1946, M.A., 1948; Ph.D., U. Utah, 1951; m. Jeannette Noble, Mar. 21, 1942; children—Nancy, Dianne, William Noble, Carol, Murray Noble (dec.). Staff scientist U. Calif., Los Alamos, 1951-52; asst. dir. explosives research group, U. Utah, Salt Lake City, 1952-55, asso. research prof., dir. high velocity research lab. 1955-58, v.p. for research, 1966-79, pres. U. Utah Research Inst., 1979—; pres., gen. mgr. Utah Research & Devel. Co., Salt Lake City, 1958-64, now cons.; staff scientist Jet Propulsion Lab., Pasadena, Calif., 1964-66; pres., gen. mgr. U. Utah Research Inst., 1972—. Served to capt. USAAF, World War II. Contbr. articles to profl. jours. Patentee in field. Home: 3927 Brockbank Way Salt Lake City UT 84117

PARZEN, EMANUEL, educator; b. N.Y.C., Apr. 21, 1929; s. Samuel and Sarah (Getzel) P.; A.B. in Math., Harvard U., 1949; M.A., U. Calif. at Berkeley, 1951, Ph.D., 1953; m. Carol Tenowitz, July 12, 1959; children—Sara Leah, Michael Isaac. Research scientist Columbia, 1953-56, asst. prof. math. statistics, 1955-56; faculty Stanford, 1956-70, asso. prof. statistics, 1959-64, prof., 1964-70; prof. statistics State U. N.Y. at Buffalo, 1970-73, prof. statis. sci., 1973-78; distinguished prof. statistics Tex. A and M U., College Station, 1978—. Guest prof. Imperial Coll., London, Eng., 1961-62; vis. prof. Mass. Inst. Tech., 1964-65, Harvard U., 1976. Fellow Internat. Statis. Inst., Am. Statis. Assn., AAAS, Royal Statis. Soc., Inst. Math. Statistics; mem. Am. Math. Soc., Soc. Indsl. and Applied Math., Math. Assn. Am., Assn. Computing Machinery, Bernoulli Soc., Biometric Soc., Econometric Soc., N.Y. Acad. Scis., Phi Beta Kappa, Sigma Xi. Author: Stochastic Processes, 1962; Modern Probability Theory and its Applications, 1960; Time Series Analysis Papers, 1967; also articles. Research in extended limit theorems probability theory to uniform convergence in a parameter; introduced reproducing kernel Hilbert space formulation founds. time series analysis; introduced Parzen window for statis. spectral analysis; developed approach to empirical time series analysis; developer theory autoregressive/maximum entropy spectral analysis, also density-quantile estimation approach to nonparametric statis. data modeling. Office: Inst Statistics Tex A & M U College Station TX 77843

PASACHOFF, JAY MYRON, educator, astronomer; b. N.Y.C., July 1, 1943; s. Samuel S. and Anne (Traub) P.; A.B., Harvard U., 1963, A.M. (NSF fellow), 1965, Ph.D. (NSF fellow, N.Y. State Regents fellow for advanced grad. study), 1969; m. Naomi Schwartz, Mar. 31, 1974; children—Eloise Hilary, Deborah Donna. Research physicist Air Force Cambridge Research Labs., Bedford, Mass., 1968-69; Menzel research fellow Harvard Coll. Obs., Cambridge, Mass., 1969-70; research fellow Hale Obs., Carnegie Instn., Washington and Calif. Inst. Tech., Pasadena, 1970-72; dir. Hopkins Obs., Williams Coll., Williamstown, Mass., 1972—, chmn. astronomy dept., 1972-77, asst. prof. astronomy, 1972-77, asso. prof., 1977—; adj. asst. prof. astronomy U. Mass., Amherst, 1975-77, adj. asso. prof., 1977—. Eclipse expdns., Mass., 1959, Can., 1963; asst. dir.

Harvard-Smithsonian-Nat. Geog. Expdn., Mex., 1970; asst. dir. Harvard-Smithsonian-Williams Expdn., Can., 1972; NSF expdn., Kenya, Africa, 1973; dir. expdns. Colombia, 1973, Australia, 1974, Pacific Ocean, 1977, Can., 1979, India, 1980; research fellow Owens Valley Radio Obs., summer 1973, U.S.-Australia Coop. Sci. Program, Australian Nat. Radio Astron. Obs., 1974; guest investigator NASA Orbiting Solar Obs.-8, 1975-79; Lockhart lectr. U. Man., 1979. Recipient Bronze medal Nikon Photo Contest Internat., 1971; photograph aboard NASA Voyagers, 1977; NSF grantee, 1973-75, 79—, Nat. Geog. Soc. grantee, 1973—, Research Corp. grantee, 1973-74, 76-79. Fellow Royal Astron. Soc.; mem. Internat. Astron. Union (U.S. nat. rep. to Commn. on Teaching Astronomy 1976—), Am. Astron. Soc., Am. Phys. Soc., N.Y. Acad. Sci., Astron. Soc. Pacific, Internat. Union Radio Sci., AAUP (chpt. pres. 1977-80), Sigma Xi (chpt. pres. 1973-74). Author: Contemporary Astronomy, 1977; (with Marc L. Kutner, Naomi Pasachoff) Student Study Guide to Contemporary Astronomy, 1977; Astronomy Now, 1978; (with M.L. Kutner, N. Pasachoff, N.P. Kutner) Student Study Guide to Astronomy Now, 1978; (with M.L. Kutner) University Astronomy, 1978, Contemporary Physics, 1981; Astronomy: From the Earth to the Universe, 1979. Asso. editor Jour. Irreproducible Results, 1972—; abstractor from Am. jours. for Solar Physics, 1968-78. Contbr. articles to profl. jours., articles and photographs to non-tech. publs. Home: 1305 Main St Williamstown MA 01267 Office: Hopkins Obs Williams Coll Williamstown MA 01267

PASAMANICK, BENJAMIN, psychiatrist, educator; b. N.Y.C., Oct. 14, 1914; s. Alex and Elizabeth (Moskalik) P.; A.B., Cornell U., 1936; M.D., U. Md., 1941; m. Hilda Knobloch, May 1, 1942. Intern, State Hosp., Bklyn., 1941, Harlem Hosp., N.Y.C., 1942; resident N.Y. Psychiat. Inst., 1943; asst. Yale Clinic Child Devel., 1944-46; chief children's in-patient and out-patient services Neuropsychiat. Inst., U. Mich. Hosp., Ann Arbor, 1946-47; chief children's psychiat. services Kings County Hosp., Bklyn., 1947-50; psychiatrist Phipps Clinic, Johns Hopkins Hosp., Balt., 1952-55, Harriet Lane Home, 1951-55; asst. prof. Johns Hopkins U. Sch. Hygiene and Pub. Health, 1950-52, asso. prof. pub. health adminstrn., 1953-55; prof. psychiatry Ohio State U., 1955-65, adj. prof. sociology and anthropology, 1963-65; clin. prof. psychiatry U. Ill. Coll. Medicine, Chgo., also Chgo. Med. Sch., asso. dir. research Ill. Dept. Mental Health, 1965-67; pres. N.Y. Sch. Psychiatry, N.Y.C., 1968-72, Sir Aubrey and Lady Hilda Lewis prof. social psychiatry, 1972—; asso. commr. N.Y. State Dept. Mental Hygiene, 1968-76; adj. prof. psychology N.Y. U., 1968—; adj. prof. epidemiology Sch. Pub. Health and Adminstrv. Medicine, Columbia, 1967—; adj. prof. pediatrics Albany Med. Coll., 1972-77, research prof., 1978—; clin. prof. preventive and community medicine N.Y. Med. Coll., 1976-77. Cutter lectr. preventive medicine Harvard, 1960; research prof. psychiatry Sch. Medicine, SUNY, Stony Brook, 1978—. Mem. Am. Psychopath. Assn. (Stratton award 1961, pres. 1967, Hamilton medal 1968), Am. Orthopsychiat. Assn. (pres. 1971), Am. Psychiat. Assn. (Hofheimer Research award 1949, 67), Am. Pub. Health Assn. (Rema Lapouse Gold medal 1977), Soc. Biol. Psychiatry, Acad. Child Psychiatry, Am. Psychol. Assn., Am. Anthrop. Assn., Am. Sociol. Assn., Am. Coll. Psychiatrists, History of Sci. Soc., Soc. for Study of Social Problems, others. Author 16 books. Contbr. numerous articles to profl. jours. Address: Feura Bush Rd Glenmont NY 12077

PASATIERI, THOMAS, composer; b. N.Y.C., Oct. 20, 1945; s. Carmelo Thomas and Marie Lucia (Carini) P.; B.Mus., Julliard Sch., 1965, M.S., 1967, D.Mus. Arts, 1969. Mem. faculty N.C. Sch. Arts, Siena, Italy, 1967; Juilliard Sch., 1967-69, Manhattan Sch. Music, 1969-71; tchr. master classes univs. throughout U.S.; composer: (operas) The Trysting Place, 1964, Flowers of Ice, 1964, The Women, 1965, La Divina, 1965, Padrevia, 1966, The Penitentes, 1967, Calvary, 1968, The Trial of Mary Lincoln, 1970, Black Widow, 1971, The Seagull, 1973, Signor Deluso, 1973, Ines de Castro, 1975, Washington Square, 1975, Before Breakfast, 1976; Three Sisters, 1979; also art songs. Recipient numerous prizes, fellowships, grants, awards. Roman Catholic. Address: 500 West End Ave New York NY 10024

PASCAL, DAVID, artist; b. N.Y.C., Aug. 16, 1918; s. Boucour and Carolina (Finor) P.; student Am. Artists Sch., 1936-38; m. Theresa Auerbach, Aug. 24, 1962; 1 son, Jeffrey B. Exhibited in one-man show Librairie Le Kiosque, Paris, 1965, Museu de Arte, Sao Paulo, Brazil, Graham Gallery, N.Y.C., 1973, Museude Arte Moderna Rio de Janeiro, Brazil, 1973, Man and His World, Montreal, 1974, 75, World Gallery, N.Y.C., 1977; group show Musee des Arts Decoratifs, 1967; drawings appeared in New Yorker, N.Y. Times, Harper's Evergreen Rev., Punch, Paris-Match, others; instr. Sch. Visual Arts, N.Y.C., 1955-58; lectr. mus., schs., congresses, N.Y., Paris, Italy, Sao Paulo, Buenos Aires (Argentina); organizer 1st Am. Internat. Congress Comics, N.Y.C., 1972; artistic counselor to bd. dirs. Lucca Internat. Comics Congresses, 1976—. Participant overseas tours for Def. Dept., 1957, 58, 61. Auditor, Coll. de Pataphysique, Paris. Served with U.S. Mcht. Marine, 1940-45. Recipient Dattero d'Oro Salone Intdelle Umorismo, Italy, 1963, Illustrator's award Nat. Cartoonists Soc., 1969, 77; Phenix award, Paris, 1971. Mem. Nat. Cartoonists Soc. (fgn. affairs sec. 1963—), Internat. Comics Orgn. (Am. rep. 1970—). Author, illustrator: The Art of Inferior Decorating, 1963, 15 Fables of Krylov, 1965 (in permanent exhibit at Congl. Library), The Silly Knight, 1967, also publ. comics: An American Expressionism (in archives Mus. of Art, Sao Paulo). Co-editor spl. internat. comics issues Graphis mag., Zurich, Switzerland; Goofus, Paris, 1975. Home and studio: 133 Wooster St New York NY 10012. *Work is adult play. Knowing what you really want to do and finding the best ways to do it are the keys to joy of life.*

PASCALE, GEORGE, diversified mfg. co. exec.; b. Bklyn., May 18, 1925; s. Victor and Josephine (Sisti) P.; B.B.A., St. John's U., Bklyn., 1949, LL.B., 1952; m. Pauline Siggia, July 14, 1956; children—Joan, Thomas, Mary-Jean, Carol, Ellen, Barbara. Admitted to N.Y. bar, 1953; atty. Diamond Internat. Corp., N.Y.C., 1962-70, asst. sec., 1970, sec., 1970-73, v.p., sec., 1973—; dir. Internat. Playing Card Co., Italpac S.p.A. Served with USAAC, 1943-46. Mem. Am., N.Y. State bar assns., Assn. Bar City of New York, Am. Soc. Corp. Secs. Home: 333 Rosedale Av White Plains NY Office: 733 3d Ave New York City NY 10017

PASCARELLA, PERRY JAMES, mag. editor; b. Bradford, Pa., Apr. 11, 1934; s. James and Lucille Margaret (Monti) P.; A.B., Kenyon Coll., 1956; postgrad. William and Mary Coll., 1957, George Washington U., 1958; m. Carol Ruth Taylor, May 4, 1957; children—Cynthia, Elizabeth. Credit reporter Dun & Bradstreet, Cleve., 1956, 60; asst. editor Steel mag., Cleve., 1961-63, asso. editor, 1963-67, bus. editor, 1968-69, mng. editor, 1969; mng. editor Industry Week mag., Cleve., 1970-71, exec. editor, 1971—; lectr. in field. Served to lt. comdr. USNR, 1957-60. Recipient Distinguished Service award Kenyon Coll., 1975; Carnegie scholar, 1952-56. Mem. N.E. Ohio Kenyon Alumni Assn. (trustee 1975-76), Soc. Profl. Journalists, Nat. Assn. Bus. Economists, World Future Soc., Am. Teilhard Assn. Future of Man, AAAS. Presbyterian (elder). Club: River Oaks Racquet. Author: Technology—Fire in a Dark World, 1979. Contbr. articles to profl. publs. Home: 29701 Wolf Rd Bay Village OH 44140 Office: Industry Week mag Penton Plaza 1111 Chester Ave Cleveland OH 44114

PASCASIO, ANNE, univ. dean; b. Pitts., Dec. 29, 1924; d. Anthony and Filomena (DiPippa) Pascasio; B.S., U. Pitts., 1946, M.Ed., 1950, Ph.D., 1966; certificate of Proficiency, D.T. Watson Sch. Phys. Therapy, 1953. Tchr. health and phys. edn. Turtle Creek Pub. Schs., 1946-52; staff phys. therapist Children's Hosp. Pitts., 1953-56; chief phys. therapist Hosp. U. Pa., Phila., 1956-59; cons. div. edn. Am. Phys. Therapy Assn., 1959-62; instr. D.T. Watson Sch. Phys. Therapy, 1962—66, part time; asso. research prof. U. Pitts. Sch. Nursing, 1967, asst. to vice chancellor health professions, 1967-68, dean Sch. Health Related Professions, 1969—. Mem. nat. adv. allied health professions Council NIH, 1971—; cons. rehab. services adminstrn. Dept. Health, Edn. and Welfare, 1971-72; mem. Nat. Commn. for Study Accreditation Selected Health Ednl. Programs, 1970-72; chmn. Gov.'s Com. on Health (Manpower) Edn., 1974-76; mem. adv. com. on accreditation and instl. eligibility U.S. Office Edn. Bd. dirs., mem. exec. com. Hosp. Council Western Pa.; mem. prof. adv. com. Nat. Soc. for Crippled Children and Adults, 1978—. Florence Strattom lectr. Boston Bouve' Coll. Northeastern U., 1968. Mem. Am. Assn. Higher Edn., Am. Soc. Allied Health Professions, A.M.A. (adv. com. on edn. for allied health professions and services Council Med. Edn. 1969-72), Pi Lambda Theta. Republican. Roman Catholic. Contbr. articles to profl. lit., chpts. to books. Office: U Pitts 106 Pennsylvania Hall Pittsburgh PA 15261

PASCH, ALAN, educator; b. Cleve., Dec. 1, 1925; s. P. Jerome and Esther (Broverman) P.; B.A., U. Mich., 1949; M.A., New Sch. Social Research, 1952; Ph.D., Princeton, 1955; Bamford fellow, 1955-56; m. Eleanor Kudlich Berna, Dec. 27, 1950; 1 dau., Rachel. Instr. Ohio State U., 1956-59, asst. prof. philosophy, 1959-60; asso. prof. U. Md., 1960-67, prof., 1967—. Served with AUS, 1944-46; PTO. Mem. Am. Philos. Assn. (exec. sec. 1969-72, sec.-treas. Eastern div., 1965-68), Metaphys. Soc. Am., Soc. Philosophy and Pub. Affairs, AAUP, Washington Philosophy Club (pres. 1978-79). Author: Experience and the Analytic, 1958. Home: 6910 Wake Forest Dr College Park MD 20740 Office: Dept Philosophy U Md College Park MD 20742

PASCH, MAURICE BERNARD, lawyer; b. Chilton, Wis., June 17, 1910; s. Jacob and Eva (Leveton) P.; student George Washington U., 1932-36; J.D., U. Wis., 1938; m. Janet Gerhardt, Nov. 26, 1936; children—Ellen, Robert, Suzy. Admitted to Wis. bar, 1938; sec. to U.S. senator, 1932-36; asst. atty. gen. Wis., 1936-40; practice in Madison, Wis., 1940—; mem. firm Pasch and Pasch. Dir., Home Savs. & Loan Assn. Mem. Wis. Coordinating Com. for Higher Edn. Bd. regents U. Wis. Served as lt. USNR, 1942-46. Mem. Am., Wis., Dane County bar assns., Mil. Order World Wars (state comdr.), Am. Legion, V.F.W., Navy League (pres.), Nat. Bd. Am. Jewish Com., Comml. Law League Am. (exec. council). Jewish (temple pres.). Mason; mem. B'nai B'rith, Elk, Lion. Home: 4834 Sherwood Rd Madison WI 53711 Office: Pasch and Pasch 30 W Mifflin St Madison WI 53703

PASCHAL, JOEL FRANCIS, educator; b. Wake Forest, N.C., Jan. 21, 1916; s. George Washington and Laura (Allen) P.; B.A., Wake Forest Coll., 1935, LL.B., 1938; M.A., Princeton U., 1942, Ph.D., 1948; m. Primrose McPherson, Dec. 21, 1949; Instr., Wake Forest Coll., 1939-40, Princeton U., 1946-47; research dir. N.C. Commn. for Improvement Adminstrn. Justice, 1947-49; admitted to N.C. bar, 1938; practice law, Raleigh, 1949-54; asso. prof. Sch. Law, Duke, 1954-59, prof. law, 1959—, chmn. acad. council, 1966-67. Pres. N.C. United World Federalists, 1952; chmn. N.C. adv. com. U.S. Civil Rights Commn., 1962-65. Served with USNR, 1942-46. Mem. Order of Coif. Democrat. Baptist. Club: Carolina Country (Raleigh). Author: Mr. Justice Sutherland, 1951. Home: 1527 Pinecrest Rd Durham NC 27705

PASCHALL, JAMES ERNEST, ret. air force officer, mgmt. cons., timber farmer; b. LaGrange, N.C., Mar. 31, 1923; s. Joshua Ernest and Claire (Hodges) P.; B.S., U.S. Mil. Acad., 1946; B.S. in Aero. Engring., USAF Inst. Tech., 1951; M.B.A., George Washington U., 1961; student Indsl. Coll. Armed Forces, 1964-65; m. Lelia Elizabeth Atkinson, June 15, 1946; children—Anne (Mrs. Eugene H. Weinheimer), Julia Elizabeth (Mrs. Harold B. Munkvold). Commd. 2d lt. USAAF, 1946, advanced through grades to maj. gen. USAF, 1973; instr. Armed Forces Spl. Weapons Sch., 1948; test officer Air Proving Ground Command, 1952; missile officer Air Force Hdqrs., 1956; devel. planner Air Force Hdqrs., 1959; chief, Policy Office, Air Force Systems Command Hdqrs., 1961; chief Office Sci. and Tech., Hdqrs. USAF, 1965, exec. officer, 1967; vice comdr. Air Force Spl. Weapons Center, 1968, comdr., 1969; dep. comdr. 22d Region N. Am. Air Def. Command, 1970, comdr. 26th Region, 1971, dep. chief of staff plans and programs Hdqrs., Ent AFB, Colo., 1973-74, comdr. 14th Aerospace Force, 1974-75; vice comdr. in chief Aerospace Def. Command, 1975-76; mgmt. cons., timber farmer, 1977—. Mem. Walnut Creek Town Council, 1979—; mem. regional adv. group pub. sci. policy and adminstrn. U. N.M., 1968-75; mem. Albuquerque Sunport Indsl. Adv. Bd., 1970, Albuquerque Armed Forces Adv. Com., 1968-70, Fed. Exec. Bd., 1968-70, Albuquerque Interagy. Bd. U.S. Civil Service, 1969-70, Ariz. Aerospace Adv. Council, 1971-73, Phoenix Armed Forces Adv. Com., 1972-73; mem. mil. adv. group for Gov. of Colo., 1974-76; bd. dirs. Pikes Peak-Colorado Springs United Way, 1974-76, Wayne County chpt. ARC, 1978—; mem. exec. bd. Tuscarora council Boy Scouts Am., 1977-79. Decorated D.S.M., Legion of Merit. Mem. Sci. Research Soc. Am., Goldsboro C. of C. (mil. affairs com. 1978-79), Order Daedalians, Air Force Assn. (pres. chpt. 1978-79), Assn. Grads. U.S. Mil. Acad., Assn. Grads. Indsl. Coll. Armed Forces. Club: Seymour Johnson AFB Officers (Goldsboro, N.C.). Home: 416 Walnut Creek Dr Goldsboro NC 27530

PASCHALL, NATHANIEL, business exec.; b. Seattle, June 11, 1912; s. Nathaniel and Bertha Cranston (Potter) P.; student U. Wash., 1932, Boeing Sch. Aeronautics, Oakland, Calif., 1934-35; m. Mary Katherine Price, Feb. 18, 1947; children—Nathaniel Price, Boeing C. Co-pilot United Airlines, Oakland, 1936-38; with Douglas Aircraft Co., Inc., Santa Monica, 1939-59, v.p., 1945-59, dir., 1951-61; chmn. bd. dirs. Fidelity Northwest, Seattle; chmn. Paschall Internat. Corp.; chmn. Bank of Montreal (Calif.), 1972-79. Clubs: Calif. (Los Angeles); Pacific Union (San Francisco); Annandale Golf (Pasadena, Calif.); Wings (N.Y.); Seattle Yacht; Mt. Royal (Montreal); Birnam Wood Golf (Montecito, Calif.). Home: 790 Fairfield Circle Pasadena CA 91106. *Died Jan. 22, 1979*

PASCOE, WILLIAM T., III, cement co. exec.; b. Wilkinsburg, Pa., 1916; grad. in engring. U. Ill., 1940. With Livingston Shipbldg. Co., 1940-41, Calif. Shipbldg. Co., 1941-42, Old World Food Co., 1946-47; chmn. bd. Pascoe Steel Corp. (acquired by Am. Cement Corp. 1968), 1947-69; dir. Am. Cement Corp., Los Angeles, 1968, pres., chief exec. officer, Newport Beach, Calif., 1970—; chmn. bd., chief exec. officer Amcord, Inc., Newport Beach, 1975; dir. Brown Co., Hollywood Park, Inc. Served with AUS, 1942-46. Mem. Calif. Thoroughbred Breeders Assn. (dir.), Oak Tree Racing Assn. (dir.). Home: PO Box 2550 Newport Beach CA 92663 Office: Amcord Inc 610 Newport Center Dr Newport Beach CA 92660

PASEWARK, WILLIAM ROBERT, educator; b. Mt. Vernon, N.Y., Sept. 9, 1924; s. William and Barbara (Hermann) P.; B.S., N.Y. U., 1949, M.A., 1950, Ph.D., 1956; m. M. Jean McHarg, Mar. 17, 1956; children—William Robert, Lisabeth Jean, Jan Alison, Carolyn Ann, Scott Graham, Susan Gayle. Instr., N.Y. U., 1949-51; asso. prof. Meredith Coll., Raleigh, N.C., 1951-52; asst. prof. Mich. State U., 1952-56; prof. Tex. Tech. U., Lubbock, 1956—; cons., lectr. in field, 1955—. Field reader research div. U.S. Office Edn., 1966—; mem. commn. to revise curricula Tex. Edn. Agy. 1974—; mem. Lubbock Vocat. Office Edn. Adv. Com.; regional bd. examiners Am. Assn. Bus. Colls.; vis. prof. Calif. State U., Fresno, 1959, No. Ariz. State U., 1969, Central Conn. State Coll., 1974. Adviser Lubbock Opportunities Industrialization Center; mem. Tex. Bus. Tchr. Edn. Council; mem. Lubbock Econ. Council; pres. Lubbock Area Presbyn. Council, 1969; chmn. Lubbock City-County Child Welfare Bd., 1973-74; active local Boy Scouts Am., United Fund. Served with USMCR, 1943-46. Recipient Founders Day award N.Y. U., 1956; Outstanding Educator of Am. award, 1970; citation Tex. Ho. of Reps., 1973; Tex. Bus. Tchr. of Year award, 1973. Mem. Nat. Bus. Edn. Assn., Nat. Assn. Bus. Tchr. Edn., Mountain-Plains, Tex. (chmn. legislative com. 1973—) bus. edn. assns., Nat. Assn. Tchr. Edn. for Bus. and Office Edn., Edn. for Bus. Coordinating Council, Bus. Edn. State Suprs. and Tchr. Educators (nat. planning com.), W. Tex. Bus. Edn. Assn. (pres. 1958), Better Bus. Bur. (edn. com.), Am. Vocat. Assn. (pres. bus. and office div. 1976-77, dir. 1976-77, nat. adv. council, award of merit 1978), Lubbock Execs. Assn., Lubbock C. of C., PTA (local pres. 1972), Delta Pi Epsilon, Phi Delta Kappa, Kappa Phi Kappa, Pi Omega Pi, Alpha Kappa Psi, Kappa Delta Pi. Lion (past dir.). Club: Lubbock Country. Author: Clerical Office Procedures, 6th edit., 1978; Rotary Calculator Course, 1962; Ten-Key Adding-Listing Machine Course, 1963, 4th edit., 1973; Key-Driven Calculator Course, 1962; Full-Keyboard Adding Listing Machine Course, 1963; Secretarial Office Procedures, 9th edit., 1977; Duplicating Machine Processes, 1971, 2d edit., 1975; Office Machines Course, 5th edit., 1979; Machine Transcription Word Processing, 1979. Editor: Individualized Instruction in Business and Office Education, 1973; Electronic and Mechanical Printing Calculator Course, 1974; Electronic Display Calculator Course, 1975. Asso. editor Am. Bus. Edn. Yearbook, 1953. Contbr. articles to profl. jours. Research in office adminstrn. and ednl. systems. Home: 4403 W 11th St Lubbock TX 79416

PASFIELD, WILLIAM HORTON, educator, chemist; b. Bklyn., Dec. 28, 1924; s. W. Ambrose and Mildred (Horton) P.; B.S., Mass. Inst. Tech., 1948; Ph.D., U. Conn., 1955; m. Fairlie Maxwell, June 21, 1947; children—Bonnie Lee, Robert H., Terry Louise, William Bruce, David N. Chemist, Hawaiian Pineapple Co., Honolulu, 1948-49; chemist Metal Hydrides, Inc., Beverly, Mass., 1949-50; chemist E.I. duPont de Nemours & Co., Wilmington, Del., 1955-58; prof. chemistry St. John's U., Jamaica, N.Y., 1958—. Served with USNR, 1943-46. Mem. Am. Chem. Soc., Sigma Xi, Phi Gamma Delta. Home: 240 Candee Ave Sayville NY 11782 Office: St Johns U Jamaica NY 11432

PASHAYAN, CHARLES, JR., congressman; b. Fresno, Calif., Mar. 27, 1941; s. Charles and Lillie P.; B.A., Pomona Coll., 1963; J.D., U. Calif., 1968; B.Litt., Oxford U., 1977. Admitted to Calif. bar, 1969, D.C. Bar, 1972, U.S. Supreme Ct. bar, 1977; spl. asst. to gen. counsel HEW, Washington, 1973-75; mem. 96th Congress from 17th Calif. Dist. Mem. Fresno County Bar Assn., Royal Inst. Internat. Affairs, Internat. Inst. Strategic Studies. Republican. Office: 1427 Longworth House Office Bldg Washington DC 20515

PASHEK, ROBERT DONALD, educator; b. The Dalles, Oreg., Feb. 27, 1921; s. Gregory and Mary M. (Bonomi) P.; A.B., Central Wash. Coll., 1949; M.A., State U. Iowa, 1950; Ph.D., U. Ill., 1955; postgrad. Columbia, 1947, Inst. Minerva, Zurich, 1947-48; children—William J., Nicole M. Asst. prof. U. Wichita, 1953-55; asst. prof. Pa. State U., 1956-58, prof., 1960—, head dept. bus. logistics, 1964-73, asso. dean Coll. Bus. Adminstrn., 1973—; acting dir. Pa. Transp. Inst., 1979—; vis. prof. San Francisco State U., 1963-64; cons. Commonwealth of Pa., U.S. AID, U.S. Dept. Commerce. Served with AUS, 1944-46. Named Transp. Man of Year, Delta Nu Alpha, 1964. Mem. Am. Soc. Traffic and Transp. (past pres., dir.), Am. Econ. Assn., Assn. I.C.C. Practitioners, Transp. Research Forum, Soc. Logistics Engrs., Beta Gamma Sigma, Alpha Kappa Psi. Author: (monographs) Land Use Planning and the Interchange Communities, 1962; Intermodal Freight Transportation, 1966; Methodological Framework for Comprehensive Transportation Planning, 1968; Community Effects of Highways Reflected by Property Values, 1973. Research on econ. and social impact hwys., transport systems planning, logistic systems design and planning. Home: 351 Oakley Dr State College PA 16801 Office: Bus Adminstrn Bldg Pa State Univ University Park PA 16802

PASHIGIAN, BEDROS PETER, educator; b. Detroit, June 12, 1932; s. George and Haiganouche (Der Bogoshian) P.; B.A., Wayne State U., 1954; Ph.D., Mass. Inst. Tech.; Ford Found., post-doctoral fellow, Northwestern U., 1960-61; m. Rose Paloian, Aug. 25, 1965; children—Melissa, Peter. Mem. faculty U. Chgo., 1961—; asst. prof. Grad. Sch. Bus., 1961-64, asso. prof., 1964-67, prof. bus. econs., 1968—; sr. research asso. Nat. Bur. Econ. Research, 1974—; research fellow Hoover Instn., Stanford U., 1976-77. Recipient doctoral dissertation series award Ford Found., 1960. Contbr. articles econ. jours. Home: 1460 E Park Pl Chicago IL 60637

PASHMAN, MORRIS, justice Supreme Ct. N.J.; b. Passaic, N.J., Sept. 27, 1912; student N.Y. U., U. Mich.; LL.B., J.D., Rutgers U., 1935; m. Tema L.; children—Linda Pashman Blair, Louis. Admitted to N.J. bar, 1936; clk. to Supreme Ct. Justice James F. Minturn; judge Passaic Police Ct., 1946-48; magistrate Passaic Mcpl. Ct., 1948-51; mayor City of Passaic, 1951-55; dir. revenue and fin., 1955-59; judge N.J. County Ct., Passaic County, 1959-61; judge N.J. Superior Ct., 1961-68, assignment judge, 1968-73; asso. justice N.J. Supreme Ct., 1973—; Mem. Passaic County Bar Assn. (pres. 1955), N.J. State Bar Assn., Am. Bar Assn. Office: Courthouse Hackensack NJ 07601*

PASINETTI, PIER-MARIA, author; b. Venice, Italy, June 24, 1913; s. Carlo and Maria (Ciardi) P.; Dottore in Lettere, U. Padua (Italy), 1935; Ph.D. in Comparative Lit., Yale, 1949. Came to U.S., 1946, naturalized, 1952. Fellow La. State U., 1935-36, U. Calif. at Berkeley, 1936-37; lectr. U. Stockholm, 1942-46; lectr. Italian and humanities U. Calif. at Los Angeles, 1949—. Recipient Fiction award Nat. Inst. Arts and Letters, 1965. Mem. Authors Guild. Club: Elizabethan Yale. Author: L'ira di Dio, 1942; Venetian Red, 1960; The Smile on the Face of the Lion, 1965; From the Academy Bridge, 1970; Suddenly Tomorrow, 1971; Dall' Estrema America, 1975; Il Centro, 1979; also articles, revs., film scripts. Home: 1421 Summitridge Dr Beverly Hills CA 90210 Office: 1259 Dorsoduro Venice Italy 30123

PASK, JOSEPH ADAM, ceramic engr., educator; b. Chgo., Feb. 14, 1913; s. Adam Poskoczem and Catherine (Ramanauskas) P.; B.S., U. Ill., 1934, Ph.D., 1941; M.S., U. Wash., 1935; m. Margaret J. Gault, June 11, 1938; children—Thomas Joseph, Kathryn Edyth. Ceramic engr. Willamina Clay Products Co. (Oreg.), 1935-36; teaching asst. ceramic engring. U. Ill., 1938, instr. 1938-41; asst. ceramic engr. electrotech. lab. U.S. Bur. Mines, 1941; asso. ceramic engr. N.W. Exptl. Sta., 1942-43, asst. prof. ceramic engring., head dept. Coll. of Mines, U. Wash., Seattle, 1941-43; research ceramist, lamp div. Westinghouse Electric Corp., N.J., 1943-46, research engr. ceramic sect., 1946-48; asso. prof. ceramic engring., head ceramic group div.

materials sci. and engring. U. Calif. at Berkeley, 1948-53, prof. 1953—, vice chmn. div., 1956-57, chmn. dept., 1957-61, asso. dean grad. student affairs Coll. Engring., 1969—, research ceramist materials and molecular research div. Lawrence Berkeley Lab. John Dorn Meml. lectr. Northwestern U., 1977. Mem. clay mineral com. NRC; mem. materials adv. bd., chmn. ad hoc com. ceramic processing, adv. commn. metallurgy div. U.S. Bur. Standards, chmn. NSF study objective criteria in ceramic engring. edn. Recipient John F. Bergerson Meml. Service award Ceramic Engring. div. U. Wash., Seattle, 1969. Fellow Am. Ceramic Soc. (hon. life mem.; v.p. 1953-54, pres. ednl. council 1954-55, trustee 1959-62, chmn. electronics div. 1959-60; John Jeppson award 1967; Ross Coffin Purdy award 1979), AAAS, Mineral. Soc. Am.; mem. Nat. Inst. Ceramic Engrs., Nat. Acad. Engring., Am. Soc. Metals, Brit. Ceramic Soc., Am. Soc. Engring. Edn. (chmn. materials com. 1961-63), Clay Minerals Soc., Keramos, Sigma Xi, Tau Beta Pi, Alpha Sigma Mu. Home: 994 Euclid Ave Berkeley CA 94708 Office: Dept Material Sci and Mineral Engring U Calif Berkeley CA 94720

PASKUSZ, GERHARD FREDERICK, univ adminstr.; b. Vienna, Austria, Jan. 21, 1922; s. Erwin J. and Rosa K. (Mraz) Paskus; came to U.S., 1938, naturalized, 1943; B.S., UCLA, 1949, Ph.D., 1961; m. Susan Melford, Mar. 20, 1943; 1 dau. Sherry Paskusz Ellingwood. Asso. in engring., dept. engring. UCLA, 1952-60, research specialist biotech., 1960-61; mem. faculty Cullen Coll. Engring., U. Houston, 1961—, prof. engring., 1968—, asso. dean engring., 1968-76, dir. minority engring. programs, 1976—. Bd. dirs. Student Competitions Relevant Engring., 1971-76. Served with AUS, 1943-46. Recipient Good Teaching award UCLA, 1957. Mem. IEEE, Am. Philatelic Soc., AAUP, Am. Soc. Engring. Edn., Assn. for Computing Machinery, Sigma Xi, Tau Beta Pi, Eta Kappa Nu, Phi Delta Kappa. Author: Linear Circuit Analysis, 1964. Home: 850 Kuhlman St Houston TX 77024

PASLAY, LE ROY CLAY, geophysicist; b. Manhattan, Kans., Dec. 26, 1907; s. Edmond B. and Minerva L. P.; B.S. in Elec. Engring., Kans. State U., 1930, M.S., 1932; m. Mary Aileen Hull, May 18, 1930; children—Robert Hull, Patricia Louise Paslay Martin. Engr., Gen. Electric Co., 1930-31; asst. prof. Kans. State U., Manhattan, 1932-35; dir. research Nat. Geophys. Co., Dallas, 1936-41; chief under water sound div. Naval Ordnance Lab., Washington, 1942-45; prin. partner Marine Instrument Co., Dallas, 1942—; exec. v.p., dir. Pan Am. Exploration Co., Dallas, 1947-55; pres., dir. Marine Seismic Surveys Inc., Dallas, 1950-63, Marine Geophys. Co. S.A., Maracaibo, Venezuela, 1950-61, Marine Petroleum Corp., Dallas, 1957—; dir. Templeton Growth Fund of Can., Toronto, Ont., Templeton World Fund, Inc., St. Petersburg, Fla., 1978—; individual trustee Tidelands Royalty Trust, 1954—; Fla. gov.'s ofcl. rep. Interstate Oil Compact Commn., 1969-70. Vice mayor Town of Manalapan, Fla., 1959-66, mayor, 1967-70, Recipient U.S. Navy Distinguished Civilian Service award, 1945. Mem. IEEE, Soc. Exploration Geophysicists (Medal award 1976), Am. Water Works Assn. Presbyterian. Clubs: La Coquille (Palm Beach, Fla.); Manalapan (Fla.) Yacht, Manalapan. Patentee in field. Home: 1020 S Ocean Blvd Manalapan FL 33462 Office: 1030 Republic Nat Bank Tower Dallas TX 75201

PASLAY, PAUL ROBERT, mech. engr.; b. New Orleans, May 9, 1931; s. Robert Cecil and Elizabeth (Westbrook) P.; B.S. in Mech. Engring., La. State U., 1950; M.S. in Mech. Engring., Rice U., 1952; Sc.D. in Mech. Engring., Mass. Inst. Tech., 1955; m. Charlotte Louise Wormuth, Dec. 29, 1951; children—Paul Westbrook, Robert Crockett. Vibration engr. Gen. Elec. Co., Schenectady, N.Y., 1955-59; prof. mech. engring. Rice U., Houston, 1959-65; prof. engring. Brown U., Providence, 1965-73; dean engring. Oakland U., Rochester, Mich., 1973-76, U. Ill. at Chgo. Circle, 1976-78; pres. Paslay, Inc., Mech. Engring. Cons., Houston, 1978—; engring. cons. NSF sr. postdoctoral fellow, Germany, 1961-62. Mem. ASME, Am. Soc. Engring. Edn., Western Soc. Engrs., Sigma Xi, Tau Beta Pi. Tech. editor Jour. Applied Mechs., 1967-70. Contbr. articles on applied mechs., machine design and bioengring. to tech. publs. Office: Paslay Inc 7417 Brompton Blvd Houston TX 77025

PASMANICK, KENNETH, bassoonist; b. Rochester, N.Y., Aug. 23, 1924; s. Philip and Rose (Levitt) P.; student Eastman Sch. Music, 1942-43, Juilliard Sch. Music, 1946-47; B.A., Am. U., 1962; m. Frances Virginia Cohen, Dec. 22, 1946; children—Philip, Anne. Performed with Martha Graham Ballet tour and at Ziegfield Theater, 1946; prin. bassoonist Nat. Symphony Orch., 1947—, also Washington Opera Soc.; performed world premiere Gian Francesca Malipiero's Serenata for Bassoon and Chamber Orch., 1962; The Windhover by Robert Evett, concerto for bassoon and orch., 1971, Bassoon Concerto by David Amram, 1972; Am. specialist abroad for Dept. State, El Salvador and Costa Rica, 1966-67; instr. bassoon Am. U., Washington; asst. prof. U. Md.; founder, mem. Nat. Symphony Wind Soloists. Served in USAAF, 1943-46. Home: 5227 Chevy Chase Pkwy Washington DC 20015

PASNICK, RAYMOND WALLACE, labor union ofcl., editor; b. New Kensington, Pa., Apr. 29, 1916; s. Stanley and Mary Ann (Grzewienska) P.; ed. pub. schs.; m. Margaret Solberg, Mar. 3, 1937; children—Victor Keith, Raymond Gene. Editor, Aluminum Workers Jour., New Kensington, 1936-37; publicity dir. Aluminum Workers Am., Pitts., 1937-44; asst. editor Steel Labor, Pitts., 1944-46, editor, 1962-78; Midwest editor, also Midwest dir. edn. United Steelworkers Am., Chgo., 1946-62, nat. editor, also dir. communications, 1962-65, dir. public relations, Pitts., 1965-78. Pub. mem. Chgo. Bd. Edn., 1955-66. Recipient of Civil Rights award Jewish Labor Com. Chgo., 1962, Man of Year award Chgo. unit Nat. Frontiersmen, 1963. Mem. Internat. Labor Press Assn. (pres. 1972-74), Am. Fedn. Tchrs., Chgo. Newspaper Guild (treas. 1948-56; v.p. 1957). Democrat. Roman Catholic. Office: 5 Gateway Center Pittsburgh PA 15222

PASQUA, PIETRO F., educator; b. Englewood, Colo., May 30, 1922; s. Frank and Josephine (Liveratti) P.; B.S. in Mech. Engring., U. Colo., 1944; M.S., Northwestern U., 1947, Ph.D., 1952; m. Madonna Louise Murphy, Feb. 21, 1945; children—Linda Louise, Randall Clyde, Michael Patrick, Karen Junell. Instr., U. Colo., 1944-45, Northwestern U., 1945-52; mem. faculty U. Tenn., 1952—, prof. nuclear engring., head dept., 1958—, ORAU councilor, chmn. nuclear engring. dept. heads, 1976-77; cons. in field. Murphy Found. fellow, 1951—. Mem. Am. Nuclear Soc. (chmn. edn. div.), Am. Soc. Engring. Edn. (chmn. nuclear div. 1966-67), Sigma Xi, Tau Beta Pi, Pi Tau Sigma, Phi Kappa Phi. Author papers in field. Home: 319 W Hunt Rd Alcoa TN 37791 Office: Nuclear Engring Bldg Univ Tenn Knoxville TN 37916

PASQUALE, ANTHONY MICHAEL, mgmt. cons.; b. Paterson, N.J., Nov. 24, 1942; s. Anthony Joseph and Theresa Constance (Salurso) P.; B.S. in Bus. Adminstrn., Seton Hall U., 1964, M.B.A., 1966; m. Karen Montagna, Aug. 21, 1965; children—Anthony J., Michael P. Wage/salary analyst Chase Manhattan Bank, N.Y.C., 1964-66; bank officer, 1971-72; 2d v.p. Hayden Stone, Inc., N.Y.C., 1966-71; cons. Marsh McLennan, N.Y.C., 1972-73; exec. v.p. Downe Communications, Inc., N.Y.C., 1973-76, also dir.; pvt. mgmt. cons., Montclair, N.J., 1976—. Former co-adj. instr. Fairleigh Dickinson U., Am. Inst. Banking, N.Y. U., Mgmt. Inst. Served with USMCR, 1966-72. Mem. Am. Compensation Assn., Am. Arbitration Assn. (arbitrator). Club: Bradford Bath and Tennis. Author: A New Dimension to Job Evaluation, 1969. Home and office: 150 Highland Ave Montclair NJ 07042

PASQUARIELLO, ANTHONY MICHAEL, educator; b. Bklyn., Sept. 3, 1914; s. Alessandro and Vincenza (Casertano) P.; B.A., Bklyn. Coll., 1938; M.A., Columbia, 1940; Ph.D., U. Mich., 1950; m. Dorothy C. Alward, Oct. 23, 1944 (dec. Apr. 1977); 1 son, Alexander A.; m. 2d, Patricia W. O'Connor, Feb. 11, 1978. Teaching fellow U. Mich., Ann Arbor, 1944-48, instr., 1948-53, asst. prof., 1953-58; asso. prof. U. Colo., Boulder, 1958-64; prof. Spanish, chmn. dept. Spanish, Italian, Portuguese, Pa. State U., University Park, 1964-69; prof. Spanish, chmn. dept. Spanish, Italian, Portuguese, U. Ill., Urbana, 1969—. Cons. Modern Lang. Assn., 1960—, Ednl. Testing Service, 1961—, Woodrow Wilson Nat. Fellowship Found., 1966—; dir. Nat. Def. Edn. Act Insts. for Tchrs. Spanish, French and German, 1961-62. Vice pres. Ann Arbor Civic Theatre, 1956-58. Rackham research fellow, 1953, Ford Found. fellow, 1955-56, U. Colo. faculty fellow, 1963. Mem. MLA, AAUP, Am. Assn. Tchrs. Spanish and Portuguese (v.p. 1971, pres. 1972), Phi Sigma Iota, Sigma Delta Pi. Author: (with F. S. Escribano) Más personajes, personas y personillas del refranero español, 1958. Editor: (with J.V. Falconieri) La otra orilla (J. López Rubio), 1958, Mi adorado Juan (M. Mihura), 1964; Escuadra hacia la muerte (A. Sastre), 1967; (with Patricia W. O'Connor) El Tragaluz (A. Buero Vallejo), 1977. Founder, co-editor Modern Internat. Drama, 1967—; asso. editor Estreno, 1974—. Home: 2208 Combes St Urbana IL 61801

PASSAGLIA, MARTIN, JR., physiologist, former naval officer, humane assn. adminstr.; b. Chgo., June 18, 1930; s. Martin and Assunta (Volpi) P.; B.S., St. Louis U., 1952, postgrad. (fellow), 1952-55; M.S. in Physiology, George Washington U., 1965; grad. Aerospace Physiology Sch., Naval Sch. Aviation Medicine, 1959, Naval Diving Sch., 1964, U.S. Naval Intelligence Sch., 1955; m. Alfreda F. Dolo, Nov. 24, 1955. Commd. ensign U.S. Navy, 1955, advanced through grades to capt., 1975; targeting officer Fleet Intelligence Center, Eastern Atlantic and Mediterranean, Port Lyautey, Morocco, 1956-57; mil. liaison officer U.S. Naval Reconnaissance and Tech. Center, Washington, 1957-59; head aerospace physiology tng. unit Naval Air Sta., Jacksonville, Fla., 1959-61; asst. head full pressure suit tng. facility Naval Air Sta., Cecil Field, Fla., 1961-63; research asso. environ. stress dept. Naval Med. Research Inst., Bethesda, Md., 1963-65; head physiology tng. dept. Naval Aerospace Med. Inst., Pensacola, Fla., 1965-69; head aerospace physiology tng. dept. Naval Regional Med. Center, San Diego, 1969-74; exec. officer Naval Regional Med. Center, Corpus Christi, 1974-76; dir. aircraft and crew systems tech. directorate, Naval Air Devel. Center, Warminster, Pa., 1976-78, ret., 1978; exec. dir. The Am. Humane Assn., Englewood, Colo., 1979—. Recipient Recognition award San Diego Humane Soc., 1974. Fellow Aerospace Med. Assn.; mem. Aerospace Physiology Soc. (pres. 1975-76, Wiley Post award 1975), Space Medicine Assn., Sigma Xi. Contbr. articles to profl. publs. Home: 7265 S Jellison Ct Littleton CO 80123 Office: 5351 S Roslyn St Englewood CO 80111

PASSALAQUA, JOSEPH ANTHONY, musician; b. New Brunswick, N.J., Jan. 13, 1929; s. Mariano and Anna (Giglotti) P.; student public schs.; m. Alison Ditwiler, May 5, 1963; children—Joseph Martin, Nina. With the Tony Pastor Orch., then Ray McKinley Orch., 1944-48, also with Duke Ellington, Ella Fitzgerald, Dizzy Gillespie, Oscar Peterson; rec. artist Pablo Records. Recipient Grammy award, Down Beat mag. award; winner Jazz Group European Jazz poll, 1974. Mem. Am. Fedn. Musicians, Nat. Acad. Rec. Artists, ASCAP. Author: Guitar Methods. Address: care Pablo Records 451 N Canon Dr Beverly Hills CA 90210

PASSANANT, RICHARD J., advt. agy. exec.; b. N.Y.C., Jan. 24, 1931; s. Charles F. and Catherine (Cunningham) P.; B.S., Seton Hall U., 1952; m. Helen Buckholz, June 26, 1954; children—James, John, Thomas, Paul, Jeanne. Mgr. mgmt. services Cooper & Lybrand, N.Y.C., 1952-59; controller Interpublic Group of Cos., N.Y.C., 1959-64; controller Doyle Dane Bernbach, N.Y.C., 1964-68; asst. treas. Harrington Righter & Parsons, N.Y.C., 1968-73; chief fin. officer, sr. v.p., sec.-treas. McCaffrey & McCall Inc., N.Y.C., 1973—, also dir. Mem. fund raising com. Eastern L.I. Hosp., 1976-77. Mem. Fin. Exec. Inst., N.Y. Creditmen's Assn., Advt. Data Processing Assn. (pres. 1964-65). Clubs: K.C. (grand knight 1965-66) (East Meadow, N.Y.); Southold Republican. Home: 2555 Elm Ct North Bellmore NY 11710 Office: 575 Lexington Ave New York NY 10022

PASSANO, EDWARD MAGRUDER, printing co. exec.; b. Towson, Md., Dec. 22, 1904; s. Edward Boetler and Eleanor (Isaac) P.; B.S. in Econs., Johns Hopkins, 1927; m. Mildred Page Nelson, Oct. 26, 1929; 1 son, Edward Magruder. With Waverly Press, Inc., Balt., 1927—, treas., 1946-68, pres., 1963-71, chmn. exec. com., 1971-75, also dir. Bd. dirs., treas. Passano Found., Inc., 1970—. Mem. Soc. Colonial Wars (treas. gen.). Republican. Episcopalian. Home: Box 534 Route 5 Easton MD 21601 Office: Waverly Press Inc Mount Royal and Guilford Aves Baltimore MD 21202

PASSANO, WILLIAM MOORE, book publisher; b. Harrisonville, Md., June 12, 1902; s. Edward Boteler and Eleanor Philips (Isaac) P.; B.Engring., Johns Hopkins, 1923; m. Ida Kemp Cockey, May 12, 1926; children—William Moore, Susan Kemp (Mrs. Samuel G. Macfarlane). Pres. Waverly Press, Inc., Balt., 1946-62; pres. Williams & Wilkins Co., pubs. med. books and sci. periodicals, Balt., 1963-70, chmn. bd., 1974—; chmn. bd. Waverly Press, 1970-74. Chief comml. printing br. WPB, 1943, dep. dir. prodn. scheduling div., 1944. Mem. bd. Balt. Urban League, 1947-55, pres., 1952-55; mem. bd. Health and Welfare Council Met. Balt., 1956-79; past chmn. planning commn. Diocese Md., P.E. Ch. Hon. chmn. Passano Found. Mem. ASME, Copyright Soc. U.S.A. (past trustee). Home: Gibson Island MD 21056 Office: 428 E Preston St Baltimore MD 21202

PASSER, HAROLD CLARENCE, economist; b. Lakefield, Minn., Nov. 27, 1921; s. Clarence Walter and Esther (Nauman) P.; S.B., Harvard, 1943, A.M., 1948, Ph.D., 1950; m. Astrid Louise Anderson, Nov. 19, 1966; children by previous marriage—Christine L., David C., Jr. Asst. prof. econs. Princeton, 1950- 52; economist Eastman Kodak Co., 1952-69; asst. sec. commerce for econ. affairs Dept. Commerce, 1969-73; asst. treas. Eastman Kodak Co., 1973—; pres. Eastman Savs. and Loan Assn., 1975-77; lectr. U. Rochester, 1953-55, Cornell U., 1955. Treas. Genesee (N.Y.) region Council Econ. Edn., 1965-69; chmn. N.Y. State Council Econ. Edn., 1974-79; mem. econ. adv. bd. Dept. Commerce, 1967-68; cons. Fed. Res. Bd., 1954-55. Served with USNR, 1943-46. Mem. Nat. Assn. Bus. Economists, Conf. Bus. Economists, Am. Econ. Assn., Nat. Econs. Club, Phi Beta Kappa. Republican. Baptist. Author: The Electrical Manufacturers, 1953; also articles. Home: 133 Imperial Circle Rochester NY 14617 Office: 343 State St Rochester NY 14650

PASSEY, GEORGE EDWARD, educator; b. Stratford, Conn., Sept. 28, 1920; s. Henry Richard and Elizabeth (Angus) P.; B.S., Springfield Coll., 1942; M.A., Clark U., 1947; Ph.D., Tulane U., 1950; m. Algie Aldridge Ashe, Nov. 18, 1950; children—Richard Ashe, Elizabeth Aldridge, Mary Louise. Asst. prof. U. Ala., Tuscaloosa, 1952-55, asso. prof., 1955-56, 57-59, prof., 1959-63, prof. psychology, chmn. div. social and behavioral scis., Birmingham, 1967-73, prof. engring., 1969—, dean Sch. Social and Behavioral Scis., 1973—; research scientist Lockheed Ga. Co., Marietta, Ga., 1956-57, 63-65, cons., 1965-67; prof. Ga. Inst. Tech., 1965-67. Served with USNR, 1942-46; PTO; with USAF, 1951-52. Fellow Am. Psychol. Assn.; mem. So. Soc. for Philosophy and Psychology, Southeastern Psychol. Assn., Ala. Psychol. Assn., Sigma Xi. Club: Terry Walker Golf and Country. Home: 3841 Spring Valley Rd Mountain Brook AL 35223. *Whatever success I have enjoyed ought to be attributed to the attempt I have made to carry out the admonitions of my parents to make choices only after having appraised the alternatives in terms of their consequences, to weigh ethical considerations above all others, never to demand of others what one is unwilling to give of himself, and to work untiringly for those causes to which one is committed.*

PASSIN, HERBERT, sociologist; b. Chgo., Dec. 16, 1916; s. Hyman and Edith (Block) P.; student U. Ill., 1935-36; M.A., U. Chgo., 1941; m. Helen Wood Latham, Dec. 18, 1964; 1 son, Thomas. Instr. Northwestern U., 1941-42; chief pub. opinion and sociol. research div., civil information and edn. G.H.Q., SCAP, Tokyo, 1946-51; prof. Far Eastern Studies U. Wash., Seattle, 1959-62; prof. sociology Columbia U., 1962—, chmn. dept., 1973-78. Chmn. bd. editorial advisers TBS-Britannica, Tokyo, 1969-73, now mem.; dir. Assn. Asian studies, 1965-68. Served to lt. AUS, 1944-47. Mem. Am. Anthrop. Assn., Soc. Applied Anthropology, Am. Sociol. Assn. Author: (with others) The Japanese Village in Transition, 1951; (with J.W. Bennett) In Search of Identity, 1958, China's Cultural Diplomacy, 1962, Society and Education in Japan, 1965, The United States and Japan, 1975; Japan and the Japanese, 1978; editor: Encounter at Shimoda, 1979; A Japan and the Japanese, 1978; editor: Encounter at Shimoda, 1979; A Season of Voting, 1979. Home: 25 Claremont Ave New York NY 10027

PASSMORE, ERIC WILLIAM, lawyer, mfr.; b. Milw., July 7, 1893; s. William and Miriam (Bloodgood) P.; student St. Johns Mil. Acad., ex 1911, U. Wis., 1911-14; LL.B., Marquette U., 1916; m. Gertrude Cole, Apr. 24, 1937. Admitted to Wis. bar, 1916; practice corporate, ins., tax, estate and trust law, Milw., 1916-56; sr. asso. Bloodgood & Passmore; exec. v.p. Simplicity Mfg. Co., Inc., Port Washington, Wis., 1937-67, cons., counsel, 1967—. Trustee Columbia Hosp., Milw. Served with USNRF, 1917-18. Mem. Am., Wis., Milw. bar assns., Sigma Nu. Clubs: University, Milwaukee Country, Milwaukee Athletic; Tavern (Chgo); Links (N.Y.C.). Home: 3510 N Lake Dr Milwaukee WI 53211 Died Nov. 6, 1979.

PASSON, RICHARD HENRY, univ. adminstr.; b. Hazleton, Pa., Aug. 18, 1939; s. Henry Richard and Grace Miriam (Bernstein) P.; B.A. (Bishop Hafey scholar), King's Coll. (Pa.), 1961; M.A., U. Notre Dame, 1963, Ph.D. (NDEA fellow), 1965; m. Margaret Rose Ferdinand, Aug. 14, 1965; children—Michael, Rebecca, Christopher. From instr. to prof. English, U. Scranton, 1964-73, chmn. English dept., 1970-73, fgn. student adviser, 1965-67; dean Coll. Arts and Scis., Creighton U., Omaha, 1973-77; acad. v.p. St. Joseph's U., Phila., 1977—. Recipient grant Nat. Assn. Fgn. Students, 1966. Mem. Modern Lang. Assn., Am. Assn. Higher Edn., Am. Assn. Acad. Deans. Democrat. Roman Catholic. Contbr. articles profl. jours. Office: St Joseph's U 54th and City Ave Philadelphia PA 19131

PASSOW, AARON HARRY, educator; b. Liberty, N.Y., Dec. 9, 1920; s. Morris and Ida (Wiener) P.; B.A. cum laude, State U. N.Y. at Albany, 1942, M.A., 1947; Ed.D. (Romiett Stevens scholar), Columbia, 1951; m. Shirley Siegel, July 2, 1944; children—Michael Joel, Deborah Miriam, Ruth Gertrude. Tchr. sci., math. Stony Point (N.Y.) High Sch., 1942-43; sci. tchr. Eden (N.Y.) Central Sch., 1946-48; instr. edn., supr. math. N.Y. State Coll. Tchrs., Albany, 1948-51; mem. faculty Columbia Tchrs. Coll., 1951—, prof. edn., 1952—, chmn. dept. curriculum and teaching, 1968-77, chmn. com. urban edn., 1965-77, Jacob H. Schiff prof. edn., 1972—, dir. div. ednl. instns. and programs, 1975—; research asso. Horace Mann-Lincoln Inst. Sch. Experimentation, 1952-65; Fulbright lectr., vis. prof. edn. U. Stockholm, 1967—68; vis. prof. Bar-Ilan (Israel) U., 1973. Dir. Study Washington Pub. Schs., 1966-67; ednl. cons., lectr. edn. disadvantaged, edn. gifted and curriculum devel. Mem. Englewood (N.J.) Bd. Edn., 1969-72, pres., 1971. Served to 1st lt. USAAF, 1943-46. Recipient Distinguished Alumnus award State U. N.Y. at Albany, 1969; Kappa Delta Pi fellow internat. edn., 1958-59. Mem. N.E.A. (life), Assn. Supervision and Curriculum Devel. (dir. 1959-62, chmn. research commn. 1961-63, co-chmn. task force edn. culturally disadvantaged 1964-66), Nat. Soc. Study Edn. (bd. dirs. 1975—), Met. Assn. Study Gifted (pres. 1957-58), Am. Ednl. Research Assn., Comparative and Internat. Edn. Assn. (dir. 1971-74), Kappa Delta Pi (Laureate chpt., hon.). Jewish (pres. temple 1966-67). Co-author: Organizing for Curriculum Development, 1953; Planning for Talented Youth, 1955; Developing a Curriculum for Modern Living, 1957; Improving the Quality of Public School Programs, 1960; author Secondary Education for All: The English Approach, 1961; also articles. Editor: Curricular Crossroads, 1962; Education in Depressed Areas, 1963; Education of Disadvantaged: A Book of Readings, 1967; Developing Programs for the Disadvantaged, 1968; Deprivation and Disadvantage: Nature and Manifestations, 1970; Reaching the Disadvantaged Learner, 1970; Urban Education in the 1970s, 1971; Opening Opportunities for Disadvantaged Learners, 1972; The National Case Study: An Empirical Study of 21 National Educational Systems, 1976; Secondary Education Reform: Retrospect and Prospect, 1976; American Secondary Education: The Conant Influence, 1977; The Gifted and the Talented: Their Education and Development, 1979. Home: 394 Eton St Englewood NJ 07631 Office: Tchrs Coll Columbia Univ New York NY 10027

PAST, RAYMOND EDGAR, educator; b. Jamestown, N.D., Dec. 14, 1918; s. Alvin Edgar and Frances Inez (Tabler) P.; A.B., U. Pa., 1941; M.A., U. Tex. at Austin, 1947, Ph.D. (U. grad. fellow), 1950; postgrad. Linguistics Inst., U. Wash., 1962; m. Frances Paracca, Sept. 23, 1942; 1 son, Alvin Wallace. Instr. English, U. Tex., Austin, 1950-51; asst. prof. English Tex. A. and M. U., 1951-52; faculty U. Tex., El Paso, 1952—, prof. English, 1961-71, prof., chmn. linguistics, 1971—, chmn. faculty council, 1964-66. Dir. NDEA Insts. in English as Second Lang., 1966-68, Experienced Tchrs. Fellowship program, 1969-70. Served to lt. USNR, 1941-46. Mem. AAUP, Nat. Council Tchrs. English, S.W. Council Fgn. Lang. Tchrs., Modern Lang. Assn., Tchrs. English to Speakers Other Langs. Democrat. Club: Campestre Juarez (Juarez, Mexico). Author (with Maria R. De Dozal) Say It in English, 1968, Vol. II, 1973, Vol. III, 1974; Language as a Lively Art, 1970. Home: 3244 Louisville Ave El Paso TX 79930

PASTA, JOHN ROBERT, govt. ofcl., physicist; b. N.Y.C., Oct. 22, 1918; s. William James and Janet (Williams) P.; B.S., Coll. City N.Y., 1946; Ph.D., N.Y. U., 1951; m. Betty Ann Bentzen, May 2, 1943; children—Diane, David. Research fellow Brookhaven Nat. Lab., 1948-51; staff mem. Los Alamos Sci. Lab., 1951-56; head math. program, div. research AEC, 1956-61; prof. physics and computer sci. U. Ill., 1961-70, head dept. computer sci., 1964-70; vis. scientist C.E.R.N., Geneva, Switzerland, 1967-68; head office computing activities NSF, 1970-74, dir. div. computer research, 1974-75, dir. div. math. and computer scis., 1975—. Liaison rep. div. math. sci. NRC, 1958-61, 70—; cons. to govt. and industry, 1961-70; adj. prof., engring. and applied sci. George Washington U., 1973-76. Mem.

math. and computer sci. research adv. com. AEC, 1961-70, chmn., 1965-67; chmn. internat. relations com. Am. Fedn. Information Processing Socs., 1965-66; Am. del. Internat. Fedn. Information Processing, 1965-66; trustee Interuniv. Communications Council, 1965-68; mem. computer sci. adv. com. Stanford, 1969-72; phys. scis. com. Ill. Bd. Higher Edn., 1969-70. Served to capt. USAAF, 1942-45. Decorated Bronze Star. Mem. Am. Phys. Soc., Am. Math. Assn., Philos. Soc. Washington. Contbr. profl. jours. and books. Asso. editor Jour. Computational Physics, 1966-74. Home: 700 New Hampshire Ave NW Washington DC 20037 Office: NSF Washington DC 20550

PASTALAN, LEON, educator; b. Newark Valley, N.Y., Feb. 7, 1930; s. John Prokof and Mary Alice (Rosowski) P.; B.S., State U. N.Y. at Cortland, 1953; Ph.D., Syracuse U., 1961; m. Alice Olive Sawyer, June 15, 1959; children—Manya Alyssa, Rebecca Ann. Asst. prof. sociology U. No. Colo., 1959-60; asso. prof. sociology, dir. Urban Studies Center, U. Toledo, 1960-66; prof. architecture, dir. research Inst. Gerontology, U. Mich., Ann Arbor, 1966—; cons. U.S. Bur. Standards, U.S. Senate Spl. Com. on Aging, Pa. Dept. Pub. Welfare, AMA, Cleve. Found.; mem. profl. adv. com. Am. Nat. Standards Inst.; mem. Mich. Task Force on Housing for White House Conf. on Aging, 1970; mem. peer rev. HEW, intergovtl. sci., engring. and tech. adv. panel Task Forces on Health and Human Resources; The Elderly; cons. VA, Medicon, Inc., Sisters of Mercy Health Care Corp. Served with U.S. Army, 1954-56. Recipient Rackham Grad. Sch. Faculty Research award U. Mich., 1971. Mem. Am. Sociol. Assn., AAAS, Gerontol. Soc., Assn. Collegiate Schs. Architecture. Author: Spatial Behavior of Older People, 1970; Man-Environment Reference, 1974; The Environmental Context of Aging, 1979. Office: 520 E Liberty St Ann Arbor MI 48109

PASTERCZYK, WILLIAM ROBERT, educator; b. Chgo., Feb. 4, 1917; s. Walter and Julia (Stachowicz) P.; B.S. in Chemistry, De Paul U., 1940, M.S. in Chemistry, 1943; Ph.D. in Biochemistry, Loyola U., 1954; m. Ardelle Jaworski, Oct. 2, 1948; children—Joan Carol, Karen Lee, Gail Ann. Faculty De Paul U., 1941—, asso. prof. chemistry, 1951-58, acting chmn. dept., 1956-58, chmn. dept., 1958-61, prof., 1958—. Mem. Am. Chem. Soc. (dir. Chgo. 1958—), AAUP, Soc. for Applied Spectroscopy, Sigma Xi. Home: 8218 N Karlov Ave Skokie IL 60076 Office: 1036 W Belden Ave Chicago IL 60614

PASTERNAK, JOSEPH, motion picture producer; b. Silagy-Somlyo, Rumania (now Hungary), Sept. 19, 1901; s. Samuel and Roza (Janovitz) P.; student High Sch. Silagy-Somlyo; came to U.S., 1921, naturalized, 1927; m. 2d, Darrell, Jan. 9, 1942; 3 sons, Michael, Jeffrey, Peter. Began as asst. dir., 1923; motion picture producer for Universal Pictures in Europe and U.S.; produced Nice Girl, The Flame of New Orleans, It Started with Eve, 1941, Seven Sweethearts, 1942, Anchors Aweigh, 1944, Thousands Cheer, Song of Russia, This Time for Keeps, and numerous others for M.G.M. including The Merry Widow, Because You're Mine, Small Town Girl, Latin Lovers, 1952, Easy to Love, Flame and the Flesh, 1953, Ask Any Girl, 1959, Please Don't Eat the Daisies, 1960, Where the Boys Are, 1961; Jumbo, 1962, A Ticklish Affair, 1963, Girl Happy, 1965, Penelope, 1966. Author: Easy the Hard Way, 1956. Address: care Metro Goldwyn Mayer 10202 W Washington Blvd Culver City CA 90230*

PASTORE, JOSEPH MICHAEL, JR., educator; b. Port Chester, N.Y., Dec. 1, 1941; s. Joseph Michael and Frances (Baviello) P.; B.B.A., St. Bonaventure U., 1963; M.B.A. (scholarship), Pace Coll., 1966; Ph.D. (scholarship), St. Louis U., 1969; m. Patricia Ann O'Brien, Aug. 21, 1965; children—Joseph Michael III, Meredith Ann, Timothy James. Instr. mgmt. scis. St. Louis U., 1967-68; instr. sch. bus. adminstrn. St. Bonaventure (N.Y.) U., 1965-66, asst. prof. mgmt. scis., 1968-70, asso. prof., 1970-76, dean Sch. Bus. Adminstrn., 1970-74, v.p. acad. planning, provost, 1974-76; prof. mgmt., dean Lubin Sch. Bus. Adminstrn., Pace U., 1976—; cons. Monsanto Co., Dresser Industries, Sylvania Electric Products, Inc., various pub. sch. systems. Mem. labor panel Fed. Mediation and Conciliation Service, 1973—. Served to 1st lt. AUS, 1963-65. Recipient Distinguished Mil. Grad. award St. Bonventure U., 1963, Niagara Mohawk Power Corp. award, 1963; Alumnus of Year award Pace U. Grad. Sch., 1975. Mem. Acad. Mgmt., Am. Arbitration Assn. (labor panel 1973—), Am. Econ. Assn., Am. Mktg. Assn., Am. Assn. Higher Edn., Middle Atlantic Assn. Colls. Bus. Adminstrn. (exec. com. 1973—), Beta Gamma Sigma. Home: 3 Woodlea Ln Scarborough NY 10510 Office: Pace U New York NY 10038

PASTORE, PETER NICHOLAS, educator, physician; b. Bluefield, W.Va., Nov. 8, 1907; s. Louis and Carmela (Ricciardulli) P.; A.B., U. Richmond, 1930; M.D., Med. Coll. Va., 1934; M.S., U. Minn., 1939; m. Julia Rourke, Sept. 14, 1939; children—Ann (Mrs. Vincent M. Cremona, Jr.), Louis, Julie, Mary (Mrs. Cyrus Dolph IV), Peter Nicholas. Intern Med. Coll. Va., 1934, resident surgery, 1935-36; fellow Mayo Clinic, 1936-39, staff asso., 1939-42; mem. faculty Med. Coll. Va., 1942—, prof., chmn. dept. otology, rhinology, laryngology, audiology and speech pathology, 1942-76, prof. emeritus, 1976—, founder, dir. Hearing and Speech Center, 1942—; chief otolaryngology McGuire VA Hosp., Richmond, 1955—; cons. U.S. Naval Hosp., Portsmouth, Va., McDonald Army Hosp., Ft. Eustis, Va. Med. dir. Richmond chpt. Am. Cancer Soc., 1959-60, pres., 1961-63; bd. dirs. Richmond Children's Aid Soc., 1944-47, Va. Soc. Crippled Children and Adults, 1954—; mem. Gov. Va. Adv. Com. Handicapped Children, 1964-72; pres. Richmond Easter Seal Soc. Crippled Children and Adults, 1967-70. Mem. bd. Benedictine High Sch., Richmond, 1959-65, pres., 1964-66. Served to 1st lt., M.C., AUS, World War II. Diplomate Am. Bd. Otolaryngology. Fellow Am. (life mem.; regent 1965-69), Internat. (life mem., pres. Va. surg. div. 1959-61) colls. surgeons, A.M.A., Am. Acad. Ophthalmology and Otolaryngology (life mem., award merit 1960); mem. Med. Soc. Va., Richmond Acad. Medicine, Va. Soc. Ophthalmology and Otolaryngology (life mem., pres. 1952-53), Richmond Eye, Ear, Nose and Throat Soc. (pres. 1945-46), Am. Otol. Soc. (life), Am. Laryngol. Assn. (life), Am. Laryng., Rhinol. and Otol. Soc. (life), Catholic Physicians Guild (pres. 1962-65), Pan-Am. Assn. Oto-Rhino-Laryngology-Broncho-Esophagology, Tidewater Otol. Med. Soc. (hon.), W.Va. (hon.), Dallas (hon.) otol. socs., Phi Beta Kappa, Sigma Xi, Alpha Omega Alpha. Lion. Club: Willow Oaks Country. Home: 5503 Riverside Dr Richmond VA 23225

PASTREICH, PETER, orch. mgr.; b. Bklyn., Sept. 13, 1938; s. Ben and Hortense (Davis) P.; A.B. magna cum laude, Yale Coll., 1959; postgrad. N.Y. U. Sch. Medicine, 1959-60: m. Ingrid Eggers; June 5, 1976; 1 son, Emanuel; 1 son by previous marriage, Michael. Mgr., Greenwich Village Symphony, N.Y.C., 1960-63; gen. mgr. Nashville Symphony, 1963-65; gen. mgr. Kansas City Philharmonic, 1965-66; asst. mgr., mgr. St. Louis Symphony, 1966-78, exec. dir., 1970-78; exec. dir. San Francisco Symphony, 1978—; bd. dirs. Nat. Com. for Symphony Orch. Support. Bd. dirs. Laumeier Sculpture Park, St. Louis. Served with U.S. Army, 1960. Recipient First Disting. Alumnus award Yale U. Band, 1977. Mem. Am. Symphony Orch. League (dir.), Assn. Calif. Symphony Orchs. (dir.), Bankers Club of San Francisco. Club: Yale (N.Y.C.). Office: 107 War Meml Veterans Bldg San Francisco CA 94102

PASTUKHIV, SERHIJ KINDZERIAVYJ, clergyman, artist, musician; b. Ukraine, July 4, 1924; s. Jacob and Kateryna (Buniak) P.; came to U.S., 1950, naturalized, 1960; ed. U. Erlangen, Germany, 1949; m. Julia Lytwynenko, Jan. 27, 1952; children—Olga, Irene, Larissa. Ordained to ministry Holy Ukranian Autocephabic Orthodox Ch. in Exile, 1965; rector Holy Trinity Cathedral, Bklyn., 1969—; adminstr. Holy Ukranian Autocephabic Orthodox Ch. in Exile, 1969—; archpriest-protopresbyter, 1976—; exhibited one-man shows, N.Y.C., Phila., Scranton, Pa. Mem. Standing Conf. of Canonical Orthodox Bishops Am., 1969—; mem. eccles. endorsing agts. Armed Forces Chaplains Bd. Home: 103 Evergreen St W Babylon NY 11704 Office: Holy Trinity Cathedral 185 S 5th St Brooklyn NY 11211

PATAI, RAPHAEL, anthropologist; b. Budapest, Hungary, Nov. 22, 1910; s. Joseph and Edith (Ehrenfeld) P.; Ph.D., U. Budapest, 1933, Hebrew U. Jerusalem, 1936; children—Ofra Jennifer (Mrs. William Wing), Daphne. Mem. faculty Hebrew U., 1937-47; dir., founder Palestine Inst. Folklore and Ethnology, 1944-48; prof. anthropology Dropsie Coll., Phila., 1948-57; vis. lectr. Columbia U., 1948, 54-56, 60-61, New Sch. Social Research, 1948; vis. prof. U. Pa., 1948-49, Ohio State U., 1956; lectr. N.Y. U., 1951-53; dir. research Theodor Herzl Inst., N.Y.C., editor Herzl Press, 1956-71; prof. anthropology Fairleigh Dickinson U., 1966-76; vis. prof. Judaic Studies Bklyn. Coll., 1971-72. Pres., Am. Friends of Tel Aviv U., 1956-68; dir. Syria-Lebanon-Jordan research project Human Relations Area Files, Inc., New Haven, 1955-56; adv. editor Judaism, Ency. Americana, 1959—. Author numerous books, including The Arab Mind, 1973; (with Jennifer Wing) The Myth of the Jewish Race, 1975; The Jewish Mind, 1977; The Hebrew Goddess, 1978; The Messiah Texts, 1979; editor: Ency. of Zionism and Israel, 1971. Home: 39 Bow St Forest Hills NY 11375

PATANE, GIUSEPPE, conductor; b. Napoli, Italy, Jan. 1, 1932; s. Franco and Giulia (Caravaglios) P.; student Naples Conservatory; m. Rita Saponaro, May 7, 1958; children—Francesca, Paola. Debuts include: Teatro San Carlo, Naples; conducted at La Scala, Rome, Palermo, Turin, Trieste, Bologna, Verona, Met. Opera, Chgo. Lyric Opera, San Francisco Opera, Cleve. Orch., Vienna State Opera, Paris Opera; prin. guest condr. Budapest Philharmonic; condr. Berlin Philharmonic, Vienna Philharmonic, Slovak Philharmonic. Office: care Robert Lombardo 30 W 60th St New York NY 10023

PATCH, PAUL FRANCIS, ret. air force officer; b. Denver, May 28, 1920; s. Pasqual and Florence (Dangelo) P.; student U. Denver, 1938-41, Air Command and Staff Sch., 1957-58; B.A., U. Md., 1961; M.A., George Washington U., 1963-64; student Air War Coll., 1963-64; m. Marguerite Helena MacMaster, Oct. 7, 1942; children—Teresa Patch Atherton, Jane, Nancy. Pilot, Pan Am. World Airways, 1946-48; commd. USAAF, 1948, advanced through grades to maj. gen. USAF, 1971; served in Germany with Berlin Airlift, then pilot, ops. officer 60th Troop Carrier Group, 1948-52; project officer Westover AFB, Mass., 1952-55; chief Air Transport Control Center, McGuire AFB, N.J., 1955-57; ops. staff officer Transport Ops. Div., Directorate Ops., Hdqrs. USAF, Washington, 1958-63; dir. transp. Hdqrs. Pacific Air Forces, Hickam AFB, Hawaii, then, chief transp. div., chief, logistics plans div., 1964-67; chief, plans div. Office of Spl. Asst. Strategic Mobility, Orgn. Joint Chiefs of Staff, Washington, 1967-69; dep. chief staff materiel Hdqrs. 7th Air Force, Vietnam, 1969-70; dep. chief staff materiel Hdqrs. Pacific Air Forces, Hickam AFB, Hawaii, 1970-72; dep. chief staff logistics Hdqrs. Mil. Airlift Command, Scott AFB, Ill., 1972-73; dir. transp. Hdqrs. USAF, Washington, 1973-75, ret., 1975. Served with USAAF, 1941-45. Decorated D.S.M., Legion of Merit with 4 oak leaf clusters. Mem. Airline Pilots Assn., Nat. Def. Transp. Assn., Order of Daedalians, Air Force Assn., Am. Def. Preparedness Assn. Roman Catholic. Home: 7 Pheasant Run Darien CT 06820 Office: Chgo Pneumatic Tool Co 6 E 44th St New York City NY 10017

PATCHAN, JOSEPH, lawyer; b. Bklyn., June 29, 1922; B.S., Miami U., Oxford, Ohio, 1943; J.D., Cleve. State U., 1952; m. Nancy Joy Letaw, Jan. 7, 1951; children—Reed, Judy, David. Merchandiser Am. Greetings Corp., Cleve., 1951-55; admitted to Ohio bar, 1952; pvt. practice law, 1955-69; judge U.S. Bankruptcy Ct., No. Dist. Ohio, 1969-75; partner Baker & Hostetler, Cleve., 1975—; mem. adj. faculty Cleve. State Law Sch., 1959-73; mem. faculty Nat. Bankruptcy Seminar, Fed. Jud. Center, Washington, 1971-77; mem. adv. com. bankruptcy rules U.S. Jud Conf., 1978—. Served with USN, 1943-46. Mem. Ohio Bar Assn., Cleve. Bar Assn., Am. Bar Assn., Nat. Conf. Bankruptcy Judges (asso.). Jewish. Clubs: Cleve. Athletic; Army and Navy (Washington). Author: Practice Comments to Rules of Bankruptcy Procedure, 1974; contbr. articles on bankruptcy law to profl. publs.; bd. editors Callaghan Bankruptcy, Practice and Procedure Treatise, 1979—; contbg. editor Nat. Survey Bankruptcy Law, Emory U., 1979—. Office: 1956 Union Commerce Bldg Cleveland OH 44115

PATCHETT, THOMAS CHARLES, television producer; b. Lansing, Mich., Apr. 16, 1940; s. Wendell Toomey and Ethel Roxanna (Perry) P.; student Albion Coll., 1958-60; B.A., Mich. State U., 1962. Advt. copywriter, 1962-66; mem. comedy team Patchett and Tarses, 1966-71; free-lance television writer, 1971-72; staff writer Carol Burnett TV show, 1972-73; staff writer Bob Newhart Show, 1973, writer, producer, 1974-76; co-creator, writer, producer The Tony Randall Show, 1976, exec. producer, 1977—; co-creator, exec. producer We've Got Each Other, 1977—. Recipient Emmy award for comedy writing Carol Burnett show, 1972. Mem. AFTRA, Writers Guild, Hollywood Acad. TV Arts and Scis. Office: care MTM Enterprises 4024 Radford Ave Studio City CA 91604*

PATE, JEROME KENDRICK, profl. golfer; b. Macon, Ga., Sept. 16, 1953; s. Patrick Jefferson and Joyce (Gallagher) P.; B.A., U. Ala.; m. Soozi Nelson, Nov. 28, 1975. Winner numerous amateur golf competitions, 1974-75; winner profl. golf competitions: U.S. Open, 1976, Canadian Open, 1976, Taiheiyo (Japan) Masters, 1976, Phoenix Open, 1977, So. Open, 1978, Mixed Team Championship, 1977. Named Rookie of Yr., 1976. Office: care Pros Inc PO Box 673 Richmond VA 23206

PATE, JOHN RALSTON, govt. ofcl., orgn. exec.; b. Scranton, S.C., Aug. 27, 1906; s. Charles H. and Nell (Singletary) P.; A.B. in Edn., A.M., U. S.C., 1927; B.S., M.D., Duke U., 1933; J.D., U. Louisville, 1945; M.P.H., Johns Hopkins U., 1948; certificate hosp. adminstrn. U. Rochester, 1933; m. Alice Drew Chenoweth, Feb. 12, 1942; 1 son, John Ralston. Instr. in English, U. S.C., 1926-27; tchr. English, Charleston (S.C.) High Sch., 1927-29; intern Strong Meml. Hosp., Rochester, N.Y.; mem. faculty George Washington U. Sch. Medicine, 1933-38; now asso. prof. community medicine and internat. health Georgetown U.; staff Ky. Dept. Health, 1938-47; with D.C. Dept. Pub. Health, 1948—, dir. bur. disease control, 1953-64, chief bur. communicable disease control, 1964—; admitted to U.S. Supreme Ct. bar, 1969. Mem. Civitan Internat., 1955—, gov. Chesapeake dist., 1961-62, v.p. zone 3, 1962-64, internat. pres.-elect, 1964-65, pres., 1965-66; nat. council Boy Scouts Am.; bd. visitors Freedoms Found. at Valley Forge; mem. Pres.'s Com. for Handicapped; mem. Gov. of Va. Com. for the Handicapped Employment; bd. dirs. Social Hygiene Soc. D.C.; adv. bd. Partridge Schs. and Rehab. Center, Gainesville, Va. Recipient 1st Albernon Sydney Sullivan medallion U. S.C., 1927; citation for service LWV D.C., 1952; scroll of honor Omega Psi Phi, 1957; named Mr. Civitan, Chesapeake dist., 1962. Fellow Am. Pub. Health Assn., Am. Coll. Legal Medicine, Royal Soc. Health; charter mem. Am. Assn. Pub. Health Physicians, Am. Venereal Disease Assn., Omicron Delta Kappa; mem. AMA, Am. Assn. Pub. Health Physicians, Assn. Tchrs. Preventive Medicine, Royal Soc. Medicine Gt. Britain, Am. Assn. History of Medicine, D.C. Med. Soc., Clin. Club Washington, Ky. Bar Assn., Am. Geriatric Soc., World Med. Assn., Acad. Medicine, SAR, Phi Beta Pi, Alpha Tau Omega. Democrat. Episcopalian. Clubs: Masons (32 deg.), Shriners. Author articles, chpts. books. Home: 1503 N Jefferson St Arlington VA 22205 Office: 1825 Connecticut Ave NW Washington DC 20009

PATE, MARTHA B. LUCAS, educator; b. Louisville, Nov. 27, 1912; d. Robert H. and Gertrude (Lasch) Lucas; A.B., Goucher Coll., Balt., 1933, LL.D., 1946; M.A., George Washington U., 1935; Ph.D., U. London, 1940; LL.D., Ala. Coll., 1946, Atlanta U., 1972; L.H.D., U. Louisville, 1950, Smith Coll., 1971; m. Maurice Pate, Oct. 1961 (dec. 1965). Asso. prof. philosophy and religion, dean of students U. Richmond (Va.), 1941-44; asso. dean Radcliffe Coll., 1944-46; pres., prof. philosophy of religion Sweet Briar Coll. (Va.), 1946-50; exec. dir. office of univ. and coll. relations Inst. Internat. Edn., 1961-62; chmn. Coll. and Sch. div. United Negro Coll. Fund, 1962—, bd. dirs., 1967—, chmn. Dana Fellowship com., 1970—; bd. dirs. Fgn. Policy Assn., 1963—, also mem. gen. ops. exec. com., nominating com.; bd. dirs. Rec. for the Blind, 1962-76, chmn. planning and devel. com., 1963—, v.p., 1967—, chmn. Nat. Scholastic awards, 1968—. Mem. nat. selections com. for Fulbright Scholarships, 1948-50, U.S. del. UNESCO Prep. Conf. of U. Reps., Utrecht, Holland, 1948, 4th Gen. Conf. UNESCO, Paris, 1949; mem. Adv. Council for Jr. Year in France, 1947-50; mem. bd. dirs. Assn. Am. Colls., 1949-50; v.p. So. U. Conf. and chmn. com. on improvement of instruction, 1949-50; 2d vice chmn. Am. Council on Edn., 1949-50; mem. adv. council on health careers United Hosp. Fund; adv. council Columbia U. Sch. Social Work, 1967—, chmn. nominations com., 1970—; mem. U.S. Nat. Adv. Commn. on Internat. Edn. and Cultural Affairs, 1970-73; mem. Nat. Com. on U.S.-China Relations, 1971—; pub. mem. selection panel for fgn. service officers USIA, 1973; mem. commn. accrediting Assn. Theol. Schs. U.S. and Can., 1978—. Bd. dirs. N.Y. Met. com. UNICEF, 1972—, incorporator nat. com., 1975—; bd. regents Georgetown U., 1974-75, bd. dirs., 1975—, vice chmn. bd. dirs., 1979—, also bd. rep. to Med. Center; trustee N.Y. Med. Coll. 1967—, chmn. ednl. policies com., 1974—, chmn. academic and student affairs com., 1975—; trustee Fund for Peace, 1967—, mem. exec. com., mem. postdoctoral fellowship com.; trustee N.Y. Sch. Psychiatry, 1971—, chmn. com. goals and acad. programs; trustee Fund for Theol. Edn., Inc., 1969-78; bd. dirs. Westchester Med. Center Found., 1969—, YWCA, Richmond, Va.; trustee L.I. U., 1969—, chmn. acad. policies com. 1970—; trustee Pierce Coll., Athens, Greece, 1962-69, chmn. acad. affairs com., 1962-69, hon. trustee, 1969—; alumnae trustee Goucher Coll., 1968-71; chmn. univs. and colls. com. bd. dirs. Ralph Bunch Meml. Project, 1976—; trustee St. Stephen's Sch. in Rome, 1977—, mem. nominations com., 1978—; mem. commn. on accreditation Assn. Theol. Schs. U.S. and Can., 1978—; bd. advisors Inst. for Study World Politics, 1977—, Center for Def. Info., 1979—. Decorated chevalier French Legion of Honor; recipient George Washington U. Alumni Citation, 1947; UN Internat. Women's Yr. award, 1975, others. Fellow Soc. Values in Higher Edn. (dir. 1976—); mem. Am. Philos. Assn., Nat. Inst. Social Scis., Council on Religion and Internat. Affairs (trustee 1968-77, chmn. 60th anniversary com. 1970-74), Acad. Religion and Mental Health, Acad. Polit. Sci., New Dramatists Soc. (dir. chmn. com. on univ. projects), Phi Beta Kappa (Bicentennial fellow 1976). Clubs: Faculty (New Haven); Vassar, Cosmopolitan (N.Y.C.). Episcopalian. Author: (with others) Religious Faith and World Culture, 1951. Lectr. on edn., philosophy and world affairs. Home: Godstow RFD 1 West Redding CT 06896 Office: 330 E 49th St New York NY 10017

PATEL, CHANDRA KUMAR NARANBHAI, research co. exec.; b. Baramati, India, July 2, 1938; s. Naranbhai Chaturbhai and Maniben P.; came to U.S., 1958, naturalized, 1970; B.Engring., Poona U., 1958; M.S., Stanford U., 1959, Ph.D., 1961; m. Shela Dixit, Aug. 20, 1961; children—Neela, Meena. Mem. tech. staff Bell Telephone Labs., Murray Hill, N.J., 1961—, head infrared physics and electronics research dept., 1967-70, dir. electronics research dept., 1970-76, dir. phys. research lab., 1976—. Recipient Adolph Lomb medal Optical Soc. Am., 1966; Ballantine medal Franklin Inst., 1968; Coblentz award Am. Chem. Soc., 1974; Honor award Assn. Indians in Am., 1975; Zworykin award Nat. Acad. Engring., 1976; Lamme medal IEEE, 1976; Founders prize Tex. Instruments Found., 1978. Fellow Am. Acad. Arts and Scis., Am. Phys. Soc., IEEE, Optical Soc. Am.; mem. Nat. Acad. Scis., Nat. Acad. Engring. Contbr. articles to tech. jours. Home: 5 Manor Hill Rd Summit NJ 07901 Office: Bell Telephone Labs 600 Mountain Ave Murray Hill NJ 07974

PATEL, VIRENDRA CHATURBHAI, mech. engr.; b. Mombasa, Kenya, Nov. 9, 1938; s. Chaturbhai S. and Kantaben N. (Rai) P.; came to U.S., 1969, naturalized, 1975; B.Sc. with honours, Imperial Coll., London, 1962; Ph.D., Cambridge (Eng.) U., 1965; m. Manjula Patel, May 29, 1966; children—Sanjay, Bindiya. Sr. asst. in research Cambridge U., 1965-69; vis. prof. Indian Inst. Tech., Kharagpur, 1966; cons. Lockheed Ga. Co., Marietta, 1969-70; mem. faculty U. Iowa, Iowa City, 1971—, prof. energy engring., 1975—, chmn. div., 1976—, chmn. mech. engring., 1978—; research engr. Iowa Inst. Hydraulic Research, 1971—; mem. Iowa Gov. Sci. Advisory Council, 1977—; mem. resistance com. Internat. Towing Tank Conf., 1978—; cons. in field. Mem. ASME, Am. Inst. Aeros. and Astronautics, Sigma Chi. Author: Three Dimensional Turbulent Boundary Layers, 1972; also articles. Home: 1212 Teg Dr Iowa City IA 52240 Office: Div Energy Engring Univ Iowa Iowa City IA 52242

PATENAUDE, JOAN, soprano; b. Can., Sept. 12, 1944; came to U.S., naturalized, 1978; d. Ernest and Rita (Mac Donald) P.; B.Mus., Ecole Vincent D'Indy, Montreal, Que., Can., 1968-70; student Kathryn Turney Long Sch., Met. Opera, 1973; Mus.M., Music Acad. of West, 1976; m. Bruce Yarnell, July 15, 1972. Leading roles in Madama Butterly, La Traviata; appeared in Am. revival Didon, Lincoln Centre, N.Y.C., 1975; appeared with N.Y.C. Opera, San Francisco Opera, Can. Opera Co.; State Dept. artist, Poland, 1977, 78, Far East, 1979; affiliate artist Westpoint Mil. Acad., 1970-72; rec. artist. Mem. AGVA, Actors Equity, Screen Actors Guild. Office: care Ludwig Lustig & Florian Ltd 111 W 57th St New York NY 10019

PATERNO, JOSEPH VINCENT, football coach; b. Bklyn., Dec. 21, 1926; s. Angelo Lafayette and Florence (de LaSalle) P.; B.A., Brown U., 1950, LL.D., 1975; m. Suzanne Pohland, May 12, 1962; children—Diana Lynne, Mary Kathryn, David, Joseph Vincent, George Scott. Asst. football coach Pa. State U., 1950-66, head football coach, 1966—. Served with AUS, 1945-46. Named Coach of Year, Walter Camp Football Found., 1972, Washington Touchdown Club, 1973. Mem. Am. Football Coaches Assn. (dir., Coach of Year 1968). Office: Pa State U University Park PA 16802*

PATERSON, BASIL ALEXANDER, sec. of state N.Y.; b. N.Y.C., Apr. 27, 1926; s. Leonard J. and Evangeline (Rondon) P.; B.S., St. John's Coll., 1948; J.D., St. John's U., 1951; m. Portia Hairston, 1953; children—Daniel, David. Admitted to N.Y. bar, 1952; partner firm

Paterson, Michael, Jones and Cherot, N.Y.C., 1956-77; mem. N.Y. State Senate, 1965-70; dep. mayor for labor relations City of N.Y., 1978; sec. of state State of N.Y., 1979—; pres. Inst. Mediation and Conflict Resolution, 1971-77; mem. N.Y. State Temporary Commn. for Revision N.Y.C. Charter. Head, Harlem br. NAACP, N.Y.C., 1966-68; del. Democratic Nat. Conv., 1972, 76; vice chmn. Dem. Nat. Com., 1972-78, mem. Dem. Nat. Com., 1972-78. Recipient Eagleton Inst. Politics award, 1967; Disting. Service award Guardians Assn. N.Y. Police Dept., 1968; City Club of N.Y. award, 1973; Black Expo award, 1973. Roman Catholic. Office: Office of Sec State Dept State 162 Washington Ave Albany NY 12231

PATERSON, KATHERINE WOMELDORF, writer; b. Tsing Kiang pu, China, Oct. 31, 1932; d. George Raymond and Mary Elizabeth (Goetchius) Womeldorf; came to U.S., 1940; A.B., King Coll., Bristol, Tenn., 1954, LL.D. (hon.), 1978; M.A., Presbyn. Sch. Christian Edn., 1957; postgrad. Kobe Sch. of Japanese Lang., 1957-60, Union Theol. Sem., 1961-62, M.R.E., 1962; m. John Barstow Paterson, July 14, 1962; children—Elizabeth Polin, John Barstow, David Lord, Mary Katherine Nah-he-sah-pe-che-a. Tchr., Lovettsville (Va.) Elementary Sch., 1954-55; missionary Presbyn. Ch., Japan, 1957-61; master sacred studies and English, Pennington (N.J.) Sch. for Boys, 1963-65. U.S. nominee for Hans Christian Anderson award, 1979. Mem. Authors Guild, Children's Book Guild Washington. Democrat. Author: Who Am I?, 1966; To Make Men Free, 1973; Justice for All People, 1973; The Sign of the Chrysanthemum, 1973; Of Nightingales That Weep, 1974; The Master Puppeteer (Nat. Book award for Children's Lit.), 1976; Bridge to Terabithia (Newbery medal 1978), 1977; The Great Gilly Hopkins (Nat. Book award for Children's Lit. 1979, Newberry honor book, Christopher award), 1978; Angels and Other Strangers, 1979.

PATERSON, PHILIP Y., physician; b. Mpls., Feb. 6, 1925; s. Donald Gildersleeve and Margaret (Young) P.; B.S., U. Minn., 1946, M.B., 1947, M.D., 1948; m. Virginia Lee Bray, Mar. 22, 1947; children—Anne, Peter, Benjamin. Intern, Mpls. Gen. Hosp., 1948-49; research fellow div. infectious diseases Tulane U. Sch. Medicine, 1949-50, instr. in medicine Am. Heart Assn. research fellow, 1950-51; Am. Heart Assn. research fellow dept. microbiology U. Va. Sch. Medicine, 1953, asst. resident and co-resident in medicine univ. hosp., 1953-55, asst. prof. microbiology, instr. in medicine, established investigator Am. Heart Assn., 1955-57; med. officer Lab. Immunology, Nat. Inst. Allergy and Infectious Diseases, NIH, Bethesda, Md., 1957-60; vis. asst. prof. microbiology N.Y. U., 1957-60, asso. prof. medicine, 1960-65; asso. prof. medicine, dir. Samuel J. Sackett Research Labs. and chief sect. infectious diseases, dept. medicine Northwestern U., 1965-66, Samuel J. Sackett prof. medicine and chief infectious diseases, hypersensitivity sect., dept. medicine Northwestern U.-McGaw Med. Center, 1966-72, Samuel J. Sackett prof. medicine and microbiology, chief infectious diseases-hypersensitivity sect., 1972-75, prof. microbiology-immunology, chmn. dept. microbiology-immunology Northwestern U. Med. and Dental Schs., 1975—; Christine Larsen lectr. Sch. Medicine, Albuquerque, 1973; Disting. lectr. Ann. Meeting Assn. Am. Physicians and Western Sect. Am. Fedn. Clin. Research, Carmel, Calif., 1974; Grace Faillace Meml. lectr. Leo Goodwin Inst. Cancer Research, Nova U., 1978; Ernest Witebsky Meml. lectr. 6th Internat. Convocation on Immunology, Niagara Falls, N.Y., 1978; Joseph E. Smadel Meml. lectr. Ann. Meeting, Infectious Diseases Soc. Am., Atlanta, 1978; mem. working group Nat. Multiple Sclerosis Soc., 1973—; mem. research study com. Am. Heart Assn., 1978-80; mem. internat. med. adv. bd. Internat. Fedn. Multiple Sclerosis Socs., 1973—; mem. adv. panel Am. Bd. Med. Lab. Immunology, 1978—. Served to capt., M.C., U.S. Army, 1951-53. Mem. Am. Fedn. Clin. Research, AAAS, Am. Soc. Microbiology, Am. Assn. Immunologists, Harvey Soc., Am. Soc. Clin. Investigation, Infectious Diseases Soc. Am. (Gold medal 1978), Central Soc. Clin. Research, Am. Rheumatism Assn., Assn. Am. Physicians, Am. Clin. and Climatol. Assn., Sigma Xi, Alpha Omega Alpha. Editor and contbg. author: (with others) The Biological and Clinical Basis of Infectious Diseases, 1975; contbr. articles to profl. jours.; mem. editorial bd. Procs. Soc. Exptl. Biology and Medicine, 1968-73, 1977—, Cellular Immunology, 1969—, Infection and Immunity, 1970—, Clin. and Exptl. Immunology, 1970—, Clin. Immunology and Immunopathology, 1978—, Jour. Clin. and Lab. Immunology, 1979—; asso. editor Jour. Infectious Diseases, 1979—. Home: 1025 Chestnut St Wilmette IL 60091 Office: 303 E Chicago Ave Chicago IL 60611

PATERSON, ROBERT ANDREW, educator; b. Reno, Jan. 23, 1926; s. Chester Arthur and Verna (Stumpf) P.; B.A., U. Nev., 1949; M.A., Stanford, 1952; Ph.D., U. Mich., 1957; m. Marion Trumbull Bergen, May 19, 1956; children—Robert Andrew, Virginia Bergen, John Arthur. Fellow U. Mich., 1954-56; from instr. to asso. prof. U. Md., 1956-67; investigator U. Mich., summers 1961-66, vis. prof., 1967; prof. botany, head dept. biology Va. Poly. Inst., 1967-79, exec. asso. dean Coll. Arts and Scis., 1979—; mem. adv. bd. Center for Study Pub. Choice, 1970—; biol. researcher in Antarctica, 1971—. Mem. Va. Water Resources Research Center; chmn Va. Biology Tchrs. Conf., 1971. Pres. Parents, Tchrs. and Students Assn., 1975-76. Served with USNR, 1944-46. NIH grantee. Mem. AAAS, Am. Inst. Biol. Sci. (pub. responsibility rep. for Va. 1972-78), Brit. Mycological Soc., Assn. Southeastern Biologists, Va. Acad. Sci. (research bd. 1973-78, chmn. 1977-78), Va. Assn. Biology Tchrs. (dir. 1976-77), Bot. Soc. Am., Mycological Soc. Am., Sigma Xi (pres. local chpt. 1975-76), Phi Kappa Phi, Phi Sigma, Sigma Nu. Author papers in field. Home: 1505 Palmer Dr Blacksburg VA 24060

PATERSON, ROBERT COWANS, banker; b. Montreal, Apr. 9, 1928; s. Alexander and Anna Cassils (Cowans) P.; B.Com., McGill U., 1949; m. Ann Skaith, Oct. 9, 1954; children—Alexander, Hartland, Elspeth, Ann. With The Royal Bank of Can., 1958—, asst. gen. mgr. investments, Montreal, exec. v.p., gen. mgr. fin. and investments; pres. RoyMor Mortgage Corp.; trustee European and Pacific Investment Trust. Bd. govs. McGill U., mem. exec. com., chmn. investment com. Mem. Can. Bankers Assn. (mem. policy and planning com.). Clubs: University, Hermitage, Badminton and Racquet (Toronto). Home: 627 Belmont Ave Westmount PQ H3Y 2W3 Canada Office: Royal Bank of Can 1 Place Ville Marie Montreal PQ H3C 3A9 Canada*

PATERSON, ROBERT WACKER, educator; b. Columbus, Ohio, Dec. 30, 1918; s. Robert Guildersleeve and Alma Henrietta (Wacker) P.; B.Sc. U. Va., 1944, M.A., 1945, Ph.D., 1953; m. Gene Vance Neff, Sept. 28, 1946; children—Ann, Ellen. Fgn. service officer Dept. State, 1945-49; instr. U. Va., Charlottesville, 1949-53; asso. prof. econs. U. S.C., Columbia, 1953-55, prof., 1955-59, dir. research, 1953-59; prof., dir. Bus. and Public Adminstrn. Research Center, U. Mo., Columbia, 1959-71, dean Coll. Bus. and Pub. Adminstrn., 1971-76, prof. econs. and pub. adminstrn., 1976—; econ. and mgt. cons. to bus. and govt. Mem. Assn. U. Burs. Econ. Research (pres. 1967), Nat. Assn. Bus. Econs., Am. Econs. Assn., Nat. Acad. Scis. Author: Forecasting Techniques for Determining the Potential Demand for Highways, 1966; The Rise of Disorganization in Metropolitan Communities, 1968. Office: Middlebush Hall Univ Missouri Columbia MO 65201

PATES, GORDON, ret. newspaper editor; b. San Francisco, Sept. 1, 1916; s. Rutherford and Louise (Ryder) P.; B.A., U. Wash., 1939; m. Lorraine Lindeberg, Aug. 24, 1941; children—Bonnie J., William G. With San Francisco Chronicle, 1939—, successively copyboy, reporter, copyreader, desk editor, editor This World mag., Sunday editor, advt. research dir., promotion dir., mng. editor, 1954-77, exec. editor, 1977-79, ret., 1979. Served as tech. sgt. AUS, USAAF, 1942-46. Recipient award for distinguished domestic news reporting, Nat. Headliners Club, 1948. Home: 3450 Tice Creek Dr Walnut Creek CA 94595 Office: Chronicle Pub Co San Francisco CA 94119

PATI, CHARLES, motion picture co. exec.; b. N.Y.C., Mar. 18, 1914; s. Natale and Mariann (Sicoli) P.; evening student Stevens Inst. Tech., Rutgers U.; student Guild Sch. Dramatic Arts; m. Helen Annis, June 14, 1942; 1 dau., Patricia Ann. With Metro-Goldwyn-Mayer, Inc., 1928-65, v.p. Metro-Goldwyn-Mayer Internat., Inc., 1945-65; exec. v.p. Banner Prodns., Inc., Los Angeles, 1965-68; exec. v.p. Technicolor, Inc., Hollywood, 1968-75; exec. v.p. Intercontinental Releasing Corp., 1976—; dir. Metro-Kalvar Corp. Mem. bd. youth council 77th Police Precinct, N.Y.C. Served with AUS, 1942-45. Mem. Acad. TV Arts and Scis., Soc. Motion Picture and TV Engrs., Acad. Motion Picture Arts and Scis.

PATI, JOGESH CHANDRA, physicist; b. Barpada, Orissa, India; s. Kailash Chandra and Indumar Pati; B.Sc. with honors, Ravenshaw Coll., Cuttack, India, 1955; M.Sc., Delhia (India) U., 1957; Ph.D., U. Md., 1960; m. Geeta Dash, Oct. 8, 1961; children—Sangeeta, Yagyensh, Sibani, Devesh. Richard C. Tolman fellow Calif. Inst. Tech., 1960-62; mem. staff Inst. Advanced Study, Princeton, N.J., 1962-63; from asst. prof. to asso. prof. U. Md., 1963-72, prof. physics, 1972—. NSF grantee, 1963-79; John Simon Guggenheim fellow, 1979-80. Mem. Am. Phys. Soc., Washington Acad. Scis. (Disting. Scientist award 1973). Home: 8604 Saffron Dr Lanham MD 20801 Office: Dept Physics U Md College Park MD 20742

PATIN, HENRY A., educator; b. St. Martinsville, La., May 11, 1919; s. Achille and Emily (Duchamp) P.; A.B., La. State U., 1939, A.M., 1941; S.M., U. Chgo., 1949, Ph.D., 1958; J.D., Northwestern U., 1977; m. Barbara Jean Anderson, June 14, 1949; children—Elaine, David, Kathy. Asst. edn. La. State U., 1939-41; instr. math. Chgo. City Coll., 1947-61; mem. faculty Chgo. State U., 1961—, prof. edn., 1963-75, chmn. dept., 1961-72, prof. emeritus, 1975—. Vice pres. Cook County Coll. Tchrs. Union, 1966. Bd. dirs. Henry N. Hart Jewish Community Center, Chgo., 1965-68. Served to 1st lt., F.A., AUS, 1942-46; ETO. Decorated Purple Heart. Mem. Philosophy Edn. Soc., Math. Assn. Am. Contbr. articles to profl. jours. Home: 9335 S Ridgeland St Chicago IL 60617

PATMOS, ADRIAN EDWARD, univ. dean; b. Paterson, N.J., June 29, 1914; s. Adrian and Myra (Van Splinter) P.; A.B. magna cum laude, N.Y.U., 1935, A.M., 1936. Penfield scholar, 1937-38; grad. study Am. U., 1936-37; m. Pearl Van Den Heuvel, Apr. 25, 1942; children—Adrian Edward III, Bruce Douglas. Asst. prof. econs. Wittenberg U., 1938-47, asso. prof., head dept., 1947-50, prof. econs., 1950—, head dept., 1950-64, dir. mgmt. devel. program, 1952—, eve. sessions, 1952—, dean Sch. Community Edn., 1955—. Jr. accountant Def. Plant Corp., Curtiss-Wright Corp., summer 1943; vis. instr. Ohio Wesleyan U., summer 1944; spl. field rep. NLRB, 1946; vis. lectr. econs. N.Y.U., 1946-47, summer 1948; vis. prof. econs. USAF Inst. Tech., 1949, 50. Chmn., Clark County Health Facilities Planning Com., 1965-66. City commr., Springfield, Ohio, 1958-62, mayor, 1960-62. Trustee United Way, Springfield and Clark County, 1960—; trustee Clark Tech. Coll., 1965—, chmn., 1969-71; trustee Springfield Community Hosp., 1975—. Recipient Wittenberg award for meritorious service to univ., Nat. Mgmt. Assn. Silver Knight award, Kiwanis award for disting. service to community, Wize award for outstanding community service. Mem. Ohio Coll. Assn. (pres. adult edn. sect. 1959-60), Am. Econ. Assn., Phi Beta Kappa, Phi Gamma Delta, Blue Key. Baptist. Kiwanian. Home: 2945 N Limestone St Springfield OH 45503

PATON, DAVID, physician, med. educator; b. Balt., Aug. 16, 1930; s. Richard Townley and Helen (Meserve) P.; grad. Hill Sch., Pottstown, Pa., 1948; A.B., Princeton, 1952; M.D., Johns Hopkins, 1956; 1 son, David Townley; 1 stepdau., Garrison Franke. Intern dept. medicine Cornell Med. Sch., N.Y.C., 1956-57; clin. asso. Nat. Inst. Neurol. Diseases and Blindness, 1957-59; resident Wilmer Inst., Johns Hopkins, 1959-64, asst. prof. ophthalmology, 1964-66, asso. prof., 1966-70; chmn., prof., ophthalmology Baylor Coll. Medicine, 1971—; chief ophthalmology Meth. Hosp., Houston; co-chmn. joint com. on recertification in ophthalmology Am. Acad. Ophthalmology and Am. Bd. Ophthalmology, 1978—. Bd. dirs. Conner Found. Served with USPHS, 1957-59. Diplomate Am. Bd. Ophthalmology (mem. bd.). Fellow A.C.S., Am. Acad. Ophthalmology (sec. continuing edn.); mem. A.M.A., Tex. Med. Assn., Tex., Houston ophthalmol. assns., Assn. U. Profs. Ophthalmology (trustee), Am. Intraocular Lens Implant Soc. (sci. adv. bd.), Am. Soc. Contemporary Ophthalmology (pres. 1976-77), Pan Am. Assn. Ophthalmology (council), Am. Soc. Order St. John (asst. hospitaller); hon. mem. S.Am. ophthal. socs. Author books. Mem. editorial bd. Ophthalmic Surgery, Annals of Ophthalmology. Contbr. articles to med. jours. Office: Cullen Eye Inst Neurosurgery Center Tex Med Center Houston TX 77030

PATON, WILLIAM DUNNING, govt. ofcl.; b. Meriden, Conn., Oct. 7, 1929; s. William Dunning and Nina Margaret (Webster) P.; M.B.A., U. Pa., 1957; LL.B., Georgetown U., 1960; m. Carol Rose, Aug. 10, 1961; children—Robert Webster, Diane C., Richard D., Andrew Kent. Admitted to Md. bar, 1961, D.C. bar, 1962, U.S. Supreme Ct. bar, 1964, gen. practice law, Montgomery County, Md., 1961-69; sec. Peoples Drug Stores, Inc., Washington, 1969-73; atty. U.S. Nuclear Regulatory Commn., Bethesda, Md., 1973—. Instr. accounting Montgomery Jr. Coll., 1964-65, U. Md., 1965. Asst. state's atty., Montgomery County, 1965-67; dep. pub. defender, Montgomery County, 1968-69. Served as 1st lt., USAF, 1952-56. Mem. Am., Montgomery bar assns. Democrat. Presbyn. Home: 9720 Whetstone Dr Gaithersburg MD 20760 Office: 7920 Norfolk Ave Bethesda MD 20015

PATRELL, OLIVER LINCOLN, ins. co. exec.; b. Springfield, Mass., Apr. 5, 1927; s. Oliver Lincoln and Mary Agnes (Doyle) P.; A.B. in Econs., Brown U., 1950; m. Catherine Frances Dolan, Nov. 27, 1950; children—Mary Ellen, Kathleen, Christopher, Michael, Margaret. With Aetna Casualty & Surety Co., 1950—, v.p. nat. accounts, Hartford, Conn., 1972-76, v.p. dept. comml. ins., 1976—, pres. subs. Aetna Tech. Services Inc., 1974-76. Trustee Hartford Easter Seal Rehab. Center; pres. Boys' Clubs of Hartford; chmn. Conn. Area Council Boys' Clubs. Served with USN, 1945-46, USCG, 1951-53. Mem. Res. Officers Assn. (pres. Conn. dept. 1965-66). Democrat. Roman Catholic. Club: Officers' of Conn. Office: 151 Farmington Ave Hartford CT 06156

PATRICELLI, LEONARD JOSEPH, broadcasting co. exec.; b. New Haven, Mar. 1, 1907; s. Liberato Leonard and Palma (Lombardi) P.; B.A., Wesleyan U., Middletown, Conn., 1929; m. Lydia Erdman, Sept. 6, 1930 (dec. Nov. 1972); children—Joan (Mrs. Garvin Bawden), Robert; m. 2d, Isabel Scoville Peterson, Aug. 11, 1973. With Broadcast-Plaza, Inc., Hartford, Conn., 1929—, exec. v.p., 1966-67, pres., 1967—; pres. 1080 Corp. (sta. WTIC-AM-FM), 1974—, chmn. bd., 1978—. Conn. chmn. P.R. Flood Relief Campaign, 1971; chmn. Bellevue Square Boys Club. Bd. dirs. Hartford Symphony Orch., Conn. Opera Assn., Conn. Citizens for Jud. Reform; trustee Hartford Rehab. Center, Conn. Cancer Soc.; bd. corporators Mt. Sinai, Hartford, St. Francis hosps., Inst. Living. Recipient Americanism award Conn. Valley council B'nai B'rith; Outstanding Citizen award VFW; James McConaughy award Wesleyan U., 1971; award editorial excellence Radio and TV News Dirs. Assn., 1970; Presdl. commendation for efforts to combat drug abuse, 1970; Civic awards Greater Hartford Bd. Realtors, Hartford Better Bus. Bur., 1973, Christopher Columbus Soc., 1977. Mem. Nat. Assn. Broadcaster (tv bd. dirs.), Broadcast Pioneers Am. and Broadcasters Found. (nat. bd. dirs., pres.), Conn. Broadcasters Assn. (pres. 1969-70), U.S. Broadcasters Com. for UN, Greater Hartford C. of C. (past v.p., dir., exec. com.). Clubs: Rotary, Hartford, Hartford Golf, Hartford Wesleyan Alumni; Stuart Yacht and Country (Fla.). Editor: Wesleyan U. Songbook, 1953. Home: 60 Norwood Rd West Hartford CT 06117 Office: 1 Financial Plaza Hartford CT 06103

PATRICK, ALLEN RUSSELL, Canadian govt. ofcl.; b. Stettler, Alta., Can., Sept. 15, 1910; s. George L. and Lavina (Ross) P.; student Camrose Normal Sch.; B.Ed., U. Alta.; m. Florence Lorene Lynn, Dec. 22, 1934; children—Lynn Allen, Terry Ross, Granton Alexander. Sch. tchr., Behrens, Alta., 1930-31; prin. Erskine Sch., 1931-42; prin. Westlock Consol. Schs., 1942-46; prin. Lacombe Schs., 1946-55; mem. legislature, Lacombe, 1952—; mem. cabinet econ. affairs, Edmonton, 1955-58, mem. cabinet provincial sec. industry and devel., 1958-62, mem. cabinet industry, devel. mines and minerals, 1962-68, minister mines and minerals, 1968-71, ret.; gov. Glen Bow-Alberta Inst., 1971—. Dir. Canadian Occidental Petroleum Ltd. Mem. Alta. Research Council, 1960-61, chmn., 1961-71. Mason, Lion. Address: 9947 Saskatchewan Dr Edmonton AB Canada

PATRICK, CARL LLOYD, corp. exec.; b. Russell County, Va., Dec. 6, 1918; s. Deward Wilmer and Virginia May (McGraw) P.; m. Frances E. Wynn, Feb. 14, 1943; children—Carl Lloyd, Michael Wynn. With Martin Theatre Cos., Columbus, Ga., 1945-70; pres., 1969-70; pres. Fuqua Industries, Inc., Atlanta, 1970—; dir. Columbus Bank & Trust Co. Chmn. bd. dirs. Columbus Pub. Safety, Columbus div. U.S. Savs. Bonds; bd. dirs. Columbus Offstreet Parking Authority; former bd. dirs. Columbus YMCA, Columbus United Fund; patron Columbus Mus., Three Arts League, Columbus Symphony Guild. Served to maj. AUS, 1941-45. Named Motion Picture Man of Yr., Motion Picture Pioneers, 1976. Mem. Nat. Assn. Theatre Owners (dir.), Assn. U.S. Army (dir.), Columbus C. of C. (dir.). Methodist (ofcl. bd.). Club: Columbus Country. Home: 3648 Peachtree Rd NE Atlanta GA 30319 Office: First Nat Bank Tower Atlanta GA 30303

PATRICK, DENNIS, actor, dir.; b. Phila., Mar. 14; s. William John and Mary Katherine (Tydings) Harrison; m. Barbara Cason, Nov. 7, 1970; children—Christine Tydings, Michaela De Paoli. Appeared in numerous plays including Harvey, The Wayward Saint; actor, dir. over 2000 television shows; film appearances include Story of Nicola Tesla with Orson Wells. Mem. Screen Actors Guild, AFTRA, Dirs. Guild Am. Club: Lambs. Office: c/o R Fisher 1801 Ave of the Stars Los Angeles CA 90067

PATRICK, JOHN, playwright; b. Louisville, May 17, 1905; s. John Francis and Myrtle (Osborne) Goggan; student pvt. schs., Holy Cross Coll., New Orleans, St. Edwards Coll., Austin, Tex., St. Mary's Sem., LaPorte Tex.; D.F.A. (hon.), Baldwin-Wallace Coll., 1972; summer student Harvard, Columbia. Radio writer NBC, San Francisco, 1933-36; first play Hell Freeze Over appeared N.Y C., 1936; freelance writer, Hollywood, 1936-38; recent plays include The Hasty Heart, 1945, Story of Mary Surratt, 1947, Curious Savage, 1950, Lo and Behold, 1951, Teahouse of the August Moon, 1953, Good as Gold, 1957, Everbody Loves Opal, 1961, Everbody's Girl, 1967, Scandal Point, 1968, Love Is a Time of Day, 1969, Barrel full of Pennies, 1970, (mus.) Lovely Ladies, Kind Gentlemen, 1971, Opal Is a Diamond, 1971, Macbeth Did It, 1972, The Dancing Mice, 1972, The Savage Dilemma, 1972, Anybody Out There?, 1972, A Bad Year for Tomatoes, 1974, Sex on the Sixth Floor, 1974, Love Nest for Three, 1974, Noah's Animals, 1975, Enigma, 1975, Roman Conquest, 1975, Opal's Husband, 1975, Divorce Anyone?, 1976, Suicide Anyone?, 1976; People!, 1977; Magenta Moth, 1978; That's Not My Mother, 1978; That's Not My Father, 1978; TV play The Small Miracle, 1972; wrote scripts for motion pictures, including Enchantment, President's Lady, Three Coins in the Fountain, 1954, Love is a Many Splendored Thing, 1955, High Society, 1956, Teahouse of August Moon, 1956, screenplay Les Girls (Royal Command Performance, London), 1957, Some Came Running, 1958, The World of Suzie Wong, 1960, Gigot, 1961, Main Attraction, 1962, Shoes of the Fisherman, 1968. Served as capt. with Am. Field Service, India, Burma, 1942-44. Received Pulitzer prize, 1954, N.Y. Drama Critics award, 1954, Perry award, Donaldson award, Aegis Theater Club award for play Teahouse of the August Moon, 1954, Fgn. Corr. award, 1957; award for best Am. musical (for Les Girls), Screen Writers Guild, 1957. Home: Fortuna Mill Estate Box 2386 St Thomas VI 00801

PATRICK, JOHN CORBIN, journalist; b. Tell City, Ind., Apr. 22, 1905; s. Norman E. and Ethel (Corbin) P.; student Notre Dame U., 1922-25; A.B., Butler U., 1927; m. Miriam L. Clapham, Nov. 15, 1930; children—Nancy D., John C. With Indpls. Star, 1925—, music, drama, books and arts editor, 1941—, critic-at-large, columnist, 1944—. Mem. Indpls. Sesquicentennial Arts Com. Bd. dirs., treas. Hoosier Salon Patrons Assn.; bd. dirs. Met. Arts Council, Community Concerts Assn. Mem. Nat. Screen Council, Soc. Am. Travel Writers, Am. Theater Critics Assn., Soc. Ind. Pioneers, Ind. Mus. Soc., Internat. Assn. Theater Critics, Sigma Delta Chi. Clubs: Indpls. Press (pres. 1939-42); Nat. Press (Washington); Internat. Skal. Home: 6829 Willow Rd Indianapolis IN 46220 Office: 307 N Pennsylvania Ave Indianapolis IN 46206

PATRICK, JOHN VERNON, JR., lawyer; b. Birmingham, Ala., May 7, 1931; s. John Vernon and Dorothy Gladys (Powell) P.; A.B. magna cum laude, Harvard, 1952, LL.B. magna cum laude, 1955; m. Sylvia Joyce Brown, May 22, 1965; children—Vera Kathryn, Virginia Gladys. Admitted to Ala. bar, 1955, D.C. bar, 1962; law clk. to Justice Hugo L. Black, U.S. Supreme Ct., 1955-56; asso. firm White, Bradley, Arant, All & Rose, Birmingham, 1959-61, 63; spl. asst., loan officer Bur. Near East and S. Asia, AID, State Dept., 1962; sr. partner firm Berkowitz, Lefkovits & Patrick, and predecessors, Birmingham, 1968—. Chmn. Am. Law Inst.-Am. Bar Assn. Conf. on Litigation under Fed. Securities Laws, 1974—; mem. adv. com. on civil rules Jud. Conf. U.S., 1978—; lectr. numerous seminars for attys. Pres., Jefferson County Assn. Mental Health, 1967-68, Jefferson-Blount-St. Clair Mental Health Authority, 1969-72. Served to 1st lt. AUS, 1956-59. Mem. Am., Ala., Birmingham bar assns., Am. Law Inst., Phi Beta Kappa. Democrat. Baptist. Clubs: The Club, Downtown (Birmingham); Mountain Brook Swim and Tennis. Contbr. articles to profl. jours. Home: 4140 Old Leeds Lane Birmingham AL 35213 Office: City Nat Bank Bldg Birmingham AL 35203

PATRICK, ROBERT, playwright; b. Kilgore, Tex., Sept. 27, 1937; s. Robert Henderson and Beulah (Goodson) O'Connor. Author numerous plays produced off-off Broadway, off-Broadway, Broadway, also abroad. Recipient Best Playwright award Show Business, 1968-69, Glasgow Citizens' Theatre Best World Playwright, 1974. Rockefeller grantee, 1974, CAPS grantee, 1975. Author: The Golden

Circle, 1965; Robert Patrick's Cheep Theatricks, 1972; One Man, One Woman, 1978; (plays) Fog, 1969, Joyce Dynel, 1969, Kennedy's Children, 1973, Judas, 1973, Play-By-Play, 1972, My Cup Runneth Over, 1976, T-Shirts, 1978, over 100 others. Address: care La Mama 74A E 4th St New York NY 10003. *Any writer works primarily on the consciousness of mankind, which works in turn on the world. Writers are working on the world, and should be careful.*

PATRICK, ROBERT MERLE, banker; b. Winthrop, Mass., Mar. 21, 1934; s. Samuel and Sybil (Wallace) P.; B.S., Va. Poly. Inst., 1955; M.S., Mass. Inst. Tech., 1968; m. Violet Nadine Hammond, Oct. 25, 1957; children—Robert, Karen, Lewis, Cheryl, Richard. Chief indsl. engr. Lockheed-Ga. Co., 1968-70; v.p., cashier Winters Nat. Bank and Trust Co., Dayton, Ohio, 1974; exec. v.p., chief financial officer Bank of Commonwealth, Detroit, 1975; sr. v.p., treas. Society Corp., Cleve., 1976—; exec. v.p. Society Nat. Bank, Cleve., 1976—; condr. workshops, speaker in field. Sloan fellow, 1968. Mem. Nat. Assn. Accountants, Planning Execs. Inst., Financial Execs. Inst., Inst. Mgmt. Scis., Am. Mgmt. Assn., Bank Adminstrn. Inst., Am. Inst. Banking. Republican. Episcopalian. Clubs: Avon Oaks Country, Westwood Country. Home: 428 Bates Dr Bay Village OH 44140 Office: 127 Public Sq Cleveland OH 44114

PATRICK, RUTH (MRS. CHARLES HODGE), limnologist, diatom taxonomist, educator; b. Topeka, Kans., d. Frank and Myrtle (Jetmore) Patrick; B.S., Coker Coll., 1929, LL.D., 1971; M.A., U. Va., 1931, Ph.D., 1934; D.Sc., Beaver Coll., 1970, PMC Colls., 1971, Phila. Coll. Pharmacy and Sci., 1973, Wilkes Coll., 1974, Cedar Crest Coll., 1974, U. New Haven, 1975, Hood Coll., 1975, Med. Coll. Pa., 1975, Drexel U., 1975, Swarthmore Coll., 1975, Bucknell U., 1976, Rensselaer Poly. Inst., 1976, St. Lawrence U., 1978; L.H.D., Chestnut Hill Coll, 1974; m. Charles Hodge, IV, July 10, 1931; 1 son, Charles, V. Asso. curator microscopy dept. Acad. Natural Scis., Phila., 1939-47, curator Leidy Micros. Soc., 1937-47, curator limnology dept., 1947—, chmn. limnology dept., 1947-73; occupant Francis Boyer Research Chair, 1973—, chmn. bd. trustees, 1973-76, hon. chmn. bd. trustees, 1976—; lectr. botany U. Pa., 1950-70, adj. prof., 1970—; guest Fellow of Saybrook, Yale, 1975; participant Am. Philos. Soc. limnology expdn. to Mexico, 1947; leader Catherwood Found. expdn. to Peru and Brazil, 1955; del. Gen. Assembly, Internat. Union Biol. Scis., Bergen, Norway, 1973. Dir. E.I. duPont, Pa. Power and Light Co. Chmn. algae com. Smithsonian Oceanographic Sorting Center, 1963-68; mem. panel on water blooms Pres.'s Sci. Adv. Com., 1966; mem. panel on water resources and water pollution Gov.'s Sci. Adv. Com., 1966; mem. nat. tech. adv. com. on water quality requirements for fish and other aquatic life and wildlife Dept. Interior, 1967-68; mem. citizen's adv. council Pa. Dept. Environ. Resources, 1971-73; mem. hazardous materials adv. com. EPA, 1971-74, exec. adv. com., 1974-79, chmn. com.'s panel on ecology, 1974-76; mem. Pa. Gov.'s Sci. Adv. Council, 1972-78; mem. exec. adv. com. nat. power survey FPC., 1972-75; mem. council Smithsonian Instn., 1973—; mem. Phila. Adv. Council, 1973-76; mem. energy research and devel. adv. council Pres.'s, Energy Policy Office, 1973-74; mem. adv. council Renewable Natural Resources Found., 1973-76; mem. adv. council Electric Power Research Found., 1973-77; mem. adv. com. for research NSF., 1973-74; mem. gen. adv. com. ERDA, 1975-77; mem. com. on human resources NRC, 1975-76; mem. adv. council dept. biology Princeton, 1975—; mem. com. on sci. and arts Franklin Inst., 1978—; mem. univ. council com. Yale Sch. Forestry and Environ. Studies, 1978—; mem. sci. adv. council World Wildlife Fund-U.S., 1978—; trustee Aquarium Soc. Phila., 1951-58, Chesnut Hill Acad., Lacawac Sanctuary Found., Henry Found.; bd. dirs. Wissahickon Valley Watershed Assn.; mem. adv. council French and Pickering Creeks Conservation Trust; bd. govs. Nature Conservancy; bd. mgrs. Wistar Inst. Anatomy and Biology. Recipient Disting. Dau. of Pa. award, 1952; Richard Hopper Day Meml. medal Acad. Natural Scis., 1969; Gimbel Phila. award, 1969; Gold medal YWCA, 1970; Lewis L. Dollinger Pure Environment award Franklin Inst., 1970; Pa. award for excellence in sci. and tech., 1970; Eminent Ecologist award Ecol. Soc. Am., 1972; Phila. award, 1973; Gold medal Pa. State Fish and Game Protective Assn., 1974; Internat. John and Alice Tyler Ecology award, 1975; Gold medal Phila. Soc. for Promoting Agr., 1975; Pub. Service award Dept. Interior, 1975; Iben award Am. Water Resources Assn., 1976, Outstanding Alumni award Coker Coll., 1977, Francis K. Hutchinson medal Garden Club of Am., 1977; Golden medal Royal Zool. Soc. Antwerp, 1978. Fellow AAAS (com. environ. alterations 1973-74) mem. Nat. Acad. Scis. (chmn. panel com. on pollution 1966, mem. com. sci. and pub. policy 1973-77, mem. environ. measurements panel of com. on remote sensing programs for earth resource surveys 1973-74, mem. nominating com. 1973-75), Nat. Acad. Engring. (com. environ. engring.'s ad hoc study on explicit criteria for decisions in power plant siting 1973), Am. Philos. Soc., Am. Acad. Arts and Scis., Bot. Soc. Am. (mem. Darbarker prize com. 1956, merit award 1971), Phycol. Soc. Am. (pres. 1954), Internat. Limnological Soc., Internat. Soc. Plant Taxonomists, Am. Soc. Plant Taxonomy, Am. Soc. Limnology and Oceanography, Pa. Zool. Soc., Water Pollution Control Fedn. (hon.), Colonial Dames Am., Soc. Study Evolution, Water Resources Assn., Del. River Basin, Am. Soc. Naturalists (pres. 1975-76), Ecol. Soc. Am., Am. Inst. Biol. Scis., Internat. Phycol. Soc., Soc. Sigma Xi. Presbyterian. Author: (with Dr. C.W. Reimer) Diatoms of the United States, Vol. 1, 1966, Vol. II, Part 1, 1975; mem. editorial bd. Science, 1974-76; American Naturalist; trustee Biological Abstracts, 1974-76; contbr. articles to profl. jours. Office: Acad Natural Scis Philadelphia PA 19103

PATRICK, UEAL EUGENE, oil co. exec.; b. Ky., Mar. 10, 1929; s. Cleveland and Maxine Patrick; B.A., Mich. State U., 1955; m. Nancy Sparrow, Mar. 7, 1953; children—Steve, Rick, Sherry, Mark. Accountant, Bond and Co., Jackson, Mich., 1955-57; controller, then exec. v.p., mgr. Midway Supply Co., Jackson, 1957-62; pres., chief exec. officer, dir. Patrick Petroleum Co., Mich., Jackson, 1962—, Patrick Petroleum Corp., Jackson, 1969—, Patrick Racing Team, Inc., 1971—; pres., chief exec. officer, sec., dir. Fayette Corp., 1966-78; pres., chief exec. officer, treas. Patrick Oil and Gas Corp., 1968—; pres., chief Nat. Bank Jackson, Mich. Nat. Bank, Lansing. exec. officer, chmn. bd. Mark Aviation, Inc., 1971—; chmn. bd., chief exec. officer Jet Way, Inc., 1971—, K & C Corp., 1974—; chief exec. officer, dir. Western Stamping Corp., 1972-79; pres., dir. Patrick Petroleum Internat., Inc., 1972—, Patrick Petroleum Internat. Australia, Inc., 1972—, Patrick Petroleum Internat. Indonesia, Inc., 1972—, Patrick Petroleum U.K. Ltd., 1974—, Patrick Petroleum Italiana, Inc. (S.P.A.), 1974—, Championship Auto Racing Teams, Inc., 1978—; chmn. bd., chief exec. officer, dir. Belibe Coal Corp., 1978—, Black Nugget Coal Co., Inc., 1978—, Patrick Coal Corp., 1978—; sec.-treas. Jackson Towing Co., 1972—; dir. Vermillion Bay Land Co., Jackson Found., Penske Corp., Nat. Bank Jackson, Mich. Nat. Bank, Lansing. Served with USAF, 1948-52. Mem. Ind. Petroleum Assn. Am. (dir. 1968—), Oil Investment Inst. (gov. 1970—), Am. Petroleum Inst. Republican. Clubs: Detroit Athletic, Detroit Renaissance; Jackson Country. Office: 744 W Michigan Ave Jackson MI 49201

PATTEN, BEBE HARRISON, clergywoman; b. Waverly, Tenn., Sept. 3, 1913; d. Newton Felix and Mattie Priscilla (Whitson) Harrison; grad. LIFE Coll., Calif., 1933; D.D., McKinley-Roosevelt Coll., 1941; D.Litt., Temple Hall Coll. and Sem., 1943; m. Carl Thomas Patten, Oct. 23, 1935; children—Priscilla Carla and Bebe Rebecca (twins), Carl Thomas. Ordained to ministry Ministerial Assn. of Evangelism, 1935; evangelist in various cities of U.S., 1934-37, 39-44; founder, pres. Patten Acad. Christian Edn., Oakland, 1944—, Patten Bible Coll., Oakland, 1945—; founder, pastor Christian Cathedral of Oakland, 1950—; condr. program The Shepherd Hour, San Francisco, 1962—. Exec. bd. Bar-Ilan U. Assn., Israel. Recipient numerous awards including medallion Ministry of Religious Affairs, Israel, 1969; medal Govt. Press Office, Jerusalem, 1971; Christian honoree of yr. Jewish Nat. Fund of No. Calif., 1975, Hidden Heroine award San Francisco Bay council Girl Scouts U.S.A., 1976, Ben-Gurion medallion Ben-Gurion Research Inst., 1977. Mem. Am. Assn. for Higher Edn., Religious Edn. Assn., Am. Acad. Religion and Soc. Bibl. Lit., Zionist Orgn. Am., Am. Jewish Hist. Soc. Author: Give Me Back My Soul, 1973. Editor: Trumpet Call, 1953—; composer 20 gospel and religious songs, 1948—. Office: 2433 Coolidge Ave Oakland CA 94601. *Go as far as you can see and when you get there you will see further.*

PATTEN, C. G., mfg. co. exec.; b. Boston, Jan. 14, 1930; s. Clyde Gowell and Helen (Keohane) P.; A.B., Harvard, 1951, LL.B., 1954; m. Judith Ann Maccready, July 9, 1960; children—Stephen W., Lisa K., Scott G. Admitted to Mass. bar, 1954, D.C. bar, 1979; with firm Tyler & Reynolds, Boston, 1956-63; with Dorr-Oliver Inc., Stamford, Conn., 1964—, sec., gen. counsel, 1969—, v.p., 1976—. Served with AUS, 1954-56. Mem. Am., Fed. bar assns. Home: 140 Breezy Hill Stamford CT 06903 Office: 77 Havemeyer Lane Stamford CT 06904

PATTEN, EDWARD JAMES, congressman; b. Perth Amboy, N.J., Aug. 22, 1905; s. Nathan and Mary (Crowe) P.; B.S. in Edn., Rutgers U., 1928, LL.B., 1926; m. Anna Quigg, Feb. 22, 1936; 1 dau., Catherine Mary. Tchr. pub. schs., Perth Amboy and Elizabeth, N.J., 1927-34; admitted to N.J. bar, 1927; practiced in Perth Amboy, 1927—; county clk. Middlesex County, 1940-54; sec. of state State of N.J., 1954-62; mem. 88th-96th congresses from 15th Dist. N.J., mem. appropriations com. Pres. Amboy Salvation Army, 1934—. Mayor, Perth Amboy, 1934-40; mem. N.J. Democratic Com., 1954—; campaign mgr. for Gov. Meyner, 1953, 57. Bd. dirs. N.J. League Municipalities. Recipient Outstanding Citizenship award Am. Heritage Found., 1960, Brotherhood award B'nai B'rith, 1958. Mem. Am. Judicature Soc., Nat. Conf. Christians and Jews, Perth Amboy C. of C., N.A.A.C.P. K.C. (N.J. advocate), Elk, Eagle, Kiwanian, Moose. Office: 2339 Rayburn House Office Bldg Washington DC 20515*

PATTEN, GERLAND PAUL, lawyer; b. Lewisville, Ark., Jan. 5, 1907; s. George Washington and Cleopatra (Sims) P.; LL.B., Ark. Law Sch., 1938; m. Ira E. Barrett, June 10, 1927; children—Gerald William, Yvonne Claire. Telegraph operator C., R.I.&P. Ry., 1923-31; admitted to Ark. bar, 1933, since practiced in Little Rock; instr. Ark. Law Sch., 1935-44, prof., 1944-67, asst. dean, 1949-67; asst. U.S. atty., Little Rock, 1948-54; v.p., gen. counsel Nat. Investors Security Co., 1957-67; sec., treas., dir. Jess Odom Enterprises, Inc., Little Rock, Marifran Investments, Inc., Little Rock, Maryco Investments, Inc., Little Rock, State Investment Corp., Little Rock, Perryco Investments, Inc., Oklahoma City, Investors Equity Corp., Oklahoma City, Royal Investments Okla., Inc.,, Oklahoma City, to 1967; pres. Gerland P. Patten & Co., Little Rock, 1960—. Chmn. budget com. of Greater Little Rock Community Chest and Council, 1938; chmn. Pulaski County Welfare Bd., 1940-46; pres. Council Social Agys., Little Rock, 1943-44. Served as 2d lt., U.S. Army, 1944 46. Mem. Am., Ark. (sec. 1947-50), Pulaski County bar assns., Ark. Trial Lawyers (pres. 1973). Methodist. Club: Little Rock, Capitol. Home: 8 Sunset Circle Little Rock AR 72207 Office: 1095 Union Nat Bank Bldg Little Rock AR 72201

PATTEN, LEWIS BYFORD, author; b. Denver, Jan. 13, 1915; s. Lewis Byford and Anna (Miller) P.; student U. Denver, 1940-42; m. Betsy Mae Lancaster, Dec. 4, 1938 (div. 1962); children—Frances A. (Mrs. Charles L. Henry), Clifford Lewis, Lewis Byford; m. 2d, Catherine Crane Wodrich, July 11, 1963. Sr. auditor Colo. Dept. Revenue, 1942-44; ranch operator DeBeque and Evergreen, Colo., 1944-49; author 95 Western novels, 1949—. Served with USN, 1933-37. Mem. Western Writers Am. Republican. Author: Red Sundown (film), 1954; Gunsmoke Empire, 1955; White Warrior, 1956; Pursuit, 1957; Five Rode West, 1958; Showdown at War Cloud, 1959; Hangman's Country, 1960; Law of the Gun, 1961; Outlaw Canyon, 1962; Guns at Gray Butte, 1963; Killer From Yuma, 1964; The Arrogant Guns, 1965; No God in Saguaro, 1966; Bones of the Buffalo, 1967; Death of a Gunfighter, 1968 (film 1969); Posse From Poison Creek, 1969; Red Runs The River, 1970; Guilt of a Killer Town, 1971; The Red Sabbath (Golden Spur award Western Writers Am.), 1969; The Meeker Massacre (Golden Spur award), 1970; The Trial of Judas Wiley, 1972; The Cheyenne Pool, 1972; A Killing in Kiowa (Golden Spur award), 1972; The Tired Gun, 1973; The Hide Hunters, 1973; The Angry Town of Pawnee Bluffs, 1974; The Gallows at Graneros, 1975; Ambush at Soda Creek, 1976; The Killings at Coyote Springs, 1977; The Law in Cottonwood, 1978; The Trail of the Apache Kid, 1979. Recipient Golden Saddleman award Western Writers Am., 1979. Address: 5995 E Iliff St Denver CO 80222

PATTEN, RONALD JAMES, univ. dean; b. Iron Mountain, Mich., July 17, 1935; s. Rudolph Joseph and Cecelia (Fuse) Pataconi; B.A., Mich. State U., 1957, M.A., 1959; Ph.D., U. Ala., 1963; m. Shirley Ann Bierman, Sept. 5, 1959; children—Christine Marie, Cheryl Ann, Charlene Denise. Accountant Price Waterhouse & Co., Detroit, 1958; instr. No. Ill. U., 1959-60; asst. prof. U. Colo., 1963-65; asso. prof. Va. Poly. Inst. and State U., 1965-67, prof., 1967-73, head dept. accounting, 1966-73; dir. research Financial Accounting Standards Bd., Conn., 1973-74; dean Sch. Bus. Adminstrn., U. Conn., Storrs, 1974—. Cons. to industry. Served to 2d lt. F.A., AUS, 1958. Recipient Nat. Quartermaster award Nat. Quartermaster, Assn., 1956. Mem. Am. Inst. C.P.A.'s, Am. Acctg. Assn., Nat. Assn. Accts. Contbr. articles to profl. jours., chpts. to books. Home: 39 Storrs Heights Rd Storrs CT 06268

PATTEN, STANLEY FLETCHER, JR., physician, educator; b. San Diego, June 23, 1924; s. Stanley Fletcher and Dorothy Amine (Bartholomew) P.; B.S., George Washington U., 1949, M.S., 1950, Ph.D. (USPHS fellow), 1953; M.D., Western Res. U., 1956; m. Cornelia Diane Golding, May 22, 1948; children—Lesley Ann, Pamela Linda, Susan Lynn. Instr. anatomy Western Res. U., 1954-56, sr. instr., 1956-57, USPHS fellow in pathology, 1957-60, sr. instr. pathology, 1960-62, asst. prof., 1962-63; intern Univ. Hosps. Cleve., 1957-58, resident pathology, 1958-60; asso. prof. U. Rochester (N.Y.), 1963-69, prof. pathology and obstetrics and gynecology, 1969—, acting chmn. dept. pathology, 1969-70, chmn. dept., 1970—; pathologist-in-chief Strong Meml. Hosp., Rochester, 1970—; cons. in field; v.p. Internat. Bd. Cytopathology. Bd. dirs. Monroe County (N.Y.) Cancer and Leukemia Assn., 1964-71, Monroe County unit Am. Cancer Soc., 1968-70. Served to capt., Med. Adminstrv. Corps, AUS, 1943-46; PTO. Fellow Internat. Acad. Cytology (Maurice Goldblatt award 1971), Am. Soc. Clin. Pathologists; mem. Am. Assn. Pathologists, Am. Soc. Cytology (pres. 1970-71, Papanicolaou award 1973), Rochester Area Assn. Pathologists (pres. 1968-69), Sigma Xi, Sigma Nu. Author: Diagnostic Cytopathology of the Uterine Cervix, 1969, 2d edit., 1978; mem. editorial bd. Am. Jour. Clin. Pathology, Analytical and Quantitative Cytology; contbr. articles to profl. jours.; patentee diagnostic equipment. Home: 49 Yarrow Hill Rd Box 80218 West Henrietta NY 14586 Office: Dept Pathology U Rochester Med Center 601 Elmwood Ave Rochester NY 14642

PATTEN, THOMAS HENRY, JR., educator; b. Cambridge, Mass., Mar. 24, 1929; s. Thomas Henry and Lydia Mildred (Lindgren) P.; A.B., Brown U., 1953; M.S., Cornell U., 1955, Ph.D., 1959; m. Jule Ann Miller, Aug. 27, 1972; 3 children. Dir. program planning Ford Motor Co., Dearborn, Mich., 1957-65; prof. mgmt. and sociology U. Detroit, 1965-67; prof. orgnl. behavior and personnel mgmt. Sch. Labor and Indsl. Relations, Mich. State U., E. Lansing, 1967—; cons. in field. Served with USMC, 1946-48. Mem. Indsl. Relations Research Assn. (chpt. pres. 1970-71), Am. Soc. Tng. and Devel. (chmn. orgn. devel. div. 1972), Am. Sociol. Assn., Internat. Personnel Mgmt. Assn., Inst. Applied Behavioral Sci., Acad. Mgmt., Am. Compensation Assn. Clubs: Fourth Estate (Boston); Mich. State U. Faculty. Author: The Foreman: The Forgotten Man of Management, 1968; Manpower Planning and the Development of Human Resources, 1971; OD-Emerging Dimensions and Concepts, 1973; A Bibliography of Compensation Planning and Administration, 1960-1974, 1975; Pay: Employee Compensation and Incentive Plans, 1977; Classics of Personnel Management, 1979. Home: 2599 Woodhill Dr Okemos MI 48864 Office: Sch Labor and Indsl Relations Mich State Univ East Lansing MI 48824. *Human values come first.*

PATTERSON, ANDREW, JR., educator; chemist; b. Texarkana, Tex., July 23, 1916; s. Andrew and Nell (Young) P.; B.A., U. Tex., 1937, M.A., 1938, Ph.D., 1942; m. Elizabeth Chambers, June 6, 1940; children—Ellen Clifton, Andrew Muir, Elizabeth Lucinda, Katherine Chambers. Asst. prof. N. Tex. Agrl. Coll., 1941-42; acting asso. prof. U. N.C., 1942-43; research asso. Harvard Underwater Sound Lab., 1943-45; physicist USN Underwater Sound Lab, 1945-46; mem. faculty Yale, 1946—, asso. prof. chemistry, 1951-68, prof., 1969—. research asso. Edwards St. Lab., 1951- 53, dir., 1953-55, Master Morse Coll., 1961-67. Mem. mine adv. com. Nat. Acad. Sci.-NRC, 1955-57, chmn. 1957-61. Mem. Am. Chem. Soc., Sigma Xi, Phi Lambda Upsilon, Alpha Chi Sigma. Author: (with H.C. Thomas) Quantitative Analysis, 1952. Contbr. articles profl. jours. Home: 175 E Rock Rd New Haven CT 06511

PATTERSON, CARRICK HEISKELL, editor; b. Little Rock, Sept. 11, 1945; s. Hugh Baskin, Jr. and Louise Caroline (Heiskell) P.; B.A. in Music, Stanford U., 1968; m. Pat Trimble Jones, June 23, 1978; children by previous marriage—Catherine Ragan, John Netherland Heiskell. With Ark. Gazette, Little Rock, 1968—, news editor, 1972-74, asst. mng. editor, 1974-77, exec. editor, 1977—; dir. Ark. Gazette Co. Mem. Am. Soc. Newspaper Editors, AP Mng. Editors Assn., Hendrix Users Group (pres. 1977), Sigma Delta Chi (chpt. pres. 1976-77). Democrat. Club: Little Rock Country. Office: PO Box 1821 Little Rock AR 72203

PATTERSON, DONALD HAMILTON, newspaper exec.; b. Balt., Sept. 2, 1916; s. Paul Chenery and Elsie Jarvis (Maclean) P.; A.B., Princeton U., 1940; m. Elizabeth Somerville Melvin, Jan. 31, 1942; children—Donald, Elizabeth B., Timothy C., Susan M. With Balt. Sun, A.S. Abell Co., Pubs., 1946—, v.p., 1964-77, pub., 1977—, pres., 1978—; dir. Sta. WMAR-TV, Inc., So. Printing Prodn., Inc. Pres. bd. trustees Sovern Sch., 1972-74; bd. dirs. Jr. Achievement Balt., 1971-79, United Way of Central Md., 1976—; pres. Nat. Alliance of Bus. of Balt., 1977. Served with USNR, 1940-46. Decorated Bronze Star. Mem. Am. Newspaper Pubs. Assn., So. Printing Prodn. Assn., Md. State C. of C. Democrat. Episcopalian. Office: 501 N Calvert St Baltimore MD 21203

PATTERSON, DOYLE, vending machine mfr.; b. Kansas City, Mo., Jan. 19, 1918; s. John Eri and Mildred (Wagner) P.; A.B., U. Mo., 1939; M.B.A., Harvard U., 1941; m. Marilyn C. Pierson, Feb. 15, 1950; children—Mildred A., Ellen A., Marguerite. With Commerce Trust Co., Kansas City, Mo., 1946-48; treas. Farm Belt Fertilizer & Chem. Co., Kansas City, 1948-51, pres., 1951-64; v.p., asst. treas. Vendo Co., 1964-66, v.p. fin., 1966-77, vice chmn., 1977—, also dir.; dir. United Funds Inc., Unitog Co. (both Kansas City). Trustee, Kansas City Research Hosp., 1958—; bd. curators U. Mo., 1959-70. Served to lt. comdr. USNR, 1942-46. Mem. Kansas City C. of C. (dir. 1964-67), Phi Beta Kappa, Beta Theta Pi. Republican. Clubs: Kansas City Country, Univ. (Kansas City), Rotary. Home: 1030 W 56th St Kansas City MO 64113 Office: 10500 Barkley St Overland Park KS 66212

PATTERSON, ELIZABETH CHAMBERS, physicist, sci. historian; b. Clarksville, Tex.; d. Clifton Ayres and Eva Ellen (Smith) Chambers; B.A., U. Tex., 1937, M.A., 1940; postgrad. Mt. Holyoke Coll., 1938-39, U. Mich., summer 1938, Oxford (Eng.) U., 1966-67, Somerville Coll., Oxford U., 1972—; m. Andrew Patterson, Jr., June 6, 1940; children—Ellen Clifton Patterson Brown, Andrew Muir, Elizabeth L., Katharine C. Teaching asst. U. Tex., 1937-38; teaching asst. physiology Mt. Holyoke Coll., 1938-39; instr. chemistry U. Tex., Arlington, 1940-41; research asst. chemistry U. N.C., Chapel Hill, 1942-44; prof. phys. sci. Albert Magnus Coll., New Haven, 1948, 58—, chmn. dept., 1970—. NSF fellow, 1963; NSF Sci. Faculty fellow, 1967; grantee Am. Philos. Soc., 1969, 72-73. Mem. Am. Phys. Soc., Am. Assn. Physics Tchrs., AAAS, Conn. Acad. Arts and Scis., History Sci. Soc., Brit. Soc. History Sci., Phi Beta Kappa, Sigma Xi, Mortar Bd. Clubs: North End, Sat. Morning (New Haven). Author: John Dalton and the Atomic Theory, 1970; (monograph) Mary Somerville, 1780-1872, 1979; also articles and revs.; editor Somerville papers, 1967—. Address: 175 East Rock Rd New Haven CT 06511

PATTERSON, ELLMORE CLARK, banker; b. Western Springs, Ill., Nov. 29, 1913; s. Ellmore Clark and Harriet Emma (Wales) P.; grad. Lake Forest Acad., 1931; B.S., U. Chgo., 1935; m. Anne Hyde Choate, Sept. 28, 1940; children—Michael Ellmore, Arthur Choate, Robert Ellmore, David Choate, Thomas Hyde Choate. With J. P. Morgan & Co., Inc., N.Y.C., 1935-39, 39-41, 46-59, v.p., 1951-59; exec. v.p. Morgan Guaranty Trust Co. N.Y. (merger J.P. Morgan and Guaranty Trust Co.), 1959-65, dir., chmn. exec. com., 1967-68, pres., 1969-71, chmn., 1971-77, chmn. exec. com., 1978; with Morgan Stanley & Co., 1939; dir. Gen. Motors Corp., Bethlehem Steel Corp., A.T. & S.F. Ry., J.P. Morgan & Co., Standard Brands, Inc., Schlumberger, Ltd., Comsat, Inc. Mem. Presdl. Commn. on Financial Structure and Regulation, 1970-72. Bd. mgrs. Meml. Hosp. Cancer and Allied Diseases, N.Y.C.; trustee Alfred P. Sloan Found., Sloan-Kettering Inst. Cancer Center, N.Y.C.; trustee U. Chgo., Mass. Inst. Tech. Served from ensign to lt. comdr., USNR, 1941-46. Mem. Council Fgn. Relations, Psi Upsilon. Episcopalian. Clubs: Links (N.Y.C.); Chicago; Bedford (N.Y.) Golf and Tennis; Jupiter Island (Hobe Sound, Fla.);

Fishers Island Country; Links Golf; Augusta Nat. Golf. Office: 23 Wall St New York NY 10015

PATTERSON, EUGENE CORBETT, editor; b. Valdosta, Ga., Oct. 15, 1923; s. William C. and Annabel (Corbett) P.; student N. Ga. Coll., Dahlonega, 1940-42; A.B. in Journalism, U. Ga., 1943; LL.D., Tusculum Coll., 1965, Harvard U., 1969, Duke U., 1978; Litt.D., Emory U., 1966, Oglethorpe Coll., 1966, Tuskegee Inst., 1966, Roanoke Coll., 1968, Mercer U., 1968, Eckerd Coll., 1977; m. Mary Sue Carter, Aug. 19, 1950; 1 dau., Mary Patterson Fausch. Reporter, Temple (Tex.) Daily Telegram and Macon (Ga.) Telegraph, 1947-48; mgr. for S.C., United Press, 1948-49, night bur. mgr., N.Y.C., 1949-53, mgr. London (Eng.) bur., also chief corr. U.K., 1953-56; v.p., exec. editor Atlanta Jour. and Constn., 1956-60; editor Atlanta Constn., 1960-68; mng. editor Washington Post, 1968-71; prof. practice of polit. sci. Duke, 1971-72; editor, pres. St. Petersburg (Fla.) Times, chief exec. officer, 1978—; editor, pres. Congl. Quar., Washington, 1972—, chief exec. officer, 1978—. Vice chmn. U.S. Civil Rights Commn., 1964-68; mem. Pulitzer Prize Bd., 1973—. Served from pvt. to capt. U.S. Army, 1943-47. Decorated Silver Star, Bronze Star with oak leaf cluster; recipient Pulitzer prize for editorial writing, 1966. Fellow Soc. Profl. Journalists; mem. Am. Soc. Newspaper Editors (pres. 1977-78), Am. Newspaper Publishers Assn. Clubs: St Petersburg Yacht, Washington Press, Federal City. Home: 1967 Brightwaters Snell Isle Saint Petersburg FL 33704

PATTERSON, FRANCIS IRVING, utility exec.; b. Chelsea, Mass., Mar. 29, 1915; s. Frederick Irving and Gladys (Haraden) P.; student N.Y. U., 1935-42; m. Elizabeth Jane Evans, Apr. 28, 1943; children—Paul L., Linda J. (Mrs. Bruce Ray French). Staff accountant Stone & Webster Mgmt. Cons., Inc., N.Y.C., 1934-46; internal auditor spl. accountant Tampa (Fla.) Electric Co., 1946-51; with Stone & Webster Mgmt. Cons., Inc. N.Y.C., 1951-70, asst. treas., accounting supr., 1954-70; v.p., treas., chief fin. officer Eastern Utilities Assos., Boston, 1971-79, sr. v.p., 1979—; dir. Eva Service Corp., Montaup Electric Co.; bd. dirs. Electric Council New Eng. Served with AUS, 1943-46. Mem. Fin. Execs. Inst., Electric Council New Eng., Edison Electric Inst. Club: Downtown (Boston). Home: 19 Arrowhead Rd Derry NH 03038 Office: PO Box 2333 Boston MA 02107

PATTERSON, FRANK PORTER, orthopedic surgeon; b. Vancouver, B.C., Can., Aug. 19, 1915; s. Frank Porter and Lillian Margaret (Sheppard) P.; student U. B.C., 1932-34; M.D.C.M., McGill U., Montreal, Que., Can., 1940; m. Dorothy Swain Grant, Dec. 23, 1960; children—Pamela, Michael. Intern, Toronto (Ont., Can.) Gen. Hosp., 1940-41; resident Shaughnessy Hosp., Vancouver, 1942-45, Hosp. for Sick Children, Toronto, 1947; practice medicine specializing in orthopedic surgery, Vancouver; head div. orthopedics, dept. surgery U. B.C. and Vancouver Gen. Hosp., 1951-73, prof. surgery, head dept. surgery, 1976—. Served with RCAF, 1941-45. Decorated Queen's Silver Jubilee medal. Fellow Brit. Orthopedic Assn. (hon.), Royal Coll. Surgeons (Can.), A.C.S.; mem. Can. Orthopedic Assn., Am. Orthopedic Assn., Am. Acad. Orthopedic Surgery, Am. Assn. Surgery of Trauma, Internat. Orthopedic Club, N.Y. Acad. Scis., Robert Jones Orthopedic Club, Can. Med. Assn., B.C. Surg. Soc., Royal Coll. Physicians and Surgeons Can. Home: Box 5 Rural Route 3 Edwards Rd Mission BC V2V 4J1 Canada Office: Dept Surgery Vancouver Gen Hosp Vancouver BC V5Z 1L5 Canada

PATTERSON, FRANKLIN KESSEL, educator; b. Ellsworth, Iowa, Sept. 14, 1916; s. Frank Harden and Olive May (Kessel) P.; B.A., Occidental Coll., 1939; M.A., U. Calif. at Los Angeles, 1941; Ph.D., Claremont Grad. Sch., 1955; LL.D., U. Mass., 1966, Amherst Coll., 1970, Brandeis U., 1972; L.H.D., Am. Internat. Coll., 1967; D.H.L., Franklin Pierce Coll., 1977; m. Jessamy Longacre, Aug. 23, 1937 (div. 1971); children—Shelley, Eric; m. 2d, Emily Goldblatt, Feb. 6, 1972; 1 son, Nicholas. Lincoln Filene prof. citizenship, pub. affairs, dir. Lincoln Filene Center for Citizenship and Pub. Affairs, Tufts U., 1957-66; pres. Hampshire Coll., Amherst, Mass., 1966-71; prof. U. Mass., Boston, 1971—, sec. to bd. trustees, 1973-74, interim pres., 1977—. Mem. Carnegie Commn. Ednl. TV, 1965-67. Served to capt. USAAF, 1942-46. Fellow AAAS, Benjamin Franklin fellow Royal Soc. Arts; mem. Acad. Polit. Sci., Am. Acad. Polit. and Social Sci., Phi Beta Kappa. Author: Youth as Citizens, 1956; High Schools for a Free Society, 1960; The Making of a College, 1966; Colleges in Consort, 1974. Editor: The Adolescent Citizen, 1960, also pamphlets. Home: 42 Antrim St Cambridge MA 02139 Office: The Library U Mass Harbor Campus Boston MA 02125

PATTERSON, FREDERICK DOUGLASS, educator; b. Washington, Oct. 10, 1901; s. William Ross and Mamie Lucille (Brooks) P.; D.V.M., Iowa State Coll., 1923, M.S., 1927; Ph.D., Cornell U., Ithaca, N.Y.; 1932; LL.D. (hon.), Va. State Coll., Ettrick, Shaw U., Tuskegee Inst. (Ala.), Atlanta U., John Marshall Coll.; H.H.D. (hon.), Wilberforce U., Xenia, Ohio, Va. Union U., Richmond; Sc.D. (hon.), Lincoln U., Pa.; D.Social Sci. (hon.), Xavier U.; D.H.L. (hon.), Morehouse Coll., N.Y. U., St. Augustine's Coll., 1977; m. Catherine Elizabeth Moton, June 12, 1935; 1 son, Frederick Douglass. Instr. vet. sci. Va. State Coll., 1923-26, dir. agr., 1927-28; head of vet. div. Tuskegee Inst., 1928-33, dir. Sch. of Agr., 1933-35, pres., 1935-53, pres. emeritus, 1953—; pres. Phelps-Stokes Fund, 1953-70; chmn. Robert R. Moton Inst., 1973—, chmn. bd., 1972—. Spl. asst. to sec. U.S. Dept. of Agr., 1944-53; cons. on higher edn. Republic of Liberia, 1954. Mem. Internat. Bank Mission to Nigeria, 1953; mem. Pres.'s Commn. on Higher Edn., 1947, Pres.'s Com. on Nat. Employment of Physically Handicapped, Fed. Def. Com., Com. on the South; founder, hon. pres. United Negro Coll. Fund. Mem. Com. on So. Regional Studies in Edn.; chmn. bd. trustees Bennett Coll., 1965-72; trustee Phelps Stokes Fund, 1953-70, Tuskegee Inst. Commd. 2d lt. O.R.C. 1923. Recipient Wilson Fairbanks award for Distinguished Service to Higher Edn., 1969; decorated Star of Africa (Liberia), 1967. Mem. Vet. Med. Soc. (Ia. chpt.), John A. Andrew Clin. Soc. (Tuskegee), Nat. Bus. League (former chmn. bd.), Phi Kappa Phi, Alpha Phi Alpha. Methodist. Author: College Endowment Funding Plan; co-author: What The Negro Wants; Economic Report of Economic Development of Nigeria of International Bank. Co-editor: Robert Russa Moton of Hampton and Tuskegee. Contbr. to Leadership for Higher Education: The Campus View; also sci. publs. Home: 124 Rockland Pl New Rochelle NY 10801 Office: 500 E 62d St 19th Floor New York NY 10021

PATTERSON, GARDNER, economist; b. Burt, Iowa, May 13, 1916; s. Charles Wendell and Trella (Gardner) P.; A.B., U. Mich., 1938, M.A., 1939; Ph.D., Harvard, 1949; m. Evelyn Roelofs, Feb. 17, 1941; 1 dau., Eliza Ruth. Teaching fellow, tutor Harvard, 1941-42; rep. in Africa and Near East for U.S. Treasury Dept., 1942-44; mem. Greek Currency Com., Athens, 1946-48; asst. prof. econs. U. Mich., 1948-49; asso. prof. econs. Princeton, 1949-54, prof., 1954-69, dir. internat. finance sect., 1949-58, dir. Woodrow Wilson Sch. Pub. and Internat. Affairs, 1958-64; Ford Found. faculty research fellow, Geneva, 1963-64; cons. to Dept. State, 1952-53, 57-59, 61-62, and adviser U.S. Mission to Turkey, 1955-56; head U.S. Economic Survey Mission to Tunisia, 1961; dir. Fgn. Bondholders Protective Council, Inc., 1963-64, 68, asst. dir.-gen. GATT, Geneva, 1966-67, 69-73, dep. dir. gen., 1973—. Cons. Pres.'s Com. Nat. Def. Policy, 1959. Served to lt. (j.g.) USNR, 1944-46. Mem. Am. Econ. Assn., Council Fgn. Relations. Club: Cosmos (Washington). Author: Survey of International Finance, 5 vols. 1950-54; Discrimination in International Trade, 1966. Editor: Essays in International Finance (series), 1949-58; Princeton Studies in International Finance (series), 1949-58. Contbr. profl. jours. Office: General Agreement on Tariffs and Trade CH-1211 Geneva 10 Switzerland

PATTERSON, GEORGE STUART, petroleum industry cons.; b. Phila., May 10, 1909; s. George Stuart and Eleanora (Willing) P.; grad. St. Paul's Sch., 1927; B.A., Yale U., 1931; m. Marguerite A. Bushnell, Dec. 9, 1933; children—George Stuart, Robert Gray, Lee W.; m. 2d, Patricia Ann Cochran, Feb. 23, 1963; 1 dau., Patricia Lee. With George H. McFadden & Bros., cotton mchts., Memphis, 1931-40; with Buckeye Pipeline Co., N.Y.C., 1940-72, exec. v.p., 1948-52, pres., 1952-70, chmn. bd., 1970-72; chmn. bd. Struthers Oil & Gas Co.; cons., dir. Vickers Energy Corp., 1973—; dir. N.W. Energy Co.; mem. adv. bd. Chem. Bank. Bd. dirs. Am. Petroleum Inst.; trustee L.I. U. Served to 1st lt. USMCR, 1943-45; PTO. Episcopalian. Home: Gin Ln Southampton NY 11968 Office: 45 Rockefeller Plaza New York NY 10020

PATTERSON, HERBERT PARSONS, cons., former banker; b. N.Y.C., Sept. 3, 1925; s. Morehead and Elsie Clews (Parsons) P.; B.S., Yale, 1948; m. Louise S. Oakey, July 30, 1949 (dec. 1968); m. 2d, Patricia Shephard, Apr. 30, 1970. With Chase Manhattan Bank, N.Y.C., 1949—, asst. mgr., 1952—, asst. treas., 1955—, asst. v.p., 1956-59, v.p., 1959-62, sr. v.p., 1962-65, exec. v.p. U.S. dept., 1965-67, internat. dept. 1967-69, pres., 1969-72; cons. Marshalsea Assos., Inc., N.Y.C., 1973-77; pres. Stonover Co., 1977—; dir. Am. Machine & Foundry Co., Ryder Systems, Inc. Trustee Brookings Instn., trustee, chmn. Community Service Soc. Mem. Newcomen Soc., Tau Beta Pi, Chi Psi. Clubs: Links, National Golf Links America, Racquet and Tennis (N.Y.C.); Bathing Corp. of Southampton, River, Brook, Shinnecock Hills Golf, Lyford Cay. Home: 44 E 67th St New York NY 10021 Office: 450 Park Ave New York NY 10022

PATTERSON, HUGH BASKIN, JR., publisher; b. Cotton Plant, Miss., Feb. 8, 1915; s. Hugh Baskin and Martha (Wilson) P.; student Henderson State Tchrs. Coll., 1933; m. Louise Caroline Heiskell, Mar. 29, 1944; children—Carrick Heiskell, Ralph Baskin. Sales dept. Smith Printing Co., Pine Bluff, Ark., 1933-36; asst. to sales mgr. Democrat Printing & Lithographing Co., Little Rock, 1936-38, promotion mgr., 1940-42; sales dept. Art Metal Constrn. Co., N.Y.C., 1938-39; planning and prodn. mgr. Rufus H. Darby Co., printers and pubs., Washington, 1939-40; with Ark. Gazette, 1946—, successively nat. advt. mgr., advt. dir. and asst. bus. mgr., pub., 1948—; pres. treas. Ark. Gazette Co.; pres. Ark. Bldg. Co. Bd. dirs. Fgn. Policy Assn., Inc.; bd. visitors U. Ark. at Little Rock. Served to maj. USAAC, 1942-46. Gazette recipient Pulitzer gold medal for pub. service, 1957, Freedom award Freedom House, 1958. Mem. Am., So. (pres. 1959-60) newspaper pubs. assns., Inter Am. Press Assn. (dir.), Council Fgn. Relations, Internat. Press Inst., Sigma Delta Chi. Democrat. Presbyterian. Clubs: Overseas Press; Nat. Press; Little Rock Country. Address: Arkansas Gazette Co 112 W 3d St Little Rock AR 72203*

PATTERSON, JAMES FULTON, medical educator; b. Xenia, Ohio, Apr. 11, 1918; s. Austin and Anne (Bailey) P.; B.S., Antioch Coll., 1941; M.D., Harvard, 1944; m. Elizabeth Hoxsie Gallagher, June 24, 1942; children—Bruce M., Sarah H., David A., Elizabeth S. Intern, Fourth Med. Service, Boston City Hosp., 1944-45; resident New Eng. Med. Center Hosp., 1948-50; sr. staff New Eng. Med. Center Hosp., 1950—, chief gastroenterology, 1961-72, chief ambulatory internal medicine, 1972—; asst. prof. medicine Tufts U. Sch. Medicine, 1950-59, asso. prof., 1960-66, prof. medicine, 1967—. Served with M.C., U.S. Army, 1946-48. Congregationalist (deacon). Home: 38 Prince St West Newton MA 02165 Office: 171 Harrison Ave Boston MA 02111

PATTERSON, JAMES MILTON, mktg. specialist, educator; b. DeQueen, Ark., Oct. 15, 1927; s. Charles Edward and Phoebe Allene (Steel) P.; B.S., U.S. Mcht. Marine Acad., 1948; M.B.A. (Teagle Found. fellow), Cornell U., 1954, Ph.D. (Ford Found. dissertation fellow), 1961; m. Della Jeanne Hays, July 3, 1964; children—J. Marshall, Julia M.; children by previous marriage—Robert T., Donald A. Third mate Esso Shipping Co., 1948-52; instr. in bus. adminstrn. Northwestern U., 1957-60; lectr. Center for Programs in Govt. Adminstrn., U. Chgo., 1959; asst. prof. mktg. Ind. U., 1960-63, asso. prof., 1963-69, prof., 1969—, chmn. dept. mktg., 1972-78; cons. petroleum mktg.; expert witness on antitrust and mktg. Served with USNR, 1945-48. Mem. Am. Mktg. Assn., Am. Econ. Assn. Democrat. Author: Marketing: The Firm's Viewpoint, 1964; Highway Robbery: An Analysis of the Gasoline Crisis, 1974; Competition Ltd.: The Marketing of Gasoline, 1972. Home: 2431 N Dunn St Bloomington IN 47401 Office: Grad Sch Bus Ind U Bloomington IN 47405

PATTERSON, JAMES NELSON, pathologist; b. Onnalinda, Pa., Feb. 15, 1902; s. Joseph S. and Catherine (Nelson) P.; B.S., Bucknell U., 1924; B.M., U. Cin., 1928, M.D., 1929, M.S. in Pathology, 1932; m. Viola Townsende Davis, Sept. 30, 1939; 1 son, Joseph P. Intern, Conemaugh Valley Meml. Hosp., Johnstown, Pa., 1928-29; resident in pathology Cin. Gen. Hosp., 1929-31; practice medicine specializing in pathology, Cin., 1931-38, Jacksonville, Fla., 1938-42, Tampa, Fla., 1946—; pathologist to coroner Hamilton County (Ohio), 1931-35; chief of lab. services Kennon Dunham Tb Hosp., Cin., 1936-38; dir. Bur. Labs, Fla. State Bd. Health, 1938-42; asst. state health officer State of Fla., 1941-42; partner Mills & Patterson Labs., Tampa, 1946-52; sr. partner Patterson & Leonard Labs., Tampa, 1952-54, Patterson & Catanzaro Labs., Tampa, 1955-61, Patterson & Eckert, Tampa, 1961-64, Patterson & Coleman & Assos., Tampa, 1964-70, cons. Patterson & Coleman Labs., Smith Kline Clin. Lab., Tampa, 1970—; asst. prof. pathology U. Cin. Coll. Medicine, 1934-38; prof., head dept. pathology Eclectic Med. Coll., Cin., 1932-34; clin. prof. pathology U. South Fla. Coll. Medicine, Tampa, 1973—; mem. staff Centro Asturiano, Centro Español, Citrus Meml. Hosps., Community Hosp. of New Port Richey (Fla.), DeSoto Meml., Jackson Meml., St. Joseph, Tampa Gen., Tarpon Springs (Fla.) Gen., Univ. Community, West Posco, G. Pierce Wood Meml. hosps; asso. dir. S.W. Fla. Blood Bank, 1946-48; med. dir., 1949-69, med. dir. emeritus, 1970—. Served from maj. to lt. col., USAAF, 1942-46. Recipient Pvt. Practitioner of Year award Am. Pathology Found., 1968; Placque awards Franciscan Sisters of St. Hosp., 1974, Cuban Med. Assn. in Exile, 1975. Diplomate Am. Bd. Pathology (trustee 1952-66, pres. 1966). Fellow Am. Coll. Pathologists; mem. Am. Assn. Blood Banks, Fla. Assn. Blood Banks (pres. 1954), Am. Soc. Pathologists, Internat. Soc. Pathologists, Fla. Soc. Pathologists (pres. 1949), Internat. Acad. Pathology, Fla. Med. Assn. (editorial bd. 1952-61, research com. 1956-58, gov. 1959), Hillsborough County Med. Assn. (pres. 1956, mem. exec. com. 1960-70), AMA, Am. Soc. Clin. Pathologists (chmn. com. on clin. chemistry 1960-62), Assn. Clin. Pvt. Practitioners Pathology Found. (past trustee), Am. Cancer Soc. (dir. Fla. div. 1967-73, v.p. 1969-70, Placque award 1975), Tampa C. of C. (health com. 1968-70), Fla. West Coast Assn. Pathologists, So. Assn. Clin. Nutrition (hon.). Republican. Episcopalian. Clubs: Rotary, Univ., Tower, Palma Cain Golf and Country. Editorial bd. Progress in Clin. Pathology, 1972—; contbr. articles on pathology and hematology to profl. jours. Home: 900 Golfview Ave Tampa FL 33609 Office: 4807 N Armenia Ave Tampa FL 33603

PATTERSON, JERE WESCOTT, mgmt. cons.; b. Chgo., Dec. 1, 1917; s. Arthur Amos and Bijou (Moffatt) P.; grad. Chgo. Latin Sch. for Boys, 1933; student Northwestern U., 1934; A.B., Princeton, 1938; student U. Paris, summer 1937; student (Rhodes scholar), Magdalen Coll., Oxford, 1938-39, London Sch. Econs., 1946; m. Betty Muggleton, Apr. 26, 1941; children—Bettina Baird (Mrs. Bettina P. Sands), Dean (Mrs. Robert Malcolm Bauer), Jere, Knight. With Ralph W. Applegate & Co., Chgo., 1939-41; with MacFarland, Aveyard & Co., advt. agy., Chgo., 1941; various positions Chgo. Metal Hose Corp. (now Flexonics Corp.), Maywood and Elgin, Ill., 1942-44; indsl. purchasing Unity Mfg. Co., Chgo., 1944; fgn. sales dir. Parker Pen Co., 1946-48; asst. to pres., account supr., mem. exec. com. Foote, Cone & Belding Internat., Inc., 1948-49; promotion mgr. Life Internat. Editions (Time, Inc.), 1949-57; exec. v.p. Erwin, Wasey & Co., 1957, combined co. Erwin, Wasey, Ruthrauff & Ryan, Inc., 1957-58; v.p. Marc Wood Internat., 1957-63, sr. partner Jere Patterson & Assos., N.Y.C., internat. bus. consultants, 1958—, partner or officer and dir. asso. cos., U.S. and abroad; partner Patterson & Wood, new product and patent advisers, 1969—; chmn. bd. Emlen, Patterson, Brazer, Inc., internat. real estate; lectr. internat. marketing mgmt. N.Y.U. Grad. Sch. Bus. Administrn., 1960-61. Chmn. 1st European Internat. Advt. Conf., Zurich, 1955, chmn. other internat. congresses and confs. including World Advt. Week, N.Y., 1970. Trustee Mus. City N.Y., 1962-70; bd. dirs. Internat. Center in N.Y., Inc., 1972-76. Served with OSS, AUS, 1944-46. Mem. Internat. Advt. Assn. (pres. 1954-56, 68-72, chmn. world congress Tokyo 1969), Am. Mgmt. Assn. (co-chmn. various internat. advt. and mktg. seminars), Inst. Mgmt. Consultants, Soc. Profl. Mgmt. Cons., Am. Mktg. Assn., Internat. C. of C. (chmn. advt. com. U.S. council; vice chmn. advt. commn. 1957-63), Real Estate Bd. N.Y., Licensing Execs. Soc., Assn. for Corp. Growth (v.p. internat.). Clubs: Union, University, Princeton (N.Y.C.); Travellers (Paris); John's Island (Fla.). Home: 480 Park Ave New York NY 10022 also 30 Wall St Southampton NY 11968 Office: 230 Park Ave New York NY 10017 also Vero Beach FL 32960

PATTERSON, JEROME CALVIN, editor; b. Chgo., Nov. 25, 1911; s. Jerome L. and Myrtle (Brooks) P.; B.A., U. Mich., 1936; m. Jane E. Edwards, June 21, 1947 (div. Nov. 1959); children—Jane Hall (Mrs. Steven Barbour), Christine Edwards (Mrs. Merlin Reichert). Reporter Port Huron (Mich.) Times Herald, 1936-39; editor Graves County Times, Mayfield, Ky., 1939-40; reporter Trenton (Mich.) Times, 1940-41; mng. editor Boating Industry Mag., St. Joseph, Mich., 1946-52; mng. editor Edn. Digest, Prakken Publs., Inc., Ann Arbor, Mich., 1952—, mng. editor book div., 1963-79; sec., dir. Arbor Lite, Inc., Ann Arbor, 1966-68. Mem. Shoreham (Mich.) Bd. Edn., 1950-52; treas. Village of Shoreham, 1950-52; mem. Ann Arbor Civic Theatre, 1952—, pres., 1963-64, treas., 1968-70. Served to capt. AUS, 1942-45. Mem. Ednl. Press Assn. (regional dir. 1975-76). Kiwanian (pres. 1974-75). Home: 426 Brookside Dr Ann Arbor MI 48105 Office: 416 Longshore Dr Ann Arbor MI 48107

PATTERSON, JERRY MUMFORD, congressman; b. El Paso, Tex., Oct. 25, 1934; B.A., Long Beach State U., 1960; J.D., U. Calif. at Los Angeles, 1966; m. Mary Jane Crisman, 1955; children—Patrick, Jane. Admitted to Calif. bar, 1967, then practice in Santa Ana, 1967-74; mem. 94th-96th Congresses from 38th Calif. Dist.; councilman, Santa Ana, 1969-74, mayor, 1973-74. Served with USCG, 1953-57. Mem. Calif. Bar Assn., Vets Club. Democrat. Conglist. Club: Toastmasters. Office: 123 Cannon House Office Bldg Washington DC 20515

PATTERSON, JOHN C., psychiatrist; b. Freehold, N.J., Dec. 1, 1918; s. William Corliss and Iris Cora (Harvey) P.; B.S., Rutgers U., 1938; M.D., Jefferson Med. Coll., 1942; m. Inez Decker, Aug. 7, 1948; children—Marie Harvey, Laura Jane, Mary Iris, John William. Intern Fitkin Hosp., Neptune, N.J., 1942-43; resident VA Hosp., Phila., 1946-48; practice medicine, specializing in psychiatry, Phila., 1948-59, Independence, Iowa, 1960-62, Augusta, Maine, 1963-71; staff mem., chief psychiatrist VA Mental Hygiene Clinic, Phila., 1949-59; staff psychiatrist Jefferson Med. Coll., 1949-59; mem. psychiat. vis. staff Phila. Gen. Hosp., 1950-59; dir. out-patient services Mental Health Inst., Independence, 1959-62; supt. Augusta State Hosp., 1963-71; dir. Freehold (N.J.) Psychiat. Clinic, 1972—; attending in psychiatry Monmouth Med. Center, Long Branch, N.J., 1972—; clin. asso. prof. psychiatry Rutgers Med. Sch., 1973—. Served to maj., M.C., AUS, 1943-46. Diplomate Am. Bd. Neurology and Psychiatry. Fellow Am. Psychiat. Assn.; mem. N.J. Psychiat. Assn. (treas.), AMA. Club: Rotary. Address: 49 E Main St Freehold NJ 07728

PATTERSON, JOHN MALCOLM, lawyer; b. Goldville, Ala., Sept. 27, 1921; s. Albert Love and Agnes Louise (Benson) P.; J.D., U. Ala., 1949; m. Mary Jo McGowin, Oct. 19, 1947; children—Albert L., Barbara Louise. Admitted to Ala. bar, 1949; practiced in Phenix City, 1949-51, 53-55; atty. gen., securities commr. State of Ala., 1955-59; gov. of Ala., 1959-63; practice law, Montgomery, Ala., 1963—; asso. prof. polit. sci. Troy State U.; cattle farmer. Served to maj., F.A., AUS, 1940-45, maj., 1951-53. Nominated one of 10 outstanding young men of U.S., 1956, one of four outstanding young men of Ala., Jr. C. of C. Mem. V.F.W., Am. Legion, Farrar Order of Jurisprudence, Woodmen of the World, Am., Ala. bar assns., Am., Ala. trial lawyers assns., Ala. Acad. of Honor, Alpha Tau Omega, Phi Alpha Delta, Sigma Delta Kappa, Phi Eta Sigma, Omicron Delta Kappa. Lion. Bd. editors Ala. Law Review, 1948-49. Home: 5315 Rexford Ct Montgomery AL 36104 Office: Bell Bldg Montgomery AL 36104

PATTERSON, JOHN MCCREADY, consultant; b. Richmond, Va., Dec. 18, 1913; s. Warren Pernet and Madge (McCready) P.; B.A., U. Va., 1934, M.A., 1936; m. Hope Cooper Wood, Feb. 3, 1945. Newspaper and mag. reporter and editor, N.Y.C. and Richmond, 1936-40; asst. dir. pub. relations Colonial Williamsburg (Va.), 1940-42; asst. regional dir. OWI, 1942-43; asst. dir. pub. relations Dept. Justice, 1943-44; information officer, asst. chief div. pub. liaison State Dept., 1944-51, chief div. pub. liaison, 1951-52; attache Am. embassy, London, Eng., 1952-54; cons. Colonial Williamsburg, 1955-56; exec. v.p. Radio Free Europe Fund (Crusade for Freedom, Inc.), N.Y.C., 1956-58, pres., 1958-61; Exec. Office of Pres., 1961-64; cons. govt. agys., 1964—. Mem. Mystery Writers Am. Democrat. Episcopalian. Clubs: Century (N.Y.C.); Metropolitan, Nat. Press (Washington). Author: Doubly Dead, 1969. Address: 4832 Hutchins Pl NW Washington DC 20007

PATTERSON, JOHN MILES, chemist, educator; b. Vineland, N.J., Nov. 5, 1926; s. James and Gladys (Barraclough) P.; B.S., Wheaton Coll., 1949; Ph.D., Northwestern U., 1953; m. E. Genevieve Christensen, Aug. 20, 1949; 1 son, John Miles. Teaching asst. Northwestern U., 1949-50, Comml. Solvents fellow, 1950-51, U.S. Rubber fellow, 1951-52, postdoctoral fellow, 1953; faculty U. Ky., Lexington, 1953—, prof. chemistry, 1967—. Mem. Am. Chem. Soc., A.A.A.S., Sigma Xi, Phi Lambda Upsilon. Contbr. articles to profl. jours. Home: 726 Della Dr Lexington KY 40504

PATTERSON, JOSEPH REDWINE, lawyer; b. Corsicana, Tex., Apr. 16, 1927; s. Joseph Isham and Caroline Anderson (White) P.; B.A. in Philosophy, So. Methodist U., 1948, M.A. in Govt., 1951, J.D., 1954; m. Ann Louise Cumber, Mar. 9, 1956; children—Joseph Redwine, Amy Cumber. Admitted to Tex. bar, 1954; asst. dist. atty.

Dallas County, 1955-56; asso. gen. counsel Traders and Gen. Ins. Co., Dallas, 1957—; partner firm Patterson, Lamberty & Kelly, Inc., Dallas, 1957—; partner PLS Properties, real estate, Dallas, 1971—; mem. profl. efficiency com. Tex. Bar. Bd. mgmt. Downtown YMCA, Dallas; founding dir. Dallas chpt. Action on Smoking and Health; adminstrv. bd., mem. chancel choir University Park United Meth. Ch., Dallas. Served with USN, 1945-46. Mem. Am., Tex., Dallas bar assns., So. Meth. U. Law Sch. Alumni Assn. (dir.). Club: Spring Valley Country. Democrat. Contbr. legal jours. Home: 6131 Meadow Rd Dallas TX 75230 Office: 2011 Cedar Springs St Dallas TX 75201

PATTERSON, KENNETH DENTON, economist; b. Omaha, Jan. 10, 1930; s. H. W. and Ruth (Meadows) P.; B.S., Iowa State U., 1951; M.A., U. Nebr., 1958, Ph.D., 1961; m. Joyce Swab, Apr. 2, 1955; children—Ann, Mary. Instr. dept. econs. Oreg. State U., 1958-60, asst. prof. econs., 1960-63, asso. prof., 1963-67, prof., 1967—, acting chmn. dept. econs., 1962, chmn., 1975—, asst. dean Sch. Humanities and Social Scis., 1965-68, asso. dean, 1968-71, acting dir. summer term, 1967-68; Ford Found. summer research fellow in econs. U. Minn., 1962; fellow acad. adminstrn. internship program Am. Council Edn. at U. N.Mex., 1965-66; mem. Cost Containment Adv. Commn. Mem. Oreg. Statewide Health Coordinating Council, 1977-79; mem. Oreg. 2000 Commn., 1978. Served with USAF, 1951-53. Mem. AAUP, Am. Econs. Assn., Western Econs. Assn. Home: 2210 NW Robinhood Corvallis OR 97330 Office: Dept Econs Oreg State U Corvallis OR 97331

PATTERSON, LYMAN RAY, lawyer, univ. adminstr.; b. Macon, Ga., Feb. 18, 1929; s. Dallas DeVotie and Ida Gertrude (Smith) P.; A.B., Mercer U., 1949, LL.B., Walter F. George Sch. Law, 1957; M.A., Northwestern U., 1950; S.J.D. (Ford fellow), Harvard U., 1966; m. Laura Adelyn, Aug. 30, 1958; children—Laura Adelyn, Barbara Ida. Admitted to Ga. bar, 1956, Tenn. bar, 1965, U.S. Supreme Ct. bar, 1969; asso. firm Matthews, Maddox, Walton & Smith, Rome, Ga., 1957-58; asst. prof. law Mercer U., 1958-63; prof. Vanderbilt U., 1963-73; prof., dean Sch. Law, Emory U., 1973—. Served with Intelligence Corps, U.S. Army, 1951-54. Mem. Am. Bar Assn. (reporter Commn. for Evaluation Profl. Standards), Atlanta Lawyers Club. Democrat. Methodist. Club: Commerce (Atlanta). Author: Copyright in Historical Perspective, 1968; (with Elliott F. Cheatham) The Profession of Law, 1971. Home: 1039 Springdale Rd NE Atlanta GA 30306 Office: Sch of Law Emory U Atlanta GA 30322

PATTERSON, MARCEL, med. educator; b. Deleon, Tex., Apr. 4, 1919; s. L. Guy and Dora Lena (Miller) P.; B.A., U. Tex., 1939; M.D., Tulane, 1943; m. Josephine Kelly, Dec. 25, 1947; children—Margaret, Guy, Robert. Intern. San Francisco Hosp. U. Calif. Service, 1943-44, resident, 1944-45; fellow Lahey Clinic, Boston, 1948, mem. staff gastroenterology div., 1949-53; instr. Med. Sch. U. Calif., San Francisco, 1954-55; mem. faculty Med. Sch. U. Tex., Galveston, 1955—, prof. medicine, 1965—, chief div. gastroenterology, 1955—; cons. USPHS Hosp., Galveston, 1957—. Pres. Friends of Rosenberg Library, Galveston, 1960. Served with M.C., AUS, 1945-47. Piper prof. Wilford Hall Lackland AFB Tex., 1962. Fellow A.C.P., Am. Gastroenterol. Assn.; mem. So. Med. Assn. (chmn. gastroenterology sect. 1964), Tex. Med. Assn. (chmn. digestive diseases sect. 1964), Tex. Acad. Internal Medicine (v.p. 1970), Sigma Xi, Alpha Omega Alpha, Delta Xi, Phi Chi. Democrat. Episcopalian. Book rev. editor Am. Jour. Digestive Diseases, 1969—. Home: 1206 Marine St Galveston TX 77550

PATTERSON, MARY MARVIN BRECKINRIDGE (MRS. JEFFERSON PATTERSON), broadcaster, photographer, writer; b. N.Y.C., Oct. 2, 1905; d. John Cabell and Isabella (Goodrich) Breckinridge; ed. schools in N.Y., Maine, S.C. and Calif., also Switzerland, Paris and Cannes (France); A.B., Vassar Coll., 1927; student photography Clarence White Sch., N.Y.C., 1936; L.H.D. (hon.), Bowdoin Coll., 1975; m. Jefferson Patterson, June 20, 1940; children—Patricia Marvin, Mark Julian. European broadcaster World News Roundup Program, CBS; photographer, film maker: The Forgotten Frontier, She Goes To Vassar, others. Mem. women's com. Corcoran Gallery Art, Smithsonian Instn. Assos.; nat. council Soc. Woman Geographers; mem. internat. council Folger Shakespeare Library, 1978—; trustee Frontier Nursing Service, 1934, gov., 1955, nat. chmn., 1960-75, hon. chmn., 1975—; mem. internat. council Folger Shakespeare Library; mem. founders bd. Transylvania U., Lexington, Ky., 1978-80; mem. Patterson Homestead Adv. Commn., Dayton, Ohio, 1978—; trustee Meridian House Internat., 1979—. Mem. Nat. Soc. Arts and Letters. Clubs: Colony, Cosmopolitan (N.Y.C.); Sulgrave, Am. Newspaper Women's (Washington). Contbr. articles to Harper's Bazaar, Vogue, Town & Country; photographs in Life and other publs. Address: 3108 Woodland Dr Washington DC 20008

PATTERSON, MERRILL REEVES, educator; b. Jersey City, Jan. 27, 1902; s. William Clifford and Maybelle Virginia (Reeves) P.; B.S., Wesleyan U., 1925; A.M., Brown U., 1930; Ph.D., Yale, 1933; Litt.D., Marietta Coll., 1967; m. Dana Robinson Rymer, June 23, 1928; children—Merrill Reeves, Barbara (Mrs. B.S. Nelson). Mng. editor New Haven (Conn.) Union, 1926-27; master Tilton Sch., N.H., 1927-28; instr. in English, Wesleyan U., Middletown, Conn., 1932-34; asst. in English, Conn. Coll. for Women. New London, Conn., 1933-34; instr. in English, Marietta (O.) Coll., 1934-36, asst. prof., 1936-38, prof., 1938-39, Hillyer prof. and chmn. dept., 1939, dean of coll., 1948-67, dean emeritus, dir. acad. advising, 1967-72; cons. Parkersburg (W.Va.) Community Coll., 1972-75, Distinguished prof., chmn. humanities div., 1975—; instr. 25th Coll. Tng. Detachment (air crew), 1943-44. Dir. pub. affairs. Marietta Civil Def. Program, 1950-51; mem. Citizens Narcotics Adv. Com. for Ohio, 1954-56; dir. Ohio Citizens Council for Health and Welfare, Marietta Meml. Hosp.: Ohio chmn. dedication Wood County (W.Va.) Airport, 1946; gen. chmn. inauguration of Pres. Shimer, Marietta Coll. 1945; dir. coll. activities for Ohio of Nat. Heritage Found.; mem. exec. com. Council of Affiliated Instns., Inst. European Studies, 1968—. Recipient award for exceptional service Crusade for Freedom, 1955; distinguished service awards Nat. Heritage Found., 1958, Inst. European Studies, Vienna, 1972; Silver Knight award Nat. Mgmt. Assn., 1967. Pres. Nat. Stillwater (Okla.) Conf. Acad. Deans, 1958-59; commr. N. Central Assn. Commn. Colls. and Univs. Mem. Modern Lang. Assn. Am., Nat. Council Tchrs. Eng. Coll. Eng. Assn. Ohio Coll. Assn. (past pres.; com. membership and inspection), Ohio Council Advanced Placement, Am. Conf. Acad. Deans (recorder, cons., group leader, exec. com., treas. 1960—), C. of C., Ohioana Library Assn. (trustee, treas.; pres. 1967—). Oratorio Soc. (violinist, concertmaster), Fine Arts Commn. (sec.), Marietta Community Concert Assn. (dir.), Internat. Platform Assn., Omicron Delta Kappa (distinguished certificate of meritorious award 1972), Alpha Psi Omega, Delta Kappa Epsilon, Beta Beta Beta, Pi Kappa Delta, Pi Delta Epsilon. Republican. Conglist. (moderator 1963-65, 1968-70, gen. chmn. sesquecentennial observance 1946). Mason (Shriner). Clubs: Rotary (past pres., dist. gov. 1956-57, consultative com. on internat. service 1958-59, mem. internat. found. fellowships com. 1959-61, Paul Harris fellow 1973), Marietta Reading (past pres.), Marietta Country. Editor and author: (booklet) Picture of an Inauguration, 1945. Contbr. to Dict. Am. Biography, 1931; Rhode Island Historical Collections, 1941; Eleusis of Chi Omega, 1938, 45; Ohio Farmer, 1939, Ohioana Quar., 1971; Script Speaking of Shakespeare, 1978; other publs. Home: 411 Fifth St Marietta OH 45750

PATTERSON, NEVILLE, chief justice Miss. Supreme Ct.; b. Monticello, Miss., Feb. 16, 1916; s. E.B. Patterson; LL.B., U. Miss., 1939; m. Catherine Stough; 3 children. Admitted to Miss. bar, 1939; practiced with father, Monticello, 1939-41; with legal dept. Fed. Land Bank, New Orleans, 1941; chancellor 15th Chancery Ct. Dist., 1947-63; asst. atty. gen. State of Miss., 1963; justice Supreme Ct. of So. Dist. Miss., 1964—, now chief justice. Prof., Jackson Sch. Law, 1966—. Chmn., Miss. Jud. Council; past chmn. Miss. Adv. Council on Rule Changes. Served to capt. inf. AUS, 1941-45. Decorated Bronze Star. Mem. Am. Legion, Miss. Bar Assn., V.F.W., 40 and 8. Democrat. Methodist. Clubs: Country of Jackson, Patio. Home: 4235 Old Orchard Pl Jackson MS 39206 Office: Supreme Court of Mississippi Jackson MS 39201

PATTERSON, RAY ALBERT, profl. basketball team exec.; b. Lafayette, Ind., Jan. 15, 1922; s. Ray Albert and Rhea A. (Walker) P.; B.S., U. Wis., 1945, M.S., 1949; m. Ruth E. Gould, Sept. 17, 1948; children—Pat, Steve, Lizabeth, Peggy, Peter. Rep., Dow Chem. Co., 1945-48; tchr., pub. relations dir. Wayland Acad., Beaver Dam, Wis., 1948-55, pres., headmaster, 1955-68; pres. Milw. Bucks Profl. Basketball Team, 1968-72, Houston Rockets Profl. Basketball Team, 1972—. Home: 639 Chevy Chase St Houston TX Office: Rockets The Summit Houston TX 77046

PATTERSON, REMINGTON PERRIGO, educator; b. Nice, France, Dec. 16, 1926 (parents Am. citizens); s. Howard Ashman and Elizabeth Mary (Perrigo) P.; grad. The Hill Sch., 1945; B.A., Yale U., 1950, M.A., 1953, Ph.D., 1957; m. Eleanor Duane Lloyd, Sept. 6, 1957; children—Burns, Sarah. Instr. English, Hill Sch., 1950-51; instr. English, Barnard Coll., Columbia U., N.Y.C., 1955-58, asst. prof., 1958-64, asso. prof., 1964-73, prof., 1973—, acting dean faculty, 1975-77. Trustee, Hall Sch., Pittsfield, Mass. Served with AUS, 1945-46; ETO. Recipient Fulbright award, 1961-62. Mem. Modern Lang. Assn., Malone Soc. Democrat. Episcopalian. Home: 280 Riverside Dr New York NY 10025

PATTERSON, RICHARD WALLACE, financial exec.; b. Cedarville, Calif., Dec. 29, 1919; s. John and Pearl (Kenyon) P.; B.S., U. Calif. at Berkeley, 1942; postgrad. Advanced Mgmt. Program, Harvard U., 1972; m. Marjorie F. North, Dec. 6, 1942; children—Richard N., Sheryl L. Asst. office mgr. real estate dept. Safeway Stores, Inc., Oakland, Calif., 1945-47; asst. treas. Otis, McAllister & Co., San Francisco, 1947-55; div. credit mgr. Durkee Famous Foods div. Glidden Co., Berkeley, asst. gen. credit mgr. parent co., 1957, gen. credit mgr., 1958-61, asst. treas., 1961-63, treas., 1963-68; v.p., treas. A-T-O Inc., 1968-79, sr. v.p., 1979—; dir. Midwest Bancorp., Midwest Bank & Trust Co., Cleve. Served to lt. USNR, 1942-45. Mem. Financial Execs. Inst. (dir.). Republican. Unitarian. Home: 2737 Sinton Pl Pepper Pike OH 44124 Office: A-T-O Inc 4420 Sherwin Rd Willoughby OH 44094

PATTERSON, ROBERT ARTHUR, physician, pharm. co. exec., ret. air force officer; b. Palestine, Ill., Sept. 3, 1915; s. Robert Bruce and Nera (McColpin) P.; student U. Ill., 1933-35; M.D., U. Louisville, 1939; m. Judith Scheirer, May 15, 1961; children—Mary Kay, Elaine Alice Mills, Robert Arthur II, Victoria Patterson Goodrum. Intern, Detroit Receiving Hosp., 1939-40; joined Mich. N.G., 1940, commd. USAAF, 1946, advanced through grades to lt. gen. USAF, 1972; rated chief flight surgeon and command pilot; assigned U.S. and ETO, 1940-45; asst. chief aviation medicine br. Office Air Surgeon, Washington, 1945-49, chief aircrew standards br., 1949-51; chief profl. services div. Office Surgeon, Offutt AFB, Nebr., 1951-53; surgeon 3090th Dep. Flt., Wright-Patterson AFB, Ohio, later Madrid, Spain, 1953-55; comdr. 7600th USAF Hosp., Madrid, 1955-57; surgeon Hdqrs. Eastern Air Def. Force, Stewart AFB, N.Y., 1957-59; comdr. Hdqrs. 1st Med. Service Wing, Tachikawa Air Base, Japan, 1959-62; Clark Air Base, Philippines, 1962-63; dep. dir. plans and hospitalization Office Surgeon Gen., USAF, Washington, 1963-65, dir. plans and hospitalization, 1965-68; surgeon Hdqrs. USAFE, Lindsey Air Sta., Germany, 1968-71; surgeon Hdqrs. SAC, Offutt AFB, 1971-72; surgeon gen. USAF, 1972-75, ret., 1975; health care cons., Arlington, Va., 1975; sr. v.p. sci. affairs Baxter Travenel Labs., Inc., Deerfield, Ill., 1976—. Decorated D.S.M. with oak leaf cluster, Legion of Merit with oak leaf cluster, Air Force Commendation medal; recipient citation of honor Air Force Assn., citation of distinction Fla. Hosp. Execs., Am. Hosp. Assn.; Diplomate aerospace medicine Am. Bd. Preventive Medicine. Fellow Am. Coll. Preventive Medicine, Aerospace Med. Assn.; mem. Assn. Mil. Surgeons (pres. 1972), AMA, Air Force Assn., Soc. Mil. Cons. to Armed Forces, Internat. Anesthesia Research Soc., Order Daedalians. Club: Mid-America. Home: 2645 Crestwood Ln Riverwoods Deerfield IL 60015 Office: One Baxter Pkwy Deerfield IL 60015

PATTERSON, ROBERT HUDSON, librarian; b. Alexandria, La., Dec. 11, 1936; s. Hubert Hudson and Beth (Jones) P.; B.A., Millsaps Coll., Jackson, Miss., 1958; M.A., Tulane U., 1963; M.L.S., U. Calif., Berkeley, 1965; m. Carol Ann Hughes; 1 dau., Jennifer Bookhart. Mem. staff Tulane U. Library, 1965-69, 73-76, asst. dir. collection devel., 1973-76; head spl. collections cataloging U. Tex., Austin, 1970-73; dir. libraries U. Wyo., Laramie, 1976—; exec. bd. Wyo. State Library Adv. Com., 1976—; mem. adv. council Bibliog. Center for Research, Denver; past mem. exec. bd. S.E. La. Library Network; cons. Gallier House Mus., Historic New Orleans Collection. Asst. fellow Am. Inst. Conservation Historic and Artistic Works; mem. ALA (bldgs. for coll. and univ. libraries com.), Mountain Plains, Wyo. (chmn. intellectual freedom com. 1976-78) library assns., Internat. Boswell Soc. Contbr. articles to profl. publns. Home: 1516 Grand Ave Laramie WY 82070 Office: Coe Library Box 3334 University Station Laramie WY 82071

PATTERSON, ROBERT PORTER, JR., lawyer; b. N.Y.C., July 11, 1923; s. Robert Porter and Margaret (Winchester) P.; A.B., Harvard U., 1947; LL.B., Columbia U., 1950; m. Bevin C. Daly, Sept. 15, 1956; children—Anne, Robert, Margaret, Paul, Katherine. Admitted to N.Y. bar, 1951, D.C. bar, 1966; law clk. Donovan Leisure Newton & Lumbard, N.Y.C., 1950-51; asst. counsel N.Y. State Crime Commn. Waterfront Investigation, 1952-53; asst. U.S. atty. Chief of Narcotics Prosecutions and Investigations, 1953-56; asst. counsel Senate Banking and Currency Com., 1954; asso. firm Patterson, Belknap, Webb & Tyler, N.Y.C., 1956-60, partner, 1960—; counsel to minority Select Com. Pursuant to House Resolution No. 1, Washington, 1967; mem. Gov's Jud. Screening Panel, 1975—, Gov.'s Sentencing Com., 1978-79. Trustee Wm. T. Grant Found., 1974—; dir. Legal Aid Soc., 1961—, pres., 1967-71; chmn. Nat. Citizens for Eisenhower, 1959-60; chmn. Scranton for Pres. (N.Y. State), 1964; trustee Millbrook Sch., 1966-78; mem. exec. com. Lawyers Com. for Civil Rights Under Law, 1968—; mem. Goldman Panel for Attica Disturbance, 1972; mem. Temporary Commn. on State Ct. System, 1971-73. Served to capt. USAAF, 1942-46. Decorated D.F.C. with cluster, Air medal with clusters. Mem. Am. Bar Assn. (ho. of dels. 1976—), N.Y. State Bar Assn. (pres. 1978-79), Assn. Bar City N.Y. (v.p. 1974-75), N.Y. County Lawyers Assn., Am. Law Inst., Am. Judicature Soc. (dir. 1979), Council Fgn. Relations. Republican. Episcopalian. Club: Century Assn. Contbr. articles to profl. jours. Home: Fair Oaks Farm Cold Springs NY 10516 Office: 30 Rockefeller Plaza New York NY 10020

PATTERSON, ROBERT STEVEN, educator; b. Ft. Macleod, Alta., Can., June 8, 1937; s. Robert Dwight and Winnifred Mary (Reach) P.; B.E., U. Alta., 1959, M.Edn., 1961; Ph.D., Mich. State U., 1966; m. Belva Emily Orr, July 2, 1957; children—Steven Kent, David Scott, Douglas Mark, Michael Robert. High sch. tchr., 1960-61; lectr. U. Alta., Edmonton, 1961-63, prof., 1966—, chmn. dept. ednl. founds., 1971—, asso. dean planning and devel. Faculty Edn., 1976—; instr. Mich. State U., 1965-66. Mem. Phi Kappa Phi. Author: (with F.H. Blackington) School, Society and the Professional Educator, 1968; (with J.W. Chalmers and John Friesen) Profiles in Canadian Education, 1975. Home: 4928 114B St Edmonton AB Canada

PATTERSON, ROBERT WILLIAM, cons. engr.; b. Ravinia, Ill., Aug. 24, 1922; s. James B. and Benice A. (Cummings) P.; B.S. in Mech. Engring., Northwestern U., 1947; m. Rae F. Spahr, Sept. 24, 1955; children—Carol L., John H. With Sargent & Lundy, cons. engrs., Chgo., 1947—, partner, 1964—, dir. engring., 1973-77, sr. partner, 1977—. Served with U.S. Army, 1943-45; ETO. Decorated Purple Heart; registered profl. engr. 14 states, including Calif., Ill., Ind., and State of Israel. Mem. Am. Nuclear Soc., ASME, Atomic Indsl. Forum, Western Soc. Engrs. Clubs: Chgo., Union League of Chgo., Park Ridge (Ill.) Country. Contbr. articles to trade press. Home: 807 Forestview Ave Park Ridge IL 60068 Office: 55 E Monroe St Chicago IL 60603

PATTERSON, ROBERT YOUNGMAN, JR., lawyer, utility exec.; b. West Palm Beach, Fla., Feb. 1, 1921; s. Robert Youngman and Christine Helene (Johnson) P.; B.A., U. Fla., 1942, LL.B., J.D., 1950; m. Lorraine Hillyer, June 14, 1952; children—Robert Youngman III, Patricia Hillyer. Admitted to Fla. bar, 1950; practiced in Jacksonville, 1950-52; successively asst. counsel, counsel, asst. gen. counsel Fla. Pub. Service Commn., Tallahassee, 1952-58; gen. atty., asst. sec.-treas. Fla. Gas Co. and subsidiaries, Winter Park, 1959-62, v.p., gen. atty., 1959—; mem. Fla. Nuclear Devel. Commn., 1957-60; chmn. Asso. Industries Fla., 1976. Served to capt. AUS, World War II; ETO. Decorated Purple Heart. Mem. Am., Fed. Power (past chmn. rate com.), Fed. Energy, Fla. (past chmn. adminstrv. law com., chmn. adminstrv. law sect. 1978), Orange County bar assns., ICC Practitioners Assn., Am. Judicature Soc., Interstate, Fla. natural gas assns., Fla., Orlando (past chmn. state legislation com.), Winter Park (dir., past chmn. congl. action com.) chambers commerce, U. Fla. Alumni Assn., Kappa Sigma, Delta Theta Phi. Democrat. Episcopalian. Clubs: Univ. (Orlando and Winter Park); Orlando Country, Capital City, Killearn Country. Home: 1225 Contessa Ct Winter Park FL 32789 Office: PO Box 44 Continental Resources Co Winter Park FL 32790. *Always have the highest respect for God, your family and your fellow man; honesty and perserverance will overcome all obstacles with such respect.*

PATTERSON, RONALD GLEN, musician; b. Los Angeles, Aug. 2, 1944; s. Leroy and Mildred (Gordon) P.; student Aspen (Colo.) Music Sch., 1960-64, U. So. Cal., 1962-64; student of Jascha Heifetz, 1964-65; m. Clare Louise Piaget, Nov. 26, 1969 (div. Jan. 1978). Concertmaster, Debut Orch., Los Angeles, 1959-64; concertmaster Greater Miami (Fla.) Philharmonic, 1965-66; asst. concertmaster St. Louis Symphony, 1966-71; concertmaster Denver Symphony Orch., 1971-72, Houston Symphony, 1972—; tchr. U. So. Calif., 1964; mem. faculty U. Miami, 1965; vis. artist MacMurray Coll., Jacksonville, Ill., 1966; artist-in-residence, asst. prof. Washington U., St. Louis, 1967-71; asso. prof., artist tchr. of violin Shepherd Sch. Music, Rice U., Houston, 1974—; soloist with orchs., in recitals and chamber music throughout U.S. Recipient certificate of merit 4th Internat. Tschaikovsky Competition Moscow, 1970; 5 times winner 1st place Coleman Chamber Music Competition, Los Angeles. Office: 615 Louisiana St Houston TX 77002

PATTERSON, ROY, physician, educator; b. Ironwood, Mich., Apr. 26, 1926; s. Donald I. and Helmi (Lantta) P.; M.D., U. Mich., 1953. Intern U. Mich. Hosp., Ann Arbor, 1953-54, med. asst. research, 1954-55, med. resident, 1955-57, instr. dept. medicine, 1957-59; attending physician VA Research Hosp., Chgo., Northwestern Meml. Hosp.; mem. faculty Northwestern U. Med. Sch., Chgo., 1959—, prof. medicine, 1964—, Bazley prof. allergy-immunology, 1967—, chmn. dept. medicine, 1973—. Served with USNR, 1944-46. Diplomate Am. Bd. Internal Medicine, Am. Bd. Allergy and Immunology. Fellow Am. Acad. Allergy (pres. 1976), A.C.P.; mem. Central Soc. for Clin. Research (pres. 1978-79). Editor Jour. Allergy and Clin. Immunology, 1973-78. Address: Dept Medicine Northwestern Univ Med Sch 303 Chicago Ave Chicago IL 60611

PATTERSON, RUSSEL HUGO, JR., neurosurgeon; b. Apr. 1, 1929; s. Russel Hugo and Virginia (Fox) P.; B.A., Stanford U., 1948; M.D., Cornell U., N.Y.C., 1952; m. Juliet Boyd, Nov. 25, 1955; children—Juliet Richie, Russel Hugo III, Alexander Canning. Intern in surgery N.Y. Hosp., N.Y.C., 1952-53, asst. resident surgeon, 1955-57, asst. resident neurosurgeon, 1957-59, resident neurosurgeon, 1959-60, provisional asst. neurosurgeon, 1960-61, asst. attending neurosurgeon, 1961-66, asso. attending neurosurgeon, 1966-71, attending surgeon-in-charge, 1971—; rotating resident in neurosurgery Meml. Hosp., 1957-60, cons. asso. neurosurgeon, 1966—, asso. attending surgeon, 1971—; practice medicine specializing in neurosurgery, N.Y.C.; asst. in surgery Cornell U. Med. Coll., 1955-59, instr., 1959-61, clin. instr., 1961-63, asst. prof. surgery, 1963-68, asso. prof., 1968-71, prof., 1971—. Served with M.C., U.S. Army, 1953-55. Diplomate Am. Bd. Neurol. Surgery. Mem. N.Y. County Med. Assn., Med. Soc. State N.Y., AMA, N.Y. Soc. Neurosurgery (pres. 1976-78), Am. Assn. Neurol. Surgeons (v.p. and chmn. sect. cerebrovascular surgery 1976-77), N.Y. Neurol. Soc., N.Y. State Neurosurg. Soc. (pres. 1972-73), Pan Am. Med. Assn., A.C.S., N.Y. Acad. Medicine, N.Y. Med. and Surg. Soc. (sec. 1973-75), Internat. Soc. Surgery, Soc. Neurol. Surgeons, Am. Acad. Neurol. Surgeons (sec. 1972-76), AAAS, Soc. Stereotaxic and Functional Surgery, Internat. Soc. Pediatric Neurosurgery, Soc. Brit. Neurol. Surgeons (corr.), Nat. Med. Vets. Soc. Contbr. numerous articles to profl. publs. Office: 525 E 68th St New York NY 10021

PATTERSON, RUSSELL, opera exec.; b. Greenville, Miss., Aug. 31, 1930; s. Dudley Russell and Elizabeth (Taylor) P.; B.A., B.Mus., S.E. La. U., 1950; M.Mus., Kansas City Conservatory of Music, 1952; D.M.A., U. Mo. at Kansas City; m. Teresa Gutierrez de Celis, Aug. 28, 1979; children—Richard Russell, Christopher Leonard. Musician with Baton Rouge Symphony, 1948-50, Brevard Music Festival, 1947-49, Kansas City Philharmonic Orch., 1951-59; Bayrische Staatsoper, Munich, Germany, 1952-53; condr. Lyric Opera of Kansas City, 1958—, Kansas City Philharmonic Orch., 1965-66, Point Lookout (Mo.) Festival, 1967—, Kansas City Ballet, 1965-66, Am. Ballet Co., European tour, 1958; gen. dir. Lyric Opera of Kansas City, 1958—; artistic dir. Missouri River Festival, 1976—; prof. music Kansas City Conservatory of Music, 1960-68; mem. profl. com. Met. Opera, 1962—; cons. Ford Found. Mem. opera com. Mo. Council Arts, 1965-69; mem. music panel Nat. Endowment Arts, 1970-72; mem. Univ. Assos. U. Mo. at Kansas City, 1970—. Mem. Friends of Art, Opera America (v.p. 1971-73), Phi Mu Alpha Sinfonia, Pi Kappa

Lambda, Mensa. Home: 4618 Warwick Blvd Kansas City MO 64112 Office: 1029 Central St Kansas City MO 64105

PATTERSON, WILLIAM BRADFORD, surg. oncologist; b. New Rochelle, N.Y., June 25, 1921; s. Arthur Henry and Gertrude Claire (Hough) P.; A.B., Harvard U., 1943, M.D., 1950; m. Helen Russell Ross, May 17, 1943; children—William Bradford, Rebecca Holmes, Linda Stevens, Stuart Ross. Chemist, E.I. DuPont Co., 1942-44; intern Peter Bent Brigham Hosp., Boston, 1950-51; resident in surgery, 1951-56; surgeon Boston City Hosp., 1956-59; practice medicine specializing in surgery, Boston, 1963-70; chief Pondville Hosp., 1959-63; prof. surgery U. Rochester (N.Y.), 1970-78; asso. dir. for cancer control Sidney Farber Cancer Inst., Boston, 1978—; vis. prof. surgery Harvard Med. Sch., 1978—; cons. Nat. Cancer Inst. Served with USNR, 1944-46. Diplomate Am. Bd. Surgery. Fellow A.C.S.; mem. Am. Assn. Cancer Research, Am. Soc. Clin. Oncology, Mass. Med. Soc., Boston Surg. Soc., New Eng. Surg. Soc., Central Surg. Soc., New Eng. Cancer Soc. Democrat. Episcopalian. Contbr. chpts. to books, articles to med. jours. Home: 405 Clinton Rd Brookline MA 02146 Office: 44 Binney St Boston MA 02115

PATTERSON, WILLIAM DUDLEY, publisher, travel and tourism cons.; b. Kernville, Calif., July 25, 1910; s. Harold Lindsay and Louise (Dudley) P.; A.B., Yale U., 1932; m. Ellen Day, Sept. 1, 1934; children—Gwen, Day, Philip. Newspaperman specializing pub. affairs, 1932-39; domestic, fgn. assignments, N.Y. dailies and Asso. Press, 1939-42; asst. to Am. ambassador, Madrid, 1942; staff New Republic, 1946-48; v.p. Fred Smith & Co., pub. relations, 1948-50; staff Sat. Rev., 1950—, asso. publisher, 1951-68, publisher, 1968—; v.p., sec. Sat. Rev., Inc., 1962-69, exec. v.p., 1970-72; v.p. pub., dir. Saturday Rev. Industries, Inc., 1972-73; cons. on travel and tourism, 1973—; chmn. bd. Travel & Tourism Consultants Internat., Inc., 1975—; ofcl. rapporteur and spl. rep. UN, Internat. Union Ofcl. Travel Orgns.; asst. dir. OWI London, ETO, 1943-44; transferred Psychol. Warfare Div., SHAEF, Germany, 1944-45; travel adv. com. Dept. Commerce, Dept. Interior; mem. U.S. delegation UN Conf. Internat. Travel, Rome, 1963; del. White House Conf. Internat. Coop., 1965; chmn. ICY Sub-Com. on Internat. Travel; mem. Pres.'s Spl. Travel Task Force, 1967-68; co-chmn. Pres.'s Travel Commn., 1971-73; mem. U.S. travel mission to USSR, 1974; chmn. adv. com. grad. program travel studies New Sch. U., 1975—. Clubs: Century, Yale, Sky, Wings (N.Y.C.); Nat. Press (Washington). Author articles current polit., internat. affairs, internat. travel and tourist industry; syndicated book column; annual Big Picture report on world travel and ann. World Tourism Overview; editor: America Miracle at Work; supervising editor Is the Common Man Too Common? Address: 11 Fairview Dr Westport CT 06880

PATTERSON, WILLIAM HENRY, JR., automotive co. exec.; b. Toledo, Dec. 16, 1921; s. William Henry and Freda (Ulmer) P.; B.B.A. cum laude, U. Toledo, 1943; m. Eleanor C. Robbins, Sept. 11, 1948; children—Janet L., William R. Accountant, City Auto Stamping Co. (now Sheller-Globe Corp.), Toledo, 1946-54, treas., 1954-65, v.p. finance, 1965-72, dir., 1968—, sr. v.p., 1972-74, exec. v.p., 1974—. Vice chmn. Toledo chpt. ARC; trustee U. Toledo Alumni Found. Served with U.S. Army, 1943-46. Decorated Army Commendation medal. Mem. Financial Execs. Inst. (pres. Toledo chpt.). Rotarian. Home: 7633 Gillcrest Rd Sylvania OH 43560 Office: 1505 Jefferson Ave Toledo OH 43624

PATTERSON, WILLIAM ROBERT, lawyer; b. Wathena, Kans., Feb. 25, 1924; s. George Richard and Jessie (Broadbent) P.; student U. Rochester, 1943-44; A.B., Lenoir-Rhyne Coll., 1947; LL.B. with distinction, Duke U., 1950; m. Lee Rhyne, Aug. 16, 1947; children—Martha, Robert, Elizabeth. Admitted to Ga. bar, 1951, D.C. bar, 1962; asso. firm Sutherland, Asbill & Brennan, Atlanta, 1950-58, partner, 1958—; lectr. in field. Mem. bd. visitors Duke U. Law Sch. 1973—, chmn., 1977—; trustee, sec. Pace Acad., Atlanta, 1958—; mem. Lenoir-Rhyne Coll. Devel. Bd., 1976-79; elder Trinity Presbyterian Ch., Atlanta. Served with USN, 1942-46. Fellow Am. Coll. Mortgage Attys.; mem. Atlanta Lawyers Club, Atlanta Bar Assn., Ga. State Bar, Am. Law Inst., So. Fed. Tax Inst. (trustee 1957—, pres. 1974-75, chmn. 1975-76), Atlanta Tax Forum (trustee 1977—), Order of Coif. Clubs: Cherokee Town and Country, Commerce. Home: 2939 Rivermeade Dr NW Atlanta GA 30327 Office: 3100 First Nat Bank Tower Atlanta GA 30303

PATTESON, ROY KINNEER, JR., ednl. adminstr.; b. Richmond, Va., Oct. 27, 1928; s. Roy Kinneer and Mary (Anderson) P.; B.A., U. Richmond, 1957; B.D., Union Theol. Sem., 1961; Th.M., Duke U., 1964, Ph.D., 1967; m. Edna Pauline Cox, Apr. 15, 1950; children—Stephen, David. Fellow, Duke U. Inst. Medieval and Renaissance Studies, 1968; pres. So. Sem. Jr. Coll., 1970-72; v.p. Mary Baldwin Coll., 1972-77; pres. King Coll., Bristol, Tenn., 1977-79; asst. to pres. Va. Wesleyan Coll., 1979—; ordained to ministry Presbyterian Ch. in U.S., 1961; pastor Pittsboro and Mt. Vernon Springs Presbyn. chs., Pittsboro, N.C., 1962-65; mem. mission council and chmn. budget com. Shenandoah Presbytery, 1973-77; mem. community adv. bd. Madison Coll., 1975-77; bd. dirs. Tenn. Ind. Coll. Fund; v.p. Mid-Appalachian Coll. Council, 1978-79. Vice pres. Rockbridge Hist. Soc., Lexington, Va., 1970-77; chmn. edn. com. Staunton-Augusta C. of C. Served with U.S. Army, 1948-49, U.S. N.G., 1949-52. Recipient Grad. Scholar award Duke U., 1966. Mem. Council Advancement and Support of Edn. Club: Rotary (Norfolk). Home: 1100 Hanover Ave Norfolk VA 23508 Office: Va Wesleyan Coll Wesleyan Dr Norfolk VA 23502

PATTILLO, CHARLES CURTIS, air force officer; b. Atlanta, June 3, 1924; s. Joseph Warren and Pearl (Stubbs) P.; student Ga. Inst. Tech., 1946-48; B.A., U. Colo., 1961; M.A., George Washington U., 1965; m. Bobbie Frances Brown, Sept. 13, 1953; children—Deborah Ann, Cheri Leigh, Jon Scott, Charles Curtis. Commd. 2d lt. USAAF, 1944, advanced through grades to lt. gen. USAF, 1968—; pilot USAF in Europe aerial demonstration team, the Skyblazers, 1949-52, aerial demonstration team Thunderbirds, 1953-54; squadron operations officer 3600th Combat Crew Tng. Group, 1954-55, squadron comdr., 1955-56, group operations officer, 1956-57; tactical squadron comdr. 366th and 401st Tactical Fighter Wings, England AFB, La., 1956-59; chief jet fighter-reconnaissance div. 4442d Standardization and Evaluation Group, Hdqrs. Tactical Air Command, Langley AFB, Va., 1962-64; dir. operations and tng. Hdqrs. 17th Air Force, Ramstein Air Base, Germany, 1965-67; comdr. 36th Tactical Fighter Wing, F-4 Phantom pilot, Bitburg Air Base, 1967-68, 8th Tactical Fighter Wing, Ubon, Thailand, 1968-69; vice comdr. Oklahoma City Air Material Area, Tinker AFB, Okla., 1969-71; dep. dir. logistics Orgn. Joint Chiefs of Staff, Washington, 1971-72; comdr. Lowry Tech. Tng. Center, Lowry AFB, Colo., 1972-74; vice comdr.-in-chief Pacific Air Forces, 1975-79; dep. comdr.-in-chief U.S. Readiness Command, McDill AFB, Fla., 1979—. Decorated D.S.M. with oak leaf cluster, Legion of Merit with 3 oak leaf clusters, D.F.C. with 1 oak leaf cluster, Air medal with 10 oak leaf clusters; Republic of Vietnam Campaign medal, Air Force Distinguished Service Order 2d Class; French Croix de Guerre with cross. Home: 405 Staff Loop McDill AFB FL 33608 Office: Dep Comdr in Chief US Readiness Command McDill AFB FL 33608

PATTILLO, CUTHBERT AUGUSTUS, air force officer; b. Atlanta, June 3, 1924; s. Joseph Warren and Pearl (Stubbs) P.; B.A. in Math., U. Colo., 1960; M.A. in Internat. Affairs, George Washington U., 1965; m. Joyce Mathews, Jan. 3, 1950; children—Robert M., Joseph W., Patricia, Peggy. Enlisted U.S. Army Air Force, 1943, commd. 2d lt., 1944; recalled to active duty, commd. 1st lt. U.S. Air Force, 1948, advanced through grades to maj. gen., 1972; wing dep. comdr. for ops. U.S. Air Force, Germany, 1965-67; dir. safety Hdqrs. U.S. Air Forces Europe, Germany, 1967-68; wing vice comdr., then wing comdr. U.S. Air Force, Vietnam, 1968-69; asst. dep. chief of staff, plans, asst. dept. chief of staff, ops. Hdqrs. Tactical Air Command, Hampton, Va., 1969-72; dep. dir., then dir. ops. Hdqrs. U.S. Air Force, Washington, 1972-74; dep. chief of staff, ops. and intelligence, sr. U.S. rep. Allied Forces Central Europe, The Netherlands, 1974-77; dir. plans and policy Hdqrs. U.S. Readiness Command, MacDill AFB, Fla., 1977-79, dep. comdr.-in-chief U.S. Readiness Command, 1979—. Decorated D.S.M. with oak leaf cluster, Silver Star, Legion of Merit with 2 oak leaf clusters, D.F.C. with oak leaf cluster, Air medal with 13 oak leaf clusters, Army Commendation medal, Air Force Commendation medal with 1 oak leaf cluster; Croix de Guerre with Palm (France); Honor Medal 1st class (Vietnam). Mem. Air Force Assn. Home: 401 Staff Loop Macdill Air Force Base FL 33621 Office: Hdqrs US Readiness Command (J5) MacDill Air Force Base FL 33608

PATTILLO, MANNING MASON, JR., univ. pres.; b. Charlottesville, Va., Oct. 11, 1919; s. Manning Mason and Margaret (Camblos) P.; student Johns Hopkins U., 1937-38; B.A. with highest honors, U. of South, 1941; student U. Calif. at Berkeley, 1941-42; A.M., U. Chgo., 1947, Ph.D., 1949; LL.D., LeMoyne Coll., 1967, St. John's U., 1968; L.H.D., U. Detroit, 1968, Coll. New Rochelle, 1967, Park Coll., 1973; Litt.D., St. Norbert Coll., 1967; m. Martha A. Crawford, June 8, 1946; children—Manning Mason III, Martha Crawford, John Landrum. From instr. to asso. prof. higher edn. U. Chgo., 1949-56; asso. dir. Lilly Endowment, Inc., Indpls., 1956-60, exec. dir. for edn., 1961-62; dir. Danforth commn. on ch. colls. and univs., 1962-66; asso. dir. The Danforth Found., 1964-66, v.p., 1966-67; pres. The Found. Center, N.Y.C., 1967-71; adj. prof. N.Y. U., 1968-71; dir. spl. projects U. Rochester, 1972-75; pres. Oglethorpe U., Atlanta, 1975—; former cons. Mary Reynolds Babcock Found., Arthur Vining Davis Found., Robert Wood Johnson Found., Charles F. Kettering Found., N.W. Area Found., W. Clement and Jessie V. Stone Found., Western Electric Fund. Tech. asst., then asso. sec. commn. on colls. and univs. North Central Assn. Colls. and Secondary Schs., 1948-56; cons. USAF Acad., 1952, Phillips Exeter Acad., 1974. Chmn. IBM Incentive awards com., 1970-75; adv. com. Brookings Instn., 1970-71; mem. pres.'s adv. council Wellesley Coll., 1969-72; trustee Seabury Press, Japan Internat. Christian U., 1970-72, Fukaishi Inst. Internat. Studies, Le Moyne Coll., 1972-75, Sacred Heart U., 1968-75; trustee Greater Rochester Community Found., 1973-75, pres., 1975; trustee, chmn. exec. com. Nat. Council on Philanthropy; trustee, chmn. bd. trustees Park Coll., 1967-74; provost St. Mary's Coll. of Md., 1975; pres. Ga. Found. for Ind. Colls., 1980—; chmn. Univ. Center in Ga.; v.p. Assn. Pvt. Colls. and Univs. of Ga. Served with AUS, 1942-46. Mem. Am. Assn. for Higher Edn., Higher Edn. Colloquium, Guild of Scholars, English Speaking Union, Atlanta Hist. Soc., Ga. Conservancy, Dekalb C. of C. (dir.), Phi Beta Kappa, Omicron Delta Kappa, Kappa Sigma. Episcopalian (vestryman, sr. warden, mem. cathedral chpt., diocesan council). Clubs: Century (N.Y.C.); Commerce (Atlanta); Rotary. Author: (with D. M. Mackenzie) Eight Hundred Colleges Face the Future; Church Sponsored Higher Education in the United States. Contbr. articles to profl. jours. Home: 1571 Windsor Pkwy NE Atlanta GA 30319

PATTINSON, RONALD RICHARD, real estate agt., mayor; b. Detroit, Oct. 7, 1932; s. Richard and Alta Ruth (Risen) P.; student E. Los Angeles Coll., 1950-51, Goldenwest Jr. Coll., 1968-72; m. Penney Forester, Nov. 1, 1971; children—Sherry, Steven, Thomas, Casey; stepchildren—Colleen Wallace, Kim Wallace, Guy Wallace. Mgr., Flagg Bros. Shoe Stores, Fresno, Calif., 1953-59; salesman Libby McNeil & Libby, San Francisco, 1959-61, Wesco Mdse., Vernon, 1961-64; police officer Maywood (Calif.) Police Dept., 1964-68, City of Huntington Beach (Calif.), 1968-75; owner Beachcliff Real Estate, Huntington Beach, 1975-77; mayor City of Huntington Beach, 1977—; mgr. Red Carpet Real Estate, Huntington Beach, 1978—; dir. Orange County (Calif.) Sanitation Dist., 1976-77, Orange County Criminal Justice Council, 1977—, Calif. Safety Com., 1977—; mem. Huntington Beach City Council, 1976, mayor protem, 1977. Mem. Republican State Central Com. Served with USAF, 1951-53. Mem. Internat. Police Officers Assn., Huntington Beach Fountain Valley Bd. Realtors. Club: Exchange. Home: 20681 Elizabeth St Huntington Beach CA 92646 Office: 9552 Hamilton St Huntington Beach CA 92646

PATTIS, S. WILLIAM, publisher; b. Chgo., July 3, 1925; s. William Robert and Rose (Quint) P.; B.S., U. Ill., 1949; postgrad. Northwestern U., 1949-50; m. Bette Z. Levin, July 16, 1950; children—Mark Robert, Robin Lynn. Exec. v.p., pub. United Bus. Publs., 1949-59; pres. The Pattis Group, 1959—, Nat. Textbook Co., Skokie Ill., 1961—; dir. Bank of Highwood (Ill.), New Century Bank, Mundelein, Ill.; pres. Wartell-Pattis Co., N.Y.C., 1970—, P-B Communications, Winnetka, Ill., 1978; mem. Pres.'s Council Youth Opportunity, 1968-70. Bd. dirs. Photography Youth Found., 1970-73, Expt. in Internat. Living, 1970. Served with C.E., U.S. Army, 1943-46. Recipient human relations award Am. Jewish Com., 1971. Clubs: Standard, Monroe, Midtown Tennis (Chgo.); Northmoor Country (Highland Park, Ill.); Tamarisk Country, Tennis (Palm Springs, Calif.). Home: 195 Elder Ln Highland Park IL 60035 Office: 4761 W Touhy Ave Lincolnwood IL 60646

PATTISHALL, BEVERLY WYCKLIFFE, lawyer; b. Atlanta, May 23, 1916; s. Leon Jackson and Margaret Simkins (Woodfin) P.; B.S., Northwestern U., 1938; J.D., U. Va., 1941; children by previous marriage—Mrs. Margaret Ann Arthur, Leslie Hansen, Beverly Wyckliffe, Paige Terhune, Woodfin Underwood; m. Dorothy Daniels Mashek, June 24, 1977. Admitted to Ill. bar, 1941, D.C. bar, 1971; practiced in Chgo., 1941—; mem. firm Pattishall, McAuliffe & Hofstetter, 1969—; lectr. trademark, trade identity and unfair trade practices law Northwestern U. Sch. Law. Dir. Juvenile Protective Assn. Chgo., 1946—, pres., 1961-63; dir. Vol. Interagy. Assn., 1975-78, sec., 1977-78; U.S. del. Diplomatic Confs. on Internat. Trademark Registration Treaty, Geneva, Vienna, 1970-73. Served to lt. comdr. USNR, 1941-46; PTO, ETO; comdr. Res. (ret.). Fellow Am. Coll. Trial Lawyers (bd. regents 1979—); mem. Internat. Patent and Trademark Assn. (pres. 1955-57, exec. com. 1955—), Am. (chmn. sect. patent, trademark and copyright Law 1963-64), Internat., Ill., Chgo., D.C. bar assns., Chgo. Bar Found. (dir. 1977—), U.S. Trademark Assn. (dir. 1963-65). Clubs: Legal, Law (exec. com. 1979—), Econ., Univ., Mid-America (Chgo.); Fox River Valley Hunt; Chicaming Country. Author: (with Hilliard) Trademarks, Trade Identity and Unfair Trade Practices, 1974. Contbr. articles to profl. jours. Home: 2244 N Lincoln Park W Chicago IL 60614 Office: Pattishall McAuliffe & Hofstetter Suite 3500 Prudential Plaza Chicago IL 60601

PATTISON, ABBOTT LAWRENCE, sculptor; b. Chgo., May 15, 1916; s. William L. and Bonnie (Abbott) P.; B.A., Yale, 1937, B.F.A., 1939; m. Mary Grant, June 2, 1945; children—William G., Grant A., Harry, Jean. Work in China and Japan, 1940, Europe, 1950-51, 55-56, 58, 60-61, Italy, 1955-56, 58, 60-61; represented in collections Art Inst. Chgo., Corcoran Gallery, Washington, Phoenix Museum, Calif. Palace Legion of Honor, others; represented permanent collections at Whitney Mus., N.Y.C., Israel State Mus. Jerusalem, San Francisco Mus., Buckingham Palace, London, Eng.; tchr. Chgo. Art Inst., 1946-51; sculptor in residence, sculptures for campus U. Ga., 1953-54; affiliated Saidenberg Gallery, N.Y.C., Feingarten Gallery, Los Angeles, Fairweather Hardin Gallery, Chgo., Alwin Gallery, London; major commns. include Mayo Clinic, Rochester, Minn., Central Nat. Bank, Cleve., U. Chgo., Chgo. State U., Ill. Capitol Bldg., Lincoln Library, Springfield, Ill., Northbrook (Ill.) Library, New Trier West High Sch., Northfield Ill., Culligan Internat. & Commerce Plaza, Oak Brook, Ill. Recipient 1st traveling fellowship Yale, 1939; 1st Logan prize and purchase Art Inst. Chgo., 1942, Eisendrath prize, 1946, 1st Pauline Palmer prize for sculpture, 1950, prize, 1953; 3d prize contemporary sculpture show Met. Mus. Art, 1951; 1st prize Chgo. Sculptor Show, Art Center, 1955; 1st prize McCormick Pl. Art Show, 1962; prize Bundy Mus., Waitsfield, Vt., 1963. Address: 334 Woodland Ave Winnetka IL 60093

PATTISON, EDWARD WORTHINGTON, former congressman; b. Troy, N.Y., Apr. 29, 1932; s. Edward Hargrave and Elisabeth (Royce) P.; A.B., Cornell U., 1953, LL.B., 1957; m. Eleanor Copley, Nov. 23, 1951; children—Mark, Lynn, Laura, Wendy. Admitted to N.Y. State bar, 1957; partner firm Smith, Pattison, Sampson & Jones, Troy, 1959-72, v.p., 1972-74; v.p. Pattison, Herzog, Sampson & Nichols, 1974; mem. 94th-96th Congresses from 29th Dist. N.Y., mem. Com. on Judiciary, Banking, Fin. and Urban Affairs Com., Adminstrn. Com.; fellow Kennedy Inst. Politics, Harvard U., 1979; sr. univ. lectr. Rensselaer Poly. Inst., 1979-80; dir. Trip Inc. Mem. Comptrollers Com. on Revision N.Y. State Real Property Tax Law, 1971-74; treas. Capital Dist. Regional Planning Commn., 1970-74, commr., 1974; mem. exec. com. Rensselaer County Inter-govtl. Council, 1972-74; chmn. Gen. Revenue Sharing Commn. Rensselaer County, 1973-74. Chmn., Town of Sand Lake Democratic Com., 1961-65; mem. exec. com. Rensselaer County Dem. Com., 1962-64; chmn. Rensselaer County Citizens for Kennedy-Johnson, 1960; Rensselaer County treas., 1969-74; candidate U.S. Congress from 30th Dist. N.Y., 1970; candidate Rensselaer County Exec., 1973. Bd. dirs. Salvation Army, adv. bd., 1964-71; bd. dirs. Family and Childrens Service, Inc., 1965-73; bd. dirs. United Community Services, sec., 1966-70, mem. exec. com., 1966-72; bd. dirs. Rensselaer County Tb. and Pub. Health Assn., pres., 1964-67; bd. dirs. Commn. on Econ. Opportunity for Rensselaer County Area, chmn., 1965-68; bd. dirs. Cornell U. Nat. Secondary Schs. Com., 1964-67; chmn. Cornell Club of Albany Secondary Schs. Com., 1962-70, HSORA, Inc., 1966-74; bd. dirs. N.Y. State Environmental Health Assn., sec., 1971-74, Home Aide Service of Eastern N.Y., Inc., 1972-74, Mohawk Hudson Community Found., 1971-74, WMHT (Channel 17 Ednl. TV), 1974, 79—; trustee Hoosac Sch., 1972-79; chmn. bd. Congl. Inst. on Future, 1979—; bd. dirs. Millay Colony for Arts, 1979—. Served to 1st lt. F.A., AUS, 1954-56. Mem. N.Y. State, Rensselaer County (exec. com. 1964-67, pres. 1974) bar assns., Assn. Bar City N.Y. (asso.). Club: Troy. Author: The Marketing of Property Acquired for Taxes, 1972; The Political Parties, Ralph Nader, Where Are You?, 1972; How to Conduct a Tax Sale, 1973. Home: West Sand Lake NY 12196

PATTISON, JAMES ALLEN, consumer services co. exec.; b. Saskatoon, Sask., Can., Oct. 1, 1928; s. Chandos W. and Julia Blue (Allen) P.; student U. B.C., 1947-50; m. Mary Ella Hudson, June 30, 1951; children—James Allen, Susan Mary Ann, Cynthia Lee. Owner, pres., chmn., chief exec. officer Jim Pattison Industries Ltd., Neonex Internat. Ltd., Jim Pattison Enterprises Ltd.; dir. Crush Internat. Ltd. Mem. Young Presidents Orgn. Club: Terminal City (Vancouver). Home: 855 Eyremount Dr West Vancouver BC Canada Office: 1600-1055 W Hastings St Vancouver BC Canada

PATTISON, JOHN NORWOOD, educator; b. Cedar Rapids, Iowa, June 1, 1919; s. Warren Berry and Laura Margaret (House) P.; B.S. in Chemistry, W.Va. U., 1941; postgrad. U. Pitts., 1943-44; Ph.D., Purdue U., 1948; m. Shirley Vivian Abendroth, Dec. 31, 1963; children—George Edgar, Kay Louise (Mrs. Fredrick Meister), Carol Anne (Mrs. John R. Stegmiller). Chemist, Am. Viscose Corp., Roanoke, Va., 1941, Mellon Inst. Indsl. Research, 1942; sr. research chemist Koppers United Co., Kobuta, Pa., 1942-46; asst. chief chem. research div. Battelle Meml. Inst., Columbus, Ohio, 1948-56; head catalyst research div. Cities Service Research & Devel. Co., Lake Charles, La., 1956-57; mgr. research and devel. Girdler Catalysts, Chemetron Corp., Louisville and Newport, Tenn., 1957-61; v.p., dir. Scott Research Labs., Inc., San Bernardino, Calif., 1961-64; cons. in air pollution control, Pasadena, Calif., 1964-66; prof. environ. engring. U. Cin., 1967—; chmn., pres. Environ. Research, Inc., Cin., 1972-74; Fulbright lectr. U. Valle, Cali, Colombia, 1974. Chmn. panel testing, inspection maintenance, commn. on motor vehicle emissions Nat. Acad. Scis., 1971-73; dir. Pristine, Inc., 1979—. Pres., Sharon Heights Civic Assn., 1952-53; bd. dirs. Air Pollution Control League Greater Cin., 1978—. Served with AUS, 1944-46. Mem. Air Pollution Control Assn. (chmn. edn. com. 1971-73, dir. E. central sect. 1968-71), Am. Chem. Soc. (chmn. Columbus sect. 1956), Internat. Standards Orgn. (vice chmn. subcom., intersoc. com. methods air sampling and analysis 1968—), Soc. Automotive Engrs., Sigma Xi, Sigma Pi Sigma, Kappa Alpha. Contbr. articles to tech. jours., chpt. to book. Home: 775 Crooked Stone Rd Cincinnati OH 45220

PATTISON, WILLIAM J., aircraft co. exec.; b. Chgo., July 18, 1914; s. William Lawrence and Bonnie Edwina (Abbott) P.; grad. Francis W. Parker Sch., Chgo., 1932; student Renssaeler Poly. Inst., 1933, Mass. Inst. Tech., 1937; m. Margaret Taylor, May 2, 1942; children—Margaret Pattison Watson, Pamela Pattison Williams, Polly Abbott, Priscilla Dudley. Eastern region diesel engine field service mgr. Fairbanks, Morse & Co., 1937; then installation engr. Buda Engine Co., and power plant engr. Grumman Aircraft Engring. Corp.; with Garrett Corp., 1948—, dir. sales and service AiResearch Mfg. div., 1953-58, v.p. charge sales parent co., 1958-69, exec. v.p., 1969—, dir., 1963—; v.p. Garrett Internat. S.A., 1964—, also dir.; dir. Normalair-Garrett (Holdings) Ltd., Garrett France, Garrett Singapore (Pte.) Ltd. Served as aviator USNR, 1941-48. Decorated Silver Star, Air medal, Presdl. citation. Registered profl. engr. Mem. Am. Ordnance Assn., Am. Instr. Aero. and Astronautics, Am. Astronautical Soc., Soc. Naval Engrs. Clubs: Cruising Am.; Camden (Maine) Yacht. Home: 12928 Evanston St Los Angeles CA 90049 Office: 9851 Sepulveda Blvd Los Angeles CA 90009

PATTON, DAVID U., lawyer; b. Livingston, Ala., Nov. 22, 1911; s. Roy Bolton and Irene Vivian (Foscue) P.; B.A., Athens Coll., 1932; J.D., Georgetown U., 1938; m. Elizabeth M. Riddle, Aug. 31, 1934; 1 dau., Elizabeth Bolton. Admitted to Ala. bar, 1938, since practiced in Athens; now partner firm Patton, Latham, Legge; mem. Ala. Senate, 1947-51. Served to capt. USMC, 1942-45. Mem. Athens (past pres.), Ala., Am. bar assns. Episcopalian. Clubs: VFW (Ala. comr. 1952-53), Rotary (past Athens club pres.). Office: PO Box 470 Athens AL 35611

PATTON, GEORGE ERWIN, landscape architect; b. Franklin, N.C., Mar. 18, 1920; s. Robert Andrew and Mamie Dickey (Slagle) P.; B.S. in Landscape Architecture, N.C. State U., 1948; m. Sydney Ott Belleville, Mar. 29, 1958. Landscape architect Simonds and Simonds, Landscape Architects, Pitts., 1948-49, 51-54; prin. George E. Patton, Inc., Landscape Architecture and Planning, Phila., 1954—; lectr. dept. landscape architecture Sch. Fine Arts, U. Pa., 1955-65. Mem. Phila. Art Commn., 1960-68; advisor Eastern Regional Office HUD, 1964-70. Served with USMCR, 1943-46. Rome prize fellow Am. Acad. in Rome, 1949-51; Fulbright scholar, 1950-51. Fellow Am. Soc. Landscape Architects (trustee, 1st v.p. 1967-69), Pa. Hort. Soc., Am. Assn. Botanic Gardens and Arboreta, Am. Rhododendron Soc. Clubs: Phila. Cricket, Peale, Art Alliance. Home: 8 Chesney Ln Philadelphia PA 19118 Office: 1725 Spruce St Philadelphia PA 19103. *The person who can learn to keep all facets of his life in harmonious balance has the best chance to lead a wholesome, happy, and long life.*

PATTON, GEORGE SMITH, army officer; b. Boston, Dec. 24, 1923; s. George Smith, Jr. and Beatrice Banning (Ayer) P.; grad. Hill Sch., Pottstown, Pa., 1942; B.S., U.S. Mil. Acad., 1946; M.P.S., George Washington U., 1965; m. Joanne Holbrook, June 14, 1952; children—Margaret, George Smith, Robert, Helen, Benjamin. Commd. 2d lt. U.S. Army, 1946, advanced through grades to maj. gen., 1973; served in Germany, 1947-51; assigned Armor Br., 1949; instr. tank offense sect. command and staff dept. Armored Sch., Fort Knox, Ky., 1952-53; comdr. Co. A, 140th Tank Bn., Korea, 1953; exec. officer I, Corps Reconnaissance Bn., Korea, 1953-54; co. tactical officer dept. tactics U.S. Mil. Acad., 1954-56; officer exec. dept. U.S. Naval Acad., 1956-57; assigned Command and Gen. Staff Coll., Fort Leavenworth, Kans., 1957-58; aide-de-camp to comdg. gen. 7th Army and comdr. in chief U.S. Army, Europe, 1958-60; exec. officer 1st squadron 11th Armored Cav. Regt., Straubing, Germany, 1960-61; assigned Armed Forces Staff Coll., Norfolk, Va., 1961-62, U.S. Army War Coll., Carlisle Barracks, Pa., 1964-65; spl. forces ops. officer Mil. Assistance Command, Vietnam, 1962-63; comdr. 2d Medium Tank Bn., 1st Armored Div., Fort Hood, Tex., 1963-64; chief Mainland S.E. Asia br. Far East-Pacific div. Office Dept. Chief Staff for Mil. Ops., Dept. Army, 1965-67; chief force devel. div. U.S. Army, Vietnam, 1967-68; comdg. officer 11th Armored Cav. Regt., Vietnam, 1968-69; assigned U.S. Army Primary Helicopter Center, Ft. Wolters, Tex. and Ft. Rucker, Ala., 1969-70; asst. div. comdr. for support 4th Armored div. Hdqrs. U.S. Army, Europe, 1970-71; comdt. U.S. Army Armor Sch., Fort Knox, 1971-73; dir. security assistance Hdqrs. U.S. European Command, 1973-74; spl. asst. to comdr. Army Readiness Region, 1974-75, comdr., 1975; comdr. 2d Armored Div., Fort Hood, 1975-77; dep. comdg. gen. U.S. VII Corps, 1977-79; dir. readiness Hdqrs. Dept. Army Materiel Devel. and Readiness Command, Alexandria, Va., 1979—; instr. history U. Md., 1960-61. Bd. fellows Norwich U. Decorated D.S.C. with oak leaf cluster, Silver Star with oak leaf cluster, Legion of Merit with two oak leaf clusters, D.F.C., Bronze Star with oak leaf cluster, Purple Heart; Cross of Gallantry with gold, silver and bronze stars (Vietnam); Army Forces Honor medal 1st class. Mem. Assn. U.S. Army, Armor Assn., Blackhorse Assn., Internat. Game Fishing Assn., Ducks Unltd., N.E. Farm Bur., Legion of Valor, Am. Legion. Club: Explorers. Office: Hdqrs Dept Army Materiel Devel and Readiness Command 5001 Eisenhower Ave Alexandria VA 22333

PATTON, GEORGE THOMAS, JR., credit agy. exec.; b. Birmingham, Ala., Sept. 22, 1929; s. George Thomas and Jewell Inez (Garner) P.; B.A., Birmingham-So. Coll., 1949; m. Hope Kirby, Dec. 20, 1953; children—Thomas Kirby, Neal Garner. With Gen. Motors Acceptance Corp., N.Y.C., 1949—, treas., 1970-72, v.p., 1972-78, exec. v.p., 1978—, dir., 1974—. Chmn. Municipal Planning Bd., Norwood, N.J., 1967-72. Trustee, Pascack Valley Hosp., Westwood, N.J., 1975—. Mem. Sigma Alpha Epsilon, Omicron Delta Kappa. Presbyn. (elder). Club: Univ. (N.Y.C.). Office: 767 Fifth Ave New York NY 10022

PATTON, JAMES GEORGE, agrl. leader; b. Bazar, Kans., Nov. 8, 1902; s. Ernest Everett and Jane Alice (Gross) P.; LL.D., Western State Coll. Colo., 1942, U. Colo., 1966; m. Velma A. Fouse, June 17, 1925 (dec. Sept. 1970); children—Marjorie Jane, James George (dec.), George Everett (dec.), Robert Lyle; m. 2d, Nathalie E. Panek, Nov. 8, 1972. Athletic dir., instr. phys. edn., Colo. and Nev., 1921-26; asst. business mgr. Western State Coll. Colo., 1927-29; organizer coop. ins. Colo. Farmers Union, 1932-34, exec. sec., 1934-37, pres., 1938-41; dir. Nat. Farmers Union, 1937-40, pres., 1940-66, ret.; pres. James G. Patton & Assos., Tucson, 1966-69; pres. United World Federalists, 1967-69; spl. cons. sec. agr., Pa., 1971-75; dir. ret. mems. dept. AFL-CIO, 1976-78; chmn. bd. dirs. Diatoms Industries, 1977-79. Formerly mem. Nat. Adv. Com. of Nat. Youth Adminstrn.; mem. Econ. Stblzn. Bd., 1942-43; mem. Nat. Labor Mgmt. Policy Commn.; former mem. adv. bd. War Moblizn. and Reconversion Bd.; rep. Carnegie Endownment for Internat. Peace, Am. Conf. of Assns. Commerce and Prodn., Montevideo, 1941; U.S. del. 2d Inter-Am. Conf. on Agrl., Mexico, 1942; U.S. adviser Inter-Am. Conf. on War and Peace, Mexico, 1945; U.S. cons. U.N. Conf. on Internat. Order, San Francisco, 1945; U.S. adv. to FAO convs., Quebec, 1945, Copenhagen, 1946, Geneva, 1947, Washington, 1948, Rome, 1949-50; del. Internat. Fedn. Agrl. Producers, 1946—; mem. exec. com. Internat. Fedn. Agrl. Producers, 1950, v.p., 1955-58, pres., 1958-61; mem. Nat. Adv. Bd. Moblzn., 1951; pres. Freedom From Hunger Found. U.S.A., 1962-63, mem. exec. com., 1973-75; cons., observer World Food Conf., Rome, 1974. Home and office: 150 Alma St 201 Menlo Park CA 94025

PATTON, JAMES GODFREY, clergyman; b. Henderson, Ky., May 22, 1896; s. James G. and Hallie (Herring) P.; B.S., Davidson Coll., 1916; B.D., Union Theol. Sem. in Va., 1921; D.D., King Coll., Bristol, Tenn., 1932; LL.D., Presbyn. Coll. S.C., 1965; m. Katherine Lynn Jones, July 27, 1918; children—Katherine Lynn (Mrs. W.B. Carssow), Samuel Joseph, James Godfrey, Claude Herbert. Ordained to ministry Presbyn. Ch., 1921; pastor in Lawrenceville, Ga., 1921-23, Atlanta, 1923-27, Abingdon, Va., 1927-39, Waynesboro, Va., 1939-42; exec. sec. Gen. Council Presbyn. Ch. in U.S., 1943-66; chmn. dept. stewardship and benevolences Nat. Councils Chs., 1950-53; moderator Synod of Ga., 1964—. Rep. U.S. at 1st World Consultation Stewardship, 1961; stated clk. Synod of Appalachia, 1936- 39. Chmn. trustees King Coll., 1932-36; adv. bd. Am. Bible Soc., 1948- 62. Served as 1st lt., inf., U.S. Army, 1917-19. Recipient Good Steward award Nat. Council Chs., 1965. Author numerous articles, pamphlets. Address: 1825 Clifton Rd NE Apt 615 Atlanta GA 30329

PATTON, JAMES RICHARD, JR., lawyer; b. Durham, N.C., Oct. 27, 1928; s. James Ralph and Bertha (Moye) P.; A.B. cum laude, U. N.C., 1948; postgrad. Yale U., 1948; J.D., Harvard U., 1951; m. Mary Margot Maughan, Dec. 29, 1950; children—James Macon, Lindsay Fairfield. Admitted to D.C. bar, 1951, also U.S. Supreme Ct.; attache of Embassy, spl. asst. to Am. ambassador to Indochina, 1952-54; with Office Nat. Estimates, Washington, 1954-55; atty. Covington & Burling, Washington, 1956-61; sr. partner firm Patton, Boggs & Blow, Washington, 1962—. Lectr. internat. law Cornell Law Sch., 1963-64, U.S. Army Command and Gen. Staff Coll., 1967-68. Mem. Nat. Security Forum, U.S. Air War Coll., 1965, Nat. Strategy Seminar, U.S. Army War Coll., 1967-70, Global Strategy Discussions, U.S. Naval War Coll., 1968, Def. Orientation Conf., 1972; mem. Com. of 100 on Fed. City, Washington; mem. adv. council on nat. security and internat. affairs Nat. Republican Com.; bd. dirs. Madeira Sch., Greenway, Va., Lawyers Com. for Civil Rights Under Law, Washington; Served with U.S. Army, 1954-55. Mem. Am. (past com. chmn.), Inter-Am. (past del.) bar assns., Internat. Law Assn., Am. Soc. Internat. Law (treas., exec. council), Washington Inst. Fgn. Affairs, Phi Beta Kappa, Alpha Epsilon Delta. Clubs: Metropolitan, International (Washington); Brook (N.Y.C.); Pacific (Honolulu). Home: 456 River Bend Rd Great Falls VA 22066 Office: 2550 M St NW Washington DC 20037

PATTON, JAMES WILLIAM, JR., lawyer; b. Columbus, Ga., July 6, 1914; s. JamesWilliam and Gertrude (Berry) P.; LL.B., U. Ala., 1937; m. Marjorie Phinizy, Aug. 2, 1941; children—Jean Patton Parker, J. William, III, Peter E. Admitted to Ala. bar, 1937; asso. firm Eyster & Eyster, Decatur, Ala., 1937-42; mem. firm Stone, Patton & Kierce and predecessors, Bessemer, Ala., 1946—. Past pres. Bessemer Salvation Army Adv. Bd.; past chmn. bd. dirs. Bessemer chpt. ARC; trustee Bessemer Meml. Hosp., 1964-73. Served with USAAF, 1942-46. Mem. Bessemer, Ala., Am. bar assns., Am. Judicature Soc., Bessemer C. of C. (pres. 1955-56). Democrat. Episcopalian. Clubs: Woodward Golf and Country, The Club; Lions (pres. local club 1962-63) (Bessemer). Home: 102 Woodland Rd Bessemer AL 35020 Office: 118 N 18th St Bessemer AL 35020

PATTON, JOHN BARRATT, geologist; b. Marion, Ind., July 1, 1915; s. Barratt Marsh and Mary Frances (Kuntz) P.; A.B. in Chemistry, Ind. U., 1938, A.M. in Geology, 1940, Ph.D. in Geology, 1954; m. Jean Glenn, 1941; children—Barratt Marsh II, Roger Craig, Frank Jamison Campbell, Ian Alastair. Geologist, Magnolia Petroleum Co., 1940-47; head indsl. minerals sect. Ind. Geol. Survey, 1947-53, prin. geologist, 1951-59, state geologist, dir., 1959—; asst. prof. geology Ind. U., 1948-52, asso. prof. econ. geology, 1952-55, prof. economic geology, 1955—, chmn. dept. geology, 1959-71, asso. dean research and advanced studies, 1973-75; commr. Am. Commn. Stratigraphic Nomenclature, 1960-63, 64-69, 75-78, vice chmn., sec., 1962-63; mem. earth scis. div. NRC, 1967-73. Fellow Geol. Soc. Am., Ind. Acad. Sci. (pres. 1975); mem. Am. Assn. Petroleum Geologists, Soc. Econ. Geologists, Soc. Econ. Paleontologists and Mineralogists, Am. Inst. Mining, Metall. and Petroleum Engrs., Ind.-Ky. Geol. Soc., Assn. Am. State Geologists (pres. 1966-67), ASTM, Interstate Oil Compact Commn., Phi Beta Kappa, Sigma Xi. Contbr. articles to profl. jours., other publs. Home: 809 Sheridan Rd Bloomington IN 47401

PATTON, LARRY DIXON, lawyer, U.S. atty.; b. Shawnee, Okla., Oct. 8, 1943; s. Guy Dixon and Eliene Leona (McCaskey) P.; B.A., U. Okla., 1965, LL.B., 1967; m. Nanette Jordan, July 17, 1971. Admitted to bar; asso. firm McClelland, Collins, Sheehan, Bailey & Bailey, 1967; asso. firm G.M. Fuller, 1967-68; asso. firm Tomerlin, High and Patton, Oklahoma City, 1972-77; U.S. atty., Western Dist. of Okla., Oklahoma City, 1978—; chmn., founder Okla. State Fed. Law Enforcement Co-Ordinating Com. Co-chmn. Okla. County Democratic Party, 1974-76; mem. state steering com. Carter-Mondale Campaign, Okla., chmn. Okla. County Campaign, 1976-77. Served to capt. U.S. Army. Mem. Okla. County Bar Assn., Okla. Bar Assn., Fed. Bar Assn., Am. Bar Assn., Am. Trial Lawyers Assn., Okla. Dist. Attys. Assn. Episcopalian. Club: Lawyers (v.p.). Office: 200 NW 4th St Oklahoma City OK 73102

PATTON, MACON GLASGOW, fin. exec.; b. Durham, N.C., Apr. 18, 1936; s. James R. and Bertha E. (Moye) P.; A.B., U. N.C., Chapel Hill, 1958, M.B.A., 1962; m. Josephine Reid Ward, June 18, 1960; children—Macon G., Josephine Reid. With Donaldson, Lufkin & Jenrette, Inc., N.Y.C., 1962-75, partner investment banking div., 1971-75; pres. Liberty Corp., Greenville, S.C., 1975—, also dir.; dir. Spartan Mills, Liberty Life Ins. Co., Cosmos Broadcasting Co., Atlantic Land Co., Hatteras Income Securities, Inc. Trustee Converse Coll., Spartanburg, S.C., Brevard (N.C.) Music Center, YMCA Camp, Greenville; bd. dirs. Bus. Found. N.C.; mem. Morehead Bus. Fellowship Com. Served with M.C. U.S. Army, 1959-60. Presbyterian. Clubs: University (N.Y.C.); Greenville Country. Address: PO Box 789 Greenville SC 29602

PATTON, MITCHELL, exec. recruiting cons.; b. Greenville, S.C., Apr. 19, 1931; s. Ernest and Margaret (Mitchell) P.; B.A., Davidson Coll., 1953; postgrad. U. N.C., 1954, Stonier Grad. Sch. Banking, Rutgers U., 1966; children—Jeffrey Leonard, Ernest Patton II. With Wachovia Bank & Trust Co., Charlotte, N.C., 1954-58; exec. v.p. Belton Bank (S.C.), 1958-65, pres., 1965-66; pres. Peoples Nat. Bank, Greenville, 1966-73, also dir.; pres. Piedmont Bank & Trust Co., Davidson, N.C., 1973-77, dir., 1973—; pres. Piedmont Corp., Davidson, 1973-77, dir., 1973—; owner Patton Assos., Charlotte, N.C., 1977—; dir. Colonial Acceptance Co., Mt. Holly, N.C. Episcopalian. Clubs: Poinsett, Cotillion (Greenville). Home: PO Box 6 Davidson NC 28036 Office: 1213 Johnston Bldg Charlotte NC 28281

PATTON, ROBERT FREDERICK, lawyer; b. New Castle, Pa., Dec. 9, 1927; s. Wylie E. and Lena Francis (Gardner) P.; A.B., Westminster Coll., New Wilmington, Pa., 1950; J.D., Harvard U., 1953; m. Virginia Lee Reehl, Aug. 15, 1952; children—Thomas E., Barbara L., Susan G., Laura L. Admitted to Pa. bar, 1954; asso. firm Buchanan, Ingersoll, Rodewald, Kyle & Buerger, Pitts., 1953-60, partner, 1960—; dir. Armstrong Cork Co., Union Nat. Bank Pitts.; adj. prof. U. Pitts. Law Sch., 1978. Trustee Westminster Coll., 1976—, sec., 1978—; elder Southminster Presbyn. Ch., 1965-68; chmn. Allegheny County Mental Health/Mental Retardation Bd., 1977—. Served with U.S. Army, 1945-47. Mem. Am. Law Inst., Am., Pa., Allegheny County bar assns. Republican. Clubs: Duquesne, Harvard-Yale-Princeton, Chartiers Country. Home: 293 Dixon Ave Pittsburgh PA 15216 Office: Buchanan Ingersoll et al 57th Floor 600 Grant St Pittsburgh PA 15219

PATTON, SELMA HICKS (MRS. CURRY PATTON), educator; b. Louisville, June 3, 1916; d. Joseph and Gertrude (Levy) Solinger; LL.B., U. Louisville, 1937, B.A., 1940; M.S., Purdue U., 1948. Ph.D., 1950; m. Grant Hicks, Dec. 23, 1938; 1 dau., Carol Sue (Mrs. Harry Papacharalambous); m. 2d, Curry Patton, Apr. 9, 1960. Admitted to Ky. bar, 1937, practiced in Louisville, 1937-40; instr. chemistry U. Ala., Tuscaloosa, 1943-44; research chemist Brown-Forman Distillers Corp., Louisville, 1950-53; sr. engr. research and devel. E.I. DuPont de Nemours Corp., Charlestown, Ind., 1953-56; asso. prof. dept. chemistry La. Tech. U., Ruston, 1956-68, prof., 1968—. Mem. vis. staff clin. chemistry Confederate Meml. Hosp., Shreveport. Recipient Erbell award U. Louisville, 1941. Fellow Am. Inst. Chemists; mem. A.A.A.S., Am. Chem. Soc., Am. Assn. Clin. Chemists, A.A.U.P., Sigma Xi, Beta Beta Beta, Sigma Delta Epsilon. Club: Women's Department (Ruston). Home: 126 Llanfair Dr Ruston LA 71270

PATTON, STUART, scientist; b. Ebenezer, N.Y., Nov. 2, 1920; s. George and Ina (Neher) P.; B.S., Pa. State U., 1943; M.S., Ohio State U., 1947, Ph.D., 1948; m. Colleen Cecelia Lavelle, May 17, 1945; children—John, Richard, Gail, Thomas, Mary Catherine, Patricia, Joseph. Chemist, Borden Co., 1943-44; research fellow Ohio State U., 1946-48; mem. faculty Pa. State U., 1949—, prof., 1959—, Evan Pugh research prof. agr., 1966—; vis. scientist Scripps Instn. Oceanography; cons. in field, 1950—. Served to lt. (j.g.) USNR, 1944-46. Recipient Borden award chemistry milk Am. Chem. Soc., 1957, Agrl. and Food Chemistry award, 1975. Mem. A.A.A.S., Am. Chem. Soc., Am. Dairy Sci. Assn. (dir. 1963-66), Am. Oil Chemists Assn., Am. Soc. Biol. Chemists, Am. Soc. Cell Biology, Sigma Xi. Author: (with Robert Jenness) Principles of Dairy Chemistry, 1959; (with Robert G. Jensen) Biomedical Aspects of Lactation, 1975. Home: 6208 Avenida Cresta LaJolla CA 92037 Office: Borland Lab University Park PA 16802

PATTON, THOMAS F., bus. cons.; b. Cleve., Dec. 6, 1903; s. John T. and Anna (Navin) P.; J.D., Ohio State U., 1926; LL.D., Cleve. Marshall Law Sch., 1953, U. Dayton, 1954, John Carroll U., 1954, Case Inst. Tech., 1961, Ohio State U., 1965, U. Akron, 1964; m. Arline Everitt, June 6, 1928; children—Arline (Mrs. Richard M. Brennan), Carol (Mrs. Michael L. Moore). Admitted to Ohio bar, 1926; mem. firm Andrews & Belden, 1926-32, partner successor firm Belden, Young & Veach, 1932-36; gen. counsel Republic Steel Corp. and subsidiary cos., 1936-44, v.p., gen. counsel, 1944-53, asst. pres., 1st v.p., 1953-56, pres., 1956-68, chief exec. officer, 1960-71, chmn. bd., 1963-71, hon. chmn. bd., 1971-76, dir., 1943-76. Trustee in bankruptcy reorgn. Erie Lackawanna Ry. Co., U.S. Dist. Ct. for No. Dist. Ohio, Eastern Div. Chmn. bd., chief exec. officer Am. Iron and Steel Inst., 1962-65, dir., 1961-71. Trustee charitable, civic and bus. assns. Mem. Bus. Council, Order of Coif, Phi Kappa Theta, Phi Delta Phi. Clubs: Union, The Country, Pepper Pike Country (Cleve.); Rolling Rock (Ligonier, Pa.). Home: 2711 Landon Rd Shaker Heights OH 44122 Office: Midland Bldg Cleveland OH 44115

PATTON, WARREN L., lawyer; b. Berkeley, Calif., Aug. 7, 1912; B.S., Calif. Inst. Tech., 1934; student Loyola U., Los Angeles, also U. So. Calif.; J.D., Mpls.-Minn. Coll. Law, 1947; m. Mildred Elizabeth Ronneberg, Dec. 29, 1943; children—Kathleen Susan, Harvey Michael. Admitted to Calif. bar, 1948, U.S. Supreme Ct., 1953, also U.S. Patent Office; partner firm Fulwider, Patton, Rieber, Lee & Utecht, Los Angeles. Mem. I.E.E.E., Am., Los Angeles County, Santa Monica Bay Dist. bar assns., State Bar Calif. (pres. patent conf. 1969-70, v.p. conf. 1968-69), Am. Patent Law Assn., Patent Law Assn. Los Angeles (pres. 1967-68). Author: An Author's Guide to the New Copyright Law, 1978. Home: 1336 Las Canoas Rd Pacific Palisades CA 90272 Office: 3435 Wilshire Blvd Los Angeles CA 90010

PATTON, WENDELL MELTON, JR., coll. pres.; b. Spartanburg, S.C., July 10, 1922; s. Wendell Melton and Emily Jane (Harris) P.; student Wofford Coll.; B.S., U. Ga., 1946, M.S., 1948; Ph.D., Purdue U., 1950; grad. Advanced Mgmt. Course, Colgate U.; LL.D., Wake Forest U., 1961; m. Martha Jane Matthews, July 5, 1944; children—Wendell III, Leland, Melissa, Brooks B. Asst. registrar U. Ga., 1946-48, asst. prof., 1946-48; prof. edn. and psychology Lander Coll., 1948, treas., dept. head, 1948-52; sr. asso. Bruce Payne & Assos., Inc., mgmt. cons., 1952-55; asst. gen. mgr. Shuford Mills, Inc., Hickory, N.C., 1955-59; pres. High Point (N.C.) Coll., 1959—; dir. Jefferson-Pilot Growth Fund, Inc., J.-P Income Fund, Furniture Library, N.C. Assn. Ind. Colls. and Univs. Served as capt. Air Transport Command, AUS, 1942-45. Licensed practicing psychologist, N.C.; licensed applied psychologist, Ga. Mem. Am. Mgmt. Assn., Am. Psychol. Assn., SAR, Phi Beta Kappa, Sigma Xi, Phi Kappa Phi, Delta Kappa Pi, Psi Chi. Methodist. Rotarian. Contbr. trade and profl. publs. Home: 2431 Gordon Rd High Point NC 27260

PATTULLO, ANDREW, found. exec.; b. Omaha, Feb. 12, 1917; s. Andrew and Dorothy Anna (Askwith) P.; B.S. in Bus. Adminstrn., U. Nebr., 1941, D.Sc. (hon.), 1979; M.B.A. in Hosp. Adminstrn., U. Chgo., 1943; m. Jean Harriet Fralick, May 1, 1941; children—Andrew, Douglas Ernest. Fellow, W.K. Kellogg Found., Battle Creek, Mich., 1943-44, asso. dir. div. hosps., 1944-51, dir. div. hosps., 1951-67, program dir., 1967-71, v.p. programs, 1971-75, v.p., 1975-78, sr. v.p., 1978—, trustee, 1972—; non-resident lectr. U. Mich. Sch. Public Health, 1960—. Mem. Fed. Hosp. Council, 1965-73; mem. Nat. Adv. Com. on Nursing Home Adminstrn., 1968-69; mem. com. on health careers Nat. Health Council, 1964-70; cons. USPHS, 1962-64, Bur. Health Services Research, Dept. HEW, 1968-78; mem. vis. com. on for sponsored research M.I.T., 1976—; mem. nat. adv. council Health Services Research Center, U. Mo.-Columbia, 1977—; mem. adv. council Mich. Mental Health Facilities, 1965-72, Gov.'s Action Com. on Health Care, 1963-66; chmn. community betterment award com. Mich. Welfare League, 1962, 63; mem. Mich. Adv. Hosp. Council, 1960-72; mem. Gov.'s Commn. on Govtl. Relations, 1954-56; mem. Adv. Commn. Prepaid Hosp. and Med. Care, 1962. Pres. Battle Creek Area United Fund, 1963, chmn. fund drive, 1960; pres. Battle Creek YMCA, 1959-60; pres. Nottawa Trails council Boy Scouts Am., 1957-60. Trustee, Calhoun County chpt. A.R.C., 1962-65; bd. dirs. Great Lakes Health and Edn. Found., 1973-74; bd. dirs. Calhoun County unit Am. Cancer Soc., 1976-78, chmn. com. on founds. Mich. div., 1978—; trustee Mich. Health Council, 1951-74, pres., 1967. Recipient Distinguished Service award U. Chgo. Hosp. Adminstrn. Alumni Assn., 1955; Tri-State Hosp. Assembly award, 1963; award of merit Am. Assn. Hosp. Planning, 1966; award for advancement edn. in hosp. adminstrn. Assn. U. Programs in Hosp. Adminstrn., 1968; Key award for meritorious service Mich. Hosp. Assn., 1970; Trustees award Am. Hosp. Assn., 1972; Distinguished Service award Mich. Health Council, 1973; Distinguished Service award Hosp. Mgmt. Systems Soc. of Am. Hosp. Assn., 1974; Silver Beaver award Boy Scouts Am. Fellow Am. Pub. Health Assn., Am. Coll. Hosp. Adminstrs. (hon.); mem. Am. Hosp. Assn. (adv. council hosp. research and ednl. trust 1960-67, mem. council research and edn. 1959-62; life mem.), Mich. Hosp. Assn. (trustee 1949-55, pres. 1954-55; life mem.), Internat. Hosp. Fedn., Mich. Pub. Health Assn., Can. Coll. Health Service Execs. (hon.). Home: 162 Feld Dr Battle Creek MI 49017 Office: WK Kellogg Found 400 North Ave Battle Creek MI 49016

PATTY, CLAIBOURNE WATKINS, JR., educator; b. Cleve., Feb. 19, 1934; s. Claibourne Watkins and Eleanor (Todd) P.; B.A., U. of South, 1955; J.D., U. Ark., 1961; m. Barbara Benton, May 4, 1968; children—Claibourne Watkins III, William Jordan. Admitted to Ark. bar, 1961; law clk. U.S. dist. judge, Ft. Smith, 1961-63; pvt. practice, Little Rock, 1963-68; asst. ins. commr. State of Ark., 1968-69; trust officer Union Nat. Bank of Little Rock, 1969-77; asst. dean U. Ark. Sch. Law, Little Rock, also exec. dir. Ark. Inst. for Continuing Legal Edn., 1977—; lectr. law Ark. Sch. Law, 1965; bd. dirs., chmn. Pulaski County Legal Aid Bur., 1966-69; bd. dirs., pres. Family Service Agy. of Central Ark., 1976-78. Served with AUS, 1955-57. Mem. Beta Theta Pi, Phi Alpha Delta. Office: U Ark Sch Law 400 W Markham St Little Rock AR 72201

PATTY, CLARENCE WAYNE, educator; b. Ringgold, Ga., Oct. 7, 1932; s. Perry M. and Ludie (Tate) P.; B.S., U. Ga., 1954, M.A., 1958, Ph.D., 1960; m. Jean O'Neal Williamson, June 9, 1976; children by previous marriage—Robert, Clarence Wayne, Christine. Research instr. U. N.C., Chapel Hill, 1960-61, asst. prof., 1961-64, asso. prof., 1964-67; prof. math. Va. Polytech. Inst. and State U., 1967—, acting chmn. dept., 1968-69, chmn., 1970—. Served with AUS, 1954-56. Mem. Am. Math. Soc., Math. Assn. Am., AAUP, Nat. Council Tchrs. Math., AAAS, Phi Beta Kappa, Sigma Xi, Phi Kappa Phi, Pi Mu Epsilon, Phi Eta Sigma. Contbr. articles math. jours. Home: 2010 Carroll Dr Blacksburg VA 24060

PATZ, ARNALL, physician; b. Elberton, Ga., June 14, 1920; s. Samuel and Sarah (Berman) P.; student U. Ga., 1940-41; B.S., Emory U., 1942, M.D., 1945; m. Ellen B. Levy, Mar. 12, 1950; children—William, Susan, David, Jonathan. Pvt. practice ophthalmology, Balt., 1951-70; faculty ophthalmology Johns Hopkins Sch. Medicine, 1955—, prof., 1973—, William Holland Wilmer prof., chmn. dept. ophthalmology, dir. Wilmer Ophthal. Inst., 1979—; dir. Med. Eye Bank of Md., Nat. Soc. Prevention Blindness; mem. Nat. Diabetes Adv. Bd., 1978-82. First recipient Edward Lorenzo Holmes award Inst. Medicine Chgo., 1954; Sight-Saving award D.C. Soc. Prevention Blindness 1954; E. Mead Johnson award Am. Acad. Pediatrics, 1956; Albert Lasker award Am. Pub. Health Assn., 1956; 1st Seeing Eye Research Prof. Ophthalmology award, 1970. Mem. AMA. (Billings silver medal 1973), Am. Acad. Ophthalmology and Otolaryngology, Assn. Research Ophthalmology, Am. Ophthal. Soc., Balt. City Med. Soc., Md. Soc. Prevention Blindness (past pres.), Pan-Am. Assn. Ophthalmology. Editorial bd. Am. Jour. Ophthalmology; sect. editor Survey of Ophthalmology. Home: 2 A Slade Ave Baltimore MD 21208 Office: Wilmer Inst Johns Hopkins Hosp Baltimore MD 21205

PATZ, EDWARD FRANK, lawyer; b. Balt., Aug. 25, 1932; s. Maurice A. and Violet (Furman) P.; B.S., U. Md., 1954, LL.B., 1959; m. Betty Seldner Levi, Nov. 18, 1956; children—Evelyn Anne, Edward Frank, Thomas L. Admitted to Md. bar, 1959; partner firm Ottenheimer, Cahn & Patz and predecessors, Balt., 1959—. Bd. dirs. Jewish Family and Children's Service, 1965-71; mem. regional bd. dirs. NCCJ. Mem. Am., Md., Balt. bar assns., Am. Judicature Soc., Comml. Law League Am. Clubs: Center, Suburban of Baltimore County (bd. govs., pres.). Home: 7917 Stevenson Rd Pikesville MD 21208 Office: Sun Life Bldg Baltimore MD 21201

PAUCK, WILHELM, educator; b. Laasphe, Westphalia, Germany, Jan. 31, 1901; s. Wilhelm and Maria (Hofmann) P.; grad. Real Gymnasium, Berlin-Steglitz, 1920; Lic. Theology, U. Berlin, 1925; Dr.Theology, h.c., U. Giessen, 1933; Litt.D., Upsala Coll., 1964, Thiel Coll., 1967; D.D., Gustavus Adolphus Coll., 1967, U. Edinburgh (Scotland), 1968; m. Olga C. Gumbel-Dietz, May 1, 1928 (dec. 1963); m. 2d, Marion Hausner, Nov. 21, 1964. Came to U.S., 1925, naturalized, 1937. Prof. ch. history Chgo. Theol. Sem., 1926-39; prof. hist. theology U. Chgo., 1939-53, prof. history, 1945-53; prof. ch. history Union Theol. Sem., 1953-60, Charles A. Briggs Grad. prof. ch. history, 1960-67; Distinguished prof. ch. history Vanderbilt U., Nashville, 1967-72, Stanford, 1972—. Exchange prof. U. Frankfurt (Germany), 1948-49. Mem. United Ch. of Christ. Fellow Am. Acad. Arts and Scis.; mem. Am. Soc. Ch. History (pres. 1936), Am. Theol. Soc. (pres. 1962-63). Author: Das Reich Gottes auf Erden, 1928; Karl Barth-Prophet of a New Christianity?, 1931; The Heritage of the Reformation, 1951, rev. edit., 1961; Luther's Lectures on Romans, 1961; Harnack and Troeltsch, Two Historical Theologians, 1968; Melanchthon and Bucer, 1969. Co-author: The Church against the World, 1935; Religion and Politics, 1946; The Ministry in Historical Perspective, 1956; (with Marion Pauck) The Life of Paul Tillich, 1976. Contbr. to Environmental Factors in Christian History, 1939; Religion and the Present Crisis, 1942; also theol. and hist. jours. Home: 1742 Willow Rd Palo Alto CA 94304

PAUL, ALDRICH KOSSUTH, educator; b. Dallas Center, Iowa, July 28, 1922; s. Harry H. and Betsy Marie (Aldrich) P.; A.B., No. U. Iowa, 1947; M.S., Drake U., 1951; Ph.D., U. Denver, 1954; m. Mary Ellen Gaedke, May 26, 1946; children—Michael Aldrich, Jeffrey Paul. Tchr. speech and drama high schs. in Eldora and Ames, Iowa, 1948-51; dir. forensics Iowa State U., 1954-56; prof., head dept. speech U. Omaha, 1956-64; prof., head dept. speech and theatre arts U. Cin., 1964-69; pres. Upper Iowa U., 1970-77; prof. orgn. communication Edinboro (Pa.) State Coll., 1977—; cons. to govt. and industry, 1957—. Pres. Omaha Radio-TV Council, 1958. Served to capt. AUS, 1943-46. Decorated Bronze Star (3). Mem. Am. Assn. U. Profs. (pres. U. Omaha chpt. 1960), Am. Council Better Broadcasts (pres. 1960, treas. 1967), Nat. Soc. Study Communication, Nat. Soc. Gen. Semantics, Speech Assn. Am., Omicron Delta Kappa, Phi Delta Kappa, Delta Sigma Rho, Sigma Phi Epsilon. Lion (pres. Westside club Omaha 1960). Author: Speech Management, 1961; also articles. Asso. editor Ohio Speech Jour., 1966. Home: 12 Terrace Dr Edinboro PA 16412. *If there is one factor in success that may be ahead of good speaking; it is the other half of speaking-which is good listening!*

PAUL, ARA GARO, univ. dean; b. New Castle, Pa., Mar. 1, 1929; s. John Hagop and Mary (Injejikian) P.; B.S. in Pharmacy, Idaho State U., 1950; M.S., U. Conn., 1953; Ph.D. in Pharmacognosy, 1956; m. Shirley Elaine Waterman, Dec. 21, 1962; children—John Bartlett, Richard Goyan. Cons. plant physiology Argonne (Ill.) Nat. Lab., 1955; asst. prof. pharmacognosy Butler U., Indpls., 1956-57; mem. faculty U. Mich., Ann Arbor, 1957—, prof. pharmacognosy, 1969—, dean Coll. Pharmacy, 1975—; vis. prof. microbiology Tokyo U., 1965-66; mem. vis. chemistry faculty U. Calif., Berkeley, 1972-73. Del. U.S. Pharmacopeial Conv., 1980. G. Pfeiffer Meml. fellow Am. Found. Pharm. Edn., 1965-66; fellow Eli Lilly Found., 1951-53, Am. Found. Pharm. Edn., 1954-56, NIH, 1972-73; recipient Outstanding Tchr. award Coll. Pharmacy, U. Mich., 1969, Outstanding Alumnus award Idaho State U., 1976. Fellow AAAS; mem. Am., Mich. pharm. assns., Am. Soc. Pharmacognosy (chmn. sci. program com. 1967, chmn. constn. and by-laws com. 1969), Acad. Pharm. Scis., Am. Assn. Colls. Pharmacy (co-chmn. tchr. seminar 1967, com. on research and grad. affairs), Washtenaw County Pharm. Soc., Am. Soc. Hosp. Pharmacists. Home: 1415 Brooklyn Ave Ann Arbor MI 48104 Office: Coll Pharmacy Univ Mich Ann Arbor MI 48109

PAUL, ARTHUR, pub. co. exec.; b. Chgo., Jan. 18, 1925; s. William and Becky (Goldenberg) P.; student Inst. Design, 1947-51; m. Beatrice Miller, Dec. 24, 1949 (div. 1973); children—William Warren, Fredric; m. 2d, Suzanne Seed, Mar. 8, 1975. Free lance illustrator, designer, 1951-53; designer 1st issue Playboy Mag., 1953; v.p., dir. art HMH Pub. Co., Chgo., 1962—, also sr. art dir., corporate art dir. Playboy Mag.; exhibited in one man shows at Etc. Gallery, 1949, 500D Gallery, 1965, U. Ill., 1965; organizer, exhibitor travelling exhbn. Beyond Illustration-The Art of Playboy, museums Europe, Asia, U.S., 1971-73, Can., 1976-77; lectr. in field. Trustee Chgo. Mus. Contemporary Art. Served with USAAF, 1943-46. Recipient numerous art awards, 1951—, including Polycube award Art Dirs. Club Phila., 1975; award Art Direction Mag., 1975; Art Inst. scholar, 1943. Hon. mem. Artist Guild Chgo., Soc. Typog. Arts, Chgo. Soc. Communicating Arts, 27 Designers Chgo.; mem. Alliance Graphique Internationale. Home: 175 E Delaware Chicago IL 60611 Office: 919 N Michigan Ave Chicago IL 60611. *Design is more than a sense of order for me. It is beauty and common sense. To draw, to paint and to look at art is in the fabric of my life. I enjoy working with ideas and seeing them develop into a reality, after which I am fortunate enough to learn whether they have performed as intended.*

PAUL, BENJAMIN DAVID, educator, anthropologist; b. N.Y.C., Jan. 25, 1911; s. Phillip and Esther (Kranz) P.; student U. Wis., 1928-29; A.B., U. Chgo., 1938, Ph.D. in Anthropology, 1942; m. Lois Fleischman, Jan. 4, 1936; children—Robert Allen, Janice Carol. Lectr., research dir. Yale, 1942-44; community orgn. expert Inter-Am. Ednl. Found., 1946; from lectr. to asso. prof. anthropology Harvard, 1946-62; dir. social sci. program Sch. Pub. Health, 1951-62; fellow Center Advanced Study Behavioral Scis., 1962-63; prof. anthropology Stanford, 1963—, chmn. dept., 1967-71, dir. program in medicine and behavioral sci., 1963-70. Cons. NIH, 1957—. Served to 2d lt. AUS, 1944-46. Travelling fellow Social Sci. Research Council, 1940-41. Fellow Am. Anthrop. Assn.; mem. Phi Beta Kappa, Sigma Xi. Editor: Health, Culture and Community: Case Studies of Pubic Reactions to Health Programs, 1955; Changing Marriage Patterns in a Highland Guatemalan Community, 1963; The Maya Midwife as Sacred Professional, 1975. Ethnographic field research in Guatemala, 1941, 62, 64, 65, 68, 69, 73-79. Home: 622 Salvatierra St Stanford CA 94305

PAUL, DAVID IRWIN, physicist; b. N.Y.C., Apr. 4, 1928; s. Philip and Frances (Wolfson) P.; A.B. in Math. with honors, UCLA, 1950, M.A. in Math., 1951, Ph.D. in Physics, 1956; m. Carolyn Keiler, Aug. 19, 1973; children—Jacob Gershon, Hannah Lisa, Sanders Michael. Research scientist Hughes Aircraft Co. Culver City, Calif., 1956-57; asst. prof. physics UCLA, 1957-62; scientist Inst. Def. Analysis, Arlington, Va., 1962-63; prof. solid state and materials sci., Sch Engring and Applied Sci., Columbia U., 1963—; vis. prof. Hebrew U., Jerusalem, 1975, Oxford (Eng.) U., 1970-71, 77-78. Served to 2d lt. USAF, 1952-53. NSF grantee, 1965-77; Office Naval Research grantee, 1959-70. Fellow Am. Phys. Soc.; mem. AIME, Magnetics Soc., Phi Beta Kappa. Jewish. Contbr. articles on solid state sci., especially magnetic properties of materials to profl. jours. Office: Sch Engring Columbia U New York NY 10027

PAUL, DAVID LEWIS, real estate developer; b. N.Y.C., May 1, 1939; s. Isadore and Ruth (Goldstein) P.; B.S. in Econs., U. Pa., Isadore and Ruth (Goldstein) P.; B.S. in Econs., Wharton Sch., U. Pa., 1951; M.B.A., Columbia U., 1965, J.D., 1967; Ph.D. in Planning, Harvard U., 1968; children—David J., Michael M. Developer Hawthorne Towers, Montclair, N.J., 1967, Colony House, Lakewood, N.J., 1968, Pequannock (N.J.) Shopping Plaza, 1969, Townhouse of Amherst (Mass.), 1971, Brandywine Village, Amherst, 1972, Shrewsbury, Mass., 1973, Regency Hyatt House, Sarasota, Fla., 1974, Tall Oaks Village, Weymouth, Mass., 1975, Somerset Village, Ft. Lauderdale, Fla., 1977, Green Knolls, Brockton, Mass., 1977, Am. Furniture Mart, Chgo., 1979, others. Trustee, Mt. Sinai Med. Center, N.Y.C., U. City N.Y., Mt. Sinai Hosp., N.Y.C., Mt. Sinai Sch. Nursing and Neustadter Convalescent Center, N.Y.C.; bd. dirs., governing mem. Lincoln Center Repertory Theatre, N.Y.C. Author: The effect of the AFL-CIO Merger on Centralization, 1961; Progressive Architecture, 1967. Office: 666 N Lake Shore Dr Chicago IL 60611

PAUL, DAVID TYLER, publisher; b. N.Y.C., Nov. 18, 1934; s. Samuel H. and Margaret (Tyler) P.; student Colgate U., 1953-54, Haverford Coll., 1954-56; B.F.A., R.I. Sch. Design, 1959; cert. in firemanics SUNY, 1976; children—Sarah, Adam David; m. Barbara Jean Bartenope, Apr. 1978. Account supr. Meriden Gravure Co. (Conn.), 1959-60; art dir., prodn. mgr. juvenile books Macmillan Co., 1960-62; art dir. Popular Boating mag., 1962-64; design dir. Parents Mag. Press, 1964-66; dir. design Random House, Inc., 1966-69; v.p., mng. editor Abelard-Schuman Ltd. & Criterion Books, 1969-70, pres., 1970-71; propr. Graphics Cons. by David T. Paul; pub. Drake Pubs., Inc., 1973-74; dir. Photo-Media, Ltd.; co-founder, editor The Fire Islander Mag., 1975-77; mng. editor Northeastern Indsl. World mag., 1977; sr. editor for video and audiovisual Cambridge Book Co., 1976-78, mng. editor, 1978—. Chief Fire Island Pines Vol. Fire Dept., 1976. Recipient awards Soc. Illustrators, Lithographers and Printers Nat. Assn., Graphic Arts Council Chgo. Mem. Am. Inst. Graphic Arts (award). Democrat. Author: Harbor Tug, 1967; Tugboat Adventure, 1967. Home: 350 W 85th St New York NY 10024. *Work hard, play hard, sleep when you have to, never be afraid to experiment or change, and always inject or respond to the humor found in every facet of life.*

PAUL, DONALD ROSS, chem. engr., educator; b. Yeatesville, N.C., Mar. 20, 1939; s. Edgar R. and Mary E. (Cox) P.; B.S., N.C. State Coll., 1961; M.S., U. Wis., 1963, Ph.D., 1965; m. Sally Annette Cochran, Mar. 28, 1964; children—Mark Allen, Ann Elizabeth. Research chem. engr. E.I. DuPont de Nemours & Co., Richmond, Va., 1960-61; instr. chem. engring. dept. U. Wis., Madison, 1963-65; research chem. engr. Chemstrand Research Center, Durham, N.C., 1965-67; asst. prof. chem. engring. U. Tex., Austin, 1967-70, asso. 1970-73, prof., 1973—, T. Brockett Hudson prof., 1978—, chmn. dept. chem. engring., 1977—; cons. in field. Recipient award Engring. News Record, 1975, Ednl. Service award Plastics Inst. Am., 1975, awards U. Tex. Student Engring. Council, 1972, 75, 76; award for engring. teaching Gen. Dynamics Corp., 1977. Mem. Am. Chem. Soc. (Doolittle award 1973), Am. Inst. Chem. Engrs., Soc. Plastics Engrs., Fiber Soc., Phi Eta Sigma, Tau Beta Pi, Phi Kappa Phi, Sigma Xi. Author: (with F.W. Harris) Controlled Release Polymeric Formulations, 1976; (with S. Newman) Polymer Blends, 2 vols., 1978. Mem. editorial adv. bds. Jour. Membrane Sci., 1976—, Polymer Engring. and Sci., 1975—, Jour. Applied Polymer Sci., 1979—; contbr. articles to profl. jours. Home: 7104 Spurlock Dr Austin TX 78731 Office: Dept Chemical Engineering U Texas Austin TX 78712

PAUL, ELIAS, food co. cons.; b. Michigan City, Ind., Nov. 16, 1919; s. Phillip P. and Esther (Kranz) P.; B.S., U. Ill., 1947; m. Gloria Payne, Aug. 24, 1942; children—Nancy E., Janet L. Exec., div. mgr. Swift & Co., Chgo., 1947-64; exec. operating com. Hygrade Food Products, Detroit, 1965; v.p., gen. mgr. meat div. Cudahy Co., Phoenix, 1966, pres., 1966-71, also chief exec. officer, dir.; chmn. bd. Am. Salt Co., Kansas City, Mo., 1966-71, Milk Specialties Co., Dundee, Ill.; ret. pres., chief exec. officer, dir. John Morrell & Co., Chgo.; chmn. bd. Golden Sun Feed Co., John Morrell & Co. Ltd.; cons. United Brands, Boston. Chmn., dir. Am. Meat Inst.; mem. Ariz. Retirement System Bd. and Investment Adv. Council Served to maj. Chem. Corps, AUS, 1941-46. Mem. Gamma Sigma Delta, Phi Kappa Phi. Home: 7017 N Desert Fairways Dr Scottsdale AZ 85253

PAUL, GABRIEL (GABE), profl. baseball club exec.; b. Rochester, N.Y., Jan. 4, 1910; s. Morris and Celia (Snyder) P.; ed. pub. schs., Rochester; m. Mary Frances Copps, Apr. 17, 1939; children—Gabriel, Warren, Michael, Jennie Lou, Henry. Reporter, Rochester Democrat and Chronicle, 1926-28; publicity mgr., ticket mgr. Rochester Baseball Club, 1928-34, traveling sec., dir., 1934-36; publicity dir. Cin. Reds Baseball Club, 1937, traveling sec., 1938-48, asst. to pres., 1948-49, v.p., 1949-60, gen. mgr., 1951-60; v.p., 1949-60; v.p., gen. mgr. Houston Astros Baseball Club, 1960-61; gen. mgr. Cleve. Indians Baseball Club, 1961-63, pres., treas., 1963-72, pres., 1978—; pres. N.Y. Yankees, 1973-77. Dir. or trustee various charitable instns. Served with inf. AUS, 1943-45. Named Major League Exec. of Year, Sporting News, 1956, 74, Sports Exec. of Year, Gen. Sports Time, 1956, Baseball Exec. of Year, Sporting News, 1974, Major League Exec. of Year, U.P., 1976; recipient J. Lewis Comiskey Meml. award Chgo. chpt. Baseball Writers Assn. Am., 1961, Judge Emil Fuchs Meml. award Boston chpt., 1967, Bill Slocum award N.Y. chpt., 1975, Sports Torch of Learning award, 1976. Clubs: Palma Ceia Country (Tampa, Fla.); Cleve. Athletic; Shaker Heights (Ohio) Country. Office: Cleveland Stadium Cleveland OH 44114. *Hard work is the greatest of all vehicles. It overcomes many inadequacies.*

PAUL, GORDON LEE, educator, psychologist; b. Marshalltown, Iowa, Sept. 2, 1935; s. Leon Dale and Ione Hickman (Perry) P.; student Marshalltown Community Coll., 1953-54, San Diego City Coll., 1955-57; B.A., U. Ia., 1960; M.A., U. Ill., 1962, Ph.D., 1964; m. Joan Marie Wyatt, Dec. 24, 1954; children—Dennis Leon, Dana Lee, Joni Lynn. Social sci. analyst VA Hosp., Danville, Ill., 1962; counseling psychologist U. Ill., Urbana, 1963; clin. psychologist VA Hosp., Palo Alto, Calif., 1964-65; pvt. practice clin. psychology, 1964-65; asst. prof. psychology U. Ill., Champaign-Urbana, 1965-67, asso. prof., 1967-70, prof., 1970—; pvt. practice psychology, Champaign, 1965—. Psychotherapy research cons., Palo Alto, 1964-65; treatment program cons. Ill. Dept. Mental Health, 1965-73; cons. NIMH, 1968-72; adviser Ontario (Calif.) Mental Health Found., 1968-69, NSF, 1968-69, Can. Council, 1969—. Served with USN, 1954-58. Recipient Creative Talent award Am. Inst. research, 1964, Teaching award U. Ill., 1968, 1975. NIMH fellow, 1963-64. Fellow Am. Psychol. Assn. (corr. com. 1965-70, pres. sect. III div. 12, 1972-73, exec. com. div. 12, 1974-77, Disting. Scientist award sect. III, div. 12, 1977); mem. Midwestern Psychol. Assn., Phi Beta Kappa, Chi Gamma Iota. Author: Insight vs. Desensitization in Psychotherapy; An Experiment in Anxiety Reduction, 1966; Anxiety and Clinical Problems, 1973; Psychosocial Treatment of Chronic Mental Patients, 1977. Editorial bd. Behavior Therapy, 1969-76. Behavior Therapy and Exptl. Psychiatry, 1969—, Schizophrenia Bull., 1971—, Jour. Abnormal Psychology, 1972-75. Cons. editor, Jour. Applied Behavior Analysis, 1968—, Psychol. Bull., 1968—, Jour. Abnormal Psychology, 1970-72, 76—, Psychosomatic Medicine, 1970—, Jour. Clin. and Cons. Psychology, 1972—. Contbr. articles to profl. jours. Home: 1817 Maynard Dr Champaign IL 61820 Office: 6th and Daniels Sts Champaign IL 61820

PAUL, JACK, lawyer; b. Los Angeles, July 31, 1928; s. Max (dec.) and Ida (Zacky) P.; B.A., U. Calif. at Los Angeles, 1950; LL.B., Stanford, 1952; LL.M. (Grad. Law scholar 1952-53), Harvard, 1953; children—Nancy Lynne, Steven Wayne, James Robert. Admitted to Cal. bar, 1953, D.C. bar, 1953, U.S. Supreme Ct. bar, 1963; atty. Beilenson & Meyer, Beverly Hills, Calif., 1956; pvt. practice law, Beverly Hills, 1956-65, Los Angeles, 1965-68; partner Paul & Gordon, Los Angeles, 1968-72, sr. member Paul & Gordon Law Corp., 1972—. Part-time instr. U. Calif., Los Angeles, 1957-67; guest speaker various univs. Mem. Beverly Hills Bd. Edn., 1967-75, pres., 1970-71, 73-74. Bd. dirs. Beverly Hills YMCA, 1967-75, Vista Del Mar, Los Angeles, 1971—; pres. Men's Club Mt. Sinai Hosp., 1958. Served with USAF, 1954-55. Fellow Nat. Contract Mgmt. Assn.; mem. Am., Fed., Calif., Beverly Hills, Los Angeles County bar assns., Beverly Hills Jr. Bar Assn. (trustee 1963-64), Phi Beta Kappa. Club: Hillcrest Country (Los Angeles). Author: United States Government Contracts and Subcontracts, 1964. Editor: Stanford Law Rev., 1952. Office: 1800 Ave of Stars Suite 822 Los Angeles CA 90067

PAUL, JAMES CAVERLY NEWLIN, univ. dean; b. Chestnut Hill, Pa., Apr. 30, 1926; s. William Allen Butler and Adelaide Sims (Newlin) P.; grad. Germantown Friends Sch., 1943; B.A., Princeton, 1948; J.D., U. Pa., 1951; m. Margaret Morris Clausen, June 25, 1948; children—Nicholas Newlin, Martha Morris, Adelaide Sims. Admitted to Pa. bar, 1952; legal sec. to Chief Justice of the U.S., 1951-53; asst. prof. U. N.C., 1953-55; asst. dir. Inst. Govt. of U. N.C., 1953-55; prof. law, dir. Inst. Legal Research, U. Pa., 1955-63; prof. law, dean faculty of law Haile Selassie U., Ethiopia, 1963-67, v.p. acad. affairs, 1967-69; exec. v.p. Ednl. and World Affairs, N.Y.C., 1969-70; dean Sch. of Law, Rutgers U., Newark, 1970-74, prof. law, 1970—; research dir. Internat. Legal Center, N.Y.C., 1974—; adj. prof. Columbia U., 1973—. Candidate for U.S. Congress from 9th Dist. Pa., 1958; del. Dem. Nat. Conv., 1960. Served with USNR, 1943-46; PTO. Recipient spl. medal for distinguished service to univ. edn. in Ethiopia, 1969. Mem. Am., N.J., Pa. bar assns., Assn. Bar City N.Y., Order of Coif. Club; Princeton (N.Y.C.). Author: Rift in the Democracy, 1951; Federal Censorship, 1961; Ethiopian Constitutional Development, 1969. Home: 417 Clark St South Orange NJ 07079 Office: 180 University Ave Newark NJ 07102. *My life in law and teaching about law gives satisfaction because it enables me to direct my energies towards thinking about social justice, individual dignity, and the possibilities of attaining more of the conditions enabling these ideals. But that satisfaction is tempered by constant realization of my own frailities and the failure everywhere of people, particularly those most fortunately endowed, to be guided by principled thinking.*

PAUL, JAMES ROBERT, energy co. exec.; b. Wichita, Sept. 10, 1934; s. Harold Robert and Zona Belle (Marlatt) P.; B.S., Wichita State U., 1956; m. Julia Ann Haigh, Aug. 14, 1955; children—John Robert, Jeffrey James, Julie Renee. With Boeing Co., Wichita, 1956-67, mgr. systems dept., 1966-67; mgmt. cons. Peat, Marwick and Co., Houston, 1967-70; v.p. fin. and adminstrn. Robertson Distribution Systems, Inc., Houston, 1970-73; treas. Colo. Interstate Gas Co., Colorado Springs, Colo., 1973-74; treas. Coastal States Gas Corp., Houston, 1974-75, v.p. fin., 1975-78, sr. v.p. fin., 1978—. Mem. Am. Petroleum Inst., Fin. Execs. Inst. Republican. Methodist. Office: 9 Greenway Plaza Houston TX 77046

PAUL, JOHN EUGENE, educator; b. Charleston, Ill., June 13, 1917; s. James Edward and Bertha Etoile (Lyon) P.; B.S., Eastern Ill. U., 1947; M.S., Purdue U., 1948, Ph.D., 1951; m. Mary Joan Shell, Aug. 22, 1943; children—John Stephen, George Franklin. Instr., asst. dir. Speech and Hearing Clinic, Purdue U., 1949-50; prof., dir. Speech and Hearing Clinic, U. Miss., 1952-56; dir. speech pathology U. Ala. Med. Coll., 1956-58; prof., chmn. dept. speech State U. N.Y., Geneseo, 1958-63, dir. div. speech, 1963-69, prof., 1969—, chmn., dir. Speech and Hearing Clinics, dept. speech pathology and audiology, 1969-76, prof., dir. Speech and Hearing Clinics, 1976—. Cons., Miss. Sch. for Deaf, Miss. Cerebral Palsy Hosp., Ala. Aid for Retarded Children, Ala. Spastic Soc., Bath (N.Y.) VA Center, 1971. Served with AUS, 1942-46, 51-52. Recipient XR Awards Purdue Research Found., 1950-51. Mem. Am. (award 1951, honors of assn. 1974), N.Y. State (founding sponsor, pres. 1961-62) speech and hearing assns., A.A.A.S., Am. Cleft Palate Assn. Episcopalian (vice deacon). Home: 17 Stuyvesant Manor Geneseo NY 14454

PAUL, JOHN JOSEPH, clergyman; b. La Crosse, Wis., Aug. 17, 1918; s. Roland Philip and Louise (Gilles) P.; B.A., Loras Coll., Dubuque, Iowa, 1939; S.T.B., St. Mary's Sem., Balt., 1943; M.Ed., Marquette U., 1959. Ordained priest, Roman Catholic Ch., 1943; prin. Regis High Sch., Eau Claire, Wis., 1948-55; rector Holy Cross Sem., La Crosse, 1955-66; rector St. Joseph's Cathedral, La Crosse, 1966-77; aux. bishop Diocese of La Crosse, 1977—. Address: Box 69 LaCrosse WI 54601

PAUL, JUSTUS FREDERICK, historian; b. Boonville, Mo., May 27, 1938; s. Firdel W. and Emma L. (Frankenfeld) P.; A.B., Doane Coll., Crete, Nebr., 1959; M.A., U. Wis., Madison, 1960; Ph.D., U. Nebr., 1966; m. Barbara Jane Dotts, Sept. 10, 1960; children—Justus, Rebecca, Ellen. Tchr., Wausau (Wis.) High Sch., 1960-62; instr. history U. Nebr., 1963-66; mem. faculty U. Wis., Stevens Point, 1966—, prof. history, 1973—, chmn. dept., 1969—. Grantee State of Wis., 1974-78, Am. Assn. State and Local History, 1968-69. Mem. Am. Hist. Assn., Orgn. Am. Historians, Hist. Soc. Wis., Nebr. Hist. Soc., U. Wis. Faculty Assn. Mem. United Ch. Christ. Author: Senator Hugh Butler and Nebraska Republicanism, 1976; editor: Selected Writings of Rhys W. Hays, 1977; co-editor: The Badger State: A Documentary History of Wisconsin, 1979. also articles. Home: 2001

Country Club Dr Stevens Point WI 54481 Office: Dept History Univ Wis Stevens Point WI 54481

PAUL, LEE GILMOUR, lawyer; b. Denver, July 27, 1907; s. Russell Barnett and Mary Ellen (Gilmour) P.; A.B., Bowdoin Coll., 1929, LL.D. (hon.), 1978; LL.B., Harvard, 1932; m. Gordon Dodge Leupp, Apr. 14, 1934; children—Jenifer (Mrs. Paul Monroe), Mary (Mrs. Dennis A. Collins), Deborah (Mrs. Robert W. Clemo). Admitted to Calif. bar, 1933; pvt. practice, Los Angeles, 1934-42; industry mem. Shipbldg. Commn., NWLB, 1942-46; partner firm Paul, Hastings & Janofsky, Los Angeles, 1946—. Pres., Pasadena (Calif.) Child Guidance Clinic, 1964-65, Los Angeles Boys Club, 1973—; chmn. Pasadena Council Alcoholism, 1966-68. Trustee Boys and Girls Aid Soc. Los Angeles County, 1968-72; bd. dirs. Pasadena's Charity Bank; bd. dirs. emeritus Emerald Bay Community Assn. Mem. Am., Los Angeles County bar assns., Sigma Nu. Clubs: California (Los Angeles); Valley Hunt (Pasadena). Home: 1064 Armada Dr Pasadena CA 91103 also 517 Emerald Bay Laguna Beach CA 92651 Office: 555 S Flower St Los Angeles CA 90071 also 18952 MacArthur Blvd Newport Beach CA 92663

PAUL, LES, entertainer, inventor; b. Waukesha, Wis., June 9, 1915; s. George and Evelyn (Stutz) Polsfuss; student pub. schs., Waukesha; children—Lester, Gene, Colleen, Robert, Mary. Appeared on numerous radio programs throughout Midwest in 1920's and 1930's; formed Les Paul Trio, 1936-37 and appeared with Fred Waring, N.Y.C.; appeared on first television broadcast with an orch. from NBC, N.Y.C., 1939; mus. dir. WJJD and WIND, Chgo., 1941; appeared with Mary Ford on own television show, Mahwah, N.J., 1953-57; host Edison 100th Anniversary of invention of phonograph at Edison Home, West Orange, N.J., 1977; recs. include Jazz at the Philharmonic, Paul Leslie and Shorty Nadiene, Lover and Brazil, 1948, Nola, 1949, Goofus, 1950, Tennessee Waltz, 1950, Little Rock Getaway, 1950, Mockin' Bird Hill, 1951, Just One More Chance, 1951, Walkin' and Whistlin' Blues, 1951, How High The Moon (Hall of Fame award 1979), 1951, Smoke Rings, 1952, The World's Waiting For The Sunrise, 1952, Tiger Rag, 1953, Meet Mr. Callaghan, 1953, Jazz Me Blues, 1952, Vaya Con Dios, 1954, Chester and Lester (Grammy award), 1976; album: Guitar Monsters (Grammy nominee), 1977. Served with Armed Forces Radio Service, World War II. Mem. Audio Engring. Soc., Am. Soc. Composers, Authors and Pubs., Screen Actors Guild, AFTRA, Am. Fedn. Musicians. Pioneer multi-track tape recorder; inventor 1st 8-track tape recorder; inventor sound-on-sound recording; creator Les Paul electric solid body guitars. . *To be successful requires hard work, determination, a positive attitude, believing in one's self, a God given talent and luck.*

PAUL, MARTIN AMBROSE, phys. chemist; b. N.Y.C., June 29, 1910; s. Martin and Rosena (Sing) P.; B.A., Coll. City N.Y., 1930; M.A., Columbia, 1931, Ph.D., 1936; m. Genevieve Wells, June 28, 1935; children—Harriet (Mrs. J. Henry Jonquiere), Dorothy (Mrs. Duvall A. Jones). Instr., Coll. City N.Y., 1930-42; research supr. Explosives Research Lab., NDRC, Bruceton, Pa., 1942-45; asst. prof. chemistry Triple Cities Coll., Syracuse U., 1946-48, asso. prof., 1948-50; prof. chemistry Harpur Coll., State U. N.Y. at Binghamton, 1950-65, chmn. dept., 1950-60; exec. sec. div. chemistry and chem. tech. Nat. Acad. Scis.-NRC, Washington, 1965-74, cons., 1974—. Vis. prof. Cornell U., several summers, U. Calif. at Los Angeles, 1957-58, Columbia, 1960-61. Exec. sec. XXIII Internat. Congress Pure and Applied Chemistry, 1971, sec. commn. on symbols, terminology and units, 1967-71, chmn., 1971-73, sec. com. on nomenclature and symbols, 1975—. Recipient Naval Ordnance Devel. award, 1946. John Simon Guggenheim fellow, 1957. Fellow A.A.A.S. (v.p., chmn. chemistry sect. 1972); Benjamin Franklin fellow Royal Soc. Arts; mem. Am. Chem. Soc., AAUP, Phi Beta Kappa, Sigma Xi, Phi Lambda Upsilon. Club: Cosmos (Washington). Author: Principles of Chemical Thermodynamics, 1951; Physical Chemistry, 1962; (with King, Farinholt) General Chemistry, 1967; also articles. Research on measurement of acidity in highly acid media, nature of indicators, catalysis by acids, thermodynamic properties of solutions, sci. policy. Home: 1772 Horatio Ave Merrick NY 11566

PAUL, OGLESBY, physician; b. Villanova, Pa., May 3, 1916; s. Oglesby and Laura Little (Wilson) P.; A.B. cum laude, Harvard, 1938, M.D. cum laude, 1942; m. Marguerite Black, May 29, 1943; children—Marguerite, Rodman. Intern. Mass. Gen. Hosp., Boston, 1942-43; asst. medicine Harvard Med. Sch., 1946-49; clin. asso. prof. medicine U. Ill., 1952-62, clin. prof. medicine, 1962; asst. attending physician Presbyn.-St. Luke's Hosp., 1951-54, asso. attending physician, 1954-59, attending physician, 1959-62; chief div. medicine Passavant Meml. Hosp., Chgo., 1963-72; prof. medicine Northwestern U., 1963-77, med. dir. Univ. Med. Assos., 1973-75, v.p. health scis., 1973-75; prof. medicine Harvard U. Sch. Medicine, Boston, 1977—, dir. admissions, 1977—; cons. U.S. Naval Hosp., Great Lakes, Ill., 1959-74. Mem. joint U.S.-U.K. Com. for Study Coronary and Pulmonary Disease, 1959—; chmn. gov.'s adv. com. Ill. Regional Med. Program on Heart Disease, Cancer and Stroke, 1967-70. dirs. Internat. Soc. Cardiology Found. Served from lt. (j.g.) to lt. M.C., USNR, 1943-46. Diplomate in cardiovascular disease Am. Bd. Internal Medicine. Fellow A.C.P., Am. Coll. Chest Physicians, Am. Coll. Cardiology, Royal Soc. Medicine (Eng.); mem. Assn. U. Cardiologists, Am. (pres. 1960-61), Chgo. (pres. 1966-67) heart assns., Am. Epidemiol. Soc., Am. Clin. and Climatol. Assn. Home: 40 Wood's End Rd Dedham MA 02026 Office: Harvard U Med Sch 25 Shattuck St Boston MA 02115

PAUL, ROBERT ARTHUR, steel co. exec.; b. N.Y.C., Oct. 28, 1937; s. Isadore and Ruth (Goldstein) P.; A.B., Cornell U., 1959; J.D., Harvard, 1962, M.B.A., 1964; m. Donna Rae Berkman, July 29, 1962; children—Laurence Edward, Stephen Eric, Karen Rachel. With Ampco-Pitts. Corp. (formerly Screw & Bolt Corp. Am.), 1964—, v.p., 1969-71, exec. v.p., 1972-79, pres., 1979—, treas., 1973—, dir., 1969—; v.p., dir. Steel Trading Corp., Dover Securities, Inc.; v.p., asst. sec., asst. treas., dir. Parkersburg Steel Corp., Louis Berkman Co., Follansbee Steel Corp., Louis Berkman Realty Co.; dir. 1st Dyna Corp., First Nat. Bank of Washington (Pa.); gen. partner Romar Trading Co. Instr., Grad. Sch. Indsl. Adminstrn., Carnegie Mellon U., 1966-69. Trustee H.L. and Louis Berkman Found.; trustee, treas. Ampco-Pitts. Found.; trustee Montefiore Hosp., Pitts.; trustee, v.p. YM & YWHA, Pitts.; trustee, treas. Pitts. Jewish Publ. and Edn. Found.; vice-chmn. bd. dirs. Vocat. Rehab. Center Allegheny County; bd. dirs., v.p. Riverview Apts. for Elderly. Mem. Am., Mass. bar assns., Soc. Security Analysts. Republican. Jewish. Clubs: Harvard (Boston and N.Y.C.); Concordia (dir.), Harvard-Yale-Princeton, Pitts. Athletic (Pitts.); Westmoreland Country (Export, Pa.). Home: 1236 Squirrel Hill Ave Pittsburgh PA 15217 Office: Porter Bldg Pittsburgh PA 15219

PAUL, ROBERT HENRY, JR., mgmt. cons.; b. Balt., Feb. 13, 1921; s. Robert Henry and Nettie Louise (Huber) P.; LL.B., U. Balt., 1941; m. Betty J. Carey, Oct. 6, 1945; children—Robert Carey, Richard Wright. Law clk. Armstrong, Machen & Allen, Balt., 1939-40; adminstrv. positions Glenn L. Martin Co., Balt., 1940-42; spl. agt. FBI, 1946-53; insp. ICA, Washington, 1953-57, regional insp., Athens, Greece, 1957-59, regional insp. Office Insp. Gen. and Comptroller, Dept. State, Athens, 1959-60, Frankfurt, Germany, 1960-62; dep. dir. mgmt. inspection staff AID, 1962-65; insp. in charge, mgmt. inspection staff USOM/Korea, Seoul, 1965-68; insp. in charge AID/Vietnam, Saigon, 1968-69; fgn. assistance insp., chief Latin Am. and Africa divs., inspection staff Office Auditor Gen., AID, Washington, 1970-74; mgmt. cons., 1974-76; realtor asso. Bethesda Realty Co., 1977—. Served from pvt. to 1st lt. USAAF, 1942-45. Decorated Air medal with clusters, D.F.C. Mem. Soc. Former Spl. Agts. FBI (treas., exec. com. mem. Washington chpt.), Montgomery County Bd. Realtors. Mason (32 deg.). Home: 9807 Inglemere Dr Bethesda MD 20034 Office: 4405 East West Hwy Bethesda MD 20014

PAUL, RODMAN WILSON, educator; b. Villa Nova, Pa., Nov. 6, 1912; s. Oglesby and Laura Little (Wilson) P.; A.B., Harvard, 1936, A.M., 1937, Ph.D., 1943; m. Anne Catherine Thomson, July 21, 1951; children—Rodman Wilson, Deborah Anne (Mrs. Charles Philip Gibbs), Judith Thomson. Asst. dean, instr. history Harvard, 1937-43; instr. history Yale, 1946-47; asso. prof. history Calif. Inst. Tech., Pasadena, 1947-51, prof., 1951-72, Edward S. Harkness prof., 1972—. Mem. Nat. Archives Adv. Council, Washington, 1968-77, chmn., 1977; mem. hist. adv. com. NASA, Washington, 1970-73. Chmn. dept. coll. work Diocese of Los Angeles, 1962-65, mem. standing com., 1965-69. Trustee, Calif. Hist. Soc. Served from lt. (j.g.) to lt. comdr. USNR, 1943-46. Huntington Library fellow, 1946, 61, Ford Fund for Advancement Edn. fellow, 1955-56, Guggenheim fellow, 1967-68. Mem. Western History Assn. (exec. council 1972-75, v.p. 1976-77, pres. 1977-78), Am. Hist. Assn., Orgn. Am. Historians. Democrat. Episcopalian. Club: Valley Hunt (Pasadena). Author: Abrogation of the Gentlemen's Agreement, 1936; California Gold, 1947; Mining Frontiers of the Far West, 1963; California Gold Discovery, 1966; A Victorian Gentlewoman in the Far West, 1972. Home: 370 California Terr Pasadena CA 91105 Office: Calif Inst Tech Pasadena CA 91125

PAUL, RON, congressman; b. Pitts., Aug. 20, 1935; grad. Gettysburg Coll.; M.D., Duke U.; m. Carol Wells, 1957; children—Ronnie, Lori, Randy, Robert, Joy Lynette. Intern, Henry Ford Hosp., Detroit, also resident in internal medicine; resident in Ob-gyn U. Pitts.; 96th Congress from Tex. 22d Dist. Bd. dirs. Community Hosp., Mem. Congl. action com. Brazosport (Tex.) C. of C.; mem. drug abuse com. Brazosport Ind. Sch. Dist.; mem. steering com. Community Conf. Tech. Vocat. Edn. Served with USAF, Air N.G. Fellow Am. Coll. Ob-Gyn.; mem. Brazoria County Med. Soc., Tex. Med. Soc. Episcopalian. Clubs: Kiwanis (past pres.), Aquatic (past pres.) (Lake Jackson, Tex.). Office: Longworth House Office Bldg Room B-227 Washington DC 20515

PAUL, RONALD STANLEY, research inst. exec.; b. Olympia, Wash., Jan. 19, 1923; s. Adolph and Olga (Klapstein) P.; student Linfield Coll., 1940-41, Reed Coll., 1943-44, Harvard, 1945; B.S., U. Oreg., 1947, M.S., 1949, Ph.D., 1951; m. Margery Jean Pengra, June 5, 1944; children—Kathleen (Mrs. Joel R. Crosby), Robert S., James N. Physicist, research mgr. Gen. Electric Co., Richland, Wash., 1951-64; asso. dir. Battelle-N.W. Labs., Richland, 1965-68, dir., 1971-72; dir. Battelle Seattle Research Center, 1969-70; v.p. ops. Battelle Meml. Inst., Columbus, Ohio, 1973-76, sr. v.p., 1976-78, exec. v.p., 1978—. Lectr. modern physics Center for Grad. Studies, Richland, 1951-62; IAEA cons. to Japan, 1962. Trustee, Linfield Coll., 1970-73, Pacific Sci. Center, 1969-74, Oreg. Mus. Sci. and Industry, 1971-72, Columbus Center Sci. and Industry, 1973—, Columbus Cancer Clinic, 1974—, Columbus Children's Hosp. Research Found., 1975—; v.p. exec. bd. Central Ohio council Boy Scouts Am., 1976—; mem. exec. bd. of fellows Seattle-Pacific Coll., 1970-73; bd. overseers Acad. for Contemporary Problems, 1971-75. Served with USAAF, 1943-46. Mem. Am. Phys. Soc., Am. Nuclear Soc., Sigma Xi, Sigma Pi Sigma, Pi Mu Epsilon. Republican. Baptist. Contbr. articles to profl. jours. Home: 803 Lookout Point Dr Worthington OH 43085 Office: 505 King Ave Columbus OH 43201

PAUL, SHERMAN, educator; b. Cleve., Aug. 26, 1920; s. Jacob and Gertrude (Leavitt) P.; B.A., U. Iowa, 1941; M.A., Harvard, 1948, Ph.D., 1950; m. Grace McDowell, May 1, 1943; children—Jared, Meredith, Erica, Jeremy. Instr. English, U. Iowa, 1946; teaching fellow Harvard, 1948-50, instr., tutor, 1950-52; asst. prof. U. Ill., Urbana, 1952-55, asso. prof., 1955-57, prof., 1957-67, past mem. Center for Advanced Study, U. Ill.; M.F. Carpenter prof. U. Iowa, Iowa City, 1967-74, Carver distinguished prof., 1974—. Vis. prof. U. Vienna (Austria), 1957-58; Fulbright lectr., 1957-58. Served to capt. USAAF, 1942-46; PTO. Recipient Bowdoin prize Harvard, 1950. Ford Found. fellow, 1952; Guggenheim fellow, 1963-64. Mem. Modern Lang. Assn. Am., Phi Beta Kappa. Author: Emerson's Angle of Vision, 1952; The Shores of America, 1958; Louis Sullivan, 1962; Edmund Wilson, 1965; Randolph Bourne, 1966; The Music of Survival, 1968; Hart's Bridge, 1972; Repossessing and Renewing, 1976; Olson's Push, 1978; editorial bd. Am. Lit., 1963-65; adv. com. PMLA, 1973—. Home: 903 E College Ave Iowa City IA 52240

PAUL, SIEGFRIED WILLIAM, orthotist, prosthetist; b. Berlin, Aug. 29, 1934; s. Otto Willi and Martha (Lehman) P.; came to U.S., 1958, naturalized, 1962; grad. Sch. Orthopedic Tech., Berlin, 1952; m. Betty L. Carter, June 3, 1962; 1 stepson, David W. Vaughn. Trainee, Tornow and Pohle, Berlin, 1949-53; orthopedic technician, 1953-56; orthotist technician Klopsch & Nesso, Berlin, 1956-58; orthopedist-prosthetist Fillauer Surg. Supplies Co., Chattanooga and Johnson City, Tenn., 1958-60, br. mgr., 1960-64; dir. orthotics and prosthetics Newington (Conn.) Children's Hosp., 1966—; instr. orthotics and prosthetics Inst. Crippled and Disabled, N.Y.C., 1964-66. Diplomate Am. Bd. Orthotics and Prosthetics. Mem. Am. Orthotic and Prosthetic Assn., Internat. Soc. Rehab. Disabled, Am. Acad. Orthotists and Prosthetists (pres. 1977-79; Spl. Service award New Eng. chpt. 1979), Internat. Soc. Orthotics and Prosthetics (sec. U.S. chpt. 1976-79), Internat. Assn. Orthotists and Prosthetists (v.p. 1976-79), Rehab. Internat. U.S.A. Lutheran. Club: Masons. Contbr. to med. jours.

PAUL, THOMAS, bass; B.A., Occidental Coll.; student Juilliard Sch. Music, N.Y.C. Carnegie Hall debut, 1960; N.Y.C. Opera debut, 1962; tour with Goldovsky Opera Co.; appearances with opera companies in Pitts., Houston, Central City, San Francisco, New Orleans, Toronto, Cin., Phila.; soloist maj. symphony orchs. music festivals U.S., Can., 1962—; prof. voice Eastman Sch. Music, Rochester, N.Y., prof. music, 1973—; debut with Chgo. Symphony Orch., 1969; artist, tchr. Aspen (Colo.) Music Festival, 1971—; European debut Zurich (Switzerland) Tonhalle, 1976; concerts, Stuttgart, Frankfurt and Mannheim, Germany, 1976; recs. for RCA, Columbia, Nonesuch, Deutsche Gramaphone. Served with AUS, 1957-59.

PAUL, WILLIAM, physicist; b. Deskford, Scotland, Mar. 31, 1926; s. William and Jean (Watson) P.; M.A., Aberdeen (Scotland) U., 1946, Ph.D., 1951; M.A. (hon.), Harvard, 1960; m. Barbara Anderson Forbes, Mar. 28, 1952; children—David, Fiona. Came to U.S., 1952. Asst. lectr., then lectr. Aberdeen U., 1946-52; mem. faculty Harvard U., 1953—, Gordon McKay prof. applied physics, 1963—. Cons. solid state physics, 1954—; Carnegie fellow, 1952-53; Guggenheim fellow, 1959-60; professeur associé U. Paris, 1966-67; fellow Clare Hall, Cambridge U., 1974-75. Fellow Am. Phys. Soc., Brit. Inst. Physics, N.Y. Acad. Scis., Royal Soc. Edinburgh; mem. AAAS, Sigma Xi. Co-editor: Solids Under Pressure, 1963. Home: 2 Eustis St Lexington MA 02173 Office: Pierce Hall Harvard Univ Cambridge MA 02138

PAUL, WILLIAM DEWITT, JR., artist, museum dir.; b. Wadley, Ga., Sept. 26, 1934; s. William Dewitt and Sonoma Elizabeth (Tinley) P.; student Emory U., summer 1952, U. Rome, summer 1953, Ga. State Coll. Bus. Adminstrn., Atlanta, spring 1953, summer 1956; B.F.A., Atlanta Art Inst., 1955; A.B., U. Ga., 1958, M.F.A., 1959; m. Dorothy Hefling, Sept. 2, 1962; children—Sarah Elizabeth, Barbara Susan, Dorothy Ann. Instr. art and art history Park Coll., Parkville, Mo., 1960-61; dir. exhbns., instr. art history Kansas City (Mo.) Art Inst., 1959-64, curator study collections, asst. prof. art, 1964-65; coordinator basic courses dept. art, asst. prof. art U. Ga., Athens, 1965-67, curator Ga. Mus. Art, asso. prof. art, 1967-69, dir. Ga. Mus. Art, asso. prof., 1969—; chmn. visual arts rev. panel Ga. Council for Arts and Humanities, 1976-77; exhibited in one man shows at Ga. Mus. Art, 1959, Atlanta Art Assn., 1959, Unitarian Gallery, Kansas City, 1960, Palmer Gallery, Kansas City, 1965, Heath Gallery, Atlanta, 1976, Hunter Mus. Art, Chattanooga, 1976, Forum Gallery, N.Y.C., 1977; exhibited group shows New Arts Gallery, Atlanta, 1961, Kansas City Art Inst., 1960-64, Park Coll,, 1960, Mulvane Art Center, Topeka, 1965, others; represented in permanent collections Gen. Mills, Inc., Mpls., Hallmark Cards, Kansas City, Little Rock Arts Center, Ga. Mus. Art, U. Ga., Art in Embassies Program USIA. Recipient numerous awards for paintings; Ford Found. faculty enrichment grantee, 1978. Mem. Am. Fedn. Arts (trustee), Coll. Art Assn., Am. Assn. Museums, Lovis Corinth Meml. Found., Ga. Alliance for Arts Edn. (dir. 1975-77), Assn. Art Mus. Dirs., Phi Kappa Phi. Guest columnist Atlanta Jour., 1968. Home: 150 Bar H Ct Athens GA 30605 Office: Ga Mus Art U Ga Athens GA 30601

PAUL, WILLIAM GEORGE, lawyer; b. Pauls Valley, Okla., Nov. 25, 1930; s. Homer and Helen (Lafferty) P.; B.A., U. Okla., 1952, LL.B., 1956; m. Barbara Elaine Brite, Sept. 27, 1963; children—George Lynn, Alison Elise, Laura Elaine, William Stephen. Admitted to Okla. bar, 1956; practiced in Norman, 1956, Oklahoma City, 1957—; partner Crowe, Dunlevy, Thweatt, Swinford, Johnson & Burdick, 1962—; asso. prof. law Oklahoma City U., 1964-68. Served to 1st lt. USMCR, 1952-54. Named Outstanding Young Man Oklahoma City, 1965, Outstanding Young Oklahoman, 1966. Fellow Am. Bar Found., Am. Coll. Trial Lawyers; mem. Am., Okla. (pres. 1976), Oklahoma County (past pres.) bar assns., U. Okla. Alumni Assn. (pres. 1973), Phi Beta Kappa, Order of Coif, Phi Delta Phi, Delta Sigma Rho. Democrat. Presbyn. Author: (with Earl Sneed) Vernon's Oklahoma Practice, 1965. Home: 13017 Burnt Oak Rd Oklahoma City OK 73120 Office: 1700 Liberty Tower Oklahoma City OK 73102

PAULEY, CLAUDE ARLINGTON, bus. exec.; b. Toledo, Nov. 23, 1898; s. Leander J. and Catherine B. (Riehm) P.; A.B., Western Res. U., 1921; m. Victoria E. Glenn, May 10, 1924 (dec. Sept. 1940); m. 2d, Kathryn MacCrae, Feb. 14, 1947. Accountant, Edison Lamp Works of Gen. Electric Co., Harrison, N.J., 1921-22; partner Wintermute, Pauley & Agler, C.P.A.'s, Cleve., 1922-27; auditor Sebring (Ohio) Pottery Co., 1927-31; accountant Firestone Tire & Rubber Co., Akron, 1931-43, comptroller, 1943-62. Regional exec. com. Boy Scouts; bd. govs. Case Western Res. U., 1962-72; trustee Children's Hosp.; treas. Old Trail Sch., 1962-73, trustee, 1973-76. C.P.A., Ohio, Mem. Am. Legion, Financial Execs. Inst., Am. Inst. C.P.A.'s, Phi Beta Kappa, Delta Upsilon. Episcopalian. Mason (32 deg., Shriner). Clubs: Union (Cleve.); Portage Country. Home: 2211 Tinkham Rd Akron OH 44313

PAULEY, EDWIN WENDELL, oil corp. exec.; b. Indpls., Jan. 7, 1903; s. Elbert L. and Ellen (Van Petten) P.; student Occidental Coll., 1919-20; B.S., U. Calif., 1922, LL.D., 1956; Litt.D., Santa Clara U., 1960; LL.D., Pepperdine Coll., 1956; m. Barbara Jean McHenry, Oct. 23, 1937; children—Edwin Wendell, Susan Jean, Stephen McHenry, Robert Van Petten. Founder Petrol Corp.; independent oil producer; real estate developer; chmn. bd. Pauley Petroleum Inc.; dir. Western Air Lines, Inc. Spl. rep. of gov. Cal. on Natural Resource Com., 1939, Interstate Oil and Compact Commn., 1940; petroleum coordinator for war in Europe on petroleum lend-lease supplies for Russia and Eng., 1941; U.S. rep. Reparations Commn., with rank of ambassador, 1945-47; adviser to sec. of state on reparations, 1947-48; spl. asst. to sec. of army 1947. Regent U. Calif., 1939—, chmn. bd., 1956—, chmn. regents, 1960—. Past sec., treas. Dem. Com.; Dem. nat. committeeman of Calif., 1944-48. Pres. Ind. Petroleum Assn., 1934-38. Home: 9521 Sunset Blvd Beverly Hills CA 90210 Office: 10000 Santa Monica Blvd Los Angeles CA 90067

PAULEY, GAY, editor. Began newspaper career with Huntington (W.Va.) Daily Advertiser; with United Press, 1943—, successively dist. and police reporter, polit. and state-house writer, bur. chief, 1943-53, editor women's new activities, 1953-76, also editor spl. page News and Features for Women; women's editor United Press Internat., until 1976, sr. editor, 1976—; also lecture tours. Recipient Nat. Headliner award Theta Sigma Phi, 1965. N.Y. Fashion Critics award, 1968. Mem. Newswomen's Club N.Y. (pres. 1969), Women in Communications (Matrix award 1976). Office: 220 E 42d St New York City NY 10017

PAULEY, JANE, TV journalist; b. Indpls., Oct. 31, 1950; B.A. in Polit. Sci., Ind. U., 1971; D. Journalism (hon.), DePauw U., 1978. Reporter, Sta. WISH-TV, Indpls., co-anchor mid-day news reports and anchor weekend news reports; co-anchor nightly news WMAQ-TV, Chgo., 1975-76; on-air staff The Today Show, 1976—; a prin. newscaster NBC News Update, 1977—. Office: care NBC 30 Rockefeller Plaza New York City NY 10020

PAULEY, ROBERT REINHOLD, investment co. exec.; b. New Canaan, Conn., Oct. 17, 1923; s. Edward Matthew and Grace Amanda (Smith) P.; student Harvard, 1946, M.B.A., 1951; D.Sc. (hon.), Curry Coll., Milton, Mass.; m. Barbara Anne Cotton, June 22, 1946; children—Lucinda Teed, Nicholas Andrew, Robert Reinhold, John Adams. With radio sta. WOR, 1951-52, NBC, 1953-56, CBS, 1956-57; account exec. ABC, 1957-59, sales mgr., 1959-60, v.p. in charge, 1960-61, pres., 1961-67; pres. MBS, N.Y.C., 1967-69; v.p. E.F. Hutton & Co., Inc., 1969—; founder, chmn. TV News Inc., N.Y.C.; dir. Butler Automatic, Inc. Bd. dirs. Curry Coll. Mem. Radio-TV Execs. Soc., S.A.R., St. Nicholas Soc. Clubs: Harvard (Boston, N.Y.C.); Myopia Hunt. Home: Box 288 Wenham MA 01984 Office: 1 Boston Plaza Boston MA

PAULEY, STANLEY FRANK, mfg. co. exec.; b. Winnipeg, Man., Can., Sept. 19, 1927; s. Daniel and Anna (Tache) P.; came to U.S., 1954, naturalized, 1961; B.E.E., U. Man., 1949; m. Dorothy Ann Ruppel, Aug. 21, 1949; children—Katharine Ann, Lorna Jane. With Canadian Industries Ltd., Kingston, Ont., 1949-53, sr. engring. asst., 1952-53; elec. controls designer Standard Machine and Tool Co. Ltd., Windsor, Ont., 1953-54; prodn. supt. E.R. Carpenter Co., Richmond, Va., 1954-57, pres., 1957—, also dir.; dir. Carpenter Chem. Co., Carpenter Oil & Gas Co., Carpenter Insulation & Coatings Co., Carpenter-Jackson Ltd., First & Mchts. Nat. Bank, 1st Mcht.'s Corp., Richmond, Am. Filtrona Corp. Trustee U. Richmond. Republican. Presbyterian. Club: Commonwealth. Home: 314 St David's Ln

Richmond VA 23221 Office: 2400 Jefferson Davis Hwy Richmond VA 23231

PAULING, LINUS CARL, educator; b. Portland, Oreg., Feb. 28, 1901; s. Herman Henry William and Lucy Isabelle (Darling) P.; B.S., Oreg. State Coll., Corvallis, 1922, Sc.D. (hon.), 1933; Ph.D., Calif. Inst. Tech., 1925; Sc.D. (hon.), U. Chgo., 1941, Princeton, 1946, U. Cambridge, U. London, Yale, 1947, Oxford, 1948, Bklyn. Poly. Inst., 1955, Humboldt U., 1959, U. Melbourne, 1964, U. Delhi, Adelphi U., 1967, Marquette U. Sch. Medicine, 1969; L.H.D., Tampa, 1950; U.J.D., U. N.B., 1950; LL.D., Reed Coll., 1959; Dr. h.c., Paris (France), 1948, Toulouse (France), 1949, Montpellier (France), 1958, Jagiellonian U., 1964; D.F.A., Chouinard Art Inst., 1958; also others; m. Ava Helen Miller, June 17, 1923; children—Linus Carl, Peter Jeffress, Linda Helen, Edward Crellin. Teaching fellow Calif. Inst. Tech., 1922-25, research fellow, 1925-27, asst. prof., 1927-29, asso. prof., 1929-31, prof. chem., 1931-64, chmn. div. chem. and chem. engring., dir. Gates and Crellin Labs. of Chemistry, 1936-58, mem. exec. com., bd. trustees, 1945-48; research prof. Center for Study Dem. Instns., 1963-67; prof. chemistry U. Calif. at San Diego, 1967-69; prof. chemistry Stanford, 1969-74; pres. Linus Pauling Inst. Sci. and Medicine, 1973-75, 78—, research prof., 1973—; George Eastman prof. Oxford U., 1948; lectr. chemistry several univs. Fellow Balliol Coll., 1948, NRC, 1925-26, John S. Guggenheim Meml. Found., 1926-27. Numerous awards in field of chemistry, including: U.S. Presdl. Medal for Merit, 1948, Nobel prize in chemistry, 1954, Nobel Peace prize, 1962, Internat. Lenin Peace prize, 1972; U.S. Nat. Medal of Sci., 1974; Fermat medal, Paul Sabatier medal, Pasteur medal, medal with laurel wreath of Internat. Grotius Found., 1957, Lomonosov medal, 1978, U.S. Nat. Acad. Sci. medal in Chem. Scis., 1979. Hon., corr., fgn. mem. numerous assns. and orgns. Author several books, 1930—, including Cancer and Vitamin C, 1979. Contbr. articles to profl. jours. Home: Salmon Creek Big Sur CA 93920 Office: Linus Pauling Inst Sci and Medicine 2700 Sand Hill Rd Menlo Park CA 94025

PAULL, RICHARD ALLEN, educator, geologist; b. Madison, Wis., May 20, 1930; s. Ethra Harold and Martha (Schaller) P.; B.S., U. Wis., 1952, M.S., 1953, Ph.D., 1957; m. Rachel Kay Krebs, Mar. 6, 1954; children—Kay Marie, Lynn Ellen, Judith Ann. Party chief Pan Am. Petroleum Co., 1955-57; research group leader Jersey Prodn. Research Co., 1957-62; mem. faculty U. Wis.-Milw., 1962—, chmn. dept. geol. scis., 1962-66, prof., 1966—; cons. in field, 1966—. Served with USAF, 1953-55. Hon. curator Milw. Museum; recipient Amoco Distinguished Teaching award, 1975. Fellow Geol. Soc. Am. (chmn. ann. meeting 1970, tech. program com. 1970, 77, membership com. 1977-80); mem. AAAS, Am. Assn. Petroleum Geologists, Soc. Econ. Paleontologists and Mineralogists, Nat. Assn. Geology Tchrs. (v.p. 1976-77, pres. 1977-78), Am. Geol. Inst. (gov. 1977-79), Nature Conservancy, Sigma Xi. Author books, papers in field. Home: 722 E Carlisle Ave Whitefish Bay WI 53217 Office: Dept Geol Scis Univ Wis Milwaukee WI 53201

PAULS, DAYTON FRANK, banker; b. Lime Ridge, Wis., Feb. 1, 1910; s. Frank Henry and Rose A. (Kirschner) P.; B.A., U. Wis., 1932; m. Margaret Stetzer, Aug. 6, 1938; children—Richard D, Mary Margaret. Accountant, Arthur Andersen & Co., Chgo., 1932-33; bank examiner State of Wis., Madison, 1933-46; exec. v.p. Cudahy State Bank (Wis.). 1946-48; pres. Citizens Bank of Sheboygan, Wis., 1948-72, chmn., 1972—; pres. Citizens Bancorp., Sheboygan; chmn. bd. Citizens North Side Bank, Sheboygan; dir. Wigwam Mills, Citizens Trust Co., Sheboygan, Wis. Physicians Service Corp., Madison. Active YMCA, United Fund, A.R.C. drives. Bd. dirs. DeLand Found.; bd. assos. Lakeland Coll.; councilor commn. med. care plans Wis. Med. Soc.; past pres. Sheboygan Arts Found. and Summer Theatre. Mem. Am., (exec. council v.p.), Wis. (pres. 1965-66) bankers assns., Nat. Conf. State Banks Suprs. (chmn. exec. council), Robert Morris Assos. Conglist. (trustee, deacon, moderator). Mason, Elk. Club: Pine Hills Country. Home: River Valley View Apts 3602 N 21st St Sheboygan WI 53081 Office: Box 171 Sheboygan WI 53081. *A man's judgment can never be any better than his information.*

PAULSEN, ALBERT, actor; b. Guayaquil, Ecuador, Dec. 13, 1929; s. Alfred and Zoila (Andrade) P.; student U. Ecuador. Broadway plans include: Night Circus, 1958, Three Sisters, 1964, Only Came in Town, 1968; appeared in off-Broadway prodns.; films include: Manchurian Candidate, 1962, Gunn, 1967, Che, 1968, Amazing Mrs. Polifax, 1969, Laughing Policeman, 1973, The Next Man, 1976; appeared in TV series, specials. Recipient Emmy award for role in One Day in the Life of Ivan Denisovitch, 1964. Address: 570 N Rossmore Ave Los Angeles CA 90004

PAULSEN, FRANK ROBERT, coll. dean; b. Logan, Utah, July 5, 1922; s. Frank and Ella (Ownby) P.; B.S., Utah State U., 1947; M.S., U. Utah, 1948, Ed.D., 1956; Kellogg Found. postdoctoral fellow U. Ore., 1958; Carnegie Found. postdoctoral fellow U. Mich., 1959-60; m. Marye Lucile Harris, July 31, 1942; 1 son, Robert Keith; m. 2d, Lydia Ransier Lowry, Nov. 1, 1969. High sch. prin., Mt. Emmons, Utah, 1948-51; supt. schs., Cokeville, Wyo., 1951-55; asst. prof., then asso. prof. edn. U. Utah, 1955-61; prof. edn., dean Sch. Edn. U. Conn., 1961-64; dean Coll. Edn. U. Ariz., Tucson, 1964—. Scholar-in-residence Fed. Exec. Inst., Charlottesville, Va., 1970; Distinguished prof. edn. U. Bridgeport, summer 1972; dir. Am. Jour. Nursing Pub. Co., N.Y.C., Am. Gen. Growth Fund, Houston, Am. Gen. Exchange Fund, Houston. Chmn., Conn. Adv. Com. Adminstrv. Certification, 1962-64; exec. com. New Eng. Council Advancement Sch. Adminstrn., 1962-64; trustee Joint Council Econ. Edn., 1962-70; v.p., dir. Southwestern Coop. Ednl. Lab., 1965-67; bd. dirs. Nat. League for Nursing, 1967-69, mem. com. on perspectives, 1966—; dir., chmn. exec. com. ERIC Clearinghouse on Tchr. Edn., 1968-70; bd. dirs. Tucson Mental Health Center, 1968-70. Served with AUS, 1942-46; PTO. Mem. Aerospace Med. Assn., NEA, Assn. Higher Edn., Am. Assn. Sch. Adminstrs., Am. Acad. Polit. and Social Sci., John Dewey Soc., Utah Acad. Letters, Arts and Scis., Am. Assn. Colls. Tchrs. Edn. (Conn. liaison officer 1962-64, mem. studies com. 1962-68, dir.), Ariz. Assn. Colls. Tchr. Edn. (pres. 1972—), AAAS, Am. Ednl. Research Assn., Kappa Delta Pi, Pi Sigma Alpha, Pi Gamma Mu. Phi Delta Kappa. Rotarian. Author: The Administration of Public Education in Utah, 1958; Contemporary Issues in American Education, 1966; American Education: Challenges and Images, 1967; Changing Dimensions in International Education, 1968; Higher Education: Dimensions and Directions, 1969; also numerous articles. Home: 2801 N Indian Ruins Tucson AZ 85715

PAULSEN, MARTIN RAYMOND, lawyer; b. Friendship, Wis., Aug. 2, 1895; s. Paul and Julia (Jacobsen) P.; student U. Dublin (Ireland), 1919; LL.B., U. Wis., 1923; m. Mary Hazen, Dec. 18, 1920. Admitted to Wis. bar, 1923; practiced in Racine, Wis., until 1931; city atty., Racine, 1928-30; practiced in Milw., 1931—; former mem. firm Shaw, Muskat & Paulsen. Past chmn. bd. Milw. Forge & Machine Co., now dir.; dir. Edward E. Gillen Co., Pima Land & Investment Co., Home Land & Trust Co. Mem. Greater Milw. Com., 1952-56. Served with USMCR, 1917-19; AEF in France, Mem. Am., Wis. bar assns., Order of Coif, Phi Kappa Phi. Home: 8165 N Casas Way Tucson AZ 85704 and 7123 N Oracle Rd Tucson AZ 85704

PAULSEN, NORMAN, JR., public relations co. exec.; b. N.Y.C., Jan. 25, 1926; s. Norman and Clara (Fuelcher) P.; student Duke U., 1942-43; B.S. in Bus. Adminstrn., Northwestern U., 1945; M.B.A., Harvard U., 1947; children—Karen, Norman, Susan. Asst. adv. mgr. Phoenix Hosiery Co., Milw., 1949-52; mgr. advt. and public relations Blue Cross of Wis., Milw., 1952-60; dir. public relations A.O. Smith Corp., Milw., 1960-68, Allied Chem. Corp., N.Y.C., 1968-70; pres. Barkin, Herman, Solochek & Paulsen, Milw., 1970—. Bd. dirs. United Way, Milw., 1973-78, Conservatory of Music, Milw., 1975-77; chmn., dir. ARC, Milw., 1977-79. Served to lt. j.g. USNR, 1944-47. Mem. Public Relations Soc. Am. (past v.p. Wis. chpt.). Congregationalist. Clubs: Univ. of Milw., Milw. Country, Rotary. Home: 8590 N Bay Ct River Hills WI 53209 Office: 777 E Wisconsin Ave Milwaukee WI 53202

PAULSEN, PAT, entertainer. Formerly host own TV show. Recipient Emmy award for individual achievement in Smothers Brothers Comedy Hour, 1967-68. Address: care William Morris Agy 151 El Camino Beverly Hills CA 90212*

PAULSEN, SERENUS GLEN, architect; b. Spooner, Wis., July 27, 1917; s. Serenus Justin and Edna Anne (Dalton) P.; student U. Ill., 1938-42; B.Arch. cum laude, U. Pa., 1947; student Architecture and City Planning, Royal Acad. Art (Sweden), 1948; m. Virginia C. Habel, Jan. 26, 1944; children—Thomas J., Nancy Lee (Mrs. John Marshall). With Carroll, Grisdale & Van Alan, Architects, Phila., 1946-47, Eero Saarinen & Assos., Bloomfield Hills, Mich., 1949-51, 53-57; chief designer Reisner & Urbahn, Architects, N.Y.C., 1951-52; archtl. coordinator Knoll Assos., N.Y.C., 1952-53; prin. Glen Paulsen Assos., Birmingham, Mich., 1958-69; prin., v.p. Tarapata-MacMahon-Paulsen Assos., Inc., Architects, Bloomfield Hills, 1969-77; pres. Cranbrook Acad. Art, head dept. architecture, 1966-70; prof., chmn. Masters Program in Architecture, U. Mich., 1976—. Mem. Nat. Com. on Urban Planning and Design, 1971-72, archtl. commn. U. Wash., Seattle, 1968-76. Trustee Cranbrook Acad. Art. Served with C.E., USAAF, 1942-46. Recipient 3d prize Bi-Nat. Competition for Design Rainbow Center Plaza, Niagara Falls, N.Y., 1972. Fellow A.I.A. (honor awards Detroit chpt. for Shapero Hall of Pharmacy, 1965, Our Shepherd Lutheran Ch., 1966, Ford Life Sci. Bldg., 1967, Birney Elementary Sch., Detroit, 1971, Fed. Bldg., Ann Arbor, Mich. 1978); mem. Mich. Soc. Architects. Home: 4820 Geddes Rd Ann Arbor MI 48105 Office: Coll Architecture and Urban Planning U Mich Ann Arbor MI

PAULSEN, WOLFGANG, educator; b. Düsseldorf, Germany, Sept. 21, 1910; s. Hans and Luise (Hunaeus) P.; ed. univs. Tübingen, Bonn, Berne, Berlin and Leipzig, 1930-34; m. Herta Schindler, June 18, 1938; 1 dau., Judith. Came to U.S., 1938, naturalized, 1943. Mem. faculty State U. Ia., 1943-47, Smith Coll., 1947-53, U. Conn., 1954-66; head dept. German, U. Mass., 1966-71, prof., 1966—. Mem. Modern Lang. Assn., Am. Assn. Tchrs. German, Deutsche Schillergesellschaft. Author: Expressionismus und Aktivismus, 1935; Georg Kaiser: Die Perspektiven seines Werkes, 1960; Die Ahnfrau: Zu Grillparzers früher Dramatik, 1962; Versuch über Rolf Bongs, 1973; Christoph Martin Wieland: Der Mensch und sein Werk in psychologischen Perspektiven, 1975; Eichendorff und sein Taugenichts, 1976; Johann Elias Schlegel und die Komödie, 1977. Editor ann. vols. Amherst Colloquium on German Lit., 1967—. Home: 49 Maplewood Dr Amherst MA 01002

PAULSON, BELDEN HENRY, polit. scientist; b. Oak Park, Ill., June 29, 1927; s. Henry Thomas and Evelina (Belden) P.; A.B., Oberlin (Ohio) Coll., 1950; M.A., U. Chgo., 1955, Ph.D., 1962; m. Louise D. Hill, Jan. 9, 1954; children—Eric, Steven. With Italian service mission, Naples, 1950-53; organizer Homeless European Land Program, Sardinia, 1957-59; with UN High Commn. Refugees, Rome, 1960-61; mem. faculty U. Wis., Milw., also U. Wis. extensions, 1962—, prof. polit. sci., 1969—, chmn. Center Urban Community Devel., 1967—. Served with USNR, 1945-46. Grantee Social Sci. Research Council, 1967-68. Mem. Am. Polit. Sci. Assn., Soc. Internat. Devel., World Futurist Soc., Latin Am. Studies Assn., AAAS, AAUP. Author: The Searchers, 1966; also articles. Home: 2602 E Newberry Blvd Milwaukee WI 53211 Office: Dept Polit Sci Univ Wis Milwaukee WI 53201

PAULSON, DONALD LOWELL, thoracic surgeon; b. St. Paul, Sept. 14, 1912; s. Joseph Bernard and Martha (Sornsen) P.; B.S., M.B., U. Minn., 1935, M.D., 1936, M.S., 1937, Ph.D. in Surgery, 1942; m. Margaret Elizabeth Willius, Mar. 16, 1938 (dec.); children—Mary Willius Paulson Cordonnier, Margaret Elizabeth Paulson Maxson, Julie Paulson Herbst. Intern, Mpls. Gen. Hosp. and U. Minn. Gen. Hosp., 1935-36; fellow anatomy U. Minn., 1936-37; fellow surgery Mayo Found., 1937-40; asst. surgery Mayo Clinic, 1940-42; pvt. practice thoracic surgery, Dallas, 1946—; chief sect. thoracic surgery Baylor U. Med. Center, 1962-77; sr. cons. Parkland Meml. Hosp., 1962—; cons. Children's Med. Center, Presbyn. Hosp.; faculty U. Tex. Southwestern Med. Sch., 1946—, clin. prof. thoracic surgery, 1962—. Vis. prof. thoracic surgery at various univs. Served to lt. col. M.C., AUS, 1942-46. Diplomate Am. Bd. Surgery, Am. Bd. Thoracic Surgery (a founder, mem. bd. 1964-73, chmn. bd. 1971-73). Fellow A.C.S., Am. Surg. Assn., Tex. Surg. Soc., So. Surg. Assn.; mem. Am. Assn. Thoracic Surgery (pres. 1981), So. Thoracic Surg. Assn. (pres. 1956), Soc. Thoracic Surgeons (pres. 1967), Am. Coll. Chest Physicians, Samson Thoracic Surg. Soc., Sigma Xi, Nu Sigma Nu. Presbyn. Author: (with R.R. Shaw) The Treatment of Bronchial Neoplasms, 1959; also articles. Mem. adv. editorial bd. Jour. Thoracic and Cardiovascular Surgery, 1963—. Home: 5359 Drane Dr Dallas TX 75209 Office: Wadley Tower Baylor Med Plaza 3600 Gaston Ave Dallas TX 75246

PAULSON, JAMES MARVIN, educator; b. Wausau, Wis., Jan. 1, 1923; s. Gustav Victor and Susanna (Dracy) P.; B.S. in Civil Engring., The Citadel, 1947; M.S. in Civil Engring., Ill. Inst. Tech., 1949; Ph.D., U. Mich., 1958; m. Marjorie Beulah Burton, May 11, 1946; children—Vicki Rae (Mrs. Charles Cruse), Michael James. Draftsman, Wausau Iron Works, 1946; engr. Charles Whitney Cons. Engr., Milw., 1948-49; faculty Wayne State U., Detroit, 1949—, prof., 1961—, chmn. dept. civil engring., 1967-72, asso. dean Coll. Engring., 1973—; v.p. Civil Engrs., Inc., 1954—; cons. in field. Served with AUS, 1943, USMCR, 1943-46. Registered profl. engr., Mich. Mem. Am. Soc. C.E., Mich. Soc. Profl. Engrs., Am. Concrete Inst., Am. Soc. for Engring. Edn., Sigma Xi, Tau Beta Pi, Chi Epsilon. Conglist. Home: 14711 Rutland Detroit MI 48227

PAULSON, JOHN DORAN, newspaper editor; b. Grand Forks, N.D., Oct. 1, 1915; s. Holger D. and Irene E. (Finkle) P.; student U.N.D., 1932-34; B.S., U. Minn., 1936; m. Zoe Y Bean Hensly, July 6, 1946; children—James L., Michael D., Christine R., David E., Patrick R. Copy editor Mpls. Star, 1936; reporter The Forum, Fargo, N.D.-Moorhead, Minn., 1937-39, polit. writer, 1939-51, mng. editor, 1951-56, editor, 1957—; v.p. Forum Pub. Co.; v.p. stas. WDAY, Inc., Fargo, 1960—; dir. S.D. Broadcasting Co., Sioux Falls, KMMJ, Grand Island, Nebr.; dir. Am. sect. Internat. Press Inst. Del. N.D. Constl. Conv., 1971-72. Served with AUS, 1942-46. Mem. Am. Soc. Newspaper Editors. Home: 1362 2d St N Fargo ND 58102 Office: Box 2020 Fargo ND 58102

PAULSON, MOSES, physician; b. Balt., May 2, 1897; s. David and Deborah (Bogatsky) P.; B.S., U. of Md., 1917, M.D., 1921; m. Helen Golden, June 9, 1926. House physician Sinai Hosp., Balt., 1921-22, chief gastroenterology, 1946-64, attending physician, 1964—; resident physician St. Agnes Hosp., 1922-23, in charge night accident service Emergency Hosp., Washington, 1923-24; resident Children's Hosp., Washington, 1923-24; gen. practice, Balt., 1924-26; full-time research in digestive diseases (gastro-enterology), Johns Hopkins U., 1926-29, part time, 1929—, asst. in medicine, 1927-28, instr., 1928-33, asso., 1933-46, asst. prof. medicine, 1946-55, asso. prof., 1955—; physician Johns Hopkins Hosp., 1930—; cons. gastroenterology Diagnostic Clinic, 1934-55; cons. pvt.-out-patient services Johns Hopkins Hosp., 1946-68, Regional Office VA, 1950; cons. gastroenterology Perry Point (Md.) VA Hosp.; practice internal medicine, specializing in gastroenterology, 1930—; vis. physician Ch. Home and Infirmary, Mercy, St. Agnes, Sinai hosps., Greater Balt. Med. Center. Cons., Council on Drugs, A.M.A., 1958—. Served as hosp. apprentice 1st class USNR, 1917-21. Fellow A.C.P., Am. Coll. Gastroenterology; mem. Am. Soc. Gastrointestinal Endoscopy, A.A.A.S., A.M.A., Am. Soc. Microbiology, So. Med. Assn., Am. Gastro-Enterol. Assn., Am. Soc. for Research in Psychosomatic Problems, Med. and Chirurgical Faculty Md., Phi Delta Epsilon. Clubs: Johns Hopkins, Masons. Author: Gastroenterologic Medicine, 1969. Editorial bd. Am. Jour. Digestive Diseases, 1934-50, Gastroenterology, 1940-55. Contbr. numerous articles to med. publs. Home: 3900 N Charles St Baltimore MD 21218 Offices: 11 E Chase St Baltimore MD 21202 also Johns Hopkins Hosp Baltimore MD 21205. *The continual maintainance of student-like proclivities; virtual unremitting industry; effort directed—at least in part—to advance knowledge in one's chosen field, as well as unquestioned integrity, bring peer recognition and other rewards, which by any of several standards would be classified as success.*

PAULSON, PAUL JOSEPH, advt. exec.; b. White Plains, N.Y., Sept. 25, 1932; s. Paul and Ann (Loughlin) P.; B.S. in Bus. Adminstrn., Ohio State U., 1954; M.B.A., Wharton Sch. U. Pa., 1959; m. Kathryn P. Keeler, June 30, 1962; children—Thomas, Mark, Kathryn, John, Clifford. With Compton Advt. Inc., N.Y.C., 1959-78, mgmt. supr., 1965-78, sr. v.p., 1968-78, also dir.; pres., dir. Doyle Dane Bernbach Inc., N.Y.C., 1978—. Chmn., Christmas for Underprivileged Children, N.Y.C., 1963—. Served to lt. (j.g.) USNR, 1955-58; M.T.O., A.T.O. Mem. Wharton Grad. Bus. Sch. (pres. N.Y.C. club 1963-65, dir. 1972—), Ohio State U. alumni assns., Wharton Grad. Bus. Sch. Clubs N.Y. (dir.), Sigma Chi. Roman Catholic. Author: Fundamentals of Consumer Goods Marketing, 1966. Home: 45 W Brother Dr Greenwich CT 06830 Office: 437 Madison Ave New York NY 10022

PAULSON, PETER JOHN, librarian; b. N.Y.C., Jan. 30, 1928; s. Peter John and Lillian Agnes Elaine (Neuman) P.; B. Social Scis. cum laude, Coll. City N.Y., 1949; M.A. in History, Columbia, 1950; M.A. in L.S., State U. N.Y., Albany, 1955; m. Josephine C. Bowen, Dec. 5, 1953; children—David, Debora. Library asst. N.Y. State Library, Albany, 1952-55, head, gift and exchange sect., 1955-65, head catalog sect., 1965-66, prin. librarian tech. services, 1966-71, dir., 1972—; adj. asst. prof. library sci. State U. N.Y. at Albany, 1960-71. Adv. com. Ohio Coll. Library Center, 1970-71; adv. council to pub. printer depository libraries, 1972-77, chairperson, 1975-77; com. fed. depository library service N.Y. State, 1960-70, chairperson, 1960-70. Mem. N.Y. (pres. 1975), Hudson-Mohawk (v.p. 1964) library assns., Phi Beta Kappa. Home: 24 Tillinghast Ave Albany NY 12204 Office: NY State Library Cultural Edn Center Albany NY 12230

PAULSON, RONALD HOWARD, educator; b. Bottineau, N.D., May 27, 1930; s. Howard Clarence and Ethel (Tvete) P.; B.A., Yale, 1952, Ph.D., 1958; m. Barbara Lee Appleton, May 25, 1957; children—Andrew Meredith, Melissa Katherine. Instr., U. Ill., 1958-59, asst. prof., 1959-62, asso. prof., 1962-63; prof. English, Rice U., 1963-67; prof. English, Johns Hopkins, 1967-75, chmn. dept., 1968-75, Andrew W. Mellon prof. humanities, 1973-75; prof. English, Yale, 1975—. Served to lst lt. AUS, 1952-54. Sterling fellow, 1957-58; Guggenheim fellow, 1965-66; Nat. Endowment for Humanities fellow, 1977-78. Author: Theme and Structure in Swift's Tale of a Tub, 1960; Fielding, 1962; Hogarth's Graphic Works, 1965, rev. edit., 1970; Fictions of Satire, 1967; Satire and the Novel, 1967; (with Thomas F. Lockwood) Fielding: The Critical Heritage, 1969; Satire: Modern Essays in Criticism, 1971; Hogarth: His Life, Art, and Times, 1971; Rowlandson: A New Interpretation, 1972; Emblem and Expression: Meaning in Eighteenth-Century English Art, 1975; The Art of Hogarth, 1975; Popular and Polite Art in the Age of Hogarth and Fielding, 1979; also numerous essays. Home: 377 St Ronan New Haven CT 06511

PAULSON, ROY RICHARD, retail exec.; b. Cin., Dec. 1, 1930; s. Irvin Joseph and Eleanor (Oser) P.; grad. Miami-Jacobs Coll., 1951; student Ind. U. Grad. Sch. Bus., 1963; m. Jane Ann Haines, Sept. 17, 1955; children—Leslie Katherine, Robert Irvin. Fin. v.p. Rike's div. Federated Dept. Stores, Dayton, Ohio, 1947-72; exec. v.p. May Dept. Stores Co., St. Louis, 1972—, pres. Eagle Stamp Co. div., 1978—. Served with U.S. Army, 1951-53. Decorated Bronze Star; named Outstanding Young Man, Dayton, 1964, State of Ohio, 1965. Mem. Nat. Retail Mchts. Assn. (dir.). Clubs: Media; Triple A Country; Town and Tennis, Old Warson. Home: 4502 Pershing Pl Saint Louis MO 63108 Office: 3100 Market St Saint Louis MO 63103

PAULSON, STANLEY FAY, educator; b. Atwater, Minn., Mar. 5, 1920; s. Adolph and Ida May (Fay) P.; B.A., in Philosophy, U. Minn., 1942, M.A., 1949, Ph.D., 1952; B.D., Bethel Theol. Sem., 1944; m. Margaret Nan Appelquist, Sept. 8, 1944; children—Richard Stanley, Lynn Edith. Instr., U. Minn., 1948-53; research asso. studies in lang. and behavior Bur. Naval Research, 1952-53; overseas instr. U. Md. Program in Germany and Eng., 1953-54; asst. prof. U. Minn., 1954-56; mem. faculty San Francisco State U., 1956-66, prof. speech, chmn. dept., 1959-62, v.p. acad. affairs, 1963-65, acting pres., 1965-66; prof., chmn. dept. speech Pa. State U., 1966-69, dean Coll. Liberal Arts, 1969—. Bd. dirs. Assn. Am. Colls., 1978—. Fulbright lectr. Kanazawa (Japan) U., 1962-63. Served to lt. (j.g.) USNR, 1945-46. Mem. Speech Communication Assn. (vice chmn. group methods sect. 1961-62), Western Speech Assn. (counselor pub. address 1961—), AAUP, Internat. Communication Assn., Council Colls. Arts and Scis. (dir. 1971—, v.p. 1972, pres. 1973). Author: (with Bystrom, Ramsland) Communicating Through Speech, 1951; also articles. Home: 439 W Park Ave State College PA 16801 Office: Pa State U University Park PA 16802

PAULSON, STEPHEN JON, bassoonist; b. Bklyn., July 13, 1946; s. Michael and Ruth (Heynick) P.; B.Mus. with honors, performers cert., Eastman Sch. Music, U. Rochester, 1968; m. Patricia Lynn Marshall, Apr. 11, 1977. Second bassoonist Rochester (N.Y.) Philharm. Orch., 1966-68, prin. bassoonist, 1968-70; co-prin. bassoonist Pitts. Symphony Orch., 1970-77; prin. bassoonist San Francisco Symphony Orch., 1977—; mem. faculty San Francisco Conservatory of Music; mem. extension faculty U. Calif., Berkeley; founder, dir. Upper Partials chamber music series, Pitts., 1972-76. Composer: Concerto for Bassoon and Orch., 1967. Office: Room 107 War Meml Vets Bldg San Francisco CA 94102

PAULSON, WILLIAM LEE, state justice; b. Valley City, N.D., Sept. 3, 1913; s. Alfred Parker and Inga Gertina (Wold) P.; B.A., Valley City State Tchrs. Coll., 1935; J.D., U. N.D., 1937; m. Jane E. Graves, Sept. 8, 1938; children—John T., Mary (Mrs. Mikal Simonson). Admitted to N.D. bar, 1937; practice in Valley City, 1937-66; state's atty., Barnes County, 1941-50, 59-66; asso. justice N.D. Supreme Ct., 1967—. Pres. N.D. States Attys. Assn., 1964; dir. for N.D., Nat. Dist. Attys. Assn., 1963-65. Pres. Valley City Jaycees, 1943; dist. v.p. U.S. Jaycees, 1945-46; bd. dirs. Valley City C. of C., 1960-61; judge Am. Legion Oratorical Contest, 1970-72; mem. nat. awards jury Freedoms Found. at Valley Forge, 1969-71, 77; chancellor Episcopal Ch. N.D., 1965—. Mem. alumni adv. bd. U. N.D. 1971—. Mem. Am. Bar Assn. State Bar N.D., U. N.D. Alumni Assn. (pres. Valley City Area 1963-65; Sioux award 1973). Elk, K.P., Eagle, Mason (Shriner) Home: 1009 E Highland Acres Rd Bismarck ND 58501 Office: Supreme Ct Chambers State Capitol Bismarck ND 58505

PAULUCCI, JENO FRANCISCO, food co. exec.; b. Aurora, Minn., July 7, 1918; s. Ettore and Michelina (Buratti) P.; student Hibbing (Minn.) Jr. Coll., 1936-37; H.H.D., Franklin Pierce Coll., 1970; D.B.A. (hon.), Mo. Valley Coll., 1970; LL.D., Coll. State Scholastica, 1974; m. Lois Mae Trepanier, Feb. 8, 1947; children—Michael J., Cynthia J., Gina J. With City Markets, Hibbing, 1933-34, Minn. Market, Hibbing, 1934-36, Hancock-Nelson Co., St. Paul, 1936-45; exec. v.p. Bean Sprouts Growers Assn., 1945-47; pres. Chun King Corp., Duluth, 1954-67, Etor Realty Co., Duluth, 1958—, Chop Chop Corp., Duluth, 1966—; chmn. bd. R.J. Reynolds Foods, Inc., N.Y.C., 1966-68, Jeno's Inc., Duluth, 1967—, Jeno F. Paulucci Enterprises, 1967—, JFP-Gray Process, Ltd., Duluth, 1967—, Central Produce and Equipment, Inc., Maitland, Fla., 1967—, 1st Sierra Corp., 1971-73; exec. com., dir. Cornelius Co., Anoka, Minn., 1969—, chmn. bd., 1971—; founder, pub. Attenzione mag., 1979—. Adv. bd. dirs. Nat. Frozen Food Assn., 1970—. Mem. Gov.'s Bus. Adv. Council; founder, pres. N.E. Minn. Orgn. Econ. Edn., 1960—; mem. nat. council USO; mem. com. U.S. Office Emergency Planning; initiated one million dollar devel. orgn. and six million dollar Duluth Arena Auditorium; gave Agrl. Research Center to Minn. Founder, chmn. Paulucci Family Found.; trustee Mo. Valley Coll., Marshall, Mo.; bd. dirs. Childrens Home Soc., St. Paul, Fla. Central Acad.; chmn. Italian Am. Found., Washington, 1976—. Named to Duluth Hall of Fame, 1962; recipient Horatio Alger award, 1965; named Outstanding Italian-Am., Italian-Am. Soc., 1965; Minn. Salesman of Yr., Mpls. Sales Exec. Club, 1967; Outstanding Industrialist award Gov. of Fla., 1967; Minnesotan of Yr., Minn. Broadcasters Assn., 1967; Distinguished Citizen award Minn. chpt. Pub. Relations Soc. Am., 1967; Rizzuto gold medal as outstanding Italian-Am. of U.S., UNICO Nat., 1968; named Employer of Year, City Duluth, 1972, Minn. Gov.'s Council Employment of Handicapped, 1972, U.S. Employer of Year Pres.'s Council Employment Handicapped-Nat. Assn. Mfrs., 1972, Wis. Rehab. Assn., 1979; hon. Swede of Year Svenskarnas Dag, Inc., 1973; mem. Minn. Bus. Hall of Fame. Presbyterian. Home: 6 Minneapolis Ave Duluth MN 55803 Office: PO Box 206 Duluth MN 55801

PAULUCCI, MICHAEL JENO, food co. exec.; b. Duluth, Minn., Oct. 26, 1948; s. Jeno Francesco and Lois Mae (Trepanier) P.; student Yampa Valley Coll., U. Colo., U. Minn.; m. Lori Jeanne Patnode, Jan. 21, 1978. Sales rep. Jeno's, Inc., later, v.p. advt., from 1970, chmn. bd., 1978—; pres. Paulucci Enterprises, Inc., 1974—; owner Grandma's Saloon and Deli, 1976—; dir. Cornelius Co., Mpls.; Crispheart Produce; v.p., dir. Kemp-Paulucci Seafoods; dir. Lyric Block Devel. Corp., Miller Hill State Bank. Served with USAF, 1973. Office: 525 Lake Ave S Duluth MN 55802

PAULUS, NORMA JEAN PETERSEN (MRS. WILLIAM G. PAULUS), state ofcl.; b. Belgrade, Nebr., Mar. 13, 1933; d. Paul Emil and Ella Marie (Hellbusch) Petersen; LL.B., Willamette U., 1962; m. William G. Paulus, Aug. 16, 1958; children—Elizabeth, William Frederick. Sec. to Harney County (Oreg.) Dist. Atty., 1950-53; legal sec., Salem, Oreg., 1953-55; sec. to chief justice Oreg. Supreme Ct., 1955-61; admitted to Oreg. bar, 1962; of counsel firm Paulus and Callaghan, Salem, 1971-76; mem. Oreg. Ho. of Reps., 1971-76; sec. of state Oreg., Salem, 1977—; fellow Eagleton Inst. Politics, 1971. Mem. Salem Human Relations Commn., 1967-70, Marion-Polk Boundary Commn., 1970-71; trustee Willamette U., 1978—. Recipient Golden Torch award Bus. and Profl. Women Oreg., 1971, Distinguished Service award City of Salem, 1971; named to Women of Future, Ladies Home Jour., 1980. Mem. Oreg. State Bar, Nat. Order Women Legislators, Nat. Soc. State Legislators (dir. 1971-72). Office: Office of Sec of State 136 State Capitol Salem OR 97310

PAULY, JOHN EDWARD, scientist, educator; b. Elgin, Ill., Sept. 17, 1927; s. Edward John and Gladys (Myhre) P.; B.S., Northwestern U., 1950; M.S., Loyola U., Chgo., 1952, Ph.D. 1955; m. Margaret Mary Oberle, Sept. 3, 1949; children—Stephen John, Susan Elizabeth, Kathleen Ann, Mark Edward. Grad. asst. gross anatomy Stritch Sch. Medicine, Loyola U., Chgo., 1953-54; research asst. anatomy Chgo. Med. Sch., 1952-54, research instr., 1954-55, instr. in gross anatomy, 1955-57, asso. gross anatomy, 1957-59, asst. prof. anatomy, 1959-63, asst. to pres., 1960-62; asso. prof. anatomy Tulane U. Sch. Medicine, 1963-67; prof., head dept. anatomy U. Ark. for Med. Scis., Little Rock, 1967—, prof., head dept. physiology and biophysics, 1978—; tech. adviser Ency. Brit. Films, 1956. Mem. safety and occupational health study sect. Nat. Inst. for Occupational Safety and Health, Center for Disease Control, 1975-79. Served with USNR, 1945-47. Recipient merit certificates AMA, 1953, 59; Bronze award Ill. Med. Soc., 1959; Lederle Med. Faculty award, 1966. Mem. Am. Assn. Anatomists (sec.-treas. 1972-80), So. Soc. Anatomists (pres. 1971-72), Assn. Anatomy Chmn. (sec.-treas. 1969-71), Am. Soc. Cancer Research, Am. Physiol. Soc., Assn. Chairmen Depts. Physiology, Assn. Am. Med. Colls., Internat. Soc. Chronobiology, Pan-Am. Assn. Anatomy, AAAS, Internat. Soc. Electrophysiol. Kinesiology, Internat. Soc. for Steriology, Sigma Xi, Sigma Alpha Epsilon. Roman Catholic. Author: (with Hans Elias) Human Microanatomy, 1960; (with Elias and E. Robert Burns) Histology and Human Microanatomy, 1978; editor: (with Lawrence E. Scheving and Franz Halberg) Chronobiology, 1974; adv. editorial bd. Internat. Jour. Chronobiology; mng. editor Am. Jour. Anatomy, 1980—; contbr. articles to profl. jours. Home: 11 Hearthside Dr Little Rock AR 72207

PAULY, JOHN WILLIAM, air force officer; b. Albany, N.Y., Mar. 12, 1923; s. John Alphonse and Ida May (Shafer) P.; student Rensselear Poly. Inst., 1940-42; B.S., U.S. Mil. Acad., 1945; M.A., George Washington U., 1965; student Nat. War Coll., 1964-65; m. Mary Francis Roberta Chatt, June 25, 1949; children—John William, Richard Lawrence, Kathleen Ann, Joanne Margaret, Karen Marie. Commd. 2nd lt., U.S. Air Force, 1945, advanced through grades to gen., 1978; purchasing and contract officer 304th Transport Carrier Squadron, Munich, Germany, 1946-47, 2029th Labor Supervision Co., 1947-48; flying instr. Central Pilots Sch., European Air Transport Service; test pilot 11th Troop Carrier Squadron, Munich; tng. officer and comdr. Hdqrs. Squadron, Mobile Air Material Area, Brookley AFB, Ala., 1948-51; test and evaluation pilot 8th Bombardment Squadron, Far East Air Forces, 1951-52, also flying safety officer, squadron ops. officer; ops. officer Directorate of Ops. and Tng. Bombardment Div., Langley AFB, Va., 1952-56, also chief ops. br.; ops. officer Light Bombardment Div. NATO, Hdqrs. 4th Allied Tactical Air Force, Ramstein Air Base, Germany, 1956-59, also exec. officer Office of Dep. Chief of Staff for Ops.; planning and programming officer in Directorate of Plans, Hdqrs. U.S. Air Force, Washington, 1959-64, asst. exec. to chief of staff; dep. comdr. ops. Hdqrs. 317th Troop Carrier Wing, Lockbourne AFB, Ohio, 1965-66; dep. chief of staff for ops. 315th Air Div., Tachikawa Air Base, Japan, 1966-68; comdr. 315th Air Commando Wing, Republic of Vietnam, 1968-69, comdr. 315th Spl. Ops. Wing, 1968-69; Air Force mem. of Chairman's Staff Group, Orgn. of Joint Chiefs of Staff, Washington, 1969-70, dep. dir. regional ops., J-3, Joint Staff, 1970-72, vice dir., J-3, Joint Staff, 1972-73; comdr. Hdqrs. 1st Strategic Aerospace Div., Strategic Air Command, Vandenberg AFB, Calif., 1973-74; asst. to chmn. Joint Chiefs of Staff, Washington, 1974-75; dep. chief staff for plans and ops. Hdqrs. U.S. Air Force, Washington, 1975-76; vice comdr. in chief U.S. Air Forces in Europe, Ramstein Air Base, Germany, 1976-78; comdr. in chief U.S. Air Forces in Europe, 1978—, comdr. Allied Air Forces Central Europe, 1978—. Decorated D.S.M. with oak leaf cluster, Air Medal with four oak leaf clusters, D.F.C. with oak leaf cluster, Legion of Merit with two oak leaf clusters; Gallantry Cross with palm (Republic of Vietnam). Mem. Am. Legion, Daedalians. Club: K.C. Home: PSC Box 8978 APO New York NY 09012 Office: Hdqrs United States Air Forces in Europe Ramstein AB Germany APO NY 09012

PAUSIG, RALPH W., communications co. exec. Vice pres. ITT. Office: ITT World Hdqrs 320 Park Ave New York NY 10022*

PAVAROTTI, LUCIANO, lyric tenor; b. Modena, Italy, Oct. 12, 1935; s. Fernando and Adele (Venturi) P.; diploma magistrale Istituto Magistrale Carlo Sigonio, 1955; studied with Arrigo Pola and Ettore Campogalliani; m. Adua Veroni, Sept. 30, 1961; children—Lorenza, Cristina, Giuliana. Formerly tchr. elementary schs.; salesman ins.; debut as Rodolfo in La Bohème, Reggio Emilia, Italy, 1961; roles include Edgardo in Lucia di Lammermoor (debut Amsterdam 1963), the Duke in Rigoletto (debut Carpi 1961), Rodolfo in La Bohème (debut Covent Garden 1963), Tonio in The Daughter of The Regiment (debut Covent Garden 1966); appeared in Lucia di Lammermoor, Australia, 1965, Am. debut, Miami, Fla., 1965; numerous European performances including La Scala, Milan, Italy, Vienna Staatsoper, Paris, Hamburg, San Francisco Opera, 1967; debut Met. Opera, N.Y.C., 1968, as Rodolfo in La Bohème; appeared in Daughter of Regiment, Met. Opera, 1971, Elisir d'Amore, Met. Opera, 1973, La Boheme, Chgo. Opera, 1973, La Favorita, San Francisco Opera, 1973, Il Trovatore, San Francisco Opera, 1975, Bellini I Puritani, Met. Opera, 1976; numerous yearly performances internationally; concert series of Am. and European cities, including Carnegie Hall, 1973; also recs. Winner Concorso Internationale, Reggio Emilia, 1961. Office: care Herbert Breslin 119 W 57th St New York NY 10019

PAVELCHEK, WALTER RAYMOND, chem. engr.; b. Johnstown, Pa., Jan. 8, 1925; s. Frank and Louise (Kudelka) P.; B.S. in Chem. Engring., Purdue U., 1945; postgrad. U. Notre Dame, 1945, Purdue U., 1946-47; M.S. in Chem. Engring., U. Ill., 1954; m. Emma Louise Hillaert, June 26, 1948; children—Edward, David, Andrew, Thomas, Louise, Mary. Tech. field man Sinclair Refining Co., East Chicago, Ind., 1947-50; mem. faculty chem. engring. Tufts U., Medford, Mass., 1951-57, asst. prof., 1954-57; process engr. Am. Viscose div. FMC Corp., Marcus Hook, Pa., 1957-60, group leader, 1960-61, sect. leader, 1961-74, project mgr., Phila., 1974-75, engring. and tech. supt., Downingtown, Pa., 1975-79, sr. project engr., Phila., 1979—. Mem. Billerica (Mass.) Town Finance Com., 1957; rep. Town Meeting, Billerica, 1957. Served to ensign USNR, 1943-46. Mem. Am. Inst. Chem. Engrs. (nat. dir. 1973-75), Sigma Nu, Tau Beta Pi. Contbg. author: Science and Technology of Packaging Films, 1971. Patentee in field. Home: 1050 S New St West Chester PA 19380 Office: FMC Corp Corp Chem Engring 2000 Market St Philadelphia PA 19103

PAVILACK, LAWRENCE LEE, lawyer; b. Wheeling, W.Va., Jan. 3, 1936; s. David and Sylvia P.; A.B., Harvard U., 1957; postgrad. W.Va. U., 1957-58, N.Y. U., 1958-59; J.D., Boston U., 1962; m. Carol Ann McGrew, June 18, 1960; children—Douglas Brooks, Joann Clements. With French-Am. Banking Corp., N.Y.C., 1958-59; admitted to Ariz. bar, 1962, since practiced in Phoenix; mem. firm Rawlins, Ellis, Burrus & Kiewit, 1962-72, 73-78, firm Pavilack, Spack & Mulchay, Scottsdale, 1978—; judge Superior Ct. Maricopa County, 1972, judge pro tem, 1979; spl. ct. commr., 1976—. Vice pres., treas., bd. dirs. Ariz. Archeol. Soc.; bd. dirs. Phoenix Archeol. Soc., Men's Arts Council of Phoenix Art Mus., Men's League of Scottsdale Center Performing Arts. Mem. Am., Ariz., Maricopa County bar assns. Clubs: University (past pres.), Harvard (past pres.), Phoenix Country (Phoenix). Home: 381 E Verde Ln Phoenix AZ 85012 Office: Suite 800 6900 E Camelback Scottsdale AZ 85251

PAVILANIS, VYTAUTAS, physician, educator; b. Kaunas, Lithuania, June 7, 1920; s. Kazys and Antonina (Eimontas) P.; M.D., U. Kaunas, 1942; diploma in microbiology Institut Pasteur, Paris, 1947, diploma in serology and hematology, 1948; m. Irene Stencelis, Mar. 8, 1947; children—Alain, Christine, Marina Pavilanis Branigan, Ingrid. Asst. prof. pathology U. Kaunas, 1942-44; resident physician, Siegbourg, Germany, 1944-45; asst. Institut Pasteur, Paris, 1945-48; asst. prof. U. Montreal (Can.), 1948; head virus dept. Institut Armand-Frappier, Ville de Laval, Que., Can., 1948-75, sci. dir., 1970-75, research coordinator, 1975-78, dir. quality control, 1976-79, asst. dir. teaching and research, 1978—; asso. prof. U. Montreal, 1956—; prof. U. Que., 1974—; cons. in field. Recipient Queen's Jubilee medal Can., 1977. Fellow Royal Soc. Can.; mem. Can. Soc. Microbiology (2d v.p. 1966), Can. Public Health Assn. (chmn. lab. sect. 1969), Virology Club Montreal (pres. 1969), Coll. Physicians and Surgeons P.Q., Can. Med. Assn., Can. Assn. Med. Microbiologists, Soc. Microbiology P.Q., N.Y. Acad. Sci. Contbr. articles to profl. jours. Home: 4742 The Boulevard Westmount PQ H3Y 1V2 Canada Office: PO Box 100 Ville de Laval PQ H7N 4Z3 Canada

PAVITT, WILLIAM HESSER, JR., lawyer; b. Bklyn., Dec. 9, 1916; s. William Hesser and Elsie (Haring) P.; A.B., Columbia, 1937, LL.B., 1939; postgrad. N.Y. U., 1943-44, Nat. U., 1947-48, U. Calif., Los Angeles, 1970, 72, 73; m. Mary Leland Oden, June 19, 1937; children—William Hesser III, Howard O., Gale Haring Palmer, Bruce M. Admitted to N.Y. bar, 1939, D.C. bar, 1947, Md. bar, 1947, Ohio bar, 1955, Calif. bar, 1958; clk. N.Y. Ct. of Appeals, N.Y.C. and Albany, 1939-40; asso. Spence, Windells, Walser, Hotchkiss & Angell, N.Y.C., 1940-44; chief procurement officer Office Naval Research, 1946-47, also lawyer Office Gen. Counsel, Navy Dept., Washington, 1947; partner Whiting & Pavitt, Washington, 1947-54; asso. Toulmin & Toulmin, Dayton, Ohio, 1954-57, Smyth & Roston, Los Angeles, 1957-59; partner Smyth, Roston & Pavitt, Los Angeles, 1960-76; mem. firm Smyth, Pavitt, Siegemund, Jones & Martella, 1976—. Pres. elementary, jr. high and high schs. P.T.A.'s, Montgomery County, Md., 1949-52. Pres. Young Republican Club, Montgomery County, 1950-51; Rep. precinct chmn., Montgomery County, 1952-53. Served from ensign to lt. (j.g.), USNR, 1944-46. Mem. Fed., Los Angeles County (vice chmn. intellectual property sect. 1970-71) bar assns., Cal. State Bar (chmn. patent conf. 1972-73), Los Angeles Patent Law Assn. (pres. 1969-70). Presbyn. (elder). Rotarian (pres. Pacific Palisades 1976-77). Club: Ambassador Tennis. Author trade secrets sect. California Continuing Education of the Bar, 1971. Home: 1334 Charmel Pl Pacific Palisades CA 90272 Office: 4262 Wilshire Blvd Los Angeles CA 90010

PAVLICK, WALTER EUGENE, home mfg. co. exec.; b. Youngstown, Ohio, Mar. 3, 1934; s. George and Jennie (Perko) P.; B.S. in Engring., Case Inst. Tech., 1956; J.D., George Washington U., 1959; M.B.A., Toledo U., 1967; m. Barbara Ann Slatsky, Sept. 8, 1956; children—Gary, Randy, Ronald. Patent examiner U.S. Patent Office, Washington, 1956; patent agt. Robertshaw-Fulton Controls Co., Washington, 1957-59; admitted to Va. bar, 1959, Ohio bar, 1960, Ind. bar, 1973; counsel Dana Corp., Toledo, 1959-72; chief counsel, sec. Nat. Homes Corp., Lafayette, Ind., 1972-79, Nat. Homes Acceptance Corp., 1972-79; v.p., gen. counsel Modine Mfg. Co., Racine, Wis., 1979—. Mem. Va., Ind., Ohio bar assns. Presbyterian. Clubs: Lafayette Country, Lafayette Tennis. Home: 623 Ridgewood Dr West Lafayette IN 47906 Office: Modine Mfg Co 1500 De Hoven Ave Racine WI 53401

PAVLIK, WILLIAM BRUCE, psychologist; b. Cleve., Feb. 29, 1932; s. William Frank and Mary (Maco) P.;B.S., Western Res. U., 1953; M.A., Ohio State U., 1955, Ph.D., 1956; m. Mary Katherine Findley, May 22, 1979; children by previous marriage—William James, Heather Ann, Russell Matthew, James Clark. Asst. prof. psychology Western Mich. U., 1956-60; asst. prof., then asso. prof. Rutgers U., 1960-68; prof. psychology Va. Poly. Inst. and State U., 1968-77, chmn. dept., 1968-72; prof., head psychology dept. U. Ga., Athens, 1977—. Mem. Am., Eastern psychol. assns., Psychonomic Soc., Animal Behavior Soc. Author articles in field. Home: 115 Georgetown Circle Athens GA 30605 Office: Dept Psychology U Georgia Athens GA 30602

PAVLIS, FRANK EDWARD, chem. co. exec.; b. Buckley, Mich., Oct. 29, 1916; s. Frank N. and Anna (Zalud) P.; B.S., Mich. Technol. U., 1938; M.S., U. Mich., 1939; postgrad. Harvard, 1957; m. Ethel A. Piehl. Nov. 27, 1947. Research and devel. engr. L.P. Pool, Detroit, 1939-40; with Air Products & Chems., Inc., and predecessor, 1940—, successively chief engr., tech. dir., tech. sales dir., treas., 1949-55, engring. v.p., 1955-56, financial v.p., 1957-60, internat. v.p., 1961—, also dir.; dir. Air Products, Ltd. Registered profl. engr., Pa. Mem. Am. Chem. Soc., Am. Inst. Chem. Engrs., Tau Beta Pi, Phi Lambda Upsilon. Home: 3544 Congress St Allentown PA 18104 Office: P O Box 538 Allentown PA 18105

PAWLEWSKI, NORMAN LEONARD, state public health ofcl.; b. Buffalo, May 28, 1934; s. William and Estelle P.; B.S. in Acct. with honors, U. Buffalo, 1960; postgrad. Nat. Center for Disease Control Tng. Program, intermittently, 1962-70; postgrad. in public adminstrn. Drake U., 1973-74; m. Rose Marie Fiscarelli, June 19, 1965; children—David Brian, Dawn Marie. Partner cocktail lounge and restaurant, Lancaster, N.Y., 1960-62; with USPHS, 1962-70, adminstrv. asst. Iowa Dept. Health, Des Moines, 1967-69, dep. chief preventive med. service, 1969-70; asst. to commr. public health Iowa Dept. Public Health, Des Moines, 1970-73, acting commr. public health, 1973, commr. public health, 1973—; dir. Sta.-KDMI-FM. Served with U.S. Army, 1953-55. Republican. Evangelical Christian. Home: 3707 SW 28th St Des Moines IA 50321 Office: Lucas Office Bldg Des Moines IA 50319

PAWLEY, THOMAS DÉSIRÉ, III, educator; b. Jackson, Miss., Aug. 5, 1917; s. Thomas Désiré and Ethel John (Woolfolk) P.; A.B. with distinction, Va. State Coll., 1937; A.M., U. Iowa, 1939, Ph.D., 1949; student U. Mo., 1957; m. Ethel Louise McPeters, Aug. 14, 1941; children—Thomas Désiré IV, Lawrence. Mem. faculty Atlanta U., summers 1939-41, 43, 44, Prairie View (Tex.) A. and M. State Coll., 1939-40; mem. faculty Lincoln U., Jefferson City, Mo., 1940—, prof. dramatic art, 1952—, head dept. communications, dean Coll. Arts and Scis., 1977—; vis. prof. U. Calif. at Santa Barbara, summer 1968, No. Ill. U., DeKalb, 1971, U. Iowa, 1976. Mem. adv. screening com. in theatre arts Com. on Internat. Exchange of Scholars, 1973-76; mem. central com. Am. Coll. Theatre Festival, 1971-75; mem. theatre adv. com. Mo. council on Arts, 1979—. Vice chmn. Jefferson City Com. Residential Standards, 1965-66; pres. Jefferson City Library Bd., 1970, 71. Chmn. Alpha Phi Alpha Edn. Found., 1967-73. Alpha Phi Alpha grad. scholar, 1947-48; Nat. Theatre Conf. fellow, 1947-48. Mem. Am. Theatre Assn. (commn. on theatre edn. 1977-79; coll. fellows 1978—), Speech and Theatre Assn. Mo. (bd. govs. 1974-79, pres. 1977-78, Outstanding Tchr. award 1977), Nat. Assn. Dramatic and Speech Arts (pres. 1953-55), Nat. Conf. Acad. Deans (dir. 1979—), Alpha Phi Alpha (dir. ednl. activities 1967-73 (v.p. Midwest region 1975-79), Iota Sigma Lambda, Omicron Delta Kappa, Purple Masque. Author: (plays) Jedgement Day, 1941; The Tumult and the Shouting, 1974. Co-editor: The Black Teacher and the Dramatic Arts, 1970. Home: 1014 Lafayette St Jefferson City MO 65101

PAXSON, CHARLES SMALL, JR., hosp. adminstr.; b. Phila., Oct. 14, 1909; s. Charles Small and Martha Kelso (Dunning) P.; B.S. in Accounting, Temple U., 1935; m. Katherine Virginia Thompson, Apr. 25, 1936; children—C. Stanley, Stephen Griffith. Office mgr. Hahnemann Hosp., Phila., 1932-41; adminstr. Delaware County Meml. Hosp., Drexel Hill, Pa., 1941-57; v.p., adminstr. Hahnemann Med. Coll. and Hosp., 1957-73; adminstrv. v.p. Temple U. Hosp., 1973-76; cons. Medicon Inc., 1976—; pres. Delaware Valley Hosp. Laundry, Inc. Treas., Phila. Health Mgmt. Corp.; dir. Greater Delaware Valley Savs. and Loan Assn. Mem. bd., past pres. Community Nursing Service Delaware County, Lansdowne Allied Youth Council; mem. bd. Delaware County chpt. Nat. Found. Infantile Paralysis, Upper Darby chpt. ARC, Greater Delaware Valley Regional Med. Program. Fellow Am. Coll. Hosp. Adminstrs. (regent 1966-72); mem. Am., Phila. (past pres.) hosp. assns., Hosp. Assn. Pa. (past pres.), Assn. Hosp. Service Phila. (bd.). Mem. Soc. of Friends. Rotarian (past pres. Upper Darby.) Home: 46 Pennock Terr Lansdowne PA 19050 Office: 222 Lancaster Park Devon PA 19333

PAXTON, FRANK, JR., corp. exec.; b. Kansas City, Mo., Nov. 14, 1918; s. Frank and Marjorie (Lane) P.; student U. Wash., 1936-37, Va. Mil. Inst., 1937-38; grad. Stanford Exec. Sch., 1967; m. 2d, Mildred Heath, Apr. 3, 1959. With Frank Paxton Co., Kansas City, 1938—, mgr., Chgo., 1947-51, pres. co., 1951—; chmn. Paxton-Nat. Inc., Overland Park, Kans., 1966—. Police commr., Kansas City, 1977-80; chmn. Thomas Hart Benton Assos., 1975-76. Served to maj. AUS, 1941-45. Mem. Nat. Wholesale Lumber Distbg. Yard Assn. (pres. 1963), Nat. Hardwood Lumber Assn. (dir. 1957-62) Philippine Mahogany Assn. (pres. 1969-71). Clubs: Kansas City Country, River (Kansas City, Mo.). Home: 800 W 52d St Kansas City MO 64112 Office: 6311 St John Ave Kansas City MO 64123

PAXTON, HAROLD WILLIAM, steel co. exec.; b. Yorkshire, Eng., Feb. 6, 1927; s. John Wilfrid and Hilda Annie (Vasey) P.; B.Sc. with 1st class honours, U. Man., 1947, M.Sc., 1948; Ph.D., U. Birmingham (Eng.), 1952; m. Ann Dorothy Davies, May 13, 1953; children—Jane Elizabeth, Sally Patricia, Anthony Charles, Nigel John. Came to U.S., 1953, naturalized, 1961. Univ. fellow U. Birmingham, 1950-53; mem. faculty Carnegie-Mellon U., 1953-74, prof. metall. engring., 1962-74, Firth Sterling prof. metall. research, 1958-63, head dept. metallurgy and materials sci., dir. Metals Research Lab., 1966-71, dir. research, 1973-74; adj. sr. fellow Mellon Inst., 1965-67; dir. div. materials research NSF, 1971-73; v.p. research U.S. Steel Corp., 1974—; vis. prof. Mass. Inst. Tech., 1970; Campbell meml. lectr., 1978; cons. to industry, 1953-74. Chmn., Internat. Conf. High Velocity Deformation, 1960, Internat. Conf. Fracture, 1962. NSF sr. postdoctoral fellow Imperial Coll., London, Eng., 1962-63. Fellow Am. Soc. Metals (Bradley Stoughton Young Tchrs. award 1960) Fellow Metall. Soc. of Am. Inst. M.E. (pres. 1976-77, v.p. inst. 1977-78); mem. AAAS, AIME, Am. Iron and Steel Inst., Nat. Acad. Engring. Author: Alloying Elements in Steel (with E. C. Bain), 3d edit., 1966; also numerous articles. Home: 115 Eton Dr Pittsburgh PA 15215 Office: Room 1365 600 Grant St Pittsburgh PA 15230

PAXTON, ROBERT OWEN, historian, educator; b. Lexington, Va., June 15, 1932; s. Matthew W. and Nell B. (Owen) P.; B.A., Washington and Lee U., Lexington, 1954, Litt.D., 1974; B.A., Oxford (Eng.) U., 1956, M.A., 1961; Ph.D., Harvard U., 1963. Asst. prof. history U. Calif., Berkeley, 1961-67; asso. prof. State U. N.Y., Stony Brook, 1967-69; prof. history Columbia, 1969—, chmn. dept., 1980—. Served with USNR, 1956-58. Rhodes scholar, 1954-56; Am. Council Learned Socs. fellow, 1974-75; Rockefeller Found. fellow, 1978-79. Mem. Am. Hist. Assn., Soc. d'histoire moderne. Author: Parades and Politics at Vichy, 1966; Vichy France: Old Guard and New Order, 1940-44, 1972; Europe in the Twentieth Century, 1975. Home: 560 Riverside Dr New York NY 10027 Office: Dept History Columbia Univ New York NY 10027

PAYCHECK, JOHNNY (DON LYTLE), country music singer and songwriter; b. Greenfield, Ohio, May 31, 1941. Guitarist with Porter Wagoner's Wagonmasters, Faron Young's Deputies, Ray Price's Band, George Jones' Jones Boys; co-founder, recorded with Little Darlin' Records; recorded for Decca, Mercury, Hilltop, Epic, numerous tours; appeared in film J.D. and the Saltflat Kid; writer songs, including Apartment Number 9, Touch My Heart; albums include 11 Months and 29 Days, Loving You Beats All, Greatest Hits, Song and Dance Man, She's All I Got, Someone to Give My Love To, Take This Job and Shove It. Address: care Glenn Ferguson 109 Courthouse Nashville TN 37201*

PAYER, ERNST DENIS, architect; b. Vienna, Austria, July 17, 1904; s. Ernst and Friederike (Dubsky) P.; came to U.S., 1936, naturalized, 1939; B.Arch., Acad. Art, Vienna, 1936; Ph.D. in Polit. Sci., U. Vienna, 1927; M.Arch., Harvard U., 1938. Architect, N.Y.C., 1939-46; architect Ernst Payer & Assos., Cleve., 1946—. Recipient 1st medal housing Ohio Soc. Architects, 1947; 1st medal craftsmanship Cleve. Mus. Art, 1951; 1st award Ohio Soc. Illuminating Engrs., 1966. Mem. Illuminating Engrs. Soc., A.I.A., Am. Soc. Landscape Architects. Clubs: Rowfant, Rotary (Cleve.). Contbr. to books, articles to profl. jours. in U.S. and Europe. Home: 4149 Giles Moreland Hills OH 44022 Office: Keith Bldg Cleveland OH 44115

PAYETTE, THOMAS MARTIN, architect; b. Grand Rapids, Mich., Aug. 9, 1932; s. Robert J. and Mary Kay (Martin) P.; B.S. in Structural Engring. magna cum laude, Mich. State U., 1956; M. Arch., Harvard U., 1960; m. Virginia Carson, Sept. 4, 1954; children—Scott Carson, Monte Martin, Shelly Kellog, Jennifer Jennings. Archtl. designer Markus & Nocka, Inc., Boston, 1960-65; pres., dir. design Payette Assos., Inc., Boston, 1965—; asst. prof. R.I. Sch. Design, Providence, 1964-65; cons. in field to Mass. Dept. Pub. Health, 1974—. Trustee Buckingham, Browne & Nichols Sch., Cambridge, Mass., 1976—. Julian Appleton Traveling fellow Harvard U. Grad. Sch. Design, 1961; registered architect, Mass., Maine, N.H., N.Y., Mich., Conn., Vt., Minn., Ky., Fla., Ga., Pa., R.I. Fellow AIA; mem. Royal Inst. Brit. Architects, Boston Soc. Architects (dir. 1972-74), Environ. Edn. Fund (dir. 1974—), Am. Hosp. Assn., N. Eng. Hosp. Assembly, Tau Beta Pi, Phi Kappa Phi, Chi Epsilon Phi. Archtl. works include: Leonard Morse Hosp., Natick, Mass., 1969; Emerson Hosp., Concord, Mass., 1970; Eastern Maine Med. Center, Bangor, Maine, 1974; Aga Khan Hosp. and Med. Coll., Karachi, Pakistan, 1976; Joslin Diabetes Found., Boston, 1977. Home: 283 Upland Rd Cambridge MA 02140 Office: 40 Isabella St Boston MA 02116

PAYETTE, WILLIAM COLIN, newspaperman; b. Aberdeen, Wash., May 13, 1913; s. Edward and Eva Lowenna (Beauchamp) P.; B.A., U. So. Calif., 1935; m. Virginia Ellis MacPherson; children—Susan, Bruce. Editor, Santa Monica (Calif.) Topics, 1935-36; staff writer Los Angeles bur. u.p., bur. mgr., Billings, Helena and Butte, Mont., state mgr. for Mont. staff Seattle bur., N.W. news editor, Portland, Oreg., mgr. Los Angeles bur., mgr. No. div. S.Am., TV mgr. U.P.I., 1936-55, asst. gen. news mgr., 1955-59, gen. sales mgr., 1959-61, S.W. div. mgr., 1961-69, dir., 1958-64; v.p. United Feature Syndicate, N.Y.C., 1968-70, gen. mgr., 1969, pres., 1970-78, chmn., 1978—. Recipient Service award So. Meth. U.: Friars award At. Bonaventure Coll.; Headliner award Women in Communications. Mem. Soc. Profl. Journalists, Sigma Delta Chi (dir. 1963-74, nat. pres. 1973). Clubs: Los Angeles Press (past pres.); Overseas Press, Dutch Treat, Players, Lambs, Deadline (past pres.), Silurians (N.Y.C.); Dallas Press (past pres.); Nantucket (Mass.) Yacht; Field, Siwanoy Country (Bronxville, N.Y.). Home: Bronxville NY 10708 Office: 200 Park Ave New York NY 10017

PAYNE, ANCIL HORACE, broadcasting exec.; b. Mitchell, Oreg., Sept. 5, 1921; s. Leslie L. and Pearl A. (Brown) P.; student Willamette U., 1939-41, U. Oreg., 1941, U. Notre Dame, Ohio State U., 1943; B.S., U. Wash., 1947; postgrad. Am. U., 1950-51; m. Valerie Dorrance Davies, Apr. 6, 1959; children—Anne Sparrow, Alison Louise, Lucinda Catherine. Adminstrv. asst. to congressman, Washington, 1949-52; gen. mgr. Martin Van Lines, Anchorage, 1952-56; gen. mgr. Frontiers-Oreg. Ltd., Portland, Oreg., 1956-59; asst. v.p. bus. div. King Broadcasting Co., Seattle, 1959-63, v.p., 1963-65, v.p. Portland stas., 1965-70, exec. v.p., Seattle, 1970-71, pres. of co., 1971—, also dir.; chmn. bd. dels. NBC. Mem. Oreg. Bd. Higher Edn., 1966-70; chmn. Bicentennial Commn. Wash. State; bd. dirs. Pacific Sci. Found. Served to lt. USNR, 1942-45; PTO. Mem. Seattle C. of C. (dir. 1973—), Phi Beta Kappa, Alpha Delta Sigma. Episcopalian. Clubs: Wash. Athletic, Monday, Ranier (Seattle); Multnomah Athletic (Portland). Home: 1356 E Boston St Seattle WA 98102 Office: 320 Aurora Ave N Seattle WA 98109

PAYNE, BRUCE, management cons.; b. Bakersfield, Calif., Feb. 6, 1911; s. James Bruce and Erma Frances (Deacon) P.; B.S., U. Calif., 1933; M.B.A., Harvard U., 1935; m. Edna Winifred Jessop, June 5, 1935; children—John Bruce, Christopher, Geoffrey Stephens. Indsl. engr. Republic Steel Corp., 1935-38; cons. Nat. City Bank of Cleve., 1938-40; v.p., dir. Dyer Engrs., Inc., Cleve., 1940-46; pres., dir. Bruce Payne Consultants Inc., 1946—, Bruce Payne & Assos. Internat., Inc., 1952—, Payne Computer Services, Inc., 1969-77, also Bruce Payne & Assos. de Sud Am. (Argentina), Bruce Payne y Associados S.A. (Mexico), Bruce Payne Associados (Brazil). Trustee Fairfield (Conn.) Country Day Sch., 1951-61. Mem. Inst. Mgmt. Cons. (dir., v.p. 1972-75, founding mem.), Council Internat. Progress in Mgmt. (dir. 1951-55, v.p. 1955-58, v.p. found. 1958—), Soc. Advancement Mgmt. (dir. 1946-50, dir.-at-large 1955, nat. treas. 1950-52, exec. v.p., 1952-53, past nat. pres., nat. adv. council), Harvard Bus. Sch. Assn. (pres. 1950-51, chmn. fund com. 1952-53, mem. fund council 1953-56), Am. Mgmt. Assn., Chief Execs. Forum, Newcomen Soc., English-Speaking Union, Alpha Sigma Phi. Clubs: Economic (N.Y.C.); Harvard (Boston, N.Y.C.); Fairfield County Hunt. Author: Planning for Company Growth, 1963; (with D.D. Swett) Office Operations Improvement, 1967. Office: Bruce Payne Consultants Inc Time-Life Bldg Rockefeller Center New York NY 10020

PAYNE, CHARLES NORVILLE, ret. naval officer, ednl. adminstr.; b. Ft. Smith, Ark., Feb. 25, 1919; s. Charles Norville and Geraldine Frances (Lambright) P.; student La. Poly. Inst., 1935-38; B.S., U.S. Naval Acad., 1941; Sc.M., Mass. Inst. Tech., 1948; m. Sunshine Venonia Shehee, May 12, 1942; children—Priscilla (Mrs. Lee Albert Cockerell), Cherry, Henry. Commd. ensign USN, 1941, advanced through grades to rear adm., 1969; controller Bur. Ships and Naval Ships Systems Command, Washington, 1964-68; comdr. Charleston Naval Shipyard, 1968-71; supr. shipbldg., Pascagoula, Miss., 1971-74; ret., 1974; pres. Webb Inst. Naval Architecture, Glen Cove, N.Y., 1974—. Faculty, Coll. William and Mary, 1949-50, U. Va., 1952-54, U.S. Naval Acad., 1954-57. Explorer chmn. Coastal Carolina council Boy Scouts Am., 1969-70, Pine Burr council, 1971-73. Decorated Legion of Merit with bronze star. Recipient Silver Beaver award Boy Scouts Am. Mem. Soc. Naval Architects and Marine Engrs. (mem. council, chmn. com. on edn.), Am. Soc. Naval Engrs. (editor Jour. 1957-60, 64-65). Methodist. Rotarian. Author: Naval Turbine Propulsion Plants, 1957. Contbr. articles to profl. jours. Address: Webb Inst Naval Architecture Glen Cove NY 11542

PAYNE, DONALD HUGHEL, chem. co. exec.; b. Indpls., June 22, 1928; s. Francis William and Mary Louise (Hughel) P.; student Butler U., 1945-47, Purdue U., 1947-49; B.S., U. Mich., M.S., 1951, Ph.D., 1953; m. E. Georgine Vallance, July 22, 1950; children—Beth Payne Ullom, William G., Lee C., Bruce W. Teaching fellow dept. chemistry U. Mich., Ann Arbor, 1949-51, du Pont fellow, 1951-52; successively research chemist, research supr., new product specialist, sr. research supr., planning mgr., research mgr., lab. dir., research and tech. dir. petroleum chems. E.I. du Pont de Nemours Co., Wilmington, Del., 1953—. Active Boy Scouts Am., Little League (past pres.). Mem. Am. Chem. Soc., Nat. Petroleum Refiners Assn., Soc. Plastics Industries, AAAS, Am. Petroleum Inst., Utes, Sigma Xi, Phi Eta Sigma, Phi Kappa Phi, Phi Lambda Upsilon, Sigma Chi. Republican. Home: 108 Stone Crop Rd Wilmington DE 19810 Office: Nemours Bldg Wilmington DE 19898

PAYNE, GERALD OLIVER, educator; b. East St. Louis, Ill., July 17, 1930; s. Amos Oliver and Suzanne Louise (Goussery) P.; B.A., Yale U., 1953; B.Music, U. Dubuque (Iowa), 1957; Ph.D., U. Wis.-Madison, 1969; m. Nancy Louise Ecklund, Aug. 8, 1959; children—Paul Clifton, Christopher Amos, Scott Eric, Miriam Louise, Susan Jeannette. Tchr. pub. schs., Aspen, Colo., 1959-61; tchr. pub. schs., Madison, 1961-65, coordinator fgn. langs., 1964-69, asst. dir. curriculum, 1967-69; asso. prof. edn. State U. N.Y. Coll. at Buffalo, 1969-71, prof. edn., 1971—, chmn. dept. curriculum and supervision, 1975-78, coordinator certificate advanced studies in adminstrn. and supervision, 1969-75, dir. Middle Sch. Inst., 1974. Mem. working com. Fgn. Lang. Educators Wis., 1968-69; mem. North Central Evaluation Teams, 1967, 68, 69; cons. Ednl. Prof. Devel. Assistance project Lackawanna (N.Y.) Pub. Schs., 1969-74; coll. rep. Coll. Assn. for Devel. Ednl. Adminstrn., N.Y. State, 1969—; mem. adv. com. career edn. Erie County (N.Y.), 1972-76; cons. middle sch. Cheektowaga (N.Y.) Central Schs., 1974; cons. Orchard Park (N.Y.) Middle Sch., 1974-76, Alden (N.Y.) Middle Sch., 1975, Geneva (N.Y.) Middle Sch., 1979. Chmn. troop com. Greater Niagara Frontier council Boy Scouts Am., Lewiston, N.Y., 1974-76, scoutmaster, 1976—, Order of Arrow, 1978—; bd. dirs., v.p. Planned Parenthood Niagara County; elder 1st Presbyterian Ch., Lewiston. Mem. NEA (life), Am. Assn. Sch. Adminstrs., Assn. for Supervision and Curriculum Devel., N.Y. State United Tchrs., Western N.Y. Yale Alumni Assn. (mem. schs. com. 1972—, dir. 1977—), Phi Delta Kappa. Republican. Contbr. articles to profl. jours. Home: 907 Escarpment Dr Lewiston NY 14092 Office: 302 Bacon State U Coll at Buffalo 1300 Elmwood Ave Buffalo NY 14222

PAYNE, HARRY MORSE, JR., architect; b. Norwood, Mass., Nov. 3, 1922; s. Harry Morse and Edna May (Beardsley) P.; student Boston Archtl. Center, 1946-49, Mass. Inst. Tech., 1949-50; m. Helen Marion Beasley, Aug. 29, 1946; children—Harry Morse, Thomas Beasley, Amelia Morse. Draftsman William G. Upham, Norwood, 1946-47; designer William Riseman Assos., Boston, 1947-49, Harry J. Korslund, Norwood, 1949-51, William Hoskins Brown, Boston, 1951-52; designer, prin. dir. The Architects Collaborative, Cambridge, Mass., 1952—, pres., 1975-77; pres. Boston Archtl. Center, 1963-65, 71-73; asst. prof. Harvard U. Grad. Sch. Design, 1954-63. Served with USN, 1943-46. Fellow AIA; mem. Boston Soc. Architects, Mass. State Assn. Architects, New Eng. Historic and Geneal. Soc., Mass. Soc. Genealogists, Lincoln Hist. Soc. Prin. works include U.S. Embassy, Athens, Greece, U. Bagdad (Iraq), Temple Israel, Boston, Quincy Sch., Boston. Home: 245 Aspen Circle Lincoln MA 01773 Office: 46 Brattle St Cambridge MA 02138

PAYNE, HARRY VERN, justice N.Mex. Supreme Ct.; b. Lordsburg, N.Mex., Aug. 13, 1936; s. Harry Vearle and Mandona (Hanchett) P.; B.A., Brigham Young U., 1961; J.D., U. N.Mex., 1964; m. Yerda Ruth Mason, June 26, 1959; children—Julie Ann, Harry Bruce, Herbert Rex., Curtis Edward, Daniel Lewis, Caroline, Thomas Mason, Sarah Dawn. Admitted to N.Mex. bar, 1964; mem. firm Hannett, Hannett & Cornish, Albuquerque, 1964-68; individual practice law, Albuquerque, 1969-70; dist. judge 2d Jud. Dist. Ct. of N.Mex., Albuquerque, 1971-76, presiding judge, 1973-74; asso. justice N.Mex. Supreme Ct., Santa Fe, 1977—; mem. N.Mex. Gov's. Council for Criminal Justice, 1971-74. Mem. exec. council Kit Carson council Boy Scouts Am., Albuquerque, 1973-74. Democrat. Mormon (lay ofcl.). Home: 105 Camino Teresa Santa Fe NM 87501 Office: Supreme Ct Bldg of N Mex Santa Fe NM 87503

PAYNE, KENYON THOMAS, educator; b. Amherst, Mass., Jan. 3, 1918; s. Loyal Frederick and Mary (Cobb) P.; B.S., Kans. State Coll., 1939; M.S., U. Nebr., 1941; Ph.D. (Conway MacMillan fellow), U. Minn., 1948; m. Jane E. Boucher, Nov. 21, 1942; children—Martha Joanna, William Samuel, Christopher Thomas. Agt., U.S. Dept. Agr., U. Nebr., 1939-41; asst. prof. Purdue U., 1948-52, asso. prof., 1952; prof. Mich. State U., 1952—, chmn. crop sci. dept., 1952-68; dean Faculty of Agr., U. Nigeria, Nsukka, 1964-66; sr. agrl. adviser, Brazil, 1969. Served from 2d lt. to lt. col., USAAF, 1941-46. Fellow AAAS, Am. Soc. Agronomy; mem. Crop Sci. Soc. Am., Internat. Turf Grass Soc., Sigma Xi, Phi Kappa Phi, Alpha Zeta, Sigma Alpha Epsilon. Home: 414 Clarendon Rd East Lansing MI 48823

PAYNE, LAWRENCE EDWARD, educator; b. Enfield, Ill., Oct. 2, 1923; s. Robert Ulysses and Harriet (Lasher) P.; student Miami U., Oxford, Ohio, 1943-44; B.S. in Mech. Engring., Iowa State U., 1946, M.S. in Applied Math., 1948, Ph.D., 1950; m. Ruth Marian Winterstein, Dec. 27, 1948; children—Steven L., John E., Marcia G., Christopher J., Michele T. Jr. engr. Linde Air Products, North Tonawanda, N.Y., 1946-47; asst. prof. math. U. Ariz., 1950-51; research asso. U. Md., 1951-52, asst. prof., 1952-55, asso. prof., 1955-60, prof., 1960-65; prof. Cornell U., Ithaca, N.Y., 1965—, dir. Center for Applied Math., 1967-71. Lectr. in field; cons. NSF, Nat. Bur. Standards 1958-65. Served with USNR, 1943-46. NSF sr. postdoctoral fellow, 1958-59. Recipient award sci. achievement math. Washington Acad. Scis., 1961. Mem. Am. Math. Soc. (Steele prize in math. 1972), Soc. Indsl. Applied Math., Math. Assn. Am., Am. Acad. Mechanics, Soc. Engring. Sci., Soc. Natural Philosophy, Sigma Xi. Editorial bd. SIAM Jour. Applied Math., Jr. Applicable Anal., Elasticity, Math. of Computation. Contbr. articles to profl. jours. Home: 103 Comstock Rd Ithaca NY 14850

PAYNE, M. LEE, banker; b. Norfolk, Va., Aug. 13, 1925; s. Robert Lee and Mary Elizabeth (Harmon) P.; grad. Woodberry Forest Sch., 1943; B.S., U. Va., 1945; M.B.A., U. Pa., 1949; m. Eunice Wortham Jenkins, July 19, 1952; children—Meriwether, John Benson, Ruth Jenkins. Investment analyst J.P. Morgan & Co., Inc., N.Y.C., 1949-51; with Seaboard Citizens Nat. Bank (now United Va. Bank/Seaboard Nat.), Norfolk, 1952—, exec. v.p., dir., 1963-67, pres., dir., 1967-74, chmn., dir., 1974—; dir. Maritime Terminals, Inc.; pres. Norfolk-Portsmouth Clearing House Assn., 1971-72. Chmn., Va. Commn. Outdoor Recreation; commr. Norfolk Area Med. Center Authority, 1969-75; mem. Commn. to Consider Matters Relating to Wetlands of State, 1974; bd. dirs. Tidewater Health Found., 1962-67, pres., 1962-67; bd. dirs. Norfolk Municipal Bond Commn., 1967-76; pres. Norfolk Symphony and Choral Assn., 1964, bd. dirs., 1959-66; bd. dirs. Norfolk United Communities Fund, 1959—, v.p., 1968-70, pres., 1971; bd. visitors Old Dominion U.; trustee Chesapeake Bay Found.; trustee, mem. exec. com. Va. Wesleyan Coll.; trustee Norfolk Acad., Va. Mus. Fine Arts, Hermitage Found.; trustee, pres. Lincoln-Lane Found.; bd. dirs., v.p. Va. Coll. Fund, 1970-74; pres. Greater Norfolk Corp.; regional v.p. Nat. Mcpl. League. Served with the USNR, 1943-46. Mem. Norfolk C. of C. (dir. 1964-77, pres. 1975). Presbyn. Clubs: Norfolk Yacht and Country, Harbor, Virginia (Norfolk); Folly Creek (Accomac, Va.). Home: PO Box 3127 Norfolk VA 23514 Office: United Va Bank/Seaboard Nat Norfolk VA 23514

PAYNE, MELVIN MONROE, sci. and ednl. exec.; b. Washington, May 23, 1911; s. Julian R. and Jeanette V. (Perry) P.; student Nat. U., 1929-30; LL.B., Southeastern U., 1939; D.Sc., S.D. Sch. Mines and Tech., 1962, Iowa Wesleyan Coll., 1969; LL.D., U. Miami, 1973; m. Ethel B. McDonnell, Sept. 1, 1938; children—Melvin Monroe (dec.), Frances, Nancy Jeanette. With N.Y. Sun, 1927; asst. to sec. Ry. Accounting Officers Assn., 1930-32; with Nat. Geog. Soc., 1932—, pres., chief exec. officer, 1967-76, chmn. bd., 1976—, also trustee, chmn. com. research and exploration; dir. Washington Mut. Investors Fund, Equitable Savs. & Loan Assn., Ethyl Corp., GEICO Corp., Criterion Ins. Co., Govt. Employees Fin. Corp., Potomac Electric Power Co.; adv. dir. Riggs Nat. Bank; admitted to D.C. bar, 1941. Mem. exec. com. Fed. City Council; council mem., adv. bd. sec. interior on Nat. Park System. Trustee, v.p. U.S. Capitol Hist. Soc.; chmn., trustee White House Hist. Assn.; vice-chmn. White House Preservation Fund; trustee Inst. Nautical Archaeology, Internat. Oceanographic Found.; bd. govs., exec. com. Nat. Space Inst.; exec. council Nat. Capital area Boy Scouts Am.; mem. internat. adv. council Louis Leakey Meml. Inst. for African Prehistory; mem. program rev. council Jane Goodall Inst. Wildlife Research, Edn., and Conservation; mem. adv. bd. Gorilla Found. Mem. Am. Bar Assn., Am. Assn. Geographers, AAAS, Supreme Ct. Hist. Soc. (trustee, exec. com.). Clubs: Alfalfa, Metropolitan, Cosmos (Washington); Chevy Chase (Md.); Burning Tree (Bethesda). Home: 8821 Burdette Rd Bethesda MD 20034 Office: 1145 17th St NW Washington DC 20036

PAYNE, MICHAEL DAVID, educator; b. Dallas, Jan. 17, 1941; s. Fred G. Payne and Jocie Marie (Kirkham) Lundberg; student U. Calif. at Berkeley, 1958-59, 61; B.A., So. Oreg. Coll., 1962; Ph.D., U. Oreg., 1969; m. Laura Asherman, Dec. 26, 1973; children—Jeffrey, Albert. Tchr. English, Medford (Oreg.) Sr. High Sch., 1962-63; instr. English, U. Oreg., Eugene, 1963-69; asst. prof. to prof. English, Bucknell U., Lewisburg, Pa., 1969—, dir. Bucknell U. Press, 1972-76, asso. editor Bucknell Rev., 1970—. Recipient Lindback award for distinguished teaching, 1976; Folger Shakespeare Library fellow, 1973, Nat. Endowment for Humanities fellow, 1974; Bucknell Alumni fellow, 1978-79. Mem. Shakespeare Assn. Am., AAUP, MLA, Dickens Fellowship, Phi Beta Kappa (hon.). Author: Contemporary Essays on Style, 1969; Irony in Shakespeare's Roman Plays, 1974; Shakespeare: Contemporary Critical Approaches, 1979; contbr. articles to profl. jours. Home: 1704 Jefferson Ave Lewisburg PA 17837

PAYNE, ROBERT WALTER, educator, psychologist; b. Calgary, Alta., Can., Nov. 5, 1925; s. Reginald William and Nora (Cowdery) P.; B.A., U. Alta., 1949; Ph.D., U. London (Eng.), 1954; m. Helen June Mayer, Dec. 1948 (div. 1972); children—Raymond William, Barbara Joan, Margaret June; m. 2d, Josephine Mary Riley Adams, Mar. 1977; children—George Reginald Alexander, Robin Charles. Lectr. psychology Inst. Psychiatry U. London, 1952-59; prof. psychology Queens U., Kingston, Ont., 1959-65; prof. psychology, chmn. dept. behavioral sci. Temple U. Med. Sch., Phila., 1965-73, prof. dept. psychiatry, 1973-78; med. research scientist III, Eastern Pa. Psychiat. Inst., Phila., 1965-78; dean Faculty Human and Social Devel., U. Victoria (B.C., Can.), 1978—. Recipient Stratton Research award, 1964. Fellow Am. Psychol. Assn., Brit. Psychol. Soc., Canadian Psychol. Assn. Contbr. articles to profl. jours. Home: 949 Pattulo Pl Victoria BC V8S 5H6 Canada

PAYNE, ROSE M., med. educator; b. Lake Bay, Wash., Aug. 5, 1909; d. Louis and Ethel (Segal) Ostroff; B.S., U. Wash., 1932, M.S., 1933, Ph.D. in Bacteriology, 1937. Research asso. Stanford U. Sch. Medicine, 1955-64, sr. scientist, 1964-72, prof. medicine, 1972-74, prof. medicine emeritus, 1975—; mem. WHO Expert Adv. Panel on Immunology, 1970; mem. adv. com. on renal dialysis and transplantation Calif. Dept. Public Health, 1972; cons. Irwin Meml. Blood Bank of San Francisco Med. Soc. Recipient John Elliott Meml. award Am. Assn. Blood Banks, 1964, Karl Landsteiner award, 1977. Mem. Transplantation Soc., Am. Soc. Hematology, Internat. Soc. Hematology, Am. Assn. Blood Banks, Internat. Soc. Blood Transfusion, Am. Assn. Clin. Histocompatibility Testing. Contbr. articles to profl. jours. Office: Rm S-135 Stanford Univ Sch Medicine Stanford CA 94305

PAYNE, SIDNEY STEWART, bishop; b. Fogo, Nfld., Can., June 6, 1932; s. Albert and Hilda May (Oake) P.; B.A., Meml. U. Nfld., 1958; L.Th., Queen's Coll. (Nfld.), 1958; B.D., Gen. Synod, 1966; m. Selma Carlson Penney, Oct. 11, 1962; children—Carla, Christopher, Robert, Angela. Ordained to ministry Anglican Ch., 1957; parish pastor, Happy Valley Labrador, 1957-65, Bay Roberts, Nfld., 1965-70, St. Anthony, Nfld., 1970-78; bishop Anglican Diocese of Western Nfld., 1978—. Home: 13 Cobb Ln Corner Brook NF A2H 2V3 Canada Office: Suite 311 Millbrook Mall Corner Brook NF A2H 4B5 Canada

PAYNE, (ORVILLE) THOMAS, polit. scientist, educator; b. Fulton, Mo., Apr. 11, 1920; s. Rufus Thomas and Addie (Kemp) P.; A.B., Westminster Coll., 1941; A.M., U. Chgo., 1948, Ph.D., 1951; m. Helen Kate Ritchie, Oct. 2, 1943 (dec. June 1974); children—David Thomas, Joseph Ritchie; m. 2d, Mora Christine MacKinnon Skari, July 10, 1975; stepchildren—Tala, Lisa Skari. Instr. U. Tenn., 1948-50; from instr. to asso. prof. U. Mont., 1951-59, prof. polit. sci., 1959—, chmn. dept., 1959-66. Mem. Mont. Commn. on Local Govt., 1974-77. Nat. commn. study jurisdiction system Meth. Ch., 1956-60. Trustee elementary sch. Dist. No. 1, Missoula, Mont., 1958-64, chmn., 1962-64; trustee Rocky Mountain Coll., Billings, Mont., 1969-76. Served from pvt. to 1st. lt. USAAF, 1942-46. Mem. Am.,

Western (exec. council 1968-70, pres. 1973-74), Pacific N.W. (pres. 1964-65) polit. sci. assns., Am. Assn. U. Profs. Republican. Methodist. Home: 3929 Timberlane Missoula MT 59801

PAYNE, TYSON ELLIOTT, JR., ins. co. exec.; b. Dallas, May 25, 1927; s. Tyson Elliott and Winnie Claris (Denman) P.; B.J., U. Tex., 1949; C.L.U., Am. Coll. Life Underwriters, 1969; m. Billie Jane Spears, Aug. 28, 1948; children—David Tyson, Sally Jane. Sports editor Lufkin (Tex.) News, 1949-51; sports editor Tyler (Tex.) Courier Times, 1951-53; with Am. Nat. Ins. Co., Galveston, Tex., 1953—, v.p. health ins. operations, St. Louis, 1965-69, exec. v.p. health ins. operations, 1969, exec. v.p. marketing, Galveston, 1970—. Pres. Lufkin Jr. C. of C., 1950, Jr. C. of C., Tyler, 1954. Served with USNR, 1945-46. Presbyn. (elder). Home: 2318 Carriage Lane La Marque TX 77568 Office: 1 Moody Plaza Galveston TX 77550

PAYNE, WILLIAM JACKSON, educator, microbiologist; b. Chattanooga, Aug. 30, 1925; s. Henry Frederick and Maude (Fonda) P.; B.S., Coll. William and Mary, 1950; M.S., U. Tenn., 1952, Ph.D., 1955; m. Jane Lindsey Marshall, June 16, 1949; children—William Jackson, Marshall, Lindsey. Instr. bacteriology U. Tenn., 1953-54; mem. faculty U. Ga., 1955—, prof. microbiology, head dept., 1962-77, acting dean Coll. Arts and Scis., 1977-78, dean, 1978—; vis. professorial fellow U. Wales, Cardiff, 1975, hon. professorial fellow, 1977—. Cons. U. Ala., 1959, 68, 70; summer research participant Oak Ridge Nat. Lab., 1960; chmn. Com. Nat. Registry Microbiologists, 1966-72; cons. U.S. EPA, 1971; mem. biol. oceanography panel NSF, 1976-77. Trustee Athens Acad., 1967-72. Served with USNR, 1943-46. Recipient M.G. Michael research award U. Ga., 1960. Fellow Am. Acad. Microbiology; mem. Am. Soc. Microbiology (pres. Southeastern br. 1963, P.R. Edwards award Southeastern br. 1972; found. lectr. 1972-73, dir. found. 1973-76, chmn. found. com. 1977—, chmn. com. undergrad. and grad. edn. 1974-77), Am. Soc. Biol. Chemists, Soc. Gen. Microbiology (Eng.), Soc. Exptl. Biology and Medicine, Ga. Acad. Sci., Sigma Xi (U. Ga. Chpt. Research award 1973), Phi Kappa Phi, Sigma Alpha Epsilon. Episcopalian. Club: Athens City. Author: (with D.R. Brown) Microbiology; A Programmed Presentation, 1968, 2d edit., 1972, (transl. to Spanish, 1975); also articles. Mem. editorial bd. Applied and Environ. Microbiology, 1974-79, U. Ga. Press, 1975-78. Home: 111 Alpine Way Athens GA 30606

PAYNE, WILLIAM WALKER, environ. engr.; b. Calverton, Va., June 1, 1913; s. Clarence Milton and Anna Laura (Day) P.; B.S., U. Va., 1935; M.S., U. Mich., 1947; M.P.H., U. Pitts., 1956, Sc.D., 1959; m. Emilie Laura Payne, Sept. 5, 1936; children—Patricia Payne Buckner, Judith Payne Taylor, Kathryn Payne Turner. San. engr. USPHS, Washington, 1943-48; engr. Nat. Cancer Inst., Bethesda, Md., 1948-62, dep. sci. dir. etiology, 1962-67; dep. dir. Nat. Inst. Environ. Health Scis., Research Triangle Park, N.C., 1967-73; sci. coordinator Frederick Cancer Research Center, Nat. Cancer Inst., Frederick, Md., 1973—. Recipient USPHS Commendation medal, 1968, USPHS Meritorious Service medal, 1972. Diplomate Am. Acad. Environ. Engrs. Mem. Conf. Fed. Environ. Engrs., Am. Indsl. Hygiene Assn., Am. Assn. Cancer Research. Contbr. sci. articles to profl. jours. Home: Box 183 Route 6 Pinecliff Frederick MD 21701 Office: Nat Cancer Inst Frederick Cancer Research Center Fort Detrick Frederick MD 21701

PAYNTER, HARRY ALVIN, trade assn. exec.; b. Miami, Ariz., July 22, 1923; s. Harry and Mabel Vera (Moore) P.; B.S., Okla. State U., 1948; M.B.A., Harvard U., 1954; postgrad. Air Command and Staff Coll., 1957, Armed Forces Staff Coll., 1961, Nat. War Coll., 1969; m. Betty Clarice Wilkins, Dec. 3, 1944; children—Harry Alvin, Steven Wilkins, Barbara Elizabeth, Susan Moore. Commd. 2d lt. AC, U.S. Army, 1943, advanced through grades to col. USAF, 1968; service as flight comdr. World War II and Berlin airlift; asst. air attache Am. embassy, Karachi, Pakistan, 1958-60; air attache Am. embassy, Quito, Ecuador, 1965-67, Vietnam, 1969; prof. aerospace studies Dartmouth, 1967-68; ret., 1970; asst. mng. dir. Gas Appliance Mfrs. Assn., Inc., N.Y.C., 1970-73, pres., Arlington, Va., 1973—. Decorated D.F.C., Air Medal with 3 oak leaf clusters, Purple Heart, Joint Services Commendation medal with oak leaf cluster (U.S.); Abdon Calderon (Ecuador); recipient Am. Bankers award, 1947; named Ecuador Hon. Command Pilot. Mem. Am. Gas Assn., Guild Ancient Suppliers (hon.), Am. Soc. Gas Engrs. (hon.), Air Force Assn., Ret. Officers Assn., Am. Soc. Assn. Execs., Am. Nat. Standards Inst. (dir.), Phi Kappa Phi. Presbyn. Club: Army and Navy (Washington). Home: 1416 N Inglewood St Arlington VA 22205 Office: 1901 N Ft Myer Dr Arlington VA 22209

PAYNTER, JOHN PHILIP, conductor; b. Dodgeville, Wis., May 29, 1928; s. Wilfred William and Minnie Elizabeth (Clark) P.; B.M., Northwestern U., 1950, N.M., 1951; m. Marietta Margaret Morgan, Sept. 10, 1949; children—Bruce David, Megan Elizabeth. Mem. faculty Sch. of Music, Northwestern U., 1951—, dir. bands, 1953—, prof. conducting, 1974—; condr., musical dir. Northshore Concert Band of Wilmette, 1958—. Mem. Am. Band Masters Assn. (past pres.), Nat. Band Assn. (co-founder, past pres.), Phi Mu Alpha Sinfonia (life), Phi Eta Sigma, Pi Kappa Lambda. Mem. United Ch. of Christ. Editor new music column Instrumentalist, 1959—. Composer and arranger numerous works. Home: 1437 Hollywood Ave Glenview IL 60025 Office: Sch of Music Northwestern U Evanston IL 60201

PAYNTER, JOHN WILLIAM, found. exec.; b. Zanesville, Ohio, Mar. 31, 1909; s. Edward Elmer and Lillie L. (Hall) P.; B.S. in Bus. Adminstrn., Ohio State U., 1932; grad. Advanced Mgmt. Program, Harvard, 1951; m. Catherine I. Thompson, Aug. 20, 1979. Staff accountant Ernst & Ernst, C.P.A.'s Cleve., 1935-40, supr. accountant, Pitts., 1940-42; with J.L. Hudson Co., Detroit, 1946-72, controller, 1948-56, financial v.p., treas., dir., 1956-68, sr. v.p. finance, treas., dir., 1968-72; treas., dir. Charles W. Warren & Co., Detroit, 1965-70, Northland Point, Inc., Detroit, 1961-70; pres., treas., dir. Vernier Properties, Inc., Detroit, 1959-69; financial v.p., treas., dir. Shopping Centers, Inc., Detroit, 1956-71, Hudson Webber Realty Co., Detroit, 1956-71, Eastland Fixtures Inc., Detroit, 1957-66; dir. Standard Fed. Savs. & Loan Assn., Troy, Mich., 1966—. Trustee, Hudson Webber Found., 1949—; treas., trustee Eloise and Richard Webber Found., 1952—; trustee, asst. treas. McGregor Fund, 1969—, exec. dir., 1973; trustee Mich. Hosp. Service, 1947—, pres., 1954-57, chmn. bd., 1962-74; pres., treas., trustee Edward C. and Hazel L. Stephenson Found., YMCA Found; bd. dirs. United Found., 1962-72; v.p., dir. Mich. United Fund, 1950-70. Served to lt. col. Ordnance Dept., AUS, 1942-46. Recipient Nat. Office Mgmt. Assn. Fellowship award, 1960; Justin Ford Kimball award Am. Hosp. Assn., 1968. C.P.A., Ohio, Pa. Mem. Tax. Execs. Inst., Am. Inst. C.P.A.'s, Mich. Assn. C.P.A.'s, Beta Gamma Sigma, Beta Alpha Psi (Outstanding Alumni award 1971). Mason. Clubs: Detroit; Grosse Pointe (Mich.) Yacht (dir. 1960-66, commodore 1966). Home: 1672 N Renaud Rd Grosse Pointe Woods MI 48236 Office: 2026 Commonwealth Bldg Detroit MI 48226

PAYSON, HENRY EDWARDS, forensic psychiatrist, educator, farmer; b. N.Y.C., May 12, 1925; s. Aurin Eliot and Lois Elizabeth (Chickering) P.; B.S., Harvard Coll., 1948; M.D., Columbia U., 1952; M.S.L., Yale U. Law Sch., 1978; m. Barbara Louise Jarvis, Mar. 29, 1958; children—Ann Elizabeth, John Eliot, Sally Lynn, Susan Gail. Research fellow in medicine Columbia U. unit Goldwater Meml. Hosp., 1952-53; intern, Osler Clinic, Johns Hopkins Hosp., 1953-54; resident in psychiatry Phipps Clinic, 1955-58; resident in internal medicine Duke U. Hosp., 1954-55; asst. prof. psychiatry and medicine Yale U. Sch. Medicine, also attending physician Yale-New Haven Med. Center, 1958-63; asst. prof. psychiatry Dartmouth Med. Sch., 1963-68, asso. prof., 1968-78, prof., 1978—; attending psychiatrist Hitchcock Clinic, Dartmouth-Hitchcock Med. Center; chief in-patient service Dartmouth-Hitchcock Mental Health Center, 1969-71; cons. VA Hosp., White River Junction, Vt., 1972—; N.H. Prison, dir. Disturbed Offender Project of N.H., 1972-73. Sec. N.H. Guardian Adv. Council, 1979—. Served with AUS, 1943-46. NIMH career tchr., 1961-63. Diplomate Am. Bd. Psychiatry and Neurology. Fellow Am. Psychiat. Assn.; mem. N.H. Psychiat. Soc. (pres. 1977-78), Am. Acad. Academic Psychiatry, Am. Acad. Forensic Scis., Am. Acad. Psychiatry and Law, Am. Psychosomatic Soc., Am. Polled Hereford Assn., Am. Soc. Psychophysiol. Study of Sleep, Grafton County Med. Soc., AAAS. Mem. Ch. of Christ. Club: Harvard (N.Y.C.). Contbr. articles to profl. publs. Office: Dartmouth Med Sch Hanover NH 03755

PAYTON, BENJAMIN FRANKLIN, found. exec.; b. Orangeburg, S.C., Dec. 27, 1932; s. Leroy Ralph and Sarah (Mack) P.; B.A., S.C. State Coll., 1955; B.D. (Danforth grad. fellow 1955-63), Harvard, 1958; M.A., Columbia, 1960; Ph.D., Yale, 1963; LL.D., Eastern Mich. U., 1972; L.H.D., Benedict Coll., 1972; Litt.D., Morgan State U., 1974; m. Thelma Louise Plane, Nov. 28, 1959; children—Mark Steven, Deborah Elizabeth. Asst. prof. sociology of religion and social ethics Howard U., Washington, also dir. Community Research-Service Project, 1963-65; dir. Office of Ch. and Race, Protestant Council, N.Y.C., 1965-66; exec. dir. dept. social justice and Commn. on Religion and Race, Nat. Council Chs. of Christ in U.S.A., 1966-67; pres. Benedict Coll., Columbia, S.C., 1967-72; program officer higher edn. and research Ford Found., 1972—. Mem. vis. com. bd. overseers Harvard; mem. nat. rev. bd. Center for Cultural and Tech. Exchange between U.S. and Asia. Bd. dirs. United Negro Coll. Fund, Liberty Corp. Recipient Billings prize Harvard, 1957; named South Carolinian of Year by statewide TV-Radio, 1972. Mem. Am. Soc. Scholars, Am. Sociol. Assn., Soc. for Religion in Higher Edn. (dir.), N.A.A.C.P., Alpha Phi Alpha, Alpha Kappa Mu. Author: (with Dr. Seymour Melman) A Strategy for the Next Stage in Civil Rights: Metropolitan-Rural Development for Equal Opportunity, 1966. Home: 12 Boulder Brook Dr Stamford CT 06903

PAYTON, CAROLYN ROBERTSON, univ. dean; b. Norfolk, Va., May 13, 1925; d. Leroy Solomon and Bertha Marie (Flanagan) Robertson; B.S., Bennett Coll., 1945; M.S., U. Wis., 1948; Ed.D., Columbia, 1962; m. Raymond Rudolph Payton (div. Feb. 1951). Asst. prof. psychology Howard U., Washington, 1959-64, dir. univ. counseling service, 1970-77, dean counseling and career devel., 1979—; dep. dir. to dir. Peace Corps, Eastern Caribbean, 1964-69, dir. Peace Corps, 1977; cons. psychologist, 1970-79; adv. council Spl. Services Disadvantaged Students; bd. dirs. Counseling Resources Center, Inc. Bd. dirs. Nat. Capital Area Big Bros. Grantee NIMH, 1961-64. Mem. Am. Psychol. Assn. (chmn. com. sci. and profl. ethics and conduct 1976-77, Task Force on Sex Bias and Sex Role Stereotyping in Psychotherapeutic Practice 1974—), Am. Personnel and Guidance Assn., Am. Orthopsychiat. Assn., Common Cause, Pi Lambda Theta, Kappa Delta Pi, Sigma Delta Epsilon. Address: 3428 Quebec St NW Washington DC 20016

PAYTON, ROBERT LOUIS, found. exec.; b. South Bend, Ind., Aug. 23, 1926; s. John Payton and Mamie (Burns) P.; student U. Ill., U. Iowa; M.A. in History, U. Chgo., 1954; Litt.D., Adelphi U., 1975; m. Pauline Schaefer, Feb. 4, 1949; children—Joseph K., Matthew W. (dec.), David E. Editor, Burlington (Ia.) Herald, 1949-51, Nat. Real Estate Jour., 1954-57; editor Washington U. mag., St. Louis, 1957-61, dir. univ. relations, 1959-61, vice chancellor for planning, 1961-66; pub. mem. Fgn. Service Insp. Corps, Ecuador, 1965; cons. Dept. State, 1966, spl. asst., 1966-67, ambassador to United Republic Cameroon, 1967-69; pres. C.W. Post Coll., L.I. U., 1969-73, Hofstra U., 1973-76; pres. Exxon Edn. Found. Served with AUS, World War II. Clubs: University (N.Y.C.); Cherry Valley (Garden City, N.Y.), Home: 15 St Paul's Crescent Garden City NY 11530 Office: 111 W 49th St New York NY 10020

PAYTON, WALTER, football player; b. Columbia, Miss., July 25, 1954; B.A. in Communications, Jackson State U. Running back with Chgo. Bears, 1975—; played Pro Bowl, 1976, 77, 78, 79. Named NFC Player of Year, The Sporting News, 1976, 77, named to NFC All-Star Team, 1976, 77, 78; named NFL Most Valuable Player, Profl. Football Writers Am., 1978; named NFC Player of Yr., UPI, 1977; Most Valuable Player, NFL, 1978. Office: care Chgo Bears 55 E Jackson St Suite 1200 Chicago IL 60604*

PAYTON-WRIGHT, PAMELA, actress; b. Pitts., Nov. 1, 1941; d. Gordon Edgar and Eleanor Ruth (McKinley) Payton Wright; B.A., Birmingham So. Coll., 1963; postgrad. Royal Acad. Dramatic Arts, London, 1963-65; m. David Arthur Butler; 1 son, Oliver Dickon Hedley. Mem. Milw. Repertory Co., 1965-66, Trinity Sq. Playhouse, 1966-67, Cin. Playhouse, 1969; appeared in A.P.A. prodns. including: Exit The King, 1968, Cherry Orchard, 1968; appeared in Lincoln Center play The Crucible; in Broadway plays: Jimmy Shine, 1969, All Over Town, 1975, Mourning Becomes Electra (Drama Desk award), 1972, Glass Menagerie, 1976, Romeo and Juliet, 1977; appeared in Off-Broadway plays: The Effect of Gamma Rays on Man-In-The-Moon Marigolds (Obie award, Clarence Derwent award), 1976, Jessie and The Bandit Queen (Obie award); in Long Wharf Theater prodns.: Lunch Girls, 1978, Summerfolk, 1979; in film Resurrection, 1979; appeared as Louisa Catherine Adams on The Adams Chronicles, TV series, 1975; guest star appearances on numerous TV shows. Mem. Actors Equity Assn., AFTRA, Screen Actors Guild. Episcopalian. Home: 21 E 93d St New York City NY 10028

PAZIK, GEORGE JAMES, editor, pub.; b. Milw., Apr. 7, 1921; s. Richard Francis and Josephine (Bartos-Bucek) P.; B.S., U. Wis., 1944; m. Bernice Emily Thiele, June 19, 1943; children—Marjorie Anne, Carol Sue. Mgr., Pazik's Delicatessen, Milw., 1946-54; owner Kitchens by Pazik, Milw., 1952-59; exec. dir. Upper 3d St Comml. Assn., Milw., 1959-64; exec. v.p., founder Northtown Planning and Devel. Council, Milw., 1964-74; editor, pub. Fishing Facts mag., Menomonee Falls, Wis., 1970—. Chmn. Milwaukee County Expressway and Transportation Commn., 1971-74; chmn. Wis. state com. of U.S. Commn. on Civil Rights, 1970-72. Served with U.S. Army, 1944-46. Recipient Human Relations award Milw. Council B'nai B'rith, 1968. Mem. Outdoor Writers Assn. Am., New Directions. Lutheran. Home: 8549 N Servite Dr Unit 204 Milwaukee WI 53223 Office: N84 W13660 Leon Rd Menomonee Falls WI 53051

PAZUR, JOHN HOWARD, educator, biochemist; b. Zubne, Czechoslovakia, Jan. 17, 1922; s. John and Mary (Bonko) P.; B.S., U. Guelph, 1944; M.S., McGill U., 1946; Ph.D., Iowa State U., 1950; m. Jean Josephine Glabais, Nov. 22, 1950; children—Robert Leslie, Barbara Jean, Beverly Ann, Carolyn Jo. Came to U.S., 1946, naturalized, 1961. Instr. chemistry Iowa State U., 1950-51; asst. prof. biol. chemistry U. Ill., 1951-52; mem. faculty U. Nebr., 1952-66, prof. biochemistry, 1959-66, chmn. dept., 1960-66; prof. biochemistry Pa. State U., 1966—, chmn. dept., 1966-74. Mem. Am. Chem. Soc., Am. Soc. Biol. Chemists. Home: 525 Nimitz St State College PA 16801 Office: 103 Althouse Lab Pa State Univ University Park PA 16802

PEABODY, GEORGE FRANCIS, lawyer; b. Houlton, Maine, Aug. 30, 1912; s. Frank A. and Fanny (Pearce) P.; grad. Hebron Acad., 1930; A.B., Bowdoin Coll., 1934; LL.B., Harvard, 1937; m. Helen E. Dill, Oct. 17, 1938; children—Sarah, Mary Helen, Jane Frances. Admitted to Maine bar, 1937; sr. partner Eaton, Peabody, Bradford & Veague, Bangor; dir. Merrill Trust Co., Hannaford Bros. Co. Mem. Bangor City Council, 1942-44, chmn., 1944. Former trustee Eastern Maine Med. Center; trustee Bangor Pub. Library; former bd. mgrs. Home for Aged Men. Fellow Am. Bar Found.; mem. Bangor Fuel Soc. (pres.), Penobscot County Bar Assn. (pres. 1959). Unitarian. Mason (33 deg., Shriner). Home: 188 W Broadway Bangor ME 04401 Office: Merrill Center Bldg Bangor ME 04401

PEABODY, ROBERT LEE, educator; b. Seattle, Dec. 23, 1931; s. Keith Royal and Pearl (Starr) P.; B.A., U. Wash., 1954, M.A., 1956; Ph.D., Stanford, 1960; m. Judith Carol Erken, Aug. 16, 1958; children—Susan, Nancy Lynn, Jennifer. Mem. faculty Johns Hopkins, 1961—, asso. prof., 1965-68, prof. polit. sci., 1969—. Asso. dir. N.Y. Times-Simulmatics Corp. election coverage project, 1962, Am. Polit. Sci. Assn. study of Congress, 1965-73; Congl. intern House Majority Whip, 1965, staff asst. to Speaker, 1975-76; film cons. An Act of Congress, 1976-78. Brookings Instn. post-doctoral research fellow, 1960-61; Social Sci. Research Council fellow, 1964-65; Ford Found. faculty fellow, 1969-70. Mem. Am. Polit. Sci. Assn., AAUP, Pub. Choice Soc., Phi Gamma Delta. Author: Organizational Authority, 1964; New Perspectives on the House of Representatives, 3d edit. 1977; Congress: Two Decades of Analysis, 1969; To Enact a Law: Congress and Campaign Financing, 1972; Education of a Congressman, 1972; Leadership in Congress: Stability, Succession and Change, 1976; Cases in American Politics, 1976. Home: 113 7th NE Washington DC 20002 Office: Dept Polit Sci Johns Hopkins Univ Baltimore MD 21218

PEABODY, WILLIAM TYLER, JR., paper mfg. co. exec.; b. Melrose, Mass., Mar. 17, 1921; s. William Tyler and Dorothy (Atkinson) P.; A.B. cum laude, Harvard, 1942, postgrad. Grad. Sch. Arts and Scis., 1946-47, LL.B., 1949; m. Florence Marshall, July 27, 1946; children—Carol (Mrs. Richard A. Moomey), William Tyler III, Janet, Marshall R. Admitted to N.Y. bar, 1950; asso. firm Root, Ballantine, Harlan, Bushby & Palmer, N.Y.C., 1949-54; with law div. Scott Paper Co., Phila., 1954-70, asst. sec., 1965-71, corporate sec., 1971—. Pres. Snohomish County Family Counseling Service, Everett, Wash., 1963-67. Bd. dirs. Nether Providence Community Assos., Inc., Wallingford, Pa., 1969-75, pres., 1969-70; bd. dirs. Nether Providence Community Centers, Inc., Wallingford, 1976—, pres., 1979—; chmn. Rose Valley Folk, 1977-78. Served to lt. USNR, 1942-46. Mem. Am. Bar Assn., Am. Soc. Corp. Secs. (dir. 1977—, pres. Middle Atlantic group 1976-77). Episcopalian. Home: 15 Rose Valley Rd Moylan PA 19065 Office: Scott Plaza Philadelphia PA 19113

PEACH, WILLIAM BERNARD, educator; b. Roslyn, Wash., June 20, 1918; s. Herman Joseph and Helen Stuart (Bowie) P.; B.A., Whitman Coll., Walla Walla, Wash., 1940; postgrad. U. Calif. at Berkeley, 1940-41; M.A., Harvard, 1949, Ph.D., 1951; m. Alice Mary Barber, Dec. 2, 1940; children—Stephanie (Mrs. Gernot S. Doetsch), Susan (Mrs. Michael H. Kelly), Sara (Mrs. Roger Sparrow), Bernard Stuart. Shipfitter, Kaiser Shipyards, Richmond, Calif., 1941-44; instr. Naval ROTC, U. Wash., Seattle, 1945-46; mem. faculty Duke, 1951—, prof. philosophy, 1963—. Served with USNR, 1944-46. Guggenheim fellow, 1957-58; grantee Am. Philos. Soc., 1958-59, Nat. Endowment Humanities, 1972-73. Mem. Am. Assn. U. Profs., Am. Philos. Assn., Mind-Aristotelian Soc. Editor: (Francis Hutcheson) Illustrations on the Moral Sense, 1971; Richard Price and the Ethical Foundations of the American Revolution, 1979. Home: 706-F Constitution Dr Durham NC 27705

PEACH, WILLIAM NELSON, educator, economist; b. Granite, Md., Oct. 21, 1912; s. Frank and Mary Anna (Nelson) P.; Ph.D., Johns Hopkins, 1939; m. Dorothy Jean Hausman, Sept. 1, 1939; children—Dorothy Jean, James Thomas, Joseph William. Instr. econs. U. Tex., 1938-42; asst. mgr. research and statistics dept. Fed. Res. Bank, Dallas, 1942-44; asst. prof. U. Tex., 1946-47; asso. prof. Syracuse U., 1947-49; prof. econs. U. Okla., Norman, 1949-65, then research prof. econs., now George Lynn Cross prof. econs.; adviser in finance U. Pa. Agy. Internat. Devel. project, Karachi, Pakistan, 1956-58; spl. cons. select com. on small bus. U.S. Ho. of Reps., 1960; fiscal and financial adviser AID, Washington, 1961. Bd. dirs. Norman Municipal Hosp. Served with USNR, 1944-46. Mem. S.W. Social Sci. Assn., Am. Soc. for Pub. Adminstrn. Author: Basic Data of the American Economy, 1948; Basic Data of the Economy of Pakistan, 1960; Principles of Economics, 1960; (with James A. Constantin) Zimmermann's World Resources and Industries, 3d edit., 1972; The Energy Outlook for the 1980's, 1973. Home: 523 Chautauqua St Norman OK 73069

PEACHER, DOUGLAS JOHN, ret. retail, catalogue order sales co. exec.; b. Hopkinsville, Ky., Nov. 33, 1912; s. Benjamin F. and Minnie (Adams) P.; LL.B., LaSalle U., Chgo.; m. Gwendolyn Edris Brown, Oct. 12, 1940; With Frederick & Nelson Dept. Store, Seattle, 1935-38; with Sears, Roebuck and Co., 1938-66, buyer, Chgo., 1946-50, mgr. mdse. div., Chgo., 1950-66; pres., dir., chmn. finance com. Simpsons-Sears, Ltd., Toronto, Ont., Can., 1966-79, ret.; pres., dir. Simpsons-Sears Acceptance Co., Ltd., Simpson Sears Properties Ltd.; dir. Allstate Ins. Co. Can., Allstate Life Ins. Co. Can., Inglis Ltd., Photo Engravers & Electrotypes Ltd., Thomson Newspapers Ltd. (all Toronto); dir., mem. exec. com. Montreal Trust Co. (Que.). Trustee, mem. investment com. Simpsons-Sears Profit Sharing Retirement Fund; hon. trustee George Williams Coll., Downers Grove, Ill.; mem. pvt. support bd. U. Toronto; past mem. res. forces policy bd. Office Sec. of Def., Washington; past nat. bd. dirs., pres. Boys Clubs Can. Served to maj. gen. USMCR. Mem. Mil. and Hospitaller Order Saint Lazarus of Jerusalem. Clubs: Royal Canadian Mil. Inst., Toronto, York (Toronto); Goodwood (Ont.); Army and Navy (Washington); La Jolla Beach and Tennis; Torry, Cuyamaca (San Diego), Ristigouche Salmon (pres., Matapedia, Que.).

PEACHEY, LEE DEBORDE, biologist; b. Rochester, N.Y., Apr. 14, 1932; s. Clarence Henry and Eunice (DeBorde) P.; B.S., Lehigh U., 1953; postgrad. U. Rochester, 1953-56; Ph.D. (Leitz fellow), Rockefeller U., 1959; m. Helen Pauline Fuchs, June 7, 1958; children—Michael Stephen, Sarah Elizabeth, Anne Palmer. Research asso. Rockefeller U., 1959-60; asst. prof. zoology Columbia U., 1960-63, asso. prof., 1963-65; asso. prof. biochemistry and biophysics U. Pa., Phila., 1965—, prof. biology, 1970—; adj. prof. molecular, cellular and developmental biology U. Colo., 1969—; mem. molecular biology study sect. NIH, 1969-73. Mem. Mayor's Sci. and Tech. Adv. Council, Phila., 1972—. Guggenheim and Fulbright-Hays fellow, 1967-68, Overseas fellow Churchill Coll., Cambridge, Eng., 1967-68; NSF grantee, 1960-72, NIH grantee, 1973—, Muscular Dystrophy Assn. Am., Inc. grantee, 1973—; Fogarty sr. internat. fellow, 1979-80; hon. research fellow Univ. Coll., London, 1979-80. Mem. AAAS,

Electron Microscope Soc. Am. (council 1975-78), Am. Soc. Cell Biology (program chmn. 1965, council 1966-69), Biophys. Soc. (program chmn. 1976, council 1976—), Internat. Union Pure and Applied Biophysics (council 1978—), Physiol. Soc. (Eng.). Editor: Third and Fourth Conferences on Cellular Dynamics, (N.Y. Acad. Scis.), 1967, First and Second Confs. on Cellular Dynamics, 1968; mem. editorial bd. Tissue and Cell, 1969—, Jour. Cell Biology, 1970-73. Contbr. articles to sci. jours. Home: 606 Old Gulph Rd Narberth PA 19072 Office: Dept Biology/G5 U Pa Philadelphia PA 19104

PEACOCK, ERLE EWART, educator, surgeon; b. Durham, N.C., Sept. 10, 1926; s. Erle Ewart and Vera (Ward).; student U. N.C., 1943-45; M.D., Harvard, 1949; m. Mary Louise Lowrey, Apr. 17, 1954; children—James Lowrey, Susan Louise, Virginia Gayle. Intern, asst. resident Roosevelt Hosp., N.Y.C., 1949-51; asst. resident, then chief resident N.C. Meml. Hosp., 1953-55; chief resident plastic surgery Barnes Hosp., St. Louis, 1955-56; from instr. to prof. surgery U. N.C. Sch. Medicine, 1956-69; prof. surgery, chmn. dept. U. Ariz. Coll. Medicine, Tucson, 1969-77; prof. surgery Tulane U., New Orleans, 1977—. Mem. surgery study sect. NIH; mem. U.S. Army Med. Research and Devel. Adv. Panel, 1974. Served with USNR, 1945; to capt. M.C., AUS, 1951-53. Named Young Man of Year, N.C. Jr. C. of C., 1961; recipient Yandell medal Louisville Surg. Soc., 1972; McGraw medal Detroit Surg. Soc., 1973; Disting. Service award U. N.C., 1979. Diplomate Am. Bd. Plastic Surgery (exec. com., chmn. bd.), Am. Bd. Gen. Surgery. Mem. Nat. Bd. Med. Examiners, Am. Bd. Med. Specialists, Am. Surg. Assn., A.C.S., Am. Assn. Plastic Surgery, Am. Soc. for Surgery Hand, Am. Assn. for Surgery Trauma, Am. Soc. Plastic and Reconstructive Surgeons, Soc. Exptl. Biology and Medicine, Soc. Univ. Surgeons (treas.), Alpha Omega Alpha. Author: Surgery and Biology of Wound Repair. Mem. editorial bd. Yearbook of Surgery, Am. Jour Surgery, Plastic and Reconstructive Surgery, connective tissue research Jour. Surg. Research. Home: 5115 Baronne St New Orleans LA 70115

PEACOCK, FRANKLIN KELLOGG, telephone co. exec.; b. Millville, N.J., Apr. 21, 1919; s. Walter Miller and Julia (Fields) P.; B.S., U. Md., 1941; grad. Northwestern U. Inst. for Mgmt., 1965; m. Patricia J. Burch, Apr. 30, 1960; children—Franklin Kellogg, Frederick, Jennifer, Julia. Traffic positions Chesapeake & Potomac Telephone Co., Washington, 1941-51, supervising accountant, 1951-52, dist. traffic mgr., 1952-54, auditor receipts, 1954-57, div. accounting mgr., 1957-62, gen. comml. engr., 1962-66, comptroller, 1966-78, gen. mgr. network ops., 1978—. Pres. Amberley Community Assn., 1965, 78; bd. dirs. Broadneck Fedn. Community Assns., 1972-73; treas. Alexander Graham Bell Assn. for Deaf, 1973—. Served with AUS, 1943-46. Mem. Nat. Assn. Accountants (dir. D.C. chpt. 1959-63), Fin. Execs. Inst. Clubs: Annapolis Yacht, Sailing of Chesapeake (commodore 1975). Home: 1698 Beech Ln Amberley Annapolis MD 21401 Office: 930 H St NW Washington DC 20001

PEACOCK, JAMES LOWE, anthropologist, educator; b. Montgomery, Ala., Oct. 31, 1937; s. James Lowe and Sara Claire (Rogers) P.; B.A., Duke U., 1959; Ph.D. (fellow), Harvard U., 1965; m. Florence Turner Fowler, Aug. 4, 1962; children—Louly, Claire, Natalie. Field researcher on Proletarian culture, Indonesia, 1962-63; asst. prof. anthropology Princeton (N.J.) U., 1965-67; asst. prof. U. N.C., Chapel Hill, 1967-69, asso. prof., 1970-72, asso. chmn. dept. anthropology, 1970-72, prof., 1973—, chmn. dept. anthropology, 1975—; field research on Muslim reformation Indonesia, 1969-70. Grantee NIMH, 1962-63, NSF, 1970-72. Mem. Am. Anthrop. Assn. (exec. bd. 1975—), Am. Ethnol. Soc. (councillor 1976—), Royal Anthrop. Soc. Gt. Britain and Ireland, Soc. for Applied Anthropology, Assn. for Asian Studies, Sigma Xi, Phi Beta Kappa. Author: Rites of Modernization, 1968; (with A. Thomas Kirsch) The Human Direction, 1970, 2d edit., 1973, Japanese transl., 1975; Consciousness and Change: Symbolic Anthropology in Evolutionary Perspective, 1975; Muslim Puritans: The Reformist Psychology in Southeast Asian Islam, 1978; Purifying the Faith: The Muhjmmadijah Movement of Indonesian Islam, 1978; mem. editorial bd. Jour. Asian Studies, 1971-74. Home: 1305 Willow Dr Chapel Hill NC 27514 Office: Dept Anthropology University North Carolina Chapel Hill NC 27514

PEACOCK, JOHN EDWARD DEAN, found. exec.; b. Flushing, N.Y., Jan. 8, 1919; s. Walter Winfreld and Hazeldean (Wood) P.; A.B., Dartmouth, 1940; m. Sylvia Griffith, June 26, 1943; children—John Edward Dean, Holly, Alexander G. With L.S. Ayres & Co., Indpls., 1945-74, v.p., sec., 1962—, pres. Ayres Found., 1965—; dir. Dean Bros. Pump Co., Indpls.; Roly's; chmn. exec. com. Guarantee Auto Stores, Inc.; cons. retail trade. Mem. Indpls. Off-Street Parking Commn., 1971; personnel chmn. Indpls. Police Dept.; trustee Indpls. Mus. Art, membership com.; bd. dirs. Nature Conservancy, Indpls. Solid Waste Task Force; mem. Public Trust Task Force; mem. Mayor's Recycle Commn.; mem. adv. com. Conner Prairie Pioneer Settlement; asst. exec. dir. Environ. Quality Control; alt. mem. citizens adv. com. of Ind. Stream Pollution Control. Served with USMCR, 1940-45. Mem. Soc. Ret. Execs. (chmn., pres. dir.). Club: Army-Navy (Indpls.). Home: 9099 Pickwick Dr Indianapolis IN 46260 Office: 1 W Washington St Indianapolis IN 46204

PEACOCK, LAMAR BATTS, physician; b. Albany, Ga., Sept. 21, 1920; s. Herbert A. and Helen Marian (LeVan) P.; B.A., Emory U., 1941; M.D., Med. Coll. Ga., 1946; m. Jane Bonner, June 7, 1947; children—Helen Lee (Mrs. Richard Paul Wade), Linda Jane, Lamar B. Intern Univ. Hosp., Augusta, 1946-47, resident, 1947-48; fellow internal medicine U. Va. Hosp., Charlottesville, 1948-49; resident Univ. Hosp., Augusta, 1949-50; practice medicine specializing in internal medicine and allergy, Atlanta, 1950—; mem. staff St. Joseph's Infirmary, Crawford Long Hosp., Piedmont Hosp., Grady Meml. Hosp., Hughes Spalding Pavilion, Doctors Meml. Hosp., Northside Hosp., West Paces Ferry Hosp., (all Atlanta), Cobb Gen. Hosp., Austell, Ga., Douglasville (Ga.) Hosp.; instr. internal medicine Ga. Bapt. Hosp., Atlanta, 1950-58, chief medicine, 1958-72; mem. faculty Emory U. Sch. Medicine, Atlanta, 1950—, asst. clin. prof. medicine, 1962—, instr. internal medicine Sch. Dentistry, 1958—. Chief med. br., health services Atlanta Met. Area Civil Def., 1960-63; mem. Ga. Pub. Health Assn., 1967-69; mem. Ga. Bd. Health, 1966-72, Ga. Vocational Rehab. Council, 1973—. Pres. trustees Med. Coll. Ga. Found., 1963. Diplomate Am. Bd. Internal Medicine. Fellow Am. Coll. Allergists (nat. pres. 1972-73), A.C.P., Am. Acad. Allergy; mem. Am., Ga. heart assns., A.M.A., Am. Soc. Internal Medicine, Ga. Soc. Internal Medicine, 5th Dist. Med. Soc., Ga. Thoracic Soc., Med. Assn. Atlanta (pres. 1965), Med. Assn. Ga. (1st v.p. 1966-67), Southeastern Allergy Assn. (pres. 1963-64), So. Med. Assn. Episcopalian. Club: Cherokee Town and Country. Home: 3120 Verdun Dr NW Atlanta GA 30305 Office: 207-A 478 Peachtree St NE Atlanta GA 30308

PEACOCK, LELON JAMES, educator, psychologist; b. Brevard, N.C., May 25, 1928; s. L.J. and Dorothy (Barrett) P.; student Emory U., 1945-47; A.B., Berea Coll., 1950; M.S., U. Ky., 1952, Ph.D., 1956; m. Marian Davis, June 8, 1945; children—Lynn Barrett, Janice Davis, Timothy Lee. Psychophysiologist, U.S. Army Med. Research Lab., Ft. Knox, Ky., 1954-56; research asso., acting dir. Yerkes Labs. of Primate Biology, Inc., Orange Park, Fla., 1956-59; asso. prof. psychology U. Ga., Athens, 1959-65, prof., 1966—. Recipient U. Ga. M.G. Michael Research award, 1964. Fellow A.A.A.S.; mem. Am. Psychol. Assn., So. Soc. for Philosophy and Psychology (pres. 1973-74), Soc. Psychophysiol. Research, Soc. Neurosci., Psychonomic Soc., Sigma Xi, Phi Kappa Phi. Author: (with R.V. Heckel) Textbook of General Psychology, 1966. Contbr. articles profl. jours. Home: 145 Woodland Way Athens GA 30601

PEACOCK, LESLIE CLARK, banker; b. Corsicana, Tex., July 24, 1930; s. Edmon Albert and Etta L. (Draper) P.; M.B.A., U. Tex., 1952, Ph.D., 1958. Financial economist Fed. Res. Bank Dallas, 1955-60; economist Republic Nat. Bank, Dallas, 1960-61; dep. mgr., dir. econs. and research Am. Bankers Assn., 1961-64; exec. v.p. Crocker-Citizens Nat. Bank, San Francisco, 1964-69, pres., 1969-77; vice chmn. Tex. Commerce Bancshares, Inc., 1974-79, Tex. Commerce Bank, N.A., 1977—; pres. Crocker Nat. Corp., 1969-73. Bd. govs. Bay Area Council. 1967—. Mem. Am. Econ. Assn., Am. Finance Assn., Newcomen Soc. Office: Route 3 Brenham TX 77833

PEACOCK, MARKHAM LOVICK, JR., educator; b. Shaw, Miss., Sept. 19, 1903; s. Markham Lovick and Mary (Patton) P.; grad. Webb Sch., 1921; B.A., Washington and Lee U., 1924, M.A., 1926; Ph.D., Johns Hopkins, 1942; m. Dora Greenlaw, Dec. 29, 1928. Mem. faculty Va. Polytech. Inst., 1926—, prof. English, 1945—, chmn. dept., 1960-66, Mem. Am. Assn. U. Profs., Nat. Council of Tchrs. English, Modern Lang. Assn., Internat. Fedn. of Modern Langs. and Lits., Modern Humanities Research Assn., Acad. Polit. Sci., N.E.A., Guild of Scholars, Omicron Delta Kappa, Lambda Chi Alpha, Sigma Upsilon, Phi Kappa Phi, Gold Triangle. Episcopalian. Clubs: Shenandoah; Tudor and Stuart, Johns Hopkins (Balt.), Princeton. Author: The Critical Opinions of William Wordsworth, 1949; also critical, ednl. and lit. articles. Home: 801 Draper Rd Blacksburg VA 24060

PEACOCK, MARY WILLA, publisher; b. Evanston, Ill., Oct. 23, 1942; d. William Gilbert and Mary Willa (Young) Peacock; B.A., Vassar Coll., 1964. Asso. lit. editor Harper's Bazaar mag., N.Y.C., 1964-69; staff editor Innovation mag., N.Y.C., 1969-70; editor in chief, co-founder, sec.-treas., pres. Rags mag., N.Y.C., San Francisco, 1970-71; co-founder, features editor Ms. mag., N.Y.C., 1971—; pub., pres. Rags mag., N.Y.C., 1977—.

PEACOCK, PETER BLIGH, educator; b. Nairobi, Kenya, Nov. 3, 1921; s. Norman Bligh and Winifred (Williams) P.; M.B., Ch.B., U. Capetown (S. Africa), 1945, D.P.H., 1947; M.D., U. Johannesburg (S. Africa), 1969, D.T.M.H., 1957; D.I.H., Royal Coll. Physicians, Eng., 1953; M.A., Samford U., 1970; m. Dorothy Selves; 1 dau., Margaret; children by previous marriage—Martin Norman, Adele. Came to U.S., 1965. Med. insp. malaria, then asst. chief health officer Union S. Africa, 1947-53; regional med. health officer, asst. prof. pub. health U. Sask. (Can.), 1953-56, 61-68; prof. pub. health, med. health officer, Johannesburg, 1956-61; prof., chmn. dept. pub. health and epidemiology U. Ala., 1966-73; chief epidemiology Am. Health Found., 1973-75; practice medicine, Fayette, Ala., 1975—. Prof., Cornell U.; vis. lectr. U. Minn. Mem. Nat. Adv. Com. Epidemiology for Stroke, Cancer and Bioradiation, 1968—; chmn. Saskatoon Gymnastic Assn., 1958-61. Fellow Royal Soc. Tropical Medicine and Hygiene; mem. Am., Canadian, S. African (pres. 1961) pub. health assns., Am., Canadian, S. African med. assns. Home: 828 4th Ave NW Fayette AL 35555

PEACOCK, WILLIAM ELDRED, govt. ofcl.; b. Salt Lake City, June 5, 1941; s. Hollis G. and Rosalind S. Peacock; A.B. cum laude, Princeton U., 1963; LL.B., J.D., Harvard U., 1966; m. Polly S. Burke, June 11, 1966; children—William Burke, Jane Hollis, Sally Spencer. Admitted to Calif. bar, 1967, D.C. bar, 1978; mgmt. cons. McKinsey & Co., Inc., San Francisco and Washington, 1966-67; asst. gen. counsel U.S. Fin. Corp., San Diego, 1970-71; with firm Chickering & Gregory, San Francisco, 1971-72; asst. to chmn. bd. Transam. Corp., San Francisco, 1972-75; v.p., corporate counsel Crocker Nat. Bank, San Francisco, 1975-77; dep. asst. sec., dir. intergovtl. affairs Dept. Energy, Washington, 1977—; prof. bus. adminstrn. Golden Gate U., San Francisco, 1976-77. Past bd. dirs. Bay Area Jr. Achievement. Served to Capt. USMCR, 1967-70; Vietnam. Recipient Distinguished Service award Exec. Office Pres., 1977. Mem. Am., D.C., Calif., San Francisco bar assns., Calif. Bankers Assn. (past vice chmn. legal affairs com.). Democrat. Episcopalian. Club: Univ. (San Francisco). Home: 3643 Tilden St NW Washington DC 20008 Office: Dept Energy Washington DC 20585

PEACOR, CARROLL NORMAN, ins. co. exec.; b. Boston, Sept. 22, 1926; s. Carroll O. and Leona (Ralph) P.; B.A., Tufts U., 1948; M.S., U. Mich., 1949; m. Dorothy Jean Andrews, Feb. 7, 1948; children—Janice Linda, Mark Alan, Grant Kenneth. With N.Y. Life Ins. Co., 1949-50; with Mass. Mut. Life Ins. Co., Springfield, 1950—, v.p., 1969-71, chief actuary, 1969—, sr. v.p., 1971-74, exec. v.p., 1974—. Mem. pension survey com., Springfield, 1958-68; exec. budget com. Pioneer Valley United Fund, 1966-69, pres. Pioneer Valley United Way, 1973-75, bd. dirs., 1975—; pres. Springfield Orch. Assn., 1975-76, bd. dirs., 1976—; chmn. bd. trustees Western New Eng. Coll.; bd. govs. Baystate Med. Center. Served to lt. comdr. USNR, 1944-46. C.L.U. Fellow Soc. Actuaries; mem. Hartford Actuaries Club, Boston Actuaries Club, Hampden County Radio Assn., Am. Radio Relay League, U.S. Chess Fedn. (past treas.), Theta Delta Chi. Home: Country Club Heights Monson MA 01057 Office: 1295 State St Springfield MA 01111

PEAIRS, RICHARD HOPE, psychologist; b. Normal, Ill., Feb. 15, 1929; s. Ralph Plummer and Myra Ann (Sinclair) P.; A.B., Occidental Coll., 1951; M.A., Ohio State U., 1956, Ph.D., 1958; m. Lillian Louise Johanna Gehrke, Dec. 18, 1954; children—Mark Andrew, John Michael, Nina Anne. Research asst. Ohio State U., 1954-55, teaching asst., 1955-56, asst. instr., 1956-57; asst. prof. psychology Colo. State U., 1957-59; asst. prof. Calif. State U., Northridge, 1959-63, asso. prof., 1963-66, chmn. dept. psychology, 1965-66; staff asso. A.A.U.P., Washington, 1966, asso. sec., dir. Western regional office, San Francisco, 1967-78; corp. psychologist, cons. Rohrer, Hibler and Replogle, Inc., Burlingame, Calif., 1978—. Served with U.S. Army, 1951-53. Mem. A.A.U.P., A.A.A.S., Am. Psychol. Assn., Sigma Xi. Club: Commonwealth of Calif. Author: (with Lillian G. Peairs) What Every Child Needs, 1974. Editor New Directions for Higher Edn., fall 1974. Home: 370 Loyola Dr Millbrae CA 94030 Office: Rohrer Hibler and Replogle Inc 1601 Old Bayshore Suite 260 Burlingame CA 94010

PEAK, PHILIP, educator; b. Estherville, Iowa, Sept. 24, 1908; s. Philip Bennett and Mary (Ross) P.; B.A., Iowa State Tchrs. Coll., 1930; M.A., U. Iowa, 1935; Ph.D., Ind. U., 1955; m. Alice Petersen, Oct. 8, 1931; children—James Bennett, Virginia Ross. Tchr. math. and agr. Mechanicsville (Iowa) High Sch., 1930-35; head dept. math. Pierre (S.D.) High Sch., 1935-38; asso. prof. math. Chadron (Nebr.) State Tchrs. Coll., 1938-42; head dept. math. Univ. Sch., Ind. U., Bloomington, 1942-62, from instr. to asso. prof. edn., 1950-59, prof. edn., 1959-79, prof. emeritus, 1979—, asst. dean edn., 1959-63, asso. dean edn., 1966-74, acting dean edn., 1963-66; mem. ednl. cons. teams for Saudi Arabia, Egypt and Pakistan. Mem. corp. Bloomington Hosp. Bd. dirs. Westminster Found. Recipient Alumni Achievement award U. No. Iowa. Fellow Ind. Acad. Sci.; mem. Central Assn. Sci. and Math. Tchrs. (pres. 1952, v.p. 1951), Nat. Council Tchrs. Math. (state rep. 1956-79, exec. com. 1958-62, chmn. com. analysis programs 1961, chmn. financial policies com. 1970-71), Ind. Tchrs. Assn. (pres. math. div. 1948, Outstanding Service award), Ind. Council Math. Tchrs., Math. Assn. Am., Nat. Assn. Research Sci. Teaching, Sigma Xi, Phi Delta Kappa. Presbyn. (elder). Club: Bloomington Exchange. Co-author: Mathematics-An Integrated Series, 9-12 math. text series; editorial bd. Math. Tchr. Contbr. articles to profl. jours. Home: 2000 E 2d St Bloomington IN 47401

PEAKE, CLIFFORD M., assn. exec.; b. Nampa, Idaho, Apr. 21, 1927; s. Clifford Henry and Frances Clare (Rands) P.; B.A., Idaho State Coll., 1950; grad. C. of C. Inst. Program Mont. State U., 1953; postgrad. Mich. State U., 1960, 65; m. Josephine Johnson, June 6, 1948; children—Christine Rae, Edward Michael, David Brian. Sec.-mgr. Jerome (Idaho) C. of C., 1950-52; mgr. C. of C., Golden, Colo., 1952-53; mgr. C. of C., North Platte, Neb., 1953-57; exec. v.p. C. of C., Belleville, Ill., 1957-66, Gary (Ind.) C. of C., 1966-69; pres. Eastern Union County C. of C., Elizabeth, N.J., 1969—; instr. C. of C. Inst., 1965-69. Pres. Ill. Assn. C. of C. Execs., 1964. Served with AUS, 1945-46. Named oustanding young man North Platte, 1955. Mem. Am. C. of C. Execs. (dir. 1979—, publs. award 1960, 63, 72), N.J., U.S. chambers commerce, N.J. Assn. C. of C. Execs. (pres. 1974-75). Presbyterian. Clubs: Masons, Rotary (pres. 1979-80). Home: 530 Montauk Dr Westfield NJ 07090 Office: 135 Jefferson Ave Box 300 Elizabeth NJ 07207

PEAKE, KIRBY, cons.; b. Detroit, Apr. 16, 1915; s. Robert Louis and Christina Josephine (DeBolt) P.; A.B., Colgate U., 1937; m. Jessie Charlotte Barnecott, Nov. 18, 1939 (div.); children—Nancy, Jonathan, Robert, Sarah, m. 2d, Hanna Mayer Johnson, Nov. 26, 1976. Reporter, Binghamton (N.Y.) Press, 1935-38; with Vick Chem. Co. div. Richardson-Merrell, Inc., 1938-59, pres., 1948-59; adminstrv. v.p. Carter-Wallace, Inc., N.Y.C., 1959-61, pres., chief exec. officer, 1961-72, chmn. bd., chief exec. officer, 1972-74, dir., 1960-75; chmn. bd., dir. Frank W. Horner, Ltd., Montreal, Que., Can., 1962-74; chmn. bd. Millmaster Onyx Corp., 1963-69. Chmn., N.Y. State Commn. for Catskills, 1972-75. Bd. dirs. Proprietary Assn., until 1970; Am. Found. for Pharm. Edn., 1965-72, Vis. Nurse Service N.Y., 1969-74; trustee Colgate U., 1962-72. Mem. Phi Beta Kappa. Clubs: Union League (N.Y.C.). Address: PO Box 506 Newtown CT 06470

PEAL, WILLIAM HUGH, lawyer; b. Bandana, Ky., Mar. 27, 1898; s. Jasper Stephen and Mary Ann (Wingo) P.; A.B., U. Ky., 1922, LL.D., 1959; B.A. in Juris. (Rhodes scholar), Oxford (Eng.) U., 1924, B.C.L., 1925, M.A., 1954; m. Margaret Jane Watson, June 4, 1932. Admitted to N.Y. bar, 1928, also fed. cts.; law clk. N.Y. firms, 1925-34; partner Chadbourne, Parke, Whiteside, Wolff & Brophy and predecessors, 1934-55; sr. partner Hardy, Peal, Rawlings & Werner, and predecessor firm, N.Y.C., 1955-73, of counsel, 1974—; expert witness ICC proc.; mem. N.Y. State Commn. Uniform State Laws, 1953-56. Asst. counsel Bur. Ships, spl. asst. to head Office of Counsel, 1942-43. Served with USNRF, 1918. Fellow Pierpont Morgan Library. Mem. U. Ky. Library Assos. (dir. 1958-59), Am., N.Y. State bar assns., Assn. Am. Rhodes Scholars, Assn. Bar City N.Y., Loudon County Hist. Soc. (pres. 1972-75), Am. Law Inst., Phi Beta Kappa, Delta Tau Delta. Democrat. Clubs: Filson (Louisville); Grolier, Cornell (N.Y.C.). Contbr. articles to legal periodicals. Home: Woodburn Leesburg VA 22075 Office: 750 3d Ave New York NY 10017

PEALE, NORMAN VINCENT, clergyman; b. Bowersville, Ohio, May 31, 1898; s. Charles Clifford and Anna (DeLaney) P.; A.B., Ohio Wesleyan U., 1920, D.D., 1936; S.T.B., Boston U., 1924, A.M., 1924; D.D., Syracuse U., 1931, Duke, 1938, Central Coll., 1964; L.H.D., Lafayette Coll., 1952, U. Cin., 1968; LL.D., Wm. Jewell Coll., 1952, Hope Coll., 1962, Brigham Young U., 1967, Pepperdine U., 1979; S.T.D., Millikin U., 1958; Litt.D., Iowa Wesleyan U., 1958, Eastern Ky. State Coll., 1964, Jefferson Med. Coll., 1955; m. Ruth Stafford, June 20, 1930; children—Margaret (Mrs. Paul F. Everett), John, Elizabeth (Mrs. John M. Allen). Ordained to ministry M.E. Ch., 1922; pastor, Berkeley, R.I., 1922-24, Kings Hwy. Ch., Bklyn., 1924-27, Univ. Ch., Syracuse, N.Y., 1927-32, Marble Collegiate Ref. Ch., N.Y.C., 1932—; Weekly Sunday radio program WOR radio; editor Guideposts, an inspirational mag. Trustee Ohio Wesleyan U., Central Coll. Mem. exec. com. Presbyn. Ministers Fund for Life Ins.; mem. Mid-Century White House Conf. on Children and Youth, Pres.'s Commn. for Observance 25th Anniversary UN; pres. Nat. Temperance Soc.; pres. Protestant Council City N.Y., 1965-69; pres. Ref. Church in Am., 1969-70; lectr. pub. affairs, personal effectiveness. Chaplain, Am. Legion, Kings County, N.Y., 1925-27. Recipient Freedom Found. award, 1952, 55, 59, 73, 74; Horatio Alger award, 1952; Am. Edn. award, 1955; Gov. Service award for Ohio, 1955; Nat. Salvation Army award, 1956; Distinguished Salesman's award N.Y. Sales Execs., 1957; Salvation Army award, 1957; Internat. Human Relations award Dale Carnegie Club Internat., 1958; Clergyman of Year award Religious Heritage Am., 1964; Paul Harris Fellow award Rotary Internat., 1972, Distinguished Patriot award Sons of Revolution, N.Y. State, 1973; Order of Aaron and Hur, Chaplains Corps U.S. Army, 1975; Christopher Columbus award, 1976; All-Time Gt. Ohioan award, 1976. Mem. Am. Found. Religion and Psychiatry (pres.), Ohio Soc. N.Y. (pres. 1952-55), Episcopal Actors Guild, Am. Authors Guild, S.A.R., Alpha Delta, Phi Gamma Delta. Republican. Clubs: Rotary, Masons (33 deg., Shriner, K.T., past grand prelate); Met., Union League. Author: The Art of Living; You Can Win; A Guide to Confident Living, 1948; The Power of Positive Thinking, 1952; The Coming of the King, 1956; Stay Alive All Your Life, 1957; The Amazing Results of Positive Thinking, 1959; The Tough-Minded Optimist, 1962; Adventures in the Holy Land, 1963; Sin, Sex and Self-control, 1965; Jesus of Nazareth, 1966; The Healing of Sorrow, 1966; Enthusiasm Makes the Difference, 1967; Bible Stories, 1973; You Can If You Think You Can, 1974; The Positive Principle Today, 1976; The Positive Power of Jesus Christ, 1980; co-author: Faith Is the Answer; Art of Real Happiness; chpt. in Am's 12 Master Salesmen. TV program: What's Your Trouble; nationally syndicated weekly TV program Guideposts Presents Norman Vincent Peale. Author newspaper column Positive Thinking appearing in many papers. Writer for various secular and religious periodicals. Tech. adviser representing Protestant Ch. in filming of motion picture One Foot in Heaven; motion picture One Man's Way, based on biography, 1963; (film) What It Takes To Be A Real Salesman. Home: 1030 Fifth Ave New York NY 10028 also Quaker Hill Pawling NY 12564 Office: 1025 Fifth Ave New York NY 10028

PEALE, RUTH STAFFORD (MRS. NORMAN VINCENT PEALE), religious leader; b. Fonda, Iowa, Sept. 10, 1906; d. Frank Burton and Anna Loretta (Crosby) Stafford; A.B., Syracuse U., 1928, LL.D., 1953; Litt. D., Hope Coll., 1962; m. Norman Vincent Peale, June 20, 1930; children—Margaret Ann (Mrs. Paul F. Everett), John Stafford, Elizabeth Ruth (Mrs. John M. Allen). Tchr. math. Central High Sch., Syracuse, N.Y., 1928-31; nat. pres. women's bd. domestic missions Ref. Ch. Am., 1936-46; sec. Protestant Film Commn., 1946-51; chmn. Am. Mother's Com., 1948-49; appeared on Nat. TV program What's Your Trouble, 1952-68; pres., editor-in-chief, gen. sec. Found. for Christian Living, 1945—. Nat. pres. bd. domestic missions Ref. Ch. in Am., 1955-56, mem. bd. N. Am. Missions, 1963-69, pres., 1967-69; mem. gen. program council Ref. Ch. in Am.,

1968—; mem. com. of 24 for merger Ref. Ch. in Am. and Presbyn. Ch. U.S., 1966-69; v.p. Protestant Council N.Y.C., 1964-66; hon. chancellor Webber Coll., 1972—. Trustee Hope Coll., Holland, Mich., Champlain Coll., Burlington, Vt., Stratford Coll., Danville, Va., Lenox Sch., N.Y.C., Interchurch Center Syracuse U., 1955-61; bd. dirs. Cook Christian Tng. Sch., Lord's Day Alliance U.S.; mem. bd. and exec. com. N.Y. Theol. Sem., N.Y.C.; sponsor Spafford Children's Convalescent Hosp., 1966—; bd. govs. Help Line Telephone Center, 1970—, Norman Vincent Peale Telephone Center, 1977. Named New York State Mother of Yr., 1963; Distinguished Woman of Yr. Nat. Art Assn.; recipient Cum Laude award Syracuse U. Alumni Assn. N.Y., 1965; Honor Iowans' award Buena Vista Coll., 1966; Religious Heritage Am. Ch. Woman of Year, 1969, Am. Mother's Com. award religion, 1970, Distinguished Service award Council Chs. N.Y.C., 1973, Distinguished Citizen award Champlain Coll., 1976, Distinguished Service to the Community and Nation award Gen. Fedn. Women's Clubs, 1977, Horatio Alger award, 1977. Mem. Insts. Religion and Health (bd. exec. com.), Am. Bible Soc. (bd.), Nat. Council Chs. (v.p. 1952-54, gen. bd.; treas. gen. dept. United Ch. Women, vice chmn. broadcasting and film commn., 1951-55; program chmn. gen. assembly 1966), N.Y. Fedn. of Women's Clubs (chmn. religion 1951-53, 57-58), Home Missions Council N.A. (nat. pres. 1942-44, nat. chmn. migrant com. 1948-51), P.E.O., Alpha Phi (Frances W. Willard award 1976). Clubs: Sorosis (pres. 1953-56, hon. life pres. 1975—), Women's National Republican (N.Y.C.), Author: I Married A Minister, 1942; The Adventure of Being a Wife, 1971. Co-editor: Guidepost Mag., 1957—. Appears on nat. radio program with husband, 1968—; co-subject with husband film One Man's Way, 1963. Home: 1030 Fifth Ave New York NY 10028 also (summer) Quaker Hill Pawling NY 12564

PEAPPLES, GEORGE ALAN, govt. ofcl.; b. Benton Harbor, Mich., Nov. 6, 1940; s. Arthur L. and Kathleen C. (Peters) P.; B.A. in Econs., U. Mich., 1962, M.B.A., 1963; m. Rebecca Dean Sowers, June 27, 1962; children—Lucia Christine, Sarah Bouton. With Gen. Motors Corp., 1964-77, staff analyst treas.' staff, N.Y.C., 1968-73, asst. divisional comptroller Delco Moraine div., Dayton, Ohio, 1973-75, asst. treas. bank relations, Detroit, 1975-77; asst. sec. of navy for fin. mgmt., Dept. Navy, Washington, 1977—. Bd. dirs. Am. Freedom Train Found., 1976-77. Mem. Am. Soc. Military Comptrollers, Phi Kappa Phi. Office: Asst Sec of the Navy Rm 4E768 Pentagon Washington DC 20350

PEARCE, CHARLES ABRAHAM, banker; b. Ft. Fairfield, Maine, Apr. 23, 1923; s. Clarence H. and Jackalena (Donaghy) P.; A.B., Colby Coll., 1949; M.Ed., Boston U., 1954; m. Virginia M. Davis, Nov. 23, 1950; children—James K., Sarah J., Catherine A. Tchr., coach Unity (Maine) High Sch., 1949-50; tchr., guidance dir. Ware (Mass.) High Sch., 1951-53; guidance dir. Northampton (Mass.) Pub. Schs., 1953-55; asst. treas., treas., exec. v.p. Ware Savs. Bank, 1955-67; pres. Quincy (Mass.) Savs. Bank, 1967—. Pres. Mutual Adv. Corp., 1975-77. Asst. chmn. Adv. Bd. Town of Hingham, 1970-71; pres. Progress for Downtown Quincy, Inc., 1975—. Bd. dirs. Mass. Taxpayers Found., Quincy YMCA, New Eng. Automated Clearing House, Mass. Automated Transfer System, William B. Eventide Home, Quincy, 1979—, St. Coletta's Day Sch., 1979—; trustee Thayer Acad., Econ. Edn. Council Mass. Served with AUS, World War II. Mem. Savs. Bank Assn. Mass. (treas. 1969-70, 2d v.p. 1970-71, 1st v.p. 1971-72, pres. 1972-74), Nat. Assn. Mut. Savs. Banks (vice chmn. 1977, chmn. 1978), Mass. Purchasing Group (steering com. 1979), Conf. State Bank Suprs. (adv. com. 1979), Mortgage Bankers Assn. Am. (legis. com.), Quincy Hist. Soc. (dir. 1979), Quincy-South Shore C. of C. (pres. 1977). Home: 957 Main St Hingham MA 02043 Office: 1200 Hancock St Quincy MA 02169

PEARCE, DONALD JOSLIN, librarian; b. Southampton, Eng., May 31, 1924; s. Alfred Ernest and Constance May (Jeffrey) P.; came to U.S., 1949, naturalized, 1952; student Sch. Oriental and African Studies, U. London, 1942-43; A.B., George Washington U., 1953; M.S. in L.S., Cath. U. Am., 1954; m. June Inez Bond, Dec. 7, 1946; children—Kristin, Kim. Part-time library asst. U.S. Dept. Agr., 1949-54; student asst. George Washington U. Library, 1950-53; circulation librarian Denison U., 1954-56; staff Ohio State U. Library, 1956-59, asst. acquisition librarian, 1958-59; head librarian, asst. prof. U. N.D., 1959-69, chief bibliographer, 1969-73, asst. dir. libraries, 1973-75, asst. prof. Oriental philosophy, 1969-75; library dir., asst. prof. philosophy U. Minn., Duluth, 1975—. Chmn. staff orgn. round table Ohio Library Assn., 1958-59. Served with Brit. Army, 1943-47. Mem. ALA, N.D. (pres. 1965-67), Minn. (sec. 1978—) library assns., Assn. Coll. Reference Librarians, A.A.U.P., Mountain Plains Library Assn. (v.p. 1968-69), Buddhist Assn., Phi Beta Kappa, Beta Phi Mu. Home: 2306 E 8th St Duluth MN 55812

PEARCE, EDWIN MCKIGNEY, JR., lawyer; b. Atlanta, Apr. 25, 1908; s. Edwin McKigney and Ella (Pope) P.; student U. Va., 1925-26; LL.B., Emory U., 1931; m. Joanne Snelson, May 1, 1949; children—Anne, Virginia, Catherine, Edwin McKigney. Admitted to Ga. bar, 1931, since practiced in Atlanta; regional price atty. Southeastern region OPA, 1944-45, regional price exec., 1946-47; lectr. law Emory U., 1941—. Dir., trustee WRC Smith Pub. Co. Mem. Atlanta C. of C., Am. (council, past chmn. labor relations), Ga. bar assns., Bryan Honor Soc., Sigma Alpha Epsilon, Phi Delta Phi. Baptist. Clubs: Atlanta Athletic, East Lake Country, Commerce, Elks (Atlanta). Home: 1475 W Paces Ferry Rd NW Atlanta GA 30327 Office: 57 Executive Park South NE Atlanta GA 30329

PEARCE, HOWARD WILLIAM, home bldg and devel. co. ofcl.; b. Oakley, Mich., Apr. 10, 1895; s. Frederick W. and Nina (Palmer) P.; student U. Alberta, U. Lyons (France); LL.D., Canisius Coll., 1958; m. Jane Seeman Lucas, Feb. 12, 1959; 1 son, Frederick W., also 1 son by previous marriage, William H. Pres., treas. Pearce & Pearce Co., Inc., Buffalo; dir. Marine Trust Co. Western N.Y. Former bd. regents Canisius Coll. Served with U.S. Army, World War I. Mem. Buffalo C. of C. (dir., chmn. exec. com., past pres.). Republican. Clubs: Buffalo (past pres.), Saturn, Country of Buffalo; Niagara Falls (Ont.). Home: 520 Klein Rd Williamsville NY 14221 Office: 900 Niagara Falls Blvd Buffalo NY 14223

PEARCE, JAMES WISHART, lawyer; b. Cin., Apr. 10, 1916; s. Charles Tabb and Jean (Wishart) P.; B.S., Mass.Inst.Tech., 1937; LL.B., U. Va., 1941; m. Helen deKay Thompson, Sept. 26, 1942; children—James W., Paula Carroll, Jeanne Tabb. Admitted to Ohio bar, 1942; atty. Atlantic Refining Co., 1941-42; asso. firm Wood, Arey, Herron and Evans, 1945-47; asso. firm Zugelter and Zugelter, Cin., 1947-59; partner firm Pearce and Schaeperklaus, Cin., 1959—. Bd. dirs. YMCA of Cin. and Hamilton County. Served with USNR, 1942-45. Mem. Cin. Patent Law Assn. (pres. 1969-70), Cin. Bar Assn., Am. Bar Assn. Episcopalian. Home: 3693 Kroger Ave Cincinnati OH 45226 Office: 1110 First National Bank Bldg Cincinnati OH 45202

PEARCE, MORTON LEE, physician, educator; b. Chgo., Aug. 22, 1920; s. James William and Lydia (Lee) P.; B.S., U. Chgo., 1941, M.D., 1944; m. Ruth Elizabeth Schwartz, Mar. 11, 1944 (div. 1977); children—Katherine, Michael, David; m. 2d, Inger Christensen, Dec. 28, 1977. Intern Los Angeles County Hosp., 1945, resident in medicine, 1945-48; research asso. U. Calif. at Los Angeles, 1948-51; fellow in medicine Johns Hopkins, 1951-52; instr. Vanderbilt U., 1952-53, asst. prof., 1953-56; asso. prof. U. Calif. at Los Angeles, 1956-63, prof. medicine/cardiology, 1963—; cons. Rand Corp., VA Hosp., Los Angeles. Mem. Los Angeles Soc. Internal Medicine (past pres.), Am. Heart Assn. (past pres. Los Angeles affiliate), Am. Fedn. Clin. Research, Western Soc. for Clin. Research, Assn. U. Cardiologists, Western Assn. Physicians, Am. Physiol. Soc., AAAS. Research in cardiology. Home: 1026 Embury St Pacific Palisades CA 90272 Office: U Calif Sch Medicine Dept Medicine Los Angeles CA 90024

PEARCE, PAUL FRANCIS, aerospace electronics co. exec.; b. Boston, Sept. 17, 1928; s. George Hamilton and Marie Louise (Duval) P.; B.S. in Elec. Engring. (Edwards scholar), Mass. Inst. Tech., 1950, M.S., 1952; postgrad. (Hughes fellow) U. Calif., Los Angeles, 1957-58, U. So., Calif., 1958-59, Inst. Mgmt. Northwestern U., 1966; m. Gilda Troisi, Apr. 11, 1953; children—Janet Theresa, Diane. Project engr. Trans-Sonics, Inc., Burlington, Mass., 1952-55; sect. head application engring., strategic systems Hughes Aircraft Co., Culver City, Calif., 1955-59; with Lockheed Electronics Co., Plainfield, N.J., 1959-67, gen. mgr. div. mil. systems, 1964-65, v.p., gen. mgr., 1965-67; v.p., div. mgr. Tele-Dynamics div. AMBAC Industries, Inc., Ft. Washington, Pa, 1967—, group v.p. comml. and aerospace electronics group, Carle Place, N.Y., 1973—. Mem. Armed Forces Communications and Electronics Assn. (pres. 1969-71), Inst. Nav., Delaware Valley Mfrs. Assn., Greater Phila. C. of C., Ft. Washington Indsl. Park Mgmt. Assn. (gov. 1973-74), Sigma Xi. Club: Mfrs'. Golf and Country (Oreland, Pa.). Home: 300 Glenn Rd Ardmore PA 19003 Office: 525 Virginia Dr Fort Washington PA 19034

PEARCE, RONALD WILLIAM, ins. co. exec.; b. Sonora, Calif., Oct. 23, 1931; s. Barthol William and Alice Elizabeth (Tell) P.; B.A., Coll. of Pacific, 1957; m. Margaret Elizabeth Alexander, Dec. 12, 1954; children—Dawn Elaine, Robin Ann, Christopher Philip. Regional mgr. Allstate Ins. Co., Sacramento, Calif., 1970-71; v.p. corp. planning, Chgo., 1971-75, sr. v.p., 1975-78, exec. v.p. Allstate Enterprises, Chgo., 1978—; dir. Allstate Savs. and Loan, Executrans, Previews, Allstate Enterprises Mortgage Corp. Bd. dirs. Sacramento Safety Council, 1971, Chgo. Met. Council on Alcoholism, 1973-75. Served with USN, 1952-54. Nat. Alliance Businessmen. Home: 15 Brunswick Ln Deerfield IL 60015 Office: Allstate Plaza Northbrook IL 60062

PEARCE, ROY HARVEY, educator; b. Chgo., Dec. 2, 1919; s. Walter Leslie and Esther (Bruesch) P.; B.A., U. Calif. at Los Angeles, 1940, M.A., 1942; Ph.D., Johns Hopkins, 1945; m. Marie Jeanette Vandenberg, Feb. 7, 1947; children—Joanna Vandenberg, Robert Elliott. Instr. English, Ohio State U., 1945-46, asso. prof., prof. English, 1949-63; asst. prof. English, U. Calif. at Berkeley, 1946-49; prof. Am. lit. U. Calif. at San Diego, 1963—, asso. dean grad. studies and research, 1968-71, dean grad. studies, 1972-75. Vis. prof., lectr. Johns Hopkins, Salzburg Seminar Am. Studies, Claremont Grad. Sch., U. Bordeaux, Tchrs. Coll. Columbia. Am. Council Learned Socs. research fellow, 1948, 58, 59, faculty study fellow, 1950-51; Fund For Advancement Edn. fellow, 1953-54; fellow Com. Midwestern Studies, 1950; Guggenheim fellow, 1975-76; mem. Com. Internat. Exchange Persons, 1963-66. Recipient Poetry Chap Book award Poetry Soc. Am., 1962. Fellow Am. Anthrop. Assn., Am. Acad. Arts and Scis.; mem. Modern Lang. Assn., Am. Hist. Assn., A.A.U.P., Am. Studies Assn., Nat. Council Tchrs. English, Internat. Assn. U. Profs. English, Modern Humanities Research Assn., Phi Beta Kappa. Club: Tudor and Stuart (Balt.). Author: The Savages of America, 1953, rev., 1965; The Continuity of American Poetry, 1961; Historicism Once More, 1969. Editor: Colonial American Writing, 1950, rev. edit., 1968; (with Cady, Hoffman) The Growth of American Literature, 1956; (with Charvat, Simpson) Centenary Edition of the Works of Nathaniel Hawthorne, 1962—; (with Miller) The Act of the Mind, 1965; Experience in the Novel, 1968; Pacific Coast Philology, 1978; bd. editors ELH, 1946-75, Am. Lit., 1969—, PMLA, 1976-79. Home: 7858 Esterel Dr La Jolla CA 92037

PEARCE, THOMAS HONE, splty. wire and metal mfg. co. exec.; b. Blackheath, Eng., Apr. 26, 1914; s. Frederick H. and Mary (Smith) P.; student Leeds Coll. Tech. (Eng.), 1933, Tech. Coll. Doncaster (Eng.), 1934, U. Sheffield (Eng.), 1935; m. Winifred M.J. Cain, Sept. 28, 1936; children—Susan R., Molly A., Jennifer M. Came to U.S., 1948, naturalized, 1956. Prodn. trainee, rep. in South Africa, Brit. Ropes, Ltd., Doncaster, 1935-48; with Nat.-Standard Co., Niles, Mich., 1948—, exec. v.p., 1957-59, pres., 1959-69, chmn. bd., chief exec. officer, 1969—, also dir.; dir. Nat.- Standard Co. Ltd., Nat. Blvd. Bank of Chgo. Asso. mem. Brit. Inst. Mgmt. Clubs: Masons, Union League (Chgo.). Home: 1115 Weesaw St Niles MI 49120 Office: National-Standard Co Niles MI 49120

PEARCE, WILLIAM MARTIN, educator; b. Plainview, Tex., Mar. 11, 1913; s. Will Martin and Annie Eugenia (Bates) P.; A.A., Kemper Mil. Sch., 1932; A.B., So. Meth. U., 1935; M.A., Tex. Tech U., 1937; Ph.D. U. Tex., 1952; m. Frances Elizabeth Campbell, Sept. 6, 1939; children—William Martin III, Richard Campbell. Instr. history Tex. Tech Coll., 1938-42, 46-47, asst. prof. history, 1949-53, asso. prof. history, 1953-55, prof., head dept. history, 1955-60, v.p. coll., 1960-68, dir. Archeol. Field Sch., Glorieta, N.Mex., 1948, Valley of Mexico, 1949; pres. Tex. Wesleyan Coll. 1968-78; ret., 1978; part-time instr. history U. Tex., 1947-49; dir. Southland Royalty Co. Served as lt. AUS, 1942-45. Decorated Bronze Star, Purple Heart; recipient Distinguished Alumnus award Tex. Tech U., 1975. Mem. Tex., Western hist. assns., Panhandle-Plains Hist. Soc. (dir.). Phi Alpha Theta, Pi Kappa Alpha, Phi Kappa Phi. Methodist. Author: The Matador Land and Cattle Company, 1964. Home: 6209 Indiana Ave Lubbock TX 79413

PEARL, MARTIN HERBERT, educator; b. N.Y.C., June 19, 1928; s. Benjamin Morris and Betty (Zimmer) P.; B.A. with honors. Bklyn. Coll., 1950; M.A., U. Mich., 1951; Ph.D., U. Wis., 1955. Mathematician, Nat. Security Agy., 1955-56; instr. U. Rochester, 1956-57; NRC postdoctoral research fellow Nat. Bur. Standard, Washington, 1957-58; mem. faculty U. Md., College Park, 1958—, prof. math., 1967—; mathematician Nat. Bur. Standards, 1966—; guest worker Mental Health Study Center, NIMH, Adelphi, Md., 1979—; vis. lectr. Imperial Coll., U. London, 1964-65. Mem. Am. Math. Soc., Soc. Indsl. and Applied Math., Sigma Xi. Home: 1002 DeVere Dr Silver Spring MD 20903 Office: Dept Math U Md College Park MD 20742

PEARL, MINNIE (SARAH OPHELIA COLLEY CANNON), entertainer; b. Centerville, Tenn., Oct. 25, 1912; d. Thomas Kelly and Fannie Tate (House) Colley; ed. Ward-Belmont Coll.; m. Henry R. Cannon. Dir. amateur plays, Atlanta and surrounding areas, 1934-40; performer WSM Grand Ole Opry, Nashville, 1940—; TV appearances include Dean Martin Show, Carol Burnett Show, Tenn. Ernie Ford Show, Operation Entertainment, Joey Bishop Show, Merv Griffin Show, Mike Douglas Show, This Is Your Life, Dinah Shore Show, Jack Paar Show, Jubilee, U.S.A., Hee Haw, The World's Largest Indoor Country Music Show, 1978; rec. artist Everest, RCA, Starday rec. cos. Recipient Woman of the Year award Billboard; All Time Great award Billboard; named to Country Music Hall of Fame, 1972. Records include: Minnie Pearl, Minnie Pearl at the Party, Answer to Giddyup and Go, Story of Country Music. Address: care WSM PO Box 100 Nashville TN 37202*

PEARL, ORSAMUS MERRILL, III, educator; b. St. Johns, Mich., May 15, 1908; s. Orsamus Merrill and Margaret (Armour) P.; A.B., U. Mich., 1929, student Law Sch., 1929-30, Ph.D., 1938; student U. Paris, 1934-35; m. Cynthia Mallory, Jan. 10, 1931 (dec. Oct. 1964); children—Devon (Mrs. David Buxbaum), John Christopher, Cynthia (Mrs. Joseph Scanio); m. 2d, Mary Jane Forsyth, May 2, 1965 (div. Sept. 1968); m. 3d, Patricia Mary Cobb, Nov. 28, 1975. Instr. Latin, Sweet Briar Coll., 1936-37; research asst. Papyrology, U. Mich., 1938-40, mem. faculty, 1940—, prof. Greek lang. and lit., 1965-78, emeritus, 1978—; spl. teaching assignment. Author articles on Greek mythology, papyrology. Home: 3200 Overridge Dr Ann Arbor MI 48104 Office: 2023 Angell Hall U Mich Ann Arbor MI 48109

PEARL, RICHARD MAXWELL, geologist, educator; b. N.Y.C., May 4, 1913; s. Morse and Etta (Stocker) P.; B.A., U. Colo., 1939, M.A., 1940; A.M., Harvard U., 1946; m. Mignon Wardell, June 13, 1941. Instr. geology U. Colo., 1940; engaged in mineral supply bus., Denver, 1941; process engr. du Pont Co., Denver, 1941-42; geologist Shell Oil Co., Tulsa, 1944; mem. faculty Colo. Coll., Colorado Springs, 1946—, prof., 1962—, curator minerals, 1977—; pub., editor-in-chief Earth Sci. mag., 1973—, Minerals mag., Mineralogy mag., Mineral Products and Resources mag., 1977—, Gem Studies mag., Cadillac mag., Zyzzogeton mag., 1978—. Vis. prof. Phoenix Coll., Denver U., Pueblo Coll.; prof. extension div. U. Colo.; geol. cons. Colo. Wonderland, Walt Disney Prodns., McGraw-Hill Book Co., Aero. Library, USAF Acad.; pres. Mineral Parks of Colo.; adviser mineralogy and geology Denver Pub. Library; mem. geology adv. panel U. Tex. at Dallas; pub. Mineral Book Co., Maxwell Pub. Co. Seigneur, May Island, Gulf Islands, Can. Bd. advs. Detroit Concert Band. Served with U.S. Army, 1942-44. Am. Fedn. Mineral. Socs. scholar, 1964. Fellow Gemological Assn. Gt. Britain and Ireland (with distinction), A.A.A.S., Meteoritical Soc., Am. Geog. Soc., Geol. Soc. Am., Mineral. Soc. Am., Gemological Assn. Australia (hon. v.p.); mem. Gemological Inst. Am. (cert.), Rocky Mountain Fedn. Mineral. Socs. (founder), Am. Fedn. Mineral. Socs. (co-founder), Colo. Mineral Soc. (co-founder), Colo. Sci. Soc. (hon.). Republican. Unitarian. Clubs: Rocky Mountain Harvard, Explorers (fellow), Winter Night, Torch, Kiwanis. Author numerous books, syndicated newspaper columns, jour. and mag. articles. Editor: Mineral Minutes. Contbr. to several encys., anthologies. Discoverer 3 Colo. minerals. Home: 16 Valley Pl Colorado Springs CO 80903

PEARLMAN, CHESTER ARTHUR, JR., psychiatrist; b. Buffalo, Jan. 8, 1934; s. Chester Arthur and Jeanette (Jacobson) P.; A.B., Harvard U., 1955; M.D., Albert Einstein Coll. Medicine, 1961; m. Edith Ann Grossman, July 2, 1967; children—Jessica, Charles. Intern, Montefiore Hosp., N.Y.C., 1961-62; resident in psychiatry Boston VA Hosp. and Beth Israel Hosp., Boston, 1962-67; clin. investigator Boston VA Hosp., 1969-72, staff psychiatrist, 1972-78, asst. chief psychiatrist, 1978—; instr. psychiatry Harvard U. Med. Sch., 1970—; asso. prof. Tufts U. Sch. Medicine, 1975—; asst. psychiatrist Beth Israel Hosp., 1977—. Mem. Brookline (Mass.) Town Meeting, 1970—, Brookline Council for Planning and Renewal, 1971—. Served with M.C., USN, 1967-69. USPHS fellow in neuropharmacology, 1957-59. Mem. Am. Psychiat. Assn., AAAS, Assn. Psychophysiol. Study of Sleep, Soc. Family Therapy and Research, Viola da Gamba Soc. Am., Lute Soc. Am. Democrat. Jewish. Contbr. articles on sleep and dream research to profl. jours. Home: 21 Elba St Brookline MA 02146

PEARLMAN, HERBERT MALCOLM, bus. exec.; b. Bklyn., Dec. 13, 1932; s. Al and Sylvia (Berger) P.; student Brown U., 1949-51, B.B.A., Adelphi Coll., 1953; m. Gail Kunen, July 17, 1954 (dec. Sept. 1971); children—Lee Roger, Julia Lynn. With Lybrand Ross Bros. & Montgomery, C.P.A.'s, N.Y.C., 1953-55, S.D. Leidesdorf & Co., C.P.A.'s N.Y.C., 1955-59; controller Kamkap Co., N.Y.C., 1960-61; controller Kalvex, Inc., N.Y.C., 1961-65, sec.-treas., 1965-68, exec. v.p., 1968-72; financial v.p. Utilities and Industries Carter Group, Inc., 1972-74; chmn. exec. com. Unimax Group Inc. (formerly Riker Maxson Inc.), N.Y.C., 1973-75, pres., chief exec. officer, 1975—; chmn. finance com., dir. Allied Artists Pictures Corp., 1967-72. Bd. dirs. Ackerman Inst., N.Y.C., 1978—. C.P.A., N.Y. State. Mem. Am. Inst. C.P.A.'s, N.Y. State Soc. C.P.A.'s. Clubs: Harmonie (N.Y.C.); Quaker Ridge Golf (Scarsdale, N.Y.). Office: 425 Park Ave New York NY 10022

PEARLMAN, JERRY KENT, electronics co. exec.; b. Des Moines, Mar. 27, 1939; s. Leo R. Pearlman; B.A., Princeton, 1960; M.B.A., Harvard, 1962; children—Gregory, Neal. Sr. v.p. fin. Zenith Radio Corp., Chgo., 1971—. Office: 1000 Milwaukee Ave Glenview IL 60025

PEARLMAN, LEONARD DAVID, electronics co. exec.; b. Fall River, Mass., Aug. 21, 1930; s. Israel and Ida (Mines) P.; B.B.A., U. Mich., 1953; m. Karen Mayersohn, Dec. 20, 1970; children—David, Karen, Janet, Laurie, Ellin, Stephanie. With Lafayette Radio Electronics Corp., Syosset, N.Y., 1955—, pres., chief exec. officer, 1973—, chmn. bd., chief exec. officer, 1976—. dir. adv. council Marine Midland Bank. Served with U.S. Army, 1953-55. Home: 3 Woodland Pl Great Neck NY 11021 Office: 11 Middleneck Rd Great Neck NY 11021

PEARLMAN, SHOLOM, univ. adminstr.; b. Ottawa, Can., July 3, 1919; s. Mendel and Rose (Mirsky) P.; D.D.S., U. Toronto, 1945; M.S., Western Res. U., 1951; m. Judith Emma Greenstein, June 24, 1945; children—Robert S., Leslie R. (Mrs. Lawrence C. Hamilton), Edward D., Philip A., Vivian A. (Mrs. Jeffrey S. Rudin), Beryl D., Marian R. Came to U.S., 1946, naturalized, 1951. Staff dentist Sask. Mental Hosp., Weyburn, 1945-46; research investigator, tchr. Western Res. U. Sch. Dentistry, also Sch. Medicine, 1947-51; asst. sec. Council Dental Therapeutics, Am. Dental Assn., Chgo., 1951-59, sec. Council Dental Research, 1959-68; asso. prof. Sch. Dentistry, U. Colo., 1968-69, prof., 1970—, dir. program devel., 1968-76, asst. dean, 1974-76. Mem. adv. bd. Oral Research Abstracts, 1965—; exec. com. Midcontinental Regional Med. Library, 1969-75; cons. Bur. Dental Health Edn., Am. Dental Assn., VA, 1968—, Indian Health Service, 1974—, Com. Internat. Exchange Scholars, 1972—; spl. adviser White House Conf. on Aging, 1961; adviser WHO, 1965; mem. NRC, 1959-68; co-chmn. Denver regional council President's Com. Health Edn., 1972-77; chmn. subcom. comprehensive health edn. Colo. Comprehensive Health Planning Council, 1973-74; mem. health adv. bd. Colo. Migrant Council, 1970—; mem. Colo. Health Dept. Task Force Venereal Disease Edn., 1970-73; pres. Denver area Vis. Nurse Assn., 1974-75; mem. biomed. library rev. com. Nat. Library Medicine, 1975-79. USPHS Research and Tng. grantee, 1960-68, 63-69; Assn. Dental Alumni of Columbia U. Research medal award, 1968. Fellow Am. Coll. Dentists; mem. AAAS (sec. sect. R Dentistry 1970—, chmn. 1978), Internat. Assn. Dental Research, Am., Colo. (mem. council and coms.) dental assns. Author: Dental Science: A Guide to Career Selection, 1969; editor several sci. publs. Contbr. articles sci., philos. jours. Home: 7 Ivy Ln Denver CO 80220

PEARLSTEIN, PHILIP, artist; b. Pitts., May 24, 1924; s. David and Libbie (Kalser) P.; B.F.A., Carnegie Inst. Tech., 1949; M.A., N.Y.U., 1955; m. Dorothy Cantor, Aug. 20, 1950; children—William, Julia, Ellen. One man shows at Tanager Gallery, N.Y.C., 1955, 59, Peridot Gallery, N.Y.C., 1956, 57, 59, Allan Frumkin Gallery, N.Y.C., 1962, 63, 65, 67, 69, 72, 74, 76, 78, Frumkin Gallery, Chgo., 1960, 65, 69, 73, 75, Kansas City Art Inst., 1962, Ceeje Gallery, Los Angeles, 1965, 66, Reed Coll., 1965, Galerie Thelen, Cologne, Germany, 1972, Galleri Ostergren, Malmo, Sweden, 1972, Galerie Kornfeld, Zurich, Switzerland, 1972, Staatliche Museen-Kupferstichkabinett, Berlin, 1972, Kunstverein, Hamburg, Germany, 1972, Editions La Tortue, Paris, 1973, Donald Morris Gallery, Detroit, 1973, 76, Gimpel Fils Ltd., London, 1975, Marianne Friedland Gallery, Toronto, Can., 1975, and numerous others; group shows at Carnegie Internat., 1955, 64, 67, Whitney Mus. Am. Art, 1955, 56, 58, 62, 65, 67, 70, 72, 73, 74, U. Ill., 1965, 67, 68, Providence Art Club, 1965, U. Mich. Mus., 1965, Corcoran Gallery, 1967, Vassar Coll., 1968, Milw. Art Center, 1969, Pa. Acad. Fine Arts, 1971-72, Indpls. Mus. Art, 1972, Galerie Lowenadler, Stockholm, Sweden, 1973, Nat. Acad. Arts and Letters, N.Y.C. (award), 1973, Yale U., 1973, 74, Hofstra U., 1973, Helsinki (Finland) Mus. Art, 1974, Art Inst. Chgo., 1974, Cleve. Mus. Art, 1974, America 1976 Bicentennial Exhbn., U.S. Dept. Interior, 1976, Wildenstein Gallery, N.Y.C., 1976, many others; retrospective exhbns. Finch Coll., 1974, U. Tex., Austin, 1974, Cranbrook Acad. Art, Mich., 1974, Notre Dame U., 1975, Grand Rapids (Mich.) Art Mus., 1975, Kalamazoo Inst. Arts, Tampa Bay Art Center, 1975, Miami Art Center, 1975; represented in permanent collections Phila. Mus. Art, San Antonio Mus. Assn., Pa. State U., Whitney Mus., Mus. Modern Art, N.Y. U., Syracuse U., James A. Michener Found., Hirshhorn Mus., Corcoran Gallery, Art Inst. Chgo., Milw. Art Center, Met. Mus. Art, Ludwig Collection, Aachen, Germany, Sydney and Frances Lewis Found., Richmond, Va., Bklyn. Mus., Cleve. Mus. Art, others; instr. Pratt Inst., 1959-63; vis. critic Yale, 1962-63; prof. art dept. Bklyn. Coll. Fulbright fellow to Italy, 1958-59, Guggenheim fellow, 1971-72; Nat. Endowment for Arts grantee, 1968. Office: Brooklyn Coll Dept Art Brooklyn NY 11210*

PEARLSTEIN, SEYMOUR, artist; b. Bklyn., Oct. 14, 1923; s. Morris Lazarus and Anna (Bassiur) P.; certificate Pratt Inst., Bklyn., 1950, Art Students League of N.Y., 1954; student Jack Potter; m. Toby Tessie Rubinstein, Mar. 21, 1943; children—Judith Helene Pearlstein Weltman, Lawrence Jonathan. Owner, artist, designer Sy Pearlstein Advt. Art Studio, N.Y.C., 1946-71; artist-painter rep. by Far Gallery, N.Y.C., 1969—; asso. prof. N.Y.C. Community Coll., Bklyn., 1971—; one-man shows: Grace Gallery, N.Y.C. Community Coll., 1971, Silvermine Guild of Artists, New Canaan, Conn., 1973, Far Gallery, 1973, 75, 78, Klitgord Center, N.Y.C. Community Coll., 1974, De Mers Gallery, Hilton Head, S.C., 1975, Adelphi U., Garden City, N.Y., 1979; group shows: A.M. Sachs Gallery, N.Y.C., 1971, Springfield (Mo.) Art Mus., 1971, Am. Acad. Arts and Letters, N.Y.C., 1975, 76, 77, NAD, N.Y.C., 1975, 76, 78, 79, Butler Inst. Art, Ohio, 1975, Ball State U., Queens Mus., N.Y.C., U.S. Dept. State Art In Embassies Program, Am. Watercolor Soc., N.Y.C., Audubon Artists, N.Y.C., Allied Artists Am., N.Y.C., Phila. Mus. Sales and Loan Gallery, Nat. Arts Club, N.Y.C., others; represented in permanent collections at Mus. N.Mex., Santa Fe, Mint Mus. Art, Charlotte, N.C., NAD, N.Y.C., Fine Arts Gallery, San Diego, Adelphi U. Served with AUS, 1942-46. Recipient Gold medal Nat. Acad. Design, 1969, Hassam Fund Purchase award Am. Acad. Arts and Letters, 1969, 77, Gold medal of honor Nat. Arts Club, 1970, Ranger Fund Purchase award NAD, 1971, Gold medal Soc. Illustrators, 1972, Nat. Inst.-Am. Acad. Arts and Letters grant, 1975. Mem. NAD, Am. Watercolor Soc. (dir. 1979-80 Watercolor U.S.A. award 1971), Art Students League of N.Y. (life), Allied Artists Am. (dir. 1976-79, E. Lowe award 1969), Audubon Artists (Grumbacher Meml. award 1971), Alliance Figurative Artists (co-chmn. 1976-77), Profl. Staff Congress. Home: 52 Dartmouth St Forest Hills NY 11375 Office: 300 Jay St Brooklyn NY 11201

PEARMAN, JEAN RICHARDSON, educator; b. Cherry, Nebr., July 15, 1915; s. William Francis and Ruth Gertrude (Richardson) P.; A.B., Nebr. State Coll., Chadron, 1938; M.A., U. Nebr., 1945; Ph.D., U. Minn., 1959; m. Alberta Valier Stevenson, July 15, 1941; children—Allen Lee, Sandra Jean, Marlene Ann, Patricia Valier. Tchr., Cherry County, Nebr., 1933-36; supr. Rose Valley (Nebr.) Sch., 1938-39; social worker Nebr. Pub. Assistance, 1939-41; asst. dir. employment WPA, Omaha, 1941-42; interviewer U.S. Employment Service, 1942-43; supt. schs. Ashby, Liberty and Chester, Nebr., 1943-46; social worker VA, 1946-47; from asst. prof. to prof. sociology and econs. No. Mich. U., 1947-64, head dept., 1961-64; prof. econs. and social work Fla. State U., Tallahassee, 1964-78, prof. econs., 1978—, head dept. social welfare, 1964-69, prof., research asso. Fla. Resources and Environ. Analysis Center, 1974-78; cons. in field. Pres. Marquette (Mich.) Council Social Agencies, 1958-62, Marquette Catholic Social Service Bd., 1959-61, Leon-Tallahassee Community Action Program Bd., 1976-78; bd. dirs. Tallahassee chpt. ARC, 1969—. HEW coop. research grantee, 1961-62; Fla. State U. summer faculty research grantee, 1969; grantee Fla. Endowment Humanities, 1977-79. Mem. Am. Econ. Assn., Assn. Evolutionary Econs., Assn. for Social Econs., Am. Pub. Welfare Assn., Am. Acad. Polit. and Social Sci., United Faculty Fla.-AFL-CIO. Democrat. Co-author: Social Services in the School, 1955; Social Science and Social Work, 1973. Contbr. to profl. jours., books. Home: 1330 Sharon Rd Tallahassee FL 32303 Office: 461 Bellamy Fla State Univ Tallahassee FL 32306. *Costs of integrity are greater than monetary benefits but the psychic income is of lasting significance.*

PEARNE, JOHN FREDERICK, lawyer; b. Los Angeles, June 13, 1912; s. Irving V. and Anna (Kwis) P.; B.S. in Mech. Engring., Calif. Inst. Tech., 1934; J.D., George Washington U., 1940; m. Jean C. Macklin, Dec. 3, 1938; children—Sally Ann, John C., Dennis H. Engr., Babcock & Wilcox Co., 1934-35; spl. agt. Pacific Nat. Fire Ins. Co., Los Angeles, 1935-36; admitted to D.C. bar, 1941, Ohio bar, 1955; examiner U.S. Patent Office, Washington, 1936-42; patent counsel Sherwin-Williams Co., Cleve., 1942-44, 46-48; practiced in Cleve., 1949—; sr. partner firm Pearne, Gordon, Sessions, McCoy & Granger, 1964—. Served to lt. USNR, 1944-46. Mem. Am., Ohio bar assns., Am., Cleve (pres. 1967-68) patent law assns. Home: 920 Stone Crab Cove Fripp Island SC 29920 Office: 1200 Leader Bldg Cleveland OH 44114

PEARSALL, GEORGE WILBUR, engr., educator; b. Brentwood, N.Y., July 13, 1933; s. Milo Dickerson and Margaret Elizabeth (White) P.; B. Metall. Engring., Rensselaer Poly. Inst., 1955; Sc.D. (Am. Soc. Metals fellow), Mass. Inst. Tech., 1961; m. Patricia Louise Stevens, Oct. 11, 1962. Research engr. Dow Chem. Co., Midland, Mich., 1955-57; research asst. Mass. Inst. Tech., 1959-60, asst. prof., 1960-64; asso. prof. Duke, 1964-66, prof., 1966—, acting dean Sch. Engring., 1969-71, dean, 1971-74. Served with AUS, 1957. Registered profl. engr., N.C. Mem. AAAS, ASME, Am. Soc. Metals, World Future Soc., World Soc. for Ekistics, Sigma Xi, Phi Lambda Upsilon, Tau Beta Pi, Pi Tau Sigma. Author: (with W.G. Moffatt and J. Wulff) The Structure and Properties of Materials, 1964. Contbr. articles to profl. jours. Home: 2941 Welcome Dr Durham NC 27705

PEARSALL, MARION, anthropologist, educator; b. Bklyn., Apr. 27, 1923; d. George Martin and Anna Laura (White) Pearsall; B.A., U. N.Mex., 1944; Ph.D., U. Calif. at Berkeley, 1950. Asst. prof. U. Ark., 1950; research fellow Rhodes-Livingstone Inst., Brit. Central Africa, 1951; asst. prof., research asso. U. Ala., 1952-56; postdoctoral social sci. resident Russell Sage Found., Boston, 1956-58; asso. rural sociologist U. Ky., Lexington, 1958-60, asso. prof., 1960-64, prof. behavioral sci. U. Ky. Med. Center, 1964—. Mem. com. on life scis. and social policy Nat. Acad. Scis. 1968—; cons. VA and USPHS, 1968—. Fellow Royal Anthrop. Inst. Gt. Britain, Am. Anthrop. Assn., Soc. for Applied Anthropology, A.A.A.S.; mem. Am. Sociol. Assn., Rural Sociol. Soc., Am. Assn. U. Profs., Soc. Med. Anthropology (pres. 1973-74), Am. Public Health Assn., Sigma Xi. Author: The Talladega Story, 1954; Little Smoky Ridge, 1959; Medical Behavioral Science: A Selected Bibliography, 1963. Editor: Human Organization, 1966-71. Contbr. articles to profl. jours. Home: 1007 Tates Creek Rd Lexington KY 40502

PEARSALL, THOMAS EDWARD, educator; b. N.Y.C., Oct. 28, 1925; s. Lewis and Anna V. (Farrell) P.; A.B. magna cum laude, Colgate U., 1949; M.A., U. Tex., 1956; Ph.D., U. Denver, 1960; m. Anne K. Chimato, Sept. 1, 1946; children—Mark, Susan, Morgan, David. Commd. 2d lt. USAF, 1949, advanced through grades to lt. col., 1969; asso. prof. English, USAF Acad., 1959-69; ret., 1969; prof. tech. communication U. Minn., St. Paul, 1969—, prof., head dept. rhetoric, 1979—; cons. Minn. Dept. Transp. Mem. MLA, Nat. Council Tchrs. English, Council Programs in Tech. and Sci. Communication (pres. 1974-78), Soc. Tech. Communication (program chmn. internat. tech. communication conf. 1978; Disting. Tech. Communication award 1974, Twin Cities Tech. Communicator of Yr. 1975), Phi Beta Kappa, Gamma Sigma Delta. Author: Teaching Technical Writing, 1975, Audience Analysis for Technical Writing, 1969; co-author: Reporting Technical Information, 4th edit., 1980, Better Spelling, 2d edit., 1978, How to Write for the World of Work, 1977. Home: 2098 Folwell St St Paul MN 55108 Office: Dept Rhetoric Univ Minn St Paul MN 55108

PEARSE, WARREN HARLAND, coll. adminstr., educator; b. Detroit, Sept. 28, 1927; s. Harry Albridge and Frances (Wressell) P.; B.S., Mich. State U., 1948; M.B., M.D., Northwestern U., 1950; m. Jacqueline Anne Langan, June 15, 1950; children—Kathryn, Susan, Laurie, Martha. Intern. Univ. Hosp., Ann Arbor, Mich., 1950-51; resident obstetrics and gynecology, 1951-53, 55-56; practice medicine specializing obstetrics and gynecology, Detroit, 1956-58; mem. faculty U. Nebr. Med. Center Omaha, 1959-71, Found. prof., chmn. dept. obstetrics and gynecology, 1962-71, asst. dean Med. Coll., 1963-71, mem. residency rev. com. obstetrics and gynecology, 1968-71; dean Med. Coll. Va., Richmond, 1971-75; exec. dir. Am. Coll. Obstetrics and Gynecology, 1975—. Chmn. research adv. group Maternal Child Health Service, Health Scis. Mental Health Adminstrn., HEW, 1967—; cons. family planning Office Econ. Opportunity, 1970—. Served from 1st lt. to capt., AUS, 1953-55. Mem. Am. Coll. Obstetrics and Gynecology (dist. sec., treas., 1964-68, vice chmn., 1968-71), Am. Gynecology Soc., Soc. Gynecology Investigation, Assn. Profs. Gynecology and Obstetrics (sec., treas., 1969—), Alpha Omega Alpha. Author: (with R.W. Stander) Obstetrics and Gynecology at the University of Michigan, 1969. Contbr. chpts., articles tech. lit. Home: 325 Abbotsford Rd Kenilworth IL 60043

PEARSON, ALBERT MARCHANT, educator; b. Oakley, Utah, Sept. 3, 1916; s. Levi and Mary (Marchant) P.; B.S., Utah State U., 1940; M.S., Iowa State U., 1941; Ph.D., Cornell U., 1949; m. Harriet Eilenberger, Nov. 16, 1946; children—Richard A., Carol Jane, Marian Beth, Donna Gay, David C. Grad. asst. Iowa State U., 1940-41, Cornell U., 1946-49; asst. prof., then asso. prof. U. Fla., 1949-54; mem. faculty Mich. State U., 1954—, prof. food sci. and human nutrition, 1961—. Served with USMCR, 1942-45; PTO. Mem. Am. Soc. Animal Sci. (sec.-treas. 1965-68, pres. 1969-70), Reciprocal Meat Conf. (chmn. 1956), Sigma Xi, Phi Kappa Phi. Spl. research body composition, muscle proteins, flavor components in meat. Home: 2525 Forest Rd Lansing MI 48910 Office: Dept Food Science and Human Nutrition Mich State U East Lansing MI 48824

PEARSON, ALLEN DAY, meteorologist; b. Mankato, Minn., July 28, 1925; s. Albert Emmanuel and Esther Luella (Day) P.; B.S., U. Calif., Los Angeles, 1946; M.S., U. Hawaii, 1968; m. Jacqueline Loretta Naujoks, Oct. 5, 1946; children—Jan Christine, Debra Day, Mark Allen, Sally Melinda. With Pan Am. Airways, San Francisco, also Honolulu, 1946-51; mem. staff U.S. Weather Bur., Honolulu and Wake Island, 1951-64, Washington, 1964-65; meteorologist Nat. Severe Storms Forecast Center, Kansas City, Mo., 1965—, also dir., 1965—; dir. Nat. Weather Service Central Region, 1979—. Mem. Nat. Acad. Sci. Geophysics Study Com. Served with USN, 1943-46. Recipient Silver medal Dept. Commerce, 1968, Gold medal, 1974. Fellow Am. Meteorol. Soc. (chmn. severe storms com. 1970, mem. ethics com. 1975—), Explorer's Club; mem. Nat. Weather Assn. Co-developer Fujita-Pearson scale for classifying tornadoes. Home: 543 W Navajo St Lake Quivira Kansas City KS 66106 Office: Room 1728 601 E 12th St Kansas City MO 64106

PEARSON, ALVIN WALDEMAR, investment trust, investment banking exec.; b. Carlton, Ore., Jan. 29, 1902; s. Nels and Ida (Lundquist) P.; B.A., Reed Coll., 1922, LL.D. (hon.), 1975; M.B.A., Harvard, 1924; m. Alveda Peterson, Sept. 1, 1924; 1 dau., Greta Christine (Mrs. James Potter Brown, Jr.). With Lehman Bros. and Lehman Corp., N.Y.C., 1924—, mgr., research staff, v.p., 1924-55, exec. v.p., 1955-63; pres. Lehman Corp., 1963-73, chmn., 1973-75; dir. Lehman Mgmt. Co., Inc.; gen. partner Lehman Bros., 1964—, mng. dir. Lehman Bros. Kuhn Loeb Inc., 1970—; hon. dir. Lehman Corp.; pres. 1 William St. Fund, 1974-75, now dir. Trustee Reed Coll., Montclair Art Mus.; trustee, pres. Robert Lehman Found. Home: 360 Highland Ave Upper Montclair NJ 07043 Office: 55 Water St New York NY 10041

PEARSON, ANDRALL EDWIN, beverage mfr.; b. Chgo., June 3, 1925; s. Andrall E. and Dorothy M. (MacDonald) P.; B.S., U. So. Calif., 1944; M.B.A., Harvard, 1947; m. Joanne Pope, Mar. 2, 1951; 1 dau., Jill Lee. Marketing mgr. Standard Brands, Inc., N.Y.C., 1948-53; asso. to prin. McKinsey & Co., Inc., N.Y.C., 1953-70, dir., 1965-70; exec. v.p. Pepsico, Inc., Purchase, N.Y., 1970-71, pres., 1971—, also dir.; dir. Warner-Lambert Inc.; dir., mem. exec. com. TWA, TWC. Trustee, Wesleyan U., 1977-79. Served as lt. (j.g.), USNR, 1943-46. Mem. Ref. Ch. of Bronxville (elder). Clubs: Harvard Bus. Sch. of N.Y. (dir.), Bronxville Field, Blind Brook, River (N.Y.C.). Contbr. articles profl. jour., chpt. in handbook. Office: Pepsico Inc Purchase NY 10577

PEARSON, CHARLES THOMAS, JR., lawyer; b. Fayetteville, Ark., Oct. 14, 1929; s. Charles Thomas and Doris (Pinkerton) P.; B.S., U. Ark., 1953, J.D., 1954; postgrad. U.S. Naval Postgrad. Sch., 1959; A.M., Boston U., 1963; m. Alice Ann Paddock, Mar. 7, 1952; children—Linda Sue, John Paddock. Admitted to Ark. bar, 1954; practice in Fayetteville, 1963—; dir., officer N.W. Communications, Inc., Dixieland Devel., Inc., Mid State Investments, Inc., GMS, Inc., Okliana Farms, Inc., N.W. Ark. Land & Devel., Inc., Garden Plaza Inns, Inc., Word Data, Inc., M.P.C. Farms, Inc., Fayetteville Enterprises, Inc., NWA Devel. Co.; dir., organizer N.W. Nat. Bank. Adviser, Explorer Scouts, 1968—; past pres. Washington County Draft Bd.; past pres. bd. Salvation Army. Served to comdr. Judge Adv. Gen. Corps, USNR, 1955-63. Mem. Am., Ark., Washington County bar assns., Judge Advs. Assn., N.W. Ark. Ret. Officers Assn. (past pres.), Methodist Men (past pres.), Housecorp. (past chmn.), Sigma Chi (pres. N.W. Ark. Alumni), Alpha Kappa Psi, Phi Eta Sigma, Delta Theta Phi. Republican. Methodist. Mason (32 deg., K.T., Shriner), Moose, Elk, Lion. Clubs: Metropolitan, Fayetteville Country, Town. Home: 500 E North St Fayetteville AR 72701 Office: 36 E Center St Fayetteville AR 72701

PEARSON, DANIEL S., lawyer; b. N.Y.C., Oct. 9, 1930; s. Joseph and Lee (Epstein) P.; B.A., Amherst Coll., 1952; J.D., Yale U., 1958; m. Beverly Danto, July 1, 1956; children—Elizabeth, William, Charles. Admitted to Fla. bar, 1959, U.S. Supreme Ct. bar, 1967; mem. firm Boardman, Bolles, Davant & Lloyd, Miami, Fla., 1959-61; asst. U.S. atty. So. Dist. of Fla., Miami, 1961-63; partner firm Pearson & Josefsberg, Miami, 1963—; lectr. U. Miami Sch. Law, Nova U. Sch. Law, Practicing Law Inst., Exec. Enterprises, Fla. Bar. Served with USCG, 1951-54. Mem. Am., Dade County bar assns., Acad. Fla. Trial Lawyers, Nat. Assn. Criminal Def. Lawyers. Home: 9266 SW 136th Circle Miami FL 33176 Office: 733 City Nat Bank Bldg Miami FL 33130

PEARSON, DAVID GENE, profl. race car driver; b. Spartanburg, S.C., Dec. 22, 1934; s. Eura A. and Lennie H. (Harris) P.; m. Helen Ray Pearson, Feb. 16, 1952; children—Larry, Ricky, Eddie. Profl. stock car racer, 1960—; owner David Pearson Garage. Winner Grand-Nat. Stock Car Champion, 3 times. Recipient Driver of Year award S.C. Hall of Fame. Mem. Nat. Assn. Stock Car Auto Racing, Screen Actors Guild. Democrat. Baptist. Clubs: Masons, Shriners. Home: Route 10 Burnett Rd Spartanburg SC 29303 Office: PO Box 4760 Spartanburg SC 29303

PEARSON, DONALD EMANUAL, educator, chemist; b. Madison, Wis., June 21, 1914; s. Gustav E. and Clara (Bjelde) P.; grad. U. Wis., 1936, U. Ill., 1940; m. Gwen Smiseth, June 5, 1950; children—Donald T., Jeanah C., Sam S. Chemist, Pitts. Plate Glass Co., Milw., 1940-42; tech. aide OSRD, 1942-45; chemist Mass. Inst. Tech., 1945-46; faculty Vanderbilt U., Nashville, 1946—, prof. chemistry, 1954—. Mem. Am. Chem. Soc. Author: (with R.C. Elderfield) Phenazines, 1956; (with C.A. Buehler) Survey of Organic Syntheses, 1970, Vol. II, 1977; also numerous articles. Discoverer new method of substitution in aromatic compounds, new rearrangement hydrazone; research on mechanisms of Beckmann rearrangement, reactions in polyphosphoric acid; structure of diuretic mercuhydrin; synthesis of barbiturates, anti-malarials, plant regulatory substances. Address: Dept Chemistry Vanderbilt U Nashville TN 37235

PEARSON, DONALD MELVIN, educator; b. Chgo., Mar. 29, 1917; s. Gustav Class and Edith (Ohlson) P.; student U. Denver, 1936; Mus.B. with distinction, Eastman Sch. Music, 1939, Mus.M., 1941; M.A., Harvard, 1956; m. Kathleen Marie Funk, Sept. 2, 1941; children—Randall Funk, Stephen Funk, Timothy Funk. Teaching fellow U. Rochester, 1939-42; mem. faculty Vassar Coll., 1946—, prof. music, 1961—, chmn. dept., 1958-61, coll. organist, 1952—, dir. coll. choir, 1952-70. Organ cons., 1954—; condr. So. Dutchess Singers, 1953-55; music dir. Danforth Found. Assos. Nat. Confs., 1956-68. Active local Community Chest campaigns. Served with AUS, 1943-46. Decorated Bronze Star; Recipient Performer's certificate U. Rochester, 1939. Danforth Found. fellow, 1955-56; Vassar faculty fellow, 1961-62, 69-70. Mem. Am. Guild Organists (dean Central Hudson Valley chpt. 1967-68), Am. Musicological Soc., Coll. Music Soc., Am. Assn. U. Profs., Am. Choral Found. Presbyn. (ruling elder 1959-61, 62-68, elder 1959—). Organ and harpsichord recitalist, U.S. and Europe; condr. maj. choral works in concert, numerous ltd. edit. recordings. Home: 9 Ivy Terr Poughkeepsie NY 12601 Office: Vassar Coll Poughkeepsie NY 12601

PEARSON, DONALD STUART, educator; b. Cleve., Feb. 19, 1905; s. David Browne and Dorothy Mathilda (Oehlhoff) P.; B.S., Case Western Res. U., 1929, M.S., 1933; Ph.D., St. Andrews U., 1958, LL.D., 1968, Ed.D. (hon.), 1973; m. 2d, Mary Jane Gorman Wagner, Dec. 19, 1964. Prof., chmn. elec. engring. dept. Ohio No. U., 1938-43; design engr. Westinghouse Electric Corp., 1944-45; mem. grad. faculty Mich. State U., 1945-49; mem. grad. faculty Pa. State U., 1949-65, emeritus prof., 1965—; prof. math. Lorain County Community Coll., 1965-76, chmn. dept. math., 1971, certificate of recognition, 1975; alumni ednl. adviser Case Western Res. U., 1972—. Examiner, Ohio State Bd. Profl. Engrs., 1939-53; founder OHIOMATYC, U. Cin., 1972. Mem. Environ. Protection Bd., Olmsted Falls, Ohio, 1972—. Charter mem. Engrs. Found. of Ohio, Columbus, 1970. Recipient Army-Navy E award, 1944, Lee Gold medal research award, 1958, certificate Nat. Council Engring. Examiners, 1970, Community Leader of Am. award, 1972. Fellow Ohio No. U., 1957, St. Andrews Res. Instn. Elec. Engrs. (London), 1958. Recipient citation 88th Congress and Library of Congress, 1964; registered profl. engr., Ariz., Ohio, Pa.; chartered engr., London. Fellow World Acad. Scholars (Australia), Royal Soc. Arts (life) (London), Instn. Elec. Engrs. (London), Intercontinental Biog. Soc., Am. Soc. Engring. Edn. (life; br. chmn. 1949); mem. IEEE (life sr. mem.), chmn. Central Pa. sect. 1953), AAUP (emeritus mem.), Math. Assn. Am., Newcomen Soc., Franklin Inst., Nat., Ohio socs. profl. engrs., N.Y. Acad. Scis., Am. Yacht Res. Soc., Amateur Yacht Research Soc. (London), IEEE nat. groups on transformers, rotating machines, radiant heating, Tau Beta Pi (eminent mem.), Eta Kappa Nu (life), Phi Delta Kappa, Pi Mu Epsilon, Theta Chi, Sigma Tau Delta. Clubs: Masons, Shriners, Kiwanis (dir. 1940); Bay View Boat (life mem.); Sun City Scots, Amateur Radio (Sun City, Ariz.). Author: Creative Image, 1959; Creativeness for Engineers, 4th edit., 1961; Basic Energy Converters, 1962. Contbr. articles profl. jours. Regional editor MATYC jour., 1970—. Home: 14014 Newcastle Dr Sun City AZ 85351. *Small bits of information are each one vital to the solution of a problem. Each of us has a duty to contribute, in his or her own way, to the betterment of our nation.*

PEARSON, DONALD WILLIAM, telephone co. exec.; b. Rochester, N.Y., Mar. 1, 1924; s. Frank William and Marian Ann (Luckman) P.; B.S. in Bus. Adminstrn., U. Rochester, 1951; m. Edna David, Feb. 1, 1947; children—Donna Pearson Werner, Michael, Mark, Steven. With Rochester Telephone Corp. (N.Y.), 1953—, dept. head computer ops., 1965-67, controller, 1967-70, v.p. adminstrn., 1970-75, v.p. fin., treas., sec., 1975—; dir. Central Trust Co. Mem. exec. bd. Otetiana council Boy Scouts Am.; past bd. dirs. Assn. for Blind of Rochester and Monroe County, N.Y.; mem. Com. to Re-evaluate County Govt., 1969-72. Served with USMC, 1942-46. Decorated Purple Heart. Mem. U.S. Ind. Telephone Assn. (investor relations com.), Nat. Assn. Accountants (past dir.), Fin. Execs. Inst., Rochester Soc. Security Analysts, Am. Soc. Corporate Secs., Better Bus. Bur. Rochester and Monroe County (dir., chmn. bd.), Rochester C. of C. Republican. Lutheran. Clubs: City Midday (N.Y.C.); Rochester. Home: 46 Larchwood Dr Pittsford NY 14534 Office: 100 Midtown Plaza Rochester NY 14646

PEARSON, DREW, profl. football player; b. Newark, Jan. 12, 1951; s. Samuel and Mary Minnie (Washington) P.; grad. Tulsa U., 1973; m. Marsha Kaye Haynes, June 24, 1972; 1 dau., Tori Nichole. Profl. football player (wide receiver) Dallas Cowboys, 1973—, also team capt., player rep. Past chmn. March of Dimes Crusade, South River, N.J.; active Carter for Pres. campaign. Named to All-State High Sch. football and baseball teams, N.J.; All-Conf. Football, 1972; name All-Pro, 1974-76; played in Pro-Bowl, 1974, 76, 77. Mem. Nat. Football League Players Assn. Baptist. Office: care Dallas Cowboys 6116 N Central Expresswy Dallas TX 75206*

PEARSON, GERALD LEON, food co. exec.; b. Mpls., June 24, 1925; s. Perry and Lillian (Peterson) P.; grad. Trimont (Minn.) High Sch., 1943; m. Beverly Mary Schultz, Nov. 10, 1946; children—Steven, Monte, Perry, Liecia. Treas. Trimont Packing Co., 1946-52; v.p. Spencer Foods (Iowa), 1952-68, pres., chief exec. officer, 1969-72, chmn. bd., chief exec. officer, 1972—; dir. Spencer Nat. Bank. Served with USNR, 1943-46. Club: Elks. Home: 528 W 4th St Spencer IA 51301 Office: Box 1228 Spencer IA 51301

PEARSON, GERALD LEONDUS, electronics engr.; b. Salem, Oreg., Mar. 31, 1905; s. David Shafer and Sarah (Allen) P.; A.B., Willamette U., 1926; Sc.D. (hon.), 1956; A.M. in Physics, Stanford, 1929; m. Mildred Oneta Cannoy, June 30, 1929; children—Ray Leon, Carol Ann. Mem. tech. staff Bell Telephone Labs., 1929-57, head applied physics solids dept., 1957-60; prof. elec. engring. Stanford, 1960-70, emeritus, 1970—, dir. Center Materials Research, 1965-66, dir. Solid-State Electronics Lab., 1970—; vis. prof. U. Tokyo, 1966; mem. ad hoc com. materials and processes for electron devices NRC, 1971-72, mem. com. on recommendations for U.S. Army basic sci. research, 1978—. Recipient John Scott award City Phila., 1956; Gold Plate award Am. Acad. Achievement, 1963; Marian Smoluchowski medal Polish Phys. Soc., 1975. Fellow Am. Phys. Soc., Am. Inst. Elec. and Electronics Engrs.; life mem. Franklin Inst. (John Price Wetherill medal 1963); mem. Nat. Acad. Scis., Nat. Acad. Engring., Telephone Pioneers Am., Sigma Xi. Author, patentee in field. Home: 501 Portola Rd Portola Valley CA 94025 Office: Stanford Electronics Labs Stanford CA 94305

PEARSON, HARRY FREDERICK, home furnishings co. exec.; b. S.I., N.Y., Oct. 20, 1927; s. Carl and Clara Josephine (Johnson) P.; student Walter Hervey Jr. Coll., 1947-49; B.S. in Bus. Adminstrn., L.I. U., 1951; m. Esther Elaine Chiurco, June 26, 1949; children—Judith Pearson Valentine, Harry Frederick. Product sales mgr. Congoleum Industries, Inc., Kearny, N.J., 1961-63, gen. sales mgr., 1963-67, v.p. sales, 1967-69, pres., 1969—, also dir.; exec. v.p., dir. Bath Industries, 1972—; exec. v.p. Congoleum Corp., 1972—. Trustee Walter Hoving Home. Served with USNR, 1945-46. Recipient Torch of Hope award, 1973. Mem. Am. Mgmt. Assn. (pres., dir.). Office: Congoleum Corp PO 195 Belgrove Dr Kearny NJ 07032

PEARSON, HENRY CHARLES, artist; b. Kinston, N.C., Oct. 8, 1914; s. A. Louis and Estelle P.; B.A., U. N.C., 1935; M.F.A., Yale U., 1938; postgrad. Art Students League, 1953-56. Stage scene designer, 1937-42; exhibitions include: Workshop Gallery, N.Y.C., 1958, Stephen Radich Gallery, N.Y.C., 1960-70, The Responsive Eye, Mus. Modern Art, 1965, 29th Biennial Exhibition, Corcoran Gallery Art, Washington, 1965; Drawings USA, Minn. Mus. Art, St. Paul, 1971-73, Betty Parsons Gallery, N.Y.C., 1971-76, Art Students League Centennial, 1975, Truman Gallery, N.Y.C., 1976-79, Marilyn Pearl Gallery, N.Y.C., 1980; represented in permanent collections: Mus. Modern Art, N.Y.C., Met. Mus. Art, N.Y.C., Whitney Mus. Am. Art, N.Y.C., Albright-Knox Gallery, Buffalo, N.C. Mus. Art, Raleigh; commd. works include: List Art Posters, 1965, N.Y. Film Festival poster, 1968; instr. art New Sch. Social Research, N.Y.C., 1965—, Pa. Acad. Fine Arts, Phila., 1973—. Served with AUS, 1942-48, USAF, 1948-53. Ford Found. fellow, 1964. Recipient gold medal for achievement in the fine arts N.C. Gov., 1970. Mem. Am. Abstract Artists, Century Assn. Illustrator: Rime of the Ancient Mariner, 1964, Five Psalms, 1969. Home: 1601 Cambridge Dr Kinston NC 28501 Office: 58 W 58th St New York NY 10019

PEARSON, HUGH JOHN SANDERS, indsl. supply co. exec.; b. Edmonton, Alta., Can., Sept. 9, 1921; s. Hugh Edward and Constance Jukes (Sanders) P.; grad. Royal Mil. Coll., Kingston, Ont., 1942; m. Kathleen Hastie, Nov. 7, 1945; children—Kathleen, Ronald, Ian. Pres., Taylor Pearson & Carson (Can.) Ltd., 1945-62, Prairie Pacific Distbrs. Ltd., 1962-67; pres., owner Century Sales & Service Ltd., Edmonton, 1967—; chmn. bd., dir. Alta. Gas Trunk Line Co. Ltd., Edmonton, 1973—, Edmonton Broadcasting, Ltd.; v.p., dir. Selkirk Holdings Ltd., 1959—; dir. Bank of Montreal, Mut. Life Assurance Co. Can., Prudential Steel Ltd., Diamond Shamrock-Alta. Gas Ltd., Beta Plastics Ltd., Calgary Power Ltd. Chmn. Bishops' Men, Edmonton, 1973—. Served with Canadian Army, 1940-45. Mem. Alta. N.W. Chamber Mines and Resources (past pres.). Clubs: Edmonton, Mayfair Golf and Country. Home: 8716 136th St Edmonton AB T5R 0B9 Canada Office: Box T1218 Edmonton AB T5J 2M6 Canada

PEARSON, JAMES BLACKWOOD, lawyer, former U.S. senator; b Nashville, May 7, 1920; s. John W. and Lillian (Blackwood) P.; LL.B., U. Va., 1950; m. Martha Mitchell, Sept. 7, 1946; children—James, Thomas, William, Laura Alice. Admitted to Kans. bar, 1950; city atty., Westwood, Fairway and Lenexa, Kans., 1950-61; asst. county atty. Johnson County, 1952-54, probate judge, 1954-56; mem. Kans. Senate from 10th Dist., 1956-60; mem. U.S. Senate from Kans., 1962-79; mem. firm Stroock, Stroock & Lavan, Washington, 1979—. Del., UN, 1972-73. Chmn., Kans. Republican Com., 1960—. Served as pilot USNR 1943-46. Office: Stroock Stroock and Lavan 1150 17th St NW Washington DC 20036*

PEARSON, JAMES EUGENE, educator, artist; b. Woodstock, Ill., Dec. 12, 1939; s. John Clarence and Arline (Harrison) P.; B.S. in Edn., No. Ill. U., 1961, M.S. in Edn., 1962, M.F.A., 1964. Tchr., Woodstock High Sch., 1961—; instr. art McHenry County Coll., Crystal Lake, Ill., 1970—; editor art The Rectangle jour., DeKalb, Ill., 1970—; one man shows include No. Ill. U., DeKalb, 1962, Elgin (Ill.) Acad., 1966; exhibited group shows, including Chgo. Artists Exhbn., 1958, U. Ill., Urbana, 1961, 69, Fine Arts Festival, Chgo., 1963, XXI Am. Drawing Biennial, Norfolk, Va., 1965, Miss. River Craft Show, Memphis, 1965, 18th, 20th N. Miss. Valley Artists exhbns., Springfield, Ill., 1965, 67, 1st, 3d annual exhbns. Ricks Coll., Rexburg, Idaho, 1965, 67, 2 eme Salon Internat. de Charleroi, Palace Fine Arts, Charleroi, Belgium, 1969, 5th Internat. Grand Prize Painting and Etching, Monte Carlo, Monaco, 1969, 2d, 3d annual McHenry County Coll. Art Fair, Crystal Lake, 1971, 1970, 71, 29th Ill. Invitational Exhbn., Springfield, 1971, Mitchell Art Mus., Mt. Vernon, Ill., 1975, several others; represented permanent collections, including No. Ill. U., DeKalb, Palis des Beaux Arts, Cherleroi, Belgium, pvt. collections. Mem. regional adv. com. Scholastic Art Award sect. Scholastic mag., 1964—. Recipient William Boyd Andrews best show award McHenry County Art Fair, 1961, 1st place Town and Country Art Exhibitors, 1961, 64, purchase award oil Waukegan News-Sun newspaper, 1969, Taft campus purchase prize No. Ill. U., 1969, 1st place sculpture award McHenry County Coll., 1970, 71, others; recipient outstanding young educator award Woodstock Jr. C. of C., 1968. Fellow Royal Soc. Arts, Mfgs. and Commerce (Eng.); mem. Centro Studi E Scambi Internazionali (Rome, Italy), Coll. Art Assn., Ill. Art Edn. Assn., Ill. Craftsmen's Council, Ill. Edn. Assn., Audubon Soc., Am. Fedn. Arts, S.A.R., Internat. Platform Assn., Kappa Pi, Phi Delta Kappa. Contbr. profl. jours. Home: 5117 Barnard Mill Rd Ringwood IL 60072 Office: 501 W South St Woodstock IL 60098

PEARSON, JERRE LEONADIS, frozen food co. exec.; b. Marion, Ala., Aug. 28, 1924; s. Jerre L. and Freddie Nichols (Hall) P.; student Marion Mil. Inst., 1941-42, Auburn (Ala.) U., 1942-47; m. Elizabeth Rainey, Oct. 25, 1949; children—Mary Elizabeth, Jerre Leonadis, Susan Patricia. Salesman, Dan Joseph Co., Columbus, Ga., 1954-58; v.p. sales, pres. So. Frozen Foods, Montezuma, Ga., 1958-66; pres., chief exec. officer Seeman Bros., Inc. (now Seabrook Foods, Inc.), Montezuma, 1966-68, chmn. bd., chief exec. officer, 1968—; pres. Montezuma Banking Co.; dir. Lionel Corp., N.Y.C. Served with USAAF, 1943-46. Mem. Montezuma C. of C., Sigma Alpha Epsilon. Baptist. Kiwanian. Office: Seabrook Foods Inc PO Box 306 Montezuma GA 31063*

PEARSON, JIM BERRY, coll. dean; b. Gilmer, Tex., Jan. 3, 1924; s. John Henry and Vera Louisa (Berry) P.; B.A., North Tex. State U., Denton, 1947, M.A., 1949; Ph.D., U. Tex., 1955; m. June Louise Young (dec.); children—Jim Berry, Terry Lee; m. 2d, Mary Frances Shields, June 1972. Asst. prof., then prof. Midwestern U., Wichita Falls, Tex., 1949-55; asso. prof. Arlington (Tex.) State U., 1955-58; asst. prof., then asso. prof. U. Tex., Austin, 1968-71, asst. dean, 1961-66, asst. v.p. acad. affairs, 1970-71; asso. v.p. acad. affairs, prof. history and edn. North Tex. State U., 1971-73, dean Coll. Arts and Scis., prof. history, 1973—; project dir. Council of Chief State Sch. Officers, Washington, 1966-68; cons. in field. Mem. Austin Com. Human Relations. Active local YMCA, United Neighbors. Served with AUS, 1943-46; CBI. Recipient Outstanding Tchr. award U. Tex. Student Assembly, 1964; Distinguished Service award Council Chief State Sch. Officers, 1968. Mem. Orgn. Am. Historians, Southwestern Social Sci. Assn., Western, Tex. (chmn. com. teaching 1969-72) hist. assns., Alpha Phi Omega. Club: Toastmasters. Author: The Maxwell Land Grant (Theta Sigma Phi award), 1961; co-author: Texas: The Land and Its People, 2d edit., 1977. Co-editor: Education in the States: Historical Developments and Outlook, 1969; Education in the States: National Development Since 1900, 1969. Book rev. editor Southwestern Hist. Quar., 1969-72; adv. editor Social Sci. Quar., Tex. Council Jour., 1968-78. Home: 915 Sherman Dr Denton TX 76201

PEARSON, JOHN EARLE, educator; b. Gilmer, Tex., Jan. 18, 1926; s. John Henry and Vera (Berry) P.; B.S., N. Tex. State U., 1948, M.S., 1948; Ph.D., Ind. U., 1956; m. Della Ann Ayecock, July 30, 1976; children by previous marriage—John Read, Monte Lee, Eric Lynn, Carla, Melissa. Teaching fellow econ. statistics Ind. U., 1948-51; Regional Faculty research fellow econ. Stanford, summer 1960; asst. prof. bus. adminstrn., asso. prof., prof. N. Tex. State U., Denton, 1957-63; prof., dir. Sch. Bus. Adminstrn., Tex. A. & M. U., College Station, 1963—, dir. Inst. Human Resources, 1965-67, dean., prof. Coll. Bus. Adminstrn., 1968-79; v.p., dir. mgmt. services 3D/Internat., Inc., 1979—; dir. City Nat. Bank, Bryan, Tex. County campaign chmn. Brazos County Heart Assn., 1964-65. Served with USAAF, 1943-45. Mem. Bryan-College Station C. of C. (dir. 1969-71), Am. Econs. Assn., Am. Statis. Assn., Southwestern Soc. Sci. Assn., Beta Gamma Sigma, Phi Kappa Phi, Sigma Iota Epsilon. Unitarian (Fellowship pres. 1968-69). Author: (with O.J. Curry) Basic Mathematics for Business Analysis, 1961, also others. Office: Suite 1200 5051 Westheimer St Houston TX 77056. *My success in life is measured only by my internal contentment. My reasons for such satisfactions are many, and include helping my fellow man, giving my best effort toward some goal, and seeing nature's wonders.*

PEARSON, JOHN EDGAR, ins. co. exec.; b. Mpls., Jan. 17, 1927; s. Edgar Clarence and Viola Esther (Quist) P.; student Gustavus Adolphus Coll., 1944-45, Northwestern U., 1945-46; B.B.A., U. Minn., 1948; m. Sharon M. Nessler, Nov. 4, 1950; children—Cynthia Lynn, Thomas Calvin. Sales trainee Minn. Mining & Mfg. Co., St. Paul, 1948-49; group rep. Northwestern Nat. Life Ins. Co., Seattle, 1949-51; salesman Marsh & McLennan Inc., Seattle, 1951-53; with Northwestern Nat. Life Ins. Co., Mpls., 1953—, pres., chief exec. officer, dir., 1975—; chief exec. officer, dir. North Atlantic Life Ins. Co., 1972—; dir. No. Life Ins. Co., Northwestern Nat. Bank. Div. chmn. United Way, 1978; Republican precinct committeeman, 1970-71; bd. dirs. Found. Health Care Evaluation, 1971-75; chmn. Mpls. Urban Coalition, 1978—, St. Marys Rehab. Center, 1975—. Served with USNR, 1944-46. Mem. Mpls. C. of C. (dir.). Clubs: Masons, Mpls.; Edina Country, Rotary. Home: 5027 Wooddale Ln Edina MN 55424 Office: 20 Washington Ave S Minneapolis MN 55440

PEARSON, KARL GUSTAV, educator; b. Lindsborg, Kans., June 14, 1908; s. Peter Henry and Esther Olivia (Lincoln) P.; B.A., Princeton, 1929; J.D., U. Mich., 1932; m. Lucy Gibson Dunn, Mar. 16, 1951. Asst. to chmn. Firestone Tire & Rubber Co., 1936-42, 45-48; chmn. dept. bus. adminstrn. Upsala Coll., 1948-59; chmn. dept. bus. adminstrn. Rider Coll., Trenton, 1959-62, dean Sch. Bus. Adminstrn., 1962-67, dir. bur. bus. research, 1963-67; prof. Grad Sch. Bus. Adminstrn., U. Mich. Ann Arbor, 1967—, also dir. real estate edn.; dean Real Estate Inst. N.J., 1954-67. Ednl. adviser N.J. Assn. Real Estate Bds., 1964-67; mem. com. edn. Nat. Assn. Real Estate Bds., 1963—; adv. com. Invest-in-Am. Council, 1963-67; pres. Middle Atlantic Assn. Colls. Bus. Adminstrn., 1962; sec. Northeastern Bus. Law Assn., 1964-66. Chmn. N.J. Employment Security Council, 1950-55; mem. Trenton Zoning Bd., 1964-66; chmn. Trenton Zoning Bd. Adjustment, 1966; mem. Gov.'s Emergency Planning Com., 1966. Trustee Upsala Coll., 1946-48; v.p. Clara Maas Hosp., Belleville, N.J., 1957-59. Served to lt. comdr. USNR, 1942-45; comdr. Res. Mem. Soc. Real Estate Appraisers, Am. Soc. Appraisers, Internat. Real Estate Fedn., Phi Beta Kappa. Rotarian. Author: Success Patterns in Real Estate, 1963; How to Succeed in Real Estate by Really Trying, 1964; Everyday Real Estate, 1966; A Broad Based Tax, 1965; Transportation, 1966; Syllabus for a Real Estate Institute, 1968; Real Estate Bibliography, 1968; Real Estate Institute I and II, 1968, II, 1969; The Real Estate Investment Boom, 1969; Big Business Discovers Real Estate, 1971; Michigan Real Estate, 2d edit., 1975; Industrialized Housing, 1972; Housing's Wave of the Future, 1972; Real Estate: Principles and Practices, 2d edit., 1976; co-author Real Estate Law, 2d edit., 1977. Home: 1050 Wall St Ann Arbor MI 48105

PEARSON, LYLE CLARENCE, ct. adminstr.; b. Montevideo, Minn., Feb. 5, 1921; s. Clarence and Mary (Ertel) P.; ed. high sch.; m. Katherine E. Fuller, Sept. 6, 1942; children—Colleen (Mrs. Joseph Bianchi), Lyle Rowland, Rosemary (Mrs. Marco Colombari), Lloyd, Ann, Gail, Kurt. Various positions Nicollet County (Minn.) Probation and Parole Dept., 1954-73; dir. Nicollet County Ct. Services, 1973—. Served with USAAF, 1943-45. Decorated Air Medal, Purple Heart, D.F.C. Named Corrections Man of Year, Minn., 1969. Mem. D.A.V. (nat. comdr. 1975—), Minn. Corrections Assn., Am. Legion, V.F.W. Roman Catholic. K.C. Home: 404 Jefferson Ave North Mankato MN 56001 Office: Ct House St Peter MN 56083

PEARSON, NATHAN WILLIAMS, investment mgmt. exec.; b. N.Y.C., Nov. 26, 1911; s. James A. and Elizabeth (Williams) P.; A.B., Dartmouth, 1932; M.B.A., Harvard, 1934; LL.D., Thiel Coll., 1972; m. Kathleen P. McMurtry, Apr. 9, 1947; children—James S. (dec.), Nathan Williams. With U.S. Steel Corp., 1939-42; mgr. research Matson Navigation Co., 1946-47; controller Carborundum Co., 1947-48; with T. Mellon and Sons, Pitts., 1948-70, v.p., gov., 1957-70; fin. exec. for Paul Mellon, 1948—; dir. Ampex Corp., Hanna Mining Co., Koppers Co., Inc., Aluminum Co. Am., Gulf Oil Corp., Mellon Nat. Corp., Mellon Bank N.A., Fed. St. Fund, Inc. Served from lt. (j.g.) to comdr. USNR, 1942-46. Republican. Presbyterian. Clubs: Duquesne, Allegheny Country, Edgeworth, Harvard-Yale-Princeton (Pitts.); Racquet and Tennis (N.Y.C.); Laurel Valley Golf, Rolling Rock (Ligonier, Pa). Home: 10 Woodland Rd Sewickley PA 15143 Office: 525 William Penn Pl Pittsburgh PA 15230

PEARSON, OLOF HJALMER, physician; b. Boston, Feb. 7, 1913; s. Nils August and Esther (Peterson) P.; A.B. magna cum laude, Harvard, 1934, M.D. cum laude, 1939; m. Barbara Farr, Dec. 30, 1942; children—Jane, Alan. John, Thomas. Asst. physiology Harvard, 1935-37, instr., 1945-46; faculty Cornell U. Med. Coll., 1949-60, asso. prof. medicine, 1952-60; asso. mem. Sloan Kettering Inst., N.Y.C., 1948-60; prof. medicine case Western Res. U. Sch. Medicine, Cleve., 1968—, Am. Cancer Soc. prof. oncology, 1973-78, head sect. endocrinology dept. medicine, 1963-70; dir. clin. labs. U. Hosps. Cleve., 1960-63, asso. attending physician, 1960-67, attending physician, 1967—. Recipient Sloan award for cancer research Sloan Kettering Inst., 1955. Fellow A.C.P.; mem. Assn. Am. Physicians, Am. Assn. for Cancer Research, Am. Fedn. for Clin. Research, Am. Soc. for Clin. Investigation, Am. Soc. Biol. Chemists, Harvey Soc., Central Soc. for Clin. Research. Author: (with C.C. Thomas) Hypophysectomy, 1957; also numerous articles. Editor: Dynamic Studies of Metabolic Bone Disease 1964. Research in endocrinology and metabolism. Home: 14111 Larchmere Blvd Shaker Heights OH 44120 Office: 2065 Adelbert Rd Cleveland OH 44106

PEARSON, PAUL BROWN, scientist; b. Oakley, Utah, Nov. 28, 1905; s. Levi and Ada (Brown) P.; B.S., Brigham Young U., 1928; M.S. (Walsh fellow), Mont. State U., 1930; Ph.D., (fellow) U. Wis., 1937; m. Emma Snow, June 20, 1933; children—Paula (Mrs. Raymond Soller), Marilyn (Mrs. Walter Johnson). Asst. prof. Mont. State U., 1930-31; research asso. U. Calif., 1932-35; prof. A. and M. Coll. Tex., 1937, distinguished prof., 1941, dean grad. sch., head dept. biochemistry and nutrition, 1947; chief biology AEC, 1949-58, cons., 1958-70; prof. Johns Hopkins, 1951-58; with program in sci. and engring. Ford Found. 1958-63; pres., sci. dir. Nutrition Found., 1963-72; chmn. dept. nutrition Drexel U., 1972-73, prof. dept. family and community medicine and dept. nutrition and food sci. U. Ariz., Tucson, 1974—; chief dept. nutrition U. Autonoma Guadalajara (Mexico), 1974—. Collaborator Bur. Animal Industry. Del. 6th Internat. Zootechnic Congress, Copenhagen, 1952, 2d Internat. Biochem. Congress, Paris, 1952, U.S.-Japan Conf. on Radiobiology, Tokyo, 1954; World Conf. Peaceful Uses Atomic Energy, Geneva, 1955, Internat. Symposium on Biochemistry of Sulphur, Roscoff, France, 1956; mem. exec. com. div. biol. and agrl. NRC, 1950-52; liaison Food and Nutrition Bd.; program com. Internat. Congress on Nutrition, 1960; cons. Pres.'s Sci. Adv. Com., Nat. Agr. Research Adv. Com., 1952-58; chmn. adv. com. P.R. Nuclear Center, 1962-73; adv. com. McCollum-Pratt Inst.; trustee Food Drug Law Inst., Nutrition Found., 1972-74. Del., White House Conf. Internat. Cooperation, 1965, White House Conf. on Food, Nutrition and Health, 1969. Fellow AAAS, Soc. for Animal Sci.; mem. Biochem. Soc. London, Am. Chem. Soc., Am. Inst. Nutrition, Brit. Nutrition Soc., Soc. Biol. Chemists. Clubs: Lochinvar, Cosmos. Author bulls. NRC; numerous sci. publs. on nutrition and biochemistry. Home: 5925 E 3d St Tucson AZ 85711 Office: Agrl Scis Bldg U Ariz Tucson AZ 85721 also Faculty Medicine U Autonoma Guadalajara Apt Postal 1-440 Guadalajara Jalisco Mexico

PEARSON, PAUL GUY, educator; b. Lake Worth, Fla., Dec. 5, 1926; s. Eric Conrad and Dora Wilma (Capen) P.; student Palm Beach Jr. Coll., 1946-47; B.S. with honors, U. Fla., 1949, M.S., 1951, Ph.D., 1954; m. Winifred Clowe, June 30, 1951; children—Thomas, Jean, Andrew. Asst. prof. U. Tulsa, 1954-55; asst. prof. Rutgers U., New Brunswick, N.J., 1955-60, asso. prof., 1960-64, prof., 1964—, asso. provost, 1972-77, exec. v.p., 1977—, acting pres., 1978, mem. bd. govs., 1971-72. Served with USNR, 1944-46. Fellow AAAS; mem. Ecol. Soc. Am. (sec. 1961-64, v.p. 1970, treas. 1974-77), Am. Inst. Biol. Scis. (gov. 1966-75, v.p. 1977, pres 1978), Am. Soc. Mammalogists. Home: 23 Hadler Dr Somerset NJ 08873

PEARSON, PAUL HAMMOND, physician; b. Bolenge, Belgian Congo (parents Am. citizens); s. Ernest B. and Evelyn (Utter) P.; B.S., Northwestern, 1944, B.Medicine, 1946, M.D., 1947; M.P.H., U. Calif. at Los Angeles, 1963. Intern, Los Angeles County Gen. Hosp., 1946-47; resident Cin. Children's Hosp., 1949-51; fellow convulsive disorders and electroencephalography Johns Hopkins Hosp., Balt., 1951-53; resident in child psychiatry U. B.C. (Can.), Vancouver, 1976-77; practice medicine specializing in pediatrics, Los Angeles, 1953-62; chief mental retardation br. USPHS div. chronic disease, 1963-65, asst. dir. mental retardation program Nat. Inst. Child Health and Human Devel., NIH, 1965-66; spl. asst. to surgeon gen. USPHS, 1966-67; C.L. Meyer prof. child health, prof. pub. health and preventive medicine, dir. Meyer Children's Rehab. Inst., mem. grad. faculty U. Nebr. Coll. Medicine, Omaha, 1967—; from instr. to asst. clin. prof. U. So. Calif. Med. Sch., 1953-62; from asso. clin. prof. pediatrics to clin. prof. pediatrics Georgetown U. Sch. Medicine, Washington, 1963-67. Cons., mem. profl. services program com. United Cerebral Palsy Assn., 1969-72, mem. nat. awards com., 1971; Am. Acad. Pediatrics liaison rep. to Am. Acad. Orthopedic Surgery, 1969-73; apptd. to Nat. Adv. Council Services and Facilities for Developmentally Disabled Dept. Health. Edn. and Welfare, 1971-75; councilor Accreditation Council Facilities for Mentally Retarded, Joint Commn. on Accreditation Hosps., 1973-74; mem. com. on accessible environments Nat. Acad. Scis., 1974-77. Served to capt. MC, AUS, 1947-49. Diplomate Am. Bd. Pediatrics. Mem. Am. Acad. Pediatrcs (com. on children with handicaps 1969-75, com. sect. on child devel. 1974—) Am. Assn. Mental Deficiency, Nat., Greater Omaha (dir.) assns. for retarded children, Am. Pub. Health Assn., Am. Acad. Cerebral Palsy and Developmental Medicine (exec. com. 1971-76, chmn. sci. program com. 1972-74, sec. 1974-77, mem. research and awards com. 1977-78), Assn. Univ.-Affiliated Facilities (exec. com. 1973—, v.p. 1974-75, pres. 1975-76, dir. 1971-78), Alpha Omega Alpha. Cons. editor Am. Jour. Mental Deficiency, 1970-72. Contbr. articles to profl. jours. Home: 503 Ridgewood Dr N Bellevue NE 68005 Office: 444 S 44th St Omaha NE 68131

PEARSON, PETER ROBB, film dir.; b. Toronto, Ont., Can., Mar. 13, 1938; s. Charles Todd and Dorothy (Robb) P.; B.A. in Polit. Sci., U. Toronto, 1961; postgrad. Centro Sperimentale di Cinematografia, Rome, 1963; m. Suzanne Nicole Vachon, June 15, 1974; 1 son, Louis-Charles de Beauce. Producer, dir. This Hour Has Seven Days, CBC, 1964-66; dir. Nat. Film Bd., Montreal, 1966-68; freelance producer, dir., writer, 1968—; films include Best Damn Fiddler From Calabogie to Kaladar (Canadian Film of Year 1969), 1969, Paperback Hero (3 Canadian Film awards 1963), 1973, Along These Lines (Best Theatrical Short 1975), 1975; author screenplay The Insurance Man From Ingersoll (Best Original Screenplay award ACTRA 1977), 1977; mem. adv. com. Canadian Sec. State, 1972-75; mem. Toronto Arts Council, 1974-76. Named Best Dir., Canadian Film Awards, 1969,

Best Producer, 1973. Mem. Dirs. Guild Can. (pres. 1972-75), Council Canadian Filmmakers (chmn. 1973-75). Address: Rural Route 3 Mansfield ON L0N 1M0 Canada

PEARSON, PHILLIP THEODORE, univ. dean; b. Ames, Iowa, Nov. 21, 1932; s. Theodore B. and Hazel C. (Christianson) P.; D.V.M., Iowa State U., 1956, Ph.D., 1962; m. Mary Jane Barlow, Aug. 28, 1954; children—Jane Catherine, Bryan Theodore, Todd Wallace, Julie Ann. Intern, Angell Meml. Animal Hosp., Boston, 1956-57; instr. Coll. Vet. Medicine Iowa State U., 1957-59, asst. prof., 1959-63, asso. prof., 1963-64, prof. vet. clin. scis. and bio-med. engring., 1965-72, dean Coll. Vet. Medicine, 1972—, dir. Vet. Med. Inst.; prof. Sch. Vet. Medicine, U. Mo., 1964-65. Bd. dirs. Ia. State Meml. Union, 1970—, v.p., 1975. Recipient Riser award, 1956; distinguished Tchr. award Norden Labs., 1962; Gaines award Gen. Foods Corp., 1966, Outstanding Tchr. award Iowa State U., 1968, Faculty citation, 1974. Mem. Am., Iowa vet. med. assns., Am. Animal Hosp. Assn., Am. Assn. Vet. Clinicians, Am. Coll. Vet. Surgeons (bd. regents 1972, pres. 1977), Sigma Xi, Phi Kappa Phi, Phi Zeta, Alpha Zeta, Gamma Sigma Delta. Kiwanian (dir., pres. Ames 1966—). Home: 621 Carr Dr Ames IA 50010

PEARSON, RALPH GOTTFRID, educator; b. Chgo., Jan. 12, 1919; s. Gottfrid and Kerstin (Larson) P.; B.S., Lewis Inst., 1940; Ph.D., Northwestern U., 1943; m. Lenore Olivia Johnson, June 15, 1941; children—John Ralph, Barry Lee, Christie Ann. Faculty, Northwestern U., 1946-76, prof. chemistry, 1957-76; prof. chemistry U. Calif., Santa Barbara, 1976—. Cons. to industry and govt., 1951—. Served to 1st lt. USAAF, 1944-46. Guggenheim fellow, 1951. Mem. Am. Chem. Soc. (Midwest award 1966, Inorganic Chemistry award 1969), Nat. Acad. Sci., Phi Beta Kappa, Sigma Xi, Phi Lambda Upsilon (hon.). Lutheran. Co-author 4 books. Originator prin. of hard and soft acids and bases. Home: 715 Grove Ln Santa Barbara CA 93105

PEARSON, RICHARD JARVIS, corp. exec.; b. Chgo., June 3, 1925; s. Andrall E. and Dorothy M. (MacDonald) P.; B.S., U. So. Calif., 1945; M.B.A., Harvard U., 1947; m. Janice L. Pope, Mar. 2, 1951; 1 son, Douglas Richard. Dir. mktg. Avery Label Co., 1960-64; v.p., gen. mgr. Avery Label N.Am., 1964-70; group v.p. Avery Internat., San Marino, Calif., 1970-76, exec. v.p., 1976—; dir. Ducommun, Inc., Kerr Glass Mfg. Co. Served to lt. USNR, 1943-45. Mem. Tag and Label Mfg. Inst., Harvard Bus. Sch. Assn. Republican. Presbyterian. Clubs: Annandale Golf; Harvard Bus. Sch. of So. Calif. (dir.). Home: 1046 Oak Grove Pl San Marino CA 91108 Office: 415 Huntington Dr San Marino CA 91108

PEARSON, ROGER, business exec.; b. St. John's Wood, London, Eng., Aug. 21, 1927; s. Edwin and Beatrice May (Woodbine) P.; came to U.S., 1965; B.S. with honors, U. London, 1951, M.S., 1954, Ph.D., 1969; m. Marion Primrose Simms, June 3, 1959; children—Edwin, Sigrid, Emma, Rupert. Chmn. Pakistan Tea Assn., 1963-64; mng. dir. Octavius Steel & Co. of Pakistan, Ltd., Chittagong, East Pakistan, 1959-65; chmn. Plummer Bros., Ltd. Chittagong, 1959-65, Chittagong Warehouses, Ltd., 1960-65; chmn. dept. sociology and anthropology Queens Coll., Charlotte, N.C., 1970-71; chmn. dept. anthropology U. So. Miss., Hattiesburg, 1971-74; dean acad. affairs, dir. research Mont. Coll. Mineral Sci. and Tech., Butte, 1974-75. Bd. dirs., sec., treas. Mont. Energy and Magnetohydrodynamics Research and Devel. Inst., 1974-75; bd. dirs. Mont. Coll. Mineral Sci. and Tech. Found., 1974-75. Served to lt. British Indian Army, 1945-48. Fellow Inst. Chartered Secs. and Adminstrs. (London), Royal Anthrop. Inst. (London), Eugenics Soc. (London); mem. Inst. of Dirs. (London), Am. Anthrop. Assn., Am. Assn. Phys. Anthropologists, Am. Ethnological Soc., Linguistic Soc. Am., Council on Am. Affairs (pres. 1975—). Clubs: Army and Navy (Washington); Oriental, Reform (London); Tollygunge (Calcutta, India). Author: Eastern Interlude, 1954; An Introduction to Anthropology, 1974; A History of Social Thought, 1978. Editor: Korea in the World Today, 1976, Sino-Soviet Intervention in Africa, 1976. Editor, Jour. Indo-European Studies, 1973—. Editor: Jour. Social and Polit. Studies, 1976—. Home: 106 Prince St Alexandria VA 22134 also Elven House Elham Kent England Office: 1716 New Hampshire Ave NW Washington DC 20009

PEARSON, ROY MESSER, JR., clergyman; b. Somerville, Mass., Mar. 10, 1914; s. Roy Messer and Bessie M. (Ricker) P.; A.B. magna cum laude, Harvard, 1935; B.D. cum laude, Andover Newton Theol. Sch., 1938; D.D. Amherst Coll., 1957, Brown U., 1971; LL.D., Emerson Coll., 1966, Colby Coll., 1967; L.H.D., Norwich U., 1968; D.S.O. Curry Coll., 1969; m. Ruth Simmons, July 12, 1936; children—Beverly, Bradford. minister, Southville (Mass.) Federated Ch., 1936-38; ordained to ministry Congl. Ch., 1938; minister First Congl. Ch. Swanzey, N.H., 1938-40, Amherst, Mass., 1940-47, Hancock Congl. Ch., Lexington, Mass., 1947-54; lectr. Andover Newton Theol. Sch., 1951-54, dean, 1954-65, pres., 1965—, also trustee; pres. Andover Theol. Sem., 1954-65, Bartlett prof. sacred rhetoric, 1954—; preacher Nat. Council Chs. in Brit. Isles, 1951; regular radio preacher Mass. Council Chs., 1952-57; preacher Internat. Congl. Council Brit. Isles, 1957. Served as 1st lt. Chaplains Corps, AUS, 1944. Recipient Churchman award for best sermon of the year, 1948. Am. Assn. Theol. Schs. fellow, 1960. Mem. Phi Beta Kappa. Club: University (Boston). Author: Here's Faith for You, 1953; This Do-And Live, 1954; The Hard Commands of Jesus, 1957; Seeking and Finding God, 1958; The Ministry of Preaching 1959. Contbg. Author: Best Sermons of 1955 (ed. G. Paul Butler), 1955; Hear Our Prayer, 1961; The Preacher: His Purpose and Practice, 1963; The Believer's Unbelief, 1963; Best Sermons of 1964, 1964; Best Sermons of 1968, 1968; also articles religious periodicals. Home: 196 Herrick Rd Newton Centre MA 02159

PEARSON, WILLARD, acad. ofcl., former army officer; b. West Elizabeth, Pa., July 4, 1915; s. John Alfred and Mary Catherine (Mehrmann) P.; student Douglass Bus. Coll., 1933-35; M.S., Columbia, 1953; postgrad. Army War Coll., 1956-57, U. Pitts., 1962; M.A., George Washington U., 1963; postgrad. Oxford U., 1964; m. Reba E. Barton, Sept. 12, 1947; children—Richard Barton, Joan Louise, Patricia Jean. Commd. 2d lt. U.S. Army Res., 1936, advanced through grades to lt. gen. U.S. Army, 1971; sr. adviser 6th Div. Korean Army KMAG, FECOM, 1950-51; regtl. exec. officer 21st Inf. Regt., FECOM, 1951; chief plans div. GI, Hdqrs. USCONARC, Ft. Monroe, Va., 1953-56; comdg. officer 1st Battle Group, 9th Inf. Regt., USARAL, 1957-59; asst. chief of staf G3, Hdqrs. U.S. Army, Alaska, 1959-61; asst. chief Western Hemisphere Div., Operations Directorate ODCSOPS, Washington, 1961-63; chief of staff Hdqrs. Allied Land Forces, Southeastern Europe, Izmir, Turkey, 1963-65; asst. div. comdr. 101st Airborne Div., Ft. Campbell, Ky., 1965-66; comdg. gen. 1st Brigade, 101st Airborne Div., Vietnam, 1966-67; J3, USMACV, Saigon, 1967-68; dep. comdr./chief of staff Hdqrs. USMACV Forward, Hue Phu Bai, 1968; dir. individual tng. ODCSPER, Hdqrs. Dept. Army, Washington, 1968-69; comdg. gen. Ft. Lewis, Wash., 1969-71; comdg. gen. V Corps U.S. Army Europe, 1971-73; supt. Valley Forge Mil. Acad. and Jr. Coll., Wayne, Pa., 1973—. Decorated D.S.M. with 2 oak leaf clusters, Silver Star medal with two oak leaf clusters, Legion of Merit with two oak leaf clusters, Bronze Star medal with two oak leaf clusters, Combat Inf. badge with star, Air medal with six oak leaf clusters; Republic of Korea Presdl. Commendation, Mil. Order of Merit (Korea); Vietnamese Order 4th and 5th Classes, Vietnamese Gallantry Cross with palm; Grand Cross Merit with star Fed. Repub. Germany; Pa. D.S.M. Mem. Assn. U.S. Army, Beta Gamma Sigma. Presbyn. Mason (33 deg.). Address: Valley Forge Mil Acad and Jr Coll Wayne PA 19087

PEART, ARTHUR FRANCIS WHITTAKER, physician; b. Freeman, Ont., Can., Feb. 9, 1915; s. Grant Somerville and Bessie Pearl (Whittaker) P.; student Ont. Agr. Coll., 1933-35; M.D., C.M., Queen's U., 1940; D.P.H., U. Toronto, 1943; postgrad. Harvard Sch. Pub. Health, 1949-50; m. Gwendolyn Stainton, Mar. 20, 1943; children—Nancy, Frances, William, James. Intern St. Joseph's Hosp., Hamilton, Ont., 1940; gen. practice medicine, Swift Current, Sask., 1947; med. officer health, region 1, Swift Current, 1946; chief div. epidemiology Dept. Nat. Health and Welfare, Ottawa, 1948-53; asst. sec. Canadian Med. Assn., Toronto, 1954-60, dep. gen. sec., 1960-66, gen. sec., 1966-70; med. dir. Traffic Injury Research Found. Can., Ottawa, 1970-75; pres., med. cons. Medifacts Ltd., Ottawa, 1970—. Served with M.C., Canadian Army, 1940-46. Decorated Order Brit. Empire. Fellow Royal Soc. Health, Royal Coll. Physicians (Can.); mem. World Med. Assn. (pres. 1971), Canadian, Ont. med. assns., AMA (hon.). Mem. United Ch. Can. Clubs: Beaver Valley Ski; Royal Ottawa Golf, Masons, Rotary. Home: 50 Rideau Terr Ottawa ON K1M 2A1 Canada Office: 471 Richmond Rd Ottawa ON K2A 0G3 Canada

PEART, DOUGLAS RUSSELL, hosp. exec.; b. Burlington, Ont., Can., Dec. 18, 1916; s. Grant Somerville and Bessie Pearl (Whittaker) P.; B.Commerce, Queen's U., Kingston, Ont., 1939; diploma hosp. adminstrn. U. Toronto, 1951; m. Helen Lawrence Daniels, Oct. 6, 1945; children—John Douglas, Grant Raymond, Susan Helen, Mary Elizabeth, Sandra Jane. Retail merchandising trainee Hudson Bay Co., Winnipeg, Man., 1939- 40; personnel and pub. relations officer Fed. Govt. Can., Ottawa, 1945-49; adminstrv. resident Toronto East Gen. Hosp., 1950-51; adminstr. Gen. Hosp. of Port Arthur, Thunder Bay, Ont., 1951-54; exec. cons. Ottawa Civic Hosp., 1954-78, exec. cons., 1978—. Served from 2d lt. to capt., Ordnance Corps, Royal Canadian Army, 1940-45. Fellow Am. Coll. Hosp. Adminstrs. (life), Royal Soc. Health; mem. Internat. Hosp. Fedn., Ont. Hosp. Assn. (Blue Cross com.), Canadian Standards Assn. (standards steering com. on health care tech.), Canadian Coll. Health Service Execs. (charter mem.), Am. Coll. Hosp. Adminstrs., Ont. Council Teaching Hosp. Adminstrs. Home: 2080 Strathmore Blvd Ottawa ON K2A 1M3 Canada Office: 1053 Carling Ave Ottawa ON K1Y 4E9 Canada

PEASE, DANIEL CHAPIN, educator; b. N.Y.C., Aug. 7, 1914; s. Marshall Carleton and Edith May (King) P.; A.B., Yale, 1936; M.S., Calif. Inst. Tech., 1938; Ph.D., Princeton, 1940; m. Phyllis Marie Frankel, Aug. 18, 1939; children—Katharine Susan, Karen. NSF research fellow Stanford, 1940-41; acting asst. prof. Columbia, 1941-42; OSRD research asso. Princeton, Stanford, 1942-44; asst. prof. anatomy U. So. Calif., Los Angeles, 1945-49, asso. prof., 1949-50; asso. prof. U. Calif. at Los Angeles, 1951-55, prof., 1955—, chmn. dept. anatomy, 1973—. Mem. Am. Soc. for Cell Biologists (council 1962-65), Am. Assn. Anatomists (council 1967-69, 78-80, pres. 1979), Electron Microscopy Soc. Am. (council 1967-69, 71-73, pres. 1972). Author: Histological Techniques of Electron Microscopy, 2d edit., 1964. Editor: Cellular Aspects of Neural Growth and Differentiation, 1971; editorial bd. Jour. Ultrastructure Research, 1956—, Jour. Submicroscopic Cytology, 1969—, Am. Jour. Anatomy, 1979—. Home: 13011 Sunset Blvd Los Angeles CA 90049

PEASE, DAVID GORDON, artist, educator; b. Bloomington, Ill., June 2, 1932; s. Gordon A. and June (Stephens) P.; B.S., U. Wis.-Madison, 1954, M.S., 1955, M.F.A., 1958; m. Julie Jensen, Mar. 29, 1956; children—Lisa Kay, Kerry Susan. Instr. art Mich. State U., 1958-60; mem. faculty Tyler Sch. Art, Temple U., Phila., 1960—, prof., 1970—, chmn. painting dept., 1970-77, dean, 1977—; vis. faculty mem. Yale U. Summer Sch. Music and Art, 1970-72; one-man exbns. include Terry Dintenfass, Inc., N.Y.C., 1969, 71, 76, Am. Acad. Arts and Letters, N.Y.C., 1970, Mpls. Mus. Art, 1971, 73, 75; exhbns. include: Carnegie Internat., Pitts., 1961, Corcoran Biennial, Washington, 1961, 63, Whitney Annual, N.Y.C., 1963; represented in permanent collections: Whitney Mus. Am. Art, Phila. Mus. Art, Pa. Acad. Fine Arts, Des Moines Art Center, Pa. State U., others. Served with U.S. Army, 1955-57. Recipient William A. Clark award Corcoran Biennial, 1963; Lindbeck Found. Disting. Teaching award, 1968; Guggenheim Found. fellow, 1965-66; Tiffany Found. grantee, 1975-76. Mem. Coll. Art Assn. Am. Home: 1497 Huntingdon Rd Abington PA 19001 Office: Tyler Sch Art Beech and Penrose Aves Philadelphia PA 19126

PEASE, DONALD JAMES, Congressman; b. Toledo, Sept. 26, 1931; s. Russell Everett and Helen Mary (Mullen) P.; B.S. in Journalism, Ohio U., Athens, 1953, M.A. in Govt., 1955; Fulbright scholar Kings Coll., U. Durham, Eng., 1954-55; m. Jeanne Camille Wendt, Aug. 29, 1953; 1 dau., Jennifer. Mem. Ohio Senate, 1965-66, 75-76; mem. Ohio Ho. of Reps., 1969-74; mem. 96th Congress from 13th Ohio Dist. Chmn. Oberlin (Ohio) Pub. Utilities Commn., 1960-61; mem. Oberlin City Council, 1961-63. Served with AUS, 1955-57. Home: 140 Elm St Oberlin OH 44074 Office: 1641 Longworth House Office Bldg Washington DC 20515

PEASE, JAMES LEWIS, JR., mfg. co. exec.; b. Cin., Feb. 3, 1921; s. James Lewis and Mary Ellen (Rieman) P.; A.B., U. Cin., 1942; M.B.A., Harvard U., 1943; m. Miriam Garrard Waters, Nov. 6, 1943; children—James Lewis, III, Thomas L., Stephen H., Richard A. With Pease Co., Hamilton, Ohio, 1946—, v.p., 1959-65, pres., 1965-78, chmn. bd., chief exec. officer, 1978—; dir. North Side Bank, First Nat. Bank of Hamilton. Vice chmn. Christ Hosp., Cin., 1977—, bd. dirs., 1959—; v.p. Hospice of Cin., 1979—, bd. dirs., 1978—; bd. dirs. Better Bus. Bur. Cin., 1979. Served to lt. (j.g.) Signal Corps, USN, 1943-46. Home: 280 Poage Farm Rd Wyoming OH 45215 Office: 900 Forest Ave Hamilton OH 45023

PEASE, JAMES NORMAN, JR., architect; b. Charlotte, N.C., Aug. 29, 1921; s. James Norman and Eddie Kilpatrick (Hunter) P.; student N.C. State Coll., 1940-43; B.Arch., Auburn U., 1955; m. Mary Carson Jones, Nov. 20, 1943; children—James Norman III, Mary Carson, Edwin Jones. With Ross Shumaker, Architect, Raleigh, N.C., 1941, Dietrick & Olsen, Charlotte, 1942; successively project architect, designer, project designer, dir. design, dir. architecture, exec. v.p. J.N. Pease Assos., Charlotte, 1947-74, pres., 1974—, chmn. bd., 1977—; prin. archtl. works include: Home Fin. Co. bldg., Charlotte, 1958; Eastern Airline Reservations Centers, Charlotte, Atlanta, Miami, Woodbridge, N.J.; Central Piedmont Community Coll., 1963—; dir. 1st Union Nat. Bank; part-time instr., vis. lectr., juror Coll. Architecture, U. N.C., Charlotte; dir. N.C. Design Found., N.C. Archtl. Found.; ambassador-at-large State of N.C., 1978—. Bd. dirs. Central Charlotte Assn., Nature Mus. Central YMCA, Univ. Research Park, Carolinas Internat. Tennis Found.; pres. Mecklenburg council Boy Scouts Am., 1975-76. Served with C.E., U.S. Army, 1942-46; PTO. Licensed architect, N.C., Ga., Mo., N.J., N.Y., S.C., Tex.; registered planner, N.J. Fellow AIA (pres. N.C. chpt. 1969); mem. Am. Correctional Assn., Archtl. League N.Y., Charlotte C. of C. (dir.), Soc. for Coll. and Univ. Planning. Presbyterian. Clubs: Charlotte City, Charlotte Country, Piedmont. Office: PO 18725 Charlotte NC 28218

PEASLEE, MARGARET MAE HERMANEK, educator; b. Chgo., June 15, 1935; d. Emil Frank and Magdalena Bessie (Cechota) Hermanek; A.A., Palm Beach Jr. Coll., 1956; B.S., Fla. So. Coll., 1959; med. technologist Northwestern U., 1958, M.S., 1964, Ph.D., 1966; m. David Raymond Peaslee, Dec. 6, 1957; 1 dau., Martha Magdelena. Med. technologist Passavant Hosp., Chgo., 1958-59, St. James Hosp., Chicago Heights, Ill., 1960-63; asst. prof. biology Fla. So. Coll., Lakeland, 1966-68; asst. prof. biology U. S.D., Vermillion, 1968-71, asso. prof., 1971-76, prof., 1976, acad. opportunity liaison 1974-76; prof., head dept. zoology La. Tech. U., Ruston, 1976—. Fellow AAAS; mem. Am. Inst. Biol. Scis., Am. Soc. Zoologists, S.D. Acad. Sci. (sec.-treas., 1972-76), AAUP, N.Y. Acad. Scis., La. Acad. Sci. (sec. 1979-81), Sigma Xi, Phi Theta Kappa, Phi Rho Pi, Phi Sigma, Alpha Epsilon Delta. Contbr. articles to profl. jours. Home: 406 Barber Dr Ruston LA 71270 Office: Dept Zoology Box 5797 La Tech U Ruston LA 71272

PEASLEE, ROBERT VICTOR, engring. and constrn. co. exec.; b. McKeesport, Pa., June 8, 1914; s. Albert Ernest and Ida (Fox) P.; B.Ch.E., Pa. State U., 1935; M.Ch.E., Bklyn. Polytech. Inst., 1937; m. Jean Montgomery Mark, Oct. 26, 1946; children—John Robert, James Mark. Engr., economist Standard Oil Co. N.J., 1935-41; chem. engr. Standard Oil Co. Venezuela, 1941-44; mgr. N.Y. office C.F. Braun & Co., N.Y.C., 1944-54, sales mgr., v.p., Los Angeles, 1954-59; v.p. Ralph M. Parsons Co., N.Y.C., 1959-63, mgr. operations Europe, Paris, 1963-67, exec. dir., exec. v.p., N.Y.C., 1967-78; exec. v.p., dir. bus. devel. The Parsons Corp., N.Y.C., 1978-79; sr. adviser Saudi Research and Devel. Corp., London, 1979—; dir. Parsons-Jurden Corp., Ralph M. Parsons Ltd., London, Ralph M. Parsons G.M.b.H., Germany, Saudi Arabia Parsons, Jeddah. Trustee Am. Sch. of Paris. Mem. Am. Chem. Soc., Am. Petroleum Inst., Alpha Chi Sigma, Phi Lambda Upsilon. Republican. Presbyn. Clubs: Petroleum (Los Angeles); Petroleum (London); Marco Polo Club (N.Y.C.); Wadawanuck (Stonington), Conn.). Home: 18 Water St Stonington CT 06378 Office: 522 Fifth Ave New York NY 10036

PECARO, DANIEL THOMAS, radio and TV sta. exec.; b. Chgo., Jan. 24, 1926; s. William and Rose Catherine Kopke P.; B.S., DePaul U., 1950; m. Nancy Jean Mihills, Apr. 15, 1950; children—Timothy Scott, Daniel Drew. Tchr., sports coach Chgo. Pub. Schs., 1950-55; radio producer, dir., writer WGN radio, Chgo., 1955-57, prodn. supr., 1957-58, asst. program mgr., 1958-60, program mgr., 1960-62, program mgr. WGN-TV, 1962-65, group P program mgr. WGN-TV, KDAL-TV, KWGN-TV, 1965-66, v.p., group program chmn., 1966-67, v.p., gen. mgr. WGN-TV, 1967-72, exec. v.p., gen. mgr., 1972-74, exec. v.p., gen. mgr., dir. WGN Continental Broadcasting Co., 1975, pres., chief exec. officer, 1975—, pres. WGN Colo. Inc., also dir.; dir. KDAL Inc., WGN Continental Sales Co. Mem. program policy adv. com. Catholic TV Network, Archdiocese Chgo., 1975—; bd. dirs. Chgo. Boys Clubs, 1976. Served with Amphibious Corps USNR. Recipient Dante award Joint Civic Com. Italian-Americans, 1978. Mem. Nat. Assn. Broadcasters (TV bd. dirs.). Clubs: Oak Park Country, Lake Shore Athletic, Metropolitan. Office: WGN 2501 N Bradley Pl Chicago IL 60618*

PECARO, GEORGE JOSEPH, bldg. materials mfg. exec.; b. Johnston City, Ill., Dec. 20, 1908, s. Frank and Anna (Fiorendino) P.; B.S. in Forestry, Iowa State Coll., 1930; m. Marjorie E. Neal, May 8, 1931; children—Annadee, George Neal. Lab. pulp tester Chgo. Mill & Lumber Co., 1930; timber buyer, hard bd. supt., plant engr. U.S. Gypsum Co., 1930-37; supr. design and constrn., insulation bd. plant Nat. Gypsum Co., 1937, asst. works mgr., 1938-40; with Flintkote Co., 1940—, v.p., gen. mgr., 1947-56, gen. v.p., 1956-57, exec. v.p., 1957-58, pres., 1958-71, chmn. bd., 1971-75, also dir., mem. financial and exec. com. Mem. Miss. Indsl. and Agrl. Commn., 1942-45; dir. Yuma Municipal Water Dist., 1973. Mem. Soc. Am. Foresters, Alpha Zeta, Chi Phi, Gamma Sigma Delta. Republican. Presbyn. Club: Pauma Valley (Cal.) Country. Home: PO Box 633 Pauma Valley CA 92061

PECHILLO, JEROME ARTHUR, clergyman; b. Bklyn., May 16, 1919; s. Arthur Salvador and Catherine (Murphy) P.; B.A., S.T.B., Catholic U. Am., 1944. Ordained priest, Roman Cath. Ch., 1947; minister provincial Franciscan Fathers, Hollidaysburg, Pa., 1956-60; prelate ordinary de Coronel Oviedo, Paraguay, 1961; consecrated titular bishop of Novasparsa, 1966; aux. bishop, Newark, 1976—. Address: 691 West Side Ave Jersey City NJ 07304

PECHMAN, JOSEPH AARON, economist; b. N.Y.C., Apr. 2, 1918; s. Gershon and Lena (Pechman) P.; B.S., Coll. City N.Y., 1937; M.A., U. Wis., 1938, Ph.D., 1942, LL.D. (hon.), 1978; m. Sylvia Massow, Sept. 29, 1943; children—Ellen Massow, Jane Elizabeth. Statistician, Nat. Research Project, Phila., 1937; research asst. econs. U. Wis., 1937-38, research asso., 1939-41; asst. dir. Wis. income tax study Wis. Tax. Commn., 1938-39; economist OPA, 1941-42; tax adv. staff Treasury Dept., 1946-53; asso. prof. finance Sch. Indsl. Mgmt., Mass. Inst. Tech., 1953-54; economist Council Econ. Advisers, 1954-56, Com. Econ. Devel., 1956-60; exec. dir. studies govt. finance Brookings Instn., 1960-69, dir. econ. studies, 1962—; Irving Fisher research prof. Yale, 1965-66; cons. Council Econ. Advisers, Treasury Dept., 1961-68; mem. Adv. Council on Social Security, 1979—; fellow Center for Advanced Study in Behavioral Scis., 1975-76. Adv. dir. Met. Opera Assn. Served with AUS, 1942-45. Mem. Am. Finance Assn. (pres. 1971), Am. Econ. Assn. (bd. editors 1960-63, exec. com. 1972-74, v.p. 1978), Nat. Tax Assn., Am. Acad. Arts and Scis., Phi Beta Kappa. Author: Federal Tax Policy, 3d edit., 1977; (with Henry Aaron and Michael Tausig) Social Security: Perspectives for Reform, 1968; (with Benjamin Okner) Who Bears the Tax Burden?, 1974; (with George Break) Federal Tax Reform: The Impossible Dream, 1975; also numerous articles, reports in field. Editor: Setting National Priorities: The 1980 Budget, 1979. Home: 7112 Wilson Ln Bethesda MD 20034 Office: Brookings Instn 1775 Massachusetts Ave NW Washington DC 20006

PECK, ABRAHAM, editor, writer; b. N.Y.C., Jan. 18, 1945; s. Jacob and Lottie (Bell) Peckolick; B.A., N.Y. U., 1965; postgrad. City U. N.Y., 1965-67; m. Suzanne Wexler Peck, Mar. 19, 1977. Engaged in community organizing and tutoring, 1962-64; with N.Y.C. Welfare Dept., 1965-67; free-lance writer, 1967—; writer, organizer Chgo. action Youth Internat. party, 1968; editor Chgo. Seed, 1968-70; treas. Seed Pub., Inc., 1968-70; mem. coordinating com. Underground Press Syndicate, 1969; asso. editor Rolling Stone mag., San Francisco, 1975, contbg. editor, 1976—; feature writer Chgo. Daily News, 1977-78; with features dept. Chgo. Sun-Times, 1978—; critic at large WBBM Radio, 1979—; editor, co-founder Sidetracks, alt. newspaper supplement, Chgo. Daily News, 1977-78. Contbr. to Radio Free Chgo., 1970—; minister Universal Life Ch. Served with AUS, 1967. Mem. Internat. Giraffe Soc. Editor: Dancing Madness, 1976; cons. editor, contbr. The Sixties, 1977; contbr. The Eighties: A Look Back, 1979. Address: care Chgo Sun-Times 401 N Wabash Ave Chicago IL 60611

PECK, ANDREW F., stock broker; b. Bklyn., Mar. 18, 1926; s. Fremont C. and Isabel (Foster) P.; A.B., Princeton, 1947; m. Louise Irons, May 10, 1952; children—Diane, Susan, Douglas. With Clark Dodge & Co., Inc., N.Y.C., 1949-74, pres., 1969-74, chief exec. officer, 1972-74; v.p., dir. Kidder Peabody & Co., N.Y.C., 1974-79; pres. Andrew Peck Assos. Inc., N.Y.C., 1979—; dir. F.W. Woolworth Co., N.Y.C.; trustee Williamsburgh Savs. Bank, Bklyn. Home: Piping Rock Rd Locust Valley NY 11560 Office: 32 Broadway New York NY 10004

PECK, AUSTIN H., lawyer; b. Pomona, Calif., Dec. 25, 1913; s. Austin H. and Helen (Templeton) P.; A.B. with distinction, Stanford, 1935, J.D., 1938; m. Jean Albertson, Nov. 9, 1939; children—Julie Peck Fleming, Francesca Peck Taylor, Lisa Peck Lindelef. Admitted to Calif. bar, 1938, since practiced in Los Angeles; mem. firm Latham & Watkins, 1946-76, of counsel, 1976—; dir. Avery Internat. Corp., San Marino, Calif., Farr Co., Los Angeles, Capital Guardian Trust Co., Los Angeles. Trustee Rose Hills Meml. Park Assn., Ear Research Inst. Mem. Am., Calif., Los Angeles bar assns., Zeta Psi, Phi Delta Phi. Clubs: California, Los Angeles Country (Los Angeles); Birnam Wood, Valley (Montecito, (Calif.); Sunset; Chancery. Home: 10375 Wilshire Blvd Apt 14F Los Angeles CA 90024 Office: 555 S Flower St Los Angeles CA 90071

PECK, BEN, shoe co. exec.; b. Balt., Mar. 9, 1918; s. Herman and Jennie (Dlin) P.; ed. pub. schs.; m. Dorothy Marie Liebtrau, Sept. 20, 1941; 1 son, Bill. With Wohl Shoe Co., St. Louis, 1937—, exec. v.p. charge mdsg., 1962-63, pres., 1963—, also chief exec. officer; mem. exec. com., dir. Brown Group, Inc.; dir. St. Louis County Nat. Bank. Trustee Jewish Community Centers Assos., Jewish Center for the Aged. Served with the inf., AUS, World War II; ETO. Decorated Purple Heart. Mem. Nat. Retail Mchts. Assn. (dir.), Nat. Shoe Retailers Assn. (dir.). Jewish (bd. dirs. temple). Home: 1845 Nettlecreek Dr Town and Country MO 63105 Office: 8350 Maryland Ave Saint Louis MO 63105

PECK, BERNARD SIDNEY, lawyer; b. Bridgeport, Conn., July 26, 1915; s. James and Sadie (Goldstein) P.; B.A., Yale, 1936, LL.B., 1939; m. Marjorie Eloise Dean, Apr. 10, 1943; children—Daniel Dean, Constance Lynn. Admitted to Conn. bar, 1939, Fla. bar, 1979; practiced in Bridgeport, 1939—; partner firm Goldstein and Peck, 1946—; judge Municipal Ct. Westport, Conn., 1951-55. Moderator town meeting, Westport, 1950-51; mem. Westport Republican Town Com., 1951—. Pres. Westport YMCA, 1957, trustee, 1964—. Served to capt. AUS, 1942-46. Fellow Am. Coll. Trial Lawyers, Internat. Acad. Trial Lawyers; mem. Am., Conn., Bridgeport bar assns., Phi Beta Kappa. Clubs: Algonquin (Bridgeport); Patterson Country (pres. 1975-76) (Fairfield, Conn.); Landmark (Stamford, Conn.); Royal Poinciana Golf (Naples, Fla.). Home: 25 Punch Bowl Dr Westport CT 06880 also 1919 Gulf Shore Blvd North Naples FL 33940 Office: 955 Main St Bridgeport CT 06604

PECK, CHARLES EDWARD, mfg. co. exec.; b. Newark, Dec. 1, 1925; s. Hubert Raymond and Helen (White) P.; grad. Phillips Acad., 1943; B.S., U. Pa., 1949; student Mass. Inst. Tech., 1943-44; m. Delphine Murphy, Oct. 15, 1949; children—Margaret, Charles Edward, Katherine, Perry Anne. With Owens-Corning Fiberglas Corp., various locations, 1949-61, sales mgr. home bldg. products, Toledo, 1961-66; v.p. home bldg. products mktg. div., 1966-68, v.p. constrn. group, 1968-75, v.p. bldg. materials group, 1976-78, exec. v.p., 1978—, also dir.; dir. Ryland Group, Inc., Columbia, Md., Producers Council, Washington, 1974-77. Mem. statutory vis. com. U.S. Nat. Bur. Standards, 1972-77; mem. adv. com. Fed. Nat. Mortgage Adminstrn., 1977-78; vice chmn. vis. com. Mass. Inst. Tech.-Harvard Joint Center for Urban Studies; chmn. Producers Adv. Forum, 1977—. Served to 2d lt. USAAF, 1944-46. Mem. U.S. C. of C. (dir. 1975—) Phi Gamma Delta. Clubs: Belmont Country (Perrysburg, Ohio); Muirfield (Columbus, Ohio); Toledo; Internat. (Washington); Metropolitan (Chgo.). Home: 29737 E River Rd Perrysburg OH 43551 Office: Owens-Corning Fiberglas Corp Fiberglas Tower Toledo OH 43659

PECK, CLAIR LEVERETT, JR., bldg. contractor; b. Los Angeles, Nov. 20, 1920; s. Clair Leverett and Viola (Curtis) P.; B.S. in Civil Engring. cum laude, Stanford U., 1942; m. Linda Haggin, Jan. 2, 1975; children—Suzanne Peck Worthington, Nancy Peck Birdwell, Clair Leverett, III. With C.L. Peck Contractor, Los Angeles, 1947—, chmn. bd., 1965—; dir. Farmers Ins. Group, Investment Co. Am., AMCAP Fund, Di Giorgio Corp., Fed. Res. Bank San Francisco, J.G. Boswell Corp.; trustee Mead Housing Trust and Devel. Corp. Past pres. YMCA Met. Los Angeles; trustee Estelle Dohony Eye Found., Huntington Library, Santa Anita Found., Brentwood Sch., Ear Research Inst. Served to lt. USNR, 1946. Recipient Humanitarian award NCCJ, 1973; Man of Year award City of Hope-Constrn. Industries Alliance, 1974; Daisy award Calif. Landscape Contractors Assn., 1975; Achievement award Los Angeles Area C. of C., 1977. Mem. ASCE, Archimedes Circle, Salerni Colegium, Stanford Assos., Republican Assos. Episcopalian. Clubs: Bohemian, Calif., Los Angeles Country, Eldorado Country, Sunset. Office: 3303 Wilshire Blvd Los Angeles CA 90010

PECK, DALLAS LYNN, geologist; b. Cheney, Wash., Mar. 28, 1929; s. Lynn Averill and Mary Hazel (Carlyle) P.; B.S., Calif. Inst. Tech., 1951, M.S., 1953; Ph.D., Harvard U., 1960; m. Tevis Sue Lewis, Mar. 28, 1951; children—Ann, Stephen, Gerritt. With U.S. Geol. Survey, 1954—, asst. chief geologist, office of geochemistry and geophysics, Washington, 1967-72, geologist, geologic div., 1972-77, chief geologist, 1977—; mem. Lunar Sample Rev. Bd., 1970-71; chmn. earth scis. adv. com. NSF, 1970-72; vis. com. dept. geol. scis. Harvard U., 1972-78. Recipient Meritorious Service award Dept. Interior, 1971, Disting. Service award, 1979. Mem. Geol. Soc. Am., Soc. Econ. Geologists, Am. Geophys. Union (pres. sect. volcancology, geochemistry and petrology 1976-78). Home: 2524 Heathcliff Ln Reston VA 22091 Office: US Geol Survey Reston VA 22092

PECK, DAVID WARNER, lawyer; b. Crawfordsville, Ind., Dec. 3, 1902; s. Dumont M. and Juliet (Warner) P.; A.B. with distinguished honors, Wabash Coll., 1922, LL.D., 1954; LL.B., Harvard, 1925; D.J.S., Suffolk U., 1952; LL.D., Union Coll., Albany, 1953; m. Elizabeth Saville, Jan. 30, 1929; children—David W., Morgan Scott. Asst. U.S. atty., 1925-28; partner firm Sullivan & Cromwell, N.Y.C., 1934-43, 58-77, of counsel, 1978—; justice Supreme Ct., N.Y., 1943-45; asso. justice appellate div. Supreme Ct., 1st dep., 1945-47, presiding justice, 1947-57; mem. Permanent Internat. Ct. Arbitration, 1957-63. Trustee Greenwich Savs. Bank. Mem. task force on legal services and procedure 2d Hoover Commn.; chmn. N.Y. State Commn. on Revision and Simplification of Constn., 1959-61. Trustee Vincent Astor Found., Wabash Coll., N.Y. U. Law Center Found. Mem. Am., N.Y. (pres. 1962) bar assns., Am. Judicature Soc., Am. Law Inst., Assn. Bar City N.Y., Am. Arbitration Assn. (chmn. bd. dirs. 1965-69), Chevaliers du Tastevin, Commanderie de Bordeaux, N.Y. County Lawyers Assn. Clubs: Quaker Hill Country (Pawling, N.Y.); Recess, Century Assn. (N.Y.C.); Metropolitan (Washington); Muirfield (Scotland). Author: The Greer Case, 1955; Decision at Law, 1961. Home: 580 Park Ave New York NY 10021 Office: 125 Broad St New York NY 10004

PECK, DONALD VINCENT, musician; b. Yakima, Wash., Jan. 26, 1930; s. Clarence Leon and Bertha A. (Compin) P.; diploma in Music, Curtis Inst. Music, 1951; student Seattle U., 1948-49. With Seattle Symphony Orch., 1947-49, Nat. Symphony Orch., Washington, 1951-52; prin. flutist Kansas City Philharmonic Orch., 1955-57, Chgo. Symphony Orch., 1957—; instr. flute and woodwind ensemble DePaul U., Chgo.; guest soloist with various orchs. Served with USMCR, 1952-55. Office: 220 S Michigan Ave Chicago IL 60604*

PECK, DOUGLAS EDWARD, mfg. co. exec.; b. Grand Rapids, Mich., Nov. 9, 1929; s. Eldon and Marion Leone (Gibson) Martin; B.A., U. Mich., 1952, LL.B., 1955; m. Mariel Joan Hamilton, Jan. 1, 1953; children—Marcia Suanne, Douglas Leland, David Hamilton. Admitted to Mich. bar, 1955; with firm Clark, Klein, Winter, Parsons & Prewitt, Detroit, 1955-66; counsel Hoover Universal, Inc. (name formerly Hoover Ball and Bearing Co.), Saline, Mich., 1966-68, sec., 1968-77, pres., 1977—; dir. Citizens Bank, Saline. Mem. Am., Mich. bar assns. Republican. Presbyterian. Home: 4207 Pleasant Lake Rd Ann Arbor MI 48104 Office: 135 E Bennett St Saline MI 48176

PECK, EARL GOODWIN, air force officer; b. Jersey City, Aug. 27, 1928; s. Earl Wilson and Dorothea May (Bliss) P.; B.A., U. Tex., 1958; student Indsl. Coll. Armed Forces, 1967-68; M.S., George Washington U., 1968; m. Margaret Raymond, June 14, 1952; children—Allen, Michael, Thomas, David, Jeffrey, Stephen, Peggy. Commd. 2d lt. U.S. Air Force, 1950, advanced through grades to maj. gen., 1977; chief programs and analysis br. Hdqrs SAC, Offutt AFB, Nebr., 1963-67; assigned F-4 Combat Crew Tng. Squadron, MacDill AFB, Fla., 1968-69; chief spl. air ops. br. Mil. Assistance Command Vietnam, Saigon, 1969-70; comdr. 3902 Air Base Wing, Offutt AFB, 1970-72; comdt. Squadron Officer Sch., Maxwell AFB, Ala., 1973-74; chief Office Air Force History, Washington, 1974-75; dep. chief of staff for personnel Hdqrs. SAC, Offutt AFB, 1975-77, DCS/Ops., Hdqrs. SAC, 1977-78, chief of staff, 1978—; command pilot, sr. missileer. Decorated Legion of Merit with 3 oak leaf clusters, Bronze Star medal. Mem. Air Force Assn., Order of Daedalians, Phi Beta Kappa, Pi Sigma Alpha. Club: Rotary. Home: Quarters 11 Offutt AFB NE 68113 Office: Chief of Staff SAC Offutt Air Force Base NE 68113

PECK, ELLEN, author, editor; b. Fairbury, Ill., Aug. 24, 1942; d. Carlton and Genevieve (Doran) Remburg; B.S. in Edn., Ill. State U., 1965; m. William Allen Peck, June 12, 1965; m. 2d, Stanley H. Allen, Apr. 8, 1979. Tchr. pub. schs., Balt., 1966-69; columnist Chgo. Tribune/N.Y. News Syndicate, 1969-74; founder, 1972, since officer Nat. Orgn. for Non-Parents, Balt.; founder, 1976, since officer Consortium on Parental Aptitude; contbg. editor Pageant, 1972-74; editor Jour. Sex Edn. and Therapy, 1975—; cons. continuing edn. div. Am. Coll. Obstetricians and Gynecologists, 1974—, Negative Population Growth, 1976; bd. dirs. Zero Population Growth; author: The Baby Trap, 1971; Sex and Birth Control: A Guide for the Young, 1973; Pronatalism: The Myth of Mom and Apple Pie, 1974; A Funny Thing Happened on the Way to Equality, 1975; The Joy of the Only Child, 1977; The Parent Test: How to Measure and Develop Your Aptitude for Parenthood, 1978. Mem. Planned Parenthood/World Population, Environ. Action, Cleveland Amory Fund for Animals, Population Inst., NOW (adv. com. task force media). Address: 177 E 77th St New York NY 10021. *I am continually surprised by any who seem in slight awe of those of us who "write." The truth is that most people I meet would, I feel, be excellent "writers;" they have ideas of worth to state in conversation and need only learn to carry on a "conversation" with a tablet or typewriter for their ideas to have a chance at a deserved wide audience. Indeed, I consider it imperative, in an age of mass communications, for every throughtful individual to learn to "write," whether what is "written" is a book or article, or perhaps a letter to the President or "the Editor." Give ideas life through written words.*

PECK, FRANKLIN BRUCE, SR., physician; b. Remington, Ind., Sept. 26, 1898; s. Frank L. and May (Tedford) P.; A.B. in Physiology, Ind. U., 1920; M.D., Jefferson Med. Coll., Phila., 1923; m. Lisbeth C. Roeder, Sept. 18, 1924; children—Franklin Bruce, Elizabeth L. (Mrs. Harry Carlson). Asst. in physiology Ind. U., 1919-20; resident physician Jefferson Med. Coll., 1923-25; clin. asst. diabetes clinic Grace Hosp., Detroit, 1927-30, asso. physician, 1930-32, physician in charge, 1932-35; staff Lilly Research Labs., Indpls., 1936-40, asso. dir. med. div., 1940-46, dir., 1946-52, dir. med. research coop., 1953-58, dir. clin. research internat., 1958-61, spl. adviser diabetes dept., clin. research div., 1961-71; asso. medicine Ind. U. Sch. Med., 1943-49, asst. prof., 1949-51, asso. prof., 1951—; physician Indpls. Gen. Hosp., 1942-50, cons. medicine, 1950-65, pres. staff, 1951; cons. White County Meml. Hosp., 1961-65. Organizing mem. Internat. Diabetes Fedn., Brussels, 1949, Am. Diabetes Assn. del., Dusseldorf, 1958; hon. pres. Indpls. Diabetes Assn. Served with U.S. Army, 1918. Recipient Davis prize Jefferson Med. Coll., 1923; named Academician of Honor, Acad. Medicine and Surgery Panama, 1957, Banting medal, 1961. Fellow A.C.P.; mem. Am. Diabetes Assn. (mng. editor jour. 1942-52, chmn. sci. publs. com., sec. 1955-58, pres. 1960-61), A.M.A.; hon. mem. numerous fgn. med. socs., diabetes assns. Contbr. articles relating to diabetes, new insulin modifications to prof. jours. Address: 8181 Lincoln Blvd Indianapolis IN 46240

PECK, GARNET EDWARD, pharmacist, educator; b. Windsor, Ont., Can., Feb. 4, 1930; s. William Crozier and Dorothy (Marentette) P.; B.S. in Pharmacy with Distinction, Ohio No. U., 1957, M.S. in Indsl. Pharmacy, Purdue U., 1959, Ph.D., 1962; m. Mary Ellen Hoffman, Aug. 24, 1957; children—Monique Elizabeth, Denise Anne, Philip Warren, John Edward. Sr. scientist Mead Johnson Research Center, 1962-65, group leader, 1965-67; asso. prof. indsl. and phys. pharmacy Purdue U., West Lafayette, 1967-73, prof., 1973—, dir. indsl. pharmacy lab., 1975—; cons. in field. Mem. West Lafayette Mayor's Advisory Com. on Community Devel., 1973—; mem. West Lafayette Citizen's Safety Com., 1974—. Served with U.S. Army, 1951-53. Recipient Lederle Faculty award Purdue U., 1976. Fellow AAAS, Acad. Pharm. Scis., Am. Inst. Chemists; mem. Am. Chem. Soc., Am. Pharm. Assn., New York Acad. Scis., Nat. Catholic Pharmacists Guild U.S., Am. Legion, Sigma Xi, Rho Chi, Phi Delta Chi, Phi Lambda Upsilon. Roman Catholic. Club: Elks. Contbr. articles to profl. jours. Office: Dept Industrial and Physical Pharmacy Pharmacy Bldg Purdue U West Lafayette IN 47907

PECK, GIRVAN, lawyer; b. N.Y.C., Nov. 30, 1923; s. Laurence Freeman and Clara Temple (Boardman) P.; B.A., Yale U., 1946, LL.B., 1949; m. Nancy Mailliard, Jan. 5, 1966; children—Natalie, Laurence F., Christie B., Sheila, Alexander M. Admitted to N.Y. bar, 1950, Calif. bar, 1952; asso. firm Debevoise Plimpton & McLean, N.Y.C., 1949-50; asst. counsel Bank of Am., San Francisco, 1952-54; asso. firm Morrison Foerster Holloway Clinton & Clark, San Francisco, 1954-60; partner firm Morrison & Foerster, San Francisco, 1961—. Bd. dirs. Katherine Branson Sch., 1963-68, Youth Law Center, 1974—, San Francisco Bail Project, 1978—. Served as navigator USAAF, 1943-45. Mem. Am. Bar Assn., Bar Assn. San Francisco (dir. 1972-73), Am. Law Inst., Phi Delta Phi. Republican. Clubs: Pacific Union: Lagunitas Country (Ross, Calif.). Home: 3633 Clay St San Francisco CA 94118 Office: 1 Market Plaza San Francisco CA 94105

PECK, GREGORY, motion picture actor; b. La Jolla, Calif., Apr. 5, 1916; ed. U. Calif., Neighborhood Playhouse Sch. Dramatics; m.; 5 children. Appeared on stage in plays including: The Doctor's Dilemma, The Male Animal, Once in a Lifetime, The Play's the Thing, You Can't Take It With You; The Morning Star; The Willow and I; Sons and Soldiers; movies, 1944—; Keys of the Kingdom, 1944; Valley of Decision, 1945; Spellbound, 1945; Duel in the Sun, 1947; The Yearling, 1947; The Macomber Affair, 1947; Gentlemen's Agreement, The Paradine Case, Yellow Sky; The Great Sinner, 1948; Twelve O'Clock High, 1949; The Gunfighter, 1950; Captain Horatio Hornblower, 1951; Only the Valiant, 1951; David and Bathsheba, 1951, Snows of Kilamanjaro, 1952; Roman Holiday, 1953; Night People, Man With a Million, Purple Plains, Moby Dick, 1954; Designing Woman, 1956; Man in the Grey Flannel Suit, 1956; Pork Chop Hill, 1959; The Bravados, 1958; On The Beach, 1959; Guns of Navarone, 1961; To Kill a Mockingbird (award as best actor 1962), Cape Fear, 1962; How the West Was Won, 1963; Captain Newman, M.D., 1963; Behold a Pale Horse, 1964; Mirage, 1965; Arabesque, 1966; Mackenna's Gold, 1967; The Chairman, 1968; The Stalking Moon, 1968; Marooned, 1969; I Walk the Line, 1970; Shootout, 1971; Billy Two-Hats, 1972; co-producer and star The Big Country, 1958; producer The Trail of the Catonsville Nine, 1972, The Dove, 1973, The Omen, 1976, MacArthur, 1977, The Boys from Brazil, 1978. Mem. Nat. Council on Arts, 1965—. Nat. chmn. Am. Cancer Soc., 1966. Recipient Presdl. Medal of Freedom; Jean Hersholt Humanitarian award, 1968. Mem. Acad. Motion Picture Arts and Scis. (gov.; pres. 1967-70), Am. Film Inst. (founding chmn. bd. trustees 1967-69). Address: PO Box 24817 Los Angeles CA 90024

PECK, JAMES STEVENSON, banker; b. Wilmington, N.C., Mar. 14, 1923; s. Oscar and Christine (Stevenson) P.; B.S., U. N.C., 1943; postgrad. Rutgers U., 1955; m. Frances Grainger Marburg, June 19, 1948; children—Frances Grainger, James Stevenson, Christine Stevenson. With Union Trust Co. of Md., Balt., 1947—, pres., 1969-72, chmn., 1972—; chmn. Union Trust Bancorp, Balt., 1972—; dir. Title Guarantee Co., U.S. Fidelity & Guaranty Co., Crown Central Petroleum Corp., Alcolac, Inc. Dir. Md. State Banking Com. Bd. dirs. Keswick Home for Incurables, United Fund, United Fund Central Md., Greater Balt. Com.; trustee Johns Hopkins Hosp. Served to lt. (j.g.) USNR, 1943-46. Clubs: Elkridge, Maryland, Merchants (Balt.). Home: 1500 Locust Ave Ruxton MD 21204 Office: Union Trust Co Baltimore and St Paul Sts Baltimore MD 21203

PECK, JOHN FREDERICK, author; b. Pitts., Jan. 13, 1941; s. Clarence Erwin and Louise Bertha (Sayenga) P.; B.A., Allegheny Coll., Meadville, Pa., 1962; Ph.D., Stanford, 1973; m. Ellen Margaret McKee, Sept. 2, 1963; 1 dau., Ingrid. Instr. English, Princeton, 1968-70, vis. lectr., 1972-75; prof. English, Mt. Holyoke Coll., 1977—. Recipient award Nat. Inst. Arts and Letters, 1975; Am. Acad. in Rome fellow in creative writing, 1978. Author: Shagbark, 1972; The Broken Blockhouse-Wall, 1978; contbr. to periodicals. Address: Dept English Mt Holyoke Coll South Hadley MA 01035

PECK, JOHN W., U.S. judge; b. Cin., June 23, 1913; s. Arthur M. and Marguerite (Comstock) P.; A.B., Miami U., 1935, LL.D., 1966; J.D., U. Cin., 1938, LL.D., 1965; LL.D., Chase Law Sch., 1971; m. Barbara Moeser, Mar. 25, 1942; children—John Weld, James H., Charles E. Admitted to Ohio bar, 1938; partner Peck, Shaffer & Williams, Cin., 1938-61; judge Ct. Common Pleas, Hamilton County, Ohio, 1950, 54; tax commr. State of Ohio, 1951-54; judge Supreme Ct. of Ohio, 1959-60, U.S. Dist. Ct., So. Dist. Ohio, 1961-66; judge U.S. Ct. Appeals, 6th Circuit, 1966—, sr. judge, 1978—; judge Temp. Emergency Ct. Appeals, 1979—; exec. sec. gov. State of Ohio, 1949; lectr. U. Cin. Coll. Law, 1948-70, Salmon P. Chase Coll. Law, 1949-51; mem. Ohio Unemployment Study Commn., 1951; mem. com. on adminstrn. criminal law Jud. Conf. U.S., 1971-79. Trustee, Miami U., 1959—, emeritus, 1975—; mem. Princeton City Sch. Dist. Bd. Edn., 1958-63, pres. bd., 1963-69. Served to capt. Judge Adv. Gen. Corps, AUS, 1942-46. Mem. Cincinnatus Assn., Gyro Club, Beta Theta Phi, Phi Delta Phi. Club: Cin. Literary. Home: 165 Magnolia Ave Glendale OH 45246 Office: US Post Office and Court House Cincinnati OH 45202

PECK, LEROY EUGENE, newspaper publisher; b. Rugby, N.D., May 16, 1922; s. LeRoy Ellsworth and Elvira (Sostrom) P.; B.A. in Journalism, U. Wyo., 1944; m. Margaret Elizabeth MacFadyen, June 29, 1946; children—John Christopher, Elizabeth Ann, David Harroun, James MacFadyen. Track coach, dir. athletic pub. U. Wyo., 1946-49; co-pub. Riverton (Wyo.) Ranger, 1949—, Kemmerer (Wyo.) Gazette, 1962—, Powell (Wyo.) Tribune, 1964—, Red Lodge (Mont.) News, Lovell (Wyo.) Chronicle, 1971—, Thermopolis Ind. Record, 1978—, Star Valley Ind., 1978—; v.p., dir. Morning Star Dairy, Inc., Riverton, 1953-72, Allied Nuclear Corp., 1957-68; v.p., dir. Western Standard Corp., 1958-68, pres., 1968—. Exec. dir. Wyo. Dept. Econ. Planning and Devel., 1967-70; a founder Wyo. Mining Assn., 1956; founder Wyo. Sugar Council, 1963; chmn. com. which started Wyo. Indsl. Devel. Corp., Riverton Indsl. Com., 1955-67; chmn. natural resources council Fedn. Rocky Mountain States, 1966-77. Republican primary candidate for Congress, 1966, for Gov., 1974; mem. Wyo. Ho. of Reps., 1970-74; mem. Wyo. Senate, 1977—. Chmn. bd. dirs. Wyo. Blue Cross, 1967-73; trustee U. Wyo., 1953-65. Served to capt., inf. AUS, 1943-46. Decorated Bronze Star, Silver Star; Croix de Guerre (France). Recipient Distinguished Service award Wyo. Kiwanis, 1965; Indsl. Leadership award Wyo. Assn. Realtors, 1967. Mem. Wyo. Press Assn. (pres. 1956), Sigma Delta Chi, Alpha Tau Omega. Methodist. Mason. Home: 1002 W Park Ave Riverton WY 82501 Office: 421 E Main St Riverton WY 82501

PECK, MERTON JOSEPH, educator, economist; b. Cleve., Dec. 17, 1925; s. Kenneth Richard and Charlotte (Hart) P.; A.B., Oberlin Coll., 1949; A.M., Harvard, 1951, Ph.D., 1954; A.M. (hon.), Yale, 1963; m. Mary McClure Bosworth, June 13, 1949; children—Richard, Katherine, Sarah, David. Teaching fellow, instr. econs. Harvard, 1951-55, asst., then asso. prof. bus. adminstrn., 1956- 61; asst. prof. econs. U. Mich., 1955-56; dir. systems analysis Office Sec. Def., 1961-63; prof. econs. Yale, 1963—, chmn. dept., 1967-74. Mem. Council Econ. Advisers, Exec. Office of Pres., 1968-69; cons. in field, 1954—. Served with AUS, 1944-46. Mem. Am. Econ. Assn., Am. Assn. U. Profs. Clubs: Lawn (New Haven); Yale (N.Y.C.). Author: (with others) The Economics of Competition in the Transportation Industries, 1959; Competition in the Aluminum Industry, 1945-58, 1961; (with F. Scherer) The Weapons Aquisition Process, An Economic Analysis, 1962; (with others) Technological Change, Economic Growth and Public Policy, 1967; (with others) Federal Regulation of Television, 1973. Contbr. articles to profl. jours. Home: 415 Humphrey St New Haven CT 06511

PECK, PAUL ARTHUR, lawyer, former naval officer; b. Birmingham, Mich., Oct. 22, 1926; s. Arthur Carl and Ruth Mae (Spencer) P.; B.S. in Indsl. Engring., Northwestern U., 1957; J.D., U. San Diego, 1971; m. Betty May Zeunert, Dec. 10, 1949; children—Donna Mary, Pamela Ann, Linda Louise. Commd. ensign U.S. Navy, 1948, advanced through grades to rear adm., 1974; admitted to Calif. bar, 1972; service in Vietnam; dep. chief staff readiness and resources on staff comdr. in chief U.S. Atlantic Fleet, 1974-76; sr. officer ship material readiness course Naval Nuclear Power Tng. Unit, Idaho, 1976; comdr. Carrier Group 3, 1976-78; ret.,

1978; pres. Two Star Internat. Inc., San Francisco, 1978—. Decorated Legion of Merit (2), D.F.C. (2), Air medal (15), Bronze Star with combat V; Vietnamese Cross Gallantry. Mem. Calif., Fed. bar assns. Lutheran. Club: Bohemian. Home: 933 Grosvenor Pl Oakland CA 94610 Office: 465 California St Suite 524 San Francisco CA 94104

PECK, RICHARD HYDE, hosp. adminstr.; b. Ft. McClelland, Ala., Aug. 30, 1941; s. Robert H. and Elizabeth M. P.; A.B. in Econs., U. N.C., 1963; M.S. in Health Adminstrn., Duke U., 1966; m. Barbara Mansfield, Dec. 27, 1964; children—Catherine, Nancy, Joanne. Adminstrv. asst. U. Hosps. Cleve., 1966-67, asst. adminstr., 1967-69; asst. dir. Duke U. Hosp., 1969-71, asso. dir., 1971-73, adminstrv. dir., 1973—; asso. prof. health adminstrn. program Duke U. Mem. exec. com. Durham, N.C. chpt. ARC, 1976-79, Duke U. Children's Classic, 1979. Mem. Am. Coll. Hosp. Adminstrs., N.C. Hosp. Assn. Democrat. Presbyterian. Home: 2833 McDowell Rd Durham NC 27705 Office: PO Box 3708 Duke Hosp Durham NC 27710*

PECK, RICHARD WAYNE, novelist; b. Decatur, Ill., Apr. 5, 1934; s. Wayne Morris and Virginia (Gray) P.; student Exeter (Eng.) U., 1954-55; B.A., DePauw U., 1956; M.A., So. Ill. U., 1959. Mem. faculty Sch. Edn., Hunter Coll., 1965-71; author books for adolescents, including: Are You in the House Alone?, 1977 (Edgar Allen Poe award 1977), Father Figure, 1978, Secrets of the Shopping Mall, 1979, (poetry anthology) Sounds and Silences, 1970; lectr. in field; asst. dir. Council Basic Edn., Washington, 1969-70. Served with U.S. Army, 1956-58. English-Speaking Union fellow Jesus Coll., Oxford (Eng.) U., 1973. Mem. Authors Guild, Authors League, Delta Chi. Republican. Methodist. Contbr. articles on architecture and local history to N.Y. Times. Home: 10 Mitchell Pl New York NY 10017 also 9 Ferriss Estate Rd New Milford CT 06776

PECK, RODERICK BUSH, coll. dean; b. Wayne, Nebr., Aug. 17, 1919; s. Errol R. and Louella (Bush) P.; A.B., Nebr. State Tchrs. Coll., Wayne, 1941; M.S., Iowa State U., 1950, Ph.D., 1952; m. Lorna Katherine Stigge, July 9, 1943; children— Roderick Bush, Marcia L. (Mrs. Stephen Noren), Michelle K. (Mrs. Kent E. Rasmussen), Jeanne A., Steven W. Supt. schs., Wynot, Nebr., 1946-49; grad. asst. Iowa State U., 1950-52; dir. summer sessions and evening div., asso. prof. sociology Midland Coll., Fremont, Neb., 1952-54; asso. dean adult edn. U. Omaha, 1954-57; dean summer sessions and continuing edn., prof. edn. Calif. State U., Long Beach, 1957—. Served with AUS, 1941-45. Mem. Phi Delta Kappa, Phi Gamma Mu, Phi Kappa Phi. Home: 5255 Tufton St Westminster CA 92683 Office: 1250 Bellflower Long Beach CA 90840

PECK, RUSSELL A., educator; b. Fremont County, Wyo., Dec. 17, 1933; s. LeRoy Ellsworth and Elvira Eugenia (Sjostrom) P.; A.B., Princeton U., 1956; Ph.D., Ind. U., 1963; m. Ruth Elaine Demaree, June 18, 1958; children—Demaree Catherine, Nathan Russell, Gunther William. Teaching asst. Ind. U., 1956-60; asst. prof. U. Rochester (N.Y.), 1961-67, asso. prof., 1968-72, prof. English, 1973—, founding dir. Medieval House; mem. adv. bd. of grad. record examiner Ednl. Testing Service; vis. prof. Hull U., 1967-68. Deacon, Brighton Presbyterian Ch. Recipient Edward Peck Curtis award, 1972; E. Harris Harbison award Danforth Found., 1972. Mem. MLA, Early English Text Soc., New Chaucer Soc., Medieval Acad. Am. Democrat. Author: Kingship and Common Profit in Gower's Confessio Amantis, 1978; asso. editor Mediaevalia. Home: 180 Crosman Terr Rochester NY 14620 Office: English Dept U Rochester Rochester NY 14627

PECK, TEMPLETON, newspaperman; b. Pomona, Cal., Aug. 26, 1908; s. Austin Hurlbut and Helena (Templeton) P.; A.B., Stanford, 1930; student U. So. Cal. Law Sch., 1935-37; m. Catherine Esther Clift, July 1, 1938; children—Templeton Clift, Caroline. Reporter, San Francisco News, 1930-31, San Diego Sun, 1931-33, Long Beach (Cal.) Press-Telegram, 1934-35, Los Angeles Daily News, 1935-37; lectr. journalism Stanford, 1937-41, lectr. communication, 1963-71; policy editor OWI, N.Y.C. and London, Eng., 1941-45; editorial writer San Francisco Chronicle, 1946-54, editor editorial page, 1954—. Fellow Wilton Park (Eng.). Republican. Episcopalian. Home: 73 Erstwild Ct Palo Alto CA 94303 Office: 901 Mission St San Francisco CA 94119

PECK, WILLIAM ARNO, physician; b. New Britain, Conn., Sept. 28, 1933; s. Bernard Carl and Molla (Nair) P.; A.B., Harvard U., 1955; M.D., U. Rochester (N.Y.), 1960; m. Nancy Wade Jones, July 24, 1961; children—Catherine, Edward Pershall, David Nathaniel. Intern, then resident in internal medicine Barnes Hosp., St. Louis, 1960-62; fellow in metabolism Washington U. Sch. Medicine, St. Louis, 1963; mem. faculty U. Rochester Med. Sch., 1965-76, prof. medicine and biochemistry, 1973-76, head div. endocrinology and metabolism, 1969-76; John E. and Adaline Simon prof. medicine, co-chmn. dept. Washington U. Sch. Medicine, St. Louis, 1976—; physician in chief Jewish Hosp., St. Louis, 1976—; chmn. endocrinology and metabolism adv. com. FDA, 1976-78; chmn. gen. medicine study sect. NIH, 1979—; chmn. Gordon Conf. Chemistry, Physiology and Structure of Bones and Teeth, 1977. Served as med. officer USPHS, 1963-65. Recipient Mosby Book award, 1960, Doran J. Stephens award U. Rochester Sch. Medicine, 1960, Lederle Med. Faculty award, 1967-70, NIH Career Program award, 1970-75. Mem. Am. Soc. Biol. Chemists, Am. Physiol. Soc., Am. Soc. Clin. Investigation, Am. Fedn. Clin. Research, Am. Diabetes Assn., Am. Soc. Bone and Mineral Research, Assn. Am. Physicians, Endocrine Soc., Orthopedic Research Soc., Sigma Xi, Alpha Omega Alpha. Contbr. med. jours. Home: 4501 Lindell Blvd Saint Louis MO 63108 Office: Sch Medicine Washington Univ Saint Louis MO 63110

PECKFORD, ALFRED BRIAN, Can. provincial premier; b. Whitbourne, Nfld., Can., Aug. 27, 1942; s. Ewart Gladstone and Allison (Young) P.; B.A., Meml. U.; m. Marina Jean, Oct. 11, 1969; 1 dau., Sue-Ann. Tchr. public high schs.; mem. Nfld. Legislature, from 1972; minister of mcpl. affairs and housing Province Nfld., 1975-76, then minister of mines and energy; premier, 1979—. Progressive Conservative. Mem. United Ch. of Canada. Office: Office of Premier Conferation Bldg Saint John's NF A1C 5T7 Canada*

PECKHAM, BEN MILLER, physician, educator; b. Milw. Mar. 8, 1916; s. John William and Mary (Peckham) Gross; B.S. in Medicine with honors, U. Wis., 1939; M.B., Northwestern U., 1941, M.D., 1942, M.S. in Physiology, 1947, Ph.D. in Physiology, 1949; m. Ann Faherty, Aug. 26, 1943; children—Mary, Roger, Gardner. Intern St. Lukes Hosp., Cleve., 1941-42: resident obstetrics and gynecology Chgo. Wesley Meml. Hosp., also Chgo. Maternity Center, 1947-50; research asst. physiology Northwestern U. Med. Sch., 1946-47, instr., 1947-48, clin. asst. obstetrics-gynecology, 1950-51, instr., then asso. and asst. prof., 1951-56; prof. gynecology and obstetrics U. Wis. Med. Sch., 1956—, chmn. dept., 1956—, asso. dean for clin. affairs, 1967-71. Mem. test com. Nat. Bd. Med. Examiners, 1957-61. Mem. Am. Assn. Obstetricians and Gynecologists, Assn. Profs. of Gynecology and Obstetrics (pres. 1964), Soc. Gynecol. Investigation (pres. 1965), Am. (sec. 1969-72, pres. 1977-78), Chgo., Milw. (hon.) gynecol. socs., Nat. Council Obstetrics and Gynecology (chmn. 1972-73), N.Y. Acad. Scis., Wis., S.D. (hon.) socs. gynecologists and obstetricians, Am. Coll. Obstetricians and Gynecologists, Am., Wis., Dane County med. socs., Sigma Xi, Chi Psi, Nu Sigma Nu. Home: 3433 Crestwood Dr Madison WI 53705

PECKHAM, DONALD CHARLES, educator; b. Bainbridge, N.Y., Sept. 11, 1922; s. Charles Henry and Josephine Marie (Palmer) P.; student Oberlin Coll., 1941-43, A.B., 1948; M.A., U. Mich., 1949; Ph.D., Pa. State U., 1954; m. Elizabeth May Doolittle, Aug. 27, 1949; children—David, Bruce, Stephen, Laura, Barbara, Christopher. Instr. physics Norwich U., 1949-51; asst. prof. St. Lawrence U., Canton, N.Y., 1954-57, asso. prof., 1957-65, prof., 1965-71, Hayward prof. physics, 1971—, chmn. dept., 1961—, acting v.p. and dean of Coll., 1976-77. Trustee Canton Central Sch. Served with AUS, 1943-46. NSF Sci. Faculty fellow, 1966-67. Mem. Am. Phys. Soc., Am. Assn. Physics Tchrs., Am. Optical Soc., AAAS, AAUP, N.Y. State Sch. Bds. Assn. (dir., v.p.), Sigma Xi. Presbyn. (elder). Home: 18 Church St Canton NY 13617

PECKHAM, DONALD EUGENE, utilities co. exec.; b. Willis, Kans., Nov. 28, 1922; s. Rolland Claude and Winona Maude (Lewis) P.; B.A. cum laude in Acctg., Eastern N.Mex. U., 1953; M.B.A., U. Ariz., 1954; m. Evelynn Darlene Dodson, Dec. 20, 1949. Acct., Ill. Power Co., Decatur, Ill., 1954-57; with Public Service Co. of N.Mex., Albuquerque, 1957—, sec., asst. treas., 1970-74, sec., treas., 1974-79, sec., asst. treas., 1979—; sec., asst. treas. Western Coal Co., Paragon Resources, Inc. Served with USMC, 1943-46. Mem. Am. Soc. Corp. Secs. Republican. Clubs: Tanoan Country, Elks. Home: 8804 Natalie St NE Albuquerque NM 87111 Office: 414 Silver Ave SW Albuquerque NM 87103

PECKHAM, HOWARD HENRY, librarian, educator; b. Lowell, Mich., July 13, 1910; s. Herman Algernon and Harriet May (Wilson) P.; A.B., U. Mich., 1931, A.M., 1933; Litt.D., Olivet Coll., 1975; m. Dorothy Koth, July 28, 1936; children—Stephen Wilson, Angela Zidana (Mrs. Thomas Hewett). Chief editorial writer Grand Rapids (Mich.) Press, 1935; curator manuscripts Clements Library of Am. History, U. Mich., 1936-44, lectr. library sci., 1942-46, univ. war historian, 1943-44; dir. Ind. Hist. Bur., Indpls., 1945-53; dir. Clements Library, prof. history U. Mich., 1953-77; cons. Office Naval History, USN Dept., 1966-78. Fellow Soc. Am. Archivists (founding mem., mem. council), Am. Assn. State and Local History (pres. 1954-56, mem. council), Am., Miss. Valley hist. assns., Mass. Hist. Soc., Bibliog. Soc. Am., Am. Antiquarian Soc., Adelphic Alpha Pi. Club: Grolier. Author: (with R.G. Adams) Lexington to Fallen Timbers, 1942; (with C. Storm) Invitation to Book Collecting, 1946; Pontiac and the Indian Uprising, 1947; William Henry Harrison, 1951; Captured by Indians, 1954; Nathanael Greene, 1956; The War for Independence, 1958; The Colonial Wars, 1964; Pontiac Young Ottawa Leader, 1963; The Making of the University of Michigan, 1967; The Toll of Independence, 1974; History of the W.L. Clements Library 1923-73, 1973; editor: George Groghan's Journal of 1767, 1939; (with L.A. Brown) Revolutionary War Journals of Henry Dearborn, 1939; Guide to the Manuscript Collections in the Clements Library, 1942; (with S.A. Synder) Letters From Fighting Hoosiers, 1948: (with C.A. Byrd) Bibliography of Indiana Imprints 1955; Narratives of Colonial America, 1971; Sources of American Independence, 1978 Ind. Hist. Bull., 1945-53; asso. editor Am. Heritage quar., 1949-54. Home: 213 London Rd Hendersonville NC 28739

PECKHAM, ROBERT FRANCIS, U.S. dist. judge; b. San Francisco, Nov. 3, 1920; s. Robert F. and Evelyn (Crowe) P.: A.B., Stanford, 1941, LL.B., 1945; postgrad. in law Yale, 1941-42; LL.D., U. Santa Clara, 1973; m. Harriet M. Behring, Aug. 15, 1953 (dec. Apr. 1970); children—Ann Evelyn, Sara Esther; m. 2d, Carol Potter, June 9, 1974. Adminstrv. asst. to regional enforcement atty. OPA, 1942-43; admitted to Calif. bar, 1945; pvt. practice in Palo Alto and Sunnyvale, 1946-48; asst. U.S. atty., 1948-53, chief asst. criminal div., 1952-53; mem. firm Darwin, Peckham & Warren, San Francisco, Palo Alto and Sunnyvale, 1953-59; judge Superior Ct. Santa Clara County, Calif., 1959-66, presiding judge, 1961-63, 65-66; U.S. dist. judge No. Dist. Calif., 1966-76, chief judge, 1976—. Trustee Foothill Coll. Dist., 1957-59, pres., 1959; mem. bd. visitors Stanford Law Sch., 1969-75, chmn., 1971-72. Recipient Brotherhood award Nat. Conf. Christians and Jews, 1968. Mem. Am., Fed., San Francisco, Santa Clara County bar assns., Am. Law Inst., Am. Judicature Soc., Soc. Calif. Pioneers (v.p. 1977—), Calif. Hist. Soc. (trustee 1974-78), Council Stanford Law Socs. (chmn. 1974-75), World Affairs Council (trustee 1979—), Phi Beta Kappa, Phi Delta Phi. Home: 101 Alma St Palo Alto CA 94301 Office: US Courthouse San Francisco CA 94102

PECKINPAH, DAVID (SAM) SAMUEL, motion picture dir.; b. Fresno, Calif., Feb. 21, 1925; s. David Edward and Fern (Chruch) P.; B.A., Fresno State Coll., 1947, M.A., U. So. Calif., 1949; m. Cecilia M. Selland, July 17, 1947 (div. Mar. 1962); children—Sharon, Kristen, Melissa, Matthew. Author, dir. Rifleman, TV series, 1960; author, producer, dir. TV series, Westerner, 1958, also Klondike; dir. Deadly Companions, 1961, Ride the High Country, (Belgian Best Film award), 1962, Ballad of Cable Hogue (Madrid Best Film award), 1970, Junior Bonner, 1972, The Getaway, 1972, Pat Garrett and Billy the Kid, 1973, Convoy, 1978; co-author, dir. Major Dundee, 1965, The Wild Bunch, 1969, Straw Dogs, 1971; author, dir. Bring Me the Head of Alfredo Garcia, 1974, The Killer Elite, 1975, Cross of Iron, 1977. Served with USMCR, 1943-46. Mem. Dirs. Guild Am., Writers Guild Am., Acad. Motion Picture Arts and Scis. Office: care Chasin-Park-Citron Agy 9255 Sunset Blvd Los Angeles CA 90069*

PECSOK, ROBERT LOUIS, chemist, educator; b. Cleve., Dec. 18, 1918; s. Michael C. and Katherine (Richter) P.; S.B. summa cum laude, Harvard, 1940, Ph.D., 1948; m. Mary Bodell, Oct. 12, 1940; children—Helen (Mrs. Norman Wong), Hansen), Katherine (Mrs. Garrett Capune), Jean (Mrs. William Tate), Michael, Ruth (Mrs. Tim Hughes), Alice (Mrs. John Dailey), Sara. Prodn. foreman Procter & Gamble Co., Balt., 1940-43; instr. chemistry Harvard, 1948; asst. prof. chemistry U. Calif. at Los Angeles, 1948-55, asso. prof., 1955-61, prof. 1961-71, vice chmn. dept., 1965-70; prof., chmn. dept. U. Hawaii, Honolulu, 1971—. Sci. adviser FDA, 1966-69. Served as lt. USNR, 1943-46. Recipient Tolman medal, 1971. Guggenheim fellow, 1956-57; Petroleum Research Fund Internat. fellow, 1963-64. Mem. Am. Chem. Soc., Am. Inst. Chemists, Phi Beta Kappa, Alpha Chi Sigma, Phi Lambda Upsilon. Author: Principles and Practice of Gas Chromatography, 1959; Analytical Methods of Organic- and Biochemistry, 1966; Modern Methods of Chemical Analysis, 1968, 2d edit., 1976; Modern Chemical Technology, 1970; Physicochemical Applications of Gas Chromatography, 1978. Home: 4775 Aukai Ave Honolulu HI 96816

PEDACE, JOHN SYLVESTER, brewing co. exec.; b. Norwich, Conn., Apr. 20, 1926; s. Bruno and Vita (LaRussa) P.; student pub. schs., Norwich; m. Estelle Olsson, Oct. 20, 1951; children—Nancy, John Sylvester, William. Gen. mgr. Conn. Beverage Co., 1952-56; dist. sales mgr. Piel Brox., 1956-63, sales promotion mgr., 1963-64; sales promotion mgr. Drewrys, Ltd., 1964-66; brand mgr. Asso. Brewing Co., 1966-72; dir. advt. G. Heileman Brewing Co., Inc., LaCrosse, Wis., 1972-73, corporate mktg. dir., 1973-74, exec. v.p. mktg., 1974—, dir., 1976—. Bd. dirs. Viterbo Coll., LaCrosse; mem. adv. bd. Salvation Army, LaCrosse. Roman Catholic. Club: Elks. Home: 2975 Longview Ct LaCrosse WI 54601 Office: 925 S 3d St LaCrosse WI 54601

PEDELAHORE, JOSEPH EARL, accountant; b. New Orleans, Sept. 30, 1910; s. Joseph W. and Maria Inez (Carreras) P.; student Tulane U.; m. Teresa Marguerite Prieto, 1931 (dec. 1933); 1 dau., Janice Myrle (Mrs. Felix Rabito); m. 2d, Julia Akers Haight, Dec. 31, 1935; 1 son, Joseph Earl. Staff supr. Sidney S. Bourgeois & Co., 1941-45; propr. J. Earl Pedelahore, C.P.A., 1945-49, 55-59; partner Pedelahore & Kiser, 1949-55, J. Earl Pedelahore & Co., 1960—; v.p., dir. Schwegmann Bank & Trust Co., 1966-68. Instr. accounting evening div. Tulane U., 1945-54; pres., sec. La. Bd. C.P.A.'s. Named La. col. Mem. Am. Inst. C.P.A.'s (council 1957-64, trial bd. 1958-60, 61-66, exec. com. 1959-61, 63-64, v.p. 1963-64), Assn. C.P.A. Examiners (pres.), So. States Conf. C.P.A.'s (pres. 1954-55), Soc. La. C.P.A.'s (pres. 1950-51), New Orleans C. of C., Beta Alpha Psi. K.C. Clubs: Young Men's Business, Internat. House, New Orleans Athletic (New Orleans). Home: 8322 Pritchard Pl New Orleans LA 70118 Office: First National Bank of Commerce Bldg New Orleans LA 70112

PEDEN, IRENE CARSWELL, elec. engr., univ. adminstr.; b. Topeka, Sept. 25, 1925; d. Jay Horton and Lena (Anderson) Carswell; B.S., U. Colo., 1947; M.S., Stanford U., 1958, Ph.D., 1962; m. Leo J. Peden, Aug. 28, 1962; stepchildren—Jefri Lyn, Jennifer. Jr. engr. Del. Power & Light Co., Wilmington, 1947-49; jr. engr. Stanford Research Inst., 1949-50, research engr. in antenna research group, 1950-52, 54-57; research engr. Midwest Research Inst., Kansas City, Mo., 1952-54; research asst. Hansen Microwave Lab. Stanford U., 1958-61; acting instr. in elec. engring. Stanford U., 1959-61; asst. prof. elec. engring. U. Wash., 1961-64, asso. prof., 1964-71, prof., 1971—, asso. dean Coll. Engring., 1973-76; mem. nat. adv. drug com. FDA, 1971-74; mem. adv. council Sch. Engring. Stanford U., 1972-78; mem. space physics bd. Nat. Acad. Scis., 1974-76; adv. bd. Alaska Geophys. Inst., 1977—; mem. adv. com. for applied sci. and research applications NSF, 1977—; mem. Army Sci. Bd., 1978—; mem. adv. bd. U.S. Mcht. Marine Acad., 1978—; regional judging panel White House Fellows Program, 1976, 77. Recipient Golden Lyre award Iota Iota alumnae chpt. Alpha Chi Omega, 1968, Nat. Achievement award, 1972; named Woman of Achievement Seattle Theta Sigma Phi, 1966, Woman of Year, Seattle sect. Quota Internat., 1971, Distinguished Contbr. to Edn., Seattle Fedn. Women's Clubs, 1971; Distinguished Alumnus award U. Colo., 1974. Fellow IEEE (chmn. Seattle sect. 1965-66, editorial bd. procs. 1965-70, 78—, mem. coms. 1966-69, 71—, v.p. ednl. activities 1976, 77, dir., exec. com., fellows com. 1978—); mem. Soc. Women Engrs. (sr., chmn. Pacific N.W. sect. 1967-68, Nat. Achievement award 1973), Engrs. Council for Profl. Devel. (engring. edn. and accreditation com. 1975—, chmn. region VII 1976-77, vice chmn. ops.-designate 1978), Internat. Union Radio Sci. (commn. on fields and waves 1976—), Am. Soc. Elec. Engrs., AAAS, Am. Geophys. Union, N.Y. Acad. Scis., Morter Bd. (hon. mem. Tolo chpt.), Sigma Xi, Tau Beta Pi. Home: 8752 Sand Point Way NE Seattle WA 98115 Office: U Wash Dept Elec Engring Seattle WA 98195

PEDEN, KATHERINE GRAHAM, indsl. cons.; b. Hopkinsville, Ky., Jan. 2, 1926; d. William E. and Mary (Gorin) Peden; student pub. schs. Vice pres. radio sta. WHOP-CBS, Hopkinsville, 1944-68; owner sta. WNVL, Nicholsville, Ky., 1961-71; commr. commerce Ky., mem. Gov. Ky. Cabinet, Frankfort, 1963-67; pres., cons. Katherine G. Peden & Assos. Inc., Louisville, indsl. and community developers; dir. Westvaco Corp., Cin., New Orleans & Tex. Pacific Ry. subs. So. Ry. System. Chmn. Louisville and Jefferson County Riverport Authority; civilian aide to Sec. of Army. Mem. com. Pres's. Commn. on Status of Women, 1961-62; mem. Pres's. Commn. on Civil Disorders, 1967; pres. Ky. Derby Festival, 1979-80. Democratic nominee U.S. Senate, 1968; mem. exec. com. Nat. Soc. to Prevent Blindness, 1979; mem. adv. council U. Ky. Coll. Bus. Named Woman of Year Hopkinsville, 1952. Mem. Fedn. Bus., Profl. Women's Clubs (pres. state 1955-56, 1st nat. v.p. 1960-61, nat. pres. 1961-62), U. Louisville Internat. Center (dir.). Mem. Christian Ch. (deaconnss 1956-59, 60-63). Home: 2118 S Virginia St Hopkinsville KY 42240 Office: Citizen's Plaza Suite 2306 Louisville KY 40202

PEDERSEN, C. RICHARD, mfg. co. exec.; b. Havre, Mont., Jan. 10, 1923; s. James G. and Anne (Walsh) P.; B.A., U. Mont., 1947; LL.B., Harvard, 1950; m. Muriel Beatrice Jones, Oct. 25, 1951; children—Charles Richard, Arthur Kirk, Lloyd Duncan, Suni, Kari Anne. Admitted to N.Y. bar, Conn. bar; with law firm Dewey, Ballantine, Bushby, Palmer & Wood, N.Y.C., 1950-57; with Am. Can Co., 1957—, asst. sec., 1958-71, asst. gen. counsel, 1960-68, v.p., gen. counsel, 1969—, sec., 1971-77, sr. v.p., 1977—. Served to capt. AUS, 1943-46. Decorated Combat Inf. Badge. Mem. Am. Bar Assn., Assn. Bar City N.Y. Home: 2 Peaceable Hill Rd Ridgefield CT 06877 Office: American Ln Greenwich CT 06830

PEDERSEN, FRANCIS D., fin. exec.; b. Hettinger, N.D., Mar. 11, 1925; s. Harry E. and Audrey M. (Andersen) P.; LL.B., U. S.D., 1949; m. Gwendolyn F. Deaton, Sept. 1, 1950; children—Richard D., Mayre T. Admitted to S.D. bar, 1949, Iowa bar, 1950; practice law, Sioux City, Iowa, 1949-50; br. mgr. Securities Acceptance Corp., Omaha, 1950-54; with Assos. Capital Corp., Nashville, 1954-63, treas., 1963-73; v.p. fin. Walter E. Heller Internat. Corp., Chgo., 1973—. Trustee Highland Park Hosp. Served with USNR, 1943-45. Clubs: Bob O'Link Golf (Highland Park, Ill.); Masons. Home: 666 Portwine Rd Deerfield IL 60015 Office: 105 W Adams Chicago IL 60603

PEDERSEN, GILBERT JOHN, lawyer; b. Buffalo, July 7, 1909; s. Hans and Eva (Soergel) P.; A.B., U. Rochester, 1930; LL.D., U. Buffalo, 1930; m. Carmen Ogden, Apr. 20, 1935; children—Lars, Ann. Admitted to N.Y. bar, 1933; partner firm Smith, Pedersen & Smith, Buffalo, 1939—; sec., dir. Pratt & Lambert Inc.; dir. Buffalo Viking Machine Tool Corp., Buerk Tool & Machine Corp. Trustee Friends Cemetery Assn. Bd. dirs. Harry Dent Family Found., Edwin Erickson Found., George and Elizabeth Smith Found. Mem. Theta Delta Chi, Phi Delta Phi. Presbyn. (past trustee, past pres.). Home: 99 Forest Dr Orchard Park NY 14127 also 5565 N Via Alcalde Tucson AZ 85718 Office: 1608 Statler Office Bldg Buffalo NY 14202

PEDERSEN, HOWARD, vehicle rental and leasing co. exec.; b. Detroit, July 12, 1931; s. Oscar Henry and Ellen Marie Pedersen; B.B.A., Gen. Motors Inst., 1954; M.B.A., U. Detroit, 1962; m. Margaret Hudson, June 20, 1953; children—Craig, Lisa, Tom Rob. Comptroller, Chrysler Chem. Co., Trenton, Mich., 1963-65; with export div. Chrysler Corp., Detroit, 1965-67, fin. exec., 1968; mgr. corp. Profit Forecasting, 1969; comptroller Chrysler Real Estate Co., Troy, Mich., 1970-71; exec. dir. Chrysler Europe, London, 1971-75; v.p., corp. officer Norton Simon, Inc., N.Y.C., 1975-78; sr. v.p. acctg. and info. services Avis, Inc., N.Y.C., 1978-79, sr. v.p., chief fin. officer, 1979—. Served with U.S. Army, 1954-56. Mem. Engring. Soc., Am. Mgmt. Assn., Nat. Assn. Accountants, Fin. Execs. Inst. Home: 4 Lakewood Circle Greenwich CT 06830 Office: 1114 Ave of Americas New York NY 10036

PEDERSEN, PAUL RICHARD, composer; b. Camrose, Alta., Can., Aug. 28, 1935; s. Richard and Anna (Rasmussen) P.; B.A., U. Sask., 1957; Mus.M., U. Toronto, 1961, Ph.D., 1970; m. Jean Frances Stollery, Aug. 6, 1956; children—Rebecca, David, Katherine, Andrew. Music dir. Camrose Lutheran Coll., 1962-64; prof. McGill U., Montreal, Que., 1966—, chmn. dept. theory, 1970-74, dir. Electronic Music Studio, 1971-74, asso. dean Faculty of Music, 1974-76, dean, 1976—; exec. producer McGill U. Records. Recipient Can. Council awards, 1958, 59, 73; Queen Elizabeth II Ont. scholar, 1965; Province of Ont. grad. fellow, 1964-65. Mem. Candian League Composers, Composers, Authors and Pubs. Assn. Can., Canadian Assn. U. Schs. Music. Contbr. articles to music jours. Composer: (chamber music) Woodwind Trio No. 1, 1956, Woodwind Trio No. 2, 1957. Chorale Prelude No. 2, 1958, Lament, 1958, Ricercare, 1958, Woodwind Quintet (commd. Saskatoon Summer Festival), 1959, Come Away, 1959, Fugue, 1959, Sonata for Violin and Piano (commd. Andrew Dawes), 1960, Serial Composition, 1965, An Old Song of the Sun and the Moon and the Fear of Loneliness, 1973, Wind Quintet No. 2, 1975; (choral works) Ecclesiastes XII, 1958, Psalm 117, 1959, All praise to Thee, 1960, Built on a Rock, 1961, Cantata and Narrative for Good Friday, 1961, God Himself is Present, 1961, O Darkest Woe, 1961, Psalm 134, 1961, On the Nativity of Christ, 1963, 12 Chorales arranged for SAB Choir, 1974; (electronic music) The Lone Tree, 1964, Themes from the Old Testament, 1966, Fantasie, 1967, Origins, 1967, For Margaret, Motherhood and Mendellssohn, 1971; (orchestral music) Concerto for Orchestra, 1961, Lament, 1962. Home: 125 Percival Ave Montreal West PQ H4X 1T7 Canada Office: 555 Sherbrooke St W Montreal PQ H3A 1E3 Canada

PEDERSEN, THOMAS AUGUST, lawyer; b. Ribe, Denmark, Aug. 26, 1908 (parents Am. citizens); s. Peder and Marie (Hahn) P.; A.B., U. Mich., 1932, J.D., 1934; m. Inez Smitherman, Apr. 28, 1940; children—Thomas Douglas, William Randolph. Admitted to Tenn. bar, 1935, since practiced in Knoxville; admitted to U.S. Supreme Ct. bar, 1938, other fed. ct. bars; law clk. TVA, 1935, jr. atty., 1936-39, asso. atty., 1939, atty., 1940, sr. atty., 1941-48, prin. atty., 1948-53, asst. gen. counsel, 1953-69, solicitor, 1969-71. Lawyer del., life mem. U.S. Jud. Conf. Mem. exec. bd., dist. chmn. Gt. Smokey Mountain council Boy Scouts Am., 1959. Served to capt. C.E., AUS, 1942-46. Fellow Am. Coll. Trial Lawyers; mem. Fed., Tenn., Knoxville bar assns., Am. Judicature Soc., Internat. Platform Assn., Order Ky. Cols. Rotarian. Clubs: Knoxville Execs., Holston Hills Country (Knoxville). Home: 5801 Marilyn Dr Knoxville TN 37914. *I believe that all useful work, properly done, is the surest way to build self-respect, character, confidence, pride and human dignity.*

PEDERSEN, WESLEY NIELS, public relations exec.; b. South Sioux City, Nebr., July 10, 1922; s. Peter Westergaard and Mary Gertrude (Sorensen) P.; student Tri-State Coll., Sioux City, Iowa, 1940-41; B.A. summa cum laude, Upper Iowa U.; postgrad. George Washington U., 1958-59; m. Angela Kathryn Vavra, Oct. 17, 1948; 1 son, Eric Wesley. Editor, writer Sioux City Jour., 1941-50; corr. N.Y. Times, Life, Time, Fortune, 1948-50; editor Dept. State, 1950-53, fgn. service officer, Hong Kong, 1960-63; fgn. affairs columnist, roving corr. USIA, 1953-60, chief, worldwide spl. publs. and graphics br., 1963-69, chief Office Spl. Projects, Washington, 1969-78; chief Office Spl. Projects, Internat. Communication Agy., 1978-79; v.p., dir. editorial services Fraser Assos., public relations, Washington, 1979—; lectr. creative communications Upper Iowa U., 1975; lectr. effective writing George Washington U., 1975, 76; lectr. Pub. Relations Inst., Am. U., 1976, Bus. and Mgmt. Div., N.Y. U., 1976, 77, 78; cons. pub. relations, editorial and design. Chmn. founding bd. dirs. Nat. Inst. for Govt. Public Info. Research, Am. U., 1977—. Served with USAAF, 1943-46. Recipient 2 awards A.P. Mng. Editors Assn. Iowa, 1949; Meritorious Service award USIA, 1963; Mead Papers award, 1969; 1st prizes Fed. Editors Assn., 1970, 74, 75; 1st prizes Soc. Tech. Communication, 1974, 75, 76; named Most Outstanding Info. Ofcl. in Exec. Br. Govt., Govt. Info. Orgn., 1975. Mem. Am. Fgn. Service Assn., Internat. Assn. Bus. Communicators (vice chmn. govt. relations com. 1976-77, chmn. nat. capital dist. conf. 1977, dir. Washington chpt. 1977-78, Communicator of Yr. award Washington chpt. 1978; awards 1973, 76, 77, 78), Nat. Assn. Govt. Communicators (pres. 1978-79, dir. profl. devel. programs 1976-77, Communicator of Year award 1977, Disting. Service award 1978, speaker nat. conf. 1979), Pub. Relations Soc. Am., Nat. Council Communications Socs. (dir. 1979—). Episcopalian. Clubs: Nat. Press, Fgn. Service (Washington). Author: Legacy of a President, 1964. Editor: Escape At Midnight and Other Stories (Pearl S. Buck), 1962; Exodus From China (Harry Redl), 1962; Education in China (K.E. Priestley), 1962; The Peasant and the Communes (Henry Lethbridge), 1962; China's Urban Communes (Henry Lethbridge), 1963; China's Men of Letters (K.E. Priestley), 1963; Children of China (Pearl S. Buck and Margaret Wylie), 1963; Early to Rise (Norbert Luciano), 1963; Macao (Richard Hughes), 1963; Quest for Greatness (Hubert H. Humphrey), 1967; The Americans and the Arts (Howard Taubman), 1969; The Dance in America (Agnes de Mille), 1969; Bounty From the Land (Dorothy Lafferty and Thomas Clemens), 1970; contbr. to American Heroes of Asian Wars, 1969, Principles and Practices of Public Relations, 1979; mem. editorial bd. Fgn. Service Jour., Public Relations Quar.; contbr. articles to profl. jours. Home: 5214 Sangamore Rd Washington DC 20006 Office: Fraser Assos 1800 K St NW Washington DC 20547. *Keenness of mind and an abundance of luck, it is said, are the key ingredients of personal success. The truth be told, however, I've performed only one act of brilliance in my lifetime: the selection of my parents. But I've had an enormous amount of good fortune, a fact manifestly clear to anyone who has ever met my wife and son. They, thank goodness, chose me.*

PEDERSON, VERNON R., judge; b. N.D., Sept. 11, 1919; s. John and Tilda (Torgerson) P.; student Minot State Coll., 1937-40; B.S., U. N.D., 1947, LL.B., 1949, J.D., 1969; m. Evelyn I. Kraby, Oct. 11, 1952; children—Kathryn, Mark (dec.), Mary. Admitted to N.D. bar, 1949; individual practice law, Minot, N.D., 1949-51; spl. agent atty. Office Price Stabilization, Fargo, N.D., 1951-53; asst. atty. gen. State of N.D., Bismarck, 1953-74; asso. justice N.D. Supreme Ct., Bismarck, 1975—; gen. counsel N.D. State Hwy. Dept., 1953-74. Bd. dirs. N.D. Community Found., 1976—. Served with U.S. Army, 1941-45. Mem. Am., N.D., Burleigh County bar assns., Am. Judicature Soc. Lutheran. Home: 2029 Second St Bismarck ND 58501 Office: Supreme Ct Capitol Bldg Bismarck ND 58505. *Every day I find more reasons to agree with Holmes who said: "I long have said there is no such thing as a hard case. I am frightened weekly but always when you walk up to the lion and lay hold the hide comes off and the same old donkey of a question of law is underneath."*

PEDICINI, LOUIS JAMES, truck trailer co. exec.; b. Detroit, June 29, 1926; s. Louis I. and Myra Ann (Bergan) P.; B.S.E.E., Wayne U., 1955; m. Ellen Sylvia Mulden, June 5, 1948; 1 son, Eric Louis. Dept. head Gen. Motors Corp., 1948-58; exec. v.p. Lester B. Knight & Assos., Inc., Chgo., 1959-76; exec. v.p. ops. Pullman Trailmobile, Chgo., 1976—. Mem. U.S. Republican Senatorial Trust. Served with U.S. Army, 1944-46. Fellow Inst. Brit. Foundrymen; mem. Am. Foundrymen's Soc. (past dir.). Republican. Roman Catholic. Clubs: Skokie Country (Glencoe, Ill.); Plaza (Chgo.). Home: 405 Sheridan Rd Kenilworth IL 60043 Office: 200 E Randolph Dr Chicago IL 60601

PEDLEY, JOHN GRIFFITHS, archaeologist, educator; b. Burnley, Eng., July 19, 1931; s. George and Anne (Whitaker) P.; came to U.S., 1959; B.A., Cambridge (Eng.) U., 1953, M.A., 1959; postgrad. (Norton fellow), Am. Sch. Classical Studies, Athens, Greece, 1963-64; Ph.D., Harvard, 1965; m. Mary Grace Sponberg, Aug. 30, 1969. Loeb research fellow in classical archaeology Harvard U., 1969-70; asst. prof. classical archaeology and Greek, U. Mich., Ann Arbor, 1965-68, asso. prof., 1968-74, acting chmn. dept. classical studies, 1971-72, 75-76, dir. Kelsey Mus. Archaeology, 1973--, prof., 1974—; mem. staff excavations, Sardis, Turkey, 1962-64, Pylos, Greece, 1964; co-dir. excavations, Apollonia, Libya, 1966-68; field dir. Corpus Ancient Mosaics Tunisia, Thysdrus, 1972-73; co-prin. investigator excavations, Carthage, N.Africa, 1975—. Am. Council Learned Socs. fellow, 1972-73; Nat. Endowment Arts Museums program grantee, 1974, 77; Nat. Endowment Humanities grantee, 1967, 75. Author: Sardis in the Age of Croesus, 1968; Ancient Literary Sources on Sardis, 1972; Greek Sculpture of the Archaic Period: the Island Workshops, 1976; co-editor: Studies Presented to GMA Hanfmann, 1971. Home: 1233 Baldwin St Ann Arbor MI 48104 Office: Kelsey Museum U Mich Ann Arbor MI 48109

PEDNEAULT, ROCH, bishop; b. Alma, Que., Can., Apr. 10, 1927; s. Leonard and Marie-Ange (Tapin) R.; B.A., Laval U., Que., 1949, B.Th., 1953, L. es Scis., 1959. Ordained priest Roman Catholic Ch., 1953; prof. chemistry Coll. of Chicoutimi (Que.), 1953-67, rector, 1967-74; aux. bishop Roman Cath. Diocese Chicoutimi, 1974—; mem. social communications commn. Canadian Conf. Cath. Bishops, 1976—. Address: 602 Racine Est Chicoutimi PQ G7H 5C3 Canada

PEDOE, DANIEL, educator; b. London, Eng., Oct. 29, 1910; came to U.S., 1962, naturalized, 1972; B.Sc., U. London, 1930; B.A., Magdalene Coll., Cambridge, Eng., 1933, Ph.D., 1937; postgrad. Princeton U., 1935-36. Instr., Southampton U., Birmingham U. (Eng.), 1936-47; Leverhulme research fellow Cambridge (Eng.) U., 1947-48; reader U. London, 1948-52; prof. U. Khartoum, 1952-59; prof. U. Singapore, 1959-62; prof. Purdue U., 1962-64; prof. math. U. Minn., Mpls., 1964—. Recipient Lester R. Ford award for expository writing Math. Assn. Am., 1968. Mem. Am. Math. Assn. Author: Methods of Algebraic Geometry, 3 vols., 1947-53; Circles, 1957; Gentle Art of Mathematics, 1958; Projective Geometry, 1963; A Course in Geometry, 1970; Geometry and the Liberal Arts, 1976. Home: 1956 E River Terr Minneapolis MN 55414

PEDRICK, WILLARD HIRAM, lawyer, educator; b. Ottumwa, Iowa, Oct. 1, 1914; s. Willard Hiram and Rachel Lumsdon P.; B.A., Parsons Coll., 1936, LL.D., 1951; J.D., Northwestern U., 1939; m. Jo Ann Glotfelty, Jan. 5, 1973; children by previous marriage—Bill, Sara, Daniel, Margo. Law clk. U.S. Ct. Appeals, Washington, 1939-40; mem. law faculty U. Cin., 1940-41, U. Tex., 1941-42, Northwestern U., 1946-66; atty., tax div. U.S. Dept. Justice, 1942-43; mem. faculty Ariz. State U., Tempe, 1966—, prof. law, founding dean Coll. of Law, 1966-75; Fulbright prof., Australia, 1956, 73. Past chmn. Cook County (Ill.) Zoning Bd. Appeals. Served with USMC, 1944-46. Decorated Commendation Ribbon; recipient Alumni Service award Parsons Coll., Northwestern U. Mem. Am. Bar Assn., Ariz. Bar Assn., Am. Judicature Soc., Iowa Bar Assn., Am. Law Inst., Ariz. State U. Law Soc., Assn. Am. Law Schs., Am. Arbitration Assn., Cello Soc. Democrat. Methodist. Club: Rotary. Author: (with others) Torts, 1977; Death, Taxes and the Living, 1979; Federal Estate and Gift Taxation, ann. edits.; contbr. articles to legal jours. Home: 2814 Bala Dr Tempe AZ 85282 Office: Ariz State U Coll Law Tempe AZ 85281*

PEDROTTI, LENO STEPHANO, educator; b. Zeigler, Ill., May 21, 1927; s. Celeste Louis and Dolores (Galeaz) P.; B.S. in Edn., Ill. State U., 1949; M.S. in Physics, U. Ill., 1951; Ph.D., U. Cin., 1961; m. Wilma Jean Sullivan, June 23, 1951; children—Daro Stephano, Michael Louis, Sandra Maria, Laura Jean, Catherine Ann, Leno Matthew, Mary Ann, John Owen. Teaching asst. U. Ill., Urbana, 1949-51; with Air Force Inst. Tech., Wright-Patterson AFB, Ohio, 1951—, prof. physics, 1964—, head dept., 1965. Lectr., coordinator physics Honor Seminars Met. Dayton (Ohio), Inc., 1962—; sr. religion tchr., high sch. prin. Confrat. Christian Doctrine Sch. of Religion, New Carlisle, Ohio, 1964-76. Mem. indsl. adv. com., cons. tech. editor Tech. Edn. Research Centers Southwest, 1972—. NSF fellow, 1957-58. Recipient Outstanding Tchr. award, 1961-63, 68; Exceptional Civilian Service award Air Force Dept., 1967; Meritorious Civilian Service award USAF, 1974. Mem. Am. Phys. Soc. chmn. Ohio sect. 1975-76), Laser Inst. Am. (dir. 1974—), Am. Assn. Physics Tchrs., Am. Soc. Engring. Edn., Am. Nuclear Soc., Am. Assn. U. Profs., Am. Optical Soc., Sigma Xi, Tau Beta Pi, Sigma Pi Sigma. Contbr. articles to profl. jours. Home: 3805 Tomahawk Dr Medway OH 45341 Office: Physics Dept Air Force Inst Tech Wright-Patterson AFB OH 45433

PEEBLER, CHARLES DAVID, JR., advt. exec.; b. Waterloo, Iowa, June 8, 1934; s. Charles David and Marry E. (Barnett) P.; student Drake U., 1954-56; m. Susie Jacobs, June 5, 1958; children—David Jacobs, Mark Walter. Asst. to exec. v.p. J.L. Brandeis & Sons, Omaha, 1956-58; with Bozell & Jacobs, Inc., 1958—, v.p., mem. plans bd., 1960-65, pres. mid-continent ops., Omaha, 1965-67, pres., chief exec. officer, 1967—, chmn. bd., to 1980. Mem. Covered Wagon council Boy Scouts Am., 1962—; asso. chmn. Coll. Worlds Series, 1966; co-chmn. primary gifts div. Creighton U. New Goals Program, 1963; chmn. Omaha area Drake U. Bldg. Fund drive, 1960, 72. Bd. dirs. United Community Services Omaha, 1963—, drive chmn., 1966-67; bd. dirs. United Funds and Councils of Am., 1967, chmn. pub. relations adv. com., mem. exec. com., 1968; bd. dirs. Omaha Jr. Achievement, 1964—, treas., mem. exec. com., 1965-66, pres., 1972-74; bd. dirs. Omaha chpt. Nat. Conf. Christians and Jews, 1962-65, chmn. ann. dinner, 1963; trustee Creighton-Omaha Regional Health Care Corp., 1972-73; pres. trustees Brownell-Talbot Sch. Mem. Young Pres.'s Orgn. (internat. dir.), Omaha Advt. Club (bd. dirs. 1964—), Omaha C. of C. (chmn. edn. com. 1962-64, bd. dirs. 1965—), Omaha Indsl. Mgmt. Club (adv. bd. mgmt. 1960-62), Omaha Sales and Marketing Execs. (bd. dirs. 1962), Ad Sell League Omaha (pres. 1972, chmn. exec. bd.), Neb. Wildlife Fedn. (pres.). Clubs: Marco Polo (N.Y.C.); Bermuda Dunes Country (Palm Springs, Calif.); Omaha Press, Omaha Plaza, Highland Country (Omaha). Office: One Dag Hammarskjold Plaza New York City NY 10017*

PEEBLES, CARTER DAVID, lawyer; b. Chgo., July 9, 1934; s. Carter Davis and Vera Virginia (Howd) P.; A.B., DePauw U., 1956; M.A., U. Stockholm (Sweden), 1955; J.D., U. Chgo., 1959; m. Donna Ruth Hostetter, Aug. 3, 1957; children—John Carter, Mary Elizabeth, Sarah Anne. Admitted to Ind. bar, 1959; partner firm Peebles, Thompson, Rogers & Hamilton, Ft. Wayne, 1976—; faculty labor relations Purdue U. Regional Campus; U.S. commr., 1961-71; U.S. magistrate, 1971—; dir. Keystone Bldg. Products Corp. Bd. dirs. Antioch Found., Religious Instrn. Assn., Religious Heritage of Am. Mem. Am., 7th Fed. Circuit, Ill., Ind., Allen County bar assns., Phi Delta Phi. Clubs: Masons, Shriners, Jesters, Kiwanis. Author: Model Business Corporation Act, 3 vols., 1960; Indiana Bankruptcy Handbook, 2d edit., 1976; Business Practice Under the UCC, 1970; (with Daniel E. Johnson) Indiana Uniform Commercial Code, Forms and Comment, 2 vols., 1970; Indiana Legal Business Forms, 2 vols., 1967; contbr. to profl. jours. Home: 137 W Lexington St Fort Wayne IN 46807 Office: 201 Commerce Bldg 127 W Berry St Fort Wayne IN 46802. *As a young man, I was passionate, and later compassionate. Now, cynicism has me. Men used to do business on a handshake; now, a lengthy contract seems made only to be broken. People seem to seek the unfair advantage, forgetting that the only "good deal" is the deal fair to both sides. Fortunately, most people don't want something for nothing, will recognize a moral obligation and, many times, possess deep moral courage. If there is revolution in this country, it will not be black against white or have against have-not, but care against care-not. It appears that compassion wins after all.*

PEEBLES, DICK, newspaper editor; b. Oil City, Pa., July 4, 1918; s. Herbert Lester and Sarah (Hagen P.; student pub. schs.; m. Mary Theresa Holman, Nov. 7, 1949; children—Michael, Timothy. With Erie Dispatch-Herald, 1936-40, Sharon (Pa.) Herald, 1940-42, San Antonio Express, 1946-58; sports editor Houston Chronicle, 1958—. Served with U.S. Army, 1942-46. Mem. Baseball Writers Assn. Am., Football Writers Assn. Am., Golf Writers Assn. Am., Delta Sigma Chi. Roman Catholic. Home: 9103 McAvoy Dr Houston TX 77074 Office: 802 Texas Ave Houston TX 77002

PEEBLES, FRED NEAL, chem. engr., univ. dean; b. Paris, Tenn., Apr. 4, 1920; s. Fred Norman and Pollye (Paschall) P.; B.S. in Chem. Engring., U. Tenn., also M.S., Ph.D. in Chem. Engring.; m. Elenor Carter, Aug. 22, 1942; children—Fred Neal, Mary, Mark, Kate. Instr. chem. engring. U. Tenn., Knoxville, 1947-50, asst. prof., 1950-54, asso. prof., 1954-57, prof., 1960-63, head engring. mechanics dept., 1963-68, dean engring., 1968—; asst. sect. chief Oak Ridge Nat. Lab., 1957-60. Served with U.S. Army, 1945-46. Registered profl. engr. Recipient Distinguished Service Professorship award U. Tenn. Mem. Am. Inst. Chem. Engrs., Knoxville Tech. Soc. (past pres.), Sigma Xi, Phi Kappa Phi, Tau Beta Pi, Omicron Delta Kappa. Contbr. articles on hydrodynamics and chem. engring. to profl. jours. Home: 522 Broome Rd Knoxville TN 37919 Office: 124 Perkins Hall University of Tennessee Knoxville TN

PEEBLES, PHILLIP JAMES EDWIN, physicist, educator; b. Winnipeg, Man., Can., Apr. 25, 1935; s. Andrew Charles and Ada Marion (Green) P.; B.Sc., U. Man., 1958; M.A., Princeton, 1959, Ph.D., 1962; m. Jean Alison Peebles, Sept. 12, 1958; children—Lesley Catherine, Margaret Ellen, Marion Ruth. Prof. physics Princeton (N.J.) U., 1965—. Mem. Am. Phys. Soc., Am. Astron. Soc., AAAS, Am. Acad. Arts and Scis., Internat. Astron. Union. Author : Physical Cosmology, 1971; The Larger Scale Structure of the Universe, 1979. Home: 24 Markham Rd Princeton NJ 08540 Office: Joseph Henry Labs Physics Dept Princeton U Princeton NJ 08540

PEEK, MERL BICKNELL, oil products co. exec.; b. Tecumseh, Nebr., Apr. 2, 1914; s. Charles William and Effa Mae (Bicknell) P.; student U. Nebr., 1931-32; B.A., Nebr. State Coll., 1935; LL.B., Georgetown U., 1948; m. Carol Jean Wherry, Feb. 6, 1943; children—Jeffrey Merl, Elizabeth Susan, Emery Jean. High sch. tchr., Nebr., Iowa, Colo., 1935-41; adminstrv. asst. to U.S. Senator Wherry of Nebr., 1946-48; admitted to Nebr. bar, 1948, Ill. bar, 1956, Calif. bar, 1962; asst. exec. sec. Nat. Reclamation Assn., Washington, 1948-51; atty. Office Chief Counsel, IRS, Washington, 1951-52, St. Paul, 1952-55; atty. Universal Oil Products Co., Des Plaines, Ill., 1955—, asst. sec., 1964-66, sec., 1966-79; exec. dir. UOP Found., 1976—, chmn. polit. action com., 1978. Bd. dirs. Ill. div. Am. Cancer Soc., N.W. Suburban unit Ill. div. Am. Cancer Soc.; mem. N.W. Suburban exec. council Boy Scouts Am., Clearbrook Center Found., Suburban United Way, Oakton Community Coll. Ednl. Found.; elder First Presbyn. Ch. Served to lt. USNR, 1941-45. Mem. Nebr., Ill. bar assns., State Bar Calif., Farmhouse Frat., Phi Delta Phi. Home: 729 B Old Barn Rd Lake Barrington Shores Barrington IL 60010 Office: 10 UOP Plaza Des Plaines IL 60016

PEEL, BRUCE BRADEN, librarian; b. Ferland, Sask., Can., Nov. 11, 1916; s. William John and Alice Annie (Switzer) P.; student Normal Sch., Moose Jaw, 1936-37; B.A., U. Sask., 1944, M.A., 1946; B.L.S., U. Toronto, 1946; m. Margaret Christina Fullerton, July 28, 1950; children—Brian David, Alison Mary. Tchr. pub. sch., Sask.; Canadian librarian charge Adam Shortt Collection, U. Sask., 1946-51; chief cataloguer U. Alta. library, 1951-54, asst. chief librarian, 1954-55, acting chief, 1955-56, chief librarian, 1956—. Asso. com. on sci. information NRC of Can., 1961-68. Mem. team Canadian U. and Coll. Libraries Study, 1966-67. Mem. Canadian Assn. Coll. and U. Libraries (past pres.), Canadian (past pres.), Alta. (past pres.) library assns., Hist. Soc. Alta. (past sec.), Bibliog. Soc. Can. (past pres.). Author: (with Eric Knowles) The Saskatoon Story, 1882-1951, 1952; A Bibliography of the Prairie Provinces to 1953, enlarged edit., 1973; Steamboats on the Saskatchewan, 1972; Early Printing in the Red River Settlement, 1974; The Rossville Mission Press, 1974. Editor: Librarianship in Canada, 1946-67, 1968. Home: 11047 83d Ave Edmonton AB T6G 0T8 Canada

PEELE, ROGER, hosp. adminstr.; b. Elizabeth City, N.C., Dec. 24, 1930; s. Joseph Emmett and Catherine (Groves) P.; certificate in counseling U. Denver, 1952; A.B., U. N.C., 1955; M.D., U. Tenn., 1960; m. Diana Egan, June 15, 1963; children—Amy, Rodney, Holly. Intern, St. Elizabeths Hosp., Washington, 1960-61, resident in psychiatry, 1961-64, tng. officer, 1964-67, chief of service William A. White div., 1967-69, dir. Area D Community Mental Health Center, 1969-73, asst. supt., 1974-75, 77—, acting supt., 1975-77, chmn. dept. psychiatry, 1979—; psychotherapist Hillcrest Adult Clinic, Washington, 1963-65; clin. instr. psychiatry George Washington U., 1965-67, asst. clin. prof., 1967-71, asso. clin. prof., 1971-79, clin. prof., 1979—; mem. faculty Washington Sch. Psychiatry, 1970—; asst. dir. NIMH, 1978-79. Served with USAF, 1950-53. Recipient 1st prize Med. Soc. St. Elizabeth's Hosp., 1963, 2d prize, 1964; Superior Service award HEW, 1967, Superior Work Performance award, 1971. Fellow Am. Orthopsychiat. Assn., Am. Psychiat. Assn.; mem. AMA, D.C. Med. Soc., Washington, World psychiat. assns., Group for Advancement Psychiatry, Med. Soc. St. Elizabeth's Hosp., Nat. Capital Med. Found., Am. Acad. Psychiatry and the Law, D.C. Mental Health Assn., Prince George's County Mental Health Assn., Washington Soc. Adolescent Psychiatry, Am. Pub. Health Assn. Episcopalian. Contbr. articles on clin. and forensic and adminstrv. issues in Am. psychiatry to profl. jours. Home: 12919 Asbury Dr Fort Washington MD 20022 Office: Saint Elizabeths Hosp Room 201 Barton Hall Washington DC 20032

PEELE, TALMAGE LEE, physician; b. Goldsboro, N.C., Aug. 16, 1908; s. Ichabod and Nora (Spence) P.; A.B., Duke U., 1929; postgrad. Sch. Medicine, Vanderbilt U., 1929-31; M.D., Duke U., 1934. Intern Duke U. Hosp., 1934-35, resident in medicine, 1935-36; resident in neurology Bellevue Hosp., 1936-37; research fellow Johns Hopkins Hosp., 1937-38; asso. anatomy U. Rochester, 1938-39; practice medicine specializing in neurology, 1947—; faculty Duke U., Durham, N.C., 1939—, asso. prof. neurology, 1963-73, prof.

neurology, 1973—, asst. prof. pediatrics, 1958—, lectr. psychology, 1958—; vis. prof. neuroanatomy Northwestern U., 1945; lectr. neurology U. N.C., 1947-50; vis. asst. prof., 1955. Recipient Golden Apple award Duke U. Sch. Medicine Students and Alumni, 1965, Distinguished Tchr. award, 1975. Mem. AMA, Am. Acad. Neurology, Med. Soc. N.C., Cajal Club, Duke Med. Alumni Assn. (sec. 1947-67), Phi Beta Kappa, Alpha Omega Alpha. Methodist. Author: Neuroanatomic Basis for Clinical Neurology, 3d edit., 1977. Contbr. articles to profl. jours. Home: K-2-D University Apts Durham NC 27701 Office: Box 3811 Duke Hospital Durham NC 27710

PEELER, JOSEPH DAVID, lawyer; b. Nashville, Sept. 29, 1895; s. Joseph David and Virginia (McCue) P.; A.B., U. Ala., 1915; LL.B. cum laude, Harvard, 1920; m. Elizabeth F. Boggess, Apr. 27, 1927; children—Stuart Thorne, Joyce Woodson. Admitted to Ky. bar, 1920, Calif. bar, 1929; practiced law in Louisville, 1920-29, Los Angeles, 1929—; mem. firm Musick, Peeler & Garrett. Bd. fellows Claremont U. Center. Served as capt. A.C., U.S. Army World War I; lt. col. USAAF, World War II. Mem. U.S.A. teams Internat. Tuna Tournament, 1939, 47, 48, 55. Mem. Am., Calif. State, Los Angeles bar assns., Phi Beta Kappa, Delta Kappa Epsilon. Republican. Conglist. Clubs: California, Tuna (past pres.), Los Angeles (past pres.), Wilshire Country, Point Mugu Game Preserve. Home: 131 N June St Los Angeles CA 90004 Office: One Wilshire Building Los Angeles CA 90017

PEELER, STUART THORNE, lawyer, petroleum service co. exec.; b. Los Angeles, Oct. 28, 1929; s. Joseph David and Elizabeth Fiske (Boggess) P.; B.A., Stanford U., 1950, J.D., 1953; m. Lenore June Thorp, Mar. 31, 1973. Admitted to Calif. bar, 1953; partner firm Musick, Peeler & Garrett, Los Angeles, 1958-73; with Santa Fe Internat. Corp., Orange, Calif., 1973—, asso. gen. counsel, 1973-74, sr. v.p., gen. counsel, 1975—, also dir.; vice chmn. bd. Supron Energy Corp., Dallas; dir. Calif. Portland Cement Co., Soldier Creek Coal Co. Trustee, J. Paul Getty Museum, Malibu, Calif. Served with U.S. Army, 1953-55. Decorated Army Commendation medal. Mem. Am. Bar Assn., State Bar Calif., Am. Judicature Soc., AIME, Theta Chi, Phi Delta Phi. Republican. Congregationalist. Clubs: Calif. (Los Angeles); Les Ambassadeurs (London). Mem. U.S. Tuna Team, 1957-67, capt., 1966. Home: 7001 E Country Club Ln Anaheim Hills CA 92807 also 72302 Blueridge Ct Palm Desert CA 92260 Office: 505 S Main St Orange CA 92668

PEEPLES, WILLIAM DEWEY, JR., educator; b. Bessemer, Ala., Apr. 19, 1928; s. William Dewey and Thelma Jeannette (Chastain) P.; B.S., Samford U., 1948; M.S., U. Wis., 1949; Ph.D., U. Ga., 1951; m. Katie Ray Blackerby, Aug. 30, 1956; children—Mary Jeannette, William Dewey III, Gerald Lewis, Stephen Ray. Research mathematician Ballistics Research Lab., Aberdeen, Md., summer 1951; mem. faculty Samford U., 1951-56, Auburn U., 1956-59; prof. math. Samford U., 1959—, head dept., 1967—; cons. Hayes Internat. Corp. Served to 1st lt. AUS, 1954-56. Fellow A.A.A.S.; mem. Am. Math. Soc., Math. Assn. Am., Nat. Council Tchrs. Math., Ala. Coll. Tchrs. Math. (pres. 1969), Sigma Xi, Pi Mu Epsilon, Phi Kappa Phi (pres. 1977), Lambda Chi Alpha. Baptist (deacon). Mason (Shriner). Co-author: Modern Mathematics for Business Students, 1969; Finite Mathematics, 1974; Modern Mathematics with Applications to Business and the Social Sciences, 1975. Contbr. articles to profl. publs. Home: 419 Poinciana Dr Birmingham AL 35209

PEER, GEORGE JOSEPH, metals co. exec.; b. St. Louis, Aug. 26, 1925; s. George J. and Melba (Rahning) P.; B.S., Purdue U., 1945, M.S., 1948; postgrad. Advanced Mgmt. Program, Harvard, 1967; m. Mary Jane Hazlewood, Feb. 14, 1948; children—Linda, Gary, Steven, Scott. Operating supr. Republic Steel Corp., Canton, Ohio, 1948-54; various sales positions to v.p. sales Basic, Inc., Chgo., Cleve., 1954-63; v.p. marketing Handy & Harman, N.Y.C., 1963-71, dir., 1971-75, group v.p. precious metals, 1972-75; chmn., pres., chief exec. officer Multi-Metal Wire Cloth, Inc., 1975—; pres. Holyoke Wire Cloth Co., 1975—, Multi-Wedge Corp., 1976—; dir. Japan Handy Harman, Tokyo, 1972-75, Technicorp Internat. Inc., Metrodyne Corp.; chmn. bd. Lucas Milhaupt, Inc., Cudahy, Wis., 1967-75. Served with USNR, 1943-46, 51-53. Mem. Am. Mgmt. Assn., Nat. Indsl. Conf. Bd., Am. Inst. Mining and Metall. Engrs., Tau Beta Pi, Kappa Delta Rho. Republican. Conglist. Clubs: Mount Kisco Country, Cornell of N.Y. Home: Route 3 Kitchel Rd Mount Kisco NY 10549 Office: 501 Route 303 Tappan NY 10983

PEERCE, JAN, tenor; b. N.Y.C.; married; children—Larry, Joyce, Susan. Studied violin and played in orchs.; debut as tenor with NBC Symphony under Toscanini; appeared on Radio City Music Hall broadcasts; leading roles in Italian operas Met., San Francisco opera cos.; Broadway debut Fiddler on the Roof, 1971, summer tours, 1972—; summer tours Rothschilds, 1971-74; concertizes extensively in U.S., Can., Europe, Mexico, C.Am., Australia, S.Am., Israel, Eng., Austria, Germany, under auspices Dept. State on tour in Russia; voted favorite male singer in poll of critics; participated Osaka (Japan) Festival; concert tour Alaska, S. Africa, Australia; recitals, soloist with Philharmonic orchs. in Sweden, Norway, West Germany, Holland, Israel, 1972; starred in 4 motion pictures; operatic debut Vienna Opera, State Opera Munich, 1970; European and Israel festivals of opera and concerts, 1968; recs. for RCA Victor, Westminster, Vanguard, United Artists; appears on TV shows Johnny Carson, Merv Griffin, Mike Douglas, spl. shows over all networks. Biography: Bluebird of Happiness, 1976. Address: care Phil Schapiro 157 W 57th St New York NY 10019

PEERMAN, DEAN GORDON, magazine editor; b. Mattoon, Ill., Apr. 25, 1931; s. Staley Jacob and Irene (Monen) P.; B.S. with highest distinction, Northwestern U., 1953; postgrad. Cornell U., 1953-54; B.D., Yale, 1959; D.D., Kalamazoo Coll., 1967. With Christian Century Found., 1959—, copy editor Christian Century mag., 1959-61, asso. editor, 1961-64, mng. editor, 1964—. Mem. Am. Civil Liberties Union, N.A.A.C.P., Fellowship of Reconciliation, Phi Beta Kappa. Democrat. Baptist. Author: (with M.E. Marty) Pen-ultimates, 1963. Editor: Frontline Theology, 1967; co-editor (with Marty) New Theology 1-10, 1964-73, A Handbook of Christian Theologians, 1965; (with Alan Geyer) Theological Crossings, 1971. Contbr.: Chile: Under Military Rule, 1974. Home: 1407 W Elmdale Ave Chicago IL 60660 Office: 407 S Dearborn St Chicago IL 60605

PEERS, MICHAEL GEOFFREY, bishop; b. Vancouver, B.C., Can., July 31, 1934; s. Geoffrey Hugh and Dorothy Enid (Mantle) P.; B.A., U. B.C., Vancouver, 1956; L.Th., Trinity Coll., Toronto, Ont., 1959, D.D. (hon.), 1978; m. Dorothy Elizabeth Bradley, June 29, 1963; children—Valerie Anne Leslie, Richard Christopher Andre, Geoffrey Stephen Arthur. Ordained to ministry Anglican Ch.; asst. curate St. Thomas Ch., Ottawa, 1959-61; chaplain U. Ottawa, 1961-66; rector St. Bede's Ch., Winnipeg, 1966-72, St. Martin's Ch., Winnipeg, 1972-74; dean of Qu'Appelle, Regina, Sask., 1974-77, bishop, 1977—; instr. Ottawa Tchrs. Coll., 1962-66, St. Paul's High Sch., Winnipeg, 1967-69. Office: 1501 College Ave Regina SK S4P 1B8 Canada

PEERY, ALLISON BOYD, architect; b. Calhoun City, Miss., May 12, 1924; s. Monroe Allison and Anne Gladys (Boyd) P.; B.Arch., Tex. A. and M. U., 1948; m. Billie Geraldine Bryant, June 2, 1946; children—Lyn Allyson, Ashton Bryant, Evan Boyd Alexander; m. 2d, Marilyn Johnson Steinert, Apr. 2, 1958. Pvt. practice architecture, San Antonio, 1948-66; dir. site devel., design and architecture Hemisfair, 1968; dir. design and engring. Ray Ellison Devels., San Antonio, 1968-72; pres. Trident Properties, Inc., 1972—; pvt. practice architecture, planning, 1972—. Guest lectr. Tex. U., Tex. A. and M. U., Rice U., Yale, U. Okla., Cal. Poly. Inst. Served with AUS, 1943-46. Mem. A.I.A., Tex. Soc. Architects, Tau Beta Pi. Prin. works include Mulberry Terrace Apts. (Honor award), Regency House Apts. (Honor award), San Antonio River Devel. (Honor award), Hemisfair '68 (Honor award). Home: 216 Acacia St San Antonio TX 78209

PEERY, THOMAS MARTIN, pathologist; b. Lynchburg, Va., Aug. 24, 1909; s. John Carnahan and Alean Emma (Martin) P.; B.A., Newberry Coll., 1928, D.M.S. (hon.), 1966; M.D., Med. Coll. of S.C., 1932; m. Eleanor Bishop, Oct. 9, 1936; children—Eleanor Peery Russell, Sue Peery Moore, Linda Peery Markin. Intern, Met. Hosp., N.Y.C., 1932-33, resident physician, 1933-34; asst. pathologist Roper Hosp., 1934-38; faculty pathology George Washington U., 1938—, prof., 1950-74, chmn. dept., 1954-74, prof. emeritus, 1974—, dir. postgrad. instrn., 1945-56; chief dept. pathology U. Hosps., 1947-74; pathologist Alexandria Hosp., 1941-47. Dir. Technicon Corp., Tarrytown, N.Y., 1963—. Mem. Bd. Health Alexandria, Va., 1944-46. Diplomate Nat. Bd. Med. Examiners, Am. Bd. Pathology. Mem. Am. Assn. Pathologists and Bacteriologists, Coll. Am. Pathologists (chmn. com. internat. exchange pathologists 1958-60, advisor to com. on anatomic pathology 1976—), A.M.A. (chmn. sect. pathology and physiology 1959, exec. com. 1958-63, chmn. exhibit lab. 1961-64), Am. Soc. Clin. Pathologists (exec. com. 1955-58, bd. schs. med. tech. 1958-61, pres. 1968-69, award for outstanding investigation 1958, award for exhibit lab. 1964, Ward-Burdick award for meritorious contbns. to clin. pathology 1974, chmn. archives com. 1976— mem. Pan Am. com. 1977—), Internat. Acad. Pathology, Am. Heart Assn., Soc. Exptl. Biology and Medicine, AAAS, Wash. Acad. Medicine, Washington Soc. Pathologists (pres. 1940-41), Sigma Xi, Alpha Omega Alpha. Clubs: Cosmos, Belle Haven Country. Sr. author: Pathology, 2d edit., 1971; Design for Med. Education, 1965. Editorial bd. Med. Annals of D.C., Pathologist, 1977—. Contbr. articles to profl. jours. Pathology cons. Random House Dictionary of English Language, 1964—. Home: 2115 Belle Haven Rd Alexandria VA 22307

PEET, JOHN CARLISLE, JR., corp. service co. exec.; b. N.Y.C., Dec. 14, 1928; s. John Carlisle and Alys Lenore (Sweeley) P.; grad. The Taft Sch., 1946; B.A., Yale, 1950; LL.B., U. Va., 1954; m. Jane Lauderman, May 26, 1951; children—John Carlisle III, Jeffrey V., Leslie A., Donald N., Sarah J. Admitted to N.Y. bar, 1954, Pa. bar, 1956; asso. White & Case, N.Y.C., 1954-56; asso. Morgan, Lewis & Bockius, Phila., 1956-63, partner, 1964-67; partner Ringe, Peet & Mason, Phila., 1967-69; v.p., gen. counsel RLC Corp., Wilmington, Del., 1969—; lectr. Temple U. Law Sch., Am. Trucking Assn., Nat. Tank Truck Assn., Am. Arbitration Assn.; dir. Philanthropic Mut. Life Ins. Co., Jarube, Inc. Served with CIC, U.S. Army, 1950-51. Mem. Am., Pa., Phila., N.Y. bar assns., Raven Soc., Order of Coif, Omicron Delta Kappa. Presbyn. Exec. editor Va. Law Rev., 1953-54. Home: 801 Brintons Bridge Rd West Chester PA 19380 Office: 1 Rollins Plaza Wilmington DE 19088

PEET, RICHARD CLAYTON, lawyer, cons.; b. N.Y.C., Aug. 24, 1928; s. Charles Francis and Florence L. (Isaacs) P.; J.D., Tulane U., 1953; m. Barbara Jean McClure, Mar. 17, 1956; children—Victoria Clementine, Alexandra Constance, Elizabeth Erica, Clarissa Barbara. Admitted to La. bar, 1955, also D.C. bar; law clk. firm Melvin M. Belli, San Francisco, 1954; with The Calif. Co., Standard Oil of Calif., 1955; atty. appellate sect. Lands div. Dept. Justice, Washington, 1956; asst. to dep. gen. counsel Dept. Commerce, 1957; with Republican policy com. U.S. Senate, 1958, office minority leader William F. Knowland, 1958; asso. counsel anti-trust subcom. House Judiciary Com., 1959-62; asso. minority counsel House Pub. Works Com., 1969-74; pres. Citizens for Hwy. Safety, 1974—; practiced in Washington, 1962-68; prin. Richard Clayton Peet & Assos., 1972—; partner Anderson, Pendleton, McMahon, Peet & Donovan, 1977—; pres., dir. Lincoln Research Center, 1965-72. Chmn. bd. Workshop Library on World Humor. Served with U.S. Army, 1946-47. Mem. Am. Bar Assn., Phi Delta Phi, Pi Kappa Alpha. Clubs: Cosmos, Tulane Alumni of Washington. Author: Goals for a Constructive Opposition, 1966; composer song: Stand Up For America, 1971 (George Washington medal Freedom's Found. 1971). Home: 8719 Woodside Ct McLean VA 22102 Office: 1000 16th St NW Suite 701 Washington DC 20036

PEETZ, JOHN EDWARD, museum adminstr.; b. McMinnville, Oreg., July 29, 1926; s. Judge Edward and Treva Claudine (Kenyon) P.; B.B.A., Armstrong Coll. Bus., 1950, postgrad. in bus. adminstrn.; m. Elizabeth McClung, Dec. 23, 1977; children—Mark Edward, Blair Evan, Paige Erin. Adminstrv. asst. Pacific Intermountain Express, Oakland, Calif., 1955-60; park ops. coordinator City of Oakland, 1960-65, dir. parks, 1965-70; dir. mus. services Oakland Mus., 1970—; lectr. cons. in field to mus.'s, colls., univs. Served with USMC, 1944-47, 50-51; PTO. Mem. Am. Assn. Mus.'s, Internat. Council Mus.'s, Western Assn. Art Mus.'s, Nat. Recreation and Park Assn., Calif. Park and Recreation Soc. Episcopalian. Club: Athenian-Nile. Office: 1000 Oak St Oakland CA 94607

PEEVER, ARTHUR JAY, food products co. exec.; b. Toledo, Jan. 23, 1933; s. Raymond A. and Doris (Goodremont) P.; B.S. with honors in Accounting, Cal. State U., Los Angeles, 1958; m. Barbara M. Davis, Jan. 2, 1953; children—Gary, Alan, Linda. Mgr. Haskins & Sells, Los Angeles, 1958-68; controller Coca-Cola Bottling Co., Los Angeles, 1968-72, v.p., treas., controller, 1972-75, sr. v.p. fin., 1975—. Served with USAF, 1950-54. C.P.A., Calif. Mem. Am. Inst. C.P.A.'s, Financial Execs. Inst. (dir. Los Angeles chpt.), Calif. Soc. C.P.A.s, World Affairs Council. Clubs: Jonathan, Town Hall (Los Angeles). Home: 327 S Reese Place Burbank CA 91506 Office: 1334 S Central Ave Los Angeles CA 90021

PEFLEY, RICHARD KRAMER, educator; b. Sacramento, June 17, 1921; s. Harold A. and Nellie (Warfel) P.; B.A., Stanford, 1944, M.S., 1951, M.E., 1960; m. Nel Annette Wentworth, May 24, 1947; children—Barbara A., William R., Steven W. Product engr. Pacific Mfg. Co., Cleve., 1945-47; research engr. Babcock & Wilcox Co., Alliance, Ohio, 1947-49; prof., head dept. mech. engring. U. Santa Clara, Calif., 1951—. Cons., Open U., Eng., 1974. Chmn. Civil Service Commn., Santa Clara, 1952-61. Served with USAAF, 1943-45. Fellow Am. Soc. M.E. (sect. chmn.); mem. Am. Soc. Engring. Edn., Am. Soc. Heating, Refrigerating and Air Conditioning Engrs., Sigma Xi, Tau Beta Pi. Author: (with R.I. Murray) Thermofluid Mechanics, 1966; (with D.G. Newnan) Mechanical Engineering License Review, 1974. Home: 2169 Bohannon Dr Santa Clara CA 95050

PEGIS, ANTON GEORGE, educator; b. Milw., Feb. 21, 1920; s. George Anton and Eugenia (Stathas) P.; A.B., Western State Coll. Colo., 1949; M.A., Denver U., 1951, Ph.D., 1956; m. Harriet Louise Stevens, June 1, 1949; children—Stefani Elizabeth, Penelope Eugenia. Jr. engr. N. Shore Gas Co., Waukegan, Ill., 1946-47; instr. Ft. Lewis Coll., 1952-53; process control technician Gates Rubber Co., Denver, 1953-54; prof. English, Colo. Sch. Mines, Golden, 1954—, asst. to pres., 1964-68, v.p. for devel., 1968-73, v.p. for external affairs, 1973-74, prof. English, 1975—. Cons. U.S. Bur. Mines, Office of Mineral Reports, Washington, Regional Tng. Center, CSC, San Francisco, 1974—. Chmn., United Way Fund; sec. Colo. Sch. Mines Found.; pres. Roland Valley Civic Assn., 1974-75. Served with AUS, 1940-46. Recipient Outstanding Prof. award Colo. Sch. Mines, 1976; Amoco Found. awards. Mem. Golden C. of C. (pres. 1968—), Am. Soc. Engring. Edn. (chmn. Rocky Mountain sect.), Am. Alumni Council (chmn. dist. VII 1971-72), Modern Lang. Assn., Blue Key, Theta Chi, Alpha Psi Omega. Republican. Presbyn. (elder). Author: Social Theory in the Novels of Ford Madox Ford, 1956; An Intensive Course in English for Foreign Engineering Students, 1957; Humanism and the Practical Order, 1964; Excellence and the Odyssean Philosophy, 1965; Platonism in the Renaissance Lyric, 1965; Education for Leadership, 1966; Totality in Engineering Education, 1968; Course Recommendations for the Resource Engineer, 1968; Encroachment of Competing Land Uses on Mineral Development, 1976. Home: 415 Scenic Ct Golden CO 80401

PEHLKE, ROBERT DONALD, educator; b. Ferndale, Mich., Feb. 11, 1933; s. Robert William and Florence Jenny (McLaren) P.; B.S. in Engring., U. Mich., 1955; S.M., Mass. Inst. Tech., 1958, Sc.D., 1960; postgrad. Tech. Inst., Aachen, Ger., 1956-57; m. Julie Anne Kehoe, June 2, 1956; children—Robert Donald, Elizabeth Anne, David Richard. Mem. faculty U. Mich., 1960—, prof. materials and metall. engring., 1968—, chmn. dept., 1973—; cons. to metall. industries. Pres., Ann Arbor Amateur Hockey Assn., 1977-79. NSF fellow, 1955-56; Fulbright fellow, 1956-57; registered profl. engr., Mich. Fellow Am. Soc. Metals (sec. metals acad. com. 1977); mem. Am. Inst. Metall. Engrs. (Gold medal sci. award extractive metallurgy div. 1976, Howe Meml. lectr. 1980), Iron and Steel Socs. of AIME (chmn. process tech. div. 1976-77, dir. 1976-79), Ger., London, Japan socs. iron and steel, Am. Foundrymen's Soc., Am. Soc. Engring. Edn., N.Y. Acad. Sci., Nat. Soc. Profl. Engrs., Sigma Xi, Tau Beta Pi, Alpha Sigma Mu (pres. 1977-78). Author: Unit Processes of Extractive Metallurgy, 1973. Editor, contbr. numerous articles to profl. jours. Home: 9 Regent Dr Ann Arbor MI 48104 Office: 2026 E Engring Bldg Univ Mich Ann Arbor MI 48109

PEI, IEOH MING, architect; b. Canton, China, Apr. 26, 1917; s. Tsu Yee Pei and Lien Kwun Chwong; B.Arch., Mass. Inst. Tech., 1940; M.Arch., Harvard 1946; D.F.A., U. Pa., 1970; LL.D., Chinese U., Hong Kong, 1970; m. Eileen Loo, June 20, 1942; children—T'ing Chung, Chien Chung, Li Chung, Liane. Came to U.S., 1935, naturalized, 1954. Practice architecture, Boston, N.Y.C., Los Angeles, 1939-42; asst. prof. Harvard Grad. Sch. Design, 1945-48; dir. archtl. div. Webb & Knapp, Inc., 1948-55; with I.M. Pei & Partners (formerly I.M. Pei & Assos.), N.Y.C., 1955—; prin. projects include: Mile High Center, Denver, Nat. Center Atmospheric Research, Boulder, Colo., Dallas Municipal Center, John Fitzgerald Kennedy Library, Cambridge, Mass., Canadian Imperial Bank of Commerce Complex, Toronto, Overseas-Chinese Banking Corp. Hdqrs. Bldg., Singapore, Grave for Robert F. Kennedy, Arlington Nat. Cemetery, Dreyfus Chemistry Bldg. at Mass. Inst. Tech., East-West Center U. Hawaii, Honolulu, Mellon Art Center, Choate Sch., Wallingford, Conn., Univ. Plaza, N.Y. U., Nat. Airlines Terminal John Fitzgerald Kennedy Internat. Airport, N.Y.C., Johnson Mus. Art at Cornell U., Ithaca, N.Y., Washington Sq. East, Phila., Everson Mus. Art, Syracuse, N.Y., Nat. Gallery Art, East Bldg., Washington, Wilmington Tower, East Campus, New Coll., Sarasota, Fla., Raffles Internat. Center, Singapore, master plan Columbia U., Bedford Stuyvesant Super Block, Bklyn., Society Hill, Phila., Mus. Fine Arts, Boston, others; planning projects: S.W. Washington Redevel. Plan, Erieview Redevel. Plan, Cleve., Govt. Center Redevel. Plan, Boston, Oklahoma City Downtown Redevel. Plan, N.Y. Conv. and Exhbn. Center. Mem. Nat. Def. Research Com., Princeton, N.J., 1943-45, Nat. Council Humanities 1966-70. Recipient Alpha Rho Psi medal Mass. Inst. Tech., A.I.A. medal, Mass. Inst. Tech. traveling fellowship, 1940; Wheelwright fellow Harvard, 1951. Fellow A.I.A. (Medal of Honor N.Y. chpt. 1963, nat. Gold Medal); hon. fellow A.I.D.; mem. Nat. Inst. Arts and Letters (Arnold Brunner award 1961), Am. Acad. Arts and Scis., Am. Acad. and Inst. Arts and Letters (chancellor), N.A.D., Urban Design Council. Office: 600 Madison Ave New York NY 10022*

PEI, MING L., educator; Peking, China, Apr. 17, 1923; s. I. Hsiang and Chao H. (Wu) P.; came to U.S., 1944; B.S., Oreg. State U., 1945; M.S., Cornell U., 1946, Ph.D., 1948; m. Yen Fen Kiang, Sept. 2, 1951; children—Victor C., Daniel C. Asst. prof. civil engring. Nat. Central U., Nanking, China, 1948-49; mem. faculty City Coll. City U. N.Y., 1950—, prof. civil engring., 1963—, chmn. dept., 1965-68, chief Computation Center, 1963-71, chmn. dept. computer sci., 1968-71; cons. to govt. and industry, 1951—. Mem. Am. Soc. C.E., Am. Inst. Aero. and Astronautics, Assn. Computing Machinery. Home: 104 River Edge Rd Bergenfield NJ 07621 Office: City Coll City U NY New York City NY 10031

PEIRCE, BROOKE, educator; b. Washington, Jan. 2, 1922; s. Charles Brooke, Jr and Nancy Ley (Bass) P.; B.A., U.Va., 1943; M.A., Harvard U., 1947, Ph.D., 1954; m. Carol Emily Marshall, July 12, 1952. Teaching fellow Harvard U., 1948-51; instr. English, U. Va., 1951-54; mem. faculty Goucher Coll., 1954—, prof. English, 1966—, chmn. dept. English and dramatic arts, 1964-69, 72-75, chmn. faculty humanities, 1964-66, 72-73. Treas., Edgar Allan Poe Soc., Balt., 1959-66, mem. bd., 1959—. Served with U.S. Army, 1943-45. Nat. Endowment for Humanities fellow, 1977-78. Mem. Modern Lang. Assn., Renaissance Soc., Classical Assn., Phi Beta Kappa. Democrat. Home: 705 Warren Rd Cockeysville MD 21030 Office: Goucher Coll Towson MD 21204

PEIRCE, GEORGE L., airport adminstr.; b. Worcester, Mass., Mar. 9, 1933; s. George Leighton and Grace Hislop (McDougall) P.; B.B.A., U. Mass., 1961; m. Carolyn Janasy, Oct. 7, 1968; children—Jennifer Lindsy, Amanda Leighton. Supr. mgmt. engring. services Port Authority of N.Y. and N.J., 1961-69; airport mgr. Stewart Airport, Newburgh, N.Y., 1970; asst. mgr. LaGuardia Airport, Flushing, N.Y., 1970-75, mgr., 1975—. Vice chmn. Queens adv. bd. Salvation Army. Served with USAF, 1954-58. Recipient Outstanding Community Service award Greater N.Y. Council Boy Scouts Am., 1978. Mem. Queens C. of C. (mem. aviation com.), Acad. Aero. (mem. adv. bd.). Club: LaGuardia Kiwanis (dir.). Home: 392 Brett Rd Fairfield CT 06430 Office: LaGuardia Airport Flushing NY 11371

PEIRCE, JAMES LORING, former mfg. co. exec.; b. Valparaiso, Ind., Sept. 13, 1907; s. Loring Hampton and Rose (Drago) P.; grad. Northwestern U., 1930; m. Marion Low Field, Feb. 12, 1938; children—Nancy (Mrs. Loren E. Pickering, Jr.), Loring. With A.B. Dick Co., Chgo., 1934-79, v.p., 1951-72, dir., 1966-79, vice chmn., 1972-79. Named to Acctg. Hall of Fame, Ohio State U., 1965. Mem. Financial Execs. Inst. (pres. 1957, trustee research found. 1956-62), Alpha Kappa Psi. Clubs: Union League (Chgo.); Westmoreland Country; Mich. Shores. Home: 3114 Harrison St Evanston IL 60201

PEIRCE, JOHN WENTWORTH, architect; b. Boston, Feb. 9, 1912; s. Thomas W. and Gabrielle (Dexter) P.; A.B. cum laude, Harvard, 1933, postgrad., Archtl. Sch., 1933-35; M.Arch., Mass. Inst. Tech., 1947; m. Grace Minot, June 27, 1934; children—Thomas W., Lucy (Mrs. David Scanlon III), John W. Individual practice architecture,

Boston, 1938-42, 75—; asso. Shepley, Bulfinch, Richardson & Abbott, Boston, 1948-60; partner Peirce & Peirce, Boston, 1960-71, Peirce Peirce & Kramer, 1971-75. Mem. Mass. Bd. Registration for Architects, 1954-59, chmn., 1957; chmn. Topsfield Conservation Commn., 1965-71; commr. Ipswich River Watershed Dist., 1968—, chmn., 1976—; bd. dirs. Ipswich River Watershed Assn., 1976—; trustee Essex County Greenbelt Assn., 1961-71, pres., 1966-77, dir., 1977—; trustee Trustees Pub. Reservations, 1966—, dir., 1976—, recipient Ann. Conservation award, 1975; bd. dirs. Plymouth County Wildlands Trust, 1973-79. Served to lt. comdr. USNR, 1942-46. Recipient Open Space award Mass. Conservation Council, 1977. Fellow AIA; mem. Mass. Assn. Architects (pres. 1968), Boston Soc. Architects (v.p. 1968, pres. 1969). Clubs: Bournès Cove Yacht (commodore 1966-68) (Wareham, Mass.); St. Botolph (Boston). Prin. archtl. works include Shields Warren Radiation Lab., N.E. Deaconess Hosp., Boston, Trinity Episcopal Ch., Topsfield, Mass., Loeb Marine Lab., Woods Hole, Mass., Art/Music Bldg., St. Mark's Sch., Southboro, Mass. Home: Witch Hill 9 Garden St Topsfield MA 01983 Office: 116 Newbury St Boston MA 02116

PEIRCE, NEAL R., journalist; b. Phila., Jan. 5, 1932; s. J. Trevor and Miriam deS. (Litchfield) P.; B.A., Princeton, 1954; postgrad. Harvard, 1957-58; m. Barbara von dem Bach-Zelewski, Apr. 18, 1959; children—Celia, Andrea, Trevor. Legis. asst. Office of U.S. Rep. Silvio Conte of Mass., 1959; polit. editor Congl. Quar., 1960-69; contbg. editor Nat. Jour., Washington, 1969—; cons. and commentator elections CBS News, 1962, 67-76, NBC News, 1964-66; lectr.; syndicated newspaper columnist Washington Post Writers Group; research fellow Urban Land Inst.; dir. Peirce-Phelps, Inc., Phila. Founder, chmn. S.W. Neighborhood Assembly and Community Council, Washington, 1963-65; mem. council Nat. Municipal League, 1975—. Trustee, South Kent (Conn.) Sch., 1968-71, Thomas Jefferson U., 1979—, Legis 50/The Center for Legis. Improvement; mem. adv. com. state and local govt. affairs Kennedy Sch. Govt., Harvard U., 1979—. Served with CIC, AUS, 1954-57. Fellow Woodrow Wilson Internat. Center Scholars, 1971-74. Mem. Nat. Acad. Pub. Adminstrn., Phi Beta Kappa. Episcopalian. Clubs: Federal City (Washington); Princeton (N.Y.C.). Author: The People's President, 1968; The Megastates of America, 1972; The Pacific States of America, 1972; The Mountain States of America, 1972; The Great Plains States America, 1973; The Deep South States of America, 1974; The Border South States, 1975; The New England States, 1976; The Mid-Atlantic States of America, 1977. Home: 610 G St SW Washington DC 20024 Office: Nat Jour 1730 M St NW Washington DC 20036

PEIRSON, WALTER R., oil co. exec.; b. 1926; grad. U. Ill. With Standard Oil Co. (Ind.), 1955-61, Gen. Gas Corp., 1961-64, Tuloma Gas Products Co., Inc., 1964-68; v.p. mktg. Am. Oil Co., Chgo., 1968-71, exec. v.p. mktg., refining, transp. and supply, 1971-74; pres. Amoco Oil Co., 1974-78; exec. v.p. Standard Oil Co. (Ind.), 1978—, also dir. Office: 200 E Randolph Dr Chicago IL 60601

PEISER, DONALD EDWARD, bus. exec.; b. Bklyn., May 6, 1919; s. Milton Alfred and Frances Jeannette (Zinman) P.; B.A., Bklyn. Coll., 1940; M.A., Columbia U., 1941; M.B.A., N.Y. U., 1948; m. 2d, Edith Sutker, Dec. 3, 1967; children by previous marriage—Robert Alan, Marlene Hope Peiser Saltzberg. Security analyst Merrill Lynch Pierce Fenner & Beane, N.Y.C., 1946-49; v.p. Central Nat. Corp., investments, N.Y.C., 1950-60; parner Andresen & Co., mems. N.Y. Stock Exchange, N.Y.C., 1961-63; investment exec. S.H. Scheuer Co., N.Y.C., 1964—; chmn. bd. Southdown, Inc., oil, gas and cement, Houston, 1976—, CLC of Am., barge transp., auto rental and leasing, Houston, 1978—; dir. Pelto Oil Co., Southwestern Portland Cement Co., Wis. Barge Co., Consol. Leasing Corp., Morgan Drive-Away, Contractors Machinery Co., Am. Dredging Co. Trustee Bklyn. Coll. Found. Served with C.E., AUS, 1941-46. Mem. N.Y. Soc. Security Analysts. Jewish. Clubs: Muttontown (N.Y.); Downtown Athletic (N.Y.C.). Office: 2 Allen Center Houston TX 77002 also 61 Broadway New York NY 10006

PEJOVIC, ILIJA, hosp. supt.; b. Podgorica, Yugoslavia, 1919; s. Kosta and Zorka (Kazic) P.; M.D., U. Belgrade, 1944; m. Grace Ann Day, 1962; children—Vesna Bliss, Michele Lorraine. Came to U.S., 1953, naturalized, 1959. Intern Main Mil. Hosp., Belgrade, 1944-48; scholar cardiology, Paris, 1952-53; resident internal medicine, Atlanta and Houston, 1953-56; asst. med. dir. Tb Hosp., Decatur, Ala., 1957-58; mem. staff W. T. Edwards Tb Hosp., Tampa, Fla., 1958—, med. supt., 1966—. Served with Yugoslavian Navy, 1948-52. Mem. Am., So., Fla. med. assns., Am., Fla. thoracic socs., Gulf Coast Tb and Respiratory Disease Assn. Author papers. Address: AG Holley State Hospital PO Box 3084 Lantana FL 33462

PEKOW, EUGENE, hotel co. exec.; b. Chgo., Aug. 11, 1930; s. Philip M. and Celia (Katz) P.; A.B. cum laude, Brown U., 1952; J.D., Northwestern U., 1955; m. Esta Bete Epstein, June 29, 1952; children—Charles Thomas Wayne, Penelope Susan, Cynthia Ann. Admitted to Ill. bar, 1955; partner Acorn Tire & Supply Co., Chgo., 1955-65, sec.-treas., dir. Acorn Tire & Supply Co. and subsidiaries, 1965—; v.p. Exec. House Hotels, Chgo., 1957-68; pres. Midland Hotel Co., Chgo., 1969—; pres. Acorn Mgmt. Co., 1974—; pres., dir. Midland Bldg. Corp., Chgo.; dir. Executive House, Inc., Asso. Tire & Battery Co., Oak Park, Ill. Mem. nat. council Bus. Execs. Move for Vietnam Peace. Bd. dirs. Deerfield Twp. Voters Assn., 1964-68; treas., bd. dirs. Bus. and Profl. People for Pub. Interest; bd. dirs. U. Chgo. Found. for Emotionally Disturbed Children; chmn. bd. dirs. Sears Roebuck YMCA. Mem. Am. Technion Soc. (dir.). Clubs: Birchwood (dir. 1973-75) (Highland Park, Ill.); Standard (Chgo.). Office: 176 W Adams St Chicago IL 60603

PEKRUHN, JOHN EDWARD, architect, educator; b. Steubenville, Ohio, May 19, 1915; s. William Frederick and Grace (Phillipson) P.; B.Arch., Carnegie Mellon U., 1938; postgrad. Harvard, 1940; m. Nancy Ingram McMahon, Aug. 1, 1942; children—Susan (Mrs. Earl Glotfelty), John Phillipson. Draftsman, Walk Jones, Memphis, 1940; designer-draftsman Shreve, Anderson & Walker, Charlestown, Ind., 1941-42, Giffels & Vallet, Texarkana, Tex., 1942-43; research group jet turbine Westinghouse Electric Corp., South Philadelphia, 1944-45; designer William Lescaze, N.Y.C., 1946; designer, head architecture Norman Bel Geddes & Co., N.Y.C., 1947; architect John Pekruhn, Pitts., 1947-67, John Pekruhn & Assos., Pitts., 1967-75. Prof., Carnegie Mellon U., Pitts., 1947—. Mem. Pitts. City Planning Commn., 1965-70. Fellow AIA. Episcopalian. Home: Colerain Spruce Creek PA 16683 Office: Carnegie Mellon U Pittsburgh PA 15213

PELADEAU, MARIUS BEAUDOIN, museum exec.; b. Boston, Jan. 27, 1935; s. Marius and Lucienne (Beaudoin) P.; B.A. cum laude, St. Michael's Coll., 1956; M.S., Boston U., 1957; M.A., Georgetown U., 1962; m. Mildred L. Cole, Feb. 26, 1972. Asso. editor Public Utilities Fortnightly, Washington, 1962-66; adminstrv. asst., press sec. to U.S. Congressman J. P. Vigorito, Washington, 1967-72; dir. Maine League Hist. Socs. and Mus.'s, Monmouth, 1972-76; dir. William A. Farnsworth Library and Art Mus., Rockland, Maine, 1976—; cons. in field. Fellow Co. Mil. Historians; mem. Am. Assn. Mus.'s, Vt. Hist. Soc. Democrat. Roman Catholic. Club: Rotary. Author: The Verse of Royall Tyler, 1968; The Prose of Royall Tyler, 1972; Chansonetta: The Life and Photographs of Chansonetta Stanley Emmons, 1858-1937, 1977. Home: Four Rod Rd Warren ME 04864 Office: PO Box 466 Rockland ME 04841

PELCZAR, MICHAEL JOSEPH, JR., educator, microbiologist; b. Balt., Jan. 28, 1916; s. Michael Joseph and Josephine (Polek) P.; B.S., U. Md., 1936, M.S., 1938; Ph.D., U. Iowa, 1941; m. Merna M. Foss, Aug. 28, 1941; children—Ann Foss, Patricia Mary, Michael Rafferty, Rita Margaret, Josephine Merna, Julia Foss. Instr. bacteriology State U. Iowa, 1940-41; asst. prof., asso. prof. bacteriology U. Md., College Park, 1946-50, prof. microbiology, 1950—, v.p. grad. studies and research, 1966-78; pres. Council Grad. Schs. in U.S., Washington, 1978—; mem. microbiology adv. panel Office Naval Research, 1965-70; spl. cons. Random House Dictionary of English Lang., 1965; councilor Oak Ridge Asso. Univs., Inc., 1959-66, also bd. dirs.; mem. So. Regional Edn. Bd., Council Grad. Edn. in Agrl. Scis., 1967; mem. departmental com. on biol. scis. U.S. Dept. Agr. Grad. Sch., 1967—; chmn. Spl. Meeting on Neisseria WHO, Geneva, Switzerland, 1964, mem. expert adv. panel on bacterial diseases, 1967—; mem. Gov.'s Sci. Adv. Bd. 1967—, chmn., 1971-72; mem. organizing com. for XVII Gen. Assembly NRC, div. biology and agr. Internat. Union Biol. Scis., 1968; chmn. bd. on human resource data and analysis Commn. on Human Resources, NRC, 1975-79, mem. exec. com. Council Grad. Schs., 1976-78. Diplomate Am. Bd. Microbiology. Mem. Am. Acad. Microbiology, AAAS, AAUP (past br. pres.) Am. Inst. Biol. Scis. (bd. govs., past vis. lectr.), Am. Soc. Microbiology (bd. govs., past com. chmn., councilor, br. pres.), Internat. Assn. Microbiology, Washington Acad. Scis., Nat. Assn. State Univs. and Land-Grant Colls. (chmn. Council for Research Policy and Adminstrn.). Phi Beta Kappa. Sigma Xi (ann. award sci. achievement 1968), Phi Kappa Phi, Sigma Alpha Omicron. Club: Cosmos (Washington). Co-author: Microbiology, 4th edit., 1977. Editorial bd. Jour. of Bacteriology, 1965—. Contbr. sect. to Ency. Brit., 1969, articles to profl. jours. Research on nutritional requirements bacteria, media for growth of bacteria, bacteriological method for assay vitamins, classification bacteria related to menigococcus and gonococcus. Home: 4318 Clagett Pineway University Park MD 20782 Office: Council Grad Schs in US One Dupont Circle NW Suite 310 Washington DC 20036

PELÉ (ARANTES DO NASCIMENTO, EDSON), soccer player; b. Tres Coracoes, Minas Gerais, Brazil, Oct. 23, 1940; s. Joao Ramos do Nascimento and Celeste Arantes; came to U.S., 1975; grad. in phys. edn. Santos U., 1972; m. Rosemari Cholby, Feb. 21, 1966 (div. 1978); children—Kelly Christina, Edson. Soccer player with Santos Football Club, Sao Paulo, 1956-74, N.Y. Cosmos, N.Y.C., 1975-77; player 4 World Cups, 1958, 62, 66, 70, won 3 times, Brazilian Nat. Team, 1957-71; chmn. Pepsi Internat. Youth Soccer Program, 1972—; pres. Empresas Pelé, Santos, Pelé N.V. (Curacao); dir. soccer clinics. Served with Brazilian Army, 1958. Author: Eu Sou Pelé, 1962; Jogando com Pelé, 1974; My Life and Beautiful Game, 1977; appeared in films: Eu sou Pelé, 1964; A Marcha, 1973; Isto Pelé, 1974; Pelé, Master and His Method, 1973; Pelé's New World, 1975; Pelé, 1977; composer numerous songs in Samba style including: Saudacao Crianca, 1969; Vexamão, 1970; soundtrack for film Pelé, 1977. Scored 1,088 goals (1,114 games) for Santos Football Club, 97 goals (111 games) for Brazilian Nat. Team, 64 goals (106 games) for Cosmos; recipient Internat. Peace award, 1978. Address: 75 Rockefeller Plaza New York NY 10019*

PELIKAN, JAROSLAV JAN, educator; b. Akron, Ohio, Dec. 17, 1923; s. Jaroslav Jan and Anna (Buzek) P.; grad. summa cum laude, Concordia Jr. Coll., Ft. Wayne, Ind., 1942; B.D., Concordia Sem., St. Louis, 1946, D.D., 1967; Ph.D., U. Chgo., 1946; D.D., Concordia Coll., 1960; Litt.D., Wittenberg U., 1960, Gettysburg Coll., 1967, Pacific Luth. U., 1967; M.A., Yale, 1961; L.H.D., Valparaiso U., 1966, Rockhurst Coll., 1967, Albertus Magnus Coll., 1973, Coe Coll., 1976, Catholic U. Am., 1977, St. Mary's Coll., 1978; H.H.D., Providence Coll., 1966; LL.D., Keuka Coll., 1967, U. Notre Dame, 1979; D.Theol., U. Hamburg (Germany), 1971; Th.D., St. Olaf Coll., 1972; m. Sylvia Burica, June 9, 1946; children—Martin, Michael, Miriam. Faculty, Valparaiso U., 1946-49, Concordia Sem., St. Louis, 1949-53, U. Chgo., 1953-62; Titus Street prof. eccles. history Yale, 1962-72, Sterling prof. history, 1972—, dir. div. humanities, 1974-75, chmn. Medieval studies, 1974-75, 78—, acting dean Grad. Sch., 1973-74, dean, 1975-78. Pres., 4th Internat. Congress for Luther Research, 1971, New Eng. Congress on Grad. Edn., 1976-77. Recipient Pax Christi award St. John's U., Collegeville, Minn., 1966; John Gilmary Shea prize Am. Cath. Hist. Assn., 1971; Nat. award Slovak World Congress, 1973; Religious Book award Catholic Press Assn., 1974; Christian Unity award Atonement Friars, 1975; Bicentennial award Czechoslovak Soc. Arts and Scis., 1976. Fellow Mediaeval Acad. Am.; mem. Am. Hist. Assn., Am. Soc. Ch. History (pres. 1965), Am. Acad. Arts and Scis. (v.p. 1976—), Am. Philos. Soc., Phi Beta Kappa. Clubs: Century Assn. (N.Y.C.); Cosmos (Washington); Elizabethan, Mory's (New Haven). Author: From Luther to Kierkegaard, 1950; Fools for Christ, 1955; The Riddle of Roman Catholicism (Abingdon award 1959), 1959; Luther the Expositor, 1959; The Shape of Death, 1961; The Light of the World, 1962; Obedient Rebels, 1964; The Finality of Jesus Christ in an Age of Universal History, 1965: The Christian Intellectual, 1966; The Preaching of Chrysostom, 1967; Spirit Versus Structure, 1968; Interpreters of Luther, 1968; Development of Doctrine, 1969; Historical Theology, 1971; The Christian Tradition, 5 vols., 1971—; The Preaching of Augustine, 1973; also introductions to works of others. Editor, translator: Luther's Works, 22 vols., 1955-71; The Book of Concord, 1959; editor Makers of Modern Theology, 5 vols. 1966-68; Twentieth-Century Theology in the Making, 3 vols., 1969-70; mem. editorial bd. Collected Works of Erasmus. Contbr. to many symposia, jours., encys. Home: 156 Chestnut Ln Hamden CT 06518 Office: Dept History Hall Grad Studies Yale New Haven CT 06520

PELL, ARTHUR ROBERT, personnel cons., author; b. N.Y.C., Jan. 22, 1920; s. Harry and Rae (Meyers) P.; A.B., N.Y. U., 1939, M.A., 1944; Ph.D., Calif. Western U., 1977; profl. diploma Cornell U., 1943; m. Erica Frost, May 19, 1946; children—Douglas, Hilary. Personnel dir. Eagle-Electric Mfg. Co., Long Island City, N.Y., 1946-50, North Atlantic Constructors, N.Y.C., 1950-53; v.p. Harper Assos., Inc., personnel consultants, N.Y.C., 1953-75; cons. Human Resources Mgmt., 1975—; adj. asso. prof. mgmt. Sch. Continuing Edn., N.Y. U., 1962—; lectr. Baruch Sch. Bus. and Pub. Adminstrn. Coll. City N.Y., 1948-67; adj. asso. prof. mgmt. Coll. Bus. Adminstrn., St. John's U., 1971—. Pres. Employment Agy. Study Group, N.Y.C., 1960-67, Brotherhood Nassau Community Temple, 1963-65. Served with AUS, 1942-46. Mem. Am. Soc. Personnel Adminstrn., Am. Soc. Tng. and Devel., Nat. Assn. Personnel Consultants. Author: (with W.B. Patterson) Fire Officer's Guide to Leadership, rev. edit., 1963; Placing Salesmen, 1963; Placing Executives, 1964; Police Leadership, 1967; How to Get the Job You Want After 40, 1967; Recruiting and Selecting Personnel, 1969; (with M. Harper) Starting and Managing an Employment Agency, 1970; Recruiting, Training and Motivating Volunteer Workers, 1972; Be A Better Employment Interviewer, 1972, rev., 1978; The College Graduate Guide to Job Finding, 1973; (with Wilma Rogalin) Women's Guide to Executive Positions, 1975; (with Albert Furbay) College Student's Guide to Career Planning, 1975; (with Dale Carnegie Assos.) Managing Through People, 1975, rev., 1978; Choosing a College Major: Business, 1978; Enrich Your Life—The Dale Carnegie Way, 1979; also articles. Office: 111 Dietz St Hempstead NY 11550

PELL, CLAIBORNE, U.S. senator; b. N.Y.C., Nov. 22, 1918; s. Herbert Claiborne and Matilda (Bigelow) P.; student St. George's Sch. (Newport, R.I.); A.B. cum laude, Princeton, 1940; A.M., Columbia, 1946; 23 hon. degrees; m. Nuala O'Donnell, Dec. 1944; children—Herbert Claiborne III, Christopher T. Hartford, Nuala Dallas, Julia L.W. Enlisted USCGR, 1941; served as seaman, ensign N. Atlantic sea duty, Africa, Italy; hospitalized to U.S., 1944; instr. Navy Sch. Mil. Govt., Princeton, 1944-45; now capt. USCGR; on loan to State Dept. at San Francisco Conf., 1945, State Dept., 1945-46, U.S. embassy, Czechoslovakia, 1946-47; established consulate gen., Bratislava, Czechoslovakia, 1947-48; vice consul, Genoa, Italy, 1949; assigned State Dept., 1950-52; v.p., dir. Internat. Rescue Com.; senator from R.I., 1961—. U.S. del. Internat. Maritime Consultative Orgn., London, 1959, 25th Gen. Assembly, 1970. Bd. dirs. World Affairs Council R.I.; trustee St. George's Sch.; trustee emeritus Brown U. Cons. Democratic Nat. Com., 1953-60; exec. asst. to chmn. R.I. State Dem. Com., 1952-54; chmn. R.I. Dem. Fund drive, 1952; Dem. nat. registration chmn., 1956, co-chmn., 1962; chief delegation tally clk. Dem. Nat. Conv., 1956, 60, 64, 68. Decorated knight Crown of Italy, grand cross Order of Merit (Italy); Red Cross of Merit (Portugal); Legion of Honor (France); comdr. Order of Phoenix (Greece); grand cross Order of Merit (Liechtenstein); grand cross Order of N. Star (Sweden); Grand Cross of Merit, Knights of Malta; Caritas Elizabeth medal (Cardinal Franz Koenig). Mem. Soc. Cin. Episcopalian. Clubs: Hope (Providence); Knickerbocker, Racquet and Tennis, Brook (N.Y.C.); Metropolitan (Washington); Travellers (Paris); Reading Room (Newport); White's (London). Author: Megalopolis Unbound, 1966; (with Harold L. Goodwin) Challenge of the Seven Seas, 1966; Power and Policy, 1972. Office: Room 325 Senate Office Bldg Washington DC 20510. *I have a seven word definition of my job and of my life: "Translate ideas into events, and help people."*

PELL, ERNEST EUGENE, fgn. corr.; b. Paducah, Ky., Mar. 15, 1937; s. Ernest Joseph and Edna Marie (Stewart) P.; B.A., Harvard U., 1959; postgrad. Boston U., 1962-63; m. Linda Winthrop, July 17, 1959; children—Anne Frances, Jennifer Susan. With Westinghouse Broadcasting Co., Inc., 1963-77, nat. corr., Washington, 1967-69, chief fgn. news service, London, 1969-74, corr. Sta. WBZ-TV, Boston, 1963-67, anchorman, 1975-77; anchorman, polit. analyst Sta. WCVB-TV, Boston, 1977-78; Moscow corr. NBC News, 1978—. Served to lt. (j.g.) USNR, 1959-62. Nieman fellow journalism Harvard U., 1974-75, vis. fellow, 1978. Mem. Am. Acad. Radio and TV Artists. Club: Harvard (Boston). Home: 38/1 Frunzenskaya Nab Kv 408 Moscow USSR Office: 3 Gruzinsky Per Kv 219-220 Moscow USSR

PELL, JOHN HOWLAND GIBBS, historian, financial cons.; b. Southampton, L.I., N.Y., Aug. 9, 1904; s. Stephen Hyatt Pelham and Sarah Gibbs (Thompson) P.; student St. Paul's Sch., 1917-21, Harvard, 1922-24; LL.D., Adelphi Coll., 1963, Chung-ang U., 1963, Fairleigh Dickinson U., 1964; L.H.D., Russell Sage Coll., 1964, New Rochelle Coll., 1976, Hamilton Coll., 1976; m. Pyrma Tilton, Sept. 3, 1929; children—Sarah Gibbs, John Bigelow. Engaged in hist. research, Ft. Ticonderoga, 1925-29; in estate mgmt., 1930-32; organizer, partner John H.G. Pell & Co., 1932—; dir. Macmillan, Inc.; trustee Dime Savs. Bank of N.Y.; chancellor L.I. U., 1962-64. Mem. Commr. Edn.'s Com. on N.Y. State Museums, 1960-69; pres. Ft. Ticonderoga Assn., 1950—; mem. Interstate Commn. on Lake Champlain Basin, 1955-65; mem. council State U. Coll. Plattsburgh, 1960-75; chmn. Fed. Hudson-Champlain Celebration Commn., 1958-59; chmn. N.Y. State Am. Revolution Bicentennial Commn., 1968—; dir. N.Y.C. Am. Bicentennial Com., 1971-76. Trustee N.Y. State Historic Trust, 1966—, Estate and Property Episcopal Diocesan Conv. N.Y., Juilliard Sch. Music. bd. mgrs., lay v.p. Seaman's Ch. Inst., 1935-70. Served from lt. to comdr. USNR, 1941-45; enlisted personnel officer 3rd Naval Dist., duty in U.S.S. Ordroneaux, 1944. Decorated officer Order of Orange Nassau (Holland); chevalier Legion of Honor (France); recipient Chauncey Depew medal, citation and gold medal S.A.R., commendation Sec. Navy. Mem. N.Y. State Hist. Assn. (trustee, v.p.), Am. Scenic and Historic Preservation Soc. (trustee, pres. 1970—), N.Y. Hist. Soc. (trustee), English Speaking Union, Soc. Colonial Wars (council), Pilgrims of U.S., Colonial Lords of Manors (pres.), Theodore Roosevelt Assn. (pres.), Soc. of Cincinnati (hon.), France Amerique (dir.). Clubs: Knickerbocker, Down Town Assn., Century Assn., Metropolitan (Washington); Newport Reading Room. Author: Life of Ethan Allen, 1929; also articles in hist., financial field. Contbr. chpt. to General Washington's Generals, 1964. Home: 870 Fifth Ave New York City NY 10021 also Fort Ticonderoga NY 12883 Office: 1 Wall St New York City NY 10005

PELL, WALDEN, II, clergyman, educator; b. Quogue, L.I., N.Y., July 3, 1902; s. Francis Livingston and Ellen Van Buren (Morris) P.; diploma St. Mark's Sch., 1920; student Princeton, 1920-23; Rhodes scholar, Oxford (Eng.) U., 1923-26, M.A., 1930; S.T.D., (hon.), U. Pa., 1945; student Union Theol. Sem., Columbia, 1958-59; m. Edith Minturn Bonsal, Aug. 25, 1928; children—Melissa, Stuyvesant Bonsal, Mary Leigh. Master, Lenox (Mass.) Sch., 1926-30; headmaster St. Andrew's Sch., Middletown, Del., 1930-57; ordained deacon P.E. Ch., 1927, priest, 1928; priest-in-charge St. Peter's Ch., Singapore, 1959-60, Anglican-Episcopal congregations of Vietnam, Cambodia and Laos, 1961-63, Augustine Parish, Chesapeake City, Md., 1963-68. Sec., Chesapeake City Dist. Civic Assn. Mem. Headmasters Assn. (hon.), Fort Ticonderoga Assn., Nat. Assn. Amateur Oarsmen, Scholastic Rowing Assn., Eastern Bird Banding Assn., Anglican Soc., Cum Laude Soc., Religious Edn. Assn., Am. Ornithol. Union, Upper Chesapeake Watershed Assn. (dir.). Democrat. Clubs: Princeton (N.Y.C.); Ivy (Princeton); Cardinal, Kilcannon (Oxford); Colonial Lords of Manors. Author: (with Powel and Dawley) The Religion of the Prayer Book. Compiler: A History of St. Andrew's School. Home: 165 Knollwood Rd Elkton MD 21921

PELL, WILBUR FRANK, JR., U.S. circuit judge; b. Shelbyville, Ind., Dec. 6, 1915; s. Wilbur Frank and Nelle (Dickerson) P.; A.B., Ind. U., 1937; LL.B. cum laude, Harvard, 1940; LL.D., Yonsei U., Seoul, Korea, 1972, John Marshall Sch. Law, 1973; m. Mary Lane Chase, Sept. 14, 1940; children—Wilbur Frank III, Charles Chase. Admitted to Ind. bar, 1940; practice law, Shelbyville, 1940-42, 45-70; spl. agt. FBI, 1942-45; sr. partner Pell & Good, 1949-56, Pell & Matchett, 1956-70; judge 7th Circuit, U.S. Ct. Appeals, 1970—; dep. atty. gen. Ind., 1953-55; dir., chmn. Shelby Nat. Bank, 1947-70. Bd. dirs. Shelbyville Community Chest, 1947-49, Shelby County Fair Assn., 1951-53; dir. Shelby County Tb Assn., 1948-70, pres., 1965-66; dist. chmn. Boy Scouts Am., 1956-57; mem. pres.'s council Nat. Coll. Edn., 1972—; dir. Westminster Found., Ind. U.; hon. dir. Korean Legal Center. Fellow Am. Coll. Probate Counsel, Am. Bar Found.; mem. Am. (Judge Edward R. Finch Law Day U.S.A. Speech award 1973, ho. of dels. 1962-63), Ind. (pres. 1962-63, chmn. ho. of dels. 1968-69), Fed., Ill., Shelby County (pres. 1957-58), 7th Fed. Circuit bar assns., Am. Judicature Soc., Am. Coun. Assn., Shelby County C. of C. (dir. 1947-49), Nat. Conf. Bar Presidents, Riley Meml. Assn., Ind. Soc. Chgo. (pres. 1978-79), Blue Key, Kappa Sigma, Alpha Phi Omega, Theta Alpha Phi, Tau Kappa Alpha, Phi Alpha Delta (hon.). Republican. Presbyn. (elder, deacon). Clubs: Chicago Rotary (dist. gov. 1952-53, internat. dir. 1959-61), Union League, Legal (pres. 1976-77) (Chgo.). Office: 219 S Dearborn St Chicago IL 60604

PELL, WILLIAM HICKS, mathematician; b. Lewisport, Ky., Oct. 15, 1914; s. William Clay and Florence Beulah (Hicks) P.; B.S., U. Ky., 1936, M.S., 1938; Ph.D., U. Wis., 1943; m. Dorothy Small, Aug. 23, 1939. Grad. asst. math. U. Ky., 1936-38, U. Wis., 1938-42; research aerodynamicist Bell Aircraft Corp., 1943-47; research asso. div. applied math. Brown U., 1947-48, asst. prof., then asso. prof., 1948-56; prof., head math. dept. U. Ky., 1952-53; mathematician Nat. Bur. Standards, Washington, 1956-58, acting chief, then chief math. physics sect., 1958-65; program dir. applied math. and statistics NSF, 1965-67, head math. scis. sect., 1967—. Postdoctoral fellow Sch. Applied Math., Brown U., 1942-43; postdoctoral fellow Inst. Fluid Dynamics and Applied Math., U. Md., 1955-56. Fellow A.A.A.S.; mem. Am. Math. Soc., Am. Soc. M.E., Soc. Indsl. and Applied Math., Math. Assn. Am., Am. Acad. Mechanics, Soc. Natural Philosophy, Phi Beta Kappa, Sigma Xi, Omicron Delta Kappa. Asso. editor Jour. Research, sect. B, Nat. Bur. Standards, 1961-65, Soc. Indsl. and Applied Math. Jour. Applied Math., 1962-68. Home: 605 Muriel St Rockville MD 20852 Office: 1800 G St NW Washington DC 20550

PELLA, MILTON ORVILLE, educator; b. Wilmot, Wis., Feb. 13, 1914; s. Charles August and Ida Marie (Pagel) P.; B.E., Milw. State Tchrs. Coll., 1936; M.S., U. Wis., 1940, Ph.D., 1948; m. Germaine Marie Reich, Dec. 9, 1944. Tchr. sci. and math. Wyler Mil. Acad., 1937-38; tchr. elementary sch. Delavan Pub. Schs., 1938-39; tchr. sci. U. Wis. High Sch., 1939-42; prof. sci. edn. U. Wis.-Madison, 1946—. With Fgn. Ednl. Service, Turkey, 1959, Iran, Turkey, Jordan, Syria, Lebanon, 1961, 62, Jordan, Lebanon, 1963, 64, 65, 66, 68, Costa Rica, 1967, Saudi Arabia, 1969, Nigeria, 1968, 69, Lebanon and Egypt, 1971-79. Served with AUS, 1942-46. Fellow A.A.A.S.; mem. Central Assn. Sci. and Math. (pres. 1955), Nat. Assn. for Research in Sci. Teaching (pres. 1966), Nat. Sci. Tchrs. Assn. (dir. 1950, 60). Mason, Rotarian. Author: Physical Science for Progress, 3d edit., 1970; Science Horizons—The Biological World (with Branley and Urban), 1965-70. Home: 5518 Varsity Hill Dr Madison WI 53705

PELLEGRIN, ROLAND JOSEPH, educator; b. Chacahoula, La., Feb. 4, 1923; s. Octave J. and Claire (LaJaunie) P.; student Southwestern La. Inst., 1940-43, Fordham U., 1943-44, Biarritz Am. U., 1945; B.S., La. State U., 1947, M.A., 1949; Ph.D., U. N.C., 1952; m. Jean Howard, Aug. 13, 1949; children—Stephen, Robert. Grad. asst., research asst. La. State U., 1947-50; grad. asst., teaching fellow, part-time instr. U. N.C., 1950-52; research asso. Inst. Research Human Relations, Washington, 1952; faculty La. State U., 1952-61, prof. sociology, 1959-61, chmn. dept., 1958-61, prof. rural sociology, 1959-61, chmn dept., 1958-61; prof. sociology, dir. Inst. Community Studies, U. Oreg., 1961-73, Center Advanced Study Ednl. Adminstrn., 1964-68; prof., head dept. sociology Pa. State U., 1973—. Vis. prof. Duke, summer 1960, U. Ga., 1971-72. Fellow Am. Sociol. Assn.; mem. Pacific Sociol. Assn., So. Sociol. Soc., Omicron Delta Kappa, Phi Kappa Phi. Author books and articles in field. Home: 1448 Park Hills Ave State College PA 16801

PELLEGRINI, ANNA MARIA, soprano; b. Pretoro, Chieti, Italy, July 15, 1944; d. Vincenzo and Giuseppina (Pietrantonio) P.; came to Can., 1959, naturalized, 1964; student U. Toronto (Ont., Can.) Faculty of Music, 1962-65; m. Steven Murray Thomas, Aug. 13, 1974; 1 son, Vincent Thomas. Debut in opera as Gilda in Rigoletto, Can. Opera Co., 1965; leading roles in: La Boheme, Turandot, I Pagliacci, Elektra, Cosi Fan Tutte; title roles in: Manon Lescaut, Madama Butterfly; appeared in maj. opera houses, throughout the world; title role of Madama Butterfly, Can. Broadcasting Corp. TV prodn., 1977; tchr. voice, Italian repertoire. Recipient prize Met. Opera Nat. Auditions, 1966; Caravello d'Oro, Ufficio Di Turismo, Genova, 1970; medallion honoring her and Puccini, Sindico di Teatro Comunale di Treviso, 1974. Mem. Can. Actors Equity, Brit. Equity, Union des Artistes (Que., Can.), Am. Guild Mus. Artists, Assn. Can. TV and Radio Artists. Office: care Christopher Melville Personal Mgr PO Box 3135 Postal Sta D Ottawa ON K1P 6H7 Canada

PELLEGRINO, EDMUND DANIEL, univ. pres., physician, educator; b. Newark, June 22, 1920; s. Michael J. and Marie (Catone) P.; B.S., St. John's U., 1941, D. Sc., 1971; M.D., N.Y. U., 1944; D.Sc., Hahnemann Med. Coll., 1971, Calif. Coll. Podiatric Medicine, 1974, N.J. Coll. Medicine and Dentistry, 1974; L.H.D., St. Benedict's Coll., Atchison, Kans., 1971, Loyola U., 1971, Med. U. S.C., 1978, Holy Family Coll., 1979, St. Leo's Coll., 1979, U. Bridgeport, 1979, Georgetown U., 1979; M.A., Yale, 1975; D.Sc., U. Ky., 1977, Adelphi U., 1977, N.Y. Med. Coll., 1979; L.D., Phila. Coll. Osteopathy, 1978; m. Clementine Coakley, Nov. 17, 1944; children—Thomas, Stephen, Virgina, Michael, Andrea, Alice, Leah. Intern, Bellevue Hosp., N.Y.C., 1944-45, asst. resident medicine, 1948-49; resident medicine Goldwater Meml. Hosp., N.Y.C., 1945-46; fellow medicine N.Y. U., 1949-50; supervising Tb physician Homer Folks Hosp., Oneonta, N.Y., 1950-53; dir. internal medicine Hunterdon Med. Center, Flemington, N.J., 1953-59, med. dir., 1955-59; prof., chmn. dept. medicine U. Ky. Med. Center, 1959-66; prof. medicine State U. N.Y. at Stony Brook, L.I., 1966—, v.p. for health scis., dir. Health Scis. Center, 1968-73, dean Sch. Medicine, 1968-72; v.p. for health affairs U. Tenn. System, chancellor U. Tenn. Med. Units, Memphis, 1973-75; prof. med. Yale, New Haven, 1975—; pres. Yale-New Haven Med. Center, 1975-78; pres. Cath. U. Am., Washington, 1978—, prof. philosophy and biology, 1978—; clin. prof. medicine and community medicine Georgetown U., Washington, 1978—. Trustee N.Y. Med. Coll., Dickinson Coll., Quinnipiac Coll. Served with USAAF, 1946-48. Diplomate Am. Bd. Internal Medicine. Fellow N.Y. Acad. Medicine, A.C.P.; mem. Am. Soc. Nephrology, Am. Assn. Pathologists, Assn. Am. Physicians, AAAS, Am. Assn. Advancement Humanities, Medieval Acad. Am., AMA, Metaphys. Soc. Am., Inst. of Medicine of Nat. Acad. Scis., N.Y. Acad. Sci., Inst. Human Values in Medicine (dir.), Am. Clin. and Climatological Assn., Soc. Health and Human Values, Assn. Acad. Health Centers (pres. 1973), Sigma Xi. Editor: Jour. Medicine and Philosophy. Home: 5812 Highland St Chevy Chase MD 20015 Office: Office of Pres Catholic U Am Washington DC 20064

PELLERZI, LEO MAURICE, lawyer; b. Cumberland, Md.; June 14 1924; s. John and Ida Lezzer (Regis) P.; A.A., George Washington U., 1947, LL.B., 1949, LL.M. 1950; m. Betty Lou Mearkle, Jan. 17, 1946; children—Cheryl M., John C., Michele S., Julie A., Laura M., Jeffrey C. Admitted to D.C. bar, 1949, also U.S. Supreme Ct.; atty. ICC, 1949-51, ECA, 1951-52; atty. Subversive Activities Control Bd., 1952-56, asst. gen. counsel, 1956-59; adminstv. law judge ICC, 1959-65; gen. counsel U.S. Civil Service Commn., 1965-68; asst. atty gen. for administrn. Dept. Justice, 1968-73; gen. counsel Am. Fedn. Govt. Employees, AFL-CIO, 1973-78; pvt. practice law, Washington, 1978—; guest lectr. Princeton, 1967, George Washington U., 1965-67; gen. counsel Lafayette Fed. Credit Union, 1956-59. Pres., Fed. Adminstrv. Law Judges Conf., 1963-65., Pres. Indian Spring Citizens Assn., 1960. Served with USAAF, 1943-45; lt. col. Res. Decorated Air medal with 4 oak leaf clusters. Recipient Commrs.'s award U.S. Civil Service Commn., 1968; Justice Tom C. Clark award Fed. Bar Assn., 1967. Mem. Am., Fed. (pres. D.C. chpt. 1962-63; chmn. com. gen. counsel 196-67) bar assns., Pub. Personnel Assn., Am. Judicature Soc., AmVets, Am. Legion, Res. Officers Assn., John Carroll Soc., George Washington U. Alumni Assn., Delta Theta Phi. Roman Catholic. Home: 106 Indian Spring Dr Silver Spring MD 20901 Office: 1325 Massachusetts Ave NW Washington DC 20005

PELLETIER, ALFRED WILLIAM, truck mfg. co. exec.; b. Toronto, Ont., Can., Jan. 22, 1922; s. William and Mildred (Goodman) P.; came to U.S., 1976; grad. Danforth Tech. Sch., 1939; m. Patricia Ann Robertson, Oct. 5, 1951; children—Janet, Douglas, Nancy. With Mack Trucks Can. Ltd., 1952-76, exec. v.p., then pres., 1971-76; pres., chief exec. officer Mack Trucks, Inc., Allentown, Pa., 1976—, chmn. bd., 1979—, also dir.; dir. Signal Cos., Inc.; chmn. Mack Can. Inc., Mack Fin. Can. Ltd. Served with Canadian Navy, 1941-45. Mem. Western Hwy. Inst., Soc. Automotive Engrs. Office: PO Box M Allentown PA 18105

PELLETIER, GERARD, Canadian govt. ofcl.; b. Victoriaville, Que., June 21, 1919; s. Achille and Leda (Dufresne) P.; B.A., Mont. U.; m. Alexandrine Leduc, Feb. 27, 1943; children—Jean, Anne-Marie, Louise, Andrée. Sec. gen. Jeunesse etudiante catholique youth movement, 1939-43; Canadian Cath. Action rep., South Am., 1945; field sec. World Student Relief Fund, Geneva, Switzerland, 1945-47; reporter Le Devoir daily, Montreal, 1947-50; dir., pub. relations ofcl. Le Travail ofcl. newspaper Nat. Trade Unions, 1950-61; editor La Presse daily, Montreal, 1961-65; M.P., 1965—, parliamentary sec. to Sec. State for external affairs, 1967, minister without portfolio, 1968, sec. state, 1968-72, minister communications, 1972-75; ambassador to France, 1975—. Mem. Privy Council. Roman Catholic. Home: 135 Rue du Faubourg St Honoré Paris 8 France

PELLETIER, JEAN, mayor; b. Chicoutimi, Qué., Can., Feb. 21, 1935; s. Burroughs and Marie (Desautels) P.; ed. Laval U., Quebec; m. Hélène Bhérer, June 3, 1961; children—Jean, Marie. Journalist, Sta. CFCM-TV, Quebec, 1957; corr. Radio Can., Qué., 1958-59; press sec. Premier's Office, 1959; exec. sec. Commn. des monuments historiques Qué., 1960-62; stock broker Levesque & Beaubien, 1964-70; v.p. Dumont Express, Québec, 1970-73; v.p. L'Action Sociale Ltée, Québec, 1973-77; mcpl. councillor, Québec, 1976-77; mayor of Québec, 1977—; mem. exec. Québec Urban Community. Pres. Assn. des scouts du Can., 1969-72, Carnaval de Québec, 1973; dir. gen. Centraide, 1973-77; v.p. Festival d'art dramatique du Can., 1961-65. Mem. Fedn. Can. Municipalities (v.p. 1979—), Union Municipalities Québec, Consel devel. econ. Quebec. Roman Catholic. Office: Hotel de Ville rue Desjardins Québec PQ G1R 4S9 Canada

PELLETIER, JOSEPH ANTHONY, internat. energy co. exec.; b. Chgo., Dec. 18, 1922; s. Joseph A. and Margaret A. (Liston) P.; B.S., Iowa State U., 1949; m. Martha I. von Schrader, May 26, 1944; children—Joseph, Norman, Monica, Martha, Karen. With No. Ind. Public Service Co., Hammond, 1949-72, v.p. engring., 1967-72, v.p. engring., constrn. and research, 1972; exec. v.p. Gasco, Inc., Honolulu, 1972-78; v.p. Pacific Resources, Inc., Honolulu, 1973-74, sr. v.p., 1974, exec. v.p., 1974-79, pres., 1979—; pres. Gasco, Inc. subs., Honolulu, 1978—. Mem. bus. adminstrn. adv. council Chaminade U., Honolulu, 1977—; mem. Dist Export Council in Hawaii, 1977—. Bd. dirs. Hawaii Employers Council, 1974—, Jr. Achievement Hawaii, 1973—, Child and Family Service, 1974—; chmn. energy recovery com. Hawaii Energy Conservation Council, 1978—. Served with U.S. Army, 1943-46, 51. Registered profl. engr., Ind., Hawaii. Mem. Am. Nuclear Soc., ASME, IEEE, Am. Gas Assn., Assn. U.S. Army (past pres. Hawaii chpt.), Hawaii Army Mus. Soc. (past pres., trustee), Navy League U.S., C. of C. Hawaii (dir.). Roman Catholic. Clubs: Oahu Country, Outrigger Canoe, Pacific, Rotary, Plaza. Home: 89 Lumahai St Honolulu HI 96825 Office: PO Box 3379 Honolulu HI 96825

PELLETIER, LAWRENCE LEE, coll. pres.; b. Farmington, N.H., Sept. 8, 1914; s. David and Marion (Leighton) P.; B.A., Bowdoin Coll., 1936, LL.D., 1962; M.A., Harvard U., 1939, Ph.D., 1947; LL.D., Colby Coll., 1963, Gannon Coll., 1974; m. Louise E. Collins, Sept. 2, 1939; children—Lawrence Lee, Mary Louise. Instr. history and govt. U. Maine, 1939-45; asst. prof. govt. Bowdoin Coll., 1946-49, asso. prof., 1949-55, prof., 1955, also asso. dir. Citizenship Clearing House, N.Y.U. Law Center, 1953-54; pres. Allegheny Coll., 1955—. Mem. Am. Polit. Sci. Assn., Phi Beta Kappa, Alpha Tau Omega. Clubs: Duquesne (Pitts.); Rotary (Meadville). Author: Financing Local Government, 1948. Home: 286 Jefferson St Meadville PA 16335*

PELLETIER, S. WILLIAM, educator, scientist; b. Kankakee, Ill., July 3, 1924; s. Anthony Amos and Estella Edith (Hays) P.; B.S. with highest honors in Chem. Engring., U. Ill., 1947, Ph.D. in Organic Chemistry, Cornell U., 1950; m. Leona Jane Bledsoe, June 18, 1949; children—William Timothy, Jonathan Daniel, Rebecca Jane, Lucy Ruth, David Mark, Sarah Lynn. Instr. chemistry U. Ill., 1950-51; mem. staff Rockefeller Inst., 1951-62, asso. prof. organic chemistry, 1961-62; prof. chemistry, head dept. U. Ga., 1962-69, Alumni Found. distinguished prof., 1969—, provost, 1969-76, Univ. prof., 1976—, dir. Inst. for Natural Products Research, 1976—. Gordon lectr., New Hampton, N.H., 1955, 59, 69; Am. Swiss Found. lectr., Zurich, Basel, Bern and Geneva (Switzerland), 1960; lectr. for internat. symposia in Berlin, Melbourne, Hong Kong, Kyoto, Prague, Stockholm, London, Riga, Latvia, Varna, Bulgaria, also other lectures in Eng., Italy, India, Israel, Taiwan, Japan; Victor Coulter lectr. U. Miss., 1965. Mem. panel equipment NSF, 1965; mem. health medicinal chemistry study panel NIH, 1968-72; cons. Walter Reed Army Inst., 1966. Pres. bd. Flushing Christian Day Sch., 1956-60; bd. advisers Ga. Mus. Art, 1968—; bd. dirs. Center for Research Libraries, Chgo., 1975—. Served with USNR, 1944-46. Fellow Royal Soc. Arts (London), Chem. Soc. (London), A.A.A.S.; mem. Am. Chem. Soc. (chmn. N.E. Ga. sect. 1968, Charles Herty medal 1971, So. Chemists award 1972), Sigma Xi, Phi Eta Sigma, Tau Beta Pi, Sigma Tau. Presbyn. (elder). Author: Chemistry of the Alkaloids, 1970; 2 monographs on Am. etcher John Taylor Arms, 1975, 76; also numerous articles in field; bd. editors Jour. Organic Chemistry, 1966-70, Heterocycles, 1979—; spl. research structure and stereochemistry diterpenoid alkaloids, applications of carbon-13 nuclear magnetic resonance to structure determination, synthesis of terpenes, X-ray crystallographic structures of natural products. Home: 555 Glenwood Dr Athens GA 30606

PELLETIER, WILFRID, symphony condr.; b. Montreal, Que., Can., June 20, 1896; s. Elzear and Zelire P.; began study of piano at age 7; won Province of Quebec prize for European study, 1914; in Paris studied piano with Isidore Philipp, 1915, harmony with Rousseau, composition with Widor, opera tradition with Bellaigue; Mus.D. (hon.), U. Montreal, 1936, U. Ottawa, Laval U., U. Alta., N.Y. Coll. Music; H.H.D., Hobart Coll.; m. Rose Bampton, May 24, 1937; children—Camille, Francois. With Met. Opera Assn., N.Y.C., 1917-50, beginning asst. condr. French and Italian repertoire; condr. Ravinia Opera Co., Chgo., 1920, San Francisco Opera Co., for 10 years, N.Y. Philharmonic Childrens Concerts, 1953-56; condr. orchs. on several radio programs; dir. Met. Opera Auditions of the Air, 12 yrs.; founder, dir. Conservatoire de Musique et Art Dramatic, Montreal, 1942-61; dir. musique Ministere des Affaires Cultureles, Quebec, P.Q., 1961-69; dir. L'Orchestre Symphonique de Quebec. Decorated Companion of Can. (Govt. Can.); Legion d'Honneur (France); Comdr. St. Michael and St. George (Eng.); Christian Den Tiendes Friheds Meds (Denmark). Author: (memoirs) Une Symphonie inachevée, 1973. Home: 322 E 57th St New York NY 10022

PELLETREAU, ROBERT HALSEY, diplomat; b. Patchogue, N.Y., July 9, 1935; s. Robert H. and Mary (Pigeon) P.; B.A., Yale U., 1957; LL.B., Harvard U., 1961; m. Pamela Day, Dec. 17, 1966; children—Katherine Day, Erica Pigeon, Elizabeth Anne. Admitted to N.Y. bar, 1961; asso. firm Chadbourne, Parke, Whiteside & Wolfe, N.Y.C., 1961-62; joined U.S. Fgn. Service, 1962; service in Morocco, Mauritania, Lebanon, Algeria, Jordan and Syria; ambassador to Bahrain, 1979—. Served with USNR, 1957-58. Mem. Am. Fgn. Service Assn., Middle East Inst. Address: American Embassy FPO NY 09526

PELLETT, THOMAS ROWAND, food co. exec.; b. Franklin, N.J., Dec. 2, 1925; s. Thomas Lawrence and Elizabeth (Rowand) P.; B.S. in Mech. Engring., Princeton, 1947; M.B.A., U. Pa., 1949; m. Anne G. Iffert, July 1, 1950; children—Nancy Anne, Deborah Rowand, Thomas Lawrence II. Financial analyst Johns-Manville Co., N.Y.C., 1949-51; asso. Lehman Bros., N.Y.C., 1951-56; asst. treas. Red Owl Stores, Inc., Mpls., 1956-59, treas., 1959-68; v.p. fin., treas. Pet, Inc., St. Louis, 1968—; dir. St. Paul Capital Fund, St. Paul Growth Fund, St. Paul Income Fund, St. Paul Securities, Inc. Served with USNR, 1944-45. Mem. Financial Execs. Inst. Home: 609 Flanders Dr Warson Woods MO 63122 Office: Pet Inc Pet Plaza 400 S 4th St St Louis MO 63166

PELLEW, JOHN C., artist; b. Cornwall, Eng., Apr. 9, 1903; s. Thomas John and Catherine Jane (Jeffrey) P.; student School Arts, Penzance, Eng.; m. Elsie Willcock, Oct. 5, 1929; 1 dau., Elma Corinne. Came to U.S., 1921, naturalized, 1927. One man shows Contemporary Arts Gallery, N.Y.C., 1934, 1941, 1948; exhibited Carnegie Internat., Corcoran Art Gallery, Washington, Pa. Acad. Art, Chgo. Art Inst., Nat. Acad. Art. N.Y.C., Whitney Mus., N.Y.C. Bklyn Mus., Detroit Art Inst.; works represented permanent collections Met. Mus., Bklyn. Mus., Newark (N.J.) Mus., Unio Cultural, Sao Paulo, Brazil, Columbia U., Butler Mus. of American Art. Awarded Vezin-James prize, Salmagundi Club 1950, Anders Jordahl prize, 1952, Mischa Lempert award, 1953, Winsor-Newton prize, Am. Water Color Soc., 1951, Gold Medal of Honor for water color, Allied Artists, 1951, Seeley award (oil) Salmagundi Club, N.Y.C., 1964; Butler award Am. Watercolor Soc., 1965, Silver medal, 1970, Antoinette Graves Goetz award, 1972, 1st Watercolor award 27th New Eng. Annual, 1976. Mem. Am. Water Color Soc., (v.p. 1953), N.A.D., Allied Artists, Audubon Artists. Club: Salmagundi (N.Y.C.). Author: Watercolor Painting; Oil Painting Outdoors; Maritime Landscape; John Pellew Paints Watercolors, 1979. Home: 123 Murray St Norwalk CT 06851

PELLI, CESAR, architect, univ. adminstr.; b. Tucuman, Argentina, Oct. 12, 1926; s. Victor V. and Teresa S. (Suppa) P.; came to U.S., 1952, naturalized, 1964; Architect cum laude, U. Tucuman, 1949; M.S. in Architecture, U. Ill., 1954; m. Diana Balmori, Dec. 15, 1950; children—Denis G., Rafael A. Asso. firm Eero Saarinen & Assos., Architects, 1954-64, Daniel, Mann, Johnson & Mendenhall, Engrs. & Architects, 1964-68, Gruen Assos. Inc., Los Angeles, 1968-77, Cesar Pelli & Assos., New Haven, Conn., 1977—; now dean Sch. Architecture, Yale U., New Haven; vis. prof. architecture U. Tucuman, U. Cordoba (Argentina), Yale U., U. Calif. at Los Angeles. Recipient 1st Design award Sunset Mountain Park, 1966, 1st prize in Competition for UN City, Vienna, Austria, 1969; Arnold Brunner Meml. prize Am. Acad. and Inst. Arts and Letters, 1978. Mem. AIA. Works include The Commons, Columbus, Ind. (Merit award So. Calif. chpt. AIA 1975); Pacific Design Center, Los Angeles (Honor award So. Calif. chpt. AIA 1976); City Hall, San Bernardino, Calif. (Honor award So. Calif. chpt. AIA 1975), U.S. Embassy, Tokyo, Japan; Rainbow Center Mall and Wintergarden, Niagara Falls, N.Y. (Progressive Architecture mag. citation 1977). Home: 95 Rogers Rd Hamden CT 06517 Office: School Architecture Yale Univ New Haven CT 06520 also Cesar Pelli & Assos 1056 Chapel St New Haven CT 06510

PELLY, FRANCIS JUSTINIAN, Brit. diplomat; b. Seattle, Mar. 31, 1913; s. Bernard and Elizabeth Montgomery (Minor) P.; grad. St. Paul's Sch., Concord, N.H., 1932; student U. Wash., 1932-34; m. Nancy Lane, June 26, 1942; children—Wendy (Mrs. Lewis McNay), Nancy Anne (Mrs. Bryan Pye). Brit. vice consul, Seattle, 1940-45; acting Brit. consul, Colon, 1945, Panama, 1946; vice consul, New Orleans, 1947-50; 2d sec., comml., Havana, 1950-51; consul, Suez, Egypt, 1951-54, Ismailia, 1954-55, Geneva, 1955-56; consul comml., N.Y.C., 1956-59; consul, Surabiya, 1959-60; 1st sec. raw materials, Washington, 1961-65; 1st sec. comml., Ottawa, Ont., Can., 1965-67; consul, Miami, Fla., 1967-70; Brit. consul gen. comml., Seattle, 1970-73; N.W. regional mktg. mgr. Frank P. Dow Co., Seattle, 1975—. Mem. Order Brit. Empire. Rotarian. Clubs: Seattle Golf, Seattle Tennis. Home: 1623 Windermere Dr E Seattle WA 98112

PELOUBET, LOUIS GERVAIS, II, chem. co. exec.; b. Orange, N.J., Apr. 18, 1927; s. Sidney Wardell and Frances (Cox) P.; B.S., Mass. Inst. Tech., 1949; M.B.A., N.Y. U., 1958; m. Mary Jane Grier, May 25, 1952; children—Louis Gervais III, Anne Lynn, William Wardell. Supr. audit staff Pogson, Peloubet & Co., N.Y.C., 1954-60; asst. controller N.Am. div. Mobil Oil Corp., N.Y.C., 1960-69; asst. controller Allied Chem. Corp., N.Y.C., 1969-72; v.p., controller Textron, Inc., Providence, 1972-75; controller Union Carbide Corp., N.Y.C., 1975—. Served with AUS, 1945-46. C.P.A., N.Y. Mem. Financial Execs. Inst., Am. Inst. C.P.A.'s, N.Y. Soc. C.P.A.'s, Delta Kappa Epsilon. Republican. Episcopalian. Clubs: Board Room (N.Y.C.); Innis Arden Golf (Old Greenwich, Conn.). Home: 3 Wahneta Rd Old Greenwich CT 06870 Office: 270 Park Ave New York NY 10017

PELS, DONALD A., broadcasting co. exec.; b. New Rochelle, N.Y., Jan. 23, 1928; s. Herbert and Alice Miriam (Brady) P.; B.S., U. Pa., 1948; J.D., N.Y. U., 1953; m. Josette Jeanne Bernard, Feb. 11, 1965; children—Juliette, Valerie, Yves. With Filene's dept. store, Boston, 1948-49, Arthur Young & Co., C.P.A.'s, N.Y.C., 1953-56; bus. mgr. sta. WABC-TV, N.Y.C., 1956-59; exec. v.p., dir. Capital Cities Communications, N.Y.C., 1959-69; chmn. bd., pres. Lin Broadcasting Co., N.Y.C., 1969—. Bd. dirs. Negro Ensemble Co., N.Y.C., Radio Advt. Bur., Nat. Health and Welfare Retirement Assn. Club: University (N.Y.C.). Home: 10 Gracie Sq New York NY 10028 Office: 1370 Ave of the Americas New York NY 10019

PELSWICK, ROSE, writer and painter. Motion picture reviewer and interviewer N.Y. Jour.-Am., 1937-66; author short stories, articles, radio scripts; radio and television appearances. Mem. Am. Newspaper Guild, N.Y. Film Critics. Clubs: Overseas Press, Nat. Arts, Salmagundi. Home: 67 Park Ave New York NY 10016

PELT, JOOST CORNELIS, ballet dancer; b. Amsterdam, Netherlands, Sept. 29, 1950; came to Can., 1977; s. Marinus and Ingetje Niesje (Van Beek) P.; student Rotterdam (Netherlands) Dance Acad., 1966-69; m. Marilyn Lewis, Feb. 28, 1976. Mem. corps de ballet Netherlands Dance Theater, 1969-71, 73-77, Ballet of Flanders, 1971-72, Ballet of XX Century, Brussels, 1972; prin. dancer Royal Winnipeg (Man., Can.) Ballet, 1977—; choreographer. Home: 722 Argue St Winnipeg MB R3L 2P2 Canada Office: 289 Portage Ave Winnipeg MB R3B 2B4 Canada

PELTASON, JACK WALTER, ednl. adminstr.; b. St. Louis, Aug. 29, 1923; s. Walter B. and Emma (Hartman) P.; B.A., U. Mo., 1943, M.A., 1944; A.M., Princeton, 1946, Ph.D., 1947; m. Suzanne Toll, Dec. 21,1946; children—Nancy Hartman, Timothy Walter H., Jill K. Faculty Smith Coll., 1947-51; faculty U. Ill., 1951-64, prof. polit. sci., 1959-64, dean Coll. Liberal Arts and Scis., 1960-64; vice chancellor acad. affairs U. Calif., Irvine, 1964-67; chancellor Urbana-Champaign campus U. Ill., Urbana, 1967-77; pres. Am. Council on Edn., Washington, 1977—. Cons. Mass. Little Hoover Commn., 1950. Mem. Am. Polit. Sci. Assn. (council 1952-54), Phi Beta Kappa, Phi Kappa Phi. Author: The Missouri Plan for the Selection of Judges, 1947; Understanding the Constitution, 7th edit., 1976; Federal Courts in the Political Process, 1957; (with James M. Burns) Government by the People, 10th edit., 1978; Fifty-eight Lonely Men, 1961; also articles, revs. Home: 1505 Dumbarton Rock Ct Washington DC 20007

PELTIER, EUGENE JOSEPH, civil engr., former naval officer, bus. exec.; b. Concordia, Kans., Mar. 29, 1910; s. Frederick and Emma Helen (Brasseau) P.; B.S. in Civil Engring., Kans. State U., 1933, LL.D., 1961; m. Lena Evelyn Gennotta, June 28, 1932; children—Marion Joyce, Eugene Joseph, Carole Josephine, Kenneth Noel, Judith Ann. Commd. lt. (j.g.) U.S. 1936, advanced through grades to rear adm., 1957; asst. public works officer, Great Lakes, Ill., 1940-42, sr. asst. supt. civil engr., Boston, 1942-44; officer in charge 137th Constrn. Bn., Okinawa, 1945, 54th Constrn. Regt., Okinawa, 1945; officer various public works assignments, Pensacola, Fla., 1945-46, Memphis, 1946-49, Jacksonville, Fla., 1949-51; dist. public works officer 14th Naval Dist., 1951-53; asst. chief maintenance and materials Bur. Docks, Washington, 1953-56; comdg. officer Pt. Hueneme, 1956-57; chief Bur. Yards and Docks, Navy Dept., Washington, 1957-62; chief of civil engrs., 1957-62; ret., 1962; instrumentman, resident engr. Kans. Hwy. Commn., Norton, Topeka, Chanute, 1934-40; v.p. Sverdrup & Parcel & Assos., Inc., St. Louis, 1962-64, sr. v.p., 1964-66, exec. v.p., 1966-67, pres., dir., 1967-75, chief exec. officer, 1972-75, partner, 1966-75, cons., 1975—; pres., dir. Sverdrup & Parcel & Assos., N.Y., Inc., 1967-75; dir. Sverdrup & Parcel Internat., Inc., 1967-75; v.p., dir. ARO, Inc., Tullahoma, Tenn., 1966-75; cons. EPA, 1976—; dir. Merc. Trust Co., St. Louis. Mem. emeritus Civic Progress, Inc.; bd. dirs. YMCA, St. Louis, 1972—. Decorated Legion of Merit; recipient citation Am. Inst. Steel Constrn., 1973; registered profl. engr., Mo., N.Y., Kans., Fla., Va., Calif. Mem. ASCE, Am. Public Works Assn. (1 of Top Ten Public Works Men of Year 1960), Soc. Mil. Engrs. (pres. 1960-61), Am. Concrete Inst., Am. Road and Transp. Builders Assn. (pres. 1972-73), Nat. Soc. Profl. Engrs., Mo. Soc. Profl. Engrs., Public Works Hist. Soc. (pres. 1977-78, trustee 1975—), Nat. Acad. Engring., Cons. Engrs. Council (award of Merit 1962), Sigma Tau, Phi Kappa Phi. Clubs: Army-Navy Country (Washington); Old Warson Country, St. Louis (St. Louis). Home: 8 Ladue Forest St Saint Louis MO 63124 Office: 800 N 12th St Saint Louis MO 63101

PELTON, JOHN FORRESTER, educator, botanist; b. Los Angeles, Mar. 15, 1924; s. George Seely and Luella (Forrester) P.; B.S. in Hort., U. Calif. at Los Angeles, 1945; M.S., U. Minn., 1948, Ph.D. in Botany, 1951; m. Jeanette Theresa Siron, Aug. 28, 1948 (dec. Oct. 1966); 1 son, George Steven; m. 2d, Mary Frances Pangborn Eudaly, July 23, 1972; stepchildren—J. Daniel, Joan. Instr., U. Minn.,, 1948-49, U. Calif. at Berkeley, 1951-52, Oberlin (Ohio) Coll., 1952-53; mem. faculty Butler U., 1953—, prof., head botany dept., 1961—. Treas. Rocky Mountain Biol. Lab., 1957-59, trustee, 1960-63. Bd. govs. Nature Conservancy, 1960-63, trustee Ind. chpt., 1960-70. NSF grantee, 1961-62. Mem. Bot. Soc. Am., Ecol. Soc. Am. (asso. editor 1959-61), AAAS, Ind. Acad. Sci. Contbr. articles to profl. jours. Home: 5028 Haynes Ave Indianapolis IN 46250

PELTON, RUSSELL GILBERT, elec. and electronics co. exec., lawyer; b. Monticello, N.Y., July 23, 1914; s. William and May (Morgan) P.; B.S. in Elec. Engring., Syracuse (N.Y.) U., 1935; J.D., George Washington U., 1944; m. Marion Gosart, Dec. 14, 1940; children—William, Marjorie, Marilyn Pelton Barringer. Engr. Gen. Electric Co., Bridgeport, Conn., 1935-40; admitted to D.C. bar, 1944, N.Y. State bar, 1947; partner firm Darby & Darby, N.Y.C., 1945-56; sr. v.p. N.Am. Philips Corp., N.Y.C., 1956-75; exec. v.p. U.S. Philips Corp., N.Y.C., 1968-75; counsel firm Rogers, Hoge & Hills, N.Y.C., 1976—; lectr. Practising Law Inst., 1953-69. Vice pres. Siwanoy council Boy Scouts Am., 1948-53; v.p. Rye Neck Bd. Edn., Mamaroneck, N.Y., 1952-62; commr. Zoning Bd. Appeals, Mamaroneck, 1966-70, town justice, 1970—. Trustee Syracuse U., 1968-74. Served with Signal Corps, U.S. Army, 1941-45. Mem. Am., N.Y. State, Westchester County bar assns., Assn. of Bar of City N.Y., Am. (chmn. com. antitrust), N.Y. (bd. govs.) patent law assns., State, County Magistrates Assns., Inst. Radio Engrs., Am. Radio Relay League, Aircraft Owners, Pilots Assn. Clubs: Wings, Cloud (N.Y.C.); Winged Foot Golf, Univ. (Mamaroneck); Waccabuc Country (South Salem, N.Y.); Masons, Elks. Contbg. author: Patent Licensing, 1969; Patentee in field. Home: 3 Oxford Rd Larchmont NY 10538 Office: 90 Park Ave New York City NY 10016 also 1 N Broadway White Plains NY 10601

PELTZ, NELSON, diversified co. exec.; b. N.Y.C., June 24, 1942; s. Maurice H. and Claire (Wechsler) P.; student Wharton Sch., U. Pa., 1964; children—Andrew, Brooke. Pres., chief exec. officer APS Food Systems, Inc., N.Y.C., 1970-72, Flagstaff Corp., N.Y.C., 1972-78, Coffee-Mat Corp., Kenilworth, N.J., 1975-76 (merged with Flagstaff Corp. 1976), FSF Industries (formerly Flagstaff Corp.), 1979—; pres., chief exec. officer, gen. partner Brook Fund. Trustee U.S. Olympic Ski Team, 1975—. Mem. Young Pres.'s Orgn. Clubs: Madison Sq. Garden, City Athletic, Old Oaks Country. Office: 600 Madison Ave New York NY 10022

PELZEL, JOHN CAMPBELL, educator; b. Harper, Kans., July 25, 1914; s. Theodore and Elizabeth (Campbell) P.; A.B., U. Chgo, 1935; postgrad. U. Pa., 1939; M.A., Harvard, 1941, Ph.D., 1950; Ph.D., Korea U., 1963. Faculty, Harvard, 1949—, prof. anthropology, 1959—; dir. vis. scholars (Far Eastern) program Harvard-Yenching Inst., 1955-64, dir. Harvard Yenching Inst., 1964-76; chief pub. opinion and sociol. research SCAP, Tokyo, 1948-49. Served to maj. USMCR, 1941-46. Decorated Legion of Merit. Fellow Am. Anthrop. Assn.; mem. Assn. Asian Studies, Am. Acad. Arts and Sci. Editor: (in Japanese) Nihonjin no yomi-kaki noryoku, 1951. Office: Peabody Mus Harvard U Cambridge MA 02138

PEMBERTON, HARRISON JOSEPH, JR., educator, philosopher; b. Orlando, Fla., Mar. 3, 1925; s. Harrison Joseph and Frances (Chappell) P.; A.B., Rollins Coll., 1949; M.A., Yale U., 1951, Ph.D., 1953. Instr., Yale U., 1951-54; asst. prof. U. Va., 1954-62; mem. faculty Washington and Lee U., 1962—, prof. philosophy, chmn. dept., 1967—; vis. prof. U. Tex., summers 1962, 66, 69, Chung Chi Coll., Chinese U. Hong Kong, 1971. Served with U.S. Army, 1943-46. Fellow Pierson Coll., Yale, 1952-54; mem. Am. Philos. Assn. Home: 602 S Main St Lexington VA 24450

PEN, RUDOLPH THEODORE, painter, lithographer; b. Chgo., Jan. 1, 1918; s. John and Agnes (Klemczak) P.; B.F.A., Art Inst. Chgo., 1943; m. Yvonne Fillis, June 29, 1946; children—Ronald Allen, Yvonne Pauline. Mem. faculty Art Inst. Chgo., 1948-63, North Shore Art League, Winnetka, Ill., 1948-79; founder, tchr., dir. Rudolph Pen Sch. Painting, Chgo., 1963—; numerous one-man shows, including: Carroll Carstairs Gallery, N.Y.C., 1944-45, Marshall Fields Gallery, Chgo., 1959, Frank Ochlschlaeger Gallery, Chgo., 1962, Vincent Price Gallery, Chgo., 1968, Art Inst. Chgo., 1977, 79; numerous group shows include: Carnegie Inst., Pitts., 1946, Art Inst. Chgo., 1966, Phila. Acad. Fine Arts, 1946, Corcoran Mus. Art, Washington, 1949, Marshall Field Art Gallery, Chgo., 1979; represented in permanent collections: Washington and Lee U., Va., Davenport (Iowa) Mus., Library of Congress, Washington, Art Inst. Chgo.; also pvt. collections; dir. Oxbow (Mich.) Summer Sch. Painting, 1964-65. Recipient prize NAD, 1946, Union League Club, Chgo., 1957, 61, 65; Joseph Ryerson traveling fellow, 1943; Huntington Hartford Found. grantee, 1958. Mem. Am. Watercolor Soc., Alumni Assn. Art Inst. Chgo. (pres. 1960-62), Union League Civic and Arts Found. (hon.). Episcopalian. Club: Arts of Chgo. Home: 55 W Schiller St Chicago IL 60610

PENA, WILLIAM MERRIWEATHER, architect; b. Laredo, Tex., Feb. 10, 1919; s. Eduardo Francisco and Clementina Contreras (Merriweather) P.; B.S., Tex. A. and M. U., 1942, B.Arch., 1948. Architect, Caudill Rowlett Scott, College Station, Tex., 1948-49, partner, College Station and Bryan, Tex., 1949-59, sr. v.p., Houston, 1959—; mem. adv. bd. CRS Design Assos. Served to capt. AUS, 1942-47; ETO. Decorated Purple Heart, Bronze Star. Recipient AIA Sch. medal, 1948. Fellow AIA; mem. Tex. Soc. Architects. Author: (with John W. Focke) Problem Seeking: New Directions in Architectural Programming, 1969; (with William Caudill and John Focke) Problem Seeking—An Architectural Programming Primer, 1977; (with Caudill and Paul Kenyon) Architecture and You: How to Experience and Enjoy Buildings, 1978. Office: 1111 W Loop S Houston TX 77027

PENALBA, ALICIA, sculptor; b. San Pedro, Buenos Aires, Argentina, Aug. 9, 1913; d. Santiago Perez and Maria de los Remedios Penalba; diplomada de Dibujo y Pintura, Escuela Superior de Bellas Artes, Buenos Aires, 1946; Ire medaille etrangere de Gravure, Ecole Superieure des Beaux Arts de Paris, 1949; student Academie de la Grande-Chaumiere, 1949-51; m. Amadeo Binci, June 25, 1939 (div.). One man exhbns. include: Galerie du Dragon, Paris, 1957, Galerie Claude Bernard, Paris, France, 1960, Otto Gerson Gallery, N.Y.C., 1960, Galerie Charles Lienhard, Zurich, Switzerland, 1961, Sixth Biennial of Sao Paulo (Brazil), 1961, Museu de Arte Moderna, Rio de Janeiro, 1962, Devorah Sherman Gallery, Chgo., 1962, Rijks museum Kröller-Müller Otterlo and Stedelijk Van Abbemuseum Eindhoven (Netherlands), Städtisches Mus. Leverkusen, Schloss Morsbroich (Germany), 1964, Galerie Creuzevault, Paris, France, 1965, Galeria Bonino, New York, 1966. Phillips Collection, Washington, 1966, Galerie d'Art Moderne, Basel, Switzerland, 1967, Galerie Pauli, Lausanne, 1967, Toninelli Arte Moderna, Milan, 1969, Galleria Nuovo Carpine, Rome, 1969, Galerie Alice Pauli, Lausanne, 1971, Galerie d'art Moderne, Basel, Switzerland, 1971, Galerie de France et du Bénélux, Brussels, 1975, Artel Galerie, Geneva, 1975, Galleria Stendhal, Milan, 1976, Arte/Contacto, Caracas, 1976, Musée d'Art Moderne de la Ville de Paris, 1977, Galerie Villand-Galanis, Paris, 1977, Museo Bellas Artes, Caracas, 1978, others; group exhbns. include: Salon de Mai, Paris, 1952, Salon de la Jeune Sculpture, Paris, 1952-57, Biennale d'Anvers, 1953, 55, 61, 69, Realites Nouvelles, 1955-58, 63, Ecole de Paris au Japon, 1956, Musee d'Angers, 1956, Musee de Tours, 1957, Kunstgewerbemuseum, Zurich, 1957, exposition internationale Musee Rodin, Paris, 1957, Hommage a Brancusi, Galerie Suzanne de Coninck, Paris, 1957, Musee de Charleroi, 1958, Kunsthalle de Recklinghausen, 1958, Pitts. Internat. Exhbn., 1958, 70, Guggenheim Mus., 1958, 62, Fine Arts Gallery, N.Y., 1959, Biennale Triveneta, Padova, 1959, Mus. Haus Lange, 1959, Documenta II, Kassel, 1959, 64, Rotterdam Kunstring, 1960, Musée de St. Etienne, 1960, 6th Biennale de Sao Paulo (1st internat. sculpture prize), 1961, Museu de Arte Moderna, Rio de Janeiro, 1961, Festival dei Due Mondi, Spoleto, 1962, Meisterwerke der Plastik, Mus. des 20. Jahrhunderts, Vienna, 1964, Pitts. Internat. Exhbn., Carnegie Inst., 1964, Hessisches Landesmuseum Darmstadt, 1964, Dallas Mus. Fine Arts, 1965, Mus. Boymans van Beuningen, Rotterdam, 1965, 8th Tokyo Biennale, 1965, Musée de Grenoble, 1966, Sonsbeek, Arnhem, 1966, Biennale d'Anvers, 1969, Hakone Open Air Mus., 1969, Fondaçao C. Gulbenkian, Lisbon, 1971, Palazzo Ducale, Venice, 1972, Seibu, Tokyo, 1973, Inst. Contemporary Art, Boston, 1973, Musée Ingres, Montauban, France, 1973, Museo de Arte Moderno, Bogota, 1974, Amos Andersonin Taidemuseo, Helsinki, 1974, Musée des Arts Décoratifs, Paris, 1975, Hetjens-Mus., Dusseldorf, 1975, Hist. Mus., Moscow, 1975, Hermitage, Moscow, 1975, Nat. Mus., Seoul, 1976, Musée Cantini, Marseilles, 1977, Cleve. Mus. Art, 1977, Centre Nat. d'Art et Culture Georges Pompidou, Paris, 1979, Fond-acao C. Gulbenkian, Lisbon, 1979, others; represented permanent collections Musée National d'Art Moderne, Paris, Musee de Tourcoing, Musee d'Art et d'Industrie, St. Etienne, France, Cleve. Mus. Art, Mus. des 20 Jahrhunderts, Vienna, Isaac Delgado Mus. Art, New Orleans, Middleheim Park, Mus. Art, Carnegie Inst., Pitts., Rijksmuseum Kröller-Müller Otterlo, Stedelijk Van Abbemuseum Eindhoven, Städtiches Mus. Leverkusen, Museu de Arte Moderna, Rio de Janeiro, Staatgalerie, Stuttgart, Centre National d'Art et de Culture Georges Pompidou Contemporain, Paris, Hirshhorn Mus. and Sculpture Garden, Washington, others; also pvt. collections; archtl. sculptures in France, U.S., Switzerland, Germany and Japan. Decorated chevalier de l'Ordre des Arts et des Lettres (France). Address: 24 rue du Roi-de-Sicile Paris 75004 France

PENCE, MARTIN, U.S. dist. judge; b. Sterling, Kans., Nov. 18, 1904; m. Eleanor Fisher, Apr. 12, 1975. Admitted to Calif. bar, 1928, Hawaii bar, 1933; practice law, Hilo, Hawaii, 1936-45, 50-61; judge 3d Circuit Ct., Hawaii, 1945-50; chief judge U.S. Dist. Ct. Hawaii, 1961-74, sr. judge, 1974—. Office: US District Court C-438 PJKK Bldg PO Box 50128 Honolulu HI 96850

PENDELL, ELMER, population economist, author; b. Waverly, N.Y., July 28, 1894; s. George and Ida (Harris) P.; LL.B., George Washington U., 1917; B.S., U. Ore., 1921; A.M., U. Chgo., 1923; studied population under James A. Field; Ph.D., Cornell, 1929; studied population under Walter F. Wilcox; m. Lucille Hunt, 1930 (div. 1946); 1 dau., Martha Jane (Mrs. James Edwin Griffin). Asst. prof. in undergrad. centers, Pa. State U., 1933-44; research for Rep. Nat. Com. and senators, 1944-45; asst. prof., Baldwin Wallace Coll., Berea, Ohio, 1946-54; exec. sec. Ashtabula County Hist. Soc., 1955-56; vis. prof. econs. Olivet Coll., 1956-57; asso. prof. econs. State U., Jacksonville, Ala., 1957-65. Served as 1st lt., inf., World War I; observer 168th Aero Squadron; awarded Purple Heart and D.S.C.; aerial observer in fire control work over Ore. forests, 1920-21. Mem. S.A.R., Legion Valor, Phi Kappa Phi, Pi Gamma Mu, Delta Mu Delta. Author: Population on the Loose, 1951; The Next Civilization, 1960; Sex Versus Civilization, 1967; Rhymed Reminders, 1970; Why Civilizations Self Destruct, 1977; (with G. I. Burch) Population Roads to Peace or War, 1945 rev. as Human Breeding and Survival, 1947. Editor: Society under Analysis, 1942, Wisdom to Guide You, 1960, Miracle (poetry), 1971. Home: care Mrs JE Griffin 4002 Old Mill Rd Alexandria VA 22309

PENDER, POLLARD EUGENE, retail trade exec.; b. Montgomery, La., Feb. 5, 1931; s. Ralph Louis and Ann Marie (Carter) P.; student Northwestern State Coll., Natchitoches, La., 1948-50, Centenary Coll., Shreveport, La., 1950-52; m. Vera Lynelle George, May 4, 1950; children—Jeffrey Scott, Gary Warren. Accountant, Pak-a-Sak Service Stores, Inc., Shreveport, 1950-52, sec.-treas., dir., 1952-71; div. controller Southland Corp., Shreveport, 1971-72, asst. corporate controller, Dallas, 1972, corporate controller, 1973—; pres. Penro Mobile Homes, Inc., Cypress River Village, Inc.; sec.-treas., dir. Highland Lakes Furniture Center, Inc.; dir. United Merc. Bank, So. Research Co., Inc. Pres., Ark.-La.-Tex. Airmens Assn., 1967-69; bd. dirs. Better Bus. Bur., 1971, Mental Health Center, 1964, United Fund. C.P.A., La., Tex. Mem. Am. Inst. C.P.A.'s, La., Tex. socs. C.P.A.'s, Fin. Execs. Inst., Q.B.'s (Keyman 1971-72). Democrat. Episcopalian. Mason. Home: 303 Stonebridge Dr Richardson TX 75080 Office: 2828 N Haskell Ave Dallas TX 75221

PENDERECKI, KRZYSZTOF, composer; b. Debica, Poland, Nov. 23, 1933; grad. State Acad. Music, Krakow, 1958; student Arthur Malawski and Stanislaw Wiechowicz; Dr. honoris causa, U. Rochester, St. Olaf Coll., Northfield, Minn.; m. 2d, Elzbieta Solecka; children—Lukasz, Dominique. Composer Psalms of David for chorus and percussion, 1958; Emanations for 2 string orchs., 1959; Strophes for soprano, narrator and 10 instruments, 1959; Dimensions of time and silence, 1960; Anaklasis, 1960; Threnody for the Victims of Hiroshima, 1960; Psalmus for tape, Fluorescences, Polymorphia, all 1961; Stabat Mater, 1962, Canon, 1962; Sonata for Cello and Orchestra, 1964; De Natura Sonoris I, 1966; St. Luke Passion, 1966; Dies Irae, 1967; Capriccio for Cello Solo, 1968; Capriccio for Violin and Orch., 1968; opera Devils of Loudun, 1969; Utrenja for double chorus, soloists and orchestra, 1970-71; Ecloga for 6 Male Voices, 1972; Partita for Harpsichord, 4 Solo Instruments and Orch., 1971-72; Actions for Jazz Ensemble, 1971; Symphony 1, 1973; Canticum Canticorum Salomonis for 30 Instruments and 16 Voices, 1970-73; Cello Concerto, 1971-72; Magnificat, 1973-74, Awakening of Jacob for Orch., 1974, others. Prof. composition Krakow State Sch. Music, 1959-65, Folkwang Hochschule für Musik, Essen, Fed. Republic Germany, 1966-68; composer-in-residence Sch. Music, Yale U., alternate years. Recipient 1st prize for Strophes, Polish Composers Assn., 1959; UNESCO award, Fitelberg prize and Polish Ministry Culture award all for Threnody, 1960; Krakow composition prize for Canon, 1961; grand prize State N. Rhine-Westphalia for St. Luke Passion, 1966; Pax prize, Poland, 1966; Jurzykowski prize Polish Inst. Arts and Scis., 1966; Sibelius award, 1967; Prix d'Italia, 1967-68; Polish 1st Class State award, 1968; grantee several founds., govts., insts. Mem. Royal Acad. Mus. London (hon.), Accademia Nazaionale di Santa Cecilia (Roma) (hon.), Royal Swedish Acad. Music, Akademie der Kuenste Berlin West (extraordinary mem.), Akademie der Kuenste E. Ger. (corr.). Creator original notational system allowing aleatory freedom for performer within sects. of precise duration. Office: care Jacques Leiser 155 W 68th St New York NY 10023*

PENDERGAST, THOMAS FRANCIS, news service exec.; b. Newburg, W.Va., Feb. 6, 1932; s. Thomas Leo and Edith Lorena (Gibson) P.; student Potomac State Coll., Keyser, W.Va., 1949-51; B.S. in Journalism, W.Va. U., 1953; m. Karen Wheeler, Feb. 14, 1963; 1 dau., Meredith Ann. City editor Hinton (W.Va.) Daily News, 1953; newsman AP, Chgo., 1955-58, regional membership exec. for La., Miss. and Ark., New Orleans, 1958-63, corr., St. Louis, 1963-65, chief of bur., Richmond, Va., 1965-67, chief of bur., Phila., 1967-69, chief of bur., Los Angeles, 1969-73, dep. personnel dir., N.Y.C., 1973-74, v.p., dir. personnel and labor relations, 1975—. Served with USNR, 1953-55. Recipient Alumni Achievement awards W.Va. Sch. Journalism, 1972, Potomac State Coll., 1977. Mem. Soc. Profl. Journalists, Sigma Delta Chi. Office: AP 50 Rockefeller Plaza New York NY 10020*

PENDERGRASS, TEDDY, musician; b. Phila., Mar. 26, 1950; student public schs.; children—Tisha, Ladonna, Teddy. Drummer for various groups, 1966-69, Harold Melvin & Blue Notes, 1969-75; solo artist, 1975—; now pres. Teddy Bear Prodns., Phila. Squire, Shelby County, Memphis. Recipient civic and public service awards. Writer hit songs. Office: 215 S Broad St Philadelphia PA 19107

PENDERGRASS, WEBSTER, ednl. adminstr.; b. Byrdstown, Tenn., Jan. 7, 1914; s. Andrew Pleasant and Maudie Mae (Bowden) P.; B.S., U. Tenn., 1936, M.S., 1947; D.P.A., Harvard, 1954; m. Mildred Knox Carter, June 20, 1937; 1 dau., Betty June. Asst. county agt., Wilson County, Tenn., 1936-37, Dickson County, 1937-39; asst. county agt., Henry County, 1940-42, county agt., 1942-44; instr. agronomy U. Tenn. Coll. Agr., 1946-47, agronomist, leader agronomy extension Agrl. Extension Service,, 1947-57, dean agr., 1957-68, vice chancellor Inst. Agr., 1968-70, v.p. for agr., 1970-79, v.p. emeritus, 1979—. Bd. dirs., v.p. internat. Fertilizer Devel. Center. Served from ensign to lt. USNR, 1944-46. Recipient Distinguished Service award for extension specialists Tenn. County Agts. Assn.; Man of Month award So. Seedman; Progressive Farmer Man of Year Tenn. Agr. award, 1964; citation for outstanding service 4-H; named Hon. State Farmer, Future Farmers Am. Mem. Tenn. Farm Bur. Fedn. (dir.), Tenn. Livestock Producers (dir.), Tenn. Edn. Assn., Assn. So. Agr. Workers (pres. 1963-64), U. Tenn. Nat. Alumni Assn. (council, pres. agrl. sec. 1959), Alpha Zeta, Phi Delta Kappa (pres. 1935-36), Phi Kappa Phi, Epsilon Sigma Phi, Gamma Sigma Delta, Omicron Delta Kappa, Phi Zeta. Mem. Christian Ch. (elder). Clubs: Block and Bridle, Rotary (pres. 1969-70, dist. gov. 1975-76). Home: 3601 Blow Dr Knoxville TN 37920 Office: PO Box 1071 Knoxville TN 37901

PENDLETON, AUSTIN, actor, dir.; b. Warren, Ohio, Mar. 27, 1940; B.A. Yale U., 1961; m. Katina Commings; 1 dau., Audrey Christine. Apprenticed at Williamstown Theatre Festival, 1957-58; N.Y.C. stage appearances: Oh Dad, Poor Dad, Momma's Hung You in the Closet and I'm Feeling So Sad, 1962, Fiddler on the Roof, 1964, Hail Scrawdyke (Clarnece Derwent award), 1966, The Little Foxes, 1967, The Last Sweet Days of Isaac (Obie award, Drama Critic's Poll award, Drama Desk award), 1970, An American Millionaire, 1974, The Sorrows of Frederick, 1976, The Three Sisters, 1977, Julius Caesar, 1978, Waiting for Godot, 1979; with Am. Conservatory Theatre, San Francisco, 1966-67; dir.: Canadian Gothic/American Modern, Manhattan Theatre Club, N.Y.C., 1972, Shelter, Broadway, 1973, Little Egolf, N.Y.C., 1974, Benita Cereno, N.Y.C., 1976, The Runner Stumbles, Broadway, 1976, The Gathering, 1977, Say Goodnight Gracie, off-Broadway, 1979, also at Williamstown (Mass.) Theatre Festival, Long Wharf Theatre, New Haven, Kennedy Center, Washington, Hardman Theatre, Stamford, Conn., Travel Light Theatre, Chgo., Acad. Festival Theatre, Chgo.; film appearances: Skidoo, 1968, Catch-22, 1970, Oven 350, 1970, Whats Up Doc, 1972, Every Little Crook and Nanny, 1972, The Thief Who Came to Dinner, 1973, The Front Page, 1974, Lovesick, 1974, The Great Smokey Roadblock, 1978, The Muppets Movie, 1979, Starting Over, 1979, Simon, 1980, First Family, 1980. Office: care Actors Equity Assn 1500 Broadway New York NY 10036

PENDLETON, BARBARA JEAN, banker; b. Independence, Mo., Aug. 14, 1924; d. Elmer Dean and Martha Lucille (Friess) P. Exec. v.p. City Bank & Trust Co., Kansas City; dir. City Bancshares, Inc. Mem. U.S. Dept. Def. Adv. Com. on Women in Service, 1965-68;

pres. bd. North Kansas City Library, 1968-73. Bd. dirs. Rehab. Inst.; nat. bd. dirs. Camp Fire Girls, Inc.; mem. Indsl. Devel. Authority of Clay County. Mem. Nat. Assn. Bank Women (pres. 1972-73), Women's C. of C. (pres. 1962), Jr. Achievement (dir.), Am. Royal Assn. Home: 1905 E 29th Ave North Kansas City MO 64116 Office: PO Box 949 Kansas City MO 64141

PENDLETON, EUGENE BARBOUR, JR., business exec.; b. nr. Louisa, Va., Apr. 2, 1913; s. Eugene Barbour and Virginia (Goodman) P.; student Va. Mil. Inst., 1930-31, Hampden-Sydney Coll., 1931-34; m. Mildred McLean, June 18, 1938; children—Barbara Jane (Mrs. Percy Wootton), Sally Anne (Mrs. Hugh Campbell), Nancy McLean (Mrs. Charles H. Wheeler IV), Susan Virginia (Mrs. Richard Riley), Martha Christina (Mrs. Cary U. Hall). Organizer, mgr. Gen. Ins. Agy., 1937-42; treas. Louisa County, Va., 1946-56; field rep. Va. Dept. Taxation, 1956-58; treas. State Va., 1958-61; treas. So. States Coop., 1961-77, v.p. fin., 1977-78; v.p. fin. Truxmore Industries Inc., Richmond, Va., 1978—; dir. So. Bank & Trust Co. Bd. dirs., pres. Richmond Businessmen's Assn.; bd. dirs. Atlantic Rural Expn., Richmond Home for Boys, Va. Edn. Fund; past bd. dirs. Richmond Symphony. Mem. bd. suprs. Louisa County, 1937-42; mem. Ho. of Dels., Va. Gen. Assembly, 1966-70. Past pres. Va. Thanksgiving Festival. Served from ensign to lt. USNR, 1942-46; ETO. Mem. Va., Richmond chambers commerce, Bond Club Va., County and City Treas. Assn. Va. (past pres.), Nat. Assn. State Treas., Mil. Order World Wars (past comdr.), Navy League U.S. (v.p.), 1st Families Va. (council), Soc. of Va. (v.p.), Am. Legion, VFW (comdr.). Mem. Christian Ch. (past elder, chmn. bd.). Mason (Shriner). Clubs: Downtown (past pres.) (Richmond); Commonwealth; Country of Va.; Army-Navy (Washington). Home: 5114 Downy Lane Richmond VA 23228 Office: PO Box 1656 Richmond VA 23213

PENDLETON, JOHNNY WRYAS, agronomist, educator; b. Hillsboro, Tenn., Jan. 1, 1922; s. Witt F. and Jo Harley (West) P.; B.S., U. Tenn., 1948; M.S., U. Ill., 1951, Ph.D., 1955; m. Eleanor Spahr, Sept. 4, 1948; children—Betsy, Don, Pam, Kip, Sandie. Asst. prof. agronomy U. Ill., Urbana, 1955-59, asso. prof., 1959-64, prof., 1964-71; prof., chmn. dept. agronomy U. Wis., Madison, 1971—. Agrl. cons. to India, Indonesia, Phillipines, 1969-71, Korea, 1975. Served with USNR, 1942-46. Recipient Research award Phi Sigma, 1951, DuPont Crop Scientist award, 1971; Australian Vis. fellow, 1969. Fellow AAAS, Am. Soc. Agronomy (dir. 1974-76, pres. 1978); mem. Am. Council Agrl. Sci. and Tech. (dir. 1973-77, mem. exec. com.), Crop Sci. Soc., Am. Inst. Biol. Sci., Soil Conservation Soc., Sigma Xi, Gamma Sigma Delta. Club: Exchange. Asso. editor Agronomy Jour., 1960-62. Contbr. numerous articles to profl. jours. Home: 4185 Nakoma Rd Madison WI 53711

PENDLETON, MOSES ROBERT ANDREW, dancer, choreographer; b. St. Johnsbury, Vt., Mar. 28, 1949; s. Nelson Augustus and Mary Elizabeth (Patchel) P.; B.A., Dartmouth Coll., 1971. Co-founder Pilobolus Dance Theatere (Edinborough Fringe Festival Scotsman award 1973, Berlin Critic's prize 1975), Washington, Conn., 1971, dir., choreographer, dancer, 1971—; choreographer, dancer numerous works, including: Pilobolus, 1971, Anendrom, 1972, Walklyndon, 1972, Ocellus, 1972, Ciona, 1973, Monkshood's Farewell, 1974, Untitled, 1975, Eve of Samhain, 1977, Alraune, 1975, Lost in Fauna, 1976, Shizen, 1977; actor, dancer film Pilobolus and Joan, 1974; choreographer and artist-in-residence at univs. throughout U.S., 1977; tchr., workshop condr. in field; choreographer Erik Satie Festival, Paris Opera, 1978; co-choreographer Molly's Not Dead, Pilobolus Dance Theater, 1978. Nat. Endowment for Arts grantee, 1975-76; Guggenheim fellow in choreography, 1977. Democrat. Home: Bell Hill Rd Washington CT 06793 Office: PO Box 233 Washington CT 06793

PENDLETON, SUMNER ALDEN, fin. exec.; b. Boston, May 2, 1918; s. Sumner Maynard and Ethel Pearl (Phinney) P.; S.B. cum laude, Harvard, 1939, M.B.A. (Baker scholar), 1941; m. Nancy Curtiss Welles, June 8, 1941; children—Nancy Alden Pendleton Dyer, John Welles. With Gen. Electric Co., 1945-50, Ford Motor Co., 1950-53; asst. to corp. controller, then controller electronics div. Curtiss-Wright Corp., 1953-60; asst. controller, financial analysis, audit and data processing methods Internat. Tel.&Tel. Corp., 1960-63; controller, asst. sec. Joy Mfg. Co., Pitts., 1963-67; v.p. finance treas. Ryan Homes, Inc., Pitts., 1967-71, v.p. corporate devel., 1971-74; v.p., sec., treas. Ryan Homes Finance Co., 1970-74; chmn., treas. Unidyne Corp., Pitts., also Bergoo Coal Co., 1975-78; asso. exec. dir. budget and fin. United Presbyterian Ch. U.S.A., 1976-78; fin. cons., 1978—; sec., dir. Hytronics Corp., Clearwater, Fla., 1978, dir., v.p. fin., 1979—. Gen. campaign chmn. Community Chest Ridgewood, Hohokus and Midland Park, N.J., 1959-60, pres., 1960-62. Served to lt. comdr. USNR, 1941-45; capt. Res. ret. Decorated Silver Star. Recipient Robert Morris Coll. Accounting Profession Exec. of Year award, 1973. Mem. Fin. Execs. Inst. (dir. Newark 1961-62), Nat. Assn. Accountants (Lybrand certificate 1955, pres. Paterson 1955-56, nat. dir. 1957-59, v.p. 1965-66, mem. exec. com. 1966-69), Stuart Cameron McLeod Soc. (pres. 1975-76), Harvard Bus. Sch. Assn. Pitts. (v.p. 1968-69, pres. 1969-70, chmn. bd. govs. 1970-71), Presbyn. (treas. 1966-76, trustee 1965-68, elder 1968-71, past deacon, head usher, Sunday Sch. tchr.). Home: 2163 Waterside Dr Clearwater FL 33516 Office: Hytronics Corp 15401 Roosevelt Blvd Box 4050 Clearwater FL 33518 also Room 1020 475 Riverside Dr New York NY 10027

PENEGAR, KENNETH LAWING, lawyer, univ. dean; b. Charlotte, N.C., May 12, 1932; s. Oscar General and Ethel Meredith (Lawing) P.; B.A. in History, U. N.C., 1954, J.D. with honors, 1961; postgrad. London Sch. Econs., 1958; LL.M., Yale U., 1962. Admitted to N.C. bar, 1961, D.C. bar, 1963; clk. to Judge Charles Fahy, U.S. Ct. Appeals, D.C. Circuit, 1962-63; asst. prof. law U. N.C., 1963-66, asso. prof., 1966-69; asso. firm Shea & Gardner, Washington, 1969-71; prof. law, dean U. Tenn., 1971—; Ford Found. vis. prof. Delhi U., India, 1967-68; v.p., dir. Fed. Tax Inst., Tenn., 1973—; cons. in field. Trustee Lawyers Com. for Civil Rights Under Law, 1976—. Mem. Am., Tenn., Knoxville bar assns., Am. Law Inst., Order of Coif, Order of Golden Fleece, Phi Kappa Phi, Omicron Delta Kappa, Phi Alpha Delta. Contbr. articles to profl. jours. Home: 3820 Woodhill Pl Knoxville TN 37919 Office: U of Tenn Coll Law 1505 W Cumberland Ave Knoxville TN 37916

PENELHUM, TERENCE MICHAEL, educator; b. Bradford-on-Avon, Eng., Apr. 26, 1929; s. Charles Arnold and Dorothy Eva (Mustoe) P.; M.A., U. Edinburgh, 1950; B.Phil., Oriel Coll., Oxford U., 1952; m. Edith Andrews, July 8, 1950; children—Rosemary Claire, Andrew Giles (dec.). Asst. prof. philosophy U. Alta., 1953-59, 1959-63; prof. philosophy U. Calgary (Alta., Can.), 1963-78, dean arts and sci., 1964-67, prof. religious studies, 1978—. Fellow Royal Soc. Can.; mem. Can. Philos. Assn., Can. Soc. Study of Religion, Am. Philos. Assn. Anglican. Author: Survival and Disembodied Existence, 1970; Religion and Rationality, 1971; Problems of Religious Knowledge, 1971; Hume, 1974. Office: Dept Religious Studies Univ of Calgary Calgary T2N 1N4 Canada

PENICK, JAMES LAL, JR., historian; b. Charleston, S.C., Aug. 22, 1932; s. James Lal and Annie Cecelia (Sheedy) P.; B.A., Coll. William and Mary, 1957; M.A., U. Calif., Berkeley, 1959, Ph.D., 1962; m. Barbara Sue Perlmutter, June 20, 1959; children—Michael Andrew, Katherine Leona. Intermediate instr. Calif. State Poly. Coll., San Luis Obispo, 1963-65; mem. faculty Loyola U., Chgo., 1965—, prof. history, 1972—. Served with USNR, 1951-54. Archbishop Riordan scholar, 1959-60; Am. Council Learned Socs. grantee, 1968. Mem. Orgn. Am. Historians. Author: Progressive Politics and Conservation: The Ballinger-Pinchot Affair, 1968, The Politics of American Science, 1939 to the Present, 1972, The New Madrid Earthquakes of 1811-1812, 1976; also articles. Home: 923 Wesley Ave Evanston IL 60202 Office: 6525 N Sheridan Rd Chicago IL 60626. *Finish something, no matter how small a task, no matter how bad you feel, everyday.*

PENICK, JOE EDWARD, oil co. exec.; b. Frederick, Okla., Nov. 8, 1920; s. Jesse Olin and Grace Ann (Lane) P.; B.S., U. Okla., 1942; grad. Exec. Devel. Program Cornell U., 1963; m. Norma Gene Scott, Oct. 18, 1942; children—Joe Edward, David Scott. Research engr. Magnolia Petroleum Co., Dallas, 1942-46; with Mobil Oil Corp., 1946—, refinery mgr., Torrance, Calif., 1961-67, v.p. mfg., N.Y.C., 1967-76, sr. v.p. for research and engring., 1977—; pres. Mobil Research and Devel. Corp., 1977—. Bd. dirs., v.p. Mobil Found., Inc.; vice chmn. adv. bd. Little Co. Mary Hosp., Torrance, 1961-67; vice chmn. bd. trustees Neighborhood Ch., Palos Verdes Estates, Calif., 1966. Mem. Nat. Petroleum Refiners Assn. (dir. 1968-76, exec. com. 1973-76), Am. Petroleum Inst., Welding Research Council (exec. com. 1976—). Club: Mt. Kisco (N.Y.) Country. Patentee petroleum refining. Office: 150 E 42d St New York NY 10017

PENICK, SYDNOR BARKSDALE, JR., business exec.; b. Bristol, Va., Sept. 7, 1905; s. Sydnor Barksdale and Margaret Henry (Dabney) P.; grad. Montclair Acad. 1921; A.B., Princeton, 1925; m. Mary Louise Schieren, Feb. 11, 1928; children—Sydnor Barksdale, Mary (Mrs. T.R. Burgin); m. 2d, Elizabeth Van Wie, Jan. 22, 1944; children—Douglas, Frank, Jeannette Elizabeth Penick Young, Margaret Lucy. With S.B. Penick & Co. (became div. Corn Products Co. (now CPC Internat., Inc., 1968), N.Y.C., 1925—, v.p., dir., 1936-42, pres., 1942-60, chmn., 1960-70, hon. chmn., 1970—, also dir., mem. exec. com. CPC Internat., Inc.; dir. Am. Nat. Bank & Trust (N.J.). Charter trustee Princeton U., 1952-76, trustee emeritus, 1976—; trustee Montclair YMCA; bd. dirs., chmn. bd. Am. Found. Pharm. Edn.; pres. Montclair Art Mus. Mem. Pharm. Mfrs. Assn. (dir., chmn. 1963-64), N.Y. Bd. Trade (chmn. drug and chem. sect. 1942), Phi Beta Kappa. Clubs: Drug and Chemical (pres. 1947), University, River, Princeton (N.Y.C.); Montclair (N.J.) Golf; Chicago; Mill Reef. Home: 40 Wayside Pl Montclair NJ 07042

PENISTEN, GARY DEAN, pharm. co. exec.; b. Lincoln, Nebr., May 14, 1931; s. Martin C. and Jayne (O'Dell) P.; B.S. in Bus. Adminstrn., U. Nebr., Omaha, 1953; m. Nancy Margaret Golding, June 3, 1951; children—Kris D., Janet L., Carol E., Noel M. With Gen. Electric Co., 1953-74, mgr. group fin. ops. power generation group, N.Y.C., 1973-74; asst. sec. navy fin. mgmt., 1974-77; v.p. fin., chief fin. officer Sterling Drug Inc., N.Y.C., 1977—. Recipient Disting. Public Service award Navy Dept., 1977; Alumni Achievement citation U. Nebr., Omaha, 1975. Mem. Fin. Execs. Inst., Navy League U.S. Republican. Unitarian. Clubs: Union League (N.Y.C.); Siwanoy Country. Home: 10 Fordal Rd Bronxville NY 10708 Office: 90 Park Ave New York NY 10016

PENLAND, JOHN THOMAS, business exec.; b. Guntersville, Ala., Mar. 31, 1930; s. James B. and Kathleen (Bolding) P.; A.A., George Washington U., 1957; m. Carolyn Joyce White, May 30, 1961; children—Jeffrey K., Mark A., Michael J. Vice pres., dir. Rouse, Brewer, Becker & Bryant, Inc., Washington, 1957-63; staff mem. SEC, Washington, 1963-67; pres., dir. INA Trading Corp., Phila., 1968-69; v.p. INA Security Corp., Phila., 1967-69; v.p. Shareholders Mgmt. Co., Los Angeles, 1969, sr. v.p., 1970, exec. v.p., 1970-73, pres., 1973-75, also dir.; pres. Shareholders Investor Service Corp., Los Angeles, 1970-75, also dir.; v.p., dir. Shareholders Mktg. Corp., Los Angeles, 1969-75; v.p. Shareholders Capital Corp., Los Angeles, 1972-73, sr. v.p., 1973-75; v.p., dir. several mut. funds managed by Shareholders Mgmt. Co., 1970-75; pres., chmn., chief exec. officer HMO Internat., Los Angeles, 1975; pres., dir. Coastal Ins. Co., Los Angeles, 1975; chmn., pres. Ins. Capital Corp., Los Angeles, 1975; chmn. bd. Pendlar Corp., Atlanta, 1977—; chmn., pres. CompuComp, Atlanta, 1977—. Served with AUS, 1948-55. Republican. Lutheran. Club: Lions. Home: PO Box 549 Social Circle GA 30279 Office: Suite 1012 Candler Bldg Atlanta GA 30303

PENN, EDWIN ALLEN, coll. pres.; b. Elkhart, Ind., Oct. 7, 1939; s. Charles Walter and Margaret Helena (Huffman) P.; B.S., Juilliard Sch. Music, 1961; M.A., Tchrs. Coll., Columbia U., 1962, Ed.D., 1966; m. Jo-Ann Ching, Aug. 24, 1961; children—Derek, Howard, Kevin. Asst. dir. student center Bklyn. Coll., City U. N.Y., 1963-64; adminstrv. asst. Tchrs. Coll. Columbia U., 1964-66; asst. dean Coll. Arts and Scis. U. Hawaii, Honolulu, 1966-70; asst. dean Coll. Arts and Scis. U. Tex., Austin, 1970-71; asst. to pres. Boston U., 1971-76; pres. Franklin (Ind.) Coll., 1976—. Mem. Am. Assn. Higher Edn., AAUP. Club: Rotary. Home: 253 S Forsythe St Franklin IN 46131 Office: Office of Pres Franklin Coll Franklin IN 46131

PENN, IRVING, photographer; b. Plainfield, N.J., June 16, 1917; s. Harry and Sonia Penn; m. Lisa Fonssagrives, 1950; 1 son, Tom. Painter, 1941; first photographs pub. in Vogue, 1943; rep. photographs permanent collections Met. Mus. Art, Mus. Modern Art, N.Y.C. Author: Moments Preserved, collection 300 photographs, 1960; Worlds in a Small Room, 1974; Inventive Paris Clothes 1909-1939: A Photographic Essay by Irving Penn with Text by Diana Vreeland, 1977. Address: Irving Penn Studios Box 934 FDR Station New York NY 10022

PENN, JOHN CLARENCE, snowmobile mfg. exec.; b. Des Moines, Dec. 18, 1939; s. Orlyn O. and Hattie R. (Harper) P.; A.B., Dartmouth, 1961, M.B.A., 1962; m. Miriam L. Fjelland, Aug. 7, 1965; children—Timothy John, Anna Marie, David Erik. Mgr., Arthur Andersen & Co., Mpls., 1962-69; treas. Arctic Enterprises, Inc., Thief River Falls, Minn., 1969-70, v.p., 1970-72, pres., 1972—, dir., 1975—; dir. 1st Fed. Savs. & Loan Assn., Thief River Falls, Dynamic Homes, Inc., Detroit Lakes, Minn. Mem. Young Pres.'s Orgn., Internat. Snowmobile Industry Assn. (dir.). Lutheran. Address: Box 635 Thief River Falls MN 56701

PENN, JOHN GARRETT, judge; b. Pittsfield, Mass., Mar. 19, 1932; s. John and Eugenie Gwendolyn (Heyliger) P.; B.A., U. Mass., 1954; LL.B., Boston U., 1957; m. Ann Elizabeth Rollison, May 7, 1966; children—John Garrett, Karen Renee, David Brandon. Admitted to bar; trial atty. tax div. Dept. Justice, from 1961, then reviewer, asst. chief gen. litigation sect.; asso. judge Superior Ct. of D.C., Washington, 1970-79; U.S. dist. judge, U.S. Dist. Ct. for D.C., Washington, 1979—. Ex officio dir. D.C. Dept. Recreation Day Care Program, 1978—. Served to 1st lt. Judge Adv. Gen. Corps, U.S. Army, 1958-61. Nat. Inst. Public Affairs fellow. Mem. Am. Bar Assn., Fed. Bar Assn., Nat. Bar Assn., Mass. Bar Assn., D.C. Bar Assn., Am. Judicature Soc., Boston U. Law Sch. Alumni Assn. Episcopalian. Clubs: Nat. Lawyers (hon.); Argyle Country. Home: 13823 N Gate Ln Silver Spring MD 20906 Office: 6315 US Courthouse 3d and Constitution Ave NW Washington DC 20001

PENN, JOHN STANLEY, educator; b. Portage, Wis., Jan. 11, 1914; s. William Henry and Alice Harriet (Inks) P.; B.A., Carroll Coll., Waukesha, Wis., 1935; M.A., U. Wis., 1938, Ph. D., 1958; m. Margaret Hjortson Thorleifson; children—Stanley Warren, Leslie Margaret, Pamela Fay. Tchr. pub. schs., Wis. and Mich., 1936-40; mem. faculty U. N.D., 1940-43, 46—, prof. speech, 1954—, chmn. dept., 1948-68, dean summer session, exec. asst. to pres.; lectr. Rockford (Ill.) Coll., 1950. Cons. Peabody Awards Com., 1942; mem. N.D. Council Ednl. TV, 1961—. Chmn. Grand Forks Bd. Budget Rev., 1963-65. Mem. Grand Forks Sch. Bd., 1960-65. Served with USNR, 1943-46. Mem. Am. Assn. U. Profs., Speech Assn. Am., Central States Speech Assn., N.D. Council Coll. Faculties (pres. 1958-61), N.D. Edn. Assn., V.F.W., Pi Kappa Delta, Pi Epsilion Delta. Republican, Conglist. Mason, Rotarian, Elk. Author: articles. Home: 2610 University Ave Grand Forks ND 58201

PENN, STANLEY WILLIAM, newspaperman; b. N.Y.C., Jan. 12, 1928; s. Murray and Lillian (Richman) P.; student Bklyn. Coll., 1945-47; B. Journalism, U. Mo., 1949; m. Esther Aronson, July 12, 1952; children—Michael, Laurel. With Wall St. Jour., 1952—, investigative reporter N.Y. bur., 1957—. Co-recipient Pulitzer prize for nat. reporting, 1967. Home: 380 Riverside Dr New York NY 10025 Office: 22 Cortlandt St New York NY 10007

PENNA, RICHARD PAUL, assn. exec.; b. Palo Alto, Calif., Sept. 7, 1935; s. Paul and Valentina Michelle (Garino) P.; B.S., U. Calif. at San Francisco, 1958, Pharm. D., 1959; m. Laura Lopez, Sept. 6, 1958; children—Theresa Lynn, Anna Marie, Richard Albert. Pharmacist, Ryan Pharmacy, Redwood City, Calif., 1958-66; asst. clin. prof. pharmacy U. Calif. Sch. Pharmacy, San Francisco, 1960-66; exec. sec. Acad. Gen. Practice Pharmacy, Am. Pharm. Assn., Washington, 1966-72, asso. exec. dir. for profl. affairs, 1972—. Mem. AAAS, Am. Pharm. Assn., Am. Pub. Health Assn. Home: 412 Victoria Ct NW Vienna VA 22180 Office: 2215 Constitution Ave NW Washington DC 20037

PENNARIO, LEONARD, concert pianist, composer; b. Buffalo, July 9, 1924; s. John D. and Mary (Chiarello) P.; student music U. So. Calif., 1942; student piano with Guy Maier, Isabelle Vengerova. Profl. debut Dallas Symphony, 1936; debut Los Angeles Philharmonic, 1939, N.Y. Philharmonic, 1943; soloist orchs. in Phila., Chgo., Boston, N.Y.C., Los Angeles, St. Louis, others; concerts in Eng., Italy, Germany, Holland, France, Scandinavian countries, Austria; on tour South Africa, 1959, Europe, 1960; featured pianist chamber music concerts, Hollywood, 1961; recorded albums Capitol Records, RCA Victor. Mem. Calif. Scholarship Fedn. Served with USAAF, World War II. Mem. Ephebian Soc., A.S.C.A.P. Roman Catholic. Composer film music Midnight on the Cliffs, also piano concerto, other pieces for piano, including March of the Lunatics, Variations on the Kerry Dance. Address: care Columbia Artists Mgmt Inc 165 W 57th St New York City NY 10019*

PENNELL, JOHN SPEAR, lawyer; b. Jackson, Mich., Jan. 7, 1916; s. Henry and Stella (Spear) P.; A.B., U. Mich., 1938, J.D. cum laude, 1940; m. Era Northcut, Nov. 30, 1946; children—William, Jeffrey, Patricia. Admitted to Ill. bar, 1941; asst. in law U. Mich. Law Sch., 1940-41; asso., partner firm McDermott, Will & Emery, Chgo., 1941—. Mem. adv. com., lectr. U. Miami Tax Conf.; lectr. U. Chgo., Tulane U. tax confs., U. So. Calif. Inst. Fed. Taxation; N.Y. U. Ann. Inst. Fed. Taxation, So. Fed. Tax Inst., others. Served to capt. U.S. Army, 1942-46. Mem. Am. (chmn. partnership com. sect. taxation 1965-68, mem. council 1970-73, vice chmn. 1971-73, chmn.-elect sect. taxation 1976-77, chmn. 1977-78), Ill. (chmn. sect. taxation 1958-60, vice chmn. adv. council Inst. on Continuing Edn. 1962-69, chmn. 1969-71), Chgo. (com. continuing legal edn. 1964-70, com. fed. taxation 1966—, chmn. 1974-75) bar assns., State Bar Mich., Am. Law Inst. Republican. Mem. Ch. of Christ. Clubs: Union League (pres. 1976-77), Mid-Day (Chgo.); Westmoreland Country (Wilmette, Ill.). Mem. editorial bd. Jour. Taxation; contbr. articles on fed. taxation to profl. publs. Home: 1030 Romona Rd Wilmette IL 60091 Office: McDermott Will & Emery 111 W Monroe St Chicago IL 60603

PENNER, PETER JOHN, farmer; b. Reedley, Calif., Aug. 28, 1932; s. Peter P. and Anna (Klippenstein) P.; student Reedley Coll., 1951; m. Ruth L. Warkentin, June 4, 1954; children—Connie, Peter, Martin. Farmer, Reedley, 1955—; pres. Penner Enterprises, Inc., 1971—, PenCo Farms, Inc., 1977—; vice chmn. bd. dirs. Sun-Maid Raisin Growers of Calif., Inc.; mem. Calif. Raisin Adv. Bd., Raisin Adv. Com. Moderator, Reedley Mennonite Brethren Ch., 1974—. Served with U.S. Army, 1953-55. Recipient Farmer of Year award Reedley C. of C., 1975. Republican. Clubs: Rotary Internat. (pres. 1973-74); Toastmasters (pres. 1967). Office: PO Box 209 Reedley CA 93654

PENNER, STANFORD SOLOMON, educator; b. Unna, Germany, July 5, 1921; s. Heinrich and Regina (Saal) P.; came to U.S., 1936, naturalized, 1943; B.S., Union Coll., 1942; M.S., U. Wis., 1943, Ph.D., 1946; m. Beverly Preston, Dec. 28, 1942; children—Merilynn Jean, Robert Clark. Research asso. Allegany Ballistics Lab., Cumberland, Md., 1944-45; research scientist Standard Oil Developing Co., Esso Labs. Linden, N.J., 1946; sr. research engr. Jet Propulsion Lab., Pasadena, Calif., 1947-50; mem. faculty Calif. Inst. Tech., 1950-63, prof. div. engring., jet propulsion, 1957-63; dir. research engring. support div. Inst. Def. Analyses, Washington, 1962-64; prof. engring. physics, chmn. dept. aerospace and mech. engring. U. Calif. at San Diego, 1964-68, vice chancellor for acad. affairs, 1968-69, dir. Inst. for Pure and Applied Phys. Scis., 1968-71, dir. Energy Center, 1973—. U.S. mem. adv. group aero. research and devel. NATO, 1952-68, chmn. combustion and propulsion panel, 1958-60; mem. adv. com. engring. scis. USAF-Office Sci. Research, 1961-65; mem. subcom. combustion NACA, 1954-58; research adv. com. air-breathing engines NASA, 1962-64; mem. coms. on gas dynamics and edn. Internat. Acad. Astronautics, 1969—; mem. coms. NRC; cons. to govt., univs. and industry, 1953—; chmn. NRC/U.S. com. Internat. Inst. Applied Systems Analysis, 1978—; nat. Sigma Xi lectr., 1977-79. Recipient spl. awards People-to-People Program, NATO, pub. service award U. Calif. San Diego. Guggenheim fellow, 1971-72. Fellow Am. Phys. Soc., Optical Soc. Am., AAAS, N.Y. Acad. Scis., Am. Inst. Aeros. and Astronautics (dir. 1964-66, past chmn. com., G. Edward Pendray award 1975), Am. Inst. Chemists, Am. Acad. Arts and Scis.; mem. Nat. Acad. Engring., Internat. Acad. Astronautics, Am. Chem. Soc., Combustion Inst., Sigma Xi. Author: Chemical Reactions in Flow Systems, 1955; Chemistry Problems in Jet Propulsion, 1957; Quantitative Molecular Spectroscopy and Gas Emissivities, 1959; Chemical Rocket Propulsion and Combustion Research, 1962; Thermodynamics 1968; Radiation and Reentry, 1968; sr. author: Energy, Vol. I (Demands, Resources, Impact, Technology and Policy), 1974, Vol. II (Non-nuclear Energy Technologies), 1975, Vol. III (Nuclear Energy and Energy Policies), 1976. Editor: Chemistry of Propellants, 1960: Advanced Propulsion Techniques, 1961: Asso. editor Jour. Chem. Physics, 1953-56; editor Jour. Quantitative Spectroscopy and Radiative Transfer. 1960—, Jour. Missile Def. Research, 1963-67, Energy, The internat. Jour., 1975—. Home: 5912 Ave Chamnez La Jolla CA 92037 Office: U Calif San Diego CA 92037

PENNEY, ALPHONSUS LIGUORI, bishop; b. St. John's, Nfld., Can., Sept. 17, 1924; s. Alphonsus Liguori and Catherine (Mullaly) P.; L.Ph., U. Ottawa, 1945, L.Th., 1949. Ordained priest Roman Catholic ch., 1949, named vicar forane, 1960, vicar gen., 1971, prelate of honour, 1971; asst. priest, then parish priest, 1949-72; bishop of Grand Falls, Nfld., 1973-79; archbishop of St. John's, Nfld., 1979. Mem. sch. bd., Burin Peninsula, Nfld., 1957-69, St. John's, 1969-71; mem. Cath. Edn. Com., 1973—. Served with RCAF, 1952-57. Address: Cathedral Residence Box 771 8a Church Rd Grand Falls NF A2A 2M4 Canada

PENNEY, CHARLES RAND, lawyer, civic worker; b. Buffalo, July 26, 1923; s. Charles Patterson and Gretchen (Rand) P.; B.A., Yale U., 1945; LL.B., J.D., U. Va., 1951. Admitted to Md. bar, 1952, N.Y. bar, 1958, U.S. Supreme Ct. bar, 1958; law sec. to U.S. Dist. Ct. Judge W.C. Coleman, Balt., 1951-52; dir. devel. office Children's Hosp., Buffalo, 1952-54; sales mgr. Amherst Mfg. Corp., Williamsville, N.Y., 1954-56, also Delevan Electronics Corp., East Aurora, N.Y.; mem. firm Penney & Penney, Buffalo, 1958-61; practiced in Niagara County, N.Y., 1961—. Served to 2d lt. AUS, 1943-46. Mem. Albright-Knox Art Gallery Buffalo (life), Buffalo Mus. Sci. (life), Buffalo and Erie County (life), Niagara County (life) hist. socs., Patteran Artists (hon. life), Old Ft. Niagara (life), Niagara County Bar Assn., Kenan Center, Cobblestone Soc., Buffalo Soc. Artists (hon. trustee), Gallery Assn. N.Y., Assn. Am. Artist, Hist. Lockport (life), Niagara Falls Area C. of C., Victorian Soc. in Am., Nat. Trust Hist. Preservation, Hist. Soc. Lewiston; mem. art com., hon. bd. mgrs. Meml. Art Gallery U. Rochester, Asso. Art Orgns. Western N.Y. (community asso.), Smithsonian Instn., Niagara Council Arts, Rochester Hist. Soc., Am. Mus. Natural History, Pierpont Morgan Library, Am. Mus. Natural History, Japan Soc., Community Music Sch., Buffalo, Internat. Mus. Photography, Calif. Palace of Legion of Honor, M.H. De Young Meml. Mus., Asian Art Mus., numerous other art assns. and museums, Chi Psi, Phi Alpha Delta. Presbyterian (deacon). Clubs: Automobile (Lockport); Intrepids, Zwicker Aquatic, Niagara County Antiques (hon.). Mem. editorial bd. Archives Am. Art. Address: 343 Bewley Bldg Lockport NY 14094. *I have tried to strive for excellence in whatever I undertake, be it small or large. What success I may have achieved has required initiative, imagination, and dedication to the task at hand. Satisfaction comes from the hard work that leads to an objective. In all that I do I adhere to the Golden Rule and to fairness, honesty, and understanding in human relationships. I try to maintain a sense of humor at all times. And I enjoy living in a small community because it is from such areas that the strength of America comes.*

PENNEY, JAMES, artist; b. St. Joseph, Mo., Sept. 6, 1910; s. John Rice and Laura Davis (Freeland) P. B.F.A., U. Kans., 1931; student Art Student's League, N.Y.C., 1931-34; m. Frances Avery, 1941 (div. 1950); 1 son, James Avery; m. 2d, Rachel Seymour Bonner, May 30, 1953. One-man shows Hudson D. Walker Gallery, N.Y.C., 1939, Kraushaar Galleries N.Y.C., 1950, 54, 57, 61, 65, 69, 74; retrospective show Munson-Williams-Proctor Inst., Utica, N.Y., 1955, 77—, Utica Coll., 1972; exhibited in group shows Corcoran Gallery, Met. Mus. Art, Art Inst. Chgo., U. Ill. annuals, U. Neb., Whitney Mus. Bklyn. Mus., Carnegie Inst., St. Louis Mus. others; represented in over 40 pub. and mus. permanent collections including: Springfield (Mass.) Mus., New Britain Inst., Kans. State U., Nelson Atkins Mus., Kansas City, Des Moines Art Center. Murdock Collection, Wichita, Lehigh U., Fort Worth Art Center, Joslyn Mus., Omaha, 1967, and others; executed murals Hamilton Coll., Flushing High Sch., N.Y.C., post offices, Union and Palmyra, Mo., in vestibule State Capitol Bldg., Lincoln, Nebr., 1963; prof. art Hamilton Coll., N.Y., 1948-55, 56-74, Margaret Bundy Scott prof. art, 1974-76, emeritus, 1976—; guest instr. Calif. Coll. Arts and Crafts, 1960; tchr. art Munson-Williams-Proctor Inst., 1948-55, also Vassar Coll. Bennington Coll., Hunter Coll., U. Kans. Recipient Kansas City Art Inst. medal, 1931; Paintings of the Year award Pepsi-Cola Co., 1948; Allbright Gallery award for graphics, 1953; purchase Hassam Fund, 1953, Audubon Artists award, 1967, 77, 78. Mem. Art Student's League N.Y.C. (life), Audubon Artists, Century Assn., Nat. Soc. Mural Painters, Am. Fedn. Art, N.A.D. Address: 312 College Hill Rd Clinton NY 13323 also care Kraushaar Galleries 1055 Madison Ave New York NY 10028. *As an artist I have always painted each new work with a determination to produce something better and more complete than ever before. I still feel that a keener visualization and a culminating realization of all my experience is just around the corner. This faith, I hope, will continue to motivate me and keep my energy going for years to come. I still feel that I am only beginning to fulfill my destiny in life while even now so many of my contemporaries are gone.*

PENNEY, NORMAN, lawyer, educator; b. Buffalo, Aug. 29, 1926; s. Norman and Bertina (von Fricken) P.; A.B., Yale U., 1950; LL.B., Cornell U., 1953; m. Sarah Elizabeth Young, Aug. 11, 1951; children—John Belding, David Wright, Celia Elizabeth, Christopher Young. Admitted to N.Y. bar, 1953; asso., then partner firm Penney, Penney & Buerger, Buffalo, 1953-57; mem. faculty Cornell U. Law Sch., 1957—, prof. law, 1962—, dean univ. faculty, 1971-74, faculty trustee, 1974-79; vis. prof. U. Khartoum (Sudan), 1965-66, univs. Melbourne and Monash (Australia), 1975; cons. N.Y. State Commrs. Uniform State Laws, 1960-63, N.Y. State Law Revision Commn., 1961, 70-72, Fed. Res. Bd., 1978—; mem. U.S. del. UNCITRAL, 1970—. Served with AUS, 1944-46. Mem. Am., N.Y. State, Tompkins County bar assns., Am. Law Inst., Order of Coif, Phi Kappa Phi, Phi Delta Phi. Author: (with W.E. Hogan) New York Annotations to the Uniform Commercial Code, 1961; (with Broude) Land Financing, 1970, 2d edit., 1977. Office: care Cornell U Law Sch Ithaca NY 14853

PENNEY, PEARCE JOHN, librarian; b. St. Anthony, Nfld., Can., Mar. 10, 1928; s. Edgar and Elsie Belle (Bussey) P.; B.A., Mt. Allison U., 1957; M.Div., Pinehill Div. Sch., 1959; M.S. in Library Scis., Syracuse U., 1968; m. Amy Parrill, Aug. 30, 1950; children—Wayne, David, Donald, Reneé. Tchr., 1946-50; ordained to ministry United Ch. of Can., 1959; pastor various chs., 1959-67; librarian, head of acquisitions Meml. U., St. John's, Nfld., 1968-71, U. Guelph (Ont.), 1971-72; chief provincial librarian Nfld. Pub. Library Services, St. John's, 1972—. Mem. Canadian, Atlantic Provinces, Nfld. library assns. Home: 24 Parsons Rd St John's NF A1A 2J1 Canada Office: Arts and Culture Centre St John's NF A1B 3A3 Canada

PENNIALL, RALPH, biochemist; b. Southampton, Eng., Dec. 25, 1922; s. George C. and Helen G. Penniall; B.A., Knox Coll., Galesburg, Ill., 1947; M.S., U. Iowa, 1950, Ph.D., 1952; NSF postdoctoral fellow Inst. Enzyme Research, Madison, Wis., 1956-58; m. Mary Jane Powell, Aug. 10, 1944; children—Susan Mary Penniall Wilson, Christopher R. asst. prof. biochemistry Baylor U. Coll. Medicine, 1954-56; mem. faculty U. N.C. Med. Sch., Chapel Hill, 1956—, prof. biochemistry, 1968—. Served with AUS, 1943-46. Decorated Bronze Star, Silver Star, Purple Heart. Advanced research fellow Am. Heart Assn., 1958-60; Fogarty Center sr. internat. fellow, 1979-80. Mem. Am. Soc. Biol. Chemists, Biochem. Soc., AAAS, Am. Soc. Cell Biology, Sigma Xi, Phi Lambda Upsilon. Contbr. articles to profl. jours. Office: Dept Biochemistry and Nutrition Univ NC Med Sch Chapel Hill NC 27514

PENNIMAN, ABBOTT LAWRENCE, JR., engring. exec.; b. nr. Bel Air, Md., Feb. 12, 1892; s. Abbott Lawrence and Frances Risteau Owings (Griffith) P.; student Bel Air Acad., 1905-07, Balt. Poly. Inst., 1907-10; m. Ethel M. Warrington, Oct. 6, 1917 (dec. Feb. 1962). With Balt. Gas & Electric Co., 1911-60, supt. power prodn., 1913-37, gen. supt. elec. ops., 1937-59, v.p., 1950-60; engring. cons., 1960—. Trustee Ch. Home and Hosp. Mem. Md. Radiation Control Adv. Bd., 1960—, Water Pollution Control Commn. Md., 1951-61, Md. State Bd. Health, 1943-61; mem. Md. State Bd. Boiler Rules, 1939, chmn., 1969, 74—; mem. Commn. for Hist. and Archtl. Preservation, 1969-76; dir. Hosp. Cost Analysis Service, Inc., 1960-66; trustee Commn. Govtl. Efficiency and Economy, Inc. (Md.), 1960-63. Recipient Karl T. Compton Modern Pioneer award, 1940; George Westinghouse gold medal, 1965. Registered profl. engr., Md., N.J., Del., N.Y. Fellow ASCE, IEEE; mem. ASME (hon.; nat. dir. 1947-51), Engring. Soc. Balt. (hon.), Nat. Soc. Profl. Engrs., Md. Hist. Soc. (chmn. bd. trustees Athenaeum 1965-73), A.A.A.S., Navy League, Naval Inst., Am. Ordnance Assn., Edison Elec. Inst. (1923-60), Newcomen Soc., Md. Acad. Scis., Braintree Hist. Soc. (hon.), Tau Beta Pi. Clubs: Univ. (hon.), Md. (Balt.). Home: 4401 Roland Ave Baltimore MD 21210

PENNIMAN, CLARA, educator, polit. scientist; b. Steger, Ill., Apr. 5, 1914; d. Rae Ernest and Alethea (Bates) Penniman; B.A., U. Wis., 1950, M.A., 1951; Ph.D., U. Minn., 1954. Legal sec., 1934-37; adminstrv. asst. Wis. Employment Service, 1937-47; mem. faculty U. Wis., 1953—, prof. polit. sci., 1961—, chmn. dept. 1963-66, dir. Center for Pub. Policy and Adminstrn., 1968-74, Oscar Rennebohm prof. pub. adminstrn., 1974—. Asso., Brookings Instn., 1972-76; examiner-cons., mem. higher edn. commn. N. Central Assn. Colls.; vis. lectr. Johns Hopkins, summer 1958. Pres., League Women Voters, Madison, 1956-58; mem. Gov. Wis. Tax Impact Study Commn., 1959, Gov.'s Higher Edn. Merger Com., 1971-73, Mayor Madison Met. Com., 1957-58, Mayor Madison Redistricting Com., 1960-63; mem. adv. com. govts. div. Bur. Census, 1962-65. Recipient Outstanding Achievement award U. Minn. Mem. Am. (v.p. 1971-72, past mem. nat. council), Midwest (pres. 1965) polit. sci. assns., Am. Soc. Pub. Adminstrn., AAUP (pres. state conf. 1972-73), Nat. Assn. Schs. Pub. Adminstrn. (mem. council 1973-75), Am. Acad. Pub. Adminstrn., Phi Beta Kappa, Phi Kappa Phi. Club: Madison Altrusa (pres. 1968-69). Co-author: The Minnesota Department of Taxation, 1955; State Income Tax Administration, 1959; Government in the Fifty States, 1960. Contbr. to Politics in the American States, 1965, 71, 76. Home: 1306 Whenona Dr Madison WI 53711

PENNIMAN, HOWARD RAE, polit. scientist; b. Steger, Ill., Jan. 30, 1916; s. Rae Ernest and Alethea (Bates) P.; A.B., La. State U., 1936, M.A., 1938; Ph.D., U. Minn., 1941; m. Morgia Anderson, Dec. 30, 1940; children—Barbara, Ruth, William, Catherine, Matthew. Social Sci. Research Council pre-doctoral field fellow, 1940-41; instr. polit. sci. U. Ala., 1941-42; instr. dept. govt. Yale, 1942-45, asst. prof., 1945-48; staff CIA, 1948-49; external research staff, asst. chief, Dept. State, 1949-52, chief external research staff, 1953-55; staff Psychol. Strategy Bd., 1952-53; chief overseas book div. USIA, 1955-57; prof. govt. Georgetown U., 1957—, head dept. govt., 1959-63; resident scholar Am. Enterprise Inst., 1971—; columnist America, 1958-64; Fulbright research grant, France, 1964-65; cons. Congl. fellowship program Am. Polit. Sci. Assn., 1959. Delegate, Md. Constl. Conv., 1967-68, chmn. com. on style; cons. to team observers on presdl. elections in Vietnam, 1967; election cons. ABC, 1968—. Co-chmn. Montgomery County Com. on Drug Abuse, 1969-70. Trustee Montgomery Coll., 1971—. With AUS, 1945-46. Mem. Am. Polit. Sci. Assn. (pres. D.C. chpt. 1958-59). Internat. Polit. Sci. Assn., Phi Beta Kappa, Pi Gamma Mu, Pi Sigma Alpha (nat. pres. 1966, nat. dir. 1975—), Sigma Delta Chi. Episcopalian. Author: Sait's American Parties and Elections, rev. edit., 1952; The American Political Process, 1962; Elections in South Vietnam, 1973. Editor: John Locke on Politics and Education, 1947; Britain at the Polls, 1974; France at the Polls, 1975; Canada at the Polls, 1975; Australia at the Polls, 1977; Italy at the Polls, 1978; Ireland at the Polls, 1978; Israel at the Polls, 1978; contbr. articles to profl. jours. Home: 6019 Neilwood Dr Rockville MD 20852 Office: Am Enterprise Inst 1150 17th St Washington DC 20036

PENNINGTON, CHESTER ARTHUR, clergyman, former educator; b. Delanco, N.J., Sept. 16, 1916; s. Chester Arthur and Emily Bolton (Lush) P.; A.B., Temple U., 1937; B.D., Drew Theol. Sem., 1940; Ph.D., Drew U., 1948; postgrad. Oxford (Eng.) U., 1949; L.H.D., Ohio No. U., 1961; D.D., McKendree Coll., 1968; m. Marjorie Elizabeth Bruschweiler, Sept. 13, 1941; children—Celeste Ann, Lawrence Arthur. Ordained to ministry Meth. Ch., 1940; with St. Andrews Meth. Ch. Spring Lake, N.J., 1941-43; asst. minister Calvary Meth. Ch., East Orange, N.J., 1945-47; prof. philosophy Centenary Coll., minister Trinity Meth. Ch., Hackettstown, N.J., 1947-51; with Ch. of St. Paul and St. Andrew Meth., N.Y.C., 1951-55; sr. minister Hennepin Av. Meth. Ch., Mpls., 1955-72; prof. preaching and worship Iliff Sch. Theology, Denver, 1972-79. Served as chaplain USNR, 1943-45. Author: Even So . . . .Believe, 1966; With Good Reason, 1967; A More Excellent Way, 1969; Half Truths or Whole Gospel?, 1972; (with Marjorie Pennington) After the Children Leave Home, 1972; Liberated Love, 1972; Christian Counter Culture, 1973; The Word Among Us, 1973; The Thunder and the Still Voice, 1974; God has a Communication Problem, 1976; A New Birth of Freedom, 1976. Home: 7515 Clinton St Los Angeles CA 90036

PENNINGTON, JAMES CLOY, army officer; b. Statesboro, Ga., Feb. 11, 1926; s. Jack Cloy and Allie (Finch) P.; B.S., Ga. So. Coll., 1950; M.S., Ind. U., 1953; grad. Command and Gen. Staff Coll., 1965, U.S. Army War Coll., 1969, Advanced Mgmt. Program, Grad. Sch. Bus. Adminstrn., Harvard U., 1971; m. Harriet Jean Donaldson, July 16, 1960; children—Kimberly, James Cloy. Commd. 2d lt. U.S. Army, 1951, advanced through grades to maj. gen., 1979; dep. adj. gen. U.S. Army Vietnam, 1970-71; exec., chief of staff to adj. gen. and comdg. gen. Adj. Gen.'s Center, Washington, 1971-73; dep. adj. gen. U.S. Army, dep. comdr. Adj. Gen.'s Center, 1973-78, adj. gen., 1978—. Decorated Legion of Merit with oak leaf cluster, D.F.C., Bronze Star medal with 4 oak leaf clusters, Purple Heart, Air medal. Home: 6015 Larkspur Dr Alexandria VA 22310 Office: Office of Adj Gen Dept Army The Pentagon Washington DC 20310

PENNINGTON, PAUL JORDAN, coll. dean; b. Deweyville, Tex., Apr. 20, 1923; s. James Franklin and Carl Christian (Jordan) P.; B.A., Henderson State U., 1948; M.A. (fellow), Okla. U., 1950; Ph.D. (fellow), La. State U., 1957; m. Virginia Dare Roach, Dec. 12, 1974; children—Paula, Caryl, Franklin. Instr., U. Okla., 1949-50; head dept. speech Okla. Southeastern State Coll., 1950-51; faculty La. Tech. U., Ruston, 1952—, prof. speech, 1955—, dept. head, 1964—, also dean Coll. Arts and Scis. Served with USAAF, 1942-46. Mem. La. Coll. Conf. (pres. 1972), La. Council of Deans Arts, Scis. and Humanities (chmn. 1977-78), So. Speech Assn., La. Speech Assn. Author: Handbook for Speaking, 1960; Speech Handbook, 1958; (poetry) If I Should Wake, 1950. Editor numerous publs. Home: 1502 Bittersweet Ln Ruston LA 71270 Office: Coll Arts and Scis La Tech U Ruston LA 71272

PENNINGTON, WELDON JERRY, newspaper exec.; b. Tacoma, Mar. 1, 1919; s. Bert Archie and Marguerite Lucille (Heraty) P.; B.A., U. Wash., 1941; m. Dorothy Grace Kinney, Oct. 6, 1945; children—Susan Diane Merry, Scott Brian, Sally Jane Ringman, Steven Kinney. Staff accountant Allen R. Smart & Co., C.P.A.'s, Seattle, 1941-42; spl. agt. FBI, 1942-46; supervising accountant Touche Ross & Co., C.P.A.'s, Seattle, 1946-51; with Seattle Times, 1951—, pres., dir., 1967—; pres., dir. Walla Walla (Wash.) Union-Bull., 1971—, Times Communications Co., 1971—; dir. Rainier Nat. Bank, Seattle, Rainier Bancorp., Paccar, Inc., Safeco Corp., Western Internat. Hotels. Pres., Seattle King County Community Chest, 1959-60, Seattle King County United Good Neighbor Fund, 1962-63, Downtown Seattle Devel. Assn., 1971-72. Mem. bd. and v.p. Virginia Mason Med. Found. Trustee Seattle Goodwill Industries, Virginia Mason Hosp.; trustee, pres. Seattle Found. Named Seattle's First Citizen of 1977 Seattle-King County Bd. Realtors. Mem. Am. Inst. C.P.A.'s (Elijah Watts Sells award 1941), Wash. Soc. C.P.A.'s (pres. 1951-52), Assn. Former Spl. Agts. FBI, Seattle C. of C. (pres. 1964-65), Sigma Delta Chi, Beta Alpha Psi. Rotarian (pres. Seattle 1966-67). Clubs: Seattle Golf (trustee 1974-77), Rainier (pres. 1968-69), Wash. Athletic, University; Desert Island Country (Palm Springs). Home: 4701 W Ruffner St Seattle WA 98199 Office: 1120 John St PO Box 70 Seattle WA 98111

PENNINGTON, WILLIAM HERBERT, former govt. ofcl.; b. Onida, S.D., July 19, 1919; s. Rohe Vester and Stella (Eller) P.; B.S., Franklin and Marshall Coll., 1940; m. Betty Jane Throckmorton, Oct. 2, 1943; children—Stephen Phillip, William Herbert, Susan Lee (dec.). Chemist, E.I. duPont de Nemours & Co., Carneys Point, N.J., 1940-42, supr., Pryor, Okla., 1942-43; supr. Oak Ridge Nat. Lab., 1943-51; engr. Phillips Petroleum Co., Idaho Falls, Idaho, 1951-55; adv. engr. Westinghouse Electric Co., Pitts., 1955-57; U.S. AEC sci. rep., atomic energy attache Am. Embassy, Tokyo, Japan, 1957-61; asst. mgr. tech. AEC, N.Y.C., 1961-62, project mgr. SNAP-50, Middletown, Conn., 1962-65, dep. mgr. AEC, N.Y.C., 1965-71; asst. dir. div. environ. affairs Dept. Energy (formerly AEC, then ERDA), Washington, 1972-73, assessments and coordination officer div. biomed. and environ. research, ERDA, 1973-76, dir. Office NEPA Coordination, Dept. Energy, 1976-79. Mem. New Eng. River Basins Commn., 1973—. Council commr. Boy Scouts Am., Idaho Falls, 1953-55, dist. vice chmn., Glastonbury (Conn.) Council, 1965-66. Fellow Am. Inst. Chemists; mem. Am. Chem. Soc., Am. Nuclear Soc. (dir.), Nat. Assn. Environ. Profls. (pres. 1976-77, dir.), Am. Inst. Aero. and Astronautics, AAAS, N.Y. Acad. Sci. Kiwanian. Club: Manor Country (Rockville, Md.). Home: 2 Boxelder Ct Rockville MD 20853

PENNY, CHARLES RICHARD, advt. exec.; b. Abilene, Tex., Dec. 22, 1934; s. Alvis Burnett and Cleo (Ward) P.; B.B.A. in Mktg.-Advt., Baylor U., 1956; grad. mktg. mgmt. and advt. seminar, Harvard, 1970, fundamentals of fin. Wharton Sch., U. Pa., 1976; m. Linda Louise Felton, Aug. 25, 1956; children—Diane Marie, Roxanne Lynne, Marianne Felton. Prodn. mgr. McCann-Erickson Advt. Agy., Dallas, 1956-58, account exec., Houston, 1959-60; account exec., v.p., stockholder Ritchie Advt. Agy., Houston, 1961-66; account exec., v.p. Weekley & Valenti Advt. Agy., Houston, 1967-70; exec. v.p., dir., stockholder Weekley, Elliott & Penny Advt. Agy., Houston, 1971-72; pres., dir., stockholder Weekley & Penny Advt. Agy., Houston, 1973—. Mem. Houston Advt. Club (dir. 1965). Clubs: Champions Country; Kingwood Country. Home: 12503 Mossycup St Houston TX 77024 Office: 3322 Richmond Ave Houston TX 77098

PENNYBACKER, ALBERT MITCHELL, JR., clergyman; b. Chattanooga, Oct. 20, 1931; s. Albert Mitchell and Agatha Lewis (Walker) P.; A.B. cum laude, Vanderbilt U., 1953; B.D., Yale, 1957; D.D. (hon.), Bethany (W.Va.) Coll., 1967; m. Martha Marian Hackney, Dec. 16, 1951; children—Susan Dabney, Janet Marie, David William. Ordained to ministry Christian Ch. (Disciples of Christ), 1954; pastor Taftville Congl. Ch., Norwich, Conn., 1954-57; sr. minister Central Christian Ch., Youngstown, Ohio, 1958-62, Heights Christian Ch., Shaker Heights, Ohio, 1963-74, Univ. Christian Ch., Ft. Worth, 1974—. W.E. Garrison lectr. Disciples House, New Haven, 1966. Chmn. bd. dirs. Council on Christian Unity, Christian Ch., 1971—; trustee Disciples Div. House, U. Chgo.; mem. exec. com. Consultation on Ch. Union, 1973—; 1st vice moderator Gen. Assembly of Christian Ch., 1968-69; del. World Council Chs. Assemblies, New Delhi, 1961, Uppsala, 1968. Trustee Tex. Christian U., Ft. Worth Country Day Sch., Brite Div. Sch. Rocker Family Found. fellow, 1972. Mem. Phi Delta Theta. Democrat. Rotarian. Clubs: Fort Worth; River Crest Country. Contbr. articles to profl. publs. Home: 2719 Greene Ave Fort Worth TX 76109 Office: 2720 University Dr Fort Worth TX 76109

PENROD, KENNETH EARL, med. edn. adminstr.; b. Blanchester, Ohio, Mar. 30, 1916; s. William F. and Josie Alma (Carman) P.; B.S., Miami (Ohio) U., 1938; Ph.D., Iowa State Coll., 1942; m. Virginia Hogue, June 29, 1942; children—Caroline, Bruce Hogue. Asst. prof. physiology Boston U. Sch. Medicine, 1946-50; asso. prof. physiology Duke U. Sch. Medicine, 1950-57, prof., 1957-59, asst. dean, 1952-59; v.p. for med. affairs, prof. physiology W.Va. U., 1959-65; provost for med. center, prof. physiology Ind. U., 1965-69; vice chancellor for med. and health scis. State U. System Fla., Tallahassee, 1969-74; dir. community hosp. grad. med. edn. program Fla. Bd. Regents, Tallahassee, 1974—. Cons. in med. edn.; spl. cons. AID, Latin Am. Served from 2d lt. to capt., aviation physiologist USAAF, 1942-46. Mem. Am. Physiol. Soc., Assn. for Acad. Health Centers, (incorporator), Assn. Am. Med. Colls., AAAS, Phi Beta Kappa, Sigma Xi, Phi Kappa Phi, Phi Kappa Tau, Alpha Omega Alpha. Presbyn. Club: Rotary. Mem. editorial bd. Jour. Med. Edn., 1957-65. Contbr. to sci. jours. in physiol. and health edn. Home: 913 Lasswade Dr Tallahassee FL 32312 Office: 107 W Gaines St Tallahassee FL 32304

PENROSE, CHARLES, JR., assn. exec.; b. Phila., Oct. 9, 1921; s. Charles and Beatrice (d,Este) P.; grad. Episcopal Acad., Overbrook, Pa., 1940; m. Ann Lucille Cantwell, Apr. 17, 1943; children—James, Thomas, John. Exec. sec. Newcomen Soc. N.Am., N.A., Phila., 1946-48; dist. sales mgr., Phila., for Fitchburg Paper Co. (Mass.), 1948-50, 52-53; sales mgr. A.M. Collins Mfg. Co., Phila., 1953-54, v.p. sales, 1954-55; sales mgr. A.M. Collins div. Internat. Paper Co., N.Y.C., 1955; asst. to sales mgr. fine paper and bleached bd. div., 1956-57; sr. v.p., chief exec. officer Newcomen Soc. in N.Am., Downingtown, Pa., 1957-61, also dir.; pres., chief exec. officer Newcomen Publs. in N.Am., Inc., 1958-61, trustee, 1948-61; pres., chief exec. officer, trustee Newcomen Soc. in N.Am., Inc., 1961—; sr. v.p. for N.Am., Newcomen Soc., London, Eng., 1957—; pres., dir. Rocaton, Inc., Darien, Conn., 1960-61. Sec., asst. treas. Chester County Investment Fund Assn., Phila., 1959-64; v.p. Brit. Am. Ednl. Found., Inc., N.Y.C., 1968-70, pres., 1970-75, trustee, 1968—. Served to capt. USAAF, 1940-46; S.W. Pacific; served to capt. AUS, 1950-52; Germany. Mem. Newcomen Soc. in N.Am., Newcomen Soc. (London), Royal Soc. Arts (Benjamin Franklin fellow 1960), Pilgrims of U.S., Franklin Inst., First Troop Phila. City Cavalry (hon.) English-Speaking Union, Nat. Inst. Social Scis., Soc. Am. Mil. Engrs., Soc. Am. Historians, Marine Hist. Assn., Peabody Mus. Salem (Mass.), Hist. Soc. Pa., N.H. Hist. Soc., Portsmouth (N.H.) Hist. Soc., Am. Precision Mus. Assn. (trustee Windsor, Vt. 1969-73), Am. Philatelic Soc., Chi Psi Omicron. Republican. Episcopalian. Clubs: Philadelphia; Metropolitan (N.Y.C.); Tokeneke (Darien). Author: They Live on a Rock in the Sea The Isles of Shoals in Colonial Days, 1957. Home: 6 Tory Hole Rd Darien CT 06820 Office: PO Box 113 Downingtown PA 19335

PENRY, JAMES KIFFIN, neurologist; b. Denton, N.C., Aug. 21, 1929; s. Robert Lee and Cordelia (Leonard) P.; B.S., Wake Forest Coll., 1951; M.D., Bowman Gray Sch. Medicine, 1955; m. Sarah Doub, Mar. 20, 1955; children—Richard Lee, Martin Doub, Denny Kiffin, Edith Catherine. Intern, Pa. Hosp., Phila., 1955-56; asst. resident in internal medicine, then asst. resident in neurology N.C. Bapt. Hosp. and Bowman Gray Sch. Medicine, 1956-58; asst. resident in neurology Boston City Hosp., also fellow neurology Harvard U. Med. Sch., 1958-60; chief applied neurologic research br., collaborative and field research Nat. Inst. Neurol. Diseases and Stroke, NIH, Bethesda, Md., 1966-75; chief epilepsy br., dir. neurol. disorders program Nat. Inst. Neurol. and Communicative Diseases and Stroke, 1975-79; prof. neurology, asso. dean neuroscis. devel. Bowman Gray Sch. Medicine Wake Forest U., 1979—; sec.-gen. Internat. League Against Epilepsy, 1973-77, pres., 1977—; cons. in field. Served to maj. M.C., USAF, 1960-66. Recipient Commendation medal USPHS, 1972; diplomate Am. Bd. Psychiatry and Neurology. Mem. Am. Acad. Neurology, AMA, Assn. Research Nervous and Mental Diseases, Phi Beta Kappa. Co-editor: Antiepilptic Drugs, 1972, Experimental Models of Epilepsy: A Manual for the Laboratory Worker, 1972, Complex Partial Seizures and Their Treatment, Epilepsy Bibliography 1900-1950, 1973; contbr. to profl. jours. Home: Route 4 Box 736 Thomasville NC 27360 Office: Bowman Gray Sch Medicine Wake Forest U Winston Salem NC 27103

PENTLAND, BARBARA LALLY, composer; b. Winnipeg, Man., Can., Jan. 2, 1912; d. Charles Frederick and Constance Lally (Howell) Pentland; studied with Cécile Gauthiez, Paris, 1929-30; student organ, Winnipeg, 1930-31, piano, 1931-36; Asso., Toronto Conservatory Music, 1931; Licentiate, Asso. Bd. Royal Schs. Music, London, 1933; fellow in composition Juilliard Grad. Sch., N.Y.C., 1936-39, studied with Frederick Jacobi and Bernard Wagenaar; studied with Aaron Copland, Berkshire Music Center, summers 1941-42; LL.D., U. Man., 1976; m. John Huberman, Oct. 10, 1958. Pvt. tchr. music, Winnipeg, 1939-42; instr. theory and composition Royal Conservatory Music, Toronto, 1943-49; instr. music U. B.C., Vancouver, 1949-63; commd. CBC, other groups, piano recitalist in own works Can., U.S., Europe, on CBC, BBC. Recipient Bronze medal XIV Olympiad, London, 1948, Can. Centennial medal, 1967; diplôme d'Honneur Canadian Conf. Arts, 1977. Mem. Can. League Composers, Juilliard Alumni Assn., Can. Music Council, Performing Rights Orgn. Can., Am. Fedn. Musicians. Composer several symphonies, concerti, other orchestral works, wind octet, septet, quintets, quartets, trios, duos, other chamber music, chamber opera, vocal and choral pieces, keyboard works, music for ballet, film, radio. Home: 4765 W 6th Ave Vancouver BC V6T 1C4 Canada

PENUELAS, MARCELINO COMPANY, educator; b. El Tovar, Cuenca, Spain, Apr. 20, 1916; s. Eusebio and Angela (Company) P.; came to U.S., 1948, naturalized, 1955; B.A., U. Valencia, Spain, 1939, M.A., 1945, M.Ed., 1940; Ph.D., U. Madrid, Spain, 1949; m. Anita Fanjul, Dec. 16, 1950; 1 dau., Anita. Asst. prof. Spanish lit. U. Denver, 1948-59, asso. prof., 1960-63; vis. prof. Stanford U., 1958-59; asso. prof. U. Wash., Seattle, 1963-67, prof., 1967—, chmn. dept. Romance langs. and lits., 1972—; chmn. devel. com. advanced placement exam. Spanish lit. Coll. Entrance Exam. Bd., 1971—, chmn., 1978. Mem. MLA, Am. Assn. Tchrs. Spanish and Portuguese. Author: Lo español en el Suroeste de Estados Unidos, 1965; Mito, literatura y realidad, 1965; Jacinto Benavente, 1968; Introducción a la literature española, 1969; Mr. Clark no toma Coca-Cola, 1960, 69; Conversaciones con Ramón J. Sender, 1970; La obra narrative de Ramón J. Sender, 1971; Cultura hispánica en Estatos Unidos: Los Chicanos, 1978; contbr. articles and short stories to profl. jours. and mags. Home: 6059 NE 61st St Seattle WA 98115 Office: U Wash Dept Romance Lang GN-60 Seattle WA 98195

PENZ, ANTON JACOB, educator; b. Cleve., Feb. 22, 1906; s. Stephen F. and Elizabeth (Prokosch) P.; B.S. in Elec. Engring., Cleve. State U., 1933; M.A. in Edn., Western Res. U., 1936; M.B.A., Northwestern U., 1942; Ph.D., Ohio State U., 1947; married; children—Alton Jeffry, David Alan. Prof. Davis and Elkins Coll., 1937-40; lectr. Rensselaer Poly. Inst., 1944; asst. prof. La. State U., 1944-47; prof. accounting, head dept. U. Ala., 1947-71, prof. emeritus, 1971—; Distinguished vis. prof. U. Nev., Reno, spring 1972, U. Colo., Boulder, spring 1973, Va. Commonwealth U., Richmond, spring 1975, U. Md., College Park, spring 1979; cons., lectr. AID, Lima, Peru, 1965-66, Guyana, 1967; del. various congresses. Mem. Nat. Assn. Accountants (Lybrand award 1951), Fin. Execs. Inst., Am. Accounting Assn. (v.p. 1962-63), Beta Alpha Psi (pres. 1955-56, editor newsletter 1953-55). Author: Manual De Contabilidad Y Costos, 1966. Editor: Accounting Teachers Guide, 1953; Professional Developments: Accounting Teachers Guide, 1953; Accountancy, A Vocation and Profession, 1958; Guide to Accounting Instruction: Concepts and Practices, 1968; Introducing the Profession: A Guide to Accounting Instruction, 1968. Home: 25 Beech Hills Tuscaloosa AL 35401 Office: Box AD University AL 35486

PENZER, MARK, lawyer, editor, publisher; b. Bklyn., Nov. 22, 1932; s. Ed and Fay (Weinberg) P.; B.B.A., Coll. City N.Y.; J.D., Fordham U.; m. Eileen Malen, Aug. 12, 1962; children—Matthew, Nicole. Free-lance writer, 1950-53; editorial asst. Hearst mags., N.Y.C., 1955, asst. editor, 1956, asso. editor, 1957-66, editor-in-chief Rudder mag., 1967-69, editorial dir., 1970-74; editor-in-chief True, 1970-73, editor-at-large, 1973-75; pub., editor-in-chief Jour. Energy Medicine, 1978—; admitted to N.Y. bar, 1968, D.C. bar, 1974. Served with AUS, 1953-55. Author: The Motorboatman's Bible, 1965; The Powerboatman's Bible, 1977. Home: 11905 NE 2d Ave Apt 311-C North Miami FL 33161 Office: 4200 Wisconsin Ave NW Washington DC 20016 also 60 E 42d St New York NY 10017 also 1175 NE 125th St North Miami FL 33161

PENZIAS, ARNO ALLAN, astrophysicist, electronics co. exec.; b. Munich, Germany, Apr. 26, 1933; s. Karl and Justine (Eisenreich) P.; came to U.S., 1940; naturalized, 1946; B.S., Coll. City N.Y., 1954; M.A., Columbia U., 1958, Ph.D., 1962; Dr. honoris causa, Observatoire de Paris, 1976; Sc.D. (hon.), Rutgers U., 1979, others; m. Anne Pearl Barras, Nov. 25, 1954; children—David Simon, Mindy Gail, Laurie Ruth. Mem. tech. staff Bell Labs., Holmdel, N.J., 1961-72, head radiophysics research dept., Holmdel, N.J., 1972-76, dir. radio research lab., 1976-79, exec. dir. research, communications scis. div., 1979—; lectr. Princeton U., 1967-72, vis. prof., 1972—; asso. Harvard Coll. Obs., Cambridge, Mass., 1968—; adj. prof. State U. N.Y., Stony Brook, 1974—; mem. astronomy adv. panel NSF, 1978-79. Trustee, Trenton (N.J.) State Coll., 1977-79; mem. vis. com. Calif. Inst. Tech., 1977-79. Served to lt. Signal Corps AUS, 1954-56. Recipient Henry Draper medal Nat. Acad. Sci., 1977; Herschel medal Royal Astronom. Soc., 1977; Nobel prize in physics, 1978. Mem. Nat. Acad. Scis., Am. Astron. Soc., Am. Acad. Arts and Scis., Am. Phys. Soc., Internat. Astron. Union, Com. Concerned Scientists (vice chmn.). Republican. Jewish. Club: E. Brunswick Country Swim. Mem. editorial bd. Ann. Rev. Astronomy and Astrophysics, 1974-78; asso. editor Astrophys. Jour., 1978—; contbr. numerous articles to profl. jours. Office: Crawford Hill Holmdel NJ 07733

PENZIEN, JOSEPH, educator; b. Philip, S.D., Nov. 27, 1924; s. John Chris and Ella (Stebbins) P.; student Coll. Idaho, 1942-43; B.S., U. Wash., 1945; Sc.D., Mass. Inst. Tech., 1950; m. Jeanne Ellen Hunson, Apr. 29, 1950; children—Robert Joseph, Karen Estelle, Donna Marie, Charlene May. Mem. staff Sandia Corp., 1950-51; sr. structures engr. Consol. Vultee Aircraft Corp., Fort Worth, 1951-53; asst. prof. U. Calif. at Berkeley, 1953-57, asso. prof., 1957-62, prof. structual engring., 1962—, dir. Earthquake Engring. Research Center, 1968-73, 77—. Cons. engring. firms; chief tech. adv. Internat. Inst. of Seismology and Earthquake Engring., Tokyo, Japan, 1964-65. NATO Sr. Sci. fellow. 1969. Fellow Am. Acad. Mechanics; mem. ASCE (Walter Huber Research award) Am. Concrete Inst., Structural Engrs. Assn. Calif., Seismol. Soc. Am., Nat. Acad. Engring. Home: 800 Solana Dr Lafayette CA 94549 Office: Davis Hall Univ Calif Berkeley CA 94720

PENZL, HERBERT, educator; b. Neufelden, Austria, Sept. 2, 1910; s. Johann and Hedwig (Schmidt) P.; grad. Gymnasium Vienna (Austria), 1929; hon. fellow Brown U., 1932-34; Ph.D., U. Vienna, 1935; m. Vera Rothmüller, Aug. 21, 1950. Came to U.S., 1936, naturalized, 1944. Editorial asst. Linguistic Atlas of U.S., Providence, 1932-34; asst. prof. Rockford (Ill.) Coll., 1936-38; asst. prof. U. Ill., Urbana, 1938-50; asso. prof. U. Mich., Ann Arbor, 1950-53, prof. German, 1953-63; prof. Germanic philology U. Calif., Berkeley, 1963—. Smith-Mundt prof. gen. linguistics U. Kabul (Afghanistan), 1958-59; vis. prof. Georgetown U., 1951-53, Northwestern U., 1960, 65, U. Calif. at Irvine, 1966, U. Colo., Boulder, 1969, Australian Nat. U., Canberra, 1970, N.Y. State U., Buffalo, 1971. Mem. German achievement com. Coll. Entrance Exam. Bd., 1965-72. Served with AUS, 1943-45. Guggenheim fellow, 1967. Mem. Modern Lang. Assn., Linguistic Soc. Am., Am. Dialect Soc., Am. Name Soc., Internationale Vereinigung für Germanistik, Am. Assn. Tchrs. German, Societas Linguistica Europaea. Author: A Grammar of Pashto, 1955; A Reader of Pashto, 1962; Geschichtliche deutsche Lautlehre, 1969; Lautsystem und Lautwandel in den althochdeutschen Dialekten, 1971; Methoden der germanischen Linguistik, 1972; Vom Urgermanischen zum Neuhochdeutschen, 1975; J. Ch. Gottsched's Deutsche Sprachkunst (edition and commentary), 1978; contbr. articles to profl. jours. Home: 1125 Grizzly Peak Blvd Berkeley CA 94708

PEOPLES, JOHN ARTHUR, JR., univ. pres.; b. Starkville, Miss., Aug. 26, 1926; s. John Arthur and Maggie Rose (Peoples) P.; B.S., Jackson State U., 1950; M.A., U. Chgo., 1951, Ph.D., 1961; m. Mary E. Galloway, July 13, 1951; children—Kathleen, Mark Adam. Tchr. math. Froebel Sch., Gary, Ind., 1951-58; asst. prin. Lincoln Sch., Gary, 1958-62; prin. Banneker Sch., Gary, 1962-64; asst. to pres. Jackson (Miss.) State U., 1964-66, v.p., 1966-67, pres., 1967—; asst. to pres. State U. N.Y., Binghamton, 1965-66; lectr. summers U. Mich., 1964, Tex. A. and M. U., 1967. Active Boy Scouts Am., Urban League; bd. govs. So. Regional Edn. Bd.; bd. visitors Air U.; adv. com. U.S. Army Command and Gen. Staff Coll.; bd. commrs. Jackson Airport Authority. Recipient Distinguished Am. award Nat. Football Found. Served with USMCR, 1944-47. Mem. Am. Council Edn. (chmn. dir. 1975), Am. Assn. Higher Edn. (dir. 1971-74), NEA, Miss. Tchrs. Assn., Jackson C. of C. (econ. council), Alpha Kappa Mu, Phi Kappa Phi, Phi Delta Kappa, Omega Psi Phi (Man of Year, Sigma Omega chpt. 1966). Club: Masons (33 deg.). Contbr. articles to profl. jours. Home: Jackson State University Jackson MS 39217

PEOPLES, THOMAS EDWARD, pub. exec., writer; b. Cleve., Oct. 26, 1915; s. Robert Stephen and Mary Frances (Box) P.; student John Carroll U., 1933-37; m. Helen Catherine Mullaney, Jan. 9, 1943; children—Michael Thomas, Mary Dennis, Thomas Edward, James Robert. Staff photographer Central Press Assn. div. Hearst Corp., 1938-41; staff photographer Internat. News Photos, Cleve., 1946, bur. mgr., Cleve., 1947-52; picture editor Newspaper Enterprise Assn., Cleve., 1953-58, comics prodn. editor, 1958-68, dir. comic art, 1968-76, v.p., 1972-76. Served to 1st lt. U.S. Army, 1941-46; PTO. Mem. Cleve. Newspaper and Newsreel Cameramens Assn. (pres. 1950-51), Newspaper Comics Council (exec. bd. 1968-76, promotion dir. 1972-73), Nat. Cartoonists Soc., Sigma Delta Chi. Democrat. Roman Catholic. Author syndicated comic page Our Boarding House with Maj. Hoople, 1959-69. Home: 1095 B Circle Terr W Delray Beach FL 33445. *Every day we should attempt to do some deed for the betterment of society and one's fellowmen. The performance of these deeds may or may not be anonymous but they must never be done with the aim of financial reward or personal or social gain. Our efforts to help our fellowmen may not be crowned with success every time, but it is in the trying we receive our reward.*

PEPE, FRANK A., anatomist; b. Schenectady, May 22, 1931; s. Rocco and Margherita (Ruggiero) P.; B.S., Union Coll., 1953; Ph.D., Yale U., 1957. Instr. anatomy U. Pa., 1957-60, asso. in anatomy, 1960-63, asst. prof., 1963-65, asso. prof., 1965-70, prof., 1970—, chmn. dept. anatomy, 1977—. USPHS research career devel. award, 1968-73. Mem. Am. Assn. Anatomists, Am. Chem. Soc., AAAS, Am. Inst. Biol. Scis., Am. Soc. Cell Biology, N.Y. Acad. Scis., Biophys. Soc., Electron Microscopy Soc. Am., Sigma Xi. Editor: Motility in Cell Function, 1979. Home: 4614 Pine St Philadelphia PA 19143 Office: Sch Medicine U Pa Philadelphia PA 19104

PEPE, PHILIP FRANCIS, sports columnist; b. N.Y.C., Mar. 21, 1935; s. Michael Paul and Lillian (Martini) P.; B.A., St. John's U., 1956; m. Adele Sbaratta, Oct. 28, 1961; children—Jayne, David, James, John. Sports reporter and columnist N.Y. World Telegram & Sun, N.Y.C., 1957-66, N.Y. World Jour. Tribune, N.Y.C., 1966-67, N.Y. News, N.Y.C., 1968—. Served with U.S. N.G., 1957. Recipient AP award, 1972; named N.Y. Sportswriter of Yr., Nat. Sportswriter and Sportscasters Assn., 1978. Mem. Baseball Writers Assn. Am. Author numerous books on sports, the most recent being: (with Zander Hollander) The Book of Sports List, 1979. Home: 83 Hampshire Hill Upper Saddle River NJ 07458 Office: 220 E 42d St New York NY 10017

PEPER, CHRISTIAN BAIRD, lawyer; b. St. Louis, Dec. 5, 1910; s. Clarence F. and Christine (Baird) P.; A.B. cum laude, Harvard, 1932; LL.B., Washington U., 1935; LL.M. (Sterling fellow), Yale, 1937; m. Ethel C. Kingsland, June 5, 1935; children—Catherine K. (Mrs. Kenneth B. Larson), Anne C. (Mrs. John M. Perkins), Christian B. Admitted to Mo. bar, 1934, since practiced in St. Louis; partner Peper, Martin, Jensen, Maichel & Hetlage. Lectr. various subjects Washington U. Law Sch., St. Louis, 1943-61; partner A.G. Edwards & Sons, 1945-67; pres. St. Charles Gas Corp., 1953-72; chmn. St. Louis Steel Casting Inc., Hydraulic Press Brick Co. Mem. vis. com. Harvard Div. Sch., 1964-70. Trustee St. Louis Art Mus. Mem. Am., Mo., St. Louis bar assns., Order of Coif, Phi Delta Phi. Roman Catholic. Clubs: Noonday, University, Harvard (St. Louis); East India, Devonshire (London). Contbr. articles to law jours. Home: 1454 Mason Rd Saint Louis MO 63131 Office: 720 Olive St Saint Louis MO 63101

PEPER, GEORGE FREDERICK, editor; b. Nyack, N.Y., Jan. 25, 1950; s. Gerhard Wilhelm and Doris Elene (Bargfrede) P.; B.A. in English and Comparative Lit., Princeton U., 1972; postgrad. Yale U., 1973; m. Elizabeth Marshall White, May 20, 1978. Asso. editor Winchester Press, N.Y.C., 1973-75; communications dir. Met. Golf Assn., N.Y.C., 1976; asso. editor, exec. editor Golf mag., N.Y.C., 1976-78, editor, 1979—. Mem. Golf Writers Assn. Am., Met. Golf Writers Assn., Golf Collectors Soc. Club: Rockaway Hunting (Cedarhurst, N.Y.). Author: Scrambling Golf, 1977. Home: 119 E 84th St Apt 2C New York NY 10028 Office: Golf Mag 380 Madison Ave New York NY 10017

PEPIN, JEAN-LUC, Canadian govt. ofcl.; b. Drummondville, Que., Can., Nov. 1, 1924; s. Victor and Antoinette (Morel) P.; B.A., U. Ottawa, 1945, L.Ph., 1946, LLL., 1956, diploma higher law studies, 1964, also hon. degree; student Inst. d'Etudes Politiques, Paris, France, 1950; hon. degrees U. Sherbrooke, U. Laval; m. Mary Brock-Smith, Apr. 12, 1952; children—Aude, Nicolas. Prof. polit. sci. U. Ottawa, 1951-56, 58-63, head dept., 1961-63; rep. Nat. Film Bd. Can. in Europe, 1956-58; M.P. for Drummond, 1963-72; parliamentary sec. to minister trade and commerce, 1963-65, minister mines and tech. surveys, 1965, energy, mines and resources, 1966-68, industry, trade and commerce, 1968-72; pres. cons. and trading firm Interimco, Ltd., Ottawa, 1972-75; chmn. Anti Inflation Bd., Ottawa, 1975-77; co-chmn. Task Force on Canadian Unity, 1977-79; polit. commentator CBC, 1958-63; Ottawa editor Le Magazine Maclean, 1961; M.P. for Ottawa-Carleton, 1979—. Decorated companion Order of Can. Home: 16 Rothwell Dr Ottawa ON Canada Office: Room 733 Confedn Bldg House of Commons Ottawa ON Canada

PEPITONE, BYRON VINCENT, mgmt. cons., former govt. ofcl.; b. New Brunswick, N.J., June 9, 1918; s. Joseph James and Sarah Frances (Byron) P.; student U.S. Army Command and Gen. Staff Coll., 1944, Air. U. Air Command and Staff Coll., 1950, NATO Def. Coll., 1955; m. Marolynn Mary Mills, June 9, 1940; children—Byron Vincent, James S. Commd. 2d lt. USAAF, 1942, advanced through grades to col. USAF, 1953; ret., 1970; dep. dir. SSS, Washington, 1970-72, acting dir., 1972-73, dir., 1973-77; ret., 1977; sr. asso. James S. Pepitone & Assos., mgmt. consultants, Greenville, S.C., Washington, 1977—. Decorated D.S.M., Legion of Merit with 2 oak leaf clusters, USAF Commendation medal, U.S. Army Commendation medal with oak leaf cluster; recipient Distinguished Service medal SSS, 1972. Mem. USAF Assn., Am. Legion. Home: 203 Yoakum Pkwy Alexandria VA 22304 Office: Greenville SC

PEPPARD, GEORGE, actor; b. Detroit, Oct. 1, 1928; B.A. in Fine Arts, Carnegie Mellon Inst. Appeared on Broadway in Girls of Summer, The Pleasure of His Company; motion pictures include The Strange One, Pork Chop Hill, Home from the Hill, The Subterraneans, Breakfast at Tiffany's, How the West Was Won, The Victors, The Carpetbaggers, Operation Crossbow, The Third Day, The Blue Max, Tobruk, Rough Night in Jericho, House of Cards, P.J., What's So Bad About Feeling Good?, Pendulum, The Executioner, Cannon for Cordoba, The Groundstar Conspiracy, Newman's Law, Damnation Alley, From Hell to Victory; TV appearances include Suspicion, U.S. Steel Hour, Alfred Hitchcock Presents, Matinee Theater, Alcoa-Goodyear Playhouse, Studio One, Hallmark Hall of Fame; films for TV include The Bravos, Banacek, Crisis in Midair, Between Two Loves; star TV series Banacek, Doctors Hosp.; author screenplay, dir., producer, star Five Days From Home, 1978. Address: PO Box 1643 Beverly Hills CA 90213

PEPPER, BEVERLY, painter, sculptor; b. Bklyn., Dec. 20, 1924; d. Irwin Edward and Beatrice Evadne (Horenstein) Stoll; studied with Fernand Leger and Andre L'Hote; student Pratt Inst., 1939-41, Art Students League, N.Y.C., 1944; m. Curtis G. Pepper, Oct. 11, 1949; children—Jorie Graham, John Randolph. One-woman shows include Galerie Hella Nebelung, Dusseldorf, Ger., 1971, Piazza Margana, Rome, 1971, Parker St. Gallery, Boston, 1971, Qui Arte Contemporanea, Rome, 1972, Marlborough Galleria d'Arte, Rome, 1972, Tyler Sch. of Art, Temple U. Abroad, Rome, 1973, Hammarskjold Plaza Sculpture Garden, N.Y.C., 1975, Andre Emmerich Gallery, N.Y.C., 1975, Met. Mus. Art, Miami, Fla., 1976, San Francisco Mus. Art, 1976, Seattle Mus. Art, 1977, Andre Emmerich Gallery, N.Y.C., 1977, 79, Princeton U., 1978, Indpls. Mus. Art, 1978, todi Piazza and Sala delle Pietra, 1979; group shows include: XXIII Biennale di Venezia, Venice, Italy, 1972, Mus. Phila. Civic Center, 1974, Finch Coll. Mus. Art, N.Y.C., 1974, Marlborough Gallery, N.Y.C., 1974, Janie C. Lee Gallery, Houston, 1975, New Orleans Mus. Art, 1976, Documenta 6, Kassel, Ger., 1977, Quadriennale di Roma, Rome, 1977, Seattle Mus., 1979; represented in numerous permanent collections including: Fogg Mus., Cambridge, Mass., Albright-Knox Art Gallery, Buffalo, Jacksonville (Fla.) Mus. Modern Art, Galleria d'Arte Moderna, Florence, Italy, Walker Art Center, Mpls., Instituto Italiano di Cultura, Stockholm, Sweden, Power Inst. Fine Arts, Sydney, Australia, Galleria Civica d'Arte Moderna, Turin, Italy, Albertina Mus., Vienna, Hirschorn Mus. and Sculpture Garden, Washington, Worcester (Mass.) Art Mus., Parkersburg (W.Va.) Art Mus., Smithsonian Inst., Washington, Dartmouth Coll., Hanover, N.H. Recipient award Nat. Endowment of Arts, 1976, 79, GSA, 1975. Author: After Five Cook Book, 1950; Potluck Cookery, 1954; See Rome and Eat, 1960; New After Five Cookbook, 1963; (with Howard Austen) Myra Breckenridge Cookbook, 1969. Home: Torre Gentile di Todi (PG) Italy 06059 Office: Andre Emmerich Gallery 41 E 57th St New York NY 10022

PEPPER, CLAUDE DENSON, congressman; b. Dudleyville, Ala., Sept. 8, 1900; s. Joseph Wheeler and Lena (Talbot) P.; A.B., U. Ala., 1921; J.D., Harvard, 1924; LL.D., McMaster U., 1941, Toronto U., U. Ala., 1942, Rollins Coll., 1944; D.Sc., U. Miami, 1974; m. Irene Mildred Webster, Dec. 29, 1936. Instr. law U. Ark., 1924-25; admitted to Ala. bar 1924, Fla. bar, 1925; practiced in Perry, Fla.; mem. Fla. Ho. Reps., 1929; practiced in Tallahassee, 1930-37; mem. Fla. Bd. Pub. Welfare, 1931-32, Fla. Bd. Law Examiners, 1933; mem. U.S. Senate from Fla., 1936-51, mem. coms. on small bus. and fgn. relations, on mil. affairs, small bus., reorgn. of congress, chmn. com. on inter-oceanic canals, Middle East sub-com. of senate fgn. relations com., 12 yrs.; mem. 88th-89th congresses from 3d Dist. Fla., 90th-92d Congresses 11th Dist. Fla., 93d-95th congress from 14th Dist. Fla., mem. house rules, chmn. subcom. No. 2 house select com. on aging. Chmn., Fla. delegation Democratic Nat. Conv., 1940-44, del., 1948, 52, 56, 60, 64, 68. Served with Armed Forces, 1918. Recipient Mary and Albert Lasker Pub. Service award, 1967, Eleanor Israel Humanities award, 1968. Mem. Internat., Inter-Am., Am., Fla. (exec. com.), Tallahassee, Miami Beach, Coral Gables, Dade County bar assns., Bar City N.Y., Am. Legion, 40 and 8, Vets. World War I, Jasons, Blue Key, Gold Key, Phi Beta Kappa, Omicron Delta Kappa, Phi Alpha Delta (Outstanding Alumnus award U. Fla. chpt. 1975), Sigma Upsilon, Kappa Alpha. Baptist. Mason (Shriner), Elk, Moose, Kiwanian, Woodman of World. Clubs: Harvard (Washington, Miami); Jefferson Island, Army and Navy (Washington); Coral Gables Country; Miami Shores Country; La Gorce Country (Miami Beach); Columbia Country (Chevy Chase, Md.); Burning Tree (Bethesda, Md.). Contbr. to periodicals. Home: 2121 North Bay Shore Dr Miami FL 33137 also 4201 Cathedral Ave NW Washington DC 20016 Office: 1701 Meridian Ave Miami Beach FL 33139 also 2239 Rayburn House Office Bldg Washington DC 20515*

PEPPERDENE, MARGARET WILLIAMS, educator; b. Vicksburg, Miss., Dec. 25, 1919; d. O.L. and Jane (Stocks) Williams; B.S., La. State U., 1941; M.A., Vanderbilt U., 1948, Ph.D., 1953; div. Instr. English, U. Oreg., 1946-47; teaching fellow Vanderbilt U., 1948-50; instr., then asst. prof. Miami U., Oxford, Ohio, 1952-56; mem. faculty Agnes Scott Coll., 1956—, prof. English, chmn. dept., 1967—. Served to lt. USNR, 1943-46. Fulbright fellow, 1950-51; Ford

Found. grad. fellow, 1951-52; AAUW fellow, 1954-55; research fellow Dublin Inst. Advanced Studies, 1954-55; Guggenheim fellow, 1956-57. Author articles. Editor: That Subtile Wreath: Lectures Presented at the Quartercentenary Celebratiom of the Birth of John Donne, 1973. Home: 418 Glendale Ave Decatur GA 30030

PEPPERELL, GERALD V. S., ins. co. exec.; b. Cardiff, Wales, Mar. 15, 1915; s. William Mayne and Kate Norman (Lane) P.; grad. London U.; m. Janet Margaret Thomas, June 11, 1942; children—John, Elisabeth. Vice pres. marine office America Corp., N.Y.C., 1964-68; exec. v.p. Talbot, Bird & Co., Inc., N.Y.C., 1965-66, pres., chmn. bd., dirs., 1966—; pres., dir. Yasuda Fire & Marine Ins. Co. Am., N.Y.C., 1966—; dir. Eagle Star Ins. Co. Am. Bd. dirs. Nat. Cargo Bur., Inc., Security Bur., Inc. Served to maj. Brit. Army, 1939-46. Fellow Chartered Ins. Inst. Gt. Britain; mem. U.S. Maritime Law Assn., Am. Inst. Marine Underwriters (chmn. 1977—), Am. Offshore Ins. Syndicate (chmn. 1978—), Am. Hull Ins. Syndicate (chmn. 1976-78). Episcopalian. Clubs: India House, Can., Met. (N.Y.C.); Montclair (N.J.) Golf. Home: 25 Old Chester Rd Essex Fells NJ 07021 Office: 156 William St New York NY 10038

PEPPLER, ALBERT PATTERSON, profl. football team exec.; b. Balt., Apr. 16, 1922; s. Walter Benjamin and Ruth Adele (Patterson) P.; B.S., Mich. State U., 1948; m. Dora Jean Peppler, Sept. 4, 1946 (div. 1977); children—Pam Nickoli, Susan Hamacheck, Walter, Terry, John, James. Coach, Grant (Mich.) High Sch., 1948-49, East Lansing (Mich.) High Sch., 1949-53; asst. coach football N.C. State U., 1954-61; asst. football coach Wake Forest Coll., 1962; dir. player personnel Green Bay Packers, 1963-72, asst. to gen. mgr., 1971-72; dir. personnel Miami Dolphins, 1972-75; gen. mgr. Atlanta Falcons, 1975-77; asst. gen. mgr. Houston Oilers, 1977—. Served with USAAF, 1943-45. Office: Box 1516 Houston TX 77001. *To paraphrase an old Western folk song "Six beautiful children came to bless this old man's heart with happiness, doubt this statement if you can this old coach was a busy man."*

PEQUEGNAT, WILLIS EUGENE, educator; b. Riverside, Calif., Sept. 18, 1914; s. Frank A. and Mary G. (Witherspoon) P.; A.B., U. Calif., 1936, A.M., 1938, Ph.D., 1942; m. Elizabeth Younghusband, 1937 (div. 1957); children—Willo Ann, John E.; m. 2d, Linda Lee Haithcock, 1957; children—Marina Lynn, William Gordon. Faculty mem. Pomona Coll., 1940-60, chmn. dept. zoology, 1944-60, prof. zoology, 1951-60; asso. program dir. NSF, 1960-61, program dir., 1962-63; prof., chmn. dept. biol. scis. State U. N.Y. at Oyster Bay, 1961-63; prof. biol. oceanography Tex. A. and M. U., College Station, 1963—, head dept. oceanography and meterology, 1964-66; chmn. bd. TerEco Corp., 1970—. Vis. prof. biology U. Chgo., 1947-48, U. Calif., summer, 1951; dir. Carnegie Conf. Progress and Horizons of Sci., 1953; dir. summer session Marine Lab., Corona Del Mar, 1948-60; Ford fellow, research asso. Scripps Instn. Oceanography, 1954-55; vis. prof. Calif. Inst. Tech., 1957, 58; Sci. Faculty fellow NSF, 1958-59. Dir. Inst. Biology for NSF. Recipient research award in oceanography Office Naval Research, 1956, 64. Fellow AAAS; mem. Am. Soc. Limnology and Oceanography, Western Soc. Naturalists, Ecol. Soc. Am., Sigma Xi. Author books; contbr. articles to sci. jours. Home: 21 Forest Dr College Station TX 77840 Office: Tex A and M U College Station TX 77843. *I have tried to keep all of my contracts and, when indicated, to do more than was called for. I found in my early employment that it was most important to do my job, whatever it was, with pride and to the best of my abilities at the time-the future, then, had a way of taking care of itself. Thus I have never had to seek an important job in life, having been recommended for satisfactory posts by former employers and professional associates.*

PERADOTTO, JOHN JOSEPH, educator, univ. ofcl., editor; b. Ottawa, Ill., May 11, 1933; s. John Joseph and Mary Louise (Giacometti) P.; B.A., St. Louis U., 1957, M.A., 1958; Ph.D., Northwestern U., 1963; m. Noreen Doran, Aug. 29, 1959; children—Erin, Monica, Noreen, Nicole. Instr. classics and English, Western Wash. State Coll., Bellingham, 1960-61; instr. Georgetown U., 1961-63, asst. prof. classics, 1963-66; asst. prof. classics State U. N.Y. at Buffalo, 1966-69, asso. prof., 1969-73; prof., chmn. classics U. Tex. at Austin, 1973-74; prof. classics SUNY, Buffalo, 1974—, chmn. dept., 1974-77, dean div. undergrad. edn., 1978—, mem. bd. editors SUNY Press, 1978—. Fellow, Center for Hellenic Studies, 1972-73. Recipient Chancellor's award for teaching excellence State U. N.Y., 1975. Mem. Am. Philol. Assn. (dir. 1974-77), Classical Assn. Atlantic States (exec. com. 1976-78), Classical Assn. Midwestern and So. States. Author: Classical Mythology: An Annotated Bibliographical Survey, 1973; also articles and revs. Founding asso. editor Arethusa, editor-in-chief, 1974—; editor: Classical Literature and Contemporary Literary Analysis, 1977; Women in the Ancient World, 1978; co-editor: Population Policy in Plato and Aristotle, 1975; The New Archilochus, 1976; Augustan Poetry Books, 1980; Indo-European Institutions: Roots of Classical Culture, 1980; Vergil: 2000 Years, 1981. Office: Dept Classics State U NY Buffalo NY 14260

PERAHIA, MURRAY, pianist, condr.; b. N.Y.C., 1947; grad. Mannes Coll. Music; student Jeanette Haien, Arthur Balsam, Mieczyslaw Horszowski. Appeared with Berlin Philharmonic, Chgo. Symphony Orch., English Chamber Orch., Boston Symphony Orch., Cin. Symphony Orch., Detroit Symphony Orch., Toronto Symphony Orch., others; performed with Budapest, Guarneri and Galimir string quartets; participant Marlboro Music Festival, Festival of Two Worlds, Spoleto, Italy, Met. Mus. series, New Sch. concerts; quest artist Lincoln Center Chamber Music Soc.; recital tours U.S., Can., Europe and Japan; recs. for Columbia Records. Recipient Avery Fisher Artist award, 1975; Kosciusko Chopin prize. Address: care Frank Salomon Assos 201 W 54th St Suite 4C New York NY 10019

PERCAS DE PONSETI, HELENA, educator; b. Valencia, Spain, Jan. 17, 1921; d. Nicolas Percas and Ana (Babenco) de Percas; came to U.S., 1940, naturalized, 1950; Baccalaureat, Paris, France, 1939; B.A., Barnard Coll., 1942; M.A., Columbia, 1943, Ph.D., 1951; m. Ignacio V. Ponseti, 1961. Tchr. lang. and lit. Barnard Coll., 1942-43, Russell Sage Coll., 1943-45, Columbia, 1945-47, Queens Coll., 1946-48; mem. faculty Grinnell Coll., 1948—, prof. lang. and lit., 1957—, Roberts Honor prof. modern fgn. langs., 1961-62, Richards prof. modern fgn. langs., 1963—. Author: La Poesia Femenina Argentina, 1810-1950, 1958; Cervantes y su concepto del arte, 1975. Home: 110 Oak Ridge Ave Iowa City IA 52240 Office: Grinnell Coll Grinnell IA 50112

PERCIVAL, WALTER CLEMENT, educator; b. Jericho, Vt., June 25, 1901; s. Charles Eugene and Sarah Jane (Nattress) P.; B.S., N.Y. State Coll. Forestry, 1923, M.S., 1926, Ph.D., 1933; m. E. Phyllis Pennington, July 14, 1928; children—Charles Leigh, Phyllis Marcia, Lillian Margaret. Silvicultural foreman U.S. Forest Service,, 1933-34, dist. ranger, 1934; mem. faculty W.Va. U., 1934—, prof. forestry and forester, 1939-66, head div. forestry, 1937-66, founder W.Va. Forestry Sch. as div. forestry Coll. Agr. and Forestry, 1937, asst. dean Coll. Agr., Forestry and Home Econs., dir. div. forestry, forester W.Va. Agrl. Expt. Sta., 1959-66, prof. emeritus, 1966—. Univ.'s new forestry bldg. named Percival Hall in his honor, 1973; named to W.Va. Agrl. Hall of Fame, 1977. Mem. W.Va. State Bd. Registration for Foresters. Fellow Soc. Am. Foresters; mem. Morgantown Power Squadron (comdr.), Sigma Xi, Sigma Nu. Republican. Methodist. Research on effects of environment during growth of wood on resistance to decay. Home: 1 Devon Rd Morgantown WV 26505. *My parents told me of the Christ. I have tried to live according to the principles which Christ taught. I have sought and carefully considered the advice of good, successful people when making decisions. For important decisions directly affecting the lives of others, I have prayed to and received help from God. I am naturally of a timid nature but God has used even me to help people and I am very glad that I have been of some constructive use.*

PERCUS, JEROME KENNETH, physicist; b. N.Y.C., June 21, 1926; s. Philip M. and Gertrude B. (Schweiger) P.; B.S.E.E., Columbia U., 1947, M.A., 1948, Ph.D., 1954; m. Ora Engelberg, May 20, 1965; children—Orin, Allon . Instr. elec. engring. Columbia U., N.Y.C., 1952-54; asst. prof. Stevens Inst. Tech., Hoboken, N.J., 1955-58; asso. prof. N.Y. U., N.Y.C., 1958-65, prof., 1965—; dir. Nat. Biomed. Research Found. Served with USN, 1944-46. Recipient Pregel award in chem. physics N.Y. Acad. Scis., 1975. Mem. Am. Math. Soc., Am. Phys. Soc., Sigma Xi. Author: Many-Body Problem, 1963; Combinatorial Methods, 1971; Combinatorial Methods in Developmental Biology, 1977; asso. editor Pattern Recognition, Statis. Physics, Jour. Math. Physics. Office: 251 Mercer St New York NY 10012

PERCY, CHARLES HARTING, U.S. senator; b. Pensacola, Fla., Sept. 27, 1919; s. Edward H. and Elisabeth (Harting) P.; A.B., U. Chgo., 1941; LL.D., Ill. Coll., 1961, Roosevelt U., 1961, Lake Forest Coll., 1962, Bradley U., 1963, Defiance Coll., 1965; H.H.D., Willamette U., 1962; D.H.L., Nat. Coll. Edn., 1964, Northwestern U., 1966; m. Jeanne Valerie Dickerson, June 12, 1943 (dec.); children—Valerie (dec.) and Sharon Lee (twins), Roger; m. 2d, Loraine Diane Guyer, Aug. 27, 1950; children—Gail, Mark. Sales trainee, apprentice Bell & Howell, 1938, mgr. war coordinating dept., 1941-43, asst. sec., 1943-46, corp. sec., 1946-49, pres., 1949-61, chief exec. officer, 1951-63, chmn. bd., 1961-66, also dir.; sales promotion Crowell-Collier Pub. Co., 1939; U.S. senator from Ill., 1967—; past dir. Harris Trust & Savs. Bank, Outboard Marine Corp. Chmn. New Ill. Com., 1965-69; spl. ambassador and personal rep. Pres. U.S. to presdl. Inauguration ceremonies in Peru and Bolivia, 1956; del. UN, 1974. Vice chmn. Republican Nat. Finance Com., 1957-59; chmn. com. platform and resolutions Rep. Nat. Conv., 1960; Rep. candidate for gov. of Ill., 1964. Nat. Conf. Christians and Jews, Chgo., 1954. Trustee, mem. citizens bd., dir. alumni found. U. Chgo.; trustee Ill. Inst. Tech., 1950-54; chmn. fund for adult edn. Ford Found., 1958-61; past trustee Calif. Inst. Tech.; bd. dirs. Chgo. Boys Club; grad. mem. Bus. Council. Served lt. USNR, 1943-45. Elected one of 10 outstanding young men of 1949, U.S. Jr. C. of C.; recipient World Trade award World Trade Award Com., 1955; Nat. Sales Execs. Mgmt. award, 1956; Bus. Man of Year award Sat. Rev., 1962; Statesmanship award Harvard Bus. Sch. Assn. Chgo., 1962; Humanitarian Service award Abraham Lincoln Center, 1962; Top-Hat award Nat. Fedn. Bus. and Profl. Women's Clubs, 1965; Bus. Adminstrn. award Drexel Inst. Tech., 1965; others; decorated officer French Legion of Honor. Mem. Chgo. Assn. Commerce, Am. Mgmt. Assn. (past dir.), Nat. Photog. Mfrs. Assn., Photog. Soc. Am., Phi Delta Phi, Alpha Dela Phi (nat. sec.). Clubs: Chicago, Economic (past dir.), Executives (past dir.), Commercial, Commonwealth (Chgo.). Author: Growing Old In the Country of the Young, 1974; I Want To Know about the United States Senate, 1976. Home: Wilmette IL 60091 Office: Senate Office Bldg Washington DC 20510

PERCY, WALKER, author; b. Birmingham, Ala., May 28, 1916; s. Leroy Pratt and Martha Susan (Phinizy) P.; B.A., U. N.C., 1937; M.D., Columbia, 1941; m. Mary Bernice Townsend, Nov. 7, 1946; children—Mary Pratt, Ann Boyd. Intern Bellevue Hosp., N.Y.C., 1942; writer, 1943—. Fellow Am. Acad. Arts and Scis.; mem. Nat. Inst. Arts and Letters. Author: The Moviegoer, 1961 (Nat. Book award 1962); The Last Gentleman, 1966; Love in the Ruins, 1971; The Message in the Bottle, 1975; Lancelot, 1976. Roman Catholic. Contbr. philos., critical and med. essays to jours., mags. Address: PO Box 510 Covington LA 70433

PERDUE, JAMES EVERETT, univ. ofcl.; b. Auburn, Nebr., June 24, 1916; s. James O. and Hazel D. Perdue; student Nebr. Wesleyan U., 1933-34; A.B., Nebr. State Tchrs. Coll., 1937; A.M., No. Colo. State U., Greeley, 1940; Ph.D., Stanford, 1952; LL.D., U. Denver, 1965; m. Raedeen Tibbetts, Apr. 9, 1939; children—Pamela Jane, Darcy Clare. Coach, tchr. social studies DeWitt (Nebr.) High Sch., 1937-38; head social sci. dept. Ft. Morgan (Colo.) High Sch., 1938-41; ednl. rep. Row, Peterson and Co., 1941-43; acting dean Coll. Arts and Scis., U. Denver, 1946-48, asso. dean, 1948-51, univ. budget officer, 1951-52, asst. to chancellor, 1952-53, prof. social sci., dean Coll. Arts and Scis., 1953-65; pres., prof. social sci. State U. N.Y., Oswego, 1965-77; asso. chancellor State U. N.Y. System, 1977-78, vice chancellor for acad. programs, policy and planning, 1978—; trustee Oswego City Savs. Bank; dir. Oswego br. Marine Midland Trust Co. Mem. adv. com. on higher edn. Legislative Council State of Colo.; mem. Colo. Mental Health Planning Com., Colo. Council on Instrn., Hosp. Review and Planning Council Central N.Y.; bd. dirs. Acad. Collective Bargaining Service, 1973—, chmn., 1974—. Chmn. Oswego County Heart Fund, 1973. Served as ops. and communications officer USNR, 1943-46. Recipient Distinguished Ednl. Service award Peru State, 1966, Outstanding Male Educator award U. N.C., 1975, Meritorious Service award Am. Assn. State Colls. and Univs., 1972, Adminstrv. Leave award Danforth Found., 1972. Mem. Am. Conf. Acad. Deans (vice chmn. 1963-64, exec. bd. 1959-64, nat. chmn. 1965-66), Am. Assn. State Colls. and Univs. (dir. 1967-72, pres. elect 1976), Phi Beta Kappa, Pi Gamma Mu, Phi Delta Kappa. Home: 159 Chestnut St Albany NY 12210

PERDUNN, RICHARD FRANCIS, mgmt. engr.; b. Trenton, N.J., Dec. 12, 1915; s. Francis R. and Edith (Nogle) P.; B.S., Lehigh U., 1939; post-grad. student U. Pitts., 1939-40, Johns Hopkins, 1941-42; m. Eugenia E. Morel, June 7, 1941; 1 dau., Justine Reneau. With U.S. Steel Co., also Glenn L. Martin, 1939-43, supt. machine and assembly, 1941-43; partner Nelson & Perdunn, engrs. and cons., also v.p. Penco Corp., 1947-49; with Merck & Co., 1949-54, mgr. adminstrn., 1951-54; with Stevenson, Jordan & Harrison, mgmt. engrs., N.Y.C., 1954-68, exec. v.p., 1962-64, pres., 1964-68; pres., chief exec. officer Bachman-Jacks, Inc., Reading, Pa., 1968-71; sr. v.p. Golightly Internat., N.Y.C., 1971—, also dir.; dir. West Point & Annapolis Text Book Pub. Co., 1948—, Indsl. Edn. Films Inc., 1966—, Eldun Corp., 1964—, Security Nat. Bank, Newark, 1964—, Surburban Life Ins. Co., 1966—, Mainstem Inc., 1965—, Greenhouse Decor Inc., 1961—, Neuwirth Mut. Fund Inc., 1975—. Lectr. on finance and mfg. in U.S., Can., Eng., Sweden. Bd. dirs. Inst. Better Confs., Internat. Inst. Bus. Devel., Inst. Urban Affairs; dir. finance Assn. Help for Retarded Children. Served with USNAF, 1942-47. Mem. N.Y.C. C. of C., Council Econ. Devel., Am. Mgmt. Assn., AIM (pres.'s council), Newcomen Soc. N.Am., Systems and Procedures Assn. Am., Soc. Advanced Mgmt. Asso. editor Systems and Procedures Quar., 1948-51. Contbr. articles to profl. publs. Home: 407 Kenli Ln Brielle NJ Office: 1 Rockefeller Plaza New York NY 10020

PEREIRA, WILLIAM L., architect, city planner; b. Chgo., Apr. 25, 1909; B.S., U. Ill., 1930; hon. degree Otis Art Inst., 1964, Art Center Coll. Design, 1971; LL.D. (hon.), Pepperdine U., 1974; m. Margaret McConnell, June 24, 1934; children—William L., Monica I. m. 2d, Bronya Kester, 1976. Began as architect, 1930; asso. Holabird & Root, Chgo., 1930-32; then pvt. practice, Chgo., also Los Angeles; designed or planned Cape Canaveral, CBS Television City, Union Oil Center, Los Angeles Mus. Art. Houston Center, African Riviera (Ivory Coast), New Eng. Center for Continuing Edn., Central Library, U. Calif., San Diego, Occidental Center, Crocker-Citizens Bldg., Los Angeles, Transamerica Hdqrs., San Francisco, Marineland of the Pacific, Palos Verdes, Doha Hotel and Conf. Center, Qatar; master planner Los Angeles Internat. Airport, Irvine Ranch, Mountain Park, U. Calif. at Irvine, U. So. Calif., others; prof. architecture U. So. Calif., 1949-57; partnership Pereira & Luckman, architects and engrs., 1950-58; prin. William L. Pereira Assos., 1958—; architect in residence Am. Acad. in Rome, 1971. Mem. adv. com. to bd. dirs. Crocker-Citizens Nat. Mem. Pres.'s Nat. Council on Arts, 1965-68; adviser Aeros. and Space Engring. Bd., 1969; chmn. Calif. Gov.'s Transp. Task Force Com., 1967-68. Bd. dirs. Urban Am., Inc. Decorated comdr. Order of Ivory Coast; recipient Scarab Medal 1940, Oscar, Acad. Motion Picture Arts and Scis., 1942, Humanitarian Medal, 1942, citation Mus. Modern Art, 1944 Phila. Art Alliance award, 1949, A.I.A. honor and merit awards, 1951-69; Man of Year award Los Angeles C. of C., 1967. Registered architect thirty-four states. Fellow A.I.A.; mem. Gargoyle Soc., Soc. Am. Mil. Engrs., Acad. Motion Picture Arts and Scis. Alpha Sigma Mu (hon.). Office: 5657 Wilshire Blvd Los Angeles CA 90036

PERELLA, NICHOLAS JAMES, educator; b. Boston, Sept. 7, 1927; s. Nicola and Maria (Giovanna) P.; B.A., Suffolk U., 1952; M.A., Harvard, 1954, Ph.D., 1957; m. Vivian Perella, Sept. 7, 1957. Mem. faculty U. Calif. at Berkeley, 1957—, now prof. Italian. Mem. Modern Lang. Assn. Am., AAUP, Am. Assn. Tchrs. Italian. Author: The Kiss Sacred and Profane: An Interpretative History of Kiss Symbolism, 1969; Night and the Sublime in Giacomo Leopardi, 1970; The Critical Fortune of Battista Guarini's Pastor Fido, 1973; Midday in Italian Literature, 1979. Home: 3 Highland Blvd Kensington CA 94707 Office: Dept Italian U Calif Berkeley CA 94720

PERELMAN, LEON JOSEPH, paper mfg. co. exec., univ. pres.; b. Phila., Aug. 28, 1911; s. Morris and Jennie (Davis) P.; B.A., LaSalle Coll., 1933, LL.D., 1978; postgrad. U. Pa. Law Sch., 1933-35; L.H.D. (hon.), Dropsie U., 1976; m. Beverly Waxman, Jan. 27, 1945 (div. Apr. 1960); children—Cynthia, David. Partner Am. Paper Products Co. (later Am. Paper Products Inc.), Phila., 1935-42, pres., 1943—; pres. Am. Cone & Tube Co. Inc., 1953—, United Ammunition Container Inc., 1961—, Ajax Paper Tube Co., 1962—; vice chmn. bd. Belmont Industries, 1963—; pres. Dropsie U., 1978—. Fin. chmn. Valley Forge council Boy Scouts Am., 1968; founder, bd. dirs. Perelman Antique Toy Museum, Phila., 1969; pres. West Park Hosp., Phila., 1975-78. Served to 1st lt. USAAF, 1942-45. Recipient citation Jewish Theol. Sem., 1965; Beth Jacob award, 1966; award Pop Warner Little Scholars Inc., 1972; Cyrus Adler award Jewish Theol. Sem., 1976. Mem. AAUP, Franklin Inst., Am. Assn. Museums. Republican. Jewish. Clubs: Union League (Phila.); Masons, Shriners. Author: Perelman Antique Toy Museum, 1972. Home: 339 Winding Way Merion PA 19066 Office: 2113-41 E Rush St Philadelphia PA 19134

PERELMAN, MELVIN, pharm. co. exec.; b. Omaha, Oct. 12, 1930; s. Ben and Sarah (Fox) P.; B.S., Northwestern U., 1952; Ph.D. (Shell Oil fellow), Rice U., 1956; postgrad. Fed. Inst. Tech., Zurich, Switzerland, 1956-57; m. Jill Louise Stott, Aug. 1, 1953; children—Steven Eric, Wendy Lynn, Kent Bryan. With Eli Lilly and Co., Indpls., 1957—, v.p. devel. research and services, 1972-73, v.p. facilities and ops. planning, 1973-76, pres. Eli Lilly Internat. Corp., 1976—, also dir.; dir. various subsidiaries Eli Lilly and Co., including Elizabeth Arden, Cardiac Pacemakers Inc., IVAC, Elanco Products Co., Eli Lilly Internat. Corp. Bd. dirs. Indpls. Zool. Soc., 1971—, pres. bd., 1977—; bd. dirs. Indpls. Visitors and Conv. Bur. Am. Cancer Soc. research fellow, Switzerland, 1956-57. Mem. Phi Beta Kappa Assos., Sigma Xi, Phi Lambda Upsilon. Contbr. articles to profl. jours.; patentee in field. Home: 3030 W 116th St Carmel IN 46032 Office: 307 E McCarty Indianapolis IN 46206

PERELMAN, SIDNEY JOSEPH, writer; b. Bklyn., Feb. 1, 1904, s. Joseph and Sophia (Charren) P.; student Brown U., 1921-25; m. Laura West, July 4, 1929; children—Adam, Abby Laura. Artist and writer Judge, 1925-29, Coll. Humor, 1929-30; writer for motion pictures, 1930—; contbr. to The New Yorker, 1931—; wrote sketches for Third Little Show, Walk a Little Faster, others. Named Best Screen Writer of 1956 for Around the World in 80 Days, also Acad. award; New York Film Critics award. Mem. Screen Writers Guild, Dramatists Guild, Nat. Inst. Arts and Letters. Club: Century Assn. Author: Dawn Ginsbergh's Revenge, 1929; Parlor, Bedlam and Bath, 1930; (play) (with Laura Perelman) All Good Americans, 1934, The Night Before Christmas, 1941; Strictly from Hunger, 1937; Look Who's Talking, 1940; The Dream Department, 1943; (play) (with Ogden Nash) One Touch of Venus, 1943; Crazy Like a Fox, 1944; Keep It Crisp, 1946; Acres and Pains; Best of S.J. Perelman, 1947; Westward Ha, 1948; Listen to the Mocking Bird, 1949; The Swiss Family Perelman, 1950; The Ill Tempered Clavichord, 1953; Perelman's Home Companion, 1955; The Road to Miltown, 1957; The Most of S. J. Perelman, 1958; The Rising Gorge, 1961; (play) The Beauty Part, 1963; Chicken Inspector No. 23, 1966; Baby, It's Cold Inside, 1970; Vinegar Puss, 1975; Eastward Ha!, 1977. Office: care Simon and Schuster 1230 Ave of the Americas New York NY 10020*

PERENCHIO, ANDREW JERROLD, film and TV exec.; b. Fresno, Calif., Dec. 20, 1930; s. Andrew Joseph and Dorothea (Harvey) P.; B.S., U. Calif. at Los Angeles, 1954; m. Robin Green, July 16, 1954 (div.); children—Candace L., Catherine M., John Gardner; m. 2d, Jacquelyn Claire, Nov. 14, 1969 (div.). Vice pres. Music Corp. Am., 1958-62, Gen. Artists Corp., 1962-64; pres., owner Chartwell Artists, Ltd., theatrical agy., Los Angeles, 1964—; chmn. bd. Tandem Prodns., Inc., also TAT Communications Co., Los Angeles, 1973—; promoter Muhammad Ali-Joe Frazier heavyweight fight, 1971, Bobby Riggs-Billie Jean King tennis match, 1973. Served to 1st lt. USAF, 1954-57. Clubs: Bel-Air Country (Los Angeles); Westchester (N.Y.) Country; Friars (N.Y.C.). Home: 23526 Malibu Colony Rd Malibu CA 90265 Office: 1901 Ave of Stars Los Angeles CA 90067

PERERA, GEORGE ALFRED, ret. physician; b. N.Y.C., Dec. 29, 1911; s. Lionello and Carolyn (Allen) P.; A.B., Princeton, 1933; M.D., Columbia, 1937, Sc.D. in Medicine, 1942; m. Anna Paxson Rhoads, Dec. 22, 1934; children—Marcia (Mrs. Nicholas B. Van Dyck), David Rhoads. Intern, Presbyn. Hosp., N.Y.C., 1937-39, resident medicine, 1941-43; asst. resident Peter Bent Brigham Hosp., Boston, 1939-40; asst. physiology N.Y. U., 1940-41; mem. staff Presbyn. Hosp., 1943-71, attending physician, 1960-71; faculty Columbia Coll. Physicians and Surgeons, 1946-71, prof. medicine, 1958-71, asst. dean, 1960-62, asso. dean, 1962-70. Lewis A. Conner meml. lectr. Am. Heart Assn., New Orleans, 1955; Lambie-Dew orator Sydney U. (Australia) Med. Soc., 1961. Trustee Riverdale Country Sch., N.Y.C., 1949—, pres., 1977—; trustee Mary Imogene Bassett Hosp., Cooperstown, N.Y., 1961—, Columbia U. Press, 1961-64, 66-69, Bridges of Understanding Found., 1973-77; trustee Concern for Dying, 1975—, v.p., 1978-79; alumni trustee Columbia, 1974—; mem. corp. Haverford Coll., 1979—. Diplomate Am. Bd. Internal Medicine (dir. 1957-64, vice chmn. 1963-64). Fellow A.C.P., AAAS; mem.

N.Y. Acad. Medicine (v.p. 1968-70, trustee 1973-78), Am. Soc. Clin. Investigation, Assn. Am. Physicians, Alpha Omega Alpha. Clubs: Century Assn., Riverdale Yacht (N.Y.C.). Contbr. profl. jours., chpts. textbooks. Editorial bd. Circulation, 1953-57, Circulation Research, 1958-60, Annals Internal Medicine, 1961-64, Jour. Med. Edn., 1962-69. Home: 4991 Henry Hudson Pkwy Bronx NY 10471

PERERA, GUIDO RINALDO, lawyer; b. Brussels, Belgium, Apr. 21, 1902; s. Gino Lorenzo and Caroline (Thacher) P.; diploma Middlesex Sch., Concord, Mass., 1920; A.B., Harvard, 1924, LL.B., 1927; m. Faith Phillips, Dec. 5, 1929; children—Guido R., Phillips, Lawrence Thacher, Ronald Christopher. Admitted to Mass. bar, 1927, since practiced in Boston; asso. firm Hutchins & Wheeler, 1927-36, partner, 1937-41; partner Hemenway & Barnes 1945-70, of counsel, 1970—; pres. Eastern Utilities Assos., 1949-72, chmn., 1972-75. Served to col. USAAF, 1942-45; col. Res. Decorated Legion of Merit, Bronze Star. Mem. Am., Boston bar assns. Home: 12 W Cedar St Boston MA 02108 Office: 60 State St Boston MA 02109

PERERA, LAWRENCE THACHER, lawyer; b. Boston, June 23, 1935; B.A., Harvard U., 1957, LL.B., 1961. Admitted to Mass. bar, 1961, U.S. Supreme Ct. bar, 1973; clk. Judge R. Ammi Cutter, Mass. Supreme Jud. Ct., Boston, 1961-62; asso. firm Palmer & Dodge, Boston, 1962-69, partner, 1969-74; judge Middlesex County Probate Ct., East Cambridge, Mass., 1974-79; partner firm Hemenway & Barnes, Boston, 1979—; faculty Nat. Jud. Coll., Reno. Chmn., Boston Fin. Commn., 1971-72; overseer Peter Bent Brigham Hosp., Boston; pres. Boston Opera Assn.; bd. dirs., v.p. Back Bay Fedn. Community Devel., Boston. Fellow Am. Acad. Matrimonial Lawyers; mem. Am. Law Inst., Am., Mass., Boston bar assns. Home: 18 Marlborough St Boston MA 01116 Office: 60 State St Boston MA 02116

PERESS, MAURICE, symphony condr.; b. N.Y.C., Mar. 18, 1930; s. Haskell Ben Ezra and Elka (Tygier) P.; B.A., N.Y.U., 1951, postgrad. Mannes Coll. Music, N.Y.U. Grad. Sch. Musicology; m. Gloria Vando, July 2, 1955; children—Lorca Miriam, Paul Avram, Anika Tygier. Asst. condr. Mannes Coll. Music, 1957-60; music dir. N.Y.U., 1958-61; asst. condr. New York Philharmonic, 1961-62; music dir. Corpus Christi (Tex.) Symphony, 1961-74; music dir. Joffrey Ballet, 1966, Austin Symphony, 1970-72; dir. Bur. Indian Affairs pilot project Communication through Music, 1968; faculty N.Y.U., 1957-61, Queens Coll., 1969-70, U. Tex., 1970-72; mus. dir. world premiere Bernstein Mass, J.F. Kennedy Center, Washington, 1971; mus. dir. Kansas City Philharmonic, 1974—. Served with AUS, 1953-55. Recipient Beethoven medal German Consul Gen., 1969; named Arts Council Artist of Year, 1969. Millicent James fellow N.Y.U., 1955, Mannes Coll. scholar, 1955-57. Mem. ASCAP. Jewish. Pub. orchestrations: Monteverdi, Tocatta and Ritornelli from Orfeo; Bernstein, West Side Story Overture; Ellington, Black Brown and Beige Suite. Author: Some Music Lessons for American Indian Youngsters, 1968. Contbr. articles profl. jours. Home: 627 E 46th St Kansas City MO 64110 Office: 210 W 14th St Kansas City MO 64105

PERETTI, ELSA, jewelry designer; b. Florence, Italy, May 1, 1940. Tchr. French and Italian pvt. schs.; mem. staff Dado Torrigiani, Architect, Milan, Italy; fashion model, Spain, France and Gt. Britain, U.S.; jewelry designer. Recipient Coty award, 1971. Office: care Tiffany and Co 727 Fifth Ave New York NY 10022

PERETTI, ETTORE ALEX JAMES, educator; b. Butte, Mont., Apr. 5, 1913; s. Charles Ludwig and Mary (Crotto) P.; B.S., Mont. Coll. Mineral Sci. and Tech., 1934, M.S., 1935; Sc.D., U. Stuttgart, 1936; Metall. Engr. (hon.), U. Mont., 1963; m. Pierina Helen Giacoletto, June 6, 1937; children—Charlene Pierre, Ettore Alex James. Inst. Internat. Edn. exchange fellow to Germany, 1935-36; instr. metallurgy Mont. Coll. Mineral Sci. and Tech., 1936-39, asst. prof., 1939-40, Columbia, 1940-46; asso. prof. U. Notre Dame, 1946-49, prof., 1949-78, head dept. metallurgy, 1951-69, asst. dean engring., 1970-78; asst. exec. dir. Nat. Consortium for Grad. Degrees for Minorities in Engring., Inc., 1978—. Cons. Bd. Econ. Warfare, 1943. Fellow Am. Soc. for Metals (past sec.-treas., past chmn. Notre Dame chpt.); mem. Am. Inst. Mining and Metall. Engrs. (past chmn. com. metallurgy courses, edn. div.), ASTM, AAUP, Am. Foundrymens Soc., Iron and Steel Inst., Am. Soc. Engring. Edn., Inst. Metals, Sigma Xi, Tau Beta Pi, Theta Tau, Alpha Sigma Mu (nat. pres. 1969-70). Author numerous tech. publs. on metallurgy. Home: 18295 Brightlingsea Pl South Bend IN 46637

PERETZ, JOHN WILLIAM, ins. co. exec.; b. Amsterdam, N.Y., Sept. 5, 1923; B.A. in Polit. Sci., Alfred U., 1951; m. Nancy L. Richtberg, Dec. 4, 1964; 1 son, Craig. With Equitable Life Assurance Soc. U.S., N.Y.C., 1951—, v.p., 1971-77, sr. v.p., 1977—. Trustee Alfred U. Served with USN, 1942-46. Home: 87 Brook St Garden City NY 11530 Office: 1285 Ave of Americas New York City NY 10019

PERETZ, MARTIN, editor, educator; b. N.Y.C., July 30, 1939; s. Julius and Ellen (Weberman) P.; B.A., Brandeis U., 1959; M.A., Harvard, 1965, Ph.D., 1966; m. Anne Labouisse, June 16, 1967; children—David, Anne Elise, Jesse, Evgenia. Instr., Harvard, 1965-68, asst. prof., 1968-72, lectr. social studies, 1972—, master South House, 1972-75; chmn. editorial bd. New Republic mag., 1974-75, editor, 1975—; dir. Dreyfus Leverage Fund, Dreyfus Money Market Instruments. Bd. govs. Hebrew U. Jerusalem; trustee Brandeis U. Woodrow Wilson fellow, 1959-61. Democrat. Jewish. Home: 20 Larchwood Dr Cambridge MA 02138 Office: 1220 19th St NW Washington DC 20036 also Com Degrees in Social Studies Harvard U Cambridge MA 02138

PEREZ, CARLOS A., radiation oncologist; b. Columbia, Nov. 10, 1934; came to U.S., 1960, naturalized, 1969; B.S., U. de Antioquia, Medellin, 1952, M.D., 1958; m. Blanca Martinez; children—Carlos S., Bernardo, Edward P. Rotating intern Hosp. U. St. Vincente de Paul, Medellin and Caldas, 1958-59; resident Mallinckrodt Inst. Radiology, Washington U. Sch. Medicine, St. Louis, 1960-63, mem. faculty, 1964—, prof. radiology, 1972—, dir. div. radiation oncology, 1976—; fellow radiotherapy M.D. Anderson Hosp. and Tumor Inst., U. Tex., Houston, 1963-64; chmn. membership com. Radiation Therapy Oncology Group, 1974—; chmn. com. radiation oncology, mem. exec. com. Southeastern Cancer Study Group, 1975; advisory com. div. cancer treatment Nat. Cancer Inst., 1979. Diplomate Am. Bd. Radiology. Fellow Am. Coll. Radiology; mem. Internat. Assn. Study Lung Cancer, Am. Soc. Clin. Oncology, Am. Soc. Therapeutic Radiologists, Am. Radium Soc., Am. Assn. Cancer Research, Am. Assn. Cancer Edn., Radiol. Soc. N.Am., Brit. Inst. Radiology, Assn. Univ. Radiologists, AAAS, AMA, Mo. Radiol. Soc., Mo. Acad. Sci., Mo., St. Louis med. socs., Greater St. Louis Soc. Radiologists, Radiation Research Soc., Soc. Surg. Yearbook Cancer, 1973—; editor Internat. Jour. Radiation and Physics, 1975—. Contbr. med. jours. Home: 9243 Clayton Rd Saint Louis MO 63124 Office: Div Radiation Oncology 4511 Forest Park Blvd Saint Louis MO

PEREZ, GERALD S. A., assn. exec.; b. Agana, Guam, Mar. 3, 1943; s. Jose B. and Veronica S. (San Agustin) P.; B.S. in Forestry, U. Idaho, 1965, M.S. in Wildlife Mgmt. (John Hay Whitney fellow, Wildlife Mgmt. Inst. fellow), 1969; m. Kathleen M. Conrow, June 14, 1966; children—Sherry, Steven, Mike. Wildlife biologist to dep. dir. Guam Dept. Agr., Agana, 1966-71, dir. Dept. Land Mgmt., 1971-74, dir. budget and mgmt. Office of Gov., 1974-75; pres. Guam C. of C., Agana, 1976—; adj. instr. ornithology U. Guam, 1967—, acting dean Land Grant Coll., 1973; instr. job devel. program Guam Economic Opportunity Commn., 1968. Exec. sec. Guam Territorial Planning Commn., Guam Hist. Site and Place Name Commn.; mem. Gov.'s Advisory Council and Legis. Rev. Com.; mem. Mental Health Advisory Bd., 1976—; mem. Internat. Council Protection of Endangered Bats, 1972—; contract officer land and water conservation funds. Govt. scholar, 1963-65; Young Men's League scholar, 1968; John Hay Whitney fellow, 1968; fellow Wildlife Mgmt. Inst., 1968. Mem. Phi Sigma, Xi Sigma Pi. Contbr. articles in field to profl. jours. Home: PO Box 2347 Agana GU 96910 Office: Chamber of Commerce PO Box 283 Agana GU 96910. *Service to mankind has been my guide to professional fulfillment. It has enabled me to better understand the diversity of man, the conditions which have formed his very being, and the journeys which are open to his choosing.*

PEREZ, GINES, army officer; b. Cuevas del Almanzora Almeria, Spain, Dec. 15, 1908; s. Indalecio Perez Asensio and Ana Lopez Melendez; came to U.S., 1919, naturalized, 1932; B.S., U. Ariz., 1932, M.S., 1933; grad. Command and Gen. Staff Coll., 1942, 48, Inf. Sch., 1947, Airborne Sch., 1952, Army War Coll., 1955, other army schs.; m. Edith Elizabeth Edwards, Oct. 16, 1937; children—Anne E., Patricia M., Gines, Carol L. Commd. 2d lt. U.S. Army, 1933, advanced through grades to maj. gen., 1960; various assignments in U.S., 1933-44; exec. officer 12th Cav., S.W. Pacific, 1944-45, 1st Cav. Brigade S.W. Pacific, 1945; instr., then student army schs., 1946-48; chief plans sect. G-3 Hdqrs. 4th U.S. Army, Ft. Sam Houston, Tex., 1948-50; comdg. officer 21st Inf., 1950-51; asst. chief staff G-3 Hdqrs. TIC, Ft. Benning, Ga., 1952, 1952-54; chief mil. missions sect., 1955-56; comdt. U.S. Army Caribbean Sch. and Army Atlantic, Ft. Gulick, C.Z., 1956-58; regtl. comdr. 3d tng. Regt., USATC, Ft. Jackson, S.C., 1958-59; dept. comdg. gen., chief staff XVIII Airborne Corps. and Ft. Bragg, N.C., 1959, asst. div. comdr. 82d Airborne Div., 1959-61; dep. chief MAAG, Madrid, Spain, 1961-64; comdg. gen. U.S. Army Tng. Center, Inf. and Ft. Jackson, 1964—. Decorated D.S.C., D.S.M., Silver Star with oak leaf cluster, Legion of Merit with oak leaf cluster, Bronze Star with V device and 4 oak leaf clusters, Joint Services Commendation medal, Commendation medal, Purple Heart (U.S.); Order Boyaca, comdr. Mil. Order of Antonio Narino (Colombia); Medal Mil. Merit (Chile); comdr. Order of Vasco Nunez de Balboa (Panama); officer Mil. Order of Ayacucho (Peru). Home: 424 Olde Woodlands Rd Columbia SC 29209

PEREZ, HENRY TAYLOR, magazine editor; b. Calgary, Alta., Can., Aug. 2, 1915 (parents Am. citizens); s. Henry Leslie and Annita (Taylor) P.; B.S. in Civil Engring., Cooper Union, N.Y.C., 1940; m. Rosanna M. Garrett, Feb. 21, 1941; children—Annita (Mrs. William B. Sawyer), Richard Garrett, Henry Taylor. Cost engr. Dry Dock Assos., Norfolk, Va., 1940-42; job engr. Merritt Chapman & Scott Corp., N.Y.C., 1942-43; cost engr. Ala. Shipbldg. and Dry Dock Co., Mobile, 1943-44; with McGraw-Hill Publs. Co., N.Y.C., 1946—, editor-in-chief Constrn. Methods & Equipment mag., 1954—. Mem. exec. com. constrn. sect. Nat. Safety Conf. Served to lt. (j.g.) USNR, 1944-46. Fellow Am. Soc. C.E.; mem. Soc. Am. Mil. Engrs., The Moles. Clubs: Engineers (N.Y.C.); Orienta Yacht (Mamaroneck, N.Y.). Home: 6 Vermont Ave White Plains NY 10606 Office: 1221 Ave Americas New York City NY 10020

PEREZ, ROBERT CLAUDE, investment co. exec.; b. Bklyn., Oct. 18, 1926; s. Claude Thomas and Gertrude (Royce) P.; B.A., Yale U., 1950; M.B.A., N.Y. U., 1956, Ph.D., 1966; m. Mary Jean Howard, Sept. 30, 1950; children—Barbara, Frederic, Moira. Vice pres. Chem. Fund, Inc., 1956—, F. Eberstadt & Co., 1950-79, Putnam Fund Distbrs., Inc., 1979—; mem. public info. and edn. com., pension com. Investment Co. Inst., Washington; adj. prof. Baruch Coll. Grad. Div. City U. N.Y., 1966-72. Club: Yale (N.Y.C.). Home: 115 Central Park W New York NY 10023 also Milbridge ME 04658 Office: 61 Broadway New York NY 10006. *The most important thing in life is to choose a career to which you can dedicate your life's efforts and ambitions. To succeed, such a career should have a moral as well as a useful purpose. In choosing the investment field, I believe I met both of these requirements.*

PEREZ GIL, EUGENIO, pipe co. exec.; b. Mexico, May 14, 1923; s. Jose and Luz (Salazar) Perez Gil Y Ortiz; m. Irma De Hoyos de Perez Gil, Feb. 7, 1949; children—Jose, Eugenio, Irma, Cecilia, Daniel. Partner, Despacho Freyssinier Morin, S.C., Mexico, also Ernst & Ernst, N.Y.C., 1943-60; exec. pres., dir. Tubos de Acero de Mexico, S.Am., Mexico City, 1960—; pres. Camara Nacional de la Industria del Hierro y del Acero; dir. Banco Serfin, S.A., Banco Internacional, S.A., Consorcio Minero Benito Juárez-Peña Colorada, S.A., Edicióny Distribución Ibero Americana de Publicaciones, S.A., Empresa Mobiliaria e Inmobiliaria Mexicana, S.A., Ferralver, S.A., Inmobiliaria Aluminio, S.A. de C.V., Icos de México, S.A., Inmobiliaria de la Zona Industrial de Framboyán, S.A., Inmobiliaria Tamsa, S.A. de C.V., Metalver, S.A., Organización Editorial Novaro, S.A.; alt. dir. Siderurgica Tamsa, S.A., Techint, S.A., Aseguradora Cuauhtémoc, S.A., many others; stockholders examiner Circuito Cine Satélite, S.A., Grupo Pliana, S.A., Industrias Polifil, S.A., Novaro Internacional, S.A., Revemex, S.A., Sidercom, S.A., Texel, S.A. de C.V. C.P.A., Mexico. Mem. Instituto de Contadores Publicos A.C., Colegio de Contadores Publicos de Mexico, A.C. Club: Mexican Racket. Home: 286 Picacho St Mexico City Mexico 20 DF Office: 15 Paris St Mexico City Mexico 4 DF

PERHAM, JOHN CARGIL, editor; b. Concord, N.H., Oct. 14, 1918; s. Harry Leavitt and Mary Florence (Norcross) P.; A.B., Harvard U., 1940, A.M., 1941; m. Mary Hull, June 20, 1942. Editorial writer Hartford (Conn.) Courant, 1942-51; asso. editor, asst. mng. editor Barrons, N.Y.C., 1951-65; sr. editor Dun's Rev., Dun & Bradstreet, N.Y.C., 1966—. Home: 26 Strawberry Hill Ave Stamford CT 06902 Office: 666 Fifth Ave New York City NY 10019

PERICOLA, JULIUS LOUIS, pharm. co. exec.; b. Union City, N.J., Jan. 2, 1929; s. Louis M. and Helen S. (Kaminsky) P.; B.S. in Acctg., Rutgers U., 1949, M.B.A. in Fin., 1956; m. Dorothy Mariani, Aug. 11, 1951; children—Patricia, Helene, Lisa. With Bristol-Myers Co., 1950-74, 76—, group gen. mgr., regional dir. Caribbean-Andean region internat. div., P.R., 1970-74, v.p., N.Y.C., 1976—; exec. v.p. Bristol Labs., Syracuse, N.Y., 1974-75, pres., 1975—; dir. Lincoln First Bank, N.A., central div., 1975—, Syracuse Research Corp., 1976—; mem. bus. adv. council U. R.I. Chmn. pacesetters div. United Way of Central N.Y., 1975; bd. dir. Greater Syracuse C. of C., Salvation Army, Syracuse, Crouse Irving Meml. Found., Syracuse, Met. Devel. Assn., Syracuse; bd. regents LeMoyne Coll.; account exec. United Way of Central N.Y., 1979—; vice chmn. long-range planning com. Hiawatha council Boy Scouts Am., 1979—. Served with USAF, 1951-52. Mem. Mfrs. Assn. Central N.Y. (dir. 1975—), Nat. Alliance of Bus. (chmn. Syracuse Met. area 1978-79). Roman Catholic. Clubs: Onondaga Country (Fayetteville, N.Y.); Century (Syracuse). Office: PO Box 657 Syracuse NY 13201

PERINI, DAVID BONFIGLIO, constrn. co. exec.; b. Framingham, Mass., May 19, 1937; s. Louis R. and Florence R. P.; B.S., Coll. Holy Cross, Worcester, Mass., 1959; LL.B., Boston Coll., 1962; m. Eileen Callahan, July 14, 1962; children—Jennifer, David Bonfiglio, Kristen, Timothy, Andrea. Admitted to Mass. bar, 1962; with Perini Corp., Framingham, 1962—, v.p., gen. counsel, 1969-71, vice chmn. bd. dirs., 1971-72, pres., 1972—. Trustee, mem. pres.'s council Coll. Holy Cross; chmn. Holy Cross Fund, 1975-77; exec. bd. Boston council Boy Scouts Am., 1976, vice chmn. property com., 1975. Mem. Am., Mass. bar assns., World Assn. Lawyers, Soc. Am. Mil. Engrs., Asso. Gen. Contractors Mass. (dir. 1973-75), The Moles (chmn. award com. 1977), Boston 200 (dir. 1975-76), Gen. Alumni Assn. Holy Cross Coll. (dir. 1973-76). Roman Catholic. Home: 3 Donnelly Dr Dover MA 02030 Office: 73 Mt Wayte Ave Framingham MA 01701

PERINI, VINCENT WALKER, lawyer; b. Ft. Worth, Feb. 22, 1939; s. Vincent Charles and Maxine Blake (Walker) P.; B.A., Yale U., 1962; LL.B., U. Tex., 1966; m. Patricia Ann Paul, Feb. 8, 1969. Admitted to Tex. bar, 1966; since practiced in Dallas. Lectr. So. Meth. U.; pres. bd. Dallas Legal Services Found. Inc., 1973. Mem. Dallas Jr. Bar Assn. (pres. 1970), Tex. Criminal Def. Lawyers Assn. (v.p. 1976-79, pres. 1979-80), Am., Dallas bar assns., Am. Judicature Soc., Nat. Assn. Criminal Def. Lawyers, State Bar Tex. (criminal law adv. commn., Tex. bd. legal specialization). Episcopalian. Club: Dallas Yale. Home: 4301 Travis St Dallas TX 75205 Office: One Turtle Creek Village Suite 300 Dallas TX 75219

PERKES, DANIEL, news agy. exec.; b. Bklyn., Feb. 17, 1931; s. A. and Edith (Sherman) P.; B.A. in Journalism, Tex. Tech U., 1957; m. Norma Jean O'Mary, Dec. 6, 1952; children—Kimberly, Daniel. Part-time reporter Amarillo (Tex.) Globe-News, 1952-54; reporter Lubbock (Tex.) Avalanche, 1954-57; with AP, 1957—, chief bur. Okla., 1964-67, Iowa-Nebr., 1967-69, gen. exec. AP Newsfeatures, N.Y.C., 1969-78, asst. gen. mgr. AP, 1978—. Served with USAF, 1950-54. Mem. Assn. Sunday and Feature Editors, Sigma Delta Chi. Clubs: N.Y. Athletic, Masons. Author: Eyewitness to Disaster, 1976. Editor-in-chief: AP Sports Almanac, 1974-77; AP News Annual, 1969-77; Century of Sports, 1971; Century of Champions, 1976. Address: 21 Lawrence Pl Pelham Manor NY 10803

PERKIN, JAMES RUSSELL CONWAY, educator; b. Northamptonshire, Eng., Aug. 19, 1928; s. William and Lily Maud (Drage) P.; B.A., Oxford U. (Eng.), 1952, M.A., 1955, D.Phil., 1955; postgrad. U. Strasbourg (France), 1954-55; m. Dorothy Joan Louise Bentley, Apr. 7, 1953; children—James Russell Bentley, John Conway, Anne Louise. Ordained to ministry Baptist Ch., 1956; minister Altrincham Bapt. Ch., Cheshire, Eng., 1956-63; lectr. New Testament Greek, New Coll., Edinburgh, 1963-65; asso. prof. New Testament, McMaster Div. Coll., Hamilton, Ont., Can., 1965-69; prof., head dept. religious studies Acadia U., Wolfville, N.S., Can., 1969-77, dean Faculty Arts, 1977—. Served with RAF, 1946-49. Mem. Soc. for New Testament Studies, Canadian Bibl. Soc., Canadian Liturg. Soc., Canadian Soc. for Study Religion. Author: Study Notes on Romans, 1957; Handbook for Biblical Studies, 1973; In Season, 1977; With Mind and Heart, 1978; editor: Theological Bull., 1966-69; Report on Theological Education in Canada, 1968; The Undoing of Babel, 1975; Chaplain Extraordinary, 1975. Home: 38 Kent Ave Wolfville NS Canada

PERKINS, ALFRED JAMES, educator; b. Elgin, Ill., Mar. 8, 1912; s. Thomas E. and Effie (Mann) P.; B.S., Kenyon Coll., 1933; Ph.D., Johns Hopkins, 1937; m. Antoinette Partridge, Feb. 1, 1944; children—Claudia (Mrs. William Schechter), Alice (Mrs. H. McCartor), James T. With E.I. duPont de Nemours & Co., Inc., Flint, Mich., 1936-38; with Underwriters Lab., Chgo., 1938-42, 45-47; asst. prof. U. Ill. Coll. Pharmacy, Chgo., 1947-51, asso. prof., 1951-61, prof, 1961-78, prof. emeritus, 1978—, also asso. dean Grad. Coll., U. Ill. Med. Center. Served from 2d lt. to maj. AUS, 1942-45. Mem. AAAS, Am. Chem. Soc., Soc. Applied Spectroscopy, AAUP, Phi Beta Kappa, Sigma Xi. Home: Windholm Farm Box 277 Burlington IL 60109

PERKINS, ANTHONY, actor; b. N.Y.C., Apr. 4, 1932; s. Osgood and Janet (Rane) P.; student Rollins Coll., 1951-53, Columbia, 1954; m. Berinthia Berenson, 1973. First profl. engagement, Brattleboro, Vt., 1946; TV appearances on Studio One, Alcoa, U.S. Steel and Armstrong hours; Broadway appearances in Tea and Sympathy, 1954, Look Homeward Angel, 1957, Greenwillow, 1960, Harold, 1962; motion pictures include The Actress, 1953, Friendly Persuasion, 1955, The Lonely Man, 1956, Fear Strikes Out, 1956, The Tin Star, 1956, The Sea Wall, 1957, Desire Under the Elms, 1957, The Matchmaker, 1957, Green Mansions 1958, On The Beach, 1959, Tall Story, 1959, Psycho, 1959, Goodbye Again, 1960, Phaedra, 1961, Five Miles to Midnight, The Trial, Two are Guilty, 1962, The Fool Killer, 1963, The Adorable Idiot, 1964, Is Paris Burning?, 1965, The Champagne Murders, 1966, Pretty Poison, 1967, Catch 22, 1968, WUSA, 1968, Someone Behind the Door, 1970, The Life and Times of Judge Roy Bean, 1972, Play It As It Lays, 1972, Lovin' Molly, 1974, Murder on the Orient Express, 1974, Mahogany, 1975, The Black Hole, 1979; theater appearance The Star-Spangled Girl, 1966, Steambath, 1972, Winterkills, 1977, Remember My Name, 1977, The Black Hole, 1978; appeared on Broadway in Equus, 1976-77. Office: care Internat Creative Mgmt 8899 Beverly Blvd Los Angeles CA 90048

PERKINS, BOB(BY) F(RANK), univ. dean; b. Greenville, Tex., Dec. 9, 1929; s. William Frank and Vela Beatrice (Richey) P.; B.S., So. Methodist U., 1949, M.S., 1950; Ph.D., U. Mich., 1956; m. Patricia Katharine Woodhull, May 25, 1954; children—Katharine Harriet, Marianna Lee, Orrin Woodhull. Instr. geology and biology So. Meth. U., 1950-51, 53-56; asst. prof. geology U. Houston, 1956-57; research paleontologist Shell Devel. Corp., Houston, 1957-66; prof. geology La. State U., Baton Rouge, 1966-75, chmn., dir. Sch. Geosci., 1973-75; prof. geology, dean Grad. Sch., U. Tex., Arlington, 1975—. Fellow Geol. Soc. Am., AAAS, Tex. Acad. Sci.; mem. Paleontol. Soc., Am. Assn. Petroleum Geologists, Palenontol. Soc. Gt. Britain, Soc. Econ. Paleontologists and Mineralologists, Malacological Soc. London. Editor 15 vol. series Geoscience and Man, 1970-75. Contbr. articles to profl. jours. Home: 1416 Creekford Dr Arlington TX 76012

PERKINS, BRADFORD, educator; b. Rochester, N.Y., Mar. 6, 1925; s. Dexter and Wilma (Lord) P.; A.B., Harvard, 1946, Ph.D., 1952; m. Nancy Nash Tucker, June 18, 1949; children—Dexter III, Matthew Edward, Martha Nash, James Bradford. From instr. to asso. prof. history U. Calif. at Los Angeles, 1952-62; prof. history U. Mich., 1962—, chmn. dept., 1971-72. Commonwealth Fund lectr. Univ. Coll., London, Eng., 1964; vis. prof. history Brandeis U., 1970; Albert Shaw lectr. Johns Hopkins U., 1979; mem. council Inst. Early Am. History and Culture, 1968-71; program dir. Nat. Endowment for Humanities Fellowships in Residence for Coll. Tchrs., 1974-75. Served with AUS, 1943-45; ETO. Decorated Bronze Star. Recipient Bancroft prize, 1965; Warren fellow, 1969-70; Social Sci. Research Council faculty research fellow, 1957-60; Guggenheim fellow, 1962-63. Mem. Am. Hist. Assn., Soc. Am. Historians, Orgn. Am. Historians (council 1969-72), Soc. Historians Am. Fgn. Relations (council 1967-72, pres. 1974), Mass. Hist. Soc. Club: Internat. Golf (Bolton, Mass.). Author: The First Rapprochement, England and the United States, 1795-1805, 1955; Youthful America, 1960; Prologue to War, England and the United States, 1805-1812, 1961; Causes of the War of 1812, 1962; Castlereagh and Adams: England and the United

States, 1812- 1823, 1964; The Great Rapprochement: England and the United States, 1895-1914, 1968. Home: 1335 W Huron River Dr Ann Arbor MI 48103

PERKINS, CARL D., congressman; b. Hindman, Ky., Oct. 15, 1912; s. J.E. and Dora (Calhoun) P.; grad. U. Louisville Sch. Law, 1935; m. Verna Johnson; 1 son, Christopher. Began practice of law, 1935; commonwealth atty. 31st Jud. Dist., 1939; mem. Ky. Gen. Assembly from 99th Dist., 1940; Knott County atty., 1941-48; counsel Ky. Dept. Hwys., Frankfort, Ky., 1948; mem. 81st-96th Congresses 7th Ky. Dist., chmn. com. edn. and labor, 1967—. Served with AUS, World War II; ETO. Democrat. Home: Hindman KY 41822 Office: House Office Bldg Washington DC 20515

PERKINS, CARL L., entertainer; b. Lake City, Tenn., Apr. 9, 1932; s. Buck and Louise Perkins; student public schs., Lake City; m. Jan. 24, 1953; 4 children. Performer at local country dances and honky tonks with Perkins Brothers; toured Britain, 1964, headliner, 1965; appeared in road show with Johnny Cash; played Brit. Country Festival, Wembley, 1976-77; formed own band with sons; recorded albums Blue Suede Shoes (Gold record), Daddy Sang Bass, Original Golden Hits, Greatest Hits, The Original Carl Perkins, Long Tall Sally. Methodist. Clubs: Masons, Shriners; Moose. Composer: Blue Suede Shoes, 1956; Honey Don't, Everybodys Trying To Be My Baby; Match Box Blues; Boppin' The Blues; Daddy Sang Bass.

PERKINS, COURTLAND DAVIS, aero. engr., educator; b. Phila., Dec. 27, 1912; s. Harry Norman and Emily Cramp (Taylor) P.; B.S., Swarthmore Coll., 1935, D.Eng. (hon.), 1977; M.S., Mass. Inst. Tech., 1941; D.Eng. (hon.), Lehigh U., 1977, Rensselear Poly. Inst., 1977; m. Jean Elizabeth Enfield, Sept. 27, 1941; children—William Enfield, Anne Taylor. Br. engr. Am. Radiator Co., Phila., 1935-39; prof. aero. engring. Princeton, 1945—, chmn. dept., 1951-63, chmn. dept. aerospace and mech. scis., sch. engring. and applied sci. 1963-74, asso. dean Sch. Engring., 1974-75; dir. Fairchild-Industries Corp., 1962-75, Am. Airlines, 1967-75 Keuffel & Esser Corp., 1969-75; trustee Mitre Corp., C. Stark Draper Labs. Aero engr. USAF, Air Materiel Command, Dayton, Ohio, 1941-45; chief scientist USAF, 1956-57, asst. sec. Research and Devel., 1960-61; mem. sci. adv. bd. USAF, chmn., 1969-73, 77-78; mem. def. sci. bd. Def. Dept., 1969-73, 77-78; chmn. adv. group for aero. research and devel. NATO, 1963-67; chmn. space systems com. NASA, 1973-77. Fellow Am. Inst. Aeros. and Astronautics (hon.; pres. 1964), Am. Acad. Arts and Scis., Royal Aero. Soc.; mem. Nat. Acad. Engring. (pres. 1975—), Nat. Acad. Sci. (mem. space sci. bd. 1964-70), Sigma Xi, Tau Beta Pi, Delta Upsilon. Author: (with Robert E. Hage) Airplane Performance Stability and Control, 1949. Home: 2700 Calvert St Washington DC 20008

PERKINS, CYRUS LEE, ret. gas pipeline co. exec.; b. Ft. Worth, Dec. 28, 1908; s. Marvin H. and Lilly M. (Turner) P.; student Hardin-Simmons U., 1928; m. Margery Smith, Feb. 5, 1930; children—Jacquelyn Perkins Cassidy, Carolyn Perkins Williams, Cyrus Lee. With transmission dept. Lone Star Gas Co., Breckenridge, Tex., 1928-29; with El Paso Natural Gas Co., 1929-74, beginning as field foreman, successively supt. dist., gen. supt., 1929-44, v.p., 1944-66, sr. v.p., 1966-74, pres. mining and exploration div., 1969-74, dir., 1945-74; ret., 1974. Methodist. Home: Del Rio TX Office: PO Box 5344 El Paso TX 79954

PERKINS, DAVID, educator; b. Phila., Oct. 25, 1928; s. Dwight Goss and Esther M. (Williams) P.; A.B., Harvard, 1951, M.A., 1952, Ph.D., 1955. Mem. faculty Harvard, 1957—, prof. English, 1964—, chmn. dept. English, 1976—. Served with AUS, 1955-57. Mem. Modern Lang. Assn., Cambridge Sci. Club. Author: The Quest for Permanence: the Symbolism of Wordsworth, Shelley and Keats, 1959; Wordsworth and the Poetry of Sincerity, 1964; English Romantic Writers, 1967; A History of Modern Poetry: From the 1890's to the High Modernist Mode, 1976; editorial adv. Keats-Shelley Jour., 1962—. Home: 23 Sparks St Cambridge MA 02138

PERKINS, DEFOREST, lawyer; b. Pullman, Wash., May 27, 1907; s. Roy T. and Emma (DeForest) P.; A.B., U. Wash., 1929, J.D., 1931; m. Jean Miller, May 18, 1947; 1 dau., Jane (Mrs. Richard Wood). Admitted to Wash. bar, 1931, since practiced in Seattle; partner firm Perkins, Coie, Stone, Olsen & Williams, and predecessors, 1942-78. Served with USNR, 1943-45. Mem. Am., Wash., Seattle-King County bar assns., Seattle Hist. Soc., Beta Theta Pi, Phi Delta Phi. Clubs: Seattle Golf, Seattle Skeet and Trap, Rainier (Seattle). Home: 117 N 130th Seattle WA 98133 Office: Washington Bldg Seattle WA 98101

PERKINS, DONALD SHELDON, diversified retail co. exec.; b. St. Louis, Mar. 22 1927; s. Arthur and Edna Ann (Meinert) P.; B.A., Yale, 1949; M.B.A., Harvard, 1951; m. Phyllis Elizabeth Babb, June 9, 1951; children—Elizabeth Perkins Hill, Jervis, Susan. With Jewel Cos., Inc., 1953—, v.p. growth and devel., 1960-61, v.p., gen. mgr. routes dept., 1961-63, exec. v.p. ops., 1963-65, pres., 1965-70, chmn. bd., 1970—, dir.; dir. Time, Inc., LaSalle St. Fund, G.B.-Inno-B.M., Brussels, Aurrera S.A., Mexico City, AT&T, Inland Steel Co., Corning Glass Works, Cummins Engine Co.; mem. internat. council Morgan Guaranty Bank. Bd. assos. Harvard Bus. Sch. Trustee Ford Found., Brookings Instn., Northwestern U. Mem. Bus. Council, Bus. Roundtable. Clubs: Chicago, Economic, Commonwealth, Commercial (Chgo.); Glen View (Golf, Ill.); Old Elm (Ft. Sheridan, Ill.); University (N.Y.C.). Office: Jewel Cos Inc 5725 E River Rd Chicago IL 60631

PERKINS, FRANCIS EATON, judge; b. Woonsocket, R.I., July 14, 1907; s. Harold W. and Mabel (Bailey) P.; student U. N.H., 1927-29, Washington Coll. Law, 1932-34; LL.B., Cleve. Law Sch., 1939; m. Mildred C. Kelley, Apr. 19, 1933; children—Harold Wilder II, Francis Eaton. Admitted to N.H. bar, 1941, D.C. bar, 1956; investigator Dept. Justice and Treasury Dept., 1934-43; enforcement atty. OPA, 1943-46; pvt. practice, Concord, N.H., 1946—; spl. justice Dist. Ct., Concord, 1955-69; asso. justice N.H. Superior Ct., 1969-77. Mem. Am., N.H. (pres. 1959-60), Merrimack County bar assns. Home: 5 Glendale Rd Concord NH 03301 Office: 10 Green St Concord NH 03301

PERKINS, FRANK CLIFFORD, III, advt. agy. exec.; b. Richmond, Va., July 19, 1941; s. Frank Clifford and Gladys G. (Pollard) P.; B.A. with honors, U. Va., 1962; m. Kathleen Mulhern., July 9, 1966; children—Colin Elizabeth, Cary Tazewell, Frank Clifford. Media planner Benton and Bowles Advt., N.Y.C., 1964-66; account exec. Compton Advt., N.Y.C., 1966-69; account dir. Ted Bates Advt., N.Y.C., 1969-76; sr. v.p., mgmt. rep. Mc Cann Erickson, N.Y.C., 1976—. Episcopalian. Club: Princeton. Office: 485 Lexington Ave New York NY 10017

PERKINS, GEORGE HOLMES, educator, architect; b. Cambridge, Mass., Oct. 10, 1904; s. George Howard and Josephine (Schock) P.; student Phillips-Exeter Acad., 1920-22; A.B., Harvard U., 1926, M.Arch., 1929; LL.D., U. Pa., 1972; m. Georgia Hencken, June 3, 1933; children—Gray H., Jennifer H. Instr. architecture U. Mich., 1929-30; instr. architecture Harvard, 1930-36, asst. prof., 1936-39, asso. prof., 1939-42, Norton prof. regional planning, chmn. dept., 1945-51; dean, chmn. dept. architecture Grad. Sch. Fine Arts, U. Pa., 1951-71, prof. architecture and urbanism, 1971—; practicing architect and city planner, 1933—; asst. regional rep., acting dir. urban devel. div. Nat. Housing Agy., 1942-45; cons. Brit. Ministry of Town and Country Planning, 1946, UN, 1946, 55-56; cons. to Govt. Turkey, 1958-60, Balt. Redevel. Authority, Cambridge Redevel. Authority, Worcester Redevel. Authority. Mem. Cambridge Planning Bd., 1950-51; dir. Phila. Housing Assn., 1951-56, pres., 1953-56; dir. Citizens Council City Planning, 1951-54; chmn. Phila. Zoning Commn., 1955-58; chmn. Phila. City Planning Comm., 1958-68; dir. Phila. Port Corp., Old Phila. Devel. Corp., Phila. Indsl. Devel. Corp. Mem. Phila. Commn. Higher Edn. Trustee Fairmount Park Art Assn., 1965—. Fellow A.I.A. (chancellor coll. fellows 1964-66); mem. Am. Inst. Planners, Am. Soc. Planning Ofcls., Nat. Assn. Housing Ofcls., World Soc. Ekistics; hon. corr. mem. Royal Inst. Architects Can. Clubs: The Country (Brookline); Franklin Inn, Rittenhouse, Philadelphia Cricket, Art Alliance (Phila.); Century (N.Y.C.). Author: Comparative Outline of Architectural History, 1937. Editor Jour. Am. Inst. Planners, 1950-52. Contbr. articles profl. journals. Home: 82 Bethlehem Pike Philadelphia PA 19118

PERKINS, GEORGE WILLIAM, II, ins. exec., film producer; b. Salem, Mass., Sept. 10, 1926; s. George William and Daisy A. (Chase) P.; student Northeastern U., 1944-49; B.Sc., Curry Coll., 1952; postgrad. Eastern Sch. Photography, Boston U.; Certificate Coll. Financial Planning, Denver, 1974; m. Mildred Boyle, Oct. 6, 1951; children—George William III, Clifton Alfred Dow, Mark Paige. Travel lectr., color cinematographer, 1946—, appearing at Carnegie Hall, N.Y. Music Hall, Phila. Symphony Hall, Nat. Geog. Soc., Washington, numerous other cities, U.S., Mexico and Can.; in charge road testing Renault auto Alcan Hwy., Alaska, 1949; narrator, film producer Burton Holmes travelogues, 1950-70; pres. Neily Film Prodns., Inc., 1953-55; Eastern regional v.p. Western Res. Life Assurance Co. Ohio, 1973-75; pres., chmn. bd. Fin. Mktg. Systems, Inc., Nashua, N.H., 1976—; registered prin. Fin. Cons., Inc., Stoneham, Mass., 1975—; div. mgr. Calif. Pacific Ins. Services Inc., 1977—; dir. Fin. Cons. Mgmt. Corp., Sonolite Corp., Contrex Co.; speaker on sales and service motivation; asso. prof. bus. adminstrn., Curry Coll., until 1963, also sr. mem. bd. trustees, mem. coll. corp., also chmn. reorgn., 1963; pvt. trustee and executor, 1972—. Served with USNR, World War II; PTO. Recipient Nat. Quality award Nat. Assn. Life Underwriters; registered investment advisor. Mem. Merrimack Valley (v.p., dir. 1968-69), Boston life underwriters assns., Advt. Club Greater Boston, Internat. Assn. Fin. Planners (charter pres. No. Mass. chpt.), Nat. Assn. Security Dealers (prin.), Northeastern U., Curry Coll. alumni assns., Mass. Brokers Assn. Mason. Rotarian (charter pres. Chelmsford, Mass. 1967-68). Contbr. articles on ins. and sales to various publ., also photographic and cinematographic publs. Designer world's largest portable cinemascope motion picture screen. Home: 278 Lowell St Lynnfield MA 01904 Office: 159 Main Dunstable Rd Nashua NH. *The bottom line in living is how you made your way from day to day.*

PERKINS, HAROLD JACKSON, univ. adminstr.; b. London, Ont., Can., July 6, 1930; s. Harold Campbell and Rita (Jackson) P.; B.A., U. B.C., 1951, M.Sc., 1953; Ph.D., Iowa State U., 1957; m. Mary Louise Kreutziger, Aug. 21, 1954; children—Campbell Jackson, Barry Nelson, David Harris, Stephanie Grace. Postdoctoral fellow NRC of Can., 1957-58; research biochemist research br. Can. Dept. Agr., Lethbridge, Alta., 1958-63; asso. prof. biochemistry State U. N.Y., Plattsburgh, 1963-64, dean faculty sci. and math., 1964-75, dean grad. studies and research, 1975-77, prof. biochemistry, 1964-77; pres. Brandon (Man., Can.) U., 1977—. Cons. N.Y. State Edn. Dept., Sci. Facilities State of N.J. Mem. editorial bd. State U. N.Y. Press, 1966-77. Mem. AAAS, Chem. Inst. Can., N.Y. Acad. Scis., Can. Soc. Plant Physiologists, Tissue Culture Assn. (exec. council 1975—). Aircraft Owners and Pilots Assn., Sigma Xi. Contbr. articles to profl. jours. Office: Brandon Univ Office of the Pres Brandon MB R7A 4P9 Canada. *I have chosen to dedicate my professional life to working in the university environment because the intellectual challenge (and fulfillment) in academe are such as to keep the "little grey cells" (of Hercule Poirot) stimulated and active.*

PERKINS, HENRY CRAWFORD, educator; b. Miami, Fla., Nov. 23, 1935; s. Henry Crawford and Dorothy Du Bois (Israel) P.; B.S., Stanford U., 1957, M.S., 1960, Ph.D., 1963; m. Barbara Joan Parvin; children—Jennifer Anne, William Bruce, Susan Elizabeth, David Parvin. Research asso. Stanford, 1962-63, acting asst. prof., 1963-64; asso. prof. aerospace and mech. engring. U. Ariz., 1964-67, prof., 1967—; vis. prof. Danish Tech. U., 1971-72, U.S. Mil. Acad., 1978-79. Recipient Teetor award Soc. Automotive Engrs., 1975. AEC fellow, 1960-61. Mem. ASME, Am. Inst. Aeros. and Astronautics, Soc. Automotive Engrs., Air Pollution Control Assn. Author: (with W.C. Reynolds) Engineering Thermodynamics, 1970, 2d edit., 1977; (with W.M. Kays) chpt. in Handbook of Heat Transfer, 1973; Air Pollution, 1974. Home: 6758 E Rosewood Circle Tucson AZ 85710

PERKINS, HERBERT ASA, physician; b. Boston, Oct. 5, 1918; s. Louis and Anna (Robinson) P.; A.B. cum laude, Harvard U., 1940; M.D. summa cum laude, Tufts U., 1943; m. Frances Snyder, Sept. 2, 1942; children—Susan, Deborah, Dale, Karen, Erin. Intern, Boston City Hosp., 1944, resident, 1947-48; practice medicine specializing in hematology, 1953—; clin. instr. Stanford Med. Sch., 1953-57, asst. clin. prof., 1957-58; hematologist Open Heart Surgery Team, Stanford Hosp., San Francisco, 1955-58; hematologist Jewish Hosp., St. Louis, 1958-59; dir. research Irwin Meml. Blood Bank, San Francisco, 1959-78, sci. dir., 1978—; asst. prof. medicine Washington U., St. Louis, 1958-59; asst. prof. medicine U. Calif. at San Francisco, 1959-66, asso. prof., 1966-71, clin. prof., 1971—. Served to maj. M.C., U.S. Army, 1944-47. Mem. Am. Assn. Blood Banks (chmn. sci. adv. com. 1972-73, chmn. standards com. 1968-71, chmn. com. on organ transplantation and tissue typing 1970—), Am. Soc. Hematology, Internat. Transfusion Soc., Transplantation Soc., Soc. Exptl. Biology and Medicine, Western Soc. Clin. Research, Am. Fedn. Clin. Research, A.A.A.S., Am. Assn. Clin. Histocompatibility Testing, Sigma Xi, Alpha Omega Alpha. Co-editor: Hepatitis and Blood Transfusion, 1972. Home: 520 Berkeley Ave Menlo Park CA 94025 Office: 270 Masonic Ave San Francisco CA 94118

PERKINS, HOMER GUY, mfg. co. exec.; b. New Haven, Oct. 23, 1916; s. Frank W. and Emily (Oesting) P.; B.A. in Internat. Relations, Yale, 1938; LL.D. (hon.), Westfield (Mass.) State Coll., 1977; m. Dorothy C. Stock, Jan. 24, 1942; children—Maribeth Perkins Grant, Homer Guy, Hazel Mary Perkins Adolphson, Dorothy Catherine Perkins Helfer, Caroline Ann Perkins Spicer, Faith Elizabeth, Ruth Emily. With Stanley Home Products, Inc., Westfield, Mass., 1939—, v.p., 1965-66, exec. v.p., 1966-70, pres., chief exec. officer, 1970-78, chmn. bd., 1978—, also dir.; officer, dir. numerous subsidiaries; dir. First Nat. Bank, Easthampton, Mass., 1958-75, Valley Bank & Trust Co., Springfield, Mass. Treas., Stanley Park of Westfield, 1949—; pres. Citizens Scholarship Found., Easthampton, 1966-67; chmn. fin. com., bd. dirs. Western Mass. Girl Scout Council, 1966-69; pres., dir. Pioneer Valley Assn., 1956-63; pres. Easthampton Community Chest, 1960-61: mem. devel. com. Clarke Sch. Deaf, Northampton, 1965—; mem. fin. com. Town of Easthampton, 1962-70, chmn., 1967-68; pres. Frank Stanley Beveridge Found., Westfield, 1966—. Trustee Cooley Dickinson Hosp., Northampton, Mass., 1963-70; Pres. bd. trustees Northampton Sch. Girls, 1964-73; bd. dirs. Porter Phelps Huntington Found., Hadley, Mass., 1960—, Guild of Holy Child, Westfield, 1969-76; bd. corporators Springfield Coll., 1957-65; bd. overseers Williston Acad., Easthampton, 1961-64, Old Sturbridge (Mass.) Village, 1970—; v.p. bd. trustees Williston-Northampton Sch., 1970-75, pres., 1975-78. Served with USAAF, 1942-46. Mem. Direct Selling Assn. (chmn. 1975, dir.). Lion (past pres. Easthampton). Home: 205 Main St Easthampton MA 01027 Office: 333 Western Ave Westfield MA 01085

PERKINS, J. STUART, automobile co. exec.; b. London, Eng., 1928; student U. Birmingham (Eng.); married, 1 dau. Student engr. Morris Car Co., Eng., 1948; later parts mgr. Brit. Motor Corp.; with Volkswagen Can. Ltd., 1952-55; with Volkswagen of Am., Inc., 1955-78, v.p., gen. sales mgr., 1960-63, gen. mgr., 1963-65, pres., 1965-78, now dir.; mem. exec. com. Volkswagen Ins. Co., 1964-78, chmn. bd. dirs., 1967-78. Home: Westchester County NY 10461

PERKINS, JACK MORTON, television corr.; b. Cleve., Dec. 28, 1933; s. Fred Morton and Ruth Lovella (Bryte) P.; B.A., Western Res. U., 1956; m. Mary Jo Keplinger, Oct. 18, 1959; children—Mark, Eric. Newsman, WGAR, Cleve., 1951-56; news dir. WEWS-TV, Cleve., 1956-61; reporter NBC, Washington, 1961-65, corr., Hong Kong, Saigon, 1965-67, corr., Los Angeles, 1967—. Office: 3000 W Alameda St Burbank CA 91505

PERKINS, JAMES ALFRED, ednl. found. exec.; b. Phila., Oct. 11, 1911; s. H. Norman and Emily Cramp (Taylor) P.; A.B., Swarthmore Coll., 1934; M.A. Princeton, 1936, Ph.D., 1937; LL.D., L.H.D. various colls. and univs.; m. Jean Bredin (dec. 1970); children—Barbara Ann (Mrs. Robert Tinker), Joan Bredin (Mrs. John Saalfield), John, David, Tracy; m. 2d Ruth B. Aall. Instr. polit. sci., Princeton, 1937-39, asst. dir. Sch. Pub. and Internat. Affairs, 1939-41; price exec. OPA, Washington, 1941-43; asst. to adminstr. FEA, Washington, 1943-45; v.p. Swarthmore (Pa.) Coll., 1945-50; v.p. Carnegie Corp., N.Y., 1950-63; pres. Cornell U., Ithaca, N.Y., 1963-69; chmn., exec. dir. Center for Ednl. Enquiry, 1969-70; chmn., chief exec. officer Internat. Council Ednl. Devel., 1970—; past trustee Rand Corp., Chase Manhattan Bank, Tchrs. Ins. and Annuity Assn., Am. Council on Edn. Founder, past chmn. Found. Library Center, Ednl. Testing Service, Inst. for Coll. and Univ. Adminstrs., Council on Higher Edn. in Am. Republics; chmn. N.Y. State Regents Adv. Com. Ednl. Leadership, 1963-67; chmn. Presdl. gen. adv. com. on Fgn. Assistance, 1965-69; co-chmn. Internat. Conf. on World Crisis in Edn., 1967; mem. Presdl. spl. adv. panel on South Asian Refugee Assistance, 1971; chmn. President's Commn. on Fgn. Lang. and Internat. Studies, 1978—; mem. Carnegie Commn. on Higher Edn., 1967-73; mem. Carnegie Council Policy Studies in Higher Edn., 1974—; sec. Carnegie Found. Advancement Teaching, 1954-55, v.p., 1955-63, trustee, 1963—; trustee Adlai Stevenson Inst. Internat. Affairs, Aspen Inst. Humanistic Studies; former trustee Atlantic Richfield Found., Inst. for Def. Analysis; bd. dirs. Center for Inter-Am. Relations, Overseas Devel. Council, Acad. for Ednl. Devel., Inst. Study Ednl. Policy; U.S. mem. adv. com. UNESCO Centre for Higher Edn., Bucharest, Rumania; mem. Am. council UN U.; founding mem. Inst. Edn., European Cultural Found.; bd. visitors Georgetown U. Sch. Fgn. Service; chmn. Ajijie Inst. for Comparative Study of Higher Edn., Autonomous U. Guadalajara, 1978—. Recipient gold medal Nat. Inst. Social Scis., 1965. Mem. Council Fgn. Relations (dir.), Nat. Acad. Pub. Adminstrn., Am. Acad. Arts and Scis., Phi Beta Kappa (hon.). Mem. Soc. of Friends. Clubs: Century, University, Coffee House (N.Y.C.). Author: The University in Transition; Higher Education: From Autonomy to Systems; The University as an Organization. Editorial bd. Higher Edn. Contbr. articles, papers to profl. and pop. publs. Home: 94 North Rd Princeton NJ 08540 Office: 680 Fifth Ave New York NY 10019

PERKINS, JOHN ALLEN, lawyer; b. New Bedford, Mass., Sept. 13, 1919; s. Ralph Chamberlain and Louise Bartlett (Allen) P.; A.B., Harvard U., 1940, LL.B., 1943; m. Lydia Bullard Bogg, Sept. 9, 1944; children—John A., Susan W., Robert C., William B. Admitted to Mass. bar; partner firm Palmer & Dodge, Boston; clk. Social Law Library, 1961—; grad. researcher Univ. Coll., Oxford U., 1978. Bd. dirs. Greater Boston Legal Services, Inc., 1972—; mem. Dedham (Mass.) Sch. Com., 1959-65, chmn., 1963-65; town counsel, Dedham, 1971-72. Mem. Am. Law Inst., Am. Coll. Probate Counsel, Mass. Bar Assn. (dir. 1973-75), Boston Bar Assn. Council. Contbr. articles to profl. jours. Home: 203 Highland St Dedham MA 02026 Office: 1 Beacon St Boston MA 02108

PERKINS, JOHN HAROLD, banker; b. Chgo., Aug. 28, 1921; s. Harold Reed and Roschen (Baker) P.; B.S., Northwestern U., 1943; m. Len Welborn, June 24, 1944; children—John Harold, Robert G., Reed F. With Continental Ill. Nat. Bank & Trust Co., Chgo., 1946—, asst. cashier, 1949-52, 2d v.p., 1952-56, v.p., 1956-65, sr. v.p. adminstrv. services, 1965-66, exec. v.p., dir., 1968-71, vice chmn., 1971-73, pres., 1973—; dir. Pillsbury Co., PEFCO; trustee Underwriters Labs., Inc. Pub. adviser, gov. Midwest Stock Exchange. Trustee Episcopalian Diocesan Found. Chgo., Chgo. Symphony Orch., Michael Reese Hosp. and Med. Center, Com. for Econ. Devel.; bd. dirs. Nat. Minority Purchasing Council. Mem. Trilateral Commn. Served with USNR, 1943-46. Mem. Econ. Club, Am. Bankers Assn. (pres.), Assn. Res. City Bankers, U.S. C. of C. (finance com.), Phi Beta Kappa, Delta Tau Delta. Clubs: Economic, University, Little La Salle Street, Chicago, Commercial, Carlton, Bond, Bankers (Chgo.); Metropolitan (Washington and Chgo.); Wall Street (N.Y.C.); Indian Hill (Winnetka); Old Elm (Ft. Sheridan). Office: 231 S LaSalle St Chicago IL 60693

PERKINS, JOHN MACIVOR, composer; b. St. Louis, Aug. 2, 1935; s. Kendall and Elizabeth Dorothy (MacIvor) P.; B.A. magna cum laude, Harvard, 1958; B.Mus. with high distinction, New Eng. Conservatory Music, 1958; M.F.A., Brandeis U., 1962; m. Anne Chenault Peper, June 24, 1961; children—Jonathan MacIvor, Andrew Baird. Instr., then asst. prof. music U. Chgo., 1962-65; lectr. music Harvard, 1965-70; asso. prof., chmn. dept. music Washington U., St. Louis, 1970—. Sheldon prize fellow, 1958-59; Woodrow Wilson Nat. fellow, 1959- 61; Nat. Inst. Arts and Letters music award, 1966. Mem. Phi Beta Kappa. Composer: Eight Songs, 1956-62; (chamber opera) Divertimento, 1958; Canons for 9 Instruments, 1958; Three Studies for Chorus, 1958; Fantasy, Intermezzo and Variations (for piano), 1959-62, (orch. version), 1961; Three Miniatures for String Quartet, 1960, Quintet Variations, 1962; Music for Carillon, 1963; (piano) Caprice, 1963; Music for 13 Players (for Fromm-Tanglewood Festival), 1964; Music for Orchestra (for St. Louis Bicentennial), 1964; Music for Brass (for Smithsonian Bicentennial), 1965; Alleluia, 1966. Office: Dept Music Washington U Saint Louis MO 63130*

PERKINS, KEITH MACINTYRE, bus. exec.; b. Providence, Oct. 12, 1931; s. Carl K. and Josephine M. (MacIntyre) P.; B.A., Rutgers U., 1962; m. Roberta R. Weny, Aug. 25, 1962; children—Scott K., Jennifer L. With ITT and subs., 1955—, v.p. corporate relations and advt., N.Y.C., 1976—; pres. Famous Solos Inc., jazz music pub. and rec. co., Saddle River, N.J., 1973—. Served with USAF, 1951-53. Mem. Air Force Hist. Assn., Nat. Jazz Educators Assn. Home: 158 Chestnut Ridge Rd Saddle River NJ 07458 Office: ITT 320 Park Ave New York NY 10022

PERKINS, LAWRENCE BRADFORD, architect; b. Evanston, Ill., Feb. 12, 1907; s. Dwight Heald and Lucy (Fitch) P.; student U. Wis., 1925-26; B.Arch., Cornell, 1930; m. Margery Blair, Jan. 1, 1932; children—Dwight Heald, Blair, Lawrence Bradford, Julia Eleanor. Practice of architecture, 1933—; partner Perkins & Will Partnership, 1935—; projects include Crow Island Sch., Winnetka, Ill., Byrd Elementary Sch., Chgo., Chgo. Tchrs. Coll. North, Riley Center Urban Devel., Indpls., U.S. Gypsum Co., Chgo., Wagner Coll. Library, S.I., Butler (Pa.) High Sch., Dundee Elementary Sch., Greenwich, Conn., Heathcote Sch., Scarsdale, N.Y., 1st Nat. Bank Bldg., Chgo., No. Bldg., Chgo., Blythe Park Sch., Riverside, Ill., Rugen Sch., Glenview, Ill., Linton High Sch., Schenectady, Evanston (Ill.) Twp. High Sch., Chute Jr. High Sch., Evanston, new campus Rockford (Ill.) Coll., Ithaca Coll. Chapel, various other schs., univ. and pub. bldgs., offices, hosps.; adj. prof. dept. architecture U. Ill. Mem. Evanston Plan Commn., 1946-62, chmn., 1946-52, 58-62. Recipient Distinguished Service award for services to edn. Am. Assn. Sch. Adminstrs., 1975. Fellow AIA; mem. Gargoyle, Sigma Phi. Clubs: Chicago, Cliff Dwellers, Chicago Yacht, Chicago, Gt. Lakes Cruising (commodore 1974-76), Cruising of Am. Author: Work place for Learning; (with Walter D. Cocking) Schools. Home: 2319 Lincoln St Evanston IL 60201 Office: 309 W Jackson Blvd Chicago IL 60606

PERKINS, MARLIN. see Perkins, R(ichard) Marlin

PERKINS, MERLE LESTER, educator; b. West Lebanon, N.H., Apr. 16, 1919; s. Charles Elisha and Ethel (Armstrong) P.; A.B., Dartmouth, 1941; A.M., Brown U., 1942, Ph.D. in French, 1950; m. Barbara Marion Cunningham, June 16, 1951; children—Elizabeth Cunningham, Janet Blair. Instr. French, Brown U., 1948-50, U. Chgo., 1950-53; mem. faculty U. Calif., Davis, 1953-67, prof. French, 1963-67, chmn. dept. fgn. langs., 1962-65, chmn. dept. Italian and French, 1965-67; prof. French, U. Wis., 1967—, chmn. grad. studies (French), 1967-74, 77—; dir. univs. Mich. and Wis. Year in France, Aix-en-Provence, 1976-77, chmn. admissions, 1979—. Served with USAAF, 1942-45. Decorated Air medal with 3 oak leaf clusters. Parker fellow Dartmouth, 1941-42; Edwards fellow Brown U., 1948-49; Penrose Fund grantee Am. Philos. Soc., 1956-57, 72-73, 74-75; Fulbright research grantee, France, 1960-61, 67-68. Mem. Am. Assn. Tchrs. French, Philol. Assn. Pacific Coast, Modern Lang. Assn. (grantee 1956-57), Internat. Assn. for 18th Century Studies, Phi Beta Kappa. Episcopalian. Author: The Moral and Political Philosophy of the Abbé de Saint-Pierre, 1959; Voltaire's Concept of International Order, 1965; J.-J. Rousseau on History, Liberty, and National Survival, 1968; Jean-Jacques Rousseau on the Individual and Society, 1974; also anthology, articles, revs. Address: Dept French 1220 Linden Dr Madison WI 53706

PERKINS, MILDRED KELLEY (MRS. FRANCIS EATON PERKINS), civic worker; b. Littleton, N.H., July 6, 1908; d. Fred and Carlotta (Kimball) Kelley; B.S., Plymouth State Coll., 1930; L.H.D. (hon.), U. N.H., 1972; m. Francis Eaton Perkins, Apr. 19, 1933; children—Harold W., Francis E. Social sci. tchr., Lisbon, N.H. and Summit, N.J., 1930-38. Mem. Civil War Centennial Commn., 1958-59; pres. N.H. Aux., 1960; mem. exec. bd. N.H. Hosp. Aux., 1960-69, also past pres.; mem. youth and govt. com. N.H. YMCA, 1965—; mem. Bd. Edn., 1960; mem. nat. bd. Med. Coll. Pa. for N.H., 1972—, Asst. treas. N.H. Republican Com., 1952, asst. chmn., 1952-57, 64-68, mem. exec. com., 1952—; mem. Rep. Nat. Com. from N.H., 1968-72; sec. arrangements com. Rep. Nat. Conv., 1972; pres. N.H. Federated Rep. Women's Clubs, 1956-57; 4th v.p. Nat. Fedn. Rep. Women, 1965-67, regional dir. New Eng. area, 1965-67, also officer and mem. various coms.; mem. Concord City Rep. Com., also mem. exec. bd. from Ward 3. Trustee N.H. U. Complex, 1967-71. Mem. Concord Alumni Plymouth State Coll., Plymouth State Coll. Alumni Assn. (hon. chmn. Robert Frost contemporary Am. award com. 1970-79). Episcopalian. Mem. Order Eastern Star. Clubs: Women's Coll.; West Concord Garden. Address: 5 Glendale Rd Concord NH 03301

PERKINS, R(ICHARD) MARLIN, former zoo dir.; b. Carthage, Mo., Mar. 28, 1905; s. Joseph Dudley and Mynta Mae (Miller) P.; student U. Mo., 1924-26, D.Sc., D.Sc., Rockhurst Coll., Northland Coll.; m. Elise More, Sept. 12, 1933 (div. Oct. 1953); 1 dau., Suzanne; m. 2d, Carol M. Cotsworth, Aug. 13, 1960. Curator of reptiles St. Louis Zoo, 1926-38; curator Buffalo Zoo, 1938-44; dir. Lincoln Park Zoo, Chgo., 1944-62; dir. St. Louis Zoo, 1962-70, dir. emeritus, 1970—. Mem. Am. Soc. Ichthyologists and Herpetologists, Internat. Union Zool. Gardens Dirs., Am. Assn. Zoo. Parks and Aquariums. Clubs: Adventurers (Chgo.); Explorers (N.Y.). Author: Animal Faces, 1944; Marlin Perkins' Zooparade, 1954; (with Carol Perkins) I Saw You from Afar (The Bushmen of the Kalahari Desert); several sci. papers on herpetology. Originator of Zoo Parade, TV program, 1949-57, winner of numerous awards including, Peabody, Look, and Sylvania; originator (with Don Meier) TV series Wild Kingdom, 1962—, winner 4 Emmy awards and numerous other awards. Address: care St Louis Zoological Park Forest Park Saint Louis MO 63110. *By knowing animals I understand people better.*

PERKINS, RALPH LINWOOD, bus. exec.; b. Orono, Me., July 17, 1914; s. Ralph L. and Zilla (Sawyer) P.; B.S. in Mech. Engring., U. Me., 1935; M.S. in Hosp. Adminstrn., Columbia, 1950; m. Hilda Beatrice Morrison, Sept. 1, 1938; children—Sylvia Lucille (Mrs. Edward Nespoli), Jacquelyn Sue (Mrs. Julian N. Lowe). With U.S. Engrs. Dept., Quoddy, Me., 1935-37, NYA in Me., Ohio and W.Va., 1937-44; with USPHS, W.Va., Miss., La., D.C. and N.Y., 1944-48, asst. adminstrv. officer, USPHS Hosp., S.I., 1949-50, adminstrv. officer, 1950-63; asso. dir. Hosp. U. Pa., 1963-64, exec. dir., 1964-74; sr. adviser Chi Systems, Inc., Ann Arbor, Mich., 1974—. Lectr., Columbia Sch. Pub. Health and Adminstrv. Medicine, 1961—. Past chmn. Delaware Valley Hosp. Council Forum. Former bd. dirs. West Phila. Community Mental Health Consortium. Recipient Commendation Medal USPHS, 1963. Fellow Am. Coll. Hosp. Adminstrs.; mem. Delaware Valley Hosp. Council (past dir., sec.-treas.), Assn. Am. Med. Colls., Hosp. Assn. Pa. (past trustee). Methodist. Home and office: 517 Fairfax Rd Drexel Hill Delaware County PA 19026

PERKINS, RAYMOND LAMONT, fgn. service officer; b. New Rochelle, N.Y., Apr. 8, 1924; s. Raymond Lamont and Dorothy Marie (Porter) P.; A.B., U. Denver, 1947, LL.B., 1948; m. Margaret M. Johnson, Aug. 25, 1946; children—Deborah, Doriane, Amy. Admitted to Colo. bar; pvt. practice, Springfield, Colo., 1949-54; joined U.S. Fgn. Service, 1954; service in Naples, Italy, Tel-Aviv, Lome, Togo, Niamey, Niger, Vietnam, Dakar, Senegal, Phnom Penh, Cambodia, Colombo, Sri Lanka; now consul gen., Calcutta, India. Served with C.E., U.S. Army, 1943-46. Mem. Am. Fgn. Service Assn. Methodist. Home: 8427 Fort Hunt Rd Alexandria VA 22313 Office: American Consulate General Calcutta India

PERKINS, REIMER ARTHUR, mfg. co. exec.; b. Waukesha, Wis., Mar. 5, 1914; s. Fred Arthur and Helen A. (Reimers) P.; B.S. in Commerce, U. Iowa, 1936, M.A., 1937; m. Clarnelle Scanlan, Aug. 31, 1940; children—Richard, James. Mgmt. cons. Ernst & Ernst, 1938-44; with Kearney & Trecker Corp., 1944-66; exec. Medalist Industries, Milw., 1966-79; ret., 1979; chmn. bd. Baker Mfg. Co. Past chmn. Milw./Waukesha ARC, West Allis (Wis.) C. of C.; past pres. Vill Oconomowoc Lake (Wis.). C.P.A., Ill., Wis. Mem. Nat. Assn. Accountants (past pres. Milw. chpt.), Fin. Execs. Inst. (past pres. Milw. chpt.), Wis. C.P.A.'s, Am. Inst. Accountants. Home: 4503 W Beach Rd Oconomowoc WI 53066 Office: 735 N 5th St Milwaukee WI 53203

PERKINS, RICHARD STURGIS, co. dir; b. Milton, Mass., June 27, 1910; s. James H. and Katherine (Coolidge) P.; ed. Brunswick, Edgewood and Berkshire Prep. Schs. With Thompson Fenn & Co., Hartford, 1929-32, Wood, Struthers & Co., N.Y. City, 1932-34; with Harris, Upham & Co., 1934-36, partner, 1936-51; exec. v.p. First Nat. City Trust Co. (formerly City Bank Farmers Trust), pres., then chmn., chief exec. officer, 1957-63; chmn. exec. com. Citycorp and Citibank, 1959-70; dir. Allied Chem. Corp., N.Y. Life Ins. Co., So. Pacific Co., ITT, New Ct. Equity Fund, Scandinavian Securities Corp., Hosp. Corp. Am.; trustee Consol. Edison Co. N.Y. Mem. staff, $1 a year man, Aircraft Prodn. Bd., 1942-45. Chmn., United Fund N.Y.; past trustee Seeing Eye, Boys' Clubs Am., Chapin Sch., Miss Porter's Sch.; trustee Carnegie Instn. Washington, Vincent Astor Found., Met. Mus. of Art; past chmn. bd. trustees N.Y. YMCA. Clubs: Racquet and Tennis, Links, Links Golf (N.Y.C.); River, Rumson Country, Seabright Lawn Tennis, Seabright Beach. Home: Box 1796 Hobe Sound FL 33455 Office: 399 Park Ave New York NY 10022

PERKINS, ROSWELL BURCHARD, lawyer, govt. ofcl.; b. Boston, May 21, 1926; s. Paul Franklin and Agnes Leeds (Burchard) P.; student Pomfret (Conn.) Sch., 1940-43; A.B. cum laude, Harvard, 1945, LL.B. cum laude, 1949; m. Joan Titcomb, Oct. 27, 1945; children—Roswell Burchard, Laura Kimball, Nancy Leeds. Admitted to Mass. bar, 1949, N.Y. State bar, 1949; asso. firm Debevoise, Plimpton, Lyons & Gates, N.Y.C., 1949-53, partner, 1957—; counsel to Gov. Nelson A. Rockefeller, 1959; asst. sec. HEW, 1954-56. asst. counsel to spl. subcom. to investigate organized crime in interstate commerce U.S. Senate Com. Interstate and Fgn. Commerce, 1950. Chmn. adv. com. Medicare adminstrn., contracting and subcontracting to sec. HEW, 1973-74; mem. Pres.'s Adv. Panel on Personnel Interchange, 1968; chmn. Mayor's Task Force on Transp. Reorgn., 1966; dir. Fiduciary Trust Co., N.Y.C., Commonwealth Fund, N.Y.C.; trustee Bowery Savings Bank, N.Y.C. Co-chmn. Nat. Lawyers Com. for Civil Rights Under Law, 1974-75; chmn. Citizen's Union Com. Transp., 1971-73; mem. Citizens Com. for Children, N.Y.C., 1962-77. Dir., sec. Greater N.Y. Fund, 1965-71, N.Y. Urban Coalition, 1967-73; mem. overseers com. to visit Harvard Coll., 1958-64, 71-77, Kennedy Sch. Govt., Harvard, 1971-77; trustee Pomfret Sch., 1961-76, Brearley Sch., 1969-75; mem. adv. council Woodrow Wilson Sch. Pub. and Internat. Affairs, Princeton U., 1967-69; adv. com. Fordham U. Sch. Social Service, 1969-74; bd. dirs. Salzburg Seminar in Am. Studies, 1970—; bd. dirs. Sch. Am. Ballet, N.Y.C., 1974—, chmn. bd., 1976—. Served as ensign USNR, 1945-46. Mem. Am. Law Inst. (council 1969—), Am. Arbitration Assn. (dir., mem. exec. com. 1966-71), Council Fgn. Relations, Am., N.Y. State bar assns., Assn. Bar City N.Y. (exec. com. 1967-71), Associated Harvard Alumni (1st v.p. 1969-70, pres. 1970-71), Harvard Law Sch. Assn. (nat. council 1969-73), Pilgrims. Republican. Clubs: Harvard (pres. 1975-77), Racquet and Tennis, Knickerbocker, Century (N.Y.C.); Capitol Hill (Washington). Home: 1120 Fifth Ave New York NY 10028 Office: 299 Park Ave New York NY 10017

PERKINS, TERRY WILLIAM, editor; b. Cleve., Mar. 19, 1936; s. Myron James and Mildred Mae (Cole) P.; B.S. in Journalism, Ohio U., 1957. Editor, Geauga Record, Chardon, Ohio, 1957-60; edn. writer News-Herald, Willoughby, Ohio, 1960-63; city editor, 1963-65; writer Scholastic Newstime, N.Y.C., 1966-69, editor, 1969-77, editorial dir. Scholastic elem. mags., 1977—. Author: Gathering the News, 1970; Understanding the News, 1970. Office: 50 W 44th St New York NY 10036

PERKINS, WILLIAM H., JR., financial co. exec.; b. Rushville, Ill., Aug. 4, 1921; s. William H. and Sarah Elizabeth (Logsdon) P.; ed. Ill. Coll.; m. Eileen Nelson, Jan. 14, 1949; 1 son, Gary Douglas. Partner, Howlett-Perkins Assos., Chgo. Mem. Ill. AEC, 1963—, sec., 1970—; mem. adv. bd. Nat. Armed Forces Mus., Smithsonian Instn., 1964—. Sgt.-at-arms Democratic Nat. Conv., 1952, 56, del.-at-large, 1964, 68, 72; spl. asst. to chmn. Dem. Nat. Com., 1960; mem. Presdl. Inaugural Com., 1961, 65, 69, 73. Served with U.S. Army, 1944-46. Mem. Health Ins. Assn. Am., Ill. Ins. Fedn. (pres. 1965—), Ill. C. of C. (chmn. legis. com. 1971), Chgo. Assn. Commerce and Industry (legis. com.), Internat. Platform Assn. Methodist. Mason (Shriner). Clubs: Ill. Athletic (Chgo.); Sangamo (Springfield, Ill.); Fed. City (Washington); Riverside Golf. Home: 52 N Cowley Rd Riverside IL 60546 Office: 208 S LaSalle St Chicago IL 60604

PERKOFF, GERALD THOMAS, educator, physician; b. St. Louis, Sept. 22, 1926; s. Nat and Ann (Schwartz) P.; M.D. cum laude, Washington U., 1948; m. Marion Helen Maizner, June 7, 1947; children— David Alan, Judith Ilene, Susan Gail. Intern Salt Lake City Gen. Hosp., 1948-49, resident, 1950-52; from instr. to asso. prof. medicine U. Utah, 1954-63; chief med. service Salt Lake VA Hosp., 1961-63; asso. prof., then prof. medicine Washington U. Sch. Medicine, St. Louis, 1963-79; chief Med. Service, St. Louis City Hosp., 1963-68, dir. div. health care research, 1968-79; Curators prof. and asso. chmn. dept. family and community medicine and prof. medicine U. Mo., Columbia, 1979—; John and Mary R. Markle scholar med. sci., 1955-60; career research prof. neuromuscular diseases Nat. Found. Neuromuscular Diseases, 1961; Henry J. Kaiser sr. fellow Center Advanced Study in Behavioral Scis., Stanford, Calif., 1976-77. Mem. Am. Soc. Clin. Investigation, Assn. Am. Physicians, Inst. Medicine (Nat. Acad. Scis.). Contbr. articles profl jours. Home: 8104 Stratford St Clayton MO 63105

PERKOVIC, ROBERT BRANKO, diversified industry fin. exec.; b. Belgrade, Yugoslavia, Aug. 27, 1925; came to U.S., 1958, naturalized, 1961; s. Slavoljub and Ruza (Pantelic) P.; M.S. in Econs., U. Belgrade, 1954; B.F.T., Am. Grad. Sch. Internat. Mgmt., 1960; grad. Stanford exec. program Stanford U., 1970; m. Jacquelyn Lee Lipscomb, Dec. 14, 1957; children—Bonnie Kathryn, Jennifer Lee. Asst. treas. Monsanto Co., St. Louis, 1971-72, Brussels, 1972-74; corp. treas. Fiat-Allis Inc. & BV, Deerfield, Ill., 1974-78; v.p., treas. TRW Inc., Cleve., 1978—; dir. Blue Cross N.E. Ohio. Served with Yugoslavian Army, 1944-47. Mem. Fin. Execs. Inst. (dir.), Cleve. Treas.'s Club. Club: Park East Racquet (Beachwood, Ohio). Home: 26 Pepper Creek Dr Pepper Pike OH 44124 Office: 23555 Euclid Ave Cleveland OH 44117

PERKS, EDWARD E., machinery co. exec.; b. Virden, Ill., May 21, 1931; s. William F. and Mary M. (Stupar) P.; A.A., Springfield (Ill.) Jr. Coll., 1957; B.S., So. Ill. U., Carbondale, 1959; m. Sandra S. Burke, Sept. 14, 1959; children—Patricia Ann, Edward E. With Arthur Young & Co., C.P.A.'s, St. Louis, 1960-63; tax adminstr. UMC Industries, Inc., Stamford, Conn., 1963-69, asst. controller gen. accounting and taxes, 1969-70, controller, 1970-71, v.p., controller, 1971-73, fin. cons., 1974—. Served with AUS, 1952-54. Mem. Nat. Assn. Accountants, Internat. Assn. Assessing Officers (mem. pres.'s ednl. adv. com.), Tax Execs. Inst. (dir. St. Louis chpt. 1969-71), VFW, Am. Legion. Elk. Home: Rural Route 5 Box 188 Murphysboro IL 62966

PERKS, HARRY MARK, SR., engring. co. exec.; b. Woodbury, N.J., Apr. 3, 1928; s. Matthew Mark and Jane (Waring) P.; B.S. in Civil Engring., Citadel, 1951; M. Engring., Yale, 1952; m. Gladys Estelle Middleton, Dec. 30, 1947; children—Harry Mark, Samuel Chris, Matthew Kent, Clark David. With Day & Zimmerman, Inc., Phila., 1952-66, v.p. engring., 1964-66, exec. v.p., dir., 1969-76, pres., 1976—; exec. dir. sch. facilities Sch. Dist. Phila., 1966-67, dep. supt. for adminstrn., 1968-69; partner Day & Zimmerman Assos., Phila., 1969—, F. G. Vittetta Assos., Westville, N.J., 1969—. Served with USNR, 1946-48. Registered profl. engr., N.J., N.Y., Pa., Fla., Mass. Mem. Nat. Soc. Profl. Engrs., Soc. Am. Mil. Engrs., ASCE. Baptist. Mason. Home: 627 Oak St Audubon NJ 08106 Office: 1818 Market St Philadelphia PA 19103

PERL, MARTIN LEWIS, physicist, educator; b. N.Y.C., June 24, 1927; s. Oscar and Fay (Rosenthal) P.; B.Chem. Engring., Poly. Inst. Bklyn., 1948; Ph.D., Columbia, 1955; m. Teri Hoch, June 19, 1948; children—Jed, Anne, Matthew, Joseph. Chem. engr. Gen. Electric Co., 1948-50; asst. prof. physics U. Mich., 1955-58, asso. prof., 1958-63; prof. Stanford, 1963—. Served with U.S. Mcht. Marine, 1944-45, AUS, 1945-46. Fellow Am. Phys. Soc.; mem. Am. Assn. Physics Tchrs., AAAS. Contbg. author: High Energy Hadron Physics, 1975. Editor: Physics and Society. Contbr. articles on high energy physics and on relation of sci. to soc. to profl. jours. Home: 525 Lincoln Ave Palo Alto CA 94301 Office: Stanford Linear Accelerator Center Stanford U Stanford CA 94305

PERLBERGER, MARTIN, lawyer; b. Amsterdam, Netherlands, Mar. 17, 1928; s. Oscar and Claire (Untermans) P.; came to U.S., 1946, naturalized, 1952; A.B. in Econs., Stanford, 1951, J.D., 1954; m. Lily Ann Barancik, Apr. 15, 1954; children—Carol, Mark. Admitted to D.C. bar, 1954, Calif. bar, 1954, also U.S. Supreme Ct. bar; asso. firm Kreeger, Ragland & Shapiro, Washington, 1954-56; asso., then partner Kaplan, Livingston, Goodwin, Berkowitz & Selvin, Beverly Hills, Calif., 1956-76; v.p. firm Slavitt, King, Weiser & Perlberger, Los Angeles, 1976-79; partner firm Marshall, Bratter, Greene, Allison & Tucker, Los Angeles, 1979—. Mem. exec. bd. Los Angeles chpt. Am. Jewish Com., 1964-70. Bd. dirs., treas. Am. Little League, Beverly Hills, 1971-73; trustee Beverly Hills Edn. Found. Mem. Internat., Inter-Am., Am. (mem. council internat. law sect.), Beverly Hills (chmn. pub. relations 1967-68), Los Angeles County (chmn. internat. law sect. 1976-77) bar assns., State Bar Calif., Am. Soc. Internat. Law, Los Angeles Copyright Soc. (trustee), Nat. Inst. Legal Aspects of Fgn. Investment in U.S. (co-chmn.), Beverly Hills C. of C. (community affairs, state and nat. affairs coms.), Fgn. Law Assn. So. Calif., Order of Coif, Phi Alpha Delta. Home: 711 N Rexford Dr Beverly Hills CA 90210 Office: One Century Plaza Los Angeles CA 90067

PERLE, EUGENE GABRIEL, lawyer; b. N.Y.C., Dec. 21, 1922; s. Philip and Simme (Meschenberg) P.; B.A., Queens Coll., 1943; LL.B. (J.D.), Yale U., 1949; m. Ellen Carlotta Kraus, Nov. 26, 1953 (dec. 1964); 1 dau., Elizabeth Anne; m. 2d, Ruth Friedberg Lerner, May 21, 1972 (div. 1977). Admitted to N.Y. bar, 1950; asso. firm Cravath, Swaine & Moore, N.Y.C., 1949-53; asst. counsel N.Y. State Moreland Commn. Investigation Harness Racing, N.Y.C., 1953-54; asso. firm Gordon, Brady, Caffrey & Keller, N.Y.C., 1954-56; asso. gen. atty. Time Inc., N.Y.C., 1956-66, pub. counsel, 1966-73, v.p. law, 1973—; trustee Baron deHirsch Fund, 1959—, sec., 1968—; commr. Nat. Commn. New Technol. Uses Copyrighted Works, 1975-78. Bd. dirs. Rowayton (Conn.) Civic Assn., 1959-62, N.Y. Sch. for Circus Arts, Inc., 1979—; justice of peace City of Norwalk (Conn.), 1960-63. Mem. Copyright Soc. U.S.A. (trustee 1962-64, 69-70, 71-74, pres. 1976-78, hon. trustee 1978—), U.S. Trademark Assn. (dir. 1969-72, 74—, v.p. 1972-73), Am. Bar Assn. (chmn. copyright div. 1970-71, chmn. com. copyright and new tech. 1971-73, chmn. com. econs. of profession 1976, council patent, trademark and copyright sect. 1979—, numerous other com. assignments), Assn. Bar City N.Y. (com. copyright and lit. property 1964-67, 70-73, 73-76), Assn. Am. Pubs. (copyright com. 1970—, lawyers com. 1978—), Am. Arbitration Assn. (dir. 1979—). Democrat. Jewish. Bd. editors Yale Law Jour., 1948-49; advisory bd. Bur. Nat. Affairs Patent, Trademark and Copyright Jour., 1972—. Home: 140 Thompson St New York NY 10012 Office: Time Inc Time and Life Bldg Rockefeller Center New York NY 10020

PERLE, GEORGE, composer; b. Bayonne, N.J., May 6, 1915; s. Joseph and Mary (Sanders) Perlman; Mus.B., DePaul U., 1938; Mus.M., Am. Conservatory Music, 1942; Ph.D., N.Y.U., 1956; m. Laura Slobe, 1940; m. 2d, Barbara Philips, Aug. 11, 1958; children—Kathy, Annette, Max Massey (stepson). Mem. faculty U. Louisville, 1949-57, U. Calif. at Davis, 1957-61, Juilliard Sch. Music, 1963, Yale, 1965-66, U. So. Calif., summer 1965, Tanglewood, summer 1967; asst. prof. Queens Coll. of City U. N.Y., 1961-63, asso. prof., 1963-66, prof., 1966—; vis. Birge-Cary prof. music State U. N.Y. at Buffalo, 1971-72; vis. prof. U. Pa., 1976, Columbia U., 1979. Served with AUS, 1943-46; ETO, PTO. Compositions include: Little Suite for piano, 1939; Two Rilke Songs, 1941; Sonata for Solo Viola, 1942; Three Sonatas for Clarinet, 1943; Piano Piece, 1945; Hebrew Melodies for Cello, 1945; Lyric Piece for Cello and Piano, 1946; Six Preludes for Piano, 1946; Sonata for Solo Cello, 1947; Solemn Procession for Band, 1947; Sonata for Piano, 1950; Three Inventions for Piano, 1957; Quintet for Strings, 1958; Wind Quintet I, 1959; Sonata I for Solo Violin, 1959; Wind Quintet II, 1960; Fifth String Quartet, 1960-67; Three Movements for Orchestra, 1960; Monody I for flute, 1960; Music for The Birds of Aristophanes, 1961; Monody II for double bass, 1962; Serenade I for Viola and Chamber Ensemble, 1962; Three Inventions for Bassoon, 1962; Sonata II for Solo Violin, 1963; Short Sonata for Piano, 1964; Solo Partita for Violin and Viola, 1965; Six Bagatelles for Orch., 1965; Concerto for Cello and Orch., 1966; Wind Quintet III, 1967; Serenade II for Chamber Ensemble, 1968; Sixth String Quartet, 1969; Toccata for Piano, 1969; Suite in C for Piano, 1970; Sonata Quasi una Fantasia for Clarinet and Piano, 1972; Seventh String Quartet, 1973; Songs of Praise and Lamentation for chorus and orch., 1974; Six Etudes for Piano, 1976; 13 Dickinson Songs, 1978; Concertino for Piano, Winds, and Timpani, 1979. Guggenheim fellow in composition, 1966-67, 74-75; commn. Koussevitzky Found., 1968, Fromm Found., 1978; Am. Council Learned Socs. grantee, 1968-69; Nat. Endowment for Arts grantee, 1978-79; Nat. Inst. Arts and Letters award, 1977. Mem. Am. Musicol. Soc., ASCAP (Deems Taylor award 1973, 78), Internat. Soc. Contemporary Music (pres. N.Y. chpt. 1968-70), Internat. Alban Berg Soc. (co-founder, dir.), Am. Acad. and Inst. Arts and Letters. Author: Serial Composition and Atonality, 4th edit., 1977; Twelve-Tone Tonality, 1977. Editorial bd. Music Forum: contbr. articles in Am., fgn. mus. jours. N.Y. Home: 333 Central Park W New York NY 10025 Office: Queens Coll Flushing NY 11367

PERLIK, CHARLES ANDREW, JR., trade union ofcl.; b. Pitts., Nov. 13, 1923; s. Charles Andrew and Theresa (Kraft) P.; B.S. in Journalism, Northwestern U., 1949, M.S., 1950; m. Marion Virginia Ford, Jan. 3, 1948; children—Paul, Lesley, Stephen. Newsman, U.P., Pitts. and Chgo., 1946-48; reporter Buffalo Eve. News, 1950-52; internat. rep. The Newspaper Guild (name formerly Am. Newspaper Guild), 1952-55, sec.-treas., 1955-69, pres., 1969—. Sec.-treas. Lowell Mellett Fund Free and Responsible Press, 1967—. Served to 1st lt. USAAF, 1943-46. Mem. Internat. Fedn. Journalists (v.p. 1970—),

Soc. Profl. Journalists, Sigma Delta Chi. Home: 2407 Barbour Rd Falls Church VA 22043 Office: Newspaper Guild 1125 15th St NW Washington DC 20005

PERLIN, BERNARD, artist; b. Richmond, Va., Nov. 21, 1918; student N.A.D., Art Students League, N.Y.C., also in Poland. Works exhibited Carnegie Inst., 1948-50, U. Ill., 1950, Brussels World's Fair, 1958, also Whitney Mus. Modern art; rep. permanent collections Mus. Modern Art, Tate Gallery, London, Springfield (Mass.) Mus. Arts, Calif. Palace Legion of Honor, Va. Mus. Fine Arts, U.S. Post Office, So. Orange, N.J., U.S.S. Pres. Hayes, S.C. Johnson and Son Collection, Racine, Wis., Art Inst. Chgo., Detroit Inst. Arts, Princeton, Smithsonian Instn., Washington, Whitney Mus. Am. Art, N.Y.C., others; illustrations appeared in Life, Fortune mags. Recipient Chaloner Found. award, 1948, 49, Nat. Inst. Arts and Letters award, 1964. Koscluszko Found. scholar, 1938; Fulbright fellow, 1950; Guggenheim fellow, 1954-55, 59. Address: 56 Shadow Lake Rd Ridgefield CT 06877*

PERLIN, SEYMOUR, educator, psychiatrist; b. Passaic, N.J., Sept. 27, 1925; s. Samuel and Fanny (Horowitz) P.; student Johns Hopkins, 1943-44; B.A. summa cum laude, Princeton, 1946; M.D., Columbia, 1950; grad. Washington Psychoanalytic Inst.; m. Ruth Joan Rudolph, Aug. 21, 1958; children—Jonathan Brian, Steven Michael, Jeremy Francis. Intern Univ. Hosp., Ann Arbor, Mich., 1951-52; resident N.Y. State Psychiat. Inst., 1950-51, 53-54, Manhattan State Hosp., 1952; practice medicine specializing in psychiatry and psychoanalysis, Bethesda, Md., 1954-59, Stanford, Calif., 1959-60, N.Y.C., 1960-63, Balt., 1964-72, Bethesda, 1974—; chief div. psychiatry Montefiore Hosp., 1960-63; dir. clin. care and tng. Henry Phipps Psychiat. Clinic, Johns Hopkins Hosp., 1964-72; sr. research scholar Center for Bioethics, Kennedy Inst., Georgetown U., Washington, 1974—; clin. prof. psychiatry U. Calif. at Los Angeles Sch. Medicine, 1973-74; clin. prof. psychiatry George Washington U. Sch. Medicine, 1974-76, prof., 1977—, also dir. residency tng. psychiatry; lectr. psychiatry Columbia, 1963-64; asso. prof. psychiatry Johns Hopkins Sch. Medicine, 1964-65, prof., 1966-72, dep. chmn. dept. psychiatry and behavioral scis., 1969-72, program dir. Fellowship Program in Suicidology, 1967-72; adv. council Univ. health services Princeton, 1970—; vis. fellow Princeton U., 1973, Oxford U., 1974; Joseph P. Kennedy fellow medicine, law and ethics, 1974-75; chief sect. psychiatry Lab. Clin. Sci., NIMH, 1955-59, mem. clin. program-project com., 1967-70; fellow Center Advanced Study in Behavioral Scis., 1959-60; chmn. mental health study sect. B, div. research grants NIH, 1964-66; cons. Community Mental Health Services, Md. Dept. Mental Hygiene, 1964-72. Served with USNR, 1944-46, USPHS, 1954-58. Recipient Meirhoff award in pathology, 1950, Bicentennial Silver medal for achievement in psychiatry, 1967 (both Coll. Phys. and Surg. Columbia). Diplomate Am. Bd. Psychiatry and Neurology. Fellow Am. Psychiat. Assn., N.Y. Acad. Medicine; mem. Washington Psychoanalytic Soc., World Fedn. Mental Health, Washington Psychiat. Soc., Am. Assn. Suicidology (pres. 1969-70, Dublin award 1978). Cons. editor Jour. Life Threatening Behavior, 1970—; editorial bd. Johns Hopkins Med. Jour., 1970-72; editor Handbook for the Study of Suicide; co-editor Ethical Issues in Death and Dying. Contbr. numerous articles to med. jours. Home: 6001 Shady Oak Ln Bethesda MD 20034 Office: Dept Psychiatry George Washington U Sch Medicine 2150 Pennsylvania Ave NW Washington DC 20037

PERLIS, ALAN J., educator, computer scientist; b. Pitts., Apr. 1, 1922; s. Louis Phillip and Zelda Anne (Gilfond) P.; B.S. in Chemistry, Carnegie Inst. Tech., 1943; postgrad. Calif. Inst. Tech., 1946-47; M.S., Mass. Inst. Tech., 1950, Ph.D. in Math., 1950; D.Sc. (hon.), Davis and Elkins Coll., 1968, Purdue U., 1973, Waterloo U., 1974; hon. doctorate Sacred Heart U., 1979; m. Sydelle Gordon, Oct. 28, 1951; children—Mark Lawrence, Robert Gordon, Andrea Lynn. Asst. prof. math., dir. computer center Purdue U., 1952-56; mem. faculty Carnegie Inst. Tech., 1956-71, prof. math., dir. computer center, 1960-71, head dept. math., 1961-64, head dept. computer sci., 1965-71; Eugene Higgins prof. computer sci. Yale U., 1971—, chmn. dept., 1976—; Gordon and Betty Moore vis. prof. engring. Calif. Inst. Tech., 1977; mem. NSF computer com. Nat. Joint Computer Com., 1954-56, Gov. Pa. Council Sci. and Tech., 1963—; com. computers research NIH, 1963—; mem. computer sci. and engring. research bd. Nat. Acad. Sci., 1968—; mem. Assembly of Engring., NRC, 1978—. Served to 1st lt. USAAF, 1942-45; ETO. Mem. Assn. Computing Machinery (pres. 1962-64, editor-in-chief jour. Communications 1958-62), Soc. Indsl. and Applied Math., Am. Math. Soc., Math. Assn., Am. Acad. Arts., Scis., Nat. Acad. Engring. Am. Home: 19 Tumblebrook Rd Woodbridge CT 06525 Office: Yale Univ New Haven CT 06520

PERLIS, DONALD M., artist; b. N.Y.C., July 29, 1941; s. Herman and Sylvia M. (Marks) P.; student Art Students League, 1961, Sch. Visual Arts, N.Y.C., 1965, Skowhegan Sch., 1965; m. Theresa Brown, June 9, 1968. Exhibited paintings at Whitney Mus., N.Y.C., Graham Gallery, 1971, 75. Home: PO Box 821 Bridgehampton NY 11932

PERLIS, HARLAN JAY, elec. engr.; b. Union City, N.J., June 12, 1924; s. William and Florence Rae (Jacobson) P.; B.E.E., Clarkson Coll. Tech., 1950; M.S., Stevens Inst. Tech., 1952; D. Engring. Sci., N.Y. U., 1963; m. Marie Josephine Lisanti, Dec. 20, 1963; children—Jay, Robert, Anthony. Broadcast engr. Sta. WICY, WMSA-AM-FM, 1947-49; jr. engr. Coles Signal Engring. Lab., 1949; sr. engr., group head A.B. DuMont Labs., 1950-56; sr. specialist Emerson Radio & Phonography Corp., 1956-58; instr., exec. asst., elec. engring. dept. N.Y. U., 1958-63; asso. Prof. Rutgers U., 1963-68; prof. elec. engring. N.J. Inst. Tech. Newark, 1968—; cons. elec. engring.; dir. Electro Mech. Corp.; co-dir. Environ. Instrumentation Systems Lab.; gen. chmn. Joint Automatic Control Conf., 1978. Scoutmaster Alexander Hamilton council Boy Scouts Am., 1946-50. Served with U.S. Army, 1942-46; PTO. Recipient Founder Day award N.Y. U., 1974; NSF grantee, 1964-72; EPA grantee, 1977-78. Fellow Instrument Soc. Am.; mem. IEEE, Armed Forces Communications and Electronics Assn., Soc. Indsl. and Applied Math., Am. Soc. Engring. Edn., N.Y. Acad. Scis., Am. Geophys. Union. Water Pollution Control Assn., Nat. Soc. Profl. Engrs. Tau Beta Pi, Eta Kappa Nu, Sigma Zi, Theta Chi. Club: Saddle H. Riding (Fairlawn, N.J.). Contbr. articles to profl. jours. Home: 791 Hartwell St Teaneck NJ 07666 Office: 323 High St Newark NJ 07102*

PERLIS, LEO, labor ofcl.; b. Bialystok, Russia, Feb. 22, 1912; s. David and Anna (Hirsch) P.; came to U.S., 1923, naturalized, 1928; student pub. schs.; D.Social Scis. (hon.), Boston Coll., 1978; m. Mimi Blatt, 1937 (dec. 1943); 1 son, Howard William; m. 2d, Betty Gantz; 1 son, Michael Fredrick. Nat. dir. CIO Community Services Com., 1945; cons. UN, 1947-48; v.p. U.S. Com. for UNICEF; sec. C.A.R.E., 1954; dir. AFL-CIO community service activities, 1955—. Mem. labor adv. com. Office Econ. Opportunity, 1965; sec. Nat. Citizens Com. Pub. Schs.; mem. adv. com. sheltered workshops Dept. Labor; hon. dir. Group Health Ins. Co.; mem. Pres.'s Citizens Adv. Com. Juvenile Delinquency and Youth Crime, Pres.'s Task Force on Prisoner Rehab., 1969; mem. exec. com. Nat. Center for Vol. Action, 1972; mem. Pres.'s Citizens Adv. Com. on Youth Fitness, 1959. Bd. dirs. Am. Heart Assn., Nat. Council Aging, Nat. Assn. Mental Health, United Community Funds and Councils Am., U.S.O., 1963-65, Nat. Assembly Social Policy and Devel.; bd. govs. United Way Am.; adv. council Sch. Social Work N.Y. U., Sch. Social Work Hunter Coll., 1964; trustee Nassau Community Coll., 1969; asso. trustee U. Pa. Recipient Page One award Newspaper Guild, 1957; first award Council Social Work Edn., 1958; award Boys Clubs Am., 1968; Silver Buffalo award Boy Scouts Am., 1970. Fellow Am. Pub. Health Assn.; mem. Health and Welfare Retirement Assn. (dir. 1968). Contbr. articles to profl. jours. Home: 6101 16th St NW Washington DC 20011 Office: 815 16th St NW Washington DC 20006. *A sense of duty, an eye for beauty, an unquenchable hope and, finally, kismet—that's it for me.*

PERLMAN, ALFRED EDWARD, railroad cons.; b. St. Paul, Nov. 22, 1902; s. Lewis H. and Leah (Levin) P.; S.B., Mass. Inst. Tech., 1923; grad. study Harvard, 1931; D.Sc., Clarkson Inst. Tech.; LL.B. (hon.), DePauw U.; m. Adele Sylvia Emrich, June 15, 1937; children—Michael L., Lee A., Constance G. With engring. and operating depts., asst. to operating v.p. N.P. Ry., Forsyth, Mont., 1923-24; with ry. div. RFC, 1934-35; with C.B. & O. R.R. 1935-36; engr. maintenance of way D. & R.G.W. R.R. Co., 1936-41, chief engr., 1941-47, gen. mgr. 1947-52, exec. v.p., 1952-54; pres., dir. N.Y. Central System, 1954-68; pres., chief adminstrv. officer Penn Central Co., 1968-69, vice chmn. bd., 1969-70; pres. Western Pacific R.R. Co., 1970-72, chmn., chief exec. officer, 1973-74, chmn. bd., 1974-76, cons., 1976—; dir., exec. com., cons. Comml. Metals Co., Dallas; cons. Israel Rys., 1950, Korean railroads for Dept. State, 1949; engr., cons. Def. Plant Corp., Las Vegas, World War II; cons. mil. airlift command USAF. Mem. council State U. at Westchester (N.Y.); vis. com. Joint Center Urban Studies, Mass. Inst. Tech. and Harvard; trustee Denver U., San Francisco Consortium; bd. dirs. San Francisco Bay Area Council; mem. corp. Mass. Inst. Tech. Mem. Econ. Devel. Council N.Y., Nat. Def. Transp. Assn. (v.p.), Commerce and Industry Assn. N.Y. (dir.), Newcomen Soc. Eng. Clubs: M.I.T., Economic (N.Y.C.); Westchester Country; Olympic. Contbr. profl. mags. Home: 3205 Ralston Ave Hillsborough CA 94010 Office: 526 Mission St San Francisco CA 94105

PERLMAN, CLIFFORD SEELEY, business exec.; b. Phila., Mar. 30, 1926; s. Bernard A. and Alfreda (Weinstein) P.; LL.B., U. Miami, 1951; children by previous marriage—Robyn Perlman Schwartz, Henry William, Jason, Clayton, Ivy Lee. Admitted to Fla. bar, 1951, Fed. bar, 1951; partner firm Perlman, Litman and Sponder, Miami Beach, Fla., 1951-61; founder Lums fast food restaurants (name changed to Caesars World, Inc. 1971), 1956, with Lums, 1956—, sec., treas., 1958-63, chmn. bd., Los Angeles, 1977—, chief exec. officer, 1977—. Trustee Mt. Sinai Hosp., Miami, Fla.; mem. athletic scholarship com. U. Miami (Fla.). Served with inf. U.S. Army, 1943-46; ETO. Mem. Am., Miami Beach bar assns., Fla. State Bar, Am. Judicature Soc. Clubs: Westview Country (Miami); Tamarisk Country (Palm Springs, Calif.); Las Vegas (Nev.) Country; Beverly Hills Tennis. Office: Caesars World Inc 1801 Century Park E Los Angeles CA 90067*

PERLMAN, D(AVID), educator; b. Madison, Wis., Feb. 6, 1920; s. Selig and Eva (Shaber) P.; B.A., U. Wis., 1941, M.S., 1943, Ph.D., 1945; m. Kató Lenárd, Aug. 18, 1968. Biochemist, Hoffmann-LaRoche, Inc., 1945; microbiologist Merck & Co., 1945-47; biochemist Squibb Inst. for Med. Research, 1947-67; prof. Sch. Pharmacy, U. Wis.-Madison, 1967—, dean, 1968-75. Chmn. 3d Internat. Congress Genetics of Indsl. Microorganisms, 1968-75, Kremers prof. pharm. biochemistry, 1979—; chmn. Conf. on Antimicrobial Agts. and Chemotherapy, 1966, 67, Gordon Research Conf. on Coenzymes and Metabolic Pathways, 1966. Guggenheim fellow, 1966. Fellow Am. Acad. Microbiology, N.Y. Acad. Scis., Acad. Pharm. Scis.; mem. Am. Chem. Soc. (Disting. Service award div. microbiol and biochem. tech. 1977, Marvin J. Johnson award (same div.) 1978), Am. Soc. Microbiology (pres. found. 1974-75, Fisher Sci. Co. award 1979, Pasteur award Ill. sect. 1979), Am. Soc. Pharmacognosists, Tissue Culture Assn., Soc. for Gen. Microbiology, Am. Pharm. Assn., Am. Soc. Biol. Chemistry, Biochem. Soc., Soc. for Indsl. Microbiology (Charles Thom award 1979), Sigma Xi. Editor: Advances Applied Microbiology, 1968—, Ann. Reports Fermentation Processes, 1977—. Contbr. articles to profl. jours. Home: 1 Chippewa Ct Madison WI 53711

PERLMAN, DANIEL HESSEL, univ. dean; b. Chgo., Dept. 24, 1935; s. Henry B. and Dorothy (Zimmerman) P.; B.A., Shimer Coll., 1954; B.A., U. Chgo., 1955, M.A., 1956, Ph.D., 1971; m. Suzanne Meyer, June 30, 1966; children—Julia, David. Psychol. counselor Roosevelt U., Chgo., 1961-64, asst. to pres., 1965-70, dir. govt. relations and planning, 1970-72, sec. bd. trustees, 1965—, prof. edn., 1974—, dean adminstrn., 1972—; spl. asst. to dep. commnr. higher and continuing edn. HEW, 1977-78. Bd. dirs. Congregation K.A.M. Isaiah Israel, Chgo., 1970-75. Mem. Am. Assn. Higher Edn., AAUP, Am. Assn. U. Adminstrs., Am. Ednl. Research Assn., Nat. Council Univ. Research Adminstrs., Soc. Coll. and Univ. Planning. Recipient Distinguished Alumnus award Shimer Coll., 1973; sr. Fulbright-hays lectr., Philippines, 1975; fellow Am. Council Edn., 1972-73; Presdl. Interchange exec., 1977-78. Contbr. profl. jours. Home: 413 Grove St Evanston IL 60201 Office: 430 S Michigan Ave Chicago IL 60605

PERLMAN, DAVID, journalist; b. Balt., Dec. 30, 1918; s. Jess and Sara P.; A.B., Columbia U., 1939, M.S., 1940; m. Anne Salz, Oct. 15, 1941; children—Katherine, Eric, Thomas. Reporter, Bismarck (N.D.) Capital, 1940; reporter San Francisco Chronicle, 1940-41, reporter, sci. editor, 1952-77, city editor, 1977-79, asso. editor, 1979—; reporter New York Herald Tribune, Paris, N.Y.C., 1945-49; European corr. Colliers mag. and New York Post, 1949-51; Regents prof. human biology U. Calif., San Francisco, 1974; cons. NSF, Ednl. TV stas. KQED and KPBS. Mem. med. com. Amnesty Internat.; bd. dirs. Planned Parenthood, 1974-76, San Francisco Social Planning Council, Squaw Valley (Calif.) Community of Writers. Served with inf., USAAF, 1941-45. Recipient Atomic Indsl. Forum award, 1975, Westinghouse Sci. Writing award, 1976, Ralph Coates Roe medal ASME, 1978. Fellow Calif. Acad. Scis.; mem. AAAS (adv. bd. Science-80 mag.), Council for Advancement Sci. Writing (pres. 1976—), Nat. Assn. Sci. Writers (pres. 1970-71), Astron. Soc. of Pacific (dir. 1976-78), Am. Assn. for Advancement Sci. Writing. Contbr. to Ency. Brit. Yearbook of Sci., 1969-73, Daedalus, 1974; Contbr. articles to major mags.; adv. bd. quar. Sci., Tech. and Human Values. Office: San Francisco Chronicle 901 Mission St San Francisco CA 94103*

PERLMAN, HAROLD LEONARD, lawyer; b. Chgo., Jan. 19, 1908; s. Morris and Kate (Colitz) P.; student U. Chgo., 1924-25; Ph.B., U. Wis., 1928; LL.B., Harvard U., 1931; m. Jane Rothschild, July 23, 1933; children—Marjorie (Mrs. Harold Feinberg), Joan (Mrs. Laurence Rosenberg). Admitted to Ill. bar, 1931, since practiced in Chgo.; partner firm Schwartz, Welfeld & Perlman, 1933-38, Cottlieb & Schwartz, 1938-51, Perlman, Schulman & Bell, 1951—; past chmn. bd. Appleton Machine Co., I-XL Furniture Co., Loftus Engring. Co., Norcor Mfg. Co.; former dir. U.S. Reduction Co., Handy Button Machine Co., VCA, Inc. Co-chmn. Jewish United Fund, Chgo., 1973—; active Michael Reese Research Found. Bd. dirs. Met. Chgo. Bd. Jewish Edn., 1940-74, Evanston (Ill.) Hosp., 1973—, Jewish Fedn. Met. Chgo., 1970—, Spertus Coll. Judaica, 1965-74; bd. dirs., sec. Michael Reese Hosp., Chgo., 1946-62; bd. dirs. Easter Seal Soc., 1970-73, co-chmn. bldg. fund campaign, 1969-70; trustee Hebrew U., 1970-75; bd. govs. Weizmann Inst. Sci., Rehovot, Israel, 1970, also donor Perlman Inst. Chem. Scis.; bd. dirs. Chgo. Med. Sch., 1953-65, donor Katie and Morris Perlman Lab.; donor Perlman Transmission Center, Chgo. Ednl. TV Assn.; donor Perlman Park, Glencoe, Ill. Recipient certificate of honor Bd. Jewish Edn.-Coll. Jewish Studies, 1960; Distinguished Service citation Michael Reese Hosp. and Med. Center, 1962; scroll of recognition Jewish United Fund, 1968; named hon. fellow Weizmann Inst. Mem. Am., Chgo., Ill. bar assns. Home: 1500 Sheridan Rd Wilmette IL 60091 Office: 135 S LaSalle St Chicago IL 60603

PERLMAN, HARVEY STUART, lawyer, educator; b. Lincoln, Nebr., Jan. 17, 1942; s. Floyd Ted and Rosalyn (Lashinsky) P.; B.A., U. Nebr., 1963, J.D., 1966; m. Susan G. Unthank, Aug. 27, 1966; children—Anne, Amy. Teaching fellow U. Chgo. Law Sch., 1966-67; admitted to Nebr. bar, 1966; mem. faculty U. Nebr. Sch. Law, 1967-74, prof., 1972-74; prof. law U. Va., Charlottesville, 1974—; exec. dir. Nebr. Commn. on Law Enforcement. Mem. Am. Bar Assn., Nebr. Bar Assn., Law-Psychology Assn. Author: (with Edmund Kitch) Legal Regulation of the Competitive Process, 1972, 79; asso. editor Jour. Law and Human Behavior, 1974—. Office: U Va Law Sch Charlottesville VA 22901

PERLMAN, ITZHAK, violinist; b. Tel Aviv, Israel, Aug. 31, 1945; s. Chaim and Shoshana P.; student Tel Aviv Acad. Music, Juilliard Sch., Meadowmount Sch. Music. Appeared with Indpls. Symphony Orch., N.Y.C. Philharmonic, Nat. Symphony Orch., Phila. Orch., Balt. Symphony Orch., Cleve. Orch., Buffalo Philharmonic Orch., Orchestre de la Suisse Romande, Geneva, Ramat-Gan Orch., Tel Aviv; participant numerous music festivals including Ravinia Festival, Berkshire Music Festival, Aspen Music Festival, Israel Festival, Wolf Trap Summer Festival; recital tours U.S., Can., S.Am., Europe, Israel, Australia, Far East; recorded for Angel, London, RCA Victor records. Recipient Leventritt prize, 1964. Address: care ICM Artists Ltd 40 W 57th St New York NY 10019

PERLMAN, LAWRENCE, lawyer; b. St. Paul, Apr. 8, 1938; s. Irving and Ruth (Mirsky) P.; B.A., Carleton Coll., 1960; J.D., Harvard U., 1963; m. Medora Scoll, June 18, 1961; children—David, Sara. Admitted to Minn. bar, 1963; law. clk. for fed. judge, 1963; partner firm Fredrikson, Byron, Colborn, Bisbee, Hansen & Perlman, Mpls., 1964-75; exec. v.p. Medtronic, Inc., Mpls., 1975-78; sr. partner firm Oppenheimer, Wolff, Foster, Shepard and Donnelly, Mpls., St. Paul, Brussels, 1978—; dir. CPT Corp.; adj. prof. Law Sch., U. Minn., 1974-76, 79—. Mem. Gov.'s Commn. on Minn.'s Future, 1973-76, Mpls. Bd. Estimate and Taxation, 1974-75; chmn. Mpls. Municipal Fin. Commn., 1978—; bd. dirs. Walker Art Center, Mpls. area br. ARC, Hennepin Center Arts; chmn. bd. visitors U. Minn. Law Sch. Mem. Am., Minn. (Outstanding Author award 1975, chmn. corps. com.), Hennepin County bar assns., Am. Judicature Soc., Health Industry Mfrs. Assn. (past dir.), Am. Law Inst., Corp. Counsel Assn. Minn. (dir.), Minn. Fgn. Policy Assn. (past pres. and dir.), Mpls. Urban League (past dir.), Phi Beta Kappa. Club: Mpls. Author: The Planning of Corporate Transactions, 1974. Home: 2366 W Lake of the Isles Pkwy Minneapolis MN 55405 Office: 4824 IDS Center Minneapolis MN 55402

PERLMAN, MARK, educator, economist; b. Madison, Wis., Dec. 23, 1923; s. Selig and Eva (Shaber) P.; B.A., M.A., U. Wis., 1947; Ph.D., Columbia, 1950; m. Naomi Gertrude Waxman, June 7, 1953; 1 dau., Abigail Ruth. Asst. prof. U. Hawaii, 1951-52, Cornell U., 1952-55; asst. prof., then asso. prof. Johns Hopkins, 1958-63; prof. econs., history and pub. health U. Pitts., 1963—, univ. prof., 1969—, chmn. dept., 1965-70; vis. fellow Clare Hall, U. Cambridge, 1977, ofcl. visitor univ. faculty econs. and politics, 1976-77. Co-chmn. Internat. Econ. Assn. Conf. on Econs. of Health in Industrialized Nations, Tokyo, Japan, 1973, Conf. on Orgn. and Retrieval Econs. Data, Kiel, West Germany, 1975. Served with AUS, 1943-46. Social Sci. Research Council fellow, 1949-50; Ford Found. fellow, 1962-63. Mem. Am. Econ. Assn. (mng. editor Jour. Econ. Lit. 1968—), Royal Econ. Soc., Internat. Union Sci. Study Population, Econ. Hist. Assn., History Econs. Soc. (v.p. 1979-80), Internat. Econ. Assn. (program com. Mexico City Congress 1980). Jewish. Club: Athenaeum (London). Author: Judges in Industry: A Study of Labor Arbitration in Australia, 1954; Labor Union Theories in America, 1958, 2d edit., 1976; The Machinists: A New Study in American Trade Unionism, 1962; (with T.D. Baker) Health Manpower in a Developing Economy, 1967; editor: The Economics of Health and Medical Care, 1974; The Organization and Retrieval of Economic Knowledge, 1977; (with G.K. MacLeod) Health Care Capital; author: Competition and Control, 1978; also articles, essays on health, population change, econ. devel., orgn. econ. knowledge and methodology, econ. productivity, history of econ. discipline; editor: Festschrifts (Sir John Barry, Edgar M. Hoover); prin. editor Cambridge Surveys of Contemporary Economics series; cons. editor, later editorial cons. USIA publ. Portfolio on Internat. Econ. Perspectives, 1972—. Home: 5622 Bartlett St Pittsburgh PA 15217

PERLMAN, RICHARD WILFRED, educator, economist; b. Mt. Vernon, N.Y., Dec. 15, 1923; s. Uriel and Annie (Feitelberg) P.; A.B., Cornell U., 1947; Ph.D., Columbia, 1953; m. Irma Lowenthal, Sept. 18, 1949; children—Abel, David, Laura, Jennifer. Asst. prof. econs. Adelphi U., Garden City, N.Y., 1953-57, asst. prof., 1957-64; prof. econs. U. Wis.-Milw., 1964—, chmn. dept., 1965-68, 74-77; NRC prof. Brookings Instn., 1958-59; Fulbright lectr. Inst. Politecnico Nacional, Mexico City, 1964, Autonomous U. Madrid, 1972. Mem. President's Com. Equal Employment Opportunity, 1963. Mem. Am. Econ. Assn., Indsl. Relations Research Assn., Phi Beta Kappa. Author: Economics of Education, 1973; Labor Theory, 1969; (with others) An Anthology of Labor Economics, 1972; Economics of Poverty, 1976. Home: 3341 N Summit Ave Milwaukee WI 53211

PERLMUTTER, ALVIN HOWARD, TV and film producer; b. Poughkeepsie, N.Y., Mar. 24, 1928; s. Fred and Jennie (Albert) P.; student Colgate U., 1945-47; B.A., Syracuse U., 1949; children—James F., Stephen H., Tom W. Dir. pub. affairs Sta. WNBC, also Sta. WNBC-TV, N.Y.C., 1957-59; program mgr. Sta. WNBC-TV, 1959-61; exec. producer Nat. Ednl. TV, 1961—, programs include series At Issue, NET Jour., The Great American Dream Machine, The Priceless Treasures of Dresden, Assignment America, various spl. programs; v.p. news documentaries NBC, 1975—; pres. Alvin H. Perlmutter, Inc.; instr. TV news and pub. affairs N.Y. U., 1957, Fairleigh Dickinson U., 1962. Served to 1st lt. AUS, 1950-53. Recipient various citations and awards, 2 Emmy awards. Mem. Acad. TV Arts and Scis. (gov. N.Y. chpt., nat. trustee, chmn. awards com. 1968), Assn. Pub. TV Producers (chmn. 1969). Club: Overseas Press (N.Y.C.). Home: 27 W 86th St New York NY 10024

PERLMUTTER, DANIEL D., educator; b. Bklyn., May 24, 1931; s. Samuel and Fannie (Kristal) P.; B.S. in Chem. Engring., N.Y. U., 1952; D.Eng., Yale, 1956; m. Felice Davidson, Oct. 23, 1954; children—Shira, Saul, Tova. Prof., U. Pa., Phila., 1965—. Guggenheim fellow, 1964; Fulbright fellow, 1968, 72. Mem. Am. Inst. Chem. Engrs., AAAS. Author: Introduction to Chemical Process Control, 1965; Stability of Chemical Reactors, 1972. Office: 311 Towne U Pa Philadelphia PA 19119

PERLMUTTER, JACK, artist, lithographer; b. N.Y.C., Jan. 23, 1920; s. Morris and Rebecca (Schiffman) P.; m. Norma Mazo, Dec. 24, 1942; children—Judith Faye, Ellen. Staff, Dickey Gallery, D.C. Tchrs. Coll., 1951-68, dir., 1962-68, now prof. art; mem. staff Corcoran Gallery Art Sch., now chmn. graphics dept., prof. art, also dir. print dept. Sch. Art; Fulbright research prof. painting and printmaking Tokyo U. Arts, 1959-60; artist-in-residence Gibbs Art Gallery, Charleston, S.C., 1974—; numerous one-man shows, U.S., Tokyo; exhibited nat. shows U.S., Switzerland, Yugoslavia; traveling exhibits Europe, S.Am., Can.; works in permanent collections Bklyn. Mus., Cin. Mus. Art, Carnegie Inst. Art, Corcoran Gallery Art, Library Congress, Met. Mus. Art, N.Y.C., Nat. Gallery Art, Washington, Phila. Mus. Art, Walker Gallery, Mpls., Nat. Mus. Modern Art, Tokyo, others. Fellow Internat. Inst. Arts and Letters; mem. Soc. Am. Graphic Artists. Club: Cosmos (Washington). Contbg. editor: Art Voices/South, 1978—. Home: 2511 Cliffbourne Pl NW Washington DC 20009

PERLMUTTER, JEROME HERBERT, former govt. ofcl., communications specialist; b. N.Y.C., Oct. 17, 1924; s. Morris and Rebecca (Shiffman) P.; A.B. cum laude, George Washington U., 1949; M.A., Am. U., 1957; m. Evelyn Lea Friedman, Sept. 19, 1948; children—Diane Muriel, Sandra Pauline, Bruce Steven. Chief editor service, prodn. editor N.E.A., Washington, 1949-50; editor in chief Jour. AAHPER, Washington, 1950-51, Rural Elec. News, REA, USDA, Washington, 1951-53; publ. writer Agrl. Research Service, 1953-56, chief, editor br. Office Info., 1956-60, sec. Outlook and Situation Bd., chief econ. reports Econ. Research Service, 1960-62; chief div. pub. and reprodn. services U.S. Dept. State, Washington, 1962-79; pres. Perlmutter Assos., 1979—; writing cons. CSC, 1956, World Bank, 1967—; faculty U. Md. Agr. Grad. Sch., also Fgn. Service Inst.; pub. cons. White House Conf. on Children and Youth, 1971. Coordinator fed. graphics Nat. Endowment for Arts, 1972-79. Served with USNR, 1943-46. Recipient award U.S. Jr. C. of C., 1963. Mem. Am. Assn. Agr. Coll. Editors, Fed. Editors Assn., Am. Farm Econ. Assn., Soc. Tech. Communication (dir.), Phi Beta Kappa, Sigma Delta Chi, Phi Eta Sigma, Artus. Author: A Practical Guide to Effective Writing, 1965. Contbr. articles profl. jours. Home: 513 E Indian Spring Dr Silver Spring MD 20901

PERLOFF, MARJORIE GABRIELLE, educator; b. Vienna, Austria, Sept. 28, 1931; d. Maximilian and Ilse (Schueller) Mintz; A.B., Barnard Coll., 1953; M.A., Cath. U., 1956, Ph.D., 1965; m. Joseph K. Perloff, July 31, 1953; children—Nancy Lynn, Carey Elizabeth. Asst. prof. English, Cath. U., Washington, 1966-68, asso. prof., 1969-71; asso. prof. U. Md., 1971-73, prof., 1973-76; Florence R. Scott prof. English, U. So. Calif., Los Angeles, 1976—. Mem. MLA (exec. council 1977-81), Comparative Lit. Assn., Coll. English Assn., Acad. Am. Poets, Am. Lit. Acad. Author: Rhyme and Meaning in the Poetry of Yeats, 1970; The Poetic Art of Robert Lowell, 1973; Frank O'Hara, Poet Among Painters, 1977. Home: 1467 Amalfi Dr Pacific Palisades CA 90272 Office: Dept English U So Calif Los Angeles CA 90007

PERLOFF, ROBERT, educator, psychologist; b. Phila., Feb. 3, 1921; s. Myer and Elizabeth (Sherman) P.; A.B., Temple U., 1949; M.A., Ohio State U., 1949, Ph.D., 1951; m. Evelyn Potechin, Sept. 22, 1946; children—Richard Mark, Linda Sue, Judith Kay. Instr. edn. Antioch Coll., 1950-51; with personnel research br. Dept. Army, 1951-55, chief statis. research and cons. unit., 1953-55; dir. research and devel. Sci. Research Assos., Inc., Chgo., 1955-59; vis. lectr. Chgo. Tchrs. Coll., 1955-56; mem. faculty Purdue U., 1959-69, prof. psychology, 1964-69, field assessment officer univ. Peace Corps Chile III project, 1962; prof. bus. adminstrn. and psychology U. Pitts. Grad. Sch. Bus., 1969—, dir. research programs, 1969-77, bd. dirs. Book Center. Cons. in field, 1959—; adv. com. assessment exptl. manpower research and devel. labs. Nat. Acad. Scis., 1972-74; mem. research rev. com. NIMH, 1976—, Stress and Families research project, 1976—; rep. to sect. social and econ. scis. AAAS. Bd. dirs., v.p. Sr. Citizens Service Corp. Served with U.S. Army, World War II; PTO. Decorated Bronze Star. Diplomate Am. Bd. Profl. Psychology. Fellow A.A.A.S., Am. Psychol. Assn. (mem.-at-large exec. com. div. consumer psychology 1964-67, 70—, pres. div. 1967-68, mem. council reps. 1965-68, 72-74, chmn. sci. affairs com., div. consumer psychology 1968—, edn. and tng. bd. 1969-72, chmn. finance com., treas., dir. 1974—, chmn. investment com. 1977—, author column Standard Deviations in jour.), Eastern (program chmn. 1974, dir. 1977-80); mem. Internat. Assn. Applied Psychology, Assn. for Consumer Research (chmn. 1970-71), Evaluation Research Soc. (pres. 1977-78), Soc. Psychol. Study Social Issues, Authors Guild, Authors League Am., Thoreau Soc., Sigma Xi, Psi Chi. Contbr. articles to profl. jours. Editor: Indsl. Psychologist, 1963-65, Evaluator Intervention: Pros and Cons; book rev. editor Personnel Psychology, 1952-55; co-editor Values, Ethics and Standards sourebook, 1979, Improving Evaluations; bd. cons. editors Am. Jour. Community Psychology, Jour. Applied Psychology; guest editor Am. Psychologist, May 1972, Education and Urban Society, 1977, Profl. Psychology, 1977. Home: 815 Saint James St Pittsburgh PA 15232. *Experiment. Innovate responsibly. Take risks judiciously. Do not shrink from new ventures for fear of failure. No one is immune from adversity. The hallmark of a successful achieving person is his or her ability to snap back after misfortune, and to benefit from and not be immobilized by failure.*

PERLONGO, DANIEL JAMES, composer; b. Gaastra, Mich., Sept. 23, 1942; s. James and Camille (Fittante) P.; Mus.B. in Composition, U. Mich., 1964, Mus.M., 1966; Corso di Perfezionamento, Accademia di S. Cecilia, Rome, 1968; m. Suzanne Elizabeth Thorin, Aug. 25, 1970. Asst. prof. music Indiana (Pa.) U., 1968—. Fulbright fellow, Italy, 1966; Italian Govt. grantee, 1967; recipient Joseph Bearns prize Columbia, 1966; Rome prize, 1971, 72; award Nat. Inst. Arts and Letters, 1975. Composer: (orch.) Myriad, 1968, Ephemeron, 1972; (chamber orch.) Variations, 1973; Voyage, a centennial rag, 1975; (chamber music) Improvision for Four (accordian, clarinet, trumpet, tuba), 1965; Improvisation #2 (piano, sax, bass, percussion), 1966, Eufonia, poetica e sonora (clarinet, horn, violin and cello, soprano voice), 1966, Intervals (string trio), 1967, Movement for 8 Players, 1967, For Bichi (percussion quartet), 1968, Movement in Brass, 1969, Process 7, 5, 3 for 6 in 12 (flute, oboe, Clarinet, 3 percussions), 1969, Semblance (string quartet), 1969-70, Tre Tempi (flute, clarinet, horn, violin, cello), 1971, Fragments (flute and cello), 1972, Structure, Semblance and Tune (tuba and percussion), 1973; (wind ensemble) Changes, 1970; (solo) Piano Sonata, 1965; 3 pieces for cello and piano, 1965, Episodes (double bass), 1966, Violin Solo, 1971. Office: Indiana Univ Pa Cogswell Hall Indiana PA 15701

PERLS, KLAUS GUNTHER, art dealer; b. Berlin, Germany, Jan. 15, 1912; s. Hugo and Kaethe (Kolker) P.; Ph.D. in Art History and Philosophy, U. Basle (Switzerland), 1933; m. Amelia Blumenthal, June 30, 1940; children—J Nicholas, Katherine Margaret. Came to U.S., 1935, naturalized, 1941. Art historian, Paris, France, 1933-35; various depts. Hallgarten & Co., stock brokers, N.Y.C., 1935-37; opened 1937, since partner, Perls Galleries, specializing in modern French paintings, N.Y.C. Mem. Art Dealers Assn. Am. (pres., dir.). Author: Jean Fouquet: Oeuvre Complet, 1938; (monograph) Viaminck, 1941. Address: 1016 Madison Ave New York City NY 10021

PERLSTEIN, HARRIS, ret. bus. exec.; b. N.Y.C., Aug. 18, 1892; s. Abram and Betsy (Cohen) P.; B.S. in Chem. Engring., Armour Inst. Tech., Chgo., 1914; LL.D., Ill. Inst. Tech., 1965; m. Anne Agazim, Mar. 11, 1929 (dec. Sept. 1956); children—Betsy Ann (Mrs. Kenneth R. Cowan) (dec.), Lawrence A.; m. 2d, Florence L. Weiss, Oct. 23, 1960 (dec. Sept. 1973). Chemist, engr., 1914-18; partner Singer Perlstein Co., cons. engrs., Chgo., 1918-24; treas., dir. Premier Malt Products Co., Peoria, Ill., 1924-27, pres. 1927-32, co. merged with Pabst Brewing Co., 1932, pres., dir. Pabst Brewing Co., Chgo., 1932-54, chmn., pres., dir., 1954-56, chmn., dir., 1956-72, chmn. exec. com., dir., 1972-79, chmn. emeritus, 1979—. Mem. adv. hosp. council Ill. Dept. Pub. Health, 1961-71; bd. dirs. U.S. Brewers Assn., 1944-79, hon. dir., 1979—; bd. dirs. Ill. Mfrs. Assn., 1945-55, 58-59; hon. chmn., life trustee, past chmn. bd. Ill. Inst. Tech.; pres., bd. dirs. Peristein Found.; past pres., dir. Jewish Fedn. Met. Chgo.; mem. Ill. Bd. Pub. Welfare Commrs., 1949-53. Mem. Am. Chem. Soc., Pi Delta Epsilon. Mason (Shriner). Clubs: Lake Shore Country, Northmoor Country, Standard (Chgo.); Chemist (N.Y.C.). Home: 1440 N Lake Shore Dr Chicago IL 60610 Office: 1 E Wacker Dr Chicago IL 60601

PERLSTEIN, MAURICE, bus. cons.; b. Phila., Aug. 21, 1915; s. Harry W. and Rae (Wiesen) P.; B.S., Syracuse U., 1937; m. Myna J. Frankel, Aug. 21, 1940; children—Marilyn (Mrs. Martin Colby), Maurice, Margo Jane (Mrs. Edward Parmacek). Textile converter, 1937-39; pres. Meadowbrook Co., mfrs. apparel, N.Y.C., 1939-49, McComb Mfg. Co. (Miss.), 1949-61; pres., chief exec. officer Kellwood Co., Chgo., 1961-65, mem. exec. com., 1965-67; pvt. investments, 1967—. Served with AUS, 1945. Home: 265 Coastal Blvd La Jolla CA 92037

PERLYN, DONALD LAURENCE, lawyer, bus. exec.; b. Bklyn., May 11, 1943; s. Irving C. and Irene R. P.; B.A. in Econs., U. Fla., 1963; J.D., U. Miami, 1968; m. Marilyn Belkin, May 2, 1971; children—Chad, Eric. Admitted to Fla. bar, 1968; atty. for legal services OEO, Miami, Fla., 1968-69; with Lums Restaurant Corp., Miami, 1969—, pres., 1975-79; pres. Wienerwald, U.S.A., Inc., Miami, 1979—. Mem. Internat. Franchise Assn. (dir.), Nat. Restaurant Assn. Democrat. Home: 7540 SW 162d St Miami FL 33157 Office: 8410 NW 53d Terr Miami FL 33166. *There are winners, there are losers, and there are survivors. Being among the survivors allows you to continue to play the game and playing is the fun of it all!*

PERMAN, NORMAN WILFORD, graphic designer; b. Chgo., Feb. 17, 1928; s. Jacob and Ida (Ladenson) P.; student Corcoran Sch. Art, Washington, 1946-47, Northwestern U., 1948-49; B.F.A., Art Inst. Chgo., 1951; m. Lorraine Shaffer, July 22, 1956; children—Jonathan Dean, Margot Bess. Asst. to designer Everett McNear, Chgo., 1951-52; ind. graphic designer specializing booklets, annual reports, exhibits, packaging and books, Chgo., 1953—; guest lectr. U. Ill. at Chgo. Circle; exhbns. include Art Inst. Chgo., 1954-62, 68, U. Ill., 1960, 62, 64, U. Wis., 1957, Am. Inst. Graphic Arts, 1958, 60, 61, 63, 64, 66, 68, 70, 72, 74, 76; exhibited in Russia for State Dept., 1964, Art Dirs. Club, N.Y.C., 1961, 63, 65, 69, HUD Art in Architecture exhibit Smithsonian Instn., 1973; 50 Yrs. Graphic Design in Chgo., 1977; lectr. in field, 1963—; juror various nat. and regional exhbns.; represented in numerous design jours. and annuals. Served with USN, 1946-47. Recipient award Art Dirs. Club, Chgo., 1960, 62, 65, 68, Art Dirs. Club, N.Y.C., 1963, Am. Inst. Graphic Arts 1961, 63, 64, Gold medal Direct Mail Assn., 1961, 64. Fellow Soc. Typog. Arts (dir., chmn. Allerton Park Conf. 1962, nat. pres. 1965-66; exhbts. 1952-79); mem. 27 Chgo. Designers, Art Inst. Chgo., Oriental Inst., Council Fgn. Relations, ACLU, NAACP, Urban League. Democrat. Club: Arts (Chgo.). Designer Invitations to Personal Reading, 165 vols., 1965; Sounds I Can Hear (records and ednl. materials), 1966; Talkstarters (ednl. material), 1967; Health and Growth, 1970; Mathematics Around Us, 1974; Good for Life (exhibit), 1978. Editor: Form and Meaning, 1962; represented in Graphis publs., Ann. Reports, Diagrams. Home: 2238 Asbury Ave Evanston IL 60201 Office: 233 E Erie St Chicago IL 60611

PERMUTT, SOLBERT, physiologist, physician; b. Birmingham, Ala., Mar. 6, 1925; s. Harry and Rachel (Damsky) P.; M.D., U. So. Calif., 1950; m. Loretta Paul, Jan. 17, 1952; children—Nina Rachel, Thomas Joshua, Lisa Ellen. Intern U. Chgo. Clinics, 1949-50, resident medicine 1952, instr. Med. Sch., 1950-52; resident medicine Montefiore Hosp., N.Y.C., 1954-56; fellow medicine and environmental medicine Johns Hopkins Med. Sch., 1956-58; chief div. cardiopulmonary physiology Nat. Jewish Hosp., Denver, 1958-61; asst. prof. physiology Sch. Medicine, U. Colo., 1960-61; mem. faculty Sch. Hygiene and Pub. Health, Johns Hopkins, 1961-72, prof. environ. health sci., 1965—, dir. respiratory div. Dept. Medicine, 1972—, prof. medicine, 1973—, prof. anesthesiology, 1978—, head physiology div. Dept. Environmental Health Scis., 1976—. Cons. space sci. bd. Nat. Acad. Sci., 1966-67, mem. com. effects atmospheric contaminants human health, 1968-70; mem. project com. Heart and Lung Program, NIH, 1970-74; mem. sci. adv. council Children's Asthma Research Inst. and Hosp., Denver, 1973-75; mem. expert panel Nat. Inst. Allergy and Infectious Diseases, 1972—; mem. vis. sci. com. Heart Assn. Md., 1970—; mem. nat. adv. com. for Cal. Primate Research Center, 1972-75; vice chmn. council on cardiopulmonary diseases Am. Heart Assn., 1974-75, chmn., 1976—, mem. membership council, 1973—, mem. research com., 1979—; nat. adviser Aspen Lung Confs., 1974—. Served with U.S. Army, 1943-46, 53-54. Fellow Nat. Found. Infantile Paralysis, 1956-58. Mem. Am. Fedn. Clin. Research, Am. Thoracic Soc., Am. Physiol. Soc., A.A.A.S., Am. Heart Assn. (bd. dirs.). Editorial bd. Am. Physiol. Soc. Circulation Research publs., 1965—, La Revue Francaise des Maladies Respiratories, 1975—. Contbr. articles to profl. jours. Home: 2303 Sulgrave Ave Baltimore MD 21209

PERNA, FRANK, JR., automotive testing equipment co. exec.; b. Detroit, Jan. 15, 1938; s. Frank and Mary (Cataldo) P.; B.S.M.E., Gen. Motors Inst., 1960; M.S.E.E., Wayne State U., 1966; M.S. in Sci. Mgmt. (Alfred P. Sloan fellow), M.I.T., 1970; m. Monika Doering, May 20, 1959; children—Laura, Renee, Christopher. Mem. engring. staff, then asst. dir. engring. Gen. Motors Corp., Detroit, 1955-72; v.p., dir. engring. Sun Electric Corp., Crystal Lake, Ill., 1972-78, exec. v.p., dir. ops., 1978, pres., chief operating officer, 1978—, also dir. Named Outstanding Young Man of Am., U.S. Jaycees, 1977; registered profl. engr., Mich. Mem. Instrumentation Soc. Am. (program chmn., treas. and sec.), Soc. Automotive Engrs. Inventor in field. Office: One Sun Pkwy Crystal Lake IL 60014

PERNECKY, JACK M(ARTIN), music educator; b. Chgo., Oct. 18, 1922; s. Paul and Marie (Orth) P.; student Rollins Coll., 1941-42, U. Chgo., 1954-55; Mus.B., Northwestern U., 1944, Mus.M., 1945, Ph.D., 1956; m. Dorothy Ehrich, Oct. 22, 1956; children—Steven, Mark. Instrumental dir. public schs., Ill., 1948-56; asst. prof. Eastern Ill. U., 1956-57; asso. prof. Mich. State U., 1957-60; asso. prof. music edn. Northwestern U., 1960-68, prof., 1968—, asso. dean univ., dir. grad. studies in music, 1969—; asso. music editor Summy-Birchard Music Pub. Co., Evanston, Ill., 1963-65; music editor M. M. Cole Music Pub., Chgo., 1965—. HEW Ill. research grantee, 1965-66; HEW Fund for Improvement of Postsecondary Edn. grantee, 1978-80. Mem. Music Educators Nat. Assn., Am. String Tchrs. Assn., Pi Kappa Lambda. Lutheran. Author: Basic Guide To Violin Playing, 1963; Growing With Strings, book I, 1966, book II, 1975; Easy String Solos, 1975; String Chamber Music, 1976; Music for Young Orchestras, 1977; contbr. numerous articles to profl. jours. Home: 2733 Princeton Ave Evanston IL 60201 Office: Sch of Music Northwestern U Evanston IL 60201

PERNICONE, JOSEPH MARIA, bishop; b. Regalbuto, Italy, Nov. 4, 1903; s. Salvatore and Petronilla (Taverna) P.; B.A., St. Joseph's Sem., Dunwoodie, Yonkers, N.Y., 1926; J.C.D., Cath. U., 1932. Ordained priest Roman Cath. Ch., 1926; asst. Our Lady Mt. Carmel, Yonkers, 1928-32; pastor Our Lady Mt. Carmel. Poughkeepsie, 1932-44, Our Lady Mt. Carmel, Bronx, 1944-66, Holy Trinity Ch., Poughkeepsie, N.Y., 1966-78; papal chamberlain, 1945, domestic prelate, 1952; aux. bishop, N.Y.C., 1954. Address: 3304 Waterbury Ave Bronx NY 10465

PEROT, H. ROSS, business exec., philanthropist; b. Texarkana, Tex., 1930; B.S., U.S. Naval Acad., 1953. Formerly with IBM Corp.; now chmn. bd. Electronic Data Systems, Inc., Dallas. Founder, United We Stand. Active Boy Scouts Am.; chmn. Perot Found. Served to lt. USNR, 1953-57. Address: 7171 Forest Ln Dallas TX 75230

PEROWNE, RONALD HERBERT, textile co. exec.; b. Montreal, Que., Can., Jan. 15, 1918; s. Herbert and Anna (Hooks) P.; B.Commerce, McGill U., 1939; m. Eunice Grant Hellyer, Oct. 4, 1945; children—Barbara Jo Ann (Mrs. Meade), Catherine Jean (Mrs. Lymburner), Margaret Elaine (Mrs. Metze), Ronald Grant, Ian Herbert. With Dominion Textile Co. Inc., 1945—, pres., 1969-74, chief exec. officer, 1969—, chmn. bd., 1974—; dir. Belding-Corticelli Ltd., DHJ Industries Inc., Howard Cotton Co., Memphis, Swift Textiles Inc., Columbus, Ga. Bd. dirs. Assos. Concordia U.; mem. corp. Bishop's U. Served with Royal Canadian Naval Vol. Res., 1941-45. Mem. Cotton Inst. Can. (pres.). Clubs: Univ., Montreal Badminton and Squash, Mount Royal (Montreal); Kanawaki Golf. Office: 1950 Sherbrooke St W Montreal PQ H3H 1H9 Canada

PERPICH, RUDY GEORGE, corp. exec., former gov. Minn.; b. Carson Lake, Minn., June 27, 1928; s. Anton and Mary (Vukelich) P.; A.A., Hibbing Jr. Coll., 1950; D.D.S., Marquette U., 1954; m. Delores Helen Simic, Sept. 4, 1954; children—Rudy George, Mary Susan. Lt. gov. State of Minn., 1971-76; gov. State of Minn., 1976-79; v.p., exec. cons. Control Data Worldtech, Inc., Mpls., 1979—. Mem. Hibbing (Minn.) Bd. Edn., 1956-62, Mem. Minn. Senate, 1962-70. Served to sgt. AUS, 1946-47. Roman Catholic. Address: Control Data Worldtech Inc 8100 34th Ave Minneapolis MN 55440*

PERRAULT, GUY, educator, engr.; b. Amos, Quebec, Can., Sept. 25, 1927; s. Rodlphe and Lorenza (Maurice) P.; B.Sc.A., Ecole Polytechnique, 1949; M.Sc., U. Toronto, 1951, Ph.D., 1955; m. Helene Lachapelle, June 24, 1957; children—Marie, Sylvie, Isabelle. Field engr. Moneta Porcupine Mines Ltd., 1955-57; prof. Ecole Polytechnique, Montreal, 1957-75, prof., 1977—; v.p. research Soquem, Sainte-Foy, Quebec, 1975-77. Recipient Prix Scientifique du Quebec, 1971. Fellow Royal Soc. Can.; mem. Can. Inst. Mining and Metallurgy, Ordre des Ingenieurs du Quebec. Roman Catholic. Contbr. articles to profl. jours. Home: 11811 Jean Masse Montreal PQ H4J 1S2 Canada Office: Ecole Polytechnique CP 6079 Succ A Montreal PQ H3C 3A7 Canada

PERRAULT, ROGER ARMAND, health assn. exec., physician; b. Amos, Que., Can., Sept. 24, 1936; s. Camille Ralph and Laurenza (Maurice) P.; B.A., Ottawa (Ont., Can.) U., 1956, M.D., 1963; Ph.D. (Can. Med. Research Council fellow), U. Uppsala (Sweden), 1972. Intern, Ottawa Gen. Hosp., 1963-64, resident, 1968-69; research fellow Def. Research Bd. Can. and Royal Canadian Navy, Ottawa, 1964-68; med. dir. Ottawa Centre, Canadian Red Cross Blood Transfusion Service, 1972-73, nat. dir., Toronto, Ont., 1974—. Served with Royal Canadian Navy, 1964-68. Mem. Canadian Med. Assn., Canadian Hematology Soc., Scandinavian Soc. Immunology. Office: 95 Wellesley St Toronto ON M4Y 1H6 Canada

PERREAULT, GERMAIN, banker; b. Montreal, Que., Can., May 23, 1916; s. Lucien and Maria (Dufault) P.; ed. Montreal. Began with Montreal Stock Exchange, 1936, Garneau, Ostiguy & Co., 1937-39; with Banque Canadienne Nationale, Montreal, 1939—, v.p., chief gen. mgr., 1972-74, pres., 1974—, chief exec. officer, 1976—, chmn. bd., 1978—; also dir.; dir. Compagnie Immobiliere BCN Limitee; dir., mem. exec. com. Sidbec, Sidbec-Dosco Ltd., pres. Soc. de la caisse de retraite de la Banque Canadienne Nationale; dir. RoyNat Ltd., Domco Industries Ltd., Laurentian Mut. Assurance Co., Commerce Gen. Ins. Co., Can. Merc. Ins. Co., Canadian Nat. Ins. Co., Corp. d'Expansion Financiere, Les Ensembles Urbains Ltee, Les Nouveaux Ensembles Urbains Ltee., Bank Can. Nat., Banque Canadienne Nationale (Europe), York Lambton Corp. Ltd., Société générale de financement du Québec; gov. Que. Hosp. Service Assn. (Blue Cross). Bd. dirs. Regie de la Place des Arts, Montreal Mus. Fine Arts, Montreal Symphony Orch.; bd. dirs., chmn. Que div. Can. Arthritis and Rheumatism Soc.; gov. Hosp. Notre Dame de Montreal. Mem. Montreal Bd. Trade (dir.), Can. C. of C., La Chambre de commerce du dist. de Montreal. Clubs: St. Denis (dir., exec. com.), Mt. Royal (Montreal); Laval-sur-le-Lac (Laval, Que.). Office: 500 Pl d'Armes Montreal PQ H2Y 2W3 Canada

PERRET, JOSEPH ALOYSIUS, credit co. exec.; b. Phila., Feb. 26, 1929; s. Joseph Henry and Mary Rose (Martin) P.; student U. Pa., 1953-57, Temple U., 1957-58, Stonier Grad. Sch. Banking, 1966; m. Nancy S. Bott, June 24, 1950; children—Kathlyne, Robert, Susan, Michael. Head analyst Phila. Nat. Bank, 1953-57; spl. banking rep. Burroughs Corp., Phila., 1957-59; v.p. First Pa. Banking & Trust Co., Phila., 1959-66; v.p. Md. Nat. Bank, Balt., 1966-70, sr. v.p., 1970-75; sr. v.p. Comml. Credit Co., Balt., 1975-78, sr. v.p. Lloyds Bank Calif., Los Angeles, 1978—. Mem. Am. Bankers Assn., Data Processing Mgmt. Assn., Balt.-Washington Regional Clearing House (chmn. 1970). Clubs: Country of Md.; Merchants (Balt.). Home: 3023 Rio Claro Dr Hacienda Heights CA 91745

PERRIN, ARTHUR MITCHELL, conveyor mfg. co. exec.; b. Bklyn., Aug. 12, 1907; s. William W. and Catherine (Mitchell) P.; ed. Pratt Inst. Sci. and Tech., Bklyn.; m. Lillian Conboy, May 1934 (dec. 1976); m. 2d, Mary-Lee J. Bolton, Dec. 1977. Vice pres. charge engring. Nat. Conveyors Co., Inc., Fairview, N.J., 1933-42, pres., 1942—; pres. Nat. Conveyors Internat. Sales Corp.; mem. Council Internat. Progress in Mgmt., 1948-52. Chmn. Englewood (N.J.) Community Chest, 1967-70. Registered profl. engr., Ill. Life fellow ASME (treas. 1968-71). Clubs: Knickerbocker Country (Tenafly, N.J.); Englewood, Skytop (Pa.) Lodge; N.J. Seniors Golf Assn.; Winter Golf League Advt. Interests, Beefeater, Elks, Venice (Fla.) Yacht; Mission Valley Golf and Country (Laurel, Fla.). Author, editor in field. Developed chipveyor system. Home: 67 Walnut Ct Englewood NJ 07631 Office: 25 Industrial Ave Fairview NJ 07022

PERRIN, FRED SMITH, soft drink co. exec.; b. Elberton, Ga., Sept. 17, 1913; s. George Grogan and Mary Elizabeth (Dye) P.; grad. Am. Inst. Banking, 1934; student Ga. State U., 1934-37; LL.B., Atlanta Law Sch., 1940. Admitted to Ga. bar, 1940; with Coca-Cola Co., Atlanta, 1940—, asst. sec., 1947-72, sec. finance com., 1962-72, corporate sec., 1972-78; ret., 1978. Bd. dirs. Met. YMCA, Atlanta,

1978—. Served to maj. Judge Adv. Gen. Corps, AUS, 1941-46. Mem. Ga. Bar Assn., Judge Adv. Gen.'s Assn., Am. Soc. Corporate Secs., Sigma Delta Kappa, Delta Kappa. Episcopalian. Mason. Club: New York Athletic. Home: 1546 Cooledge Rd Tucker GA 30084

PERRIN, JAMES, fgn. service officer; b. Boston, Jan. 27, 1930; s. Hugh and Helen Frances (Baxter) P.; A.B., Harvard, 1950; M.A., Institut des Hautes Etudes Cinematographiques, 1960; m. Martha Bodel, Mar. 21, 1959. Free-lance performer TV, theatre, night clubs, 1950-55; stage mgr., asso. producer CBS-TV, N.Y.C., 1955-63, producer, 1963-64; exec. producer Nat. Ednl. TV, 1964-66; asst. info. officer USIS, Kinshasa, Zaire, 1966-68; pub. affairs officer, Ndjamena, Chad, 1968-70; dep. pub. affairs officer, Jakarta, Indonesia, 1970-73; pub. affairs officer, Abidjan, Ivory Coast, 1973-74, counselor embassy for pub. affairs, 1974-75; detailed Nat. War Coll., 1975-76; country affairs officer France and Germany, ICA, 1976-78, dep. dir. TV and film service, 1978—. Fulbright fellow, 1958-60. Recipient Fulbright honors award, 1959. Mem. Am. Fgn. Service Assn. Home: 3700 Prince William Dr Fairfax VA 22030 Office: ICA 1776 Pennsylvania Ave NW Washington DC 20547

PERRIN, RICHARD WILLIAM EDMUND, architect; b. Milw. Mar. 14, 1909; s. Richard and Emily (Tischer) P.; student U. Wis., 1927-29, Layton Sch. Art, 1929-31, Beaux Arts Inst. Design, 1934-35; m. Adeline Pucyloski, Oct. 22, 1932. Apprentice architect Richard Philipp, Milw., 1927-34; supr. Hist. Am. Bldgs. Survey Milw., 1934-35; practice architecture with Elliott B. Mason, Milw., 1934-42, Smith, Hinchman & Grylls, Detroit, 1942-43; cartographic engr. U.S. Army Mapping Service, 1943-44; asst. dir. Housing Authority City Milw., 1944-46, exec. dir., 1946-71; exec. dir. Milw. Redevel. Authority, 1961-71; exec. sec. City Plan Commn., also commr. dept. city devel., 1961-71; historic Am. bldgs. survey adv. bd. Dept. Interior; bd. dirs. Wis. Archtl. Archive. Mem. Wis. Com. Historic Sites Preservation, 1968-74, Wis. Historic Preservation Rev. Bd.; chmn. Milw. Landmarks Commn., 1964-71; mem. Wis. Capitol and Exec. Residence Bd., 1966-74; hon. curator history Milw. Pub. Mus. Recipient numerous citations, awards. Fellow AIA (vice chmn. nat. com. historic bldgs. preservation 1961); mem. Nat. Assn. Housing Ofcls. (life), Soc. Archtl. Historians, Wis. Acad. Scis., Arts and Letters (v.p. arts, pres. 1973), Internat. Council Monuments and Sites (U.S. com. 1968-73), Arbeitskreis für Hausforschung (Germany). Author numerous articles; also books. Address: 9825 W Concordia Ave Milwaukee WI 53222. *I hope that I may never lose the capacity for learning, retaining an open mind in all things and at all times, in the further hope that I will continue to be called upon to serve in such capacities for which I may have some competence.*

PERRINE, BEAHL THEODORE, lawyer; b. Monticello, Iowa, July 4, 1902; s. John H. and Minnie (Ryan) P.; student U. Mich., 1922-27, J.D., 1927; m. Irene L. Hall, Oct. 27, 1934. Admitted to Iowa bar, 1927, since practiced in Cedar Rapids; sr. mem. firm Simmons, Perrine, Albright and Ellwood, 1943—; asst. atty. Linn County, 1942-44; former pres. and chmn. bd. Iowa Mfg. Co.; sec., dir. Amana Refrigeration, Inc. Regional war Bond dir. Treasury Dept., World War II. Trustee Herbert Hoover Presdl. Library Assn., Mercy Hosp., Cedar Rapids, bd. dirs. Mercy Hosp. Endowment Found.; bd. dirs., chmn. bd. Hall Found.; trustee YMCA, past pres. bd.; former bd. dirs. Episcopal Corp. Diocese of Iowa. Mem. Am., Iowa, Linn County (pres. 1936) bar assns., Am. Judicature Soc., Cedar Rapids C. of C., Alpha Kappa Lambda, Delta Theta Phi. Clubs: Pickwick, Elks, Cedar Rapids Country. Home: 2222 1st Ave NE Cedar Rapids IA 52402 Office: Merchants Nat Bank Bldg Cedar Rapids IA 52401

PERRINE, LAURENCE, educator; b. Toronto, Ont., Can., Oct. 13, 1915; s. Ren Brown and Mary (Dollins) P.; B.A., Oberlin Coll., 1937, M.A., 1939; Ph.D., Yale, 1948; m. Catherine Lee Stockard, Sept. 17, 1949; children—David, Douglas. Mem. faculty So. Meth. U., 1946—, prof. English, 1960—. Served with AUS, 1942-46; ETO. Mem. Tex. Inst. Letters, Nat. Council Tchrs. English (bd. dirs. 1962-65), S. Central Modern Lang. Assn. (pres. 1970-71), Tex. Conf. Coll. Tchrs. English (pres. 1973-74), Phi Beta Kappa. Author: Sound and Sense: An Introduction to Poetry, 5th edit., 1977; Story and Structure, 5th edit., 1978; Poetry: A Closer Look (with J.M. Reid, J. Ciardi), 1963; 100 American Poems of the Twentieth Century (with J.M. Reid), 1966; Literature: Structure, Sound and Sense, 1970, 3d edit., 1978; The Art of Total Relevance: Papers on Poetry, 1976. Home: 7616 Royal Pl Dallas TX 75230

PERRINE, RICHARD LEROY, educator, environ. engr.; b. Mountain View, Calif., May 15, 1924; s. George Alexander and Marie (Axelson) P.; A.B., San Jose State Coll., 1949; M.S., Stanford U., 1950, Ph.D. in Chemistry, 1953; m. Barbara Jean Gale, Apr. 12, 1945; children—Cynthia Gale, Jeffrey Richard. Research chemist Calif. Research Corp., La Habra, 1953-59; asso. prof. U. Calif. at Los Angeles, 1959-63, prof. engring. and applied sci., 1963—, chmn. environ. sci. and engring., 1971—; cons. environ. sci. and engring., energy resources, flow in porous media; mem. Los Angeles County Energy Commn., 1973—; mem. adv. council South Coast Air Quality Mgmt. Dist., 1977—; mem. air conservation com. Los Angeles County Lung Assn., 1970—. Served with AUS, 1943-46. Recipient Outstanding Engr. Merit award in environ. engring. Inst. Advancement Engring., 1975. Mem. Am. Chem. Soc., Soc. Petroleum Engrs., Am. Inst. Chem. Engrs., Can. Inst. Mining and Metallurgy, Nat. Assn. Environ. Edn., Nat. Assn. Environ. Profls., Air Pollution Control Assn., Am. Water Resources Assn., AAAS, N.Y. Acad. Scis., Explorers Club, Calif. Tomorrow, Sierra Club, Wilderness Soc., Audubon Soc., Sigma Xi, Tau Beta Pi, Phi Lambda Upsilon. Home: 22611 Kittridge St Canoga Park CA 91307 Office: Engring I Room 2066 U Calif Los Angeles CA 90024

PERRINE, VALERIE, actress; b. Galveston, Tex., Sept. 3, 1943; d. Kenneth and Renee (McGinley) Perrine; student U. Ariz., 1961. Film appearances include Slaughterhouse Five, The Last American Hero, Lenny, W.C. Fields and Me, Mr. Billion, Superman, The Magician of Lublin; The Electric Horseman, 1979; TV movies include Ziegfeld: The Man and His Women, The Couple Takes a Wife. Recipient Best Actress award for Lenny, Cannes Film Festival, 1975; Best Supporting Actress, N.Y. Film Circle, 1975, Nat. Bd. Ofcls. Motion Pictures, 1975; Actress of Year award United Motion Pictures Assn., 1975; award most promising newcomer to leading film roles Brit. Acad., 1975. Mem. Screen Actors Guild, A.F.T.R.A. Address: care Bernie Francis 328 S Beverly Dr Beverly Hills CA 90212*

PERRING, RAYMOND T., banker; b. Detroit, Apr. 16, 1905; s. Walter and Charlotte (Brown) P.; student Wayne U., 1922-24; A.B., U. Mich., 1926, M.B.A., 1927; m. Viola J. Chubb, Aug. 9, 1928; 1 dau., Kay. With Union Trust Co., 1927; with Detroit Bank & Trust Co. (formerly The Detroit Bank), 1928—, exec. v.p., 1951, pres., dir., 1952-63, chmn. bd., 1963-75; former dir. Detroit Edison Co., Chrysler Corp., Reliance Ins. Co., Phila. Bd. dirs. United Found., Detroit Symphony Orch.; trustee Harper/Grace Hosp., Cranbrook Acad. Art, Citizen's Research Council Mich., YWCA Detroit, Detroit Press Club Found.; past trustee, treas. Met. Fund; past chmn., dir. Detroit chpt. A.R.C. Mem. Am. Inst. Banking, Mich. Bankers Assn., Greater Detroit Bd. Commerce (past pres.), Mich. C. of C. (past dir., past chmn. bd.), Detroit Grand Opera Assn. (dir.), Detroit Mus. Art Founders Soc., Delta Phi, Beta Gamma Sigma. Clubs: University of Mich., Detroit Athletic (past pres.), Detroit, Econ. (dir.) (Detroit); Pine Lake Country (past pres.) (Pontiac, Mich.); Bloomfield Hills Country (past pres., bd. govs.); John's Island; Yondotega. Home: 4220 Wabeek Lake Dr Bloomfield Hills MI 48013 Office: care Detroit Bank & Trust Co Fort St at Washington Detroit MI 48231

PERROS, THEODORE PETER, educator, chemist; b. Cumberland, Md., Aug. 16, 1921; s. Peter G. and Christina (Sioris) P.; B.S., George Washington U., 1946, M.S., 1947, Ph.D., 1952; postgrad. Technische Hochschule, Munich, Germany; m. Electra Paula Zolotas, July 21, 1973. Analyst research div. U.S. Naval Ordnance Lab., 1943-46; faculty George Washington U., Washington, 1946—, prof. chemistry and forensic scis., 1960—, chmn. dept. forensic sci., 1971-73; v.p. Meridian-West Assos., 1978—. Research chemist Bur. Ordnance, 1949; research dir. Air Force Office Sci. Research and Devel., 1958-59; cons. U.S. Naval Ordnance Lab., 1953-56; sec. Ahepa Ednl. Found., 1969-78. Pres. So. Intercollegiate Athletic Conf., 1968, Hellenic Republican Club of Washington, 1968-70; campaign chmn. Nat. Republican Heritage Groups Council, 1977-78. NSF fellow, 1959; AEC grantee, 1951-53; Research Corp. grantee, 1953-54. Fellow Am. Inst. Chemists, Am. Acad. Forensic Scis., Washington Acad. Scis.; mem. Am. Chem. Soc., Soc. Applied Spectroscopy, German Lang. Soc., Chem. Soc. London, Gesellschaft Deutscher Chemiker, Philos. Soc. Washington, Ahepa (pres. Inst. Arts and Scis., pres. Washington chpt. 1976-78), Sigma Xi, Omicron Delta Kappa, Alpha Chi Sigma (pres. 1964). Author: (with William F. Sager) Chemical Principles, 1961; (with C.R. Naeser, W. Harkness) Experiments in General Chemistry, 1961; College Chemistry, 1966. Contbr. articles to profl. jours. Research on stabilities of inorganic coordination polymers, preparation and characterization fluorine containing compounds transition metals. Home: 5825 3d Pl NW Washington DC 20011

PERROT, PAUL NORMAN, museum dir.; b. Paris, France, July 28, 1926; s. Paul and K. Norman (Derr) P.; came to U.S., 1946, naturalized, 1954; student Ecole du Louvre, 1945-46, N.Y. U. Inst. Fine Arts, 1946-52; m. Joanne Stovall, Oct. 23, 1954; children—Paul Latham, Chantal Marie Claire, Jeannine, Robert. Asst., The Cloisters, Met. Mus. Art, 1948-52; asst. to dir. Corning (N.Y.) Mus. Glass, 1952-54, asst. dir. mus., 1954-60, dir., 1960-72; editor Jour. Glass Studies, 1959-72; asst. sec. for mus. programs Smithsonian Instn., Washington, 1972—; lectr. glass history, aesthetics, museology; v.p. Internat. Council Mus.; past pres. N.E. Conf. Mus.; v.p. Internat. Centre for Study of Preservation and Restoration of Cultural Property, Rome, mem. council, 1974—. Mem. Am. (v.p., council 1967-78), N.Y. State (past pres.) assns. museums, Internat. Assn. History Glass (v.p.), Corning Friends of Library (past pres.), So. Tier Library System (past pres.), Archeol. Inst. Am. Author: Three Great Centuries of Venetian Glass, 1958; also numerous articles on various hist. and archael. subjects. Home: 308 A St NE Washington DC 20002 Office: Smithsonian Instn Washington DC 20560

PERRY, ANTHONY JOHN, hosp. adminstr.; b. Dighton, Mass., Oct. 19, 1919; s. Antone and Jessie P.; B.S. in Edn., State Coll. Mass. at Bridgewater, 1942; M.S. in Hosp. Adminstrn., Northwestern U., 1952; m. Harriet M. McGirr, Nov. 26, 1949; children—Joan Perry, Martha. Flight supt. Trans World Airlines, Lisbon, Portugal, 1946-47; sta. mgr. Peruvian Internat. Airlines, N.Y.C., 1947-49; with adminstrn. Decatur and Macon County Hosp. (now Decatur Meml. Hosp.), Decatur, Ill., 1952—, adminstr., 1961—, exec. v.p., 1969-74, pres., 1974—; dir. Multihosp. Mut. Ins. Ltd. Pres. Mental Health Assn. Macon County, 1957; mem. Tech. Council Means and Methods of Financing Health Care for Ill. Bd. dirs. Macon County chpt. ARC, 1960-66, South Central Ill. Health Planning Council, 1969—, United Way Decatur and Macon County, 1960-66, Voluntary Hosps. Am., 1977—. Served with USAAF, 1942-46. Fellow Am. Coll. Hosp. Adminstrs.; mem. Am. Hosp. Assn. (chmn. council on financing 1977-79), Ill. Hosp. Assn. (pres., del. to Am. Hosp. Assn.). Clubs: Decatur Country, Decatur. Home: 421 Hackberry Dr Decatur IL 62521 Office: 2300 N Edward St Decatur IL 62526

PERRY, BENJAMIN LUTHER, JR., univ. pres.; b. Eatonville, Fla., Feb. 27, 1918; s. Benjamin Luther and Annie (Gordan) P.; B.S., Fla. A. and M. Coll., 1940; M.S., Iowa State Coll., 1942; Ph.D., Cornell U., 1954; m. Helen N. Harrison, Aug. 12, 1944; 1 dau., Kimberly V. Dean students, Mich. State adviser U. Nigeria, 1962-64; dir. research and grants Fla. A. and M. U., Tallahassee, 1965-67, dean adminstrn., 1967-68, pres., 1968-77, dir. Agrl. Research and Extension Center, 1977—; prof. econs., cons. U.S. Dept. Treasury, Pub. Instn. Higher Learning in So. States. Asso. commr. Boy Scouts Am., 1967; pres. Mayor's Commn. on Urban Renewal, 1968—, Frontiers Internat., 1969. Served with AUS, 1942-46. Recipient Gold Key plaque-Man of Year, 1970, Phi Delta Kappa of Year award, 1970, Eastern Star award, 1970; Danforth grantee. Mem. Nat. Assn. Personnel Workers (pres. 1968), Am. Assn. Higher Edn. (founder, adviser), Fla. Assn. Colls. and Univs. (pres.), So. Assn. Land-Grant Colls. and Univs., Tallahassee Urban League, Kappa Alpha Psi, Alpha Phi Omega. Author: Higher Education for Disadvantaged Students, 1969. Contbr. articles to profl. jours. Home: 1446 Perry St Tallahassee FL 32304

PERRY, BERNARD BERENSON, cons. editor; b. Boston, Dec. 16, 1910; s. Ralph Barton and Rachel (Berenson) P.; student U. N.C., 1932-33; A.B., Harvard, 1934; m. Marian Wynn, Oct. 10, 1941 (div. 1947); m. 2d, Elizabeth B. Jennings, Nov. 22, 1947; children—Marjorie Elizabeth, David Jennings, Rachel Berenson. With W.W. Norton & Co., 1934-35; asso. editor E.P. Dutton & Co., 1936-40; asso. editor, sales mgr. Vanguard Press, 1940-45; gen. mgr. A.A. Wyn, Inc., 1945-49; founder, dir. Ind. U. Press, Bloomington, 1950-76, cons. editor, 1976—; vis. prof. creative writing U. N.Mex., summer 1950; cons. editor W.D. Howells Edit.; panelist Nat. Endowment for Humanities, 1978; editorial cons. Univ. Press New Eng.; reader Book-of-the-Month Club. Mem. Assn. Am. Univ. Presses (v.p. 1973-74), Phi Kappa Sigma. Clubs: Harvard (N.Y.C.); Harvard of Ind.; Arts (Chgo.). Contbr. chpts. How To Write for Pleasure and Profit, also to N.Y. Times Book Rev., Saturday Rev., Scholarly Pub. Address: Indiana University Press 10th and Morton Sts Bloomington IN 47401. *The work ethic didn't really take hold at first; but later followed the principle of substituting dogged persistence and long hours of hard work for lack of brilliance. Today I should say that happiness in life is greatly preferable to "making it." Advice to retirees: do not retire from something but into something which may or may not be a new field of endeavor.*

PERRY, CHARLES E., bus. exec.; b. Holden, W.Va., July 25, 1937; s. Lester and Ethel (White) P.; B.A. with honors, B.S. (Distinguished Service grad.), M.A., L.H.D., Bowling Green State U.; postgrad. U. Mich.; LL.D., Bethune-Cookman Coll.; m. Betty Laird, Sept. 17, 1960; children—Thomas Edward, Lynnette Eleanor. Tchr. English and history East Detroit pub. schs.; admissions counselor Bowling Green State U., 1959-61, dir. admissions, 1961-64, dir. devel., 1964-67, asst. to pres., 1965-67; spl. asst. to gov. Fla. for edn., 1967-68; vice chancellor Fla. U. System, 1968-69; pres. Fla. Internat. U., 1969-75; pres., pub. Family Weekly mag., 1976; pres. Golden Bear, Inc., 1977—, Golforce, Inc.; partner Jack Nicklaus & Assos.; chmn. bd. dirs. Golden Bear Communications; chmn., chief exec. CEPCO; dir. Am. Bankers Life Assurance Co., Jack Nicklaus Eyeware, Inc., B.C. Devel. Corp., Orange Bowl. Past exec. dir. Fla. Commn. Quality Edn.; past chmn. Gov. Fla. Edn. Adv. Council; past dir. So. Regional Edn. Bd.; past chmn. Council Fla. Jr. Coll. Affairs; past chmn. Fla. Edn. Council, Fla. del. Edn. Commn. States; past mem. Select Council Post High Sch. Edn.; past chmn. com. on internat. programs Am. Assn. State Colls. and Univs.; past mem. Nat. Com. Utilization Ednl. TV, Southeastern Ednl. Lab. Council, Commn. Latin Am. Affairs, Miami Commn. Fgn. Relations, Dade Marine Inst., UN U.S.A., UN World Edn. Commn., U.S. commn. UNESCO; past mem. exec. com. Fla. Am. Revolution Bicentennial Commn., James E. Scott Community Assn. Past trustee Cultural Alliance Greater Miami, United Way Dade County, Council Internat. Visitors, Fla. Council 100, Internat. Center, Miami, Fla. Hist. Soc., Community TV Found. S. Fla., Third Century U.S.A., Mus. Sci. and Space Transit Planetarium; past mem. planning adv. bd. Capital Improvement Commn. Met. Dade County. Named Outstanding Young Man of Bowling Green, 1966; One of 10 Outstanding Young Men of Am., U.S. Jr. C. of C., 1971, Outstanding Young Man of Achievement, 1965; recipient Silver Anvil award Pub. Relations Soc. Am., 1964; Spl. Appreciation award for outstanding contbns. to Fla., 1968; Certificate of Merit award Edinboro State Coll., 1972; Diamond Jubilee Celebration award City of Miami, 1971; 1st Ann. Service award N.O.W.; Man of Year award Phi Delta Kappa, 1972; Community Service award Christian Migrant Assn., 1973; Medal of Honor, Acción Pro Darien Soc., Colombia, 1973; Distinguished Service award Marshall U. Alumni Assn., 1973; Distinguished Alumnus award Bowling Green State U., 1975. Mem. Am. Assn. Higher Edn., Internat. Assn. U. Pres.'s, Young Pres.'s Orgn., So. Assn. Colls. and Schs., Fla. C. of C., Pi Sigma Alpha, Alpha Kappa Delta, Phi Delta Kappa. Address: Golden Bear Inc 1208 US Hwy #1 North Palm Beach FL 33408

PERRY, CHARLES OWEN, sculptor; b. Helena, Mont., Oct. 19, 1929; s. Owen Hindmarch and Margaret Carroll (Bache) P.; student Columbia U., 1953; M.Arch., Yale U., 1958; m. Sheila Alicia Henry, June 22, 1962; children—Paul, Carlo, Daniela, Patrick, Marc. Architect, Skidmore Owings & Merrill, San Francisco, 1958-64, Prix de Rome Architecture, 1964-66; one-man shows: Hansen Gallery, San Francisco, 1964, Waddell Gallery, N.Y.C., 1967, 70, Dartmouth Coll., 1973, Arts Club, Chgo., 1973; group shows include: Whitney Mus., 1964, 66, Spoleto Festival, 1967, Venice Biennale, 1970, Quadrienalle di Arte de Roma, 1977; represented in permanent collections: Mus. Modern Art, N.Y.C., Art Inst. Chgo., San Francisco Mus. Art, Dartmouth Coll., U. Mich. Served with U.S. Army, 1951-53. Decorated Bronze star. Fellow Am. Acad. Rome; mem. Sculptors Guild. Roman Catholic. Club: Century Assn. (N.Y.C.). Address: Shorehaven Rd Norwalk CT 06855

PERRY, DOUGLAS, opera singer; B.M., Wittenberg U.; M.A., Ball State U. Apprentice artist Santa Fe; debut with N.Y.C. Opera as Don Basilio in Marriage of Figaro; other roles include King Kaspar in Amahl and the Night Visitors, Timothy in Help! Help! The Globolinks, the Tenor in Opera, The Sec. in Melasine; featured soloist on tours and recordings with Gregg Smith Singers and Camerata Singers; with Sante Fe Opera, 1966—; also performed with Ft. Worth Opera, Chatauqua Opera, N.Y.C. Opera, Opera Co. of Boston, Houston Grand Opera, Balt. Opera. Recordings: Celestial Country, Music of Heinrich Schutz, The Mother of US AU-Thaddeus Stevens. Address: 170 West End Ave New York NY 10023

PERRY, EDMUND FRANKLIN, educator; b. Chickamauga, Ga., May 18, 1923; s. James McDaniel and Rubye (Griffin) P.; student Reinhardt Jr. Coll., 1942; A.B., U. Ga., 1944; B.D., Emory U., 1946; Ph.D., Northwestern U., 1950; D.Litt. (hon.), U. Ceylon, 1968; m. Lena Bowers, Dec. 22, 1946; children—Stephen, Philip, Peter. Ordained to ministry Meth. Ch.; student pastor, 1942-46; dir. Wesley Found., 1946-48; instr. Duke, 1950-51, asst. prof., 1951-52, dir. undergrad. studies, 1952-54; asso. prof. dept. religion Northwestern U., 1954-60, prof. religion, 1960—, chmn. dept., 1954-72, 78—, on leave as Fulbright prof. comparative religions Vidyodaya U. of Ceylon, 1967-68. Chmn., Internat. Studies Council, 1973-75; dir. Richter Internat. Scholars Program, 1974-76. Mem.-at-large Univ. Senate of Meth. Ch., 1956-60, chmn. gen. faculty com., 1970-71; exec. dir. Soc. Buddhist-Christian Friends, 1968—; chmn. exec. com. N.Am. Ecumenical Inst., 1958-60; chmn. Bd. Ministerial Tng. and Qualifications of Meth. Ch., 1964-66. Chmn. exec. com. Evanston Human Relations Commn., 1966-67. Trustee Kendall Coll., 1966-78, John Wesley Theol. Inst., 1974—. Mem. Am. Soc. Study Religions, Internat. Assn. History Religions, Am. Acad. Religion, Am. Theol. Soc. (pres. 1975-76), Am. Oriental Soc., Am. Civil Liberties Union, Am. Assn. U. Profs. (pres. chpt. 1971-72), Inst. Religion and Ethics (trustee). Author: Confessing the Gospel Mark Preached, 1957; The Gospel in Dispute, 1958. Co-editor: Buddhist Studies in Honour of Walpola Rahula, 1979; editorial bd. Jour. Religion and the Religions. Contbr. chpts.-to books, articles to book revs. periodicals. Home: 2036 Ewing Ave Evanston IL 60201

PERRY, ELEANOR BAYER, author; m. Frank Perry. Author play Third Best Sport; screen plays David and Lisa, 1963, Ladybug, Ladybug, 1964, Last Summer, 1969, The Swimmer, 1968, Trilogy, 1968, Diary of a Mad Housewife, 1970, The Lady in the Car, 1970, (with Truman Capote) A Christmas Memory, 1966, The Man Who Loved Cat Dancing, 1973; author: Blue Pages, 1978. Address: care Writers Guild Am 8955 Beverly Blvd Los Angeles CA 90048*

PERRY, ERMA JACKSON MCNEIL, journalist; b. Winthrop, Mass.; d. Hooper Martyn and Henrietta D. (Jackson) McNeil; B.S., Boston U., 1936; m. Irving C. Perry, Apr. 29, 1939; children—Dorothy Gayle Perry Toy, Irving C. With Phila. Daily News, 1954-56; feature writer Phila. Inquirer, 1956, Phila. Bull., 1963—; syndicated writer Copley News Service, San Diego, 1967—; v.p. Arkwright-Boston Ins. Co.; free-lance contbr. nat. mags., newspapers. Mem. women's com. Internat. House, 1951-56; mem. Friends Social Order Com., 1956-66, Friends Prison Service Com., 1965-67; trustee Phila. Center Older People, 1960-67; mem. bd. Quaker Women, 1964-69. Named hon. citizen Tex., 1972; winner nat. article writing contest Writer's Digest Mag., 1971, 72. Mem. Bucks County Writers (pres. 1970), Phila. Pub. Relations Assn., Soc. Am. Travel Writers (Photography award 1979), Am. Soc. Journalists and Authors. Quaker. Clubs: Jenkintown Women's (sec. 1964-66); Mfrs. Golf and Country (Oreland, Pa.); N. Conway Country. Address: 134 Greenwood Ave Jenkintown PA 19046 also West Side Rd North Conway NH 03860

PERRY, EUGENE RUSSELL, mfg. co. exec., chem. engr.; b. Independence, Mo., Sept. 11, 1905; s. William Frederick and Flora (Leachman) P.; A.B. in Chemistry, Hastings (Nebr.) Coll., 1926; M.S. in Chemistry, Carnegie Inst. Tech., 1927; postgrad. U. Pitts., 1927-29; m. Anne Margaret Orr, June 19, 1929; 1 son, Peter W. Engring. mgr. Micarta div., factory supt., div. mgr. Westinghouse Electric Corp., 1929-53; pres., gen. mgr. Nat. Vulcanized Fibre Co. (now NVF Co.), Wilmington, Del., 1953—, pres., 1953-70, chmn., 1966-67, chief exec. officer, 1967-70, vice chmn., 1970-73, asst. to chmn., 1974—; dir. DWG Corp., Southeastern Pub. Service Co., Sharon Steel Co. Bd. dirs. Wilmington YMCA, Delmarva council Boy Scouts Am. Mem. Del. C. of C. (dir.), Am. Chem. Soc., Nat. Elec. Mfrs. Assn. (past pres., dir.), NAM. Presbyn. Rotarian. Home: Kendal at Longwood Box 82

Kennett Square PA 19348 Office: 501 W 11th St Wilmington DE 19801

PERRY, FRANK, motion picture dir.; b. N.Y.C., 1930; m. Barbara Goldsmith. Apprentice Conn. County Playhouse, Westport, then stage mgr., prodn. mgr., mng. dir.; dir. Actors Studio, 1955-79, Theatre Guild, 1956-60; dir. films David and Lisa, 1963, Last Summer, 1969, Ladybug, Ladybug, 1964, The Swimmer, 1968, Trilogy, 1968, Diary of a Mad Housewife, 1970, Doc, 1971, Play It as It Lays, 1972, Man on a Swing, 1974, Rancho Deluxe, 1975, A Christmas Memory-Truman Capote, Thanksgiving Visitors, Dummy, 1978; author screenplay Matinee, 1978; dir. Broadway prodn. Ladies At The Alamo, 1978; pres. F.P. Films, Inc. Trustee Actor's Studio, 1978—. Served with AUS, 1952-54. Recipient Peabody award, 1st prize Venice Film Festival, 1st prize Mar del Puata Film Festival, Acad. Award nomination for best dir., Emmy Award nomination for best dir. Mem. Dirs. Guild of Am., Writers Guild of Am. Author screenplays: Irwin Shaw's Nightwork, David Waggoner's The Road to Many A Wonder and others. Address: care Frank Pervy Films 667 Madison Ave New York NY 10021

PERRY, GAYLORD JACKSON, profl. baseball player; b. Williamston, N.C., Sept. 15, 1938; ed. Campbell Coll. Pitcher San Francisco Giants, 1962-71, Cleve. Indians, 1972-75, Tex. Rangers, 1975—. Recipient Cy Young Meml. award Am. League, 1972; Cy Young award Nat. League, 1978; mem. Nat. League All-Star team, 1966, 70, Am. League All-Star team, 1972, 74. Author: Me and the Spitter: An Autobiographical Confession, 1974. Address: Arlington Stadium PO Box 1111 1500 Copeland Rd Arlington TX 76010*

PERRY, GEORGE MCDONALD, food co. exec.; b. Bury, Eng., Nov. 12, 1921; s. Robert and Rose (McDonald) P.; came to U.S., 1923; naturalized, 1929; B.S. in Indsl. Mgmt., U. R.I., 1943; M.S. in Bus. Adminstrn., Columbia U., 1947; m. Blenda Cheshire, May 13, 1943; children—Jordice, Beth, Robert. Engr., Western Electric Co., N.Y.C., 1947-49; with Gen. Foods Corp., 1949-70, v.p., gen. mgr. Birds Eye, 1966-67, group v.p. food services, 1967-70; pres. Dobbs Life Savers, Inc., N.Y.C., 1970—; group v.p., dir. Squibb Corp., N.Y.C., 1970—. Served with USAAF, 1943-46. Mem. Tau Kappa Epsilon. Home: 21 Canoe Trail Darien CT 06820 Office: 40 W 57th St New York City NY 10019

PERRY, HAROLD OTTO, dermatologist; b. Rochester, Minn., Nov. 18, 1921; s. Oliver and Hedwig Clara (Tornow) P.; A.A., Rochester Jr. Coll., 1942; B.S., U. Minn., 1944, M.B., 1946, M.D., 1947; B.S. in Dermatology, Mayo Grad. Sch. Medicine, 1953; m. Loraine Thelma Moehnke, Aug. 27, 1944; children—Preston, Oliver, Ann, John. Intern, Naval Hosp., Oakland, Calif., 1946-47; resident in dermatology Mayo Grad. Sch. Medicine, 1949-52; practice medicine specializing in dermatology, Rochester, 1953—; mem. staff Mayo Clinic, 1953—; instr., asst. prof., asso. prof. Mayo Med. Sch., 1953-70, prof., 1970-78, Robert H. Kieckhefer prof. dermatology, 1978—, head dept. dermatology, 1975—. Served with USN, 1943-45, 46-49. Mem. AMA, Am. Acad. Dermatology (v.p. 1976), Am. Dermatol. Soc., Noah Worcester Dermatol. Soc. (pres. 1969), Minn. Dermatol. Soc. (pres. 1967), Chgo. Dermatol. Soc., Internat. Soc. Tropical Dermatology, Minn. Med. Assn., French Dermatol. Soc. (hon.), Spanish Acad. Dermatology (hon.), Brazilian Dermatol. Soc. (hon.), Ga. Dermatol. Soc. (hon.), Iowa Dermatol. Soc. (hon.). Contbr. articles to med. jours. and chpts. to books. Home: 3625 SW Bamber Valley Rd Rochester MN 55901 Office: Mayo Clinic Rochester MN 55901

PERRY, HAROLD TYNER, dentist, educator; b. Bismarck, N.D., Jan. 26, 1926; s. Harold Tyner and Isabel (McGillis) P.; student Bismarck Jr. Coll., 1946-47, U. N.D., 1948; D.D.S., Northwestern U., 1952; m. Mary Lynn Moss, 1952; children—Harold Tyner III, Dana Lynn. USPHS research fellow, 1952-56; practice dentistry, Elgin, Ill., 1956—; faculty Northwestern U. Dental Sch., 1954—, prof., chmn. dept. orthodontics, 1961—; research asso. Mooseheart (Ill.) Hosp.; guest lectr. U. Nebr.; dental cons. Middle East sect. WHO. Dir. Union Nat. Bank & Trust Co., Elgin; cons. VA. Bd. dirs. Fox Valley council Boy Scouts Am., Elgin YMCA; bd. govs. United Community Fund, Elgin. Served with inf., AUS, 1944-46; ETO. Decorated Bronze Star medal, Combat Inf. badge, Croix de Guerre; named Young Man of Year, Elgin Jr. C. of C., 1961. Fellow Internat., Am. colls. dentists, Inst. Medicine Chgo.; mem. ADA, Am. Assn. Orthodonists, AAAS, Sigma Xi, Alpha Tau Omega, Delta Sigma Delta, Omicron Kappa Upsilon. Methodist. Club: Elgin Riverside. Home: 413 N Alfred St Elgin IL 60120 Office: 100 E Chicago St Elgin IL 60120

PERRY, HART, investment banking exec.; b. York, Nebr., June 18, 1918; s. Benton and Elizabeth (Hart) P.; M.A. in Polit. Sci. and Econs., U. Chgo., 1940; LL.D., U. Nebr., 1967; m. Beatrice Gaidzik, Aug. 30, 1941; 1 son, Hart II. With U.S. housing agys., 1941-46; sec. Am. Community Builders, Inc., Park Forest, Ill., 1946-51; with U.S. Bur. Budget, 1951-57; with Devel. Loan Fund, 1957-61, dep. mng. dir., 1960-61; pres. ITT Credit Corp. subs. ITT, 1961-62, dir., 1964—, treas. parent co., 1963, sr. v.p., treas., dir., 1964-72, exec. v.p. fin., treas., 1966-67, exec. v.p. fin., 1967-73; pres., chief exec. officer, dir. Sogen-Swiss Internat. Corp., N.Y.C., 1973—; chmn. bd. Energy Assets Internat. Corp., N.Y.C. dir. Syracuse China Co. Trustee Bard Coll., U. Chgo. Served with AUS, 1943-46. Recipient Honor award exceptional service Devel. Loan Fund, 1961; Profl. Achievement award U. Chgo., 1970; Bard medal, 1978. Mem. Council Fgn. Relations, Asia Soc. (treas., trustee), Fgn. Policy Assn. (past dir.), Alpha Delta Phi. Democrat. Congregationalist. Clubs: Econ., River (N.Y.C.); Edgewood (Tivoli, N.Y.). Office: Energy Assets Internat Corp 405 Lexington Ave Suite 3104 New York NY 10017

PERRY, J. WARREN, univ. dean; b. Richmond, Ind., Oct. 25, 1921; s. Charles Thomas and Zona M. (Ohler) P.; B.A., DePauw U., 1944; postgrad. Harvard, 1948-49; M.A., Northwestern U., 1952, Ph.D., 1955. Instr., St. John's Mil. Acad., Delafield, Wis., 1944-47; counselor, asst. prof. psychology U. Ill. at Chgo., 1953-56; dir. prosthetic-orthotic edn., asst. prof. orthopaedic surgery Northwestern U. Med. Sch., 1957-61; lectr. psychology U. Chgo., 1957-61; asst. chief div. tng. Vocational Rehab. Adminstrn., HEW, 1961-64, dep. asst. commr. research and tng., 1964-66; prof. health scis. adminstrn. State U. N.Y. at Buffalo, 1966—, dean Sch. Health Related Professions, 1966-77. Mem. Task Force for Legislation for Allied Health Professions; mem. com. edn. allied health professions and services, council med. edn. A.M.A., 1968-73; mem. nat. adv. com. Am. Dietetic Assn., 1970-75, chmn., 1972-75; mem. nat. rev. com., regional med. programs HEW, 1969-72; mem. Inst. Medicine, Nat. Acad. Scis., 1973—, mem. steering com. on manpower policy for primary care; mem. spl. med. adv. com. VA, 1974-77; mem. task force on manpower for prevention Fogarty Internat. Inst., NIH, 1975-76; mem. acad. planning com. Mass. Gen. Hosp., 1978—. Bd. dirs. Lyric Opera Guild, Chgo., 1957-61, dir. com. opera edn., 1957-61; chmn. acad. div. drive, council of trustees Buffalo Philharmonic, 1970—; bd. dirs. Goodwill Industries Buffalo, 1969-76; trustee Community Music Sch. Buffalo, 1977—; mem. men's bd. Sisters of Charity Hosp., Buffalo, 1969—; bd. visitors U. Pitts., 1977—; mem. council trustees D'Youville Coll., Buffalo, 1978—. Recipient Sustained Superior Service award HEW, 1965; Distinguished Service award Am. Orthotics-Prosthetics Assn., 1966; Chancellor's award for adminstrv. service State U. N.Y., 1977; Disting. Author award Jour. Allied Health, 1978; Mary E. Switzer Meml. lectr., Dallas, 1977; named Ky. col., 1969, Nebr. adm., 1964. Mem. Am. Soc. Allied Health Professions (pres. 1969-70, certificate of merit 1977, Pres.'s award 1978), Am. Dietetics Assn. (hon.), Am. Psychol. Assn., Am. Personnel and Guidance Assn., Nat. Rehab. Assn., Phi Beta Kappa, Phi Delta Kappa (pres. 1955), Delta Tau Delta. Contbr. articles to profl. jours. Editor: Jour. Allied Health, 1972-78.

PERRY, JACQUELIN, orthopedic surgeon; b. Denver, May 31, 1918; d. John F. and Tirzah (Kuruptkat) P.; B.E., U. Calif., Los Angeles, 1940; M.D., U. Calif., San Francisco, 1950. Intern, Children's Hosp., San Francisco, 1950-57; resident in orthopedic surgery U. Calif., San Francisco, 1951-55; orthopedic surgeon Rancho Los Amigos Hosp., Downey, Calif., 1955—, chief pathokinesiology, 1968—, chief stroke service, 1972-75; mem. faculty U. Calif. Med. Sch., San Francisco, 1966—, clin. prof., 1973—; mem. faculty U. So. Calif. Med. Sch., 1969—, prof. orthopedic surgery, 1972—; Distinguished lectr. for hosp. for spl. surgery and Cornell U. Med. Coll., N.Y.C., 1977-78; Packard Meml. lectr. U. Colo. Med. Sch., 1970; Osgood lectr. Harvard Med. Sch., 1978; Sumner lectr., Portland, 1977; cons. USAF; guest speaker symposia. Served as phys. therapist U.S. Army, 1941-46. Named Woman of Year for Medicine in So. Calif., Los Angeles Times, 1959. Mem. Am. Acad. Orthopedic Surgeons (Kappa Delta award for research 1977), Am., Western orthopedic assns., AMA, Calif., Los Angeles County med. socs., Am. Phys. Therapy Assn. (hon. Golden Pen award 1965), Am. Acad. Orthotists and Prosthetists (hon.), Scoliosis Research Soc., LeRoy Abbott Soc., Am. Acad. Cerebral Palsy. Home: 12319 Brock Ave Downey CA 90242 Office: 7601 Imperial Hwy Downey CA 90242

PERRY, JOHN DOUGLAS, educator; b. Jeffersonville, Ind., July 4, 1901; s. Claud Walter and Anna Mary (McCauley) P.; A.B., Butler U., 1926; A.M., U. Chgo., 1932; student U. Pa., 1936-41; m. Billie Nash, Nov. 17, 1922 (div. 1926); m. 2d, Miriam Cosand, Dec. 23, 1933 (dec. Oct. 1958); children—Judith Anne (Mrs. Arthur McCaffrey), John Douglas; m. 3d, Elizabeth Savidge Rodewald, Aug. 11, 1962. Newspaper writer, editor Ky. News Bur., 1919, Indpls. Star, 1926, 36, 42, 43, Indpls. News, 1927, Capitol News Service, 1930, Phila. Evening Bull., 1944; pastor Disciples of Christ chs., 1922-24; instr., asst. prof., asso. prof. and head dept. journalism Butler U., 1927-36; lectr. Indpls. Coll. Pharmacy, 1931-33; asst. prof., asso. prof., prof. and chmn. dept. journalism and communications Temple U., 1937-68, prof. emeritus, 1968—, acting dean Sch. Communications and Theater, 1966-68, univ. historian, 1970-78; vis. prof. journalism Ind. U., 1955, Rider Coll., Trenton, N.J., 1968-70; pub. relations cons.; NBC journalist covering Dem. and Rep. Nat. Convs., 1952. Recipient Lindback Found. award (teaching), 1961. Mem. Am. Soc. Journalism Sch. Adminstrs. (pres. 1954), Assn. Edn. Journalism, Phila. Regional Writers Conf. (dir. 1956-59), Sigma Delta Chi (dir. Greater Phila. Profl. chpt. 1962-69), Phi Kappa Phi, Kappa Tau Alpha, Pi Delta Epsilon, Sigma Pi. Mem. Soc. Friends. Author: The People's University, Temple's First Eighty Years. News editor: Journalism Educator, 1958-61; asso. editor Econs. and Bus. Bull., 1963-66. Home: 9 Hathaway Circle Wynnewood PA 19096 Office: Temple U Philadelphia PA 19122

PERRY, JOHN HOLLIDAY, JR., newspaper exec.; b. Seattle, Jan. 2, 1917; s. John Holliday and Dorothy Lilly P.; A.B., Yale U., 1939; postgrad. Harvard Sch. Bus. Adminstrn., 1940; m. Jeanne See, 1946 (div. 1966); children—John Holliday III, Henry A., Stanton See; m. 2d, Marina Rosati, Nov. 5, 1966; children—Christiana, Francesca, Alessandra. Chmn. bd. Perry Oceanographics, Inc., Martin County Cable TV, Perry Submarine Builders, Perry Ocean Products, Inc., Palm Beach Cable TV, St. Lucie Cable Co., Inc.; pres. Bahama Pubs. Ltd., Bahamas Undersea Research Found., Perry Found., Fiscal Policy Council; v.p. Perry Communications, Inc.; former mem. Pres.'s Commn. on Marine Scis., Engring. and Resources; mem. Am. Bur. Shipping, Caribbean Conservation Corp, Fla. Commn. Marine Scis. and Tech., Sea Space Symposium. Trustee, Internat. Oceanographic Found. Commd. 1st lt. USAAF, 1942-45. Mem. Inter Am. Press Assn. (dir. 1959-69), Zeta Psi. Presbyterian. Clubs: Racquet and Tennis (N.Y.C.); Bath and Tennis, Everglades, Beach (Palm Beach, Fla.). Author: The National Dividend. Office: Perry Oceanographics Inc 100 E 17th St Riviera Beach FL 33404. *Two principle thoughts have always governed my life. First, always put more into life than you take out. Second, make decisions based on a hierarchy of values which puts wisdom at the top.*

PERRY, JOHN RICHARD, educator; b. Lincoln, Nebr., Jan. 16, 1943; s. Ralph Robert and Ann (Roscow) P.; B.A., Doane Coll., 1964; Ph.D. (Woodrow Wilson fellow 1964, Danforth fellow 1964-68), Cornell U., 1968; m. Louise French, Mar. 31, 1962; children—James, Sarah, Joseph. Asst. prof. philosophy UCLA, 1968-72, asso. prof., 1972-74; asso. prof. Stanford U., 1974-77, prof., chmn. dept. philosophy, 1977—. Bd. dirs. Ocean Park Community Center, 1971-72; pres. Santa Monica Democratic Club, 1973-74. Guggenheim fellow, 1975-76. Mem. Am. Philos. Assn., AAUP. Author: A Dialogue on Personal Identity and Immortality, 1978. Home: 545 Hilbar Palo Alto CA 94303 Office: 91B Stanford U Stanford CA 94305*

PERRY, JOSEPH EARL, ret. banker, lawyer; b. Shelburne Falls, Mass., Dec. 30, 1884; s. Joseph Charles and Miriam Holbrook (Packard) P.; A.B. Williams Coll., 1906; J.D., Harvard U., 1909; B.B.A., Boston U., 1922; m. Bessie Luella Stanford, June 24, 1911 (dec. Oct. 1968); children—Miriam Elizabeth Perry Bell, Joseph Earl, Walter Stanford; m. 2d, Florence S. Kuhn, May 24, 1969. Admitted to Mass. bar, 1908; practiced law, Boston, 1909—; income tax assessor Mass. State, 1917-19; mem. Mass. Ho. of Reps., 1925-30, chmn. com. on taxation and on constl. law, vice chmn. recess com. on taxation; commr. banks State of Mass., 1940-44; pres. Newton Savs. Bank, 1944-59; chmn. Mass. Bd. Bank Inc., 1940-44; sometime mem. faculty Boston U., Northeastern U., Grad. Sch. Banking, Rutgers U. Mem. Belmont Sch. Com., 1919-22; pres. Mass., R.I. State assns. YMCA, 1936-37; mem. budget com. Newton Community Chest, 1944; incorporator New Eng. Deaconess Hosp.; bd. dirs. Nat. Thrift Assn.; nat. bd. field advisers Fed. Small Bus. Adminstrn. Pres., Nat. Assn. Suprs. State Banks, 1943; mem. council Harvard Law Sch. Assn., 1942-44; trustee Boston U., 1946-64, hon. trustee, 1964—, mem. exec. com., 1953-64, treas., 1954-57; trustee DeMolay Found. Mass., Internat. Coll., Beirut; trustee, pres. Masonic Edn. and Charity Trust. Mem. Mass. Savs. Bank Life Ins. Council (pres. 1949-50), Am. Bankers Assn. (pres. savs. and mortgage div. 1951-52, mem. exec. council 1951-52), Newton Bankers Assn. (pres. 1951-52, Boston Execs. Assn. (charter), Phi Kappa Assn. Greater Boston (past sec.), Beta Gamma Sigma (hon.). Methodist (chmn. bd. trustees, hon. chmn. 50th anniversary com.). Mason (33 deg., grand master Mass. 1938-40, dir. grand lodge Mass., only Western Hemisphere Mason to have official part in Duke of Kent installation as Eng. Grand Master by King George VI, London, 1939), Rotarian (past pres.). Author: The Masonic Way of Life, 1968; also many articles and brochures on law, banking and masonry. Home: 18 Holt St Belmont MA 02178

PERRY, JOSEPH SAMUEL, judge; b. Carbon Hill, Ala., Nov. 30, 1896; s. Barnabas Jackson and Mary (Brown) P.; A.B., U. Ala., 1923; M.A., U. Chgo., 1925, J.D., 1927; m. Nelle Brookman, June 9, 1928; children—John Thomas, Maribeth Ann. Admitted to Ill. bar, 1927; coal miner, farmer, tchr. country schs., Brilliant, Ala., 1910-17; tchr. high sch., Mobile, 1923-24, Riverside (Ill.)-Brookfield High Sch., 1926-28; with Legal Aid Bur. United Charities, Chgo., summer 1928; asso. Cannon & Poague, 1928-29, Dunbar & Rich, 1929-33; master in chancery DuPage County, Wheaton, Ill., 1933-37; also pvt. law practice; mem. Ill. Gen. Assembly 41st Senatorial Dist., 1937-43; mem. Perry & Elliott, Wheaton, 1943-51; pub. adminstr. DuPage County, 1949-51; U.D. dist. judge, 1951—, Chmn. DuPage County Democratic Central Com., 1934-42. Served as q.m. U.S. Navy, landing force duties, N. Russia, 1918, Near East service, 1919. Mem. Am., Ill., DuPage County bar assns., V.F.W., Am. Legion (judge adv. DuPage County), 40 et 8, Phi Beta Kappa. Episcopalian. Mason (32 deg., Shriner). Home: Riford Rd Glen Ellyn IL 60137 Office: US Ct House 219 S Dearborn St Chicago IL 60604

PERRY, JOSEPH WILLIAM, ret. ins. co. exec.; b. Youngstown, Ohio, Apr. 25, 1903; s. John William and Clara (Boyer) P.; student Ohio State U., 1921-25; m. Katherine Tansey, July 17, 1943; 1 son, Joseph William. With Ohio State Jour., Columbus, 1925-28; sales promoter RCA, 1928-31; with Western and So. Life Ins. Co., Cin., 1931-76, sec., 1956-63, v.p., 1964-66, v.p., sec., 1966-76. Served to lt. comdr. USNR, 1942-46. Mem. Pi Kappa Alpha. Club: Queen City (Cin.). Home: 1130 Beverly Hills Dr Cincinnati OH 45226

PERRY, KENNETH WILBUR, educator; b. Lawrenceburg, Ky., May 21, 1919; s. Ollie Townsend and Minnie (Monroe) P.; B.S., Eastern Ky. U., 1942; M.S., Ohio U., 1949; Ph.D., U. Ill., 1953; m. Shirley Jane Kimball, Sept. 5, 1942; 1 dau., Constance June (Mrs. Linden Warfel). Instr., Berea Coll., 1949-50, U. Ky., summer 1950; teaching asst. U. Ill. at Champaign, 1950-53, asst. prof. accounting, 1953-55, asso. prof., 1955-58, prof., 1958—, Alexander Grant prof., 1975—; vis. prof. Northeastern U., summer 1966, Parsons Coll., 1966-67, Fla. A. and M. U., fall 1971; Carman G. Blough prof. U. Va., fall 1975; dir. Illini Pub. Co. Served to maj. AUS, 1942-46; col. Res. ret. Named outstanding alumnus Eastern Ky. U., 1969. C.P.A., Ill. Mem. Am. Accounting Assn. (v.p. 1963, Outstanding Educator award 1974), Am. Inst. C.P.A.'s, Am. Statis. Assn., Nat. Assn. Accountants (dir. 1969-71), Ill. Soc. C.P.A.s (chair in accountancy), Beta Alpha Psi, Beta Gamma Sigma (Distinguished scholar 1977-78), Omicron Delta Kappa. Methodist. Author: Accounting: An Introduction, 1971; Passing the C.P.A. Examination, 1964; (with N. Bedford and A. Wyatt) Advanced Accounting, 1960; contbg. author: Complete Guide to a Profitable Accounting Practice, 1965; C.P.A. Review Manual, 1971. Editor The Ill. C.P.A., 1968-70; contbg. editor Accountants' Cost Handbook, 1960. Home: 2314 Fields South Dr Champaign IL 61820 Office: Commerce W U Ill Champaign IL 61820

PERRY, LEE ROWAN, lawyer; b. Chgo., Sept. 23, 1933; s. Watson Bishop and Helen (Rowan) P.; B.A., U. Ariz., 1944, LL.B., 1961; m. Barbara Ashcraft Mitchell, July 2, 1955; children—Christopher, Constance, Geoffrey. Admitted to Ariz. bar, 1961, since practiced in Phoenix; clk. Udall & Udall, Tucson, 1960-61; mem. firm Carson, Messinger, Elliott, Laughlin & Ragan, 1961—. Mem. bd. edn. Paradise Valley Elementary and High Sch. Dists., Phoenix, 1964-68, pres., 1968; treas. troop Boy Scouts Am., 1970-72; mem. Ariz. adv. bd. Girl Scouts U.S.A., 1972-74, mem. nominating bd., 1978-79; bd. dirs. Florence Crittenton Services Ariz., 1967-72, pres., 1970-72; bd. dirs. U. Ariz. Alumni, Phoenix, 1968-72, pres., 1969-70; bd. dirs. Family Service Phoenix, 1974-75, Vol. Bur. Maricopa County, 1975—, Ariz. div. Am. Cancer Soc., 1978—, Florence Crittenton div. Child Welfare League Am., 1976—; bd. dirs. Crisis Nursery for Prevention of Child Abuse, 1978—, pres., 1978-79. Served to 1st lt. USAF, 1955-58. Mem. State Bar Ariz. (conv. chmn. 1972), Am., Maricopa County bar assns., Phi Delta Phi, Phi Delta Theta (pres. 1954). Republican (precinct capt. 1970). Episcopalian (sr. warden 1968-72). Rotarian (dir. 1971—, pres. 1975-76). Club: Ariz. Mem. law rev. staff U. Ariz., 1959-61. Office: United Bank Bldg PO Box 33907 Phoenix AZ 85067

PERRY, LOUIS BARNES, ins. co. exec.; b. Los Angeles, Mar. 4, 1918; s. Louis Henry and Julia (Stoddard) P.; B.A., U. Calif. at Los Angeles, 1938, M.A., 1940, Ph.D., 1950; fellow econs. Yale, 1941; LL.D., Pacific U., 1964; L.H.D., Whitman Coll., 1967; D.C.S., Willamette U., 1977; m. Genevieve Patterson, Feb. 8, 1942; children—Robert Barnes, Barbara Ann, Donna Lou. Teaching asst. U. Calif. at Los Angeles, 1940-41, research teaching asst., 1946-47; faculty Pomona Coll., 1947-59, asst. to pres., 1955-57, prof. econs., 1957-59; pres. Whitman Coll., Walla Walla, Wash., 1959-67; v.p., treas. Standard Ins. Co., Portland, Oreg., 1967-68, exec. v.p., 1968-71, pres., 1972—, also dir. Dir. 1st Nat. Bank Oreg., Pacific Power & Light Co., Oreg. Portland Cement Co., Tektronix, Inc., Willamette Industries, N.W. Energy Co.; investment counselor, broker Wagenseller & Durst, Los Angeles, 1951-59; research coordinator So. Calif. Research Council, 1952-54; cons. Carnegie Survey Bus. Edn., 1957-58. Pres. Oreg. Bd. Higher Edn. Served to maj. AUS, World War II; lt. col. Res. Mem. Am. Coll. Life Underwriters (trustee), Am. Econ. Assn., Phi Beta Kappa, Phi Delta Kappa, Pi Gamma Mu, Alpha Gamma Omega, Artus. Methodist. Rotarian. Club: Arlington (Portland). Author: (with others) Our Needy Aged, 1954; A History of the Los Angeles Labor Movement, 1963. Contbr. articles to profl. jours. Home: 1238 SW Davenport St Portland OR 97201 Office: 1100 SW 6th St Portland OR 97207. *In looking back over the years, an unspoken and oftentime subliminal guiding principle has been to reach beyond one's realistic grasp. This concept coupled with an interest in treating others as one would like to be treated has made it possible to react to new challenges. Successfully meeting the latter has provided a varied career in a number of different fields of activity.*

PERRY, MARGARET NUTT, ednl. adminstr.; b. Waynesboro, Tenn., Apr. 23, 1940; d. Trester S. and Evelyn M. (Brewer) Nutt; B.S., U. Tenn. at Martin, 1961; M.S. (NDEA fellow), U. Tenn. at Knoxville, 1963, Ph.D., 1965; m. Randy L. Perry, Oct. 30, 1965; children—Paul Andrew and Samuel Jason. Asst. prof., asst. to dean Coll. Home Econs., U. Tenn., Knoxville, 1966-67, asst. prof., asst. dean, 1967-68, asso. dean, 1968-73, dean for grad. studies, 1973-79; asso. v.p. for acad. affairs Tenn. Technol. U., Cookeville, 1979—. Mem. exec. com. Conf. So. Grad. Schs. Bd. dirs. Knoxville Early Child Devel. Center. Mem. Council Grad. Schs. (exec. com.), Am., Tenn. home econs. assns., Inst. Food Technologists, Assn. Home Econs. Adminstrs., Sigma Xi, Omicron Nu. Office: Box 5316 Tenn Technol University Cookeville TN 38501

PERRY, MARVIN BANKS, JR., coll. pres.; b. Powhatan, Va., Sept. 29, 1918; s. Marvin Banks and Elizabeth (Gray) P.; A.B., U. Va., 1940; A.M., Harvard, 1941, Ph.D., 1950; LL.D., Washington Coll., 1967, Washington and Lee U., 1977; D.Litt., Oglethorpe U., 1978; m. Ellen Coalter Gilliam, Apr. 6, 1950; children—Elizabeth Gray, Margaret McCluer. Grad. asst. Harvard, 1946-47; instr. English, U. Va., 1947-51, prof. English, dean admissions, 1960-67; asst. prof. English, Washington and Lee U., 1951-53, asso. prof., 1953-56, prof., chmn. dept., 1956-60; pres. Goucher Coll., Towson, Md., 1967-73, Agnes Scott Coll., Decatur, Ga., 1973—; mem. Polish Seminar (Dept. State), U. Krakow, Poland, 1966. Past trustee Mary Baldwin Coll., Gilman Sch., Bryn Mawr Sch., Md. Acad. Sci., Balt. Symphony Orch.; trustee Atlanta Arts Alliance, Lovett Sch. Served to lt. USNR, 1942-46; comdr. Res. Mem. Modern Lang. Assn. Am., Coll. English Assn. (past dir., past pres. N.C.-Va.), Assn. Pvt. Colls. and Univs. in Ga., Keats-Shelley Assn. Am., Bibliog. Soc. U. Va., Raven Soc., Phi Beta Kappa, Omicron Delta Kappa, Phi Gamma Delta. Presbyn. (elder). Rotarian. Clubs: Executive (Decatur); Hamilton St. (Balt.); Colonnade (U. Va.); Harvard (N.Y.C.). Author, editor: Modern Minds, 1949; Nine Short Novels, 1952. Contbr. articles profl. jours. Address: Agnes Scott Coll Decatur GA 30030

PERRY, MERVYN F., investment co. exec.; b. Brockton, Mass., Feb. 20, 1923; s. Mervyn Elsworth and Marie (Therien) P.; A.B., Boston U., 1950, J.D., 1951; m. Marian D. Sprong, June 9, 1949; children—Richard Caverhill, Cynthia B., Susan Van Dake, Janet Horton. Mgr., Conn. Gen. Life Ins. Co., Cleve., 1956-62; v.p., dir. Mass. Gen. Life Ins. Co., Boston, 1962-65; pres., chief exec. officer, dir. Mass. Co. Distbr., Inc., Boston, 1965-69; pres., chmn. bd., chief exec. officer Mass. Fund for Income, 1973-78; pres., chief exec. officer, dir. Mass. Co., Inc., to 1978; chmn. bd., pres., chief exec. officer, dir. Independence Fund, Inc., Freedom Fund, Inc.; chmn. bd., dir. T.M.C. Ins. Agy., Inc.; pres., dir. Massco Investment Mgmt. Corp., 1969-78, chmn. bd., 1978—, also dir.; pres., chief exec. officer Ready Reserves Trust, 1975-78; pres., chmn. bd., chief exec. officer Investment Mgmt. Assos., Inc., Denver, 1978—. Served with USNR, 1942-45, USAAF, 1946-48. Episcopalian. Mason. Clubs: Union, University (Boston); Aspen (Colo.); Pinehurst Country (Denver). Home: 4725 W Quincy Ave Denver CO 80236 Office: 5600 S Syracuse Circle Englewood CO 80111

PERRY, MURVIN HENRY, educator; b. Bruce, S.D., Apr. 28, 1922; s. Earl Henry and Lorraine (Eichel) P.; B.S., S.D. State Coll., 1950; M.A., U. Iowa, 1954, Ph.D. in Mass Communications, 1959; m. Rita Clare Kaefring, Aug. 23, 1952; children—Gail, Mark, Scott, Todd, Chris. High sch. tchr., Gregory, S.D., 1947-48; publicist, tchr. S.D. State Coll., 1949-51; with VA, 1952-56; asst. to dir. Sch. Journalism, State U. Iowa, 1956-59; asst. prof. journalism Kans. State U., 1950-69; prof., dir. journalism Kent State U., 1963-79; chmn. dept. mass communications E. Tenn. State U., Johnson City, 1979—. Served with USNR, 1943-46. Mem. Sigma Delta Chi. Home: 307 Oak Ln Johnson City TN 37601

PERRY, PERCIVAL, educator; b. Chesterfield, S.C., Aug. 30, 1916; s. William Joel and Essie (Buchanan) P.; A.B., Wake Forest Coll., 1937; A.M., Rutgers U., 1940; Ph.D., Duke, 1947; m. Margaret Erma Ruthven, Sept. 17, 1942; children—William Percival. Alexander Ruthven. Mem. faculty Wake Forest Coll., 1947—, prof. history, 1957—, dean summer session, 1960—. Served with AUS, 1942-45; ETO. Fellow history Rutgers U., 1937-39, Duke, 1941-42; fellow econs. Case Inst. Tech., summer 1952. Mem. Hist. Soc. N.C. (pres. 1968-69), So. Hist. Assn., Forest History Soc., N.C. Assn. Coll. and U. Summer Session Deans (pres. 1971-72), Phi Alpha Theta. Contbr. articles to profl. jours. Home: 121 Belle Vista Ct Winston-Salem NC 27107

PERRY, RALPH BARTON, III, lawyer; b. N.Y.C., Mar. 17, 1936; s. Ralph Barton and Harriet Armington (Seelye) P.; A.B., Harvard U., 1960; LL.B., Stanford U., 1963; m. Mary Elizabeth Colburn, Sept. 2, 1961; children—Katherine Suzanne, Daniel Berenson. Admitted to Calif. bar, 1964; asso. and mem. Keatinge & Sterling, Los Angeles, 1963-68; mem. firm Grossman Graven & Perry, Los Angeles, 1968—. Bd. dirs. Planning and Conservation League, 1968—; pres. Coalition for Clean Air, 1972—. Served with U.S. Army, 1956-58. Mem. State Bar Calif., Am., Los Angeles County bar assns., Lawyers Club Los Angeles County (gov. 1968—), Planning and Conservation League (gov. 1968—), Keep Tahoe Blue, Nat., Internat. wildlife fedns., Sierra Club. Club: Los Angeles Athletic. Home: 296 Redwood Dr Pasadena CA 91105 Office: One Wilshire Bldg Suite 2420 Los Angeles CA 90017

PERRY, RICHARD HERBERT, athletic dir.; b. Long Beach, Calif., July 13, 1929; s. Paul I. and Marguerite (Holliday) P.; B.A., Coll. Emporia (Kans.), 1951; M.S., Kans. State Tchrs. Coll., 1958; Ph.D., U. So. Calif., 1968; m. Donna Veryl Silven, Sept. 1, 1949; children—James, Joan, John, Janelle. Tchr., coach Mayetta (Kans.) Rural High Sch., 1951-52, St. John (Kans.) High Sch., 1953-55, Hays (Kans.) High Sch., 1955-56; head basketball coach, asso. prof. phys. edn., asst. football coach Calif. State Coll., Long Beach, 1958-67; asso. prof. U. So. Calif., Los Angeles, 1967—, dir. athletics, 1975—. Republican. Presbyterian. Author: Basketball: Progressive Fundamentals, 1969. Home: 6562 Pickett Ave Garden Grove CA 92645 Office: University Park Los Angeles CA 90007

PERRY, ROBERT WILLIAM, educator, mech. engr.; b. Niagara Falls, N.Y., Apr. 2, 1921; s. Robert William and Marie Elizabeth (Hirschle) P.; B.Mech. Engring., Cornell U., 1943, M.M.E., 1947, Ph.D., 1951; m. L. Esther Sheperdson, Apr. 21, 1945 (dec. Mar. 1965); 1 son, Robert William III. Mgr. hypervelocity br. Gas Dynamics Facility, Arnold Engring. Devel. Center, Tullahoma, Tenn., 1953-59; chief hyperaerodynamic research Republic Aviation Corp., Farmingdale, N.Y., 1959-65; prof. aerospace engring. Poly. Inst. Bklyn., 1965-67; sr. staff cons. Liquid Metal Engring. Center, Canoga Park, Calif., 1968-70; Henry Vogt Distinguished prof. dept. mech. engring. U. Louisville, 1971—. Mem. NASA research adv. com. for fluid mechanics, 1959-60; cons. adv. group for aerospace research and devel. NATO, Brussels, 1966. Registered profl. engr., N.Y., Tenn., Ky. Asso. fellow Am. Inst. Aeros. and Astronautics; mem. Am. Soc. M.E., Am. Phys. Soc., Ky. Soc. Profl. Engrs., Sigma Xi. Home: 8918 Marksfield Rd Louisville KY 40222

PERRY, ROGER LEE, actor; b. Davenport, Iowa, May 7, 1933; s. Lee Marion and Corrinne Norma (Miller) P.; B.A., Grinnell Coll., 1954; m. JoAnne Worley, May 11, 1975; children—Christopher, Dana. Appeared in over 200 TV shows, including: The Man with the Power, 1977, Conspiracy of Terror, 1976, Most Wanted, 1978; TV series Harrigan and Son, 1961-62, Arrest and Trial, 1963-64. Served with USAF, 1955-57. Democrat. Office: care Fred Amsel and Assos 321 S Beverly Dr Suite R Beverly Hills CA 90212

PERRY, RUFUS PATTERSON, cons.; b. Brunswick, Ga., June 4, 1903; s. Harry P. and Nannie Alice (Williams) P.; B.A., Johnson C. Smith U., 1925, LL.D., 1956; M.S., U. Iowa, 1927, Ph.D., 1939; m. Thelma Davis, Nov. 30, 1945; children—Margaret Maribeth, Dorothy Patricia. Chmn. natural sci. dept., prof., head dept. chemistry Prairie View (Tex.) A. and M. Coll., 1927-43, dir. div. arts and scis., 1939-43; adminstrv. dean, prof. chemistry, v.p. Langston U., 1943-57; pres. Johnson C. Smith U., 1957-69; cons., 1969—; pres. Perry Drug & Chem. Co., Oklahoma City, 1947—; sec.-treas. 1725 T St. Co-op. Assn., 1973—. Mem. exec. com. Council Protestant Colls. and Univs., 1963-68; v.p. Presbyn. Coll. Union, 1965, pres., 1966; 1st v.p. N.C. Council Ch. Related Colls., 1965-66; mem. adv. council N.C. Commn. Higher Edn. Facilities. Bd. dirs. United Arts Council, So. Fellowship Fund; mem. bd. nat. missions U.P. Ch. U.S.A., 1964-70, del. World Presbyn. Alliance, Frankfurt, Germany, 1964. Fellow Am. Inst. Chemists, AAAS, Okla. Acad. Sci.; mem. N.C. Acad. Sci., Am. Chem. Soc., Nat. Inst. Sci., Sigma Xi, Alpha Phi Alpha, Sigma Pi Phi. Democrat. Mason (32 deg.). Contbr. articles to profl. jours. Address: 1725 T St NW Washington DC 20009

PERRY, RUSSELL H., ins. co. exec.; b. Cornell, Ill., Nov. 8, 1908; s. Walter O. and Mabel (Hilton) P.; student N.Y. U., 1937; J.D. cum laude, Bklyn. Law Sch., 1940; D.C.L., Atlanta Law Sch., 1973; m. Phoebe Sherwood, June 2, 1956. Admitted to N.Y. bar, 1941, Tex. bar, 1963; clk. Chgo. Fire & Marine Ins. Co., 1925-32; underwriter Republic Ins. Co., N.Y.C., 1934-38, charge Eastern dept. underwriting, 1939-42, asst. to v.p., 1942-43, spl. agt. L.I., Westchester, 1943-44, mgr. Eastern dept., 1945-47, resident sec., 1947-49, v.p., 1949-59, exec. v.p., 1959-61; pres., dir. Republic Financial Services, Inc., Republic Ins. Co. Group, 1961-71, chmn. bd., pres., chief exec. officer, 1971-72, chmn. bd., chief exec. officer, 1972—; dir. KERA-TV, Dallas, Allied Finance Co., Taca, Inc., Dallas, Bonanza Internat., Inc., Met. Fed. Savs. and Loan Assn., Union Bank & Trust Co., Dallas, Ins. Information Inst.; trustee Murray Mortgage Investors, Dallas. Mem. exec. adv. council N. Tex. State U. Coll. Bus. Adminstrn.; mem. exec. com. Assn. Tex. Fire-Casualty Cos.; mem. adv. council Airline Passengers Assn. Dir. Dallas Citizens Council; chmn. exec. com. Dallas Postal Customers Council; mem. exec. com. Tex. Good Rds. Transp. Assn.; mem. Dallas Bapt. Coll. Devel. Bd.; v.p. finance Tex. Soc. Prevention Blindness. Chmn. bd. trustees Salvation Army Adv. Bd. Dallas; chmn. bd. dirs. Dallas Council on World Affairs; bd. dirs. Ins. Info. Inst.; bd. dirs. Dallas Crime Commn.; nat. bd. dirs. Am. Cancer Soc.; bd. dirs. Tex. Research League, Big Bros./Big Sisters Am., Citizen's Choice, Washington, Tex. Assn. Taxpayers, Trinity Improvement Assn.; trustee, v.p. Tex. Bur. Econ. Understanding; trustee Dallas Bar Found., Center for Internat. Bus.; bd. dirs., mem. exec. com. Dallas Citizens Council. Recipient G. Mabry Seay award Dallas Assn. Ins. Agts., 1970; Headliner of Year award Press Club of Dallas, 1975; Person of Vision award Tex. Soc. Prevention of Blindness, 1977, Linz award for Dallas civic service, 1978, Torch of Liberty award Anti-Defamation League, others. Mem. U.S. (dir., chmn. pub. affairs com., vice chmn. S.W. div.), E. Tex. (dir., past chmn.), Tex. (dir.), Dallas (chmn., dir.), N.Y. chambers commerce, Am. Ins. Assn. (dir., exec. com.), La. Ins. Adv. Assn. (exec. com.), Tex. Property and Casualty Adv. Assn. (chmn.), Tex. Catastrophe Property Ins. Assn. (dir.), Philonomic Soc., Am., N.Y. bar assns., State Bar Tex., Lawyers Club N.Y., Navy League U.S. (dir. Dallas), Philonomic Soc., Newcomen Soc. N.Am., Delta Theta Phi. Rotarian. Clubs: New York University, Insurance, Dallas Petroleum, Dallas Country, Dallas Knife and Fork (dir., mem. exec. com.), Lancers, Lawyers of N.Y., Rock Creek Barbecue; Austin, 2001 Club. Home: 3437 Gillespie St Dallas TX 75219 Office: 2727 Turtle Creek Blvd Dallas TX 75219

PERRY, SEYMOUR MONROE, oncologist-hematologist; b. N.Y.C., May 26, 1921; s. Max and Manya (Rosenthal) P.; B.A. with honors, U. Calif. at Los Angeles, 1943; M.D. with honors, U. So. Calif., 1947; m. Judith Kaplan, Mar. 18, 1951; children—Grant Matthew, Anne Lisa, David Bennett. Intern, Los Angeles County Hosp., 1946-48, resident, 1948-51, mem. staff outpatient dept., 1951; examining physician Los Angeles Pub. Schs., 1951-52; sr. asst. surgeon Phoenix Indian Gen. Hosp., USPHS, 1952; charge internal medicine USPHS Outpatient Clinic, Washington, 1952-54; fellow hematology U. Calif. at Los Angeles, 1954-55, asst. research physician atomic energy project, 1955-57, asst. prof. medicine, head Hematology Tng. Program, Med. Center, 1957-60; instr. medicine Coll. Med. Evangelists, 1951-57; attending specialist internal medicine Wadsworth VA Hosp., Los Angeles, 1958-61; sr. investigator, medicine br. Nat. Cancer Inst., 1961-65, chief medicine br., 1965-68, mem. clin. cancer tng. com., 1966-69, chief human tumor cell biology br., 1968-71, asso. sci. director clin. trials, 1966-71, asso. sci. dir. for program, div. cancer treatment, 1971-73, dep. dir., 1973-74, acting dir., 1974; spl. asst. to dir. NIH, 1974-78, asso. dir., 1978—; acting dep. asst. sec. health (tech.) and acting dir. Nat. Center Health Care Tech., OASH, 1978-80, dir., 1980—; mem. adv. com. research therapy cancer Am. Cancer Soc., 1966-70, mem. adv. com. chemotherapy and hematology, 1975-77, chmn. epidemiology, diagnosis and therapy com., 1971, grantee, 1959-60; med. dir. USPHS, 1961—; mem. radiation com. NIH, 1963-70, co-chmn., 1971-73; pres. Nat. Blood Club, 1971; chmn. Interagy. Com. on New Therapies for Pain and Discomfort, 1978—. Decorated commendador Order of Merit (Peru); Pub. Health Service commendation, 1967. Diplomate Am. Bd. Internal Medicine. Fellow A.C.P. (adv. com. to gov. Md. on coll. affairs 1969-76); mem. Am. Fedn. Clin. Research, Am. Assn. Cancer Research, Am. Soc. Hematology (chmn. leukocyte subcom. 1969-71, mem. sci. affairs com. 1969-70, chmn. 1971), AMA, Am. Soc. Clin. Oncology. Club: Cosmos. Office: Nat Insts Health Bldg 1 Bethesda MD 20205

PERRY, VINCENT ALOYSIUS, bus. exec.; b. Weehawken, N.J.; s. Edwin Robert and Florence Loretta (Gutberlet) P.; A.B., N.Y. U., 1948, M.A., 1949; m. Doris Lucille Wanckel, Dec. 3, 1944; children—Cynthia Jeanne, Bradford Kimball. Asst. prof. fin. Lehigh U., Bethlehem, Pa., 1949-51; mgr. econs. and fin. analysis div. Gen. Foods Corp., White Plains, N.Y., 1951-59; v.p., treas. Universal Match Corp., St. Louis, 1959-61; asst. treas. Internat. Paper Co., N.Y.C., 1961-71; v.p., treas. Bangor Punta Corp., Greenwich, Conn., 1971-75; fin. v.p., treas. Ziff-Davis Pub. Co., N.Y.C., 1975-77; v.p. fin. The Viguerie Co., Inc., Falls Church, Va., 1977—. Treas., Workshop for Bus. Opportunities, N.Y.C., 1969—. Served to capt. AUS, 1942-46; ETO. Mem. Lambda Chi Alpha. Club: Union League (N.Y.C.). Home: 120 Maywood Rd Darien CT 06820 Office: 7777 Leesburg Pike Falls Church VA 22043

PERRY, WILLIAM JAMES, govt. ofcl.; b. Vandergrift, Pa., Oct. 11, 1927; s. Edward Martin and Mabelle Estelle (Dunlap) P.; B.S. in Math., Stanford U., 1949, M.S., 1950; Ph.D., Pa. State U., 1957; m. Leonilla Mary Green, Dec. 29, 1947; children—David Carter, William Wick, Rebecca Lynn, Robin Lee, Mark Lloyd. Instr. math. Pa. State U., 1951-54; sr. mathematician HRB-Singer Co., State College, Pa., 1952-54; dir. electronic def. labs. GTE Sylvania Co., Mountain View, Calif., 1954-64; pres. ESL, Inc., Sunnyvale, Calif., 1964-77; tech. cons. Dept. Def., Washington, 1967-77, dir. def. research and engring., now under sec. def. for research and engring. Served with U.S. Army, 1946-47. Recipient Outstanding Civilian Service medal U.S. Army, 1962, Exceptional Civilian Service medal Def. Intelligence Agency, 1976. Mem. Am. Math. Soc., Nat. Acad. Engring., Sigma Xi. Home: 3645 N Monroe St Arlington VA 22207 Office: care Dept Def Pentagon Washington DC 20301

PERRY, YVONNE SCRUGGS, educator; b. Niagara Falls, N.Y., June 24, 1933; d. Leonard Andrew and Geneva Ellen (Byrd) Scruggs; B.A., N.C. Central U., 1955; postgrad. Free U., Berlin, 1956; M.A.P.A., U. Minn., 1958; postgrad. U. Pa., 1972-74; children—Cathryn Diane, Rebecca Scruggs. Asso. dir. Phila. Council Community Advancement, Phila., 1964-67; fed. liaison officer U.S. Model Cities, Phila., 1967-70; coordinator field research U. Pa. Human Resources Center, 1970-74, mem. faculty U. Pa., 1972-74; chmn. dept. city planning Howard U., 1974-77, 79—; dep. asst. sec. HUD, Washington, 1977-79; mem. Pennsylvania Ave. Devel. Corp.; mem. U.S. Water Resources Council; lectr. in field; fgn. lectr. USIA, Africa; del. head OECD/Paris, Urban Concerns, 1979; with Econ. Commn. Europe, Comprehensive Planning, Geneva, 1978-79; v.p. Pa. Housing Fin. Corp., 1973-74, Assn. Collegiate Schs. Planning, 1976. Recipient Leadership award Nat. Council Negro Women, 1975, Outstanding Achievement award HUD, 1979, also spl. achievement certificate, 1979; named Outstanding Planner, Am. Inst. Planners, 1978; Fulbright fellow, 1955-56. Mem. Am. Planning Assn., Nat. Assn. Planners, Pi Gamma Mu. Democrat. Office: Dept City and Regional Planning Howard U Washington DC 20059

PERRYMAN, ERIC CHARLES WILLIAM, nuclear energy co. exec.; b. Stanwell, Middlesex, Eng., Feb. 7, 1922; s. Frederick and Violet (Plow) P.; M.A., Cambridge (Eng.) U., 1943; m. Gladys Winifred Field Taylor, May 21, 1945; children—Gavin, Marcia, Anthony, Roger. Jr. research officer metallurgy dept. Royal Aircraft Establishment, Eng., 1943-46; research officer Brit. Non-Ferrous Metals Research Assn., 1946-51, Aluminum Labs. Ltd., Kingston, Ont., Can., 1951-54; with Atomic Energy of Can. Ltd., Chalk River, Ont., 1954-60, 63— (on attachment 1954-57), dir. fuels and materials, 1967-70, dir. applied research and devel., 1970-78, gen. mgr. comml. ops, 1979—; dep. head reactor materials lab. U.K. Atomic Energy Assn., Culcheth, Eng., 1960-63. Fellow Royal Soc. Can.; mem. Can. Inst. Mining and Metallurgy, Brit. Nuclear Energy Soc. (corr.), Can. Welding Devel. Inst. (dir.). Anglican. Club: Deep River Yacht and Tennis. Contbr. numerous articles to profl. jours. Home: 17 Beach Ave Deep River ON K0J 1P0 Canada Office: Chalk River Nuclear Labs Chalk River ON K0J 1J0 Canada

PERSHING, FRANCIS WARREN, broker; b. Cheyenne, Wyo., June 24, 1909; s. John Joseph and Helen Frances (Warren) P.; student Philips Exeter Acad., 1923-27, Inst. Carnal, Switzerland, 1924-25; B.S., Yale, 1931; m. Muriel Bache Richards, Apr. 22, 1938 (dec. June 1978); children—John Warren, Richard Warren (killed in action Vietnam 1968). Chmn. emeritus Pershing & Co. div. Donaldson, Lufkin & Jenrette Securities Co., N.Y.C.; dir. Dome Mines, Ltd. Mem. Assn. Stock Exchange Firms (past gov.). Home: 830 S County Rd Palm Beach FL 33480 Office: 120 Broadway New York City NY 10005

PERSHING, ROSCOE LOUIS, mfg. co. exec.; b. Washington, Ind., Oct. 8, 1940; s. John Carl and Mabel Harriet (Morris) P.; B.S. in Agrl. Engring., Purdue U., 1962; M.S., U. Ill., 1964, Ph.D., 1966; m. Annette Elvina Bauling, Aug. 22, 1964; children—Michael, Pamela, Kimberly. Instr., teaching fellow U. Ill., Urbana, 1962-66; with Deere & Co., Moline, Ill., 1966-73, exec. asst. chmn.'s office, 1973-74, project mgr. parts distbn., 1974-76, div. engr. advanced products John Deere Ottumwa (Iowa) Works, 1976-79; mgr. engring. systems Deere & Co., Moline, 1979—; part-time instr. Black Hawk Jr. Coll., Moline, 1968-71. Mem. agrl. engring. adv. com. U. Ill., 1974—. Mem. Am. Soc. Agrl. Engrs. (Nat. paper award 1970, Young Researcher award 1973), Soc. Automotive Engrs. (gov. bd. Miss. Valley sect. 1972-73), Sigma Xi (chpt. pres. 1968). Methodist (lay leader 1969-73, adminstrv. bd. 1971-72). Author, patentee in field. Home: 3003 36th St Moline IL 61265 Office: Deere & Co Moline IL 61265

PERSICHETTI, VINCENT, composer; b. Phila., June 6, 1915; s. Vincent R. and Martha (Buch) P.; B.Mus., Combs Conservatory Music, 1936; diploma conducting Curtis Inst., 1939; M.Mus., Phila. Conservatory, 1940, D.Mus., 1945; m. Dorothea Flanagan, June 3, 1941; children—Lauren, Garth. Head composition dept. Juilliard Sch. Music, 1947—; dir. publs. Elkan-Vogel Co., Inc., 1952—; adv. Nat. Endowment for Arts, 1977; sculptor in marble, granite and wood, 1926—. Recipient Juilliard Pub. award, 1943, Blue Network award, 1945; grantee Nat. Inst. Arts and Letters, 1948; medal Italian Govt., 1958; citation Am. Bandmasters Assn., 1964; commns. from Juilliard Music Found., 1948, Martha Graham Company, 1949, Louisville Orch., 1950, Samaroff Found., 1952, Koussevitzky Found., 1955, St. Louis Symphony, 1959, Naumburg Found., 1960, Lincoln Center, 1962, N.Y. Philharmonic, 1977; recipient Kennedy Center Friedheim award, 1978; Guggenheim fellow, 1959, 69, 73. Mem. ASCAP (dir.), Phila. Art Alliance (dir.). Compositions include 11 piano sonatas, 9 symphonies, 4 string quartets, 13 serenades for miscellaneous instruments, 11 band works, 65 songs, 17 choral works, 33 piano works, 25 chamber works, Stabat Mater, The Creation, Te Deum for chorus and orch., Harmonium Cycle for soprano and piano. Home: Hillhouse Wise Mill Rd Philadelphia PA 19128 Office: Juilliard Sch Lincoln Center Plaza New York NY 10023

PERSKY, MORDECAI (MORT), mag. editor; b. Savannah, Ga., Oct. 28, 1931; s. Nathan and Esther (Surasky) P.; A.B., U. S.C., 1953; m. Janet P. Holley, Oct. 1953 (div. 1962); 1 dau., Lisa; m. 2d, Yolanda P. Kelley, Apr. 9, 1964 (div. 1974); m. 3d, Judith P. Rossner, Jan. 7, 1979; stepchildren—Jean Rossner, Daniel Rossner. Sports writer Augusta (Ga.) Herald, 1953-54, Atlanta Constn., 1954-56; editor, columnist Augusta Herald, 1956-58; copy editor Miami (Fla.) Herald, 1958-62; Sunday layout editor N.Y. Herald Tribune, 1962-64; Sunday editor Detroit Free Press, 1964-67, asst. mng. editor, 1967-70; asst. to exec. editor Phila. Inquirer, 1970-71; editor-in-chief, v.p. Family Weekly Mag., N.Y.C., 1971-76; mng. editor Phila. Daily News, 1976-77; editorial dir. new publs. Playboy Enterprises, Inc., Chgo. and N.Y.C., 1977—. Recipient Boyd Martin award for editing nation's best entertainment pages, 1965; medal Art Dirs. Club Detroit, 1965, 66; certificate of merit Art Dirs. Club N.Y., 1966-67; participant (as editor) Pulitizer prize for Detroit Free Press coverage of 1967 riots. Mem. Am. Soc. Mag. Editors, Am. Assn. Sunday and Feature Editors, Sigma Delta Chi. Home: 145 Central Park W New York NY 10023 Office: 747 Third Ave New York NY 10017

PERSOFF, NEHEMIAH, actor; b. Jerusalem, Aug. 14, 1920; s. Samuel and Paula (Holman) P.; came to U.S., 1929; student Hebrew Tech. Inst., 1934-37; m. Thia Persov, Aug. 22, 1951; children—Jeffrey, Dan, Perry, Dahlia. Stage appearances include Montserrat, Galileo, Sundown Beach, Richard III, Peter Pan, King Lear, Tiger at the Gates, Flahooly, Camino Real, Reclining Figure, Mlle. Colombe, Peer Gynt, Only in America, Golden Boy, Detective Story, Road to Rome, Hay Fever, Room Service, The Devil's Disciple, Too Many Thumbs, Rosebloom, Sholem-Aleichem, Cages, The Dybbuk, The Glass Managerie, The Big Knife; appeared in numerous films including On the Waterfront, The Wrong Man, The Harder They Fall, Men in War, The Street of Sinners, The Day of the Outlaw, The Badlanders, Some Like It Hot, Al Capone, This Angry Age, Green Mansions, Never Steal Anything Small, The Commancheros, Fate is the Hunter, The Power, The Treasure of San Bosco Reef, Red Sky at Morning, Mrs. Pollifax Spy, The Money Jungle, The People Next Door, The Kirlin Force, Voyage of the Dammned; TV shows include G.E. Theatre, Philco Playhouse, Goodyear Playhouse, Kraft Theater, Climax, The Goldbergs, You Are There, Captain Video, Playhouse 90, Camera 3, The Witness, Producers Showcase, Untouchables, Route 66, Naked City, Wagon Train, Rawhide, Gunsmoke, Bus Stop, For Whom the Bell Tolls, Last Days of Benito Mussolini, Killers of Leon Trotsky, Missiles of October, Wild Wild West, Dan August, Big Valley, Mission Impossible, Bill Cosby Show, Love American Style, Name of the Game, Streets of San Francisco, Marcus Welby, Hawaii 5-0, McCloud, Cool Million, Mannix, The Twilight Zone, The Man From Uncle, It Takes A Thief, The Trials of O'Brien, Search, High Chaparral, Police Story, Police Surgeon, Columbo, Wonder Women, Six Million Dollar Man, Invisible Man, Hunter, Baretta, Francis Gary Powers Story, Killing Stone, numerous others; appeared in TV miniseries The French Atlantic Affair. Recipient Sylvania award for best supporting actor in TV drama, 1958. Served with AUS, 1942-45. Columnist: My Friends and Others. Office: Care Contemporary-Korman Artists Ltd Contemporary Artists Bldg 132 Lasky Dr Beverly Hills CA 90212. *I suspect that one of the most* *powerful forces shaping my life when I was growing up in the U.S.A. was that German with the small mustache who questioned the right of my people (and therefore me) to live. He put the burden of proof on me, personally. I was then determined to develop whatever talent I had to prove worthy of the gift of life. The habit of work remained with me in later years.**

PERSON, CLAYTON OSCAR, geneticist; b. Regina, Sask., Can., May 16, 1922; s. Oscar and Alma (Eriksson) P.; B.A., U. Sask., 1949; M.A., Ph.D., U. Alta. (Can.), 1953; m. Mary Meyer, Feb. 9, 1946; children—Jens, Joan, Lisa. Asst. prof. genetics U. Alta., 1953-54, prof., 1961-66; postdoctoral fellow U. Lund (Sweden), 1954-55, John Innes Inst., Hartford, Eng., 1955-56; research officer Can. Dept. Agr., Winnipeg, Man., 1956-61; prof. botany U. B.C., Vancouver, 1966—; cons. on diseases of coffee FAO, Rome, Ethiopia. Served with Royal Can. Navy, 1941-47. Fellow Royal Soc. Can.; mem. Am. Phytopath. Soc., Can. Genetics Soc. Contbr. articles to profl. jours. Office: Dept Botany U BC Vancouver BC V6T 1W5 Canada

PERSON, EVERT BERTIL, newspaper and radio exec.; b. Berkeley, Calif., Apr. 6, 1914; s. Emil P. and Elida (Swanson) P.; student U. Calif., Berkeley, 1937; m. Ruth Finley, Jan. 26, 1944. Co-publisher, sec.-treas. Press Democrat Pub. Co., Santa Rosa, Calif., 1945-72, editor, 1972-73, pres., pub., editor-in-chief, 1973—; sec.-treas. Finley Broadcating Co., Santa Rosa, 1945-72, pres., 1972—; pres. Person Properties Co., Santa Rosa, 1945-70; v.p. Finley Ranch & Land Co., Santa Rosa, 1947-72, pres., 1972-79; pres. Baker Pub. Co. (Oreg.), 1957-67, Sebastopol (Calif.) Times, 1978—, Russian River News, Guerneville, Calif., 1978—. Bd. dirs. Empire Coll., Santa Rosa, 1972—, Sonoma County Taxpayers Assn., 1966-69, San Francisco Spring Opera Assn., 1974-79; chmn. Santa Rosa Civic Arts Commn., 1961-62; pres. Santa Rosa Sonoma County Symphony Assn., 1966-68, Luther Burbank Meml. Found., 1979, Santa Rosa Symphony Found., 1967—; adv. bd. Santa Rose Salvation Army, 1959-67; commodore 12th Coast Guard Dist. Aux., 1969-70. Mem. Am. Soc. Newspaper Editors, Internat. Press Inst., Calif. Newspaper Pubs. Assn. (pres. elect 1980-81), Inst. Newspaper Controllers and Fin. Officers (pres. 1961-62), Navy League U.S., Calif. Broadcasters Assn., Nat. Assn. Broadcasters, Sigma Delta Chi. Episcopalian. Clubs: Press, Bohemian, St. Francis Yacht (San Francisco); Sonoma County Press; Santa Rosa Golf and Country, Santa Rosa Rotary (past pres.); Masons (32 deg., Shriner), Elks. Home: 1020 McDonald Ave Santa Rosa CA 95404 Office: 427 Mendocino Ave Santa Rosa CA 95401

PERSON, ROBERT JOHN, fin. mgmt. cons.; b. Mpls., Mar. 7, 1927; s. Otto Carl and Alice Kathryn (Kasper) P.; B.B.A., U. Minn., 1947; M.S., Columbia, 1953; m. Jeanette Haines, Mar. 11, 1948; 1 dau., Julie Ann. Financial analyst Equitable Life Assurance Soc. U.S., N.Y.C., 1947-53; asst. v.p. bus. devel. met. banking dept. Bankers Trust Co., N.Y.C., 1953-64; v.p. bus. devel. div. Union Bank, Los Angeles, 1964-67; v.p., dir. mktg. Bank of Calif., San Francisco, 1967-70; sr. v.p. Central Nat. Bank of Chgo., 1970-72, 1st v.p., 1973-76; 1st v.p. Central Nat. Chgo. Corp., 1973-76; v.p., regional mgr. Lester B. Knight & Assos., Inc., San Francisco, 1976-77; dir. bank cons. Western States Coopers & Lybrand, San Francisco, 1977—; instr. salesmanship sch. pub. relations N.Y. Bankers Assn., 1960-63; instr. mktg. research Stonier Grad. Sch. Banking, Rutgers U., 1964-65, 73, 75-77, Brown U., 1964; instr. Agrl. Lending Sch., Ill. Bankers Assn., 1973-76, Nat. Comml. Lending Sch., Am. Bankers Assn., 1973-76. Vice chmn. mgmt. effectiveness com. Community Fund Chgo.; chief crusader Crusade of Mercy, Chgo. Treas. Sch. Bd., Huntington, N.Y., 1957-59. Bd. dirs. Am. Cancer Soc., Chgo. Served with USNR, 1944-46. Recipient Florence McNeil Stanley award Columbia, 1953. Mem. Am. Bankers Assn., Bank Mktg. Assn., Am. Mgmt. Assn. (mktg. planning council), Mgmt. Centre-Europe (fin. mgmt. adv. com. 1971—), Sales and Mktg. Execs. Internat. Republican. Presbyn. Elk. Clubs: Executives, University (Chgo.); Eastward Ho! (Cape Cod); University, Presidio Yacht (San Francisco); Sunset Ridge (Winnetka, Ill.); Marin Country (Novato, Calif.). Home: 4 Flamingo Ln San Rafael CA 94901 Office: 1 Bush St San Francisco CA 94104

PERSON, ROBERT TALLMAN, utilities exec.; b. Des Moines, Aug. 6, 1914; s. Howard A. and Caroline M. (Tallman) P.; student N.Y. U., 1932; B.S., U. N.Mex., 1936; grad. mgmt. course U. Idaho, 1954; m. Marian Elizabeth Clark, June 6, 1936; children—Nancy Joanne Person Morton, Robert Tallman, Howard Clark. With sales dept. Albuquerque Gas & Electric Co., 1936-40; comml. mgr. Pueblo Gas & Fuel Co., Colo., 1940-47, v.p., gen. mgr., 1947-53, pres., chief exec. officer, chmn. bd., from 1959; v.p. public relations Public Service Co. Colo., Denver, 1953-58, dir., 1957—, exec. v.p., 1958-59, pres., chief exec. officer, from 1959, now chmn. bd., mem. exec. com.; chmn. bd. FUELCO; pres., chief exec. officer Cheyenne Light, Fuel & Power Co. (Wyo.), 1959-66, chmn. bd., 1966; pres. Western Slope Gas Co., Denver, from 1959; chief exec. officer Fuel Resources Devel. Co., from 1959, pres., from 1971; dir. Fed. Res. Bank of Kansas City. Co-chmn. Rocky Mountain region NCCF; bd. dirs. Nat. Western Stock Show; pres. Mile High United Fund, Denver; trustee Denver Mus. Natural History. Served to lt., j.g., USNR, 1944-46, 50; PTO. Mem. Edison Electric Inst. (pres.), Colo. Assn. Commerce and Industry (dir.), Rocky Mountain Elec. League (pres.), Denver C. of C. (pres.), Nat. Assn. Electric Cos. (dir., chmn.), Am. Gas Assn. (dir.). Clubs: Denver County, Denver Athletic, Denver, Am. Legion, Elks, Rotary. Office: 550 15th St Denver CO 80202

PERSON, ROBERT TALLMAN, utilities exec.; b. Des Moines, Aug. 6, 1914; s. Howard A. and Caroline M. (Tallman) P.; student N.Y. U., 1932; B.S., U. N.Mex., 1936; mgmt. course U. Idaho, 1954; m. Marian Elizabeth Clark, June 6, 1936; children—Nancy Joanne (Mrs. Max Morton), Robert Tallman, Howard Clark. With sales dept. Albuquerque Gas & Electric Co., 1936-40; comml. mgr. Pueblo Gas & Fuel Co., Colo., 1940-47, v.p., gen. mgr., 1947-53; v.p. pub. relations Pub. Service Co. Colo., Denver, 1953-58, dir., 1957—, exec. v.p., 1958-59, pres., 1959-76, chief exec. officer, 1959—, chmn., 1976—; pres., dir. Cheyenne Light, Fuel & Power Co. (Wyo.), 1959-76; dir. Western Slope Gas Co. (Denver), 1959-77; chief exec. officer Fuel Resources Devel. Co., 1959-77, chmn. bd., dir., 1977—; dir. Fed. Res. Bank of Kansas City, 1971-77, chmn. bd., 1975-76. Co-chmn. Rocky Mountain region NCCJ; bd. dirs. Mountain States Employers Council, Nat. Western Stock Show; past pres. Mile High United Fund; trustee Denver Mus. Natural History. Served to lt. (j.g.) USNR, 1944-46, 50; PTO. Mem. Edison Electric Inst. (past pres.), Colo. Assn. Commerce and Industry (dir.), Rocky Mountain Elec. League (past pres.), Denver C. of C. (past pres.), Nat. Assn. Electric Cos. (past dir., chmn.), Am. Gas Assn. (past dir.), Am. Legion. Elk, Rotarian. Clubs: Denver Country, Denver Athletic, Denver Press, Denver. Home: 116 Krameria St Denver CO 80220 Office: 550 15th St Denver CO 80202

PERSONS, CLAYTON HENRY, clergyman; b. Altura, Minn., Oct. 7, 1915; s. Henry Roy and Esther Margaret (Koepsel) P.; B.A., Moravian Coll., 1937; B.D., Moravian Theol. Sem., 1940, D.D., 1969; m. Helen Lillie Frankenfield, Sept. 28, 1940; children—Margaret M. (Mrs. Britton Wiley Sanders), Charles Clayton. Ordained to ministry Moravian Ch. in Am., 1940; pastor Daggett (Mich.) Home Moravian Ch., 1940-47, Kernersville Moravian Ch., 1947-57, Trinity Moravian Ch., Winston-Salem, N.C., 1957-68; chief adminstr. Moravian Ch., So. Province, Winston-Salem, 1968-74; pastor Immanuel Moravian Ch., Winston-Salem, 1974—. Past mem. exec. com. U.S. Conf., World Council Chs.; mem. gen. bd. Nat. Council Chs.; mem. exec. bd. N.C. Council Chs. Bd. dirs. Moravian Home, Inc.; trustee Salem Coll., Moravian Coll. Home: 1912 Peachtree St Winston-Salem NC 27107 Office: 2009 Peachtree St Winston-Salem NC 27107

PERSONS, STOW SPAULDING, educator, historian; b. Mt. Carmel, Conn., June 15, 1913; s. Frederick Torrell and Florence Isabel (Cummings) P.; B.A., Yale U., 1936, Ph.D., 1940; m. Dorothy Mae Reuss, Sept. 4, 1943; 1 dau., Catherine. Instr. history Princeton U., 1940-45, asst. prof., 1945-50, acting chmn. Am. civilization program, 1947-48; prof. history U. Iowa, 1950—, research prof., 1956-57, acting chmn. history dept., 1957-58, acting dean Grad. Coll., 1960-61, Carver Disting. prof., 1978—; sr. research fellow Nat. Endowment for Humanities, 1967-68. Vis. prof. Salzburg (Austria) Seminar, 1955, 61, Stetson U., 1957, San Francisco Coll., 1959, U. Wyo., 1960, U. Colo., 1964. Fellow Fund Advancement Edn., 1954-55. Mem. Am. Hist. Assn., Orgn. Am. Historians (exec. com. 1960-63), Am. Studies Assn. (pres. Central Miss Valley chpt. 1958-59). Author: Free Religion, 1947; American Minds, 1958; Decline of American Gentility, 1973. Editor: Evolutionary Thought in America, 1950; (with D. Egbert, T.D.S. Bassett) Socialism and American Life, 1952; Social Darwinism: Selected Essays of William Graham Sumner, 1963; The Cooperative Commonwealth (Laurence Gronlund), 1965. Editorial bd. Am. Quar., 1958-61, Miss. Valley Hist. Rev., 1954-57. Home: 1433 Oaklawn Ave Iowa City IA 52240

PERTSCHUK, MICHAEL, chmn. FTC; b. London, Jan. 12, 1933; s. David and Sarah (Baumander) P. (parents Am. citizens); B.A., Yale U., 1954, LL.D., J.D., 1959; m. Carleen Joyce Dooley, Sept. 1954 (div. Dec. 1976); children—Mark, Amy; m. 2d, Anna Phillips Sofaer, Apr. 1977. Asst. in instruction Yale U. Law Sch., 1957; admitted to Oreg. bar, 1959; law clk. to U.S. Dist. Ct. Judge Gus O. Solomon, Portland, Oreg., 1959-60; assoc. firm Hart, Rockwood, Davies, Biggs & Strayer, Portland, 1960-62; legis. asst. to Senator Maurine B. Neuberger of Oreg., 1962-64; trade relation counsel Senate Commerce Com., Washington, 1964-68, chief counsel, staff dir., 1968-77; chmn. FTC, Washington, 1977—; professorial lectr. Am. U.; adj. prof. Georgetown U. Sch. Law; lectr. pub. law seminars Brookings Instn.; pub. mem. Nat. Interagy. Council Smoking and Health, 1973-76; commr. Nat. Commn. Product Safety, 1967-70; mem. council Adminstrv. Conf. U.S.; mem. Nat. Commn. for Rev. of Antitrust Laws and Procedures. Mem. Nat. Acad. Pub. Adminstrn. Served with AUS, 1954-56. Home: 3411 Rodman St NW Washington DC 20008 Office: FTC Pennsylvania Ave at 6th St NW Washington DC 20580

PERUSSE, ROLAND IRVING, educator; b. Springfield, Mass., May 18, 1921; s. Alfred and Louise (Maheu) P.; student N.Y. U., 1943-44, Sorbonne, 1945, 46; B.A., U. Wis., 1947; Ph.D. in Internat. Relations and Orgn., Am. U., 1955. Research analyst Dept. Def., 1947-49; pub. affairs officer U.S. High Commn. Germany, Am. embassy, Bonn, 1949-53; fgn. affairs officer USIA, Washington, 1954-57; press officer NATO, Paris, France, 1957-59; asst. dir. UNESCO relations staff Dept. State, 1959-60, mass communications officer, 1961; pub. information officer Pharm. Mfrs. Assn., 1962-64; asso. prof. polit. sci. U. Md., 1954-64, U. Tex., El Paso, 1964-66; prof., chmn. dept. polit. sci., dir. Inter-Am. studies Inter-Am. U., San Juan, P.R., 1966-69; spl. asst. to gov. P.R., 1969-70; exec. dir. Corp. Caribbean Econ. Devel., 1971; acting dir. North-South Center for Tech. and Cultural Interchange, 1971-72; prof. polit. sci., dir. Inter-Am. studies Inter-Am. U., San Juan, P.R., 1972—; dir. Inter Am. Inst., Hato Rey, P.R., 1975—. Adviser, Rockefeller Presdl. Mission to Latin Am., 1969, U.S. delegation Atlantic Congress, London, Eng., 1959; research dir. Caribbean Community Project, 20th Century Fund, 1970-71; pub. mem. U.S. delegation 21st session UN Social Devel. Commn., 1970; gov. bd. Council State Govts., 1969-70; adv. council Hampshire Coll.; mem. Americas Found.; past chmn. Md. Citizens Commn. Fair Congl. Redistricting. Dir. Scholars for Scranton, 1964. Served with M.I., AUS, 1943-46. Decorated Legion of Merit. Mem. Am. Assn. UN, Am. Polit. Sci. Assn., Internat., Caribbean (founder, pres.) studies assns., Fgn. Service Assn. Home: El Monte Hato Rey PR 00918 Office: PO Box 1293 Hato Rey PR 00919

PERUTZ, GERALD ERIC ALEXANDER, mfg. co. exec.; b. Vienna, Austria, Sept. 8, 1929; s. George and Helen (Traill) P.; D.L.C., Loughborough (Eng.) Coll., 1948; m. Dinah Fyffe Pope, Sept. 19, 1953; children—Sandra, Simon, Timothy. Engr. Harbour & Gen. Works Ltd., London, Eng., 1950-51; project engr. Foster Wheeler refinery contractors, London, 1951-57; gen. mgr. internat. ops. photo div. Rank Orgn., London, 1957-63; with Bell & Howell, Ltd., various locations, 1963—, mng. dir., London, corporate v.p., chief exec. Europe, now exec. v.p. Office: 7100 McCormick Rd Chicago IL 60645

PERVIN, WILLIAM JOSEPH, educator; b. Pitts., Oct. 31, 1930; s. Abraham and Stella (Greenberger) P.; B.S., U. Mich., 1952, M.S., 1952; Ph.D., U. Pitts., 1957; m. Gilda Fuss, June 13, 1954; children—Edward, James, Sharon. Prof., Pa. State U., 1957-63; vis. prof. Heidelberg (Germany) U., 1963-64; prof., chmn. U. Wis.-Milw., 1964-67; dir. Computer Center, prof. math. Drexel U., Phila., 1967-73; dir. Regional Computer Center, U. Tex., Dallas, 1973-78, prof. math. scis., 1973—. Mem. Assn. Computing Machinery, Am. Math. Soc., Soc. Indsl. and Applied Math., Math. Assn. Am. Mason. Author: Foundations of General Topology, 1964. Office: Box 688 UTD-Sta JO 42 Richardson TX 75080

PESCH, LEROY ALLEN, physician, educator, health and hosp. cons.; b. Mt. Pleasant, Iowa, June 22, 1931; s. Herbert Lindsey and Mary Clarissa (Tyner) P.; student State U. Iowa, 1948-49, Iowa State U., 1950-52; M.D. cum laude, Washington U., St. Louis, 1956; m. Donna J. Stone, Dec. 28, 1975; children from previous marriage—Christopher Allen, Brian Lindsey, Daniel Ethan; stepchildren—Christopher Scott Kneifel, Linda Suzanne Kneifel. Intern, Barnes Hosp., St. Louis, 1956-57; research asso. NIH, Bethesda, Md., 1957-59; asst. resident medicine Grace-New Haven Hosp., New Haven, 1959-60; clin. fellow Yale Med. Sch., New Haven, 1960-61, instr. medicine, 1961-62, asst. prof. medicine, 1962-63, asst. dir. liver study unit, 1961-63; asso. physician Grace-New Haven Hosp., 1961-62; asso. prof. medicine Rutgers U., New Brunswick, N.J., 1963-64, prof., 1964-66, chmn. dept. medicine, 1965-66; asso. dean, prof. medicine Stanford Sch. Medicine, 1966-68; mem. gen. medicine study sect. NIH, 1965-70, chmn., 1969-70; dean, dir. univ. hosps. State U. N.Y., Buffalo, 1968-71; spl. cons. to sec. for health HEW, 1970—; prof. div. biol. scis. and medicine U. Chgo., 1972-77; prof. pathology Northwestern U., 1977—; health and hosp. cons.; pres. Concept Group, Inc., Chgo., 1976-77; pres. L.A. Pesch Assos., Inc., Chgo., 1977—; dir. Lakeside Bank. Bd. dirs. Buffalo Med. Found., 1969-72, Health Orgn., Western N.Y., 1968-71; trustee Michael Reese Hosp. and Med. Center, Chgo., 1971-76, pres., chief exec. officer, 1971-77; mem. exec. bd. Auditorium Theatre Council, Chgo.; trustee W. Clement and Jessie V. Stone Found. Served with USPHS, 1957-59. Mem. Am. Assn. Study of Liver Diseases, Am. Fedn. Clin. Research, Am. Soc. Biol. Chemists, AAAS, Sigma Xi, Alpha Omega Alpha. Clubs: Buffalo, Standard, Internat. Quadrangle, Mid-Am., Capitol Hill, Acapulco Yacht, Chicago Yacht. Contbr. articles on internal medicine to profl. jours. Home: 333 N Mayflower Rd Lake Forest IL 60045 Office: 303 E Ohio St Chicago IL 60611

PESCH, PETER, astronomer; b. Zurich, Switzerland, June 29, 1934; s. Roland Henry and Hildegard May (Stoecklin) P.; B.S. in Physics, U. Chgo., 1955, M.S., 1956, Ph.D. in Astronomy, 1960; m. Donna Marie Lehmann, July 25, 1975; children—Marina, Ada Ines. Research asso. Case Western Res. U., 1960-61, mem. faculty, 1961—, prof. astronomy, 1974—, chmn. dept., dir. Warner and Swasey Obs., 1975—; on leave with Kitt Peak Nat. Obs., Tucson, 1970-71; program dir. astron. instrumentation and devel. program NSF, summer 1972. Mem. Am. Astron. Soc., Internat. Astron. Union. Home: 2361 Euclid Heights Blvd Cleveland Heights OH 44106 Office: 1975 Taylor Rd East Cleveland OH 44112

PESCHKA, THOMAS ALAN, banker; b. Great Bend, Kans., Oct. 15, 1931; s. William A. and Elsie (Austin) P.; student Coll. Holy Cross, 1949-50; B.S., U. Kans., 1953, LL.B., 1958; m. Betty Joan Gaunt, June 3, 1954. Admitted to Kans., Mo. bars; since practiced in Kansas City; law clk. to U.S. dist. judge Kans., 1958-60; with Commerce Bancshares, 1960—, v.p., gen. counsel, 1966-72, sec., 1968-78, sr. v.p., gen. counsel, 1972—; gen. counsel, sec. Commerce Bancshares, Inc., v.p., 1973—, treas., 1978—; sec.-treas., dir. Tower Properties Co., 1964-74; sec., dir. Capital for Bus., Inc., Commerce Mortgage Co.; sec. CBI Ins. Co., 1973-78, pres., 1978—; sec. COMPAC Services, Inc. Served to 1st lt. USAF, 1953-55. Mem. Am., Mo., Kans., Kansas City bar assns., Lawyers Assn. Kansas City, Phi Delta Theta, Phi Delta Phi. Roman Catholic. Club: University (Kansas City). Home: 4401 Somerset Dr Shawnee Mission KS 66207 Office: 720 Main St Kansas City MO 64105

PESCOW, DONNA GAIL, actress; b. Bklyn., Mar. 24; student Am. Acad. Dramatic Arts, 1975. Toured in play Ah, Wilderness, summer 1975; appeared in TV series One Life to Live; co-star movie: Saturday Night Fever; appeared in TV films: Human Feelings, Rainbow; star TV series Angie, 1979—. Office: care ABC Public Relations 1330 Ave of Americas New York NY 10019*

PESEK, JOHN THOMAS, JR., agronomist; b. Hallettsville, Tex., Nov. 15, 1921; s. John Thomas and Elizabeth Georgia (Kallus) P.; B.S. in Agrl. Edn., Tex. A&M Coll., 1943, M.S. in Agronomy, 1947; Ph.D. in Agronomy, N.C. State Coll., 1950; m. Isabel Lorraine Christensen, Aug. 7, 1952; children—Brian John, Cynthia Anne, Rebecca Lynne. Grad. teaching asst. Tex. A&M Coll., 1946-47; grad. research and teaching asst. N.C. State Coll., 1947-50; asst. prof. agronomy Iowa State U., 1950-52, asso. prof., 1952-58, prof., 1958—, head dept. agronomy, 1964—; trustee Com. for Agrl. Devel., Iowa State U. Agrl. Found.; participant Pontifical Acad. Scis. Study Week, 1972; spl. guest Soil Sci. Soc. So. Africa Congress, 1975. Served with U.S. Army, 1943-45. Decorated Air medal with 2 oak leaf clusters, D.F.C. Fellow Am. Soc. Agronomy (pres. 1979), Soil Sci. Soc. Am., AAAS; mem. Crop Sci. Soc. Am., Internat. Soil Sci. Soc., Soil Conservation Soc. Am., Nat. Catholic Rural Life Conf., Iowa Acad. Scis., Iowa Crop Improvement Assn. (dir.), Sigma Xi, Phi Kappa Phi, Gamma Sigma Delta, Epsilon Sigma Phi. Democrat. Roman Catholic. Club: Farm House (asso.). Contbr. articles on fertilizer use and crop prodn., econs. of fertilizer use to profl. and popular publs. Home: 1304 Marston St Ames IA 50010 Office: 120 Agronomy Iowa State U Ames IA 50011

PESHKIN, ALAN, educator; b. Chgo., Jan. 6, 1931; s. Morris and Harriet (Casty) P.; B.A., U. Ill., 1952, M.Ed., 1954; Ph.D., U. Chgo., 1962; m. Maryann Rotberg, Aug. 15, 1953; children—Nancy, David, Julie. Tchr. social studies Barrington (Ill.) Consol. High Sch., 1954-57; adminstr., adviser U. Chgo.-Pakistan Edn. Project, Karachi and Dacca, 1958-61; asst. prof. edn. U. Wis., 1962-64; coordinator No. Nigeria Tchr. Edn. Project, Maiduguri, 1965-66; faculty U. Ill., Urbana, 1967—, prof. comparative edn., 1969—, dir. African studies, 1968-71, chmn. dept. ednl. policy studies, 1975-79. Guggenheim fellow, 1973-74; Center for Advanced Study asso., 1979-80. Mem. Council on Anthropology and Edn., Comparative Edn. Soc., Am. Ednl. Research Assn., Am. Anthropology Assn. Author: The Kanuri Schoolchildren—Education and Social Mobilization in Nigeria, 1972; Growing Up American: Schooling and the Survival of Community, 1978; also papers. Home: 704 S Prospect St Champaign IL 61820 Office: Coll Edn Univ Ill Urbana IL 60801

PESHKIN, MURRAY, physicist; b. Bklyn., May 17, 1925; s. Jacob and Bella Ruth (Zuckerman) P.; B.A., Cornell U., 1946, Ph.D., 1951; m. Frances Julie Ehrlich, June 12, 1955; children—Michael, Sharon, Joel. Instr., then asst. prof. physics Northwestern U., 1951-59; physicist, then sr. scientist, asso. dir. physics div. Argonne (Ill.) Nat. Lab., 1959—. Fellow Weizmann Inst. Sci., Rehovoth, Israel, 1959-60, 68-69. Served with AUS, 1944-46. Home: 838 Parkside Ave Elmhurst IL 60126 Office: Argonne Nat Lab Argonne IL 60439

PESHKIN, SAMUEL DAVID, lawyer; b. Des Moines, Oct. 6, 1925; s. Louis and Mary (Grund) P.; B.A., State U. Iowa, 1948, J.D., 1951; m. Shirley R. Isenberg, Aug. 17, 1947; children—Lawrence Allen, Linda Ann. Admitted to Iowa bar, 1951, since practiced in Des Moines; partner firm Bridges & Peshkin, 1953-66, Peshkin & Robinson, 1966—. Mem. Iowa Bd. Law Examiners, 1970—. Bd. dirs. State U. Iowa Found., 1957—, Old Gold Devel. Fund, 1956—, Sch. Religion U. Iowa, 1966—. Fellow Am. Bar Found., Internat. Soc. Barristers; mem. Am. (chmn. standing com. membership 1959—, ho. of dels. 1968—, bd. govs. 1973—), Iowa (bd. govs. 1958—, pres. jr. bar sect. 1958-59, award of merit 1974), Inter-Am., Internat. bar assns., Am. Judicature Soc., State U. Iowa Alumni Assn. (dir., pres. 1957). Home: 3000 Grand Ave Des Moines IA 50312 Office: Fleming Bldg Des Moines IA 50309

PESKY, ALAN DONALD, advt. exec.; b. N.Y.C., Dec. 17, 1933; s. Louis I. and Belle (Silverstein) P.; A.B., Lafayette Coll., 1956; M.B.A., Dartmouth Coll., 1960; m. Wendy Stern, Mar. 30, 1961; children—Heidi, Lee, Greg. Product mgr. Standard Brands, N.Y.C., 1960-63; account supr. Papert, Koenig, Lois, Inc., Advt. Agency, N.Y.C., 1963-67; founding partner, pres. Scali, McCabe, Sloves, Internat. Advt. Agency, N.Y.C., 1967—, also chief fin. officer Scali, McCabe, Sloves, Inc.; dir. Bickmore, Inc., Glamour Care, Inc. Bd. trustees New Canaan (Conn.) Country Sch., Environ. Def. Fund. Served to lt. U.S. Army, 1956-58. Mem. Am. Assn. Advt. Agencies, Lafayette Coll. Alumni Assn. (exec. com.). Clubs: City Athletic, Pound Ridge Tennis. Home: 874 Rockrimmon Rd Stamford CT 06903 Office: Scali McCabe Sloves 800 3d Ave New York NY 10022

PESMEN, SANDRA (MRS. HAROLD WILLIAM PESMEN), reporter; b. Chgo., Mar. 26, 1931; s. Benjamin S. and Emma (Lipschultz) P.; B.S., U. Ill., 1952; m. Harold W. Pesmen, Aug. 16, 1952; children—Bethann, Curtis. Reporter, Radio and Community News Service, Chgo., 1952-53; wire reporter Champaign-Urbana (Ill.) Courier, 1953; reporter, feature writer Lerner Chgo. N. Side Newspapers, 1953-55; stringer corr. Wayne (Mich.) Eagle, 1958-61; reporter, feature writer Chgo. Daily News, 1968-78; features editor Crain's Chgo. Business mag., 1978—; tchr. feature writing Northwestern U. Eve. Sch., 1972-73. Recipient Golden Key award Ill. Mental Health Dept., 1966, 71; Inst. Psychoanalysis award, 1971; Penny Mo. award, 1978; Stick o' Type award Chgo. Newspaper Guild,

1978; AP award, 1975. Home: 2811 Fern Ave Northbrook IL 60062 Office: care Crain Communications 740 N Rush St Chicago IL 60611

PESQUERA, HERNAN G., fed. dist. judge; b. San Juan, P.R., May 25, 1924; s. Angel M. and Ines F. (Guillermety) P.; B.A., U. P.R., 1944; LL.D., Cornell U., 1948; m. Sonia Marty, Aug. 22, 1951; children—Sonia Pesquera Galligan, Maria M., Hernan G., Isabel. Partner firm Geigel, Silva & Pesquera, San Juan, 1952-72; chmn. P.R. Racing Commn., 1971-72; Judge U.S. Dist. Ct. for P.R., 1972—. Decorated Meritorious Service medal. Mem. Am., P.R., Fed. bar assns., Am. Judicature Soc., Am. Trial Lawyers Assn., Am. Legion, Mil. Order World Wars, Nu Sigma Beta. Roman Catholic. Club: Elks. Home: Apt R-5 Dostorres Condominium Santurce PR 00907 Office: US Post Office and Ct Bldg San Juan PR 00904

PESTANA, CARLOS, physician, educator; b. Tacoronte, Tenerife, Canary Islands, Spain, June 10, 1936; s. Francisco and Blanca (Suarez) P.; came to U.S., 1968, naturalized, 1973; B.S., Nat. U. Mex., 1952, M.D., 1959; Ph.D. in Surgery, U. Minn., 1965; m. Myrna Lorena Serrato, Aug. 25, 1966; children—Becky Elizabeth, George Byron. Intern, St. Mary of Nazareth Hosp., Chgo., 1959-60; resident Mayo Clinic, Rochester, Minn., 1961-65; surgeon Hosp. 20 de Noviembre Mexico City, asst. prof. surgery Nat. U. Mex., 1966-67; asst. prof. surgery U. Tex. Med. Sch. at San Antonio, 1968-70, asso. prof., 1970-74, prof., 1974—, asso. dean for acad. devel., 1971-73, asso. dean for student affairs, 1973--; chief gen. surgery service Audie Murphy VA Hosp., San Antonio, 1973-78. Recipient Edward John Noble Found. award, 1965, Piper Prof. award Minnie Stevens Piper Founds., 1972. Mem. Assn. Acad. Surgery, AMA, A.C.S., N.Y. Acad. Scis., Tex. Med. Soc., Bexar County Med. Soc., Western Surg. Soc., San Antonio Surg. Soc., Soc. for Surgery Alimentary Tract, Assn. Am. Med. Colls., Priestley Soc., Allen O. Whipple Surg. Soc., Sigma Xi, Alpha Omega Alpha. Home: 10123 N Manton St San Antonio TX 78213 Office: 7703 Floyd Curl Dr San Antonio TX 78284

PETACQUE, ART, journalist; b. Chgo., July 20, 1924; s. Ralph David and Fay Nora (Brauner) P.; student U. Ill., 1940-42; m. Regina Battinus, Dec. 10, 1944; children—Susan Wendy (Mrs. James Bradley Leshin), William Scott. With Chgo. Sun, 1942-47; with Chgo. Sun-Times, 1947—, investigative reporter, 1957—, columnist, 1974—. Crime editor World Book Ency., 1970-75; lectr. various univs. and civic orgns. Recipient Page One awards for outstanding journalism Chgo. Newspaper Guild, 1949, 57, 59, 62, 63, 65, 68; Joseph M. Fay Meml. award Chgo. Newspaper Reporters Assn., 1960; Prof. Jacob Scher-Theta Sigma Phi Daily Newswriting award Chgo. chpt. Theta Sigma Phi, 1964; John Baptist Scalabrini award for leadership Am. Community Italian Ancestry, 1966; awards for investigative reporting and spot news Asso. Press, 1963, 66, 68, (2) 74, 76; Marshall Field award for outstanding editorial contbn. in behalf of Chgo. Sun-Times, 1968; Pulitzer Prize for gen. reporting, 1974; State of Israel Prime Minister's medal, 1976. Mem. Chgo. Newspaper Guild, Jewish War Vets. (hon.), Sigma Delta Chi, Sigma Alpha Mu. Jewish. Club: B'nai B'rith. Home: 4075 Chase Ave Lincolnwood IL 60646 Office: 401 N Wabash Ave Chicago IL 60611. *Have tried to be fair, careful and objective in my profession, realizing that what we say about the person we write about has not only an effect on the subject but his family and friends.*

PETCH, HOWARD EARLE, physicist, educator; b. Agincourt, Ont., Can., May 12, 1925; s. Thomas Earle and Edith (Painter) P.; B.Sc., McMaster U., 1949, M.Sc., 1950, D.Sc., 1974; Ph.D., U. B.C., 1952; m. Rosalind June Hulet, Aug. 13, 1949 (dec.); children—Stephen, Patricia; m. 2d, Linda Jean Schlechte, Mar. 27, 1976; 1 son, Jeremy. Postdoctoral fellow McMaster U., Ont., 1952-53, faculty, 1954-67, prof. metallurgy and metall. engring., 1960-67, dir. research, 1961-67, prin. Hamilton Coll., 1963-67, chmn. interdisciplinary materials research unit, 1964-67; prof. dept. physics, acad. v.p. U. Waterloo (Ont.), 1967-74, pres. pro tem, 1969; prof. dept. physics, pres. U. Victoria (B.C., Can.), 1975—. Mem. Sci. Council Can., 1966-72, Def. Research Bd. Can., 1973-78. Rutherford Meml. fellow Cambridge U., 1953-54, Research Council Ont. and NRC scholars; B.C. Acad. Scis. grantee; NRC fellow. Mem. Am. Crystallographic Assn., Am. Phys. Soc., Canadian Assn. Physicists, Canadian Research Mgmt. Assn., Internat. Union Crystallography, Royal Soc. Can. A developer fast coincidence circuit to measure lifetimes of excited nuclear states and other nuclear properties; pioneer in exptl. studies of the nuclear elec. quadrupole interaction in single crystals and applications of method to elucidating phys. properties of crystals; contbns. to understanding crystal chemistry of hydrated borates, atomic mechanism of order-disorder type of hydrogen-bonded ferroelec., dynamics of small groups in solids. Office: U Victoria PO Box 1700 Victoria BC V8W 2Y2 Canada

PETCHENIK, EDWARD, surgeon; b. Clinton, N.Y., Dec. 25, 1908; s. Patrick and Bridget (McCabe) P.; grad. sch., Plattsburg, N.Y.; student Plattsburgh Normal Sch.; M.D., Albany Med. Coll., 1936; post-grad. Postgrad. Med. Sch. and Hosp., N.Y. Polyclinic; m. Nora Loomis, Oct. 15, 1940. Practiced at Kingston, N.Y., 1940; mem. staff Augustana Hosp.; mem. bd. mgrs. Tng. Sch. for Boys, Hudson, N.J.; v.p. bd. mgrs. Tb Hosp. 1959—; chmn. clinics County Com. for Prevention Tb; chmn. County Pub. Health Co. Democrat. Clubs: K.C., Elks. Home: 335 Lincolnwood Rd Highland Park IL 60035*

PETER, EDWARD COMPSTON, II, army officer; b. Washington, May 8, 1929; s. Edward and Anita (Smith) P.; B.S., U.S. Mil. Acad., 1951; M.S., U. Mich., 1955; grad. Indsl. Coll. Armed Forces, 1969; m. Jean Foresteire, May 9, 1953; children—Jean Peter Larsen, Edward Compston, III, Mary A., Anita S. Commd. 2d lt. U.S. Army, 1951, advanced through grades to maj. gen., 1979; service in Korea and Vietnam; asst. comdr. 25th Inf. Div., Hawaii, 1976-78; chief legis. liaison Dept. Army, 1978—. Decorated Silver Star with oak leaf cluster, Legion of Merit with oak leaf cluster, Bronze Star with oak leaf cluster, Meritorious Service medal, Air medal with 6 oak leaf clusters, Army Commendation medal. Mem. Assn. U.S. Army. Roman Catholic. Home: 12B Jackson Ave Ft Myer VA 22211 Office: Office Sec Army Washington DC 20310

PETER, FRANK ALFRED, power co. exec.; b. Waterloo, Iowa, Apr. 15, 1917; s. Louis W. and Ella (Pries) P.; B.S., U. Ill., 1940, M.S., 1941; m. Marjorie L. Webber, Sept. 8, 1940; children—William M., Marjorie Kay. Pub. accounting audit staff Arthur Andersen & Co., Chgo., 1941-49, audit mgr., 1946-49; asst. controller Gen. Telephone Co. Ind., Lafayette, 1949-50, controller, 1950-55; controller-elect Gen. Telephone Co. Calif., Santa Monica, 1955-56, controller, 1956-59, v.p. fin., 1959-65; asst. to comptroller Pacific Gas & Electric Co., 1965-66, comptroller, 1966—, v.p., 1970—. Served with Supply Corps, USNR, 1943-46. C.P.A., Ill. Mem. Am. Inst. C.P.A.'s, Calif. Soc. C.P.A.'s, Fin. Execs. Inst., San Francisco C. of C., Pacific Coast Electric Assn., Edison Electric Inst., Pacific Coast Gas Assn., Alpha Kappa Psi, Beta Gamma Sigma, Phi Kappa Phi. Republican. Clubs: Commonwealth of Calif., Commercial, Electric (San Francisco); Diablo Country. Home: 77 Beale St San Francisco CA 94106 Office: 77 Beale St San Francisco CA 94106

PETER, LAURENCE JOHNSTON, educator, author; b. Vancouver, B.C., Can., Sept. 16, 1919; s. Victor C. and Vicenta (Steves) P.; B.A., Western Wash. State Coll., 1957, M.Ed., 1958; Ed.D., Wash. State U., 1963; m. Ireene J. Howe, Feb. 25, 1967; children—John, Edward, Alice, Margaret. Tchr., B.C., 1941-47; instr. B.C. Prison, Burnaby, 1947-48; guidance counselor, Vancouver, 1948-64; instr. U. B.C., 1964; asst. prof. U. So. Calif., Los Angeles, 1964-66, asso. prof., 1966-69, prof., 1969-70, dir. Evelyn Frieden Center for Prescriptive Teaching, 1967-70; ret., 1970; ind. research and writing projects, 1970—; adj. prof. U. Calif., Turlock. Panel mem. rev. bd. HEW; 1969-70. Vice pres. B.C. div. Canadian Mental Health Assn., 1959-61. Bd. dirs. Big Bros. Greater Los Angeles. Recipient Phi Delta Kappa research award U. So. Calif., 1970, Canadian Fed. Health grant for one year multidisciplinary study mental health services for children. 1955. Mem. Canadian Psychol. Assn., AAUP, P.E.N., AFTRA, Authors Guild, Council Exceptional Children, Phi Delta Kappa. Author: Prescriptive Teaching, 1965; (with Raymond Hull) The Peter Principle: Why Things Always Go Wrong, 1969; The Peter Prescription: How to Make Things Go Right, 1972; The Peter Plan: A Proposal for Survival, 1975; Competencies for Teaching, 4 vols., 1975; Peter's Quotations: Ideas for Our Time; Peter's People and Their Marvelous Ideas, 1979. Home: 2332 Via Anacapa Palos Verdes Estates CA 90274

PETER, PHILLIPS SMITH, elec. product co. exec.; b. Washington, Jan. 24, 1932; s. Edward Compston and Anita Phillipa (Smith) P.; B.A., U. Va., 1954, J.D., 1959; m. Jania Jayne Hutchins, Apr. 8, 1961; children—Phillips Smith Peter Jr., Jania Jayne Hutchins. Admitted to Calif. bar, 1959; asso. firm McCutchen, Doyle, Brown, Enerson, San Francisco, 1959-63; with Gen. Electric Co. and subs., various locations, 1963—, v.p. corp. bus. devel., 1973-76, v.p., Washington, 1976—. Mem. leadership com. United Fund, Darien, Conn., 1974—; mem. fin. com. Republican Town Com., Darien, 1974—; v.p. Federal City Council, Washington. Served with Transp. Corps, U.S. Army, 1954-56. Mem. Calif. Bar Assn., Elfun Soc., Order of Coif, Omicron Delta Kappa. Episcopalian. Clubs: Wee Burn (Darien); Eastern Yacht (Marblehead, Mass.); Farmington Country (Charlottesville, Va.); Ponte Vedra (Fla.); Lago Mar (Ft. Lauderdale, Fla.); Racquet (Miami Beach, Fla.); Landmark (Stamford, Conn.); Congl. Country (Bethesda, Md.); Georgetown, F Street (Washington); Coral Beach and Tennis (Bermuda). Mem. editorial bd. Va. Law Rev., 1957-59. Home: 10805 Tara Rd Potomac MD 20854 Office: 777 14th St NW Washington DC 20005

PETERA, FRED B., credit co. exec.; b. Czechoslovakia, Mar. 5, 1916; student in bus. adminstrn. Charles U., Prague, Czechoslovakia. Interpreter, Brit. Army, 1939-47; with UN, 1946-47; self-employed, 1947-50; sales rep. Baronet Corp., 1950-52; with Am. Express Co., N.Y.C., 1953—, successively v.p., pres. travel div., vice chmn. travel div. Served with Brit. Army, 1946-47. Home: 200 E 72d St New York NY 10021 Office: 125 Broad St New York NY 10004

PETERDI, GABOR F., printmaker, painter; b. Budapest, Hungary, 1915; s. Andor and Zseni (Varnai) P.; student Hungarian Acad., Budapest, Academia delle Belle Arte, Roma, Italy, also Studio 17, Paris, France; m. Maria, Sept. 17, 1941. Exhibited U.S. and abroad, including Library of Congress, Mus. Modern Art, N.Y.C., Art Inst. of Chgo., Tate Gallery, London, Am. Graphics, Paris, Am. Fedn. Arts traveling show, others; works rep. in collections Sao Paulo Mus., Brazil, Whitney Mus., Firestone Library, Detroit, Art Inst. of Chgo., Phila. and Bklyn. museums, Mus. Modern Art, N.Y.C., Mus. Boymans, Rotterdam, Rijksmuseum, Amsterdam, Kunstmuseum, Dusseldorf, Bibliotheque Nat. Paris, Victoria and Albert, London, Nat. Gallery of Victoria, Melbourn, Australia, numerous others; exhibited retrospective show Bklyn. Mus., 1959, Salt Lake City Art Center, 1961, Cleve. Mus. Art, 1962. Asso. prof. art Yale, 1961-65, prof. art, 1965—. Recipient Prix de Rome, 1930; gold medal for mural (with Lurcat), Paris, 1937; graphic prize Brooklyn Biennial, 1950; Am. Color Print ann., 1951, New England ann., 1952, 53, 55, 57; Sesnan Gold Medal, Pa. Acad. Art, 1958; grand prize Bklyn. Annual, 1956; 1st prize Allied Artists Am. internat. graphic competition, 1959; prize Bklyn. Mus. Biennial, 1960; Adele Hyde Morrison medal Bay Printmakers, 1960; Ford Found. grant, 1960; Phila. Mus. Prize, 1961; Pennel medal Pa. Acad., 1961; purchase award Internat. Graphic Show, Lugano, 1962; Mus. of Western Art prize, Tokyo, 1964; purchase prize Duane Coll., 1971, Mus. of Anchorage, 1972, Davidson Coll., 1972, Honolulu Acad. Arts, 1971, 75, U. Wis., 1972, Nat. Print Exhbn., 1973; 1st prize in painting New Eng. Ann., Silvermine, 1976. Guggenheim fellow, 1964-65. Mem. Florentine Acad. Design (hon.). Author: Printmaking 1959. Home: 108 Highland Ave Rowayton CT 06853

PETERFREUND, HERBERT, educator; b. Mildred, Pa., Mar. 5, 1913; s. Otto and Sarah (Groag) P.; A.B., Pa. State U., 1933; LL.B., Harvard, 1936; LL.M., Columbia, 1942; m. Clara Sidney. Admitted to N.Y. bar, 1937; pvt. practice, N.Y.C., 1937-41; faculty N.Y. U. Sch. Law, 1946-78, prof., 1953-78, Frederick I. and Grace A. Stokes prof. law, 1969-78; Disting. vis. prof. law U. San Diego Sch. Law, 1978—; U.S. commr. of jurors, So. Dist. N.Y., 1954-68; mem. adv. com. N.Y. Jud. Conf., 1966-78. Served from pvt. to capt. AUS. 1942-46. Recipient Great Tchr. award N.Y. U. Alumni Fedn., 1968. Mem. Order of Coif (hon.), Phi Kappa Phi, Pi Gamma Mu. Author: Manual of New York Practice, 2d edit., 1959; Appleton's New York Practice, 6th edit., 1960; (with Joseph M. McLaughlin) Cases and Other Materials on New York Practice, 4th edit., 1978. Home: 10400 Caminito Cuervo 227 San Diego CA 92108

PETERFREUND, SHELDON PAUL, educator; b. Camden, N.J., Dec. 3, 1917; s. Otto and Sarah (Groag) P.; B.S., Harvard, 1939; M.A., U. Chgo., 1940; Ph.D., U. Pa., 1948; m. Josephine A. Rogowicz, 1949. Faculty, Suffolk U., Boston, 1948-49; faculty Syracuse (N.Y.) U., 1949—, now prof. Served with USAAF, 1942-45. Decorated Air medal. Mem. Am. Philos. Assn., AAUP. Author: (with T.C. Denise and E. Albert) Great Traditions in Ethics, 1953; An Introduction to American Philosophy, 1959; (with T.C. Denise) Contemporary Philosophy and its Origins, 1967. Home: 20 Erregger Terr Syracuse NY 13224

PETERING, RALPH EDWIN, ret. elec. mfg. co. exec.; b. LaPorte, Ind., Apr. 26, 1908; s. George H. and Magdalena (Droege) P.; B.S., U. Ill., 1931; postgrad. Loyola U., Chgo., 1938; m. Ernestine Hohengarten, Oct. 14, 1939; children—Nancy Jane, Elizabeth Anne, Robert R. Sr. accountant Lybrand, Ross Bros. & Montgomery, Chgo., 1931-33, 35-42; comptroller Silver Fleet Motor Express, Inc., Louisville, 1933-35; auditor Fed. Res. Bank, Chgo., 1935; comptroller Emerson Electric Co. (formerly Emerson Electric Mfg. Co.), St. Louis, 1942-46, comptroller, asst. sec., 1946-50, comptroller, asst. sec., asst. treas., 1950-51, v.p., asst. treas., 1951, v.p., treas., 1952-65, sr. v.p., 1965-73, also dir.; dir. Mattel Inc. C.P.A., Ill. Mem. Am. Inst. C.P.A.'s (Elijah Watts Sells Gold medal 1938), Ill. Soc. C.P.A.'s (Gold medal 1938), Beta Gamma Sigma. Home: 1220 Hampton Park Dr Richmond Heights Saint Louis MO 63117

PETERKIN, DEWITT, JR., banker; b. Webster Groves, Mo., June 6, 1913; s. DeWitt and Margaret (O'Brien) P.; grad. Kent (Conn.) Sch., 1933; A.B., Yale, 1937; m. Jane Parks (dec.); 1 dau., Clare; m. 2d, Katharine Urban, Oct. 23, 1948; children—DeWitt III, George Urban, Kate, Christopher (dec.), Patrick. With J.P. Morgan & Co., Inc. (now Morgan Guaranty Trust Co. N.Y.), N.Y.C., 1937—, v.p., 1953-64, sr. v.p., 1964-65, exec. v.p., 1965-71, vice chmn., 1971-76, advisor to mgmt., 1976-78, also mem. adv. council; dir. Champion Internat., Inc., Stauffer Chem. Co., Trane Co. Dir. Yale Alumni Fund, Yale Devel. Bd.; cons. chmn. St. Luke's-Roosevelt Hosp. Center. Trustee, pres. Roosevelt Hosp., N.Y.C.; bd. dirs. Nat. Audubon Soc. Served to capt. USNR, 1941-45. Decorated Silver Star, Bronze Star (2). Episcopalian. Clubs: Wee Burn Country (Darien); Ekwanok Golf (Manchester, Vt.); Links, Yale (N.Y.C.); Bohemian (San Francisco); Noroton (Conn.) Yacht. Home: 224 Long Neck Point Rd Darien CT 06820 Office: 23 Wall St New York City NY 10015

PETERKIN, GEORGE ALEXANDER, JR., diversified co. exec.; b. Baton Rouge, Apr. 12, 1927; s. George Alexander and Genevieve (Favrot) P.; B.B.A., U. Tex., 1948; m. Nancy Girling, Jan. 27, 1965; children—George Alexander III, Julie, John Thomas, Susan Lynn. With Dixie Carriers, Inc., Galveston, Tex., New Orleans, Houston, 1949-53, pres., 1953-72; pres. Kirby Industries, Inc., Houston, 1972-76, Kirby Exploration Co., 1976—. Bd. dirs. Tex. Med. Center, 1973—, Living Bank, 1968—; trustee Tex. Children's Hosp., 1966—. Served with USN, 1945-46. Mem. Young President's Orgn. (pres. 1971), World Bus. Council, Chief Execs. Forum. Home: 4931 Tilbury St Houston TX 77056 Office: PO Box 1745 Houston TX 77001

PETERLE, TONY JOHN, educator; b. Cleve., July 7, 1925; s. Anton and Anna (Katic) P.; B.S., Utah State U., 1949; M.S., U. Mich., 1950, Ph.D. (Univ. scholar), 1954; Fulbright scholar, U. Aberdeen, Scotland, 1954-55; postgrad. Oak Ridge Inst. Nuclear Studies, 1961; m. Thelma Josephine Coleman, July 30, 1949; children—Ann Faulkner, Tony Scott. With Niederhauser Lumber Co., 1947-49, Macfarland Tree Service, 1949-51; research biologist Mich. Dept. Conservation, 1951-54, asst. dir. Rose Lake Expt. Sta., 1955-59; leader Ohio Coop. Wildlife Research unit U.S. Fish and Wildlife Service, Dept. Interior, 1959-63; asso. prof., then prof. zoology Ohio State U., Columbus, 1959—, chmn. faculty population and environmental biology, 1968-69, chmn. dept. zoology, 1969—, dir. program in environ. biology, 1970-71; co-organizer XIII Internat. Congress Game Biology, chmn. internat. affairs com., mem. com. ecotoxicology, 1979-80; mem. com. rev. EPA pesticide decision making Nat. Acad. Scis.-NRC; mem. vis. scientists program Am. Inst. Biol. Scis.-ERDA, 1971-77; mem. com. pesticides Nat. Acad. Scis.; mem. ecology com. of sci. adv. council EPA, 1979—; mem. research units coordinating com. Ohio Coop. Wildlife and Fisheries, 1963—. Served with AUS, 1943-46. Fellow AAAS, Am. Inst. Biol. Scis., Ohio Acad. Sci.; mem. Wildlife Disease Assn., Wildlife Soc. (regional rep. 1962-67, v.p. 1968, pres. 1972), Ecol. Soc., INTECOL-NSF panel U.S.-Japan Program, Xi Sigma Pi, Phi Kappa Phi. Editor: Jour. of Wildlife Management, 1969-70. Home: RFD 3 Delaware OH 43015 Office: Dept Zoology Ohio State U 1735 Neil Ave Columbus OH 43210

PETERMANN, JOHN BERNHARD, lawyer; b. Wellston, Okla., Oct. 26, 1910; s. Conrad Bernhard and Bessie (Gleckler) P.; student San Diego State Coll., 1928-32; B.S. in Bus. Adminstrn., U. So. Calif., 1934, LL.B., 1937; m. Roberta Kessner, Sept. 3, 1937 (dec. 1949); 1 son, Conrad D.; m. 2d, Bette Jane Woolsey, June 30, 1954. With Calif. Cotton Oil Corp., Los Angeles, 1933-40; admitted to Calif. bar, 1937; practiced law, Los Angeles, 1940—; city judge, Hawthorne, Calif., 1951; dir. Industria Americana & Co., Inc., Los Angeles. Pres., So. Calif. Lions Eye Inst.; bd. dirs. Lions Hear Program. Mem. Am. Arbitration Assn. (arbitrator). Mason (Shriner), Lion (past dist. gov.). Home: 6435 Sherbourne Dr Los Angeles CA 90056 Office: 700 S Flower St Los Angeles CA 90017

PETERS, ALAN, scientist, educator; b. Nottingham, Eng., Dec. 6, 1929; s. Robert and Mabel (Woplington) P.; B.Sc., Bristol (Eng.) U., 1951, Ph.D., 1954; m. Verona Muriel Shipman, Sept. 30, 1955; children—Ann Verona, Sally Elizabeth, Susan Clare. Came to U.S., 1966. Lectr. anatomy Edinburgh (Scotland) U., 1958-66; vis. lectr. Harvard, 1963-64; prof., chmn. dept. anatomy Boston U., 1966—. Mem. anatomy com. Nat. Bd. Med. Examiners, 1971-75; mem. neurology B study sect. NIH, 1975, chmn., 1978-79. Served to 2d lt. Med. Corps, Royal Army, 1955-57. Mem. Anat. Soc. G.B. and Ireland (Symington prize anatomy 1962, overseas mem. council 1969), Assn. Anatomy Chmn. (pres. 1976-77), Am. Anat. Assn., Am. Soc. Cell Biology, Soc. Neuroscis. Author: (with S.L. Palay and H. deF Webster) The Fine Structure of the Nervous System, 1970, 2d edit., 1976; (with A.N. Davison) Myelination, 1970. Contbr. articles profl. jours. Editorial bd. Jour. Neurocytology, Anat. Record. Home: 16 High Rock Circle Waltham MA 02154 Office: Dept Anatomy Boston Univ Sch Medicine 80 E Concord St Boston MA

PETERS, ALTON EMIL, lawyer; b. Albany, N.Y., Mar. 21, 1935; s. Emil and Winifred (Rosch) P.; A.B. cum laude, Harvard U., 1955, LL.B., 1958; m. Elizabeth Irving Berlin, Feb. 27, 1970; 1 dau., Rachel Canfield; 1 stepdau., Emily Anstice Fisher. Admitted to N.Y. bar, 1958, U.S. Dist. Ct. for So. Dist. N.Y., 1963; asso. firm Bleakley, Platt, Schmidt & Fritz, N.Y.C., 1958-65, partner, 1965—. Bd. dirs. Am. Friends of Covent Garden and Royal Ballet, N.Y.C., 1971—, v.p., 1971—; chmn. U.S. council Am. Museum in Britain, Bath, Eng., 1970—; bd. dirs. Goodwill Industries of Greater N.Y., Inc., 1966—, pres., 1971—; mem. adv. com. Lamont Gallery, Phillips Exeter Acad., Exeter, N.H., 1970—; bd. dirs. Met. Opera Assn., N.Y.C., 1968—, sec., 1974—; bd. dirs. Met. Opera Guild, 1965—, 1st v.p., 1971—; hon. trustee Signet Asso., Cambridge, Mass. Mem. Assn. Bar City N.Y., N.Y. State Bar Assn., Am. Judicature Soc., Am. Bar Assn., English-Speaking Union U.S. (dir. 1968—, mem. exec. com. 1973—, chmn. N.Y. br. 1972—). Episcopalian (mem. adv. council Episcopal Ch. Found. 1967—). Clubs: Church, Century Assn., Downtown Assn., Knickerbocker, The Pilgrims (N.Y.C.); Odd Volumes (Boston). Home: 1185 Park Ave New York NY 10028 Office: 80 Pine St New York NY 10005

PETERS, ARTHUR KING, import-export co. exec.; b. Charleston, W.Va., Oct. 17, 1919; s. Arthur Cushing and Jessie (King) P.; A.B., Cornell U., 1940; M.A., Columbia, 1954, Ph.D., 1969; m. Sarah Jebb Whitaker, Oct. 21, 1943; children—Robert Bruce, Margaret Allen, Michael Whitaker. With W.R. Grace & Co., 1940-50; pres., owner A.K. Peters Co., N.Y.C., 1950—; pres. French-Am. Found., N.Y.C., 1977—, chmn., 1978—; asst. prof. French lit. Hunter Coll. City U. N.Y., 1971-74; speaker internat. trade confs., radio and TV. Mem. U.S. Trade Mission to Peru, Argentina, 1957; pres. Nat. council Am. Importers, 1965, sr. counselor, 1966—. Chmn. Westchester com. Sarah Lawrence Coll., 1961-63; chmn. com. selection sch. trustees Bronxville, N.Y., 1965; bd. dirs. Community Fund Bronxville, 1962-65. Served to maj. U.S. Army, 1941-46. Mem. U.S. C. of C. (internat. com.), Modern Lang. Assn., Assn. Am. Tchrs. French, Am. Arbitration Assn. (internat. trade panel), Phi Delta Theta. Mem. Ref. Ch. (deacon). Clubs: Am. Alpine, Coffee House, University (N.Y.C.); Bronxville Field. Author: Cocteau and Gide, 1973. Critic, author scholarly articles. Translator French lit., mountaineering works. Home: 14 Village Ln Bronxville NY 10708 Office: A K Peters Co 230 Park Ave New York NY 10017 also French-Am Found 680 Park Ave New York NY

PETERS, BERNADETTE (BERNADETTE LAZZARA), actress; b. Queens, N.Y., Feb. 28, 1948; d. Peter and Marguerite (Maltese) Lazzara; student Quintano Sch. Young Profls., N.Y.C. Regular on TV series All's Fair, 1976-77; frequent guest appearances on TV; films include: The Longest Yard, 1974, Silent Movie, 1976, Vigilante Force, 1976, W.C. Fields and Me, 1976, The Jerk, 1979; stage appearances include: The Most Happy Fella, 1959, Gypsy, 1961, This is Google, 1962, Riverwind, 1966, The Penny Friend, 1966, Curly McDimple, 1966, Johnny No-Trump, 1967, George M!, 1968, Dames at Sea, 1968, La Strada, 1969, W.C., 1971, On the Town, 1971, Tartuffe, 1972, Mack and Mabel, 1974. Recipient Drama Desk award for Dames at Sea, 1968. Office: care Agy for Performing Arts 9000 Sunset Blvd Suite 315 Los Angeles CA 90069*

PETERS, BROCK, actor, singer; b. N.Y.C., July 2, 1927; s. Sonnie and Alma A. (Norford) Fisher; student U. Chgo., 1944-46, City Coll. N.Y., 1946-47; student acting with Betty Cashman, Michael Howard, Robert Lewis, Harry Wagstaff Gribble; D.Performing Arts (hon.), Sienna Hts. Coll., 1975; m. Dolores Daniels, July 29, 1961; 1 dau. Theatrical appearances include Porgy and Bess, 1943 (also on tour), South Pacific, 1943, Anna Lucasta, 1944-45, My Darlin' Aida, 1952, Head of a Family, 1950, The Year Round, 1956, Mister Johnson, 1956, King of the Dark Chamber, 1961, Kwamina, 1961, Othello, 1963, 65, Great White Hope (nat. tour), 1970, Lost in the Stars, 1972; numerous stock engagements; bass soloist DePaur Inf. Chorus, 1947-50; films include Carmen Jones, 1954, Porgy and Bess, 1959, To Kill a Mockingbird, 1962, Heavens Above, 1962, The L-Shaped Room, 1963, The Pawnbroker, 1963, Major Dundee, 1964, P.J., 1966, The Daring Game, 1966, The Incident, 1968, The MacMasters, 1969, Black Girl, 1972, Soylent Green, 1973, Slaughter II, 1973, Lost in the Stars, 1974; co-producer Five on the Black Hand Side, 1973, Two-Minute Warning, 1976; TV movie: SST-Death Flight, 1977; numerous TV and nightclub appearances. Chmn. Cal. Arts Commn., 1975. Recipient All Am. Press Assn. award; Box Office Blue Ribbon award; Allen AME award; Am. Soc. African Culture Emancipation award, 1962; Man of Year award Douglas Jr. High Sch., 1964; Drama Desk award, 1972; Outer Circle Critics award, 1972; Tony nomination, 1973. Mem. Actors Equity Assn., A.F.T.R.A., Screen Actors Guild, Am. Guild Variety Artists. Address: care Diamond Artists Ltd 9200 Sunset Blvd Suite 909 Los Angeles CA 90069. *The quality of whatever I try to do as an actor, singer, etc., is directly related to my primary concern, which isto be a fully matured sensitive, flexible individual in heart and mind.**

PETERS, BRUCE HARRY, neurologist; b. Ft. Dodge, Iowa, July 18, 1937; s. Harry Bertus and Bess Anne (Rachuy) P.; B.A., U. Iowa, 1959, M.D., M.S., 1963; m. Nancy J. Harban, July 3, 1964; children—Thomas, Elizabeth, Benjamin. Intern, U. Calif., San Francisco, 1963-64; resident in neurology U. Iowa, 1966-69; asst. prof. neurology U. Tex., Galveston, 1969-72, asso. prof., 1972-75, prof., 1975—; cons. in field. Served with M.C. USAF, 1964-66. Diplomate Am. Bd. Psychiatry and Neurology. Fellow Am. Acad. Neurology; mem. Soc. Neurosci., Internat. Neuropsychol. Soc., Brit. Brain Inst., Am. Med. Soc., Tex. Neurol. Soc. (pres.). Club: Galveston Raquet. Contbr. numerous articles to med. jours., 1961—; bd. editors Tex. Reports on Biology and Medicine, 1976—; research on behavioral neurology and memory augmentation; inventor quantitative neurol. test battery, 1976. Home: 2958 Dominique Galveston TX 77551 Office: 915 Strand Galveston TX 77550

PETERS, C. WILBUR, retail fabric chain exec.; b. Hospers, Iowa, Dec. 16, 1922; s. Cornelius and Tena (Mulder) P.; B.B.A., U. Minn., 1947; D. Humanities (hon.), Pillsbury Baptist Bible Coll., 1979; m. Bessie Van Essen, Dec. 20, 1943; children—Judith Ann Peters Becklund, Roger. Chief indsl. engr. McQuay, Inc., Mpls., 1947-60; pres. Minnesota Fabrics Inc., Charlotte, N.C., 1960—, also chief exec. officer; dir. Nat. City Bank, Mpls.; bus. cons. Pillsbury Bapt. Bible Coll. Baptist. Home: 45 Fairway Ridge Clover SC 29710 Office: PO Box 32606 Charlotte NC 29710

PETERS, CHESTER EVAN, univ. adminstr.; b. Mpls., Oct. 15, 1922; s. Robert Earl and Gladys (Kresky) P.; B.S., Kans. State U., 1947, M.S., 1950; Ph.D., U. Wis., 1953; m. Doris Lerene Clow, Jan. 24, 1943; children—Karen Sue Peters Hartner, Stephen Chester. Asst. dean Kans. State U. Sch. Arts and Sci., Manhattan, 1947-51, dir. placement, 1953-62, dean students, 1962-67, v.p. student affairs, 1967—. Reader, U.S. Office Edn.; pres. Coll. Placement Council. Served to capt., inf. AUS, 1943-46. Mem. Nat. (pres. 1971-72), Kans. (pres.) assns. student personnel adminstrs., Nat. Woodcarvers Am., Farmhouse. Methodist. Kiwanian. Home: 3140 Bermudalane St Manhattan KS 66502. *The commitment to serve others through whatever talents I possess has been a rewarding and fulfilling way of living.*

PETERS, CLYDE PHILIP, publishing co. exec.; b. Harrisburg, Pa., Dec. 10, 1929; s. Clyde Chester and Helena May (Zorger) P.; student Harvard Bus. Sch., 1974; children—Kathleen, Patricia, Colleen, Maureen. Prodn. asst. Stackpole Books, Harrisburg, 1953-59, asst. to sales mgr., 1959-62, sales mgr., 1962-64, dir. mktg., 1964-72, exec. v.p., 1972-75, pres., 1975—; lectr. Radcliffe Pub. Procedures Course, Denver Pub. Inst., Pubmart Seminars; lectr. mktg. Harrisburg Area Community Coll. Served with USMCR, 1950-52, Res. AUS, 1952-73. Mem. Assn. Am. Pubs. (chmn. smaller pub. com., dir. 1977—), Outdoor Writers Assn. Am. Republican. Home: 704 Cedar Ridge Ln Mechanicsburg PA 17055 Office: Stackpole Books Cameron & Kelker Sts Harrisburg PA 17105

PETERS, DENNIS GAIL, chemist; b. Los Angeles, Apr. 17, 1937; s. Samuel and Phyllis Dorothy (Pope) P.; B.S. cum laude, Calif. Inst. Tech., 1958; Ph.D., Harvard U., 1962. Mem. faculty Ind. U., 1962—, prof. chemistry, 1974—, Herman T. Briscoe prof., 1975—. Woodrow Wilson fellow, 1958-59; NIH predoctoral fellow, 1959-62; recipient Ulysses G. Weatherly award distinguished teaching Ind. U., 1969; grantee NSF, Am. Chem. Soc. Mem. Am. Chem. Soc., N.Y. Acad. Scis. Co-author textbooks, contbr. articles profl. jours. Home: 1401 Nancy St Bloomington IN 47401 Office: Dept Chemistry Ind Univ Bloomington IN 47405

PETERS, DONALD CAMERON, constrn. co. exec.; b. Milw., Mar. 25, 1915; s. Simon C. and May (Gnewuch) P.: B.S. in Civil Engring., Marquette U., 1938; m. Twila Bingel, Dec. 7, 1940; children—Susan (Mrs. Douglas Ingram), David C., Bruce C., Douglas C. Engr., Siesel Constrn. Co., Milw., 1938-44; v.p., dir. Crump, Inc., Pitts., 1944-51; pres., dir. Mellon-Stuart Co., Pitts., 1951—, chmn., 1973—; chmn. Cameron Constrn. Co., Pitts.; dir. Overly Mfg. Co., Liberty Mut. Life Ins. Co., Michael Baker, Inc.; v.p. Pitts. Realty Investment Trust. Mem. 5 man gen. com. rewriting Pitts. Bldg. Code, 1947; mem., vice chmn. Pa. Registration Bd. Profl. Engrs., 1962—; chmn. bd. standards and appeals Pitts. Bur. Bldg. Inspection, 1960-72; past pres. Pitts. Builders Exchange. Chmn. bd. suprs. Pine Twp., Allegheny County, 1953—. Chmn. Constrn. Industry Advancement Program Western Pa., 1975—; trustee LaRoche Coll., Pitts.; dir. North Pitts. Community Devel. Corp., 1971-76; mem. corporate bd. North Hills Passavant Hosp. Registered profl. engr., Wis., Pa. Fellow ASCE; mem. Nat. (nat. dir. 1954-57, chmn. bd. ethical rev. 1978-79), Pa. (pres. 1953-54) socs. profl. engrs., Asso. Gen. Contractors Am. (nat. dir.), Pitts. C. of C. (chmn., dir.), Master Builders Assn. Western Pa. (past pres.), Triangle, Tau Beta Pi, Alpha Sigma Nu. Club: Duquesne (Pitts.). Home: RD 3 Pearce Mill Rd Wexford PA 15090 Office: 1425 Beaver Ave Pittsburgh PA 15233

PETERS, DOUGLAS DENNISON, economist, banker; b. Brandon, Man., Can., Mar. 3, 1930; s. Wilfrid Seymour and Mary Gladys (Dennison) P.; B.Com., Queen's U., Kingston, Ont., Can.; Ph.D., U. Pa.; m. Audrey Catherine Clark, June 26, 1954; children—David Wilfrid, Catherine Elaine Peters Dixon. With Bank of Montreal, 1950-60; chief economist, dir. econ. research dept. Toronto-Dominion Bank, Toronto, 1966—, v.p., chief economist, 1972—. Trustee The Fraser Inst., Vancouver. Mem. Can. (mem. exec. council), Am. econs. assns., Toronto Assn. Bus. Economists (past pres.), Nat. Assn. Bus. Economists, Royal Econs. Assn. Co-author: The Monetarist Counter-Revolution, 1979. Home: 28 Admiral Rd Toronto ON Canada Office: Toronto Dominion Bank PO Box 1 Toronto Dominion Centre Toronto ON M5K 1A2 Canada

PETERS, DOYLE BUREN, educator, govt. ofcl.; b. Chester, Tex., Nov. 23, 1922; s. Sam B. and Ellie E. (Handley) P.; B.S., Tex. A. and M. Coll., 1949, M.S., 1951; Ph.D., U. Calif. at Berkeley, 1954; m. Norma Rider, Feb. 4, 1950; children—Carol Peters, David, Scott, John. Soil scientist USDA, Urbana, Ill., 1954—; asst. prof. soil physics U. Ill., Urbanna, 1954-59, asso. prof., 1959-65, prof., 1967—. Served with AUS, 1943-45. Fellow Am. Soc. Agronomy; mem. Soil Sci. Soc. Am. (chmn. div. 1964), Sigme Xi, Phi Kappa Phi. Research and publs. in mass and energy transport in soil-plant-atmosphere continuum especially evapotranspiration and photosynthesis of crop communities problems of soil water flow related to ion and water absorption by plant roots. Home: 401 Evergreen Ct Urbana IL 61801

PETERS, EDWARD MURRAY, educator; b. New Haven, May 21, 1936; s. Edward Murray and Marjorie (Corcoran) P.; B.A., Yale, 1963, M.A., 1965, Ph.D., 1967; m. Patricia Ann Knapp, July 8, 1961; children—Nicole, Moira, Edward. Instr. in English and history Quinnipiac Coll., Hamden, Conn., 1964-67; asst. prof. history U. Calif. at San Diego, 1967-68; Henry Charles Lea asst. prof. medieval history U. Pa., 1968-70, Henry Charles Lea asso. prof. medieval history, 1970—, curator Henry Charles Lea Library, 1968—. Served with AUS, 1956-59. Woodrow Wilson fellow, 1963-64, Woodrow Wilson dissertation fellow, 1966-67; hon. Sterling fellow, 1966-67. Fellow Royal Hist. Soc.; mem. Am. Hist. Assn., Mediaeval Acad. Am. Author: The Shadow King, 1970; (with A.C. Kors) Witchcraft in Europe, 1100-1750, 1972; Europe: The World of the Middle Ages, 1977; The Magician, the Witch and the Law, 1978; TV series The World of the Middle Ages, 1974; The World Around the Revolution, 1977; also articles, revs., introductions. Editor, translator: (with Jeanne Krochalis) The World of Piers Plowman, 1975; Heresy and Authority in Medieval Europe, 1980. Home: 4225 Regent Sq Philadelphia PA 19104 Office: Dept History U Pa Philadelphia PA 19104

PETERS, ELLEN ASH, justice Conn. Supreme Ct.; b. Berlin, Mar. 21, 1930; d. Ernest Edward and Hildegard (Simon) Ash; came to U.S., 1939, naturalized, 1947; B.A. with honors, Swarthmore Coll., 1951; LL.B. cum laude, Yale U., 1954, M.A. (hon.), 1964; m. Phillip I. Blumberg; children—David Bryan Peters, James Douglas Peters, Julie Peters. Admitted to Conn. bar, 1957; law clk. to judge U.S. Circuit Ct., 1954-55; asso. in law U. Calif., Berkeley, 1955-56; asst. prof. Yale U. Law Sch., 1956-59, asso. prof., 1959-64, prof., 1964-75, Southmayd prof., 1975-78, adj. prof., 1978—; asso. justice Conn. Supreme Ct., Hartford, 1978—. Bd. mgrs. Swarthmore Coll.; mem. Conn. Permanent Commn. on Status of Women, 1973-74, Conn. Bd. Pardons, 1978—, Conn. Law Revision Commn., 1978—. Mem. Conn. Bar Assn., Am. Law Inst. Author: Commercial Transactions: Cases, Texts, and Problems, 1971; Negotiable Instruments Primer, 1974; contbr. articles to profl. jours. Office: 235 Church St New Haven CT 06510

PETERS, EMIL EDWARD, law enforcement ofcl.; b. San Antonio, Feb. 7, 1918; s. Edward Albert and Constance (Bozetta) P.; student St. John's Sem., FBI Nat. Acad., 1956, FBI Nat. Exec. Inst., 1977; m. Mary Ellen Bonugli, May 21, 1939; children—Ronald Thomas, Paul James, Jerome David. Salesman, 1938-41; joined San Antonio Police Dept., 1941, successively sgt., lt., capt., insp., apptd. chief of police, 1971—; mem. Atty. Gen.'s Council on Organized Crime, Gov.'s Com. Standards and Goals for Law Enforcement, Tex. Commn. on Law Enforcement Standards and Edn.; dir. City Employees Credit Union, San Antonio. Recipient citations K.C., Optimist Club, Sigma Delta Chi of Tex., Bexar County Shields Assn.; Dir.'s award U.S. Secret Service. Mem. Internat. Assn. Chiefs of Police, Tex. (past pres.), San Antonio police assns., Tex. Municipal League (chiefs of police div.). Roman Catholic. Clubs: Lions, Fathers'. Contbr. articles on law enforcement to profl. publs. Home: 1510 Greer Ave San Antonio TX 78210 Office: PO Box 9346 San Antonio TX 78285

PETERS, FARNSLEY LEWELLYN, assn. exec.; b. Louisville, Aug. 11, 1929; s. Floyd P. and Freda E. (Meyer) P.; B.S., U. Wis., 1952; m. Jean Davies, June 28, 1952; children—Susan, David. Vice pres. F.P. Peters Moving & Storage Co., Joliet, Ill., 1954-62; dept. mgr. Madison (Wis.) C. of C., 1962-65; mgr. Greater Aurora (Ill.) C. of C., 1965-70; exec. v.p. Rockford (Ill.) Area C. of C., 1970-78, Cin. C. of C., 1978—. Served as 1st lt. U.S. Army, 1952-54. Recipient Outstanding Citizen award DuKane Valley Council, 1971. Mem. Am. (dir.), Ill. (pres.) assns. chamber commerce execs., Insts. for Orgn. Mgmt. (bd. regents), Ill. Jr. C. of C. (life), Alpha Chi Rho. Rotarian. Club: Nat. W (U. Wis.). Home: 5909 Lengwood Dr Cincinnati OH 45244 Office: 120 W Fifth St Cincinnati OH 45202

PETERS, FRANK C., univ. pres.; b. Russia, July 5, 1920; s. Cornelius C. and Mrs. (Hildebrandt) P.; B.A., Tabor Coll., 1947; M.Sc., Kans. State U., 1948; B.D., U. W. Ont., 1950; M.Th., Victoria U., 1952; Th.D., Central Baptist Coll., Kansas City, 1956; Ph.D., U. Kans., 1959; m. Melita Krause, Aug. 15, 1943; children—Robert James, Edward Allen, Gerald Franklin, Marianne Joyce, John Wesley. Instr. psychology Waterloo Coll., 1949-53; pres. Tabor Coll., 1953-56; dean Mennonite Brethren Coll. of Arts, 1957-65; prof. psychology Wilfrid Laurier U. (formerly Waterloo (Ont.) Lutheran U.), 1965-68, pres., 1968—, acting dean arts and sci., 1967-68, also vice chancellor. Mem. Canadian, Ont. psychol. assns. Mennonite. Rotarian. Co-author: History of the Mennonites, 1967; The Compassionate Community, 1969. Home: 76 Shuh Ave Kitchener ON Canada Office: Wilfrid Laurier U Office of Pres Waterloo ON N2L 3C5 Canada*

PETERS, FRANK LEWIS, JR., music critic; b. Springfield, Mo., Oct. 19, 1930; s. Frank Lewis and Mary (Frissell) P.; A.B., Drury Coll., 1951; postgrad. State U. Iowa, 1953-55; m. Alba Manciani, Jan. 20, 1963; children—Carl Nathaniel, Adrian Frissell. Copy editor Ark. Gazette, Little Rock, 1958-59, Springfield (Mo.) Leader & Press, 1960-61; mng. editor Rome (Italy) Daily Am., 1962-64; music editor St. Louis Post-Dispatch, 1967—. Served with AUS, 1951-52. Recipient Pulitzer prize distinguished criticism, 1972. Mem. SAR, Lambda Chi Alpha. Episcopalian. Home: 1400 S Rock Hill Rd Saint Louis MO 63119 Office: 1133 Franklin Ave Saint Louis MO 63101

PETERS, FRED, lawyer; b. N.Y.C., Dec. 7, 1925; s. Samuel and Frieda P.; B.J., U. Mo., 1949; LL.B., Bklyn. Law Sch., 1952, J.D., 1952; m. Florence Berler, June 27, 1948; children—Franne, Jeffrey, Jonathan. Admitted to N.Y. bar, 1952; atty., chief trial counsel Allstate Ins. Co., N.Y.C., 1952-57; partner firm Berger & Peters, Bklyn., 1957-75; pres. Peters, Berger & Koshel P.C., Bklyn., 1975—; lectr. law and trial technique Bklyn. Law Sch., St. Johns Law Sch., Hofstra Law Sch., Practicing Law Inst. Mem. Charter Revision Commn., Glen Cove, N.Y.; master Civil Ct., N.Y.C. Served with USNR, 1943-46. Mem. Assn. Trial Lawyers Am., Def. Assn. N.Y., Bklyn. Bar Assn., Am. Bar Assn., Nassau County Bar Assn., Met. Trial Lawyers Assn., Nassau-Suffolk Trial Lawyers, Inner Circle of Advocates (pres.). Club: K.P. (past chanceller comdr.). Home: 43 Highland Rd Glen Cove NY 11542 Office: Peters Berger & Koshel PC 26 Court St Brooklyn NY 11242

PETERS, GORDON BENES, musician; b. Oak Park, Ill., Jan. 4, 1931; s. Arthur George and Julia Anne (Benes) P.; student Northwestern U., 1949-50; Mus.B., Eastman Sch. Music, 1956, Mus.M., 1962; m. Catherine Ann Kemper, Sept. 15, 1962; children—Renee, Erica. Percussionist, Rochester (N.Y.) Philharmonic Orch., 1955-58, Grant Park Symphony Orch., Chgo., 1955-58; faculty Rochester Bd. Edn., 1956-57, Geneseo State Tchrs. Coll., 1957-58; prin. percussionist Chgo. Symphony Orch., 1959—; condr., adminstr. Civic Orch. Chgo., 1966—; condr. Elmhurst Symphony Orch., 1968-73. Instr. percussion instruments Northwestern U., 1963-68. Served with U.S. Mil. Acad. Band, 1950-53. Recipient Pierre Monteux disciple award conducting, 1962. Mem. Percussion Arts Soc. (pres. 1962-66), Am. Symphony Orch. League, Common Cause, Condrs. Guild (treas., exec. com. 1979—). Author-pub.: The Drummer: Man; arranger-pub. Marimba Ensemble arrangements; composer-pub. Swords of Moda-Ling. Editor percussion column Instrumentalist mag., 1963-69. Contbr. articles profl. jours. Home: 824 Hinman Ave #2N Evanston IL 60202 Office: 220 S Michigan Ave Chicago IL 60604

PETERS, HENRY AUGUSTUS, neurologist; b. Oconomowoc, Wis., Dec. 21, 1920; s. Henry Augustus and Emma N. P.; B.A., M.D., U. Wis.; m. Jean McWilliams, 1950; children—Henry, Kurt, Eric, Mark. Prof. dept. neurology and rehab. medicine U. Wis. Med. Sch., Madison; mem. med. adv. bd. Muscular Dystrophy Assn. Served to lt. M.C., U.S. Navy. Fellow A.C.P.; mem. Wis. Med. Assn., Am. Acad. Neurology. Club: Rotary. Office: 600 Highland Ave Madison WI 53706

PETERS, HENRY BUCKLAND, educator, optometrist; b. Oakland, Calif., Nov. 2, 1916; s. Thomas Henry and Eleanor Bernice (Hough) P.; A.B., U. Calif. at Berkeley, 1938; M.A., U. Nebr., 1939; D.O.S., So. Coll. Optometry, 1971; m. Anne Zara Ledin, Feb. 3, 1968; children—Lynn (Mrs. Joseph P. McDonough), Thomas Henry, James Clifton, Christopher Patrick, Elizabeth Anne. Pvt. practice optometry, Chico, Calif., 1939-40, Oakland, 1946-59; instr., asst. prof. U. Calif. at Berkeley, 1947-62, asso. prof., asst. dean Sch. Optometry, 1962-69; prof., dean Sch. Optometry, prof. pub. health Sch. Medicine, Med. Center, U. Ala., Birmingham, 1969—; pres. Nat. Health Council, 1978-79; cons. So. Regional Edn. Bd., S.C. Commn. Higher Edn., Calif. Dept. Pub. Health, Lawrence Radiation Lab., Aerojet Gen., Nat. Acad. Sci. Inst. Medicine; v.p. Children's Vision Center, Oakland, 1963-69; dir. Calif. Vision Service, 1953-59; mem. optometric rev. com. Bur. Health, Manpower and Edn., HEW, 1970-73, Rev. and Program Council, Medicaid, Calif., 1966-69; dir. Community Service Council, Birmingham, 1969-76; mem. deans com. VA Hosp., Birmingham; bd. dirs. Birmingham Health Services Agy., 1976-79, chmn. manpower com., 1976—; chmn. optometry services adv. com. VA, 1977—, chmn. spl. adv. com. on legally blind, 1977—. Served to lt. USNR, 1942-46. Named Optometrist of Year, Calif. Optometric Assn., 1959. Fellow Am. Pub. Health Assn., Am. Acad. Optometry (pres. 1973-74, Carel C. Koch medal 1974); mem. Am., Ala. (Optometrist of Year 1973) optometric assns., Assn. Schs. and Colls. Optometry (pres. 1967-68, dir.), Phi Beta Kappa, Sigma Xi, Phi Delta Kappa, Beta Sigma Kappa. Author: (with Blum, Bettman) Vision Screening for Elementary Schools, 1959; also articles. Home: 712 Vestavia Lake Dr Birmingham AL 35216

PETERS, HENRY JOHN, baseball club exec.; b. St. Louis, Sept. 16, 1924; s. Henry J. and Estelle (Biehl) P.; m. Dorothy Kleimeier, Nov. 21, 1950; children—Steven, Sharon. Asst. farm dir. St. Louis Browns, 1946-53; gen. mgr. Burlington (Iowa) Baseball Club, 1954; farm dir. Kansas City A's, 1955-60, asst. gen. mgr., 1962-64, gen. mgr., 1965; farm dir. Cin. Reds, 1961; v.p., dir. player personnel Cleve. Indians, 1966-71; pres. Nat. Assn. Profl. Baseball Leagues, St. Petersburg, Fla., 1972-75; exec. v.p., gen. mgr. Balt. Orioles, 1976—. Served with AUS, 1943-45. Recipient Good Guy award Cleve. chpt. Baseball Writers Assn., 1970, Maj. League Exec. of Yr. award Sporting News-UPI, 1979. Republican. Lutheran. Elks. Club: St. Petersburg Yacht. Home: 12 Hume Ct Towson MD 21204 Office: Meml Stadium Baltimore MD 21218

PETERS, HOWARD NEVIN, univ. adminstr.; b. Hazleton, Pa., June 29, 1938; s. Howard Eugene and Verna Catherine (Miller) P.; B.A., Gettysburg Coll., 1960; Ph.D., U. Colo., 1965; m. Judith Anne Griessel, Aug. 24, 1963; children—Elisabeth Anne, Nevin Edward. Asst. prof. fgn. langs. Valparaiso (Ind.) U., 1965-75, dir. grad. div., 1967-70, acting dean Coll. Arts and Scis., 1970-71, asso. dean, 1971-74, dean, 1974—, prof. fgn. langs., 1975—. NDEA fellow, 1960-63. Mem. Midwest MLA, Phi Beta Kappa, Phi Sigma Iota. Lutheran. Home: 860 N CR 500 E Valparaiso IN 46383 Office: Heritage Hall Room 20 Valparaiso Univ Valparaiso IN 46383

PETERS, JAMES ALEXANDER, ofcl. HEW; b. Pensacola, Fla., Oct. 7, 1928; s. Alex George and Carrye Sue (Spencer) P.; D.V.M., Auburn (Ala.) U., 1954; M.P.H., U. Mich., 1968; m. Martha Long, Nov. 24, 1949; 1 son, James R. Veterinary asst. Agrl. Research Service, U.S. Dept. Agr., Beltsville, Md., 1952; pvt. practice veterinary medicine, New Iberia, La., 1954-56, Panama City, Fla. 1956-64; vis. lectr. Gulf Coast Jr. Coll., 1956-64; commd. sr. veterinary officer Regular Corps, USPHS, 1964, promoted veterinary dir., 1969; with epidemiology br. Nat. Cancer Inst., NIH, Bethesda, Md., 1964-68, staff asst. Office Asso. Sci. Dir., 1968-69, head program and data analysis unit, 1970, asst. to sci. dir. etiology, 1970-71, dep. sci. dir., 1971, acting sci. dir., 1972, acting dir. div. cancer cause and prevention, 1972, dir., 1973-78; med. dir. Cystic Fibrosis Found., Atlanta, 1978—; cons. V Pan Am. Congress Veterinary Medicine and Zootechnic, 1966, Veterinary Edn. Com. for Latin Am., 1966, animal health com. NRC-Nat. Acad. Scis., 1966, Pan Am. Health Orgn., 1966, WHO, 1966, XVIII World Vet. Congress, 1967, Am. Assn. for Cancer Research, 1971; corr. Smithsonian Instn., Center for Short-lived Phenomena, 1971. Mem. AAAS, Am. Pub. Health Assn., Am., Fla. veterinary med. assns., Commd. Officers Assn. USPHS, Drug Info. Assn., Nat. Cancer Inst. Assembly Scientists, Pub. Health Cancer Assn., Omega Tau Sigma. Contbr. articles to profl. jours. Home: 7550 Westlake Terr Bethesda MD 20034

PETERS, JOHN DONALD, ret. air force officer, research exec.; b. Mars, Pa., May 25, 1922; s. John Boyd and Mary (Hazlett) P.; B.S., U. Ill., 1956, M.S., 1960, Ph.D., 1963; m. Verda Mae Schlictman, May 12, 1951; children—Sallie, Stephen, Donald Scott. Commd. 2d lt. U.S. Army, 1945, advanced through grades to brig. gen., 1970; various engring. assignments, 1945-56; project engr. Hdqrs. Ballistic Systems, Los Angeles, 1956-60, spl. scientist, 1962-63; dep. dir. research Arnold Engring. Devel. Center, Tullahoma, Tenn., 1963-65; dep. for Project Turnkey and Heavy Repair Squadron Operations, Hdqrs. 7th Air Force, South Vietnam, 1966-67; chief engring. div. Directorate

Civil Engring., Hdqrs. USAF, 1967-69; dep. chief staff civil engring. Hdqrs. Air Force Systems Command, Andrews AFB, Md., 1969-72; dep. chief staff civil engring. Hdqrs. Pacific Air Forces, Hickam AFB, Hawaii, 1972-73; ret., 1973; cons. to dir. regulation AEC, 1973-74; dir. energy devel. Mechanics Research Inc., McLean, Va., 1974-77; mgr. energy and resources dept. Systen Devel. Corp., 1977-78; founder, pres. Energy Systems Assos., Inc., Washington, 1978—; mem. adv. bd. Tenn. Space Inst., U. Tenn., 1969-73. Decorated D.S.M., Legion of Merit with oak leaf cluster, Bronze Star, Air Force Commendation medal with 1 oak leaf cluster; recipient Outstanding Author award Air Force Assn., 1970; named Distinguished Grad., U. Ill., 1973. Fellow ASCE; mem. Am. Soc. Mil. Engrs., Sigma Xi. Mason. Contbr. articles engring. jours. Inventor gage to measure dynamic pore pressure, in porous media, 1962, solar grain dryer, 1974. Home: 3158 Cantrell Ln Fairfax VA 22030 Office: 918 16th St SW Washington DC 20006

PETERS, JOHN JAMES, hosp. adminstr.; b. Balt., Mar. 26, 1925; s. John James and Madelyne (Tracey) P.; B.S. in Bus. Adminstrn., U. Balt., 1956; B.S. in Acctg., U. Del., 1958; m. Frances Rohe, Sept. 16, 1945; children—John C., Francine Peters Montgomery, Karen Peters Cutler, Lisa. Fiscal officer VA Center, Wilmington, Del., 1956-60; with VA Dept. Medicine and Surgery, Washington, 1960-70, spl. asst. to dep chief med. dir., 1967-69, dir. planning, programming and budget service, 1969-70; hosp. adminstrn. officer VA Hosp., Richmond, Va., 1970-71; hosp. dir. VA Hosp., Altoona, Pa., 1971-72, VA Hosp., Indpls., 1972-77; med. center dir. VA Med. Center, Palo Alto, Calif., 1977—; med. dist. dir. VA Med. Dist. #27, San Francisco, 1977—; asst. prof. health care adminstrn. Med. Coll. Va., 1970-71; asso. prof. Sch. Public Health, Ind. U., 1972-77; preceptor George Washington U. Grad. Program in Health Care Adminstrn.; Council of Teaching Hosps. rep. to Assembly of Assn. Am. Med. Colls., 1978—; mem. VA Chief Med. Dir.'s Adv. Com. of Dirs., 1978—; mem. VA Chief Med. Dir.'s Task Force on Reorgn., 1978—; mem. faculty VA Leadership Program, Ann Arbor, Mich., 1978; mem. VA Central Office Med. Research Adv. Com., 1978—; chmn. VA Ambulatory Care Field Adv. Group, 1978-79; bd. dirs. Santa Clara County Health Systems Agy., 1977—. Mem. rehab. rev. com. United Way of Santa Clara County, 1977-78. Served with USAAF, 1943-46. Recipient Outstanding Performance award VA Adminstr., 1971, 72, award for exec. leadership, 1979. Mem. Am. Hosp. Assn., Am. Coll. Hosp. Adminstrs., Ind. Hosp. Assn., Assn. Mil. Surgeons, Ind. Comprehensive Health Planning Agy. Roman Catholic. Clubs: Am. Legion (life mem.), DAV (life mem.), Elks. Home: 611 Willow Rd Menlo Park CA 94025 Office: 3801 Miranda Ave Palo Alto CA 94304*

PETERS, JOSEPH HARLAN, savs. and loan exec.; b. Coffeyville, Kans., Feb. 21, 1920; s. Phillip John and Florence (Harris) P.; A.A., Coffeyville Jr. Coll., 1940; A.B., Baker U., 1942; m. Geraldine Carr, Feb. 8, 1947; children—Susan Jo, Julie Lynn. With Blue Valley Fed. Savs. & Loan Co., Kansas City, Mo., 1946—, v.p., 1952-61, dir., 1955—, pres., mng. officer, 1961—; dir. United Mo. Bank Blue Valley, Kansas City, Mo.; past mem. Fed. Savs. and Loan Adv. Council, Washington. Trustee, Jackson County 4-H Found.; hon. fellow Harry S. Truman Library Inst. Nat. and Internat. Affairs; trustee Baker U., Baldwin, Kans., Mt. Washington Cemetery; bd. govs. Am. Royal Assn. Served with USNR, 1943-46. Recipient Distinguished Service award Independence Jr. C. of C., 1954. Mem. Mil. Order World Wars (life), Am. Savs. and Loan Inst. (pres. 1948), Kansas City Savs. and Loan League (pres. 1965-66), Kansas City Bd. Realtors (dir.), Kansas City, Independence (pres. 1957) chambers commerce, Blue Valley Mfrs. and Bus. Men's Assn. (pres. 1966-67), Am. Legion, V.F.W., Delta Tau Delta (Nat. Achievement award 1976). Democrat. Presbyn. (elder). Mason. Home: 673 Red RD Independence MO 64055 Office: 6515 Independence Ave Kansas City MO 64125

PETERS, JOSEPH JOHN, educator, clergyman, scientist; b. Chgo., Aug. 5, 1907; s. Joseph and Mary (Savicha) P.; A.M., St. Louis U., 1934; M.S., U. Detroit, 1936; Ph.D., Fordham U., 1945. Ordained priest Roman Cath. Ch., 1940; mem. faculty Xavier U., Cin., 1946—, prof. biology, chmn. dept., 1947—. Fellow Acad. Zoology, Central Electroencephalographic Assn., Ohio Acad. Sci.; mem. Am. Physiol. Soc., Soc. Devel. and Growth, Am. Soc. Zoologists, Sigma Xi. Contbr. articles neurophysiology and elec. activity cerebral lobes in developing chicks subjected to various environ. conditions. Address: Xavier U Cincinnati OH 45207

PETERS, LYNN HERMAN, educator; b. Marion, Wis., Feb. 21, 1928; s. Herman Carl and Mabel (Mierswa) P.; B.A., U. Wis., 1949, LL.B., 1951, M.B.A., 1956, Ph.D., 1959. Asst. prof. mgmt. U. Detroit, 1957-59; asst. prof. mgmt. San Diego State Coll., 1959-62, asso. prof., 1962-66, prof., 1966—, chmn. dept., 1962-65, 68-70, chmn. Sch. Nursing, 1975-76; vis. prof. U. Wash., 1966-67; mem. Calif. State Acad. Senate. cons. in field. Mem. Indsl. Relations Research Assn., Econ. History Assn., AAUP, Soc. Advancement Mgmt. (regional dir. univ. div.), Acad. Mgmt. (chmn. publs. com., chmn. div. social issues), Nat. Alliance Businessmen, Phi Eta Sigma, Phi Kappa Phi, Beta Gamma Sigma, Delta Epsilon. Author: The Acquisitive Motivation of the Business Man, 1966; Management and Society, 1968. Home: 9702 Alto Dr La Mesa CA 92041 Office: Coll Bus Adminstrn San Diego State U San Diego CA 92182

PETERS, MAX STONE, educator; b. Delaware, Ohio, Aug. 23, 1920; s. Charles Clinton and Dixie Mae (Stone) P.; B.S. in Chem Engring., Pa. State U., 1942, M.S., 1947, Ph.D. (Shell Oil Co. grad. fellow 1949-51), 1951; m. Laurnell Louise Stephens, June 29, 1947; children—Margaret Dixie, M. Stephen. Prodn. supr. Hercules Powder Co., 1942-44; research asst. Pa. State U., 1946-47; tech. plant supr. George I. Treyz Chem. Co., 1947-49; mem. faculty U. Ill., 1951-62, prof. chem. engring., 1957-62, head dept., 1958-62; dean engring. U. Colo., 1962-78, prof. chem. engring., 1978—; spl. research distillation, kinetics, mechanisms. Mem. adv. com. engring. div. NSF, 1962-66; chmn. Pres.'s Nat. Medal Sci. Com., 1969—, Colo. Environmental Commn., 1970-72. Served with AUS, 1944-46. Recipient Merit award Am. Assn. Cost Engrs., 1969; Distinguished Alumnus award Pa. State U., 1974. Registered profl. engr., Pa., Colo. Mem. Nat. Acad. Engring., Am. Inst. Chem. Engrs. (dir. 1961-64, pres. 1968, Founders award 1974), Am. Soc. Engring. Edn. (chmn. chem. engring. div. 1962, sec. engring. coll. adminstrn. council 1965-67, George Westinghouse award 1959, Lamme award 1973), Am. Chem. Soc. (adv. bd. jour. 1956-59), Am. Assn. Cost Engring., Sigma Xi, Alpha Chi Sigma, Phi Eta Sigma, Phi Lambda Upsilon, Tau Beta Pi, Sigma Tau. Author: Elementary Chemical Engineering, 1954; Plant Design and Economics for Chemical Engineers, rev. edit., 1968. Cons. editor McGraw-Hill series chem. engring., 1960—. Home: 1965 Vassar Circle Boulder CO 80303

PETERS, MICHAEL BARTLEY, editorial cartoonist; b. St. Louis, Oct. 9, 1943; s. William Ernst and Charlotte Burt (Wiedeman) P.; B.F.A., Washington U., St. Louis, 1965; m. Marian Connole, Sept. 11, 1965; children—Marci Michelle, Tracy Patricia, Molly Martha. Polit. cartoonist Chgo. Daily News, 1965-66, 68, Dayton (Ohio) Daily News, 1969—; syndicated with United Features Syndicate, 1971—; author: The Nixon Chronicles, 1976; Clones You Idiot, I Said Clones, 1978; inventor editorial animation features Motion Punctures; lectr. Bd. dirs. Dayton Living Arts Center, 1975—. Served with AUS, 1966-68. Recipient Sigma Delta Chi award, 1975. Mem. Am. Assn. Editorial Cartoonists (dir. 1973—), Social Health Assn. (dir. 1970—), Civitan (dir. 1969-73), Sigma Chi. Home: 1421 Coolwood Ct Xenia OH 45385 Office: 4th and Ludlow Sts Dayton OH 45401

PETERS, MITCHELL THOMAS, musician; b. Red Wing, Minn., Aug. 17, 1935; s. Thomas Tushi and Fillona Miti (Bosho) P.; B.Mus., performer's cert., Eastman Sch. Music, Rochester, N.Y., 1957, M.Mus., 1958; m. Beverely Ann Cross, Apr. 29, 1962 (div.); children—Michelle Kristol, Mitchell Thomas, II; stepchildren—Karen Suzanne, John Mack. Drummer, Dallas Summer Musicals, 1962-69; prin. percussionist Dallas Symphony Orch., 1960-69; co-prin. timpanist and percussionist Los Angeles Philharm. Orch., 1969—; instr. UCLA, Calif. State U., Los Angeles; owner music pub. co. Served with AUS, 1958-60. Mem. ASCAP. Composer: (for marimba and piano) Sonata Allegro, 1968; (for marimba) Yellow After the Rain, 1971; also instrn. materials. Home: 3231 Benda Pl Los Angeles CA 90068 Office: 135 N Grand Ave Los Angeles CA 90012

PETERS, PHILIP HOMER, ins. co. exec.; b. Oak Park, Ill., Dec. 11, 1915; s. Frank and Minerva (Thompson) P.; B.S., Mass. Inst. Tech., 1937, M.S., 1939; grad. Advanced Mgmt. Program, Harvard, 1953; m. Ruth Bell, June 24, 1939; children—Philip Homer, Gregory B., Jeffrey B. Mgr. group pension sales John Hancock Mut. Life Ins. Co., 1940-43, dir. group sales and services, 1946-50, 2d v.p., 1950-56, v.p., 1956-66, sr. v.p., 1966-78, exec. v.p., 1979—, also dir.; dir. John Hancock Internat. Services, S.A., Brussels, Maritime Life Assurance Co. Mem. corp. Mass. Inst. Tech., 1969-75, Babson Coll., 1974—; bd. dirs. Assn. Internationale Etudiants en Scis. Economiques et Commercials, United Way Massachusetts Bay; bd. dirs., pres. World Affairs Council; trustee Babson Coll., 1975—. Served to lt. (j.g.) USNR, 1943-46. Mem. Assn. C.L.U., Greater Boston (dir. 1967-69, v.p. 1970-74, pres. 1974-75, chmn. 1975-76), U.S. chambers commerce, Alumni Assn. Mass. Inst. Tech. (pres. 1969-70), Sigma Nu, Tau Beta Pi. Clubs: Rotary, Algonguin (Boston); Wellesley; The Country (Brookline, Mass.); Appalachian Mountain; University (N.Y.C.). Home: 14 Cushing Rd Wellesley Hills MA 02181 also Juniper Hill Tin Mountain Jackson NH 03846 Office: Hancock Pl Boston MA 02117

PETERS, RALPH FREW, investment banker; b. Mineola, N.Y., Mar. 21, 1929; s. Ralph and Helen Louise (Frew) P.; B.A., Princeton U., 1951; postgrad. Stonier Grad. Sch. Banking, Rutgers U., 1962; m. Diana Joyce Clayton, Dec. 19, 1969; children—Louise Frew, Jean Reid, Ralph Frew, Melvyn T., Richard Clayton. With Corn Exchange Bank & Trust Co., 1947-52; pres., dir. Discount Corp. N.Y., N.Y.C., 1955—; trustee Lincoln Savs. Bank, N.Y.C. Served with USNR, 1948-55. Mem. Public Securities Assn. Episcopalian. Clubs: Anglers, Creek, Leash, Links, North Woods, Recess. Office: 58 Pine St New York NY 10005

PETERS, RALPH MARTIN, educator; b. Knoxville, Tenn., May 9, 1926; s. Tim C. and Alma (Shannon) P.; B.S., Lincoln Meml. U., 1949; M.S., U. Tenn., 1953, Ed.D., 1960; m. Lorraine Daniel, 1949; children—Teresa, Marta. Tchr. pub. schs.; prof., dept. chmn., v.p. Lincoln Meml. U., 1956-63; prof. edn., dean students, dean Grad. Sch., Tenn. Tech. U., Cookeville, 1963—. Served with Armed Forces, World War II. Mem. Phi Kappa Phi, Phi Delta Kappa. Baptist. Club: Rotary. Editor publs. Home: 927 Mt Vernon Rd Cookeville TN 38501 Office: Tenn Tech U Dean Grad Sch Cookeville TN 38501

PETERS, ROBERT LEE, architect; b. Brownsville, Tex., Nov. 23, 1920; s. R. Lee and Mary E. (Saunders) P.; B.Arch., U. Tex., 1951; m. Helen Frances Smith; children (by previous marriage)—Lynn Ellen, Lee Edward, Steven Robert. Pvt. practice architecture, Odessa, Tex., 1953-55; partner Peters & Fields, Odessa and Austin, Tex., 1955-78; pvt. practice, Austin, 1979—. Mem. Odessa City Bldg. Commn., 1958-65, City Tax Equalization Bd., 1963-66; vice chmn. Bldg. Bd. Appeals, 1964-72; mem. adv. council Tex. Dept. Community Affairs; 1972-73. Precinct chmn. Democratic Party, 1956-58. Pres., bd. dirs. Odessa Symphony Assn., Permian Council for Mentally Retarded; bd. dirs. Tex. Fine Arts Soc., Permian Basin Rehab. Center, Austin Symphony Orch. Soc. Served with USAAF, 1942-46; PTO. Decorated Air medal; recipient numerous archtl. awards; named Boss of Year, Jr. C. of C., 1960. Mem. AIA (past pres., dir. W.Tex. chpt.), Tex. Soc. Architects (past v.p., dir.), Constrn. Specifications Inst. (dir., pres.), Odessa C. of C. (past dir.). Presbyn. Lion. Clubs: Odessa Country; Country of Austin. Important works include Ector County Courthouse, Odessa City Hall, Rehab. Bldg. Big Spring State Hosp., Odessa Coll. Composite Tech. Bldg., John Ireland Elementary Sch., Odessa, U. Tex. Land Office Bldg., Ballinger First Nat. Bank, Odessa Family YMCA, Ft. Leaton Restoration, Lake Somerville State Park, Criss Cole Rehab. Center for Blind, Austin, U. Tex. Permian Basin Gymnasium. Home: 6002 Highlandale Austin TX 78731 Office: 9027 Northgate Blvd Austin TX 78758

PETERS, ROBERT REVEDD, hydrologist; b. Mathews County, Va., Nov. 15, 1928; s. Elmer Amos and Amy (Morgan) P.; grad. Coll. William and Mary, Norfolk, Va., 1955, Mass. Inst. Tech., 1967; m. Irene Marie Wood, June 29, 1951; children—Amy, Paul. Exec. pilot Layne Atlantic Co., Norfolk, 1952-55, sales engr., then v.p., 1955-69; v.p., regional mgr. water resources div. Layne Atlantic Co., div. Singer Co., 1969-75; v.p. Layne Western Co., Inc., Norfolk, 1975—. Bd. govs. Capital Fedn. Cosmopolitan Internat., 1973; mem. jr. bd. Central YMCA, Norfolk, 1955. Served with USMCR, 1946-48. Registered profl. engr., Va. Mem. Am. Water Works Assn. (pres. 1977), Nat. Water Well Assn. (pres. 1974), Nat. Soc. Profl. Engrs., Am. Soc. Mil. Engrs. Democrat. Episcopalian. Clubs: Cosmopolitan (past pres.), Shriners (Norfolk). Author manual, articles. Address: PO Box 7095 Norfolk VA 23509

PETERS, ROBERTA, soprano; b. N.Y.C., May 4, 1930; d. Sol and Ruth (Hirsch) Peters; ed. privately; Litt.D., Elmira Coll., 1967; Mus. D., Ithaca Coll., 1968; L.H.D., Westminster Coll., 1974, Lehigh U., 1977; m. Bertram Fields, Apr. 10, 1955; children—Paul, Bruce. Met. Opera debut as Zerlina in Don Giovanni, 1950, also appeared in Rigoletto, The Magic Flute, The Barber of Seville, The Marriage of Figaro, Lucia di Lammermoor, Die Fledermaus, Don Pasquale, L'Elisir d'Amore Lakme, Cosi ops., Tutte, La Sonnambula, Martha, Richard Strauss' Ariadne auf Naxos; recorded several operas; appeared motion pictures Tonight We Sing, Barber of Seville; frequent appearances radio and TV; sang at Royal Opera House, Convent Garden, London, Eng., summers 1951-60, Cin. Opera, summers 1952-53, 58, Vienna State Opera, 1963, Salzburg Festival, 1963, 64; debuts at festivals in Vienna and Munich, 1963, 64; concert tours in U.S., Soviet Union, Scandinavian countries, Israel; debut Kirov Opera, Leningrad, USSR, 1972, Bolshoi Opera, Moscow, 1972. Named Woman of Yr., Fedn. Women's Clubs, 1964; 1st Am. to receive Bolshoi medal. Author: Debut at the Met. Home: Scarsdale NY 10583 Office: ICM Artists Ltd 40 W 57th St New York NY 10019. *I believe that life is a series of just one darn thing after another. If we can learn that we must expect, meet, and solve.*

PETERS, SVETLANA ALLILUYEVA, author; b. Moscow, USSR, Feb. 28, 1926; d. Joseph Stalin and Nadezhda Alliluyeva; came to U.S., 1967; student Moscow U., Acad. Social Scis., Moscow; m. William Wesley Peters, 1970 (div.); 1 dau., Olga; children by previous marriage—Joseph, Katherine. Author: Twenty Letters to a Friend; Only One Year. Address: care Harper and Row 10 E 53d St New York NY 10022*

PETERS, WILLIAM, author, film and TV producer-dir.; b. San Francisco, July 30, 1921; s. William Ernest and Dorothy (Wright) P.; B.S., Northwestern U., 1947; m. Mercy Ann Miller, Oct. 12, 1942 (div. 1968); children—Suzanne Peters Hilton, Geoffrey Wright, Jennifer, Gretchen. Account exec. pub. relations J. Walter Thompson Co., Chgo., 1947-51; mem. fiction staff Ladies' Home Jour., 1951-52; article editor Woman's Home Companion, 1952-53; freelance writer, 1953-62; producer CBS Reports for CBS News, 1962-66; freelance writer, film dir. and TV producer/exec. producer, N.Y.C., 1966—; cons. race relations, 1959—, hist. TV documentaries, 1976—. A founder, 1946, North Shore Citizens Com., bd. dirs., 1946-51; a founder, 1963, Pelham Com. Human Relations, vice chmn., 1963-65, chmn., 1965-66. Served to capt. USAAF, 1942-45; ETO. Decorated Air medal with 2 oak leaf clusters, D.F.C.; recipient Benjamin Franklin mag. award, 1954; Peabody TV award, 1963, 70, 76, Golden Gavel award Am. Bar Assn., 1963; Sch. Bell award N.E.A., 1964. Democrat. Author: Passport to Friendship-The Story of the Experiment in International Living, 1957; The Southern Temper, 1959; (with Mrs. Medgar Evers) For Us, The Living, 1967; A Class Divided, 1971; producer, writer, dir. documentaries The Eye of the Storm, 1971; Suddenly an Eagle, 1976; Death of a Family, 1979; others. Home: One Lincoln Plaza-20 T New York NY 10023

PETERS, WILLIAM CHARLES, banker; b. Bridgeport, Conn., Sept. 19, 1920; s. Henry LeBaron and Marguerite A. (Bishop) P.; student Kent (Conn.) Sch., 1933-38; B.S. in Econs., U. Pa., 1942; m. Mary Eileen Neary, Jan. 26, 1946; children—Kathleen Louise (Mrs. Gregory T. Thompson), Susan Karen (Mrs. Thomas M. Gutner), Kimberly Ann. With Conn. Nat. Bank, Bridgeport, 1945—, asst. v.p., comptroller, 1956-60, v.p., comptroller, 1960-66, sr. v.p., comptroller, 1966-71, sr. v.p. ops., 1971—. Mem. Easton (Conn.) Republican Town Com., 1969-76, Easton Bd. Fire Commrs., 1970—; vestryman Parish of Christ's Ch., Easton, 1971-74, 77—. Served to capt., inf. AUS, 1942-45; ETO; lt. col. Res. (ret.). Decorated Combat Inf. Badge. Mem. Conn. Yankee Conf., Bank Adminstrn. Inst., Conn. Bankers Assn., Am. Legion (comdr.). Home: Judd Rd Easton CT 06468 Office: 888 Main St Bridgeport CT 06601

PETERS, WILLIAM HENRY, educator; b. Kansas City, Mo., Apr. 7, 1928; s. William Henry and Orra Adell (Hoobler) P.; A.B., William Jewell Coll., 1951; M.S. in Journalism, Columbia U., 1952; M.B.A., U. Mich., 1966, Ph.D. in Bus. Adminstrn., 1968; m. Virginia Louise Stauffer, Apr. 24, 1953; children—Anne Louise, Alison Lee. Asst. mgr. public relations Lederle Lab. div. Am. Cyanamid Co., 1952-54; advt. asst. AT&T, 1954-55; div. advt. mgr. Pfizer, Inc., 1955-59, div. dir. advt., 1959-65; asst. study dir. Inst. for Social Research, U. Mich., 1967-68; asso. prof. mktg. U. Wis.-Madison, 1968-76; dean, prof. mktg. Sch. of Bus., U. Louisville, 1976—; mktg. cons. Bd. dirs., mem. exec. com. Ky. Council on Econ. Edn.; bd. dirs. Better Bus. Bur. Louisville. Served with USN, 1946-47. NDEA fellow, 1965-68; New Careers fellow, 1965-66. Mem. Am. Mktg. Assn., Am. Assn. Higher Edn., Am. Assembly of Collegiate Schs. of Bus. (sec. mid-continent east region), Phi Kappa Phi, Beta Gamma Sigma. Unitarian. Club: Rotary. Contbr. articles to profl. jours. Office: Strickler Hall Univ of Louisville Louisville KY 40208

PETERS, WILLIAM WESLEY, architect and planner; b. Terre Haute, Ind., June 12, 1912; s. Frederick Romer and Clara (Margedant) P.; ed. Evansville Coll., 1929-30, D.Sc. (hon.), 1971; ed. Mass. Inst. Tech., 1930-32; D.F.A. (hon.), Centre Coll. Ky., Danville, 1973; m. Svetlana Wright, Apr. 1, 1935 (dec. Sept. 1946); children—Brandoch, Daniel (dec.); m. 2d, Svetlana Allilueva, Apr. 7, 1970 (div. May 1973); 1 dau., Olga Margedant. Practice architecture, Evansville, Ind., 1936; with Frank Lloyd Wright Found., Taliesin, Spring Green, Wis. and Taliesin West, Scottsdale, Ariz., 1936—, sec.-treas., 1943-59, v.p., 1959—; chief architect Taliesin Asso. Architects, 1959—; mem. ednl. staff Frank Lloyd Wright Sch. Architecture; structural engr. Guggenheim Mus., N.Y.C., Adminstrn. and Research Tower, Johnson Wax Co., Racine, Wis., Price Tower, Bartlesville, Okla.; completed works designed by Frank Lloyd Wright: Beth Sholom Synagogue, Phila., Annunciation Greek Orthodox Ch., Milw., Marin County Civic Center, San Raphael, Calif., Grady Gammage Auditorium, Tempe, Ariz.; designing architect San Jose (Calif.) Community Theater, Lewis and Eugenia Van Wezel Performing Arts Hall, Sarasota, Fla., Vets. Meml. Auditorium, San Raphael, Music bldg. Ariz. State U., Tempe, Lincoln Income Life Ins. Office Bldg. and Bank, Louisville, Monona Basin Master Plan, Madison, Wis., Golden Rondelle for S.C. Johnson & Son, Racine, feasibility study and projection for Island of Minoo, Imperial Govt. Iran Palace at Mehrdasht nr. Tehran, and residential complex in Chalus nr. Caspian Sea for Her Imperial Highness Princess Shams Pahlavi of Iran, Ascension Luth. Ch., Scottsdale, St. Mary's Roman Cath. Ch., Alma, Mich., Bank of Spring Green (Wis.), Mount Damavand Coll., Tehran, Club Xanadu, Costa Rica, Our Lady of Fatima Ch., Tucson, Ariz. Biltmore restoration, Phoenix, Regional Art Center, Centre Coll., Danville, Ky., master plan and recreational devel. for Ricardo Bordallo, Agana, Guam, master plan Bartlesville (Okla.) Community Center. Address: Taliesin West Scottsdale AZ 85258 also Taliesin Spring Green WI 53588

PETERSDORF, ROBERT JAMES, labor union exec.; b. Cannon Falls, Minn., Jan. 9, 1921; s. Willus H. and Cora (Haas) P.; student pub. schs., Zumbrota, Minn.; m. Margaret McGregor Hankins, Dec. 28, 1969; children by previous marriage—David, Diana, Sherry, Terry, Denise; stepchildren—Timothy, Daniel. Painter, 1938-46; bus. rep. Rochester (Minn.) Bldg. Trades Council, 1946-55; sec. Minn. State Bldg. Trades, Rochester, 1952-55; gen. organizer Brotherhood of Painters, Rochester and Mpls., 1955-66, gen. v.p., 1966-76; gen. sec.-treas. Internat. Brotherhood Painters and Allied Trades, Washington, 1976—. Served with U.S. Army, 1941-45. Democrat. Roman Catholic. Editor: Painters and Allied Trades jour., 1976—. Home: 17000 Teal Ct Rockville MD 20855 Office: Internat Brotherhood Painters and Allied Trades 1750 New York Ave NW Washington DC 20006

PETERSEN, BURTON BRADFORD, advt. agy. exec.; b. Omaha, Oct. 19, 1927; s. Burton Bradford and Marie Marguerite (Jensen) P.; B.S. in Bus., U. Nebr., Omaha, 1949; m. Marjorie Claire Chambers, Sept. 4, 1948; children—Bradford William, Craig Douglas. Salesman advt. dept. Omaha World Herald, 1951-56, Denver Post., 1956-59; with World Wide Agy., Inc., Los Angeles, 1959—, gen. mgr., 1960-65, pres., 1965—. Served with USN, 1945-46. Mem. Am. Newspaper Classified Mgrs. Assn. Lutheran. Club: Masons. Office: 514 Shatto Pl Los Angeles CA 90020

PETERSEN, DONALD EUGENE, automobile co. exec.; b. Pipestone, Minn., Sept. 4, 1926; s. William L. and Mae (Pederson) P.; B.M.E., U. Wash., 1946; M.B.A., Stanford U., 1949; m. Jo Anne Leonard, Sept. 12, 1948; children—Leslie Carolyn, Donald Leonard. With Ford Motor Co., Dearborn, 1949—, asst. to v.p. N.Am. ops., 1965-66, car product planning mgr., 1966-69, exec. dir. adminstr. engring. and indsl. design, 1969, v.p. car planning and research, 1969-71, v.p. truck and recreation products ops., 1971-75, exec. v.p.

diversified products ops., 1977—, exec. v.p. internat. automotive ops., 1977—, dir., 1977—. Bd. trustees Cranbrook Ednl. Community, Bloomfield, Mich., 1973—. Served with USMCR, 1946-47, 51-52. Mem. Soc. Automotive Engrs., Engring. Soc. Detroit, Phi Beta Kappa, Sigma Xi, Tau Beta Pi. Episcopalian. Clubs: Renaissance, Bloomfield Hills Country. Home: 1318 Country Club Dr Bloomfield Hills MI 48013 Office: Am Rd Dearborn MI 48121

PETERSEN, FORREST SILAS, naval officer; b. Holdrege, Nebr., May 16, 1922; s. Elmer Louis and Stella Bell (Nickels) P.; student U. Nebr., 1939-40; B.S., U.S. Naval Acad., 1944; B.S. in Aero. Engring., U.S. Naval Postgrad. Sch., 1952; M.S. in Engring., Princeton U., 1953; m. Jean Baldwin Carter, June 17, 1978. Commd. ensign USN, 1944, advanced through grades to vice adm., 1976; designated naval aviator, 1947; assigned fighter squadrons, 1947-50, 53-56; instr. Naval Test Pilot Sch., 1956-58; research pilot X-15 plane, 1958-62; comdg. officer Fighter Squadron 154, 1962; with naval reactors br. AEC, 1963; exec. officer nuclear powered aircraft carrier U.S.S. Enterprise, 1964-66; with Office Chief Naval Operations, Washington 1966-67; comdg. officer U.S.S. Bexar, 1967-68, U.S.S. Enterprise, 1969-71; asst. dir. strategic and support systems test and evaluation DDR&E, Dept. Def., 1972-74; comdr. attack carrier striking forces 6th Fleet, 1974-75; vice chief Naval Material, 1975-76; dep. chief naval ops. (air warfare), 1976; comdr. Naval Air Systems Command, 1976—. Decorated D.S.M., Legion of Merit, D.F.C., Bronze Star medal; recipient Disting. Service medal NASA, 1962, Collier trophy Look mag., 1962. Fellow AIAA; mem. Soc. Exptl. Text Pilots, Nat. Soc. Aerospace Profls. (Montgomery award 1962), Nat. Aero. Assn. Home: Gibbon NE 68840 Office: Naval Air Systems Command Dept Navy Washington DC 20361

PETERSEN, FRANK EMMANUEL, JR., marine corps officer; b. Topeka, Mar. 2, 1932; s. Frank Emmanuel and Edith (Sutthard) P.; B.A., George Washington U., 1968, M.S., 1973; m. 2d Alicia Joyce Downes, Sept., 1974; children—Gayle Marie, Dana Charlette, Frank Emmanuel III, Lindsay Charlette, Monique. Served as enlisted man U.S. Navy, 1950-52; commd. 2d lt. U.S. Marine Corps., 1952, advanced through grades to brig. gen., 1979; dep. dir. ops. Nat. Mil. Command Center, Washington, 1980—. Decorated Legion of Merit with combat V, D.F.C., Air medal, Purple Heart; named Man of Yr., NAACP., 1979. Office: Pentagon NMCC S-3 Washington DC 20301

PETERSEN, HOWARD CHARLES, lawyer, banker; b. East Chicago, Ind., May 7, 1910; s. Hans Christian and Silvia Anna (Charles) P.; A.B., De Pauw U., Greencastle, Ind., 1930, LL.D., 1953; J.D., U. Mich., 1933; LL.D., St. Joseph's Coll., 1962, Swarthmore Coll., 1968; D.S.C., Drexel Inst., 1962, U. Pa., 1974; m. Elizabeth Watts, Sept. 3, 1936; children—Elizabeth, Howard Charles (dec.). Asso. Cravath, Gersdorff, Swaine & Wood (now Cravath, Swaine & Moore), N.Y.C., 1933-40. Mem. Nat. Emergency Com. Mil. Tng. Camps Assn., 1940, counsel to com. apptd. by Pres. Roosevelt to draft Selective Service Regulations, 1940; successively spl. asst. and exec. asst. to under-sec. of war; spl. asst. to sec. of war, 1945; asst. sec. of war, 1945-47; spl. asst. to Pres. U.S. on trade legislation, 1961-62; exec. v.p., dir. Fidelity Bank, Phila., 1947-50, pres., 1950-66, chmn. bd., 1966-78, chief exec. officer, 1966-75, also dir.; dir. ADELA, Fidelity Bank (France), Ins. Co. N. Am. Headed U.S. del. to London Conf. with Commonwealth nations on Japanese trade relations, 1948; 3d Fed. Res. Dist. rep. Fed. Adv. Council, 1960-63; mem. Adv. Com. Monetary Reform. Active Greater Phila. Movement. Nat. finance chmn. Eisenhower pre-conv. campaign, 1952. Trustee Carnegie Endowment for Internat. Peace; chmn. bd. trustees Inst. for Advanced Studies; chmn. bd. mgrs. U. Pa. Mus.; mem. econs. vis. com. Harvard, 1967-73; trustee Com. on Econ. Devel., Eisenhower Exchange Fellowships, Marshall Found. Recipient Medal for Merit, 1945, War Dept. Exceptional Civilian Service award, 1945, Selective Service medal, 1946. Mem. N.Y., Ind. bars, Assn. Bar City N.Y., Am. Philos. Soc., Am. Bankers Assn. (exec. council), Pa. Bankers Assn. (past pres.), Phila. Com. on Fgn. Relations, Council Fgn. Relations, Wistar Assn., Am. Acad. Polit and Social Sci. (dir.), Phi Gamma Delta. Republican. Episcopalian. Clubs: Phila., Fourth St., Merion Cricket (Phila.); Met. (Washington). Author: Selective Service Manual (edited with annotations), 1940. Home: Radnor PA 19087 Office: Fidelity Bank 135 S Broad St Philadelphia PA 19109

PETERSEN, JOHN CHRESTEN, community coll. adminstr.; b. Modesto, Calif., Jan. 21, 1931; s. Laurits M. and Ella W. (Lundø) P.; A.A., Modesto Jr. Coll., 1951; A.B., U. Calif., Berkeley, 1953, Ph.D., 1969; M.S., U. N.Mex., 1960; m. Norma Lambert, June 13, 1954; 1 son, Daniel L. Tchr. biology Ceres (Calif.) High Sch., 1954-62; instr. Cabrillo Coll., 1962-67, dean students, 1969-72, supt./pres., 1977—; asst. dir. jr. coll. leadership program U. Calif., Berkeley, 1968-69; pres. Skyline Coll., 1972-77; mem. accrediting commn. community and jr. colls. and accrediting commn. sr. colls. and univs. Western Assn. Schs. and Colls. Active Easter Seal Soc., United Way. Kellogg fellow. Mem. Calif. Community and Jr. Coll. Assn. (dir.; v.p. 1979-80), Assn. Calif. Community Coll. Adminstrs., C. of C. Democrat. Presbyterian. Home: 106 Florence Dr Aptos CA 95003 Office: 6500 Soquel Dr Aptos CA 95003

PETERSEN, MARSHALL ARTHUR, fin. exec.; b. Whittier, Calif., June 21, 1938; s. Arthur J. and Esther V. (Jensen) P.; B.S., U. Redlands, 1960; M.B.A., Stanford, 1962; m. Georgia Lea Higgins, Aug. 21, 1960; children—David M., Steven L., Karen E., Jennifer L. Mgr. investor relations TRW Inc., Cleve., 1967-69, dir. investor relations, 1969-71, asst. treas., 1971-73, treas., 1973—, v.p., 1976—; treas. Cin. Milacron Inc., 1977—. Danforth fellow, 1960-64. Mem. Fin. Execs. Inst., Nat. Investor Relations Inst. (past pres.), Omicron Delta Kappa. Club: Anderson Hills Tennis. Home: 800 Old Orchard Rd Cincinnati OH 45230 Office: 4701 Marburg Ave Cincinnati OH 45209

PETERSEN, RAYMOND INGVARD, airline exec.; b. York, Nebr., Aug. 10, 1912; s. John and Rose Marie (Becker) P.; m. Jan. 7, 1939; children—Rosemarie, Charles Edward, Susan Virginia, Raymond Frederick. Partner, Ray Petersen Flying Service, Bethel, Alaska, 1934-47; pres. No. Consol. Airlines, Inc., Anchorage, 1947-68; pres., chmn. bd. Wien Consol. Airlines, Inc., Anchorage, 1968-76; chmn. bd., chief exec. officer Wien Air Alaska, Inc., Anchorage, 1976—; dir. Goodhews Bay Mining Co., Seattle; regional dir. designate Dept. Transp. Nat. Def. Exec. Res., ret.; consulaire agt. at Anchorage, Republic of France, ret. Chmn. Anchorage Telephone Utility, 1962-75; trustee Alaska Methodist U. Mem. Airline Transport Assn., Assn. Local Transport Airlines (past chmn.), Anchorage C. of C. (chmn. aviation com.), Assn. Internat. des Skal Clubs. Roman Catholic. Clubs: Elks, Quiet Birdmen, Conquistadores del Cielo, Rotary, Wings, OX-5 Aviation Pioneers. Office: Wien Air Alaska Inc 4100 Internat Airport Rd Anchorage AK 99502*

PETERSEN, RAYMOND JOSEPH, mag. publisher; b. West Orange, N.J., May 9, 1919; s. Raymond O. and Ellen (Bond) P.; student Newark U., evenings 1938-39, N.Y. U., 1953; Dr. Journalism (hon.), St. Joseph's Coll., Phila., 1966; m. Rosalie Iovin, July 22, 1949 (dec. Nov. 1970); children—Raymond Jeffery, Gregory Eugene, Michael Joseph, Mary, John Kevin, Teresa, Cathy Anne, Jeanne Marie, Matthew James; m. 2d, Abbey Darer, Sept. 13, 1975; children—Pamela, Johnathan. With N.J. Assn. Credit Men, 1938-40, Carnrick Co., Newark, 1940-42; space salesman Street & Smith Publs., 1945-48; with Hearst Mags., Inc., N.Y.C., 1948—, sr. v.p., 1967-74, exec. v.p., 1973—, advt. dir. Good Housekeeping mag., 1958-60, v.p., pub., 1960-74; dir. Hearst Corp., Supermarkets Gen. Corp. Bd. dirs., mem. exec. bd. Boy Scouts Am., recipient Good Scout award, 1973; bd. dirs. USO; bd. govs. St. Vincent's Hosp., Montclair, N.J.; testamentary trustee estate William Randolph Hearst, Sr.; trustee Jr. Essex Troop of Cavalry; bd. govs. Acad. Food Marketing, St. Joseph's Coll., Phila.; bd. dirs. Council Better Bus. Burs., Consumer Research Inst. of Grocery Mfg. Industry; mem. bus. com. Montclair State Coll., St. Lawrence U.; adv. bd. Weber Coll. Served with AUS, 1942-45; Africa, ETO. Decorated Bronze Star medal; Knight of Malta (Vatican). Mem. Am. Advt. Fedn. (exec. com., sec.-treas. 1976-77, chmn. 1977-78), Mag. Pubs. Assn. (mem. mktg. com.). Home: Khakum Wood Greenwich CT 06830 Office: Hearst Inc 959 8th Ave New York City NY 10019

PETERSEN, ROBERT E., publisher; b. Los Angeles, Sept. 10, 1926; s. Einar and Bertha (Putera) P.; m. Margie McNally, Jan. 26, 1963. Founder, chmn. bd. Petersen Pub. Co., pubs. Hot Rod, Motor Trend, Car Craft, Motorcyclist, Photog., Skin Diver, Teen, Hunting, Guns & Ammo mags., Los Angeles, 1948—; owner Robert E. Petersen Prodns., producers TV series, commls., auto shows, trade shows; owner Petersen Galleries, Beverly Hills, Calif. Mem. Los Angeles Library Commn., 1963-64. Bd. dirs. Boys Club Am., past pres. Hollywood br.; bd. dirs. Thalians. Served with USAF. Clubs: So. Calif Safari, Balboa Bay, Catalina Island Yacht. Office: 8490 Sunset Blvd Los Angeles CA 90069

PETERSEN, ROBERT V., educator; b. S. Jordan, Utah, Apr. 21, 1926; s. Edgar Ray and Martha (Smith) P.; B.S., U. Utah, 1950; Ph.D., U. Minn., 1955; m. Betty Jayne Bigler, Oct. 23, 1950; children—Robyn, Kent Earl, Susan, Marilyn. Teaching asst. U. Minn., 1951-54; asst. prof. pharm. chemistry Oreg. State Coll., 1955-57; asst. prof. pharmacy U. Utah, 1957-61, asso. prof., 1961-67, chmn. dept. applied pharm. scis., 1965-78, chmn. dept. pharms., 1978—, prof., 1967—; exec. com. Am. Assn. Colls. Pharmacy, 1968-74, v.p., 1971-72, pres., 1972-73. Served with AUS, 1944-46. Mem. Am. Chem. Soc., Am., Utah pharm. assns., Acad. Pharm. Sci., Am. Inst. History Pharmacy, Sigma Xi, Rho Chi (exec. council 1970-72, 74-76), Phi Lambda Upsilon. Research field nonaqueous emulsions, plastics composition and toxicology, biodegradable polymers as drug delivery devices. Contbr. articles sci., scholastic jours. Home: 4639 Meadow Rd Murray UT 84107 Office: Coll Pharmacy U Utah Salt Lake City UT 84112

PETERSEN, ROLAND, painter, printmaker; b. Endelave, Horsens, Denmark, 1926; came to U.S., 1928; B.A., U. Calif. at Berkeley, 1949, M.A., 1950; postgrad. Han Hofmann's Sch. Fine Arts, summers 1950-51, S.W. Hayter's Atelier 17, Paris, 1950, 63, 70, Islington Studio, London, 1976; m. Sharane Havlina, Aug. 12, 1950; children—Dana Mark, Maura Brooke, Julien Conrad, Karena Caia. Tchr., State Coll. Wash., Pullman, 1952-56; mem. faculty U. Calif. at Davis, 1956—, now prof. art; exhibited one-man shows Gump's Gallery, San Francisco, 1962, Staempfli Gallery, N.Y.C., 1963, 65, 67, Adele Bednarz Gallery, Los Angeles, 1966, 69, 70, 72, 73, 75, 76, Crocker Art Gallery, Sacramento, 1965, de Young Mus., San Francisco, 1968, La Jolla Mus., 1971, Phoenix Mus., 1972, Santa Barbara Mus., 1973, USIS sponsored touring one-man exhbn., Turkey, U. Reading (Eng.), 1977, U. Calif., Davis, 1978, Brubaker Gallery, Sarasota, Fla., 1979; exhibited group shows including Calif. Palace Legion of Honor, San Francisco Art Inst., 1962, Mus. Art, Carnegie Inst., Pitts., 1964, Obelisk Gallery, Washington, John Herron Art Inst., Indpls., 1964, Pa. Acad. Fine Arts, Phila., Crocker Art Gallery, Sacramento, 1965, Art Inst. Chgo., 1965, Va. Mus. Fine Arts, Richmond, 1966, U. Ariz. Art Gallery, Tucson, 1967, Am. Cultural Center, Paris, 1971, Nat. Gallery, Washington, 1972, Otis Art Inst. Gallery, Los Angeles, 1974, Auerbach Fine Art Gallery, London, 1977, U. Wis., Madison, 1977, Bklyn. Mus., 1978, U. Ill., 1978; represented in permanent collections: de Young Mus., San Francisco, Va. Mus. Fine Arts, Richmond, Mus. Modern Art, N.Y.C., Phila. Mus. Art, Whitney Mus. Am. Art, Phoenix Mus., Santa Barbara Mus., Musée Municipal, Brest, France, Smithsonian Instn. Nat. Collection Fine Arts, others. Served with USN, 1944-46; PTO. Recipient numerous prizes and awards, 1950—; Guggenheim fellow, 1963; U. Calif. creative arts fellow, 1967, 70, 77; Fulbright grantee, 1970. Mem. Print Council Am., AAUP, San Francisco Art Assn., Calif. Soc. Printmakers, Nat. Soc. Lit. and Arts. Address: care Staempfli Gallery 47 E 77th St New York NY 10021

PETERSEN, SYDNEY R., oil co. exec.; b. Oakland, Calif., 1930; B.S., U. Calif., Berkeley, 1953; married. With Getty Oil Co., 1955—, group v.p. refining, distbn. and fin., 1974-77, group v.p. fin., 1977-79, pres., chief operating officer, Los Angeles, 1979—; also dir.; dir. Nuclear Fuel Services, Mitsubishi Oil Co. Served with U.S. Army, 1953-55. Office: 3810 Wilshire Blvd Los Angeles CA 90010*

PETERSEN, ULRICH, educator, geologist; b. Zorritos, Peru, Dec. 1, 1927; s. Georg and Harriet (Bluhme) P.; Mining Engr., Escuela Nacional de Ingenieros, Lima, Peru, 1954; M.A., Harvard, 1955, Ph.D., 1963; m. Edith Martensen, Apr. 27, 1952 (dec. Aug. 1978); children—Erich, Heidi. Geologist, Instituto Geológico del Peru and Instituto Nacional de Investigación y Fomento Mineros, 1946-51; geologist Farro de Pasco Corp., Peru, 1951-54, asst. chief geologist, 1956-57, chief geologist, 1958-63; lectr. Harvard, 1963-66, asso. prof., 1966-69, prof. mining geology, 1969—; cons. geologist, 1963—. Named comendador de la orden al Merito por Servicios Distinguidos (Peru), 1968. Mem. Soc. Econ. Geologist, Geol. Soc. Am., Soc. Geologica del Peru, Mineral. Soc. Am., Am. Inst. Mining and Metall. Engrs., AAAS, Geochem. Soc. Home: 414 Marsh St Belmont MA 02178 Office: 20 Oxford St Cambridge MA 02138

PETERSEN, WILLIAM JOHN, writer, educator; b. Dubuque, Iowa, Jan. 30, 1901; s. Charles Lewis and Bertha Louise (Helm) P.; B.A., U. Dubuque, 1926; M.A., U. Iowa, 1927, Ph.D., 1930; LL.D., Iowa Wesleyan Coll., 1958; m. Bessie Josephine Rasmus, Sept. 25, 1937. Grad asst., fellow U. Iowa, 1926-30, instr. history, 1930-36, lectr. history, 1936—, asso. prof., 1948-69; research asso. State Hist. Soc. Iowa, 1930-47, supt., 1947-72; hist. lectr. Am. Sch. Wild Life, summers 1932, 36-40, Drake U. Tours, summers 1933, 34; prof. history Washington U., St. Louis, summers 1940, 41, 65, Iowa Wesleyan Coll., summers 1962, 63. Bd. dirs. Alvord Meml. Commn., 1940; mem. Iowa Centennial Com., 1946; chmn. Johnson County Red Cross War Fund, 1945. Recipient Iowa Library Assn. award for best contbn. to Am. lit. by an Iowan, 1937. Mem. Am., So., Miss. Valley (editorial bd. 1953-56) hist. assns., Soc. Am. Archivists, Am. Acad. Polit. and Social Sci., Minn., Kans. hist. socs., State Hist. Soc. Iowa, Phi Kappa Delta, Pi Gamma Mu, Zeta Sigma Pi, Delta Upsilon. Republican. Presbyn. Mason (32 deg.). Clubs: Iowa Author (pres. 1940-42); Propeller (Quad City); Westerners, Cliff Dwellers, Caxton (Chgo.); Research (sec.-treas. 1944-46) Triangle, S.P.C.S. Rotary, C. of C. (Iowa City). Author: True Tales of Iowa (with Edith Rule), 1932; Two Hundred Topics in Iowa History, 1932; Steamboating on the Upper Mississippi, 1937, rev. edit., 1968; Iowa: The Rivers of Her Valleys, 1941; A Reference Guide to Iowa History, 1942; Iowa History Reference Guide, 1952; The Story of Iowa, 2 vols., 1952; Mississippi River Panorama: Henry Lewis Great National Work, 1979; Towboating on the Mississippi, 1979. Editor: (John Plumbe, Jr.) Sketches of Iowa and Wisconsin, 1948; (Isaac Galland) Galland's Iowa Emigrant, 1950; (John B. Newhall) A Glimpse of Iowa in 1846, 1957; author-editor: The Pageant of the Press, 1962; The Annals of Iowa-1863; Illustrated Historical Atlas of the State of Iowa in 1875 (A.T. Andreas), 1970; Towboating on the Mississippi, 1979; contbr. to profl. mags. Home: 329 Ellis Ave Iowa City IA 52240

PETERSMEYER, CHARLES WREDE, ret. corp. exec.; b. Los Angeles, Jan. 28, 1919; s. Harry Frederick and Florence (Quayle) P.; A.B. with honors, U. Calif., 1941; M.B.A. with high distinction, Harvard, 1943; m. Frances Carolyn Gregg, Apr. 12, 1944; children—Susan Calhoun (Mrs. Ben G. Henneke, Jr.), Charles Gregg, Nancy Quayle. Asso. McKinsey & Co., 1946-47; asso. J. H. Whitney & Co., 1947-51, partner, 1951-59; founder, chmn. until 1977 of Corinthian Broadcasting Corp., N.Y., owner stas. KOTV, Tulsa, KHOU-TV, Houston, KXTV, Sacramento, WANE-TV, Fort Wayne, WISH-TV, Indpls., TVS Television Network; trustee Greenwich Savs. Bank. Trustee, Pine Manor Coll., chmn. bd., 1975-78; bd. dirs. and overseers Sweet Briar Coll.; advisor Sprout Funds; chmn. Harvard Bus. Sch. Fund, 1976-78. Served from pvt. to capt. AUS, 1943-46. Mem. Nat. Inst. Social Scis., Nat. Assn. Broadcasters (past dir.), Assn. Maximum Service Telecasters (past dir.), Com. Econ. Devel. (trustee), Phi Beta Kappa Assos. (dir.), Phi Beta Kappa, Delta Kappa Epsilon. Clubs: University, Harvard Business School (N.Y.C.); John's Island (Fla.); Augusta (Ga.) Nat. Golf; Bronxville (N.Y.) Field. Home and Office: 6 Northway Bronxville NY 10708

PETERSON, BARTLETT, clergyman; b. Boston, Oct. 29, 1908; s. Ansel Lee and Charlotte B. (Anderson) P.; grad. Christie U., 1928; LL.B., U. Minn., 1943; B.Th., N. Central Coll., 1946; D.D., Northwest Coll., 1973; m. Lydia E. Espeseth, Sept. 24, 1930; children—Denny Lee, Wilson B., Don S. Ordained to ministry Assemblies of God, 1927; pastor in Minn., 1929-40; sec. Minn. Dist., 1940-43, supt., 1943-48; gen. presbyter Gen. Council Assemblies of God, 1942—, exec. presbyter, 1945-53, gen. sec., 1960-75; pres. Central Bible Coll., 1948-58, bd. dirs., 1942-48, 60-75; editor Gospel Broadcast, 1940-44; sec. So. Mo. Dist. Council Assemblies of God, 1958-60; dir. Nat. Religious Broadcasters, 1960-68, dir. Pulpit mag., 1960—. Com. mem. dept. radio Assemblies of God, 1960—. Mem. Greene County Planning Commn. Bd. dirs. N. Central Bible Coll., 1937-48, Assemblies of God Grad. Sch. Theology, 1973-75. Mem. Springfield C. of C., Nat. Sheriffs Assn., Nat. Assn. Evangelicals (dir. 1969-75, mem. radio and TV commn., evang. action com.). Contbr. articles to religious mags.; poet; composer songs and hymns. Home: Route 3 Box 223-A Rogersville MO 65742 Office: 1445 Booneville Ave Springfield MO 65802

PETERSON, BEN, lawyer; b. Boise, Idaho, Sept., 23, 1910; s. Joseph H. and Eva T. (Rogers) P.; student Utah State Coll., 1931-33; LL.B., U. Utah, 1936; m. Louise Lauck, June 1, 1940; children—Linda, Ben, Keith. Admitted to Idaho bar, 1936, also U.S. Supreme Ct.; practice in Pocatello, 1936-57; city atty., Pocatello, 1948-57; U.S. atty., Boise, 1957-60; mem. firm Baum & Peterson, Pocatello, 1959—. Mem. Am. Bar Assn., Idaho State Bar, Sigma Chi. Elk. Home: 540 Fiarway Dr Pocatello ID 83201 Office: 504 Center 151 Bldg Pocatello ID 83201

PETERSON, BEN ANTON, constrn. co. exec.; b. Portland, Oreg., Jan. 25, 1942; s. Anton F. and Margaret (Gadsby) P.; B.B.A., U. Oreg., 1964, M.B.A., 1968. Sr. accountant Peat Marwick Mitchell & Co., San Jose, Calif., 1965-67; controller Bosie Cascade Properties, Honolulu, 1968-69; dir. budgets financial planning Fairchild Camera & Instruments, Mountain View, Calif., 1969-70; controller Swinerton & Walberg Co., San Francisco, 1970-78, v.p. fin., 1979—. Treas., Young Republicans, Palo Alto, 1970-71. C.P.A., Calif., Oreg. Mem. Am. Inst. C.P.A.'s, Fin. Execs. Inst., Alpha Kappa Psi (v.p. 1963), Kappa Sigma. Clubs: San Francisco Yacht, Rotary. Home: 55 Corte Real Greenbrae CA Office: 100 Pine St San Francisco CA 94111

PETERSON, BETTELOU, journalist; b. Richmond, Va.; d. Carl and Marion Edith (Thomson) P.; student Wayne State U., 1948-50, U. Mich., 1950-55; m. Laurence M. Middlemas, Jr., July 1, 1955. With Detroit Free Press, 1944—, now television writer, Sunday TV supplement editor. Office: Detroit Free Press 321 W Lafayette Blvd Detroit MI 48231

PETERSON, BRUCE BIGELOW, educator; b. Boston, Mar. 26, 1935; s. Thomas Howard and Rhea (deCoudres) P.; B.A., Middlebury Coll., 1956; M.A., Syracuse U., 1958, Ph.D., 1962; m. Judith Frances Allen, Aug. 25, 1956; children—Thomas, Kristin, Donald. Instr. math. Syracuse U., 1960-62; mem. faculty Middlebury Coll., 1962—, prof. math., 1972—, chmn. dept., 1968—, dean men, 1967-70; lectr. Assn. Tchrs. Math. in New Eng., 1964—; reader advanced placement Coll. Entrance Exam. Bd., 1966—; mem. faculty Colby Coll. Summer Sci. Inst., 1966—; vis. scholar U. Wash., Seattle, 1970-71; with NATO Advanced Study Inst., 1972. Mem. adv. com. Vt. Tchrs. Edn., 1966—. Bd. dirs. Middlebury Union High Sch., 1965-70. Recipient NSF awards, 1960, 61, 63. Mem. Am. Math. Soc., Math. Assn. Am. (vis. lectr. 1977—), AAUP, Sigma Xi. Author articles profl. jours. Home: RD 2 Peet Rd Cornwall VT 05753

PETERSON, C(ARL) DONALD, state justice; b. Mpls., Feb. 2, 1918; s. Karl Emil and Emma Marie (Sellin) P.; B.A. cum laude, U. Minn., 1939; J.D. with honors (mem. Law Rev.), U. Ill., 1941; grad. Appellate Judges Seminar, N.Y. U., 1967, Nat. Coll. State Trial Judges, 1969; m. Gretchen Elaine Palen, Dec. 6, 1952; children—Barbara Elaine, Craig Donald, Mark Bradley, Polly Suzanne, Todd Douglas, Scott Jeffrey. Admitted to Minn. bar, 1941, also U.S. Supreme Ct.; practice in Mpls., 1941-66; partner firm Howard, Peterson, LeFevere, Lefler, Hamilton & Pearson, 1953-66; justice Supreme Ct. Minn., 1967—. Co-chmn. task force study creating Nat. News Council, 20th Century Fund, 1972-73; bd. dirs. state youth in govt. project YMCA, 1968-78. Mem. Minn. Ho. Reps., 1959-62, minority whip, 1961-62; Republican nominee for lt. gov. Minn., 1962. Served to maj. USAAF, 1942-45, USAF, 1951-52. Decorated Bronze Star. Mem. Am., Minn. bar assns., Inst. Jud. Adminstrn., Am. Law Inst., Am. Judicature Soc., Minn. Press Council (chmn. 1971—), Am.-Swedish Inst., Delta Sigma Rho. Presbyn. (elder 1963—, pres. 1964, 79). Clubs: Minnesota (St. Paul); Torske Klubben (Mpls.). Home: 4809 Wilford Way Edina MN 55435 Office: Minn Supreme Ct State Capitol Saint Paul MN 55155

PETERSON, CARL RUDOLF, lawyer; b. Newark, Apr. 8, 1907; s. Carl Emil Rudolf and Elin (Lindholm) P.; A.B., Princeton, 1928; LL.B., Columbia, 1931; m. Dorothy McNicholas, July 7, 1934; 1 dau., Elsa. Admitted to N.Y. bar, 1932, D.C. bar, 1942; research asst. Columbia Law Sch., 1931-33; asso. firm Hawkins, Delafield & Longfellow, N.Y.C., 1933-37; with Office Chief Counsel, Bur. Internal Revenue, 1937-42, asst. head legislation and regulation div., 1941-42; partner firm Alvord & Alvord, Washington, 1942-50, Lee, Toomey & Kent, Washington, 1950—; lectr. tax and law insts.; condr. occasional seminars Harvard Law Sch., 1950-54; tech. adviser nat. tax com. Fin. Execs. Inst., 1950—. Mem. Am., N.Y. State, D.C. bar assns., Am. Law Inst. Internat. Acad. Law and Sci., Phi Beta Kappa. Clubs: Chevy Chase (Md.); Princeton, Met. (Washington); Chatham (Mass.) Beach and Tennis. Contbr. to legal publs. Home: 5115 Rockwood Pkwy NW

Washington DC 20016 Office: 1200 18th St NW Washington DC 20036

PETERSON, CHARLES EMIL, architect; b. Madison, Minn., Aug. 23, 1906; s. Charles Emil and Mae (Nisbit) P.; B.A., U. Minn., 1928. Landscape architect Western field hdqrs. U.S. Nat. Park Service, San Francisco, 1929-30, resident landscape architect, Yorktown, Va., 1930-33, dep. chief architect, Washington, 1933-35, sr. landscape architect riverfront project, St. Louis, 1936-48, regional architect, Richmond, Va., 1948-49, resident architect independence Nat. Hist. Project, Phila., 1950-54, supervising architect historic structures Eastern U.S., 1954-62; assisted numerous projects, including Skyline Drive, Va., Great Smoky Mountains Nat. Park, Colonial Nat. Hist. Park, Williamsburg to Yorktown; restorations include Moore House, Yorktown, Va., Peirce Mill., Washington, Tempe Wicke House, Morristown, N.J., Andrew Johnson Home, Greenville, Tenn., Hampton Mansion, Balt., Independence Hall, Phila.; cons. archtl. historian, restorationist and planner, Phila., 1962—; adj. prof. architecture Columbia U., 1964—; pioneered Hist. Am. Bldgs. Survey, 1933; mem. Phila. Hist. Commn., 1956-64; conducted devel. studies Easter Island for UNESCO, 1966-68; A.I.A. del. II Internat. Congress Architects and Technicians Hist. Monuments, Venice, 1964, 1st assembly Internat. Council Monuments and Sites, Warsaw-Cracow, 1965, Oxford, Eng., 1969, Budapest, 1972; contbr. to Conf. on Edn. Restorationists, Pistoia, Italy, 1968; organized forums on restoration historic bldgs. Bldg. Research Inst., 1964, Nat. Trust, 1966, A.I.A., 1969; founder St. Louis Hist. Documents Found.; corr. mem. com. Tng. Architects for Conservation (Gt. Britain). Served to comdr. C.E.C., USNR, 1942-46. Recipient Distinguished Service award Dept. Interior, 1961; Louise du Pont Crowninshield award Nat. Trust Hist. Preservation, 1965; Conservation Service award, 1976. Fellow AIA (medal 1979), Athenaeum of Phila.; Benjamin Franklin fellow Royal Soc. Arts; mem. Soc. Archtl. Historians (dir. 1950-64, past pres., v.p. editor Am. notes 1950-67), Mo. Hist. Soc. (dir.), Assn. Studies in Conservation Historic Bldgs. (Gt. Britain), William Clark Soc. (founder), Soc. Hill Civic assns. (dir. 1957-68), Carpenters' Co. of City and County Phila. (co. historian), Assn. Preservation Tech. (past pres.), Phi Kappa Sigma. Club: Franklin Inn (Phila.). Author: Colonial St. Louis, 1948. Contbg. author: Historic Philadelphia, 1953; Philadelphia Architecture in the 19th Century, 1953; The French in the Mississippi Valley, 1965; editor: The 1786 Carpenters' Company Rule Book, 1971; Building Early America, 1976. Contbr. articles profl. jours. Address: 332 Spruce St Society Hill Philadelphia PA 19106

PETERSON, CHARLES LOREN, agrl. engr.; b. Emmett, Idaho, Dec. 27, 1938; s. Clarence James and Jane (Shelton) P.; B.S., U. Idaho, 1961, M.S., 1965; Ph.D. in Engring. Sci., Wash. State U., Pullman, 1973; m. Julianne Rekow, Sept. 7, 1962; children—Val, Karl, Marianne, Cheryl Ann, Charles Lauritz, Brent. Exptl. engr. Oliver Corp., Charles City, Iowa, 1961; farmer, Emmett, 1962-65; instr. math. Emmett High Sch., 1962-63; instr. freshman engring., then extension agrl. engr. U. Idaho, Moscow, 1963-67, prof. agrl. engring., 1973—; asst. prof. Wash. State U., 1968-73; cons. in field. Republican precinct committeeman, 1972-75, sec. 5th legis. dist. Idaho, 1976-79. Grantee Wash. Potato 1971-73, U & I, Inc., 1974, Amalgamated Sugar Co., 1974, Beet Sugar Devel. Found., 1975-78, Phillips Chem. Co., 1976-78, Dept. Agr., 1976-78, Star Found., 1978; registered profl. engr., Idaho. Mem. Am. Soc. Agrl. Engrs. (chmn. Inland Empire chpt. 1978-79, chmn. nat. environ. stored products com. 1978-80; Engr. of Year award Inland Empire chpt., nat. Blue Robbin award 1975), Nat. Soc. Profl. Engrs., Am. Soc. Engring. Edn., Potato Assn. Am., Am. Soc. Sugarbeet Technologists, Idaho Soc. Profl. Engrs., Sigma Xi. Mormon. Contbr. numerous articles profl. jours. Home: Route 3 Box 271 Moscow ID 83843 Office: Agrl Engring BEL 318 Univ Idaho Moscow ID 83843

PETERSON, CHASE N., univ. adminstr.; b. Logan, Utah, Dec. 27, 1929; s. E.G. and Phebe (Nebeker) P.; A.B., Harvard, 1952, M.D., 1956; m. Grethe Ballif, 1956; children—Erika Elizabeth, Stuart Ballif, Edward Chase. Asst. prof. medicine U. Utah Med. Sch., 1965-67; asso. Salt Lake Clinic; dean admissions and fin. aids to students Harvard, 1967-72, v.p. univ., 1972-78; v.p. health scis. U. Utah, Salt Lake City, 1978—. Diplomate Am. Bd. Internal Medicine. Home: 1532 Arlington Dr Salt Lake City UT 84103 Office: U Utah Salt Lake City UT 84112

PETERSON, CLIFFORD LYLE, mfg. co. exec.; b. Moline, Ill., Jan. 17, 1919; s. Emor William and Ora (Bowles) P.; B.S., U. Ill., 1941; m. Roberta Jane Morrison, Sept. 1, 1941; children—Jeffrey Howard, Sally Lynn. With Deere & Co., Moline, 1941—, mgr. cost dept., 1956-59, comptroller, 1959-64, v.p. charge fin., 1964-70, sr. v.p., 1970—, also dir. Bd. dirs. Farm and Indsl. Equipment Inst. Chmn. advanced gifts Moline United Appeal; bd. suprs. Rock Island County, Ill.; treas. Moline Girl Scouts; dir. athletic bd. U. Ill. Bd. dirs. Moline YMCA, Arrowhead Boys Ranch, Coal Valley, Ill. Served with USNR, 1943-46. Mem. Fin. Execs. Inst., U. Ill. Alumni Assn. (dir.), Ill. C. of C. (bd. dirs.), Delta Tau Delta. Conglist. (council). Mason. Club: Union League (Chgo.). Home: 3429 28th Ave Ct Moline IL 61265 Office: John Deere Rd Moline IL 61265

PETERSON, COURTLAND HARRY, educator; b. Denver, June 28, 1930; s. Harry James and Courtney (Caple) P.; B.A., U. Colo., 1951, LL.B., 1953; M.C.L., U. Chgo., 1959; J.D., U. Freiburg (Ger.), 1964; m. Susan Schwab, Gisvold, Jan. 28, 1966; children—Brooke, Linda, Patrick. Admitted to Colo. bar, 1953; mem. faculty U. Colo. Law Sch., 1959—, prof., 1963—, dean, 1974-79; vis. prof. U. Calif. Law Sch., Los Angeles, 1965, Max Planck Inst., Hamburg, Ger., 1969-70, U. Tex. Law Sch., Austin, 1973-74; bd. dirs. Continuing Legal Edn. in Colo., 1974-77. Served to 1st lt. USAF, 1954-56. Fgn. Law fellow U. Chgo., 1957-59; Ford Found. Law Faculty fellow, 1964; Alexander von Humboldt Stiftun fellow, 1969-70. Mem. Am., Colo. (bd. govs. 1974-79), Boulder County bar assns., Am. Soc. Internat. Law, Am. Assn. Comparative Study Law (dir., bd. editors, treas.). Author: Die Anerkennung Auslaendischer Urteile, 1964. Translator: (Bauer) An Introduction to German Law, 1965. Home: 205 Camden Pl Boulder CO 80302 Office: Law Sch Univ Colo Boulder CO 80309

PETERSON, DEAN FREEMAN, JR., civil engr., univ. adminstr.; b. Delta, Utah, June 3, 1913; s. Dean Freeman and Lucille (Crookston) P.; B.S., Utah State U., 1934, D.Sc. (hon.), 1978; M.S. in Civil Engring., Rensselaer Poly. Inst., 1935, Dr. Civil Engring. (Russell Sage fellow 1937-39), 1939; m. Bessie Virginia Carter, Sept. 16, 1938; children—Linda Peterson Thorne, Doris Peterson Rusch, Dean Freeman III, Lucille Peterson Randall, Nicholas R. Jr. engr. Utah WPA, 1935-36; road engr. Indian Service, 1936-37; jr. hydraulic engr. U.S. Geol. Survey, 1937-39; instr. U. Wash., 1939-40; project engr. Upper Potomac River Commn., 1940-41; progress engr. Sanderson & Porter, Pine Bluff, Ark., 1941-44; asso. prof., prof. civil engring. Utah State U., 1946-49, prof., dean engring. Coll. Agrl. and Applied Sci., 1957-73, v.p. for research, 1973-76; chief soil and water div. AID, Washington, 1976-76, dir. Office of Agr., 1978—; prof., head civil engring. Colo. State U., 1949-57; cons. engr., 1946—; tech. asst., office sci. and tech. Exec. Office Pres., 1965-66; dir. Office of Water for Peace, 1968-69; mem. advisory com. on soil, water and fertilizer research Dept. Agr., 1952-59; chmn. panel weather modification NSF, 1963-65; irrigation cons. Near East-S.Asia, AID, 1959-64, 67—; sr. U.S. del. 3d-5th Near East-S.Asia irrigation seminars, Lahore, Pakistan and Ankara, Turkey, 1960, 62, New Delhi, 1964; cons. water resources Office Sci. and Tech., Exec. Office of Pres., 1963, 64, chmn. com. water resources research Fed. Council Sci. and Tech., 1965-66, chief Agrl. Rev. Team, Afghanistan, 1967; chmn. Utah Advisory Council on Sci. and Tech., 1973—. Mem. Cache Valley council Boy Scouts Am. Served to lt. USNR, 1944-46; capt. Res. Fellow Am. Geophys. Union; mem. AAAS (mem. and chmn. com. arid lands 1970-78), ASCE (v.p. 1972-74, mem. exec. com. irrigation and drainage div. 1963-66, vice chmn. 1964, chmn. exec. com. 1966, Royce J. Tipton award 1968), Am. Geophys. Union; mem. Univs. Council on Water Resources (dir., chmn. 1965), Am. Soc. Engring. Edn. (chmn. civil engring. div. 1956-57, mem. commn. on grad. edn. 1956-58), AAUP, Nat. Acad. Engring., Am. Acad. Arts and Scis., Sigma Xi, Phi Kappa Phi, Chi Upsilon, Sigma Tau. Mormon. Club: Cosmos (Washington). Author publs. on irrigation and drainage, hydraulic engring. Home: 765 E 7th N Logan UT 84321 Office: Office of Agr AID Washington DC 20523

PETERSON, DONALD BULLEN, hosp. cons., psychiatrist; b. Mpls., Feb. 16, 1911; s. Will Herbert and Berenice (Bullen) P.; B.S., M.B., U. Minn., 1934, M.D., 1935; m. Catherine Louise Quigley, Sept. 27, 1935; children—Martin Quigley, Karen (Mrs. K. Eric Nelson), Will Thatcher. Intern U. Minn. Gen. Hosps., 1934-35; detached service psychiat. tng. St. Elizabeth's Hosp., Washington, 1941-42; commd. 1st lt. M.C., U.S. Army, 1935, advanced through grades to col.; assigned Letterman Army Hosp., San Francisco, 1936-37, Fitzsimons Army Hosp., Denver, 1938-41, 48-51, St. Elizabeth's Hosp., Washington, 1941-42, Camp Berkeley, Abilene, Tex., 1942-45, army hosps., Calcutta, India, 1945-46, Ft. Lewis, Wash., 1946-47; chief cons. psychiatry and neurology Far East Command, Tokyo, Japan, 1951-54; chief cons. to surgeon gen. U.S. Army, Washington, 1954-56; ret., 1956; supt. Anoka (Minn.) State Hosp., 1956-62, State Hosp. No. 1, Fulton, Mo., 1962-76, cons., 1976—. Decorated Legion of Merit. Diplomate Am. Bd. Psychiatry and Neurology. Fellow A.C.P., Am. Psychiat. Assn.; mem. AcA, Callaway County Med. Soc., Group Advancement Psychiatry (past chmn. com. govtl. agencies), Assn. Med. Supts. Mental Hosps. (council 1965-68), Mid-Continent Psychiat. Assn. Contbr. articles profl. jours. Home: 1 Country Club Dr Fulton MO 65251

PETERSON, DONALD ROBERT, educator, psychologist, univ. dean; b. Pillager, Minn., Sept. 10, 1923; s. Frank Gordon and Ruth (Friedland) P.; B.A., U. Minn., 1948, M.A., 1950, Ph.D., 1952; m. Jean Hole, Feb. 10, 1951 (div.); children—Wendy, Jeffrey, Roger, Lisa; m. 2d, Jane Snyder Salmon. Mem. faculty U. Ill. at Urbana, 1952-75, prof. clin. psychology, 1963-75, head div., 1963-70, dir. Psychol. Clinic, 1961-70, dir. D. Psychology program, 1970-75; dean Grad. Sch. Applied and Profl. Psychology, Rutgers U., New Brunswick, 1975—. Served with AUS, 1943-46. Mem. Am., Eastern, N.J. psychol. assns. Author: The Clinical Study of Social Behavior, 1968; also articles; editor Jour. Abnormal Psychology, 1970-72. Office: Grad Sch Applied and Profl Psychology Rutgers U New Brunswick NJ 08903

PETERSON, EDWARD ADRIAN, lawyer; b. St. Louis, May 19, 1941; s. Adrian J. and Virginia (Hamlin) P.; B.S. in Bus. Adminstrn., Washington U., St. Louis, 1963; LL.B., So. Methodist U., 1966; m. Catherine Frances Younghouse, Dec. 17, 1960; children—Kristin, Kendra. Admitted to Tex. bar, 1966; instr. bus. law and accounting Midwestern U., Wichita Falls, Tex., 1967; practice law, Dallas, 1967—; partner firm Moore & Peterson, 1976—. Bd. dirs. Leukemia Soc., 1970-71. Mem. Am. Bar Assn., Dallas Bar Assn., State Bar Tex., Real Estate Fin. Execs. Assn., Phi Alpha Delta, Sigma Alpha Epsilon. Lutheran. Club: Dallas. Contbr. legal jours. Home: 9442 Spring Hollow Dr Dallas TX 75243 Office: 28th Floor Republic Nat Bank Tower Dallas TX 75201

PETERSON, EDWARD DALE, educator; b. Marshalltown, Iowa, Apr. 18, 1929; s. Thomas Lars and Mildred Olive (Medhus) P.; B.A., U. No. Iowa, 1951; M.B.A., Ind. U, 1953, D.B.A., 1960; m. Neoma Jean Lovig, Aug. 19, 1951; children—Brian, Mark, Jon, Kristin, Reid. Tchr., Radcliffe pub. schs., 1951-52, Clinton (Iowa) Jr. Coll., 1953-56; mem. faculty Ind. U., 1957-59; mem. faculty Mankato (Minn.) State U., 1959—, prof. econs., 1962—, chmn. dept., 1963—. Treas. Mankato Higher Edn. Ministry, 1963—; mem. Blue Earth Med. Adv. Com., 1969—, Tech. Rev. Panel for State of Minn. Title I, 1968-70. Bd. dirs. Mankato YMCA, Twin Valley council Boy Scouts Am. Mem. Am., Midwest, Minn. (pres. 1973) econ. assns., Faculty Assn. (pres. 1979—), AAUP (pres. 1971-76). Home: 6 Capri Dr Mankato MN 56001

PETERSON, ESTHER, consumer adviser; b. Provo, Utah, Dec. 9, 1906; d. Lars and Annie (Nielsen) Eggertsen; A.B., Brigham Young U., 1927; M.A., Columbia Tchrs. Coll., 1930; hon. degrees Smith Coll., Bryant Coll., Carnegie Inst. Tech., Montclair Coll., Hood Coll., Maryhurst Coll., Simmons Coll., Northeastern U., U South Utah, Western Coll. Women, Oxford, Ohio, Mich. State U., U. Mich., U. Utah, Williams Coll.; m. Oliver A. Peterson, May 28, 1932; children—Karen Kristine, Eric N., Iver E., Lars E. Tchr., Branch Agr. Coll., Cedar City, Utah, 1927-29, Winsor Sch., Boston, 1930-36, Bryn Mawr Summer Sch. for Women Workers in Industry, 1932-39; asst. dir. edn. Amal. Clothing Workers Am., 1939-44, Washington legis. rep., 1945-48; legis. rep. indsl. union dept. AFL-CIO, 1958-61; dir. Women's Bur., U.S. Dept. Labor, 1961-64, asst. sec. labor for labor standards, 1961-69; exec. vice chmn. Pres.'s Commn. on Status of Women, 1961-63, Interdeptl. Com. Status Women, 1963-65; chmn. Pres.'s Com. Consumer Interests, 1964-67, spl. asst. to President for consumer affairs, 1964-67; legis. rep. Amal. Clothing Workers Am., Washington, 1969-70; consumer adviser Giant Food Corp., 1970-77; spl. asst. to Pres. for consumer affairs, 1977—; mem. Fed. Commn. on Fed. Paperwork, 1975-77; lectr. Mem. adv. com. Women's Bur., Dept. Labor, 1945-48; mem. D.C. Minimum Wage Bd., 1945. Bd. dirs. Nat. Center for Resource Recovery, Inst. Pub. Interest Representation, Center Sci. in Pub. Interest, Fair Campaign Practices Com.; hon. chmn. Nat. Com. Household Employment; mem. Women's Nat. Democratic Club. Mem. AAUW, Am. Newspaper Women's Club (asso.), Am. Home Econs. Assn. (hon.), Nat. Consumers League (pres. 1974-76), Phi Chi Theta (hon.), Delta Sigma Theta (hon.). Home: 7714 13th St NW Washington DC 20012 Office: White House Washington DC 20500

PETERSON, EVAN TYE, educator; b. Phoenix, Oct. 12, 1925; s. Harold Anton and Juna (Tye) P.; B.S., Brigham Young U., 1952, M.S., 1953; Ph.D., U. Mich., 1959; m. Elnora Nuttall, Sept. 1, 1950 (div.); children—Carol J., Mary E., Mark E., Steven B., Eric A., Helen E.; m. 2d, Gail Winther, June 5, 1978. Instr., U. Mich., 1956-57, research appointments, 1957-58; asst. prof. Miss. State U., 1958-59; asst. prof. Brigham Young U., Provo, Utah, 1959-62, asso. prof., 1962-67, prof., 1967—, chmn. dept. sociology, 1970-75, dir. Survey Research Center, 1975—; research appointments U. Utah, 1963-67; vis. prof. San Diego State Coll., summers 1966-67, Ariz. State U., 1968; cons. Coll. Nursing, U. Utah, Engring. Corp. Am., Phoenix. Served with M.C., AUS, 1944-46. Mem. Am., Pacific sociol. assns., Nat. Council Family Relations, Soc. Study Social Problems, Am. Assn. U. Profs., Sigma Xi, Alpha Kappa Delta, Phi Kappa Phi. Mem. Ch. of Jesus Christ of Latter-day Saints (bishop). Author: (with others) Introductory Sociology, 1960; Notes on Methods of Sociological Research, 1969. Home: 1075 E Grove Creek Dr Pleasant Grove UT 84062

PETERSON, FLOYD DELNER, utilities exec.; b. Mpls., Feb. 21, 1907; s. Charles Gustav and Dorothea (Listul) P.; B.S., U. Minn., 1930, postgrad., 1931-32; postgrad. Western Res. U., 1934-35, Columbia, 1940-41; L.H.D., Gettysburg Coll., 1968; m. Eva Eleanore Kjellstrand, Nov. 11, 1939; Hydraulic engr., architect, surveyman, Mpls., 1924-30; with C.E., Duluth, Minn., 1930-33, asst. div. engr., Cleve., 1934-35, chief engring. div., N.Y.C., 1936-44; chief civil works U.S. Bur. of Budget, Washington, 1944-54; chief Fed. Pub. Works Office and spl. asst. to pres. for pub. works, Washington, 1955-61; cons. engr., planner, cons. dir. research Nat. Assn. Elec. Cos., 1961-70; chmn., commr. Washington Suburban San. Commn., Hyattsville, Md., 1971-76; cons. engr., 1976—. Mem. exec. bd., chmn. fin. com. Md. Synod Lutheran Ch. in Am., 1962-68; mem., sec., chmn. fin. com. Bd. Am. Missions, Luth. Ch. in Am., 1964-72; chmn. bd. Columbia (Md.) Coop. Ministry, 1966-72; chmn. bd. dirs. Luth. Social Services, Washington, 1960-67, pres., 1967; treas. Peter Muhlenberg Meml. Assn., 1960-75, Luth. Resources Commn., 1970—. Precinct chmn. Montgomery County, Md., 1970-71. Trustee, Theol. Sem., Gettysburg, Pa.; bd. assos. Gettysburg Coll. Recipient Distinguished Service medal Pres. of U.S., 1961. Registered profl. engr., Washington. Mem. ASCE (pres. Nat. Capital sect., Civil Govt. award 1976, Bartholomew Urban Planning and Devel. award 1978), Am. Acad. Polit. and Social Scis., Am. Pub. Works Assn., Am. Soc. Pub. Adminstrn., Am. Inst. Planners, Soc. Am. Mil. Engrs., Permanent Internat. Nav. Congresses, Road Gang, Am.-Scandinavian Found., Norwegian-Am. Hist. Assn., Am. Judicature Soc., Nat. Lawyers Club. Republican. Kiwanian. Home and Office: 873 Teryl Rd Naples FL 33942

PETERSON, FRANK DEWEY, business exec.; b. Taylor County, Ky., Sept. 1, 1899; s. John Artibury and Lou Vinie (Sinclair) P.; A.B., Centre Coll., 1924; student Bowling Green Bus. Coll., 1924, U. Chgo., 1932, U. Ky., 1934; LL.D., Georgetown U., 1953; m. Audrey Whitlock, May 22, 1924. Dir. sch. finance Ky. Dept. Edn., 1925-36; adminstr. for Ky., NYA, 1935-36; dep. commr. finance, comptroller, Ky., 1936-41; comptroller U. Ky., 1941-55, sec. bd. trustees, 1942-63, treas. univ., 1944-63, sec. bd. trustees, 1942-63, treas. univ., 1944-63, v.p. bus. adminstrn., 1955-64, founder Coll. Bus. Mgmt. Inst., 1953; sec., treas., dir. Southeastern States Securities, Inc., 1963—, Royce Blevins Constrn., Inc., 1963—; treas., sec. R.L. Saunders Co., 1968—; pres. 7-Kings, Inc., Franchise Jiffy Franchise System, also Salty Bay Oyster House, 1969-71; treas., dir. Town & Country Realty Co., Gen. Tire Service (both Lexington, Ky.); dir. Spindletop Research, Inc., Ky. Family Security Ins. Co., Inc.; dir., sec. Lexington Fire Protection Corp., 1975—, Saylor's Corp., 1976—, Bellaire Enterprises Gen. Partnership, 1977—; fin. cons. Rep. rural states before NYA, 1936; chmn. Ky. Fair Wage Scale Commn., 1937; mem. nat. com. uniform distbn. fed. aid to distressed sch. dists. in U.S., 1934-35; pres. Internat. Book Project, 1969; mem. City-Fayette County Merger Com., 1972-73; mem. state adv. council SBA. Pres. bd. trustees Central Baptist Hosp., Lexington, 1955-64; pres. Carnhan House of U. Ky., 1956-61, United Community Fund, Lexington, 1959-62; mem. Bapt. Hosp. Commn. Ky., 1955-64; bd. overseers Centre Coll., 1944; mem. bd. Am. Family Security Found.; sec., treas. Ky. Research Found., 1949-63, founder, dir., adminstr., 6 years; treas. Thomas P. Cooper Agrl. Found., 1952-63; pres. Spindletop Hall, U. Ky., 1961-63; pres. bd. dirs. Internat. Book Project, U. Ky., 1966—, bd. dirs. Coll. Bus. Mgmt. Inst., U. Ky., 1952-63; life mem. Pres.'s Club Georgetown U. Recipient certificate appreciation So. Assn. Coll. and Univ. Bus. Officers, 1956, Campbellsville (Ky.) Coll., 1953, City of Louisville, 1937, Taylor County, Ky., 1958; Distinguished Service award U. Ky., 1974; named Ky. col., 1938. Mem. So. Assn. Coll. and Univ. Bus. Officers (pres. 1952), Ky. Edn. Assn., Central Assn. Coll. and Univ. Bus. Assn., Civil War Round Table, Chamberlain Lit. Soc., Thoroughbred Club Am., Phi Delta Kappa, Omicron Delta Kappa, Beta Gamma Sigma, Kappa Sigma. Baptist (trustee). Clubs: Spindletop, Lafayette, Masons, Shriners, Kiwanis (pres., dist. lt. gov. 1975-76, Distinguished Service award), Lexington Country. Author: Uniform Financial Accounting System for County, City and Graded School Districts for Kentucky, 1933; also articles. Editorial cons. Coll. and Univ. Bus. mag. Home: 1557 Tates Creek Rd Lexington KY 40502

PETERSON, FRANK THURSTON, engring. co. exec.; b. Napanoch, N.Y., Jan. 18, 1921; s. Frank I. and Marta K. (Gustafson) P.; B.S.M.E., Syracuse U., 1942; m. Janet Boeppler, Feb. 1, 1952; children—Kim, Kurt, Lars. Design engr. Black Clawson Co., 1945-47, v.p., 1947-50, exec. v.p., 1950-54, pres., 1954-64; pres. Brown Co., 1964-72; sr. v.p. Parsons & Whittemore, 1972-76, Rust Engring. Co., Birmingham, Ala., 1976-77; pres. Rust Internat., Inc., Stamford, Conn., 1977—. Served to maj. U.S. Army, 1943-45. Mem. ASME. Clubs: Union League, N.Y. Athletic (N.Y.C.); Burning Tree Country (Greenwich, Conn.). Home: 48 Old Mill Rd Greenwich CT

PETERSON, FRED MCCRAE, librarian; b. Mpls., Dec. 29, 1936; B.A., U. Minn., 1958, M.S., 1960; Ph.D. in Library Sci., Ind. U., 1974. Asst. to dir. Iowa State U. Library, 1961-64, head catalog dept., 1964-67, asso. dir. library, 1969-70; with Cath. U. Am., Washington, 1970—, asst. prof., asso. chairperson, 1973-77, acting dir. libraries, 1977-78, dir. libraries, 1978—; vis. lectr. U. Minn., U. Iowa. Mem. ALA, Assn. Am. Library Schs., Cath. Library Assn., D.C. Library Assn. Home: 2210 Greenery Ln #302 Silver Spring MD 20906 Office: Mullen Library Cath U Am Washington DC 20064

PETERSON, FRITZ FRED, profl. baseball player; b. Oak Park, Ill., Feb. 8, 1942; s. Fred Joseph and Annette Ester (Ingels) P.; B.S. in Edn., No. Ill. U., 1965, M.S. in Edn., 1967, certificate advanced study, 1973; children—Gregory Todd, Eric Brett, Lindsay Annette, Tobie Nora. Player with N.Y. Yankees, 1963-74, Cleve. Indians, 1974-75, Tex. Rangers, from 1976; tchr. phys. edn. Morehead (Ky.) State U., 1967, No. Ill. U., 1968-71; commentator N.Y. Raiders Hockey Team, 1972-73; now host TV program Winning Athletes, WCFC, Chgo.; speaker on Christianity. Mem. Baseball Chapel Inc. Mem. Inter Sports Assn., Tau Kappa Epsilon, Phi Delta Kappa. Home: 245 Thomas St Cary IL 60013 Office: 20 N Wacker Dr Suite 1345 Chicago IL 60606. *My entire life was spent searching for happiness but it wasn't until I had "everything" that I realized that true happiness could not be found apart from Jesus Christ. Now, instead of fearing the future, I look forward to each and every day as a new experience "in the Lord" and since the Bible says "All things work together for good for those who love the Lord and are called accordingly to His purpose" I can accept any circumstance of life with assurance that it is THE best for me and my family.*

PETERSON, GEORGE EMANUEL, JR., lawyer, corp. exec.; b. Mt. Vernon, N.Y., Mar. 8, 1931; s. George E. and Lydia Evelyn (Peterson) P.; B.A., Yale, 1953; LL.B., U. Va., 1958; m. Barbara Ritter, Aug. 30, 1957; children—Lisa Manvel, George Emanuel III. Admitted to N.Y. State bar, 1959, Conn. bar, 1974; asso. firm Reid & Priest, N.Y.C., 1958-68, partner, 1968-70; v.p., gen. counsel Insilco Corp., Meriden, Conn., 1970-72, v.p. finance, 1972-76, v.p., sec., 1976—; dir. Hazeltine Corp., 1975—. Trustee Hamden Hall Country Day Sch., 1975—. Served as lt. USNR 1953-55. Mem. Am., N.Y. State bar assn.

Home: 275 Chestnut Ln Hamden CT 06518 Office: 1000 Research Pkwy Meriden CT 06450

PETERSON, GEORGE HAROLD, univ. adminstr.; b. San Francisco, Apr. 11, 1931; s. Harold George and Margaret (Steinacher) P.; B.S., U. Calif. at Berkeley, 1953, Ph.D., 1957. Asst. prof. botany and plant pathology Purdue U., 1957-63; mem. faculty Calif. State Coll., Hayward, 1963—, dean acad. planning, 1970-79, asso. v.p. acad. resources, 1979—, prof. biol. scis., 1971—, faculty rep. Far Western Intercollegiate Conf., 1967—. Chmn. soil enzymes symposium 8th Internat. Congress Microbiology, Montreal, 1962. Fellow AAAS; mem. Am. Soc. Microbiology, N.Y. Acad. Scis., Am. Inst. Biol. Scis., Sigma Xi. Co-editor: Soil Biochemistry, 1967. Home: 401 Monte Vista Ave Oakland CA 94611

PETERSON, GEORGE LESTER, editor; b. Olivia, Minn., Dec. 2, 1902; s. George and Martha (Broberg) P.; B.A., Hamline U., 1926, LL.D., 1957; postgrad. U. Minn., 1927-28, 41-42; m. Marguerite Littel, June 18, 1929 (dec.); children—Mary E., Nils Peter; m. 2d, Rose Littel, Nov. 14, 1953 (dec.); m. 3d, Florence Windemuth Lanning, Dec. 18, 1976. Country newspaper editor, 1926-27; copyreader, later copy desk editor Mpls. Morning Tribune, 1927-29, news editor, 1929-41; journalism instr. U. Minn., Hamline U., 1930-40; mem. editorial page staff Mpls. and Tribune, 1941-70, editorial page editor until 1970, now writer weekly farm column; sec., staff editor Experience Inc., cons. firm, 1970—; corr. in Alaska, World War II. Pres. bd. trustees Hamline U., 1970-76. Mem. Soil Conservation Soc. Am. (hon.). Home: 19390 Park Ave Wayzata MN 55391 Office: Dain Tower Minneapolis MN 55402. *My early blind faith in technology has eroded over the years. I now realize that technology raises about as many questions as it answers. As a convert to organic gardening I have learned that the simple way is often the best way in the long run.*

PETERSON, GEORGE RAYMOND, JR., publisher; b. Mankato, Minn., June 15, 1938; s. George Raymond and Catherine Gladys (Blickan) P.; B.A., St. John's U., Collegeville, Minn., 1960; m. Sandra Lee Vint, June 23, 1962; children—Thomas Jay, Michael George, Kristin Lee, Timothy James. Exec. trainee Prentice-Hall Co., 1964; officer Creative Edn., Inc., Mankato, 1964-68, pres., owner, 1968—; v.p. Amecus St., Inc.; treas. Child's World, Inc.; pres. Instructional Aids Co.; dir. Northwestern Nat. Bank, Mankato. Bd. dirs. Mankato YMCA; treas. Newman Center, Mankato. Served to 1st lt. AUS, 1962-64. Mem. Minn. Golf Assn. (dir.). Roman Catholic. Club: Mankato Golf (dir.). Home: 1574 Sherwood Dr North Mankato MN 56001 Office: 123 S Broad St Mankato MN 56001

PETERSON, HARDING WILLIAM, baseball club ofcl.; b. Perth Amboy, N.J., Oct. 17, 1929; s. Louis Christian and Gladys (Jenkins) P.; B.S. in Edn., Rutgers U., 1950; m. Gladys Marie Dudics, June 4, 1952; children—Eric Harding, Amy Beth. Player, Pitts. Pirates, 1950-59, mgr. Pirate Farm System, 1959-67, minor league dir., 1967-76, scouting dir., 1968-76, v.p., 1976-78, exec. v.p., 1979—. Mem. Profl. Baseball Players Assn. Club: Allegheny. Office: Three Rivers Stadium Pittsburgh PA 15212

PETERSON, HAROLD OSCAR, educator, radiologist; b. Dalbo, Minn., Apr. 13, 1909; s. Adolph Oscar and Hulda (Forslund) P.; B.S., U. Minn., 1930, M.D., 1934; m. Margaret Dorothy Ferris, Sept. 22, 1934; children—John F., F., Judith Ann (Mrs. David P. Lyons), Richard H., James R. Intern Kansas City (Mo.) Gen. Hosp., 1933-34; resident radiology Mass. Gen. Hosp., Bostón, 1935-36; mem. faculty U. Minn. Med. Sch., 1937—, prof. radiology, emeritus prof., 1977—, chmn. dept., 1957-70; radiologist, head dept. Charles T. Miller Hosp., St. Paul, 1941-57, Children's Hosp., St. Paul, 1948-57; cons. Mpls. Gen. Hosp., 1958—; radiologist Bethesda Hosp., St. Paul, 1941-44, St. Joseph's Hosp., St. Paul, 1941-43, Interstate Clinic, Red Wing, Minn., 1940-57; chief staff Univ. Hosp., U. Minn., 1966—; Pancoast lectr., Phila., 1956; Friedman lectr. U. Cin., 1959; Caldwell lectr. and gold medal Am. Roentgen Ray Soc., 1961; Hodges lectr., Ann Arbor, Mich., 1962; Carmen lectr. St. Louis Med. Soc., 1962; ann. lectr. Canadian Assn. Radiologists, 1962; Manville lectr. La. Med. Soc., 1961; Golden lectr. N.Y. Roentgen Soc., 1964; Rigler lectr., Tel Aviv, Israel, 1965; Holmes lectr. New Eng. Roentgen Ray Soc., 1965; Kirklin Weber Meml. lectr. Mayo Clinic, 1965; Dyke lectr. Columbia, 1971; Stauffer lectr. Temple U., 1972; Rigler lectr. U. Minn., 1972; vis. prof. U. Tex. Med. Br., Galveston, 1979-80. Diplomate Am. Bd. Radiology (trustee 1959-65, 65-71). Fellow Am. Coll. Radiology (chancellor 1958-62, 65-69, v.p. 1963-64, chmn. com. tech. affairs 1965-69; gold medal St. Louis meeting 1971), Am. Coll. Chest Physicians; mem. Am. Roentgen Ray Soc. (dir. instructional courses 1957-76, exec. council 1954-57, chmn. council 1956-57, pres. 1964), Am. Soc. Neuroradiology (charter, founding mem., pres. 1967), A.M.A., Minn., Ramsey County med. socs., Minn. Radiol. Soc., Minn. Trudeau Soc., Radiol. Soc. N.Am., AAUP, Am. Trudeau Soc., AAAS, Assn. Am. Med. Colls., Minn. Soc. Neurol. Scis., Am. Soc. Pediatric Radiology (charter, founding mem.), Pan Am. Med. Assn., Minn. Acad. Medicine, Am. Acad. Neurology, Sigma Xi; hon. mem. numerous med. socs. Republican. Methodist. Club: Midland Hills Country (St. Paul). Sr. author: Introduction to Neuroradiology, 1972. Author numerous articles med. jours. Home: 1995 W County Rd B Saint Paul MN 55113

PETERSON, HARRIES-CLICHY, financial cons.; b. Boston, Sept. 7, 1924; s. Edwin William and Annekathe (Lieske) P.; A.B., Harvard, 1946, M.B.A., 1950. Sci. officer Ronne Antarctic Expdn., 1947-48; staff asst. Kidder Peabody & Co., N.Y.C., 1952-53, Devel. and Resources Corp., N.Y.C., 1959-61; dir. indsl. devel. W.R. Grace & Co., Lima, Peru, 1953-57; staff asst. Devel. & Resources Corp., N.Y.C. 1959-61; bus. cons., Lima, 1961-65; v.p. internat. div. Foremost Dairies, Inc. (now Foremost-McKesson, Inc.), San Francisco, 1965-67; v.p. H.K. Porter Co., Inc., Pitts., 1967-68, also dir. overseas affiliates, 1967-68; independent fin. adviser, San Francisco and Los Angeles, 1968—. Served to col. USMCR, 1943-45, 51-52, 57-59. Decorated Silver Star. Mem. Colegio de Economistas del Peru (past dir.), Am. Mgmt. Assn. (conf. chmn.). Author: Development of Titanium Metals Industry, 1950; Che Guevara on Guerrilla Warfare, 1961; Petróleo: Hora Céro, 1964; Islamic Banking, 1979. Contbr. articles gen. interest, bus., mil. publs. Address: Box 2916 San Francisco CA 94126. *I am grateful to classical education for having shown me truth and beauty. But the challenge to apply ideals and innovation into tradition and hierarchy requires endless self-appraisal and adjustment, sometimes exhilarating, sometimes disheartening, sometimes edifying, sometimes extracting great sacrifices from self and others I might have better served. Yet, the pursuit of uncynical truth and harmonious beauty remains an unshakeable mistress needed to satisfy soul and spirit.*

PETERSON, HERBERT K., banker; b. Manistique, Mich., May 9, 1934; s. Herbert K. and Edith (Thomas) P.; B.A., Albion Coll., 1956; m. Barbara J. Borsenik, Apr. 18, 1964; 1 son, Peter Thomas. With Mich. Nat. Bank, Saginaw, 1956—, asst. v.p. comml. loan dept., 1959-71, v.p., dir., 1964-74, sr. v.p., 1970-74; sr. v.p. Mich. Nat. Bank, Grand Rapids, 1974-77, sr. v.p. Central Adminstrv. Office, Lansing, 1977—. Served with AUS, 1957-59. Named Outstanding Young Man of Year, Saginaw Jr. C. of C., 1963. Mem. Robert Morris Assos. Presbyn. Home: 1225 Farwood Dr East Lansing MI 48823 Office: 124 W Allegan St Lansing MI 48901

PETERSON, J. DWIGHT, investments; b. Decatur, Ind., May 25, 1897; s. John Samuel and Olive (Hale) P.; A.B., Ind. U., 1919, LL.D.; m. Mary Irene Frisinger, July 19, 1921; children—Patricia (Mrs. Donald C. Danielson), Sally (Mrs. Robert A. Ravensberg), John. Bond salesman City Trust Co., Indpls., 1919-24; bond salesman City Securities Corp., Indpls., 1924-28, asst. mgr., 1928-30, v.p., 1930-34, pres., 1934-63, chmn. bd., 1963-70, 71-79, hon. chmn. bd., 1979—; pres., dir. Lianhurst Realty Corp.; dir. City Discount Corp., Lilly Indsl. Coatings, Inc., Central Newspapers, Inc.; hon. dir. Am. States Ins. Co., Am. States Life Ins. Co., Am. Economy Ins. Co. Trustee Pub. Employee's Retirement Fund Indi and Hanover Coll.; bd. govs. James Whitcomb Riley Hosp.; treas., dir. Ind. U. Found. Served as 2d lt. F.A., U.S. Army, World War I. Mem. Am. Legion, Sigma Chi (past grand consul), Beta Gamma Sigma, Sigma Delta Chi. Republican. Presbyn. (elder). Mason, Rotarian. Clubs: Columbia, Service, Contemporary, Highland Golf and Country (Indpls.). Home: 4200 N Pennsylvania St Indianapolis IN 46205 Office: Circle Tower Indianapolis IN 46204

PETERSON, J. W., savs. and loan assn. exec.; b. Dallas; s. James William and Cora Leona (Buder) P.; student City Coll. Law and Fin., Jefferson Coll.; diploma Savs. and Loan Inst.; m. Helen Borne, July 29, 1940; children—Rochelle, Larry. Ct. abstractor, title examiner Title Ins. Corp., St. Louis, about 1933-35; partner St. Louis Tax Service, 1935-36; sec. Community Fed. Savs. & Loan Assn., St. Louis, 1936—, v.p., 1953-68, exec. v.p., 1968—, mem. exec. com., 1977—, also dir., mem. other coms. Mem. Ritenour Consol. Sch. Bd., St. Louis County, 1953-70, v.p., 1951-59, pres., 1959-67. Recipient Friends of Scouting award Boy Scouts Am., 1977-79, Century award YMCA, 1978. Mem. Community C. of C. (an organizer, pres. 1953-54, dir. 1951-71, exec. com. 1968-69), Mo. C. of C., U.S. C. of C., Greater St. Louis Savs. and Loan League, Mo. Savs. and Loan League (40 Yr. Service award 1976), U.S. Savs. and Loan League, Nat. Savs. and Loan League, Friends of Scouting. Club: Lions (20 Yr. Membership award 1964). Home: 2440 Hartland Ave Saint Louis MO 63114 Office: 1 Community Fed Center Saint Louis MO 63131. *I have found the three ingredients of achievement are desire, determination and time.*

PETERSON, JAMES ALFRED, marriage counselor; b. Glendive, Mont., May 11, 1913; s. John Martin and Hilda (Moline) P.; A.B., Ripon (Wis.) Coll., 1934; B.D., Chgo. Theol. Sem., 1938; Ph.D., U. So. Calif., 1950; m. Audrey Mount Crawford, June 2, 1936; children—Jon Chrispin, Mary Louise (Mrs. Peter Hamlet), Nancy Lea. Ordained to ministry Conglist. Ch., 1936; pastor Manhattan Beach (Calif.) Community Ch., 1939-50; prof. sociology U. So. Calif., 1950-58, chmn. dept., 1962-65, 70, acting dir. Sch. Gerontology, founding dir. Rossmoor Cortese Inst. Study Retirement and Aging, 1963-65; exec. dir. Peterson-Guedel Family Center, Beverly Hills, Calif., 1960—; pres. Gerontol. Cons. Assos., Los Angeles, El Dorado Corp. for Mining and Recreation, Helena, Mont.; exec. v.p. Christian Services Inc., Kansas City, Mo.; lectr. U. Oreg., 1975. Mem. Am. (pres. 1967-68), So. Calif. (pres. 1962) assns. marriage counselors, So. Calif. Conf. Family (pres. 1961). Author: Education for Marriage, 1964; (with Eleanor Metheny) The Trouble with Women, 1956; Toward a Successful Marriage, 1962; Married Love in the Middle Years, 1968; Marriage and Family Counseling, 1968; Counseling and Values: A Philosophical Examination, 1970; Finding and Preparing Precious and Semi-Precious Stones, 1974; (with Barbara Payne) Love in the Later Years, 1975; (with Michael Briley) Widows and Widowhood, 1977. Home: 2428 N Highland St Altadena CA 91001 Office: 8530 Wilshire Blvd Beverly Hills CA 90211. *In a world of rapid technological and ideational change it is critical for the leader to measure his contribution both against the past and in anticipation of the social system that is evolving. The person who lives only in the current hour is already an anachronism.*

PETERSON, JAMES ALGERT, geologist, educator; b. Baroda, Mich., Apr. 17, 1915; s. Djalma Hardaman and Mary Avis (McAnally) P.; student Northwestern U., 1941-43, U. Wis., 1943; B.S. magna cum laude, St. Louis U., 1948; M.S. (Shell fellow), U. Minn., 1950, Ph.D., 1951; m. Gladys Marie Pearson, Aug. 18, 1944; children—James D., Wendy A., Brian H. Mem. staff U.S. Geol. Survey, Spokane, Wash., 1949-51; instr. geology Wash. State U., Pullman, 1951; geologist Shell Oil Co., 1952-65; geologist div. stratigrapher, 1958-63, sr. geologist, 1963-65; instr. geology N. Mex. State U., San Juan, (P.R.), br., 1959-65; prof. geology U. Mont., Missoula, 1965—; cons. U.S. Geol. Survey, 1976—. Served to 1st lt., USAAF, 1943-46. Recipient Alumni Merit award St. Louis U., 1960. Fellow AAAS, Geol. Soc. Am.; mem. Am. Assn. Petroleum Geologists (pres. Rocky Mountain sect. 1964), Four Corners Geol. Soc. (pres. 1962), Am. Inst. Profl. Geologists (pres. Mont. sect. 1971), Soc. Econ. Paleontologists and Mineralogists (sec.-treas. 1969-71, editor 1976-78), Mont., Utah geol. socs. Editor: Geology of East Central Utah, 1956; Geometry of Sandstone Bodies, 1960; Rocky Mountain Sedimentary Basins, 1965; (with others) Pacific Geology. Contbr. articles to profl. jours. Home: 301 Pattee Canyon Dr Missoula MT 59801

PETERSON, JAMES BYRON, educator; b. Omaha, Feb. 26, 1913; s. Byron S. and Anna V. (Armstrong) P.; B.F.A., U. Omaha, 1938; M.Mus., Eastman Sch. Music, 1941; Ph.D., State U. Iowa, 1953; m. Patricia Bush, Jan. 16, 1944; 1 dau., Zoe Ann. Tchr. music Coll. Emporia (Kans.), 1938-40, Colby Jr. Coll., New London, N.H., 1941-42, Miss. So. Coll., Hattiesburg, 1946-47, Shorter Coll., Rome, Ga., 1947-49, Midland Coll., Fremont, Nebr., 1945-51; mem. faculty U. Omaha, 1953—, prof., 1955—, head music dept., 1953—; violinist, conductor, 1938—; music critic, columnist Omaha World Herald, 1966-70. Pres. Met. Arts Council, 1966-68. Served with AUS, 1942-45; ETO. Decorated Bronze Star. Mem. Nebr. Music Tchrs. Assn. (pres. 1959-61), Music Tchrs. Nat. Assn. (pres. West Central div. 1956-58, nat. pres. 1963—), AAUP (pres. U. Omaha 1962-63), Am. String Tchrs. Assn., Omaha Musicians Assn., Phi Mu Alpha, Sinfonia. Home: 528 Parkwood Ln Goldsboro NC 27530

PETERSON, JAMES ROBERT, holding co. exec.; b. Momence, Ill., Oct. 28, 1927; s. Clyde and Pearl (Deliere) P.; student St. Thomas Coll., 1945, Iowa State U., 1945-46, U. Colo., 1946, Northwestern U., 1946; B.S. in Mktg. cum laude, U. Ill., 1952; grad. exec. program Stanford, 1967; m. Betty Windham, May 12, 1949; children—Richard James, Lynn Peterson Anderson, Susan Kathryn, John Windham. With Pillsbury Co., Mpls., 1952-76, brand mgr. grocery products, 1953-57, brand supr. flour, 1957-61, dir. mktg., 1961-66, v.p. mktg., 1966-68, v.p., gen. mgr. Grocery Products Co., 1968-71, group v.p. consumer cos., 1971-73, pres., dir., 1973-76; exec. v.p., dir. R.J. Reynolds Industries, Inc., Winston-Salem, N.C., 1976—; dir. Shedd-Brown, Inc., Mpls., Avon Products, Inc., N.Y.C., Dun & Bradstreet Corp., N.Y.C. Mem. nat. council Boy Scouts Am., mem. exec. bd. S.E. region, past pres. Viking council; bd. regents St. Olaf Coll., 1974—; trustee Moravian Music Found., 1977—; bd. visitors Wake Forest U., 1977—. Served to lt. USN, 1945-50. Recipient Bronze Tablet award U. Ill. Mem. Nat. Soft Wheat Millers (past pres.), Beta Gamma Sigma, Dir.'s Table. Methodist. Club: Old Town. Home: 2832 Bartram Rd Winston-Salem NC 27106 Office: Reynolds Blvd Winston-Salem NC 27102

PETERSON, JOHN BOOTH, soil chemist; b. Salem, Oreg., July 18, 1905; s. Victor Allen and Bertha (Booth) P.; B.S., Oreg. State U., 1928; M.S., Iowa State U., 1929, Ph.D., 1936; NRC fellow geology, U. Calif. at Berkeley, 1939-40; m. Elizabeth L. Fogel, June 7, 1930; children—John Robert, Mary Jean (Mrs. Robert J. Brown). Mem. faculty Iowa State U., Ames, 1929-48, prof. agronomy, 1933-48; head dept. agronomy Purdue U., 1948-71, prof. agronomy, 1948—, asso. dir. Lab. Applications Remote Sensing, 1971—; vis. Distinguished prof. N.Mex. State U., 1977; cons. Rockefeller Found., Latin Am., 1961-62, Greek Govt., 1963, Ford Found., Argentina, 1964—, FAO, 1970, U.S./Saudi Arabia Joint Commn. on Econ. Cooperation, 1977. Fellow Am. Soc. Agronomy (Stevenson award research soil sci. 1948, Agronomic Service award 1978; pres. 1958-59, hon. mem. 1976), AAAS; mem. Sigma Xi. Home: Rd 10 East 650 North West Lafayette IN 47907 Office: Purdue Park Purdue U Lafayette IN 47907. *Objective, honest research, reported without bias and communicated to the citizens is essential to an effective and lasting democracy.*

PETERSON, JOHN DWIGHT, investment co. exec.; b. Indpls., July 20, 1933; s. J. Dwight and Mary Irene (Frisinger) P.; B.S., Ind. U., 1955; m. Nancy Jane Browning, July 16, 1955; children—Debbra Lee, John Dwight III, Penny Anne. With City Securities Corp., Indpls., 1955—, dir., 1966—, v.p., 1968-70, pres., 1970—, chmn., chief exec. officer, 1979—; dir. Lilly Indsl. Coatings, Inc., Mutz Corp., Bowes Seal Fast Corp. Mem. James Whitcomb Riley Meml. Assn., 1965—, Ind. Bd. Vocational and Tech. Edn., 1973—; mem. career edn. action com. Indpls. Pub. Schs., 1974—. Mem. Ind. U. Athletic Bd., 1971-74; pres. bd. dirs. Jr. Achievement Central Ind., 1979. Served as capt. U.S. Army, 1956. Mem. Young Presidents Orgn., Nat. Assn. Securities Dealers (dist. com. 8, 1975-78), Indpls. Bond Club (pres. 1969), Sigma Chi. Presbyn. (elder). Clubs: Marion County Varsity (chmn. 1961-71); Columbia, University (Indpls.), Masons, Rotary; Highland Golf and Country. Home: 97 E 73d St Indianapolis IN 46240 Office: 400 Circle Tower Indianapolis IN 46204

PETERSON, JOHN EDWIN, hosp. adminstr.; b. Ottumwa, Iowa, Aug. 11, 1918; s. Harry E. and Lorene A. (Johnson) P.; B.B.A. with distinction, U. Minn., 1948; M.B.A., U. Chgo., 1951; m. Margaret L. Youngdahl, June 5, 1948; children—Todd, Janis, Catherine. Adminstrv. resident Highland-Alameda County Hosp., Oakland, Calif., 1949-50, adminstrv. asst., 1950-51, asst. supt., 1951-53; asst. adminstr. Alta Bates Hosp., Berkeley, Calif., 1953-54, adminstr., 1954-67; exec. v.p., adminstr. Eisenhower Med. Center, Palm Desert, Calif., 1967-68; exec. v.p., dir. Valley Hosp., Ridgewood, N.J., 1968—; preceptor course in hosp. adminstrn. U. Calif., Berkeley. Served with USNR, 1942-46. Mem. Am. Hosp. Assn., N.J. Hosp. Assn., Am. Coll. Hosp. Adminstrs., Nat. Council Community Hosps., Am. Public Health Assn., N.J. Public Health Assn., Am. Health Planning Assn., Am. Assn. Hosp. Planning. Home: 320 Cupsaw Dr Ringwood NJ 07456 Office: Valley Hosp Linwood and N Van Dien Ave Ridgewood NJ 07451

PETERSON, JOHN ERIC, physician, educator; b. Norwalk, Ohio, Oct. 26, 1914; s. Charles Augustus and Fannie Helen (Stanford) P.; student Columbia Jr. Coll., 1932-34; M.D., Coll. Med. Evangelists, 1938; m. Lodene C. Pruett, Aug. 18, 1938; children—Carol Peterson Haviland, John Eric. Intern, Henry Ford Hosp., Detroit, 1938-39, resident, 1939-42; practice medicine specializing in internal medicine, Los Angeles, 1942-56, Loma Linda, Calif., 1956—; mem. staff Los Angeles County Hosp., Riverside (Calif.) County Gen. Hosp.; mem. faculty Sch. Medicine, Loma Linda U., 1942—, prof. medicine, 1967—, chmn. dept., 1969—, asso. dean Sch. Medicine, 1965-75; mem. staff Loma Linda U. Hosp., 1967—, chief medicine service, 1969—; cons. to univs. and fgn. govts. Diplomate Nat. Bd. Med. Examiners, Am. Bd. Internal Medicine. Fellow A.C.P.; mem. AMA, Calif., San Bernardino County med. assns., Am. Heart Assn., Calif., Inland socs. internal medicine, Am. Diabetes Assn., Western Soc. Clin. Research, Assn. Profs. of Medicine, Los Angeles Acad. Medicine, Diabetes Assn. Co. Calif., Sigma Xi, Alpha Omega Alpha. Contbr. articles to various publs. Home: 24317 Lawton Ave Loma Linda CA 92354

PETERSON, JOHN LAWRENCE, ednl. adminstr.; b. Waseca, Minn., Jan. 24, 1929; s. Lawrence Reuben and Lida Matilda (Ericson) P.; B.A., Grinnell Coll., 1951; M.A., Case-Western Res. U., 1952; Ph.D., Northwestern U., 1959; m. Carolyn Johnson, July 18, 1953; children—Mark, Elinor. Asst. prof. speech U. Wis., Madison, 1959-62, prof., 1975—, dean sch. allied health professions, 1975—; asst. prof. La. State U., New Orleans, 1962-64, asso. prof., 1964-70, prof., 1970-75; cons. audiologist Ochsner Found., New Orleans, 1963-70, NASA, 1965-68; chmn. manpower com. La. Regional Med. Program, 1970-73; mem. health scis. adv. council U. Wis. System, 1975—; bd. dirs. Cottage Sch. for Deaf, New Orleans, 1963-75. Served with USAAF, 1952-54. Rehab. Services Adminstrn. grantee, 1967-70. Mem. Am., Wis. speech and hearing assns., Acoustical Soc. Am., Soc. Internationale d'Audiologie, Am. Soc. Allied Health Professions. Home: 3605 Sunset Dr Madison WI 53705 Office: 610 N Walnut St Madison WI 53706

PETERSON, JOHN MARSHALL, educator; b. Ft. Worth, Jan. 6, 1922; s. Walter Leonard and Elizabeth (Hudson) P.; A.B., U. Wash., 1942; M.B.A., Harvard, 1947; M.A., U. Chgo., 1950, Ph.D., 1956; m. 2d, LaVerne Gutteridge, Feb. 1, 1960; children by previous marriage—Wendy (Mrs. Dennis Negley), Rhonda Lee. Economist, U.S. Bur. Labor Statistics, 1951-53, TVA, 1953-55; asso. dir. Indsl. Research and Extension Center, U. Ark., Little Rock, 1955-62; prof. U. Ark., Fayetteville, 1962-67; adminstrv. asst. Office Gov. Ark., 1967-70; dean Coll. Bus. Adminstrn., Ohio U., Athens, 1970-76, prof. econs., 1976—. Served with AUS, 1943-46. Mem. Am. Econ. Assn. Author: (with Ralph Gray) Economic Development of the United States, 1969; (with Charles T. Stewart Jr.) Employment Effects of Wage Minimums, 1969. Home: 130 LaMar Dr Athens OH 45701

PETERSON, JOHN MERRIAM, chem. co. exec.; b. Council Bluffs, Iowa, Mar. 3, 1903; s. Ernest Walter and Mary (Merriam) P.; B.S., Iowa State U., 1923, M.S., 1924; Ph.D., U. Ill., 1927; postdoctoral student U. Del., 1937-38; m. Flora E. Bailey, June 10, 1926; children—Robert B., Glenn M., Dan W., Martha J. Research and devel. chem. engr., head dept. Hercules, Inc., 1927-40; prof. chem. engring. Cooper Union, 1940-68, asst. dean Sch. Engring. and Sci., 1964-68, emeritus, 1968—; v.p., dir. Chemtree Corp., 1968—; dir. Green Engring. Camp., Ringwood, N.J., 1942-55; vis. prof. Grad. Sch., Stevens Inst. Tech., 1948-57, Yeshiva U., 1957-58; cons. in field, 1940—; dir. Nat. Water Corp. Dir. N.Y. State Info. and Tech. Services Center Air Pollution Control, 1967-68. Registered profl. engr., N.Y. State. Mem. Am. Inst. Chem. Engrs., Am. Nuclear Soc., Am. Chem. Soc., Atomic Indsl. Forum, Am. Soc. Engring. Edn., AAAS, AAUP, Am. Forestry Assn., Sigma Xi. Author, Patentee in field. Home: Toleman Rd Rock Tavern NY 12575 Office: Chemtree Corp Chemtree Park Central Valley NY 10917

PETERSON, JOHN WILLARD, composer; b. Lindsborg, Kans., Nov. 1, 1921; s. Peter Ephraim and Adlina Marie (Nelson) P.; student Moody Bible Inst., Chgo., 1947-48; B.Mus., Am. Conservatory Music, Chgo., 1952; D.Mus. (hon.), John Brown U., Siloam Springs, Ark., 1967; D.D. (hon.), Western Conservative Bapt. Sem., 1970; D.F.A. (hon.), Grand Canyon Coll., Phoenix, 1979; m. Alta Marie Addis,

Feb. 11, 1944; children—Sandra (Mrs. Thomas Catzere), Candace (Mrs. Rodger Strader), Pamela. Broadcaster, WMBI radio, Chgo., 1950-55; editor-in-chief, pres. Singspiration, Inc., Grand Rapids, Mich., 1955-71, exec.-composer, Carefree, Ariz., 1971—; mus. dir. Day of Discovery Telecast, 1974—; pres. Good Life Prodns., Scottsdale, Ariz., 1977—; music reviewer Moody Monthly Mag., 1975—. Dir. Gospel Films, Inc., Muskegon, Mich. Bd. dirs. Grand Rapids Sch. Bible and Music. Served with USAF, 1942-45. Decorated Air medal; recipient Sacred Music award Nat. Evang. Film Found., 1966; Internat. Gospel Composer of Year award, 1975. Mem. Nat. Ch. Music Leadership Conf. (dir.), Hump Pilots Assn. Author: (autobiography) The Miracle Goes On, 1976. Composer sacred cantatas and musicales, also numerous sacred songs. Address: 6350 Naumann Dr Paradise Valley AZ 85253

PETERSON, KARL LEE, newspaperman; b. Kansas City, Mo., June 29, 1919; s. Karl Leonard and Zora Lee (Evans) P.; B.A., U. Kansas City, 1940; m. Dorothy Jean Carter, Feb. 8, 1946; children—Karl Lee, Kristine Lynn, Ingrid Ellen. Gen. assignment reporter Kansas City Star, 1945-63, river editor, 1947—, editorial writer, 1963—. Served with USAAF, 1941-45. Mem. Sigma Delta Chi. Clubs: Kansas City Press (pres. 1966-67). Home: 13960 Falkirk Circle Grandview MO 64030 Office: 1729 Grand Ave Kansas City MO 64108

PETERSON, KENNETH GERARD, librarian; b. Bklyn., May 30, 1927; s. Walter Gunnar and Gertrude Marguerite (Haberstock) P.; B.A., Drew U., 1946; M.Div., Yale, 1949; M.L.S., U. Calif., Berkeley, 1963, Ph.D., 1968; m. Jane Elizabeth Shumaker, Oct. 15, 1949; children—David, Matthew, Martha, John, Ruth. Ordained to ministry Congregational Ch., 1949; pastor chs., Ohio, Calif., 1949-62; librarian Pacific Luth. Theol. Sem., Berkeley, 1962-67; asso. univ. librarian U. Va., Charlottesville, 1968-76; dean library affairs So. Ill. U., Carbondale, 1976—; mem. Ill. State Archives Adv. Bd.; mem. adv. council U. Ill. Grad. Sch. Library Sci. Mem. ALA, Ulysses S. Grant Assn. (dir.). Author: The University of California Library at Berkeley, 1900-45, 1970; An Introductory Bibliography for Theological Students, 1964; contbr. articles to profl. jours.; editor ACRL Publs. in Leadership, 1972-77. Home: 911 Briarwood Dr Carbondale IL 62901 Office: Morris Library So Ill U Carbondale IL 62901

PETERSON, KIRK CHARLES, ballet dancer; b. New Orleans, Dec. 10, 1949; s. John Lawrence and Dorothy Ann (Wagner) P.; student public schs.; scholar Harkness House for Ballet Arts. Charter mem. Harkness Youth Dancers, 1968-69; prin. dancer Harkness Ballet, 1970, Nat. Ballet, Washington, 1971-74, London Festival Ballet, 1973; mem. Am. Ballet Theatre, 1974—, soloist, 1975-78, prin. dancer, 1978—; choreographer: Metamorphosis, Floating Weeds; tchr. master classes, condr. lecture demonstrations; prin. roles include: Albrecht in Giselle, James in La Sylphide, Cinderella, Billy the Kid, Petrouchka, Prodigal Son, Theme and Variations, Sphinx, Pierrot Lunaire, Le Sacre du Printemps, Macumba, Idylle, Serenade, Fancy Free, The River, At Midnight, Les Patineurs, Le Corsaire Pas de Deux, The Maids. Recipient Bronze medal Internat. Ballet Competition, Varna, Bulgaria, 1972, Cultural award Dept. State, 1972, key to City of New Orleans, 1965, 66, 67. Mem. Am. Guild Musical Artists, Screen Actors Guild, AFTRA, Epiphyllum Soc. Am. Office: Ballet Theatre Found 888 7th Ave New York NY 10019. *In my work I strive for the purest and truest artistic goals within the standards that I have set and continually reset for myself. Ideals fluctuate within one's own framework of perception as one matures as an artist. The creative impulse within one, if it does exist, should be explored to its maximum. The great gift of expressionistic creativity through which one distills, restructures, and evolves the elements concerned is an unmatched phenomenon in the striving of higher civilized ideals. It is an endeavor in which I am continually involved and which I continually respect and learn from in others.*

PETERSON, LAURENCE E(LMER), physicist; b. Grantsburg, Wis., July 26, 1931; s. Elmer T. and Mary E. (Grant) P.; student Stout Inst., 1949-50; B.S., U. Minn., 1954, Ph.D. (NSF fellow), 1960; m. Elenor E. Gleason, Feb. 18, 1978; children—Mark L., Daniel F., Lynn M., Julianne, Jan K., Patricia E., William T. Research technician U. Minn., 1951-54, research asst., 1954-60, research asso., 1960-62; research physicist U. Calif., San Diego in La Jolla, 1962-63, asst. prof. physics, 1963-67, asso. prof., 1967-71, prof., 1971—; cons. to NASA and aerospace industry. Recipient Space Sci. award AIAA, 1978; Exceptional Sci. Achievement award NASA, 1978; Guggenheim fellow, 1973-74. Mem. Am. Astron. Soc., Internat. Astron. Union, Am. Phys. Soc., Am. Geophys. Union, AAAS. Contbr. numerous articles on cosmic rays, x-ray and gamma-ray astronomy, balloon and spacecraft instrumentation to profl. publs.; editor: (with W. A. Baity) X-Ray Astronomy, vol. 3 of Advances in Space Exploration, 1979. Home: 4739 Ingraham St San Diego CA 92109 Office: Dept Physics C-011 U Calif at San Diego La Jolla CA 92093

PETERSON, LOUIS ROBERT, consumer products co. exec.; b. Racine, Wis., Nov. 11, 1923; s. Edward J. and Effie (Buenning) P.; student Utah State Agrl. Coll., 1943-44, U. Wis.-Racine, 1945-46; m. Marian Francis Barber, Nov. 22, 1947; children—Karen Jean, Kathleen Alice, Jill Ann. With Johnson Wax Co., Racine, Wis., 1947—, v.p. internat. ops., 1972-75, exec. v.p. internat. ops., 1975-76, exec. v.p. U.S. household products, partner in office of the chmn., 1976—; dir. Heritage Bank-Mt. Pleasant. Trustee Racine Environment Com.; dir. Racine Area United Way. Served with U.S. Army, 1943-46. Republican. Roman Catholic. Clubs: Racine Country, Somerset (Racine, Wis.); Pinnacle Peak Country (Scottsdale, Ariz.). Home: 4511 Pleasant Ave Racine WI 53405 Office: 1525 Howe St Racine WI 53403

PETERSON, LOWELL EUGENE, chem. co. exec.; b. Keokuk, Iowa, Apr. 20, 1926; s. Albert Sanford and Myrtle Elizabeth (Anderson) P.; B.S., U. Minn., 1950, Ph.D., 1954; m. Gloria Skordahl, June 19, 1948; children—David L., Paul D., Kenneth A., Steven R., Deborah A. With Gen. Mills Chems., Inc. (name now Henkel Corp.), Mpls., 1954—, dir. research indsl. chems., 1972-75, dir. basic devel., 1975—. Served with USNR, 1944-46. Mem. Am. Chem. Soc., Comml. Devel. Assn., Sigma Xi. Mem. Evang. Free Ch. Club: Decathlon Athletic (Mpls.). Author, patentee in field. Home: 610 W Minnehaha Pkwy Minneapolis MN 55419 Office: 2010 E Hennepin Ave Minneapolis MN 55413

PETERSON, LYSLE HENRY, physician, educator; b. Mpls., Jan. 21, 1921; s. Oscar Emil and Lucy Rie (Ireland) P.; B.S., U. Minn., 1943; M.D. (Haynes scholar), U. Pa., 1950; m. Sara Meredith, July 1, 1967; children—Christopher Alan, Nancy (Mrs. Robert Ward Hallett), Douglas Randall, Hope Sutton. Instr. physiology U. Pa., Phila., 1950-51, asst. prof., 1952-55, asso. prof., 1955-61, prof., 1961-75, dir. Bockus Research Inst., 1961-75, pres. Univ. City Sci. Inst., 1967-70; v.p. acad. affairs U. Tex. Health Sci. Center, Houston, 1975-77, prof. physiology, 1975—; dir. Houston Cardiovascular Rehab. Center, 1978—; chmn. aeromed. bioscis. panel USAF Sci. Adv. Bd., 1970-77; dir. MDC Corp., 1972-77. Mem. Gov.'s Panel on Health Services Devel., 1968-71; chmn. Model Health City Task Force for Phila. Bicentennial, 1969-72. Served with USNR, 1943-46. Decorated Bronze stars; Haynes scholar, 1946-50; recipient award Am. Physiol. Soc., 1950; Borden Research award, 1950, others. Fellow Am. Coll. Cardiology, A.A.A.S., Phila. Coll. Physicians; mem. Am. Physiol. Soc. (chmn. circulation sect. 1956-58 temperature regulation sect. 1958-60), Am. Soc. Clin. Investigation, Am. Heart Assn. (v.p. 1965-68, chmn. basic sci. council 1964-65, chmn. research com. 1965-66, dir. 1964-68), Internat. Soc. Cardiology (pres. 1974-76), Internat. Acad. Astronautics, Soc. Med. Cons. to Armed Forces, Sigma Xi. Clubs: Racquet (Phila.); Cosmos (Washington). Author books and articles. Cons. editor Macmillan Co., 1971—; mem. editorial bd. Am. Jour. Physiology, 1961-66, Jour. Applied Physiology, 1958-63, Internat. Jour. Biomed. Computing, 1970—, Circulation, 1965-70, Circulation Research, 1965-70, others. Home: 3435 Meadow Lake Ln Houston TX 77027 Office: 6418 Fannin Houston TX 77030

PETERSON, MARTHA ELIZABETH, coll. pres.; b. Jamestown, Kans., June 22, 1916; d. Anton R. and Gail (French) P.; A.B., U. Kans., 1937, M.A., 1943, Ph.D., 1959; postgrad. Northwestern U., Columbia U.; L.H.D., Chatham Coll., 1968, Med. Coll. Pa., 1970, Molloy Coll., 1971, Mundelein Coll., 1972, Pace Coll., 1974, U. Wis., Madison, 1975, Temple U., 1975; D. Letters and Laws, Columbia, 1968, Douglas Coll., 1968; LL.D., Hofstra U., 1969, Austin Coll., 1972, Hamilton Coll., 1974, Drury Coll., 1975, W.Va. Wesleyan Coll., 1976; Dr. Pedagogy, R.I. Coll., 1975. Instr., U. Kans., 1942-46, asst. dean women, 1946-52, dean women, 1952-56; dean women U. Wis., 1956-63, asst. to pres., 1963, univ. dean students, 1963-67; pres. Barnard Coll., also dean Columbia U., 1967-75; pres. Beloit Coll., 1975—; dir. Met. Life Ins. Co., Exxon Corp., First Wis. Corp., United Banks Ill., R.H. Macy & Co., Beloit Bldg. & Loan Assn. Mem. exec. com. commn. Ind. colls. and univs.; mem. Pres.'s Commn. White House Fellowships, Rhodes Scholarship Com. Wis.; trustee U. Notre Dame, Chatham Coll., Pitts., 1965—; mem. Com. Econ. Devel.; mem. vis. com. Am. Council Learned Socs. Recipient Charles Evans Hughes award, 1975, Spirit of Achievement award Albert Einstein Coll. Medicine, 1975; named to U. Kans. Women's Hall Fame, 1972. Mem. Am. Council Edn. (student personnel commn. 1956-59, commn. acad. affairs 1970—, chmn. exec. com. 1971—), Nat. Assn. Women Deans and Counselors (exec. bd. 1959-61, pres. 1965-67), Nat. Assn. Ind. Colls. and Univs. (dir. 1976-77), Intercollegiate Assn. Women Students (nat. adviser 1953-55, 59-61), Am. Arbitration Assn. (dir.), Phi Beta Kappa, Sigma Xi, Mortar Bd., Pi Lambda Theta, Phi Kappa Phi. Office: Beloit Coll Beloit WI 53511

PETERSON, MAURICE LEWELLEN, educator; b. Lyons, Nebr., Dec. 30, 1913; s. C.O.A. and Edna M. (Carlson) P.; B.S., U. Nebr., 1938; M.S., Kan. State U., 1940; Ph.D., Iowa State U., 1946; m. Katharine A. Jones, Aug. 27, 1938; children—David M., James L., Gary R. Research with Dept. Agr., 1938-43, Iowa State U., 1943-48; mem. faculty U. Calif. at Davis, 1948—, prof. agronomy, 1955—, dir. expt. sta., 1962-65, dean agr., 1963-67. Mem. Am. Soc. Agronomy, Am. Soc. Plant Physiology. Home: 1922 Amador Ave Davis CA 95616

PETERSON, MENDEL LAZEAR, underwater exploration cons.; b. Moore, Idaho, Mar. 8, 1918; s. Hans Jordan and Fannie (Lish) P.; B.S. with honors, Miss. So. Coll., 1938; M.A., Vanderbilt U., 1940; grad. student Lowell Textile Inst., 1945-47; m. LaNelle Walker, July 5, 1937 (div. May 1962); children—LaNelle Hampton (Mrs. Gerald Spence), Mendel L.; m. 2d, Gertrude A. Auvil, Aug. 19, 1962; 1 dau., Anna Victoria. Camp edn. adviser Civilian Conservation Corps, 1939-42; div. merchandiser Montgomery Ward & Co. 1942-43; curator dept. history Smithsonian Inst., 1948-56, chmn. dept. armed forces history, 1956-69, dir. underwater exploration project, 1969-73; cons. underwater exploration, treasure trove, 1973—. Served from ensign to comdr. USNR, 1943—. Mem. Am. Numis. Assn., Am. Numis. Soc., Nautical Research Assn. Clubs: Explorers, Club de Exploraciones y Deportes Acuaticos de Mexico (hon. life). Author: History Under the Sea, 1965; Funnel of Gold, 1975. Contbr. numerous articles in field to profl. jours., UNESCO publs. Address: PO Box 404 McLean VA 22101

PETERSON, MERRILL DANIEL, educator; b. Manhattan, Kans., Mar. 31, 1921; s. William Oscar and Alice Dwinell (Merrill) P.; student Kans. State Coll., 1939-41; A.B., U. Kans., 1943; Ph.D. in History of Am. Civilization, Harvard, 1950; m. Jean Humphrey, May 24, 1944; children—Jeffrey Ward, Kent Merrill. Teaching fellow Harvard, 1948-49; instr., then asst. prof. history Brandeis U., 1949-55; asst. prof., bicentennial preceptor Princeton, 1955-58; mem. faculty Brandeis U., 1958-62, dean students, 1960-62, Harry S. Truman prof. Am. history, 1961-63; Thomas Jefferson Found. prof. U. Va., 1963—, chmn. dept. history, 1966-72. Guggenheim fellow, 1962-63; fellow Center Advanced Study Behavioral Scis., 1968-69. Served with USNR, 1943-46. Mem. Am., So. hist. assns., Soc. Am. Historians, Orgn. Am. Historians, Phi Beta Kappa. Author: The Jefferson Image in the American Mind (Bancroft prize, Gold medal Thomas Jefferson Meml. Assn.), 1960; Democracy, Liberty and Property: The State Constitutional Convention Debates of the 1820's; Thomas Jefferson and the New Nation, 1970; Adams and Jefferson: A Revolutionary Dialogue, 1976. Editor: Major Crises in American History; Thomas Jefferson: A Historical Profile, 1967; James Madison: A Biography in His Own Word, 1974; The Portable Thomas Jefferson, 1975. Home: 1817 Yorktown Dr Charlottesville VA 22901

PETERSON, MILDRED OTHMER (MRS. HOWARD R. PETERSON), lectr., writer, librarian, civic leader; b. Omaha, Oct. 19, 1902; d. Frederick George and Freda Darling (Snyder) Othmer; student U. Iowa, 1919, U. Nebr., 1921-23, Northwestern U., 1935, U. Chgo., 1943, m. Howard R. Peterson, Aug. 25, 1923 (dec. Feb. 1970). Asst. Central High Sch. Library, Omaha, 1915-19; asst. Tech. High Sch. Library, 1919-20; asst. purchasing agt. Met. Utilities Dist., 1920-21; asst. U. Nebr. Library, 1921-23; tchr. piano, dir. choir, Harlan, Iowa, 1924-26; dir. pub. relations and gen. asst. Des Moines Pub. Library, 1928-35; broadcaster weekly book programs WHO and other Iowa radio stas.; columnist, writer Mid-West News Syndicate, Des Moines Register and Tribune, editor Book Marks, 1929-35; writer for Drug Topics, Drug Trade News, others, No. Ill., 1935; writer, spl. asst. ALA, Chgo. 1935-59, Chgo. Tribune, 1941-59; travel writer Hyde Park Herald, 1974—; lectr. on travel, fgn. jewelry and internat. relations, 1940—; lectr. SS. Rotterdam of Holland Am. Line, 1971; lectr. tours U.S., Can., Mexico, 1970—; Del. 1st Assembly Librarians Ams., Washington, 1947. Chgo. Chmn. India Famine Relief, 1943; a founder, pres. Pan Am. Bd. Edn., 1955-58; a founder, pres. Internat. Visitors Center, 1952-56; rep. Chgo. at State Dept. Conf. on Community Services to Fgn. Visitors, also a founder COSERV (Nat. Council for Community Services to Internat. Visitors), Washington, 1957; mem. exec. bd., awards com. Mayor's Com. on Chgo. Beautiful; mem. Ill. Gov.'s Com. on Sao Paulo (Brazil), Partners of Am., chancellor's com. U. Nebr. Former bd. dirs. council, troop leader Girl Scouts U.S.A.; mem. centennial com. Hyde Park Union Ch., also 75th anniversary com.; bd. dirs. YWCA, recipient Outstanding Service award; women's bd. Camp Brueckner-Farr, Grad. Bapt. Student Center. Decorated Uruguayan medal, 1952; Internat. Eloy Alfaro medal, 1952, Order of Carlos Manuel de Cespedes (Cuba); Order of Vasco Nunez de Balboa (Panama); cited by Chgo. Sun, Ill. Adult Edn. Council, 1953; recipient scholarship in Latin-Am. field U. Chgo. and Coordinator Inter-Am. Affairs, U.S. Govt., 1943; world understanding merit award Chgo. Council on Fgn. Relations, 1955; Distinguished Service award Hospitality Center, 1958; Distinguished Service medal U. Nebr., also U. Nebr. Alumni Assn., 1963, Distinguished Achievement award, 1975; Ambassador of Friendship award Am. Friendship Club, 1963; merit award YWCA, 1964, Distinguished Service award, 1975; Civic salute WMAQ radio, Chgo., 1965; Distinguished Service award Pan-Am. Bd. Edn., 1966, also founders award, 1968; Laura Hughes Lunde Meml. award Citizens Greater Chgo., 1968; Friendship award Philippine Girl Scouts, 1971; Distinguished Service award OAS, 1971; named Woman of Year, Friends of Chgo. Sch. and Workshop for Retarded, 1975; Distinguished Service trophy Fedn. Latin Am. Orgns., 1976. Fellow Am. Internat. Acad. (life mem.); mem. Nat. Council Women U.S., English Speaking Union, Japan-Am. Com., U.S.-China Friendship Assn., Internat. House Assn. (v.p.), Pan-Am. Bd. Edn., Chgo. Better Films and TV Council, U.S.-China Friendship Assn., U.S. Capitol, Ill., Nebr., Chgo., Hyde Park (charter mem. award 1978) hist. socs., Field Mus. Natural History, Lincoln Park Zool. Soc., Citizenship Council Met. Chgo., Oriental Inst., Am. Heritage Council, Am., Ill. (local arrangements conf. com. 1976, 78) library assns., Soc. Woman Geographers (pres. Chgo. chpt., v.p. internat. 1978—), Council Fgn. Relations (speakers bur.), Nat. Assn. Travel Ofcls. (Chgo. Tribune rep.), Pan. Am. Council (a a founder), Library Internat. Relations, U. Nebr. Alumni Assn. (past pres. local chpts.), U. Nebr. Found., U. Chgo. Internat. House Assn. (v.p. 1976—), Art Inst. Chgo., U. Chgo. Service League (past bd. mem.), Am. Legion Aux. (mem. state bds. Iowa and Ill.), AAUW, League Women Voters, Children's Benefit League, United Negro Coll. Fund Bd., Renaissance Soc., Peruvian Arts Soc., Hispanic Soc. Chgo., Chgo. Acad. Scis. (woman's bd.), Chgo. Chamber Orch. Assn., John G. Shedd Soc., Japan Am. Soc., Friends Chgo. Pub. Library, Chgo. Symphony Soc., Citizens Greater Chgo., Found. for Ill. Archaeology, Cook County Hosp. Aux., Dyslexia Guild, Lyric Opera Guild, Crossroads Student Center, Internat. Platform Assn., Alpha Delta Pi (past pres. local alumnae chpts., editor Adephean 1938-39, woman of year award U.S. and Can. 1955), Xi Delta. Mem. Order Eastern Star. Clubs: South Shore Country, College, Quadrangle, Ill. Athletic, University of Chicago Dames, Iowa Authors, Lakeside Lawn Bowling, Hyde Park Neighborhood, Travellers Century. Contbr. articles to newspapers, periodicals, encys. and yearbooks; lectr. Travelled to 125 countries, including China. Address: 5834 Stony Island Ave Chicago IL 60637

PETERSON, NAD ALMA, lawyer; b. Mt. Pleasant, Utah, May 6, 1926; s. Angus Alma and Crystal (Olsen) P.; A.B., George Washington U., 1950, J.D., 1953; m. Martha Peterson, Sept. 7, 1948; children—Anne Carroll (Mrs. Stanford P. Darger, Jr.), Christian, Elizabeth, Robert and Lane (twins). Admitted to D.C. bar, 1953, Calif. bar, 1960, U.S. Supreme Ct. bar, 1958; with firm Pierson, Ball & Dowd, Washington, 1953-60; sec., asst. gen. counsel Dart Industries, Los Angeles, 1960-67; chief counsel Fluor Corp., Irvine, Calif., 1967-73, gen. counsel, 1973—. Mem. Am., Orange County, D.C. bar assns., State Bar of Calif., George Washington Law Rev., Phi Delta Phi. Clubs: Big Canyon Country, Balboa Bay (Newport Beach, Calif.). Office: 3333 Michelson Dr Irvine CA 92730

PETERSON, NADEEN ANN, advt. exec.; b. McKeesport, Pa., Dec. 3, 1934; d. Michael James and LaVerna Peal (Long) Powell; student U. Fla., 1952-53; m. Robert Glenn Kilzer, Dec. 24, 1966; 1 son, Douglas Robert; m. 2d, Peter A. Schweitzer, Dec. 31, 1977. Copywriter, Ellington & Co., N.Y.C. 1961-64; v.p., asso. creative dir. Tatham-Laird, N.Y.C., 1964-65; v.p., asso. creative dir. Foote, Cone & Belding, Inc., N.Y.C., 1966-69; v.p., sr. asso. creative dir. Norman, Craig & Kummell, N.Y.C., 1969-70, sr. v.p., creative dir., 1975-77; sr. v.p., creative dir. Doyle, Dane, Bernbach, Inc., N.Y.C., 1978—. Recipient Matrix award, 1977. Home: 15 W 81st St New York NY 10024 Office: 437 Madison Ave New York NY 10022

PETERSON, OSCAR EMMANUEL, pianist; b. Montreal, Que., Can., Aug. 15, 1925; LL.D. (hon.), Carleton U., 1973; studied classical music. Began music career on weekly radio show, then with Johny Holmes Orchestra, Can., 1944-49; appeared with Jazz at the Philharmonic, Carnegie Hall, 1949, toured the U.S. and Europe, frequently, 1950—; leader trio with Ray Brown, Irving Ashby, later Barney Kessel, Herb Ellis, Ed Thigpen, Sam Jones, Louie Hayes; concert appearances with Ella Fitzgerald, Eng., Scotland, 1955; appeared Stratford (Ont.) Shakespeare Festival, Newport Jazz Festival; recorded and performed solo piano works, 1972—; toured USSR, 1974; recordings with Billie Holiday, Fred Astaire, Benny Carter, Count Basie, Roy Eldridge, Lester Young, Ella Fitzgerald, Joe Pass, Orsted Pederson, Dizzy Gillespie, Harry Edison, Clark Terry; recorded for Verve, BASF (Germany); now with Pablo Records. Recipient award for piano Down Beat mag., 1950-54, 60-63, 65, critics poll, 1953; award Metronome mag., 1953-54; Service medal Order of Can., 1973; Grammy award, 1974, 75, 77; 10-time jazz poll winner Playboy mag.; named number one (piano) Jazz and Pop 3d Ann. Readers Poll, 1968. Author: Jazz Exercises and Pieces: Oscar Peterson New Piano Solos. Office: care Pablo Records 451 N Canon Dr Beverly Hills CA 90210*

PETERSON, OSCAR JAMES, III, utility exec.; b. Clinton, N.C., Aug. 26, 1935; s. Oscar James, Jr. and Elizabeth Julia (Collins) P.; B.S. in Bus. Adminstrn., U. N.C., Chapel Hill, 1962; m. Amanda Louisa Wade, Dec. 29, 1962; children—Amanda Leigh, Oscar James, Windley Collins. With Carolina Tel. & Tel. Co., 1962-70, fin. staff asst., Taboro, N.C., 1966-70; exec. asst. fin., then asst. treas. Va. Electric and Power Co., Richmond, 1970-75, treas., 1975—, v.p., chief fin. officer, 1978—; pres., dir. Thermopress Corp., Richmond; dir. Colonial Plastics, Inc., Richmond; past chmn. fin. sect., accounting and fin. div. Southeastern Electric Exchange, Atlanta. Bd. dirs., exec. com. Va. Coll. Bldg. Authority, 1973-77; fin. adv. bd. Va. Commonwealth U., 1978—. Served with USNR, 1957-59. Mem. Edison Electric Inst., Va. C. of C., Atomic Indsl. Forum. Presbyterian. Club: Commonwealth (Richmond). Patentee insulating window. Home: 5 Bellona Arsenal Midlothian VA 23113 Office: 1 James River Plaza Richmond VA 23219

PETERSON, PAUL AMES, lawyer; b. Los Angeles, Feb. 17, 1928; s. Thaddeus and Norma (Brown) P.; A.B. in Econs., U. Calif., Berkeley, 1953, J.D., 1956; m. Barbara Jean Henderson, Sept. 12, 1976; children—Daniel Comer, Andrew Grant, Matthew Ames, James Frederick. Admitted to Calif. bar, 1956; atty. George W. Phillips, Jr., Castro Valley, Calif., 1956-57; partner firm Peterson, Gamer, Muns, Branton & Price, San Diego, 1958—; dir. Price Co., 1976—; mem. faculty U. San Diego Law Sch., 1958-60, Calif. Western U. Law Sch., San Diego, 1960-63; chmn. com. bar examiners State Bar Calif., 1973-74, chmn. com. law sch. edn., 1975-76, chmn. continuing edn. of bar com., 1967; del. Jud. Conf. 9th Circuit, 1976-78. Chmn. San Diego Stadium Bd., 1974; past bd. dirs. Arthritis Found., San Diego County Lung Assn., San Diego Human Relations Commn., San Diego 200th Anniversary Com.; chmn. San Diego County Democratic Central Com., 1964-66. Served with AUS, 1946-48. Walter Perry Johnson scholar, 1954. Fellow Am. Bar Found.; mem. Am. (chmn. treasury com., adminstrv. sect. 1964-65), Calif., Alameda County, San Diego County (chmn. ad hoc exam. procedure com. 1977), Fed. bar assns., Am. Judicature Soc., Phi Beta Kappa, Order of Coif. Presbyterian. Club: City (San Diego). Home: 1875 Caminito Marzella La Jolla CA 92037 Office: 530 B St Suite 2300 San Diego CA 92101

PETERSON, PAUL KENNETH, judge; b. Mpls., Apr. 13, 1915; s. Karl Emil and Emma Maria (Sellin) P.; A.A., North Park Coll., 1934; B.A., U. Minn., 1936; LL.B., Minn. Coll. Law, 1950; J.D., William Mitchell Coll. Law, 1969; m. Jean A. Erickson, May 1955; children—Jane, Paula, Carol. Mem. Minn. Legislature, 1946, re-elected, 1948, 50, 52, chmn. civil adminstrn. com., serving on jud., edn., gen. legislation and elections coms.; selected by Minn. Legislature to serve on Council State Govts.; chmn. Republican Party in Minn., 1949-53; mem. Rep. Nat. Com., 1952-54; Rep. nominee for lt. gov. Minn., 1954; mayor Mpls., 1957-61; Rep. nominee for U.S. Senator from Minn., 1960; regional counsel Lee Higginson Corp., 1961-63; engaged in practice of law, Mpls., 1963-67; adminstrv. law judge Bur. Hearings and Appeals, HEW, 1974—. Mem. Fed. Civil Def. Adv. Bd., 1959-62; chmn. Minn. Pub. Service Commn., 1967-73; mem. Minn. Corrections Authority, 1973-74; pres. Minn. Prisoners Aid Soc., 1965-67; mem. Mpls. Bd. Park Commrs.; commr. Met. Airports Commn., 1957-67. Mem. U.S. Near East Refugee Commn., 1953-54; mem. UN Conf. on Trade and Devel., Geneva, 1970. Served to lt. (s.g.), air combat intelligence, USN, World War II; ret. lt. comdr., USNR. Am.-Scandinavian Found. fellow Uppsala U., Lund U., 1937; voted Outstanding Young Man in Mpls., 1949; named in 100 Leaders of Tomorrow, Time mag. Mem. Council State Govts., Interstate Coop. Commn. Minn., Delta Sigma Rho, Delta Theta Phi. Presbyn. (elder). Author: Minnesota Presidential Primary Law, 1949; Civil Defense Law, 1951; Minnesota Narcotic Control Act, 1953. Represented U.S. univs. European Good Will Mission, 1937; spl. mission to Iran, Iraq, Egypt, 1954. Home: 3332 Edmund Blvd Minneapolis MN 55406 Office: 830 Plymouth Bldg Minneapolis MN 55402

PETERSON, PAUL QUAYLE, univ. dean; b. Marissa, Ill., June 30, 1912; s. Charles Logan and Phoebe (Lewis) P.; B.S., U. Ill., 1933, M.D., 1937; M.P.H., U. Mich., 1946; m. Kathryn Lentz, Aug. 1936; children—Philip Lewis, Frances Anne; m. 2d, Mildred Cook Allison, Dec. 7, 1957; foster children—Patricia Elaine Allison, Susan Claire Allison. Intern Bethesda Hosp., Cin., 1936-37; gen. resident Meml. Hosp., Lima, Ohio, 1937-38; pvt. practice gen. medicine, McLeansboro, Ill., 1939-40, specializing preventive medicine, 1940-46; health officer Breckenridge, Meade and Hancock counties, Ky., 1940-41, Warren, Simpson and Allen counties, 1942-45; regional cons., div. local health Ky. Health Dept., 1946-47; chief bur. direct services, asst. to dir. Ohio Dept. Health, 1948-51; asst. prof. preventive medicine Ohio State U., 1948-51; chief health div. Mut. Security Mission to China, Taipei, Taiwan, 1952-53; chief health and sanitation div. USOM, asso. states Cambodia, Laos and Vietnam, 1954; chief program services, div. internat. health USPHS, Washington, 1955, chronic disease program, 1957; asst. dir. Nat. Inst. Allergy and Infectious Diseases, NIH, 1958-61; dep. chief div. pub. health methods Office Surgeon Gen., 1961-62, chief div., 1962-64; asst. surgeon gen. USPHS, 1964, asso. chief bur. state services (community health) USPHS, 1964-67, dep. dir. Bur. Health Services, 1967-68, asso. adminstr. Health Services and Mental Health Adminstrn., 1968-70; dep. surgeon gen., 1970; dean Grad. Sch. Pub. Health, U. Ill., Chgo., 1971—; dir. Ill. Dept. Pub. Health, 1977—; dir. Am. Bur. Med. Aid to China; mem. residency rev. com. Liaison Com. Grad. Med. Edn., 1976—. Diplomate Am. Bd. Preventive Medicine (service mem., vice chmn. 1976—). Fellow Am. Pub. Health Assn. (chmn. program area com. pub. health adminstrn.); mem. Am. Assn. Pub. Health Physicians (pres. 1975-76), AMA (interspity. adv. bd. 1975-77), Assn. Schs. Pub. Health (exec. com. 1975—), Pub. Health Service Commd. Officers Assn. (sec. D.C. 1959), AAAS, Assn. Mil Surgeons, Am. Coll. Preventive Medicine (regent 1975—), Ill. Hosp. Assn. (exec. bd. 1974-77), Phi Beta Pi (pres. 1935), Delta Omega. Methodist. Editorial bd. Pub. Health Service World, Mil. Medicine. Home: 1110 N Lake Shore Dr Chicago IL 60611 Office: 160 N LaSalle St Room 1100 Chicago IL 60601

PETERSON, PETER G., former sec. commerce U.S., co. exec.; b. Kearney, Nebr., June 5, 1926; s. George and Venetia (Paul) P.; student Mass. Inst. Tech., 1944-45; B.S. summa cum laude, Northwestern U., 1947; M.B.A. with honors, U. Chgo., 1951; m. Sally Hornbogen, May, 1953; children—John Scott, James S., David, Holly, Michael. Market analyst Market Facts, Inc., Chgo., 1947-49, asso. dir., 1949-51, exec. v.p., 1951-53; dir. marketing services McCann-Erickson, 1953, v.p., 1954-58, gen. mgr. Chgo. office, 1955-57, dir., asst. to pres. coordinating services regional offices, 1957-58; exec. v.p., dir. Bell & Howell Co., 1958-61, pres., 1961-63, pres., chief exec. officer, 1963-68, chmn. bd., chief exec. officer, 1968-71; asst. to Pres. for internat. econs. affairs, Washington, 1971-72, also exec. dir. Council on Internat. Econ. Policy; sec. of commerce, 1972-73; mem. Ind. Commn. on Internat. Devel. Issues, Trilateral Commn.; chmn. bd. Lehman Bros. Kuhn Loeb, Inc., N.Y.C., 1973—; dir. RCA, Lehman Corp., Black & Decker Mfg. Co., Cities Service Co., 3M Co., Gen. Foods, Federated Dept. Stores. Chmn. planning com. Ill. Citizens for Eisenhower, 1952; chmn. U.S. council Internat. C. of C. Trustee Mus. Modern Art, Council Fgn. Relations, U. Chgo. Named outstanding young man of Chgo., Jr. C. of C., 1955, U.S., Jr. C. of C., 1961. Clubs: Chicago, Economics (Chgo.); Links, Blind Brook, Burning Tree Golf, Maidstone, Augusta Nat. Golf. Editor, contbr.: Readings in Market Organization and Price Policies, 1952. Home: 10 Gracie Sq New York City NY Office: Lehman Bros Kuhn Loeb Inc One William St New York City NY 10004

PETERSON, PHILIP EVERETT, legal educator; b. Galena, Ill., July 10, 1922; s. Everett Marvin and Marie Isabelle (Greeson) P.; student Loras Coll., 1948; B.S., U. Ill., 1950, J.D., 1952; LL.M., Harvard, 1958; m. Jeanne Rosanna Payette, Nov. 17, 1947; children—Christine Marie, Barbara Ellen, Claudia Ann, Patricia Eileen, Eric Karl, Kurt Kevin. Admitted to Ill. bar, 1951, Idaho bar, 1955, U.S. Supreme Ct. bar, 1958; practice in Urbana, Ill., 1951-52; mem. faculty U. Idaho Law Sch., 1952—, prof. law, 1961—, dean, 1962-67; legal cons., 1955—. Served with AUS, 1942-48; lt. col. USAF Res. Decorated Purple Heart, D.F.C. with cluster, Air medal with 3 clusters. Mem. Am., Ill., Idaho bar assns., AAUP. Home: 318 5th St Lewistown ID 83501

PETERSON, RALPH EDWARD, educator, physician; b. Paola, Kans., Aug. 21, 1918; s. William O. and Alice (Merrill) P.; B.S., Kans. State U., 1940; M.S., Brown U., 1941; M.D., Columbia, 1946; children—Susan, Merrill, Lawrence, Patricia, Dean, Sandra. Intern U. Minn. Hosp., 1946-47, resident medicine, 1947-48; scientist NIH, 1952-58; dir. endocrinology div. Cornell Med. Center, N.Y.C., 1958—; mem. faculty Cornell U. Med. Sch., 1958—, prof. medicine, 1968—. Served to capt. M.C., AUS, 1948-52. Fulbright scholar Melbourne (Australia) U., 1964-65. Research in endocrinology, adrenals, gonads, abnormalities of sexual devel. and hypertension. Home: 450 E 63d St New York City NY 10021 Office: 1300 York Ave New York City NY 10021

PETERSON, RALPH EDWARD, clergyman; b. Duluth, Minn., Apr. 12, 1932; s. Harold Edward and Muriel (Miller) P.; B.A., U. Minn., 1954; M.A.T., Harvard U., 1955, grad. Advanced Mgmt. Program, 1977; student Episcopal Theol. Sch., Cambridge, Mass., 1955-56; M.Div., Lutheran Sch. Theology, Rock Island, Ill., 1960; postgrad. Columbia U., 1962-63; D.D., Gettysburg Coll., 1971; m. Karen Birgitta Esselius, May 31, 1969; 1 son, Kristofer Amandus Esselius. Ordained to ministry Lutheran Ch. in Am., 1960; pastor Christ Ch., Hammond, Ind., 1960-62; exec. dir. dept. ministry Nat. Council Chs. of Christ, 1962-64; exec. dir. dept. ministry, vocation and pastoral services Nat. Council Chs., 1965-66; pastor St. Peter's Ch., N.Y.C., 1966—; lectr. N.Y. Theol. Sem., 1965-67. Mem. Citizens Com. N.Y.C. Mem. bd. theol. edn. Luth. Ch. Am., 1967-72; adv. com. Christian ministries Episcopal Ch., 1965-68; exec. bd. Met. N.Y. Synod, Luth. Ch. Am., 1966-70; del. assembly World Council Ch., Uppsala, 1968; chmn. religion and vocation sect. Nat. Vocat. Guidance Assn., 1965; pres. The Common at the Intersection, 1977—. Trustee, chmn. N.Y. Theol. Sem., 1966-78; trustee Inst. Advanced Pastoral Studies Bloomfield Hills, Mich., 1967-71, Gettysburg Theol. Sem., 1968-74; mem. Am. com. for Mansfield Coll., Oxford (Eng.), U., 1965-74. Bd. dirs. Religious Communities, the Arts and Am. Revolution, 1975. Mem. Inst. Religion and Mental Health (profl. bd. 1964-76), Am. Scandinavian Found., Forum on Investment Responsibility, Am. Mgmt. Assn., Am. Coll. Personnel Assn., Luth. Human Relations Assn., Soc. Worship, Music and Arts, Acad. Parish Clergy (pres. 1967-71), Phi Delta Kappa. Clubs: Harvard, University (N.Y.C.). Home: 417 Park Ave New York NY 10022 Office: 619 Lexington Ave New York NY 10022

PETERSON, RANDOLPH LEE, educator; b. Roanoke, Tex., Feb. 16, 1920; s. Omas Anthony and Margaret (Francisco) P.; B.Sc., Tex. A. and M. Coll., 1941, postgrad., 1945; Ph.D., U. Toronto (Ont., Can.), 1950; m. Elizabeth Fairchild Taylor, Dec. 25, 1942; children—Penny Elizabeth, Bernard St. Louis. Came to Can., 1946, naturalized, 1964. Acting curator dept. mammalogy Royal Ont. Mus., Toronto, 1946-50, curator, 1950—; mem. faculty dept. zoology U. Toronto, 1949—, asso. prof., 1962-68, prof., 1968—; pres. Sci. Borealis Ltd., Mississauga, Ont., 1961-74, Boreal Biol. Ltd., Rockwood, Ont., 1974—. Bd. dirs. Met. Toronto Zool. Soc., 1972—, chmn. bd., 1977—. Served with USAAF, 1942-46. Mem. Am. Soc. Mammalogists (past pres.), Soc. Systematic Zoology (councillor 1965-69). Author: North American Moose, 1955; The Mammals of Eastern Canada, 1966. Home: RR 3 Rockwood ON Canada Office: 100 Queen's Park Toronto ON Canada

PETERSON, RICHARD HAMLIN, utility exec., lawyer; b. Berkeley, Calif., May 6, 1914; s. Otto Wallace and Gladys (Grinstead) P.; A.B., U. Calif. at Berkeley, 1935, J.D., 1940; m. Marianne Hammond, May 17, 1957; children—John, Stephen, Richard Hamlin. Admitted to Calif. bar, 1941; asso. firm McCutchen, Olney, Mannon & Greene, Los Angeles, 1940-43, McCutchen, Thomas, Matthews, Griffiths & Greene, San Francisco, 1946-47; atty. law dept. Pacific Gas & Electric Co., San Francisco, 1947-54, asst. gen. counsel, 1954-55, gen. counsel, 1955-69, sr. v.p., gen. consel, 1965-69, exec. v.p., 1969-72, vice chmn. bd., 1972-76, chmn. bd., 1976-79, also dir.; chmn. bd. Pacific Gas Transmission Co., 1974-79; dir. Alta. Natural Gas Co., Ltd., Indsl. Indemnity Co. Served with USNR, 1943-46; lt. comdr. Res. Mem. Am., Calif. bar assns., Bar Assn. San Francisco, Phi Beta Kappa, Order of Coif, Delta Tau Delta, Phi Delta Phi. Clubs: Pacific Union, Bohemian. Office 77 Beale St San Francisco CA 94106

PETERSON, RICHARD STANE, economist; b. Seattle, July 18, 1930; s. William Stane and Mabel (Bock) P.; B.A., wash. State U., 1953; postgrad. U. Calif., Berkeley, 1955-59; children—Kirsten Marie, Suzanne. Economist, Bank of Am., San Francisco, 1959-69; sr. v.p. Continental Bank, Chgo., 1969—, editor Continental Comment. Treas., Lake Bluff (Ill.) Park Bd., 1974-76. Served with U.S. Army, 1953-55. Mem. Nat. Assn. Bus. Economists, Am. Econ. Assn., Econ. Club Chgo. Home: 1550 N State Pkwy Chicago IL 60610 Office: 231 S LaSalle St Chicago IL 60693

PETERSON, RICHARD WILLIAM, lawyer, magistrate; b. Council Bluffs, Iowa, Sept. 29, 1925; s. Henry K. and Laura May (Robinson) P.; B.A., U. Iowa, 1949, J.D., 1951; postgrad. U. Nebr., Omaha, 1972-80; m. Patricia Mae Fox, Aug. 14, 1949; children—Kathryn Ilene Peterson Sherbondy, Jon Eric, Timothy Richard. Admitted to Iowa bar, 1951; individual practice law, Council Bluffs, 1951—; U.S. commr. U.S. Dist. Ct. So. Dist. Iowa, 1958-70, U.S. magistrate, 1970—; mem. nat. faculty Fed. Jud. Center, Washington, 1972—; dir. Western Fed. Savs. and Loan, Council Bluffs; legal adv., trustee Christian Home Assn. Bd. dirs. Pottawattamie County (Iowa) chpt. ARC, state fund chmn., 1957-58; state chmn. Radio Free Europe, 1960-61; dist. chmn. Trailblazer dist. Boy Scouts Am., 1952-55, mem. exec. council Mid-Am. council, 1976—. Served with inf. U.S. Army, 1943-46. Decorated Purple Heart, Bronze Star; named Outstanding Young Man, Council Bluffs C. of C., 1959. Mem. Pottawattamie County Bar Assn. (pres. 1979-80), Iowa Bar Assn. (chmn. com. fed. practice 1978-80), Am. Bar Assn., Fed. Bar Assn., Inter-Am. Bar Assn., Nat. Council U.S. Magistrates (pres. 1978-79), Phi Delta Phi, Delta Sigma Rho, Omicron Delta Kappa. Republican. Lutheran. Clubs: Kiwanis (pres. club 1957) (Council Bluffs); Masons. Contbr. articles to legal pubis. Home: 317 Burr Oak Rd Council Bluffs IA 51501 Office: 208 First Nat Bank Bldg Council Bluffs IA 51501

PETERSON, ROBERT AUSTIN, mower mfg. co. exec.; b. Sioux City, Iowa, July 5, 1925; s. Austen W. and Marie (Mueller) P.; B.S., U. Minn., 1946, B.B.A., 1947; m. Carol May Hudy, May 19, 1925; children—Roberta, Richard, Thomas, Bruce. Credit mgr. New Holland Machine div. Sperry Rand Corp., Mpls., 1952-61; credit mgr. Toro Co., Mpls., 1961-68, treas., 1968-70, v.p., internat. fin., 1970—; pres. Toro Credit Co., 1978—; dir. Clapper Co., Boston, Norton Corp., Phoenix, State Bond & Mortgage Co., State Bond Ins. Co., New Ulm, Autoturfcare, Darlington, Eng., Gulf Shore Turf Equipment, Pensicola, Fla., Wislar Co., Atlanta. Chmn. Prior Lake Spring Lake Watershed Dist., 1970—. Chmn., mem. bd. dirs. Prior Lake Bd. Edn., 1965-71; chmn. Scott County Republican Party, 1969-70. Bd. dirs. Scott Carver Mental Health Center, 1969-73, Minn. Watershed Assn., 1972-76. Served to ensign USNR, 1943-46. Mem. Fin. Execs. Inst. Clubs: Prior Lake Yacht; Decathlon Athletic (Mpls.). Home: 14956 Pixie Point Circle SE Prior Lake MN 55372 Office: 8111 Lyndale Ave S Minneapolis MN 55420

PETERSON, ROBERT L., meat processing co. exec.; b. Nebr., July 14, 1932; ed. U. Nebr., 1951; married; children—Mark R., Susan P. With Wilson & Co., Jim Boyle Order Buying Co.; cattle buyer R&C Packing Co., 1956-61; cattle buyer, plant mgr., v.p. carcass prodn. IBP, 1961-69; exec. v.p. ops. Spencer Foods, 1969-71; founder, pres. Madison Foods; 1971-76; pres., dir. Iowa Beef Processors, Inc., Dakota City, Nebr., 1976—. Served with Q.M.C., U.S. Army, 1952-54. Club: Sioux City Country. Office: Iowa Beef Processors Inc Dakota City NE 68731

PETERSON, ROBERT LEWIS, educator; b. Memphis, July 28, 1927; s. Arthur and Elsie (Turner) P.; B.A., Baylor U., 1949, M.A., 1950; Ph.D., U. Tex., 1960; m. Dorothy Beth Shaw, May 21, 1949; children—Robert Erik, Gretchen, Kendra. High sch. tchr., Tex., 1950-51; county librarian Nueces County Library, Tex., 1955- 58; asst. prof. U.S. history Del Mar Coll., Corpus Christi, Tex., 1958- 60; research fellow bus. history Harvard Grad. Sch. Bus. Adminstrn., 1960-62, asst. prof. bus. history, 1961-62; U.S. econ. historian U. Oreg., 1962-66; Hill prof. bus history U. Mont., 1966—, chmn. dept. history, 1967-69. Served with USNR, 1944-46. Mem. Am. Hist. Assn., Orgn. Am. Historians, Econ. History Assn., Bus. and Econ. History Soc. (pres. 1976-77). Contbr. profl. jours. Home: 200 Woodworth St Missoula MT 59801

PETERSON, ROGER ERNEST, journalist; b. Mpls., Apr. 10, 1937; s. John Waldemar and Rose Cecelia Peterson; B.A., U. Minn., 1962; m. Karen Stokoe, Nov. 6, 1966; 1 son by previous marriage, Christopher Eric. Corr. various radio-TV stas.; with ABC News, 1965—, now energy corr., Washington. Served with USAR, 1959-60. Mem. White House Corr. Assn., House-Senate Radio-TV Gallery. Office: 1124 Connecticut Ave NW Washington DC 20036

PETERSON, ROGER TORY, ornithologist, artist; b. Jamestown, N.Y., Aug. 28, 1908; s. Charles Gustav and Henrietta (Bader) P.; student Art Students League, 1927-28, N.A.D., 1929-31; D.Sc., Franklin and Marshall Coll., 1952, Ohio State U., 1962, Fairfield U., 1967, Allegheny Coll., 1967, Wesleyan U., 1970, Colby Coll., 1974, Gustavus Adolphus Coll., 1978; Dr. H., Hamilton Coll., 1976; D.H.L., Amherst Coll., 1977; m. Mildred Warner Washington, Dec. 19, 1936; m. 2d, Barbara Coulter, July 29, 1943; children—Tory, Lee; m. 3d, Virginia Westervelt, 1976. Decorative artist, 1926; instr. sci. and art River Sch., Brookline, Mass., 1931-34; engaged in bird painting and illustration bird books, 1934—; mem. adminstrv. staff Nat. Audubon Soc., charge ednl. activities; art editor Audubon mag., 1934-43; Audubon screen tour lectr., 1946—; editor Houghton-Mifflin Co. Field Guide Series, 1946—; art dir. Nat Wildlife Fedn.; distinguished scholar-in-residence Fallingwater-Western Pa. Conservancy, 1968; del. 11th Internat. Ornithol. Congress, Basel, Switzerland, 1954, 12th, Helsinki, 1958, 13th, Ithaca, N.Y., 1962, 14th, Oxford, Eng., 1966, 15th, The Hague, Netherlands, 1970, Internat. Bird Protection Conv., Tokyo, 1960, Cambridge, Eng., 1966; mem. Internat. Galapagos Sci. Project, 1964, USARP-Operation Deepfreeze (Antarctica), 1965; chmn. Am. sect. Internat. Bird Protection Com. Hon. trustee Uganda (Africa) Nat. Parks; sec. Nat. Audubon Soc., 1960-64; mem. council Cornell Lab. Ornithology; bd. dirs. World Wildlife Fund, 1962-76; 1st v.p. Am. Ornithologists Union, 1962-63. Served with C.E., U.S. Army, 1943-45. Recipient Brewster Meml. medal Am. Ornithologists Union, 1944; John Burroughs medal exemplary nature writing, 1950; Geoffrey St. Hilaire gold medal, French Natural History Soc., 1958; gold medal N.Y. Zool. Soc., 1961; Arthur A. Allen medal Lab. Ornithology, 1967; White Meml. Found. Conservation award, 1968; Gold medal Safari Club Phila., 1968; Paul Bartsch award Audubon Naturalist Soc., 1969; Frances Hutchinson award Garden Club Am., 1970; Gold medal N.J. Garden Club, 1970; Gold medal World Wildlife Fund, 1972, Joseph Wood Krutch medal, 1973; Explorers Club medal, 1974; Tchr. of Year award, 1974, Distinguished Pub. Service award Conn. Bar Assn., 1974, Cosmos Club award, 1976, Linné Gold medal Royal Swedish Acad. Scis., 1976, Green World award N.Y. Bot. Garden, 1976; Sarah Joseph Hale award Richards Library, 1977; Master Bird Artist medal Leigh Yankee Mus., 1978; named Swedish-Am. of 1977 Vasa Order of Am.; officer Order of Golden Ark (Holland), 1978; fellow Davenport Coll., Yale, 1966—. Fellow AAAS, N.Y. Zool. Soc., Am. Ornithologists Union, Linnaean Soc. N.Y. (hon.), London Zool. Soc. (hon.); mem. Nat. Audubon Soc. (life; dir. 1958-60, 65-67, Audubon medal 1971, spl. cons. 1972—), Soc. Wildlife Artists (Eng.) (v.p.), Wilson Ornithol. Soc. (life pres. 1964-65), Brit. Ornithologists Union (hon.), Cooper Ornithol. Soc., Nat. Assn. Biology Tchrs. (hon.). Clubs: Nuttall (Cambridge, Mass.); Cosmos, Biologists Field (Washington); Century Assn., Explorers (N.Y.C.); Intrepids (pres.). Author: Field Guide to the Birds, 1934; Junior Book of Birds, 1939; A Field Guide to Western Birds, 1941; Birds Over America, 1948; How to Know the Birds, 1949; Wildlife in Color, 1951; A Bird-Watchers Anthology, 1957; A Field Guide to the Birds of Texas, 1959; Penguins, 1979; Illustrator: Birds of South Carolina, 1949; Birds of Newfoundland, 1951; Arizona and Its Bird Life, 1952; Birds of Nova Scotia, 1961; Birds of Colorado, 1965; ltd. edit. prints of birds Mill Pond Press, 1974. Co-author: The Audubon Guide to Attracting Birds, 1941; Field Guide to Birds of Europe, 1953; Wild America, 1955; The World of Birds, 1964; The Birds, 1963; Field Guide to Wildflowers, 1968; Field Guide to Birds of Mexico, 1973. Editor: American Naturalist series, 1965—. Contbr. articles to natural history and popular publs.; lectr. in field. Home: Old Lyme CT 06371

PETERSON, RUDOLPH A., banker; b. Svenljunga, Sweden, Dec. 6, 1904; s. Aaron and Anna (Johannson) P.; B.S. in Commerce, U. Calif., 1925, LL.D., 1968; L.H.D., U. Redlands, 1967; m. Barbara Welser Lindsay, Dec. 25, 1962; children—Linnea (Mrs. Stephen W. Bennett), R. Price; stepchildren—Robert I. Lindsay, Lorna Lindsay Burke, Anne Lindsay Grubb, Margaret Lindsay Rude. With Comml. Credit Co., 1925-36, successively asst. mgr., San Francisco, v.p., gen. mgr., Mexico City, div. operations mgr., Chgo.; dist. mgr. Bank Am. Nat. Trust & Savs. Assn., Fresno, Calif., 1936-41, v.p., San Francisco, 1941-46, vice chmn. bd, 1961-63, pres., 1963-70, chmn. exec. com., 1970-75, also dir., hon. dir., 1975—; pres. Allied Bldg. Credits, 1946-52, Bank of Hawaii, Honolulu, 1956-61; v.p. Transam. Corp., San Francisco, 1952-55; pres. BankAm. Corp., San Francisco, 1968-70, chmn. exec. com., 1970-76, also dir.; adminstr. UN Devel. Programme, 1972-76; chmn. policy com. Becker & Warburg-Paribas Group, 1976—; chmn. S.G. Warburg N.Am. Ltd., 1977—, Paribas N.Am., 1977—; dir. Alza Corp., Di Giorgio Corp., Scandinavian Airlines System, Inc. Trustee Calif. Acad. Scis., Calif. Berkeley Found., Calif. Inst. Tech., Asia Found.; hon. trustee Com. Econ. Devel.; bd. dirs. Children's Hosp. Med. Center, James Irvine Found. Decorated comdr. Royal Order Vasa (Sweden); Grand Cross of Civil Merit (Spain); Order of Merit (Italy); named Swedish-Am. of Year, Vasa Order, 1965, Man of Year, Cons. Engrs. Assn. Calif., 1968, U. Calif. Alumnus of Year, 1968, Calif. Industrialist of Year, Calif. Mus. Sci. and Industry, 1969; recipient Capt. Robert Dollar Meml. award for contbn. to advancement Am. fgn. trade, 1970. Clubs: Bohemian, Pacific-Union, Villa Taverna (San Francisco); Cypress Point (Pebble Beach, Calif.); Links (N.Y.C.). Home: 86 Sea View Ave Piedmont CA 94611 Office: Bank Am Center San Francisco CA 94137

PETERSON, RUSSELL WILBUR, assn. exec., former gov. Del.; b. Portage, Wis., Oct. 3, 1916; s. John Anton and Emma (Anthony) P.; B.S., U. Wis., 1938, Ph.D., 1942; D.Sc. (hon.), Williams Coll., 1975; hon. doctorates Butler U., Springfield Coll., Stevens Inst. Tech., 1979; m. E. Lillian Turner, June 30, 1937; children—Russell Glen, Peter Jon, Kristin, Elin. With E. I. DuPont de Nemours & Co., Inc., 1942-69, research dir. textile fibers dept., 1954-55, 56-59, merchandising mgr. textile fibers, 1955-56, dir. new products div. textile fibers, 1959-62, dir. research and devel. div. devel. dept., 1963-69; bd. dirs. Textile Research Inst., Princeton, N.J., 1956-69, chmn. exec. com., 1959-61, chmn. bd. dirs., 1961-63; gov. of Del., 1969-73; mem. Nat. Commn. Critical Choices for Am., 1973-74, chmn. exec. com., 1973; chmn. U.S. Council on Environ. Quality, 1973-76; pres. New Directions, Washington, 1976-77; dir. Office Tech. Assessment, U.S. Congress, 1978-79; pres. Nat. Audubon Soc., 1979—; pres. New Directions, Washington, 1976-77. Regional v.p. Nat. Municipal League, 1968—; chmn. Edn. Commn. States, 1970; chmn. com. nuclear energy and space tech. So. Govs. Conf., 1970-71; chmn. Nat. Adv. Commn. on Criminal Justice Standards and Goals, 1971-73; chmn. com. law enforcement, justice and pub. safety Nat. Govs. Conf., 1970-73; v.p. Council State Govts., 1970-71; chmn. Del. River Basin Commn., 1971-72; bd. dirs. World Wildlife Fund, Population Crisis Com., Alliance to Save Energy; chmn. adv. bd. Solar Energy Research Inst., 1979—; mem. Pres.'s Commn. on Accident at Three Mile Island, 1979. Recipient Gold medal World Wildlife Fund, 1971; Ann. award Comml. Devel. Assn., 1971; Gold Plate award Nat. Acad. Achievement, 1971; Parsons award Am. Chem. Soc., 1974;

Audubon award Nat. Audubon Soc., 1977; Proctor prize Sigma Xi, 1978; named Conservationist of Year, Nat. Wildlife Fedn., 1972. Hon. fellow Textile Research Inst., Am. Inst. Chemists; mem. North-South Round Table, Am. Ornithologists' Union, Fedn. Am. Scientists, AAAS (dir.), Am. Chem. Soc., Phi Beta Kappa, Sigma Xi (Proctor prize 1978), Phi Lambda Upsilon. Unitarian. Clubs: Kiwanis, Masons, U.S. Assn. for Club of Rome (dir.) Office: Nat Audubon Soc 950 3d Ave New York NY 10022

PETERSON, SPIRO, educator; b. New Haven, Dec. 25, 1922; s. Walter and Anastasia (Morris) P.; A.B., Trinity Coll., Hartford, 1947; M.A., Harvard, 1947, Ph.D., 1953; m. Yerevan Sarkisian, June 10, 1951; children—Ellen Dorothea, Anastasia Lynne, Andrew Townsend. Mem. faculty Miami U., Oxford, Ohio, 1952—, asso. prof., 1958-62, prof., 1962—, also chmn. dept. English, 1964-73, dean Grad. Sch. and Research, 1972—. Mem. Woodrow Wilson Fellowship Selection Com., 1964-71. Served with inf. AUS, 1943-46. Decorated Bronze Star. Mem. Coll. English Assn. Ohio (pres. 1971-72, exec. council), Modern Lang. Assn., Am. Soc. for 18th Century Studies, Phi Beta Kappa, Phi Kappa Phi. Editor, annotator: The Counterfeit Lady Unveiled and Other Criminal Fiction of Seventeenth-Century England, 1961. Home: 115 N University Ave Oxford OH 45056

PETERSON, STEPHEN LEE, librarian; b. Lindsborg, Kans., Jan. 31, 1940; s. Donald Gordon and Grace C. (Forsberg) P.; B.A., Bethel Coll., St. Paul, 1962; B.D., Colgate Rochester Div. Sch., 1965; M.A., U. Mich., 1967, M.A. in L.S., 1968; Ph.D., Vanderbilt U., 1975; m. Mabel Jean Moen, Aug. 31, 1963; children—Anne Davina, Matthew Robert Moen. Head divinity librarian Joint Univ. Libraries, Nashville 1969-70, asst. dir. Univ. Library, 1971; divinity librarian Yale U., 1972-79, librarian Beinecke Rare Book and Manuscript Library, 1979—. Xerox grad. fellow info. sci. Beta Phi Mu, 1968; Sealantic fellow, 1970-71; Lilly fellow, 1975-76; fellow Council Library Resources, 1975-76. Mem. Am. Theol. Library Assn., Am. Soc. Missiology. Home: 57 Northside Rd North Haven CT 06473 Office: Yale Sta Box 984 New Haven CT 06520

PETERSON, THEODORE BERNARD, educator; b. Albert Lea, Minn., June 8, 1918; s. Theodore B. and Emilie (Jensen) P.; B.A., U. Minn., 1941; M.S., Kans. State Coll., 1948; Ph.D., U. Ill., 1955; m. Helen M. Clegg, Sept. 13, 1946; children—Thane Eric, Kristin, Megan, Daniel Alan. Instr., then asst. prof. journalism Kans. State Coll., 1945-48, head coll. news bur., 1945-48; instr. journalism U. Ill., 1948-55, asso. prof., 1955-57, prof., 1957—, dean Coll. Communications, 1957-79; judge Nat. Mag. Awards, 1967—. Recipient award for distinguished research journalism Sigma Delta Chi, Kappa Tau Alpha, 1956; Outstanding Achievement award U. Minn., 1973. Mem. Assn. Edn. Journalism (1st v.p. 1962, pres. 1963), Am. Council on Edn. Journalism (accrediting com. 1961-70, 72—), Am. Assn. Schs. and Depts. Journalism (pres. 1965), Kappa Tau Alpha, Phi Kappa Phi, Alpha Delta Sigma. Author: Writing Nonfiction for Magazines, 1949; Magazines in the Twentieth Century, 1956, rev., 1964; (with F.S. Siebert, Wilbur Schramm) Four Theories of the Press, 1956; (with J.W. Jensen, Wm. L. Rivers) The Mass Media in Modern Society, 1965, rev., 1971. Home: 103 E George Huff Dr Urbana IL 61801

PETERSON, VICTOR HERBERT, assn. exec.; b. Rockford, Ill., Oct. 9, 1916; s. Herbert T. and Mary Olive (Lind) P.; B.A., Beloit Coll., 1938; M.A., U. Chgo., 1939; m. Ruth-Elizabeth Colman, Dec. 30, 1939 (div. 1968); children—Sager Lynn, Harriett Vicki, Elizabeth Ann; m. 2d, Sonia d'Ancona, 1968. Tchr. pub. schs., Rockford, 1939, Kingsport, Tenn., 1940-42; reporter-photographer Indpls. Times, 1943-50, city editor, 1950-52, asst. mng. editor, 1952-53, mng. editor, 1953-54; mem. pub. relations dept. Socony Mobil Oil Co., Inc., N.Y.C., 1954-57, asst. mgr., 1957-59; asst. mgr. pub. relations dept. Standard-Vacuum Oil Co., White Plains, N.Y., 1959-62; mgr. pub. relations Mobil Petroleum Co., Inc., also Mobil Oil Corp. (formerly Socony Mobil Oil Co., Inc.), 1962-64, mgr. information, 1964-67; dir. pub. relations Hooker Chem. Corp., 1967-69; v.p. pub. relations and edn. Chem. Mfrs. Assn., Washington, 1969—; adj. prof. Am. U., Washington, 1979—; owner PR Counseling, pub. relations firm. Mem. Phi Beta Kappa, Sigma Delta Chi, Sigma Alpha Epsilon. Clubs: Deadline, By-line, Circumnavigators, Overseas Press (N.Y.C.); Nat. Press. Author: MCA 1872-1972, A Centennial History; co-author: The Exercise Prescription for Musculoskeletal Problems; Fifty Plus and Holding. Home: 2306 California St NW Washington DC 20008 Office: 1825 Connecticut Ave NW Washington DC 20009. *I learn something from everyone I meet. Hopefully, I give back as much or more.*

PETERSON, VINCENT R., bus. exec.; b. 1919; B.A., U. Wis., 1940; m. With Peat, Marwick, Mitchell & Co., C.P.A.'s, 1946-50, Haskins & Sells, C.P.A.'s, 1950-55; with Koehring Co., from 1955, v.p. fin., treas., from 1967, sec., from 1968; now with Johnson Controls, Inc., Milw. Served to 1st lt. AUS, World War II. C.P.A., Wis., Minn. Address: 507 E Michigan Milwaukee WI 53202

PETERSON, WALLACE CARROLL, educator, economist; b. Omaha, Mar. 28, 1921; s. Fred Nels and Grace (Brown) P.; B.A., U. Nebr., 1947, M.A., 1948, Ph.D., 1953; m. Eunice V. Peterson, Aug. 16, 1944; children—Wallace Carroll, Shelley Lorraine. Reporter, Lincoln (Nebr.) Jour., 1946; faculty U. Nebr., 1951—, prof. econs., 1962—, chmn. dept., 1965-75, George Holmes prof. econs., 1966—, v.p. faculty senate, 1972-73, pres., 1973-74. Fulbright research scholar, France, 1957-58; Fulbright lectr., Greece, 1964-65. Mem., vice chmn. Nebr. Polit. Accountability and Disclosure Commn.; mem. Nebr. Democratic Central Com., 1968-74. Served to capt. USAAF, 1942-46. Mem. Assn. for Evolutionary Econs. (pres. 1976), AAUP (pres. Nebr. 1963-64, nat. council), Am., Midwest (pres. 1968-69) econs. assns., Assn. Social Econs., AAAS, Fedn. Am. Scientists, Common Cause, ACLU, UN Assn. U.S.A. (state pres.), Nebr. Council Econ. Edn. (chmn. 1976-77). Author: Income, Employment and Economic Growth, 4th edit., 1978; The Welfare State in France, 1960; Elements of Economics, 1973. Editor: Nebr. Jour. Econs. and Bus.; editorial bd. Jour. Post Keynesian Econs., Social Sci. Jour.; author bi-weekly newspaper column Money in Am.; contbr. articles to profl. jours. Home: 4549 South St Lincoln NE 68506

PETERSON, WALTER FRITIOF, univ. pres.; b. Idaho Falls, Idaho, July 15, 1920; s. Walter Fritiof and Florence (Danielson) P.; B.A., State U. Iowa, 1942, M.A., 1948, Ph.D., 1951; m. Barbara Mae Kempe, Jan. 13, 1946; children—Walter Fritiof III, Daniel John. Instr., State U. Iowa, 1949-51, Buena Vista Coll., 1951-52; asst. prof. history, chmn. dept. history Milw. Downer Coll., 1952-57, asso. prof. history, chmn. social sci. div., 1957-64; asso. prof. history Lawrence U., Appleton, Wis., 1964-67, prof. history, Alice G. Chapman librarian, 1967-70; pres. U. Dubuque, 1970—. Vis. lectr. summers Ball State U., Muncie, Ind., 1954, 56, Drake U., Des Moines, 1962, U. Wis.-Milw., 1959, 61, 63, 64; regional tng. officer Peace Corps, 1965-68, dir. India project, 1965. cons. history Allis-Chalmers Mfg. Co., 1959—, Home Mut. Ins. Co., 1968—. Dir. Home Mut. Ins. Group. Vice-chmn. World Affairs Council Milw.; mem. exec. com. council theol. sems. U.P. Ch. U.S.A.; chmn. Assn. Theol. Faculties of Iowa, 1975-76. Bd. dirs. Finley Hosp., Dubuque Symphony Orch., Dubuque Art Assn. Served with USAAF, 1942-45; PTO. Mem. Am. Studies Assn. (pres. Wis.-Ill. chpt.), UN Assn. U.S.A. (pres. Milw. chpt., v.p. Wis. div. 1968-70, bd. Iowa div.), Iowa Assn. Coll. and Univ. Presidents (pres. 1975-76), A.A.U.P., Milwaukee County Hist. Soc. (dir.), A.L.A., Am. Hist. Assn., Orgn. Am. Historians, Phi Alpha Theta, Kappa Delta Pi, Phi Delta Kappa. Editor: Transactions of Wis. Acad. Scis., Arts and Letters, 1965-72; The Allis-Chalmers Corporation: An Industrial History, 1977. Contbr. articles to profl. jours. Office: Office of Pres Univ Dubuque 2050 University Ave Dubuque IA 52001

PETERSON, WALTER RUTHERFORD, coll. pres., real estate exec.; b. Nashua, N.H., Sept. 19, 1922; s. Walter Rutherford and Helen (Reed) P.; B.A., Dartmouth, 1947; m. Dorothy Donovan, Nov. 24, 1949; children—Margaret Joanna, Andrew Reed. Tchr., N.H. Country Day Sch., 1948-49; partner Petersons, Inc., realtors, Peterborough, N.H., 1949-68, 73—, mem. N.H. Gen. Ct. from Hillsborough Country, 1961-69, majority leader, 1963-64, speaker, 1965-69; gov. N.H., 1969-73; pres. Franklin Pierce Coll., Rindge, N.H., 1976—; trustee Monodnock Bank, Jaffrey, N.H. Bd. dirs. Peterborough Indsl. Devel. Corp., N.H. Council World Affairs. Chmn., Hillsborough County Republican Com., 1952-64. Trustee New Hampton Sch. Served as officer UNSR, World War II. Mem. Nat. Assn. Real Estate Bds. N.H. Bd. Realtors (pres. 1960-61), Am. Legion, VFW, Grange. Episcopalian. Lion, Elk, Eagle. Office: Franklin Pierce Coll Rindge NH 03461*

PETERSON, WILLIAM HERBERT, economist; b. N.Y.C., Feb. 26, 1921; s. George C. and Ann (Erickson) P.; B.S., N.Y. U., 1943, Ph.D., 1952; M.S., Columbia, 1948; m. Mary Jean Bennett, Feb. 17, 1949; children—Mark, Laura. Part-time instr. Rutgers U., 1948-50, Columbia, 1948; asst. prof. econs. Poly. Inst. Bklyn., 1948-53; prof. econs. N.Y. U., 1953-64; economist U.S. Steel Corp., 1964-71; sr. econ. adviser U.S. Dept. Commerce, Washington, 1972-74; John David Campbell prof. Am. bus. Am. Grad. Sch. Internat. Mgmt., Glendale, Ariz., 1974-76; Burrows T. Lundy prof. philosophy of bus. Campbell Coll., Buies Creek, N.C., 1976-78; Scott L. Probasco, Jr. chair of free enterprise, dir. Center Econ. Edn., U. Tenn., Chattanooga, 1979—; mem. Conf. Bd. Econ. Forum, 1964-71; adv. com. to sec. commerce. Mem. nat. campaign staff Nixon for Pres., 1960. Served to lt. (j.g.) USNR, World War II. Mem. Am., So. econs. assns., Nat. Assn. Bus. Econs., Am. Statis. Assn., Mont Pelerin Soc. Author: The Great Farm Problem, 1959; also monographs, articles. Home: 700 New Hampshire NW Washington DC 20037 Office: Center Econ Edn U Tenn Chattanooga TN 37402

PETERSON, WILLIS LESTER, educator; b. Mpls., Mar. 3, 1932; s. Lester Wilfred and Valeria Leone (Slatoski) P.; B.S., U. Minn., 1960, M.S., 1962; Ph.D., U. Chgo., 1966; m. Dorothy Feiertag, July 5, 1969. Research fellow U. Chgo., 1962-65; mem. faculty U. Minn., 1965—, prof. econs., 1972—. Served with U.S. Army, 1952-54. Author: Principles of Economics: Macro, 1971, 74, 77, 80; Principles of Economics: Micro, 1971, 74, 77, 80; Introduction to Economics, 1977. Home: 500 Constance Blvd Anoka MN 55303 Office: 337 Cla-Off Bldg Univ Minn Saint Paul MN 55108

PETGEN, ELIZABETH AHERN, library adminstr.; b. Norfolk, Va., July 24, 1931; d. Christopher Hugh and Lucile Elizabeth (Draper) Ahern; B.A. in Edn., U. N.C., 1953; M.S. in L.S., Columbia, 1961; m. Albert Bennett Petgen, Jr., Sept 3, 1955; 1 son, Richard Bennett. Librarian, tchr. Ft Bragg (N.C.) Dependents Sch., 1953-56, Arlington (Va.) Bd. Edn, 1957, Fairfax County (Va.) Bd. Edn., 1957-58; librarian N.Y.C. Bd. Edn., 1960-61, TV Info. Office, N.Y.C., 1963, Pub. Library of Charlotte and Mecklenburg County, Charlotte, N.C., 1964-66; med. librarian Med. Library of Mecklenburg County, Charlotte, 1966-71; asso. dir. midcontinental regional med. library program Library of Medicine, U. Nebr. Med. Center, Omaha, 1971-79; asso. dir. Library of Rush U., 1979—. Mem. ALA, Spl. Libraries Assn., Med., N.C., Nebr. library assns., AAUP, AAUW, Chi Omega. Club: Faculty Women's. Address: 1506 W Polk Chicago IL 60607

PETHICK, CHRISTOPHER JOHN, physicist; b. Horsham, Sussex, Eng., Feb. 2, 1942; s. Richard Hope and Norah Betty (Hill) P.; came to U.S., 1966; B.A., Magdalen Coll., Oxford (Eng.) U., 1962, D. Phil., 1966. Fellow by examination Magdalen Coll., Oxford U., 1965-70; research asso. U. Ill., 1966-68, research asst. prof., 1968-69, asso. prof. physics, 1970-73, prof., 1973—; prof. physics Nordita, Copenhagen, 1975—. A. P. Sloan research fellow, 1970-72. Fellow Am. Phys. Soc.; mem. Am. Astron. Soc. Office: Dept Physics U Ill Urbana IL 61801

PETICOLAS, WARNER LELAND, educator; b. Lubbock, Tex., July 29, 1929; s. Warner Marion and Beulah Francis (Lowe) P.; B.S., Tex. Technol. Coll., 1950; Ph.D., Northwestern U., 1954; m. Virginia Marie Wolf, June 30, 1969; children—Laura M., Alicia B.; children by previous marriage—Cynthia M., Nina P., Phillip W. Research asso. DuPont Co., Wilmington, Del., 1954-60; research div. IBM, San Jose, Calif., 1960-67, cons., 1967-69, mgr. chem. physics group, 1965-67; prof. phys. chemistry U. Oreg., 1967—; cons. in field. Committeeman Democratic party, Eugene, Oreg., 1967-70. Served with USPHS, 1955-57. Guggenheim fellow Max von Laue-Paul Langevin Inst., Grenoble, France, 1973-74. Mem. Am. Chem. Soc., Am. Phys. Soc., Sigma Xi, Alpha Chi Sigma, Tau Beta Pi. Episcopalian. Home: 2829 Arline Way Eugene OR 97403

PETIT, HERBERT HANLEY, educator; b. Lexington, Ky., Aug. 16, 1911; s. Harry H. and May (Hanley) P.; A.B., Transylvania Coll., 1932, M.A., U. Ky., 1934; Ph.D., Western Res. U., 1952, Instr. English, asst. prof., registrar John Carroll U., 1937-47; asso. prof., then prof. English, U. Detroit, 1947-58; faculty Duquesne U., 1958—, prof. English philology, 1958—, distinguished service prof., 1976—, dean Grad. Sch., 1965-68, provost, 1968-70. Mem. Linguistic Soc., Modern Lang. Assn., Am. Dialect Soc., Modern Humanities Research Assn. Editor: Annuale Mediaevale, 1959-76. Home: 245 Melwood Ave Pittsburgh PA 15213

PETITO, FRANK A., investment banker; b. Trenton, N.J., Sept. 2, 1914; A.B., Princeton, 1936; grad. Babson Inst. Bus. Adminstrn., 1937; m. Laura Haven Flock, Feb. 21, 1941; children—Frank A., A. Robert, David, John. With Morgan Stanley & Co. Inc., and predecessor, N.Y.C., 1937—, partner, 1954—, chmn., 1973—. Bd. dirs. Am.-Italy Soc.; trustee Alfred P. Sloan Found. Served with AUS, 1940-45. Club: University (N.Y.C.). Office: Morgan Stanley and Co 1251 Ave of Americas New York NY 10020*

PETRAK, IVOR, hotel exec.; b. Czekoslovakia, Feb. 3, 1922; s. Jan and Marie P.; student Charles U., Prague, 1945-47, Hotel Sch., Lausanne Switzerland, 1947-49; m. Phyllis B. Bausher, June 7, 1958; children—Maria, Ian, Jean-Pierre. Mgr., v.p. The Lodge at Smugglers, 1955-64; gen. mgr., v.p. Hotel Corp. Am., Nassau, Bahamas and Megeve, France, 1964-71; gen. mgr., v.p. Can. Pacific Hotels, Coral Gables, Fla., 1971—. Mem. Innkeeping Inst. Am. (gov.), So. Inst. Tech. Alberta (bd. trustees), Lausanne Hotel Sch. Alumni Assn. Clubs: Skal, Rotary, Chaine des Rotisseurs, Chevaliers Du Tastevin. Home: Balmoral Beach Hotel Cable Beach Nassau Bahamas Office: 255 Alhambra Circle Suite 455 Coral Gables FL 33134

PETRAKIS, HARRY MARK, author; b. St. Louis, June 5, 1923; s. Mark E. and Stella (Christoulakis) P.; student U. Ill., 1940-41, L.H.D., 1971; m. Diane Perparos, Sept. 30, 1945; children—Mark, John, Dean. Freelance writer, tchr., lectr.; tchr. workshop classes in novel, short story; McGuffey vis. lectr. Ohio U., Athens, 1971; writer-in-residence Chgo. Pub. Library, 1976-77, Chgo. Bd. Edn., 1978-79. Mem. Authors Guild, P.E.N. Recipient awards Friends of Am. Writers, Friends of Lit., Soc. Midland Authors, all 1963. Mem. Writers Guild Am.-West. Author: Lion at My Heart, 1959; The Odyssey of Kostas Volakis, 1963; Pericles on 31st Street (nominated for Nat. Book award), 1965; The Founder's Touch, 1965; A Dream of Kings (Nat. Book award nomination), 1966; The Waves of Night, 1969; Stelmark: A Family Recollection, 1970; In the Land of Morning, 1973; The Hour of the Bell, 1976; A Petrakis Reader, 28 Stories, 1978; Nick the Greek, 1979. Contbr. short stores to mags. including Atlantic Monthly, Sat. Eve. Post, Harper's Bazaar, Country Beautiful. Story included in Prize Stories, also O. Henry Award 1966. Address: 80 East Rd Dune Acres Chesterton IN 46304

PETRANEK, STEPHEN LYNN, editor; b. Washington, Aug. 19, 1944; s. Chester J. and Mabel Oleta (Mercer) P.; student U. Okla., 1962-63; B.S., U. Md., 1970; M.A., U. Mo., 1975. Editor-in-chief The Diamondback, U. Md., 1969-70; reporter Democrat and Chronicle, Rochester, N.Y., 1972, financial writer, 1972-73, asst. Sunday editor, 1973; mng. editor Upstate mag., 1974-75, editor, 1975-77; editor Tropic Mag. The Miami Herald, 1977-78; dep. editor Washington Post Mag., 1978—. Recipient John Hancock award for fin. writing, 1972, Bus. Journalism award U. Mo., 1973, Frank Tripp Newswriting award, 1973. Mem. Sigma Delta Chi, Kappa Tau Alpha, Omicron Delta Kappa, Pi Delta Epsilon. Methodist. Club: Genesee Yacht. Author newspaper series Decline and Fall of Stirling Homex, 1972. Home: 11438 Stewart Ln Silver Spring MD 20904 8fOffice: 1150 15th St NW Washington DC 20071

PETRAZIO, EDWARD GLENN, architect; b. Emporium, Pa., Jan. 29, 1921; s. Filipo Joseph and Helen Mary (Ippoliti) P.; B.Arch., M.Arch., Pa. State U., 1942; m. Rosanne Edwards, Feb. 27, 1947; Plant engr. Chevrolet Motor div., Buffalo, 1942-44; plant architect Carbide and Carbon Chems. Corp., Oak Ridge, Tenn., 1944-48; asso. partner Skidmore Owings & Merrill, Oak Ridge, N.Y.C., Germany, Chgo., 1948-74; adminstr. dept. profl. practice AIA, Washington, 1974-77; asso. Meltzer Assos., Real Estate, New Orleans, 1977—; mem. Nat. Council Archtl. Bds. Mem. AIA, Friends of Cabildo New Orleans, Coll. of Fellows of AIA, Patio Planners of New Orleans. Democrat. Roman Catholic. Club: Internat. (New Orleans). Home: 925 Saint Peter St New Orleans LA 70116 Office: 316 S Rampart St New Orleans LA 70112

PETREE, WILLIAM HORTON, lawyer; b. Winston-Salem, N.C., Nov. 4, 1920; s. Elbert Heaton and Ethel (Tucker) P.; B.S., U. N.C., 1944, LL.B., 1948; m. Lena Morris, Dec. 23, 1943; children—William Horton, Mary Jo. Admitted to N.C. bar, 1948, since practiced in Winston-Salem; partner firm Hudson, Petree, Stockton, Stockton & Robinson, and predecessors, 1956—. Dir. Northwestern Bank, Winston-Salem; dir., mem. exec. com. Old Salem, Inc.; dir. numerous other corps. Chmn. found. com. Winston-Salem Found.; past pres. Forsyth County Tb and Health Assn.; past bd. dirs. Moravian Home; past trustee, exec. com. Salem Coll. Served to 1st lt. USMCR, 1944-46. Mem. Forsyth County Bar Assn. (past pres.), Alpha Tau Omega, Phi Delta Phi. Democrat. Mem. Moravian Ch. (trustee, elder). Kiwanian (dir. Winston-Salem, pres. 1976-77). Club: Forsyth Country (past dir.). Home: 729 Westover Ave Winston-Salem NC 27104 Office: Reynolds Bldg Winston-Salem NC 27101. *Enthusiasm, coupled with proper motivation, contributes most to a successful, happy and fulfilling life.*

PETREK, WILLIAM JOSEPH, univ. pres.; b. Arcadia, Wis., Feb. 26, 1928; s. Roman Casper and Agnes (Jankowski) P.; B.A. cum laude, St. John's U., Minn., 1948; S.T.L. magna cum laude, Gregorian U., Rome, 1952; Ph.D. with great distinction, Higher Inst. Philosophy, U. Louvain (Belgium), 1956; m. Sandra Lucille Nash, Nov. 24, 1961; children—Michele, Søren. Asst. prof. philosophy, chmn. dept. philosophy Holy Cross Coll., La Crosse, Wis., 1956-60; from asst. prof. to prof. philosophy and religion DePauw U., Greencastle, Ind., 1961-71, dir. internat. edn., asst. dean internat. edn. and off-campus programs, 1966-71; v.p. Gt. Lakes Colls. Assn., Ann Arbor, Mich., 1971-72; dean Coll. Liberal Arts, Hofstra U., Hempstead, N.Y., 1972-74, provost, dean faculties, 1974-76; acad. v.p. Southeast Mo. State U., Cape Girardeau, 1976-80; pres. Richmond Coll., London, 1980—. Trustee Nassau Higher Edn. Consortium, 1973-76; exec. com. bd. Council Intercultural Studies and Programs, 1974—; bd. nat. cons. Nat. Endowment Humanities, 1974—; bd. dirs. Word Univ. Service, 1976-80. Danforth asso., 1964; recipient Best Prof. award DePauw U., 1965; Ford Found. humanities grantee, 1970; Gt. Lakes Colls. Assn. Non-Western research grantee, 1965; hon. fellow Inst. Am. Univs., Aix-en-Provence, France, 1973. Mem. Soc. Phenomenology and Existential Philosophy. Translator, author introduction: (Jean Nabert) Elements for an Ethic, 1969. Office: Richmond Coll Queens Rd Richmond Surrey TW10 6JP England

PETREQUIN, HARRY JOSEPH, JR., fgn. service officer; b. Ste. Genevieve, Mo., July 1, 1929; s. Harry Joseph and Cresentia Ellen (Bechter) P.; A.B., Westminster Coll., 1950; B.Fgn. Trade, Am. Grad. Sch. Internat. Mgmt., 1954; postgrad. Johns Hopkins, 1960; M.A., Fletcher Sch. Law and Diplomacy, 1970. Joined U.S. Fgn. Service, 1955; assigned AID and predecessor agys., 1955—, dep. dir. S.E. Asia Regional Econ. Devel. Office, Thailand, 1970-74, U.S. coordinator Senegal River Basin Authority, Dakar, 1975-76, dir. Office Indonesian, Asian and South Pacific Affairs, 1977—. Served to lt. (j.g.) USCGR, 1951-53; comdr. Res. Mem. Soc. Internat. Devel., Am. Acad. Polit. and Social Sci., Acad. Polit. Sci., Am. Fgn. Service Assn., Cousteau Soc., Common Cause, Center for Study Democratic Instns., World Future Soc., Amnesty Internat., Phi Alpha Theta. Home: 375 N 5th St Ste Genevieve MO 63670 Office: AID Washington DC 20523

PETRI, LOUIS, bus. exec.; b. San Francisco, Oct. 13, 1912; s. Angelo and Amelia (Guidi) P.; student San Jose State Tchrs. Coll., U. Calif., also med. sch. U. St. Louis; m. Flori Cella, July 21, 1935; 1 dau., Patricia Mary. Began as gen. winery worker Petri Wine Co., 1934, pres., 1944-64, chmn. bd., 1964-68; pres., chief exec. officer United Vintners; dir., mem. exec. com., compensation and pension com. Foremost-McKesson, Inc.; dir. Bank of Am. NT & SA, Bankam. Corp., Edward D. Sultan Co., Honolulu, John Burton Machine Co., Concord, Calif. Decorated Gran Ufficiale, Order of Merit (Italy). Mem. Am.-Italy Soc. (chmn. bd. San Francisco). Clubs: World Trade, Pacific, Villa Taverna, Bohemian, St. Francis Yacht, Olympic (San Francisco); Eldorado Country, Thunderbird Country (Palm Springs, Calif.). Home: 1000 Mason St San Francisco CA 94108 Office: 220 Montgomery St Room 407 San Francisco CA 94104

PETRI, THOMAS E(VERT), U.S. congressman; b. Marinette, Wis., May 28, 1940; B.A., Harvard U., 1962, J.D., 1965. Admitted to Wis. bar, 1965; law clk. to U.S. Dist. Judge, James Doyle of Western dist. Wis., 1965-66; practiced law, Fond du Lac, Wis., 1970—; vol. Peace Corps, Somalia, 1966-67; dir. crime and drug studies Pres.'s Nat. Adv. Council on Exec. Orgn., 1969; mem. Wis. State Senate, 1972-79;

mem. 96th Congress from 6th Dist. Wis. Mem. Fond du Lac County Bar Assn., State Bar Wis., Am. Bar Assn. Republican. Office: Longworth House Office Bldg Washington DC 20515

PETRICH, BEATRICE ANN, educator; b. Glencoe, Minn., Apr. 13, 1925; d. Otto Edward and Clara Blanche (Johnson) P.; B.S., U. Minn., 1947; M.S. in Edn., Colo. State U., 1958; Ph.D., Iowa State U., 1964. Tchr. high sch. home econs., Minn., 1947-58; asst. prof. S.D. State U., 1958-60; asso. prof., chmn. Stout State U., Menomonie, Wis., 1961-63; asso. prof. No. Ill. U., DeKalb, Ill., 1965-71; prof., coordinator home econs. edn., dept. continuing and vocat. edn. U. Wis., Madison, 1971—; cons. to ednl. instns., state agys.; nutrition edn. cons. March of Dimes. Vocat.-Tech. and Adult Edn. Bd. Wis. grantee, 1971-72; Grad. Sch. U. Wis. grantee, 1972-73; Bd. Vocat. Edn. and Rehab. Ill. grantee, 1969-70; Dept. Pub. Instrn. Wis. grantee, 1972-80. Mem. Am. Ednl. Research Assn., AAUP, Nat. Council for Measurement in Edn., Am. Home Econs. Assn., Am. Vocat. Assn., Am. Vocat. Edn. Research Assn., Soc. for Nutrition Edn., Am. Council for Consumer Interests, Adult Edn. Assn., Wis. Home Econs. Assn. (chmn. research sect. 1974-76), Omicron Nu (hon.), Phi Kappa Phi (pres. elect U Wis chpt.), Pi Lambda Theta (treas., advisor). Club: Order of Eastern Star. Home: 3125 Grandview Blvd Madison WI 53713 Office: U Wis 1300 Linden Dr Madison WI 53713

PETRICK, ERNEST NICHOLAS, mech. engr.; b. Pa., Apr. 9, 1922; s. Aurelius and Anna (Kaschak) P.; B.S. in Mech. Engring., Carnegie Inst. Tech., 1943; M.S., Purdue U., 1953, Ph.D., 1955; m. Magdalene Simcoe, June 13, 1946; children—Deborah Petrick Healey, Katherine Petrick Niver, Denise, Victoria. Faculty, Purdue U., 1946-53; dir. heat transfer research Wright Aero. div. Curtiss-Wright Corp., Woodridge, N.J., 1953-56, chief advanced propulson systems Curtiss-Wright Research div., Quehanna, Pa., 1957-60; chief research engr. Kelsey-Hayes Co., Detroit, 1960-65; chief scientist U.S. Army Tank-Automotive Research and Devel. Command, Warren, Mich., 1965—; adj. prof. engring., guest lectr. Wayne State U.; guest lectr. U. Mich., Oakland U.; panel mem. combat vehicles NATO, 1973—; mem. adv. bd. on basic combustion research NSF, 1973; chmn. advanced transp. systems com. White House Energy Project, 1973; mem. adv. com. NSF Project, Wayne State U., 1975—; mem. vis. adv. com. NSF-RANN research program Drexel U. Coll. Engring., 1976—. Mem. adv. bd. U. Detroit Coll. Engring.; bd. visitors Oakland U., Rochester, Mich. Served to lt. USN, 1942-46, to lt. comdr. USNR, 1946-54. Recipient certificate of achievement U.S. Army, 1967, Outstanding Performance awards, 1970, 71, 76; named Disting. Engring. Alumnus, Purdue U., 1966. Registered profl. engr., Ind., Mich. Fellow AIAA; mem. Soc. Automotive Engrs. (chmn. Arch T. Colwell award com. 1975, dir. 1978—), Am. Def. Preparedness Assn., Sigma Xi, Pi Tau Sigma. Contbr. articles on transp., ground vehicles, flight propulsion and project mgmt. to profl. jours. Home: 1540 Stonehaven Rd Ann Arbor MI 48104 Office: US Army Tank-Automotive Command Warren MI 48090

PETRIDES, GEORGE ATHAN, educator, ecologist; b. N.Y.C., Aug. 1, 1916; s. George Athan and Grace Emeline (Ladd) P.; B.S., George Washington U., 1938; M.S., Cornell U., 1940; Ph.D., Ohio State U., 1948; postdoctoral fellow U. Ga., 1963-64; m. Miriam Clarissa Pasma, Nov. 30, 1940; children—George H., Olivia L., Lisa B. Naturalist, Nat. Park Service, Washington and Yosemite, Calif., 1938-43, Glacier Nat. Park, Mont., 1947, Mt. McKinley Nat. Park, Alaska, 1959; game technician W.Va. Conservation Commn., Charleston, 1941; instr. Am. U., 1942-43, Ohio State U., 1946-48; leader Tex. Coop. Wildlife unit, asso. prof. wildlife mgmt. Tex. A. and M. Coll., 1948-50; asso. prof. wildlife mgmt., zool. and African studies Mich. State U., 1950-58, prof., 1958—; research prof. U. Pretoria, S. Africa, 1965; vis. prof. U. Kiel (Germany), 1967; del. sci. confs., Warsaw, 1960, Nairobi and Salisbury, 1963, Sao Paulo, Aberdeen, 1965, Lucerne, 1966, Varanasi, India, Nairobi, 1967, Oxford, Eng., Paris, 1968, Durban, 1971, Mexico City, 1971, 73, Banff, 1972, Nairobi, Moscow, The Hague, 1974, Johannesburg, 1977, Sydney, 1978, Kuala Lampur, 1979; participant NSF Expdn., Antarctic, 1972, FAO mission to Afghanistan, 1972, World Bank mission to Malaysia, 1975. Fulbright research awards in E. Africa, Nat. Parks Kenya, 1953-54, Uganda, 1956-57; N.Y. Zool. Soc. grantee, Ethiopia, Sudan, 1957, Thailand, 1977; Mich. State U. grantee, Nigeria, 1962, Zambia, 1966, Kenya, 1969, Africa, 1970, 71, 73, Greece, Iran, 1974, Botswana, 1977, Papua, New Guinea, Thailand, 1979; Iran Dept. Environment grantee, 1977; Smithsonian Instn. grantee, India and Nepal, 1967, 68, 75, 77; World Wildlife Fund grantee, W. Africa, 1968. Served to lt. USNR, 1943-46. Mem. Am. Ornithologists Union, Am. Soc. Mammalogists, Wildlife Soc. (exec. sec. 1953), Wilderness Soc., Am. Comm. Internat. Wildlife Protection, Ecol. Soc., Fauna Preservation Soc., E. African Wildlife Soc., Internat. Union Conservation Nature, Zool. Soc. So. Africa, Sigma Xi. Presbyn. Author: Field Guide to Trees and Shrubs, 1958, 2d edit., 1972. Editor wildlife mgmt. terrestial sect. Biol. Abstracts, 1947-72. Contbr. articles to biol. publs. Home: 4895 Barton Rd Williamston MI 48895 Office: Dept Fisheries and Wildlife Mich State U East Lansing MI 48824

PETRIE, DANIEL MANNIX, film, theatre and TV dir.; b. Glace Bay, N.S., Can., Nov. 26, 1920; s. William Mark and Mary (Campbell) P.; came to U.S., 1945; B.A., St. Francis Xavier U., Antigonish, N.S., 1942, Litt.D.(hon.), 1974; M.A., Columbia U., 1945; postgrad. Northwestern U., 1947-48; m. Dorothea Grundy, Oct. 27, 1946; children—Daniel Mannix, Donald Mark, Mary Susan and June Anne (twins). Broadway actor, 1945-46; TV dir., 1950—; TV shows include: Eleanor and Franklin, ABC, 1976 (Outstanding Drama award 1976, Emmy award 1976, Critics Circle award 1976, Peabody award 1976), Harry Truman Plain Speaking, Pub. Broadcasting Sta., 1976, Sybil, NBC, 1976 (Emmy award for Outstanding Spl. 1977, Peabody award 1976), Eleanor and Franklin, The White House Years, ABC, 1977, Silent Night, Lonely Night; film dir., 1958—; films include: A Raisin In The Sun, 1960 (Cannes Film Festival Humanitarian award 1963), Buster And Billie, 1973 (London Film Festival Outstanding Film award 1974), Lifeguard, 1975, The Betsy, 1977, Resurrection, 1979; theatre dir., 1958—; plays include: Volpone, 1971, The Cherry Orchard, 1960, Who'll Save The Plowboy, 1961, Monopoly, 1966, Mornin' Sun, 1965, A Shadow of My Enemy, 1958; lectr. U. So. Calif., U. Iowa, U. Calif., San Diego. Served as lt. Canadian Army, 1942. Recipient numerous awards, the most recent being: Emmy award, 1977, Peabody award, 1977, Critics Circle award, 1977. Mem. Acad. Motion Picture Arts Scis., Writer's Guild Am., Dir's. Guild Am. (award 1977), Acad. TV Arts. Office: care Internat Creative Mgmt 8899 Beverly Blvd Los Angeles CA 90048

PETRIE, MRS. DONALD A. (ELIZABETH M. PETRIE), civic worker; b. Camden, N.J.; d. Walter Eugene and Janet (Harbage) Murphy; LL.D., Drexel Inst. Tech., 1964; L.H.D., Ursinus Coll., 1965; LL.D., Temple U., 1972; m. Albert Greenfield, Jan. 14, 1952 (dec. 1967); children—Theodore Hallstrom II, Janet Scurria; m. 3d, Donald A. Petrie, Sept. 12, 1973. Exec. dir. Phila. br. Fgn. Policy Assn., 1947-49, World Affairs Council Phila., 1949-52; chmn. Bd. Trade and Convs., Phila., 1952-54; bd. mgrs. Savs. Fund of Germantown, 1971-73; dir. Blue Cross Phila., 1959-73. Mem. Phila. Bd. Pub. Edn., 1957-71, Pa. Bd. Pub. Edn., 1963-71; mem. Internat. Exhbns. Com.; bd. govs. U. Pa. Mus.; v.p. Phila. Museum Art; trustee Corcoran Gallery, Washington; asso. trustee U. Pa., bd. overseers faculty arts and scis.; co-chmn. nat. adv. com. John F. Kennedy Center for Performing Arts, Washington. Unitarian. Club: Cosmopolitan (Phila.).

PETRIE, DONALD ARCHIBALD, lawyer, investment banker; b. Charleston, W.Va., Apr. 27, 1921; s. James MacFarlin and Emma (Leunig) P.; B.A., U. Chgo., 1942, J.D., 1947; m. Ruth Elfrieda Hauser, June 28, 1942 (div. 1971); children—Ann Elizabeth, James MacFarlin; m. 2d, Elizabeth M. Greenfield, Sept. 12, 1973. Admitted to Ill. bar, 1947, N.Y. bar, 1961, D.C. bar, 1970; partner firm D'Ancona, Pflaum, Wyatt & Riskind, Chgo., 1947-55; v.p. Hertz Corp., 1955-59, exec. v.p., dir., 1959-60; pres. Hertz Am. Express Internat., Ltd., 1960-61; chmn. exec. com. Avis Rent A Car, 1962-66; partner Lazard Freres & Co., N.Y.C., 1967-71, 78—; of counsel Coudert Bros., Washington, 1973-74; pub. Washington Monitor, 1975-77; dir. Harcourt Brace Jovnnovich, Inc., Fin. Fedn., Inc. Treas., Democratic Nat. Com., 1972. Unitarian. Clubs: Univ. (N.Y.C.); Nat. Press (Washington).

PETRIE, DONALD JOSEPH, banker; b. N.Y.C., Sept. 2, 1921; s. John and Elizabeth (Thomson) P.; B.B.A., Manhattan Coll., 1950; m. Jane Adams, Aug. 27, 1949; children—R. Scott, Anne, Elizabeth, Douglas, Susan. Personnel mgr. Otis Elevator Co., N.Y.C., 1951-59; personnel dir. Brown Bros. Harriman & Co., N.Y.C., 1959-68; exec. v.p. U.S. Trust Co., N.Y.C., 1968—; lectr., Baruch Sch. Bus., Coll. City N.Y., 1955-58; pres., chmn. exec. and fin. coms., dir. Webster Apts., N.Y.C., BanCap Corp., N.Y.C. Mem. fin. devel. com. YMCA Greater N.Y. Served to capt. USAAF, 1942-46. Mem. N.Y. Chamber Commerce and Industry (chmn. mgmt. edn. and adv. com. 1964—), N.Y. Personnel Mgmt. Assn. Author: Explaining Pay Policy, 1969; Handling Employee Questions About Pay, 1976. Home: 11 Fairview Ave Great Neck NY 11023 Office: 45 Wall St New York City NY 10005

PETRIK, EUGENE VINCENT, coll. pres.; b. Little Ferry, N.J., May 25, 1932; s. Ferdinand Vincent and Anna Agnes (Komarek) P.; B.S., Fairleigh Dickinson U., 1955; M.A., Columbia U., 1957, Ed.D., 1959; postdoctoral student Stevens Inst. Tech., 1961-62; m. Helen Veliky, June 26, 1955; children—John, Mark, Thomas, James. Instr. physics Fairleigh Dickinson U., 1957-59; asst. prof. gen. sci. N.Y. U., N.Y.C., 1959-60; asso. prof. Seton Hall U., 1960-65, prof., 1965-68; v.p. Mt. St. Mary's Coll., Los Angeles, 1968-73; pres. Bellarmine Coll., Louisville, 1973—. Mem. adv. council TRY Found., Los Angeles, 1971-73. Bd. dirs. Kentuckiana Metroversity, 1973—, Chaminade Prep. Sch., Los Angeles, 1971-73, Bright Future Child Devel. Center, Compton, Calif., 1971-73. Sci. Manpower fellow Columbia, 1957, 59; Am. Council Edn. fellow acad. adminstrn. internship program, 1966-67. Mem. Council Ind. Ky. Colls. and Univs. (dir. 1973—), Ky. Ind. Coll. Found. (dir. 1973—). Author: Modern High School Physics, 1959; Inductive Calculus, 1967. Home: 1609 Dundee Way Louisville KY 40205

PETROCELLI, FRANK JOHN, pharm. co. exec.; b. Astoria, N.Y., Dec. 3, 1933; s. Frank John and Gelsy (Nappi) P.; B.S., St. John's U., Jamaica, N.Y., 1969; m. Jeanne Therese Anatrella, June 7, 1958; children—Frank John III, Lynne, Gerard. Chief accountant d-Con Co. Inc., N.Y.C., 1957-61; with Sterling Drug Inc., N.Y.C., 1961—, asst. treas., 1972, treas., 1973—; dir. Zimpro Inc. Mem. Carmel (N.Y.) Indsl. Devel. Agy. Served with U.S. Army, 1953-55. Mem. Commerce and Industry Assn., Stock Transfer Assn. Republican. Roman Catholic. Home: MacGregor Dr Mahopac NY 10541 Office: 90 Park Ave New York NY 10016

PETRONE, ROCCO A., business exec.; b. Amsterdam, N.Y., Mar. 31, 1926; s. Anthony and Theresa (DeLuca) P.; B.S., U.S. Mil. Acad., 1946; degree Mech. Engring., Mass. Inst. Tech., 1952; D.Sc. (hon.) Rollins Coll., 1969; m. Ruth Holley, Oct. 29, 1955; children—Teresa, Nancy, Kathryn, Michael. Devel. officer Redstone Missile Devel., Huntsville, Ala., 1952-55; mem. army gen. staff Dept. Army, Washington, 1956-60; mgr. Apollo program Kennedy Space Center, 1960-66, dir. launch ops., 1966-69, Apollo program dir. NASA, Washington, 1969-73, dir. Marshall Space Flight Center, Huntsville, Ala., 1973-74, asso. adminstr. NASA, Washington, 1974-75; pres., chief exec. officer Nat. Center for Resource Recovery, Washington, 1975—. Decorated D.S.M. with 2 clusters NASA; Commendatore Ordine al Merito (Italy). Fellow Am. Inst. Aeros. and Astronautics; mem. Nat. Acad. Engring., Sigma Xi. Home: 1353 Macbeth St McLean VA 22101

PETROU, PIERRE JEAN, fishing industry exec.; b. Alexandria, Egypt, July 23, 1914 s. Jean and Marie (Gabriel) P.; student Am. Mission Sch., 1928-31; m. Tahani Elezaby, Mar. 15, 1948; children—Said, Mona Petrou Harchetts, Laila; came to U.S., 1946, naturalized, 1953. Pres., Internat. Proteins Corp., Fairfield, N.J., 1955—, Pasco Foods Corp., Fairfield, 1976—; pres., dir., chmn. bd. Animalfeeds Internat. Corp., Panama, Pesquera Taboguilla S.A., Panama, Xcellent Products S.A., Panama, Empacadora Nacional S.A., Guayaquil, Ecuador, Atlantic Shippers Balt., Inc., Atlantic Shippers, Inc., Morehead City, N.C., Atlantic Shippers of Tex., Inc., Port Arthur, Petrou Fisheries, Inc., Empire, La. Home: 123 Fairfield Rd Fairfield NJ 07006 Office: 123 Fairfield Rd Fairfield NJ 07006. *Learning from one's failures is the road to success.*

PETRY, HERBERT CHARLES, JR., lawyer; b. Carrizo Springs, Tex., Aug. 10, 1917; s. Herbert C. and Florence (Votaw) P.; diploma Trinity U., 1936; LL.B., U. Tex., 1947; m. Josephine L. White, July 17, 1947; children—Boothe, John. Admitted to Tex. bar, 1940; since practiced in Carrizo Springs; mem. law firm Petry & Petry. Real estate and bus. holdings; chmn. bd. Union State Bank, Tri Motor Sales, Inc., 1975—; dir. Central Power & Light Co., Dimmit Supply Co., Secon, Inc., LaMantia, Cullom, Collier & Co. Mem. Tex. Economy Commn. Trustee Southwest Research; regent Inst. Tex. Cultures, 1977—. Recipient Bernardo O'Higgins medal Pres. Chile, 1950, Distinguished Alumni award Trinity U., 1968. Mem. Am., Tex., Dimmit County (pres.) bar assns., Tex. (pres. 1972), South Tex. (exec. com., Mr. South Tex. 1966) chambers commerce, Delta Theta Phi. Methodist (trustee). Club: Lions (dist. gov. 1944-45, internat. dir. 1945-47, v.p. 1947-50, chmn. bd. internat. relations 1946-50, pres. 1950-51). Home: Petry Pl Carrizo Springs TX 78834 Office: Petry Law Bldg Carrizo Springs TX 78834

PETRY, RAY C., educator; b. Eaton, Ohio, July 2, 1903; s. Benjamin F. and Jennie (Kitterman) P.; A.B., Manchester Coll., 1926, LL.D., 1948; A.M., U. Chgo., 1927, Ph.D. (fellow), 1932; m. Ruth Mertz, May 29, 1930 (dec. Feb. 1965). Asst. prof. history McPherson (Kans.) Coll., 1929-30, prof. religion, 1933-37; faculty Manchester Coll., 1930-31; asst. prof. ch. history Duke Div. Sch., 1937-43, asso. prof., 1943-45, prof., 1945-72, James B. Duke prof. ch. history, 1964-72, emeritus, 1972—. Sr. fellow Southeastern Inst. Medieval and Renaissance Studies, U. N.C., 1965; prof. ch. history summers Union Theol. Sem., also Columbia, 1947, 55, Iliff Sch. Theology, 1949, 75, So. Meth. U., 1953; found. lectr. Crozer Theol. Sem., 1948; Lilly Found. lectr. Goshen (Ind.) Coll., 1958; lectr. ch. history U. Oreg., West Coast colls., 1959; European editorial researcher Library Christian Classics, 1954; Gheens hist. lectr. So. Bapt. Theol. Sem., 1966; Centennial lectr. U. Chgo. Div. Sch., 1967; Carver-Barnes Meml. lectr. Southeastern Bapt. Theol. Sem., 1971; James A. Gray lectr. Duke, 1972; vis. prof. Pacific Luth. U., 1977; guest mem. Mansfield Coll., Oxford (Eng.) U., 1968. Mem. council Duke, 1952-54, acad. council, 1963-65, Duke library council, 1957-60, exec. com., 1958-60; participant Roman Cath.-Protestant Colloquium, Harvard U., 1963. Joint grantee Duke U. Research Council, Carnegie Found. for Advancement Teaching. Mem. Am. Soc. Ch. History (pres. 1951; hon. mem. council 1952—; editorial bd. 1947-74), Phi Beta Kappa. Author: Francis of Assisi, 1941, 2d edit., 1964; No Uncertain Sound, 1948; Preaching in the Great Tradition, 1950; Christian Eschatology and Social Thought, 1956; Late Medieval Mysticism, 1957; History of Christianity, vol. I, 1962; (with others) Medieval and Renaissance Studies, 1966, The Impact of the Church Upon Its Culture, 1968. Contbr. to jours., Commissio Internationalis Bonaventuriana Centenary, Vol. II, 1973, Festschrift Duke University, 1974, Ency. Brit. Home: 1301 Highlands Pkwy N Apt 429 Tacoma WA 98406

PETRY, THOMAS EDWIN, mfg. co. exec.; b. Cin., Nov. 20, 1939; s. Edwin Nicholas and Leonora Amelia (Zimpelman) P.; B.S., U. Cin., 1962; M.B.A., Harvard, 1964; m. Mary Helen Gardner, Aug. 25, 1962; children—Thomas Richard, Stephen Nicholas, Daniel Gardner. Sales engr. Air Products & Chems., Inc., Allentown, Pa., 1964-68; group v.p. Eagle-Picher Industries, Inc., Cin., 1968—. Republican. Clubs: Queen City, Terrace Park Country. Home: 4 Lexington Circle Terrace Park OH 45174 Office: 580 Walnut St Cincinnati OH 45202

PETRYSHYN, WALTER VOLODYMYR, educator; b. Lviv, Ukraine, Jan. 22, 1929; s. Vasyl and Maria (Pasirska) P.; B.A., Columbia, 1953, M.S., 1954, Ph.D., 1961; m. Arcadia Olenska, Sept. 2, 1956. Came to U.S., 1950, naturalized, 1956. Instr. math. Notre Dame Coll., S.I., N.Y., 1954-56; lectr. Columbia, 1956-57, Coll. City N.Y., 1959-61; temporary mem. Courant Inst. Math. Sci., N.Y. U., 1961-64; asst. prof. U. Chgo., 1964-66, asso. prof., 1966; prof. math. Rutgers U., New Brunswick, N.J., 1967—. Mem. Am. Math. Soc., Soc. Indsl. and Applied Math., Shevchenko Sci. Soc., Ukrainian Acad. Arts and Scis. Contbr. articles to profl. jours. Originator theory of P-compact and A-proper mappings and application to ordinary and partial differential equations. obtained most gen. fixed point theorem for I-set and I-ball contractions; developed degree and index theories for multivalued noncompact mappings. Home: 167 Willowbrook Dr North Brunswick NJ 08902

PETSCHEK, HARRY EWALD, physicist; b. Prague, Czechoslovakia, Sept. 12, 1930; came to U.S., 1938, naturalized, 1945; s. Hans and Eva (Epler) P.; student Cornell U., 1952, Ph.D., 1955; children—Dell Salza, Bruce, Kim, Philip. Instr., Princeton U., 1955-56; prin. research scientist Avco Everett Research Lab., Everett, Mass., 1956-68; asso. dir., 1968-72, pres., 1973-78; v.p. Avco Corp., Greenwich, Conn., 1973—; chmn., chief exec. officer Avco Everett Research Lab., Inc., 1978—; dir. Jersey Nuclear-Avco Isotopes, Inc., Bellevue, Wash. Fellow Am. Phys. Soc., AIAA; mem. Am. Geophysical Union, AAAS, Am. Soc. Artificial Internal Organs, Indsl. Research Inst. Office: 2385 Revere Beach Pkwy Everett MA 02149

PETTENGILL, BEATON FRANCIS, paper co. exec.; b. Englewood, N.J., July 18, 1923; s. Francis Wilbur and Elizabeth (Smith) P.; B.A., Muskingum Coll., 1947; postgrad. Ohio State U., 1947-48; m. Margaret Frances Bradley, Sept. 2, 1944; children—John Bradlev, Matthew Beaton. With Corco, Inc., Columbus, Ohio, 1948-54, 66—, gen. mgr., exec. v.p., 1970-75, pres., 1975-77 also dir.; pres. Corco div. Western Kraft paper group Williamette Industries, Inc., Portland, Oreg., 1977—. with W.Va. Corrugated Container Co., Huntington, 1954-62, v.p., gen. mgr., 1956-60, pres., 1960-62. Bd. dirs. United Appeal, 1960-62, YMCA, 1959-62, Boys Club Huntington, 1960-62; bd. dirs. Jr. Achievement Central Ohio, 1972—, also pres.; trustee Muskingum Coll., New Concord, O., 1971—. Served with USMCR, 1942-46. Mem. Central Ohio Mgmt. Assn. (dir. 1972—). Rotarian. Clubs: Scioto Country, Athletic, Newcomen (Columbus). Home: 4305 Waybourn Rd Columbus OH 43220 Office: PO Box 494 Worthington OH 43085. *Press on. Persistence. Set goals. Single-minded purpose. The Golden Rule.*

PETTENGILL, GORDON H(EMENWAY), physicist; b. Providence, Feb. 10, 1926; s. Rodney Gordon and Frances (Hemenway) P.; B.S., M.I.T., 1948; Ph.D., U. Calif., Berkeley, 1955; m. Pamela Anne Wolfenden, Oct. 28, 1967; children—Mark Robert, Rebecca Jane. Staff mem. Lincoln Lab., M.I.T., Lexington, 1954-63, 65-68; asso. dir. Arecibo (P.R.) Obs., 1963-65, dir., 1968-71; prof. planetary physics, dept. earth and planetary scis. M.I.T., Cambridge, 1971—; Served with inf., Signal Corps, AUS, 1944-46. Decorated Combat Inf. badge. Mem. Am. Phys. Soc., Am. Astron. Soc., AAAS, Internat. Astron. Union, Internat. Radio Sci. Union, Nat. Acad. Sci., Am. Acad. Arts and Sci., Nat. Audubon Soc., Mass. Audubon Soc. Pioneer several techniques in radar astronomy for describing intrinsec properties of planets and satellites; discovered 59-day rotational period of planet Mercury. Office: Room 54-620 Mass Inst Tech Cambridge MA 02139

PETTENGILL, KROGER, investment counselor; b. Cin., Nov. 4, 1922; s. Irving Wilbert and Gertrude (Kroger) P.; B.A., Princeton U., 1943; m. Kathryn W. Mitchell, Oct. 6, 1945; children—Adele Pettengill Bunker, Thomas Kroger, Charles Abbott. With Provident Bank, Cin., 1946-49; with 1st Nat. Bank Cin., 1949-68, v.p., 1958-64, pres., 1964-68; pres. C/B Fin. Counsel, Inc. Cin., 1973-76, Kroger, Pettengill Fin. Counsel, Inc., 1976—; dir. Cin. br. Fed. Res. Bank Cleve., 1965-67. Gen. budget com. Community Chest and Council Cin. Area, 1960-66; trustee, chmn. bd., chmn. investment com. Children's Hosp. Med. Center, Cin.; chmn. adv. com. to dean U. Cin. Coll. Medicine; trustee, chmn. bd. Berea (Ky.) Coll. Republican. Episcopalian. Clubs: Commercial, Commonwealth, Queen City, Camargo (Cin.). Home: 4750 Willow Hills Ln Cincinnati OH 45243 Office: 1831 Carew Tower Cincinnati OH 45202

PETTERSEN, KJELL WILL, stock broker; b. Oslo, Norway, June 19, 1927; s. Jens Will and Ragna O. (Wickstrom) P.; came to U.S., 1946, naturalized, 1957; student Zion Theol. Sch., 1945-46, N.Y. Inst. Finance, 1955-56; m. Marilyn Ann Stevens, Aug. 16, 1952; children—Thomas W., Maureen, Kevin W., Maryann, Kathleen. Mgr., A.M. Kidder & Co., N.Y.C., 1954-64; sr. v.p., sec., dir. Halle & Stieglitz, Fillor Bullard Co., Inc., 1964-73; sr. v.p., dir. mktg. Parrish Securities, Inc., N.Y.C., 1973-74; cons. Loeb, Rhoades & Co., N.Y.C., 1974-79; v.p., div. mgr. Bache Halsey Stuart Shields Inc., N.Y.C., 1979—; dir. Scandinavian Systems, Inc., Atlanta. Allied mem. N.Y. Stock Exchange, Am. Stock Exchange, Chgo. Bd. Trade. Dir. Norwegian affairs N.Y. World Fair, 1964-65. Democratic candidate N.Y. State Assembly, Nassau County, 1962. Served with U.S. Army, 1949-53. Mem. N.Y. C. of C., Security Industry Assn., Nat. Assn. Security Dealers, Scandinavian Found., Bankers Club of Am., Norwegian-Am. C. of C. (dir.). Club: Norwegian (N.Y.C.). Home: North Shore Towers 270-22L Grand Central Pkwy Floral Park NY 11005 Office: 100 Gold St Bache Plaza New York NY 10038

PETTERSON, DONALD K., fgn. service officer; b. Huntington Park, Calif., Nov. 17, 1930; s. Walter H. and Muriel Frances (McIntyre) P.; student San Luis Obispo Jr. Coll., 1952-53; B.A., U. Calif., Santa Barbara, 1956, M.A., 1960; postgrad. UCLA, 1959-60, Stanford U.,

1967-68; m. Julieta Rovirosa Argudin, Aug. 26, 1961; children—Susan, Julie, John. Personnel analyst State of Calif., 1958-59; teaching asst. UCLA, 1959-60; commd. fgn. service office Dept. State, 1960; vice consul Am. Consulate, Mexico City, 1961-62; vice consul Am. Consulate, Zanzibar, 1963-64, prin. officer, 1964-65; polit. officer Lagos, 1966-67; served in personnel office Dept. State, Washington, 1968-70; dep. chief of mission U.S. Mission, Freetown, Sierra Leone, 1970-72; polit. counselor, Pretoria, 1972-75; mem. policy planning staff Dept. State, Washington, 1975-77, dir. Office So. African Affairs, 1977-78, dep. asst. sec. of state, 1978; U.S. ambassador to Somalia, Mogadiscio, 1978—. Served with USN, 1948-52. Recipient Superior Honor award Dept. State, 1964, 71; named Alumnus of Yr., U. Calif., Santa Barbara, 1965. Mem. Am. Fgn. Service Assn. Home: 204 N Chorro Apt 30 San Luis Obispo CA 93401 Office: Mogadiscio Dept State Washington DC 20520

PETTERSON, RODNEY RUSSELL, ins. co. exec.; b. Paxton, Ill., Oct. 6, 1932; s. Charles Russell and Ella (Hanson) P.; B.A., DePauw U., 1954; postgrad. Ind. U. Law Sch., 1963-64; m. Merry Ann Chester, July 2, 1955; children—Russell, Polly. Pres., Duval Water Conditioning, Inc., Jacksonville, Fla., 1957-58; asst. dir. personnel Am. United Life Ins. Co., Indpls., 1959-61, dir. methods and procedures, 1961-63, with reins. sales, 1963-65, regional v.p. reins. sales, 1965-69, sr. v.p. reins. 1969—; dir. Affiliated Services Corp., AUL Equity Sales Corp. Served to 1st lt. USAF, 1954-57. Mem. Indpls. C. of C., Phi Kappa Psi (dir.). Republican. Methodist. Mason (Shriner), Rotarian. Club: Highland Golf and Country. Home: 12035 Hampton Ct Carmel IN 46032 Office: 1 W 26th St Indianapolis IN 46206

PETTERSON, VERNON TENNANT, mfg. co. exec.; b. Marshalltown, Iowa, Sept. 27, 1915; s. Oscar L. and Lillian (Tennant) P.; student U. Chgo., 1934-35; B.A., Denison U., 1937; m. Ellen Dorothy Petersen, Dec. 14, 1940; children—Karen Louise, Lynn E. (Mrs. Robert E. Bender). Indsl. engr. George S. May Co., 1939-41; mgr. priorities and prices, then asst. plant mgr. C.A. Dunham Co., 1941-50; with Joy Mfg. Co., 1951—, treas., 1968—, v.p., 1971—; dir. Aero Mecanica Darma S.A., Sao Paulo, Brazil, Maquina de Proceso, Mexico City, Mustang Equipment Co., Los Angeles, Western Steel Co., Salt Lake City, Smith & Harris Machine Co., Cleve. Bd. dirs. Little Lake Dinner Theatre, Allegheny Trails council Boy Scouts Am., Pitts. Council for Internat. Visitors. Served with U.S. Army, 1944-46; ETO. Mem. Internat. Platform Assn. Elk. Clubs: Chartiers Country, Fellows, Amen Corner, Downtown of Pitts. (dir.). Home: 361 Orchard Dr Pittsburgh PA 15228 Office: Joy Mfg Co Henry W Oliver Bldg Pittsburgh PA 15222

PETTEWAY, SAMUEL BRUCE, coll. pres.; b. Fayetteville, N.C., July 18, 1924; s. Walter Bernard and Margaret Maysie (Cole) P.; B.S., N.C. State U., 1949, M.Ed., 1966, Ed.D., 1968; m. Eleanor Glenn Sugg, Nov. 27, 1948; children—Margaret Petteway Small, Samuel Bruce. Gen. mgr. Homeowners Ins. and Realty Co., 1960-63; engring. tech. dept. chmn., dean occupational and transfer programs, dir. evening programs Lenoir County Community Coll., 1963-68; pres. Coll. of the Albemarie, Elizabeth City, N.C., 1968-75, N.C. Wesleyan Coll., Rocky Mount, 1975—; dir. 1st Union Nat. Bank, Elizabeth City, 1970-75; adj. prof. Va. Poly. Inst. and State U., 1973-75. Pres. chpt. Am. Cancer Soc., 1960-61; bd. dirs. Rocky Mount Acad., 1979—; chmn. deferred giving com. N.C. Methodist Found., 1979—; chmn. council on ministries 1st United Meth. Ch., Rocky Mount, 1980-81. Served with USNR, 1941-46. Named Tar Heel of Week, News and Observer, 1975, Today's Outstanding N.C. Citizen, WNCT-TV, 1975. NSF fellow U. Ill., 1963. Mem. N.C. Assn. Colls. and Univs., N.C. Conf. United Meth. Ch. (chmn. bd. trustees 1973-79), Rocky Mount C. of C. (dir. 1980—), Phi Kappa Phi, Theta Alpha Phi. Democrat. Clubs: Benvenue Country, Galaxy Social, Rotary (pres.-elect 1980-81). Home: NC Wesleyan Coll Rocky Mount NC 27801

PETTI, ANTHONY GAETANO, educator; b. London, Feb. 12, 1932; s. Gaetano and Letizia (Terroni) P.; B.A., Univ. Coll., London, 1955, M.A., 1957, D.Lit., 1970; m. Lorna Virginia Rowsell, Aug. 10, 1957; children—Gregory Richard, Lydia Mary, Jeremy John, Damian Andrew. Asst., Univ. Coll., London, 1955-57, Quain student, 1957-59, lectr. dept. English, 1960-69; prof. U. Calgary, Alta., Can., 1969—, head dept. English, 1971-74, Killam residential fellow, 1977; dir. U. London Catholic Choir and Orch., 1953-67; bd. dirs. studies in English, music and palaeography U. London, 1965-69; dir. Calgary Renaissance Singers and Players, 1970—. Examiner, external expert Civil Service Commn. Gt. Britain, 1963-69. Sec. Joseph Crabtree Found., 1965. Served with Royal Arty., 1950-52, Hon. Arty. Co., 1952-55. Can. Council grantee, 1971, leave fellow, 1974-75; Harkness Commonwealth Fund fellow, 1959-60; Huntington Library fellow, 1970; hon. research fellow Univ. Coll., London, 1974-75; vis. fellow Clare Hall, Cambridge U., 1976-77. Fellow Royal Hist. Soc., Soc. Antiquaries; mem. MLA, Learned Socs. Can., Cath. Record Soc. (council), Pacific N.W. Renaissance Conf., Victorian Studies Assn. Western Can., Hopkins Soc., Malone Soc. Author: Letters of Richard Verstegan, 1959; Ellesmere Manuscripts, 1968; New Catholic Hymnal, 1971; English Literary Hands from Chaucer to Dryden, 1977; Catholicism in Elizabethan Staffordshire, 1979. Editor: Glapthorne's Lady Mother, 1959; Anerio, Requiem Mass, 1966; Western Wind Mass (John Shepherd), 1976; The Latin Motet: Italy, 1977; The Latin Motet: England, 1977; The Latin Motet: Spain, 1977; The Latin Motet: Germany, 1977; The Latin Motet: Low Countries, 1977; The Latin Motet: Christmas and Advent, 1977; The Latin Motet: Three Voices, 1979; The Latin Motet: France, 1979, numerous others. Editorial bd. Ariel; exec. bd. Records of Early English Drama. Contbr. articles to profl. jours.; composer choral music. Home: 1445 24th St SW Calgary AB Canada

PETTIGREW, RICHARD ALLEN, govt. ofcl.; b. Charleston, W.Va., June 10, 1930; s. Grady Lewis and Otella Lee (Overton) P.; B.A. in Polit. Sci., U. Fla., 1953, LL.B., 1957; m. Ann Moorhead, Mar. 8, 1954; children—Jill Elizabeth, Grady Lewis. Admitted to Fla. bar, 1957; mem. firm Pettigrew & Bailey, Miami, 1969-76, Pettigrew, Arky, Freed, Stearns, Watson & Greer, Miami, 1976-77; asst. to Pres. for reorgn., White House, Washington, 1977—. Active, Met. Dade County Community Relations Bd., 1974-76, chmn., 1976-77; mem. Fla. Ho. of Reps., 1963-72, chmn. govtl. reorgn. and efficiency com., 1968-70, speaker, 1970-72; mem. Constl. Revision Commn., 1965-67; mem. Fla. Senate, 1972-74, chmn. Com. on Criminal Justice, 1973-74; past pres. Young Democrats of Fla., Dade County Young Dems.; state chmn. Young Citizens for Johnson-Humphrey; bd. dirs. Hist. Assn. So. Fla.; trustee Legis 50. Served with USAF, 1953-55. Recipient St. Petersburg Times award, 1967; named Most Valuable Mem. of House (Allen Morris award), 1969, architect of Fla.'s Exec. Br. Reorgn., 1969, Outstanding Fla. Democrat, Fla. Young Dems., 1971, Lawmaker-Newsmaker of Year, Capitol Press Corps, 1971. Mem. Am., Fla., Dade County (past pres. young lawyers sect.) bar assns. Congregational. Home: 5108 Wehawken Rd Bethesda MD 20016 Office: 134 Old Exec Office Bldg Washington DC 20500

PETTIGREW, THOMAS FRASER, educator, social psychologist; b. Richmond, Va., Mar. 14, 1931; s. Joseph Crane and Janet (Gibb) P.; A.B. in Psychology, U. Va., 1952; M.A. in Social Psychology, Harvard, 1955, Ph.D., 1956; m. Ann Hallman, Feb. 25, 1956; 1 son, Mark Fraser. Research asso. Inst. Social Research, U. Natal, Republic South Africa, 1956; asst. prof. psychology U. N.C., 1956-57; asst. prof. social psychology Harvard, 1957-62, lectr., 1962-64, asso. prof., 1964-68, prof. social psychology, 1968-74, prof. social psychology and sociology, 1974—. Chmn., Episcopal presiding Bishop's Adv. Com. on Race Relations, 1961-63; v.p. Episcopal Soc. Cultural and Racial Unity, 1962-63; mem. Mass. Gov.'s Adv. Com. on Civil Rights, 1962-64; social sci. cons. U.S. Commn. Civil Rights, 1966-71; mem. White House Task Force on Edn., 1967. Guggenheim fellow, 1967-68; NATO sr. scientist fellow, 1974; fellow Center Advanced Study in Behavioral Scis., 1975-76; Sydney Spivack fellow in intergroup relations Am. Sociol. Assn., 1978. Fellow Am. Psychol. Assn., Am. Sociol. Assn.; mem. Soc. Psychol. Study Social Issues (council 1962-66, pres. 1967-68). Author: (with E.Q. Campbell) Christians in Racial Crisis: A Study of the Little Rock Ministry, 1959; A Profile of the Negro American, 1964; Racially Separate or Together?, 1971. Editor: Racial Discrimination in the United States, 1975; The Sociology of Race Relations: Reflection and Reform, 1978; editorial bd. Jour. Social Issues, 1959-64, Sociometry, 1977-80; asso. editor Am. Sociol. Rev., 1963-65; adv. bd. Integrated Edn., 1963—, Phylon, 1965—, Edn. and Urban Society, 1968—, Ethnic and Racial Studies, 1978—. Contbr. articles to profl. publs. Home: 5 Follen St Cambridge MA 02138 Office: 1330 William James Hall Harvard Univ Cambridge MA 02138

PETTIJOHN, FRANCIS JOHN, geologist; b. Waterford, Wis., June 20, 1904; A.B., U. Minn., 1924, A.M., 1924, Ph.D., 1930; D.H.L., Johns Hopkins U., 1978; m. Dorothy Bracken, 1930; children—Norma Pettijohn Friedemann, Clare Pettijohn Maher, Loren. Instr., Macalester Coll., 1924-25, Oberlin Coll., 1925-29, U. Minn., 1928-29; instr. U. Chgo., 1929-31, asst. prof., 1931-39, asso. prof., 1939-46, prof., 1946-52; prof. Johns Hopkins U., Balt., 1952-73, prof. emeritus, 1973—, chmn. dept. geology, 1963-68, acting chmn. dept. earth and planetary scis., 1970; geologist U.S. Geol. Survey, 1943-53; cons. Shell Oil Co., 1953-63; mem. adv. panel for earth scis. NSF, 1959-62; mem. adv. bd. Petroleum Research Found., 1963-65. Recipient Twenhofel medal Soc. Econ. Paleontologists and Mineralogists, 1974; Wollaston medal Geol. Soc. London, 1974, Penrose medal Geol. Soc. Am., 1975. Fellow AAAS, Geol. Soc. London, Geol. Soc. Am.; hon. mem. Soc. Econ. Paleontologists and Mineralogists (pres. 1955-56); corr. mem. Geol. Soc. Finland; mem. Am. Assn. Petroleum Geologists, Am. Acad. Arts and Scis., Nat. Acad. Scis., Phi Beta Kappa, Sigma Xi. Author numerous books in field including: Sedimentary Rocks, 1949, 3d edit., 1973; (with P.E. Potter) Paleocurrents and Basin Analysis, 1963, 2d edit., 1977; (with P.E. Potter, R. Siever) Sand and Sandstone, 1972; contbr. articles to profl. jours.; editor Jour. Geology, 1947-52. Home: 512 Woodbine Ave Towson MD 21204 Office: Dept Earth and Planetary Scis Johns Hopkins U Baltimore MD 21218

PETTINE, RAYMOND JAMES, judge; b. Providence, July 6, 1912; s. James and Alvina (Caruole) P.; student Providence Coll., 1931-34; LL.B., Boston U., 1937, LL.M., 1940; LL.D., Our Lady of Providence Seminary, 1967; m. Lidia Golini, Sept. 6, 1941; 1 dau., Lydia A. Admitted to R.I. bar, 1940, also U.S. Supreme Ct., U.S. Ct. Mil. Appeals, ICC; practiced in Providence, 1946-61; spl. counsel atty. gen. Dept. State R.I., 1948-52; asst. atty. gen., 1952-61; U.S. atty. dist. R.I., Providence, 1961-66; U.S. Dist. Court judge for R.I., 1966—, now chief judge. Vice pres., treas. Italian Collection and Reading Room Com., 1957-58; mem. R.I. Commn. to Encourage Morality in Youth, 1958-60, R.I. Family Ct. Study Commn., 1956-57. Bd. dirs., exec. com. R.I. Philharmonic Orch. Served to maj. AUS, 1941-46. Mem. R.I. Bar Assn., Italian-Am. Vets., Res. Officers Assn. R.I. (past pres.), Nat. Assn. Christians and Jews (dir.), Amvets (past judge adv. R.I.), Order Sons Italy. Club: Serra Internat. Office: Federal Bldg Providence RI 02903*

PETTINGA, CORNELIUS WESLEY, pharm. co. exec.; b. Mille Lacs, Minn., Nov. 10, 1921; s. R.C. and Adrianna (Landaal) P.; A.B., Hope Coll., 1942; postgrad. Syracuse U., 1943; Ph.D. in Chemistry, Iowa State Coll., 1949; m. Yvonne Imogene Svoboda, Dec. 22, 1943; children—Julie, Steven, Mark, Tom, Jennifer. With Eli Lilly & Co., 1949—, v.p. research, devel. and control, 1964-70, v.p., asst. to pres., 1970-72, exec. v.p., 1972—, dir., 1966—; pres. Elizabeth Arden, Inc., 1971-72, now dir.; dir. Elanco Products, Eli Lilly Internat. Corp. Bd. overseers Sweet Briar Coll.; chmn. chancellor's adv. bd. Ind. U./Purdue U.; trustee, bd. govs., finance com., exec. com. Indpls. Mus. Art; mem. med. explorer post com. Crossroads Am. council Boy Scouts Am.; bd. dirs. Hanover Coll.; trustee Park-Tudor Sch., Coe Coll.; mem. corp. vis. com. dept. nutrition and food science Mass. Inst. Tech. Served with USNR, 1943-45. Fellow Nat. Cancer Inst., 1949. Mem. Am. Chem. Soc., Bus. Com. for Arts, Indpls. C. of C. (new bus. devel. com.), Newcomen Soc. N.Am., Sigma Xi. Clubs: Lambs, University, Columbia, Woodstock, Meridian Hills Country (Indpls.); Piedmont (Lynchburg, Va.); John's Island (Vero Beach, Fla.). Contbr. articles to profl. jours. Home: 445 Somerset Dr Indianapolis IN 46260 Office: 307 E McCarty St Indianapolis IN 46206

PETTINGILL, OLIN SEWALL, JR., zoologist, ornithologist; b. Belgrade, Maine, Oct. 30, 1907; s. Olin Sewall and Marion Bradbury (Groves) P.; student U. Mich. Biol. Sta., summer 1928; A.B., Bowdoin Coll., 1930, Sc.D. (hon.), 1956; Ph.D., Cornell U., 1933; Sc.D. (hon.), Colby Coll., 1979; m. Eleanor Rice, Dec. 31, 1932; children—Polly-Ann, Mary-Ann. Instr. ornithology Ithaca (N.Y.) Night Sch., 1933; teaching fellow biology Bowdoin Coll., 1933-34; instr. ornithology N.H. Nature Camp at Lost River, summers 1934, 36; instr. biology Westbrook Jr. Coll., Portland, Maine, 1935-36; faculty U. Mich. Biol. Sta., summers 1938-45, 47-57, 59-74; dir. Lab. Ornithology, Cornell U., 1960-73; faculty Carleton Coll., 1936-54, asso. prof. zoology 1946-54. Leader expdn. Falkland Islands, 1953-54, 71-72; lectr. Audubon Screen Tours, 1943—; research asso. Cranbrook Inst. Sci., 1940-45; mem., leader ornithol. expdns Can., Iceland, Argentina, Falkland Islands, Antarctica, N.Z., Mexico for various groups, 1941—; del. 12th Internat. Ornithol. Congress, Helsinki, Finland, 1958, 14th, Oxford, Eng., 1966. Trustee Kents Hill Sch., 1975—. Recipient Arthur A. Allen award Cornell U., 1974. Mem. Wilson Ornithol. Soc. (past pres., sec.), Nat. (dir. 1955-66, 67-75, sec. 1957-59, 63-66), Me. (pres. 1959-60), Audubon socs., Am. Ornithologists Union (sec. 1946-51), Sigma Xi, Pi Delta Epsilon, Psi Upsilon. Author ornithol. works including: The American Woodcock, 1936; Bird Life of the Grand Manan Archipelago, 1939; Ornithology in Laboratory and Field, 4th edit., 1970; A Guide to Bird Finding East of the Mississippi, 1951, 2d edit., 1977; A Guide to Bird Finding West of the Mississippi, 1953; Another Penguin Summer, 1975; author-photog. 10 motion pictures on birds (for Coronet Instructional Media), 1941, 3 for Walt Disney Prodns., 1951. Co-author: Birds of the Black Hills, 1965. Editor-in-chief: Audubon Illustrated Handbook of American Birds, 1968; editor sect. on Aves on Biol. Abstracts, 1942-53, The Bird Watcher's America, 1965; editor The Living Bird, 1962-64, co-editor, 1965-73; rev. editor Wilson Bull., 1959-69; columnist Audubon mag., 1957-71, contbg. editor, 1978—; adv. editor Nature Books, McGraw-Hill Book Co., 1963-68. Office: Wayne ME 04284

PETTIS-TAKAMINE, SHIRLEY NEIL, former congresswoman; b. Mountain View, Calif., July 12, 1924; d. Harold Oliver and Dorothy Susan (O'Neil) McCumber; student Andrews U., 1942, U. Calif., 1943-44; m. John J. McNulty, Dec. 14, 1943 (dec. Dec. 1945); m. 2d, Jerry L. Pettis, Mar. 2, 1947 (dec. Feb. 1975); children—Peter Dwight, Deborah Neil; m. 3d, Jokichi Takamine, Oct. 21, 1978. Mgr., Magnetic Tape Duplicator, Hollywood, Calif., 1953-67, Audio-Digest Co., Los Angeles, 1951-55; sec.-treas. Pettis, Inc., Hollywood, 1958-64; mgr. citrus and avocado ranch, Pauma Valley, Calif., 1950—; mem. 94th-95th Congresses from 37th Calif. Dist., mem. Internat. Relations Com., Com. on Edn. and Labor; dir. Kemper Corp. Bd. dirs. Women's Research and Edn. Inst.; trustee Redlands U. Mem. adv. council on nat. security and internat. affairs Republican Nat. Com. Mem. Am. Hist. Soc., Nat. Womens Polit. Caucus, Calif. Elected Womens Assn. for Edn. and Research. Republican. Seventh-day Adventist. Clubs: Capitol Hill (Washington); Pauma Valley Country. Home: 616 Firth Ave West Los Angeles CA 90049

PETTIT, ARCH PAULL, electric co. exec.; b. Wheeling, W.Va., May 1, 1928; s. Arch E. and Carolyn P. (Zimmerman) P.; B.S., Case Inst. Tech., 1951; m. Ida Marie Volpe, Oct. 15, 1951; children—Pamela Ann, David Bruce, Jeffery Scott, Timothy Brook, Jason Blair, Robin Lynn. Field supt. Electric Furnace Co., Salem, Ohio, 1951-59; gen. mgr. sales and engring. Tampa (Fla.) Electric Co., 1959-69; gen. sales mgr. Ark. Power and Light Co., Little Rock, 1969-72, v.p. mktg., 1972-73, sr. v.p. customer services, 1973-76, pres., chief operating officer, 1976-77, pres., chief exec. officer, 1977—, dir., 1976—; bd. dirs. Middle South Services, Middle South Utilities, Middle South Energy, Systems Fuels, Inc. Bd. dirs. Ark. Boys Choir, chmn. bd., 1975—; bd. dirs. United Way, Pulaski County, Ark., 1976—, Ark. Symphony Orch., 1977—. Mem. Am. Mktg. Assn., Edison Electric Inst., Energy Mgmt. Commn., Am. Inst. Energy Resource Mgmt. (bd. govs.). Club: Masons. Office: PO Box 551 Little Rock AR 72203*

PETTIT, JOSEPH MAYO, inst. pres.; b. Rochester, Minn., July 15, 1916; s. Joseph Asahel and Florence (Anderson) P.; B.S., U. Calif. at Berkeley, 1938; E.E., Stanford, 1940, Ph.D., 1942; m. Florence Rowell West, June 8, 1940; children—Marjorie Pettit Wilbur, Joseph Roy, Marilyn Pettit Backlund. Instr., U. Calif. at Berkeley, 1940-42; spl. research asso., asst. exec. engr. radio research lab. Harvard, 1942-45; tech. observer USAF, India-China, 1944; asso. tech. dir. Am. Brit. Lab., ETO, 1945; supervising engr. Airborne Instruments Lab., Inc., N.Y.C., 1945-46; faculty Stanford, 1947-72, prof. elec. engring., 1954-72, asso. dean engring., 1955-58, dean Sch. Engring., 1958-72; pres. Ga. Inst. Tech., Atlanta, 1972—. Dir. Varian Assos., Sci. Atlanta, Inc., Ga. Motor Club, Inc. Mem. Army Sci. Adv. Panel, 1957-63; mem. Nat. Sci. Bd., 1977—. Recipient Presdl. certificate Merit; Electronics Achievement award I.R.E. Registered profl. engr., Calif. Fellow IEEE, AAAS; mem. Nat. Acad. Engring., Am. Soc. Engring. Edn. (pres. 1972-73), Ga. Acad. Scis. Congregationalist. Clubs: Rotary; Univ. (N.Y.C.); Cosmos. Author: Electronic Switching, Timing and Pulse Circuits, 1959, 2d edit. (with M.M. McWhorter) 1970; (with others) Very-High-Frequency Techniques, 1947; (with F.E. Terman) Electronic Measurements, 1952; (with McWhorter) Electronic Amplifiers, 1961. Home: 292 10th St NW Atlanta GA 30318

PETTIT, LAWRENCE KAY, univ. system adminstr.; b. Lewistown, Mont., May 2, 1937; s. George Edwin and Dorothy Bertha (Brown) P.; B.A., U. Mont., 1959; A.M., Washington U., St. Louis, 1962; Ph.D. (Univ. fellow, Vilas fellow), U. Wis., 1965; m. Sharon Lee Anderson, June 21, 1961 (div. Oct. 1976); children—Jennifer Anna, Matthew Anderson, Allison Carol, Edward McLean. Legis. asst. U.S. Senate, 1959-60, 62; mem. faculty dept. polit. sci. Pa. State U., 1964-67; mem. adminstrv. staff Am. Council Edn., Washington, 1967-69; chmn. dept. polit. sci. Mont. State U., 1969-72; adminstrv. asst. to gov. State Mont., 1973; commr. higher edn. Mont. Univ. System, Helena, 1973—; mem. various nat. and regional bds. and coms. on higher edn. Mem. Mont. Democratic Reform Commn., 1971. Served with U.S. 1955-63. Mem. Am. Polit. Sci. Assn., AAUP, State Higher Bd. Exec. Officers (exec. com.), ACLU, Sigma Chi. Presbyterian. Clubs: Rotary, Masons, Shriners, Eagles. Author: (with H. Albinski) Political Processes, 2d edit. 1974; (with E. Keynes) Legislative Process in the U.S. Senate, 1969; (with S. Kirkpatrick) Social Psychology of Political Life, 1972; (with Herb Pace) The Invasion of Canada, 1978. Home: 109 S Montana Ave Helena MT 59601 Office: 33 S Last Chance Gulch Helena MT 59601

PETTIT, MANSON BOWERS, psychiatrist; b. Waco, Tex., May 26, 1902; s. Benjamin Franklin and Nancy (Phillips) P.; A.B., Trinity U., 1923; M.D., Vanderbilt U., 1928; m. Dagny Rudback, Mar. 26, 1930; children—Marjorie Pettit James), John Whitney. Intern, Meth. Hosp. So. Calif., 1928-29; rotating gen. intern St. Elizabeth's Hosp., Washington, 1930-31, resident psychiatry, 1931-33, staff psychiatrist, 1933-58, clin. dir., 1958-60; med. supt. State Hosp. Number 2, St. Joseph, Mo., 1960-66; supt. Southwestern State Hosp., Thomasville, Ga., 1966-73; cons. clin. psychiatry Community Mental Health Center, Archbold Meml. Hosp., Thomasville, 1974-79; psychotherapist Washington Inst. Mental Hygiene, 1930-58; organizer Arlington County Mental Hygiene Center, 1947-60. Lectr. mental health, hygiene asso. clin. prof. psychiatry Georgetown U., 1941-60. Mem. St. Joseph Community Welfare Council, 1960—. Diplomate Am. Bd. Psychiatry and Neurology. Fellow Am. Psychiat. Assn.; mem. Interprofl. Inst., AMA, Buchanan County Med. Soc. Methodist. Mason (Shriner), Kiwanian. Club: Shrine. Contbr. to Biol. Abstracts; articles, book revs. to profl. jours. Home: 15311 Pine Orchard Dr Silver Spring MD 20906

PETTIT, ROWLAND, educator, chemist; b. Adelaide, S. Australia, Feb. 6, 1927; s. George William and Selina T. (Underwood) P.; B.Sc., U. Adelaide, 1949, M.Sc., 1950, Ph.D., 1953; Ph.D., U. London, 1957; m. Flora V. Hunter, July 21, 1959; children—George H., Nancy S. Came to U.S., 1957, naturalized, 1969. Faculty, U. Tex., Austin, 1957—, prof. chemistry, 1963—. Seydel-Wooley lectr. Ga. Inst. Tech., 1966; Venable lectr. U. N.C., 1967; Reilly lectr. U. Notre Dame, 1968. Exhbn. of 1851 fellow, 1952-54; I.C.I. research fellow, 1954-57; Sloan research fellow, 1960-64. Fellow Chem. Soc. (London); mem. Nat. Acad. Sci., Am. Chem. Soc. (sec. organometallic div. 1968, S.W. regional award 1968), Am. Acad. Arts and Scis., Alpha Chi Sigma, Phi Lambda Upsilon. Home: 2900 Wade Ave Austin TX 78703

PETTIT, TOM, television news corr.; b. Cin.; grad. U. No. Iowa, 1953; M.A., U. Minn., 1958. Reporter, Sta. WOI-TV, Ames, Iowa, Sta. KCRG-TV, Cedar Rapids, Iowa, Sta. WCCO-TV, Mpls.; with NBC, 1959—, corr. West Coast, 1962-75, Washington corr. NBC News, 1975—. Recipient Peabody award, 3 Emmy awards for reporting. Office: care NBC News 30 Rockefeller Plaza New York NY 10020*

PETTIT, WILLIAM DUTTON, investment counselor; b. Bklyn., May 8, 1920; s. Karl Dravo and Estelle (Fitch) P.; B.A., Princeton, 1941; postgrad. N.Y. U., 1946-49; m. Carole Helene Earle, Dec. 27, 1941; children—Carole Fitch (Mrs. Joseph E. Lovelock, Jr.), Penelope Sherwood (Mrs. Robert Lee Kreinberg, Jr.), William Dutton, Jonathan Earle, Donald Stevenson. With Karl D. Pettit & Co., N.Y.C., 1946-74, partner, 1947-74; pres., treas., dir. Knickerbocker Shares, Inc., 1967-74; pres., dir. Knickerbocker Growth Fund, Inc., 1960-75; v.p., dir. Knickerbocker Fund, 1972-75; exec. v.p., dir. Schuster Fund, 1975—, Liberty Fund, 1975—; v.p.

CNA Mgmt. Co., N.Y.C., 1974-79, CNA Investment Counselors, 1974-79, Neuberger & Berman Mgmt., 1979—. Served from 2d lt. to maj., F.A., AUS, 1941-46; ETO. Decorated Bronze Star. Clubs: Springdale Golf; Princeton Cannon. Home: Ridgeview Rd Princeton NJ 08540 Office: 522 Fifth Ave New York NY 10036

PETTIT, WILLIAM SCHUYLER, ret. coll. pres.; b. Burlington, N.J., Mar. 19, 1909; s. Ivans and Irene (Schuyler) P.; B.S. in Chemistry, U. Pa., 1932, M.S., 1933; Sc.D. (hon.), Ursinus Coll., 1969; m. Marion Burgstresser, June 17, 1939; 1 dau., Isabelle Schuyler Seeman. Chemist, Baeder Adamson Co., Phila., 1928-29; engaged in ind. chem. research and cons., 1935-52; instr. Engring. Def. Tng. Corps, Pa. State U., 1941—; mem. faculty Ursinus Coll., Collegeville, Pa., 1933-76, prof. chemistry, 1944-76; dean coll., 1954-76, v.p. for academic affairs, 1969-72, pres., 1970-76; cons. exptl. program tchr. edn. Temple U., 1955-70. Pres. Worcester Sch. Authority, 1955—; chmn. Worcester-Lower Providence Sch. Authority, 1959—. Recipient Lindback award. Mem. Montgomery County Hist. Soc. (trustee), Am. Chem. Soc., Am. Conf. Acad. Deans, Newcomen Soc., Sigma Xi, Alpha Chi Sigma. Republican. Episcopalian. Clubs: Midday (Phila.); University (N.Y.); Manufacturer's Golf and Country (Oreland, Pa.). Home: 8 Lanai Circle Naples FL 33942 also Quidnet Rd Nantucket MA 02554

PETTIT, WILLIAM THOMAS, reporter; b. Cin., Apr. 23, 1931; s. William Porter and Kathryn (Neely) P.; B.A., Iowa State Tchrs. Coll., 1953; M.A., U. Minn., 1958; m. Betty Trimble, Dec. 22, 1951; children—Debra Lynn, Anne Eileen, William James, Robert Thomas. Reporter, WOI-TV, Ames, Iowa, 1953-55, KCRG-TV, Cedar Rapids, Iowa, 1955-56, WCCO-TV, Mpls., 1956-59; reporter NBC News, Phila., 1959-61, N.Y.C., 1961-62, Los Angeles, 1962-67, Pub. Broadcast Lab., 1967-68; reporter NBC News, Los Angeles, 1968-75, Washington, 1975—. Recipient Emmy award, 1969, 70, 74; Peabody award, 1970; DuPont-Columbia award, 1970, 75; Polk award, 1970; Robert F. Kennedy Journalism award, 1970, 76; Med. Journalism award AMA, 1971. Mem. AFTRA (nat. v.p., bd. dirs.). Office: 4001 Nebraska Ave NW Washington DC 20016

PETTITT, ROGER CARLYLE, lawyer; b. Riverside, Calif., Oct. 27, 1927; s. Thomas Alexander and Edna Victoria (Merrick) P.; grad. Riverside Coll., 1948; B.A., U. Calif. at Berkeley, 1951; LL.B., U. Calif. at Los Angeles, 1954; m. Judith A. Whitman, Aug. 25, 1950; children—Reid, Sally, Susanne. Admitted to Calif. bar, 1955; individual practice law, Los Angeles; partner firm Brant & Pettitt, Los Angeles, 1960—. Chmn., U. Calif. at Los Angeles Found., 1964-66; mem. bd. regents U. Calif., 1968-69; mem. select com. Master Plan Calif. Higher Edn., 1971-72; mem. Calif. Postsecondary Edn. Com., 1974—, chmn., 1976-77; trustee UCLA Found., 1978—. Mem. Order of Coif (pres. law sch. student body 1953-54), U. Calif. at Los Angeles Alumni Assn. (dir. 1960-69; pres. 1966-69). Home: 7555 Jalmia Way Los Angeles CA 90046 Office: 550 Flower St Los Angeles CA 90017

PETTUS, ERLE, JR., lawyer; b. Birmingham, Ala., Feb. 12, 1911; s. Erle and Ellelee (Chapman) P.; A.B., Princeton, 1932; LL.B., Duke, 1935; m. Eleanor Pryor Agee, Nov. 29, 1947; children—Erle III, Suzanne C., Jeffrey H. Admitted to Ala. bar, 1935, D.C. bar, 1947; practice in Birmingham, 1935-41, 49—, Washington, 1947-49; mem. firm Rives, Peterson, Pettus, Conway, Elliott & Small, 1949—; dir. Bank of the Southeast. Served with AUS, World War II; ETO. Mem. Am., Ala., Birmingham bar assns. Episcopalian. Club: Birmingham Country. Home: 4004 Lenox Rd Birmingham AL 35213 Office: 800 First Nat-Southern Natural Bldg Birmingham AL 35203

PETTWAY, GEORGE HOLMES, textile mfg. co. exec.; b. Chattanooga, Sept. 29, 1943; s. William D. and Anne Elizabeth (Patten) P.; B.A., U. Va., 1965; M.B.A., U. Pa., 1969; m. Kathryn Dade Wall, Aug. 8, 1967; children—Patten, Townshend, Anne Elizabeth. Mgmt. cons. Cresap, McCormick & Paget, N.Y.C., 1969-70; mgr. distbn. Standard-Coosa-Thatcher Co., Chattanooga, 1971-74, asst. treas., 1975-77, v.p. fin., 1977-79, div. pres., 1980—. City commr., Lookout Mountain, Ga., 1976—; v.p. Jr. Achievement, 1979. Served with USNR, 1965-67. Mem. Am. Textile Mfg. Assn., Am. Apparel Mfg. Assn., Ga. Textile Mfg. Assn. Republican. Episcopalian. Club: Rotary. Home: 1404 Lule Lake Rd Lookout Mountain TN 37350 Office: 18th and Watkins Sts Chattanooga TN 37404

PETTY, CHARLES SUTHERLAND, pathologist; b. Lewistown, Mont., Apr. 16, 1920; s. Charles Frederic and Mae (Reichert) P.; B.S., U. Wash., 1941, M.S., 1946; M.D., Harvard U., 1950; m. Lois Muriel Swenson, Dec. 14, 1957; children—Heather Ann, Charles Sutherland II; children by previous marriage—Daniel S., Carol L. Intern, Mary Imogene Bassett Hosp., Coopertown, N.Y., 1950-52; resident in pathology Peter Bent Brigham Hosp., Children's Med. Center, New Eng. Deaconess Hosp., Boston, 1952-55; instr. pathology La. State U. Sch. Medicine, 1955-56, asst. prof., 1956-58; asst. med. examiner State of Md., 1958-67; asst. prof. forensic pathology U. Md. Sch. Medicine, 1958-64, asso. prof., 1964-67; lectr., then asso. Johns Hopkins U. Sch. Hygiene and Public Health, 1959-67; adj. prof. police adminstrn. U. Louisville, 1978—; dir. Balt. Regional ARC Blood Program, 1959-67; prof. forensic pathology Ind. U. Sch. Medicine, Indpls., 1967-69; dir. lab. Ind. Commn. on Forensic Scis., 1967-69; chief med. examiner Dallas County, 1969—; prof. forensic scis., pathology U. Tex. Southwestern Med. Sch., Dallas, 1969—; dir. Southwestern Inst. Forensic Scis., 1969—. Served from ensign to lt. comdr. USNR, 1941-45. Fellow Coll. Am. Pathologists, Am. Soc. Clin. Pathologists, A.C.P., Am. Acad. Forensic Scis. (pres. 1967-68); mem. Sigma Xi. Episcopalian. Home: 3964 Goodfellow Dr Dallas TX 75229 Office: 5230 Medical Center Dr Dallas TX 75235

PETTY, DAN SHERMAN, assn. exec.; b. Texarkana, Tex., Nov. 3, 1939; s. N.S. and Gladene M. (Stephens) P.; B.S.C.E., U. Tex., Austin, 1961, M.A. in Public Adminstrn., 1966; M.B.A., U. Pa., 1964; m. Kay Lacewell, Aug. 8, 1959; children—Adrienne Anne, Kent Sherman. Asst. city mgr., Lubbock, Tex., 1963; dir. urban affairs North Central Council of Govts., 1967-69; dir. planning coordination, exec. asst. to Govt. of Tex., 1969-73; dir. public affairs U. Tex. System, 1973-74; asst. city mgr., Dallas, 1974-77; pres. Dallas C. of C., 1977—. Chmn. univ. relations com. U. Tex.; bd. dirs. Hope Cottage; mem. budget com. United Way, Dallas. Mem. Internat. City Mgmt. Assn., Am. C. of C. Execs., Tex. C. of C. Execs. Methodist. Office: 1507 Pacific Dallas TX 75201

PETTY, RICHARD, auto racer; s. Lee and Elizabeth T. Petty; m. Lynda Owens; children—Kyle, Sharon, Lisa, Rebecca. Auto racer 21 years; entered 803 Grand Nat. Races, winner 190, 1958-79, with 45 Superspeedway wins; winner Daytona 500, 1964, 66, 71, 73, 74. Mem. Pres.'s Council Fitness and Sport. Named Grand Nat. Rookie of Year, 1959; Most Popular Driver in Grand Nat., 1962, 64, 68, 70, 74, 75, 76, 77, 78; Martini & Rossi Am. Driver of Year, 1971; Driver of Year, Nat. Motorsport Press Assn., 1974-75; inducted into N.C. Athletic Hall of Fame, 1973. Mem. Nat. Assn. Stock Car Auto Racing (6 time champion; Winston Cup grand nat. champion 1964, 67, 71, 72, 74, 75). Address: Route #3 Box 621 Randleman NC 27317

PETTY, THOMAS LEE, physician, educator; b. Boulder, Colo., Dec. 24, 1932; s. Roy Stone and Eleanor Marie (Kudrna) P.; B.A., U. Colo., 1955, M.D., 1958; m. Carol Lee Piepho, Aug. 7, 1954; children—Caryn, Thomas, John. Intern, Phila. Gen. Hosp., 1958-59; resident U. Mich., 1959-60; resident U. Colo., Denver, 1960-62, pulmonary fellow, 1962-63, chief resident medicine, 1963-64, instr. medicine, 1962-64, asst. prof., 1964-68, asso. prof., 1968-74, prof. medicine, 1974—; practice medicine, specializing in internal medicine, pulmonary medicine, Denver, 1962—. Cons., Fitzsimmons Army Hosp., 1970—. NIH and Found. grantee, 1966-77. Mem. Am. Lung Assn. Colo. (pres.), Phi Beta Kappa, Phi Delta Theta, Alpha Omega Alpha, Phi Rho Sigma (pres. 1976). Author: For Those Who Live and Breath, 1967; Intensive and Rehabilitative Respiratory Care, 1971; Pulmonary Diagnostic Techniques, 1975; Chronic Obstructive Pulmonary Disease, 1978. Contbr. articles to profl. jours. Home: 1940 Grape St Denver CO 80220 Office: 4200 E 9th Ave Denver CO 80262

PETTY, TRAVIS HUBERT, pipeline co. exec.; b. Clarksville, Tex., July 31, 1928; s. Joseph H. and Kathleen (Mauldin) P.; student U. Tex., 1945-46; m. Berenice Wieland, Feb. 10, 1948; children—Brian, Paul, David, Kevin, Sean, Karen, Michael. With El Paso Natural Gas Co., 1946—, asst. controller, 1961-65, controller, 1965-69, v.p., 1969-73, exec. v.p., 1973-76, pres., 1976-78, chmn., 1978—; dir. The El Paso Co., 1974—, exec. v.p., 1974-78, vice-chmn., 1974-78, chmn., 1979—; dir. Public Utilities Reports, Inc., El Paso Nat. Bank, Trans Tex. Bancorp. Mem. Am. Gas Assn. (dir.), Gas Research Inst. (dir.), Pacific Coast Gas Assn. (dir., past chmn.), Interstate Natural Gas Assn. (dir.), The Conf. Bd., So. Gas Assn. (past chmn. adv. council). Office: The El Paso Co PO Box 2185 Houston TX 77001

PETTY, WILBERT CORNELIUS, fgn. service officer; b. Asheville, N.C., Oct. 12, 1928; s. Herman Wakefield and Julia Hattie (Murray) P.; B.A. cum laude, Howard U., 1951; M.F.A., Catholic U., 1955; postgrad. Universite de Paris, 1955, Inst. Langs., Georgetown U., 1956, U. Calif. at Los Angeles, 1968-69; m. Irene Mae Powell, May 30, 1959. Tchr. art pub. schs., Washington, 1954-59; with USIA, 1959—, asst. cultural affairs officer USIA, Tunis, Tunisia, 1959-60, asst. pub. affairs officer USIS, Conakry, Guinea, 1960-61, cultural affairs officer USIS, DaKar, Senegal, 1962-65, pub. affairs officer USIS, 1st sec. Am. embassy, Abidjan, Ivory Coast, 1965-68; cultural affairs officer, USIS, 1st sec. Am. embassy, Lagos, Nigeria, 1970-71, Stockholm, 1971-74; spl. asst. Office Pub. Info., USIA, Washington, 1974-76, program officer Africa area, 1976-78; dir. EEO Office, ICA, Washington, 1978—; tchr. ceramic sculpture Ecole des Beaux Arts, Dakar, Senegal, Abidjan, Ivory Coast. Trustee, cons. Expt. in Internat. Living; trustee, chmn. bd. Fine Arts Chamber Orch., N.Y.C. Served with AUS, 1951-53. Decorated Purple Heart, Bronze Star medal; recipient Superior Service award USIA. Mem. N.E.A., Scabbard and Blade, Alpha Phi Omega. Home: 1443 Kennedy St NW Washington DC 20011 Office: EEO Office ICA Washington DC 20547

PETUCHOWSKI, JAKOB JOSEF, clergyman, educator; b. Berlin, Germany, July 30, 1925; s. Siegmund and Lucie Recha (Loewenthal) P.; B.A., U. London (Eng.), 1947; B.H.L., Hebrew Union Coll., 1949, M.A., 1952, Ph.D., 1955; Fellow Humane Letters, Maimonides Coll., Winnipeg, Man., Can., 1959; Dr.phil.h.c., U. Cologne (W. Ger.), 1978; D.Lit. (hon.), Brown U., 1979; m. Elizabeth Rita Mayer, Nov. 28, 1946; children—Samuel Judah, Aaron Mark, Jonathan Mayer. Came to U.S., 1948, naturalized, 1954. Rabbi, 1952; rabbi Beth Israel, Washington, Pa., 1955-56; asst. prof. Rabbinics, Hebrew Union Coll., Cin., 1956-59, asso. prof., 1959-63, prof., 1963-65, prof. Rabbinics and theology, 1965-74, research prof. Jewish theology and liturgy, 1974—; vis. prof. philosophy, religion Antioch (Ohio) Coll., 1961; dir. Jewish studies Hebrew Union Coll., Jerusalem, 1963-64; vis. prof. Jewish philosophy Tel-Aviv U., 1971; rabbi Temple B'nai Israel, Laredo, Tex., part-time 1956—. Heinsheimer Meml. fellow Hebrew Union Coll., 1952-55. Fellow Am. Acad. for Jewish Research; mem. Am. Acad. Religion. Author: The Theology of Haham David Nieto, 1954, 70; Ever Since Sinai, 1961, 68, 79; Prayerbook Reform in Europe, 1968; Heirs of the Pharisees, 1970; Contributions to the Scientific Study of Jewish Liturgy, 1970; Understanding Jewish Prayer, 1972; Beten im Judentum, 1976 Es Lehrten Unsere Meister, 1979; Theology and Poetry, 1978; editor: New Perspectives on Abraham Geiger, 1975; editorial bd. Judaism, Hebrew Union Coll. Ann. Contbr. articles to profl. jour. Home: 7836 Greenland Pl Cincinnati OH 45237

PETZAL, DAVID ELIAS, editor, author; b. N.Y.C., Oct. 21, 1941; s. Henry and Aline Born (Bixer) P.; B.A., Colgate U., 1963; m. Arlene Ann Taylor, May 29, 1974. Editor, Maco Publs., N.Y.C., 1964-69; mng. editor Davis Publs., N.Y.C., 1969-70; features editor Hearst Publs., N.Y.C., 1970-72; mng. editor CBS Publs., N.Y.C., 1972-79, editor, 1979—; author: The .22 Rifle, 1972; editor: The Experts Book of the Shooting Sports, 1972; The Experts Book of Upland Game and Waterfowl Hunting, 1975; The Experts Book of Big-Game Hunting in North America, 1976. Home: PO Box 219 Bedford NY 10506 Office: 1515 Broadway New York NY 10036

PETZOLD, ROBERT GEORGE, educator; b. Milw., Sept. 25, 1917; s. George Arthur and Ruth Helen (Blackmun) P.; B.S., Milw. State Tchrs. Coll., 1938; Mus.M., U. Wis., 1947, Ph.D., 1950; m. Elsbeth H. Dobbs, June 20, 1942; children—Susan Jean, Sara Jane, Cynthia Joan, Robin Beth. Pub. sch. music tchr., Wis., 1938-50; prof. music edn. U. Wis.-Madison, 1951—, chmn. dept. curriculum, instr., 1965-67, asso. dean Sch. Edn., 1967-70. Vis. lectr. music edn. U. Tex., 1955, U. Ill., 1962, Western Res. U., 1966; research Wis. Research and Devel. Center for Cognitive Learning. Served with USAAF, 1942-46; PTO. Research grantee U.S. Office Edn., 1959, 60, 61-66, Nat. Center Endowment in Arts, 1968-71. Mem. Music Educators Nat. Conf. (nat. commn. instrn.), NEA, Am. Ednl. Research Assn., Ill. Council Research in Mus. Edn., Internat. Soc. Mus. Edn. (mem. Commn. on Research). Editor: Jour. Research in Music Edn., 1972-78. Contbr. articles to profl. jours. Home: 14 N Whitney Way Madison WI 53705

PEW, GEORGE THOMPSON, investments co. exec.; b. Phila., Mar. 30, 1917; s. J. Howard and Helen (Thompson) P.; grad. M.I.T., 1939; m. Constance Delk Clarke, May 4, 1940; children—George Thompson, Margaret Clarke (Mrs. William H. Moorhouse, Jr.). With Sun Oil Co., 1939-50; chmn. Aero Design & Engring. Co., 1950-57, pres., chmn., 1957-59, pres., 1958-61; pres. George T. Pew Enterprises, 1961—; chmn. Par Truck Leasing, Inc., 1961-73, Joe Hodge Transp., Inc., 1963-71. Mem. Am. Inst. Aeros., Am. Ordnance Assn., Sportsman Pilot Assn., Quiet Birdmen, Nat. Pilots Assn. Clubs: Merion Cricket (Haverford, Pa.); Merion Golf (Ardmore, Pa.); Bay Head (N.J.) Yacht; Racquet, Corinthian Yacht, Philadelphia Aviation Country (past pres.), Union League (Phila.); Key Largo Anglers (Fla.). Home: 231 Cheswold Hill Rd Haverford PA 19041

PEW, ROBERT ANDERSON, oil corp. officer; b. Phila., Aug. 22, 1936; s. Arthur Edmund and Mary Elizabeth (Elliott) P.; student Princeton U., 1954-56; B.S., Temple U., 1959; M.S. in Mgmt. (Alfred P. Sloan fellow), Mass. Inst. Tech., 1970; m. Joan Ferguson, Feb. 1, 1958; children—Robert Anderson (dec.), James Cunningham, Glenn Edgar, Joan Elliott. Ops. asst. prodn. div. Sun Oil Co., Premont, Tex. and Morgan City, La., 1959-60, auditor internal audit dept., Phila., 1960-65, staff asst. treasury dept., 1965-69, asst. to exec. v.p. corp. projects group, 1970-71, sec.-treas., mgr. financial control of products group, 1971-74, corp. sec., 1974-77; pres. Helios Capital Corp., Radnor, Pa.; dir. Sun Co., Inc., Radnor, Glenmede Trust Co., Alliance Enterprise Corp. (all Phila.), Narco Sci., Inc., Ft. Washington, Pa. Bd. dirs. Children's Hosp. Phila., 1968—, vice-chmn., 1973—; bd. govs. Health Systems Agy. S.E. Pa., 1979—; chmn. Health Services Council, Phila., 1975—; trustee Bryn Mawr (Pa.) Coll. Mem. Pa. Air N.G., 1956-59. Recipient R. Kelso Carter award Widener Coll., 1971. Mem. Aircraft Owners and Pilots Assn. (trustee, chmn. 1974-77, vice-chmn. 1979—), Am. Hosp. Assn. (hon.). Republican. Presbyn. Clubs: Union League; Rittenhouse; Seal Harbor; Phila. Aviation Country; Bar Harbor; Merion Cricket; Northeast Harbor Fleet. Home: 916 Muirfield Rd Bryn Mawr PA 19010 Office: 100 Matsonford Rd Radnor PA 19087

PEW, ROBERT CUNNINGHAM, II, office equipment mfg. co. exec.; b. Syracuse, N.Y., June 4, 1923; s. Robert Carroll and Bernice (Evans) P.; B.A., Wesleyan U., Middletown Conn.; m. Mary Bonnell Idema, Aug. 23, 1947; children—Robert Cunningham, John Evans, Kate Bonnell. Labor relations exec. Doehler-Jarvis Corp., Grand Rapids, Mich., 1948-51; with Steelcase Inc., Grand Rapids, 1952—, exec. v.p., 1964-66, pres., 1966-75, chmn. bd., pres., 1975—; dir. Old Kent Financial Corp., Kirsch Co., Wometco Enterprises. Trustee Aquinas Coll., Grand Rapids; bd. dirs. Econ. Devel. Corp. Grand Rapids. Served to 1st lt. USAAF, 1942-45, to capt. USAF, 1951-52. Decorated Purple Heart, Air medal with 2 oak leaf clusters. Mem. Grand Rapids C. of C. (dir.), Grand Rapids Employers Assn. (dir.), Chi Psi. Episcopalian. Clubs: Kent Country, Lost Tree, Peninsular, Univ. (Grand Rapids). Home: 210 Greenwich Rd NE Grand Rapids MI 49506 Office: 1120 36th St SE Grand Rapids MI 49506

PÉWÉ, TROY LEWIS, educator, geologist; b. Rock Island, Ill., June 28, 1918; s. Richard E. and Olga (Pomrank) P.; A.B. in Geology, Augustana Coll., 1940; M.S., State U. Iowa, 1942; Ph.D., Stanford, 1952; m. Mary Jean Hill, Dec. 21, 1944; children—David Lee, Richard Hill, Elizabeth Anne. Head dept. geology Augustana Coll., 1942-46; civilian instr. USAAC, 1943-44; instr. geomorphology Stanford, 1946; geologist Alaskan br. U.S. Geol. Survey, 1946—; chief glacial geologist U.S. Nat. Com. Internat. Geophys. Year (Antarctica), 1958; prof. geology, head dept. U. Alaska, 1958-65; prof. geology Ariz. State U., 1965—, chmn. dept., 1965-76, dir. Mus. Geology, 1976—; lectr. in field, 1942—. Mem. organizing com. 1st Internat. Conf. Permafrost, 1962-63, chmn. U.S. planning com. 2d Internat. Permafrost Conf., Nat. Acad. Sci., 1972-74; chmn. U.S. del. 3d Internat. Permafrost Conf., Nat. Acad. Sci., 1978, chmn. 4th internat. conf., 1979—; com. study Good Friday Alaska Earthquake, Nat. Acad. Scis., 1964-70, mem. glaciological com. polar research bd. 1971-73, chmn. permafrost com., 1975—, mem. polar research bd., 1973-78; organizing chmn. Internat. Assn. Quarternary Research Symposium and Internat. Field Trip Alaska, 1965; mem. Internat. Commn. Periglacial Morophology, 1964-71; mem. polar research bd. NRC, 1975-78, late Cenozoic study group, sci. com. Antarctic research, 1977—. Recipient Antarctic Service medal, 1966; Outstanding Achievement award Augustana Coll., 1969. Fellow AAAS (pres. Alaska div. 1956, com. on arid lands 1972—), Geol. Soc. Am. (editorial bd. 1975—, chmn. cordilleran sect. 1979-80, chmn. elect geomorphology div. 1979), Arctic Inst. N.Am. (bd. govs. 1969-74, exec. bd. 1972-73), Iowa, Ariz. acads. sci.; mem. Assn. Geology Tchrs., Glaciological Soc., N.Z. Antarctic Soc., Am. Soc. Engring. Geologists, Internat. Geog. Union. Contbr. numerous papers to profl. lit. Home: 538 E Fairmont Dr Tempe AZ 85282

PEYRE, HENRI MAURICE, educator; b. Paris, Feb. 21, 1901; s. Brice and Marie (Tuvien) P.; came to U.S., 1925; grad. Ecole Normale Superieure, Paris, 1920; 1 son, Brice. Mem. faculty French univs., also Bryn Mawr Coll., Yale U.; distinguished prof. French, Grad. Center, City U. N.Y., 1969—. Mem. Am. Philos. Soc., Am. Acad. Arts and Scis. Author: The Failures of Criticism, 1967; Historical and Critical Essays, 1968; Dostoevsky and French Literary Imagination, 1975; What is Romanticism, 1977. Contbr. articles to profl. jours. Address: 290 North Ave Westport CT 06880

PEYSER, JOSEPH LEONARD, educator; b. N.Y.C., Oct. 19, 1925; s. Samuel and Sadye (Quinto) P.; B.A., Duke U., 1947, M.A., 1949; profl. diploma, Columbia U., 1955; postgrad. U. Nancy (France), 1949-50; Ed.D., N.Y. U., 1965; m. Julia Boxer, May 30, 1948; children—Jay Randall, Jan Ellen. Tchr., chmn. fgn. langs. Nancy pub. schs., 1949-50, Monroe (N.Y.) pub. schs., 1951-54, Uniondale (N.Y.) pub. schs., 1954-61; asst. high sch. prin., Plainview, N.Y., 1961-63; mem. faculty Hofstra U., Hempstead, N.Y., 1963-68, asso. prof. edn., 1966-68, asst. dean, then asso. dean Sch. Edn., 1964-66, interim dean, 1966-68; dean acad. affairs, prof. French and edn. Dowling Coll., Oakdale, N.Y., 1968-70, v.p. acad. affairs, dean faculty , 1970-73; prof. edn. and French, Ind. U., South Bend, 1973—, dean faculties, 1973-75; vis. prof. N.Y. U., 1964-66; adj. asst. prof. L.I. U., 1961-63; cons. in field. Active No. Ind. council Boy Scouts Am., 1973-76; mem. alumni admissions com. Duke U., 1969-73. Served with USN, 1943-46. Teaching fellow French Ministry Edn., 1949-50; recipient Founders Day award N.Y. U., 1966. Mem. AAUP, NEA, Phi Delta Kappa, Kappa Delta Pi, Pi Delta Phi. Editor: Pathescope-Berlitz Foreign Language Series, 1960; Israel, Crossroads of History, 1971; Fort St. Joseph Manuscripts, 1978. Contbr. profl. publs. Office: Dept Fgn Langs Ind Univ South Bend IN 46615

PEYSER, PETER A., congressman; b. Cedarhurst, N.Y., Sept. 7, 1921; s. Percy A. and Rubye (Hoeflich) P.; B.A., Colgate U., 1943; m. Marguerite Richards, Dec. 23, 1949; children—Penny, Carolyn, Peter, James, Tommy. Mgr., Mut. N.Y. Ins. Co., N.Y.C., 1956-70; mem. 92d congress from 25th N.Y. Dist., mem. Edn. and Labor Com.; mem. 93d, 94th and 96th Congresses from 23d N.Y. Dist., mem. Edn. and Labor Com., Adminstrn. Com. Mayor, Irvington, N.Y., 1963-70. Served with U.S. Army, 1943-46. Decorated Bronze Star (U.S.); Belgian Fourragere. Episcopalian. Home: Sunnyside Ln Irvington NY 10533 Office: 301 Cannon House Office Bldg Washington DC 20515

PEYTON, DONALD LEON, assn. exec.; b. Portland, Oreg., May 5, 1925; s. Bernard Thomas and Nelle (Moses) P.; student Mont. State Coll., 1946-47; B.A., No. Colo. U., 1950; m. Jane Frances Kirkman, Aug. 26, 1950; children—Patrick Philip, James Allen. Civilian edn. specialist USAF, 1951-56; engaged in real estate, Cheyenne, Wyo., 1956-57; adminstrv. asst. to congressman, 1957-60; with U.S. C. of C., 1960-66, gen. mgr. govt. relations, 1965-66; exec. v.p. Am. Nat. Standards Inst., Inc., 1966—. Lectr. govt. bus. relations Am. U., 1965-66, Amos Tuck Sch., Dartmouth, 1965—. Pres. Cheyenne Jr. C. of C., 1955-56. Mem. Am. Soc. Assn. Execs., Council Engring. Soc. Secs., Internat. Orgn. Standardization (exec. com.), N.Y. Soc. Assn. Execs. Clubs: Capitol Hill, Univ. (Washington); N.Y. Athletic. Author monographs. Home: 23 Fenimore Rd Scarsdale NY 10583 Office: 1430 Broadway New York NY 10018

PEYTON, PATRICK JOSEPH, clergyman; b. Carracastle, County Mayo, Ireland, Jan. 9, 1909; s. John and Mary (Gillard) P.; grad. Holy Cross Sem., Notre Dame, 1932; A.B., U. Notre Dame, 1937; postgrad. Holy Cross Coll., Washington; LL.D. (hon.), Stonehill Coll., 1963. Came to U.S., 1928, naturalized, 1938. Mem. Congregation Holy Cross; ordained priest Roman Catholic Ch., 1941; founder, dir. Family Rosary Crusade, Can., U.S., Eng., Spain, Africa, India, Burma, Ceylon, Australia, New Zealand, Ireland, Venezuela, Philippines, Argentina, Colombia, Chile, Brazil, Panama, Dominican Republic,

1942—; founder, producer Family Theater, weekly MBS program, 1947; producer local Rosary programs, 1942—, world-wide Rosary programs, Joyful Hour, Triumphant Hour, 1945—, Matter of Faith TV series, 1972-73; producer, filmer 9 feature TV programs, 1950—; producer TV series Prayer of the Ages, 1964; producer 15 films on Rosary for TV, theaters in Madrid, 1956, Marian Theater, half-hour, weekly radio program MBS, 1956; dir. Family Rosary Newspaper, Time, 1948—; exec. dir. Rosary Theater, Brussels World Fair, 1958, Family Rosary Crusade, Belgium, 1959, Ecuador and Canary Islands, 1966, Bethelehem, Nazareth and Jerusalem, 1971, El Salvador, 1971, Guatemala, Mexico, Costa Rica, 1970, P.R., Mexico City, Rio de Janeiro, 1973-75; producer TV programs Family Hour, 1966, Search, 1966; producer feature Redeemer, 1964, Somewhere Along the Line, 1969, Father Pat, 1970, The Day the Clocks Stopped, 1976; producer TV series Prince of Peace, 1967-68; founder Families for Prayer, 1972. Recipient George Washington honor medal Freedoms Found., 1954; Nat. Mass Media award Thomas Alva Edison Found., 1955; Bronze medal Venice Internat. Film Festival for TV film, The Soldier, 1964; recipient Pro Ecclesia et Pontifice papal medal, 1966; hon. citizen Guanabara, Brazil, 1970. K.C. (4 deg.). Author: The Ear of God, 1951; Father Peyton's Rosary Prayer Book, 1954; Family Prayer Book, 1964; (autobiography) All for Her, 1967. Originator slogan The Family That Prays Together Stays Together; televised Pope Paul's Christmas Mass, Easter Mass to U.S., Can., 1973. Address: 7201 Sunset Blvd Hollywood CA 90046

PEYTON, WESLEY GRANT, JR., newspaper editor; b. San Luis Obispo, Calif., May 22, 1925; s. Wesley Grant and Jessie (Jolly) P.; student La. State U., 1943-44; B.A. in Journalism, San Jose State Coll., 1948; m. Jewel Schneider, Dec. 24, 1950; children—Evelyn Anne, Carolyn Sue, David Wesley. With San Jose Mercury, 1943—, editorial page editor, 1957-73; chief editorial writer San Jose Mercury and News, 1973—; subeditor Stars and Stripes, Paris and Hoescht (Germany), 1945-46; copyreader Fresno (Calif.) Bee, 1949-50. Part-time asst. prof. journalism San Jose State Coll., 1958-59. Served with inf. AUS, 1943-46. ETO. Decorated Belgian Fourragere. Recipient McQuaide Meml. award, 1955; 7th ann. Calif. Press-Bar award, 1959-60; spl. award Santa Clara Valley Council City Civic Unity for work leading to creation City San Jose Commn. Human Rights, 1956; certificate merit City San Jose for work leading to receiving All-Am. City award, 1961; Calif. Press-Bar award, 1969. Mem. Nat. Conf. Editorial Writers, Sigma Delta Chi. Democrat. Jewish. Contbr. articles to profl. jours. Home: Los Gatos CA 95030 Office: 750 Ridder Park Dr San Jose CA 95190

PEZZILLO, ALBERT ROBERT, consumer goods co. exec.; b. Phila., Oct. 23, 1928; s. Albert R. and Josephine (Melo) P.; B.S. in Bus., La Salle Coll., Phila., 1959; m. Kathryn Holmes, June 16, 1951; children—Susan, Kathy. Asst. to pres. Colgate Palmolive Co., N.Y.C., 1968-69, pres., gen. mgr., Mexico, 1970-72; pres. personal products div. Warner-Lambert Co., Morris Plains, N.J., 1972-77, pres. consumer products group, 1977-79, corp. exec. v.p., 1979—. Served with U.S. Army, 1950-52. Office: Warner-Lambert Co 201 Tabor Rd Morris Plains NJ 07950

PFAELZER, MARIANA R., fed. judge; b. 1926; A.B., U. Calif.; LL.B., UCLA Sch. Law. Admitted to bar, 1958; judge U.S. Dist. Ct. for Dist. Central Calif. Mem. Am. Bar Assn. Office: US Dist Ct 312 N Spring St Los Angeles CA 90012*

PFAELZER, MORRIS, lawyer; b. Phila., Apr. 12, 1913; s. Frank A. and Elsie (Levy) P.; grad. Mercersberg Acad., 1931; A.B., Harvard, 1935; LL.B., U. Pa., 1938; m. Marjorie Lesser, Apr. 12, 1938 (div. 1959); children—Fay (Mrs. Jon Abrams), Betty (Mrs. Michael Rauch); m. 2d, Mariana Richardson, Oct. 14, 1961. Admitted to Calif. bar, 1946, Pa. bar, 1939; practice in Los Angeles, 1946—; partner Kadison, Pfaelzer, Woodard, Quinn & Rossi, 1967—. Lectr. law U. So. Calif., 1960-64. Pres., Los Angeles County Bar Found., 1972-74. Pres., trustee Resthaven Psychiat. Hosp., 1961-69; bd. councilors U. So. Calif. Law Center, 1971—, chmn., 1976—. Served with USNR, 1942-45. Fellow Am. Bar Found.; mem. Am., Los Angeles County, Pa., Phila. bar assns., Calif. State Bar. Home: 230 N Carmelina Ave Los Angeles CA 90049 Office: 707 Wilshire Blvd 40th Floor Los Angeles CA 90017

PFAFF, WARREN GEORGE, advt. exec.; b. N.Y.C., Nov. 26, 1929; s. Frederick William and Lydia (Anton) P.; B.A., Dartmouth Coll., 1951; m. Kathryn Allen, Aug. 1, 1959; children—Frederick Warren, Christopher Walker, Sandra Bentley. Actor, comml. artist, muralist, set designer, N.Y.C., 1956-57; art dir. Bryan Houston, Inc., N.Y.C., 1957-58; graphic arts cons. U.S. Commn. Civil Rights, 1961; with J. Walter Thompson Co., N.Y.C., 1958-70, sr. v.p., creative supr., 1969-70; pres. Warren Pfaff Inc., N.Y.C., 1970—. Served to lt. (j.g.) USNR, 1953-56. Recipient numerous awards Venice Film Festival, N.Y. Art Dirs. Club N.Y.C., Outdoor Advt. Club, Hollywood Internat. Broadcasting, Am. Advt. Fedn. Mem. A.S.C.A.P. Club: Players. Home: 106 Stamford Ave Stamford CT 06902 Office: 505 Park Ave St New York NY 10022

PFAFF, WILLIAM WALLACE, physician, educator; b. Rochester, N.Y., Aug. 14, 1930; s. Norman Joseph and Elcanor Blakesley (Wells) P.; A.B., Harvard U., 1952; M.D., U. Buffalo, 1956; m. Patricia Ann Clark, June 25, 1960; children—Nancy, Karen, Margaret, Mary Catherine. Intern, U. Chgo., 1956-57, resident, 1957-58; resident in surgery Stanford U. Med. Center, 1960-65, instr. surgery, 1965; faculty U. Fla., Gainesville, 1965—, prof. surgery, 1971—, dir. gen. surgery residency; chmn. Fla. Med. Coll. Admissions Com., 1969-71. Served with USPHS, 1958-60. Mem. A.C.S., Southeastern Surg. Congress, Fla. Kidney Found., Alachua County Med. Soc. (pres. 1977-78), Alpha Omega Alpha. Contbr. numerous articles to profl. jours. Home: 1624 N W 7th Pl Gainesville FL 32610 Office: Dept Surgery U Fla PO Box J 286 Gainesville FL 32610

PFAFFMANN, CARL, educator; b. Bklyn., May 27, 1913; s. Charles and Anna (Haaker) P.; Ph.B., Brown U., 1933, M.A., 1935; B.A., Oxford (Eng.) U., 1937; Ph.D. (Rhodes scholar), Cambridge (Eng.) U., 1939; D.Sc., Brown U., 1965, Bucknell U., 1966, Yale, 1972; m. Hortense Louise Brooks, Dec. 26, 1939; children—Ellen Anne, Charles Brooks (dec.), William Sage. Research asso. Johnson Found., U. Pa., 1939-40; instr. psychology Brown U., 1940-42, asst. prof., 1945-48, asso. prof., 1949-51, prof., 1951-65, Florence Pirce Grant U. prof., 1960; vis. prof. Yale, 1958-59, Harvard, 1962-63; Nat. Sigma Xi lectr., 1963; v.p. Rockefeller U., 1965-78, prof., 1965—; chmn. div. behavorial scis. NRC, 1962-64; chmn. 17th Internat. Congress Psychology, 1963; mem. exec. com. Internat. Union Psychol. Scis., 1966-72; chmn. sect. exptl. psychology and animal behavior Internat. Union Biol. Scis., 1969-76; chmn. com. olfaction and taste Internat. Union Physiol. Scis., 1971-77. Bd. fellows Brown U., 1968—. Served from lt. (j.g.) to comdr. USNR, 1942-45. Recipient Kenneth Craik Research award St. John's Coll., Cambridge U., 1968. Guggenheim fellow, 1960-61. Fellow Am. Psychol. Assn. (Distinguished Sci. Contbn. award 1963, pres. div. exptl. psychology 1956-57), AAAS, Am. Acad. Arts and Scis.; mem. Am. Philos. Soc., Nat. Acad. Sci., Soc. Exptl. Psychologists (Howard Crosby Warren medal research psychology 1960), Am. Physiol. Soc., Eastern Psychol. Assn. (pres. 1958-59). Home: One Gracie Terr New York City NY 10028 also Pond Meadow Rd Killingworth CT 06417

PFANN, JOHN P., corp. exec.; b. Nebraska City, Nebr., May 17, 1929; B.S. in Bus. Admistrn., U. Nebr.; m. Donna, May 27, 1951; children—Teresa Lee, Joanna Donna. Asst. comptroller ITT, N.Y.C., 1965-71, v.p., 1971—, dep. treas., 1973-76, treas., 1976—, sr. v.p., 1979—. Served with USN, 1945-46. C.P.A. Mem. Am. Inst. C.P.A.'s, Fin. Exec. Inst. Office: 320 Park Ave New York NY 10022*

PFANN, WILLIAM GARDNER, scientist; b. N.Y.C., Oct. 25, 1917; s. John G. and Anna F. (Liedtke) P.; B.Chem.Engring., Cooper Union, N.Y.C., 1940; m. Mary L. Gronewold, May 31, 1946; children—Jean L., Susan D., Anna V. Lab. asst. Bell Telephone Labs., Murray Hill, N.J., 1935-43, staff scientist, 1943-59, dept. head research, 1959-74, cons., 1975—; vis. scientist dept. metallurgy Cambridge (Eng.) U., 1962. Recipient Clamer medal Franklin Inst., 1957; Moisson medal Sch. Chemistry U. Paris, 1962; 1st award for Creative Invention, Am. Chem. Soc., 1968; award for Excellence, Carborundum Co., 1972; award in Solid State Sci. and Tech., Electrochem. Soc., 1973; Profl. Progress award Am. Inst. Chem. Engrs., 1960. Fellow AIME (Mathewson medal 1955), Am. Soc. Metals (Sauveur achievement award 1958); mem. Nat. Acad. Scis., Soc. Cryobiology, Am. Phys. Soc. (award for New Materials 1976). Author: Zone Melting, 2d edit., 1966. Patentee in field. Office: Bell Labs Murray Hill NJ 07974

PFAU, JOHN M(ARTIN), coll. adminstr.; b. Gakovo, Yugoslavia, Apr. 28, 1918; A.B., U. Chgo., 1947, A.M., 1948, Ph.D. in History, 1951; married; 2 children. Instr. Am. history North Central Coll., Naperville, Ill., 1948-50; asso. prof. history Chgo. Tchrs. Coll., 1951-59, adminstrv. asst. to dean, 1955-56, asst. dean in charge Foreman br., 1956-59; prof. history, chmn. dept. social scis. Chico (Calif.) State Coll., 1959-61, Sonoma State Coll., Rohnert Park, Calif., 1961-62; pres. Calif. State Coll. at San Bernardino, 1962—. Mem. Calif. Council for Humanities in Public Policy, 1977—. Mem. Am. History Assn., Orgn. Am. History, Am. Assn. State Colls. and Univs. (com. on culture). Address: Calif State Univ at San Bernardino 5500 State College Pkwy San Bernardino CA 92407

PFEFFER, EDWARD ISRAEL, supt. schs.; b. Newark, July 1, 1914; s. Jacob and Fannie Bessie (Fisher) P.; B.S., N.Y. U., 1937; M.A., N.J. State Tchrs. Coll., Montclair, 1942; Ed.D., Rutgers U., 1954; m. Anna Chinich, July 14, 1940; children—Cynthia Roberta, Bruce Paul. Tchr., Abington Ave. Sch., Newark, 1937-46; vice prin. Warren St. Sch., 1946-53; prin. Monmouth St. and Coes Pl. schs., 1953-57, Robert Treat Jr. High and Elem. Sch., 1957-64; asst. supt. spl. services Newark Dist. Pub. Schs., 1964-67, dep. supt., 1967-72, 73—, acting supt., 1972-73. Commr., Newark Sr. Citizens Commn., 1967—; mem. Newark Juvenile Problems Commn., 1958-62; chmn. Children's Resources Commn., Council Social Agys., 1955-60, mem. exec. bd. Family and Children's Div., 1955-62; mem. Newark Commn. for UN Week, 1962—, Newark Disaster Com., 1967—; mem. Bd. Edn., Temple B'nai Abraham, Essex County, N.J., 1964-65. Mem. exec. bd. Newark Central Community Council; mem. adv. bd. Essex County Tech. Sch. Recipient citations Newark Assn. Dirs. and Suprs., 1973, Newark Title I Central Parents Council, 1973. Mem. Newark Pub. Sch. Prins. Assn. (pres. 1963-64), N.J. Elementary Sch. Press Assn. (pres.), Congress Parents and Tchrs. (life), NEA (life), Am., N.J. assns. sch. adminstrs., Newark Schoolmens Assn. (bd. govs., named Outstanding Schoolman of Year 1972-73), Columbia Scholastic Press Assn. (v.p.; Gold Key 1948), Urban League, NAACP, Phi Delta Kappa. Contbr. articles profl. publs. Home: 507 Clinton Pl Newark NJ 07112 Office: 2 Cedar St Newark NJ 07102

PFEFFER, J. ALAN, educator; b. Bklyn., June 26, 1907; s. Isaac and Henny (Halpern) P.; A.B. magna cum laude, U. Buffalo, 1935, M.A., 1936; Ph.D., Columbia, 1946; m. Bertha Manoff, Feb. 27, 1938; children—Robert I., JoAnne. Grad. asst. U. Buffalo, 1935-36, instr. German, 1939-46, asst. prof., 1946-48, asso. prof., 1948-49, prof., 1949-62, exec. officer German sect. modern lang. dept., 1952-62; prof. chmn. dept. Germanic langs., lit. U. Pitts., 1962-72, chmn. humanities council, 1968-69, dir. Inst. Basic German, 1960—; instr. German, Buffalo Collegiate Center, 1936-37, Columbia extension div., 1937-39; cons. prof. Stanford U., 1976—; cons. N.D. Lang. Insts.; lectr. various European univs. Recipient Gold medal Goethe Inst. Germany, 1972. Mem. AAUP (local pres.), N.Y. State Conf. U. Profs. (councilor), Am. Assn. Tchrs. German (pres. Western zone), Modern Lang. Assn. (adv. com. Publ. German Tchrs. Guides), N.Y. Fedn. Fgn. Lang. Tchrs. (pres.), Nat. Fedn. Modern Lang. Tchrs. Assn. (chmn. state survey acad. preparation tchrs. modern lang., exec. council, pres.), Delta Phi Alpha (nat. 1st v.p.), Phi Beta Kappa (local pres.). Author, editor: Civil and Military German, 1943; German-English and English-German Dictionary of Everyday Usage, 1947; The Proverb in Goethe, 1948; Essays on German Language and Literature in Honor of Theodore B. Hewitt 1952; Modern German-Civilization, Composition and Conversation, 1953; German Review Grammar, rev. edit., 1969; Basic Spoken German Series: vol. I, Word List, Level I, 1962, vol. II, Index of English Equivalents, Lcvcl I, 1965, vol. III, Idiom List, Level I, 1968, vol. IV, Dictionary of Basic (Spoken) German, 1970, vol. V, World List, Level II, 1970, vol. VI, German-English Glossary of 2000 Utility Words, 1974; Basic Spoken German Grammar, 1974, Taiwan edit., 1975; Grunddeutsch: Erarbeitung und Wertung dreier deutscher Korpora, 1975; Kontexte, 1976; Studien zur deskriptiven deutschen Grammatik, 1980. Asst. editor Modern Lang. Jour., 1954-59, mng. editor, 1959-62; asso. editor German Quar., 1958-62; editorial bd. Zielsprache Deutsch, 1970-72. Contbr. articles, revs. to profl. publs. Home: 685 Cowles Rd Santa Barbara CA 93108

PFEFFER, LEO, lawyer, educator; b. Hungary, Dec. 25, 1910; s. Alter Saul and Hani (Yaeger) P.; came to U.S., 1912, naturalized, 1917; B.S.S., Coll. City N.Y., 1930; J.D., N.Y. U., 1933; L.H.D. (h.c.), Hebrew Union Coll.-Jewish Inst. Religion, 1979; m. Freda Plotkin, Sept. 18, 1937; children—Alan Israel, Susan Beth. Admitted to N.Y. bar, 1933; practice in N.Y.C., 1933—; pvt. tchr. law, N.Y.C., 1933-45; lectr. New Sch., 1954-58, Mt. Holyoke Coll., 1958-60; David W. Petergorsky prof. constl. law Yeshivah U., 1962-63; gen. counsel Am. Jewish Congress, 1958-64, spl. counsel, 1964—; prof. polit. sci., chmn. dept. L.I. U., 1964—. Vis. prof. constl. law Rutgers U., 1965; frequent radio and TV appearances, 1954—. Pres., Lawyers Constl. Def. Com., 1964-66, gen. counsel, 1966—; cons. counsel Religious Coalition for Abortion Rights, 1976—; adv. com. Nat. Project Center for Film and the Humanities, 1974—; mem. religious liberty com. Nat. Council Chs. of Christ in U.S.A. Recipient Religious Freedom award Ams. for Separation Ch. and State, 1955; citation contbns. to civil rights Minn. Jewish Community Council, 1962; Thomas Jefferson Religious Freedom award Unitarian-Universalist Ch. N.Y., 1967; Bklyn. Civil Liberties award, 1968; citation for contbns. to pub. edn. Horace Mann League, 1972; award Com. for Pub. Edn. and Religious Liberty, 1972; Townsend Harris medal Coll. City N.Y., 1974; Rabbi Maurice N. Eisendrath Meml. award Union of Am. Hebrew Congregations, 1977; George Brussel Meml. award Stephen Wise Free Synagogue, 1978; Trustee award for Scholarly Achievement, L.I. U., 1978; Ams. United Fund, 1979. Mem. Am. Jewish Congress, Am. Acad. Religion, Am. Acad. Polit. and Social Scis., AAUP (pres. L.I. U. chpt. 1967-68), ACLU (cons., cooperating atty.), Soc. Sci. Study Religion, N.Y. U. Law Rev. Assn. (pres. 1964-66), Am. Judicature Soc., Am. Polit. Sci. Assn., Am. Arbitration Assn. (panel arbitrators), Nat. Assn. Intergroup Relations Ofcls., Horace Mann League U.S. (gen. counsel), Am. Soc. for Legal History, Com. for Pub. Edn. and Religious Liberty (founder 1967, gen. counsel 1967—). Author: Church, State and Freedom, 1953; The Liberties of an American, 1956; Creeds in Competition, 1958; (with Anson Phelps Stokes) Church and State in the United States, 1964; This Honorable Court, 1965; God, Caesar and the Constitution, 1975; Religious Freedom, 1976. Editorial bd. jour. Ch. and State, 1958—, Judaism, 1964—. Contbr. to various books, encys. Home: 29 Ridge Terr Central Valley NY 10917 Office: 15 E 84th St New York NY 10028

PFEFFER, RICHARD LAWRENCE, educator; b. Bklyn., Nov. 26, 1930; s. Lester Robert and Anna (Newman) P.; B.S. cum laude, CCNY, 1952; M.S., Mass. Inst. Tech., 1954, Ph.D., 1957; m. Roslyn Ziegler, Aug. 30, 1953; children—Bruce, Lloyd, Scott, Glenn. Research asst. Mass. Inst. Tech., 1952-55, guest lectr., 1956; atmospheric physicist Air Force Cambridge Research Center, Boston, 1955-59; sr. scientist Columbia, 1959-61, lectr., 1961-62, asst. prof. geophysics, 1962-64; asso. prof. meteorology Fla. State U., Tallahassee, 1964-67, prof., dir. Geophys. Fluid Dynamics Inst., 1967—; cons. NASA, 1961-64, N.W. Ayer & Son, Inc., 1962, Ednl. Testing Service, Princeton, N.J., 1963, Voice of Am., 1963, Grolier, Inc., 1963, Naval Research Labs., 1971-76. Mem. Internat. Commn. for Dynamical Meteorology, 1972-76. Bd. dirs. B'nai B'rith Anti-Defamation League; chmn. religious concern and social action com. Temple Israel, Tallahassee, 1971-72. Mem. Am. Meteorol. Soc. (program chmn. ann. meeting 1963), Am. Geophys. Union, N.Y. Acad. Scis. (chmn. planetary scis. sect. 1961-63), Sigma Xi, Chi Epsilon Pi, Sigma Alpha. Editor: Dynamics of Climate, 1960. Contbr. articles to profl. jours. Home: 926 Waverly Rd Tallahassee FL 32312

PFEFFER, ROBERT FREDERICK HERMAN, equipment mfg. co. exec.; b. Milw., Jan. 17, 1921; s. John and Marie (Wiedenhoeft) P.; student Marquette U., 1956-57; m. Margaret Lucille Siegel, June 29, 1940; children—Peter, Steven, Robert Pfeffer Carlson. Factory worker James Shoe Factory, Milw., 1937-40; plant mgr. Mercury Engring. Co., Milw., 1940-48; with Badger Meter, Inc., Milw., 1948—, pres., chief operating officer, 1974—; seminar discussion leader U. Wis., 1962-65, Am. Mgmt. Assn., 1963-65. Mem. Brown Deer (Wis.) Planning Commn., 1955-57; mem. Brown Deer Bldg. Bd., 1956-58. Recipient certificate of achievement U. Wis., 1965, Am. Mgmt. Assn. Mem. Brown Deer Businessmen's Assn. (pres. 1954). Republican. Lutheran. Club: Ozaukee Country (pres. 1967-68) (Mequon, Wis.). Home: 9424 N Waverly Dr Milwaukee WI 53217 Office: 4545 W Brown Deer Rd Milwaukee WI 53223

PFEIF, WILLIAM JAMES, elec. appliance co. exec.; b. Schenectady, Apr. 11, 1917; s. George H. and Etta (Bostock) P.; Ph.B., U. Wis., 1940; m. Marjorie Emma Tafel, Sept. 6, 1941; children—Wynne Whittles, Steven G., Joann Thatcher. With housewares div. Gen. Electric Co., Bridgeport, Conn., 1940-69; pres. internat. div. Sunbeam Corp., Oakbrook, Ill., 1969-70, v.p. Sunbeam Corp., 1970, exec. v.p., dir., 1970-71, pres., chief operating officer, 1971-77, vice chmn. bd., chief adminstrv. officer, 1977—; dir. Am. Nat. Bank, Chgo. Mem. Chgo. Assn. Commerce and Industry (dir. 1972—), Phi Delta Theta. Methodist. Clubs: Chicago; Finn & Feather (Oak Brook). Home: 124 Carriage Way Dr B-111 Burr Ridge IL 60521 Office: 2001 S York Rd Oak Brook IL 60521

PFEIFER, C. E., JR., aluminum co. exec.; b. St. Louis, Dec. 9, 1932; s. Carl E. and Lois D. (Dodge) P.; B.S.Ch.E., Washington U., St. Louis, 1954, M.S., 1958; M.B.A., U. Pitts., 1964; m. Joan Anne Balise, Dec. 31, 1958; children—Samantha Mae, Thomas James, Antony Peter, Benjamin Charles. With Aluminum Co. of Am., 1954—, fin. dir. Alcoa of Australia Ltd., 1966-75, asst. treas. parent co., 1975-78, treas., 1978—. Served with U.S. Army, 1956. Mem. Am. Inst. Chem. Engrs., Fin. Execs. Inst., Machinery and Allied Products Inst., Fin. Council II. Clubs: Duquesne, Pitts. Field; Melbourne Australian, Royal Melbourne (Australia) Golf. Office: 1501 Alcoa Bldg Pittsburgh PA 15219

PFEIFER, ELLEN CLAIRE (MRS. DANIEL M. POLVERE), music critic; b. St. Louis, June 23, 1947; d. George Edwin and Audrey Louise (McIntosh) Pfeifer; student U. Colo., 1964-65; B.S. in Journalism, Northwestern U., 1968; postgrad. U. So. Calif., 1968-70; m. Daniel M. Polvere, Apr. 8, 1973. Asst. music critic Boston Globe, 1970-72; music critic Boston Herald-Am., 1972—; guest critic Urban Arts, Sta. WNAC-TV, Boston, 1974-75. Participant, Rockefeller Found. project for tng. music critics, 1969-71. Rockefeller fellow, 1969-71. Mem. Music Critics Assn., Charlestown Preservation Soc. (sec.). Contbr. to Musical Am., High Fidelity, Opera News, Music Jour. Home: 33 Monument Sq Charlestown MA 02129 Office: 300 Harrison Ave Boston MA 02106

PFEIFER, SUSAN ELIZABETH (MRS. ANASTASIOS C. SOUTZOS), lawyer; b. Frederick, Md., Dec. 10, 1943; d. Charles Ernest and Catherine Virginia (Sanbower) Pfeifer; B.A., Am. U., 1964, J.D., 1967; m. Anastasios C. Soutzos, Nov. 16, 1969. Law clk. firm Fulbright, Crooker, Freeman, Bates & Jaworski, Washington, 1964-68; admitted to Md. bar, 1967, D.C. bar, 1968; mem. firm Richey & Clancy, Washington, 1968-71, Clancy & Pfeifer, Chevy Chase, Md., 1971—. Mem. Am., Md., D.C. bar assns., Am. Judicature Soc., Kappa Beta Pi (dean 1968, vice dean 1972). Home: 11812 Hunting Ridge Ct Potomac MD 20854 Office: Suite 750 5454 Wisconsin Ave Chevy Chase MD 20015

PFEIFFER, CARL CURT, pharmacologist; b. Peoria, Ill., May 19, 1908; s. Curt Richard and Minnie D. (Meiers) P.; A.B., U. Wis., 1931, A.M., 1933, Ph.D., 1935; M.D., U. Chgo., 1937; m. Lillian H. Twenhofel, June 13, 1930; children—Helen Nancy, Edward Carl. Asst. instr. pharmacology U. Wis., 1930-35; instr. pharmacology U. Chgo., 1936-37, 38-40; intern Wis. Gen. Hosp., Madison, 1937-38; asso. prof. pharmacology Wayne U. Coll. Medicine, 1940-41; chief pharmacology Parke Davis & Co., Detroit, 1941-43; prof., head dept. pharmacology U. Ill. Coll. Medicine, Chgo., 1945-54; prof., chmn. dept. pharmacology Emory U., 1954-57, dir. div. basic health scis., 1956-60; head sect. psychopharmacology Bur. Research, N.J. Neuropsychiat. Inst., 1960-74; dir. Brain Bio Center, 1974—. Sec.-treas. N.J. Mental Health Research and Devel. Fund, Inc.; trustee Brain Research Found.; sci. adv. bd. Am. Schizophrenic Assn. Served as lt. USNR, charge pharmocology and toxicology Naval Med. Research Inst., Bethesda, Md., 1943-45. Mem. A.M.A., Am. Soc. Pharmacol. and Exptl. Therapeutics (pres. 1961-62), Am. Soc. Exptl. Biology and Medicine, AAAS, Am. Chem. Soc. (medinial div.), Acad. Neurology and Biol. Psychiatry, N.Y. Acad. Sci., Assn. Research

Nervous and Mental Diseases, Sigma Xi. Author articles in med. jours.; former editor Internat. Rev. Neurobiology. Home: RD 5 169 Cherry Hill Rd Princeton NJ 08530 Office: 1225 State Rd Princeton NJ

PFEIFFER, ERIC ARMIN, psychiatrist, gerontologist; b. Rauental, Ger., Sept. 15, 1935; s. Fritz and Emma (Saborowski) P.; came to U.S., 1952, naturalized, 1957; A.B., Washington U., 1956, M.D., 1960; m. Natasha Maria Emerson, Mar. 21, 1964; children—Eric Alexander, Michael David, Mark Armin. Intern Albert Einstein Coll. Medicine, Bronx, 1960-61; resident in psychiatry U. Rochester (N.Y.), 1961-64; practice medicine specializing in psychiatry, Durham, N.C., 1966-76, Denver, 1976-78; asst. prof. Duke U., Durham, 1966-69, asso. prof., 1969-72, prof., 1971-76, project dir. OARS program, 1971-76, asso. dir. Center for Study Aging, 1974-76; dir. Davis Inst. for Care and Study Aging, Denver, 1976-77; prof. psychiatry U. Colo., Denver, 1976-78; prof. psychiatry, chief div. geriatric psychiatry U. South Fla. Coll. Medicine, Tampa, 1978—; chief psychiatry service Tampa VA Med. Center, 1979—; cons. in field; chmn. bd. Social Systems, Inc., 1975-76; chmn. com. on mental health and mental illness of elderly HEW, 1976-77. Served with USPHS, 1964-66. Markle Found. scholar academic medicine, 1968-73. Fellow Gerontol. Soc. (chmn. clin. medicine sect. 1975-76), Am. Psychiat. Assn.; mem. Am. Geriatrics Soc. (Allen Gold medal 1977), So. Psychiat. Soc., Phi Beta Kappa. Author: Disordered Behavior, 1968; (with E. W. Busse) Behavior and Adaptation in Late Life, 1970, 2d edit., 1977; Successful Aging, 1974; Multidimensional Functional Assessment, 1977. Home: 5140 Longfellow Ave Tampa FL 33609 Office: 12901 N 30 St Tampa FL 33612

PFEIFFER, J(OHN) DOUGLAS, mag. editor; b. Quebec City, Can., Oct. 29, 1927; s. Gordon Edward and Dorothy Douglas (Young) P.; came to U.S., 1950, naturalized, 1955; student Sir George Williams Coll., Montreal, 1945-48, Pasadena City Coll., 1952-53, Pomona Coll., 1951-52, Los Angeles State Coll., 1953-55, Redlands U., 1955; B.A., Long Beach State Coll., 1961; m. Virginia Mae Sturgess, Nov. 8, 1958. Dir. ski sch. Snow Summit, Big Bear Lake, Cal., 1953-63; tchr. Big Bear Lake, 1955-56, Newport Beach (Cal.) pub. schs., 1960-63; nat. editor Skiing mag., N.Y.C., 1963-64; dir. ski sch., Loveland Basin, Colo., 1964-65; editor-in-chief Skiing, Skiing Area News, Skiing Area Guide, Skiing Internat. Yearbook, Skiing Trade News, N.Y.C., 1965-74, editor-at-large, 1975-76, contbg. editor Ski Mag. Mem. Far West (pres. 1961-62), Rocky Mountain ski instrs. assns., Profl. Ski Instrs. Am. (founding dir., treas. 1961-65). Clubs: Los Angeles Athletic; City Island Yacht (N.Y.C.). Author: Skiing with Pfeiffer, 1958, 62; Skiing Simplified, 1972; Ten Secrets of Skiing (for Bob Beattie), 1965; Skiing—The Killy Way, 1972. Writer, narrator film Freestyle, Prostyle, 1975. Contbr. articles to mags.; TV sports commentator; performer ski films. Home: 200 E 36th St New York City NY 10016 Office: Ski Mag 380 Madison Ave New York City NY 10017. *Had always wanted to be the world's best ski instructor. I love teaching, any subject. Skiing is more a way of life than merely a sport for me. Relinquished administrative and office responsibilities in N.Y.C. to be free to spend more time in mountains, to write, and to get back in touch with the roots of life.*

PFEIFFER, JANE CAHILL, broadcasting exec.; b. Washington, Sept. 29, 1932; d. John Joseph and Helen (Reilly) Cahill; B.A., U. Md., 1954; m. Ralph A. Pfeiffer, Jr., June 3, 1975. With IBM Corp., Armonk, N.Y., 1955-76, sec. mgmt. rev. com., 1970, dir. communications, 1971, v.p. communications and govt. relations, 1972-76; bus. cons., 1976-78; chmn. bd. NBC, Inc., N.Y.C., 1978—; dir. Chesebrough-Ponds, Inc., Internat. Paper Co., J.C. Penney Co. Participant, White House Fellows program, 1966; mem. Council on Fgn. Relations; mem. Pres.'s Commn. Mil. Compensation, Pres.'s Commn. White House Fellows. Trustee Rockefeller Found., U. Notre Dame. Office: NBC 30 Rockefeller Plaza New York NY 10020

PFEIFFER, JOHN EDWARD, author; b. N.Y.C., Sept. 27, 1914; s. Edward Heyman and Jeannette (Gross) P.; B.A., Yale U., 1936; m. Naomi Ranson, Sept. 9, 1939; 1 son, Anthony John. Sci. editor Newsweek mag., N.Y.C., 1936-42; sci. dir. CBS, N.Y.C., 1946-48; mem. editorial bd. Sci. Am., N.Y.C., 1948-50; free-lance writer, editor, 1950—; adj. prof. anthropology Livingston Coll., Rutgers U., 1968—; cons. NSF, U. Chgo., Princeton, Tulane U., Ednl. Testing Service, Princeton, N.J. Trustee Solebury Sch., New Hope, Pa. Recipient CBS TV Writing award, 1959, Wenner-Gren Found. grant, 1961, Carnegie Corp. of N.Y. grants, 1965, 69; Guggenheim fellow, 1952, 54, Fulbright fellow, 1958. Mem. AAAS, Am. Anthrop. Assn., Soc. Am. Archeologists, Nat. Assn. Sci. Writers, Prehistoric Soc. London. Author: Science in Your Life, 1939; The Human Brain, 1955; The Changing Universe, 1956; From Galaxies to Man, 1959; The Thinking Machine, 1962; The Search For Early Man, 1963; The Cell, 1964; New Look at Education, 1968; The Emergence of Man, 1969, 3d edit., 1978; The Emergence of Society...A Prehistory of the Establishment, 1977. Home: 170 N Main St New Hope PA 18938 Office: 28 W Bridge St New Hope PA 18938

PFEIFFER, JOHN WILLIAM, publisher, writer; b. Wallace, Idaho, July 10, 1937; s. John William and Mary Loretta (Schmidt) P.; B.A., U. Md., 1962; Ph.D. (fellow), U. Iowa, 1968; m. Judith Ann Cook, Dec. 14, 1973; children—Heidi Erika, Charles Wilson. Instr. U. Md., 1965-67; dir. adult edn. Kirkwood (Iowa) Community Coll., 1967-69; dir. ednl. resources Ind. Higher Edn. Telecommunications Systems, Indpls., 1969-72; pres. Univ. Assos., San Diego, 1972—; adj. tchr. Ind. U., 1969-72, Purdue U., 1971-72. Served with U.S. Army, 1958-62. Author: Instrumentation in Human Relations Training, 1973, 2d edit., 1976; Reference Guide to Handbooks and Annuals, 1975, 2d edit., 1977. Editor: A Handbook of Structured Experiences for Human Relations Training, 7 vols., 1969-79; The Annual Handbook for Group Facilitatiors, 8 vols., 1972-79; editor Group and Organizations Studies: Internat. Jour. for Group Facilitators, 1976—. Home: 369 Mesa Way La Jolla CA 92037 Office: 8517 Production Ave San Diego CA 92121

PFEIFFER, RALPH ALOYSIUS, JR., mfg. co. exec.; b. Fordyce, Ark., Mar. 19, 1927; s. Ralph Aloysius and Catherine (Winter) P.; B.B.A., John Carroll U., 1950; postgrad. John Marshall Law Sch., 1951-52; m. Maryruth Price, Sept. 3, 1949 (div. Mar. 1974); children—Mary Ellen, Karen, Christine, JoAnne, Ralph Aloysius III, Elizabeth, John, William, Nancy, Thomas E.; m. 2d, Jane Pennington Cahill, June 3, 1975. With IBM Corp., 1949—, data processing div. v.p., regional mgr. for govt.-edn.-med. region, 1963-69, corp. dir. mktg., 1969-70, corp. v.p. ops. staff, 1970, pres. data processing div., 1970-74, corp. sr. v.p., chmn., chief exec. officer IBM W.T. Ams./Far East Corp., 1974—; dir. Riggs Nat. Bank, Washington; vice chmn. U.C. Bus. and Industry Adv. Com. to OECD. Trustee, Ind. Coll. Funds Am., vice chmn., 1974—; trustee Manhattanville Coll.; trustee, mem. exec. com. Council of the Americas; bd. dirs., mem. exec. com. Center for Inter-Am. Relations, 1975—; mem. adv. bd., mem. Internat. Council on Future of Bus., Center Strategic and Internat. Studies; advisory council Japan-U.S. Econ. Relations, Council Fgn. Relations; Nat. Com. on U.S.-China Relations. Served with USNR, 1945-46. Mem. Asia Soc. (trustee 1974—), U.S.-Mex. C. of C. (dir.), Internat. C. of C. (trustee, mem. exec. com. U.S. council 1976—), Nat. Planning Assn. (com. changing internat. realities). Clubs: Internat. (bd. govs. 1964-65), Congressional Country, F St. (Washington); Econ., Univ. (N.Y.C.); Apawamis Country (Rye); Belle Haven (Greenwich); Pinnacle (N.Y.C.). Home: Field Point Circle Greenwich CT 06830 Office: Town of Mt Pleasant Route 9 North Tarrytown NY 10591

PFEIFFER, RICHARD CLAIR, univ. pres.; b. Kenton, Ohio, Dec. 12, 1915; s. Henry Albert and Ruth (Borland) P.; B.C.S., Tiffin U., 1954; LL.D., Heidelberg Coll., 1972; m. Jean Elizabeth Homan, Oct. 4, 1941; children—Dan E., Marc A. (dec.), Amy Lou (Mrs. Dennis Day Turner). Jr. accountant W. Leslie King & Co., C.P.A.'s, Cleve., 1940-43; partner Deinzer-Pfeiffer & Co., pub. accountants, Tiffin, Ohio, 1946-67; pres. Tiffin U., 1953—. Dir. Tri-County Nat. Bank, Tiffin. Mem. Ohio Advisory Council Vocat. Edn., 1974-77. Served to capt. AUS, 1943-46, 51-52. Registered pub. accountant, Ohio. Mem. Nat., Ohio pub. accountants socs., Ohio Bus. Tchrs. Assn., Am. Assn. Ind. Coll. and Univ. Pres.'s, Am. Legion, Tiffin U. Alumni Assn., Tiffin C. of C. (past treas.). Mem. United Ch. of Christ (moderator Gen. Synod 1969-71, treas. N.W. Ohio Assn. 1963—). Mason (Shriner), Rotarian, Elk. Home: 74 W Perry St Tiffin OH 44883. *Having devoted most of my sixty-three years to a life of service and concern, I am frequently asked by my friends, "Why do you do what you do when you get nothing for it?" While many people look at reward only in terms of money, my philosophy has been, to do what needed to be done, those things for which I had the ability and would devote the time.*

PFEIFFER, ROBERT JOHN, business exec.; b. Suva, Fiji Islands, Mar. 7, 1920; s. William Albert and Nina (MacDonald) P.; came to U.S., 1921, naturalized, 1927; grad. high sch., Honolulu, 1937; m. Mary Elizabeth Worts, Nov. 29, 1945; children—Elizabeth Pfeiffer Tumbas, Margaret Pfeiffer Colbrandt, George, Kathleen. With Inter-Island Steam Navigation Co., Ltd., Honolulu (re-organized to Overseas Terminal Ltd. 1950, merged into Oahu Ry. & Land Co. 1954), 1937-55, v.p., gen. mgr., 1950-54, mgr. ship agy. dept., 1954-55; v.p., gen. mgr. Pacific Cut Stone & Granite Co., Inc., Alhambra, Calif., 1955-56; v.p., gen. mgr. Matcinal Corp., Alameda, Calif., 1956-58; mgr. div. Pacific Far East Line, Inc., San Francisco, 1958-60; with Matson Nav. Co., San Francisco, 1960—, v.p., 1966-70, sr. v.p., 1970-71, exec. v.p., 1971-73, pres., 1973-79, chmn. bd., 1979—; v.p. The Matson Co., San Francisco, 1968-70, pres., 1970—; chmn. bd. Matson Terminals, Inc., 1970-78, Matson Services Co., 1973—, Matson Agys., Inc., 1973-78; sr. v.p. Alexander & Baldwin, Inc., Honolulu, 1973-77, exec. v.p., 1977-79, pres., 1979—, also dir., dir. all Matson Cos., Sierra R.R. Co. Past chmn. maritime transp. research bd. Nat. Acad. Sci.; former mem. select com. Am. Mcht. Marine Seamanship Trophy Award; former mem. commn. sociotech. systems NRC. Bd. dirs. San Francisco Bay Area Council. Served to lt. USNR, World War II; comdr. Res. ret. Mem. Nat. Assn. Stevedores (past pres.), Nat. Cargo Bur. Internat. (bd. dirs.), Internat. Cargo Handling Coordination Assn. (past pres. U.S. nat. com.), Propeller Club U.S. (past pres. Honolulu), Nat. Def. Transp. Assn. (life), U.S., Calif., Los Angeles, San Francisco, Hawaii Island, Hawaii, Maui chambers commerce, Nat. Maritime Museum Assn. (trustee), World Affairs Council No. Calif. (trustee), Am. Bur. Shipping (bd. mgrs.), Pacific Maritime Assn. (dir., mem. exec. com.), Navy League U.S. (adv. bd.), Aircraft Owners and Pilots Assn., San Francisco Area World Trade Assn. (dir.). Republican. Mason (32 deg., Shriner). Clubs: Pacific, Outrigger (Honolulu); Pacific Union, Bohemian, World Trade (San Francisco). Home: 535 Miner Rd Orinda CA 94563 Office: 822 Bishop St Honolulu HI 96813

PFENNING, CHARLES RICHARD, assn. exec.; b. Buhl, Minn., May 21, 1920; s. Charles Earl and Mae (Lyons) P.; student Virginia (Minn.) Jr. Coll., 1939, Denver City Coll., 1947-48, Am. River Coll., 1956-57, Sacremento City Coll., 1958-59, Sacramento State Coll., 1959-60; m. Nola Fern Cluett, Oct. 6, 1940; children—Charles Richard, Gary L., Terrence Allen. With G.N. Ry., 1937-41; freight-passenger agt., night chief dispatcher, asst. chief dispatcher W.P. R.R. Co., 1948-63; trustee Am. Train Dispatchers Assn., Chgo., 1963, v.p. Midwest, 1964-69, pres., 1969—. Served with AUS, 1941-47; PTO. Mem. Ry. Labor Execs. Assn. (exec. bd.). Mason; mem. Order Eastern Star. Home: 325 N Lombard Ave Oak Park IL 60302 Office: 1401 S Harlem Ave Berwyn IL 60204*

PFEUFFER, ROBERT JOHN, musician; b. Cleve., Dec. 25, 1925; s. Henry Vincent and Elmo Alice (Burger) P.; B.Mus. in Edn., U. Mich., 1950, M.Mus. in Edn., 1951; m. Betty June Weller, Sept. 21, 1946; children—Barbara (Mrs. Steven Mosley), Jeanne, Susan, Catherine. Contrabassoonist, bassoonist Detroit Symphony Orch., 1951-61, Phila. Orch., 1962—; instr. bassoon Wayne State U., 1957-61, New Sch. Music, Phila., 1969—. Served with AUS, 1942-44. Mem. U.S. Power Squadron, Kappa Kappa Psi, Pi Mu Alpha. Roman Catholic. Home: 29 Mountwell Ave Haddonfield NJ 08033 Office: care Phila Orchestra 230 S 15th St Philadelphia PA 19102

PFISTER, EDWARD JOSEPH, pub. broadcasting exec.; b. N.Y.C., Apr. 9, 1934; s. Paul A. and Caroline (Safranck) P.; B.A., St. Peter's Coll., 1957; M.A., Seton Hall U., 1965; m. Kathryn M. Luchsinger, June 18, 1960; children—Eddie, Therese, Anthony. Mgr. info. services Nat. Ednl. TV, N.Y.C., 1960-65; dir. info. services Agy. for Instructional TV, Bloomington, Ind., 1965-70; dir. pub. relations and info. services Nat. Assn. Ednl. Broadcasters, Washington, 1970-72, dir. chmn.'s coordinating com., 1972-73; exec. asst. to chmn. bd. Pub. Broadcasting Service, 1973-76; pres. Pub. Communication Found. N. Tex., Dallas, 1976—; tchr. Greek, Latin and English, high schs., N.Y., 1957-60; reporter Reno Evening Gazette, 1960, The Record, Hackensack, N.J., 1954-57. Mem. fin. com. Pub. Broadcasting Service; mem. Eastern Ednl. TV Network. Mem. So. Ednl. Communications Assn. (vice-chmn., exec. com.), Nat. Assn. Ednl. Broadcasters, Public TV Mgrs. Council, Assn. Public Broadcasting (dir., incorporator). Author: The People's Business: A Review of Public TV, 1974; The Financial Status of Public Broadcasting Stations in the U.S., 1968-69, 1970; also articles. Home: 4818 Melissa Ln Dallas TX 75229 Office: 3000 Harry Hines Blvd Dallas TX 75201

PFISTER, RICHARD GEORGE, agrl. engr., educator; b. Lake City, Mich., July 15, 1926; s. Emil E. and Anna C. Pfister; B.S., Mich. State U., 1950, M.A., 1953, Ph.D., 1960; m. Lydia M. Venta, Sept. 9, 1950; children—Linda, Mary, Nancy. Grad. asst. dept. Mich. State U., East Lansing, 1950-51, instr. agrl. engring. extension div., 1955-60, asst. prof. agrl. engring., 1960-70, asso. prof., 1970-72, prof., 1972—; cons. Bur. Labor Standards, Occupational Safety and Health Adminstrn., U.S. Dept. Labor; chmn. standards adv. com. on agr. U.S. Dept. Labor, 1977-78; chmn. Mich. Bd. Health and Safety Compliance and Appeals, 1975—; mem. Nat. Adv. Com. on Safety in Agr., 1975-76; tchr. Imlan (Mich.) public schs., 1951-55. Served with USN, 1946-48. Recipient Outstanding Extension Specialist award Mich. State U., 1972. Mem. Am. Soc. Agrl. Engrs., Am. Soc. Safety Engrs. (pres. Lansing chpt. 1965-66), Nat. Inst. for Farm Safety, Mich. Rural Safety Council (sec. 1955—), Mich. State U. Extension Specialists Assn. (pres. 1970-71), Alpha Zeta, Kappa Delta Pi. Co-author: Agricultural Machinery Safety; contbr. numerous articles on agrl. engring. and safety to various mags. and jours. Home: 1134 Sunset Ln East Lansing MI 48823 Office: Agricultural Engring Dept Mich State Univ East Lansing MI 48824*

PFISTER, ROBERT KENNETH, drug co. exec.; b. Newark, Jan. 17, 1919; s. Richard and Viola (Kaufmann) P.; student Syracuse U., 1937-40; B.S., N.Y. U., 1941; m. Doris Crane, May 15, 1943; children—Jeffrey, Carol, Richard, Nancy, Greg. With Mfrs. Hanover Trust Co., 1941-42; accountant Hurdman & Cranstoun, 1942-44, Price Waterhouse & Co., 1944-47; staff Sterling Drug, Inc., N.Y.C., 1947—, treas., asst. sec., 1960-66, dir., v.p. finance, treas., 1966-71, exec. v.p., 1971-74, vice chmn. bd., 1974—; dir. Dentsply Internation, Inc., York, Pa., Am. Union Ins. Co., Am. States Ins. Co., Indpls. Served with AUS, 1941. C.P.A., N.Y. Mem. Drug Chem. and Allied Trade Assn. (dir.), Delta Kappa Epsilon. Club: Canoe Brook Country. Home: 67 Browning Rd Short Hills NJ 07078 Office: 90 Park Ave New York City NY 10016

PFISTER, ROBERT MARTI, educator, microbiologist; b. Bellrose, N.Y., Feb. 25, 1933; s. Robert and Edna Agatha (Beuscher) P.; B.S., Syracuse (N.Y.) U., 1957, M.S., 1960, Ph.D., 1964; m. Jeanne Deborah Nordheim, Nov. 13, 1954; children—Ellen, Alison, Valerie, Robert. Research asst. Syracuse U. Research Corp., 1958-63; research asso. Lamont Geol. Lab., Columbia U., 1964-66; mem. faculty Ohio State U., Columbus, 1966—, prof. microbiology, chmn. dept., 1973—. Served with U.S. Army, 1952-54. NSF grantee, 1966, Dept. Interior grantee, 1971. Mem. Am. Soc. Microbiology (v.p. Ohio br. 1973—), Sigma Xi. Author articles in field. Home: 1325 Wren Lane Powell OH 43605 Office: 484 W 12th St Columbus OH 43210

PFLANZE, OTTO PAUL, educator; b. Maryville, Tenn., Apr. 2, 1918; s. Otto Paul and Katrine (Mills) P.; B.A., Maryville Coll., 1940; M.A., Yale U., 1942, Ph.D., 1950; m. Hertha Maria Haberlander, Feb. 20, 1951; children—Stephen, Charles, Katrine. Historian, Dept. State, 1948-49; instr. N.Y. U., 1950-51; asst. prof. U. Mass., 1952-58, U. Ill., 1958-61; prof. history U. Minn., 1961-76, Ind. U., 1977—; editor Am. Hist. Rev., 1977—; chmn. Conf. Group Central European History, 1978; mem. exam. bd., grad. record exam Ednl. Testing Service, 1972-76; mem. Inst. Advanced Study, 1970-71. Served to 1st lt. U.S. Army, 1942-46. Fulbright research fellow, 1955-57; fellow Am. Council Learned Socs., 1951-52, Guggenheim Found., 1966-67, Nat. Endowment Humanities, 1975-76, Internat. Research and Exchanges Bd., 1976; recipient Humanities award McKnight Found., 1962. Mem. Am. Hist. Assn., AAUP. Author: Bismarck and the Development of Germany, The Period of Unification, 1815-1871 (Biennal Book award Phi Alpha Theta), 1964; co-author: A History of the Western World: Modern Times, 3d edit., 1975. Co-editor: Documents on German Foreign Policy, 1918-1945, Vols. I-III, 1949-50; bd. editors Jour. Modern History, 1971-73, Central European History, 1972-74. Home: 4195 S Gran Haven Dr Bloomington IN 47401 Office: Dept History Ballantine Hall Ind Univ Bloomington IN 47401

PFLUEGER, EDWARD MAXIMILIAN, chem. co. exec.; b. Frankfort, W. Ger., June 23, 1905; s. Heinrich and Amalie (Ude) P.; came to U.S., 1926, naturalized, 1935; grad. gymnasium, Frankfurt, 1923; m. Kathleen Isabel Powers, Sept. 16, 1943. Owner, pres. Metachem, Inc., N.Y.C., 1953—; hon. chmn. Mobay Chem. Corp., Pitts., 1975—, Cutter Labs., Inc., Berkeley, Calif., 1973—. Clubs: Links, Racquet and Tennis (N.Y.C.); Duquesne (Pitts.). Home: 760 Park Ave New York NY 10021 Office: 425 Park Ave New York NY 10022

PFNISTER, ALLAN OREL, educator; b. Mason, Ill., July 23, 1925; s. Ardon Orel and Rose Margaret (Sandtner) P.; A.B. summa cum laude, Augustana Coll., 1945; M.Div. summa cum laude, Augustana Theol. Sem., 1949; A.M. with honors, U. Chgo., 1951, Ph.D., 1955; LL.D. (hon.), U. Denver, 1978; m. Helen Edith Klobes, Dec. 18, 1948; children—Alicia Ann, Jonathan Karl, Susan Elaine. Instr. in religion Augustana Coll., 1946-47; instr. in philosophy and German, Luther Coll., Wahoo, Nebr., 1949-52, dean, 1953-54; research asst., univ. fellow U. Chgo., 1952-53, instr., 1954-57, asst. prof., 1957-58; dir. research joint bds. parish edn. Lutheran Ch. Am., 1958-59; vis. asso. prof. U. Mich., 1959-62, asso. prof., 1962-63; dean Coll. Liberal Arts, prof. philosophy Wittenberg (Ohio) U., 1963-67, provost, prof., 1967-69, acting pres., 1968-69; prof. higher edn. U. Denver, 1969-77, 78—, exec. vice chancellor and acting chancellor, 1977-78; dir. study fgn. study programs Fedn. Regional Accrediting Commns. Higher Edn., 1970-72; cons. in field. Recipient Outstanding Achievement Alumni award Augustana Coll., 1963. Mem. AAAS, Am. Acad. Polit. and Social Sci., Am. Studies Assn., Am. Assn. Higher Edn., Assn. for Study Higher Edn., Comparative and Internat. Edn. Soc., Blue Key, Phi Delta Kappa. Democrat. Author: Teaching Adults, 1967; Trends in Higher Education, 1975; Planning for Higher Education, 1976; contbr. numerous articles on higher edn. to profl. jours. Home: 7231 W Linvale Pl Denver CO 80227 Office: GCB 136 U Denver Denver CO 80208

PFOHL, JAMES CHRISTIAN, musician; b. Winston-Salem, N.C., Sept. 17, 1912; s. Bishop John Kenneth and Bessie (Whittington) P.; Mus.B., U. Mich., 1933, Mus.M., 1939; Mus.D. (hon.), Cin. Conservatory Music; m. Carolyn Day, Aug. 16, 1968; children—Alice Keith, James Christian, David Nelson. Dir. music Davidson Coll., 1933-52; dir. Moravian Ch. Chorus, Winston-Salem, 1933-66; organist, choir dir. Myers Park Presbyn. Ch., Charlotte, N.C., 1941-61; founder, condr. Mint Mus. Art Orch., Charlotte, 1944-46; founder, dir. Brevard (N.C.) Music Center and Transylvania Music Camp, 1936-64, Reston (Va.) Music Center, 1966-77, York (Pa.) Music Center for Young Musicians, 1977—; condr. No. Va. Youth Orch., 1967-77; artistic dir. No. Va. Music Center, Reston, 1968; dir. choral music Robert E. Lee High Sch., Fairfax County, Va.; asst. dir. fine and performing arts Inter-Suburban Planning Project, Alexandria, Arlington, Falls Church sch. dists., 1966; music dir., condr. Brevard Music Festival Orch., 1946-64, York (Pa.) Youth Symphony, 1976, condr. Charlotte Symphony, 1949-56, Charlotte Opera Assn., 1950-52, Jacksonville Symphony, 1952-61; music dir., condr. York (Pa.) Symphony Orch., 1971—; musician-in-residence York Coll., 1978; organist, choir dir. Washington Plaza Ch., Reston, 1969—; founder, dir. Reston Chorale and Reston Chamber Orch., 1966—; music dir. United Christian Parish of Reston. Regional v.p. Am. Symphony Orch. League. Mem. Am., N.C. bandmasters assns., Am. Guild Organists, Music Tchrs. Nat. Assn., N.C. Music Educators Assn., N.C. Orch. Dirs. Assn., Reston Chorale and Mus. Soc. (founder, dir. 1966), Am., N.C. choral dirs. assns., Music Educators Nat. Conf., Fedn. Music Clubs, Delta Omicron, Phi Mu Alpha, Phi Kappa Phi, Omicron Delta Kappa, Phi Kappa Lambda, Scabbard and Blade, Sigma Chi. Mason, Rotarian. Home: Brockie Green 1000 Country Club Rd York PA 17403

PFORZHEIMER, CARL HOWARD, JR., investment banker; b. N.Y.C., July 17, 1907; s. Carl H. and Lily Maud (Oppenheimer) P.; A.B., Harvard, 1928, M.B.A., 1930; H.H.D., Capital U., Columbus, 1969; D.C.S., Pace Coll., N.Y.C., 1959; m. Carol Jerome Koehler, Sept. 1, 1931; children—Nancy (Mrs. Edgar D. Aronson), Carl Howard III. Faculty, Centre de Preparation aux Affaires, Paris, 1930; banking apprentice, France, Germany, Eng., 1930-32; sr. partner investment banking firm Carl H. Pforzheimer & Co., N.Y.C., 1934—; pres., dir. Petroleum & Trading Corp. Mem. N.Y. State Bd. Regents, 1958-78, vice chancellor, 1975-78, emeritus, 1978—; chmn. Nat. Conf. on Govt., 1979—; pres. Carl and Lily Pforzheimer Found.; treas. Neustadter Found., 1950-58; mem. research libraries com. N.Y.

Pub. Library; mem. exec. com. Nat. Council on Ednl. Research, rep. to Edn. Commn. of States, 1971-74; past pres. Nat. Assn. State Bds. Edn.; vis. com. Harvard Grad. Sch. Edn., Univ. Library; mem. Temp. State Commn. Campus Unrest, 1969-73; mem. Nat. Reading Council, 1969-74; trustee, hon. chmn. investment com. Mt. Sinai Hosp.; bd. dirs. Econ. Devel. Corp., N.Y.C.; hon. trustee Horace Mann Sch., Boys Club of N.Y.; mem. council Rockefeller U. Served as col. War Dept. Gen. Staff, AUS, World War II; expert cons. sec. war, 1947. Decorated Legion of Merit; officer Legion Honor, Medaille de la Reconaissance (France). Mem. N.Y. Chamber Commerce and Industry (dir.), Nat. Mcpl. League (treas. 1958-75, pres. 1975-78), Keats-Shelley Assn. (pres.), Am. Assn. Community and Jr. Colls. (dir.), Am. Soc. French Legion, Newcomen Soc., Asso. Harvard Alumni (pres.), Signet Soc. Clubs: Union Interalliée (Paris); Westchester Country (Purchase, N.Y.); Century Assn., City Midday, Harvard, Grolier (council) (N.Y.C.); Harvard, Union Boat (Boston); Army and Navy (Washington); Ft. Orange (Albany, N.Y.). Office: 70 Pine St New York NY 10005. *Being fortunate enough to lead a life that is privately happy and being able also to lead a life that hopefully is publicly useful, to me the most satisfying condition is to spread this philosophy to the upcoming generations for their future guidance.*

PFOUTS, RALPH WILLIAM, educator; b. Atchison, Kans., Sept. 9, 1920; s. Ralph Ulysses and Alice (Oldham) P.; B.A., U. Kans., 1942, M.A., 1947; Ph.D., U. N.C., 1952; m. Jane Hoyer, Jan. 31, 1945; children—James William, Susan Jane, Thomas Robert, Elizabeth Ann. Research asst., instr. econs. U. Kans., 1946-47; instr. econs. U. N.C., 1947-50, lectr., 1950-52, asso. prof., 1952-58, prof., 1958—, chmn. grad. studies Sch. Bus. Adminstrn. and dept. econs., 1957-62, chmn. dept. econs., 1962-68. Social Sci. Research Council fellow U. Cambridge, 1953-54; Ford Found. Faculty Research fellow, 1962-63. Served as deck officer USNR, 1943-46. Mem. AAAS, Am., N.C. (past pres.) statis. assns., Am., So. (past pres.) econ. assns., Atlantic Econ. Soc. (v.p. 1973-76, pres. 1977-78), Population Assn. Am., Econometric Soc., Phi Beta Kappa, Pi Sigma Alpha, Alpha Kappa Psi, Omicron Delta Epsilon. Author: Elementary Economics-A Mathematical Approach, 1972; editor So. Econ. Jour., 1955-75; editor, contbr.: Techniques of Urban Economic Analysis, 1960; Essays in Economics and Econometrics, 1960; editorial bd. Metroeconimica, 1961—, Atlantic Econ. Jour., 1973—. Contbr. articles to profl. jours. Home: 502 Ransom St Chapel Hill NC 27514

PFRETZSCHNER, PAUL ALFRED, educator; b. Pelham Manor, N.Y., Nov. 6, 1922; s. Alfred and Rheta (Isaacs) P.; A.B., U. Buffalo, 1947; M.A., Yale, 1948; Ph.D., State U. Iowa, 1953; m. Caroline Putnam, Sept. 3, 1948; children—Margaret B., Susan C., Ellen P. Faculty govt. Lafayette Coll., Easton, Pa., 1949—, prof., 1959—, chmn. dept. govt. and law, 1960-63, 76—; Fulbright lectr. U. Dublin, 1963-64; vis. lectr. U. Buffalo, 1948, 56, 60, U. Pa., 1955-56; cons. Pa. Dept. Commerce, 1958-70. Impartial chmn. Pa. Blouse Industry, 1959—; commr. Easton Housing Authority, 1957-62, 65-71, Northampton County Park Bd., 1974—. Bd. dirs. Lehigh-Del. Devel. Council, Easton, chmn., 1972—. Served with AUS, 1943-46. Mem. AAUP, Am. Polit. Sci. Assn., Pa. Polit. Sci. and Pub. Adminstrn. Assn., Inst. Pub. Adminstrn. (Ireland). Author: Procedural Guide for Planning Commissions, 1960; Capital Improvements Programming, 1961; Community Renewal, 1962; County and Regional Planning, 1963; The Dynamics of Irish Housing, 1965; Political Culture in Ireland, 1976. Editor: Mid-Eastern Counties Boroughs Reporter, 1955-60. Home: 132 Reeder St Easton PA 18042

PFUND, HARRY WILLIAM, educator; b. Phila., Jan. 3, 1900; s. William J. and Anna M. (Erb) P.; A.B., Haverford Coll., 1922; A.M., Harvard, 1926, Ph.D., 1931; postgrad. univs. Munich, Berlin, Heidelberg; m. Friederike Marie Haufe, July 4, 1931; children—Peter Harry, Helga Friederike (Mrs. Helmut Gutmann). Instr. German, Harvard, 1924-26; instr., tutor Harvard, Radcliffe Coll., 1928-30; instr. German, Haverford Coll., 1926-27, asst. to asso. prof., 1930-48, prof., 1948-67, prof. emeritus, 1965—, chmn. dept. German, 1955-65, Exchange lectr. German univs., summer 1966; Ottendorfer traveling fellow N.Y. U., 1927-28. Vis. lectr. U. Colo., summer 1954, West Chester (Pa.) State Coll., 1967-72, Villanova U., 1972-73. Asst. sec. Carl Schurz Meml. Found., Phila., 1931-33, dir., mem. exec. com., 1946-49, v.p., 1949-56, pres., 1956-62. Relief work Am. Friends Service Com. (Quakers), Germany, also head mission French Zone, 1946-47. Named hon. citizen Freiburg, Germany, 1949; decorated Officer's Cross, Order of Merit (Republic Germany). Mem. Am. Assn. Tchrs. German (pres. Phila. chpt. 1968-70), Modern Lang. Assn. Am., German Soc. Pa. (v.p.), Nat. Carl Schurz Assn. (pres. 1962-71), Phi Beta Kappa. Author: Studien zu Wort und Stil bei Brockes, 1935; A History of the German Society of Pennsylvania, 1944, rev. edit., 1964. Co-editor: Studies in Honor of John Albrecht Walz, 1941. Founder, mem. editorial bd. Am.- German Rev., 1934-70. Contbr. articles, revs. to mags. Home: 624 Overhill Rd Ardmore PA 19003

PFUNDER, MALCOLM GILKEY, banker; b. Miles City, Mont., Nov. 11, 1919; s. Malcolm C. and Edna (Gilkey) P.; B.S. cum laude, Harvard U., 1942, M.B.A., 1947; m. Helen Marie Wash, June 12, 1943; children—Malcolm R., Elizabeth G. With Northwestern Nat. Bank, Mpls., 1947—, now sr. v.p. trust dept.; sec., dir. Shawmut Co.; dir. Mpls., Northfield and So. Ry. Past pres. Citizens League. Past v.p., bd. dirs. Family and Childrens Service, Mpls.; past treas. Minn. Orchestral Assn.; sec., treas., bd. dirs. Sumner T. McKnight Found. Served to capt. USAAF, 1942-45; ETO. Mem. Am. Inst. Banking, Am. Legion (past post comdr.). Episcopalian. Clubs: Minneapolis; Minnetonka Racquet, Woodhill Country. Home: 3360 Hill Ln Wayzata MN 55391 Office: Northwestern Nat Bank of Mpls 7th and Marquette Minneapolis MN 55480

PHAIR, GEORGE, research geologist; b. Washington, Nov. 15, 1918; s. Harry Gau and Eva (Weston) P.; B.S., Hamilton Coll., 1940; M.S., Rutgers U., 1942; M.A. (NRC-Rockefeller Found. fellow), Princeton, 1947, Ph.D., 1949; m. Cecil Alice MacQuaid, Sept. 27, 1946; children—Susan Marie, Raymond Weston. Asst. phys. chemist Geophys. Lab., Carnegie Instn., 1942-45; geologist, party chief Nfld. Geol. Survey, 1945-47; geologist, geochemist U.S. Geol. Survey, 1949—. Mem. earth scis. div. NRC, 1957-61, exec. com. div., 1958-61. Fellow Geol. Soc. Am., Mineral. Soc. Am. (archivist 1966-74), A.A.A.S., Wash. Philos. Soc.; mem. Geol. Soc. Washington, Geochem. Soc., Sigma Xi. Contbr. sci. papers to profl. lit., chpts. to tech. books. Editor: U.S. Geol. Survey Research, 1964-65. Home: 14700 River Rd Potomac MD 20854 Office: US Geol Survey Washington DC 20007

PHALEN, GEORGE ELMER, JR., banker; b. Norwood, Mass., Dec. 11, 1923; s. George Elmer and Eva (Welch) P.; B.S., Bentley Coll., 1943; postgrad. Grad. Sch. Credit and Financial Mgmt., Dartmouth, 1955, Stonier Grad. Sch. Banking, Rutgers, 1961; m. Veronica Daunt, June 14, 1947; children—Mary Phalen Hood, James, Ann Phalen Flaherty, Joan, Patricia, David, Stephen, Earl. Accountant Herbert French Co., Boston, 1946-48, with 1st Nat. Bank Boston, 1948—, sr. v.p., 1967-70, exec. v.p., 1970—; dir. First Nat. Boston Corp., Ludlow Corp., Needham, Mass.; trustee Edn. Devel. Corp., Waltham, Mass. Trustee, Bentley Coll., 1968. Served to capt. AUS, 1945. Mem. Nat. Assn. Credit Mgmt. (dir. 1962), New Eng. Credit Assn. (pres. 1955), Am. Bankers Assn. (chmn. comml. lending div. 1974). Clubs: Algonquin (Boston); Union League (N.Y.C.); Internat. (Washington). Home: 34 Chickering Rd Norwood MA 02062 Office: 100 Federal St Boston MA 02110

PHARES, E. JERRY, educator; b. Glendale, Ohio, July 21, 1928; s. Bruce and Gladys (West) P.; B.A., U. Cin., 1951; M.A., Ohio State U., 1953, Ph.D., 1955; m. Betty L. Knost, Aug. 6, 1955; 1 dau., Lisa M. Faculty, Kans. State U., Manhattan, 1955—, prof. psychology, 1964—, head dept., 1967—. Vis. asso. prof. Ohio State U., Columbus, Ohio Wesleyan U., 1961-62. Research grantee NIMH, 1960, NSF, 1964-76, Population Council, 1971. Fellow Am. Psychol. Assn. Author, co-author books. Contbr. articles to profl. jours. Office: Psychology Dept Kan State U Manhattan KS 66506

PHAUP, BERNARD HUGO, clergyman; b. Farmville, Va., July 17, 1912; s. George Leroy and Minnie (Dunkum) P.; student Central (S.C.) Wesleyan Coll., 1930-32; D.D., Houghton Coll., 1961; m. Dorothy Mae Foster, Oct. 16, 1935; 1 son, Gary Bernard. Ordained to ministry Wesleyan Meth. Ch., 1936; pastor, Radford, Va., 1932-35, Charlotte, N.C., 1935-38, 48-53, Altavista, Va., 1938-41, High Point, N.C., 1941-46, Thomasville, N.C., 1973—; gen. evangelist, 1946-48; v.p. N.C. Conf. Wesleyan Meth. Ch., 1950-53, pres., 1953-59; gen. supt. Wesleyan Ch., 1959-73, mem. bd. adminstrn., 1955-73, 76—, chmn. bd., 1959-69, 72-73, chmn. bd. trustees all corp., 1959-69, chmn. commn. world missions, 1959-68, 72-73, chmn. commn. extension and evangelism, 1968-72, supt. Eastern zone, 1959-63, Western zone, 1963-68, 72-73, So. zone, 1968—72; world-wide adminstrv. and preaching ministry, 1962. Chmn. bd. Hephzibah Children's Home, 1959—; pres. Wesleyan Investment Found., 1968—; bd. dirs. Central Wesleyan Coll., 1976—, Houghton Coll., 1976—, Kernersville Wesleyan Acad., 1976—. Home: 908 Lake Dr W Thomasville NC 27360

PHEIFFER, CHESTER HARRY, coll. dean; b. Louisville, Feb. 10, 1921; s. Frederick Philip and Frieda Anna (Lichtenberger) P.; A.B. with honors in Psychology, U. Louisville, 1943; M.A. (Seagram fellow), Ohio State U., 1944, Ph.D. in Psychology, 1949; O.D., So. Coll. Optometry, 1954; m. Catherine Ann Temple, Dec. 27, 1949; 1 dau., Anne Louise. Research asst., then research asso. Ohio State U., 1947-49; prof. psychology So. Coll. Optometry, 1949-54; practice optometry, Brownfield, Tex., 1955, Galveston, Tex., 1957; faculty U. Houston Coll. Optometry, 1954—, prof. optometry, 1959-61, 78—, dean coll., 1961-78; chmn. div. optometry Northeastern State U., Tahlequah, Okla., 1979—; cons. Nat. Bd. Examiners Optometry, 1953-60, Bur. Health Manpower, HEW, 1974-75; mem. adv. panel study cost of educating health profls. Inst. Medicine, 1972-74; mem. research adv. Com. Optometric Extension Program, 1972—. Bd. dirs. S.W. Contact Lens Soc., 1962-64, postgrad. chmn., 1960-66, program chmn., 1962-66; mem. adv. research council Am. Optometric Found. Recipient Service award Tex. Optometric Assn., 1977; named Tex. Optometrist of Year, 1971. Mem. Am. Optometric Assn. (cons. com. on edn. 1969-72, reviewer for jour.), AAAS, Am. Acad. Optometry, AAUP, Am. Pub. Health Assn., S.W. Contact Lens Soc. (program. chmn. 1969, plaque), Am. Assn. Higher Edn., Assn. Schs. and Colls. Optometry (v.p. 1969-71, pres. 1971-73, mem. exec. com. 1973-74, dir. 1973-78), Tex. Assn. Children with Learning Disabilities, Sigma Xi, Beta Sigma Kappa (gold medal award, regent 1964—, chmn. research adv. com. 1971—), Phi Kappa Phi. Mem. editorial council Jour. Optometric Edn., 1974, editor, 1975-78. Contbr. articles to profl. jours. Home: 508 Wheeler St Tahlequah OK 74464

PHEIFFER, WILLIAM TOWNSEND, former ambassador, former congressman; b. Purcell, Okla., 1898; grad. U. Okla., LL.B., 1919; m. Frances Uihlein, Mar. 20, 1954. Mem. state bars Okla., Tex., N.Y.; mem. 77th Congress (1941-43), 16th N.Y. Dist.; U.S. ambassador to Dominican Republic, 1953-57. Capt. cav. U.S. Army Res. Corps; vet. World Wars I and II. Mem. Counsel for Petroleum Adminstrn. for War; exec. asst. to chmn. Republican Nat. Com. Recipient award of Merit, World War II. Mem. Am. Bar Assn., Assn. Bar City N.Y., Am. Legion (past post comdr.), Chi Phi, Phi Alpha Delta, Delta Sigma Rho. Republican. Unitarian. Mason. Clubs: Metropolitan (N.Y.C.); Everglades, Beach (Palm Beach, Fla.). Home: 480 Park Ave New York NY 10022 Office: 110 E 59th St New York NY 10022. *I have endeavored to make the Golden Rule the yardstick of my daily conduct. Moreover, it is my credo to be kind to, and considerate of, people in the humblest stations of life who could never possibly bestow any benefit on me. To that end I have borne in mind those inspiring words of Goethe: "Kindness is the golden chain by which society is bound together."*

PHELAN, ARTHUR JOSEPH, business exec.; b. N.Y.C., Oct. 26, 1915; s. Arthur Joseph and Josephine Adelaide (Barrett) P.; student Am. Inst. Banking, 1934-35, N.Y. U., 1935-36; m. Mary Frances Ryan, Feb. 11, 1939; children—Jane Carolee, Leslie Diane, Sandra Christine. With Guaranty Trust Co. of N.Y., 1933-37; accountant N.Y. Post, 1937-38; accountant Webb & Knapp, Inc., N.Y.C., 1938-41, asst. sec., 1941, comptroller, 1942-44, treas., 1944-53, v.p., treas., 1953-55, sr. v.p., 1955-65, also trustee employees profit sharing plan; exec. v.p. David Greenewald Assos., Inc., 1965-66; fin. v.p. Lefrak Organization, Inc., Forest Hills, N.Y., 1966—; v.p., dir. LOGO Inc., Tulsa, 1976—. Roman Catholic. Club: North Hempstead Country. Home: 88 Summit Rd Port Washington NY 11050 Office: 97-77 Queens Blvd Forest Hills NY 11374

PHELAN, HAROLD LEON, lawyer; b. Smyer, Tex., Mar. 6, 1934; s. Jay Alfred and Phearby (Wynn) P.; B.S., Sul Ross State Coll., 1958; J.D., U. Tex., 1962; m. Marilyn E. Guetersloh, Sept. 1, 1960; children—Jay Michael, Randal Scott, Kimberley Kaye. Admitted to Tex. bar, 1961; pvt. practice law, 1962-64; county atty. Hockley County, Tex., 1964—. Founder Little Dribblers Basketball, Inc. Served with AUS, 1962. Mem. Tex., 121st Jud. bar assns. Baptist. Home: 1929 S Ave H Levelland TX 79336 Office: 518 Ave H Levelland TX 79336

PHELAN, JOHN DENSMORE, ins. co. exec., bus. cons.; b. Kalamazoo, Aug. 31, 1914; s. John and Ida (Densmore) P.; B.A. magna cum laude, Carleton Coll., 1935; m. Isabel McLaughlin, July 31, 1937; children—John Walter, William Paul, Daniel Joseph. With Hardware Mut. Ins. Co., Stevens Point, Wis., 1936-45; with Am. States Ins. Co., Indpls., 1945—, pres., 1963-76, chmn., 1976-79, also dir., dir. numerous subs.'s; dir. Mchts. Nat. Bank & Trust Co., Mchts. Nat. Corp., Indpls., Indpls. Power and Light; mem. adv. com. Timberland Co., Newmarket, N.H. Past pres. Marion County Assn. Mental Health; chmn. Harry J. Loman Found.; bd. dirs. United Way of Greater Indpls. C.P.C.U. Mem. C.P.C.U. Soc. (past nat pres.), C.L.U. Soc., Ind. State C. of C. (dir.), Phi Beta Kappa. Presbyterian. Clubs: Indpls. Athletic, 100 Club, Woodland Country (Indpls.). Author: Business Interruption Primer, 1949; contbr. articles to profl. jours. Home: 307 Woodland Ln Carmel IN 46032 Office: 500 N Meridian St Indianapolis IN 46207

PHELAN, MARTIN DUPONT, ret. film co. exec.; b. Chgo., Dec. 25, 1913; s. Martin Anthony and Margaret Crespo (DuPont) P.; A.B., DePauw U., 1934; m. Mary Katharine Harris, Aug. 14, 1937; children—Richard H., Jeremy D. Mdse. exec. Montgomery Ward, Chgo., 1934-42, Butler Bros., Chgo., 1946-47; corporate officer Eastin-Phelan Corp., Davenport, Iowa, 1947-77; dir. Citizens Fed. Savs. & Loan Assn., Citizens Service Corp. Trustee Davenport Area Found., Marycrest Coll. Served to col. U.S. Army, 1942-46. Mem. Am. (dir.), Iowa (pres. 1972) library trustee assns., Davenport C. of C. (pres. 1959). Republican. Episcopalian. Rotarian. Clubs: Davenport Country, Outing, Davenport. Home: 2524 Lorton Ave Davenport IA 52803 Office: 1235 W 5th St Davenport IA 52808

PHELAN, RICHARD MAGRUDER, mech. engr.; b. Moberly, Mo., Sept. 20, 1921; s. Frederick William and Ethel Ray (Magruder) P.; student Moberly Jr. Coll., 1939-41; B.S. in Mech. Engring., U. Mo., Columbia, 1943; M.M.E., Cornell U., 1950; postgrad. U. Mich., 1956-57; m. Olive Bernice McIntosh, May 25, 1951; children—William James, Susan Ray. Instr., Cornell U., 1947-50, asst. prof. mech. engring., 1950-56, asso. prof., 1956-62, prof., 1962—. Served with USNR, 1943-46. Mem. ASME, Am. Soc. Engring. Edn., Soc. Exptl. Stress Analysis, Am. Gear Mfrs. Assn., AAUP, AAAS, N.Y. Acad. Scis., Sigma Xi, Phi Kappa Phi, Pi Tau Sigma, Tau Beta Pi. Author: Fundamentals of Mechanical Design, 1957, 3d rev. edit., 1970; Dynamics of Machinery, 1967; Automatic Control Systems, 1977. Home: 4 Cornell Walk Ithaca NY 14850 Office: Upson Hall Cornell U Ithaca NY 14853

PHELAN, ROBERT CLARENCE, former cigar co. exec.; b. Bklyn., Feb. 25, 1916; s. Clarence J. and Julia (Flannery) P.; A.B., St. Peter's Coll., Jersey City, 1936; postgrad. N.Y. U. Grad. Sch. Bus., 1950-55; m. Rose A. Dougherty, July 31, 1943; children—Robert J., Gerard A., Brian P., Maureen A., John M. With Consol. Brokers, N.Y.C., 1936-39, R.H. Squire, ins., 1939-48; with Consol. Cigar Corp., 1948-78, sr. v.p., 1965-78, also dir. Chmn., No. Valley council Boy Scouts Am. Served to lt. USNR, 1942-46. Mem. Holy Name Soc. (pres. Mt. Carmel Ch. 1957, mem. bd. edn.). Home: 233 Engle St Tenafly NJ 07670

PHELAN, ROY LAWRENCE, bus. equipment mfg. co. exec.; b. Phila., Dec. 23, 1924; s. Edward R. and Frieda (Waizenegger) P.; B.E.E., Drexel Inst. Tech., 1949; m. Cecilia Boyle, Feb. 5, 1954; children—Kathleen, R. Kevin, Patrick E., Craig L. Jr. engr. Philco Co., Phila., 1949-50; devel. engr. IBM Corp., Vestal, N.Y., 1950-53; research engr. Burroughs Research Center, Paoli, Pa., 1953-58; mgr. systems engring., then mgr. engring. Burroughs Corp., Plymouth, Mich., 1958-69, mgr. advanced planning, Detroit, 1969-70; pres. Victor Research Center, Chgo., 1970-74; v.p. research and devel. NCR Corp., Dayton, Ohio, 1974—; dir. Synertek Corp., 1972-74; CBEMA, 1974—, chmn., 1978. Served with USAAF, 1943-45. Mem. Research Soc. Am. Methodist-Episcopalian. Patentee in field. Home: 908 Windom Sq Dayton OH 45429 Office: NCR Corp Dayton OH 45479

PHELPS, ALVA W., banker; b. Buena Vista, Ga.; s. Isaac E. and Georgia (Maddox) P.; student W. Ga. Coll., Columbia U.; m. Veva Whetstone (dec.); 1 dau., Sylvia (Mrs. James Moore); m. 2d, Genevieve Farls; 1 foster son, Robert E. Phelps. Formerly engr. U.S. Navy Arsenal, Dayton, O., Willys Overland Co., Toledo, O.; sales engr. Match & Merryweather Mfg. Co., Cleve.; mfg. exec., then asst. v.p. Gen. Motors Corp.; pres., chief exec. officer Oliver Corp., Chgo., then chief exec. officer, chmn. bd. dirs., pres.; now chmn. exec. com., chmn. bd. emeritus Old Orchard Bank, Skokie, Ill.; dir. Colt Industries, Inc.; cons. Hess Oil & Chem. Co. Mem. Am. Soc. M.E., Soc. Automotive Engrs. Mason (32, Shriner), Elk. Clubs: Chicago, University (Chgo.); Glen View (Golf, Ill.). Home: 100 Oxford Rd Kenilworth IL 60043 Office: Old Orchard Bank Old Orchard Plaza Skokie IL 60076

PHELPS, ASHTON, publisher; b. New Orleans, Dec. 30, 1913; s. Esmond and Harriott K. (Barnwell) P.; A.B., Tulane U., 1935, LL.B., 1937; postgrad. U. Mich. Law Sch., summer 1936; m. Jane C. George, Nov. 21, 1939 (dec.); 1 son, Ashton. Admitted to La. bar, 1937, since practiced in New Orleans; mem. firm Phelps, Dunbar, Marks, Claverie & Sims, 1946-67; pres., pub. Times-Picayune Pub. Corp., New Orleans, 1967—, also dir. Mem. bd. Christian edn. Presbyn. Ch. U.S., 1958-61, also mem. com. wills and bequests. Pres., New Orleans Community Health Assn., 1945-49, Howard Meml. Library Assn., 1950—; chmn. adv. bd. Female Orphan Soc., New Orleans, 1946-59; bd. visitors Tulane U., 1953-55, v.p. bd. administrs., 1955-72, adv. administr., 1972—. Active New Orleans chpt. ARC, 1954-60, Oschner Found. Hosp.; mem. Bd. of Liquidation City Debt, 1962-74, New Orleans Sewerage and Water Bd., 1964-67. Served from ensign to lt. USNR, 1942-45. Mem. Am. (spl. com. antitrust sect. on revision rules FTC), La., New Orleans bar assns., Assn. Bar City N.Y., Am. Law Inst., Am. Newspaper Pubs. Assn. (dir. 1972—, trustee found., chmn. press/bar com.), Order of Coif, Phi Beta Kappa, Delta Tau Delta, Phi Delta Phi, Omicron Delta Kappa. Clubs: Boston, La. (New Orleans). Presbyn. (elder, trustee). Home: 2100 Saint Charles Ave New Orleans LA 70140 Office: 3800 Howard Ave New Orleans LA 70140

PHELPS, CHARLTON YARNALL JACOBS (MRS. STOWE C. PHELPS), assn. exec.; b. Ardmore, Pa., May 24, 1926; d. Reginald R. and Sophia (Yarnall) Jacobs; student Smith Coll., 1943-44; m. Stowe C. Phelps, June 24, 1944; children—Sophia Y. Phelps Payne, Meredith C. Phelps Rugg. Dir. Planned Parenthood Manhattan and Bronx, 1950-56; dir. N.Y. State League for Planned Parenthood, 1951-56, pres., 1954-56; dir. Planned Parenthood Fedn. Am., 1953-65, past 1st v.p., chmn. exec. com., sec.; vice chmn. Child Care and Adoption Service; chmn. child adoption service Children's Aid Soc., 1965-68, pres. service, 1968—, trustee soc., 1968-74, chmn. city and country branches com., pres., 1975—; pres. bd. trustees Margaret Sanger Research Bur., 1969-72; dir. Reed St. Neighborhood House, Phila., 1945-48; mem. bd. Amateur Needlework Guild Am.; v.p. Les Boutiques de Noel; past treas. Spence Sch. Parents' Assn.; bd. dirs. Concern for Dying, 1973—, Boys' Clubs Am., 1976—; chmn. BCA Nat. Health Adv. Council, 1977—. Club: Cosmopolitan. Home: 149 E 73d St New York NY 10021

PHELPS, DAVID MICHAEL, journalist; b. Oakland, Calif., Feb. 16, 1950; s. Frank Wilbur and Frances Louise (Jones) P.; B.A. in Journalism, Mankato State U., 1972; m. Patricia Ann Maki, Sept. 11, 1971; 1 son, Nathan. Reporter, Mankato (Minn.) Free Press, 1972-76; press aide U.S. Rep. Tom Hagedorn, 1976; reporter Jackson (Miss.) Clarion-Ledger, 1977; reporter Mpls. Tribune, 1977—. Recipient Heywood Broun award Newspaper Guild, 1977; Disting. Service award Sigma Delta Chi, 1977; Frank Premack public affairs reporting award, 1978. Home: 1928 Cleveland St NE Minneapolis MN 55418 Office: 425 Portland Ave Minneapolis MN 55488

PHELPS, EDMUND STROTHER, economist; b. Evanston, Ill., July 26, 1933; s. Edmund Strother and Florence Esther (Stone) P.; B.A., Amherst Coll., 1955; M.A., Yale U., 1956, Ph.D., 1959; m. Viviana Regina Montdor, Oct. 1, 1974. Economist, Rand Corp., Santa Monica, Calif., 1959-60; asst. prof. Yale U., Cowles Found., 1960-62, asso. prof., 1963-66; vis. asso. prof. M.I.T., 1962-63; prof. econs. U. Pa., Phila., 1966-71; prof. econs. Columbia U., 1971-78, 79—; prof. N.Y. U., 1978-79; fellow Center for Advanced Study in Behavioral Scis., 1969-70; sr. advisor Brookings Inst., 1976—. Guggenheim fellow, 1978; Social Sci. Research Council fellow, 1966; Econometric Soc. fellow. Mem. Am. Econ. Assn. (mem. exec. com. 1976-78), Soc. Philosophy and Public Affairs, Phi Beta Kappa. Author numerous books including: Golden Rules of Economic Growth, 1966;

Microeconomic Foundations of Employment and Inflation Theory, 1970; Economic Justice, 1973; Studies in Macroeconomic Theory, 1979. Home: 45 E 89th St New York NY 10028 Office: Dept Econs Columbia U New York NY 10027

PHELPS, EDWIN RICE, coal cons.; b. Leavenworth, Kans., Jan. 12, 1915; s. Edwin Rice and Thekla (Wulfekuhler) P.; B.S., Kans. U., 1937; postgrad. Mass. Inst. Tech., 1942; m. Yvonne White, June 18, 1938; children—Edwin Rice III, Janet L. Phelps Karr, Jonathan F., William Bruce. Engr., Southwestern Ill. Coal Co., Percy, 1937-42; supt. constrn. Constant Constrn. Co., Lawrence, Kans., 1946-48; gen. supt. Pittsburg and Midway Coal Mining Co., Pittsburg, Kans., 1948-51, v.p. ops., 1951-59, pres., 1959-60; chief engr. Peabody Coal Co., St. Louis, 1960-62, v.p. engring., 1962-68, sr. v.p. ops., 1968-71, pres., chief exec. officer, 1971-78, vice-chmn., 1978-79; cons., 1979—; dir. Bank of St. Louis; mem. Dept. Interior Coal Adv. Com., 1976, World Energy Conf. Adv. Com., 1976; bd. mem. U.S. Nat. Com. of World Energy Conf., 1977—. Mem. advisory com. Sch. Engring., Kans. U. Served to lt. comdr. USNR. Recipient Disting. Service award U. Kans., 1976; registered profl. engr., Kans., Ky. Mem. Am. Inst. Mining, Metall. and Petroleum Engrs. (Howard N. Eavenson award 1972, Erskine Ramsey award 1978), Nat. Coal Assn. (dir. 1971—, chmn. 1974-75), Am. Mining Congress (dir. 1972-78, chmn. ad hoc exec. com. on surface mining), Bituminous Coal Ops. Assn. (dir. 1972-78), Nat. Soc. Profl. Engrs., Kans. U. Alumni Assn. (dir. 1955-60), U.S. C. of C. (natural resources com. 1958-60), Chi Epsilon (hon.). Presbyterian. Home: 12000 Heatherdane Saint Louis MO 63131 Office: 301 N Memorial Dr Saint Louis MO 63102

PHELPS, HUGH VAUGHN, supt. schs.; b. Montpelier, Idaho, Aug. 12, 1925; s. Hugh Morris and Irene Mae (Kunz) P.; B.E., U. So. Calif., 1946; B.S., U. Nebr., 1961, M.S., 1964, Ed.D., 1968; m. Margaret Ann Bowman, June 23, 1946; children—Kenneth V., Pamela Jean, Ronald H. Tchr. pub. schs., Pleasanton, Nebr., 1947-55; tchr. research project, Mullen, Nebr., 1955-57; coordinator community resources U. Nebr., Lincoln, 1957-58; supt. schs. Westside Community Schs., Omaha, 1959—. Vis. prof. Colo. State U., 1960—. Bd. dirs. Doane Coll., 1974—. Served with USN, 1943-46. Recipient Distinguished Service award Nebr. Council Sch. Adminstrs., 1973; Dr. Norman Thorpe award U. Nebr., 1973. Mem. Am. Assn. Sch. Adminstrs. (pres. 1975-76), Assn. Pub. Sch. Systems (pres. 1973-74), Omaha C. of C. (pres.'s council). Congregationalist (past moderator). Kiwanian. Home: 231 S 96th St Omaha NE 68114 Office: 909 S 76th St Omaha NE 68114

PHELPS, JAMES CARL, petroleum co. exec.; b. Lindsay, Okla., Oct. 14, 1922; s. Thomas and Alma (Thornton) P.; B.S. in Indsl. Engring., Okla. State U., 1949, M.S., 1951; m. Cora Marie Erwin, Apr. 25, 1942; children—Robert R., Ronald C. Refinery engr. Deep Rock Oil Corp., Cushing, Okla., 1950-51; pipeline engr. Service Pipe Line Co., Tulsa, 1951-53; v.p. Continental Pipe Line Co., Ponca City, Okla., 1953-62; v.p. Continental Oil Co., Houston, 1965-66, group v.p., 1966-67, sr. v.p., 1967-70, exec. asst. to pres., 1970-71; pres. Tesoro Petroleum Co., San Antonio, 1971—; dir. Citizens Nat. Bank. Mem. adv. com. Okla. State U., 1968; trustee Tex. S.W. Meth. Hosp., 1974—; vice-chmn. bd. San Antonio chpt. Am. Heart Assn.; vice-chmn. United Way San Antonio and Bexar County; chmn. S.W. Tex. Meth. Hosp. Fund Devel. Found.; mem. adv. com. U. Tex. at San Antonio, 1978-79. Served with USAF, 1943-46. Mem. San Antonio C. of C. (vice-chmn. 1979-80). Methodist (trustee ch.). Home: 208 Chattington Ct San Antonio TX Office: Tesoro Petroleum Corp 8700 Tesoro Dr San Antonio TX 78286

PHELPS, JAMES RAY, lawyer, pharm. co. exec.; b. East Bernstadt, Ky., Dec. 1, 1938; s. Fredrick and Evelyn (Bowling) P.; A.B. with honors in History, U. Cin., 1960, LL.B., 1962; m. Sophia Peter Sideroff, Mar. 20, 1965; children—Evan Parker, James Morgan, Michael Peter Frederick. Admitted to Ohio bar, 1962, Ky. bar, 1965, D.C. bar, 1967, U.S. Supreme Ct. bar, 1967, Ill. bar, 1970; trial atty. food and drug div. Office of Gen. Counsel, HEW, Washington, 1965-67; asst. U.S. atty. for D.C., 1967-69; asso., then partner firm Burditt & Calkins, Chgo., 1969-77; v.p., gen. counsel G.D. Searle & Co., Skokie, Ill., 1977—; instr. John Marshall Law Sch., 1970-73. Served with U.S. Army, 1962-64. Mem. D.C., Ill., Ky., Chgo. bar assns. Clubs: Union League (Chgo.); Skokie Country (Glencoe, Ill.). Home: 43 Crescent St Glencoe IL 60022 Office: PO Box 1045 Skokie IL 60076

PHELPS, JOSEPH BARNWELL, lawyer; b. New Orleans, July 25, 1916; s. Esmond and Harriott Kinloch (Barnwell) P.; grad. Woodberry Forest Sch., 1934; B.A., Tulane U., 1938, LL.B., 1940; m. Euphemie Labatut Tobin, Mar. 26, 1942; 1 son, Esmond II. Admitted to La. bar, 1940, since practiced in New Orleans; partner firm Phelps, Dunbar, Marks, Claverie & Sims, and predecessor, 1951—. Chmn. spl. donors div. New Orleans Heart Fund drive, 1963-64; capt. Tulane U. Forward Fund drive, 1965; adviser Christian Women's Exchange, New Orleans, 1965—. Served to maj. F.A., AUS, 1941-46. Decorated Bronze Star. Mem. Am., La. bar assns., Phi Delta Phi, Delta Tau Delta. Clubs: Boston, Louisiana, Stratford, New Orleans Country (New Orleans). Home: 1416 Valmont St New Orleans LA 70115 Office: Hibernia Bank Bldg New Orleans LA 70112

PHELPS, JOSEPH WILLIAM, banker; b. Richmond, Ky., Jan. 6, 1927; s. Ben and Hannah (Blunschi) P.; student pub. schs.; m. Mary Margaret Culton, Jan. 2, 1954; children—Melanie Jean, Joseph William. Nat. bank examiner U.S. Treasury Dept., 1950-58; asst. cashier Liberty Nat. Bank & Trust Co., Louisville, 1958-59, asst. v.p., 1959-62, v.p., 1962-67, head corr. bank dept., sec. to bd., exec. com., 1967-68, sr. v.p., 1968-70, exec. v.p., 1971-73, pres., chief adminstrv. officer, 1973—, also dir.; dir. Lincoln Income Life Ins. Co., One Hour Cleaners, Spartanburg, S.C., Neenah-Menasha, Wis., Badger One Hour Cleaners. Mem. exec. bd. Old Ky. Home council Boy Scouts Am.; dir. Ky. Council Econ. Edn.; bd. dirs. Ky. div. Am. Cancer Soc., Louisville Med. Research Found., YMCA, Associated Industries Ky.; gen. campaign chmn. Metro United Way, 1978; bd. regents Eastern Ky. U.; mem. Gov.'s Council Econ. Devel., Gov.'s Council Land Use Planning. Served with AUS, 1945. Mem. Am. Inst. Banking, Am. Bankers Assn., Ky. (dir.), Louisville (chmn. com. econ. edn.) chambers commerce, Res. City Bankers, Filson Club, English Speaking Union, Newcomen Soc. Episcopalian (vestryman). Clubs: Pendennis, Louisville Boat (Louisville). Home: 5015 Dunvegan Rd Louisville KY 40222 Office: 416 W Jefferson St Louisville KY 40202

PHELPS, MALCOM ELZA, physician, surgeon; b. El Reno, Okla., Oct. 16, 1905; s. James I. and Lydia (Malcom) P.; student U. Okla., 1922-26; M.D., State U. Ia., 1929; m. Maxine Hicks, Mar. 22, 1925; children—James V., Joseph M. Intern, U. Okla. Hosp., 1929-30, resident surgeon, 1930-31; asst. in urology Dr. W.J. Wallce, Oklahoma City, 1932-33; practice medicine, El Reno, 1931-68; founder Phelps Clinic, El Reno, 1948; cons. surgeon U.S. Indian Hosp., Concho, Okla., 1938-50; chief of staff El Reno Sanitarium, 1945-54; mem. staff Park View Hosp., El Reno, 1954—; div. surgeon, examiner C.R.I.&P. R.R., 1953—. Mem. Nat. Adv. Com. Poliomyelitis Vaccine, 1955-57; mem. adv. com. dependents med. care Dept. Def., 1956-68; spl. adviser to surgeon gen. army, 1957, 59; mem. adminstrs. med. adv. com. FAA, 1960-66; field dir. AMA Vol. Physicians Vietnam, 1966-67; dir. Supporting Assistance Health Office AID, Dept. State, 1968-74; clin. prof. family practice and community medicine U. Okla. Sch. Medicine, Oklahoma City, 1974—; cons. U.S.S.W. Reformatory (Bur. Prisons), USPHS. Licensed judge Am. Kennel Dog Show, 1945—. Decorated Medal of Health 1st class (Vietnam); named to Okla. Hall of Fame, 1967. Trustee, pres. Shepherd Found.; bd. dirs. Am. Bd. Family Practice, 1968-72, treas., 1972-74. Founding mem., sr. fellow S.W. Surg. Congress; mem. A.M.A. (poliovaccine com. 1957, com. preparation gen. practice 1957-58, v.p. 1967-68), So. Med. Assn., Okla. Med. Soc. (v.p. 1950), Am. Acad. Gen. Practice (founding mem., v.p., chmn. bd. 1952-56, pres. 1957, treas. 1962-66, pres. Family Health Found. Am. 1958-62), Am. Med. Writers Assn., Am. Soc. Clin. Hypnosis, Am. Assn. Physicians and Surgeons, Am. Assn. Ry. Surgeons, Flying Physicians Assn. (founding mem.), Delta Tau Delta, Phi Chi. Mem. Christian Ch. Mason, Elk. Clubs: Oklahoma City Kennel (pres. 1945-56), Bulldog of America (pres. 1958-60). Editorial Bd. Worldwide Abstracts of Gen. Medicine. Home: 801 S Hoff St El Reno OK 73036 Office: Phelps Clinic 1801 Parkview Dr El Reno OK 73036. *Kindness, courtesy, consideration of others and gentlemenly conduct are always in order regardless of circumstances. These attributes are present in those we admire and respect the most. Rudeness, arrogance and lack of consideration of others are often apparent in insecure individuals with an inferiority complex and are rarely seen in individuals of stature.*

PHELPS, MASON, corp. exec.; b. Evanston, Ill., Jan. 18, 1925; s. Mason and Louise Lamb (Cowles) P.; B.A., Yale, 1948; m. Margaret Taylor, July 5, 1947; children—Mason, Evans (Mrs. Michelson), Taylor. With VSI Corp., Pasadena, Calif., 1947—, pres., chief exec. officer, 1958—, also dir.; dir. Marshall Industries, San Marino, Calif., 1961—, Clow Corp., Chgo., 1968—. Office: VSI Corp 600 N Rosemead Blvd Pasadena CA 91107*

PHELPS, ORME WHEELOCK, educator; b. Hobart, Okla., July 5, 1906; s. William Andrews and Kate Mae (Forman) P.; A.B., U. Chgo., 1937, M.B.A., 1939, Ph.D., 1945; m. Jean Wright, Aug. 18, 1940; children—John Jackson, Sarah Hamilton. Asst prof. bus. adminstrn. U. Chgo., 1942-47; prof. econs. Claremont (Calif.) Men's Coll. and Grad. Sch., 1947-63, sr. prof., 1963-76, emeritus, 1976—, dean faculty, 1970-74; vis. prof. UCLA, 1950, State U. N.Y. at Brockport, 1968-69; Fulbright research prof. Univ. Coll. of W.I., Kingston, Jamaica, 1957-58; Brookings research prof., Washington, 1962-63. Pub. mem., regional vice-chmn. Wage Stblzn. Bd., 1951-53; labor arbitrator, mem. various govt. bds. Ford found. fellow, 1953-54. Mem. Indsl. Relations Research Assn., Am., Western econ. assns., Am. Assn. U. Profs. Democrat. Episcopalian. Author: Introduction to Labor Economics, 4th edit., 1967; Discipline and Discharge in the Unionized Firm, 1959; Union Security, 1954; Legislative Background of the Fair Labor Standards Act, 1939. Contbr. articles, book revs. to profl. jours. Home: 807 Noth College Claremont CA 91711

PHELPS, RICHARD FREDERICK, basketball coach; b. Beacon, N.Y., July 4, 1941; s. Richard Bruce and Margaret Adelle (Sullivan) P.; B.S. in Commerce, Rider Coll., 1963; M.A. in Bus. Edn., 1964; m. Teresa K. Godwin, June 25, 1965; children—Karen, Richy, Jennifer. Head basketball coach St. Gabriel's High Sch., Hazleton, Pa., 1965-66; asst. basketball coach U. Pa., 1966-70; head basketball coach Fordham U., N.Y.C., 1970-71, U. Notre Dame, 1971—. Named Coach of Year, N.Y. Coll. Basketball Writers Assn., 1971, Phila. Coll. Basketball Writers Assn., 1971. Office: U Notre Dame Notre Dame IN 46556*

PHELPS, ROBERT HOWARD, newspaper editor; b. Erie, Pa., July 19, 1919; s. Harry Vernon and Ruth Edwina (Fox) P.; A.B., U. Mich., 1941; M.S., Columbia U., 1950; m. Elizabeth Rita King, Jan. 10, 1947. Reporter, Ambridge (Pa.) Citizen, 1941-42, UP, Harrisburg, Pa., 1942-43, 46-49; copy editor Providence Jour.-Bull., 1952-54; asst. to nat. editor, then asst. met. editor,Washington editor N.Y. Times, 1954-74; exec. editor Boston Globe, 1974—. Served with USNR, 1943-46. Mem. Am. Soc. Newspaper Editors. Club: St. Botolph (Boston). Co-author: Libel: Rights, Risks, Responsibilities, 1967; editor: Men in the News, 2d edit., 1959, Witness to History, 1975. Home: PO Box 145 Lincoln MA 01773 Office: 135 Morrissey Blvd Boston MA 02107

PHELPS, THOMAS WILLIAM, former investment counsel; b. Chester, Minn., June 15, 1902; s. Thomas L. and Nellie (Coulson) P.; A.B., U. Minn., 1923; m. Rosalie Greenleaf Bailey, Apr. 22, 1933 (dec. Sept. 1965); children—Thomas W., Rosalie G. (Mrs. R.L. Thomas), Lucinda B. (Mrs. James C.S. Buckley); m. 2d, Christine Reed Cameron, Oct. 8, 1966. City editor Rochester (Minn.) Post and Record, 1919; reporter, city editor Mpls. Jour., 1923-25; free lance writer, 1925-27; reporter, news editor, chief Washington Bur. Wall St. Jour., 1927-35; editor Barron's Nat. Financial Weekly, 1936-38; partner, economist Francis I. du Pont & Co., 1938-49; mgr. econs. dept., asst. to bd. chmn. Socony Mobil Oil Co., Inc., 1949-60; partner Scudder, Stevens & Clark, N.Y.C., 1960-70. Life trustee Am. Schs. Oriental Research. Recipient Outstanding Achievement award U. Minn., 1956. Mem. N.Y. Soc. Security Analysts (past dir.), Phi Beta Kappa Assos. (past trustee), Beta Theta Pi. Clubs: Deadline, Pilgrims, University, Explorers, (N.Y.C.); Nantucket (Mass.) Yacht. Author: Your Securities Under Social Security, a Handbook of the Labor Factor in Investments, 1936; 100 to 1 in the Stock Market, 1972. Asso. editor: Financial Analysts Jour., 1964-66. Contbr. to periodicals. Home: 1111 N Ocean Blvd Delray Beach FL 33444 also 19 Orange St Nantucket MA 02554

PHELPS, WILLIAM CUNNINGHAM, lt. gov. Mo.; b. Nevada, Mo., Apr. 5, 1934; s. Dean Henry and Julia Irene (Myers) P.; A.B., U. Mo., 1956, LL.B., 1959; m. Joanne Ronchetto, July 22, 1972. Admitted to Mo. bar, 1959; partner firm Morrison, Hecker, Cozad, Morrison & Curtis, Kansas City, Mo., 1959-73; mem. Mo. Ho. of Reps., 1961-73, mem. appropriations, jud. and econ. coms., Republican whip, mem. joint legis. coms. fiscal affairs and correctional insts.; lt. gov. State of Mo., 1973—. Chmn. Gov.'s Conf. on Edn.; vice chmn. Nat. Conf. Lt. Govs.; state chmn. YMCA's Youth in Govt. Program, 1966-73; hon. bd. dirs. Rockhurst Coll.; trustee Kansas City Philharmonic Orch.; bd. govs. Citizens Assn., Kansas City. Served as capt. U.S. Army, 1957. Mem. Am., Mo. bar assns., Mo. Assn. Reps. (pres. 1963), Omicron Delta Kappa, Phi Eta Sigma, Beta Theta Pi, Phi Delta Phi. Episcopalian. Home: 5016 Grand St Kansas City MO 64112 Office: State Capitol Bldg Box 563 Jefferson City MO 65102

PHELPS, WILLIAM WALTER, JR., banker; b. Washington, Mar. 18, 1918; s. William Walter and Nina (Paris) P.; grad. St. Marks Sch., 1935; B.A., Yale, 1939; m. Olive Richards Perry, May 28, 1942; children—William Walter III, Rosamond Lea, Ellen Sheffield. Served with U.S. Fgn. Service, Havana, Oslo, Frankfurt, 1946-53; with First Nat. Bank. Boston in London, Eng. and Boston, 1953-63; with Mellon Bank N.A., Pitts., 1963—, sr. v.p., 1967—; dir. Mellon Bank Internat., N.Y.C. Bd. dirs. World Affairs Council Pitts. Served to maj. AUS, 1941-46. Decorated Bronze Star, Soldiers medal. Home: 712 St James St Pittsburgh PA 15232 Office: Mellon Bank NA Mellon Sq Pittsburgh PA 15230

PHENIX, PHILIP HENRY, educator; b. Denver, Mar. 1, 1915; s. Henry Vinton and Bessie Thorson (Manning) P.; B.A., Princeton, 1934; M.Div., Union Theol. Sem., 1942; Ph.D., Columbia, 1950; L.H.D., Alderson-Broaddus Coll., 1970; m. Gena Tenney, June 14, 1943; children—Roger Branscombe, Morgan Scott. Head ordinary math. sect., actuarial div. Met. Life Ins. Co., N.Y.C., 1937-39; instr. meteorology USAAF, 1943-45; asst. prof. philosophy and religion, counselor religion Carleton Coll., 1946-48, asso. prof. religion, chaplain, 1950-53, coll. dean, 1958-60; lectr. philosophy Columbia, 1949-50, lectr. edn. Tchrs. Coll., 1953-54, asso. prof., 1954-56, prof. edn., 1956-58, 60-62, prof. philosophy, 1962-73, Arthur I. Gates prof. Philosophy and edn., 1973—, chmn. dept. philosophy and social scis., 1974-77, also dir. div. philosophy, social scis. and edn., 1974-77; program asso., asst. treas. Edward W. Hazen Found., New Haven, 1953-54. Served as 1st lt. Chaplain Corps, AUS, 1945-46. Fellow Philosophy Edn. Soc. (pres. 1971), Soc. Values in Higher Edn.; mem. Religious Edn. Assn., NEA, Phi Beta Kappa, Sigma Xi. Author: Intelligible Religion, 1954; Philosophy of Education, 1958; Religious Concerns in Contemporary Education, 1959; Education and the Common Good, 1961; Realms of Meaning, 1964; Man and His Becoming, 1964; Education and the Worship of God, 1966. Editor: Philosophies of Education, 1961; transl. from Spanish: Frontiers in the Americas: A Global Perspective (Jorge Mañach), 1975. Home: 70 LaSalle St Apt 13G New York City NY 10027

PHIBBS, HARRY ALBERT, interior designer; b. Denver, Jan. 9, 1933; s. Harry Andrew and Mary May (Perriam) P.; B.A., U. Colo., 1954, B.F.A., 1957; m. Alice Conners Glynn, Oct. 23, 1957; children—Kathleen Ann, Paul Robert, Mary Alice, Michael John, Peter James, Daniel Edward. Interior designer Howard Lorton, Inc., Denver, 1957-68; interior designer, v.p. Ronald Ansay Inc., Wheatridge, Colo., 1969-71; interior designer, pres. Phibbs Design Assos., Inc., Denver, 1972-78; interior designer, mgr. Howard Lofton, Inc., Colorado Springs, Colo., 1979—; pres. Interior Designers Housing Devel. Corp., 1969-72. Vice-pres. Arvada (Colo.) Hist. Soc., 1973. Served with U.S. Army, 1954-56. Fellow Am. Soc. Interior Designers (nat. pres. 1977); mem. (pres. Colo. chpt. 1964-65), Nat. Trust Historic Preservation, Am. Arbitration Assn., Nat. Fedn. Ind. Businessmen, Theta Xi (pres. Denver Area alumni club 1958-64). Democrat. Roman Catholic. Home: 3430 Clubheights Dr Colorado Springs CO 80906 Office: 10 N Sierra Madre Colorado Springs CO 80903

PHIBBS, PHILIP MONFORD, univ. pres.; b. Bemidji, Minn., Oct. 2, 1931; s. Clifford Matthew and Dorothy Ethel (Wright) P.; B.A. with highest honors, Wash. State U., 1953; postgrad. (Rotary Found. fellow), Cambridge (Eng.) U., 1953-54; M.A., U. Chgo., 1956, Ph.D. (Edward Hillman fellow), 1957; m. Gwen Willis, Aug. 29, 1954; children—Kathleen, Jennifer, Diana, Dirk (dec.). Congl. fellow Am. Polit. Sci. Assn., Washington, 1957-58; instr. polit. sci. Wellesley Coll., 1961-63, asst. prof., 1963-68, asso. prof., 1968-73, exec. v.p., 1968-73, acting pres., 1973; pres. U. Puget Sound, Tacoma, 1973—. Dir., Wellesley-Vassar Washington Internship Program, 1962-73; asso. Danforth Found., 1963—; mem. Wash. Council Postsecondary Edn., Seattle Found., Seattle Com. on Fgn. Relations. Trustee Pacific Sci. Center, Tacoma Art Mus.; mem. public policy com. United Methodist Bd. Higher Edn. and Ministry. Served to 1st lt. USAF, 1958-61. Fulbright grantee, India, 1963; Rockefeller grantee, India, 1966-67. Mem. AAUP, Am. Bar Assn. (asso.), Am. Polit. Sci. Assn., Am. Council on Edn. (commn. internat. edn. relations), Phi Beta Kappa, Phi Kappa Phi, Pi Sigma Alpha, Phi Kappa Delta. Contbr. to publs. in field. Home: 3500 N 18th St Tacoma WA 98406 Office: 1500 N Warner St Tacoma WA 98416

PHIFER, KENNETH GALLOWAY, clergyman; b. Lewisburg, Tenn., Dec. 21, 1915; s. William Everette and Blanche (Wyatt) P.; A.B., Centre Coll., Danville, Ky., 1939, Litt.D., 1961; B.D. (Walter Kennedy Patterson scholar), Louisville Presbyn. Theol. Sem., 1942; M.A., Vanderbilt U., 1944; D.D., Hampden-Sydney Coll., 1957; m. Mary Agnes Penney, June 17, 1941; children—Anne Penney (Mrs. James W. Carneal, Jr.), Lynn Cameron, William Riker. Ordained to ministry Presbyn. Ch., 1942; minister First Presbyn. Ch., Franklin, Tenn., 1942-45, Oakland Av. Presbyn. Ch., Rock Hill, S.C., 1945-50, Old Presbyn. Meeting House, Alexandria, Va., 1950-59; prof. homiletics Louisville Presbyn. Theol. Sem., 1959-65; pastor St. Charles Av. Presbyn. Ch., New Orleans, 1965—. Bd. dirs. Greater New Orleans Fedn. Chs. Mem. Met Crime Commn. New Orleans. Mem. Beta Theta Pi, Omicron Delta Kappa. Democrat. Rotarian. Author: A Star is Born, 1952; A Protestant Case for Liturgical Renewal, 1965; (with others) Stories for Christmas, 1967; Tales of Human Frailty and the Gentleness of God, 1974. Contbr. articles to jours. Home: 1644 State St New Orleans LA 70118 Office: 1545 State St New Orleans LA 70118

PHILARET (GEORGE VOZNESENSKY), primate Russian Orthodox Ch.; b. Kursk, Russia, Mar. 22, 1903; s. Nicholas and Lydia (Vinogradova) Voznesensky; came to U.S., 1964. Elec. Engr., Russian-Sino Politech. Inst., Harbin, China, 1929; grad. pastoral theol. sch., Harbin, 1931. Ordained priest Russian Orthodox Ch., 1931, took vows of monkhood, 1931, named archimandrite, 1937; consecrated Bishop of Brisbane, Australia; vicar bishop Australian Diocese Russian Orthodox Ch., 1963; elected metropolitan, primate of Russian Orthodox Ch. Outside Russia, 1964. Address: 75 E 93d St New York NY 10028*

PHILBIN, JOHN ARTHUR, lawyer; b. Shawnee, Okla., July 2, 1934; s. Floyd Austin and Challie (Calhoun) P.; student Modesto Jr. Coll., 1953; B.B.A., U. Okla., 1957; J.D., Oklahoma City U., 1961; m. Diane L. Douglass, June 15, 1957; children—John Arthur, Douglass. Admitted to Okla. bar; with IRS, Oklahoma City, 1957-62; practice law, Oklahoma City, 1962—; mem. firm Speck, Fleig & Hewett, 1962-64, Speck, Philbin, Fleig, Trudgeon & Lutz, and predecessor, 1964—. Mem., past pres. Oklahoma City Estate Planning Council. Active YMCA, United Fund; mem. devel. com. Baptist Med. Center of Okla. Bd. dirs. Oklahoma City All Sports Assn., Intrognene Found.; pres. Beta Kappa Found.; bd. advisers Mercy Hosp. Named Young Man of Year, Oklahoma City Jaycees, 1969, Outstanding Young Man Am., Jaycees, 1970. Mem. Am. (past pres. Oklahoma City chpt.), Am., Fed., Okla., Oklahoma County bar assns., Oklahoma City Art Center, Southwestern Legal Fedn., Lawyers' Tax Group (past pres.), U. Oklahoma City Alumni Club (past pres.), C. of C., Sigma Chi, Phi Delta Phi. Republican. Methodist. Clubs: Touchdown, Sooner Dinner (pres., dir.), Men's Dinner, Young Men's Dinner (past pres.). Home: 1209 Glenwood Ave Oklahoma City OK 73116 Office: 800 City National Bank Tower Oklahoma City OK 73102. *To be a success or to be able to make a situation successful, knowing myself is vital. To know and accept my feelings, my beliefs, my faults, enables me to deal with each problem, each goal realistically. To be patient and to respect the thoughts and feelings of those who live around me, understanding that if I had strong beliefs, then I must try to be understanding of those opinions that differ from mine.*

PHILBRICK, DONALD LOCKEY, lawyer; b. Portland, Maine, May 3, 1923; s. Donald Ward and Ruth (Lockey) P.; A.B., Bowdoin Coll., 1944; J.D., Harvard U., 1948; m. Marjorie Helene Sloat, May 3, 1963 (div. 1973); children—Deborah Palmer, Sarah Peyton; adopted children—Paul Sloat, Mark Whitfield, Andrew Hunter; m.

2d, Barbara Frances Crockett, Nov. 10, 1973 (div. 1978). Admitted to Maine bar, 1948, since practiced in Portland; partner firm Verrill & Dana, 1951—. Selectman, Cape Elizabeth, Maine, 1957-63. Served with AUS, 1943-45, with USAF, 1951-53. Mem. Maine Hist. Soc. (past pres.), N.E. Hist. Gen. Soc., Delta Kappa Epsilon. Republican. Congregationalist. Home: 340 Eastern Promenade Portland ME 04101 Office: 2 Canal Plaza Portland ME 04112

PHILBRICK, DONALD WARD, lawyer; b. Skowhegan, Maine, Mar. 16, 1896; s. Samuel White and Mabel Emma (Ward) P.; A.B., Bowdoin Coll., 1917; LL.B., J.D., Harvard, 1922; m. Ruth Lockey, Apr. 17, 1922; children—Donald L., Jean P. (Mrs. Cushing Strout), John W. Admitted to Maine bar, 1922, since practiced in Portland; partner firm Verrill, Dana, Philbrick, Putnam & Williamson, 1924—; corporator Maine Savs. Bank. Mem. local SSS Bd., 1940-46; moderator, mem. budget com., charter com., adv. council Town Meeting, 1940-58; chmn. Cape Elizabeth Sch. Com., 1933-39; mem. Bowdoin Alumni Council; pres. Pine Tree council Boy Scouts Am.; bd. corporators Maine Med. Center; mem. Maine Ho. of Reps. from Cape Elizabeth, 1935-40, speaker, 1939-40; chmn. Maine Office Bldg. Authority; del. Republican Nat. Conv., 1944, 52; col. gov. Maine staff, 1941-44; chmn. Cumberland County Rep. Com., 1940-46. Trustee North Yarmouth Acad.; chmn. bd. dirs. Bowdoin Alumni Fund, Portland Salvation Army; bd. dirs. Asso. Charities Portland. Served to 1st lt., inf. U.S. Army, 1917-19; AEF in France. Mem. Am., Maine, Cumberland County (pres. 1958) bar assns., Am. Legion, Phi Beta Kappa, Delta Kappa Epsilon. Mason. Clubs: Lincoln (pres.), Exchange (pres.), Portland (v.p.), Bowdoin (pres.) (Portland). Home: 21 Oakhurst Rd Cape Elizabeth ME 04107 Office: 2 Canal Plaza Portland ME 04112

PHILDIUS, PETER P., health care exec.; b. Bklyn., Mar. 22, 1930; s. George Philip and Ada (Bunkin) P.; B.B.A., Hofstra Coll., 1957; m. Marlene Drexler, Aug. 28, 1954; children—Cathy, Lisa, Kristi. Pres., artificial organs div. Baxter Travenol Labs., Inc., Chgo., 1973-75; v.p. Travenol Labs., Chgo., 1975-76; group v.p. Baxter Labs., Inc., 1976-78; pres., chief operating officer Nat. Med. Care, Inc., Boston, 1978—. Served with USN, 1951-55. Mem. Health Industries Mfg. Assn. (dir.), High Tech. Council. Republican. Clubs: University, Greater Boston Running (Boston). Home: 81 Westerly Rd Weston MA 02181 Office: 200 Clarendon St Boston MA 02116

PHILIP, CORNELIUS BECKER, former pub. health officer, entomologist; b. Ft. Lupton, Colo., June 12, 1900; s. Smith Durie and Mattie (Shoemaker) P.; B.Sc., U. Nebr., 1923, Sc.D., 1952; M.S., U. Minn., 1925, Ph.D., 1930; postgrad. Johns Hopkins, 1940, Harvard, 1940; m. Gladys Helen Hill, Nov. 11, 1922; children—Robert, Bonnie Dee (Mrs. Harold L. Holt), Jo Joyce (Mrs. William D. Dratz), Gordon. Asst. entomology U. Nebr., 1922-23; grad. instr. U. Minn., 1923-26; asst. entomologist Expt. Sta., Mont. State Coll., 1926-27; staff Mont. Bd. Entomology, 1928; entomologist Rockefeller W. Africa Yellow Fever Commn., 1928-29; asso. to prin. med. entomologist Rocky Mountain Lab., USPHS, Hamilton, Mont., 1930-70, asst. dir., 1950-62, dir., 1962-64. Asso. mem. Armed Forces Epidemology Bd., 1947-49; cons. Chem. Corps Biol. Warfare Lab., Ft. Detrick, 1951-61, Air Forces Arctic Aeromed. Lab., Fairbanks, Alaska, 1952-56, U.S. Naval Med. Res. Unit, Cairo, Egypt, 1953-70; sec. Internat. Northwest Conf. Diseases Nature Communicable to Man, 1947, pres., 1952; sec. Internat. Conf. Great Plains Entomologists, 1947; Mayo Found. lectr., 1940, Theobald Smith lectr. N.Y. Acad. Tropical Medicine, 1948; vis. lectr. Ohio State U., 1951, U. Ill., 1952, U. Mont., 1958-59, Wash. State U., 1958, U. Ga., 1961, Ft. Sam Houston Med. Officers Sch., 1954-56, Communicable Disease Center Pub. Health Service Tng. Sch., 1959- 60; mem. scrub typhus unit U.S. Army, Malaya, 1948; sect. pres. 6th Internat. Congress Microbiology, Rome, 1953; mem. Internat. Commn. Bacteriological Nomenclature, 1958-66, jud. commn., 1963-66; mem. expert panel tickborne diseases FAO, 1959-70, chmn., 1966; interagy. adv. com. Dugway Proving Ground, 1959-63; adv. panel biol. and chem. def. Dept. Def., 1960-69; chmn. WHO Conf. Typhus-like Diseases, 1963, 11th Pacific Sci. Congress, 1966, Symposium on Tsutsugamushi Diseases, Niigata, Japan. Served as pvt. U.S. Army, 1918; from maj. to col. San. Corps, AUS, 1942-46. Guggenheim fellow, 1941-42. Recipient medal U.S.A. Typhus Commn., 1945; Outstanding Achievement Alumnus award U. Minn., 1960; Superior Service award Dept. Health, Edn. and Welfare, 1968. Mem. Western Mont. Fed. Business Men's Assn. (pres. 1957), AAAS, Am. Soc. Parasitology (v.p. 1948, pres. 1953), Entomol. Soc. Am. (bd. govs. 1959-62), Am. Soc. Tropical Medicine and Hygiene (council 1960), Pacific Coast Entomol. Soc. (pres. 1974), Am. Legion (past post comdr.), Phi Beta Kappa, Sigma Xi, Delta Chi. Lion. Contbr. chpts. to Pullen's Communicable Diseases, 1950, Yearbook of Agr., 1952, Manual Tropical Medicine, 1966, McGraw-Hill Ency. Sci. and Tech., 1966, Bergey's Manual of Determinative Bacteriology, 8th edit., 1974, others. Bd. editors Folia Parasitologica, Prague, 1953—. Contbr. numerous sci. articles to profl. jours. Home: 50 Chumasero Dr San Francisco CA 94132 Office: Calif Acad Sci Golden Gate Park San Francisco CA 94118. *Life is action and passion, therefore it is required of a man that he should share the passions and action of his time, at the peril of being judged not to have lived.*

PHILIP, PETER VAN NESS, securities co. exec.; b. N.Y.C., Feb. 23, 1925; s. Van Ness and Lilian (Davis) P.; A.B., Yale U., 1945; M.B.A., N.Y. U., 1950; m. Sabina FitzGibbon, May 3, 1952; children—William Van Ness, Thomas Winslow, Peter Sandys. With Price, Waterhouse & Co., N.Y.C., 1947-52; W.H. Morton & Co., Inc., N.Y.C., 1952-73, pres., chief exec. officer, 1970-73; sr. v.p., dir. White Weld & Co., Inc., N.Y.C., 1974-76; v.p. Morgan Guaranty Trust Co., N.Y.C., 1977—; dir. Seaboard Surety Co., N.Y.C. Served with 86th inf. div. AUS, 1943-45. Decorated Purple Heart. Clubs: Racquet and Tennis, Yale, Downtown Assn., Bond (N.Y.C.); Bedford (N.Y.) Golf and Tennis; Ekwanok (Manchester, Vt.). Home: 1088 Park Ave New York City NY 10028 Office: 23 Wall St New York City NY 10015

PHILIP, WILLIAM WARREN, banker; b. Tacoma, Oct. 26, 1926; s. Warren F. and Lillian (Lehman) P.; student U. Wash., Seattle; m. Dorothy Mary Mitchell, Oct. 14, 1954; children—Cynthia Ann, Susan Kelly. With Puget Sound Nat. Bank, Tacoma, 1951—, pres., 1971—; v.p. bd. dirs. Econ. Devel. Council Puget Sound.; chmn. Pierce County, Savs. Bond div. Treasury Dept.; past mem. regional adv. com. to comptroller of currency. Trustee U. Puget Sound.; bd. dirs. Lakewood Water Dist., Downtown Tacoma Assn., Tacoma Gen. Hosp.; past chmn. bd. Mary Bridge Children's Hosp.; pres. Tacoma-Pierce County Econ. Devel. Bd. Mem. Wash. Bankers Assns. (past dir.), Tacoma C. of C. (pres.). Clubs: Tacoma, Tacoma Golf and Country (dir.); Rainier (Seattle). Home: 7602 Langlow St Tacoma WA 98498 Office: 1119 Pacific Ave Tacoma WA 98402

PHILIPP, ALICIA ANNE, found. exec.; b. Balt., Aug. 17, 1953; d. William Henry and Alice (Connor) P.; student Dunbarton Coll., 1971-73; B.A., Emory U., 1975; m. William C. Piontek, Sept. 4, 1976. Asst. dir. Ga. Spl. Olympics, Atlanta, 1975-76; asst. to pres. Central Atlanta Progress, Inc., 1976-77; exec. dir. Met. Found. of Atlanta, 1977—. Mem. Fulton County Democratic Com., 1978—; treas., bd. dirs. Feminist Action Alliance, 1978; active United Way of Met. Atlanta, Inc. Mem. Council on Founds., Inc., Women and Founds./Corp. Philanthropy, Southeastern Council of Founds. Roman Catholic. Home: 270 Colonial Homes Dr Atlanta GA 30309 Office: 1132 Healey Bldg Atlanta GA 30303

PHILIPP, HOWARD JOHN, chem. co. exec.; b. Vienna, Austria, July 23, 1912; s. Max and Stephanie (Beral) P.; Ph.D. in Chemistry, U. Vienna, 1935; m. Henriette Janice Kahn, Sept. 13, 1941; children—Lynne, Gail. Came to U.S., 1939, naturalized, 1942. Research asst. Chem. Inst., U. Vienna, 1935-38, U. Zurich Phys. Inst., 1938; research chemist Raymond Labs., St. Paul, 1939; chemist J.T. Gibbons, Inc., New Orleans, 1939-41, prodn. mgr., 1941-42; research chemist So. regional research lab. Dept. Agr., New Orleans, 1942-45; research group leader Celanese Corp. Am., Cumberland, Md., also Summit, N.J., 1945-51, tech. control supt., Narrows, Va., 1951; tech. coordinator Celanese Fibers Co., N.Y.C., also Charlotte, N.C., 1952-53, spl. projects mgr., Charlotte, 1954-55, asst. tech. dir., Charlotte, 1955-59, planning dir., 1960, v.p. planning, 1960-62; corporate planning dir. Celanese Corp. Am., N.Y.C., 1962-64, v.p. planning, 1964-66; dir. corporate planning W.R. Grace & Co., N.Y.C., 1966-77; mgmt. cons., 1977—. Mem. Am. Chem. Soc., N.Am. Soc. Corporate Planning, Assn. Corporate Growth. Home and office: 1621 Gulf Blvd Apt 507 Clearwater FL 33515

PHILIPP, ROBERT, painter; b. N.Y.C., Feb. 2, 1895; s. Paul and Yanka (Phillipp) P.; student Art Students League, 1910-14, N.A.D., 1914-17; m. Rochelle Politziner, June 3, 1935. Carnegie vis. prof. art, resident painter U. Ill., 1940; tchr. N.A.D., Art Students League; rep. permanent collections Bkyn. Mus., Whitney Mus., Met. Mus. Art, N.Y.C., Houston, Dallas museums fine arts, Corcoran Mus. (Washington), Omaha Mus., Miami Mus., Atlanta High Mus., IBM Corp., Akron (Ohio) Mus., Dayton (Ohio) Art Inst., Parrish Mus., South Hampton, L.I., Municipal Art Gallery (Davenport), Ency. Brit. collection, Toledo Mus., Wichita Mus., Springfield (Mass.) Mus., Dayton Mus., Norton Gallery (Palm Beach), U. Ill., USAF Acad., Colorado Springs. Recipient 2d Hallgarten prize N.A.D., 1922, first Logan prize, $500 Chgo. Art Inst., 1936; 1st hon. mention, $400 Carnegie Internat., 1937; Clarke prize, $1,500 and silver medal, Corcoran Gallery; hon. award and medal IBM, 1939; 1st Altman prize $1,000, N.A.D., 1951, 62, 67; 1st prize, $1,000 Laguna Beach, Cal., 1951, Allied Artists prize, 1960, W. C. Osborne award Am. Water Color Soc., 1967, others. N.Am. Benjamin Franklin fellow Royal Soc. of Art London. Sec. N.A.D. Club: Lotos (life mem.). (N.Y.C.). Office: 881 7th Ave New York NY 10019*

PHILIPP, WALTER VIKTOR, educator, mathematician; b. Vienna, Dec. 14, 1936; s. Oskar and Anna Julie (Krasucky) P.; came to U.S., 1963, naturalized, 1974; M.S. in Math. and Physics, U. Vienna, 1960, Ph.D. in Math., 1960; m. Barbara Paula Wallner, July 6, 1963; children—Petra, Robert. Asst., U. Vienna, 1960-63, 65-67, dozent, 1967; asst. prof. U. Mont., 1963-64; vis. asst. prof. U. Ill., Urbana, 1964-65, mem. faculty, 1967—, prof. math., 1973—; vis. prof. U. N.C., Chapel Hill, 1972. Fellow Inst. Math. Statistics; mem. Am. Math. Soc. Asso. editor Annals of Probability. Home: 2009 Cureton Dr Urbana IL 61801

PHILIPPI, HARLAN ANTON, univ. dean; b. Milw., June 8, 1926; s. Albert Matthew and Delilia (Liester) P.; B.S., U. Wis., 1949, M.S., 1953; Ph.D., Northwestern U., 1962; m. Dorothy Collette, Aug. 2, 1947; children—Sandra Collette, John Christopher. Tchr., Lanesboro, Minn., 1949-53; tchr., Highland Park, Ill., 1953-55, counselor, 1956-57, guidance dir., 1957-60; prin., Deerfield, Ill., 1960-63; chmn. dept. secondary edn. Boston U., 1963-65, asso. dean, dir. grad. studies, 1965-70, asso. dean research and devel., 1970-72, acting dean, 1972; dean U. Maine-Portland-Gorham, 1972-77; dir. planning Univ. Coll., U. Maine System, 1977—, dir., interim dean, 1977; cons. in field; mem. Nat. Humanities Faculty, 1971—, trustee, 1973—. Mem. Bd. Family Service Highland Park, 1959-61; mem. Mass. Task Force Racial Imbalance, 1966-67. Served with USNR, 1944-46. NIMH grantee, 1966-70; named Outstanding Tchr., Boston U. Sch. Edn., 1967. Author: Challenges to American Youth, 1958. Home: RFD 3 Gorham ME 04038 Office: Corthell Hall U So Maine Gorham ME 04038

PHILIPPS, LOUIS EDWARD, hosp. data system mfg. co. exec.; b. Duluth, Minn., Feb. 7, 1906; s. Carl Frederick Ferdinand and Sarah Marguerithe (Mortenson) P.; student pub. schs., Duluth; m. Gladys Victoria Monsen, Nov. 13, 1930. Engr., Cleve. Radioelectric Co., 1946-48; v.p., gen. mgr. Radio Systems, Inc., Cleve., 1948-50, Royal Communications, Inc., Cleve., 1950-56; dir. engring. Auth Electric Co., N.Y.C., 1956-59; chief engr. hosp. products div. Motorola-Dahlberg Co., Mpls., 1959-63; founder, pres., chmn. bd. Medelco Inc., Schiller Park, Ill., 1964-74; founder, 1975, since chmn. bd., dir. Datx Corp., Chgo. Named Father of Hosp. Systems Industry, Am. Hosp. Assn., 1974. Sr. mem. IEEE. Republican. Presbyterian. Clubs: Anvil (E. Dundee, Ill.); Order Eastern Star, Masons (Robbinsdale, Minn.); Masons, Shriners (Chgo.). Patentee pulsed audio signaling, radio nurse system, data handling system. Contbr. to profl. jours. Home: 402 6th Ave Addison IL 60101 Office: 303 E Ohio St Chicago IL 60611. *My wife's faith and encouragement to use defeat as a stepping stone to success made it possible for me to reach my goals. Encouraging and teaching employees also played an important part.*

PHILIPPS, PAUL DAVID, manpower cons.; b. Denver, Mar. 9, 1918; s. Floyd Earl and Josephine (Scurman) P.; B.S., U.S. Mil. Acad., 1940; M.A., George Washington U., 1963; grad. Command and Gen. Staff Coll., 1951, Nat. War Coll., 1960; m. Rita Anne Ruzicka, June 15, 1940; children—Nancy-Jo Phillips Michel, Rita Anne Philipps Tschfielly, Paul David. Commd. 2d lt. U.S. Army, 1940, advanced through grades to brig. gen.; dir. force planning and analysis Office Chief Staff U.S. Army, 1965-66; ret., 1966; dept. head Research Analysis Corp., 1966-68, 70-71; prin. dep. asst. sec. army for manpower, 1969-70, 71-79; manpower cons., Denver, 1979—. Decorated D.S.M., Silver Star, Legion of Merit, Bronze Star, Army Commendation medal; Philippine Legion of Honor; recipient Disting. Civilian Service award Dept. Army. Mem. Assn. U.S. Army, Nat. Assn. Armed Forces, Ret. Officers Assn., Defenders of Bataan and Corregidor. Republican. Roman Catholic. Address: Unit 5 Court 17 Meadow Dr Winter Park CO 80482

PHILIPS, ABRAM LEWIS, JR., lawyer; b. Columbus, Ga., Dec. 31, 1934; s. Abram Lewis and Mary Louise (Rice) P.; A.B. in English and Polit. Sci., U. Ala., 1957, LL.B., 1959, J.D., 1969; grad. Practicing Law Inst. Sch. Admiralty and Maritime Law, 1960; m. Frances Carolyn Tingen, Aug. 23, 1957; children—Abram Lewis III, Sidney Tingen, Scott Rice, Lee Bradley. Owner, operator water ski sch., Lake Martin, Ala., 1954-55; circulation mgr. newspaper, Tuscaloosa, Ala., 1956; mgmt. trainee Shell Oil Co., 1957; credit investigator Dunn & Bradstreet, 1958; admitted to Ala. bar, 1959, since practiced in Mobile; mng. partner firm Pillans, Reams, Tappan, Wood, Roberts & Vollmer, 1965—; v.p., dir., gen. counsel Exotics, Inc., Sidney W. Tingen Co., Inc.; v.p., dir. the Philips Agy., Inc. Bd. dirs. Mobile Jr. C. of C., 1961-72, pres., 1969; Mobile Jazz Festival; bd. dirs. Greater Gulf State Fair, 1965-72, v.p., 1967. Mem. Gov. Ala. Indsl. Adv. Com., 1965, Mayor Mobile Charter Commn., 1966-67, Mobile's Historic and Cultural Mission to Spain, 1965, Council So. Sch. Attys., 1967—; campaign chmn. Mobile Mental Health drive, Multiple Sclerosis Assn.; gen. chmn. America's Jr. Miss Pageant, 1963; dir. Ala. Guatemala Partners of Alliance for Progress, 1965-68; del. 1st inter-am. conf. Partners of Alliance, Rio de Janeiro, 1967; mem. council attys. Nat. Sch. Bds. Assn., 1968-71, Ala. Council Sch. Attys. Mem. Mobile County Democratic Exec. Com., 1960-66, 70-74. Named outstanding chmn., Mobile Jr. C. of C., 1967, outstanding dir., 1968; named one of outstanding young men Am., U.S. Jr. C. of C., 1968. Mem. Maritime Law Assn. U.S., Am. Trial Lawyers Assn., Ala., Mobile bar assns., Delta Tau Delta, Phi Alpha Delta, Phi Mu Alpha. Methodist (ofcl. bd. 1968-71). Clubs: Mystics of Time, Gulf Pines, Country (Mobile). Home: 4160 N Carmel Dr Mobile AL 36608 Office: 3662 Dauphin St Mobile AL 36608

PHILIPS, JESSE, mfg. co. exec.; b. N.Y.C., Oct. 23, 1914; s. Simon and Sara (Berkowitz) P.; A.B. magna cum laude, Oberlin Coll., 1937; M.B.A., Harvard, 1939; m. Carol Jane Frank, Dec. 23, 1945 (div. 1971); children—Ellen Jane, Thomas Edwin; m. 2d, Caryl Ann Dombrosky, Sept. 11, 1978. With G. Fox & Co., Hartford, Conn., 1939-40; gen. mdse. mgr. Worth's, Waterbury, Conn., 1940-44; exec. v.p. Big Store Co., Cin., 1944-46; gen. mdse. mgr. Wurzburg's, Grand Rapids, Mich., 1946-47, Stark's Dept. Store, Canton, Ohio, 1947-49; exec. v.p. Johnston Shelton Dept. Store, Dayton, Ohio, 1949-56; pres. Philips Industries, Inc., Dayton, 1957-68, chmn. bd., chief exec. officer, 1968—; dir. Third Nat. Bank & Trust Co., Dayton. Chmn., Dayton Found. Ind. Colls., Dayton Jewish Community Devel. Council; asso. chmn. Dayton Community Chest drive. Bd. dirs. Good Samaritan Hosp., Dayton, Dayton Jr. Achievement, Dayton Better Bus. Bur., Miami Valley council Boy Scouts Am., Dayton council Salvation Army, Jewish Community Council; trustee Oberlin Coll., U. Dayton, Ohio Found. Ind. Colls., Arthritis Found., Wright State U. Found.; Andrew Wellington Cordier fellow Columbia U.; vis. com. Harvard Grad. Sch. Bus. Adminstrn. Mem. Conn. N.G., 1930-33; served with USAAF, 1942-43. Decorated comdr. Ordre Souvenain de Chypre; recipient Free Enterprise award, 1965. Mem. Dayton C. of C. (dir.), Dayton Retail Mchts. Assn. (dir.), Nat. Retail Dry Goods Assn., Joint Distbn. Com. Clubs: Columbia Yacht (Chgo.); Meadowbrook Country (Dayton); Cavendish Bridge (N.Y.C.); St. Moritz (Switzerland) Tobogganing; Motor Yacht of Cote D'Azur (Cannes, France). Author: International Stabilization of Currencies, 1936; British Rationalization, 1937; contbg. author: Chief Executive Handbook. Office: 4801 Springfield St Dayton OH 45401

PHILIPS, JOHN NASH, energy co. exec.; b. Pitts., July 18, 1921; s. Samuel Kniess and Irma Dell (Nash) P.; A.B., Harvard, 1942; LL.B., Boston U., 1949; m. Virginia Lee Shade, Jan. 27, 1946; children—Lisa Graydon (Mrs. Steven Turner), Janice Lee. Admitted to Mass. bar, 1949; with Eastern Gas & Fuel Assos., Boston, 1946—, v.p., 1960-63, sr. v.p., treas., 1963-66, sr. v.p. adminstrn. and finance, 1966-69; exec. v.p., 1969-73, pres., 1973-76, chmn., 1976—, also trustee; dir. EG&G Inc., Gulfstream Banks Inc., Gulfstream First Bank and Trust N.A. Trustee, Boca Raton Community Hosp. Served to capt., F.A., AUS, 1942-46. Clubs: Somerset (Boston); Royal Palm (Boca Raton). Home: Boca Raton FL Office: 855 S Federal Hwy Suite 212 Boca Raton FL 33432

PHILIPSBORN, JOHN DAVID, banker; b. Chgo., Sept. 8, 1919; s. Martin Max and Amy (Dinkelspeil) P.; grad. Francis W. Parker Sch., Chgo., 1938, Harvard U., 1942; m. Edwige Auffret, Dec. 16, 1963; children—John Timothy, Christopher. With Office of Sec. Dept. Army, 1947-49; joined U.S. fgn. service, 1949; vice consul Am. embassy, Paris, France, 1949-50, asst. comml. attache, 1950-51, asst. labor attach, 1951-55; 1st sec., 1958-64; assigned Dept. State, Washington, 1955-58; v.p. Europe, Chase-Manhattan Bank, N.Y.C., 1964—. Served to maj. USAAF, 1941-47. Clubs: Cercle Interallie, Travelers, Cercle de Deauville (Paris); Harvard (N.Y.C.); University (Washington); Hurlingham, American, Bucks (London, Eng.). Home: 52 Egerton Crescent London SW3 England Office: Chase Manhattan Bank Woolgate House Coleman St London EC 2P 2HD England

PHILIPSON, HERMAN LOUIS, JR., investment banker; b. Dallas, May 14, 1924; s. Herman Louis and Lillian (Adler) P.; B.S., Tex. A. and M. Coll., 1946; postgrad. Harvard Sch. Bus. Adminstrn., 1947-48; m. Sonia Topletz, July 20, 1955; children—Cynthia Ann, Leslie, Nancy, Julie. Pres., Philipson's, Inc., 1946-56; pres. Nat. Data Processing Corp., 1957-60, chmn. bd., 1960-61; pres. Recognition Equipment Inc., Dallas, 1961-73, chmn. exec. com., 1973-76, vice chmn., 1976—; pres. Internat. Bus. Devel. Ltd., Dallas; dir. Datacraft Corp., Ft. Lauderdale, Fla.; chmn. bd. Corp S, Dallas. Mem. Dallas Citizens Council, also v.p., mem. exec. com. Bd. dirs. Dallas County Camp Fire Girls, recipient Ernest Thompson Seton award, 1975; trustee So. Meth. U. Found. for Sci. and Engring. Served to 1st lt. AUS, 1943-46. Decorated Bronze Star, Purple Heart with cluster, Combat Infantryman's badge; recipient Dallas Exporter of Year award, 1970. Mem. Dallas C. of C. (world trade com.), Japan-Tex. Assn. Mason (Shriner). Patentee in field. Home: 9100 Rockbrook Dr Dallas TX 75220 Office: 1545 W Mockingbird Ln Dallas TX 75235

PHILIPSON, MORRIS, univ. press dir.; b. New Haven, June 23, 1926; s. Samuel and Edith (Alderman) P.; diploma U. Paris, 1947; B.A., U. Chgo., 1949, M.A., 1952; Ph.D. in Philosophy, Columbia, 1959; m. Susan Antonia Sacher, Apr. 26, 1961, children—Nicholas, Jenny, Alex. Instr. English lit. Hofstra Coll., 1954-55; instr. philosophy Juilliard Sch. Music, 1955-56, 57-58; lectr. Hunter Coll., 1957-60; editor Vintage Books, Alfred A. Knopf, Inc., N.Y.C., 1959-61; editor Modern Library, also trade books Random House, Inc., Pantheon Books, 1961-65; sr. editor Basic Books, N.Y.C., 1965-66; exec. editor U. Chgo. Press, 1966-67, dir., 1967—. Served with AUS, 1944-46. Clubs: Arts, Caxton, Tavern, Quadrangle (Chgo.). Author: Outline of Jungian Aesthetics, 1963; Bourgeois Anonymous, 1964; The Count Who Wished He Were a Peasant: A Life of Leo Tolstoy, 1967; Paradoxes, 1969; Everything Changes, 1972; The Wallpaper Fox, 1976; A Man in Charge, 1979; also short stories, articles; editor: Aldous Huxley on Arts and Artists, 1960; Aesthetics Today, 1961; Automation: Implications for the Future, 1962; (with Clapp, Rosenthal) Foundations of Western Thought, 1962. Office: 5801 S Ellis Ave Chicago IL 60637

PHILLABAUM, LESLIE ERVIN, editor; b. Cortland, N.Y., June 1, 1936; s. Vern Arthur and Beatrice Elizabeth (Butterfield) P.; B.S., Pa. State U., 1958, M.A., 1963; m. Roberta Kimbrough Swarr, Mar. 17, 1962; children—Diane Melissa, Scott Christopher. Editor, Pa. State U. Press, 1961-63; editor-in-chief U. N.C. Press, 1963-70; asso. dir., editor La. State U. Press, Baton Rouge, 1970-75, dir., 1975—. Served to 1st lt. AUS, 1959-61. Mem. Assn. Am. Univ. Presses (dir. 1978—), Am., So. hist. assns., Orgn. Am. Historians, Acacia, Omicron Delta Kappa, Alpha Kappa Psi. Democrat. Home: 670 Burgin Ave Baton Rouge LA 70808 Office: La State U Press Baton Rouge LA 70803

PHILLIP, LEE JUNE, TV personality; b. Chgo.; d. James A. and Helen (Novak) Phillip; B.S., Northwestern U., 1950; m. William Joseph Bell, Oct. 23, 1954; children—William J., Bradley, Lauralee. Appearances on TV, 1951—; with CBS-TV, 1952—; shows include Lee Phillip Show, 1952—, Lady and the Tiger Show, WBBM-Radio, from 1962; woman's dir. WBBM-TV, Chgo., Ill., 1964—; former columnist Chgo. Am. Dir. Phillip's Flowers, Inc. Bd. dirs. Chgo. Foundlings Home Bldg. Fund, United Cerebral Palsy, Chgo. Unlimited, Northwestern U. Hosp., Chgo. Heart Assn. Mem. Chgo. Maternity Center. Recipient Top Favorite Female award TV Guide mag., 1956; Outstanding Woman of Radio and TV award McCall's mag., 1957-58, 65; Emmy awards, 1959-67, 71; Alumni Merit award Northwestern U., 1961. Mem. Am. Woman Radio and TV (Golden Mike award 1968), Fashion Group Am., Acad. TV Arts and Scis. (dir.), Dacowits, Delta Delta Delta. Office: CBS-TV 630 N McClurg Ct Chicago IL 60611*

PHILLIPPI, WENDELL CRANE, editor; b. Zionsville, Ind., July 4, 1918; s. Jesse F. and Bernice (Brock) P.; A.B., Ind. U., 1940; m. Georgiana Pittman, Jan. 10, 1942; children—Frank, Ann. Copy editor Indpls. News, 1940-46, state editor, 1946-47, city editor, 1947-52, asst. mng. editor, 1952-62, mng. editor, 1962—. Pres., Ind. A.P., 1957; bd. dirs. A.P. Mng. Editors Assn., 1963-66, 69-72, v.p. 1971, pres., 1972; mem. Pulitzer Prize in Journalism Jury, 1971, 75, 76. Pres. Ind. Armory Bd., 1968-73; maj. gen. 38th Div., Ind. N.G., 1962-63. Bd. dirs. 500 Festival, v.p., 1963-65; mem. Ind. U. Daily Student Bd., 1968-77. Served to maj. AUS, 1941-45; maj. gen. Res. Decorated Silver Star, Bronze Star with cluster. Mem. N.G. Assn. U.S. and Ind. (pres. 1953-55), Army Assn. Ind. (pres. 1957-58), Assn. U.S. Army, Indpls. C. of C., Am. Soc. Newspaper Editors, Am. Legion, Ind. U. Alumni Assn. (mag. bd. 1967—), Blue Key, Sigma Nu, Sigma Delta Chi. Episcopalian. Clubs: Contemporary, Indpls. Athletic. Home: 2240 D Rome Dr Indianapolis IN 46208 Office: 307 N Pennsylvania St Indianapolis IN 46204

PHILLIPS, A(NDREW) CRAIG, ednl. adminstr.; b. Greensboro, N.C., Nov. 1, 1922; A.B., U. N.C., 1943, M.A., 1946, Ed.D. in Sch. Adminstrn., 1956; m. 1943; 4 children. Tchr., asst. supt. Winston-Salem (N.C.) City Schs., 1946-55, supt. schs., 1957-62; supt. Charlotte-Mecklenburg (N.C.) Schs., 1962-67; adminstrn. v.p. Richardson Found., 1967-68; supt. pub. instrn. State of N.C., Raleigh, 1969—. Mem. steering com. N.C. Gov.'s Com. To Study N.C. Pub. Sch. System, 1967-68; mem. Pres.' Commn. on Mental Health for Children. Mem. NEA, N.C. Assn. Edn., N.C. Edn. Assn., Am. Assn. Sch. Adminstrs. (dir., nat. acad. sch. exec. 1969), So. Assn. Colls. and Schs. Home: 2200 Barfield Ct Raleigh NC 27612 Office: State Dept Public Instruction State Capitol Raleigh NC 27611

PHILLIPS, ALFREDO, govt. ofcl., banker; b. Mexico, Sept. 2, 1935; s. Howard S. and Dolores (Olmedo) P.; student U. Mexico, U. London: m. Maureen Greene, Sept. 6, 1960; children—Alfredo, Ricardo, Adriana. With ministry finance and pub. credit, Mexico City, 1960-65; sr. loan officer InterAm. Devel. Bank, 1965-66; alternate exec. dir. Internat. Monetary Fund, 1966-68, exec. dir., 1968-70; adviser to gov. Bank of Mexico, 1970-71, mgr., 1971-75, dep. dir. in charge internat. affairs, 1975—; treas., bd. govs. Latin Am. Export Bank, 1978—; treas. Bladex, 1978; chmn. Deps. Group of 24, 1979; chmn. deps. Intergovtl. Group of 24 on Internat. Monetary Affairs, 1979—; prof. trade cycles Sch. Bus. Adminstrn., InterAm. U., Mexico City. Home: Palacio de Versalles 185 Lomade Chapultepec Mexico 10 DF Mexico Office: Banco de Mexico SA 5 de Mayo 2 Mexico City Mexico

PHILLIPS, ALMARIN, educator; b. Port Jervis, N.Y., Mar. 13, 1925; s. Wendell Edgar and Hazel (Billett) P.; B.S., U. Pa., 1948, M.A., 1949; Ph.D., Harvard, 1953; m. Dorothy Kathryn Burns, June 14, 1947 (div. 1976); children—Almarin Paul, Frederick Peter, Thomas Rock, David John, Elizabeth Linett, Charles Samuel; m. 2d, Carole Cherry Greenberg, Dec. 19, 1976. Instr. econs. U. Pa. at Phila., 1948-50, 51-53, asst. prof. econs., 1953-56, prof. econs. and law, 1963—, chmn. dept. econs., 1968-71, 72-73, asso. dean Wharton Sch., 1973-74, dean Sch. Pub. and Urban Policy, 1974-77; teaching fellow Harvard, 1950-51; asso. prof. U. Va, 1956-61, prof., 1961-63; vis. prof. U. Hawaii at Honolulu, summer 1968, U. Warwick, London, Grad. Sch. Bus. Studies, U. Ohio, 1972, McGill U., 1978; cons. Bur. Budget, 1955, Bd. Govs., Fed. Res. System, 1962-73, Rand Corp., 1964—; cons. Pa. Commn. Banking Law, 1965-66; co-dir. Pres.'s Commn. Fin. Structure and Regulation, 1970-71; mem. Nat. Commn. Electronic Fund Transfers, 1976-77; economist mem. Va. Milk Commn., 1958-59. Served with AUS, 1943-45. Decorated Purple Heart, Bronze Star; Ford Found. faculty research fellow, 1967-68; sr. fellow Brookings Instn., 1970-75. Fellow Am. Statis. Assn., AAAS; mem. Am., So. (editor jour. 1963-65) econ. assns., Econometric Soc. Author: (with R.W. Cabell) Problems in Basic Operations Research Methods for Management, 1961; Market Structure, Organization and Performance, 1962; Technology and Market Structure: A Study of the Aircraft Industry, 1971. Editor: Perspectives on Antitrust Policy, 1965; (with O.E. Williamson) Prices: Issues in Theory, Practice and Policy, 1968; Promoting Competition in Regulated Markets, 1975. Editor The Am. Statistician, 1953-56, asso. editor, 1965-70, acting editor, 1959-60; editor Jour. Indsl. Econs., 1974—. Contbr. articles to tech. lit. Home: 1115 Remington Rd Wynnewood PA 19096

PHILLIPS, ARIS, educator; b. Smyrna, Asia Minor, Nov. 30, 1915; s. Herakles and Julia (Stamatiadis) Philippidis; diploma engring. Nat. Tech. U., Athens, Greece, 1937; Dr.Ing., Tech. U., Berlin, 1939; M.A. (hon.), Yale, 1960; m. Bessie Barbikas, Nov. 20, 1949; children—John Aristotle, Dean Aris. Came to U.S., 1947, naturalized, 1950. Asst. prof. engring. mechanics Stanford, 1947-54; mem. faculty Yale, 1954—, prof. civil engring., 1960-63, prof. engring. and applied sci., 1963-79, Robert Higgin prof. mech. engring., 1979—; dir. grad. studies dept. engring. and applied sci., 1963-70. Fellow ASME, Am. Acad. Mechanics; mem. Soc. Engring. Sci., Sigma Xi. Author: Introduction to Plasticity, 1956; also research papers. Editor: Acta Mechanica, 1965—. Home: 45 Round Hill Rd North Haven CT 06518 Office: Yale Univ New Haven CT 06520

PHILLIPS, ARTHUR, investment analyst; b. Montreal, Que., Can., Sept. 12, 1930; s. Frederick William and Renee Josephine (Snakers) P.; B.Comm., U. B.C., 1953; m. Carole Goss Taylor, June 3, 1977; children—Susan, Norman, John, David, Lisa. With A.E. Ames & Co. Ltd., Vancouver, B.C., 1951-54; co-founder, dir. Capital Mgmt. Ltd., Vancouver, 1954-64; pres., chmn. Phillips, Hager & North Ltd., investment counsellors, Vancouver, 1965-76, dir., 1977—; pres. Phillips Cons. Services Ltd., Vancouver, 1977—; mem. Parliament for Vancouver Centre, 1979—. Alderman, City of Vancouver, 1969-72, mayor, 1973-76. Mem. Vancouver Fin. Analysts Soc., Assn. Profl. Economists, Vancouver Bd. Trade. Liberal. Author: How to Win at the Stock Market, 1971. Address: 801 Ferry Row Vancouver BC V5Z 3Z5 Canada

PHILLIPS, ARTHUR HYDE, found. cons.; b. Wenham, Mass., June 7, 1920; s. John C. and Eleanor (Hyde) P.; A.B., Harvard, 1942, J.D., 1948; m. Elizabeth Elliott Sass, Aug. 22, 1943; children—Marion R., John C. II, Elizabeth E. Admitted to Mass. bar, 1949; with firm Tyler & Reynolds, Boston, 1948-55; with Cabot Corp., and predecessor, Boston, 1955-75, various positions including sec., gen. counsel, financial v.p. corp. and subsidiaries; dir. Cabot Found., Inc., 1964—; trustee Godfrey L. Cabot Charitable Trust, 1970—; dir. devel. Peabody Mus. of Salem (Mass.), 1977-79. Chmn. Boston Indsl. Mission, 1970-74; pres. Asso. Found. Greater Boston, 1969-72; mem. adv. council Trustees of Reservations. Bd. dirs. Federated Dorchester Neighborhood Houses, Lena Park Community Devel. Corp. Episcopalian. Home: 148 Argilla Rd Ipswich MA 01938 Office: 125 High St Boston MA 02110

PHILLIPS, ASA EMORY, JR., lawyer; b. Washington, Dec. 7, 1911; s. Asa Emory and Virginia N. (Boyd) P.; A.B. cum laude, Harvard Coll., 1934; LL.B., Harvard U., 1938; m. Anne Wight, 1956; children—Asa Emory III, Anne Crocker. Admitted to Mass. bar, 1939, D.C. bar, 1938, Maine bar, 1953, U.S. Supreme Ct. bar, 1944; sr. partner firm Asa E. Phillips, Jr., Boston, 1952—; dep. head atty. Compliance div. War Prodn. Bd., Washington, 1942-44; asst. to sec. state and vice pres. U.S., 1945-47. Vice chmn. lawyers div. Greater Boston Community Fund, 1948-50, dist. dir. Federal St. dist., 1947; chmn. Heart Fund for Brookline, 1958-60; chmn. adv. com. Gov. of Commonwealth U.S.S. Mass. Relics, 1965; chmn. com. of mgmt. YMCA, Charlestown, Mass., 1969-71; sec.-treas. Friends of Chamber Music, Inc., 1954-64; chmn. Gov.'s Prayer Breakfast, 1978; mem. council Freedom Trail Found., 1977—; mem. advisory bd. Salvation Army Greater Boston, 1977—; bd. dirs. Youth Found., Inc., N.Y.C.; founder, pres. bd. trustees Thomas W. Sidwell Meml. Scholarship, Mrs. Asa E. Phillips Meml. Fund; founder, chmn. bd. trustees Charles Francis Adams Meml. Trophy; trustee Mass. Trustees of Internat. Com. of YMCA for Army and Navy Work, Inc.; corporator Brookline Savs. Bank; mem. overseers com. to visit mil. depts. Harvard U., 1960-66. Served as ensign USN, World War II. Decorated knight Order St. Lazarus; recipient Meritorious Pub. Service citation Sec. Navy, 1960. Mem. Am. (moderator weekly radio broadcasts), Boston bar assns., Friends Sch. Alumni Assn. (past pres.), Greater Boston C. of C., Navy League of U.S. (nat. v.p. 1962-68, pres., chmn. bd. Boston council, nat. chmn. Navy Day, mem. nat. exec. com.), Soc. Colonial Wars (past treas., gov. Mass., nat. gov. gen. 1969-72), Order Founders and Patriots Am. (gov. Mass. Soc. 1964—, gov. gen. Gen. Ct. 1972—), Soc. of Lees of Va. (nat. v.p.), Huguenot Soc. Mass. (pres. 1966-68), Mass. Com. of Patriotic Socs. (founder, chmn. 1962—), Soc. of Cin., Roger Williams Family Assn., Soc. Descs. of Colonial Clergy, U.S. Naval Acad. Alumni Assn. Boston, Order of Lafayette (nat. dir. 1966—, pres. gen. 1974—), U.S. Flag Found., Inc. (counselor), SAR (pres. Mass. Soc. 1975-77, chmn. Ann. Congress 1975, trustee 1977—, chmn. state pres.' caucus Nat. Soc. 1976-78, nat. trustee 1977-79, historian gen. 1978—), S.R. (pres. Mass. 1974—, regional gen. v.p. 1977—), New Eng. Historic Geneal. Soc., Sovereign Mil. Order Temple of Jerusalem. Clubs: Rotary of Boston (dir. 1975—, pres. 1979—), Country, Union, Eastern Yacht, Harvard, Bostonian Soc., Essex Inst., Supper Dance (Boston); St. Nicholas Soc., Colonial Order of Acorn, New York Yacht, Squadron A, Univ. (N.Y.C.); Met., Chevy Chase (Washington); Bar Harbor, Bar Harbor Yacht, Seal Harbor Yacht, Harbor (Seal Harbor) (Mt. Desert Island); Cumberland (Portland, Maine); Hope (Providence); Ends of the Earth. Home: Westover Seal Harbor ME 04675 also Seawold Ogunquit ME 03907 Hilltop 90 Sargent Rd Brookline MA 02146 Office: 60 State St Boston MA 02109

PHILLIPS, BERT EUGENE, mfg. co. exec.; b. Quincy, Ill., May 8, 1919; s. John Herbert, and Zella Mae (Long) P.; student U. Ill., 1938-39, Quincy Coll., 1940-41; m. Helen Joyce Grummon, Jan. 23, 1943. Aircraft salesman, 1945-47; with Clark Equipment Co., Battle Creek, Mich., 1948—, v.p., gen. mgr. indsl. truck div., 1959-65, group exec. mobile products divs., 1965-66, gen. mgr. constrn. machinery div., 1966-67, exec. v.p., 1967-70, pres. 1970—, also dir.; vice chmn. bd., dir. Clark Leasing Corp., Clark Equipment Credit Corp., Clark Rental Corp., Clark Equipment Overseas Finance Corp.; v.p., dir. Clark Internat. Marketing, S.A., Clark Realty Corp., Clark Equipment Can., Ltd.; dir. Whirlpool Corp., Amsted Industries, Mass. Mut. Life Ins. Co. Trustee Tri-State Coll. Served as flight instr. USAAF, World War II. Mem. Indsl. Truck Assn. (past pres.), Material Handling Inst. (past pres.). Home: Route 5 Sandy Beach Diamond Lake Cassopolis MI 49031 Office: Circle Dr Buchanan MI 49107

PHILLIPS, BRUCE JOHNSON, food wholesale co. exec., lawyer; b. Norwich, Conn., Oct. 15, 1933; s. George Dwight and Alice Elizabeth (Johnson) P.; B.A., Yale U., 1954; LL.B., Harvard U., 1957; m. Gail Nuckolls, Jan. 17, 1959; children—Ethan, Morgan. Admitted to Mass. bar, N.H. bar; practiced in Boston, 1959-61, Nashua, N.H., 1962-64; with Dead River Co., Bangor, Me., 1965-70, Certain-Teed Products Corp., Valley Forge, Pa., 1970-78, Fox Industries, Inc., Pitts., 1979—. Home: 3060 Hartswood Dr Allison Park PA 15101 Office: 400 Penn Center Pittsburgh PA 15235

PHILLIPS, BURRILL, composer, educator; b. Omaha, Nov. 9, 1907; s. LeRoy Grey and Anna (Burrill) P.; student Denver Coll. Music, 1924-28; Mus.B., Eastman Sch. Music, 1932, M.Mus., 1933; m. Alberta Mayfield, Nov. 17, 1928; children—Stephen, Ann (Mrs. Robert Basart). Faculty, Eastman Sch. Music, 1933-34, faculty theory and composition, 1933-49, vis. prof. composition, 1965-66; prof. music U. Ill., 1949-64, chmn. div. theory and composition, 1957-60; Fulbright lectr. U. Barcelona (Spain), 1960-61; vis. composer East West Center, U. Hawaii, 1965; vis. prof. Juilliard Sch. Music, 1968-69, Cornell U., 1972-73. Recipient Am. Acad. Arts and Letters award, 1944; Fromm Found. Commn., 1956-57; Elizabeth Sprague Coolidge Found. Commn., 1959; Guggenheim fellow, 1942-43, 61, 62; Nat. Endowment for Arts grantee, 1976. Mem. ASCAP. Compositions include: Selections from McGuffey's Reader (suite for orch.); Courthouse Square (orch.); Play Ball (ballet for stage, orch.); American Dance (bassoon, strings); String Quartet; Dance Overture (sch. orch.); Tom Paine (overture); Don't We All (opera buffa); Triple Concerto, String Quartet 2, First Day of the World; The Return of Odysseus (baritone solo, chorus and orch.); Soleriana Concertante; Sonata in Two Movements (violin, harpsichord), 1966; That Time May Cease (men's voices, piano), 1966; La Piñata (for dance, commd. by José Limón), 1969; Canzona V (chorus, solo piano); Yellowstone, Yates and Yosemite (tenor saxophone, concert band); Eve Learns a Little (soprano, piano and 5 wind instruments); Huntingdon 2's and 3's (flute, oboe, cello); Intrada (for seven instruments); Just a Minimal Bite, said Eve (2 alto saxophones and actress); If I Am Persephone (actress, alto saxophone, two pre-recorded tape tracks); The Recesses of My House (soprano, clarinet, percussion, piano); Scena da Camera (violin and cello). Compositions performed by orchs. under Hanson, Stokowski, Thor Johnson, Kubelik, Wallenstein, Reiner, Ormandy, Fennell, Bales, Shaw, Sherman and Slonimsky, Barati; compositions performed by chamber ensembles: Paganini String Quartet, Walden String Quartet, Eastman Piano Quartet, Heritage Piano Quartet, Huntingdon Trio. Home: Italy Hill Turnpike Branchport NY 14418

PHILLIPS, CHANNING EMERY, clergyman, former univ. adminstr.; b. Bklyn., Mar. 23, 1928; s. Porter W. and Dorothy A. (Fletcher) P.; student U. Utah, 1945-46; A.B., Va. Union U., 1950; M.Div., Colgate Rochester Div. Sch., 1953; postgrad. Drew U., 1953-56; m. Jane Celeste Nabors, Dec. 22, 1956; children—Channing Durward, Sheilah Nahketah, Tracy Jane, Jill Celeste, John Emery. Instr., Howard U., 1956-58; ordained to ministry United Ch. of Christ, 1952; sr. minister Lincoln Temple, Washington, 1961-70; pres. Housing Devel. Corp., 1967-74; v.p. Va. Union U., 1974-75; congressional liaison officer Nat. Endowment for Humanities, Washington, 1978—. Chmn., D.C. delegation Nat. Democratic Conv., 1968; D.C. Dem. Nat. committeeman, 1968-72. Mem. adv. bd. ACLU. Served with USAAF, 1945-47. Mem. Alpha Phi Alpha. Home: 3501 Moss Side Ave Richmond VA 23222

PHILLIPS, CHARLES DILL, assn. exec.; b. Drew, Miss., July 4, 1930; s. Ephraim Fant and Vennie Lee (Dill) P.; B.A. summa cum laude, Miss. Coll., 1952; M.Div., So. Baptist Theol. Sem., 1956, M.Th., 1957; M.R.E., New Orleans Bapt. Theol. Sem., 1965, Ed.D., 1972; m. Sarah Shirley Cooper, Apr. 5, 1952; children—Charles Dill, Deborah Lynn, Max Randall. Ordained to ministry So. Bapt. Ch., 1951; pastor chs. in Miss., 1957-61, 61-64; prof. Bibl. studies Copiah-Lincoln Coll., Miss., 1957-61; chaplain So. Bapt. Hosp., New Orleans, 1964-67; exec. dir. Coll. Chaplains, Chgo., 1967-73; pres. Am. Protestant Hosp. Assn., Schaumburg, Ill., 1973—. Active local A.R.C., Boy Scouts Am. Mem. Coll. Chaplains (Disting. Service award 1975), Am. Hosp. Assn., Assn. Clin. Pastor Edn., Am. Soc. Assn. Execs., Assn. Mental Health Clergy, Royal Soc. Health. Clubs: Lions, Civitan. Office: 1701 E Woodfield Rd Schaumburg IL 60195

PHILLIPS, CHARLES EMORY, life ins. co. exec.; b. Md., Oct. 2, 1902; s. Asa Emory and Estelle (Randall) P.; LL.B., George Washington U., 1925, LL.M., 1926; m. Laura E. Ludwig, July 24, 1937. With Equitable Life Ins. Co., Washington, 1922—, asst. sec., 1933-43, bd. trustees, 1936—, sec.-treas., 1943-48, pres., chief exec. officer, 1948-68, chmn. bd., chmn. exec. com., 1968—, also dir.; pres., chief exec. officer Equitable Gen. Corp., McLean, Va.; dir. emeritus, mem. investment trust com. Nat. Savs. & Trust Co.; former dir. Am. Life Ins. Assn. Past pres., Life Insurers Conf.; state v.p. Am. Life Conv., 1961; pres. Met. Washington Bd. Trade, 1962-63. Gen. campaign chmn. United Givers Fund, Nat. Capital area, 1959, pres., 1960-61, dir., 1962; pres. Clark-Winchcole Found., 1964—; mem. finance com. The Washington Home. Charter mem., chmn. bd. trustees, chmn. exec. com. George Washington U.; bd. dirs. Met. Police Boys Club; past dir. Benjamin Franklin Found., Berlin, Germany, Kiwanis Found., Am. Life Ins. Council. Mem. Life Underwriters Tng. Council (treas.). Clubs: Congressional Country (pres. 1963-65), Kiwanis (pres. Washington 1962), University (Washington); Mid-Ocean (Bermuda). Office: 1700 Old Meadow Rd PO Box 900 McLean VA 22101*

PHILLIPS, CHARLES FRANKLIN, econ. cons.; b. Nelson, Pa., May 25, 1910; s. Frank G. and Emily Catherine (Stevens) P.; A.B., Colgate U., 1931, LL.D., 1945; Ph.D., Harvard, 1934; LL.D., Colby Coll., 1949, Bowdoin Coll., 1952, Northeastern U., 1953, Shaw U., 1966, Bates Coll., 1967; L.H.D., U. Maine, 1954; Litt.D., Western New Eng. Coll., 1959, Nasson Coll., 1959, Morehouse Coll., Atlanta, 1963; m. Evelyn Minard, June 22, 1932; children—Charles Franklin Jr., Carol Ann. Asst. econs. Hobart Coll., Geneva, N.Y., 1933-34; instr. econs. Colgate U., 1934-36, asst. prof., 1936-39, prof., 1939-44; on leave of absence, 1941-44 to serve as cons. counsumers div. Nat. Def. Adv. Com., 1941, asst. price exec. OPA, 1941-42, chief tire rationing div., 1942-43, dir. automotive supply rationing div., 1943-44, dep. adminstr. charge rationing dept., 1944; pres. Bates Coll., 1944-67, pres. emeritus, 1967—; chmn., dir. Central Maine Power Co., Augusta, 1965—, Hannaford Bros. Co., 1978—; dir. Union Mut. Life Ins. Co., Sperry & Hutchinson Co., Allied Maintenance Corp., others; former pub. gov. Am. Stock Exchange. Pres., New Eng. Colls. Fund, 1954. Mem. Phi Beta Kappa, Phi Delta Theta. Author: Marketing, 1938; (with Jasper V. Garland) Government Spending and Economic Recovery, 1938, Discussion Methods, 1938, The American Neutrality Problem, 1939; (with Delbert J. Duncan and Stanley C. Hollander) Modern Retailing Management, rev. edit., 1972; (with others) Marketing Principles and Methods, rev. edit., 1973, Marketing by Manufacturers, rev. edit., 1951; A Tax Program to Encourage the Economic Growth of Puerto Rico, 1958. Contbr. articles to acad., trade jours. Address: Maple Hill Ln Auburn ME 04210

PHILLIPS, CHARLES FRANKLIN, JR., economist, educator; b. Geneva, N.Y., Nov. 5, 1934; s. Charles Franklin and Evelyn (Minard) P.; B.A., U. N.H., 1956; Ph.D., Harvard, 1960; m. Marjorie Hancock, June 22, 1957; children—Charles Franklin, Susan Hancock, Anne Davis. Asst. prof. economics Washington and Lee U., Lexington, Va., 1959-63, asso. prof., 1963-66, prof., 1966—; adv. bd. 1st Nat. Exchange Bank, Lexington, 1971—; econ. cons. pub. utilities. Mem. city council, Lexington, 1969-71, mayor, 1971—; trustee Hebron Acad., Maine, 1971—; mem. Commn. on Rev. of Nat. Policy Toward Gambling, 1972-76; bd. dirs. Hist. Lexington Found. Recipient McKinsey Found. award 1962; Outstanding Regional Dir. award Omicron Delta Epsilon, 1971. Mem. Am., So. econ. assns., Am. Mktg. Assn., Phi Beta Kappa, Omicron Delta Epsilon (pres. 1976-77, 78-79). Republican. Presbyterian. Author: Competition in the Synthetic Rubber Industry, 1963; The Economics of Regulation, 1965, rev. edit., 1969; editor: Competition and Monopoly in the Domestic Telecommunications Industry, 1974; Competition and Regulation-Some Economic Concepts, 1976; Expanding Economic Concepts of Regulation in Health, Postal and Telecommunications Services, 1977; Regulation, Competition and Deregulation-An Economic Grab Bag, 1978. Home: 414 Morningside Dr Lexington VA 24450 Office: Dept Economics Washington and Lee Univ Lexington VA 24450

PHILLIPS, CHRISTOPHER HALLOWELL, assn. exec.; b. The Hague, Netherlands, Dec. 6, 1920 (parents Am. citizens); s. William and Caroline A. (Drayton) P.; A.B., Harvard, 1943; m. Mabel B. Olsen, May 11, 1943; children—Victoria A. (Mrs. Andrew J. Corbett, Jr.), Miriam O. (Mrs. Charles N. Eley, Jr.), David W. Reporter, Beverly (Mass.) Evening Times, 1947-48; mem. Mass. Senate from 2d Essex dist., 1948-53; spl. asst. to asst. sec. UN affairs Dept. State, 1953, later dep. asst. sec. of state for internat. orgn. affairs; apptd. U.S. Civil Service commr., vice chmn. U.S. Civil Service Commn., 1957; U.S. rep. to UN Econ. and Social Council, 1958-61; Chase Manhattan Bank rep. for UN affairs, 2d v.p., mgr. Canadian div., 1961-65; pres. U.S. council Internat. C. of C., 1965-69; ambassador, dep. U.S. rep. UN Security Council, 1969-70; dep. U.S. rep. UN, ambassador, 1970-73; pres. Nat. Council for U.S.-China Trade, Washington, 1973—. Mem. adv. council Sch. Advanced Internat. Studies, Johns Hopkins; Mass. dist. del. Republican Nat. Conv., 1952, 60. Served to capt. USAAF, 1942-46. Mem. Council Fgn. Relations N.Y., Am. Acad. Arts and Scis., U.S. Com. for UNICEF, UN Assn. U.S.A. (dir.). Episcopalian. Clubs: Metropolitan (Washington); Tavern (Boston); River (N.Y.C.). Home: 2801 New Mexico Ave NW Washington DC 20007 Office: Nat Council US-China Trade 1050 17th St NW Washington DC 20036

PHILLIPS, CLARENCE DELBERT, lawyer; b. Superior, Wis., May 8, 1903; s. Charles D. and Eva E. (White) P.; J.D., Willamette U., 1925; m. Mildred I. Tomlinson, Dec. 31, 1928; children—Shirley K., James D. With Spokane Title Co. (Wash.), 1919-21; sec. to judge Supreme Ct. Oreg., 1924-25; admitted to Oreg. bar, 1925; asst. dist. atty., Jackson County, Oreg., 1925-26; with Griffith, Peck & Coke, Portland, Oreg., 1926-40; partner Phillips, Coughlin, Buell, Stoloff and Black; sec., gen. counsel Portland Gen. Electric Co., 1940-74, ret., 1974; treas. Pacific N.W. Power Co.; ret. gen. counsel Crown Zellerbach Corp. in Oreg., Oreg. Bank, Willamette Western Co., several ins. cos. Past mem. bd. San Francisco Theol. Sem.; chmn. bd. govs. Shriners Hosp. for Crippled Children. Mem. Am., Oreg. (past bd. govs.) bar assns., Geol. Soc. Oreg. Country (past pres.). Presbyn. Mason (K.T., Shriner), Rotarian (past pres.). Clubs: City (past pres.), Arlington (Portland), Waverly Country. Home: 1485 SW Cardinell Dr Portland OR 97201 Office: Electric Bldg Portland OR 97205

PHILLIPS, CLAUDE FRANK, accountant; b. Forsyth County, N.C., Nov. 26, 1914; s. John Henry and Lula Ethel (Hampton) P.; grad. Draughon Bus. Coll., Winston-Salem, N.C., 1934; postgrad. U. N.C., U. Ga.; m. Margaret Smith, Nov. 9, 1940 (dec.); children—C. Frank, Mary Ann, Elaine Phillips Gwin; m. 2d, Margaret B. Edwards, Nov. 17, 1973. Bookkeeper, Mendenhalls, Inc., Greensboro, N.C., 1934-42; officer mgr. Jones-Onslow Electric Membership Corp., Jacksonville, N.C., 1943; with A.M. Pullen & Co., C.P.A.'s, Greenboro, 1943-79, partner in charge Winston-Salem office, 1962-79, also mem. exec. com., chmn. practice aquisitions com. Mem. provincial elders conf. So. province Moravian Ch. Am., 1941-44; bd. elders Calvary Moravian Ch., Winston-Salem, 1975—; trustee Salem Acad. and Coll., 1970—, fin. chmn., 1975—, exec. com., 1978—; bd. dirs., mem. exec. com. Red Shield Boys' Club, 1962—. C.P.A., N.C. Mem. Am. Inst. C.P.A.'s, N.C. Assn. C.P.A.'s (past dir., chmn. pub. relations com.), Winston-Salem C. of C. (past dir.), Newcomen Soc. N.Am. Clubs: Winston-Salem Civitan (pres. 1959-60); Forsyth Country (dir. 1969-72, v.p. 1972), Twin City, Hound Ears. Home: 405 Gloucestershire Rd Winston-Salem NC 27104

PHILLIPS, CLIFTON J., educator; b. Olean, N.Y., Apr. 11, 1919; s. Charles Clifton and Edith (Grey) P.; B.A., Hiram Coll., 1941; Th.B., Starr King Sch. Religious Leadership, 1944; M.A., Harvard, 1950, Ph.D., 1954; m. Rachel Jacqueline Martin, July 19, 1952; children—Peter Martin, Elaine Abigail, Alexis Anne, Patience Cecily. Civil edn. officer Dept. Def., Kobe, Japan, 1946-49; faculty history De Pauw U., 1954—, prof., 1965—, chmn. dept. history, 1969-72, 78—. Served with inf. AUS, 1944-46; PTO. Fulbright-Hays fellow Chinese civilization, Taiwan, summer 1962; lectr. Am. Studies, Korea, 1968-69. Mem. Am. Hist. Assn., Assn. Asian Studies, Orgn. Am. Historians, Ind. Hist. Soc. Author: Indiana in Transition: The Emergence of an Industrial Commonwealth, 1880-1920, 1968; Protestant America and the Pagan World: The First Half Century of the American Board of Commissioners for Foreign Missions, 1810-1860, 1969; (with others) The Missionary Enterprise in China and America, 1974. Home: 422 Anderson St Greencastle IN 46135

PHILLIPS, DANIEL MILLER, lawyer; b. Cleve., Mar. 21, 1933; s. Clovis H. and Lillian (Miller) P.; student Wesleyan U., Middletown, Conn., 1951-53; B.S., Ohio State U., 1958, J.D., 1961; m. Joyce C. Hamilton, July 26, 1958 (div. 1976); children—Meegan M., Sarah H., Anthony J.; m. 2d, Ann Molony Desmond, Aug. 10, 1976. Admitted to Ohio bar, 1961, since practiced in Toledo; mem. firm Robison, Curphey & O'Connell, 1961-77, partner, 1967-77; mem. legal dept. Owens-Corning Fiberglas Corp., Toledo, 1977-78, sr. counsel, 1978—; lectr. Ohio Legal Center Inst., 1969-70, 73; pres. Found. for Practice Law in Pub. Interest, Toledo, 1976. Pres., Toledo Florence Crittenton Services, 1971-72. Mem. Lucas County Mental Health and Retardation Bd., 1975-76; trustee Toledo Legal Aid Soc., 1977—, Community Planning Council of Northwestern Ohio. Served with AUS, 1953-55. Mem. Am., Ohio (chmn. negligence law com. 1971-73, mem. ins. law com. 1974—), Toledo (exec. com. 1971—, sec. 1974, pres. 1978-79), Toledo Jr. (pres. 1970-71) bar assns., Fedn. Ins. Counsel, Def. Research Inst., Ohio Def. Assn. (pres. 1971-72), U.S. Jud. Conf. (life). Home: 2464 Scottswood Ave Toledo OH 43620 Office: 1 Lewis Sq Toledo OH 43659

PHILLIPS, DAVID ATLEE, lectr.; b. Ft. Worth, Oct. 31, 1922; s. Edwin Thomas and Mary Louise (Young) P.; student William and Mary Coll., 1940-41, Tex. Christian U., 1941-42, U. Chile, 1948-49; m. Helen Hausman Haasch, June 5, 1948 (div. Dec. 1967); children—Maria, David Atlee, Christopher, Atlee (dec.); m. 2d, Virginia Pederson Simmons, Mar. 28, 1969; 1 son, Todd Phillips; stepchildren—Deborah, Bryan, Wynne. Actor, writer, 1942-48; editor, pub. South Pacific Mail, Santiago, Chile, 1949-54; lectr. on Latin Am., 1954-57; propr. David A. Phillips Assos., pub. relations, Havana, Cuba, 1958-61; joined U.S. Fgn. Service, 1961; assigned Mexico City, 1961-65, Santo Domingo, 1965-67, Washington, 1968-69; 1st sec. Am. embassy, Rio de Janeiro, Brazil, 1970-72, Caracas, Venezuela, 1972; mem. staff Dept. State, Washington, 1973-75, ret., 1975; lectr. Keedick Lecture Bur., 1975—. Served with USAAF, 1943-45. Decorated Purple Heart, Air medal. Mem. Assn. Former Intelligence Officers (founder, chmn. bd. 1978—). Democrat. Club: Kenwood Golf and Country. Author: The Night Watch, 1977; The Carlos Contract, 1978. Address: 8224 Stone Trail Dr Bethesda MO 20034

PHILLIPS, DAVID COLIN, chemist; b. Rhosllanerchrugog, Wales, Sept. 6, 1940; s. John and Sarah Elizabeth (Dodd) P.; came to U.S., 1968; B.Sc., U. Wales, 1965, Ph.D. in Phys. Chemistry, 1968; m. Irfonwy Lloyd Thomas, Sept. 21, 1968; children—Tudur Joseph Colin, Gareth John Gwilym. Chemist, Shell Chem. Co., Eng., 1962-63, Monsanto Chems. Ltd., Ruabon, Wales, 1963-64; sr. scientist Westinghouse Research Labs., Pitts., 1968-76, mgr. chem. reaction dynamics, 1976—; mem. faculty U. Wales, 1965-68. Recipient Indsl. Research-100 award Indsl. Research Mag., 1976. Mem. Royal Inst. Chemistry, Am. Chem. Soc. Author, patentee gas reaction kinetics, laser chemistry, electropolymerization, photopolymerization, particulate chemistry. Home: 825 Garden City Dr Monroeville PA 15146 Office: Westinghouse Research and Devel Center 1310 Beulah Rd Pittsburgh PA 15235

PHILLIPS, DAVID SHELBY, univ. adminstr., former govt. ofcl.; b. Grand Saline, Tex., Oct. 15, 1912; s. David Shelby and Georgia P. (Clifford) P.; B.S., N. Tex. State U., Denton, 1934, M.S., 1938; m. Glenna M. Lemon (div. July 1954); children—David Shelby, Lillian Glyn, William Lawrence; m. 2d, Gloria Smith Bauknight, Sept. 22, 1955. 1975. Supr., sch. ofcl., Grand Saline, Denton and Ft. Worth, 1934-40; student work officer Nat. Youth Adminstrn., FSA, Austin, 1940-42; chief adminstrv. services div. Bur. Census, Dept. Commerce, Washington, 1946-50; dir. adminstrv. services div. OPS, Econ. Stblzn. Agy., Washington, 1950-53; exec. asst. to asst. commr. adminstrn., dir. operating facilities div. IRS, Washington, 1953-56; asst. commr. bldgs. mgmt. Pub. Bldgs. Service, GSA, Washington, 1956-59; regional adminstr. GSA, Dallas, 1959-64, Washington, 1964-69; asst. supt. for support services Fairfax County Pub. Schs., Fairfax, Va., 1972-73; dir. Dallas Center, N. Tex. State U., 1975; task force leader, supply and support services Pres.'s Reorgn. Project, Washington, 1977-78. Chmn., Ft. Worth-Dallas Fed. Exec. Bd., 1962-64; chmn. S.W. D.C. Employment Area Transp. Exec. Com., 1966-69. Bd. dirs. Belle Haven Citizens Assn. Served from lt. (j.g.) to lt. comdr. USNR, 1942-46. Episcopalian. Club: Belle Haven Country. Home: 3101 S Ocean Blvd Apt 318 Highland Beach FL 33451

PHILLIPS, DEAN, assn. exec.; b. Collbran, Colo., Aug. 23, 1916; s. James Lester and Elsie Irene (Cox) P.; A.A. in Chem. Engring., Compton Coll., 1936; certificate corporate accounting Walton Sch. Commerce, 1940; m. Audrey Maxine Crain, Jan. 27, 1940 (dec.); children—Michael D., William L., Jeffrey C. With Rockwell Internat. (formerly North Am. Aviation Co.), Los Angeles, 1937-41, 46-50, Kansas City, Kans., 1941-44, Columbus, Ohio, 1951-73, dir. personnel and pub. relations, 1956-71, mgr. pub. affairs, 1971-73; pres., chief exec. officer Goodwill Industries Am., Inc., Washington, 1973—; pres., bd. dirs. Nat. Center for Barrier-Free Environment; mem. exec. com. Pres's. Commn. on Employment of Handicapped. Served with USN, 1944-46. Bd. dirs. Nat. Industries for Severly Handicapped (exec. com.), Nat. Assembly Voluntary Health, Social Welfare Orgns. (treas.). Club: Bethesda (Md.) Country. Author books, the most recent being: Man in Flight, 1963; Book of Satellites, 1965. Office: 9200 Wisconsin Ave Washington DC 20014

PHILLIPS, DUDLEY COOMBS, investment co. exec.; b. Bartlesville, Okla., July 13, 1922; s. Dudley Collings and Mary Elizabeth (Coombs) P.; B.S., U. Okla., 1947, LL.B., 1949; m. Nan Elizabeth Burg, Mar. 16, 1944; children—Dudley Collier, Jan Clare, Lynn Elizabeth. Admitted to Okla. bar, 1949, N.Y. bar, 1965, Kans. bar, 1954; atty. Sinclair Oil & Gas Co., Tulsa, Okla., 1949-54, gen. counsel Sinclair Pipeline Co., Independence, Kans., 1954-64, asso. gen. counsel Sinclair Oil Corp., N.Y.C., 1964-69; chief house counsel BP Oil Co., N.Y.C., 1969-70; v.p., gen. counsel Bangor Punta Corp., Greenwich, Conn., 1970-75, sr. v.p., gen. counsel, 1975—; v.p., gen. counsel, dir. Piper Aircraft Corp., 1970—; dir. Producers Cotton Oil Co., Fresno, Calif. Served with USAAF. Decorated Air medal. Mem. Okla., Kans., N.Y. bar assns., Order of Coif, Phi Gamma Delta, Phi Delta Phi. Mem. Ch. Christ Scientist (trustee). Home: 871 Weed St New Canaan CT 06840 Office: 1 Greenwich Plaza Greenwich CT 06830

PHILLIPS, EDWARD EVERETT, III, ins. co. exec.; b. Orange, N.J., Sept. 14, 1927; s. Edward Everett, Jr. and Margaret (Jaffray) P., Jr.; B.A. cum laude, Amherst Coll., 1952; LL.B., Harvard U., 1955; m. Margaret Whitney, Sept. 7, 1952; children—John Whitney, Margaret Jaffay, Nancy Osborne. Admitted to Mass. bar, 1955; with firm Mirrick, O'Connell, De Mallie & Lougee, Worcester, Mass., 1955-57; with John Hancock Mut. Life Ins. Co., Boston, 1957-69, v.p. agy. dept., 1965-69; with New Eng. Mut. Life Ins. Co., Boston, 1969—, adminstrs. v.p. home office ops., 1971-72, exec. v.p. home office ops., 1972-77, sec., 1969-77, pres., 1977—, chmn., chief exec. officer, 1979—, dir., 1973—; dir. New Eng. Life Equity Services Corp., 1973—, Butler Aviation Internat., Inc., 1967-71. Chmn. Weston chpt. United Fund; mem. adv. com. positive program N.A.A.C.P., Boston; mem. sch. com., Weston, 1966-73, chmn., 1972—. Bd. dirs. Big Bros. Boston Inc.; dir., mem. exec. com. Mass. Taxpayers Found., Inc., Mass. Safety Council; trustee Berkshire Boys Choir. Served with USMCR, 1945-48. Brookings Inst. pub. affairs fellow, 1965. Mem. Life Ins. Agy. Mgmt. Assn. (combination cos. exec. com. 1968-69), Inst. Life Ins. (life ins. pub. relations council). Office: 501 Boylston St Boston MA 02117*

PHILLIPS, EDWIN ALLEN, educator; b. Lowell, Fla., Mar. 18, 1915; s. William Henry and Jane (Goodman) P.; A.B., Colgate U., 1937, M.A., U. Mich., 1940, Ph.D., 1948; m. Margaret Ellen Knight, Jan. 16, 1942; children—Ellen Knight, Nancy Jane. Instr. botany Colgate U., Hamilton, N.Y., 1946-48; prof. botany Pomona Coll., Claremont, Calif., 1948—, chmn. dept. botany, 1973-77; vis. prof. plant ecology U. Mich. Biol. Sta., summers 1955-56, 58, 70-71; cons., mem. steering com. U. Hawaii Fundamental Approach to Sci. Teaching Study, 1969—; sci. cons. Govt. India, AID, summers 1964-65; mem. research adv. bd. San Dimas Exptl. Forest, 1957—; participant AID Sci. Edn. Survey, State Dept., Indonesia, 1972; researcher Kenya Nat. Parks, 1972. Served with USNR, 1941-45; comdr. Res. Recipient Wig Distinguished Prof. award Pomona Coll., 1966. NSF fellow Harvard, summer 1959, Oxford U., 1961-62. Fellow AAAS; mem. Am. Inst. Biol. Scis. (steering com. biol. sci. curriculum study, film com., lab. innovation com.), Bot. Soc. Am., Am., Brit. bryological socs., Ecol. Soc. Am., Soc. Am. Naturalists, Phi Beta Kappa (pres. local chpt. 1958, 65), Sigma Xi (pres. local chpt. 1966). Author: Methods of Vegetation Study, 1959; Field Ecology, 1964; Basic Ideas in Biology, 1971; Co-author: Basic Demonstrations in Biology, 1971; The Environment and Organisms; an Ecosystem Approach, 1971-74; revision plant sects. 4th edit. Biological Science, An Inquiry into Life, 1977. Editorial bd. Vegetatio, 1955-74. Home: 1201 N College Ave Claremont CA 91711

PHILLIPS, EDWIN CHARLES, gas transmission co. exec.; b. Saskatoon, Sask., Can., Oct. 19, 1917; s. Charles Henry and Beatrice Grace (Johnson) P.; student Lethbridge Collegiate Inst., 1931-35; m. Elizabeth Winnifred Johnston, June 27, 1942; children—Diane, Carol, Glen, Earl, Jane, Sue. Asst. buyer Loblaw Groceries Co. Ltd., Toronto, 1938-42; advt. mgr. Can. and Dominion Sugar Co., Chatham, Ont., 1945-47; asst. to gen. mgr. Consumers Gas Co., Toronto, 1947-52; with Trane Co. Can., Ltd., 1952-68, exec. v.p., gen. mgr., 1964-65, pres., 1966-68; group v.p. Westcoast Transmission Co., Ltd., Vancouver, 1968-70, exec. v.p., 1971-72, pres. 1972—, Chief exec. officer, 1976—, also dir., mem. exec. com.; dir. Pacific No. Gas Ltd., Emco Ltd., Mac Millan Bloedel Ltd., Can. Western C0rdage Co. Ltd., Westcoast Petroleum Ltd., Saratoga Processing Co. Ltd.; sr. v.p., dir. Foothills Pipe Lines (Yukon) Ltd.; pres., dir. Foothills Oil Pipe Line Ltd.; dir. Barclays Can. Ltd., Dynalectron Corp. Served with RCAF, World War II. Mem. Ch. of Christ. Clubs: Shaughnessy Golf, Vancouver, Southlands Polo and Riding. Home: 4458 W 2d Ave Vancouver BC V6R 1K5 Canada Office: 1333 W Georgia St Vancouver BC V6E 3K9 Canada

PHILLIPS, ELLIOTT HUNTER, lawyer; b. Birmingham, Mich., Feb. 14, 1919; s. Frank Elliott and Gertrude (Zacharias) P.; A.B. cum laude, Harvard U., 1940, J.D., 1947; m. Gail Carolyn Isbey, Apr. 22, 1950; children—Elliott Hunter, Alexandra. Admitted to Mich. bar, 1948, since practiced in Detroit; partner firm Hill, Lewis, Adams, Goodrich & Tait, 1953—. Pres., dir., sec. Detroit & Can. Tunnel Corp.; pres., dir. Detroit and Windsor Subway Co.; dir., sec. Enterform, Inc. (radio sta. WPHM), Palmer-Shile Co., Palmer-Shile Internat. Co. Mem. Mich. Bd. Accountancy. Treas., bd. dirs. Detroit chpt. ARC; pres., trustee McGregor Fund; trustee Boys Republic, Detroit Orthopaedic Clinic; mem. corp. Cottage Hosp., Grosse Pointe, Mich.; mem. Harvard overseers com. to visit Law Sch., also overseers com. univ. resources; trustee, pres. Ch. Youth Service. Served to lt. comdr. USNR, 1946. Mem. Detroit, Am. bar assns., State Bar Mich., Harvard Law Sch. Assn. (fund chmn. Mich. 1969-72), Asso. Harvard Alumni (v.p., exec. com.), Lincoln's Inn Soc. (Harvard). Episcopalian (vestryman, sr. warden). Clubs: Country, Detroit, Renaissance, Yondotega (Detroit); Harvard Eastern Mich. (pres. 1955-56); Harvard (N.Y.C.). Contbr. to legal and accounting jours. Home: 193 Ridge Rd Grosse Pointe Farms MI 48236 Office: 32d Floor 100 Renaissance Center Detroit MI 48226

PHILLIPS, ELLIS LAURIMORE, JR., ednl. cons.; b. N.Y.C., Feb. 26, 1921; s. Ellis Laurimore and Kathryn (Sisson) P.; A.B., Princeton, 1942; LL.B., Columbia, 1948; LL.D., Keuka Coll., N.Y., 1956; m. Marion Grumman, June 13, 1942; children—Valerie Rose Phillips Parsegian, Elise M. Phillips Watts, Ellis Laurimore, Kathryn Noel Phillips Zimmermann, Cynthia Louise. Admitted to N.Y. bar, 1948; with firm Burke & Burke, N.Y.C., 1948-53; mem. staff Pres.'s Com. Internat. Info. Activities, 1953; asst. dean Columbia Sch. Law, 1953-61, asso. prof. law, 1953-56, prof., 1956-70, dir. univ. budget, 1961-64; pres. Ithaca (N.Y.) Coll., 1970-75. Spl. asst. to U.S. ambassador to Eng., 1957-58; dir. Grumman Corp., Bethpage, N.Y., Wiltek, Inc., Norwalk. Pres., Bd. Edn. Union Free Sch. Dist. 15, Jericho, L.I., 1950-53, Ellis L. Phillips Found., 1959—; trustee Inc. Village Brookville, L.I., 1958-64; pres. Action Com. for L.I., Inc., 1978—; trustee Drew U., Ithaca Coll. Served to capt. AUS, USAAF, 1942-45. Republican. Author: (with others) Cases and Materials in Accounting for Lawyers, 1964, The Legal Profession, 1970, Information Services for Academic Administration, 1971; Look Back from Forty, 1967; A New Approach to Academic Administration, 1969; (with others) Accounting and the Law: Cases and Materials, 1978. Home: 687 Donna Dr Oyster Bay NY 11771 Office: 420 Jericho Turnpike Jericho NY 11753

PHILLIPS, ETHEL C. (MRS. LLOYD J. PHILLIPS), writer; b. N.Y.C., Mar. 16, 1908; d. Henry and Minnie (Hirshfeld) Cohen; B.A., Vassar Coll., 1930; M.A., Columbia U., 1932; m. Lloyd Jay Phillips, June 26, 1930; children—Lloyd James, Anne. Publs. dir. Am. Jewish Com., Inst. Human Relations, N.Y.C., 1939-65. Bd. dirs., mem. exec. com. Nat. Information Bur., N.Y.C., 1966—. Mem. N.Y. Soc. for Ethical Culture (trustee 1977—), Nat. Council Women U.S. (pres. 1972-74, hon. pres. 1974-76, UN rep. 1976—). Clubs: Vassar, Harvard, Women's City (N.Y.C.). Author: Mind Your World, 1964; Record and the Vision, 1965; You in Human Rights, 1968; also pamphlets and media features on civil rights, internat. cooperation, human rights, volunteerism. Home: 120 E 79th St New York NY 10021

PHILLIPS, EUAN HYWEL, pub. co. exec.; b. Chipstead, Surrey, Eng., Mar. 31, 1928; s. Edgar Aneurin and Elsie Llewella (Davies) P.; B.A., Emmanuel Coll., Cambridge, Eng., 1949, M.A., 1965; m. Margaret June Savage, June 12, 1954; children—David John, Janet Margaret. Cost acct. J. Lyons & Co. Ltd., London, 1950-53; dispatch mgr. Pickerings Produce Canners Ltd., Manchester, Eng., 1953-56; mgmt. cons. P.A. Mgmt. Cons. Ltd., London, 1956-65; mng. dir. Unwin Bros. Ltd., Old Woking, Eng. 1965-73; univ. printer designate Cambridge (Eng.) U. Press, 1973-74, univ. printer, 1974-76, dir. Am. br., N.Y.C., 1977—. gov. Guilford Sch. Art, 1966-69; gov. Cambridge Coll. Arts and Tech., 1974-76; dir. East Asian History of Sci., Inc., 1978—. Served with Royal Navy, 1946-48. Mem. Brit. Printing Industries Fedn. (mem. council 1966-73, pres. Home Counties alliance 1970-71). Clubs: Hayling Island Sailing, Cedar Point Yacht, Pubs. Lunch. Home: 68 White Oak Ln Stamford CT 06905 Office: 32 E 57th St New York NY 10022

PHILLIPS, FRANCES MARIE, educator; b. Hale Center, Tex., Nov. 8, 1918; d. Clyde C. and Ada (Stutzman) Phillips; B.A., West Tex. State Coll., 1940, M.A., 1946; Ph.D. (Univ. fellow), U. N.Mex., 1956; postgrad. (Fulbright scholar), U. London, 1954-55. Tchr. public schs., Channing, Tex., Miami, Tex., Palisade, Colo., Tucumcari, N.Mex., 1940-46; supr. State Tchrs. Coll. Campus High Sch., Wayne, Nebr., 1947-51; instr. U. Md. Overseas Program, Eng., 1955; grad. asst. U. N.Mex., 1955-56; asst., asso. prof. history Sul Ross State Coll., Alpine, Tex., 1956-60, prof. history, dean grad. div., 1962-71; program dir. sr. colls. Coordinating Bd. Tex. Coll. and Univ. System, Austin, 1971—; asst. prof. Mankato (Minn.) State Coll., 1960-62. Chmn. bd. Carlsbad dist. Wesley Found., 1962-66; mem. Adv. Council for Ednl. Personnel Devel., 1972—, State Bd. Examiners for Tchr. Edn., 1972—, Tex. Com. on Early Childhood Devel. Careers, 1976—. Mem. Am. Assn. U. Women, Am. Hist. Assn., Orgn. Am. Historians, N.Mex. Hist. Soc., N.E.A., Tex. State Tchrs. Assn., Assn. Tex. Grad. Schs. (v.p. 1967-69, pres. 1969-70), Alpha Chi, Phi Kappa Phi, Phi Alpha Theta, Delta Gamma Kappa. Democrat. Methodist (mem. N.Mex. Conf. Bd. Edn., mem. ofcl. bd.). Research in Anglo-Am. relations, 1954-56, 1962. Home: 8700 Millway Dr Austin TX 78758

PHILLIPS, GERALD BAER, physician, scientist; b. Bethlehem, Pa., Mar. 20, 1925; s. Abel H. and Cecilia (Blum) P.; A.B., Princeton U., 1948; M.D., Harvard U., 1948; m. Maria Bonzi Lewis, July 15, 1970; children—Abigail, Elizabeth. Intern, Presbyn. Hosp., N.Y.C., 1948-50; research fellow Thorndike Meml. Lab., Harvard Med. Sch., 1950-53; vis. fellow in biochemistry Coll. Phys. and Surgs., Columbia, N.Y.C., 1954-56, from asso. in medicine to prof. medicine, 1956—; attending in medicine Roosevelt Hosp., 1968—. Sr. asst. surgeon USPHS at Nat. Inst. Arthritis and Metabolic Diseases, NIH, 1952-54. Recipient Lederle Med. Faculty award, 1963-66. Diplomate Am. Bd. Internal Medicine. Mem. Am. Fedn. for Clin. Research, Soc. for Exptl. Biology and Medicine, Am. Soc. for Clin. Investigation, Am. Soc. Biol. Chemists, Am. Assn. for Study Liver Diseases, Alpha Omega Alpha. Home: 196 E 75th St New York City NY 10021 Office: 428 W 59th St New York City NY 10019. *I attribute any success I may have had to heredity and luck.*

PHILLIPS, GIFFORD, publisher; b. Washington, June 30, 1918; s. James Laughlin and Alice C. (Gifford) P.; student Stanford U., 1939, Yale U., 1942; m. Joann Grace Kocher, Feb. 14, 1953; children—Alice Katherine, James Laughlin, Marjorie G. Pub., Frontier mag., Los Angeles, 1949-67; partner Pardee-Phillips Homebuilders, Los Angeles, 1952—; asso. pub. Nation mag., N.Y.C., 1967-73. Del. Democratic Nat. convs., 1952, 56, 60, 64; mem. McCarthy Steering Com., Calif., 1968. Trustee Mus. Modern Art, N.Y.C., Phillips Collection, Washington, Rothko Found., N.Y.C.; trustee Pasadena Art Mus., 1971—, pres., 1973-74, sec.-treas., 1975-76; bd. dirs. Nat. Urban League, 1950-53, chmn. regional office, 1952-56. Served with AUS, 1942-43. Recipient Merit awards Nat. Urban League, 1956, U. So. Calif. Sch. Arts, 1973. Author: The Arts in a Democratic Society, 1966. Home: 2501 La Mesa Santa Monica CA 90402 Office: 11777 San Vicente Blvd Suite 636 Los Angeles CA 90049. *I have endeavored to find out what the good life is and how more people can share in it. The answers sometimes seem contradictory, but in our times one must learn to live with ambiguity.*

PHILLIPS, GUY BERRYMAN, JR., ins. co. exec.; b. Oxford, N.C., May 25, 1918; s. Guy Berryman and Annie (Craig) P.; B.S., U. N.C., 1938; m. Bernice Brantley, Nov. 10, 1974; children by previous marriage—Guy Berryman III, Patricia Anne. With Jefferson Standard Life Ins. Co., Greensboro, N.C., 1938— sec., 1957—, 2d v.p., 1960-64, v.p., 1964-75, sr. v.p., 1975—; asst. sec. Jefferson Pilot Corp., 1968-69, sec., 1969—. Chmn. ann. campaign Greensboro United Fund, 1960-61; v.p. N.C. Bus. Edn. Council, 1957-58; chmn. Greensboro Citizens for Greensboro Coll., 1963-64; trustee Pfeiffer Coll., 1979—. Served to maj. USAAF, 1942-46, USAF, 1951-52. Mem. Nat. Office Mgmt. Assn. (past pres. Greensboro chpt.), Personnel Assn. Greensboro Area (past pres.), Life Office Mgmt. Assn. (dir., past com. chmn.), Delta Pi Epsilon. Methodist. Home: 4120 Dogwood Dr Greensboro NC 27410 Office: PO Box 21008 Greensboro NC 27420

PHILLIPS, HARRY, judge; b. Watertown, Tenn., July 28, 1909; s. Norman Cates and Bernice (Neal) P.; A.B., Cumberland U., 1932, LL.B., 1933, LL.D., 1951; m. Virginia Major, Nov. 26, 1936; children—Harriet (Mrs. Robert E. Scott), Rachel (Mrs. Sidney S. Eagles, Jr.), Caroline (Mrs. Robert M. Ligon), Martha (Mrs. James M. Robinson). Admitted to Tenn. bar, 1933; practiced in Watertown, 1933-37; asst. atty. gen. Tenn., 1937-43, 46-50; mem. firm Phillips, Gullett & Steele, and predecessors, Nashville, 1950-63; exec. sec. Tenn. Code Commn., 1953-63; judge U.S. Ct. of Appeals, 6th Circuit, 1963—, chief judge, 1969-79, sr. judge, 1979—. Served to lt. comdr. USNR, 1943-46. Recipient award of merit Bar Assn. Tenn., 1960. Fellow Am. Bar Found. (hon.); mem. Am. Bar Assn. (spl. com. coordination of fed. jud. improvements 1978—), S.A.R., Order of Coif (hon.), Sigma Alpha Epsilon. Baptist. Clubs: Cumberland, University (Cin.); Exchange. Author: Phillips' Family History, 1935; Phillips' Prichard on Wills and Administration of Estates, 1955; co-author: History of Wilson County, Tennessee, 1962, History of the Sixth Circuit, 1976. Home: 2809 Wimbledon Rd Nashville TN 37215

Office: US Courthouse Nashville TN 37203 also US Courthouse Cincinnati OH 45202

PHILLIPS, HOWARD, public policy analyst; b. Boston, Feb. 3, 1941; s. Fred N. and Gertrude P.; A.B., Harvard Coll., 1962; m. Margaret E. Blanchard, July 5, 1964; children—Douglas, Amanda, Bradford, Jennifer, Alexandra. Mem. exec. staff Republican Com. of Boston, 1966-68; acting exec. dir. Pres.'s Council on Youth Opportunity, 1969-70; acting dir. OEO, Washington, 1973; nat. dir. Conservative Caucus, Falls Church, Va., 1974—; pres. Conservative Caucus Research Analysis and Edn. Found., 1977—. Bd. dirs. Young Americans for Freedom, 1960; candidate for Democratic nomination to U.S. Senate from Mass., 1978. Jewish. Club: Harvard (Boston). Contbr. articles to mags., including Human Events, Nat. Rev., N.Y. Times, Conservative Digest, Campus Digest. Home: 30 Radnor Rd Brighton MA 02135 Office: 422 Maple Ave Vienna VA 22180 also 47 West St Boston MA 02115

PHILLIPS, HOWARD WILLIAM, investment banker; b. N.Y.C., May 16, 1930; s. Louis and Helen (Klein) P.; B.A., Dartmouth Coll., 1951, M.B.A., 1952; LL.B., Harvard U., 1957; m. Ellen Birk, July 15, 1956; children—Jan Leslie, Richard Louis. Admitted to N.Y. bar, 1957; asso. Cahill, Gordon, Reindel & Ohl, N.Y.C., 1957-64; v.p., gen. counsel McCall Corp., N.Y.C., 1964-68, sr. v.p., 1968-69; partner Oppenheimer & Co., N.Y.C., 1969—; dir. Lou Ana Industries, New Orleans, Big Bears Stores Co., Columbus, Ohio, Automatic Service Co., Atlanta, Shirley of Atlanta, Havatampa Corp., Tampa, Fla., Reliable Stores, Balt., Walls Industries, Cleburne, Tex. Served to lt. (j.g.) USNR, 1952-54. Clubs: Noyac (N.Y.) Golf and Country; Sky (N.Y.C.); Easthampton (N.Y.) Tennis. Home: 1070 Park Ave New York City NY 10028 Office: 1 New York Plaza New York City NY 10004

PHILLIPS, IVAN EDWARD, engring. and constrn. co. exec.; b. Gloucester, Eng., July 31, 1926; s. Edward Charles and May Victoria (Webb) P.; came to U.S., 1960; B.Sc. in Chemistry, Southampton (Eng.) U., 1952; postgrad. Advanced Mgmt. Program, Harvard, 1974; m. Christine Pearl Fripp, Mar. 28, 1948; children—John Christopher, Clare Elisabeth, David Anthony. Prodn. mgr. Fisons Ltd., Stanford-le-Hope, Eng., 1954-59; mgr. chem. ops. Internat. Minerals & Chem. Corp., Bartow, Fla., 1961-63, mgr. gen. ops., Esterhazy, Sask., Can., 1966-68; exec. v.p. Davy Powergas Inc., Lakeland, Fla., 1970-74, pres., 1974—, also dir. Served with Royal Navy, 1944-47. Asso. mem. Royal Inst. Chemistry, Lakeland C. of C. (dir.). Clubs: Lakeland Yacht and Country, Lone Palm Golf, Univ. Home: 210 Lake Hollingsworth Dr Lakeland FL 33803 Office: PO Drawer 5000 4715 S Florida Ave Lakeland FL 33803

PHILLIPS, JAMES ARCHIBALD, JR., educator; b. Harford County, Md., Sept. 13, 1930; s. James Archibald and Ida Lucille (Taylor) P.; B.S., Salisbury (Md.) State Tchrs. Coll., 1951; M.Ed., U. Md., 1956; Ed.D., Mich. State U., 1961; m. Mildred Mae Bluett, Aug. 11, 1956; children—James Archibald III, Stephen W., Beatrice Ann. Tchr. pub. schs. Baltimore County (Md.), 1951-57; instr. Mich. State U., 1957-59; asso. prof. Towson (Md.) State Coll., 1959-62; asst. prof. Kent (Ohio) State U., 1962-65, asso. prof., 1965-69, prof. secondary edn., coordinator grad. programs in curriculum, instrn. and supervision, 1969-76, prof., chmn. dept. curriculum and instrn., 1976—. Co-dir. Soviet Edn. Seminar, 1972, E. European Edn. Seminar, 1973; curriculum cons. Am. Sch. Health Assn. Served with AUS, 1952-54. Mem. Assn. Supervision and Curriculum Devel. (dir. 1973—), Ohio Assn. Supervision and Curriculum Devel. (pres. 1973-74), Profs. Curriculum, Am. Ednl. Research Assn., Phi Delta Kappa (Leadership award 1974), Kappa Delta Pi. Cons. author: Medicines, Drugs and Healthful Living, 1973. Editor: Developing Value Constructs in Schooling: Inquiry into Process and Product, 1972. Home: 549 Ivan Dr Kent OH 44240

PHILLIPS, JAMES CHARLES, educator, physicist; b. New Orleans, Mar. 9, 1933; s. William D. and Juanita (Hahn) P.; B.A., U. Chgo., 1952, B.S., 1953, M.S., 1955, Ph.D., 1956; m. Erika Muehl, Oct. 24, 1976. Mem. tech. staff Bell Labs., 1956-58; NSF fellow U. Calif. at Berkeley, 1958-59, Cambridge (Eng.) U., 1959-60; faculty U. Chgo., 1960-68, prof. physics, 1965-68; mem. tech. staff Bell Labs., 1968—. Sloan fellow, 1962-66; Guggenheim fellow, 1967. Fellow Am. Phys. Soc. (Buckley prize 1972); mem. Nat. Acad. Scis. Home: 204 Springfield Ave Summit NJ 07901

PHILLIPS, JAMES DICKSON, JR., fed. judge; b. Scotland County, N.C., Sept. 23, 1922; s. James Dickson and Helen (Shepherd) P.; B.S. cum laude, Davidson Coll., 1943; J.D., U. N.C., 1948; m. Jean Duff Nunalee, July 16, 1960; children—Evelyn Phillips Perry, James Dickson, III, Elizabeth Duff, Ida Wills. Admitted to N.C. bar; asst. dir. Inst. Govt., Chapel Hill, N.C., 1948-49; partner firm Phillips & McCoy, Laurinburg, N.C., 1949-55, Sanford, Phillips, McCoy & Weaver, Fayetteville, N.C., 1955-60; from asst. prof. to prof. law U. N.C., 1960-78, dean Sch. Law, 1964-74; circuit judge U.S. Ct. Appeals, 4th Circuit, 1978—. Mem. N.C. Wildlife Resources Commn., 1961-63; mem. N.C. Cts. Commn., 1963-75, also vice chmn.; chmn. N.C. Bd. Ethics, 1977-78. Served with parachute inf. U.S. Army, 1943-46. Decorated Bronze Arrowhead, Bronze Star, Purple Heart; recipient John J. Parker Meml. award; Thomas Jefferson award. Mem. Am. Law Inst., N.C. Bar Assn., Am. Bar Assn. Democrat. Presbyterian. Home: 529 Caswell Rd Chapel Hill NC 27514 Office: 209 PO Bldg 323 E Chapel Hill St Durham NC 27701

PHILLIPS, JAMES DONALD, former coll. pres. and chancellor; b. S. Lyon, Mich., July 17, 1907; s. James M. and Ada Jane (Cole) P.; student Mercersburg (Pa.) Acad., Detroit Coll. Law; B.S., Mich. State Normal Coll., 1938; M.A., U. Mich., 1940; LL.D., Franklin Coll., 1952; D.Sc. (hon.), Cleary Coll., 1966; L.H.D., Hillsdale (Mich.) Coll., 1971; m. Elizabeth Jane Pellett, Dec. 20, 1940; children—James Donald, MacWain, Sally Ada, Juliann, David. Rural sch. tchr., 1925-26; salesman, 1926-27; sch. prin., Salem, Mich., 1927-29; supt. schs., Sherwood, Mich., 1930-36; lectr., adult edn. cons. U. Mich., 1938-40; mem. staff A.R.C., Washington, 1940-41; Mich. rep. FSA, 1941-42; dir. civilian war services, Lansing, Mich., 1943-44; dir. adult edn. Mich. State Coll., 1944-51; pres. Hillsdale Coll., 1952-71, chancellor, 1971-72; ednl., bus. cons., originator various group communication techniques; lectr., conf. leader, trainer. Mem. Adult Edn. Assn., Mich. Acad. Sci., Arts and Letters, Phi Delta Kappa, Phi Kappa Phi, Delta Theta Phi, Pi Kappa Delta, Omicron Delta Kappa. Baptist. Home: Edgewood Dr Lake Wilson Hillsdale MI 49242. *No hill is worth the climb if the effort requires the use of steps formed by the broken spirits of others.*

PHILLIPS, JAMES LINFORD, agrl. journalist, editor; b. Bristol, Pa., Nov. 27, 1943; s. James Henry and Dorothy (Morgan) P.; student Pa. State U., 1961-63; B.A., Brigham Young U., 1973; m. Judith Lynne Bylund, May 31, 1968; children—James Bruce, Scott Linford, Mark Kevin, Deborah Eleanor, Rheanna Lynne. Editor, Mich. Farm News, Lansing, 1974-76; asst. editor Mich. Farmer, Lansing, 1976-77; asso. editor livestock Farm Jour. mag., Phila., 1977—. Mem. Am. Agrl. Editors Assn., Kappa Tau Alpha, Sigma Delta Chi. Mormon. Office: 230 W Washington Sq Philadelphia PA 19105

PHILLIPS, JAMES PAUL, II, former fgn. service officer, internat. communications cons.; b. Jellico, Tenn., July 7, 1927; s. James Paul and Myrtle Edith (Harris) P.; B.S., U. Tenn., 1948; postgrad. internat. relations Georgetown U., 1950-51, Am. U., 1955-56; m. Patricia Adelaide Neeld, July 12, 1952; 1 son, Mark Neeld. Copy editor Knoxville (Tenn.) News-Sentinel, 1947-48; textbook writer Dept. Navy, 1949-51; social scientist Internat. Info. Adminstrn., 1951-56; info. officer Am. embassy, Mexico, 1957-59, Republic China, 1960-61, Vietnam, 1961-63; spl. asst. to asst. sec. state for internat. orgn. affairs, 1963-66; asst. regional dir. III Corps, Vietnam, 1967-69; program officer USIS, India, 1970-71; dir. Office Pub. Info., Dept. State Bur. Ednl. and Cultural Affairs, Washington, 1971-73; dep. dir. USIS, Manila, 1973-77; dir. USIA, Hong Kong, 1977-78; internat. communications cons., Bethesda, Md., 1978—. Bd. govs. Am. Internat. Sch., New Delhi, 1970-71. Served to lt. comdr. USNR, 1945-46. Decorated medal of Honor 1st class, Psychol. Ops. medal (Vietnam); recipient Meritorious Honor award USIA, 1970. Mem. U.S. Naval Inst., Am. Fedn. Govt. Employees, Phi Delta Kappa. Unitarian. Author: Electronic Aids to Navigation, 1949; Naval Search and Fighter-Director Radar, 1950; Electronics Technician, 1951. Address: 4849 Broad Brook Dr Bethesda MD 20014

PHILLIPS, JANET COLLEEN, assn. exec.; b. Pittsfield, Ill., Apr. 29, 1933; d. Roy Lynn and Catherine Amelia (Wills) Barker; B.S., U. Ill., 1954; m. David Lee Phillips, Feb. 7, 1954; children—Clay Cullen, Sean Vincent. Reporter, Quincy (Ill.) Herald Whig, summers 1951, 52, society editor, summer 1953; editorial asst. Pub. Info. Office, U. Ill., 1953-54, asst. editor Library, 1954-61; asst. editor Assn. Am. Library Schs., State College, Pa., 1960-61, mng. editor, 1961—, exec. sec., 1970—; cons. in field. Mem. AAUW, PTA, State College Weavers Guild, Faculty Needlecraft Group, Embroiderers Guild Am., Theta Sigma Phi Delta Zeta. Presbyterian. Clubs: Pa. State U. Faculty Women's, Penn State Blue Course. Address: 471 Park Ln State College PA 16801

PHILLIPS, JERRY JUAN, lawyer; b. Charlotte, N.C., June 16, 1935; s. Vergil Ernest and Mary Blanche (Wade) P.; B.A., Yale U., 1956, J.D., 1961; B.A., Cambridge (Eng.) U., 1958, M.A. (hon.), 1964; m. Anne Butler Colville, June 6, 1959; children—Sherman Wade, Dorothy Colville. Admitted to Tenn. bar, 1961; asso. firm Miller, Martin, Hitching, Tipton & Lenihan, Chattanooga, 1961-67; asst. prof. law U. Tenn., 1967-72, asso. prof., 1972-73, prof., 1973—; adv. Tenn. Law Revision Commn., 1968-70; mem. Tenn. Jud. Council, 1970-74; adv. Fed. Interagy. Task Force on Products Liability, 1976-77; lectr. in field. U. Tenn. grantee, 1978. Mem. Am. Law Inst., Knoxville Bar Assn. Democrat. Episcopalian. Club: Knoxville Racquet. Author: (with Dix W. Noel) Products Liability in a Nutshell, 1974, Products Liability Cases and Materials, 1976; adv. Tenn. Law Rev., 1977—. Home: 3919 Kingston Pike Knoxville TN 37919 Office: 1505 W Cumberland Knoxville TN 37916

PHILLIPS, JOHN CHARLES, oil co. exec., lawyer; b. Metcalfe, Ont., Can., 1921; student U. Toronto (Ont.), 1940, Osgoode Hall Law Sch., 1949. Called to Ont. bar, 1949; with Gulf Can. Ltd., Toronto, 1949—, asst. gen. counsel, 1960-69, gen. counsel, 1969-71, v.p., sec., gen. counsel, 1971-76, sr. v.p., 1976-77, exec. v.p., 1977-79, chmn., 1979—, also dir. Office: Gulf Can Ltd 800 Bay St Toronto ON M5S 1Y8 Canada*

PHILLIPS, JOHN DAVID, communications co. exec.; b. Exeland, Wis., June 29, 1920; s. Mathew Frank and Iva (Bryant) P.; B.S., U. Wis., 1937; m. Estelle Margaret Pautsch, July 19, 1941; 1 son, John David. Partner, Miss Wis. Cheese, 1946-56; dir. marketing Armour & Co., 1956-60; v.p. Am. Home Corp., 1960-66; founder, pres. R.J. Reynolds Foods, Inc., 1966-72; pres. CBS/Columbia Group, N.Y.C., 1973—; dir. CBS Inc., Glenmore Distillers Co., Cornelius Co. Past pres. Assn. Corp. Growth, N.Y.C., Hamilton Coll. Parents Assn.; trustee N.Y.C. Pub. Library, Juniata Coll.; adv. bd. Howard U. Served with USAAF, 1944-46. Conglist. (trustee). Clubs: Greenwich Country, Riverside Yacht, N.Y. Yacht; Links (N.Y.C.); Petroleum (Corpus Christi, Tex.). Home: Pilot Rock Riverside CT 06878 Office: 51 W 52d St New York City NY 10019

PHILLIPS, JOHN DAVISSON, lawyer; b. Clarksburg, W.Va., Aug. 21, 1906; s. Robert Bruce and Lela (Davisson) P.; student Washington and Lee U., 1924-25; A.B., W.Va. U., 1928, LL.B., 1930; postgrad. Oxford U., 1930-32; m. Virginia Maxwell, Nov. 12, 1932; children—John Davisson, Julia Anne. Admitted to W.Va. bar, 1932; gen. practice law, Wheeling, W.Va., 1932—; mem. firm Phillips, Gardill & Hazlett; asst. pros. atty. Ohio County, 1937-40; city solicitor City of Wheeling, 1942-47; dir. Wheeling Dollar Savs. & Trust Co., M. Marsh & Son, Wesbanco, Inc., Wheeling; hon. dir. Fostoria Glass Co.; past mem. W.Va. State Bd. Law Examiners. Served as capt. USMCR, World War II. Fellow Am. Bar Founds.; mem. Am. Law Inst., Am., W.Va. (pres. 1955-56) bar assns., Am. Judicature Soc., Phi Kappa Psi, Phi Delta Phi. Episcopalian. Clubs: Wheeling Country, Fort Henry. Home: 4 Arlington Dr Howard Pl Wheeling WV 26003 Office: Bd Trade Bldg Wheeling WV 26003

PHILLIPS, JOHN EDWARD, zoologist; b. Montreal, Que., Can., Dec. 20, 1934; s. William Charles and Violet Mildred (Lewis) P.; B.Sc., Dalhousie U., 1956, M.Sc., 1957; Ph.D., Cambridge (Eng.) U., 1961; m. Eleanor Mae Richardson, Sept. 8, 1956; children—Heather Anne, Jayne Elizabeth, Jonathan David, Catherine Melinda, Wendy Susannah. Asst. prof. zoology Dalhousie U., 1960-64; asso. prof. U. B.C. (Can.), Vancouver, 1964-71, prof., 1971—; vis. researcher dept. zoology Cambridge U., 1972, 76; chmn. grant selection com. on animal biology Nat. Research Council Can., 1969-71. Mem. Vancouver Bach Choir. Fellow Royal Soc. Can.; mem. Can. Soc. Zoology (pres. 1978-79, editorial bd. Can. Jour. Zoology 1971-75), Am. Physiol. Soc. (editorial bd. Am. Jour. Physiology), Am. Soc. Zoologists, Soc. Exptl. Biology U.K. Contbr. articles to profl. jours. Home: 2033 W 58th Ave Vancouver BC V6P 1X3 Canada Office: 2075 Wesbrook Pl Vancouver BC V6T 1W5 Canada

PHILLIPS, JOHN GARDNER, educator, astrophysicist; b. New Haven, Jan. 9, 1917; s. Ray Edmund and Dora (Larson) P.; B.A., Carleton Coll., 1939; M.A., U. Ariz., 1942; Ph.D., U. Chgo., 1948; m. Margaret Ann Butler, June 11, 1944; children—Mary Jane, Cynthia Ann, Gail Elizabeth. Instr., Yerkes Obs., U. Chgo., 1948-50; faculty U. Calif. at Berkeley, 1950—, prof. astrophysics, 1960—, chmn. dept. astronomy, 1964-67, 71-75, dir. Leuschner Obs., 1964-67, 71-75. Cons. NASA, Ames Lab. Guggenheim fellow, 1956. Mem. Am. Astron. Soc., Internat. Astron. Union (pres. commn. 14 1979—), Astron. Soc. Pacific (sec.-treas. 1968—), AAAS. Author: (with S.P. Davis) The Red System of the CN Molecule, 1963, The Swam System of the C2 Molecule; The Spectrum of the HgH Molecule; (with Alter, Cleminshaw) Pictorial Astronomy, 1963, rev., 1969, 75. Asso. editor Ann. Revs. Astronomy and Astrophysics, 1966—. Home: 1234 Lawrence St El Cerrito CA 94530 Office: Dept Astronomy U Calif Berkeley CA 94720

PHILLIPS, JOHN GURLEY, oil co. exec.; b. Camden, Ark., Sept. 8, 1922; s. John Gurley and Thalia (DuBose) P.; B.S., U. Ark., 1948; m. Evelyn Richards, Dec. 16, 1950; children—Fran Evelyn (Mrs. Roger Alan Grayson), Cherry Thalia. Staff accountant Peat, Marwick, Mitchell & Co., 1948-51; with La. Land & Exploration Co., 1951—, exec. v.p., 1962-67, dir., 1962—, pres., 1967-74, chief exec. officer, 1972—, chmn. bd., 1974—; dir. Bank of N.Y., Whitney Nat. Bank, Travelers Corp.; mem. nat. adv. bd. Comml. Nat. Bank, Little Rock, Nat. Petroleum Council; trustee Com. Econ. Devel. Bd. dirs. Am. Petroleum Inst.; nat. exec. bd. Boy Scouts Am.; chmn. Tulane Bd. Adminstrs.; trustee Tax Found., Inc. Served to 1st lt. USAAF 1942-45. Mem. Am. Inst. C.P.A.'s. Clubs: Country, Boston, Pickwick (New Orleans); Racquet and Tennis (N.Y.C.); River Oaks Country (Houston); Wildcat Cliffs Country (Highlands, N.C.). Home: 5658 Evelyn Ct New Orleans LA 70124 Office: 225 Baronne St New Orleans LA 70112 also PO Box 60350 New Orleans LA 70160

PHILLIPS, JOHN PIERSON, lawyer; b. Phoenix, Mar. 3, 1925; s. Ralph A. and Clara (Pierson) P.; J.D., U. Ariz., 1948; m. Virginia I. Merritt, July 19, 1948; children—Ralph M., John P., Mary Patricia. Admitted to Ariz. bar, 1948, since practiced in Phoenix; mem. firm Phillips, Jones & Phillips, 1948-63, Snell & Wilmer, 1964—. Pres., bd. dirs. Family Service of Phoenix; treas., bd. dirs. Maricopa County chpt. ARC; bd. dirs. Maricopa County chpt. Am. Cancer Soc. Mem. Am., Ariz., Maricopa County (treas., dir.) bar assns., Sigma Chi, Phi Alpha Delta. Episcopalian (vestryman). Home: 240 E Orangewood St Phoenix AZ 85020 Office: Valley Bank Center Phoenix AZ 85073

PHILLIPS, JOSEF CLAYTON, ins. co. exec.; b. Seattle, June 27, 1908; s. Joseph Clinton and Margaret Janet (Branlund) P.; student U. Wash., 1925-28, U. Paris (France), 1928-29; m. Ada May Gummer, Sept. 24, 1931; 1 dau., Barbara Lee (Mrs. Charles Huffman). With Merrill, Lynch, Pierce, Fenner & Bean, Seattle, 1930-35; with United Pacific Corp., 1936—, pres., 1960-63, chmn. bd., 1963-67; dir., chmn. exec. com. United Pacific Ins. Co., 1957-68; dir. N.W. Bldg. Co., Met. Bldg. Co., Pelican Corp. Clubs: Seattle Golf (Seattle); Wailea Golf (Maui, Hawaii). Home: 326 NW 137th St Seattle WA 98177

PHILLIPS, JOSEPH DEXTER, economist; b. Buena Park, Calif., Dec. 5, 1914; s. Joseph Dexter and Ivy (Yates) P.; A.B., U. Calif., 1937, postgrad., 1937-40; Ph.D. (Univ. fellow, Social Sci. Research Council fellow), Columbia U., 1951; m. Genevieve Rae Ferguson, July 30, 1938; children—Joan Rae, James Harold, Elizabeth Hunt, William Yates, Ann Louise. Sr. labor economist Recruitment and Manning Orgn., War Shipping Adminstrn., Washington, 1942-44; asst. prof. econs. Wesleyan U., 1946-49; lectr. in econs. U. Calif., Santa Barbara, 1949-51; asso. prof. Champlain Coll., 1951-53; prof. econs., chmn. dept. econs. and bus. Idaho State Coll., 1953-56; prof. U. Ill., Urbana-Champaign, 1956—; cons. in field. Served with AUS, 1945. Mem. Am. Econ. Assn., AAAS, AAUP, Am. Fedn. Tchrs. Editor: Little Business in the American Economy, 1958; The Self-employed in the United States, 1962; (with Herbert Schiller) Superstate, Readings in the Military-Industrial Complex, 1970; editor Quar. Rev. Econs. and Bus., 1970-79. Home: 802 Brighton Dr Urbana IL 61801 Office: 419 Commerce W U Ill Urbana IL 61801

PHILLIPS, JULIA, film producer; b. N.Y.C., April 7, 1944; d. Adolph and Tanya Miller; grad. Nicolet high sch.; B.A., Mt. Holyoke Coll., 1965; m. Michael Phillips (div.); 1 dau., Kate Elizabeth. Former prodn. asst. McCall's Mag.; later advt. copywriter MacMillan Publs.; editorial asst. Ladies Home Journal, later asso. editor; East Coast story editor Paramount Pictures, N.Y.C.; head Mirisch Prodns., N.Y.; creative exec. First Artists Prodns., N.Y.C.; founded (with Tony Bill and Michael Phillips) Bill/Phillips Prodns., 1970; films include Steelyard Blues, 1972. The Sting (Acad. award for best picture of yr.), 1973, Taxi Driver (Palme d'or for best picture), 1976, The Big Bus, 1976, Close Encounters of the Third Kind, 1977; dir. The Estate of Billy Buckner for Women Dirs. Workshop, Am. Film Inst., 1974. Recipient Phi Beta Kappa award for ind. work, 1964; Katherine McFarland Short Story award, 1964. Mem. Acad. Motion Picture Arts and Scis. Home: Beverly Hills CA

PHILLIPS, KEVIN PRICE, newspaper columnist; b. N.Y.C., Nov. 30, 1940; s. William Edward and Dorothy Virginia (Price) P.; A.B., Colgate U., 1961; postgrad. U. Edinburgh (Scotland), 1959-60; LL.B., Harvard, 1964; m. Martha Eleanor Henderson, Sept. 28, 1968; children—Andrew, Alexander. Admitted to N.Y. bar, 1965; adminstrv. asst. to Congressman Paul Fino, 1964-68; spl. asst. atty. gen. U.S., 1969-70; newspaper columnist syndicated King Features, 1970—; lectr.; pres. Am. Polit. Research Corp., 1971—; commentator CBS (Spectrum), 1978—. Spl. asst. to campaign mgr. Nixon for Pres. Com., 1968. Mem. N.Y., D.C. bars, Phi Beta Kappa. Author: The Emerging Republican Majority, 1969; Electoral Reform and Voter Participation, 1975; Mediacracy, 1975; editor and pub. The American Political Report, 1971—, Business and Public Affairs Fortnightly, 1979—. Home: 5115 Moorland Ln Bethesda MD 20014 Office: 4312 Montgomery Ave Bethesda MD 20014

PHILLIPS, LAUGHLIN, mus. ofcl.; b. Washington, Oct. 20, 1924; s. Duncan and Marjorie Grant (Acker) P.; student Yale U., 1942-43; M.A., U. Chgo., 1949; m. Elizabeth Hood, Mar. 17, 1956; children—Duncan Vance, Elizabeth Laughlin; m. 2d, Jennifer Stats Cafritz, Aug. 13, 1975. Fgn. service officer, 1949-64; vice consul, Hanoi, Vietnam, 1950-53; 2d sec., Tehran, Iran, 1957-59; co-founder Washingtonian mag., 1965, editor, 1965-74, editor-in-chief, 1974-79; pres. Washington Mag., Inc., 1965-79; pres. Phillips Collection, 1967—, also dir. Washington trustee Fed. City Council, 1974—. Bd. dirs. MacDowell Colony, 1977-79. Mem. Nat. Com. for an Effective Congress, 1966—. Served with AUS, 1943-46; PTO. Decorated Bronze Star medal. Mem. Am. Assn. Mus. Dirs. Clubs: Cosmos, Metropolitan, Chevy Chase (Washington). Home: 3044 O St NW Washington DC 20007 Office: 1600 21st St NW Washington DC 20009

PHILLIPS, LAWRENCE S., bus. exec.; b. 1927; s. Seymour J. Phillips; B.A., Princeton; m. With Phillips-Van Heusen Corp., 1948—, v.p., 1951-59, exec. v.p., 1959-68, pres., 1968—, also dir. Mem. Am. Apparel Mfrs. (dir.). Address: 1290 Ave of Americas New York NY 10016*

PHILLIPS, LOUIE MARTIN, banker; b. Lebanon, Tenn., May 6, 1908; s. Jesse Martin and Nancy (Potter) P.; B.A., Vanderbilt U., 1930; m. Elizabeth Gould Moore Buntin, Jan. 1, 1944; stepchildren—Daniel C. Buntin, Thomas C. Buntin, Roger C. Buntin. With Commerce Union Bank, Nashville and Gallatin, Tenn., 1930-35; v.p., partner Temple Securities, investment bankers, Nashville, 1935-42; v.p., dir. Broadway Nat. Bank, Nashville, 1946-47, pres., 1947-62; bank merged with Commerce Union Bank, Nashville, 1962, vice chmn. bd., dir., 1962-68, now cons., dir., mem. exec. com.; dir. Tenn. Valley Bancorp., Inc., mem. exec. com.; sec.-treas., dir. 6th Ave. Realty Co.; owner Fairfield Co.; pres. Union Corp.; dir., mem. exec. com. Am. Health Profiles, Inc.; chmn. bd., dir. Nat. Automated Petroleum Services Corp. Mem. staff gov. Tenn., 1953, 59, 63, 69-72. Past pres., dir. Nashville Boys Club; hon. lifetime chmn., mem. bd. Nashville Polio Found.; founder, original trustee Nashville United Givers Fund; chmn. spl. gifts com. Rural Life Found.; dir. Council of Community Agys.; chmn. Broadway Bus. Men's Assn.; past chmn. budget com. Tenn. Bot. Gardens and Fine Arts Center; treas., dir., mem. exec. com. Tenn. Mental Health Assn.; bd. dirs., chmn. budget com., past campaign chmn. Nashville Salvation Army; Middle Tenn. chmn. Radio-Free Europe. Bd. dirs. Day Care Center and Sch. for Retarded Children; bd. govs. Sewanee (Tenn.) Acad. Served to lt. col.

USAAF, 1942-46; ETO. Decorated Order Orange Nassau with crossed swords (Netherlands); Golden Boy award Boys Club, 1960. Mem. Tenn. Motor Transp. Assn., Am. Inst. Banking, Am. Bankers Assn., N.A.M., Navy League (treas., dir. Nashville), Am. Ordnance Assn., Night Fighters Assn. Mem. Christian Ch. (deacon, vice chmn. ofcl. bd.). Mason (32 deg.). Clubs: Sports Car of America; Gatlinburg (Tenn.) Ski; Cumberland, Belle Meade Golf and Country, Pheasant (Nashville); Harbor Island Yacht, Jaguar Owners America. Home: 5527 Stanford Dr Nashville TN 37215 Office: 400 Union St Nashville TN 37219

PHILLIPS, LOYAL, newspaper exec.; b. Cullman, Ala., Apr. 11, 1905; s. Monroe and Lucy Ann (Bailey) P.; B.A., Howard Coll. (now Samford U.), 1928; m. Evelyn Caldwell, Apr. 8, 1928; children—Sharon Kay, Terry Lynn. Promotion mgr. Atlanta Georgian-Am. 1929; classified advt. mgr. Birmingham (Ala.) Post, 1930, Nashville Banner, 1931-32, Omaha World-Herald, 1933-34; classified advt. mgr. Washington Daily News, 1936, acting advt. dir., 1937-38; co-founder, partner, editor Parish-Phillips Newspaper Advt. Syndicate, Miami, Fla., 1939-43, also spl. cons. Tampa Times, Miami News, Washington Post; columnist Editor and Pubs. mag., N.Y.C., 1940; advt. dir. New Orleans Item, 1945-49; gen. mgr., treas. St. Petersburg Ind., Inc., 1950-59, editor, pub., sec., treas., 1952-59, pres., 1959-62; pres. Petersburg (Va.) Newspaper Corp., 1959-62; sec.-treas. Punta Gorda Herald and Clewiston News, 1953—; gen. mgr. Southwest Citizen; pres. Laurel (Miss.) Leader-Call, 1959-62, Independent, Inc., 1962—, WCCF radio sta., 1960; pub., v.p. Ocala (Fla.) Star-Banner, 1963-67; gen. mgr. Elizabeth City (N.C.) Daily Advance, 1967—, co-pub., 1970—; asst. to pres. Dear Publ. & Radio, Inc., 1971-72; gen. mgr. Seabag Newspaper for Norfolk Navy Base, 1967—; roving columnist Gannett Fla. Newspapers, 1973; dir. Citizens Pub. Co. Active ARC, Goodwill Industries, Childrens Service Bur., Salvation Army, Boy Scouts Am.; treas. New Orleans Art Acad.; chmn. Gov.'s Traffic Safety Adv. Com. State Fla., 1956; chmn. Elizabeth City United Fund, 1969, pres., 1970. Bd. dirs. Greater New Orleans. Served as lt. (j.g.) USNR, 1943-47. Mem. Nat. Assn. Newspaper Classified Advt. Mgrs. (v.p. 1933—), So. Newspaper Pubs. Assn. (dir., chmn. pub. relations), Sales Exec. Council, Assn. Commerce, Newspaper Advt. Execs. Assn., Internat. House, Elizabeth City C. of C. (pres. 1972), Lambda Chi Alpha. Rotarian. Clubs: Metairie Country, Quarterback, New Orleans Advertising (pres. 1945-46). Author: Newspaper Advertising, 1946; Fifty Successful Advertising Ideas, 1948. Home: 102 4th Ave Ft Walton Beach FL 32548 Office: Gannett Pennsacola News-Jour 113 4th St SE Ft Walton Beach FL 32548

PHILLIPS, LYMAN COLLVER, utility exec.; b. Toledo, Sept. 22, 1939; s. Milton E. and Harriet A. (Collver) P.; B.B.A., U. Toledo, 1962; m. Barbara Ann Turner, Aug. 18, 1962; children—Kimberly Avo, Andrea Lynn, Daria Marie. With Toledo Edison Co., 1962—, asst. treas., then treas., 1972-77, v.p. adminstrv. services, 1976—. Bd. dirs., treas. Toledo Methadone Clinic; bd. dirs. Maumee Valley council Girl Scouts U.S.A. Mem. Fin. Analysts Fedn. (dir.), Fin. Analysts Soc. Toledo. Home: 2755 Tarrytowne Dr Toledo OH 43613 Office: 300 Madison Ave Toledo OH 43652

PHILLIPS, MATT JAY, artist; b. N.Y.C., Aug. 12, 1927; s. Louis and Pearl E. P.; student Barnes Found., 1950-52; M.A., U. Chgo., 1952; postgrad. Stanford U., 1952-54; m. Sandra Sammataro, June 28, 1968; 1 son, Joshua; children by previous marriage—Katherine, Elizabeth, Miriam. Chmn. art dept. Bard Coll., 1964—; one-man shows include: 15 yr. retrospective Balt. Mus. Art, 1976, Peter Deitsch Gallery, N.Y.C., 1962, 65, Marilyn Pearl Gallery, N.Y.C., 1977, Phillips Collection, Washington, 1978, William Sawyer Gallery, San Francisco, 1978, Des Moines Art Center, 1978, Donald Morris Gallery, Detroit; group shows: Smithsonian Instn. Traveling Exhbn., 1972-73, 78-79, Indpls. Mus. Art, 1972, Santa Barbara (Calif.) Mus. Art, 1976, Impressions Workshop, Boston, 1977, Smith Andersen Gallery, Palo Alto, Met. Mus., 1980, Boston Mus., 1980; represented in permanent collections, including: Met. Mus. Art, N.Y.C., Nat. Gallery Art, Washington, Phillips Collection, Whitney Mus. Art, N.Y.C., Phila. Mus. Art. John Simon Guggenheim Found. grantee, 1974; Nat. Endowment for Arts grantee, 1975. Home: Kidd Ln Tivoli NY 12583 Office: Bard Coll Annandale-on-Hudson NY 12504

PHILLIPS, MERRILL COCHRAN, advt., pub. relations exec.; b. Warren, Pa., May 21, 1910; s. Clair Clifford and Nell Jane (Cochran) P.; A.B., Colgate U., 1934; m. Mary Wilhelmina Slaght, June 5, 1937; children—Elizabeth Cochran, Katherine Augusta (Mrs. M. Douglas Cameron), Margaret Wilhelmina. Sales rep. Milton C. Powell Co., Inc., Rochester, N.Y., 1935-39; broadcast exec. Gen. Electric Co., Schenectady, San Francisco, 1939-42; broadcast mgr. U.S. Office Inter-Am. Affairs, San Francisco, 1942-47; broadcast exec. CBS Internat. div., N.Y.C., 1947-48; information officer U.S. Dept. State, N.Y.C., 1948-55; exec. v.p., dir. John Moynahan & Co., Inc., N.Y.C., 1955-73; owner, propr. Merrill Cochran Phillips, advt., pub. relations agy., Mt. Kisco, N.Y., 1973—. Mem. Bd. Edn., Bedford (N.Y.) Pub. Schs., 1958-63, pres., 1962; mem. Bd. Edn., Bd. Coop. Ednl. Services, Westchester and Putnam counties, N.Y., 1971-74; mem. exec. com. Westchester County Sch. Bds. Assn., 1971-74. Bd. dirs. Boys Club of Mt. Kisco, 1967-71, N.Y. State Citizens Com. for Pub. Schs., 1964-69, Colgate U. Alumni Corp., 1947-50; trustee Human Rights Commn. Mt. Kisco, 1965-67. Mem. Pub. Relations Soc. Am. (accredited), Sigma Chi. Episcopalian. Home: 82 Grandview Dr Mount Kisco NY 10549 Office: PO Box 171 Mount Kisco NY 10549

PHILLIPS, MICHAEL KEITH, lawyer, state legislator; b. Huntingburg, Ind., Sept. 2, 1943; s. Lowell T. and Ida Ruth (Kelley) P.; B.A., DePauw U., Greencastle, Ind., 1965; J.D., Ind. U., 1969; m. Julie Mahon, June 8, 1963; children—Mark, Jennifer, Stephanie, Jeffrey, Emily. Admitted to Ind. bar, 1969, since practiced in Boonville; individual practice law, 1973-78; with firm Phillips & Long, P.C., 1978—; mem. Ind. Ho. of Reps. from 71st Dist., 1970-72, 74—, majority leader, 1974-77, minority leader, 1977—; adminstrv. asst. to chmn. Ind. Democratic Central Com., 1965-69; asst. voter registration chmn. Dem. Nat. Com., 1968. Mem. Am., Ind., Warrick County bar assns., Am. Trial Lawyers Assn., Boonville, Boonville Jr. chambers commerce, Beta Theta Pi. Clubs: Masons, Kiwanis, Lions, Elks. Home: 1441 S 1st St Boonville IN 47601 Office: 117 W Main St Boonville IN 47601

PHILLIPS, MICHAEL STEVEN, motion picture producer; b. Bklyn., June 29, 1943; s. Lawrence Ronald and Shirley Lee (Fischer) P.; A.B., Dartmouth U., 1965; J.D., N.Y. U. Law Sch., 1968; 1 dau., Kate Elizabeth. Admitted to N.Y. bar, 1969; securities analyst, N.Y.C., 1968-70; independent motion picture producer, 1971—; films include Steelyard Blues, 1973, The Sting (Academy Award, 1973), 1973, Taxi Driver (1st prize Cannes Film Festival 1976), 1976, Close Encounters of the Third Kind, 1977. Mem. Acad. Motion Picture Arts and Scis., N.Y. Bar Assn. Office: Michael Phillips Productions Universal Studios Universal City CA 91608

PHILLIPS, NORMAN EDGAR, univ. dean; b. Detroit, Dec. 20, 1928; s. Norman C. and Elma (Watson) P.; B.A., U. B.C., 1949, M.A., 1950; Ph.D., U. Chgo., 1954; m. Paula M. McCreery, July 3, 1951; children—N. Christopher, Susan M. NRC postdoctoral fellow, 1954-55; from instr. to prof. chemistry U. Calif. at Berkeley, 1955—, asso. dean, 1966-70, dean Coll. Chemistry, 1975—. Guggenheim fellow Oxford U., 1963-64; NSF sr. postdoctoral fellow Tech. U. at Helsinki, 1970-71. Fellow Am. Phys. Soc.; mem. Am. Chem. Soc., AAAS, Sigma Xi. Home: 1168 Glen Rd Lafayette CA 94549 Office: U Calif Berkeley CA 94720

PHILLIPS, OAIL ANDRES (BUM), football coach; b. Orange, Tex., Sept. 29, 1923; student Lamar Jr. Coll.; B.S., Stephen F. Austin State Coll., 1949. High sch. coach, 1950-56, 58-64; asst. coach football Tex. A. and M. U., 1957, U. Houston, 1965-66, San Diego Chargers, 1967-71, So. Meth. U., 1972, Okla. State U., 1973; asst. coach Houston Oilers, 1974, gen. mgr., head coach, 1975—. Office: Houston Oilers 6910 Fannin St Houston TX 77030*

PHILLIPS, ORLEY OLIVER, archtl. engring. cos. exec.; b. Victor, Colo., Nov. 24, 1903; s. Harry William and Lydia Ann (Roby) P.; B.C.E., U. Colo., 1926; m. Bernice Mahon, Jan. 28, 1929; 1 son, Ronald Warren. Draftsman, Old Dominion Copper Co. and Miami Copper Co., 1926-27; draftsman, engr. Am. Smelting & Refining Co., 1927-31; engr. Buffalo Exploration & Mining Co., 1932-33; asst. city engr. Colorado Springs, Colo., 1933-36; chief structural engr. Holly Surgar Co., 1936-37; partner Sanford & Phillips, cons. engrs., Colorado Springs, 1937-40; chief engr. Prouty Bros. Engring. Co., Denver, 1941-44; mem. firm R.J. Tipton & Assos., Denver, 1944-49, v.p., 1949-57; prin. Western Hemisphere Corp., Denver, 1952-56; mem. firm Tipton & Hill, Denver, 1955-59; pres. Phillips-Carter-Osborne Inc., Denver, 1949-73, Phillips-Carter-Reister & Assos., Inc., Denver, 1966-73; exec. v.p. DMJM-Phillips-Reister Inc., Denver, 1973—; v.p. Daniel, Mann, Johnson & Mendenhall, Los Angeles, 1973—, Henningson, Durham & Richarson de Espana, Denver and Madrid, 1962-67; chmn. bd. Phillips-Carter-Durham & Richarson, Denver and Rio de Janeiro, 1962-67; chmn. Colo. State Bd. Registration for Profl. Engrs. and Land Surveyors, 1962-75; nat. v.p., dir. Western zone Nat. Council Engring. Examiners, 1973-75; mem. Denver Bd. Appeals, 1954-60, chmn., 1957-58; chmn. Denver Bldg. Code Advisory Com., 1947-63; mem. U. Colo. Engring. Devel. Found., 1954-72, chmn., 1958-59. Recipient Distinguished Alumnus award U. Colo., 1970; Gold Medal award Colo. Engrs. Council, 1978; registered profl. engr., Colo., N. Mex., Mont., Nev. Fellow ASCE (life mem., past pres. Colo. chpt., Recognition award 1970), Am. Concrete Inst., Am. Cons. Engrs. Council; mem. Profl. Engrs. Colo. (past pres.), Nat. Soc. Profl. Engrs. (past bd. dirs.), Cons. Engrs. Council U.S. (past bd. dirs., past v.p.), Structural Engrs. Colo., ASTM, Colo. Constn. League (past pres.), Am. Water Works Assn., Denver C. of C. Home: 1176 S Jackson St Denver CO 80210 Office: 910 15th St Denver CO 80202

PHILLIPS, OWEN MARTIN, oceanographer; b. Parramatta, Australia, Dec. 30, 1930; s. Richard Keith and Madeline (Lofts) P.; B.Sc., Sydney (Australia) U., 1952; Ph.D., U. Cambridge (Eng.), 1955; m. Merle Winifred Simons, Aug. 8, 1953; children—Lynette Michelle, Christopher Ian, Bronwyn Ann, Michael Stuart. Research fellow Imperial Chem. Industries, U. Cambridge, 1955-57; asst. prof., then asso. prof. Johns Hopkins, 1957-61; asst. dir. research U. Cambridge, 1961-64; prof. geophys. mechanics Johns Hopkins, 1964—, chmn. dept. earth and planetary scis., 1971-77, Decker prof. sci. and engring., 1975—. Cons. to industry, 1960—. Mem. council mems. Nat. Center Atmospheric Research, 1964-67, chmn. rev. and goals, 1965-67; mem. com. global atmospheric research project Nat. Acad. Sci., 1967-69; mem. Waterman award com. NSF, 1975—. Trustee Roland Park Country Sch., 1974—; trustee Chesapeake Research Consortium, 1972-76, sec., 1972. Recipient Adams prize U. Cambridge, 1965, Sverdrup Gold medal Am. Meteorol. Soc., 1974. Fellow Royal Soc. (London); mem. Am. Meteorol. Soc. (publs. commn. 1971-77), Am. Geophys. Union, Md. Acad. Sci. (sci. council 1974—), Sigma Xi, Pi Tau Sigma. Author: The Dynamics of the Upper Ocean, 1966, 2d edit., 1968, 3d edit., 1977, Russan edit., 1969; The Heart of the Earth, 1968, Italian edit., 1970, 74; The Last Chance Energy Book, 1979; contbr. numerous articles to profl. jours. Asso. editor Jour. Fluid Mechanics, 1964—. 23 Merrymount Rd Baltimore MD 21210

PHILLIPS, PRESSLY CRAIG, aquarium adminstr.; b. Buffalo, May 23, 1922; s. Pressly Craig and Adelia Grace (Vergith) P.; A.B., U. Miami (Fla.), 1951; M.S., U. Md., 1971; m. Fanny Bradford Lee, Oct. 21, 1953. Asst. to curator Marineland of Fla. 1946-47; research aide U. Miami (Fla.), 1951-53; curator Miami Seaquarium, 1954-59; asst. curator Nat. Aquarium, Washington, 1959-72, dir., 1976—; chief prodn. and distbn. Nat. Fish Hatcheries, 1972-76; co-founder Fla. Gulfarium, 1954. Served with USN, 1942-46. Mem. Nat. Soc. Ichthyologists, Herpetologists, Am. Assn. Zool. Parks, Aquariums. Author (with Winfield Brady) and illustrator: Sea Pests, 1953; author, illustrator The Captive Sea, 1964; contbr. artwork to Nat. Geog. mag., 1952, 56, Websters Internat. Dictionary, 1960. Home: 10109 Grant Ave Silver Spring MD 20910 Office: B-037 Commerce Bldg Washington DC 20230

PHILLIPS, RALPH SAUL, educator; b. Oakland, Calif., June 23, 1913; s. Isadore and Mary (Shaw) P.; A.B., U. Calif. at Los Angeles, 1935; Ph.D., U. Mich., 1939; m. Jean Adair, Oct. 11, 1942; 1 child, Xanthippe. Instr., U. Wash., 1940-41, Harvard, 1941-42; group leader Radiation Lab., Mass. Inst. Tech., 1942-46; asst. prof. math. N.Y. U., 1946-47; asso. prof. U. So. Calif., 1947-53, prof., 1953-58; prof. U. Calif. at Los Angeles, 1958-60, Stanford U., 1960—. Rackham fellow Inst. Advanced Study, 1939-40, mem., 1950-51; research asso. Yale U., 1953-54; Guggenheim fellow, 1954, 74; research asso. N.Y. U., 1958; vis. prof. U. Aarhus, 1968; mem. interacad. exchange program mission to USSR, 1975. Mem. Am. Acad. Arts and Scis. Co-author: Theory of Servomechanisms, 1947; Functional Analysis and Semigroups, 1957; Scattering Theory, 1967; Scattering Theory for Automorphic Functions, 1976. Co-editor Jour. Functional Analysis. Home: 2140 Santa Cruz Ave Menlo Park CA 94025 Office: Stanford U Stanford CA 94305

PHILLIPS, RALPH WILBUR, dental educator; b. Farmland, Ind., Jan. 12, 1918; s. J. Stanley and Effie Mae (Berger) P.; B.S., Ind. U., 1940, M.S., 1950; D.Sc., U. Ala., 1960; m. Dorothy E. McCleaster, Aug. 21, 1943; 1 dau., Cheryl D. (Mrs. William J. Dale). Mem. faculty Ind. U. Sch. Dentistry, Indpls., 1940—, research prof. dental materials, 1962—, asst. dean research, 1966-74, asso. dean research, 1974—; dir. Oral Health Research Inst., 1974—; vis. prof. U. Calif. at San Francisco, U. Tenn., La. State U.; mem. rev. com. research grants Am. Fund Dental Health, 1979—; cons. bioengring. programs Rensselaer Poly. Inst., U. Va., N.Y. U. Past chmn. dental study sect. Nat. Inst. Dental Research, chmn. bio-materials research adv. com., 1962—; mem. dental panel FDA, 1977—, chmn., 1978—. Recipient Callahan award Ohio Dental Assn., 1964; research award Chgo. Dental Soc., 1948, 54; gold medal research award Alumni Assn. Columbia Dental Sch., 1960; distinguished citation Washington U., St. Louis, 1958; ann. recognition award Ind. U. Student Union Bd., 1959; Hollenback award Am. Acad. Operative Dentistry, 1977; Spanedel award N.Y. Dental Assn., 1977; Internat. Research award Mass. Dental Assn., 1979; Gold Medal award Pierre Fauchard Acad., 1979. Fellow Am. (Gies award 1976), Internat. colls. dentists, AAAS (past dir. dentistry sect.); hon. mem. Am. Acad. Restorative Dentistry, Am. Dental Assn.; mem. Internat. Assn. Dental Research (past pres., Souder award 1964), Am. Chem. Soc., Am. Assn. Dental Schs., Am. Assn. Dental Editors, Belgian Dental Assn. (hon.), Indpls. Dental Soc., Ind. Acad. Sci., Ind. U. Alumni Assn. (dir.), Sigma Xi, Omicron Kappa Upsilon, Phi Lambda Epsilon, Alpha Chi Sigma, Phi Eta Sigma. Author: Skinner's Science of Dental Materials, 7th edit., 1973; Elements of Dental Materials for Dental Hygienists and Assistants, 3d edit., 1977; also articles, sects. in books; co-author: Materials for the Practicing Dentist, 1969; Modern Day Practice in Crown and Bridge, 3d edit., 1971. Editorial bds. numerous dental jours. Home: 735 E 70th Pl Indianapolis IN 46220 Office: 1121 W Michigan Ave Indianapolis IN 46202

PHILLIPS, RAMON J., combustion engine mfg. co. exec.; b. Woodward, Okla., June 12, 1926; s. Jewell William and Catharine Lura (Allison) P.; B.B.A., U. Okla., 1951; grad. exec. program Stanford U., 1974; m. Katharine E. Cope, Nov. 25, 1949; children—Janet, Deborah, Scott, Evalyn. Personnel dir. Ryan Aero. Co., San Diego, 1954-66; v.p. indsl. relations Continental Motors Corp., Muskegon, Mich., 1966-72; v.p., asst. gen. mgr. Teledyne Continental Motors Co., Muskegon, 1972-74, pres. indsl. products div., 1974—; dir. Muskegon Bank & Trust Co. Bd. dirs. Muskegon chpt. ARC, 1966-70, Miss Mich. Program, 1968-70, United Appeal, Muskegon, 1968-72. Served with USAAF, 1944-46; PTO. Mem. Nat. Mgmt. Assn. (Silver Knight of Mgmt. 1974, Golden Knight of Mgmt. 1977), Mfrs'. Assn. (dir.), Nat. Personnel Mgmt. (dir. 1966-70), Muskegon Area C. of C. (dir. 1976-79), Pres.'s Club. Republican. Mem. United Ch. of Christ. Clubs: Rotary, Optimists. Home: 670 Lyncott Ave North Muskegon MI 49445 Office: 700 Terrace St Muskegon MI 49443

PHILLIPS, RANDALL CLINGER, clergyman, univ. adminstr.; b. Santa Maria, Calif., Dec. 3, 1924; s. Glenn Randall and Ruth (Clinger) P.; B.S. cum laude, U. So. Calif., 1946, M.Th., 1951, Th.D., 1966; D.Arts, Willamette U., 1963; D.D., Calif. Western U., 1964; children—Ruth Ann Phillips McKercher, Janet Lee Phillips Kessler, Melinda Lee. Ordained to ministry Meth. Ch., 1947; minister, Sherman Oaks, Calif., 1949-55, Burbank, Calif., 1955-59, Wilshire United Meth. Ch., 1959-78; v.p. U.S. Internat. U., San Diego, 1978—; mem. exec. com. nat. bd. publs. United Meth. Ch.; pres. Inter-religious Council Los Angeles. Vice pres. bd. trustees Sch. Theology, Claremont, Calif.; bd. dirs., v.p. Portals House, Los Angeles; pres., chmn. bd. dirs. Midnight Mission Los Angeles, Wilshire YMCA; chmn. bd. Pacific Homes. Served to lt. (j.g.) USNR, 1943-47. Recipient Freedoms Found. award, 1967, 68. Mem. Los Angeles Council Chs. (pres. 1970-71), Kappa Alpha. Republican. Mason (33 deg., Shriner). Club: Wilshire Area Sertoma (chaplain, pres.). Home and Office: 10455 Pomerado Rd San Diego CA 92131

PHILLIPS, RICHARD IDLER, govt. ofcl.; b. Artesia, N.Mex., Apr. 2, 1911; s. Edward F. and Florence (Idler) P.; student U. Nebr., 1928-29; A.B., U. So. Calif., 1932, J.D., 1934; m. Irene Shields, Feb. 7, 1942 (dec. Sept. 1964); m. 2d, Katharine H. Mayberry, Apr. 23, 1965. Admitted to Calif. bar, 1934; practiced in Los Angeles, 1934-36; auditor Singer Sewing Machine Co., Buenos Aires, Argentina, 1936-38; partner law firm Marval, Rodriguez, Larreta & O'Farrell, Buenos Aires, 1938-41; exec. sec. Coordination Com. of Uruguay, Montevideo, 1941-46; 2d sec. Am. embassy, Montevideo, 1946-48, Caracas, Venezuela, 1948-51; adviser U.S. delegation to UN, 1951-52; consul, Nairobi, Kenya, 1952-54; adviser Bur. Inter-Am. Affairs, Dept. State, 1954-57, 58-61; consul, Guadalajara, Mexico, 1957-58; spl. asst. Bur. Pub. Affairs, 1962-63, dir. Office News, 1963-64, dep. asst. sec. state for pub. affairs, 1964-69, acting asst. sec. state for pub. affairs, 1969-70; consul gen., Monterrey, Mexico, 1970-71; indsl. community relations adviser Nat. Inst. on Alcohol Abuse and Alcoholism, Dept. Health, Edn. and Welfare, Washington, 1972—. Mem. Calif. Bar Assn., Phi Beta Kappa, Sigma Nu. Rotarian. Clubs: American (treas. Buenos Aires 1940-41). Home: 2801 New Mexico Ave NW Washington DC 20007 Office: NIAAA 5600 Fishers Ln Rockville MD 20852

PHILLIPS, RICHARD LEE, ins. co. exec.; b. Newcomerstown, Ohio, May 13, 1926; s. David Rees and Ethel (Rees) P.; B.S. in Bus. Adminstrn., Ohio State U., 1950; m. Virginia Grace Hoawischer, Sept. 17, 1950; children—Douglas Richard, Joy Lynn. With Shelby (Ohio) Mut. Ins. Co., 1950—, spl. agt., 1950-56, asst. sec., 1956-61, sec., 1961-67, v.p. sales, 1967-71, v.p., sec., 1971-76, pres., chief exec. officer, 1976—, also dir.; pres., chmn. bd. dirs. Shelby Mut. Ins. Co., Shelby Life Ins. Co., IPBS, Inc., Shelby Fin. Corp.; trustee Griffith Found. Ins. Edn.; instr. Sch. Mut. Ins. Agts. Oberlin Coll., 1967—. Chmn., Mansfield br. fund raising drive Ohio State U., 1961; bd. dirs. Mansfield U. Found., 1962; chmn. citizens' adv. bd. Mansfield campus Ohio State U., 1963; pres. Shelby (Ohio) chpt. Am. Field Service, 1965; pres. Shelby Jr. Achievement, 1967; bd. dirs., chmn. Shelby United Fund, 1971; mem. alumni adv. bd. Ohio State U., 1975; vice chmn. community bldg. fund drive Shelby YMCA, 1976; trustee Richland County Found. Served with USN, 1943-46. C.P.C.U., Ohio. Mem. Soc. C.P.C.U.'s (pres. Akron/Canton chpt. 1968), Ohio Ins. Inst. (vice-chmn. elect 1979), Ins. Fedn. Ohio (pres. 1979), Sigma. Republican. Methodist. Home: 58 Louise Dr Shelby OH 44875 Office: 19 Mansfield Ave Shelby OH 44875

PHILLIPS, RICHARD MYRON, lawyer; b. N.Y.C., Sept. 8, 1931; s. Morris and Henrietta (Schatz) P.; B.A., Columbia U., 1953; LL.B., Yale, 1956; m. Elda Marie Torres, June 11, 1955; children—Laurie, David, Steven. Admitted to D.C. bar, 1957, N.Y. State bar, 1961; atty. Office Gen. Counsel, Bur. Aeros., Navy Dept., Washington, 1956-57; with SEC, 1960-68, spl. counsel Office Gen. Counsel, 1964-66, asst. gen. counsel, 1966-68; mem. firm Surrey, Karasik, Greene & Hill, Washington, 1968-71, Hill, Christopher & Phillips, Washington, 1971—; lectr. in field, 1966—; cons. Brazilian securities markets AID, 1970-71. Served to lt. USNR, 1957-60. Mem. Am. Bar Assn. Co-author: Regulation of Brokers, Dealers and Securities Markets, 1977. Contbr. articles to profl. jours. Home: 10603 Vantage Ct Potomac MD 20854 Office: 1900 M St NW Washington DC 20036

PHILLIPS, ROBERT FRANCIS, ins. co. exec.; b. Springfield, Mass., Jan. 5, 1936; s. John Francis and Margaret Agnes (Shiel) P.; B.B.A., U. Mass., 1957; m. Elizabeth Karels, Nov. 19, 1960; children—Elizabeth, Laura, Robert. With Aetna Life and Casualty Co., Hartford, Conn., 1957—, agy. supr., Cleve., 1964-66, adminstr. agy. dept., Hartford, 1966-68, asst. sec. personnel adminstrn., 1968-72, dir. personnel adminstrn., 1972-74, asst. v.p. personnel and tng., 1974-76, v.p. corp. personnel, 1976—. Mem. adv. com. Grad. Sch. of Bus., U. Mass. Mem. Chartered Property Casualty Underwriters, Hartford C. of C. (chmn. human resources com.). Office: Aetna Life and Casualty Co 151 Farmington Ave Hartford CT 06156

PHILLIPS, ROBIN, actor, director; b. Haslemere, Surrey, Eng., Feb. 28, 1942; s. James William and Ellen Anne (Barfoot) P.; student Bristol Old Vic Theatre Sch. Debut as Mr. Puff in The Critic at Theatre Royal, Bristol Old Vic Co., 1959; appeared as Romeo Konstantin in The Seagull and Geoffrey in A Taste of Honey, 1959-60; asso. dir. Bristol Old Vic Co., 1960-61; played Eric MacClure in South, 1961, Curio in The Chances and Prophilus in The Broken Heart, 1962; appeared in Six Characters in Search of an Author, 1963; with Oxford Playhouse Co., 1964; asst. dir. Royal Shakespeare Co., Stratford, 1965; dir. The Ballad of the False Barman, Hampstead,

1966; asso. dir. Northcott Theatre, 1967-68; dir. The Seagull, Leatherhead, 1969; Tiny Alice, RSC, Aldwych, 1970; Sing a Rude Song, 1970; Abelard and Heloise, 1970; The Two Gentlemen of Verona, Strafford and Aldwych, 1970; first New York prodn. Abelard and Heloise, 1970; dir. Dear Antoine (Chichester and London), Caesar and Cleopatra (Chichester), Miss Julie (London), 1971, Notes on a Love Affair (London), The Beggars Opera, The Lady's Not For Burning (both Chichester) also played Louis Dubedat in The Doctors Dilemma, 1972; artistic dir. Company Theatre, Greenwich, 1973, Stratford Festival, Ont., Can., 1974; co-dir. Comedy of Errors and The Two Gentlemen of Verona on nat. tour, adding own prodns. of Measure for Measure, Trumpets and Drums and The Importance of Being Earnest to Festival season, 1975; dir. Antony and Cleopatra, A Midsummer Night's Dream and The Way of the World, 1976; co-dir. Hamlet and The Tempest and restaged Measure and Measure and The Importance of Being Earnest, 1976; dir. Richard III, The Guardsman, A Midsummer Nights Dream, As You Like It, Hay Fever, 1977, Macbeth, The Winter's Tale, Uncle Vanya, The Devils, Judgement, Private Lives, As You Like It, 1978, Love's Labours Lost, King Lear, The Importance of Being Earnest, 1979; appeared in numerous films since 1967, including leads in Decline and Fall and David Copperfield; TV performances include The Seagull, Forsyte Saga. Address: Stratford Festival of Can Festival Theatre Box 520 Stratford ON N5A 6V2 Canada

PHILLIPS, ROGER WILLIAM FREDERICK, aluminum co. exec.; b. Ottawa, Ont., Can., Dec. 17, 1939; s. Norman William Frederick and Florence Elizabeth (Marshall) P.; B.Sc., McGill U., Montreal, 1960; m. Ann Wilson, June 9, 1962; children—Andree, Claire. Asst. to treas. Aluminum Co. Can. Ltd., 1965-66, exec. v.p., 1975—, also dir.; v.p., gen. mgr. mill products, then exec. v.p. Alcan Can. Products Ltd., 1966-75, also dir.; chmn. bd., dir. Raberval & Saquency Ry. Co.; pres., dir. Alcan Smelters and Chems. Ltd., 1975—. Bd. dirs. Fondation Quebeçoise d'Edn. Economique; bd. govs. Conseil du Patronat du Que. Mem. Que. C. of C. (v.p.). Clubs: St. Denis, University (Montreal). Home: 1 de Casson Montreal PQ H3Y 2G9 Canada Office: 1 Pl Ville Marie Montreal PQ H3C 3H2 Canada

PHILLIPS, RONALD LEWIS, geneticist; b. Huntington County, Ind., Jan. 1, 1940; s. Philemon Lewis and Louise Alpha (Walker) P.; B.S. in Crop Sci., Purdue U., 1961, M.S. in Plant Breeding and Genetics, 1963; Ph.D. in Genetics, U. Minn., 1966; postgrad. Cornell U., 1966-67; m. Judith Lee Lind, Aug. 19, 1962; children—Brett, Angela. Research and teaching asst. Purdue U., 1961-62; research and teaching asst. U. Minn., St. Paul, 1962-66, research asso., 1967-68, asst. prof., 1968-72, asso. prof., 1972-76, prof. genetics and plant breeding, 1976—; NIH trainee Cornell U., 1966-67; program dir. USDA Competitive Research Grants Office, Washington, 1979; mem. NSF and USDA adv. grant panels. Mem. chmn. council on ministries, lay leader United Methodist Ch., 1968—; Cub Scout pack co-chmn. Boy Scouts Am., 1976-77; judge Minn. Regional and State Sci. Fair, 1970—. Recipient Purdue Agrl. Alumni Achievement award, 1961. NSF fellow, 1961, NIH fellow, 1966-67. Mem. Genetics Soc. Am., Am. Soc. Agronomy (Student Sect. award, Caleb-Dorr award), Crop Sci. Soc. Am. (awards com.), AAAS, Biol. Stain Commn., Sigma Xi, Gamma Alpha (nat. treas.), Gamma Sigma Delta, Alpha Zeta. Co-editor: Cytogenetics, 1977, Molecular Genetic Modification of Eucaryotes, 1977, Molecular Biology of Plants, 1979, The Plant Seed: Development, Preservation and Germination, 1979, Emergent Techniques for the Genetic Improvement of Crops; asso. editor, Genetics, 1978—; mem. editorial bd. Maydica, 1978—. Contbr. chpt. to Maize Breeding and Genetics, 1978. Contbr. sci. articles to profl. jours. Office: Dept Agronomy and Plant Genetics U Minn 1509 Gortner Ave Saint Paul MN 55108

PHILLIPS, ROSS FERGUSON, oil co. exec.; b. Winnipeg, Man., Can., Oct. 21, 1926; s. Albert Sidney and Olive Ford (Hawkin) P.; Chartered Accountant degree, U. Man., 1949; m. Mary Robinson King, July 28, 1956; children—David Ferguson, Janet King. With accounting dept. Millar, Macdonald and Co., 1943-49; internal auditor Traders Fin. Corp. Ltd., Toronto, Ont., Can., 1949-53; chief accountant Oilwell Operators Ltd., Calgary, Alta., Can., 1953; comptroller Home Oil Co. Ltd., Calgary, after 1959, v.p. adminstrn., 1966-71, sr. v.p. fin., 1971-73, pres., chief exec. officer, 1973-79, chmn., chief exec. officer, 1979—, also dir.; dir. Consumers Gas Co., Calgary Power Ltd., Crown Trust Co., Comml. Life Assurance Co. of Can., Halifax Ins. Co., Air Can.; pres., dir. Scurry-Rainbow Oil Ltd.; mem. adv. council Calgary Club of U. Western Ont. Bus. Sch.; mem. Calgary adv. bd. Crown Trust Co.; bd. govs. Canadian Petroleum Assn.; dir., hon. treas. Calgary Exhbn. and Stampede. Fellow Inst. Chartered Accountants Man.; mem. Inst. Chartered Accountants Alta., Fin. Execs. Inst. (pres. Alta. chpt. 1966-67), Petroleum Accountants Soc. Western Can. (v.p. 1960-61), Canadian Inst. Chartered Accountants. Mem. Anglican Ch. of Can. Clubs: Glencoe, Earl Grey Golf, Ranchmen's, Calgary Golf and Country, Calgary Petroleum (Calgary); Canadian of N.Y., Met. (N.Y.C.). Home: 6925 Lefroy Ct SW Calgary AB T3E 6H1 Canada Office: 2300 Home Oil Tower 324 8th Ave SW Calgary AB T2P 2Z5 Canada

PHILLIPS, RUFUS COLFAX, III, cons. co. exec.; b. Middletown, Ohio, Aug. 10, 1929; s. Rufus Colfax and Williamina (Chamberlayne) P.; B.A., Yale U., 1951; postgrad. U. Va. Law Sch., 1952; M.S. in City and Regional Planning, Cath. U., 1971; m. Barbara Hubner, May 28, 1960; children—Rufus IV, Anne, Edward, Patricia. With MAAG, Vietnam, 1954-56, ICA, Laos, 1957-59; asst. pres. Airways Engring. Corp., cons., Washington, 1959-62, pres., 1963—; pres. Intercontinental Cons., Inc., Washington, 1963—. Counterinsurgency cons. Rand Corp., 1962; cons. AID on Vietnam, 1962; asst. dir. rural affairs AID mission to Vietnam, Saigon, 1962-63; cons. Dept. State, 1965-68; chmn. Pres.'s Bus. Adv. Panel on Export Issues to Nat. Commn. for Rev. Antitrust Laws and Procedures, 1978. Chmn., No. Va. Transp. Commn., 1973—; supr. Dranesville dist. Fairfax County Bd. Suprs., 1972-76; mem. Council of Govt.'s Transp. Planning Bd., 1972, chmn., 1975; mem. No. Va. Planning Dist. Commn.; alt. mem. Washington Met. Area Transit Authority Bd., 1975. Served 1st lt. AUS, 1953-55. Mem. Am. Inst. Planners (Washingtonian of Year award 1975). Home: 6520 Ridge St McLean VA 22101 Office: 1700 N Moore St Arlington VA 22209

PHILLIPS, RUSSELL ALEXANDER, JR., found. exec.; b. Charlotte, N.C., Sept. 19, 1937; s. Russell Alexander and Robmae (Black) P.; A.B., Duke U., 1959; LL.B. (Edward John Noble fellow), Yale U., 1962. Admitted to N.C. bar, 1962, D.C. bar, 1966; clk. to Sr. Judge, U.S. Ct. Appeals, 4th Circuit, 1962-63; legal adv. Ministry of Fin., Govt. No. Nigeria, 1963-65; asst. commr. income tax (legal) East African Common Services Orgn., Nairobi, Kenya, 1965-66; asso. firm Wilmer, Cutler & Pickering, Washington, 1966-68; corp. sec. Rockefeller Bros. Fund, N.Y.C., 1973—, v.p., 1979—; trustee Martha Baird Rockefeller Fund for Music. Pres. Bd. Trustees of Lingnan U. Recipient Benjamin N. Cardozo prize Yale U., 1960. Mem. N.C. Bar Assn., D.C. Bar, Council Fgn. Relations, Phi Beta Kappa. Democrat. Presbyterian. Club: Univ. (N.Y.C.). Home: 40 E 88th St Apt 5D New York NY 10028 Office: Room 3450 1290 Ave of Americas New York NY 10019

PHILLIPS, RUTH H., govt. ofcl.; b. Bklyn., Sept. 2, 1918; d. Harry and Beatrice (Jacobson) P.; A.B., Bklyn. Coll., 1939; postgrad. Columbia U., 1939-49. Dep. dir. Bur. European Affairs, Dept. State, Washington, 1969-74, econ. comml. counsellor Am. Embassy, Brussels, Belgium, 1974-77; dir. Office Internat. Telecommunications Affairs, Dept. State, 1977-78, dep. asst. sec. Bur. of Econ. and Bus. Affairs, 1978—. Home: 4701 Willard Ave Chevy Chase MD 20015 Office: Dept State 22d and C Sts NW Washington DC 20520

PHILLIPS, SAMUEL J., corp. exec.; b. North Vandergrift, Pa., Sept. 17, 1931; s. Samuel and Margaret (Solomon) P.; B.S., U. Md., 1953; M.B.A., Xavier U., 1960; LL.D. (hon.), Franconia Coll., 1978; m. Matina Fidanis, Jan. 28, 1953; children—Diana M., Samuel T., Candice A., Tracy L., Daniel J. With Procter & Gamble Co., Cin., 1956-67, mgr. cost acctg. dept., food products div., 1964-65, controller, chief fin. officer Folger Coffee Co. div., Kansas City, Mo., 1965-67; controller film div. Polaroid Corp., Waltham, Mass., 1967-69, group controller, Cambridge, Mass., 1969-70; v.p. ops. Healthcare Corp., Boston, 1970; v.p. ops. Parkwood Laminates, Inc., Lowell, Mass., 1971-74, pres., 1972-74; pres., chmn. Acton Corp., (Mass.), 1975—; dir. Phillips Corp., College Park, Md. Trustee Cin. Summer Opera, 1964-65; chmn. exec. com., trustee Franconia (N.H.) Coll., 1976-78; trustee N.H. Coll., Manchester, 1979—; trustee Phillips Found., Annapolis, Md. Served to 1st. lt. U.S. Army, 1953-56. Recipient Kansas City Boy Scout award for community service, 1966. Office: Acton Corp Box 407 Acton MA 01720

PHILLIPS, SILAS BENT, JR., utilities exec.; b. Portland, Oreg., Feb. 3, 1915; s. Silas Bent and May (Stevenson) P.; B.S. in Econs., Harvard, 1937; m. Frances May Rau, Jan. 17, 1943; children—Dabney Carr, Elizabeth May, Jane Rowland, William Stevenson. With W. Tex. Utilities Co., 1939-65, v.p., 1960-64, pres., 1964-65; pres., dir. Central and S.W. Corp., Dallas, 1965-76, chmn., chief exec. officer, 1976—; pres., dir. Central & S.W. Services, Inc., Dallas, 1969-76, chmn., chief exec. officer, 1976—. Served with USAAF, 1941-46. Home: 4711 N Lindhurst Ave Dallas TX 75229 Office: 2700 One Main Pl Dallas TX 75250

PHILLIPS, THEODORE LOCKE, radiologist; b. Phila., June 4, 1933; s. Harry Webster and Margaret Amy (Locke) P.; B.Sc., Dickinson Coll., 1955; M.D., U. Pa., 1959; m. Joan Cappello, June 23, 1956; children—Margaret, John, Sally. Intern, Western Res. U., 1960; resident in therapeutic radiology U. Calif., 1963, clin.instr., San Francisco, 1963-65, asst. prof. radiation oncology, 1965-68, asso. prof., 1968-70, prof., 1970—, chmn. dept. radiation oncology, 1973—; research radiobiologist U.S. Naval Radiologic Def. Lab., San Francisco, 1963-65; research asso. Cancer Research Inst. and Lab. Radiobiology, research physician Lawrence Berkeley Lab. and Donner Lab., U. Calif., Berkeley. Served with USNR, 1963-65. Nat. Cancer Inst. grantee, 1970-81. Mem. Am. Soc. Therapeutic Radiologists, Am. Soc. Clin. Oncologists, Radiol. Soc. N.Am., Radiation Research Soc. (pres. 1978), Am. Assn. Cancer Research, Calif. Med. Assn., Am. Coll. Radiology, Radium Soc., No. Calif. Radiotherapy Assn., Phi Beta Kappa, Alpha Omega Alpha. Republican. Contbr. numerous articles to profl. publs. Home: 10 Marinita Ave San Rafael CA 94901 Office: Dept Radiation Oncology M-330 U Calif San Francisco CA 94143

PHILLIPS, THOMAS L., corp. exec.; b. May 2, 1924; B.S., Va. Poly. Inst., 1947, M.S., 1948; hon. doctorates Stonehill Coll., 1968, Northeastern U., 1968, Lowell Technol. Inst., 1970, Gordon Coll., 1970, Boston Coll., 1974. With Raytheon Co., Lexington, Mass., 1948—, exec. v.p., 1961-64, pres., chief operating officer, 1964-68, chief exec. officer, 1968—, chmn. bd., 1975—, dir., 1962—; dir. John Hancock Life Ins. Co., State St. Investment Corp. Trustee, Gordon Coll., Northeastern U., Joslin Diabetes Found. Recipient Meritorious Pub. Service award for work in Sparrow III missile system, U.S. Navy, 1958. Mem. Nat. Acad. Engring., Bus. Council, Bus. Roundtable, Com. Econ. Devel. Clubs: Pilgrims U.S., Algonquin, Comml. (Boston); Weston Golf. Home: 60 Black Oak Rd Weston MA 02193 Office: Raytheon Co 141 Spring St Lexington MA 02173

PHILLIPS, THOMAS PORTER, lawyer; b. Los Angeles, Dec. 25, 1940; s. Thomas P. and Patricia (Tucker) P.; B.A. in Econs., Pomona Coll., 1962; J.D., Hastings Coll. Law, U. Calif., 1965; m. Evgenia A. Phillips. Admitted to Calif. bar, 1966, since practiced in Los Angeles; asso. firm Meserve, Mumper & Hughes, 1965-70; prin., dir. Rodi, Pettker, Galbraith & Phillips, Law Corp., 1970—; lectr. U. Calif. Continuing Edn. of Bar, 1976; judge pro tem Los Angeles Mcpl. Ct., 1977—; mem. bench and bar council Los Angeles Superior Ct., 1976-77, mem. spl. com. to prepare civil trial manual, 1975-76; spl. hearing officer Los Angeles Community Coll. Dist., 1975-78. Bd. dirs., pres. San Marino (Calif.) Men's Republican Club; bd. dirs. Pasadena (Calif.) Lincoln Club; bd. dirs., v.p. Lan Jordan Inst. Counseling Psychotherapy, 1973-79; bd. dirs. Pasadena Child Guidance Clinic, 1975-79, v.p., 1977-79. Mem. State Bar Calif., Am., Los Angeles County (sec. 1973-75, vice chmn. 1975-76, chmn., 1976-77, mem. bd. exec. com. trial lawyers sect. 1973—, founding mem., vice-chmn. appellate cts. com. 1977—, lawyer referral service com. 1978—) bar assns., Assn. Bus. Trial Lawyers, Los Angeles Trial Lawyers Assn. Club: Univ. (Los Angeles). Office: Suite 1600 611 W 6th St Los Angeles CA 90017

PHILLIPS, VEL, state ofcl.; b. Milw., Feb. 18, 1924; d. Russell Lowell and Thelma (Payne) Rodgers; B.S., Howard U., 1946; LL.B., U. Wis., 1951; grad. Summer Coll. Juvenile Ct. Judges, U. Nev., 1971; m. W. Dale Phillips, Nov. 7; children—Dale Franklin, Michael Damon. Admitted to Wis. bar; legislator Milw. Common Council, 1956-71; county judge Milwaukee County Children's Ct., Br. 13, 1971-73; now sec. of state State of Wis., Madison; lectr. dept. Afro-Am. studies U. Wis., Milw.; vis. prof. law U. Wis., Carroll Coll. Bd. dirs. Milw. Council Alcoholism, Sojourner Truth House, NAACP, Art Exchange; nat. bd. dirs. Day Care and Child Devel. Council Am.; trustee YWCA. Recipient Jr. Achievement award, 1957; Alumni Achievement award Howard U., 1960; Delta Sigma Theta award, 1962; Hadassah award, 1964; Milw. Star award, 1967; Alumni award Elks, 1968; named Woman of Yr., C. of C., 1958, Milw. Sentinel, 1967; named Woman of Yr., Theta Sigma Phi, 1968, Doer of Decade. Mem. Wis. Bar Assn., Milw. Bar Assn., Wis. Bd. Juvenile Ct. Judges, Nat. Council Juvenile Ct. Judges, AAUW. Democrat. Home: 2237 N Booth St Milwaukee WI 53212 Office: 244 W Washington Ave Madison WI 53702

PHILLIPS, WALLACE WATTS, JR., food processing co. fin. exec.; b. Seattle, July 14, 1936; s. Wallace Watts and Doris Lucille (Talkington) P.; B.A. in Bus. Adminstrn., U. Wash., 1958; postgrad. U. Oreg., 1962-66; m. Kay Maurine McLaren, Sept. 16, 1961; children—Ann, Susan, Karen, Carol. Staff acct. Touche, Ross & Co., Portland, Oreg., 1963-66; v.p. fin. Lamb-Weston div. Amfac Foods, Inc., Portland, 1966-78, sr. v.p., controller Amfac Foods, Inc., Portland, 1978—. Served with U.S. Army, 1959-60. C.P.A., Oreg. Mem. Oreg. Soc. C.P.A.'s, Am. Inst. C.P.A.'s, Fin. Execs. Inst. (sec., dir. Portland chpt.), Am. Frozen Foods Inst. (chmn. com. acctg.). Republican. Presbyterian. Club: Multnomah Athletic. Home: 7905 SW Linden Rd Portland OR 97225 Office: 6600 SW Hampton St Portland OR 97223

PHILLIPS, WALTER RAY, lawyer, educator; b. Democrat, N.C., Mar. 19, 1932; s. Walter Yancey and Bonnie (Wilson) P.; A.B., U. N.C., 1954; LL.B., Emory U., 1957, LL.M., 1962, J.D., 1970; postgrad. Yale U., 1965-66; m. Patricia Ann Jones, Aug. 28, 1954; children—Bonnie Ann, Rebecca Lee. Admitted to Ga. bar, 1957, Fla. bar, 1958, Tex. bar, 1969, U.S. Supreme Ct. bar; with firm Jones, Adams, Paine & Foster, West Palm Beach, Fla., 1957-58; law clk. to chief judge U.S. Dist. Ct., Atlanta, 1958-59; with firm Powell, Goldstein, Frazer & Murphy, Atlanta, 1959-60; bankruptcy judge U.S. Cts., Atlanta, 1960-64; prof. law U. N.D., 1964-65; teaching fellow Yale U., 1965-66; prof. law Fla. State U., 1966-68; prof. law Tex. Tech. U., Lubbock, 1968-71; Disting. vis. prof. law Baylor U., 1971; atty. Commn. on Bankruptcy Laws of U.S., Washington, 1971-72; dep. dir., adminstrv. officer, 1972-73; prof. Sch. Law, U. Ga., 1973—, asso. dean, 1975—, acting dean, 1976, Joseph Henry Lumpkin prof., 1977—, also dir. univ's self. study, 1978; reporter Gov.'s Legislation for Ga., 1973; v.p., dir. Killearn Estates, Inc. Bd. dirs. Lubbock Day Nurseries, 1969, pres., 1970-71; trustee Joseph Henry Lumpkin Found., Inst. Continuing Legal Edn. Served with USAF, 1950. Mem. Am. Bar Assn. (consumer bankruptcy com. 1973—), Fed. Bar Assn., Fla. Bar Assn., Tex. Bar Assn., Athens Bar Assn., Ga. Bar Assn. (vice chmn. publs. com. 1977—), Am. Judicature Soc., Phi Alpha Delta (chief tribune). Presbyterian. Club: Rotary. Author: Florida Law and Practice, 1960; Encyclopedia of Georgia Law, 1962; Seminar for Newly Appointed Referees in Bankruptcy, 1964; (with James William Moore) Debtors' and Creditors' Rights, Cases and Material, 1966, 5th edit., 1979; The Law of Debtor Relief, 1969, 2d edit., 1972, supplement, 1975; Rule 6, Moore's Federal Practice, 1969; Adjustment of Debts for Individuals, 1979. Home: 310 Red Fox Run Athens GA 30605

PHILLIPS, WARREN HENRY, newspaperman; b. June 28, 1926; s. Abraham and Juliette (Rosenberg) P.; A.B., Queens Coll., 1947; J.D. (hon.), U. Portland, 1973; m. Barbara Anne Thomas, June 16, 1951; children—Lisa, Leslie, Nina. Copyreader, Wall St. Jour., 1947-48, fgn. corr., Germany, 1949-50, chief London Bur., 1950-51, fgn. editor, 1951-53, news editor, 1953-54, mng. editor Midwest edit., 1954-57, mng. editor, 1957-65; exec. editor Dow Jones & Co., pub. Wall St. Jour., 1965-70, v.p., gen. mgr., 1970-71, editorial dir., 1971—, exec. v.p., 1972, pres., 1972-79, chief exec. officer, 1975—, chmn. bd., 1978—, also dir.; copyreader Stars & Stripes European edit., 1949. Pres., Am. Council Edn. for Journalism, 1971-73; mem. Pulitzer Prizes Bd., 1976—. Served with AUS, 1943-45. Named One of Ten Outstanding Young Men in U.S., U.S. Jr. C. of C., 1958. Mem. Am. Newspaper Pubs. Assn. (dir.), Am. Soc. Newspaper Editors (pres. 1975-76). Clubs: Reform (London, Eng.); Economic, River (N.Y.C.); Cosmos (Washington). Author: (with Robert Keatley) China: Behind the Mask, 1973. Office: 22 Cortlandt St New York NY 10007

PHILLIPS, WILLIAM, educator, editor, author; b. N.Y.C.; s. Edward and Marie (Berman) P.; B.S., Coll. City N.Y.; M.A., N.Y. U.; postgrad. Columbia; m. Edna M. Greenblatt. Editor, Partisan Rev., 1934—; former cons. editor Dial Press, Criterion Books, Random House, Chilmark Press; asso. prof. N.Y. U., 1960, 61-63; instr. Columbia, 1945; lectr. New Sch. Social Research; vis. lectr. U. Minn., 1953, Sarah Lawrence Coll., 1951-54, 56-57; prof. English, Rutgers U., 1963-78; prof. Boston U., 1978—. Mem. Gov. N.J. Com. on Arts, 1964-66; mem. arts advisory group Bus. Com. for Arts; mem. Pres. Carter's Task Force for Arts and Humanities. Guggenheim fellow, 1977; Rockefeller Found. grantee, 1977-78; Nat. Endowment for Humanities fellow, 1978—. Mem. Assn. Lit. Mags. Am., Coordinating Council Lit. Mags. Am. (chmn. 1967-75, hon. pres. and chmn. 1975—), Author's League, AAUP, PEN. Clubs: Lotos, Century, N.Y. U. Author: A Sense of the Present, 1967. Editor: Best American Short Novels; Art and Psychoanalysis; Short Stories of Dostoyevsky; co-editor: Modern Writing, 1, 2, 3, 4,; Stories in the Modern Manner, 1, 2; The Partisan Reader; The New Partisan Reader; The Partisan Review Anthology. Home: 263 W 11th St New York NY 10014 Office: 128 Bay State Rd Boston MA 02215 also 522 Fifth Ave New York NY 10036

PHILLIPS, WILLIAM EUGENE, advt. exec.; b. Chgo., Jan. 7, 1930; s. William E. and Alice P.; B.S., Cornell U., 1951; M.B.A., Northwestern U., 1955; m. Elizabeth Earl, Aug. 13, 1971; children by previous marriage—Michael, Tom, Sarah. Brand mgr. Procter & Gamble, Cin., 1955-59; with Ogilvy & Mather, Inc., N.Y.C., 1959—, chmn., 1978—; dir. Ogilvy & Mather Internat. Inc., Gen. Housewares Corp.; former partner Snowbird Ski Area. Mem. N.Y.C. Mayor's Com. on Pub. Interest; mem. alumni council Cornell U.; trustee P.A.L., Bus. Mktg. Corp. N.Y.C., Outward Bound, Wells Coll. Served to lt. (j.g.) USNR, 1951-54; Korea. Clubs: Cornell, Black Hall Golf, Murray Hill, Racquet. Home: 1 Beekman Pl New York NY 10022 Office: 2 E 48th St New York NY 10017

PHILLIPS, WILLIAM GEORGE, business exec.; b. Cleve., Mar. 3, 1920; s. Edward George and Ina Marie (Cottle) P.; A.B., Antioch Coll., 1942; m. Laverne Anne Evenden, Aug. 7, 1943; children—Karen Anne (Mrs. David F. Berry), Connie Allynette (Mrs. Richard Tressel), Scott William. Pub. accountant Price Waterhouse & Co., Cleve., 1945-48; tax accountant Glidden Co., Cleve., 1948-52, asst. treas., 1952, treas., dir., 1953-67, adminstrv. v.p., 1963-64, pres., 1964-67, chief exec. officer, 1967, pres. Glidden-Durkee div. SCM Corp., 1967-68; pres., chief exec. officer Internat. Multifoods Corp. (formerly Internat. Milling), Mpls., 1968-70, chmn. bd., 1970—; dep. chmn. Mpls. Fed. Res. Bank, 1979—; dir. Northwestern Nat. Bank Mpls., 1969-78, Soo Line R.R. Co., 1971—, N.Am. Life and Casualty Co., 1975—, Fed. Res. Bank Mpls., 1979—. Bd. overseers U. Minn. Coll. Bus. Adminstrn.; nat. corp. adv. bd. United Negro Coll. Fund; exec. com. U.S.-Iran Joint Bus. Council; adv. bd. Nat. Alliance Businessmen; bd. dirs. Mpls. Downtown Devel. Corp., Minn. State Council on Econ. Edn.; mem. Mpls. YMCA investment com.; mem. pres.'s adv. bd. Am. Diabetes Assn.; adv. bd. Inst. Internat. Edn.; trustee Baldwin-Wallace Coll.; bd. dirs. Mpls. Found.; trustee Mpls. Soc. Fine Arts, Nat. Jewish Hosp. at Denver, Ednl. Research Council Am. Served to lt., inf. AUS, 1942-45. Mem. Conf. Bd., C. of C. of U.S. (dir., mem. U.S.-Can. com.), Ohio Soc. C.P.A.'s, Grocery Mfrs. Am. (dir.), Conf. Bd. Mem. Community Ch. Clubs: Lafayette, Minneapolis (bd. govs.), Woodhill Country. Home: 2610 W Lafayette Rd Excelsior MN 55331 Office: 1200 Multifoods Bldg Minneapolis MN 55402

PHILLIPY, LESTER NEWTON, constrn. co. exec.; b. Greencastle, Pa., Nov. 28, 1897; s. Newton Shank and Rebecca Susan (Eshleman) P.; B.Engring., Johns Hopkins U., 1920; m. Anna Katherine Krause, Mar. 31, 1923; 1 son, Lester Newton. With Whiting Turner Contracting Co., Balt., 1920—, gen. supt., estimator, 1928-39, sec., 1939—, dir., 1940—, v.p., 1947-51, exec. v.p., 1951—; dir. Whiting Turner Consultants. Vice pres. Carroll County Hist. Soc. Served with U.S. Army, 1918. Registered profl. engr., Md. Fellow ASCE. Republican. Lutheran. Club: Kiwanis (past lt. gov. internat.). Home: 1029 Sullivan Rd Westminster MD 21157 Office: 300 E Joppa Rd Baltimore MD 21204

PHILLPOT, CLIVE JAMES, art librarian; b. Thornton Heath, Surrey, Eng., June 26, 1938; came to U.S., 1977; s. Cyril Frederick and Beatrice Barbara Jane (Crosby) P.; A.L.A., Poly. of North London, 1967; Dip. H.A. with distinction, U. London, 1974; m. Jean Barbara Webb, June 29, 1961; children—Melanie Carol, Belinda Saffron.

Librarian, Westminster (Eng.) Public Library, 1960-63, Hastings (Eng.) Public Library, 1963-70, Chelsea Sch. Art, London, 1970-77; librarian of the museum Mus. Modern Art, N.Y.C., 1977—; mem. nat. adv. com. Archives of Am. Art, 1979—. Library Assn. U.K., Art Libraries Soc. U.K. (sec. and mem. council 1970-74), Art Libraries Soc. N.Am. (sec. 1979—), Spl. Libraries Assn. Contbr. numerous articles to profl. publs.; editor (with T. Fawcett) and contbr.: The Art Press, Two Centuries of Art Magazines, 1976. Office: 11 W 53d St New York NY 10019

PHILOS, CONRAD DONALD, lawyer; b. Chgo., Nov. 3, 1913; s. James D. and Sophia (de Gaweck) P.; student U. Ill., 1934; J.D., Chgo.-Kent. Coll. Law, 1939; postgrad. Oxford U., U. London, 1946, U. Vienna, 1947-49, U. Chgo., 1951, George Washington U., 1961; m. Helen Katherine Staley, Dec. 21, 1944 (div. June 6, 1969); children—Daphne Ann, Diane Lee, Valerie Jean; m. My Dung Diep, Aug. 1, 1969. Admitted to Ill. bar, 1939, U.S. Supreme Ct. bar, 1964, D.C. bar, 1967, Mass. bar, 1972, Va. bar, 1976; practice in Chgo., 1939-42, Washington, 1952; asso. atty. Petit, Olin & Overmyer, 1939-40; asso. atty. McConnell & Leaton, 1941-42; chief mil. justice U.S. Forces, Austria, 1946; dep., acting chief legal div. Allied Commn., Austria, 1947-50; pres. Ct. Civil and Criminal Appeals U.S. Zone, Austria, 1946-50; asso. atty. McConnell, Lutkin & Van Hook, Chgo., 1952; spl. asst. litigation and pub. affairs Office Judge Adv. Gen., U.S. Army, 1953-60, employment policy officer to chief of staff, chief civilian personnel law div., 1960-65, spl. asst. for intelligence, 1965-67; spl. asst. to chief AID Mission to Vietnam, 1967-68; dir. Study Ministry Pub. Works, Communication and Transp., Republic South Vietnam, 1967-68; spl. asst. procurement litigation, chief legis. relief div. office Judge Adv. Gen. Army, 1969-75; of counsel firm McNutt, Dudley Easterwood & Losch, 1975-78; prof. Internat. Sch. Law, 1978-79, George Mason U. Sch. Law, 1979—; asst. judge adv. gen. army (res.) 1968-70; dir. Option Writers Investment Mut. Fund, 1st & Mchts. Bank, No. Va. Lectr., Judge Adv. Gen.'s Sch., U. Va. Dir. Fed. Bar Bldg. Corp. Mem. Conf. on Crime of U.S. Atty. Gen., 1967. Bd. dirs., chmn., treas. Research Found. Fed. Bar Assn. Served to lt. col. AUS, 1942-46; brig. gen. AUS, ret. Recipient Exceptional Civilian Service award, 1951; Outstanding Service awards with Commendation certificates, 1957-67, 70-75. Mem. Fed. Bar Assn. (past pres.), Inst. for Advancement Pub. Adminstrn. (pres.), Inter-Am. (chmn. com. on govt. service), Am. (ho. of dels. 1965-67) bar assns., Nat. Lawyers Club (gov.), Inst. Mil. Law (gov.). Author: Digest of Military Law, 1953. Gen. editor Fed. Bar Jour., 1956-62; civil rights, collective bargaining and fed. legislation editor West's Federal Practice Manual, 1969—. Contbr. articles to profl. jours. Home: 9601 Atwood Rd Beau Ridge VA 22180 Office: 3401 N Fairfax Dr Arlington VA 22203

PHILOTHEOS, Bishop of Meloa; b. Istanbul, Turkey, Sept. 1, 1924; s. George and Lambrini Karamitsos; came to U.S., 1960, naturalized, 1965; M.S.T., U. Athens, 1959; postgrad. Hunter Coll., N.Y.C., 1960-61, U. Scranton, 1962-64, Latin Am. Inst., N.Y.C., 1966-67. Ordained deacon Greek Orthodox Ch., 1950, priest, 1961; consecrated bishop, 1971; priest Annunciation Ch., Scranton, Pa., 1961-65, St. Eleftherios Ch., N.Y.C., 1965-71; aux. bishop to Archbishop Iakovos, N.Y.C., 1971—, dir. Eccles. Ct.; chief sec. Greek Orthodox Synod of Bishops in Ams.; former v.p. Greek Orthodox Clergy Fellowship Greater N.Y.; trustee, former gen. dir. St. Basil's Acad., Garrison, N.Y.; gen. dir. Archdiocese Registry and Philanthropies; elected to episcopate by Holy Synod of Ecumenical Patriarchate of Constantinople, 1971. Address: 8-10 E 79th St New York NY 10021

PHILPOTT, HARRY MELVIN, univ. pres.; b. Bassett, Va., May 6, 1917; s. Benjamin Cabell and Daisy (Hundley) P.; A.B., Washington and Lee U., 1938, LL.D., 1966; Ph.D., Yale, 1947; D.D., Stetson U., 1960; LL.D., U. Fla., 1969, U. Ala., 1970; H.H.D., Samford U., 1978; m. Pauline Breck Moran, Sept. 15, 1943; children—Harry Melvin, Jean Todd, Benjamin Cabell II, Virginia Lee. Ordained to ministry Bapt. Ch., 1942; dir. religious activities Washington and Lee U., 1938-40; prof. religion U. Fla., 1947-52, v.p., 1957-65; dean, head dept. religion and philosophy Stephens Coll., 1952-57; pres. Auburn U., 1965—. Dir. First Ala. Bank, Montgomery, Ala., West Point Pepperell. Mem. So. Regional Edn. Bd., 1966—, vice chmn., 1973-75; chmn. Ala. Edn. Study Commn., 1967-69; pres. Southeastern Conf., 1972-74. Served to 1st lt. Chaplains Corps., USNR, 1943-46. Mem. Nat. Assn. State Univs. and Land-Grant Colls. (chmn. council presidents 1972-73, exec. com. 1973—, pres. 1976-77), Fla. Blue Key, Kappa Alpha, Omicron Delta Kappa, Kappa Delta Pi, Phi Kappa Phi. Club: Kiwanis. Home: 430 S College St Auburn AL 36830

PHILPOTT, LARRY LA FAYETTE, horn player; b. Alma, Ark., Apr. 5, 1937; s. Lester and Rena (Owens) P.; B.S., Ga. So. Coll., 1962; Mus.M., Butler U., 1972; m. Elise Robichaud, Nov. 24, 1962; Daniel. Mem. N.C. Symphony, 1960, Savannah (Ga.) Symphony, L'Orchestre Symphonique de Quebec (Que., Can.), 1962-64; prin. horn player Indpls. Symphony Orch., 1964—, Flagstaff Summer Festival, 1968—; instr. in horn Butler U., De Pauw U.; artist in-residence Ind.-Purdue Indpls.; appeared with Am. Shakespeare Theatre, summer 1965, Charlottetown Festival, summers 1967-68. Served with USN, 1956-60. Mem. Am. Fedn. Musicians, Internat. Conf. Symphony and Opera Musicians, Phi Mu Alpha Sinfonia. Home: 740 Spring Mill Ln Indianapolis IN 46240 Office: Indpls Symphony 4600 Sunset Ave Indianapolis IN 46208

PHINNEY, HARTLEY KEITH, JR., library adminstr.; b. Ames, Iowa, Nov. 15, 1938; s. Hartley Keith and Fenella (Ainslie) P.; B.A. in Geology, U. Conn., 1960; M.L.S., U. Pitts., 1966; m. Mary Alice Braudwell, Feb. 9, 1962; children—Hartley Kenneth, Leslie Mary, Ruth Alice. Geology-biology librarian Princeton U., 1966-70; supr. tech. info. center Chevron Oil Field Research Co., La Habra, Calif., 1970-74; chief reference and circulation U.S. Geol. Survey Library, Reston, Va., 1974-77; dir. library Arthur Lakes Library Colo. Sch. Mines, Golden, 1977—. Served to lt. U.S. Navy, 1960-65. Mem. Colo. Library Assn., Geoscience Info. Soc. (pres. 1973), Spl. Libraries Assn., Am. Geol. Inst. (bd. govs. 1974). Office: Arthur Lakes Library Colo Sch of Mines Golden CO 80401

PHINNEY, ROBERT ALDEN, geophysicist; b. Rochester, N.Y., Oct. 7, 1936; s. Robert Morris and Margaret (Smith) P.; B.S. in Geology and Geophysics, Mass. Inst. Tech., 1959, M.S., 1959, Ph.D., Calif. Inst. Tech., 1961; m. Caroline Manning Emont, 1977; children—Carolyn, Christopher. Asst. prof. Calif. Inst. Tech., 1961-63; asso. prof. Princeton, 1963-69, prof. geophysics, 1969—, dir. geophys. fluid dynamics program, 1975-78. Cons. lunar and planetary sci. NASA, 1966—; mem. space sci. bd. NAS/NRC, 1973-77. Fellow Am. Geophys. Union; mem. Geol. Soc. Am., Seismol. Soc. Am. Editor: History of the Earth's Crust, 1968. Asso. editor Jour. Geophys. Research, 1966-69, Rev. Geophysics, 1969—. Home: 22 Lake Ln Princeton NJ 08540

PHINNEY, WILLIAM CHARLES, geologist; b. South Portland, Maine, Nov. 16, 1930; s. Clement Woodbridge and Margaret Florence (Foster) P.; B.S., Mass. Inst. Tech., 1953, M.S., 1956, Ph.D., 1959; m. Colleen Dorothy Murphy, May 31, 1953; children—Glenn, Duane, John, Marla. Faculty geology U. Minn., 1959-70; chief geology br. NASA Lyndon B. Johnson Space Center, Houston, 1970—; NASA prin. investigator lunar samples. Served with C.E., AUS, 1953-55. Recipient NASA Exceptional Sci. Achievement medal, 1972. NSF research grantee, 1960-70. Mem. Am. Geophys. Union, A.A.A.S., Mineral. Soc. Am., Geol. Soc. Am., Minn. Acad. Sci. (dir.), Sigma Xi. Contbr. articles to profl. jours. Home 18523 Barbuda Ln Houston TX 77058 Office: SN 6 NASA Lyndon B Johnson Space Center Houston TX 77058

PHIPPS, ALLAN ROGERS, lawyer; b. Denver, Oct. 3, 1912; s. Lawrence Cowle and Margaret (Rogers) P.; A.B., Williams Coll., 1934; B.A. in Jurisprudence, Oxford (Eng.) U., 1936; J.D., U. Denver, 1937; m. Clara Mitchell Van Schaack, Nov. 21, 1955; children by previous marriage—Graham Rogers, Antony Allan, Margaret Doreen Mignonette. Admitted to Colo. bar, 1938, since practiced in Denver; partner firm Hughes & Dorsey, 1950—. Pres., Denver Bears Baseball Club, Broncos Football Club; dir. Cherry Creek Nat. Bank, Van Schaack Corp., South Denver Nat. Bank. Trustee U. Denver, Winter Park Recreational Assn.; pres. bd. trustees Denver Mus. Natural History, Denver Symphony Soc., Graland Country Day Sch. Served to lt. comdr. USNR, 1942-46. Mem. Am., Colo., Denver bar assns., Newcomen Soc., Gargoyle Soc., Phi Beta Kappa, Chi Psi, Phi Delta Phi. Home: 3481 E Kentucky Ave Denver CO 80209 Office: 1600 First of Denver Plaza Bldg Denver CO 80202

PHIPPS, GERALD H., business exec.; b. Denver, 1915; grad. Williams Coll., 1936. Pres., dir. Gerald H. Phipps, Inc., Denver; dir. So. Calif. Edison Co.; prin. owner, chmn. bd. Rocky Mountain Empire Sports, Inc.; dir. 1st Nat. Bank Denver, 1st Nat. Bancorp. Denver, D. & R.G.W. R.R. Co., Rio Grande Industries. Office: 1530 W 13th Ave Denver CO 80204

PHIPPS, JOHN H. (BEN), television exec.; b. London, Nov. 3, 1904 (parents Am. citizens); s. John Shafer and Marguerita (Grace) P.; Ph.B., Yale U., 1928; m. Elinor Klapp, June 26, 1928; children—John Eugene, Colin. Salesman, Ingersoll Rand Co., Boston, N.Y.C., 1929-31; v.p. Dugas Fire Extinguisher Co., N.Y.C., 1931-32; engaged in gen. bus. under name Westbury Corp., N.Y., Fla., 1932-42; owner John J. Phipps Radio Stas. throughout S.E. including WTVS, Marianna, Fla., 1943—, WCTV, WKTG, Thomasville, Ga., WPTV, Palm Beach, Fla; pres. John H. Phipps Agy., ins., 1936—; chmn. bd. South Eastern Shares, Inc.; dir. Bessemer Truste Co., Ingersoll-Rand Co., W.R. Grace & Co. Pres., Carribean Conservation Corp.; mem. region 3 adv. bd. OCDM. Patron, Am. Mus. Natural History; mem. Fla. State U. Found. Bd. Served as col. USAAF, 1942-45; ETO, 1943-45. Decorated Bronze Star medal. Named chevalier d'Agr., 1971. Mem. N.Y. Zool. Soc. (trustee), Am. Internat. Charolais Assn. (standards com.), Am. Charbray Breeders Assn. (dir.), Am. Legion. Democrat. Clubs: Pinnacle, Meadow Brook. Home: Ayavalla Plantation Tallahassee FL 32303 Office: John Phipps Broadcasting Stas Box 3166 Tallahassee FL 32303. *"It is not whom you know, but how you know them."*

PHIPPS, JOHN RANDOLPH, adj. gen. Ill.; b. Kansas, Ill, May 16, 1919; s. Charles Winslow and Kelsey Ethel (Torrence) P.; B.S. in Econs. with honors, U. Ill., 1941; M.P.A., Sangamon State U., 1976; asso. course Command and Gen. Staff Coll., 1959, nuclear weapons employment course, 1962; course U.S. Army War Coll., 1973, U.S. Nat. Def. U., 1978; m. Pauline M. Prunty, Feb. 8, 1946; children—Charles W., Kelsey J. Phipps-Selander. Owner, operator chain shoe stores in Eastern Ill., 1946-70; commd. 2d lt. F.A., U.S. Army, 1941, advanced through grades to capt., 1943; service in Philippines and Japan; discharged as maj., 1946; organizer, comdr. Co. E, 130th Inf., Ill. N.G., Mattoon, 1947, comdg. officer 2d Bn., 130th Inf., 1951, lt. col., 1951; called to fed. service, 1952; adv. 29th Regt., 9th Republic of Korea Div., 1952-53; comdr. officer 1st Bn., 130th Inf., Ill. N.G., 1954, col., 1959, comdg. officer 2d Brigade, 33d Div., 1963-67, asst. div. comdr. 33d Inf. Div., 1967, brig. gen., 1967, comdr. 33d Inf. Brigade, Chgo., 1967-70, comdr. Ill. Emergency Ops. Hdqrs., 1970, asst. adj. gen. Ill., 1970-77, acting adj. gen., 1977-78, adj. gen., 1978—, promoted to maj. gen., 1978. Decorated Silver Star, Bronze Star, various Philippine and Korean decorations; State of Ill. Long and Honorable Service medal. Mem. VFW, Adj. Gens. Assn. U.S., N.G. Assn. U.S., N.G. Assn. Ill. Methodist. Home: 114 Golf Rd Springfield IL 62704 Office: 1301 N MacArthur Blvd Springfield IL 62702

PHIPPS, OGDEN MILLS, banker; b. N.Y.C., Sept. 18, 1940; s. Ogden and Lillian (Bostwick) P.; B.A., Yale U., 1963; m. Andrea Broadfoot; children—Lillian Mills, Diana Hunt, Samantha, Ogden. Chmn. bd. Bessemer Trust Co. Fla. (formerly Palm Beach Trust Co.), 1976—, Bessemer Trust Co., Newark, 1976—, Bessemer Trust Co., N.A., N.Y.C., 1976—; chmn. N.Y. Racing Assn., Jamaica, N.Y., 1976—. Bd. govs. Soc. N.Y. Hosps.; trustee Miami Heart Inst., U. Miami; treas. Internat. Gamefish Assn.; chmn. Fla. Game and Freshwater Fish Commn., 1974-75. Episcopalian. Clubs: Racquet and Tennis, Links (N.Y.C.); Indian Creek Country (Miami, Fla.). Office: Bessmer Trust Co 245 Park Ave New York City NY 10017

PHLEGER, ATHERTON MACONDRAY, lawyer; b. San Francisco, Feb. 5, 1926; s. Herman and Mary Elena (Macondray) P.; A.B., Stanford, 1949; LL.B., Harvard, 1952; m. Joan Cudahy Casserly, June 20, 1953; children—Michael Atherton, Elena Dean, Peter Macondray, Mariana. Admitted to Calif. bar, 1953; asso., partner Brobeck, Phleger & Harrison, San Francisco, 1958—. Dir., Almaden Vineyards, Inc., Wells Fargo & Co., Wells Fargo Bank. Trustee Childrens Hosp., San Francisco, William G. Irwin Charity Found., Bancroft Library. Served with USMCR, 1943-46. Mem. Am., Calif. bar assns. Clubs: Pacific-Union, Bohemian (San Francisco). Home: 319 Walnut St San Francisco CA 94118 Office: Spear Street Tower One Market Plaza San Francisco CA 94105

PHLEGER, HERMAN, lawyer; b. Sacramento, Sept. 5, 1890; s. Charles W. and Mary (McCrory) P.; B.S., U. Calif., 1912; postgrad. Harvard Law Sch., 1913-14; LL.D., Mills Coll., 1935, U. Cal., 1957; m. Mary Elena Macondray, Apr. 2, 1921; children—Mary Elena (Mrs. William Goodan), Atherton Macondray, Anne (Mrs. Milo S. Gates). Partner, Brobeck, Phleger & Harrison, San Francisco; legal adv. Dept. State, 1953-57; dir. Moore Dry Dock Co., various other cos. Mem. U.S. delegation Inter-Am. Conf., Caracas, 1954, Indo-China and China confs., 1954, Summit, Fgn. Ministers confs., Geneva, 1955, Suez Conf., London, 1956, Bermuda Conf., 1957; a U.S. mem. Permanent Ct. Arbitration under Hague Treaties, 1957-63, 70-76; U.S. rep. 13th UN Gen. Assembly, 1958; chmn. U.S. delegation with rank of ambassador, chmn. Antartica Conf., Washington, 1959; mem. gen. adv. com. U.S. Arms Control and Disarmament Agy., 1960-68. Trustee Stanford U., 1944-64, emeritus, 1964—; trustee William G. Irwin Charity Found. (both San Francisco). Served as lt. USN, 1917-18; asso. dir. legal div. Office Mil. Gov. (Germany), 1945. Fellow Am. Bar Assn.; mem. Council on Fgn. Relations, Am. Soc. Internat. Law, Internat. Law Soc. Clubs: Pacific Union, Bohemian, Burlingame Country (San Francisco); Links (N.Y.C.); Metropolitan (Washington). Home: Woodside Redwood City CA 94062 Office: Spear St Tower One Market Plaza San Francisco CA 94105

PHYPERS, DEAN PINNEY, computer co. exec.; b. Cleve., Jan. 13, 1929; s. Fordham S. and Grace Ellen (Pinney) P.; B.A. in Physics, Harvard U., 1950; postgrad. U. Mich. Sch. Bus., 1952; children—Dean A., Toni T., William C., Jonathan W., Katharine L. With IBM, 1955—, v.p. bus. plans, Armonk, N.Y., 1972-74, v.p. fin. and planning, 1974-79, sr. v.p. fin. and planning, 1979—; dir. Church & Dwight Co., Inc., N.Y.C. Mem. econ. adv. council Columbia U.; bus. adv. council Carnegie Mellon U. Served with USNR, 1952-55. Mem. U.S. C. of C. (dir.). Home: 831 Oenoke Ridge Rd New Canaan CT 06840 Office: IBM Old Orchard Rd Armonk NY 10540

PIACSEK, BELA EMERY, physiologist, educator; b. Budapest, Hungary, Apr. 17, 1937; s. Stephen E. and Adrienne A. (Vasarhelyi) P.; came to U.S., 1952, naturalized, 1958; B.S., U. Notre Dame, 1959, M.S., 1961; Ph.D., Mich. State U., 1966; m. Eniko Mary DePottyondy, June 9, 1962; children—Kristina Marie, Steven Bela, Kathleen Elizabeth, Thomas Charles. Research fellow Harvard Med. Sch., 1966-68; asst. prof. Marquette U., Milw., 1968-72, asso. prof., 1972-79, prof., 1979—. Active Boy Scouts Am.; mem. sex edn. panel New Berlin (Wis.) Pastors Assn., 1969-71; mem. St. Luke Community Choir. USPHS research grantee, 1969—. NIH predoctoral trainee, 1964-66; NIH postdoctoral fellow, 1966-68. Mem. Am. Physiol. Soc., Endocrine Soc., Soc. for Study Reprodn., Internat. Soc. Neuroendocrinology, Sigma Xi. Roman Catholic. Club: New Berlin Frontrunners. Contbr. articles to profl. jours. Office: 530 N 15th St Milwaukee WI 53233

PIAN, RULAN CHAO, scholar, musicologist; b. Cambridge, Mass., Apr. 20, 1922; d. Yuen-ren and Buwei (Yang) Chao; B.A., Radcliffe Coll., 1944, M.A., 1946, Ph.D., 1960; m. Theodore Hsueh-huang Pian; Oct. 3, 1945; 1 dau., Canta Chao-po Pian Lent. Teaching asst., instr. in modern Chinese, Harvard, 1947-60, lectr. Chinese and Chinese music, 1961-74, prof. E. Asian langs., civilization and music, 1974—, coordinator modern Chinese lang. instruction, 1962-68, mem. council E. Asian studies, 1975—, master of South House, 1975-78; vis. prof. music Chung Chi Coll., Chinese U. Hong Kong, 1975. Recipient Caroline Wilby dissertation prize Radcliffe Coll., 1960; NDEA Fulbright-Hayes research grantee Chinese Music, Taiwan, 1964; Nat. Endowment Humanities grantee, Hong Kong, 1978-79. Mem. Am. Musicol. Soc. (Otto Kinkeldey book award 1968), Internat. Musicol. Soc., Soc. Ethnomusicology, Conf. Chinese Oral Performing Lit. Author: A Syllabus for the Mandarin Primer, 1961; Sonq Dynasty Musical Sources and Their Interpretation, 1967; contbr. articles to scholarly jours. Home: 14 Brattle Circle Cambridge MA 02138 Office: 2 Divinity Ave Cambridge MA 02138

PIANKA, ERIC RODGER, population biologist; b. Hilt, Calif., Jan. 23, 1939; s. Walter Henry and Virginia Lincoln (High) P.; B.A., Carleton Coll., 1960; Ph.D. (NIH fellow), U. Wash., 1965; m. Helen Louise Dunlap, Dec. 20, 1965; children—Karen Elizabeth, Gretchen Anna. NIH postdoctoral fellow Princeton U., 1965-68, U. Western Australia, Nedlands, 1966-67; asst. prof. zoology U. Tex., Austin, 1968-72, asso. prof., 1972-77, prof., 1977—; vis. prof. U. Kans., 1978. Guggenheim fellow, 1978-79; NSF grantee, 1966-77; Nat. Geog. Soc. grantee, 1975-79. Mem. Am. Soc. Naturalists, Ecol. Soc. Am., Am. Soc. Ichthyologists and Herpetologists, Soc. for Study Evolution, Herpetologists League, AAAS, Am. Inst. Biol. Scis., Western Australian Naturalists. Author: Evolutionary Ecology, 2d edit., 1978; mng. editor The Am. Naturalist, 1971-74, mem. editorial bd., 1975-77; mem. editorial bd. BioSci., 1975-79; contbr. articles to profl. publs.; research on ecology and diversity of desert lizards. Office: Dept Zoology U Tex Austin TX 78712

PIASECKI, FRANK NICHOLAS, corp. exec., aero. engr.; b. Phila., Oct. 24, 1919; s. Nikodem and Emilia (Lotocki) P.; student U. Pa., 1936-39; B.S. in Aero. Engring., N.Y. U., 1940, Dr. Aero. Engring. (hon.), 1955; D.Aero. Sci., Pa. Mil. Coll., 1953; D.Sci., Alliance Coll., 1970; m. Vivian O'Gara Weyerhaeuser, Dec. 1958; children—Lynn, Nicole, Frederick, Frank, John, Michael, Gregory. Aircraft designer Platt-LePage Aircraft Corp., Eddystone, Pa., 1940-41; aerodynamicist Edward G. Budd Mfg. Co., Phila., 1941-43; founded an engring. research group, 1940, inc. as P-V Engring. Forum, 1943, became Piasecki Helicopter Corp., 1946, later chmn. bd.; founded Piasecki Aircraft Corp., 1955, pres.; dir. Crown Cork Internat. Corp. Mem. indsl. cons. com. NACA; adv. com. Daniel Guggenheim Sch. Aeros, N.Y. U.; mem. NSF Commn. on Innovation; mem. Citizens' Adv. Com. Transp. Quality Dept. Transp.; mem. adv. com. indsl. innovation presentation, subcom. sci., tech. and space Senate Com. on Commerce, Sci. and Transp. Trustee, Kosciuszko Found., N.Y.C. Recipient Lawrence Sperry award Inst. Aero. Scis., 1951; Mendel award Villanova U., 1954; Philip H. Ward, Jr. medal Franklin Inst., 1979; chosen one of nation's ten outstanding young men of year U.S. Jr. C. of C., 1952; registered profl. engr., Pa. Fellow Inst. Aero. Scis.; hon. fellow Am. Helicopter Soc. (past pres.); mem. Soc. Automotive Engrs., Am. Soc. Profl. Engrs., Helicopter Assn. Gt. Britain, Am. Soc. Quality Control, Aircraft Industries Assn., Soc. Exptl. Test Pilots. Clubs: Wings (N.Y.C.); Merion Cricket (Haverford, Pa.); Engineers, Corinthian Yacht (Phila.); Twirly Birds (founder mem.); Racquet. Home: Tunbridge Rd and Andover Rd Haverford PA 19041 Office: Island Rd Internat Airport Philadelphia PA 19153

PIATT, WILLIAM MCKINNEY, III, cons. engr.; b. Durham, N.C., Nov. 17, 1918; s. William McKinney and Marion Adele (Sheppard) P.; B.S. in Elec. Engring., Lafayette Coll., 1940; postgrad. Rutgers U., 1940-42; m. Lois Jewel Keast, Apr. 22, 1943; children—William McKinney IV, Raymond Keast, Joseph Wood. Instr. elec. engring. Rutgers U., New Brunswick, N.J., 1942-44; with W.M. Piatt and Co., Cons. Engrs., and predecessors, Durham, N.C., 1946—, elec. engr., 1946-57, partner, 1957-64, sole owner, 1964-66, pres., 1966—; guest lectr. water supply, waste treatment U. N.C., Duke U. Served to lt. comdr. USNR, 1944-46, 51-53. Registered profl. engr., N.C. Fellow Am. Cons. Engrs. Council; mem. ASCE, Water Pollution Control Fedn., Am., New Eng. waterworks assns., Am. Pub. Works Assn., ASTM, Cons. Engrs. Council N.C. (pres. 1973-74), N.C. Soc. Engrs. (pres. 1971), N.C. Wildlife Fedn. (dir. 1966-69, v.p. 1970-76). Democrat. Christian Scientist. Clubs: Kiwanis, Durham Engrs. (pres. 1962), Durham County Wildlife (pres. 1964-65). Home: 5321 Lakeview Dr Durham NC 27712 Office: W M Piatt Co 111 Corcoran St Durham NC 27702

PIAZZA, MARGUERITE, opera singer, actress, supper club entertainer; b. New Orleans, May 6, 1926; d. Albert William and Michaela (Piazza) Luft; Mus.B., Loyola U. of South; Mus.M., La. State U.; D.Mus. (hon.), Christian Bros. Coll., Memphis, 1973; L.H.D. honoris causa, Loyola U. at Chgo., 1975; m. William J. Condon, July 15, 1953 (dec. Mar. 1968); children—Gregory, James (dec. Oct. 1975), Shirley, William J., Marguerite P., Anna Becky; m. 2d, F.H. Bergtholdt, Nov. 8, 1970. Soprano, N.Y.C. Center Opera, 1948, Met. Opera Co., 1950; TV artist Show of Shows, NBC, 1950-54; founder Marguerite Piazza Thanksgiving Gala for the benefit of St. Jude's Hosp., 1976. Dir. Cemrel, Inc. Bd. dirs. St. Jude Found., Found. World Literacy, NCCJ, Memphis Symphony Orch. Nat. chmn. Soc. for Cure Epilepsy; nat. crusade chmn. Am. Cancer Soc., 1971. Recipient Sesquicentennial medal for Carnegie Hall Concert, 1952; service award Chgo. Heart Assn., 1956, Fedn. Jewish Philanthropies of N.Y., 1956; named Queen of Memphi, Memphis Cotton Carnival, 1973, Person of the Year Los Angeles Council for Performing Arts, 1975. Mem. Woman's Exchange, Beta Sigma Omicron, Phi Beta. Roman Catholic. Clubs: Memphis Country, Memphis Hunt and Polo. Home: 1720 Central Ave Memphis TN 38104

PICARD, ROBERT (GEORGE), psychologist; b. Edmonton, Alta., Can., Mar. 27, 1905; s. Joseph Henri and Martine (Voyer) P.; B.A., Xavier Coll., Edmonton, Ph.D., Immaculate-Conception Coll., Montreal, Que., Can., 1929; Diploma, Inst. Psychology, Sorbonne, U. Paris, 1940. Joined S.J., Roman 1923; prof. psychology Immaculate-Conception Coll., 1940-70, rector, 1957-63; prof. U. Montreal, Ecole Normale, 1941-57, Institut de Psychologie, 1948-57; editor Education et Societe, Montreal, 1970-75; pres. Editions Bellarmin, Montreal, 1976-78; ret., 1978. Mem. Am. Psychol. Assn., Am. Anthropl. Assn. Contbr. articles to profl. jours. Home: 25 Jarry W Montreal PQ H2P 1S6 Canada

PICCARD, JEANNETTE RIDLON, clergywoman, former aerospace cons; b. Chgo., Jan. 5, 1895; d. John and Emily Caroline (Robinson) Ridlon; B.A. in Philosophy and Psychology, Bryn Mawr Coll., 1918; M.S. in Organic Chemistry, U. Chgo., 1919; Ph.D. in Edn., U. Minn., 1942; D.D. (hon.), Hobart Coll., 1977; D.H.L. (hon.), Carlton Coll., 1979; m. Jean Piccard, Aug. 19, 1919 (dec. 1963). Exec. sec., housing sect. Minn. Office Civilian Def., 1942-43; counselor Waldorf Paper Products, St. Paul, 1943-44; nurse's aid ARC, 1944-46; aerospace cons. Aerospace Research Dept., Gen. Mills, Inc., 1947; cons. Office Naval Research, 1955, Tex. Gulf Coast Sci. Ednl. Resources Center, 1966-70; cons. to dir. NASA Johnson Space Center, 1964-70; holder spherical balloon pilot's license Fedn. Aero. Internat., 1934; pilot stratosphere balloon flight, altitude 57,559 feet, 1934. Ordained deacon Episcopal Ch., 1971, priest, 1974. Pres. bd. dirs. St. Paul Episcopal Day Sch., St. Paul, 1961-65; hon. bd. dirs. Seabury-Western Theol. Sem., 1968—; bd. govs. Nat. Space Inst., 1975—; bd. dirs. St. Barnabas Day Sch., Houston, 1966-70; adv. council Dayton Ave. Motivational-Tutorial Program, St. Paul, 1966-70. Recipient Certificate of Performance, Nat. Aero. Assn., 1934, Certificate of Honor, 1964; named One of Minn.'s Women of Distinction, 1956; recipient Harmon trophy Ligue Internat. des Aviateurs, 1934; Bronze plaque in memory of 1934 stratospheric balloon flight, Dearborn, Mich.; 1st recipient W. Randolph Lovelace II award Am. Astronautical Soc., 1965, Outstanding Achievement award U. Minn., 1968, award for personal contbns. to manned space flight NASA Manned Spacecraft Center, 1970. Asso. fellow Am. Inst. Aero. and Astronautics; mem. Bryn Mawr Coll., U. Chgo., U. Minn., Gen. Theol. Sem. alumnae assns., Soc. Women Engrs., LWV, AAUW, Am. Meteorol. Soc. (hon.; past sec. and pres. Twin City chpt.); hon. mem. Wingfoot-Lighter-than-Air Soc., Minn. Aerostate Soc., Balloon Fedn. Am., Iota Sigma Pi, Sigma Delta Upsilon. Clubs: Soroptomists; New Century (St. Paul); Faculty Women's (U. Minn.). Author technical papers. Home: 1445 E River Rd Minneapolis MN 55414. *My husband, Jean Piccard, and I made our Stratosphere balloon flight to 57,559 feet on Oct. 23, 1934. The first verse of the psalm for Evening Prayer that night read: "Not unto us, O Lord, not unto us but to Thy Name give the praise for Thy loving kindness and Thy truth's sake." If I have had success, do not praise me. Praise God and give thanks for God's love and truth.*

PICCHIONI, ALBERT LOUIS, educator; b. Klein, Mont., Aug. 28, 1921; s. William Joseph and Josephine Marie (Medici) P.; B.S., U. Mont., 1943; M.S., Purdue U., 1950, Ph.D., 1952; m. Theresa Marie Scott, Dec. 27, 1953; children—Mary Jane, William Joseph, Geno Anthony, Ann Marie. Pharmacist Staley Drug Co., Harlowton, Mont., 1945-46; pharmacist supr. U. Mich. Hosp., Ann Arbor, 1946-48; prof. pharmacology U. Ariz., Tucson, 1952—, head dept. pharmacology and toxicology Coll. Pharmacy, 1970—, dir. Ariz. Poisoning Control Information Center, 1957—. Served with M.C., AUS, 1943-45. Am. Found. Pharm. Edn. fellow, 1948-52; named Ariz. Pharmacist of Year, Ariz. Pharm. Assn., 1956. Mem. Am. Soc. Pharmacology and Exptl. Therapeutics, N.Y. Acad. Scis., AAAS, Acad. Pharm. Scis., Internat. Soc. Biochem. Pharmacology, Western Pharmacology Soc. Research with activated charcoal as antidote to poisoning. Home: 2510 N Santa Lucia St Tucson AZ 85715

PICHA, KENNETH GEORGE, univ. ofcl.; b. Chgo., July 24, 1925; s. George and Sylvia (Beran) P.; B.Mech. Engring., Ga. Inst. Tech., 1946, M.S. in Mech. Engring., 1948; Ph.D., U. Minn., 1957; m. Vivien O. Crawford, May 1, 1948; children—Kenneth George, Kevin Crawford, Katrina Alison. Research scientist NACA, 1948-49; instr., then asso. prof. Ga. Inst. Tech. Sch. Mech. Engring., 1949-58, dir. Sch., 1960-66; program dir. engring. sci. program NSF, 1958-60; dean U. Mass. Sch. Engring., Amherst, 1966-76, dir. Office To Coordinate Energy Research and Edn., 1977—; dir. Office Univ. Programs, ERDA, 1976-77; cons. in field, 1959—; cons. Govt. Singapore on U. Singapore master planning, 1970-71; mem. adv. bd. Internat. Tech. Edn. Cons., 1978; chmn. engring. edn. and accreditation com. Engrs. Council for Profl. Devel., 1973-74; chmn. commn. edn. engring. profession Nat. Assn. Land Grant Colls. and Univs.; chmn. manpower devel. com. Nat. Air Pollution Control Agy., 1970-71; vice chmn. Council for Specialized Accreditation, 1973-77; vice-chmn. mem. exec. com. Council on Post Secondary Accreditation, 1974-77; NSF adv. com. Worcester Poly. Inst., 1972-75. Bd. govs. Mass. Sci. and Tech. Found., 1970-76; bd. visitors Sch. Engring. U. Pitts. Served with USNR, 1943-46. Fellow ASME, AAAS; mem. Am. Soc. Engring. Edn. (dir., mem. exec. com. 1974-76), Ga. Inst. Tech. Nat. Alumni Assn., Nat. Soc. Profl. Engrs. (affiliate), Sigma Xi, Tau Beta Pi, Phi Kappa Phi, Pi Tau Sigma. Club: Cosmos. Home: 56 Oak Knoll Amherst MA 01002

PICHÉ, ALPHONSE, poet; b. Chicoutimi, Que, Feb. 14, 1917; s. Mendoza and Marie Celeste (Velleneuve) P.; student Sem. St. Joseph, 1930-35. Accountant, Delisle Ltd., Montreal, Que.; collections of poetry include: Ballades de la petite extrace, 1946, Remous, 1947, Voie d'eau, 1950, Poèmes, 1946-68; contbr. poetry to lit. jours. and anthologies; lectr. writers symposiums. Recipient Prix David, Que., 1947, Lit. Prize, Trois-Rivières St. Jean Baptist Soc., 1956, Priz. Gouverneur General du Canada, 1976, Priz Duvernay St. Jean Baptiste Soc., 1966. Mem. Liberal Party. Roman Catholic. Club: St Maurice Yacht. Home and Office: Case Postale 1942 Trois-Rivières PQ Canada

PICHE, MARCEL, lawyer; b. Les Eboulements, Que., Can., Feb. 16, 1914; s. Odilon and Antonia (Cousineau) P.; grad. Sem., Quebec, 1932; B.A., U. Ottawa, 1935; LL.B., Laval U., 1938; m. Beatrice Foster, Sept. 28, 1940; 1 dau., Helene. Admitted to Que. bar, 1938, queen's counsel; superior Sch. Commerce, Que.; gen. practice, Quebec City, 1938-44, Montreal, 1944—; sr. partner firm Blain, Piche, Emery & Assos.; prof. law U. Montreal. Chmn. bd. Corby Distillery, Ltd.; pres. Havre Champlain Inc.; sec. Reynolds Aluminum Co. Can., Ltd.; dir. Hugo Stinnes, Inc., ITT Industries of Can. Ltd., Transmaris Holding & Investment, Inc., Trust Gen. du Can., La Presse Newspaper, Tele-Metropole Corp.; solicitor Reynolds Aluminum Co. Can. Ltd.; mem. bd., v.p. Gen. Trust Can. Pres., Clin. Research Inst., Montreal; hon. chmn. bd. Regie de la Place des Arts. Chancellor, mem. bd., exec. com. U. Montreal, 1976-77. Mem. C. of C. Roman Catholic. Clubs: St. Denis, Mount Stephen, Mt. Bruno Country. Home: 8 Springgrove Crescent Outremont Montreal PQ H2V 3H9 Canada Office: 1010 Sherbrooke St W 25th Floor Montreal PQ H3A 1S6 Canada

PICHE, PAUL, bishop; b. Gravelbourg, Sask., Can., Sept. 14, 1909; s. Joseph Amedee and Eleonore (Pratte) P.; B.A. in Anthropology, Ottawa (Ont.) U., 1931; Scholasticate of Sacred Heart, Lebret, Sask., 1935. Ordained priest Roman Cath. Ch., 1934; prof. holy scripture, liturgy and history of ch. Lebret Sem., 1935-39; prof. social economy Oblates Scholasticate, Lebret, 1939-41; superior Juniorate of Holy Family, St. Boniface, Man., Can., 1941-43; superior, prin. Qu'Appelle Indian Residential Sch., Lebret, 1943-51; provincial superior Oblate Fathers of Mary Immaculate, St. Boniface, Man., 1951-56; gen. dir. Oblate Indian and Eskimo Commn., Ottawa, Ont., 1956-59; bishop of MacKenzie, 1959—. Decorated Centennial medal, 1967. K.C. Author writings on Indian edn. Address: Bishop's Residence Fort Smith NT X0E 0P0 Canada. *Fulfill duties with honesty, courage and perseverance.*

PICHETTE, CLAUDE, univ. adminstr.; b. Sherbrooke, Que., Can., June 13, 1936; s. Donat and Juliette (Morin) P.; B.A., U. Sherbrooke, 1956; M.Sc.Soc. (Econ.), U. Laval, 1960; Doct. d'Etat es Sc. Econ., U. D'Aix-Marseille (France), 1970; m. Renee Provencher, Sept. 5, 1959; children—Anne-Marie, Martin, Philippe, Prof., U. Sherbrooke, 1960-70; civil servant Govt. Que., 1970-75; vice rector adminstrn. and fins. U. Que., Montreal, 1975-77, rector, 1977—; with Found. U. Que., Montreal; mem. cons. com. Commission d'initiative et de developpement economique de Montreal; pres. Que. Found. Econ. Edn., 1979-80. Can. Council grantee, 1958; Federation nationale des cooperatives de consommation de France grantee, 1973. Mem. Que. Assn. Econs. (pres. 1977-78), Can. Econs. Assn., Societe canadienne de Science Economique. Club: St.-Denis (Montreal). Author: Analyse micro-economique et cooperative, 1972; editorial bd. Gestion. Home: 745 Hartland Outremont PQ H2V 2X5 Canada Office: CP 8888 1193 (Carre Philippe) Montreal PQ H3C 3P8 Canada

PICHLER, JOSEPH ANTON, univ. dean, educator; b. St. Louis, Oct. 3, 1939; s. Anton Dominick and Anita Marie (Hughes) P.; B.B.A. (Woodrow Wilson fellow), U. Notre Dame, 1961; M.B.A., U. Chgo., 1963, Ph.D. (Ford Found. fellow, Standard Oil Indsl. Relations fellow), 1966; m. Susan Ellen Eyerly, Dec. 27, 1962; children—Gretchen, Christopher, Rebecca, Josh. Asst. prof. bus. U. Kans., 1964-68, asso. prof., 1968-73, prof., 1973—, dean Sch. Bus., 1974—. Spl. asst. to asst. sec. for manpower U.S. Dept. Labor, 1968-70; chmn. Kans. Manpower Services Council; dir. Dillon Cos., Inc.; mem. nat. bd. cons.'s Nat. Endowment for Humanities; indsl. cons. Bd. dirs. Kans. Charities, 1973-75, Benedictine Coll., Atchison, Kans. Recipient Performance award U.S. Dept. Labor Manpower Adminstrn., 1969. Mem. Kans. Assn. Commerce and Industry. Author: (with Joseph McGuire) Inequality: The Poor and the Rich in America, 1969; contbg. author: Creativity and Innovation in Manpower Research and Action Programs, 1970; Contemporary Management: Issues and Viewpoints, 1973; Institutional Issues in Public Accounting, 1974. Co-editor, contbg. author: Ethics, Free Enterprise, and Public Policy, 1978. Contbr. articles to profl. jours. Home: 1108 Sunset Dr Lawrence KS 66044 Office: Sch of Bus 202 Summerfield Hall U Kans Lawrence KS 66045

PICIRILLI, ROBERT EUGENE, clergyman, coll. adminstr.; b. High Point, N.C., Oct. 6, 1932; s. Eugene and Lena (Harrell) P.; B.A., Free Will Bapt. Bible Coll., Nashville, 1953; M.A., Bob Jones U., 1955, Ph.D., 1963, D.D., 1967; m. Clara Mae Lee, June 14, 1953; children—Annina Jean, Myra Jane, Mary June, Celina Joy, Roberta Jill. Ordained to ministry Free Will Bapt. Ch., 1952; grad. asst. Bob Jones U., 1954-55; prof. N.T., Free Will Bapt. Bible Coll., 1955—, registrar, 1960-79, dean, 1979—; clk. Nat. Assn. Free Will Baptists, 1961-65, moderator, 1966-71. Mem. testing com. Accrediting Assn. Bible Colls., 1959-72; sec.-treas. So. region Evang. Theol. Soc., 1964-68, vice chmn., 1972-73, chmn., 1973-74. Pres., Ransom Elementary Sch. P.T.A., 1965-67. Fellow Inst. for Bibl. Research; mem. NEA, Am. Assn. Collegiate Registrars and Admissions Officers, Delta Epsilon Chi. Home: 301 Greenway Ave Nashville TN 37205

PICKARD, GEORGE LAWSON, former oceanographer; b. Cardiff, Wales, July 5, 1913; s. Harry Lawson and Phoebe (Crosier) P.; B.A., Oxford (Eng.) U., 1935, D.Phil., 1937, M.A., 1947; m. Lilian May Perry, Apr. 26, 1938; children—Rosemary Ann Pickard McAfee, Andrew Lawson. Sci. officer Royal Aircraft Establishment, Farnborough, Eng., 1937-42; prin. sci. officer operational research sect. coastal command RAF, Eng., 1942-47; faculty U. B.C., Vancouver, Can., 1947—, prof. physics, 1954—, dir. Inst. Oceanography, 1958-79. Mem. Fisheries Research Bd. Can., 1963-72. Bd. mgmt. B.C. Research Council. Fellow Royal Soc. Can., AAAS; mem. B.C. Acad. Scis. (past pres.), Am. Soc. Limnology and Oceanography (past v.p.), Am. Geophys. Union. Author: Descriptive Physical Oceanography, S. Pond) Introductory Dinamic Oceanography, 1978; also articles. Research on circulation in estuaries and seas relating to anti-pollution studies. Home: 4546 W 5th Ave Vancouver BC V6R 1S7 Canada

PICKARD, JOHN BENEDICT, educator; b. Newton, Mass., Oct. 4, 1928; s. Greenleaf Whittier and Helen (Liston) P.; B.A., Holy Cross Coll., 1950; postgrad. Boston Coll., 1950-51; Ph.D., U. Wis., 1954; m. Margaret Suzanne Dederich, Nov. 24, 1956; children—Stephen, Ellen, Nathaniel, Thaddeus, John Samuel. Instr. U. Calif., Far East Extension, 1956; asst. prof. English, Rice U., 1956-63; asso. prof. U. Fla., Gainesville, 1963-68, prof., 1968—. Vice pres. Nat. Newman Orgn., 1962-63; bd. dirs. Hist. Gainesville, Inc., 1971-72; bd. dirs. St. Augustine Sch. Religion, 1971-72, Fla. Trail Assn., 1977-80. Served with U.S. Army, 1954-56. Named Outstanding Tchr., Rice U., 1958; Am. Philos. Soc. grantee, 1962, 67, 69. Mem. MLA, South Central MLA, Fla. Coll. Tchrs. English, Am. Film Inst., Fla. Trail Assn. Democrat. Roman Catholic. Author: J.G. Whittier: an Introduction and Interpretation, 1961; Legends of New England by J.G. Whittier, 1965; Emily Dickinson, 1967; Memorabilia of J.G., 1968; The Letters of John Greenleaf Whittier, 3 vols., 1975; Whittier and Whittierland, 1976. Office: Dept English U Fla Gainesville FL 32611

PICKARD, LOWERY BLAINE, newsprint mfr.; b. Jasper, Tex., Sept. 28, 1942; s. Arthur Vernon and Berniece (Lowery) P.; B.B.A. in Accounting, Tex. A. and M. U., 1965; m. Myna Flo Baldree, May 29, 1965; children—Ronald Todd, David Michael. Accountant Pan Am. Petroleum Corp., Tulsa, 1965-67; accounting supr. Southland Paper Mills, Inc., Lufkin, Tex., 1967-73, treas., Houston, 1973—. Mem. Nat. Assn. Fin. Mgmt., Nat. Assn. Accountants. Home: 11250 Pompano St Houston TX 77072 Office: 1111 Fannin St Houston TX 77002

PICKELS, DONALD GEORGE, newspaper editor; b. Fishers Is., N.Y., May 10, 1925; s. Wayne McVeigh and Hallie Mae (Cochran) P.; B.A., Tex. A. and M. U., 1949; m. Joy Ruth Taylor, Aug. 12, 1948; children—Donald Wayne, Steven Jack, Wanda Lisa. Reporter, San Antonio Light, 1949-58; with Houston Chronicle, 1958—, asst. mng. editor, 1966-71, mng. editor, 1971—. Served with USNR, 1943-44, AUS, 1944-45. Democrat. Episcopalian. Home: 2015 Willowmoss Houston TX 77008 Office: 801 Texas Ave Houston TX 77002

PICKENS, BUFORD LINDSAY, archtl. historian, educator; b. Coffeyville, Kans., Jan. 15, 1906; s. Samuel Milton and Emily (Grigson) P.; B.Arch., U. Ill., 1930; A.M., U. Chgo. (fellow), 1937; m. Mabel Grönner, June 2, 1934; children—Lindsay Lloyd, Grigson Buford. Archtl. work, Chgo., 1925-28, 30-35; instr. Ohio U., 1937-38; pvt. practice residential architecture, community planning cons., 1938—; asst. prof. Wayne U., Detroit, 1938-45; prof., dir. Coll. Architecture, Tulane U., 1946-53; prof. Washington U., 1953-74, prof. emeritus, 1974—, dean Sch. Architecture, 1953-56, dir. campus planning, 1956-63; vis. lectr. U. Minn., summer 1940; cons. Detroit City Planning Commn., 1944-45. Mem. Vieux Carre Commn., New Orleans, 1947-52; mem. Fulbright Adv. Screening Com., 1958-60, Joint AIA/ACSA Award Com., 1976-79; hist. bldg. commr. Mo., 1960-73, St. Louis County, 1964-74. Served U.S. Army as instr. Univ. Tng. Command, Florence, Italy, 1945. Fellow A.I.A.; mem. Soc. Archtl. Historians (pres. 1950), Assn. Collegiate Schs. Architecture (pres. 1957-59), Alpha Rho Chi. Contbr. articles to Am., English, Italian jours. Home: 1122 Warson Woods Dr Saint Louis MO 63122

PICKENS, MARSHALL IVEY, trust adminstr.; b. Pineville, N.C., Jan. 23, 1904; s. Corneliuus Miller and Emma (Watts) P.; A.B., Duke, 1925, M.A., 1926; LL.D., Davidson Coll. 1962; m. Sarah Wakefield, Dec. 17, 1932; children—Lucinda Watts (Mrs. H.B. Lockwood, Jr.), Sarah Wakefield (Mrs. J. Worth Williamson, Jr.), Marshall Ivey. With Duke Endowment, Charlotte, N.C., 1928—, field rep., asst. sec., 1946-61, sec., 1961-66, asso. dir., 1948-50, dir. hosp. and child care sects., 1950-62, exec. dir. hosp. and child care sects., 1962-66, trustee, 1951—, vice chmn. trustees, 1966-73, chmn., 1973-74, hon. chmn., 1975—; dir. Duke Power Co. Trustee emeritus Duke U.; past pres. United Community Services, Charlotte and Mecklenburg County, N.C., also Social Planning Council of Charlotte; past pres., bd. mgrs. Meth. Home for Aged; bd. visitors Davidson (N.C.) Coll. Fellow Am. Coll. Hosp. Adminstrs. (hon.); mem. Am., N.C., S.C. hosp. assns., Am. Assn. Hosp. Cons., A.I.A. (hon. asso. mem.), Newcomen Soc., Omicron Delta Kappa, Pi Kappa Phi. Methodist. Clubs: Charlotte Country, City (Charlotte). Home: 1730 Brandon Rd Charlotte NC 28207 Office: 200 S Tryon St Charlotte NC 28202

PICKENS, ROBERT BRUCE, electronics mfg. co. exec.; b. Uniontown, Pa., May 20, 1926; s. Joseph Abraham and Margaret Gertrude (Brown) P.; B.S. in Bus. Adminstrn., Waynesburg Coll., 1950; m. Mary Ellen Evans, Sept. 9, 1950; children—Laura Gail (Mrs. Dean Darin Martin), Rachel Diane, David Bruce. Vice pres. Home Bottle Gas Corp., Uniontown, 1950-51; jr. accountant to sr. accountant Tenney & Co., Uniontown, 1951-56; mgr. Hosp. Service Assn. Western Pa., Pitts., 1956-57; auditor U. Pitts., Pitts., 1957-58; sr. accountant, Eugene A. Conniff Co., Pitts., 1958-59; mgr. Sheppard & Co., Pitts., 1959-63; supr. Alexander Grant & Co., Chgo., 1963-65; asst. to treas. CTS Corp., Elkhart, Ind., 1965, gen. auditor, controller, 1966—. Mem. Bower Hill Civic League, 1956-62; active Boy Scouts Am., 1938-62. Served to cpl. USAAF, 1944-45. C.P.A., Pa., Ill., Ind. Mem. Am. Inst. C.P.A.'s, Pa. Inst. C.P.A.'s, Ill. C.P.A. Soc., Ind. Assn. C.P.A.'s, Accounting Research Assn. Republican. Presbyn. (elder, trustee 1959-61, treas. 1960-61). Home: 3322 Calumet Ave Elkhart IN 46514 Office: 905 N West Blvd Elkhart IN 46514

PICKENS, SLIM (LOUIS BERT LINDLEY, JR.), actor; b. Kingsberg, Calif., June 1919; ed. public schs., Hanford, Calif. Numerous film appearances, including: Boy Oklahoma, Last Command, One-Eyed Jacks, Dr. Strangelove, Major Dundee, Rough Night in Jericho, The Cowboys, Pat Garrett and Billy the Kid, Blazing Saddles, Rancho Deluxe, White Line Fever, Mr. Billion, The Apple Dumpling Gang, The White Buffalo, The Swarm, Beyond the Poseidon Adventure; regular on TV series The Outlaws, The Legend of Custer; numerous other TV appearances, including: Wagon Train, Wide Country, Bonanza, Gunsmoke, Alias Smith and Jones, Men from Shiloh, The Mary Tyler Moore Show, Partridge Family, Hawaii Five-O, World of Disney, Baretta, McMillan and Wife; also TV film appearances.

PICKENS, THOMAS BOONE, JR., oil co. exec.; b. Holdenville, Okla., May 22, 1928; s. Thomas Boone and Grace Marclen Molonson P.; B.S. in Geology Okla. State U., 1951; m. Beatrice Louise Carr, Apr. 21, 1972. Geologist Phillips Petroleum Co., 1951-55; founder, pres., chmn. bd. Mesa Petroleum Co., Amarillo, Tex.; dir. 1st. Nat. Bank Amarillo. Mem. Nat. Petroleum Council, 1970—. Home: Woodstone One Amarillo TX 79106 Office: Mesa Petroleum Co Box 2009 300 S Polk St Amarillo TX 79189

PICKER, HARVEY, univ. ofcl., mfg. co. exec.; b. N.Y.C., Dec. 8, 1915; s. James and Evelyn (Feil) P.; B.A. magna cum laude, Colgate U., 1936, D.Sc., 1968; student Oxford (Eng.) U., 1936-37; M.B.A., Harvard, 1938; m. Jean Sovatkin, Sept. 23, 1947; children—Frances, Gale. With Picker Corp., mfrs. x-ray apparatus and nuclear instruments, White Plains, N.Y., 1938—, pres., 1945-70, chmn. bd., 1968—, also dir.; dir. C.I.T. Fin. Corp.; prof. polit. sci. Colgate U., 1970-72; dean Columbia Sch. Internat. Affairs, prof. internat. relations, 1972—. U.S. del. IAEA, 1967; chmn. tech. transfer panel Econ. Policy Council, UNA; mem. Nat. Sci. Bd., 1965-70; Dept. State Selection Bd., 1968. Trustee Conn. Coll., 1958-72, Colgate U., 1964-72, Hudson Inst., Internat. House, 1973-78, Lenox Hill Hosp., 1960-65, N.Y. Philharmonic Soc., Eisenhower Exchange Fellowships, Found. Child Devel., UNITAR. Served to lt. comdr. USNR, 1940-45. Fellow Am. Coll. Radiology (hon.); mem. Am. Phys. Soc., Am. Assn. Physics Tchrs., Am. Polit. Sci. Assn., N.Y. Acad. Scis., A.A.A.S., Council Fgn. Relations, Soc. Nuclear Medicine, Pub. Mems. Assn., Phi Beta Kappa, Sigma Chi. Mem. Soc. Friends. Clubs: Century Assn., Corinthians, Harvard (N.Y.C., Boston); Army-Navy (Washington); Explorers (N.Y.C.). Home: 1327 Flagler Dr Edgewater Point Mamaroneck NY 10543 Office: Sch Internat Affairs Columbia 420 W 118th St New York NY 10027

PICKER, JEAN SOVATKIN, educator, former diplomat; b. N.Y.C., Mar. 7, 1921; d. Edward and Frances (Sklar) Sovatkin; B.A., Smith Coll., 1942; m. Harvey Picker, Sept. 23, 1947; children—Frances, Gale. News corr. Life mag., various locations U.S., Eng., 1942-47; spl. projects Westchester County govt., White Plains, N.Y., 1952-53; vol. UN office pub. info., N.Y.C., 1953-61; co-founder, 1962, since v.p. Interchange Found., N.Y.C., pres., 1978; U.S. del. 23d Gen. Assembly, UN 1968; permanent rep. UN Commn. for Social Devel., 1969-77, spl. adviser U.S. del. 25th, 27th-31st Gen. Assemblies, 48th 50th, 52d 54th, 56th, 58th, 60th, 62d ECOSOC; dir. Union Savs. Bank of N.Y., 1977—, Bank of Tokyo Trust Co., 1978—; mem. nominating com. Am. Stock Exchange, 1977-78. Dir. Com. of Corr., N.Y.C., 1958-66, chmn. bd., 1965-67; mem. exec. com. U.S. Nat. Commn. UNESCO, 1967, 71, 72. Mem. Presdl. Task Force on Suburban Problems, 1967; U.S. del. assemblies World Fedn. UN Assn., 1964, 66, 68-70, v.p. World Fedn., 1968-71; bd. mem. Council on Religion and Internat. Affairs, 1973-79. Bd. dirs. Inst. World Order, 1959—; bd. overseers Friends World Coll., 1963-72; mem. adv. council Hampshire Coll.; trustee Colgate U., 1975—, Smith Coll., 1977—; sec. James Picker Found.; pres. Branta Found. Mem. UN Assn. (sec., gov. 1970-75, vice chmn. 1975—), Fgn. Policy Assn. (vice chmn. bd. 1968-71, dir.). Mem. Soc. of Friends. Clubs: Cosmopolitan (N.Y.C.); Smith College. Author, pub. text books. Home: Edgewater Point Mamaroneck NY 10543 Office: Interchange Found 300 E 42d St New York NY 10017

PICKERELL, ALBERT GEORGE, educator; b. Cherryvale, Kans., May 7, 1912; s. Albert Newton and Opal M. (Guist) P.; B.S., Kans. State Tchrs. Coll., Pittsburg, 1934, M.S., 1935; M.A., Stanford U., 1948, Ph.D. in Polit. Sci., 1952; m. Betty J. Johnson, Apr. 20, 1954; children—Blair, Lynn. Reporter, copyreader Joplin (Mo.) Globe and News Herald, also other papers in Midwest, 1936-41; with Washington Post, also A.P., 1946; news editor U.P.I., 1947-50, USIA,

1950-51; faculty U. Calif. at Berkeley, 1951—, prof. journalism, 1960—, chmn. dept. journalism, 1967-69, acad. asst. to pres., 1960. Statewide dir. info. for U. Calif., 1961-65. Served to maj. AUS, 1942-45. Fulbright lectr., Thailand, 1954-55, India, 1979; Social Sci. Research Council grantee, Thailand, 1959. Mem. Assn. Edn. Journalism, AAUP, Sigma Delta Chi. Democrat. Clubs: London Press, San Francisco Press. Co-author: The University of California: A Pictorial History, 1968; The Courts and the News Media, 1974, 2d edit., 1979; contbr. articles to profl. jours. Home: 56 Gipsy Ln Berkeley CA 94705

PICKERELL, JAMES HOWARD, photo-journalist; b. Dayton, Ohio, June 9, 1936; s. Howard and Frances (Harrison) P.; student Ohio U., 1954-56; B.A., U. Calif. at Los Angeles, 1963; m. Mary Louise Fisher, June 26, 1965; children—Cheryl Elizabeth, Stacy Rae. Free-lance photographer Black Star Pub. Co., N.Y.C., 1963—; photographer in S. Vietnam, 1963-67. Served with USNR, 1956-60. Mem. Nat. Press Photographers Assn. (1st Pl. Spot News award 1965), Am. Soc. Mag. Photographers, Profl. Photographers Am., Beta Theta Pi. Author: Vietnam in the Mud, 1966. Address: 8104 Cindy Ln Bethesda MD 20034

PICKERING, GORDON LANGSDALE, hosp. adminstr.; b. Glen Valley, B.C., Can., June 2, 1913; s. Hugh Langsdale and Catharine Anna Alice (Norgrove) P.; B.A., U. Man. (Can.), 1935; B.Sc., U. Sask., 1937; m. Marie B. Gamache, Nov. 8, 1941; children—Wayne, Joan, Bryan, Ray. Acct., Regina Hosp., 1937-40; cost acct. Asso. Textiles, 1946-48; bus. adminstr. St. Boniface Hosp., Winnipeg, Can., 1949-57; chmn. Man. Hosp. Commn., 1958-65; dir. Can. Pension Plan, Ottawa, 1965-68; chief exec. officer, chmn. bd. Edmonton (Alta.) Gen. Hosp., 1968—. Served with RCAF, 1941-45. Mem. Cath. Health Care Conf. Alta. (pres.), Coll. Health Services Execs. Office: Edmonton Gen Hosp Edmonton AB Canada

PICKERING, JAMES HENRY, coll. ofcl.; b. N.Y.C., July 11, 1937; s. James H. and Anita (Felber) P.; B.A., Williams Coll., 1959; M.A., Northwestern U., 1960, Ph.D., 1964; m. Patricia Paterson, Aug. 18, 1962; children—David Scott, Susan Elizabeth. Instr. English, Northwestern U., 1963-65; mem. faculty Mich. State U., East Lansing, 1965—, prof. English, 1972—, grad. and asso. chmn. dept., 1968-75, dir. Honors Coll., 1975—. Mem. Coll. English Assn. (pres. 1980), Phi Beta Kappa, Phi Kappa Phi, Omicron Delta Kappa. Author: Fiction 100, 1974, 78; The World Turned Upside Down: Prose and Poetry of the American Revolution, 1975; The City in American Literature, 1977; also articles, revs. Home: 1830 Bramble Dr East Lansing MI 48823

PICKERING, JOHN HAROLD, lawyer; b. Harrisburg, Ill., Feb. 27, 1916; s. John Leslie and Virginia Lee (Morris) P.; A.B., U. Mich., 1938, J.D., 1940; m. Elsa Victoria Mueller, Aug. 23, 1941; children—Leslie Ann, Victoria Lee. Admitted to N.Y. bar, 1941, D.C. bar, 1947; practiced in N.Y.C., 1941, Washington, 1946—; asso. Cravath, de Gersdorff, Swaine & Wood, 1941; law clk. to Justice Murphy, Supreme Ct. U.S., 1941-43; asso. firm Wilmer & Broun, 1946-48, partner, 1949-62; partner firm Wilmer, Cutler & Pickering, 1962-79, Wilmer & Pickering, 1979—; vis. lectr. U. Va. Law Sch., 1958; mem. com. visitors U. Mich. Law Sch., 1962-68, chmn. devel. com., 1973—; chmn. adv. com. on procedures U.S. Ct. Appeals for D.C. Circuit, 1976—; bd. govs. D.C. Bar, 1975-78, pres. 1979-80. Served to lt. comdr. USNR, 1943-46. Mem. Am., D.C. bar assns., Am. Law Inst., Barristers Washington, Order of Coif, Phi Beta Kappa, Phi Kappa Phi. Democrat. Mem. United Ch. Christ. Clubs: Lawyers, Metropolitan, Chevy Chase, Internat.; Wianno (Mass.). Home: 4708 Jamestown Rd Washington DC 20016 Office: 1666 K St NW Washington DC 20006

PICKERING, JOHN MAYLIN, editor; b. Phila., Apr. 25, 1916; s. Maylin Joseph and Nelle Audrey (Pontz) P.; A.B., Washington U., St. Louis, 1938; M.B.A., Harvard U., 1943; m. Gudrun Gisela Rest, Mar. 22, 1952; children—David Maylin, Philip Rest. Writer, book salesman, 1947-52; sr. editor Rinehart & Co., N.Y.C., 1952-60; sr. editor Holt, Rinehart & Winston, N.Y.C., 1960-65; v.p. Chandler Pub. Co., San Francisco, 1965-70; sr. editor Intext Ednl. Pubs., Scranton, Pa. and N.Y.C., 1970-73; editorial dir. Pa. State U. Press, University Park, 1973—. Edn. chmn. Urban League of Bergen County, N.J., 1963-65; sec. Marin County (Calif.) Joint Peace Council, 1967-68. Bd. mem. Lackawanna County (Pa.) Citizens for McGovern, 1972. Served to capt. AUS, 1943-46; PTO. Decorated Army Commendation medal; recipient Tom Paine award Nat. Emergency Civil Liberties Com., 1958. Mem. Abington Players, Waverly, Pa., Omicron Delta Kappa. Episcopalian. Club: Pa. State U. Faculty. Editor: Rinehart Edits. series, 1952-60, Henry Holt Edits. in Psychology, 1964-65, Chandler Edits. in Drama, 1965-70, Pennsylvania State Bicentennial Book, 1976. Home: 1000 Plaza Dr State College PA 16801 Office: 215 Wagner Bldg University Park PA 16802. *Communication is the nervous system of the democratic body politic. Vocationally, as a book editor, my goal is to help authors in communicating their ideas and emotions with maximum effectiveness. Avocationally, as a citizen, my concern is to protect our first amendment rights of free association and expression.*

PICKERING, THOMAS REEVE, diplomat; b. Orange, N.J., Nov. 5, 1931; s. Hamilton R. and Sarah C. (Chasteney) P.; A.B., Bowdoin Coll., 1953; M.A., Fletcher Sch. Law and Diplomacy, 1954, U. Melbourne (Australia), 1956; m. Alice J. Stover, Nov. 24, 1955; children—Timothy R., Margaret S. Joined U.S. Fgn. Service, 1959; fgn. affairs officer ACDA, 1961; polit. adviser U.S. delegation 18 Nation Disarmament Conf., Geneva, Switzerland, 1962-64; consul, Zanzibar, 1965-67; counselor of embassy, dep. chief mission Am. embassy, Dar es Salaam, Tanzania, 1967-69; dep. dir. Bur. Politico-Mil. Affairs, State Dept., 1969-73; spl. asst. to Sec. of State, exec. sec. Dept. of State, 1973-74; ambassador to Jordan, Amman, 1974-78; asst. sec. of state for Bur. Oceans, Internat. Environ. and Sci. Affairs, Washington, 1978—. Served to lt. comdr. USNR, 1956-59. Mem. Council Fgn. Relations, Internat. Inst. Strategic Studies, Phi Beta Kappa. Address: OES Room 7831 Dept State Washington DC 20520

PICKERING, WILLIAM HAYWARD, educator, scientist; b. Wellington, N.Z., Dec. 24, 1910; s. Albert William and Elizabeth (Hayward) P.; B.S., Calif. Inst. Tech., 1932, M.S., 1933, Ph.D. in Physics, 1936; hon. degrees Clark U., 1966, Occidental Coll., 1966, U. Bologna, 1974; m. Muriel Bowler, Dec. 30, 1932; children—William B., Anne E. Mem. Cosmic Ray Expdn. to India, 1939, Mexico, 1941; faculty Calif. Inst. Tech., 1940—, prof. elec. engring., 1946—, dir. jet propulsion lab., 1954-76. Mem. sci. adv. bd. USAF, 1945-48; chmn. panel on test range instrumentation Research and Devel. Bd., 1948-49; mem. U.S. nat. com. tech. panel Earth Satellite Program, 1955-60; mem. Army Sci. Adv. Panel, 1960-64. Decorated Order of Merit (Italy); knight comdr. Order Brit. Empire; recipient James Wyld Meml. award Am. Rocket Soc., 1957; Columbus medal Genoa, 1964; Prix Galabert for Astronautics, Goddard award Nat. Space Club, 1965; NASA Distinguished Service medal, 1965; Army Distinguished Civilian Service award, 1959, Spirit of St. Louis medal, 1965; Crozier medal Am. Ordnance Assn., 1965; Man of Year award Indsl. Research Inst., 1968; Interprofl. Coop. award Soc. Mfg. Engrs., 1970; Marconi medal Marconi Found., 1974; Nat. Medal of Sci., 1976; Fahrney medal Franklin Inst., 1976; award of merit Am. Cons. Engrs. Council, 1976. Fellow Am. Inst. Aeros. and Astronautics (pres. 1963, Louis W. Hill Transp. award 1968), Am. Acad. Arts and Sci.; mem. AAAS, Nat. Acad. Scis., IEEE (Edison medal 1972), Am. Geophys. Union, Internat. Astronautical Fedn. (pres. 1965-66), Royal Soc. N.Z., Nat. Acad. Engring., AAUP. Home: 292 St Katherine Dr Flintridge CA 91011

PICKETT, BETTY HORENSTEIN, psychologist; b. Providence, R.I., Feb. 15, 1926; d. Isadore Samuel and Etta Lillian (Morrison) Horenstein; A.B. magna cum laude, Brown U., 1945, Sc.M., 1947, Ph.D., 1949; m. James McPherson Pickett, Mar. 10, 1952. Asst. prof. psychology U. Minn., Duluth, 1949-51; asst. prof. U. Nebr., 1951; lectr. U. Conn., 1952; profl. asso. psychol. scis. Bio-Scis. Info. Exchange, Smithsonian Instn., Washington, 1953-58; exec. sec. behavioral scis. study sect. exptl. psychology study sect. div. research grants, NIH, Washington, 1958-61; research cons. to mental health unit HEW, Boston, 1962-63; exec. sec. research career program NIMH, 1963-66, chief cognition and learning sect. div. extramural research program, 1966-68, dep. dir., 1968-74, dir. div. spl. mental health programs, 1974-75, acting dir. div. extramural research program, 1975-77, asso. dir. for extramural and collaborative research program Nat. Inst. Aging, 1977-79; dep. dir. Nat. Inst. Child Health and Human Devel., Bethesda, Md., 1979—; mem. health scientist adminstr. panel Civil Service Commn. Bd. Examiners, 1970-76. Mem. Am. Psychol. Assn., Eastern Psychol. Assn., Psychonomic Soc., Assn. Women in Sci., AAAS, Soc. Research for Child Devel., Phi Beta Kappa, Sigma Xi. Contbr. articles to profl. jours. Home: 2561 Waterside Dr NW Washington DC 20008 Office: Bldg 31 Rm 2A/04 Bethesda MD 20205

PICKETT, GEORGE EASTMAN, health and welfare adminstr.; b. Cleve., July 28, 1935; s. Justus C. and Frances (Snyder) P.; B.A., Harvard U., 1957; M.D., C.M., McGill U., Montreal, 1961; M.P.H., U. Mich., 1966; m. Anne Ferrante, Nov. 2, 1960; children—Alan Francis, Stephen Vincent. Dir. chronic disease control State of Nebr., 1962-64; asst. chief spl. project sect., cancer control program USPHS, 1964-65; dir. health City of Detroit and Wayne County, Mich., 1968-70; dir. health and welfare County of San Mateo (Calif.), 1970-77; dir. health State of W.Va., Charleston, 1977—; clin. prof. W.Va. U. Sch. Medicine and Marshall U. Sch. Medicine; mem. Milbank Commn. Study Higher Edn. in Pub. Health. Epidemiology tng. grantee U. Mich., 1965-66. Fellow Am. Coll. Preventive Medicine, Royal Soc. Health (hon.), Am. Pub. Health Assn. (past pres.); mem. Nat. Assn. County Health Officers (dir.), Delta Omega. Democrat. Co-author: Hanlon's Public Health Administration and Practice, 7th edit., 1979; contbr. articles to profl. jours. Address: 1549 Virginia St E Charlston WV 25311

PICKETT, GEORGE EDWARD, assn. exec., former army officer; b. Palestine, Tex., May 26, 1918; s. James D. and Helen (Mackey) P.; B.S., U.S. Mil. Acad., 1939; grad. Armed Forces Staff Coll., 1951, Nat. War Coll., 1957, Advanced Mgmt. Program, Harvard, 1961; m. Jane M. Stanton, June 14, 1939; children—George Edward, Jane Gray, Thomas D'Aubigne, Sharon Stanton. Commd. 2d lt. U.S. Army, 1939, advanced through grades to lt. gen., 1972; signal officer 1st Signal Co., 1st Inf. Div., Ft. Monmouth, N.J., 1939-42; div. signal officer 1st Inf. Div., North Africa and ETO campaigns, 1942-46; staff officer G-3 sect., Army Ground Forces, Ft. Monroe, Va., 1946-49; chief signal corps. career mgmt. br. Office Chief Signal Officer, U.S. Army, 1949-51; plans officer, plans office Office Asst. Chief Staff Logistics, Dept. Army, 1951-52; exec. officer Office Undersec. Army, 1952-56; asst. chief staff, J-5, also chief signal officer U.S. Taiwan Def. Command/Mil. Assistance Adv. Group, Taiwan, 1957-59; signal officer U.S. Army Ordnance Missile Command, Redstone Arsenal, Ala., 1959-62, Hdqrs. 8th Army, Korea, 1962-63; chief combat support div., also dir. officer personnel Office Personnel, Dept. Army, 1963-65; dep. dir. def. communications system Def. Communications Agy., Washington, 1965-67, vice dir. agy., 1967-68; asst. chief staff for communications-electronics Dept. Army, Washington, 1968-72; dep. asst. sec. def. mgmt. Office Telecommunications, 1972-74, ret., 1974; exec. v.p. Armed Forces Communications and Electronics Assn., 1974-76, U.S. Ind. Telephone Assn., 1977—. Decorated D.S.M., Silver Star, Legion of Merit, Bronze Star with V device; Croix de Guerre, Fourragere (France); War cross (Czechoslavakia); Fourragere (Belgium). Mem. Soc. 1st Inf. Div. (pres. D.C. chpt. 1962-63), Assn. U.S. Army, Nat. War Coll. Alumni Assn. (v.p. 1965-66), Clubs: Army-Navy Country (Arlington, Va.); International (Washington). Home: PO Box 3221 Alexandria VA 22302

PICKETT, LAWRENCE KIMBALL, physician, educator; b. Balt., Nov. 10, 1919; s. Herbert E. and Emily (Ames) P.; B.A., Yale U., 1941, M.D., 1944; m. Pauline Ferguson, Dec. 17, 1943; children—Lawrence Kimball, Nancy Lee, Paul F., Stephen B. Intern Peter Bent Brigham Hosp., Boston, 1945-46; resident surgery Boston Childrens Hosp., 1959-60; practice medicine specializing in pediatrics and surgery, Syracuse, N.Y., 1950-64, New Haven, 1964—; clin. asso. prof. surgery Upstate Med. Center, 1953-64; prof. surgery and pediatrics Yale U. Sch. Medicine, 1964—, asso. dean, 1973—; chief of staff Yale-New Haven Hosp., 1973—. Served to capt. M.C., AUS, 1951-53. Fellow A.C.S., Am. Acad. Pediatrics (past sect. chmn.); mem. Am. Surg. Assn. Mem. United Ch. of Christ. Home: 205 Blake Rd Hamden CT 06517 Office: 789 Howard Ave New Haven CT 06504

PICKETT, MORRIS JOHN, bacteriologist; b. Beloit, Kans., Dec. 3, 1915; s. John A. and Mabel A. (Hall) P.; A.A., U. Chgo., 1936; B.A., Stanford, 1938, Ph.D., 1942; m. Marion Maurice Newcombe, Mar. 21, 1946; children—Linda N., David H., Charles H., Roger E. Faculty U. Calif. at Los Angeles, 1947—, prof., 1957—, acting chmn. bacteriology, 1957-59. Cons., Olive View Hosp., 1963-71, Space Gen. Corp., 1963-65; sci. adviser FDA, 1971—; mem. sci. adv. bd. Nat. Center Toxicol. Research, 1978—. Mem. Am. Soc. Microbiology, N.Y. Acad. Scis., Soc. Gen. Microbiology, Am. Acad. Microbiology, Sigma Xi. Author: (with C.R. Manclark and H.B. Moore) Laboratory Manual for Medical Bacteriology, 1972; adv. editor Lab. World, 1961-78, Jour. Infectious Diseases, 1964-67; contbr. numerous articles to profl. jours. Developed, improved procedures for med. bacteriology; research on immunity to undulant fever and other chronic diseases. Office: Dept Microbiology U Calif at Los Angeles 5304 Life Scis Bldg Los Angeles CA 90024

PICKETT, WILLIAM STEPHEN, automotive co. exec.; b. Toledo, Apr. 1, 1920; s. Clarence and Myra P.; student U. Toledo, 1938-42; B.B.A., U. Tex., 1942, B.M.E., 1943; m. Marian Cannan, Aug. 14, 1949; children—Stephen, Michael, Anna. Asst. to pres. Willys Overland Co., Toledo, 1946-49, sales mgr., 1949-50, v.p. def. prodn., 1950-53; v.p. Internat. Kaiser Jeep Co., Toledo, 1953-60; v.p. Internat. Am. Motors Corp., Detroit, 1960-67, v.p. sales Am. Motors Corp., 1967-71, pres., gen. mgr. Am. Motors (Can.) Ltd., Brampton, Ont., 1971—. Home: 1300 Bloor St Suite 307 Mississauga ON L4Y 3Z2 Canada Office: 350 Kennedy Rd S Brampton ON L6V 2M3 Canada

PICKHARDT, CARL EMILE, JR., artist; b. Westwood, Mass., May 28, 1908; s. Carl Emile and Louise (Fowler) P.; B.A., Harvard U., 1931; studied with Harold Zimmerman, 1931-37; m. Marjorie Sachs, June 15, 1935 (div. 1952); children—Nancy Louise (Mrs. Paul Narkiewicz), Carl Emile III, Sally Anne; m. 2d, Rosamond Forbes Wyman, Mar. 28, 1953. Tchr., Fitchburg Art Mus., 1951-62, Worcester Mus. Sch., 1949-50, Sturbridge Art Sch., 1952-60; one-man shows: Berkshire Art Mus., 1941, Doris Meltzer Gallery, N.Y.C., 1961, 68, 70, 71, 72, Jacques Seligmann Gallery, N.Y.C., 1935, 51, 52, 54, Stuart Gallery, Boston, 1946, Margaret Brown Gallery, Boston, 1951, Fitchburg Art Mus., 1951, Lawrence Gallery, Kansas City, Mo., 1955, Artek Gallery, Helsinki, Finland, 1959, Laguna Gloria Art Mus., Austin, Tex., 1966; exhibited in group shows at Carnegie Internat., 1951, Mus. Modern Art, N.Y.C., 1940, 63, 64, Whitney Mus., 1936, Nat. Acad., 1942, 49, Internat. Biennial of Color Lithography Ill. Show, 1951, Boston Inst. Contemporary Art, 1941, Internat. Exhbn., Japan. 1952, Exhbn. Am. Drawings, France, 1955, Art Inst. Chgo., Calif. Palace of Legion of Honor, 1953, Boston Arts Festival, 1950, Am. Drawing Biennial, Norfolk, 1964, Pa. Acad. Fine Arts, 1968, Laguna Gloria Art Mus., 1973, Fitchburg Art Mus., 1974; represented in permanent collections Mus. Modern Art N.Y.C., Boston Mus. Fine Arts, Bklyn. Art Mus., Worcester Art Mus., Library of Congress, N.Y. Pub. Library, Newark Art Mus., Fogg Art Mus., Addison Gallery, Finch Coll. Art Mus., Fitchburg Art Mus., Wadsworth Athenaeum, De Cordova Mus. Served with USNR, 1942-45. Ford Found. and Am. Fedn. Arts artist-in-residence Laguna Gloria Art Mus., 1966. Recipient Shope prize Nat. Acad., 1942. Author: Portfolio of Etchings, 1942. Address: 66 Forest St Sherborn MA 01770. *My life-long purpose has been to create in visual images a new language and to express order in asymetrical terms. My life-long purpose has been to create in visual images a new language and to express order in assymmetrical terms.*

PICKHOLZ, JEROME WALTER, advt. agy. exec.; b. N.Y.C., Sept. 11, 1932; s. Solomon and Miriam (Schussler) P.; B.B.A., CCNY, 1953; m. Phyllis Plump, July 11, 1954; children—Keith, Michelle. Sr. accountant Eisner & Lubin, C.P.A.'s, 1957-60; controller Hodes-Daniel Co., Elmsford, N.Y., 1960-65, v.p., 1965-70, pres., mgr. direct mail ops. Cordura Corp. div. Hodes Daniel Co., Elmsford, 1970-74; exec. v.p. Ogilvy & Mather Direct Response, Inc., N.Y.C., 1974-77, pres., 1978—; sr. v.p., treas. Ogilvy & Mather Inc., N.Y.C., 1978. Served with USN, 1953-56. C.P.A., N.Y. Mem. N.Y. State Soc. C.P.A.'s, Direct Mail/Mktg. Assn. Home: 39 Annandale Dr Chappaqua NY 10514 Office: 675 3d Ave New York NY 10017

PICKLE, J.J., congressman; b. Roscoe, Tex., Oct. 11, 1913; s. J.B. and Mary Pickle; B.A., U. Tex.; m. Beryl Bolton McCarroll; children—Mrs. James Norris, Dick McCarroll, Graham McCarroll. Area dir. Nat. Youth Adminstrn., 1938-41; co-organizer Radio Sta. KVET, Austin; later entered pub. relations, advt. bus.; mem. 88th-96th congresses from 10th Dist. Tex.; mem. Ways and Means Com., chmn. subcom. social security; dir. Tex. Democratic Exec. Com., 1957-61; mem. Tex. Employment Commn., 1961-63. Address: 242 House Office Bldg Washington DC 20515

PICKLE, ROBERT DOUGLAS, lawyer, diversified industry exec.; b. Knoxville, Tenn., May 22, 1937; s. Robert Lee and Beatrice Jewel (Douglas) P.; A.A., Schreiner Mil. Inst., Kerrville, Tex., 1957; B.S. in Bus. Adminstrn., U. Tenn., Knoxville, 1959, J.D., 1961; honor grad. seminar Nat. Def. U., 1979; m. Rosemary Elaine Noser, May 9, 1964. Admitted to Tenn. bar, 1961, Mo. bar, 1964, U.S. Ct. Mil. Appeals bar, 1962, U.S. Supreme Ct., 1970; atty. Brown Shoe Co., Inc., St. Louis, 1963-69, asst. sec., atty., 1969-74; sec., gen. counsel Brown Group, Inc., St. Louis, 1974—. Provisional judge Municipal Ct., Clayton, Mo., summer 1972; chmn. Clayton Region attys. sect., profl. div. United Fund Greater St. Louis Campaign, 1972-73, team capt., 1974—. Served to lt. col. JAG Corps, U.S. Army, 1961-63. Mem. Am., Tenn., Mo., St. Louis County bar assns., Bar Assn. Met. St. Louis, St. Louis Bar Found. (dir. 1979—), Am. Soc. Corp. Secs. (treas. St. Louis regional group 1976-77, sec. 1977-78, v.p. 1978-79, pres. 1979-80), U. Tenn. Gen. Alumni Assn. (pres., dir. St. Louis chpt. 1974-76), U.S. Trademark Assn. (dir. 1978—), Tenn. Soc. St. Louis, Scabbard and Blade, Kappa Sigma, Phi Delta Phi, Phi Theta Kappa, Beta Gamma Sigma, Phi Kappa Phi. Republican. Presbyn. Club: University (dir. 1976—, v.p. 1976-77, sec. 1977—) (St. Louis). Home: 214 Topton Way Saint Louis MO 63105 Office: 8400 Maryland Ave Saint Louis MO 63105

PICKRAL, GEORGE MONROE, educator; b. Gretna, Va., Jan. 2, 1922; s. George Monroe and Elizabeth (Gay) P.; B.S., Va. Mil. Inst., 1943; M.A., Miami U., Oxford, O., 1950; Ph.D., U. Cin., 1953; m. Edna Moore McCormick, Mar. 10, 1945; children—James C., Robert M., Thomas M., Janet G., Elizabeth A. Faculty, Va. Mil. Inst., 1946-49, 53—, prof. chemistry, 1960—. Active local Boy Scouts Am., Little League Baseball. Served to 1st lt. USMCR, 1943-46. Mem. Am. Chem. Soc. (chmn. Va. Blue Ridge sect. 1971), Va. Acad. Scis., Sigma Xi, Phi Lambda Upsilon. Kiwanian. Home: 501 Brooke Lane Lexington VA 24450

PICKREL, PAUL, educator; b. Gilson, Ill., Feb. 2, 1917; s. Clayton and Inez (Murphy) P.; A.B., Knox Coll., 1938; M.A., Yale, 1942, Ph.D., 1944. Instr. English, Lafayette Coll., 1941-42; instr. Yale, 1943-45, asst. prof., 1945-50, lectr. English, 1954-66, chmn. Scholar of House Program, 1959-60, 61-66, fellow Morse Coll., 1962-66, adviser John Hay fellows, 1959-66; vis. prof. English, Smith Coll., Northampton, Mass., 1966-67, prof., 1967—, chmn. dept., 1972-75. Mem. Aurelian Honor Soc., Phi Beta Kappa. Clubs: Elizabethan, Faculty (Northampton). Author: (novel) The Moving Stairs, 1948; also essays on fiction, numerous book revs. Mng. editor Yale Rev., 1949-66; chief book critic Harper's mag., 1954-65. Office: Wright Hall Smith Coll Northampton MA 01060

PICKRELL, KENNETH LEROY, plastic surgeon; b. Old Forge, Pa., June 6, 1910; s. Thomas and Anna May (Williams) P.; B.S., Franklin and Marshall Coll., 1931; M.D., Johns Hopkins, 1935; m. Katharine Council, June 11, 1935; children—Judith, Katharine Lee, Anna May, Elizabeth. Fellow surgery Johns Hopkins Hosp., 1935-36, instr. pathology, instr. neurosurgery, instr. plastic surgery, instr. gen. surgery, asso. surgery, 1936-44; asst. prof. plastic surgery Duke Sch. Medicine and Hosp., 1944-46, asso. prof. plastic surgery, 1946-50, prof. plastic and reconstructive surgery, 1950—; cons. plastic surgeon VA hosps., Durham, Fayetteville, N.C., Womack Army Hosp., Fort Bragg, N.C. Diplomate Am. Bd. Plastic Surgery (chmn. 1962-63), Am. Bd. Surgery. Fellow A.C.S., So. Surg. Assn.; mem. Soc. U. Surgeons, Soc. U. Profs., Am. Soc. Surgery of Hand, Am. Soc. Plastic and Reconstructive Surgery (pres. 1960), Am. Assn. Plastic Surgeons, Am. Surg. Assn., Internat. Soc. Surgery, Japanese Soc. Plastic Surgeons. Contbr. sect. Sabiston's Textbook of Surgery, 1977; also numerous articles to surg. jours., chpts. to books. Home: 3 Sylvan Rd Durham NC 27701 Office: Duke U Hosp Durham NC 27710

PICKUS, ALBERT MAURICE, motion picture theatre owner; b. New Haven, Mar. 20, 1903; s. Jacob David and Rose (White) P.; B.S., Washington and Lee U., 1924; m. Lelia Victoria Elliott, Dec. 21, 1939; children—Lois Francine (Mrs. E. Harrison), Reyna Sue (Mrs. Richard Hassell), Ross Gary, Addie Lee. Engaged in motion picture exhbns., 1925—; accountant, auditor Albert M. Pickus, New Haven, 1925-40; pres. Stratford Theatre, Inc. (Conn.), 1926—, chmn. bd., 1961—; pres. Whippoorwill Crest Co., real estate, Stratford, 1947—; builder, owner Colonial Sq. Shopping Center, Stratford. Mem. Theatre Owners Am.,

1948—, v.p., 1953-57, asst. to pres., 1957-58, pres., 1959-61, chmn. bd., 1961-63; mem. exec. com. Council Motion Picture Orgns., 1957-61. Bd. dirs. Motion Picture Owners Conn. Dir. Civil Def., Stratford, 1950-77; chmn. Stratford War Finance Com., 1944-48, Conn. Brotherhood Week, 1949, Stratford Econ. Devel. Commn., 1970-73; pres. Sterling House Community Center, Stratford, 1950-52; Past chmn., now bd. dirs. local A.R.C., Community Chest, Cerebral Palsy Assn.; bd. dirs. Will Rogers Meml. Hosp., Saranac Lake, N.Y., Fairfield County Symphony. Named Man of Year, Stratford V.F.W., 1950; recipient Distinguished service award Treasury Dept., 1943; Golden Deeds award Stratford Exchange Club, 1950; Citizen's award Stratford Police Dept., 1976; Golden Crown award Stratford Oldtimers Athletic Assn., 1977; named Man of Year, Stratford Civitan Club, 1973. Republican. Clubs: Mill River Country, Cupheag (pres. Stratford 1945-46), Masons, Oddfellow. Home: Whippoorwill Ln Stratford CT 06497 Office: 2424 Main St Stratford CT 06497

PICO, RAFAEL, geographer; b. Coamo, P.R., Dec. 29, 1912; s. Arturo and Maria Teresa (Santiago) P.; A.B. with high honors, U. P.R., 1932; A.M., Clark U. Sch. Geography, 1934, Ph.D., 1938, LL.D., 1962; LL.D., Eastern Mich. U., 1962; Litt.D., Cath. U. P.R., 1966; m. Maria Teresa Vidal, Feb. 12, 1938; children—Maria Teresa, Isabel Victoria. Instr. geography U. P.R., 1934-38, asso. prof., 1940-42, prof., 1943-50, prof. ad honorem, 1950—. Vis. instr. geography Northwestern U., summer 1938; on leave as instr., asst. prof. geography Cath. U. Am., 1938-40; cons. geographer P.R. Reconstrn. Adminstrn., 1935-36; cons. U.S. Census Bur., Washington, 1939-40; chmn. P.R. Planning Bd., 1942-55; sec. treasury P.R., 1955-58; mem. gov. bd. Land Authority P.R., 1941-42, 58-64; chmn. bd. dirs. Govt. Devel. Bank for P.R., 1953-58, pres., 1958-64; dir. Tropigas Internat. Corp., 1970-74, Grand Union Co., 1973—, Commonwealth Oil Refining Co., 1973—; vice chmn. bd. Banco Popular, San Juan, P.R., 1968-78, dir., 1965—; senator at large, 1964-68. Cons., del. many internat. confs., congresses of govts., socs.; rep. P.R. at 1st West Indian Conf., Barbados, 1944, 2d, St. Thomas, 1946; attended conf. to draft agreement for orgn. Caribbean Commn., Washington, 1947; mem. U.S. delegation 3d extraordinary session Inter-Am. Econ. and Social Council, Caracas, 1953; pres. adv. com. for devel. sci. OAS, 1958; planning adviser Govt. Honduras, 1957, 77, Venezuela, 1958, Colombia, Cuba, 1959; vice chmn. ad hoc adv. group on presdl. vote P.R., 1970-71, mem. adv. council financial aid to students HEW, 1973-75. Trustee, treas. Inst. Social Tech., 1970-74; trustee Cath. U. P.R. Fellow Am. Geog. Soc.; mem. Assn. Am. Geographers, Am. Soc. Planning Ofcls. (pres. 1949-51), Am. Inst. Planners, Am. Soc. Pub. Adminstrn. (pres. P.R. chpt. 1956-57), Municipal Finance Officers Assn. (chmn. P.R. 1956-58), Inter-Am, Planning Soc. (pres. 1956-60), P.R. Bankers Assn. (pres. 1972). Popular Democrat. Roman Catholic. Author, co-author books on P.R.; lectr. Home: Box 1028 Hato Rey PR 00919. *Public service and assistance to my fellow men have been the highest goals of my life. Essential to my devotion to public service have been absolute honesty and selflessness as well as hard work.*

PICON, LEON, ret. diplomat; b. Reading, Pa., Aug. 16, 1917; s. Simon and Edith (Schwartzberg) P.; A.B., Bklyn. Coll., 1938; postgrad. Dropsie Coll. for Hebrew and Cognate Learning, 1938-41, Ph.D., 1952; m. Elizabeth Lucy Long, Sept. 11, 1944; children—Ellen (Mrs. Thomas E. Tucker), Louise (Mrs. Masaharu Shimizu), William J. Tchr., Pa. Instn. Instrn. Blind, 1938-39; counselor Foster Home, Phila., 1939-41; analyst Def. Dept., 1946-48; research analyst State Dept., 1949-52; with Am. embassy, London, Eng., 1952-54; with USIA, 1954—; cultural officer Am. embassy, Tokyo, 1955-65; spl. asst. cultural affairs Dept. State, 1965-69; cultural attache Am. embassy, Ankara, Turkey, 1969-72; dir. overseas speakers div. USIA, 1972-—. Mem., treas. Commn. Ednl. Exchange Between U.S. and Turkey; mem. numerous spl. task forces in govt. Served with AUS, 1942-46. Recipient Meritorious Service award Fgn. Service, 1961, 72. Author: A Linguistic Analysis of the Sinuhe Romance, 1952. Translator from Japanese: Rediscovery (Kawabata); The Counterfeiter and Other Stories (Inoue), 1964. Home: 10318 Fleming Ave Bethesda MD 20014

PICOT, JULES JEAN CHARLES, educator; b. Edmundston, N.B., Can., July 23, 1932; s. J. Ernest and Marie Blanche (Lebel) P.; B.E., N.S. Tech. Coll., Halifax, 1955; M.S., Mass. Inst. Tech., 1957; Ph.D., U. Minn., 1966; m. Mary Carol Creaghan, Aug. 25, 1956; children—Mary Nicole, Andre Joseph. Control engr. Consol. Bathurst Mills (N.B.), 1955-59; asst. prof., asso. prof., prof. U. N.B., Fredericton, 1959—, chmn. dept. chem. engring., 1970-76; vis. prof., Poitiers, France, 1974; research asst. U. Minn., 1963-66. Mem. asso. com. on heat transfer NRC of Can., 1969-71, mem. grants selection com. for chem. and metall. engrs., 1970-73; mem. selection com. scholarships Can. Council, 1970-72. Fellow Chem. Inst. Can.; mem. Can. Soc. Chem. Engrs., Assn. Profl. Engrs. N.B. Contbr. articles profl. jours. Home: 29 Simcoe Ct Fredericton NB Canada

PICOTT, JOHN RUPERT, assn. exec.; b. Suffolk, Va., Aug. 25, 1916; s. William C. and Mary V. (White) P.; B.A., Va. Union U., 1938, Pd.D., 1950; M.Ed., Temple U., 1940; LL.D., Va. State Coll., 1960; D.H.L., Va. Sem. and Coll., 1972; m. Altia Hodges, June 19, 1937; children—John Rupert, Hodges. Exec. sec. Va. Tchrs. Assn., 1944-66; asst. dir. membership N.E.A., 1967—; exec. dir. Assn. Study Afro-Am. Life and History, Washington, 1972—. Del., White House Confs. on Children, 1955, 60, 65, White House Conf. on Youth, 1970. Pres. Va. Statewide Independent Voters League, 1965-70. Chmn. bd. mgmt. Leigh St. YMCA, Richmond, Va., 1965-67; state treas. Richmond br. Va. Council on Human Relations; bd. dirs. Richmond Urban League, 1960-66, Richmond Friends Assn. for Children, 1958-67; bd. visitors Mary Washington Coll., 1975—. Mem. NEA (v.p. 1955-56), Am. Tchrs. Assn. (pres. 1963-64), Assn. Study Negro Life and History (pres. 1967-70), Nat. Council State Tchrs. Assn. (chmn. 1957-63), Fed. Schoolmens Club, Alpha Phi Alpha, Alpha Beta Boule, Sigma Pi Phi. Editor: Negro History Bull., 1972—. Home: Waterside Towers Apt 811-C 907 6th St SW Washington DC 20024 Office: 1401 14th St NW Washington DC 20005

PIDGEON, JOHN ANDERSON, headmaster; b. Lawrence, Mass., Dec. 20, 1924; s. Alfred H. and Nora (Regan) P.; grad. Hebron Acad., 1943; B.A., Bowdoin Coll., 1949; Ed.D., Bethany Coll., 1973; D.Litt., Washington and Jefferson Coll., 1979; m. Judith Shepar, Aug. 4, 1951; children—John Anderson, Regan S., Kelly. Instr. Latin, adminstrv. asst. to headmaster Deerfield Acad., 1949-57; headmaster Kiskiminetas Springs Sch., Saltsburg, Pa., 1957—; dir. Saltburg Savs. & Trust. Served as ensign USNR, 1943-46. Mem. New Eng. Swimming Coaches Assn. (pres. 1956-57), Cum Laude Soc., Delta Upsilon. Home: Kiskiminetas Springs School Saltsburg PA 15681

PIEDMONT, EUGENE BERNARD, sociologist, univ. dean; b. Holley, N.Y., June 29, 1932; s. John Leonard and Mary (Yoffredo) P.; B.S. summa cum laude, SUNY, Buffalo, 1956; M.A., U. Rochester, 1959; Ph.D. (Roswell Park Meml. Inst. fellow 1959, NIMH fellow 1960-62), U. Buffalo, 1962; m. Joan Kathryn Leonard, Sept. 26, 1952; children—Robert Eugene, Brian Scott, Steven Leonard, Nancy Jane, Donald James. Instr. sociology U. Buffalo, 1958-62; asst. prof. sociology, dept. psychiatry SUNY at Buffalo, 1962-63; asst. prof. dept. neurology and psychiatry, lectr. sociology U. Va., 1963-64; NIMH postdoctoral fellow, research asso. Washington U., St. Louis, 1964-65; asst. to prof. sociology U. Mass., 1965—, asso. grad. dean, 1972-76, acting dean Grad. Sch., 1977—; chmn. grad. adv. com. Mass. Bd. Higher Edn., 1973—; cons. USPHS health care tech. study sect. Nat. Center for Health Services Research and Devel., 1971-76. Vestryman, Grace Episcopal Ch., 1972—; charter mem. Community Mental Health and Retardation Bd. Greater Hampshire-Franklin Area, 1967-70; research dir. Franklin County Pub. Hosp., 1968-69; mem. Woodrow Wilson Nat. Fellowship Found. Selection Com. for Eastern U.S. and Can., 1968-69; founder Valley Health Plan, 1976; pres. New Eng. Council on Grad Edn., 1977—; troop chmn., instl. rep. Boy Scouts Am., 1969-76; bd. dirs. Valley Light Opera. Fellow Am. Sociol. Assn.; mem. AAUP, AAAS. Home: 36 King Philip Ave South Deerfield MA 01373 Office: U Mass Grad Sch Amherst MA 01003

PIEL, GERARD, editor, publisher; b. Woodmere, L.I., N.Y., Mar. 1, 1915; s. William F.J. and Loretto (Scott) P.; A.B. magna cum laude, Harvard U., 1937; D.Sc., Lawrence Coll., 1956, Colby Coll., 1960, U. B.C., Brandeis U., 1965, Lebanon Valley Coll., 1977, L.I. U., 1978, Bard Coll., 1979, City U. N.Y., 1979; Litt.D., Rutgers U., 1961, Bates Coll., 1974; L.H.D., Columbia, 1962, Williams Coll., 1966, Rush U., 1979; LL.D., Tuskegee Inst., 1963, U. Bridgeport, 1964, Bklyn. Poly. Inst., 1965, Carnegie-Mellon U., 1968; m. Mary Tapp Bird, Feb. 4, 1938; children—Jonathan Bird, Samuel Bird (dec.); m. 2d, Eleanor Virden Jackson, June 24, 1955; 1 dau., Eleanor Jackson. Sci. editor Life mag., 1938-44; asst. to pres. Henry J. Kaiser Co. (and asso. cos.), 1945-46; organizer (with Dennis Flanagan, Donald H. Miller, Jr.), pres. Sci. Am., Inc., 1946—; pub. mag. Sci. Am., 1947—. Chmn., Commn. Delivery Personal Health Services City N.Y., 1967-68. Trustee Am. Mus. Nat. History, Radcliffe Coll., Phillips Acad., N.Y. Bot. Garden, N.Y. U., Henry J. Kaiser Family Found., Mayo Found.; chmn. trustees Found. for Child Devel.; bd. overseers Harvard U., 1966-68, 73-79. Recipient George Polk award, 1961, Kalinga prize, 1962, Bradford Washburn award, 1966, Arches of Sci. award, 1969, Rosenberger medal U. Chgo., 1973; named Pub. of Yr., Mag. Pubs. Assn., 1980. Fellow Am. Acad. Arts and Scis.; mem. Council Fgn. Relations, Am. Philos. Soc., Nat. Acad. Scis. Inst. Medicine, Phi Beta Kappa, Sigma Xi. Clubs: Harvard, Century, Coffee House (N.Y.C.); Cosmos (Washington); Somerset (Boston); Duquesne (Pitts.). Author: Science in the Cause of Man, 1961; The Acceleration of History, 1972. Home: 320 Central Park W New York NY 10025 Office: 415 Madison Ave New York NY 10017

PIEL, WILLIAM, JR., lawyer; b. N.Y.C., Nov. 28, 1909; s. William Loretto (Scott) P.; A.B., Princeton U., 1932; LL.B., Harvard U., 1935; m. Eleanor Green, Dec. 1, 1951; children by former marriage—Michael, Anthony, Thomas. Admitted to N.Y. bar, 1935, practiced in N.Y.C.; partner firm Sullivan & Cromwell, 1945—; expert cons. mil. intelligence service War Dept. Gen. Staff, 1944-45; dir. Am. Re-Ins. Co., Campbell Soup Co., Phillips Petroleum Co. Mem. adv. council Romance lang. Princeton U. Fellow Am. Coll. Trial Lawyers, N.Y. State Bar Found.; mem. Am. Judicature Soc., Am. Bar Assn., Bar Assn. City N.Y. (chmn. judiciary com.), N.Y. County Lawyers Assn. Clubs: Century Assn., Down Town Assn., Coffee House, Princeton (N.Y.C.), Squadron A Assn. Home: 248 W 11th St New York City NY 10014 also Tree House Briggs Hill Rd Sherman CT 06784 Office: 125 Broad St New York NY 10004

PIELOU, EVELYN C., educator; b. Eng.; B.Sc., U. London, 1950, Ph.D., 1962, D.Sc., 1975; m. Patrick Pielou, June 22, 1944; three children. Research scientist Canadian Govt., 1963-67; vis. prof. N.C. State U., 1968, Yale, New Haven, 1969; prof. biology Queen's U., Kingston, Ont., 1969-71, Dalhousie U., Halifax, N.S., 1971—; vis. prof. U. Sydney (Australia), 1975. Author: Introduction to Mathematical Ecology, 1969; Population and Community Ecology, 1974; Ecological Diversity, 1975; Mathematical Ecology, 1977; Biogeography, 1979; contbr. articles to profl. jours. Home: 6755 Jubilee Rd Halifax NS Canada Office: Biology Dept Dalhousie U Halifax NS Canada

PIENE, OTTO, artist, educator; b. Laasphe, Westphalia, Germany, Apr. 18, 1928; s. Otto and Anne (Niemeyer) P.; student Acad. Fine Arts, Munich, Germany, 1949-50, Acad. Fine Arts, Dusseldorf, Germany, 1950-52; Staatsexamen in Philosophy, U. Cologne, Germany, 1957; m. Mira Cantor, July 17, 1976; children—Annette, Herbert, Claudia, Chloe. Co-founder Group Zero, Dusseldorf, Germany, 1957; vis. prof. Grad. Sch. Art, U. Pa., Phila., 1964; prof. environ. art Sch. Architecture and Planning, M.I.T., Cambridge, Mass., 1972—, dir. Center for Advanced Visual Studies, 1974—; vis. artist, guest prof. numerous univs.; one man exhbns. include: Galerie Heseler, Munich, 1971, 72, 75, 77, 78, 79, MIT, 1975, Galerie Schoeller, Düsseldorf, W.Ger., 1977, 79, Fitchburg (Mass.) Art Mus., 1977; numerous group exhbns. U.S. and abroad including Guggenheim Mus., N.Y.C., 1964, 66, Albright-Knox Gallery Buffalo, 1968, Nat. Mus. Modern Art, Tokyo, 1969, Tate Gallery, London, 1974, Smithsonian Instn., Washington, 1978, others; also represented in numerous permanent collections. Recipient award Internat. Exhibition Graphic Art, Ljubljana, Yugoslavia, 1967, 69; prize 8th Internat. Biennial Prints Nat. Mus. Modern Art, Tokyo, Japan, 1972. Mem. Deutscher Kunstlerbund, The Lighter Than Air Soc. Author: (with Heinz Mack) Zero 1, 2, 3, 1958, 61; More Sky, 1970; Rainbows, 1971; Zero, 1973; More Sky, 1973. Home: 1129 Beacon St #4 Brookline MA 02146 Office: 40 Massachusetts Ave Cambridge MA 02139

PIEPER, HEINZ PAUL, educator; b. Wuppertal, W. Ger., Mar. 24, 1920; came to U.S., 1957, naturalized, 1963; s. Heinrich Ludwig and Agnes Marie (Koehler) P.; M.D., U. Munich (Germany), 1948; m. Rose Irmgard Hackl, Apr. 23, 1945. Resident, 2d Med. Clinic, U. Munich, 1948-50, asst. prof. dept. physiology, 1950-57; asst. prof. dept. physiology Coll. Medicine, Ohio State U., Columbus, 1957-60, asso. prof., 1960-68, prof., 1968—, chmn. dept. physiology, 1974—. Mem. Am. Physiol. Soc., German Physiol. Soc., Ohio Acad. Scis., Biophys. Soc., Sigma Xi. Clubs: Columbus Med. Rev., Columbus Maennerchor. Mem. editorial bd. Am. Jour. Physiology, 1973—; contbr. articles on cardiovascular physiology to profl. jours. Home: 1563 Fishinger Rd Columbus OH 43221 Office: Coll Medicine Ohio State U 333 W 10th Ave Columbus OH 43210

PIEPER, JAY BROOKS, brewing co. exec.; b. Atlantic, Iowa, Sept. 11, 1943; s. Elmer Paul and Leona Bertha (Knop) P.; B.A., Cornell Coll., Iowa, 1965; M.B.A., Washington U., St. Louis, 1967; m. Beverly Jeanne Schultz, Aug. 12, 1967; 1 dau., Cynthia. Staff accountant Pabst Brewing Co., Milw., 1967-69, corporate finance mgr., 1969-72, treas., 1972-76, treas., asst. to pres., 1976-79, v.p. corp. devel., treas., 1979—; instr. acctg. and fin. Milw. Tech. Coll., 1967-70. Pres., Luther Meml. Chapel. Mem. Fin. Execs. Inst., Beta Gamma Sigma. Lutheran. Home: 5742 N Bay Ridge Ave Whitefish Bay WI 53217 Office: 917 W Juneau Ave Milwaukee WI 53201

PIEPER, RAYMOND FRANCIS, constrn. co. exec.; b. St. Louis, Mar. 3, 1926; s. Frank Henry and Rose Elizabeth (Wessels) P.; B.S.C.E., Washington U., St. Louis, 1949; m. Elizabeth M. Strubhart, Oct. 14, 1950; children—Joan, Diane, Kathryn, Stephen. With J.S. Alberici Constrn. Co. Inc., St. Louis, 1949—, pres., 1975—, also dir.; dir. Mark Twain Northland Bank; treas., dir. E.B. Jones Constrn. Co. Inc. Served with USN, 1943-46. Mem. ASCE, Nat. Soc. Profl. Engrs. Republican. Roman Catholic. Clubs: Bellerive Country, St. Louis Engrs. Home: 51 Muirfield Ct Saint Louis MO 63141 Office: 2150 Kienlen Ave Saint Louis MO 63121

PIEPER, SAMUEL JOHN LOUIS, JR., psychiatrist; b. Beeville, Tex., Oct. 14, 1931; s. Samuel John Louis and Buelah S.N. (Pullin) P.; student Rice U., 1948-51; M.D. cum laude, Baylor U., 1955; m. Joan Bruce Woods, July 14, 1962; children—Wanda Lynne, Melanie Ruth, Cheryl Yvonne, Karen Lee, John Samuel, David Bernard. Intern, Meth. Hosp., Houston, 1955-56; resident in neurology Baylor U. Hosp., 1958-61, psychiatry Northwestern U., Evanston, Ill., 1966-68; fellow, 1968-69; instr. neurology Baylor U. Coll. Medicine, Houston, 1961-64; dir. med. and neurol. service Big Spring (Tex.) State Hosp., 1964-66; med. dir. Regional Mental Health Center, Oak Ridge, 1969-75; asst. commr. for Mental Health Services Tenn. Dept. Mental Health and Mental Retardation, Nashville, 1975—. Mem. med. adv. bd. Mid-East Tenn. Area, Tenn. Mid-South Regional Med. Program, 1971-73, med. adv. bd. Oak Ridge Nat. Epilepsy Found., 1973, Tenn. Neuropsychiat. Inst., 1975—. Served with USPHS, 1956-58. Diplomate Am. Bd. Psychiatry and Neurology. Mem. Am. Coll. Psychiatry, Am. Acad. Neurology, AMA, Am. Psychiat. Assn., Commd. Officers Assn. USPHS, Alpha Omega Alpha. Office: Tenn Dept Mental Health and Mental Retardation 501 Union Bldg Nashville TN 37219

PIERCE, ALAN KRAFT, physician, educator; b. Houston, Sept. 3, 1931; s. Fred Allan and Esther Beth (Schmidt) P.; student Rice U., 1948-51; M.D., Baylor U., 1955; m. Dorothy Louise Manes, Dec. 23, 1958; children—Katherine Neal, Alan Kent. Intern, Univ. Hosps. of Cleve., 1955-56; resident Parkland Meml. Hosp., Dallas, 1958-61; practice medicine, specializing in pulmonary diseases, Dallas, 1962—; from instr. to prof. U. Tex. Southwestern Med. Sch., Dallas, 1963—. Served to capt. USAF, 1956-58. Fellow A.C.P.; mem. Am. (pres. 1972-73), Tex. (pres. 1969-70) thoracic socs., Am., Central, So. socs. for clin. research, Am. Assn. Physicians. Home: 3537 Vilanova St Dallas TX 75225 Office: 5323 Harry Hines Blvd Dallas TX 75235

PIERCE, BRUCE JOHN, banker, investment exec., cons.; b. Westchester, Pa., Jan. 21, 1938; s. Melvin E. and Sara Elizabeth (Wentzel) P.; B.S. in Econs., U. Pa., 1960; M.B.A., U. Mich., 1963; m. Barbara Ann Woodward, June 25, 1960; children—Lisa Anne, Brian John, Valerie Lee, Andrew MacIntosh. Credit analyst trainee, then sr. credit analyst Nat. Bank Detroit, 1960-64; with Bank of N.Mex., Albuquerque, 1964—, exec. v.p., 1970-71, pres., 1971—, chief exec. officer, 1973-77, also dir.; pres. Bruce J. Pierce & Assos., Inc., 1977—; chmn. bd. Funds Mgmt., Inc., 1978—; gen. partner Rosenwald, Ltd., 1978—; dir. Devel. Credit Corp. Vice chmn. Joint Council Econ. Edn.; advisory council Chapparal council Girl Scouts U.S.; trustee St. Joseph's Hosp., Albuquerque; mem. Gov.'s Council Econ. Advisers, chmn. fin. com.; advisory council U. N.Mex. Sch. Bus. and Adminstrv. Sci.; bd. dirs. United Way, Neighborhood Housing Services Albuquerque; bd. dirs., sec. Albuquerque Indsl. Devel.; mem. Albuquerque Center Inc. Task Force. Served as officer AUS, 1961. Mem. Am., N.Mex. (past chmn. investment com., past mem. edn. com., mem. exec. council, mem. budget com., past mem. legis. com.) bankers assns., Robert Morris Assos. (past chmn. Upper Rio Grande area), Am. Inst. Banking, Conf. Bd. (Rocky Mountain regional advisory council), Fedn. Rocky Mountain States (human resources council), Newcomen Soc. N.Am. Clubs: Petroleum, Panorama Golf and Country (Albuquerque). Office: 40 First Plaza NW Suite 70 Albuquerque NM 87102

PIERCE, CHARLES CURRY, investment banker; b. Colorado City, Tex., Dec. 14, 1904; s. Charles Albert and Jessie (Curry) P.; student Wayland Coll., 1922-24; B.B.A., U. Mo., 1927; m. Melverne Rawson, Mar. 28, 1932; children—Charles Curry, Marian Susan. Securities dept. Merc. Nat. Bank, 1927-33; organizer Rauscher, Pierce & Co., investment bankers, Dallas, 1933, v.p., 1933-64, pres., 1964-69, chmn., 1969—; dir. Henry Miller Real Estate Trust. Past vice chmn. Midwest Stock Exchange. Trustee Tex. Scottish Rite Hosp. for Crippled Children; former trustee Wayland Coll. Mem. Investment Bankers Assn. (bd. govs., mem. legis. com., chmn. legis. com. Tex., v.p. 1964), Nat. Assn. Securities Dealers (past dist. chmn), Assn. Stock Exchange Firms (bd. govs.), Delta Sigma Pi. Methodist. Mason (33 deg.). Clubs: Dallas, Dallas Country (Dallas); Petroleum. Home: 4331 Beverly Dr Dallas TX 75205 Office: Mercantile Dallas Bldg Dallas TX 75201

PIERCE, CHARLES DUANE, judge; b. Wadena, Minn., Mar. 27, 1926; s. Charles Harrison and Sylvia Fay (Hinds) P.; student Hamline U., 1946-48, U. Colo., 1949; J.D., U. Colo., 1952; m. Florence Jane Gillis, Sept. 10, 1949; children—Kathryn, Cynthia, John Pierce. Admitted to Colo. bar, 1955; individual practice law, La Jara, Colo., 1956-58; city clk., town atty., treas., La Jara, 1956-58; dep. dist. atty., Conejos County, Colo., 1956-58; individual practice law, Pueblo, Colo., 1958-70; public trustee, Pueblo County, Colo., 1968-69; judge Colo. Ct. of Appeals, Denver, 1970—. Served with U.S. Army, 1944-46; ETO. Mem. Am. Bar Assn., Colo. Bar Assn., Denver Bar Assn., Pueblo County Bar Assn., Am. Judicature Soc., Am. Law Inst. Methodist. Club: Rotary. Home: 865 Steele St Denver CO 80206 Office: 2 E 14th Ave Denver CO 80203

PIERCE, CHARLES R., utility exec.; b. Bar Harbor, Maine, 1922; A.B., Hofstra Coll., 1947; LL.B., Columbia, 1949. Chmn., chief exec. officer L.I. Lighting Co. Home: 21 Wayside Ln Huntington NY 11743 Office: 250 Old Country Rd Mineola NY 11501

PIERCE, CHESTER MIDDLEBROOK, psychiatrist, educator; b. Glen Cove, N.Y., Mar. 4, 1927; s. Samuel Riley and Hettie Elenor (Armstrong) P.; A.B., Harvard U., 1948, M.D., 1952; Sc.D. (hon.), Westfield Coll., 1977; m. Jocelyn Patricia Blanchet, June 15, 1949; children—Diane Blanchet, Deirdre Anona. Instr. psychiatry U. Cin., 1957-60; asst. prof. psychiatry U. Okla., 1960-62, prof., 1965-69; prof. edn. and psychiatry Harvard U., 1969—; pres. Am. Bd. Psychiatry and Neurology, 1977-78; mem. Polar Research Bd.; cons. USAF. Advisor, Children's TV Workshop, Child Devel. Asso. Consortium; bd. dirs. Action Children's TV. Served with M.C., USNR, 1953-55. Mem. Inst. Medicine, Black Psychiatrists Am. (chmn.). Democrat. Author publs. on sleep disturbances, media, polar medicine, sports medicine, racism; mem. editorial bds. Home: 17 Prince St Jamaica Plain MA 02130

PIERCE, CLAUDE CONNOR, JR., lawyer; b. Colon, Panama, Dec. 7, 1913; s. Claude Connor and Shirley (Reeves) P.; A.B., Princeton, 1935; LL.B., Harvard, 1938; m. Katherine M. Goodwin, Aug. 2, 1942; children—Daniel G., David M. Admitted to N.Y. bar, 1939, N.C. bar, 1949; practiced in N.Y.C., 1938-40, Washington, 1940-47, Greensboro, 1947—; atty. Smart & Von Sneidern, 1938-40; atty. Office Chief Counsel, Bur. Internal Revenue, 1940-47; atty., mem. firm Brooks, Pierce McLendon, Humphrey & Leonard, 1947—. Served to lt. col. C.E., AUS, 1941-46. Decorated Legion of Merit, Mem. Am., N.C. (bd. govs.), Greensboro (pres.) bar assns. Rotarian. Clubs: M. and M. (bd. govs.), Greensboro Country (past dir., pres. 1972-73) (Greensboro). Home: 2004 Dalton Rd Greensboro NC 27408 Office: Suite 1400 Wachovia Bldg Greensboro NC 27402

PIERCE, DANIEL MARSHALL, lawyer, state legislator; b. Chgo., Mar. 31, 1928; s. Hyman A. and Thelma (Udwin) P.; A.B., Harvard U., 1949, LL.B., 1952; children—Andrew, Anthony, Theodore.

Admitted to Ill. bar, 1952, since practiced in Chgo.; partner firm Altheimer & Gray, 1966—; mem. Ill. Ho. of Reps. from 32d Dist., 1964—, chmn. environ. com., 1975-77, chmn. revenue com., 1977—; mem. Ill. Reapportionment Commn., 1963, Ill. Democratic Central Com., 1962-66, 70—; chmn. Ill. Energy Resources Commn., 1979—; chmn. renewable energy sub-com. Nat. Conf. State Legislatures, 1978—. Bd. dirs. Cove Sch., Evanston, Ill., 1975. Served to 1st. lt. USAF, 1952-54. Mem. Am., Ill., Chgo. bar assns. Club: Harvard (Chgo.). Home: 630 Sheridan Rd Highwood IL 60040 Office: 1 IBM Plaza Chicago IL 60611

PIERCE, DAREN LAINE, textile and interior designer; b. Lebanon, Oreg., May 23, 1922; s. Frederick Franklin and Frances Alice (Frum) P.; student Wolfe Sch. Costume Design, Los Angeles, 1940-41, U. Oreg., 1941-42. Textile designer Dorothy Liebes Textiles, San Francisco, 1945-48; interior designer William Pahlmann Assos., Inc., N.Y.C., 1948-64; pres., designer, Woolworks, Inc., N.Y.C., 1964—; designer Edward Fields Carpets, N.Y.C., Philip Graf Wallpapers, N.Y.C., Eaglesham Fabrics, N.Y.C.; bd. dirs. Franciscan Fabrics, San Francisco. Fellow Am. Soc. Interior Designers; mem. Indian Inst. Interior Designers (hon.). Republican. Author cookbooks and design publs. Home: 405 E 54th St New York City NY 10022

PIERCE, EDWARD FRANKLIN, coll. pres.; b. Cambridge, Mass., July 15, 1927; s. John and Kathleen (McCue) P.; B.S., Boston Coll., 1949, M.A., 1950; Ph.D., Columbia U., 1959, Ed.D., 1959; m. Sandra Lea, June 8, 1958; children—Valerie, Marc, Adrienne. Research chemist AEC, 1950-51; mem. faculty Skagit Valley Coll., Mt. Vernon, Wash., 1954; instr. chemistry SUNY, Geneseo, 1959-66, chmn. dept., 1962, dean, 1964; dean U. N.H. System, Keene, 1966-72; pres. Quincy (Mass.) Jr. Coll., 1972—; mem. New Eng. Dist. Scholarship Com.; cons. in field, seminar lectr. Chmn. United Fund, 1968, Dist. com. Boy Scouts Am., 1951-54, Council for Children, Quincy, 1972—; pres., treas. South Shore Day Care Services, 1972-76. Served to ensign USNR, 1944-46. Fellow Am. Inst. Chemists; mem. AAAS, N.Y. Acad. Sci. Club: Quincy Kiwanis (past pres.). Author: Selected Quantitative Studies in Physical Science, 1962; Modern Chemistry, 1960; Historical Perspectives in the Physical Sciences, 1964; also articles. Home: 14 Seagull Rd Quincy MA 02169 Office: 34 Coddington St Quincy MA 02169

PIERCE, FREDERICK S., broadcasting exec.; grad. Baruch Sch. Bus. Adminstrn., Coll. City N.Y.; m. Marion; children—Richard, Keith, Linda. With ABC, 1956—, supr. audience measurements TV network research dept., 1957, mgr. audience measurements, 1958-61, dir. research, 1961, dir. research and sales devel., 1962, dir. sales planning and sales devel., 1962-64, v.p., nat. dir. sales for TV network, 1964-68, v.p. planning, 1968-70, v.p. charge planning, asst. to pres. TV network, 1970-72, v.p. charge TV planning and devel., 1972-74, sr. v.p. ABC TV, 1974, pres., 1974—, also dir. Am. Broadcasting Cos., Inc. Served with U.S. Army Combat Engrs., Korea.

PIERCE, GEORGE FOSTER, JR., architect; b. Dallas, June 22, 1919; s. George Foster and Hallie Louise (Crutchfield) P.; student So. Meth. U., 1937-39; B.A., Rice U., 1942, B.S. in Architecture, 1943; diplome d'architecture, Ecoles d'Art Americaines, Ecole des Beaux-Arts, 1958; m. Betty Jean Reistle, Oct. 17, 1942; children—Ann Louise (Mrs. Robert G. Arnett), George Foster III, Nancy Reistle. Pvt. practice architecture, 1946—; sr. partner Pierce, Goodwin, Alexander, architects, engrs. and planners, 1947—. Design cons. Dept. Army, 1966-70; instr. archtl. design Rice U., 1945, preceptor dept. architecture, 1962-67, trustee, exec. com. Rice Center for Community Design and Research; projects include 8 bldgs. Rice U. Campus, Exxon Brook Hollow Bldg. Complex, Houston Mus. Natural Sci. and Planetarium, Michael Debakey Center Biomed. Edn. and Research, Baylor Coll. Medicine, Houston Intercontinental Airport, S.W. Bell Telephone Co. office bldg., Petroleum Club of Houston, U. Tex. Med. Sch. Hosp., Galveston, U. Houston Continuing Edn. Center and Hotel, U. Houston Student Center, 2 Houston Center 40 story office bldg., others. Mem. exec. bd. Sam Houston area council Boy Scouts Am.; mem. grad. council Rice U.; past pres., chmn. bd. trustees Contemporary Arts Mus., Houston; trustee Houston Mus. Natural Sci.; trustee, past pres. Tex. Archtl. Found. Served as ensign USNR, World War II. Recipient Outstanding Young Texan award Jr. C. of C., 1954; also numerous nat., state, local archtl. awards for design. Fellow A.I.A. (past nat. chmn. com. on aesthetics, student affairs and chpt. affairs), La Sociedad de Architectos Mexicanos (hon.); mem. Tex. Soc. Architects (past pres.), Houston C. of C. (chmn. future studies), Rice U. Pres.'s Club (founding chmn. 1970-72), Rice U. Assos., Kappa Alpha. Methodist. Clubs: Rotary, Houston Country, Petroleum (Houston); Riverhill (Kerrville, Tex.). Contbr. articles to profl. publs. Home: 5555 Del Monte N 1103 Houston TX 77056 Office: PO Box 13319 Houston TX 77019

PIERCE, GORDON BARRY, physician, educator; b. Westlock, Alta., Can., July 21, 1925; s. Gordon Barry and Helen Mary (Jones) P.; M.Sc., U. Alta., 1950, M.D., 1952; postgrad. (Markle scholar), U. Pitts., 1959-64; m. Donna J. Turner, Oct. 4, 1952; children—Donald B., C. Helen, Gordon B., Patricia L., Thomas A. Lectr., U. Alta., 1953-55; Sarah Mellon Scaife fellow pathology U. Pitts., 1955-59, asst. prof. pathology, 1958-61; asso. prof. pathology U. Mich., Ann Arbor, 1961-65, prof., 1965, Am. Cancer Soc. prof. pathology, 1964—, prof., chmn. dept. pathology U. Colo. Med. Center, Denver, 1968—. Diplomate Am. Bd. Pathology. Mem. Internat. Acad. Pathology, Fedn. Am. Socs. Exptl. Biology (pres. 1978-79), Soc. Developmental Biology, Am. Soc. Cell Biology, Am. Assn. for Cancer Research, A.A.A.S., Am. Soc. for Exptl. Pathology, Am. Assn. Pathologists (pres. 1977-78), Internat. Soc. Developmental Biology, Internat. Soc. Differentiation (pres. 1978—), Ewing Soc. Club: Pluto. Contbr. articles to profl. jours. Research in testicular cancer, basement membranes. Home: 21 S Kearney Denver CO 80222

PIERCE, HARVEY FENN, ret. elec. engr.; b. Apalachicola, Fla., Oct. 18, 1909; s. Albert and Maude (Fenn) P.; B.S. in Elec. Engring., U. Fla., 1932; m. Mary Littledale, May 1, 1937; children—Harvey Allan, Brian Kenneth. With Fla. Power & Light Co., 1932-37; partner Maurice H. Connell & Assos., Miami, Fla., 1937-46, sec.-treas., 1946-67; pres. Connell Assos., Inc., 1967-71, chmn., 1971-73; partner Connell, Pierce, Garland & Friedman, 1956-74, ret., 1974. Mem. nat. council Boy Scouts Am., 1968-72; mem. adv. bd. Salvation Army, 1960-71; bd. dirs. Boys Clubs of Miami, 1960-72. Recipient citation for work at Cape Canaveral, C.E., 1960. Registered profl. engr., Fla., N.C. Fellow IEEE, Fla. Engring. Soc. (Outstanding Tech. Achievement award 1961, past pres.); mem. Nat. Soc. Profl. Engrs. (award 1968, v.p. 1961-62, pres. 1962-63), Am. Inst. Cons. Engrs. (v.p. 1969), Am. Def. Preparedness Assn. (life), Blue Key, Phi Kappa Phi, Phi Eta Sigma, Sigma Tau, Tau Beta Pi. Club: Kiwanis. Home: PO Box 1149 Highlands NC 28741

PIERCE, HENRY HILL, JR., former banker; b. N.Y.C., June 12, 1908; s. Henry Hill and Katharine Robinson (Curtis) P.; B.A., Cambridge (Eng.) U., 1931, M.A., 1935; M.A., Trinity Coll., 1964; m. Mildred Pope, June 10, 1938; children—Katharine C., Margot (Mrs. Elmer H. Close), Thomas H., Evelina L. (Mrs. David Sarles), Patience P. Bank commr., Conn., 1955-60; with Union & New Haven Trust Co., 1960-69, pres., 1963-69, also dir.; chmn. bd. Union Trust Co., New Haven, 1969-77, N.E. Bancorp., 1975-79; pres. Community Progress, Inc., 1962-66; police commr. City New Haven, 1968-73; mem. stockholders adv. com. Fed. Res. Bank Boston, 1963-65, chmn. com., 1964-65; faculty Rutgers U. Grad. Sch. Banking, 1959-60; pres. New Haven Clearing House, 1966-68; exec. com. Nat. Assn. Suprs. State Banks, 1957-60. Mem. Conn. Tchrs. Retirement Bd., 1955-60; mem. Conn. Adv. Council on Banking, 1967-71; mem. Commn. Conn.'s Future, 1977—. First selectman Clinton, 1951-55; Democratic candidate U.S. Ho. of Reps., 2d Dist. Conn., 1954. Chmn. trustees com. New Haven Found., 1968-69; trustee Hopkins Grammar-Day Prospect Sch., 1974-79; Asso. fellow Ezra Stiles Coll., Yale U. Mem. Am. Bankers Assn. (pres. state bank div. 1968-69). Episcopalian (exec. council Conn. Diocese 1971-73). Clubs: Lawn, Quinnipiack (New Haven); Madison (Conn.) Beach; Players (N.Y.C.); Oxford and Cambridge University (London). Home: 240 St Ronan St New Haven CT 06511

PIERCE, JAMES CLARENCE, surgeon; b. Huron, S.D., Aug. 5, 1929; s. Henry Montraville and Carrie Bernice (Matson) P.; B.A., Carleton Coll., 1951; M.D., Harvard U., 1955; M.S., U. Minn., 1963, Ph.D. in Surgery, 1966; m. Carol Sue Wilson, 1967; children—Henry MacDonald, Richard Matson, Elizabeth Gail. Surg. intern Peter Bent Brigham Hosp., Boston, 1955-56; surg. fellow U. Minn., 1959-66; instr. surgery Med. Coll. Va., Richmond, 1972, prof. surgery and microbiology, 1972-75, dir. Tissue Typing Lab., 1969-75; attending surgeon, dir. surg. research, dir. transplantation service St. Luke's Hosp. Center, N.Y.C., 1975-78; prof. surgery Columbia U., 1976, Ailsa Mellon Bruce prof. surgery, 1977-78; clin. prof. surgery Pa. State U. and chmn. dept. surgery Geisinger Med. Center, Danville, Pa., 1979—. Served with M.C., USAF, 1957-59. NIH fellow, 1963-65; Royal Soc. Medicine Found. travelling fellow, 1971; James IV Assn. Surg. traveller, 1978. Diplomate Am. Bd. Surgery. Mem. Am. Assn. Pathologists, A.C.S., Transplant Soc., Am. Fedn. for Clin. Research, Am. Soc. Nephrology, Am. Soc. Transplant Surgeons, Assn. for Acad. Surgery, Assn. Am. Med. Colls., Eastern Surg. Soc., N.Y. Surg. Soc., N.Y. Clin. Soc., Soc. Univ. Surgeons, Sigma Xi, Phi Lambda Upsilon. Republican. Presbyterian. Contbr. articles to profl. jours. Home: 101 N Huntington Ave Danville PA 17821 Office: Geisinger Med Center Danville PA 17821

PIERCE, JOHN GRISSIM, educator; b. San Jose, Calif., May 9, 1920; s. James Lester and Elise (Furst) P.; A.A., San Jose State Coll., 1939; B.A., Stanford U., 1941, M.A., 1942, Ph.D., 1944; m. Elizabeth Copeland, Dec. 18, 1949; children—Sarah Thurston, John Pieronnet, Anne Moore, James Lester. Instr. to asst. prof. Cornell U. Med. Coll., 1948-52; from asst. prof. to prof. biochemistry U. Calif. at Los Angeles, 1953—, vice chmn. dept. biol. chemistry, 1963-79, chmn., 1979—; Eli Lilly lectr. Endocrine Soc., 1971. Served from ensign to lt. (j.g.) USNR, 1944-46. Fellow Nutrition Found., 1942-44, Am. Chem. Soc., 1946-47, Arthritis and Rheumatism Found., 1952-53, Guggenheim Found., 1960-61, 75-76. Mem. Am. Chem. Soc., Am. Soc. Biol. Chemists, Harvey Soc., A.A.A.S., Phi Beta Kappa. Editorial bd. Jour. Biol. Chemistry, 1969-74, 78—. Research in chemistry, biology of pituitary hormones. Home: 23330 Calvert St Woodland Hills CA 91367 Office: U Calif Center Health Scis Los Angeles CA 90024

PIERCE, JOHN ROBINSON, educator, elec. engr.; b. Des Moines, Mar. 27, 1910; s. John Starr and Harriet Anne (Robinson) P.; B.S., Calif. Inst. Tech., 1933, M.S., 1934, Ph.D., 1936; D.Engring., Newark Coll. Engring., 1961; D.Sc., Northwestern U., 1961, Yale, Poly. Inst. Bklyn., 1963, Columbia U., 1965, U. Nev., 1970, U. So. Calif., 1977; E.D., Carnegie Inst. Tech., 1964; D.Elec. Engring., U. Bologna (Italy), 1974; LL.D., U. Pa., 1974; m. Martha Peacock, Nov. 5, 1938 (div. Mar. 1964); children—John Jeremy, Elizabeth Anne; m. 2d, Ellen R. McKown, Apr. 1, 1964. With Bell Telephone Labs., Inc., 1936-71, mem. tech. staff, dir. electronics research, 1952-55, dir. research, communication principles, 1958-62, exec. dir. research, communications principles and systems div., 1963-65, exec. dir. research, communications scis. div., 1965-71; prof. engring. Calif. Inst. Tech., Pasadena, 1971—, chief technologist Jet Propulsion Lab., 1979—; trustee Aerospace Corp.; past mem. Pres.'s Sci. Adv. Com., Pres.'s Com. of Nat. Medal of Sci. Trustee Battelle Meml. Inst. Recipient Morris Liebmann meml. prize I.R.E., 1947; Stuart Ballantine medal, Franklin of Year, Air Force Assn., 1962; Golden Plate award Acad. Achievement, 1962; General Hoyt S. Vandenberg trophy Arnold Air Soc., 1963; Nat. Medal of Sci., 1963; Edison medal Am. Inst. E.E., 1963; Valdemar Poulsen Gold medal, 1963, H.T. Cedergren medal, 1964, Marconi award, 1974, John C. Scott award, 1975; Marconi Internat. fellow, 1979. Fellow Acoustical Soc. Am., Am. Phys. Soc., I.E.E.E. (medal of honor 1976); mem. Nat. Acad. Engring. (Founders award 1977), Am. Acad. Arts and Scis., Air Force Assn., Nat. Acad. Scis., Royal Acad. Sci. (Sweden), Am. Philos. Soc. Author: Theory and Design of Electron Beams, rev. edit., 1954; Traveling Wave Tubes, 1950; Electrons, Waves and Messages, 1956; Man's World of Sound, 1958; Symbols, Signals and Noise, 1961; (with A.G. Tressler) The Research State: A History of Science in New Jersey, 1964; Electrons and Waves, 1964; Quantum Electronics, 1966; Waves and Messages, 1967; The Beginnings of Satellite Communications, 1968; Science, Art and Communication, 1968; Almost All About Waves, 1973; also articles on popular sci., short stories. Home: 961 Canon Dr Pasadena CA 91106 Office: Steele Lab Calif Inst Tech Pasadena CA 91125

PIERCE, KENNETH RAY, educator; b. Snyder, Tex., May 21, 1934; s. Clois Vernon and Ellen (Goolsby) P.; D.V.M., Tex. A. and M. U., 1957, M.S., 1962, Ph.D. (NSF fellow), 1965; m. Anne Stasney, Aug. 31, 1956; children—Cynthia Cae, Meloney Rae. Instr. vet. anatomy Tex. A. and M. U., College Station, 1957-59, asst. prof., 1961-65, asso. prof., 1965-69, prof., 1969—, head dept., 1978—, chief sect. vet. clin. pathology, 1967-75; comparative pathologist Inst. Comparative Medicine, Tex. A. and M. U.-Baylor Coll. Medicine, Houston, 1976-79; pvt. vet. practice San Angelo (Tex.) Vet. Hosp., 1959-61; cons. dept. vet. medicine and surgery M.D. Anderson Tumor Inst. and Hosp., Houston, 1971—. Diplomate Am. Coll. Vet. Pathologists. Mem. Am. Soc. Vet. Clin. Pathologists, Internat. Acad. Pathology, AVMA, Tex. Vet. Med. Assn., N.Y. Acad. Sci., Sigma Xi, Phi Kappa Phi, Phi Zeta, Gamma Sigma Delta. Presbyterian (deacon, elder). Co-editor Vet. Pathology Jour., 1971—; contbr. articles to profl. jours. Home: 1500 Laura Ln College Station TX 77840 Office: Dept Veterinary Pathology Tex A&M U College Station TX 77843

PIERCE, LAWRENCE WARREN, judge; b. Phila., Dec. 31, 1924; s. Harold Ernest and Leora (Bellinger) P.; B.S. Bus. Adminstrn., St. Joseph's Coll., 1948, D.H.L., 1967; J.D., Fordham U., 1951; LL.D., Fairfield U., 1972; m. Cynthia Straker, July 8, 1979; children—Warren Wood, Michael Lawrence, Mark Taylor. Admitted to N.Y. State bar, 1951, U.S. Supreme Ct. bar, 1968; civil law practice, N.Y.C., 1952-61; asst. dist. atty. Kings County (N.Y.), 1954-61; dep. police commr., N.Y.C., 1961-63; dir. N.Y. State Div. for Youth, Albany, 1963-66; chmn. N.Y. State Narcotic Addiction Control Commn., 1966-70; vis. prof. Sch. Criminal Justice, State U. N.Y. at Albany, 1970-71; U.S. dist. judge So. dist. N.Y., 1971—; mem. 2d Circuit Com. on Reduction Burdens and Costs in Civil Litigation; mem. U.S. Fgn. Intelligence Surveillance Ct., 1979; mem. planning and program com. 2d Circuit Jud. Conf. Bd. dirs. St. Joseph's U.; bd. mgrs. Lincoln Hall for Boys. Served with AUS, 1943-46, MTO. Mem. Urban League, NAACP, Am. Bar Assn. (commn. on correctional services and facilities 1970—, commn. on jud. adminstrn.), 2d Circuit Hist. Soc., Fordham Law Alumni Assn. (dir.), SAR, Supreme Ct. Hist. Soc. (founding). Roman Catholic. Home: Canaan NY 12060

PIERCE, LEONARD AUGUSTUS, JR., pulp and paper co. exec.; b. Houlton, Maine, Oct. 13, 1916; s. Leonard Augustus and Anna Mitchell (Putnam) P.; B.S., Bowdoin Coll., 1938; student pulp and paper Internat. Corr. Schs., 1946; m. Helen B. Wormwood, Feb. 23, 1943; 1 dau., Susan B. With St. Regis Paper Co., 1946-56, mgr. kraft paper mill., 1950-52, mgr. paper mill, Kalamazoo, 1952-54, asst. to v.p. charge mfg., N.Y.C., 1955-56; asst. to pres., v.p. ops. Penobscot Chem. Fibre Co., Boston and Old Town, Maine, 1956-60; pres. Brown Co., 1960-67; exec. v.p. James W. Sewall Co., Old Town, 1968—; dir. Depositers Bank Bangor, Inc. Served to maj., inf. U.S. Army, 1940-46. Decorated Bronze Star medal. Mem. Delta Kappa Epsilon. Home: Box 401 Route 2 Carmel ME 04419

PIERCE, LOUIS, educator, chemist; b. Ely, Minn., May 22, 1929; s. John and Angela (Bolka) P.; B.S., Western Res. U., 1951, M.S., 1952, Ph.D., 1954; m. Geraldine Caroline Ustar, May 29, 1954; children—Nancy, Louis, Jerome, John, Susan. Research fellow Harvard, 1954-56; asst. prof. U. Notre Dame, 1956-59, asso. prof., 1959-62, prof. chemistry, 1962—, asst. and acting dir. Computing Center, 1962-64. Alfred P. Sloan Found. fellow, 1961-65, NSF Sr. Postdoctoral fellow, 1965-66. Mem. Am. Chem. Soc., Am. Phys. Soc. Home: 116 S Hawthorne Dr South Bend IN 46617 Office: U Notre Dame Dept Chemistry Notre Dame IN 46556

PIERCE, LOVICK, former pub. co. exec.; b. Sparta, Ga., Oct. 17, 1903; s. Walter Flournoy and Sarah (Alfriend) P.; grad. Ga. Mil. Coll., 1921; Dr. Bus. Adminstrn., Morningside Coll., 1952; Litt.D., Ohio No. U., 1961; m. Florence Eugenia Couch, Jan. 30, 1926; children—Eugenia Carter (Mrs. Andrew W. Young, Jr.), Lovick Pierce. Mdse. mgr. The Methodist Pub. House, Richmond, Va., 1921-29; regional mgr. Methodist Pub. House and Cokesbury Book Store, Dallas, 1929-46, pres., pub. Meth. Pub. House of Meth. Ch., Nashville, 1946-70, 71-77; chmn. bd. Aurora Pubs., Inc., Nashville, 1970-78; dir. First Am. Nat. Bank (Nashville). Treas., S. Central Jurisdictional Conf., 1940-46; mem. Joint Commn. of Meth. E.U.B., Union. Trustee Scarritt Coll. Mem. Am. Booksellers Assn. (v.p.), Nat. Council Churches Christ, Protestant Church-Owned Pub. Assn., U.S., Nashville chambers of commerce, AIM (pres.'s council), Am. Book Pubs. Council. Methodist. Mason. Clubs: Union League, Rotary, Belle Meade Country, Cumberland, Chgo. Press. Home: 620 Enquirer Ave Nashville TN 37205

PIERCE, MARGARET HUNTER, govt. ofcl.; b. Weedsport, N.Y., June 30, 1910; d. Thomas Murray and Ruby (Sanders) Hunter; B.A., Mt. Holyoke Coll., 1932; J.D., N.Y. U., 1939; m. John R. Pierce, Nov. 4, 1950 (div. May 1959); 1 dau., Barbara Hunter. Admitted to N.Y. bar, 1941, D.C. bar, 1958; atty. Office Alien Property Custodian, Washington, 1942-43, 45, Office Solicitor, Dept. Labor, 1943-45, NLRB, 1946, 47-48; atty.-adviser U.S. Ct. Claims, 1947-48, 48-59, reporter decisions, 1959-68; commr. U.S. Indian Claims Commn., 1968-78; pvt. practice, Washington, 1978—. Mem. D.C. (ct. claims com. 1958—, mil. law com. 1967), Fed. (Indian law com. 1955—), Am. (sec. adminstrv. law-vets. com., mil. law com., immigration and nationality com.), D.C., Women's bar assns., Nat. Assn. Women Lawyers, Zonta Internat. (pres. Washington 1977-78), Exec. Women in Govt., Bus. and Profl. Women (Cosmopolitan br.). Home: 3829 Garfield St NW Washington DC 20007

PIERCE, PONCHITTA ANNE, journalist; b. Chgo., Aug. 5, 1942; d. Alfred Leonard and Nora (Vincent) P.; student Cambridge (Eng.) U., summer 1962; B.A. cum laude, U. So. Calif., 1964. Asst. editor Ebony mag., 1964-65, asso. editor, 1965-67, editor N.Y.C. office, 1967-68; chief N.Y.C. editorial bur. Johnson Pub. Co., 1967-68; spl. corr. CBS news div. N.Y.C., 1968-71; contbg. editor McCall's mag., 1971-77; editorial cons. Philps Stokes Fund, 1971—; WNBC-TV co-host Sunday, 1973—, The Prime of Your Life, 1976—; staff writer Reader's Digest, 1976—, roving editor, 1977—; free lance writer. Mem. Gov. N.Y. Com. Minority Groups News Media, Manhattan adv. com. N.Y.C. Urban League. Del. to WHO Conf., Geneva, 1973; bd. dirs. Am. Freedom from Hunger Found., African Student Aid Fund, Voice Found., Inner-City Scholarship Fund. Recipient Penney-Mo. mag. award excellence women's journalism, 1967; John Russwurm award N.Y.C. Urban League, 1968; AMITA Nat. Achievement award in communications, 1974. Life mem. Calif. Scholarship Fedn., Nat. Honor Soc.; mem. Nat. Acad. TV Arts and Scis., Women in Communications (Woman Behind the News award 1969), Nat. Headliner award 1970), Mortar Bd. Alumnae. Author: Status of American Women Journalists on Magazines, 1968; History of the Phelps Stokes Fund 1911-1972. Home: 780 Madison Ave New York NY 10021 Office: NBC 30 Rockefeller Plaza New York NY 10020

PIERCE, ROBERT NASH, educator; b. Greenville, Miss., Dec. 5, 1931; student U. Mo., 1950; B.A., Ark. State U., 1951; M.J. in Journalism, U. Tex., Austin, 1955; Ph.D., U. Minn., 1968; m. Ann Courter, 1953 (div. 1978); children—Douglas, Diana. Reporter, asst. state editor, acting state editor Ark. Democrat, Little Rock, 1953-55; reporter, real estate editor Sarasota (Fla.) News, 1956-60; news editor, asso. editor San Angelo (Tex.) Standard-Times; dir. public relations Fla. Presbyn. Coll., St. Petersburg, 1960-62, adviser, chmn. bd. student publs., 1960-62; asst. city editor St. Petersburg Evening Independent, 1962-63; legis. corr. Shreveport Jour., La. Legislature, summer 1970; freelance writer, Gainesville, Fla., 1970—; copy editor Miami Herald, 1972; asst. prof. La. State U., 1965-70; asso. prof. U. Fla., Gainesville, 1970-76, prof., 1976—, dir. grad. studies, 1978—; Fulbright-Hays lectr. journalism U. Argentina de la Empresa, 1973; vis. lectr. Cath. U. Minas Gerais, Belo Horizonte, Brazil, 1973; guest lectr. Panamanian Syndicate of Journalists, Panama City, Colombian-Am. Cultural Inst.; research grantee Fulbright-Hays Faculty Research Abroad Program, U.S. Office Edn., 1976. Deacon, Presbyterian Ch., 1968—. Mem. Assn. for Edn. in Journalism, Sigma Delta Chi, Kappa Tau Alpha. Author: Keeping the Flame: Media and Government in Latin America, 1979; contbr. chpts. to Internat. Communication as a Field of Study, 1970; Mass Communication in Mexico, 1975; also monograph, articles. Home: 2824 SW 14th Dr Gainesville FL 32608 Office: Coll Journalism and Communications U Fla Gainesville FL 32611

PIERCE, SAMUEL RILEY, JR., lawyer; b. Glen Cove, L.I., N.Y., Sept. 8, 1922; s. Samuel R. and Hettie E. (Armstrong) P.; A.B. with honors, Cornell U., 1947, J.D., 1949; postgrad. (Ford Found. fellow) Yale Law Sch., 1957-58; LL.M. in Taxation, N.Y. U., 1952, LL.D., 1972; m. Barbara Penn Wright, Apr. 1, 1948; 1 dau., Victoria Wright. Admitted to N.Y. bar, 1949, Supreme Ct. bar, 1956; asst. dist. atty. County N.Y., 1949-53; asst. U.S. atty. So. Dist. N.Y., 1953-55; asst. to under sec. Dept. Labor, Washington, 1955-56; asso. counsel, counsel Jud. Subcom. on Antitrust, U.S. Ho. Reps., 1956-57; pvt. practice law, 1957-59, 61-70, 73—; faculty N.Y. U. Sch. Law, 1958—; guest speaker colls., univs.; judge N.Y. Ct. Gen. Sessions, 1959-60; gen. counsel, head legal div. U.S. Treasury, Washington, 1970-73. Cons. Fund Internat. Social and Econ. Edn., 1961-67; chmn. impartial disciplinary rev. bd. N.Y.C. Transit System, 1968—. Chmn., N.Y.

State Minimum Wage Bd. Hotel Industry, 1961; mem. N.Y. State Banking Bd., 1961-70, N.Y.C. Bd. Edn., 1961, Adminstrv. Conf. U.S., 1968-70, Battery Park City Corp. Authority, 1968-70, N.Y.C. Spl. Commn. Inquiry into Energy Failures, 1977; mem. nat. adv. com. comptroller of currency, 1975—; adv. group commr. IRS, 1974-76; mem. Nat. Wiretapping Commn., 1973-76. Dir. N.Y. 1964-65 World's Fair Corp., Prudential Ins. Co., U.S. Industries, Inc., Internat. Paper Co., Gen. Electric Co., Internat. Basic Economy Corp., Rand Corp., 1st Nat. Boston Corp., 1st Nat. Bank of Boston; gov. Am. Stock Exchange, 1977—. Trustee, Inst. Civil Justice, Mt. Holyoke Coll., 1965-75, Hampton Inst., Inst. Internat. Edn., Cornell U., Howard U.; bd. dirs. Tax Found. U.S. del. Conf. on Coops., Georgetown, Brit. Guiana, 1956; mem. panel symposium Mil.-Indsl. Conf. on Atomic Energy, Chgo., 1956; fraternal del. All-African People's Conf., Accra, Ghana, 1958; mem. Nat. Def. Exec. Res., 1957—; mem. nat. exec. bd. Boy Scouts Am., 1969-75; mem. N.Y.C. U.S.O. Com., 1959-61; mem. panel arbitrators Am. Arbitration Assn. and Fed. Mediation and Conciliation Service, 1957—. Bd. dirs. Louis T. Wright Meml. Fund, Inc., Nat. Parkinson Found., Inc., 1959-61; sec., dir. YMCA Greater N.Y., 1960-70. Mem. N.Y. State Republican Campaign Hdqrs. Staff, 1952, 58; gov. N.Y. Young Rep. Club, 1951-53. Served with AUS, 1943-46, as 1st lt. J.A.G.C. Res., 1950-52. Recipient N.Y.C. Jr. C. of C. Ann. Distinguished Service award, 1958, Alexander Hamilton award Treasury Dept., 1973. Fellow Am. Coll. Trial Lawyers; mem. Cornell Assn. Class Secs., Telluride Assn. Alumni, Cornell U. Amumni Assn. N.Y.C. (gov.), C.I.D. Agts. Assn. (gov.), Am. Bar Assn., Assn. N.Y.C. Bar, N.Y. County Lawyers Assn., Inst. Jud. Adminstrn., Phi Beta Kappa, Phi Kappa Phi, Alpha Phi Alpha, Alpha Phi Omega. Methodist (mem. commn. on interjurisdictional relations Meth. Ch. in U.S.). Contbr. articles to profl. jours. Home: 16 W 77th St New York NY 10024 Office: 280 Park Ave New York NY 10017

PIERCE, WALLACE LINCOLN, mcht.; b. Boston, Mar. 4, 1912; s. Walworth and Marie Burr (Harmon) P.; B.S., Harvard U., 1934; m. Mary Markle Bannard, Feb. 22, 1936 (dec. 1978); children—Mary Markle (Mrs. John W. Adams), Patricia Stillman (Mrs. David C. Garre). With S.S. Pierce Co., 1934—, clk. of corp., v.p., 1947-54, pres., 1954-67, chmn. bd., 1967-69, also dir., hon. chmn., 1970—; pres. S.S. Pierce Realty Co., Pierce Co., Inc.; trustee Suffolk-Franklin Savs. Bank, William Underwood Co., Watertown, Mass.; dir. New Eng. Mchts. Nat. Bank; former v.p. Boston Retail Trade Bd. Trustee, Univ. Hosp., Michael Anagnos Agrl. Coll., Konista, Greece; mem. corp. Boston Children's Friend Soc., Mus. Sci.; bd. overseers Robert Breck Brigham Hosp. Served from lt. (j.g.) to lt. comdr. USNR, 1942-45. Decorated chevalier Ordre Mérite (France). Mem. Am. Soc. for Friendship with Switzerland (past dir.). Episcopalian. Clubs: Country (Brookline); Harvard, Wardroom (N.Y.C.); Boston. Home: 60 Fernwood Rd Chestnut Hill MA 02167

PIERCE, WALTER SMITH, architect; b. Bklyn., Feb. 10, 1920; s. Stanley Woodward and Sallie (Smith) P.; student Bowdoin Coll., 1937-38; B.S. in Archtl. Engring., Va. Poly. Inst., 1941; M.Arch., Mass. Inst. Tech., 1947; m. Marianne Fisker, Sept. 14, 1951; children—Steffen Fisker, Christian Smith. Partner firm Compton & Pierce, Cambridge, Mass., 1952-60, firm Pierce, Pierce & Kramer, and predecessor, Boston, 1962—; instr. Mass. Inst. Tech., Cambridge, 1947-50, Kongelige Kunstakademiet, Copenhagen, 1951. Mem. Design Adv. Group, Lexington Mass. Planning Bd., 1967—. Served to maj. C.E., AUS, 1941-46; ETO, PTO. Recipient several AIA awards, including Honor award for AVCO Everett (Mass.) Research Lab., 1971, 1st Honor award for Peacock Farms housing, Lexington, 1957. Fellow AIA; mem. Boston Soc. Architects, Mass. Assn. Architects. Home: 16 Trotting Horse Dr Lexington MA 02173 Office: 116 Newbury St Boston MA 02116

PIERCE, WILLIAM JAMES, educator; b. Flint, Mich., Dec. 4, 1921; s. Francis Scott and Ellen (Pelton) P.; A.B. in Econs., U. Mich., 1947, J.D., 1949; m. Betty Kathren Wise, Nov. 20, 1954; children—Darrell William, Margery Marie, Constance Ellen, Kathren Elizabeth. Faculty, U. Mich., 1953—, prof. law, dir. Legislative Research Center, 1958—, asso. dean, 1971-79; exec. sec. Mich. Law Revision Commn., 1966-69; chmn. Citizens Adv. Com. Juvenile Ct., 1964-66; pres. Nat. Conf. Commrs. Uniform State Laws, 1966-69, exec. dir., 1969—. Mem. Pres.'s Consumer Adv. Council, 1967-69, Mich. Gov.'s Commn. on Mental Health Laws, 1969-72; mem. exec. com. Inst. Continuing Legal Edn., 1964—. Served with AUS, 1943-45. Decorated Bronze Star medal. Mem. Am. Law Inst., Am. Bar Assn. (ho. of dels. 1966-69), State Bar Mich. Author: (with Estep, Stason) Atomic Energy and the Law, 1957; (with Lamb, White) Apportionment and Representative Institutions, 1963; (with Read, MacDonald, Fordham) Materials on Legislation, 1973. Home: 1505 Roxbury Rd Ann Arbor MI 48104

PIERCY, GEORGE TOBIAS, petroleum co. exec.; b. Eau Claire, Wis., Nov. 29, 1915; s. Thomas and Margaret Jane (Patterson) P.; B.Chem. Engring., U. Minn., 1938; m. Virginia Budrow, Mar. 2, 1940; children—Nancy Ann (Mrs. Michael L. Murray), Susan Jane (Mrs. Thomas E. McCarthy). With Standard Oil Co. of La., Baton Rouge, 1938-51, coordinator crude oil, 1944-47, asst. mgr., 1947-51; with Esso Standard Oil Co., N.Y.C., 1951-58, gen. mgr. supply dept., 1955-58; with Exxon Corp. (formerly Standard Oil Co. N.J.), various locations, 1958—, dir., 1966—, v.p., N.Y.C., 1967-70, sr. v.p., 1970—; dir. Chem. Bank, Chem. N.Y. Corp. Mem. nat. council Near East Found., N.Y.C., 1966—; trustee, mem. exec. com. Ednl. Broadcasting Corp., N.Y.C., 1967—; trustee U. Minn. Found. Bd., Mpls., 1976. Mem. Am. Petroleum Inst., Am. Inst. Chem. Engrs., Council on Fgn. Relations. Clubs: 25 Yr. of Petroleum Industry; Econ., University, River (N.Y.C.); Lansdowne (London). Home: 870 United Nations Plaza New York NY 10017 Office: Exxon Corp 1251 Ave of the Americas New York NY 10020

PIERCY, MARGE, poet, novelist, essayist; b. Detroit, Mar. 31, 1936; d. Robert Douglas and Bert Bernice (Bunnin) P.; A.B., U. Mich., 1957; M.A., Northwestern U., 1958. Instr., Ind. U., Gary extension, 1960-62; poet-in-residence U. Kans., 1971; Distinguished vis. lectr. Thomas Jefferson Coll., Grand Valley State Colls., fall 1975; cons. N.Y. State Council on Arts, 1971, Mass. Found. for Humanities and Council on Arts, 1974; bd. advisors Feminist Book Club, 1971-72; sponsor Sagaris Coll., 1973-76. Active Students for Democratic Soc., 1965-69, N.Am. Congress on Latin Am., 1966-67, Women's Caucus of Students for Democratic Soc., 1967-68, Movement for Dem. Soc., 1968-69, W.I.T.C.H., 1969-70, Women's Center N.Y., 1969-71, Cape Cod Women's Liberation, 1971—, Feminist Party, 1971—, Cambridge Women's Edn. Center, 1972—, Lower Cape Women's Center, 1973-76, Jewish Socialist Community, 1973—, Nine to Five, 1973—, Mass. Fed. Feminist Credit Union, 1974—; bd. dirs. Transition House, Mass. Found. Humanities and Public Policy, 1978. James B. Angell scholar; Lucinda Goodrich Downs scholar; recipient Orion Scott award in Humanities; maj. and minor awards in poetry and fiction Avery Hopwood Contest, 1956, 57; Borestone Mountain Poetry award, 1968, 74; Lit. award Gov. Mass. Commn. on Status of Women, 1974; Nat. Endowment Arts award, 1978. Mem. Authors Guild, Authors League, PEN, Poetry Soc. Am., Feminist Writers Guild, Nat. Audubon Soc., Mass. Audubon Soc., Am. Rose Soc. Author: Breaking Camp, 1968; Hard Loving, 1969; Going Down Fast, 1969; Dance the Eagle to Sleep, 1970; (with Bob Hershon, Emmett Jarrett and Dick Lourie) 4-Telling, 1971; Small Changes, 1973; To Be of Use, 1973; Living in the Open, 1976; Woman on the Edge of Time, 1976; The High Cost of Living, 1978; The Twelve-Spoked Wheel Flashing, 1978; (play) (with David Ira Wood) The Last White Class, 1978; adv. editor APHRA, 1975-78, Poetry on the Buses, 1979—; adv. bd. Sojourner, 1976—, Nat. Forum, 1979—. Address: Box 943 Wellfleet MA 02667

PIERNO, ANTHONY ROBERT, lawyer; b. Uniontown, Pa., Apr. 28, 1932; s. Anthony Michael and Mary Jane (Saporita) P.; B.A. summa cum laude, Whittier (Calif.) Coll., 1954; J.D., Stanford U., 1959; m. Beverly Jean Kohn, June 20, 1954; children—Kathryn Ann, Robert Lawrence, Linda Jean, Diane Marie. Admitted to Calif. bar, 1960; practice in Los Angeles, 1960-67; chief dep. commr. corps. State Calif., 1967-69, commr. corps., 1969-71; partner firm Wyman, Bautzer et al, Los Angeles, 1971-74; sr. partner firm Memel, Jacobs, Pierno & Gersh, Los Angeles, 1976—; founder, dir. Exec. Savs. & Loan Assn., Century City, Calif., 1974-76; lectr. Am. Mgmt. Assn., 1979—. Mem. Gov. Calif. Council, 1969-71, Gov. Calif. Task Force Higher Edn., 1970-71, Atty. Gen.'s Vol. Adv. Com., 1971-78. Mem. legal adv. bd. N.Y. Inst. Finance, 1971—; mem. adv. bd. Legal Edn. Inst., 1975—; adv. dir. Whittier Coll. Sch. Law, 1975—, vice-chmn., 1979—; trustee Marymount Palos Verdes Coll., 1976—, Whittier Coll., 1977—. Served with AUS, 1954-56. Recipient Outstanding Alumni award Whittier Coll., 1970. Mem. Am. Bar Assn., State Bar Calif. (chmn. com. corps. 1971-75, exec. com. bus. law sect. 1977—), N.Am. Securities Adminstrs. (exec. com. 1969-71), Delta Theta Phi. Clubs: Palos Verdes Yacht; Peninsula Racquet. Home: 2901 Via Anacapa Palos Verdes Estates CA 90274 Office: 1801 Century Park E Los Angeles CA 90067

PIEROTTI, JOHN, cartoonist; b. N.Y.C., July 26, 1911; s. Roger and Emily (Brucato) P.; student Mechanics Art Inst., 1930, Cooper Union, 1931, Art Students League, 1932-33; m. Helen Mastrangelo, June 5, 1938 (dec.); children—Melba, John, Pamela; m. 2d, Orla Smith Pierotti. Copy boy, illustrator, sports, news cartoons, portraits N.Y. Telegram, 1927; engaged in drawing for N.E.A. Syndicate, Sporting News, St. Louis, advt. for Gen. Foods; sports cartoonist Washington Post, 1933; movie animation work Popeye and Betty Boop, N.Y.C., 1936-37; joined United Features Syndicate, 1937, sports editor, 1943; artist comic strip Hippo and Hookie, King Features Syndicate, 1939; staff cartoonist N.Y. daily PM, 1940; sports cartoonist N.Y. Star (successor to PM), 1948-49; sports editor, cartoonist McClure Syndicate, 1949-51; syndicated own strip Nutcracker U., 1950; sports, cartoonist N.Y. Post, 1951—; illustrator children's, sports, polit. books. Recipient nat. recognition for portrait Georges Clemenceau, 1928; 2d prize award for best editorial cartoon Los Angeles Pub. Assn., 1955; Page One award for best sports cartoon Graphic Arts, 1955; Silurian award for best editorial cartoon, 1965, 67, 68, 71, 72; Page One award for best sports cartoon, 1965, for best editorial cartoon, 1967, 68, 70, 71, 72, 73, 75. Mem. Nat. Cartoonists Soc. (pres. 1957-59, named Best Editorial cartoonist 1975), Baseball Writers Assn., Banshees Artists and Writers Assn., Newspaper Reporters Assn. N.Y.C., U.S. Harness Writers Assn. (pres. N.Y. chpt.). Contbr. cartoons to popular mags., U.S., Can., Gt. Britain, France, S.Am. Home: 2004 Ocean Ave Brigantine NJ 08203

PIEROTTI, ROBERT AMEDEO, educator; b. Newark, Nov. 13, 1931; s. Amedeo and Maria-Pia (Pisani) P.; B.A. in Chemistry, Pomona Coll., 1954; Ph.D. (Leonard and Rose Chudacoff scholar) U. Wash., 1958; m. Dorothy Clare Soper, June 22, 1959; children—Margaret-Marie, Stephen Robert. Instr., U. Nev., Reno, 1958-60; faculty Ga. Inst. Tech., Atlanta, 1960—, prof. chemistry, 1968—. NATO sr. fellow Bristol (Eng.) U., 1968. Mem. Am. Chem. Soc., Am. Phys. Soc., Faraday Soc., AAAS, AAUP, Sigma Xi (M.A. Ferst Research prize 1962). Home: 3689 Cochise Dr NW Atlanta GA 30339

PIEROTTI, ROLAND, banker; b. N.Y.C., Sept. 3, 1905; s. Ubaldo and Rosina (Gualla) P.; A.B., Cornell U., 1927; postgrad. Harvard Law Sch., 1927-28; J.D., N.Y. U., 1936; m. Alice Jackson, Aug. 27, 1941. With Bank of Am., N.A., 1928-31, Bancamerica-Blair Corp., N.Y.C., 1931-34, Waller & Co., N.Y.C., 1934-35; atty. SEC, N.Y.C., 1937-47, chief. atty., 1945-47, chief econ. warfare div., 1941-45; asst. v.p. Washington rep. Bank of Am., N.T. & S.A., 1947-49, v.p., Washington rep., 1949-53, asst. to pres., San Francisco, 1953-64, exec. v.p., 1964-70, mem. adv. council, 1953, ret.; sr. rep. Europe, dir. First Boston Corp., London, 1970-72; cons. Bank of Calif., San Francisco, 1973-76; dir. Investment Bank of Greece, Athens, Rumianca s.p.a., Turin, Italy, Alumnio de Mexico, Editorial Novarro, Mexico City. Trustee St. Francis Hosp., San Francisco. Mem. N.Y. State Bar. Clubs: Union, Racquet and Tennis, Grolier, Harvard, Knickerbocker (N.Y.C.); Metropolitan (Washington); Pacific Union (San Francisco). Home: 1100 Sacramento St San Francisco CA 94108

PIERPOINT, POWELL, lawyer; b. Phila., Apr. 30, 1922; s. James Reynolds and Ruth (Powell) P.; B.A., Yale, 1944, LL.B., 1948; m. Margaret Shaw Sagar, Mar. 24, 1950; 1 dau., Harriet Pierpoint Bos. Admitted to N.Y. bar, 1949; asso. firm Hughes, Hubbard & Reed, and predecessors, N.Y.C., 1948-53, partner, 1955-61, 63—; asst. U.S. atty. So. Dist. N.Y. 1953-55; gen. counsel Dept. Army, 1961-63; pres. Legal Aid Soc., 1979—. Mem. N.Y.C. Bd. Ethics, 1972—. Served with USNR, 1943-46. Fellow Am. Coll. Trial Lawyers; mem. Am., N.Y. State bar assns., Am. Judicature Soc., Assn. Bar City N.Y., N.Y. County Lawyers Assn. Home: 155 E 72d St New York NY 10021 Office: 1 Wall St New York NY 10005

PIERPOINT, ROBERT CHARLES, journalist; b. Redondo Beach, Calif., May 16, 1925; s. Charles O. and Emma Estelle (Adkins) P.; student Calif. Inst. Tech., 1943-44; B.A., U. Redlands, 1947, D.Journalism (hon.), 1976; postgrad. U. Stockholm (Sweden), 1947-48, U. Zurich (Switzerland), 1948; m. Patricia Jean Adams, Oct. 3, 1959; children—Alan, Eric, Kim, Marta. Reporter, Swedish Broadcasting Corp., 1948-51; free-lance reporter, Scandinavia, also stringer CBS News, 1949-51; war corr. CBS News, Korea, 1951-54, chief Far East bur., Tokyo, Japan, 1954-57, White House corr., Washington, 1957—. Served with USNR, 1943-45. Recipient Distinguished Services award U. Redlands, 1963; Drew Pearson award for investigative reporting Drew Pearson Found., 1973; Emmy award (2) Nat. Acad. TV Arts and Scis., 1974; award for best radio interpretation fgn. affairs Overseas Press Club Am., 1975. Mem. AFTRA. Office: 2020 M St Washington DC 20036

PIERPONT, ROBERT, med. service adminstr.; b. Somers Point, N.J., Jan. 27, 1932; s. Robert E. and Elise D. (White) P.; B.S. in Bus. Adminstrn., Pa. Mil. Coll., 1954; postgrad. Inst. Ednl. Mgmt., Harvard Grad. Sch. Bus. Adminstrn., 1970; m. Marion J. Welde, Oct. 11, 1958; children—Linda J., Nancy L., Robert W., Richard F. Comml. sales rep. Atlantic City (N.J.) Electric Co., 1956-58; asst. dir. devel. Widener Coll. (formerly Pa. Mil. Coll.) Chester, 1958-61, asst. to pres., 1961-62, dir. devel., 1962-68, v.p. for devel., 1968-70; sr. cons. v.p. and dir. Brakeley, John Price Jones, Inc., N.Y.C., 1970-79; v.p. devel. Mt. Sinai Med. Center, N.Y.C., 1979—; guest faculty mem. Big 10 Fund Raisers Inst., Mackinac Island, Mich., 1971; mem. adv. com. on application of standards, Philanthropic Adv. Service, Council of Better Bus. Burs., Washington, 1978—. Mem. bishops adv. com. on stewardship Diocese of Pa., 1968-69; vestryman Trinity Episcopal Ch., Swarthmore, 1970-72. Served to 1st lt. inf. U.S. Army, 1954-56. Mem. Nat. Soc. Fund Raising Execs. (dir.-at-large 1970-78, pres. inst. 1977-79, chmn. bd. 1979—), Nat. Assn. Hosp. Devel. Office: 19 E 98th St 2B New York NY 10029

PIERPONT, WILBUR K., educator; b. Winn, Mich., Mar. 15, 1914; s. Clarence N. and Ethel (Kent) P.; A.B., Central Mich. Coll. Edn., 1934; M.B.A., U. Mich. (Univ. scholar), 1938, Ph.D., 1942; LL.D., Central Mich. U., 1958, Hope Coll., 1977; m. Maxine Sponseller, Feb. 7, 1941; children—Ann (Mrs. Kenneth Mack), James. Brookings Instn. fellow, 1941; price analyst Ordnance Dept., Washington, 1942-44; teaching fellow U. Mich., 1938-40, instr. Sch. Bus. Adminstrn., 1941-42, asst. prof., 1946-51, controller, 1947-51, v.p., chief financial officer prof., 1951-76, prof. accounting, 1977—; trustee Ex-Cell-O Corp., Tecumseh Products Corp. Trustee, Kresge Found., Coll. Retirement Equities Fund. Served as lt. (j.g.) Bur. Ordnance, USNR, 1944-46. Recipient Delta Sigma Pi, Phi Kappa Phi awards, 1938. Mem. Am. Accounting Assn., Beta Gamma Sigma, Phi Kappa Phi. Methodist. Clubs: Golf and Outing, Rotary (Ann Arbor); Economic (Detroit). Conbr. articles to numerous jours. Home: 2203 Devonshire Rd Ann Arbor MI 48104

PIERRE, JEANNE (SARAH JEANNETTE DECEVÉE), fashion exec.; b. Harrisburg, Pa., Apr. 29, 1908; d. Edwin J. and Anna Mary (Patterson) Decevée; grad. Irving Coll., Mechanicsburg, Pa., 1923-27; m. John Russel Delaney, July 21, 1951. Actress, 1927-35; designer, dressmaker, 1935-38; asst. design Sohon System, N.Y.C. 1938-39; fashion dir. Arnold Constable, 1940-44; fashion coordinator J.L. Hudson Co., Inc., Detroit, 1944-1946; fashion dir. A.D. Juillard & Co., Inc., N.Y.C., 1946-53, Am. Rayon Inst., 1953-72; v.p. Papert, Koenig, Lois, Inc., advt., 1959-65; account supr., v.p. Hockaday Assos., Inc., 1965-72; editor Merchandising Motivation Inc., 1972—, v.p., 1976—; instr. textiles Tobe-Coburn Sch. Fashion Careers; fashion advt. cons. textile adv. com. Fashion Inst. Tech. Mem. Fashion Group (gov. 1949, 53, v.p. 1950, chmn. bd. 1951-52, pres. 1969), N.Y. Fashion Designers (adv. council), Advt. Women of N.Y. Contbr. articles to profl. publs. Home: 163 E 36th St New York NY 10016

PIERRE, PERCY ANTHONY, govt. ofcl.; b. nr. Donaldsville, La., Jan. 3, 1939; s. Percy John and Rosa (Villavaso) P.; B.S., U. Notre Dame, 1961, M.S., 1963; Ph.D., Johns Hopkins, 1967; postgrad. U. Mich., 1968; m. Olga Agnes Markham, Aug. 7, 1965; children—Kristin, Allison. Asst. prof. So. U., 1963; instr. Johns Hopkins, 1963-64; instr. Morgan State Coll., 1964-66; instr. U. Mich., 1967-68; instr. U. Calif. at Los Angeles, 1968-69; staff mem. RAND Corp., 1968-71; White House fellow, 1969-70; dean Sch. Engring., Howard U., Washington, 1971-77; asst. sec. for research, devel. and acquisition U.S. Dept. Army, 1979—; program officer, cons. project on expanding opportunities in minority engring. edn. Alfred P. Sloan Found., 1973-75; formerly cons. Center for Naval Analysis, Energy Research & Devel. Adminstrn., BDM Corp., NSF. Lectr. Mass. Inst. Tech., Yale, U. Calif., Berkeley, Purdue U., U. N.Y., Buffalo, U. Calif., San Diego, Johns Hopkins. Trustee U. Notre Dame, Nat. Fund for Minority Engring. Student; mem. adv. bd. scholars for reviewing proposed grad. programs within Ill. System; mem. adv. panel Nat. Bur. Standards for Inst. Applied Tech. Mem. Inst. Math. Statistics, I.E.E.E., Nat. Acad. Engring. (chmn. com. on minorities in engring., co-chmn. Symposium on Minorities in Engring., Washington 1973), Tau Beta Pi. Contbr. articles to profl. jours. Home: 8412 Carlynn Dr Bethesda MD 20034 Office: Pentagon Washington DC 20310

PIERROT, GEORGE FRANCIS, editor, TV producer, writer; b. Chgo., Jan. 11, 1898; s. George Francis (M.D.) and Aloyse (Martin) P.; A.B. in Journalism, U. Wash., 1920; L.H.D., Wayne State U., 1978; m. Kathryn Barnhisel, Aug. 31, 1922 (div. 1929); 1 son, George Francis Jr. (dec. 1929); m. 2d, Helen Hay Reck, Aug. 3, 1935; children—Nancy Ann, Helen Jeanne, Alan Hay, Robert Charnley. Reporter, Yakima Valley Am., 1919; editor U. Wash. Daily, 1920, Canning Age, 1920; reporter Seattle Times, 1920-21; publicity sec. Seattle C. of C., 1921-22; lectr. journalism U. Wash. Extension Div., 1921-22; asso. editor Bus. Mag., Detroit, 1922; asst. mng. editor Am. Boy mag., 1922-24; editor Am. Boy-Youth's Companion, 1924-36, staff writer travelling around world, 1931; world traveller as corr. World Letters, Inc., 1937-38; pres., dir. World Adventure Series Lectures, 1933-79; pres. George F. Pierrot Prodns., Inc. (TV), 1959—; pres. GFP, Inc., TV syndicated shows, 1966-73; publicity dir. Ford Motor Co. Expn., N.Y. World's Fair, 1939-40; pres., editor Sprague Publs., Inc., 1940-41; traveled in Europe, Africa, Asia making ednl. films USAF, 1952; chmn. Intra-Film, 1975-76; roving editor Mich. AAA mag. Mich. Living, 1975—. Mng. dir. Met. Detroit USO, 1942-43; exec. sec. Med. Sci. Center of Wayne U., 1943-47; mem. Regional Loyalty Bd., U.S. Civil Service Commn. Candidate Central Inf. O.T.S., Camp McArthur, Tex., 1918. Trustee Cranbrook Sch. for Boys, 1935-45; trustee, v.p. Internat. Film Found., 1946-49; journalism adv. bd. Wayne State U., 1949—; pres. Circumnavigators Club Found., 1964—; bd. dirs. Mich. Humane Soc., 1964—. Recipient Distinguished Service award Wayne State U., 1961; Stenius award for audio-visual service to internat. relations, 1961; award of merit Circumnavigators Club, 1964; MUCC State Conservation award, 1965; World Trader of Year award World Trade Club, Detroit, 1966; Minute Man award Gov. Mich., 1967; Significant Sig citation Sigma Chi, 1969; citation Mich. Senate, 1971, 75; Plaque Merit in Tourism, Austria, 1972; Merit award, W. Germany, 1972; Macomb Mr. Zip award, 1975; Pioneer award Detroit Producers Assn., 1978; chevalier Ordre Nationale du Merite, France, 1976, others. Mem. Detroit Zool. Soc. (dir.), Gamma Theta Epsilon, Sigma Delta Chi (internat. treas. 1923, sec. 1924, pres. 1925, editorial bd. Quill, Wells Key 1924). Dir., Am. Platform Guild, Am. Platform Assn., Archives Am. Art; hon. life trustee Detroit Inst. Arts Founders' Soc. Mem. Am. Polar Soc., English-Speaking Union, Ducks Unltd., Friends Detroit Pub. Library, Wilderness Soc. (life), Am. Mus. Nat. History (asso.), Mich. Outdoor Writers Assn., Detroit, Mich. hist. socs., Nat. Wildlife Fedn., Soc. Am. Travel Writers, Midwest Travel Writers Assn., Sons of Whisky Rebellion (comdr. in chief 1966—), Profl. Travel Film Dirs. Assn. (pres. 1972). Clubs: Explorers (co-comdr. El Paricutin volcano expdn., Mex. 1944); Circumnavigators (Mich. pres. 1962, internat. pres. 1962-63, Magellan award 1973), Adventurers, Overseas Press (N.Y.C.); Detroit Press; Torch, Prismatic (Detroit); Mich. Polar Equator; Internat. Skal; Economic. Author: Yea, Sheriton, 1925; The Vagabond Trail, 1935; producer World Adventure Series, WXYZ-TV, 1948-68, George Pierrot Show, WWJ-TV, 1953-76, George Pierrot Presents, WWJ-TV, 1958-75. Home: 2224 Burns Ave Detroit MI 48214 Office: 1507 Industrial Bldg Detroit MI 48226

PIERSON, ALBERT CHADWICK, educator; b. Pierson, Ill., Jan. 3, 1914; s. Charles Cleveland and Gertrude Fannie (Gale) P.; B.A. in Liberal Arts and Scis., U. Ill., 1935; M.B.A. with distinction, Harvard U., 1947; Ph.D., Columbia U., 1963; m. Evelyn Matilda Swanson, Sept. 13, 1952; 1 stepson, Jay F. Lynch. Merchandiser, Montgomery Ward & Co., Chgo., 1935-41; mgmt. cons., N.Y.C., 1947-53; prof. mgmt. San Diego State U., 1954—; cons. in field; pub. accountant, Calif.; research editor Jour. Travel Research, 1967—. Vice-pres. Nat. Arts Found., Lichenstein; mem. accreditation vis. teams Am. Assembly Collegiate Schs. Bus., 1977—. Served to col. AUS, 1941-46. Decorated Bronze Star. Fellow Soc. Applied Anthropology; mem. Acad. Mgmt. (pres. Western div. 1974-75), Western Council Travel Research (dir. 1965-67), Acad. Internat. Mgmt., Mil. Logistics Soc.,

James Joyce Soc., Beta Gamma Sigma, Sigma Iota Epsilon, Tau Sigma. Democrat. Methodist. Clubs: Harvard (Chgo.); Columbia (N.Y.C.); Marine Corps Officers (San Diego). Author: Trends in Lodging Enterprises, 1939-1963, 1963. Home: 1245 Park Row La Jolla CA 92037 Office: Coll Bus San Diego State U San Diego CA 92182

PIERSON, EARL WENDELL, accountant; b. Elgin, Ill., July 15, 1910; s. Per Algot and Emma (Johnson) P.; B.A., U. Wis., 1933; m. Hazel C. Nelson. Nov. 29, 1934; 1 son, Earl Wendell. With Arthur Andersen & Co., C.P.A.'s, Chgo., 1933-37, Houston, 1937-73, partner, 1949-73, adv. group, 1956-65, Chmn., 1957-58, partner charge Houston office, 1961-68, partners bd., 1968-69, ret., 1973; pres., dir. HCRC Corp. Past pres., dir. River Oaks Property Owners; treas., mem. exec. com. Houston Assn. Retarded Children, 1965-66; life mem., past chmn. bd. govs. Harris County Center for the Retarded; past trustee, treas. Mus. Fine Arts; mem. U. Wis. Found. Life mem. bd. dirs. St. Joseph Hosp. Found.; past trustee St. Joseph Hosp. Mem. Am. Inst. C.P.A.'s, Tex. Soc. C.P.A.'s, Beta Gamma Sigma, Alpha Kappa Psi, Beta Alpha Psi. Methodist (bd. adminstrn.). Clubs: River Oaks Country (past trustee, treas.), Ramada, Coronado (past dir.) Home: 2204 Chilton Rd Houston TX 77019 also Eagle River WI Office: 711 Louisiana St Suite 700 Houston TX 77002

PIERSON, FRANK COOK, educator, economist; b. Denver, Nov. 4, 1911; s. Silas Gilbert and Grace (Tisdale) P.; B.A., Swarthmore Coll., 1934; M.A., Columbia U., 1938, Ph.D., 1942; m. Marguerite Cannon Tamblyn, Mar. 16, 1940; children—John Halsey, Frank Cook. Asst. bank examiner, econ. research asst. Fed. Res. Bank N.Y., 1934-36; faculty Swarthmore Coll., 1940—, prof. econs., 1951—, chmn. dept., 1967-75, Joesph N. Wharton prof. polit. economy, 1968-79, prof. emeritus, 1979—. Spl. arbitrator NLWB, 1943, vice chmn. 3d region, 1944-45; vis. lectr., research asso. Inst. Indsl. Relations U. Cal. at Los Angeles, 1948-50; cons., pub. panel mem. WSB, 1952; research prof. Brookings Instn., 1961-62; cons. Dept. Labor, 1966-68, Council Econ. Advisers, 1965-68; dir. survey bus. edn. Carnegie Corp., 1957-59; dir. survey community manpower programs Upjohn Inst., 1970-71, unemployment control, 1975-77. Bd. dirs. White William Found. Mem. Am. Econ. Assn., Indsl. Relations Research Assn. (exec. com. 1962-65). Author: Collective Bargaining Systems, 1942; Community Wage Patterns, 1953; (with others) The Education of American Businessmen, 1959; Unions in Postwar America, 1967; Community Manpower Services for the Disadvantaged, 1972. Editor: (with G.W. Taylor) New Concepts in Wage Determination, 1957. Home: 740 Ogden Ave Swarthmore PA 19081

PIERSON, FRANK ROMER, writer, dir.; b. Chappaqua, N.Y., May 12, 1925; s. Harold C. and Louise (Randall) P.; grad. Harvard U., 1950; divorced; children—Michael, Eve. Journalist, Time/Life mags., 1950-58; TV writer, dir., producer, 1960—; prodns. include Have Gun-Will Travel, 1960-62, Naked City, 1963, Route 66, 1963; co-author screenplays: Cat Ballou (Oscar nomination), 1964, Dog Day Afternoon (Oscar award Acad. Motion Picture and Arts and Scis.), 1975; author screenplay Cool Hand Luke (Oscar nomination), 1967; dir. TV movie Neon Ceiling (San Francisco Film Festival award), 1972; dir., co-author film A Star Is Born, 1976; dir., writer film King of the Gypsies, 1978. Served with U.S. Army, 1943-46. Mem. Writers Guild Am. West (v.p. 1979—). Address: care Adams Ray and Rosenberg 9200 Sunset Blvd Los Angeles CA 90069

PIERSON, GEORGE ALLEN, banker; b. Fairview Park, Ind., June 13, 1916; s. Bert and Nellie (Henkel) P.; student Walsh Inst. Acctg., 1937-38, U. Detroit, 1939-41; certificate U. Wis. Grad. Sch. Banking, 1958-60; m. Hazel Harrison Elliott, Jan. 12, 1940. Accountant, Gen. Motors Corp., Detroit, 1935-40; field rep. Gen. Motors Acceptance Corp., Detroit, 1940-42; with Mich. Bank, Nat. Assn. (name now Mich. Nat. Bank of Detroit), 1946—, sr. v.p., 1968-70, pres., 1970-74, vice chmn. bd., 1974—, also dir., chmn. bd. Mich. Nat. Bank of Oakland, 1970—, Mich. Nat. Bank of West Metro, 1973—, Mich. Nat. Bank of Dearborn, 1977—, Mich. Nat. Bank Port Huron; chmn., dir. Mich. Nat. Corp., Bloomfield Hills; dir. Mich. Nat. Bank of North Metro, Mich. Nat. Bank of Sterling, Mich. Nat. Bank of Lansing, Wayne By-Products Co., Armada Corp., Hoskins Mfg. Co. Mem. exec. bd. advisers Mt. Carmel Mercy Hosp. and Med. Center; trustee Redford (Mich.) Community Hosp.; mem. exec. bd., asst. treas. Detroit Area council Boy Scouts Am., 1976—. Served with AUS, 1942-46. Decorated Bronze Star medal. Mem. Greater Detroit C. of C., Econ. Club Detroit, Robert Morris Assos. Clubs: Oakland Hills Country, Renaissance, Standard. Home: 2620 Endsleigh Dr Birmingham MI 48010 Office: 21 E Long Lake Rd PO Box 704 Bloomfield Hills MI 48013

PIERSON, GEORGE WILSON, historian; b. N.Y.C., Oct. 22, 1904; s. Charles Wheeler and Elizabeth Granville (Groesbeck) P.; B.A., Yale U., 1926, Ph.D., 1933; H.H.D., Merrimack Coll., 1974; m. Mary Laetitia Verdery, Sept. 10, 1936; children—Norah, Laetitia Deems. Faculty, Yale U., 1926—, prof. history, 1944-46, Larned prof. history, 1946-73, emeritus, 1973—, also historian of univ., chmn. dept. history, 1956-62, dir. div. humanities, 1964-70. Fellow Davenport Coll., 1933—. Guggenheim fellow, 1955-56. Recipient Porter prize Yale U., 1933; Wilbur Lucius Cross medal Yale U. Grad. Sch. Assn., 1973; Alumni medal Yale U., 1975. Fellow Am. Acad. Arts and Scis.; mem. Century Assn., Am. Hist. Assn., Phi Beta Kappa (pres. Yale U. chpt. 1965-73, W.C. DeVane medal 1974). Author: Tocqueville and Beaumont in America, 1938, (abridged) Tocqueville in America, 1959; Yale College, An Educational History, 1871-1921, 1952; Yale: The University College, 1921-1937, 1955; The Education of American Leaders: Comparative Contributions of United States Colleges and Universities, 1969; The Moving American, 1973; Yale: a short history, 1976; contbr.: American Universities in Nineteenth Century: The Formative Period to The Modern University (editor Margaret Clapp), 1950. Co-editor: Gustave de Beaumont: Lettres d' Amérique, 1973. Contbr. articles to hist., ednl. publs. Home: 176 Ives St Mount Carmel CT 06518 Office: PO Box 1691 Yale Sta New Haven CT 06520

PIERSON, GORDON KEITH, fgn. service officer; b. Billings, Mont., July 30, 1930; s. Eric A. and Florence (Birch) P.; B.B.A., U. Wash., 1952, Ph.D., 1963; postgrad. U. Stockholm, 1957-58; m. B. Patricia Walker, Oct. 23, 1953; 1 dau., Andria Kathleen. Research analyst, Larry Smith Real Estate Cons., Seattle, 1955-56; instr. econs. U. Wash., 1958-61; asst. prof. U. N.M., 1961-62; program economist USOM, Thailand, Bangkok, 1962-66; internat. relations officer Asian Devel. Bank, Manila, Philippines, 1966-67; chief Thailand-Burma AID desk, 1968-71, program officer, Tunis, 1971, asst. dir. Tunis, 1972-73; program officer, Amman, Jordan, 1974-77, asst. dir., 1977; AID rep., Khartoum, Sudan, 1977-79; AID mission dir., Khartoum, Sudan, 1979—. Pres. Am. Community Sch. Bd., Amman; mem. Khartoum Am. Sch. Bd., 1978-80. Trustee SEATO Grad. Sch. Engring., Bangkok, 1966-67. Served to 1st lt. USAF, 1952-54. Recipient award Am. Scandinavian Found., 1957. Mem. Am. Econs. Assn., Am. Fgn. Service Assn., Theta Chi. Address: Khartoum Dept State Washington DC 20520

PIERSON, HERBERT FLETCHER, musician; b. Trenton, N.J., May 9, 1914; s. John Ewing and Margaret (Fletcher) P.; B.M., Curtis Inst. Music, 1937; m. Betty G. Wayda, Aug. 25, 1951; children—Herbert, Lisa. French hornist Trenton Symphony, 1930-36, Kansas City, 1937-38, Phila., 1938-74; faculty Temple U., Phila. Coll. Performing Arts. Served with AUS, 1942-46. Home: 28 Endicott Rd Trenton NJ 08690. *Success is no accident, it comes to the person who does his job a little better than the other fellow.*

PIERSON, JOHN THEODORE, JR., mfr.; b. Kansas City, Mo., Oct. 13, 1931; s. John Theodore and Helen Marguerite (Sherman) P.; B.S.E., Princeton U., 1953; M.B.A., Harvard U., 1958; m. Susan K. Chadwick, Apr. 16, 1977; children by previous marriage—Merrill Sherman, Karen Louise, Kimberly Ann. With Vendo Co., Kansas City, Mo., 1960—, gen. automatic products salesman, 1960-61, mgr. new products, 1961-63, v.p. sales equipment for Coca-Cola, 1963-66, pres. Vendo Internat., 1966-69, exec. v.p., chief operating officer, 1969-71, pres., chief exec. officer, 1971-74; pres. Preco Industries, Inc., 1974—, chmn., 1977—; dir. Leawood Nat. Bank. Mem. Regional Export Expansion Council; dir. Fgn. Trade Zone of Greater Kansas City. Past dir. Civic Council, Kansas City. Trustee, mem. exec. com. Midwest Research Inst.; past trustee Pembroke-Country Day Sch., Barstow Sch.; past mem. adv. council U.S.-Japan Econ. Relations; bd. dirs. Youth Symphony Kansas City, 1965-69; mem. council Chmn. for Exploring; mem. Nat. Scout Council. Served as lt. intelligence USNR, 1953-56. Mem. Kansas City (v.p. internat.), U.S. (dir. 1970-74) chambers commerce. Clubs: River, Kansas City Country. Co-author: Linear Polyethylene and Polypropylene: Problems and Opportunities, 1958. Home: 5908 Reinhardt Dr Shawnee Mission KS 66205 Office: 4719 Merriam Dr Shawnee Mission KS 66203

PIERSON, LEON H.A., lawyer; b. Balt., Apr. 12, 1901; s. Samuel B. and Minnie (Mondress) P.; LL.B., U. Md., 1923; m. Jane Garner Michel, May 2, 1947; children—Marcia J., William Michel, Joanna, David, Robert, Dorothy, Barbara. Admitted to Md. bar, 1923; partner Pierson & Pierson, 1931-57, 61—; gen. counsel Pub. Service Commn. Md., 1956-57; U.S. atty. Dist. Md., 1957-61. Pres., Md. Soc. Mentally Retarded Children, 1957-58; chmn. Gov.'s Commn. to Revise Mental Health Laws Md., 1966-69; bd. dirs. Balt. Assn. Retarded Citizens, Sch. of Chimes. Fellow Am. Coll. Trial Lawyers; mem. Am., Md., Balt. (pres. 1962-63) bar assns. Jewish. Home: 2210 Chilham Rd Baltimore MD 21209 Office: 10 Light St Baltimore MD 21202

PIERSON, ROBERT JAMES, JR., controls co. exec.; b. Evanston, Ill., Sept. 30, 1923; s. Robert J. and Hildur (Milroy) P.; B.B.A., U. Wis., 1950; m. Janet L. Williams, June 23, 1950; children—Linda, Elizabeth, Robert James III. Account exec. Merrill Lynch, Pierce, Fenner & Smith, Inc., Chgo., 1950-53; marketing exec. Rheem Mfg. Co., Chgo., 1953-69, pres. environmental group, 1969-73; exec. v.p. Robertshaw Controls Co., Richmond, Va., 1973—, also dir.; dir. Robertshaw Controls Co., Central Nat. Bank Richmond. Served in USAAF, 1942-45. Mem. Phi Gamma Delta. Republican. Presbyterian. Clubs: Hermitage Country, Glenview. Home: 201 Walsing Dr Richmond VA 23229 Office: 1701 Byrd Ave PO Box 26544 Richmond VA 23261

PIERSON, WILLIAM MICHEL, lawyer; b. Balt., Jan. 11, 1950; s. Leon H.A. and Jane Garner (Michel) P.; B.A. with honors, U. Md., 1970, J.D. with honors, 1973; m. Linda Gayle Bowler, Sept. 8, 1973. Admitted to Md. bar, 1973; law clk. to Judge C. Stanley Blair, 1973-74; asso. firm Pierson & Pierson, 1974—. Mem. Am., Md., Balt. bar assns., Am. Soc. Legal History, Order of Coif. Home: 4107 Roland Ave Baltimore MD 21211 Office: 10 Light St Baltimore MD 21202

PIETENPOL, WILLIAM JOHN, business exec., educator; b. Boulder, Colo., July 15, 1921; s. William B. and Helen (Carson) P.; B.S. in Elec. Engring., Colo. U., 1943, B.A. in Physics, 1943; Ph.D. in Physics, Ohio State U., 1949; m. Marlea Jo Roberts, Mar. 11, 1950; children—Lynn Jo, David John. Devel. engr. RCA, 1943-46; dir. devel. semiconductor devices Bell Telephone Labs., 1950-58; v.p., gen. mgr. semiconductor div. Sylvania Electric Products, Inc., Woburn, Mass., 1958-61; mgr. components devel. components div. IBM Corp., 1961-64; v.p. engring. tech. Bell & Howell Co., Chgo., 1964-74; cons., 1974—; vis. lectr. U. Colo., Boulder, 1976-78, dean engring. and applied sci., 1978—. Eastman Kodak fellow, 1947; Westinghouse fellow, 1948. Mem. Phi Beta Kappa, Sigma Xi, Tau Beta Pi. Office: Coll Engring U Colorado Boulder CO 80310

PIETRACK, LEO WALTER, mfg. co. exec.; b. Calumet City, Ill., July 16, 1928; s. Leo W. and Margaret (Woznica) P.; A.B., U. Ill., 1954; C.P.A., 1958; m. Josephine Valenti, June 13, 1953; children—Scott L., Judy A., David A., Thomas J. With Ernst & Ernst, C.P.A.'s, Chgo., 1954-61; with Rockwell Mfg. Co., 1961-73, controller, 1967-73; v.p. finance, treas., sec. AVM Corp., Jamestown, N.Y., 1973—. Served with U.S. Army, 1946-48. Mem. Nat. Assn. Accountants, Financial Execs. Inst., Am. Inst. C.P.A.'s. Home: 1243 Holy Cross Dr Monroeville PA 15146 Office: 525 William Penn Pl Suite 3729 Pittsburgh PA 15219

PIETSCH, CHARLES JOSEPH, JR., fin. co. exec.; b. Honolulu, Feb. 5, 1919; s. Charles Joseph and Florence Alison (McCulloch) P.; student U. Hawaii-Wheaton Coll., 1937-39; m. Fern Lucille Prohaska, May 2, 1941; children—Charles Joseph, III, Diana Alison Pietsch Hewett. Real estate salesman, Honolulu, 1940-41; real estate broker, builder, Honolulu, 1947-54; pres., chmn. bd. Honolulu Mortgage Co., Ltd., 1954—; chmn. bd. Bishop Investment Co., 1970—. Served from 2d lt. to maj., USAAF, 1941-46. Episcopalian. Clubs: Masons; Shriners; Oahu Country; Outrigger Canoe. Home: 59-777 Pupukea Rd Haleiwa HI 96712 Office: PO Box 1060 Honolulu HI 96808

PIETTE, LAWRENCE HECTOR, educator, biophysicist; b. Chgo., Jan. 4, 1932; s. Gerald John and Lillian (Bumgardner) P.; B.S., Northwestern U., 1953, M.S., 1954; Ph.D., Stanford, 1957; m. Mary Irene Harris, Aug. 15, 1957; children—Jeffrey, Martin. Mgr. research biochemistry and biophysics Varian Assos., 1956-65; prof. biophysics U. Hawaii, 1965—, chmn. dept., 1968—, dir. Cancer Research Lab., 1970—; exec. dir. Cancer Center Hawaii, 1974. Chmn. cancer adv. com., regional med. program, research com. Hawaii div. Am. Cancer Soc. Mem. Am. Chem. Soc., Biophys. Soc., A.A.U.P. Contbr. articles to profl. jours. Asso. editor Archives Biochemistry and Biophysics, Jour. Spectroscopy Letters, Jour. Organic Magnetic Resonance. Home: 4954 Kolohala Ave Honolulu HI 96816

PIETZ, ERVIN, mfg. and engring co. exec.; b. Eureka, S.D., Oct. 4, 1912; s. John J. and Margaret (Preszler) P.; B.S. in Elec. Engring., S.D. Sch. Mines and Tech., 1934, D.Engring. (hon.), 1966; m. Helen F. Moffatt Feb. 2, 1939; children—Merle, Peter, Paul, William. Pres., chief exec. officer, chmn. bd., dir. Barry Wright Corp., Watertown, Mass.; dir. Bay Bank Middlesex, Waltham, Mass.; past pres., now dir. Asso. Industries Mass. Trustee, Lesley Coll.; bd. dirs. Boys' Club Watertown; mem. corp. Babson Coll. Mem. Am. Assn. Indsl. Mgmt. N.E. (dir., past pres.), Chief Execs. Forum, Watertown C. of C. (dir.), Newcomen Soc. N.Am., Am. Helicopter Soc. Home: 75 Grove St Wellesley MA 02181 Office: 680 Pleasant St Watertown MA 02172

PIFER, ALAN (JAY PARRISH), found. exec.; b. Boston, May 4, 1921; s. Claude Albert and Elizabeth (Parrish) P.; A.B., Harvard U., 1947; Lionel de Jersey Harvard student Emmanuel Coll., Cambridge (Eng.) U., 1947-48; LL.D., Mich. State U., 1971, Hofstra U., 1974, Notre Dame U., 1975; D. of Univ., Open U., Eng., 1974; m. Erica Pringle, June 20, 1953; children—Matthew, Nicholas, Daniel. Exec. sec. U.S. Ednl. Commn. in U.K., London, 1948-53; exec. asst. Carnegie Corp. N.Y., 1953-57, exec. asso., 1957-63, v.p. 1963-65, acting pres., 1965-67, pres., 1967—, v.p. Carnegie Found. for Advancement of Teaching, 1963-65, acting pres., 1965-67, pres., 1967—; dir. McGraw-Hill Inc.; mem. mgmt. com. U.S.-South Africa Leader Exchange Program, 1957—; chmn. mayor's adv. com. Bd. Higher Edn., N.Y.C., 1966-69; chmn. Pres.'s Task Force on Edn., 1968-69; mem. adv. council Columbia Sch. Social Work, 1963-69; dir. N.Y. Urban Coalition, 1967-71, Nat. Assembly Social Policy and Devel., 1967-71; mem. sr. execs. council Conf. Bd., 1973-74; mem. Commn. on Pvt. Philanthropy and Pub. Needs, 1973-75. Trustee Found. Library Center, 1967-70, chmn., 1968-70; trustee African-Am. Inst., 1957-72, U. Bridgeport (Conn.), 1973—, Am. Ditchley Found., 1973—; bd. dirs. Council on Founds., 1970-76; bd. overseers Harvard U., 1969-75; mem. Pres.'s Commn. White House Fellowships, 1975-77. Served from pvt. to capt. AUS, 1942-46. Fellow Am. Acad. of Arts and Scis.; mem. Council Fgn. Relations. Clubs: Pilgrims of U.S., Harvard, Century Assn. Home: 311 Greens Farms Rd Greens Farms CT 06436 Office: 437 Madison Ave New York City NY 10022

PIGEON, GILLES, physician, educator; b. Montreal, Que., Can., Mar. 16, 1931; s. Leopold and Juliette (Groulx) P.; B.A., Sem. Philosophie Montreal, 1950; M.D., U. Montreal, 1956; m. Suzanne Roy, Nov. 7, 1959; children—Marie, Marc, Nicole, Jean, Anne. Asst. prof. medicine U. Montreal, 1964-69; intern U. Montreal and affiliated hosps., 1955-56; resident U. Montreal, Yale, 1956-62; chmn. dept. nephrology Hôpital Général, de Verdun (Que., Can.), 1966-69; prof. medicine U. Sherbrooke, Que., 1969—, dean faculty medicine, 1972-79. Bd. dirs. Centre Hospitalier Universitaire de Sherbrooke. Home: 431 Duvernay St Sherbrooke PQ J1L 1J3 Canada Office: U Sherbrooke Sherbrooke PQ J1H 5N4 Canada

PIGEON, LOUIS PHILIPPE, judge; b. Henryville, Que., Can., Feb. 8, 1905; s. Arthur and Maria (Demers) P.; B.A., Petit Seminaire de Que., 1925; LL.L., Laval U., Quebec, Que., 1928, LL.D.; LL.D. U. Ottawa (Ont.); m. Madeleine Gaudry, Aug. 29, 1936; children—Jacques, Madeleine, Louise, Francois, Yves, Michel. Called to bar Que., 1928, created queen's counsel, 1940; asso. firm St.-Laurent, Gagne, Devlin & Taschereau, 1928-37; partner firm Hudon & Pigeon, 1938-40, Germain, Pigeon, Thibeaudea & Lesage, 1946-67; law clk. Legis. Que., 1940-44; justice Supreme Ct. Can., Ottawa, from 1967, then puisne judge; prof. constl. law Laval U., 1942-67; legal adv. Prime Minister Que., 1960-66; batonnier Dist. Que., 1960-61; chmn. Nat. Council Adminstrn. Justice, 1963-67; v.p. Conf. Commrs. Uniformity Legis. in Can., 1966-67; chmn. Nat. Profl. Conduct Com., 1966-67. Mem. Can. Bar Assn. (v.p. Province Que. 1966-67). Roman Catholic. Clubs: Rideau; Cercle Universitaire (Quebec). Office: Supreme Ct Bldg Wellington St Ottawa ON K1A 0J1 Canada*

PIGFORD, ROBERT LAMAR, chem. engr.; b. Meridian, Miss., Apr. 16, 1917; s. Lamar and Zula Vivian (Harrington) P.; B.S., Miss. State Coll., 1938; M.S., U. Ill., 1940, Ph.D., 1942; m. Marian Gray Pinkston, Aug. 30, 1939; children—Nancy Marie, Robert Harrington. Research engr., exptl. sta. E.I. duPont de Nemours & Co., Inc., Wilmington, Del., 1941-47; Allan P. Colburn prof. chem. engring., chmn. dept. U. Del., 1947-66, Univ. prof., 1975—; prof. chem. engring. U. Calif. at Berkeley, 1966-75; Vis. prof. U. Wis., 1957, Cambridge U., 1959; part-time cons. indsl. chem. cos., 1946—. Mem. sci. adv. bd. USAF, 1956-60. Recipient Francis Alison award U. Del., 1979. Mem. Am. Inst. Chem. Engrs. (Profl. Progress award 1955, William H. Walker award 1958, W.K. Lewis award 1970, Founders award 1973), Nat. Acad. Engring., Nat. Acad. Scis., Am. Chem. Soc. (editor Fundamentals Quar., Indsl. and Engring. Chemistry), Sigma Xi, Tau Beta Pi. Author: (with W.R. Marshall, Jr.) Applications of Differential Equations to Chemical Engineering Problems, 1946; (with T.K. Sherwood) Absorption and Extraction, 1951; (with T.K. Sherwood and C.R. Wilke) Mass Transfer, 1974; sects. on diffusional operations, gas absorption and distillation in J.H. Perry's Chemical Engineers' Handbook (with A.P. Colburn), 1950. Home: 300 Wilson Rd Newark DE 19711

PIGFORD, THOMAS HARRINGTON, nuclear engr.; b. Meridian, Miss., Apr. 21, 1922; s. Lamar and Zula Vivian (Harrington) P.; B.S. in Chem. Engring., Ga. Inst. Tech., 1943; S.M. in Chem. Engring., M.I.T., 1948, Sc.D. in Chem. Engring., 1952; m. Catherine Kennedy Cathey, Dec. 31, 1948; children—Cynthia Pigford Naylor, Julie Pigford Earnest. Asst. prof. chem. engring., dir. Sch. Engring. Practice, M.I.T., 1950-52, asst. prof. nuclear and chem. engring., 1952-55, asso. prof., 1955-57; head engring., dir. nuclear reactor projects and asst. dir. research lab. Gen. Atomic Co., La Jolla, Calif., 1957-59; prof. nuclear engring., chmn. dept. nuclear engring. U. Calif., Berkeley, 1959—; cons. in field. Served with USNR, 1944-46. Named Outstanding Young Man of Greater Boston, Boston Jaycees, 1955; E. I. DuPont DeNemours research fellow, 1948-50; Japan Soc. for Promotion Sci. fellow, 1974-75; NSF grantee, 1960-75; EPA grantee, 1973-78; Dept. Energy grantee, 1976-79; Ford Found. grantee, 1974-75; Electric Power Research Inst. grantee, 1974-75. Fellow Am. Nuclear Soc. (Arthur H. Compton award 1971); mem. Nat. Acad. Engring., Am. Chem. Soc., Am. Inst. Chem. Engrs., AIME, Sigma Xi, Phi Kappa Phi, Tau Beta Pi. Author: (with Manson Benedict) Nuclear Chemical Engineering, 1958; contbr. numerous articles to profl. jours.; patentee in field. Home: 1 Garden Dr Kensington CA 94708 Office: Dept Nuclear Engring U Calif Berkeley CA 94720

PIGNATARO, LOUIS JAMES, educator; b. Bklyn., Nov. 30, 1923; s. Joseph and Rose (Capi) P.; B.C.E., Poly. Inst. Bklyn., 1951; M.S., Columbia U., 1954; Dr. Tech. Sci., Tech. U. Graz, Austria, 1961; m. Edith Hoffmann, Sept. 12, 1954; 1 dau., Thea. Faculty, Poly. Inst. N.Y., 1951—, prof. civil engring., 1965—, dir. div. transp. planning, 1967—, head dept. transp. planning and engring., 1970, dir. Transp. Tng. and Research Center, 1975; cons. govtl. agys., pvt. firms.; expert examiner N.Y.C. Dept. Traffic. Mem. Gov.'s Task Force Advisers on Transp. Problems, commr.'s council advisers N.Y. State Dept. Transp. Served with AUS, 1943-46. Recipient Distinguished Tchr. citation Poly. Inst. Bklyn., 1965, Dedicated Alumnus award, 1971, Distinguished Alumnus award, 1972; citation for distinguished research Poly. chpt. Sigma Xi, 1975; named Engr. of Year, N.Y. State Soc. Profl. Engrs., 1974. Registered profl. engr., N.Y., Calif., Fla. Fellow ASCE (dir.), Inst. Transp. Engrs.; mem. Am. Rd. and Transp. Builders Assn. (div. dir.), Transp. Research Bd. (univ. liaison rep.), Transp. Research Forum, Sigma Xi, Chi Epsilon, Tau Beta Pi. Sr. author: Traffic Engineering-Theory and Practice, 1973. Contbr. articles to profl. jours. Home: 230 Jay St Brooklyn NY 11201 Office: 333 Jay St Brooklyn NY 11201

PIGOTT, CHARLES MCGEE, mfr. transp. equipment; b. Seattle, Apr. 21, 1929; s. Paul and Theiline (McGee) P.; B.S., Stanford U., 1951; m. Yvonne Flood, Apr. 18, 1953. With PACCAR Inc, Seattle, 1959—, exec. v.p., 1962-65, pres., 1965—, also dir.; dir. Safeco Corp.,

Boeing Co., Citibank, Citicorp, Standard Oil Calif. Bd. dirs. United Good Neighbors, Seattle, SRI Internat. Mem. Bus. Council. Office: Business Center Bldg 777 106th NE PO Box 1518 Bellevue WA 98004

PIKAART, LEN, mathematician, educator; b. Nutley, N.J., Jan. 4, 1933; s. Leonard Gascoigne and Janette Theodora (Hendricks) P.; B.A. with distinction, U. Va., 1959, M.Ed., 1960, Ed.D., 1963; m. Constance Natalie Headapohl, Nov. 6, 1954; children—Leonard Frederick, William Edward, Lori Janette, Lucinda Corinne. Tchr. math. jr. and sr. high schs., Arundel County, Md., 1955-56; sr. research asst., instr. div. ednl. research U. Va., 1960-62, instr. div. math. Sch. Engring., 1962-63; mem. faculty U. Ga., Athens, 1963-74, prof. math. edn., 1971-74, dir. Ednl. Profl. Devel. Act Program for math. suprs., 1969-70, dir. program doctoral study in math edn., 1964-74; Robert L. Morton prof. math. edn. Ohio U., Athens, 1974—; participant internat. confs., cons. to govt. and industry. Pres. Athens County unit Am. Cancer Soc., 1977-79. Served with U.S. Army, 1956-58. Postdoctoral fellow N.Y. U., 1970-71. Mem. Math. Assn. Am., Am., Nat., Ohio, Ga. (pres. 1972-73) councils tchrs. math., AAUP, Am. Ednl. Research Assn., Phi Delta Kappa (chpt. pres. 1967-68). Club: Kiwanis. Co-author: Mathematics Teaching, 1977. Asst. editor The Arithmetic Teacher, 1967-70; mem. editorial com. Investigations in Math. Edn., 1968-79. Contbr. articles to profl. jours. Home: 27 Utah Pl Athens OH 45701 Office: McCracken Hall Ohio Univ Athens OH 45701

PIKARSKY, MILTON, transp. ofcl.; b. N.Y.C., Mar. 28, 1924; s. Abraham J. and Celia (Kaufman) P.; B.C.E., Coll. City N.Y., 1944; postgrad. Ill. Inst. Tech., 1947-56, M.S. in Civil Engring., 1969; postgrad. DePaul U., 1959-60; m. Sally Nesal, Aug. 9, 1947; children—Joel Jay, Amy Jo. Asst. engr. New York City R.R., Chgo., 1944-57; cons. civil engr., Chgo., Gary, Ind., Dearborn, Mich., 1955-60; engr. Dept. Pub. Works, Chgo., 1960-64, commr., 1964-73; chmn. Chgo. Transit Authority, 1973-75; chmn. Regional Transp. Authority, Chgo., 1975-79; dir. transp. research Ill. Inst. Tech. Research Inst., also research prof., 1979—. Mem. steering com. Urban Mass Transp. Adv. Council, U.S. Dept. Transp.; mem. Engrs. Joint Council Panel on Tech. Assessment, 1973; mem. adv. com. basic transp. research studies Mass. Inst. Tech. Center Transp. Studies; mem. indsl. adv. com. Coll. Engring. U. Ill.; mem. transp. adv. com. FEA, 1976. Trustee Children's World Montessori Sch. Park Ridge. Named Chicagoan of Year in Architecture and Engring., Chgo. Jr. Assn. Commerce and Industry, 1967, One of Top 10 Pub. Works Men-of-Year, 1969; recipient Townsend Harris medal Coll. City N.Y., 1969, Chgo's. Outstanding Leader in Transp. award Soc. Little Flower, 1969. Registered profl. engr., Ill. Fellow ASCE (Civil Govt. award 1973); mem. Nat. (Outstanding Engring. award for Chgo. Central Filtration Plant), Ill. socs. profl. engrs., Am. Ry. Engring. Assn., Am. Rd. Builders Assn. (chmn. council urban mass transp.), Western Soc. Engrs. (past pres.), Transp. Research Bd. (exec. com.), Chgo. Engrs. Club, Nat. Acad. Engring. (com. BART impact, com. pub. engring. policy), Am. Pub. Transit Assn., Chi Epsilon, Lambda Alpha. Clubs: Economic, Ground Hog (pres.). Home: 300 N State St Apt 5321 Chicago IL 60610 Office: 10 W 35th St Chicago IL 60616

PIKE, ALBERT RAYMOND, banker; b. Orwell, Ohio, Jan. 2, 1916; s. Granville E. and Nellie (Squibbs) P.; student Hiram Coll., 1934; B.S., Ohio State U., 1938; postgrad. U. Wis., 1960-63; m. Katherine Virginia Stevens, June 15, 1941; children—Gregory Stevens, Byron Albert. With Central Nat. Bank, Cleve., 1939-55; asst. v.p. Lake County Nat. Bank, Painesville, Ohio, 1955-68, pres., chief exec. officer, 1968-74, chmn. bd., chief exec. officer, 1974—. Campaign chmn. United Fund of Central and Eastern Lake County, Ohio, 1962-63, pres., 1963; pres. Credit Bur. Painesville; campaign chmn. Salvation Army and YMCA Capital Fund, 1969. Trustee Cleve. Dist. Golf Assn. Caddie Found.; pres. East Suburban Concerts, Inc. Served to 1st lt. Q.M.C., AUS, 1942-45. Mem. Painesville Area C. of C. (pres.), Ohio Bankers Assn. (past v.p., pres. 1976-77, chmn. 1977—, chmn. polit. action com. 1975-77), Am. Bankers Assn. (chmn. nat. bankers polit. action com. 1979). Rotarian (pres.). Clubs: Madison Country (North Madison, Ohio); Mentor Harbor Yachting; Kirtland Country (Willoughby, Ohio), Cleveland Treasurers, Cleveland Athletic, Clevelander. Home: 535 Barrington Ridge Painesville OH 44077 Office: 30 S Park Pl Painesville OH 44077

PIKE, BERTRAM N., actuary; b. N.Y.C., July 7, 1927; s. Morris and Kate (Plotkin) P.; B.Mgmt. E., Rensselaer Poly. Inst., 1948, M.Mgmt. E., 1949; m. Sonya A. Averbach, Sept. 9, 1951; children—Suzanne, Carl. With John Hancock Mut. Life Ins. Co., Boston, 1949—, v.p., 1970-72, sr. v.p. and group actuary, 1972—. Served with AC, U.S. Army, 1946-47. Soc. Actuaries, Am. Acad. Actuaries. Club: Algonquin. Office: Hancock Tower John Hancock Pl Boston MA 02116

PIKE, BURTON, educator; b. Boston, June 12, 1930; s. Leslie Arthur and Marian (Levin) P.; B.A., Haverford Coll., 1952; postgrad. U. Strasbourg (France), 1953-54; M.A., Harvard, 1955, Ph.D., 1958; Lectr. English, U. Hamburg (Germany), 1957-59; faculty Cornell U., 1959-69, asso. prof. comparative lit. and German, 1966-69, chmn. dept. comparative lit., 1964-68; prof., chmn. dept. German and comparative lit. Queens Coll., City U. N.Y., 1969-72, prof. comparative lit. Queens Coll., also City Univ. Grad. Center, 1970—. Fellow Am. Council Learned Socs., 1952-53; Fulbright fellow, 1953-54; Guggenheim fellow, 1966-67. Mem. Modern Lang. Assn., Am. Comparative Lit. Assn. (sec. 1967-71), Phi Beta Kappa. Author: Robert Musil: An Introduction to His Work, 1961. Home: 2 Charlton St Apt 6C New York City NY 10014

PIKE, FREDERICK ERNEST, bus. devel. co. exec.; b. Salt Lake City, Mar. 15, 1904; s. Edward Ernest and Louise (England) P.; grad. Am. Inst. Banking, Salt Lake City, Grad. Sch. Banking of Rutgers U., 1942; m. Ella Robison, July 14, 1926; children—Barbara Ann, Fred R. With Walker Bank & Trust Co., Salt Lake City, 1920-69, mgr. credit dept., 1931-46, v.p., 1948-56, sr. v.p. in charge loans, 1956-65, exec. v.p., 1965-69; exec. v.p. Utah Bus. Devel. Corp., Salt Lake City, 1969—; dir. Deseret Trust Co., Salt Lake City. Pres. Credit Bur., Salt Lake City, 1938. Mem. Robert Morris Assos. (nat. pres. 1958-59; pres. Mountain States chpt. 1955-57), Utah Bankers Assn. (exec. com.), Intermountain Assn. Credit Men (pres. 1941-42), Salt Lake City C. of C. (mem. bd., treas. 1955-58). Mem. Ch. of Jesus Christ of Latter-day Saints. Clubs: East Mill Creek Lions (pres. 1946-47); Ambassador Athletic (mem. bd., treas. 1956-59), Fort Douglas-Hidden Valley Country (Salt Lake City). Home: 6559 S 1615 E Salt Lake City UT 84121 Office: 115 S Main St Salt Lake City UT 84111

PIKE, KENNETH LEE, linguist; b. Woodstock, Conn., June 9, 1912; s. Ernest Reginald and Hattie May (Grannis) P.; Th.B., Gordon Coll. Theology and Missions, Boston, 1933; Ph.D., U. Mich., 1942; L.H.D., U. Chgo., 1973; hon. degree U. Paris, 1978; m. Evelyn Griset, Oct. 20, 1939; children—Judith, Barbara, Stephen. Engaged in field trips for research aboriginal langs. to Mexico, Guatemala, Ecuador, Peru, New Guinea, Ghana, Nigeria, Philippines, Irian Java, Java, Nepal, 1935—; asso. prof. linguistics U. Mich., 1948-55, prof., 1955-79; pres. Summer Inst. Linguistics, 1942-79, emeritus, 1979—; bd. dirs. Wycliffe Bible Translators, Inc., 1942-79. Recipient Presdl. medal of merit Govt. of Philippines, 1974. Mem. Linguistic Soc. Am. (pres. 1961); Internat. Phoenetic Assn. (council), Am. Anthrop. Assn. (liaison fellow), Phi Alpha Chi, Phi Kappa Phi. Author: Phoenetics, 1943; Phonemics, 1947; The Intonation of American English, 1945; Tone Languages, 1948; Language in Relation to a Unified Theory of the Structure of Human Behavior, vols. I-III, 1954, 55, 60, 2d edit., 1967; With Heart and Mind, 1962; Stir-Change-Create, Poems and Essays, 1967; Mark My Words, 1971; (with R. Young and A. Becker) Rhetoric, Discovery and Change, 1971; Selected Writings (Ruth M. Bend, editor), 1972; (with Evelyn G. Pike) Grammatical Analysis, 1977; (with Stephen B. Pike) Songs of Fun and Faith, 1977. Translator: (with D. Stark) New Testament into Mixtec. Address: Inst Linguistics 7500 W Camp Wisdom Rd Dallas TX 75236. *In my view, integrity is more important than "success".*

PIKE, THOMAS POTTER, corp. exec.; b. Los Angeles, Aug. 12, 1909; s. Percy M. and Elizabeth (Potter) P.; A.B. in Econs., Stanford U., 1931; m. Katherine Keho, June 15, 1931; children—John Keho, Josephine (Mrs. Craig S. Barnes), Mary Katherine Potter (Mrs. David Coquillard). Asso. Republic Supply Co. Cal., 1931-38, former pres., chmn. bd., organized T.P. Pike Drilling Co., 1938, pres., 1938-53; dep. asst. sec. of def., for supply and logistics, 1953-54, asst. sec. def., 1954-56; spl. asst. to the Pres., 1956, to sec. def., 1957-58; chmn. bd., chief exec. officer Pike Corp. of Am., 1961-69; hon. vice chmn., dir. Fluor Corp., Los Angeles, 1970—; dir. Hewlett-Packard Co., Channel 28 KCET Community TV of So. Calif. Chmn. State Alcoholism Adv. Council Bd. dirs. Nat. Council on Alcoholism; founder, dir. Alcoholism Council Greater Los Angeles; trustee Loyola Marymount U., Los Angeles; trustee, past pres. bd. Stanford U. Mem. Alpha Delta Phi. Roman Catholic. Clubs: California (Los Angeles); Valley Hunt (Pasadena, Calif.); Bohemian (San Francisco); Dana Strand Beach and Tennis (Dana Point, Cal.), Home: 1475 Circle Dr San Marino CA 91108 Office: 707 Wilshire Blvd Los Angeles CA 90017

PIKE, WILLIAM EDWARD, banker; b. Ft. Collins, Colo., Jan. 25, 1929; s. Harry H. and Alice Francis (Swinscoe) P.; student U. Colo., 1947-48; B.S., U.S. Naval Acad., 1952; M.B.A., Harvard, 1960; m. Catherine Broward Crawford, June 26, 1965; children—Elizabeth Catherine, Robert Crawford, Daniel William. Commd. ensign USN, 1952, advanced through grades to lt., 1958; ret., 1958; asst. treas. Morgan Guaranty Trust Co., N.Y.C., 1962-64, asst. v.p., 1964-66, v.p., 1966-71, sr. v.p., 1971-74, chmn. credit policy com., 1974—; dir. VF Corp., Am. Union Ins. Co. Bd. dirs. N.Y. Blood Center. Episcopalian. Club: Country (New Canaan, Conn.). Home: Indian Waters Dr New Canaan CT 06840 Office: 23 Wall St New York NY 10015

PILAFIAN, SUREN, architect; b. Izmir, Turkey, July 20, 1910; s. Harutune and Arshalous (Tatian) P.; brought to U.S., 1912, naturalized, 1921; student Pratt Inst., 1928-29, Columbia, 1929-30, N.Y.U., 1930-35; m. Grace Elizabeth Jones, Sept. 6, 1940 (dec. July 1969); children—Peter, Sherry, Michael, Christopher. Designer firm Cass Gilbert, N.Y.C., 1928-35; partner firm Barton and Pilafian, architects, Teheran, Iran, 1935-38; designer firm Norman Bel Geddes, N.Y.C., 1938-39; project planner Fed. Works Agy., 1939-41; designer firm Shreve, Lamb & Harmon, N.Y.C., 1941-42; pvt. practice, Detroit, 1942-47, 50-69, 72—; partner of Frank Montana, Detroit, 1947-50; designer firm Albert Kahn Assos., architects and engrs., Detroit, 1969-72; prin. works include Wayne State U. master plans, 1942-54, State Hall, 1947, Coll. Engring., 1952, Community Arts Center, 1955, Gen. Library, 1954, Kresge Sci. Library, 1953; master plans Auburn Hills (Mich.) campus Oakland Community Coll., 1968; St. John's Armenian Ch., Southfield, Mich., 1968; Eshleman Library at Henry Ford Community Coll., 1967; Sr. High Sch., Holland, Mich., 1962; Keating, Columbian, St. Clair, Stark Elementary Schs., Detroit, 1963-70. Vice pres. Mich. Archtl. Found., 1956-60. Vice pres. Detroit Sci. Museum Soc., 1950—, pres., 1960-61; mem. adv. com. Detroit Bd. Edn., 1956-59; mem. Detroit Armenian Cultural Assn., 1953—, pres., 1953-54; mem. Rosedale Park Players, 1969—, Rackham Symphony Choir, 1970, Dearborn Symphony Orch., 1970. Bd. dirs. Will-o-Way Performing Arts Center. Recipient Presdl. citation N.Y.U., 1958; Spl. citation Am. Assn. Sch. Adminstrs., 1960. Fellow AIA (past pres. Detroit; Honor award Detroit chpt. 1955, 59); mem. Mich. Soc. Architects, Architects Civic Design Group (past exec. com.), N.Y.U. Alumni Club (past pres.), Unitarian-Universalist. Contbr. articles to profl. jours. Home: 19820 Florence Av Detroit MI 48219

PILAR, FRANK LOUIS, educator; b. Verdigre, Nebr., Aug. 28, 1927; s. Henry and Lydia (Holan) P.; B.S., U. Nebr., 1951, M.S., 1953; Ph.D., U. Cin., 1957; m. Anita Hooper, June 16, 1954; children—Marcella, Mark, Deborah, Stacie, David. Research chemist Standard Oil Co. (Ind.), Whiting, 1954-55; prof. chemistry U. N.H., Durham, 1957—; vis. scientist Oxford (Eng.) U., 1963-64; vis. prof. U. Wis., 1970-71. Served with USMCR, 1945-46. Recipient U. N.H. sr. key faculty award, 1970. Mem. Am. Chem. Soc., Am. Phys. Soc., Sigma Xi, Phi Lambda Upsilon, Phi Kappa Phi. Author: Elementary Quantum Chemistry, 1968; Chemistry: The Universal Science, 1978. Patentee in field. Home: 26 Newmarket Rd Durham NH 03824

PILARCZYK, DANIEL EDWARD, bishop; b. Dayton, Ohio, Aug. 12, 1934; s. Daniel Joseph and Frederica Susanna (Hilgefort) P.; student St. Gregory Sem., Cin., 1948-53; Ph.B., Pontifical Urban U., Rome, 1955, Ph.L., 1956, S.T.B., 1958, S.T.L., 1960, S.T.D., 1961; M.A., Xavier U., 1965; Ph.D., U. Cin., 1969. Ordained priest Roman Catholic Ch., 1959; asst. chancellor Archdiocese of Cin., 1961-63, synodal judge Archdiocesan Tribunal, 1971—; mem. faculty Athenaeum of Ohio, St. Gregory Sem., 1963-74, v.p. Athenaeum of Ohio, also rector St. Gregory Sem., 1968-74; archdiocesan dir. ednl. services, 1974—; aux. bishop of Cin., 1974—; vicar gen., 1974—. Ohio Classical Conf. scholar to Athens, 1966. Mem. Am. Philol. Assn. Author: Praepositini Cancellarii de Sacramentis et de Novissimis, 1964-65. Home: 5418 Moeller Ave Cincinnati OH 45212 Office: 100 E 8th St Cincinnati OH 45202

PILAT, OLIVER, newspaperman; b. N.Y.C., Aug. 7, 1903; s. Oliver I. and Emma (Ramsay) P.; B.A., Amherst Coll., 1926; m. Avice Riddle, Apr. 11, 1930; children—Carl Jeffrey, Betsy. With Bklyn. Eagle, 1926-36, European corr., 1930-34; with New York Post, 1937-65, Washington corr., 1943-49, polit. reporter, N.Y.C., 1949-65; asst. to Mayor Lindsay, N.Y.C., 1966-67; asst. to council Pres. Garelik, N.Y.C., 1970-71; writer-in-residence New Sch. for Social Research, 1974—. Vice pres. N.Y. Liberal party, 1974—. Mem. Authors Guild, Inner Circle, N.Y. Newspaper Guild (pres. 1965), Silurians (pres. 1972), Phi Beta Kappa, Phi Gamma Delta. Author: Sea-Mary, 1936; The Mate Takes Her Home, 1939; (with Jo Ranson) Sodom by the Sea, 1942; The Atom Spies, 1952; Pegler: Angry Man of the Press, 1963; Lindsay's Campaign, 1968; Drew Pearson: An Unauthorized Biography, 1973. Office: 24 Fifth Ave New York City NY 10011

PILCH, JUDAH, educator; b. Kiev, Ukraine, Sept. 8, 1902; s. Joseph H. and Bat Sheba (Milstein) P.; came to U.S., 1923, naturalized, 1928; B.S., Lewis Inst., Chgo., 1932; M.A., Columbia, 1946; Ph.D., Dropsie Coll., Phila., 1951; m. Bernice Shapery, June 24, 1933; children—Yosef Hayim, Ben Z. Lectr., Coll. Jewish Studies, Chgo., 1929-39; ednl. dir. Jewish Edn. Assn., Rochester, N.Y., 1939-44; dist. cons. Jewish Edn. Com. N.Y., 1944-49; exec. dir. Am. Assn. Jewish Edn., 1949-60; dir. Nat. Curriculum Research Inst., N.Y.C., 1960-62; lectr. edn. N.Y. U., also Dropsie Coll., 1959—. Pres. Nat. Council Jewish Edn., 1948-50, Nat. Conf. Jewish Social Service, 1954-55; v.p. Religious Edn. Assn. U.S. and Can., 1952-59, chmn. exec. com., 1959—; chmn. Nat. Bible Contest Com., 1958—. Recipient Alumni citation Dropsie Coll., 1957. Mem. Acad. Religion and Mental Health, Soc. Sci. Study Religion, Histadrut Ivirt Am. Author: Jewish Life in Our Times, 1943; Teaching Modern Jewish History, 1948. Editor Jewish Education Register and Directory, Vol. 1, 1951, Vol. 2, 1959, Vol. 3, 1965; Readings in Jewish Educational Philosophy, 1960; The Contemporary Jewish Scene, 2 vols., 1962; A History of Jewish Education in the United States, 1969; The Weak Against the Mighty, 1973; Between Two Generations, 1977. Editorial bd. Jewish Edn., The Reconstructionist. Editor: The Nazi Holocaust, 1967. Co-editor: Judaism and the Jewish School, 1966. Home: 520 S Burnside Ave Los Angeles CA 90036

PILCHER, GEORGE WILLIAM, historian; b. Chillicothe, Ohio, Sept. 30, 1935; s. George William and Elia (Huizinga) P.; B.A., U. Dayton (Ohio), 1957; M.A., Okla. State U., 1959; Ph.D., U. Ill., 1963; m. Jean Elizabeth Rickstrew, May 20, 1959; children—Ian-Christopher, Crystal-Dawn. Asst. prof. Okla. State U., 1963-65; mem. faculty U. Colo., Boulder, 1965—, prof. history, 1973—, chmn. dept., 1975—; sr. Fulbright-Hays prof. U. Bordeaux III (France), 1973-74; lectr.-cons. Benjamin Franklin Library, Paris, also U. Aix, 1973-74; cons. to acad. and comml. publishers. Grantee Inst. Early Am. History and Culture, 1965, Am. Philos. Soc., 1970, U. Colo., 1969-70, 73-74, Council Internat. Exchange Scholars, 1973-74. Mem. Orgn. Am. Historians, Inst. Early Am. History and Culture, Am. Hist. Assn., Soc. 18th Century Studies, AAUP, Sierra Club, Phi Alpha Theta, Pi Gamma Mi, Phi Kappa Phi. Club: Colo. Mountain. Author: The Reverend Samuel Davies Abroad, 1967, Samuel Davies, Apostle of Dissent in Colonial Virginia, 1971; also articles, revs.; editorial bd. The Historian, 1966-73, book rev. editor, 1966-73. Home: 16 Pine Brook Hills Boulder CO 70302 Office: Dept History CB 234 Univ Colo Boulder CO 80309

PILCHIK, ELY EMANUEL, clergyman; b. Russia, June 12, 1913; s. Abraham and Rebecca (Lipovitch) P.; came to U.S., 1920, naturalized, 1920; A.B., U. Cin., 1935; M.Hebrew Lit., Hebrew Union Coll., 1936, D.D., 1964; m. Ruth Schuchat, Nov. 20, 1941; children—Susan Pilchik Rosenbaum, Judith Pilchik Zucker. Ordained rabbi, 1939; founder, dir. Hillel Found. at U. Md., 1939-40; asst. rabbi Harssinal Temple, Balt., 1940-41; rabbi Temple Israel, Tulsa, 1942-47, Temple B'nai Jeshurun, Short Hills, N.J., 1947—; prof. Jewish thought Upsala Coll., 1969—; pres. Jewish Book Council Am., 1957-58. Served as chaplain USNR, 1944-46. Mem. N.J. Bd. Rabbis (pres. 1955-57), Central Conf. Am. Rabbis (pres. 1977-79). Author books, including: Hillel, 1951; From the Beginning, 1956; Judaism Outside the Holy Land, 1964; Jeshurun Essays, 1967; author play: Toby, 1968; lyricist 6 cantatas; contbr. articles to profl. and gen. jours. Home: 5 Cherrywood Circle West Orange NJ 07052 Office: 1025 S Orange Ave Short Hills NJ 07078. *I have been influenced by the advice of the 3rd Century head of the Academy in Babylonia, Rab, to his pompous colleague Kahana: "Deal in carcasses, not in words. Flay a carcass in the market-place and sell its hide rather than boasting, 'I am Kahana, I am a great man'."*

PILE, ROBERT BENNETT, advt. exec.; b. Pierre, S.D., May 27, 1918; s. Homer Bennett and Ruth (Gleckler) P.; B.A., U. Minn., 1941; m. Cynthia Way, Feb. 28, 1953; children—Timothy, Benjamin, Robert, Michael, Cynthia, Anthony. Asst. advt. mgr. Red Owl Stores, Mpls., 1946-47; advt. mgr. Lactona, St. Paul, 1947-48; account exec., partner Olmsted & Foley Advt. Agy., Mpls., 1948-55; account exec. Campbell-Mithun, Inc., Mpls., 1955—, sr. v.p., 1969—, also dir. and mem. exec. com. Bd. dirs. Big Brothers Mpls., Minn. Heart Assn., St. Mary's Hosp.; bd. dirs., chmn. 4-A's of Twin Cities, bd. govs. Central Region. Served with USAAF, 1941-46. Recipient spl. award Mpls. Spruce Up Drive, 1965. Mem. Northwest Advt. Golf Assn. (pres. 1977-78, gov.), Am. Assn. Advt. Agencies (chmn. Twin City council), Phi Kappa Psi. Clubs: Interlachen Country, Ham and Eggs Breakfast, Minneapolis. Home: 4315 E Lake Harriet Blvd Minneapolis MN 55409 Office: 1000 Northstar Center Minneapolis MN 55402

PILECKI, FRANCIS JOHN, coll. pres.; b. Rochester, N.Y., Aug. 4, 1934; s. Frank Walter and Rose P. (Meyer) P.; A.B., St. John Fisher Coll., 1955; M.Ed., U. Rochester, 1964, D.Ed., 1967; m. Juliana Helena Mueller, Oct. 19, 1957; children—Jane Frances, Mary Alice, Francis John, Rita Louise; Henry and Joseph Connors (Wards). Tchr., Aquinas Inst., Rochester, 1960-64; dir. Title III Program, Bd. Edn., Bellefonte, Pa., 1966-68; asst. prof., acting dir. Human Relations Center, Boston U., 1968-71; dean Laboure Jr. Coll., Boston, 1971-73; dean edn., acad. v.p. Fitchburg State Coll., 1973-78; pres. Westfield (Mass.) State Coll., 1978—. Organist, choir dir. Roman Catholic Ch., 1948-78. Served with USAF, 1956-60. Mem. Soc. for Gen. Systems Research, Am. Assn. Sch. Adminstrs., ACLU, Nat. Soc. for Study Edn., Phi Delta Kappa. Democrat. Club: Kiwanis. Author: Mass for High Festival Occasions, 1964; (with Glenn L. Immegart) An Introduction to Systems for Educational Adminstrators, 1973. Contbr. chpt. to Planned Change in Education: A Systems Approach, 1971. Contbr. articles to profl. jours. Hom 531 Western Ave Westfield MA 01085 Office: Westfield State Coll Westfield MA 01085

PILKEY, ORRIN H., educator; b. N.Y.C., Sept. 19, 1934; s. Orrin H. and Elizabeth (Street) P.; B.S., Wash. State U., 1957; M.S., Mont. State U., 1959; Ph.D., Fla. State U., 1962; m. Sharlene M. Greenaa, Dec. 29, 1956; children—Charles, Linda, Diane, Keith, Kerry. Research asso. U. Ga. Marine Inst., Sapelo Island, 1962-65; asso. prof. geology Duke, 1965-72, prof., 1972—; vis. prof. U. P.R. at Mayaguez, 1972-73; sr. marine scientist U.S. Geol. Survey, Woods Hole, Mass., 1975-76. Active shoreline conservation. Editor: (with D.J. Swift and D.B. Duane) Shelf Sediment Transport, 1972; author: (with O.H. Pilkey Sr.) How to Live with an Island, 1975; (with O.H. Pilkey Sr. and William Neal) Currituck to Calabash, 1978; (with Wallace Kaufman) The Beaches are Moving, 1979; editor: (with S. Fritz) Marine Atlas of Puerto Rico, 1976; Jour. Sedimentary Petrology, 1977—; (with Larry J. Doyle) Geology of Continental Slopes, 1979; contbr. articles to profl. jours. Research on geol. oceanography. Home: Route 4 Box 426 Hillsborough NC 27278 Office: Dept Geology Duke Univ Durham NC 27708

PILKINTON, JAMES HARVEY, lawyer; b. Hope, Ark., Jan. 15, 1914; s. Ivison Lane and Louise (Betts) P.; B.A., Henderson State Coll., 1936; postgrad. Ark. Law Sch., 1936-37; m. Marguerite Crumpler, Sept. 9, 1939; children—Tena Louise (Mrs. Thomas F. Carter), James Harvey. Admitted to Ark. bar, 1937, since practiced in Hope; mem. Ark. Senate, 1939-41; dist. atty. 8th Jud. Dist. Ark., 1947-51; chancellor 6th Chancery Circuit Ark., 1951-61; city atty., Hope, 1961-78; dir. First Nat. Bank of Hope. Democrat nominee for lt. gov. Ark., 1966. Pres., Pioneer Washington (Ark.) Restoration Found. Served with USNR, 1942-45. Mem. Am., Ark. bar assns. Home: 402 E 19 St Hope AR 71801 Office: 116-118 E 2d St Hope AR 71801

PILLA, ANTHONY MICHAEL, bishop; b. Cleve., Nov. 12, 1932; s. George and Libera (Nista) P.; student St. Gregory Coll. Sem., 1952-53, Borromeo Coll. Sem., 1955, St. Mary Sem., 1954, 56-59; B.A. in Philosophy, John Carroll U., Cleve., 1961, M.A. in History, 1967. Ordained priest Roman Catholic Ch., 1959; asso. St. Bartholomew Parish, Middlebury Hts., Ohio, 1959-60; prof. Borromeo Sem., Wickliffe, Ohio, 1960-72, rector-pres., 1972-75; mem. Diocese Cleve. Liturical Commn., 1964-69, asst. dir., 1969-72; sec. for services to clergy and religious personnel Diocese Cleve., 1975-79; titular bishop of Scardona, aux. bishop of Cleve. and vicar Eastern region Diocese of Cleve., 1979—; trustee Borromeo Sem., 1975-79; trustee, mem. bd. overseers St. Mary Sem., 1975-79; adv. bd. permanent diaconate program Diocese of Cleve., 1975-79, mem. hospitalization and ins. bd., 1979. Mem. Nat. Cath. Edn. Assn. (dir. 1972-75), U.S. Cath. Conf., Nat. Conf. Cath. Bishops, Cath. Conf. Ohio. Address: 28700 Euclid Ave Wickliffe OH 44092

PILLA, FELIX MARIO, hosp. adminstr.; b. Phila., Sept. 22, 1932; s. Domenick and Carmela (DiPalma) P.; diploma profl. nursing Pa. Hosp. Sch. Nursing, 1956; B.S. in Bus. Adminstrn., LaSalle Coll., Phila., 1959; M.S. in Hosp. Adminstrn., Columbia U., 1961; m. Sally Irene Bixler, Oct. 2, 1953; children—Mark, Beth Ann, Michael, Matthew. Mgr. central supply dept. Jefferson Med. Coll. Hosp., Phila., 1957-59; asst. adminstr. Hackensack (N.J.) Hosp., 1961-64; mgr. hosp. relations Md. Blue Cross, Balt., 1964-66; asst. dir. Hosp. Planning Assn. Allegheny County, Pitts., 1966; asso. dir. Presbyn.-Univ. Hosp., Pitts., 1966-67; asst. dir. planning Med. Center Bklyn. and Queens, N.Y.C., 1967-69; asso. adminstr. Monmouth Med. Center, Long Branch, N.J., 1969-70, adminstr., 1970—, exec. dir., 1977—. USPHS tng. grantee, 1961. Fellow Am. Pub. Health Assn., Royal Soc. Health (Gt. Britain); mem. Am., N.J. (chmn. 1979—) hosp. assns., Am. Coll. Hosp. Adminstrs. Office: 300 2d Ave Long Branch NJ 07740

PILLAI, KRISHNAPILLAI CHENNAKKADU SREEDHARAN, statistician; b. Veliyanadu, Kerala, India, Feb. 24, 1920; s. K. Padmanabha and Kutti (Amma) P.; came to U.S., 1962, naturalized, 1966; B.Sc., Kerala U., 1941, M.Sc., 1945; postgrad. Princeton U., 1951-52; Ph.D., U. N.C., 1954; m. Kamalakshi Amma, Aug. 1941; children—Mohanan, Anandan, Sudha. Research scholar, dept. stats. Kerala U., 1941-45, lectr., 1945-51; research asst. Princeton U., 1951-52; research asso. U. N.C., 1952-53; asst. statistician UN, N.Y.C., 1954-55, statistician, 1960-62; UN sr. statis. adv., vis. prof. stats. U. Philippines, Manila, 1956-59; prof. math. and stats., dept. stats. Purdue U., 1962—. NSF grantee, Aerospace Research Labs., USAF. Fellow Inst. Math. Stats., Am. Statis. Assn.; mem. Internat. Statis. Inst., Biometric Soc., Philippine Statis. Assn. (life). Hindu. Author 2 books, numerous research papers, also articles. Home: 214 Forest Hill Dr West Lafayette IN 47906 Office: Math Sci Bldg Dept Stats Purdue U West Lafayette IN 47907

PILLARD, CHARLES HARRY, union ofcl.; b. Buffalo, Oct. 26, 1918; s. Harry Alvin and Elizabeth Frances (Bates) P.; grad. high sch.; m. Helen May Bratten, Apr. 7, 1944; children—Jane Elizabeth (Mrs. Fred Carollo), Linda Charles (Mrs. James Voye). Mem. Internat. Brotherhood of Elec. Workers, 1940—, bus. mgr. local union 41, 1952-68, mem. internat. exec. council, 1961-68, internat. pres., 1968—, co-chmn. council on indsl. relations for elec. industry, 1968—, co-chmn. nat. joint apprenticeship and tng. com. for elec. industry, 1968—; pres. N.Y. State Assn. Elec. Workers, 1954-68; v.p. maritime trades dept. Buffalo Port Council, AFL-CIO, 1955-68, v.p. bldg. and constrn. trades dept., 1968—, also mem. exec. council dept., 1968—, v.p. metal trades dept., 1968—, also mem. exec. council dept., 1968—, v.p. indsl. union dept., 1968—, also mem. exec. council dept., 1968—, mem. exec. council ry. employees' dept., 1968—; mem. social security com. AFL-CIO, 1970, mem. econ. policy com., 1971—, mem. exec. bd. council of unions for sci. and cultural employees, 1971—, mem. adv. bd. task force for Burke-Hartke, 1972-73, v.p. exec. council AFC-CIO, 1976—, mem. standing com. on housing, 1976—. Pres. Buffalo Bldg Trades Council, 1958-68; v.p. N.Y. State Bldg. & Constrn. Trades Council, 1959-68; mem. Nat. Elec. Benefit Bd., 1968; mem. nat. adv. com. Jobs for Vets., 1970; mem. exec. bd. Nat. Council of Sr. Citizens, 1970; labor rep. Constrn. Industry Stablzn. Com., 1971-74; mem. exec. adv. com. Nat. Power Survey, FPC, 1972—; mem. adv. bd. Elec. Power Research Inst., 1973-77; mem. People to People Com. for Handicapped, 1972—; mem. Nat. Council Alcoholism; mem. Pres.'s Com. Employment of Handicapped, 1974; mem. Fed. Com. on Apprenticeship, 1974; mem. constrn. adv. com. Fed. Energy Adminstrn., 1974; mem. Nat. Health Ins. Com., 1974; mem. Collective Bargaining Com. in Constrn., 1975-76; chmn. Adv. Com. for Trade Negotiations, 1975; mem. adv. com. Nat. Commn. on Supplies and Shortages, 1976; mem. Nat. Adv. Com. on Trade Negotiations, 1976-79; mem. Nat. Inst. Bldg. Scis., 1976; vice chmn. industry-labor council White House Conf. on Handicapped Individuals, 1976-78; mem. Nat. Com. for Full Employment, 1976. Mem. econ. council UN Assn., 1976; bd. dirs. Rural Telephone Bank, 1971-78, Lab. Inst. Human Enrichment, 1978; co-chmn. Industry-Labor Council for Nat. Center Employment Handicapped, 1978; mem. Future Directions Com., 1978, Labor Adv. Com. to Spl. Trade Rep., 1979; nat. steering com. Bob Hope USO Center, 1979; mem. Nat. Citizens Coalition for Windfall Profits Tax, 1979. Served to capt. AUS, 1941-45. Recipient Civil Rights award Anti-Defamation League, B'nai B'rith, 1970, Heritage of Liberty award, 1976; Bishop's Plaque for Outstanding work labor-mgmt. Buffalo area, also others. Mem. Am. Legion, Duane Ford Elec. Post. Home: 3481 S Leisure World Blvd Silver Spring MD 20906 Office: 1125 15th St NW Washington DC 20005

PILLIOD, CHARLES JULE, JR., rubber co. exec.; b. Cuyahoga Falls, Ohio, Oct. 20, 1918; s. Charles Jule and Julia (Sullivan) P.; student Muskigum Coll., 1937-38, Kent State U., 1938-40; m. Marie Elizabeth Jacobs, June 15, 1946; children—Christine Marie Pilliod Earhart, Charles Jule, Mark Alan, Stephen Matthew, Renee Elizabeth. With prodn. squadron Goodyear Tire & Rubber Co. 1941; salesman Goodyear Internat. Corp., 1945-47, mgr., dir. Panama, field rep. Costa Rica, 1947-51, field rep., Chile, Bolivia, Peru, 1951-53, asst. sales mgr., Peru, 1953, sales mgr., Colombia, 1954-56, comml. mgr., Brazil, 1956-59, mng. dir., Brazil, 1959-63, sales dir., Eng., 1963-64, mng. dir., Eng., 1964-66, dir. ops., Akron, Ohio, 1966-67, v.p., 1967-71, pres., 1971-72; v.p. Goodyear Tire & Rubber Co., 1971, exec. v.p., dir., 1971-72, pres., 1972-74, chmn. bd., 1974— chief exec. officer, 1973—; dir. CPC Internat., Inc., Mfrs. Hanover Corp., Mfrs. Hanover Trust Co., Communications Satellite Corp., Continental Group, Inc. Trustee U. Akron, Mt. Union Coll., Alliance, Ohio. Served to capt. USAAF, 1942-45. Mem. U.S.-Mex. C. of C., Rubber Mfrs. Assn., Bus. Council, Bus. Roundtable. Office: 1144 E Market St Akron OH 44316

PILLSBURY, DONALD MARION, physician; b. Omaha, Nebr., Dec. 29, 1902; s. Marion Albert and Amanda (Johnson) P.; student Creighton U., Omaha, 1919-20; A.M., U. Nebr., 1925, M.D., 1926; grad. tng. in dermatology and syphilology, U. Pa., 1928-33; m. Charlotte Forsman Denny, Sept. 3, 1929 (dec. 1970); children—Katherine Esmond, Donald Marion, David Chamberlain; m. 2d, Susan Peebles Cooper, Feb. 26, 1972. Intern U. Nebr. Hosp., 1926-28; engaged in research in bacteriology and chemistry of skin; pvt. practice, Phila., 1933—; prof. dermatology and syphilology U. Pa. Med. Sch., 1945—, chmn. dept. dermatology, 1945-65, prof. Grad. Sch. Medicine, 1946—; cons. to surgeon gen. U.S. Army, 1946—. Cons. dermatology to com. on medicine NRC, 1940-42, chmn. sub. com. dermatology, 1951—. Served with AUS, 1942-45. Decorated Legion of Merit, Bronze star (U.S.); Bronze medal of honor Health Service France. Mem. Internat. Congress Dermatology (pres. 1958-62), Am. Dermatol. Assn., Coll. Physicians Phila., AMA, Soc. Investigative Dermatology, Soc. U.S. Med. Consultants in World War II (treas.), Assn. Am. Physicians, Am. Acad. Dermatology, Sigma Xi, Alpha Omega Alpha, Phi Rho Sigma. Independent Republican. Presbyn. Sr. author: Manual of Dermatology (prepared for Armed Forces), 1942; author: A Manual of Dermatology, 1971; co-author: Dermatology, 1956, A Manual of Cutaneous Medicine, 1961, Dermatology, 1975. Home: 1019 Great Springs Rd Rosemont PA 19010

PILLSBURY, FREDERICK HOBART, elec. co. exec.; b. St. Louis, Aug. 19, 1908; s. Edwin Staunton and Harriette Marie (Brown) P.; B.S., Washington U., 1930; m. Anne M. Larsen, June 29, 1940; children—Cynthia Anne (Mrs. Dickinson), Elizabeth Marie, Linda Jane (Mrs. Roos), Evelyn Lucy (Mrs. Shepherd). Student engr. factory tng. course Gen. Electric Co., Schenectady, 1930-31; lab. instr. Washington U., St. Louis, 1932; joined Century Electric Co., St. Louis, 1932, pres., dir., chmn. bd., 1943-71, chmn. bd., 1971-72; v.p., cons., dir. Gould Inc., 1972-75; dir. Allen Organ Co., Mark Twain State Bank. Trustee William Jewell Coll., Liberty, Mo. Mem. Am. Theatre Organ Soc., IEEE Clubs: Engineers (St. Louis); Harbor Point Yacht (West Alton, Mo.); Venice (Fla.) Yacht. Home: 680 S McKnight Rd Saint Louis MO 63124 also 852 Whitecap Circle Venice FL 33595 Office: 1831 Chestnut St St Louis MO 63166

PILLSBURY, GEORGE STURGIS, investment adviser, state senator; b. Crystal Bay, Minn., July 17, 1921; s. John S. and Eleanor (Lawler) P.; A.B., Yale U., 1943; m. Sally Whitney, Jan. 4, 1947; children—Charles Alfred, George Sturgis, Sarah Kimball, Katharine Whitney. Pres. Sargent Mgmt. Co.; dir. Pillsbury Co., Fiduciary Trust Co., N.Y.C., Whitney Land Co. Mem. Minn. Senate from 42d dist. Mem. nat. bd. Smithsonian Assos. Clubs: Seminole Golf (Palm Beach, Fla.); Minnesota, Woodhill, Minnetonka Yacht, Mpls. Athletic, Mpls.; River (N.Y.C.). Home: 1320 Bracketts Point Rd Wayzata MN 55391 Office: 930 Dain Tower Minneapolis MN 55402

PILLSBURY, JOHN SARGENT, JR., ins. co. exec.; b. Mpls., Oct. 28, 1912; s. John Sargent and Eleanor (Lawler) P.; B.A., Yale U., 1935; LL.B., U. Minn., 1940; m. Katharine Harrison Clark, June 11, 1936; children—John Sargent III, Donaldson Clark, Lynde Harrison, Katharine (Mrs. Wood). Various positions Pillsbury Mills, Inc., 1936-37; admitted to Minn. bar, 1940; asso. Faegre & Benson, Mpls., 1940-45, partner, 1946-56; pres. Northwestern Nat. Life Ins. Co., 1956-69, chmn., chief exec. officer, 1969-77, chmn. bd., 1978—, also dir.; dir. Northwestern Bell Telephone Co., Boise Cascade Corp., Pillsbury Co.; trustee Wells Fargo Mortgage and Equity Trust. Bd. dirs. Minn. Orchestral Assn.; trustee Dunwoody Indsl. Inst. Served from lt. (j.g.) to lt. comdr., air combat intelligence USNR, 1942-45. Mem. Am., Minn., Hennepin County bar assns., Order of Coif, Phi Delta Phi. Republican. Conglist. Clubs: Mpls., Minn. Yacht, Woodhill Country (Mpls.); Yale (N.Y.C.). Office: 930 Dain Tower Minneapolis MN 55402

PILLSBURY, PHILIP WINSTON, flour mfg. co. exec.; b. Mpls., Apr. 16, 1903; s. Charles Stinson and Nelle Pendleton (Winston) P.; A.B., Yale U., 1924; LL.D., Grinnell Coll., 1948; m. Eleanor Bellows, July 5, 1934; children—Philip Winston, Henry Adams; m. 2d, Corinne Griffith, Nov. 7, 1977. Began with The Pillsbury Co., 1924, dir., 1928—, treas., 1940, pres., dir., 1940-52, chmn. bd., 1952-65, chmn. finance, exec. coms., 1965-70, hon. chmn., 1970-74, chmn. emeritus, 1974—; dir. Kewatin Mining Co., Sargent Mining Co. Past mem. Chgo. Bd. Trade, Nat. Com. for Immigration Reform, Com. for Nat. Trade Policy; mem. adv. com. Export-Import Bank of Washington, 1962-64; mem. adv. com. bus. programs The Brookings Instn., Washington; mem. adv. council Jr. Achievement of Mpls., 1956-64; mem. adv. council Indsl. Relations Center, U. Minn., 1945-71, Inst. Agr., U. Minn., 1950-62; former mem. Child Welfare League Am., Council on Social Work Edn. Trustee Food Law Inst., Mpls. Found.; mem. exec. com. Yale Alumni Bd., bd. chmn., 1960-62, bd. dirs. Family and Children's Service, Mpls., 1939-60, pres., 1952-53; hon. French consul, 1960-79. Decorated officer Legion of Honor (France). Mem. Minn. Orchestral Assn. (past trustee; pres. 1956-58, now dir.), Mpls. Soc. Fine Arts (trustee), Met. Opera Assn., Jamestown Soc., Newcomen Soc., Soc. of the Cincinnati, Nat. Audubon Soc. (dir. 1968-74). Clubs: Racquet (Chgo.); University (St. Paul); Woodhill (Wayzata, Minn.); Minneapolis, Skylight (Mpls.). Home: 300 W Ferndale Rd Wayzata MN 55391 Office: Pillsbury Bldg Minneapolis MN 55402

PILON, JEAN-GUY, entomologist; b. Ste. Therese, Que., Can., Apr. 7, 1931; s. Amaury and Simone (Brunet) P.; B.A., U. Montreal (Que.), 1953, B.Sc., 1956; M.Sc., McGill U., Montreal, 1960; Ph.D., Yale U., 1965; m. Denise Lagace, Apr. 30, 1960; children—Louis, Stephane. Scientist I, Can. Agr., Quebec City, 1956-60; scientist II, Forests Can., Quebec City, 1960-65; prof. entomology U. Montreal, 1965—, dir. biol. sta., 1966-75, now dir. dept. biol. scis.; cons. James Bay, Que. Mem. Entomol. Soc. Am., Entomol. Soc. Can., Entomol. Soc. Que., Can. Assn. Zoologists, Assn. Canadienne Francaise pour l'Avancement des Scis., Societas Internationalis Odonatologice. Contbr. numerous articles to profl. jours. Office: U Montreal Montreal PQ H3C 3J7 Canada

PILPEL, HARRIET FLEISCHL, lawyer; b. N.Y.C.; d. Julius and Ethel (Loewy) Fleischl; B.A., Vassar Coll.; M.A. in Internat. Relations and Pub. Law, LL.B. (Kent scholar), Columbia U.; m. Robert Cecil Pilpel; children—Judith Ethel (Mrs. Alan Appelbaum), Robert Harry. Research asst. Columbia Law Sch., 1934-35; admitted to N.Y. bar, 1936, since practiced in N.Y.C.; sr. partner Greenbaum, Wolff & Ernst; co-author column You Can Do That, Publisher's Weekly mag. Past mem. Citizen's Adv. Com. to N.Y.C. Dept. Correction; spl. counsel U.S. Govt. com. for Oliver Wendell Holmes Devise; panel experts U.S. Govt. Copyright Office; cons. Spl. Com. Divorce and Marriage Laws of Nat. Conf. Commrs. Uniform State Laws; gen. counsel Planned Parenthood-World Population; past mem. adv. bd. Arthur and Elizabeth Schlesinger Library on History of Women in Am., counsel Sex Info. and Edn. Council of U.S.; counsel Assn. for Voluntary Sterilization; chmn. panel law and planned parenthood Internat. Planned Parenthood Fedn.; mem. internat. adv. com. AID Programme on Law and Population; mem. com. on polit. and civil rights Pres. Kennedy's Commn. on Status Women; mem. spl. task force on status women Pres. Johnson's Citizens' Adv. Com.; dir. HEW Study on Laws and Policies Relating to Contraception and Vol. Sterilization; mem. exec. com. bd. visitors Columbia U. Sch. Law; co-chairperson com. on law, social action and urban affairs Am. Jewish Congress; bd. dirs. Population Resource Center, Women's Forum; mem. N.Y. core group of nat. bd. YWCA; past trustee N.Y. Ethical Culture Soc., Women's Law Fund. Recipient SIECUS award, 1973; Margaret Sanger award, 1974; Louise Waterman Wise Laureate award, 1978; Earl Warren Civil Liberties award, 1978. Mem. Am. Assn. Marriage Counselors (affiliate), Am. Acad. Matrimonial Lawyers, Copyright Soc. U.S.A. (past trustee), Assn. Bar City N.Y., Am., Fed. bar assns., N.Y. County Lawyers Assn., ACLU (1st vice chmn. nat. adv. council, chmn. communications media com.), Am. Law Inst., Authors League Am., PEN Club, Am. Soc. Journalists and Authors, Phi Beta Kappa. Author: (with Theodora Zavin) Your Marriage and the Law, 1952, 64; Rights and Writers, 1960; (with Morton D. Goldberg) A Copyright Guide, 1960; (with Minna Post Peyser) Know Your Rights, 1965. Writer, lectr. on marriage and family law, lit. and entertainment law, constl. law, civil liberties, birth control, abortion, and related subjects, status of women, problems of sr. citizens and legal profession, also of communications media. Mem. editorial adv. bd. Jour. Marriage and Family Counseling; bd. editors Performing Arts Rev. Home: 70 E 96th St New York City NY 10028 Office: 437 Madison Ave New York City NY 10022. *To me, the most important thing of all is the capacity to keep learning. There is so much to know about so much-and so little any one person can know even about one subject. One of the reasons the law is such an exciting profession is that it is ever old and ever new. Snakelike it sheds its old skin while simultaneously and constantly growing a new one. It is thus always one of the world's newest professions.*

PILPEL, ROBERT, orgn. exec.; b. N.Y.C., Mar. 27, 1905; s. Emanuel and Cècile (Meyer) P.; student Ethical Culture Schs., 1910-22, Reed Coll., 1922-23; A.B., Harvard, 1926; LL.B., N.Y. Law School, 1931; m. Harriet F. Fleischl, June 15, 1933; children—Judith E. Pilpel Appelbaum, Robert H. Admitted to N.Y. bar, 1932, practiced law, N.Y.C., 1932-39; exec. asst., gen. counsel Am. Jewish Joint Distbn. Com., Inc., 1939-52; exec. sec. Am. Booksellers Assn., 1952-53; v.p. Robert Joseph & Co., Inc., indsl. real estate, 1953-63; asst. to exec. dir. Hudson Guild Neighborhood House, 1963-68; cons. div. on aging Fedn. Protestant Welfare Agys., 1968-71; asst. to pres. Nat. Assn. on Drug Abuse Problems, Inc., 1974—. Bd. govs. Ethical Culture Schs., 1933-51; trustee Ednl. Alliance (N.Y.C.), 1949—. Vice pres. Central Bur. for Jewish Aged, Inc. Home: 70 E 96th St New York City NY 10028 Office: 355 Lexington Ave New York City NY 10017

PIMENTEL, DAVID, educator; b. Fresno, Calif., May 24, 1925; s. Frank and Marion V. (Sylva) P.; student St. John's U., Collegeville, Minn., 1943, Clark U., summer 1946; B.S., U. Mass., 1948; Ph.D., Cornell U., 1951; postdoctoral investigator, U. Chgo., winters 1954-55; OEEC research fellow Oxford (Eng.) U., 1961; NSF computer scholar, Mass. Inst. Tech., summer 1961; m. Marcia R. Hutchins, July 16, 1949; children—Christina, Susan, Mark David. Chief tropical research lab. USPHS, San Juan, P.R., 1951-54, project leader tech. devel. lab, Savannah, Ga., 1954-55; mem. faculty Cornell U., 1955—, prof. insect ecology, 1963—, head dept. entomology and limnology, 1963-69, prof. entomology, ecology and systematics, 1969-76, prof. insect ecology and agrl. scis., 1976—; prof., core faculty Center Environ. Quality Mgmt., 1973-74. Cons. Office Sci. and Tech., Exec. Office Pres., 1964-67, 69-70, EPA, 1971. Co-chmn. Commn. on Mosquito Control for Developing Countries, Nat. Acad. Sci., 1972-73, mem. commn. on pesticides and pest mgmt. in Inter-Am., 1973—; mem. Nat. Adv. Council on Environ. Edn., 1973-74; chmn. panel on environ. impact of herbicides EPA, 1972-74, pesticide adv. council, 1975-78; nat. adv. council environ. edn. Office Edn., HEW, 1975-78, chmn., 1975; chmn. study team on interdependence of food, population, health, energy and environment World Food and Nutrition Study, Nat. Acad. Scis., 1976—, mem. environ. studies bd., 1979—. Trustee Village of Cayuga Heights. Served to 2d lt., pilot, USAAF, 1943-45. Mem. Entomol. Soc. Am. (governing bd., chmn. editorial bd., pres. Eastern br. 1974-75), Ecol. Soc. Am., Am. Soc. Naturalists, Soc. Study Evolution, Entomol. Soc. Can., Am. Soc. Zoologists, AAAS (climate com. 1979—), Nat. Acad. Scis. (chmn. panel biology and renewable resources, exec. bd. com. life scis. 1966-68, com. on world food, health and population 1974-75, chmn. panel on econ. and environ. aspects of pest mgmt. in C.Am., 1974-76, chmn. bd. on sci. and tech. for internat. devel. 1975—, mem. com. on food and food prodn. 1974-76), Sigma Xi, Phi Kappa Phi, Gamma Alpha (nat. recorder 1960-62). Asso. editor Am. Midland Naturalist. Contbr. articles to profl. jours. Office: Dept Entomology Comstock Hall Cornell U Ithaca NY 14853

PIMENTEL, GEORGE CLAUDE, chemist, govt. exec.; b. Rolinda, Calif., May 2, 1922; s. Emile J. and Lorraine Alice (Reid) P.; A.B., UCLA, 1943, Ph.D. in Chemistry, 1949; children—Anne Christine, Tess Loren, Janice Amy. From instr. to asso. prof. chemistry U. Calif., Berkeley, 1949-59, prof., 1959—; dep. dir. Nat. Sci. Found., Washington, 1977—; participant U.S.-Japan Eminent Scientists Exchange Program, 1973-74. Served with USNR, 1944-46. Recipient Campus Teaching award U. Calif., Berkeley, 1968, Coll. Chemistry Teaching award Mfg. Chemists Assn., 1971, Joseph Priestley Meml. award Dickinson Coll., 1972, Spectroscopy Soc. Pitts., 1974, Alexander von Humboldt Sr. Scientist award, 1974; Guggenheim fellow, 1955. Fellow Am. Acad. Arts and Sci.; mem. Nat. Acad. Scis., Am. Chem. Soc. (Precision Sci. award 1959, award Calif. sect. 1957), Am. Phys. Soc. Earle K. Plyer prize 1979), Optical Soc. Am., Phi Beta Kappa, Sigma Xi, Phi Eta Sigma, Phi Lambda Epsilon, Alpha Chi Sigma. Author: Chemistry—An Experimental Science, 1963; co-author: Understanding Chemistry, 1971, Introductory Quantitative Chemistry, 1956; editor Chem. Study, 1960; contbr. papers to profl. jours. Home: 6118 Massachusetts Ave Bethesda MD 20016 Office: Nat Sci Found Washington DC 20550

PIMSLER, ALVIN J., artist; b. N.Y.C., May 17, 1918; s. Adolph and Jennie (Freedman) P.; grad. Pratt Inst. Sch. Fine and Applied Art, 1938, Art Students League, 1939-40; m. Norma Moran, Aug. 3, 1947; children—Meade, Paul S. Free lance illustrator; fashion artist; portrait painter; one man show Soc. Illustrators Gallery, 1972; exhibited in group shows Art Students League, 1958, Art Dirs. Exhbn., 1956, Soc. Illustrators fashion illustration exhbn., 1964, portrait painting, 1967, Portraits, Inc., 1968, 11th, 12th, 16th and 21st Ann. Exhbns.-Illustration, 1969, 70, 74, 76, 79, C.C. Price Gallery, 1970, N.Y. Hist. Soc., 1976, Soc. Ill. Ann., 1978, Smithsonian Instn., 1973, Salmagundi Club, 1973; tchr. fashion illustration Sch. Visual Arts, 1966-67; tchr. Parsons Sch. Design, 1974—, Fashion Inst. Tech., 1975—; trustee Artists Fellowship, 1978. Served to capt. AUS, 1941-46; ETO. Decorated Combat Inf. Badge; recipient William Collins award Hudson Valley Art Assn., 1971. Mem. Soc. Illustrators (v.p. 1970, pres. 1974—). Club: Lake Success Golf (pres. 1967-68). Home: 101 Central Park W New York City NY 10023

PINARD, MAURICE, sociologist, educator; b. Drummondville, Que., Can., Apr. 25, 1929; s. J. Ernest and Aline (Masson) P.; B.A., U. Montreal, 1951, LL.L., 1954, M.A. in Law, 1955; Ph.D., Johns Hopkins U., 1967; m. Minola Saragea, June 10, 1967; Pierre. Asst. prof. U. Montreal, 1959-60; asst. prof. sociology McGill U., Montreal, 1963-67, asso. prof. 1967-71, prof., 1971—. Fellow Royal Soc. Can. Roman Catholic. Author: The Rise of a Third Party: A Study in Crisis Politics, 2d edit., 1975. Home: 3467 Vendome Ave Montreal PQ H4A 3M6 Canada Office: Dept Sociology McGill U 855 Sherbrooke St W Montreal Canada

PINAULT, H. ROGER, engr., assn. exec.; b. Roberval, Que., Can., Dec. 2, 1926; s. Henri and Valerie (St. Laurent) P.; B.Sc. in Applied Metallurgy, Laval U., 1953; postgrad. Queen's U.; m. Nini Bouchard, Aug. 14, 1951; children—Pierre, Helene. Prodn. supr. Que. Iron and Titanium Co., Sorel, 1953-54; with Aluminum Co. Can., Arvida,

Kingston and Montreal, 1954-64, metall supr., quality controller; chief non-ferrous metals div. dept. of industry Trade and Commerce, Ottawa, Can., 1964-67, dir. materials br., 1967-71; mng. dir. Assn. Cons. Engrs. Can., Ottawa, 1971—. Bd. dirs. Montfort Hosp., Ottawa. Mem. Inst. Gen. Mgmt. (past pres.), Nat. Constrn. Industry Devel. Found. (past dir.), Assn. Profl. Engrs. Ont., Engring. Inst. Can., Inst. Assn. Execs. Clubs: Cercle Universitaire d'Ottawa (dir.), Ottawa Ski Club (past pres.). Home: 1996 Garfield Ave Ottawa ON K2C 0W8 Canada Office: 130 Albert St Suite 616 Ottawa ON K1P 5G4 Canada

PINCOCK, CAROLYN SNYDER, pediatrician; b. Kingston, N.Y., Oct. 9, 1910; d. Howard E. and Carrie (Bortz) Snyder; student U. Wis.; B.A., George Washington U., 1931, M.D., 1934; m. Glen Pincock, June 6, 1934; children—David, Diane R., Douglas G. Intern Jr. Kingston Hosp., 1933, George Washington U. Hosp., Washington, 1934-35; resident Children's Hosp., Washington, 1935-36; pvt. practice pediatrics, Silver Spring, Md., 1936-77; mem. staff Children's Washington, Columbia, Doctors, George Washington U., Suburban, Providence hosps. Bd. dirs. Cynthia Warner Sch. Recipient Togetherness award McCall's mag., 1957. Mem. AMA, Am. Med. Women's Assn. (Med. Women of Year award, 1956, pres. 1975), D.C., Montgomery County (pres. 1970), George Washington U. med. socs., D.A.R., Alpha Epsilon Iota, Chi Sigma Gamma. Home: 14602 Edelmar Dr Silver Spring MD 20906

PINCOCK, RICHARD EARL, educator; b. Ogden, Utah, Sept. 14, 1935; s. Earl Samuel and Virginia (Christenson) P.; B.S., U. Utah, 1956; A.M., Harvard U., 1957, Ph.D., 1960; m. Elke Gertrud Hermann, Aug. 20, 1960; children—Christina, Gordon, Jennifer. Postdoctoral research fellow Calif. Inst. Tech., 1959-60; faculty U. B.C., Vancouver, Can., 1960—, prof., 1969—. Mem. Phi Beta Kappa, Sigma Pi. Office: U BC Chemistry Dept Vancouver BC V6T 1Y6 Canada

PINCOFFS, EDMUND LLOYD, educator; b. Chgo., June 7, 1919; s. Edmund Peter and Rosalind Marie (Posey) P.; A.B., U. N.C., 1941; Ph.D., Cornell U., 1957; m. Mary Elizabeth Zimmerman, Oct. 1, 1948; children—Ruth Posey, Peter, Mary. Partner, Maurice Pincoffs Co., Houston, 1946-50; instr. U. Houston, 1955-56, asst. prof., 1956-60, asso. prof., 1960-65, chmn. dept. philosophy, 1959-65; vis. fellow Princeton, 1962-63; asso. prof. U. Tex. at Austin, 1965-67, prof., 1967—, asso. dean Grad. Sch., 1967-68, chmn. dept. philosophy, 1976—. Served with USCGR, 1941-45. Recipient Am. Council Learned Socs. grant-in-aid, 1969-70, U. Research Inst. grantee, 1969-70. Mem. Am. (past com. chmn.), Southwestern (past pres.), philos. assns., Am. Soc. for Polit. and Legal Philosophy, Internat. Assn. for Philosophy of Law and Social Philosophy (past mem. exec. com. Am. sect.), Am. Assn. U. Profs. (past mem. nat. council, past pres. Tex. conf., past pres. U. Tex. chpt.), Am. Civil Liberties Union (past dir. Central Tex. chpt.), Omicron Delta Kappa, Phi Kappa Phi, Phi Eta Sigma. Unitarian. Author: The Rationale of Legal Punishment, 1966. Editor: The Concept of Academic Freedom, 1975. Contbr. articles to profl. jours. Home: 2607 Wooldridge Dr Austin TX 78703

PINCUS, GEORGE, educator; b. Havana, Cuba, July 5, 1935; s. Max and Ana (Slutzkaya) P.; student U. Havana, 1953-56; B.C.E. with honors, Ga. Inst. Tech., 1959, M.S., 1959; Ph.D., Cornell U., 1963; M.B.A., U. Houston, 1974; m. Dora Dzubquevich, June 8, 1958; children—Cynthia Judith, David Nathan, Karen Joy. Came to U.S., 1957, naturalized, 1966. Asst. prof. structural engring. U. Ky., Lexington, 1963-66, asso. prof. civil engring., 1966-69; prof. civil engring. U. Houston, 1969—, also dir. structural mechanics lab., 1972-75, chmn. civil engring., 1975—; chief of party, grad. engring. program AID, Rio de Janeiro, Brazil, also prof. Fed. U., Rio de Janeiro, 1967-68; cons. in field. Recipient W.T. Kittinger prize, 1975; registered profl. engr., Ky., Tex., Fla., N.Mex., W.Va., Calif.; system design fellow NASA/U. Houston, 1969; Aeros. and Space Research fellow, 1970. Mem. ASCE (D.V. Terrell award 1965), Am. Soc. Engring. Edn., AAUP, Am. Concrete Inst., Phi Kappa Phi. Author 2 books; contbr. articles to profl. jours. Home: 9722 Checkerboard St Houston TX 77096 Office: Dept Civil Engring U Houston Houston TX 77004. *It is surprising to find some who underestimate the value of living in this country with its principles of reward for hard work, full equal opportunity for all, personal liberty, and its tradition for world moral leadership. My primary goals have been: to show continued improvement and growth in my academic career and to prepare myself for greater administrative responsibilities in higher education. I hope that these goals will produce tangible benefits for my adopted country.*

PINCUS, HOWARD JONAH, geologist, educator; b. N.Y.C., June 24, 1922; s. Otto Max and Gertrude (Jankowsky) P.; B.S., Coll. City N.Y., 1942; A.M., Columbia, 1948, Ph.D., 1949; m. Maud Lydia Roback, Sept. 6, 1953; children—Glenn David, Philip E. Mem. faculty Ohio State U., 1949-67, successively instr., asst. prof., asso. prof., 1949-59, prof., 1959-67, chmn. dept. geology, 1960-65; geologist, research supr. U.S. Bur. Mines, 1967-68; prof. geol. sci. and civil engring. U. Wis-Milw., 1968—, dean Coll. Letters and Sci., 1969-72; research asso. Lamont Geol. Obs., Columbia, 1949, 50, 51; geologist Ohio Dept. Natural Resources, summers 1950-61; cons. geology and rock mechanics, 1954-67, 68—; research geologist U.S. Bur. Mines, summers 1963-67. Mem. U.S. nat. com. on tunnelling tech. Nat. Acad. Scis.-Nat. Acad. Engring., 1972-74; mem. U.S. nat. com. on rock mechanics Nat. Acad. Scis., 1975-78. Sr. postdoctoral fellow NSF, 1962. Served to 1st lt. C.E., AUS, 1942-46. Recipient award for teaching excellence U. Wis.-Milw. Alumni Assn., 1978. Fellow Explorers Club, Geol. Soc. Am., Royal Astron. Soc. (London), AAAS; mem. ASTM, AAUP (pres. Ohio State U. chpt. 1955-56, council 1965-67, pres. U. Wis.-Milw. chpt. 1976-77), Am. Geophys. Union, Geol. Soc. Am. (chmn. engring. geology div. 1973-74), Internat. Assn. Math. Geologists, Soc. Mining Engrs., Internat. Assn. Engring. Geology, Internat. Soc. Rock Mechanics, Assn. Engring. Geologists, Am. Inst. Profl. Geologists (pres. Ohio sect. 1965-66), Phi Beta Kappa (pres. Ohio State U. chpt. 1959-60, pres. U. Wis. Milw. chpt. 1976-77), Sigma Xi. Contbr. articles profl. jours. Home: 5755 N Santa Monica Blvd Whitefish Bay WI 53217 Office: Sabin Hall U Wis-Milw Milwaukee WI 53201

PINCUS, JOSEPH, economist, educator; b. N.Y.C., Apr. 17, 1919; s. Samuel and Lillian (Sirotkin) P.; B.S.S., Coll. City N.Y., 1941; M.A., Am. U., 1947, Ph.D., 1953; m. Ethel Frances London, July 6, 1952; children—Terri Ellen, Sally Neila, Robert Alan. Internat. economist Latin Am. studies project U.S. Tariff Commn., Washington, 1946-47, 61-62; economist, fgn. affairs analyst Div. Research Am. Republics, Dept. State, Washington, 1949-58; tariff adviser ICA, USOM, Honduras, 1958-60, rep. with Continental Allied Co. to study indsl. devel., 1961; program officer, econ. adviser AID, Costa Rica, 1962-64, acting dir. mission, 1964, econ. adviser, pvt. enterprise adviser Am. embassy, Paraguay, 1964-66, acting embassy econ. officer, 1967, pvt. enterprise devel. officer, El Salvador, 1967-69, acting program officer, 1968, loan economist, 1968-69; dir. research Brokers Internat. Ltd., Miami, Fla., 1972-73; adj. prof. econs. Fla. Internat. U., also Embry-Riddle Aero. U., 1974-75; vis. prof. econs. U. Miami, 1974, 79, Fla. Meml. Coll., 1975; pres. Common Market Devel. Corp., Miami, 1975—; partner, chief economist Brown and Pincus Assos.; dir. Enterprise Devel. Program, Center for Advanced Internat. Studies, U. Miami; mem. Fla.-Colombia Partners Program. Mem. Am. Fgn. Service Assn., Latin Am. Studies Assn., Soc. Internat. Devel., Acad. for Internat. Bus., Caribbean Studies Assn., U. Miami Consortium on Hunger and Poverty, Omicron Delta Epsilon, Beta Gamma Sigma. Home and Office: 14525 SW 85th St Miami FL 33183. *To those involved in corporate or governmental bureaucracies, my advice is to exercise initiative, go as far as you can on your own, and then seek advice. If you're wrong, someone in authority will stop you eventually. But you could be RIGHT.*

PINCUS, THEODORE HENRY, public relations exec.; b. Chgo., Sept. 15, 1933; s. Jacob T. and F. (Engel) P.; B.S. in Fin., Ind. U., 1955; m. Donna Forman, Mar. 12, 1961; children—Laura, Mark, Susan. Free-lance bus. writer, 1955-58; sr. exec. Harshe Rotman & Druck, Chgo., 1958-62; communications dir. Maremont Corp., Chgo., 1962-64; chmn. chief exec. officer Fin. Relations Bd., Chgo., 1964—; dir. 5 corps. Public affairs adv. to Nelson Rockefeller, N.Y.C., 1960, 68; active presdl. nomination campaigns; vice-chmn. Am. Jewish Com.-Midwest. Served to 1st lt. USAF, 1955-57. Recipient numerous awards including Silver Anvil award Public Relations Soc. Am., 1966. Mem. Young Pres.'s Orgn., Nat. Investor Relations Inst. (founding). Club: Union League. Author books, the most recent being: Giveaway Day, 1977. Office: 150 E Huron St Chicago IL 60611

PINCUS, WALTER HASKELL, editor; b. Bklyn., Dec. 24, 1932; s. Jonas and Clara (Glassman) P.; B.A., Yale, 1954; m. Betty Meskin, Sept. 12, 1954; 1 son, Andrew John; m. 2d, Ann Witsell Terry, May 1, 1965; children—Ward Haskell, Adam Witsell, Cornelia Battle. Cons., Senate Fgn. Relations Com., 1962-63; spl. writer Washington Evening Star, 1963-66; editor, reporter Washington Post, 1966-69; chief cons. Symington subcom. Senate Fgn. Relations Com., 1969-70; asso. editor New Republic, 1972-74, exec. editor, 1974-75; spl. writer Washington Post, 1975—. Cons., NBC News, 1971—. Served with AUS, 1955-57. Recipient Page One award, 1960, George Orwell award, 1977, George Polk award, 1978. Mem. Council Fgn. Relations. Clubs: Federal City, Yale (Washington). Home: 3202 Klingle St NW Washington DC 20008 Office: Washington Post 1155 15th St NW Washington DC 20036

PINCUS, WILLIAM, found. exec., lawyer; b. Phila., Apr. 29, 1920; s. Louis and Dora (Labunsky) P.; B.A., Bklyn. Coll., 1941; M.A., Am. U., 1948; J.D., George Washington U., 1953; m. Elsa Bronson, Sept. 22, 1940; children—Lanni B. Pincus Tama, Jillian R., S. Rachel Pincus Kozan. In various positions U.S. govt. agys., 1941-57; admitted to Md. bar, 1954, D.C. bar, 1955, N.Y. bar, 1959; program officer Ford Found., N.Y.C., 1957-68; pres. Council on Legal Edn. for Profl. Responsibility, Inc., N.Y.C., 1968—. Mem. Am. Bar Assn., N.Y. State Bar Assn., Assn. Bar City N.Y., Am. Jewish Com., Am. Jewish Congress.

PINDELL, HOWARDENA DOREEN, artist; b. Phila., Apr. 14, 1943; s. Howard Douglas and Mildred Edith (Lewis) P.; B.F.A., Boston U., 1965; M.F.A., Yale U., 1967. Curatorial asst. Mus. Modern Art, N.Y.C., 1969-71, asst. curator, 1971-77, asso. curator dept. prints and illus. books, 1977-79; asso. prof. art SUNY, Stony Brook, 1979—; exhbns. include: Mus. Modern Art, Stockholm and 5 European museums, 1973, Fogg Art Mus., Cambridge, Mass., 1973, Indpls. Mus., Taft Mus., Cin., 1974, Gerald Piltzer Gallery, Paris, 1975, 9th Paris Biennale, Mus. Modern Art, Paris, 1975; Vassar Coll. Art Gallery, 1977; represented in permanent collections: Mus. Modern Art, N.Y.C., Fogg Art Mus., Met. Mus., N.Y.C., Whitney Mus. Am. Art, N.Y.C. Nat. Endowment Arts grantee, 1972-73. Mem. Coll. Art Assn., Am. Assn. Museums, Internat. Assn. Art Critics. Contbr. articles to profl. jours. Studio: 322 7th Ave New York NY 10001 Office: Dept Art SUNY Stony Brook NY 11794

PINDER, GEORGE FRANCIS, educator; b. Windsor, Ont., Can., Feb. 6, 1942; s. Percy Samuel and Stella Marie B.Sc., U. Western Ont., 1965; U. Ill., 1968; m. Phyllis Marie Charlton, Sept. 14, 1963; children—Wendy Marie, Justin George. Research hydrologist U.S. Geol. Survey, 1968-72; mem. faculty dept. civil engring. Princeton U., 1972—, prof., 1977—, dir. water resources program, 1972—. Recipient O.E. Meinzer award Geol. Soc. Am., 1975. Mem. Am. Geophysical Union, ASCE, Soc. Petroleum Engrs. Home: 343 Prospect Princeton NJ 08540 Office: Princeton Univ Princeton NJ 08540

PINDERA, JERZY TADEUSZ, mech. engr.; b. Czchow, Poland, Dec. 4, 1914; s. Jan Stanislaw and Natalia Lucia (Knapik) P.; immigrated to Can., 1965, naturalized, 1975; B.S. in Mech. Engring., Tech. U., Warsaw, 1936; M.S. in Aero. Engring., Tech. U., Warsaw and Lodz, 1947; D.Tech.Scis., Polish Acad. Scis., 1959; D.Habil. in Applied Mechanics, Tech. U., Cracow, 1962; m. Aleksandra-Anna Szal, Oct. 29, 1949; children—Marek Jerzy, Maciej Zenon. Asst., Lot Polish Airlines, Warsaw, 1947; head lab. Aero. Inst., Warsaw, 1947-52, Inst. Metallography, Warsaw, 1952-54; dep. prof., head lab. Polish Acad. Scis., 1954-59; head lab. Bldg. Research Inst., Warsaw, 1959-62; vis. prof. mechanics Mich. State U., E. Lansing, 1963-65; prof. mechanics U. Waterloo (Ont., Can.), 1965—; chmn. Internat. Symposium Exptl. Mechanics at univ., 1972; vis. prof. in France and W. Ger.; cons. in field. Served with Polish Army, 1939. Registered profl. engr., Ont. Mem. Canadian Soc. Mech. Engring., Gesellschaft angewandte Mathematik und Mechanik, Soc. Exptl. Stress Analysis (N.M. Frocht award 1978), ASME, Soc. Française des Mécaniciens, Assn. Profl. Engrs. Ont. Author tech. books, also articles, chpts. in books. Editorial adv. bd. Mechanics Research Communications, 1974—. Home: 310 Grant Crescent Waterloo ON N2K 2A2 Canada Office: Dept Civil Engring 200 University Ave Waterloo ON N2L 3G1 Canada

PINE, GRANVILLE MARTIN, lawyer; b. Okmulgee, Okla., Aug. 21, 1915; s. Roswell Dean and Mary Louise (Harder) P.; A.B., U. Okla., 1936; LL.B., Harvard, 1939; m. Elide Anna de Teisseyre, Feb. 7, 1976; children—Granville, Donald. Admitted to N.Y. bar, 1941; partner firm Morgan, Finnegan, Pine, Foley & Lee, N.Y.C., 1946—. Home: 945 Fifth Ave New York City NY 10021 also Villa Belvedere Vallecchia (Lucca) Italy Office: 345 Park Ave New York NY 10022

PINE, IRVING, psychiatrist; b. Bklyn., May 5, 1909; s. Jacob and Dora (Katz) P.; student N.Y. U., 1925-28; M.D., N.Y. Med. Coll., 1932; m. Helen M. Zukas, Feb. 26, 1939; children—Janet Helen, Evelyn Jean. Intern Met. Hosp., N.Y.C., 1932-33; resident medicine Seaview Hosp., S.I., N.Y., 1933-35; practice medicine, Otisville, N.Y., 1935-37, Chenango Bridge, N.Y., 1937-39; specialist in psychiatry and medicine VA Hosp., North Little Rock, Ark., 1939-40, Oteen VA Hosp., 1946-47; resident in psychiatry Duke Hosp., Durham, 1947-49, acting chief electroencephalographic lab., asst. psychiatry, 1949-51; practice medicine specializing in psychiatry, Columbus, Ohio, 1952—; asso. prof. psychiatry Ohio State U. Coll. Medicine, Columbus, 1952-69, asst. clin. prof. medicine, 1959-68, clin. prof. psychiatry, 1969—; cons. psychiatry, tchr. Columbus State Hosp., Harding Hosp. Charter mem. Franklin County (Ohio) Mental Health and Retardation Bd. Served to capt., M.C., AUS, 1942-45. Decorated Purple Heart. Fellow Am. Psychiat. Assn., Am. Acad. Psychosomatic Medicine, Am. Group Psychotherapy Assn. (dir. 1968-69); mem. AMA, Ohio Psychiat. Assn. (pres. 1963-64), Neuropsychiat. Soc. Central Ohio (pres. 1958-59). Contbr. articles to profl. jours. Home: 288 Charleston Ave Columbus OH 43214 Office: Riverside Medical Bldg 3545 Olentangy River Road Columbus OH 43214. *The practice of psychiatry like the practice of medicine is a trust between patient and doctor that transcends the pragmatic and beckons the spiritual relationship between two people. This alliance utilizes every possible means to help sustain and develop a more meaningful life for each individual to encourage and strengthen both physical and mental well-being. To this end a physician-psychiatrist is aware of values: purpose, responsibility, decision-making, constructive cooperation, productivity, and creativity.*

PINE, MAX, restaurant chain exec.; b. Cin., Apr. 17, 1934; s. Ben and Rose (Berkman) P.; B.A. in Polit. Sci., Northwestern U., 1956; M.B.A. in Mktg., Harvard U., 1958; m. Barbara Goldman, Feb. 7, 1963. Exec. asst. State Dept., 1958-61; with Interstate United Corp., 1961-68, v.p., asst. gen. mgr. subs. at N.Y. World's Fair, 1964-65, v.p., dir. bus. devel. restaurant div., N.Y.C., 1966-68; v.p. corp. planning Restaurant Assos. Industries, Inc., N.Y.C., 1968-73, sr. v.p., chief fin. officer, 1973-76, pres., chief operating officer, 1976—; bd. dirs. N.Y. Visitors and Conv. Bur.; mem. bd. overseers Center for Study of Foodservice Mgmt., N.Y. U.; trustee Culinary Inst. Am. Bd. dirs. Henry St. Settlement, N.Y.C., 1976; mem. exec. council Harvard Bus. Sch. Assn., 1979. Club: Harvard Bus. Sch. of N.Y. Office: 1540 Broadway New York NY 10036

PINE, RALPH JONATHAN, pub. co. exec.; b. Paterson, N.J., Apr. 30, 1939; s. Maurice M. and Molly (Margulies) P.; student Rutgers U., 1957-58, Boston U., 1960; B.S., Emerson Coll., 1961; M.A., U. Cal. at Los Angeles, 1963. Writer, dir. theatrical agt., N.Y.C., 1963-67; pres., editor-in-chief Drama Book Specialists (Publishers), N.Y.C., 1967—; pres. Razzmatazz Rags Ltd.; gen. partner Props and Practicals, N.Y.C. lectr. in theatre at various colls. and univs. Mem. Players Club N.Y.C., Am. Theatre Assn., U.S. Inst. theatre Tech. Contbr. articles to various publs. Home: 151 E 80th St New York City NY 10021 Office: 150 W 52d St New York City NY 10019

PINE, SIDNEY ROBERT, lawyer; b. Newark, Mar. 2, 1910; B.S., N.Y. U., 1930, J.D., 1932; m. Lee Hayes, May 16, 1943. Admitted to N.J. bar, 1933, N.Y. bar, 1946; asso. firm, partner McCarter & English, Newark, 1933-43; partner firm Sidney R. Pine, N.Y.C., 1943-67, Valicenti, Leighton, Reid & Pine, N.Y.C., 1968-75; counsel Trubin Sillcocks Edelman & Kanpp, N.Y.C., 1976—. Mem. N.J. Bar Assn., N.Y. State Bar Assn., Am. Bar Assn. (past chmn. fgn. tax subcom., past chmn. tax sect. subcom. internat. legal exchange program). Club: Manhattan. Contbr. articles to profl. jours. Home: 530 Park Ave New York NY 10021 Office: 375 Park Ave New York NY 10022

PINES, DAVID, physicist; b. Kansas City, Mo., June 8, 1924; s. Sidney and Edith (Adelman) P.; A.B., U. Calif. at Berkeley, 1944; M.A., Princeton, 1948, Ph.D., 1950; m. Aronelle Siegerman, June 15, 1948; children—Catherine Deirdre, Jonathan David. Instr., U. Pa., 1950-52; research asst. prof. U. Ill. at Urbana, 1952-55; asst. prof. Princeton U., 1955-58; mem. Inst. Advanced Study, Princeton, 1958-59; prof. physics and elec. engring. U. Ill., 1959—, dir. Center Advanced Study, 1967-70, asso., 1972-73, prof., 1978—; prof. asso. Faculty des Scis., U. Paris (France), 1962-63; vis. prof. NORDITA, Copenhagen, 1970; Lorentz prof. U. Leiden (Netherlands), 1971; Fritz London Meml. lectr. Duke, 1972; Guilio Racah Meml. lectr. Hebrew U., Jerusalem, 1974; Marchon lectr. Newcastle-Upon-Tyne U., 1976; Sherman Fairchild distinguished scholar, Calif. Inst. Tech., 1977-78; exchange prof. U. Paris, 1978. Dir. W.A. Benjamin, Inc., N.Y.C., 1963-71. Mem. physics survey com. Nat. Acad. Scis., 1963-65; v.p. Aspen Center for Physics, 1968-76, chmn. exec. com. bd. trustees, 1976-77; mem. council for biology and human affairs Salk Inst., 1969-73; co-chmn. Joint Soviet-U.S. Symposia on Theory of Condensed Matter, 1968, 70, 71, 73, 74, 76; mem. NRC Commn. Internat. Relations, 1974—; mem. Com. Scholarly Communication with People's Republic of China, 1974-78. Chmn. Nat. Acad. Scis.-NRC Bd. Internat. Sci. Exchange, 1974—; chmn. Working Group on Physics US-USSR Joint Commn. on Sci. and Tech. Coop., 1974—. NSF sr. postdoctoral fellow, 1957-58; Guggenheim fellow, 1962-63, 70. Fellow AAAS, Am. Phys. Soc., Am. Astron. Soc.; mem. Assn. U. Research Astronomy (trustee 1975-78, cons. 1978—), Nat. Acad. Scis., Internat. Astron. Union, Phi Beta Kappa, Sigma Xi. Author: The Many Body Problem, 1961; Elementary Excitations in Solids, 1963; (with P. Nozières) Theory of Quantum Liquids, 1967. Editor: Frontiers of Physics, 1961—; Lecture Notes and Supplements in Physics, 1962—; Revs. of Modern Physics, 1973—. Mem. editorial adv. bd. Jour. Physics and Chemistry of Solids; Collective Phenomena, Jour. of Non-Metals; editorial adviser Jour. Low Temperature Physics. Home: 403 W Michigan St Urbana IL 61801

PINES, NED LEWIS, ins. co. exec.; b. Malden, Mass., Dec. 10, 1905; s. Joseph and Dora (Goldes) P.; student Columbia, 1923-24; m. Jacquelyn Sangor, Aug. 29, 1938 (div. 1959); children—Judith Ann (Mrs. E. Anthony Bernard), Susan Jane; m. 2d, Maxine Firestone, Nov. 19, 1967. Pres. Pines Publs., Inc., 1928-61; pres. Popular Library, Inc., 1942-66, chmn., 1966-68; chmn. bd., dir. mem. finance and exec. coms. Eastern Life Ins. Co. N.Y., 1949-71; cons. U.S. Life Corp., N.Y.C., 1971-76. Mem. coordinating com. Columbia U. Inst. Research, 1945-47. Bd. dirs. Jewish Guild for Blind, 1950-73; life trustee Fedn. Jewish Philanthropies N.Y., 1968; mem. nat. judging com. Boys' Clubs Am. Adv. bd. Commentary mag., 1970—, Merce Cunningham Dance Found., 1970-74, Am. Friends of Israel Mus., Jerusalem, 1976—. Founder, United Jewish Appeal, 1940. Recipient U.S. Treasury award, 1945; award Bur. Intercultural Edn., 1949; Nat. Mass Media award Thomas Alva Edison Found., Inc., 1956; gold medallion and certificate Boys' Clubs Am., 1956. Clubs: La Conferie des Chevaliers du Tastevin, Harmonie (N.Y.C.); Noyac Golf (Sag Harbor, N.Y.); Southampton (N.Y.) Golf; American (Paris, France). Home: New York NY also Paris France also East Hampton NY Office: 355 Lexington Ave New York NY 10017

PING, CHARLES JACKSON, univ. pres.; b. Phila., June 15, 1930; s. Cloudy J. and Mary M. (Marion) P.; B.A., Southwestern at Memphis, 1951; B.D., Louisville Presbyn. Theol. Sem., 1954; Ph.D., Duke, 1961; m. Claire Oates, June 5, 1951; children—Andrew, Ann Shelton. Asso. prof. philosophy Alma Coll., 1962-66; prof. philosophy Tusculum Coll., 1966-69, v.p., dean faculty, 1967-68, acting pres., 1968-69; provost Central Mich. U., Mt. Pleasant, 1969-75; pres. Ohio U., Athens, 1975—. Adv. bd. Ind. Coll. Program Northwest Area Found. Mem. Am. Philos. Assn., Am. Council Acad. Deans, Am. Assn. Higher Edn. Author: Meaningful Nonsense, 1966, also articles. Office: Ohio U Office of Pres Athens OH 45701

PINGEL, JOHN SPENCER, advt. exec.; b. Mt. Clemens, Mich., Nov. 6, 1916; s. George F. and Margaret (Dalby) P.; student U.S. Mil. Acad.,1936; B.A., Mich. State U., 1939; m. Isabel Hardy, Dec. 12, 1939; children—John S., Roy Hardy. Asst. dir. truck merchandising Dodge div. Chrysler Corp., 1940-41, fleet sales rep., 1949; adminstrv. asst. Mich. State U., 1945-46; dir. advt. Reo Motors, Inc., 1947-48; with mdsg. dept. Brooke, Smith, French & Dorance, Inc., 1949-55, v.p., account supr., 1955-57, v.p., asst. to pres., 1957-60, exec. v.p., 1960; exec. v.p. Ross Roy-BSF & D, Inc., Detroit, 1960-62; exec. v.p. Ross Roy, Inc., 1962-64, pres., 1964—. Exec. bd., pres., chmn. orgn. and extension com. Detroit area council Boy Scouts Am; pres. Inst.

for Econ. Edn., 1971; mem. adv. bd. United Found., 1970-71; mem. Pres.'s Council on Phys. Fitness and Sports, 1975—. Trustee Alma Coll., New Detroit, Inc., Grace Hosp., Oakland U. Found.; mem. exec. com. Grosse Pointe U. Sch., 1957-58, trustee, 1959—; bd. dirs. Boys Republic, Inc., Greater Met. Detroit Project Hope, Greater Mich. Found.; trustee emeritus Mich. State U. Served from 2d lt. to lt. col. 95th Inf. Div., AUS, 1941-45. Decorated Bronze Star, Purple Heart; named to Nat. Football Hall of Fame, 1968, to Mich. Sports Hall of Fame, 1973. Mem. Detroit Sales Execs. Club (v.p. 1951), Am. Assn. Advt. Agys. (chmn. Mich. 1960, chmn. East Central Region 1978-79), Mich. (dir.), Greater Detroit (dir. 1970-71, chmn. 1977-78), chambers commerce. Presbyterian (elder). Clubs: Detroit Athletic, Country of Detroit, Adcraft (pres. 1960-61), Detroit, Economic, Yondotega (Detroit); Seminole Golf (Palm Beach, Fla.); Jupiter Hills. Home: 582 Peach Tree Lane Grosse Pointe Woods MI 48236 Office: 2751 E Jefferson Ave Detroit MI 48207

PINGS, VERN MATTHEW, librarian; b. Sauk City, Wis., Apr. 10, 1923; s. Frank Christ and Viola Suzanne (Neis) P.; Ph.B., U. Chgo., 1946; B.A., U. Wis., 1947, M.A. in L.S., 1955, Ph.D., 1958; M.A., Columbia U., 1952; m. Joan Louise Gilmore, Oct. 6, 1963. Refugee relief work Am. Friends Service Com., Gaza, Palestine, 1949-50; works officer UN Relief and Works Agy., Beirut, 1950-51; dir. univ. farms Sch. Agr., Am. U., Beirut, 1952-54; asst. engring. librarian Coll. Engring., U. Wis., 1955-58; librarian Ohio No. U., Ada, 1959; asso. prof. Sch. Librarianship, U. Denver, 1960; med. librarian Wayne State U., Detroit, 1961-71, dir. libraries, 1971—; dir. Ky., Ohio., Mich. Regional Med. Library, Detroit, 1969-75; acting dir. Mich. Library Consortium, Detroit, 1974-76, trustee, 1974—; prof. Wayne State U. Med. Sch., 1966—; vis. com. library sci. Case Western Res. U., 1971—; mem. facilities and resources com. Nat. Library Medicine, USPHS, 1966-70; mem. U.S.-Argentine study panel on sci. info. Nat. Acad. Sci., 1970-71; mem. nat. adv. com. Nat. Serials Data Program, 1972. Mem. tech. com. Mich. Adv. Council Comprehensive State Health Planning, 1969-70; bd. overseers Oakland Community Coll., Farmington Hills, Mich., 1970-75. Mem. Med., Mich. library assns., Spl. Libraries Assn., AAAS, Assn. Am. Library Schs. Author: Nursing Literature, 1964; also articles. Home: 1248 Navarre St Detroit MI 48207 Office: 130 Purdy Library Wayne State Univ Detroi MI 48202

PINION, DWIGHT JAMES, lawyer; b. Nebr., Mar. 12, 1911; s. Paul Andrew and Mabel (Anderson) P.; LL.B., Southeastern U., 1937; m. Kathryn Martin, Nov. 8, 1937; children—Carolyn Pinion Elkins, Nancy (Mrs. James B. Stehman, Jr.), Pauline. Admitted to D.C. bar, 1937; atty. SEC, 1938-42; asst. counsel Office Legis. Counsel, U.S. Senate, 1942-66, legis. counsel, 1967-69. Mem. D.C., Fed. bar assns. Baptist. Club: Nat. Lawyers (Washington). Home: 6910 Bright Ave McLean VA 22101

PINKE, EDGAR AEBLI, airline exec.; b. St. Louis, May 23, 1919; s. Edgar and Mabel M. (Aebli) P.; B.S., Westminster Coll., Fulton, Mo., 1941; m. Julia R. Wilke, Aug. 15, 1942; children—Becky J., Cynthia S., Julia A. Capt., check pilot Slick Airways, 1946-49; with Flying Tiger Line, 1949—, v.p. ops. and maintenance, 1965-67; sr. v.p. ops., 1967-74, sr. cons., 1974—, also dir. Bd. dirs. Daniel Freeman Regional Hosp., Inglewood, Calif., 1967—. Served with Air Transp. Command, USAAF, 1941-46. Mem. Kappa Alpha. Presbyn. Home: 4 Lighthouse St Marina del Rey CA 90291 Office 7401 World Way W Los Angeles CA 90009

PINKERMAN, JOHN HORTON, editor, writer; b. Meridian, Miss., Mar. 25, 1914; s. Harold Cochrane and Mabel Kate (Horton) P.; student U.S. Army Gen. Edn. Devel. Program, 1947-49; m. Gladys Besse, Oct. 29, 1949. Reporter, Bridgeport (Conn.) Post, 1933-35, Bridgeport Times-Star, 1935-41, Hartford (Conn.) Times, 1949-56, San Diego Union, 1956-63; news editor hdqrs. Copley News Service, San Diego, 1963-65, exec. news editor, 1965-68, v.p., 1970-77; founder, pres., editor News Assos., Idyllwild, Calif., 1977—; world affairs columnist, 1971—; lectr. Mt. San Jacinto Coll., U. So. Calif. Served with U.S. Army, 1941-49, 50-52; officer Calif. Mil. Res., 1979. Decorated Presdl. citation. Mem. Internat. Press Inst., Audubon Soc., Izaak Walton League, Ret. Officers Assn., Assn. U.S. Army. Congregationalist. Clubs: Optimists (pres. San Diego 1966-67), Am. Legion. Author: History of Southern Japan, 1948; contbr. articles to Asia Mail. Home: 53255 Deerfoot Ln Idyllwild CA 92349 Office: PO Drawer J Idyllwild CA 92349

PINKERTON, WILLIAM STEWART, JR., journalist; b. Mpls., Nov. 30, 1942; s. William Stewart and Dorothy Naomi (Wilson) P.; A.B. in English, Princeton U., 1964; postgrad. N.Y. Law Sch., 1978—; m. Ann-Byrd Platt, Oct. 7, 1978. Copy editor, reporter Wall St. Jour., San Francisco, 1964-66, staff reporter, Los Angeles, 1966-69, staff reporter, N.Y.C., 1969-71, asst. N.Y. bur. mgr., 1975, bur. mgr., 1975—; mng. editor Can. Dow Jones, Ltd., Montreal, 1971-75. Sec., Princeton Class of '64, 1979—. Republican. Episcopalian. Clubs: Princeton, Doubles (N.Y.C.). Home: 30 Waterside Plaza Apt 26J New York NY 10010 Office: 22 Cortlandt St New York NY 10007

PINKHAM, DANIEL, composer; b. Lynn, Mass., June 5, 1923; s. Daniel R. and Olive C. (White) P.; A.B., M.A., Harvard, 1944; Litt.D. (hon.), Nebr. Wesleyan U., 1976; Mus.D. (hon.), Adrian Coll., 1977, Westminster Choir Coll., 1979. Mem. faculty New Eng. Conservatory Music, 1959—; music dir. King's Chapel, Boston, 1958—; co-founder Cambridge Festival Orch., 1948. Fellow Am. Acad. Arts and Scis.; mem. Am. Guild Organists (past dean Boston chpt.). Composer: Sonatas for Organ and Strings, 1943, 54; Piano Concertino, 1950; Concerto for Celesta and Harpsichord, 1954; Wedding Cantata, 1956; Christmas Cantata, 1958; Easter Cantata, 1961; Symphonies, 1961, 64, Signs of the Zodiac, 1964; St. Mark Passion, 1965; Jonah, 1966; In the Beginning of Creation, 1970; Ascension Cantata, 1970; Organ Concerto, 1970; When the Morning Stars Sang Together, 1971; the Other Voices of the Trumpet, 1971; Safe in Their Alabaster Chambers, 1972; To Troubled Friends, 1972; Daniel in the Lions' Den, 1973; The Seven Deadly Sins, 1974; Four Elegies, 1974; The Passion of Judas, 1975; Garden Party, 1976; Blessings, 1977; Company at the Creche, 1977; Miracles, 1978; Epiphanies, 1978; Proverbs, 1979. Home: 150 Chilton St Cambridge MA 02138

PINKHAM, FREDERICK OLIVER, govt. ofcl., ednl. adminstr., bus. exec.; b. Ann Arbor, Mich., June 16, 1920; s. Frederick Oliver and Leah Winifred (Hallett) P.; A.B., Kalamazoo Coll., 1942, LL.D., 1958; M.A., Stanford U., 1947, Ed.D., 1950; LL.D. (hon.), Lawrence Coll., 1957; m. Helen Kosta, June 20, 1943; children—Peter James, Gail Louise, Steven Howard. Tchr., counselor Sequoia Union High Sch., Redwood City, Calif., 1947-49; researcher Sanford Consultation Service, 1949-50; asst. to pres. George Washington U., 1950-51; exec. sec. Nat. Commn. on Accrediting, 1951-55; pres. Ripon (Wis.) Coll., 1955-66; dir. The Yardstick Project, nation-wide ednl. project, Cleve., 1966-68; v.p., dir. Western Pub. Co., 1967-70; founder, pres. Edn. Mgmt. Services, Inc., 1970—; pres. Capital Higher Edn. Service, 1975-76; asst. adminstr. for population and humanitarian affairs AID, Dept. State, 1976-77, chmn. Population Crisis Com., 1977—; pres. The Omni Group, 1977—; dir. Omniflight Helicopters, Inc., 1978—. Vice pres., co-founder World Bus. Council, 1970—; v.p., dir. research Ednl. Records Bur., Darien, Conn., 1970-72; cons. HEW, AID, corps., founds. and assns. Chmn. Wisconsin adv. com. Nat. Commn. on Civil Rights. Mem. bd. visitors Air U.; pres. Wis. Found of Ind. Colls.; chmn. Asso. Colls. Midwest; chmn. Midwest Coll. Council; sec., trustee, mem. exec. com. Young Pres.'s Found. Served from cpl. to 1st lt. AUS, 1942-45, ETO. Decorated Bronze Star, Purple Heart. Mem. Young Pres. Orgn. (nat. sec., dir., mem. exec. com.). Home: 4374 Westover Pl NW Washington DC 20016

PINKIN, JAMES EDWARD, advt. agy. exec.; b. Elizabeth, N.J., Feb. 21, 1947; s. Wallace M. and Alice (Mann) P.; student The Citadel, 1965-67; B.S., Fairleigh Dickinson U., 1969; M.B.A., Seton Hall U., 1971; m. Lois M. Pushman, 1966; children—Steven, Jeffrey, Brett, Drew. Acct., S.D. Feldman, C.P.A., Caldwell, N.J., 1968-69; mgr. Peat Marwick, Mitchell & Co., Newark and N.Y.C., 1969-73; corp. dir. fin. planning Faberge, Inc., N.Y.C., 1973-78; v.p. Canyon Energy Co., Houston, 1978; sr. v.p., treas. Benton & Bowles, Inc., N.Y.C., 1978—. Mem. Am. Inst. C.P.A.'s, N.J. Soc. C.P.A.'s, Fin. Execs. Inst., Nat. Assn. Accts., Assn. Corp. Growth, Am. Mgmt. Assn. Republican. Presbyterian. Clubs: Toastmasters, Westfield Tennis Assn., Westfield Soccer Assn., Westfield Coll. Men's, Jaycees (past dir.). Home: 20 Barchester Way Westfield NJ 07090 Office: 909 3d Ave New York NY 10022

PINKNEY, DAVID HENRY, historian; b. Elyria, Ohio, July 2, 1914; s. David Henry and Zaida Margaret (Fulmer) P.; A.B., Oberlin Coll., 1936; M.A., Harvard U., 1937, Ph.D., 1941; m. Helen Dorothy Reisinger, Nov. 14, 1942; children—Janet Sloss, David Henry (dec.). Research analyst, coordinator info. OSS, Washington and London, 1941-43; asst. prof. history U. Mo., Columbia, 1946-51, asso. prof., 1951-57, prof., 1957-66, chmn. dept. history, 1956-59; prof. U. Wash., 1966—, Disting. Univ. Lectr., 1977; bd. dirs. Am. Council on Edn., 1979-80. Served to lt., j.g., USNR, 1943-46. Fund for Advancement Edn. fellow, 1954-55; Guggenheim fellow, 1960-61; Nat. Endowment for Humanities fellow, 1977-78. Mem. Am. Hist. Assn. (pres. 1980), Soc. French Hist. Studies (pres. 1975-76), Western Soc. French History, Societe d'Histoire moderne, Phi Beta Kappa. Author: Napoleon III and the Rebuilding of Paris, 1958; The French Revolution of 1830, 1972; The Nineteenth Century, 1978; editor: A Festschrift for Frederick B. Artz, 1964; editor French Hist. Studies, 1966-75. Home: 3812 48th Ave NE Seattle WA 98105 Office: Dept History DP-20 U Wash Seattle WA 98195

PINKNEY, JAMES FAULKNER, lawyer; b. Fayette County, W.Va., Aug. 27, 1906; s. Harry H. and Ann May (Dixon) P.; A.B., Davidson Coll., 1927; LL.B., U. Colo., 1930; grad. Command and Gen. Staff Sch., 1942; m. Dorris Vallette Hands, Dec. 26, 1935; children—James Faulkner, Edgar Hands. Admitted to Colo. bar, 1930, N.C. bar, 1948, D.C. bar, 1953; practiced in Denver, 1930-34; with Grant, Ellis, Shafroth & Toll; litigation div. Nat. Recovery Adminstrn., 1934-35; asst. chief examiner bur. motor carriers ICC, 1935-37, chief examiner, 1937-41; prof. polit. sci. and law Davidson Coll., 1946-50; vis. prof. law U. Colo., 1947; gen. counsel Am. Trucking Assns., Inc., 1952-59, chief counsel, 1961—, sr. v.p., 1970-72; v.p. law, Ryder System, Inc., 1959-61. Bd. visitors Davidson Coll. Served as col. USAAF, 1942-46, asst. chief staff A-2, 10th Air Force; col. USAF, 1950-52. Decorated Legion of Merit, Bronze Star, Air medal. Mem. Assns. ICC Practitioners (pres. 1954-55), Transp. Assn. Am. (dir.), Beta Theta Pi, Phi Delta Phi, Omicron Delta Kappa, Presbyn. Clubs: Burning Tree (Washington); Belle Haven Country (Alexandria). Home: 6401 Olmi-Landrith Dr Alexandria VA 22307

PINKSTON, JOHN WILLIAM, JR., hosp. supt.; b. Valdosta, Ga., Aug. 11, 1924; s. John William and Fannie L. (Smith) P.; B.B.A., Emory U., 1946; m. Jane G. Grant, Nov. 12, 1959; children—Carol Grant, John William III. Trainee, Western Electric Co., 1947-48; with Grady Meml. Hosp., Atlanta, 1948—, exec. dir., 1964—. Sec. health and social service adv. council Atlanta Regional Commn., 1975. Served with C.E., AUS, 1944-46. Mem. Am. (chmn. elect pub. hosp. sect. 1975, mem. council on legis. 1975-77, ho. of dels. 1978—), Ga. (treas. 1975, pres.-elect 1976, pres. 1977) hosp. assns., Assn. Am. Med. Colls. (mem. adminstrv. bd. council of teaching hosps. 1974-75). Home: 3176 Verdun Dr NW Atlanta GA 30305 Office: 80 Butler St SE Atlanta GA 30303

PINNELL, GEORGE LEWIS, office equipment co. exec.; b. Caterville, Mo., Mar. 2, 1921; s. George Lewis and Elma (Fly) P.; student Eastern Okla. Coll. Edn., 1943; m. Joan Russell, Jan. 31, 1942; children—Richard Vance, James Lunsford. Partner, Jaynes Bus. Machines, Walla Walla, Wash., 1945-50; owner Pinnell Office Machines, Yakima, Wash., 1950-57; pres. Pinnell, Inc., Yakima, 1957—, Pinnell World Processing Systems Co., 1973—, Diversified Office Equipment Inc., Yakima, 1970—. Pres. United Good Neighbors, Yakima, 1962, Oreg.-Wash.-B.C. Community Chests and Councils, 1963. Campaign chmn. for Congresswoman Catherine May, 1958. Bd. govs. Am. Nat. Red Cross, 1966—. Served with AUS and USAAF, 1942-45. Recipient Distinguished Service award U.S. Jr. C. of C., 1953. Mem. Nat. Office Machine Dealers Assn. (bd. dirs. 1949), N.W. Office Machine Dealers (pres. 1947). Republican. Elk, Rotarian (pres. Yakima 1965-66). Club: Cameratta (pres. 1952) (Yakima). Home: 6909 Englewood Terr Yakima WA 98902 Office: 805 Summitview Ave Yakima WA 98902

PINNEY, EDMUND, educator, mathematician; b. Seattle, Aug. 19, 1917; s. Henry Lewis and Alice (Joy) P.; B.S., Calif. Inst. Tech., 1939, Ph.D., 1942; m. Eleanor Russell, Mar. 10, 1945; children—Henry Russell, Gail Shiela. Research asso. Radiation Lab., Mass. Inst. Tech., 1942-43; research analyst Consol.-Vultee Aircraft Corp., 1943-45; instr. Ore. State Coll., 1945-46; mem. faculty U. Calif. at Berkeley 1946—, prof. math., 1959—; cons. in field. Fellow AAAS; mem. Am. Math. Soc., Am. Phys. Soc. Author: Ordinary Difference-Differential Equations, 1958. Home: 66 Scenic Dr Orinda CA 94563 Office: 841 Evans Hall Univ Calif Berkeley CA 94720

PINNEY, EDWARD LEE, educator; b. Jacksonville, Fla., Nov. 2, 1930; s. Edward Lee and Caroline (Bruner) P.; B.S., Auburn U., 1952; M.A., U. N.C., 1956, Ph.D., 1960; m. Winston Reese Withers, Apr. 27, 1956; children—Reese Bruner, Edward Lee. Instr. U. N.C. at Chapel Hill, 1956-59; mem. faculty La. State U. at Baton Rouge, 1959-63; prof. politics Washington and Lee U., Lexington, Va., 1963—. Mem. Baton Rouge Symphony Bd., 1960-64. Chmn. Rockbridge County (Va.) Citizens for Johnson- Humphrey, Democratic Party, 1964. Served to 1st lt., AUS, 1952-54. Mem. Am., So. (exec. council, rec. sec.) polit. sci. assns., AAUP. Author: Federalism, Bureaucracy and Party Politics in West Germany, 1963. Editor: Comparative Politics and Political Theory: Essays Written in Honor of Charles Baskervill Robson, 1966. Bd. pubs. Shenandoah, 1970-76, chmn., 1973-76. Home: 207 White St Lexington VA 24450

PINNEY, SIDNEY DILLINGHAM, JR., lawyer; b. Hartford, Conn., Nov. 17, 1924; s. Sydney Dillingham and Louisa (Griswold) Wells P.; student Brown U., 1943, also Mass. Inst. Tech., 1943-44; B.A. cum laude, Amherst Coll., 1947; LL.B., Harvard U., 1950; m. Sarah Tinsley Sather, July 7, 1956; children—William Griswold, David Rees. Admitted to Conn. bar, 1950, since practiced in Hartford,; asso. firm Shepherd, Murtha and Merritt, Hartford, 1950-53, partner (name changed to Murtha, Cullina, Richter and Pinney 1967), 1953—. Dir. Greater Hartford Area Tb and Respiratory Diseases Health Soc., 1956-69, pres., 1966-67. Mem. Wethersfield (Conn.) town council, 1958-62. Trustee Hartford Conservatory Music, 1967-71, 75—; trustee, pres. Historic Wethersfield Found., 1961—; bd. dirs. Hartford Hosp., 1971—; corporator Hartford Pub. Library, 1969—; Renbrook Sch., West Hartford, Conn., 1970-75. Served to 1st lt. USAF. Fellow Am. Coll. Probate Counsel; mem. Conn., Hartford County bar assns., Republican. Congregationalist. Contbr. to Estate Planning mag. Home: 1 Woodside Circle Hartford CT 06105 Office: 101 Pearl St Hartford CT 06103

PINNIX, ROBERT HENRY, bldg. contractor; b. Greensboro, N.C., Feb. 8, 1901; s. Major Henry and Lula (Brooks) P.; student Mercersburg (Pa.) Acad.; A.B., Duke, 1924; m. Jennie Mae Henry, Oct. 21, 1925; 1 dau., Joan Henry (Mrs. Henry Monroe Whitesides). Pres., Robert H. Pinnix, Inc., bldg. contractors, 1927—; dir. Citizens Nat. Bank, Gastonia; N.C. adv. bd. Liberty Mut. Ins. Co. Pres. N.C. Indsl. Council, 1964-66, N.C. Bldg. Code Council, 1945-50. Bd. mgrs., mem. exec. com. Meth. Home for Aged, Charlotte, N.C.; trustee Duke U., also chmn. bd. visitors Sch. Engring.; mem. exec. com. Duke U. Nat. Council, 1963-69; bd. dirs. Ednl. Found. for Commerce and Industry N.C., v.p., 1968—. Mem. Newcomen Soc., Asso. Gen. Contractors Am. (nat. dir., past pres. Carolinas br.), N.C. (past pres.), Gastonia (pres.) chambers commerce, Alpha Tau Omega. Methodist (trustee, mem. bd. stewards). Clubs: Rotary (pres.); Charlotte City; Gaston Country (pres.). Home: 215 W 10th Ave Gastonia NC 28052 Office: PO Box 100 Gastonia NC 28052

PINO, JOHN ANTHONY, found. exec.; b. Tyler, Pa., Jan. 26, 1923; s. Antonio and Dolores (Reino) P.; B.S., Rutgers U., 1943, Ph.D., 1951; m. Edith Mary Norman, Aug. 14, 1944; children—Susanne E. (Mrs. Lebrija), John Norman, Eugene David, Thomas Michael. Instr., Rutgers U., 1947-51, asst. prof., 1951-54, asso. prof., 1954-55; with Mexican Agrl. Program, Rockefeller Found., 1955-65, asso. dir. agrl. scis., N.Y.C., 1965-70, dir. agrl. scis., 1970—. Mem. Nat. Acad. Scis. com. on animal health, 1968-72, mem. agrl. bd., 1971—; mem. FAO expert panel on animal breeding and climatology, 1965—; mem. President's Sci. Adv. Com. panel on world food supply, 1967; mem. Nat. Agrl. Research and Extension Users Adv. Bd., 1978—. Chmn. bd. trustees Internat. Lab. for Research on Animal Diseases, 1973—; vice chmn. bd. trustees Internat. Center Tropical Agr., 1974—; trustee Internat. Agrl. Devel. Service, 1979—; vice chmn. bd. dirs. Winrock Internat. Livestock and Tng. Center, 1976—. Served to capt., inf. U.S. Army, 1943-46. Mem. World Soc. Animal Prodn., AAAS, Assn. Advancement Agrl. Scis. in Africa, N.Y. Acad. Scis., World Poultry Sci. Assn., Poultry Sci. Assn., Pacific Sci. Congress. Home: 28 Compo Pkwy Westport CT 06880 Office: 1133 Ave of Americas New York NY 10036

PINOLA, JOSEPH JOHN, banker; b. Pittstown, Pa., May 13, 1925; B.A. in Econs., Bucknell U., 1949; postgrad. Dartmouth Coll., 1960; grad. Advanced Mgmt. program, Harvard Brad. Sch. Bus. Adminstrn., 1971; H.L.D., Wilkes Coll., 1978; m. Doris Jean Walker; children—Mary, James. With Bank of Am., 1953-76, sr. v.p. 1970-74, exec. v.p. N.Am. div., 1974-76; pres., dir. United Calif. Bank, 1976-77; dir. Western Bancorporation, Los Angeles, 1977—, chmn., chief exec. officer, 1978—; dir. Fed. Res. Bank, San Francisco, Los Angeles br., 1st Nat. Bank Ariz., 1st Nat. Bank Nev., United Calif. Bank. Chmn. advisory bd. Salvation Army, Los Angeles; mem. campaign cabinet United Way of Los Angeles County. Served with USNR. Mem. Assn. Res. City Bankers. Clubs: California, Los Angeles Country, Stock Exchange, Virginia Country. Office: 707 Wilshire Blvd Los Angeles CA 90017

PINSKY, LAWRENCE STEVEN, physicist, educator; b. Kew Gardens, N.Y., Aug. 9, 1946; s. Bernard and Kathrine June (Collins) P.; B.S., Carnegie-Mellon U., 1968; M.A., U. Rochester, N.Y., 1970, Ph.D. (fellow), 1973; m. Brenda Joyce Wilson, Aug. 21, 1971. With physics br. NASA, Johnson Space Center, Houston, 1970-72; postdoctoral fellow U. Houston, 1972-75, asst. prof. physics, 1975—; designer hist. simulation games Avalon Hill Co., Simulations Publs., Inc. Head coach NASA Area Saints Football Team, 1970—. Served from 2d lt. to capt. C.E., AUS, 1969-72. Research grantee NASA, 1974—. Mem. Am. Phys. Soc., Am. Inst. Physics (pres. Carnegie-Mellon U. Student chpt. 1967-68). Contbr. articles to profl. jours. Home: 15518 Penn Hills Ln Houston TX 77058

PINSKY, MARK ALLAN, mathematician; b. Phila., July 15, 1940; s. Harry A. and Helen V. (Marker) P.; B.A., Antioch Coll., Yellow Springs, Ohio, 1962; Ph.D., M.I.T., 1966; m. Joanna K. Leff, Dec. 23, 1963; children—Seth, Jonathan, Lea. Instr. math. Stanford U., 1966-68; mem. faculty Northwestern U., 1968—, prof. math., 1976—, dir. integrated sci. program, 1977—; prof. associe U. Paris, 1972-73; vis. prof. U. Chgo., 1979. Fellow Inst. Math. Stats.; mem. Am. Math. Soc., Math. Assn. Am., AAUP. Home: 1223 Grant St Evanston IL 60201 Office: Dept Math Northwestern Univ Evanston IL 60201

PINSOF, NATHAN, advt. co. exec.; b. Havana, Cuba, July 16, 1926; s. Oscar and Rose (Newman) P.; came to U.S., 1928, naturalized, 1952; student City Jr. Coll., Chgo., 1944-46; M.B.A., U. Chgo., 1949; m. Barbara Cohn, Oct. 28, 1956; children—Ellen, Diane. Asst. controller Stineway Drugs, 1949-51; mgr. media dept. Weiss & Geller, 1953-60; sr. v.p., media dir. Edward H. Weiss & Co., 1960-67; v.p., mgr. media dept. J. Walter Thompson, 1967-69; sr. v.p., dir. media and fin. Grey-North, Inc., Chgo., 1969-75, exec. v.p., 1975—. Bd. dirs. Off The Street Club; trustee North Shore Cong. Israel. Bd. dirs. Jewish Children's Bur.; chmn. communications div. Jewish United Fund, 1978-79. Served with U.S. Army, 1951-53. Mem. Broadcast Advt. Club, Mental Health Assn., Art Inst. Chgo. Clubs: B'nai B'rith, The Arts of Chicago. Home: 445 Sunset Ln Glencoe IL 60022 Office: Merchandise Mart Chicago IL 60654

PINSON, ELLIS REX, JR., chemist; b. Wichita, Kans., Oct. 23, 1925; s. Ellis Rex and Vivian (Neal) P.; B.Sc., U. of South, 1948; Ph.D., U. Rochester, 1951; m. Betty Ann Hogarth, Dec. 4, 1954; children—Matthew, Martha, Thomas. Research chemist Pfizer Inc., Groton, Conn., 1951-59, project leader, 1959-61, sect. mgr., 1961-65, asst. dir. pharmacology research, 1965-67, dir. pharmacology research, 1967-71, dir. research, 1971-72, v.p. medicinal products research and devel., 1972—. Served with USNR, 1943-46. Fellow N.Y. Acad. Scis.; mem. Am. Chem. Soc., A.A.A.S., Am. Soc. Pharmacology and Exptl. Therapeutics, Internat. Soc. Biochem. Pharmacology, Phi Beta Kappa, Sigma Xi. Club: Baker Street Irregulars. Contbr. articles to profl. jours. Patentee in field. Office: Pfizer Inc Eastern Point Groton CT 06340

PINTAR, MILAN MIK, physicist; b. Celje, Yugoslavia, Jan. 17, 1934; s. Richard and Milena (Kovac) P.; came to Can., 1966, naturalized, 1973; B.Sc., U. Ljubljana, 1958, M.Sc., 1964, Ph.D., 1966; m. Sandra Dawn Burt, Nov. 7, 1974; children—Richard, Katarina, Andrej. Research fellow Inst. J. Stefan, Ljubljana, 1957-66; postdoctoral fellow McMaster U., Hamilton, Ont., Can., 1966-67; mem. faculty U. Waterloo (Ont.), 1967—, prof. physics, 1975—; chmn. Internat. Summer Sch. Nuclear Magnetic Resonance, 1969—; cons. Ont. Cancer Found. Recipient Nat. Sci. award B. Kidric, Ljubljana, 1965, Presern Student Research award U. Ljubljana, 1956; grantee Nat. Research Council Can., 1967—, NIH, 1973-76, Med. Research Council Can., 1973-74. Mem. Canadian Assn. Physicists, Am. Phys. Soc., Internat. Soc. Magnetic Resonance (dir., sec.-gen.),

Ampere Soc. Editor: NMR Introductory Essays, 1976. Home: 134 Dunbar St S Waterloo ON N2L 2E9 Canada Office: Dept Physics Univ Waterloo ON N2L 3G1 Canada

PINTER, HAROLD, playwright; b. London, Oct. 10, 1930; s. Hyman and Frances (Mann) P.; student Brit. schs.; D.Litt. (hon.), U. Reading, 1970, U. Birmingham, 1971; m. Vivien Merchant, Sept. 14, 1956; 1 son, Daniel. Actor in repertory theatres, 1949-57; dir. plays and films, 1970—; asso. dir. Nat. Theatre, 1973—; author: (plays) The Room, The Birthday Party, Dumb Waiter, 1957, Slight Ache, 1958, A Night Out, The Caretaker, 1959, Night School, The Dwarfs, 1960, The Collection, 1961, The Lover, 1962, Tea Party, 1963, The Homecoming, 1964, The Basement, 1966, Landscape, 1968, Silent Night, 1969, Old Times, 1971, Monologue, 1972, No Man's Land, 1975, Betrayal, 1979; (screenplays) The Caretaker, 1962, The Servant, 1962, The Pumpkin Eater, The Quiller Memorandum, 1966, Accident, 1967, The Go-Between, 1969, Langrishe Go Down, 1970, A la Recherche du Temps Perdu, 1972, The Last Tycoon, 1974; also TV and radio plays. Decorated comdr. Order Brit. Empire; recipient Italia prize for TV play The Lover, 1963, Shakespeare prize, Hamburg, W. Ger., 1970, Australian State prize lit., 1973. Mem. Soc. Authors, Dramatists Club. Address: care ACTAC 16 Cadogan Ln London SW1 England

PINTOFF, ERNEST, film dir. and producer, writer, composer; b. N.Y.C., Dec. 15, 1931; s. Joseph and Sylvia (Kokol) P.; B.F.A., Syracuse U., 1953; M.A., Mich. State U., 1955; m. Caroline Webb-Carter, May 21, 1970; children—Jonathan, Gabrielle. Instr. painting and design Mich. State U., East Lansing; instr. screenwriting Sch. of Visual Arts, N.Y.C.; guest lectr. on film production and screenwriting to various univs. and art schs.; pres. Pintoff Productions, N.Y.C.; dir. TV films, CBS, films include: Kojak, Hawaii Five-O, The Blue Knight, Young Dan'l Boone; writer, composer, dir. films including: The Violinist (Am. Film Festival award, Brit. Acad. award, Edinburgh Film Festival award), The Old Man and the Flower (London Film Festival citation), Harvey Middleman, Fireman (Montreal Film Festival award), The Shoes (Venice Film Festival award, Edinburgh Film Festival award), The Wild Wild East; dir. and producer films including: The Critic (Academy award, Brit. Academy award, Oberhausen Film Festival award), The Interview (Edinburgh Film Festival award, Stratford Internat. Film Festival award), Dynamite Chicken, Blade; writer, designer and dir. of documentary and live action comml. films including: Aquarium, Good Ole Country Music, Performing Painter, Lion Hunt; dir. films NBC-TV; films include: Police Woman, Ellery Queen, Big Hawaii, James At Fifteen; Am. juror at Oberhausen Film Festival, Film Festival, Annecy, France. Mem. Writers Guild of Am., Dirs. Guild of Am., Acad. of Motion Picture Arts and Scis. Writer, illustrator (books): Travel With Your Pet, Tennis Anyone?, Always Help a Bird. Office: care Irv Schechter 404 N Roxbury Dr Beverly Hills CA 90210*

PIORE, EMANUEL RUBEN, physicist; b. Wilno, Russia, July 19, 1908; s. Ruben and Olga (Gegusin) P.; came to U.S., 1917, naturalized, 1924; A.B., U. Wis., 1930, Ph.D., 1935, D.Sc. (hon.), 1966; D.Sc. (hon.), Union U., 1962; m. E. Nora Kahn, Aug. 26, 1931; children—Michael Joseph, Margot Deborah, Jane Ann. Asst. instr. U. Wis., 1930-35; research physicist RCA, 1935-38; engr. in charge TV lab. CBS, 1938-42; head spl. weapons group, bur. ships U.S. Navy, 1942-44; head electronics br. Office Naval Research, 1946-47, dir. phys. sci., 1947-48, dep. for natural sci., 1949-51, chief sci., 1951-55; v.p., dir. Avco Mfg. Corp., 1955-56; dir. research IBM Corp., 1956-61, v.p. research and engring., 1961-63, v.p., group exec., 1963-65, v.p., chief scientist, 1965—, also dir.; physicist research lab. electronics Mass. Inst. Tech., 1948-49. Dir. Sci. Research Assos., Inc., Health Advancement, Inc., Paul Revere Investors, Guardian Mut. Fund. Mem. Pres.'s Sci. Adv. Com., 1959-62; mem. Nat. Sci. Bd., 1961—; bd. dirs. N.Y. State Found. for Sci.; past bd. dirs. NSF; chmn. vis. com. Nat. Bur. Standards; chmn. bd. Hall of Science, N.Y.C.; mem. corp. Woods Hole Oceanographic Instn.; mem. exec. com. Resources for Future; bd. dirs. Stark Draper Lab., Nat. Info. Bur.; mem. vis. com. to elec. engring. dept. Mass. Inst. Tech., 1956-57, vis. com. Harvard Coll., 1958-70; trustee Sloan-Kettering Inst. Cancer Research; mem. N.Y.C. Bd. Higher Edn., 1976—. Served to lt. comdr. USNR, 1944-46. Recipient Indsl. Research Inst. award, 1967; Distinguished Civilian medal Dept. Navy; Kaplun award Hebrew U., 1975. Fellow AAAS, Royal Soc. Arts (London, Eng.), Am. Phys. Soc., IEEE, Am. Acad. Arts Scis.; mem. Sci. Research Soc. Am., Sci. Research Assn. (dir.), Nat. Acad. Sci., Nat. Acad. Engring., Am. Inst. Physics (dir.), Am. Philos. Soc., Sigma Xi. Clubs: University (N.Y.C.); Cosmos (Washington). Home: 115 Central Park W New York City NY 10023 Office: Armonk NY 10504

PIORE, MICHAEL JOSEPH, economist; b. N.Y.C., Aug. 14, 1940; s. Emanuel R. and Nora (Kahn) P.; B.A., Harvard U., 1962, Ph.D., 1966; m. Nancy Kline, Aug. 6, 1966; children—Adam Alejo, Ana Leah. Mem. faculty M.I.T., 1966—, prof. econs., 1975—; cons. Dept. Labor, Commonwealth of P.R., NAACP Legal Def. Fund. Mem. Am. Econ. Assn., Indsl. Relations Research Assn., Union Radical Polit. Econs. Democrat. Jewish. Author: Birds of Passage, Migrant Labor and Industrial Societies, 1979; co-author: Internal Labor Markets and Manpower Adjustment, 1971; editor: Inflation and Unemployment, Institutionalist and Structuralist Views, 1979. Home: 19 Cortes St Apt 9 Boston MA 02116 Office: E 52-271 B Mass Inst Tech Cambridge MA 02139

PIOTROWSKI, JOHN LOUIS, air force officer; b. Detroit, Feb. 17, 1934; s. John and Mary P.; student Ariz. State U., 1959-61, Fla. State U., 1963-64; B.S., U. Nebr., 1965; postgrad. U. So. Calif., 1969-70, Auburn U., 1974-75; grad. program for mgmt. devel. Harvard U., 1970, Air Command and Staff Coll., 1966, Armed Forces Staff Coll., 1968, RAF Coll. Air Warfare, 1971; m. Sheila Dee Frederickson, Dec. 22, 1961; children—Denise, Scott, Jon. Served as enlisted man U.S. Air Force, 1952-54, commd. 2d lt., 1954, advanced through grades to maj. gen., 1978; assigned to 67th Tactical Reconnaissance Wing, Korea and Japan, 1955-57; pilot trainee Marana Air Base, Ariz., Bainbridge Air Base, Ga., and Bryan AFB, Tex., 1957-58; aircraft advanced gunnery trainee, Williams AFB, Ariz., 1958-59; armament and electronics maintenance officer, Williams AFB Base, Luke AFB, Ariz., 1961; with initial cadre Project Jungle Jim (later 1st Air Commando Wing), Eglin AF Aux. Field 9, Fla., 1961, S.E. Asia, 1961-63; served at USAF Fighter Weapons Sch. Nellis AFB, Nev., 1965; action officer Hdqrs. USAF, Washington, 1968-70; dep. comdr. for ops. 36th Tactical Fighter Wing, Bitburg Air Base, Germany, 1971-72; comdr. 40th Tactical Group, Aviano Air Base, Italy, 1972-74; chief USAF Six-Man Group, 1974-75; vice comdr. Keesler Tech. Tng. Center, Keesler AFB, Miss., 1975-76; comdr. 552d Airborne Warning and Control Wing, Tactical Air Command, Tinker AFB, Okla., 1976-79; dep. comdr. for air def. Tactical Air Command, Peterson AFB, Colo., 1979—. Decorated Legion of Merit, D.S.M., Meritorious Service medal with 2 oak leaf cluster, Air medal with 2 oak leaf cluster, Air Force Commendation medal with oak leaf cluster. Mem. Daedalians. Contbr. articles on counter-insurency and aircraft weapons requirements to mil. jours. Office: ADTAC/CD Peterson AFB CO 80914

PIPAL, GEORGE HENRY, journalist; b. Lafayette, Ind., Oct. 14, 1916; s. Francis John and Belle (Kadavy) P.; B.A., U. Nebr., 1937; M.S., Columbia, 1939; m. Caroline Dunsmore, Aug. 17, 1946; children—John, Susan, Philip, Frank. Corr. various bureaus U.P.I., 1937-41, bur. mgr., Prague, 1946, mgr. for Eastern Europe, 1947, mgr. for Germany, 1948, dir. European Services, 1949-51, gen. European bus. mgr., Europe, Middle East, Africa, 1952-65, gen. sales exec., N.Y.C., 1966-68, gen. mgr. fgn. features div., 1968-78; mng. dir. UPI (U.K.), Ltd., 1964-65; v.p. United Features Syndicate, 1978—. Served as lt. USNR, 1942-46. Mem. Sigma Delta Chi, Chi Phi. Home: 12 Cove Ridge Ln Old Greenwich CT 06870 Office: 200 Park Ave New York NY 10017

PIPER, ANSON CONANT, educator; b. Newton, Mass., Aug. 14, 1918; s. Luther Warren and Elizabeth (Smith) P.; B.A., Williams Coll., 1940; M.A., U. Wis., 1947, Ph.D., 1953; m. Miriam Etna Simms, Nov. 12, 1945; children—Jonathan, Victoria, Gregory. Grad. asst. Spanish, U. Wis., 1941-42, 46-49, mem. staff NDEA Summer Inst., 1961; mem. faculty Williams Coll., 1949—, prof. Romanic langs., 1961—; mem. staff Colby Coll. Summer Sch. Langs., 1956-58, 60, 62, 68. Fulbright lectr., Brazil, 1963-64. Co-dir. of study radiophonic teaching in Latin Am. for Internat. Research Assos., 1961-63. Co-dir. Williamstown United Fund. Served with USNR, 1942-46. Williams Found. grantee for study in Argentina, 1951-52; Gulbenkian grant for Portuguese studies, 1967. Mem. Am. Assn. Tchrs. Spanish and Portuguese (pres. Western Mass. chpt. 1966-68), Inst. Internat. Edn. (mem. nat. screening com. 1973-74, 76-77), Phi Beta Kappa. Conglist. (moderator 1959-61, 72-75). Author: Asi es la vida, 1958; also articles. Co-editor: Portuguese: A Fundamental Vocabulary, 1968. Home: Baxter Rd Williamstown MA 01267

PIPER, DON COURTNEY, educator; b. Washington, July 29, 1932; s. Don Carlos and Alice (Courtney) P.; B.A., U. Md., 1954, M.A., 1958; Ph.D. (James B. Duke fellow), Duke, 1961; m. Rowena Inez Wise, July 6, 1956; children—Sharon, Valarie. Research asso. Duke, 1961-62, exec. sec. Commonwealth-Studies Center, 1962-64; asst. prof. dept. govt. and politics U. Md., College Park, 1964-67, asso. prof., 1967-69, prof., 1969—, head dept. govt. and politics, 1968-74, chmn. faculty council College Park Faculty Assembly, 1974-75, chmn. campus senate, 1975-77. Research asst. Am. Council on Edn., 1966-68; mem. faculty adv. com., planning adv. com. Md. State Bd. Higher Edn., 1977—. Served to 1st lt. USAF, 1955-58. Recipient U. Md. Regents award for excellence in teaching, 1966. Mem. Am. Assn. U. Profs., Am. (chmn. com. dept. chmn. 1973-75), So. (council 1970-72, chmn. Chastain award com. 1973-75) polit. sci. assns., Am. Soc. Internat. Law, Internat. Law Assn., Internat. Studies Assn., Am. Peace Soc. (dir.), Phi Beta Kappa (pres. Gamma chpt. 1978-79), Phi Kappa Phi, Pi Sigma Alpha. Methodist. Author: International Law of Great Lakes, 1967; contbg. author: International Law Standard and Commonwealth Developments, 1966; De Lege Pactorum, 1970; Foreign Policy Analysis, 1975. Editor: (with R. Taylor Cole) Post-primary Education and Political and Economic Development, 1964. Bd. editors World Affairs; editorial adv. com. Internat. Legal Materials, 1977-78. Home: 4323 Woodberry St Hyattsville MD 20782 Office: Dept Govt and Politics U Md College Park MD 20742

PIPER, HENRY DAN, educator; b. Haskell, N.J., Feb. 20, 1918; s. Henry Anson and Blanche (Guy) P.; B.A., Princeton, 1939; Ph.D., U. Pa., 1950; m. Roberta Bicknell, July 3, 1953; children—Andrew Dan, Jonathan Bicknell. Research chemist E. I. duPont de Nemours & Co., 1939-42, prodn. supr., 1942-45; historian AEC, 1947-48; instr. Grad. Sch. Philosophy, Columbia, 1950-52; asso. prof. English humanities div. Calif. Inst. Tech., 1952-62; vis. prof. Am. civilization univs. Lille and Clermont (France), 1953-54, U. Kent (Eng.), 1967-68; sr. cons. Tech. Communications, Inc., engring., Los Angeles; cons. communications Shell Oil Co., 1957-58, Union Oil Co., 1961-62; Cons. Nat. Endowment for Humanities, 1970—, USIS, Dept. State, 1974-75, also cultural affairs, India, Pakistan, Bangladesh, Afghanistan; prof. English, So. Ill. U., 1962—, dean Coll. Liberal Arts and Scis., 1962-66; vis. disting. Mellon prof. English, Lafayette Coll., 1979-80. Bd. dirs. Ill. Bd. Natural Resources. Asst. to dir. research div. Manhattan Project, U.S. Army, 1947-48. Harrison fellow U. Pa., 1949-50, Guggenheim fellow, 1957-58; grantee Am. Council Learned Socs., 1961-62. Mem. Am. Studies Assn. (exec. bd. 1953-54, pres. So. Calif. chpt. 1957-58), Coll. English Assn. (pres. So. Cal. chpt. 1961-62), Modern Lang. Assn. (acting chmn. library resources com. 1958-59). Author: Guide to Technical Reports, 1958; American Literary Manuscripts, 1961; F. Scott Fitzgerald: A Critical Portrait, 1965; Land Between the Rivers: The Southern Illinois Country, 1973. Editor: Dimensions in Drama: Six Plays of Crime and Punishment, 1964; Think Back on Us: A Literary Chronicle of the 1930s, 1966; The Great Gatsby: The Novel, the Critics, the Background, 1970; A Many-Windowed House, Essays by Malcolm Cowley, 1970. Contbr. articles popular and scholarly jours. Home: Route 1 Murphysboro IL 62966

PIPER, HOWARD, aviation cons.; b. Bradord, Pa., Nov. 3, 1917; s. William T. and Marie (Vandewater) P.; B.S., Harvard, 1939; m. Helen Wann, Dec. 29, 1939; children—David, Patricia, Howard. With Piper Aircraft Corp., 1939-73, v.p., 1950-73, also dir.; cons. Beech Aircraft Corp., 1973-76; gen. aviation cons., 1976—; dir. aviation mgmt. program Wichita State U., 1978—. Treas., Lock Haven (Pa.) Hosp., 1965-73. Served with USNR, 1942-45. Home: 7736 Dublin St Wichita KS 67206

PIPER, MARK HARRY, banker; b. Flint, Mich., Apr. 17, 1931; s. James U. and Dorothy (Weed) P.; B.S., St. John's Mil. Acad., 1949; A.B. with distinction and honors in Econs., U. Mich., 1953, J.D. cum laude, 1956; m. Wanda L. Hubbard, June 20, 1953; children—Mark T., Kathryn L. Admitted to Mich. bar, 1956; with firm Clark, Klein, Winter, Parsons & Prewitt, Detroit, 1956-57; with Genesee Mchts. Bank & Trust Co., Flint, 1957—, v.p., sr. trust officer, 1966-72, sr. v.p., 1972—; sr. v.p. United Mich. Corp., 1975—; dir. Fidelity Abstract & Title Co., Flint; adj. instr. bus. adminstrn. U. Mich., Flint, 1976—. Pres. Flint Estate Planning Council, 1969-70; mem. Flint citizens adv. com. U. Mich., 1974—, vice chmn., 1975—. Dir. Retirement Homes of Detroit Ann. Conf. Methodist Ch., 1968-76, vice chmn. profl. ministry and support, 1975, mem. bd. support systems, 1975, mem. council fin. and adminstrn., 1976—; trustee Flint YMCA Boysfarm Found., 1964-78, chmn., 1976-78; bd. mgmt. Flint YMCA Boysfarm, 1964-74; mem. Detroit Conf. Bd. P. United Meth. Ch., 1968-76, chmn., 1972-75; dir., sec. Flint Area Young Life Found., 1979—. Mem. Am., Mich., Genesee County bar assns., Inst. Continuing Legal Edn., Am. Judicature Soc., Fin. Execs. Inst., Flint C. of C. Clubs: U. Mich. (dir., pres. 1973-74), City, Flint, Flint Golf, University (Flint). Home: 1378 Oxyoke Dr Flint MI 48504 Office: Genesee Mchts Bank Flint MI 48502

PIPER, ROBERT JOHNSTON, architect, urban planner; b. Byron, Ill., Feb. 2, 1926; s. Leo Edward and Helen Anna (Johnston) P.; B.S. in Archtl. Engring., U. Ill., 1951; M. City and Regional Planning, Cornell U., 1953; m. Carol Jane White, June 23, 1951; children—Christopher White, Brian Douglas, Eric Johnston. Architect, planner Orput & Assos., Rockford, Ill., 1953-61; dir. profl. services AIA, Washington, 1961-67; partner, v.p. Perkins & Will, Chgo., 1967-74; dep. dir. Northeastern Ill. Planning Commn., Chgo., 1974-76; asso. Metz, Train, Olson & Youngren, Inc., Chgo., 1976—; pres. Landmarks Preservation Council and Service, Chgo., 1976—; trustee Village of Winnetka, Ill., 1978—; mem. Potomac Planning Task Force Dept. Interior, 1967-68, Commn. on Fed. Procurement, Washington, 1970-71; mem. nat. advisory bd. community characteristics HEW, 1970-78; Served with USNR, 1944-46; PTO. Fellow AIA (mem. Task Force Future of Inst. 1974-75, various coms.); mem. Am. Soc. Planning Ofcls., Am. Inst. Planners (chpt. pres. 1971-72), Lamdba Alpha. Episcopalian. Club: Rotary. Author: Careers in Architecture, vocat. guidance manuals, 1967, 71, 75, 79; author, editor: Architect's Handbook of Professional Practice, 7th edit., 1963; prin. works include Ministry of Info. Bldg., Riyadh, Saudi Arabia, Regional Open Space Plan, Northeastern Ill., Spring Valley Operations Breakthrough Housing Complex, Kalamazoo, YMCA Isham Center, Chgo.; Home: 972 Elm St Winnetka IL 60093 Office: 1 E Wacker Dr Chicago IL 60601. *My most significant contributions, and most rewarding compensations, have consistently resulted from those assignments that provided opportunities to advocate, develop, refine and support more meaningful linkages between private interests and public policies - linkages that reflected our time, respected our place and realized our limitations.*

PIPER, THOMAS LAURENCE, III, investment banker; b. Washington, June 20, 1941; s. Thomas Laurence and Edna (Milewski) P.; student U. Va., 1959-61; m. Ann Runnette, Apr. 8, 1967; children—Thomas Laurence IV, Andrew Kerr. Asso., Hodgdon & Co., Inc., Washington, 1962-65; sr. v.p., dir. Hayden Stone Inc., N.Y.C., 1966-73; mng. dir. New Court Securities Corp., N.Y.C., 1974—. Chmn. fund drive New Canaan chpt. ARC, 1978. Mem. Investment Assn. N.Y. (pres. 1974), Bond Club N.Y. Clubs: Racquet and Tennis (N.Y.C.); New Canaan (Conn.) Field. Home: 99 Mariomi Rd New Canaan CT 06840 Office: 1 Rockefeller Plaza New York NY 10020

PIPES, RICHARD EDGAR, educator, historian; b. Cieszyn, Poland, July 11, 1923; s. Mark and Sophia (Haskelberg) P.; came to U.S., 1940, naturalized, 1943; student Muskingum (Ohio) Coll., 1940-43; A.B., Cornell U., 1945; Ph.D., Harvard, 1950; m. Irene Eugenia Roth, Sept. 1, 1946; children—Daniel, Steven. Mem. faculty Harvard, 1950—, prof. history, 1963-75, Frank B. Baird Jr. prof. history, 1975—, asso. dir. Russian Research Center, 1962-64, dir., 1968-73; sr. cons. Stanford Research Inst., 1973-78. Mem. exec. com. Com. on Present Danger, 1977—; chmn. Govt. Team B to Rev. Intelligence Estimates, 1976. Served with AUS, 1943-46. Guggenheim fellow, 1956, 65; fellow Am. Council Learned Socs., 1965, Center for Advanced Study in Behavioral Scis., Stanford, Calif., 1969-70. Fellow Am. Acad. Arts and Scis.; mem. Council Fgn. Relations. Author: Formation of the Soviet Union, rev. edit., 1964; Karamzin's Memoir on Ancient and Modern Russia, 1959; Social Democracy and the St. Petersburg Labor Movement, 1963; Europe Since 1815, 1970; Struve: Liberal on the Left, 1870-1905, 1970; Russia Under the Old Regime, 1974; Struve: Liberal on the Right, 1905-1944, 1980; editor: Russian Intelligentsia, 1961; (with John Fine) Of the Russe Commonwealth (Giles Fletcher), 1966; Revolutionary Russia, 1968; Collected Works in Fifteen Volumes (P.B. Struve), 1970; Soviet Strategy in Europe, 1976. Home: 17 Berkeley St Cambridge MA 02138

PIPES, SAMUEL WESLEY, III, lawyer; b. Mobile, Ala., Feb. 28, 1916; s. Samuel Wesley, Jr. and Miriam (Larkin) P.; LL.B., U. Ala., 1938; m. Maude Beeland, June 19, 1940; children—S. Wesley, Prather (Mrs. Norton Brooker, Jr.). Admitted to Ala. bar, 1938, since practiced in Mobile; mem. firm Lyons, Pipes & Cook, 1940—; lectr. seminar on oil and gas Fla. State U., 1974; dir. Comml. Guaranty Bank, Title Ins. Co.; spl. justice Supreme Ct. Ala., 1971, mem. standing com. on civil practice and procedure. Bd. dirs. U. Ala. Law Sch. Found., 1964, pres., 1966-68; bd. visitors Ala. Law Inst.; chmn. bldg. fund Ala. Bar Found., 1966—. Recipient Daniel J. Meador Outstanding Alumnus award U. Ala., 1973. Fellow Am. Coll. Trial Lawyers; mem. Ala. State Bar (pres. 1969), Mobile Bar Assn. (pres. 1959). Episcopalian (vestryman, past treas.). Club: Athelstan (pres. 1964-65) (Mobile). Contbr. articles to profl. jours. Home: Point Clear AL Office: 2 N Royal St Mobile AL 33601

PIPES, WESLEY O'FERAL, educator; b. Dallas, Jan. 28, 1932; s. Wesley O'Feral and Lunnette (Waller) P.; B.S., North Tex. State U., 1953, M.S., 1955; Ph.D., Northwestern U., 1959; m. Karin Sergel Schultz, July 11, 1970; children by previous marriage—Phylis, Victoria, Wesley; children—Susan, Gordon. Research engr. U. Calif. at Berkeley, 1955-57; asst. prof. Northwestern U., 1959-62, asso. prof., 1962-67, prof. civil engring., 1967-74, prof. biol. scis., 1969-74; L. Drew Betz prof. ecology Drexel U., 1975—; cons. water pollution and wastewater treatment Met. San. Dist. Greater Chgo., 1967—, Commonwealth Edison Co., 1968-78, Republic Steel, 1973-77, TVA, 1974-75. Mem. tech. adv. com. on water resources Northeastern Ill. Planning Commn., 1968-74. Named one of 10 Outstanding Young Men of Chgo., Chgo. Jr. Assn. Commerce and Industry, 1963. Mem. Assn. Environ. Engring. Profs. (dir. 1970-76, v.p. 1974, pres. 1975), ASCE, Ecol. Soc. Am., Am. Water Works Assn., Water Pollution Control Fedn., Am. Soc. Microbiology, Sigma Xi, Tau Beta Pi. Research and publs. on microbiology of water and wastewater. Office: Dept Biol Scis Drexel U Philadelphia PA 19104

PIPKIN, ALLEN COMPERE, II, mathematician; b. Mena, Ark., May 21, 1931; s. Allen Compere and Leyland (Chambers) P.; Sc.B., Mass. Inst. Tech., 1952; Ph.D., Brown U., 1959; m. Ann Brittain, May 26, 1956; children—Janet Louise, Lee Ann, Allen Brittain. Research asst. Brown U., Providence, 1955-58, asst. prof. applied mathematics, 1960-63, asso. prof., 1963-66, prof., 1966—; research asso. Inst. for Fluid Dynamics and Applied Mathematics U. Md., College Park, 1958-60. Served with U.S. Army, 1952-54. Guggenheim fellow, 1968; NSF grantee, 1969—; sr. vis. fellow Sci. Research Council (U.K.), 1978. Mem. Soc. Rheology, Soc. for Natural Philosophy. Author: Lectures on Viscoelasticity Theory, 1972; mem. editorial bd. Jour. Applied Mathematics, 1970-76; contbr. articles in field to profl. jours. Home: 87 Greenwood Ave Rumford RI 02916 Office: Div Applied Mathematics Brown Univ Providence RI 02912

PIPKIN, FRANCIS MARION, educator, physicist; b. Marianna, Ark., Nov. 27, 1925; s. Larry Stewart and Augusta Pearl (Hill) P.; student U. Kan., 1943-44, Morningside Coll., Sioux City, Ia., 1946-47; B.A., State U. Ia., 1950; M.A., Princeton, 1952, Ph.D., 1954; m. Phyllis Burr, June 14, 1958; children—Jane, Augusta. Jr. fellow Soc. Fellows, Harvard, 1954-57, mem. faculty, 1957—, prof. physics, 1964—, Baird prof. sci., 1976—, asso. dean Harvard and Radcliffe colls., 1974-77, Alfred P. Sloan fellow, 1959-63; spl. research atomic physics, nuclear orientation, high energy nuclear physics. Served with U.S. Army, 1944-46. Mem. Am. Phys. Soc., Am. Acad. Arts and Scis., Sigma Xi. Author research papers. Home: 10 Kilburn Rd Belmont MA 02178 Office: Dept Physics Harvard Univ Cambridge MA 02138

PIPPIN, DONALD W., musical dir., composer; b. Macon, Ga., Nov. 25; s. Earl C. and Irene L. (Ligon) P.; student U. Ala., Julliard Sch. Music, 1953; m. Marie B. Santell, Jan. 27, 1974. Staff pianist ABC-TV, N.Y.C., 1950-54; condr., vocal arranger for Broadway musicals Mame, Oliver, Irma La Douce, Applause, Seesaw, A Chorus Line; exec. mus. dir. Radio City Music Hall. Served with AUS. Decorated Bronze Star. Composer for Off-Broadway shows The Contrast, 1972, Fashion, 1974; guest condr. pop concerts Cleve., Pitts., Vancouver,

London Royal Philharm. orchs. Recipient Tony award for Oliver. Home: 270 West End Ave New York NY 10023

PIQUET, HOWARD S., economist; b. Bklyn., July 4, 1903; s. Samuel D. and Laura E. (Mann) P.; B.S., N.Y. U., 1924; M.A., U. Calif., 1926; Ph.D., Princeton, 1930; m. Dorothy Virginia Burke, Dec. 23, 1930; children—Dorothy Vanna, Howard S., Barbara. Instr. Princeton, 1928-32; asst. prof. econs. N.Y. U., 1932-34; economist U.S. Tariff Commn., 1934-43, chief econ. div., 1937-43; sec. sect. on distbn. UN Conf. on Food and Agr., Hot Springs, Va., 1943; exec. sec. UN Interim Commn. on Food and Agr., 1943-45; adj. prof. econ. theory Grad. Sch., Am. U., Washington, 1934-56. Spl. adviser Office of War Moblzn. and Reconversion, 1945-46, exec. sec. Inter-agy. policy com. on rubber, 1945-46, sr. specialist on internat. econs. Congl. Research Service, Library of Congress, 1946-69; mem. profl. staff Com. on Fgn. Affairs, Ho. of Reps., dep. staff dir. Ho. Select Com. on Fgn. Aid. Mem. Am. Econ. Assn., Phi Beta Kappa. Clubs: Nat. Press, Cosmos (Washington). Author: Building and Loan Associations in New Jersey, 1930; Outline of the New Deal Legislation, 1933; Functional International Organization in Annals Am. Acad. Polit. and Social Sci., 1945; Charter for an International Trade Organization in Proceedings of the Economic Institute, U.S. Chamber of Commerce, 1948; Aid, Trade and the Tariff, 1953; Trade Agreements Act and the National Interest, 1958; The European Free Trade Association: Implications for U.S. Exports, 1960; Gold and the U.S. Balance of Internat. Payments, 1961; Foreign Trade and Foreign Policy, 1962; The Trade Expansion Act of 1962: How Will It Affect Canadian American Trade?, 1963; Some Consequences of Dollar Speculation in Gold, 1962; The European Common Market in Economic Perspective, 1964; U.S. Balance of Payments and International Monetary Reserves, 1966; Some Important Issues in Foreign Aid, 1966; U.S. Foreign Trade Policy After the Kennedy Round, 1967; Trends in International Trade of the U.S., 1968; Payments Deficits versus Free Trade, 1968; The Export-Import Bank of the U.S., 1970; Free Trade Truths—and Myths, 1971; Balance of Payments and U.S. Trade Policy, 1971; The Balance-of-Payments Breakdown: Treating the Symptoms, 1972. Co-author The Common Market: Friend or Competitor?, 1964; The Economic Axioms, 1978. Home: 2045 Yorktown Rd NW Washington DC 20012

PIRANI, CONRAD LEVI, pathologist, educator; b. Pisa, Italy, July 29, 1914; s. Mario Giacomo Levi and Adriana Pirani; came to U.S., 1939; naturalized, 1945; diploma Ginnasio-Liceo Beccaria, 1932; M.D., U. Milano, Italy, 1938; m. Luciana Nahmias, Mar. 12, 1955; children—Barbara, Sylvia, Robert. Intern, Columbus Meml. Hosp., Chgo., 1940-42; resident Michael Reese Hosp., Chgo., 1942-45; instr. pathology U. Ill., Chgo., 1945-48, asst. prof., 1948-52, asso. prof., 1952-55, prof., 1955-70; chmn. dept. pathology Michael Reese Hosp., Chgo., 1965-72; prof. pathology Coll. Physicians and Surgeons, Columbia U., N.Y.C., 1972—, dir. Renal Pathology Lab., 1972—; cons. Armed Forces Inst. Pathology; mem. sci. com. Kidney Found. N.Y., 1973—. USPHS, NIH grantee. Mem. Am. Assn. Pathologists, AAAS, Internat. Acad. Pathology (counselor 1966-69), Am., Internat. socs. nephrology. Contbg. author various books. Asso. editor: Laboratory Investigation, 1972—, Nephron, 1975—. Contbr. numerous articles to profl. jours. Home: 101 California St Ridgewood NJ 07450 Office: 630 W 168th St New York NY 10032

PIRET, EDGAR LAMBERT, energy resources co. exec.; b. Winnipeg, Man., Can., July 1, 1910; s. Hubert and Maria Celine (Dutilleux) P.; came to U.S., 1922, naturalized, 1927; B. Ch.E., U. Minn., 1932, Ph.D., 1937; France-Am. fellow, 1935-36; Docteur in Biochemistry, U. Lyon (France), 1936; m. Alice Moeglein, Sept. 4, 1945; children—Mary Louise, Marguerite, Jacqueline, John, Robert, James. Instr. chem. engring. U. Minn., 1937-41, asst. prof., 1941-43, prof., 1945-65, dir. chem. products from peat project, 1954-59; chief chem. engr. Minn. Mining & Mfg. Co., 1943-45, cons., 1937-65; sci. attaché Dept. State, Am. embassy, Paris, 1959-67, counselor sci. and technol. affairs, 1967-75; asst. exec. dir. Am. Chem. Soc., Washington, 1975-77; dir. European ops. Energy Resources Co., Cambridge, Mass., 1977—; adminstr. chem. catalysis program U.S.-USSR, 1976—; guest of inst., vis. prof. Mass. Inst. Tech., 1965-66; cons. U.S. Naval Research Lab., 1951-55. Recipient Freidel medal U. Paris, 1951; medallist U. Liege, Belgium, 1951; Palms Acadèmiques, Officier d'Acadèmie, France, 1951; Bronze medal Swedish Assn. Engrs., 1954, lectr. Gothenburg, 1954, Royal Inst. Engrs., Holland, 1954; chevalier Legion of Honor (France), 1957; Fulbright research prof. univs. Nancy and Paris, 1950-51. Fellow AAAS, N.Y. Acad. Scis., Am. Inst. Chem. Engrs. (nat. program com. 1948-49-50; Walker award 1955); mem. Chemists Club, Am. Inst. Chem. Engrs. (awards com. 1958-63), Am. Soc. Engring. Edn., AAUP, Alpha Chi Sigma, Sigma Xi, Phi Lambda Upsilon, Tau Beta Pi. Clubs: Automobile Club de France; Cosmos (Washington). Author of numerous papers on continuous reactor theory and design, theory of crushing, leaching, heat and mass transfer. Editor: Chemical Engineering around the World, 1957. Editorial bd. Jour. Am. Inst. Chem. Engrs., 1957-70, Chem. Engring. Progress, 1957-70, Jour. Internat. Chem. Engring., 1961-70. Patentee in field. Office: 185 Alewife Brook Pkwy Cambridge MA 02138

PIRIE, JAMES WILLIAM, ret. librarian; b. N.Y.C., Sept. 22, 1913; s. Robert and Ellen (Phipps) P.; B.S., N.Y. U., 1939; B.L.S., Pratt Inst., 1940; Harvard, 1949; M.A., Western Res. U., 1955; m. Elizabeth Marshall Waller, May 1, 1943; children—Catherine Ross, Robert Waller, Ellen, James Marshall (dec.). Cataloguer Pratt Inst. Library, 1940-41; adminstrv. asst. Harvard Univ. Library, 1946-47, head duplicate and exchange div., 1947-49, reference librarian Lamont Library, 1949-50; librarian Youngstown Coll., 1950-57; dir. Charles Stewart Mott Library, Flint Coll., U. Mich. Flint Jr. Coll., 1957-66; librarian Lewis and Clark Coll., Portland, Oreg., 1966-79, ret., 1979. Mem. adv. com. on libraries State of Oreg., 1973-77. Mem. Lewis and Clark Trail Heritage Com., 1972-77. Served with AUS, 1941-46. Mem. ALA, Oreg. Library Assn., Assn. Coll. and Research Libraries (com. to revise coll. library standards 1973-75), ACLU. Democrat. Editor: Books for Junior College Libraries, 1969. Home: 3203 SW Mitchell Ct Portland OR 97201

PIRIE, JOHN T., JR., mcht.; b. Evanston, Ill., May 22, 1903; s. John T. and Sophie (Hunter) P. Chmn. exec. com. Carson Pirie Scott & Co., Chgo., now hon. chmn. exec. com.; dir. Universal Resources Corp. Adv. bd., officer Salvation Army; hon. trustee The Seeing Eye, Inc.; life trustee Field Mus. Natural History. Home: 1351 E Westleigh Rd Lake Forest IL 60045 Office: 1 S State St Chicago IL 60603

PIRIE, ROBERT BURNS, JR., govt. ofcl.; b. San Diego, Sept. 10, 1933; s. Robert Burns and Gertrude May (Freeman) P.; student Princeton U., 1950-51; B.S., U.S. Naval Acad., 1955; B.S., Magdalen Coll., Oxford U., 1959, M.A., 1963; m. Joan Adams, Dec. 23, 1960; children—John Winthrop, Carl Joseph Emil, Susan Gilman. Commd. ensign U.S. Navy, 1955, advanced through grades to comdr., 1969; comdg. officer U.S.S. Skipjack, 1969-72; dep. asst. dir. Congressional Budget Office, 1975-77; prin. dep. asst. sec. for manpower, res. affairs and logistics Dept. Def., Washington, 1977-79, asst. sec., 1979—. Vestryman, St. John's Ch., Chevy Chase, Md., 1973-76. Rhodes scholar, 1956. Mem. U.S. Naval Inst., Internat. Inst. Strategic Studies, U.S. Naval Acad. Alumni Assn. (trustee 1967-70). Episcopalian. Clubs: Vincent's, Kenwood. Office: Room 3E80B The Pentagon Washington DC 20301

PIRIGYI, ANDREW ALEXANDER, educator; b. Perth Amboy, N.J., Apr. 30, 1921; s. Andrew and Mary (Marcy) P.; A.B. cum laude, Drew U., 1942; M.S., Rutgers U., 1948, Ph.D., 1950; m. Pauline Skoyec, Apr. 12, 1946. Asst. prof. biology Utica Coll. of Syracuse U., 1950-56; prof. biol. scis., chmn. dept. Fairleigh Dickinson U. 1956-64, chmn. dept. clin. microbiology Sch. Dentistry, 1956—. Served with M.C., U.S. Army, 1942-46. Mem. Am. Soc. Microbiology, Am. Inst. Biol. Sci., Am. Assn. Dental Schs. Author: Laboratory Manual for General Microbiology, 1959; Laboratory Manual for Pathogenic Microbiology, 1960; Laboratory Manual of Applied Microbiology, 1961; Laboratory Manual of Microbiology, 1974. Office: Fairleigh Dickinson U Sch Dentistry 110 Fuller Pl Hackensack NJ 07601

PIRKL, JAMES JOSEPH, indsl. designer; b. Nyack, N.Y., Dec. 27, 1930; s. James and Ida Bertha (Gigrich) P.; cert. Advt. Design, Pratt Inst., 1951, B.Indsl. Design, 1958; m. Sarah B. Woolsey, June 8, 1974; children—Theo, James, Philip. With design staff Gen. Motors Corp., Warren, Mich., 1958-65, sr. designer, 1961-64, asst. chief designer, 1964-65; instr. indsl. design Center for Creative Studies, Detroit, 1963-65; faculty dept. design Syracuse (N.Y.) U., 1965—, asso. prof., 1969-73, prof. indsl. design, 1974—, chmn. indsl. design program, 1979—, exec. council chmn. Sch. Art, 1976-78; prin. James J. Pirkl/Design, Cazenovia, N.Y., 1965—; cons. Fed. Prison Industries, 1974, Gen. Electric Co., 1967-70, Genesee Labs., Inc., 1968, N.Y. State Council on Arts, 1968-69, Stettner-Trush, Inc., 1972—, Strathmore Chem. Coatings, Inc., 1969, Syracuse U. Gerontology Center, 1972, Village of Cazenovia, 1979—, Xerox Corp., 1975. Mem. Everson Mus. Art, 1977—. Served with SeaBees, USNR, 1951-55. Mem. Indsl. Designers Soc. Am. (chmn. Central N.Y. chpt. 1977-78, v.p. Mid-East region 1979—, dir.), AAUP, Human Factors Soc. Club: Willow Bank Yacht. Co-editor: State of the Art and Science of Design, 1971. Patentee 4-way handle; co-designer Gen. Motors Futurama Exhbn., N.Y. World's Fair, 1964-65. Home: Meadow Hill Rd Cazenovia NY 13035 Office: Dept Design Syracuse U Syracuse NY 13210

PIRKLE, EARL CHARNELL, educator; b. nr. Buckhead, Ga., Jan. 8, 1922; s. Early Charnell and Eva Lee (Collins) P.; A.B., Emory U., 1943; M.S., 1947; postgrad. U. Tenn., 1947-50; Ph.D., U. Cin., 1956; m. Valda Nell Armistead, July 9, 1942; children—Betty Jean, William A., Fredric L. Prodn. coordinator, research crystallographer Pan-Electronics Labs., Inc., Atlanta, 1942-45; instr. geology U. Tenn., 1947-50; mem. faculty dept. phys. scis. and geology U. Fla., Gainesville, 1950—, prof., 1963—, chmn. dept. phys. scis., 1972-79, dir. Phys. Scis., 1979—; cons. in field; vis. prof. geology Emory U., summers, 1959-65; research cons. Fla. Dept. Natural Resources Bur. Geology. Served with AUS, 1945-46. Certified profl. geologist. Fellow Geol. Soc. Am.; mem. Am. Assn. Petroleum Geologists, Am. Soc. Mining, Metall. and Petroleum Engrs., Soc. Econ. Geologists, Fla. Acad. Scis., Southeastern Geol. Soc., Phi Beta Kappa, Sigma Gamma Epsilon, Sigma Chi. Democrat. Methodist. Author: Natural Regions of the United States, 1977. Editor: Physical Science- Our Environment, 1968; Our Physical Environment, 1979. Contbr. articles to profl. jours. Home: 2219 NW 17th Ave Gainesville FL 32605 Office: 3141 GPA Bldg U Florida Gainesville FL 32611

PIRLOT, PAUL LEON, educator, biologist; b. Mettet, Belgium, Mar. 17, 1920; s. Leon and Frumence (Quinet) P.; Licence Philosophie et Lettres, Brussels, 1942; License Sci., U. Louvain, 1946, Agrege Enseignement, 1949; Ph.D., In Zoology, U. London, 1949, D.Sc., 1960; children—Marie-Antoinette, Jean-Paul, Brigitte. Research asso. Inst. Recherche Scientifique Afrique Centrale, Zaire, 1949-57; asso. prof. U. Montreal, 1958-63, prof. vertebrate biology, 1963—. Mem. Can. Soc. Zoologists, Soc. Scientifique de Bruxelles, N.Y. Acad. Sci., Soc. Study of Evolution, Can. Soc. History and Philosophy of Sci., Am. Soc. Anatomists, Am. Soc. Naturalists, Assn. Ecrivains de Langue Francaise. Roman Catholic. Author 4 books in field; contbr. articles to profl. jours. Home: Abercorn Brome County PQ J0E 1B0 Canada Office: Dept Biol Sci U Montreal Box 6128 Station A Montreal PQ H3C 3J7 Canada

PIRNIE, ALEXANDER, former congressman; b. Pulaski, N.Y., Apr. 16, 1903; s. Roscoe C. and Mary R. (Price) P.; grad. Pulaski Acad.; A.B., Cornell U., 1924, J.D., 1926; m. Mildred Silvernail, July 7, 1938; children—Bruce R., Douglas J. Admitted to N.Y. bar, 1926; pres. Duofold, Inc.; mem. 86th to 87th Congresses, 34th Congl. Dist. N.Y., 88th to 93d Congresses, 32d Dist. N.Y. Past pres. Utica Community Chest. Past chmn. bd. mgrs. Faxton Hosp.; v.p. Utica Found. Served from 2d lt. inf. to col. Judge Adv. Gen. Corps, U.S. Army, 1942-46. Decorated Bronze Star, Legion of Merit. Mem. Am. Legion. Republican. Presbyterian. Club: Masons (33 deg.). Home: 12 Slaytonbush Ln Utica NY 13501

PIRNIE, MALCOLM, JR., cons. engr.; b. Mount Vernon, N.Y., Mar. 15, 1917; s. Malcolm and Gertrude (Knowlton) P.; A.B., Harvard U., 1939, S.M., 1941; m. Jane Purse, Nov. 7, 1942; children—Malcolm III, Pamela. With Malcolm Pirnie Engrs., 1946—, asso., 1948-51, partner, 1952-70, chmn. bd., 1970—. Pres. Berkeley Assn., Scarsdale, 1954; mem. non-partisan com., Scarsdale, N.Y., 1954-57; bd. dirs. White Plains, YMCA, 1967-70, Westchester County Assn., 1978—; mem. Hoover Medal Bd. Award, 1976—; mem. Pres.'s Advisory Council Coll. of New Rochelle, 1977-79. Served from lt. (j.g.) to lt. comdr. USPHS, 1941-45. Diplomate Am. Acad. Environ. Engrs. Fellow ASCE (dir. Met. sect. 1956-57, v.p. 1960-62, pres., 1962-63, nat. dir. 1967-70), Am. Cons. Engrs. Council (v.p. 1973-75); mem. Am. Inst. Cons. Engrs. (councilor 1964-66, v.p., 1965-66, 71-72), Inter-Am. Assn. San. Engrs., Am. Shore and Beach Preservation Assn., Fla. Engring. Soc., Water Resources Congress (project com.), Harvard Engring. Soc. (v.p. 1955), Engrs. Joint Council (planning com. 1955-58; mem. engring. manpower commn. 1965-70), Am. Water Works Assn. (chmn. planning com. 1966), Engrs. Council for Profl. Devel. (guidance com. 1953-58), N.Y. Assn. Cons. Engrs. (dir. 1971-75). Clubs: Harvard (N.Y.C.); Town (Scarsdale, N.Y.); Scarsdale Golf. Home: 15 Windsor Ln Scarsdale NY 10583 Office: 2 Corporate Park Dr White Plains NY 10602

PIRO, ANTHONY JOHN, radiologist; b. Boston, May 28, 1930; s. John Anthony and Josephine (Pepe) P.; A.B., Boston U., 1952, M.D., 1956; m. Marian Giallombardo, Sept. 5, 1955; children—Anthony John, Janet, Jacquelyn. Intern, Mass. Meml. Hosp., Boston, 1956-57; resident Boston VA Hosp., 1959-62; practice medicine specializing in internal medicine, Framingham, Mass., 1962-63; staff physician Boston VA Hosp., 1963-66; sr. asso. Children's Cancer Research Found., 1966-70; radiotherapist Harvard Joint Center for Radiation Therapy, 1970-77; prof. therapeutic radiology, chmn. dept. therapeutic radiology Tufts-New Eng. Med. Center Hosp., 1977—. Served with USAF, 1957-59. Nat. Cancer Inst. grantee, 1977-79. Diplomate Am. Bd. Internal Medicine, Am. Bd. Radiology. Fellow A.C.P.; mem. AAAS, Am. Soc. Clin. Oncologists, Am. Soc. Therapeutic Radiologists, Am. Assn. Cancer Research, Radiation Research Soc., Am. Coll. Radiology, Phi Beta Kappa, Alpha Omega Alpha. Unitarian. Contbr. articles to profl. jours. Home: 43 Norwich Rd Wellesley MA 02181 Office: 171 Harrison Ave Boston MA 02111

PIROFSKY, BERNARD, educator, physican; b. N.Y.C., Mar. 27, 1926; s. Hyman and Yetta (Herman) P.; A.B., N.Y. U., 1946, M.D., 1950; m. Elaine Friedwald, June 19, 1953; children—Daniel Niles, Tandy Ellen, Jillann Yetta. Intern Bellevue Hosp., N.Y.C., 1950-52, resident medicine, 1954-55; research fellow U. Oreg., 1955-56; dir. Pacific N.W. Regional Blood Center, 1956-58; instr. medicine U. Oreg., 1956-59, asst. prof., 1959-63, asso. prof., 1963-66, prof., 1966—, prof. microbiology, 1973—, head div. immunology, allergy and rheumatology, 1965—; cons. immunohematologist Portland VA, Barnes VA hosps., Pacific N.W. Regional Blood Center; mem. Med. Adv. Bd. of Leukemia Soc., 1965-69; vis. prof. Nat. Inst. Nutrition, Mexico, 1966-67, Med. Research Council, S. Africa, 1977; vis. scientist Nat. Acad. Sci., Japan, 1978-79. Served as capt., USAF, 1952-54. Commonwealth Fund fellow, 1966-67; recipient Gov.'s N.W. Sci. Award, 1968; Emily Cooley award Am. Assn. Blood Banks, 1972. Fellow A.C.P.; mem. Internat. Soc. Hematology, Internat. Soc. Blood Transfusions, Am., Mexican (hon.) socs. hematology, Transplantation Soc. Author: Autoimmunization and the Autoimmune Hemolytic Anemias, 1969; Blood Banking Principles, 1973. Contbr. articles to profl. jours. Research on immunology and hematology. Home: 10370 SW Ridgeview Ln Portland OR 97219

PIRONE, THOMAS PASCAL, plant pathologist; b. Ithaca, N.Y., Jan. 3, 1936; s. Pascal Pompey and Loretta Muriel (Kelly) P.; B.S., Cornell U., 1957; Ph.D., U. Wis., 1960; m. Sherrill Sevier, Aug. 1, 1961; children—John Sevier, Catherine Sherrill. Asst. prof. La. State U., Baton Rouge, 1960-63, asso. prof., 1963-67; asso. prof. U. Ky., Lexington, 1967-71, prof., 1971—, chmn. plant pathology, 1978—. Sr. Fulbright research fellow, U.K., 1974-75. Mem. Am. Phytopathol. Soc., AAAS, Entomol. Soc. Am. Contbr. articles on plant virology to profl. jours.; mem. editorial bd. Virology, 1974-76; mem. editorial bd. Phytopathology, 1971-73, sr. editor, 1977-78. Office: Dept Plant Pathology U Ky Lexington KY 40546

PIRRUNG, GILBERT ROBINSON, corp. exec.; b. Columbus, Ohio, July 12, 1911; s. Henry Casper and Catherine Manley (Robinson) P.; grad. Choate Sch., Wallingford, Conn., 1930; B.S., Yale, 1934; m. Lila Marshall Childress, 1937 (div. 1941); m. 2d, Joan D.H. Burgess, July 9, 1947; children—Lynette R.H. Lillstrom, Clifford Mark, Henriette Christine, Timothy Burgess. Owner and mgr. Pirrung Racing Team, Indpls., 1934-36; prodn., sales depts. Gaylord Container Corp., St. Louis, 1936-39, budget dir., asst. to treas., 1939-41, dir. 1950-56; owner, mgr. Aragon Farms, Bainbridge, Ga., 1950—; chmn. bd. Vada Corp., Bainbridge, Ga., 1977—; dir. Nat. Transactions Network, St. Louis. Trustee Aiken Prep. Sch., 1962-74. Mem. nat. exec. bd. Boy Scouts of Am., 1960-73, internat. commr., 1968-72, pres. Interamerican Scout Com., 1968-70, v.p., 1970—, mem. adv. council, 1973-77; v.p., sec. U.S. Found. for Internat. Scouting; chmn. Gen. Council Presbyterian Church of U.S., 1962-71; chmn. Ga. Found. Ind. Colls., 1971-73. Trustee Ga. Conservancy, Inc., 1969—. Served as col. C.E., AUS, 1941-45. Decorated Silver Star, Bronze Star with two oak leaf clusters; Croix de Guerre; recipient Silver Beaver, Silver Antelope, Silver Buffalo award Boy Scouts of Am., Scout decorations from Japan, Paraguay, Chile, Guatemala, Ecuador, Venezuela, Peru, Inter-Am. Region, World Conf. Presbyn. (elder). Clubs: St. Louis Country, Racquet (St. Louis); St. Anthony, Yale (N.Y.C.); Capitol City (Atlanta); Little Harbor (Mich.). Home: Aragon Farms Bainbridge GA 31717

PIRSIG, ROBERT MAYNARD, author; b. Mpls., Sept. 6, 1928; s. Maynard Ernest and Harriet Marie (Sjobeck) P.; B.A., U. Minn., 1950, M.A., 1958; m. Nancy Ann James, May 10, 1954 (div. Aug. 11, 1978); children—Christopher (dec. Nov. 18, 1979), Theodore; m. 2d, Wendy L. Kimball, Dec. 28, 1978. Author: Zen And The Art of Motorcycle Maintenance, 1974. Served with AUS, 1946-48. Recipient Award, AAAL, 1979; Guggenheim fellow, 1974—. Mem. Soc. Tech. Communicators (sec. Minn. chpt. 1970-71, treas. 1971-72). Office: care william Morrow and Co Inc 105 Madison Ave New York NY 10016*

PISACANO, NICHOLAS JOSEPH, physician, educator; b. Phila., June 6, 1924; s. Joseph Harry and Rafaella (Sequella) P.; B.A., Western Md. Coll., 1947; M.D., Hahnemann Med. Coll., 1951; children—Toni Ann, Nicki Rae, Dean Alan, Don Arlie, Lorie Sue. Intern, Stamford (Conn.) Hosp., 1951-52, resident, 1952-53; gen. practice medicine, South Royalton, Vt., 1953-55, Phila., 1955-62; asst. prof. medicine Med. Sch., U. Ky., Lexington, 1962-65, asso. prof., 1965—, asso. prof. biology, 1966—, dir. continuing med. edn., 1962-66, asst. dean Coll. Arts and Scis., 1966, asst. v.p. Med. Center, 1968—, prof., chmn. dept. allied health edn. and research, 1971—; exec. dir., sec. Am. Bd. Family Practice, 1969—; mem. exec. com. Am. Bd. Med. Specialties; med. dir. Phila. div. Am. Cancer Soc., 1958-62. Vice pres. Ky. Mental Health Assn., 1977—. Served with U.S. Army, 1943-46. Recipient Most Popular Prof. award, 1965; Distinguished Teaching award U. Ky., 1967; Spl. Recognition plaque Student Am. Med. Assn., 1967; Spokewheel award, 1968; Spl. Recognition for Family Practice Edn., Ky. Acad. Family Physicians; Max Cheplove M.D. award N.Y. Acad. Family Physicians, 1975. Mem. Pan Am., So., Ky. med. assns., Am. Acad. Family Physicians (Thomas Johnston award 1977), Can. Coll. Family Physicians (hon., W. Victor Johnson orator 1977), AAAS, N.Y. Acad. Scis., Assn. Am. Med. Colls., Soc. Health and Human Values. Office: Univ Kentucky Medical Center Annex 2 Room 224 Lexington KY 40506

PISANI, JOSEPH MICHAEL, physician; b. N.Y.C., Mar. 22, 1919; s. Antonio David and Josephine Catherine (Walsh) P.; A.B., Fordham Coll., 1938; M.D., N.Y.U., 1942; grad. Army Sch. Tropical Medicine, 1943; m. Agatha Rita Evaskitis, Nov. 11, 1942; children—Michael, Robert, Richard. Intern, Bellevue Hosp., 1942-43; resident medicine Bronx (N.Y.) VA Hosp., 1946-48, asst. chief chest service, 1948-49; dep. exec. dir. Com. on Med. Scis., Research and Devel. Bd., Washington, 1949-50, exec. dir., 1950-51; asst. dean and instr. medicine State U. Coll. of Medicine at N.Y., Bklyn., 1951-54, asst. dean, asst. prof. medicine, 1954-57; asst. vis. physician Kings County Hosp., 1951-57; med. dir. Bankers Trust Co., N.Y.C., 1957-60, Union Family Med. Fund of Hotel Industry of N.Y.C., 1960- 64; dep. med. dir. FDA, Dept. Health, Edn. and Welfare, Washington, 1965-66, industry liaison rep. FDA-OTC rev. panels, 1972-76; v.p. for med.-sci. affairs and med. dir. Proprietary Assn., Washington, 1966—; clin. instr. medicine George Washington U. Sch. Medicine, and asso. in medicine, George Washington U. Hosp., 1949-51; adj. asso. prof. adminstrv. medicine Columbia U., N.Y.C., 1960-64; asso. clin. prof. adminstrv. medicine George Washington U., 1964-67, asso. clin. prof. medicine, 1968—. Exec. sec. Spl. Com. on Med. Research, NSF, 1955, cons. on med. research, 1956. Served as capt. M.C., U.S. Army, 1943-46; overseas in N. Africa and Italy with 5th Army, Field and Hosp. Med. Service. Recipient Alumni Achievement award in medicine Fordham U., 1959. Fellow Am. Pub. Health Assn., Indsl. Med. Assn.; mem. A.M.A., Am. Soc. Clin Pharmacology and Therapeutics, D.C. Med. Soc., N.Y. Acad. Scis., Soc. Alumni of Bellevue Hosp., Alumni Assn. N.Y. Univ. Coll Medicine, Celtic Med. Soc., Soc. Med. Consultants to Armed Forces. Roman Catholic. Contbr. articles on adminstrv. aspects med. care, med. edn. and med. research, drug evaluation. Home: 5404 Ridgefield Rd Bethesda MD 20016 Office: 1700 Pennsylvania Ave NW Washington DC 20006. *Whatever small success I may have thus far achieved can be completely attributed to my good fortune in being blessed by a fine heritage, both past and present. The principles of conduct, discipline, ideals and goals in life to which my dear wife and I were exposed in our respective families, have guided us in our own family. No matter* *how trite it may seem to some, our basic philosophy of life is centered on the golden rule. This involves a fundamental interest in people and trust in them despite disappointments in this regard from time to time.*

PISCHEL, DOHRMANN KASPAR, physician; b. San Francisco, Nov. 22, 1895; s. Kaspar and Minna (Dohrmann) P.; A.B., U. Calif. at Berkeley, 1918; M.D., Stanford U., 1923; m. Margery Lovegrove, June 7, 1923; children—Dohrmann Kaspar, Eleanor (Mrs. Peter McAndrew), Elizabeth (Mrs. Ivan Heisler). Intern Lane Stanford Hosp., San Francisco, 1922-23; resident 1st Univ. Eye Clinic, Vienna, Austria, 1924-26; practice ophthalmology, San Francisco, 1926—; mem. staff Children's Hosp., San Francisco Marshal Hale Hosp., Presbyn. Hosp., San Francisco; clin. instr. ophthalmology U. Calif. at San Francisco, 1926-28; mem. faculty Sch. Medicine, Stanford, 1928-61, prof., head. div. ophthalmology, 1955-61, prof. emeritus, 1961—. Bd. dirs. Nat. Soc. Prevention Blindness, 1960-70. Diplomate Am. Bd. Ophthalmology. Mem. Am. Ophthal. Soc. (Howe medal 1966; pres. 1970), AMA (chmn. ophthalmology sect. 1958), Calif. med. assns., San Francisco County Med. Soc., Pacific Coast Oto-Ophthal. Soc. (pres. 1960), Pan Pacific Surg. Assn., Pan Am. Ophthal. Soc., Am. Acad. Ophthalmology and Otolaryngology (pres. 1960), Societe Ophtamologique Francais, New Zealand and Australian Ophthal. Soc. (hon.), Internat. Council Ophthalmology (past v.p. 1962-70). Clubs: Bohemian (San Francisco); Lagunitas (Ross, Calif.). Home: Box 113 Ross Marin County CA 94957 Office: 490 Post St San Francisco CA 94102

PISCHL, ADOLPH JOHN, concert mgr.; b. East Orange, N.J., Mar. 28, 1920; s. Adolph and Anna (Ellerman) P.; certificate Drake Coll., 1940; m. Tennessee Wild, Sept. 9, 1947; 1 dau., Sallyann. With Juilliard Sch. of Music, N.Y.C., 1962—, asst. to concert mgr. 1962-66, dir. pub. relations, 1966-68, concert mgr., 1966—. Pub. dir. Am. Dance Festival, Conn. Coll., 1964-68; mgr. Betty Jones Dances I Dance, 1966-68, Ruth Currier Dance Co., 1966-68, Anna Sokolow Dance Co., 1966—; mgr. Juilliard Sch. Bookstore, 1971—. Bd. dirs. Dance Notation Bur.; sec. bd. dirs. Walter W. Naumburg Found., Inc. Served with AUS, 1940-46. Founder, editor Dance Perspectives, 1958-64, Dance Data, 1977; editor Juilliard News Bull. and Rev. Ann., 1964—; pub. Dance Horizons, 1965—. Contbr. articles to dance mags. Home: 1801 E 26th St Brooklyn NY 11229 Office: Juilliard Sch 144 W 66th St New York City NY 10023

PISCIOTTA, ANTHONY VITO, physician, educator; b. N.Y.C., Mar. 3, 1921; s. Andrew and Mary (Zinnanti) P.; B.S., Fordham U., 1941; M.D., Marquette U., 1944, M.S., 1952; m. Lorraine Gault, June 15, 1951; children—Robert Andrew, Nancy Marie, Anthony Vito. Intern Jersey City Med. Center, 1944-45; resident pathology Fordham Hosp., N.Y.C., 1947-48; resident medicine Milwaukee County Gen. Hosp., 1948-51; research fellow hematology New Eng. Center Hosp., 1951-52; instr. medicine Tufts U., 1951-52; mem. faculty Marquette U., 1952—, prof., 1966—; dir. blood research lab., staff hematologist Milwaukee County Gen. Hosp., 1952; cons. hematology U.S. Naval Hosp., Great Lakes, Ill., 1960; mem. hematology research evaluation com. VA, 1968-70; vis. prof. Mayo Clinic, 1967. Served to capt. M.C., AUS, 1945-47. Diplomate Am. Bd. Internal Medicine. Fellow A.C.P.; mem. AMA, Wis., Milw. County med. socs., Assn. Am. Physicians, AAAS, Am. Assn. Immunologists, Am. Soc. for Exptl. Pathology, Am. Soc. Hematology, Central Soc. Clin. Research, Internat. Soc. Hematology, Milw. Acad. Medicine, Milw. Soc. Internal Medicine, N.Y. Acad. Sci., Soc. Exptl. Biology and Medicine, Nat. Blood Club (sec. 1970-71), Alpha Omega Alpha. Mem. adv. editorial bd. of Transfusion, 1960-67; mem. editorial bd. of Jour. Lab. and Clin. Medicine, 1967-70. Home: 12550 W Grove Terr Elm Grove WI 53122 Office: 8700 W Wisconsin Ave Milwaukee WI 53226

PISETZNER, EMANUEL, civil engr.; b. N.Y.C., July 13, 1926; s. Alter and Esther (Kramer) P.; B.C.E., Coll. City N.Y., 1948; m. Stella Martin, Jan. 22, 1949; children—Joel, Jeffrey, Barry, Ann. Designer draftsman Allied Chem. & Dye Corp., Hopewell, Va., 1948-50; structural engr. Baskerville & Son Architects, Richmond, Va., 1950-52; structural engr. Weiskopf & Pickworth, Cons. Engrs., N.Y.C., 1953-57, asso., 1957-60, partner, 1960—; dir. Design Profl. Financial Corp., San Francisco; mem. spl. study com. on selection architects and engrs. GSA, 1974. Served with AUS, 1944-46. Recipient Prestressed Concrete Inst. Excellence in Design of Structures award, 1971, 73, Concrete Reinforcing Steel Inst. Design award, 1974; 1st award Lincoln Arc Welding Found., 1979. Fellow Am. Cons. Engrs. Council (v.p. 1972-73, dir. 1967-69), ASCE; mem. N.Y. Assn. Cons. Engrs. (pres. 1965-66, Distinguished Service to Profession award 1976), Nat. Assn. Profl. Engrs., Chi Epsilon, others. Jewish. Important works include John F. Kennedy Meml. Library, Boston, Nat. Gallery Art-East Bldg., Washington, Christian Sci. Center, Boston, Credit Lyonaiss Tower, Lyon, France, Commerce Ct. Project, Toronto, Can., UN Devel. Corp. Hotel-Office Bldg., N.Y.C., L'Enfant Plaza Devel., Washington. Office: Weiskopf & Pickworth 200 Park Ave New York NY 10017

PISHKIN, VLADIMIR, psychologist; b. Belgrade, Yugoslavia, Mar. 12, 1931; s. Vasili and Olga (Bartosh) P.; came to U.S., 1946, naturalized, 1951; B.A., Mont. State U., 1951, M.A., 1951, Ph.D., U. Utah, 1958; m. Dorothy Louise Martin, Sept. 12, 1953; children—Gayle Ann, Mark Vladimir. Dir. neuropsychiat. research labs. VA Hosp., Tomas, Wis., 1959-62; chief research psychologist VA Hosp., Oklahoma City, 1962—; prof. psychiatry Coll. Medicine, U. Okla. Health Scis. Center, Oklahoma City, 1973--, chmn. research council dept. psychiatry and behavioral scis., 1972-75. Served with USAF, 1952-54. Recipient Disting. Service award Jr. C. of C. Fellow Am. Psychol. Assn.; mem. Southwestern Psychol. Assn. (pres. 1973-74), Okla. Psychol. Assn., Midwestern Psychol. Assn., AAAS. Clubs: Masons, Shriners. Author: (with Mathis and Pierce) Basic Psychiatry, rev. edit., 1972; editor in chief Jour. Clin. Psychology, 1974—; contbr. articles to profl. jours. Home: 3113 NW 62d St Oklahoma City OK 73112 Office: VA Hosp 921 NE 13th St Oklahoma City OK 73104

PISKOR, FRANK PETER, univ. pres., polit. scientist; b. Turners Falls, Mass., Jan. 5, 1916; s. Stephen and Blanche (Frak) P.; A.B., Middlebury Coll., 1937, LL.D., 1959; Ph.D., Syracuse U., 1950, L.H.D., 1970; LL.D., Alfred U., 1969; m. Anne Moore Calder, Dec. 29, 1945; children—Joanne Mariett, Nancy Calder. Personnel counselor Syracuse (N.Y.) U., 1939-41, dir. freshman counselling, 1941-43, acting dean of men, 1943-46, dean of men, 1946-53, instr. polit. sci., 1941-50, asst. prof., 1950-53, asso. prof., v.p. and dean student services, 1953-59, prof., v.p. acad. affairs, 1959-69, vice chancellor and provost, 1969; pres. St. Lawrence U., Canton, N.Y., 1969—. Lectr. pub. personnel adminstrn. Maxwell Sch. Citizenship, 1945-68. Dir., St. Lawrence Nat. Bank, Niagara Mohawk Power Corp.; dir., sec. Thousand Islands Corp., 1974-77; trustee Syracuse Savs. Bank. Commr. Middle States Commn. Higher Edn., 1961-71, vice chmn., 1964-67, chmn., 1968-71, trustee, 1974—; vice chmn. Fedn. Regional Accreditation Commn., 1967-70; mem. sub-com. of govs. sponsoring com. on N.Y. State's Pub. Adminstrn. Interneship Program, 1948-56; mem. N.Y. Commn. on Grad. Edn., 1959-69; mem. joint ad hoc com. on accreditation Dept. Edn. and Assn. Colls. and Univs. N.Y. State; mem. exec. com. Citizens Found. Inc. of Syracuse, 1948-54; mem. alumni council Middlebury Coll.; mem. N.Y. State Regents Adv. Council on Ednl. TV, 1965-70, N.Y. State Regents Adv. Com. on Higher Edn. Facilities and Planning, 1971-76, N.Y. State Adv. Council on Higher Edn., 1970-78; mem. exec. com. Assn. Colls. and Univs. State N.Y., 1972-78; mem. long-range financing com. Commn. on Ind. Colls. and Univs. Bd. dirs. Commn. on Ind. Colls. and Univs. State N.Y., 1970-74, mem. com. on pub. affairs, 1974-77; trustee North County Hosps., Noble Found., Sculpture in Environment, Syracuse U. Library Assos., Citizens Pub. Expenditure Survey, Inc., N.Y.; bd. dirs., mem. exec. com. Canton-Potsdam Hosp.; bd. dirs. St. Lawrence council Boy Scouts Am., 1978—. Mem. Am. Soc. for Pub. Adminstrn., Am. Polit. Sci. Assn., Nat. Assn. Student Adminstrs., Am. Assn. Univ. Adminstrs. (dir. 1971-75), N.Y. State Assn. Deans and Other Guidance Personnel, Eastern Assn. Deans and Advisers Men, Am. Assn. Presidents Ind. Colls. and Univs. (dir. 1974—), Phi Beta Kappa, Omicron Delta Kappa, Beta Gamma Sigma, Chi Psi, Alpha Phi Omega, Tau Theta Upsilon. Rotarian. Clubs: University, Century. Home: 54 E Main St Canton NY 13617

PISONI, DAVID B., psychologist; b. N.Y.C., Nov. 25, 1945; s. David C. and Leanora L. P.; A.B., Queens Coll., U. City N.Y., 1968; Ph.D. (Rockham Prize fellow), U. Mich., 1971; m. Beth Gail Greene, Nov. 25, 1971. Asst. prof. to prof. psychology Ind. U. Guggenheim fellow, 1978-79. Mem. Acoustical Soc. Am., Linguistic Soc. Am., Soc. Research in Child Devel., Psychonomic Soc. Research in cognitive psychology. Home: 1114 Nancy St Bloomington IN 47401 Office: Psychology Dept Ind U Bloomington IN 47405*

PISTNER, STEPHEN LAWRENCE, retail store chain exec.; b. St. Paul, Mar. 14, 1932; s. Leopold and Prudence Charolette (Selcer) P.; B.S.B.A., U. Minn., 1953; m. Jane Evelyn Golden, Sept. 30, 1971; children—Paul David, John Alan, Betsy Ann. Pres., chief exec. officer Target Stores, Inc., Mpls., 1973-76, chmn., chief exec. officer, 1976; exec. v.p. Dayton Hudson Corp., Mpls., 1976-77, pres., chief operating officer, 1977—, also dir.; dir. Northwestern Nat. Bank. Bd. govs. Mt. Sinai Hosp., Mpls.; dir., mem. exec. com. Minn. Orchestral Assn.; trustee Mpls. Soc. Fine Arts, KTCA Public TV. Home: 5109 Ridge Rd Edina MN 55436 Office: 777 Nicollet Mall Minneapolis MN 55402

PISTOR, CHARLES HERMAN, JR., banker; b. St. Louis, Aug. 26, 1930; s. Charles Herman and Virginia (Brown) P.; B.B.A., U. Tex., 1952; M.B.A., Harvard U., 1956, So. Meth. U., 1961; grad. Stonier Sch. Banking, Rutgers U., 1964; m. Regina Prikryl, Sept. 20, 1952; children—Lori Ellen, Charles Herman III, Jeffrey Glenn. Pres., dir. Republic Nat. Bank, Dallas, to 1980, chmn., chief exec. officer, 1980—; dir. Republic Financial Services, Inc., Dallas. Trustee Dallas Found.; chmn. SMU Bus. Sch. Found. Served to lt. USNR, 1952-54. Mem. Assn. Res. City Bankers. Presbyn. (elder). Club: Dallas Country. Home: 4200 Belclaire St Dallas TX 75205 Office: PO Box 225961 Dallas TX 75265

PISTORIUS, GEORGE, educator; b. Prague, Czechoslovakia, Mar. 19, 1922; s. Theodor and Blazena (Jiranek) P.; student Charles U., Prague, 1945-48; postgrad. Universite de Paris, France, 1948-50; certificats d'etudes superieures Universite de Strasbourg, France, 1950, 1951, Ph.D., U. Pa., 1963; m. Marie Skokan, June 30, 1945; 1 dau., Erika. Came to U.S., 1958, naturalized, 1964. Asst. dept. comparative lit. Charles U., 1946-48; instr. Lafayette Coll., Easton, Pa., 1958-61; asst. prof. French, 1961-63; asso. prof. Williams Coll., 1963-68, prof. Romanic langs., 1968—, chmn. dept. Romanic langs., 1971—; instr. French, Colby Coll. Summer Sch. Lang., 1959-65. Mem. Modern Lang. Assn. Am., Am. Comparative Lit. Assn., Am. Assn. Tchrs. of French, Assn. Internationale des Etudes Francaises. Author: Bibliography of the works of F.X. Salda, 1948; Destin de la culture francaise dans une democratie populaire, 1957; L'Image de l'Allemagne dans le roman francais entre les deux guerres (1919-1939), 1964. Home: Cluett Dr Williamstown MA 01267

PITBLADO, JOHN M., mfg. co. exec.; b. Mpls., Jan. 25, 1918; s. James M. and Jennie S. (Bark) P.; B.S. in Chem. Engring., U. Minn., 1940; m. Jeanne F. Oistad, Jan. 21, 1942; children—James M., Judy Pitblado Skoglund. Chem. engr. U.S. Steel South Works, Chgo., 1940-41; chem. engr. Mobil Oil Co., Milw., 1941-43; with 3M Co., 1946—, gen. sales and mktg. mgr. coated abrasives and related products div., 1966-68, gen. mgr. bldg. service and cleaning products div., 1968-70, div. v.p., 1970-75, group v.p., 1975-79, pres. U.S. ops., 1979—. Served with USNR, 1943-46. Mem. Chem. Mfrs. Assn. (bd. dirs.). Office: 3M Co 3M Center St Paul MN 55101

PITCHELL, ROBERT J., business exec.; b. N.Y.C.; A.B., Fordham U., 1939; Ph.D., U. Calif., 1955; m. Louise Clark Oct. 26, 1974; 1 dau. Mem. faculty Purdue U.; lectr. polit. sci. Butler U.; prof. Ind. U., to 1963; pres. Roosevelt U., 1963-65; formerly dep. adminstr. Fed. Extension Service, Dept. Agr.; later exec. dir. Nat. U. Extension Assn., Washington; now pres. Robert Pitchell Assos., Fairfax, Va., also Postsecondary Edn. Resources, Inc., Fairfax; cons., past dir. Ind. Tax Study Commn. Assisted senatorial campaign Birch Bayh, 1962. Author books on taxation and continuing edn. Home and Office: 3134 Prosperity Ave Fairfax VA 22031

PITCHER, ARTHUR EVERETT, mathematician, educator; b. Hanover, N.H., July 18, 1912; s. Arthur Dunn and Wilimina (Everett) P.; A.B., Western Res. U., 1932, D.Sc. honoris causa, 1957; M.A., Harvard, 1933, Ph.D., 1935; m. Sarah Hindman, July 2, 1936 (dec. Oct. 1972); children—Joan (Mrs. Robert Morrison), Susan Sarah (Mrs. John L. Cooper); m. 2d, Theresa Sell, June 8, 1973. Asst., Inst. Advanced Study, 1935-36, mem. 1945-46, 47-50; Benjamin Peirce instr. Harvard, 1936-38; mem. faculty Lehigh U., 1938—, distinguished prof., 1963-78, chmn. dept. math. and astronomy, 1960-78, cons. to pres., 1978—, acting dir. Center for Application of Math., 1965-66. Guggenheim fellow, 1952-53. Served to capt. AUS, 1942-45. Fellow AAAS; mem. Am. Math. Soc. (sec. 1967—), Soc. Indsl. and Applied Math. (trustee 1960-63), Math. Assn. Am., Phi Beta Kappa, Sigma Xi, Pi Kappa Alpha. Home: 1237 Dalehurst Dr Bethlehem PA 18018

PITCHER, EVELYN GOODENOUGH, educator; b. Lansing, Ohio, June 15, 1915; d. Bert and Edna (Jackson) Wiltshire; B.A., Wilson Coll., 1937; M.A., Yale, 1939, Ph.D., 1956; LL.D., New Eng. Coll., 1962; m. Erwin R. Goodenough, Jan. 29, 1942 (div. Aug. 1962); children—Ursula W., Daniel A.; m. 2d, Robert B. Pitcher, Aug. 1962. Co-dir. nursery sch., also pre-sch. psychol. examiner and dir. pre-sch. services Gesell Inst. Child Devel., New Haven, 1951-59; asso. prof. New Haven State Tchrs. Coll., 1956-59; lectr. Quinnipiac Coll., 1957-59; chmn. Eliot-Pearson dept. child study Tufts U., prof., 1965—. Cons. Mass. Council Children and Youth, White House Conf. Children and Youth, 1960. Trustee James Jackson Putnam Children's Center. Mem. Am. Assn. U. Profs., Am. Assn. U. Women, Am., Mass. psychol. assns., Soc. Research Child Devel., Boston Assn. Nursery Edn. Author: (with Ernst Prelinger) Children Tell Stories: An Analysis of Fantasy, 1963; (with Louise B. Ames) The Guidance Nursery School, 1964, 2d edit., 1974; (with Lasher, and others) Helping Young Children Learn, 1966, 3d edit., 1979. Author articles. Home: 91 Somerset St Belmont MA 02178 Office: Eliot-Pearson Dept Child Study Tufts U Medford MA 02155. *Unusually intimate personal relations with my parents and children, and mentor relationships with my two husbands provoked and nurtured a curiosity and caring for people. The study of young children and their families proved to be the exciting route for me to pursue an understanding of myself and others, and the education of students in the multi-disciplinary field of child study is a natural corollary to my professional interests.*

PITCHER, GEORGE WILLARD, educator, philosopher; b. Newark, May 19, 1925; s. Edward Arthur and Helen (Porter) P.; B.S., U.S. Naval Acad., 1946; M.A. in Philosophy, Harvard, 1954, Ph.D. in Philosophy, 1957; spl. student Magdalen Coll., Oxford (Eng.) U., 1955-56. Instr. philosophy Princeton, 1956-60, asst. prof., 1960-63, asso. prof., 1963-70, prof., 1970—. Served to lt. USNR, 1946-49, 51-53. Guggenheim fellow, 1965-66. Mem. Am. Philos. Assn. Author: The Philosophy of Wittgenstein, 1964; A Theory of Perception, 1971; Berkeley, 1977; also several articles. Editor: Truth, 1964; Wittgenstein, 1966; (with O.P. Wood) Ryle, 1970. Home: 18 College Rd W Princeton NJ 08540

PITCHER, TOM STEPHEN, educator; b. Wenatchee, Wash., Apr. 17, 1926; s. Edwin K. and Grace (Peterson) P.; B.A., U. Wash., 1949; Ph.D., Mass. Inst. Tech., 1953; m. Bettz J. Bolender, June 17, 1950; children—Ellen, Katharine, Stephen. Mathematician, Lincoln Lab., Lexington, Mass., 1953-65; prof. math. U. So. Calif., 1965-70, U. Hawaii, 1970—. Served with USAAF, 1944-45. Mem. Am. Math. Soc. Home: 2140 Lanihuli Dr Honolulu HI 96822 Office: U Hawaii Honolulu HI 96822

PITCHFORD, DEAN S(TANLEY), actor; b. Honolulu, July 29, 1954; s. William Myron and Marie Rita (Paluch) P.; B.A. in English and Drama, Yale, 1972. Mgr. Ticket Service for Groups, N.Y.C., 1971-76; cons. Conn. Dept. Edn., 1970-71; artist-in-residence Cath. U. Am., 1972; appearances on Broadway include Godspell, 1971-73, Pippin, 1973-77, Umbrellas of Cherbourg, 1978-79. Author: Budget Guide to Hawaii, 1969. . *Don't look back; your history will take care of itself. Successes will speak louder than you ever could; as for failures, learn from them but don't live with them. No, don't ever look back.*

PITELKA, FRANK ALOIS, zoologist, educator; b. Chgo., Mar. 27, 1916; s. Frank Joseph and Frances (Laga) P.; B.S. with highest honors, U. Ill., 1939; summer student U. Mich., 1938, U. Wash., 1940; Ph.D., U. Calif. at Berkeley, 1946; m. Dorothy Getchell Riggs, Feb. 5, 1943; children—Louis Frank, Wenzel Karl, Vlasta Kazi Helen. Mem. faculty U. Calif. at Berkeley, 1944—, prof. zoology, 1958—, chmn. dept., 1963-66, 69-71, Miller research prof., 1965-66, curator birds Mus. Vertebrate Zoology, 1949-63, exec. com. Miller Inst. Basic Research in Sci., 1967-71, chmn., 1967-70. Panel environ. biology NSF, 1959-62, panel polar programs, 1978—; mem. panel biol. and med. scis., com. polar research Nat. Acad. Scis., 1960-65; research asso. Naval Arctic Research Lab., Barrow, Alaska, 1951-78; adv. coms. U.S. Internat. Biol. Program, 1965-68, dir. Tundra Biome Program, 1968-69; mem. U.S. Tundra Biome Program, 1970-73; mem. U.S. Commn. for UNESCO, 1970-72. Guggenheim fellow, 1949-50; NSF sr. postdoctoral fellow Oxford (Eng.) U., 1957-58; Research fellow Center for Advanced Study in Behavioral Scis., Stanford, 1971. Fellow Arctic Inst. N.Am., Am. Ornithologists Union, Calif. Acad. Scis., A.A.A.S.; mem. Ecol. Soc. Am. (Mercer award 1953), Cooper Ornithol. Soc. (hon. mem.; pres. 1948-50), Brit. Ecol. Soc., Am. Soc. Mammalogists, Am. Soc. Naturalists, Am. Inst. Biol. Scis., Western Soc. Naturalists (pres. 1963-64), Japanese Soc. Population Ecology, Alaska Conservation Soc., Mendocino (Calif.) Art Assn., Phi Beta Kappa, Sigma Xi. Contbr. research papers in field. Editorial bd. Ecology, 1949-51, 60-62, editor, 1962-64; editorial bd. U. Cal. Press., 1953-62, chmn., 1959-62; editorial bd. Ecol. Monographs, 1957-60, Systematic Zoology, 1961-64; asst. editor Condor, 1943-45, asso. editor, 1945-62. Home: PO Box 9278 Berkeley CA 94709

PITERNICK, ANNE BREARLEY, librarian, educator; b. Blackburn, Eng.; d. Walter and Ellen (Harris) Clayton; came to Can., 1956, naturalized, 1965; B.A., U. Manchester (Eng.), 1948; A.L.A., 1955; m. George Piternick, May 6, 1971. Mem. library staff U. B.C., Vancouver, Can., 1956—, head sci. div., 1960-61, head social scis. div., 1965-66, prof. Sch. Librarianship, 1966—; mem. Nat. Com. Bibliog. Services Can., 1975—; Can. Council Adv. Group Research Instruments, 1976; mem. adv. bd. Nat. Library Can.; organizer Nat. Conf. on State of Canadian Biblio., 1974. Mem. Canadian Library Assn. (pres. 1976-77), Canadian Assn. Spl. Libraries Info. Services (pres. 1969-70), Spl. Libraries Assn., Library Assn. (Gt. Britain), Am. Soc. Info. Scis., others. Author manuals and articles on availability of library materials. Home: 1849 W 63rd Ave Vancouver BC V6P 2H9 Canada Office: Sch Librarianship U BC Vancouver BC V6T 1W5 Canada

PITKIN, DONALD STEVENSON, educator; b. Boston, Jan. 6, 1922; s. Donald Stevenson and Dorothy (Bacon) P.; B.A., Harvard U., 1947, M.A., 1950, Ph.D., 1954; m. Emily Knapp, Dec. 28, 1948 (dec. 1964); children—Donald Stevenson II, Roxanna Elizabeth Farwell; m. 2d, Mary Lincoln Coolidge, Aug. 20, 1975. Research asso. Mass. Inst. Tech., 1953; prof., chmn. dept. sociology and anthropology Northeastern U., 1954-64, Amherst Coll., 1965—. Served with U.S. Army, 1942-46. Fellow Am. Anthrop. Assn., Am. Sociol. Soc. Home: 61 Lincoln Ave Amherst MA 01002

PITKIN, EDWARD THADDEUS, educator; b. Putnam, Conn., Dec. 14, 1930; s. Thaddeus Eugene and Florence Mabel (Brown) P.; B.S., U. Conn., 1952; M.S. (Guggenheim fellow), Princeton, 1953; Ph.D. (NASA fellow), U. Cal. at Los Angeles, 1964; m. Clara Lucy Modliszewski, June 13, 1953; children—Gayle Linda, Dale Edward. Project engr. Astro Div. Marquardt Co., Los Angeles, 1956-59, mgr. space propulsion, 1959-61; engring. cons., Los Angeles, 1961-64; asso. prof. aerospace engring. U. Conn., Storrs, 1964-70, prof. mech. and aerospace engring., 1970—, asst. dean, 1977—. Served as lt. USAF, 1953-55. Asso. fellow Am. Inst. Aeros. and Astronautics; mem. Am. Astronautical Soc., Solar Energy Soc. Contbr. articles to tech. pubs. Home: 115 Brookside Ln Mansfield Center CT 06250 Office: U 139 U Conn Storrs CT 06268

PITKIN, MILO JAMES, assn. exec.; b. Forest City, Iowa, Jan. 16, 1936; s. Milo James and Lucille Marie (Bonar) P.; B.S. in Econs., Drake U., Des Moines; m. Carol Jane Kline, Dec. 25, 1956; children—Stephen, Susan, Shelly. With Bankers Life Co., 1963-67, Metal Fabricating Inst., 1967-70; founder, exec. dir., editor publ. Fabricating Mfrs. Assn., Inc., Rockford, Ill., 1970—. Bd. dirs. Protestant Community Services. Mem. Am. Soc. Assn. Execs. Clubs: Toastmasters Internat., Rotary Internat. Home: 5809 Hillsbrough St Rockford IL 61109 Office: 7811 N Alpine Rd Rockford IL 61111

PITKIN, ROBERT BOLTER, writer, ret. magazine editor; b. Dover, N.J., Dec. 27, 1910; s. Walter B. and Mary B. (Gray) P.; B.S., Columbia Tchrs. Coll., 1941; m. Emily B. Greif, Jan 24, 1936; children—Patricia Gray (Mrs. G. Penfield Jennings), Robert Bolter. Asst. author's agt. N.Y.C., 1933-34; asst. track coach, Columbia, 1935-42, also editor Columbia Alumni News, 1936-38; asso. editor Am. Legion mag., 1946-53, mng. editor, 1953-63, editor, 1963-76, ret., 1976; freelance writer, 1976—. Mem. editorial com. Boy Scouts Am., 1968—; bd. dirs. Found. Sci. Relaxation, Chgo.; sponsor Am.

Assn. Advancement Tension Control, Louisville. Served to lt. comdr. USNR, 1942-46. Mem. Am. Legion, Theta Xi. Clubs: Dutch Treat (N.Y.C.); ANAVICUS (Can.); Post Mortem (Washington); Tarpon Springs (Fla.) Yacht. Contbr. numerous articles to mags. Home: 308 Hillpoint Dr PO Box 477 Ozona FL 33560

PITLIK, NOAM, television producer, dir.; b. Phila., Nov. 4, 1932; s. Samuel and Eva P.; student Swarthmore Coll., 1950-51; B.A. in Theatre, Temple U., 1954; M.A. in Theatre, N.Y. U., 1958; m. Linda Smith, June 23, 1973; stepchildren—Ian, Carrie. Actor numerous films including: The Graduate, Fortune Cookie, Hallelujah Trail, Front Page; actor numerous TV shows, commercials; dir. TV series including: Dick Van Dyke Show, 1973, The Practice, 1974, Barney Miller, 1975—; now producer, dir. Barney Miller. Served with U.S. Army, 1955-57. Recipient Emmy for Best Direction of Comedy Series, 1979. Mem. Dirs. Guild Am., Screen Actors Guild, AFTRA.

PITMAN, BENJAMIN FRANKLIN, JR., investment banker; b. Chadron, Nebr., May 27, 1898; s. Benjamin F. and Emma (Morgan) P.; student U. Nebr., 1914-17, Sorbonne, Paris, 1918-19, U. Wash., 1919-20; m. Virginia W. Pitman; children—Benjamin Franklin III, Peggy. Sec., Chadron Bldg. & Loan Assn., 1920-22, Pitman & Co., real estate, Sarasota, Fla., 1921-24; mgr. El Paso (Tex.) br. Henry L. Doherty & Co., investment bankers, 1924-29; pres. Pitman & Co., San Antonio, 1929—; dir. Dean & Co. Republican. Episcopalian. Clubs: Argyle; San Antonio Country, St. Anthony. Contbr. articles to profl. publs. Home: 5425 New Braunfels Ave Apt 1A San Antonio TX 78209 Office: 900 NE Loop 410 C-104 San Antonio TX 78209

PITMAN, WALTER GEORGE, ednl. adminstr.; b. Toronto, Ont., Can., May 18, 1929; s. Ernest George and Elsie (Kendrick) P.; B.A., U. Toronto, 1952, M.A., 1955; postgrad. (Inst. fellow) Ont. Inst. for Studies in Edn., Toronto, 1976; m. Florence Ida Collingi; children—Wade George, Cynthia Lynn, Mark Donald, Anne Lorraine. Tchr. secondary schs. North York (Ont.) Bd. Edn., 1952-56; head history dept. Kenner Collegiate, Peterborough, 1956-60; master tchr. York Central Bd. Edn., 1965; asso. registrar Trent U., Peterborough, 1964-67, dean arts and sci., 1972-75, dir. part-time studies, 1965-67; pres. Ryerson Poly. Inst., Toronto, 1975—; mem. Can. Parliament, Ottawa, 1960-62, Ont. Provincial Parliament, 1967-71. Dep. leader Nat. Democratic Party Ont.; elder Lawrence Park Community Ch.; bd. dirs. Can. Civil Liberties Assn., Nat. Survival Inst.; chmn. Metro Toronto Commn. on Racism. Decorated Centennial medal. Mem. Can. Assn. Adult Edn. (pres.), Ont. Ednl. Assn. (pres. 1967-68). Home: 2 Fidelia Ave Toronto ON M4N 3E8 Canada Office: 50 Gould St Toronto ON M5B 1E8 Canada

PITNEY, JAMES CARRINGTON, lawyer; b. N.Y.C., Aug. 21, 1926; s. Shelton and Etta C. (Brown) P.; A.B., Princeton, 1947; LL.B., Columbia, 1950; m. Madeline L. Stevens, June 28, 1947; children—James Carrington, John Hoffman Stevens, Theodora Shelton (dec.), Henry Cooper. Admitted to N.J. bar, 1951; law sec. to Hon. William J. Brennan, Jr., 1951-52; asst. U.S. atty., 1954-55; asso., then partner firm Pitney, Hardin & Kipp, Newark, 1955—; dir. Nat. Investors Corp., Broad St. Investing Corp., Union Income Fund, Inc., Union Capital Fund, Inc., Union Cash Mgmt. Fund, Inc., Automatic Switch Co. Former mem. sch. bd. planning bd., twp. com., Harding Twp., N.J. Pres., Morristown (N.J.) Meml. Hosp., 1968-69, also bd. mgrs.; trustee Marcus L. Ward Home. Served with USNR, 1944-46. Mem. Am., N.J., Essex County, Morris County bar assns. Clubs: Essex (Newark); N.Y. Yacht; Morristown (past pres.); Somerset Hills Country (bd. govs.) (Bernardsville, N.J.). Asso. editor N.J. Law Jour. Home: Glen Alpine Rd Morristown NJ 07960 Office: 33 Washington St Newark NJ 07102 also 163 Madison Av Morristown NJ 07960

PITOT, HENRY CLEMENT, physician, educator; b. N.Y.C., May 12, 1930; s. Henry Clement and Bertha (Lowe) P.; B.S. in Chemistry, Va. Mil. Inst., 1951; M.D., Tulane U., 1955, Ph.D. in Biochemistry, 1959; m. Julie S. Schutten, July 29, 1954; children—Bertha, Anita, Jeanne, Cathy, Henry, Michelle, Lisa, Patrice. Instr. pathology Tulane U. Med. Sch., 1955-59; postdoctoral fellow McArdle Lab., U. Wis.-Madison, 1959-60; mem. faculty U. Wis. Med. Sch.-Madison, 1960—, prof. pathology and oncology, 1966—, chmn. dept. pathology, 1968-71, acting dean Sch. Medicine, 1971-73, dir. McArdle Lab., 1973—; mem. Nat. Cancer Adv. Bd., 1976-82, chmn., 1979-80. Recipient Borden undergrad. research award, 1955; Lederle Faculty award, 1962; Career Devel. award, 1965; Parke-Davis award in exptl. pathology, 1968. Mem. AAAS, Am. Soc. Cell. Biology, Am. Assn. Cancer Research, Am. Soc. Biol. Chemists, Am. Chem. Soc., Am. Assn. Pathologists (pres. 1976-77), N.Y. Acad. Scis., Soc. Exptl Biology and Medicine, Soc. Developmental Biology. Roman Catholic. Home: 1812 Van Hise Ave Madison WI 53705

PITT, CARL ALLEN, educator; b. Three Forks, Mont., Sept. 6, 1911; s. John Marshall and Clara Rebecca (Biggs) P.; B.A., Intermountain Union Coll., 1933; M.A., Wash. State Coll., 1946; summer postgrad. U. Iowa, 1947, U. Mich., 1949; Ph.D., Purdue U., 1952; m. Olive Marguerite MacGillivray, June 29, 1935 (dec. Feb. 1963). Salesman, Nat. Biscuit Co., Butte, Mont., 1933-40; dir. forensics Highline High Sch., Seattle, 1942-46; dir. resources discussion U. Wash., 1946-48; faculty speech U. Ill., Chgo., 1950-73, prof., 1967-73, ret. Lectr. on communication problems to coll. and civic groups. Air Age fellow, 1946. Mem. Speech Communication Assn. Am., Central States Speech Assn., Western Speech Communication Assn., Am. Forensic Assn., Internat. Communication Assn., Am. Assn. for Higher Edn., Am. Inst. Parliamentarians, Am. Platform Assn., Phi Delta Kappa, Pi Kappa Delta. Mason (Shriner). Editor: Chgo. Circle Studies, 1964-68. Mem. editorial staff Parliamentary Jour., Central States Speech Jour.; contbr. articles to profl. jours. Home: 6326 37th SW Seattle WA 98126

PITT, COURTNAY, economist; b. Cuba, N.Y., May 29, 1908; s. David Alexander and Maud E. (Hanna) P.; grad. Peddie Sch.; A.B., Princeton U., 1929, A.M., 1934, Ph.D., 1935; m. Elizabeth Findley Buchanan, Aug. 14, 1935; children—Courtnay, William. Faculty, Princeton U., 1935-36; partner Ivy Lee & T.J. Ross, pub. relations counsel, N.Y.C., 1936-41; joined Philco Corp., Phila., 1941, chief economist, 1947, v.p. finance, 1948-56, dir., 1949-56; dir. research Baker, Weeks & Co., Phila., mems. N.Y. Stock Exchange, 1956-60, partner, 1960-70; v.p., 1970-71; ltd. partner W.H. Newbold's Son & Co., 1971-74, voting stockholder, 1975-78; with A.G. Edwards & Sons, Abington, Pa., 1978—; dir. Canadian Hydrocarbons, Ltd., Calgary, Can., 1956-74. Chmn., Pitt-Buchanan Charitable Trust, Jenkintown, Pa. Recipient Peddie Alumni citation, 1955. Mem. Financial Analysts of Phila., Am. Econ. Assn., Newcomen Soc. Presbyn. (trustee). Clubs: Princeton, Union League (Phila.); Huntingdon Valley Country; Nassau (Princeton, N.J.). Author: Currency History of Guatemala, 1935. Home: 429 Clement Rd Jenkintown PA 19046 Office: 1301 Highland Ave Abington PA 19001

PITT, HARVEY LLOYD, lawyer; b. Bklyn., Feb. 28, 1945; s. Morris Jacob and Sara (Sapir) P.; B.A., Bklyn. Coll., City U. N.Y., 1965; J.D. with honors (Univ. scholar), St. John's U., N.Y.C., 1968; m. Phyllis Yagerman, Aug. 13, 1966; children—Emily Laura, Jonathan Bradley. Admitted to N.Y. State bar, 1969, U.S. Supreme Ct. bar, 1972; with SEC, Washington, 1968-78, legal asst. to commr., 1969, editor Instl. Investor Study, 1970-71, spl. counsel Office Gen. Counsel, 1971-72, chief counsel div. market regulation, 1972-73, exec. asst. to chmn., 1973-75, gen. counsel, 1975-78; partner firm Fried, Frank, Harris, Shriver & Kampelman, Washington, 1978—; adj. prof. law George Washington U., Georgetown U. Vice pres. Glen Haven Civic Assn., Silver Spring, Md., 1972-73, pres., 1974. Mem. Am., Fed. (Outstanding Young Lawyer award 1975) bar assns., Edwick Jones Assn. (sec. bd. dirs.), Delta Sigma Rho, Tau Kappa Alpha, Phi Delta Phi. Home: 11204 Bedfordshire Ave Potomac MD 20854 Office: 600 New Hampshire Ave Washington DC 20039

PITT, PAUL ARTHUR, engring. exec.; b. Lovelock, Neb., May 27, 1917; s. George Earl and Irene (Rasmussen) P.; B.S.M.E., U. Calif., Berkeley, 1940; m. June Marie Craft, July 16, 1943; children—Paulette June, James William, Lauren Irene. Weight engr. Lockheed Aircraft Co., Burbank, Calif., 1941-42; project engr. Solar Aircraft Co., San Diego, 1942-47; chief engr., 1947-60; v.p. engring. and research solar div. Internat. Harvester, San Diego, 1960-77, sr. v.p. Solar Group, 1977—; dir. Solar Aircraft Co. Fellow ASME; mem. Soc. Automotive Engrs., Am. Soc. Archeology. Republican. Home: 5730 Lancaster Dr San Diego CA 92120 Office: 2200 Pacific Hwy San Diego CA 92138

PITT, ROBERT HEALY, II, internat. mktg. exec.; b. Richmond, Va., Dec. 30, 1924; s. Alfred Taylor and Adele (Ott) P.; B.S., U. Pa., 1949. Dean of admissions U. Pa., 1954-61; partner Atlantic Devel. Co., 1961-68; pres., chmn. bd. dirs. Club Internationale Mgmt. Corp., 1968-70; pres. Diners Club Internat., Ltd., N.Y.C., 1970-75; chmn. bd., pres. Domino Internat. Inc., 1976—; pres. TAG Systems USA Inc., 1978—. Served with USAAF, 1943-45. Decorated Air medal, Purple Heart with oak leaf cluster. Mem. Phi Gamma Delta, Beta Gamma Sigma. Democrat. Episcopalian. Clubs: Country of Va., Commonwealth (Richmond). Home: 624 S St Asaph St Alexandria VA 22314 Office: 424 N Washington St Alexandria VA 22314

PITTENDRIGH, COLIN STEPHENSON, biologist; b. Whitley Bay, Eng., Oct. 13, 1918; s. Alexander and Florence Hemy (Stephenson) P.; B.Sc. with 1st class honors (Lord Kitchener nat. meml. scholar), U. Durham (Eng.), 1940; A.I.C.T.A., Imperial Coll., Trinidad, B.W.I., 1942; Ph.D. (Univ. fellow), Columbia, 1947; m. Margaret Dorothy Eitelbach, May 1, 1943; children—Robin Ann, Colin Stephenson. Came to U.S., 1945, naturalized, 1950. Biologist internat. health div. Rockefeller Found., 1942-45; adviser Bromellad-malaria, Brazilian govt., 1945; asst. prof. biology Princeton, 1947-50, asso. prof., 1950-57, prof., 1957-69, Class of 1877 prof. zoology, 1963-69, dean Grad. Sch., 1965-69; profl. biology Stanford, 1969—, Bing prof. human biology, 1970-76; Miller prof. biology, dir. Hopkins Marine Sta., Stanford U., 1976—; vis. prof. Rockefeller Inst., 1962; Phillipps lectr. Haverford Coll., 1956; Timothy Hopkins lectr. Stanford, 1957; Phi Beta Kappa nat. lectr., 1976-77; Sigma Xi nat. lectr., 1977-78, 78-79. Adviser Brit. colonial office on Bromeliad-malaria, 1958; mem. Nat. Acad. Scis.-NRC Com. oceanography. Past v.p., trustee Rocky Mountain Biol. Lab. Guggenheim fellow, 1959. Fellow Am. Acad. Arts and Scis.; mem. Am. Inst. Biol. Scis., Am. Soc. Zoologists, Am. Soc. Naturalists (pres. 1968), Nat. Acad. Sci., AAAS (v.p. for zoology 1968), Soc. Study Evolution, Sigma Xi. Author: (with George Gaylord Simpson, L. H. Tiffany) Life, 1957. Contbr. to books, profl. jours. Home: 26240 Jeanette Rd Salinas CA 93908

PITTINGER, CHARLES BERNARD, physician, educator; b. Akron, Ohio, Apr. 27, 1913; s. Charles B. and Mary (Leininger) P.; B.S. in Chemistry, U. Akron, 1935; M.D., U. Cin., 1949; M.S. in Anesthesiology, U. Iowa, 1952; m. Gertrude Anne Cramer, June 20, 1949; children—Suzanne, Charles, Catherine. Tchr. sci. and math. Akron high schs., 1935-37; chemist USAAF, Wright Field, Dayton, Ohio, 1937-45; instr. chemistry U. Akron, summers 1947-48; intern U. Iowa Hosps., 1949-50, resident anesthesiology, 1950-52, mem. faculty, 1952-62, prof. anesthesiology, 1960-62, acting chmn. div., 1961-62; prof. anesthesiology Vanderbilt U. Sch. Medicine, 1962-78, chmn. dept., 1962-68, asso. prof. pharmacology, 1963-75, prof. pharmacology, 1975-78, prof. anesthesiology emeritus, 1978—; anesthesiologist-in-chief Vanderbilt U. Hosp., 1962-68, cons., 1979—; cons., research collaborator Brookhaven Nat. Lab., 1954-56; cons. VA Hosp., Nashville, 1962-70, Bur. Medicine, HEW, 1966-70, St. Thomas Hosp., Nashville, 1965—; mem. scope panel on anesthesiology Rev. Com. U.S. Pharmacopeia, 1966-70. Diplomate Am. Bd. Anesthesiology. Fellow Am. Coll. Anesthesiologists; mem. AAAS, AAUP, Am. Chem. Soc., Am., So., Tenn. med. assns., Am. Soc. Pharmacology and Exptl. Therapeutics, Am. Soc. Anesthesiologists, Assn. U. Anesthetists, Central Soc. Clin. Research, Central Surg. Assn., Davidson County Med. Soc., Internat. Anesthesia Research Soc., Nashville Acad. Medicine, N.Y. Acad. Scis., Soc. Exptl. Biology and Medicine, So., Tenn. socs. anesthesiologists, Sigma Xi, Kappa Delta Pi, Alpha Kappa Kappa. Roman Catholic. Author: Hyperbaric Oxygenation, 1966; numerous sci. articles on pharmacology of anesthesia. Home: 201 Vaughns Gap Rd Nashville TN 37205

PITTLE, R. DAVID, govt. ofcl.; b. Washington, Oct. 7, 1938; B.S. with high honors, U. Md.; M.S., Ph.D. in Elect. Engring., U. Wis. Tchr. elect. engring. U. Wis., 1963-69, Wis. Sch. Electronics, 2 yrs.; tchr. elect. engring., pub. affairs Carnegie-Mellon U., 1969-73; mem. Consumer Product Safety Commn., Washington, 1973—; mem. consumer adv. com. Pa. Ins. Dept. Recipient Eastern Consumer Conf. award, 1977; NSF grantee. Mem. Nat. Assn. Homebuilders (consumer relations panel), Consumer Fedn. Am., Am. Council Consumer Interests, ASTM (consumer standards com.), Am. Nat. Standards Inst. Office: Consumer Product Safety Commn 1111 18th St NW Washington DC 20207

PITTMAN, JAMES ALLEN, JR., physician; b. Orlando, Fla., Apr. 12, 1927; s. James Allen and Jean C. (Garretson) P.; B.S., Davidson Coll., 1948; M.D., Harvard, 1952; m. Constance Ming-Chung Shen, Feb. 19, 1955; children—James Clinton, John Merrill. Intern, asst. resident medicine Mass. Gen. Hosp., Boston, 1952-54; teaching fellow medicine Harvard, 1953-54; clin. asso. NIH, Bethesda, Md., 1954-56; instr. medicine George Washington U., 1955-56; chief resident U. Ala. Med. Center, Birmingham, 1956-58, instr. medicine, 1956-59, asst. prof., 1959-62, asso. prof., 1962-64, prof. medicine, 1964-71, dir. endocrinology and metabolism div., 1962-71, co-chmn. dept. medicine, 1969-71, also asso. prof., physiology and biophysics, 1966-71, prof. medicine, 1973—, dean Sch. Medicine, 1973—, exec. dean med. edn. program U. Ala. System, 1974—; asst. chief med. dir. research and edn. in medicine U.S. VA, 1971-73; prof. medicine Georgetown U. Med. Sch., Washington, 1971-73; mem. endocrinology study sect. NIH, 1963-67; mem. pharmacology, endocrinology fellowships rev. coms., 1967-68; chmn. Liaison Com. Grad. Med. Edn., 1976; mem. Grad. Med. Edn. Nat. Adv. Com., 1977-78. Fellow A.C.P. (life); mem. Assn. Am. Physicians, Endocrine Soc., Am. Thyroid Assn., N.Y. Acad. Scis. (life), Soc. Nuclear Medicine, Am. Diabetes Assn., Am. Chem. Soc., Wilson Ornithol. Club (life), Am. Ornithologists Union, Am. Fedn. Clin. Research (pres. So. sect., mem. nat. council 1962-66), So. Soc. Clin. Investigation, Phi Beta Kappa, Alpha Omega Alpha, Omicron Delta Kappa. Author: Diagnosis and Treatment of Thyroid Diseases, 1963. Contbr. articles in field to profl. jours. Office: School of Medicine Univ Alabama University Station Birmingham AL 35294

PITTMAN, RICHARD FRANK, JR., newspaper publisher; b. Tampa, Fla., Mar. 12, 1923; s. Richard Frank and Jette (Robinson) P.; B.S. in Bus. Adminstrn., U. Fla., 1944; m. Dada Andrews, Apr. 15, 1952; children—Richard Andrews, Dada Katherine. With IRS, 1946; with Tribune Co., Tampa, 1946—, bus. mgr., 1965-69, v.p., gen. mgr., 1970-77, pub. Tampa Tribune and Tampa Times, 1978—, also v.p., dir.; dir. Barnett Bank of Tampa. Elder, 1st Presbyn. Ch., 1976-79; past pres. Tampa chpt. ARC; campaign chmn., pres., dir., treas. United Way of Greater Tampa; past v.p., bd. dirs. United Cerebral Palsy; vice chmn. S.W. Fla. Blood Bank; bd. dirs. Community Coordinating Council, Fla. Gulf Coast Symphony Assn., Family Service Assn., Sta. WEDU. Served to 1st lt., Tank Corps, AUS, 1942-46; PTO. Recipient Vol. Activist award, 1977. Mem. Am. Newspaper Pubs. Assn., So. Newspaper Pubs. Assn., Fla. Press Assn., Inst. Newspaper Controllers and Finance Officers, Tampa C. of C. (dir., mem. exec. com.), Pi Kappa Alpha. Clubs: Rotary (past pres.), Tampa Yacht and Country (commodore), Univ. (past dir.), Merrymakers (past pres.), Tower (dir.) (Tampa); Ye Mystic Krewe of Gasparilla (past king and capt.). Home: 3120 Morrison Ave Tampa FL 33609 Office: Tribune Co 202 S Parker St PO Box 191 Tampa FL 33601

PITTMAN, STEUART LANSING, lawyer; b. Albany, N.Y., June 6, 1919; s. Ernest Wetmore and Estelle Young (Romeyn) P.; grad. St. Paul's Sch., Concord, N.H., 1937; A.B. cum laude, Yale, 1941, LL.B., 1948; children by previous marriage—Andrew Pinchot, Nancy Steuart, Rosamond Pinchot, Tamara Pickering; m. 2d, Barbara Milburn White, Mar. 29, 1958; children—Patricia Milburn, Steuart Lansing, Anne Romeyn. With Pan Am. Airways, Egypt, 1941-42, China Nat. Aviation Co., Calcutta, India, 1942; admitted to N.Y. bar, 1948, D.C. bar, 1954; with firm Cravath, Swaine & Moore, N.Y.C., 1948-50; with govt. agys. ECA, Mut. Security Agy. and FOA, 1950-54; partner firm Shaw, Pittman, Potts & Trowbridge and predecessors, Washington, 1954-61, 64—; asst. sec. of def., 1961-64. Cons., 2d Hoover Commn., 1954-55, Dept. State, 1955, Devel. Loan Fund, 1958-59. Mem. bd. Freedom House Books U.S.A.; co-chmn. Civil Def. Forum. Trustee Hudson Inst. Served to 1st lt. USMCR, World War II; CBI. Decorated Silver Star. Club: Metropolitan (Washington). Office: 1800 M St NW Washington DC 20036

PITTMAN, VIRGIL, fed. judge; b. Enterprise, Ala., Mar. 28, 1916; s. Walter Oscar and Annie Lee (Logan) P.; B.S., U. Ala., 1939, LL.B., 1940; m. Floy Lasseter, 1944; children—Karen Pittman Gordy, Walter Lee. Admitted to Ala. bar, 1940; spl. agt. FBI, 1940-44; practice law, Gadsden, Ala., 1946-51; judge Ala. Circuit Ct., Circuit 16, 1952-66; U.S. dist. judge Middle and So. Dist. Ala., 1966-71; chief judge U.S. Dist. Ct. for Ala. So. Dist., 1971—; lectr. bus. law, econs. and polit. sci. U. Ala. Center, Gadsden, 1948-66. Mem. Ala. Bd. Edn., 1951. Served to lt. (j.g.) USN, 1944-46. Mem. Ala. State Bar, Etowah County Bar Assn. (pres. 1949), Omicron Delta Kappa. Democrat. Baptist. Author: Circuit Court Proceedings in Acquisition of a Tract of Right of Way, 1959; A Judge Looks at Right of Way Condemnation Proceedings, 1960; Technical Pitfalls in Right of Way Proceedings, 1961. Office: 247 US Courthouse and Fed Bldg Mobile AL 36602

PITTS, CHARLES FRANKLIN, mfg. co. exec.; b. Belton, Mo., Jan. 26, 1925; s. P. H. and Mary (Taylor) P.; B.S. in Bus. Adminstrn., Central Mo. State Coll., 1949; m. Mary Anna Vest, June 8, 1947; children—Charles Franklin, Debra Lynn, Kevin Scott. Accountant, Mo. Gas & Electric Service Co., Lexington, 1949-51; supr. financial analysis and pricing, aircraft plant Ford Motor Co., Claycomo, Mo., 1951-56; with Lear Siegler, Inc., Santa Monica, Calif., 1956—, pres., gen. mgr. astronics div., 1967-68, v.p. comml. products group, 1968-70, v.p. comml. and indsl. group, 1971-73, v.p. climate control and housing group, 1973-75, sr. v.p., 1975—. Served with USN, 1942-46. Mem. Am. Mgmt. Assn., Air Force Assn., Am. Ordnance Assn., Assn. U.S. Army, Am. Legion, Kappa Sigma Kappa. Elk. Methodist. Club: Bel Air Country. Home: 1227 Villa Woods Dr Pacific Palisades CA 90272 Office: 3171 S Bundy Dr Santa Monica CA 90406

PITTS, CURTIS HARDAMAN, aircraft mfg. co. exec.; b. Stillmore, Ga., Dec. 9, 1915; s. Drew Lee and Amanda (Dickerson) P.; student pub. schs., Americus, Ga.; m. Willie Mae Lord, Oct. 29, 1938. Instr., mechanic Laurie Young Flying Service, Jacksonville, Fla., 1940-41; aircraft quality control insp. U.S. Navy, 1941-45; self-employed all phases civil aviation, 1945; pres. Pitts Aviation Enterprises, Homestead, Fla., 1964—. Recipient Gold medal Fed. Aeronautique Internat., 1976. Mem. Nat. Assn. Designated Engring. Reps., Aerobatic Club Am., Internat. Aerobatic Club, 0X5 Aviation Pioneers, Exptl. Aircraft Assn. Home: 1500 NW 10th St Homestead FL 33030 Office: 31901 SW 212th St Homestead FL 33030

PITTS, EUGENE, III, editor; b. Louisiana, Mo., Aug. 3, 1940; s. Eugene II and Leora Mae (Shetley) P.; grad. Northwestern U., 1962; m. Sharon Lee Green, May 5, 1973. Editor, Audio mag., Phila. Mem. Audio Engring. Soc. Office: Audio 401 N Broad St Philadelphia PA 19108

PITTS, GUY HARVEY, diversified industries exec.; b. Painted Post, N.Y., May 20, 1918; s. Guy Harvey and Della (Chase) P.; B.S., U. Mich., 1940; postgrad. A.P. Sloan Sch. Mgmt., Mass. Inst. Tech., 1965; m. Barbara Backus, June 20, 1942; children—Thomas, Nancy. Plant mgr. Bohn Aluminum & Brass Co., Detroit, 1950-53, div. mgr., 1954-57, v.p. mfg., 1958-65, exec. v.p., 1966-68, pres., 1969; v.p. Gulf & Western Industries, Inc., N.Y.C., 1969-72, sr. v.p., 1972—; pres. Gulf & Western Mfg. Co., Southfield, Mich., 1969—, chmn., 1978—. Trustee Citizens Research Council Mich.; mem. exec. bd. Detroit Area council Boy Scouts Am. Mem. Soc. Automotive Engrs., Greater Detroit C. of C. Clubs: Economic, Recess (Detroit); Bloomfield Hills Country. Home: 1730 Hammond Ct Bloomfield Hills MI 48013 Office: Clausen Bldg North 23100 Providence Dr Southfield MI 48075

PITTS, HENRY LARUE, lawyer; b. McLean, Ill., Dec. 12, 1910; s. Lewis Edgar and Caroline (LaRue) P.; B.S., U. Ill., 1934; J.D., U. Mich., 1939; student Ill. State U., 1929-31; m. Alberta G. Van Petten, Mar. 29, 1941; children—Albert Lewis, Sarah Jeanne Pitts Eldridge, Emily LaRue Pitts Dixon. Admitted to Ill. bar, 1939; mem. firm Rooks, Pitts, Fullagar & Poust, and predecessor firms, Chgo., 1939—. Dir. Mojonnier Bros. Co., Mohr Lino-Saw Co. Chmn., Ill. State Bd. Investment, 1970-73; mem. Chgo. Crime Commn., v.p., bd. dirs., 1976—; trustee Union League Found. for Boys Clubs; trustee Union League Civic and Arts Found.; bd. dirs. Forest Found. of DuPage County. Served to lt. USNR, 1943-46; MTO, PTO. Fellow Am. Coll. Probate Counsel, Am. Bar Found.; mem. Am. (ho. dels. 1967-74, chmn. spl. com. on nat. coordination disciplinary enforcement 1970-73, council gen. practice sect. 1971-76, 79—) Ill. (bd. govs. 1960-71, pres. 1969-70; Merit award 1979) Chgo. bar assns., Chgo. Assn. Commerce and Industry (dir., v.p. govtl. affairs 1974—), Am. Judicature Soc. (dir. 1972-74), Bar Assn. 7th Fed. Circuit, Nat. Conf. Bar Pres.'s (exec. council 1970-72), Am. Legion (past comdr.), Order of Coif, Kappa Delta Pi. Republican. Episcopalian (mem. diocesan council 1962-65). Clubs: Law, Legal, Union League (past pres., v.p., dir.), Metropolitan (Chgo.). Home: Leask Ln Wheaton IL 60187 Office: 208 S LaSalle St Chicago IL 60604

PITTS, LLOYD FRANK, oil co. exec.; b. Wesson, Miss., Oct. 7, 1910; s. John L. and Addie Mae (Sandifer) P.; student Copiah-Lincoln Jr. Coll., 1925-31, Northwestern U., 1932; m. Mary Martha McCann, Dec. 28, 1935; children—Lloyd F. (dec.), Linda Pitts Custard. With Nu-Enamel Corp., 1931-48, pres., dir., 1939-48; pres., dir. Nu-Enamel Internat., 1947-48; owner Pitts Oil Co., Dallas, 1948—; v.p., dir. Star Oil Co., Dallas, 1946-60; pres., dir. Longhorn Prodn. Co., Dallas, 1960—; chmn. bd., chief exec. officer Exploration Surveys Inc., Dallas, 1961—, pres., 1967-71, dir., 1957-71; chmn. bd. Dallas Prodn., Inc., 1968—; mem. Nat. Petroleum Council. Pres., Park Cities Rotary Club Found., Inc., 1967-68; mem. Baylor U. Devel. Council, Waco, 1966—, Golden Gate Sem. Devel. Council, Mill Valley, Calif., 1966—; bd. dirs. Dallas Civic Opera, 1970—, v.p., 1972—. Mem. Am. Assn. Petroleum Landmen, Am. Petroleum Inst. (chmn. industry adv. forum), Ind. Petroleum Assn. Am., Tex. Mid-Continent Oil and Gas Assn., Tex. Ind. Producers and Royalty Owners Assn. (exec. com., Pres.'s council). Baptist (deacon). Clubs: Park Cities Rotary (pres. 1966-67, dir.), Dallas Petroleum, Dallas, Brookhollow Golf, Preston Trails Golf. Home: 4938 DeLoache St Dallas TX 75200 Office: Meadows Bldg Dallas TX 75206

PITTS, NATHAN ALVIN, govt. ofcl.; b. Macon, Ga., June 29, 1913; s. Willis Norman and Roberta Irene (Jackson) P.; B.S., Xavier U., New Orleans, 1936; M.A. (Penfield fellow), Catholic U., Washington, 1944, Ph.D., 1950; postdoctoral Harvard U., 1953, Boston U., 1955; m. Mary Alma Williams, June 14, 1939; 1 dau., Mitra Anne. Mem. faculty N.C. Coll., Durham, 1944-45; chmn. social sci. dept. Shaw U., Raleigh, N.C., 1946-50, Coppin State Coll., Balt., 1950-61; program officer U.S. Dept. Edn., Washington, 1961-70; attache, U.S. del. to UNESCO, Paris, France, 1970-75; spl. asst. to the dir. Div. Tng. and Facilities Bur. Postsecondary Edn. USOE, 1975-76, chief Internat. Exchange br. Div. Internat. Edn., 1976—. Tchr. tng. adviser, Tabriz, Iran, 1957-59. Mem. Nat. Urban League, YMCA, Alpha Phi Alpha. Author: Cooperative Movement Among Negro Communities of North Carolina, 1950. Home: 3310 Dorchester Rd Baltimore MD 21215 Office: US Office Edn Washington DC 20202

PITTS, WILLIAM REID, ret. neurosurgeon; b. Glen Alpine, N.C., 1909; B.A., Duke, M.D., Harvard U., 1933. From intern to resident surgery L.I. Coll. Hosp., 1933-40; resident neurosurgery Kings County Hosp., Bklyn., 1935-36, Bklyn. Hosp., 1936-37; practice medicine specializing in neurosurgery, Charlotte, N.C., 1940-42, 45-79, ret., 1979; mem. surg. staff Mercy, Presbyn., hosps., chief neurosurgery Charlotte Meml. Hosp.; past instr. surgery L.I. Coll. Medicine. Trustee Duke, Charlotte County Day Sch., bd. visitors Duke Med. Center, Davidson Coll.; mem. parents' com. Princeton. Served to lt. col., M.C., U.S. Army, 1942-45. Mem. Congress Neurol. Surgeons, So. Neurol. Soc., AMA, Harvey Cushing Soc. Address: 429 Eastover Rd Charlotte NC 28207

PITZELE, MERLYN STUART, educator; b. Chgo., Nov. 18, 1911; s. William A. and Gertrude (Klein) P.; A.B., U. Chgo., 1933, then postgrad.; postgrad. U. Wis., 1938; m. Patricia Lowe, July 7, 1950; 1 son, Peter Ascher. Econ. analyst Ill. Emergency Relief Commn.; tchr. Chgo. Fedn. Labor Sch., A.F. of L.; field rep. Steel Workers Organizing Com. C.I.O.; faculty dept. econs. U. Wis., 1938-40; mgmt. cons., N.Y.C., 1940—; labor editor Business Week, 1940-55, sr. editor, 1955-57; mem. faculty Tchrs. Coll. Columbia U., 1969—. Mem. N.Y. Bd. Mediation, 1945-57, chmn., 1950-57; mediator, arbitrator; chief cons. N.Y. Legislative Joint Com. on States Economy; lectr. N.Y. U., Princeton, Harvard, others; labor adviser Thomas E. Dewey, 1944, 48, Dwight D. Eisenhower, 1952; exec. dir. Retirement Advisers, 1958—. Trustee, Daytop Village Inc.; v.p. Moreno Inst. Author articles, spl. studies on labor, econs. and aging. Editor: McGraw-Hill Labor-Mgmt. series, 1955-57. Cons. editor The Personnel Jour. Address: PO Box 311 Beacon NY 12508

PITZER, KENNETH S., chemist, educator; b. Pomona, Calif., Jan. 6, 1914; s. Russell K. and Flora (Sanborn) P.; B.S., Calif. Inst. Tech., 1935; Ph.D., U. Calif., 1937; D.Sc., Wesleyan U., 1962; LL.D., U. Calif. at Berkeley, 1963, Mills Coll., 1969; m. Jean Mosher, July 1935; children—Ann, Russell, John. Instr. chemistry U. Calif., 1937-39, asst. prof., 1939-42, asso. prof., 1942-45, prof., 1945-61, asst. dean letters and sci., 1947-48, dean coll. chemistry, 1951-60; pres., prof. chemistry Rice U., Houston, 1961-68, Stanford (Calif.), 1968-70; prof. chemistry U. Calif. at Berkeley, 1971—; tech. dir. Md. Research Lab. for OSRD, 1943-44; dir. research U.S. AEC, 1949-51, mem. gen. adv. com., 1958-65, chmn., 1960-62; Centenary lectr. Chem. Soc. Gt. Britain, 1978; mem. adv. bd. U.S. Naval Ordnance Test Sta., 1956-59, chmn., 1958-59; mem. commn. chem. thermo-dynamics Internat. Union Pure and Applied Chemistry, 1953-61; dir. Owens-Ill., Inc.; mem. Pres.'s Sci. Adv. Com., 1965-68. Trustee, Pitzer Coll. Guggenheim fellow, 1951, Precision Sci. Co. award in petroleum chemistry, 1950; 1 of 10 Outstanding Young Men, U.S. Jr. C. of C., 1950; Clayton prize Instn. Mech. Engrs., London, 1958; Priestley Memorial award Dickinson Coll., 1963; Priestley medal Am. Chem. Soc., 1969; Nat. medal for sci., 1975. Mem. program com. for phys. scis. Sloan Found., 1955-60. Fellow Am. Nuclear Soc., Am. Inst. Chemists (Gold medal award 1976), Am. Acad. Arts and Scis., Am. Phys. Soc.; mem. Am. Chem. Soc. (award pure chemistry 1943, Gilbert N. Lewis medal 1965, William Gibbs medal 1976), Faraday Soc., AAAS, Nat. Acad. Scis. (councilor 1964-67, 73-76), Am. Philos. Soc., Chem. Soc. (London), Am. Council Edn. Clubs: Chemists' (hon.); Bohemian; Cosmos (Washington). Author: Selected Values of Properties of Hydrocarbons (with others), 1947; Quantum Chemistry, 1953; (with L. Brewer) Thermodynamics, rev. 1961. Editor: Prentice-Hall Chemistry series, 1955-61. Contbr. articles to profl. jours. Home: 12 Eagle Hill Berkeley CA 94707 Office: Coll Chemistry U Calif Berkeley CA 94720

PITZNER, A. FREDERICK, banker; b. Chgo., May 8, 1936; s. Alwin Frederick and Alice (Girard) P.; B.A., Dartmouth, 1958; m. Nancy Christine Gulin, Sept. 1, 1962; children—Christina Erika, Alexander Caldwell. With Am. Nat. Bank & Trust Co., Chgo., 1958-75, v.p., 1966-68, adminstrv. v.p., 1968-75; corp. v.p. ops. Exchange Bancorp., Tampa, Fla., 1975—, also pres., chief exec. officer, dir. Exchange Operating Corp., Tampa. Mem. Tampa Com. 100. Mem. Sigma Alpha Epsilon. Clubs: University, Carrollwood Golf and Tennis (Tampa). Home: 3118 Belmore Rd Tampa FL 33618

PIVEN, FRANCES FOX, polit. scientist, educator; b. Calgary, Alta., Can., Oct. 10, 1932; d. Albert and Rachel (Paperny) F.; came to U.S., 1933, naturalized, 1953; B.A., U. Chgo., 1953, M.A., 1956, Ph.D., 1962; 1 dau., Sarah. Mem. faculty Columbia, 1966-72; prof. polit. sci. Boston U., 1972—. Bd. dirs. Movement for Econ. Justice, Com. for Pub. Justice. Recipient C. Wright Mills award Soc. Study Social Problems, 1971. Guggenheim fellow, 1973-74. Mem. Am. Polit. Sci. Assn., Union Radical Polit. Economists, ACLU (dir.). Co-author: Regulating the Poor: The Functions of Public Welfare, 1971; The Politics of Turmoil: Essays on Poverty, Race and the Urban Crisis, 1974; Poor People's Movements, 1977. Home: 3 Medford St Chelsea MA 02215 Office: 232 Bay State Rd Boston MA 02215

PIVIROTTO, RICHARD ROY, retail exec.; b. Youngstown, Ohio, May 26, 1930; s. Arthur M. and Ruth (Erhardt) P.; A.B., Princeton, 1952; M.B.A., Harvard, 1954; m. Mary Burchfield, June 27, 1953; children—Mary B., Richard Roy, Susan W., Nancy P., David H., Jennifer P. Pres., Joseph Horne Co., Pitts., 1954-70; vice chmn. Associated Dry Goods Corp., N.Y.C., 1970-72, pres., 1972-76, chmn. bd., 1976—; dir. Westinghouse Electric Corp., Pitts., Gen. Am. Investors Co., N.Y.C., NRMA, N.Y.C., N.Y. Life Ins. Co., Chem. N.Y. Corp., Chem. Bank; trustee Bowery Savs. Bank. Charter trustee Princeton U., 1977—. Served with AUS, 1955-56. Mem. Am. Retail Fedn. (dir. 1968—). Clubs: Union League, Princeton (N.Y.C.); Duquesne (Pitts.); Greenwich Country. Home: 111 Clapboard Ridge Rd Greenwich CT 06830 Office: 417 Fifth Ave New York NY 10016

PIXLEY, CHARLES CALVIN, army med. officer; b. Grants Pass, Oreg., Aug. 8, 1923; s. Charles and Ruby Clark (Best) P.; B.A., U. Oreg., 1945, M.D., 1947; M.S. in Surgery, Baylor U., 1953; m. Marian E. Vanderbrook, June 1, 1951; children—Mary Louise, Teresa Ann. Intern, Guthrie Clinic, Sayre, Pa., 1948-49; commd. 1st lt. M.C., U.S. Army, 1949, advanced through grades to lt. gen., 1976; resident in surgery Brooke Army Med. Center, 1949-54; service in Korea; comdr. William Beaumont Army Hosp., El Paso, Tex., 1975-77, U.S. Army Acad. Health Scis., Ft. Sam Houston, Tex., 1977-79; surgeon gen. U.S. Army, 1979—. Decorated Legion of Merit (3), Army Commendation medal (3). Diplomate Am. Bd. Surgery. Fellow A.C.S.; mem. Assn. Mil. Surgeons U.S., AMA, Am. Hosp. Assn., Tex., Bexar County med. socs. Home: Quarters 1 Walter Reed Army Med Center Washington DC 20012 Office: Office of Surg Gen Pentagon Washington DC

PIZER, DONALD, author, educator; b. N.Y.C., Apr. 5, 1929; s. Morris and Helen (Rosenfeld) P.; B.A., U. Calif. at Los Angeles, 1951, M.A., 1952, Ph.D., 1955; m. Carol Hart, Apr. 7, 1966; children—Karin, Ann, Margaret. Mem. faculty Tulane U., 1957—, prof. English, 1964-72, Pierce Butler prof. English, 1972—, Mellon prof. humanities, 1978-79. Served with AUS, 1955-57. Guggenheim fellow, 1962; Am. Council Learned Socs. fellow, 1971-72; Nat. Endowment Humanities fellow, 1978-79. Mem. Modern Lang. Assn. Author: Hamlin Garland's Early Work and Career, 1960; Realism and Naturalism in Nineteenth-Century American Literature, 1966; The Novels of Frank Norris, 1966; The Novels of Theodore Dreiser, 1976. Home: 6320 Story St New Orleans LA 70118

PLAA, GABRIEL LEON, pharmacologist, toxicologist; b. San Francisco, May 15, 1930; s. Jean and Lucienne Matilde (Chalopin) P.; B.S., U. Calif., 1952, M.S., 1956, Ph.D., 1958; m. Colleen Brasefield, May 19, 1951; children—Ernest, Steven, Kenneth, Gregory, Andrew, John, Denise, David. Asst. prof. pharmacology Tulane U. Sch. Medicine, 1958-62; asso. prof. U. Iowa Coll. Medicine, 1962-68; prof., chmn. dept. pharmacology Faculty Medicine U. Montreal (Que., Can.), 1968—; cons. toxicology. Served with U.S. Army, 1952-54; Korea. Recipient Claude Bernard medal U. Montreal, 1971, Thienes Meml. award Am. Acad. Clin. Toxicology, 1977. Mem. Soc. Toxicology (Achievement award 1967), Am. Soc. Pharmacology and Exptl. Therapeutics, Am. Acad. Forensic Scis., Pharmacol. Soc. Can. (past pres.), Soc. Toxicology Can. Roman Catholic. Contbr. numerous articles to sci. jours.; editor Toxicology and Applied Pharmacology, 1972—; editorial bd. numerous jours. Home: 236 Meredith St Dorval PQ H9S 2Y7 Canada Office: PO Box 6128 Montreal PQ H3C 3J7 Canada

PLACE, EDWIN BRAY, educator; b. La Harpe, Ill., Aug. 20, 1891; s. John and Anna (Bray) P.; A.B., U. Colo., 1913, A.M., 1916, Litt.D. (hon.), 1955; Ph.D., Harvard U., 1919; postgrad. research, Paris, Madrid, Rome, 1920, 25-26; m. Lula May Streamer, Aug. 5, 1914 (dec. Nov. 1956); children—Charles E., Dorothy-Lou (Mrs. J. D. Whicker), William O.; m. 2d, Marian Fredine, June 7, 1957. Instr., U. Colo., 1916-18, asst. prof. Romance langs., 1919-21, asso. prof., 1921-24, prof., 1924-35, head dept., 1931-35; instr. French, Harvard, 1918-19; prof. Romance langs. Northwestern U., 1935-56, emeritus, 1956—, chmn. dept., 1935-45. Vis. prof. Spanish, U. Pa., 1934; vis. lectr. Spanish, U. Calif. at Berkeley, 1956-58, vis. prof., 1966-68; vis. prof. Romance langs. U. Chgo., 1963-64. Mem. Am. Assn. Tchrs. Spanish (pres. 1937), Mediaeval Acad. Am. (councillor 1942-45), MLA (exec. council 1946-47), Am. Assn. Tchrs. French (v.p. 1939-40), Am. Assn. Tchrs. Italian (councillor 1939), Phi Beta Kappa, Sigma Chi, Phi Sigma Iota (nat. pres. 1940-46); mem. Hispanic Soc. Am. Named Officier d'Academie (France). Author: María de Zayas, 1923; (with C.C. Ayer) Un viaje por España, 1924; Manuel elemental de novelística española, 1926; (with N.B. Adams) Lecturas modernas, 1939; (with A. Torres-Rioseco) Contemporary Spanish Grammar, 1943; contbg. author: A Critical Bibliography of Old French Literature, 1947. Editor: Así se escribe la historia, 1926; La casa del placer honesto, 1927, 68; Madame Corentine, 1927; Don Gonzalo González de la Gonzalera, 1931; Gilles de Chyn, 1941; Processo de cartas, 1950; Amadís de Gaula, 1959, 62, 65, 68. 69. Translator: (with H.C. Behm) Translation of Amadís de Gaula, Books I and II, 1974, III and IV, 1975. Contbr. Am., fgn. jours., encys. Home: 110 41 St Oakland CA 94611

PLACE, MARY KAY, actress, singer; d. Bradley E. Place; grad. U. Tulsa, 1969. Scriptwriter for TV shows including The Mary Tyler Moore Show, Phyllis, MASH; regular TV series Mary Hartman, Mary Hartman, 1976-77, Fernwood Forever, 1977-78; films include: Bound for Glory, 1976, New York, New York, 1977, More American Graffiti, 1979. Recipient Emmy award for Mary Hartman, Mary Hartman, 1977. Albums: Tonite! At the Capri Lounge Starring Loretta Haggers; Aimin' to Please. Office: care Century Artists 9477 Wilshire Blvd Beverly Hills CA 90212*

PLACZEK, ADOLF KURT, librarian; b. Vienna, Austria, Mar. 9, 1913; s. Oswald and Pauline (Selinko) P.; student U. Vienna Med. Sch., 1931-34, Inst. Fine Arts, U. Vienna, 1934-38; B.L.S., Columbia, 1942; m. Jan Struther, Mar. 1, 1948 (dec. July 1953); m. 2d, Laura Beverley Robinson, Jan. 5, 1957. Came to U.S., 1940, naturalized, 1943. Asst. librarian Avery Archtl. Library, Columbia, 1948-60, Avery librarian, 1960—, adj. prof. architecture, 1971—. Served with AUS, 1943-46. Mem. Soc. Archtl. Historians (sec. 1963-67 dir. 1968-71, 2d v.p. 1974-75, 1st v.p. 1976-77, pres. 1978—), Am. Council Learned Socs. (del. 1971-74). Contbr. to Ency. Brit., Columbia Ency., also to books, mags. Home: 176 W 87th St New York NY 10024 Office: Avery Library Columbia Univ New York NY 10027

PLAGENZ, GEORGE RICHARD, clergyman, journalist; b. Lakewood, Ohio, Dec. 11, 1923; s. George William and Edith Louise (Fenner) P.; B.A. cum laude, Western Res. U., 1945; S.T.B., Harvard, 1949; m. Faith Hanna, Sept. 12, 1953; children—Joel, George William II, Martha, Sarah. Sports writer Cleve. Press, 1943-46; ordained to ministry Unitarian Ch., 1951; asst. minister King's Chapel, Boston, 1951-54; news broadcaster Radio Sta. WEEI, Boston, 1955-63; writer Boston Sunday Advertiser, 1963-70; religion editor Cleve. Press, 1970—; syndicated columnist Scripps-Howard Newspapers, 1974—. Mem. Beta Theta Pi. Club: Harvard (Boston). Home: 16913 Clifton Blvd Lakewood OH 44107 Office: 901 Lakeside Ave Cleveland OH 44114

PLAGER, SHELDON JAY, educator; b. Long Branch, N.J., May 16, 1931; s. A.L. and Clara L. (Matross) P.; A.B., U. N.C., 1952; J.D., U. Fla., 1958; LL.M., Columbia U., 1961; children—Anna Katherine, David Alan, Daniel Tyler. Admitted to Fla. bar, 1958, Ill. bar, 1964; asst. prof. law U. Fla., 1958-62, asso. prof., 1962-64; asso. prof. law U. Ill. at Urbana-Champaign, 1964-65, prof., 1965-77, dir. Office Environ. and Planning Studies, 1972-74, 75-77; dean, prof. law Ind. U. Sch. Law, Bloomington, 1977—. vis. research prof. law U. Wis., 1967-68. Chmn., Gainesville (Fla.) Planning Commn., 1962-63; mem. Urbana Plan Commn., 1966-70; mem. nat. air pollution manpower devel. adv. com., 1971-75; cons. Ill. Inst. for Environ. Quality, U.S. EPA; chmn. Ill. Task Force on Noise, 1972-76. Served with USN, 1952-55. Author: (with Maloney and Baldwin) Water Law and Administration, 1968; Social Justice Through Law-New Approaches in the Law of Property, 1970. Home: Bloomington IN 47401 Office: Law Bldg Ind U Bloomington IN 47401

PLAISTED, ROBERT LEROY, plant breeder, educator; b. Hornell, N.Y., Jan. 1, 1929; s. Robert A. and Eva B. (Gitchell) P.; B.S., Cornell U., 1950; M.S., Ia. State U., 1954, Ph.D., 1956; m. Ellen B. Overbaugh, Feb. 10, 1951; children—Deborah, Kathleen, Thomas, Diane. Grad. asst. Ia. State U., 1953-56; asst. prof. Cornell U., 1956-60, asso. prof., 1960-64, prof., 1964—, chmn. dept. plant breeding and biometry, 1964-79. Served with AUS, 1951-53. Mem. Crop Sci. Soc. Am., Potato Assn. Am. (pres. 1971). Home: 536 Ellis Hollow Creek Rd Ithaca NY 14850

PLAMBECK, HERBERT HENRY, ret. govt. ofcl., agrl. cons.; b. Davenport, Iowa, Mar. 1, 1908; s. Herman Theodore and Lydia (Keller) P.; student Iowa State U., 1931-36; m. Frances Marie Hahn, June 23, 1937; children—Mary Frances Plambeck Munger, James. Farm worker, 1924-29; Scott County (Iowa) youth leader, 1930; Scott County youth extension dir., 1931-32; asst. county extension agt., Boone County, Iowa, 1934; farm editor Davenport Democrat, 1935; farm editor radio sta. WHO, Des Moines, 1936-42; U.S. war corr., 1943-45; farm service dir. sta. WHO-TV, 1946-69; food observer UN FAO, 1967; asst. to sec. Dept. Agr., Washington, 1970-74, ret., 1974; farm observer Peoples Republic China, 1976. Founding mem., bd. dirs. Nat. Farm Inst., now chmn.; bd. govs. Nat. Agrl. Hall of Fame, Living History Farms. Recipient citations from U.S. War Dept., Netherlands and Norwegian govts. for combat reporting; Hoover Citizenship award, Heritage Found. award, Reuben Brigham Journalism award, Nat. 4-H Alumni award, Nat. Livestock Conservation award, Nat. Easter Seal Soc. award, Iowa State U. award of merit; Distinguished Service awards from Am. Farm Bur., Nat. Conservation Dists., Nat. Future Farmers, Nat. Assn. U.S. Plowmen, Nat. Farm Broadcasters Assn.; Oscar in Agr.; World Citizenship award. Mem. Nat. Assn. Farm Broadcasters (past pres., historian), Am. Farm Bur., Soil Conservation Soc., Am., Nat. Corn Growers Assn., Alpha Gamma Rho, Sigma Delta Chi. Presbyterian (elder). Mason, Kiwanian (internat. agrl. chmn. 1948, 59, pres. Des Moines 1952, gov. Neb.-Iowa dist. 1965). Author: Heritage of Community Service, 1970; Fifty Golden Years, 1971. Contbr. articles to profl. publs. Home: 4909 Harwood Dr Des Moines IA 50312 Office: Des Moines Savs and Loan Assn Des Moines IA 50307

PLANE, DONALD RAY, educator; b. Evansville, Ind., July 17, 1938; s. Edward L. and Margaret I. (Downen) P.; M.E., U. Cin., 1961; M.B.A., (NDEA fellow), Ind. U., 1963, D.B.A. (NDEA fellow), 1965; m. Rosemary Bieber, Sept. 4, 1961; children—Brian Russell, Dennis Lowell, Margaret Diane. Instr. econs. U.S. Air Force Acad., 1965-67, asst. prof. econs., 1967-68; asso. prof. mgmt. sci. U. Colo., 1968-72, prof., 1972—, head div. mgmt. sci., 1976—; vis. Fulbright prof. mgmt. sci. U. Nairobi, 1978-79; cons. in field. Elder, St. Andrew Presbyterian Ch., Boulder, Colo. Served with USAF, 1965-68. Ford Found. fellow, 1965. Mem. Am. Inst. Decision Scis. (mem. council 1977—). Co-author 4 books, including: (with E.B. Oppermann) Statistics for Management Decision, 1977; (with J. Dinkel and G. Kochenberger) Management Science: Text and Applications, 1978; research, publs. in field. Home: 2700 Iliff St Boulder CO 80303 Office: Grad Sch Bus Adminstrn U Colo Boulder CO 80309

PLANE, ROBERT ALLEN, coll. pres.; b. Evansville, Ind., Sept. 30, 1927; s. Allen George and Altha (Warren) P.; A.B., Evansville Coll., 1948; M.S., U. Chgo., 1949, Ph.D., 1951, D.Sc., U. Evansville, 1968; m. Mary Moore, July 2, 1963; children—David Allen, Martha Lu, Ann Marie, Jennifer. With Oak Ridge Nat. Lab., 1951-52; mem. faculty Cornell U., 1952-74, prof. chemistry, 1962-74, chmn. dept. chemistry, 1967-70, acting provost, 1969-70, provost, 1970-73; pres. Clarkson Coll., Potsdam, N.Y., 1974—; vis. scientist U. Calif., Berkeley, 1969; vis. prof. enology N.Y. State Experiment Sta., 1979. Mem. N.Y. State Commr.'s Adv. Council on Higher Edn., 1976-78; chmn. Commn. on Ind. Colls. and Univs., 1976-78; dir. Nat. Assn. Ind. Colls. and Univs., 1978—; trustee Cazenovia Coll., 1978—. NIH Spl. fellow Nobel Med. Inst., Stockholm, Sweden, 1960, Oxford (Eng.) U., 1961. Mem. Am. Chem. Soc., Am. Soc. Enologists, Empire State C. of C. (dir.), Sigma Xi. Author: (with M.J. Slenko) Chemistry, 1957, Experimental Chemistry, 1958, Physical Inorganic Chemistry, 1963, Chemistry: Principles and Properties, 1966; (with R.E. Hester) Elements of Inorganic Chemistry, 1965. Contbr. articles to profl. jours. Address: Clarkson Coll Potsdam NY 13676

PLANJE, THEODORE JOHN, univ. dean; b. St. Louis, Mar. 17, 1919; s. George and Edna (Johnston) P.; B.S. in Ceramic Engring., Mo. Sch. Mines and Metallurgy, 1940; postgrad. Mass. Inst. Tech., 1940-41; Ph.D. in Ceramic Engring., U. Mo., 1950; m. Miriam Louise Kelting, Aug. 8, 1942; children—Theodore John, Curtis E. Instr. ceramic engring. U. Mo. at Rolla (formerly Mo. Sch. Mines and Metallurgy), 1946-50, asst. prof., 1950-52, asso. prof., 1952-55, prof., chmn. dept. ceramic engring., 1955-64, dir. Sch. Mines and Metallurgy, 1964-65, dean, 1965—, also dir. of Space Sci. Research Center. Served to capt. USAAF, 1941-46. Registered profl. engr., Mo. Fellow Am. Ceramic Soc. (past pres.); mem. Am. Inst. Mining, Metall. and Petroleum Engrs., Nat. Inst. Ceramic Engrs., Am. Soc. for Engring. Edn., Rolla C. of C., Keramos, Sigma Xi, Tau Beta Pi, Sigma Gamma Epsilon. Contbr. articles tech. publs. Patentee in field. Home: 2 McFarland Dr Rolla MO 65401

PLANK, BETSY ANN (MRS. SHERMAN V. ROSENFIELD), pub. relations counsel; b. Tuscaloosa, Ala., Apr. 3, 1924; d. Richard Jeremiah and Bettye (Hood) Plank; student Bethany (W.Va.) Coll., 1940-43; A.B., U. Ala., 1944; m. Sherman V. Rosenfield, Apr. 10, 1954. Continuity dir. radio sta. KQV, Pitts., 1944-47; account exec. Mitchell McKeown Orgn., Chgo., 1947-54; pub. relations counsel Chgo. chpt. A.R.C., 1954-57; dir. pub. relations Chgo. Council on Fgn. Relations, 1957-58; v.p. Ronald Goodman Pub. Relations Counsel, Chgo., 1958-61; exec. v.p., treas., dir. Daniel J. Edelman, Inc., Chgo., 1961-73; dir. pub. relations planning Am. Tel. & Tel. Co., N.Y.C., 1973-74; asst. v.p. pub. relations Ill. Bell Telephone Co., Chgo., 1974—. Dep. chmn. VII World Congress Pub. Relations, 1976. Pres., Assn. House of Chgo., 1968-70, United Christian Community Services, Chgo., 1970; chmn. pub. relations com. Chgo. Met. Crusade of Mercy, 1972, 78. Trustee Chgo. YWCA, 1972-73, Betsy Plank chpt. Pub. Relations Student Soc. Am., No. Ill. U.; trustee Found. for Pub. Relations Research and Edn., 1975—; nat. bd. dirs. Girl Scouts U.S.A., 1975—. Recipient medal of merit Pi Delta Epsilon. Mem. Pub. Relations Soc. Am. (nat. pres. 1973, chmn. pub. utilities sect. 1977, outstanding service award 1974, 77), Publicity Club Chgo. (pres. 1963-64; Outstanding Service award 1961), Ill. Council on Econ. Edn. (v.p. 1977—), Econ. Club Chgo., Welfare Pub. Relations Forum Chgo. (pres. 1966-67), Chgo. Network, Bon Vivant Soc., Chgo. Power Squadron Aux. (pres. 1958), Nat. Pub. Relations Council (dir.

1973-75), Burnham Park Yacht Club Aux., Zeta Tau Alpha. Presbyterian. Mem. adv. bd. Ill. Issues, PR News, PR Rev. Home: 421 Melrose Ave Chicago IL 60613 Office: 225 W Randolph St Chicago IL 60606

PLANK, JOHN NATHAN, polit. scientist; b. Dayton, Ohio, July 22, 1923; s. Laurance Robbins and Grace (Ganssle) P.; A.B., Harvard, 1949, Ph.D., 1959; M.A., Haverford Coll., 1953; m. Eleanor McVay Bent, Aug. 23, 1952; children—David Nathan, Margaret Hopkins, Geoffrey Gilbert. Dir. Am. Friends Service Com. project community devel., El Salvador, 1953-54; teaching fellow govt. Harvard, 1955-57, 58, asst. prof., 1959-62, vis. prof., 1962; vis. asst. prof. Northwestern U., 1959; research asso. Harvard Center Internat. Affairs, 1959-63; prof. Latin Am. affairs Fletcher Sch. Internat. Law and Diplomacy, 1962-63; dir. Office Research and Analysis Am. Republics, Bur. Intelligence and Research, State Dept., 1963-64; mem. sr. staff Brookings Instn., 1964-70; prof. polit. sci. U. Conn., Storrs, 1970—, dir. Inst. Internat. and Intercultural Studies, 1971—. Cons. to govt., founds., assns., 1959—. Mem. com. on internat. exchange of persons Sr. Fulbright Hays Program, 1970—, also chmn. Latin Am. Sub-com.; bd. overseers Moses Brown Sch., 1975—. Served with AUS, 1941-45. Scholar, Harvard, 1941-42, grad. fellow, 1955-56, Doherty fellow, 1957-58, Bliss fellow, 1960-61; sr. asso. mem. St. Anthony's Coll., Oxford (Eng.) U., 1979; recipient Superior Honor award State Dept., 1964. Mem. Am., Internat. polit. sci. assns., Am. Soc. Pub. Adminstrn., New Eng. Council Latin Am. Studies (pres. 1974-75), Soc. Internat. Devel., Inter-Am. Assn. Democracy and Freedom, Am. Friends Service Com., Council on Fgn. Relations, Latin Am. Studies Assn. (treas. 1965-70), Council on Hemispheric Affairs (trustee 1976—). Author articles in field. Editor: Cuba and the United States; Long Range Perspectives, 1967. Home: 99 Dog Ln Storrs CT 06268

PLANK, RAYMOND, corp. exec., b. Mpls., May 29, 1922; s. Raby and Maude (Howe) P.; B.A., Yale U., 1944; m. Louise Benz Cobb, Mar. 19, 1976; children by previous marriage—Katherine, Michael, Pamela, Roger, Dana. Founder, partner Plank & Somekawa, accounting, Mpls., 1946-53; founder, 1954; since chmn., chief exec. officer Apache Corp., Mpls.; dir. Fabri-Tek, Inc., St. Paul Securities, Inc., Questor Corp. Past pres. Mpls. Boys Club; trustee Carleton Coll., U. Minn. Found. Served 1st lt., pilot USAAF, World War II. Mem. Beta Theta Pi. Republican. Clubs: Minneapolis; Woodhill Country. Home: 550 E Long Lake Rd Wayzata MN 55391 Office: Foshay Tower Minneapolis MN 55402

PLANO, RICHARD JAMES, educator, physicist; b. Merrill, Wis., Apr. 15, 1929; s. Victor James and Minnie (Hass) P.; A.B., U. Chgo., 1949, B.S., 1951, M.S., 1953, Ph.D., 1956; m. Louise Sylvia Grevillius, July 3, 1956; children—Linda Sylvia, Robert James. Faculty, Columbia, 1956-60; faculty Rutgers U., New Brunswick, N.J., 1960—, prof. physics, 1962—. Mem. Am. Inst. Physics, Am. Assn. Physics Tchrs., AAUP. Studies on properties of elementary particles. Home: PO Box 306 Middlebush NJ 08873 Office: Physics Dept Rutgers U New Brunswick NJ 08903

PLANT, FORREST ALBERT, lawyer; b. Sacramento, Dec. 17, 1924; s. Forrest A. and Marie (Phleger) P.; A.B., U. Cal., 1944, J.D., 1949; m. Shirley J. Boles, Oct. 15, 1949; children—Forrest Albert, Randall B., Gregory M., Brian J. Admitted to Cal. bar, 1950, since practiced in Sacramento; partner Diepenbrock, Wulff, Plant & Hannegan; prof. law U. of Pacific, 1952-61; dir. Ludry Stores Inc. Mem. Jud. Council State Cal., 1972-76. Pres. Legal Aid Soc. Sacramento County, 1961-62. Trustee, dir. Golden Empire council Boy Scouts Am., 1963-67. Bd. dirs. Sacramento Children's Home; trustee, exec. com. Sutter Community Hosps.; trustee Cal. Mus. Assn., pres., 1968-69; bd. visitors Stanford Law Sch. Served with USNR, World War II. Fellow Am. Bar Found., Am. Coll. Probate Counsel, Am. Coll. Trial Lawyers (bd. regents); mem. State Bar of Cal. (bd. govs. 1968-71, pres. 1970-71), Sacramento County Bar Assn. (pres. 1966, mem. council), Phi Beta Kappa. Clubs: Sutter (past dir.), Rotary (past pres. and dir.). Home: 1515 13th Ave Sacramento CA 95818 Office: 455 Capitol Mall Sacramento CA 95814

PLANT, MARCUS LEO, educator; b. New London, Wis., Nov. 10, 1911; s. George Henry and Margaret (McGinty) P.; B.A., Lawrence Coll., 1932, M.A., 1934; J.D., U. Mich., 1938; m. Geraldine Hefter, Dec. 27, 1944; children—Margaret, Elizabeth, Mark, Nancy. Admitted to Wis. bar, 1939, N.Y. bar, 1946, Mich. bar, 1949; pvt. practice Miller, Mack & Fairchild, Milw., 1938-44, Cahill, Gordon, Zachry & Reindel, N.Y.C., 1944-46; prof. law U. Mich., Ann Arbor, 1946—. Rep., U. Mich. in Intercollegiate Conf. Faculty Reps., 1955-79, sec., 1956-79; mem. U.S. Olympic Com., 1969-72. Mem. Nat. Collegiate Athletic Assn. (pres. 1967-69). Order of Coif, Tau Kappa Alpha, Delta Tau Delta. Author: Cases on the Law of Torts, 1953; (with Burke Shartel) The Law of Medical Practice, 1959; (with Wex S. Malone) Cases and Materials on Workmen's Compensation, 1962; (with Wex S. Malone and Joseph W. Little) Cases and Materials on the Employment Relation; also various articles law jours. Home: 2311 Woodside Rd Ann Arbor MI 48104

PLANT, ROBERT ANTHONY, singer, composer; b. Bromwich, Staffordshire, Eng., Aug. 20, 1948. Previously sang with rock group Joy and with Alexis Korner; with rock group Led Zeppelin, 1968—; world-wide concert tours; performed in film The Song Remains the Same, 1976; songs composed include: (with J. Page) Stairway to Heaven, Immigrant Song, Black Dog; albums include: Led Zeppelin I, Led Zeppelin II, Led Zeppelin III, Led Zeppelin IV, Houses of the Holy, Physical Graffiti, Presence, In Through the Out Door. Office: Swan Song Inc 444 Madison Ave New York NY 10022*

PLANTE, INGE RUDLOFF, psychiatrist, instl. dir.; b. Leipzig, Germany, Sept. 20, 1929; d. Erich A. and Hildegard (von Kienitz) Rudloff; came to U.S., 1955, naturalized, 1960; student U. Wuerzburg (Germany), 1949, Ursinus Coll., Collegeville, Pa., 1950; D. Medicine Surgery, U. Munich (Germany), 1954; m. Marc A. Plante, Dec. 28, 1957 (dec. Feb. 1967); children—Sabrina, Michele Andree, Marc Rudloff. Intern McKinley Hosp., Trenton, N.J., 1955-56; resident psychiatry Trenton Psychiat. Hosp., 1956-59, asst. med. dir. west hosp., 1970-73, med. dir., chief exec. officer, 1973-74; med. dir., chief exec. officer N.J. Neuropsychiat. Inst., Princeton, 1974—. Address: New Jersey Neuropsychiatric Institute Box 1000 Princeton NJ 08540

PLANTE, PETER PAUL, lawyer; b. Gracefield, Que., Can., Aug. 3, 1920; s. Edgar M. and Georgiana (Monahan) P.; B.A., U. Western Ont. (Can.), 1943; J.D., U. Detroit, 1949; m. Rita Mary Donahue, Sept. 4, 1948; children—Therese (Mrs. Gary Wood), Kathleen, Thaddeus, Maura Ellen, Maryanna, Christina, Stephen, Margaret, Robert, Anthony, Jeanne Marie. Admitted to Vt. bar, 1950; partner firm Pierce & Plante, Newport, Vt., 1950-52; asso. Henry F. Black, White River Junction, Vt., 1952-54; partner firm Black & Plante, White River Junction, 1954—; dir. Woodstock Nat. Bank, 1973—. Town auditor, Norwich, Vt., 1957-60, moderator, 1977—; sch. dir. Norwich, 1957-62; justice of peace, Norwich, 1960-63; judge Harford Municipal Ct., 1962-67; mem. Jud. Selection Bd., 1967-78; chmn. Vt. Parole Bd., 1968-75. Trustee Mary Hitchcock Meml. Hosp., Hanover, N.H., 1968-71; trustee U. Vt., 1975—. Served with AUS, 1943-46. Fellow Am. Bar Found.; mem. Am., Vt. (pres. 1973-74) bar assns., Am. Coll. Trial Lawyers, Am. Judicature Soc., Internat. Soc. Barristers, Windsor County Bar Assn. K.C. Home: 12 Church St Norwich VT 05055 Office: 24 North Main White River Junction VT 05001

PLASBERG, COEN CHRISTIAN, hosp. adminstr.; b. Venlo, Netherlands, Mar. 8, 1933; s. Jaques I. and Anne Gertruda P.; came to U.S., 1958, naturalized, 1966; B.S. in Math., U. Delfzyl (Netherlands), 1955; student U. Md., 1972-73, Balt. Coll. Commerce, 1967-72; M.H.A., George Washington U., 1974; m. Elizabeth May Somerville, Nov. 16, 1957; children—Diana, Christian, Laura. Bus. mgr. dept. medicine, adminstrv. asst. to physician-in-chief Johns Hopkins Hosp., Johns Hopkins U., 1961-64; asst. adminstr. Sinai Hosp. Balt., 1964-67; asst. supt. Clifton T. Perkins State Hosp., Jessup, Md., 1967-73, on spl. assignment to Commr. Mental Health of Md., 1973; supt. Mental Health Inst., Mt. Pleasant, Iowa, 1974-77, Mental Health Inst., Clarinda, Iowa, 1976; dir. Western State Hosp., Staunton, Va., 1977—; asso. prof. psychiatry U. Va., 1979—; preceptor George Washingtin U. Served with Dutch Mcht. Marines, 1955-58. Recipient cert. commendation Iowa Mental Health Assn., 1977, cert. appreciation Va. Kiwanis Club, 1977; lic. nursing home adminstr., Va. Mem. Assn. Mental Health Adminstrs., Am. Public Health Assn., Am. Hosp. Assn., Am. Coll. Hosp. Adminstrs. Roman Catholic. Initiated delivery comprehensive mental health services S.E. Iowa, 1975. Home: 531 Thornrose Ave Staunton VA 24401 Office: Western State Hosp PO Box 2500 Staunton VA 24401

PLASKETT, THOMAS GEORGE, airline exec.; b. Raytown, Mo., Dec. 24, 1943; s. Warren E. and Frances S. (Winegar) P.; B.Indsl. Engring., Gen. Motors Inst., Flint, Mich., 1966; M.B.A., Harvard U., 1968; m. Linda Lee Maxey, June 8, 1968; children—Kimberly Ann, Keith Thomas. With Gen. Motors Corp., 1961-73, sr. staff asst. treas. dept., N.Y.C., 1973; asst. controller, then v.p. mktg. adminstrn. Am. Airlines, Inc., N.Y.C., 1974-76, sr. v.p. fin., chief fin. officer, 1976—. Mem. Am. Mgmt. Assn., Fin. Execs. Inst., Theta Xi. Club: Las Colinas (Irving, Tex.). Home: 3911 Fox Glen Dr Irving TX 75062 Office: Am Airlines PO Box 61616 DFW Airport TX 75261

PLASS, GILBERT NORMAN, physicist, educator; b. Toronto, Ont., Can., Mar. 22, 1920 (parents Am. citizens); s. Norman and Annette (Sunier) P.; B.S. summa cum laude, Harvard, 1941; Ph.D., Princeton, 1947; m. Thyra Nichols Pliske, Oct. 6, 1962; children—Gordon Marc, Lucie Susan. Asso. physicist Metall. Lab., U. Chgo., 1942-45; asst. prof. Johns Hopkins, 1946-54, asso. prof., 1954-55; mgr. theoretical physics, research fellow Aeronutronic, Ford Motor Co., Newport Beach, Calif., 1955-63; prof. Southwest Center Advanced Studies, Dallas, 1963-68; prof. chmn. dept. physics Texas A. and M. U., College Station, 1968—; vis. prof. Northwestern U., 1947, Mich. State U., 1954-55. Fellow Am. Phys. Soc., Optical Soc. Am., AAAS; mem. Am. Geophys. Union, Am. Meteorol. Soc., Am. Astron. Soc., Am. Assn. Physics Tchrs. Author: Infrared Physics and Engineering, 1963; Advances in Molecular Spectroscopy, 1962; Scientific American Resource Library: Earth Sciences, Vol. 1. Carbon Dioxide and Climate, 1969; Electrochemistry of Cleaner Environments, 1972. Cons. editor Infrared Physics, 1960—. Home: 914 Park Ln Bryan TX 77801 Office: Dept of Physics Texas A & M Univ College Station TX 77843

PLATH, DAVID WILLIAM, educator; b. Elgin, Ill., Dec. 8, 1930; s. Ernest Karl and Laura Emadele (Baumgardt) P.; B.S. in Journalism, Northwestern U., 1952; M.A. in Anthropology and Far Eastern Langs., Harvard, 1959, Ph.D., 1962; m. Marilyn Ann Lusher, Aug. 25, 1956; children—Mark Ernest, Gail Christine. Lectr. anthropology U. Calif. at Berkeley, 1961-63; asst. prof. U. Iowa, 1963-64, asso. prof., 1964-66; asso. prof. anthropology and Asian studies U. Ill. at Urbana, 1966-68, prof., 1969—, head dept. anthropology, 1970-72; vis. prof. Kyoto U., 1972-73, Konan U., 1972-73, 76; field dir. Internat. Sch. Am., 1969-70, Konan-Ill. Center, 1976-78; mem. joint com. Japanese studies Am. Council Learned Socs./Social Sci. Research Council, 1978—. Mem. sci. rev. com. Milton Olive III Meml. Corp., 1968-72. Served with USNR, 1952-55; PTO. Ford Found. Fgn. Area fellow, 1959-61; grantee Am. Council Learned Socs. and Social Sci. Research Council, 1965-66; Guggenheim fellow, 1972-73. Fellow Am. Anthrop. Assn.; mem. Am. Ethnol. Soc., Assn. for Asian Studies (mem. N.E. Asia regional council 1971-74), Central States Anthrop. Soc. Author: The After Hours: Modern Japan and the Search for Enjoyment, 1964; (with Yoshie Sugihara) Sensei and His People: The Building of a Japanese Commune, 1969; Long Engagements: Maturity in Modern Japan, 1980; editor: Aware of Utopia, 1971; Adult Episodes in Japan, 1975; editorial bd. Jour. Asian Studies, 1963-66; contbg. editor Japan Interpreter, 1975—. Home: 1302 Briarwood Dr Champaign IL 61820 Office: Dept Anthropology Davenport Hall U Ill Urbana IL 61801

PLATNER, WARREN, architect; b. Balt., June 18, 1919; s. Warren Kelly and Alice Darling (Chapman) P.; B.Arch., Cornell U., 1941; m. Joan Payne, 1945; children—Bronson, Joan, Sharon, Madeleine. Assos., Eero Saarinen and Assos., architects, 1950-65; propr. Warren Platner Assos., architects, New Haven, 1965—; vis. lectr. archtl. schs.; prin. works include Kent Meml. Library, Suffield, Conn., 1972, Princeton U. Prospect Center, 1970, MGIC Hdqrs., Milw., 1973, Am. Restaurant, Kansas City, Mo., 1974, malls at Water Tower Pl., Chgo., 1975, Windows on the World, N.Y.C., 1976, Standard Brands Research Center, Wilton, Conn., 1979. Recipient Rome prize architecture, 1955; advanced research Fulbright award architecture, 1955; Graham Found. award advanced studies fine arts, 1962; 1st ann. award Designers Lighting Forum, 1975; also several internat. design awards. Fellow AIA, Am. Acad. in Rome. Address: 18 Mitchell Dr New Haven CT 06511

PLATOU, CARL NICOLAI, hosp. exec.; b. Bayridge, N.Y., Nov. 10, 1923; s. Alfred Stoud and Anna Sofia (Arveschoug) P.; B.A., U. Minn., 1949; M.H.A., Concordia Coll., 1951, LL.D. in Hosp. Adminstrn. (hon.), 1969; m. Susan Kumpf, Apr. 11, 1977; children—Priscilla, Kenneth, Patricia, Nancy. Asst. adminstr. N.W. Hosp., Mpls., 1951-52; adminstr. Fairview Hosp., Mpls., 1952-63, exec. v.p. Fairview and Fairview-Southdale Hosps., 1963-70, pres. Fairview Hosps. (name changed to Fairview Community Hosps. 1973), 1970—; preceptor U. Minn. Program Hosp. Adminstrn., 1956—, Concordia Coll. Program Hosp. Adminstrn., 1968—, Ohio State U. Program Hosp. Adminstrn., 1974—; lectr. Harvard U. Health Seminars Summer Series, 1973—; dir. F & M Savs. Bank, Mpls., 1969—, bd. dirs. Augsburg Coll., 1972—, Sons of Norway Found., Mpls., 1976—, Vinland Nat. Center, Mpls., 1976—, Guthrie Theater, 1978—. Served with U.S. Army, 1943-46. Decorated Purple Heart, Bronze Star (U.S.); knight 1st class Order St. Olav (Norway); named 1 of 100 Mpls. Newsmakers of Tomorrow, Time Mag., 1953, Outstanding Man of Year, Mpls. Jr. C. of C., 1957, commodore Mpls. Aquatennial, 1966. Mem. Am. Hosp. Assn., Minn. Hosp. Assn., Hosp. Research and Devel. Inst., Am. Protestant Hosp. Assn., Am. Coll. Hosp. Adminstrs., U. Minn. Alumni Assn., Greater Mpls. C. of C. Lutheran. Clubs: Rotary, Mpls., Interlachen Country, Lafayette, U. Minn. Alumni, Skylight, Sons of Norway, Torske Klubben. Home: 4516 Wooddale Ave Minneapolis MN 55424 Office: 2312 S 6th St Minneapolis MN 55454

PLATT, ALEXANDER BRADFORD, cons. psychologist; b. N.Y.C., Mar. 2, 1935; s. Leonard Scranton and Rachel Mary (McClurg) P.; B.A., Washington and Lee U., 1957; M.A., Columbia, 1958, Ph.D., 1966; m. Patricia Ann Edwards, June 18, 1960; children—Alexander Bradford, Corinne Patricia. Vocational counselor YMCA Vocat. Service Center, N.Y.C., 1959-60; asst. to dean students Sch. Gen. Studies, Columbia U., 1960-62, dean students, 1962-66; prof. psychology Briarcliff Coll., Briarcliff Manor, N.Y., 1966-67; asso. dean student affairs Columbia Coll., Columbia U., 1967-68; mgmt. cons. Rohrer, Hibler & Replogle, N.Y.C., 1968-69; v.p., dir. instructional systems div. Grolier Ednl. Corp., N.Y.C., 1969-77; gen. partner Keyes, Platt & Dineen, Darien, Conn. 1977—. Mem. Am. Psychol. Assn. Home: 30 Willowmere Ave Riverside CT 06878

PLATT, CHARLES ADAMS, architect, planner; b. N.Y.C., May 16, 1932; s. William and Margaret (Littell) P.; A.B., Harvard, 1954, M.Arch., 1960; m. Joan Mathieson, June 20, 1958; children—Sylvia, Ethan, Virginia Lippincott. Gen. partner Smotrich & Platt, N.Y.C., 1965—. Mem. nat. panel arbitrators Am. Arbitration Assn.; bd. dirs. Municipal Art Soc., N.Y.C., 1966-78; pres. bd. trustees Augustus St.-Gaudens Mus.; mem. N.Y.C. Landmarks Preservation Commn. Recipient nat. honor award for excellence in architecture AIA, 1969, Bard award for civic architecture and urban design, 1969, Record Interiors award, 1970, 73, 75, Record House awards, 1971, 78. Mem. AIA. Club: Century (N.Y.C.). Home: 1261 Madison Ave New York NY 10028 Office: 227 E 45 St New York NY 10017

PLATT, CHARLES MICHAEL, author, educator; b. Tehran, Iran, Apr. 18, 1949; adopted s. Robert Moriah Platt; student Churchill Coll., Cambridge (Eng.) U., 1967; m. Leah Wallach, Apr. 7, 1971 (div. 1977); 1 son, Joseph Richard; m. 2d, Nancy Weber, May 31, 1977; 1 dau., Rose. Came to U.S., 1969. Author: Garbage World, 1967; The City Dwellers, 1970; The Gas, 1970; Planet of the Voles, 1971; The Power and the Pain, 1971; The Image Job, 1971; T-Shirting, 1975; Outdoor Survival, 1976; Sweet Evil, 1976; A Song for Christina, 1977; Twilight of the City, 1977; Universe of Pain, 1978; Brain Damage, 1978; personal asst. to mng. dir. Sidgwick & Jackson Pubs., London, Eng., 1968; editor New Worlds mag., 1969—; cons. editor Avon Books, N.Y.C., 1972; sci. fiction editor Condor Books, N.Y.C., 1977-78; asst. prof. creative writing S.I. Community Coll., 1972; instr. New Sch., N.Y.C., 1971—, Apple Skills Exchange, N.Y.C., 1977. Labor councillor for Colville Ward, Royal Borough Kensington and Chelsea, London, 1968. Recipient William Travis award for excellence in poetry, 1971; Cornelius prize for best speculative short fiction, 1978. Doubleday fellow, summer 1970. Mem. Sci. Fiction Writers Am., Churchill Coll. Scholars Assn. (hon.). Club: British North America (Oxford, Eng.). Address: Box 556 Old Chelsea Station New York NY 10011

PLATT, FRANKLIN DEWITT, historian; b. Marion, La., Nov. 15, 1932; s. Robert Baxter and Ethel Estelle (White) P.; B.A., La. State U., 1955; Rockefeller Bros. Theol. fellow Union Theol. Sem., 1955-56; A.M., Washington U., St. Louis, 1963, Ph.D., 1969; m. Dixie Ferguson, Aug. 4, 1956; 1 dau. Dixie. Instr. dept. humanities Mich. State U., 1964-69, asst. prof., 1969-72, asso. prof., 1972-77, prof., 1977—, asst. chmn. dept. humanities, 1971-78, chmn., 1978—. Served with USNR, 1956-60. Mem. Am. Hist. Assn., Assn. for Gen. and Liberal Studies, Archeol. Inst. Am. Club: University (East Lansing). Home: 1134 Southlawn St East Lansing MI 48823 Office: Dept Humanities Mich State U East Lansing MI 48824

PLATT, GEOFFREY, architect; b. Cornish, N.H., Aug. 6, 1905; s. Charles A. and Eleanor (Hardy) P.; grad. St. Mark's Sch., 1923; A.B., Harvard, 1927; B.Arch., Columbia, 1930; m. Helen Choate, Dec. 20, 1932 (dec. June 1974); children—Penelope, Nicholas, Geoffrey; m. 2d, Alice Doubleday Holbrook, June 26, 1976. Mem. firm William & Geoffrey Platt, N.Y.C., and predecessor, 1934-72; with firm Platt, Wyckoff & Coles, 1972—; works include bldgs. for Deerfield Acad., Smith Coll., Bennett Coll., Middlesex Sch., Princeton U., chapel at Am. Mil. Cemetery (France), houses throughout U.S., particularly N.Y. and N.E. area., Gen. Douglas MacArthur Meml., Norfolk, Va., Rye City Hall., Garden Center Cleve., addition to Pierpont Morgan Library, N.Y.C. Chmn. N.Y.C. Landmarks Preservation Commn., 1962-68; v.p. N.Y. Landmarks Conservancy. Served from lt. to maj., USAAF, 1942-45. Decorated Order Brit. Empire; recipient Gold medal N.Y. Municipal Art Soc., 1968, medal N.Y. Archtl. and Engring. Socs., 1972—. Fellow AIA; asso. NAD. Home: Harris Rd Bedford Hills NY 10507 Office: 305 E 46th St New York NY 10017

PLATT, HARRISON GRAY, writer, editor; b. Portland, Oreg., Apr. 27, 1902; s. Harrison Gray and Nelly (Durham) P.; grad. Punahou Acad., Honolulu, 1920; B.A., Reed Coll., 1925; postgrad. Yale, 1925-26; M.A., Harvard, 1927, postgrad., 1928-30; m. Rhoda Failing Burpee, Aug. 19, 1925; children—Harrison Gray III, William Brewster; m. 2d, Mary Alice Kaye, Dec. 30, 1943. Faculty dept. lang. and lit. Reed Coll., 1927-28, dept. English, Brown U., 1930-38; editor Reilly & Lee Co., 1941-43; asso. editor Bobbs Merrill Co., Inc., 1944-54, editor gen. pub. dept., 1954-60; tech. editor C.L. Barnhart, Reference Books, 1960-61, mng. editor, 1961-63; chief dictionary editor for Harcourt Brace Jovanovich, N.Y.C., 1963-78, ret., 1978; free-lancer writer, editor, 1978—. Democrat. Episcopalian. Author: Current Expressions of Fact and Opinion (with Porter G. Perrin), 1941; other books and articles. Exec. editor Dictionary of Army Terms, 1944, World Book Ency. Dictionary, 1963. Editor in chief: Harcourt Brace School Dictionary, 1968 (rev. as HBJ Sch. Dictionary 1977); Harcourt Brace Intermediate Dictionary, 1968. Contbr.: American College Dictionary, 1947. Home: 160 E 48th St New York NY 10017

PLATT, HOWARD, shoe mfg. co. exec.; b. Bayonne, N.J., Dec. 10, 1926; A.B., U. Rochester (N.Y.), 1946; m. Sue Ellen Sezzin, June 17; children—Jeffrey, Marc, Wendy. Gen. mdse. mgr. Hochschild Kohn, Balt.; with William Hahn & Co., retail shoe div. U.S. Shoe Corp., 1968-79; sr. v.p. U.S. Shoe Corp., Cin., 1979—. Served to lt. USNR, 1944-47, 50-52. Jewish. Home: 3543 Amber Acres Dr Cincinnati OH 45237 Office: 1658 Herald Ave Cincinnati OH 45219

PLATT, JOSEPH BEAVEN, coll. pres.; b. Portland, Oreg., Aug. 12, 1915; s. William Bradbury and Mary (Beaven) P.; B.A., U. Rochester, 1937; Ph.D., Cornell U., 1942; LL.D., U. So. Calif., 1969; m. Jean Ferguson Rusk, Feb. 9, 1946; children—Ann Ferguson Walker, Elizabeth Beaven Garrow. Instr. physics U. Rochester, 1941-43, successively asst. prof. to prof. physics, 1946-56, asso. chmn. dept., 1954-56; staff mem. radiation lab. Mass. Inst. Tech., 1943-46; pres. Harvey Mudd Coll., 1956-76, Claremont U. Center (Calif.), 1976—; dir. Bell & Howell, Jacobs Engring. Group; chmn., trustee Analytic Services, Inc.; vice chmn., trustee Aerospace Corp. With Office Field Service, NDRC, 1944-46; chief physics br. AEC, 1949-51; cons. NSF, U.S. Office Ordnance Research, 1953-56; mem. com. on sci. in UNESCO, Nat. Acad. Scis.-NRC, 1960-62, com. on internat. orgns. and programs, 1962-64; chmn. subcom. on Sino-Am. Sci. Cooperation, 1965—; sci. adviser U.S. del. UNESCO Gen. Conf., Paris, 1960; mem. panel on internat. sci. Pres.'s Sci. Adv. Com., 1961; alt. del. U.S. delegation UNESCO Gen. Conf., Paris, 1962; chmn. select com. Master Plan for Higher Edn. Calif., 1971-73; mem. NSF Adv. Com. Sci. Edn., 1973—, chmn., 1974; mem. Los Angeles Com. on Fgn. Relations, 1973—. Trustee, China Found. for Promotion of

Edn. and Culture; trustee Carnegie Found. for Advancement Teaching, 1970-78, mem. Carnegie Council for Policy Studies in Higher Edn.; bd. dirs. Los Angeles World Affairs Council, 1973—. Governing bd. Am. Inst. Physics, 1957-60. Fellow Am. Phys. Soc.; mem. Am. Assn. Physics Tchrs., IEEE, Am. Soc. Engring. Edn., Automobile Club So. Calif. (dir.), Phi Beta Kappa, Sigma Xi, Phi Kappa Phi. Clubs: California, Sunset, Town Hall (Los Angeles); Twilight (Pasadena); Cosmos (Washington); Bohemian (San Francisco). Home: President Claremont Univ Center Claremont CA 91711

PLATT, JOSEPH SWAN, lawyer; b. Columbus, Ohio, Jan. 8, 1902; s. Rutherford Hayes and Maryette (Smith) P.; grad. Hotchkiss Sch., 1920; B.A., Yale, 1924; LL.B. cum laude, Harvard, 1927; m. Margaret Hubbell Day, Feb. 24, 1930; children—Emily (Mrs. Roy L. Hilburn), Robert Day, William Rutherford, David Day, Elizabeth Swan (Mrs. Charles R. Carmalt). Admitted to Ohio bar, 1927, since practiced in Columbus; partner firm Porter, Wright, Morris and Arthur and predecessor firms, 1946—; with AAA, 1933-34, Bd. Econ. Warfare, 1943; chief criminal and compromise sects. tax div. Dept. Justice, 1944-46; lectr., adj. prof. Coll. Law, Ohio State U., 1946-73. Mem. commr.'s adv. com. IRS, 1953-55; conferee estate and gift tax project Brookings Instn. Fellow Am., Ohio bar founds.; mem. Am., Ohio, Columbus bar assns., Am. Law Inst., Phi Beta Kappa, Order of Coif, Alpha Delta Phi, Phi Delta Phi. Contbr. articles to profl. jours. Home: 112 Stanbery Ave Columbus OH 43209 Office: 37 W Broad St Columbus OH 43215

PLATT, ROBERT HOLMES, railroad exec.; b. Bklyn., Apr. 1, 1920; s. Foster Holmes and Marie (Quigley) P.; A.B., Colgate U., 1941; m. Colette M. Gaffney, Sept. 20, 1941; children—J. Garry, Laura L., Marion C. With Gen. Electric Co., 1941-63, bus. recruit, Schenectady, 1941-47, traveling auditor, 1947-52, mgr. finance, 1952-56, treas., mgr. finance Gen. Electric Credit Corp., N.Y.C., 1956-63; v.p. finance Magnavox Co., N.Y.C., 1963-68, pres., 1968-75, also dir.; vice chmn. Lone Star Industries, Inc., 1975-77; exec. v.p. Consol. Rys. Corp. (Conrail), 1977—; dir. Lincoln Nat. Corp., Goodyear Tire and Rubber Co., U.S. Industries, Inc. Trustee Colgate U. Served with USNR, 1943-46. Mem. Econ. Club N.Y.C., Am. Mgmt. Assn., Alpha Tau Omega. Home: 33 Tower Rd Riverside CT 06878 Office: 6 Penn Center Plaza Philadelphia PA 19103

PLATT, SHERMAN PHELPS, JR., publisher; b. N.Y.C., Mar. 29, 1918; s. Sherman Phelps and Penelope (Sears) P.; grad. Taft Sch., 1936; B.A., Yale, 1940; m. Leila Bronson, Jan. 11, 1941 (div. 1968); children—Sherman Phelps III, John, Bronson; m. 2d, Margaret McClure Smithers, 1968. With Dodd, Mead & Co., N.Y.C., 1940—, beginning as editor, successively salesman, prodn. mgr., sec., dir., exec. v.p., pres., 1964—; v.p., dir. Apollo Editions, Inc., N.Y.C., 1962—. Served as 1st lt. inf. U.S. Army, 1943-46. Mem. Century Assn. Club: Yale (N.Y.C.). Home: 6 Academy Ln Old Lyme CT 06371 Office: 79 Madison Ave New York NY 10016

PLATT, WILLIAM, architect; b. N.Y.C., Feb. 6, 1897; s. Charles Adams and Eleanor (Hardy) P.; A.B., Harvard, 1919; B.Arch., Columbia, 1923; m. Margaret Littell, June 3, 1922; children—Eleanor, Clarissa, Charles Adams. Began as architect in 1924, pvt. practice, 1928-33; mem. firm Charles A. Platt, William and Geoffrey Platt, 1933; mem. firm William & Geoffrey Platt, 1934-72; mem. firm Platt, Wyckoff & Coles, 1972—; recent works include bldgs. for Deerfield Acad., Smith Coll., Chapel at Am. Mil. Cemetery, Suresnes, France, Nat. Acad. Sch. Fine Arts, N.Y.C., Gen. MacArthur Meml., faculty housing, Princeton, N.J., N.Y. Bot. Garden, Garden Center Greater Cleve., Bennett Coll. Arts Center, Norfolk Mus. Arts and Scis.; cons. architect Vanderbilt U., 1957-69. Hon. pres. Saint Gaudens Mus.; trustee emeritus Am. Acad. in Rome. Comdg. ensign, naval aviation, World War I; lt. comdr. USNR, 1942, comdr., 1945. Recipient 1st prize internat. competition, Replanning Central Bus. Dist., City of Stockholm, 1933. Fellow AIA, Archtl. League. Club: Century Assn. (N.Y.C.). Home: Star Route 4 Cornish NH Post Office Windsor VT 05089 Office: 305 E 46 St New York NY 10017

PLATTEN, DONALD CAMPBELL, banker; b. N.Y.C., Sept. 18, 1918; s. John Homer and Katherine Campbell (Viele) P.; B.A., Princeton, 1940; grad. Advanced Mgmt. Program, Harvard, 1966; m. Margaret Leslie Wyckoff, June 24, 1940; children—Katherine L. (Mrs. Randolph S. Naylor), Peter W., Alison C. (Mrs. Alfred G. Vanderbilt, Jr.). With Chem. Bank N.Y.C., 1940—, sr. v.p., 1964-67, exec. v.p., 1967-70, 1st v.p., 1970-72, pres., 1972-73, chmn. bd., 1973—; chmn. bd. Chem. N.Y. Corp., 1973—; dir. CPC Internat., Inc., Thomson Newspapers, Inc., Asso. Dry Goods Corp., Consol. Edison Co. N.Y. Inc. Chmn. bd. dirs. Goodwill Industries Greater N.Y.; bd. dirs. United Fund Greater N.Y.; bd. dirs. Econ. Devel. Council N.Y., Dana Found., Nat. Fgn. Trade Council; trustee Collegiate Sch., N.Y.C., Am. U. Beirut, United Student Aid Funds; charter trustee Princeton. Served to 1st lt. AUS, 1944-46. Mem. Japan Soc., Council on Fgn. Relations, Internat. C. of C. (trustee U.S. council), Res. City Bankers Assn. Clubs: University, Blind Brook, Links, Downtown Assn., Presidents, Bond (N.Y.C.), Economic (N.Y.); Laurel Valley Golf (Ligonier, Pa.). Office: Chem NY Corp 20 Pine St New York NY 10015

PLATTS, JOHN H., appliance co. exec.; b. Detroit, Nov. 19 1917; s. Ralph E. and Mary E. (Snyder) P.; student U. Toledo, 1938-39; m. Dorothea M. Sleeper, Nov. 24, 1940; children—Pamela, Polly, Melissa. With Whirlpool Corp., St. Joseph, Mich., 1941—, successively assemblyman, tool engr., buyer, dir. purchases, gen. sales mgr. Sears Products, gen. mgr. refrigeration plant, v.p. refrigeration product group, Evansville, Ind., 1941-62, corporate pres., Benton Harbor, Mich., 1962-77, chmn., chief exec. officer, 1971—, also dir.; dir. Shell Oil Co., Houston, Sears Bank & Trust Co., Chgo., Area Resources Improvement Council, St. Joseph, Clark Equipment Co. Mem. adv. council Coll. Engring. U. Notre Dame. Mem. Am. Soc. Heating, Refrigerating and Air-conditioning Engrs., Conf. Bd. (trustee), Citizens Research Council Mich. Clubs: Chicago, Union League, Metropolitan (Chgo.); Point O'Woods (Benton Harbor). Office: Whirlpool Corp Administrative Center Benton Harbor MI 49022

PLATZMAN, GEORGE WILLIAM, educator, geophys. scientist; b. Chgo., Apr. 19, 1920; s. Alfred and Rose I. (Kaufman) P.; B.S., U. Chgo., 1940, Ph.D., 1948; M.S., U. Ariz., 1941; m. Harriet M. Herschberger, Feb. 19, 1945. Instr., U. Chgo., 1942-45, research asso., 1947-48; mem. faculty, 1949—, head phys. scis. in coll., 1959-60, prof. meteorology, 1960—, chmn. dept. geophys. scis., 1971-74; hydrologic engr. C.E., U.S. Army, 1945-46; cons. Inst. Advanced Study, Princeton, 1950-53. Guggenheim fellow, 1967-68. Fellow Am. Geophys. Union, Am. Meterol. Soc. (editor jour. 1948-49, chmn. publs. com. 1966-70; Meisinger award 1966; Editor's award 1973). Contbr. articles to profl. jours. Office: Dept Geophys Scis U Chgo 5734 Ellis Ave Chicago IL 60637

PLAUT, ERIC ALFRED, state ofcl.; b. N.Y.C., Nov. 16, 1927; s. Alfred and Margaret (Blumenfeld) P.; B.S., Columbia U., 1949, M.D., 1953; m. Eloine Raab, Sept. 5, 1976. Intern, Montefiore Hosp., Bronx, N.Y., 1953-54; psychiat. resident State Hosp., Worcester, Mass., 1954-55, Mass. Meml. Hosp., Boston, 1956-57; cons. psychiatrist Mass. Dept. Corrections, 1957; fellow student health psychiatry U. Calif., Berkeley, 1957-58; practice medicine specializing in psychiatry, Berkeley, 1958-74; staff psychiatrist Kaiser Hosp., Oakland, Calif., 1958-62, Cowell Meml. Hosp., U. Calif., Berkeley, 1958-62; cons. psychiatrist Bur. Indian Affairs, Dept. Interior, 1967-68; program chief Berkeley Mental Health Services, 1968-71; dep. commr. Ind. Dept. Mental Health, Indpls., 1974-76; commr. Conn. Dept. Mental Health, Hartford, 1976—; asst. clin. prof. psychiatry U. Calif. Med. Sch., San Francisco, 1958-74; asso. clin. prof. psychiatry U. Ind. Med. Sch., Indpls., 1975-76; clin. prof. psychiatry U. Conn. Med. Sch., Farmington, 1978—, Yale U. Med. Sch., 1979—; cons. Assembly Sci. Advisory Council, Calif. Legislature, 1970; chmn. Bay Area region Calif. Conf. Local Mental Health Dirs., 1970-71; mem. Task Force on Access and Barriers, Pres.'s Commn. on Mental Health, 1977—; gen. partner Vanguard Investments, Berkeley, 1971-78. Bd. dirs. ACLU, Berkeley, 1960-65; mem. psychiatry panel Grad. Med. Edn. Nat. Adv. Com., 1979—. Served with USN, 1944-46. Diplomate Am. Bd. Psychiatry and Neurology. Fellow Am. Psychiat. Assn. (cons. Task Force on Govt. Relations 1973-76, chmn. com. on pub. info. 1975-76, com. on certification in adminstrv. psychiatry 1979—); mem. No. Calif. Psychiat. Soc. (chmn. com. on law and legislation 1968-72, fed. legis. rep. 1972-74, councillor 1972-73, pres. elect 1973-74), Calif. Med. Assn. (alt. del. 1968-71), Alameda-Contra Costa Med. Assn. (chmn. mental health com. 1972), Conn. Med. Soc., Nat. Assn. State Mental Health Program Dirs. (dir.). Mem. editorial bd. Yale Psychiat. Quar., 1976—; contbr. articles to profl. jours. Home: 81 Iroquois Rd West Hartford CT 06117 Office: Dept Mental Health 90 Washington St Hartford CT 06115

PLAUT, GERHARD WOLFGANG EUGEN, biochemist; b. Frankfurt, Germany, Jan. 9, 1921; s. Max and Clara (Mayer) P.; came to U.S., 1937, naturalized, 1944; B.S., Iowa State U., 1943; M.S., U. Wis., 1949, Ph.D., 1951. Asst. prof. biochemistry U. Wis., 1951-54; asso. prof. biochemistry N.Y.U., 1954-58; asso. prof. biochemistry, asso. research prof. medicine U. Utah, Salt Lake City, 1958-60, prof. biol. chemistry, research prof. medicine, 1960-66; prof. biochemistry, chmn. dept. Rutgers U. Med. Sch., 1966-70, Temple U. Med. Sch., 1970—. Established investigator Am. Heart Assn., 1954-58. Recipient Research Devel. award USPHS, 1959-62, Research Career award, 1962-66. Mem. Am. Chem. Soc., Am. Soc. Biol. Chemists, Biochem. Soc., Am. Inst. Nutrition. Research and numerous publs. in mode of action of vitamins, biosynthesis of pteridines and riboflavin, phosphorylation reactions, mechanism of enzyme action. Office: Dept Biochemistry Temple U Med Sch Philadelphia PA 19140

PLAUT, JAMES SACHS, found. exec.; b. Cin., Feb. 1, 1912; s. Jacob M. and Alice S. (Sachs) P.; student Auteuil Day Sch., Paris, 1925-26, Taft Sch., Watertown, Conn., 1927-28; A.B., Harvard, 1933, A.M., 1935; D.F.A. (hon.), Wheaton Coll., 1974; m. Mary E. Friedlander, May 24, 1933; children—Susan, Thomas. Asst. dept. of fine arts, Harvard U., 1934-35; asst. to curator of paintings Mus. Fine Arts, Boston, 1935-39; dir. Inst. Contemporary Art, Boston, 1938-56, trustee and dir. emeritus, 1956-61, cons. indsl. design for State of Israel; chmn. Exhbn. Services Internat.; dir. devel., trustee New Eng. Aquarium, Boston, New Eng. Conservatory Music; sec. gen. World Crafts Council, 1967-76; pres. Aid. to Artisans, Inc., 1976—; dep. commr. gen. of U.S. to Brussels World Expn., 1958. Vice pres. Old Sturbridge Village, Mass., 1959-61. Served with USNR, 1942-46; ETO, North Africa; lt. comdr. Res. Decorated Legion of Merit; Chevalier, Legion d'Honneur; knight 1st Class, Order of St. Olav (Norway); comdr. Royal Order of Leopold (Belgium). Gen. chmn. Cambridge Community Fund, 1950 campaign; mem. vis. com. Mus. Fine Arts, Boston, Sch. Artisanry, Boston U.; chmn. vis. com. Wheaton Coll.; mem. council for arts Mass. Inst. Tech. Clubs: Country, Badminton and Tennis (Boston); Harvard, Century Assn. (N.Y.C.). Author: Steuben Glass, 1948; Oskar Kokoschka, 1948; (with Octavio Paz) In Praise of Hands, 1974; also catalogues for exhbns. Inst. Contbr. to Saturday Rev. Lit., Atlantic Monthly, bulls. of art museums, others. Home: 64 Fairgreen Pl Chestnut Hill MA 02167

PLAUT, W. GUNTHER, clergyman, author; b. Muenster, Germany, Nov. 1, 1912; s. Jonas and Selma (Gumprich) P.; LL.B., U. Berlin (Germany), 1933, J.D., 1934; M.H.L., Hebrew Union Coll., Cin., 1939, D.D., 1964; LL.D., U. Toronto, 1978; D.Litt., Cleve. Coll. Jewish Studies, 1979; m. Elizabeth Strauss, Nov. 10, 1938; children—Jonathan, Judith. Came to Can., 1961. Rabbi, 1939; rabbi B'nai Abraham Zion, Chgo., 1939-48, Mt. Zion Temple, St. Paul, 1948-61; sr. rabbi Holy Blossom Temple, Toronto, Ont., Can., 1961-78, sr. scholar, 1978—. Chmn., Minn. Gov.'s Commn. on Ethics in Govt., 1958-61; pres. St. Paul Gallery and Sch. Art (name changed to Minn. Mus.), 1953-59, World Federalists Can., 1966-68; nat. pres. Can. Jewish Congress, 1977—; vice chmn. Ont. Human Rights Commn.; bd. govs. World Union for Progressive Judaism, 1970—, Union Am. Hebrew Congregations, 1974—; fellow York U., 1979—. Served to capt. AUS, 1943-46. Decorated Bronze Star. Author: The Jews in Minnesota, 1959; The Book of Proverbs - A Commentary, 1961; Judaism and the Scientific Spirit, 1962; The Rise of Reform Judaism, 1963; The Growth of Reform Judaism, 1964; The Case for the Chosen People, 1965; Your Neighbour is a Jew, 1967; Page 2, 1971; Genesis, A Modern Commentary, 1974; Time to Think, 1977; Hanging Threads, 1978; Numbers, A Modern Commentary, 1979, others. Contbr. to encys., anthologies, other books, articles to mags., newspapers. Editorial contbr. Toronto Globe and Mail, 1967—. Clubs: York Racquets, Oakdale Golf and Country. Office: 1950 Bathurst St Toronto ON M5P 3K9 Canada

PLAXICO, JAMES SAMUEL, educator, economist; b. Chester, S.C., Oct. 2, 1924; s. James S. and Mary Belle (Hood) P.; B.S., Clemson U., 1945, M.S., 1948; Ph.D., U. Minn., 1953; m. Jackie Lee Edwards, Dec. 29, 1945; children—James Samuel, Alan Thomas, David Emory, Cheryl Lynn. Asst. agrl. economist Clemson U., 1945-46; asst. prof., then asso. prof. agrl. econs. Va. Poly. Inst., 1947-54; prof. agrl. econs. Okla. State U., 1955-61, head dept., 1961—; program adviser Ford Found., 1968-69; state exec. dir. A.S.C.S., 1979—; cons. pub. and pvt. agys. and instns. Trustee Coll. of Ozarks. Mem. Am., So. (pres. 1972) agrl. econs. assns., Am., So. econ. assns. Presbyterian (elder). Contbr. articles to profl. jours.

PLAYER, GARY JIM, profl. golfer; b. Johannesburg, South Africa, Nov. 1, 1936; ed. King Edward Sch., Johannesburg; m. Vivienne Verwey, 1956; children—Jennifer, Mark, Wayne, Michelle, Theresa, Amanda. Turned profl. golfer, 1953; joined PGA, 1957; winner South African Open, 1956, 60, 65, 66, 67, 68, 69, 72, 75, 76, 77, Australian Open, 1958, 62, 63, 65, 69, 70, 74, Australian PGA, 1957, South African Dunlop Masters, 1976, U.S. Open (1st foreigner to win in 45 yrs.), 1965, Ky. Derby Open, 1958, Lucky Internat., 1961, Sunshine Open, 1961, San Diego Open, 1962, Pensacola Open, 1963, 500 Festival, 1964, Greater Greensboro Open, 1970, Nat. Airlines, 1971, Jacksonville Open, 1971, New Orleans Open, 1972, Memphis Classic, 1974, Brazil Open, 1974, So. Open, 1974, Gen. Motors Classic, 1976, Masters, 1961, 74, 78, Brit. Open, 1959, 68, 74, Profl. Golfers Assn. championship, 1962, 72, Picadilly Match Play, 1965, 66, 68, 71, 73, South African PGA, World Series of Golf, 1965, 68, 72, NTL Challenge Cup, Tournament of Champions, 1969, 78, World Cup, 1965, 77, Houston Open, 1978. Named Christian Athlete of Year, So. Baptist Conv., 1967; Richardson award Golf Writers Assn. Am., 1975; named to World Golf Hall of Fame. Address: care Internat Mgmt Group One Erieview Plaza Cleveland OH 44114

PLEASANTS, HENRY, music critic; b. Wayne, Penn., May 12, 1910; s. Henry and Elizabeth Washington (Smith) P.; student Phila. Music Acad.; D.M. (hon.), Curtis Inst. Music, 1977; m. Virginia V. Duffey, Aug. 31, 1940. Music critic Phila. Evening Bulletin, 1930-42; Central European music corr., N.Y. Times, 1945-55; with U.S. Fgn. Service, Munich, 1950-52, Bern, 1952-56, Bonn, 1956-64; London music critic Internat. Herald Tribune (Paris), 1967—; London editor Stereo Review, (N.Y.C.), 1967—; lectr. in field; appearances on T.V., U.K., U.S.A., Europe. Served in U.S. Army, 1942-50, Alaska, ETO, NATOUSA. Decorated Bronze Star (twice). Mem. Authors Guild. Author: The Agony of Modern Music, 1955, Death of a Music; 1961, The Great Singers, 1966, Serious Music-And All That Jazz!, 1969, The Great American Popular Singers, 1974; translator, editor various books in field; contbr. articles to musical, lit. jours. Home: 95 Roebuck House Palace St London SW1E 5BE United Kingdom

PLEASANTS, SAMUEL AUGUSTUS, educator; b. Oakland, Calif., Sept. 26, 1918; s. Samuel Augustus and Fay (Crawford) P.; B.A., Columbia, 1940, M.A., 1941, Ph.D., 1947; m. Elsie Marie Walter, Sept. 22, 1947; children—Ellen, Elizabeth, Samuel. Faculty, Walter Hervey Jr. Coll., N.Y.C., 1946-52; faculty Fairleigh Dickinson U., Teaneck, N.J., 1952—, prof. history, 1963—, travel grantee to North Africa, Middle East, USSR, 1959. Served with USNR, 1942-45. Mem. Soc. Am. Historians, Am. Soc. Legal History, Delta Chi. Author: Fernando Wood of New York, 1947. The Declaration of Independence, 1967; The Bill of Rights, 1968; The Articles of Confederation, 1969. Home: 27 Linden Terr Leonia NJ 07605 Office: Fairleigh Dickinson U Teaneck NJ 07666

PLEASENCE, DONALD, actor; b. Workshop, Eng., Oct. 5, 1919; s. Thomas Stanley and Alice (Armitage) P.; m. Miriam Raymond (div.); children—Angela Daphne, Jean Denise; m. 2d, Josephine Martin Crombie; children—Lucy Maria, Polly Jo, Alexis Helena; m. 3d, Meira Shore; 1 dau., Miranda. Made 1st appearance on stage in Wuthering Heights at Playhouse, Jersey, Eng., 1939, 1st London appearance in Twelfth Night; actor on London stage in Vicious Circle, Saint's Day, Hobson's Choice, The Rules of the Game, The Lark, Ebb Tide (his own play), The Caretaker, The Man in the Glass Booth, Wise Child, The Basement, Tea Party, Wise Child; motion picture actor, 1953—, films include Manuela, 1957, The Man in the Sky, Heart of a Child, 1958, Tale of Two Cities, 1958, The Shakedown, 1959, Battle of the Sexes, 1959, Hell Is a City, 1960, The Flesh and the Fiends, 1960, The Horsemaster, Spare the Rod, 1961, No Love for Johnnie, 1961, The Hallelujah Trail, 1965, Cul-de-Sac, 1966, Fantastic Voyage, 1966, Matchless, 1966, Night of Generals, 1967, You Only Live Twice, 1967, Will Penny, 1968, Soldier Blue, 1970, Cutback, 1971, THX 1138, 1971, The Jersusalem File, 1972, The Pied Piper, 1972, Henry VIII and His Six Wives, 1972, Goldenrod, Arthur! Arthur, Wedding in White, 1973, Innocent Bystanders, 1973, Death Line, The Rainbow Boys, The Black Windmill, 1974, Journey into Fear, Escape to Witch Mountain, 1975, Hearts of the West, 1975, The Devil within Her, 1975, Passover Plot, 1976, The Last Tycoon, 1976, Trial by Combat, The Eagle Has Landed, 1977; TV appearances include Fate and Mr. Browne, Small Fish and Sweet, The Silk Purse, A House of His Own, The Traitor, The Millionaires, The Cupboard Machinal, The Count of Monte Cristo, 1975, The Hatchet Man, The Bandstand, Ambrose, Thou Good and Faithful Servant, Call Me Daddy, Taste, The Fox Trot, Omnibus, Julius Caesar, Occupations, The Joke, The Cafeteria, The French Atlantic Affair, 1979, Colombo, Centennial, The Bastard, Mrs. Colombo, others. Served with RAF, 1942-46. Named Stage Actor of Yr., London Variety, 1968. Address: care Film Artists Assos 5730 Sunset Blvd Hollywood CA 90028

PLEASURE, HYMAN, physician, state ofcl.; b. N.Y.C., Mar. 31, 1908; s. Joseph and Goldie (Heimowitz) P.; B.S. summa cum laude, N.Y. U., 1931, M.D., 1935; m. Edith Schlank, Nov. 25, 1932; children—David E., Robert J., Judith G. Intern, Cumberland Hosp., Bklyn., 1935-37; asst. physician Dannemora (N.Y.) State Hosp., 1937-41, clin. dir., 1948-49; supervising psychiatrist Central Islip (N.Y.) State Hosp., 1941-48; postgrad. in psychiatry and neurology N.Y. Med. Coll., 1943-45, Mt. Sinai Hosp., N.Y.C., 1945-46, Columbia Postgrad. Med. Coll. Psychiat. Inst., 1946; asst. dir. Pilgrim State Hosp., Brentwood, N.Y., 1949-55; dir. Middletown (N.Y.) State Hosp., 1955-66; dep. commr. N.Y. State Dept. Mental Hygiene, 1966-71; dir. Rockland State Hosp., Orangeburg, N.Y., 1971-77; asso. clin. prof. psychiatry N.Y. Med. Coll., 1974-76, clin. prof., 1976—. Cons. psychiatrist New Hampton State Tng. Sch., 1958-59, Eastern Correctional Inst., Naponoch, N.Y., 1959-61; med. dir. epilepsy project N.Y. State Correction Dept., 1961-63; mem. Rockland County Mental Health Bd., 1971-76; cons. in psychiatry N.Y. Dept. Mental Hygiene, 1977—. Bd. dirs. Am. Lung Assn. Lower Hudson Valley, Richmond Fellowship Am. Diplomate Am. Bd. Psychiatry and Neurology. Life fellow Am. Psychiat. Assn. (past pres. West Hudson Dist. br.); mem. N.Y. State, Rockland County med. socs., Am. Assn. Mental Hosp. Supts., Phi Beta Kappa. Contbr. articles to med. jours. Address: 8 Fern Oval East Orangeburg NY 10962

PLEDGER, THOMAS, constrn. co. exec.; b. Piedmont, Ala., Jan. 13, 1938; s. John Edward and Mary Susan (Wright) P.; student Auburn U., 1955-56, U.S. Armed Forces Inst., 1956-58; ed. U. Ala., 1958-59, Pensacola Jr. Coll., 1959-62; m. Phyllis Rounell Reeves, Oct. 23, 1959; children—Susanne Sheree, Thomas Rolon. With Burnup & Sims, West Palm Beach, Fla., 1960-76, v.p., asst. dir. overseas operations, 1967-68, v.p., 1968-69, exec. v.p., 1969-70, pres., gen. mgr., 1970-76, also chief exec. officer, dir., until 1976; chmn. bd., chief exec. officer Rubin Constrn. Co., West Palm Beach, 1976—; dir. Flagship Banks, Inc. Adv. bd. Boys Club of Palm Beach County, Inc., Stetson U. Sch. Bus., Goodwill Industries; bd. dirs. Fla. Council of 100. Served with USNR, 1956-59. Republican. Southern Baptist. Mason (32 deg.). Clubs: Lost Tree Village Country, Mayacoo Country, Sailfish of Fla. Home: 11265 Old Harbour Rd North Palm Beach FL 33408 Office: Southern Blvd at Rubin Rd West Palm Beach FL 33411

PLEISSNER, OGDEN MINTON, artist; b. Bklyn., 1905; s. George Bradford and Christine (Minton) P.; student Bklyn. Friends Sch., Art Students League (N.Y.C.); m. Marion Williams Gould, Mar. 9, 1977. Represented by paintings in Met. Mus. (N.Y.C.), Bklyn. Mus., Mpls. Mus., Swope Gallery (Terre Haute, Ind.), Canajoharie Art Gallery, New Britain (Conn.) Art Gallery, Toledo Art Ins., U. Idaho, U. Nebr., N.Y. Public Library, War Dept. Collection, Phila. Mus., U. Ga., N.A.D., I.B.M. Collection, Chrysler Collection War Art, Library of Congress, Sarasota (Fla.) Art Mus., Norton Gallery, Palm Beach, Fla., Mus. Fine Arts, St. Petersburg, Fla., Am. Embassy London, Phoenix Art Mus., Fitchburg (Mass.) Art Mus., Columbus (Ohio) Gallery Fine Arts, in colls. and univs., and many municipal museums and galleries throughout U.S. Mem. art commn. Nat. Collection of Fine Arts; v.p. Louis C. Tiffany Found.; trustee Shelburne Mus., Vt. Served as capt. with USAAF. Recipient Hallgarten prize N.A.D., 1938, Altman prize, 1952, 61; bronze and gold medals Allied Artists, Chandler prize, 1951, Gold medal, 1969, Emily Lowe award, 1970, Meml. prize, 1974; John Singer Sargent prize St. Botolph Club, 1942; Audubon award

Audubon Artists, 1945, Klein award, 1947, medal of honor, 1950, Grumbacher prize, 1955, Pres.'s prize; medal of honor Concord Art Assn., 1953; medal Nat. Arts Club, 1953, 60, Silver medal in watercolor, 1970, Gold medal of honor, 1972, 1st prize, 1973; Saportas prize Am. Watercolor Soc., 1961, Bronze medal honor, 1973, Herb Olsen award, 1975, High Winds award, 1978; Joseph Pennell medal Phila. Water Color Club, 1954; Howard Penrose prize, Gedney Bunce prize Conn. Acad. Fine Arts, 1955; gold medal, silver medal, gold medal and $1,000 for Water Color of Year, 1956; gold medal of honor, Hudson Valley Art Assn., 1956; medal of honor Century Assn., 1960, Popular prize, 1965; gold medal Nat. Arts Club, 1963, Gold medal Painting, 1972, Best in Show Watercolor, 1973, First prize, 1976; Watercolor prize Salmagundi Club, 1965, Macowin Tuttle prize, 1976, Ellis fellowship prize, 1975; Frank V. DuMond prize Hudson Valley Art Assn.; medal for watercolor Nat. Arts Club, 1969, D'Arches award, 1969, 70, Bronze medal, 1971, Gold medal Knickerbocker Artists, 1974, Dale Meyers prize, 1977; award Mex. Inst. Art, 1979; Nat. academician. Mem. N.A.D. (v.p., Morse medal of honor 1959), Phila. Water Color Club, Am. Water Color Soc. (hon.), Allied Artists Am., Balt. Water Color Club, Audubon Artists Am., So. Vt. Artists, Nat. Arts Club, Art Students' League (life), Conn. Acad. Fine Arts (hon.), Royal Soc. Art (London). Clubs: Century Assn., Salmagundi (N.Y.C.); Equanok (Manchester, Vt.). Address: Box 513 Manchester VT 05254

PLENTY, ROYAL HOMER, editor, writer; b. Phila., Aug. 28, 1918; s. Royal Homer and Florence (Gehman) P.; B.S. in Econs., U. Pa., 1941; m. Evelyn Treaster, Dec. 15, 1945 (dec. 1958); 1 dau., Evelyn Ann; m. 2d, Mildred Craig, Sept. 12, 1959 (div. 1970); m. 3d, Gladys Ann Muller, Nov. 14, 1970. Clk., H.M. Byllesby & Co., investment bankers, 1941; jr. underwriter New Amsterdam Casualty Co., 1941-42; reporter Phila. office Wall St. Jour., 1942-46; mem. staff Phila. Inquirer, 1946-72, financial editor, 1957-72; dir. pub. relations Levitz Furniture Corp., 1972-73; pub. relations account exec. Aitkin-Kynett Co., Inc., Phila., 1973-75; dir. pub. info. Securities Industry Assn., N.Y.C., 1975-77; corporate relations Merrill Lynch & Co., 1977-78; free-lance editor, writer, 1978—. Mem. Phila. Econ. Assn., Phila. Press Assn., Nat. Investor Relations Inst., Phila. Investment Traders Assn., Sigma Delta Chi. Unitarian (treas. 1958-65). Home: Harrison Towers Somerset NJ 08873

PLESENT, STANLEY, lawyer; b. N.Y.C., Nov. 4, 1925; s. Lester and Kate (Titefsky) P.; B.S.S., Coll. City N.Y., 1948; LL.B., M. Internat. Affairs, Columbia, 1952; m. Gloria Guberman, Jan. 30, 1949; children—Leslie, Nora, Mark, John. Admitted to N.Y. bar, 1953; with firm Paul, Weiss, Rifkind, Wharton & Garrison, N.Y.C., 1952-54; asst. counsel Young & Rubicam, Inc., advt., 1954-61; gen. counsel, congl. liaison USIA, 1961-65; partner firm Squadron & Plesent, N.Y.C., 1966-70, Squadron, Ellenoff, Plesent & Lehrer, 1971—. TV panelist, 1958-59. Chmn. bd. trustees Alvin Ailey Dance theater Found. Served with AUS, 1943-46; ETO. Decorated Silver Star, Bronze Star, Purple Heart; recipient Legacy award Anti-Defamation League, 1964. Mem. Bar Assn. N.Y.C. (Fed. legislation com., matrimonial law com.), Fed. Bar Assn. (gov. council 1964-65), Am. Soc. Internat. Law, Am. Arbitration Assn. (panelist). Democrat. Jewish. Mem. B'nai B'rith (v.p. Jackson Heights chpt. 1958-60). Home: 6 Walnut Ave Larchmont NY 10538 Office: 551 Fifth Ave New York City NY 10017

PLESHETTE, EUGENE, TV prodn. and mktg. co. exec.; b. Bklyn., Jan. 7, 1914; s. Maximillian and Gertrude (Sklarew) P.; B.S., Coll. City N.Y., 1933; m. Geraldine Kaplan, Oct. 29, 1934; 1 dau., Suzanne. Producer off Broadway prodns., 1932-34; v.p. Reid-Singer Music Pub. Co., 1934; exec. v.p. Lucky Record Co., 1934-36; treas. N.Y. Paramount Theatre, 1936-42, mgr., 1942-46; exec. mgr. Bklyn. Paramount Theatre, 1946-52, mng. dir., 1952-62; v.p. merchandising ABC, 1962-63, Am. Broadcasting-Paramount Theatres, Inc., 1963—; exec. v.p. MSG-ABC Productions, Inc., 1965—; exec. v.p. Don Reid TV Prodns.; pres. Pleshette Assos., Beverly Hills, Calif., 1975—. Chmn. bd. dirs. Knights Before Christmas; bd. dirs. precinct coordinating council N.Y.C. Police Dept. Youth Program, Navy Yard Boys Club, Bklyn. Center Psychotherapy; adv. com. youth fund Am. Guild Variety Artists. Recipient awards from Nat. Council Combat Blindness, Treasury Dept., Anglo-Jewish Publs., A.R.C., Boy Scouts Am., United Cerebral Palsy, Nat. Found. Muscular Dystrophy, Assn. Nat. Tb, NCCJ, Motion Picture Herald. Home: 9908 1/2 Durant Dr Beverly Hills CA 90212 Office: 9489 Dayton Way Beverly Hills CA 90210

PLESHETTE, SUZANNE, actress; b. N.Y.C., Jan. 31; d. Eugene Pleshette and Geraldine Pleshette (Rivers); student Syracuse (N.Y.) U., Finch Coll., N.Y.C.; m. Thomas Joseph Gallagher, III, Mar. 16, 1968. Star in Broadway prodns. Compulsion, Cold Wind and The Warm, The Golden Fleecing, Two for the Sea-Saw, The Miracle Worker; star numerous TV prodns. latest being Bob Newhart Show, 1972-78; star 30 feature films; TV movie Flesh and Blood, 1979, If Things Were Different, 1979.

PLESKOW, ERIC, motion picture co. exec.; b. Vienna, Austria. Film officer U.S. War Dept., 1946-48; asst. gen. mgr. Motion Picture Export Assn., Germany, 1948-50; continental rep. for Sol Lesser Prodns., 1950-51; with United Artists Corp., 1951—, Far Eastern sales mgr., 1951-52, South African mgr., 1952-53, German sales mgr., 1953-58, exec. asst. to continental mgr., 1958-59, asst. continental mgr., 1959-60, continental mgr., 1960-62, v.p. in charge fgn. distbn., 1962, exec. v.p., chief operating officer, 1973, pres., chief exec. officer, 1973-78; pres., chief exec. officer Orion Pictures Co., N.Y.C., 1978—. Office: 75 Rockefeller Plaza New York NY 10019

PLETCHER, DAVID MITCHELL, historian; b. Faribault, Minn., June 14, 1920; s. Nuba Mitchel and Jean (Hutchinson) P.; B.A., U. Chgo., 1941, M.A., Ph.D., 1946. Asst., U. Chgo., 1943; instr. history U. Iowa, 1944-46; asso. prof. Knox Coll., Galesburg, Ill., 1946-56; asso. prof., then prof. Hamline U., St. Paul, 1956-65; prof. history Ind. U., 1965—. Recipient McKnight Found. award, 1962; grantee Social Sci. Research Found., 1950-51, 62-63, Nat. Archives, 1972; Fulbright sr. research fellow, 1953-54. Mem. Am. Hist. Assn. (Albert J. Beveridge award 1957), Soc. Historians Am. Fgn. Relations (v.p. 1979). Author: Rails, Mines and Progress, Seven American Promoters in Mexico, 1867-1911, 1958, The Awkward Years, American Foreign Relations Under Garfield and Arthur, 1962, The Diplomacy of Annexation, Texas, Oregon and the Mexican War, 1973. Home: 509 N Fess Ave Bloomington IN 47401 Office: Dept History Ballantine Hall Ind Univ Bloomington IN 47401

PLETCHER, ELDON, editorial cartoonist; b. Goshen, Ind., Sept. 10, 1922; s. Arthur and Dora (Cripe) P.; student Chgo. Acad. Fine Arts, 1941-42, U. Aberdeen (Scotland), 1945, John Herron Art Sch., Indpls., 1946-47; m. Barbara Jeanne Jones, Jan. 29, 1948; children—Thomas Lee, Ellen Irene. Editorial cartoonist Sioux City (Iowa) Jour., 1949-66, New Orleans Times-Picayune, 1966—; editorial cartoon and panel cartoon First the Good News distributed by Rothco Cartoons Inc.; rep. permanent exhbns. Syracuse U., U. South Miss., U. Cin., Boston Mus. Art, Harry S. Truman Library, Lyndon B. Johnson Library, Wichita State U. Served with AUS, 1943-46. Recipient Christopher award, 1955, Freedoms Found. award, 12 years. Mem. Assn. Am. Editorial Cartoonists. Democrat. Presbyterian. Home: 331 Tiffany St Slidell LA 70458 Office: 3800 Howard Ave New Orleans LA 70140

PLETSCH, GEORGE BURGESS, lawyer; b. Tonica, Ill., June 24, 1921; s. Ernest Phillip and Grace (Burgess) P.; A.B., U. Chgo., 1942, J.D., 1944; m. Joan E. Hammerschmidt, Feb. 16, 1946; children—George William, James Burgess. Admitted to Ill. bar, 1943, D.C. bar, 1977, U.S. Supreme Ct., 1958; asso. Pam, Hurd & Reichmann (now Schiff Hardin & Waite), Chgo., 1943-51, partner, 1952—; dir. Groman Corp., Hamler Industries, Inc., Head, Inc., Hartmann-Sanders Co., Inca Plastics, Inc., Michael-Leonard, Inc., Planmetrics, Inc., Porcelain Products Co., Pub. Communications Inc., United Steel Service, Inc., Tonica State Bank. Trustee Millikin U., chmn., 1975-78; trustee, exec. com., sec., gen. counsel Ill. Inst. Tech.; trustee, exec. com., sec., gen. councel IIT Research Inst.; trustee Asso. Colls. Ill. Mem. Am., Fed. Energy, Ill., Chgo. bar assns., Law Club Chgo., Legal Club Chgo. Clubs: Mid-Am., Union League, Metropolitan (Chgo.). Home: 826 S Western Ave Park Ridge IL 60068 Office: 7200 Sears Tower Chicago IL 60606 also 1101 Connecticut Ave NW Washington DC 20036

PLETZ, FRANCIS GREGORY, banker; b. Lakefield, Minn., Aug. 23, 1917; s. John F. and Anna (Pietsch) P.; A.B. summa cum laude, Coll. St. Thomas, St. Paul, 1940; M.B.A. with distinction (Arthur Andersen accounting fellow), U. Mich., 1942; J.D. magna cum laude, U. Toledo, 1950; grad. Stonier Sch. Banking, Rutgers U., 1956; m. Virginia E. Connell, Sept. 12, 1942 (dec. 1977); children—Thomas G., John F.; m. 2d, Florence B. Haynes, Sept. 29, 1978. Teller, First Nat. Bank, Lakefield, 1937-38; research asst. Bur. Bus. Research, U. Mich., 1940-41; accountant Ernst & Ernst, Detroit, summer 1941; with Toledo Trust Co., 1946—, sr. v.p., head trust dept., 1968—, sec., 1973—; admitted to Ohio bar, 1950; former dir. Alloy Founders, Inc., Mather Co. Trustee Toledo Soc. for Blind, Stranahan Charitable Found., St. Vincent Hosp. Served to lt. USNR, 1942-46; ETO. Mem. Ohio, Lucas County, Toledo bar assns., Toledo C. of C. Lion. Clubs: Toledo, Sylvania Country (Toledo). Home: 3605 Orchard Trail Toledo OH 43606 Office: 245 Summit St Toledo OH 43603

PLEWS, GEORGE MONTAGUE, publishing cons.; b. Montreal, Que., Can., July 9, 1910; s. William John and Aileen Gertrude (McAdoo) P.; came to U.S., 1916, naturalized, 1942; student pvt. schs.; m. Jean Elizabeth McCorkell, Jan. 9, 1946; children—Elizabeth Aileen (Mrs. Robert Reinhart), Barbara Jean (Mrs. Malcolm Clay), George McCorkell, Margaret Lougheed. With Plews Processes Lab., Hoboken, N.J., 1932-33; prodn. mgr. Plews Puffed Products, Niagara Falls, N.Y., 1934-36; food prodn. devel., lab. technician, sales Plews Processes, subs. Quaker Oats Co., 1936-40, Ferguson Assos., 1940-54; pres. J.G. Ferguson Pub. Co., Chgo., 1954-75; pres., dir. Career Guidance Assos., Charlotte, N.C., 1974-75; cons., 1975—. Mem. Bd. Edn. Crystal Lake (Ill.) Dist. 47, 1952-55. Served to capt. U.S. Army, 1943-46. Decorated Soldiers medal, Silver Star, Bronze Star. Congregational (deacon 1960, mem. fin. com. 1974—, trustee 1979—). Club: Racket (dir.) (Crystal Lake). Home: 1936 South Shore Dr Crystal Lake IL 60014 Office: 111 E Wacker Dr Chicago IL 60601

PLEXICO, PHILIP SPRATT, lawyer, investment banking co. exec.; b. Toledo, June 15, 1931; s. Robert S. and Marian L. (Jefferson) P.; A.B., Princeton U., 1953; LL.B., Harvard U., 1958; children—Robert B., Duncan B. Admitted to N.Y. bar, 1959; asso. firm Breed, Abbott & Morgan, N.Y.C., 1958-69; sr. v.p., sec., gen. counsel Blyth Eastman Dillon & Co. Inc., N.Y.C., 1969—. Served to 1st lt. F.A., U.S. Army, 1953-55. Mem. N.Y. State Bar Assn., Fed. Bar Assn. So. Dist. N.Y. Republican. Clubs: Quaker Hill Country (Pawling, N.Y.); Wall St; Princeton (N.Y.C.). Home: Leach Hollow Rd Sherman CT 06784 Office: Blyth Eastman Dillon & Co Inc 1221 Ave of Americas New York NY 10020

PLIMPTON, CALVIN HASTINGS, physician; b. Boston, Oct. 7, 1918; s. George Arthur and Fanny (Hastings) P.; B.A. cum laude, Amherst Coll., 1939; M.D. cum laude, Harvard, 1943, M.A., 1947; Med. Sci.D., Columbia, 1951; LL.D., Williams Coll., 1960, Wesleyan U., 1961, Doshisha U., Kyoto, Japan, 1962, St. Lawrence U., 1963, Amherst U., 1971; L.H.D., U. Mass., 1962; D.Sc., Rockford Coll., 1962, St. Mary's, 1963, Trinity Coll., 1966, Grinnell (Iowa) Coll., 1967; Litt.D., Am. Internat. Coll., 1965, Mich. State Coll., 1969; m. Ruth Talbot, Sept. 6, 1941; children—David, Thomas, George (dec.), Anne, Edward. Intern, asst. resident, resident medicine Presbyn. Hosp., N.Y.C., 1947-50; asst. attending physician Columbia-Presbyn. Med. Center, 1950-60; asso. medicine Coll. Phys. and Surg., 1950-59, asst. prof. clin. medicine, 1959-60; prof. medicine, chmn. dept. Am. U. Beirut, Am. U. Hosp., Beirut, Lebanon, 1957-59; pres. Amherst Coll., 1960-71; pres. Downstate Med. Center, State U. N.Y., 1971-79, dean med. sch., 1971-74, 76-79, prof. medicine, 1971—; vis. prof. Columbia Presbyn. Med. Center, 1976-77; dir. Bankers Trust Co. Trustee Am. U., Beirut, 1960—, World Peace Found., 1962-77, Phillips Exeter Acad., 1963-76, Commonwealth Fund, 1962—, Hampshire Coll., 1963-71, U. Mass., 1962-70, L.I. U., 1972—, N.Y. Law Sch., 1976—; bd. overseers Harvard, 1969-75. Served from 1st lt. to capt. U.S. Army, 1944-46. Decorated comdr. Order of Cedars (Lebanon); recipient award Nat. Geog. Soc., award New Eng. Soc. Diplomate Nat. Bd. Med. Examiners, Am. Bd. Internal Medicine. Fellow A.C.P.; mem. Soc. Mayflower Descs., Harvey Soc., Am. Acad. Arts and Scis., Council Fgn. Relations, Alpha Omega Alpha, Sigma Xi. Clubs: Century, Grolier, Charaka, Riverdale Yacht, Pilgrims, University, Coffee House (N.Y.C.); Tavern Boston: Address: Downstate Med Center 450 Clarkson Ave Brooklyn NY 11203

PLIMPTON, FRANCIS T.P., lawyer, diplomat; b. N.Y.C., Dec. 7, 1900; s. George Arthur and Frances Taylor (Pearsons) P.; grad. Phillips Exeter Acad., 1917; A.B. magna cum laude, Amherst Coll., 1922; J.D., Harvard, 1925; LL.D., Colby Coll., 1960, Lake Forest Coll., 1964, N.Y. U., 1970, Yale U., 1972, Vt. Law Sch., 1979; L.H.D., Pratt Inst., 1967, Adelphi U., 1972, Amherst Coll., 1973; m. Pauline Ames, June 4, 1926; children—George Ames, Francis T.P., Oakes Ames, Sarah Gay. Admitted to bar, 1926; asso. with Root, Clark, Buckner & Ballantine, N.Y.C., 1925-32, in charge of Paris office, 1930-31; gen. solicitor RFC, Washington, 1932-33; partner Debevoise, Plimpton, Lyons & Gates, and predecessor firms, 1933-61, 1965—; ambassador, dep. U.S. rep. to UN, 1961-65, mem. U.S. delegations 15th-19th gen. assemblies, mem. UN adminstrv. tribunal, 1st v.p.; mem. State Dept. Adv. Com. on Internat. Orgns., 1965-69; trustee (now hon.) U.S. Trust Co. of N.Y., Met. Mus. Art; trustee Bowery Savings Bank, 1948-75, Teachers Ins. and Annuity Assn. (TIAA), 1946-68, trustee TIAA stock; mem. Coll. Retirement Equity Fund, 1949-75, pres., 1951-75; chmn. N.Y.C. Mayor's Commn. for Distinguished Guests, N.Y.C. Bd. Ethics; trustee emeritus Amherst Coll.; trustee (now adv.) St. Luke's-Roosevelt Hosp.; dir. emeritus Union Theol. Sem.; trustee Barnard Coll., Athens (Greece) Coll., Lingnan U. (China); dir. Adlai Stevenson Inst. Internat. Affairs, 1965-76, Center for Law and Social Policy, Am.-Italy Soc., N.Y. Lawyers for Pub. Interest; dir. French Inst.-Fedn. French Alliances, former pres.; trustee Phillips Exeter Acad., 1935-65, pres. or chmn. bd., 1956-65; overseer Harvard, 1963-69; dir. Philharmonic-Symphony Soc. N.Y., Theodore Roosevelt Assn., U.N. Assn. U.S.A. Decorated chevalier Legion of Honor (France); comdr. Order of Merit (Italy); asso. knight Order of St. John of Jerusalem; recipient Distinguished Pub. Service awards New Eng. Soc. N.Y., 1963, Fed. Bar Council, 1964, St. Nicholas Soc., 1974, Inst. Man and Sci., 1975; Bronze medal N.Y.C., 1975; Gold medal N.Y. State Bar Assn., 1977; Barnard Coll. medal of distinction 1979. Fellow Am. Acad. Arts and Scis., Am. Bar Found.; Benjamin Franklin fellow Royal Soc. Arts; mem. Am. (mem. ho. of dels.), N.Y. State, Internat., Inter-Am. bar assns., Am. Law Inst., Bar Assn. City N.Y. (pres. 1968-70), Union Internat. des Avocats (hon. v.p.), Washington Inst. Fgn. Affairs, Am. Soc. Internat. Law, Internat. Law Assn., Fgn. Policy Assn. (dir. 1935-49), Council Fgn. Relations, Acad. Polit. Sci., Exec. Council Diplomats (hon. dir.), Pilgrims, Soc. Mayflower Descs., Colonial Soc. Mass., Phi Beta Kappa, Delta Kappa Epsilon, Delta Sigma Rho. Presbyterian. Clubs: Union, Century, Brook, River, Down Town, Grolier, Coffee House, Economic (N.Y.C.); Piping Rock, Cold Spring Harbor Beach (L.I.); Metropolitan (Washington); Ausable (Adirondacks); Mill Reef (Antigua, W.I.). Contbg. author: As We Knew Adlai; also mag. articles. Home: 131 E 66th St New York NY 10021 also 168 Chichester Rd West Hills Huntington NY 11743 Office: 299 Park Ave New York NY 10017

PLIMPTON, GEORGE AMES, author, editor; b. N.Y.C., Mar. 18, 1927; s. Francis T.P. and Pauline (Ames) P.; student Phillips Exeter Acad., 1944; A.B., Harvard, 1948; M.A., Cambridge (Eng.) U., 1950; L.H.D., Franklin Pierce Coll., 1968; Litt.D. (hon.), Hobart Smith Coll., 1978; m. Freddy Medora Espy, 1968; children—Medora Ames, Taylor Ames. Editor-in-chief Paris Review, 1953—, Paris Rev. Edits., subsidiary Doubleday and Co., 1965-72; instr. Barnard Coll., 1956-58; asso. editor Horizon mag., 1959-61; dir. Am. Lit. Anthology program, 1967—; asso. editor Harper's mag., 1972—; contbg. editor Food and Wine Mag., 1978; editorial adv. bd. Realities, 1978; spl. contbr. Sports Illustrated, 1968—. Commr. fireworks N.Y.C., 1973. Trustee WNET, 1973—, Nat. Art Mus. Sport, 1967—, Police Athletic League, 1976—; bd. dirs. Dynamite Mus., Nat. Tennis Found., 1979, N.Y. Philomusica. Served to 2d lt. AUS, 1945-48. Asso. fellow Trumbull Coll., Yale, 1967; recipient Distinguished Achievement award U. So. Cal., 1967. Mem. NFL Alumni Assn. Clubs: Century Assn., Racquet and Tennis; Brook; Piping Rock; Dutch Treat; Coffee House; Devon Yacht; Travellers (Paris). Author: Rabbit's Umbrella, 1956; Out of My League, 1961; Paper Lion, 1966; The Bogey Man, 1968; Mad Ducks and Bears, 1973; One for the Record, 1974; Shadow-Box, 1976; One More July, 1976; (with Neil Leiffer) Sports!, 1978; also numerous articles. Editor: Writers at Work, Vol. 1, 1957, Vol. 11, 1963, Vol. 111, 1967, Vol. IV, 1976; American Journey: The Times of Robert Kennedy, 1970; Pierre's Book, 1971; The Fancy, 1973. Address: 541 E 72d St New York NY 10021

PLISCHKE, ELMER, educator, polit. scientist; b. Milw., July 15, 1914; s. Louis and Louise (Peterleus) P.; Ph.B. cum laude, Marquette U., 1937; M.A., Am. U., 1938; certificate Carnegie summer session internat. law, U. Mich., 1938; Ph.D. (fellow), Clark U., 1943; certificate Naval Sch. Mil. Govt. and Civil Affairs, Columbia, 1944; m. Audrey Alice Siehr, May 30, 1941; children—Lowell Robert, Julianne. Instr., Springfield Coll., 1940; dist. supr., state dir. Wis. Hist. Records Survey, 1940-42; exec. sec. War Records Commn., Wis. Council Def., 1942; asst. prof. DePauw U., 1946-48; asst. prof. U. Md., 1948-49, asso. prof., 1949-52, prof., 1952-79, prof. emeritus, 1979—, head dept. govt. and politics, 1954-68; adj. prof. Gettysburg (Pa.) Coll., 1979—; spl. historian Office U.S. High Commr. for Germany, 1950-52; cons. Dept. State, summer 1952; adj. scholar Am. Enterprise Inst. Pub. Policy Research, 1978—; lectr. Air War Coll., Armed Forces Staff Coll., Army War Coll., Def. Intelligence Sch., Indsl. Coll. Armed Forces, Inter-Am. Def. Coll., Nat. War Coll., Sr. Officers Seminar Fgn. Service Inst., Instituto de Altos Estudios Nacionales, Quito, Ecuador. Mem. adv. com. fgn. relations of U.S. Dept. State, 1967-72, chmn., 1969-70. Served from ensign to lt. USNR, 1943-46; exec. asst., then exec. officer Civil Affairs div., comdr. U.S. Naval Forces for Europe, London, 1944-45; charge de- Nazification policy coordination Office Dir. Polit. Affairs, Office Mil. Govt. for Germany, 1945. Recipient research awards U. Md. Gen. Research Bd., 1956, 58, 69; elected knight Mark Twain. Mem. Am. (council), D.C. (council, pres. 1961), So. (council) polit. sci. assns., Internat. Studies Assn., AAUP, Am. Soc. Internat. Law, Phi Beta Kappa, Phi Kappa Phi, Pi Sigma Alpha, Sigma Tau Delta. Author: Conduct of American Diplomacy, 3d edit., 1967, reissued, 1975; (with Robert G. Dixon, Jr.) American Government: Basic Documents and Materials, 1950, reissued, 1971; Berlin: Development of Its Government and Administration, 1952, reissued, 1970; The Allied High Commission for Germany, 1953; International Relations: Basic Documents, rev., 1962; American Foreign Relations: A Bibliography of Official Sources, 1955, reissued, 1966; American Diplomacy: A Bibliography of Biographies, Autobiographies and Commentaries, 1957; Summit Diplomacy: Personal Diplomacy of the President of the United States, 1958, reissued, 1974; Contemporary Governments of Germany, 1961, rev. edit., 1969; Government and Politics of Contemporary Berlin, 1963; Foreign Relations Decisionmaking: Options Analysis, 1973; United States Diplomats and Their Missions: A Profile of American Diplomatic Emissaries Since 1778, 1975; Microstates in World Affairs: Policy Problems and Options, 1977; Neutralization as an American Strategic Option, 1978; Modern Diplomacy: The Art and the Artisans, 1979; others. Contbr. articles to profl. jours., also Americana Ann., 1972-79. Editor, contbr. to Systems of Integrating the International Community, 1964; bd. editors Jour. Politics, 1966-68. Home: 227 Ewell Ave Gettysburg PA 17325 Office: Gettysburg Coll Gettysburg PA 17325

PLISKOFF, STANLEY STEWART, educator; b. N.Y.C., Jan. 24, 1930; s. Philip and Gertrude (Levy) P.; B.A., N.Y. U., 1951, M.A., 1953, Ph.D., 1956; m. Elizabeth M. Duff, June 14, 1957. From instr. to asso. prof. U. Md., 1957-58, 61-65; research psychologist Army Chem. Center, 1958-61; asso. prof. Ariz. State U., 1965-67; asso. dir. Inst. Behavioral Research, 1967-69; mem. faculty U. Maine, 1969—, chmn. dept. psychology, 1969-74. Served with AUS, 1955-57. Fellow AAAS; mem. Eastern Psychol. Assn., Psychonomic Soc. Editor Jour. Exptl. Analysis of Behavior, 1969-72. Contbr. articles profl. jours. Home: Chase Rd MRB Bangor ME 04401 Office: Univ Maine Orono ME 04473

PLITT, HENRY G., theatre chain exec.; b. N.Y.C., Nov. 26, 1918; s. Charles B. and Anna (Klein) P.; grad. Syracuse U., St. Lawrence U. Law Sch.; m. Edna Marie Sedgwick, Aug. 14, 1954; children—Edward M., Sam M., Sedgie M. Plitt Helpern. Admitted to N.Y. State bar; with ABC, 1946—, v.p. Paramount-Richards div. (later named ABC Mid-South Theatres, Inc.), New Orleans, 1951-55, pres. div., 1955-59, pres. ABC Films, Inc., N.Y.C., beginning 1955, pres. ABC Gt. States, Inc., Midwest motion picture theatre circuit, beginning 1966, left ABC, 1973; pres., chief exec. officer Plitt Theatres, Chgo., 1974—. Mem. exec. com. State St. Council, Chgo.; area chmn. amusement div. ann. Reach Out program, Chgo.; 1st chmn. Joseph Jefferson Awards Fellowship Chgo.; chmn. amusement div. Israel Bonds; bd. dirs. Will Rogers Meml. Hosp. Served to maj. Paratroops, U.S. Army, 1940-46; Normandy. Decorated Silver Star with oak leaf cluster, Bronze Star with oak leaf cluster, Purple Heart with 2 oak leaf clusters (U.S.); Croix de Guerre (France and Belgium); Order Dutch Lanyard; honoree Israel Bonds, 1969; named Exhibitor of Yr., Internat. Film Importers and Distbrs. Am., Inc., Motion Picture Pioneer of Yr., Found. Motion Picture Pioneers, 1979; recipient Will Rogers Meml. Hosp. statue, 1971. Mem. Nat. Assn. Theatre Owners, TV Acad. Arts and Scis., Nat. Assn. Broadcasters.

Clubs: Friars, Chgo. Press. Office: Plitt Theatres 175 N State St Chicago IL 60601

PLOESER, WALTER CHRISTIAN, bus. cons., former ambassador; b. St. Louis, Jan. 7, 1907; s. Christian D. and Maud Elizabeth (Parr) P.; student City Coll. of Law and Finance, St. Louis; LL.D. (hon.), Norwich U., 1948; Dr. hon. causa, Nat. U. Asuncion, Paraguay; m. Dorothy Annette Mohrig, Aug. 17, 1928; children—Ann (Mrs. Don Bergan), Sally (Mrs. William L. Chapel III). In ins. business, St. Louis, 1922—; founded firm Ploeser, Watts & Co. (now Alexander & Alexander), bus. cons., 1933; organized subsidiary Marine Underwriters Corp., 1935, former pres.; now dir. Webster Groves Trust Co.; founder Ins. Inst. Mo., 1938, pres., 1938-40; past pres. Grant, Ploeser & Assos., Inc., nat. and internat. pub. relations; U.S. ambassador to Republic of Paraguay, 1957-59, to Costa Rica, 1970-72. Mem. Mo. Legislature, 1931-32; chmn. 5th dist. com. finance and budget Rep. Nat. Program Com., 1937-39; mem. 77th-80th Congresses from 12th Mo. Dist.; mem. appropriations com., Rep. steering com., chmn. select com. on small business, chmn. subcom. on govt. corps.; mem. econ. adv. com. U.S. Senate com. on banking and currency, 1953-54; Rep. nat. committeeman for Mo., 1964-66. Former bd. dirs. St. Louis unit Shriners Hosp. for Crippled Children, Scottish Rite Found. Mo.; chmn. bd. Salvation Army St. Louis, 1967-70; mem. pres.'s council Sch. of Ozarks. Recipient Freedoms Found. award, 1949; decorated Grand Cross Republic of Paraguay, 1959. Mem. Miss. Valley Assn. (chmn. bd. 1956; pres.), DeMolay Legion of Honor, Ins. Bd. of St. Louis, St. Louis C. of C. (chmn. nat. affairs com. 1964-66). Mason (33 deg., Shriner; sovereign grand insp. gen. Mo. Scottish Rite); mem. Order of DeMolay (Supreme council exec., grand master internat. 1952). Clubs: Mo. Athletic, Triple A Golf and Tennis. Home: 275 Union Blvd Saint Louis MO 63108 Office: 3633 Lindell Blvd Saint Louis MO 63108

PLONSEY, ROBERT, elec. and biomed. engr., educator; b. N.Y.C., July 17, 1924; s. Louis B. and Betty (Vinograd) P.; B.E.E., Cooper Union, 1943; M.S. in Elec. Engring., N.Y. U., 1948; Ph.D., U. Calif. at Berkeley, 1955; postgrad. Med. Sch., Case Western Res. U., 1969-71; m. Vivian V. Vucker, Oct. 1, 1948; 1 son, Daniel. Asst. prof. elec. engring. U. Calif. at Berkeley, 1955-57; asst. prof. elec. engring. Case Inst. Tech., Cleve., 1957-60, asso. prof., 1960-66, prof., 1966-68, dir. bioengring. group, 1962-68; prof. biomed. engring. Sch. Engring. and Sch. of Medicine, Case Western Res. U., 1968—, chmn. dept., 1976—. Mem. biomed. fellowships rev. com. NIH, 1966-70, mem. tng. com. Engr. in Medicine and Biology, 1972-73, cons., 1974—; cons. NSF, 1973; mem. com. on electrocardiography Am. Heart Assn., 1976—. Vice pres. Your Schs., Cleveland Heights, Ohio, 1968-69, 73-75; provisional trustee Am. Bd. Clin. Engrs., 1973-74, pres., 1975, trustee, 1976—. Served with AUS, 1944-46. Registered profl. engr., Ohio. Fellow IEEE (chmn. Cleve. chpt. group on biomed. electronics 1962-63, chmn. publs. com. group on engring. in medicine and biology 1968-70; v.p. adminstrv. com. 1970-72, pres. 1973-74, chmn. fellows com. 1977-79; William S. Morlock award 1979); mem. Alliance for Engring. in Medicine and Biology (treas. 1976-78), Biophys. Soc., Biomed. Engring. Soc. (dir. 1975-78, 79—), AAUP, Am. Physiol. Soc., Am. Soc. Engring. Edn. (dir. biomed. engring. div. 1978—), AAAS. Author: (with R. Collin) Principles and Applications of Electromagnetic Fields, 1961; Bioelectric Phenomena, 1969. Mem. editorial bd. Trans. IEEE Biomed. Engring., 1965-70, asso. editor, 1977-79; editorial bd. T.I.T. Jour., 1971—, Electrocardiology Jour., 1974—; proc. editor Engring. in Medicine and Biology, 17th Ann. Conf., 1964; co-editor Biomed. Engring. Series. Home: 3055 Scarborough Rd Cleveland Heights OH 44118 Office: Case Western Res U 10900 Euclid Ave Cleveland OH 44106. *External recognition of success is not nearly so important as the inner awareness of coming to full grips with life, to be fully involved, bending all strengths to fulfill one's goals and philosophies. And of all involvements, those with people are most meaningful (to be aware of and share the feelings of colleagues, students, friends, and family—and to enrich these relationships)—and for me most difficult.*

PLONSKY, ANDREW W., elec. engr., educator; b. Harford, Pa., Dec. 19, 1912; s. Walter and Eleanore (Norek) P.; B.S., U. Scranton, 1940; B.S. in Elec. Engring., Mass. Inst. Tech., 1943, M.S., 1945; postgrad. Am. U., summer 1960, U. Mo., summer, 1961. Tex. A. and M. Coll., summer 1963, U. Calif. at Los Angeles, summer 1964; m. Dorothy Leslie, Feb. 23, 1941; children—Carl, Matthew, Kenneth. Elec. engr. N.Y., N.H. & H. R.R., 1945-47; prof. U. Scranton, Pa., 1947—; tech. editor Intext, 1950-57. Mem. Bldg. Code Com., Scranton, 1965-69. Registered profl. engr., Pa. Mem. IEEE, Math. Assn. Am., AAUP, Nat. Soc. Profl. Engrs. Author: Calculus for Engineers, 1968. Home: 620 Taylor Ave Scranton PA 18510

PLONUS, MARTIN ALGIRDAS, educator; b. Trumpininken, Lithuania, Dec. 21, 1933; s. Christopher and Anna (Sliupas) P.; came to U.S., 1949, naturalized, 1955; B.S., U. Ill., 1956, M.S., 1957; Ph.D., U. Mich., 1961; m. Martina Rauer, Feb. 20, 1965; children—Sabine, Jacqueline, Marcus, Michelle. Asst. prof. elec. engring., Northwestern U., Evanston, Ill., 1961-64, asso. prof., 1964-69, prof., 1969—; research mathematician U. Mich., summers, 1964, 65, 66. Dir. Nat. Electronics Corp., Inc., 1962-68. Nat. Champion Shields Sailboat class, 1974. NSF grantee, 1967, 75-77 OSRD grantee, 1964. Mem. Internat. Sci. Radio Union, IEEE (chmn. group antennas and propagation Chgo. sect. 1966-67, spl. recognition award 1971), AAUP, U. Mich. Research Club, Sigma Xi, Eta Kappa Nu, Sigma Tau, Tau Beta Pi. Asso. editor trans. IEEE, 1968-72. Author: Applied Electromagnetics, 1978. Contbr. articles profl. jours. Home: 9120 Austin Ave Morton Grove IL 60053

PLOTKIN, HARRY MORRIS, lawyer; b. Athol, Mass., May 18, 1913; s. Louis and Fannie (Coffman) P.; A.B. magna cum laude, Harvard, 1934, LL.B. magna cum laude, 1937; m. Esther Lipsez, Dec. 25, 1937; children—Ira L., Judith Deborah (Mrs. Jonathan Wilkenfeld). Admitted to Ill. bar, 1937, D.C. bar, 1951; asso. firm Topliff & Horween, Chgo., 1937-39; atty. FCC, 1940-51, asst. gen. counsel, 1943-51; partner firm Arnold, Fortas & Porter, Washington, 1951-56, Arent, Fox, Kintner, Plotkin & Kahn, and predecessor, Washington, 1956—; dir. Viacom Internat. Inc. Trustee, Washington United Jewish Appeal Fedn., also v.p. Mem. Fed., Fed. Communications, D.C., Am. bar assns., Phi Beta Kappa. Clubs: Harvard (Washington, N.Y.C.); Nat. Lawyers, Nat. Broadcasters (Washington). Home: 3719 Harrison St NW Washington DC 20015 Office: 1815 H St NW Washington DC 20006

PLOTKIN, MANUEL D., former govt. ofcl., economist; b. Chita, Russia, May 16, 1923; s. Jacob and Bella (Katz) P.; came to U.S., 1929, naturalized, 1938; B.S. with honors, Northwestern U., 1948; M.B.A., U. Chgo., 1949; m. Diane Fern Weiss, Dec. 17, 1967; 1 dau., Lori Ann. Price economist, survey coordinator U.S. Bur. Labor Statistics, Washington, 1949-51, Chgo., 1951-53; sr. economist Sears Roebuck & Co., Chgo., 1953-61, mgr. market research, 1961-66, chief economist, mgr. economic and market research, 1966-73, asso. dir. corporate planning and research, 1973-77; dir. U.S. Bur. Census, Washington, 1977-79; instr. statistics Ind. U., 1953-54; instr. economics Wilson Jr. Coll., Chgo., 1954-55; instr. quantitative methods and managerial economics Northwestern U., 1955-63; mem. conf. bd. Mktg. Research Adv. Council, 1968-77, chmn., 1977; chmn. adv. com. U.S. Census Bur., 1974-75; trustee Mktg. Sci. Inst., 1968-77; mem. Nat. Commn. Employment and Unemployment Stats., 1978-79, Adv. Council Edn. Stats., 1977-79, Interagy. Com. Population Research, 1977-79. Trustee, U.S. Travel Data Center, 1977-79. Served with AUS, 1943-46; ETO. Decorated Bronze Star medal with oak leaf cluster. Mem. Am. Mktg. Assn. (pres. Chgo. 1968-69, nat. dir. 1969-70, nat. v.p. mktg. research 1970-72), Am. Statis. Assn. (pres. Chgo. 1966-67, Forecasting award 1963), Am. Econ. Assn., Nat. Assn. Bus. Economists, Planning Execs. Inst., World Future Soc., Midwest Planning Assn., U. Ill. Businessmen Research Adv. Group, Chgo. Assn. Commerce and Industry, Beta Gamma Sigma, Alpha Sigma Lambda. Contbr. articles to profl. jours. Office: US Bureau Census Washington DC 20233

PLOTKIN, STANLEY ALAN, med. virologist; b. N.Y.C., May 12, 1932; s. Joseph and Lee (Fishbein) P.; B.A., N.Y. U., 1952; M.D., State U. N.Y., N.Y.C., 1956, M.A. (hon.), U. Pa., 1974; m. Susan Lannon, Nov. 24, 1979; children—Michael, Alec. Intern, Cleve. Met. Gen. Hosp., 1956-57; resident pediatrics Childrens Hosp., Phila., 1961-62; registrar Hosp. for Sick Children, London, 1962-63; asso. mem. Wistar Inst., Phila., 1963-74, prof., 1974—; dir. div. infectious diseases, sr. physician Childrens Hosp., Phila., 1969—; asst. prof. pediatrics U. Pa., 1966-71, asso. prof., 1971-74, prof., 1974—. Served as med. officer USPHS, 1957-60. Joseph P. Kennedy Found. grantee, 1964-66; Hartford Found. grantee, 1971-73; NIH grantee, 1973—. Diplomate Am. Bd. Pediatrics, Am. Acad. Pediatrics. Mem. Soc. Pediatric Research, Am. Pediatric Soc., Infectious Diseases Soc. Am., Am. Epidemiology Soc., Am. Soc. Microbiology. Asso. editor, Am. Jour. Epidemiology, 1967—. Pioneer vaccine strains for protection against polio, rubella and cytomegalovirus. Home: 3940 Delancey St Philadelphia PA 19104 Office: Childrens Hosp 34th and Civic Center Blvd Philadelphia PA 19104

PLOTNICK, HARVEY BARRY, pub. co. exec.; b. Detroit, Aug. 5, 1941; s. Isadore and Esther (Sher) P.; B.A., U. Chgo., 1963; m. Susan Regnery, Aug. 16, 1964 (div. Apr. 1977); children—Andrew, Alice. Editor, Contemporary Books, Inc., Chgo., 1964-66, pres., 1966—. Home: 305 W Fullerton Chicago IL 60614 Office: 180 N Michigan Ave Chicago IL 60601

PLOTNIK, ARTHUR, editor; b. White Plains, N.Y., Oct. 1, 1937; s. Michael and Annabelle (Taub) P.; B.A., State U. N.Y., Binghamton, 1960; M.A., U. Iowa, 1961; M.S. in L.S., Columbia U., 1966; m. Meta Von Borstel, Sept. 6, 1960 (div. 1979); children—Julia Nicole, Katya Michelle. Gen. reporter, reviewer Albany (N.Y.) Times Union, 1963-64; freelance writer, 1964-66; editor Librarians Office, Library of Congress, 1966-69; asso. editor Wilson Library Bull., Bronx, N.Y., 1969-74; editor-in-chief Am. Libraries, Chgo., 1975—; editorial devel. dir. ALA, Chgo., 1979—; speaker in field. Served with U.S. Army, 1962. Fellow Iowa Writers Workshop Creative Writing, 1961; recipient award Ednl. Press Assn. Am., 1973 (3), 77; certificate excellence Internat. Reading Assn., 1970. Mem. ALA. Author: Library Life-American Style: A Journalist's Field Report, 1975; also fiction, articles, photography. Home: 2014 N Kenmore Ave Chicago IL 60614 Office: 50 E Huron Ave Chicago IL 60611

PLOTT, CHARLES R., economist; b. Frederick, Okla., July 8, 1938; s. James Charles and Flossie Ann (Bowman) P.; B.S., Okla. State U., 1961, M.S., 1964; Ph.D., U. Va., 1965; m. Marianna Brown Cloninger, May 30, 1961; children—Rebecca Ann, Charles Hugh. Asst. prof. econs. Purdue U., 1965-68, asso. prof., 1968-70; vis. prof. econs. Stanford U., 1968-69; prof. econs. Calif. Inst. Tech., Pasadena, 1970—, dir. Program for Study of Enterprise and Public Policy, 1979—; vis. prof. law U. So. Calif. Law Center, 1976; vis. prof. U. Chgo., 1980; dir. Lee Pharms., Mobile Recreation Systems, Inc.; cons. Gen. Motors Corp., Analytical Assessments Corp., Polinomics Research Lab., FTC, CAB. Ford Found. fellow, 1968; NSF grantee, 1972, 74, 78, 79, 80. Mem. Am. Econ. Assn., So. Econ. Assn. (exec. com. 1978-79), Public Choice Soc. (pres. 1977-78), Royal Econ. Assn., Econometric Soc., Am. Polit. Sci. Assn. Author works in fields of econs., polit. sci., philosophy, exptl. methods, math. methods; contbr. articles to profl. jours. Bd. editors Social Sci. Research, 1976-77, Public Choice, 1973—. Home: 881 El Campo Dr Pasadena CA 91107 Office: Div Humanities and Social Scis Calif Inst Tech Pasadena CA 91125

PLOTZ, CHARLES MINDELL, physician; b. N.Y.C., Dec. 6, 1921; s. Isaac and Rose (Bluestone) P.; B.A., Columbia U., 1941, D.Sc., 1951; M.D., L.I. Coll. Medicine, 1944; m. Lucille Weckstein, Aug. 5, 1945; children—Richard, Thomas, Robert. Intern New Haven Hosp., 1944-45; resident internal medicine Kings County Hosp., 1945-46, Maimonides Hosp., 1948-49; postdoctoral research fellow USPHS, Columbia Coll. Phys. and Surgs., 1949-50; practice medicine, specializing in internal medicine, Bklyn., 1950—; chief Arthritis Clinic, attending physician Kings County Hosp. Center, 1950—; attending physician L.I. Coll. Hosp., chief Arthritis Clinic, 1950-65; asst. attending physician Mt. Sinai Hosp., 1955—, chief Arthritis Clinic, 1955-65; chief Arthritis Clinic, State U., Hosp., 1967—; asst. physician Columbia-Presbyn. Med. Center, 1949-71; attending physician Bklyn. State Hosp.; cons. physician Peninsula Gen. Hosp.; cons. rheumatology VA Hosp., Bklyn.; cons. family practice Lutheran Med. Center; vis. cons. internal medicine Jewish Gen. Hosp., Montreal, Que., Can., 1965; cons. internal medicine Avicenna Hosp. and Wazir Akbar Hosp., Kabul, Afghanistan, 1965; prof. medicine, dir. continuing edn., chmn. dept. family practice State U. N.Y. Downstate Med. Center. Mem. nat. bd. govs. Arthritis Found., 1964—, bd. govs. N.Y. chpt., 1965—, v.p., 1971—; trustee, 1977—, N.Y. chpt. sr. v.p., 1977—; trustee Leo N. Levi Meml. Nat. Arthritis Hosp., Alumni Fund-Alumni Assn. State U. N.Y. Downstate Med. Center, Bklyn. Inst. Arts and Scis.; trustee Bklyn. Botanic Garden; mem. adv. bd. MEDICO, corporate mem., 1977—. Served to capt. AUS, 1946-48. WHO fellow U. Negev, 1974. Diplomate Am. Bd. Internal Medicine. Fellow A.C.P., Am. Acad. Family Physicians (Charter), N.Y. Acad. Medicine (chmn. edn. com. 1976-78); mem. AMA, N.Y. State, Kings County med. socs., Am. Fedn. Clin. Research, Harvey Soc., N.Y. State, Bklyn. socs. internal medicine, AAUP, Am. (past sec.-treas.), N.Y. (past pres., exec. com.) rheumatism assns., Soc. Tchrs. Family Medicine, Am., N.Y. State acads. family physicians, Mystery Writers of Am., Soc. Urban Physicians, Sigma Xi, Alpha Omega Alpha. Editorial adv. bd. Am. Family Physician, Pakistan Med. Forum. Club: Heights Casino. Home: 184 Columbia Heights Brooklyn NY 11201 Office: 161 Marlborough Rd Brooklyn NY 11226 also 450 Clarkson Ave Brooklyn NY 11203

PLOURDE, GERARD, auto parts co. exec.; b. Joliette, Que., Can., Feb. 12, 1916; s. Louis-George and Rose de Lima (Jolicoeur) P.; B.A., Brébeuf Coll., 1936; M. Commerce, U. Montreal (Que.), 1939, D. Honoris Causa, 1973; m. Jeannine Martineau, Dec. 4, 1943; children—Monique, Pierre, Marc-André. Accountant, UAP Inc., Montreal, from 1941, pres., gen. mgr., 1951-70, chmn. bd., chief exec. officer, 1970—, mgr. subs. Internat. Electric Co. Ltd., 1945-51; v.p., dir. Toronto-Dominion Bank, Alliance Compagnie Mutuelle d'assurance-vie; dir. Bell Can., Gulf Oil Can. Ltd., No. Telecom Ltd., Rolland Paper Co. Ltd., Steinberg's, Ltd., Molson Cos. Ltd. Decorated Order of Can. Mem. Montreal Bd. Trade, Montreal C. of C., Soc. Automotive Engrs. Clubs: Laval-sur-le-Lac, Saint-Denis, Mount Bruno Country; Can. (N.Y.C.). Home: 6065 DeVimy St Montreal PQ H3S 2R2 Canada Office: 7025 Ontario St E Montreal PQ H1N 2B3 Canada

PLOURDE, J-AURELE, bishop; b. St. Francois, N.B., Can., Jan. 12, 1915; s. Antoine and Suzanne (Albert) P.; B.A., St. Joseph's U., Moncton, 1939; student Halifax Maj. Sem., 1939-44, Cath. Inst. Paris, 1947-48; Licentiate Social Scis., Ottawa U., 1948-50; L.M. in Theology, Gregorian U., Rome, 1960. Ordained priest Roman Cath. Ch., 1944; asst. St. Quentin, N.B., 1944-46; sec. to bishop Edmundston, N.B., 1946-47; prof. philosophy St. Louis Coll., Edmundston, 1950-55; pastor St. Leonard Parish, N.B., 1955-59; aux. bishop of Alexandria, 1964-67; archbishop Ottawa, 1967—. Address: 256 King Edward Ave Ottawa ON Canada

PLOWDEN, LORD EDWIN NOEL, corp. exec.; b. Strachur Argyll, Scotland, Jan. 7, 1907; s. Roger Herbert and Helen (Haseltine) P.; Degree in Econs., Pembroke Coll., Cambridge, Eng., 1929; D.Sc. (hon.), Pa. State U., 1958; D.Sc. (hon.), U. Aston, Birmingham, Eng., 1972; D.Litt. (hon.), Loughborough U. Tech., Eng., 1976; m. Bridget Richmond, June 20, 1933; children—William, Anna, Penelope, Francis. Temp. civil servant Ministry Econ. Warfare, 1939-40; with Ministry Aircraft Prodn., 1940-46, chief exec., mem. aircraft supply council, 1945-46; treasury chief planning officer, chmn. Econ. Planning Bd., 1947-53; vice chmn. temp. council com. NATO, 1951-52; chmn. U.K. Atomic Energy Authority, 1954-59; chmn. Tube Investments, Ltd., 1963-76, pres., 1976—; mem. Ford European Adv. Council; chmn. Equity Capital for Industry Ltd.; 1977—. Chmn. com. of enquiry Treasury Control of Pub. Expenditure, 1959-61, Orgn. Representational Services Overseas, 1963-64, Aircraft Industry, 1964-65, structure of electricity supply industry, 1974-75; chmn. standing advisory com. Pay of Higher Civil Services, 1968-70; chmn. Police Complaints Bd. dep. chmn. Com. Enquiry into Orgn. of Police; chmn. Police Negotiating Bd., 1979—. Hon. fellow Pembroke Coll., 1958; vis. fellow Nuffield Coll., Oxford, 1956-64. Hon. pres. London Grad. Sch. Bus. Studies, chmn. governing body, 1964-76. Decorated knight comdr. Brit. Empire; knight comdr. of Bath. Home: Marteis Manor Dunmow Essex England Office: Bridgewater House Cleveland Row St James's London SW1A 1DG England

PLOWMAN, BOYD REX, mfg. co. exec.; b. Logan, Utah, Aug. 2, 1943; s. Rex G. and Barbara (Wiser) P.; B.S. cum laude, Utah State U., 1965; m. Eldene Dahle, Sept. 21, 1964; children—Terri Lyn, Michael Boyd, Robert Neil, Kristen Rae. Asst. accountant semi-sr., then sr. accountant on audit and tax staffs Arthur Andersen & Co., Phoenix, 1965-67; tax sr. Ernst & Ernst, Salt Lake City, 1967-69; asst. controller, controller, treas., fin. v.p. Fleetwood Enterprises, Inc., Riverside, Calif., 1969—, now sr. v.p. C.P.A., Utah. Mem. Am. Inst. C.P.A.'s, Utah Assn. C.P.A.'s (award as outstanding accounting grad. and highest achievement on exam 1965), Phi Kappa Phi. Office: 3125 Myers St Riverside CA 92523

PLOWMAN, F(REDERICK) BLAIR, advt. agy. exec.; b. St. Paul, Nov. 14, 1938; s. C. W. and Mary E. (Stutz) P.; student Amherst Coll., 1956-58; B.S. in Journalism, U. Minn., 1962; m. Elizabeth A. Murphy, Feb. 5, 1959; children—Catherine S., Sarah S. Salesman, Nat. Life Ins. Co. Vt., 1959-60; asst. account exec. BBD&O, Mpls., 1961-62; with Grey Advt., Inc., N.Y.C., 1962-72, 76—, mgmt. supr., 1962-72, exec. v.p., mgmt. rep., 1976—; dir. client services McCann-Erickson Ltd., London, 1973-74; sr. v.p. coordination McCann-Erickson Europe, London, 1974-76. Served with U.S. Army, 1958. Home: 440 E 79th St New York NY 10021 Office: 777 Third Ave New York NY 10017

PLOWMAN, LAURENCE CARRINGTON, former real estate and indsl. devel. co. exec.; b. Berkeley, Cal., Aug. 13, 1906; s. George Taylor and Maude (Bell) P.; student Wentworth Inst., 1925-27; m. Mabel Christie, June 23, 1930; 1 dau., Anne Christie. Indsl., gen. real estate exec., Boston, also Portland, Me., 1933-45; pres. Industries, Inc., Portland, 1945-52; propr. Laurence C. Plowman Co., Portland, 1950-52; v.p. Textron Inc., Providence, 1952-58; pres. Hawaiian Textron, Inc., 1957-59; exec. v.p. R.I. Devel. Co., 1953-57; exec. v.p., regional mgr. Arthur Rubloff & Co. of Cal., 1972-76. Adv. Greater Portland Pub. Devel. Commn., 1945-52; mem. Gov.'s Adv. Com. Indsl. Devel., N.H., 1949-57; chmn. planning bd., City of Portland, 1951-52; commr. Greater Portland Regional Planning Bd., 1956-58. Mgr. Nashua (N.H.) Found., 1948-52. Office: 55 Chumasero Dr San Francisco CA 94132. *I have always tried to give my employers and/or my clients more than bargained for. In other words, compensation has and is secondary to service and results. In public life I have given many hours to committees, commissions, and boards, while also giving my share of time to church activities and boards.*

PLUCKER, ORVIN LOWELL, supt. schs.; b. Emery, S.D., July 18, 1922; s. John E. and Johannah (Olthoff) P.; student Sioux Falls Coll., 1940-41; B.A. cum laude, Augustana Coll., 1943; M.Ed., U. S.D., 1948; Ed.D., U. Colo., 1951; m. Mavis Appleton, Mar. 3, 1945; 1 dau., Mary Kathryn. Tchr. pub. schs., Alexandria, S.D., 1943-44, Canton, S.D., 1944-48; dir. curriculum pub. schs., Yankton, S.D., 1948-49; instr. U. Colo., Boulder, 1949-51; dir. instrn., Independence, Mo., 1951-54, supt. schs., 1954-62; pres. Kansas City (Kans.) Jr. Coll., 1962-66; supt. schs., Kansas City, Kans., 1962—; educator in residence U. Kans., 1973. Bd. dirs. Mid-continent Ednl. Lab., Kansas City, Mo., 1965—, v.p., 1967, pres., 1968—. Dir. Anchor Savs. & Loan Co., Kansas City, Kans. Mem. Kans. Gov.'s Commn. Sch. Fin., 1968. Bd. dirs., exec. com. West Central Area YMCA, Kansas City, pres., 1964, sec., 1966-69; bd. dirs., v.p. YMCA of Rockies, Estes Park, Colo.; bd. dirs. Urban League Kansas City (Mo.), Sci. Pioneers, Kansas City, Mo., Heart Assn. Kansas City (Kans.), United Fund Kansas City (Kans.), Heart of Am. council Boy Scouts Am.; bd. dirs. Kansas City (Kans.) March of Dimes, chmn., 1979-80; bd. dirs., exec. com. Central Baptist Sem.; mem. nat. bd. Am. Bapt. Ch., 1976; mem., vice chmn. human resources com. Mid Am. Regional Council. Recipient Distinguished Service award Jr. C. of C., Independence, Mo., 1958, YMCA of Rockies, 1979; YMCA Man of Yr. award, 1972. Mem. Kans. C. of C. (dir. 1965-68, 70-72, 76-79), Am. Assn. Sch. Adminstrs., Wyandotte County Council Govts. (founder, pres. 1967—), Met. Sch. Supts. Assn. Kansas City (charter mem., dir.), United Sch. Adminstrs. of Kans. (dir. 1970—, pres. 1973-74, distinguished service award 1977), Nat. Conf. City Supts. (chmn. 1976—), NAACP, Horace Mann League (nat. dir.), Kans. Sch. Masters (pres. 1973-74), Phi Delta Kappa. Baptist (deacon). Mason, Rotarian (pres. Kansas City 1968-69, dir. 1968-72, chmn. internat. group study exchange com. 1967-69). Home: 2235 Washington Blvd Kansas City KS 66102 Office: 625 Minnesota St Kansas City KS 66101

PLUGGE, WILFRED ROBERT, internat. research orgn. exec.; b. Hartman, Ark., Apr. 28, 1924; s. John and Marie (Eveld) P.; student U. Tulsa, 1946-53, Harvard Bus. Sch., 1956-57; m. Mary Josephine Scott, Sept. 5, 1946. With Am. Arlines, Inc., Tulsa, 1946-53, dir. financial analysis and budgets, asst. v.p., v.p. mgmt. research, N.Y.C., 1954-70; sr. v.p. Avis, Inc., Garden City, N.Y., 1970-75; dir. Stanford Research Inst., Menlo Park, Calif., 1975—. Served with USAAF, 1942-45. Decorated Bronze Star medal. Mem. Spl. Fellows Soc., Nat. Def. Transp. Assn. Clubs: Tulsa University; Sleepy Hollow Country (Briarcliff Manor, N.Y.); Indian Springs Country (Broken Arrow, Okla.); Cloud (N.Y.C.). Home: Suite 1 17 Davies St Berkeley Sq

London W1 England Office: Stanford Research Inst 333 Ravenswood Ave Menlo Park CA 94025

PLUM, CHARLES WALDEN, bus. educator; b. Circleville, Ohio, Apr. 13, 1914; s. Horace Walden and Anna Frances (Eaton) P.; B.S., Ohio State U., 1936; M.B.A., Western Res. U., 1951; postgrad. Advanced Mgmt. Program, Harvard, 1954; m. Margaret E. McCollister, Sept. 17, 1939; children—David Walden, Donald Alan. Sr. accountant Coopers and Lybrand, N.Y.C., 1936-42; supr. acctg. Amertorp Corp., Naval Ordnance Plant, St. Louis, 1942-45; various positions to v.p. acctg. and mgmt. systems Standard Oil Co. (Ohio), Cleve., 1945-78; prof. acctg. Tex. A. and M. U., College Station, 1978—; dir., chmn. audit com. Hospitality Motor Inns, Inc., Cleve., 1976-79; Sohio vis. prof. Kent State U., 1977; sec.-treas., dir., mem. mgmt. com. Am. Assembly Collegiate Schs. Bus., 1977-78; lectr. acctg. Western Res. U., 1946-54; bus. exec. in residence, disting. lectr. Tex. A. and M. U., 1976. Mem. bus. adv. council Kent State U., 1967-77. C.P.A., N.Y., Tex., Ohio. Mem. Fin. Execs. Inst., Am. Petroleum Inst. (certificate of appreciation 1964, chmn. com. on cooperation with Am. Inst. C.P.A.'s 1955-68), Am. Inst. C.P.A.'s, Tex. Soc. C.P.A.'s, Am. Acctg. Assn., Ohio Soc. C.P.A.'s, Planning Execs. Inst., Sigma Phi Epsilon, Beta Gamma Sigma, Beta Alpha Psi. Home: 5 Forest Dr College Station TX 77840 Office: Tex A and M U College Station TX

PLUM, FRED, neurologist; b. Atlantic City, Jan. 10, 1924; s. Fred and Frances (Alexander) P.; B.A., Dartmouth, 1944, postgrad., 1944-45; M.D., Cornell U., 1947; m. Jean Houston, July 15, 1950 (div. 1978); children—Michael, Christopher, Carol. Intern, N.Y. Hosp., 1947-48, asst. resident, 1948-50, physician to outpatients, 1950-53, neurologist-in-chief, 1963—; Niles fellow neurology Cornell U.-Bellevue Hosp., 1950-51; instr. neurology Sch. Medicine Cornell U., 1950-53, Anne Parrish Titzell prof. neurology, 1963—, chmn. dept. neurology, 1963—; head neurology sect. U.S. Naval Hosp., St. Albans, N.Y., 1951-53; asst. prof., asso. prof., prof. neurology Sch. Medicine U. Wash., 1953-63; vis. scientist U. Lund (Sweden), 1970-71, vis. physician Rockefeller U. Hosp., 1975—; asso. neuroscis. research program Mass. Inst. Tech.; mem. neurology study sect. Nat. Inst. Neurol., Communicative Disorders and Stroke, 1964-68, mem. grad. tng. com., 1959-63, 71, mem. adv. council, 1977—. Mem. Am. Neurol. Assn. (v.p. 1974-75, pres. 1976-77), Am. Acad. Neurology (past mem. council), Soc. Neurosci., Am. Soc. Clin. Investigation, Assn. Research Nervous Mental Diseases (pres. 1973), Assn. Am. Physicians, Harvey Soc. (pres. 1977-78), Alpha Omega Alpha. Author: Diagnosis of Stupor and Coma, 1966, 72, 80; Clinical Management of Seizures, 1976; asso. editor: neurology sect. Cecil's Textbook of Medicine, 1968, 72, 75, 79; chief editor: Contemporary Neurology series; editor: Recent Trends in Neurology, 1969, Brain Dysfunction in Metabolic Disorders, 1974. Mem. editorial bd. Archives Neurology, 1958-68, chief editor, 1972-76; editor Annals of Neurology, 1977—. Contbr. articles to scientific and profl. jours. Research in brain metabolism, epilepsy and stroke. Office: 525 E 68th St New York NY 10021

PLUMB, JOHN JAY, ins. cons.; b. Hackensack, N.J., Apr. 4, 1916; s. Carmen and Mary (Anthony) P.; B.A., Duke U., 1938; M.B.A., N.Y. U., 1948; children—Stephen J., David L. Exec. dir. Prudential Life Ins. Co., Newark, 1938-55; sr. v.p. Paul Revere Life Ins. Co., Worcester, Mass., 1955-66; successively sr. v.p., pres. Channing Mut. Funds; pres. Variable Annuity Life Ins. Co. subs. Am. Gen. Group, staff cons. to Am. Gen. Group, Houston, 1966—. Served to lt. USCG, World War II. Mem. Am. Soc. C.L.U.'s, Nat. Assn. Life Underwriters, Phi Beta Kappa. Home: 3601 Allen Pkwy Apt 281 Houston TX 77019 Office: 2727 Allen Pkwy Houston TX 77019

PLUMB, VALWORTH RICE, educator; b. Schenectady, Sept. 19, 1914; s. Henry Hammond and Rilla (Rice) P.; B.A. cum laude, U. Colo., 1936; Ph.M. in Edn., U. Wis., 1942, Ph.D., 1950; m. Genevieve Eleanor Morsch, June 19, 1937; children—Judith Ann (Mrs. John T. Saunders), Gerald Morsch, David Richard, Diane Susan (Mrs. Thomas R. Roalstad). Tchr., Denver, 1936-42; research asst. edn., lectr. physics U. Wis., 1942-43; tchr., Beloit, Wis., 1945-46; mem. faculty U. Minn., Duluth, 1951-79, prof. edn., 1954-79, chmn. dept., 1949-79, dir. student personnel services, 1947-48, chmn. div. edn. and psychology, 1948-72; technologist U.S. Forest Products Lab., Madison, Wis., 1943-45; ednl. cons. Ford Found., Calcutta, India., Kathmandu, Nepal, 1966-68. Mem. bd. world ministries United Ch. Christ, 1965-70. Mem. Am. Edn. Research Assn., John Dewey Soc., Comparative and Internat. Edn. Soc., Phi Beta Kappa, Phi Delta Kappa, Sigma Pi Sigma, Kappa Delta Pi. Lion. Cons. editor Jour. Ednl. Research, Jour. Exptl. Edn. Contbr. to books and jours. Home: 4902 London Rd Duluth MN 55804

PLUMER, PAUL SOUTHWORTH, ret. newspaper editor; b. Union, Maine, Sept. 12, 1907; s. Herbert Hall and Alice Linda (Southworth) P.; grad. Mount Hermon Prep. Sch., 1925; A.B., Conn. Wesleyan U., 1929; m. Claire E. Miller, Aug. 25, 1935; children—Paul, Stephen Hall, Timothy Carl. Mem. staff Kenebec Jour., Augusta, Maine, 1931-72, editor 1949-72, also asst. gen. mgr., 1950-56, editor, gen. mgr., 1956-72; v.p. Guy Gannett Pub. Co., 1959-72. Pres., Kennebec Valley Community Chest, 1960; vice chmn. Maine. State Mus. Com., 1966-72. Mem. New Eng. Asso., Press News Execs. Assn. (pres. 1958), Maine Daily Newspaper Pubs. Assn. (pres. 1965-66), Augusta Area C. of C. (pres. 1959), Sigma Nu. Methodist. Rotarian. Home: 20 Star Route 64 Damariscotta ME 04543. *Finding my aptitude early in life and staying with it. Placing the satisfaction of doing a job of importance to our social structure above monetary gain. Staying within my limitations instead of reaching for greedy goals. The rewards proved beyond expectations.*

PLUMLY, STANLEY ROSS, poet, educator; b. Barnesville, Ohio, May 23, 1939; s. Herman Ross and Esther P. (Wellbaum) P.; B.A., Wilmington Coll., 1961; M.A., Ohio U., 1968, postgrad., 1968-69. Instr. creative writing La. State U., Baton Rouge, 1968-70; prof. English, Ohio U., Athens, 1970-74; vis. lectr. Writers' Workshop, U. Iowa at Iowa City, 1974—. Recipient Guggenheim Meml. Found. award in poetry, 1973-74, Delmore Schwartz Meml. award in poetry, 1973. Author: In the Outer Dark, 1970; How the Plains Indians Got Horses, 1973; Giraffe, 1974; Out-of-the-Body Travel, 1977. Editor poetry Ohio Rev., 1970—, Iowa Rev., 1975-76. Address: Princeton U 185 Nassau St Princeton NJ 08540

PLUMMER, CHRISTOPHER, actor; b. Toronto, Ont., Can., Dec. 13, 1929; s. John and Isabella Mary (Abbott) P.; ed. pub. and pvt. schs., Can.; pupil Iris Warren, C. Herbertcasari; m. Tammy Grimes (div.); 1 dau., Amanda; m. Particia Audrey Lewis, May 4, 1962 (div.); m. 3d, Elaine Taylor. First appeared on stage in The Rivals with Canadian Repertory Theatre, 1950; actor Canadian Repertory Theatre, 1950-52; Broadway debut in Starcross Story, 1954; London debut in Becket, 1961; performed with Stratford (Ont.) Shakespeare Festival, Nat. Theatre Co., London; radio roles in Shakespeare, Canada; plays include Home is the Hero, 1954, Dark is Light Enough, The Lark, Julius Caesar, The Tempest, 1955, Arturo Ui, 1963, The Royal Hunt of the Sun, 1965, Danton's Death, 1971, Amphitryon 38, 1971, (musical) Cyrano, 1973, The Good Doctor, 1973, Love and Master Will, 1975; made TV debut, 1971; TV prodns. include Little Moon of Alban, Johnny Belinda, 1958, Cyrano de Bergerac, 1962, Oedipus Rex, After the Fall, 1974, The Doll's House, The Prince and the Pauper, Prisoner of Zenda, Macbeth, Time Remembered, Capt. Brassbound's Conversion; star TV series The Moneychangers, 1977; made film debut in 1957; films include Stage Struck, 1958, The Fall of the Roman Empire, 1964, Inside Daisy Clover, 1965, Sound of Music, 1965, Triple Cross, 1967, The Battle of Britain, 1969, The Royal Hunt of the Sun, 1969, Lock up your Daughters, 1969, The Phyx, 1970, Waterloo, 1971, The Man Who Would Be King, 1975, The Return of the Pink Panther, 1975, Conduct Unbecoming, 1975, International Velvet, 1978, Murder By Decree, 1979, Starcrash, 1979, The Silent Partner, 1979. Decorated companion Order of Can.; recipient Theatre World award, 1955, Evening Standard award, 1961, Antoinette Perry award, 1974, Emmy award Nat. Acad. TV Arts and Scis., 1977. Address: care Stanley Gorrie Whitson and Co 9 Cavendish Sq London W1M 0DU England*

PLUMMER, FRANK ARTHUR, banker; b. Richland, N.Y., June 18, 1912; s. Charles Eugene and Nettie (Dwight) P.; B.S., Syracuse U., 1932, M.S., 1933; grad. Rutgers U. Grad. Sch. Banking; m. Elizabeth Higgins, Sept. 10, 1938. Exec. v.p., dir. Marine Bank & Trust Co., Tampa, Fla.; sr. v.p., dir. First Nat. Bank Montgomery, 1953-58, pres., 1964-69, chmn. bd., pres., 1969—, also chief exec. officer; pres., dir. Birmingham Trust Nat. Bank, 1959-61, chmn. bd., pres., 1961-64; pres., chmn. bd., chief exec. officer First Ala. Bancshares, Inc.; dir. Alabama Power Co., Maytag Corp.; mem. fed. adv. council Fed. Res. Bd., Washington. Chmn., United Appeal, Montgomery, 1957; bd. visitors Berry Coll.; mem. adv. bd. U. Ala. Med. Center; chmn. bd. regents Stonier Grad. Sch. Banking, Rutgers U.; bd. dirs. So. Research Inst., Jackson Hosp. Found. Served lt. to lt. col., AUS, 1940-46. Mem. Montgomery C. of C. (past pres.), C. of C. U.S. (fin. com.), Beta Theta Phi, Delta Phi Sigma, Alpha Kappa Psi, Betta Gamma Sigma. Home: 2215 Allendale Pl Montgomery AL 36111 Office: First Ala Bancshares Montgomery AL 36102

PLUMMER, GLADYS EMILY SERENA, assn. exec.; b. N.Y.C., May 17, 1894; d. Carl and Elena (De La Pena) Müller; student Cathedral Sch. for Girls, Havana, Cuba, 1906-12; student Sch. of Journalism, Columbia, 1927; m. George W. Plummer Dec. 25, 1936 (dec. Jan. 23, 1944). Sec.-gen. Societas Rosicruciana in Am. (Soc. of Rosicrucians, Inc.), 1933-44, pres. (for life), 1944—; pres. Met. Consistory, Sociétas Rosicruciana in Am., N.Y., 1944—. Trustee Holy Orthodox Ch. in Am. Mem. Sem. Bibl. Research, N.Y.C. Writer of books, pamphlets, lessons on Rosicrucian philosophy. Lecturer on Christian Mysticism, Metaphysics. Home: 321 W 101st St New York City NY 10025

PLUMMER, JAMES WALTER, aerospace industry exec.; b. Idaho Springs, Colo., Jan. 29, 1920; s. Edwin Leroy and Mary Frances (Halliday) P.; B.S. in Elec. Engring., U. Calif. at Berkeley, 1942; M.S. in Elec. Engring., U. Md., 1953; m. Mary Anderson, Sept. 10, 1949; children—Robert, John, Janet, Julia. Br. head electronics test div. U.S. Naval Test Center, 1947-55; Lockheed Missiles & Space Co., 1955-73, dir. mil. programs, 1962-65, v.p., asst. gen. mgr. space systems, 1965-68, v.p., asst. gen. mgr. research and devel., 1968-69, v.p., gen. mgr., space systems, 1969-73, exec. v.p., 1976—; under sec. U.S. Dept. Air Force, Washington, 1973-76. Mem. adv. bd. Naval Weapons Center, China Lake, Calif., 1971-72; mem. summer task force Def. Sci. Bd., 1972; cons. Office Sec. Def., 1972-73. Chmn. camping com. Stanford (Calif.) Area council Boy Scouts Am., 1971; bd. visitors Def. Systems Mgmt. Coll., 1979. Served to lt. comdr. USNR, 1942-46. Decorated Air medal; Order Nat. Security Merit Guk-Seon medal (Korea); recipient USAF Meritorious Service award for Discoverer space program, 1960, Exceptional Civilian Service award, 1975; Silver Knight of Mgmt. award Nat. Mgmt. Assn., 1967; Distinguished Public Service award with oak leaf palm Dept. Def., 1975, others. Fellow Am. Inst. Aeros. and Astronautics, Am. Astronautical Soc.; mem. Nat. Acad. Engring. Author: (with others) UHF Propagation, 1953. Home: 1999 Deodora Dr Los Altos CA 94022 Office: Lockheed MSD Sunnyvale CA

PLUMMER, JOSEPH THORNTON, JR., advt. agy. exec.; b. Lewistown, Pa., Feb. 21, 1941; s. Joseph Thornton and Harriet Louise (Durben) P.; B.A., Westminster Coll., 1963; M.A., Ohio State U., 1963, Ph.D. (Nat. Assn. Broadcasters Fellowship grantee), 1967; m. Katharine Elizabeth Slagel, Sept. 9, 1966; children—John Christen, Joseph Benjamin, Suzanne Blymer. Asst. dean Ohio State U., 1964-67; with Leo Burnett Co., Chgo., 1967—, v.p. mktg. worldwide, 1974-76, sr. v.p. in charge research, 1976-77, also dir.; sr. v.p. research services Young & Rubicam Co., N.Y.C., 1979—; mem. grad. faculty Northwestern U., 1969; reviewer NSF, 1974-77. Bd. dirs. Youth Guidance Bd., Chgo., 1968-79, pres., 1970-73; trustee Episcopal Charities, Chgo., 1974-79; adv. campaigns Daniel Walker, 1975, William Singer, 1976; pres. Grace Nursery Sch. Bd., Hinsdale, Ill., 1976-78. Mem. Assn. Consumer Research (chmn. ann. conf. 1974), Am. Mktg. Assn. (chmn. attitude conf. 1978), Internat. Communication Assn., Am. Acad. Advt., Am. Statis. Assn., Assn. Public Opinion Research. Contbr. numerous articles, chpts. to profl. publs.; editorial bd. Jour. Bus., 1977—, Jour. Advt., 1977—, Jour. Mktg., 1979—; developer life style research. Home: 77 Indian Head Rd Riverside CT 06878 Office: Young & Rubicam 285 Madison Ave New York NY 10017

PLUMMER, RAYMOND EUGENE, U.S. judge; b. Harlan, Iowa, Mar. 27, 1913; s. Joseph Carl and Stella Mae (Keldgord) P.; A.B., U. Nebr., 1937, LL.B., 1939; m. Mary Marjorie Provost, Dec. 28, 1941; children—Raymond E., Marjorie Jane. Admitted to Nebr. bar, 1939; practiced in Lincoln, 1941-44; asst. U.S. atty., Anchorage, 1944-46, U.S. atty., 1946-49; pvt. practice, 1949-61; U.S. judge Dist. Ct. Alaska, 1961-74, sr. judge, 1974—. Former mem. Ty. Bd. Bar Examiners. Past pres. Boys' Club of Alaska, Inc. Former mem. Democratic Nat. Com.; Mem. Territorial Legislature, 1955. Mem. Am., Fed., Alaska, Nebr. bar assns., Am. Jud. Soc., Phi Alpha Delta. Roman Catholic. Home: 1729 W 11th Ave Anchorage AK 99501 Office: PO Box 1080 US District Ct Anchorage AK 99501

PLUMMER, RISQUE WILSON, lawyer; b. Mobile, Ala., Oct. 13, 1910; s. Frederick Harvey and Caroline (Wilson) P.; J.D., U. Va., 1933; m. Constance M. Burch, Feb. 21, 1939; children—Risque Wilson, Richard Randolph. Admitted to Va. bar, 1932, Md. bar, 1938; atty. in charge of litigation HOLC, 1933-38; pvt. practice law, 1938—; counsel U.S. Maritime Commn., 1942; partner firm Griffin & Plummer, 1951-73; counsel O'Connor, Preston, Glenn & Smith, Balt., 1979—; prof. law Am. Inst. Banking, 1948-52. Exec. sec. Md. Commn. on Anti-Subversive Activities, 1949-50; co-founder, pres. Roland Park Baseball Leagues, Inc., 1956-57; founder, pres. Wyndhurst Improvement Assn., Inc., 1957-59; mem. Selective Service Adv. Bd., 1940-42. Served to lt. USNR, 1943-46; PTO. Fellow Internat. Acad. Law and Sci.; mem. Am. Judicature Soc., Am. Bar Assn. (council sect. of family law 1966-70), Md. Bar Assn. (council sect. of family and juvenile law 1968-70), Md. Plaintiffs Bar Assn. (gov. 1966-67), Bar Assn. Balt. City (com. on grievances 1966-69, chmn. com. on profl. ethics 1969-70, exec. com. 1969-70) Delta Tau Delta (pres. U. Va. chpt.), Phi Delta Phi. Episcopalian. Contbr. articles to profl. jours. Home: 6003 Lakehurst Dr Baltimore MD 21210 Office: Law Bldg 425 St Paul Pl Baltimore MD 21202

PLUNK, JAMES HAROLD, retail chain store exec.; b. Bethel Spring, Tenn., May 17, 1931; s. William Elvis and Pearl Hazel (Wilks) P.; B.S. in Accounting, Memphis State U., 1957; m. Ruby Nell Holyfield, Nov. 26, 1954; children—Paula Ann, Linda Faith. Office mgr. Nat. Tea Co., Memphis, 1957-58; chief accountant T.G. & Y. Stores Co., Oklahoma City, 1958-64, office mgr., 1964-66, controller, 1966-70, v.p. fin., 1970-78, sr. v.p., 1978—. Served with USMCR, 1951-53. Mem. Nat. Assn. Accountants, Fin. Execs. Inst., Delta Sigma Pi. Republican. Home: 2801 Camelot Dr Oklahoma City OK 73120 Office: 3815 N Santa Fe Oklahoma City OK 73118

PLUNKETT, JAMES WILLIAM, JR., profl. football player; b. San Jose, Calif., Dec. 5, 1947; grad. Stanford, 1971. Quarterback Boston (now New England) Patriots, NFL, 1971-76, San Francisco 49ers, NFL, 1976-78, Oakland Raiders, NFL, 1978—. Recipient Heisman trophy, Maxwell trophy, both 1970; named Am. Football Conf. Rookie of Year, 1971. Address: care Oakland Raiders 7811 Oakport St Oakland CA 94621*

PLUNKETT, ROBERT, mech. engr., educator; b. N.Y.C., Mar. 15, 1919; s. Charles Robert and Helen Rebecca (Edwards) P.; B.C.E., Mass. Inst. Tech., 1939, Sc.D. in Mech. Engring., 1948; Docteur (hon.), U. Nantes (France), 1966; m. Helen Catharine Bair, May 11, 1946; children—Christopher Robert, Brian Charles, Margaret Louise. Research asst. in elec. engring. Mass. Inst. Tech., Cambridge, 1939-41, instr. mech. engring., 1941, asst. prof., 1946-48; asst. prof. mech. engring. Rice U., Houston, 1948-51; cons. engr. acoustics and mechanics Gen. Electric Co., Schenectady, 1951-60; prof. applied mechanics U. Minn., Mpls., 1960—; cons. engr. Hughes Tool Co., Hamilton Standard Co., Ford Co., USN, U.S. Army, USAF, Honeywell Corp., Control Data Corp., Worthington Corp., Westinghouse Co. Served to maj. C.E., AUS, 1942-46. Fulbright scholar Nantes, 1964, Technion, Israel, 1971. Fellow ASME, AAAS, Acoustical Soc. Am., Am. Inst. Aeros. and Astronautics (asso.); mem. Nat. Acad. Engring. Home: 3122 W Owasso Blvd Saint Paul MN 55112 Office: Aero 107 U Minn Minneapolis MN 55455

PLUSK, RONALD FRANK, mfg. co. exec.; b. Chgo., Mar. 30, 1933; s. Frank and Ann (Petrauskas) P.; B.S.C., Loyola U., Chgo., 1954; postgrad. Northwestern U., 1957-59; m. Rose Marie Pawlikowski, May 25, 1957; children—Frank A., Ronald S., Cynthia Marie. Mgmt. cons. Peat, Marwick, Mitchell & Co., Chgo., 1963-66; corp. controller Varo, Inc., Garland, Tex., 1966-69; dir. planning and mgmt. systems Rucker Co. (merged with NL Petroleum Services Co. 1977), Oakland, Calif., 1969-72, dir. ops., audit and systems, 1972-76, v.p. ops., audit and systems, 1976-77, v.p. fin. adminstrn., Houston, 1977—. Served to 1st lt. AUS, 1954-56; ETO. Mem. Am. Mgmt. Assn., Planning Execs. Inst. Roman Catholic. Contbr. articles to profl. jours. Home: 6151 Middlefield Rd Littleton CO 80123 Office: 1717 St James Pl Houston TX 77056

PLYM, LAWRENCE JOHN, mfg. exec., newspaper pub.; b. Kansas City, Mo., June 28, 1906; s. Francis J. and Jennie (Barber) P.; student U. Ill., 1928; grad. Babson Inst., 1929; m. Mary P. Lippincott, Nov. 28, 1933; children—Sarah (Mrs. Murray C. Campbell), John Eric, Andrew Joseph. Pres., Kawneer Co., Niles, Mich., 1940-62; pres. Plym Co., Star Pub. Co.; pub. Niles Daily Star; dir. Am. Metal Climax, Inc., N.Y.C.; dir. 1st Nat. Bank of Southwestern Mich.; pres. Niles Broadcasting Co. Trustee Lake Forest Acad. Mem. Phi Gamma Delta. Republican. Presbyn. Clubs: Tavern, Chicago, Glen View, Old Elm (Chgo.); Gulf Stream Golf, Country of Florida, Delray Beach Yacht (commodore) (Delray Beach, Fla.). Home: 969 S Ocean Blvd Delray Beach FL 33444

POAGE, WILLIAM ROBERT, congressman; b. Waco, Tex., Dec. 28, 1899; s. William Allan and Helen Wheeler (Conger) P.; student U. Tex., summer 1919, U. Colo., summer 1923; A.B., Baylor U., 1921, LL.B., 1924, LL.D., 1967; L.H.D., Mary Hardin-Baylor Coll., 1973; m. Frances Cotton, Feb. 14, 1938. Farmer, Throckmorton County, Tex., 1920-22; instr. geology Baylor U., 1922-24, instr. law, 1924-28; admitted to Tex. bar 1924, practiced in Waco; mem. firm Poage and Neff, 1928-35; mem. Tex. Ho. of Reps., 1924-28, Tex. Senate, 1930-36; mem. 75th-95th congresses from 11th Tex. Dist., chmn. com. on agr., 1967-74, vice chmn., 1953-66, 75—; Am. del. Inter-Parliamentary Union, 1947—. Served with USNRF, 1918. Mem. Am. Legion. Democrat. Universalist. Mason. Home: 600 Edgewood Ave Waco TX 76708

POATS, RUTHERFORD MELL, govt. ofcl.; b. Spartanburg, S.C., Aug. 8, 1922; s. Thomas Grayson and Anna Laura (Mell) P.; A.B., Emory U., 1943; m. Esther A. Smith, July 16, 1946; children—Penfield E., Huntley E., Rutherford S., Grayson M. Reporter, Internat. News Service, Atlanta, 1941-42; info. div. chief Hdqrs. Far East Command, Dept. Army, 1946-47; reporter UPI, Japan, Philippines, China, Korea, 1947-51, chief Tokyo Bur., 1951-57, fgn. service editor, reporter, Washington, 1957-61; area specialist AID, Washington, 1961-63, dep. asst. adminstr. Far East, 1963, asst. adminstr., 1964-67, dep. adminstr. agy., 1967-70; Fed. exec. fellow Brookings Instn., 1970-71; v.p. Overseas Pvt. Investment Corp., 1972-74; exec. dir. steering group for joint commns. Dept. State, 1975, sr. econ. adviser to dep. sec. state, 1976-77; acting pres. Overseas Pvt. Investment Corp., 1977-78; mem. Nat. Security Council, 1978—. Served with AUS, 1942-46. Mem. Soc. of Cincinnati, Phi Beta Kappa. Author: Decision in Korea, 1954; Technology for Developing Nations, 1972. Home: 6352 Crosswoods Dr Falls Church VA 22044 Office: Exec Office of Pres Washington DC 20506

POBOISK, DONALD PAUL, agrl. co. exec.; b. St. Paul, Apr. 24, 1926; s. David Peter and Daphne (Mulvaney) P.; B.A., U. Minn., 1951; M.A., Fletcher Sch. Law and Diplomacy, 1953; postgrad. N.Y. U. Grad. Sch. Bus. Administrn., 1954; m. JoAnn Amunson, July 26, 1952; 1 son, David Arthur. Fgn. affairs officer U.S. State Dept., Washington, 1951-52; financial analyst Standard Oil Co. (N.J.), N.Y.C., 1953-56; asst. sec., asst. treas. Minn. & Ont. Paper Co., Mpls., 1956-64; mgr. internat. devel. Boise Cascade Corp. (Ida.), 1964-66; asst. treas. Archer Daniels Midland Co., Mpls., 1966-68, treas., Decatur, Ill., 1969—, also v.p., 1973—. Served with CIC, AUS, 1945-47. Mem. Phi Beta Kappa, Phi Delta Theta. Clubs: Decatur, Decatur Country, Southside Country. Home: 455 Shoreline Dr Decatur IL 62521 Office: 4666 Faries Pkwy Decatur IL 62526

POCHYLY, DONALD FREDERICK, physician, univ. adminstr.; b. Chgo., June 3, 1934; s. Frank J. and Vlasta (Bezdek) P.; M.D., Loyola U., 1959; M.Ed., U. Ill., 1971; m. Diane Dilelio, May 11, 1957; children—Christopher, Jonathan, David. Intern, Resurrection Hosp., Chgo., 1959-60; resident in internal medicine Hines VA Hosp., 1960-61; USPHS trainee in infectious disease Univ. Hosp., U. Ill., 1964-66, chief resident dept. medicine, 1966-67, asst. prof. med. edn. U. Ill., 1967-72, asso. prof., 1972-74; chmn. dept. health scis. edn. U. of Health Scis., Chgo. Med. Sch., 1975-77, provost, acting pres., 1977-79; v.p. Ill. Council Continuing Med. Edn., 1977-79; cons. Nat. Library Medicine, Bur. Health Manpower, WHO; bd. dirs. Suburban Cook County Health Systems Agency. Served with USAF, 1961-63. Diplomate Am. Bd. Internal Medicine; mem. Assn. Am. Med. Colls., AAAS, AMA, Chgo. Med. Soc., Inst. Medicine Chgo., Alpha Omega Alpha. Roman Catholic. Contbr. articles to med. jours. Home: 555

Monroe St River Forest IL 60305 Office: 2020 W Ogden Ave Chicago IL 60612

POCKER, YESHAYAU, educator, chemist, biochemist; b. Kishineff, Rumania, Oct. 10, 1928; s. Ben Zion and Esther (Sudit) P.; M.Sc., Hebrew U., Jerusalem, 1949; Ph.D., U. Coll., London, 1953; D.Sc., U. London, 1960; m. Anna Goldenberg, Aug. 8, 1950; children—Rona, Elon I. Came to U.S., 1961, naturalized, 1967. Research asso. Weizmann Inst. Sci., Israel, 1949-50; Humanitarian Trust fellow U. Coll., London, Eng., 1951-52, asst. lectr., 1952-54, lectr., 1954-61; examiner sci. Russian U. London, 1960; vis. asso. prof. Ind. U., 1960-61; prof. chemistry U. Wash., Seattle, 1961—; Bicentennial lectr. Mont. State U., Bozeman, 1976; Horizons in Chemistry lectr. U. N.C., Chapel Hill, 1977. Mem. Am. Chem. Soc. (nat. speaker 1970, 74; plaque awards 1970, 74, chmn. Pauling award com. 1978), Am. Soc. Biol. Chemists, Chem. Soc. (London), AAAS, N.Y. Acad. Scis., AAUP, Sigma Xi (nat. lectr. 1971). Research and publs. on chem. dynamics especially organic reaction mechanisms, rearrangements, catalysis, hydration and hydrolysis, structure and function of metalloenzymes, deuterium isotope effects, kinetics of fast reactions, enzyme mechanisms, biophys. chemistry, storage and release of solar energy. Home: 3515 NE 42d St Seattle WA 98105

POCOCK, JOHN GREVILLE AGARD, historian; b. London, Mar. 7, 1924; s. Lewis Greville and Antoinette (Legros) P.; came to U.S., 1966; B.A., U. N.Z., 1945, M.A., 1946; Ph.D., Cambridge (Eng.) U., 1952; Litt.D. (hon.), U. Canterbury (N.Z.), 1973; m. Felicity Willis-Fleming, Mar. 27, 1958; children—Stephen Greville, Hugh Edward. Lectr. history U. Otago (N.Z.), 1953-55; research fellow St. John's Coll., Cambridge U., 1956-58; from sr. lectr. to prof. polit. sci. U. Canterbury, 1959-65; prof. history and polit. sci. Washington U., St. Louis, 1966-74; prof. history Johns Hopkins U., 1974—. Overseas fellow Churchill Coll., Cambridge U., 1969; sr. fellow Am. Council Learned Soc., 1969; vis. fellow Australian Nat. U., 1973. Mem. Am. Soc. 18th Century Studies (pres. 1977-78), Am. Acad. Arts and Scis., Royal Hist. Soc., Am. Hist. Assn., Am. Polit. Sci. Assn., Conf. Study Polit. Thought, Conf. Brit. Studies. Author: The Ancient Constitution and The Feudal Law, 1957; Politics, Language and Time, 1971; The Machiavellian Moment, 1975; The Political Works of James Harrington, 1977. Home: 4721 Keswick Rd Baltimore MD 21210 Office: Dept History Johns Hopkins Univ Baltimore MD 21218

POCOCK, JOHN WILLIAM, tech. cons.; b. Akron, Ohio, May 20, 1916; s. Eugene William and Bess (Livenspire) P.; student Western Res. U., 1937; B.A., Coll. of Wooster, 1938; M.S., Mass. Inst. Tech., 1939; m. Mary Elizabeth Snavely, Dec. 6, 1941; children—Carol Ann, Peter William, Lynn Elizabeth, John Steven and Mary Patricia (twins). Indsl. engr. Armstrong Cork Co., 1939-41, asst. chief aircraft engr., 1941-44; partner Booz, Allen & Hamilton, 1944-59; pres., chief exec. officer Booz, Allen Applied Research, Inc., 1955-57, 59-71; dir. Booz, Allen & Hamilton, Inc., 1964-71, sr. v.p. Booz, Allen & Hamilton, Inc., 1970-72; chmn. bd. Asso. Consultants Internat. Corp., Bethesda, Md., 1972-78; dir. West Coast Chain Mfg., Bergstralh Assos., Inc. Chmn. bd. trustees Coll. Wooster; dir. Assn. Governing Bds. Univs. and Colls., 1972—, vice chmn., 1975-76, chmn., 1976-77. Fellow AAAS; asso. fellow Am. Inst. Aeros. and Astronautics; mem. Ops. Research Soc. Am., Phi Beta Kappa, Sigma Pi Sigma. Home: 1029 Green Bay Rd Winnetka IL 60093

POCOCK, PHILIP F., archbishop; b. St. Thomas, Ont., Can., July 2, 1906; s. Stephen Bernard and Sarah-May (McCarthy) P.; student Assumption Coll., 1922-23; A.B., U. Western Ont., 1926; grad. St. Peter's Sem., 1930; postgrad. Cath. U. Am., 1931-32; J.C.D., Angelicum, Rome, 1934. Ordained priest Roman Catholic Ch., 1930; prof. moral theology and canon law St. Peter's Sem., 1934-44; consecrated bishop, 1944; installed as bishop of Saskatoon, Sask., Can., 1944; named apostolic adminstr. Archdiocese of Winnipeg, 1951; titular archbishop Apro and coadjutor archbishop of Winnipeg, 1951, succeeded to See, 1952; titular archbishop of Isauropoli and coadjutor archbishop of Toronto, 1961; succeeded to See, 1971; resigned, 1978. Address: St Mary's Ch 3 Woodbrook Dr Brampton ON L6W 3P2 Canada

PODELL, IRWIN LESTER, chem. co. exec.; b. N.Y.C., July 29, 1924; s. Max and Ida (Lester) P.; B.S. in Chemistry, Polytech. Inst. Bklyn., 1952; m. Pauline Cohen, Aug. 31, 1947; children—Linda (Mrs. David Bachrach), Craig, Barbara, Nancy. Chemist, Rand Rubber Co., Bklyn., 1946-50; chief chemist Pantasote Co., Passaic, N.J., 1950-56; founder Irwin L. Podell, Inc., Clifton, N.J., 1956—, pres., cons.; founder, pres. Podell Industries, Inc., Clifton, 1960—. Tchr. plastics courses Stevens Inst. Tech., Newark Coll. Engring., U. Mass.; cons. Gulf Oil Co., Nat. Lead Co., Esso Research and Engring., Quaker Oats Co., Vulcan Materials, Reichhold Chems., others. Pres., Jewish Community Orgn., Wyckoff, N.J., 1967-69. Served with USAAF, 1942-45; PTO. Decorated D.F.C. with oak leaf cluster, Air medal with 1 silver, 2 bronze oak leaf clusters; recipient N.Y. State medal of Valor. Mem. Am. Chem. Soc., N.Y. Pigment Club, N.Y. Rubber Group, Soc. Plastics Engrs. (v.p. 1969-71, pres. 1971—). Contbr. to textbooks on plastics and pigment usage in plastics. Home: 436 Weymouth Dr Wyckoff NJ 07481 Office: 3 Entin Rd Clifton NJ 07014

PODESTA, ROBERT ANGELO, investment banker; b. Chgo., Oct. 7, 1912; s. Angelo D. and Agnes (Fraser) P.; student Loyola U., Chgo., 1930-33; B.S., B.A., Northwestern U., 1944; LL.D., St. Mary's Coll., 1969; m. Corrine A. Murnighan, Dec. 26, 1936; children—Carol Ann (Mrs. Brian F. Foley), Mary Ellen (Mrs. C. Kevin Burke), Kathleen (Mrs. John T. Mehigan), Robert Anthony. Vice pres., treas., dir. Julien Collins & Co., 1945-49; mng. partner Cruttenden, Podesta & Miller, 1949-63; sr. v.p., dir. Walston & Co., Inc., 1963-65; sr. v.p., treas., dir. Chgo. Corp., until 1969, now vice chmn. bd.; chmn. exec. com. Altorfer, Podesta, Woolard & Co., 1979—; asst. sec. for econ. devel. Dept. Commerce, 1969; now investment banker; dir. Pay TV Corp., Calumet Industries, Inc., Wieboldt Stores, Inc. Bd. govs. Am. Stock Exchange, 1962-64, Midwest Stock Exchange, 1954-57. Chmn. Nat. Pub. Adv. Com. for Regional Econ. Devel.; mem. Chgo. Mayor's Council Manpower and Econ. Advisors; bd. dirs. Nat. Council for Urban Econ. Devel. Mem. Nat. Assn. Securities Dealers. Roman Catholic. Clubs: Chicago, Mid-Day, Mid-Am., Chicago Golf (Chgo.); Bohemian (San Francisco). Home: 505 N Lake Shore Dr Chicago IL 60611

PODHORETZ, NORMAN, editor, writer; b. Bklyn., Jan. 16, 1930; s. Julius and Helen (Woliner) P.; A.B., Columbia, 1950; B.H.L., Jewish Theol. Sem., 1950; B.A. (Kellett fellow), Cambridge (Eng.) U., 1952, M.A., 1957; L.H.D., Hamilton Coll., 1969; m. Midge Rosenthal Decter, Oct. 21, 1956; children—Rachel, Naomi, Ruth, John. Asso. editor Commentary, 1956-58, editor-in-chief, 1960—; editor-in-chief Looking Glass Library, 1959-60. Mem. U. Seminar Am. Civilization, Columbia, 1958. Served with AUS, 1953-55. Fulbright fellow 1950-51. Mem. Council on Fgn. Relations, Com. on the Present Danger. Author: Doings and Undoings, The Fifties and After in American Writing, 1964; Making It, 1968; Breaking Ranks, 1979. Editor: The Commentary Reader: Two Decades of Articles and Stories; The Commentary Reader, 1966. Home: 120 E 81st St New York NY 10028 Office: 165 E 56th St New York NY 10022

PODLECKI, ANTHONY JOSEPH, educator; b. Buffalo, Jan. 25, 1936; s. Anthony Joseph and Eugenia Evelyn (Jendrasiak) P.; B.A., Holy Cross Coll., Worcester, Mass., 1957; B.A. (Woodrow Wilson fellow, Fulbright scholar, James C. Cumming research fellow), Oxford U., 1960, M.A., 1963; M.A., U. Toronto, 1961, Ph.D., 1963; m. Jennifer Julia Grube, July 28, 1962; children—Christopher, Julia, Antonia. Instr. to asst. prof. classics Northwestern U., 1963-66; from asso. prof. classics to prof., head dept. Pa. State U., University Park, 1966-75; prof. classics, head dept. U. B.C. (Can.), Vancouver, 1975—; asst. dir. Vergilian Soc. Am. summer sch., Italy, 1965; lectr. Greek archeology Seton Hill U. Summer Inst., Greece, 1968. Vis. fellow Wolfson Coll., Oxford, 1970. Mem. Am. Philol. Assn., Joint Assn. Classics Tchrs., classical assns. Can., Gt. Britain, Pacific Northwest (pres. 1977-78). Author: Political Background of Aeschylean Tragedy, 1966; The Life of Themistocles, 1975; editor and translator: The Persians (Aeschylus) 1970; also contbr. to classical lit. Home: 4524 W 7th Ave Vancouver BC V6R 1X3 Canada

PODSHADLEY, ARLON GEORGE, dental educator; b. Farmersville, Ill., Jan. 5, 1928; s. William and Louise (Fuchs) P.; D.D.S., St. Louis U., 1951, M.S. in Dentistry, 1964; m. Callista Mahoney, Dec. 26, 1949; children—Maureen, Susan, Joan, Ann, Mary. Practice gen. dentistry, Jacksonville, Ill., 1953-62; asst. prof. Coll. Dentistry, U. Ky., 1965-69; prof., chmn. dept. restorative dentistry Sch. Dentistry, U. Louisville, 1969—; cons. Am. Dental Assn., WHO, U.S. Army, Served with USAF, 1950-53. Alpha Omega scholar, 1951; USPHS postdoctoral fellow, 1962. Mem. Am., Ky. dental assns., Louisville Dental Soc., Omicron Kappa Upsilon, Alpha Sigma Nu. Author: (with James D. Harrison) Cavity Preparation and Impression Taking, 1965. Home: 305 Rannoch Ct Louisville KY 40243

POE, BRYCE, II, air force officer; b. Wichita, Kans., Oct. 10, 1924; s. Bryce and Aileen (Keith) P.; student Colo. Sch. Mines, 1941, Kans. U., 1942; B.S., U.S. Mil. Acad., 1946; M.A., U. Nebr., 1964; M.S., George Washington U., 1965; postgrad. Nat. War Coll., 1965; m. Kari Rollum, Mar. 24, 1955; children—Susan, Karen, Bryce III. Commd. 2d lt. USAAF, 1946, advanced through grades to gen. USAF, 1978; jet tactical recon. pilot, U.S., Japan, Korea, 1946-52; pilot Allied Air Forces, No. Europe, 1952-56; strategic missile research and devel. and operations, 1956-64; legislative liaison, 1965-66; tactical recon. comdr., U.S., S.E. Asia, Germany, 1967-69, Hdqrs. USAFE, 1970-73; comdr. Ogden Air Materiel Area, Hill AFB, Ogden, Utah, 1973-74; vice comdr. in chief U.S. Air Forces in Europe, 1974-76; comdr. acquisition logistics div. Wright-Patterson AFB, Ohio, 1976-78, comdr. Air Force Logistics Command, 1978—. Chmn. bd. U.S. Army/Air Force European Exchange and Motion Picture Service, 1970-72; bd. mem. World-Wide Army/Air Force Exchange and Motion Picture Service, 1970-72. Pres. European area. Protestant Men of the Chapel, 1972, Transatlantic Council Boy Scouts Am. 1974. Decorated D.S.M. with oak leaf cluster, Legion of Merit, D.F.C. with 3 oak leaf clusters, Bronze Star, Air medal with 19 oak leaf clusters, Air Force Commendation medal with 3 oak leaf clusters; Korean Order of Nat. Security Merit 1st Class; Vietnamese Honor medal 1st class. Mem. West Point Alumni Assn., Air Force Assn., Order of Daedalians, Phi Alpha Theta, Sigma Alpha Epsilon. Clubs: Army and Navy Country; Assn. Am. Rod and Gun Clubs (v.p. Europe 1970-71, pres. 1971-72). Home: 531 Lahm Circle Wright-Patterson AFB OH 45433 Office: AFLC/CC Wright-Patterson AFB OH 45433

POE, JAMES, screenwriter; b. Dobbs Ferry, N.Y., Oct. 4, 1921; s. James and Peggy (Bobbit) P.; student St. John's Coll.; children-Lorna, Adam, Jonathan. Engaged in motion picture industry, 1941—; pres. James Poe Co., Inc., 1967—; credits include Around the World in 80 Days, Cat on a Hot Tin Roof, Attack!, Big Knife, Hot Spell, Summer and Smoke, Toys in the Attic, The Bedford Incident, Lilies of the Field, They Shoot Horses, Don't They?, The Gathering. Bd. dirs. Nat. Council Arts and Govt., 1965—. Served as aviator USNR, World War II; ETO. Recipient award Am. Acad. Motion Picture Arts and Scis., 1957, also 3 nominations; award Screen Writers Guild, 1957, 63, Writers Guild Am. West, 1957, 63, 69; Laurel award, 1971. Mem. Writers Guild Am. West (pres. screen br. 1965-67), Acad. Motion Picture Arts and Scis., Screen Dirs. Guild, Film Editors Guild, Am. Film Inst. Address: 760 N La Cienga Blvd Los Angeles CA 90069*

POE, JERRY, educator; b. Springfield, Mo., Oct. 3, 1931; s. Carlyle and Eunice P.; A.B., Drury Coll., 1953; M.B.A. (Weinheimer fellow), Washington U., St. Louis, 1957; D.B.A. (Ford Found. fellow), Harvard U., 1963; m. Carol J. Mussler, Sept. 9, 1959; children—Cheryl Marie, Jennifer Brenna. Instr., U. Ark., spring 1957; indsl. engr. McDonnell Aircraft Corp., St. Louis, 1957; lectr. on fin. Boston U., 1959-61; asst. prof. bus. adminstrn. Drury Coll., 1961-64, asso. prof., 1964-68, prof., 1968-74, dir. Breech Sch. Bus. Adminstrn., 1968-74; prof. fin., chmn. dept. fin. Ariz. State U., 1974—; vis. prof. Fla. Tech. Coll., 1971; examiner North Central Assn. Colls. and Schs.; bd. dirs. NDEA Inst. Econs.; cons. in field; mem. Regional Manpower Adv. Com.; mem. bus. and profl. adv. council Empire Bank. Served to lt. comdr. USNR, 1953-55. Mem. Am. Fin. Assn., Fin. Mgmt. Assn., Midwest Fin. Assn., Beta Gamma Sigma, Omicron Delta Kappa. Methodist. Author: An Introduction to the American Business Enterprise, 1969, 4th rev. edit., 1980; Cases in Financial Management, 1977. Office: Dept Fin Coll Bus Adminstrn Ariz State U Tempe AZ 85281

POE, LUKE HARVEY, JR., lawyer; b. Richmond, Va., Jan. 29, 1916; s. Luke Harvey and Alice Colburn (Reddy) P.; B.S. in Math., U. Va., 1938, J.D., 1941; postgrad. (Rhodes scholar) Oxford (Eng.) U., 1939, D.Phil., Christ Ch., 1957. Admitted to Va. bar, 1940, D.C. bar and D.C. Ct. Appeals bar, 1967, U.S. Supreme Ct. bar, 1969, Md. bar, 1974; asso. firm Cravath, Swaine & Moore, N.Y.C., 1941-42; tutor St. John's Coll., Annapolis, Md., 1946-50, asst. dean, 1947-49, tenure tutor, 1953-60, dir. physics and chemistry lab., 1959-60; asst. chmn. Nat. Citizens Com. for Kennedy and Johnson and chmn. Citizens Com., Pres.'s Inaugural Com., 1960-61; asst. to chmn. bd. Aerojet-Gen. Corp., El Monte, Calif., 1961-63; div. pres. Internat. Tech. Assistance and Devel. Co., Washington, 1963-66; partner firm Howard, Poe & Bastian, Washington, 1966—; dir. 1st Am. Bank of Md., 1979—; cons., lectr. in field; guest panelist Panel on Sci. and Tech. of Com. on Sci. and Astronautics, U.S. Ho. of Reps., 1970; pres. bd. dirs. Watergate East, Inc., 1976-79. Chmn. Annapolis Bd. Zoning Appeals, 1966-75; mem. Annapolis Mayor's Task Force, 1967-74; mem. Md. Gov's Commn. on Capital City, 1970-76. Served to lt. comdr. USNR, 1942-46. Mem. Am. Law Inst., AAUP, Soc. Cin., Phi Beta Kappa, Phi Delta Phi. Episcopalian. Clubs: Met., Nat. Capital Democratic (Washington); Travellers (London); Brook (N.Y.C.); New Providence (Annapolis); Vincent's (Oxford). Author: The Combat History of the Battleship U.S.S. Mississippi, 1947; lab. manuals (with others) Einstein's Theory of Relativity, 1957, Electro-Magnetic Theory, 1959; editor Va. Mag., 1936-38, U. Va. Law Rev., 1940-41. Home: 139 Market St Annapolis MD 21401 also 2500 Virginia Ave NW Washington DC 20037 Office: 1701 Pennsylvania Ave NW Washington DC 20006

POE, WILLIAM FREDERICK, former mayor, ins. agy. exec.; b. Tampa, Fla., July 22, 1931; s. Fred Holland and Zula Blanche (Willoughby) P.; student Duke U., 1950; B.S., U. Fla., 1953; m. Elizabeth Ann Blackburn, June 21, 1954; children—William, Keren, Janice, Marilyn, Charles. Founder, pres. Poe and Assos., Ins. Agency, Tampa, Fla., 1956-74, chmn., 1979—; mayor City of Tampa, 1974-79. Mem. Hillsborough County Port Authority, 1961, chmn., 1963; pres. chpt. ARC. Served with USAF, 1955-56. Mem. Tampa Assn. Ins. Agents, Young Pres. Orgn. Democrat. Baptist. Club: Yacht. Home: 70 Ladoga Tampa FL 33606 Office: PO Box 1348 102 W Whiting St Tampa FL 33601

POETTCKER, HENRY, sem. pres.; b. Rudnerweide, South Russia, Mar. 27, 1925; s. John and Margaretha (Voth) P.; A.B., Bethel Coll., North Newton, Kans., 1950; B.D., Mennonite Bibl. Sem., Chgo., 1953; Th.D., Princeton Theol. Sem., 1961, converted Ph.D., 1973; m. Aganetha Baergen, July 4, 1946; children—Victoria (Mrs. D. Ross McIntosh), Ronald, Martin. Ordained to ministry Mennonite Ch., 1948; instr. Can. Mennonite Bible Coll., Winnipeg, Man., 1954-59, pres., 1959-78; pres. Mennonite Bibl. Sem., Elkhart, Inc., 1978—; interim dean Bluffton (Ohio) Coll., 1965-66; vis. lectr. Taiwan Theol. Coll. and Tainan Theol. Coll., Taiwan, 1973-74. Pres., Gen. Conf. Mennonite Ch., Newton, Kans., 1968-74. Mem. Soc. Bibl. Lit. and Exegesis, Can. Soc. Bibl. Studies. Editor: (with Rudy A. Regehr) Call to Faithfulness, 1972; Alumni Bull. Can. Mennonite Bible Coll., 1960-73. Home: 58358 Valley View Dr Elkhart IN 46514 Office: 3003 Benham Ave Elkhart IN 46514

POETTMANN, FRED HEINZ, oil co. exec.; b. Germany, Dec. 20, 1919; s. Fritz and Kate (Hussen) P.; B.S., Case Western Res. U., 1942; M.S., U. Mich., 1944, Sc.D., 1946; grad. Advanced Mgmt. Program, Harvard U., 1966; m. Anna Bell Hall, May 29, 1952; children—Susan Trudy, Phillip Mark. Research chemist Lubrizol Corp., Wickliffe, Ohio, 1942-43; mgr. production research Phillips Petroleum Co., Bartlesville, Okla., 1946-55, asso. research dir., 1955-72; mgr. comml. devel. Marathon Oil Co., Littleton, Colo., 1972—. Chmn. S. Suburban Met. Recreation and Park Dist., 1966-71; chmn. Littleton Press Council, 1967-71; bd. dirs. Hancock Recreation Center, Findlay, Ohio, 1973-77. Registered profl. engr., Colo., Okla. Mem. Nat. Acad. Engring., Soc. Petroleum Engrs., Am. Inst. Chem. Engring., Am. Chem. Soc., Am. Petroleum Inst., Sigma Xi, Tau Beta Pi, Alpha Chi Sigma, Phi Kappa Phi. Republican. Co-author, editor 5 books in field; holder 45 patents. Home: 47 Eagle Dr Littleton CO 80123 Office: PO Box 269 Littleton CO 80160

POFF, RICHARD HARDING, justice; b. Radford, Va., Oct. 19, 1923; s. Beecher David and Irene Louise (Nunley) P.; student Roanoke Coll., 1941-43; LL.B., U. Va., 1948, LL.D., 1969; m. Jo Ann R. Topper, June 24, 1945; children—Rebecca, Thomas, Richard Harding. Admitted to the Va. bar, 1947; partner law firm Dalton, Poff, Turk & Stone, Radford, 1949-70; mem. 83d-92d congresses, 6th Dist. Va.; justice Supreme Ct. Va., 1972—. Vice chmn. Nat. Commn. on Reform Fed. Crime Laws; chmn. Republican Task Force on Crime; sec. Rep. Conf.; sec. House Rep. Leadership. Named Va.'s Outstanding Young Man of Year, Jr. C. of C., 1954; recipient Nat. Collegiate Athletic Assn. award, 1966, Roanoke Coll. medal, 1967, Distinguished Virginian award Va. Dist. Exchange Clubs, 1970, Presdl. certificate of appreciation for legislative contbn., 1971, legislative citation Assn. Fed. Investigators, 1969, Thomas Jefferson Pub. Sesquicentennial award U. Va., 1969, Japanese Am. Citizens League award, 1972. Mem. Am., Va. bar assns., Am. Judicature Soc., V.F.W., Am. Legion, Pi Kappa Phi, Sigma Nu Phi. Mason, Moose, Lion. Home: 2910 W Brigstock Rd Midlothian VA 23113 Office: Supreme Ct Bldg Richmond VA 23210

POFFENBERGER, PAUL ROUTZAHN, educator; b. Hagerstown, Md., Jan. 28, 1913; s. George F. and Elizabeth (Routzahn) P.; B.S., U. Md., 1935, M.S., 1937; Ph.D., Am. U., 1953; m. Gladys Maud Leonard, Apr. 5, 1947; children—Linda Lee, Gail Patrice. Asst. prof. dept. agrl. econs. U. Md., College Park, 1940-43, asso. prof., 1946-54, prof., head dept., 1954-61, asst. dean instrn. Coll. Agr., 1956-69, prof. agrl. econs., asso. dean Coll. Agr., 1969—. Pres., Columbia Rd. Citizen's Assn., 1963. Served with USNR, 1943-46. Fellow AAAS; mem. Am. Agrl. Econs. Assn., Alpha Gamma Rho, Alpha Zeta, Omicron Delta Kappa, Pi Delta Epsilon, Phi Kappa Phi. Lutheran. Club: Toastmasters International (ednl. v.p. 1965, pres. 1966) (Silver Spring). Contbr. articles profl. jours. Home: 2400 Fairland Rd Silver Spring MD 20904 Office: Coll Agr U Md College Park MD 20742

POGGEMEYER, HERMAN, JR., mgmt. co. exec., former marine corps officer; b. Leavenworth, Kans., Apr. 22, 1919; s. Herman Henry and Dorcas Echo (Thompson) P.; B.S., U.S. Naval Acad., 1942; M. Engring. Adminstrn., George Washington U., 1960; m. Claudine Leslie Gamble, June 20, 1942; children—Herman III, Frederick W. Commd. 2d lt. U.S. Marine Corps, 1942, advanced through grades to maj. gen., 1967; asst. chief staff, G-3 Marine div., Fleet Marine Force, Viet Nam, 1966-67, Pacific, Hawaii, 1967-68; dep., then asst. chief staff G-4, Marine Hdqrs., Navy Dept., Washington, 1968-71; base comdr. Camp Pendleton, Calif., 1971-73, comdg. gen. III MAF, 1973-74; comdg. gen. Camp LeJeune, N.C., 1975-77, ret., 1977; gen. mgr. New River Mgmt. Co. div. North Hills, Inc., Raleigh, N.C., 1977—. Decorated Legion of Merit with 3 stars, Navy Commendation with star, Purple Heart. Mem. U.S. Naval Inst. (bd. control 1968-71), Kappa Sigma. Methodist. Clubs: Masons, Shriners. Office: PO Box 5083 Jacksonville NC 28540

POGGIO, GIAN FRANCO, educator; b. Genoa, Italy, Sept. 21, 1927; came to U.S., 1954, naturalized, 1970; s. Alberto and Angela (Castagnino) P.; M.D., U. Genoa, 1951. Mem. faculty, dept. neurology U. Genoa Sch. Medicine, 1951-54; fellow in neurol. surgery Johns Hopkins Hosp., 1954-56; asso. prof. physiology Johns Hopkins Med. Sch., 1957-76, prof., 1976—. Home: 2 Elmhurst Rd Baltimore MD 21210*

POGO, BEATRIZ TERESA GARCIA-TUNON, cell biologist, virologist; b. Buenos Aires, Argentina, Dec. 24, 1932; came to U.S., 1964, naturalized, 1976; d. Dario and Maria Teresa (Vergnory) Garcia-Tunon; B.S., Lycee No. 1, Buenos Aires, 1950; M.D., Sch. Medicine, Buenos Aires, 1956; D.M.Sci., 1961; m. Angel Oscar Pogo, Jan. 13, 1956; children—Gustavo, Gabriela. Asst. prof. cell biology Inst. Cell Biology, Cordoba (Argentina) U., 1962-64; research asso. Rockefeller U., N.Y.C., 1964-67; asst. Public Health Research Inst., N.Y.C., 1967-69, asso., 1969-73, asso. mem., 1973—; prof. exptl. cell biology and microbiology Mt. Sinai Sch. Medicine, City U. N.Y., 1978—. Damon Runyon Fund fellow, 1964-65; Am. Cancer Soc. grantee, 1970-73; NIH grantee, 1975—. Mem. Am. Assn. for Cancer Research, N.Y. Acad. Sci., Am. Soc. Cell Biology, Harvey Soc., Assn. for Women in Sci., Am. Microbiol. Soc. Contbr. articles to profl. jours. Home: 237 Nyac Ave Pelham NY 10803 Office: Mt Sinai Sch Medicine 1 Gustave Levy Pl New York NY 10029

POGREBIN, LETTY COTTIN, magazine editor, author; b. N.Y.C., June 9, 1939; d. Jacob and Cyral (Halpern) Cottin; A.B. cum laude with spl. distinction in English and Am. Lit., Brandeis U., 1959; m. Bertrand B. Pogrebin, Dec. 8, 1963; children—Abigail and Robin (twins), David. Vice pres. Bernard Geis Assos., book pubs., N.Y.C., 1969-70; columnist The Working Woman column Ladies Home Jour., 1971—; editor Ms mag., N.Y.C., 1971—; author: How to Make It in a Man's World, 1970; Getting Yours: How to Make the System Work for the Working Woman, 1975; cons. Women's Action Alliance, 1971, Free to Be, You and Me projects, 1972—; lectr. women's issues, employment. Bd. dirs. Action for Children's TV, Ms. Found., Pub. Action Coalition on Toys. Mem. NOW, Nat. Women's Polit. Caucus (a founder), Women's Equity Action League, ACLU. Contbr. articles to mags., newspapers. Address: Ms Magazine 370 Lexington Ave New York NY 10017

POGUE, FORREST CARLISLE, historian; b. Eddyville, Ky., Sept. 17, 1912; s. Forrest Carlisle and Frances (Carter) P.; A.B., Murray (Ky.) State Coll., 1931; M.A., U. Ky., 1932; Ph.D., Clark U., 1939, L.H.D., 1975; Litt.D., Washington and Lee U., 1970; LL.D., Murray State U., 1970; Am. Exchange fellow, Inst. des Hautes Etudes Internationales, U. Paris (France), 1937-38; m. Christine Brown, Sept. 4, 1954. Instr., Western Ky. State Coll., 1933; from instr. to asso. prof. Murray State Coll., 1933-42; mem. hist. sect. U.S. Forces, ETO, 1944-46; with Office Chief Mil. History, Dept. Army, 1946-52; sometime professorial lectr. George Washington U.; ops. research analyst Ops. Research Office, Johns Hopkins, U.S. Army, Hdqrs. Europe, Heidelberg, Germany, 1952-54; prof. history Murray State Coll., 1954-56; dir. George C. Marshall Research Center, Arlington, Va., 1956-64, George C. Marshall Research Library, 1964-74; exec. dir. George C. Marshall Research Found., 1965-74, biographer, 1974—, also life trustee, mem. adv. com., dir. Dwight D. Eisenhower Inst. Hist. Research, Nat. Mus. History and Tech., Smithsonian Instn., 1974—, also adv. com. on Eisenhower papers; adj. fellow Woodrow Wilson Internat. Center Scholars, 1974-77; Disting. vis. prof. Va. Mil. Inst., 1972; Past chmn., Am. Com. on History 2d World War; mem. adv. groups Air Force and Navy Hist. Office; chmn. adv. com. Senate Hist. Office; adv. com. Former Mems. Congress; mem. exec. com. Ky. Bicentennial Oral History Commn. Trustee, Harry S. Truman Inst. of Truman Library; mem. adv. com. Nat. Hist. Soc. Served with U.S. Army, 1942-45; ETO. Recipient Distinguished Alumni Centennial award U. Ky., 1965; decorated Bronze Star; Croix de Guerre (France); Harmon Meml. lectr. U.S. Air Acad., 1968, Distinguished Bicentennial lectr. U.S. Mil. Acad., 1974. Hon. fellow U.S. Mil. History Research Collection (past adv. group); fellow Am. Mil. Inst. (trustee, past pres.); mem. Oral History Assn. (past pres.), U.S. Commn. on Mil. History (trustee), Am., So. hist. assns., Orgn. Am. Historians, Soc. Am. Historians, NEA (life), English Speaking Union, Am. Legion, Murray State U. Alumni Assn. (past pres.). Democrat. Presbyterian. Club: Cosmos. Author: The Supreme Command, 1954; George C. Marshall: Education of a General, Vol. 1, 1963, Ordeal and Hope, 1939-42, Vol. 2, 1966, Organizer of Victory, 1943-45, Vol. 3, 1973. Co-author: The Meaning of Yalta, 1956. Contbr.: Command Decisions, 1960; Total War and Cold War, 1962; D Day: The Normandy Invasion in Retrospect, 1970; America's Continuing Revolution, 1975; The War Lords, 1976; Bicentennial History of the United States, 1976. Address: 1111 Army-Navy Dr Arlington VA 22202

POGUE, LLOYD WELCH, lawyer; b. Grant, Iowa, Oct. 21, 1899; s. Leander Welch and Myrtle Viola (Casey) P.; A.B., U. Nebr., 1924; LL.B., U. Mich., 1926; S.J.D., Harvard Law Sch., 1927; m. Mary Ellen Edgerton, Sept. 8, 1926; children—Richard Welch, William Lloyd, John Marshall. Admitted to Mass., N.Y., D.C., Ohio, U.S. Supreme Ct. bars; asso. Ropes, Gray, Boyden and Perkins, 1927-33; partner firm Searle, James and Crawford, N.Y.C., 1933-38; asst. gen. counsel CAA (now CAB), 1938-39, gen. counsel, through 1941, chmn. bd., 1942-46; now mem. firm Jones, Day, Reavis & Pogue, Washington. Mem. U.S. dels. Chgo. Internat. Civil Aviation Conf., 1944, Bermuda United Kingdom-U.S. Conf., 1946 (vice-chmn.), Interim Assembly PICAO, 1946 (vice chmn.), 1st Assembly ICAO, 1947. Served with AUS, 1918. Fellow Am. Helicopter Soc.; Benjamin Franklin fellow Royal Soc. Arts; hon. mem. Nat. Inst. Aeronautic Scis.; mem. Council on Fgn. Relations, Am. Legion, Phi Delta Phi, Delta Sigma Rho, Acacia. Mason. Clubs: Nat. Aviation, Metropolitan, University (Washington); Wings (N.Y.C.); Bohemian (San Francisco). Home: 5204 Kenwood Ave Chevy Chase MD 20015 Office: 1735 Eye St NW Washington DC 20006

POGUE, WILLIAM REID, ret. astronaut; b. Okemah, Okla., Jan. 23, 1930; s. Alex W. and Margaret (McDow) P.; B.S. in Secondary Edn., Okla. Bapt. U., 1951, D.Sc. (hon.), 1974; M.S. in Math., Okla. State U., 1960; m. Jean Ann Pogue; children—William Richard, Layna Sue, Thomas Reid. Commd. 2d lt. USAF, 1952, advanced through grades to col., 1973; combat fighter pilot, Korea, 1953; gunnery instr., Luke AFB, Ariz., 1954; mem. acrobatic team USAF Thunderbirds, Luke AFB and Nellis AFB, Nev., 1955-57; asst. prof. math. USAF Acad., 1960-63; exchange test pilot Brit. Royal Aircraft Establishment, Ministry Aviation, Farnborough, Eng., 1964-65; instr. USAF Aerospace Research Pilots Sch., Edwards AFB, Calif., 1965-66; astronaut NASA, Manned Spacecraft Center, Houston, 1966-75; v.p. High Flight Found., Colorado Springs, Colo., 1975—, pilot 3d manned visit to Skylab space sta. Decorated Air medal with oak leaf cluster, Air Force Commendation medal, D.S.M., USAF; named to Five Civilized Tribes Hall of Fame, Choctaw descent; recipient Distinguished Service medal NASA, Collier trophy Nat. Aero. Assn.; Robert H. Goddard medal Nat. Space Club, Gen. Thomas D. White USAF Space Trophy Nat. Geog. Soc., Halley Astronautics award, 1975, de laVaalx medal Fedn. Aeronautique Internat., 1974, V.M. Komarov diploma, 1974; Fellow Acad. Arts and Scis. of Okla. State U., Am. Astron. Soc.; mem. Soc. Exptl. Test Pilots, Sigma Xi, Pi Mu Epsilon. Baptist (deacon). Club: Explorers. Home: 1109 Oak Dr Fayetteville AR 72701 Office: Code CB NASA Johnson Spacecraft Center Houston TX 77058

POHAN, ARMAND, trucking co. exec., profl. hockey club exec.; b. Langley Field, Va., Apr. 28, 1944; s. Armen and Helen (Turner) P.; A.B., Harvard U., 1964, LL.B., 1967; m. Margaret A. Neigel, Dec. 18, 1976; 1 son, Andrew Stephen. Admitted to N.J. bar, 1967; asso. firm McCarter & English, Newark, 1968-70; asst. prosecutor Hudson County, N.J., 1970-72; asso. firm McCarter & English, 1973-76, partner firm, 1976-77; v.p. A-P-A Transport Corp., North Bergen, N.J., 1977—; pres. Colo. Rockies Hockey Club, Denver, 1978—. Mem. Fort Lee (N.J.) Bd. Adjustment, 1977-78; mem. Fort Lee Planning Bd., 1979; borough atty., Fort Lee, 1973-76. Mem. Nat. Hockey League (bd. govs.), N.J. State Bar Assn. Office: 2100 88th St North Bergen NJ 07047

POHL, FREDERIK, editor, author; b. N.Y.C., Nov. 26, 1919; s. Fred George and Anna Jane (Mason) P.; m. Carol Metcalf Ulf, Sept. 15, 1952; children—Ann, Karen, Frederik IV (dec.), Frederik IV, Kathy. Editor, Popular Publs., 1939-43; advt. copywriter Thwing & Altman, Inc., 1946; editor book dept., also asst. circulation mgr. Popular Sci. Pub. Co., 1946-49; lit. agt., 1949-53; free-lance writer, 1953-60; editor Galaxy Pub. Corp., N.Y.C., 1960-69; sr. editor Ace Books, 1971-72; editorial cons. Bantam Books, 1973—; lectr. Mem. exec. bd. Monmouth County (N.J.) Civil Liberties Union, 1966—. Mem. Monmouth Democratic County Com., 1956-66. Trustee Harbour Sch., Red Bank, N.J., 1972—. Served with USAAF, 1943-45; ETO. Recipient Edward E. Smith meml. award, 1966; Internat. Sci. Fiction Achievement award, 1966, 67, 68, 73, H.G. Wells award, 1975. Mem. Sci. Fiction Writers Am. (pres. 1974-76), A.F.T.R.A., Am. Astronautical Soc., N.Y. Acad. Scis., Brit. Interplanetary Soc. Unitarian (trustee 1973—), Authors Guild (council 1976—). Club: Hydra (N.Y.C.). Author (with C.M. Kornbluth) The Space Merchants, 1953; The Case Against Tomorrow, 1957; Drunkard's Walk, 1960; The Age of the Pussyfoot, 1967; Practical Politics, 1971; Day Million, 1970; The Gold at the Starbow's End, 1972; The Early Pohl, 1976; Man Plus, 1976; Gateway, 1977. Editor: Star Science Fiction Stories; The Expert Dreamers; Galaxy Reader; Nightmare Age, 1970; (with Carol Pohl) Science Fiction: The Great Years, 1973; Jupiter, 1973. Home: 386 W Front St Red Bank NJ 07701

POHL, HERBERT ACKLAND, chemist, educator; b. Lisbon, Portugal, Feb. 17, 1916; s. Lucien Charles and Emily May (Williams) P.; came to U.S., 1916; A.B. magna cum laude, Duke, 1936, Ph.D., 1939; m. Eleanor Kathleen Rich, Aug. 23, 1941; children—Douglas, Patricia (Mrs. Robert Langdon), Elaine (Mrs. Thomas Shelby Johnson), Charles, William. Rockefeller fellow in anatomy Johns Hopkins Med. Sch., 1939; Carnegie Instn. of Washington fellow, 1940; NDRC fellow chem. engring. Johns Hopkins, 1941-42; sr. chemist Naval Research Lab., 1942-45; research asso. E.I. duPont de Nemours & Co., 1945-57; sr. research asso., lectr. plastics dept. Sch. Engring., Princeton, 1957-62; vis. prof. materials sci. Poly. Inst. Bklyn., 1962-63; vis. prof. quantum chemistry group Uppsala U. (Sweden), 1963-64 prof. physics Okla. State U., Stillwater, 1964—; vis. prof. U. Calif., Riverside, 1970; vis. prof. Cavendish Lab., U. Cambridge (Eng.), 1971; NATO sr. sci. fellow, 1971. Vice pres. Sci-Tech. Corp., N.Y.C. Pres. Princeton chpt. United World Federalists, 1959-61; v.p. Stillwater Unitarian Ch., 1978-79. Recipient Rensselaer award in sci., 1933, Soc. Plastics award, 1959; A. & K. Wallanberg fellow, 1963-64. Fellow Am. Inst. Chemists, Explorers Club; mem. Am. Phys. Soc., AAAS, Am. Assn. Physics Tchrs., AAUP, Am. Chem. Soc., Okla. Acad. Sci. (past chmn.), Philos. Soc. Author: Semiconduction in Molecular Solids, 1960; Quantum Mechanics, 1967; (with W.F. Pickard) Dielectrophoretic and Electrophoretic Deposition, 1969; How to Tell Atoms from People, 1970; Dielectrophoresis-The Behavior of Matter in Nonuniform Electric Fields, 1978. Editor: Jour. Biol. Physics, 1977—; editorial bd. Jour. Electrostatics, Jour. Cell Biophysics. Contbr. articles to profl. jours. Patentee in field.

POHL, JOHN FLORIAN, orthopedic surgeon; b. Saint Cloud, Minn., Aug. 25, 1903; s. Francis William and Mary Ellen (Heartz) P.; B.S., U. Minn., 1926, M.B., 1928, M.D., 1929; student Carleton Coll., Northfield, Minn., 1922-23, Harvard, 1934-35, U. Manchester (Eng.), 1935-36; m. Alice Elizabeth Croze, June 16, 1941; children—Mary Ellen, Peter Jon, John Martin DeLand. Interne, City Hosp., St. Louis, 1928-29; pediatrician's asst., Mpls., 1929-31; house surgeon, Childrens Hosp., Boston, 1931-34, neuro-surg. asst., 1936-37; house surgeon, Mass. Gen. Hosp., Boston, 1934-35; orthopedic surgeon, Mpls., 1937—; med. supr. Elizabeth Kenny Inst., 1940-48; clin. asst. prof. orthopedic surgery U. Minn., 1937-48; orthopedic surgeon Michael Dowling Sch. for Crippled Children, Mpls.; attending orthopedic surgeon Mpls. Gen., Abbott, Northwestern, Maternity and Asbury hosps. (all Mpls.), Glen Lake Sanatorium for Tuberculosis; orthopedic cons. Mpls. Bd. Edn. Served as lt. comdr. USNR, 1942-43. Travelling fellow WHO, Europe, 1951. Mem. Hennepin County, Minn. State med. socs., Mpls. Acad. Medicine, Acad. Orthopedic Surgeons, Theta Chi, Nu Sigma Nu. Club: Harvard. Author: The Kenny Concept of Infantile Paralysis and Its Treatment, 1943; Cerebral Palsy, 1950. Contbr. articles to med. jours. Home: 1708 South Irving Ave Minneapolis MN 55403 Office: Med Arts Bldg Minneapolis MN 55402

POHL, RICHARD WALTER, botanist; b. Milw., May 21, 1916; s. Herman John and Flora Marie (Philipp) P.; B.S. summa cum laude, Marquette U., 1939; Ph.D., U. Pa., 1947; postgrad. U. Calif., Berkeley, 1952-53; m. Marjorie E. Conley, Aug. 15, 1941; children—Katherine E., Richard Wilson, Ann Marie D. Asst. instr. U. Pa., 1939-42, 45-47; range conservationist, soil conservationist Soil Conservation Service, Tex., 1942-45; asst. prof. botany Iowa State U., Ames, 1947-51, asso. prof., 1951-56, prof., 1956—, Disting. prof., 1975—, curator Herbarium, 1950—; research asso. in botany Field Mus. Natural History, 1968—. Served with AUS, 1943. NSF grantee, 1959—. Mem. Internat. Assn. Plant Taxonomy, Am. Soc. Plant Taxonomists (treas. 1959-65, mem. council 1966-72, pres. 1973), Bot. Soc. Am., Am. Inst. Biol. Scis., AAAS, Iowa Acad. Sci. Author: How to Know the Grasses, 1954, 3d edit., 1975; Keys to Iowa Vascular Plants, 1975; Grasses of Costa Rica, 1980; contbr. articles to sci. jours. Office: Dept Botany Iowa State U Ames IA 50011

POILLON, ARTHUR JACQUES, ret. marine corps officer; b. Boston, Aug. 27, 1925; s. Arthur and Lena Riley (Curtis) P.; B.A. in History, Princeton U., 1952; m. Natalie J. Tisdale, Aug. 21, 1954; 1 dau., Jeanette Evans. Enlisted USMC, 1943, commd. 2d lt., 1945, advanced through grades to maj. gen., 1975; service in China, Korea, Vietnam and Pacific area; assigned G-1 Div., Hdqrs. USMC, 1969-72, exec. officer div., 1972; asst. div. comdr., then comdg. gen. 2d Marine Div., Camp Lejeune, N.C., 1972-73; comdg. gen. 8th Marine Amphibious Brigade, 29 Palms, Calif., 1973, Force Troops, Atlantic, Camp Lejeune, 1973-75, Marine Corps Recruit Depot, Parris Island, S.C., 1975—, dep. chief staff (manpower), also dir. Manpower Plans and Policy Div., Hdqrs. U.S. Marine Corps, 1978-79; ret., 1979. Decorated Legion of Merit with combat device and star, Army Commendation medal; Vietnam Cross of Gallantry with palm and silver star. Mem. Soc. Colonial Wars, Hueguenot Soc. N.Y., Mil. Order Fgn. Wars, Holland Soc. N.Y. (v.p.). Republican. Episcopalian. Clubs: Belle Haven Country (Alexandria, Va.); Army and Navy (Washington); Shriners. Home: Shipyard Hilton Head Island SC 29928

POINDEXTER, CHARLES WEBER, banker; b. Jeffersonville, Ind., Nov. 12, 1923; s. James Edgar and Mabel L. (Walker) P.; B.S., Ind. U., 1948; M.B.A., U. Louisville, 1950; m. Elizabeth S. Willey, Oct. 6, 1961; children—C. Read, Graham S., James W., Philip S., John W. With Citizens Fidelity Bank & Trust Co., Louisville, 1948—, mgr. trust div., 1973—. Lectr. econs. U. Louisville, 1950-61. Pres. Metro United Way, 1975—. Bd. dirs. United Cerebral Palsy. Served with AUS, 1942-45. Republican. Episcopalian. Home: 411 Jarvis Ln Louisville KY 40207 Office: Citizens Fidelity Bank & Trust Co PO Box 1140 Louisville KY 40201

POINDEXTER, HILDRUS AUGUSTUS, bacteriologist, educator; b. Memphis, May 10, 1901; s. Fred and Luvenia (Clarke) P.; A.B. cum laude, Lincoln U., Pa., 1924, D.Sc., 1946; M.D., Dartmouth-Harvard, 1929; A.M., Columbia, 1930, Ph.D. in Pure Sci., 1932, M.S. in Pub. Health, 1937; D.Sc., Dartmouth Coll., 1956, Howard U., 1961; m. Ruth Viola Grier, June 11, 1924; 1 dau., Patchechole B.B. Asst. prof., prof., head dept. bacteriology, pub. health and preventive medicine Howard U., 1931-46; med. dir. USPHS, Washington, 1947-65; div. chief FOA, Indochina, 1953-56; dir. Med. Research Lab. and Point IV Div., Liberia, 1947-52; div. chief ICA, Surinam, 1956-58, Iraq, 1959, Libya, 1960-61, Jamaica, 1961, Sierra Leone, 1962-64; prof. preventive medicine and pub. health Howard U., Washington; prof., spl. cons. on tropical diseases Dept. State, Dept. Def. Bd. dirs. Nat. Finance & Investment Corp. Washington. Trustee Lincoln U. Served from maj. to lt. col. M.C., AUS, 1943-47. Decorated Bronze Star (U.S.); knight comdr. Order Human Redemption (Liberia); Career Service award Nat. Civil Service League, 1963; Distinguished Service award AID, 1963; Meritorious Service award USPHS, 1965, Commendation for Excellence, Omega Frat., 1974; Human Service award Nat. Grad. U., 1975. Diplomate Nat. Bd. Med. Exam., Am. Bd. Preventive Medicine and Public Health, Am. Bd. Microbiology. Fellow AAAS, Am. Pub. Health Assn. (chmn. internat. health sect.; Edward W. Browning Achievement award 1973), AMA, Am. Found. Tropical Medicine, Am. Soc. Tropical Medicine, Am. Soc. Parasitology, Am. Soc. Protozoologists, Soc. Am. Bacteriologists, Sigma Xi, Alpha Omega Alpha. Author: My World of Reality, 1973. Contbr. to tech. papers. Home: 9507 Piscataway Rd Clinton MD 20735 Office: Howard University Washington DC 20059. *I have always tried to make my labor or services justify the remuneration. In selecting priorities for labor or services, I have tried to select as number one priority the one that responds best to the real needs.*

POINDEXTER, JOSEPH BOYD, editor; b. N.Y.C., July 4, 1935; s. Everton Gentry and Elinor (Fuller) P.; A.B., Harvard U., 1957; m. Holly McNeely, Oct. 20, 1976; 1 son, Matthew McNeely. Asst. mgmt. editor Bus. Week, 1963-67; sr. editor Dun's Rev., 1967-70, asst. mng. editor, 1970-73; editor MBA Mag., 1973-76, exec. editor, 1974-76; exec. editor Juris Doctor, 1974-76, Med. Dimensions, 1974-76, New Eng., 1974-76; sr. editor East/West Network, N.Y.C., 1976-77, exec. editor, 1977—. Served in U.S. Army, 1958-59. Club: Harvard (N.Y.C.). Home: 213 Warren St Brooklyn NY 11201 Office: East/West Network 488 Madison Ave New York NY 10022

POINDEXTER, ROBERT DOWNS, oil field supply co. exec.; b. Vivian, La., Nov. 10, 1915; s. Robert Newton and Gladys Zuleika (Downs) P.; student Okla. U., 1933, 36-37, Centenary Coll., Shreveport, 1933-36, U. Houston, 1938; B.S. in Bus. Adminstrn., La. State U., 1941; m. Mary Alice Pendleton, Sept. 3, 1937; 1 dau., Pricilla Louise. Sec.-treas., Superior Iron Works & Supply Co., Inc., Shreveport, 1941, pres., 1941-69, chmn. bd., chief exec. officer, 1969—; chmn. bd., chief exec. officer div. Pelican Supply Co., also Paramount Pipet Machinery Co., 1969—; pres. Apex Properties, Inc., Shreveport, 1957—, Excello Land & Improvement Co., Inc., Shreveport, 1956—, Excelsior Co., Shreveport, 1953—, Acme Equipment Leasing Corp., Shreveport, 1960—. Past div. v.p. NAM. Bd. dirs. United Fund of Caddo-Bossier Parishes; chmn. bd. Business-Industry Polit. Action Com.; nat. asso. Boys Club Am., Shreveport area, 1926. Bd. dirs. Jr. Achievement, ARC, Pub. Solicitation Rev. Council, Public Affairs Research Council La. Mem. Am. Petroleum Inst., Petroleum Equipment Suppliers Assn., Ind. Petroleum Assn. Am., Shreveport C. of C., Delta Upsilon, Delta Sigma Pi. Roman Catholic. Clubs: Shreveport Country, Shreveport; Petroleum (Dallas and Shreveport). Home: 4805 Tacoma Dr Shreveport LA 71107 Office: PO Box 7002 Shreveport LA 71107

POINDEXTER, WILLIAM MERSEREAU, lawyer; b. Los Angeles, June 16, 1925; s. Robert Wade and Irene M. (Mersereau) P.; B.A., Yale U., 1946; postgrad. U. Chgo., 1946-47; LL.B., U. Calif. at Berkeley, 1949; m. Cynthia Converse Pastushin, Nov. 10, 1979; children—James Wade, David Graham. Admitted to Calif. bar, 1952; practiced in San Francisco, 1952-54, Los Angeles, 1954—; mem. firm Poindexter & Doutre, Inc., 1964—. Pres. Consol. Brazing & Mfg. Co., Riverside, Calif., 1949-52; dir. Trio Metal Stampings, Inc. Pres. South Pasadena-San Marino (Calif.) YMCA, 1963. Mem. San Marino Sch. Bd., 1965-69, pres., 1967; pres. Conf. of Ins. Counsel, 1975. Served with USMCR, 1943. Fellow Am. Coll. Probate Counsel; mem. Am., Los Angeles County bar assns., State Bar Calif. Republican. Presbyn. Clubs: Yale of So. Calif. (pres. 1961), California. Home: 1825 Braemar Rd Pasadena CA 91103 Office: 1 Wilshire Bldg Suite 2920 Los Angeles CA 90017

POINIER, ARTHUR BEST, editorial cartoonist; b. Oak Park, Ill., Feb. 9, 1911; s. Edward Wesley and Alta Louise (Best) P.; A.B., Ohio Wesleyan U., L.H.D., 1955; student Drake U., 1934; m. Lola Marie McColloch, Nov. 29, 1941; children—Lois, John E. Sports cartoonist Columbus (Ohio) Dispatch, 1929-32; cartoonist Des Moines (Iowa) Register and Tribune, 1934-36; drew nationally syndicated comic strip. Jitter, 1936-43; polit. cartoonist Detroit Free Press, 1940-51, Detroit News, 1951-76; with Bell-McClure Syndicate and United Features Syndicate, 1958—. Served lt., USNR, 1943-46. Mem. Assn. Am. Editorial Cartoonists (past pres.), Sigma Phi Epsilon, Pi Delta Epsilon, Omicron Delta Kappa. Home: 5470 Miller Rd Ann Arbor MI 48103

POINSETT, ALEXANDER CAESAR, journalist; b. Chgo., Jan. 27, 1926; s. Alexander A. and Adele Leola (Prindle) P.; B.S. in Journalism, U. Ill., 1952, M.A. in Philosophy, 1953; postgrad. U. Chgo., 1953-54; m. Norma Ruth Miller, Aug. 24, 1951; children—Pierrette Mimi, Alexis Pierre. Asso. editor Jet Mag., Chgo., 1954-61; asso. editor Ebony Mag., Chgo., 1961-67, sr. staff editor, 1967—; lectr. numerous colls. and univs. Served with USNR, 1944-47. Recipient Penny-U. Mo. journalism award; award P.U.S.H. Found., Chgo., 1977, Fla. A&M U., 1977. Unitarian (past ch. trustee). Author: Common Folk in an Uncommon Cause; Black Power: Gary Style; contbg. author: Ebony Pictorial History; The Ebony Success Library; Black Americans and the Political System (Lucius J. Barker and Jesse J. McCorry, Jr.), 1976. Home: 8532 S Wabash Ave Chicago IL 60619 Office: 820 S Michigan Ave Chicago IL 60605

POINTER, SAM CLYDE, JR., judge; b. Birmingham, Ala., Nov. 15, 1934; s. Sam Clyde and Elizabeth Inzer (Brown) P.; A.B., Vanderbilt U., 1955; J.D., U. Ala., 1957; LL.M., N.Y. U., 1958; m. Paula Purse, Oct. 18, 1958; children—Minge, Sam Clyde III. Admitted to Ala. bar, 1957; partner Brown, Pointer & Pointer, 1958-70; U.S. dist. judge No. Dist. Ala., Birmingham, 1970—. Vice chmn., gen. counsel Ala. Rep. Party, 1965-69. Bd. dirs. Ala. Found. Hearing and Speech, 1965-70, Vol. Bur. Greater Birmingham, 1966-72; trustee Crippled Children's Clinic, 1967-72. Mem. Am., Ala., Birmingham bar assns., Am. Law Inst., Farrah Order of Jurisprudence, Phi Beta Kappa. Episcopalian. Home: 4139 Appomattox Ln Birmingham AL 35213 Office: Federal Courthouse Birmingham AL 35203

POIRIER, JACQUES CHARLES, chemist, educator; b. Mehun sur Yevre, France, Jan. 3, 1927; s. Anthony Joseph and Renee Berthe (Potier) P.; came to U.S., 1927; Ph.B., U. Chgo., 1947, S.B., 1948, S.M., 1950, Ph.D., 1952; m. Marsha London, June 22, 1951; children—Marc Raymond, Charles Joseph, Julia Eve. NSF postdoctoral fellow Yale, New Haven, 1952-53; Corning Glass Works Found. postdoctoral fellow U. Calif. at Berkeley, 1953-55; asst. prof. chemistry Duke, 1955-60, asso. prof., 1960-67, prof., 1967—. Vis. asso. prof. Ind. U., Bloomington, 1961; cons. Union Carbide, Charleston, W.Va., 1955-57. Served with USNR, 1944-45. Alfred Sloan fellow, 1959-63; research grantee Research Corp., 1964, NSF, 1967-69, Army Research Office-Durham, 1970-71, NIH, 1970-76. Mem. Am. Chem. Soc., Am. Phys. Soc., Phi Beta Kappa, Sigma Xi. Home: 210 W Lavender Ave Durham NC 27704

POIRIER, RICHARD, educator, writer; b. Gloucester, Mass., Sept. 9, 1925; s. Philip and Annie (Kiley) P.; A.B., Amherst Coll., 1949; M.A., Yale, 1951; Ph.D., Harvard, 1959; student U. Paris (France), 1944-45; postgrad. Cambridge (Eng.) U., 1952-53; H.H.D., Amherst Coll., 1978. Editor, Partisan Rev., 1963-73, O Henry Prize Stories, 1961-65; mem. faculty Williams Coll., 1950-52, Harvard U., 1953-63; Disting. prof. English, Rutgers U., 1963—; v.p. Lit. Classics of U.S., Inc. Served with AUS, 1943-46. Mem. Am. Acad. Arts and Scis., Phi Beta Kappa. Club: Century. Author: The Comic Sense of Henry James, 1960; In Defense of Reading, 1962; A World Elsewhere, 1966; The Performing Self, 1971; Norman Mailer, 1973; Robert Frost: The

Work of Knowing, 1977; also articles, revs. Home: 16 W 11th St New York NY 10011

POIS, JOSEPH, educator, lawyer; b. N.Y.C., Dec. 25, 1905; s. Adolph and Augusta (Lesser) P.; A.B., U. Wis., 1926; M.A., U. Chgo., 1927, Ph.D., 1929; J.D., Chgo.-Kent Coll. Law, 1934; m. Rose Tomarkin, June 24, 1928; children—Richard Adolph (dec.), Robert August, Marc Howard. Admitted to Ill. bar, 1934, Pa. bar, 1978; staff mem. J.L. Jacobs & Co., Chgo., 1929-35, jr. partner, 1946-47; gen. field supr. Pub. Adminstrn. Service, Chgo., 1935-38; chief adminstrv. studies sect. U.S. Bur. Old Age and Survivors Ins., 1938-39; chief adminstrv. and fiscal reorgn. sect. Exec. Office of Pres., U.S. Bur. Budget, 1939-42; dir. finance State of Ill., 1951-53; counsel, asst. to pres., v.p., treas., dir. Signode Corp., 1947-61; prof. U. Pitts., 1961-76, emeritus, 1976—, chmn. dept. pub. adminstrn., 1961-71, asso. dean, 1973-75; cons. ECA, 1948, Dept. State, 1949, 62-65, U.S. Dept. Def., 1954, Brookings Instn., 1962-63, AID, 1965, Indian Inst. Pub. Adminstrn., 1972, Commn. on Operation Senate, 1976, Pitts. Citizens' Task Force on Refuse Disposal, 1976-78; mem. cons. panel Comptroller Gen. of U.S., 1967-75. Mem. Chgo. Bd. Edn., 1956-61; pres. Chgo. Met. Housing and Planning Council, 1956-57, Immigrants Service League, Chgo., 1960-61; dir. Pitts. Council Pub. Edn., 1965-67; mem. citizens bd. U. Chgo., 1958-78; mem. Pitts. Bd. Pub. Edn., 1973-76; bd. dirs. Pitts. Arts and Crafts Center, 1977—. Served from comdr. to capt. USCGR, 1942-46. Recipient alumni citation for pub. service, U. Chgo., 1960; award for pub. service U.S. Gen. Accounting Office, 1971. Mem. Am. Acad. Polit. and Social Sci., Am. Accounting Assn., Am., Chgo., Fed., Pa., Allegheny County bar assns., Am. Polit. Sci. Assn., Am. Soc. Pub. Adminstrn., Fin. Execs. Inst., Nat. Assn. Accountants, Royal Inst. Pub. Adminstrn., Phi Beta Kappa, Pi Lambda Phi, Phi Delta Phi. Clubs: Economic (Chgo.); Army and Navy, Federal City (Washington); Downtown (Pitts.). Author: The School Board Crisis: a Chicago Case Study, 1964; Financial Administration in the Michigan State Government, 1938; Kentucky Handbook of Financial Administration, 1937; Public Personnel Administration in the City of Cincinnati, 1936; (with Edward M. Martin and Lyman S. Moore) The Merit System in Illinois, 1935; Watchdog on the Potomac, 1979; contbr. articles to profl. jours. Home: 825 Morewood Ave Pittsburgh PA 15213

POISTER, ARTHUR (WILLIAM), organist, educator; b. Galion, Ohio, June 13, 1898; s. Theodore Henry and Sarah Caroline (Ricker) P.; B.Mus., Am. Conservatory of Music (academic work U. of Chgo.), 1925, M.Mus., 1931; student Marcel Dupré, France, 1925-26, 27-28, of Karl Straube, Leipzig, Germany, 1933-34; Mus.D. (hon.), Southwestern U., 1960, Morningside Coll., 1967; L.H.D. (hon.), Syracuse U., 1967; D.F.A. (hon.), Drake U., 1975; m. Dorothy Broeland, Dec. 20, 1941; children—Theodore Henry, Wendy. Dir. music Central High Sch., Sioux City, Iowa, also organist and dir. music First Congl. Ch., 1920-27; prof. organ and theory U. of Redlands, Calif., 1928-37; prof. organ and univ. organist U. Minn., 1937-38; prof. organ Oberlin (Ohio) Conservatory Music, 1938-48; prof. organ and univ. organist Syracuse U. 1948-67, prof. emeritus, 1967—; vis. prof. organ Oberlin Conservatory Music, Drake U., Morningside Coll., U. Colo. at Boulder, Longwood Coll.; organ recitalist making concert tours throughout U.S. and Can., 1935—; artist in residence Hollins (Va.) Coll., 1967-68, Meredith Coll., Raleigh, N.C., 1975—. Asso. Am. Guild Organists; mem. Phi Mu Alpha, Pi Kappa Lambda, Phi Delta Theta. Methodist. Lectr. Arthur Porster endowed lectureship established Oberlin Coll. Conservatory, 1967; endowed Poister Scholarship Syracuse U. and St. Olaf Coll. Address: Meredith Coll Raleigh NC 27611

POITIER, SIDNEY, actor; b. Miami, Fla., Feb. 20, 1927; s. Reginald and Evelyn (Outten) P.; 3 yrs. elementary sch. in Bahamas, 1 yr. jr. high sch., Nassau; m. Juanita Hardy, Apr. 29, 1950 (div.); children—Beverly, Pamela, Sherri, Gina; m. Joanna Shimkus; children—Anika, Sydney. Appeared Am. Negro Theater in Days of Our Youth, Strivers Road, You Can't Take it With You, others; various roles Broadway prodn. Anna Lucasta, 1948; star A Raisin in the Sun, 1959; films include From Whom Cometh My Help, No Way Out, 1950, Cry, the Beloved Country, 1951, Red Ball Express, 1952, Blackboard Jungle, 1955, Something of Value, 1957, Edge of the City, Band of Angels, 1958, The Defiant Ones, 1958, film adaptation of Porgy and Bess, 1959, A Raisin in Sun, 1960, Paris Blues, 1960, Pressure Point, 1962, The Long Ships, 1964, Lilies of the Field, 1963, The Greatest Story Ever Told, 1965, Slender Thread, 1965, Duel of Diablo, To Sir With Love, 1967, In the Heat of the Night, 1967, Guess Who's Coming to Dinner, 1967, The Lost Man, 1968, For the Love of Ivy, 1968, They Call Me Mr. Tibbs, 1969, The Organization, 1971, Brother John, Buck and the Preacher, The Wilby Conspiracy, 1975, Let's Do It Again, 1975; star, dir. A Patch of Blue, A Warm December, 1973, Uptown Saturday Night, 1974, Let's Do It Again, 1975, A Piece of the Action, 1977. Served with 1267th Med. Detachment, AUS, World War II; physiotherapist. Decorated knight comdr. Order Brit. Empire; recipient Silver Bear award Berlin Film Festival, 1958, N.Y. Film Critics award and Acad. award nomination for The Defiant Ones, 1958, Acad. award best actor for film Lilies of the Field, 1963, San Sebastian Film Festival award best actor For Love of Ivy, 1968. Address: care Verdon Prodns Ltd 9350 Wilshire Blvd Beverly Hills CA 90212

POITRAS, PIERRE, leisure and transp. products co. exec.; b. Quebec, Que., Can., July 8, 1934; s. Adrien and Simone (Talbot) P.; M.C.S., Laval U., 1957; M.B.A., Am. U., 1958; m. Micheline Gagnon, Oct. 25, 1958; children—Richard, Lucie, Guy, Denis. Vice pres., treas. Bombardier Inc., Montreal, Que., 1964-68; dir. fin. Bombardier Ltd., 1968-71, v.p. fin., 1971—; past pres. Creditel of Can. Ltd. Mem. Can. Chartered Accountants Inst., Fin. Execs. Inst. Club: K.C. Home: 386 Arlington Circle Beaconsfield PQ Canada Office: Bombardier Inc Montreal PQ Canada

POJETA, JOHN, JR., geologist; b. N.Y.C., Sept. 9, 1935; s. John and Emilie (Pilat) P.; B.S., Capital U., Columbus, Ohio, 1957; M.S., U. Cin., 1961, Ph.D., 1963; m. Mary Louise Eberz, June 23, 1957; children—Kim Louise, John Martin. Teaching fellow U. Cin., 1957-63; geologist U.S. Geol. Survey, 1963—, chief lower paleozoic studies unit, 1969-74; asso. prof., lectr. George Washington U., 1965—; research asso. Smithsonian Instn., 1969—; U.S. Geol. Survey-Australian Bur. Mineral Resources exchange scientist, 1974-75. Pres. Potomac Woods Citizens Assn.; mem. area 4 council Montgomery County (Md.) Bd. Edn.; mem. bd. Citizens for Good Govt.; trustee Paleontol. Research Instn., 1976—. Fellow Geol. Soc. Am., AAAS (council); mem. Paleontological Soc. Am., Assn. Australasian Paleontologists. Author papers in field. Home: 1492 Dunster Ln Rockville MD 20854 Office: US Geol Survey E-501 US Nat Museum Washington DC 20560

POKEMPNER, JOSEPH KRES, lawyer; b. Monessen, Pa., June 11, 1936; s. Leonard and Ethel Lee (Kres) P.; A.B., Johns Hopkins, 1957; LL.B., U. Md., 1962; m. Judith Montague Stephens, Aug. 23, 1970; children—Elizabeth, Jennifer, Amy. Law clk. to Supreme Bench Balt., 1960-62; admitted to Md. bar, 1962; field atty. 5th region NLRB, 1962-64; individual practice labor law, Balt., 1964—; partner firm Wolf, Pokempner & Hillman, Balt., 1972—. Served to capt. AUS, 1969-74. Mem. Am., Fed. (pres. Balt. 1979-80), Md., Balt. (treas. 1977) bar assns. Jewish. Club: Serjeant's Inn Law (Balt.). Contbr. articles to legal jours. Home: 5518 N Charles St Baltimore MD 21210 Office: 810 WR Grace Bldg Baltimore MD 21202

POKORNY, JAN HIRD, architect; b. Brno, Czechoslovakia, May 25, 1914; s. Jaroslav and Theresia (Harrer) P.; Engr.-Architect, Poly. U., Prague, 1937; M.S. in Architecture, Columbia, 1941; m. Marise Angelucci, 1967; 1 son, Stefan Alexander. Came to U.S., 1940, naturalized, 1945. Gen. practice architecture, Prague, 1938-39; designer Winn-Roensch & Brezner, Detroit, 1942, Leo Bauer, Detroit, 1942-44, Skidmore, Owings & Merrill, N.Y.C., 1944-45; owner firm Jan Hird Pokorny, architect, N.Y.C., 1945-71, 77—; partner Pokorny & Pertz, 1971-77. Asso. prof. Columbia Sch. Architecture, 1958-74, dir. evening program in architecture, 1957-73, prof. architecture Grad. Sch. Architecture and Planning, 1974—; architect mem. Art Commn. City N.Y., 1973-77. Bd. dirs. Am. Fund for Czechoslovak Refugees, 1959—, sec., 1964-71, chmn. 1971—. Fellow A.I.A. (awards of merit 1955, 61); mem. Nat. Inst. Archtl. Edn., Columbia Archtl. Alumni Assn. (v.p. 1960-63, dir.). Club: Century Assn. Contbr. articles to profl. jours. Prin. works include Taylor Meml. Library and Reeves Student Union Bldg. at Centenary Coll. for Women, Hackettstown, N.J.; Lewisohn Hall at Columbia; (with Damaz and Weigel) Student Union, Adminstrn. Bldg., Library and Fine Arts Bldg. at N.Y. State U., Stony Brook; (with David Todd Assos.) master plan, Library, Auditorium, Speech and Theatre Bldg., renovated Student Hall at Lehman Coll.-City U. N.Y.; housing at Grasslands, Westchester Med. Center, (for Urban Devel. Corp.) in Middletown, Elmira and Wayne County, N.Y.; N.Y. Maritime Mus. in Schermerhorn Row Block, N.Y.C. Home and office: 306 E 51st St New York City NY 10022

POKROSS, DAVID R., lawyer; b. Fall River, Mass., Dec. 30, 1906; s. Israel and Jennie (Lucksniansky) P.; A.B., Harvard, 1927, LL.B., 1930; m. Muriel R. Kohn, June 17, 1936; children—Joan (Mrs. Ronald C. Curhan), William R., David R. Admitted to Mass. bar; mem. firm Peabody, Brown, Rowley & Storey, Boston, 1932—, now sr. partner. Trustee Northeast Utilities: Mem. Hosp. Planning for Greater Boston, Inc.; chmn. bd. United Community Planning Corp., Boston; mem. corp. Mus. Sci., Boston. Chmn. bd. overseers Florence Heller Grad. Sch. for Advanced Studies in Social Welfare, Brandeis U.; bd. mgrs. trust property Combined Jewish Philanthropies of Greater Boston; trustee, mem. exec. com. Beth Israel Hosp.; trustee, past pres. Combined Jewish Philanthropies of Greater Boston; bd. dirs. United Way Mass. Bay; bd. overseers Boston Symphony Orch.; hon. pres. Jewish Family and Children's Service; trustee Cambridge Sch., Weston, Mass., 1955-60, now mem. corp.; mem. Harvard Fund Council, 1964-65. Served with USNR, 1943-46. Mem. Am., Fed. Power, Boston (council) bar assns., Am. Jewish Hist. Soc. (exec. council, pres.), Am. Law Inst. Clubs: Harvard (Boston and N.Y.C.); Downtown; Belmont Country; New Century (past pres.). Home: 125 Rutledge Rd Belmont MA 02178 Office: 1 Boston Pl Boston MA 02108

POLACK, JOSEPH ALBERT, educator; b. New Orleans, Sept. 11, 1920; s. Robert Henry and Miriam Berthelot (Lemann) P.; B.E., Tulane U., 1941; S.M., Mass. Inst. Tech., 1943, Sc.D., 1948; certificate mgmt. Northwestern U. Sch. Bus., 1959; m. Anne Godchaux, June 26, 1943; children—Robert, Susan. Research asso., instr. Mass. Inst. Tech., 1943-48; with Esso Research Labs., Humble Oil & Refining Co., Baton Rouge, 1948-70, asst. dir., 1957-66, dir., 1966-70; prof., head chem. engring. dept. La. State U., 1970-76; dir. Audubon Sugar Inst., 1976—; dir. Leon Godchaux Clothing Co., New Orleans. Mem. La. Bd. Nuclear Energy, 1966-72; bd. dirs. Capital Area United Givers, 1971; pres. United Cerebral Palsy Assn. Baton Rouge, 1972, Baton Rouge Crisis Intervention Center, 1974-75. Mem. Am. Inst. Chem. Engrs., Sigma Xi, Phi Lambda Upsilon, Tau Beta Pi, Omicron Delta Kappa. Jewish (pres. congregation 1972-74).

POLAK, ELIJAH, elec. engr., computer scientist; b. Bialystok, Poland, Aug. 11, 1931; s. Isaac and Fruma (Friedman) P.; came to U.S., 1957, naturalized, 1977; B.S.E.E., U. Melbourne (Australia), 1957; M.S.E.E., U. Calif., Berkeley, 1959, Ph.D., 1961; m. Virginia Ann Gray, June 11, 1961; children—Oren, Sharon. Instrument engr. ICIANZ, Melbourne, Australia, 1956-57; summer student IBM Research Labs., San Jose, Calif., 1959-60; vis. asst. prof. M.I.T., fall 1964; asso. dept elec. engring. and computer scis. U. Calif., Berkeley, 1958-61, asst. prof. elec. engring. and computer scis., 1961-66, asso. prof., 1966-69, prof., 1969—. Guggenheim fellow, 1968; U.K. Sci. Research Council sr. fellow, 1972, 76. Fellow IEEE; mem. Soc. Indsl. and Applied Math. (asso. editor Jour. Control and Optimization 1972—), Soc. Math. Programming. Author: (with L.A. Zadeh) System Theory, 1969; (with E. Wong) Notes for a First Course on Linear Systems, 1970; (with others) Theory of Optimal Control and Mathematical Programming, 1970; Computational Methods in Optimization, 1971. Home: 38 Fairlawn Dr Berkeley CA 94708 Office: Dept Elec Engring and Computer Scis U Calif Berkeley CA 94720

POLAKOFF, ABE, baritone; b. Bucharest, Rumania; s. Sam and Mary P. Ousherenkova; student CCNY, N.Y. Coll. Music, 1955-57; m. Ethel Zevin, Mar. 22, 1953; children—David Fred, Mark Evan, Robert Ira. Debuts include Marcello in La Boheme, Milan, Florence, 1960; leading baritone Zurich Opera, 1961-63; numerous appearances with N.Y. Met. Opera, City Opera N.Y., Phila. Lyric Opera, Pitts. Opera, Seattle Opera, Berlin Deutsche Opera, Frankfurt Opera, Hamburg, Munich Staatsoper, Netherlands Opera, others; dir. Island Opera Players; opera lectr. Arts Councils and Municipalities on L.I. Rockefeller Found. grantee, 1961-62; 1st prize winner Am. Opera auditions, 1960, Vercelli (Italy) Internat. singing contest, 1960. Mem. Central Opera Service, Am. Guild Musical Artists, Actors Equity Assn. Address: 134-45 166th Pl 11G Jamaica NY 11434

POLAN, MORRIS, librarian; b. St. Louis, Jan. 24, 1924; s. Jacob and Fannie (Poe) P.; student So. Ill. U., 1941-42; B.A., U. Calif., Los Angeles, 1949; postgrad., 1949-50; M.S. in L.S., U. So. Calif., 1951; m. Cecelia Hassan, Nov. 16, 1947 (div. 1974); children—Miriam, Ruth; m. 2d, Nancy Wilsford Percy, Mar. 17, 1978. Librarian, Municipal Reference Library, Los Angeles, 1951-52; serials and reference librarian Hancock Library of Biology and Oceanography, U. So. Calif., Los Angeles, 1952-55; periodicals librarian Calif. State U., Los Angeles, 1955, supervising reference librarian, 1956-57, chief reader services, 1958-64, acting coll. librarian, 1965, univ. librarian, 1966-77, dir. library and media resources, 1977—; lectr. library sci. U. So. Calif., 1967; mem. chancellor's library personnel study com. Calif. State Univs. and Colls., 1969, mem. adv. com. library devel., 1974—; chmn. Council Calif. State Univ. and Colls. Library Dirs., 1967-68, 70, 74. Mem. adv. bd. U. So. Calif. Library Sch., 1966-69; mem. library edn. adv. com. U. Calif. System, 1966-70; mem. U. Calif.-Calif. State Univ. and Colls. Task Force on Library Co-op., 1974—; mem. Com. to Advise Gov. on State Librarian, 1972; mem. planning com. Calif. Library Authority for Systems and Service, 1973-75, adv. council, 1977—, long range planning group, 1979—, pres. congress of mems., 1979—; mem. adv. bd. Arnold Schoenberg Ins., U. So. Calif., 1974—; exec. com. Roy Harris Archive, 1978—; mem. Mayor's Blue Ribbon Com. on Los Angeles Pub. Library, 1976—; chmn. White House Conf. on Libraries and Info. Services, 1979. Served with USAF, 1943-46. Mem. Am., Calif. (pres. 1975, chmn. govt. relations com. 1977) library assns., AAUP. Editor: California Librarian, 1971-74. Home: 1128 Rosa Del Rio Way Sacramento CA 95812 Office: California State University 5151 State University Dr Los Angeles CA 90032

POLAND, BURDETTE CRAWFORD, educator; b. Phila., Nov. 24, 1926; s. Burdette Kerkhoff and Georgiana Bell (Crawford) P.; B.A., Swarthmore Coll., 1948; certificat d'etudes, U. Grenoble (France), 1949; M.A., Princeton U., 1951, Ph.D., 1954; m. Nancy Jean Aubrey, Sept. 7, 1949; children—Bruce Crawford, Amy Evelyn, Thomas Edwin. Instr., then asst. prof. history Denison U., 1953-55; asst. prof. U. Nebr., 1955-58; mem. faculty Pomona Coll., Claremont, Calif., 1958—, prof. history, 1966—, E. Wilson Lyon prof. humanities, 1969—; mem. faculty Claremont Grad. Sch., 1958—. Served with USNR, 1945-46. Mem. Am. Hist. Assn., Soc. French Hist. Studies, Western Slavic Assn., Kappa Sigma. Author: French Protestantism and the French Revolution, 1957. Home: 1404 Niagara Ave Claremont CA 91711

POLANSKI, ROMAN, film dir., writer; b. Paris, France, Aug. 18, 1933; ed. Art Sch. in Cracow, State Film Coll., Lodz; m. Sharon Tate (dec.). Dir. films Two Men and a Wardrobe, 1958, When Angles Fall, Le Gros et le Maigre, Knife in the Water, The Mammals, Repulsion, Cul-de-Sac, The Vampire Killers, Rosemary's Baby, Macbeth, What?, Chinatown, The Tenant; actor in films A Generation, The End of the Night, See You Tomorrow, The Innocent Sorcerers, Two Men and a Wardrobe, The Vampire Killers, What?, Chinatown, The Tenant. Address: care Carlin Levy & Co 265 N Robertson Blvd Beverly Hills CA 90211

POLANYI, JOHN CHARLES, chemist, educator; b. Jan. 23, 1929; B.Sc., Manchester (Eng.) U., 1949, M.Sc., 1950, Ph.D., 1952, D.Sc., 1964; D.Sc. (hon.), U. Waterloo, 1970, Meml. U., 1976, McMaster U., 1977; LL.D. (hon.), Trent U., 1977; m. Anne Ferrar Davidson, 1958; 2 children. Mem. faculty dept. chemistry U. Toronto (Ont., Can.), 1956—, prof., 1962—, Univ. prof., 1974—; William D. Harkins lectr. U. Chgo., 1970; Reilly lectr. U. Notre Dame, 1970; Purves lectr. McGill U., 1971; F.J. Toole lectr. U. N.B., 1974; Philips lectr. Haverford Coll., 1974; Kistiakowsky lectr. Harvard U., 1975; Camille and Henry Dreyfus lectr. U. Kans., 1975; J.W.T. Spinks lectr. U. Sask., Can., 1976; Laird lectr. U. Western Ont., 1976; Disting. lectr. Simon Fraser U., 1977; Gucker lectr. Ind. U., 1977; Jacob Bronowski meml. lectr. U. Toronto, 1978; Hutchinson lectr. U. Rochester (N.Y.), 1979. Decorated officer Order of Can., companion Order of Can.; recipient Marlow medal Faraday Soc., 1962; Centenary medal Chem. Soc. Gt. Brit., 1965; (with N. Bartlett) Steacie prize, 1965; Noranda award Chem. Inst. Can., 1967; award Brit. Chem. Soc., 1971; medal Chem. Inst. Can., 1976; Henry Marshall Tory medal Royal Soc. Can., 1977; Sloan Found. fellow, 1959-63; Guggenheim fellow, 1979-80. Mem. Nat. Acad. Scis. U.S. (fgn.), Am. Acad. Arts and Sci. (hon. fgn.). Co-editor: (with F.G. Griffiths) The Dangers of Nuclear War, 1979; contbr. articles to jours., mags., newspapers; producer film: Concepts in Reaction Dynamics, 1970. Home: A6 3 Rosedale Rd Toronto ON M4W 2P1 Canada Office: U Toronto Dept Chemistry Toronto ON M5S 1A1 Canada

POLASEK, THEO LOUIS, pipeline transp. co. exec.; b. Wharton, Tex., July 9, 1933; s. Theodore Otto and Agnes Marie (Kucera) P.; B.S., U. Tex., 1956, M.S. in Petroleum Engring., 1957; m. Mary Ann Konvicka, Sept. 12, 1955; children—Carla, Thomas, John. Mgr., N. Slope unitization Atlantic Richfield Co., Dallas, 1970-72, mgr. corporate resource planning, Los Angeles, 1972-75, mgr. planning and N. Slope coordination transp. div., Los Angeles, 1975-76, pres. ARCO Pipe Line Co., Independence, Kans., 1976—, also dir.; dir. La Sal Pipe Line Co. Dist. pres. Jr. Achievement of Independence (Kans.), 1978-80; mem. United Sch. Dist. #446 of Montgomery County (Kans.), 1979—. Registered profl. engr., Tex. Mem. Soc. Petroleum Engrs., Am. Petroleum Inst., Assn. Oil Pipe Lines, Kans., Independence chambers of commerce, PRIDE. Roman Catholic. Clubs: Independence Country, Rotary, Elks. Home: 311 Rajah Rd Independence KS 67301 Office: ARCO Pipe Line Co ARCO Bldg Independence KS 67301

POLENBERG, RICHARD, educator; b. N.Y.C., July 21, 1937; s. Morris and Leah (Lieber) P.; B.A., Bklyn. Coll., 1958; M.A., Columbia, 1959, Ph.D., 1964; m. Marcia Linda Weiss, July 12, 1959; children—Lisa, Amy, Michael. Lectr. history Queens Coll., N.Y.C., 1960-61; lectr. Bklyn. Coll., 1961-64, instr. history, 1964-65, asst. prof., 1965-66; asst. prof. history Cornell U., 1966-68, asso. prof., 1968-70, prof., 1970—. Mem. grants com. Eleanor Roosevelt Meml. Inst., 1974-76; cons. Nat. Endowment for Humanities, 1974—. Soc. Sci. Research Council grantee, 1970-71, Am. Council Learned Socs. grantee, 1970-71. Author: Reorganizing Roosevelt's Government, 1966: War and Society: U.S., 1941-45, 1972; (with others) The American Century, 1975. Editor: America at War, 1968, Radicalism and Reform in the New Deal, 1972. Home: 101 Orchard Pl Ithaca NY 14850

POLESKIE, STEPHEN FRANCIS, artist, educator; b. Pringle, Pa., June 3, 1938; s. Stephen Francis and Antoinette Elizabeth (Chludzinski) P.; B.S., Wilkes Coll., 1959; postgrad. New Sch. for Social Research, 1961. Owner Chiron Press, N.Y.C., 1961-68; instr. Sch. Visual Arts, N.Y.C., 1968; prof. art Cornell U., Ithaca, N.Y., 1969—; vis. critic Pratt Graphic Arts Center, N.Y.C., 1965-68; vis. artist Colgate U., Hamilton, N.Y., 1973; vis. artist USSR, 1979, others; vis. prof. U. Calif. at Berkeley, 1976; works represented in collections at Met. Mus., N.Y.C., Mus. Modern Art, N.Y.C., Whitney Mus., N.Y.C., Walker Art Center, Mpls., Fort Worth Art Center, others. Am. Fedn. of Arts grantee, 1965; Carnegie Found. grantee, 1967; Nat. Endowment for Arts grantee, 1973; N.Y. State Council on Arts grantee, 1973; Creative Artists Public Service Program grantee, 1978. Mem. Exptl. Aircraft Assn., Aircraft Owners and Pilots Assn., Internat. Aerobatic Club. Home: 306 Stone Quarry Rd Ithaca NY 14850

POLESKY, HERBERT FRED, physician; b. Los Angeles, Jan. 31, 1933; s. Fred A. and Jeanne (Neugroschl) P.; A.B., Stanford, 1953, M.D., 1957; m. Nancy Staley, Nov. 26, 1964. Intern Phila. Gen. Hosp., 1957-58; resident Cedars of Lebanon Hosp., Los Angeles, 1958-59, Yale-New Haven Hosp., 1961-64; practice medicine, specializing in blood banking, Mpls., 1964—; dir. Mpls. War Meml. Blood Bank, 1964—; prof. lab. medicine and pathology U. Minn., Med. Sch., 1974. Mem. blood resource br. program sci. adv. bd. Nat. Heart and Lung Inst. Served with USNR, 1959-61. Mem. Am. Soc. Clin. Pathology (council on immunohematology), Am. Assn. Blood Banks (dir. 1971-72, sec. 1972-73, pres. 74), Coll. Am. Pathologists. Address: 2304 Park Ave Minneapolis MN 55404

POLETTI, CHARLES, lawyer; b. Barre, Vt., July 2, 1903; s. Dino and Carolina (Gervasini) P.; A.B summa cum laude, Harvard, 1924, LL.B. cum laude, 1928; Eleanor Duse fellow U. Rome, 1924-25; student U. Madrid, 1928; LL.D., U. Palermo, U. Rome; m. Jean Knox Ellis, June 2, 1934 (dec. Feb. 1974); children—Carla Knox (Mrs. Kyril R. Tidmarsh), Charles Ellis, Joanna Shattuck (Mrs. Philip Todisco); m. 2d, Elizabeth Munn Vanderloo, Sept. 1, 1975. Admitted to N.Y. bar, 1930; asso. Davis, Polk, Wardwell, Gardiner & Reed, N.Y., 1928-33; legal asst. St. Lawrence Power Devel. Commn., 1930; counsel to gov. of N.Y., 1933-37; apptd. justice N.Y. Supreme Ct., 1937, resigned to run for lt. gov., 1938; lt. gov. State of N.Y., 1939-42, gov., 1942; spl. asst. sec. war, 1943; allied mil. gov., Sicily, 1943, Naples, Italy, 1944, Rome, Italy, 1944-45, Milan, Italy, 1945-46; now counsel to Poletti, Freidin, Prashker, Feldman & Gartner. Vice pres. charge internat. relations and exhibits N.Y. World's Fair Corp., 1960-66; counsel N.Y. State Commn. on Ednl. Finances, 1955-56; vice chmn. N.Y. State Commn. on Constl. Conv., 1956-58; chmn. Governor's Conf. on Crime, Criminal and Soc., 1935; mem. N.Y. Bd. Social Welfare, 1936; chmn. N.Y. Constl. Conv. Com., 1937-38; del.-at-large N.Y. Constl. Com., 1938; vice chmn. N.Y. State Def. Council and State War Coordinator, 1941-42; impartial chmn. Coat and Suit Industry, N.Y.C., 1946-48. Counsel, Democratic Nat. Com., 1932-37. Mem. bd. overseers Harvard; bd. dirs. Syracuse Sch. Forestry; trustee Cornell U.; trustee N.Y. State Power Authority (builders St. Lawrence Power Project, Niagara Power Project), 1955-60. Served with N.Y. N.G., 1941; from lt. col. to col. AUS, 1943-46; MTO. Decorated Bronze Star with 2 oak leaf clusters (U.S.); knight Order Grand Cross Crown of Italy; comdr. Papal Order of St. Gregory the Great; officer Brit. Empire; Legion of Merit (U.S.); named hon. citizen, Naples, Rome, Milan (Italy); Star of Jordan decoration of 1st Order. Mem. Council Fgn. Relations Atlantic Council U.S., Council Against Intolerance in Am. (exec. com.), Italian Welfare League (adv. com.), Nat. Urban League (treas.), Am., N.Y. State bar assns., Assn. Bar City N.Y., N.Y. Law Soc., Phi Beta Kappa. Democrat. Presbyn. Editor: Reports of N.Y. State Constitutional Conv. Com., 12 vols., 1938. Address: 1185 Ave of Americas New York City NY 10036

POLI, KENNETH JOSEPH, editor; b. Bklyn., June 8, 1921; s. Joseph H. and Irene (Seeman) P.; student Goddard Coll., 1938-40; m. Virginia Osk, Dec. 14, 1946; 1 son, Bruce. Writer, photographer Am. Red Cross, N. Atlantic Area Office, N.Y.C., 1946-49; editor External House Mag., Internat. Nickel Co., N.Y.C., 1949-53, Leica Photography Mag., E. Leitz, Inc., N.Y.C., 1953-65; asso. editor Popular Photography Mag. Ziff-Davis Pub. Co., N.Y.C., 1965-69, sr. editor, 1969-70, editor, 1970—. Editorial cons., 1965—. Served with AUS inf., 1942-45; PTO. Decorated Purple Heart medal. Mem. Soc. Photog. Scientists and Engrs., ACLU, Photographic Adminstrs., Circle of Confusion, Am. Soc. Mag. Editors, Internat. Center Photography, Photographic Hist. Soc. Am., Mensa. Contbr. articles to photog. jours. and encys. Home: 362 Middle Rd Bayport NY 11705 Office: 1 Park Ave New York NY 10016

POLICOFF, LEONARD DAVID, physician, educator; b. Wilmington, Del., Apr. 22, 1918; s. David and Rosalie (Rockkind) P.; B.S., U. Richmond, 1938; M.D., Med. Coll. Va., 1942; m. Naomi Lewis, June 25, 1942; children—Susan, Stephen. Asst. prof. Med. Coll. Va., 1948-55; prof., chmn. dept. phys. medicine and rehab. Albany Med. Coll. Union U., 1955-67; prof., chmn. dept. phys. medicine and rehab. Temple U., Phila., 1967-70; prof., chmn. Hahnemann Med. Coll., Phila., 1970-71; prof. clin. phys. medicine U. Pa., chmn. dept. rehab. medicine Princeton (N.J.) Hosp., 1971-75, cons., 1975-78; dir. rehab. medicine Somerset Hosp., Somerville, N.J., 1975-78; acting chmn., prof. clin. phys. medicine Rutgers Med. Sch., 1976-78; chmn. dept. rehab. medicine Pacific Med. Center, San Francisco, 1978—. Bd. med. examiners N.Y. State, 1962-67. Bd. dirs. Commn. on Edn. in Phys. Medicine and Rehab., 1968—, com. for Handicapped People-to-People Program, 1967—. Served to maj., M.C., AUS, 1943-46. Nat. Inst. Neurologic Diseases fellow, 1953-55. Diplomate Am. Bd. Internal Medicine, Am. Bd. Phys. Medicine and Rehab. (mem. 1968—). Fellow A.C.P., Am. Acad. Phys. Medicine and Rehab., Am. Acad. Cerebral Palsy; mem. Am. Congress Rehab. Medicine (pres. 1971), Assn. Acad. Physiatrists, AMA (chmn. phys. medicine sect. 1965-66), Am. Rheumatism Assn., Calif. Med. Assn., Phi Beta Kappa, Alpha Omega Alpha, Sigma Zeta. Contbr. articles to profl. jours., textbooks. Home: 72 Upper Briar Rd Kentfield CA 94904 Office: Pacific Med Center PO Box 7999 San Francisco CA 94120

POLIER, JUSTINE WISE, lawyer, ret. judge; b. Portland, Oreg., Apr. 12, 1903; d. Stephen S. and Louise (Waterman) Wise; student Bryn Mawr Coll., 1920-22, Radcliffe Coll., 1922-23; A.B., Barnard Coll., 1924; LL.B., Yale U., 1928, LL.D., 1979; LL.D., Princeton U., 1976, Kenyon Coll., 1977, City U. N.Y., 1978; m. Leon Arthur Tulin, June 14, 1927 (dec. Dec. 12, 1932); 1 son, Stephen Wise; m. 2d, Shad Polier, Mar. 26, 1937; children—Trudy H., Jonathon W., Michael W. (dec. Mar. 10, 1945). Admitted to Conn. bar, 1928, N.Y. State bar, 1929, and began practice in N.Y.; referee N.Y. State Dept. Labor, 1929-34; asst. corp. counsel N.Y.C., 1934-35; counsel and sec. Mayor's Com. on Relief, 1934-35; counsel Emergency Relief Bur., 1935; justice Domestic Relations Ct., N.Y., 1935-62; judge N.Y. State Family Ct., 1962-73; dir. program for juvenile justice Children's Def. Fund-Washington Research Project Fund, 1973-76; cons. Office Civilian Def., 1941-42. Mem. N.Y. Citizens Com. Foster Care Children; v.p. N.Y.C. Citizens Com. for Children; vice-chairperson Eleanor Roosevelt Inst.; mem. Joint Commn. Inst. Juvenile Adminstrn.-Am. Bar Assn.; mem. adv. rev. bd. Human Resources Adminstrn.; mem. Commr.'s adv. council for children with handicapping conditions N.Y. State Dept. Edn.; mem. N.Y. State Task Force on Mental Health Services for Children and Youth. Bd. dirs., pres. Wiltwyck Sch.; trustee N.Y. Sch. Nursery Years, Ch. Peace Union; v.p. Field Found.; bd. dirs. Marshall Field Awards, Inc., Research Center of Human Relations; pres. Louise Wise Services; hon. pres. women's div., chmn. exec. com. Am. Jewish Congress; mem. exec. com. World Jewish Congress. N.Y. del. White House Conv. on Children, 1960; mem. White House Planning Conf. on Civil Rights, 1965; bd. visitors Antioch Sch. Law; bd. dirs. Children's Def. Fund. Named Woman of Month Dec. 1948, Am. Women's Assn.; recipient Isaac Ray award Am. Psychiat. Assn., 1964, Naomi Lehman award Fedn. Jewish Philanthropies, 1965, Distinguished Service award City N.Y., 1973; Human Services award N.Y. and Bronx Mental Health Assn., 1973, N.Y. Assn. U. Women, 1973; Hannah G. Solomon award Nat. Council Jewish Women, 1975; Eleanor Roosevelt Humanitarian award bd. dirs. Wiltwyck Sch., 1975; Gertrude F. Zimand Meml. award Nat. Child Labor Com., 1976; Marion E. Kenworthy award Columbia U. Sch. Social Work, 1979. Mem. Assn. Bar City N.Y., Am. Orthopsychiat. Assn. Jewish. Author: Everyone's Children, Nobody's Child, 1941; Back to What Woodshed, 1956; Parental Rights, The Need for Law and Social Action, A View From the Bench, The Rule of Law and the Role of Psychiatry, 1968. Co-editor Personal Letters of Stephen Wise, 1956. Contbr. to social and sci. jours. Home: 175 E 64th St New York NY 10021 Office: 100 E 85th St New York NY 10028

POLIER, REX JOSEPH, journalist; b. Rock Island, Ill., Dec. 13, 1916; s. Joseph Leo and Lala (Applegate) P.; student St. Ambrose Coll., Davenport, Iowa, 1941; m. Emily Kathryn Shaw, Oct. 31, 1942; children—Suzanne, Rex Joseph, Mary Clare, Emily, John L., Peter A. With Davenport Times, 1941-42, Gen. News Service, Washington, 1943, Balt. Sun, 1943-44; columnist, TV editor Phila. Bull., 1963—. Ford Found. grantee to research Brit. TV, 1966. Mem. Phila. Press Club. Roman Catholic. Contbr. articles to newspapers and mags. Home: 625 Aronimink Pl Drexel Hill PA 19026 Office: Phila Bull 30th and Market Sts Philadelphia PA 19101

POLIN, ALBERT TERRENCE, savs. and loan co. exec.; b. N.Y.C., Sept. 29, 1924; s. Lewis and Polly (Talkoff) P.; B.A., U. Wis., 1947, M.A., 1948; M.A., Columbia U., 1952, Ph.D. in Psychology, 1955; m. Elane C. Cohen, May 3, 1947; children—Linda Gale, Lawrence Robert, Liza Beth, Jonathan Lewis. Research psychologist Columbia U., 1950-53; mgr. mgmt. devel. Gen. Electric Co., 1955-61; dir. Research Inst. for Bus. and Econs., U. So. Calif., 1961-64, asso. prof. orgn. behavior, 1961-75; pres. Gibraltar Savs. & Loan Assn., Beverly Hills, Calif., 1975—; mgmt. cons.; practice psychology for exec. career devel. Bd. dirs. Calif. State Univs. and Colls. Fund, Beverly Hills YMCA; mem. bd. overseers Hebrew Union Coll., 1979—; mem. univ. adv. bd. Calif. State U., Los Angeles; mem. Western region United Way Planning Council Bd. Served with USN, 1943-45. Mem. Am. Psychol. Assn., Am. Mgmt. Assn., Sigma Xi. Office: 9111 Wilshire Blvd Beverly Hills CA 90213

POLIN, CLAIRE, musician; b. Phila.; d. Josef and Celia (Dolgien) P.; B.Mus., Phila. Conservatory Music, 1948, M.Mus., 1950, D.Mus., 1955; Mus.D., Temple U., Juilliard Sch. Music, Dropsie U., Gratz Coll., Berkshire Music Center; m. Merle Schaff (dec.); children—Josef, Gabriel. Mem. faculty Phila. Conservatory-Phila. Mus. Acad., 1955-65; mem. faculty Rutgers U., 1957—, dir. Univ. Exchange Concerts, 1960—; free-lance flutist, 1955—; Leverhulme fellow to U.K., 1968-69; mem. Pan Orphic Duo (flute and harp); vis. lectr., composer, performer, Gt. Britain, France, Israel. Recipient award-commn. Ga. Brass Symposium, 1970, numerous prizes for composition. Faculty Study grant Rutgers U., 1973-74, 76-77. Mem. AAUP, Am. Soc. Composers, Soc. Ethnomusicology, Am. Music Center, Phila. Art Alliance, Am. Musicol. Soc., Composers Guild Gt. Britain, Bibliotheque Internat. de Musique Contemporaine, Welsh Guild, ASCAP, Delta Omicron (award 1953, 59). Author: Music of the Ancient Near East, 1954; (with William Kincaid) 5 vol. Flute Method, 1967—; The Ap How Ms, 1980; also articles in Welsh and Yiddish on early Am. music. Composer: The Journey of Owain Madoc (brass quintet, piano and percussion; commd. N.Y. Brass Quintet), 1971; Infinito (saxophone, soprano, chorus, narrator-dancer?), 1972; Aderyn Pur (flute, saxophone, tape), 1972; Eligmos Archaios (solo harp), 1973; Procris (flute tuba), 1973; Biblical Madrigals SSATB, 1973; Paraselene (song cycle for soprano flute), 1976; Ma'alet (viola and percussion), 1976; Klockwrk (saxophone, horn, bassoon), 1977; Amphion (symphony orch.), 1978; Gilgamesh (flute, string orch.), 1967; Windsongs (voice and guitar), 1978; numerous solo works. Home: Dragon Hill Baird and Heath Rds Merion PA 19066 Office: Rutgers Univ Dept Music Camden NJ 08102

POLING, FORREST KENNETH, automobile mfg. co. exec.; b. Dixon, Ohio, Feb. 26, 1923; s. Clarence Simon and Bertha Zorado (Bayles) P.; B.S. in Mech. Engring., Ohio State U., 1948; M.S. in Indsl. Mgmt., M.I.T., 1957; m. Betty Louise Rhine, Oct. 6, 1945; children—Philip Terrence, Steven Clark. With Ford Motor Co., Dearborn, Mich., 1949—, chassis design exec. engr., 1971-75, vehicle design exec. engr., 1975—. Chmn. fin. com. Cherry Hill United Presbyn. Ch., Dearborn, 1977-79. Served to capt. USAAF, 1942-46, USAF, 1950-53; Korea. Decorated D.F.C., Air medal; recipient Texnikoi Outstanding Alumnus award Ohio State U., 1965, Disting. Alumnus award, 1976. Mem. Soc. Automotive Engrs., Sigma Xi, Pi Tau Sigma, Tau Beta Pi. Republican. Home: 8 Parkside Ct Dearborn MI 48124 Office: 20000 Rotunda Dr Dearborn MI 48121

POLING, HAROLD ARTHUR, corp. exec.; b. Troy, Mich., Oct. 14, 1925; s. Plesant Arthur and Laura Elizabeth (Thompson) P.; B.A., Monmouth (Ill.) Coll., 1949; M.B.A., Ind. U., 1951; m. Marian Sarita Lee, 1957; children—Pamela Lee, Kathryn Lynn, Douglas Lee. With Ford Motor Co., Dearborn, Mich., 1951-59, 60—, controller product devel. group, 1968-72, v.p. finance, Ford of Europe, 1972-75, pres. Ford of Europe, Inc., Brentwood, Eng., 1975-77, chmn. bd., 1977—, exec. v.p. corp. staffs Ford Motor Co., Dearborn, Mich., 1979—, also dir.; with Tait Mfg. Co., Dayton, Ohio, 1959-60. Mem. dean's adv. Council Ind. U. Sch. Bus. Served with USNR, 1943-45. Mem. Fin. Execs. Inst. (Detroit chpt.), Nat. Assn. Accountants (Detroit chpt.). Clubs: Birmingham (Mich.) Athletic; Bloomfield Hills (Mich.) Golf; Masons; Thorndon Park Golf (Brentwood); Marks (London). Home: 1565 N Glengarry St Birmingham MI 48010 Office: Ford Motor Co Dearborn MI

POLISHOOK, WILLIAM MARTIN, emeritus educator; b. Boston, Sept. 21, 1909; s. Harry and Celia (Goldsmith) P.; B.S., Mass. State Tchrs. Coll., Salem, 1931; Ed.M., Harvard, 1935; Ed.D., N.Y. U., 1945; Pe.D., Widener Coll., 1978; m. Eleanor Halladay Delano, Aug. 21, 1937; children—Robert Delano, Margaret Louise. High sch. tchr. Dedham, Mass., 1931-37; head dept. bus. edn., dir. guidance Clifford J. Scott High Sch., East Orange, N.J., 1937-47; dir. dept. of bus. edn., prof. of bus. edn. Temple U. Phila., 1947-53, prof. edn., 1953-66, asst. dean Tchrs. Coll., 1950-64, asso. dean Grad. Sch., 1964-66; v.p. charge acad. affairs Brandwine Jr. Coll., 1966-77, acting pres., 1974-76, ret., 1977. Chmn. joint com. on tests Nat. Bus. Entrance Tests, 1948-50. Trustee Husson Coll. Mem. United Bus. Edn. Assn., Nat. Office Mgmt. Assn. (dir. extension sch.), Nat. Bus. Tchrs. Tng. Assn., Eastern (pres. 1957), Pa. bus. tchrs. assns., Phi Delta Kappa, Delta Pi Epsilon (research award 1945), Alpha Phi Omega. Author: Workbook for Secretarial Training, 1942; Elements of General Business, 1945, rev., 1953; Comml. Arithmetic, 1948; Today's General Business, 1959. Cons. editor: (office mgmt. series) McGraw-Hill Pub. Co., 1958—; editor; Tchrs. College News, Temple Univ., 1948—; editor Organization, Administration and Supervision of Business Education. Home: Blakely Rd Haverford PA 19041

POLITZ, ALFRED, consumer and indsl. researcher; s. Alfred and Martha (Arlt) P.; student exptl. psychology, doctorate in Physics, U. Berlin; m. Martha Bruszat, Mar. 28, 1939. Founder, Alfred Politz Research Orgn., N.Y.C., 1943, dir. incorporation, 1947, pres. Alfred Politz Research, Inc., 1947-64, chmn. bd., 1964-67; lectr. Columbia, Yale, N.Y. U. Recipient leadership award for devel. sci. standards, mktg. research techniques Am. Mktg. Assn., 1946, for devel. econs., sci. sampling procedures, 1947; ann. award for creativeness Media-Scope mag., 1960, ann. award for creative media research, 1963; named to Mktg. Hall of Fame, 1953, Transit Advt. Hall of Fame, 1977. Mem. World Assn. Pub. Opinion Research, Market Research Council (life). Contbr. articles to profl. and sci. publs. Home: 55 Copeland Rd Odessa FL 33556

POLK, CHARLES, elec. engr., educator; b. Vienna, Austria, Jan. 15, 1920; s. Heinrich and Amalie (Canar) P.; student U. Paris (Sorbonne), 1939; B.S., Washington U., 1948; M.S., U. Pa., 1953, Ph.D., 1956; m. Dorothy R. Lemp, Apr. 27, 1946; children—Dean F., Gerald W. Came to U.S., 1940, naturalized, 1943. Engr., RCA Victor div., Camden, N.J., 1948-52; research and teaching asso. U. Pa., 1952-57; prof. elec. engring. Drexel Inst. Tech., Phila., 1957-59; tech. staff RCA Labs., Princeton, N.J., 1957-59; prof. elec. engring., chmn. dept. U. R.I., 1959—; head elec. scis. and analysis sect. engring. div. NSF, Washington, 1975-76, acting dir. engring. div., 1976-77; vis. prof. elec. engring. Stanford, 1968-69. Organized 1st microwave closed circuit television link for grad. edn. in U.S., 1962, mem. R.I. Legis. Commn. on Electricity Rates, 1974-75. Served with AUS, 1943-46. Mem. IEEE (chmn. Phila. chpt. profl. group antennas and propagation 1954-55, vice chmn. Providence sect. 1963-64, chmn., 1964-65), Am. Geophys. Union (nat. com. on space electricity 1974-75), AAAS, Am. Soc. for Engring. Edn., AAUP, N.Y. Acad. Scis., Internat. Assn. Meteorology and Atmospheric Physics (joint com. on atmospheric electricity), Internat. Sci. Radio Union, Sigma Xi, Tau Beta Pi. Contbr. articles to profl. publs. Home: 21 Springhill Rd Kingston RI 02881

POLK, CHARLES HENRY, coll. pres.; b. Lufkin, Tex., July 11, 1942; s. John Marcus and Eva Mae (Wilmon) P.; B.S., Stephen F. Austin State U., 1963, M.A. in Sociology Psychology, 1965; Ed.D., N.C. State U., 1970; m. Ann Paula Tricomi, Jan. 23, 1965; children—John, Anthony. Instr. sociology Odessa (Tex.) Coll., 1965-66; instr. sociology, psychology Sandhills Community Coll., Southern Pines, N.C., 1966-68; dir. adult and continuing edn. Wilkes Community Coll., Wilkesboro, N.C., 1970; asst. dean for adult and continuing edn., exec. dean to downtown campus Fla. Jr. Coll., Jacksonville, 1970-74; pres. Daytona Beach (Fla.) Community Coll., 1974—. Bd. dirs. United Way, East Volusia; bd. govs. Daytona Beach Community Coll. Found.; bd. counselors Bethune-Cookman Coll., Daytona Beach; mem. Flagler-Volusia Coordinating Council for Vocat. Edn.; mem. exec. com. of 100, Daytona Beach. Mem. Am. Assn. Community and Jr. Colls., Assn. Community Coll. Trustees, Council for Advancement and Support of Edn., Nat. Coop. Edn. Commn., Daytona Beach Area C. of C. (bd. govs.), Halifax Hist. Soc. Presbyterian. Clubs: Masons, Scottish Rite, Rotary. Home: 885 Willow Run Ormond Beach FL 32074 Office: PO Box 1111 Welch Blvd Daytona Beach FL 32015

POLK, HIRAM CAREY, JR., surgeon; b. Jackson, Miss., Mar. 23, 1936; s. Hiram Carey and Dorris (Hemby) P.; B.S., Millsaps Coll., 1956; M.D., Harvard U., 1960; m. Wanda Waddell, Sept. 1, 1956; children-Susan Elizabeth, Hiram Cary. Intern, Barnes Hosp., St. Louis, 1960-61, resident, 1961-65; instr. in surgery Washington U., St. Louis, 1964-65; asst. prof. surgery U. Miami (Fla.), 1965-69, asso. prof., 1969-71; prof. chmn. dept. surgery U. Louisville, 1971—; pres., chmn. bd. dirs. Univ. Surg. Assos., P.S.C., 1971—; chmn. bd. Clin. Services Assn., Inc., bd. govs. Louisville Gen. Hosp., Trover Clinic Found., Madisonville, Ky. Mem. Allen O. Whipple Soc. (exec. council 1977-80), Am. Assn. Cancer Edn. (exec. council 1968-72) Am. Assn. Surgery of Trauma, Am. Burn Assn., Am. Cancer Soc., A.C.S. (gov. 1972-78, commn. on cancer 1975-80), AMA, Am. Surg. Assn., Acad. Surgery (pres. 1975-76), Central Surg. Assn., Assn. Am. Med. Colls. (chmn. ad hoc com. on Medicare and Medicaid 1978—), Collegium Internationale Chirurgiae Digestivae, Council on Public Higher Edn. (task group on health scis. Halsted Soc., Internat. Soc. Burn Injuries, Jefferson County Med. Soc., Ky. Med. Assn., Ky. Surg. Soc., Louisville Surg. Soc., Société Internationale de Cirurgie, Soc. Surgery Alimentary Tract (treas. 1975-78), Soc. Clin. Surgery. Soc. Surg. Chairmen, Soc. Surg. Oncology, Soc. Univ. Surgeons (treas. 1971-74, pres. 1979-80), Southeastern Surg. Congress, So. Med. Assn. (vice chmn. sect. on surgery 1969-70, chmn. sect. 1972-73, sec. 1970-72, exec. council for Ky. 1971-77, So. Surg. Assn., Alpha Omega Alpha (faculty). Author: (with H.H. Stone) Contemporary Burn Management, 1971, Hospital-Acquired Infections in Surgery, 1977; (with N.J. Ehrenkranz) Therapeutic Advances and New Clinical Implications: Medical and Surgical with Betadine Microbicides, (with others) Basic Surgery: A Problem Oriented Text, 1978; contbr. numerous articles to profl. publs.; editorial bd. So. Med. Jour., 1970-72, Jour. Surg. Research, 1970-72, 75—, Current Problems in Surgery, 1973—, Surgery, 1975—, Current Surgery, 1977—, Current Surg. Techniques, 1977—, Emergency Surgery: A Weekly Update, 1977—, Collected Letters in Surgery, 1978—. Home: 18 River Hill Rd Louisville KY 40207 Office: Dept Surgery U Louisville Sch Medicine PO Box 35260 Louisville KY 40232

POLK, JAMES HILLIARD, ret. army officer, cons.; b. Philippine Islands, Dec. 13, 1911 (parents U.S. citizens); s. Harding and Esther (Fleming) P.; B.S., U.S. Mil. Acad., 1933; grad. Nat. War Coll., 1952; m. Josephine Leavell, Nov. 7, 1936; children—Josephine W. (Mrs. Jonathan D. Schwartz, Jr.), James Hilliard III. Commd. 2d lt. U.S. Army, 1933, advanced through grades to gen., 1967; comdr. armored regt. in Patton's 3d Army, World War II; staff officer, Korea 1951; mem. NATO staff, 1957-59; U.S. comdt. in Berlin during Autobahn crisis, 1963; comdg. gen. 5th U.S. Army Corps, Frankfurt, Germany, 1964-66; comdg. gen. U.S. Army in Europe, Heidelberg, 1966-71; ret.; cons. industry and research agys. including Los Alamos Labs., Army Materiel Command System Analysis Agy., Vought Corp. Pres. Army Emergency Relief Soc. 1971—. Decorated D.S.M. with oak leaf cluster, Silver Star with oak leaf cluster, Bronze Star, Legion of Merit with 2 oak leaf clusters; comdr. Legion of Honor, Croix de Guerre (France); Grand Cross (Germany). Mem. Soc. Cincinnati, Order Carabao, Washington Inst. Fgn. Affairs, Army War Coll. Alumni Assn. Clubs: Chevy Chase (Md.); Army-Navy (Washington). Home: 4355 Lowell St NW Washington DC 20016 Office: Vought Corp 1745 Jefferson Davis Hwy #612 Arlington VA 22202

POLK, JAMES RAY, journalist; b. Oaktown, Ind., Sept. 12, 1937; s. Raymond S. and Oeta (Fleener) P.; B.A., Ind. U., 1962; m. Bonnie Becker, Nov. 4, 1962; children—Geoffrey, Amy. With A.P., Indpls., 1962-65, Milw., 1965, Madison, Wis., 1966-67, Washington, 1967-71; investigative reporter Washington Star, 1971-75, NBC News, Washington, 1975—. Chmn., dir. Internat. News, Inc., 1968-71. Adv. bd. Fund for Investigative Journalism, Washington; pres., dir. Investigative Reporters and Editors, Inc. Recipient Raymond Clapper Meml. award, 1972, 74. Pulitzer prize for nat. reporting, 1974, Sigma Delta Chi award, 1974. Mem. Phi Kappa Psi. Contbr. articles to polit. jours. Home: 2124 Florida Ave NW Washington DC 20008 Office: 4001 Nebraska Ave NW Washington DC 20016

POLK, LEE, TV prodn.-syndication co. exec.; b. Bklyn., Oct. 24, 1923; s. David and Becky (Truskinoff) P.; student N.Y. U., 1946-48; m. Lois Steinhauer, Jan. 16, 1949 (dec.); children—Bonnie, Joanne, David. Staff dir. Dumont TV Network, N.Y.C., 1950-55; dir. Sta.-WCBS-TV, N.Y.C., 1955-58; producer-dir. ednl. TV project Sta.-WPIX-TV, N.Y.C., 1958-62; dir. news and public affairs Sta.-WNET-TV, N.Y.C., 1962-70; dir. children's programs Nat. Ednl. TV, N.Y.C., 1970-72; dir. children's programs ABC-TV Network, N.Y.C., 1972-76; v.p. Kin Features TV Prodns., Inc., N.Y.C., 1976-79; v.p. program devel. Gold Key Entertainment, N.Y.C., 1979—; mem. faculty N.Y. U.; instr. New Sch. Social Research; lectr. Fordham U.; cons. TV, HEW; workshop leader White House Conf. on Children, 1970; moderator of hearings on children's programs FCC, 1972. Mem. Greenburgh Sch. Dist. 7 Bd. Edn., Hartsdale, N.Y., 1970-75; bd. overseers Emerson Coll. Served with USAAF, 1942-46. Mem. Nat. Acad. TV Arts and Scis. (pres. N.Y.C. chpt. 1976-81, nat. trustee 1977-81), Internat. Radio and TV Soc. Author: (with Eda LeShan) Incredible Television Machine, 1978; contbr. articles on TV to profl. jours. Home: 150 E 69th St New York NY 10021 Office: 159 W 53d St New York NY 10019. *The key element in my work is enjoying fully the field that I am in. The world of children, where I have spent most of my career personally and professionally, is the most satisfying one that exists for me. To contribute to a child's growth helps me develop as well.*

POLK, LOUIS FREDERICK, bus. exec.; b. Dayton, Ohio; A.B., Sc.D., Miami U., Oxford, Ohio, 1926; D.Eng. (hon.), U. Dayton, 1966; Sc.D. (hon.), Comml. U. Cin., 1971; m. Pauline Chaney, 1926; children—Louis Frederick, Paula Lou. With Sheffield Corp. and its predecessors, 1926-63, pres., 1941-60, chmn., 1960-63; corporate v.p. Bendix Corp., 1956-63, dir., 1956-75; pres. Pirm, Inc.; chmn. bd., dir., exec. com. State-Fidelity Fed. Savs. & Loan, 1949-77, ret.; dir.

Winters Nat. Bank, Dayton, Ohio, 1947-75, Leisure Dynamics, Mpls.; past chmn., dir. Round Hill Devel., Inc., Jamaica, W.I. Past chmn. Cox Heart Inst.; pres. Polk Found.; mem. panel engring. and commodity standards U.S. Dept. Commerce, 1963-65, chmn. task force on measurement and systems, past chmn. nat. metric advisory panel; chmn. U.S. Metric Bd., 1977—, U.S. Interagy. Com. on Metric Policy, 1978—; cons. U.S. chmn. ABC Internat. Conf. for unification engring. standards, 1945-62; mem. bd. ABC Internat.; mem., past chmn., chmn. def. com. APC; cons. metrology USAF; mem. USAF AFLC Adv. Bd., 1959-77; bd. dirs., v.p., chmn. metric adv. com. Am. Nat. Standards Inst., 1965—; chmn. U.S. Standards Mission to USSR, 1967; past mem. adv. com. on metrology Nat. Acad. Scis.-Nat. Bur. Standards. Past mem. bd. U. Dayton; bd. dirs. Air Force Mus. Found.; chmn. bd. Sinclair Community Coll. Found.; past mem. bd. Miami Valley Hosp., Dayton Art Inst., Nat. Aviation Hall of Fame, Engring. and Sci. Inst. of Dayton. Recipient citation Sec. of War, 1946; Ordnance gold medal, 1945, 69; citation Am. Soc. Tool Engrs., 1957; Howard Coonley ANSI gold medal, 1961; Gen. Levin H. Campbell, Jr. gold medal Am. Ordnance Assn., 1962, Charles L. Harrison medal 1971, USAF Exceptional Service award, 1975, Astin-Polk Internat. Standards medal Am. Nat. Standards Inst., 1975. Fellow Am. Soc. M.E. (former mem. council, dir., chmn. bd. codes and standards); hon. life fellow Standards Engrs. Soc.; mem. Nat. Machine Tool Builders Assn. (pres. 1955-56), Am. Ordnance Assn. (pres. 1959-60, mem. exec. com., life dir.), N.Y. Acad. Scis., ASTM (hon.), Soc. Mfg. Engrs. (hon.), Am. Soc. Tool Engrs., Newcomen Soc. N.Am., Delta Kappa Epsilon. Clubs: Engineers, Moraine Country, Miami Valley Hunt and Polo (Dayton); Metropolitan (N.Y.C.); Detroit Athletic; Union League (Chgo.); Camargo, Queen City (Cin.); Rolling Rock (Ligonier, Pa.); Metropolitan (Washington). Author: Vision in Metrology; Review of Peneumatic Dimensional Gages; co-author: Dimensional Control; Common Systems of Measurement; Inch vs. Millimeter. Contbr. to Am. Tech. Press. Home: 333 Oakwood Ave Dayton OH 45409 Office: Winters Bank Tower PO Box 967 Dayton OH 45401

POLK, LOUIS FREDERICK, JR., bus. exec.; b. Dayton, Ohio, Mar. 7, 1930; s. Louis Frederick and Pauline (Chaney) P.; grad. Phillips Acad., Andover, Mass., 1949; B.S. in Elec. and Indsl. Engring., Yale, 1954; M.B.A. in Finance and Mfg., Harvard, 1956; m. Sally Boyd, July 1, 1954 (div. Nov. 1969); children—Christy Kennard, Louis Frederick III, Mary Lees, Stephen Boyd. With Sheffield Corp., subsidiary Bendix Corp., 1956-60, v.p., mgr. operations instruments and systems div., machine tool div., cutting tool div., contract services div., 1960; with Gen. Mills, Inc., 1960-68, comptroller, 1961-68, fin. v.p., dir. 1962-66, group v.p. fin. internat. and devel., 1965-68; pres., chief exec. officer Metro-Goldwyn Mayer, Inc., N.Y.C., 1968-69; chmn. bd., founder Kreisler Group, Leisure Dynamics, Inc., Carey Corp., Children's World; dir. Wolverine World Wide, Inc., Greylock Mgmt. Corp., Exec. Jet Aviation, Inc. Former mem. U. Minn. Sch. Bus. Adminstrn.; former trustee Phillips Andover Acad.; founder, past trustee Minn. Outward Bound Schs., Inc.; adv. bd. Macalester Coll., 1962-65, Mpls. Soc. Fine Arts; mem. Yale Devel. Bd. Mem. Harvard Bus. Sch. Assn. (exec. council), Book and Snake, Delta Kappa Epsilon. Clubs: River, Racquet and Tennis, Piping Rock (N.Y.C.); Metropolitan (Washington); Minneapolis. Author articles in field. Office: 375 Park Ave New York NY 10022

POLK, RALPH LANE, JR., publishing co. exec.; b. Detroit, Jan. 14, 1940; s. Ralph Lane and Winifred E. (Pike) P.; grad. Taft Sch., 1958; B.A., Hillsdale Coll., 1963; m. Nancy Knorr, Aug. 29, 1964; children—Katherine Lynn, Susan Elizabeth, Julie Ann. With R.L. Polk & Co., Detroit, 1963—, v.p., dir., 1966—, treas., 1969—, chief fin. officer, 1978—. Mem. Detroit Econ. Club, Detroit Adcraft Club. Clubs: Bloomfield Hills Country, Detroit, Detroit Athletic. Home: 3805 Lahser Rd Bloomfield Hills MI 48013 Office: 431 Howard St Detroit MI 48231

POLK, WILLIAM MECKLENBURG, ednl. adminstr.; b. N.Y.C., Nov. 1, 1939; s. Frank Lyon and Katharine (Salvage) P.; student Groton Sch., 1953-58; B.A., Trinity Coll., 1962; M.Div. (Rockefeller Bros. fellow), Union Theol. Sem., 1966; m. LuAnn Smith, June 17, 1966; children—Malinda, Gillian. Teaching intern St. Paul's Summer Sch., 1961; teaching fellow Athens Coll., 1965; chmn. dept. religion Lawrenceville (N.J.) Sch., 1967-70, dir. social service programs 1967-70, asst. dean students, 1970-78, asst. coach football, hockey and baseball, 1967-78, tchr. Lawrenceville Summer Sch., 1967, 68, dir. Upward Bound Program, 1970-71, dir. Lawrenceville Counseling Inst., 1976-78; headmaster Groton (Mass.) Sch., 1978—, mem. standing com., 1971-73; mem. bd. fellows Trinity Coll., 1970, trustee, 1971-78; trustee Fay Sch., 1979—; internat. fellow Columbia U., 1966; Groton Sch. sr. prefect, 1957-58. Recipient award Pi Gamma Mu, 1962; Don Porter award Trinity Coll., 1959. Mem. Nat. Assn. Ind. Schs., Nashua River Watershed Assn. (trustee), Phi Beta Kappa. Democrat. Episcopalian. Home: Headmaster's House Groton Sch Farmers Row Groton MA 01450 Office: Headmaster's Office Groton Sch Farmers Row Groton MA 01450

POLK, WILLIAM ROE, educator; b. Ft. Worth, Mar. 7, 1929; s. George Washington and Adelaide (Roe) P.; student U. Nacional de Chile, 1945-46; B.A. with honors, Harvard U., 1951, Ph.D., 1958; postgrad., Am. U. Beirut, 1951-52; B.A. with honors, Oxford (Eng.) U., 1955, M.A., 1959; LL.D., Lake Forest Coll., 1969; m. Joan Cooledge, Dec. 15, 1950 (div. Dec. 1960); children—Milbry Catherine, Alison Elizabeth; m. 2d, Ann Cross, June 9, 1962; children—George W. IV, Eliza Forbes. Asst. prof. Harvard U., 1955-62; sr. partner Polk-Robinson Assos., Boston, 1958-61; sr. editor, dir. Arlington Books, Inc., Cambridge, Mass., 1959-61; adv. editor Beacon Press, Boston, 1960—; mem. Policy Planning Council, Dept. State, 1961-65; prof. Middle Eastern history U. Chgo., 1965-75, dir. Center for Middle Eastern Studies, 1965-69; dir. Adlai Stevenson Inst. Internat. Affairs, 1967-70, pres., 1970-74, sr. fellow, 1975-75; pres. Rabia Ltd., 1975—; Dir. Perkins & Will Internat. Ltd., Chgo., Microform Data Systems, Mountain View, Calif., Hyde Park Bank, 1967-74. Mem. Permanent Class of 1951, Harvard U., bd. dirs. Central YMCA Community Coll., Chgo. Rockefeller fellow, 1951-55; Guggenheim fellow, 1961-62. Fellow Acad. on Pub. Policy; mem. Middle Eastern Studies Assn. (dir.), Council Fgn. Relations, Am. Oriental Soc., Am. Hist. Soc. Clubs: Arts, Wayfarers (Chgo.); Federal City, Cosmos (Washington); Century (N.Y.C.). Author: Perspective of Arab World, 1956, Backdrop to Tragedy: The Struggle for Palestine, 1957, Generations, Classes and Politics, 1962, The Opening of South Lebanon, 1963, The Developmental Revolution, 1964, The United States and the Arab World, 1965, 2d edit., 1969, 3d edit., 1975; Passing Brave, 1973; also articles, bulls. Editor: (with Stanford Shaw) Studies on the Civilization of Islam (Gibb), 1962; Developmental Revolution, 1964; (with Richard Chambers) Beginnings of Modernization, 1969; The Golden Ode, 1973, 2d edit., 1977; The Elusive Peace: The Middle East in the Twentieth Century, 1979. Home: Poste Restante Varkiza Attica Greece

POLL, HEINZ, choreographer, artistic dir.; b. Oberhausen, West Germany, Mar. 18, 1926; s. Heinrich and Anna Margareta (Winkels) P.; came to U.S., 1965, naturalized, 1975. Dancer with Gottingen Mcpl. Theatre, 1946-48, Deutsches Theatre Konstanz, 1948-49, East Berlin State Opera, 1949-50, Nat. Ballet of Chile, 1951-62, Ballet de la Jeunesse Musicales de France, 1963-64; guest appearances with Nat. Ballet Chile, 1964, Am. Dance Festival, 1965; choreographed works for Nat. Ballet Chile, Paris Festival Ballet, Ballet de la Jeunesse Musicales de France, Nat. Ballet Can., Pa. Ballet, Ohio Ballet; co-founder, dir. The Dance Inst., U. Akron, 1967-77; founder, artistic dir., choreographer Ohio Ballet, Akron, 1968—; tchr. Chilean Instituto de Extension Musical, 1951-61, N.Y. Nat. Acad., 1965-66. Nat. Endowment for the Arts grantee, 1974-75. Office: 354 E Market Akron OH 44325

POLL, MARTIN HARVEY, film producer; b. N.Y.C., Nov. 24, 1923; s. David and Fay (Tamber) P.; student Wharton Sch. Bus. U. Pa., 1940; B.S., N.Y. U., 1943; m. Lee Lindenberg, May 21, 1954 (div. Oct. 10, 1967); children—Mark, Jonathan; m. 2d, Gladys Peltz Jaffe, Oct. 31, 1976. Asst. to gen. mgr. Paramount Music Corp., N.Y.C., 1947-50, partner Artists Mgmt. Assn., N.Y.C., 1950; pres. Inter-Continental TV Films Inc., N.Y.C., 1952; exec. producer Theatre Network TV Inc., N.Y.C., 1953; pres. Gold Medal Studios, Bronx, N.Y., 1954-62; ind. producer, 1962—; films include Love is a Ball, 1962, Sylvia, 1964, The Appointment, 1968, The Lion in Winter (Best Picture award), 1968, The Magic Garden of Stanley Sweetheart, 1970, Night Watch, 1972, The Man Who Loved Cat Dancing, 1973, Love and Death, 1975, The Sailor Who Fell From Grace with The Sea, 1976, The Dain Curse, Somebody Killed her Husband. Served with AUS, 1944-47. Named Hon. Commr. Motion Picture Arts N.Y.C., 1958; recipient David Di Donatello Best Film Producer award Pres. Italy, 1968, N.Y. Film Critics award, 1968, Hollywood Fgn. Press Assn. Golden Globe award, 1968, Brit. Acad. award, 1968. Mem. Producers Guild of Am., Acad. Motion Picture Arts and Scis., Cinema Circulus, Friends of Library U. So. Calif. Home: 911 Park Ave New York NY 10021 Office: 919 3d Ave New York NY 10022

POLLACK, GERALD LESLIE, educator, physicist; b. Bklyn, July 8, 1933; s. Herman and Jennie (Tenenbaum) P.; B.S., Bklyn. Coll., 1954; Fulbright scholar, U. Gottingen, 1954-55; M.S., Calif. Inst. Tech., 1957, Ph.D., 1962; m. Antoinette Amparo Velasquez, Dec. 22, 1958; children—Harvey Anton, Samuela Juliet, Margolita Mia, Violet Amata. Physics student trainee Nat. Bur. Standards, Washington, 1954-58, solid state physicist, 1961-65, cons., Boulder, Colo., 1965-70; asso. prof. dept. physics Mich. State U., East Lansing, 1965-69, prof., 1969—; cons. NRC; physicist Naval Med. Research Inst., Bethesda, Md., summer 1979. Fellow Am. Phys. Soc.; mem. Biophys. Soc., Am. Assn. Physics Tchrs., AAAS. Jewish. Contbr. articles to profl. jours. Home: 253 Highland Ave East Lansing MI 48823

POLLACK, HENRY NATHAN, geophysicist; b. Omaha, July 13, 1936; s. Harold Myron and Sylvia (Chait) P.; A.B., Cornell U., 1958; M.S., U. Nebr., 1960; Ph.D., U. Mich., 1963; m. Lana Beth Schoenberger, Jan. 29, 1963; children—Sara Beth (dec.), John David. Lectr., U. Mich., 1962, asst. prof., asso. prof., prof. geophysics, 1964—; research fellow Harvard U., 1963-64; sr. lectr. U. Zambia, 1970-71; vis. scientist U. Durham, U. Newcastle-on-Tyne (U. K.), 1977-78. Mem. AAAS, Am. Geophys. Union, Seismol. Soc. Am., Geol. Soc. Am. Research on thermal evolution of the earth. Office: Dept Geology and Mineralogy U Mich Ann Arbor MI 48109

POLLACK, HERMAN, cons., educator; b. N.Y.C., Oct. 22, 1919; s. Phillip and Molly (Mareine) P.; B.S. in Social Sci., Coll. City N.Y., 1940; postgrad. Columbia, 1940-41; M.A. in Internat. Relations, George Washington U., 1965; m. June Rae Cohen, Nov. 19, 1949. With agys. U.S. Govt., 1941-46; with State Dept., 1946-74; chief, mgmt. staff, 1958-61, dep. asst. sec. state personnel, 1961-63, Nat. War Coll., 1963-64, acting dir. Internat. Sci. Affairs, 1964-67, dir. internat. sci. and tech. affairs, 1967-74; cons. to govt., research prof. George Washington U., 1974—. Mem. commerce tech. adv. bd. CTAB, 1975-77; mem. Weather Modification Advisory Bd., 1977-78. Served with AUS, 1943. Mem. AAAS. Club: Cosmos (Washington). Home: 7000 Selkirk Dr Bethesda MD 20034 Office: George Washington U Washington DC 20052

POLLACK, IRWIN WILLIAM, educator, psychiatrist; b. Phila., Aug. 14, 1927; s. Nathan and Rose (Bergman) P.; A.B., Temple U., 1950; M.A., Columbia, 1951; student U. Pa., 1951-52; M.D., U. Vt., 1956; m. Lois Madlyn Franco, Feb. 9, 1957; children—Nathaniel Edward, Joshua Frank, Jonathan Daniel. Intern Grad. Hosp. U. Pa., 1956-57; asst. resident psychiatry Henry Phipps Psychiat. Clinic, John Hopkins Hosp., 1957-60; chief resident psychiatry Johns Hopkins Hosp., 1960-61, adminstr. psychosomatic clinic, psychiat. liaison service, 1961-64; psychiatrist-in-chief Sinai Hosp., Balt., 1964-68; mem. faculty psychiatry Coll. Medicine and Dentistry N.J., Rutgers Med. Sch., 1968—, asso. prof. psychiatry, 1968-70, also dir. Community Mental Health Center, prof. psychiatry, 1970—, chmn. dept. Coll. Medicine and Dentistry, exec. dir. Community Mental Health Center, 1970-77; spl. research problems time and space perception, time limited psychiat. treatment, doctor-patient relationships. Bd. dirs. Balt. Mental Health Assn. Served with USNR, 1945-46. Diplomate Am. Bd. Psychiatry and Neurology. Fellow Am. Psychiat. Assn.; mem. N.J. Psychiat. Assn., Am. Psychosomatic Soc., Alpha Omega Alpha. Home: 324 Lincoln Ave Highland Park NJ 08904 Office: Dept Psychiatry Rutgers Med Sch/Coll Medicine and Dentistry Piscataway NJ 08854

POLLACK, JEROME MARVIN, univ. pres.; b. Chgo., Apr. 16, 1926; s. David and Sylvia (Marcus) P.; B.S., U. Okla., 1949, M.S., 1951, Ph.D., 1959; m. Ruth Mary Stephens, Aug. 2, 1952; children—Eric, Cassy, Nancy, Michael. Geologist, Humble Oil & Refining Co., 1951-55; instr. geology U. Okla., 1955-58; asst. prof. Oklahoma City U., 1958-59, Harpur Coll., Binghamton, N.Y., 1959-61; asso. prof. geology, chmn. dept. geology and geography U. N.H., 1961-65; dean Coll. Arts and Scis., prof. geology U. R.I., Kingston, R.I., 1965-68, v.p. for acad. affairs, 1968-69, dean Coll. Arts and Scis., 1969-71; v.p. acad. affairs Fairleigh Dickinson U., 1971-73, exec. and acad. v.p., 1973-74, acting pres., 1974, pres., 1974—. Mem. Geol. Soc. Am., Am. Assn. Petroleum Geologists, Soc. Econ. Mineralogists and Paleontologists, AAUP, AAAS, Sigma Xi. Home: PO Box 900 Teaneck NJ 07666 Office: Fairleigh Dickinson U Rutherford NJ 07070

POLLACK, JOSEPH, labor union ofcl.; b. N.Y.C., Nov. 21, 1917; s. George and Martha (Miller) P.; student pub. schs., N.Y.C.; m. Theresa Keenan, Dec. 17, 1941; 1 son, Terry. Agt., Prudential Ins. Co., N.Y.C., 1946-52; pres. Local 19, Ins. Workers Internat. Union AFL-CIO, N.Y.C., 1952-61, v.p. Washington, 1961-76, pres., 1976—; mem. exec. bd. dept. profl. employees AFL-CIO. Bd. dirs. Labor Inst. Human Enrichment; mem. Pres.'s Com. Employment Handicapped. Served with AUS, 1941-45. Democrat. Jewish. Editor: Insurance Worker, 1976. Office: 1017 12th St NW Washington DC 20005. *The price of leadership is hard work and a willingness to accept responsibility. The main attribute of continued elected leadership is total fairness under all circumstances. Dignity in leadership and a dedication to the dignity of all mankind makes for a worthwhile organization.*

POLLACK, MILTON, judge; b. N.Y.C., Sept. 29, 1906; s. Julius and Betty (Schwartz) P.; A.B., Columbia U., 1927, J.D., 1929; m. Lillian Klein, Dec. 18, 1932, (dec. July 1967); children—Stephanie P. Pollack Singer, Daniel A.; m. 2d, Moselle Baum Erlich, Oct. 24, 1971. Admitted to N.Y. bar, 1930; asso. atty. firm Gilman & Unger, N.Y.C., 1929-38; partner firm Unger & Pollack, N.Y.C., 1938-44; propr. Milton Pollack, N.Y.C., 1945-67; U.S. dist. judge So. Dist. N.Y., 1967—. Pres., Prospect Park So. Assn., Bklyn., 1948-50, counsel, 1950-60, bd. dirs., 1945-60; mem. local SSS, 1952-60. Chmn. lawyers div. Fedn. Jewish Philanthropies, 1957-61, vice chmn., 1954-57; chmn. lawyers div. Am. Jewish Com., 1964-66, bd. dirs., 1967—. Bd. dirs. Beth Isreal Hosp.; trustee, Temple Emanu-El, 1977—, v.p., 1978—. Recipient Learned Hand award Am. Jewish Com., 1967; Proskauer medal lawyers div. Fedn. Jewish Philanthropies, 1968. Mem. Am., N.Y. State, New York County, Kings County bar assns., Assn. Bar City N.Y., Columbia Law Sch. Alumni Assn. (pres. 1970-72). Home: 480 Park Ave New York NY 10022 Office: US Courthouse Foley Sq New York NY 10007

POLLACK, NORMAN, educator; b. Bridgeport, Conn., May 29, 1933; s. Benjamin and Mary (Beimel) P.; B.A., U. Fla., 1954; M.A., Harvard, 1957, Ph.D., 1961; m. Nancy Bassing, Feb. 2, 1957; 1 son, Peter Franklin. Instr. history Yale, 1961-62, asst. prof., 1962-65; asso. prof. Wayne State U., 1965-68; prof. Mich. State U., 1968—. Guggenheim fellow, 1968-69. Author: The Populist Response to Industrial America, 1962; The Populist Mind, 1967. Home: 929 Roxburgh East Lansing MI 48823 Office: Dept of History Mich State U East Lansing MI 48824

POLLACK, REGINALD MURRAY, painter; b. Middle Village, L.I., N.Y., July 29, 1924; grad. High Sch. Music and Art, N.Y.C., 1941; student with Wallace Harrison, Moses Soyer, Boardman Robinson; student Academie de la Grande Chaumiere, 1948-52; m. Kerstin Birgitta Soederlund; children by previous marriage—Jane Olivia, Maia Jaquine. Exhibited one man shows Charles Fourth Gallery, N.Y.C., 1948, Peridot Gallery, 1949, 52, 55-57, 59, 60, 62, 63, 65, 67, 69, Galerie Saint-Placide, Paris, 1952, Dwan Gallery, 1960, Jefferson Gallery, LaJolla, Calif., 1963, 68, 69, Goldwach Gallery, Chgo., 1964, 65, 56, Gallery Z, Beverly Hills, Calif., 1973, David Alexander Gallery, 1974, Washington Gallery Arts, 1974, Cosmos Club, Washington, 1976, Washington Project for Arts, 1976, Everhart Mus., Scranton, Pa., 1977, Pa. State U., 1977, Jack Rasmussen gallery, 1978, 79, Art Washington, 1979; exhibited group shows including Whitney Mus. Am. Art, 1953, 55, 56, 58, 62, U. Nebr., 1951, 56, 57, 60, 63, Chgo. Art Inst., Carnegie, Pitts., Salon du Mai, Paris, U. Ill., Salon des Artistes Independants, Paris, 1955-58, numerous others; multi-media theatrical prodns. The War of The Angels, 1974, The Twelve Gifts of Christmas, 1974; commns. include Jacob's Ladder painting Washington Cathedral; represented in permanent collections Bezalel Mus., Bklyn. Mus., Collection de L'Etat, France, U. Glasgow, Haifa, Mus. Modern Art, U. Nebr., Newark Mus., Rockefeller Inst., Whitney Mus. Am. Art, Worcester Art Mus., numerous other pub. and pvt. collections. Tchr., Yale, 1962-63, Cooper Union, 1963-64; mem. staff Human Relations Tng. Center U. Calif. at Los Angeles, 1966; instr. Quaker Half-way House, Los Angeles, 1968; cons. staff Lighthouse Child Guidance Center Presbyn. Hosp., Los Angeles, 1966-69; pvt. instr., 1966-69; vis. artist Materials Research Lab., Pa. State U., 1977. Trustee Washington Project for Arts, 1976—. Served with AUS 1941-45. Recipient Prix Neumann, Paris, 1952, Prix Othon Friesz, Paris, mention, 1954, 57, Prix de Peintres Etrangeres, 2d prize Paris Moderne, 1958; Ingram-Merrill Found. grantee, 1964, 70-71. Author and illustrator: The Magician and the Child, 1971. Illustrator: Get a Horse (Steven Price), 1974; Visions from the Ramble (John Hollander), 1964; The Quest of the Gole (John Hollander), 1966; O is for Overkill, A Survival Alphabet (Merrill Pollack), 1968; The Blessed Ones (Ulla Isaksson), 1970; Oedipus (Seneca, transl. Ted Knight), 1973, also mag. cover, posters, record albums. Address: 205 River Bend Rd Great Falls VA 22066

POLLACK, SYDNEY, film dir.; b. Lafayette, Ind., July 1, 1934; s. David and Rebecca (Miller) P.; grad. Neighborhood Playhouse Theatre Sch., N.Y.C., 1954; m. Claire Griswold, Oct. 22, 1958; children—Steven, Rebecca, Rachel. Asst. to Sanford Meisner, Neighborhood Playhouse Theatre, 1954, instr. acting, 1954-60; appeared in Broadway prodns. The Dark Is Light Enough, 1954, A Stone For Danny Fisher, 1955; appeared on live TV programs Playhouse 90, Kraft Television Theater, Goodyear Playhouse, Alcoa Presents, others; toured in Stalag 17; dir. TV programs Naked City, Route 66, The Defenders, Ben Casey, Dr. Kildare, The Chrysler Theatre, others, 1960-65; dir. motion pictures The Slender Thread, 1965, This Property Is Condemned, 1966, The Scalphunters, 1967, Castle Keep, 1968, They Shoot Horses, Don't They?, 1969-70, Jeremiah Johnson, 1971-72, The Way We Were, 1972-73, The Yakuza, 1974, Three Days of the Condor, 1974-75, Bobby Deerfield, 1976, The Electric Horseman, 1978-79; exec. dir. West Coast br. The Actors Studio. Nominated for numerous Acad. and Emmy awards. Served with AUS, 1957-59. Office: 4000 Warner Blvd Burbank CA 91505

POLLACK, WILLIAM, research found. exec.; b. London, Eng., Feb. 26, 1926; s. David and Rose (Weis) P.; B.S., Imperial Coll. Sci. and Tech., 1948; M.S., St. George's Hosp. Med. Sch., London U., 1950; Ph.D., Rutgers U., 1964; m. Alison Elizabeth Calder, Dec. 4, 1954; children—Malcolm Trevor, David Calder. Sci. officer dept. hematology and bacteriology, serologist, immunologist St. George's Hosp. Med. Sch., 1950-54; head blood bank and serology dept. Royal Columbian Hosp., B.C., Can., 1954-56; sr. scientist dept. immunology Ortho Research Found., Raritan, N.J., 1956-61, dir. div. immunochemistry, 1968-69, asso. dir. research, diagnostics, 1969, v.p., dir. Ortho Research Inst. Med. Scis., 1975—; asso. clin. prof. pathology Coll. Phys. and Surg., Columbia, 1969—, asso. prof. Rutgers U. Med. Sch. Served with Brit. Royal Navy, 1943-46. Recipient John Scott award Bd. Dirs. City Trusts, City of Phila., 1976; Joseph Bolivar DeLee Humanitarian award, Chgo., 1979. Fellow N.Y. Acad. Scis., N.Y. Acad. Medicine; mem. A.A.A.S., Am. Soc. Clin. Pathologists, Am. Assn. Blood Banks (Karl Landsteiner award 1969), Brit., Am. socs. immunology, Sigma Xi. Co-developer of vaccine to prevent Rh disease of babies. Contbr. articles immunology, immunochemistry to sci. jours. Home: Sunset Rd Belle Mead NJ 08509 Office: Ortho Research Inst Med Scis Raritan NJ 08869

POLLAK, HARRY HAMILTON, fgn. service officer, diplomat; b. Passaic, N.J., Mar. 12, 1921; s. Sigmond and Molly (Katz) P.; B.A., Rutgers U., 1948; M.A., U. Chgo., 1951; m. Suzette Lois Aldon, June 29, 1950; children—Mollyann Pollak Gassel, Daniel. Asso. dir. internat. dept. CIO, 1951-55; asso. Inter-Am. rep. AFL-CIO, 1956-58, Asian rep., 1958-62; labor adviser Am. embassy, Tokyo, 1962-65; labor editor Voice of Am., 1956-66; labor attache, polit. officer U.S. Mission to European Communities, Brussels, Belgium, 1967-73; labor attache, first sec. Am. embassy, London, 1973-77; dep. coordinator internat. labor affairs Dept. of State, 1977—; vis. lectr. Am. U., 1961; pub. mem. U.S. Fgn. Service Selection Bd., 1951; labor adviser Peace Corps, 1961; mem. trade union advisory com. Dept. Labor and Fgn. Operations Adminstrn., 1951-55. Vice pres. Burgundy Farm Country Day Sch., Alexandria, Va., 1960; hon. sec. Tokyo Jewish Community Center, 1963. Served with USAAC, 1942-45. Decorated D.F.C., Air medal with 3 oak leaf clusters; recipient cert. of merit Labor Dept., 1959. Mem. Fgn. Service Assn., Phi Beta Kappa. Jewish. Editor Am. Labor Rev., Tokyo, 1962-64; asst. editor Inter-Am. Labor Bull., 1956-58. Office: Dept State (S/IL) Washington DC 20520

POLLAK, HENRY OTTO, utility research exec.; b. Vienna, Austria, Dec. 13, 1927; s. Ludwig and Olga (Weil) P.; came to U.S., 1940, naturalized, 1945; B.A., Yale, 1947; M.A., Harvard U., 1948, Ph.D., 1951; D.Sc., Rose Poly. Inst., 1964, Monmouth Coll., 1975, Bowdoin Coll., 1977; m. Ida Jeanne Tobias, May 7, 1949; children—Katherine, James. With Bell Telephone Labs., Murray Hill, N.J., 1951—, mem. tech. staff, 1951-59, head dept. communications fundamentals II, 1959-61, acting dir. math. and mechanics research center, 1961-62, dir. math. and statistics research center, 1962—. Mem. sch. math. study group, com. on undergrad. program in math. Internat. Commn. on Math. Instrn., 1970-74; mem. adv. bd. Unified Sci. and Maths. for Elementary Schs., 1969-77; mem. adv. com. for sci. edn. NSF, 1977-80, chmn., 1978-80. Mem. Am. Math. Soc., Math. Assn. Am. (pres. 1975-76), Nat. Council Tchrs. Math., AAAS, Elizabethan Club, Austria Philatelic Soc. N.Y., Austrian Stamp Club of Gt. Brit., Phi Beta Kappa, Sigma Xi. Mem. Christ Ch. Home: 40 Edgewood Rd Summit NJ 07901 Office: Bell Labs 600 Mountain Ave Murray Hill NJ 07974

POLLAK, LOUIS HEILPRIN, judge; b. N.Y.C., Dec. 7, 1922; s. Walter Heilprin and Marion (Heilprin) P.; A.B., Harvard, 1943; LL.B., Yale, 1948; m. Katherine Weiss, July 25, 1952; children—Nancy, Elizabeth, Susan, Sarah, Deborah. Admitted to N.Y. bar, 1949, Conn. bar, 1956, Pa. bar, 1976; law clk. to U.S. Supreme Ct. Justice Rutledge, 1948-49; with firm Paul, Weiss, Rifkind, Wharton & Garrison, N.Y.C., 1949-51; atty. Dept. State, spl. asst. to ambassador-at-large, 1951-53; vis. lectr. Howard U. Sch. Law, 1953; asst. counsel Amalgmated Clothing Workers Am., 1954-55; mem. faculty Yale Law Sch., 1955-74, prof., 1961-65, 70-74, dean of Law Sch., 1965-70; Greenfield prof. U. Pa., 1974-78; dean Law Sch., 1975-78; U.S. dist. judge for Eastern dist. Pa., 1978—; vis. prof. U. Mich. Law Sch., 1961, Columbia Law Sch., 1962. Mem. New Haven Bd. Edn., 1962-68; chmn. Conn. adv. com. U.S. Civil Rights Commn., 1962-63; mem. bd. NAACP Legal Def. Fund, 1960-78, v.p., 1971—; chmn. New Haven Human Rights Com., 1963-64. Served with AUS, 1943-46. Mem. Assn. Bar City N.Y., Am. (chmn. sec. individual rights 1970-71), Pa., Phila. bar assns., Am. Law Inst. (council 1978—), Soc. Am. Law Tchrs. (bd. govs. 1975-78), Author: The Constitution and the Supreme Court: A Documentary History, 1966. Office: 13613 US Courthouse 601 Market St Philadelphia PA 19106

POLLAK, RICHARD, editor; b. Chgo., Apr. 5, 1934; s. Robert and Janet (Spitzer) P.; student Knox Coll., 1952-54; B.A. in English, Amherst Coll., 1957; m. Merle Ann Winer, Mar. 26, 1961; 1 dau., Amanda. Reporter Worcester (Mass.) Telegram & Gazette, 1957; polit. reporter Evening Sun, Balt., 1959-64; asso. editor Newsweek, N.Y.C., 1964-67; asst. editor Honolulu Star Bull., 1967-68; freelance writer, N.Y.C., 1968-71; co-founder, editor More mag., N.Y.C., 1971-76; editor press dept. The Nation, 1978—; tchr. Yale U., spring 1977, N.Y. U., fall 1977. Cons. Ford Found., 1970-72. Served with AUS, 1957-59. Poynter fellow Yale U., 1977. Mem. P.E.N. Editor: Stop The Presses, I Want To Get Off!, 1975. Home: 404 Riverside Dr New York NY 10025

POLLAK, STEPHEN JOHN, lawyer; b. Chgo., Mar. 22, 1928; s. Maurice August and Laura (Kramer) P.; A.B., Dartmouth, 1950; LL.B., Yale, 1956; m. Ruth Scheinfeld, June 22, 1951; children—Linda Jan, David Michael, Roger Lincoln, Eve Juliette. Admitted to Ill. bar, 1956, D.C. bar, 1957; asso. firm Covington & Burling, Washington, 1956-61; asst. to solicitor gen. Dept. Justice, 1961-64; counsel President's Task Force War Against Poverty, 1964; dep. gen. counsel Office Econ. Opportunity, 1964-65; 1st asst. civil rights div. Dept. Justice, 1965-67, asst. atty. gen., 1968-69; President's adviser for Nat. Capital affairs, 1967; mem. firm Shea & Gardner, Washington, 1969—. Chmn., Washington Lawyers Com. for Civil Rights under Law, 1970-72, D.C. Circuit Jud. Conf. Com. on Adminstrn. of Justice under Emergency Conditions, 1971-73; mem. exec. com. Nat. Lawyers' Com. for Civil Rights Under Law, 1969—, co-chmn., 1975-77. Bd. dirs. Washington Planning and Housing Assn., 1958-67, pres., 1965-66; trustee Black Student Fund, 1969—, chmn., 1977—. Served to lt. (j.g.) U.S. Navy, 1950-53. Recipient Jewett prize Yale, 1955. Mem. Am. Bar Assn. (ho. of dels. 1978—), D.C. Bar (bd. govs. 1972-73, sec. 1974-75, pres.-elect 1979—), Order of Coif, Phi Beta Kappa. Home: 3314 Newark St NW Washington DC 20008 Office: 1800 Massachusetts Ave NW Washington DC 20036

POLLARD, BRAXTON, educator; b. Hannibal, Mo., Oct. 8, 1908; s. William Braxton and Nancy Elizabeth (Robinson) P.; student Washington U., St. Louis, 1926-27; B.J., U. Mo., 1930; m. Maj-Britt Larsson, May 29, 1963 (div. 1974); children—Elizabeth Kristina, Braxton Erik W. Mem. research dept. D'Arcy Advt. Co., St. Louis, 1930-33; dir. publicity Nat. Mark Twain Centennial, 1934-35; writer Selznick Internat. Pictures, Inc., 1935-36; theatre reviewer, feature writer N.Y. Sun, 1936-37; advt. mgr. A.P. Green Co., St. Louis, 1938-47; mem. central advt. dept. Monsanto Chem. Co., 1947-54, mgr. internat. advt., 1954-65, mgr. advt. media, 1965-68, mgr. advt. design and prodn., 1968-69, mgr. corporate promotion, 1969-71; prof. internat. advt. Sch. Journalism, U. Mo., Columbia, 1971—; founder, editor-in-chief Monsanto Internat. mag., 1948-65; condr. workshops for Assn. Nat. Advertisers, also Am. Mgmt. Assn.; instr. Inst. Advt., St. Louis U., 1951-52. Publicity chmn. Fgn. Trade Bur., St. Louis C. of C., 1950-60; mem. advt. activities com. 50th Anniversary Celebration, U. Mo. Sch. Journalism, 1959; panel judges McKinsey Found. award Harvard Bus. Rev., 1963. Distinguished lectr. U. Mo. Sch. Journalism 50th Anniversary Celebration, 1959. Mem. Internat. Advt. Assn. (Internat. Advt. Man of Year award 1962, Best Chem. advt. award 1954), Assn. Nat. Advertisers, Indsl. Advertisers Assn. (past pres. St. Louis), Hist. Soc. Mo., Municipal Theatre Assn. St. Louis, Kappa Sigma, Kappa Tau Alpha. Baptist. Author: A Basic Guide to International Advertising, 1959; also articles; contbr. to International and Intercultural Communications, 1976. Home: 204 W Stewart Rd Columbia MO 65201 Office: Sch Journalism U Mo Columbia MO 65201

POLLARD, CHARLES WILLIAM, health care services co. exec.; b. Chgo., June 1, 1938; s. Charles W. and Ruth Ann (Humphrey) P.; A.B., Wheaton Coll., 1960; J.D., Northwestern U., 1963; m. Judith Ann, June 8, 1959; children—Julie Ann, Charles W., Brian, Amy. Admitted to Ill. bar, 1963; mem. firm Wilson and McIlvaine, 1963-67; mem. firm Vescelus, Perry & Pollard, Wheaton, Ill., 1968-72; prof., v.p. Wheaton Coll., 1972-77; sr. v.p. Service Master Industries, Downers Grove, Ill., 1977-80, exec. v.p., 1980—; dir. Gary-Wheaton Bank. Bd. dirs. Wheaton Coll., Stewards Found. Home: 716 N Wheaton Wheaton IL 60187 Office: 2300 Warrenville Rd Downers Grove IL 60515

POLLARD, DARRELL HENRY, coll. adminstr.; b. Terre Haute, Ind., Apr. 9, 1921; s. James Henry and Iva (Payne) P.; A.B., Albion (Mich.) Coll., 1943; M.A., U. Mich., 1949, Ph.D., 1959; m. Alice Katherine Hampton, Oct. 31, 1943; children—Alicia G., Dennis D., Craig J., Leslie S. Instr. history and polit. sci. Sault br. Mich. Sch. Mines, 1950-51; prof. history and polit. sci. Albion Coll., 1951-64, chmn. dept., 1959-64; dean coll. Adrian Coll., 1964—, v.p., 1966—, dir. personnel and labor relations, 1978—. Vice pres. Adrian Bd. Edn., 1967-68, pres., 1968—. Mem. Mich. Constl. Reform Study Commn., 1960-61. Bd. dirs. profl. div. Adrian United Fund; pres. Southeastern Mich. Goodwill LARC Industries, 1976—; bd. dirs. Lenawee Assn. for Retarded Children Activities Center, Lenawee Country Club. Served with AUS, 1943-46. Recipient citation for Community service Adrian United Fund, 1967. Mem. Assn. Colls. and Univs. for Internat. and Intercultural Studies (pres. 1967—), Am. Hist. Assn., Am. Polit. Sci. Assn., Am. Council Edn., Am. Assn. Colls. and Univs. Republican. Presbyn. Rotarian (pres. Adrian 1970—). Home: 1717 Southgate St Adrian MI 49221

POLLARD, DAVID EDWARD, editor; b. Columbus, Ohio, Oct. 7, 1927; s. James Edward and Marjorie Olive (Pearson) P.; B.S., Ohio State U., 1950; postgrad. in cotton econs. Memphis State U., 1967; m. Ilse Knack, Dec. 24, 1960; children—Walter Thomas, Marcus Andreas, Michael David, Christopher James. With Columbus Citizen, 1943-50; with Army Times Pub. Co., 1952-60, mng. editor U.S. Coast Guard Mag., Washington, 1956-57, asso. editor Am. Weekend, Washington, also Frankfurt, Ger., 1957-60; info. specialist Air Forces Europe Exchange, Wiesbaden, Ger., 1961-63; reporter Comml. Appeal, Memphis, 1963-66, fin. writer, 1967-68; news-desk editor U.S. News & World Report, Washington, 1968-76, chief news desk, 1976—. Served with USMC, 1945-46, 51-52. Mem. White House Corrs. Assn., Sigma Delta Chi, Alpha Delta Sigma, Alpha Tau Omega. Roman Catholic. Patentee garden implement. Office: 2300 N St NW Washington DC 20037

POLLARD, FRED DON, bus. exec.; b. Proctorsville, Vt., Sept. 15, 1931; s. Bryant Frank and Millie Viola (Brobst) P.; B.A., Dartmouth Coll., 1953; M.B.A., Tuck Sch. Bus. Adminstrn., 1954; m. Sandra Jean Norton, Oct. 19, 1957; children—Fred Don, Bruce Gardiner, Mark Bryant. Staff auditor Touche, Niven, Bailey & Smart, Chgo., 1954-55, 57-58; with Hertz Corp., Chgo., 1958-60, London, 1960-62, Paris, France, 1962-64, N.Y.C., 1964-65; European controller Avis Rent A Car, London, 1965-69, internat. treas., 1969-71, asst. v.p., dir. fin., Garden City, N.Y., 1971-72, asst. treas., 1972-75; treas. Garcia Corp., Teaneck, N.J., 1975-78; v.p. fin., treas. Augsbury Orgn., Inc., Ogdensburg, N.Y., 1978-79, sr. v.p. fin., treas., 1979—, also dir.; dir. Augsburg Corp., Hall Corp., Montreal, Que., Can., Carlton Holding Co./N.Y. Casualty, Watertown, N.Y. Mem. adv. bd. Clarkson Sch. Mgmt., Potsdam, N.Y.; mem. exec. bd. St. Lawrence council Boy Scouts Am. Served with U.S. Army, 1955-57. C.P.A., N.Y. Mem. Fin. Execs. Inst. Presbyterian. Clubs: Toastmasters Internat. Home: Little River Farm Star Route Canton NY 13617 Office: 100 Lafayette St Ogdensburg NY 13669

POLLARD, GEORGE MARVIN, economist; b. St. Joseph, Mo., Oct. 5, 1909; s. James Coleman and Ethel (Mallory) P.; A.B., George Washington U., 1934, A.M., 1939; student Columbia, 1940-41, sch. mil. govt. U. Va., 1944, Stanford, 1944-45; m. Jean Mary Campion, Apr. 15, 1939; 1 dau., Elizabeth G. Mem. staff U.S. Dept. Agr., 1928-41, WPB, 1941-43; sr. economist U.S. Dept. Army, 1946-49; internat. economist, 1949-51; fgn. service officer Dept. State, 1955-64, internat. economist, 1951-55, 64—; consul, chief polit. and econ. affairs Am. Consulate Gen., Düsseldorf, Germany, 1956-58; 1st sec. econ. affairs U.S. Mission to European Communities, Luxembourg, 1958-61; supervisory officer econ. affairs Bur. Internat. Orgn. Affairs, Dept. State, Washington, 1961-63; assigned to Bur. Internat. Commerce, U.S. Dept. Commerce, Washington, 1964-76. Mem. planning and zoning commn., Vienna, Va., 1953-56. Served as lt. USNR, 1943-46, mil. govt. officer Occupation of Japan, 1945-46, mem. U.S. rep. Far Eastern Commn., Washington, 1947-49; lt. col. U.S. Army Res., 1949-63, ret. Mem. Phi Theta Kappa, Phi Sigma Kappa, Alpha Kappa Psi. Lion. Home: 9369 Campbell Rd Vienna VA 22180

POLLARD, HARRY, educator; b. Boston, Feb. 28, 1919; s. David and Rebecca (Bell) P.; grad. Boston Latin Sch., 1935; A.B., Harvard U., 1939, A.M., 1940, Ph.D., 1942; m. Helen May Rickard, May 13, 1943; children—Joel, Carl Jesse, Betsy Helen (Mrs. Kenneth Williams), Harry Seth, Amy Hester (Mrs. Andrew Ryan). Mem. faculty Cornell U., 1946-61, prof., 1956-61; prof. math. Purdue U., 1961-77, prof. math. and edn., 1977—; vis. prof. Harvard, 1970-71, 73, So. Meth. U., 1978; cons. projects applied math., space projects; dir. New Directions, Monitor, Ind. Mem. Am. Math Soc., Math. Assn. Am., Soc. for Indsl. and Applied Math. Author: Theory of Algebraic Numbers, 1950, rev. edit., 1975; Introduction to Celestial Mechanics, 1966; Applied Mathematics, An Introductions, 1972; Celestial Mechanics, 1977. Home: 1425 Ravinia Rd West Lafayette IN 47906 Office: Purdue U West Lafayette IN 47907

POLLARD, HENRY, lawyer; b. N.Y.C., Jan. 10, 1931; s. Charles and Sarah (Lanster) P.; A.B., Coll. City N.Y., 1953; LL.B., Columbia, 1954; m. Adele Brodie, June 16, 1954; children—Paul Adam, Lydia Sara. Admitted to N.Y. bar, 1954, Calif. bar, 1962; practice in N.Y.C., 1954-61, Beverly Hills, 1961—; asso. Sullivan & Cromwell, 1954, 56-61; asso. Kaplan, Livingston, Goodwin, Berkowitz & Selvin, 1961-63, partner, 1963—. Served with AUS, 1954-56. Mem. Am., Los Angeles County, Beverly Hills bar assns., State Bar Calif., State Bar N.Y. Mem. editorial bd. Columbia Law Rev., 1953-54. Home: 224 S Bundy Dr Los Angeles CA 90049 Office: 450 N Roxbury Dr Beverly Hills CA 90210

POLLARD, HERMAN MARVIN, physician, educator; b. Lamar, Colo., 1906; M.D., U. Mich., 1931, M.S., 1938; 1 son, William Lee. Intern, U. Mich. Hosp., Ann Arbor, 1931-33, instr. internal medicine, 1933-38, asst. prof., 1938-45, asso. prof., 1945-51, prof., 1951—; cons. in gastroenterology VA Hosp., Ann Arbor, 1953. Diplomate Am. Bd. Internal Medicine. Fellow A.C.P. (pres. 1968-69); mem. AMA, Central Soc. Clin. Research, Am. Fedn. Clin. Research, Am. Gastroenterology Soc., Am. Cancer Soc. (pres. 1970—), Am. Gastroent. Assn. (pres. 1959), World Orgn. Gastroenterology (pres. 1970—), Am. Assn. for Cancer Research. Home: 2012 Vinewood Blvd Ann Arbor MI 48104 Office: Dept Internal Medicine U Mich Med Center Ann Arbor MI 48104

POLLARD, JAMES JOSEPH, civil engr., architect, educator; b. Greenwood, Miss., Nov. 23, 1907; s. Robert Van Buren and Bettie Freear (Young) P.; B.S. cum laude, Emory U., 1929; B.Arch., Harvard Grad. Sch. Design, 1942; M.S. in Civil Engring., Ga. Sch. Tech., 1948; diplome Fontainebleau Ecole des Beaux Arts, 1939; m. Caralisa Putnam Barry, Nov. 7, 1937 (div. 1962), remarried Apr. 3, 1969; children—Caralisa Hallonquist (Mrs. Thomas Hastings Hughes), Margaret Freear. Timekeeper, asst. supt., supt. Barge-Thompson Co., Atlanta, 1929-34; engr., contractor, Greenwood, Miss., 1935-38; studies and research, concrete structural framing systems for sports stadia, 1944-45; pvt. practice civil and archtl. engring., Atlanta, 1944-47, 51-52; partner Pollard & Altobellis, architects and engrs., 1949-51; instr., asst. prof. mech. engring. Tulane U., 1941-44; asso. prof. archtl. engring. Ga. Sch. Tech., 1944-47, prof. archtl. engring., 1949-52; prof. archtl. engring. U. Tex., 1948-49, 52-61, chmn. dept., 1948-49, 54-60; vis. prof. civil engring. Chulalongkorn U., Bangkok, Thailand, chief adviser Engring. Coll., 1956-57; NSF faculty fellow Columbia, 1960-61; prof. engring. Washington and Lee U., 1961—. Lt. col., C.E., AUS, Res., 1949-61. Fellow ASCE; mem. Nat. Soc. Profl. Engrs., Phi Beta Kappa, Sigma Xi, Tau Beta Pi, Chi Epsilon, Omicron Delta Kappa, Kappa Sigma. Contbr. articles to archtl. and engring. jours. Home: Shellmound Plantation Greenwood MS 38930

POLLARD, MORRIS, microbiologist, educator; b. Hartford, Conn., May 24, 1916; s. Harry and Sarah (Hoffman) P.; D.V.M., Ohio State U., 1938; M.S., Va. Poly. Inst., 1939; Ph.D. (Nat. Found. Infantile Paralysis fellow), U. Calif. at Berkeley, 1950; m. Mildred Klein, Dec. 29, 1938; children—Harvey, Carol, Jonathan. Mem. staff Animal Disease Sta., Nat. Agrl. Research Center, Beltsville, Md., 1939-42; asst. prof. preventive medicine Med. br. U. Tex., Galveston, 1946-48, asso. prof., 1948-50, prof., 1950-61; prof. biology U. Notre Dame, Ind., 1961-66, prof., chmn. microbiology, 1966—, dir. Lobund Lab., 1961—; vis. prof. Fed. U. Rio de Janeiro (Brazil), 1977; mem. tng. grant com. NIH, 1965-70; mem. adv. bd. Inst. for Lab. Animal Resources, 1965-68; mem. adv. com. microbiology Office Naval Research, 1966-68, chmn., 1968-70; mem. sci. adv. com. United Health Found., 1966-70; cons. U. Tex., M.D. Anderson Hosp. and Tumor Inst., 1958-66; mem. project rev. com. United Cancer Council, 1966-70, 74—; mem. colon cancer com. Nat. Cancer Inst., 1972—, chmn. tumor immunology com., 1976-79; mem. com. cancer cause and prevention NIH, 1979—; lectr. Found. Microbiology, 1978. Served from 1st lt. to lt. col. Vet. Corps, AUS, 1942-46. McLaughlin Faculty fellow Cambridge U., 1956; Raine Found. prof. U. Western Australia, 1975; Disting. Alumnus, Ohio State U., 1979. Mem. Am. Acad. Microbiology (charter), Brazilian Acad. Scis., Soc. Exptl. Biology and Medicine, Am. Soc. Microbiology, Am. Assn. Pathologists, Assn. for Gnotobiotics (pres.), AAAS, Sigma Xi. Editor: Perspectives in Virology Vol. I to X 1959-77. Contbr. articles to profl. jours. Home: 3540 Hanover Ct South Bend IN 46614 Office: Lobund Lab Notre Dame IN 46556

POLLARD, THOMAS DEAN, med. scientist; b. Pasadena, Calif., July 7, 1942; s. Dean Randall and Florence (Dierker) P.; B.A., Pomona Coll., 1964; M.D., Harvard U., 1968; m. Patricia E. Snowden, Feb. 7, 1964; children—Katherine, Daniel. Intern, Mass. Gen. Hosp., 1968-69; staff asso. Nat. Heart and Lung Inst., Bethesda, Md., 1969-72; asst. prof. anatomy Harvard Med. Sch., Boston, Mass., 1972-75, asso. prof., 1975-78; Bayard Halsted prof., dir. dept. cell biology and anatomy Johns Hopkins U. Sch. Med., Balt., 1977—; mem. adv. com. Nat. Inst. Gen. Med. Scis., 1977—. Served with USPHS, 1969-72. NIH grantee, 1972—. Mem. Am. Soc. Cell Biology (council 1976—), Biophys. Soc. (council 1977—), Soc. Gen. Physiology, Woods Hole Marine Biol. Lab. (corp. mem.). Office: Dept Cell Biology and Anatomy Johns Hopkins U Sch Med 725 N Wolfe St Baltimore MD 21205

POLLARD, WILLIAM APPLEBY, ins. co. exec.; b. Boston, Dec. 22, 1927; s. Albert Ashworth and Edith (Appleby) P.; A.B., Brown U., 1950; m. Jeannette Jones, May 26, 1951; children—Jenny, Judy, Wendy, Dede. Exec. sec. Nat. Assn. Ins. Agents, N.Y.C., 1958-60; with Reliance Ins. Co., Phila., 1960—, asst. v.p., 1967-69, asst. to pres., 1969-70, v.p., 1970-73, exec. v.p., 1973-74, pres., 1974-76, pres., chief exec. officer, 1977—, also dir.; dir. Old Phila. Devel. Corp., Ins. Services Office, N.Y., Pilot Ins. Co. Can., United Pacific, Tacoma, Reliance Standard Life Ins. Co., Chgo., Gen. Casualty, Madison, Wis., Commonwealth Land Title Co., Phila. Trustee United Way, Phila., 1972—, Pa. Acad. Fine Arts, World Affairs Council of Phila. bd. dirs. Boy Scouts Am., Phila., Phila. Indsl. Devel. Corp., Pa. Economy League; trustee Princeton Theol. Sem., Presbyn.-U. Pa. Hosp., Phila.; dir. Ins. Info. Inst., Am. Fgn. Ins. Co. Mem. Phila. C. of C. (dir.), Ins. Fedn. Pa. (chmn.), Am. Ins. Assn. (dir. N.Y.), Pa. Savs. Fund Soc. Clubs: Annapolis (Md.) Yacht, Sailing of Chesapeake (Annapolis); Union Leage, Brown U. (Phila.); Waynesborough Country (Paoli, Pa.). Home: 577 Timberlane St Devon PA 19333 Office: Reliance Ins Co 4 Penn Center Plaza Philadelphia PA 19103

POLLARD, WILLIAM SHERMAN, JR., cons. engr.; b. Oak Grove, La., Jan. 1, 1925; s. William Sherman and Carrie Lois (Horner) P.; B.S. in Civil Engring., Purdue U., 1946, M.S., 1948; m. Gloria Louise Ponder, June 29, 1946; children—William Sherman, III, Katherine Lynn. Instr. civil engring. Purdue U., 1948-49, U. Ill., 1949-51, asso. prof., 1951-55; with Harland Bartholomew & Assos., St. Louis, 1955-71, asso. partner, chief civil engr., 1956-58, partner, Memphis, 1958-71, head ops., 1958-60, head Memphis office, 1960-71; pres. William S. Pollard Cons., Ins., Memphis, 1971—; adj. prof. urban planning Memphis State U., 1973—; chmn. WKNO-TV, Memphis. Mem. adv. commn. Downtown Memphis Center, U. Tenn.; mem. pres.' council Southwestern U., Memphis; bd. dirs. Greater Memphis State, Central Midwestern Regional Ednl. Lab.; Served with USMC, 1942-46. Named Distinguished Engring. Alumnus, Purdue U., 1969. Fellow Am. Cons. Engrs. Council, ASCE (state of the art award 1970), Inst. Transp. Engrs.; mem. Am. Rd. Builders Assn., Cons. Engrs. Memphis, Nat. Assn. Environ. Profls., Nat. Soc. Profl. Engrs., Soc. Am. Mil. Engrs., Urban Land Inst., Transp. Research Bd., Navy League, Presbyterian. Clubs: Rotary (pres. 1979-80), Engrs., Summit. Home: 5035 Barfield Rd Memphis TN 38117 Office: 1395 Madison Ave Memphis TN 38104

POLLEY, EDWARD HERMAN, anatomist; b. Chgo., Sept. 20, 1923; s. Sam and Anna (Revzin) P.; B.A., DePauw U., Greencastle, Ind., 1947; M.S., St. Louis U., 1949, Ph.D., 1951; m. Jo Ann Welsh, Aug. 11, 1953; children—Lisa, Eric. Instr., then asst. prof. anatomy Hahnemann Med. Coll., Phila., 1953-59; asst. prof., then asso. prof. U. Md. Med. Sch., 1964-70; research biologist Edgewood (Md.) Arsenal, 1959-70; prof. anatomy, neurosurgery and ophthalmology U. Ill. Med. Sch., Chgo., 1970—; vis. prof. dept. pharm. and physiol. scis. U. Chgo., 1979-80; mem. hearing and vision coms. Nat. Acad. Sci.-NRC, 1964—. Served to lt. (j.g.) USNR, 1942-46. Mem. Am. Assn. Anatomists, Midwest Assn. Anatomists, AAAS, Am. Soc. Neurosci., Midwest Soc. Electron Microscopists, Sigma Xi. Clubs: Cajal, Chgo. Literary. Office: Dept Anatomy Univ Ill Med Sch 1853 W Polk St PO Box 6998 Chicago IL 60680

POLLEY, HOWARD FREEMAN, physician; b. Columbus, Ohio, Nov. 12, 1913; s. David William Latimer and Mary Ann (Lakin) P.; A.B., Ohio Wesleyan U., 1934, Sc.D., 1965; M.D., Ohio State U., 1938; M.S., U. Minn., 1945; m. Georgiana Alice Redrup, June 5, 1938; children—Alice Lynne (Mrs. Fred Breimyer), Mary Ann (Mrs. Dale McCoy), William Redrup. Intern, St. Luke's Hosp., Chgo., 1938-39, resident medicine, 1939-40; fellow medicine Mayo Grad. Sch. Medicine, 1940-43; cons. in medicine Mayo Clinic, 1943—, head sect., 1962-66, chmn. div. rheumatology and internal medicine, 1966-76, sr. cons., 1976—; instr. U. Minn., 1946-50, asst. prof. medicine, 1950-54, asso. prof. medicine, 1954-60, prof. medicine, 1960—; asso. Doctors Hench, Kendall and Slocumb in original clin. research cortisone and ACTH for rheumatoid arthritis, rheumatic fever. Bd. dirs. Arthritis Found., 1963-69, exec. com., 1963-68, v.p., 1966-68; trustee Ohio Wesleyan U., 1967—, exec. bd., 1970-72. Mem. adv. council Nat. Inst. Arthritis, Metabolism and Digestive Diseases, NIH, 1972-76; mem. Nat. Arthritis Commn., 1975—. Recipient Alumni Achievement award Ohio State U., 1958. Fellow A.C.P.; mem. AMA (spl. cons. council phys. medicine and rehab. 1946-50), Central Soc. Clin. Research, Am. Rheumatism Assn. (v.p. 1962-64, pres. 1964-65), Uruguay Soc. Rheumatology (hon. mem.), All-Union (USSR) Rheumatol. Soc. (hon.), Indian (hon.), Japan (hon.) rheumatism assns., Sigma Xi, Alpha Omega Alpha, Omicron Delta Kappa, Phi Mu Alpha, Pi Delta Epsilon, Phi Delta Theta, Alpha Kappa Kappa. Sr. author: Rheumatologic Interviewing and Physical Examination of Joints, 2d edit., 1978. Asso. editor Arthritis and Rheumatism, 1960-64. Contbr. articles to med. jours. Co-author

Physical Examinations of Joints, 1965. Home: 1015 Plummer Circle Rochester MN 55901 Office: Mayo Clinic Rochester MN 55901

POLLIN, ABE, profl. basketball exec., builder; b. Phila., Dec. 3, 1923; s. Morris and Jennie (Sack) P.; B.A., George Washington U., 1945; student U. Md., 1941-44; m. Irene S. Kerchek, May 27, 1945; children—Robert Norman, James Edward. Engaged in home bldg. bus., 1945—; pres. Abe Pollin, Inc., Balt., 1962—; pres. Balt. Bullets Basketball Club, Inc. (now Washington Bullets), 1964—; dir. County Fed. Savs. & Loan Assn., Rockville, Md. Bd. dirs. United Jewish Appeal, Nat. Jewish Hosp., Jewish Community Center; bd. dirs., adv. com. John F. Kennedy Cultural Center. Mem. Nat. Assn. Home: Builders, Asso. Builders and Contractors Md., Washington Bd. Trade. Jewish. Office: 6101 16th St Washington DC 20011 also Washington Bullets Capital Centre Landover MD 20786*

POLLIN, WILLIAM, psychiatrist, psychoanalyst, govt. adminstr.; b. Phila., May 13, 1922; s. Samuel and Fannie (Glassman) P.; B.A., Bklyn. Coll., 1947; M.D., Columbia U., 1952; grad. Wash. Psychoanalytic Inst., 1965; m. Marilyn Joyce Federman, June 23, 1951; children—David Joshua, Laura Joanne. Tutor, lectr. dept. biology Bklyn. Coll., 1947-51; teaching fellow dept. psychiatry U. Pitts., 1953-56; intern Columbia Med. Div., Bellevue Hosp., W.Y.C., 1952-53; resident Western Psychiat. Research Inst., Pitts., 1953-56; with NIMH, 1956-74, chief clin. research Research Task Force, Bethesda, Md., 1972-74, coordinator research programs, div. narcotic addiction and drug abuse, Rockville, Md., 1973-74; research dir. White House Spl. Action Office on Drug Abuse Prevention, 1974-75; dir. div. research Nat. Inst. Drug Abuse, Rockville, Md., 1975-79, dir. inst., 1979—; research coordinator U.S.-USSR Joint Schizophrenia Research Project, 1972-73; advisor WHO, 1969. Served with U.S. Maritime Service, 1942-46. Fellow Am. Psychiat. Assn.; mem. Psychiat. Research Soc., Am. Psychopathol. Assn., Assn. Research Child Devel., Behavioral Genetics Assn., Washington Psychiat. Soc., Md. Psychiat. Soc., Washington Psychoanalytic Soc., Soc. Life History Research in Psychopathology, Am. Psychoanalytic Assn. (asso.), Am. Coll. Neuropsychopharmacology (adminstrv. mem.), Alpha Omega Alpha. Contbr. articles to profl. publs. Home: 7720 Sebago Rd Bethesda MD 20034 Office: 5600 Fishers Ln Rockville MD 20857

POLLINI, FRANCIS, author; b. West Wyoming, Pa., Sept. 9, 1930; s. Sem and Assunta (Ciani) P.; B.A. in Psychology, Pa. State U., 1951; m. Gloria Ann Swann, Sept. 12, 1959; children—Susanne, Lisa. Served to 1st lt. USAF, 1952-57. Mem. Soc. Authors (London). Author: Night, 1959; Glover, 1965; Excursion, 1966; The Crown, 1967; Pretty Maids All In a Row, 1968; Three Plays, 1967; Dubonnet, 1973, The Hall, 1975. Address: 41 Sunningdale Norwich England

POLLOCK, DAVID, lawyer; b. Mpls., Jan. 14, 1910; s. Harry and Anna (Waller) P.; LL.B., Southwestern U., 1936; m. Herlinda Miller, Sept. 19, 1941. Admitted to Cal. bar, 1937, since practiced in Los Angeles; sr. mem. firm Pollock and Pollock and predecessor. Arbitrator, Los Angeles County Superior Ct., 1972; conv. speaker. Dir. Specialty Records, Fidelity Records. Bd. dirs. Bay Crest Convalescent Hosp. Mem. Los Angeles County Bar Assn., Cal. (bd. govs. 1965-70, asso. editor jour.), Western (bd. govs. 1969), Los Angeles (pres. 1965) trial lawyers assns., Lawyers Club Los Angeles, Comml. Law League Am., Wilshire Bar Assn. Home: 3626 Crownridge Dr Sherman Oaks CA 91403 Office: 1888 Century Park E Suite 1520 Los Angeles CA 90067

POLLOCK, EDWARD ISADORE, lawyer; b. Mpls., Jan. 14, 1910; s. Harry and Anna (Waller) P.; J.D., Southwestern U., 1935; m. Ann Hemmel, Sept. 2, 1933. Admitted to Calif. bar, 1936, U.S. Supreme Ct. bar, 1946; practiced in Los Angeles, 1936—; sr. mem. firm Pollock, Pollock & Fay, 1946-79, Pollock and Pollack, 1979—; judge pro tem Los Angeles Municipal Ct., 1953, Los Angeles Superior Ct., 1963. Lawyer cons. on Calif. Practice, Bancroft Whitney Co., 1966-71; mem. faculty Assn. Trial Lawyers Am., 1966—, v.p., trustee Dean Roscoe Pound-Assn. Trial Lawyers Am. Found., 1964-67; lectr. tort subjects and trial tactics to bar assn. convs. and seminars, 1950—; arbitrator Los Angeles Atty.'s Spl. Arbitration Plan, 1972—; mem. Calif. Atty. Gen.'s Vol. Adv. Council, 1972-78. Bd. dirs. Century Park East Homeowners Assn., 1975-76. Served with AUS, 1943-45. Fellow Internat. Acad. Trial Lawyers; mem. State Bar Calif. (chmn. jury instrns. com. 1974—), Los Angeles County Bar Assn. (trustee 1972-74), Assn. Trial Lawyers Am. (gov. 1958-60, chmn. amicus curiae com. 1975-78), Western (pres. 1968), Calif. (pres. 1963, founder, mem. amicus curiae com. 1964—, chmn. 1964-69, chmn. jury instrns. com. 1969-74), Los Angeles (pres. 1955, Theodore A. Horn Meml. award 1973) trial lawyers assns., Am. Arbitration Assn. (arbitrator 1963—). Author: California Tort Claims Act-The Key to the Maze, 1973. Co-editor: California Jury Instructions, Civil, 4th rev. edit., 1956; founder, asso. editor Calif. Trial Lawyers Jour., 1962-74. Home: 2170 Century Park East Los Angeles CA 90067 Office: 1888 Century Park East Suite 1808 Los Angeles CA 90067

POLLOCK, GEORGE HOWARD, psychoanalyst; b. Chgo., June 19, 1923; s. Harry J. and Belle (Lurie) P.; B.S., U. Ill., 1944, M.D. cum laude, 1945, M.S., 1948, Ph.D., 1951; m. Beverly Yufit, July 3, 1946; children—Beth L. (Ungar), Raphael E., Daniel A., Benjamin B., Naomi R. Intern Cook County Hosp., Chgo., 1945-46; resident Ill. Neuropsychiat. Inst., Chgo., 1948-51; practice medicine, specializing in psychiatry, Chgo., 1948—. Clin. asso. prof. dept. psychiatry Coll. Medicine U. Ill., 1955-64, clin. prof., 1964-72; prof. psychiatry Northwestern U., 1972—; staff mem. Inst. for Psychoanalysis, Chgo., 1956—, asst. dean edn., 1960-67, tng. analyst, 1961—, supervising analyst, 1962—, dir. research, 1963-71, dir., 1971—; Exchange Program participant Hampstead Child-Therapy Clinic, 1962-63; pres. Center for Psychosocial Studies, 1972—. Mem. med. adv. com. Planned Parenthood Assn., 1966-70. Pres. governing bd. Parents Assn. Lab. Schs. U. Chgo., 1966-70; mem. med. adv. council Asthma and Allergy Found. for Greater Chgo. Bd. dirs. Erikson Inst. for Early Edn. Served from 1st lt. to capt. AUS, 1946-48. Commonwealth fellow, 1951; research grantee Founds. Fund for Research in Psychiatry, 1960-65. Diplomate Am. Bd. Psychiatry and Neurology (examiner 1972—). Fellow Am. Coll. Psychiatrists, Am. Orthopsychiat. Assn., Am. Psychiat. Assn.; mem. Am. Acad. Polit. and Social Sci., Am. Anthrop. Assn., Nat. Council on Family Relations, AAAS, AAUP, Profs., Am. Electroencephalographic Soc., Am. Heart Assn., Assn. for Research in Nervous and Mental Disease, Soc. for Exptl. Biology and Medicine, Ill., N.Y. acads. scis., Chgo. Psychoanalytic Soc., Soc. for Gen. Systems Research, AMA, World Med. Assn., Am. Name Soc., Am. Psychoanalytic Assn. (pres. 1974-75), Am. Psychol. Assn., Am. Psychosomatic Soc., Am. Pub. Health Assn., Am. Sociol. Assn., Assn. Am. Med. Colls., Ill. Psychiat. Soc. (pres. 1973), Sigma Xi, Alpha Omega Alpha, numerous others. Chmn. bd. editors Ann. of Psychoanalysis, 1971—; editorial bd. Jour. Am. Psychoanalytic Assn., 1971-74; editorial bd. sect. psychoanalysis Psychiat. Jour. U. Ottawa Faculty Medicine, 1976—; corr. editor Jour. Geriatric Psychiatry, 1975—. Contbr. articles to profl. jours. Home: 5759 S Dorchester Ave Chicago IL 60637 Office: 180 N Michigan Ave Chicago IL 60601

POLLOCK, JAMES VALIANT, constrn. co. exec.; b. Raton, N.Mex., Jan. 20, 1937; s. William Dunne and Edith Eleanor (Nims) P.; B.S., U. Denver, 1958; m. Janice Leilani Alexander, July 1, 1961; children—Laurie Kehaulani, Julie Kauilani, James Alexander. Sr. accountant Peat, Marwick, Mitchell & Co., Honolulu, 1958-62; chief accountant Dillingham Corp., Honolulu, 1962-64, asst. controller, 1964-70, controller, 1970-76, gen. auditor, 1976—. Served with AUS, 1959. C.P.A., Hawaii. Mem. Am. Inst. C.P.A.'s, Hawaii Soc. C.P.A.'s, Fin. Execs. Inst., Acacia. Home: 46-426 Hololio St Kaneohe HI 96744 Office: Box 3468 Honolulu HI 96801

POLLOCK, JOHN PHLEGER, lawyer; b. Sacramento, Apr. 28, 1920; s. George Gordon and Irma (Phleger) P.; A.B., Stanford, 1942; J.D., Harvard, 1948; m. Juanita Irene Gossman, Oct. 26, 1945; children—Linda Pollock Fellows, Madeline Pollock Chiotti, John, Gordon. Admitted to Calif. bar, 1949, U.S. Supreme Ct. bar, 1954; partner Musick, Peeler & Garrett, Los Angeles, 1953-60, Pollock, Williams & Berwanger, Los Angeles, 1960—. Active Boy Scouts Am., former trustee Pitzer Coll., Claremont, Calif., 1968-76, Jones Found., Good Hope Med. Found. Served with AUS, 1942-45. Fellow Am. Coll. Trial Lawyers; mem. Am., Interam., Internat., Los Angeles County (trustee 1964-66) bar assns., Am. Judicature Soc. Contbr. articles to profl. publs. Home: 1021 Oak Grove Ave San Marino CA 91108 Office: 800 W 6th St Los Angeles CA 90017

POLLOCK, ROBERT ELWOOD, nuclear physicist; b. Regina, Sask., Can., Mar. 2, 1936; s. Elwood Thomas and Harriet Lillian (Rooney) P.; B.Sc. (Hons.), U. Man., Can., 1957; M.A., Princeton U., 1959, Ph.D., 1963; m. Jean Elizabeth Virtue, Sept. 12, 1959; children—Bryan Thomas, Heather Lynn, Jeffrey Parker, Jennifer Lee. Instr., Princeton U., 1961-63; Nat. Research Council Can. postdoctoral fellow, Harwell, Eng., 1963-64; asst. prof. Princeton U., 1964-69, research physicist, 1969-70; asso. prof. Ind. U., 1970-73, prof., 1973—, dir. Ind. U. Cyclotron Facility, 1973—; mem. Nuclear Sci. Adv. Com. Fellow Am. Phys. Soc.; mem. Can. Assn. Physicists. Home: 1261 Winfield Rd Bloomington IN 47401 Office: Swain Hall West Ind U Bloomington IN 47405

POLOMÉ, EDGAR CHARLES, educator; b. Brussels, Belgium, July 31, 1920; s. Marcel Félicien and Berthe (Henry) P.; came to U.S., 1961, naturalized, 1966; B.A., Université Libre de Bruxelles, 1941, Ph.D., 1949; M.A., Cath. U. Louvain, 1943; m. Julia Josephine Schwindt, June 22, 1944 (dec. May 1975); children—Monique (Mrs. John Ellsworth), André. Instr. Germanic lang. Athénée Ville de Bruxelles, 1942-56; prof. Dutch, Belgian Nat. Broadcasting Corp., Brussels, 1954-56; prof. linguistics U. Belgian Congo (now Zaire), 1956-61; prof. Germanic, Oriental, African langs. and lits. U. Tex., Austin, 1962—, chmn. dept., 1969-76. Served with Belgian Aux. Aerodrome Police, 1945. Fulbright prof. U. Kiel, 1968; Ford Found. team dir. Tanzania survey, 1969-70. Mem. Linguistics Soc. Am., Am. Oriental Soc., Modern Lang. Assn., African Studies Assn., Am. Anthrop. Assn., Indogermanische Gesellschaft, Societas Linguistica Europea, Société de Linguistique de Paris, Am. Inst. Indian Studies (chmn. lang. com. 1972-78). Author: Swahili Language Handbook, 1967; Language in Tanzania, 1980; editor: Old Norse Literature and Mythology, 1969; co-editor: Jour. Indo-European Studies, 1973—. Home: 2701 Rock Terr Austin TX 78704 Office: 2601 University Ave Austin TX 78712

POLONIS, DOUGLAS HUGH, educator; b. North Vancouver, B.C., Can., Sept. 2, 1928; s. William and Ada (Burrows) P.; came to U.S., 1955, naturalized, 1963; B.A.Sc., U. B.C., 1951, Ph.D., 1955, M.A.Sc., U. Toronto, 1953; m. Vera Christine Brown, Jan. 30, 1953; children—Steven Philip, Malcolm Eric, Douglas Hugh, Christine Virginia. Metall. engr. Steel Co. Can., Hamilton, Ont., 1951-52; mem. faculty U. Wash., Seattle, 1955—, prof. metall. engring., 1962—, chmn. dept. mining, metall. and ceramic engring., 1969-71, 73—; metall. cons., 1955—. Mem. Am. Soc. Metals, AIME, Am. Soc. Engring. Edn., Tau Beta Pi, Alpha Sigma Mu, Sigma Phi Delta. Mem. Christian Ref. Ch. Contbr. articles to profl. jours. Home: 19227 46th Ave NE Seattle WA 98155

POLONSKY, ARTHUR, artist, educator; b. Lynn, Mass., June 6, 1925; s. Benjamin and Celia (Hurwitz) P.; diploma with highest honors, Sch. of Mus. Fine Arts, Boston, 1948; m. Lois Tarlow, Mar. 15, 1953; children—Eli, D.L., Gabriel. One-man shows: Stedelijk Mus., Amsterdam, Netherlands, 1950, Boris Mirski Gallery, Boston, 1950, 54, 56, 64, 66, Boston Public Library, 1969, Durlacher Gallery, N.Y.C., 1965, Mickelson Gallery, Washington, 1966, 74; group shows include: Met. Mus., N.Y.C., 1950, Carnegie Internat. Expn., 1951, Inst. Contemporary Art, Boston, 1960, Mus. Fine Arts, Boston, 1976; represented in permanent collections: Mus. Fine Arts, Boston, Fogg Mus., Harvard U., Addison Gallery of Am. Art, Andover, Mass., Stedelijk Mus.; instr. art Boston Mus. Sch., 1950-60, Brandeis U., 1964-65; asso. prof. Sch. Arts, Boston U., 1965—. Recipient Louis Comfort Tiffany award for painting, 1951; 1st prize Boston Arts Festival, 1954. Mem. Artists Equity Assn. (founding mem. New Eng. chpt.), Boston Visual Artists Union, AAUP. Address: 364 Cabot St Newtonville MA 02160. *The most familiar companions have been: doubt, duality, reversibility, and their humanizing influence. Art, merged with living, has been the centering strength. This restless fabrication of the visible remains an urgent labor by which origins and fragile goals are joined.*

POLSBY, NELSON WOOLF, educator, polit. scientist; b. Norwich, Conn., Oct. 25, 1934; s. Daniel II and Edythe (Woolf) P.; grad. Pomfret (Conn.) Sch., 1952; A.B., Johns Hopkins, 1956; M.A., Yale U., 1958, Ph.D., 1961; m. Linda Dale Offenbach, Aug. 3, 1958; children—Lisa, Emily, Daniel R. Instr., U. Wis., 1960-61; from asst. prof. to prof. Wesleyan U., Middletown, Conn., 1961-68; prof. polit. sci. U. Calif. at Berkeley, 1967—; mem. vis. faculty Columbia, 1963, Yale, 1963, 67, 75, Hebrew U. of Jerusalem, 1970, Stanford, 1977. Mem. com. on pub. engring. policy Nat. Acad. Engring., 1973-76; mem. commn. on vice presdl. selection Democratic Nat. Com., 1973-74; mem. Yale U. Council, 1978—. Fellow Social Sci. Research Council, 1959, Brookings Instn., 1959-60, Center Advanced Study Behavioral Scis., 1965-66, Ford Found., 1970-71, John Simon Guggenheim Found., 1977-78. Mem. AAAS, Am. Polit. Sci. Assn. (council 1971-77), Am. Sociol. Assn., Council on Fgn. Relations, Phi Beta Kappa. Author: Community Power and Political Theory, 2d edit., 1980; Congress and the Presidency, 3d edit., 1976; (with Aaron Wildavsky) Presidential Elections, 5th edit., 1980; Congress: An Introduction, 1968; Political Promises, 1974. Editor: (with R.A. Dentler and P. Smith) Politics and Social Life, 1963; (with R.L. Peabody) New Perspectives on the House of Representatives, 3d edit., 1977; Congressional Behavior, 1971; Reapportionment in the 1970's, 1971; The Modern Presidency, 1973; (with F.I. Greenstein) Handbook of Political Science, 8 vols., 1975. Book rev. editor Transaction, 1968-71; mng. editor Am. Polit. Sci. Rev., 1971-77; editorial adv. bd. Polit. Sci. Quar., Jour. Polit. and Mil. Sociology, Policy Analysis, Am. Polit. Sci. Review. Home: 1500 Leroy Ave Berkeley CA 94708

POLSKY, LEON BERNARD, lawyer; b. N.Y.C., June 21, 1931; s. Joseph A. and Annette P.; B.S., N.Y. U., 1952, LL.B., 1954; m. Cynthia Hazen, Apr. 19, 1957; children—Alexander, Nicholas. Admitted to N.Y. State bar, 1956, U.S. Supreme Ct. bar, 1961; chief appellate counsel Legal Aid Soc., N.Y.C., 1960-69, atty.-in-charge civil div., 1972-73, atty.-in-charge criminal def. div., 1978—; judge N.Y. State Ct. of Claims and acting justice Supreme Ct. of State of N.Y., 1973-78; chief counsel Temporary State Commn. to Evaluate Drug Laws, 1970-72. Served with U.S. Army, 1955-57. Mem. Am. Law Inst., Am. Bar Assn., N.Y. State Bar Assn., Assn. Bar of City of N.Y. Office: 15 Park Row New York NY 10038

POLUNIN, NICHOLAS, sci. author, editor; b. Checkendon, Oxfordshire, Eng., June 26, 1909; s. Vladimir and Elizabeth Violet (Hart) P.; B.A., Christ Church, U. Oxford, 1932 (1st class honors), M.A., 1935, D. Phil., 1935, D.Sc., 1942; M.S., Yale, 1934; m. Helen Lovat Fraser, 1939 (dec.); 1 son, Michael; m. 2d, Helen Eugenie Campbell, Jan. 3, 1948; children—April Xenia, Nicholas V. C., Douglas H. H. Participant or leader numerous sci. expdns., 1930-65, primarily in arctic regions, including Spitsbergen, Greenland, Canadian Arctic, North Pole; curator, tutor, demonstrator, lectr. various instns., especially Oxford U., 1933-47; vis. prof. botany McGill U., 1946-47, Macdonald prof. botany, 1947-52; Guggenheim fellow, research fellow Harvard U., 1950-53, also fgn. research asso., USAF research project dir., lectr. plant sci. Yale, also biology Brandeis U., 1953-55; prof. plant ecology and taxonomy, head dept. botany, dir. U. Herbarium and Botanic Garden, Baghdad, Iraq, 1955-58; guest prof. U. Geneva, 1959-61, 75—; adviser establishment, founding prof. botany, dean faculty sci. U. Ife, Nigeria, 1962-66; founding editor plant sci. monographs and world crops books, 1954-78, Biol. Conservation, 1967-74, Environ. Conservation, 1974—; chmn. internat. steering com., editor proc. Internat. Conf. Environ. Future, Finland, 1971, Iceland, 1977, sec.-gen., editor proc., 1977; pres. Found. for Environ. Conservation, 1975—; participant Internat. Bot. Congresses, Stockholm, 1950, Paris, 1954, Edinburgh, 1964, Seattle, 1969, Leningrad, 1975. Decorated comdr. Order Brit. Empire; recipient undergrad., grad. student scholarships, fellowships, research associateships Harvard U., 1936-37; Rolleston Meml. prize, 1938, D.S.I.R. spl. investigator, 1938; Leverhulme Research award, 1941; sr. research fellow New Coll., Oxford; Arctic Inst. N.A. research fellow, 1946-47, Guggenheim fellow, 1950-52; recipient Ford Found. award, Scandinavia, USSR, 1966-67; Marie-Victorin medal (Can.). Fellow Royal Geog. Soc., Royal Hort. Soc., Linnean Soc. London, AAAS, Arctic Inst. N.A.; mem. Torrey Bot. Club (life), various fgn. and nat. profl. and sci. socs. Clubs: Harvard (life) (N.Y.C.); Canadian Field Naturalists (Ottawa); Lake Placid (N.Y.); Reform (London) (life). Author: Russian Waters, 1931; The Isle of Auks, 1932; Botany of the Canadian Eastern Arctic, 3 vols. 1940-48; Arctic Unfolding, 1949; Circumpolar Arctic Flora, 1959; Introduction to Plant Geography, 1960 (various fgn. edits.); Eléments de Géographie botanique, 1967; The Environmental Future, 1972. Editor: Growth Without Ecodisasters?, 1979; Environ. Monographs and Symposia, 1979—; Contbr. to various jours. Research plant life and ecology of artic, subartic and high-altitude regions; discoverer plants in Greenland introduced from N.Am. by Vikings, microscopic life over North Pole, last maj. islands to be added to world map. Home: 15 chemin F-Lehmann 1218 Grand-Saconnex Geneva Switzerland

POLYCHRON, JOHN PHILIP, consumer products co. exec.; b. Oceanside, N.Y., Aug. 9, 1936; s. Harry Robert and Lucille Elizabeth (McLaughlin) P.; B.S., U. Pa., 1958; M.B.A., N.Y. U., 1970; m. Adrienne Lecraw, Oct. 8, 1977; children—Leslie Dale, Jason John. Salesman, Proctor & Gamble, 1958-62; dir. sales Thomas J. Lipton, Inc., 1962-74; pres. Popsicle Industries, Englewood, N.J., 1974-79; pres. R.J. Reynolds Tabacos do Brasil Ltda., Rio de Janeiro, 1979—. Clubs: Knickerbocker Country, Gavea Golf and Country, Yacht, Jockey (Rio de Janeiro). Office: Praia de Botafogo 440 22250 Rio de Janeiro Brazil

POLZER, GEORGE FRANCIS, JR., chem. co. exec.; b. S.I., N.Y., Dec. 21, 1918; s. George F. and Louise (Schaffer) P.; B.Chemistry in Chem. Engring., Cornell U., 1940, M.A. in Inorganic Chemistry, 1942; m. Doris McEnerney, Feb. 23, 1941; children—Penelope Ann, Jo Ann, George. With Texaco, Inc., 1942-51, Am. Cyanamid Co., 1951-56; with Witco Chem. Corp., N.Y.C., 1956—, group v.p. comml. services, 1972-75, exec. v.p., dir., 1975—. Mem. Alpha Chi Sigma, Tau Kappa Epsilon. Club: Cornell of N.Y. Home: 27 Park Ln Fairhaven NJ 07701 Office: 277 Park Ave New York City NY 10017

POMERANCE, EUGENE C., advt. agy. exec.; b. Chgo., Nov. 15, 1921; s. Isaac S. and Grace F. (Smith) P.; student Wilson Jr. Coll., 1938-40; S.B., U. Chgo., 1942, M.B.A., 1947; m. Virginia I. Lus, Apr. 8, 1944; children—Lynne Pomerance Attaway, Diane Pomerance Koenker, Roger. Research analyst McCann-Erickson Advt., Chgo., 1947-50; with Foote, cone & Belding Advt., Chgo., 1950—, sr. v.p. mktg. services, Comr., Elmhurst (Ill.) Park Dist., 1959-65, 67-73, pres., 1962-65, 69-70; trustee Ill. Park and Recreation Found., 1978—; dir. Ill. Prairie Path, 1968-73. Served with U.S. Army, 1942-46. Mem. Ill. Assn. Park Dists. (hon. life, dir. 1969-73, pres. 1970-71), Ill. Park and Recreation Soc. (hon. life), Am. Mktg. Assn. Home: 561 Fern Ave Elmhurst IL 60126 Office: 401 N Michigan Ave Chicago IL 60611

POMERANCE, NORMAN, mfg. co. exec.; b. Greensburg, Pa., June 24, 1926; s. Isaac and Esther (Cohen) P.; B.S. (Evan Pugh scholar), Pa. State U., 1950; M.S., Ohio State U., 1951; m. Carol Joan Raynor, Mar. 29, 1953; children—John, Jane, Jason. Dir. planning and analysis Gen. Precision, Inc., Tarrytown, N.Y., 1954-66; dir. bus. planning IT&T, N.Y.C., 1966-69; sr. v.p. Macmillan, Inc.; pres., dir. Macmillan Pub. Co., N.Y.C., 1969-74; group v.p. Arlen Realty and Devel. Corp., N.Y.C., 1974-76; v.p., dir. Am. Optical Corp., Southbridge, Mass., 1976—, pres. internat. div., 1976—. Served with USNR, 1944-46. Mem. Tau Beta Pi, Eta Kappa Nu, Pi Mu Epsilon, Phi Kappa Phi, Phi Eta Sigma. Home: 49 Lawrence Rd Scarsdale NY 10583 Office: 14 Mechanic St Southbridge MA 01550

POMERANCE, RALPH, architect; b. N.Y.C., Sept. 1, 1907; s. Harry and Esther (Perlstein) P.; B.Arch., Carnegie Inst. Tech., 1930; m. Josephine A. Wetheim, June 8, 1934; children—Pamela (Mrs. Brian Johnson), Stephen M., Ralph. Archtl. practice as Ralph Pomerance, 1933-38, Pomerance & Breines, N.Y.C., 1938—; prin. works include Bronx Municipal Hosp. Center, N.Y.C., 1955, Rose Fitzgerald Kennedy Research Center at Albert Einstein Coll. Medicine, 1969, Riis Houses Plaza and Amphitheatre, N.Y.C., 1966, Bellevue Hosp., 1970, N.Y. U. Dental Coll., 1976. Chmn. Greenwich (Conn.) Housing Authority, 1947-53. Served to capt. AUS, 1942-45. Decorated knight 1st class Royal Order Vasa (Sweden), 1939. Fellow AIA (treas. N.Y. chpt. 1950-51, exec. com. 1954-57). Home: 101 Orchard St Cos Cob CT 06807 Office: 30 E 42d St New York NY 10017

POMERANTZ, ABRAHAM L(OUIS), lawyer; b. Bklyn., Mar. 22, 1903; s. Louis and Lena (Betz) P.; LL.B. cum laude, Bklyn. Law Sch., 1924; m. Phyllis Cohen, Jan. 10, 1926; children—Dan, Charlotte. Admitted to N.Y. State bar, 1924, since practiced N.Y.C.; mem. firm Pomerantz, Levy, Haudek & Block; instr. law Bklyn. Law Sch., 1925; lectr. Columbia U., U. Pa., Harvard U. Law Sch., Yale U. Law Sch., Northwestern U. Law Sch., U. London; dep. chief counsel in prosecution of Nazi War Criminals, Nuremburg Trials, 1946. Mem. adv. com. rules of practice and procedure U.S. Supreme Ct.; mem. com. on qualifications to practice before U.S. cts. 2d Circuit Jud. Council of 2d Circuit; mem. Anglo-Am. Exchange, 1973; participants seminars Am. Bar Assn., Am. Law Inst., Practicing Law Inst., N.Y. Law Jour. Home: 146 Central Park W New York NY 10023 Office: 295 Madison Ave New York NY 10017

POMERANTZ, CHARLOTTE, writer; b. Bklyn., July 24, 1930; d. Abraham L. and Phyllis (Cohen) Pomerantz; B.A., Sarah Lawrence Coll., 1953; m. Carl Marzani, Nov. 12, 1966; children—Gabrielle Rose, Daniel Avram. Children's books include: The Bear Who Couldn't Sleep, 1965; The Moon Pony, 1967; Ask the Windy Sea, 1968; Why You Look Like You Whereas I Look Like Me, 1968; The Day They Parachuted Cats on Borneo (chosen for Internat. Year of the Child), 1971; The Princess and the Admiral (Jane Addams Children's Book award), 1974; The Piggy in the Puddle, 1974; The Ballad of the Long Tailed Rat, 1975; Detective Poufy's First Case, 1976; The Mango Tooth, 1977; The Downtown Fairy Godmother, 1978; contbr. stories to mags.; spl. editorial asst. Einstein on Peace, 1960; editor: A Quarter Century of Un-Americana, 1963. Address: 260 W 21st St New York NY 10011

POMERANTZ, LOUIS, art conservator; b. Bklyn., Sept. 26, 1919; s. Jacob and Gussie (Watnick) P.; student Art Students League, N.Y.C., 1938-40, Academie Julian, Paris, 1949-50; apprenticeships with T.G. Satinover, Paris, 1949-50, H.H. Mertens, chief restorer, Rijksmuseum, Amsterdam, 1950-51, G.L. Stout, dir. Worcester Art Mus., 1951, Bklyn. Mus., 1952-54, Inst. Royal du Patrimoine Artistque, Brussels, 1963, Central Lab. Belgium Mus., Brussels, 1954, 56, 58; m. Elisabeth C. Picard, Oct. 5, 1951; children—Carrie, Johanna, Lonnie Roberta. Founder conservation studio, N.Y.C., 1952; instr., lab. asst. Bklyn. Mus., 1954; founder dept. conservation, apptd. conservator dept. painting and sculpture Art Inst. Chgo., 1956-61; ind. art conservator, Evanston, Ill., 1961—; cons. Milw. Art Center, 1958, Nat. Gallery Can., 1961, George F. Harding Mus., Chgo., 1965-68; UNESCO cons., 1968; cons. Smithsonian Instn. Travelling Exhbn. Services, Iowa Mus. Art, State Hist. Soc. Minn.; vis. lectr. in field. Mem. bd. advisors Urban Gateways, 1975-79; dir. Art Commn. City of Evanston, 1968-75, pres., 1975-76. Served with U.S. Army, 1941-45. Fellow Internat. Inst. Conservation of Historic and Artistic Works, Am. Inst. Conservation (past chmn.), mem. Internat. Commn. Museums, Am. Assn. Museums, Midwest Mus. Conf. Unitarian. Home: 6300 Johnsburg Rd Spring Grove IL 60081

POMEROY, BENJAMIN SHERWOOD, educator; b. St. Paul, Apr. 24, 1911; s. Benjamin A. and Florence A. (Sherwood) P.; D.V.M., Iowa State U., 1933; M.S., Cornell U., 1934; Ph.D., U. Minn., 1944; m. L. Margaret Lyon, June 25, 1938; children—Benjamin A., Sherwood R., Catherine A., Margaret D. Diagnostician, U. Minn., 1934-38, faculty, 1938—, prof., 1948—, head dept. vet. microbiology and public health, 1953-73, asso. dean, 1970-74, acting dean, 1979. Mem. adv. com. FDA; cons. animal scis. div. and animal health div., meat insp. service Dept. Agr. Republican precinct officer, 1958-60, ward chmn., 1960-61; chmn. Ramsey County (Minn.) Rep. Com., 1961-65, 4th Congl. Dist., 1961-63, 67-69; mem. Minn. Rep. Central Com., 1961-71; del. Minn. Rep. Conv., 1960-71, Rep. Nat. Conv., 1964. Named Veterinarian of Year in Minn., 1970; recipient Eminent Citizen award St. Anthony Park Legion Post and Aux., 1955; Alumni Merit award for preeminent service Iowa State U., 1973, Stange award for meritorious service in veterinary medicine, 1977. Fellow Poultry Sci. Assn.; mem. Nat. Turkey Fedn. (Research award 1950; life), Am. Poultry Hall of Fame (life), Tex. Poultry Assn. (life), Minn. Turkey Growers Assn. (life); mem. Soc. Exptl. Biology and Medicine, Am. Assn. Avian Pathologists (life), Am. Coll. Vet. Microbiologists, Am. Acad. Microbiology, Am. Soc. Microbiology, Am. (council research 1963-73), Minn. (sec.-treas. 1950-75, pres. 1979) vet. med. assns., Sigma Xi, Phi Kappa Phi, Alpha Gamma Rho, Phi Zeta, Gamma Sigma Delta. Presbyn. (elder). Co-author: Diseases and Parasites of Poultry, 1958; contbg. author: Diseases of Poultry, 1978. Home: 1443 Raymond Ave Saint Paul MN 55108

POMEROY, CHARLES A., justice Maine Supreme Ct.; b. 1914; grad. Columbia U. Admitted to Maine bar, 1936; justice Maine Supreme Ct. Mem. Am. Bar Assn. Office: Maine Supreme Court Augusta ME 04330*

POMEROY, EARL, educator; b. Capitola, Calif., Dec. 27, 1915; s. Earl Spencer and Hazel B. (Keesling) P.; B.A., San Jose State Coll., 1936; M.A., U. Calif. at Berkeley, 1937, Ph.D., 1940; m. Mary Catherine Rentz, July 7, 1940 (dec. Aug. 1977); children—Susan Margaret (Mrs. R.E. Guilford), Peter Rentz, James George, Caroline Jane. Instr. U. Wis., 1940-42; asst. prof. U. N.C., 1942-45; asst. prof. Ohio State U., 1945-49; asso. prof. U. Oreg., 1949-54, prof., 1954-61, Beekman prof. history, 1961-76; prof. U. Calif. at San Diego, 1976—; vis. prof. Johns Hopkins U., Bologna center, 1963-64; vis. prof. Stanford, 1967, U. Calif. at San Diego, 1975-76. Recipient A.J. Beveridge award Am. Hist. Assn., 1942. Ford fellow, 1953-54; Guggenheim fellow, 1956-57, 72; Nat. Endowment for Humanities fellow, 1968; fellow Center for Advanced Study in Behavioral Scis., 1974-75. Mem. Orgn. Am. Historians, Am. (pres. Pacific Coast br. 1969-70), Agrl., Western hist. assns. Episcopalian. Author: The Territories and the U.S., 1861-1890, 1947, 69; Pacific Outpost; Guam and Micronesia in American Strategy, 1951; In Search of the Golden West: The Tourist in Western America, 1957; The Pacific Slope: a History, 1965, 74. Home: 2475 Van Ness St Eugene OR 97403 also 376 Serpentine Dr Del Mar CA 92014 Office: Dept History U Calif San Diego LaJolla CA 92093

POMEROY, EDWARD COFFIN, assn. exec.; b. Westfield, Mass., July 26, 1916; s. Silas C. and Minnie (Coffin) P.; A.B., Am. Internat. Coll., 1939, L.H.D., 1976; M.A., Columbia U., 1947, Ed.D., 1949; Litt.D., Trenton State Coll., 1961, Eastern Ky. U., 1968; m. Pauline E. Head, June 24, 1940 (dec. July 1966); 1 dau., Judith E. (Mrs. Larry Reynolds); m. 2d, Letha E. Walters, Feb. 28, 1967. Asst. to pres. Am. Internat. Coll., 1939-43; asst. to gen. sec. Tchrs. Coll., Columbia, 1949-51; asso. sec. Am. Assn. Colls. for Tchr. Edn., 1951-53, exec. sec., 1953-69, exec. dir., 1969—; pres. Internat. Council on Edn. for Teaching, 1972-76, bd. dirs., 1976—; mem. Nat. Commn. on Competency—based Edn., 1974-77. Alumni trustee Am. Internat. Coll., 1954-57; trustee Colo. Women's Coll., 1969-77, Joint Council on Econ. Edn., 1976—; mem. adv. com. on child abuse and neglect Edn. Commn. of the States, 1976-78. Served from ensign to lt. (j.g.), Supply Corps, USNR, 1943-46. Mem. N.E.A., Am. Assn. Sch. Adminstrs., Am. Ednl. Research Assn., Phi Delta Kappa, Kappa Delta Pi, Sigma Alpha Phi. Club: University (Washington). Home: 5402 Trent St Chevy Chase MD 20015 Office: 1 DuPont Circle Washington DC 20036. *Encouraging the growth and development of people to the full extent of their capabilities is, in my opinion, the basic cornerstone of a democratic society. My professional career has been built around this concept and the fact that those who serve children and youth in educational situations perform a key role in a world that is constantly changing.*

POMEROY, LAWRENCE HITCHCOCK, mfg. co. exec.; b. Cleve., Oct. 17, 1927; s. Lawrence H. and Cathrine (Schwind) P.; B.S. in Bus., Miami U., Oxford, Ohio, 1951; m. Mary Virginia Reinhart, Aug. 18, 1951; children—Lawrence Hitchcock III, William R., Jeffrey S. With Wolverine Tractor Co., Detroit, 1952, Magic Tractor & Implement Co., Jerome, Idaho, 1952-53; with Ford Motor Co., 1953-57, dealer placement mgr., regional continental sales mgr., 1954-57; with Massey-Ferguson, Ltd., 1957-71, exec. v.p., gen. mgr. recreation and farmstead equipment, 1969-71, also dir.; corp. v.p. mktg. and bus. devel. B.F. Goodrich Co., Akron, Ohio, 1971-72, sr. v.p., 1978-79, pres. B.F. Goodrich Indsl. Products Co. div., 1972-74, B.F. Goodrich Engring. Edn. Systems Div., 1974-78, exec. v.p., pres. Engring. Products Group, 1979—; dir. mktg. Massey-Ferguson (Australia) Ltd., 1958-60; dir. mktg. Massey-Ferguson (U.K.) Ltd., 1960-62, v.p. mktg. N.Am. ops., 1962-69; pres. Badger Northland Inc., Kaukauna, Wis. Trustee Akron Art Inst.; mem. bus. adv. council Miami U., Oxford, Ohio. Served with USAAF, 1946-47. Mem. Rubber Mfrs. Assn. (past chmn. exec. com., indsl. div. 1974-76), Phi Delta Theta (chpt. pres. 1949-50). Episcopalian. Home: 4135 Granger Rd Akron OH 44313 Office: 500 S Main St Akron OH 44318

POMEROY, THOMAS WILSON, JR., lawyer, former state supreme ct. justice; b. Crafton, Pa., Nov. 20, 1908; s. Thomas Wilson and Marion Elizabeth (Bradbury) P.; A.B., Lafayette Coll., 1929; LL.B., Harvard, 1933; m. Maria Frances Whitten, July 6, 1935; children—Anne Whitten (Mrs. Richard B. Martin), George Robinson, Helen F. (Mrs. John Alden Hopkins), Benjamin Bradbury. Instr. pub. speaking Lafayette Coll., 1929-30; admitted to Pa. bar, 1933, practiced in Pitts.; partner firm Kirkpatrick, Pomeroy, Lockhart & Johnson, 1946-68; gen. counsel Pitts. & W.Va. Ry. Co., 1946-65; justice Supreme Ct. Pa., 1968-78; of counsel firm Kirkpatrick, Lockhart, Johnson & Hutchison, Pitts., 1979—. Pres., Pitts. Council Intercultural Edn., 1943-44; pres. Pitts. YMCA, 1964-66, now emeritus dir.; elder Ben Avon Presbyterian Ch.; former mem. bd. Christian edn. United Presbyn. Ch. U.S.A.; trustee Lafayette Coll. Served to lt. comdr. USNR, 1944-46. Fellow Am. Bar Found.; mem. Am., Pa. (pres. 1961), Allegheny County (pres. 1959) bar assns., Am. Law Inst., Am. Judicature Soc., Inst. Jud. Adminstrn., World Affairs Council Pitts. (pres. 1940-44), Scotch-Irish Soc. U.S. (pres. 1962-64), Phi Kappa Psi, Tau Kappa Alpha. Clubs: Harvard-Yale-Princeton, Univ., Shannopin Country (Pitts.). Home: 53 Newgate Rd Pittsburgh PA 15202 Office: 1500 Oliver Bldg Pittsburgh PA 15222

POMEROY, WARDELL BAXTER, psychotherapist; b. Kalamazoo, Dec. 6, 1913; s. Percy Wardell and Mary Adelia (Baxter) Pa.; A.B., Ind. U., 1935, M.A., 1941; Ph.D., Columbia, 1952; m. Catherine Sindlinger, Sept. 4, 1937; children—David Wardell, John Eric, Mary Lynne. Clin. psychologist Mental Hygiene Clinic, St. Joseph County, Ind., 1938-39, 41-42; clin. psychologist Ind. Reformatory, 1940-41; with Inst. Sex Research Ind. U., 1943-63, dir. field research, 1956-63; psychotherapist N.Y.C., 1963-76; acad. dean Inst. Advanced Studies in Human Sexuality, 1976—. Fellow Am. Psychol. Assn., Soc. For Sci. Study Sex (pres. 1969); mem. Am. Assn. Marriage Counselors (pres. 1970). Author: (with others) Sexual Behavior in the Human Male, 1948; (with others) Sexual Behavior in the Human Female, 1953; (with others) Pregnancy, Birth, and Abortion, 1958; (with others) Sex Offenders, 1965; Boys and Sex, 1968; Girls and Sex, 1969; Dr. Kinsey and the Institute for Sex Research, 1972; Your Child and Sex, 1974. Address: 1611 Vallejo St San Francisco CA 94123

POMEROY, WILLIAM TAMPLIN, mfg. co. exec.; b. East Liverpool, Ohio, Feb. 28, 1908; s. Charles C. and Mabel Irene (Roberts) P.; student Kiski Prep. Sch., 1923-25; B.S., U. Pitts., 1930; m. Helen Elizabeth Miller, Feb. 11, 1929; children—William Tamplin, Ann, Jean Miller. With Sterling China Co., 1930—, sales mgr., 1934-36, v.p., sales mgr., 1936-42, pres., dir., 1943—; dir. Central Fed. Savings & Loan, Wellsville, 1944-79, pres., 1950-65, chmn., 1965-79, dir. emeritus, 1979—; pres., dir. Caribe China Corp., Vega Baja, P.R., 1951—. Mem. Am. Resturant China Mfrs. Assn. (dir.), Am. Cermaic Soc., Phi Delta Theta. Clubs: East Liverpool Country; University (Pitts.); Youngstown (Ohio) Country. Home: Elysian Way East Liverpool OH Office: Sterling China Co Wellsville OH 43968 also Caribe China Corp Vega Baja PR 00763

POMFRET, JOHN DANA, newspaper exec.; b. Princeton, N.J., Jan. 30, 1928; s. John Edwin and Sara Cornelia (Wise) P.; A.B., Princeton U., 1949; grad. Advanced Mgmt. Program, Harvard U., 1976; m. Margaret Elizabeth Haas, Apr. 19, 1952; children—Dana Katherine, John Edwin II. Reporter, Milw. Jour., 1949-50, 52-60, editorial writer, 1961-62; labor reporter Washington Bur., N.Y. Times, 1962-65, White House corr., 1965-66, asst. to dir. indsl. relations, 1966-67, dir. indsl. relations, 1967-71, asst. to pub., 1971-75, v.p., 1971-73, sr. v.p., 1973—, coordinator planning, 1973-75, asst. gen. mgr., 1975-79, gen. mgr., 1979—. Served with AUS, 1950-52. Nieman fellow, 1960-61. Contbr. to books, anthologies. Office: 229 W 43d St New York NY 10036

POMMERENING, EDWIN CARLTON, bus. exec.; b. Milw., Oct. 7, 1938; s. Edwin Carl and Emily (Schink) P.; B.S., U. Wis., 1961, J.D., 1964; m. Sandra Lee Bloom, Sept. 13, 1969; children—Bradford William, Douglas Edwin. Admitted to Wis. bar, 1964; with Legis. Reference Bur., State of Wis., 1966-67; asst. corporate counsel Ansul Co., Marinette, Wis., 1967-68, asst. to pres., 1968-69, mgr. subs. ops., 1969-70, gen. mgr. chem. div., 1970-72, gen. mgr. internat. div., 1972-73, corporate sec., 1973-77, gen. counsel, corporate sec., 1977—, v.p., 1978—. Served to capt., Transp. Corps, U.S. Army, 1964-66. Mem. Am., Inter Am., Wis., Marinette bar assns., Nat. Investor Relations Inst., Am. Soc. Corporate Secs. Lutheran. Clubs: Elks; Riverside Country; Twi Cees. Home: 813 Barbara Ln Marinette WI 54143 Office: 1 Stanton St Marinette WI 54143

POMPADUR, I. MARTIN, communications exec.; b. Bklyn., June 25, 1935; s. Jack and Florence (Raitbord) P.; B.A., Williams Coll., 1955; LL.B., U. Mich., 1958; m. Joan Lynn Krassner, Dec. 18, 1960; children—F. Douglas, Jana Sue. Admitted to Conn. bar, 1958, N.Y. bar, 1961; mem. firm Wofsey, Rosen, Kweskin & Kuriansky, Stamford, Conn., 1958-60; atty. ABC-TV Network, N.Y.C., 1960-61, 61-66, chief adminstrv. officer TV network, v.p., 1966-68, gen. mgr. TV network, 1968-70, v.p. broadcast div., 1970-72, corp. v.p., 1972, pres. ABC Leisure Group I, 1973-75, asst. to pres. parent co., 1975-76, also dir. parent co.; sr. v.p. Ziff Corp., 1977-78, pres., 1978—; atty. Young & Rubicam, Inc., advt. agy., N.Y.C., summer 1961. Mem. Stamford bd. reps., chmn. legis. and rules com., 1959-60. Home: 33 Dorset Rd Scarsdale NY 10583 Office: Ziff Corp 1 Park Ave New York City NY 10016

POMPER, VICTOR HERBERT, mgmt. cons.; b. White Plains, N.Y., July 17, 1923; s. Anthony Louis and Martha (Manzek) P.; B.S. in Elec. Engring., Mass. Inst. Tech., 1948, M.S., 1950; grad. Advanced Mgmt. Program, Harvard, 1973; m. Anne Ritchie, 1959; children—Anthony Scott, Michael Louis, Martha Anne. Engr., Philco Corp., 1948-49; sales engr. H.H. Scott, Inc., Maynard, Mass., 1950, sales mgr., 1951, asst. gen. mgr., 1952-57, v.p., 1957-59, exec. v.p., 1959-68, pres., dir., 1968-73; pres. Levco, Inc., 1973—. Pres. Bio-Behavioral Inst., 1977—; instr. Worcester Poly. Inst., 1977—. Designer products selected for exhbn. at Milan Triennale, U.S. Pavilion, Brussels Worlds Fair. Mem. adv. bd. Boston Salvation Army, 1963-69. Trustee Childrens Hosp., Fund Urban Negro Devel. Served as sgt. Signal Corps, AUS, 1943-46. Named one of ten oustanding young men Boston Jr. C. of C., 1959. Registered profl. engr., Mass. Mem. Acad. Applied Scis. (v.p., dir. 1963—), Am. Mgmt. Assn., I.E.E.E. (sr.), Acoustical Soc. Am., Am. Inst. Physics, Inst. High Fidelity Mfrs. (dir. 1962-66), Audio Engring. Soc., Am. Assn. Indsl. Mgmt. (pres. Boston 1964-66), Internat. Soc. Gen. Semantics, Soc. Gen. Systems Research, Tau Beta Pi, Eta Kappa Nu. Contbr. articles tech. lit. Home: 740 Country Way North Scituate MA 02060

POMPEY, MAURICE DALE, judge; b. South Bend, Ind., May 14, 1923; s. Luther Martin and Thelma (Findlay) P.; student Howard U., Washington, 1940-41, Roosevelt U., Chgo., 1947; LL.B., J.D., DePaul U., 1951; grad. Nat. Coll. of State Judiciary, 1975; m. Josephine Marie Galloway, Aug. 1, 1945; children—Maurice Dale, Tina Marie. Admitted to Ill. bar, 1951, also Fed. Ct. bar; asst. corp. counsel City of Chgo., 1963; judges trial asst. Mcpl. Ct. of Chgo., 1963; magistrate Circuit Ct. of Cook County, 1964-70, circuit judge, 1970—. Bd. dirs. Woodlawn Chgo. Boys Club. Served to 1st lt. USAAF, 1943-45. Mem. Am., Nat., Ill., Cook County, Chgo. bar assns. Club: Original Forty. Office: 2600 S California St Chicago IL 60608

POMRINSE, SIMOUR DAVID, hosp. adminstr.; b. N.Y.C., May 24, 1916; s. Harry and Rebecca (Schuldiner) P.; B.S., Rensselaer Poly. Inst., 1937; M.D., Western Res. U., 1941; M.P.H., Columbia, 1959; m. Catherine Sortino, June 25, 1959. Intern Cleve. City Hosp., 1941-42; resident internal medicine Cleve. City Hosp., 1942-43, Sunny Acres Sanatorium, Cleve., 1944; practice medicine specializing in internal medicine, Springfield, Ohio, 1946-55; med. dir. USPHS, 1956-61; asso. dir. Mt. Sinai Hosp., N.Y.C., 1961-69, dir., 1969-75, exec. v.p., 1975-77; prof. adminstrv. medicine Mt. Sinai Sch. Medicine, 1969-77, prof. emeritus, 1977—; exec. v.p. hosp. affairs Mt. Sinai Med. Center, 1969-77; co-chmn. adv. com. health care adminstrn. Baruch Coll., 1969-77; pres. Greater N.Y. Hosp. Assn., 1977—; sec. Hosp. Assn. N.Y. State, 1977. Fellow N.Y. Acad. Medicine, A.C.P., Am. Pub. Health Assn., Am. Coll. Hosp. Adminstrs.; mem. Sigma Xi, Alpha Omega Alpha. Home: 530 E 72d St New York NY 10021 Office: Greater NY Hosp Assn 3 E 54th St New York NY 10022

POMROY, JESSE HERBERT, JR., educator; b. St. Paul; s. Jesse Herbert and Marion Ann (Clos) P.; B.S. in Agrl. Engring., U. Minn., 1950, M.S. in Agrl. Engring., 1952; m. Patricia Lewellyn Burleson, Nov. 29, 1945; children—Pamela, Jon, William, Elizabeth, Robert. With Nicols, Dean & Gregg Co., hardware, 1936-41, VA, 1945-46; mem. faculty dept. agrl. engring. U. Minn., St. Paul, from 1946, now prof. Cons. on farm, agrl. structures. Served with inf., AUS, 1941-45. Decorated Bronze Star, Purple Heart; NSF grantee. Mem. Minn. Fedn. Engrs. Soc., Am. Soc. Agrl. Engrs. (chmn. sect.). Home: 841 E Cook Ave Saint Paul MN 55106 Office: U Minn Agrl Engring Dept Saint Paul MN 55108

PONCE DE LEON, MICHAEL, artist, lectr., educator; b. Miami, Fla., July 4, 1922; s. Manuel and Joan (Cobos) P. de L.; student U. Mexico, 1939, N.A.D., N.Y.C., 1942, Art Students League, N.Y.C., 1947, Bklyn. Mus. Art Sch., 1949, also in Europe. Cartoonist, Sat Eve. Post, Colliers, New Yorker mags., 1942-49; tchr. Vassar Coll., 1953, Pratt Graphic Art Center, 1957-71, Cooper Union, 1962-67, Hunter Coll., 1959-67, U. Pa., 1966—, Art Students League, 1966-75, Pratt 1968-75, Calif. State Coll., 1969, Hayward State Coll., 1970, Columbia, 1972, N.Y. U., 1976-77; one-man show Corcoran Gallery, Washington, 1966; exhibited numerous cities throughout Can., S.Am., Mexico, Middle East, Russia, Europe, India, Australia, Japan, Korea, Taiwan; represented in permanent collections numerous Am. museums, including Whitney Mus., Jewish Mus., N.A.D., Mus. Modern Art, Met. Mus. Art, Bklyn. Mus., Pa. Acad., Dallas Mus., Cin. Art Mus., U. Ill., U. Mich., U. Nebr., U. N.C., Norfolk Mus., Smithsonian Instn., Library Congress, Phila. Mus., N.Y.U., Acherbach Found., San Francisco, Cleve. Mus., Columbia (S.C.) Mus., UN, Nat. Gallery, Washington, Boston Mus., Sarasota (Fla.) Art Mus., Walker Art Center, Mpls., Auckland (New Zealand) Art Mus., Nat. Gallery, Stockholm, Nat. Gallery, Oslo, Musee de l'Art Moderne, Paris, Victoria and Albert Mus., London, Am. embassies in Bonn, Germany, Belgrade, Moscow, Prague, New Delhi, White House, Washington; v.p. Nelson Rockefeller Collection; Shah of Iran collection; John F. Kennedy collection; commd. by P.O. Dept. to design U.S. stamp honoring fine arts, 1964, by USIA on cultural missions to Yugoslavia, 1965, Pakistan, India, 1967, Venzuela, 1966, Spain, 1971; represented U.S. at Symposium of 1st Indian Triannial of Art in New Delhi, Venice Biennale, 1970 Served with USAAF, 1943-46. Recipient Gold medal Oakland Art Mus., 1958, Nat. Acad. Design prize, 1963, 78, Medal of Honor, Audubon Artists, 1964, 66, 67, 68, 70, Alice McFadden Eyre medal Pa. Acad. Design, 1965, 65 purchase prizes from U.S. museums and colls. Included in Archives Am. Art; Tiffany fellow, 1953-55, Fulbright fellow, 1955-57; Guggenheim fellow, 1967. Mem. Soc. Am. Graphic Artists (past. treas.). Contbr. to 13 books on printmaking, including Printmaking, 1971, Printmaking Today, 1972, Etching, 1973, Mexican-American Artists, 1973, History of Pictorial Illusion, 1975, the Art of the Print, 1976; Printmaking, 1977; History of Prints, 1980. Address: 463 West St New York NY 10014

POND, ALONZO WILLIAM, anthropologist; b. Janesville, Wis., June 18, 1894; s. William Samuel and Marie (Olson) P.; grad. Wayland Acad. Beaver Dam, Wis., 1914; B.S., Beloit (Wis.) Coll., 1920, C.S.C., 1978; studied Am. Sch. in Europe for Prehistoric Research, 1921-22, Ecole d'Anthropologie, Paris, 1922; M.A., U. Chgo., 1928; m. Dorothy Helen Long, July 20, 1926; children—Chomingwen Dorothy, Arthur Alonzo. Asst. curator Logan Museum, Beloit Coll., 1925-31; leader of Logan Sahara Expedition of Beloit College, 1925-26; asso. with Dr. George L. Collie, dir. Logan Museum, in excavation at Dordogne, France, 1926, asst. in charge paleolithic excavations at Mechta el Arbi, Algeria, 1926-27; archaeologist for Dr. Roy Chapman Andrews on Central Asiatic Expdn. of Am. Museum Natural History, 1928; leader of 2 Logan Museum Expdns. to Africa, 1929, 30; directed eastern group of Rainbow Bridge-Monument Valley Expdn., 1933; archaeologist Nat. Park Service, June-Sept. 1935, in charge of excavation and study of desiccated body of prehistoric miner found in Mammoth Cave, Ky. Mgr. newly discovered Cave of the Mounds, Blue Mounds, Wis., 1940-45; owner-mgr. Wisconsin Gardens, scenic attraction. Editorial research specialist USAF Arctic Desert Tropic Info. Center, chief desert sect.; prof. desert geography Air U., 1949-58. French Army and U.S. Ambulance Service, France, 1917-19. Mem. Wis. Archaeol. Soc., Am. Legion, Sigma Xi. Republican. Clubs: Adventurers (Chgo.); Explorers (N.Y.). Wrote bulletins, A Contribution to the Study of Prehistoric Man in Algeria, North Africa, Primitive Methods of Working Stone Based on Experiments of H.L. Skavlem; Interotate Park and Dalles of the St. Croix; Prehistoric Habitation Sites in the Sahara and North Africa; Illustrated Guide Book to Cave of the Mounds; Afoot in the Desert; Climate and Weather in Central Gobi of Mongolia. Author of scenario (ednl. motion picture) Lime Stone Caverns; tech. adv. A.F. tng. film, Sun, Sand, and Survivial. Author: (with Nesbitt and Allen) The Survival Book, 1959; A Pilots Survival Manual, 1978; The Desert World, 1962; Deserts, 1964; Caverns of the World, 1969; Survival in Sun and Sand, 1969; (with Lafferty and Eady) Desert Survival Problem, 1970; Andrews: Gobi Explorer, 1972; Dr. Kate & the Million Penny Parades, 1974. Address: Wis Gardens 8953 Minch Dr Minocqua WI 54548. *Experience is a harsh teacher from whom we learn reluctantly but the lessons make the ups and downs of history repeating itself less frustrating. Man hasn't changed his nature since Adam ate the apple. We still listen to sweet words of bad advice. Wishful thinking and tinkering with words have not changed laws of Nature. Despite our power over Nature and our* *wishful thinking on the "rights" of Man, Tennison was closer to TRUTH when his little brook sang: "Men may come and men may go, but I go on forever."*

POND, BYRON OLIVER, JR., automotive parts mfg. co. exec.; b. Royal Oak, Mich., July 6, 1936; s. Byron Oliver and Irene Alma (Torikka) P.; B.S. in Bus. Adminstrn., Wayne State U., 1961; m. Margaret J. Kenney, Dec. 17, 1960; children—Douglas, David, Byron, Eric. Dist. sales mgr. Fed. Mogul Corp., Cleve., 1965-68; v.p., gen. mgr. nat. accounts Maremont Corp., Chgo., 1974-76, sr. v.p., 1976-78, exec. v.p., dir., 1978, pres., chief exec. officer, 1979—. Served with U.S. Army, 1954-56. Mem. Automotive Parts and Accessories Assn. (dir.). Republican. Office: 200 Randolph Chicago IL 60601

POND, MARTIN ALLEN, educator; b. Ansonia, Conn., Oct. 17, 1912; s. Clifford A. and A. Louise (Hafner) P.; grad. Loomis Sch., 1930; B.S., Yale, 1935, M.P.H., 1936; m. Madeleine Huson Davidson, May 28, 1938; children—Sarah L. (Mrs. Gary K. Williams), Jonathan D., Roger A. Successively asst., instr., asst. prof. pub. health Yale, 1936-42; commd. officer USPHS (res.), 1942-46, (regular), 1948-68; asst. prof. pub. health Yale, 1946-1948; prof. pub. health U. Pitts., 1968—, asso. dean, 1969-74. Adviser U.S. delegation WHO, 1965, 67; mem. Nat. Adv. Health Council, 1970-73. Mem. alumni council Loomis Sch. Recipient Meritorious service medal USPHS, 1965; spl. citation Sec. Health, Edn. and Welfare, 1968; Sedgwick Meml. medal, 1978. Fellow, life mem. Am. Pub. Health Assn. Home: 5125 5th Ave Pittsburgh PA 15232

POND, ROBERT BARRETT, SR., educator; b. Franklin, Va., Dec. 1, 1917; s. Charles Ellsworth and Josie Edwards (Barrett) P.; B.S., Va. Poly. Inst., 1942; m. Mary Palmer Wright, June 27, 1942; children—Robert Barrett, Mary (Mrs. John Mac Winter), Bertie, William, Edward, Margaret (Mrs. D. Shifler). Prodn. foreman Bethlehem Steel Co., Sparrows Point, Md., 1942-47; asst. prof. Johns Hopkins, 1947-60, asso. prof. metallurgy, 1960-71, prof. metallurgy, 1971—, chmn. dept. mechanics, materials sci., 1973—. Founder, chmn. bd. dirs. Marvalaud Inc. Cons. numerous firms, including U.S. Army, Mendes & Mount, Battelle Meml. Inst., Cities Service Corp., Balt. Gas & Electric Co.; mem. sci. adv. com. Univ. Space Research Agy. NASA, 1975-78; lectr. to profl. orgns., young people. Served with USN, 1935-38. Fellow Am. Soc. Metals (chmn. chpt. 1953, Pres's. award 1967, Albert Easton White Distinguished Tchr. award 1974, award of Merit, 1974); mem. Md. Inst. Metals (pres. 1955), Alpha Sigma Mu, Tau Beta Pi, Phi Kappa Phi, Omicron Delta Kappa. Republican. Methodist (chmn. Council on Ministries 1970-73). Contbg. author: Hypervelocity Impact Phenomena, 1970; Response of Metals to High Velocity Deformation, 1960; Metal Progress, 1966, High-Velocity Impact Phenomena, 1970, The Inhomogeneity of Plastic Deformation, 1973. Patentee in field; lectr. movies: Plasticity of Metals, Wright Air Devel. Command, 1955, Fun in Metals, Johns Hopkins Quar., Am. Soc. Metals, 1966. Home: 299 Ridge Rd Westminster MD 21157 Office: Dept of Mechanics and Materials Sci Johns Hopkins U Baltimore MD 21218

POND, THOMAS ALEXANDER, educator, physicist; b. Los Angeles, Dec. 4, 1924; s. Arthur Francis and Florence (Alexander) P.; A.B., Princeton, 1947, A.M., 1949, Ph.D., 1953; m. Barbara Eileen Newman, Sept. 6, 1958; children—Arthur Phillip Ward, Florence Alexandra. Instr. physics Princeton, 1951-53; asst. prof., then asso. prof. physics Washington U., St. Louis, 1953-62; prof. physics, chmn. dept. State U. N.Y. at Stony Brook, 1962-67, exec. v.p., prof. physics, 1968—, acting pres., 1970, 75, 78. Bd. dirs. Action Com. for L.I., 1978—, Tri-State Regional Planning Commn., 1979—. Served to ensign USNR, 1943-46. Mem. Fedn. Am. Scientists (council 1964-66), Am. Phys. Soc., Phi Beta Kappa, Sigma Xi. Home: 8 Flax Pond Woods Old Field Setauket NY 11785 Office: State Univ New York Stony Brook NY 11794

PONDER, THOMAS C., pub. co. exec.; b. nr. Tuckerman, Ark., Dec. 6, 1921; s. Harry Lee and Ruth Lee (Hopper) P.; B.S., U. Ark., 1948; m. Catherine Frances Cahill, Nov. 26, 1942; children—Thomas C., Stephen Cahill, Harry Lee. With Pitts. Plate Glass Co., 1948-51; process engr. Foster Wheeler Corp., Houston, 1951-54; project engr. the Lummus Co., engring. and constrn., Houston, 1954-55; with Hydrocarbon Processing tech. jour. Gulf Pub. Co., Houston, 1955—. Served with USAAF, 1944-46. Registered profl. engr., Tex.; certified cost engr. Mem. Am. Inst. Chem. Engrs., Am. Chem. Soc., ASME, Am. Assn. Cost Engrs. (nat. sec., nat. pres. 1965, award of merit 1971). Home: 10227 Raritan Dr Houston TX 77043

PONITZ, DAVID HENRY, coll. pres.; b. Royal Oak, Mich., Jan. 21, 1931; s. Henry John and Jeanette (Bouwman) P.; B.A., U. Mich., 1952, M.A., 1954; Ed.D., Harvard U., 1964; m. Doris Jean Humes, Aug. 5, 1956; children—Catherine Anne, David Robinson. Formerly prin., later supt. Waldron (Mich.) Area Schs.; later Harvard U. cons. Boston Sch. Survey; supt. Freeport (Ill.) public schs., 1962-65; pres. Freeport Community Coll., 1962-65; pres. Washtenaw Community Coll., 1965-75, Sinclair Community Coll., 1975—; cons. to community colls. Chmn. Dayton Mayor's Council on Econ. Devel., 1977—; campaign chmn., chmn. fin. resources devel. council Dayton Area United Way; vice chmn. Dayton Citizens Adv. Council for Desegregation Implementation; mem. Area Progress Council, Dayton; bd. dirs. Leadership Dayton, Miami Valley Hosp.; pres. Portage Trails council Boy Scouts Am. Served with U.S. Army, 1954-56. Named Outstanding Alumnus, U. Mich. Mem. Am. Assn. Community and Jr. Colls., Ohio Tech. and Community Coll. Assn. (pres. 1979-80), Acad. Collective Bargaining Info. Service. Methodist. Club: Rotary. Mem. editorial adv. bd. Nations Schs., 1963-70; chmn. adv. bd. Community Coll. Rev., 1978—. Home: 5556 Viewpoint Dayton OH 45459 Office: 444 W 3d St Dayton OH 45402

PONKA, JOSEPH LUKE, surgeon; b. Gary, W.Va., May 18, 1913; s. John and Barbara (Visoglant) P.; A.B., B.S., W.Va. U., 1940; M.D., Washington U., St. Louis, 1942; M.S.C., U. Mich., 1953; m. Clara Margaret Straub, June 8, 1938; children—Joseph Luke, George J., Clare Suzette, Carol Jo. Intern, then resident in surgery Henry Ford Hosp., Detroit, 1942-50, mem. staff, dir. surg. edn. program, 1965—, now dir. West Bloomfield Center Satellite; practice medicine specializing in surgery, Detroit, 1951—; mem. faculty U. Mich., 1970—, clin. prof. surgery, 1977—. Bd. dirs. Children's Orthogenic Sch., Detroit, 1960-64. Served with AUS, 1943-46. Mem. A.C.S. (Sci. award 1966), AMA, Am. Proctologic Soc., Am. Surg. Assn., Detroit Surg. Soc. (pres. 1968-69), Detroit Acad. Surgery (pres. 1967-68), Am. Soc. Colon and Rectal Surgeons, Am. Med. Writers Assn., Am. Geriatric Soc., Am. Assn. Med. Clinics, Colegium Internat. Chirurgiae Digestivae, Detroit Gasteroenterol. Soc., Detroit Physiol. Soc., Detroit Acad. Medicine, Mich., Wayne County med. socs., Soc. de Chirugie Internat., Soc. Surgery Alimentary Tract, Pan Pacific, Western, Central surg. assns. Editor Detroit Med. News, 1975-76. Contbr. to med. jours. Home: 1520 W Boston Blvd Detroit MI 48206 Office: Henry Ford Hosp 2799 W Grand Blvd Detroit MI 48202 also West Bloomfield Center West Bloomfield MI 48033

PONSETI, IGNACIO VIVES, orthopaedic surgeon; b. Cuidadela, Balearic Islands, Spain, June 3, 1914; s. Miguel and Margarita (Vives) P.; B.S., U. Barcelona, 1930, M.D., 1936; 1 son, William Edward; m. 2d, Helena Percas, June 21, 1961. Became naturalized U.S. citizen, 1948. Instr. dept. orthopaedic surgery State U. Iowa, 1944-57, prof., 1957—. Served as capt. M.C., Spanish Army, 1936-39. Recipient Kappa Delta award for orthopaedic research, 1955. Mem. Assn. Bone and Joint Surgeons, Am. Acad. Cerebral Palsy, Soc. Exptl. Biology and Medicine, Internat. Coll. Surgeons, N.Y. Acad. Sci., AMA (Ketoen gold medal 1960), Am. Acad. Orthopedic Surgeons, A.C.S., Am. Orthopedic Assn., Iowa Med. Soc., Orthopedic Research Soc. (Shands award 1975), Chgo. Orthopedic Soc., Midwest Orthopedic Club, La Sociedad Mexicana de Ortopedia, Sigma Xi; hon. mem. Asociacion Argentina de Cirugia, Sociedad de Cirujanos de Chile. Author papers on congenital and developmental skeletal deformities. Home: 110 Oak Ridge Iowa City IA 52240 Office: Carver Pavilion U Iowa Hosps Iowa City IA 52242

PONT, JOHN, educator, football coach; b. Canton, Ohio, Nov. 13, 1927; s. Bautista and Susie (Sikurinec) P.; B.S., Miami U., Oxford, Ohio, 1952, M.S., 1956; m. H. Sandra Stoutt, June 23, 1956; children—John W., Jennifer Ann, Jeffrey David. Profl. football player, Can., 1952-53; instr., freshman football and basketball coach Miami U., 1953-55, asst. prof., head football coach, 1955-62; head football coach Yale, 1963-65; prof., head football coach Ind. U., Bloomington, 1965-73; head coach Northwestern U., Evanston, Ill., 1973-77, athletic dir., 1974—; athletic dir. Jewish Community Center, Canton, 1953. Mem. Pres.'s Council on Phys. Fitness. Chmn., Ind. Easter Seal, 1968-69, Ind. div. Cancer Crusade, 1969. Bd. dirs. Multiple Sclerosis, N.E. Ill. council Boy Scouts Am. Served with USNR, 1945-47. Named Coach of Year, Coaches Assn., 1967, Football Writers, 1967; recipient Significant Sig award, 1968. Mem. Am. Football Coaches Assn. (chmn. ethics com.), Blue Key, Sigma Chi, Phi Epsilon Kappa, Omicron Delta Kappa. Republican. Home: 2520 Sheridan Rd Evanston IL 60201

PONTE, VINCENT DE PASCIUTO, city planning cons.; b. Boston, Oct. 27, 1919; s. Salvatore R. and Marie (Mitrano) Pasciuto; A.B., Harvard, 1943, M. City Planning, 1949. With HHFA-FHA, 1950, N.Y.C. Planning Dept., 1951-52, Webb & Knapp Inc., 1956-58; mem. planning div. I.M. Pei & Assos., 1959-63; propr. Vincent Ponte, planning cons., Montreal, 1963-73; partner Cossutta & Ponte, Architects, Planners, 1973-77; prin. works include sites for central bus. dists., underground pedestrian systems for downtown Montreal, Dallas, Melbourne, Paris, Madrid, Ottawa and Winnipeg; parks, blvds. and above-grade walkways, Charlotte, N.C. and Columbus, Ohio. Mem. Am., Can. insts. planners, Corp Professionnelle des Urbanistes duQue. Home: 3450 Drummond St Montreal PQ Canada Office: 600 Madison Ave New York NY 10022

PONTON, MARK, bus. cons.; b. Providence, R.I., Nov. 23, 1931; s. Oscar O. and Anne G. P.; B.S., Providence Coll., 1953; children—Anne Ponton, Christine. With AT&T, 1954-61; with IBM, 1961-68, program mgr., to 1968; with Citicorp, 1968-76, v.p., 1973-76; with European Am. Bank and Trust Co., N.Y.C., 1976-79, exec. v.p., 1979-80; pres. Mark Ponton Co., N.Y.C. Office: 505 Main St New York NY 10044

PONTY, JEAN-LUC, violinist, composer; b. Avranches, Normandy, France, Sept. 29, 1942; grad. Conservatoire National Superieur de Musique, Paris, 1960. Classical violinist, to 1964; played with Concerts Lamoureux Symphony Orch.; jazz violinist, Europe, 1964-69; night club and music festivals with George Duke Trio, U.S., 1969; toured with own group, France and Europe, 1970-72; recorded with Elton John, Honky Chateau, 1972; with Frank Zappa and the Mothers of Invention, 1973, Mahavishnu Orch., 1974-75; frequent appearances at music festivals, including Monterey, Newport, Berlin and Montreux jazz festivals; albums include: Sunday Walk, Open Strings, Sonata Erotica, Ponty/Grappelli, Cantaloupe Island, Upon the Wings of Music, Aurora, Imaginary Voyage, Enigmatic Ocean, Cosmic Messenger, Live and A Taste for Passion; with Mahavishnu Orch.: Apocalypse, Visions of the Emerald Beyond. Winner Downbeat Readers and Critics polls, 1971-79. Office: care JLP Prodns Inc PO Box 46425 Los Angeles CA 90046

POOL, ITHIEL DE SOLA, educator; b. N.Y.C., Oct. 26, 1917; s. David de Sola and Tamar (Hirshenson) P.; B.A., U. Chgo., 1938, M.A., 1939, Ph.D., 1952; m. Jean MacKenzie, Mar. 3, 1956; children—Jonathan, Jeremy, Adam. Chmn. div. social scis. Hobart Coll., 1942-49; asso. dir. RADIR project Hoover Inst., Stanford, 1949-53; vis. lectr. Yale U., 1953-54; prof. polit. sci. Mass. Inst. Tech., 1953—, chmn. polit. sci. dept., 1959-61, 65-69; vis. prof. Keio U., Tokyo, 1976. Sci. adv. bd. USAF, 1961-64; mem.-at-large Def. Sci. Bd., 1968-71. Fellow Churchill Coll., Cambridge (Eng.) U., 1977—. Fellow Am. Acad. Arts and Scis.; mem. Council Fgn. Relations, Am. Polit. Sci. Assn., Am. Assn. Pub. Opinion Research. Club: Cosmos. Author: Satellite Generals. 1955; American Business and Public Policy, 1963; The People Look at Educational Television, 1963; Candidates Issues and Strategies, 1964; Contemporary Political Science, 1967; The Prestige Press, 1970; Talking Back, 1973; Handbook of Communication, 1973; The Social Impact of the Telephone, 1977. Home: 105 Irving St Cambridge MA 02138

POOL, JAMES LAWRENCE, physician; b. N.Y. City, Aug. 23, 1906; s. Eugene H. and Esther (Hoppin) P.; A.B., Harvard, 1928; M.D., Columbia, 1932, D.M.S., 1941; m. Angeline K. James, June 14, 1940; children—James Lawrence, Eugene H. II, Daniel S. Intern N.Y.-Cornell, 1932-33, Presbyn. Hosp., N.Y.C., 1934-36; Neurol. Inst., 1936-38, chief resident neurol. surgery, 1938-39; neurosurgeon, N.Y.C., 1939—; neurosurgeon Bellevue Hosp., 1939-47, Neurol. Inst., 1947—; prof. neurol. surgery and dir. dept. Presbyn. Hosp. and Columbia Coll. Physicians and Surgeons, 1949-72, emeritus, 1972—; cons. Englewood (N.J.) Hosp. Trustee St. Pauls Sch., Concord, N.H., 1954-64; Am. Mus. Natural History, 1956-60; bd. overseers Harvard Coll., 1948-54. Served to lt. col. M.C., AUS, World War II. Diplomate Am. Bd. Neurol. Surgery. Fellow A.C.S. (gov. 1959-62; mem. AMA, Am. Neurology Assn., Am. Acad. Neurol. Surgery (pres. 1952-53), Harvey Cushing Soc., Neurosurg. Soc., World Fedn. Neurol. Surgeons (treas. 1965-73), Harvard Alumni Assn. (pres. 1958-59). Clubs: Anglers, Century, Harvard (N.Y.C.); British Royal Ocean Racing. Author: Neurosurgical Treatment of Paraplegia, 1951; (with Arthur Pava) Acoustic Nerve Tumors, 1957, 2d edit., 1971; (with Gordon Potts) Aneurysms and AVM of the Brain, 1965; Your Brain and Nerves, 1973, paperback edit., 1978; Izaak Walton, Life and Times, 1975; The Neurological Institute of N.Y.: 1909-1972, 1974. Home: Box 31 Cherry Hill Rd West Cornwall CT 06796

POOL, JOHN LAWRENCE, cancer surgeon; b. N.Y.C., Dec. 12, 1907; s. John Lawrence and Maud Gordon (Fleming) P.; B.S., Princeton, 1930; M.D., Columbia Coll. phys. and Surg., 1934; m. Patricia Matthews Martin, June 25, 1938 (div. 1953); children—Christopher Fleming, Julia Lawrence (Wald), Martin Van Dyke; m. 2d, Doris Kelley Yerkes, June 20, 1957. Intern surgery Presbyn. Hosp., N.Y.C., 1934-37, asst. attending surgeon, 1948-54; resident surgery Meml. Hosp., N.Y.C., 1937-40, asst. attending thoracic surgeon, 1946-48, asso. attending thoracic surgeon, 1948-65, attending thoracic surgeon, 1965-72, cons. surgeon, 1972—; first and then chief surgeon Tata Meml. Hosp., Bombay, India, 1940-43; clin. asst. prof. surgery Cornell U. Med. Sch., 1948-66, clin. asso. prof. surgery, 1966-72; sr. surgeon, dir. surg. edn. Norwalk (Conn.) Hosp., 1972-76; asso. clin. prof. surgery Yale, 1972-75, emeritus; cons. surgery Meml. Sloan Kettering Inst., 1972—, Interagy. Council on Smoking and Health, HEW. Trustee Wilton Library, Norwalk, Conn. Served to maj. M.C., AUS, 1943-46. Decorated Bronze Star. Diplomate Am. Bd. Surgery. Fellow A.C.S., Am. Coll. Chest Physicians; mem. Am. Assn. Thoracic Surgery, Eastern Surg. Soc. (pres. 1969-70), N.Y. Surg. Soc., James Ewing Soc. (pres. 1960), Am. Radium Soc. (v.p. 1963, pres. 1967-68), Am. Broncho-esophagological Soc., N.Y. Thoracic Soc. (pres. 1957), N.Y. Cancer Soc. (pres. 1964), N.Y. Acad. Medicine (pres. 1969-70). Contbr. articles on thoracic disease and cancer. Home and Office: 560 Belden Hill Rd Wilton CT 06897

POOL, MARY JANE, magazine editor; b. La Plata, Mo.; d. Earl Lee Pool and Dorothy (Matthews) Pool Evans; student St. de Chantal Acad., 1942; B.A. with honors in Art, Drury Coll., 1946. Mem. staff Vogue mag., N.Y.C., 1946-69, asso. merchandising editor, 1948-57, promotion dir., 1958-66, exec. editor, 1966-68; editor-in-chief House and Garden mag., 1970—. Mem. com. of friends of environ. design collections Cooper-Hewitt Mus. of Smithsonian Instn.; mem. industry adv. council, dept. interior design Fashion Inst. Tech.; bd. govs. Fashion Group, Inc., N.Y.C., 1966—; trustee Drury Coll., 1971; v.p., bd. dirs. 34557 Corp., 1974-77; bd. dirs. Isabel O'Neil Found., 1978; mem. bus. com. N.Y. Zool. Soc. Recipient Vogue Prix de Paris, 1946; award Nat. Soc. Interior Designers. Mem. Am. Soc. Mag. Editors. Editor: Billy Baldwin Decorates; House and Garden's 26 Easy Little Gardens. Office: 350 Madison Ave New York NY 10017

POOL, TAMAR DE SOLA, lecturer, educator; b. Jerusalem, Israel; d. Chaim and Eva (Cohen) Hirschenson; brought to U.S., 1904; A.B., Hunter Coll., 1913; student U. Paris, 1913-14 (traveling fellowship); grad. student Columbia, 1914-17; m. Rev. David de Sola Pool, Feb. 6, 1917; children—Ithiel de Sola, Naomi de Sola (Mrs. Rodstein). Tutor English lang. and lit. Lycée Lamartine, Paris, 1913-14; instr. French, Latin and Greek, Hunter Coll., 1914-17; faculty adviser Menorah Socs., Hunter Coll., 1914-17; editor Hadassah Newsletter; nat. pres. Hadassah, 1939-43, pres. N.Y. chpt., 1929-35, life hon. v.p.; chmn. world praesidium Henrietta Szold Centennial, 1960; Hadassah chmn. Szold Inst.; dir. Nat. Council of Women of U.S.; hon. chmn. Jewish Nat. Fund; mem. gen. council World Zionist Orgn.; sometime mem. exec. Am.-Jewish Com.; vice chmn. Am. Jewish Conf.; mem. gov. bd. Youth Aliyah; mem. exec. com. Children to Palestine; chmn. Hebrew U.-Hadassah Med. Sch. Com.; co-founder, chmn. Am. Mothers Com.; mem. bd. Sisterhood of Spanish and Portuguese Synagogue of N.Y.; pres., later hon. pres. Sifriot Libraries for Youth in Israel and U.S.; bd. govs. Hebrew U., Jerusalem; organizer Arab-Jewish Peoples Amity Commn. of World Sephardi and Am. Sephardi Fedns., 1976; mem. bd. Union Sephardic Congregations, Am. Sephardi Fedn.; women's div. Alliance Israelite Universelle. Named Life Virilist, World Zionist Congress. Author: Israel and the United Nations: In the Spirit of '76 (a drama); Triple Cord (novel); (with David de Sola Pool) An Old Faith in The New World, 1955; The Passover Haggadah; Is There an Answer? An Inquiry into Some Human Dilemmas; Haggadah (art edit.), 1975; (with Nima Adlerblum) David de Sola Pool-Portrait of a Rabbinic Family. Address: 91 Central Park W New York NY 10023 Office: 8 W 70th St New York NY 10023

POOLE, ALBERT TERENCE, wire and cable mfg. co. exec.; b. Corner Brook, Nfld., Can., Dec. 5, 1942; s. C. George and Ada (Tipple) P.; B.Comm., Dalhousie U., Halifax, N.S., 1965; m. Louise Marion Burry, Sept. 11, 1964; children—Sue Ellen, Stephanie, Andrew. Audit mgr. Clarkson, Gordon & Co., Montreal, 1965-71; comptroller Ogilvie Mills Ltd., Montreal, 1971-73; treas. Laura Secord Ltd., Toronto, 1973-75; v.p. fin. Phillips Cables Ltd., Brockville, Ont., 1976—. Mem. Can. Inst. Chartered Accountants, Elec. and Electronic Mfrs. Assn. Can., Fin. Execs. Inst., Conf. Board Can., Montreal Bd. Trade. Club: Brockville Country. Home: 37 James St E Brockville ON K6V 1K3 Canada Office: Phillips Cables Ltd King St W Brockville ON K6V 5W4 Canada

POOLE, CECIL AVERY, assn. exec.; b. Monmouth, Oreg., Aug. 11, 1907; s. Archie N. and Ora Pearl (Halleck) P.; grad. So. (Ashland) Oreg. Coll. Edn., 1931; m. Corda Elise Stewart, Oct. 12, 1928. Sch. prin., Jackson County, Oreg., 1929-34; field rep., lectr. for Rosicrucian Order, Amorc, San Jose, Calif., 1934-36, dir. Latin-Am. div., 1936-39, supreme sec., 1939-63; bd. dirs. Supreme Grand Lodge of Amorc, Inc., v.p., treas., 1963-72, v.p., cons., dir., 1972—. SCORE counselor, 1973-78. Bd. dirs. Better Bus. Bur. Santa Clara County, 1966-72, treas., 1971-72. Mem. Soc. Study Evolution (charter), AAAS, Am. Ornithologists Union, Calif. Acad. Sci., San Jose Round Table (pres.), Cooper Ornithol. Soc. Clubs: Kiwanis, Ottawa Field Naturalists. Author: The Eternal Fruits of Knowledge, An Introductory Philosophy, 1975; Cares that Infest, 1978. Contbr. mag. articles, essays on philosophy, edn. and psychology. Home: 125 N Mary Ave #15 Sunnyvale CA 94086 Office: Rosicrucian Park San Jose CA 95191. *Whether or not an individual develops an individual philosophy of life based upon an established premise, form, doctrine, or creed, we should realize that living is an obligation as well as a necessity. To find out more about that process of life and its purpose should be an obligation of the intelligent human being.*

POOLE, CECIL F., judge; b. Birmingham, Ala.; LL.B., U. Mich.; LL.M., Harvard, 1939; children—Gayle, Patricia. Practice of law, San Francisco; formerly asst. dist. atty., San Francisco, also clemency sec. to Gov. Brown of Calif.; U.S. atty. No. Dist. Calif., 1961-70; Regents prof. Law U. Calif. at Berkeley, 1970; counsel firm Jacobs, Sills & Coblents, San Francisco, 1971-76; judge U.S. Dist. Ct. No. Dist. Calif., 1976-79, U.S. Ct. of Appeals for 9th Circuit, 1979—. Served to 1st lt. AUS, World War II. Office: PO Box 547 US Ct Appeals and Post Office Bldg San Francisco CA 94101

POOLE, DANIEL ARNOLD, biologist; b. N.Y.C., Apr. 11, 1922; s. Thomas Harvey and Ursula Elizabeth (Wynne) P.; student Kent State U., 1944; B.S. in Wildlife Tech., U. Mont., 1950, M.S., 1952; m. Dorothy C. Sepure, June 1, 1946; children—Wynn A., Kathleen M. With Gen. Electric Co., 1939-44; biol. aide U.S. Fish and Wildlife Service, 1950-52; waterfowl biologist Mont. Fish and Game Dept., 1952; with Wildlife Mgmt. Inst., 1952—, sec., 1963—, pres., 1970—, columnist Am. Rifleman mag., 1960-70, also free-lance writer. Sec. Natural Resources Council Am., 1966-70, vice chmn., 1971-73, chmn., 1973-75. Trustee N.Am. Wildlife Found., Stronghold (Sugarloaf Mountain) Inc., 1974—; chmn. Citizens Com. on Natural Resources, 1972-79; chmn. nat. conservation com. Boy Scouts Am. Mem. Nat. Rifle Assn. Am. (life), Wildlife Soc., Nat. Audubon Soc., Outdoor Writers Assn. Am. (chief Jades award 1969), Internat. Assn. Fish and Wildlife Agys., Mason Dixon Outdoor Writers Assn., Phi Sigma. Clubs: Cosmos, West River Sailing. Home: 7120 Wolftree Ln Rockville MD 20852 Office: Wire Bldg Washington DC 20005

POOLE, FRANK HARRISON, tobacco co. exec.; b. Watertown, Mass., May 30, 1920; s. Ava Winifred and Agnese Josephine (Peckham) P.; B.S., Harvard U., 1943; m. Jane F. Hardesty, Sept. 2, 1972; 1 dau., Josephine H.; children by previous marriage—Scott H., Laurie M. Credit analyst Chase Nat. Bank, N.Y.C., 1948-52; v.p., dir. Hayward Hosiery Co., Ipswich, Mass., 1952-55; asst. to pres. White & Wyckoff Inc., Holyoke, Mass., 1955-57; asst. to v.p. Philip Morris

Inc., N.Y.C., 1957-60, dir. planning, 1960-76, treas., 1976—, v.p., 1978—; dir. Switzerland Gen. Ins. Co., Christiania Gen. Ins. Co., 860 West Tower, Inc.; trustee Union Dime Savs. Bank. Trustee Silvermine Guild Artists, 1973-75, Kips Bay Boys Club, 1978—; treas. Wilson Point Beach, Inc., 1966-75; mem. adv. bd. Norwalk Hosp., 1966-75. Served to capt. U.S. Army, 1943-46. Decorated Air medal, Bronze Star, Purple Heart. Mem. Assn. for Corp. Growth (pres. 1975-76), N.Y.C. C. of C. and Industry (members council 1977), Newcomen Soc. N.Am., Treasurers Club, Sales Execs. Club N.Y. Republican. Clubs: River, Union League (N.Y.C.). Home: 860 United Nations Plaza New York NY 10017 Office: Philip Morris Inc 100 Park Ave New York NY 10017

POOLE, FRAZER GLENDON, librarian; b. Federalsburg, Md., Nov. 5, 1915; s. Earle Glendon and Norma (Brower) P.; A.B. cum laude, Catawba Coll., 1937; B.S. in L.S., U. Calif. at Berkeley, 1949; L.H.D., St. John Fisher Coll., 1975; m. Rebecca Claire Veach, Mar. 24, 1946; 1 son, Glendon Frazer. Asst. univ. librarian U. Calif. at Santa Barbara, 1956-59; dir. library tech. project ALA, 1959-63; dir. library, prof. library adminstrn. U. Ill. Chgo. Circle, 1963-67; asst. dir. for preservation Library of Congress, 1967-78, coordinator bldg. planning, 1970-76; cons. nat., internat. library bldg. Served to comdr. USNR, 1942-46, 50-52. Mem. Internat. Inst. Conservation Artistic and Hist. Objects, ALA, Am. Inst. Conservation, Sierra Club. Club: Cosmos. Contbr. articles to profl. jours. Home: 1502 River Farm Dr Alexandria VA 22308

POOLE, JAMES EDWIN, natural resources exec.; b. Toledo, May 23, 1924; s. Alfred Edwin and Margaret (Brown) P.; student Ohio Wesleyan U., 1946; B.B.A., Western Res. U., 1949; m. Judy M. Holder, May 24, 1978; children—Carol Christine, James Edwin. Asst. to chief engr. Pickands Mather & Co., Cleve., 1949-54; v.p. sales and mktg. Huron Portland Cement Co., Detroit, 1955-65; v.p. mktg., dir. Medusa Portland Cement Co., Cleve., 1965-70, exec. v.p., 1970, pres., 1970-72; v.p., dir. Cement Transit Co., Manitowoc Portland Cement Co. (Wis.), 1970-72; v.p. Medusa Products Co. Can., Ltd., 1970-72; pres., chmn. bd., chief exec. officer Marquette Co. (formerly Marquette Cement Mfg. Co.), Chgo., 1972-74, Nashville, 1974—; pres. Natural Resources Group, Gulf & Western Industries, Inc., 1977—; dir. Third Nat. Bank, Nashville, Que. Iron & Titanium Corp., N.Y.C. Bd. dirs. Tenn. Bot. Gardens and Fine Arts, St. Thomas Hosp. Devel. Found. Served with USMC, 1943-46. Mem. Nashville C. of C. (dir.), Portland Cement Assn. (dir.), Delta Tau Delta. Episcopalian. Clubs: Union (Cleve.); Chgo. (Chgo.); Cumberland, Belle Meade Country (Nashville); Tamarron (Durango, Colo.). Home: 4117 Legend Hall Nashville TN 37215 Office: Gulf & Western Inc 1st American Center Nashville TN 37238

POOLE, JOHN BAYARD, broadcasting exec., lawyer; b. Chgo., May 17, 1912; s. John Eugene and Edna (Carpenter) P.; student U. Chgo., 1929-32; LL.B., Detroit Coll. Law, 1936, J.D., 1968; m. Evelyn Singer, Apr. 10, 1979; 1 dau., Leah Kathleen. Admitted to Mich. bar, 1936; partner Poole, Littell & Sutherland, Detroit, 1936-76; of counsel Butzel, Long, Gust, Klein & VanZile, 1976-79; sec., v.p., dir. Storer Broadcasting Co., Detroit, 1945-55; chmn. exec. com. Capital Cities Communications, N.Y.C., 1960-64; chmn. Poole Broadcasting Co. WJRT-TV, Flint, Mich., WPRI-TV, Providence, WTEN-TV, Albany, N.Y., 1964-78; dir. Knight Ridder Newspapers, Inc., Mich. Nat. Corp., Mich. Nat. Bank of Detroit. Trustee, chmn. William Beaumont Hosp., 1960-72; trustee U. Chgo., 1974—, Cranbrook Ednl. Community, 1976—. Fellow Am. Bar Found.; mem. Am., Detroit, Mich. bar assns., Am. Judicature Soc. Episcopalian (vestryman 1959-62). Clubs: Key Largo Anglers; Marco Polo (N.Y.C.); Detroit; Bloomfield Hills Country (bd. govs., pres.); Indian Creek, Surf (Maimi); Cat Cay (Bahamas). Home: 229 Barden Rd Bloomfield Hills MI 48013 also 8 Indian Creek Island Miami Beach FL 33154 Office: 1700 N Woodward Ave Bloomfield Hills MI 48013

POOLE, JOHN JORDAN, lawyer; b. Fulton County, Ga., May 19, 1906; s. James Stubbs and Etta Ida Lou (Porter) P.; Ph.B., Emory U., 1927, J.D., 1929; m. Jeannette Harper, July 21, 1931. Admitted to Ga. bar, 1929; partner firm Poole, Pearce, Cooper & Smith, specializing in civil law, Atlanta, 1934—; dir. Bass Furniture Co., Peachtree on Peachtree Inn, Simons-Eastern Internat., Inc. Bd. dirs. Atlanta Union Mission Corp. Served as lt. comdr. USNR, 1942-45. Decorated Letter of Commendation. Mem. Am., Ga., Atlanta bar assns. Baptist. Clubs: Masons (Shriner), Optimists (pres. 1949; sec.-treas. 21st dist. internat. 1957), 13, Lawyers, Atlanta Athletic, Commerce (Atlanta). Home: 1128 Oakdale Rd NE Atlanta GA 30307 Office: 57 Executive Park South NE Suite 310 Atlanta GA 30329

POOLE, RICHARD WILLIAM, educator; b. Oklahoma City, Dec. 4, 1927; s. William Robert and Lois (Spicer) P.; B.S., U. Okla., 1951, M.B.A., 1952; postgrad. George Washington U., 1957-58; Ph.D., Okla. State U., 1960; m. Bertha Lynn Mehr, July 28, 1950; children—Richard William, Laura Lynne, Mark Stephen. Research analyst Okla. Gas & Electric Co., Oklahoma City, 1952- 54; mgr. sci. and mfg. devel. dept. Oklahoma City C. of C., 1954-57; mgr. Office of J.E. Webb, Washington, 1957-58; instr., asst. prof., asso. prof., prof. econs. Okla. State U., Stillwater, 1960-65, dean Coll. Bus. Adminstrn., prof. econs., 1965-72, v.p., prof. econs., 1972—; cons. to adminstr. NASA, Washington, 1961-69; adviser U.S. Senate subcommittee on govt. research, 1966-69. Mem. Gov.'s Com. on Devel. Ark.-Verdigris Waterway, 1970-71. Past v.p., bd. dirs., mem. exec. com. Okla. Council on Econ. Edn.; past bd. dirs. Mid-Continent Research and Devel. Council (past chmn.) Served to 2d lt., arty., U.S. Army, 1946-48. Recipient Delta Sigma Pi Gold Key award Coll. Bus. Adminstrn., U. Okla., 1951. Mem. Southwestern Econ. Assn. (past pres.), Am. Assn. Collegiate Schs. Bus. (past dir.), Nat. Assn. State Univs. and Land Grant Colls. (past chmn. commn. on edn. for bus. professions), Southwestern Bus. Adminstrn. Assn. (past pres.), Okla. (dir.), Stillwater (past dir., past pres.) chambers commerce. Author: (with others) The Oklahoma Economy, 1963, County Building Block Data for Regional Analysis, 1965. Home: 124 Georgia Ave Stillwater OK 74074

POOLE, WILLIAM, economist; b. Wilmington, Del., June 19, 1937; s. William and Louise Hemstreet (Hiller) P.; A.B. with high honors, Swarthmore Coll., 1959; M.B.A., U. Chgo., 1963, Ph.D., 1966; m. Mary Lynne Ahroon, June 26, 1960; children—William, Lester Allen, Jonathan Carl. Asst. prof. econs. Johns Hopkins U., 1963-69; economist Bd. Govs. of FRS, Washington, 1969-73; adv. Fed. Res. Bank Boston, 1973-74, cons., 1974—; prof. Brown U., 1974—; mem. research adv. bd. Com. Econ. Devel.; mem. bus. and industry adv. bd. Opportunities Industrialization Center R.I. Mem. Am. Econ. Assn., Am. Fin. Assn., Phi Beta Kappa. Author: Money and the Economy: A Monetarist View, 1978; contbr. numerous articles and notes to profl. jours.; asso. editor Jour. Money, Credit and Banking, 1976—. Office: Dept Econs Brown U Providence RI 02912

POOR, ALFRED EASTON, architect; b. Balt., May 24, 1899; s. Charles Lane and Anna Louise (Easton) P.; student St. George's Sch., Newport, R.I., 1911-16; A.B., Harvard, 1920; B. Arch., U. Pa., 1923, M. Arch., 1924; Woodman travelling fellow architecture, 1925; m. Janet Sheppard, Oct. 26, 1929; children—Charles Lane, John Sheppard, Anna Easton. Draftsman Peabody, Wilson & Brown, John Russell Pope, 1923-25; ind. practice architecture, 1925-27; partner Rodgers & Poor, N.Y.C., 1927-32; architect Army bldgs., labs., Ft. Monmouth, Ft. Jay, Lowry Field, 1932-40, Rio de Janeiro Airport, 1933; chief architect Red Hook (N.Y.) Houses, 1938; architect Army bldgs., labs., Rome (N.Y.) Air Depot, 1941, banks of Chem. Bank, Nat. City Bank, Bank of Manhattan Co., 1946—, Parke-Bernet Gallery, 1949, airfield and assembly plant for U.S.N., L.I., two air bases in France for U.S. A.F.E., Queens Co. Ct. House and prison for City of N.Y., 1953; alterations and addition to the New House Office Building and Capitol of U.S., Washington; Washington; partner Walker & Gillette and Alfred Easton Poor, N.Y.C., 1946-47, Walker & Poor, 1947-52, Office of Alfred Easton Poor 1952; asso. architect Queens County Courthouse and Prison, 1961; partner Poor and Swanke, 1972-75, Poor, Swanke, Hayden & Connell, 1975—; asso. architect U.S. Customs Ct. and Fed. Office Bldg., N.Y.C., James Madison Meml., Library of Congress; architect McGraw-Hill Home Office Bldg., N.Y.C., restoration and extension E. front U.S. Capitol, restoration old Supreme Ct. Chamber and old Senate Chamber, 1975; adv. architect Johns Hopkins, Balt.; architect Annenberg Sch. Communications, U. Pa. Trustee Met. Mus. Art, Burke Found. Fellow, Morgan Library. Ensign USN, 1918-19, flight instr. Air Sta., Key West, Fla.; comdr. USNR, 1942-46, Bur. Aeor. rep. Trenton, N.J., 1943-45. Awarded Commendation ribbon. Winner open competition award Meml. to Wright Bros., Kitty Hawk, N.C., 1928; hon. mention apt. house design, N.Y. chpt. AIA, 1928; open competition low cost housing, N.Y.C., 1933; Olympic medal for architecture, 1936; Archtl. award Fifth Ave. Assn., 1950, 52, 54, 63; 75th Anniversary medal Nat. Sculpture Soc., 1968; Herbert Adams Meml. medal Nat. Sculpture Soc., 1974. N.A. Fellow AIA, Internat. Inst. Arts and Letters, Royal Soc. Arts; mem. Nat. Inst. Archtl. Edn., N.A.D. (pres.), Am. Water Color Soc., Fedn. Alliances Francaises (dir.), Delta Phi. Republican. Episcopalian. Clubs: Metropolitan (Washington); Knickerbocker (pres.), N.Y. Yacht, U. of Washington, Century (N.Y.C.): Author: Colonial Architecture of Cape Cod, Martha's Vineyard and Nantucket, 1932. Home: 850 Park Ave New York NY 10021 Office: 14 E 60th St New York NY 10022

POOR, ANNE, painter; b. N.Y.C., Jan. 2, 1918; d. Henry Varnum and Bessie (Breuer) P.; student Bennington Coll., 1936, 38, Art Students League, 1935. Works exhibited Am. Brit. Art Center, 1944, 45, 48, Maynard Walker Gallery, 1950, Graham Gallery, 1957-59, 62, 68-71; executed murals P.O., Gleason, Tenn., DePew, N.Y.; South Solon (Maine) Free Meeting House, 1957, others; represented permanent collections Whitney Mus., Bklyn. Mus., Wichita Mus., Art Inst. Chgo.; mem. faculty Skowhegan Sch. Painting and Sculpture, 1947-61. Artist corr. WAC, 1943-45. Edwin Austin Abbey Meml. fellow, 1948; grantee Nat. Inst. Arts and Letters, 1957; recipient Benjamin Altman 1st prize landscape painting N.A.D., 1971. Mem. Artists Equity Assn. Illustrator: Greece, 1964. Home: 92 S Mountain Rd New York City NY 10956 Office: Graham Gallery 1014 Madison Ave New York City NY 10021

POOR, HUSTACE HUBBARD, ret. mfg. co. exec.; b. Yonkers, N.Y., Nov. 9, 1914; s. Frederic Hedge and Elizabeth Van Winkle (Hubbard) P.; A.B. cum laude in Physics, Harvard U., 1936, M.S. in Mech. Engring., 1938; m. Katharine Littlefield, Nov. 1, 1947; children—Margaret H., Bancroft R. With engring. dept. Babcock & Wilcox Co., N.Y.C., 1938-56, project mgr. atomic energy div., Lynchburg, Va., 1956-61, lab. mgr. research and devel. div., Alliance, Ohio, 1962-63, dir. Alliance Research Center, 1963-67, gen. mgr. research and devel. div., 1967-70, v.p. research and devel. div., 1970-77, v.p. contract research div., 1976-79. Mem. Hudson (Ohio) Bd. Edn., 1966-70, pres., 1970; trustee Seven Hills Sch., Lynchburg, 1959-61. Fellow ASME; mem. Harvard Engring. Soc., Am. Nuclear Soc., Newcomen Soc. Eng., Am. Mgmt. Assn., Nature Conservancy (treas. Va. chpt. 1960-61, vice chmn. Ohio chpt. 1971-73, treas. 1973-79), Nat. Audubon Soc., Am. Ornithologists Union (life mem.). Home: 36 Baldwin St Hudson OH 44236

POOR, JOHN BARTON, broadcasting exec.; b. Phila., Aug. 29, 1915; s. Samuel Smith and Elsie (Preston) P.; grad. Western Res. Acad., Hudson, O., 1934; A.B., Wesleyan U., 1938; LL.B., Harvard, 1941; m. Mary Elizabeth Rome, Apr. 17, 1943; children—Nancy Preston, John Barton, Penelope Mason, Pamela Elizabeth, Lisbeth Rome. Admitted to Mass. bar, 1941; partner firm Dalton & Poor, Boston, 1949-52; gen. counsel, dir. Gen. Teleradio, Inc., N.Y.C., 1952-55, v.p., 1954; exec. v.p., dir. MBS, N.Y.C., 1955, pres., 1956-57; v.p., treas. RKO General, Inc., 1956-62, pres., treas., 1962-75, vice chmn., 1975—; mem. fin. com., dir. Frontier Airlines, Inc.; dir. Cablecom-Gen., Inc.; trustee Met. Savs. Bank. Served to lt. USCGR, 1942-45. Mem. Am. Bar Assn., Am. Judicature Soc., Radio and Television Execs. Soc., Phi Beta Kappa, Delta Kappa Epsilon. Clubs: N.Y. Athletic, Yale (N.Y.C.). Home: 58 3d St Garden City NY 11530 Office: 1440 Broadway New York NY 10018

POOR, PETER VARNUM, producer, dir.; b. N.Y.C., May 17, 1926; s. Henry Varnum and Bessie (Breuer) P.; B.A., Harvard U., 1947; postgrad. (Fulbright scholar) Centro Sperimentale di Cinematografia, Rome, 1951-52; m. Eloise Marcovicci Miller, Sept. 27, 1950; children—Candida Eustacia, Anna Maria, Graham Varnum. Various positions in documentary film work, N.Y.C., 1948-51; film editor, dir. and producer CBS News-Airpower, N.Y.C., 1954-57, 7 Lively Arts, N.Y.C., 1957-58, Twentieth Century, N.Y.C., 1958-66, 21st Century, N.Y.C., 1966-69, 60 Minutes, CBS, N.Y.C., 1970-71, CBS Reports, N.Y.C., 1971-75; producer-dir. NBC News, N.Y.C., 1977 ; instr. in TV journalism Fordham U., 1976-78; mem. Screening Com. for Fulbright Grants in Film, TV and Radio, 1961-66, chmn., 1963. Served with USAAF, 1944-45. Recipient Emmy award Acad. TV Arts and Sci., 1960, 61, 67, Lasker TV award Lasker Found., 1968, 69, hon. mention Robert Kennedy Journalism Award in TV, 1976. Mem. Dirs. Guild Am., Film Editors Union. Producer-dir. numerous documentary films broadcast on network TV in U.S. and abroad, including: What's New at School, 1972; The IQ Myth, 1975. Home: 1150 Fifth Ave New York NY 10028 Office: 30 Rockefeller Plaza New York NY 10020

POORE, JEANETTE, coll. pres.; b. Centralia, Wash., Jan. 22, 1924; d. Jack Ralph and Mable Mary (Clark) P.; B.A., Wash. State U., 1946, M.Ed., 1957; LL.D. (hon.), Seattle U., 1970. Counselor, sec. to supt. schs., Port Townsend, Wash., 1946-50; counselor Snohomish (Wash.) High Sch., 1950-54; dir. guidance and spl. edn. Moses Lake (Wash.) Sch. Dist., 1954-57; counselor, instr. psychology Everett (Wash.) Community Coll., 1957-59, registrar and coordinator student services, then dean students, 1959-69, acting pres., then pres., 1969-75; pres. Coll. of Alameda (Calif.), 1975—; mem. faculty Community Coll. Inst., Danforth Found., 1972; mem. Carnegie Commn. Nat. Appraisal Student Personnel, 1964; adv. com. to state chancellor Calif. Community Colls., 1978. Recipient Recognition award Wash. Home Econs. Assn., 1971, President's medal Everett Community Coll., 1971, Luther Gulick award Camp Fire Girls, 1974. Mem. Am. Assn. Community and Jr. Colls., Calif. Assn. Community and Jr. Colls. Office: 555 Atlantic St Alameda CA 94501

POORMAN, PAUL ARTHUR, newspaper editor; b. Lock Haven, Pa., Aug. 29, 1930; s. Wilson Paul and Margaret (Heylmun) P.; B.A., Pa. State U., 1952; m. Sylvia Elizabeth Powers, Nov. 22, 1952; children—Pamela (Mrs. Robert Phillips), Cynthia (Mrs. Donald Paul), Peter, Stephen, Thomas, Andrew, Robert, William. Reporter State College (Pa.) Centre Daily Times, 1953-57, news editor, 1957-62; news editor Harrisburg (Pa.) Patriot, 1962-63; news editor Phila. Bulletin, 1963-66; asst. mng. editor Detroit News, 1966-69, mng. editor, 1969-75; vis. prof. Northwestern U., 1975-76; editor, v.p. Akron Beacon Jour., 1976—. Served with USAF, 1951-53. Mem. Am. Soc. Newspaper Editors. Office: 44 E Exchange St Akron OH 44328

POORMAN, ROBERT LEWIS, coll. pres.; b. Germantown, Ohio, Dec. 9, 1926; s. Dale Lowell and Bernice Velma (Krick) P.; student Ohio Wesleyan U., 1944-45, U. Va., 1945-46; B.S.Ed., Ohio State U., 1948; M.A., 1950; postgrad. U. So. Calif., 1951-53; Ed.D. (Kellogg fellow 1960-62, Disting. Scholar Tuition grantee 1960-62), UCLA, 1964; m. Lois May Romer, Dec. 26, 1949; children—Paula Beth, Janice Marie, Mark Leon, John Alex, Lisa Ann, Daniel Romer. Tchr., counselor, adminstr., secondary schs. Colo., Mo., Ariz., 1948-57; registrar Phoenix Coll., 1957-60; intern Bakersfield Coll., 1960-63, asst. to pres., 1963-64, asso. dean instrn., 1964-65, dean students, 1965-67; founding pres. Lincoln Land Community Coll., 1967—. Bd. dirs. United Way of Springfield, Urban League of Springfield, Good Will Industries of Springfield, Springfield (Ill.) Symphony, Catholic Youth Orgn., Springfield, Ill. Gov.'s Prayer Breakfast, Springfield Mental Health. Served with USNR, 1944-46. Mem. Am. Assn. Community and Jr. Colls., Ill. Council Public Community Coll. Pres. (sec. 1973-74, vice chmn. 1974-75, chmn. 1975-76), Council North Central Community and Jr. Colls. (exec. bd. 1979-81). Republican. Roman Catholic. Contbr. articles to profl. jours. Home: 2324 Willemoore Springfield IL 62704 Office: Lincoln Land Community Coll Shepherd Rd Springfield IL 62708

POOVEY, WILLIAM ARTHUR, educator, theologian; b. Balt., Sept. 20, 1913; s. William Arthur and Opal (Holland) P.; B.A., Capital U., Columbus, Ohio, 1934; certificate Evang. Lutheran Sem., Columbus, 1939; M.A., Northwestern U., 1939; D.D., Wartburg Coll., Waverly, Iowa, 1972; m. Mary Virginia Smith, June 29, 1940. Ordained to ministry Am. Luth. Ch., 1939; instr. speech Capital U., 1935-39; pastor in Monterey Park, Cal., 1939-45, San Antonio, 1945-53, Memphis, 1953-57; prof. homiletics Wartburg Theol. Sem., Dubuque, Iowa, 1957-76, acting pres., 1970, 71. Mem. commn. research and social action Am. Luth. Ch., 1960-72, chmn. 1963-72, mem. bd. pensions, 1972—. Author: Hymn Dramatizations, 1942; Questions That Trouble Christians, 1946; Problems That Plague Saints, 1950; No Hands But Ours, 1954; Your Neighbor's Faith, 1961; And Pilate Asked, 1965; Cross Words, 1967; Lenten Chancel Dramas, 1967; What Did Jesus Do?, 1968; Chancel Dramas for Lent, 1968; The Christian in Society, 1969; Mustard Seeds and Wine Skins, 1972; Let Us Adore Him, 1972; Stand Still and Move Ahead, 1973; Signs of His Coming, 1973; Six Faces of Lent, 1974; Banquets and Beggars, 1974; the Power of the Kingdom, 1974; Celebrate with Drama, 1975; The Days Before Christmas, 1975; The Wonderful Word Shalom, 1975; The Days Before Easter, 1976; The Prayer He Taught, 1976; Letting the Word Become Alive, 1977; Six Prophets for Today, 1977; Planning a Christian Funeral, 1978; The Days of Pentecost, 1979; Faith is the Password, 1979. Home: 10418 Applegate San Antonio TX 78230

POPE, ALEXANDER H., county ofcl., lawyer; b. N.Y.C., June 4, 1929; s. Clifford H. and Sarah H. (Davis) P.; A.B. with honors, U. Chgo., 1948, J.D., 1952; children—Stephen C., Virginia L., Daniel M. Admitted to Ill. bar, 1952, Republic of Korea bar, 1953, Calif. bar, 1955, U.S. Supreme Ct. bar, 1970; practice in Los Angeles, 1955-77; asso. firm David Ziskind, Los Angeles, 1955; partner firm Shadle, Kennedy & Pope, Los Angeles, 1956, Fine & Pope, Los Angeles, 1957-77; Los Angeles County assessor, 1978—. Pres. Westchester Mental Health Clinic, 1963. Nat. bd. mem. Vols. for Stevenson, 1952; vice-chmn. Los Angeles County Democratic Central Com., 1958-59; legis. sec. gov. Calif., 1959-61; mem. Calif. Hwy. Commn., 1966-70; mem. Los Angeles Bd. Airport Commrs., 1973—, v.p., 1973-75, pres., 1975-76. Served with U.S. Army, 1952-54; Korea. Mem. U. Chgo. Alumni Club Greater Los Angeles (pres. 1970-71), ACLU, Zero Population Growth, Ams. United, Calif., Los Angeles, Southwest Dist. bar assns. (pres. 1967). Democrat. Unitarian. Home: 800 W 1st St Apt 2502 Los Angeles CA 90012 Office: Hall of Adminstrn 500 W Temple St Suite 320 Los Angeles CA 90012

POPE, ALFRED, physician, educator; b. Cleve., Jan. 23, 1915; s. Carlyle and Mary Slade (Kline) P.; grad. Milton Acad., 1932; A.B., Harvard, 1937, M.D., 1941; m. Maria Lorenz, Aug. 19, 1950. House officer pathology Children's Hosp., Boston, 1941-42; research asst. medicine Mass. Gen. Hosp., Boston, 1943, research fellow medicine, 1944; teaching fellow biol. chemistry, research fellow medicine Harvard, 1943-44. Austin teaching fellow biol. chemistry, 1944-45, asst. neuropathology, 1946-49, tutor biochem. scis., 1947-49, instr. neuropathology, 1949-51, asso., 1951-52, asst. prof., 1953-56, asso. prof., 1956-63, prof. neuropathology, 1964—; fellow med. sci. NRC, Montreal Neur. Inst., Can., 1945-46; research asso. neuropathology McLean Hosp., Belmont, Mass., 1946-55, asso. neuropathologist, 1955-56, neuropathologist, 1956—; mem. neurology field investigations com. Nat. Inst. Neur. Diseases and Blindness, 1957- 61; mem. neurology study sect., div. research grants NIH, 1961-65. Mem. research adv. com. United Cerebral Palsy Research and Ednl. Found., Inc., 1963-69; adv. com. on epilepsies USPHS, 1966-69; neurology program project com. Nat. Inst. Neurol. Diseases and Stroke, 1969-73; mem. adv. com. on fundamental research Nat. Multiple Sclerosis Soc., 1968-74; Trustee Longy Sch. Music, Cambridge, 1968—. Mem. Assn. Research Nervous and Mental Disease, Am. Soc. Biol. Chemists, Am. Assn. Neuropathologists, Am. Acad. Neurology, Am. Neur. Assn., Am. Acad. Arts and Scis., Internat. Brain Research Orgn., Internat. Soc. Neurochemistry, Soc. Neurosc., Am. Soc. Neurochemistry. Editorial bd. Jour. Neurochemistry, 1955-69, Neurology, 1959-63, Archives of Neurology, 1961-66. Contbr. numerous sci. articles to profl. lit. Home: Longwood Towers Brookline MA 02146 Office: McLean Hosp Belmont MA 02178

POPE, ANDREW JACKSON (JACK), JR., justice state supreme ct.; b. Abilene, Tex., Apr. 18, 1913; s. Andrew Jackson and Ruth Adelia (Taylor) P.; B.A., Abilene Christian Coll., 1934; LL.B., U. Tex., 1937; m. Allene Esther Nichols, June 11, 1938; children—Andrew Jackson III, Walter Allen. Admitted to Tex. bar, 1937; practice law, Corpus Christi, 1937-46; judge 94th Dist. Ct., Corpus Christi, 1946-50; justice Ct. Civil Appeals, San Antonio, 1950-65, Supreme Ct. of Tex., Austin, 1965—. Pres. Met. YMCA, San Antonio, 1956-57. Trustee Abilene Christian Coll. Served with USNR, 1944-46. Recipient Silver Beaver award Alamo council Boy Scouts Am., 1961; Rosewood Gavel award St. Mary's U., San Antonio, 1962. Mem. Am. Bar Assn., State Bar Tex., Order of Coif, Nueces County (pres. 1946), Travis County, Bexar County bars, Am. Judicature Soc., Alpha Chi, Phi Delta Phi. Mem. Ch. of Christ. Mason, K.P. (grand chancellor 1946-47). Home: 2803 Stratford Dr Austin TX 78746 Office: PO Box 11248 Capitol Station Austin TX 78711*

POPE, BILL JORDAN, educator, business exec.; b. Salt Lake City, Sept. 12, 1922; s. Louis Albert and Ruth (Jordan) P.; B.S. in Chem. Engring., U. Utah, 1947; M.S., U. Wash., 1949, Ph.D., 1959; m. Margaret McConkie, Sept. 10, 1943; children—Louis, Leslie (Mrs. Alan S. Layton), Kathryn (Mrs. Richard D. Hoopes), Patrice (Mrs. Wayne L. Tew). Project chem. engr. Utah Oil Refining Co., 1951-58; mem. faculty Brigham Young U., 1958-59, 62—, prof. chem. engring.,

1962-66, chmn. dept., 1966-70; prof. chem. engring., acting pres. Abadan (Iran) Inst. Tech., 1959-62; exec. v.p. Megadiamond Corp., Provo, 1970-73, pres., 1973-79; pres. Megadiamond Industries N.Y., 1976-79, U.S. Synthetic Corp., 1979—; cons. to industry. Del. Utah Republican Conv., 1958, 74. Served to 1st lt., C.E., AUS, 1942-46. Research fellow U. Wash., 1947-49; Keysor Chem. Research grantee, 1964-70. Mem. Am. Inst. Chem. Engrs., Am. Chem. Soc., Am. Soc. Profl. Engrs., Am. Soc. Engring. Edn., Utah Acad. Arts and Scis., Utah Soc. Profl. Engrs., Sigma Xi, Tau Beta Pi. Mem. Ch. of Jesus Christ of Latter Day Saints (bishop 1965-72, stake pres., counsellor 1972-76, stake pres. 1976—). Home: 1866 N 1450th E Provo UT 84601

POPE, EVERETT PARKER, banker; b. Milton, Mass., July 16, 1919; s. Laurence Everett and Ruth Parker (Pope) P.; B.S. magna cum laude, Bowdoin Coll., 1941, M.A. (hon.), 1946; m. Eleanor Hawkins, Feb. 21, 1942; children—Laurence E., Ralph H. With Workingmens Co-op. Bank, Boston, 1947—, asst. treas., 1949-52, asst. v.p., 1952, pres., dir., 1953—; dir. Money Markets/Options, Inc., Boston, Co-op. Central Bank, Boston. Trustee, Bowdoin Coll., Brunswick, Maine, Children's Hosp. Med. Center, Boston; bd. dirs. Mass. Higher Edn. Assistance Corp. Served with USMC, 1941-46, 50-51. Decorated Congl. Medal of Honor, Bronze Star, Purple Heart. Mem. Phi Beta Kappa. Home: 78 Green St Canton MA 02021 Office: 30 Congress St Boston MA 02109

POPE, GENEROSO PAUL, JR., publisher; b. N.Y.C., Jan. 13, 1927; s. Generoso and Catherine (Richichi) P.; B.S. in Gen. Engring., Mass. Inst. Tech., 1946; m. Lois Frances Berrodin, May 29, 1965; children—Generoso Paul, III, Michele, Maria, Gina, Paul, Lorraine. Vice pres. Forange, Inc., N.Y.C., 1945-51; v.p., treas. Colonial Sand and Stone Co., Inc., N.Y.C., 1946-51; v.p. Empire Sand and Stone Corp., N.Y.C., 1946-51; exec. v.p., gen. mgr. Sta. WHOM, N.Y.C., 1946-51; editor Il Progresso Italo-Americano, N.Y.C., 1947-51; v.p. Coastal Sales Corp., N.Y.C., 1947-51; sec.-treas., v.p. Progress Mdsg. Corp., N.Y.C., 1947-51; dir. Pope Found., Inc., N.Y.C., 1947—; v.p. Roslyn Sand and Gravel Corp., N.Y.C., 1948-51, Coastal Brokerage Co., Inc., N.Y.C., 1948-51, Colonial Blue Diamond Mortar Corp., N.Y.C., 1949-51; intelligence officer CIA, 1951; pub. Nat. Enquirer, Inc., Lantana, Fla., 1952—, chmn. bd., 1976—; pres. Generoso Pope Jr. Found., Lantana, 1963—; chmn. bd. Distbn. Services, Inc., 1976—. Mem. N.Y.C. Mayor's Com. Unity, 1949-52, N.Y.C. Mayor's Com. Mgmt. Survey, 1950, N.Y.C. Bd. Higher Edn., 1950-54, Grand St. Boys Assn., N.Y.C., 1948-51; co-chmn. spl. groups div. March of Dimes, N.Y.C., 1949-50; chmn. N.Y.C. Mayor's Com. Police Dept. vs. Fire Dept. Baseball Championship, 1950; pres. Columbus Citizens Com., N.Y.C., 1950-51; trustee Library Presdl. Papers, N.Y.C., 1965-70, Englewood (N.J.) Hosp., 1965-71, John F. Kennedy Meml. Hosp., Atlantis, Fla., 1972—; bd. dirs. Three Sch. Devel. Found., Englewood, 1965-71; bd. lay advisers St. Joseph's Village for Children, Rockleigh, N.J., 1965-71. Mem. Sachem, Soc. of Tammany, Columbia Assn. N.Y. Post Office, (hon. pres.), Columbian Assn. Bd. Transp. City N.Y., Columbia Assn. Police Dept. City N.Y. Democrat. Roman Cath. Address: 600 SE Coast Ave Lantana FL 33464

POPE, JOHN ALEXANDER, sinologist, ret. museum dir.; b. Detroit, Aug. 4, 1906; s. Gustavus Debrille and Mary Theresa (Soper) P.; grad. Phillips Exeter Acad., 1921-25; A.B., Yale, 1930; M.A., Harvard, 1940, Ph.D., 1955; D.Litt., Middlebury Coll., 1972; m. Helen Rees Hebbard, Jan. 31, 1931; children—John Alexander, Sara Merchant (Mrs. Richard T. Cooper) m. 2d, Annemarie Henle, Dec. 10, 1947. Trainee, Chase Nat. bank, N.Y.C., 1930-32; exec. sec. People's M''seum Assn., Detroit Inst. Arts, 1932-34; lectr. Chinese art Columbia, 1941-43; asso. research Freer Gallery Art, Washington, 1943-46, asst. dir., 1946-62, dir., 1962-71; research prof. Oriental art U. Mich., 1962-71; adviser in Oriental art Va. Mus. Fine Arts, 1972—. Chmn. Am. selection com. for exhbn., Chinese Art Treasures, sent by Govt. Republic China, 1960; chmn. com. grants research on Asia, Am. Council Learned Socs., 1960-66. Mem. com. to visit dept. East Asian langs. and civilizations Harvard Bd. Overseers, 1957-62, 69-75. Recipient Hills Gold medal Oriental Ceramic Soc., 1971; decorated comdr. Royal Order No. Star (Sweden). Served as capt. USMCR, 1945-46. Mem. Am. Oriental Soc. (chmn. Louise Wallace Hackney scholarship com. 1962-71), Assn. Asian Studies, Oriental Ceramic Soc. (London, Eng.). Office: Freer Gallery Art Washington DC 20560. *The best thing that can happen to a man is to be born lucky.*

POPE, JOHN EDWIN, III, journalist; b. Athens, Ga., Apr. 11, 1928; s. Henry Louis and Rose (McAfee) P.; B.A. in Journalism, U. Ga., 1948. Sports editor Banner-Herald, Athens, Ga., 1944-48; So. sports editor UPI, Atlanta, 1948-50; sports writer Atlanta Constn., 1950-54; exec. sports editor Atlanta Jour., 1954-56; asst. sports editor Miami (Fla.) Herald, 1956-67, sports editor, 1967—. Recipient Bill Corum Meml. award Thoroughbred Racing Assn., 1962; Top Sports Column award Nat. Headliners Club, 1962, 79; Eclipse award Thoroughbred Racing Assn., 1962, 77; named to Internat. Churchmen's Sports Hall Fame, 1976. Mem. Profl. Football Writers Am. (pres. 1968-69). Presbyterian. Author: Football's Greatest Coaches, 1956; Baseball's Greatest Managers, 1960; Encyclopedia of American Greyhound Racing, 1963; Ted Williams: The Golden Year, 1970; (with Norm Evans) On the Line, 1976. Contbr. articles to popular mags. Office: Miami Herald 1 Herald Plaza Miami FL 33101

POPE, LEAVITT JOSEPH, broadcasting co. exec.; b. Boston, Apr. 2, 1924; s. Joseph and Charlotte (Leavitt) P.; B.S., Mass. Inst. Tech., 1947; m. Martha Pascale, Nov. 20, 1948; children—Joseph, Daniel, Patricia, Elizabeth, Nancy, Maria, Joan, Christopher, Virginia, Matthew, Charles. Adminstrv. asst. N.Y. Daily News, N.Y.C., 1947-51; asst. to gen. mgr. Sta. WPIX-TV, N.Y.C., 1951-56, v.p. ops., 1956-72; v.p. ops. Sta. WPIX-FM, N.Y.C., 1956-72; sec. WPIX, Inc., N.Y.C., 1958-75, exec. v.p., 1972-75, pres., 1975—, also dir.; sec., exec. v.p. Conn. Broadcasting Co., Bridgeport, 1967-75, pres., 1975—, also dir.; dir. Tribune Co., Chgo., N.Y. News. Mem. N.Y. State Regents Ednl. TV Adv. Council, 1958; bd. govs. Daytop Village, 1972—; trustee Catholic Communications Found., St. Thomas Aquinas Coll., 1968-75, Flower Hosp., 1979—. Served with Signal Corps, U.S. Army, 1942-46. Mem. Assn. Ind. TV Stas. (pres. 1976—, dir.), ASME, Internat. Radio and TV Soc., N.Y. State Broadcasters Assn. (pres.), Sigma Nu. Clubs: Univ. (N.Y.C.); Internat. (Washington); Knights of Malta. Home: 173 Dorchester Rd Scarsdale NY 10583 Office: 220 E 42d St New York NY 10017

POPE, MICHAEL, elec. engr.; b. N.Y.C., May 16, 1924; s. Philip and Anna (Frimet) P.; B.E.E., Coll. City N.Y., 1944; m. Sally Ganong Farrell, May 1, 1977; children—Barbara Lisa, Joseph David, Michele Burton; stepchildren—Jackson Elliott Dube, Ian Hans Farrell. With Pope, Evans and Robbins and predecessor firms, N.Y.C., 1946—, partner, 1951, pres., 1954-69, chief exec. officer, chmn. bd., 1969—; dir. Fluidized Combustion Co., N.Y.C.; mem. N.Y. State Temp. Study Commn. to Rev. Procedures of State U. and State U. Constrn. Fund, 1971, N.Y. State Ad Hoc Com. on Energy Conservation in Large Bldgs., 1973. Trustee Manhattan Country Sch., N.Y.C., 1966—, chmn., 1974-78; bd. dirs. City Coll. Fund, 1965—, pres., 1976-79. Served with U.S. Maritime Service, 1944-46. Recipient 125th Anniversary medal to distinguished alumni CCNY, 1973; award of Honor, Am. Cons. Engrs. Council, 1979. Fellow Am. Cons. Engrs. Council; mem. ASME, Nat. Soc. Profl. Engrs., IEEE. Club: Univ. Research in fluidized bed combustion of coal (pollution free). Home: 1133 Fifth Ave New York NY 10028 Office: 1133 Ave of Americas New York NY 10036

POPE, THOMAS HARRINGTON, lawyer; b. Kinard, S.C., July 28, 1913; s. Thomas H. and Marie (Gary) P.; A.B., The Citadel, 1935, LL.D., 1977; LL.B., U. S.C., 1938; grad. Command and Gen. Staff Coll., 1951; LL.D., Newberry Coll., 1969; m. Mary Waties Lumpkin, Jan. 3, 1940; children—Mary Waties (Mrs. Robert H. Kennedy), Thomas Harrington III, Gary Tusten. Admitted to S.C. bar, 1938, U.S. Supreme Court; practice in Newberry, 1938—; spl. circuit judge Richland and Lexington counties, 1955-56. Dir. Citizens and So. Nat. Bank S.C., State Record Co., Am. Sentinel Life Ins. Co., Carolina Motor Club. Mem. S.C. Ports Authority, 1957-65; mem. Jud. Council S.C., 1957—, chmn., 1979—; mem. S.C. Archives Commn., 1965-75, vice chmn., 1974-75; chmn. Newberry County Sesqui-Centennial Commn., 1939. Mem. S.C. Ho. of Reps. from Newberry County, 1936-40, 45-50, speaker, 1949-50; chmn. S.C. Democratic Party, 1958-60; del. at large Dem. Nat. Conv., 1956, 60; pres. S.C. Dem. Conv., 1958, 62. Mem. S.C. Tricentennial Commn., 1966-71. Trustee U. of South, 1965-70, Newberry Coll., 1965-75; chmn. S.C. Found. Ind. Colls.; bd. visitors The Citadel, 1939-40, 46. Served to lt. col. AUS, 1941-45; ETO; brig. gen. ret. S.C. N.G. Recipient Algernon Sydney Sullivan award Newberry Coll., 1976. Fellow Am. Coll. Trial Lawyers, Am. Bar Found.; mem. Am., S.C. (pres. 1964, chmn. exec. com. 1956-58), Newberry County (pres. 1951) bar assns., Am. Law Inst. (life), Am. Judicature Soc., So. Hist. Assn., Nat. Trust for Historic Preservation (adv. bd.), U. South Carolina Soc. (curator 1968-72), South Carolina (curator 1968-74), Newberry County Hist. Soc. (pres. 1966), Phi Beta Kappa. Omicron Delta Kappa, Phi Delta Phi, Alpha Tau Omega. Episcopalian (sr. warden 1963-65, 70). Mason (grand master S.C. 1958-60; Albert Gallatin Mackey medal Grand Lodge S.C. 1965, Henry Price medal Grand Lodge Mass. 1960). Clubs: Newberry Country; Palmetto, Summit, Pine Tree Hunt (Columbia); Army-Navy (Washington). Author: The History of Newberry County, South Carolina, Vol. 1, 1973. Home: 1700 Boundary St Newberry SC 29108 Office: 1508 College St Newberry SC 29108

POPE, WILFRED STUART GEORGE, music pub. co. exec.; b. Folkestone, Eng., Aug. 9, 1921; s. Wilfred Lefevre and Mabel Mary (Goodenough) P.; came to U.S., 1964; attended London (Eng.) Coll. Choristers, Boy Singers' Sch., Royal Coll. Organists, 1947; m. Doris Eveline Marshall, Apr. 11, 1942; children—Judith (Mrs. Jeffrey Taylor Browne), John Stuart, Brenda Ann. Accounts clk. Boosey & Hawkes Ltd., until 1948, mgr. depts. electronics and organ, 1948-58, mng. dir. Boosey & Hawkes (South Africa) Ltd., 1958-64, mng. dir. Boosey & Hawkes Inc., N.Y.C., 1964—, pres., 1975—. Dir. music, organist Crown Ct. Ch., London, 1947-58; organist St. Mary's Anglican Cathedral, Johannesburg, South Africa, 1960-64. Bd. dirs. Am. Music Center. Served with Royal Air Force, 1940-46. Mem. Royal Coll. Organists, ASCAP (dir.), Music Pubs'. Assn. U.S. (pres. 1971-72). Home: 6 Old Mill Rd Great Neck NY 11023 Office: 30 W 57th St New York City NY 10019

POPE, WILLIAM KENNETH, bishop; b. Hale, Mo., Nov. 21, 1901; s. William Mumford and Victoria (LaRue) P.; student Clarendon (Tex.) Coll., 1917-20; B.A., So. Methodist U., 1922, B.D., 1924, LL.D., 1964; student Yale Grad. Sch., 1927-29; D.D. (hon.), Southwestern U., Georgetown, Tex., 1937, Hendrix Coll., 1961; m. Kate Sayle, Mar. 16, 1930; children—Katherine Victoria, Kenneth Sayle. Ordained to ministry Methodist Ch., 1925, consecrated bishop, 1960; pastor in Milford, Tex., 1924-26, Breckenridge, Tex., 1929-33, Georgetown, Tex., 1933-36, Springfield, Mo., 1936-40, Austin, Tex., 1940-49, Houston, 1949-60; bishop Ark. area Meth. Ch., 1960-64, Dallas-Ft. Worth area, 1964—; bishop-in-residence Perkins Sch. Theology, So. Meth. U., 1972-76. Mem. gen. bd. evangelism, bd. Christian social concerns Meth. Ch.; mem. program council United Meth. Ch.; chmn. bd. Western Meth. Assembly, Fayetteville, Ark., 1960-64; vis. lectr. Perkins Sch. Theology, So. Meth. U., 1949; del. World Conf. on Life and Work, Oxford, Eng., 1937, World Meth. Conf., Oxford, 1951; vis. preacher Gen. Conf. Meth. Ch. in Mexico, 1946; rep. Meth. Ch. in U.S. to centennial celebration Methodism in India, 1956; pres. Tex. Council Chs., 1968, Tex. Conf. Chs., 1969. Chmn. bd. trustees So. Meth. U., 1971-72. Mem. Lambda Chi Alpha, Theta Phi, Tau Kappa Alpha. Author: A Pope at Roam, the Confessions of a Bishop, 1976. Contbr. Christian Advocate, Adult Student, Prayer for Today. Home: 3131 Maple St Dallas TX 75201 Office: Perkins Sch theology So Meth Univ Dallas TX 75205

POPE-HENNESSY, JOHN WYNDHAM, art historian; b. Dec. 13, 1913; ed. Balliol Coll., Oxford (Eng.) U. Mem. staff Victoria and Albert Museum, 1938-73, keeper dept. architecture and sculpture, 1954-66, dir., sec., 1967-73; dir. Brit. Mus., 1974-76; consultative chmn. dept. European Paintings Met. Mus. Art, 1977—; Slade prof. fine art Oxford U., 1956-57, Cambridge (Eng.) U., 1964-65; Robert Sterling Clark prof. art Williams Coll., Williamstown, Mass., 1961-62; prof. art Inst. Fine Arts N.Y. U., 1977—. Decorated comdr. Brit. Empire; created knight, 1971. Fellow Brit. Acad., Soc. Antiquaries, Royal Soc. Lit.; mem. Am. Acad. Arts and Scis.; fgn. mem. Am. Philos. Soc. Author: Giovanni di Paolo, 1937; Sassetta, 1939, Sienese Quattrocento Painting, 1947; A Sienese Code of the Divine Comedy, 1947; The Drawings of Domenichino at Windsor Castle, 1948; A Lecture on Nicholas Hilliard, 1949; Paolo Uccello, 1950, rev. edit., 1969; Fra Angelico, 1952, rev. edit., 1974; Italian Gothic Sculpture, 1955, rev. edit., 1972; Italian Renaissance Sculpture, 1958, rev. edit., 1971; Italian High Renaissance and Baroque Sculpture, 1963, rev. edit., 1970; Catalogue of Italian Sculpture in the Victoria and Albert Museum, 1964; Renaissance Bronzes in The Kress Collection, 1965; The Portrait in the Renaissance, 1967; Essays on Italian Sculpture, 1968; The Frick Collection, Sculpture, 1970; Raphael, 1970; Luca della Robbia, 1980. Address: 1130 Park Ave New York NY 10028

POPELKA, ROBERT JOSEPH, lawyer; b. Madison Lake, Minn., May 9, 1920; s. Charles Joseph and Gertrude Helen (Mape) P.; A.B., Coll. of St. Thomas, 1940; J.D., U. Calif., 1948; m. Dorothy Popelka; children—Robert, Robin, John, James, Mark (dec.). Admitted to Calif. bar, 1949; practice law, San Francisco, 1949-51; founder, sr. partner firm Popelka, Allard, McCowan & Jones, San Jose, Calif., 1951—. Served with USMC, 1942-46; PTO. Mem. Am., Calif. bar assns., Am. Coll. Trial Lawyers, Trial Attys. Am. (v.p.), Am. Bd. Trial Advocates, Internat. Soc. Barristers. Republican. Roman Catholic. Clubs: San Jose Country; Commonwealth of Calif. Home: 574 Kumquat Dr San Jose CA Office: Popelka Allard McCowan & Jones 777 N 1st St San Jose CA 95112

POPHAM, ARTHUR COBB, JR., lawyer; b. Louisville, Mar. 31, 1915; s. Arthur Cornelius and Ethel (Estes) P.; B.A., U. Ariz., 1937; J.D., U. Mo., 1939; m. Mary Corzine, July 6, 1939; children—Carole Popham McKnight, Melinda Popham Benton, Arthur Connor; m. 2d, Phoebe T. Kennedy, Nov. 13, 1969. Admitted to Mo. bar, 1939, since practiced in Kansas City; mem. firm Popham, Conway, Sweeny, Fremont & Bundschu, and predecessors. Pres., trustee, bd. govs., lectr. Kansas City Mus. History and Scis. Served to 1st lt. USAAF, 1943-45. Mem. Am., Mo., Kansas City bar assns., Sigma Nu, Phi Delta Phi. Clubs: Boone and Crockett (1st v.p., conservation and judge big game competition) (N.Y.C.); Campfire of America (Chappaqua, N.Y.). Home: 5521 Mission Dr Mission Hills KS 66208 Office: Commerce Bank Bldg Kansas City MO 64106

POPHAM, RICHARD ALLEN, educator, botanist; b. Charleston, Ill., Sept. 29, 1913; s. Frank and Charlotte (Kluge) P.; B.Ed., Eastern Ill. U., 1936; M. Sc., Ohio State U., 1937, Ph.D., 1940. Mem. faculty Ohio State U., 1940—, asso. prof. botany, 1950-68, prof. botany, 1968—; chief ballistician Scioto Ordnance Plant, 1942-43; supt. atomic bomb mfg. plant, Los Alamos, 1943-45; cons. Battelle Meml. Inst., 1958-70; research collaborator Brookhaven Nat. Lab., 1964—. Recipient Alfred J. Wright award Ohio State U., 1966. Mem. Bot. Soc. Am. (bus. mgr. Am. Jour. Botany 1972—), Internat. Soc. Plant Morphologists, Ohio Acad. Sci. (pres. 1965-66, patron 1971—), Soc. Econ. Botany, Can. Soc. Plant Physiologists, Columbus Numis. Soc. (pres. 1973, treas. 1974-77), Sigma Xi, Gamma Alpha (nat. treas., pres. 1956-60, nat. editor 1968-73). Author: Developmental Plant Anatomy, 1952; Laboratory Manual for Plant Anatomy, 1966; also sci. papers. Home: 1519 Neil Ave Columbus OH 43201 Office: Dept Botany Ohio State U 1735 Neil Ave Columbus OH 43210

POPHAM, WAYNE GORDON, lawyer; b. Florence, S.D., Oct. 23, 1929; s. Samuel Russell and Vera (Monahan) P.; B.S., U. Minn., 1951, LL.B., 1953; m. Joan Marian Nelson, Dec. 10, 1955; children—Todd Gordon, Kathryn Elizabeth, Geoffrey Nelson, Stephanie Ann, John William. Admitted to Minn. bar, 1953; partner firm Popham, Haik, Schnobrich, Kaufman & Doty, Mpls., 1955—; mem. Minn. Senate, 1962-72. Mem. Commn. on Minn.'s Future, 1974-77; trustee Mpls. Soc. Fine Arts, 1975—. Served with AUS, 1953-55. Mem. Am., Minn., Hennepin County bar assns., Am. Judicature Soc., Mpls. C. of C. (v.p., dir. 1978—), Citizens League (pres. 1978-79). Republican. Methodist. Club: Minneapolis. Home: 1550 E Minnehaha Pkwy Minneapolis MN 55417 Office: IDS Center Minneapolis MN 55402

POPJÁK, GEORGE JOSEPH, educator, biochemist; b. Kiskundorozsma, Hungary, May 5, 1914; s. George and Maria (Mayer) P.; M.D., Royal Francis Joseph U., Szeged, Hungary, 1938; D.Sc., U. London, 1961; m. Hasel Marjorie Hammond, Apr. 9, 1941. Came to U.S., 1968. Intern U. Szeged Clinics, 1937-38; postdoctoral Brit. Council scholar Postgrad. Med. Sch., U. London, 1939-41; lectr. pathology St. Thomas's Hosp., London, 1941-47; mem. sci. staff Nat. Inst. Med. Research, London, 1947-53; dir. M.R.C. Exptl. Radiopathology Research Unit, Hammersmith Hosp., London, 1953-62; joint dir. chem. enzymology lab. Shell Research Ltd., Sittingbourne, Eng., 1962-68; prof. biochemistry and psychiatry U. Calif. at Los Angeles Med. Sch., 1968—; vis. scientist Nat. Heart Inst., Bethesda, Md., 1960-61; hon. sr. lectr. biochemistry Royal Postgrad. Med. Sch., U. London, 1953-68; prof. molecular scis. U. Warwick (Eng.), 1965-68; hon. mem. med. adv. com. Nat. Heart Found., 1968. Recipient Ciba medal Brit. Biochem. Soc., 1965, Davy medal Royal Soc., London, 1968, Stouffer prize Stouffer Found., 1967, Lipid Biochem. award Am. Oil Chemists Soc., 1977; Vanderbilt Centenary medal Vanderbilt U., 1978; Disting. Sci. Achievement award Los Angeles affiliate Am. Heart Assn., 1979; Beit Meml. fellow med. research, 1943-47; Harvey lectr., 1970. Fellow Royal Inst. Chemistry, Royal Soc.; mem. Am. Acad. Arts and Scis., Royal Flemish Acad. Scis. and Fine Arts (fgn.), Am. Soc. Biol. Chemists (hon.), N.Y. Acad. Scis., Alpha Omega Alpha (hon.). Contbr. profl. jours. Home: 511 Cashmere Terr Los Angeles CA 90049

POPLINGER, LOUIS L., corp. exec.; b. N.Y.C., 1916; B.A., U. Mich., 1939; LL.B., Harvard, 1942. Vice pres., sec., gen. counsel, dir. Western Auto Supply Co.; sec., dir. Midland Internat. Corp., Eva Gabor Internat. Ltd. Home: 8504 Ensley Pl Leawood KS 66206 Office: 2107 Grand Ave Kansas City MO 64108

POPOV, EGOR PAUL, educator; b. Kiev, Russia, Feb. 19, 1913; s. Paul T. and Zoe (Derabin) P.; B.S., U. Calif., 1933; M.S., Mass. Inst. Tech., 1934; Ph.D., Stanford, 1946; m. Irene Zofia Jozefowski, Feb. 18, 1939; children—Katherine, Alexander. Structural engr., bldg. designer, Los Angeles, 1935-39; asst. prodn. engr. Southwestern Portland Cement Co., Los Angeles, 1939-42; machine designer Goodyear Tire & Rubber Co., Los Angeles, 1942-43; design engr. Aerojet Corp., Calif., 1943-45; asst. prof. civil engring. U. Calif. at Berkeley, 1946-48, asso. prof., 1948-53, prof., 1953—, chmn. structural engring. and structural mechanics div., dir. structural engring. lab., 1956-60; Miller research prof. Miller Inst. Basic Research in Sci., 1968-69. Registered civil, structural and mech. engr., Calif. Mem. Am. Soc. Metals, Internat. Assn. Shell Structures (v.p., mem. exec. council), ASCE (Ernst E. Howard award 1976), Soc. Exptl. Stress Analysis, Am. Soc. Engring. Edn., AAAS, Am. Concrete Inst., Nat. Acad. Engring., Soc. Engring. Sci., Internat. Assn. Bridge and Structural Engring., Am. Inst. Steel Constrn. (adv. com. specifications), Sigma Xi, Chi Epsilon, Tau Beta Pi. Author: Mechanics of Materials, 1952, 2d edit., 1976; Introduction to Mechanics of Solids, 1968. Contbr. articles profl. jours. Home: 2600 Virginia St Berkeley CA 94709

POPOVA, NINA, former ballerina, teacher, ballet co. exec.; b. Novorossisk, USSR, 1922; ed. in Paris; studied ballet with Olga Preobrajenska, Lubov Egorova, Anatole Vilzak, Anatole Oboukhov, Igor Schwezoff. Ballet debut with Ballet de la Jeunesse, Paris, London, 1937-39; soloist Original Ballet Russe, 1939-41, Ballet Theatre (now Am. Ballet), 1941-42, Ballet Russe de Monte Carlo, 1943, 47, Ballet Alicia Alonso, Cuba; mem. faculty Sch. Performing Arts, N.Y.C., from 1954; later artistic dir. Houston Ballet Found., until 1975; tchr. Nat. Acad. Arts, Champaign, Ill., also N.Y.C., 1975—, now Eglevsky Ballet Sch., L.I.; tchr. ballet Mexico City, Mex.; asst. choreographer Girls Against the Boys, N.Y.C., 1959; stage dir., choreographer mus. comedy Birmingham So. Coll., Ala., 1960; numerous appearances on Broadway stage, TV; former mem. regular cast Your Show of Shows. Address: 33 Adams Sea Cliff NY 11579 also 17 E University Champaign IL 61820

POPOVICH, MILOSH, ret. univ. administr.; b. Pittsburg, Calif., Sept. 3, 1917; s. Nick D. and Mika (Rakich) P.; B.S. in Chem. Engring., Oreg. State Coll., 1939, M.S. in Mech. Engring., 1941; m. Jeanne F. Hartman, Sept. 30, 1939; 1 dau., Judy. Asst. prof. mech. engring. Oreg. State Coll., 1945-46; engr. Union Oil Co. Calif., 1946-47; asst., then asso. prof. mech. engring. Oreg. State U., 1947-50, chmn. dept. mech. engring., 1950-54, asst. dean engring., 1954-59, dean adminstrn., 1959-76, v.p., 1976-79; dir. Cascade Fed. Savs. and Loan Assn., Corvallis. Served from 2d lt. to maj. Ordnance Corps, AUS, 1941-45. Decorated Legion of Merit, Bronze Star medal; Croix de Guerre with gold star, with silver star. Registered profl. engr., Oreg. Fellow ASME (chmn. Oreg. 1956); mem. Benton County (dir. 1954), Corvallis (dir. 1965-67) chambers commerce, Sigma Xi. Home: 1390 NW 14th St Corvallis OR 97330

POPPA, RYAL ROBERT, computer co. exec.; b. Wahpeton, N.D., Nov. 7, 1933; s. Ray Edward and Annabelle (Phillips) P.; A.A., Chaffey Jr. Coll., 1955; B.B.A., Claremont Men's Coll., 1957; m. Ruth Ann Curry, June 21, 1952; children—Sheryl Lynn, Kimberly Marie. Sales trainee IBM Corp., Los Angeles, 1957-59, sales rep., 1959-62, product Mktg. rep., 1963, sales mgr., 1964-66; v.p., gen. mgr. Comml. Computers Inc., Los Angeles, 1966-67; v.p. Greyhound Computer Corp., Chgo., 1967-68, pres., chief exec. officer, dir., 1969-70; pres., chief exec. officer, dir., mem. exec. com. Data Processing Fin. & Gen.,

Hartsdale, N.Y., 1970-72; exec. v.p., chief fin. officer, dir., mem. exec. com. Mohawk Data Scis. Corp., Utica, N.Y., 1972-73; chmn., pres., chief exec. officer Pertec Computer Corp., Los Angeles, 1973—; dir. Spacelabs, Inc. Trustee, mem. exec. com., mem. pres.'s adv. council Claremont Men's Coll. Mem. Computer and Communications Industry Assn., (dir., vice chmn., mem. exec. com.), Am. Electronic Assn. (past dir., mem. exec. com.), Young Pres.'s Orgn., USC Assos., Golden Circle, Los Angeles County Mus. Arts (sustaining). Home: 1533 Via Leon Palos Verdes Estates CA 90274 Office: 12910 Culver Blvd Los Angeles CA 90066

POPPE, FRED CHRISTOPH, advt. agy. exec.; b. Bklyn., Dec. 26, 1923; s. Fred G. and Laura (Funk) P.; student Bklyn. Poly. Inst., 1941-42; A.B., Princeton, 1948; m. Inez Hanssen, Oct. 10, 1952; children—Steven Hammond, Ellen Jane. Copywriter, Fuller & Smith & Ross, Inc., N.Y.C., 1948-51; advt. mgr. Yale & Towne Mfg. Co., 1951-53; group account supr. G.M. Basford Co., N.Y.C., 1953-59; mgr. account devel. Donahue & Coe, Inc., N.Y.C., 1959-60; exec. v.p. T.N. Palmer, Inc., N.Y.C., 1960-63; pres. Complan, Inc., N.Y.C., 1963-74; pres., chief exec. officer Poppe Tyson Inc., N.Y.C., 1974—; dir. de Garmo Inc. Served with USNR, 1941-46. Named Advt. Agy. Man of Year, N.Y. Bus./Profl. Advertisers Assn., 1966-67. Mem. Pub. Relations Soc. Am., Bus./Profl. Advertisers Assn. (internat. 1st v.p., N.Y. past pres.), Great South Bay Yacht Racing Assn. Republican. Clubs: Princeton (N.Y.C.); Stuart (Fla.), Yacht and Country; Princeton (N.J.) Elm; Babylon Yacht (Babylon, N.Y.); Southward Ho Country (Bay Shore, N.Y.); Magoun Landing Yacht (commodore) (West Islip, N.Y.). Home: 133 Tahlulah Ln West Islip NY 11795 also 2800 SE Fairway W Yacht and Country Stuart FL 33494 Office: 475 Park Ave S New York NY 10016

POPPENSIEK, GEORGE CHARLES, educator; b. N.Y.C., June 18, 1918; s. George Frederick and Emily Amelia (Miller) P.; student Cornell U., 1936-37, M.S., 1951; student U. Pa., 1937-42, V.M.D., 1942; m. Edith M. Wallace, July 3, 1943; children—Neil Allen, Leslie Marion. Asst. instr. medicine U. Pa. Sch. Vet. Medicine, 1943; asst. prof. vet. sci. U. Md., 1943-44; head dept. vet. virus vaccine prodn. Lederle Labs. div. Am. Cyanamid Co., 1944-49; dir. diagnostic lab. N.Y. State Coll. Vet. Medicine, Cornell U., 1949-51, research asso. Vet. Virus Research Inst., 1951-55; veterinarian Plum Island Animal Disease Lab., animal disease and parasite research div. Agrl. Research Service, Dept. Agr., 1955-56, acting-in-charge diagnostic investigations, 1956-58, charge immunological investigations, 1958-59; dean and prof. microbiology N.Y. State Coll. Vet. Medicine, Cornell U., 1959-74, James Law prof. comparative medicine, 1974—; guest prof. U. Bern (Switzerland), 1975. Mem. exam. com. Nat. Bd. Vet. Med. Examiners, 1974—; bd. dirs. Cornell Research Found., 1963-74; chmn. bd. dirs. Cornell Veterinarian, Inc., 1976—. Recipient Certificate of Merit award Dept. Agr., 1958; citation Sch. Vet. Med., U. Pa., 1978, others. Diplomate Am. Bd. Microbiology, Am. Coll. Vet. Microbiology. Charter fellow Am. Acad. Microbiology; fellow AAAS; mem. Am. Vet. Med. Assn., N.Y. State Vet. Med. Soc., Am. Bd. Microbiology, U.S. Animal Health Assn., N.Y. Acad. Scis., Assn. Am. Vet. Med. Colls. (pres. 1970-71), So. Tier Vet. Med. Assn., Am. Vet. Radiology Soc., Am. Soc. for Microbiology, N.Y. Agrl. Soc. (life), Societas Polona Medicinae Veteriariae (hon.), Sigma Xi, Phi Kappa Phi, Alpha Psi, Omega Tau Sigma, Phi Zeta. Baptist. Club: Rotary. Home: 122 E Remington Rd Ithaca NY 14850

POPPER, DAVID, lawyer; b. Detroit, Dec. 12, 1925; s. Harry Lewis and Celia (Marron) P.; student Ohio State U., 1943, U. Mo., 1945; B.S., U. Ariz., 1949; J.D., U. Miami, 1952; m. Joanne MacGillivray, Jan. 30, 1954; children—David Harry, Richard Charles, Bruce Allen, Jodi Eleanor. Admitted to Fla. bar, 1952; practice in Miami Shores, Fla., 1952, Miami, Fla., 1952-54; mem. firm Popper, Tittle & Weston, Coral Gables, Fla., 1954-56; pvt. practice law, Coral Gables, 1957-58; mem. firm. Bennett & Popper, Miami, 1958-59, Popper & Scheiss, South Miami, Fla., 1960-61, Brunstetter & Popper, 1961-67, Virgin, Whittle & Popper, 1977-78, Leib & Popper, 1978—; mcpl. judge, South Miami, Fla., 1966-67; circuit judge 11th Jud. Circuit Fla., Miami, 1967-77. Bd. govs. South Miami Hosp., 1970-78. Served with AUS, 1944. Recipient award of merit Am. Trial Lawyers Assn., 1970, Good Govt. award Jr. C. of C., 1968, certificate of appreciation City of South Miami, 1967. Mem. Fla., Dade County bar assns., Khoury League Coral Gables (commr. 1969), Sigma Chi, Phi Alpha Delta. Republican. Roman Catholic. Elk, K.C. Clubs: Exchange of South Dade (pres. 1959); Coral Gables Country; Highlands (N.C.) Country; Calusa Country (Miami, Fla.). Home: 5900 SW 85th St South Miami FL 33143 Office: Flager Center Bldg 100 N Biscayne Blvd Miami FL 33132

POPPER, DAVID HENRY, fgn. service officer; b. N.Y.C. Oct. 3, 1912; s. Morris and Lilliam (Greenbaum) P.; A.B., Harvard, 1932, A.M., 1934; m. Florence C. Maisel, Mar. 8, 1936; children—Carol, Lewis, Katherine, Virginia. Research asso. Fgn. Policy Assn., Inc., N.Y.C., 1934-40, asso. editor publs., 1941-42; specialist internat. orgn. affairs Dept. of State, 1945—, asst. chief div. internat. orgn. affairs, 1948-49, officer in charge UN Gen. Assembly affairs, 1949-51, dept. dir. Office UN Polit. and Security Affairs, 1951-54, dir., 1954-55; Nat. War Coll., Washington, 1955-56; dep. U.S. rep. for internat. orgns., Geneva, 1956-59; adviser U.S. delegation to UN Gen. Assembly, 1946-53, prin. exec. officer, 1949-50; dep. U.S. rep. Conf. on Discontinuance Nuclear Weapons Tests, Geneva, 1959-61; sr. adv. disarmament affairs U.S. Mission to UN, 1961-62; dir. Office Atlantic Polit. and Mil. Affairs, Dept. State, 1962-65, dep. asst. sec. state for internat. organizational affairs, 1965-69; U.S. ambassador to Cyprus, 1969-73, to Chile, 1974-77; dep. for Panama Canal Treaty Affairs, Dept. of State with rank of ambassador, 1977-78; spl. rep. of sec. of state for Panama Treaty Affairs, 1978—; asst. sec. state for internat. orgn. affairs, 1973-74. Mem. U.S. delegations to NATO Ministerial Meetings, 1962-65. Served as capt. C.W.S., M.I. Service, AUS, 1942-45. Mem. Latin Am. Studies Assn., Am. Soc. Internat. Law, Am. Acad. Polit. and Social Sci. Author: The Puzzle of Palestine, 1938. Contbr. profl. publs. Home: 6116 33d St NW Washington DC 20015

POPPER, HANS, pathologist; b. Vienna, Austria, Nov. 24, 1903; s. Carl and Emma (Gruenhaum) P.; M.D., U. Vienna, 1928; M.S., U. Ill., 1941, Ph.D., 1944; M.D. (hon.), Catholic U. Louvain, 1965, U. Bologna, 1965, U. Hannover, 1974, U. Turin, 1975, U. Tuebingen, 1977, Cath. Coll., Seoul, Korea; Ph.D. (hon.), U. Vienna, 1965; D.Sc. (hon.), Mt. Sinai Med. Sch., 1979; m. Lina Billig, June 4, 1942; children—Frank, Charles. Resident, asst., dept. pathology and medicine U. Vienna, 1928-38; practice medicine, specializing in pathology, Chgo., 1938-57, N.Y.C., 1957—; research fellow Cook County Grad. Sch. Medicine, 1938-42; dir. labs. Cook County Hosp., 1944-46, dir. dept. pathology, 1946-57; sci. dir. Hektoen Inst. Med. Research, 1943-57; asst. prof., asso. prof., prof. pathology Med. Sch. Northwestern U., 1946-57; pathologist-in-chief Mt. Sinai Hosp., 1957-72, cons. pathologist, dir. emeritus dept., 1972—; prof. pathology Columbia, 1957-67; dean acad. affairs, prof. pathology, chmn. dept. pathology Mt. Sinai Sch. Medicine, City U. N.Y., 1965-72, pres., dean, 1972-73, pres. and dean emeritus, 1973—, Gustave L. Levy Distinguished Service prof., 1972—; hon. prof. U. Arequipa (Peru), 1965; cons. VA Hosp., Bronx, USPHS Hosp., S.I., Communicable Disease Center, Atlanta, 1957—. Served to maj. M.C., U.S. Army, 1944-46. Fellow Am. Acad. Arts and Scis.; mem. Nat. Acad. Scis., Internat. Assn. for Study of Liver (past pres.), Am. Assn. Study Liver Diseases (past pres.), Chgo., N.Y. (past pres.) pathol. socs., Deutsche Akademie der Naturforscher Leopoldina. Author: Clinical Pathological Conferences of Cook County Hospital, 1948; Liver: Structure and Function, 1957. Editor: Progress in Liver Diseases, 1961, 65, 70, 73, 76, 79; Clinical Pathological Conferences of Mount Sinai Hospital, 1963; Trends in New Medical Schools, 1967; Collagen Metabolism in the Liver, 1975; Intrahepatic Cholestasis, 1975; Chronic Hepatitis, 1976; Membane Alterations as Basis of Liver Injury, 1977; Primary Liver Tumors, 1978; Problems in Intrahepatic Cholestasis, 1979. Contbr. articles to med. jours. Home: 8 E 83d St New York NY 10028 Office: Mt Sinai Hosp 100th St and Fifth Ave New York NY 10029

POPPER, PETER, textile engr.; b. Vienna, Austria, Apr. 16, 1937; s. Paul and Cilli (Wettenstein) P.; came to U.S., 1939, naturalized, 1956; B.S., Lowell Tech. Inst., 1957; S.M., Mass. Inst. Tech., 1959, Mech.E., 1964, Sc.D., 1966; m. Rosalie Ann Lemberger, Sept. 6, 1958; children—Lisa, Linda, Laura. Engr., Bonnie Briar Knitting Mills, N.Y.C., 1957; research engr. Coates & Clark Research Labs., Newark, 1959; sr. research asso. engring. tech. lab. engring. dept. E.I. DuPont de Nemours & Co., Wilmington, Del., 1966—. Served to lt. USAF, 1959-62; materials lab. Recipient Cotton medal Lowell Tech. Inst., 1957; Coates & Clark fellow, 1958; Camille Dreyfus fellow, 1958. Mem. Fiber Soc. (award 1977), Textile Research Inst., Sigma Xi. Patentee in field. Home: 3319 Morningside Rd Wilmington DE 19810 Office: Exptl Sta 304 EI duPont Nemours Wilmington DE 19898

PORADA, EDITH, educator, archeologist; b. Vienna, Austria, Aug. 22, 1912; Ph.D., U. Vienna, 1935. Mem. faculty Queens Coll., 1950-58; mem faculty Columbia U., 1958—, prof. art history and archaeology, 1964—; hon. curator seals and tablets Pierpont Morgan Library, 1956—. Recipient award for disting. achievement Archaeol. Inst. Am., 1977. Fellow Am. Acad. Arts and Scis., Brit. Acad. (corr.); mem. Am. Philos. Soc. Author: Alt Iran, 1963; The Art of Ancient Iran, 1965; also monographs, articles. Office: 815 Schermerhorn Hall New York NY 10027

PORCH, RALPH DOUGLAS, JR., lawyer; b. Sylacauga, Ala., July 9, 1920; s. Ralph Douglas and Laurine (Liles) P.; student U. So. Calif., 1940; A.B., Emory U., 1941; J.D., U. Ala., 1947; m. Jean Lance, Sept. 19, 1942; children-Ralph Douglas III, Mark Liles. Admitted to Ala. bar, 1947, since practiced in Anniston; partner Merrill, Porch, Doster & Dillon, 1947—; lectr. corp. law, continuing legal edn. Ala. Bar Assn.; dir. So. Machinery & Supply Co. Chmn. Internat. House Program, Jacksonville State U., 1965-67; mem. Ala. Edn. Survey Commn., 1969; pres. Calhoun County Heart Fund, Anniston Little Theater; chmn. adv. bd. Salvation Army; dir. Calhoun-Cleburne Mental Health Bd. Served to capt. USMCR, World War II; to maj., Judge Adv. Gen. Dept., AUS, Korean War; col. Res. ret. Named Man of Year, Anniston Rotary Club, 1966. Mem. Am., Ala. bar assns., Anniston C. of C. (past dir.), Chi Phi, Phi Delta Phi. Episcopalian. Rotarian (gov. Dist. 686, 1958-59). Club: Anniston Country. Home: 7 Ruby Ridge Rd Anniston AL 36201 Office: First Nat Bank Bldg Anniston AL 36201

PORGES, WALTER RUDOLF, TV news producer; b. Vienna, Nov. 26, 1931; s. Paul and Charlotte (Posamentier) P.; B.A., City Coll. N.Y., 1953; m. Jean Belle Mlotok, Dec. 22, 1953; children—Donald F., Marian E., Lawrence M. News writer radio sta. WOR, N.Y.C., 1955-56, WCBS Radio and TV, N.Y.C., 1956-57; news writer ABC Radio Network, N.Y.C., 1958-60, news editor, 1960-63, asst. dir. radio news, 1963-65; asst. assignment mgr. ABC-TV, 1965-68; asso. producer ABC-TV Evening News, 1968-70, sr. producer, 1973-75; European producer ABC News, London, 1970-73; producer ABC-TV spl. events, N.Y.C., 1975-76; coordinating producer ABC News, Republican Nat. Conv., 1976; editorial producer, chief writer ABC Evening News, 1976—, sr. producer ABC Evening News, 1977—. Served with U.S. Army, 1953-55. Jewish. Home: 15 Burkeley Pl Hastings-on-Hudson NY 10706 Office: 7 W 66th St New York City NY 10023

PORILE, NORBERT THOMAS, educator, chemist; b. Vienna, Austria, May 18, 1932; s. Irving and Emma (Intrator) P.; came to U.S., 1947, naturalized, 1952; B.A., U. Chgo., 1952, M.S., 1954, Ph.D., 1957; m. Miriam Eisen, June 16, 1957; 1 son, James. Research asso. Brookhaven Nat. Lab., Upton, N.Y., 1957-59, asso. chemist, 1959-63, chemist, 1963-64; vis. prof. chemistry McGill U., 1963-65; asso. prof. chemistry Purdue U., Lafayette, Ind., 1965-69, prof. chemistry, 1969—; research collaborator Brookhaven Nat. Lab., Argonne Nat. Lab., Los Alamos Sci. Lab.; vis. prof. Facultes des Scis., Orsay, France; fellow Soc. Promotion of Sci. in Japan, Inst. Nuclear Study, U. Kyoto, 1961. John Simon Guggenheim meml. fellow, Institut de Physique Nucleaire Orsay, 1971-72; recipient F.D. Martin Undergraduate Teaching award, 1977. Mem. Am. Chem. Soc., Am. Phys. Soc., AAAS. Office: Dept Chemistry Purdue U Lafayette IN 47907

PORIS, GEORGE JAY, advt. exec.; b. N.Y.C., Feb. 15, 1924; s. Sidney F. and Elynor (Bregmen) P.; A.B., Columbia, 1948; m. Florence L. Kirschenbaum, May 30, 1947; children—James, Andrew, Dana. Asst. dir. creative services SSC & B, Inc., N.Y.C., 1957-68, sr. v.p., creative dir., 1971—; v.p. Revlon, Inc., N.Y.C., 1968-71. Served with USAAF, 1942-45. Decorated Air medal with 2 oak leaf clusters. Mem. Phi Beta Kappa. Home: 285 Whitman St Haworth NJ 07641 Office: 1 Dag Hammarskjold Plaza New York City NY 10017

POROPAT, ANTHONY RICHARD, banker; b. Chgo., Sept. 18, 1919, s. Anton and Martha (Herczeg) P.; student South Bend Coll. Commerce, 1939; grad. Sch. Bank Adminstrn. U. Wis., 1971; m. Sherron P. Gooch, June 24, 1945; children—Richard K., Julia E. Miller. Vice pres., treas. First Bank & Trust Co., South Bend, 1968-76; with Smith-Zeisz Co., South Bend, 1976-77; dir. ops. Valley Bank & Trust Co., Mishawaka, Ind., 1977—. Served with AUS, 1941-45. Lion. Home: 4902 Blackford Dr W South Bend IN 46614 Office: 202 Lincolnway E Mishawaka IN 46544

PORRETTO, JOHN PAUL, hosp. adminstr.; b. Galveston, Tex., Dec. 19, 1942; s. Paul Dominick and Elizabeth P.; B.B.A., Sam Houston State U., 1965; m. Nina Carolyn Hiroms, May 31, 1974; children—Robin Lynn, John Paul. Auditor GAO, 1966; acct., bus. mgr. U. Tex. Med. Br., Galveston, 1966-69, asst. to bus. mgr., 1969-70, dir. fiscal services, 1970-77, asst. v.p. for hosp. affairs, 1977-79; v.p. for adminstrn. and fin. U. Tex. Health Sci. Center, Houston, 1979—. Mem. adv. bd. Salvation Army; bd. dirs. Galveston Airport Commn. Served with U.S. Army, USAF. Mem. Hosp. Fin. Mgmt. Assn., Fin. Mgmt. Assn., Nat. Hosp. Fin. Mgmt. Assn., Assn. Am. Med. Colls., Nat. Assn. So. Colls. and Univ. Bus. Officers, Am. Hosp. Assn., Tex. Assn. Hosp. Accts., Tex. Assn. So. Colls. and Univ. Bus. Officers. Home: 6 Park Ln Circle Galveston TX 77551 Office: PO Box 20036 Houston TX 77025*

PORRITT, RUTH KILBURN, librarian; b. Goffstown, N.H., Oct. 6, 1908; d. William Wells and Bessie (Libbey) Porritt; B.S., Simmons Coll., 1930; A.M., Boston U., 1944. Asst. acquisition dept. Baker Library, Harvard Bus. Sch., 1930-42, reference librarian, 1942-49; librarian Radcliffe Coll., 1949-71; librarian Hilles Library, Harvard, 1971-73, asso. South House, 1973—. Library cons. Salzburg Seminars Am. Studies, 1957; visitor to library Mus. Fine Arts, Boston, 1969—. Mem. ALA. Congregationalist. Club: Appalaehian Mountain (Boston). Home: 20 Standish Rd Melrose MA 02176 Office: Hilles Library Harvard U Cambridge MA 02138

PORT, EDMUND, U.S. judge; b. Syracuse, N.Y., Feb 6, 1906; s. Abraham M. and Clara (Alderman) P.; LL.B., Syracuse U., 1929; m. Barbara Streeter, Jan 2, 1945; children—Alan David, Linda Kay. Admitted to N.Y. bar, 1930; asst. U.S. atty. No. Dist. N.Y., 1943-51, U.S. atty., 1951-53; U.S. judge No. Dist. N.Y., 1964—. Home: Townhouse 6 Standart Woods Auburn NY 13021 Office: US Court House Auburn NY 13021

PORT, FREDERICK JAMES, corp. exec.; b. Parkston, S.D., Oct. 13, 1914; s. Frederick James and Gretchen (Bleser) P.; B.S., U. Ill., 1936; Sc.D., Mass. Inst. Tech., 1940; M.B.A., U. Chgo.,1946; m. Edith Ann Whitney, Sept. 14, 1940 (div. 1964); children—Robert, Thomas, Eric, David, Anthony; m. 2d, Rolanda DeWinter, Sept. 10, 1971; children—Jason, Hannah. Works mgr. Cribben & Sexton Co., 1946-49; gen. mgr. Hein-Werner Corp., 1949-50; dir. battery ops. Solar Corp., 1950-55; dir. engring. ESB, Inc., Cleve., 1955-56, mgr. mfg. and engring., 1956-58, gen. mgr. automotive div., 1958-60, v.p. automotive group, 1960-69, pres., chief exec. officer, 1971—, also chmn.; dir. Provident Nat. Bank, SKF Industries Inc Provident Nat. Corp., INCO (U.S.), Inc.; trustee Penn Mut. Life Ins. Co. Served from 2d lt. to capt., Ordnance Dept., U.S. Army, 1942-46. Mem. Assn. Am. Battery Mfrs. (dir., pres. 1964-65), Soc. Automotive Engrs., Electrochem. Soc. Clubs: Aronimink Golf, Pine Valley Golf. Home: 1333 S Concord Rd West Chester PA 19380 Office: 5 Penn Center Plaza Philadelphia PA 19103

PORT, SIDNEY CHARLES, educator, mathematician; b. Chgo., Nov. 27, 1935; s. Isadore and Sarah (Landy) P.; A.B., Northwestern U., 1957, M.S., 1958, Ph.D., 1962; m. Idelle Jackson, Mar. 24, 1957; children—Ethan, Jonathan, Daniel. Staff mathematician Rand Corp., 1962-66; asso. prof. math. U. Calif. at Los Angeles, 1966-69, prof., 1969—. Fellow Inst. Math. Statistics; mem. Am. Math. Soc. Author: (with P. Hoel and C. Stone) Probability, Statistics and Stochastic Processes, 1971; (with C. Stone) Browman Motion and Classical Potential Theory, 1978. Contbr. articles to profl. jours. Home: 680 Kingman Ave Santa Monica CA 90402 Office: Univ Calif Los Angeles Los Angeles CA 90024

PORTE, ANDREW JAY, editor; b. Chgo., June 21, 1944; s. Ned Hart and Blossom P.; B.A., Syracuse U., 1965; m. Judy Lieberman, Apr. 27, 1974. Asst. dir. pub. relations Crusade for Opportunity, Syracuse, N.Y., 1965-66; copy editor Syracuse Post-Standard, 1966-68; reporter N.Y. Post, 1968-69, asst. city editor, 1969-73, city editor, 1973-76, met. editor, 1976-77; assignment editor ABC News, N.Y.C., 1977-78, asst. assignment mgr., 1978—. Served with U.S. Army, 1967. Office: ABC News 7 W 66th St New York NY 10023

PORTEOUS, MARK, ballet co. exec.; b. Montreal, Que., Can., June 1, 1952; s. John Geoffrey and Millicent S. (Asselman) P.; student Paul Smith's Coll., N.Y.C., 1970-71, Ryerson Poly. Inst., Toronto, Ont., Can., 1971-72. With Shaw Festival, 1972-75, Theatre London, 1974, Toronto Arts Prodns., 1973; theatre mgr. Centaur Theatre, Montreal, 1975-77; asst. co. mgr. Nat. Ballet of Can., 1977-78; co. mgr. Royal Winnipeg Ballet, Man., Can., 1978—. Office: care Royal Winnipeg Ballet 289 Portage Ave Winnipeg MB R3B 2B4 Canada

PORTER, ABRAHAM, lawyer; b. N.Y.C., Mar. 21, 1911; s. Harry and Rachel (Pfeiffer) P.; B.A. cum laude, Coll. City N.Y., 1930; J.D. (editor law rev.), Columbia 1933; m. Edith Indenbaum, Apr. 27, 1935; 1 son, Kenneth J. Admitted to N.Y. bar, 1933, since practiced in N.Y.; partner firm Hays, Porter, Spanier & Curtis, 1942-79, cons., 1979—. Mem. N.Y. County Lawyers Assn., N.Y. Law Inst., Phi Beta Kappa. Home: 515 Ave I Brooklyn NY 11230 Office: 445 Park Ave New York NY 10022

PORTER, ANDREW BRIAN, writer; b. Cape Town, South Africa, Aug. 26, 1928; came to U.S., 1972; s. Andrew Ferdinand and Vera Sybil (Bloxham) P.; B.A., M.A., Univ. Coll., Oxford, Eng., 1952. Music critic Fin. Times, London, 1950-74; music critic New Yorker, N.Y.C., 1972—; mem. music panel Arts Council of Great Britain, 1962-74; mem. music adv. panel Brit. Council, 1966-74; vis. fellow All Souls Coll., Oxford, 1973-74. Mem. Royal Musical Assn., Am. Music Center, ASCAP. Author: A Musical Season, 1974; Wagner's Ring, 1976; Music of Three Seasons, 1978; editor: Musical Times, 1960-67; editorial bd. Grove's Dictionary of Music and Musicians, 6th edit. Office: The New Yorker 25 W 43d St New York NY 10023

PORTER, ARTHUR, educator, cons. engr.; b. Ulverston, Eng., Dec. 8, 1910; s. John William and Mary Anne (Harris) P.; student U. Manchester, 1930-37, (Commonwealth Fund fellow) M.I.T., 1937-39; m. P. Patricia Dixon, July 26, 1941; 1 son, John Arthur Harris. Sci. officer Brit. Admiralty, 1939-45; prin. sci. officer Nat. Phys. Lab., 1946; prof. instrument tech. Mil. Coll. Sci., 1946-49; head research div. Ferranti Electric Ltd., Toronto, 1949-55; prof. elec. engring. U. London, 1955-58; dean engring. U. Sask. (Can.), 1958-61; prof., chmn. dept. indsl. engring. U. Toronto, 1961-75; chmn. Royal Commn. on Electric Power Planning, Toronto, 1975—; dir. Sask. Power Corp., 1960-61. Bd. govs. Seneca Coll., 1968-75; chmn. adv. council for sci. and medicine Expo '67, Montreal, 1964-67; chmn. Can. Environ. Adv. Council, 1972-75. Recipient Centennial medal (Can.), 1967; Jubilee medal (Can.), 1977. Fellow Royal Soc. Arts (London), Royal Soc. Can., Instn. Elec. Engrs. (London); mem. Assn. Profl. Engrs. Ont., Can. Operational Research Soc. Anglican. Clubs: Arts and Letters (Toronto); Athenaeum (London). Author: An Introduction to Servomechanisms, 1950; Cybernetics Simplified, 1969; Towards A Community University, 1971. Contbr. articles to profl. jours. Home: Belfountain ON L0N 1B0 Canada Office: 14 Carlton St Toronto ON M5B 1J2 Canada. *Metaphor has been central in my thought processes since the early 1930's when I was first involved in building mechanical models of physical entities. The perception that metaphor and concomitantly poetry, as well as art and science, are synonymous has given rise to an unquenchable curiosity. And above all it has powerfully influenced my approach to teaching, and this has been the greatest joy of all.*

PORTER, ARTHUR RENO, economist, arbitrator; b. Poland, Ohio, Nov. 14, 1918; s. Arthur Reno and Grace (Schoeller) P.; B.S., Washington and Lee U., 1940; M.A., U. Pa., 1948, Ph.D., 1955; m. Ruth Stottler, June 23, 1945; children—Stephen Warren, Mark Schoeller, David Rankin, Malcolm James. Instr. econs. U. Pa., Phila., 1940-42, 45-48; mem. staff regional WLB, Phila., 1943-45; prof. econs. Hanover (Ind.) Coll., 1948-67; prof. econs., dean coll. Heidelberg Coll., Tiffin, Ohio, 1967-79. Arbitrator labor disputes. Mem. Nat. Acad. Arbitrators, Indsl. Relations Research Assn., Phi Beta Kappa. Mem. U.P. Ch. Author: Job Property Rights, 1954. Contbr. articles to Labor Law Jour. Office: 2520 E Township Rd Suite 122 Tiffin OH 44883

PORTER, BARRY LAVON, state librarian; b. Cedar City, Utah, Oct. 3, 1942; s. LaVon and Alta (Haycock) P.; B.S., So. Utah State Coll., 1967; M.L.S., Brigham Young U., 1970; m. Gayle Willis, Sept. 3, 1965; children—Donald, Michelle, Jeffrey, Steven, Jared. Bookmobile librarian Utah State Library Commn., 1967-68; reference librarian, 1968-73; dir. Iowa State Library Commn., 1973—. Exec. sec. Utah Library Assn., 1972; trustee Bibliog. Center for Research, Rocky Mountain region, 1973—, pres. bd., 1978. Mormon. Home: 521 31st St West Des Moines IA 50265 Office: Historial Bldg Des Moines IA 50319

PORTER, BARRY SCHUYLER, ins. co. exec.; b. Cin., Jan. 25, 1937; s. Clarence Andrew and Marjorie Lillian (Dewey) P.; B.A. in Econs., Denison U., 1959; M.B.A., U. Cin., 1968; m. Susan Macke, Aug. 21, 1971; children—Bari Susan, Holly Lynn and Joseph Macke (twins). With Sawbrook Steel Castings Co., Lockland, Ohio, 1959-60, 64-72, controller, asst. treas., 1969-72; asst. treas. Ohio Casualty Ins. Co., Hamilton, 1972-76, treas., since 1976. Pres. Hamilton County Council Retarded Children, 1975-76, treas., 1977-79. Served as officer USAF, 1960-63. Mem. Beta Theta Pi. Home: 385 Oliver Rd Cincinnati OH 45215 Office: 136 N 3d St Hamilton OH 45025

PORTER, BLAINE ROBERT MILTON, educator; b. Morgan, Utah, Feb. 24, 1922; s. Brigham Ernest and Edna (Brough) P.; student Utah State U., 1940-41; B.S., Brigham Young U., 1947, M.A., 1949; Ph.D. (Grant Found. fellow family life edn. 1951-52), Cornell U., 1952; m. Elizabeth Taylor, Sept 27, 1943 (dec.); m. 2d, Barbara Duessler, June 12, 1975; children—Claudia Black, Roger B., David T., Patricia A. Hintze, Corinna. Instr. sociology Iowa State Coll., 1949-51; asst. prof. sociology and child devel. Iowa State U., 1952-55; prof., chmn. dept. human devel. and family relationships Brigham Young U., 1955-65, dean Coll. Family Living, 1966—; vis. prof., Fulbright research scholar U. London, 1965-66. Pres. elect Iowa Council Family Relations, 1954-55; pres. Utah Council Family Relations, 1957-58; chmn. sect. marriage counseling Nat. Council Family Relations, 1958-59, bd. dirs., 1957-60, exec. com., 1958-72, pres., 1963-64; bd. dirs. Am. Family Soc., 1975—. Served as pilot USAAF, 1942-45. Named Prof. of Year, Brigham Young U., 1964. Mem. Am. Home Econs. Assn. (vice chmn. sect. family relations and child devel. 1955-56), Am. Sociol. Assn. (sec. sect. on family 1964-67), Am. Assn. Marriage and Family Counselors, Am. Psychol. Assn., Soc. Research in Child Devel., Sigma Xi, Phi Kappa Phi (chpt. pres. 1969-71), Psi Chi, Alpha Kappa Delta. Mem. Ch. of Jesus Christ of Latter-day Saints (bishop). Editor: The Latter-day Saint Family, 1963, rev. edit., 1966. Contbr. articles to profl. jours. Home: 1675 Pine Ln Provo UT 84601

PORTER, CLYDE HENRY, coal and coke co. exec.; b. Birmingham, Ala., Apr. 29, 1906; s. John William and Bertha Catherine (Albes) P.; student U. Ala., Birmingham; m. Sadie Gay Graves, June 5, 1930; children—Marguerite Richards, Elizabeth Martin, Clyde Henry, Warren G. Asst. treas. Lincoln Res. Life Ins. Co., Birmingham, 1928-32; with Ala. By-Products Corp., Birmingham, 1932—, asst. sec., 1954-60, sec., 1960—, exec. com., 1968—; sec. Smokeless Fuel Co. Mem. exec. com., past pres. Birmingham area council Boy Scouts Am. Mem. Nat. Assn. Purchasing Mgmt. (Corcoran award 1975), Commerce Execs. Soc., Purchasing Mgmt. Assn. Ala. (past pres. Ala. chpt.), Ala. C. of C., Birmingham C. of C. Republican. Presbyterian. Clubs: Birmingham Kiwanis (past pres.), Masons (past master). Author monthly mag. column, 1966—. Home: 3125 Warrington Rd Mountain Brook AL 35223 Office: PO Box 10246 Birmingham AL 35202

PORTER, DARRELL RAV, profl. baseball player; b. Joplin, Mo., Jan. 17, 1952. With Milw. Brewers, 1971-76, Kansas City (Mo.) Royals, 1976—; mem. Am. League All-Star Team, 1974, 78. Office: care Kansas City Royals Royals Stadium PO Box 1969 Kansas City MO 64141*

PORTER, DAVID HUGH, pianist, harpsichordist, educator; b. N.Y.C., Oct. 29, 1935; s. Hugh B. and Ethel K. (Flentye) P.; B.A. with highest honors, Swarthmore Coll., 1958; Ph.D. (Danforth Grad. fellow), Princeton U., 1962; student Phila. Conservatory Music, 1955-61; m. Laudie Ernestine Dimmette, June 21, 1958; children—Hugh, Everett, Helen, David. Instr. in classics and music Carleton Coll., 1962-63, asst. prof. classics and music, 1963-68, asso. prof., 1968-73, prof., 1973—, William H. Laird prof. liberal arts, 1974--; recitalist, lectr., especially on contemporary music, at colls., univs. throughout U.S., Europe, on radio and TV; mem. Minn. Humanities Council, music panel Minn. Arts Bd. Nat. Endowment for Humanities research fellow, 1969-70; Am. Council Learned Socs. research fellow, 1976-77. Mem. Am. Philos. Assn., Classical Assn. M.W. and South, Coll. Music Soc. Democrat. Mem. United Ch. Christ. Contbr. articles on classics, music to profl. jours. Home: 202 Elm St Northfield MN 55057 Office: Carleton Coll Northfield MN 55057

PORTER, DAVID STEWART, U.S. dist. judge; b. Cin., Sept. 23, 1909; s. Charles Hamilton and Caroline (Pemberton) P.; A.B., U. Cin., 1932, J.D., 1934; m. Marjorie Bluett Ellis, July 26, 1956; children by previous marriage—Mary Stewart, Margaret Lee, Elizabeth Sue. Admitted to Ohio bar, 1934; practice in Troy, 1936-49; judge Common Pleas Ct., Miami County, Ohio, 1949-66; U.S. dist. judge So. Dist. Ohio, 1966—. Active Ohio Jud. Conf.; past pres. Ohio Common Pleas Judges Assn.; faculty adviser Nat. Coll. State Trial Judges, 1964-65. Past bd. dirs. Ohio Blue Cross, Dettmer Hosp., Troy. Mem. Am., Ohio, Cin. bar assns., Am. Judicature Soc. Presbyn. (elder). Office: US Post Office and Court House Cincinnati OH 45202

PORTER, DUDLEY, JR., ins. co. exec., lawyer; b. Paris, Tenn., May 10, 1915; s. Dudley and Mary (Bolling) P.; student Murray (Ky.) State Coll., 1933-34; LL.B., Cumberland U., 1936; m. Mary Rhoda Montague, Oct. 21, 1950. Admitted to Tenn. bar, 1937; asst. atty. gen Tenn., 1937-40; mem. firm Tyne, Peebles, Henry & Tyne, Nashville 1940-49; with law dept. Nat. Life & Accident Ins. Co., Nasvhille, 1940-49, asso. gen. counsel, 1948; with Provident Life & Accident Ins. Co., Chattanooga, 1949—, gen. counsel, 1954-72, sr. v.p., 1958-72, sec., 1965-72, vice chmn., sr. counsel, 1972-76, now dir., mem. exec. com.; of counsel Chambliss, Bahner, Crutchfield, Gaston & Irvine, Chattanooga, 1977—; dir. Coca-Cola Bottling Corp., Cin. Mem. Hamilton County Juvenile Ct. Commn., 1958-64, chmn., 1964; mem. Tenn. Health Planning Council, 1968-76, Tenn. Hist. Commn., 1976—; an incorporator, mem. bd. Sr. Neighbors Chattanooga, 1960-66; v.p., trustee Maclellan Found. Served with AUS, 1942-46; judge adv. 100th Inf. Div., ETO. Mem. Am., Tenn., Chattanooga bar assns., Am. Life Conv. (chmn. legal sect. 1958), Assn. Life Ins. Counsel (exec. com. 1970—, pres. 1974-75), Newcomen Soc., Sigma Alpha Epsilon. Presbyterian. Clubs: Mountain City (Chattanooga); Belle Meade Country (Nashville). Home: 1125 Healing Springs Rd Elder Mountain Chattanooga TN 37409 Office: 1014 Maclellan Bldg Chattanooga TN 37402

PORTER, DWIGHT JOHNSON, electric co. exec.; b. Shawnee, Okla., Apr. 12, 1916; s. Dwight Ernest and Gertrude (Johnson) P.; A.B., Grinnell Coll., 1938, LL.D., 1968; student Am. U., 1938-40, 46-48, Nat. War Coll., 1957-58; m. Adele Ritchie, Oct. 6, 1942; children—Dwight A., James G., Ellen Jean, Barbara Adele, Joan Anne. Ritchie Johnson. Govt. intern Nat. Inst. Pub. Affairs, Washington, 1938-39; personnel officer U.S. Housing Authority, 1939-41; exec. officer Dept. Agr., San Francisco, 1941-42; asst. personnel dir. Bd. Econ. Warfare, 1942; dir. adminstrv. services Rural Electrification Adminstrn., 1946-48; mgmt. officer Dept. State, 1948; dep. dir. Displaced Persons Commn., 1949; adminstrv. officer U.S. High Commn., Germany, 1949-54; 1st sec. Am. embassy, London, 1954-56; exec. officer econ. area Dept. State, 1956-57, coordinator Hungarian Refugee Relief, 1957, spl. asst. to dep. under-sec., and under-sec. state, 1958-59; counsellor Am. embassy, Vienna, 1959-62, minister, 1962, dep. chief of mission, 1962-63; asst. sec. of state for adminstrn., 1963-65; ambassador to Lebanon, 1965-70; permanent U.S. rep. IAEA, Vienna, 1970-75; dir. internat. govt. affairs Westinghouse Electric Corp., Washington, 1975—. Served to capt. USMCR, 1942-45. Recipient alumni award Grinnell Coll., 1958. Home: 5131 Edgemoor Ln Bethesda MD 20014

PORTER, ELIOT FURNESS, photographer; b. Winnetka, Ill., Dec. 6, 1901; s. James Foster and Ruth Wadsworth (Furness) P.; B.S., Harvard, 1924, M.D., 1929; D.F.A. (hon.), Colby Coll., 1969; Litt.D., U. Albuquerque, 1974; m. Marian Brown, 1927 (div. 1934); children—Eliot Furness, Charles Anthony; m. 2d, Aline Kilham, May 8, 1936; children—Jonathan, Stephen, Partick Eliot. Tchr. biochemistry and bacteriology Harvard, also Radcliffe Coll., 1929-39; engaged in photography, 1939—; exhbns. include Stielglitz's An Am. Place, 1939, Mus. Modern Art, 1943, 52, George Eastman House, Rochester, N.Y., 1960, Art Inst. Chgo., 1953, Nelson Gallery, Kansas City, Mo., 1959, Met. Mus. Art, N.Y.C., 1979, numerous others. Asso. fellow Morse Coll., Yale, 1967; bd. dirs. Sierra Club, until 1971. Recipient Conservation Service award U.S. Dept. Interior, 1967; Maine Commn. on Arts and Humanities award, 1968; Distinguished Son of Maine award, 1969; Newhouse citation Syracuse U., 1973; Gov.'s award N.Mex. Arts Commn., 1976; Guggenheim fellow, 1941, 46. Fellow Am. Acad. Arts and Scis.; mem. Am. Ornithol. Union, Cooper, Wilson ornithol. socs. Publs. include: In Wildness is the Preservation of the World, 1962; The Place No One Knew-Glen Canyon on the Colorado, 1963; Forever Wild—The Adirondacks, 1966; Summer Island, 1966; Baja California—the Geography of Hope, 1967; Galapagos—The Flow of Wildness, 1968; Appalachian Wilderness, 1970; Birds of North America—A Personal Selection, 1972; also contbr. books ornithology, natural history. Co-author: Down The Colorado, 1969; The Tree Where Man Was Born—An African Experience, 1972; Antarctica, 1978; Intimate Landscapes, 1979. Address: Rt 4 Box 33 Santa Fe NM 87501

PORTER, ELSA ALLGOOD, ofcl. Dept. Commerce; b. Amoy, China, Dec. 19, 1928 (parents Am. citizens); d. Roy and Petra S. (Johnsen) Allgood; B.A., Birmingham-So. Coll., 1949; M.A., U. Ala., 1959; M. Pub. Adminstrn., Harvard U., 1971; m. G. Hinckley Porter, Nov. 22, 1962; children by previous marriage—Barbara E. Liles, Janet R. Liles; stepchildren—David H., Brian F., Wendy E. With HEW, Washington, 1960-73, chief career devel. br., 1969-70, chief manpower planning, 1970-71, asst. adminstr. orgn. devel. Social and Rehab. Service, 1971-73; dir. clearinghouse on productivity and organizational effectiveness U.S. Civil Service Commn., Washington, 1973-77; asst. sec. Dept. Commerce, Washington, 1977—. Home: 400 S Lee St Alexandria VA 22314 Office: Dept Commerce 14th St between Constitution Ave and E St NW Washington DC 20230

PORTER, FELIX NATHANIEL, banker; b. Caddo, Okla., Dec. 23, 1915; s. Hafford and Zelma (Porter) P.; B.S., Okla. State U., 1937; ed. Wharton Sch. Fin., U. Pa., 1956; LL.D. (hon.), Oklahoma City U., 1975; m. Jane Ward Harreld, Oct. 19, 1946. Vice pres. The First Nat. Bank and Trust Co., Oklahoma City, 1958-66, exec. v.p., 1966-69, pres., 1969-74, chmn. exec. com., 1974-75, vice chmn. bd., 1975—, also dir.; exec. v.p., sec., dir. 1st Okla. Bancorp., Inc.; v.p., dir. 1st Nat. Leasing Inc.; dir., mem. exec. com. Scrivner, Inc.; dir. 1st Okla. Investments Corp., 1st Nat. Found., Inc., 1st Nat. Mgmt. Corp., GHF Agy., Inc., FNB Indsl. Co., Inc., Am. Mortgage and Investment Co., 1st Okla. Realty Investment Corp.; adv. dir. N.W. Bank, Oklahoma City; trustee, mem. exec. com. Okla. Blue Cross. Mem. exec. com. Frontiers of Sci. Found.; trustee Oklahoma City U., Jr. Achievement Greater Oklahoma City, Oklahoma City Airport Trust; mem. Appeals and Rev. Bd. Oklahoma City; bd. dirs. Better Bus. Bur. Central Okla.; treas. Presbyn. Hosp. Served with U.S. Army, 1941-46. Mem. Oklahoma City C. of C. (treas., dir.), Assn. Res. City Bankers, Pi Kappa Alpha, Alpha Kappa Psi. Democrat. Episcopalian. Clubs: Beacon (treas., dir.), Economics, Men's Dinner, Bond of Okla. Home: 3233 N Harvey Pkwy Oklahoma City OK 73118 Office: 120 N Robinson St Oklahoma City OK 73102

PORTER, GENE HUNTLEY, govt. ofcl.; b. Little Falls, N.Y., Aug. 27, 1936; s. Eugene F. and Mildred C. (Johnson) P.; B.S., U.S. Naval Acad., 1958; M.S., U. Wash., 1962; m. Mary Katherine Dugan, Aug. 22, 1959; children—Katherine, Geoffrey, Laura. Commd. ensign U.S. Navy, 1958, advanced through grades to comdr., 1972; exec. officer nuclear submarine USS Jack, 1964-71; res., 1973; with Dept. Def., 1971—, dep. asst. sec. gen. purpose programs Office of Program Analysis and Evaluation, 1977—. Office: Pentagon Washington DC 20301

PORTER, GEORGE ALVIN, physician; b. Medford, Oreg., Dec. 22, 1931; s. Jack Luther and Rosalie (Jones) P.; B.S., Oreg. State U., 1953; M.S., M.D., U. Oreg., 1957; m. Marthel Drysdale, June 12, 1953; children—Jack, Robert, Douglas, David. Intern, U. Oreg. Health Scis. Center, 1957-58; resident U. Oreg. Med. Sch., 1958-60, fellow cardiology, 1960-62, asst. prof. medicine, 1964-69, asso. prof., 1969-73, prof., head div. nephrology, 1973-77, prof., chmn. dept. medicine, 1977—; fellow in nephrology U. Calif., San Francisco, 1962-64; practice medicine, specializing in nephrology, Portland, Oreg., 1970—; chmn. NIH Workshop on Drug and Environ. Toxins; chmn. med. adv. bd. Roseburg VA Med. Center; chmn. operating com. VA Nat. Coop. Program for Dialysis; vice chmn. Network Coordinating Council #2; mem. Intersoc. Com. Renal Research, Nat. Acad. Sci. Adv. Com. to VA Hosp. Safety officer Mt. Sylvania Community Coll., 1964-69, pres., 1967; active Twin Creek Promotion Com., 1964-66, Wilson Hi Dad's Club, 1970-74. Recipient Career Devel. award NIH, 1965-70. Fellow A.C.P.; mem. Am. Heart Assn. (chmn. council on kidney cardiovascular disease, dir.), Am. Fedn. Clin. Research, Am. Soc. Clin. Investigation, Am. Soc. Nephrology, Am. Physiol. Soc., Endocrine Soc., Internat. Soc. Nephrology, Nat. Kidney Found., Western Assn. Physicians, Western Soc. Clin. Investigation, Inter-Am. Soc. Hypertension, Portland Acad. Medicine, Alpha Omega Alpha. Republican. Episcopalian. Club: Multnomah Athletic. Mem. editorial bd. Western Jour. Medicine, 1979. Home: 3545 SW Jerald Ct Portland OR 97221 Office: 3181 SW Sam Jackson Park Rd Portland OR 97201

PORTER, GERALD JOSEPH, mathematician; b. Elizabeth, N.J., Feb. 27, 1937; s. Fred and Tillie Florence (Friedman) P.; A.B., Princeton U., 1958; Ph.D., Cornell U., 1963; M.A. (hon.), U. Pa., 1971; m. Judith Deborah Revitch, June 26, 1966; children—Daniel, Rebecca, Michael. Instr., Mass. Inst. Tech., 1963-65; Office Naval Research postdoctoral fellow Brandeis U., 1965-66; asst. prof. math. U. Pa., Phila., 1965-69, asso. prof., 1969-75, prof., 1975—, chmn. undergrad. affairs dept. math., 1971-73. Co-chmn. Phila. Acad. Com. for Soviet Jewry, 1975-78; vice chmn. math. Com. Concerned Scientists, 1977-78, nat. dir., 1979—; mem. Democratic Com., Haverford Twp., Pa., 1976—. Mem. Am. Math. Soc., Math. Assn. Am. (exec. com. Phila. sect. 1976-79), Assn. Computing Machinery, Democrat. Jewish. Contbr. articles on math. to profl. jours. Home: 161 Whitemarsh Rd Ardmore PA 19003 Office: 4N63 DRL/E1 U Pa Philadelphia PA 19104

PORTER, HELEN VINEY (MRS. LEWIS M. PORTER, JR.), assn. exec., lawyer; b. Logansport, Ind., Sept. 7, 1935; s. Charles Lowry and Florence Helen (Kunkel) V.; A.B., Ind. U., 1957; J.D., U. Louisville, 1961; m. Lewis Morgan Porter, Jr., Dec. 26, 1966; children—Alicia Michelle, Andrew Morgan. Admitted to Ind. and Ill. bars, 1961, U.S. Supreme Ct. bar, 1971; atty. office chief counsel Midwest regional office IRS, Chgo., 1961-73; asso. regional atty. litigation center Equal Employment Opportunity Commn., Chgo., 1973-74; practice in Northbrook, Ill., 1974-79; partner firm Porter & Andersen, Chgo., 1979—; lectr. Law in Am. Found., Chgo., summer, 1973, 74; asso. prof. Lewis U. Coll. Law, Glen Ellyn, Ill., 1975-79; lectr. women's rights and fed. taxation to bar assns. Fellow Am. Bar Found.; mem. Women's Bar Assn. Ill. (pres. 1972-73), Fed. (pres. Chgo. chpt. 1974-75), Ill. (del. 1972-78) bar assns., Nat. Assn. Women Lawyers (pres. 1973-74) Home: 225 Maple Row Northbrook IL 60062 Office: 120 S LaSalle St Suite 820 Chicago IL 60603

PORTER, HENRY HOMES, JR., bus. exec.; b. Chgo., Nov. 13, 1934; s. Henry H. and Mary (Kinney) P.; A.B., Yale U., 1956; M.B.A., Harvard U., 1962; m. Louisa Catherine Perkins, June 10, 1961; children—Mary Kinney, Louisa Catherine. With Gen. Mills, Inc., Mpls., 1962-76, asst. treas., 1964-67, treas., 1967-76, v.p. fin., 1969-76; sr. v.p., chief fin. officer, dir. Brown & Williamson Industries, Inc., 1977—; dir. Greenwich Research Assos. (Conn.). Trustee Carleton Coll., Hazen Found. Served to lt. (j.g.) USNR, 1957-60. Home: 3720 Hillsdale Rd Louisville KY 40222 Office: 2000 Citizens Plaza Louisville KY 40202

PORTER, JOHN ARTHUR, educator; b. Vancouver, B.C., Can., Nov. 12, 1921; s. Arthur and Ethel (Cuffin) P.; B.Sc. in Econs., London U., 1949, D.Sc., 1966; LL.D. (hon.), McMaster U., 1973; D.Litt. (hon.), Waterloo U., 1977; m. Marion Ruth Lyons, Oct. 5, 1951; children—Charles Anthony, Ann Veronica. Lectr. to prof. dept. sociology Carleton U., 1949—, v.p. academic, 1977-78; research asso. U. Toronto, 1957-58, prof., 1968-69; fellow Inst. Labor Studies, Geneva, 1966-67; vis. prof. Harvard U., 1973-74. Served with Can. Army, 1941-46. Recipient Centennial medal Can., 1967. Fellow Royal Soc. Can.; mem. Am. Sociol. Assn. (MacIver award 1966), Can. Sociology and Anthropology Assn. (hon. pres.). Author: The Vertical Mosaic: An Analysis of Social Class and Power in Canada, 1965; Canadian Social Structure a Statistical Profile, 1967; (with others) Towards 2000: Post Secondary Education in Ontario, 1971; Does Money Matter? Prospects for Higher Education, 1973; editor: (with others) Canadian Society: Sociological Perspectives, 1961. Home: 92 Powell Ave Ottawa ON K1S 2A3 Canada Office: Carleton U Ottawa ON K1S 5B6 Canada

PORTER, JOHN EDWARD, congressman; b. Evanston, Ill., June 1, 1935; s. Harry H. and Beatrice V. Porter; attended M.I.T. and Northwestern U., received B.S. and B.A. degrees; J.D. with distinction, U. Mich., 1961; m. Kathryn Porter; 3 children. Admitted to Ill. bar, 1961, U.S. Supreme Ct. bar, 1968; former honor law grad. atty., appellate div. Dept. Justice, Washington; partner firm Porter and Keating, Evanston; mem. Ill. Ho. of Reps., 1973-79; mem. 96th Congress from 10th Dist. Ill. Trustee, Cove Sch. for Perceptually Handicapped Children. Recipient Best Legislator award League Conservative Voters, 1973; Best Legislator award Ind. Voters Ill., 1974. Mem. Am. Bar Assn., Chgo. Bar Assn., Ill. Bar Assn., N.W. Suburban Bar Assn. Republican. Past editor Mich. Law Rev. Office: US Ho of Reps Washington DC 20515*

PORTER, JOHN FINLEY, JR., educator, physicist; b. Birmingham, Ala., Aug. 22, 1927; s. John Finley and Janice (Nowell) P.; B.S., U. Ala., 1950, M.S., 1956; Ph.D., Johns Hopkins, 1966; m. Jacqueline Christine Harbin, Dec. 27, 1949; children—Gayle P. Barnett, John Finley III, Paul William, Adam Michael, David Wade. Research staff asst. Radiation Lab., Johns Hopkins, 1956-59, research asso. Carlyle Barton Lab., 1959-66, research scientist, 1966, lectr. elec. engring., 1965-66; asso. prof. physics U. Ala., Huntsville, 1966-69, chmn. physics faculty, 1968-69, prof. physics, dean faculty, 1969-70, prof. physics, dean grad. programs and research, 1970-72; dep. exec. dir. Ala. Commn. on Higher Edn., 1972-73, exec. dir., 1973—; cons. Catlayst Research Corp., Balt., Environmental Sci. Service Adminstrn., Washington; chmn. State Council Grad. Deans, 1971-72; mem. planning bd. Edn. Commn. of States, 1975-77; mem. Ala. Right To Read Adv. Council, 1974-76, Ala. Post Secondary Edn. Planning Commn., 1974-76; mem. Gov.'s Budget Adv. Com., 1976-77. Active Boy Scouts Am. Served to 1st lt., arty., U.S. Army, 1945-47, 50-54. Mem. State Higher Edn. Exec. Officers Assn. (fed. relations com. 1975-76, 78-79, audit and fin. com. 1977-78), Am. Assn. Higher Edn., Sigma Xi. Methodist. Clubs: Montgomery Country, Capital City. Contbr. articles to profl. jours. Home: 2517 Darrington Rd Montgomery AL 36111 Office: Suite 221 One Court Square Montgomery AL 36104

PORTER, JOHN FRANCIS, III, banker; b. Wilmington, Del., Sept. 17, 1934; s. John Francis, Jr. and Eloise Wilhelmina (Berlinger) P.; B.A., U. Va., 1956, M.B.A., U. Del., 1965; m. Ann Mayfield, Sept. 8, 1956; children—Leslie Gibson, Nina Covington, Sophie Ernst. With Del. Trust Co., Wilmington, 1958—, asst. treas., 1960-66, sec., 1966-68, v.p., sec., 1968-72, sr. v.p., sec., 1972-75, exec. v.p., 1975-79, pres., 1979—; pres., dir. Wilmington Auto Sales Co., Wilmington Appliance Co. Mem. bank adv. bd. State of Del., 1969-71; mem. Council on Banking for State of Del., 1971—, chmn., 1976—; bd. dirs. Alfred I. duPont Inst. of Nemours Found., Wilmington and Brandywine Cemetery; bd. dirs., trustee Wilmington Med. Center. Served to capt., arty., U.S. Army, 1957. Clubs: Wilmington Country (dir.), Wilmington, Vicmead Hunt. Home: 4821 Kennett Pike Wilmington DE 19807 Office: 900 Market St Wilmington DE 19899

PORTER, JOHN STEPHEN, TV exec.; b. Avoca, N.Y., Sept. 2, 1932; s. Frank R. and Margaret H. (McGreel) P.; B.A. in English, St. John Fisher U., 1958; M.S. in Radio/TV, Syracuse U., 1959; postgrad. in Edn., U. Rochester, 1960-61; m. Marie C. Eiffert, Sept. 6, 1958; children—Stephen, David, Mark, Kevin, Matthew. Producer, broadcaster weekly news analysis N.Y. State Empire State FM Sch. of Air, 1962-64; producer, narrator weekly series sta. WROC-FM, Rochester, N.Y., 1964-65; pres., gen. mgr. sta. WXXI-TV, Rochester, 1966-69; trustee Eastern Ednl. TV Network, Boston, 1966-68, mem. exec. com., 1967-68, exec. dir., 1969—. Served to 1st lt. AUS, 1952-56. Mem. N.Y. State Ednl. Radio/TV Assn. (treas. 1962-64), Pub. TV Sta. Mgrs. New York State (chmn. 1968-69), Nat. Assn. Ednl. Broadcasters (adv. com.). Home: 200 Downer Ave Hingham MA 02043 Office: 131 Clarendon St Boston MA 02116

PORTER, JOHN WESLEY, JR., ret. judge; b. Eufaula, Okla., Nov. 7, 1911; s. John Wesley and Mary Elizabeth (Baskett) P.; LL.B., Cumberland U., 1935; m. Nanabel Blankenship, June 18, 1937; children—Janita (Nita) (Mrs. Paul Williams), John Wesley III, Mary Jane. Admitted to Okla. bar, 1935, U.S. Supreme Ct. bar, 1948;

practiced in Muskogee, Okla., 1935, 76—; police judge, Muskogee, 1948-53; asst. county atty. Muskogee County, 1953-61, county judge, 1961-69, judge dist. ct., 1969-76. Leader Explorer Scouts, 1959-60. Bd. dirs. Muskogee Salvation Army, 1967-69. Mem. Fed., Am., Okla., Muskogee County (sec. 1938) bar assns., Am., Okla. trial lawyers assns., Am. Judicature Soc., Lambda Chi Alpha. Democrat. Baptist. Clubs: Muskogee Knife and Fork (dir.); Lions, Kiwanis. Contbr. articles to profl. jours.; also inventor. Home: 301 S 30th St Muskogee OK 74401

PORTER, JOHN WILLARD, educator, biochemist; b. Mukwonago, Wis., June 12, 1915; s. George Willard and Josephine (Gunderson) P.; B.S., U. Wis., 1938, Ph.D., 1942; m. Helen Reynolds, June 12, 1941; children—John Willard, Mary Grace, Susan Ann, James Alvin. Asst. chemist Purdue U., 1942-45, asst. prof., 1945-49; asst. chemist Armed Services Med. Nutrition Lab., Chgo., 1945; sr. scientist Gen. Electric Co., Hanford, Wash., 1949-54; Enzyme Inst. fellow U. Wis., Madison, 1954-56, asso. prof. dept. physiol. chemistry, 1956-64, prof., 1964—; asst. chief Radioisotope Service, VA Hosp., Madison, 1956-64, chief Lipid Metabolism Lab., 1964—. Chmn. subcom. Nat. Acad. Sci., 1964-76. Mem. Am. Soc. Biol. Chemists, Am. Chem. Soc., Am. Soc. Plant Physiologists, AAAS, Am. Inst. Chemists, Sigma Xi. Author: (with E.T. Mertz) Laboratory Experiments in Biochemistry, 1948; Plant and Animal Biochemistry, 1949. Research, numerous publs. primarily in field of elucidation of pathways and mechanisms of control of biosynthesis of carotenes, cholesterol and fatty acids. Home: 1710 Baker Ave Madison WI 53705 Office: VA Hosp 2500 Overlook Terr Madison WI 53705

PORTER, JOHN WILSON, univ. pres.; b. Fort Wayne, Ind., Aug. 13, 1931; s. James Richard and Ola (Phillips) P.; A.B., Albion Coll., 1953, D.Pub. Adminstrn., 1973; M.A., Mich. State U, 1957, Ph.D., 1962, LL.D., 1977; L.H.D., Adrian Coll., 1970; LL.D., Western Mich. U., Kalamazoo, 1971, Eastern Mich. U., Ypsilanti, 1975; H.H.D., Kalamazoo Coll., 1973, Madonna Coll., 1977; D.Ed. (hon.), Detroit Inst. Tech., 1978; m. Lois Helen French, May 27, 1961; children—Stephen James, Donna Agnes. Counselor, Lansing Pub. Schs., 1953-58; cons. Mich. Dept. Pub. Instrn., 1958-61; dir. Mich. Higher Edn. Assistance Authority, 1961-66; asso. supt. for higher edn. Mich. Dept. Edn., 1966-69, state supt. schs., 1969-79; pres. Eastern Mich. U., 1979—. Mem. Nat. Commn. Reform of Secondary Edn., 1972—, Nat. Commn. Financing Post-Secondary Edn., 1972—, Nat. Commn. on Manpower Policy, 1974—; pres. Council Chief State Sch. Officers, 1976. Trustee Nat. Urban League; mem. commn. on ednl. credit Am. Council Edn., 1977, Pres.'s Commn. on Mental Health, 1977, Adv. Council on Social Security, 1978; adv. bd. Women's Ednl. Equity Communications Network, 1977; bd. dirs. Council Chief State Sch. Officers, 1978—, Nat. Sch. Vol. Program, 1978—. Recipient Outstanding Achievement award Phi Beta Sigma, 1970; resolution of recognition Mich. Legislature, 1970, 79; Distinguished Service award Mich. Assn. Secondary Sch. Prins., 1974; Distinguished Alumni award Coll. Edn., Mich. State U., 1974; Elementary Sch. Prins. Outstanding Service award, 1976; Pres.'s award Nat. Alliance Black Sch. Educators, 1977; recognition awards Mich. Assn. Sch. Bds., 1979, Mich. Assn. Sch. Bds., 1979, Mich. Assn. Sch. Adminstrs., 1979. Home: 622 Camelot Dr East Lansing MI 48823 Office: Michigan National Tower Lansing MI 48933

PORTER, JULIAN DONALD, ins. co. exec.; b. Pleasanton, Kans., Jan. 19, 1919; s. Clarence Henry and Minnie (DeForest) P., B.A. in Bus. Adminstrn., Baker U., 1940; m. Martha Jane Parkhurst, Mar. 22, 1945; children—Nancy Porter Eller, Richard, Cynthia, Bradley. With Unigard Ins. Group, Seattle, Washington, 1940—, office mgr., spl. agt., 1940-58, asst. div. mgr., 1958-62, div. mgr., 1962-63, Western div. mgr., 1963-66, v.p., 1964-73, mktg. v.p., 1966-68, exec. v.p. Unigard Olympic Life Ins. Co., 1968-73, pres., 1973—, chief operating officer, 1974—, chief exec. officer, 1975—, chmn. bd., 1978—, also dir. Mem. governing com. Improved Risk Mutuals; mem. Citizens Adv. Com. Financial Instns., 1973-74. Mem. bus. and industry adv. council Seattle Opportunities Industrialization Center, 1973—. Bd. dirs. Jr. Achievement, 1975-78, United Way of King County; hon. bd. dirs. Internat. Yr. of Child; mem. adv. bd. Salvation Army; sr. bd. dirs. Safety Tng. and Research Assn. Wash.; trustee Indsl. Conf. Bd., 1974-75; v.p. bd. trustees Downtown Seattle Devel. Assn. Served with USNR, 1942-45. C.P.C.U. Mem. Seattle C. of C. (v.p. membership) Wash. Ins. Council and Ins. Fund Found. (treas. 1970-73), Wash. Life and Disability Ins. Guaranty Assn. (sec.-treas. 1971-72), Health Ins. Inst. (dir. 1973), Health Ins. Assn. Am., Pacific Ins. and Surety Conf. (pres. 1977-78), Nat. Assn. Casualty and Surety Execs., Alliance Am. Insurers (dir.). Clubs: Rainier, U. Wash. President's Wash. Athletic, Seattle Golf, Masons, Rotary (dir.). Home: 4240 Crestwood Pl Mercer Island WA 98040 Office: 1215 4th Ave Seattle WA 98161

PORTER, KARL HAMPTON, musical dir., condr.; b. Pitts., Apr. 25, 1939; s. Reginald and Naomi Arzetta (Mitchell) P.; student Carnegie-Mellon U., 1958-60, Peabody Conservatory, 1960-62, Juilliard Sch. Music, 1962-63, Domaine Sch. Condrs., 1961-63, Am. Symphony Orch. League Sch. Condrs./Tanglewood, 1962-72. Mem. Denver Symphony Orch., 1963-64, Met. Opera Nat. Co., 1965-67, Gil Evans Band, 1967-69; formed Harlem Youth Symphony, 1968, Harlem Philharmonic Orch., 1969, New Breed Brass Ensemble, Harlem String Quartet, Harlem Woodwind Quintet, 1970; condr. Balt. Symphony, 1970; mus. dir., condr. Harlem Philharmonic Orch., 1970—, N.Y.C. Housing Authority Orch., 1972—, Massapequa (N.Y.) Symphony Soc., 1974—; condr. Northeastern Philharmonic of Pa., Scranton Philharmonic, Ridgefield Symphonette, 1971; mus. dir. for Josephine Baker, 1972; free lance bassoonist Am. Symphony, Bklyn. Philharmonic, N.J. Symphony, 1967—. Judge for Congress of Strings, BMI Composers Competition, 1970-74; instr. theory Mt. Morris Park, 1969-73; instr. woodwind L.I. Inst. Music, 1969-75, U. Denver, 1963-64; tchr. bassoon Newark Community Arts Center, 1969-71; instr. Afro Am. music N.Y.C. Community Coll., 1972—. Mem. nat. adv. bd. Dance Theatre of Harlem. Recipient Martha Baird Rockefeller Found. grant, 1969, Nat. Endowment grant, 1970. Mem. Nat. Soc. Lit. and Arts, N.Y. State Assn. Jr. Colls., Am. Symphony Orch. League, Performing Arts Assn. N.Y., Soc. Black Composers. Club: The Bohemians. Home: 425 Central Park W New York NY 10025 Office: PO Box 445 New York NY 10025

PORTER, KATHERINE ANNE, writer; b. Indian Creek, Tex., May 15, 1890; d. Harrison Boone and Mary Alice (Jones) Porter; student in various pvt. schs.; D.Litt., Maryville Coll., St. Louis, 1968; L.H.D., U. Mich., 1954, U. Md., 1966; m. Albert Russel Erskine, Jr., Apr. 19, 1938; (div. 1942). Writer-in-residence and lectr. on lit. Stanford U., Calif., 1949; writer in residence U. Va., 1958- 59; first Glasgow prof. Washington and Lee U., 1959. From 1920 to 1937 lived in N.Y. or in Europe and Mexico. Awarded Guggenheim fellowship for creative writing, 1931, 38; fellow of regional Am. lit. library of Congress, 1944. Recipient Book-of-the-Month Club award, 1937; first ann. gold medal for lit. Soc. for Libraries of N.Y.U., 1940, for Pale Horse, Pale Rider; Ann. prize lit. work Tex. Inst. Lit., Dallas, 1950; Emerson-Thoreau Bronze medal Am. Acad. of Arts and Sci., 1962; Nat. Book award for fiction, 1966; Pulitzer prize for fiction, 1966; gold medal for fiction Nat. Inst. Arts and Letters, 1967. Guest lectr. English dept. U. Mich. 1953-54; Fulbright lectr. U. Liege, Belgium, 1955; Ford Found. grant in literature, 1959-60. Vice pres. Nat. Inst. Arts and Letters, 1950-52. Mem. Am. Acad. Arts and Letters, Phi Beta Kappa. Author: (short story collections) Flowering Judas, 1930, Hacienda: A Story of Mexico, 1934, Noon Wine, 1937; Pale Horse, Pale Rider: three Short Novels, 1938, the Leaning Tower and Other Stories, 1944, Holiday (1st prize O'Henry Awards), 1962, Collected Stories of Katherine Anne Porter, 1964 (Book-of-the-Month Club); (novel) Ship of Fools, 1962 (Book of Month Club); (non-fiction) the Days Before: Collected Essays and Occasional Writing, 1952 (augmented edit. 1970), A Defense of Circe, 1955; The Never-Ending Wrong, a memoir of the Sacco Vanzetti case, 1977; compiler, translator French Song Book, Paris, 1933; translator the Itching Parrot (Fernandez de Lizardi), 1942.

PORTER, KEITH ROBERTS, educator, cytologist; b. Yarmouth, N.S., Can., June 11, 1912; s. Aaron C. and Josephine (Roberts) P.; B.S., Acadia U., 1934, D.Sc., 1964; M.A., Harvard, 1935, Ph.D., 1938; LL.D., Queen's U., 1966; D.Sc. (hon.), Med. Coll. Ohio, 1975, Rockefeller U., 1976, U. Toronto, 1978; m. Elizabeth Lingley, June 16, 1938. NRC fellow Princeton, 1938-39; research asst. Rockefeller Inst., 1939-45, asso., 1945-50, asso. mem., 1950-56, mem., prof., 1956-61; prof. biology Harvard, 1961-70, chmn. biology dept., 1965-67; prof., chmn. molecular, cellular and developmental biology U. Colo., Boulder, 1968-74. Cons. Armed Forces Inst. Pathology, 1957-75; mem. adv. panel developmental biology NSF, 1964-66. Dir. Marine Biol. Lab., Woods Hole, Mass., 1975-76. Recipient (with George Palade) Warren Triennial award, 1962; (with Palade) Passano award, 1964; Gairdner Found. Ann. award, 1964; (with Palade and Albert Claude) Louisa Gross Horwitz prize, 1970; Nat. medal of sci., 1978; Waterford Biomed. award Scripps Clinic and Research Found., 1979; Guggenheim fellow, 1967-68; (with Palade) Dickson prize, 1971; (with Claude, F.S. Sjostrand) Paul Ehlich-Ludwig Darmstaedter prize, 1971; Robert L. Stearns award U. Colo., 1973; Nat. Medal Sci., 1977; Waterford Bio-Med. award Scripps Clinic and Research Found., 1979. Mem. Am. Soc. Zoologists, Am. Assn. Anatomists, Harvey Soc., Electron Microscope Soc. Am. (pres. 1962-63, award 1975), Tissue Culture Assn. (1st pres. 1946, pres. 1978-80), Am. Soc. Cell Biology (1st pres. 1961, pres. 1977-78), Am. Acad. Arts and Scis., Internat. Inst. Embryology, Internat. Soc. for Cell Biology, Am. Assn. Pathologists and Bacteriologists, Nat. Acad. Scis. (adv. com. on USSR and Eastern Europe 1962-65), Sigma Xi. Mng. editor Jour. Biophys. and Biochem. Cytology (now Jour. Cell Biology), 1955-64; co-editor Protoplasma, 1964—; cons. editor McGraw-Hill Ency. Sci. and Tech., 1960-76. Office: Molecular Cellular and Developmental Biology Dept U Colo Boulder CO 80309

PORTER, PAUL BERGGREN, educator; b. Morrill, Nebr., Oct. 7, 1917; s. David A. and Signa M. (Berggren) P.; B.A., U. Wyo., 1941; M.A., Stanford, 1947, Ph.D., 1950; m. Jean Norman, Aug. 19, 1943; children—Paul Henry, James Norman. Mem. faculty U. Utah, 1950—, prof. psychology, 1962—, head dept., 1962-65. Served AUS, 1941-45. Mem. Am., Western, Rocky Mountain (pres. 1960-61), Utah psychol. assns., N.Y. Acad. Scis., AAAS, Phi Beta Kappa, Sigma Xi, Phi Kappa Phi. Contbr. papers in field. Home: 1571 Michigan Ave Salt Lake City UT 84105

PORTER, PHILIP WAYLAND, educator; b. Hanover, N.H., July 9, 1928; s. Wayland Robinson and Bertha Maria (LaPlante) P.; A.B., Middlebury Coll., 1950; M.A., Syracuse U., 1955; Ph.D., U. London, 1957; m. Patricia Elizabeth Garrigus, Sept. 5, 1950; children—Janet Elizabeth, Sara Louise, Alice Catherine. Instr. geography U. Minn., Mpls., 1957-58, asst. prof., 1958-64, asso. prof., 1964-66, prof., 1966—, chmn. dept., 1969-71, asso. to v.p. acad. affairs, also dir. Office Internat. Programs, 1979—. Mem. geography panel Com. on Space Programs for Earth Observations, Nat. Acad. Scis., 1967-71. Served with AUS, 1952-54. Central Research Fund (London) grantee, 1955-56; NSF grantee 1961-62, 78-80; Social Sci. Research Council grantee, 1966-67; Rockefeller Found. grantee, 1969, 71-73. Mem. Assn. Am. Geographers, Am. Geog. Soc., Pierce County (Wis.) Geog. Soc., African Studies Assn., Am. Soc. Photogrammetry, Am. Congress Surveying and Mapping. Contbr. articles, monographs to profl. lit. Home: 86 Arthur Ave SE Minneapolis MN 55414 Office: Office Internat Programs U Minn Minneapolis MN 55455

PORTER, RICHARD FRANCIS, chemist; b. Fargo, N.D., Feb. 8, 1928; s. Richard C. and Alice (Gillies) P.; student N.D. State U., 1945-46; B.S., Marquette U., 1951; Ph.D., U. Calif. at Berkeley, 1954; m. Dolores L. Bolger, Sept. 1, 1955; children-Patricia, Thomas. Research asso. dept. physics U. Chgo., 1954- 55; faculty Cornell U., Ithaca, N.Y., 1955—, prof. dept. chemistry, 1964—; vis. prof. U. Fla., 1964; vis. collaborator Brookhaven Nat. Lab., 1978. Served with AUS, 1946-47. Alfred P. Sloan fellow, 1960-64; John Simon Guggenheim fellow, 1964; NATO sr. postdoctoral fellow U. Freiburg (Germany), 1970. Mem. Am. Chem. Soc., N.Y. Acad. Scis., Sigma Xi. Contbr. articles profl. jours. Home: 142 N Sunset Dr Ithaca NY 14850

PORTER, RICHARD WILLIAM, elec. engr.; b. Salina, Kan., Mar. 24, 1913; s. Thomas F. and Dora Mimi (Schermerhorn) P.; B.S., U. Kan., 1934; Ph. D., Yale, 1937, Sc.D. (hon.), 1947; m. Edith Wharton Kelly, Oct. 5, 1946; children—Susan Jane, Mary Elizabeth, Thomas Andrew. With Gen. Electric Co., 1937-76, successively student engr., supr. advanced course in engring., supr. aircraft equipment devel., project engr. Hermes Missile, mgr. engring. guided missiles, 1937-52, gen. mgr. guided missiles dept., 1952-55; cons. communication and control Engring. Services, 1955-60, cons. adv. devel., 1960-63, cons. aerospace sci. and tech., 1963-70, mgr. sci. and tech. affairs, aerospace group, 1970-76; independent cons., 1976—. Chmn. tech. evaluation group Research and Devel. Bd., Dept. Def., 1947-49; sci. adv. bd. USAF, 1950-51, 60-75, 76-78; chmn. tech. panel on earth satellite program IGY, 1956-58, dir. Am. Scientific satellite projects; chmn. internat. relations com., space sci. bd. Nat. Acad. Scis., 1959-70; v.p. com. space research Internat. Council Sci. Unions, 1959-71; mem. Nat. Council Scholars, 1968-72; mem. A.I.B.S. Planetary Quarantine Adv. Com., 1970-75; mem. Sci. and Tech. Adv. Council to Mayor N.Y.C., 1966-72. Recipient outstanding young engr. award Eta Kappa Nu, 1944, Charles A. Coffin award Gen. Electric Co., 1946, alumni award U. Kans., 1950, Exceptional Civilian Service award USAF, 1975. Fellow Am. Inst. Aeros. and Astronautics; mem. Am. Soc. Engring. Edn., IEEE (sr. mem.), Am. Geophys. Union, A.A.A.S., N.Y. Acad. Scis. Home: 164 Cat Rock Rd Cos Cob CT 06807 Office: PO Box 28 Riverside CT 06878

PORTER, ROBERT CHAMBERLAIN, lawyer, investment adv.; b. Pitts., Feb. 13, 1912; s. Horace C. and Helen (Dana) P.; A.B., Bowdoin Coll., 1934; LL.B., U. Pa., 1939; m. Elizabeth Pattison Watkins, Feb. 28, 1941; children—Robert Chamberlain, Marion Dana. With Bankers Trust Co., N.Y.C., 1934-36; admitted to N.Y. bar, 1939; asso. Cravath, Swaine & Moore, 1939-42, 1945-50; v.p. Chem. Bank & Trust Co., N.Y.C., 1950-51; sec., counsel, dir. Pfizer Inc., Bklyn., 1951-56; gen. partner Eberstadt & Co., 1956-62, Shearson, Hammill & Co., 1962-65, F. Eberstadt & Co., 1965-69; pres. F. Eberstadt & Co., Inc., 1969-77, chmn., 1977-78, also dir.; chmn. Eberstadt Asset Mgmt., Inc., 1979—; chmn., dir. Chem. Fund, Inc., Surveyor Fund; dir. Marsh & McLennan Mgmt. Co.; trustee Am. Savs. Bank. Bd. overseers Bowdoin Coll., 1975—; trustee Drew U., 1978—; bd. govs. Investment Co. Inst., 1976—. Served as lt. comdr. USNR, 1942-45. Mem. Am. Bar Assn. Clubs: University, Baltusrol Golf, Lost Tree Golf, Recess, Bond, Economic (N.Y.). Home: 105 Whittredge Rd Summit NJ 07901 Office: 61 Broadway New York NY 10006

PORTER, ROBERT GEORGE, union ofcl.; b. East St. Louis, Ill., Aug. 11, 1927; s. Joseph and Lillian Pearl (Wells) P.; B.S., Washington U., St. Louis, 1953; m. Patricia Sue Penn, Aug. 23, 1952; children—Stephen, Paula, Rudolph. Tchr., East St. Louis Jr. High Sch., 1953-60; adminstrv. aide Am. Fedn. Tchrs., Washington, 1960-63, sec.-treas., 1963—; mem. exec. bd. Profl. Employee dept. AFL-CIO. Chmn. bd. St. John's Luth. Pre-Sch. Served with U.S. Army, 1945-47. Democrat. Lutheran. Home: 13511 Oriental St Rockville MD 20853 Office: 11 Dupont Circle Washington DC 20036

PORTER, ROBERT KEITH, business exec.; b. Medicine Hat, Alberta, Can., Mar. 7, 1918; s. Richard Earl and Clara (Bumgardner) P.; grad. U. B.C., 1942; m. Agnes Merle Turnbull, July 11, 1942; children—Lawrence, Robert, William Barbara. Salesman Lever Bros., Ltd., Vancouver, B.C., 1946, field supr., Toronto, 1946-47; advt. mgr. Pepsodent Co. Can., Toronto, 1947-48; gen. mgr. H.H. Ayer Can., Ltd., Montreal, 1948-50, pres. H.H. Ayer, N.Y.C., 1950-54; v.p., gen. mgr. Thomas J. Lipton, Ltd., Toronto, 1959-64, pres., 1964-78, chief exec. officer, 1964—, chmn., 1978—; chmn., dir. Dineen Constrn. Ltd.; dir. Thomas J. Lipton, Ltd., Lever Bros. Ltd. Mem. Bd. Trade (Toronto); dir. Tea Council Can., Canadian council Internat. C. of C. Hon. life mem. bd. trustees Canadian Hunger Found.; bd. dirs. Canadian Exec. Service Overseas. Mem. Tea and Coffee Assn. Can., Newcomen Soc. (mem. Canadian com.), Beta Theta Pi (pres. 1941-42), Sigma Tau Chi (pres. 1941-42). Clubs: Canadian (N.Y.C.); Rosedale Golf, Granite, Toronto (Toronto); Lyford Cay (New Providence, Bahamas). Home: 7 Valleyanna Dr Toronto ON M4N 1J7 Canada Office: 2180 Yonge St Toronto ON M4S 2C4 Canada

PORTER, ROBERT WILLIAM, U.S. dist. judge; b. Monmouth, Ill., Aug. 13, 1926; s. William Benson and Vieva Laurel (Drew) P.; A.B. cum laude, Monmouth Coll., 1949; J.D., U. Mich., 1952; m. Lois Virginia Freeman, July 4, 1956; children—Robert William, William Benson, John David. Admitted to Tex. bar, 1953; home office counsel Res. Life Ins. Co., Dallas, 1952-54; asso. and partner Thompson, Coe, Cousins, & Irons, Dallas, 1954-74; judge U.S. Dist. Ct., No. Dist. Tex., 1974—; spl. counsel County of Dallas, 1972-74; lectr. Robert A. Taft Inst. of Govt., U. Tex., Arlington, 1972-73. Vice chmn. bd. trustees Lamplighter Sch. Inc., 1967-74; councilman, Richardson, Tex., 1965-66, mayor pro tem., 1966, mayor, 1967; pres. Tex. Assn. Mayors, Councilmen and Commrs., 1965-66; pres. Greater County League of Municipalities, 1966-67; mem. exec. com. N. Central Tex. Council of Govts., 1966-67, 70-72, regional citizen rep., 1967-72; mem. Dallas County Election Bd., 1972-74; original conferee Goals for Dallas, chmn. neighboring communities com., mem. task force com., vice chmn. task force on transp. and communications, chmn. achievement com. for transp. and communications, 1965-74; mem. State Rep. Exec. Com., 1966-68, chmn. Task Force on Modernization of State and Local Govts., 1967; dep. state chmn. Rep. Party of Tex., 1969-71; Dallas County Rep. chmn., 1972-74; mem. adv. council S.W. Center Advanced Study, 1966-69. Served in USN, 1944-46; PTO. Mem. Richardson, Dallas bar assns., State Bar Tex., Am. Law Inst., Barristers Soc., Delta Theta Phi, Alpha Tau Omega. Presbyterian. Home: 3300 Beverly Drive Dallas TX 75205 Office: 1100 Commerce St Dallas TX 75242

PORTER, ROGER STEPHEN, educator; b. Windom, Minn., June 2, 1928; s. Sherman Clarence and Cora Ruth (Rogers) P.; B.S. in Chemistry, U. Calif., Los Angeles, 1950; Ph.D., U. Wash., 1956; m. Catharine Crow, Aug. 3, 1968; children—Margaret Davis, Stephen Cady; children by previous marriage—Laura Jean, Ruth Anne. Sr. research asso. Chevron Research Co., Richmond, Calif., 1956-66; prof., dept. polymer sci. and engring. U. Mass., Amherst, 1966—, head dept., 1966-76, asst. to pres. for research, 1979—; plastics cons. to maj. U.S. cos.; co-dir. NSF Materials Lab., 1972—; study group head U.S./USSR Commn. on Sci.; mem. Nat. Acad. Scis. coms., 1969—; mem. adv. panels NSF; mem. adv. bds. for various sci. jours.; lectr. Russian, Brazilian and Romanian acads. scis.; bd. dirs. Plastics Inst. Am., Gordon Research Confs. Recipient Polyolefins award Soc. Plastics Engring., 1977; also awards Polymer research. Fellow Am. Phys. Soc.; mem. Am. Chem Soc. (award in plastics 1979), Sigma Xi, Alpha Chi Sigma, Phi Gamma Delta. Editor: Polymer Engineering and Science; co-editor books. Home: 220 Rolling Ridge Rd Amherst MA 01002

PORTER, RUTHERFORD B., educator; b. Crawford County, Pa., June 17, 1909; s. Burchard H. and Anna (Anderson) P.; B.S., Allegheny Coll., Meadville, Pa., 1930; M.Ed., U. Pitts., 1934; Ed.D., Pa. State U., 1942; m. Grace Johnson, July 2, 1934; children—Susanne Porter Hoagland, Andrew C. Tchr., Union City (Pa.) Pub. Sch., 1930-34; guidance counselor Meadville Pub. Sch., 1935-39; supr. spl. edn. 3 counties, Huntingdon, Pa., 1939-44; dir. student personnel, chmn. psychology dept. Fairmont (W.Va.) State Coll., 1946-47; chmn psychology dept. No. Mich. U., Marquette, 1947-48; chmn. spl. edn. dept. Ind. State U., Terre Haute, 1948—; cons. in field, 1950—; pvt. practice psychology, 1975—. Dir., sec.-treas. Vigo County Adult and Child Guidance Clinic, 1959-68. Served with USNR, 1944-46. Recipient citation Merit, Ind. Rehab. Assn., 1962; Distinguished Service award Ind. Council Exceptional Children, 1966, Distinguished Service in Sch. Psychology award, div. sch. psychology Ind. Psychol. Assn., 1969; Gordon A. Barrows Meml. award for distinguished contbn. in psychology, 1974; award for outstanding contbn. in edn. for handicapped Ind. Council Adminstrs. Spl. Edn., 1976. Diplomate Am. Bd. Profl. Psychology. Mem. Am., Ind. (sec. treas. 1949-52, pres. 1952-54) psychol. assns., Nat. Rehab. Counseling Assn., Council Exceptional Children, Phi Delta Kappa. Author: (with others) American School Intelligence Tests, 1960; sr. author Handbook and Tests for Children's Personality Questionnaire, Inst. Personality and Ability Testing, 1959, 68, 79; also articles, chpt. in book. Contbr. numerous articles to profl. jours. Home: Rural Route 24 Box 60 Terre Haute IN 47802

PORTER, SYLVIA FIELD, writer; b. Patchogue, L.I., N.Y., June 18, 1913; d. Louis and Rose (Maisel) Feldman; B.A. magna cum laude, Hunter Coll., 1932; student Grad. Sch. Bus. Adminstrn., N.Y. U.; 14 hon. degrees; m. Reed R. Porter, 1931; m. 2d, G. Sumner Collins, 1943; 1 dau., Chris Sarah, 1 stepson, Sumner Campbell Collins; m. 3d, James F. Fox, 1979. Editor weekly news letter, Reporting on Governments; asso. N.Y. Post, 1935-77, N.Y. Daily News, 1978—; syndicated columnist Field Newspaper Syndicate; contbg. editor Ladies' Home Jour. Named one of Am.'s 25 Most Influential Women, World Almanac, 1977-79; Woman of the Decade, Ladies Home Jour., 1979. Mem. Phi Beta Kappa. Author: How to Make Money in Government Bonds; If War Comes to the American Home; How to Get More for Your Money; Sylvia Porter's Income Tax Guide (pub. annually 1960—); Sylvia Porter's Money Book-How to Earn It, Spend It, Save It, Invest It, Borrow It, and Use It to Better Your Life, 1975, paperback edit., 1976; Sylvia Porter's New Money Book for the 80's, 1979; co-author: (with J.K. Lasser) How to Live Within Your Income, Managing Your Money; bd. editors World Book Encyclopedia Yearbook, 1961-79. Home: 2 Fifth Ave New York NY 10011 Office: 30 E 42d St New York NY 10017

PORTER, THOMAS ARTHUR, univ. ofcl.; b. Eldora, Iowa, July 28, 1934; s. Clyde Andrew and Velma Amelia (Bryan) P.; B.A., Yale U., 1956; LL.B., U. Calif., at Berkeley, 1959; Ph.D., Harvard U., 1966; m. Judith Barry Monroe, Feb. 2, 1967. Admitted to Calif. bar, 1960; dep. county counsel Los Angeles County, 1960; asst. prof. polit. sci. Calif. State U. at Long Beach, 1963-65; asst. prof. polit. sci. U. Calif. at Berkeley, 1965-66; asst. to v.p. acad. affairs, U. Calif. State-Wide System, 1966-70; dean Sch. Arts and Scis., Central Conn. State Coll., New Britain, 1970-75; v.p. acad. affairs State U. N.Y. Coll. Arts and Scis., Plattsburgh, 1975-77; exec. officer acad. and student affairs Conn. State Coll. System, New Britain, 1978—. Woodrow Wilson fellow Harvard, 1960-61. Mem. State Bar Calif. Home: 22 Plymouth Rd West Hartford CT 06107

PORTER, VERNON L., hotel exec.; b. Visalia, Calif., Sept. 29, 1945; s. Vernon L. and Vera Mae (Janzen) P.; B.S., Calif. State U., Northridge, 1972; m. Christine Ann Morgan, Sept. 25, 1971; 1 son, Shawn Porter. Sales rep. Zellerbach Paper Co., Los Angeles, 1964-68; acct. Price Waterhouse, Los Angeles, 1972-77; v.p. Biltmore Hotel, Los Angeles, 1977—. Mem. Am. Inst. C.P.A.'s, Calif. Hotel and Motel Assn., Los Angeles Hdqrs. Assn., Can. Soc. Republican. Office: 515 S Olive St Los Angeles CA 90013

PORTER, WALTER ARTHUR, lawyer; b. Dayton, Ohio, June 6, 1924; s. Claude and Estella (Raymond) P.; B.S. in Engring., U. Cin., 1948, LL.B., 1949; m. Patricia Reeves Higdon, Dec. 3, 1947; children—Scott Paul, David Bryant. Admitted to Ohio bar, 1949; legal dep. Montgomery County Probate Ct., 1949-51; asst. pros. atty. Montgomery County, 1951-56; with Albert H. Scharrer, atty., Dayton, 1956-61; partner firm Smith & Schnacke, Dayton, 1962—. Served with inf. U.S. Army, 1943-45; ETO. Mem. Am., Ohio (pres. 1973-74), Dayton bar assns., Am. Coll. Trial Lawyers, Phi Alpha Delta, Omicron Delta Kappa. Democrat. Presbyterian. Mason. Home: 6050 Mad River Rd Dayton OH 45459 Office: Mead Tower Dayton OH 45402

PORTER, WILLIAM LYMAN, univ. dean; b. Poughkeepsie, N.Y., Feb. 19, 1934; s. William Quincy and Lois (Brown) P.; B.A., Yale U., 1955, M.Arch., 1957; Ph.D., Mass. Inst. Tech., 1969; m. Lynn Rogers Porter; children—Quayny Lyman, Zoe Lynn, Eve Lyman. Designer, job capt. Louis I. Kahn, architect, Phila., 1960-62; urban designer, asst. chief of design Ciudad Guayana project Joint Center for Urban Studies of Harvard and Mass. Inst. Tech., Caracas, Venezuela, 1962-64; Mellon fellow dept. urban studies and planning Mass. Inst. Tech., 1964-65; Samuel Stouffer fellow Joint Center for Urban Studies, Harvard and Mass. Inst. Tech., 1966-67; asst. prof. urban design, depts. architecture and urban studies and planning Mass. Inst. Tech., 1968-70, asso. prof. urban design, 1970-71, prof. architecture and urban planning, 1971—, dean Sch. Architecture and Planning, 1971—; cons. in field. Mem. Nat. Archtl. Accrediting Bd., 1978—, pres., 1979; mem. Mass. Designer Selection Bd., 1978-79, chmn., 1979; mem. steering com. Aga Khan Award for Architecture, 1977—. Served with U.S. Army, 1958-60. Mem. AIA, Boston Soc. Architects (dir. 1969-73, 77—), AAUP. Club: St. Botolph (Boston). Home: 34 Holden Ln Concord MA 01742 Office: Mass Inst Tech Sch Architecture and Planning Cambridge MA 02139

PORTERFIELD, JAMES H., pub. relations co. exec.; b. Willow Bend, W.Va., Sept. 21, 1910; s. Isaac L. and Roxie L. (Fisher) P.; B.A. in Journalism, W.Va. U., 1936; m. Irene Smith, Oct. 4, 1930; children—Christopher, Karen. Reporter, Morgantown (W.Va.) Post, 1936-37; city editor-mng. editor Morgantown Dominion-News, 1937; successively reporter, writer, state editor AP, Phila., 1937-43, writer-editor, N.Y.C., 1943-47; account exec., then v.p., account exec. Carl Byoir & Assos., Inc., N.Y.C., 1947-65, exec. v.p., 1965—, also dir. Mem. Pub. Relations Soc. Am. (chmn. counselors sect. 1977; citation meritorious service counselors sect. 1976, chmn.'s citation 1977). Episcopalian. Clubs: Pinnacle (N.Y.C.); Royal Palm Yacht (Ft. Myers). Author articles, detective stories. Home: 1405 Whiskey Creek Dr Fort Myers FL 33907 Office: 380 Madison Ave New York NY 10017

PORTERFIELD, NEIL HARRY, landscape architect, planner; b. Murrysville, Pa., Aug. 15, 1936; s. Phil Frank and Alvira Clare (Rea) P.; B.S. in Landscape Architecture, Pa. State U., 1964; M. Landscape Architecture, U. Pa., 1964; m. Sandra Jean Beswarick, Aug. 9, 1958; children—Eric Jon, Jennifer Jane, Garrett Andrew. Landscape architect Pitts. Dept. Parks and Recreation, 1958-59; land planner Neil H. Porterfield & Assos., Murrysville, 1961-64; dir. landscape architecture and planning Hellmuth, Obata & Kassabaum, Inc., St. Louis, 1964-70, prin., v.p., dir., 1977—; exec. v.p. HOK Assos., St. Louis, 1970-72, pres., 1972—; lectr. in field; prof. Washington U., 1979; chmn. Landscape Archtl. Accreditation Bd. Recipient honor award Married Student Housing, U. Mich., Am. Soc. Landscape Architects, 1969, Merit award Parkside Campus Study U. Wis. at Kenosha, Am. Soc. Landscape Architects, 1969, others. Mem. Am. Soc. Landscape Architects, Council of Edn. Presbyterian. Contbr. articles to profl. orgns., anthologies. Home: 920 Singlepath Ln Saint Louis MO 63122 Office: HOK Assos 100 N Broadway Saint Louis MO 63102

PORTERFIELD, WILLIAM WENDELL, educator; b. Winchester, Va., Aug. 24, 1936; s. Donald Kennedy and Adelyn (Miller) P.; B.S., U. N.C., 1957, Ph.D., 1962; M.S., Calif. Inst. Tech., 1960; m. Dorothy Elizabeth Dail, Aug. 24, 1957; children—Allan Kennedy, Douglas Hunter. Sr. research chemist Hercules, Inc., Cumberland, Md., 1962-64; asst. prof. chemistry Hampden-Sydney (Va.) Coll., 1964-65, asso. prof., 1965-68, prof. chemistry, 1968—, chmn. natural sci. div., 1973-77. Mem. Am. Chem. Soc., Chem Soc. (London, Eng.), Phi Beta Kappa, Sigma Xi. Author: Concepts of Chemistry, 1972. Contbr. articles to profl. jours. Home: Box 697 Hampden-Sydney VA 23943

PORTES, ALEJANDRO, educator; b. Havana, Cuba, Oct. 13, 1944; s. Helio B. and Eulalia (Cortada) P.; came to U.S., 1960, naturalized, 1968; student U. Havana, 1959, Cath. U. Argentina, 1963; B.A., Creighton U., 1965; M.A., U. Wis., 1967, Ph.D., 1970. Lectr., U. Wis., Madison, 1969-70; asst. prof. sociology U. Ill., Urbana, 1970-71; asso. prof. U. Tex., Austin, 1971-75, asso. dir. Inst. Latin Am. Studies, 1973-75; prof. Duke U., Durham, N.C., 1975—, dir. grad. tng. program in immigration and ethnicity studies, 1979—, chmn. Hispanic council, 1979—; past chmn. nat. dissertation fellowship com. for Latin Am. and Caribbean, Social Sci. Research Council; mem. social scis. tng. rev. com. NIMH, 1973—, project dir. The Recent Assimilation of Latin Am. Immigrants in U.S., 1973—; mem. rev. bd. Internat. Program Population, Smithsonian Inst., 1972-74; program advisor Ford Found., Brazil, 1976; mem. fellowship selection bd. Inter-Am. Found., 1979—. Council on Fgn. Relations internat. fellow, 1972-73. Mem. Am. Sociol. Assn., So. Sociol. Assn., Latin Am. Studies Assn. Author: Urban Latin America, 1976; Current Perspectives in Latin American Urban Research, 1976; editor spl. issue on Mexican immigration Internat. Migration Rev., 1978; asso. editor Am. Sociol. Rev., 1979—; contbr. articles to profl. jours. Home: 2322 Dawn Trail Durham NC 27712 Office: Dept Sociology Duke U Durham NC 27706

PORTFOLIO, ALMERINDO GERARD, ophthalmologist; b. Union City, N.J., May 10, 1923; s. Pasquale and Angela (Falasca) P.; B.A., St. Peters Coll., 1943; M.D., N.Y. U., 1947, M.S. in Ophthalmology, 1954; m. Claire Enright, Nov. 22, 1947; children—Deidre, Almerindo, Drew, Maura, Melissa. Intern, Kings County Hosp., Bklyn., 1947-49; resident in pathology Cleve. City Hosp., 1949-50, resident in ophthalmology N.Y. U.-Bellevue Hosp., N.Y.C., 1951-53; practice medicine specializing in ophthalmology, Ridgewood, N.J., 1956—; mem. staffs Valley Hosp., Ridgewood, N.J., Bellevue and Univ. hosps., N.Y.C.; clin. prof. ophthalmology N.Y. U. Served as capt., M.C., USMC, 1954-56. Diplomate Am. Bd. Ophthalmology. Fellow A.C.S.; mem. AMA, N.J. Acad. Ophthalmology, Am. Acad. Ophthalmology and Otolaryngology, N.J., Bergen County (N.J.) med. socs. Roman Catholic. Home: 330 Algonquin Rd Franklin Lakes NJ 07417 Office: 20 Wilsey Sq Ridgewood NJ 07450

PORTH, DONALD LESTER, mfg. co. exec.; b. Calamus, Iowa, Oct. 10, 1916; s. Yengel C. and Theresa C. (Pewe) P.; B.S. in Chem. Engring., Iowa State U., 1938; m. Vira L.; children by previous marriage—Donald Lester, Robert John, Patricia Anna Porth Reebie, Linda Jean. With Culligan Internat. Co., Northbrook, Ill., 1938—, exec. v.p., line officer internat. and staff mktg., research and devel. and product planning, 1968-77, pres., chief operating officer, 1977—; mem. N. Central regional export expansion council Dept. Commerce, 1969-73; mem. Ill. Mfg. Export Advisory Com., 1969—. Pres. North Shore area council Boy Scouts Am., 1953-55, Northbrook Civic Assn., 1942, Northbrook Fire Dept., 1941; mem. exec. com. Library Internat. Relations Chgo.; trustee Highland Park (Ill.) Hosp. Assn. Recipient Silver Beaver award Boys Scouts Am., 1957; D.L. Pettit award Water Conditioning Assn. Internat., 1968. Mem. Sales and Mktg. Execs. Internat., Internat. Trade Club Chgo. (past pres., dir.), Water Quality Assn. (bd. govs., Hall of Fame award 1979), Water Conditioning Found. (past pres., exec. com.), Water Quality Research Council (past pres.). Clubs: Execs. (Chgo.); Evanston (Ill.) Golf; Tucson Nat. Golf. Office: Culligan Internat Co 1 Culligan Pkwy Northbrook IL 60062*

PORTHOUSE, CYRIL ROUTLEDGE, business exec.; b. Ravenna, Ohio, Jan 1, 1911; s. David Routledge and Iva Belle (Moncrief) P.; B.Chem. Engring., Ohio State U., 1932, M.Sc., 1933; m. Roberta Elizabeth Diehl, Oct. 21, 1933; children—Dian (Mrs. William Kottinger III), John David, Roberta Ann (Mrs. J.J. Benich, Jr.), Jean Routledge (Mrs. J.L. Hunt). Joined Questor Juvenile Products Co. (formerly Pyramid Rubber Co.), Ravenna, 1937, pres., 1950-73, ret., 1973—; dir. Questor Corp., 1967—; chmn. bd., dir. Fred Arbogast Co., Inc., Akron, Ohio, 1952—; dir. Banc One, Ravenna, Carboline Corp. Pres., dir. Porthouse Found. Trustee emeritus Kent State U. Mem. Am. Chem. Soc., Akron Rubber Group, Ohio Engrs. Assn., Soc. Plastics Industry, Nat., Ohio mfrs. assns., Rubber Mfrs. Assn., Sigma Xi, Sigma Phi Epsilon, Phi Eta Sigma, Tau Beta Pi, Omicron Delta Kappa. Conglist. Club: Twin Lakes Country (Kent). Home: 1243 Lake Roger Dr Sugar Bush Knolls Kent OH 44240 Office: 313 W North St Akron OH 44303

PORTIER, WIM, banker; b. Kediri, Indonesia, Oct. 8, 1927; s. Hendrik Daniel and Louise (Wintersteyn) P.; student State Coll., Indonesia, 1945-47, Police Acad., Indonesia, 1948-49; B.S., Bentley Coll. Accounting and Finance, 1968; m. Elisabeth Jansen, Feb. 25, 1953; children—Gerard E.H., George P., Sylvia, Robert William. Insp. of police, Indonesia; with Maclean, Watson & Co., Indonesia, Skandia Import, Indonesia, Amsterdam Police, The Netherlands, Dept. Pub. Works, The Netherlands; asst. v.p. Mut. Bank for Savs., Newton, Mass. Treas., Boy Scouts Am., 1967-69, Cub Scouts, 1970-73. Mem. Nat. Assn. Accountants Accountants. Home: 20 Charles River Rd Medway MA 02053 Office: 1188 Centre St Newton MA 02159

PORTIS, ALAN MARK, physicist, educator; b. Chgo., July 17, 1926; s. Lyon and Ruth (Libman) P.; Ph.B., U. Chgo., 1948; A.B., U. Calif., Berkeley, 1949, Ph.D., 1953; m. Beverly Aline Levin, Sept. 5, 1948; children—Jonathan Marc, Stephen Robert, Lori Ann, Frederick Sean. Mem. faculty, U. Pitts., 1953-56; mem. faculty U. Calif. Berkeley, 1956—, prof. physics, 1964—, asst. to chancellor for research, 1966-67, asso. dean grad. div., 1967-68, dir. Lawrence Hall Sci., 1969-72. Fulbright fellow, 1961, 67; Guggenheim fellow, 1965. Fellow Am. Phys. Soc., AAAS; mem. Am. Assn. Physics Tchrs. (Robert Andrews Millikan award 1966), Sigma Xi. Contbg. author: Berkeley Physics Laboratory, 1964, 65, 66, 71; author: Electromagnetic Fields/Sources and Media, 1978. Home: 2723 Marin Ave Berkeley CA 94708

PORTMAN, JOHN CALVIN, JR., architect, developer; b. Walhalla, S.C., Dec. 4, 1924; s. John Calvin and Edna (Rochester) P.; midshipman U.S. Naval Acad., 1944; B.S. in Architecture, Ga. Inst. Tech., 1950; m. Joan Newton, Dec. 23, 1944; children—Michael Wayne, John Calvin III, Jae Phillip, Jeffrey Lin, Jana Lee, Jarel Penn. With Ketchum, Gina and Sharp, H.M. Heatly, Asso. Architects, N.Y.C. and Atlanta, 1945-49, Stevens & Wilkinson, Atlanta, 1950-53; individual practice, Atlanta, 1953-56; partner Edwards and Portman, Architects, Atlanta, 1956-68; prin. John Portman & Assos., 1968—, Portman Properties, Atlanta, 1971—; chmn. Atlanta Mdse. Mart. Dir. C & S Nat. Bank. Pres. Central Atlanta Progress, 1970-72; sponsor Atlanta Symphony; hon. consul Denmark. Mem. nat. adv. bd. Ga. Inst. Tech., trustee Atlanta Arts Alliance, Nat. Jewish Hosp. and Research Center; adv. bd. Agnes Scott Coll. Served with USNR, 1942-44. Decorated knight Royal Order Knights of Dannenburg (Denmark); officer Royal Order of the Crown (Belgium); recipient Ivan Allen award N. Ga. chpt. A.I.A., 1964, award excellence Am. Inst. Steel Constrn., 1973, Design in Steel award Am. Iron and Steel Inst., 1975, others; named Outstanding Young Man of Year, Ga. Jr. C. of C. 1959, Salesman of Year Sales and Mktg. Execs. Atlanta, 1968. Registered architect, Ga. Fellow A.I.A.; mem. Nat. Council Archtl. Registration Bds., Ga. Archtl. and Engring. Soc., Omicron Delta Kappa, Tau Sigma Delta Prin. works include: Peachtree Center, Atlanta, Embarcadero Center, San Francisco, Hyatt Regency O'Hare Hotel, Chgo., Atlanta Decorative Arts Center, Hyatt Regency Hotel, Atlanta, Blue Cross-Blue Shield Bldg., Chattanooga, Ft. Worth Nat. Bank Bldg. and Garage, Brussels Trade Mart, Dana Fine Arts Bldg. at Agnes Scott Coll. (Decatur), Kennedy Community Center and Middle Sch., Atlanta, Renaissance Center, Detroit, Los Angeles Bonaventure Hotel, Los Angeles, Peachtree Center Plaza Hotel, Atlanta. Co-author: The Architect as Developer. Office: 225 Peachtree St NE Room 1800 Atlanta GA 30303

PORTNOFF, COLLICE HENRY, educator; b. San Luis Obispo, Calif., Dec. 9, 1898; d. James H. and Kate E. (Wilson) Henry; A.B., U. Calif. at Berkeley, 1921, M.A., 1922; Ph.D., Stanford, 1927; Carter Meml. fellow, also fellow acad., Am. Acad. in Rome, 1927-30, M.A., 1930; m. George E. Portnoff, Aug. 16, 1931; 1 dau., Lisa (Mrs. James Crehan). Instr., Belmont (Calif.) Mil. Acad., 1922-23; teaching asst. Stanford, 1923-27; instr. Ariz. State Coll., Flagstaff, 1930-41; cryptanalyst U.S. Signal Corps, Washington, 1942; translator Allied Mil. Govt., Washington, 1942-43; prof. English, Ariz. State U., Tempe, 1945-69, prof. emeritus, 1969—, chmn. dept., acting head div. lang. and lit., 1957-58, chmn. English dept., 1957-64. Dir. pageant Miracle of the Roses, Scottsdale, Ariz., 1960, gen. chmn., 1961. Bd. dirs. Phoenix Chamber Music Soc., Valley Shakespeare Theatre. Recipient medal for achievement in drama Nat. Soc. Arts and Letters; Distinguished Tchr. award Ariz. State U. Alumni Assn. Mem. AAUP, Ariz. Coll. Assn., Soc. Gen. Semantics, Nat. Soc. Arts and Letters, Washington, Nat. Council Tchrs. English, Conf. Coll. Communication and Composition, Centro Studié E Scambi Internazionali, Bus. and Profl. Womens Club Tempe, Cath. Bus. Assn., Am. Translators Assn., Alumni Assn. Am. Acad. in Rome, Rocky Mountain Modern Lang. Assn. (pres. 1964), Pi Sigma, Sigma Delta Pi, Alpha Lambda Delta, Gamma Phi Beta, Phi Kappa Phi. Clubs: Faculty, Women's Faculty (Ariz. State U.); Dinner, Paradise Valley Country (Scottsdale). Author: (play, with Samuel R. Golding) Naked Came I, 1957. Ofcl. translator Gregorio and Maria Martinez Sierra, 1949—. Contbg. editor: The Ariz. Republic, Phoenix; co-translator The Cursillo Movement (from Spanish); columnist Scottsdale Daily Progress, 1978—. Home: 6310 Quail Run Rd Paradise Valley AZ 85253 Office: English Dept Ariz State U Tempe AZ 85281. *My constant faith in God, together with the cultural background acquired from my family and the outstanding educators I have had the good fortune to be associated with, the distinguished and loyal friends whose ideals I have had the good fortune to share, all these have contributed to whatever success I have achieved. And a bit of the luck of the Irish has helped also.*

PORTNOY, WILLIAM MANOS, educator; b. Chgo., Oct. 28, 1930; s. Joseph and Bella (Saltzman) P.; B.S., U. Ill., 1952, M.S., 1952; Ph.D., 1959; m. Alice Catherine Walker, Sept. 9, 1956; children—Catherine Ann, Michael Benjamin. Mem. tech. staff Hughes Aircraft Co., Newport Beach, Calif., 1959-61, Tex. Instruments Inc., Dallas, 1961-67; mem. faculty Tex. Tech. U., Lubbock, 1967—, prof. biomed. engring., 1973, prof. elec. engring., 1972; adj. asso. prof. Baylor Coll. Medicine and Inst. Health Services research, Houston, 1969-73; resident cons. Hughes Research Labs., Malibu, Calif., 1972. Bd. dirs. Am. Heart Assn., Lubbock County, 1972-75. Nat. Heart Inst. postdoctoral trainee, 1969; NASA sr. postdoctoral resident research asso. Manned Spacecraft Center, Houston, 1968; Fulbright prof., 1975. Mem. IEEE (sr.), Am. Soc. Engring. Edn., Internat. Soc. Hybrid Microelectronics, Am. Phys. Assn. Sigma Xi. Contbr. articles to profl. jours.; patentee in field. Office: Dept Electrical Engring Tex Tech U Lubbock TX 79409

PORTOGHESE, PHILIP SALVATORE, educator; b. N.Y.C., June 4, 1931; s. Philip A. and Constance (Antonelli) P.; B.S., Columbia, 1953, M.S., 1958; PH.D., U. Wis., 1961; m. Christine L. Phillips, June 11, 1960; children—Stephen, Stuart, Philip. Asst. prof. Coll. Pharmacy, U. Minn., Mpls., 1961-64, asso. prof., 1964-69, prof. medicinal chemistry, 1969—, head dept., dir. grad. study in medicinal chemistry, 1974—; cons. NIMH. 1971-72; mem. med. chemistry B sect. NIH, 1972-76; mem. pharmacology, substance abuse and environ. toxicology interdisciplinary cluster President's Biomed. Research Panel, 1975. Served with U.S. Army, 1954-56. Fellow Acad. Pharm. Scis.; mem. Am. Pharm. Assn., Am. Chem. Soc., Am. Soc. Pharm. Exptl. Therapeutics, Internat. Union Pure and Applied Chemistry (commn. on medicinal chemistry 1978—), AAAS, Sigma Xi, Rho Chi, Phi Lambda Upsilon. Mem. editorial adv. bd. jour. Med. Chemistry, 1969-71, editor, 1972—; editorial adv. bd. Med. Chem. series, 1972—. Home: 2165 W Hoyt Ave Saint Paul MN 55108 Office: Coll Pharmacy U Minn Minneapolis MN 55455

PORTUGAL, DECOROSO M., steel trading co. exec.; b. Laredo, Tex., Oct. 18, 1925; s. Jose De Jesus and Dolores (Medina) P.; B.B.A., U. Houston, 1949; m. Florence R. Bradfield, Feb. 26, 1949; children—Dolores, Richard, Christopher, Phillip, Theresa, Mary, David. Passenger service rep. Pan Am. Airways, 1943-46; exec. v.p., dir. Crispin Co., Houston, 1950—; v.p. dir. Tube Central, Inc., Saddle Brook, N.J.; dir. Steel Sales & Service, Inc., Shreveport, La., Bd. dirs. Houston World Trade Club, 1972-74. Served with USAAF, 1944-45. Decorated Air medal with 2 oak leaf clusters, chevalier de L'Ordre de Leopold II. Chancellor of Consulate of Belgium, Houston, 1951-60. Roman Catholic. Clubs: Petroleum (Houston); Champions Golf. Home: 11910 Coblestone St Houston TX 77024 Office: 22 World Trade Center Houston TX 77002

PORZIO, RALPH, lawyer; b. Bklyn., Aug. 27, 1914; A.B., Drew U., 1938; J.D., Harvard, 1942. Admitted to N.J. bar, 1943; U.S. Supreme Ct.; sr. partner law firm Porzio & Bromberg, Morristown, 1962—. Counsel, bd. trustees Internat. Coll. Angiology; internat., nat. and local lectr., London, Copenhagen, Dublin, Rome, San Juan, Libson, Geneva, Montreal and U.S. Mem. Boonton Charter Commn., 1952-53, Bd. Edn., 1953-56. Trustee Drew U., N.J. Conservation Found., Holmes Library, Boonton. Recipient Freedoms Found. citation for writings advancing Am. way of life, 1951, Outstanding Achievements award in arts Drew U., 1956. Fellow Internat. Acad. Law and Sci. (pres., bd. regents), Internat. Soc. Barristers; mem. Am., N.J., Morris County (pres. 1970-71), Fed. bar assns., Am. Judicature Soc., N.Y. State, N.J. plaintiffs trial lawyers assns., Law-Sci. Acad. Am., Am. Coll. Legal Medicine, Am. Soc. Law and Medicine, Trial Attys. of N.J. (charter, ann. award for disting. service in cause of justice 1979), Assn. Trial Lawyers of Am., N.J. Assn. Sch. Attys. Club: Optimist (pres.) (Morristown). Author: The Transplant Age—Reflections on the Legal and Moral Aspects of Organ Transplants, 1969. Editor-in-chief Lex et Scientia, Internat. Jour. Law and Sci., asso. editor, 1969-75. Contbr. articles to profl. jours. Home: 123 Glover St Boonton NJ 07005 Office: 163 Madison Ave Morristown NJ 07960. *Learning is the beginning of living. When one stops learning, one may, at least for most purposes, be pronounced dead. Beyond the spiritual, this "brief candle" still casts some shadows of awareness: the need for compassion; the brevity of life; the fragility of man. And life's greatest reward is not to be loved but to be needed.*

POSER, ERNEST GEORGE, psychologist; b. Vienna, Austria, Mar. 2, 1921; s. Paul and Blanche (Furst) P.; came to Can., 1942, naturalized, 1946; B.A., Queen's U., Kingston, Ont., 1946, M.A., 1949; Ph.D., U. London, 1952; m. Maria Jutta Cahn, July 3, 1953; children—Yvonne, Carol, Michael. Asst. prof. U. N.B., 1946-48; chief psychologist N.B. Dept. Health, 1952-54; prof. psychology McGill U., Montreal, 1954—; asso. prof. psychiatry Faculty Medicine, 1963—; dir. behavior therapy unit Douglas Hosp. Center, Montreal, 1957—; hon. fellow Middlesex Hosp., London, 1964. Diplomate Am. Bd. Profl. Psychologists. Fellow Canadian Psychol. Assn.; mem. Am. Psychol. Assn., Que. Corp. Psychologists. Author: Adaptive Learning: Behavior Modification with Children, 1973; Behavior Therapy in Clinical Practice, 1977. Office: 1205 McGregor St Montreal PQ H3C 3G1 Canada

POSER, NORMAN STANLEY, stock exchange exec.; b. London, May 28, 1928; came to U.S., 1939, naturalized, 1946; s. Jack and Margaret (Salomon) P.; A.B. cum laude, Harvard U., 1948, LL.B. cum laude, 1958; m. Miriam Kugelman, Sept. 1, 1957 (div. 1979); children—Samuel Marc, Susan. Admitted to N.Y. bar, 1958; asso. firm Greenbaum, Wolf & Ernst, N.Y.C., 1958-61; atty. SEC, Washington, 1961-64, asst. dir. div. trading and markets, 1964-67; asso. firm Rosenman, Colin, Kaye, Petschek, Freund & Emil, N.Y.C., 1967-68; v.p. Am. Stock Exchange, N.Y.C., 1968-72, sr. v.p., 1972-75, exec. v.p., 1975—; adj. prof. law N.Y. U., 1975—; cons. in field. Served with U.S. Army, 1951-53. Mem. N.Y. County Lawyers Assn., Am. Bar Assn., N.Y.C. Bar Assn. Clubs: Harvard (N.Y.C.);

Dunes Racquet (East Hampton, N.Y.). Mem. adv. bd. BNA Securities Regulation & Law Report, 1979—, Rev. Securities Regulation, 1975—. Office: 86 Trinity Pl New York NY 10006

POSERT, HARVEY PERES, inst. exec., pub. relations counselor; b. Memphis, May 29, 1930; s. Hardwig Peres and Natlee (Isenberg) P.; B.A., Yale, 1951; m. Myra Gail Gainsboro, June 28, 1958; children—Harvey Peres III, Robert Lee, Peter David. Reporter, Comml. Appeal, Memphis, 1950-54; with Daniel J. Edelman, Inc., Chgo., N.Y.C., San Francisco, 1955-58, 61-75; pres. Harvey Posert & Assos., Memphis, 1958-61; exec. v.p. Edelman of Cal., San Francisco, 1961-75; pub. relations dir. Wine Inst.; pres. Reading Records Inc.; dir. Fin. Resources, Inc.; asso. prof. mktg. San Francisco State Coll., 1968-69. Vice pres. Memphis Cotton Carnival, 1961. Served with CIC, U.S. Army, 1951-54. Mem. Pub. Relations Soc. Am. (pres. Midsouth chpt. 1961), Pub. Relations Round Table. Contbr. articles to profl. jours. Home: 48 Lagoon St Belvedere CA 94920 Office: 165 Post St San Francisco CA 94108

POSES, JACK I., perfume co. exec.; b. Russia, Dec. 28, 1899; s. Moses and Selma (Rivin) P.; came to U.S., 1911, naturalized, 1928; B.C.S., N.Y. U., 1923, M.B.A., 1924; L.L.D., Brandeis U., 1968; D.H.L., City U. N.Y., 1976; m. Lillian L. Shapiro, Aug. 27, 1930; 1 dau., Barbara Joan (Mrs. Ernest Kafka). Pres. Jack I. Poses Assos.; pres. Zanadu Mfg. Corp. N.Y.C., 1932—, Condon Products Corp., N.Y.C., 1952—. Vice chmn. Bd. Higher Edn. N.Y.C., 1963-74; mem. Citizens Adv. Com. FDA, 1962; chmn. industry drives United Jewish Appeal, 1943—. Trustee, treas. N.Y. Studio Sch. Drawing, Painting and Sculpture; trustee Brandeis U., also chmn. investment com., mem. edn. and budget coms., chmn. constrn. fund City U. N.Y., chmn. Council Fine Arts and founder Poses Inst. Fine Arts at univ.; bd. dirs. Fragrance Found.; bd. govs. Joint Def. Appeal; founder Einstein Med. Sch.; mem., contbr. to Detroit Inst. Art, Mus. Modern Art, Guggenheim Mus., Whitney Mus.; life fellow, contbr. Met. Mus. Art; established scholarships and/or fellowships at Harvard, Yale Law Sch., Radcliffe Coll., Bryn Mawr Coll., Brandeis U.; mem. N.Y.C. Bd. Correction, 1978—, Dormitory Authority, 1979. Decorated chevalier Legion of Honor (France); recipient Madden award N.Y. U., 1970; Pres.'s medal City U. N.Y. grad. div., 1970. Mem. Toilet Goods Mfrs. Assn. (v.p., dir.), Perfume Importers Assn., Quill Soc. Clubs: Harmony (N.Y.C.); Birchwood Country (past pres.) (Westport, Conn.). Home: 1107 Fifth Ave New York City NY 10028 also Colyetown Rd Westport CT 06880 Office: 400 Madison Ave New York City NY 10017

POSEY, ELDON EUGENE, educator; b. Oneida, Tenn., Jan. 25, 1921; s. Daniel M. and Eva (Owens) P.; B.S., East Tenn. State U., 1947; M.A., U. Tenn., 1949, Ph.D., 1954; m. Christine K. Johnson, Dec. 25, 1943; children—Margaret (Mrs. Robert Snider), Daniel Marion. Instr. W.Va. U., 1954-55, asst. prof., 1955-59; asso. prof. Va. Poly. Inst., 1959-61, prof., 1961-64; prof., head dept. math. U. N.C., 1964—. Served to capt. USAAF, 1941-46. Decorated Air medal with 18 oak leaf clusters, D.F.C., Silver Star, Purple Heart. Mem. Am. Math. Soc., Math. Assn. Am., Sigma Xi, Pi Mu Epsilon. Home: 4311 Dogwood Dr Greensboro NC 27410

POSEY, ROLLIN BENNETT, ret. educator; b. Mankato, Minn., June 10, 1907; s. Chesley Justin and Maude (Johnston) P.; A.B., U. Kan., 1927; M.B.A. with distinction, Harvard, 1930; Ph.D., U. Pa., 1942; m. Elizabeth Sylvester Dykstra, Dec. 24, 1931; children—Stephen Dykstra, Jonathan, Robert. Asst. dir. Cin. Bur. Govt. Research, 1933-34; dir. Dept. Municipal Research, City of Hartford, 1934-35; cons. U.S. Bur. of Budget, 1936, J.L. Jacobs & Co., 1936-37; research asso. Inst. Local and State Govt., U. Pa., 1937-40; exec. sec. Phila. Charter Commn., 1937-38; dir. Pub. Service Inst. Pa., 1938-39; asst. to dean faculties Northwestern U., 1940-42, dir. summer session, 1942-43, dir. Civil Affairs Tng. Sch., 1943-45, asso. prof. polit. sci., 1940-47, prof., 1947-57, lectr., 1957-62, dean Univ. Coll., 1943-48, chmn. dept. polit. sci., 1948-53; editor coll. publs. Row, Peterson & Co., Evanston, Ill., 1955-62, v.p., 1961-62; editor Harper & Row, N.Y.C., 1962-65; chmn. social scis. New Coll., 1965-67; dean Sch. Profl. Studies, U. Wis. at Green Bay, 1968-72, prof. and dean emeritus, 1972—. Mem. Chgo. Crime Commn., 1948-62; pres. Sarasota Civic League, 1975-77. Mem. Am. Polit. Sci. Assn., Alpha Sigma Lambda (founder 1946, nat. chmn. 1947-53). Episcopalian. Clubs: Ivy League (pres. 1978—); Bird Key Yacht. Author: American Government, 1977; The Illinois Constitution, 1977; The Voter's Handbook, 1973. Bd. editors Jour. Criminal Law and Criminology, 1944-64. Contbr. articles to profl. jours. Home: 217 Bird Key Sarasota FL 33577

POSIN, DANIEL Q., educator, TV lectr.; b. Turkestan, Aug. 13, 1909; s. Abram and Anna (Izritz) P.; came to U.S., 1918, naturalized, 1927; A.B., U. Cal., 1932, A.M., 1934, Ph.D., 1935; m. Frances Schweitzer, 1934; children—Dan, Kathryn. Instr. U. Cal., 1932-37; prof. U. Panama, 1937-41; dean natural scis. U. Mont., prof., 1941-44, chmn. dept. physics and math., 1942-44; staff Mass. Inst. Tech., 1944-46; prof. physics, chmn. dept. N.D. State Coll., Fargo, 1946-55; prof. dept. physics DePaul U., 1956-67; prof. phys. sci. dept., Cal. State U., San Francisco, 1967—, chmn. dept. interdisciplinary scis., 1969—; appearances CBS Radio-TV, WTTW-WGN-TV, 1956-67, NET; ABC TV series Dr. Posin's Universe; dir. Schwab Sci. Lecture Series, Atoms for Peace exhibit Mus. Sci. and Industry, Chgo. Chief cons. Borg Warner Sci. Hall and Allied Chem. Sci. Hall, Times Square; scientific cons. CBS-TV; chmn. edn. com. Chgo. Heart Assn., 1963-67. Trustee Leukemia Soc. Recipient 6 Emmy awards for best educator on TV in Chgo., and best ednl. TV programs; James T. Grady award Am. Chem. Soc., 1972. Fellow Am. Phys. Soc.; mem. A.A.A.S., Phi Beta Kappa, Sigma Xi. Author: Fisica, Fisica Experimental, Trigonometria, 1937-41; Mendeleyev—The Story of a Great Scientist, 1948; I Have Been to the Village, 1948, rev. edit., 1974; Out of This World, 1959; What is a Star, 1961; What is Chemistry, 1961; What is a Dinosaur, 1961; The Marvels of Physics, 1961; Find Out, 1961; Chemistry for the Space Age, 1961; Experiments and Exercises in Chemistry, 1961; What is Matter, 1962; What is Electronic Communication, 1962; What is Energy; Dr. Posin's Giants, 1962; Life Beyond our Planet, 1962; Man and the Sea, 1962; Man and the Earth, 1962; Man and the Jungle, 1962; Man and the Desert, 1962; Science in the Age of Space, 1965; Rockets and Satellites; Our Solar System; 20th Century Physical Science; College Physics; The Next Billion Years, 1973. Contbr. to Phys. Rev., Chemtech, Today's Health; sci. cons. World Book Ency., Ency. Brit., Jr., Compton's Yearbook. Contbr. feature articles Chgo. Tribune. Home: 726 Crestview Dr Millbrae CA 94030 Office: California State Univ San Francisco CA 94132

POSIN, KATHRYN OLIVE, choreographer, dancer; b. Butte, Mont., Mar. 23, 1945; d. Daniel Q. and Frances (Schweitzer) P.; B.A. in Dance, Bennington (Vt.) Coll., 1966. Dancer with cos. of Anna Sokolow, Valerie Bettis, Lotte Goslar, Dance Theatre Workshop, Am. Dancer Theatre, 1967-72; artistic dir. Kathryn Posin Dance Co., 1972—; prin. works for co. include Days, Bach Pieces, Nuclear Energy I and II, Waves, Light Years, Soft Storm, Windowsill; choreographer rock mus. Salvation, 1970, The Cherry Orchard, 1977; guest choreographer Ballet West, 1978, Nederlans Dance Theatre, 1978; mem. faculty U. Colo., Boulder, 1967, Am. U., 1968, U. Wis., Milw., 1968, Princeton U., 1970-72, Etudes et Rencontres Artistique, Geneva, 1973, Harvard U., summers 1974-75, Conn. Coll., 1976, Washington U., St. Louis, 1977. Grantee Bennington Coll., 1967, Jerome Robbins Found., 1972, N.Y. State Council Arts, 1971-77, Nat. Endowment Arts, 1973-75, 77; Doris Humphrey fellow, 1967; Guggenheim fellow, 1977-78. Mem. AFTRA, Am. Guild Mus. Artists, Actors Equity, Soc. Stage Dirs. and Choreographers. Home: 20 Bond St New York NY 10012 Office: 130 W 56 St New York NY 10019

POSNER, AARON SIDNEY, scientist, educator; b. Newark, Nov. 10, 1920; s. Benjamin and Ida Helen (Falbaum) P.; B.S. in Chemistry, Rutgers U., 1941; M.S. in Chemistry, Poly. Inst. Bklyn., 1949; Ph.D. in Phys. Chemistry, U. Liege, 1954; m. Rita Sylvia Nussbaum, Nov. 1, 1944; children—Jane Sarah, Nancy Ann. Research crystal chemist Squier Signal Lab., Ft. Monmouth, N.J., 1948-50; research chemist Am. Dental Assn. Research div. Nat. Bur. Standards, 1950-61; chief crystal chemistry sect. Nat. Inst. Dental Research NIH, Bethesda, Md., 1961-63; asso. dir. research Hosp. for Spl. Surgery, N.Y.C., 1963—; prof. biochemistry Cornell U. Med. Coll., 1963—; cons. in field. Served to 1st lt. USAAF, 1942-46. Named Claude Bernard Guest prof. U. Montreal (Can.), 1962. Recipient Kappa Delta award Am. Acad. Orthopaedic Surgeons, 1977; Basic Research in Biol. Mineralization award, 1978. Mem. Am. Chem. Soc., Am. Crystallographic Assn., Biophys. Soc., Internat. Assn. Dental Research (mineralized tissue group, sci. award 1978), Am. Dental Assn., N.Y. Acad. Scis. (chmn. biophysics sect. 1969-71), AAAS, Am. Inst. Biol. Scis., Fedn. Am. Scientists, Soc. Exptl. Biology and Medicine, Orthopedic Research Soc., Am. Soc. Biol. Chemists, Am. Soc. Bone and Mineral Research, AAUP. Contbr. articles, chpts. profl. jours., sci. books; editorial bd. Calcified Tissue Internat., Clin. Orthopedics and Related Research, Biol. Abstracts. Home: 2 Longview Dr Scarsdale NY 10583 Office: 535 E 70th St New York NY 10021

POSNER, ADOLPH, ophthalmologist; b. Poland, Mar. 19, 1906; s. Joseph and Elsie (Friedman) P.; brought to U.S., 1920, naturalized, 1926; B.S., Coll. City N.Y., 1926; M.D., N.Y. U., 1930; m. Edna Olian, Mar. 16, 1941 (dec. Aug. 1968); children—Ellen Dana (Mrs. Richard M. Romano) and George Jeremy; m. 2d, Florence Helfant, June 18, 1970. Intern Lebanon Hosp., 1930-32; practice of medicine, N.Y.C., 1932—, specializing ophthalmology, 1933—; attending surgeon Manhattan Eye Ear and Throat Hosp., N.Y.C., dir. Glaucoma clinic, 1951—; attending opthalmologist Montefiore Hosp., 1950—; attending ophthalmologist Bronx Municipal Hosp. Center; prof. Albert Einstein Med. Coll., Yeshiva U., cons. Health Ins. Plan N.Y., Mem. med. adv. bd. N.Y. State Commn. for Blind; mem. Com. for Standardization of Tonometers; founder, dir. Inst. Glaucoma Research. Served as capt. AUS, World War II. Recipient Schoenberg Meml. award for research in glaucoma, 1951; Lucien Howe prize N.Y. State. Diplomate Am. Bd. Opthalmology. Fellow Am. Acad. Ophthalmology and Otolaryngology, N.Y. Acad. Medicine, Am. Coll. Surgeons, Soc. Eye Surgeons; mem. A.M.A., N.Y. Soc. Clin. Ophthalmology (pres. 1951), Pan-Am. Ophthal. Soc., Soc. for Research in Ophthalmology, French Ophthal. Soc. (hon.), Manhattan Ophthal. Soc. (cofounder, past pres.). Co-author: Slit Lamp Gonioscopy. Editor, translator; Slit Lamp Examinations of fundus and vitreous. Author articles med. journals. Contributing editor: Eye, Ear, Nose and Throat Monthly. Co-discoverer Posner-Schlossman Syndrome. Home: 425 E 51st St New York City NY 10022 Office: 667 Madison Ave New York City NY 10021. *A sense of humor, or the ability to laugh at oneself, makes our lives more enjoyable and helps those who come in contact with us derive more pleasure from theirs.*

POSNER, DONALD, art historian; b. N.Y.C., Aug. 30, 1931; s. Murray and Frances (Teitel) P.; A.B., Queens Coll., 1956; M.A., Harvard U., 1957; Ph.D., N.Y. U., 1962; m. Leslie Marion Jones, Jan. 16, 1976; 1 dau., Anne Tyre. Lectr., Queens Coll., 1957; asst. prof. art history Columbia U., 1961-62; mem. faculty Inst. Fine Arts, N.Y. U., 1962—, Ailsa Mellon Bruce prof. fine arts, 1975—, acting dir. Inst. Fine Arts, 1978-79; Robert Sterling Clark prof. Williams Coll., 1973; William R. Kenan, Jr. prof. U. Va., 1976-77. Served with USAF, 1951-55. Am. Acad. in Rome fellow, 1959-61; Inst. for Advanced Study fellow, 1976; recipient Charles Rufus Morey award, 1972. Mem. Coll. Art Assn. Am. (dir. 1970-74), Am. Soc. 18th Century Studies, Société Francaise d'Etude du XVIII siécle, Renaissance Soc. Am. Author: Annibale Carracci, 1971; Watteau: A Lady at Her Toilet, 1973; (with J. Held) Seventeenth and Eighteenth Century Art, 1971. Office: 1 E 78th St New York NY 10021

POSNER, HARRY A., JR., research inst. exec.; b. Watsonville, Calif., Oct. 10, 1931; s. Harry A. and Lucy G. (Nash) P.; B.S.E.E. magna cum laude, U. So. Calif., 1958; M.S.E.E., N.Mex. State U., 1960; m. Betty L. Siverson, Aug. 24, 1955; children—Cheryl Ann, Harry A. III, Randall L. Supr. advanced system design group Bell Telephone Labs., Whippany, N.J., 1958-66; dir. phys. chemistry lab. Phys. Sci. Lab., N.Mex. State U., 1966-68; dir. systems research Stanford Research Inst., Menlo Park, Calif., 1968-74; pres. Inst. Paper Chemistry, Appleton, Wis., 1974—. Served with USN, 1950-54. Home: 2425 W Prospect Ave Appleton WI 54911 Office: 1043 E South River St Appleton WI 54911

POSNER, JAMES, retail cons.; b. N.Y.C., Jan. 25, 1927; s. Alex J. and Elizabeth (Schattman) P.; student Purdue U., 1943; B.S. in Bus. Adminstrn., Ind. U., 1948; m. Joan Darter, Oct. 19, 1952; children—Carol Lynn, Ronni Jo. Asso. with Asso. Mdse. Co., 1948-53, Bambergers, Newark, R.H. Macy, N.Y.C., 1953-58; asst. to v.p. Allied Stores Corp., N.Y., 1959-63; pres. Fashion of Columbus (Ohio), 1963-65; pres. Dey Bros. & Co., Syracuse, N.Y., 1965-70; pres. Bond Stores, Inc., N.Y.C., 1970-72; pres. James Posner Assos. Ltd., N.Y.C., retail cons., 1972—; dir. Unity Mut. Life Ins. Co., 1969-74, Syracuse Transit Corp., 1968-70, N.Y. Bd. Trade, 1979—; chmn. bd. WCNY-TV, 1970; pres. Market Monitor, 1977. Chmn. bd. Syracuse Credit Bur., 1968-70; bd. dirs. YMCA Syracuse and Onondaga County, Met. Devel. Assn., Cultural Resources Council; trustee Everson Mus., 1968-70. Served with USNR, 1944-46. Mem. Mchts. Assn. (dir.), Syracuse C. of C. (exec. com., v.p. 1968-70). Home: 66 Indian Rock Rd Stamford CT 06903 Office: 30 Park Ave New York NY 10016. *Set your goals for personal or business achievements, then rationally plan to reach that goal, adjust the plan to new conditions, react to setbacks with greater resolve, keep thinking, thinking, and thinking. Believe if anyone can achieve these goals, you can.*

POSNER, JAMES STUART, mfg. co. exec.; b. N.Y.C., Jan. 7, 1937; s. Lewis Bernard and Valeria (Shapiro) P.; B.A., Washington and Jefferson Coll., 1958; J.D., St. John's U., Bklyn., 1961; m. Renee C. Bruckenthal, Nov. 24, 1965 (dec.); children—Jennifer Elizabeth, David Braden. Admitted to N.Y. bar, 1961; pvt. practice, N.Y.C., 1961-66; asso. gen. atty. U.S. Trucking Corp., N.Y.C., 1966-67; sr. staff atty. Bristol-Myers Co., N.Y.C., 1967-73, counsel, 1973-74, 77-78, sec., 1975-77, 79—. Mem. N.Y. State Bar Assn., N.Y. County Lawyers Assn., Assn. Bar City N.Y., Am. Soc. Corp. Secs. Club: Board Room (N.Y.C.). Home: 2500-G Johnson Ave Riverdale NY 10463 Office: 345 Park Ave New York NY 10022

POSNER, MICHAEL LOUIS, newspaperman; b. Providence, Jan. 15, 1932; s. Eli and Minnie (Jacobson) P.; student U. Maine, 1949-51; B.S., Boston U., 1953; m. C. Andrea Mattson, June 21, 1964. Mem. staff U.P.I., 1956-72, Reuters, 1972—; Congl. corr., Washington, 1959—; free-lance writer, 1953—; radio and TV panelist. Former officer Environ. Communications Corp. Served with inf. AUS, 1953-55. Mem. Newspaper Guild, Wire Service Guild (nat. committeeman), Standing Com. Washington Corrs. (chmn. 1979), White House Corr. Assn., Tau Epsilon Phi. Club: Nat. Press (gov.) (Washington). Home: 3500 36th St NW Washington DC 20016 also 6 Grasmere Rd Portland ME 04101 Office: Nat Press Bldg Washington DC 20004

POSNER, ROY EDWARD, corp. exec.; b. Chgo., Aug. 24, 1933; s. Lew and Julia (Cvetan) P.; student U. Ill., 1951-53, Internat. Accountants Soc., 1956-59, Loyola U., Chgo., 1959; grad. Advanced Mgmt. Program, Harvard U., 1976; m. Donna Lea Williams, June 9, 1956; children—Karen Lee, Sheryl Lynn. Public accountant Frank W. Dibble Co., Chgo., 1956-61; supr. Harris, Kerr, Forster & Co., C.P.A.'s, Chgo., 1961-66; with Loews Corp., N.Y.C., 1966—, v.p. fin. services, chief fin. officer, 1973—. Pres. No. Regional Valley High Sch. Music Parents Assn., 1978-79. Served with U.S. Army, 1953-55. C.P.A., Ill. Mem. Am. Inst. C.P.A.'s, Fin. Execs. Inst., Ins. Acctg. and Stats. Assn., Internat. Hospitality Accountants Assn., Am. Hotel and Motel Assn., Ill. Soc. C.P.A.'s, N.Y. State Soc. C.P.A.'s, Delta Tau Delta. Club: Alpine Country. Home: 273 Whitman St Haworth NJ 07641 Office: 666 Fifth Ave New York NY 10019

POSNER, SIDNEY, advt. exec.; b. Syracuse, N.Y., Jan. 14, 1924; s. Harry and Fannie (Hoffman) P.; B.S., Syracuse U., 1947; m. Miriam Frances Kaplowitz, June 8, 1952; children—Steven Charles, Peter Scott, Robert Keith. Pres. Newmark, Posner & Mitchell, Inc., N.Y.C., 1959—, Bus. Counselors Corp.; dir. Communicorp, Tech., Indsl. & Sci. Marketing, Inc., Domestic Sci. Found. Mem. Sale Execs. Club, Financial Writers Club. Alpha Delta Sigma, Alpha Kappa Psi. Home: 454 Broadway Cedarhurst NY 11516 Office: 300 E 42 St New York NY 10017

POSNER, VICTOR, industrialist; b. Balt., Sept. 18, 1918; s. Morris and Marry (Dopkin) P.; LL.D. (hon.), Norwich U., Vt., 1975; divorced; children—Steven and Gail Posner Cohen (twins), Tracy, Troy. Chmn. bd. Security Mgmt. Corp., 1951—; chmn. bd., pres., chief exec. officer NVF Co., 1966—, Sharon Steel Corp., 1969—, Pa. Engring. Corp., 1967—, Nat. Propane Corp., 1967—, Birdsboro Corp., 1968—, Southeastern Pub. Service Co., 1966—, Wilson Bros., 1967—. Founder, Mt. Sinai Hosp., Miami Beach, Fla., 1956. Office: DWG Corp 6917 Collins Ave Miami Beach FL 33141

POSNICK, ADOLPH, chem. co. exec.; b. Yellow Creek, Sask., Can., May 3, 1926; s. Frank and Joanne (Shimko) P.; came to U.S., 1947; B.S. in Ceramic Engring., U. Sask., 1947; m. Sarah Anne Briggs, May 16, 1947; children—Joann Elizabeth, Barbara Ellen. Research engr. Ferro Corp., Cleve., 1947-50; tech. dir. Ferro Enamel-Brazil, Sao Paulo, 1950-56, mng. dir., 1956-65, v.p. internat. ops. Ferro Corp., Cleve., 1965-74, sr. v.p. ops., 1974-75, exec. v.p., 1975-76, pres., chief exec. officer, 1976—; dir. fgn. subsidiaries. Mem. Am., Brazilian ceramic socs., Cleve. World Trade. Clubs: Clevelander, Mid Day, Chagrin Valley Country, Union, Pepper Pike Country. Office: Ferro Corp 1 Erieview Plaza Cleveland OH 44144*

POSPISIL, JOSEPH LAWRENCE, credit co. exec.; b. N.Y.C., June 4, 1929; s. Joseph Lawrence and Mary (O'Dowd) P.; student Fordham U., 1947-51; m. Helen Marie Koleda, Sept. 11, 1954; children—Mark, Michael, Lori. With Bank of Manhattan Co., N.Y.C., 1947-54; credit analyst Interchemical Corp., N.Y.C., 1954-55; asst. credit mgr. Fedders Corp., 1955-57; pres., dir. ITT Credit Corp., East Meadow, N.Y., 1957—; pres., dir. Kellogg Credit Corp., N.Y.C., ISE Finance Holdings S.A., Luxembourg; asst. treas. ITT. Served with AUS, 1951-54. Office: 1900 Hempstead Turnpike East Meadow NY 11554

POSPISIL, LEOPOLD JAROSLAV, educator; b. Olomouc, Czechoslovakia, Apr. 26, 1923; s. Leopold and Ludmila (Petrlak) P.; came to U.S., 1949, naturalized, 1954; J.U.C. in Law, Charles U., Prague, 1947; B.A. in Sociology, Willamette U., Salem, Oreg., 1950; M.A. in Anthropology, U. Oreg., 1952; Ph.D. (Ford Found, fellow, Sr. Sterling fellow), Yale, 1956; Sc.D. (hon.), Willamette U., 1969; m. Zdenka Smyd, Jan. 31, 1945; children—Zdenka, Mira. Instr., Yale, New Haven, 1956-57, asst. prof., 1957-60, asst. curator Peabody Mus., 1956-60, asso. prof., 1960-65, prof., curator, 1965—, dir. div. anthropology, 1966—. Guggenheim fellow, 1962, NSF fellow, 1962, 64-65, 1967-71, SSRC grantee, 1966, NIMH fellow, 1973-79. Mem. Am. Anthrop. Assn., N.Y. Acad. Scis., Czechoslovakian Acad. Arts and Scis. in Am. Author: Kapauku Papuans and Their Law, 1958; Kapauku Papuan Economy, 1963; Kapauku Papuans of West New Guinea, 1963; Anthropology of Law, 1971; Ethnology of Law, 1972. Contbr. articles to profl. jours. Home: 554 Orange St New Haven CT 06511

POSSIEL, NORMAN CHARLES, civil engr.; b. Newark, June 27, 1927; s. Philip Albert and Margaret (Veradi) P.; B.S., N.J. Inst. Tech., 1949; m. Pauline Lucille Pariso, Apr. 29, 1950; children—Norman Charles, Nancy Ann, Eileen Lucille. With Edwards & Kelcey, Inc., Newark, 1949—, now sr. v.p., treas., gen. mgr., dir.; dir. Wyer, Dick & Co., Edwards & Kelcey Internat. Inc., Transource, Inc. Registered profl. engr., N.Y., Conn. Fellow Am. Cons. Engrs. Council; mem. ASCE, Nat. Soc. Profl. Engrs., Cons. Engrs. Council of N.J. (past pres.), Adv. Com. for Civil and Environmental Engring., N.J. Inst. Tech. Home: 15 Hickory Pl Murray Hill NJ 07974 Office: 70 S Orange Ave Livingston NJ 07039

POST, ALLEN, lawyer; b. Newnan, Ga., Dec. 3, 1906; s. William Glenn and Rosa Kate (Muse) P.; A.B. summa cum laude, U. Ga., 1927; B.A., 1st honors, Oxford U. (Rhodes scholar), 1929, B.C.L., 2d honors, 1930, M.A., 1933; Ph.D.; m. Mary Chastaine Cook, Dec. 27, 1934; 1 son, Allen W. Admitted to Ga. bar, 1930; spl. atty. gen. Ga., 1933, 1935; asst. atty. gen. assigned Ga. Pub. Service Commn., 1934; partner Moise, Post & Gardner, Atlanta, 1942-61, specializing in bus. and corp. law; partner Hansell, Post, Brandon & Dorsey, 1962—; dir., exec. com. Atlanta Gas Light Co.; dir. Am. Cast Iron Pipe Co., Atlantic Am. Corp., Thomaston Mills, other corps.; hon. dir. 1st Nat. Bank Atlanta, 1st Atlantic Corp.; lectr., writer on legal subjects. Pres. Atlanta Estate Planning Council, 1960; trustee Ragan and King Charitable Found., W. N. Banks Found., The Howell Fund; mem. State Democratic Exec. Com.; mem. com. to rewrite election laws and revise primary rules of Ga., 1956; Dem. presdl. elector. Mem. Governor's Staff; mem. State Com. to Revise Income Tax Laws of Ga., 1956; mem. Ga. Income Tax Study Commn. Chmn. Northside Hosp. Served as lt. comdr. USNR, World War II. Mem. Atlanta (exec. com., pres. 1956), Am., Ga. bar assns., Am. Coll. Probate Counsel, Am. Coll. Trial Lawyers, Am. Judicature Soc., Atlanta Claims Assn., S.A.R., Navy League, Res. Officers Naval Services (1st pres. Atlanta chpt.), Mil. Order World Wars, Am. Legion (comdr.), Am. Assn. Rhodes Scholars, Sphinx, Phi Beta Kappa, Phi Kappa Phi, Phi Delta Phi, Kappa Alpha. Methodist (chmn. ofcl. bd., trustee). Clubs: Capital City, Piedmont Driving, Lawyers (Atlanta); Old War Horse Lawyers (pres. 1962); Commerce, Rotary. Home: 620 Peachtree Battle Ave

NW Atlanta GA 30327 Office: 1st Nat Bank Tower Atlanta GA 30303. *Be right; be thorough; be on time.*

POST, ALTON GUSTAV, cons., ret. army officer; b. Zumbrota, Minn., Dec. 26, 1920; s. Henry Edolph and Mathilda (Nelson) P.; B.A., U. Nebr., 1961; M.S., George Washington U., 1968; m. Leimomi R. Buchanan, June 9, 1973; children—Patricia Lynn, Christopher Alton. Commd. 2d lt. U.S. Army, 1942, advanced through grades to maj. gen., 1973; comdr. 34th Aviation Group, Vietnam, 1968-69; asst. comdt. U.S. Army Transp. Sch., Fort Eustis, Va., 1969-70; chief of staff for logistics U.S. Army, Vietnam, 1970-71; chief staff security assistance Pacific Command Hdqrs., 1971-72, chief of staff for logistics U.S. Army, Pacific, 1972-74; chief of staff logistics Tng. and Doctrine Command, Ft. Monroe, Va., 1974-75; comdg. gen. U.S. Army Transp. Center, also comdt. U.S. Army Transp. Sch., Fort Eustis, 1975-78, ret., 1978; cons. Boeing Vertol Co., Honolulu, Hawaii, 1978—. Decorated D.S.M. with oak leaf cluster, Legion of Merit with oak leaf cluster, D.F.C., Bronze Star with V device and oak leaf cluster, Air medal with 8 oak leaf clusters, others. Mem. Assn. U.S. Army, Army Aviation Assn. Am., Nat. Def. Transp. Assn., VFW. Lutheran. Clubs: Outrigger Canoe, Polo (Hawaii), Masons. Home: 581 Kamoku St Apt 3108 Honolulu HI 96826

POST, AVERY DENISON, ch. ofcl.; b. Norwich, Conn., July 29, 1924; s. John Palmer and Dorothy (Church) P.; B.A., Ohio Wesleyan U., 1945; B.D., Yale U., 1949, S.T.M., 1952; L.H.D. (hon.), Lakeland Coll., Sheboygan, Wis., 1977; D.D. (hon.), Chgo. Theol. Sem., 1978, Middlebury (Vt.) Coll., 1978, Defiance (Ohio) Coll., 1979; m. Margaret Jane Rowland, June 8, 1946; children—Susan Macalister Post Roszkowksi, Jennifer Campbell Post Quinn, Elizabeth Champlin, Anne Denison Post Proudman. Ordained to ministry Methodist Ch., 1949; pastor chs. in Vt., Ohio, Conn. and N.Y., 1946-63; sr. minister Scarsdale (N.Y.) Congl. Ch., 1963-70; minister, pres. Mass. conf. United Ch. Christ, 1970-77; pres. United Ch. Christ, N.Y.C., 1977—; mem. central com. World Council Chs., 1978—; exec. com., bd. govs. Nat. Council Chs., 1977—; lectr. Bible, Adelphi Coll., Garden City, N.Y., 1958-59; Luccock lectr. Yale U. Div. Sch., 1961; lectr. homiletics Union Sem., N.Y.C., 1967-69, bd. dirs., 1967-77; trustee Andover Newton Theol. Sem., 1970—; del. numerous internat. ch. meetings. Served with USNR, 1943-45. Recipient 1st Ecumenical award Mass. Council Chs., 1976; life mem. PTA, Norwich, N.Y. Fellow Soc. Arts, Religion and Contemporary Culture; mem. Acad. Am. Poets, Boston Athenaeum. Democrat. Clubs: Yale, Appalachian Mountain; Randolph (N.H.) Mountain. Home: 421 Martling Ave Tarrytown NY 10591 Office: 105 Madison Ave New York NY 10016

POST, CHARLES DAYTON, lawyer; b. Syracuse, N.Y., Mar. 9, 1910; s. Dr. Charles D. and Mary (McMahon) P.; A.B., Harvard, 1931, LL.B., 1934; m. Cynthia Dudley, Aug. 12, 1935; children—Penelope, Dudley, Allan, Alison, Carolyn. With Goodwin, Procter & Hoar, counsellors at law, Boston, 1934—, partner, 1942—; seminar lectr. Harvard, others; lectr. tax insts. N.Y.U., U. Mich.; dir. Keystone Custodian Funds, Inc. Mem. adv. com. Commr. Internal Revenue, Washington, 1953-55; chmn. adv. com. Wellesley, Mass., 1953-54; treas. Fed. Tax Inst. of New England. Mem. exec. com. pre-union chmn. Harvard 25th Reunion, 1956; treas., trustee Keystone Charitable Found.; bd. dirs. Internat. Bus. Center NE; pres. Boston Tax Forum. Served as air combat intelligence officer USN, 1943-46. Decorated Bronze Star, Air Medal. Pres. Boston Jr. C. of C., 1941-42. Mem. Am. (chmn. com. fed. income taxes 1952-55, chmn. com. on extraterritorial application of taxes 1950-52), Mass. (fed. tax rep.), Boston (chmn. internat. law sect. 1973-77) bar assns., World Affairs Council Boston (pres. 1967-69), Mass. Civic League (dir.). Republican. Episcopalian. Clubs: Union (Boston); Harvard (N.Y.C.) (Boston); Weston Country. Home: 71 Meadowbrook Rd Weston MA 02193 Office: 28 State St Boston MA 02109

POST, ELIZABETH LINDLEY (MRS. WILLIAM G. POST), author; b. Englewood, N.J., May 7, 1920; d. Allen L. and Elizabeth (Ellsworth) Lindley; grad. high sch.; m. William G. Post, Aug. 5, 1944; children—Allen C., William G., Lucinda Ann, Peter L. Dir. Emily Post Inst., 1965—; author syndicated newspaper column Doing the Right Thing, 1966—. Republican. Episcopalian. Author: Emily Post's Book of Etiquette for Young People, 1968; Wonderful World of Weddings, 1970; Please Say Please, 1972; Revised Emily Post's Etiquette, 1965, 69, 75. Contbg. editor Goodhousekeeping Mag. Home: Waterbury Center VT 05677 Office: 120 E 36th St New York NY 10016

POST, GERALD JOSEPH, air force officer; b. Braintree, Mass., Sept. 27, 1925; s. Robert Z. and Marjorie F. (Dunn) P.; M.B.A., U. Chgo., 1958; m. Jane Stewart Curry, May 4, 1945; children—Sharyn Post Hodgdon, Gerald J., Steven M., Richard J., Sean C., David D., Tracy M. Commd. 2d lt. U.S. Air Force, 1945, advanced through grades to lt. gen., 1978; comptroller, dir. materiel mgmt. San Antonio Air Materiel Area, 1970-73; dep. chief of Staff for Materiel Mgmt., Wright-Patterson AFB, Ohio, 1973-75; chief of staff Air Force Logistics Command, Wright-Patterson AFB, 1975-77; asst. dep. chief of staff for systems and logistics Hdqrs. USAF, 1977-78, dir. Def. Logistics Agy., 1978—. Decorated Legion of Merit with oak leaf cluster, D.F.C., Air medal with 2 oak leaf clusters, others. Mem. Am. Soc. Mil. Comptrollers, Air Force Assn., Am. Inst. Aeros. and Astronautics, Am. Def. Preparedness Assn., Phi Beta Kappa, Beta Gamma Sigma. Home: 7212 Doncaster St Springfield VA 22150 Office: HQ/DCA Alexandria VA 22314

POST, JACKIE EDITH, bus. exec.; b. Lakewood, Ohio, Nov. 17, 1928; d. Sidney Walter and Della N. (Korver) Jackson; B.S. cum laude, Miami U., Oxford, Ohio, 1950; 1 dau., Deborah Downs Cottingham Dryer. Sec. (to Henry Laribee), Laribee & Cooper, Lawyers, Medina, Ohio, 1955-69, (to Baya M. Harrison), Harrison, Greene, Mann, Davenport, et al, Lawyers, St. Petersburg, Fla., 1970-72; corporate sec., sec. to chmn. bd. Jack Eckerd Corp., Clearwater, Fla., 1972—. Mem. Beta Gamma Sigma. Republican. Home: 8A Imperial Ct 1433 S Belcher St Clearwater FL 33516 Office: PO Box 4689 Clearwater FL 33518

POST, RICHARD FREEMAN, physicist; b. Pomona, Calif., Nov. 14, 1918; s. Freeman and Miriam Jocelyn (Colcord) P.; B.A., Pomona Coll., 1940, D.Sc. (hon.), 1959; Ph.D., Stanford U., 1950; m. Marylee Armstrong, Aug. 7, 1946; children—Stephen, Marjorie, Rodney. Grad. asst., then instr. physics Pomona Coll., 1940-42; civilian physicist Naval Research Lab., 1942-46; research asso. Stanford U., 1947-50; research group leader controlled thermonuclear research U. Calif. Lawrence Livermore Lab., 1951-74, dep. asso. dir. magnetic fusion energy, 1974—; prof.-in-residence U. Calif., Davis/Livermore, 1963—. Recipient Meritorious Civilian Service award U.S. Navy, 1945, Disting. Asso. award ERDA, 1977. Fellow Am. Phys. Soc. (chmn. plasma physics div.; James Clerk Maxwell prize 1978), Am. Nuclear Soc. (Outstanding Achievement award controlled nuclear fusion div. 1978). Congregationalist. Author articles in field; holder more than 25 patents in fields of nuclear fusion, particle accelerators, electronics and mech. energy storage; asso. editor Phys. Rev. Letters, 1978—; bd. editors Nuclear Fusion, 1976—. Home: 1630 Orchard Ln Walnut Creek CA 94595 Office: Univ Calif Lawrence Livermore Lab PO Box 808 Livermore CA 94550

POST, RICHARD SAINT FRANCIS, govt. ofcl.; b. Spokane, Dec. 11, 1929; s. Harry Grant and Mary (Brinker) P.; grad. Phillips Exeter Acad., 1947; A.B. cum laude, Harvard, 1951; M.S., George Washington U., 1969; student Boston U. African research program, 1957-58; m. Ann Hawks, June 13, 1952; children—Brian, Jonathan, Bridget, Patrick. With State Dept., Ethiopia, 1952-55, Hong Kong, 1955-57, Somalia, 1958-60, Swaziland, Bechuanaland and Basutoland, 1964-66 Lesotho, 1966-68; officer charge Libya affairs State Dept., 1961-62, Ethiopia and Somalia affairs, 1962-64; charge d'affairs, Lesotho, 1966-68; consul gen., Angola, 1969-72; minister-counselor of embassy, Lisbon, Portugal, 1972-75; polit. counselor Am. embassy, Ottawa, Ont., Can., 1975-76; dir. for East African affairs State Dept., 1976-78; mem. Exec. Seminar in Nat. and Internat. Affairs, 1978-79; consul gen. Karachi, Pakistan, 1979—. Recipient Meritorious Honor award State Dept., 1966. Mem. Am. Fgn. Service Assn. Clubs: Washington Lacrosse (pres. 1963-64); Harvard of Hong Kong (v.p. 1956-57); Karachi Polo. Home: 1630 Davidson Rd McLean VA 22101 Office: Dept State Karachi Washington DC 20520

POST, TED, film, TV and theatre dir.; b. Bklyn.; s. Jacob C. and Dina Post; m. Thelma Feifel, July 6, 1941; children—Robert Charles, Laurie Margaret. Films include: Go Tell the Spartans, Good Guys Wear Black, Magnum Force, Hang 'Em High, Beneath the Planet of the Apes, The Harrad Experiment; dir. films for TV including: Dr. Cook's Garden, Do Not Fold, Spindle, or Mutilate, The Girls in the Office; producer, dir. Coney Island of the Mind, NBC-TV; plays include: The Glass Menagerie, Mal Entendu, The Heiress, Watch on the Rhine, The Eagle Has Two Heads, A Midsummer Night's Dream, Burlesque; stage dir. for Norwich Summer Theatre, Suffern Summer Theatre, Yardley Summer Theatre, Marblehead Playhouse, The American Negro Theatre; lectr. acting and directing UCLA, New Sch. for Social Research, N.Y.C. Served with U.S. Army, 1943-45. Named Dir. of Year, Western Heritage, also Limelight Mag. Mem. Dirs. Guild Am. (nominated Best Dir.), TV Acad. Arts and Scis. (Best Dir. nomination), Acad. of Motion Picture Arts and Scis. Office: 10889 Wilshire Blvd Los Angeles CA 90024

POSTE, LESLIE IRLYN, librarian, educator; b. St. Catharines, Ont., Aug. 26, 1918; s. Leslie and Isabella L. (Sparling) P.; A.B., Wayne State U., 1941; B.S., Columbia, 1942; Ph.D., U. Chgo. Grad. Library Sch., 1958; m. Virginia Beryl Lloyd, May 11, 1946; 1 dau., Linda Jean. Page, desk asst. Detroit Pub. Library, 1932-41; acting librarian Columbia Coll. Library, Columbia U., 1942-43; editorial asso. A.N. Marquis Co., 1949; prof., head dept. library sci. U. Ky., 1949-53; prof., dir. sch. librarianship U. Denver, 1953-55; asst. dir. Toledo Pub. Library, 1955-58; acting coll. librarian, 1960; prof. Sch. of Library and Information Sci., State U. of N.Y. Coll. of Arts and Sci. at Geneseo, N.Y., 1958—; antiquarian book dealer, 1971—; vis. prof. Sch. Library and Info. Scis. North Tex. State U., summers 1968, 69; arts-monuments-archives specialist officer U.S. Army Civil Affairs Sch., Fort Bragg, N.C., 1959-68, dir. instrn., 1968-72; cons. faculty U.S. Army Command and Gen. Staff Coll., Ft. Leavenworth, Kans., 1968—; cons. U.S. Army John F. Kennedy Center for Mil. Assistance, Ft. Bragg, N.C., 1970-72; Indsl. Coll. Armed Forces, Washington, 1974; cons. U.S. Army Sergeants Maj. Acad., Ft. Bliss, Tex., 1972—; conducted 1st library travel seminar Europe, summer 1961. Pvt. to 1st lt., AUS, 1943-46; col. USAR; counselor Armed Forces Inst., ETO, 1944; librarian-instr. Army Info.-Edn. Staff Sch., 1944-45; specialist officer German libraries and archives. U.S. Zone of Occupation in Germany, 1945-46, dep. dir. pub. relations, Land Wuerttemberg-Baden, 1946; dir. U.S. info. Centers, Land Hesse, 1946-47; Recipient Newsboy award Horatio Alger Soc., 1974. Fellow Library Assn. Gt. Britain; mem. A.L.A., Assn. Am. Library Schs., Am. Booksellers Assn., Spl. Libraries Assn., Assn. of Coll. and Research Libraries, Bibliog. Soc. Am., Ky. (2d v.p. 1952-53), N.Y., Mountain-Plains (chmn. intellectual freedom com. 1954-55) library assns., Livingston County C. of C., Res. Officers Assn., Horatio Alger Soc. (dir. 1973—), N.E.A., Beta Phi Mu. Club: N.Y. Library. Author: The Development of U.S. Protection of Libraries and Archives in Europe during World War II, 1958, rev. edit., 1964; Arts, Monuments and Archives, 1960. Contbr. articles to profl. jours. Home: 4222 Lakeville Rd Geneseo NY 14454 Office: Fraser Hall State U NY Coll Geneseo NY 14454

POSTL, ANTON, educator; b. Graz, Austria, June 16, 1916; s. Anton and Louise (Postl) Kurz; B.S., U. Hawaii, 1940, M.S., 1942; Ph.D., Oreg. State U., 1955; m. Mildred Louise Walker, June 16, 1942; children—Sylvia Louise (Mrs. James T. McGill), William Anton, Andrea Grace (Mrs. John J. McDonnell, Jr.). Staff, Mid-Pacific Inst., Honolulu, 1941-43; instr. chemistry U. Hawaii, Honolulu, 1943-45; mem. faculty Ore. Coll. Edn., Monmouth, 1947—, prof. chemistry, 1958—, chmn. div. sci. and math., 1955-72. Fellow AAAS; mem. Am. Chem. Soc. (sect. chmn., 1963-64), Oreg. Acad. Sci. (pres. 1968-69, citation 1973), Austrian Geol. Soc., History Sci. Soc., Sierra Club, Phi Kappa Phi. Club: Rotary. Author: Laboratory Experiments in Physical Sciences, 1970; also articles, chpt. in book. Home: 916 E Jackson St Monmouth OR 97361

POSTMA, HERMAN, research instn. exec.; b. Wilmington, N.C., Mar. 29, 1933; s. Gilbert and Sophie Hadrian (Verzaal) P.; B.S. summa cum laude, Duke, 1955; M.S., Harvard, 1957, Ph.D., 1959; m. Patricia Dunigan, Nov. 25, 1960; children—Peter, Pamela. Summer staff Oak Ridge Nat. Lab., 1954-57, physicist thermonuclear div., 1959-62, co-leader DCX-1 Group, 1962-66, asst. dir. thermonuclear div., 1966, asso. dir. div., 1967, dir. div., 1967-73, dir. nat. lab., 1974—; vis. scientist FOM-Instituut voor Plasma-Fysica, The Netherlands, 1963; cons. Lab. Laser Energetics, U. Rochester. Bd. dirs. The Nucleus; chmn. bd. trustees Hosp. of Meth. Ch.; mem. adv. bd. Coll. Bus. Adminstrn., U. Tenn., 1976—, Energy Inst., State of N.C. Registered profl. engr., Calif. Fellow Am. Phys. Soc. (exec. com. div. plasma physics), AAAS; mem. Am. Nuclear Soc. (dir.), Phi Beta Kappa, Beta Gamma Sigma, Sigma Pi Sigma, Omicron Delta Kappa, Sigma Xi, Pi Mu Epsilon, Phi Eta Sigma. Editorial bd. Nuclear Fusion, 1968-74. Home: 104 Berea Rd Oak Ridge TN 37830 Office: Oak Ridge Nat Lab PO Box X Oak Ridge TN 37830

POSTMAN, LEO JOSEPH, psychologist; b. St. Petersburg, Russia, June 7, 1918; s. Joseph and Elizabeth (Leites) P.; came to U.S., naturalized, 1944; B.S.S., Coll. City N.Y., 1943; M.A., Harvard U., 1944, Ph.D., 1946; m. Dorothy Lerman, June 27, 1945. Instr. Harvard U., 1946-47, asst. prof., 1948-50; asst. prof. Ind. U., 1947-48; mem. faculty U. Calif., Berkeley, 1950—, prof. psychology, 1957—. Mem. Nat. Acad. Scis., Soc. Exptl. Psychologists (Warren medal 1974), Am. Psychol. Assn. (past pres. div. exptl. psychology, gen. psychology), Psychoonomic Soc., AAAS (past v.p.). Co-author: Experimental Psychology, 1949; editor: Psychology in the Making, 1962; co-editor: Verbal Learning and Memory, 1969; editor Jour. Verbal Learning and Verbal Behavior, 1961-68, Am. Jour. Psychology, 1976—; asso. editor Jour. Exptl. Psychology, 1968-74; contbr. articles to profl. jours., chpts. to books. Home: 632 Grizzly Park Blvd Berkeley CA 94708 Office: Dept Psychology U Calif Berkeley CA 94720

POSTON, ERSA HINES, govt. ofcl.; b. Paducah, Ky., May 3, 1921; d. Robert S. and Adele (Johnson) Hines; A.B., Ky. State Coll., 1942; M.S.W., Atlanta U., 1946; LL.D., Union Coll., Schenectady, 1978, Fordham U. Community orgn. sec. Hartford (Conn.) Tb and Health Assn., 1946-47; teen-age program dir. W. side br. YWCA, N.Y.C., 1947-48, adult dir., 1948-49; asst. dir. Clinton Community Center, N.Y.C., 1949-50, dir., 1950-53; field sec. N.Y.C. Welfare and Health Council, 1953-55; field project supr. N.Y.C. Youth Bd., 1955, asst. dir. program rev., 1955-57; area dir. N.Y. State Div. for Youth, 1957-62, youth work coordinator, 1962-64; confidential asst. to Gov. Rockefeller, 1964; dir. N.Y. State Office Econ. Opportunity, 1964-67; pres. N.Y. State CSC, 1967-75, commr., 1975-77; commr. U.S. CSC, 1977-79; vice-chmn. U.S. Merit Systems Protection Bd., 1979—; mem. Internat. CSC; mem. adv. council Federally Employed Women; dir. Panama C.Z. Co. Former mem. Nat. Commn. to Study Goals for State Colls. and Univs.; chmn. Pres.'s Adv. Council Intergovtl. Personnel Policy; v.p. Nat. Urban League; U.S. del. UN Gen. Assembly, 1976; vice presiding officer U.S. Commn. on Observance of Internat. Woman's Year Bd. govs. Albany Med. Center Hosp.; bd. dirs. Whitney M. Young Meml. Found. Recipient Achievement awards Bklyn. club Nat. Assn. Negro Bus. and Profl. Women's Clubs; Dutchess of Paducah award; Dau. of Paducah plaque; named Ky. col.; Distinguished Alumni award Ky. State Coll.; Distinguished Service award Greater N.Y. chpt. Links; Woman of Year award Central Jersey club Nat. Assn. Negro Bus. and Profl. Women's Clubs; Achievement award Phi Delta Kappa; Populus Dei award Mercy Coll.; Woman of Year award Utility Club; Outstanding Woman of Year award Iota Phi Lambda.; Nat. Achievement award Nat. Assn. Negro BPW Clubs, 1967; Outstanding Service award 26th A.D. Rep. Orgn. Queens County; Trail Blazer award Jamaica Club Nat. Assn. Negro BPW Clubs; Benjamin Potoker Brotherhood award, 1970; named 1970 Woman of Year, BPW Club Albany; Equal Opportunity Day award Nat. Urban League, 1976; Spl. award Psi Nu chpt. Omega Psi Phi, 1977; Disting. Public Servant award Capital Press Club, 1978; Founders' Day award Alpha Kappa Alpha, 1978; First award Nat. Black Personnel Assn., 1978; many others. Mem. Nat. Assn. Social Workers, Acad. Certified Social Workers, Nat. Acad. Public Adminstrn., Am. Soc. Public Adminstrn., Internat. Personnel Mgmt. Assn., N.A.A.C.P., Nat. Council Negro Women, Links, Nat. Bus. and Profl. Women, Girlfriends, Inc., Lambda Kappa Mu (hon.; Achievement award Nu chpt.), Alpha Kappa Alpha (outstanding awards Bklyn. chpt. 1960, 65). Club: Zonta. Office: US Merit Systems Protection Bd 1717 H St NW Washington DC 20419

POSTON, FREDDIE LEE, air force officer; b. Jacksonville, Fla., Sept. 16, 1925; s. Lora Dalphus and Essie (Mock) P.; student Jacksonville Jr. Coll., 1948-50; m. Norma Mildred Smith, May 10, 1946; children—Freddie Lee, Constance Engelhardt, David. Served as enlisted man U.S. Air Force, 1948-50, commd., 1950, advanced through grades to lt. gen.; comdr. 309th Tactical Fighter Squad, Homestead AFB, Fla. and Vietnam, 1966-68; dir. ops 58th Tactical Fighter Wing, Luke AFB, Ariz., 1968-70; comdr. 57th Tactical Fighter-Weapons Wing, Nellis AFB, Nev., 1970-71; dep. dir. ops U.S. Strike Command, MacDill AFB, Fla., 1972-74; dep. chief of staff for plans and ops Hdqrs., Pacific Air Forces, Hickam AFB, Hawaii, 1974-75, dep. chief of staff for ops. and intelligence, 1975-76; comdr. 13th Air Force, Clark Air Base, Philippines, 1976-79; chief of staff Pacific Command, Camp H. M. Smith, Hawaii, 1979—. Decorated Silver Star, Legion of Merit, D.F.C. with oak leaf cluster, Air Force Commendation medal with 3 oak leaf clusters (U.S.); Order Nat. Security Merit, Cheon Su (Korea); Air Service medal, honor class (Vietnam); Air Force Command Pilot badge (gold) (Philippines). Home: 201 8th St Honolulu HI 96818 Office: Chief of Staff PACOM PO Box 41 Camp H M Smith HI 96861*

POSTON, GRETCHEN, govt. ofcl.; b. Mpls., Feb. 14, 1932; d. George and Katharene (Walsh) Householder; B.S., St. Mary's Coll., Leavenworth, Kans., 1952; m. Raymond L. Poston, Jr., Dec. 30, 1960; children—Jeffrey, Carol, Ramsey, Katharene. Sch. tchr. in Mo., France, Germany and Va., 1952-60; co-founder Washington Whirl-Around, Inc., 1967-77; founder Wonderful Weddings, Inc., 1965-77; social sec. to White House, Washington, 1977—; organizer social events Democratic Nat. Convs., 1964, 72, 76. Mem. exec. bd. Woman's Nat. Dem. Club; bd. dirs. Goodwill Industries. Roman Catholic. Author: (with others) The Wonderful Wedding Workbook, 1966. Home: 3215 Ellicott St NW Washington DC 20008 Office: The White House Washington DC 20050

POSTON, MET RAY, mfg. co. exec.; b. Chattanooga, Mar. 11, 1920; s. Arthur Julian and Lillian (Smith) P.; B.S., U. Chattanooga, 1942; LL.B., George Washington U., 1951; m. Francella Redwine, May 21, 1946; children—Frederick, Met Ray, George, Wendy, Shelly. Research chemist Reilly Tar & Chem. Corp., Indpls., 1942-43; engaged in research Oak Ridge Nat. Lab., 1946-48; patent counsel AEC, 1948-51; admitted to D.C. bar, 1952, N.C. bar, 1962; with Am. Enka Corp. (N.C.), 1951-70, sec., 1960-70, gen. counsel, 1962-70; v.p., gen. counsel Akzona Inc., Asheville, N.C., 1970—. Trustee Ariz. Found. Served to lt. USNR, 1943-46; PTO. Mem. Am., N.C. bar assns., Phi Alpha Delta. Methodist. Mason. Clubs: Asheville Downtown, City, Country of Asheville; University (N.Y.). Home: 5 W Avon Pkwy Asheville NC 28804 Office: Akzona Inc Asheville NC 28802

POSTON, TOM, actor; b. Columbus, Ohio, Oct. 17, 1927; s. George and Margaret Poston; student Bethany Coll., 1938-40, Am. Acad. Dramatic Arts, 1945-47; m. Kay Hudson, June 8, 1968; children—Francesca, Hudson, Jason. First appeared on stage as a tumbler with The Flying Zebleys; acting and Broadway debuts in Cyrano de Bergerac, 1947; appeared on Broadway, regional theaters and in summer stock; stage appearances include: The Insect Comedy, King Lear, Will Success Spoil Rock Hunter?, Goodbye Again, Best of Burlesque, Romanoff and Juliet, Drink to Me Only, Golden Fleecing, The Conquering Hero, Come Blow Your Horn, Mary, Mary, Forty Carats, But, Seriously..., A Funny Thing Happened on the Way to the Forum, The Odd Couple, Bye, Bye, Birdie, Mother Courage; host WABC-TV series Entertainment, 1955; regular on TV show The Steven Allen Show, 1956-58 (Emmy award for best supporting actor in comedy series 1959); host TV show Split Personality, 1959-60; panelist on TV show To Tell The Truth; appeared in TV series On the Rocks, 1975-76, We've Got Each Other, 1977, Mork and Mindy, 1978—; other TV appearances include: Merman on Broadway, You Sometimes Get Rich, U.S. Steel Hour, The Enchanted, The Tempest, The Bob Newhart Show; film appearances include: The Tempest, The Sleeps, Zotz, The Old Dark House, Cold Turkey, The Happy Hooker, Rabbit Test. Served with USAAF, World War II. Office: care ABC Public Relations 1330 Ave of Americas New York NY 10019*

POSTYN, SOL, financial cons.; b. N.Y.C., May 22, 1934; s. Jacob and Tillie (Goldman) P.; B.S., U. Conn., 1956; m. Jo Kirschner, May 22, 1964; children—Sarah, Noah. With Seidman & Seidman, C.P.A.'s, 1959-65; controller Renauld Internat., San Francisco, 1965-67, Koret of Calif., San Francisco, 1967-69; treas. Koracorp. Industries, San Francisco, 1969-73; financial cons., San Francisco, 1973—. Bd. dirs. Festival Theatre, Marin County, Calif., 1963-65; bd. dirs. Homewood Terrace, San Francisco, 1974—, pres. bd., 1976—; chmn. exec. com. Jewish Family and Children's Services, San Francisco, 1977—; bd. dirs. Jewish Welfare Fedn., San Francisco, 1976-78. Served with U.S. Army, 1957-59. Home: 370 Franklin St San Mateo CA 94402 Office: 433 California St San Francisco CA 94104

POSVAR, WESLEY WENTZ, univ. pres.; b. Topeka, Sept. 14, 1925; s. Vladimir L. and Marie (Wentz) P.; B.S., U.S. Mil. Acad., 1946; B.A. (Rhodes scholar), Oxford (Eng.) U., 1951, M.A., 1954; M.P.A., Ph.D. (Littauer fellow), Harvard U., 1964; LL.D.; L.H.D.; research asso. Center Internat. Studies, Mass. Inst. Tech., 1963-64; m. Mildred Miller, Apr. 30, 1950; children—Wesley William, Margot Marina, Lisa Christina. Commd. officer USAAF, later USAF; fighter test pilot Air Proving Ground, Fla., 1946-48; pilot Berlin airlift, 1949; command pilot; asst. prof. social scis. U.S. Mil. Acad., 1951-54; mem. long range strategic planning group Hdqrs. USAF, 1954-57; prof. polit. sci., head dept. USAF Acad., 1957-67, chmn. div. social scis., 1960-62, 66-67; chancellor (pres.), prof. polit. sci. U. Pitts., 1967—; dir. Eastern Air Lines, Inc., Federated Investors, Group Mut. and Money Mgmt. Funds. Former mem. vis. com. Harvard U., M.I.T., Nat. War Coll.; exec. com. Allegheny Conf. on Community Devel.; cons. various fed. agencies; trustee Rand Corp., Pitts. Symphony Soc., Presbyn.-Univ. Hosp., U. Health Center, U. Pitts., Carnegie Endowment for Internat. Peace, numerous civic orgns. Named one of ten outstanding young men U.S. Jr. C. of C., 1959. Mem. Am. Polit. Sci. Assn., Assn. Am. Rhodes Scholars, Internat. Studies Assn. (pres. 1961-62), Pa. Assn. Colls. and Univs. (pres. 1971-72), Internat. Inst. Strategic Studies, Council Fgn. Relations, Arms Control Assn. Clubs: Cosmos, Duquesne, Univ. (N.Y.C.). Contbr. articles to books and publs. on mgmt. planning, fgn. affairs, higher edn. Address: University of Pittsburgh Pittsburgh PA 15260

POTASHNER, PAUL, mfg. co. exec.; b. N.Y.C., July 8, 1930; s. Jacob and Mae (Sachs) P.; B.B.A., CCNY, 1951; M.B.A., Harvard U., 1960; m. Evelyn Lubliner, Oct. 27, 1951; children—Kenneth, Dean. Staff v.p., group v.p. RCA Corp., N.Y.C.; dir. Banquet Foods, Random House Inc., Oriel Foods. Served with USMC. Clubs: Harvard Bus. Sch.; Les Ambassadeurs (London). Office: 30 Rockefeller Plaza New York NY 10020

POTCHEN, EDWARD JAMES, radiologist, educator; b. Queens County, N.Y., Dec. 2, 1932; s. Joseph Anton and Eleanore (Joyce) P.; B.S., Mich. State U., 1954; M.D., Wayne State U., 1958; postgrad. (fellow) Harvard, 1964-66; M.S. in Mgmt. (Sloan fellow), Mass. Inst. Tech., 1972; m. Geraldine J. Jeplawy, Sept. 1, 1956; children—Michelle M., Kathleen A., Michael J., Joseph E. Intern Butterworth Hosp., Grand Rapids, Mich., 1958-59; pvt. practice gen. medicine, Grand Rapids, Mich., 1959-61; resident radiology Peter Bent Brigham Hosp., Boston, 1961-64, chief resident radiologist, 1964; dir. div. nuclear medicine Harvard Med. Sch. dept. radiology, 1965; asso. radiologist Barnes Hosp., St. Louis, 1966; dir. nuclear medicine div. Edward Mallinckrodt Inst. Radiology, Washington U. Sch. Medicine, St. Louis, 1967; chief diagnostic radiology Edward Mallinckrodt Inst., 1971-73; prof. radiology, dean mgmt. resources Johns Hopkins U. Sch. Medicine, 1973-75; prof. radiology and health systems mgmt. Mich. State U., East Lansing, 1975—, chmn. dept. radiology, 1973—; prof. radiology Washington U. Sch. Medicine, 1969-73. Cons. Nat. Heart Inst., Nat. Inst. Gen. Med. Scis., div. biology and medicine U.S. AEC; examiner Am. Bd. Radiology. Trustee Soc. Nuclear Medicine. Recipient John J. Larkin award for basic med. research, 1963; James Picker Found. fellow in acad. radiology Nat. Acad. Scis.-NRC, 1965-66; Sloan fellow, Mass. Inst. Tech., 1972-73. Mem. AMA (mem. ho. of dels., sect. on nuclear medicine 1976—, council on med. edn. 1979), Am. Fedn. Clin. Research, Central Soc. Clin. Research, Am. Soc. Clin. Investigation, Soc. Nuclear Med. (nat. pres. 1975-76), Am. Physiol. Soc., Am. Radium Soc., Assn. of Univ. Radiologists, Alpha Omega Alpha. Editor: Endocrine Radiology, 1966; Frontiers of Chest Radiology, 1969: Diagnostic Radiology, 1971; Introduction to the Tracer Method, 1972; Neuro-Nuclear Medicine, 1972; Current Concepts in Radiology, 1972, 3d edit., 1977; also contbr. to jours. Home: 4810 Arapaho Dr Okemos MI 48864 Office: Dept Radiology Mich State U B220 Clinic Center East Lansing MI 48824

POTEAT, WILLIAM HARDMAN, educator; b. Kaifeng, Honan, China, Apr. 19, 1919; s. Edwin McNeill and Wilda (Hardman) P.; student Mars Hill Jr. Coll., 1936-37; A.B., Oberlin Coll., 1941; B.D., Yale Div. Sch., 1944; Ph.D., Duke U., 1951; m. Marian Kelley, Sept. 8, 1943; children—Anne Carlyle, Susan Colquitt, Edwin McNeill. Asso. sec. YMCA, U. N.C., 1944-46, acting sect., 1946-47, instr. dept. philosophy, 1947-49, asst. prof., 1950-54, asso. prof., 1954-57; Quin prof. philos. theology and Christian criticism Episcopal Theology Sem. of S.W., 1957-60; asso. prof. Christianity and culture Duke U., 1960-66, prof., 1966-69, prof. religion and culture, 1969-71, prof. religion and comparative studies, 1971—, chmn. dept. religion, 1972—; vis. prof. Stanford U., 1970, U. Tex., 1971; cons. spl. com. liberal studies Am. Assn. Colls., 1967; mem. Nat. Humanities Faculty, 1969—; mem. devel. bd. Lenoir Rhyne Coll., 1968-70; mem. council grad. studies Danforth Found., 1967—; cons. lectr. World Student Christian Fedn., 1953-56; cons. research and devel. Gov. Terry Sanford, 1961-64; chmn. central com. Nat. Council Religion and Higher Edn., 1954-55. Disting. Humanities scholar Haverford (Pa.) Coll., 1969. Mem. Am. Philos. Assn., Am. Acad. Polit. and Social Sci., Phi Beta Kappa. Democrat. Episcopalian. Co-editor, contbg. author: Intellect and Hope: Essays in the Thought of Michael Polanyi, 1968; contbr. articles to profl. jours. Home: 621 Greenwood Rd Chapel Hill NC 27514

POTEETE, ROBERT ARTHUR, editor; b. Perry, Ark., Aug. 29, 1926; s. Arthur and Ruby (Farish) P.; B.A., U. Central Ark., 1948; postgrad. Medill Sch. Journalism, Northwestern U., 1948-49; m. Frances Reynolds, Feb. 15, 1951 (dec. Mar. 1969); children—Anthony R., Julia Anne, Richard A.R. (dec. Sept. 1973). Reporter, Ark. Gazette, 1949; reporter, day city editor, asst. news editor, asst. Sunday editor N.Y. Herald Tribune, 1950-66, mng. editor European edit., Paris, 1963-65; sr. editor Sat. Eve. Post, N.Y.C., 1966-69; mng. editor, editor Psychology Today, Del Mar, Cal., 1969-73; mng. editor New Publs., Playboy Enterprises, Inc., Chgo., 1973-74; sr. editor Money mag., 1974-76; editor-in-chief Am. Illustrated mag. U.S. Internat. Communication Agy., Washington, 1976—. Editorial cons. Episcopal Diocese L.I., Garden City, N.Y., 1967-68; mem. bd. United Youth Ministry, La Jolla, Cal., 1971-72. Recipient Citizens Budget Commn. citation for articles on N.Y.C. govt. purchase of real estate, 1958. Mem. Inner Circle. Contbr. articles popular mags. Home: 2500 Q St NW Washington DC 20007 Office: Am Illustrated 1776 Pennsylvania Ave NW Washington DC 20547

POTH, EDGAR JACOB, physician, surgeon; b. Seguin, Tex., Feb. 1, 1899; s. Edward William and Josephine Olga (Schwab) P.; B.A., U. Tex., 1922, M.A., 1923; Ph.D., U. Calif., 1925; M.D., Johns Hopkins, 1931; m. Gaynelle Robertson, Dec. 22, 1928. Intern Stanford Hosp., 1931-32, resident, 1932-36; research fellow chemistry Am. Petroleum Inst. of Nat. Research Council, 1926-28, research asso., 1928-30; instr. pharmacology Johns Hopkins, 1927, asst., 1927-30, research asso., 1940-41, asso., 1941-42; research fellow Stanford U., 1932-34, asst., 1932-36, instr., 1939; prof. surgery, head dept. U. Ark., 1939-40; asso. prof. surgery U. Tex., 1942-43, prof., 1943-64, chief div. gen. surgery, 1962-64, Ashbel Smith prof., 1964—, dir. surg. research lab., 1943-61; hon. cons. gen. surgery Lackland Air Force Base; nat. cons. surgery Surgeon Gen. U.S., USAF, 1958-62, mem. chancellor's council U. Tex., 1969; sec.-treas., dir. Isle Hotels of Galveston, Inc. Trustee Robertson Poth Found., 1952-69. Recipient Modern Medicine award for distinguished achievement, 1966. Fellow A.C.S. (gov.), Am. Soc. Colon and Rectal Surgeons (hon.); mem. Southwestern Surg. Congress (pres. 1962-63), A.M.A., Johns Hopkins Med. and Surg. Soc., Tex., Stanford, Hollywood, Kansas City, Mo., Singleton surg. socs., So. Med. Assn., Western (v.p.), So., Am. surg. assns., Internat. Soc. Surgeons, AAAS, Am. Physiol. Soc., Soc. Surgery of Alimentary Tract, Am. Geriatrics Soc., Phi Beta Kappa, Sigma Xi, Phi Beta Pi. Contbr. articles to profl. jours. Home: 7310 Seawall Blvd No 1108 Galveston TX 77551. *Whatever you undertake, do it to the best of your ability. When the task is completed, judge it with complete honesty and criticize it to determine how one should do it subsequently so it will be improved upon. Be tolerant, but do not accept mediocracy.*

POTOK, CHAIM, author, editor; b. N.Y.C., Feb. 17, 1929; s. Benjamin Max and Mollie (Friedman) P.; B.A., summa cum laude, Yeshiva Coll., 1950; M.H.L., Jewish Theol. Sem., 1954; Ph.D., U. Pa., 1965; m. Adena S. Mosevitzky, June 8, 1958; children—Rena, Naama, Akiva. Ordained rabbi, 1954; Nat. dir. Leaders Tng. Fellowship, 1954-55; dir. Camp Ramah, Ojai, Cal. 1957-59; scholar-in-residence Har Zion Temple, Phila., 1959-63; mem. faculty Tchrs. Inst., Jewish Theol. Sem., 1963-64; editor Jewish Publ. Soc., 1965-74, spl. projects editor, 1974—. Served as chaplain AUS, 1955-57; Korea. Mem. P.E.N., Author's Guild. Rabbinical Assembly. Author: The Chosen, 1967; The Promise, 1969; My Name is Asher Lev, 1972; In the Beginning, 1975; Wanderings, 1978; also short stories, articles. Address: 20 Berwick Rd Merion PA 19131

POTT, HERMAN THEODORE, mfr.; b. Sheboygan, Wis., June 14, 1895; s. August W. and Marie (Bruns) P.; B.S., U. Wis., 1916; m. Phenie Ryals, Oct. 16, 1937. Asst. gen. mgr. Dravo Corp., Pitts., 1923-26; v.p. St. Louis Structural Steel Co., East St. Louis, Ill., 1927-33; pres., dir. St. Louis Shipbldg.-Fed. Barge, Inc., 1933-59, chmn. bd., 1959—; dir. Federal Barge Lines, Inc.; chmn. bd. Pott Industries, Inc., St. Louis. Mem. Am. Waterways Operators, Inc. (dir.), Miss. Valley Assn. (exec. com.) Office: Pott Industries Inc 611 E Marceau St St Louis MO 63111*

POTTER, BRADLEY ORVILLE, advt. cons.; b. Bradley Beach, N.J., Aug. 19, 1915; s. Joseph R. and Helen (Capes) P.; A.B., Oberlin Coll., 1936; m. Bethia Jakeman, Sept. 2, 1944; children—Nancy A. (Mrs. Gary L. Testa), Bradley J., Pamela T. Accounting control supr. E.R. Squibb & Sons, N.Y.C., 1939-47; with Klemtner Advt. Inc. (name now Klemtner & Compton), N.Y.C., 1947—, v.p., 1955-64, sec.-treas., 1964-69, exec. v.p., 1969-70, chmn., chief exec. officer, 1970-79, cons., 1979—. Mem. Nat. Advt. Rev. Bd., 1971-78. Trustee A.A.A.A. Pension and Profit Sharing Plan. Served to maj. USAAF, 1942-46. Conglist. (trustee). Club: Red Fox Country (Tryon, N.C.). Home: Rt 1 Box 373A Landrum SC 29356

POTTER, CARY, assn. exec.; b. N.Y.C., June 4, 1915; s. Alonzo and Elsie (Nicholas) P.; A.B., Yale, 1937, postgrad., 1937-39; m. Julia K. Macy (div.); children—C. Nicholas, Dick Macy (dec.); m. 2d, Edith G. Betts, Oct. 10, 1946. Personnel dir. Rockefeller Center, Inc., N.Y.C., 1939-46; asst. headmaster Roxbury (Mass.) Latin Sch., 1948-57; asst. exec. sec. Nat. Council Ind. Schs., 1957-62; pres. Nat. Assn. Ind. Schs., Boston, 1964-78. Asso. in edn. Harvard Grad. Sch. Edn. Bd. dirs. Council for Am. Pvt. Edn., Big Bro. Movement, Manhattan; trustee Advent Sch., Roxbury Latin Sch., A Better Chance; incorporator Children's Hosp. Med. Center. Served with USNR, 1943-46. Mem. New Eng. History Tchrs. Assn., Nat. Council Social Studies Tchrs. Republican. Episcopalian (trustee). Clubs: Tavern (Boston); Yale, Racquet and Tennis (N.Y.C.); Brookline (Mass.) Country; Shinnecock Hills Golf (Southampton, N.Y.); U.S. Srs. Golf Assn. Home: 16 Cedar Rd Chestnut Hill MA 02167

POTTER, CHARLES JACKSON, coal mining co. exec.; b. Greenfield, Mo., July 16, 1908; s. Henry Arthur and Effie May (Evans) P.; B.S., U. Mo., Rolla, 1929, M.S., 1930; Ph.D., W.Va. U., 1932; D.Eng. (hon.), U. Mo., 1950; m. Jane Elizabeth Griffith, Jan. 24, 1948; children—Susan, Charles, Carolyn. Combustion engr. Continental Coal Co., Fairmont, W.Va., 1934-38; chief mktg. div. Dept. Interior, Washington, 1938-40; with Rochester & Pittsburgh Coal Co., Indiana, Pa., 1940—, chmn., 1970—; dep. adminstr. Solid Fuels Adminstrn., Washington, 1943-46; chmn., dir. Savs. & Trust Co. of Pa. dir. Rochester & Pittsburgh Coal Can., United Eastern Coal Sales Corp. Recipient Merit medal Pres. Truman; named hon. comdr. Order British Empire. Mem. Am. Inst. Mining and Metall. Engrs. (Erskine Ramsay medal 1975, Howard N. Eavenson award 1976), Am. Mining Congress (dir.). Republican. Home: 330 N Carpenter Ave Indiana PA 15701 Office: Rochester Pittsburgh Coal Co 655 Church St Indiana PA 15701

POTTER, CHARLES STEELE, investment co. exec.; b. N.Y.C., Feb. 29, 1912; s. Joseph Wiltsie Fuller and Mary Barton (Atterbury) P.; student St. Bernard's Sch., N.Y.C., Groton Sch., Mass.; m. Barbara Ogden McClurg, Nov. 6, 1954; children—Barbara Fuller, Trevor, Helen, Charles Steele. Co-trustee Prince Charitable Trusts, 1979—; vice chmn., dir. Central Nat. Bank Chgo.; dir. F.H. Prince & Co., Inc., Kysor Indsl. Corp. Served to comdr. USNR, 1942-45. Clubs: Chicago, Racquet, Mid Day (Chgo.). Home: 1500 N Lake Shore Dr Chicago IL 60611 Office: 1 First Nat Plaza Room 4950 Chicago IL 60603

POTTER, CLARKSON NOTT, publishing co. exec.; b. Mendham, N.J., May 17, 1928; s. John Howard Nott and Margaretta (Wood) P.; B.A., Union Coll., 1950; m. Ruth Delafield, June 14, 1949 (div. Aug. 1965); children—Howard Alonzo, Christian, Margaretta, Edward Eliphalet; m. 2d, Pamela Howard, Nov. 26, 1973 (div. Apr. 1976); 1 son, Jack Rohe Howard-Potter. With Doubleday & Co., N.Y.C., 1950-57; sr. editor, advt. mgr., mng. editor Dial Press, N.Y.C., 1958-59; founder, editor-in-chief Clarkson N. Potter Inc., N.Y.C., 1959-76; dir., editor-in-chief Barre Pub. Co. Inc. (Mass.), 1974-76; pres. The Brandywine Press, 1976—. Bd. dirs., v.p. Pub. Center for Cultural Resources Inc., N.Y.C., 1973—. Clubs: University, Century, Coffee House. Home: 750 Park Ave New York NY 10021 Office: New York NY 10021

POTTER, DAN MARTIN, clergyman; b. Omaha, Nov. 22, 1916; s. Frank A. and Martha (Hutchenson) P.; B.A., Drew U., 1939, M.Div., 1942; D.D., Wagner Coll., 1959; grad. student Columbia, Union Theol. Sem., Boston U.; m. Jeannette Charlotte Ackerson, Aug. 22, 1943; children—Eric W., Janet L., Ruth A., Nelson D. Ordained to ministry Presbyn. Ch., 1943; minister, White Oak Ridge (N.J.) Community Ch., 1939-41, Nefoundland Presbyn. Ch., Oak Ridge, N.J., 1941- 43; chaplain Bellevue Hosp., Rochester State Hosp., Fed. Detention Hdqrs., also Lorton Reformatory, 1943-48; exec. sec. Attleboro (Mass.) Dist. Council Chs., 1948-52; dean Sch. Ecumenical Adminstrn., Boston U. Sch. Theology, 1950-52; exec. dir. Protestant Council City N.Y., 1952-55; exec. dir. Council Chs. City N.Y., 1955—, Soc. for the Family of Man, 1963—. Mem. White House Conf. Youth, 1950, 60, White House Conf. Aged, 1955, Gov. N.Y. Commn. Youth and Aged, 1962-64; co-chmn. Mayor N.Y.C. Com. Religious Leaders, 1957—, N.Y.C. Conf. Religion and Race, 1964; chmn. com. Moral Standards N.Y.C., 1959—, Inter-faith Com. Motion Pictures, 1958—; del. Nat. Council Chs., 1951. Pres. Community Guidance Service, N.Y.C., 1957-79. Recipient Interfaith Service award Va. chpt. V.F.W., 1948, Outstanding Citizen award Mayor N.Y.C., 1963, Outstanding Protestant award Nat. St. George Assn., 1963, Distinguished Service award Interfaith Movement, 1963, Clergyman of Yr., Wisdom Hall Fame, 1970, Disting. Service award CCNY, 1977. Mem. Assn. Council Secretaries, Nat. Assn. Ecumenical Staff, Presbytery N.Y.C., Council Clin. Tng., Am. Protestant Hosp. Chaplains Assn., N.Y. State Council Chs. Clubs: Old Westbury (L.I.) Golf and Country; Garden City (N.Y.) Country. Office: 475 Riverside Dr New York NY 10027

POTTER, DAVID SAMUEL, automotive co. exec.; b. Seattle, Jan. 16, 1925; B.S., Yale, 1945; Ph.D., U. Wash., 1951; children—Diana (Mrs. Paul Bankston), Janice (Mrs. Robert Meadows), Tom, Bill. Mem. staff Applied Physics Lab., U. Wash., 1946-60, asst. dir., 1955-60; with Gen. Motors Corp., 1960-73, chief engr. Milw. ops. GM Delco Electronics div., 1970-73, dir. research and devel. Detroit Diesel Allison div., 1973; asst. sec. for research and devel. Dept. Navy, 1973-74, under sec., 1974-76; v.p. environ. activities staff Gen. Motors Corp., Detroit, 1976-78, v.p. and group exec. public affairs group, 1978—. Mem. Gov. Calif. Adv. Commn. Ocean Resources, 1964-68; mem. adv. panel Nat. Sea Grant Program, 1966; adv. bd. Naval Postgrad. Sch., Dept. Energy. Served to ensign USNR, 1943-46. Mem. Nat. Acad. Engring., NSF, Marine Tech. Soc., Am. Phys. Soc., AIAA, Am. Acoustical Soc., Nat. Oceanographic Assn. (v.p. 1966), Soc. Automotive Engrs. (chmn. tech. bd. 1978-79). Club: Cosmos (Washington). Research cosmic rays, magnetics, underwater acoustics. Office: 14th Floor Gen Motors Bldg 3044 W Grand Blvd Detroit MI 48202

POTTER, DONALD ALBERT, mfg. co. exec.; b. Indpls., May 9, 1922; s. Donald Holmes and Gertrude Antoinette (Sullivan) P.; B.S. magna cum laude, Notre Dame U., 1943; m. Marian Helen Loughery, Feb. 6, 1943; children—Donald V., Mary J., Richard J., Ann T., Robert A., William M., James P. Chief engr. Universal Castings Corp., Chgo., 1946-47; with Stewart-Warner Corp., Chgo., 1947—, gen. mgr. electronics div., 1959—, v.p., dir. subsidiary Datafax Corp., 1959—, v.p. corp., 1960—; pres., dir. Stewart Warner Microcircuits, Inc., 1963—. Chmn. citizens bd. Loyola U., 1975-77, named hon. alumnus, 1978. Served to ensign USNR, 1943-45. Registered profl. engr., Ind. Mem. ASME, Am. Def. Preparedness (dir. 1977—), Soc. Automotive Engrs., Ill. C. of C., Armed Forces Communications and Electronics Assn. (dir. Chgo. area 1963-67), Chgo. Research and Devel. Council, Loyola U. devel. council. Club: Chgo. Athletic, Economics. Patentee heat transfer, elec. controls. Home: 250 Franklin Rd Glencoe IL 60022 Office: 1300 N Kostner Ave Chicago IL 60651

POTTER, GUY DILL, radiologist, educator; b. Greensboro, N.C., Jan. 24, 1928; s. Guy Dill and Frances Tanner (Porter) P.; B.S., U. Chgo., 1957, M.D., 1960; m. Pearl Baer, May 11, 1951. Intern, Blodgett Meml. Hosp., Grand Rapids, Mich., 1960-61; resident U. Chgo. Clinics, 1961-64; instr. to prof. radiology Coll. Physicians and Surgeons, Columbia U., N.Y.C., 1964-78; asst. to attending radiologist Presbyn. Hosp., N.Y.C., 1964-78; dir. dept. radiology mem. med. bd. Lenox Hill Hosp., N.Y.C., 1979—; prof. clin. radiology Cornell U. Coll. Medicine, N.Y.C., 1979—; cons. USPHS, 1966—, VA, 1975. Served with AUS, 1946-47. Named Hickey Lectr., Mich. Radiol. Soc., 1973. Fellow Am. Coll. Radiology (chmn. com. head and neck evaluation, dir. N.Y. State chpt.), mem. Radiol. Soc. N. Am., AMA, N.Y. Otol. Soc., N.Y. State Med. Soc., N.Y. County Med. Soc., N.Y. Roentgen Soc., Am. Roentgen Ray Soc. Author: Sectional Anatomy and Tomography of the Head, 1971; numerous articles on radiology of the ear, sinuses and skull; editor: Radiology of the Ear, 1974; co-editor: Disorders of the Head and Neck, 1977. Office: 100 E 77th St New York NY 10021

POTTER, JAMES LEE, investment banker; b. Gardiner, Maine, 1889; s. James E. and Nellie (Jackins) P.; student pub. schs.; m. Bessie G. Thayer, Sept. 1915. Apprentice, engr. electric plant, 1906-14; salesman, head comml. dept. Greenfield Electric Light & Power Co., 1914-17; supt. Amherst Gas Co., 1917-18; gen. mgr. Newburyport Gas & Electric Co., 1918-25; salesman, statistician Arthur W. Wood Co., investment bankers, Boston, 1925-28, v.p., dir., 1928-35, now chmn. bd. Home: 360 High St Newburyport MA 01950 Office: 19 Congress St Boston MA 02110

POTTER, JOSEPH DENTON RAND, steel co. exec.; b. Digby, N.S., Can., Dec. 18, 1942; s. E. Keith and Ruberta (Rand) P.; student Acadia U., 1962-65; LL.B., Dalhousie U., 1968; m. Edith B. Evenden, Aug. 21, 1965; children—Janet Lynn, Jennifer, Sarah. Called to Ont. bar, 1970; with Algoma Steel Corp., Ltd., Sault Ste. Marie, Ont., 1968—, asst. sec., 1970-71, sec., 1971-76, v.p. corporate services, 1976-77, group v.p. fin. and corp. services, 1977—. Mem. Law Soc. Upper Canada, Canadian Bar Assn. Home: 118 Leo Ave Sault Ste Marie ON Canada Office: 503 Queen St E Sault Ste Marie ON P6A 5P2 Canada

POTTER, KARL HARRINGTON, educator; b. Oakland, Cal., Aug. 19, 1927; s. George Reuben and Mabel (Harrington) P.; grad. Taft Sch., 1942-45; A.B., U. Cal. at Berkeley, 1950; M.A., Harvard, 1952, Ph.D., 1955; m. Antonia Fleak, June 26, 1957; children—David Fleak, Julie Ann. Instr. philosophy Carleton Coll., 1955-56; mem. faculty U. Minn., 1956-71, prof. philosophy, 1965-70, chmn. dept. philosophy, 1964-67, dir. S. Asia Center, 1967-70; prof. philosophy and S. Asian studies U. Wash., 1971—, asso. dir. S. Asia program, 1972—. Served with USNR, 1945-46. Fulbright fellow, India, 1952-53, 59-60; Am. Inst. Indian Studies fellow, India, 1963-64. Mem. Assn. for Asian Studies (bd. dirs., mem. S. Asia regional council 1971-74, chmn. council 1972-74), Am. Philos. Assn. U. Profs., Am. Oriental Soc., Soc. for Asian and Comparative Philosophy (pres. 1968-70). Author: The Padarthatattvanirupanam of Raghunatha Siromani, 1957; Presuppositions of India's Philosophies, 1963; Ency. of Indian Philosophies, 1970, 77. Home: 19548 47th Ave NW Seattle WA 98155 Office: Dept Philosophy Univ Washington Seattle WA 98105

POTTER, LOREN DAVID, educator; b. Fargo, N.D., June 23, 1918; s. John Henning and Jessie Alice (Payne) P.; B.S., N.D. State U., 1940; student Ia. State U., 1941; M.A., Oberlin Coll., 1946; Ph.D., U. Minn., 1948; m. Elvira V. Heuer, June 10, 1941; children—Claudia Ann, Nancy Ellen, Audrey Louise, Janet Lynn. With N.D. Game and Fish Dept., 1941; research div. Goodyear Tire & Rubber Co., 1943-45; from asst. prof. to prof. biology N.D. State U., 1948-58; chmn. biology dept. U. N.Mex., 1958-72; prof. plant ecology, 1972—, also Radiation Biol. Insts. Recipient numerous research grants plant ecology. Fellow A.A.A.S.; mem. Ecol. Soc. Am., Am. Soc. Range Mgmt., Sigma Xi, Phi Kappa Phi. Home: 1612 Lafayette Dr NE Albuquerque NM 87106

POTTER, PHILIP ALFORD, clergyman, assn. exec.; b. Dominica, West Indies, Aug. 19, 1921; s. Clement and Violet (Peters) P.; student Caenwood Theol. Coll., Jamaica, 1944-47, Richmond Coll., Eng., 1947-48; B.D., London U., 1947, M.Th., 1954; Th.D., U. Hamburg (Germany), 1971; LL.D., U. West Indies, 1974; m. Doreen Cousins, Apr. 7, 1956. Missionary, overseas sec. Student Christian Movement, Gt. Britain, 1948-50; ordained to ministry Methodist Ch.; pastor Meth. Ch., Haiti, 1950-54; sec. World Council Chs. Youth Dept., 1954-57, exec. sec. youth dept., 1957-60, dir. Commn. World Mission and Evangelism, 1967-72, gen. sec. World Council Chs., Geneva, Switzerland, 1972—; sec. for West Africa and West Indies Meth.

Missionary Soc., London, 1961-66. Author: (with Hendrikus Berkhof) Key Words to the Gospel, 1963; contbg. author Explosives Latein-Amerika. Editor Ecumenical Rev.; contbr. editorials to Internat. Rev. Mission. Home: 6 chemin de Tavernay 1218 Geneva Switzerland Office: 150 route de Ferney 1211 Geneva 20 Switzerland*

POTTER, RALPH BENAJAH, JR., educator; b. Los Angeles, May 19, 1931; s. Ralph Benajah and Vivian Irene MacNabb (Borden) P.; B.A., Occidental Coll., 1952; postgrad. Pacific Sch. Religion, 1952-53; B.D., McCormick Theol. Sem., 1955; Th.D. (Presbyn. Grad. fellow 1958-63, Rockefeller fellow 1961-62, Kent fellow 1963-63), Harvard, 1965; m. Jean Ishbel MacCormick, Aug. 15, 1953; children—Anne Elizabeth, Ralph Andrew, James David, Margaret Jean. Ordained to ministry Presbyn. Ch., 1955; dir., pastor Clay County Presbyn. Larger Parish, Manchester, Ky., 1955-58; sec. social edn. Bd. Christian Edn., United Presbyn. Ch. in U.S.A., Phila., 1963-65; asst. prof. social ethics Harvard Div. Sch., mem. Center for Population Studies, Harvard, Cambridge, Mass., 1965-69, prof., 1969—. Theologian-in-residence Am. Ch. in Paris, France, 1975; sr. research scholar Kennedy Inst. for Bio-ethics Georgetown U., 1974. Fellow Inst. Soc., Ethics and Life Scis.; mem. Am. Soc. Polit. and Legal Philosophy, Am. Soc. Christian Ethics, Soc. for Values in Higher Edn., Societe Europeene de Culture, War-Nation-Ch. Study Group. Author: War and Moral Discourse, 1969. Contbr. chpts. to The Religious Situation: 1968, 1968; Religion and the Public Order, 1968; Toward a Discipline of Social Ethics, 1972; The Population Crisis and Moral Responsibility, 1973. Office: 45 Francis Ave Cambridge MA 02138

POTTER, RICHARD CARTER, coll. dean; b. Ekalaka, Mont., May 19, 1919; s. Martin James and Inez (Reishus) P.; B.S., Purdue U., 1940, M.S., 1947, Ph.D. (research fellow), 1950; m. Eleanor Ann Stimson, Aug. 18, 1948; children—Rosann Enes Potter Lopez-Balbontin, Ellen Wells Potter Hervey, Joan Carter Potter Adan, Martin Cody, Richard Carter, Curtis Jeffrey. Asst. research engr. Crane Co., Chgo., 1940-46; asso prof., asst. dean Kans. State U., Manhattan, 1949-52, asso. dean, prof. mech. engring., 1952-59; research staff mem. Gen. Atomic div. Gen. Dynamics, San Diego, 1959-60; mgr. tech. staff devel. Ramo-Wooldridge div. Thompson Ramo-Wooldridge, Canoga Park, Calif., 1960; mgr. profl. placement and devel. Space Tech. Labs., Inc., Los Angeles, 1960-63; dir. Inst. Indsl. Research, prof. research U. Louisville, 1963-65; pres. Northrop Inst. Tech., Inglewood, Calif., 1966-67; dir. ednl. services Calif. State U., Long Beach, 1967-69, dean Sch. Engring., 1969—. Cons. mem. selection com. NSF fellowships, 1960-62. Coll. chmn. United Fund, Manhattan, 1956; coll. chmn. St. Mary's Hosp. Fund, Manhattan, 1958. Served with AUS, 1941-46; PTO; col. Res. Ret. Recipient Silver Anniversary award Sports Illustrated Mag., 1964; named to Purdue U. R.O.T.C. Hall of Fame, 1975. Registered profl. engr., Kans. Mem. Am. Soc. Engring. Edn., ASME, Western Coll. Assn. (mem. exec. com.), Sigma Xi, Phi Gamma Delta, Sigma Tau, Phi Kappa Phi, Pi Tau Sigma, Tau Beta Pi. Republican. Episcopalian. Rotarian. Home: 209 N Hillcrest Blvd Inglewood CA 90301 Office: 1250 Bellflower Blvd Long Beach CA 90840

POTTER, ROBERT JOSEPH, capital good mfg. exec.; b. N.Y.C., Oct. 29, 1932; s. Mack and Ida (Bernstein) P.; B.S. cum laude (Kroner scholar), Lafayette Coll., 1954; M.A. in Physics, U. Rochester, 1957, Ph.D. in Optics, 1960; m. Natalie Joan Silverstein, Sept. 9, 1956; children—Diane Gail, Suzanne Lee, David Craig. Cons., ANPA Research Inst., AEC Brookhaven Nat. Lab., RCA Labs., U.S. Naval Research Labs., 1952-60; mgr. optical physics and optical pattern recognition IBM Thomas J. Watson Research Center, Yorktown Heights, N.Y., 1960-65; asso. dir. Applied Research Lab., Xerox Corp., Rochester, N.Y., 1965-67, v.p., mgr. advanced engring., 1967-68, v.p., mgr. devel. and engring. Info Systems div., 1968-69, v.p., gen. mgr. Spl. Products and Systems div., Stamford, Conn. and Pasadena, Calif., 1969-71, v.p. info. tech. group, mgr. devel. dept., Rochester, 1971-73, v.p. info. tech. group, mgr. info. systems, Dallas, 1973-75, pres. Office Systems div., 1975-78; sr. v.p., chief tech. officer Internat. Harvester Co., Chgo., 1978—. Bd. dirs. So. Meth. U. Found. Sci. and Tech., Xerox Center for Health Care Research, Baylor Sch. Medicine, Houston, United Way Met. Dallas; trustee Ill. Inst. Tech. Recipient IBM Outstanding Tech. Contbn. award, 1964. Fellow Optical Soc. Am., Am. Phys. Soc., Phi Beta Kappa, Sigma Xi. Contbr. articles to profl. jours. Home: 170 Enid Ln Northfield IL 60093 Office: 401 N Michigan Ave Chicago IL 60611

POTTER, VAN RENSSELAER, scientist; b. Day County, S.D., Aug. 27, 1911; s. Arthur Howard and Julia Eva (Herpel) P.; B.S. with high honors, S.D. State Coll., 1933, D.Sc. (hon.), 1959; M.S., U. Wis., 1936, Ph.D., 1938; m. Vivian Christensen, Aug. 3, 1935; children—Karin, John, Carl. Nat. Research fellow U. Stockholm, 1938-39, Rockefeller fellow Univ. of Sheffield and Chgo., 1939-40, Bowman fellow U. Wis., 1940-42, asst. prof. oncology, U. of Wis., 1942-45, asso. prof., 1945-47, prof., 1947—; asst. dir. McArdle Lab., 1959—; vis. prof. Andean biology U. San Marcos, Lima, Peru, 1952-53. Recipient Paul Lewis award in enzyme chem., 1947, Bertner award cancer research, U. Tex., 1961; Clowes award Am. Assn. for Cancer Research, 1964; Hubert lectr. Brit. Assn. Cancer Research, 1978; Fellow AAAS, Nat. Acad. Scis.; mem. Am. Soc. Biol. Chemists, Am. Assn. for Cancer Research (pres. 1974-75), Am. Chem. Soc., Am. Soc. Cell Biology (pres. 1964-65), Japan Biochem. Soc. (hon.), Japanese Cancer Assn. (hon.), Am. Acad. Arts and Scis., Sigma Xi, Gamma Alpha. Author: Nucleic Acid Outlines, Vol. 1, 1960; Bioethics Bridge to the Future, 1971; editor: Methods in Medical Research, vol. 1, 1948. Home: 163 N Prospect Ave Madison WI 53705

POTTER, WILLIAM BARTLETT, trucking co. exec.; b. Washington, Jan. 4, 1938; s. George Holland and Virginia (Bartlett) P.; A.B., Princeton, 1960; M.B.A., Emory U., 1962; m. Simone Robert, June 6, 1964; children—Eva Simone, William Bartlett. With Merc.-Safe Deposit & Trust Co., Balt., 1962—, asst. sec., asst. treas., 1964-66, asst. v.p., 1966-68, v.p., 1968-69, sr. v.p., 1969-76, exec. v.p., 1976; exec. v.p. Preston Trucking Co., 1976-77, pres., 1977—; dir. EASCO Corp., Mercantile Bankshares Corp. Bd. govs. Chesapeake Bay Maritime Mus. Clubs: Maryland (Balt.); Greenspring Valley Hunt. Home: Route 4 Peach Blossom Point Easton MD 21601 Office: Preston MD 21655

POTTER, WILLIAM SAMUEL, lawyer; b. Clarksburg, W.Va., Jan. 10, 1905; s. Dorsey Read and May (Wheat) P.; LL.B., U. Va., 1927; m. Alice H. Harvey, June 28, 1930; children—Mary Harvey (Mrs. William L. Kitchel), Florence Allen (Mrs. David Robb), Renee DuPont (Mrs. Peter M. Siegaff). Admitted to Del. bar, 1928. Dir. Shapdale, Inc., Wilmington Trust Co., Del. Wild Lands, Inc. Mem. Del. Racing Commn., 1939-45; Democratic state chmn. Del., 1942-45; mem. Dem. Nat. Com., 1955-72; bd. dirs. Copeland Andelot Found., Del. Racing Assn., Del. Park; trustee Episcopal Ch. Sch. Found., Inc., 1948—, Winterthur Mus., 1952—, U. Va. Law Sch. Found.; mem. bd. visitors U. Va., 1967-79; Mem. Am., Del. (pres. 1942-44) bar assns., Assn. Bar City of N.Y., Soc. Colonial Wars, Am. Judicature Soc., Order of Coif, Phi Beta Kappa. Episcopalian (vestryman; chancellor Diocese of Del.). Clubs: Wilmington, Wilmington Country; Vicemead Hunt; Blue Ridge Country (Milwood, Va.); Raven Soc. Author: Delaware Corporation Law Annotated (with Leahy and Anderson), 1936. Home: 5826 Kennett Pike Wilmington DE 19807 Office: Delaware Trust Bldg Wilmington DE 19801

POTTHOFF, CARL JOHN, physician; b. Morgan, Minn., Jan. 14, 1904; s. Henry Anthony and Florence Amelia (Baechtold) P.; B.S., Hamline U., 1926; M.D., U. Minn., 1933; M.P.H., 1941. High sch. prin., Slayton, Minn., 1926-28; supt. schs., Welcome, Minn., 1928-29; intern Asbury Hosp., Mpls., 1932-33; pvt. practice medicine, Hallock, Minn., 1934-36; asst. prof. biol. sci. and pub. health U. Minn., 1937-41; asso. prof., 1941-45; supr. emergency and admitting service Mpls. Gen. Hosp.; asso. med. dir. A.R.C., Washington, 1945-52; med. dir. Albuquerque Area Bur. Indian Affairs, 1952-53; prof. preventive medicine and pub. health U. Neb., 1954-70, also former chmn.; asst. commr. health, Omaha, 1954-55. Diplomate Am. Bd. Preventive Medicine. Fellow Am. Coll. Preventive Medicine, A.A.A.S., Am. Pub. Health Assn. Author: American Red Cross First Aid Textbook, rev. 1957; American Red Cross First Aid Textbook for Juniors. Columnist Todays Health in Safety & First Aid, 1950-71, Am. Jour. Public Health, 1964-67, Sun City News-Sun, 1973—. Author articles on health. Home: 13830 Whispering Lake Dr Sun City AZ 85351

POTTINGER, JOHN STANLEY, lawyer, former govt. ofcl.; b. Dayton, Ohio, Feb. 13, 1940; s. John Paul and Eleanor Louise (Zeller) P.; B.A. with honors in Govt., Harvard, 1962, LL.B., 1965; LL.D., Lincoln U., 1975, children—Paul, Kathryn, Matthew. Admitted to Calif. bar, 1965; asso. mem. law firm Broad, Khourie and Schulz, San Francisco, 1965-69; cons. HEW, Washington, 1969-70, dir. Office for Civil Rights, also asst. to sec. for civil rights, 1970-73; asst. atty. gen. civil rights div. U.S. Dept. Justice, Washington, 1973-77, spl. asst. to atty. gen., Feb.-Apr., 1977; mem. firm Troy, Malin and Pottinger, Washington, Los Angeles, Paris, 1977—. Pres., Richmond Dist. Community Council, San Francisco, 1968. Bd. dirs. Lighthouse for Blind, San Francisco, 1968; trustee Lawyers' Com. for Civil Rights Under Law, 1979. Named as Future Leader of Am., Time Mag., 1974; recipient award Mexican-Am. Educators Assn., 1972, Nat. Assn. Retarded Citizens, 1975. Contbr. articles to profl. jours. Home: 7107 Helmsdale Rd Bethesda MD 20034 Office: Suite 300 1300 19th St NW Washington DC 20036

POTTS, ALBERT MINTZ, physician, educator; b. Balt., June 8, 1914; s. Isaac and Leah (Mintz) P.; A.B. in Chemistry, Johns Hopkins, 1934; Ph.D. in Biochemistry, U. Chgo., 1938; M.D., Western Res. U., 1948; m. Esther Topkis, June 14, 1938; children—William Topkis, Leah Susan, Deborah. Research asst. U. Chgo., 1938-42, research asso., instr., 1942-44; biochemist Metall. Lab., Manhattan Project, 1944-45; resident ophthalmology Univ. Hosps., Cleve., 1948-50; sr. instr. biochemistry Western Res. U., 1951-54, assos. prof. opthal. research, 1954-59; asst. ophthalmologist Univ. Hosps., Cleve., 1951-59; prof. ophthalmology, dir. research ophthalmology, dept. ophthalmology U. Chgo. Sch. Medicine, 1959-75; prof. ophthalmology, chmn. dept. ophthalmology U. Louisville, 1975—. Mem. sensory diseases study sect. NIH, 1958-63, vision research tng. com., 1962-66, surgeon gen.'s adv. com. smoking and health, 1963-64; mem. com. vision Armed Forces NRC. Mem. Assn. Research Vision and Ophthalmology (Jonas S. Friedenwald Meml. award 1961, pres. 1974), Am. Ophthal. Soc., Am. Acad. Ophthalmology and Otolaryngology, Am. Chem. Soc., Am. Soc. Biol. Chemists, Soc. Exptl. Biology and Medicine, AAAS, AAUP, Chgo. Ophthal. Soc. (program chmn. 1964-65, councillor 1966-67, pres. 1971-72), Soc. Med. History Chgo. Contbr. articles to profl. jours. Address: Dept Ophthalmology U Louisville Sch Medicine 301 E Walnut St Louisville KY 40202

POTTS, DEAN, grocery chain exec.; b. Blairsville, Pa., Aug. 31, 1926; s. Samuel M. and Helen (Bergman) P.; B.S., U. Pitts., 1948. With Great Atlantic & Pacific Tea Co., 1948-77, comptroller, 1968-77, v.p., sec., 1970-75, v.p. finance, treas., 1975-77; sr. v.p. finance, treas. First Nat. Supermarkets Inc., 1977-78, pres., 1978—. Served with USAAF, 1945. Mem. Fin. Execs. Inst. Clubs: Harvard (N.Y.); Stamford Yacht (Conn.). Home: 39 MacArthur Ln Stamford CT 06902 Office: 1 Myrtle St Hartford CT 06105

POTTS, DOUGLAS GORDON, neuroradiologist; b. New Zealand, Jan. 27, 1927; s. Leslie Andrew and Vera (Morgan) P.; B.Sc., Canterbury Univ. Coll., Christchurch, New Zealand, 1946; M.B., Ch.B., U. Otago, Dunedin, New Zealand, 1951; M.D., U. New Zealand, 1960; m. Ann Jean Frank, June 16, 1962; children—David Andrew, Kenneth Morgan, Alison Jean. Came to U.S., 1960, naturalized, 1966. Intern Auckland (New Zealand) Hosp., 1952-53, resident radiology, 1954-55; sr. registrar Atkinson Morley's Hosp., London, England, 1958-59, Nat. Hosp., London, England, 1959-60; radiologist Presbyn. Hosp., N.Y.C., 1960-67, N.Y. Hosp., 1967—; prof. radiology Cornell U. Med. Coll., 1970—. Mem. Am. Soc. Neuroradiology (pres. 1970-71). Author: (with Pool) Aneurysms and Arteiovenous Anomalies of the Brain, 1965 Editor: (with T.H. Newton) Radiology of the Skull and Brain, Vol. 1, 1971, Vol. 2, 1974, Vol. 3, 1977, Vol. 4, 1978. Home: 239 Mountain Rd Englewood NJ 07631 Office: New York Hospital 525 E 66th St New York City NY 10021

POTTS, GERALD NEAL, mfg. co. exec.; b. Franklin, N.C., Apr. 10, 1933; s. Joseph Thomas and Virgie (Bryant) P.; B.S., U. N.C., 1954; grad. Advanced Mgmt. Program, Harvard, 1973; m. Ann Eliza Underwood, Dec. 21, 1956; children—Catherine Ann, Thomas Underwood, Alice Ann. Purchasing agt. Vulcan Mold & Iron Co., Chgo., 1957-59, sales engr., 1959-62, gen. sales mgr. Latrobe, Pa., 1963-65, v.p. sales, 1965-68; v.p. Vulcan, Inc., Latrobe, 1968-72, exec. v.p., 1972-73, pres., 1973—, chief exec. officer, 1977—, also dir. Bd. dirs. Latrobe Area Hosp., 1967—; trustee Greater Latrobe Community Chest, 1970—, pres., 1978-79; adv. bd. U. Pitts. at Greensburg, 1974—; trustee Seton Hill Coll., Greensburg, 1978—. Served with AUS, 1954-55. Mem. Am. Iron and Steel Inst., Am. Inst. Metall. Engrs., Young Presidents Orgn., Chi Phi. Mason (Shriner, 32 deg.). Clubs: Rolling Rock (Ligonier, Pa.); Duquesne (Pitts.); Olympia Fields (Ill.) Country. Home: 800 Spring St Latrobe PA 15650 Office: PO Box 70 Latrobe PA 15650

POTTS, JOSEPH MCKEAN, II, mfg. co. exec.; b. Pottstown, Pa., Sept. 3, 1918; s. Lemuel Eastburn and Sara P. (Root) P.; B.A., Princeton, 1941; m. Helen Cashwell Bolling, July 22, 1949; children—Joseph McKean III, Thomas Bolling. With Bonney Forge & Tool Works, Allentown, Pa., 1949-65, pres., 1959-65; pres. Miller Mfg. Co., Detroit, 1965—; pres. Bonney Forge & Foundry, Inc., Allentown, 1965-69, chmn., 1969-74; pres. Bonney Group and v.p. Gulf and Western Mfg. Co., Allentown, 1972-74; pres. Taylor-Bonney Internat. and v.p. G & W Energy Products Group, 1974-77; v.p., gen. mgr. splty. products div. G & W Energy Products Group, 1977—; chmn. Bonney Forge Internat. Ltd., Irvine, Scotland; dir. TF de Mexico, S.A., Mexico City, Metalmeg, S.A., Caracas, Venezuela, Bonney Forge Italia, Albano, Italy, Tubacex Taylor Accesorios, S.A., Llodio, Spain, John M. Henderson & Co. (Holdings) Ltd., London, 1974-77. Trustee, Hill Sch., Pottstown Pa. and Allentown YMCA, 1979—. Served to maj. AUS, 1941-46. Mem. Allentown-Lehigh County C. of C. (bd. govs. 1964-69), Newcomen Soc., Pa. Soc. Republican. Presbyn. Mason. Clubs: Livingston, Lehigh Country, Lehigh Valley (Allentown); Mid Ocean (Bermuda); Country of N.C.; Princeton (N.Y.C.). Home: RD 2 Riverbend Rd Allentown PA 18103 Office: 1444 Hamilton St Allentown PA 18105

POTTS, KEVIN T., educator; b. Sydney, Australia, Oct. 26, 1928; B.Sc., U. Sydney, 1950, M.Sc., 1951; D. of Philosophy in Organic Chemistry, Oxford U. (Eng.), 1954, D.Sc., 1973; married, 1959; children—Mary Ellen, Jeannette, Karen, Susan. Demonstrator chemistry, U. Sydney, 1950, teaching fellow, 1951; research asst. organic chemistry Oxford U., 1951-54; scientist Med. Research Council of Eng., 1954-56; research asst. organic chemistry Harvard, 1956-58; lectr. Adelaide, 1958-61; asso. prof. chemistry Louisville U., 1961-65; prof. chemistry Rensselaer Poly. Inst., 1966—, chmn. dept., 1973—. Nat. Cancer Inst. grantee, Nat. Heart Inst. grantee, AEC grantee, NSF grantee. Mem. A.A.A.S., Am., Brit. chem. socs., Royal Inst. Chemistry. Contbr. articles in field organic chemistry to sci. jours. Home: 1199 Godfrey Lane Schenectady NY 12309 Office: Dept Chemistry Rennselaer Poly Inst 110 Eighth Troy NY 12181

POTTS, MERLE DEAN, grocery chain exec.; b. Blairsville, Pa., Aug. 31, 1926; s. Samuel M. and Helen (Bergman) P.; B.S., U. Pitts., 1948. With Great Atlantic & Pacific Tea Co., 1948—, comptroller, 1968—, v.p.. sec., 1970-75, v.p. finance, treas., 1975-77; sr. v.p., chief fin. officer, treas. First Nat. Supermarkets Inc., 1977—. Served with USAAF, 1945. Home: 39 MacArthur Ln Stamford CT 06902 Office: 1 Myrtle St Hartford CT 06105

POTTS, NADIA, ballet dancer; b. London, Apr. 20, 1948; d. Robert E. and Lucy N. (Creed) P.; came to Can., 1952; student Nat. Ballet Sch. Can., Toronto, Ont., 1960-66; m. Harold Gomez, June 11, 1975. With Nat. Ballet of Can., Toronto, 1966—, soloist, 1968-69, prin., 1969—. Recipient Bronze medal and 1st prize for best pas de deux Internat. Ballet Competition, Varna, Bulgaria, 1970. Danced opposite Barishnikov in his first Swan Lake, 1975, also with Nureyev, Bruhn. Office: 157 King St E Toronto ON M5C 1G9 Canada

POTTS, RAMSAY DOUGLAS, lawyer; b. Memphis, Oct. 24, 1916; s. Ramsay Douglas and Ann Clifton (VanDyke) P.; B.S., U. N.C., 1941; LL.B., Harvard U., 1948; m. Veronica Hamilton Raynor, Dec. 22, 1945; children—Ramsay Douglas, David Hamilton, Lesley Ann, Lindsay Veronica. Commd. 2d lt. USAAF, 1941, advanced through grades to maj. gen. Res., 1961; squadron and group comdr. 8th Air Force, Eng., 1942-44, dir. bomber operations, 1944-45; exec. officer mil. analysis div. U.S. Strategic Bombing Survey, 1945; staff, faculty Air War Coll., Montgomery, Ala., 1948-49; dep. exec. officer, exec. officer Sec. Air Force, 1950-51; wing comdr. 459th Troop Carrier Wing, 1955-60; chmn. Sec. Air Force Air Res. Policy Com., 1967-68; admitted to D.C. bar, 1954; practice in Washington, 1955—; spl. asst. to chmn. Nat. Security Resources Bd., 1951; pres. Ind. Mil. Air Transport Assn., 1952-55; partner Shaw, Pittman, Potts & Trowbridge, 1956—. Mem. State Council Higher Edn. for Va., 1968-71. Trustee Air Force Hist. Found. (pres. 1971-75). Decorated D.S.C., Silver Star medal with oak leaf cluster, Legion of Merit, Bronze Star medal, D.F.C. with 2 oak leaf clusters, Air medal with 5 oak leaf clusters, Brit. D.F.C., French Croix de Guerre. Mem. Am., D.C. bar assns., Phi Beta Kappa. Clubs: City Tavern, Metropolitan (Washington); Harvard (N.Y.C.); Army Navy Country (Arlington, Va.). Contbr. articles to profl. jours. Home: 1650 30th St NW Washington DC 20007 Office: 1800 M St NW Washington DC 20036

POTTS, ROBERT ANTHONY, publisher; b. Chester, Pa., Sept. 11, 1927; s. William James and Sara Louise (Watson) P.; B.A., Pace Coll., 1952; m. Eva A. Morra, Sept. 8, 1955; children—Mark, Matthew, Amy, Abby. Vice pres. Cahners Pub. Co., Inc., N.Y.C., 1952-72, Intercontinental Publs., Stamford, Conn., 1972-75; exec. v.p., pub. Dun's Review Mag. Dun & Bradstreet Publs., N.Y.C., 1975—. Served with USAAF, 1945-47. Club: Wings (N.Y.C.). Contbr. articles on sales and publ. mgmt. for Folio Mag. Office: 666 Fifth Ave New York NY 10019

POTTS, ROBERT HENDERSON, bank exec.; b. Wayne, Pa., Feb. 1, 1924; s. Joseph and Mabel C. (Green) Potts; B.A., Yale U., 1945; student Am. Mgmt. Assn. Sch.; postgrad. U. Pa., 1949-52; m. Edith Halsey Ligget, July 6, 1946; children—Susan Potts Bloom, Robert Henderson, Thomas H., David L. Vice chmn., dir. Phila. Nat. Bank, 1949-74; with City Nat. Bank & Trust Co. of Columbus (Ohio), 1974—, pres., 1974-77, chmn., chief exec. officer, 1977—; dir. First Banc Group Ohio, Inc., VISA, U.S.A. and Internat., Alco Standard Corp., Ironsides Co., Potts Ice Cream Co. Bd. dirs. Devel. Com. for Greater Columbus; trustee United Way, Columbus. Served to maj. USMC, 1942-46, 52-53. Decorated Air medal. Mem. Columbus Area C. of C. (dir.). Republican. Clubs: Yale of Columbus, The Golf, Columbus, Rocky Fork Hunt and Country, Pine Valley Golf. Office: City Nat Bank and Trust Co 100 E Broad St Columbus OH 43215*

POTVIN, DENIS CHARLES, hockey player; b. Hull, Que., Can., Oct. 29, 1953; s. Armand Jean and Lucille (St. Louis) P.; came to U.S., 1973; student pub. schs., Hull; m. Deborah Anne Taylor. June 22, 1974. Hockey player Ottawa 67s Jr. Hockey League, 1967-73, New York Islanders, Nat. Hockey League, 1973—; part prin. in mktg. firm People & Properties. Inc., 1973-77. Recipient Calder trophy as Rookie of Year, 1973-74, Norris trophy as best defenseman, 1975-76; mem. All Star Team, 4 times in 6 years. Author: Power on Ice, 1977. Office: 914 3d Ave New York NY 10022

POTVIN, PIERRE, educator; b. Quebec City, Que., Can., Jan. 5, 1932; s. Rosario and Eva (Montreuil) P.; B.A., Laval U., Que., 1950, M.D., 1955; Ph.D., U. Toronto, 1962; m. Louise Dube, Aug. 31, 1963; children—Aline, Bernard. Intern Ste.-Foy Hosp., Quebec City, 1955-56; asst. prof. physiology Laval U., 1960-66, asso. prof., 1966-69, prof., 1969—, dir. preclin. med. studies, 1970-75, pres. health scis. com., 1970-74, sec. faculty of medicine, 1975—, exec. asst. dean, 1977—. Asst. editor of Laval Med., 1960-70. Médecine Moderne du Canada, 1957-61. Home: 1915 rue Bourbonniere Quebec City PQ G1S 1N3 Canada Office: Faculte de medecine Universite Laval Quebec City PQ 10 Canada

POTVIN, RAYMOND HERVE, educator, author; b. Southbridge, Mass., Oct. 28, 1924; s. Cleophas R. and Eva (Beauvais) P.; S.T.B., U. Montreal, 1948; Ph.D., Catholic U. Am., 1958. Ordained priest Roman Cath. Ch., 1948; asst. pastor, Springfield, Mass., 1948-53; mem. faculty Cath. U., 1958—, prof. sociology, 1967—, chmn. dept., 1968-71, 77—, dir. Inst. Social and Behavioral Research, 1972-74; sr. researcher Boys Town Center, 1974—. Fellow Population Council, 1966-67. Fellow Am. Sociol. Assn., Population Assn. Author: (with Charles Westoff) College Women and Fertility Values, 1967; (with Antanas Suziedelis) Seminarians of the Sixties, 1970; (with Antanas Suziedelis) Vocational Challenge and Seminary Response, 1971; (with D. Hoge and H. Nelson) Religion and American Youth, 1976; (with Hart Nelsen and Joseph Shields) The Religion of Children, 1977. Address: Box 1264 Catholic Univ Washington DC 20017

POU, EMILY HOTCHKISS QUINN, educator; b. Pitts.; d. Leonard B. and Thelma (Jennings) Hotchkiss; B.S., Ga. State Coll. for Women, 1948; M.S., U. Wis., 1962, Ph.D., 1964; m. Robert Earl Quinn, Aug. 25, 1955 (div. June 1958); 1 son, David Michael; m. 2d, John William Pou, Oct. 6, 1973. Extension home economist U. Ga., Athens, 1955-56, U. Ariz., Tucson, 1956-61; fellow U. Wis., Madison,

1961-63; asso. prof. edn. N.C. State U., Raleigh, 1964-67, prof. edn., state leader tng., 1967-71; dean Coll. Home Econs., U. Ga., 1971—. Recipient Friend of Extension in Home Econs. award Ga. Coop. Extension Service, 1976; Ag Hill Council Disting. Service award, 1978, others. Mem. Adult Edn. Assn. U.S., Ga. Adult Edn. Assn., Ga. Nutrition Council, Am. Home Econs. Assn., Ga. Home Econs. Assn., So. Assn. Home Econs. Adminstrs., Assn. Adminstrs. Home Econs. (exec. bd.), Phi Upsilon Omicron, Omicron Nu, Delta Kappa Gamma. Author: (with E.J. Boone and E.H. Quinn) Curriculum Development in Adult Basic Education, 1967; cons. editor Adult Edn. Jour. Home: 379 Sandstone Dr Athens GA 30605

POUGH, FREDERICK HARVEY, mineralogist; b. Bklyn., June 26, 1906; s. Francis H. and Alice H. (Beckler) P.; S.B., Harvard, 1928, Ph.D., 1935; M.S., Washington U., 1932; student Ruperto Carola, Heidelberg, Germany, 1932-33; m. Eleanor C. Hodge, Oct. 14, 1938 (dec. May 1966); children—Frederick Harvey, Barbara Hodge. Asst. curator mineralogy Am. Mus. Natural History, N.Y.C., 1935-40, acting curator, 1941, curator, 1942-44, curator phys. geology and mineralogy, 1942-52, cons. mineralogist, 1953-64, 66—; gem cons. Jewelers Circular-Keystone, 1940—; dir. Santa Barbara Mus. Natural History, 1965-66; pres. Mineralogy, Inc., 1978—. Recipient Bronze medal Royal Geol. Soc., Belgium, 1948, Derby medal Brazilian Geol. Survey; named Mineralogist of Year, Am. Fedn. Mineral. Soc., 1966. Fellow Mineral Soc. Am., Geol. Soc. Am.; mem. Mineral Soc. Gt. Britain. Clubs: Harvard (N.Y.C.); Explorers. Author: Jewelers Dictionary, 1945, 50, 76; Field Guide to Rocks and Minerals, 1953, 76; All About Volcanoes and Earthquakes, 1953, Hindi translation, 1958, Persian translation, 1959, Bengali translation, 1959, Italian translation, 1960, Arabic translation, 1962, Portuguese translation, 1964; Our Earth, 1961; The Story of Gems and Semi-Precious Stones, 1967; Guide des Roches et Mineraux, 1969. Contbg. editor: Lapidary jour. Address: Box 7004 Reno NV 89510

POUGH, RICHARD HOOPER, conservationist; b. Bklyn., Apr. 19, 1904; s. Francis Harvey and Alice (Beckler) P.; student Washington U., 1921-24; B.S., Mass. Inst. Tech., 1926; postgrad. Harvard, 1926-27; LL.D., Haverford Coll., 1970; m. Moira Flannery, Dec. 3, 1937; children—Edward Warren, Tristram Hooper. Chem. and mech. engrng. positions So. Acid & Sulphur Co., Port Arthur, Tex., Fulton Iron Works, St. Louis, 1927-31; propr. MacCallum Stores, Phila., 1932-36; staff Nat. Audubon Soc., N.Y.C., 1936-48; chmn. dept. conservation and gen. ecology Am. Mus. Natural History, N.Y.C., 1948-56; pres. Natural Area Council, Inc., 1957; pres. Open Space Int., Inc., 1957-74. Dir. Center for the Hudson Valley, Inc. Mem. exec. com. Scenic Hudson Preservation Conf.; vice chmn. Marine Resources Com. Dir. Feinstone Environmental Awards, Spirit of Stockholm Found.; chmn. Am. the Beautiful Fund; adv. council Trust for Pub. Lands; mem. assembly, Inst. of Ecology, trustee Nat. Sci. Youth Found., Thorne Ecol. Inst., Sapelo Island Research Found.; pres. Goodhill Found., Vineyard Open Land Found., Charles A. Lindbergh Meml. Fund. Recipient medal Federated Garden Clubs Conn., 1958; Frances Hutchinson medal Garden Club Am., 1961; Conservation award, Am. Motors Corp., 1962; Horace M. Albright medal, Am. Scenic and Historic Preservation Soc., 1963; Man of Yr. award Pelham Men's Club; Silver medal Federated Garden Clubs N.Y. State; Distinguished Service medal Bklyn. Bot. Garden. Fellow AAAS, Linnaean Soc. (pres. 1943-45); mem. Internat. Council Bird Preservation (sec. 1950- 60, chmn. U.S. sect. 1954-60), 1943-45), Defenders of Wildlife (past pres., dir.), Am. Ornithologists' Union (past chmn. bird protection com.), Nature Conservancy (gov., past pres.), John Burroughs Meml. Assn. (past pres., dir.), Island Beach Nat. Monument Com. (past chmn.), Assn. Protection of Adirondacks (past pres., hon. trustee), Am. Scenic and Historic Soc. (trustee), National Parks and Conservation Assn. (trustee), Vineyard Conservation Soc. (adviser), Alpha Tau Omega, Alpha Chi Sigma, Tau Beta Pi. Clubs: Men's Garden (N.Y.C.); Boone and Crockett; Explorers. Author: Audubon Bird Guides, 3 vols. 1946, 51, 57, also sci. papers and mag. articles. Home: 33 Highbrook Ave Pelham NY 10803 Office: 145 E 52d St New York NY 10022

POUL, FRANKLIN, lawyer; b. Phila., Nov. 6, 1924; s. Boris and Anna P.; student U. Pa., 1942-43, Haverford Coll., 1943-44; LL.B. cum laude, U. Pa., 1946; m. Shirley Weissman, June 26, 1949; children—Leslie R., Alan M., Laurie J. Admitted to Pa. bar, 1949, U.S. Supreme Ct., 1955; asso. firm Gray, Anderson, Schaffer & Rome, Phila., 1948-56; asso. firm Wolf, Block, Schorr and Solis-Cohen, Phila., 1956-60, partner, 1960—. Bd. dirs. ACLU, Phila., 1955—, pres., 1975-76. Served with AUS, 1943-46. Mem. Am. Law Inst., Am. Bar Assn., Order of Coif. Office: 12th Fl Packard Bldg Philadelphia PA 19102

POULIOT, JEAN A., broadcasting exec.; b. Quebec, Que., Can., June 6, 1923; s. Adrien and Laure (Clark) P.; ed. Seminaire de Quebec and Laval U., Quebec, received C.M., B.A., B.A.Sc.; m. Rachel Lebel, Sept. 8, 1945; children—Jean, Vincent, Louise, Adrien, Martin. Electronic research engr. Can. Army, Ottawa, Ont., 1945-49; supt. Can. Navy Labs., Ottawa, 1949-52; exec. engr. TV dept. Famous Players Co., Toronto, 1952-57; gen. mgr. Television de Que. (Can.) Ltd., 1957-62, mng. dir., 1962-71; pres., chief exec. officer Tele-Capitale Ltee., 1971-78; pres., chief exec. officer CFCF Inc., Montreal, Que., 1979—; pres. Red Carpet Aero Services Inc., Quebec Aviation Ltd., Quebec Aviation Air Services Ltd., Broadcast News, No. Multicorp Ltd., Unicom Broadcast Sales Ltd., Electromedia Sales Ltd., Cine-Capitale Ltee; v.p. CHRC Ltee., Cin-Video Inc., Les Productions du Verseau, Radio Laval Inc.; dir. Tele-Metropole Inc., Cite-Jardin Vantadour Quebec Inc., Television de la Baie des Chateurs; mem. cons. com. Royal Trust Co. Mem. Can. Assn. Broadcasters (pres. 1965-67), Assn. Profl. Engrs. Roman Catholic. Clubs: The Garrison, Royal Quebec Golf, Mt. Royal. Home: 1677 Place de Bruyere Quebec PQ G1W 3G9 Canada Office: 405 Ogilvy Ave Montreal PQ H3N 1M4 Canada

POULOS, MICHAEL JAMES, life ins. co. exec.; b. Glens Falls, N.Y., Feb. 13, 1931; s. James A. and Mary P.; B.A., Colgate U., 1953; M.B.A., N.Y. U., 1963; m. Bessie Kefalas, Aug. 15, 1951; children—Denise, Peter. With sales and mgmt. depts. U.S. Life Ins. Co., N.Y.C., 1958-65, asst. v.p., 1965-67, 2d v.p., chief adminstrv. officer for sales, 1967-68, sec., treas., dir., 1968, v.p. adminstrn., 1969, mem. exec. com., 1970; v.p. adminstrn. Calif.-Western States Life Ins. Co., Sacramento, 1970, dir., 1971, sr. v.p., 1972, exec. v.p., chmn. investment com., 1974, pres., chief exec. officer, dir., 1975—; sr. v.p. div. head life ins. Am. Gen. Ins. Co., 1979; chmn. bd. AG Life Ins. Co., AG Life Ins. Co. Del., Cal-Western States Life Ins. Co., Hawaiian Life Ins. Co., Variable Annuity Life Ins. Co., Assn. Calif. Life Ins. Co.; dir. Nat. Pub. Service Ins. Co., Ins. Systems Am., Mem. Am. Soc. C.L.U.'s, Nat. Assn. Life Underwriters, Life Office Mgmt. Assn., Am. Mgmt. Assn., Assn. Calif. Life Ins. Cos., Beta Gamma Sigma, Delta Sigma Pi. Greek Orthodox. Clubs: Houston. Home: 5555 Del Monte Dr Apt 105 Houston TX 77056 Office: 2727 Allen Pkwy Houston TX 77019

POULSON, DONALD FREDERICK, biologist; b. Idaho Falls, Ida., Oct. 5, 1910; s. Christian Frederick and Esther (Johnson) P.; B.S., Cal. Inst. Tech., 1933, Ph.D., 1936; M.A., Yale, 1955; m. Margaret Judd Boardman, June 18, 1934; children—Donald Boardman, Christian Frederick. Teaching fellow biology Cal. Inst. Tech., 1934-36, Gosney research fellow biology, 1949; research asst. dept. embryology Carnegie Inst. Washington, 1936-37; instr. biology Yale, 1937-40, asst. prof., 1940-46, asso. prof., 1946-55, prof., 1955—, chmn. dept. biology, 1962-65; research collaborator Brookhaven Nat. Lab., 1951-55. Fulbright com. NRC, 1958-60; vis. lectr. developmental biology U. Chgo., 1959. Fellow Calhoun Coll., Yale, 1954—; Fulbright sr. research scholar Commonwealth Sci. and Indsl. Research Orgn., Canberra, Australia, 1957-58, 66-67; Guggenheim fellow, 1957-58. Central qualifications bd. Nat. Insts. Health, 1961-63. Fellow A.A.A.S. (council 1960-62); mem. Internat. Soc. Developmental Biologists, A.A.U.P., Am. Soc. of Naturalists (treas. 1951-53), Am. Soc. Zoologists, Genetics Soc. Am., Soc. Developmental Biology, Conn. Acad. Arts and Scis., Sigma Xi. Author: The Embryonic Develoment of Drosophila Melanogaster, 1937; contbr. Biology of Drosophila, 1950. Contbr. articles sci. jours. Home: 96 Green Hill Rd Orange CT 06477 Office: Kline Biology Tower Yale U New Haven CT 06520

POULSON, ROBERT DEAN, lawyer; b. Valparaiso, Ind., June 10, 1927; s. Frank Ferlin and Esther Marie P.; LL.B., Drake U., 1953, J.D., 1974; m. Betty Lou Caroline Mercer, Aug. 19, 1950; children—Richard D., Thomas C., John R. Admitted to Iowa bar, 1953, Ill. bar, 1954, Colo. bar, 1957; staff atty. Texaco, Chgo. and Denver, 1953-59; divisional atty. Superior Oil Co., Denver, 1959-64; sr. partner firm Poulson, Odell & Peterson, Denver, 1964—. Mem. Bow Mar (Colo.) City Council, 1968-72. Served with USN, 1945-47. Mem. Denver, Atapaboe County (Colo.), Colo., Am. bar assns., Rocky Mountain Mineral Law Found. (pres. 1975-76), Rocky Mountain Oil and Gas Assn. (chmn. gen. legal com. 1963-66, trustee 1963—), Ind. Petroleum Assn. Am. (dir.), Phi Alpha Delta. Republican. Methodist. Clubs: Univ. (Denver); Masons. Home: 5455 Lakeshore Dr Littleton CO 80123 Office: 1776 Lincoln St Denver CO 80203

POULTON, BRUCE ROBERT, univ. system chancellor; b. Yonkers, N.Y., Mar. 7, 1927; s. Alfred Vincent and Ella Marie (Scanlon) P.; B.S. with honors, Rutgers U., 1950, M.S., 1952, Ph.D., 1956; m. Elizabeth Charlotte Jerothe, Aug. 26, 1950; children—Randall Lee, Jeffrey Jon, Cynthia Sue, Peter Gregory. Research instr., then asst. prof. Rutgers U., 1952-56; asso. prof., then prof., chmn. dept. animal and vet. sci. U. Maine, 1958-66, dir. Bangor campus, 1967-68, dean, dir. Coll. Life Scis. and Agr., 1968-71, v.p. research and pub. service, 1971-75; chancellor Univ. System N.H., 1975—, also trustee; vis. prof. Mich. State U., 1966-67: Mem. regional adv. com. Farm and Home Administrn.; mem. exec. com., council on research policy and grad. edn. Nat. Assn. State Univs. and Land Grant Colls., also mem. senate; mem. Gov.'s Econ. Advisory Council (N.H.); mem. selection com. Kellogg Found. Lectureship in Agr.; mem. policy devel. com. New Eng. Innovation Group; adv. com. U.S. Command and Gen. Staff Coll. Trustee Unity Coll. Served with AUS, 1944-46. Am. Council Edn. fellow acad. adminstrn., 1966-67. Mem. Am. Inst. Nutrition, Brit. Nutrition Soc., Fedn. Am. Soc. Exptl. Biology, Ams. for Energy Independence (pres. N.H. chpt.), Am. Soc. Exptl. Biology, Am. Soc. Animal Sci., Am. Dairy Sci. Assn. (past pres. Eastern div.), A.A.A.S., Sigma Xi, Alpha Zeta. Author articles in field. Office: Univ System of NH Office Chancellor Durham NH 03824

POULTON, CHARLES EDGAR, natural resources cons.; b. Oakley, Idaho, Aug. 2, 1917; s. Richard and Narrie Jane (Queen) P.; B.S. with high honors, U. Idaho, 1939, M.S., 1948; postgrad. Mont. State Coll., 1946-47; Ph.D., Wash. State U., 1955; postdoctoral U. Calif. at Berkeley, 1967-68; m. Marcile Belle McCoy, Sept. 29, 1939; children—Richard C., Robert J., Mary Jane Poulton Daberkow, Betty Jean Poulton Petrone. Adminstr., researcher U.S. Forest Service, Western states, 1937-46, dist. forest ranger, 1941-46, cons. forest ecology, Ala., Fla., 1958-59; asst. prof. range mgmt. Mont. State Coll., Bozeman, 1946-47; instr. range mgmt. U. Idaho, Moscow, 1947-49; prof., dir. range mgmt. program Oreg. State U., Corvallis, 1949-70, prof. range ecology, 1970-73, dir. Environ. Remote Sensing Applications Lab., 1972-73; dir. range and resource ecology div. Earth Satellite Corp., Berkeley, Calif., 1974-75; sr. officer Rangeland Resources and Pasture, Food and Agr. Orgn. UN, Rome, Italy, 1976-77. Cons. Benton County (Oreg.) in land use planning, 1972-73, NASA, 1967-71. Served with USNR, 1945-46. Recipient merit certificate for outstanding service to grassland agr. Am. Grassland Council, 1963. Mem. Am. Soc. Range Mgmt. (charter, pres. pacific N.W. sect. 1962, nat. dir. 1965-68), Soc. Am. Foresters (chmn. range mgmt. div. 1955), Nat. Acad. Sci. (panels 1969, 73-74), Am. Soc. Photogrammetry, Sigma Xi, Phi Eta Sigma, Xi Sigma Pi. Mem. Christian Ch. Elks. Asso. editor Range Mgmt. Jour. Forestry, 1956-62. Editorial bd. Ecology, 1965-67. Contbr. articles to profl. jours. Home: 121 Muir Ave Santa Clara CA 95051 Office: NASA-Ames Research Center Mail Stop 240-7 Moffett Field CA 94035

POUND, GLENN SIMPSON, univ. dean; b. Hector, Ark., Mar. 7, 1914; s. Leroy and Maude (Bullock) P.; B.A. magna cum laude, U. Ark., 1940; Ph.D., U. Wis., 1943; m. Daisy Cole; children—Robert Arthur, Elizabeth Jane. Mem. faculty U. Wis., 1946—, prof. plant pathology, 1954—, chmn. dept., 1954—, now also dean emeritus agrl. and life scis., acting chancellor, 1977; asso. in pathology U.S. Dept. Agr., 1943-46, collaborator, 1952—. Dir. Merck Co. Rockefeller traveling fellow in Europe, 1959. Mem. Am. Phytopathol. Soc. (sec. 1953-56, pres. 1959, chmn. golden jubilee anniversary celebration 1958), Am. Inst. Biol. Scis., A.A.A.S., Phi Beta Kappa, Sigma Xi, Phi Eta Sigma, Phi Kappa Phi. Baptist. Kiwanian (past lt. gov.). Author tech. publs. vegetable diseases and plant virology. Home: 5377 La Jolla Blvd La Jolla CA 92037

POUND, GUY MARSHALL, educator; b. Portland, Ore., Apr. 2, 1920; s. Guy Aubrey and Besse (Marsh) P.; B.A., Reed Coll., 1941; M.S., Mass. Inst. Tech., 1943; Ph.D., Columbia, 1949; m. Barbara Ann Corbly, June 17, 1944; children—Stephen M., James W., Alexandra W., Guy N., Howard K. Prof. metallurgy and materials sci. Carnegie Inst. Tech., 1949-66, Alcoa prof., dir. metals research lab., 1960-66; prof. materials sci. Stanford, 1966—; v.p. Failure Analysis Assos., Inc., Palo Alto, Calif., 1968—; dir. Stanford/Ames-NASA Inst. for Surface and Microstructure Studies, 1976—; spl. research theory phase transition kinetics. Vis. prof., sr. Fulbright research scholar, Guggenheim fellow U. Sheffield (Eng.), 1959-60; Gastprofessor an der Technischen, U. Berlin, 1964-65, U. Wien (Austria), 1972-73. Mem. Am. Chem. Soc., Am. Soc. Metals (Albert Easton White award 1978), Am. Inst. Metall. Engrs. Author: (with J.P. Hirth) Condensation and Evaporation, 1963. Home: 3003 Country Club Ct Palo Alto CA 94304 Office: Peterson Hall Stanford Univ Stanford CA 94305

POUND, HAROLD DELMAR, govt. ofcl.; b. Empress, Alta., Can., Jan. 22, 1925; s. Edwin Delmar and Leone (Buxton) P.; student pub. schs., Empress; m. Phyllis Mary Sunstrum, May 16, 1948; children—Edwin Andrew, James Donald. Farm mgr. McCabe Grain Co., Brooks, Alta., 1944-53, seed plant mgr., elevator supt., 1953-60; sales coordinator Oliver Indsl. Supplies, Lethbridge, Alta., 1960-68, exec. v.p., gen. mgr., Calgary, Alta., 1968-70; mem. bd. Grain Commrs., Winnipeg, Can., 1970-71; chief commr. Canadian Grain Commn., Winnipeg, 1971—. Dir., Alta. Liberal Party, 1966-68. Mem. Alta. (dir. 1954), Winnipeg chambers commerce. Mem. United Ch. of Canada. Home: 45 Stillwater Rd Winnipeg MB R2J 2R2 Canada Office: 600 303 Main St Winnipeg MB R3C 3G8 Canada

POUND, RICHARD WILLIAM DUNCAN, lawyer, accountant; b. St. Catharines, Ont., Can., Mar. 22, 1942; s. William Thomas and Jessie Edith Duncan (Thom) P.; B.Commerce, McGill U., Montreal, 1962, B.C.L., 1967; B.A., Sir George Williams U., Montreal, 1963; chartered accountant, 1964; m. Julie Houghton Keith, Nov. 4, 1977. Auditor, Riddell, Stead, Graham & Hutchinson, Montreal, 1963-65; law clk.; then atty. firm Laing, Weldon, Courtois, Clarkson, Parsons & Tétrault, Montreal, 1965-71; called to bar, 1968; mem. firm Stikeman, Elliott, Tamaki, Mercier & Robb, Montreal, 1972—; lectr. taxation McGill U. Faculty Law; lectr. Que. Real Estate Assn.; editorial bd. Can. Tax Service. Pres. Canadian Olympic Assn., 1977—, sec., 1968-76; mem. Internat. Olympic Com., 1978—; trustee Martlet Found., Stanstead Wesleyan Coll., McGill U. Athletic Bds. Named to Canadian Swimming Hall of Fame, 1969, Sports Fedn. Can. Hall of Fame, 1976; chartered accountant. Mem. Canadian Bar Assn., Canadian Tax Found., Internat. Fiscal Assn., Canadian Squash Racquets Assn., Royal Life Sav. Soc., Grads. Soc. McGill U. (v.p.). Clubs: Montreal Amateur Athletic Assn., Racket, Badminton and Squash (Montreal); Hillside Tennis, Jesters. Gen. editor: Doing Business in Canada. Home: 87 Arlington Ave Westmount PQ H3Y 2W5 Canada Office: 1155 Dorchester Blvd W Suite 3900 Montreal PQ H3B 3V2 Canada

POUND, ROBERT VIVIAN, physicist; b. Ridgeway, Ont., Can., May 16, 1919; s. Vivian Ellsworth and Gertrude C. (Prout) P.; came to U.S., 1923, naturalized, 1932; B.A., U. Buffalo, 1941; A.M. (hon.), Harvard, 1950; m. Betty Yde Andersen, June 20, 1941; 1 son, John Andrew. Research physicist Submarine Signal Co., 1941-42; staff mem. radiation lab. Mass. Inst. Tech., 1942-46; jr. fellow Soc. Fellows, Harvard, 1945-48, asst. prof. physics, 1948-50, asso. prof., 1950-56, prof., 1956-68, Mallinckrodt prof. physics, 1968—, chmn. dept. physics, 1968-72, dir. Physics Labs., 1975—; Fulbright research scholar Oxford, 1951; vis. prof. Coll. de France, 1973; vis. fellow Joint Inst. Lab. Astrophysics, U. Colo., 1979-80; vis. research fellow Merton Coll., Oxford U., 1980. Trustee, Asso. Univs., Inc., 1976—. Recipient B. J. Thompson Meml. award Inst. Radio Engrs., 1948; John Simon Guggenheim fellow, 1957-58, 1972-73; Fulbright lectr., Paris, 1958; Eddington medal Royal Astron. Soc., 1965. Fellow Am. Phys. Soc., Am. Acad. Arts and Scis.; mem. Nat. Acad. Scis., Soc. Franc. De Physique (membre du conseil 1958-61), Acad. des Scis. (fgn. asso.) (France), Phi Beta Kappa, Sigma Xi. Author, editor: Microwave Mixers, 1948. Contbr. articles to profl. jours. Home: 87 Pinehurst Rd Belmont MA 02178

POUND, RUSSELL FOWLER, JR., banker; b. Plainfield, N.J., Jan. 30, 1932; s. Russell Fowler and Ruth D. (Moffitt) P.; A.S., Mitchell Coll., 1957; grad. Williams Sch. Banking, 1964; postgrad. Sch. Credit and Financial Mgmt., Dartmouth, 1973, postgrad. in bus. Sch. Banking; m. Carol Ann Dunning, Feb. 23, 1957; children—Debra Ann, Sandra Lee, Lee Ann. With Hartford Nat. Bank & Trust Co. (Conn.), 1957—, sr. v.p., mgr. ops. div., 1973—. Trustee Mitchell Coll. Served with AUS, 1950-53. Recipient Outstanding Alumni award Mitchell Coll., 1967; named One of Outstanding Young Men of Am., 1967. Mem. OCR Users Assn. (dir.). Club: Hartford Lions. Home: 133 Hyde Rd West Hartford CT 06117 Office: 150 Windsor St Hartford CT 06120

POUNDER, ELTON ROY, physicist, educator; b. Montreal, Que., Can., Jan. 10, 1916; s. Roy M. and Norval (McLeese) P.; B.Sc., McGill U., Montreal, 1934, Ph.D., 1937; m. Marion Crane Wry, Feb. 15, 1941; children—David Crane, Norval Gillian. Field engr. Bell Telphone Co. Can., Ottawa, Ont., Montreal, 1937-39; faculty McGill U., 1945—, prof. physics, 1959—. Fellow Royal Soc. Can.; mem. Canadian Assn. Physicists (past pres.), Am. Phys. Soc., Am. Geophys. Union. Author: (with J.S. Marshall and R.W. Stewart) Physics, 2d edit., 1967; The Physics of Ice, 1965; also numerous articles. Research on constrn. cyclotron, neutron prodn., doppler radar used mid-Can. line, geophysics of sea ice. Office: Physics Dept McGill U 3600 University St Montreal PQ H3A 2T8 Canada

POUNDS, WILLIAM FRANK, univ. dean; b. Fayette County, Pa., Apr. 9, 1928; s. Joseph Frank and Helen (Fry) P.; B.S. in Chem. Engring., Carnegie Inst. Tech., 1950, M.S. in Math. Econs., 1959, Ph.D. in Indsl. Adminstrn., 1964; m. Helen Ann Means, Mar. 6, 1954; children—Thomas McClure, Julia Elizabeth. Indsl. engr. Eastman Kodak Co., 1950-51, 55-57; cons. Pitts. Plate Glass Co., 1958-59, asst. to gen. mgr. Forbes finishes div., 1960-61; mem. faculty Sloan Sch. Mgmt., Mass. Inst. Tech., 1961—, prof. mgmt., dean, 1966—; cons. to industry, 1958—. Dir. EG&G, Inc., Putnam Funds, Sun Co., Inc., Gen. Mills Inc., M/A COM Inc., Stop and Shop Co., Inc. Served as Naval aviator U.S.N. (j.g.) USNR, 1951-55. Fellow Am. Acad. Arts and Scis.; mem. Inst. Mgmt. Sci. (pres. Boston 1965-66). Home: 33 Prince St West Newton MA 02165 Office: 50 Memorial Dr Cambridge MA 02139

POUNDSTONE, WILLIAM NICHOLAS, coal co. exec.; b. Morgantown, W.Va., Aug. 12, 1925; s. James Stanley and Lena Grace (Robison) P.; B.S., W.Va. U., 1949; m. Doris Mae Jamison, June 11, 1949; children—William N., Scott L., Kathy A. Sect. foreman Christopher Coal Co. div. Consolidation Coal Co., 1949-55, supt., 1955-60, gen. supt., 1960-61, asst. v.p. operations Consolidation Coal Co., 1961-65, exec. v.p. engring., exploration, research and devel., Pitts., 1965—, dir.; dir. Conoco Coal Devel. Co. Served with AUS, 1943-46. Mem. Nat. Acad. Engring., Am. Inst. Mining Engrs., Engrs. Soc. Western Pa., Tau Beta Pi, Sigma Gamma Epsilon. Methodist. Clubs: Duquesne, St. Clair Country. Patentee in field. Home: 268 Trotwood Dr Pittsburgh PA 15241 Office: 1800 Washington Rd Consol Plaza Pittsburgh PA 15241

POURCIAU, LESTER JOHN, JR., librarian; b. Baton Rouge, La., Sept. 6, 1936; s. Lester John and Pearlie M. (Hogan) P.; B.A., La. State U., 1962, M.S., 1964; Ph.D. (Higher Edn. Act fellow), Ind. U., 1975; m. Rebecca Anne Thomas, 1975; 1 son, Lester John III. Asst. reference librarian U. S.C., Columbia, 1963-64; reference librarian Florence County Pub. Library, Florence, S.C., 1964-65; reference services coordinator U. Fla., Gainesville, 1966-67; dir. libraries Memphis State U., 1970—. Served with USAF, 1955-59. Mem. Am., Southeastern, Tenn. library assns. Home: 4320 Sequoia Rd Memphis TN 38117 Office: Memphis State U Libraries Memphis TN 38152

POUR-EL, MARIAN BOYKAN, mathematician; b. N.Y.C.; d. Joseph and Mattie (Caspe) Boykan; A.B., Hunter Coll.; A.M., Ph.D., Harvard U., 1958; m. Akiva Pour-El; 1 dau., Ina. Asst. prof. math. Pa. State U., 1958-62, asso. prof., 1962-64; mem. faculty U. Minn., Mpls., 1964—, prof. math., 1968—; mem. Inst. Advanced Study, Princeton, N.J., 1962-64; mem. council Conf. Bd. Math. Scis., 1977—, trustee, 1978—; lectr. internat. congresses in logic and computer sci., Eng., 1971, Czechoslovakia, 1973, Hungary, 1967; lectr. Polish Acad. Sci., 1974. Trustee Conf. Bd. Math. Scis., 1978—. Named to Hunter Coll. Hall of Fame, 1975; Nat. Acad. Scis. grantee, 1966. Mem. Am. Math. Soc. (lectr. nat. meeting 1976, also spl. sessions 1971, 78, chmn. spl. session on recursion theory 1975), Assn. Symbolic Logic, Math. Assn. Am., Phi Beta Kappa, Sigma Xi, Pi Mu Epsilon, Sigma Pi Sigma. Author papers math. logic, analog computers, women in sci. Home:

1389 Keston St Saint Paul MN 55108 Office: Dept Math U Minn Minneapolis MN 55455. *In order to practice our careers our family has evolved a pattern of life at variance with the norm. For the past twenty years we have lived apart most of the time. Our strong emotional and personal ties were intensified by this absence of continuous physical nearness. It is my belief that one can succeed personally, socially and professionally without having to accept the constraints of an existing social order.*

POUS, RAMON MANUEL, advt. exec.; b. Mexico City, June 12, 1941; s. Ramon Pous and Carolina Herrerias; grad. U. Iberoamericana, 1964; B.A. in Bus. Adminstrn., U. of the Ams., 1969; m. Patricia Landa, June 9, 1965; children—Ramon Manuel, Ana Patricia, Ana Paula, Eduardo Xavier. Mktg. trainee Colgate-Palmolive, Mexico City, 1963-65; accounting supr. McCann, Erickson & Stanton, Mexico City, 1965-69; group production mgr., mktg. mgr. Johnson & Johnson, Mexico City, 1969-71; mktg. dir. Ekco, S.A., Mexico City, 1971-73; pres., gen. mgr. Publicidad D'Arcy, S.A. de C.V., Mexico City, 1973—; adj. prof. U. Iberoamericana. Pres. Settlers' Assn., Arboledas, Edo. de Mexico, 1971-72. Served with Mex. Army, 1959. Mem. Assn. de Ventas y Mercadotecnia, Better TV for Children. Clubs: Club de Golf La Hacienda, Club Hipico La Hacienda, Club de Industriales. Home: 68 San Miguel Regla Club de Golf La Hacienda Edo de Mexico Office: Publicidad D'Arcy SA de CV Homero 1933 Mexico 10 DF

POUSETTE-DART, RICHARD, artist; b. St. Paul, June 8, 1916; s. Nathaniel and Flora Pousette-Dart; student Bard Coll., 1934, L.H.D., 1965; m. Evelyn Gracey, June 2, 1946; children—Joanna, Jonathan. First one-man exhbn. Artists Gallery, N.Y.C., 1939, others include Marion Williard Gallery, 1941, 42, 44, 45, Peggy Guggenheim Gallery Art of This Century, 1946, Betty Parsons Gallery, 1948-52, 55, 58, 59, 61, 67, Obelisk Gallery, Boston, 1970, Whitney Mus. Am. Art, 1971, 74-75, Harkus, Krakow, Rosen, Sonnabend Gallery, Boston, 1974, 75, Edwin A. Ulrich Mus. Art, Wichita, Kans., 1975, Andrew Crispo Gallery, N.Y.C., 1976, 78, Arts Club Chgo., 1978; group exhbns. include Pa. Acad. Ann., 1947-48, Whitney Mus. Ann., 1950-51, 53, 56, 57-58, 78, Toledo Mus., 1950-54, Corcoran Gallery, Va. Mus. Fine Arts, Detroit Inst., Chgo. Art Inst., Whitney Mus., 1959, Brooks Meml. Art Gallery, Memphis, John Heron Art Inst., Indpls., St. Louis City Art Mus., Mus. Legion of Honor, San Francisco, Mus. Modern Art, N.Y.C., 1969, Mpls. Art Mus., Cornell U., Carnegie Internat. Exhbn., Nat. Gallery Art, Washington, 1974, Allentown (Pa.) Art Mus., 1975, Ulrich Mus. Art, Wichita, Kans., 1975, Andrew Crispo Gallery, 1975, 76, 77, 78, 79, Herbert F. Johnson Mus. Art, 1978, Seibu Mus., Tokyo, 1978; retrospective exhbn. Whitney Mus. of Am. Art, 1963, others Germany, Japan, S.A., Rome; travelling exhbn. Mus. Modern Art, 1968-70; mural commn. East Bronx Hosp., 1970, North Bronx Hosp., 1974; lectr. Boston Mus. Sch. Fine Arts, 1959, Mpls. Inst. Fine Arts, 1965; instr. painting New Sch. Social Research, 1959-61; prof. art Sarah Lawrence Coll., 1971-74; guest critic Columbia, 1968; represented in permanent collections Mus. Modern Art, Whitney Mus. Am. Art, Addison Gallery, Albright Art Gallery, Buffalo; pvt. collections. Recipient Comstock prize Art Inst. Chgo., 1961, silver medal award Corcoran Biennial, Washington, 1965, Nat. Arts Council award, 1966, also others. Guggenheim Found. grantee, 1951; Ford Found. grantee, 1959. Home: 286 Haverstraw Rd Suffern NY 10901

POUSHTER, DAVID LEON, physician; b. Syracuse, N.Y., Jan. 14, 1925; s. Julius and Libby (Sacks) P.; A.B., Syracuse U., 1945, M.D., 1947; m. Phyllis Margaret Freeman, June 23, 1946; children—Linda, Susan, Karen. Intern, Harper Hosp., Detroit, 1947-48, resident, 1948-51; asst. resident in otolaryngology City Detroit Hosp., 1949; resident in otolaryngology Children's Hosp., Detroit, 1950-51; clin. instr. otolaryngology SUNY, Syracuse, 1953-56, clin. asst. prof., 1956-64, clin. prof., 1977—; practice medicine specializing in otolaryngology, Syracuse, 1953—; pres. staff Crouse Irving Hosp., Syracuse, 1963, chief ear, nose and throat, 1965-68; chief ear nose and throat Crouse Irving Meml. Hosp., 1968-74. Bd. dirs. Am. Cancer Soc., 1960-66; pres. Temple Adath Yeshurun, Syracuse, 1973-75; pres. Jewish Family Service Bur., 1968-69. Served with USAF, 1951-53. Mem. AMA, N.Y. Med. Soc., Onondaga County Med. Soc. (pres. 1977-78), Central N.Y. Eye, Ear, Nose and Throat Soc., Am. Triological Soc., Jacobson-Eisner Med. Soc. (pres. 1965), Pan Am. Otol. and Bronchoesophagological Soc. Club: Lafayette Country. Contbr. articles to profl. jours. Home: 219 Bradford Pkwy Syracuse NY 13224 Office: 406 University Ave Syracuse NY 13210. *The key to success is closely intertwined with one's relationship to fear. One should never be afraid of work, for without it man is nothing. One should not be fearful of saying he does not know; the admission of lack of knowledge should be an incentive and catalyst for learning. One must never be afraid of failure; failures must be absorbed to provide the foundation for success.*

POUSSAINT, ALVIN FRANCIS, psychiatrist, educator; b. N.Y.C., May 15, 1934; s. Christopher Thomas V. and Harriet (Johnston) P.; B.A., Columbia, 1956; M.D., Cornell U., 1960; M.S., U. Calif. at Los Angeles, 1964. Intern U. Calif. at Los Angeles Center Health Sci., 1960-61, resident psychiatry Neuro. Psychiat. Inst. 1961-64, chief resident, 1964-65, So. field dir. Med. Com. Human Rights, Jackson, Miss., 1965-66; asst. prof. psychiatry Tufts U. Med. Sch., 1966-69; asso. prof. psychiatry, asso. dean students Harvard Med. Sch., 1969-75, 78—, dean students 1975-78. Nat. treas. Black Acad. Arts and Letters, 1969-70, Med. Com. Human Rights, 1966—. Recipient Michael Schwerner award, 1968. Fellow Am. Psychiat. Assn.; mem. Nat. Med. Assn. Author numerous articles in field. Office: Judge Baker Guidance Center 295 Longwood Ave Boston MA 02115

POUST, JOHN G., lawyer; b. Sycamore, Ill., Nov. 27, 1920; B.S., Northwestern U., 1942, J.D., 1946. Admitted to Ill. bar, 1946, U.S. Supreme Ct. bar, 1960; mem. firm Rooks, Pitts, Fullagar and Poust, Chgo. Mem. Ill. Supreme Ct. Com. on Pattern Jury Instrns. Fellow Am. Coll. Trial Lawyers (Ill. chmn. 1976-77); mem. Am. (chmn. mfrs. liability com.), Ill., Chgo. mem. civil practice, ins. law coms.; mem. bd. mgrs. 1969-71) bar assns., Soc. Trial Lawyers, Internat. Assn. Ins. Counsel. Clubs: Legal, Law, Univ. (Chgo.); Westmoreland Country (Wilmette, Ill.). Office: 208 S La Salle St Chicago IL 60604

POVICH, SHIRLEY LEWIS, columnist, ret. sports editor; b. Bar Harbor, Me., July 15, 1905; s. Nathan and Rosa (Orlovich) P.; student Georgetown U., 1922-24; m. Ethyl Friedman, Feb. 21, 1932; children—David, Maurice R., Lynn. Reporter, Washington Post, 1923-25, sports editor, 1926-33, columnist, 1933-45, war corr., PTO, 1945; columnist Washington Post, 1946—; adj. prof. communications Am. U., 1975—. Recipient citation for outstanding service as war corr., 1945; Nat. Headliners Grantland Rice award for sportswriting, 1964; elected to Baseball Hall of Fame, Cooperstown writers div., 1976. Mem. Baseball Writers Assn. Am. (pres. 1955). Author: The Washington Senators, 1954; All These Mornings, 1969; also articles in mags. Home: 2801 New Mexico Ave NW Washington DC 20007 Office: Washington Post & Times-Herald 1515 L St NW Washington DC 20005

POVISH, KENNETH JOSEPH, bishop; b. Alpena, Mich., Apr. 19, 1924; s. Joseph Francis and Elizabeth (Jachcik) P.; A.B., Sacred Heart Sem., Detroit, 1946; M.A., Cath. U. Am., 1950; grad. student No. Mich. U., 1961, 63. Ordained priest Roman Cath. Ch., 1950; asst. pastorships, 1950-56; pastor in Port Sanilac, Mich., 1956-57, Munger, Mich., 1957-60, Bay City, Mich., 1966-70; dean St. Paul Sem., Saginaw, Mich., 1960-66, vice-rector, 1962-66; bishop of Crookston, Minn., 1970-75, Lansing, Mich., 1975—; bd. consulators Diocese of Saginaw, 1966-70; instr. Latin and U.S. history St. Paul Sem., 1960-66. Bd. dirs. Cath. Charities Diocese Saginaw, 1969-70. Mem. Mich., Bay County hist. socs. Kiwanian. Weekly columnist Saginaw and Lansing diocesan newspapers. Home: 1348 Cambridge Lansing MI 48910 Office: 300 W Ottawa St Lansing MI 48933

POVOLNY, MOJMIR, educator; b. Menin, Czechoslovakia, Nov. 25, 1921; s. Antonin and Marie (Konecna) P.; Jur.D., Masaryk U., Brno, Czechoslovakia, 1947; postgrad. U. Paris, 1948-49; Ph.D., U. Chgo., 1954; m. Joyce Wuesthoff, July 15, 1956; children—David, Daniel. Came to U.S., 1950, naturalized, 1956. Exec. sec. Benes Party, Prague, 1947-48; asst. dir. Am. Friends Service Com., Phila., Tokyo, 1954-57; instr. U. Chgo., 1957-58; asst. prof. govt. Lawrence U., Appleton, Wis., 1958- 62, asso. prof., 1962-67, prof., 1967—, Henry M. Wriston prof. social scis., 1970—, acting v.p. acad. affairs, 1976-77, dean univ. faculty, 1979—. Chmn. exec. com. Council Free Czechoslovakia, Washington, 1974—. Bd. dirs. Fox Valley Human Rights Council, Appleton, Wis., Czechoslovak Fgn. Inst. in Exile, Chgo. Fellow Mid.-European Studies Center, 1951-54; mem. Am. Polit. Sci. Assn., Internat. Studies Assn., Czechoslovak Soc. Arts and Scis., Am. Assn. Advancement Slavic Studies. Home: 31 S Meadows Dr Appleton WI 54911

POWELL, ALAN, engr., govt. ofcl.; b. Buxton, Derbyshire, Eng., Feb. 17, 1928; s. Frank and Gwendolen Marie (Walker) P.; came to U.S., 1956; student Buxton Coll., 1939-45; diploma in aeros., Loughborough Coll., 1948; B.Sc. in Engring. with 1st class honors, London U., 1949; honours diploma 1st class, Loughborough U. Tech., 1949; Ph.D., U. Southampton, 1953; m. June Sinclair, Mar. 28, 1956. Engr., Percival Aircraft Co., Luton, Eng., 1949-51; research asst. U. Southampton (Eng.), 1951-53, lectr., 1953-56; research fellow Calif. Inst. Tech., Pasadena, 1956-57; asso. prof. UCLA, 1957-62, prof. engring., 1962-65, head Aerosonics Lab., 1957-65; asso. tech. dir. David Taylor Model Basin, Dept. Navy, Washington, 1965-66, tech. dir., 1966-67; tech. dir. David Taylor Naval Ship Research & Devel. Center, Bethesda, Md., 1967; mem. Undersea Warfare Research & Devel. Council, 1966-76, chmn., 1971; mem. council on Fed. Labs., 1972—; mem. com. on hearing Bioacoustics and Biomechs. Nat. Acad. Sci.-NRC, 1961, exec. council, 1963-65, chmn., 1965-66. Cons. Douglas Aircraft Co., 1956-65. Recipient Navy Meritorious Civilian Service award, 1970. Chartered mech. engr. Fellow Royal Aero. Soc. London (Baden-Powell prize 1948, Wilbur Wright prize 1953), Phys. Soc. London, Inst. Physics (London), Acoustical Soc. Am. (biennial award 1962, asso. editor Jour. 1962-67, chmn. edn. com. 1964-66, exec. council 1966-69, chmn. medals and awards com. 1979—) Instn. Mech. Engrs.; asso. fellow Am. Inst. Aeros. and Astronautics; mem. Inst. Noise Control Engrs. (initial mem., dir. 1974-77), Soc. Naval Architects and Marine Engrs., IEEE (sr. mem.), Inst. Acoustics, Am. Soc. Naval Engrs., Am. Mgmt. Assn. (research council 1979—), Am. Soc. Engring. Edn. (mem. research council), Sigma Xi, Tau Beta Pi (hon.). Contbr. articles on acoustics and aeronautics to profl. jours. Home: 9328 Winterset Dr Potomac MD 20854 Office: Bethesda MD 20084

POWELL, ALLEN LARUE, govt. ofcl.; b. Nacogdoches, Tex., July 12, 1915; s. Joe Allen and Minnie Eugenia (Larue) P.; B.S., U. Tex., 1938; m. Neta Menefee, Mar. 25, 1939; children—Allen Larue, Leilani Ann. Commd. ensign U.S. Marine Corps, 1944, advanced through grades to rear adm., 1969; chief ship constrn., 1963-69; dir. Atlantic Marine Center, Norfolk, Va., 1969-71; chief Office Fleet Ops., 1971-72, dir. Nat. Ocean Survey, Commerce Dept., Rockville, Md., 1972—; mem. Miss. River Commn., 1972—. Mem. Soc. Am. Mil. Engrs. (dir.), Am. Shore and Beach Preservation Assn. Home: 1453 Trombone Ct Vienna VA 22180 Office: Nat Ocean Survey 6001 Executive Blvd Rockville MD 20852

POWELL, BENJAMIN EDWARD, ret. librarian; b. Sunbury, N.C., Aug. 28, 1905; s. Willis Warren and Beatrice (Franklin) P.; A.B., Duke U., 1926; B.L.S., Columbia U., 1930; Ph.D., U. Chgo., 1946; m. Elizabeth Graves, Mar. 6, 1940; 1 dau., Lisa Holland. Athletic dir. Bethel (N.C.) High Sch., 1926-27; asst. Duke U., Library, 1927-29, reference librarian and supt. circulation, 1930-34, 1935-37; librarian U. Mo. Library, 1937-46; librarian Duke U., 1946-75; ret., 1975; vis. prof. U. N.C. Sch. Library Sci., 1961, 62, 68, 70. Chmn. bd. trustees Durham Pub. Library. Mem. ALA (council 1947-54, v.p., 1958-59, pres. 1959-60, mem. exec. bd., 1956-58; chmn. com. Co-op. Microfilm Project, 1950-54; joint com. Govt. Publs., 1955-56, Govt. Documents, 1956-59; Spl. Com. Reorgn. 1957), Assn. Research Libraries (dir. 1950-55, 62-64), Southeastern Library Assn., N.C. Library Assn., Assn. Coll. and Reference Libraries (sec. 1940-44, pres. 1948-49), Mo. Library Assn. (pres. 1938-39), N.C. Lit. and Hist. Assn., So. Hist. Assn., James Madison Meml. Commn., Bibliog. Soc. Am., AAUP, Sigma Nu, Phi Beta Kappa. Democrat. Methodist. Clubs: Hope Valley Country, University, Rotary (Durham, N.C.). Home: 3609 Hathaway Rd Hope Valley Durham NC 27707

POWELL, BENJAMIN HARRISON, IV, corp. exec.; b. Huntsville, Tex., Feb. 2, 1915; s. Benjamin Harrison and Marian Leigh (Rather) P.; B.A., Va. Mil. Inst., 1936; LL.B., U. Tex., 1939; LL.M., Harvard U., 1940; m. Kitty King Corbett, Aug. 5, 1939; children—Nancy (Mrs. Harvin C. Moore III), Marian (Mrs. James E. Osborne), Benjamin Harrison V, Katherine. Admitted to Tex. bar, 1939; with firm Powell, Wirtz, Rauhut & McGinnis, and predecessor, Austin, 1940-41, 46-55, partner, 1947-55; asso. prof. bus. law U. Tex., 1940-41; exec. v.p., dir., gen. counsel Brown & Root, Inc., and domestic and fgn. subsidiaries, Houston, 1955—; sr. v.p., dir., gen. counsel Highlands Ins. Co., Southwestern Pipe, Inc., Prestressed Concrete Products Co., Inc., Jackson Marine Corp.; sr. chmn. bd. dirs. Am. Nat. Bank, Austin; dir. Halliburton Co., Dallas, Merc. Tex. Corp., Dallas, Brown & Root-Wimpey Highlands Fabricators, Ltd., Scotland. Served to lt. col. U.S. Army, 1941-45. Decorated Legion of Merit. Mem. Phi Delta Phi, Phi Delta Theta, Friars. Episcopalian. Lion (past dir.). Home: 3451 Del Monte Dr Houston TX 77019 Office: 4100 Clinton Dr Houston TX 77001

POWELL, BOLLING RAINES, lawyer, educator; b. Florala, Ala., Aug. 10, 1910; s. Bolling Raines and Marie (Arnold) P.; B.A., Birmingham-So. Coll., 1930; M.A., LL.B., J.D., U. Va., 1934; m. Mary Vilette Spaulding, Dec. 10, 1949; children—Bolling Raines, James Spaulding. Asst. prof. law U. Va., 1938-39; partner firm Paul V. McNutt, Washington and N.Y.C., 1947-50; partner firm Powell, Dorsey and Blum, Washington, 1950-62, Powell, Horkan and Powell, Washington, 1962-75; prof. Wythe Sch. of Law, Coll. William and Mary, 1969—; individual practice law, Gloucester, Va., 1975—; spl. counsel to bd. govs. Fed. Res. System, 1956-62; bd. advisors Ct. Practice Inst., 1973-78. Chmn. Gloucester United Taxpayers, 1978—; dir. Boy Scouts Am. Fund Raising Campaign, Gloucester County, 1965. Served to lt. col. AUS, 1942-46. Decorated Legion of Merit. Mem. Va. State Bar (bd. govs. adminstrv. law sect.), Ala. Bar Assn., D.C. Bar Assn., Am. Bar Assn., Phi Beta Kappa, Omicron Delta Kappa. Episcopalian. Clubs: Metropolitan (Washington), Farmington Country (Charlottesville, Va.). Editor-in-chief Va. Law Rev., 1934. Home: Warner Hall Plantation Gloucester VA 23061 Office: PO Box 800 Gloucester VA 23061 PO Box 2750 Williamsburg VA 23185

POWELL, BOONE, univ. adminstr.; b. Etowah, Tenn., July 15, 1912; s. N.C. and Savannah (Smith) P.; student U. Ga., 1931-33, U. Tenn., 1934-36; LL.D., Baylor U., 1958; m. Ruth Galloway, Nov. 30, 1935; children—Boone, Jerry Aileen, James Lawrence. Mgr. pub. service TVA, Norris, Tenn., 1936-41; asst. chief Govt. Project of War Housing, 1941; asst. regional dir. S.W. Region Fed. Works Agy., 1942-45; bus. mgr. Baylor U. Hosp., 1945-47, asst. adminstr., 1947-48, adminstr., 1948—, adminstr. Baylor U. Med. Center, 1948—; chmn. bd. Lakewood Bank & Trust Co.; dir. Abbott Labs. Active Boy Scouts Am. Recipient Gold medal award Am. Coll. Hosp. Adminstrs.; Silver Beaver award, Distinguished Eagle Scout award Boy Scouts Am.; Disting. Service award Am. Hosp. Assn.; named to Hall of Fame, North Ga. Coll. Fellow Am. Coll. Hosp. Adminstrs. (past pres.); mem. Tex. Hosp. Assn. (past pres.), Dallas C. of C. Home: 6563 Blanch Circle Dallas TX 75214 Office: 3500 Gaston Ave Dallas TX 75246

POWELL, CHARLES GREGORY, JR., ins. co. exec.; b. Oxford, N.C., Sept. 4, 1922; s. Charles Gregory and Lois (Parker) P.; B.S., Wake Forest U., 1948, LL.B., 1950; m. Roselyn Griffin Miller, Aug. 20, 1945; children—Gregory Whitford, Roselyn G. Admitted to N.C. bar, 1950; individual practice law, Raleigh, N.C., 1950-51; asst. atty. gen. State of N.C., 1951-55; atty. Jefferson Standard Life Ins. Co., Greensboro, N.C., 1955-57, asst. gen. counsel, 1958-71, sr. v.p., gen. counsel, 1972—, v.p., gen. counsel Jefferson-Pilot Corp., 1972—, also dir. Served with USAF, 1942-45. Mem. Am., N.C. bar assns., Assn. Life Ins. Counsel. Home: 3710 Friendly Ave Greensboro NC 27410 Office: PO Box 21008 Greensboro NC 27420

POWELL, CLINTON COBB, physician, univ. adminstr.; b. Hartford, Conn., Mar. 9, 1918; s. Harry Havey and Nita Florence (Nass) P.; B.S., Mass. Inst. Tech., 1940; M.D., Boston U., 1944; student U. Chgo., 1947-48; m. Francis Arlene Collins, Apr. 2, 1944; children—Pamela Powell Kellogg, Brenda Joyce, Donna Sue. Intern U.S. Marine Hosp., Boston, 1944-45; commd. asst. surgeon USPHS, 1946, med. dir., 1956; staff mem. indsl. hygiene research lab. NIH, 1946-47; radiation safety officer NIH, 1948-51; resident radiology USPHS Hosp., Balt., 1951-52; fellow radiology U. Pa. Hosp., 1952-54; staff physician radiation therapy, clin. center NIH, 1954-55; grants analyst, research grants and fellowship br. Nat. Cancer Inst., 1955-56; chief radiol. health med. program, div. spl. health services USPHS, 1956-58; exec. sec. radio and surgery study sect., div. research grants NIH, 1958-59, asst. chief research grants rev. br., div. research grants, 1959-60, dep. chief div., 1960-61; asst. dir. Nat. Inst. Allergy and Infectious Diseases, 1961-62; dir. Nat. Inst. Gen. Med. Scis., NIH, 1962-64; asso. coordinator med. and health scis. U. Cal., 1964-66, coordinator, 1966-71, spl. asst. to pres. for health affairs, 1971-79, spl. asst. emeritus, 1979—. Mem. Internat. Commn. Radiol. Protection, 1965-68; mem. com. Nat. Com. Radiation Protection, 1956-68, exec. com., 1957-67, ad hoc subcom. wide-spread radioactive contamination, 1958-60, subcom. 1, 1960—; mem. radiol. physics fellowship bd. AEC, 1958-63; com. radiation effects Am. Thoracic Soc., 1957—; com. use radioisotopes in hosps. Am. Hosp. Assn., 1953—; subcom. radiol. health Assn. State and Territorial Health Officers, 1956-58. Served with USNR, 1945-46. Diplomate Am. Bd. Radiology, Nat. Bd. Med. Examiners. Fellow A.A.A.S.; mem. Am. Coll. Radiology (commn. radiol. units, standards and protection 1957—, chmn. com. radiation exposure of women), A.M.A., Am. Pub. Health Assn. (program area com. radiol. health 1959), Radiol. Soc. N.Am., Radiation Research Soc., Health Physics Soc., Assn. for Acad. Health Centers (dir. 1969-70). Contbr. numerous articles profl. jours. Home: 542 Tahos Rd Orinda CA 94563 Office: Univ Hall Berkeley CA 94720

POWELL, DON GRABER, banker; b. Hutchinson, Kans., Oct. 19, 1939; s. Wilbur L. and Esther E. (Graber) P.; B.S., Kans. U., 1961; M.B.A. with distinction, U. Mich., 1966; m. Nancy Kay Hertzler, Nov. 18, 1961; children—Michael Scott, Jeffrey John. Fin. analyst treas.'s dept. Exxon Corp., 1966-68; asst. v.p. TSAI Investment Services, 1968-69; v.p. Mackay Shields Fin. Corp., 1969-71, Standard & Poors/Intercapital Co., N.Y.C., 1971-73, Citicorp, N.Y.C. and Houston, 1973-77; exec. v.p. State St. Bank & Trust Co., Boston, 1977—. Served to lt. USN, 1961-65. Recipient Achievement award Sec. of Navy, 1965. Mem. Chartered Fin. Analysts, Beta Gamma Sigma. Office: 225 Franklin St Boston MA 02101

POWELL, DONALD CLIFTON, forest products co. exec.; b. Argentina, May 14, 1932; s. Gerard Clifton and Eleanor Elizabeth (Wernert) P.; B.S. in Commerce, U. Ill., 1954; M.B.A., Harvard U., 1959; m. Helen Muriel Fry, Aug. 8, 1954; children—Douglas, Jennifer. With Goodyear Tire & Rubber Co., Akron, Ohio, 1954-55; with Champion Internat. Corp., Stamford, Conn., 1959—, successively v.p. fin., mgr.-dir. Brazilian subs., pres. Timberlands div., v.p. corporate planning and devel., now sr. v.p. adminstrn., Stamford, Conn., 1974—. Bd. dirs. Stamford Museum and Nature Center, Hartman Theatre; bd. visitors U. Conn. Bus. Sch. Served as 1st lt. arty., U.S. Army, 1955-57. Mem. U.S. C. of C. of Sao Paulo (Brazil) (hon., 1st v.p. 1971). Clubs: Greenwich (Conn.) Country; Econ. of N.Y. Home: 28 Boulder Brook Rd Greenwich CT 06830 Office: 1 Landmark Sq Stamford CT 06921

POWELL, DREXEL DWANE, JR., editorial cartoonist; b. Lake Village, Ark., Nov. 7, 1944; s. Drexel Dwane and Minnie Louise (Ruth) P.; B.S. in Agri-Bus., U. Ark. at Monticello, 1970; m. Janice Sue Lovell, Apr. 10, 1971. Cartoonist, Sentinel Record, Hot Springs, Ark., 1970-72; cartoonist San Antonio Light, 1973-74; editorial cartoonist Cin. Enquirer, 1974-75; editorial cartoonist News and Observer, Raleigh, N.C., 1975—, syndicated Los Angeles Times Syndicate, 1979—; free lance artist; designer book jackets; lectr. Served with N.G., 1967-68. Recipient Overseas Press Club citation, 1978, Headliners Club award, 1978; named Disting. Alumnus, U. Ark. at Monticello, 1979. Mem. Assn. Am. Editorial Cartoonists. Author: Is That All You Do?, 1979. Office: 215 S McDowell St Raleigh NC 27602

POWELL, EDMUND WILLIAM, lawyer; b. St. Paul, Dec. 23, 1922; s. George L. and Mary (Sexton) P.; student St. Thomas Coll., St. Paul, 1941-43, U. Minn., 1943, 46; LL.B., Marquette U., 1948; m. Ellen M. Williams, May 7, 1949; children—Susan Marie, Sarah Anne, Daniel. Admitted to Wis. bar, 1948, since practiced in Milw.; pres. firm Borgelt, Powell, Peterson & Frauen, and predecessors, 1955—. Served with USNR, 1943-45; to capt. USMCR, 1945-46, 52-53. Fellow Am. Coll. Trial Lawyers; mem. Am., Milw. (exec. com. 1959-62) bar assns., State Bar Wis. (sec. 1964-65, bd. govs. 1961-63, 65-67; sec., dir. ins. sect. 1962-69), Internat. Assn. Ins. Counsel, Marquette Law Alumni Assn. (pres., dir. 1957-60). Clubs: Town, University (Milw.). Home: 4611 N Lake Dr Milwaukee WI 53211 Office: 735 N Water St Milwaukee WI 53202

POWELL, EDWARD ANGUS, wood products mfg. co. exec.; b. Richmond, Va., Mar. 20, 1914; s. Louis F. and Mary Lewis (Gwathmey) P.; B.S. in Commerce, Washington and Lee U., Lexington, Va., 1936; M.B.A., Harvard U., 1938; m. Helen Elizabeth Bryson, Aug. 31, 1940; children—Helen Elizabeth, Katherine Powell Rolph, Edward Angus, Earl Bryson. With Lea Industries, Inc., and predecessor, Richmond, Va., 1938—, pres., 1951-70, chmn. bd., 1970—; pres., chmn. bd. Chesterfield Land & Timber Co., Midlothian, Va., 1959—; dir. Waste Combustion Corp., 1968—, First & Mchts. Nat. Bank, Richmond, 1960-73; dir. Fed. Res. Bank Richmond, 1973—, chmn., 1976-77; bd. dirs. So. Exposition Bldg., Inc., 1970-72, U.S. Indsl. Council, 1975—, So. Indsl. Relations Council, 1952-68. Pres. bd. dirs. Collegiate Schs., Richmond, 1959-62; vice chmn. trustees Union Theol. Sem., Richmond, 1969-72; rector bd. Longwood Coll., Farmville, Va., 1967-70; pres. bd. Rich-Met. YMCA, 1955-57; co-chmn. fund raising campaign Westminster-Canterbury Home, retirement home, Richmond, 1972; past elder, deacon River Rd. Presbyn. Ch., Richmond. Served to lt. A.C., USNR, 1942-45. Recipient Silver Brotherhood medallion NCCJ, 1972. Mem. Metro Richmond C. of C. (past dir.), So. Furniture Mfrs. Assn. (past dir.), Va. Mfrs. Assn. (past dir.), Phi Kappa Sigma (pres. 1935), Omicron Delta Kappa (pres. 1936). Clubs: Country of Va. (past dir.); Commonwealth (past dir.) (Richmond). Home: 3 Hillaire Ln Richmond VA 23229 Office: 1005 Sycamore Sq Suite 202 Midlothian VA 23113. *A major goal I have always strived to achieve as a business executive is to deal fairly with all - customers, stockholders, employees, and suppliers. I do not believe any business can achieve its maximum potential unless each of these groups recognizes the contribution each makes to the success of the enterprise.*

POWELL, EDWIN LLOYD, JR., state ofcl., ret. army officer; b. Washington, Jan. 11, 1920; s. Edwin Lloyd and Kathryn (Denny) P.; B.S., U.S. Mil. Acad., 1941; M.S., U. Calif. at Berkeley, 1948; m. Clelia Helene Pez, May 11, 1946; children—Jill Kathryn (Mrs. Richard H. Sargent), Denny Wood, Douglas Lloyd. Commd. 2d lt. U.S. Army, 1941, advanced through grades to brig. gen., 1968; instr. U.S. Mil. Acad., 1941, 44-47; comdr. 118th Combat Engr. Bn., Germany, 1952-53; dir. devel. guidance Army Aviation Bd., Ft. Rucker, Ala., 1956-59; area engr., Hamadan, Iran, 1960-61; mil. asst. to asst. dir. Def. Research and Engring., sec. DDR&E panel on limited war, 1962-63; mil. asst. to NATO asst. sec. gen. sci. affairs, Paris, 1965-66; dir. Army Aviation, Pentagon, 1967-69; asst. comdr. Americal Div., Vietnam, 1969-70; dep. comdr. Army Test and Evaluation Command, Aberdeen Proving Ground, Md., 1970-71, ret., 1971; dep. sec. state planning, Md., 1972-74; staff specialist Md. State Colls., 1974-79; dir. adminstrv. services Md. Dept. Econ. and Community Devel., 1979—. Cons. Sikorsky Aircraft, 1972-74. Decorated D.S.M., Silver Star, D.F.C., Legion of Merit with oak leaf cluster, Air medal with 16 oak leaf clusters, Bronze Star; Vietnamese Cross of Gallantry; recipient Sikorsky award for helicopter rescue, 1969. Mem. Am. Helicopter Soc. (chmn. Forum 1962), Assn. U.S. Army, Army Aviation Assn. Am. (nat. exec. bd. 1962-67 v.p. 1970-73), Govt. Employees Assn. (v.p. 1972-74, pres. 1974-77, dir. 1977—), Mil. Order of Purple Heart, Ret. Officers Assn. (dir. Annapolis chpt. 1976—). Episcopalian (vestryman 1975-78). Home: 1740 Long Green Dr Annapolis MD 21401 Office: Dept Econ and Community Devel 2525 River Rd Annapolis MD 21401

POWELL, EVAN ARNOLD, editor; b. Asheville, N.C., Sept. 5, 1937; s. Arnold Elmore and Mary Elizabeth (Reighard) P.; student N.C. State U., 1954-55; B.A., Furman U., 1958; m. Cema Sitton Chapman, Dec. 20, 1969; children—Angela, Trip, Scott. Tech. service dir. product engring. and tng. Sears Roebuck & Co., 1959-73; feature writer Popular Sci. mag., N.Y.C., 1969-73, S.E. editor, Greenville, S.C., 1973—. Instr., Greenville Tech. Coll., 1967-70; producer, commentator television features Update, Bill Wheless Show, Road Test, Scrunch, Weekend Ramblers, Handyman, Checkpoint, WFBC-TV, Multimedia, Alcare. Recipient ALMA awards Assn. Home Appliance Mfrs., 1972, 73, 75, 77-78, award Major Appliance Consumer's Action Panel, 1975, Nat. Endowment for Humanities, 1978. Mem. Am. Soc. Journalists and Authors. Presbyn. Author: The Complete Guide to Home Appliance Repair, 1974, rev. edit., 1980; contbr. to Homeowner's How to Treasury, 1976, Popular Sci. Homeowner's Ency., 1975, 78, Areté Encyclopedia, 1980, also mags. Off Duty, Energy Horizons, Sci. and Mechanics, Sandlapper, Carolina Outdoors; contbg. editor How-To Homeowner's Handbook, Motorcamping Handbook; columnist Housepower, Checkpoint. Home: 108 Morningdale Dr Greenville SC 29609 Office: Chestnut Mountain Travelers Rest SC 29690. *It's often expected of those of us engaged in scientific and technical fields to express a cynical and agnostic viewpoint. My own observations have led to the opposite conclusion—that the only explanation for events that occur in our world and universe lies within and points to the logical plan of a divine Creator. Recognition and acknowledgment of this as fact, coupled with the influence of wise and loving parents and the patience and instruction of those with whom I work, have allowed my dreams and ambitions to come true.*

POWELL, GEORGE EVERETT, JR., motor freight co. exec.; b. Kansas City, Mo., June 12, 1926; s. George Everett and Hilda (Brown) P.; student Northwestern U.; m. Mary Catherine Kuehn, Aug. 26, 1947; children—George Everett III, Nicholas K., Richardson K., Peter E. With Riss & Co., Inc., Kansas City, Mo., 1947-52, treas., 1950-52; with Yellow Freight System, Inc., Kansas City, Mo., 1952—, pres., 1957-68, chmn. bd., 1968—; dir. 1st Nat. Charter Corp., Butler Mfg. Co. Trustee, mem. exec. com. Mid-West Research Inst., Kansas City, Mo., 1961—, chmn. bd. trustees, 1968—; bd. govs. Kansas City Art Inst., 1964—, chmn. bd. trustees, 1973-75. Served with USNR, 1944-46. Mem. Kansas City C. of C. (bd. dirs. 1965-68). Home: 1040 W 57th St Kansas City MO 64113 Office: Yellow Freight System Inc 10990 Roe Overland Park KS 66207

POWELL, GEORGE VAN TUYL, lawyer; b. Seattle, May 14, 1910; s. John Havard and Elizabeth Sargent (Gastman) P.; grad. Phillips Exeter Acad., 1927; A.B., Princeton, 1931; LL.B., U. Wash., 1934; m. Katherine Jaynes, Aug. 22, 1933; children—Jane (Mrs. Robert Walton Thomas), George Van Tuyl, Lisa Katherine (Mrs. John Preston Gibson). Admitted to Wash. bar, 1935, since practiced in Seattle; mem. firm Lane, Powell, Moss & Miller. Mem. Wash. Ho. of Reps., 1947-53. Commr. Uniform State Laws, 1952-64. Regent U. Wash., 1965-77. Served to lt. USNR, 1944-46. Mem. Am. (past del.), Wash. (past bd. govs.) bar assns. Clubs: Seattle Golf (past pres.), University (past pres.), Rainier (Seattle). Home: Route 8 Box 8580 Bainbridge Island WA 98110 Office: Rainier Bank Tower Seattle WA 98101

POWELL, HAMPTON OLIVER, furniture mfr.; b. Lynch Station, Va., Mar. 19, 1911; s. George C. and Mary Susan (Wood) P.; ed. high sch., Altavista, Va.; m. Beverly Andrews Wilkinson, May 30, 1936. With Lane Co., Inc., 1927—, beginning in sales and advt. div., successively staff credit and prodn. depts., gen. adminstrv. officer, exec. v.p. and dir., 1927-56, pres., 1956-76, chmn. bd., 1976—. Dir Furniture Found., Inc. Recipient Outstanding Citizen award Altavista C. of C., 1966; James T. Ryan award for outstanding service to furniture industry, 1974. Mem. So. Furniture Mfrs. Assn. (past pres., dir., chmn. govt. relations com.), Va. C. of C. Baptist. Mason (Shriner). Home: Lynch Station VA 24571 Office: Lane Co Inc Altavista VA 24517

POWELL, HAROLD FRYBURG, co. fin. exec.; b. Corry. Pa., Oct. 18, 1932; s. Harold K. and Freda F. P.; B.S. in Econs., Wharton Sch., U. Pa.; postgrad. Western Res. U.; m. Jacqueline Williams, May 14, 1955; children—Jeffery, Stephen. Securities analyst Central Nat. Bank, Cleve., 1955-61; asst. treas. Carling Brewing Co., Cleve., 1961-63, divisional controller, St. Louis, 1963-67; mgr. corp. planning Philip Morris Inc., N.Y.C., 1967-69, asst. to corp. pres., 1969-71; v.p. Benson & Hedges (Can.) Ltd., Toronto, Ont., 1971-74; v.p. fin. Standard Brands Ltd., Montreal, Que., Can., 1974-76; v.p. fin. Internat. Standard Brands Inc., N.Y.C., 1976-77; v.p., treas. Standard Brands Inc., N.Y.C., 1977-79, v.p., corp. comptroller, 1979—. Home: 1062 Smith Ridge Rd New Canaan CT 06840 Office: Standard Brands Inc 625 Madison Ave New York NY 10022

POWELL, HARVARD WENDELL, bus. cons.; b. Duluth, Minn., Feb. 1, 1915; s. Edgar S. and Leona (Bush) P.; B.S., U. Minn., 1950, J.D., 1951; grad. Indsl. Coll. Armed Forces, 1956; m. Audrey Barker, June 18, 1941; children—Mark Horton, Anne Bush. Commd. 2d lt. USAAF, 1940, advanced through grades to brig. gen. USAF, 1959; command pilot, comdr. China, 1943-45; dir. procurement and prodn. USAF, 1958; vice comdr. Air Force Space Systems Div., 1960; retired, 1963; v.p. mgmt. planning and service N.Am. Rockwell, 1963-70; pres., chief exec. officer A.J. Industries, Inc., Los Angeles, 1970—, also dir.; pres. A.J. Land Co., Juneau Hydroelectric, Inc.; dir. Devel. Services, Inc., Sargent Engring. Co., Roberts-Gordon Appliance Ltd., Calif. Bankers Trust Corp. Mem. Gov. Calif. Commn. Ednl. Reform; dir. small bus. and econ. utilization policy Office Sec. Def., 1971-77; internat. bus. cons., 1977—. Decorated D.F.C., Air medal with 2 oak leaf clusters, Legion of merit with oak leaf cluster. Mem. Fed. Bar Assn., State Bar Minn., Air Force Assn. Home: 1001 Wilson Blvd Arlington VA 22209 Office: 1100 Connecticut Ave Suite 510 Washington DC 20036

POWELL, JACK BERNARD, sugar co. exec.; b. Norfolk, Va., Mar. 29, 1920; s. Bernard H. and Ocie L. (Hall) P.; student W.Va. U., 1940-43; B.S. in Mech. Engring., U. Ill., 1947; m. Elizabeth Ann Wright, Jan. 2, 1944; children—Margaret Lenore, Deborah Jean. Engr., Gt. Western Sugar Co., Denver, 1947-57, factory mgr., 1957-64, ops. exec., 1964-69, v.p., gen. mgr. No. Ohio Sugar Co. subs., 1969-71, v.p. mfg., 1971-74, exec. v.p., chief operating officer parent co., 1974-75, pres., chief exec. officer, 1975—, also pres., chief exec. officer, dir. all subsidiaries. Bd. dirs. United Way, Ft. Morgan, Colo. Served with Signal Corps, U.S. Army, 1943-46. Mem. Beet Sugar Devel. Found. (dir.), Am. Soc. Beet Sugar Technologists, U.S. Beet Sugar Assn. (trustee). Colo. Assn. Commerce and Industry (dir.). Republican. Congregationalist. Contbr. sect. to Beet-Sugar Technology, 2d. edit. Home: 7877 E Mississippi St Apt 302-E Denver CO 80231 Office: 1530 16th St Denver CO 80202

POWELL, JAMES FREDERICK, lawyer; b. Birmingham, Ala., Jan. 2, 1936; s. Lewis W. and Louise (DeArman) P.; B.S., U. Ala., 1957, LL.B., 1959; m. Bette Weaver, Sept. 8, 1959; children—Wesley Weaver, James Frederick. Admitted to Ala. bar, 1959, since practiced in Birmingham; asso. Moore, Thomas, Taliaferro, Forman & Burr, 1962-65; partner Thomas, Taliaferro, Forman, Burr & Murray, 1966—. Served to capt. Judge Adv. Gen.'s Corps, AUS, 1959-62. Mem. Am., Ala., Birmingham bar assns., Newcomen Soc. in N.Am., Pi Kappa Alpha, Phi Alpha Delta. Presbyn. Clubs: Birmingham Country, Kiwanis, Relay House (Birmingham). Home: 3744 E Fairway Dr Birmingham AL 35213 Office: 16th Floor Bank for Savs Bldg Birmingham AL 35203

POWELL, JAMES LAWRENCE, coll. provost; b. Berea, Ky., July 17, 1936; s. Robert Lain and Lizena (Davis) P.; A.B., Berea Coll., 1958; Ph.D., Mass. Inst. Tech., 1962; divorced; children—Marla, Dirk. Mem. faculty Oberlin (Ohio) Coll., 1962—, also prof. geology, asso. dean, 1973-75, v.p., provost, 1976—. Fellow Geol. Soc. Am. Author: Strontium Isotope Geology, 1972. Home: 76 S Professor St Oberlin OH 44074

POWELL, JAMES MILTON, police exec.; b. Chapel Hill, Tenn., May 13, 1914; s. Milton Thomas and Aurora Ethel (Ralston) P.; student Southeastern U., 1955; grad. FBI Nat. Acad., 1955; m. Dorothy Elizabeth Forsht, June 4, 1938; children—James, John, Joseph. With D.C. Met. Police, 1940-58, 3d dist. supr., 1953-58, capt., 1958; mem. detail U.S. Capitol Police, 1958-65, chief of police, 1965—. Mem. Internat. Assn. Chiefs of Police, D.C. Police Assn., FBI Nat. Acad. Assn. (pres. D.C. chpt. 1964-65). Club: Lions. Office: 331 First St Washington DC 20510

POWELL, JANE (SUZANNE BURCE), actress, singer; b. Portland, Oreg., Apr. 1, 1929; d. Paul and Eileen Burce; student pub. schs., Portland; m. Geary Steffen, 1953 (div.); children—Geary, Suzanne; m. 2d Pat Nerney (div. 1963); 1 dau., Lindsey; m. 3d, James Fitzgerald, June 27, 1965; m. 4th, David Parlour, 1978. Under contract Metro-Goldwyn Mayer to 1957; numerous motion pictures including Holiday in Mexico, Royal Wedding, Athena, Seven Brides for Seven Brothers, Three Daring Daughters, Luxury Liner, Date With Judy, Nancy Goes to Rio, Two Weeks With Love, Rich, Young and Pretty, Small Town Girl, Three Sailors and a Girl, Deep in My Heart, Hit the Deck, Girl Most Likely, The Enchanted Island; night club engagements, Las Vegas, N.Y.C.; star TV version Meet Me in St. Louis, 1959; appeared in play Irene, N.Y.C., 1974. Address: 1364 Stradella Rd Los Angeles CA 90024*

POWELL, JOSEPH LESTER, JR. (JODY), govt. ofcl.; b. Cordele, Ga., Sept. 30, 1943; s. Joseph Lester and June (Williamson) P.; student U.S. Air Force Acad., 1961-64; B.A., Ga. State U., 1966; postgrad. Emory U., 1966-70; m. Nan Sue Jared, Apr. 23, 1966; 1 dau., Emily Claire. Group claims adjuster Life Ins. Co. of Ga., 1966-67; personal aide to State Sen. Jimmy Carter in gubernatorial campaign, Atlanta, 1970; press sec. to Gov. Jimmy Carter of Ga., 1970-74, to presdl. candidate Jimmy Carter, 1975-76, to Pres. Jimmy Carter, Washington, 1977—. Mem. Sigma Nu. Democrat. Baptist. Office: The White House 1600 Pennsylvania Ave Washington DC 20050*

POWELL, JULIUS CHERRY, univ. pres.; b. Harriman, Tenn., Jan. 23, 1926; s. Julius K. and Lucille L. (Cherry) P.; B.A., U. Ky., 1950, D.Ed., 1970; M.Ed., U. Louisville, 1952; m. Elizabeth D. Case, Nov. 22, 1950; children—Karen, Julia. Tchr. Louisville Pub. Sch. System, 1950-57; with Ky. Dept. Edn., 1957-60; exec. asst. to pres. Eastern Ky. U., Richmond, 1960-62, dean bus. affairs, 1962-65, exec. dean, 1965-69, v.p. for adminstrn., 1969-76, pres., 1976—. Mem. Council on Pub. Higher Edn. Served with AUS, 1944-47. Mem. Phi Delta Kappa, Kappa Delta Pi. Democrat. Club: Rotary. Home: 507 Lancaster Ave Richmond KY 40475 Office: Eastern Ky U Lancaster Ave Richmond KY 40475

POWELL, LESLIE CHARLES, JR., educator; b. Beaumont, Tex., Dec. 13, 1927; s. Leslie Charles and Tillie Bee (Wallace) P.; B.S., So. Meth. U., 1948; M.D., Johns Hopkins U., 1952; children—Jeffrey Johns, Randall Gardner, Daniel Charles, Gerard Paul. Intern, then resident U. Tex., Galveston, 1952-55; instr. Ob-Gyn 1957-59, asst. prof., 1959-63, asso. prof., 1963-68, prof., 1968—; cons., Richmond State Sch., 1969—. Pres., Am. Cancer Soc., Galveston County, 1972-73. Served with M.C., AUS, 1955-57. Recipient Hannah award Tex. Assn. Ob-Gyn, 1955; research grantee HEW, 1969-71; Fulbright scholar, Burma, 1975; diplomate Am. Bd. Ob-Gyn. Mem. Alpha Tau Omega, Phi Beta Pi. Republican. Dir. S.W. Conf. Unitarian Ch. Editorial cons. Tex. Reports Biology and Medicine, 1975, Psychosomatics, 1977; contbr. articles to profl. jours. Home: 7517 Leeward St Galveston TX 77551 Office: 800 Ave B U Tex Med Sch Galveston TX 77550

POWELL, LEWIS FRANKLIN, JR., asso. justice U.S. Supreme Ct.; b. Suffolk, Va., Sept. 19, 1907; s. Lewis Franklin and Mary Lewis (Gwathmey) P.; B.S., Washington and Lee U., 1929, LL.B., 1931, LL.D., 1960; LL.M., Harvard, 1932; hon. degrees: LL.D., Hampden Sydney Coll., 1959, Coll. William and Mary, 1965, U. Fla., 1965, U. Richmond, 1970, U.S.C., 1972, Wake Forest U., 1974, Brigham Young U., 1975, Yeshiva U., 1976, Columbia U., 1978; m. Josephine M. Rucker, May 2, 1936; children—Josephine Powell Smith, Ann Pendleton Powell Carmody, Mary Lewis Gwathmey Powell Sumner, Lewis Franklin, III. Admitted to Va. bar, 1931, U.S. Supreme Ct. bar, 1937; practiced law in Richmond, 1932-71; mem. firm, Hunton, Williams, Gay, Powell and Gibson 1937-71; asso. justice, U.S. Supreme Ct., 1972—. Chmn. emeritus Colonial Williamsburg Found.; mem. Nat. Commn. on Law Enforcement and Adminstrn. Justice, 1965-67; mem. Blue Ribbon Def. Panel to study Def. Dept., 1969-70. Served from lt. to col. USAAF, 1942-46, 33 months overseas: Decorated Legion of Merit, Bronze Star (U.S.); Croix de Guerre with palms (France). Trustee emeritus Washington and Lee U.; hon. bencher Lincoln's Inn. Fellow Am. Bar Found. (pres. 1969-71), Am. Coll. Trial Lawyers (pres. 1969-70); mem. Am. (gov., pres. 1964-65), Va., Richmond (pres. 1947-48) bar assns., Bar Assn. City N.Y., Nat. Legal Aid and Defender Assn. (v.p. 1964-65), Am. Law Inst., Soc. Cin., Sons Colonial Wars, Phi Beta Kappa, Phi Delta Phi, Omicron Delta Kappa, Phi Kappa Sigma. Presbyterian. Clubs: Alfalfa; Century, University (N.Y.C.). Office US Supreme Ct Washington DC 20543

POWELL, LORING WEBSTER, life ins. co. exec.; b. Melrose, Mass., Nov. 23, 1918; s. Webster H. and Laurena (Vander Pyl) P.; A.B., Harvard U., 1940, M.B.A., 1942; m. Winifred Saurwein, Dec. 28, 1943; children—Anne S. Powell Ball, Robert Loring. With John Hancock Mut. Life Ins. Co., Boston, 1942—, v.p. group pensions, 1970—; trustee West Newton Savs. Bank. Chmn., mem. exec. com. United Methodist Ch. Pension Fund Investment Com.; pres. Ministers Retirement Mut. Fund; corp. mem. Morgan Meml. Inc.; mem. vis. com. Boston U. Mem. Am. Pension Conf., Ins. Accounting and Statis. Assn., Squirrel Island Maine Land Assn. (pres.). Clubs: Brae Burn Country, Longwood Covered Cts. Home: 226 Kent Rd Waban MA 02168 Office: John Hancock Pl Boston MA 02116

POWELL, LOYD EARL, JR., plant physiologist, educator; b. Ravenwood, Mo., Oct. 17, 1928; s. Loyd Earl and Myrtle Emma (Freeman) P.; B.S. in Agr., U. Mo., 1951; M.S., Ohio State U., 1952; Ph.D., Cornell U., 1955; m. Betty Elaine Balduf, Aug. 4, 1956; children—David, Brian, Eric. Asst. prof. N.Y. State Agrl. Expt. Sta., Cornell U., Geneva, 1955-61; asso. prof. pomology Cornell U., Ithaca, 1961-74, prof. pomology, 1974—; research asso. biology Yale, 1962-63; NATO vis. prof. U. Pisa (Italy), 1974. Fellow Am. Soc. Hort. Sci. (J.H. Gourley award 1974); mem. Am. Soc. Plant Physiologists, Scandinavian Soc. Plant Physiologists. Unitarian. Contbr. articles to profl. jours. Home: 1685 Ellis Hollow Rd Ithaca NY 14850

POWELL, NORBORNE BERKELEY, urologist; b. Montgomery, Ala., July 24, 1914; s. Floyd Berkeley and Eloise (Sadler) P.; M.D., Baylor U., 1938; m. Elizabeth Mary Balas, Dec. 18, 1939; children—Norborne Berkeley, Barbara Key. Intern, Duke Hosp., Durham, N.C., 1938-39, Charity Hosp., New Orleans, 1939-40; resident Tulane Service, Charity Hosp., 1940-42; practice medicine, specializing in urology, Houston, 1942—; mem. staff Ben Taub Gen. Hosp.; mem. staff Twelve Oaks Hosp., Houston, chief staff, 1974; mem. cons. staff Meth. Hosp., St. Luke's Episc. Hosp.; clin. prof. urology Baylor Coll. Medicine, 1964—. Trustee Baylor Med. Found., 1945-55; pres. Twelve Okas Med. Found., 1976—. Diplomate Am. Bd. Urology. Fellow A.C.S., Internat. Coll. Surgeons; mem. Mexican Urol. Assn. (corr.), Am. Urol. Assn. (Sci. Exhbn. 1st prize 1951), Houston Urol. Soc. (pres. 1955). Club: River Oaks Country. Contbr. articles to profl. jours. Home: 2410 Avalon Pl Houston TX 77019 Office: 4126 Southwest Freeway Houston TX 77027

POWELL, PHILIP WAYNE, educator, author; b. Chino, Calif., Oct. 30, 1913; s. Robert Chester and Muriel June (Holcomb) P.; student Occidental Coll., 1930-32; B.A., U. Calif. at Berkeley, 1936, Ph.D., 1941; m. Mariá Luisa Vanegas Guarín, Jan. 22, 1942; children—Diana Linda (Mrs. Larry M. Fornas), Lilia Patricia (Mrs. James A. Rochester). With State Dept., 1941-43; vis. prof. history U. Pa., 1943-44; asst. prof. Northwestern U., 1944-48; prof. history U. Calif. at Santa Barbara, 1948—, chmn. dept., 1958, 62-64, dir. univ. study center at U. Madrid (Spain), 1964-66. Chmn. Nat. Conf. Latin Am. History, 1947; spl. adviser 9th Internat. Conf. Am. States, Bogota, 1948. Served with USMCR, 1942-43. Decorated comdr. Order Isabel the Catholic (Spain). Mem. Phi Beta Kappa, Phi Gamma Delta. Author: Soldiers, Indians and Silver: The Northward Advance of New Spain, 1550-1600, 1952; Ponzoña en Las Nieves, 1966; Tree of Hate: Propaganda and Prejudices Affecting United States Relations with the Hispanic World, 1971; Arbol de Odio, 1972; Mexico's Miguel Caldera: The Taming of America's First Frontier, 1548-1597, 1977; La Guerra Chichimeca, 1977. Adv. editor The Americas, 1953—. Home: 1216 Shoreline Dr Santa Barbara CA 93109

POWELL, RICHARD GORDON, lawyer; b. Rochester, N.Y., Jan. 7, 1918; B.S., Harvard U., 1938; LL.B., Columbia U., 1941. Admitted to N.Y. bar, 1941, U.S. Supreme Ct. bar, 1955; asso. firm Sullivan & Cromwell, N.Y.C., 1941-52, partner, 1952—; dir. DeLaval Separator Co., Liberian Iron Ore, Ltd., Orinoka Mills; vice chmn. bd. Colloids, Inc.; chmn. bd. Hedwin Corp., Solvay Am. Corp. Former mem. bd. mgrs. Englewood (N.J.) Community Chest; trustee, elder 1st Presbyterian Ch. Mem. Am., N.Y. State bar assns., Assn. Bar City N.Y., Am. Law Inst., N.Y. Law Inst. (pres.), Am. Soc. Internat. Law. Home: 555 Park Ave New York NY 10021 Office: 125 Broad St New York NY 10004

POWELL, RICHARD PITTS, author, writer; b. Phila., Nov. 28, 1908; s. Richard Percival and Lida Catherine (Pitts) P.; grad. Episcopal Acad., 1926; A.B., Princeton, 1930; m. Marian Carleton Roberts, Sept. 6, 1932; children—Stephen Barnes, Dorothy Louise. Reporter Phila. Evening Ledger, 1930-40; with N.W. Ayer & Son, Phila., 1940-58, mem. pub. relations dept., 1940-42, charge info. services, 1949-58, v.p., 1951-58. Served as lt. col. AUS, 1942-46; chief news censor S.W. Pacific Theatre, 1945. Club: Royal Palm Yacht (Fort Myers, Fla.). Author: (mystery books) Don't Catch Me, 1943; All Over but the Shooting, 1944; Lay That Pistol Down, 1945; Shoot If You Must, 1946; And Hope to Die, 1947; Shark River, 1950; Shell Game, 1950; A Shot in the Dark, 1952; Say It with Bullets, 1953; False Colors, 1955; (novels) The Philadelphian, 1957; Pioneer, Go Home, 1959; The Soldier, 1960; I Take This Land, 1963; Daily and Sunday, 1965; Don Quixote, U.S.A., 1966; Tickets to the Devil, 1968; Whom the Gods Would Destroy, 1970; Florida: A Picture Tour, 1972; (novel under pen name Jeremy Kirk) The Build-Up Boys, 1951. Contbr. short stories, articles, serials to mags. Home: 1201 Carlene Ave Fort Myers FL 33901

POWELL, ROBERT MORGAN, trucking co. exec.; b. Cleve., Sept. 28, 1934; s. David Kelso and Rachel Kirk (Alford) P.; B.S., U. N.C., 1956; m. Janice Hobbs, Sept. 2, 1973. With Ark.-Best Freight System, Inc., 1960— ops. mgr., St. Louis, 1960-62, asst. dir. terminals, Fort

Smith, Ark., 1962-63, br. mgr., St. Louis, 1963-67, dir. research and planning, Fort Smith, 1967-68, v.p. spl. commodities, 1968-69, v.p. ops., 1969-73, exec. v.p., 1973—. Past bd. dirs. Fort Smith Art Center; past treas., bd. dirs. Salvation Army; active fund-raising drives United Way. Served with USN, 1956-60, 61-62. Mem. Am. Trucking Assn. (dir. ops. council). Club: Fort Smith Town (dir., past pres.). Office: Ark-Best Freight System Inc PO Box 48 Fort Smith AR 72901

POWELL, ROBERT NICHOLAS, ins. co. exec.; b. Detroit, June 14, 1928; s. Nicholas Miles and Helen (Davis) P.; B.B.A., U. Mich., 1951, M.A., 1952; m. Patricia Tashjian, Apr. 18, 1953; children—Pamela Rose, Laura Jean, Lucy Anne. With Calif.-Western State Life Ins. Co., Sacramento, 1952-69, asst. actuary, 1957-59, asso. actuary, 1959-61, actuary, 2d v.p., 1961-62, v.p., actuary, 1962—, chief actuary, 1969—; v.p. Nationwide Corp., 1969—, Nat. Service, Inc., 1969—. Served with AUS, 1946-47. Fellow Soc. Actuaries; mem. Tri-State Actuarial Club. Home: 1526 Bridgeton Dr Columbus OH 43220 Office: One Nationwide Plaza Columbus OH 43216

POWELL, STANLEY, JR., mgmt. cons.; b. Oakland, Calif., Feb. 3, 1917; s. Stanley and Esther (Bentley) P.; B.A., U. Calif. at Berkeley, 1940; m. Mary Elizabeth Winstead, July 3, 1942; children—Robert, Katherine, Nancy, Georgia. With Matson Nav. Co., 1941-42, 45-70, sec.-treas., 1958-59, v.p. freight div., 1959-61, exec. v.p., 1961-62, pres., dir. 1962-70; v.p. Oceanic Steamship Co., 1959-62, pres., dir., 1962-66, chmn. bd., 1966-70; chmn. bd. Matson Research Corp., 1965-70; v.p., dir. Matson Terminals, Inc., 1962-67; v.p. Alexander & Baldwin, Inc., 1965-66, pres., dir., 1966-70; mem. exec. com., dir. U.S. Leasing Internat., Inc., 1970—; chmn. bd. Ship Funding Internat., Inc., 1972-73; ind. mgmt. cons., 1970—. Mem. U.S. Shipbldg. Commn. Served to lt. (s.g.) USNR, 1942-45. Mem. Alpha Delta Phi. Clubs: Bohemian (San Francisco); Pacific-Union, Meadow Calif.). Home: 130 Barber Ave San Anselmo CA 94960 Office: 215 Market St Room 901 PO Box 7990 San Francisco CA 94120

POWELL, SUMNER CHILTON, educator; b. Northampton, Mass., Oct. 2, 1924; s. Chilton Latham and Theodora Duval (Sumner) P.-Hall; grad. Taft Sch., 1942; B.A., Amherst Coll., 1946; Ph.D., Harvard U., 1956. Vice pres. Ewen Knight Electronic Research Corp., Cambridge, Mass., 1953-54; instr. History and English Choate Sch., 1954-60; mem. faculty Yale U., New Haven, 1960-62; instr. history Barnard Sch. Boys, Riverdale, N.Y., 1962-63; intr. history Iona Coll., New Rochelle, 1964-67, asst. prof. history and polit. sci., 1967-69; co. historian William Underwood Co., 1969-71; pres. Powell Assos., research and devel. in edn., 1971—. Served to lt. (j.g.) USNR, 1943-46. Mem. Am. Hist. Assn., Mass. Colonial Soc., Phi Beta Kappa, Phi Alpha Psi. Author: From Mythical to Mediaeval Man, 1957; Venture to Windward, 1958; Puritan Village (Pulitzer prize history 1964), 1963; Venture to the Windward Isles, 1969; When I Was Five, 1974. Address: 349 Homeland South Way Apt 1A Baltimore MD 21212

POWELL, WALTER HECHT, labor arbitrator; b. N.Y.C., Apr. 13, 1915; s. Arthur Lee and Stella (Hecht) P.; B.S., N.Y. U., 1938, J.D., 1940; M.A., U. Pa., 1948; m. Dorothy Meyer, Mar. 15, 1945; children—Lawrence L., Alan W., Lesley A., Steven H. Asst. prof. Temple U., 1946-51; asst. dir. personnel Am. Safety Razor, Kingsbury, Ind., 1951-53; v.p., dir. operations Internat. Resistance Co., Phila., 1953-69, v.p., dir. indsl. relations, 1956-69; sr. v.p. First Pa. Banking & Trust Co., Phila., 1969-73; v.p. for personnel resources Temple U., Phila., 1973-78; ind. labor arbitrator, 1978—; panel mem. Am. Arbitration Assn., Fed. Mediation and Conciliation Service, Pa., N.J. labor relation bds.; lectr. U. Pitts., Temple U., U. Richmond, Vanderbilt U., Am. U., others; dir. Auerbach Corp., Phila. Commr., Phila. Commn. on Human Relations, 1969—. Bd. dirs. Opportunities Industrialization Center. Served to capt. AUS, 1942-46. Recipient award Phila. C. of C., 1968. Mem. Am. Mgmt. Assn. (adv. council 1963—), Indsl. Relations Assn., Indsl. Relations Research Assn. (local pres. 1966). Contbr. articles to mag., chpts. to books. Home: 2200 Benjamin Franklin Pkwy Philadelphia PA 19130

POWELL, WILLARD REES, mfg. co. exec.; b. Scranton, Pa., May 3, 1926; s. Arthur Rees and Helen (Lord) P.; B.A., Pa. State U., 1947; M.B.A., Columbia U., 1949; m. Margaret Auten Coughlin, Aug. 1, 1953; children—D. Scott, Doug, Greg, Ridgway. With Ernst & Ernst, N.Y.C., 1949-63; v.p., treas. Amerace Corp., N.Y.C., 1963-69; v.p. Paine, Webber, Jackson & Curtis, N.Y.C., 1969-71; v.p. fin. ITT Continental Baking Co., Rye, N.Y., 1971-76; sr. v.p. UMC Industries, Inc., Stamford, Conn., 1976—. Vice pres. Washington Irving council Boy Scouts Am., 1963-70. Served with USNR, 1944-45. C.P.A., N.Y. Mem. Fin. Execs. Inst., Am. Inst. C.P.A.'s. Home: 60 Ludlow Dr Chappaqua NY 10514 Office: PO Box 1090 High Ridge Park Stamford CT 06904

POWELL, WILLIAM ARNOLD, JR., banker; b. Verbena, Ala., July 7, 1929; s. William Arnold and Sarah Frances (Baxter) P.; B.S. in Bus. Adminstrn., U. Ala., 1953; grad. Sch. Banking of South, La. State U., 1966; m. Barbara Ann O'Donnell, June 16, 1956; children—William Arnold III, Barbara Ann McCaleb, Susan Frances, Patricia Baxter. With First Nat. Bank Birmingham (Ala.), 1953—, asst. v.p., 1966, v.p., 1967, v.p., br. supr., 1968-72, sr. v.p., br. supr., 1972-73, exec. v.p., 1973—, dir., 1979—; dir. Alabanc Fin. Corp., Engel Mortgage Co., Inc., 1st Nat. Bank of Birmingham. Trustee Ala. Banking Sch.; bd. dirs., v.p. Warrior-Tombigbee Devel. Assn.; bd. dirs. Big Bros. Birmingham; pres. Met. Devel. Bd. Served to lt. AUS, 1954-56. Mem. Birmingham Area C. of C. Kiwanian (pres. 1970). Clubs: The Club, Downtown, Riverchase Country, Birmingham Country, Green Valley Country (Birmingham). Home: 3309 Thornton Dr Birmingham AL 35226 Office: 1st Nat Bank of Birmingham 5th Ave and 20th St (PO Box 11007) Birmingham AL 35288

POWELL, WILLIAM ROSSELL, JR., lawyer; b. Evansville, Ind., Aug. 4, 1926; s. William R. and Nellie M. (Springer) P.; B.A., Western Ky. U., 1950; J.D., South Tex. Coll. Law, 1961; m. Jeri Lacy, Apr. 30, 1955. Claims mgr. Agrl. Ins. Group, Houston, 1954-61; admitted to Tex. bar, 1961, practiced in Houston; asso. firm Foreman, Dyess, Prewett, Hendeson & Cantey, 1961-67; mem. firm Schulman & Powell, 1967-69, Prappas, Caldwell & Moncure, 1969-73, Funderburk, Powell & Gibson, 1973-76. Served with USAAF, 1944-46, USAF, 1950-51. Mem. Houston, Tex. bar assns., Houston Assn. Claims Men, Tex. Assn. Def. Counsel. Contbr. articles to profl. jours. Home: 2025 South Blvd Houston TX 77098 Office: 711 Polk Ave Houston TX 77002

POWELL, WILLIAM WINTERSMITH, corp. exec.; b. Woodbury, N.J., May 18, 1937; s. William and Marcia Bledsoe (Wintersmith) P.; A.B. magna cum laude, Princeton U., 1959. With Colgate Palmolive Co., 1959-64, 65—, gen. mgr., Milan, Italy, 1972-74, v.p., gen. mgr. household products div., N.Y.C., 1974-75, group v.p., 1978—, dir. various subs.; pres., chief exec. officer Kendall Co., Boston, 1975-78. Bd. dirs. Mass. Taxpayer's Assn., 1976-79; mem. Mayor's Adv. Council Cultural Affairs, Boston, 1976-79; trustee Children's Hosp., Boston, 1976—. Served with U.S. Army, 1960. Mem. Health Industry Mfrs. Assn., Soap and Detergent Assn. (past dir.), Am. C. of C. of Italy (past dir.). Clubs: Princeton (N.Y.C.); Harvard, Longwood Cricket (Boston); Wianno (Osterville, Mass.). Home: 125 E 72d St New York NY 10021 Office: 300 Park Ave New York NY 10021. *While business environments may change, the basic requirements for success do not. There are no substitutes for intelligence, enthusiasm and hard work.*

POWELSON, JOHN PALEN, economist; b. N.Y.C., Sept. 3, 1920; s. John Abrum and Mary Elizabeth Rennie (Stephen) P.; grad. Phillips Acad., 1937; A.B., Harvard U., 1941, A.M., 1947, Ph.D., 1950; M.B.A., U. Pa., 1942; m. Alice Williams Roberts, May 31, 1953; children—Cynthia, Judith, Kenneth, Carolyn, Lawrence. Accountant, Haskins & Sells, C.P.A.'s, N.Y.C., 1942-44; instr. accounting U. Pa., 1944-45; teaching fellow econs. Harvard U., 1946-48; sr. accountant Price, Waterhouse & Co., C.P.A.'s, Paris, France, 1948-49; asst. prof. accounting U. Buffalo, 1949-50; economist Internat. Monetary Fund, 1950-54, asst. chief tng., 1954-58; prof. econs. Sch. Advanced Internat. Studies, Johns Hopkins U., 1958-64; prof. econ. devel. U. Pitts., 1964-66; prof. econs. U. Colo., 1966—; chmn. econs. dept. Inter-Am. U. Air, 1966-67; dir. tng. program nat. accounts Centro de Estudios Monetarios Latinamericanos, Mexico City, 1963-64; econ. adviser Govt. Bolivia, 1960; vis. prof. econs. U. San Andres, La Paz, Bolivia, 1960; cons. Inter-Am. Devel. Bank, Washington, 1967-68; econ. adviser Minstry of Finance and Planning, Kenya, 1972-74. Treas. Internat. Student House, Washington, 1952-59. C.P.A., N.Y. Mem. Am. Econ. Assn., Soc. Internat. Devel. Author: Economic Accounting, 1955; National Income and Flow-of-Funds Analysis, 1960; Latin America-Today's Economic and Social Revolution, 1964; Institutions of Economic Growth, 1972; A Select Bibliography on Economic Development, 1979; co-editor: Economic Development, Poverty, and Income Distribution, 1977. Home: 45 Bellevue Dr Boulder CO 80302

POWELSON, ROBERT JAMES, food co. exec.; b. Plainfield, N.J., May 31, 1928; s. Edward Francis and Margaret C. (Johnson) P.; grad. Rutgers U., 1961; grad. Advanced Mgmt. Program, Harvard U., 1970; m. Patricia Ann Wetherwax, May 27, 1950; children—Patricia, Gregory, Christopher, Kevin. With Nabisco, Inc., 1949—, adminstrv. asst. to pres., then exec. asst. to pres., 1971-73, pres. biscuit div., corp. v.p., 1973-78; group v.p. with responsibility for U.S. Biscuit div., total Can. ops., Nabisco Confections. Mem. advisory bd. Salvation Army. Served with USNR, 1945-46. Mem. Biscuit and Cracker Mfrs. Assn. (alt. dir.), Sales Execs. Club N.Y., Am. Logistics Soc. Home: 8 Woodland Rd Brookside NJ 07926 Office: Nabisco Inc River Rd East Hanover NJ 07936. *The ultimate test of any manager is simply "Did he do what he said he would do?" Are the objectives achieved? Are the goals fulfilled?*

POWER, ALOYSIUS FRANCIS, lawyer; b. Worcester, Mass., July 11, 1902; s. James David and Mary (Creamer) P.; A.B., Coll. Holy Cross, Worcester, 1923; student Sch. Bus., N.Y. U., 1923-24; LL.B., Fordham U., 1927; LL.D., Iona Coll., New Rochelle, N.Y., 1964; Dr. Civil Jurisprudence, Coll. Holy Cross, 1967; m. Eleanor G. Hurley, June 30, 1934; children—Patricia A. (dec.), Mary Power Monaghan, John A. Instr. math. Fordham Prep. Sch., N.Y.C., 1923-27; admitted to N.Y. bar, 1928, Mich. bar, 1938; with Gen. Motors Corp., 1927-67, v.p., gen. counsel, 1961-67. Mem. Am., Mich., Detroit bar assns., Knights of Malta. Roman Catholic. Clubs: Detroit Athletic, Recess (Detroit); Bloomfield Hills Country. Home: 420 Dunston Rd Bloomfield Hills MI 48013

POWER, CORNELIUS MICHAEL, archbishop; b. Seattle, Dec. 18, 1913; s. William and Kate (Dougherty) P.; student St. Patrick Sem., 1933-35, St. Edward Sem., 1935-39; J.C.D., Cath. U. Am., 1943. Ordained priest Roman Catholic Ch., 1939; asst. pastor St. James Cathedral, Seattle, 1939-40; resident chaplain Holy Names Acad., Seattle, 1943-52; adminstr. Parish of Our Lady of Lake, Seattle, 1955-56, pastor, 1956-69; vice chancellor Archdiocese of Seattle, 1943-51, chancellor, 1951-69; apptd. domestic prelate, 1963; 2d bishop of Yakima, 1969, bishop of Yakima, 1969-74; archbishop, Portland, Oreg., 1974—. Address: Archdiocese Portland PO Box 351 Portland OR 97207*

POWER, EUGENE BARNUM, microphotographer, bus. exec.; b. Traverse City, Mich., June 4, 1905; s. Glenn Warren and Annette (Barnum) P.; A.B., U. Mich., 1927, M.B.A., 1930, L.H.D., 1971; L.H.D., St. John's U., 1966; m. Sadye L. Harwick, June 17, 1929; 1 son, Philip H. With Edwards Bros., Inc., Ann Arbor, Mich., 1930-38, v.p., 1935-38; engaged in expts. with methods and uses of microfilm technique for reprodn. materials for research, 1935; founder Univ. Microfilms (merged Xerox Corp., 1962), 1938-70; dir. Xerox Corp., 1962-68, organized Microfilms, Inc., as distbn. agency, using microfilm as reprodn. medium for sci. and tech. materials, 1942-62; organized Projected Books, Inc., a non-profit corp., for distbn. of reading and entertainment materials in photog. form to physically incapacitated, 1944-70; organized Eskimo Art, Inc. (non-profit corp.), Univ. Microfilms, Ltd., London, 1952; owner Park Pl. Motor Inn, Traverse City; dir. Daedalus Enterprises Inc., Ann Arbor. Past chmn. Mich. Coordinating Council State Higher Edn. Regent U. Mich., 1956-66; del. Internat. Fedn. Documentation Conf., 1939, Paris, 1946, Berne, 1947; pres. Internat. Micrographic Congress, 1964-65, Nat. Microfilm Assn., 1946-54; spl. rep. Coordinator of Info. and Library of Congress, London, 1942, OSS, 1943-45; mem. Nat. Council on Humanities, 1969-73; trustee Carleton Coll., 1966-75, St. John's U., 1966-71, Detroit Inst. Art Founders Soc.; pres., chmn. The Power Found. Recipient award merit Nat. Microfilm Assn., 1956, fellow, 1963; hon. fellow Magdalene Coll., Cambridge, 1967, Northwestern Mich. Coll., 1967; decorated hon. Knight Comdr. Order of British Empire (Eng.), 1977. Asso. fellow Royal Photog. Soc.; mem. Am. Philos. Soc. Rotarian. Club: American (London). Author numerous articles. Organized 1st large microfilming project for libraries, copying all books printed in Eng. before 1640; during war directed large scale copying important Brit. manuscript materials in pub. and pvt. archives, also enemy documents. Home: 989 Forest Rd Barton Hills Ann Arbor MI 48105 Office: 2929 Plymouth Rd Ann Arbor MI 48105

POWER, FREMONT ALVIN, newspaper editor; b. Home Place, Ind., Dec. 19, 1915; s. Alvin S. and Harriett (Elliott) P.; student Ind. U., 1933-37; m. Marjorie Ethlyn Snider, Aug. 16, 1942; children—Michael, Stephen. Amusements editor, sports and feature writer Indpls. Times, 1938-42; exec. editor Indpls. News, 1965—. Bd. dirs. Northside YMCA, Indpls., 1954. Served with U.S. Maritime Service, 1942-45. Named to Race Relations Honor Roll, Indpls. Recorder, 1953; recipient award for articles racial integration Indpls. pub. schs. Health and Welfare Council Indpls; Casper award Community Services Met. Indpls.; Community Services award Flanner House and Bd. Fundamental Edn., 1978; Lamp of Learning award Ind. region B'nai B'rith Anti-Defamation League, 1969; Best Columnist award Indpls. Press Club, 1969, 70, 76, named Newsman of Year, 1973; Brotherhood award Ind. region NCCJ, 1973; Isadore Feibleman Man of Year award Indpls. chpt. B'nai B'rith, 1978. Presbyterian (deacon 1965-67). Club: Indpls. Press (pres. 1958). Office: 307 N Pennsylvania St Indianapolis IN 46206

POWER, GEORGE C., JR., investment analyst; b. St. Paul, Mar. 31, 1914; s. George C. and Anna (Dawson) P.; B.A., Carleton Coll., 1935; m. Jeanne Rogers, Feb. 24, 1944; children—George C., Margaret P. Power Klema. Mem. investment research dept. 1st Bank Systems, 1937-42; partner Mairs & Power Investment Counsel, St. Paul, 1946-61; pres., dir. Mairs and Power, Inc., Investment Counsel, St. Paul, 1961—; pres., dir. Mairs & Power Growth Fund, Inc., Mairs & Power Income Fund, Inc. Pres., dir. St. Lukes Hosp., St. Paul, 1963-72; dir. United Hosps., Inc., chmn., 1972-77; dir. Bush Found., St. Paul; treas. Episcopal Diocese of Minn., 1973-78, mem. investment com., 1973—. Served to capt. AUS, 1942-46. Mem. Twin City Soc. Security Analysts (past pres.), Fin. Analysts Fedn. Clubs: Univ., Pool and Yacht, Athletic. Home: 1700 S Lexington St Paul MN 55118 Office: W-2062 1st Nat Bank Bldg St Paul MN 55101

POWER, JOHN FRANCIS, investment banker; b. N.Y.C., June 3, 1906; s. James F. and Adelaide (Schultz) P.; A.B., Holy Cross Coll., 1928; m. Margaret Morrissey, Oct. 12, 1933; children—Mary Power Donovan, John, Patricia Power Moore, Margaret Power Mulry, Cathy Power Schibil, James, Elizabeth Power Maloney. Financial writer, publicist N.Y. News Bur., Wall St. News, 1928-33; statistician, sales exec. Boettcher, Newton & Co., also Harris, Upham & Co., N.Y.C., 1933-36; sales mgr. Eastman Dillon & Co., 1936-44, gen. partner, 1944-56; gen. partner Eastman Dillon, Union Securities & Co., 1956-72; sr. v.p. Blyth, Eastman, Dillon and Co., Inc., mem. N.Y. Stock Exchange, 1972—. Clubs: Creek (Locust Valley); University, Stock Exchange Luncheon (N.Y.C.); St. Andrews (Gulfstream, Fla.); Eqwanok Country (Manchester, Vt.); Country of Fla. (Delray); Everglades (Palm Beach, Fla.); Quail Ridge Golf (Delray Beach, Fla.). Contbr. to Ethics of Banking. Home and Office: 2727 N Ocean Blvd Gulfstream Delray Beach FL 33444

POWER, JOSEPH THOMAS, labor orgn. exec.; b. Chgo., Feb. 22, 1920; s. Joseph and Mary (Kelly) P.; grad. high sch.; m. Mary Kathryn Powers, Oct. 12, 1943; children—John J., Kathryn E., Mary Ann, Joan, Joseph, Sheila. Vice pres. Plasterers' Local 5, Chgo., 1954-55, pres., 1955-56; internat. v.p. Operative Plasterers' and Cement Masons' Internat. Assn., Washington, 1956-59, exec. v.p., 1959-70, gen. pres., 1970—, editor ofcl. monthly publ. Plasterer and Cement Mason. Mem. Nat. Joint Bd. for Settlement of Jurisdictional Disputes, 1961-71, v.p., mem. exec. council bldg. and constrn. trades dept., 1970—; del. ILO, Geneva, Switzerland, 1971, 1972, Japanese Confedn. Lab., Tokyo, 1972, Japan/Korea, 1974, Washington, 1975; mem. Dept. State mission to South Am., 1973; pub. mem. Dept. State Fgn. Service Selection Bd. III, 1974—. Bd. visitors U.S. Mil. Acad., 1977—. Served with USCGR, 1941-46. Roman Catholic. Home: 3327 Pensa Dr Falls Church VA 22041 Office: 1125 17th St NW Washington DC 20036

POWER, JULES, TV producer; b. Hammond, Ind., Oct. 19, 1921; grad. cum laude (Hardy scholarship in speech and communications) Northwestern U., 1944; m. Dorothy Kutchinsky; children—Robert, Robin. Sr. producer AM America, ABC-TV; former producer TV show Watch Mr. Wizard, NBC-TV; exec. producer ABC-TV News and Pub. Affairs; exec. producer TV prodn. Discovery, 1962-71; exec. producer TV spl. How Life Begins, 1968, The Unseen World, 1970, producer AM America, 1975; now sr. producer Over Easy; exec. producer ednl. films for ABC-McGraw-Hill. Served with USAAF, World War II. Recipient Emmy award, Peabody award, Thomas Alva Edison award (3), Ohio State award (5). Mem. Writers Guild Am. East, Nat. Acad. Television Arts and Scis. (past nat. nat. vice-chmn., past pres. N.Y. chpt.). Club: Friars (gov.) (N.Y.C.). Author: How Life Begins. Home: 48 Lyford Dr Tiburon CA 94920

POWER, PHILIP HARWICK, publisher; b. Ann Arbor, Mich., June 3, 1938; s. Eugene Barnum and Sayde (Harwick) P.; B.A. summa cum laude, U. Mich., 1960; M.A. (Marshall Scholar), Univ. Coll., Oxford (Eng.) U., 1964; m. Sarah Hutchins Goddard, July 5, 1971. Sports editor, acting city editor Fairbanks (Alaska) Daily News-Miner, 1961-62; fgn. stringer Chgo. Daily News, 1962-64; mem. gubernatorial campaign staff U.S. rep., 1964; adminstrv. asst. to U.S. rep., 1965-66; founder, pub. Observer Newspapers, Inc., Livonia, Mich., 1966-74; founder, chmn. bd. Suburban Communications Corp., 1974—. Bd. dirs. Power Found.; chmn. Mich. Found. for Arts. Mem. Council on Fgn. Relations. Club: American (London). Office: 36251 Schoolcraft Rd Livonia MI 48150

POWER, ROBERT HARBISON, bus. exec.; b. Woodland, Calif., Apr. 19, 1926; s. Edward Ignatius and Helen Melissa (Harbison) P.; A.A., San Francisco City Coll., 1948; m. Margaret Mary Casey, June 25, 1949; children—Diane, Mark, Linda, Julie, John, Brian. Partner, Nut Tree Restaurant, Nut Tree, Calif., 1948—; dir. Buttes Gas & Oil Co., Oakland, Calif., 1961—, chmn., 1974—, cons. Nut Tree Assos., 1974—. Pres. Calif. Republican Assembly, 1955-56; treas. Calif. Rep. Central Com., 1958-60; del. Rep. Nat. Conv., Chgo., 1960; bd. dirs. Calif. State Parks Found., 1968—, chmn., 1976-77; bd. dirs. Library Assos. U. Calif., Davis, 1968-73, pres., 1968-69; mem. Calif. Heritage Preservation Commn., 1968-77, chmn., 1970-77; bd. dirs. Nat. Inst. Foodservice Industry, mem. Sir Francis Drake Commn., Sacramento, 1974—; mem. Solano County Planning Commn., 1951-63, chmn., 1956. Served with USAR, 1943-45; ETO. Decorated Purple Heart. Mem. Calif. State (dir. 1965—, pres. 1975-76), Calif. (dir. 1978—), Nat. (dir. 1971—, treas. 1976-77, v.p. 1978-79, pres. 1979-80) restaurant assns., Calif. Hist. Soc. (pres. 1976-78, dir.), Royal Geog. Soc., Hakluyt Soc., Friends of Bancroft Library, Book Club of Calif., Brit. Museum Soc. Clubs: Commonwealth of Calif., Rotary (pres. Vacaville 1964-65), Press of San Francisco, Sacramento Book Collectors (pres. 1971-72). Author: Pioneer Skiing in California, 1960; Francis Drake and San Francisco Bay: A Beginning of the British Empire, 1974. Home: Nut Tree CA 95688 Office: Nut Tree Restaurant Nut Tree CA 95688

POWER, WILLIAM EDWARD, bishop; b. Montreal, Que., Can., Sept. 27, 1915; s. Nicholas Walter and Bridget Elizabeth (Callaghan) P.; B.A., Montreal Coll., 1937; student Grand Sem., Montreal. Ordained priest Roman Catholic Ch., 1941; parish asst., Montreal, 1941-47; vice-chancellor Diocese Montreal, 1947-50; diocesan chaplain Young Christian Workers and Christian Family Movement, 1950-53; nat. chaplain Young Christian Workers, 1953-59; chaplain, mgr. Cath. Men's Hostel, Montreal, 1957-59; pastor St. Barbara's Ch., Lasalle, Que., 1959-60; bishop of Antigonish, N.S., 1960—; chancellor St. Francis Xavier U., 1960-77. Bd. dirs. Canadian Catholic Conf. of Bishops, 1975—, pres., 1971-73. Address: 155 Main St Box 1330 Antigonish NS B26 2L7 Canada

POWERS, ALAN GILBERT, bldg. maintenance co. exec.; b. N.Y.C., Apr. 13, 1931; s. Benjamin and Fannie (Fink) P.; B.S. in Bus. Adminstrn., L.I. U., 1952; m. Rita Ginsberg, Nov. 22, 1951; children—Benay M., Marc D., Steven L., David S. Pres. Regent Window Cleaning Co., N.Y.C., 1952-54; supr., salesman Prudential Bldg. Maintenance Corp., N.Y.C., 1954-67, v.p., sec., 1967-72, pres., 1972—. Home: Woodhollow Court Muttontown NY 11791 Office: 1430 Broadway New York City NY 10018

POWERS, ANNE, author; b. Cloquet, Minn., May 7, 1913; d. John Patrick and Maud (Lynch) Powers; student U. Minn., 1932-33; m. Harold A. Schwartz, Aug. 22, 1938; children—Weldon, Lynn. Lectr., instr. writing Marquette U., Milw., instr. creative writing Coll. Journalism. Marquette U. Recipient ann. award best gen. book submitted Nat. Fedn. Press Women, 1946; matrix citation fiction writing Theta Sigma Phi, 1951. Mem. Allied Authors, Fictioneers, Sigma Kappa. Roman Catholic. Club: Shorewood Woman's (Milw.). Author: The Gallant Years, 1946; Ride East, Ride West, 1947; No

Wall So High, 1949; The Ironmaster, 1951; The Only Sin, 1953; The Thousand Fires, 1957; Ride With Danger, 1958; No King But Caesar, 1960; Rachel, 1973; The Four Queens, 1977; The Royal Consorts, 1978; The Young Empress, 1979; Possession, 1979. Home: 3800 N Newhall St Milwaukee WI 53211 Office: care Bobbs-Merril Co Inc 1720 E 38th St Indianapolis IN 46218

POWERS, DARDEN, educator; b. Holly Springs, Miss., Nov. 15, 1932; s. Percy Harmon and Irene (Mathews) P.; B.S. with spl. distinction, U. Okla., 1955; M.S., Calif. Inst. Tech., 1957, Ph.D., 1961; m. Patricia Ann Walls, July 6, 1957; children—Susan Lynne, John Darden, David Michael, Peter Daniel. With Hughes Aircraft Co., 1955-57; research asst. Calif. Inst. Tech., 1957-61; asst. prof. Baylor U., Waco, Tex., 1961-64, asso. prof., 1964-68, prof. physics, 1968—, dir. Van De Graaff Lab., 1965—. Served to sgt. 1st class AUS, 1951-53. Mem. Am. Assn. Physics Tchrs., Am. Phys. Soc., Phi Beta Kappa, Sigma Xi, Sigma Pi Sigma. Contbr. articles to profl. jours. Home: 3217 Forrester Ln Waco TX 76708

POWERS, DAVID PRICE, TV dir.; b. Los Angeles, Dec. 2, 1932; s. Dwight Henry and Marion Alice (Ryf) P.; m. Jacquelyn C. Cowman, May 12, 1968; children—Debra, Timothy, Gregory. Prodn. asst. CBS-TV, Los Angeles, 1953-57, stage mgr., 1957-64, asso. dir., 1964-68, dir., 1968—. Recipient Emmy award for Carol Burnett Show, 1973, 74. Office: care CBS Entertainment 51 W 52d St New York NY 10019*

POWERS, DUDLEY, musician; b. Moorhead, Minn., June 25, 1911; s. James Harold and Mary Phoebe (Brainard) P.; student Juilliard Musical Found., 1926-30; Mus.B., Northwestern U., 1942, Mus.M., 1945; m. Dorothy Louise Dasch, May 14, 1935; children—Jean Powers Todd, Eileen Powers Buchanan, Arthur, Anita Powers Palant. Cellist, Little Symphony of Chgo., 1931-33; with Chgo. Symphony, 1933-53, prin. cellist, 1943-53; prof. cello Northwestern U., 1933—; mem. Mischakoff String Quartet, 1935-38, Chgo. Symphony Quartet, 1940-53, Sheridan String quartet, 1960-72; condr. Youth Symphony Greater Chgo., Eckstein String Quartet, 1972—; also cello recitalist. Home: 1856 Sherman Ave Evanston IL 60201

POWERS, EDWARD ALTON, clergyman; b. Jamestown, N.Y., Oct. 26, 1927; s. Leslie Edgar and Mabelle Florence (Alton) P.; B.A., Coll. Wooster, 1948; B.D., Yale U., 1952; Ed.D., Columbia U. Tchrs. Coll., 1973; m. Rey O'Day; children—Randall Edward, Christopher Alan, Ann Lynn. Ordained to ministry Congl. Ch., 1951; pastor in Hamden, Conn., 1949-53, Pleasant Hill, Ohio, 1953-56; sec. dept. youth work Congl. Christian Ch. Bd. Home Missions, 1956-60; gen. sec. div. Christian edn., bd. home missions Congl. and Christian Chs., 1960-61, div. Christian edn., bd. homeland ministries United Ch. of Christ, 1962-73; gen. sec., div. evangelism, edn., ch. extension United Ch. Bd. Homeland Ministries, 1973—. Mem. program bd., exec. com. div. edn. and ministry Nat. Council Chs., 1963—; chmn., Peace Priority Team, United Ch. of Christ, 1970-75, adminstr., editor sexuality study, 1977. Author: Journey Into Faith, 1964; Signs of Shalom, 1973; (with Rey O'Day) Theatre of the Spirit, 1980; also articles. Home: 215 E 24th St New York City NY 10010 Office: 132 W 31st St New York NY 10001

POWERS, EDWARD DAVID, mfg. co. exec.; b. N.Y.C., Apr. 6, 1932; s. Joseph T. and Catherine M. (Martin) P.; B.S., St. John's U., Jamaica, N.Y., 1954; M.B.A., Fairleigh Dickinson U., 1964; m. Doris M. Oshinski, May 5, 1954; children—Gregg, Claudia, Chris, Richard, Steven, Donna. Buyer, Lever Bros. Co., N.Y.C., 1956-65; dir. purchasing UOP Co., Des Plaines, Ill., 1965-69; corp. dir. purchasing ITT Grinnell Co., Providence, 1970-71, product line mgr., 1971-73; pres. ITT Grinnell Valve Co., Elmira, N.Y., 1973-78; pres. Mueller Co., Decatur, Ill., 1978—. Bd. dirs. St. Mary's Hosp., Decatur. Served with U.S. Army, 1954-56. Mem. Valve Mfrs. Assn. (dir.). Home: 2965 Lewallen Pl Decatur IL 62521 Office: 500 W Eldorado St Decatur IL 62525

POWERS, EDWARD LATELL, accountant; b. Birmingham, Ala., Jan. 21, 1919; s. Jesse Franklin and Clara (Kircus) P.; student Wayne State U., 1944-45, U. Ala., 1952-53; m. Frances Gail Watters, Aug. 2, 1939; children—Karen Sue Powers Hoss, Linda Gail Powers Nix. Accountant, So. Cotton Oil Co., Birmingham, 1937-42; examiner pub. accounts Ala. Dept. Examiners Pub. Accounts, 1942; chief accountant Refuge Cotton Oil Co., Columbus, Miss., 1942-43; chief warrant officer, auditor Detroit Ordnance Dist., 1943-46; pub. accountant Screven, Turner & Co., Birmingham, 1946-48; pub. accountant Scarborough, Thomas & Co., Birmingham, 1948-49; sr. partner Blankenship & Powers, Birmingham, 1950-51; sr. partner Scarborough & Powers, Birmingham, 1951-56; mng. partner Birmingham office, Haskins & Sells, 1956—. Mem., chmn. Ala. Bd. Pub. Accountancy; mem. Mayor's Fact Finding Com., Birmingham, 1964-65. Recipient Army Commendation award Detroit Ordnance Dist., 1945. C.P.A., Ala., N.Y., La., N.C. Trustee Baptist Medical Centers. Mem. Am. Inst. C.P.A.'s, Ala. Soc. C.P.A.'s (past pres.), Soc. States Conf. C.P.A.'s (past mem. exec. com.), Nat. Assn. Accountants, Am. Accounting Assn., Newcomen Soc. N.Am., N.Y. Soc. of C.P.A.'s, Beta Alpha Psi. Baptist (deacon). Clubs: Rotary, Vestavia Country, Downtown, The Club, Relay House. Contbr. articles profl. jours. Home: 3812 Dunbarton Dr Birmingham AL 35223 Office: First Alabana Bank Bldg Birmingham AL 35203

POWERS, EDWARD LAWRENCE, biologist; b. Columbia, S.C., Dec. 30, 1915; s. Edward Lawrence and Emilie (Devereux) P.; student U. Notre Dame, 1933-34; B.S., Coll. Charleston (S.C.), 1938, Litt.D., 1974; Ph.D., Johns Hopkins, 1941; m. Mary Eleanor Fogarty, Dec. 27, 1939; children—Mary Eugenia (Mrs. Russell Anderson), Emilie Devereux (Mrs. L. Dacunto), Judith Ann (Mrs. Russell Cykoski), Catherine (Mrs. Joseph Schourek), Patricia, Christina, Barbara Clare. Teaching asst. Coll. Charleston, 1936-38; asst. zoology Johns Hopkins, 1938-41; vis. lectr. genetics Fordham U., 1941, vis. lectr. biology, 1943; instr., then asst. prof. U. Notre Dame, 1941-45; asso. biologist Argonne Nat. Lab., 1946-49, sr. biologist, 1949-65, asso. dir. div. biol. and med. research, 1950-59; spl. research expt. and theory radiation damage biol. systems; prof. zoology, dir. Lab. Radiation Biology, dir. Center for Fast Kinetics Research, U. Tex., Austin, 1965—. Mem. Park Forest (Ill.) Planning and Zoning Commn., 1949-52, chmn., 1950-52; mem. Park Forest Zoning Bd. Appeals, 1951-52, Park Forest Bldg. Code Bd. Appeals, 1951-52. Bd. dirs. Park Forest Family Counseling Services, 1951-52. Tomlinson fellow Coll. Charleston, 1937; Guggenheim fellow, 1958; Douglas Lea Meml. lectr. U. Leeds (Eng.), 1961; vis. prof. Christie Hosp., Holt Radium Inst., Manchester, Eng., 1972. Fellow A.A.A.S.; mem. Am. Soc. Human Genetics, Am. Soc. Microbiologists, Am. Soc. Naturalists, Am. Soc. Zoologists, Brit. Assn. Radiation Research, Genetic Assn. Am., Genetics Soc., Am., Internat. socs. cell biology, Radiation Research Soc. (pres. 1964-65), Soc. Protozoology, Phi Beta Kappa, Sigma Xi. Contbr. articles to profl. jours. Home: 2504 Inwood Pl Austin TX 78703

POWERS, FRANCIS FOUNTAIN, educator; b. Hastings, Nebr., Sept. 12, 1901; s. John Thomas and Lenore Julia (Fountain) P.; A.B., U. Wash., 1923, Ph.D., 1928; A.M., U. Oreg., 1927; m. Oma Beryl Meyer, July 17, 1926. Tchr. Latin, Moran (Wash.) Sch., 1922-25, teaching fellow U. Oreg., 1925-27; instr. edn. U. Wash., 1928-30, asst. prof., 1930-35, asso. prof., 1935-39, prof., 1939—, dean Coll. Edn., 1939-61, dir. Office Ednl. Research, 1961-66, dir. Office Publs. and Spl. Projects, 1966—. Mem. Municipal League Seattle and King County. Mem. Council Basic Edn., AAUP, Wash. State Council on Econ. Edn. (dir.), N.W. Assn. Secondary and Higher Schs. (pres. 1950-56, chmn. higher com. 1946-50, chmn. com. research and service 1961—), U.S. Naval Inst., Navy League U.S., Phi Beta Kappa, Phi Delta Kappa (nat. sec., 1935-39), Pi Sigma. Conglist. Clubs: Faculty, College, Swedish, Rainier (Seattle). Author or co-author books relating to field; latest publs: Educational Psychology (with Edwin R. Guthrie), 1950; How to Improve Your Reading (booklet), 1950. Home: 4225 Brooklyn Ave NE Seattle WA 98105

POWERS, GENE ROY, speech pathologist; b. White Deer, Tex., Feb. 10, 1928; s. Lee Roy and Julia Marion (Wright) P.; B.A., Tex. Tech. U., 1949; M.A., U. Iowa, 1958, Ph.D., 1960; m. Rosa Glynn Ellerbe, May 18, 1952; children—James Lee, Carolyn Rose, William Edward, Charles Ellerbe. Research asso. U. Iowa, 1958-61; asst. prof. speech pathology U. Conn., 1961-64, asso. prof., 1964-68, prof., 1968-74, head dept. speech, 1967-74; prof. U. Tex., Austin, 1974—, dir. program in communication disorders, 19—; chmn. Am. Bd. Examiners in Speech Pathology and Audiology, 1975-78. Served with USAF, 1950-55. Fellow Am. Speech and Hearing Assn. (cert. clin. competenence; chmn. edn. and tng. bd. 1973-75); mem. Am. Cleft Palate Assn. (v.p. 1971-72), Conn. Speech and Hearing Assn. (pres. 1964-66), Tex. Speech and Hearing Assn., Tex. Dirs. Tng. Programs in Communication Disorders (pres. 1977-79), Sigma Xi. Democrat. Methodist. Research, publs. in speech pathology. Home: 11521 Spicewood Pkwy Austin TX 78750 Office: Dept Speech Communication U Tex Austin TX 78712

POWERS, GEORGIA MONTGOMERY DAVIS, govt. ofcl., state senator; b. Springfield, Ky., Oct. 29, 1923; d. Ben G. and Frances (Walker) Montgomery; student Louisville Municipal Coll., 1940-42; m. James L. Powers, Aug. 17, 1973; 1 son by previous marriage, William F. Davis; stepchildren—Cheryl Campbell, Carlton, Deborah (Mrs. Dan Rattle). Supr., U.S. Census Bur., Jeffersonville, Ind., 1958-61, Louisville, 1969—; asst. hosp. adminstr. Red Cross Hosp., Louisville, 1964-65; mem. Ky. Senate, 1968—, chmn. labor and industry com. Active in civil rights, 1961-68; mem. SCLC, NAACP, Urban League. Mem. Jefferson County Democratic Exec. Com., 1964-66. Recipient King-Kennedy award Young Democrats of Ky., 1968; Achievement award Alpha Kappa Alpha, 1970; Ky. Congress Beauticians and Barbers award, 1971; Woman of Year award Women's Coalition, 1978; Achievement award Zion Baptist Ch., 1973; Recognition award Ky. chpt. NAACP, 1979; Achievement award Watson Meml. Bapt. Ch., 1979. Home: 733 Cecil Ave Louisville KY 40211

POWERS, HAROLD STONE, musicologist, educator; b. N.Y.C., Aug. 5, 1928; s. William Stuart and Charlotte de Sers (Stone) P.; B.Mus. in Piano, Syracuse (N.Y.) U., 1950; M.F.A. in Composition, Princeton U., 1952, Ph.D. in Musicology, 1959; m. Elizabeth Connor, Aug. 3, 1957; children—Stuart, Cornelia. Instr. music Princeton U., 1955-58, Harvard U., 1958-60; mem. faculty U. Pa., 1961-73, prof. music and S. Asia regional studies, 1971-73, adj. prof. S. Asian regional studies, 1973—; vis. prof. NDEA Summer Sch., U. Rochester (N.Y.), 1970, U. Calif., Berkeley, 1971; prof. music Princeton U., 1973—. Fulbright fellow, India, 1952-54; jr. fellow Princeton Council Humanities, 1954-55; Am. Council Learned Socs. scholar in linguistics, 1955; Rockefeller Found. grantee, 1960-61; Fulbright-Hayes grantee, 1967-68; Nat. Endowment Humanities grantee, 1975-76. Mem. Am., Internat. musicol. socs., Soc. Ethnomusicology, Am. Oriental Soc. Contbr. articles to profl. publs. Home: 11 University Pl Princeton NJ 08540 Office: Dept Music Princeton Univ Princeton NJ 08540

POWERS, HARVEY MARCELLUS, JR., educator; b. Washington, May 3, 1923; s. Harvey Marcellus and Helen May (Davis) P.; A.B., Tufts U., 1947; A.M., Johns Hopkins U., 1949; Ph.D., Cornell U., 1968; m. Betsy Louise Kinsella, June 28, 1947; children—Christina Powers Van Buskirk, Dianne Powers Early, Harvey Marcellus III. Instr. English, Bucknell U., 1949-53, asst. prof., 1954-62, asso. prof., 1963-69, prof., 1970—, dir. Univ. Theatre, 1959—, dir. Inst. Fgn. Students, 1958—; cons. Inst. Internat. Edn., 1961, 63; chmn. theatre dept. Pa. Gov.'s Sch. Arts, 1974—. Served with USNR, 1943-45. Recipient Lindback award for distinguished teaching, 1973. Mem. Am. Theatre Assn., Theatre Assn. Pa. (pres. 1977—), Phi Kappa Phi, Theta Alpha Phi, Theta Delta Chi. Democrat. Methodist. Home: 20 S Water St Lewisburg PA 17837

POWERS, HENRY MARTIN, JR., oil co. exec.; b. Bath, Maine, July 18, 1932; s. Henry Martin and Eva (Saunders) P.; B.S., Maine Maritime Acad., 1954; m. Hepzibah Hinchey Reed, June 20, 1959; children—Henry Martin III, Carlton Reed. Marine engr. Am. Export Lines, N.Y.C., 1954-58; staff engr. Bull & Roberts Inc., N.Y.C., 1958-59; gen. sales mgr. Williams Bros., Inc., Portland, Maine, 1959-61; v.p. C.H. Sprague & Son Co., Boston, 1961-72, pres., 1972—, also dir.; dir. Portsmouth Trust Co. (N.H.), Petroleum Heat & Power Co. R.I., Shanley Corp., Strawbery Banke Inc. Vice pres. Seacoast United Fund, 1967-69; chmn. fuels, energy com. New England Council, 1974-75; pres. Portsmouth Council, 1966-67; bd. visitors Maine Maritime Acad. Served to lt., USNR, 1956-58. Mem. Navy League, Mechanic Fire Soc. Mason. Clubs: Fort Hill, Algonquin (Boston), Taratine (Bangor, Maine); Cumberland (Portland). Home: 845 South Portsmouth NH 03801 Office: One Parade Mall Portsmouth NH 03801

POWERS, HOWARD FRANCIS, pharm. co. exec.; b. Boston, May 30, 1932; s. Howard and Mary F. (Sullivan) P.; B.S., Boston Coll., 1958; M.B.A., Harvard U., 1960; m. Aug. 19, 1960; children—Howard Francis, Jenniffer, Bradford. With Merck & Co. Inc., Rahway, N.J., group v.p.-environ. indsl. Served with U.S. Army, 1952-54. Home: 120 Audubon Ln Princeton NJ Office: Merck & Co Rahway NJ 07065*

POWERS, HUGH WILLIAM, newspaperman; b. Slaton, Tex., Dec. 20, 1926; s. James J. and Myrtle (Black) P.; student W. Va. U., 1944-47; m. Constance Cornwall, Aug. 30, 1952; children—Nan Margaret, Sarah Ann. Mng. editor Houston chpt. Asso. Gen. Contractors News Service, until 1957; with Houston Press, 1957-64, city editor, 1964; mem. staff Houston Chronicle, 1964—, now asso. editor. Mem. Phi Kappa Psi. Club: Press (pres. 1973-74) (Houston). Home: 10818 Hillcroft St Houston TX 77096 Office: 801 Texas Ave Houston TX 77002

POWERS, JACK WESLEY, univ. adminstr.; b. Ft. Wayne, Ind., Oct. 28, 1929; s. Dorsey Byrl and Winnifred (Kundred) P.; B.S., Purdue U., 1952, M.S., 1956, Ph.D., 1957; student Ill. Inst. Tech., 1952-54; m. Ruth Margaret Ollhoff, Aug. 23, 1952; children—Tod, David, Alicia, Laura. Chemist, Phelps-Dodge Corp., 1947-48, Corn Products Co., 1952-54; prof. chemistry, chmn. dept. Ripon (Wis.) Coll., 1957-69; regional dir. Research Corp., 1969-75, v.p. program support, 1975-79; v.p. external affairs Rensselaer Poly. Inst., 1979—; vis. scientist Nat. Center Atmospheric Research, Boulder, Colo., 1964-65; cons. to industry, 1958-68. Recipient Severy award teaching Ripon Coll., 1963; Uhrig Found. award excellence teaching, 1962. Mem. Am. Chem. Soc., Midwest Assn. Chemistry Tchrs., Indsl. Research Inst., Sigma Xi, Phi Lambda Upsilon, Pi Kappa Phi. Mason. Home: 105 Corlies Ave Pelham NY 10803

POWERS, JAMES BASCOM, banker; b. Laurens, S.C., May 30, 1924; s. John Bascom and Ollie Esther (Ellenburg) P.; B.A., Furman U., 1955; postgrad. Carolina Sch. Banking, Chapel Hill, N.C., 1957-59, Sch. Banking of South, La. State U., 1959-61, Exec. Program Profl. Bus., U. N.C., 1970-71; m. Julia Weskett, Dec. 7, 1963; children—James S., Deborah, John. Accountant, Daniel Constrn. Co., Greenville, S.C., 1945-50; v.p. nat. accounts div. Wachovia Bank & Trust Co., Raleigh, N.C., 1955-67; exec. v.p., dir., mem. exec. com. Planters Nat. Bank & Trust Co., Rocky Mount, N.C., 1967-72, pres., chief exec. officer, dir., mem. exec. com., 1972—, chmn., 1975—; dir. New Bern Oil & Fertilizer Co. (N.C.); chmn. Carolina Sch. Banking, Chapel Hill, 1965-68. Chmn., Nash County Med. Devel. Authority; past bd. dirs. Rocky Mount YMCA, United Community Services; past pres., dir. N.C. Wesleyan Coll. Area Found.; del. White House Conf. on Small Bus.; mem. adv. council Furman U.; trustee Peace Coll.; pres., dir. Sch. Banking of South, Baton Rouge, La. Served with USNR, 1942-45, 50-52. Mem. Am. Banking Assn. (governing council, state v.p.), Am. Inst. Banking, Bank Adminstrn. Inst., N.C. Bankers Assn. (past pres.), Newcomen Soc. N.Am., Robert Morris Assos. (past chpt. dir.), Furman U. Alumni Assn. (past dir.), Rocky Mount C. of C. (past pres.). Democrat. Baptist. Rotarian (past dir.), Mason. Club: Benvenue Country (Rocky Mount). Home: 307 Shady Circle Dr Rocky Mount NC 27801 Office: 131 N Church St Rocky Mount NC 27801

POWERS, JAMES FARL, author; b. Jacksonville, Ill., July 8, 1917; s. James Ansbury and Zella (Routzong) P.; student Northwestern U., 1938-40; m. Elizabeth Alice Wahl, Apr. 22, 1946; children—Katherine, Mary, James, Hugh, Jane. Tchr. writing courses St. John's U., Collegeville, Minn., 1947, 75, 76, 77, Marquette U., 1949-51, U. Mich., 1956-57; writer-in-residence Smith Coll., 1965-66. Guggenheim fellow, 1948; grantee Nat. Inst. Arts and Letters, 1948; Rockefeller fellow, 1954, 57, 67. Mem. Nat. Inst. Arts and Letters. Author: Prince of Darkness and Other Stories, 1947; The Presence of Grace (short stories), 1956; Morte d'Urban (Nat. Book award 1963, Thormod Monsen award Soc. Midland Authors 1963), 1962, Look How the Fish Live (short stories), 1975. Office: care Random House 201 E 50th St New York NY 10022*

POWERS, JAMES JOSEPH ALOYSIUS, sports columnist; b. Cleve., Feb. 9, 1903; s. James Joseph and Catherine Cecilia (Kearns) P.; m. Winona Smyser, Jan. 12, 1930; children—Patricia, Michael, Mary Ann. Commentator, NBC 1935-60; mem. faculty Marymount Coll., 1947-55. Served as comdr. USNR, World War II. Home: 10178 Collins Ave Bal Harbour FL 33154

POWERS, JOHN GEDROICE, lawyer; b. Mt. Vernon, N.Y., Aug. 5, 1916; s. John J. and Constance (Gedroice) P.; A.B., Princeton, 1938; LL.B., Harvard, 1941; m. Elaine Prentice Ettinger, June 13, 1940; (div. July 1965); children—Jean Prentice (dec.), Lynn Prentice, John Prentice; m. 2d, Kimiko, Mar. 1966. Admitted N.Y. bar, 1941; with Chadbourne, Hunt, Jaeckel & Brown, N.Y.C., 1941-43; with Prentice-Hall, Inc., 1943-64, successively gen. counsel, editor-in-chief, v.p., dir., 1947-54, pres., 1954-64; cons., 1964—; faculty asso. Colo. State U.; chmn. Mid-Valley Land Co.; dir. Eastern Book Service, Inc., Tokyo, The Greystone Corp., Springer-Vering, N.Y., Inc. Bd. dirs. Adviser to pres. Aspen Inst. Humanistic Studies. Aspen Center Contemporary Art; fine arts vis. com. Harvard; East Asian vis. com. Harvard, mem. joint library subcom.; trustee Denver Art Mus. Mem. Japan Soc., Asia Soc., Am. Bar Assn., Nat. Tax Assn. Office: 680 Fifth Ave New York NY 10019

POWERS, ODELL EUGENE, turbine and elec. equipment co. exec.; b. Peoria, Ill., May 2, 1928; s. Clarence O. and Beulah (Fernandez) P.; B.S., Bradley U., 1952; m. Elizabeth Marie Johnson, Mar. 12, 1950; children—Mark Daniel, Kristin Lynne, Julianne Lynne, Elizabeth M. Mng. dir. Caterpillar Mitsubishi, Inc., Tokyo, Japan, 1963-67; dir. internat. finance and adminstrn. Honeywell, Inc., Mpls., 1967-69, v.p., Brussels, Belgium, 1969-71, v.p. Honeywell, Inc., exec. v.p. Honeywell-Europe, Brussels, 1971-73; pres., chief exec. officer Turbodyne Corp., Mpls., 1973-76, chmn. bd., chief exec. officer, 1976-78; pres., chief operating officer, dir. McGraw-Edison Co., Elgin, Ill., 1979—; dir. Internat. Multifoods, Mpls. Trustee Bradley U. Served with AUS, 1946-47. Mem. U.S. C. of C. (internat. trade subcom.). Republican. Presbyterian. Clubs: Mpls.; Met. (N.Y.C.); Barrington Hills Country (Barrington, Ill.). Home: 214 Maple Rd Barrington IL 60010 Office: 333 W River Rd Elgin IL 60120

POWERS, PHILIP NATHAN, educator; b. Terre Haute, Ind., Aug. 17, 1912; s. Samuel Ralph and Eda (Olds) P.; B.A., Columbia U., 1932, Ph.D., 1940; Gen. Edn. Bd. fellow U. Chgo., 1940-41; m. Eleanor Ritchie, Apr. 25, 1936 (div.); 1 son, Cameron; m. 2d, Evelyne Schanze, May 22, 1959; stepchildren—Jacques le Sourd, Liliane Maginot. Asso. sci. New Coll. Tchrs. Coll., Columbia, 1932-35; asso. New Coll. Community, 1937-38; instr. natural scis. Stephens Coll., 1939-42; physicist Naval Ordnance Lab., 1942-44, tng. dir., 1944-46; chief sci. edn. br. Office Naval Research, 1946; adviser sci. personnel Pres.' Sci. Research Bd., 1947, AEC, 1947-50; manpower specialist, sec. sci. manpower adv. com. NSRB, 1950-51, cons., 1953; dir. atomic project Monsanto Chem. Co., 1951-55; chmn. bd. Internuclear Co., Clayton, Mo., 1955-59, pres., 1955-60; prof., head dept. nuclear engring., Purdue U., 1960-73, dir. Energy Engring. Center, 1973-78, prof. emeritus, 1978—, acting dir. Coal Research Lab., 1977-78, asso. dir. engring. expt. sta., 1960-61, dir. engring. expt. sta., 1961-68, also v.p. Purdue Research Found., 1961-62. Chmn. council Asso. Midwest Univs., 1964-65, chmn. nuclear engring. edn. com. 1964-65; trustee, exec. com. Argonne Univs. Assn., 1965-72, pres., 1966-72; dir. Atomic Indsl. Forum, 1968-74; chmn. Great Lakes-Great Plains advisory council, 1973-74; cons. com. on specialized personnel ODM, 1951-63, mem. com. manpower resources 1953; cons. NSF, 1952-57, AEC, 1964-68, AEC Fellowship Bd., 1964-66, Select Com. Govt. Research, Ho. of Reps., 1964-65, Pres.'s Com. Scientists and Engrs., 1956-58, Dept. of State, 1957; cons. N.Y. Univ. planning internat. activities, 1958-59; series editor Energy, Power and the Environment, Marcel-Dekker, Inc., 1976—. Mem. Commn. on Survey of Dentistry; chmn. atomic energy panel Engrs. Joint Council, 1956-58; ex-officio mem. Ind. Gov.'s Energy Com., 1973-76; mem. Congressmen Landgrebe's Energy Crisis Study Commn., 1973-74; mem. panel Nat. Acad. Scis. for Korea-U.S. Joint Com. for Sci. Cooperation, 1973; mem. exec. com. Ind. Gov.'s Energy Com., 1974-78; mem. ad hoc panel on mechanisms for providing sci. advice to State Ind., 1974-76; chmn. Ind. Select Com. on Energy Research and Devel., 1977; dir. U.S. Nat. Com. World Energy Conf., 1977—; cons. Commonwealth Edison Co., 1978—. Recipient Meritorious Civilian Service award USN, 1946; Robert C. Morris award State of Ind., 1978; named Sagamore of the Wabash, 1978. Fellow AAAS; mem. Am. Nuclear Soc. (dir. 1963-66, mem. exec. com. aerospace div. 1963-65), Am. Soc. for Engring. Edn. (chmn. atomic energy edn. com. 1953-57; chmn. com. on space engring. 1962-66, chmn. grad. studies div. 1965-66), U.S. C. of C. (nat. def. com. 1953-59, com. on comml. uses atomic energy, 1959-62, com. on new frontiers of tech. 1960-63), Am. Nuclear Soc., Am. Soc. Engring. Edn., Ind. Acad. Scis., Sigma Xi. Home: 200 E 64th St New York NY 10021

POWERS, RAYMOND EDWIN, JR., distillery exec.; b. Aurora, Ill., Sept. 17, 1937; s. Raymond Edwin and Alma Malinda (Knapp) P.; B.S., No. Ill. U., 1959; M.B.A., U. Chgo., 1968; m. Nancy Jo Kein, Aug. 28, 1936; children—Dawn, Stacy, Raymond Edwin III. Sr. accountant U.S. Gypsum Co., Chgo., 1959-62; accounting mgr. Paper Mate Co., Chgo., 1962-66; controller Leaf Brands div. W.R. Grace Co., Chgo., 1966-70, Barton Brands, Ltd., Chicago, 1970—; sec. bd. dirs. Manning Savs. & Loan. Treas., Western Springs Service Club. C.P.A., Ill. Mem. Am. Inst. C.P.A.'s, Ill. Soc. C.P.A.'s. Home: 4208 Hampton St Western Springs IL 60558 Office: 55 E Monroe Ave Chicago IL 60603

POWERS, RICHARD RALPH, city adminstr.; b. Orange, Calif., May 22, 1940; s. Ralph and Murl Helen P.; A.A., Fullerton Jr. Coll., 1960; B.A. with honors, U. Calif., Santa Barbara, 1962; M.P.A., Calif. State U., Fullerton, 1968; m. Marlene Hruby, May 15, 1971; 1 son, Justin. Research grant asst. Ford Found.; adminstrv. intern City of Anaheim (Calif.), 1964-65; asst. city mgr., dir. planning City of LaMirada (Calif.), 1965-69; urban devel. coordinator City of Garden Grove (Calif.), 1969-70, dir. urban planning, 1970-71, asst. city mgr., 1971-72, acting city mgr., 1972, city mgr., 1972—; mem. Orange County Econ. Devel. Commn. Recipient Man of Distinction award Fullerton Jr. Coll., 1960, Outstanding Community Service award La Mirada Jr. C. of C., 1965, Disting. Services award Garden Grove Jaycees, 1973. Mem. Internat. City Mgmt. Assn., Am. Soc. Public Adminstrn. (pres. Orange County chpt. 1972-73, program chmn. chpt. 1979), Garden Grove C. of C. Club: Rotary. Office: 11391 Acacia Pkwy Garden Grove CA 92640

POWERS, RICHARD WALLACE, petroleum co. exec.; b. Boise, Idaho, Jan. 20, 1926; s. Wallace Henry and Rosa Elizabeth (Ulmer) P.; A.B. in Geology, U. So. Calif., 1947; M.S., Yale U., 1960, Ph.D., 1961; m. Marte Marie Ledahl, Jan. 20, 1951; children—Cydnie Christin, Dirk Frederick. With Aramco, 1947—, dir., Dhahran, Saudi Arabia, 1970—, sr. v.p. fin. and relations, 1971-73, pres., 1973-78, vice chmn. bd., 1978—; pres., chief exec. officer Tapline, 1972-73, dir., 1972—. Served to 1st lt. USMC, 1942-45, 51-52. Mem. Am. Assn. Petroleum Geologists, Geol. Soc. Am., AAAS, Soc. Econ. Paleontologists and Mineralogists, Am. Inst. Mining and Metall. Engrs., Sigma Xi. Contbr. sci. articles to profl. jours. Address: c/o Aramco Box 2574 Dhahran Saudi Arabia

POWERS, ROBERT THROOP, chem. co. exec.; b. Brookline, Pa., Mar. 27, 1921; s. Heman T. and Margaret (Reynolds) P.; B.A., Wabash Coll., 1943; m. Helen Bagge, July 31, 1943; children—Elizabeth, Susan, Robert. With Nalco Chem. Co., Chgo., 1946—, exec. v.p., 1965-70, pres., 1970-77, chmn. bd., 1971—; dir. Bliss & Laughlin Inc., Amsted Ind. Trustee, George Williams Coll., Downers Grove, Ill., Wabash Coll., Crawfordsville, Ind., Glenwood (Ill.) Sch. for Boys; vice chmn. Jr. Achievement; bd. govs. Briarwood Lakes Assn. Served with USNR, 1943-46. Mem. Mfg. Chemists Assn., Phi Gamma Delta. Presbyn. Clubs: Chicago, Mid-Am.; Hinsdale Golf; Butler Nat. Golf. Home: 179 Briarwood Loop Oak Brook IL 60521 Office: 2901 Butterfield Rd Oak Brook IL 60521

POWERS, RONALD CLAIR, educator; b. Wagner, S.D., Dec. 26, 1934; s. Claude M. and Fern (Carpenter) P.; B.S., Iowa State U., 1957, M.S., 1960, Ph.D. in Rural Sociology, 1963; m. Myrna Cecelia Finken, June 20, 1959; children—Jeanene, Kenneth, Sonya, Kristin. Extension youth asst. Iowa State U., 1958-59, extension sociologist, 1961-67, prof., head, dept. family environment, 1967-73, asst. dir. agrl. and home econs. expt. sta., asst. dir. coop. extension service, dir. North Central Regional Center Rural Devel., 1974-79, asst. dean Coll. of Agr., 1979—; Vis. lectr. Ariz. State U., 1964, 65, Colo. State Coll., 1966, 67. Served with AUS, 1957-58. Mem. AAAS, Am. Home Econs. Assn., Rural Sociol. Soc., Community Devel. Soc. Am., Alpha Kappa Delta. Author: (with George M. Beal and R.C. Blount) Social Interaction, 1966; (with George M. Beal and E.W. Coward) Sociological Perspectives of Domestic Development, 1971. Home: 1835 Coolidge Dr Ames IA 50010

POWERS, RONALD DEAN, TV critic; b. Hannibal, Mo., Nov. 18, 1941; s. Paul Sidney and Elvadine (Toalson) P.; B.J., U. Mo., 1963; Reporter, St. Louis Post-Dispatch, 1963-69; reporter Chgo. Sun Times, 1969-70, TV critic, 1970-77; critic-at-large WMAQ-TV, Chgo., 1977-79; commentator Spl. Edit., WNET-TV, N.Y.C., 1979—. Recipient Pulitzer prize for criticism, 1973. Author: The Newscasters, 1977; Face Value, 1979. Office: WNET-TV 356 W 58th St New York NY 10019

POWERS, SAMUEL JOSEPH, JR., lawyer; b. Ellicott City, Md., July 26, 1917; s. Samuel J. and Irene (McDonald) P.; A.B., Loyola Coll., Balt., 1939; J.D., Catholic U. Am., 1942; m. Marion W. Locke, Jan. 15, 1945; children—Richard S., Thomas E. Admitted to Fla. bar, 1946, since practiced in Miami; partner firm Blackwell, Walker, Gray, Powers, Flick & Hoehl; municipal judge City North Miami, 1952-53. Counsel to Pres. Nixon in case Hon. John J. Sirica, U.S. Dist. Ct., D.C. vs. Richard N. Nixon, Pres. of U.S., 1973. Served lt. with USNR, 1942-45. Fellow Am. Coll. Trial Lawyers, Am. Coll. Probate Counsel, Am. Bar Found.; mem. Am., Fla. (chmn. bar grievance com. 1957), D.C., Fed., Dade County (pres., past dir., mem. exec. com.) bar assns., Internat. Assn. Ins. Counsel (pres. 1970), Am. Judicature Soc., Am. Law Inst., Def. Research Inst. (regional v.p. 1965-66, dir. 1966, 69-71), Fla. Council Bar Assn. Presidents, S. Fla. Inter-Profl. Council (charter), Dade County Def. Bar Assn. (pres. 1965-66), Fla. Soc. Prevention Blindness (chmn. Dade County com. 1966). Kiwanian (dir. Miami 1963-65, pres. 1968). Home: 290 Bal Bay Dr Bal Harbour FL 33154 Office: 2400 First Federal Bldg 1 SE 3d Ave Miami FL 33131

POWERS, SAMUEL RALPH, surgeon; b. Mpls., Sept. 25, 1919; B.A. with honors, Swarthmore Coll., 1941; M.D., Columbia U., 1945, D.Sc., 1954. Intern, Columbia Presbyn. Med. Center, N.Y.C., 1945-46, asst. resident, resident, 1949-54; NRC fellow in surgery Johns Hopkins Hosp., 1948-49; Beekman fellow in surg. research Columbia U., N.Y.C., 1953-54; practice medicine specializing in surgery, Albany, N.Y.; attending surgeon Albany Med. Center Hosp., 1954—, surgeon-in-chief, 1974—; cons. surgeon Albany VA Hosp., 1954—, Mary McClellan Hosp., Cambridge, N.Y., 1976—, St. Peter's Hosp., Vassars Bros. Hosp., Poughkeepsie, N.Y., 1975; prof. surgery dept. surgery Albany Med. Coll., 1964—, chmn. dept. surgery, 1974—, prof. physiology dept. physiology, 1977—; adj. prof. bioengring. Rensselaer Poly. Inst., 1968—; surg. cons. Office Naval Research. Served to capt., M.C., U.S. Army, 1946-48. Recipient Albion O. Bernstein award AMA, 1972, Golden Apple award Albany Med. Coll.; diplomate Am. Bd. Surgery. Mem. A.C.S. (bd. govs. 1966—), Am. Surg. Assn., Central Surg. Assn., Eastern Surg. Assn. (pres. 1972-74), So. Surg. Soc., Soc. for Vascular Surgery, Internat. Cardiovascular Soc., Kansas City Surg. Soc. (hon. mem.), B.C. Surg. Soc. (hon. mem.), Am. Fedn. Clin. Research, Am. Trauma Soc., Am. Assn. for Surgery of Trauma, Am. Heart Assn., N.Y. Heart Assn., Alden March Soc., Allen O. Whipple Surg. Soc. (pres. 1970-72), N.Y. Acad. Scis., AAAS, Pan Am. Med. Soc., N.Y. State Med. Soc., Soc. for Critical Care Medicine, Alpha Omega Alpha. Author: (with C.S. Welch) The Essence of Surgery, 1958; contbr. numerous articles on cardiovascular surgery to profl. jours.; contbr. chpts. in field to texts on surgery and medicine; editorial bd. Archives of Surgery. Office: Albany Med Coll 47 New Scotland Ave Albany NY 12208

POWERS, STEFANIE, actress; b. Hollywood, Calif., 1942. Appeared in: (films) Experiment in Terror, The Interns, If A Man Answers, Palm Springs Weekend, McLintock, The New Interns, Love Has Many Faces, Die! Die! My Darling, Stagecoach, Warning Shot, Herbie Rides Again, Fanatic; (TV shows) Bonanza, Love American Style, Mod Squad, Streets of San Francisco, Cannon, Escape to Athena, The Swarm; (TV movies) Sky Hei$t, 1975, Return to Earth, 1976, Nowhere to Run, 1978; (TV series) The Girl From U.N.C.L.E., The Feather and Father Gang, Once Upon A Dead Man, Washington: Behind Closed Doors, Hart to Hart. Address: care ABC Public Relations 1330 Ave of Americas New York NY 10019*

POWERS, THOMAS MOORE, author; b. N.Y.C., Dec. 12, 1940; s. Joshua Bryant and Susan (Moore) P.; B.A., Yale, 1964; m. Candace Molloy, Aug. 21, 1965; children—Amanda, Susan, Cassandra. Reporter, Rome (Italy) Daily American, 1965-67, U.P.I., N.Y.C., 1967-70; freelance writer, 1970—. Recipient Pulitzer prize for nat. reporting, 1971. Author: Diana: The Making of a Terrorist, 1971; The War at Home, 1973; The Man Who Kept the Secrets: Richard Helms and the CIA, 1979. Home: 43 W 10th St New York NY 10011 Office: care Karen Hitzig 34 Gramercy Park New York NY 10003

POWERS, WILLIAM SHOTWELL, lawyer, former mem. Republican Nat. Com.; b. Elizabeth, N.J., June 7, 1910; s. James P. and May B. (Staats) P.; B.S. in Bus., Rutgers U., 1933, LL.B., 1936; m. Arlene M. Crane, Oct. 4, 1940; children—Jean P., Patricia C. Admitted to N.J. bar, 1937, Colo. bar, 1946; practice in Denver, 1946—; partner firm Rothgerber, Appel & Powers, 1946—. Mem. Rep. Nat. Com. for Colo., 1960-72. Served to col. U.S. Army, 1940-46. Decorated Legion of Merit, Bronze Star medal. Mem. Colo., Denver bar assns., Delta Upsilon. Home: 745 S Steele St Denver CO 80209 Office: Colorado State Bank Bldg Denver CO 80202

POWIS, ALFRED, mining co. exec.; b. Montreal, Que., Can., Sept. 16, 1930; s. Alfred and Sarah Champe (McCulloch) P.; B. Commerce, McGill U., 1951; m. Shirley Haldenby. Aug. 8, 1953; children—Timothy Alfred, Nancy Alison, Charles Robert. Mem. staff investment dept. Sun Life Assurance Co. Can., 1951-55, now dir.; with Noranda Mines Ltd., Toronto, Ont., Can., 1956, asst. treas., 1958-62, asst. to pres., 1962-63, exec. asst. to pres., 1963-66, v.p., 1966-67, exec. v.p., 1967-68, pres., 1968—, dir., 1964—; dir. B.C. Forest Products; dir. Noranda subsidiaries, Canadian Imperial Bank Commerce, Gulf Oil Can. Ltd., Placer Devel. Ltd., Kerr Addison Mines Ltd., Simpsons-Sears Ltd., Sun Life Assurance Co. Can. Trustee Toronto Gen. Hosp. Anglican. Clubs: York; Rosedale Golf; Mount Royal (Montreal). Home: 70 Woodlawn Ave W Toronto ON Canada Office: Commerce Ct W Toronto ON Canada

POWLEY, GEORGE REINHOLD, educator; b. New London, O., Mar. 7, 1916; s. George Starling and Rose (Maier) P.; B.S. in Elec. Engring., Va. Poly. Inst., 1938, M.S. in Elec. Engring., 1939; m. Beverly Carper, July 20, 1940; children—Rosemary, George, Robert, Ann. Engaged in induction motor design, electro-dynamic works, Electric Boat Co., 1939; test engr., control engr. Gen. Electric Co., 1939-41, control engr., 1945-48; prof. elec. engring. Va. Polytech. Inst., 1949—, head dept., 1958-64, Westinghouse prof. elec. engring., 1964—, chmn. elec. engring. tech. program, 1974—. Pres. Giles Gideon Camp, Giles County, Va., 1959-60. Served to capt. AUS, 1941-45; lt. col. Res. Recipient W.E. Wine-award for faculty achievement Va. Polytech. Inst., 1957, named to Acad. for Teaching Excellence, 1974. Mem. IEEE (sr.), Virginia Gideons (1st v.p. 1968, state pres. 1971-73), Omicron Delta Kappa, Tau Beta Pi, Eta Kappa Nu, Phi Kappa Phi (local pres. 1960-61). Home: 1401 Hillcrest Dr Blacksburg VA 24060

POYDOCK, MARY EYMARD, nun, ednl. adminstr., biologist, educator; b. Sykesville, Pa., Dec. 3, 1910; d. John Andrew and Anna Mary (Dryna) P.; B.A. (NSF grantee), Mercyhurst Coll., 1943; M.A., U. Pitts., 1947; Ph.D. (Sperti fellow), St. Thomas Inst., 1965. Joined Sisters of Mercy, Roman Cath. Ch.; tchr. elementary sch., Erie Diocese, 1935-41; tchr. high sch. Pitts. Diocese, 1941-47; instr. biology 1947-49, Mercyhurst Coll., Erie, Pa., asst. prof. biology, asso. prof. biology, 1949-55, prof., 1955-64, prof., chmn. dept. biology, 1964-70, dir. Undergrad. Research, 1960-65, dir. Cancer Research, 1960—; also artist. Mem. AAAS, Pa. Acad. Sci., Internat. Oceanographic Found., Am. Assn. Cancer Research, Am. Cancer Soc. (mem. exec. bd. Erie Unit 1966-75), Cancer Prevention Study (gen. chmn. Erie unit 1973-74), Zonta Club of Erie II, Beta Beta Beta. Author: Outline of Histology, 1956; Guidelines for Biotechnique, 1970; Guidelines for Microbiology, 1971, and others. Contbr. articles to profl. jours. Home and office: 501 E 38th St Erie PA 16501

POYNER, JAMES MARION, lawyer; b. Raleigh, N.C., Sept. 18, 1914; s. James Marion and Mary (Smedes) P.; B.S. in Chem. Engring., N.C. State U., 1935, M.S., 1937; J.D., Duke, 1940; m. Florence I. Chan, Feb. 25, 1945; children—Susan (Mrs. Vic C. Moore), Chan (Mrs. Joseph D. Pike), Margaret, Edythe, James Marion III. Orch. leader, trombonist, arranger Jimmy Poyner and His Orch., 1933-38; admitted to N.C. bar, 1940, since practiced in Raleigh; sr. partner firm Poyner, Geraghty, Hartsfield & Townsend, 1946—; co-founder Cameron-Brown Co.; life dir. 1st Union Corp., 1st Union Nat. Bank; dir. First Fed. Savs. & Loan Assn., Eastern Standard Title Ins. Co. Mem. N.C. Senate, 1955-59. Past chmn. bd. trustees St. Mary's Coll.; chmn. bd. World Golf Hall of Fame; past chmn. trustees N.C. Symphony Soc. Served to lt. col. AUS, 1942-46. Decorated Legion of Merit. Mem. Am., N.C. (pres. 1967-68) bar assns., Am. Judicature Soc. (dir.), Phi Kappa Phi. Episcopalian. Home: 710 Smedes Pl Raleigh NC 27605 Office: 615 Oberlin Rd Raleigh NC 27605

POZEN, WALTER, lawyer, former govt. ofcl.; b. East Orange, N.J., Oct. 17, 1933; s. Irving Joseph and Berte (Protter) P.; B.A., U. Chgo., 1952, grad. student, 1952-53; J.D., 1956; m. Elizabeth Klupt, June 19, 1955; children—Agatha Elizabeth, Jonathan Walter, Thorn Lord; m. 2d, Joan Kennan, Apr. 24, 1971. Admitted Md. bar, 1963; with Strasser, Spiegelberg, Fried & Frank, Washington and N.Y.C., 1956-58; mem. campaign staff Harrison A. Williams for U.S. Senator, 1958; legislative counsel Home Rule Com., Inc., Washington, 1959-60; counsel, asso. dir. Fgn. Policy Clearing House, Washington, 1960-61; asst. to sec. interior, 1961-67; partner Stroock & Stroock & Lavan, N.Y.C., 1967—, in charge Washington office. Ofcl. rep. U.S. del. GATT Ministerial Meeting, Geneva, 1963. Mem. Gov.'s Commn. on Historic Preservation, Md.; mem. D.C. Bd. Elections and Ethics. Del. Democratic Nat. Conv., 1964, counsel credentials com., 1968, counsel compliance rev. com. Dem. Nat. Com. Mem. vis. com. Coll. of U. Chgo. Mem. Fed., Am., D.C., Md. bar assns. Clubs: City Tavern, Harmonie, Fed. City. Author: (with Dr. J.H. Cerf) Strategy for the Sixties, 1960; also articles, book reviews. Home: 3806 Klingle Pl NW Washington DC 20016 Office: 1150 17th St NW Washington DC 20036

POZZATTI, RUDY OTTO, artist; b. Telluride, Colo., Jan. 14, 1925; s. Innocente and Mary L. (Mimiolla) P.; B.F.A., U. Colo., 1948, M.F.A., 1950, D.H.L., 1973; m. Dorothy I. Pozzatti, May 20, 1946; children—Valri Marie, Rudy Otto, Gina Maria, Mia Ines, Illica Lara. One-man exhibitions include: Cleve. Mus. Art., 1955, Whitney Mus. Am. Arts., N.Y.C., 1961, Tyles Sch. Art, Rome, 1969, Sheldon Meml. Art. Gallery U. Nebr., 1969; represented in permanent collections: Mus. Modern Art, N.Y.C., Library of Congress, Washington (D.C.), Art Inst. Chgo., Cleve. Mus. Art; mem. faculty dept. art U. Nebr., Lincoln, 1950-52, 53-56; mem. faculty dept. art Ind. U., Bloomington, 1956—, prof. fine arts, 1964—, Disting. prof., 1975—; artist-in-residence Roswell Mus. and Art Center. Served with AUS, 1943-46. Recipient George Norlin silver medal U. Colo., 1974; Fulbright grantee, 1952-53, 63-64; Guggenheim fellow, 1963-64; Ford Found. fellow, 1963. Mem. Soc. Am. Graphic Artists, Am. Color Print Soc., Coll. Art Assn. (bd. dirs., Artists Equity Assn. Roman Catholic. Office: Dept Art Indiana U Bloomington IN 47401

PRADO, GERALD M., retail co. exec.; b. Langeloth, Pa., Jan. 19, 1946; s. Caesar S. and Anita A. Prado; B.A., Washington and Jefferson Coll., 1963-67; m. Judith A. Pompe, May 20, 1967; children—Dennis, Eric, Lynn, Christopher. Sr. accountant Haskins and Sells, Pitts., 1967-72; auditor G.C. Murphy Co., McKeesport, Pa., 1972-76, asst. controller, 1976-78, treas., 1979—. Mem. Pa. Inst. C.P.A.'s, Am. Inst. C.P.A.'s, Tri-State Controllers Assn., Washington and Jefferson Alumni Assn., McKeesport C. of C. Roman Catholic. Home: 205 Overlook Dr McMurray PA 15317 Office: 531 5th Ave McKeesport PA 15132

PRAEGER, FREDERICK AMOS, book publisher; b. Vienna, Austria, Sept. 16, 1915; s. Max Meyer and Manya (Foerster) P.; student law and polit. sci. U. Vienna, 1933-38; student Sorbonne, Paris, 1934; m. Cornelia E. Blach, May 8, 1946 (div. Mar. 1959); children—Claudia Elizabeth, Andrea Maxine; m. 2d, Heloise Babette Arons, Feb. 5, 1960; children—Manya Margaret, Alexandra Yael. Came to U.S., 1938. Asso. editor R. Loewit Verlag, Vienna, 1935-38, also sports writer; various positions, including jewelry salesman, asst. merchandising mgr. jewelry store chain, U.S., 1938-41; civilian head publs. br., info. control div. U.S. Mil. Govt., Hesse, Germany, 1946-48; pres. Frederick A. Praeger, Inc., specializing books on politics and contemporary world affairs, art, architecture, archeology, until 1968; pres. Phaidon Pubs., Inc., N.Y.; chmn. Phaidon Pubs., Ltd., London; pres., editorial dir. Westview Press, Boulder, Colo., 1975—; dir. Pall Mall Press, London. Adj. prof. Grad. Sch. Librarianship, Denver U., asso. dir. The Publishing Inst., 1976. Served to 1st lt., AUS, 1942-46; research and editorial asst. Command and Gen. Staff Sch., Ft. Leavenworth, Kans.; mil. intelligence instr. specializing German Army orgn. and tactics; charge German-Austrian desk, intelligence br. G-2 div., Hdqrs. U.S. Armed Forces, Frankfurt-am-Main. Decorated Bronze Star medal; recipient Carey-Thomas award for creative publishing R.R. Bowker Co., 1957. Club: Reform (London); Boulder Valley Racquet, Meadows Tennis (Boulder). Office: 5500 Central Ave Boulder CO 80301

PRAETORIUS, WILLIAM ALBERT, advt. and real estate exec.; b. Forty-Fort, Pa., Oct. 7, 1924; s. George Albert and Elizabeth (Madden) P.; student Biarittz (France) Am. U., 1945-46, N.Y. U., 1947-48; m. Theresa M. Barnes, June 25, 1949; children—Kathleen Ann, William Albert, Gregg Douglas. With L.W. Frohlich Intercon Internat., Inc., 1946-72, sr. v.p., dir. ops., 1969-71, chmn. operating com., 1972; sr. v.p., dir. ops. Deltakos div. J. Walter Thompson Co., N.Y.C., 1972-73; sr. v.p. adminstrn. J.W.T. Affiliated Cos., 1973-75; pres. Healthmark Communications, Inc., N.Y.C., 1975-77; dir. Clause Comml. div. Donald J. Clause, Southampton, N.Y., 1977-78; dir. comml. div. Meadow Real Estate, 1978—. Served with AUS, 1942-45. Mem. Pharm. Advt. Assn., Nat. Wholesale Drug Assn., Pharm Mfrs. Assn., Barns Landing Assn. Democrat. Catholic. Contbr. column to East End Bus. Rev., articles to profl. jours. Home: 30 Captains Walk East Hampton NY 11937 Office: 60 Windmill Ln Southampton NY 11968

PRAGER, DAVID, justice Kans. Supreme Ct.; b. Ft. Scott, Kans., Oct. 30, 1918; s. Walter and Helen (Kishler) P.; A.B., U. Kans., 1939, LL.B., 1942; m. Dorothy Schroeter, Sept. 8, 1945; children—Diane, David III. Admitted to Kans. bar, 1942; practiced in Topeka, 1946-59; dist. judge Shawnee County (Kans.) Dist. Ct., 1959-71; asso. justice Kans. Supreme Ct., 1971—; lectr. Washburn Law Sch., 1948-68. Served to lt. USNR, 1942-46; ETO, PTO. Mem. Kans. Dist. Judges Assn. (past pres.). Order of Coif, Phi Beta Kappa, Phi Delta Theta. Club: Lions. Home: 5130 SW 53d St Topeka KS 66610 Office: Supreme Ct Bldg State Capitol Topeka KS 66612

PRAGER, STEPHEN, educator; b. Darmstadt, Germany, July 20, 1928; s. William and Gertrude Ann (Heyer) P.; came to U.S., 1941, naturalized, 1950; B.Sc., Brown, 1947; Ph.D., Cornell, 1951; m. Julianne Heller, June 7, 1948. Mem. faculty U. Minn., Mpls., 1952—, asso. prof. chemistry, 1956-62, prof., 1962—. Cons., Union Carbide Corp., Oak Ridge, 1954-74. Fulbright scholar and Guggenheim fellow, 1958, 59, Fulbright lectr. and Guggenheim fellow, 1966-67. Mem. Am. Chem. Soc., Am. Phys. Soc., Soc. Rheology. Asso. editor Jour. Phys. Chemistry, 1970-79. Home: 3320 N Dunlap St St Paul MN 55112 Office: Chemistry Dept U Minn Minneapolis MN 55455

PRAGER, WILLIAM, educator; b. Karlsruhe, Germany, May 23, 1903; s. Willy and Helen (Kimmel) P.; state certificate as civil engr., 1925; Dr. Engring. Scis., Inst. of Tech., Darmstadt, 1926; hon. degrees U. Liège (Belgium), 1962, U. Poitiers (France), 1962, Case Inst. of Tech., 1963, Politeconico di Milano, 1964, U. Waterloo (Ont., Can.), 1969, U. Stuttgart (Germany), 1969, Tech. U., Hannover, Germany, 1969, Brown U., 1973, U. Manchester (Eng.), 1974, U. Brussels (Belgium), 1975; m. Gertrude A. Heyer, Sept. 16, 1925; 1 son, Stephen. Came to U.S., 1941. Instr. Mechanics, Inst. of Tech., Darmstadt, 1927-29; acting dir. Inst. Applied Mechanics, U. of Göttingen, 1929-32; prof. mechanics, Tech. Inst., Karlsruhe, 1933; structural insp. German Airsport League, Berlin, 1929-33; sci. adviser Fieseler Aircraft Co., Kassel, Germany, 1933; prof. mechanics, U. of Istanbul, 1934-41; mng. editor Revue de la Faculté des Sciences de l'Université d'Istanbul, 1935-41; prof. applied mechanics, Brown U., 1941-63, chmn. grad. div. of applied math., 1946-52, chmn. phys. scis. council, 1953-59, L. Herbert Ballou univ. prof. 1959-63, prof. engring. and applied math., 1968-73, prof. emeritus, 1973—; cons. IBM Research Lab., Zürich, Switzerland 1963-65; prof. applied mechanics U. Calif. at San Diego, 1965-68. Recipient of Worcester Reed Warner medal ASME, 1957, Timoshenko medal, 1966; Theodore Von Karman award, ASCE, 1960; Panetti prize Turin Acad. Scis., 1963. Fellow Am. Acad. Arts and Scis.; mem. ASCE, ASME (hon.), Nat. Acad. Sci., Nat. Acad. Engring., Polish Acad. Scis., Soc. Indsl. and Applied Math. (editor jour.), Am. Math. Soc., Groupe Français de Rhéologie (hon.), Groupe pour l'Avancement des Méthodes Numériques de l'Ingénieur (hon.), Académie des Sciences de L'Institut de France (corr.). Author: (with K. Hohenemser) Dynamik der Stabwerke, 1933; Mécanique des solides isotropes, 1937; Tersimi Hendese, 1937; (with F. Gürsan) Mihanik, 1941; (with P. G. Hodge, Jr.) Theory of Perfectly Plastic Solids, 1951; Probleme der Plastizitaetstheorie, 1955; An Introduction to Plasticity 1959; Introduction to Mechanics of Continua, 1961; Introduction To Basic Fortran Programming and Numerical Methods; Introduction to APL, 1971. mng. editor, Quar. Applied Math., 1943-65. Tech. editor Jour. Applied Mechanics, 1969-72; editor Computer Methods in Applied Mechanics and Engring., 1972—. Address: 7451 Savognin Switzerland

PRALL, VICTOR OSCAR, JR., banker; b. Cambridge, Mass., July 31, 1912; s. Victor O. and Rena (Ray) P.; B.A. in Econs., Wesleyan U., 1934, M.A. in Econs., 1935; postgrad. Cornell U., 1935-36; m. Hedwiga Modzeleski, Mar. 13, 1943; 1 son, Victor Oscar, III. With N.Y. Trust Co., 1936, Bank Monrovia, Liberia, 1938-41, State Bank Ethiopia, Addis Ababa, Ethiopia, 1945-49; joined First Nat. City Bank, N.Y.C., 1949—, mgr., Buenos Aires, Argentina, 1956-63, v.p. in charge Argentina, Paraguay, Uruguay, 1963-68, sr. v.p. internat. banking group, N.Y.C., 1968-77, also dir. various subsidiaries; chief exec. officer Grindlays Bank Ltd., London, 1975-77. Served to lt. comdr. USNR, 1941-45. Mem. Phi Beta Kappa, Delta Tau Delta. Club: Timber Trails. Home: Timber Trails Pepper Pond Rd Sherman CT 06784 also 5757 Gulf of Mexico Dr Longboat Key FL 33548

PRAMER, DAVID, microbiologist; b. Mt. Vernon, N.Y., Mar. 25, 1923; s. Coleman and Ethel (Toback) P.; student St. John's U., 1940-41, Tex. A&M Coll., 1941; B.Sc., Rutgers U., 1948, Ph.D., 1952; m. Rhoda Lifschutz, Sept. 6, 1950; children—Andrew, Stacey. Vis. investigator Butterwick Research Labs., Imperial Chem., Ltd., Eng., 1952-54; asst. prof. microbiology Rutgers U., New Brunswick, N.J., 1954-57, asso. prof., 1957-60, prof., 1960-67, disting. prof., 1967—, chmn. dept. biochemistry and microbiology, 1965-69, dir. biol. scis., 1969-73, dir. univ. research, 1973-75, asso. v.p. for research, 1975—; dir. New Brunswick Sci. Co., N.J. Marine Scis. Consortium, R&D Council N.J., N.J. Ednl. Computer Network; Am. del. Internat. Commn. on Microbial Ecology, 1970-73; dep. mem. UNESCO/UNEP/ICRO Panel on Microbiology, 1973; chmn. life scis. adv. com. Council for Internat. Exchange Scholars. Committeman, Democratic Party, Highland Park, N.J., 1960-65. Served with USAAF, 1943-46. Recipient Fulbright award, 1969, 72. Fellow Am. Acad. Microbiology; mem. Internat. Assn. Ecology, Am. Soc. Microbiology, AAAS, Phi Beta Kappa, Sigma Xi, Alpha Zeta. Author: (with E.L. Schmidt) Experimental Soil Microbiology, 1964; Life in the Soil, 1965; (with H.A. Lechevalier) The Microbes, 1971; editor Internat. Jour. Soil Biology and Biochemistry, Soil Sci., BioScis. Home: 37 Grant Ave Highland Park NJ 08904 Office: 116 College Ave New Brunswick NJ 08903. *Do your best, don't settle for less.*

PRANGE, HENRY CARL, retail co. exec.; b. Sheboygan, Wis., July 22, 1927; s. H. Carl and Laura (Neuses) P.; student Villanova Coll., 1945-46; B.B.A., U. Wis., 1949; m. Laura Vollrath, Sept. 3, 1949; children—Laura Lee, Henry Carl, William, John, Thomas. With Mut. Buying Syndicate, Inc., N.Y.C., 1950; buyer H.C. Prange Co., Sheboygan, 1951-52, divisional mdse. mgr., 1953-58, gen. mdse. mgr., 1959-63, store mgr., 1964, pres., 1965-73, chmn. bd., 1973—; dir. Wis. Power & Light Co., Asso. Merchandising Corp. Mem. Sheboygan Employment Opportunities Commn.; bd. dirs. Wis. Taxpayers Alliance, Wigwam Hills. Served with USNR, 1945-46. Republican. Roman Catholic. Clubs: Sheboygan Yacht (dir.); Naples (Fla.) Bath and Tennis. Home: 3703 N 6th St Sheboygan WI 53081 Office: 727 N 8th St Sheboygan WI 53081

PRANSES, ANTHONY LOUIS, electric co. exec., orgn. exec.; b. Claracq, France, May 3, 1920 (parents Am. citizens); s. Anthony Kasimer and Georgette (Pilon) F.; student Sorbonne, Paris, France, 1937-39; B.S. in Metall. Engring., Carnegie Inst. Tech., 1942, grad. student, 1946-48; m. Margaret Louise Hamill, July 24, 1943; children—Anthony Randolph, Terry Jay, Renee Louise. With Westinghouse Electric Corp., 1945—, mgr. mfg. planning, Lima, O., 1954-57, plant mgr., Lima, 1958-59, mgr. mfg. services, Lima, 1959-72, mgr. mfg., 1972—. Joined Am. Youth Hostels, 1935, founder Pitts. council, 1947, pres. council, 1947-50, mem. nat. bd. dirs., 1954-72, Midwest regional v.p., 1957-59, nat. pres., 1959-62, pres. Lima council, 1962-75, chmn. nat. bd. dirs., 1963-67. Served to capt., C.E., AUS, 1942- 45. Mem. Am. Soc. Tool Engrs., Nat. Mgmt. Assn., Am. Soc. Metals. Home: Rural Route 2 6005 Poling Rd Elida OH 45807 Office: Box 566 Lima OH 45802

PRASAD, ANANDA SHIVA, medical educator; b. Buxar, Bihar, India, Jan. 1, 1928; s. Radha Krishna and Mahesha (Kaur) Lall; B.Sc. with honors, Patna (India) Sci. Coll., 1946, M.B. B.S., 1951; Ph.D., U. Minn., 1957; m. Aryabala Ray, Jan. 6, 1952; children—Rita, Sheila, Ashok, Audrey. Came to U.S., 1952, naturalized, 1968. Intern Patna Med. Coll. Hosp., 1951-52; resident St. Paul's Hosp., Dallas, 1952-53, U. Minn., 1953-56, VA Hosp., Mpls., 1956; instr. dept. medicine Univ. Hosp., U. Minn., Mpls., 1957-58; vis. asso. prof. medicine Shiraz Med. Faculty, Nemazee Hosp., Shiraz, Iran, 1960; asst. prof. medicine and nutrition Vanderbilt U., 1961-63; mem. faculty, dir. div. hematology dept. medicine Wayne State U., Detroit, 1963—, asso. prof., 1964-68, prof., 1968—; mem. staff Detroit Gen. Hosp., VA Hosp., Allen Park, Mich. Mem. trace elements subcom. Food and Nutrition Bd., NRC-Nat. Acad. Scis., 1965-68; reviewer several profl. jours. Trustee Detroit Internat. Inst., Detroit Gen. Hosp. Research Corp., 1969-72. Pfizer scholar, 1955-56. Recipient research recognition award Wayne State U., 1964, award Am. Coll. Nutrition, 1976. Diplomate Am. Bd. Nutrition. Fellow A.C.P., Internat. Soc. Hematology; mem. Am. Soc. Clin. Nutrition (awards com. 1969-70), Am. Fedn. Clin. Research (pres. Mich. 1969-70), Am. Inst. Nutrition (trace elements panel), Am. Physiol. Soc., Am. Soc. Clin. Investigation, Am. Soc. Hematology, Assn. Am. Physicians, Central Soc. Clin. Research, Soc. Exptl. Biology and Medicine (councillor Mich. 1967-71), Wayne County Med. Soc., AMA (Goldberger award 1975), Internat. Soc. Internal Medicine, Sigma Xi. Club: Cosmos (Washington). Author: Zinc Metabolism, 1966; Trace Elements in Human Health and Disease, 1976; Trace Elements and Iron in Human Metabolism, 1978; Zinc in Human Nutrition, 1979; editor Am. Jour. Hematology; co-editor Zinc Metabolism, Current Aspects in Health and Disease, 1977. Contbr. articles to profl. jours. Home: 4710 Cove Rd Orchard Lake MI 48033 Office: 540 E Canfield Ave Detroit MI 48201

PRASHKER, HERBERT, lawyer; b. N.Y.C., July 10, 1922; s. Louis and Sarah (Solomon) P.; B.A., Columbia, 1942, LL.B., 1943; m. Betty Arnoff, Dec. 10, 1950 (div. 1974); children—Susan, Lucy, Martha Louise. Admitted to N.Y. bar, 1943, Mass. bar, 1971, D.C. bar, 1972; atty. Dept. Justice, 1943-44; law clk. to chief judge N.Y. Ct. Appeals, 1944-45; law clk. to chief justice U.S., 1945-46; asso., then partner firm Poletti Freidin Prashker Feldman & Gartner, and predecessors, N.Y.C., 1946—. Pres. N.Y. Young Democratic Club, 1952-53. Bd. dirs. Northside Center Child Devel., 1964—, Am. Civil Liberties Union, 1964-70. Mem. Bar Assn. City N.Y., Am., N.Y. State bar assns., N.Y. County Lawyers Assn. Home: 512 E 87th St New York NY 10028 and Seekonk Cross Rd Great Barrington MA 01230 Office: 1185 Ave of Americas New York NY 10036

PRASIL, ANTONE GEORGE, utility exec.; b. Friendship, Wis., Aug. 24, 1922; B.S. in Chem. Engring., U. Wis., 1946; m. Frances Williams, Sept. 19, 1974; children—Antone G., Edward R., Peggy Ann, Richard A., James R. Engr., Wis. Public Service Corp., Oshkosh, 1946-58; with So. Union Gas Co., Dallas, 1958—, v.p., ops. mgr., 1972-73, sr. v.p. utility ops., 1973—, dir., 1974—. Active local Boy Scouts Am., Camp Fire Girls. Served with A.C., USN, 1943-45. Registered profl. engr., Ariz., Colo., N.Mex., Okla., Tex., Wis. Mem. Am. Gas Assn. (chmn. ops. sect. 1978-79, award of merit 1970), Nat. Soc. Profl. Engrs., Interstate Natural Gas Assn. Am., Tex. Mid-Continent Oil and Gas Assn., ASME, Am. Inst. Chem. Engrs., Nat. Assn. Corrosion Engrs., NAM, Am. Mgmt. Assn., So. Gas Assn. Presbyterian. Clubs: Dallas Petroleum, Royal Oaks Country, Freestone Country, Masons, Elks. Home: 10042 Coppedge St Dallas TX 75229

PRATER, CHARLES DWIGHT, scientist, engr.; b. Sylacauga, Ala., Jan. 2, 1917; s. Rubin Walker and Mary Hunt (Corley) P.; B.S., Auburn U., 1940; postgrad. U. Chgo., 1940-41; Ph.D., U. Pa., 1951; m. Willie Lee Miller, May 28, 1938; children—Anne Marie, Linda Lee. Physicist, Bartol Research Found., Franklin Inst., 1941-46; research asso. Johnson Found. of Med. Physics, U. Pa., 1946-51; sr. research physicist research dept. Mobil Oil Corp., 1951-57, research asso., 1957-62, sr. research asso., 1962-67, mgr. process research and devel., 1967-77, sr. scientist, research advisor, 1977—. Recipient Alpha Chi Sigma in Chem. Engring. research Am. Inst. Chem. Engrs., 1972. Mem. AAAS, Am. Inst. Chem. Engrs., Am. Chem. Soc., Nat. Acad. Engring., Sigma Xi. Home: 112 Monroe Ave Pitman NJ 08071 Office: Mobil Research and Devel Corp Paulsboro NJ 08066

PRATHER, ELBERT CHARLTON, physician, state ofcl.; b. Jasper, Fla., Mar. 13, 1930; s. Walter J. and Myrtle (Wetherington) P.; B.S. in Bacteriology, U. Fla., 1952, M.S., 1954; M.D., Bowman Gray Sch. Medicine, 1959; M.P.H. in Epidemiology, U. N.C., 1963; m. Lou Leigh, Feb. 14, 1954; children—Elbert Charlton, Walter F. Research epidemiologist Fla. State Bd. Health, 1959-61; intern Jackson Meml. Hosp., Miami, Fla., 1961-62; pub. health resident Hillsborough County Health Dept., Tampa, Fla., 1963-64; state epidemiologist Fla. Div. Health, Jacksonville, 1964-70, chief bur. preventable disease, 1970-74, staff dir. health program office Dept. Health and Rehab. Services, Tallahassee, 1974-78, state health officer, 1978—; asso. clin. prof. schs. medicine U. Fla., U. Miami. Mem. Am., Fla. (Meritorious Service award 1975) pub. health assns., Assn. State and Territorial Health Ofcls., AMA, Fla. Med. Assn., Delta Omega. Presbyterian. Home: 2816 Terry Rd Tallahassee FL 32303 Office: 1323 Winewood Rd Tallahassee FL 32301

PRATHER, JACK LEON, mfg. co. exec.; b. Sherman, Tex., Apr. 9, 1918; s. William Henry and Emma Virginia (Graham) P.; B.S. in Mech. Engring., Tex. A. and M. U., 1941; J.D., So. Meth. U., 1948; m. Louise Vehle, July 4, 1937; 1 dau., Virginia Lou. Sales engr. Crane Co., Dallas, 1941-42; with U.S. C.E., Denison, Tex., 1942-43; admitted to D.C. bar, 1949; examiner Patent Office, Washington, 1948-49; patent atty., gen. counsel, 1949-54; asst. to Pres., 1955-62; v.p. Fuller Co., Catasauqua, Pa., 1962—, also dir.; dir. Indsl. Devel. Corp., Indsl. Devel. Authority. Served to lt. (j.g.) USNR, 1943-46. Mem. Internat. Bar Assn., Hon. 1st Defenders. Club: Lehigh Country (Allentown). Home: 3754 Congress St Allentown PA 18104 Office: 2040 Ave C Industrial Park #1 Bethlehem PA 18018 also PO Box 2040 Bethlehem PA 18018

PRATHER, WILFRED CLARENCE, broadcasting exec.; b. Buffalo, Feb. 7, 1921; s. Alfred C. and Carolyn (Sears) P.; student U. Chgo., 1942, Northwestern U., 1943; m. Irma Charlotte Hess, Oct. 7, 1941; children—Philip Brian, Daniel Putnam, Paul Bradley, Jan Ellen. Studio technician radio sta. WBNY, Buffalo, 1939-41; with NBC, 1941—, sta. mgr. WMAQ-TV, 1965-74, dir. engring. NBC Radio div., 1974—. Pres. bd. edn., Wood Dale, Ill., 1963-68; mem. Broadcast Skills Com., 1967—, Gen. Bd. Ch. Fedn. Chgo., 1966—; mem. TV, radio and film commn. United Methodist Ch., 1969—. Served with USNR, 1943-46. Mem. Nat. Assn. TV Arts and Scis., Soc. Motion Picture and TV Engrs. Methodist (lay leader). Office: NBC Radio Div 30 Rockefeller Plaza New York City NY 10020

PRATOR, RALPH, educator; b. LaVeta, Colo., Nov. 16, 1907; s. Charles and Isabella (Duncan) P.; A.B., U. Colo., 1929, A.M., 1933; Ed.D., U. Calif., 1947; m. Lois Skinner, June 17, 1937; children—Bruce, Lewis, Roxanna. Prin. and coach, Flagler, Colo., 1929-30, MacAlister, N.M., 1931-33; athletic coach, tchr. Huerfano County High Sch., Walsenburg, Colo., 1933-34; athletic coach, tchr., Del Norte, Colo., 1934-36; dean of men and athletic dir., Mesa Coll., Grand Junction, Colo., 1936-39; dir. alumni relations, U. Colo., Boulder, 1940-42, dir. admissions and records, 1942-50; pres. Bakersfield (Calif.) Coll., 1950-58; pres. San Fernando Valley State Coll., 1958-68, pres. emeritus, prof. higher edn., 1968-78, ret., 1978; vis. lectr., summers 1952, 53, 54, 55; vis. prof. Fresno State Coll., Summer 1956, 57, U. Calif. at Los Angeles, 1968-69, U. Guam, spring 1979; mem. accrediting commn. Western Coll. Assn. Dir. Valley Fed. Savs. & Loan Assn. Bd. dirs. San Fernando Valley council Boy Scouts Am., Los Angeles Devel. Assn. (pres. 1971). Served as lt. comdr., USNR, 1942-46, now capt. Mem. Los Angeles C. of C. (ednl. com.), Phi Delta Kappa (emeritus), Sigma Phi Epsilon. Presbyn. Clubs: Executive (past pres.), Rotary, Saticoy Country. Author: College President, 1963. Home: 13203 Village 13 Camarillo CA 93010

PRATT, ALBERT, investment banker; b. Newton, Mass., May 23, 1911; s. Frederick Sanford and Ella Winifred (Nickerson) P.; grad. Country Day Sch., Newton, 1929; A.B., Harvard, 1933, J.D., 1936; m. Alice Mathea Lee, May 24, 1940 (dec. 1976); children—Alice Mathea (Mrs. John Hughes), Cornelia S. (Mrs. Paul Mandelstein), Nina L., Frederick H., Kate Nickerson; m. 2d, Fanny Gray Morgan, Jan. 2, 1977. Admitted to Mass. bar, 1936; with firm Goodwin, Procter & Hoar, Boston, 1936-40; investment banker Paine, Webber, Jackson & Curtis, Inc., Boston, 1946—, vice chmn., 1970-76, cons., 1976—, gen. partner, 1950-54, 57-70, ltd. partner, 1954-57; dir., chmn. exec. com. Paine Webber Properties, Inc.; asst. sec. navy personnel and res. forces, 1954-57. Dir. Itek Corp., Asia Mgmt. Corp., Japan Fund, Inc., Ludlow Corp., Paine Webber Inc. Bd. govs. N.Y. Stock Exchange, 1963-66. Pres. United Fund Boston, 1962-64. Served to comdr. USNR, 1940-45. Mem. Investment Bankers Assn. (chmn. N.E. group 1952-53, gov. 1957-60, 64-67, chmn. securities act com. 1959-63, pres. 1965-66), Assn. Harvard Alumni (dir. 1964-70), Boston C. of C. (dir. 1958-61), Asso. Harvard Clubs (pres. 1962-63), Harvard Alumni Assn. (dir. 1958-63). Clubs: Somerset (Boston); Crusing of America; Knickerbocker, N.Y. Yacht (N.Y.); Bounty Bay Yacht. Home: Dam Pond House Box 508 Osterville MA 02655 Office: 100 Federal St Boston MA 02101

PRATT, ARNOLD W., govt. ofcl., physician; b. Binghamton, N.Y., Nov. 24, 1920; s. Donald Patrick and Agnes Kate (Smith) P.; Sc.D., Hobart Coll., 1973; M.D., U. Rochester, 1946; m. Mary Durfee, June 17, 1945; children—Mary Pratt Grant, Susan Broomfield, Janet Pratt Oliver. Mem. house staff N.Y. Hosp., Cornell U. Med. Center, N.Y.C., 1946-47; research asso. Cornell U. Med. Sch., 1947-48; head sect. energy metabolism lab. physiology Nat. Cancer Inst., NIH, Bethesda, Md., 1948-66, dir. div. computer research and tech., 1966—. Editorial bd. Computers and Biomed. Research, 1967—, Methods of Info. in Medicine, 1970—, Computer Programs in Biomedicine, 1972—. Home: 6 North Dr Bethesda MD 20014 Office: 9000 Rockville Pike Bldg 12A Room 3033 Bethesda MD 20014

PRATT, BURT CARLTON, found. exec.; b. Lititz, Pa., May 13, 1911; s. William A. and Laura G. (Becker) P.; B.S. in Chem. Engring., Bucknell U., Lewisburg, Pa., 1933; Ph.D. in Organic Chemistry, Cornell U., 1938; m. Dorothy M. McCaslin, May 23, 1931; 1 dau., Patricia Pratt Knodel. With E.I. duPont de Nemours & Co., Wilmington, Del., 1938-73, asso. dir. central research dept., 1951-64, exec. sec. com. ednl. aid, 1964-73; dir. Crystal Trust, Wilmington, 1973—. Bd. dirs., treas. Wilmington Coll., 1976—, Wilmington Music Sch., 1970—. Mem. Am. Chem. Soc., AAAS, Sigma Xi. Patentee synthetic organic chemistry, polymers, radiation-absorptive films. Address: 1088 Du Pont Bldg Wilmington DE 19898

PRATT, CHARLES ANDERSON, entertainment production exec.; b. Chgo., Oct. 17, 1923; s. Charles Reid and Marion (Anderson) P.; B.A., Amherst Coll., 1949; m. Joan Broughton, June 12, 1948; children—Marion, Andrew, Charles Anderson. Vice pres. advt. Alberto Culver Corp., 1959-64; dir. broadcast services Gen. Foods Corp., 1964-65; dir. corporate devel. Cox Broadcasting Corp., 1965-68; v.p. devel. Bing Crosby Productions Inc., Los Angeles, 1968-69, pres., 1969—. Served with U.S. Army, 1942-45; PTO. Decorated Bronze Star, Purple Heart. Republican. Presbyterian. Club: Bel Air Country (Los Angeles). Office: 1041 N Formosa Ave Los Angeles CA 90046

PRATT, DOUGLAS MCLAIN, transp. co. exec.; b. Omaha, 1911. Pres., Balt. Transit Co., 1952-55, Phila. Transit Co., 1955-62; pres., chief exec. officer, gen. mgr. Nat. City Lines, Inc., Denver, 1962—; chmn. exec. com., chief exec. officer, dir. TIME-DC Inc. Office: 5 Denver Technological Center Denver CO 80217*

PRATT, EDMUND TAYLOR, JR., pharm. co. exec.; b. Savannah, Ga., Feb. 22, 1927; s. Edmund Taylor and Rose (Miller) P.; B.S. in Elec. Engring. magna cum laude, Duke U., 1947; M.B.A., U. Pa., 1949; m. Jeanette Louise Carneale, Feb. 10, 1951; children—Randolf Ryland, Keith Taylor, With IBM Corp., 1949-51, 54-57, asst. to exec. v.p., 1956-57; with IBM World Trade Corp., 1957-62, controller, 1958-62; asst. sec. financial mgmt. Dept. Army, 1962-64; controller Pfizer Inc., N.Y.C., 1964-67, v.p. operations internat. subsidiaries, 1967-69, chmn. bd., pres. internat. subsidiaries, 1969-71, exec. v.p. Pfizer Inc., 1970-71, pres., 1971-72, chmn., chief exec. officer, 1972—; also chmn. exec. com.; dir. Chase Manhattan Corp., Internat. Paper Co., Gen. Motors Corp. Trustee Com. for Econ. Devel., U.S. council Internat. C. of C.; bd. dirs. Internat. Exec. Service Corps, Econ. Devel. Council N.Y.C.; chmn. Emergency Com. for Am. Trade; trustee Duke U.; bd. overseers Wharton Sch. Commerce and Finance. Served to lt. (j.g.) USNR, 1952-54. Mem. Bus. Council, Bus. Roundtable (policy com.), N.Y. Chamber Commerce and Industry (dir.), Phi Beta Kappa. Home: Port Washington NY 11050 Office: 235 E 42d St New York NY 10017

PRATT, EDWARD LOWELL, physician, educator; b. Great Barrington, Mass., Dec. 19, 1913; s. Albert Stone and Anna (Lowell) P.; grad. Peddie Sch., 1932; B.S., Mass. Inst. Tech., 1936; M.D., Harvard U., 1940; m. Esther Fillmore, Aug. 28, 1940; 1 son, Lowell Albert. Intern bacteriology and pathology Infants and Childrens Hosp., Boston, 1940-41; asst. resident pediatrics Childrens Hosp., Boston, 1942-43, sr. resident pediatrics, 1943-44; sr. fellow pediatrics NRC at Yale, 1946-48, Cambridge (Eng.) U., 1948-49; asso. prof. pediatrics N.Y. U. Coll. Medicine; vis. physician Bellevue Hosp. and attending physician Univ. Hosp., 1949-54; prof. pediatrics, chmn. dept. U. Tex. Southwestern Med. Sch., also chief staff Childrens Med. Center and Parkland Meml. Hosp., Dallas, 1954-63; B. K. Rachford prof. pediatrics, dir. dept. U. Cin., Coll. Medicine, 1963-79, prof. pediatrics, 1979—; physician exec. dir. Childrens Hosp., Cin., also dir. Childrens Hosp. Research Found., 1963-79; dir. pediatrics and contagious div. Cin. Gen. Hosp., 1963-79. Mem. med. exchange teams to Greece and Italy, 1947, Turkey, Lebanon and Israel, 1958. Diplomate Am. Bd. Pediatrics. Mem. Am. Pediatric Soc. (pres. 1976), Soc. Pediatric Research (pres. 1958), Am. Soc. Clin. Investigation, Alpha Omega Alpha. Home: 922 Rookwood Dr Cincinnati OH 45208 Office: Childrens Hosp Elland Ave and Bethesda Cincinnati OH 45229

PRATT, GEORGE CHENEY, judge; b. Corning, N.Y., May 22, 1928; s. George Wollage and Muriel (Cheney) P.; B.A., Yale U., 1950, LL.B., 1953; m. Carol June Hoffman, Aug. 16, 1952; children—George W., Lisa M., Marcia S., William T. Admitted to N.Y. bar, 1953, U.S. Supreme Ct. bar, 1964, U.S. Ct. Appeals bar, 1974; law clk. to Charles W. Froessel, Judge of N.Y. Ct. Appeals, 1953-55; asso., then partner firm Sprague & Stern, Mineola, N.Y., 1955-60; partner firms Andromidas, Pratt & Pitcher, 1960-65, Pratt, Caemmerer & Cleary, 1965-75, Farrell, Fritz, Pratt, Caemmerer & Cleary, 1975-76; judge U.S. Dist. Ct., Eastern Dist. of N.Y., Westbury, 1976—; adj. prof. St. John's U. Law Sch., 1978—. Mem. Am., N.Y. State, Nassau County bar assns., Nassau Lawyers Assn. Mem. United Ch. of Christ. Home: 363 Split Rock Rd Syosset NY 11791 Office: 900 Ellison Ave Westbury NY 11590

PRATT, GERALD HILLARY, surgeon, educator, author; b. Montello, Wis., Dec. 15, 1906; s. Martin Henry and Margaret Anne (Farr) P.; B.S., U. Minn., 1924; M.D., State U. Iowa, 1928; hon. degrees U. Bordeaux (France), U. Madrid (Spain), U. Barcelona (Spain); m. Mae Dolores Gargin, Mar. 19, 1935; children—Margaret Anne (Mrs. Thomas Taylor), Judith (Mrs. Martin Kingsley), Gerald Hillary; m. 2d, Nancy Hildegarde Brown, Mar. 22, 1956; children—Dennis Gerald, James Martin. Intern, resident L.I. Coll. Med. Sch. and Hosp., Bklyn., 1928-30; chief resident Louisville U. Med. Sch. and Hosp., 1930-31; fellow, personal asst. to W. Wayne Babcock, prof. surgery Temple U. Hosp. Med. Sch., Phila., 1931-35; instr., asst. prof., surg. tng. New York Postgrad. Hosp. and Med. Sch., Columbia, 1935-48; asso. prof. N.Y. U. Sch. Medicine, 1948—; lectr. N.J. Coll. Medicine and Dentistry, 1965—; mem. surg. staff St. Vincent's Hosp. and Med. Center City N.Y., St. Clare's Hosp. and Health Center, Doctors Hosp., N.Y.C. Mem. Armed Forces Cons. to U.S., 1950—. Served to maj. M.C., AUS, 1939-41; from lt. comdr. to capt. M.C., USNR, 1941—; PTO. Recipient Service citation for 25 years service N.Y. U., 1973; citation N.Y. State Med. Soc., 1978. Diplomate Am. Bd. Surgery. Fellow A.C.S., Internat. Coll. Surgeons, Am. Coll. Chest Physicians, Am. Geriatrics Soc. (cons. med. adv. bd.), Am. Heart Assn. (council on circulation), Coll. Internat. de Chirurgiens; mem. N.Y. Acad. Scis., Pan Am. Med. Assn. (v.p.; chmn. vascular surgery sect.), Internat. Cardiovascular Soc. (founder), Am. Therapeutic Soc. (v.p., pres. 1955-57), N.Y. Heart Assn. (dir.), N.Y. Acad. Medicine, Soc. Med. Cons.'s to Armed Forces (certificate 1978, surg. com. 1978), Navy League U.S., Nu Sigma Nu, Tau Upsilon Kappa, Phi Gamma Delta. Club: Century. Author: (textbooks) Surgical Management of Vascular Diseases, 1949; Tratamiento Quirurgico de las Enfermedades Vasculares, 1952; Cardiovascular Surgery, 1954; Vascular Surgery: Guide and Handbook, 1976; Saga of a Surgeon, 1976. Contbr. chpts. to med. and surg. books, also articles to profl. jours. Cons. for manuscripts various med. jours. Home: 211 Ocean Ave Sea Girt NJ 08750 Office: Dept Surgery St Clare's Hosp and Health Center 415 W 51st St New York City NY 10019. *I was taught my life should be one of service without desire for acclaim or financial reward. I thank God for giving me the opportunity to help others by prolonging their lives or alleviating pain. The opportunity to teach others in my chosen field of cardiovascular surgery was accepted eagerly. If I have succeeded in this aim I have accomplished my purpose in life.*

PRATT, JAMES REECE, architect; b. Stamford, Tex., Mar. 25, 1927; s. James Reece and Margaret Louise (Barret) P.; B.Arch., U. Tex., 1950; M.Arch., Harvard, 1953; m. Joanne Henderson, Nov. 2, 1955; children—Sabrina Vittoria, Alexandra Barret, Ilya Cristy. Staff architect Edward D. Stone and A.L. Aydelott, Memphis, 1952; staff architect I.M. Pei, N.Y.C., 1953; designer Haefeli, Moser & Steiger, Zurich, 1954; staff architect Broad & Nelson, Dallas, 1955-57; pvt. practice architecture, Dallas, 1955-57; pvt. practice architecture, Dallas, 1957—; now partner Pratt, Box, Henderson & Partners. Mem. Allied Profl. Ednl. Cons. Services; chmn. Nat. Com. on Pub. Edn., 1970, 72. Chmn. Urban Design Task Force, multidisciplinary adv. body to Dallas City Mgr., 1969-71. Mem. Dallas County Democratic Exec. Com., 1962-66. Bd. dirs. Pub. TV Found. N.Tex.; trustee Dallas Mus. Health and Sci.; past chmn. adv. com. U. Tex. Sch. Architecture Found. Served with USNR, 1945-46. Recipient Enrico Fermi Meml. Archtl. Competition shared prize, 1957, shared Grand prize Homes For Better Living Competition, 1959, grants Tex. Architecture Found., 1957, Tex. Soc. Architects awards, 1965-77. Fellow AIA (pres. Dallas chpt. 1969); mem. Tex. Soc. Architects (chmn. urban planning and design com.). Prin. works include St. Stephen Meth. Ch., Brookhaven Community Coll., Greenhill Sch. Theater and Middle Sch., Gt. Hall of Apparel Mart Dallas, Quadrangle Shopping Center Dallas. Co-author: Environmental Encounter, 1978. Editor: AIA Guide to Environmental Education, 1970. Office: 3526 Cedar Springs St Dallas TX 75219

PRATT, JOHN HELM, judge; b. Portsmouth, N.H., Nov. 17, 1910; s. Harold Boswell and Marguerite (Rockwell) P.; A.B. cum laude, Harvard, 1930, LL.B., 1934; m. Bernice G. Safford, Oct. 25, 1938; children—Clare, Lucinda (Mrs. Daniel D. Pearlman), John Helm, Patricia (Mrs. George Moriarty), Mary (Mrs. William DeLong). Admitted to D.C. bar, 1934, since practiced in Washington; partner firm Morris, Pearce, Gardner & Pratt, 1954-68; asst. counsel Boys Club Greater Washington, 1948-68; U.S. dist. judge, Washington, 1968—. Chmn. Montgomery County (Md.) Housing Authority, 1950-53. Chmn. bd. trustees D.C. Legal Aid Agy., 1967-68. Served to capt. USMCR, 1942-46; PTO. Decorated Bronze Star, Purple Heart; recipient Army citation for civilian service in field prosthetics, 1948. Mem. Am. Bar Assn. (ho dels. 1963-64), Am. Bar Found., Bar Assn. D.C. (pres. 1963-64), Harvard Law Sch. Assn. (pres. Washington 1952-53), Asso. Harvard Clubs (pres. 1952-53), Marine Res. Corps Officers Assn. (judge adv. gen. 1961-68). Democrat. Roman Catholic. Clubs: Barristers (pres. 1969), Lawyers, Harvard (pres. 1949-51); Chevy Chase. Home: 4119 Rosemary St Chevy Chase MD 20015 Office: US Courthouse Washington DC 20001

PRATT, JOHN HELM, JR., armored car co. exec.; b. Washington, Nov. 23, 1943; s. John Helm and Bernice (Safford) P.; B.A., Harvard U., 1966; postgrad. U. Hawaii, 1969-70; m. Mary E. Sullivan, Sept. 16, 1972; children—Erin, John. Regional mgr. Purolator Armored, Inc., Chgo., 1974-75, divisional v.p., 1975-76, sr. v.p., Dallas, 1976-79, pres., Piscataway, N.J., 1979—. Served with USNR, 1966-72. Mem. Nat. Armored Car Assn. (dir.). Republican. Roman Catholic. Home: 185 Pelican Rd Middletown NJ 07748 Office: 255 Old New Brunswick Rd Piscataway NJ 08854

PRATT, JOHN WINSOR, educator; b. Boston, Sept. 11, 1931; s. Frederic Wolsey and Theresa (Winsor) P.; A.B., Princeton, 1952; Ph.D., Stanford, 1956; M.A. (hon.), Harvard, 1966; m. Joy A. Wilmunen, Nov. 15, 1958; children—Maria Theresa Winsor, Samuel Frederick Wolsey. Research asso. U. Chgo., 1955-57; member faculty Harvard, 1957—, prof. bus. adminstrn., 1966; vis. research prof. Kyoto U., 1972-73; dir. Social Sci. Research Council, 1971-76; chmn. study group on environ. monitoring NRC, 1975-77. Guggenheim fellow, 1971. Trustee Middlesex Sch., Concord, Mass., 1964-67. Fellow Am. Statis. Assn. (editor jour. 1965-69), Inst. Math. Statistics, Econometric Soc., AAAS (chmn. sect. U., 1977); mem. Bernoulli Soc. for Math. Statistics and Probability, Math. Assn. Am. Co-author: Introduction to Statistical Decision Theory, 1965; Social Experimentation, a Method for Planning and Evaluating Social Intervention, 1974. Editor: Statistical and Mathematical Aspects of Pollution Problems, 1974. Home: 2 Gray Gardens E Cambridge MA 02138 Office: Morgan Hall 325 Harvard Bus Sch Boston MA 02163

PRATT, JOSEPH HYDE, JR., surgeon; b. Chapel Hill, N.C., Mar. 9, 1911; s. Joseph Hyde and Mary (Bayley) P.; grad. Choate Sch., 1929; A.B., U. N.C., 1933; M.D., Harvard, 1937; M.S., U. Minn., 1947; m. Hazel Housman, Dec. 11, 1943; children—Judith Housman, Lisa Mary, Joseph Hyde. Intern Boston City Hosp., 1938-39; fellow surgery Mayo Found., 1940-43; mem. staff Mayo Clinic, 1943—, head sect. in surgery, 1945-72, sr. gynecol. surgeon, 1958—; prof. clin. surgery Mayo Grad. Sch. Medicine, U. Minn., 1963—; prof. surgery Mayo Med. Sch., 1973—. Diplomate Am. Bd. Surgery, Am. Bd. Obstetrics and Gynecology. Mem. A.C.S. (bd. govs. 1966-71, bd. regents 1971—), AMA, Am. Coll. Obstetricians and Gynecologists, Am., Central assns. obstetrics and gynecology, Western Surg. Assn., Obstet. and Gynecol. Travel Club, Soc. Vaginal Surgeons (pres. 1979-80), Soc. Pelvic Surgeons (pres. 1968), So. Surg. Assn., Minn. Obstet. and Gynecol. Soc., Minn. Surg. Soc., Sigma Xi, Nu Sigma Nu. Republican. Episcopalian. Contbr. articles to med. jours. Home: 1425 20th St SW Rochester MN 55901 Office: 200 1st St SW Rochester MN 55901

PRATT, LAWRENCE ARTHUR, thoracic surgeon, fgn. service officer; b. Paris, Ill., Dec. 20, 1907; s. Luther F. and Katherine (Kaufman) P.; B.S., Wayne State U., Detroit, 1930, M.B., M.A., M.D., 1934, Master Edn., 1960; LL.B. Woodrow Wilson Coll. Law, Atlanta, 1943; m. Alice E. Palmer, Sept. 3, 1935 (div. Jan. 1971); children—Lawrence Alice, Dorothy Jane; m. 2d, Mai Thi Ngoc Suong, May 7, 1973; 1 child, Mai Chi. Intern Grace Hosp., 1934-35; practice thoracic surgery, Detroit 1935-41, 46-63; attending thoracic surgeon Grace, Detroit Meml. hosps.; courtesy staff St. John's Hosp.; cons. thoracic surgeon Holy Cross, Highland Park Gen. hosps., Detroit; U.S. fgn. service officer, 1963—; vis. prof. medicine U. Saigon, Viet- Nam, 1963—; exec. v.p. Am. Fedn. Med. Centers, Inc., 1953-54; chief med. dental edn. div. AID/PH, Vietnam. Cons. to Vietnam Minister Edn., 1974-75; asso. dean Minh Duc Med. Sch., Saigon, 1974-75; cons. HEW, 1975—, spl. asst. Div. Medicine Bur. Health Manpower, 1976; cons., mem. White House Task Force Internat. Health Policy, 1977; mem. World Bank Task Force Internat. Health Policy and Manpower, 1977; leader design team Health Care Program, Mauritania, W.Africa, 1978. Served as lt. col., M.C., AUS, 1941-46. Recipient Unit citation; Medal of Culture and Edn., Medal of Merit (Govt. of Vietnam). Diplomate Am. Board of Surgery, also the Am. Board of Thoracic Surgeons. Fellow A.C.S. (life), Am. Coll. Chest Physicians; mem. AMA, Mich., Wayne County med. socs., Internat. (founder), Am. bronchoesophagol. assns., 4th Aux. Surg. Group Assn. (pres. 1955-56), Wayne State U. Med. Alumni Assn. (pres. 1956-57), Ga. Bar Assn. Clubs: Essex Cricket (Eng.); Lambs (N.Y.C.); Scarab, Detroit Skating (Detroit); Grosse Pointe Yacht, Grosse Pointe Hunt; Am. Radio Relay League; El Cajon (Calif.) Radio. Home: 9908 Helixmont Dr La Mesa CA 92041

PRATT, MATTHEW, forest products co. exec.; b. Seattle, Feb. 26, 1928; s. Dudley and Virginia (Claflin) P.; B.A. magna cum laude, Yale U., 1949; certificate Stanford Exec. Program, 1977; m. Branwen Bailey, June 25, 1949; children—Sarah Claflin, Susannah Farrell, Anthony Whittlesey; m. 2d, Polly Propp, Sept. 12, 1970. Mill laborer, trainee Potlatch Forest, Inc., Lewiston, Idaho, 1953; mill laborer, trainee Weyerhaeuser Co., Everett, Wash., 1954, sales rep., Distbn. Center mgr., Western region mgr., nat. sales ops. mgr., 1955-75; exec. v.p. Am. Forest Products Corp., San Francisco, after 1975; now officer, dir. Bendix Forest Products Corp. Mem. Am. Plywood Assn. (trustee), Am. Wood Council (treas.), Phi Beta Kappa. Republican. Clubs: San Francisco Tennis, Dolphin Swimming and Boating. Home: 237 Upper Toyon Dr Kentfield CA 94904 Office: 2740 Hyde St San Francisco CA 94109

PRATT, NORMAN TWOMBLY, JR., educator; b. Providence, July 29, 1911; s. Norman T. and Annie (Rounds) P.; A.B., Brown U., 1932; M.A., Princeton, 1934, Ph.D., 1935; m. Barbara Frances Fisher, Apr. 2, 1936; children—David Wixon, Martha Anne (Mrs. Presley T. Buntin), Deborah Frances (Mrs. Raymond J. Maloni). From instr. to asst. prof. Princeton, 1935-42; mem. faculty Ind. U., 1946—, chmn. dept. Classics, 1946-71, prof., 1950-76, emeritus, 1976—; vis. asso. prof. Columbia, 1949-50; vis. prof. Am. Sch. Classical Studies, Athens, Greece, 1962-63, 1969-70. Served with USNR, 1942-46. Bollingen fellow, 1962-63. Mem. Am. Philol. Assn., Archaeol. Inst. Am., Classical Assn. Middle West and South (pres. 1964-65), Am. Classical League (pres. 1966-69), Phi Beta Kappa. Episcopalian. Author: Dramatic Suspense in Seneca and in His Greek Precursors, 1939; also articles, Editor Classical Jour., 1956-61. Home: 772 Marbury Lane Longboat Key FL 33548

PRATT, PHILIP, judge; b. Pontiac, Mich., July 14, 1924; s. Peter and Helen (Stathis) P.; student (Alumni scholar) U. Mich., 1942-43, LL.B., 1950; student U. Chgo., 1943-44; m. Mary C. Hill, July 26, 1952; children—Peter, Laura, Kathleen. Admitted to Mich. bar, 1951; title examiner Abstract & Title Co., Pontiac, 1951; asst. pros. atty., Oakland County (Mich.), 1952; mem. firm Smith & Pratt, Pontiac, 1953-63; circuit judge 6th Jud. Circuit of Mich., Pontiac, 1963-70; U.S. dist. judge, Eastern Dist. Mich., 1970—. Served with OSS, AUS, 1943-46. Decorated Bronze Star medal. Mem. Am., Oakland County (pres. 1961) bar assns., State Bar Mich., Am. Judicature Soc. Office: US Courthouse Detroit MI 48226

PRATT, PHILIP CHASE, pathologist; b. Livermore Falls, Maine, Oct. 19, 1920; s. Harold Sewell and Cora Johnson (Chase) P.; A.B., Bowdoin Coll., 1941; M.D., Johns Hopkins U., 1944; m. Helen Clarke Deitz, Feb. 4, 1975; children—William Clarke (dec.), Charles Chase. Intern in pathology Johns Hopkins Hosp., 1944-45, asst. resident in pathology, 1945-46; pathologist Saranac Lab., Saranac Lake, N.Y., 1946-52, asst. dir., 1952-55; instr. Ohio State U., 1955-57, asst. prof. pathology, 1957-62, asso. prof., 1962-66; asso. prof. Duke U. Med. Center, 1966-71, prof., 1971—. Diplomate Am. Bd. Pathology. Fellow Am. Coll. Chest Physicians; mem. Am. Thoracic Soc., Am. Soc. Exptl. Pathology, Am. Assn. Pathologists and Bacteriologists, Internat. Acad. Pathology, Royal Soc. Health. Unitarian. Contbr. numerous articles to profl. publs. Home: 2707 Sevier St Durham NC 27706 Office: Duke Med Center Davison Bldg Durham NC 27710. *The innovative idea is the essential commodity of the academic life. Origins of such ideas are varied but for me usually begin with realization that an existing concept does not adequately explain observed phenomena. When direct reasoning does not produce a new, better concept, the problem is put aside. Weeks later a return to the question often promptly reveals a logical new solution which has arisen without conscious effort. Of course, this must then be subjected to investigation to be either confirmed or refuted.*

PRATT, RICHARD HOUGHTON, educator; b. N.Y.C., May 5, 1934; s. Karl Chapman and Gertrude (Gennis) P.; A.B., U. Chgo., 1952, S.M., 1955, Ph.D., 1959; m. Elizabeth Ann Glass, Nov. 1, 1958; children—Jonathan Peter, Kathryn Eileen, Mary Caroline, Paul Chapman. Research asso. Stanford, 1959-61, asst. prof., 1961-64; asso. prof. physics U. Pitts., 1964-69, prof., 1969—. Cons. Nat. Bur. Standards, Naval Research Lab., Lawrence Livermore Lab.; prin. investigator Dept. Energy, NSF, HEW; mem. Pa. Gov.'s Sci. Advisory Com. Bd. dirs. Pa. Environ. Council. Fellow Am. Phys. Soc., AAAS, Phi Beta Kappa, Sigma Xi. Club: Sierra (chmn. Pa. chpt. 1976—). Home: 1131 Shady Ave Pittsburgh PA 15232

PRATT, RICHARDSON, JR., coll. pres.; b. N.Y.C., Mar. 25, 1923; s. Richardson and Laura C. (Parsons) P.; A.B., Williams Coll., 1946, LL.D. (hon.), 1978; M.B.A., Harvard U., 1948; m. Mary Esterbrook Offutt, Aug. 12, 1944; children—Laura Pratt Gerrity, Thomas R., David O. Econ. analyst, sec. com. on human relations Exxon Co., 1948-52, dist. mktg. mgr., 1953-63, mktg. planning and evaluation, 1964-71; mng. partner Charles Pratt & Co., 1971—; pres. Pratt Inst., Bklyn., 1972—, Dime Savs. Bank N.Y.; dir. Bklyn. Union Gas Co. Trustee African Wildlife Leadership Found., Fedn. Protestant Welfare Agys.; mem. governing bd. Bklyn. Mus., Bklyn. Bot. Gardens. Served to ensign USNR, 1943-46. Mem. Bklyn. C. of C. Presbyterian. Home: 30 Dock Hollow Rd Cold Spring Harbor NY 11724 Office: 215 Ryerson St Brooklyn NY 11205

PRATT, ROBERT CRANFORD, polit. scientist; b. Montreal, Que., Can., Oct. 8, 1926; s. Robert Goodwin and Henrietta (Freeman) P.; B.A., McGill U., Montreal, 1947; postgrad. Inst. Polit. Sci., Paris, 1948; B.Phil. (Rhodes scholar), Oxford (Eng.) U., 1952; m. Renate Hecht, July 15, 1956; children—Gerhard, Marcus, Anna. Lectr., McGill U., 1952-54, 56-58, Makerere (Uganda) U., 1954-56; research officer Oxford Inst. Commonwealth Studies, 1958-60; prin. Univ. Coll., Dar-es-Salaam, Tanzania, 1961-65; chmn. internat. studies program U. Toronto (Ont., Can.), 1966-71, prof. polit. sci., 1966-; spl. asst. to pres. Tanzania, 1965; research fellow Internat. Devel. Research Centre, 1978; commonwealth vis. prof. U. London, 1979-80. Recipient Killam award Can. Council, 1968. Fellow Royal Soc. Can.; mem. Can. Polit. Sci. Assn., Canadian African Studies Assn., Ecumenical Forum Can. Mem. New Democratic Party. Author: (with Anthony Low) Buganda and British Overrule, 1960; The Critical Phase in Tanzania; Nyerere and the Emergence of a Socialist Strategy, 1976; Towards Socialism in Tanzania, 1979. Home: 205 Cottingham St Toronto ON M4V 1C4 Canada Office: Dept Polit Economy U Toronto Toronto ON M5S 1A1 Canada

PRATT, WALLACE EVERETTE, cons. geologist; b. Phillipsburg, Kans., Mar. 15, 1885; s. William Henry and Olive Belle (Bostetter) P.; A.B., U. Kans., 1908, B.S., 1908, M.A., 1909, Engr. of Mines in Geology, 1914; m. Pearl M. Stuckey, Dec. 30, 1912 (dec.); children—Fletcher Stuckey, Nancy Jane, Houston Wallace; m. 2d, Iris Calderhead, Jan. 3, 1941 (dec.); m. 3d, Suzanne d'Autremont, Nov. 4, 1966. Asst., Kans. U. Geol. Survey, 1908-09; asst. geologist Div. Mines, Bur. Sci., Govt. Philippines, Manila, 1910, geologist, 1911-12, chief div. mines, 1913-15; geologist Texaco, Houston, 1916-17; chief geologist Humble Oil & Refining Co., Houston, 1918-23, dir., 1924-33, v.p., 1933-36; dir., mem. exec. com. Standard Oil Co. (N.J.), N.Y.C., 1937-45, v.p., 1942-45, ret., 1946; spl. asst. to chmn. N.S.R.B., cons. AEC, Washington, 1948; cons. geologist, Frijole, Culberson County, Tex., 1949-66, Tucson, 1966—. Chmn., Tex. Engrs. for Hoover, 1928; elector from Tex. to Electoral Coll., 1928. Recipient Anthony F. Lucas Gold medal Am. Inst. Mining and Metall. Engrs., 1948; James Furman Kemp medal Columbia U., 1950; Am. Petroleum Inst. Gold medal, 1954; elected to Permian Basin Hall of Fame, 1969; presented as "Grand Old Man of Exploration" Internat. Petroleum Exposition, 1976. Fellow Geol. Soc. Am.; mem. Am. Assn. Petroleum Geologists (founder mem. 1917, hon. mem. 1958; Sidney Powers Meml. medal 1945, Gold medal for Service through Geology to Human Needs 1972, pres. 1920), Soc. Econ. Geologists, Soc. Exploration Geophysicists (hon.), Houston (hon.), West Tex. (hon.) Sigma Xi. Author: Oil in the Earth, 1941. Editor: (with Dorothy Good) World Geography of Petroleum, 1950. Author papers in fields of econ. and areal geology, iron ores in Philippines, petroleum in the Arctic, 1948, petroleum on Continental shelves, 1945, distbn. of petroleum in earth's crust, vulcanology, non-metallic minerals, coal, Portland cement raw materials. Address: 2820 N Torino Ave Tucson AZ 85712

PRATT, WILLIAM CROUCH, JR., educator; b. Shawnee, Okla., Oct. 5, 1927; s. William Crouch and Irene (Johnston) P.; B.A., U. Okla., 1949; M.A., Vanderbilt U., 1951, Ph.D., 1957; m. Anne Cullen Rich, Oct. 2, 1954; children—Catherine Cullen, William Stuart, Randall Johnston. Rotary Internat. fellow U. Glasgow, Scotland, 1951-52; instr. English, Vanderbilt U., 1955-57; instr. English, Miami U., Oxford, Ohio, 1957-59, asst. prof., 1959-64, asso. prof., dir. Freshman English, 1964-68, prof., 1968—; adviser Ohio Poetry Circuit, 1964—; Fulbright-Hays lectr. Am. lit., prof. Am. lit. Univ. Coll., Dublin, Eire, 1975-76; resident scholar Miami U. European Center, Luxembourg, fall 1976; lectr. Yeats Internat. Summer Sch., Sligo, Eire, 1979. Served to lt., USNR, 1953-55. Mem. MLA, Nat. Council Tchrs. English (Ohio awards chmn. 1967-69), Coll. Conf. on Composition, Communication, Internat. Contemporary Lit. and Theatre Soc., Soc. Study So. Lit., Phi Beta Kappa, Sigma Alpha Epsilon. Republican. Episcopalian. Club: Butler County (Ohio) Torch. Author: The Imagist Poem, 1963; The Fugitive Poets, 1965; The College Writer, 1969. Contbr. essays, translations, poems, rev.s to lit. jours., books. Home: 212 Oakhill Dr Oxford OH 45056. *The capacities to love, and to believe, are the greatest gifts God can give. Fortunate indeed is the man who can live in the contemplation of what he loves.*

PRATTE, YVES, lawyer; b. Quebec, Que., Can., Mar. 7, 1925; B.A., Coll. Garnier, Quebec, 1944; LL.L., Laval U., 1947; postgrad. U. Toronto, 1947-48. Admitted to Que. bar, 1947; mem. firm St. Laurent, Taschereau, Noel and Pratte, Quebec, 1948-53; sr. partner firm Pratte, Cote, Tremblay, Beauvais, Bouchard, Garneau & Truchon, Quebec, 1954-68; dean Faculty of Law Laval U., 1962-65; spl. legal counsel Prime Ministers Jean Lesage and Daniel Johnson, 1965-68; mem. Royal Commn. Security, 1966-68; bd. dirs. Can. Nat. Railways, 1968-75; sr. partner Desjardins, Ducharme, Bourque & Pratte, Quebec, 1976-77; justice Supreme Ct. of Can., Ottawa, 1977-79; partner firm Courtois, Clarkson, Parsons & Tetrault, Montreal, Que., 1979—; chmn. bd., chief exec. officer Air Can., 1968-75. Home: 1321 Sherbrooke Apt A-110 Montreal PQ H2L 1M3 Canada Office: 630 Dorchester Blvd W Montreal PQ H3B 1V7 Canada

PRAUSNITZ, JOHN MICHAEL, chem. engr., educator; b. Berlin, Germany, Jan. 7, 1928; s. Paul Georg and Susi (Loewenthal) P.; came to U.S., 1937, naturalized, 1944; B.Chem. Engring., Cornell U., 1950; M.S., U. Rochester, 1951; Ph.D., Princeton, 1955; m. Susan Bergmann, June 10, 1956; children—Stephanie, Mark Robert. Mem. faculty U. Cal. at Berkeley, 1955—, prof. chem. engring., 1963—; cons. to cryogenic, polymer, petroleum and petrochem. industries. Guggenheim fellow, 1962, 73; Miller research prof., 1966, 78. Recipient Alexander V. Humboldt Sr. Scientist award, 1976. Mem. Am. Inst. Chem. Engrs. (Colburn award 1962, Walker award 1967), Am. Chem. Soc. (E.V. Murphree award 1979), Nat. Acad. Engring., Nat. Acad. Scis. Author: (with others) Computer Calculations for Multicomponent Vapor-Liquid Equilibria, 1967; (with P.L. Chueh) Computer Calculations for High-Pressure Vapor-Liquid Equilibria, 1968; Molecular Thermodynamics of Fluid-Phase Equilibria, 1969; (with others) Regular and Related Solutions, 1970; (with others) Properties of Gases and Liquids, 1977. Contbr. to profl. jours. Home: 52 the Crescent Berkeley CA 94708

PRAY, LLOYD CHARLES, geologist, educator; b. Chgo., June 25, 1919; s. Allan Theron and Helen (Palmer) P.; B.A., Carleton Coll., 1941; M.S., Calif. Inst. Tech., 1943, Ph.D. (NRC fellow 1946-49), 1952; m. Carrel Myers, Sept. 14, 1946; children—Lawrence Myers, John Allan, Kenneth Palmer, Douglas Carrel. Geologist, Magnolia Petroleum Co., summer 1942, U.S. Geol. Survey, 1943-44, part time 46-56; instr. to asso. prof. geology Calif. Inst. Tech., 1949-56; sr. research geologist Denver Research Center, Marathon Oil Co., 1956-62, research asso., 1962-68; prof. geology U. Wis., Madison, 1968—. Short course vis. prof. U. Tex., 1964, U. Colo., 1967, U. Miami, 1971, U. Alta., 1969; vis. scientist Imperial Coll. Sci. and Tech., London, 1977. Pres. Colo. Diabetes Assn., 1963-67, v.p., 1968; mem. adv. panel earth scis. NSF, 1973-76. Served as hydrographic officer USNR, 1944-46. Named Layman of Year, Am. Diabetes Assn., 1968. Fellow Geol. Soc. Am. (research grants com. 1965-67, com. on nominations 1973, com. Penrose medal 1979—), AAAS; mem. Am. Assn. Petroleum Geologists (research com. 1958-61, lectr. continuing edn. program, 1966-69, Matson Trophy, 1967; continuing edn. com. 1978—), Soc. Econ. Paleontologists and Mineralogists (sec.-treas. 1961-63, v.p. 1966-67, pres. 1969-70, hon. life mem. Permian Basin sect. 1977), Am. Inst. Profl. Geologists, Am. Geol. Inst. (edn. com. 1966-68, ho. bd. of dels. 1970-72), Phi Beta Kappa. Author articles sedimentary carbonates, the Permian Reef complex, stratigraphy and structural geology So. N.M. and W. Tex., porosity of carbonate facies, Calif. rare earth mineral deposits. Home: 7664 Tumbledown Trail Verona WI 53593 Office: U Wis Madison WI 53706

PREBLE, W. JAMES, ins. co. exec.; b. Mpls., Oct. 4, 1926; s. Max W. and Ada (James) P.; B.A., Wooster Coll., 1948; m. Virginia Duvall, Feb. 13, 1949; children—Stephen, Susan. With Acacia Mut. Life Ins. Co., Washington, 1949-52; with Nat. Life Ins. Co., Montpelier, Vt., 1952—, asst. to pres., 1958-64, adminstrv. v.p., 1964-69, sr. v.p. ins. ops., 1969—; dir. Equity Services, Inc., Nat. Life Investment Mgmt. Co., Inc. Co-chmn. Montpelier chpt. A.R.C., 1966, chmn., 1967-69; Washington County chmn. Heart Fund spl. gifts campaign, 1965-66; dir. Washington County United Way, 1976—. Served with USAAF, 1945-46. Fellow Soc. Actuaries; mem. Am. Acad. Actuaries. Home: RFD #1 Montpelier VT 05602 Office: Nat Life Ins Co Nat Life Dr Montpelier VT 05602

PRECKSHOT, GEORGE WILLIAM, educator, chem. engr.; b. Collinsville, Ill., Nov. 18, 1918; s. Mike and Agness (Dietchmann) P.; B.S. in Chem. Engring., U. Ill., 1940; M.S., U. Mich., 1941, Ph.D., 1951; m. Amy Dorothy Enss, July 12, 1942; children—George Garrell, Judith Elise, Nancy Evelyn, Geoffrey William. Asst. metallurgist Am. Zinc Co., summers 1937, 39; oil field chemist Standard Oil Co., summer 1941; research asso. chem. engring. U. Mich., 1946-48; asst. prof. U. Minn., 1948-56, asso. prof., 1956-64; prof. chem. engring., chmn. dept. U. Mo., Columbia, 1964—. Research scientist 3M Co., summers 1959-60; cons. in field. Vice pres., dir. research Atmotron Corp., Mpls., 1963. Served to maj. AUS, 1942-46. Decorated Bronze Star. Recipient research award Fatty Acid Producers and Am. Oil Chemistry Soc., 1956; Standard Oil Co. (Cal.) fellow U. Mich., 1940, 41, Horace H. Rackham grad. fellow, 1942, Am. Chem. Soc. fellow, 1946; Guggenheim research scholar U. Edinburgh (Scotland), 1957-58. Registered profl. engr., Mo., Minn. Mem. Am. Inst. Chem. Engrs., Am. Chem. Soc., Am. Soc. Engring. Edn., A.A.A.S., St. Louis Engrs. Club, A.A.U.P., Sigma Xi (pres. Mo. chpt. 1970-71). Clubs: University (pres. 1970-71 Columbia). Home: 1101 Parkridge Dr Columbia MO 65201

PREDMORE, RICHARD LIONEL, educator; b. Tottenville, N.Y., Dec. 21, 1911; s. Royal Lionel and Jennie (Trowbridge) P.; B.A., Rutgers U., 1933, M.A., 1935; postgrad. U. Madrid (Spain), 1935-36, Columbia, 1936-37, 41-42; D. Modern Langs., Middlebury Coll., 1941; m. Catherine Pennock, Mar. 27, 1937; children—Michael, Richard, James. Teaching fellow Rutgers U., 1933-35, instr. Romance langs., 1937-41, asst. prof., 1941-45, asso. prof., chmn. dept., 1947-50; vis. asst. prof. Romance langs. Duke, 1945-46, prof., 1950—, sec., 1961-62, dean Grad. Sch. Art and Scis., 1962-69, vice provost, 1966-69; chief grad. acad. programs br. Bur. Higher Edn., U.S. Office Edn., 1966-67. Mem. Modern Lang. Assn. Am., Am. Assn. Tchrs. Spanish and Portuguese, Internat. Assn. Hispanists. Author: An Index to Don Quijote, 1938; Topical Spanish Review Grammer, 1954; El Mundo del Quijote, 1958; The World of Don Quixote, 1967; Cervantes, 1973. Editor: Incidents of Travel in Central America, Chiapas and Yucatan, 1949. Contbr. numerous articles and revs. to profl. jours. Home: 7 Glenmore Dr Durham NC 27707

PREECE, SHERMAN JOY, JR., educator; b. Salt Lake City, May 2, 1923; s. Sherman J. and Alice M. (Lawrence) P.; student U. Colo., 1943-44; B.A., U. Utah, 1945, M.S., 1950; postgrad. U. Mont., summer 1949; Ph.D., Wash. State U., 1956. Instr. botany dept. Wash. State U., 1954-56; mem. faculty botany dept. U. Mont., 1956—, asso. prof., 1963-68, prof., 1968—, chmn. dept., 1966—. Active Met. Opera Guild. Served with USNR, 1943-45. NSF grantee, 1961—. Mem. Bot. Soc. Am., Am. Inst. Biol. Scis., A.A.A.S. (exec. com. Pacific div.), Am. Soc. Plant Taxonomists, Internat. Soc. Plant Taxonomy, Am., Brit. iris socs., Northwest Sci. Assn., Mont. Acad. Scis., Audubon Soc., Cal. Bot. Soc., Wilderness Soc. Author: Laboratory Introduction to Biology, 1967; also numerous articles. Home: 3329 Darrell Lane Missoula MT 59801

PREECE, WARREN EVERSLEIGH, editor; b. Norwalk, Conn., Apr. 17, 1921; s. Everett Lowe and Ethel (Miles) P.; B.A. cum laude, Dartmouth Coll., 1943; M.A., Columbia U., 1947; m. Deborah Weeks, July 12, 1947; children—Scott Everett, Mark William, Thayer Evelyn. Instr. English, U. Chgo., 1947-49; reporter Norwalk Hour, 1949-50, writer, copy editor, 1952-56; campaign aide, publicity dir. to U.S. Senator Dodd, 1956-57; exec. sec. bd. editors Ency. Brit., 1957-64, editor, 1964-65, editor-in-chief, 1965-68, gen. editor, 1968-73, editor, 1973-75, vice chmn. bd. editors, 1974-79, bd. editors, 1979—; cons. Center Study Democratic Instns. Ninth ann. C.N. Williamson lectr. Peabody Coll., Nashville. Bd. dirs., sec. Conn. chpt. ARC, 1955-57; bd. dirs. Protestant Youth Homes, Baldwinville, Mass. Served with arty. U.S. Army, 1943-46, 50-52. Mem. AAAS, Soc. for History of Tech., Phi Beta Kappa Assos., Phi Beta Kappa, Sigma Nu. Democrat. Episcopalian. Clubs: Caxton, Arts of Chicago; Quadrangle (Chgo.). Author: (with others) The Technological Order, 1962. Editor: Encyclopaedia Britannica College Preparatory Series, 1964. Home: 10 Main St North Orange RFD 2 Orange MA 01364 Office: Ency Britannica 425 N Michigan Ave Chicago IL 60611

PREER, JOHN RANDOLPH, JR., zoologist, educator; b. Ocala, Fla., Apr. 4, 1918; s. John Randolph and Ruth (Williams) P.; B.S., U. Fla., 1939; Ph.D., Ind. U., 1947; m. Louise Bertha Brandau, Nov. 17, 1941; children—James Randolph, Robert William. Asso. dept. zoology U. Pa., Phila., 1947-48, asst. prof., 1948-51, asso. prof., 1951-58, prof., 1958-68; prof. dept. zoology Ind. U., Bloomington, 1968—, chmn. dept. biology, 1977—. Served with U.S. Army, 1942-45. NRC fellow, 1946-47; NSF fellow, 1967-68; Guggenheim fellow, 1976-77. Mem. Nat. Acad. Scis., AAAS, Genetics Soc. Am., Am. Soc. Protozoologists, Am. Soc. Naturalists. Democrat. Contbr. articles to profl. jours. Home: 1414 Maxwell Ln Bloomington IN 47401 Office: Dept Biology Ind U Bloomington IN 47401

PREFONTAINE, ROBERT RODOLPHE, publishing co. exec.; b. Montreal, Que., Can., Jan. 2, 1929; s. Armand and Yvonne (Henault) P.; M.A., U. Montreal; children by previous marriage—Kateri, Dominique, Genevieve. Editor, pres. Le Sablier Inc., Varennes, Que.; pres. Pubications Graficor Inc., Hourglass Pub. Ltd.; tchr., cons. in field. Author books. Home: 705 Pere Le Jeune Boucherville PQ J4B 5E6 Canada Office: Le Sablier Inc Varennes PQ Canada

PREGERSON, HARRY, U.S. judge; b. Los Angeles, Oct. 13, 1923; s. Abraham and Bessie (Rubin) P.; B.A., UCLA, 1947, LL.B., Boalt Hall, Berkeley, 1950; m. Bernardine Seyma Chapkis, June 28, 1947; children—Dean Douglas, Kathryn Ann. Admitted to Calif. bar, 1951; partner William M. Costley, Van Nuys, 1953-65; judge Los Angeles Municipal Ct., 1965-66, Los Angeles Superior Ct., 1966-67; judge U.S. Dist. Ct. Central Dist. Calif., 1967—; faculty mem., seminar for newly appointed distr. Judges Fed. Jud. Center, Washington, 1970-72; mem. faculty Am. Soc. Pub. Adminstrn., Inst. for Ct. Mgmt., Denver, 1973—. Served to 1st lt. USMCR, 1944-46. Decorated Purple Heart. Mem. Am. (vice-chmn., com. on fed. rules of criminal procedure and evidence sect. of criminal law, 1972—), Los Angeles County, San Fernando Valley bar assns., State Bar Calif., Marines Corps Res. Officers Assn. (pres. San Fernando Valley 1966-78). Office: 312 N Spring St Los Angeles CA 90012

PREIS, ROBERT JOHN, advt. exec.; b. N.Y.C., July 11, 1923; s. John and Elizabeth (Weinspach) P.; B.S. in Econs., Wharton Sch. Fin., U. Pa., 1948; m. Rosemary C. Drucker, Sept. 4, 1948; children—Elizabeth, David, Deborah, Marylou, Roberta. Accountant, Arthur Andersen & Co., N.Y.C., 1948-53, budget dir. CBS-Columbia, N.Y.C., 1953-56; sr. v.p., chief fin. officer Ted Bates & Co., Inc., N.Y.C., 1956—, also dir., mem. exec. com. Served to lt. (j.g.) USNR, 1943-45. C.P.A., N.Y. Mem. Am. Inst. C.P.A.'s, N.Y. Soc. C.P.A.'s, N.Y. Credit and Fin. Mgmt. Assn. (pres. 1978-80), Am. Assn. Advt. Agencies chmn. fiscal control com. 1976-78). Home: 47 Lafayette Pl Greenwich CT 06830 Office: One Astor Plaza New York NY 10036

PREISER, STANLEY, educator; b. N.Y.C., Nov. 25, 1927; s. Sam and Ray (Sklar) P.; B.S., Coll. City N.Y., 1949; M.S., N.Y. U., 1950, Ph.D., 1958; m. Jeannette Schneidman, June 17, 1951; 1 dau., Irene Lynn. Mathematician, Nuclear Devel. Assos., White Plains, N.Y., 1950-60; sr. mathematician United Nuclear Corp., East View, N.Y., 1960-66; asst. prof. math. Poly. Inst. N.Y. (formerly Poly. Inst. Bklyn.), 1965-66, asso. prof., 1966-68, prof., 1969—, now prof. math. and computer sci., former dir. computer sci. div.; lectr. Coll. City N.Y., 1959-65; cons. IBM, 1966-68, Radioptics, 1965-68, Bridgeport Engring. Inst., 1970—. Mem. Assn. for Computing Machinery, Soc. for Indsl. and Applied Math., Am. Math. Soc., Math. Assn. Am., AAAS. Mem. B'nai B'rith, K.P. Home: 5700 Arlington Ave New York NY 10471 Office: 333 Jay St New York NY 11201

PREISKEL, BARBARA SCOTT, lawyer, assn. exec.; b. Washington, July 6, 1924; d. James and B. Beatrix Scott; B.A., Wellesley Coll., 1945; LL.B., Yale U., 1947; m. Robert H. Preiskel, Oct. 28, 1950; children—John S., Richard A. Admitted to D.C. bar, 1948, N.Y. bar, 1948. U.S. Supreme Ct. bar, 1960; law clk. US. Dist. Ct., Boston, 1948-49; asso. firm Poletti, Diamond, Roosevelt, Freidin & Mackay, N.Y.C., 1949-50; asso. firm Dwight, Royall, Harris, Koegel & Caskey, N.Y.C., 1950-54, cons., 1954-59; cons. Ford Found. Fund for the Republic, N.Y.C., 1954; dep. atty. Motion Picture Assn. Am., Inc., N.Y.C., 1959-71, v.p., legis. counsel, 1971-77, sr. v.p., gen. atty., 1977—; dir. Jewel Cos., Inc., Amstar Corp., Textron Inc. Mem. Pres.'s Commn. on Obscenity and Pornography, 1968-70; bd. dirs. Citizens Com. for Children, 1966-72, Child Adoption Service of State Charities Aid Assn., 1961-68, Hillcrest Center for Children, 1958-61, Fedn. Prot. Welfare Agys., 1959-61, 64—, N.Y. Philharmonic Soc., 1971—; bd. dirs. Wiltwyck Sch., 1950—, chm. bd., 1969-78; mem. N.Y.C. Bd. Ethics; successor trustee Yale Corp., 1977—; mem. distbn. com. N.Y. Community Trust, 1978—. Mem. Am. Bar Assn., Bar Assn. City N.Y. (exec. com. 1972-76), ACLU (dir.). Home: 300 West End Ave New York NY 10023 Office: 522 Fifth Ave New York NY 10036

PREISS, DAVID LEE, pub. co. exec.; b. Milw., June 22, 1935; s. Elmer Charles and Dolores Eileen (Creuz) P.; student U. Wis., 1953-57, Art Students League N.Y., 1965, New Sch. Social Research, 1969-71; m. Eleanor Grace Osborne, Feb. 15, 1958 (div.); children—Nora Susan, Jennifer Emily; m. 2d, Jean Marie Nicolle, Jan. 27, 1979. Coll. bur. mgr. Playboy mag., Chgo., 1957-60; editor Collage mag., Chgo., 1960-61, Grune & Stratton, N.Y.C., 1961-63; prodn. editor Motor Boating mag., N.Y.C., 1963-66; prodn. editor Am. Artist mag., N.Y.C., 1966-68, mng. editor, 1969-78; pres. Old Block Books, N.Y.C., 1978—. Pres. Boerum Hill Assn., Bklyn., 1967. Bd. dirs. Bklyn. Heights Youth Center, 1967-69, Found. for the Community of Artists, N.Y.C., 1972-76. Recipient Editorial award Billboard Publs., 1977. Mem. Internat. Soc. Artists, Theta Chi. Home: 61 S Oxford St Brooklyn NY 11217 Office: Old Block Books 240 W 10th St New York NY 10014

PRELL, ARTHUR ELY, educator; b. Los Angeles, Mar. 2, 1924; s. Maurice F. and Bertha (Frischling) P.; B.A., U. Redlands, 1946; B.S., U.S. Mcht. Marine Acad., 1942; M.A., Washington U., St. Louis, 1949; Ph.D., U. Minn., 1955; m. Joyce Merle Prelutsky, June 12, 1949 (dec.); children—Michael Gary, Stacy Beth, Melissa Ann; m. 2d, Gerry Ettlinger, Apr. 2, 1978. Profl. engr. Waterman Co., Mobile, Ala., Matson Nav. Co., San Francisco, 1946-47; instr. U. N.H., 1949-50, asst. prof. sociology and anthropology, 1953-54; asst. prof. sociology Washington U., 1955-57; cons., St. Louis, 1955-60, 72—; exec. v.p., dir. Compumatix, Inc., St. Louis, 1957-58; exec. v.p., dir. French Advt., Inc., St. Louis, 1958-63; mktg. dir. Maritz, Ins., 1962-63; prof. mktg., dir. Bur. Bus. Research, So. Ill. U., 1963-68, chmn., prof. mktg. and mgmt. sci., 1973-78; dean Sch. Bus., Calif. State Coll., Long Beach, 1968-73. Chmn. fin. Greater Egyptian council Boy Scouts Am., 1963-68; bd. dirs., acting dir. mktg. Family Health Program, Long Beach; chmn. bd. dirs. Behavioral Health and Therapy Center. Served to lt. (j.g.) USNR, 1942-45, to lt., 1950-52. Mem. Am. Sociol. Soc. (membership chmn.), Am. Mktg. Assn. (past v.p.), Am. Anthrop. Soc., Am. Statis. Soc., Long Beach C. of C. Mason, Rotarian. Author: (with David J. Luck) Market Strategy, 1968. Contbr. articles profl. jours. Home: 24 Twin Springs Ln St Louis MO 63124 Office: So Ill U Edwardsville IL 62026

PRELOCK, EDWARD PATRICK, motion picture exec.; b. Cleve., Sept. 1, 1934; s. Nicholas and Sophie E. (Sabo) P.; B.A., U. Kans., 1958, J.D., 1963; m. Mary Ann Constant, May 22, 1971. Admitted to Kans. bar, 1964; dir. labor relations Walt Disney Prodns., Burbank, Calif., 1964-75; mem. bd. dirs. Assn. Motion Picture and TV Producers, Hollywood, Calif., 1973—, chief exec. officer, 1975—; pres. Central Casting Corp., 1976; chmn. bd. Contract Services Adminstrn. Trust Fund, 1976—; bd. dirs. Permanent Charities Com. Entertainment Industries, 1976—. Served as 1st lt. Mil. Police U.S. Army, 1958. Mem. Animated Film Producers Assn. (pres. 1971—), Acad. Motion Picture Arts and Scis., Nat. Acad. TV Arts and Scis. Office: 8480 Beverly Blvd Los Angeles CA 90048*

PREMACK, DAVID, psychologist; b. Aberdeen, S.D., Oct. 26, 1925; s. Leonard B. and Sonja (Liese) P.; B.A., U. Minn., 1949, Ph.D., 1955; m. Ann M. James, Oct. 26, 1951; children—Ben, Lisa, Timothy. Research asso. Yerkes Labs. Primate Biology, Orange Park, Fla., 1955; research asso., asst. prof. psychology U. Mo., Columbia, 1956-58, asso. prof., 1959-62, prof., 1963-64; prof. U. Calif., Santa Barbara, 1965-75; vis. prof. Harvard U., 1970-71; prof. U. Pa., 1975—. Served with U.S. Army, 1943-46. Ford Found. teaching intern, 1954; USPHS postdoctoral fellow, 1956-59; Social Sci. Research Council fellow, summer 1963; Center for Advanced Study in Behaviorial Scis. fellow, 1972-73; Guggenheim fellow, 1979-80; NSF grantee, 1961-80; USPHS grantee, 1960-80. Fellow AAAS; mem. Soc. Exptl. Psychologists. Author: Intelligence in Ape and Man, 1976; editorial bd. Jour. Exptl. Psychology: Animal Processes, 1976—, Cognition, 1977—, Jour. Human Evolution, 1977—, Brain and Behavior Sci., 1978—. Office: 3815 Walnut St Philadelphia PA 19174

PREMINGER, EVE M., judge; b. Vienna, Austria, Sept. 20, 1935; d. Ingo and Kate Maria (Musil) P.; student Antioch Coll.; LL.B., Columbia U., 1960; m. Theodore H. Friedman, Dec. 6, 1962; children—Wendy Kate, Sarah Elizabeth. Admitted to N.Y. State bar, 1961, U.S. Supreme Ct. bar, 1967; asso. firm William G. Mulligan, N.Y.C., 1960-62; trial counsel Marshall & Morris, N.Y.C., 1965-70; dir. legal services bur. Correctional Assn. City of N.Y., 1971-76, pres., 1971-76; legal advisor Columbia U., N.Y.C., 1971-73; mem. faculty Columbia U. Law Sch., 1972-76; spl. asst. atty. gen., State of N.Y.-Inquiry on Attica Prosecution, 1975; judge Criminal Ct., City of N.Y., 1976-78; acting justice Supreme Ct. State of N.Y., N.Y.C., 1978—. Mem. Am. Law Inst., Assn. Bar of City of N.Y. (chairperson com. on sentencing), N.Y. County Lawyers Assn., Women in Criminal Justice, Am. Bar Assn. Office: 100 Centre St New York NY 10007

PREMINGER, OTTO, motion picture and stage producer and dir.; b. Vienna, Austria, Dec. 5, 1906; LL.D., U. Vienna; m. Marion Mill; m. 2d, Mary Gardner (div.); m. 3d, Patricia Hope Bryce, Mar. 1960; children—Erik, Victoria and Mark (twins). Came to U.S., 1935. Producer, dir. Max Reinhardt Theatre in der Josefstadt, Vienna; dir. Libel, In Time To Come, Howard Koch play about Woodrow Wilson, Outward Bound, The Moon is Blue, Critic's Choice, Full Circle; dir., starred in Margin For Error (all N.Y.C.); producer, dir. motion pictures, including: Laura, Fallen Angel, Centennial Summer, A Royal Scandal, Forever Amber, Daisy Kenyon, Whirlpool, Where The Sidewalk Ends, The Thirteenth Letter, The Moon Is Blue, Angel Face, River of No Return, Carmen Jones, The Man with the Golden Arm, Saint Joan, Bonjour Tristesse, Porgy and Bess, Anatomy of a Murder, Exodus, Advise and Consent, The Cardinal, In Harm's Way, Bunny Lake is Missing, Hurry Sundown, Skidoo, Tell Me That You Love Me, Junie Moon, Such Good Friends, Rosebud, The Human Factor; appeared in Hollywood on Trial, 1977. Author: Preminger: An Autobiography, 1977. Office: Sigma Prodns Inc 129 E 64th St New York NY 10021

PREMO, DAVID JOHN, mag. editor, educator; b. Troy, N.Y., Dec. 25, 1946; s. John Joseph and Helen Catherine (Scott) P.; B.S. in Biology, Siena Coll., Loudonville, N.Y., 1968; M.S. in Journalism, Boston U., 1972. Dir. advt. and pub. relations Wang Labs., Inc., Tewksbury, Mass., 1969-72; editor Hudson News, 1972; founding editor Clin. Lab. Products, Amherst, N.H., 1972-, also officer, dir.; lectr. journalism grad. program sci. communications Boston U., 1974-; pres., chief exec. officer Horizon Aircraft Corp., Nashua, N.H., 1977—; flight instr. Nashua Aviation & Supply, 1978—; Vol. writer Easter Seal Found., 1972-73. NSF scholar, 1968-69; recipient numerous awards for advt. readership. Mem. Am. Assn. Bus. Press Editors (v.p. New Eng. chpt. 1975, nat. dir. 1976-), Am. Med. Writers Assn. (pres. New Eng. chpt. 1976, nat. dir. 1978—), Pharm. Advt. Club, Biomed. Mktg. Assn. Clubs: Isaac Davis Toastmasters (v.p. 1975), Hampshire Hills Racket. Contbr. articles to profl. jours. Home: Brook Rd Amherst NH 03031 Office: Route 101 A Amherst NH 03031

PREMO, DAVID JOHN, mag. editor, educator; b. Troy, N.Y., Dec. 25, 1946; s. John Joseph and Helen Catherine (Scott) P.; B.S. in Biology, Siena Coll., Loudonville, N.Y., 1968; M.S. in Journalism, Boston U., 1972. Dir. advt. and pub. relations Wang Labs., Inc., Tewksbury, Mass., 1969-72; editor Hudson News, 1972; founding editor Clin. Lab. Products, Amherst, N.H., 1972—, also officer, dir.; lectr. journalism grad. program sci. communications Boston U., 1974—; pres., chief exec. officer Horizon Aircraft Corp., Nashua, N.H., 1977—; flight instr. Nashua Aviation & Supply, 1978—; Vol. writer Easter Seal Found., 1972-73. NSF scholar, 1968-69; recipient numerous awards for advt. readership. Mem. Am. Assn. Bus. Press Editors (v.p. New Eng. chpt. 1975, nat. dir. 1976—), Am. Med. Writers Assn. (pres. New Eng. chpt. 1976, nat. dir. 1978—), Pharm. Advt. Club, Biomed. Mktg. Assn. Clubs: Isaac Davis Toastmasters (v.p. 1975), Hampshire Hills Racket. Contbr. articles to profl. jours. Home: Brook Rd Amherst NH 03031 Office: Route 101 A Amherst NH 03031

PREMONT, JACQUES, librarian; b. Que., Can., Oct. 10, 1926; s. Robert and Simone (Boivin) P.; B.A., Jesuits Coll., Que., 1946; LL.L., Laval U., 1949; M.A., Oxford (Eng.) U., 1960; m. Raymonde Jean, June 1, 1957; 1 dau., Sylvie. Admitted to Que. bar, 1950; with Dept. Justice, Ottawa, 1950-51; practice law, 1951-58; asst. clk. of law Que. Legislature, 1960-62; clk. Que. Exec. Council, 1962-69; chief librarian, dir. Library of Legislature of Province of Que., 1969—. Mem. Standing Com. on Reform of Electoral Dists., 1971—. Mem. Bar Assn. Club: Cercle Universitaire de Quebec. Home: 2308 Chapdelaine Apt 202 Quebec PQ G1V INI Canada Office: Office of Chief Librarian Nat Assembly Parliaments Bldgs Quebec PQ G1A 1A5 Canada

PRENDERGAST, CHARLES J., JR., journalist; b. Providence, Nov. 4, 1918; s. Charles and Bertha (Doll) P.; B.A., Providence Coll., 1941; M.S., Columbia U., 1942; m. Margaret McSoley; 1 dau., Judith Doll; m. 2d, Helen Morgan; children—Charles J. III, William Allen. Reporter St. Louis Post-Dispatch, 1942-51, editorial writer, 1951-71, exec. city editor, 1971-76, mem. editorial bd., 1976—. Served to capt. U.S. Army, 1942-46; officer-in-charge CBI army newspaper Roundup, 1945. Unitarian. Home: 1954 Briargate Ln Kirkwood MO 63122 Office: care Pulitzer Publishing Co 1133 King Dr St Louis MO 63101

PRENGLE, HERMAN WILLIAM, JR., chem. engr.; b. Connellsville, Pa., Nov. 6, 1919; s. Herman William and Irene Florence (Smith) P.; B.S. in Chem. Engring., Carnegie-Mellon U., 1941, M.S., 1947, D.Sc., 1949; m. Ruth Elizabeth Hamilton, Dec. 6, 1941; children—Pixie Prengle Sykes, Karl (dec.), Scott. Jr. research engr. Linde Air Products Co., Tonawanda, N.Y., 1941; from sr. research engr. to sr. technologist Shell Oil Co., Houston, 1949-52; mem. faculty U. Houston, 1952—, prof. chem. engring., 1959—; a founder Prengle, Dakler & Crump, Houston Research Inst., Inc.; cons. engr. Houston Research, Inc., 1952—; advisor U.S. Dept. Energy, U.S. EPA, others; vis. scholar Cambridge (Eng.) U., 1971-72. Mem. Charter Study Com., Friendswood, Tex., 1969-70; chmn. Charter Commn., Friendswood, 1970. Served to lt. col. AUS, 1941-46. Decorated Bronze Star with oak leaf cluster; recipient W.T. Kittinger excellence in teaching award U. Houston, 1971; registered profl. engr., Tex. Fellow Am. Inst. Chemists; mem. Am. Inst. Chem. Engrs., Am. Chem. Soc. London, Am. Chem. Soc., Houston Engring. and Sci. Soc., Sigma Xi, Phi Kappa Phi. Episcopalian (past vestryman and sr. warden). Contbr. articles to profl. jours. Patentee in field. Home: 512 Falling Leaf Ln Friendswood TX 77546 Office: Chem Engring Univ Houston Cullen Coll Engring Houston TX 77004

PRENTICE, DIXON WRIGHT, state justice; b. Sellersburg, Ind., June 3, 1919; s. Walter E. and Maude (Wilson) P.; LL.B., Ind. Law Sch., 1942; m. Phyllis Catherine Ropa, Dec. 20, 1941; children—Penelope (Mrs. Robert L. Rauzi), Peter K., William W. Admitted to Ind. bar, 1942, U.S. Supreme Ct., 1949; practice law, Jeffersonville, Ind., 1946-70; partner Green Tree Assos., Jeffersonville, 1967-70; asso. justice Supreme Ct. Ind., Indpls., 1971—; commr. Nat. Conf. Uniform State Laws, 1979—. Served to lt. comdr. USNR, 1942-46, ret. Mem. Clark County (pres. 1953), Ind. (ho. dels. 1954-66, bd. mgrs. 1964-66), Indpls., Am. bar assns., Am. Judicature Soc., Jeffersonville Jr. C. of C. (pres. 1949). Clubs: Meridian Hills Country, Gyro (Indpls.), Elks. Office: 306 State House Indianapolis IN 46204

PRENTICE, NORMAN MACDONALD, clin. psychologist; b. Yonkers, N.Y., Feb. 25, 1925; s. Lester M. and Islay (Macdonald) P.; A.B. in Psychology, Princeton U., 1949; M.A. in Clin. Psychology, Harvard U., 1952, Ph.D., 1956; m. Marilyn E. Shepherd, Dec. 24, 1953; children—Wendy Elizabeth, Lisa Shepherd. Research fellow child psychiat. unit Mass. Gen. Hosp., Boston, 1953-55; NIMH fellow Judge Baker Guidance Center, Boston, 1955-57; chief adolescent sect. psychologist Children's Hosp., Boston, 1957-58; staff psychologist to coordinator of training Judge Baker Guidance Center; 1958-65; asso. prof. psychology U. Tex., Austin, 1965-68, prof. psychology and ednl. psychology, 1968—; cons. VA, 1966—. Bd. dirs. Austin Community Nursery Sch., 1966-69; trustee Austin-Travis County Mental Health Retardation Center, 1971-73; trustee Art Inst. Boston, 1968—. Served with AUS, 1943-45. Decorated Purple Heart. Fellow Am. Psychol. Assn., Am. Orthopsychiat. Assn. (v.p. 1979—), Soc. for Personality Assessment; mem. Phi Beta Kappa. Contbr. articles to profl. jours. Home: 505 Terrace Mountain Dr Austin TX 78746 Office: Dept Psychology Univ of Tex Austin TX 78712

PRENTICE, TIM, sculptor, architect; b. N.Y.C., Nov. 5, 1930; s. T. Merrill and Theodora (Machado) P.; B.A., Yale U., 1953, M.Arch., 1960; m. Marie Truesdale Bissell, Aug. 23, 1960; children—Nora L., Phoebe A. Gen. partner Prentice & Chan, Ohlhausen, Architects and predecessor, N.Y.C., 1966-74; one-man show Inst. Architecture and Urban Studies, N.Y.C., 1975; group shows: New Britain Mus. Am. Art, 1978, Carlson Art Gallery U. Bridgeport, 1978, S.C.A.F. Gallery, Sharon, Conn., 1978, Indpls. Mus. Art, 1978, Conn. Painting, Drawing and Sculpture Today, 1977; kinetic sculpture represented in permanent collections: Am. Express Co., N.Y.C., AT&T Long Lines, Bedminster, N.Y., Henry St. Settlement, N.Y.C.; adj. prof. archtl. design Columbia U., 1974—. Served to lt., j.g., USNR, 1954-58. Dept. State cultural exchange grantee, 1963-64. Fellow AIA (pres. N.Y. chpt. 1973-74); mem. Nat. Council Archtl. Registration Bds., Mcpl. Arts Soc. N.Y. (pres. 1974-76). Club: Century Assn. Home: 210 Riverside Dr New York NY 10025 Studio: RFD 114 W Cornwall CT 06796

PRENTICE, WILLIAM COURTNEY HAMILTON, coll. pres.; b. E. Aurora, N.Y., Aug. 4, 1915; s. Bryant Hawk and Susan Selden (Dimmock) P.; B.A., Swarthmore Coll., 1937, LL.D., 1968; Rhodes scholar, Univ. Coll., Oxford, Eng., 1937-38; M.A., Harvard, 1941, Ph.D., 1942; LL.D., Stonehill Coll., 1967, Wheaton Coll., 1975; D.Litt., Southeastern Mass. U., 1973; m. Elsie Benton Doty, June 24,

1939; children—Dorothy Doty (Mrs. Richard Ziegler), Susan Selden (Mrs. Richard H. Brainard), William Courtney Hamilton, Benton Doty. Asst. tutor Harvard and Radcliffe colls., 1938-41; vis. prof. Harvard, summer 1951; vis. instr. Coll. William and Mary, 1940; instr. psychology U. Vt., 1941-42; instr. Swarthmore Coll., 1942-43, asst. prof., asso. prof., then prof. psychology, 1947-62, chmn. dept., 1953-56, dean, 1956-62; pres. Wheaton Coll., Norton, Mass., 1962-75; Bryant and Stratton Bus. Inst., 1975—; instr., asst. prof. Johns Hopkins, 1943-47; research psychologist NDRC, Princeton, 1943-44, U. Wis., 1944-45; vis. prof. New Sch. Social Research, 1955. Dir. Attleboro Trust Co. Mem. R.I. and dist. selection coms. Rhodes scholarships, 1965-70; chmn. trustees Coll. Entrance Exam. Bd., 1968-72, mem. commn. tests; sci. adv. panel Research to Prevent Blindness, Inc.; bd. mgrs. Swarthmore Coll., 1979—. Guggenheim fellow, 1952-53. Fellow Am. Psychol. Assn., AAAS; mem. Psychonomic Soc., Eastern Psychol. Assn., United World Federalists, Phi Beta Kappa, Sigma Xi, Phi Kappa Psi. Clubs: Harvard (N.Y.C.), Highland Country, Acoaxet. Contbg. editor Am. Jour. Psychology, 1957-72. Contbr. sci. articles to profl. jours. Home: 646 River Rd Westport MA 02790

PRENTISS, LOUIS WATKINS, JR., army officer; b. Washington, Dec. 25, 1927; s. Louis Watkins and Helen (Bowie) P.; B.S., U.S. Military Acad., 1950; M.S.E., Princeton U., 1956; m. Margaret Ruth Thomas, June 8, 1950; children—Barbara J. Prentiss Balascio, Jacquelyn B. Prentiss Markusic, Martha M. Prentiss Morris. Commd. officer C.E., U.S. Army, 1950, advanced through grades to maj. gen., 1977; dist. engr., Balt. dist., 1972-74; brigade comdr., Germany, 1974-75; div. engr. European div. C.E., Ger., 1975-76; dep. chief of staff engrs. U.S. Army Europe, Ger., 1976-78; div. engr. Ohio River div., Cin., 1978-79; comdg. gen. U.S. Army Tng. Center Engrs., Fort Leonard Wood, Mo., 1979—. Decorated Bronze Star, Legion of Merit, air medal and others. Mem. ASCE, Nat. Soc. Profl. Engrs., Soc. Am. Mil. Engrs. Home: 1 Mackenzie Dr Fort Leonard Wood MO 65473 Office: Office of Comdg Gen USATC Engr Fort Leonard Wood MO 65473

PRESCHLACK, JOHN EDWARD, office equipment mfg. co. exec.; b. N.Y.C., May 30, 1933; s. William and Anna M. (Hrubesch) P.; B.S.E.E., M.I.T., 1954; M.B.A., Harvard U., 1958; m. Lynn A. Stanley, Dec. 29, 1962; children—John Edward, James S., David C. Partner, McKinsey & Co., Inc., N.Y.C., London, Dusseldorf, W. Ger., 1958-73; pres. ITEK Graphic Products Co., Lexington, Mass., 1973-77; pres., chief exec. officer Gen. Binding Corp., Northbrook, Ill., 1977—; dir. House of Vision, Inc., Chgo. Trustee, Chgo. Hort. Soc., 1978—. Served to 1st lt. USAF, 1954-56. Decorated Air Force Commendation medal; recipient Corp. Leadership award M.I.T., 1978. Mem. Bus. Record Mfrs. Assn. (dir.). Republican. Roman Catholic. Clubs: Onwentsia, Winter of Lake Forest (Ill.). Office: One GBC Plaza Northbrook IL 60062. *Focus on what's right, not who's right; be honest and candid in dealing with others; don't get hung up on who gets credit for what you've done; select and reward outstanding people.*

PRESCOTT, DAVID MARSHALL, molecular biologist; b. Clearwater, Fla., Aug. 3, 1926; s. Clifford Raymond and Lillian Florence (Moore) P.; B.A., Conn. Wesleyan U., 1950; Ph.D. in Zoology, U. Calif. at Berkeley, 1954; m. Gayle Edna Demery, June 20, 1969; children—Lavonne Marie, Jason David, Ryan Michael, Ingrid, Christopher, Peter, Trine. Research asso., fellow Rask-orsted Found., U. Copenhagen, 1951-52; asst. prof. dept. anatomy Sch. Medicine, U. Calif. at Los Angeles, 1955-59; biologist Oak Ridge Nat. Lab., 1959-63; chmn., prof. dept. anatomy U. Colo. Med. Sch., Denver, 1963-66, prof. Inst. Developmental Biology, Boulder, 1966-68, prof. dept. molecular, cellular and developmental biology, Boulder, 1968—; lectr. in field.; exchange scientist to USSR, 1969. Lectr. local unit Am. Cancer Soc., 1970—. Served in U.S. Mcht. Marine, 1944-47. Recipient Humboldt award Alexander von Humboldt Found., W. Ger., 1979-80. Fellow Am. Acad. Arts and Scis.; mem. Nat. Acad. Scis., Am. Soc. Cell Biology. Author: Cancer: The Misguided Cell, 1972; Reproduction of Eukaryotic Cells, 1976; editor: Methods in Cell Biology, 1964—; co-editor: Advances in Cell Biology, vol. 1, 1970, vol. 2, 1971; Cell Biology: A Comprehensive Treatise, vol. 1, 1978, vol. 2, 1979. Home: Magnolia Star Route Nederland CO 80466 Office: Dept Molecular Cellular and Developmental Biology U Colo Boulder CO 80309

PRESCOTT, JOHN HERNAGE, marine biologist, aquarium adminstr.; b. Corona, Calif., Mar. 16, 1935; s. Arthur J. and Henrietta I. (Hernage) P.; A.B., U. Calif., Los Angeles, 1957, postgrad., 1959; postgrad. U. So. Calif., 1961; m. Jacquelyn L. Prescott, Oct. 22, 1954; children—Craig C., Blane R. Curator, Marineland of the Pacific, Palos Verdes Peninsula, Calif., 1957-71, v.p., mgr., dir., 1971; v.p., exec. dir. New Eng. Aquarium, Boston, 1972—; chmn. com. sci. advisers Marine Mammal Commn.; cons. environ. ichthyology, whales and dolphins. Corporator Provident Instn. for Savs., Woods Hole Oceanographic Instn.; mem. advisory bd. underwater parks State of Calif., 1968-72; sci. advisory bd. Moorpark Coll., Am. Cetacean Soc., Am. Littoral Soc., Ocean Research and Edn. Soc. Bd. dirs. Greater Boston Conv. and Tourist Bur., Boston Harbor Assn., Met. Cultural Internat. Union Dirs. Zool. Gardens, Alliance Boston. Fellow Am. Assn. Zool. Parks and Aquariums; mem. Internat. Assn. Aquatic Animal Medicine, Am. Soc. Icthyologists and Herpetologists, Am. Fisheries Soc., Am. Inst. Fishery Research Biologists, Am. Assn. Mammalogists. Clubs: Explorers (N.Y.C.); Danvers Fish and Game. Author: Aquarium Fishes of the World, 1976. Office: New Eng Aquarium Central Wharf Boston MA 02110

PRESCOTT, JOHN MACK, univ. adminstr., biochemist; b. San Marcos, Tex., Jan. 22, 1921; s. John Mack and Maude (Raborn) P.; B.S. in Chemistry, S.W. Tex. State Coll., 1941; M.S. in Biochemistry and Nutrition, Tex. A. and M. U., 1949; Ph.D. in Biochemistry U. Wis., 1952; m. Kathryn Ann Kelly, June 8, 1946; children—Stephen Michael, Donald Wyatt. Lab. asst. Dow Chem. Co., Freeport, Tex., 1942-43; faculty Tex. A. and M. U., College Station, 1946-49, 52—, prof. biochemistry, 1959-69, dean Coll. Sci., 1970-77, v.p. for acad. affairs, 1977—; research asst. U. Wis., Madison, 1949-51, U. Tex., Austin, 1951-52; cons. to indsl. orgns.; dir. Brazos Savs. Assn. of Tex. Mem. Tex. Bd. Examiners in Basic Scis., 1974-79. Served to lt. USAAF, 1943-46; lt. col. USAF Res. 1946-68. Mem. Am. Chem. Soc., Am. Soc. Biol. Chemists, Am. Inst. Nutrition, Soc. for Exptl. Biology and Medicine, Sigma Xi, Phi Kappa Phi, Phi Lambda Upsilon. Contbr. articles profl. jours. Home: 31 Forest Dr College Station TX 77840 Office: Vice Pres for Acad Affairs Tex A & M U College Station TX 77843

PRESCOTT, KENNETH WADE, educator; b. Jackson, Mich., Aug. 9, 1920; s. Edward E. and Harriett Mae (McInerney) P.; B.S., Western Mich. Coll. Edn., 1942; M.A., U. Mich., 1948, Ph.D., 1950; Ed.M., U. Del., 1954; m. Emma-Stina Johnsson, Jan. 13, 1947; children—Kristina Lisen, Gertrude Mae. Dir. Kansas City Mus., 1954-58; mng. dir. Acad. Natural Scis., Phila., 1958-63; dir. State Mus. N.J., 1963-71; program officer, div. humanities and arts Ford Found., 1971-74; chmn. dept. art U. Tex., Austin, 1974—; mus. cons. Harry S. Truman Library, 1958, Lee Chapel Mus., Washington and Lee U., 1963; cons. Ford Found., Kennedy Galleries, N.Y.C., Jewish Mus., N.Y.C.; adj. prof. dept. edn. Temple U. Sch. Grad. Studies, Phila., 1959-70; mem. Cornell Ornithology Lab., 1966—; juror regional and nat. art exhbns. Exec. com. Trenton Symphony, 1964-65; pres. Kansas City Camp Fire Girls, 1956-59, regional exec. com., 1957, 58; bd. dirs. Urban League, Kansas City, 1957-58, Ben Shahn Found., 1970-71, Dermatology Found., 1974—; adv. com. continuing adult edn. U. Kansas City, 1956-58; chmn. Jr. Red Cross, So. Pa. chpt., 1959-62; mem. White House Conf. on Children and Youth, 1970-71, adv. com. U. Pa. Dental Sch., 1972-74, Sec. of Navy's Adv. Bd. on Edn. and Tng., 1972-75. Served with USNR, 1942-46, 51-54; comdg. officer motor torpedo boats SW Pacific; exec. officer U.S.S. Jamestown; instr. Naval Res. Officer Candidate Sch.; asst. officer-in-charge Naval Prep. Sch.; edn., tng. officer Service Sch., Bainbridge, Md.; capt. ret. Mem. Mid-West Museums Conf. (mem. council 1955-56, pres. 1957-58), AAAS (chmn. Jr. Scientists Assembly 1962), Sci. Pioneers (1st v.p. 1957, 58, 59), Am. Acad. Dermatology (council 1972—), Westerners, Coll. Art Assn. (life), C. of C., Nat. Council Art Adminstrs. (dir. 1977—), Coll. Art Assn. (life), Tex. Assn. Schs. Art (dir. 1977-79), Friends of Art, Greater Kansas City Art Assns., Am. Ornithol. Union, Wilson Ornithol. Club, N.E., Eastern, Inland bird banding assns., Art Alliance (Phila.), N.J. Audubon Soc., Navy League, Sigma Xi, Phi Sigma. Club: Scandinavian (Kansas City). Author: Life History of the Scarlet Tanager, 1965; co-author: Domjan the Woodcutter, 1966; The Complete Graphic Works of Ben Shahn, 1973; also intros. for art exhbn. catalogues, numerous articles on art, orinthology and museology. Editorial bd. Am. Art Jour., 1976—. Home: 2526 Tanglewood Trail Austin TX 78703 Office: Dept Art U Tex 23d and San Jacinto Austin TX 78712

PRESCOTT, NORM, film producer; b. Boston, Jan. 31, 1927; s. Edward and Edith (Riskin) Pransky; student Emerson Coll., 1946-47; m. Elaine Barbara Shumrack, Oct. 6, 1951; children—Jeffrey David, Michael Robert. Radio performer, producer and dir. various stas., Boston and N.Y.C., 1947-59; v.p. in charge post production and music Embassy Pictures, N.Y.C., 1959-60; pres. Norm Prescott Productions, Boston, 1960-65; chmn. bd., exec. producer Filmation Studios, Hollywood, Calif., 1965—, producer children's motion pictures and TV films; numerous network TV series include Star Trek, Fat Albert, Jason of Star Command, Tarzan and the Super Seven. Recipient Emmy award for animated Star Trek TV series; Ann. award for Fat Albert TV series Ohio State U. Mem. Acad. Motion Picture Arts, Scis., Screen Actors Guild, Hollywood Radio, TV Soc., Screen Cartoonist Guild, Nat. Acad. TV Arts, Scis. Author feature film: Journey Back to Oz, 1962.*

PRESCOTT, ORVILLE, author; b. Cleve., Sept. 8, 1906; s. Orville Wilbur and Eda (Sherwin) P.; B.A., Williams Coll., 1930, LL.D., 1963; m. Lilias Ward-Smith, Nov. 1, 1933; children—Peter Sherwin, Jennifer (Mrs. Edward C. McLean, Jr.). Mng. editor, sports, art, and book columnist Cleve. Town Tidings, 1931-33; mem. editorial staff Newsweek mag., 1933-36; asso. editor, lit. editor Cue mag., 1936-47; co-editor N.Y. Times Books of the Times, 1942-66; lectr. lit. subjects, 1940-54; fiction reviewer Yale Rev., 1943-49. Mem. Authors League, P.E.N., Soc. of Am. Historians, Royal Soc. of the Arts. Clubs: Century Assn. (N.Y.C.); Country (New Canaan); Yeamans Hall (North Charleston). Author: In My Opinion: An Inquiry into the Contemporary Novel, 1952; The Five-Dollar Gold Piece: The Development of a Point of View, 1956; Mid-Century: An Anthology of Distinguished Contemporary American Short Stories, 1958; The Undying Past, 1961; A Father Reads To His Children, 1965; Princes of the Renaissance, 1969; History as Literature, 1971; Lords of Italy: Portraits from the Middle Ages, 1972. Home: 13 Hatfield Mews New Canaan CT 06840

PRESCOTT, PETER SHERWIN, writer; b. N.Y.C., July 15, 1935; s. Orville Wilbur, Jr. and Lilias (Ward-Smith) P.; A.B. magna cum laude, Harvard, 1957; m. Anne Courthope Kirsopp Lake, June 22, 1957; children—David Sherwin, Antonia Courthope. Editor, E.P. Dutton Co., N.Y.C., 1958-67; lit. editor, syndicated columnist Women's Wear Daily, N.Y.C., 1964-68; mem. faculty Pubs. Sch. for Writers, N.Y.C., 1965-66; lit. editor, columnist Look mag., 1968-71; book critic Newsweek mag., N.Y.C., 1971—, sr. writer, 1978—; lectr. U.S. State Dept., 1978; asso. Grad. Sch. Journalism, Columbia U., 1979—. Mem. Democratic Town Com., New Canaan, 1969-72; constable Town of New Canaan, 1969-73. Pres. Authors Guild Found. Served with USAR, 1958-64. Recipient George Polk award criticism, 1978. Guggenheim fellow, 1977. Mem. P.E.N. Am. Center (exec. bd. 1974-76), Authors League Am. (exec. bd. 1974-76), Authors Guild (exec. bd.), Nat. Book Critics Circle (adv. bd. 1974-76), Phi Beta Kappa. Clubs: Century Assn., Coffee House (N.Y.C.); Country (New Canaan). Author: A World of Our Own: Notes on Life and Learning in a Boys' Preparatory School, 1970; Soundings: Encounters with Contemporary Books, 1972; A Darkening Green: Notes from the Silent Generation, 1974. Contbr. articles and revs. to newspapers and mags. Home and Office: 81 Benedict Hill Rd New Canaan CT 06840

PRESCOTT, ROBERT WILLIAM, airline exec.; b. Ft. Worth, May 5, 1913; s. George Washington and Una Victoria (Stewart) P.; A.A., Compton (Cal.) Jr. Coll., 1934-36; law student Loyola U., Los Angeles, 1937-39; m. Anne- Marie Bennstrom, July 16, 1962; children (by previous marriage)—French, Kirsten. With Goodyear Tire & Rubber Co., Los Angeles, 1934-36, Challenge Cream & Butter Co., 1937-39; pilot for Transcontinental & Western Airlines, 1942-43; capt. for China Nat. Aviation Corp., transporting supplies over The Hump, 1943-44; engaged in purchasing planes and supplies for a Mexican airline, 1944-45; founder, 1945, since pres., dir. Flying Tiger Line, Inc. (formerly Nat. Skyway Freight Corp.), Los Angeles. Served as ensign, instr., U.S. Naval Flying Sch., Pensacola, Fla., 1939-41; mem. Am. Vol. Group (Flying Tigers), 1941-42; flight leader participating in five maj. campaigns and shooting down 6 Japanese planes, 1942. Mem. Flying Tigers A.V.G. Group Air Transp. Assn. (dir.). Home: 4356 Clybourn St Burbank CA 91505 Office: Los Angeles Internat Airport Los Angeles CA 90009

PRESCOTT, WILLIAM GOODWIN, lawyer; b. Colorado Springs, Colo., Sept. 24, 1906; s. William Chester and Pearl Eva (Cummings) P.; student Westminster Coll. and Law Sch. (later merged with U. Denver), 1926-27, LL.B., 1930; m. Frances Jeanne Dutton, Mar. 2, 1931 (dec. May 1974); m. 2d, Mona B. Henne, Aug. 31, 1974 (dec. June 1976); m. 3d, Bonnie Helen Ellis, Jan. 1, 1977 (dec. Dec. 1977); m. 4th, Royallene L. Kanan, Feb. 10, 1978. With Gt. Western Sugar Co., Denver, 1925, Nat. Cash Register Co., Denver, 1926; sales record clk. E.I. duPont de Nemours & Co., Inc., Denver, 1926-27; clk. Justice Charles C. Butler, Supreme Ct. of Colo., 1927-31; admitted to Colo. bar, 1930; atty. Denver & Rio Grande Western R.R. Co., Denver, 1931-55, asst. gen. atty., 1955-56, corp. sec., 1956-71, dir., 1961; sec., treas., dir. Northwestern Terminal R.R. Co., 1956-69; dir. Rio Grande Land Co., 1956-71; practice law, 1971—. Mem. Colo., Denver bar assns., Am. Soc. Corp. Secs. (asso.). Mason. Home and Office: 2610 Tennyson St Denver CO 80212

PRESCOTT, WILLIAM THEODORE, mag. publisher; b. Lacona, N.Y., Mar. 10, 1915; s. Maurice Sheldon and Flora Elizabeth (Stone) P.; B.S., Cornell U., 1938; m. Anita Mizener, Dec. 7, 1977; children—Peter, John, Martha. Mem. editorial staff Holstein-Friesian World, Lacona, N.Y., 1938—, advt. mgr., 1954-64, mng. editor, 1964-70, pub., 1970—; dir. 1st Nat. Bank, Lacona, 1955-64; adv. bd. Mchts. Nat. Bank, Syracuse, 1964—. Chmn. United Fund Drive, 1953-54; bd. dirs. Oswego County Health Planning Council, 1972—; pres. bd. trustees No. Oswego County Health Bldg., 1968-77; mem. coll. council State U. Coll. at Oswego, 1966-73; trustee Eastern States Expn., 1965—. Mem. Printing Industry Assn., Nat. Composition Assn., Am. Holstein-Friesian Assn., N.Y. Holstein-Friesian Assn., Pulaski C. of C., Sandy Creek Service Club (pres. 1950-52), Delta Upsilon. Republican. Methodist. Club: Elms Golf. Author: (with Allen N. Crissey, J.W. Bartlett) Selling Purebreds for Profit, 1958. Home: 8103 Harwood Dr Sandy Creek NY 13145 Office: Holstein-Friesian World Lacona NY 13063

PRESENT, ARTHUR JEROME, physician, educator; b. Rochester, N.Y., May 24, 1905; s. Morris and Sarah (Straws) P.; B.A., Yale U., 1927, M.D., 1932; Sc.D. in Medicine, Columbia U., 1937; m. Barbara Kennard, Oct. 7, 1961. Surg. intern Duke Hosp., Durham, N.C., 1932-33; med. intern Strong Meml. Hosp., Rochester, 1933-34; resident radiology Presbyn. Hosp., N.Y.C., 1934-37; asso. radiologist Scripps Meml. Hosp. and Scripps Clinic, La Jolla, Calif., 1937-40; pvt. practice radiology, Tucson, 1946-70; asso. prof. radiology Coll. Medicine, U. Ariz., 1970-71, prof., 1971—; cons. Tuscon Med. Center, St. Mary's Hosp., St. Joseph's Hosp., VA Hosp. Tucson, USAF Hosp. Tucson. Vice pres. Tucson Festival Soc., 1958-61, pres., 1961-62; pres. Ariz. Corral Theatre, 1958-63. Served to lt. col. U.S. Army, 1940-46. Fellow Am. Coll. Radiology (chmn. bd. chancellors 1960-61, pres. 1962-63, Gold medal 1975)); mem. Am., Ariz. med. assns., Radiol. Soc. N.A., Am. Roentgen Ray Soc., AAAS, Am. Cancer Soc. (pres. Ariz., 1958-59; nat. bd. dirs., exec. com. 1963-67), Sigma Xi. Club: Old Pueblo (Tucson). Home: 6322 N Calle del Caballo Tucson AZ 85718

PRESENT, RICHARD DAVID, educator; physicist; b. N.Y.C., Feb. 5, 1913; s. David and Blanche (Wertheimer) P.; B.S., Coll. City N.Y., 1931; M.A., Harvard, 1932, Ph.D., 1935; m. Thelma Cohen, July 31, 1943; children—Irene Naomi, Constance Sarah. Instr. physics Purdue U., Lafayette, Ind., 1935-40; research asso. Harvard, 1940-41; asst. prof. physics N.Y.U., 1941-43; mem. div. war research Manhattan Project, Columbia, 1943-46; asso. prof. physics U. Tenn., 1946-48, prof. physics 1948-69, Distinguished prof., 1969—. Cons. Clinton Nat. Labs., 1946-48; NSF vis. scientist, 1958-71. Fellow Inst. Internat. Edn., Paris, 1937-38. Fellow Am. Phys. Soc. (chmn. S.E. sect. 1964-65); mem. Am. Assn. U. Profs., Phi Beta Kappa, Sigma Xi. Author: Kinetic Theory of Gases, 1958. Research nuclear theory, molecular structure, statis. mechanics. Home: 421 Circle Hill Dr Knoxville TN 37919

PRESENT, ROBERT TUCKER, banker; b. N.Y.C., Feb. 1, 1927; s. Jack and Katherine (Tucker) P.; student Ariz. State Coll., 1948-49; B.S. with distinction, Ind. U., 1951; m. Mary Jean Oren, Apr. 30, 1949; children—Richard Criag, Randall Clay. With 1st Nat. Bank, Dallas, 1952-70, sr. v.p., 1966-70; pres. Capital Nat. Bank, Austin, Tex., 1970-73, chmn. bd., chief exec. officer, since 1973—; chmn. sr. bank mgmt. case Southwestern Grad. Sch. Banking, 1975—; chmn. Tex. Bankers Conf., 1976. Trustee, Baylor Coll. Dentistry, Dallas, St. David's Hosp., Austin; mem. adv. bd. Salvation Army; area fund raising chmn. United Negro Coll. Fund; bd. dirs., treas. Austin Aqua Festival, 1971; bd. dirs. United Way; vice chmn. Tex. Research League. Served with U.S. Army, 1945. Mem. Am. Inst. Banking, Robert Morris Assos., Austin C. of C. (dir. 1974). Lutheran. Clubs: Headliners, Tarry House, Citadel, Austin. Home: 2900 Willowbridge Circle Austin TX 78703 Office: PO Box 550 Austin TX 78789

PRESLEY, BOBBY WAYNE, air force officer; b. Fort Smith, Ark., Feb. 5, 1931; s. Edwin West and Ada Mae P.; student U. Ark., 1949-52; B.S., U. Colo., 1962, M.S. in Fin. Mgmt., 1966 m. Audrey JoAnn Smith, Sept. 30, 1956; children—Robert, Rand, Robin. Commd. 2d lt. U.S. Air Force, 1952, advanced through grades to maj. gen., 1977; comptroller USAF Europe, 1972-74; dep. dir. budget and asst. comptroller Hdqrs. U.S. Air Force, 1974-77; comdr. Army and Air Force Exchange Service, Dallas, 1977—. Decorated D.F.C., Air medal. Mem. Am. Soc. Mil. Comptrollers, Oak Cliff C. of C. (dir.). Democrat. Presbyterian. Club: Masons. Office: 400 S Zang Dallas TX 75208

PRESNICK, WALTER JOHN, editor, photographer; b. N.Y.C., Dec. 22, 1942; s. Walter and Jean (Mrsnik) P.; A.A. cum laude, Los Angeles Valley Coll., 1969. Eastern editor Business Automation; editor Innovation Newsletter; asso. editor Industrial Distribution; chief editor Industrial Bulletin, N.Y.C., 1974—. Mem. Am. Bus. Press, N.Y. Bus. Press Editors, Am. Soc. Bus. Press Editors. Home: 271 Cedarhurst Ave Cedarhurst NY 11516 Office: 205 E 42d St New York City NY 10017. *Let's hear it for the individual who believes in himself. The present-day temptation is to have everyone conform to the common denominator, for everyone to yield their creativity for the purpose of uniformity. Allow the human spirit to grow and explore, to seek out all that it needs to be at peace with itself. We alone are the instruments of our happiness.*

PRESS, CHARLES, educator; b. St. Louis, Sept. 12, 1922; s. Otto Ernst and Laura (Irion) P.; student Elmhurst (Ill.) Coll.; B. Journalism, U. Mo., 1948, M.A., U. Minn., 1951, Ph.D., U. Minn., 1953; m. Nancy Miller, June 10, 1950; children—Edward Paul, William David, Thomas Leigh, Laura Mary. Faculty, N.D. Agrl. Coll., 1954-56; dir. Grand Rapids Area Study, 1956-57; with Bur. Govt., U. Wis., 1957-58; faculty Mich. State U., East Lansing, 1958—, prof. polit. sci., 1964—, chmn. dept., 1966-73. Cons. Mich. Constl. Conv., 1962-63. Supr., Ingham County, 1966-68; sec. Ingham County Bd. Health, 1966-72; chmn. or mem. East Lansing Bd. Rev., 1966—. Bd. dirs. Urban League, 1971-73. Served with AUS, 1943-45. Mem. Am., Midwest (pres. 1974-75), So. polit. sci. assns., Mich. Conf. Polit. Scientists (pres. 1972-73), Nat. Municipal League. Author: Main Street Politics, 1962; (with C. Adrian) The American Government Process, 1965: (with C. Adrian) Governing Urban America, 1968, 5th edit., 1977; (with Charles Adrian) American Politics Reappraised, 1974; (with Kenneth Ver Burg) States and Communities in a Federal System, 1979. Home: 987 Lantern Hill Dr East Lansing MI 48823 Office: 315 S Kedzie Hall Mich State Univ East Lansing MI 48824

PRESS, EDWARD, physician; b. N.Y.C., May 4, 1913; s. Louis and Anna (Karpas) P.; B.A., Ohio U., 1934; M.D., N.Y. U., 1937; M.P.H., Harvard U., 1947; m. Ruth Scheffer, July 8, 1951; children—Stephen, Phyllis. Intern, Beth Israel Hosp., N.Y.C., 1938-40; resident Lincoln Hosp., Bronx, N.Y., 1940; asst. dir. maternal and child health div. W.Va. Health Dept., 1941-42; pediatric cons. Mich. Health Dept., 1946; regional med. dir. U.S. Children's Bur., Chgo., 1947-50; asso. dir. div. services crippled children U. Ill., 1950-55; field dir. Am. Public Health Assn., N.Y.C., 1955-59; dir. Dept. Public Health, Evanston, Ill., 1959-64; med. asst. to dir. Ill. Dept. Public Health, 1964-67; state health officer Oreg. Health Div., Portland, 1967-79; public health cons., 1979—; asst. prof. preventive medicine U. Ill., 1950-55; asst. prof. pediatrics Northwestern U., 1964-67; clin. prof. pub. health, preventive medicine and pediatrics Med. Sch., U. Oreg., 1967—; organizer Poison Control Center, Chgo., 1953; mem. Poison Control Com., N.Y.C., 1955-57, Nassau County, N.Y., 1957-59. Trustee Underwriters' Labs., Inc., 1969-79. Served to maj. USAAF, 1942-46. Recipient Clifford G. Grulee award Am. Acad. Pediatrics, 1961; recognition award Am. Assn. Poison Control Centers, 1975.

Diplomate Am. Bd. Pediatrics, Am. Bd. Preventive Medicine. Mem. AMA, Am. Public Health Assn., Nat. Soc. Prevention of Blindness, Am. Assn. Public Health Physicians (pres. 1971-72), Conf. State and Provincial Health Authorities N.Am. (pres. 1971-72), Assn. State and Territorial Health Officers (mem. exec. com. 1972-75). Clubs: Rotary, Portland City, Multnomah Athletic (Portland). Mem. editorial bd. Pediatric News, 1966—, Family Practice News, 1972—; contbr. articles to profl. jours. Home: 2211 SW 1st Ave Apt 905 Portland OR 97201 Office: 1400 SW 5th Ave PO Box 231 Portland OR 97201

PRESS, FRANK, educator, geophysicist; b. Bklyn., Dec. 4, 1924; s. Solomon and Dora (Steinholz) P.; B.S., Coll. City N.Y., 1944, LL.D., 1972; M.A., Columbia U., 1946, Ph.D., 1949; D.Sc., Notre Dame U., 1973; m. Billie Kallick, June 9, 1946; children—William Henry, Paula Evelyn. Research asso. Columbia, 1946-49, instr. geology, 1949-51, asst. prof. geology, 1951-52, asso. prof., 1952-55; prof. geophysics Cal. Inst. Tech., 1955-65, dir. seismol. lab., 1957-65; prof. geophysics, chmn. dept. earth and planetary scis. Mass. Inst. Tech., 1965-77; sci. advisor to Pres., dir. Office Sci. and Tech. Policy, Washington, 1977—; cons. USAF, 1958, U.S. Geol. Survey, 1957, USN, 1957—, Office Spl. Asst. for Sci. and Tech., 1961-64, Office Sci. and Tech., 1964—, ACDA, 1961-68, AID, 1961-64. Dir. United Electro Dynamics. Expert, UNESCO Tech. Assistance Adminstrn., 1953; seismology and glaciology panel U.S. nat. com. IGY, 1955; chmn. U.S. del. Nuclear Test Ban Conf., 1960; mem. Pres.'s Sci. Adv. Com. and Internat. Geophysics Com., 1961-64; mem. Lunar and Planetary Mission Bd., 1965-70; chmn. adv. bd. Nat. Center Earthquake Research, 1966—; mem. Nat. Sci. Bd., 1970—. Recipient Columbia medal for excellence, 1960, pub. service award U.S. Dept. Interior, 1972, gold medal Royal Astron. Soc., 1972, pub. service medal NASA, 1973. Mem. Am. Acad. Arts and Scis., Geol. Soc. Am. (councilor), Am. Geophys. Union (pres. 1973), Soc. Exploration Geophysicists, Seismol. Soc. Am. (pres. 1963), AAUP, Nat. Acad. Scis. (councilor), Phi Beta Kappa. Author: (with M. Ewing, W.S. Jardetzky) Propagation of Elastic Waves in Layered Media, 1956; (with R. Siever) Earth, 1974. Co-editor: Physics and Chemistry of the Earth, 1957—. Home: 3315 Wisconsin Ave NW Apt 605 Washington DC 20016 Office: Exec Office Bldg Washington DC 20500

PRESSLER, HERMAN PAUL, lawyer; b. Austin, Tex., Dec. 12, 1902; s. Herman P. and Veannis (Maddox) P.; student Va. Mil. Inst, 1919-20; LLB., U. Tex. at Austin, 1925; student advanced mgmt. program, Harvard, 1951; m. Elsie W. Townes, Nov. 20, 1928; children—Herman Paul III, Townes Garrett. Admitted to Tex. bar, 1925; gen. practice, Houston, 1925-33, 68—; mem. law dept. Humble Oil and Refining Co., Houston, 1933-55, dir., 1955-59, v.p., mem. bd. mgmt. Humble div., 1959-60, v.p. pub. relations, 1960-67; dir. Humble Pipe Line Co., 1948-55. Chmn. Houston and Harris County chpt. A.R.C., 1952-54; chmn. bd. trustees Tex. Childrens Hosp.; pres. Tex. Med. Center; adv. bd. Salvation Army; mem. Houston Com. on fgn. Relations. Mem. Tex., Miss., Houston (pres. 1950-51) bar assns., Philos. Soc. Tex., Chi Phi, Phi Delta Phi. Democrat. Baptist. Clubs: Houston, Houston Country, Bayou (Houston); Eagle Lake Rod and Gun. Home: 2133 Pine Valley Dr Houston TX 77019 Office: 603 San Jacinto Bldg Houston TX 77002

PRESSLER, LARRY, U.S. Senator; b. Humboldt, S.D., Mar. 29, 1942; s. Antone Lewis and Loretta Geneive (Claussen) P.; B.A., U. S.D., 1964; diploma (Rhodes scholar) Oxford (Eng.) U., 1966; M.A., Kennedy Sch. Govt., Harvard U., 1971, J.D., 1971. Atty., Office of Legal Adviser, State Dept., 1971-74; mem. 94th-95th Congresses from 1st S.D. Dist.; mem. U.S. Senate from S.D., 1979—, mem. Budget Com., Commerce, Sci. and Transp. Com., Environ. and Public Works Com., Select Com. on Small Bus.; mem. Republican Nat. Senatorial Campaign Com., Nat. Transp. Policy Study Commn.; summer legal aide firm Dana, Moore, Golden & Rasmussen, Sioux Falls, S.D. All-Am. del. 4-H agrl. fair, Cairo, 1961. Aide S.D. Rep. Central Com., 1962; bd. visitors U.S. Mcht. Marine Acad. Served to 1st lt. AUS, 1966-68; Vietnam. Recipient Nat. 4-H Citizenship award, 1962, Report to the Pres. 4-H award, 1962. Mem. Am. Assn. Rhodes Scholars, VFW, Am. Bar Assn., Am. Legion, Audubon Soc., S.D. Hist. Soc., Phi Beta Kappa. Club: Lions. Home: 700 New Hampshire Ave NW Washington DC 20037 Office: US Senate Washington DC 20510

PRESSLER, SYLVIA BRODSKY, judge; b. N.Y.C., Apr. 10, 1934; d. Norman and Bella (Gofsaof) Brodsky; student Queens Coll., 1952-54; B.A., Boston U., 1955; J.D. with high honors, Rutgers U., 1959; m. David A. Pressler, Aug. 22, 1954; children—Jessica Anne, Noah Stephen. Partner firm Okin Pressler & Shapiro, Ft. Lee, N.J., 1960-73; city atty. City of Englewood (N.J.), 1969-73; hearing examiner N.J. Div. Civil Rights, 1964-73; 1st asst. county counsel Bergen County (N.J.), 1965-66; judge County Ct., 1973-76; judge law div. Superior Ct. N.J., 1976-77, judge appellate div., 1977—. Committeewoman Democratic Party, vice chmn. Bergen County. Mem. Am. Law Inst., N.J. State Bar Assn., Bergen County Bar Assn., ACLU (past dir. N.J.), LWV. Jewish. Author: New Jersey Court Rules, Annotated; mem. editorial bd. N.J. Law Jour.*

PRESSLY, THOMAS JAMES, educator; b. Troy, Tenn., Jan. 18, 1919; s. James Wallace and Martha Belle (Bittick) P.; A.B., Harvard, 1940, A.M., 1941, Ph.D., 1950; m. Lillian Cameron, Apr. 30, 1943; children—Thomas James II, Stephanie (Mrs. Kaoruhiko Suzuki). Instr. history Princeton, 1946-49; asst. prof. U. Wash., 1949-54, asso. prof., 1954-60, prof., 1960—. Vis. asso. prof. Princeton, 1953-54, Johns Hopkins, 1969-70. Served with AUS, 1941-45. Ford Found. Faculty fellow, 1951-52; Center for Advanced Study in Behavioral Scis. fellow, 1955-56. Mem. Am., So. (editorial bd. Jour. So. History 1973-77) hist. assns., Orgn. Am. Historians. Author: Americans Interpret Their Civil War, 1954. Editor: (with W. H. Scofield) Farm Real Estate Values in the United States, 1965; (with others) American Political Behavior, 1974. Home: 4545 E Laurel Dr NE Seattle WA 98105 Office: Dept of History U of Wash Seattle WA 98195

PRESSMAN, DAVID, immunochemist; b. Detroit, Nov. 24, 1916; s. Jacob and Lottie (Frankfort) P.; B.S., Calif. Inst. Tech., 1937, Ph.D., 1940; M.S., U. Calif., Los Angeles, 1938; m. Reinie Mildred Epstein, July 11, 1940; children—Jeffrey Leonard (dec.), Adele Rhea. Sr. fellow in research Calif. Inst. Tech., Pasadena, 1940-47; head sect. immunochemistry Sloan-Kettering Inst., N.Y.C., 1947-54; asso. prof. biochemistry Sloan-Kettering div. Cornell U. Med. Sch., 1952-54; dir. cancer research in biochemistry Roswell Park Meml. Inst., Buffalo, 1954-73, asso. inst. dir., 1967—, dir. cancer research in immunology, 1973—; research prof. chemistry Roswell Park div. State U. N.Y., Buffalo, 1955—, research prof. microbiology Sch. Medicine, 1968—; research prof. grad. faculty Niagara U., 1968—, Canisius Coll., 1968—; bd. sci. counselors, div. biologics standards NIH, USPHS, 1967-71; mem. breast cancer diagnostic com. Nat. Cancer Inst., 1973-75. Recipient Bertha Teplitz award Ann Langer Cancer Research Found., 1958; Service to Mankind award Sertoma Internat., 1973. Fellow AAAS, N.Y. Acad. Scis.; mem. Am. Chem. Soc. (Schoellkopf medal 1965, Morley medal 1967), Am. Soc. Biol. Chemists, Am. Assn. Cancer Research, Soc. Exptl. Biology and Medicine (pres. Western N.Y. sect. 1964-65), Am. Assn. Immunolgists, Sigma Xi, Tau Beta Pi. Author: (with Howard J. Lucas) Principles and Practice in Organic Chemistry, 1949; (with A.L. Grossberg) Structural Basis of Antibody Specificity, 1968; editorial bd. Transplant Bull., 1954-56; asso. editor Jour. Immunology, 1959-63, 65-72; editorial bd. Jour. Medicine and Pharm. Chemistry, 1962-65, Immunochemistry, 1964-71; Transplantation, 1975-78; editorial adv. bd. Immunol. Communications, 1972—. Home: 76 Edge Park Buffalo NY 14216 Office: 666 Elm St Buffalo NY 14263

PRESTAGE, JEWEL LIMAR, polit. scientist; b. Hutton, La., Aug. 12, 1931; d. Brudis L. and Sallie Bell (Johnson) Limar; B.A., So. U., Baton Rouge, 1951; M.A., U. Iowa, 1952, Ph.D., 1954; m. James J. Prestage, Aug. 12, 1953; children— Terri, James, Eric, Karen, Jay. Asso. prof. polit. sci. Prairie View (Tex.) Coll., 1954-55, 56; asso. prof. polit. sci. So. U., 1956-57, 58-62, prof., 1962—, chairperson dept., 1965—. Chairperson La. adv. com. to U.S. Commn. on Civil Rights, 1975—. Rockefeller fellow, 1951-52; NSF fellow, 1964; Ford Found. postdoctoral fellow, 1969-70. Mem. Am. Polit. Sci. Assn. (v.p. 1974-75), So. Polit. Sci. Assn. (pres. 1975-76), Nat. Conf. Black Polit. Scientists (pres. 1976-77). Author: (with M. Githens) A Portrait of Marginality: Political Behavior of the American Woman, 1976; contbr. articles to profl. jours. Home: 2145 77th Ave Baton Rouge LA 70807 Office: Box 9222 Southern University Baton Rouge LA 70813. *Commitments which guide my life are: (1) maximum development of personal potential through pursuit of excellence in all endeavors; (2) fair play, respect, compassion and quest of community in relations with fellow human beings; (3) utilization of personal talents in the interest of removing impediments to the good life "for all persons"; (4) pursuit of truth as the pervasive concern in academia; and (5) transmission of the above as priority goals to all with whom I have contact.*

PRESTEGAARD, PETER, automobile leasing co. exec.; b. Mpls., Mar. 15, 1942; s. Paul G. and Doris L. (Kretzschmar) P.; B.S.B. in Indsl. Adminstrn., U. Minn., 1965; M.B.A., N.Y. U., 1971; m. Barbara J. Anderson, June 25, 1965; children—Richard Paul, Daniel Peter, Jennifer Jean. Vice pres. Irving Trust Co., N.Y.C., 1965-74; sr. v.p., treas. Avis Inc., N.Y.C., 1974-76, chief fin. officer, 1976-79, group v.p. leasing, 1979—. Trustee Nauraushaun Presbyn. Ch. Recipient Ski-U-Mah award U. Minn., 1965. Mem. Fin. Execs. Assn. Address: 300 Strawtown Rd New City NY 10956

PRESTELE, JOSEPH ALAN, research inst. exec.; b. Phila., Mar. 21, 1928; s. Joseph Alan and Marian Elizabeth (Herling) P.; M.E., Stevens Inst. Tech., 1949, M.S. in Indsl. Engring., 1957; m. Sally Elizabeth Fuller, Apr. 13, 1957. Sr. engr. Consol. Edison Co. N.Y., N.Y.C., 1949-58, mgr. Indian Point nuclear power plant, Buchanan, N.Y., 1958-69, mgr. nuclear power generation dept., N.Y.C., 1969-73; dir. nuclear engring. and ops. Electric Power Research Inst., Palo Alto, Calif., 1973—; cons. Gen. Electric Co. Knolls Atomic Power Lab.; advisor Fed. Energy Adminstrn. Early Action Program. Served with Chem. Corps, U.S. Army, 1950-52. Fellow Am. Nuclear Soc. (dir., past chmn. standards com.); mem. ASME. Home: 1 Parkwood Dr Atherton CA 94025 Office: 3412 Hillview Ave Palo Alto CA 94304

PRESTHUS, ROBERT GRANNING, polit. scientist, educator, author; b. St. Paul, Feb. 25, 1917; s. Andrew and Edla (Granning-Farmen) P.; B.A., U. Minn., 1940, M.A., 1941; Ph.D., U. Chgo., 1948; postgrad. U. London, 1948; m. Anita Larsen, June 1, 1941; m. 2d, Sara Churchill, Sept. 1, 1966; children—Lesley Ann, Tonia Lynn, Jeffrey Vance, Robert Churchill. Asst. prof. polit. sci. U. So. Calif., 1948-50; asso. prof. polit. sci. Mich. State U., 1951-56; prof. polit. sci. Cornell U., 1956-66; vis. prof. U. Oreg., 1966-67; prof., chmn. dept. polit. sci. York U., Toronto, 1967—, Univ. prof., 1969—; research dir. UN Inst. Pub. Adminstrn., Ankara, Turkey, 1954-55; cons. U.S. Civil Def. Agy., CSC, lectr. Inst. Social Sci., The Hague and U. Amsterdam, 1963; vis. prof. U. Sussex, 1973, U. Goteborg, 1974. Served with USNR, 1943-46; PTO. Ford fellow, 1959; Social Sci. Research Council fellow, 1950, 63-64; research fellow Can. Council, 1968-72. Mem. Internat. Polit. Sci. Assn., Can. Polit. Sci. Assn., Am., Can. socs. public adminstrn., Am. Sociol. Assn., Am. Acad. Polit. and Social Sci., Pi Sigma Alpha, Lambda Phi. Author: The Turkish Conseil d'Etat, 1958; Men at the Top: a Study in Community Power, 1964; Behavioral Approaches to Public Administration, 1965; Individual and Organisation: Typologie der Anpassung, 1966; Public Administration, 6th edit., 1975; Elite Accommodation in Canadian Politics, 1973; Elites in the Policy Process, 1974; Interest Groups in International Perspective, 1974; Cross-National Perspectives: United States and Canada, 1977; The Organizational Society, 1978. Editor: Adminstrv. Sci. Quar., 1956-66; Behavioral Polit. Sci. series, 1968-75; editorial bd. Comparative Polit. Studies, Theory and Decision. Home: 14 Green Valley Rd Toronto ON Canada

PRESTINI, JAMES LIBERO, sculptor, designer, educator; b. Waterford, Conn., Jan. 13, 1908; s. Claude and Angelina (Buzzi) P.; B.S., Yale, 1930, student Sch. Edn., 1932; student, Sweden, 1938, Ill. Inst. Tech. Inst. Design, 1939, Italy, 1953-56. Master, Lake Forest (Ill.) Acad., 1933-42; instr. Ill. Inst. Tech. Inst. Design, 1939-46; research engr. Armour Research Found., Chgo., 1943-53; mem. faculty U. Calif. at Berkeley, 1956—, prof. design architecture, 1962—; Bauhaus-Archiv research prof., W. Berlin, 1977; cons. univs., research instns. in U.S., India, Germany, 1946—; exhbns. prin. U.S. museums and univs., 1938—; represented in permanent collections Mus. Modern Art, N.Y.C., Cleve. Mus. Art, Art Inst. Chgo., Met. Mus. Art, N.Y.C., San Francisco Mus. Art, Smithsonian Instn., Buffalo Albright-Knox Art Gallery, Seattle Art Mus., Milw. Art Inst., Mpls. Walker Art Center, Chgo. Hist. Soc., U. Calif. at Berkeley Art Mus., U. Ill. Krannert Art Mus., N.Y. Cooper-Hewitt Mus. Design, Bauhaus Archive Mus., Berlin, Pompidou Centre, Paris, Phila. Mus. Art. Co-recipient Best Research Paper prize Internat. Competition Low-Cost Furniture, N.Y. Mus. Modern Art, 1949; diploma D'Onore 10th Triennale, Milan, Italy, 1954; Am. Iron and Steel Inst. award for excellence in fine art in steel, 1971, award for excellence in craft in steel, 1973; R.S. Reynolds Meml. Sculpture award, 1972, U. Calif. Berkeley award, 1975. Ford Found. grantee, 1962-63; Graham Found. co-grantee, 1962; U. Cal. Creative Arts Inst. fellow, 1967-68, 70-71, 73-74; Guggenheim Found. fellow, 1972-73; N.Y. Met. Mus. Art life fellow, 1969; Deutscher Akademischer Austauschdienst grantee, Bonn, W. Ger., 1977. Home: 2324 Blake St Berkeley CA 94704

PRESTON, BILLY, musician, songwriter, singer; b. Houston, Sept. 9, 1946. Began playing piano at age 3; at age 10 played W. C. Handy in film St. Louis Blues, 1958; toured with Little Richard and Sam Cooke, 1962; made first record Sixteen Year Old Soul, 1964; musician on TV show Shindig, 1964-66; toured with Ray Charles, 1967; recorded with the Beatles, 1967; signed to Apple Records, then A&M Records as solo artist, 1971—; performed at Concert for Bangladesh, 1969; session musician for Steve Stills, 1971, Rolling Stones, 1972-74, 76-77, Peter Frampton, 1972, George Harrison, 1972, 74-76, John Lennon, 1970, Ringo Starr, 1973-74; songs composed include: That's the Way God Planned It, Outa Space, Will It Go Round in Circles. Recipient Grammy award, 1972, Office: care DePasse-Jones Mgmt 6255 Sunset Blvd Los Angeles CA 90028*

PRESTON, CHARLES B., mfg. co. exec.; b. Mishawaka, Ind., Nov. 1, 1928; s. Everett R. and Esther (Glenn) P.; B.B.A. magna cum laude, U. Miami (Fla.), 1949; m. Evalyn McClelland, Aug. 18, 1951. Audit mgr. Price Waterhouse & Co., C.P.A.'s, N.Y.C. and Hartford, 1949-58; with United Techs. Corp., 1958—, controller, 1968—, v.p., 1978—. C.P.A., N.Y. Mem. Am. Inst. C.P.A.'s, Fin. Execs. Inst. Office: United Techs Corp United Techs Bldg Hartford CT 06101

PRESTON, CONRAD SMITH, oil co. exec.; b. Bartlesville, Okla., Oct. 21, 1926; s. Carl Leon and Katy Elizabeth (Smith) P.; B.S. in Geology, U. Okla., 1949; m. Betty Jeanne Stark, Dec. 21, 1947; children—John D., Thomas K., Suzanne. Geologist, Sunray Oil Corp., Midland, Tex., 1949-54, sr. geologist, Oklahoma City, 1954-57; chief geologist Eason Oil Co., Oklahoma City, 1956-66, v.p., 1966-69, exec. v.p., 1969, also dir.; group v.p. Tesoro Petroleum Corp., San Antonio, 1969-77, exec. v.p., 1977—; pres. Tesoro Coal Co., San Antonio, 1976—, also dir.; dir. Land & Marine Rental Co., Petroleum Distbg. Co., La. Barrelling Co.; trustee Preston-Chouteau Trust. Served with AC, U.S. Army, 1945-46. Mem. Am. Assn. Petroleum Geologists, So. Tex. Geol. Soc., Am. Petroleum Inst., Soc. Petroleum Engrs., Am. Mining Congress, Ky. Coal Assn., Delta Upsilon. Republican. Mem. Christian Ch. (Disciples of Christ). Club: Oak Hills Country (San Antonio). Home: 2630 Country Hollow San Antonio TX 78209 Office: 8700 Tesoro Dr San Antonio TX 78276

PRESTON, DAVID MICHAEL, lawyer; b. Detroit, Apr. 15, 1930; s. David Harold and Ruth (MacDonald) P.; B.A., U. Mich., 1952, J.D., 1955; m. Judith Ann Hillner, Aug. 19, 1961; children—Matthew MacDonald, Sarah Elizabeth, Melissa Ann. Admitted to Mich. bar, 1955; partner firm Long, Preston, Kinnaird & Avant, Detroit and Birmingham, 1965—. Pres., Tim-Ro-Nan-Go Center for Emotionally Disturbed Children, Birmingham, 1972-74; trustee, Oakland Community Coll., 1969-70. Mem. Am., Mich., Oakland County bar assns., Beta Theta Pi, Phi Delta Phi. Club: Birmingham Athletic (pres. 1977-78). Home: 577 Westwood Dr Birmingham MI 48009 Office: 100 W Long Lake Rd Bloomfield Hills MI 48013 also 4300 City Nat Bank Bldg Detroit MI 48226

PRESTON, DON ALAN, free lance editor, writer; b. Louisville, Apr. 6, 1930; s. Leonard and Edna (Dupin) P.; B.A., U. Louisville, 1952; m. Sue Fisher, Aug. 7, 1953; children—Rachel, Laura, Amy. Asso. editor Prentice-Hall, Inc., Englewood Cliffs, N.J., 1952-55, sr. editor Trade div., 1973-76; asso. fiction editor Am. mag., 1955-56; mng. editor Gold Medal Books, Fawcett, 1956-58; exec. editor Avon Books, 1958-61; exec. editor, v.p. Bernard Geis Assos., 1963-71. Home: High Falls NY 12440

PRESTON, EDWARD FRANCIS, govt. ofcl.; b. Boston, May 10, 1919; s. Patrick and Martha (Reed) P.; student Northeastern U., 1939-42; B.A., Syracuse U., 1947, M.A. (grad. fellow), Maxwell Sch. Citizenship and Pub. Affairs, 1948; m. Maria Escribano Ortiz, Sept. 16, 1945; children—Phyllis, Richard. Jr. mgmt. asst. Office Sec. Treasury, 1948-49, mem. treasury mgmt. staff, 1949-50; mem. mgmt. staff IRS, 1950-52, asst. to asst. commr. operations, 1952-55, asst. to dep. commr., 1955-60, asst. commr. adminstrn., 1960-71, asst. commr. stablzn., 1971-74; asst. dir. Office Mgmt. and Budget, Exec. Office Pres., 1974—. Named Outstanding Young Man, Treasury Dept., 1954; recipient Exceptional service award Treasury Dept., 1972 Commr.'s award, 1973; Nat. Civil Service League award, 1973. Mem. Am. Soc. Pub. Adminstrn. Home: 1604 Fitzgerald Ln Alexandria VA 22302 Office: 6233 New Executive Office Bldg Washington DC 20037

PRESTON, FRANCES W., performing rights orgn. exec.; m. E.J. Preston; children—Kirk, David, Donald. Vice pres. Broadcast Music, Inc., Nashville. Dir. United Am. Bank. Vice pres. Pub. TV Council. Chmn. Cerebral Palsy Telethon, Nashville, 1970; hon. chmn. Christmas Seal Campaign, Nashville, 1968, 69, chmn., 1970; past mem. pub. info. com. Tenn. div. Am. Cancer Soc. Bd. dirs. Davidson County (Tenn.) Anti-Tb Assn., Tenn. Arts Commn., Oak Hill Sch., Univ. Sch., Nashville Better Bus. Bur., Goodwill Industries, Leadership Nashville, John Work Meml. Found.; advisory bd. Tenn. Performing Arts Found.; advisory council Belmont Coll.; trustee Country Music Found., Inc., Gospel Music Hall of Fame, 1978-79. Mem. Country Music Assn. (past chmn. bd., past pres., life dir.), Nashville Symphony Assn. (past sec., dir.), Gospel Music Assn. (chmn. 1978-79), Am. Symphony Orch. League, Nashville Symphony Guild, Nat. Acad. Recording Arts and Scis. (past dir. Nashville chpt.), Nashville Songwriters Assn. (life), Nat. Am. Women in Radio and TV (past dir.), Nashville Advt. Fedn. (past sec.), Nashville C. of C. (past dir.), Nashville Jr. Achievement (past dir.). Presbyterian. Address: care Broadcast Music Ins 10 Music Sq E Nashville TN 37203

PRESTON, FREDERICK WILLARD, surgeon; b. Chgo., June 27, 1912; s. Frederick Augustus and Margaret (Atwater) P.; B.A., Yale, 1935; M.D., Northwestern U., 1940, M.S., 1942; M.S., U. Minn., 1947; m. Gertrude Eldred Bradford, June 23, 1942 (div. 1961); children—Frederick Willard, David E., William B. Preston; m. 2d, Barbara Gay Hess, July 30, 1961. Intern Presbyn. Hosp., Chgo., 1940-41; fellow surgery Mayo Clinic, 1941-48; practice surgery, Chgo., 1950-75; instr. surgery Northwestern U. Med. Sch., 1950-51, asso. surgery, 1951-53, asst. prof., 1953-58, asso. prof., 1958-60, prof. surgery, 1960-75; asso. attending surgeon Chgo. Wesley Meml. Hosp., 1950-75; attending surgeon Skokie Valley Community Hosp., 1964-75, Henrotin Hosp., 1950-75; chief surg. service VA Research Hosp., Chgo., 1953-68; chmn. dept. Surgery Santa Barbara Gen. Hosp., 1975-78; dir. surg. edn. Santa Barbara Gen. and Cottage hosps., 1975—. Bd. dirs. Schweppe Found.; gov. mem., mem. planning com. Shedd Aquarium, 1968-75. Served to maj. M.C., AUS, 1942-46. Fellow A.C.S. (chpt. pres. 1965-66); mem. A.M.A., Chgo. Surg. Soc. (sec. 1961-64, pres. 1968-69), Chgo. Acad. Scis. (sec. 1963-67), Am. Assn. Cancer Research (pres. Chgo. sec. 1963-64), Am. Geriatrics Soc., Am. Fedn. Clin. Research, A.A.A.S., Am., Central, Pan Pacific, Western surg. assns., Société Internationale de Chirurgie, Soc. Surgery Alimentary Tract. Clubs: University (Chgo.); La Cumbre Golf and Country. Author, editor: Basic Surgical Physiology. Editor: Loose-Leaf Practice of Surgery. Contbr. 123 articles to profl. jours. Home: 755 Via Airosa Santa Barbara CA 93110 Office: Santa Barbara County Health Care Services 300 N San Antonio Rd Santa Barbara CA 93110

PRESTON, HUBERT MAX, telephone co. exec.; b. Brownfield, Tex., Oct. 6, 1933; s. C.A. and Myrtle Christine (Mosley) P.; B.A., Tex. Technol. Coll., 1954; J.D., U. Tex., 1959; m. Norma Jean Wren, Jan. 31, 1958; children—Brian Kurt, Grant Lang. Admitted to Tex. bar, 1959; asst. gen. atty. Gen. Telephone Co. of SW., San Angelo, Tex., 1959-65, sec., gen. counsel, 1965-70, v.p., sec., gen. counsel, 1970-75, v.p., gen. counsel, 1975-77; v.p. marketing and customer service Gen. Telephone Co. of S.E., Durham, N.C., 1977—. Mem. Tom Green County Library Bd., 1971-77, chmn., 1972-73, chmn. long-range planning com., 1974-77; past pres. San Angelo Civic Theater; past v.p. W. Tex. Therapy Center Bd.; mem. San Angelo Lake Bd.; past chmn. Tom Green County Republican Party; regional campaign coordinator U.S. Senator John Tower, 1972; mem. Tex. Campaign Finance Com., 1976-77. Served in U.S. Army, 1954-56. Mem. Am., Tex., Tom Green bar assns., Tex.-Okla. Telephone Assn. Episcopalian. Home: 2806 DeKalb St Durham NC 27705 Office: 3632 Roxboro Rd Durham NC 27702

PRESTON, JOHN FREDERICK, JR., telephone co. exec.; b. Missoula, Mont., June 18, 1917; s. John Frederick and Maud (Hunicke) P.; B.A., Washington and Jefferson Coll., 1938; J.D.,

Georgetown U., 1947; m. Barbara Pogue, Aug. 19, 1942 (dec. Aug. 1963); children—John Frederick, Thomas Pogue; m. 2d, Sue Marshall Schell, Nov. 28, 1964. Spl. agt. FBI, 1942-47; admitted to D.C. bar, 1941, Md. bar, 1955, N.Y. bar, 1959; counsel Joint Congl. Com. Labor-Mgmt., 1947-49; trial counsel NLRB, 1949-52; atty. Chesapeake & Potomac Telephone Companies, 1952-55; gen. atty. Chesapeake & Potomac Telephone Co. Md., 1955-58; atty. A.T.&T., 1958-61, gen. atty., 1963-74, gen. solicitor, 1974-76, asso. gen. counsel, 1976—; v.p., gen. counsel Ohio Bell Telephone Co., 1961-63. Mem. Am., N.Y. State, N.Y. County, Fed. Communications bar assns., Am. Judicature Soc., Phi Beta Kappa, Phi Gamma Delta. Home: 11 Calhoun Dr Greenwich CT 06830 Office: 195 Broadway New York City NY 10007

PRESTON, KENDALL, JR., electro-optical engr.; b. Boston, Oct. 22, 1927; s. Kendall and Dorothy Fletcher (Allen) P.; grad. Milton Acad., 1945; B.A. cum laude, Harvard U., 1950, M.S., 1952; m. Sarah Malcolm Stewart, Aug. 23, 1952; 1 dau., Louise. Mem. tech. staff Bell Telephone Labs., Murray Hills, N.J., 1952-60, sect. head scanning and data processing, 1960, mgr. new product devel., 1961; sr. staff scientist Perkin-Elmer Corp., Norwalk, Conn., 1961-74; prof. engring. and bioengring. Carnegie-Mellon U., Pitts., 1974—; prof. radiation health Grad. Sch. Pub. Health, U. Pitts., 1977—; chmn. Internat. Optical Computing Conf., Zurich, Switzerland, 1974; U.S. chmn. U.S.-Japan Seminar on Digital Processing of Biomed. Images, Pasadena, Calif., 1975; faculty NATO Advanced Study Inst. on Digital Image Processing and Analysis, Bonas, France, 1976; mem. Tech. Audit Bd., Inc., N.Y.C., 1976—. Chmn. Ecclesia, YMCA, Summit, N.J., 1958-60; chmn. conf. automatic cytology Engring Found., N.Y.C., 1971-72, chmn. conf. coherent radiation systems, 1973, chmn. conf. on comparative productivity of non-invasive techniques for med. diagnosis, 1976; chmn. health services industry com. Automation Research Council, Am. Automatic Control Council, N.J., 1973-76; mem. NSF Fact Finding Team on Egyptian Scientific Instrumentation, 1974-75. Served with arty. AUS, 1946-47. Fellow IEEE (chmn. Conn. PTGEC 1966-67); mem. AAAS, Biol. Engring. Soc. Gt. Britain, Biomed. Engring. Soc. (charter), Harvard Engrs. and Scientists (pres. students 1952), N.Y. Acad. Sci., Cum Laude Soc. Clubs: D.U., Hasty Pudding Inst. 1770; Harvard of Western Pa.; Country (Brookline, Mass.); Lake (Dublin, N.H.); Hillsboro (Pompano Beach, Fla.); Lawn (New Haven); Capitol Hill (Washington). Author: Coherent Optical Computers; 1972; Kogeretnye Optiches (in Russian), 1974; editor: (with Dr. Onoe) Digital Processing of Biomedical Images, 1976; (with Drs. Ayers, Johnson and Taylor) Medical Imaging Techniques: A Comparison, 1979. Patentee blood smear spinning, laser location of chromosomes on microscope slide, acoustic holography, others. Asso. editor Pattern Recognition; editorial adviser Biocharacterist; editorial adviser Analytical and Quantitative Cytology; contbr. articles to profl. jours. Office: Carnegie Mellon U Dept Elec Engring Schenley Park Pittsburgh PA 15213

PRESTON, LEE EGAN, educator; b. Dallas, July 28, 1930; s. Lee E. and Cecil (Degan) P.; B.A., Vanderbilt U., 1951; M.A., Harvard U., 1953, Ph.D., 1958; m. Patricia Louise Leahy, Jan. 27, 1957; children—Katherine, James, Mary Jane. Asst. prof. to prof. bus. adminstrn. U. Calif., 1958-69, asso. dean Sch. Bus. Adminstrn., 1967-69; Melvin H. Baker prof. Am. enterprise State U. N.Y. at Buffalo, 1969—, dir. Center for Policy Studies, 1973—; staff economist Council Econ. Advisers, Exec. Office of Pres., 1961-62; cons. Served with Aus, 1954-56. Author: (with Norman R. Collins) Concentration and Price-Cost Margins in Manufacturing Industries, 1968; Markets and Marketing: an Orientation, 1970; Industry and Enterprise Structure for the U.S. Economy, 1971; (with James E. Post) Private Management and Public Policy, 1975. Home: 25 Eltham Dr Buffalo NY 14226

PRESTON, LEWIS THOMPSON, banker; b. N.Y.C., Aug. 5, 1926; s. Lewis Thompson and Priscilla (Baldwin) P.; grad. Harvard U., 1951; m. Gladys Pulitzer, Apr. 17, 1959; children—Linda Pulitzer Bartlett, Victoria Maria Bartlett, Lucile Baldwin, Lewis Thompson, Priscilla Munn, Electra. With J.P. Morgan & Co. (merged with Guaranty Trust Co., named Morgan Guaranty Trust Co. 1959), 1951—, vice chmn. bd., dir. J. P. Morgan & Co. and Morgan Guaranty Trust Co., N.Y.C., 1976-78, mem. corporate office, mem. exec. com., 1976—, pres. J.P. Morgan and Morgan Guaranty Trust Co., 1978—. Trustee Foxcroft Sch., Middleburg, Va., N.Y. U. Served with USMC, 1944-46. Mem. The Pilgrims, Council Fgn. Relations, Res. City Bankers Assn. Republican. Episcopalian. Clubs: White's (London); The Brook, The River (N.Y.C.); Bedford Golf and Tennis. Office: 23 Wall St New York NY 10015*

PRESTON, MALCOLM, educator; b. N.J., May 25, 1919; s. Frank and Anniece (Landau) P.; B.S., U. Wis., 1940; M.A., Columbia, 1945, Ph.D., 1951, student New Sch. Social Research, N.Y.C., 1940-42; m. Mary Alice Bales, Nov. 27, 1942; children—Jennifer, Amanda. Display artist and designer, free lance artist, 1939-41; fellow, asst. instr. painting New Sch. Social Research, 1940-41; high sch. tchr., 1944-49; art supr. Manhasset pub. schs., 1945; part-time instr. Adelphi Coll., 1947; chmn. dept. fine arts Hofstra Coll., 1949-74, prof. fine arts, 1954-74, chmn. div. humanities, 1959-74, coordinator arts, 1961-74, dir. Inst. Arts, 1962-74; radio, television shows Met. area; developed and carried out television series Ford Found. grant, Nat. Ednl. Radio and Television Center, Arts Around Us, Am. Art Today, 1956; art critic Newsday, 1968—, Boston Herald Traveler, 1970-72. One man shows Ward Eggleston Gallery, N.Y.C., 1950-51, 54, 56, A.C.A. Gallery, 1959, S.A.G., 1962, Palm Beach, 1968, St. Mary's Coll., 1978, Benson Gallery, 1979; group shows New Art Gallery, 1948-49, Ward Eggleston Gallery, 1949-50, also L.I. Artists Exhibit, Nat. Water Color Exhibit, San Diego, Am. Artists Assn. Gallery group shows, 1951, Roosevelt Field Art Center, 1957, Art U.S.A., 1958, Hansa Gallery Group Show, 1958, Shore Studio Gallery, Provincetown, 1957-58, Kendall Art Gallery, Wellfleet, Mass., 1974, 75, 76, 77, 78, Roko Gallery, 1978, Himelfarb Gallery, 1978. Lowe Found. research grantee, 1950, Ford Found. grantee, 1958; recipient Emily Lowe award, 1949, 50, 52, 54, 56; 1st prize oil, Utica, N.Y.; Shell Research award, 1963. Served as 2d lt. F.A. AUS, World War II. Mem. Coll. Art Assn., Am. Fedn. Arts, AAUP. Contributor articles to newspapers and magazines. Home: Box 182 Truro MA 02666

PRESTON, MELVIN ALEXANDER, physicist, educator; b. Toronto, Ont., Can., May 28, 1921; s. Gardener Alexander and Hazel (Melvin) P.; B.A., U. Toronto, 1942, M.A., 1946; Ph.D., U. Birmingham, 1949; m. Mary Whittaker, Aug. 16, 1947; children—Jonathan, Richard; m. 2d, Eugene Shearer, June 25, 1966. Asst. lectr. math. physics U. Birmingham, 1947-49, Nuffield fellow, 1957; faculty U. Toronto, 1949-53; faculty McMaster U., Hamilton, Ont., 1953-77, prof. physics, 1959-77, prof. applied math., 1967-77, chmn. dept., 1975-77, dean grad. studies, 1965-71; exec. vice chmn. adv. com. on acad. planning Council of Ont. Univs., 1971-75; prof. physics, acad. v.p. U. Sask., Saskatoon, 1977—; pres. Canadian Assn. Grad. Schs., 1971. Decorated Canada decoration, Centennial medal. NRC Sr. fellow U. Inst. Teoretisk Fysik, Copenhagen, 1963-64. Fellow Am. Phys. Soc., Royal Soc. Can.; mem. AAAS, Phys. Soc. London, Canadian Assn. Physicists. Author: Physics of the Nucleus, 1962; Structure of the Nucleus, 1975. Contbr. articles profl. jours. Office: University of Saskatchewan Saskatoon SK S7N 0W0 Canada

PRESTON, PHILIP COTTLE, accounting firm exec.; b. Sturgis, S.D., Aug. 12, 1930; s. Charles Elliott and Martha Luella (Cottle) P.; B.S. in Bus. Adminstrn., U. Denver, 1949, M.B.A., 1957, J.D., 1961; m. Rachel Yoshiko Ono, Aug. 29, 1953; children—Dawn, Kenneth, Martha, Joanne. Mgmt. trainee Hilton Hotels, Chgo., 1949-50; accountant Von Tobel & Carr, C.P.A.'s, Denver, 1954-58; with Alexander Grant & Co., Denver, Chgo., San Francisco, N.Y.C., Atlanta, 1958—, mng. partner, Atlanta, 1978—; disting. practitioner, lectr. U. Ga., 1979—. Bd. dirs. San Francisco Spring Opera, 1972-74, N.Y.C. Opera, 1976—, Atlanta Ballet, 1978—; co-pres. Atlanta Civic Opera Co., 1979—. Served with USAF, 1950-54. Mem. Am. Inst. C.P.A.'s, Am. Bar Assn., Planning Execs. Inst. (internat. pres. 1974-75), Ga. C. of C. (indsl. devel. com. 1979—), Internat. Assn. Planning Socs. (sec. 1976—), Accts. for Public Interest (nat. dir. 1978—). Republican. Episcopalian. Clubs: Metropolitan, Cherokee Town and Country, Commerce, Masons. Contbr. articles to mags. Home: 5825 Winterthur Dr Sandy Springs GA 30328 Office: 1111 South-Omni Internat Atlanta GA 30303

PRESTON, ROBERT, actor; b. Newton Highlands, Mass., June 8, 1918; s. Frank W. and Ruth (Rea) Meservey; m. Catherine Craig, Nov. 8, 1940. Motion pictures include: Union Pacific, 1938; Northwest Mounted Police, 1939; Beau Geste, 1940, Wake Island, 1941, The Macomber Affair, 1946, The Bride Comes to Yellow Sky, 1951, The Dark at the Top of the Stairs, 1960, The Music Man, 1962, How the West Was Won, 1963, All The Way Home, 1963, Junior Bonner, 1972, Child's Play, 1972, Mame, 1973, Semi-Tough, 1977; Broadway plays include: Twentieth Century, 1951, The Male Animal, 1952, His and Hers, 1953, The Magic and the Loss, 1954, The Tender Trap, 1954, Janus, 1955, The Hidden River, 1957, The Music Man (musical), 1957, Too True to be Good, 1963, Nobody Loves an Albatross, 1963, Ben Franklin in Paris (musical), 1964-65, A Lion in Winter, 1966, I Do, I Do (musical), 1966-67, Mack and Mabel (musical), 1974; stage appearances include Sly Fox, 1977, The Prince of Grand Street (musical), 1978; TV film The Chisholms, 1979; star TV series The Chisholms II, 1980—. Mem. gov. bd. Actors' Equity. Served from pvt. to capt., USAAF, World War II. Recipient Antoinette Perry award as best musical male star, 1958, 67. Office: care John Springer Assos 667 Madison Ave New York NY 10021

PRESTON, SEYMOUR STOTLER, III, mfg. co. exec.; b. Media, Pa., Sept. 11, 1933; s. Seymour Stotler and Mary Alicia (Harper) P.; B.A., Williams Coll., 1956; M.B.A., Harvard U., 1958; m. Jean Ellen Holman, Sept. 8, 1956; children—Courtney J., Katherine E., Alicia D., Shelley S. With Pennwalt Corp., Phila., 1961—, exec. v.p. in charge of chems. and equipment ops., worldwide, 1975-77, pres., chief operating officer, 1977—, also dir.; dir. Phila. Nat. Corp., Phila. Nat. Bank. Trustee, Shipley Sch., Bryn Mawr, Pa., 1976—; elder, mem. session First United Presbyterian Ch., Paoli, Pa. Served to 1st lt., USAF, 1958-61. Mem. Soc. for Chem. Industry, Chem. Mfrs. Assn. (dir.), Greater Phila. C. of C. (dir. 1979—). Clubs: Union League, Urban (Phila.). Office: Pennwalt Corp Three Pkwy Philadelphia PA 19102

PRESTON, WILBUR DAY, JR., lawyer; b. Balt., May 29, 1922; s. Wilbur Day and Rena (Ehrlich) P.; B.A., Western Md. Coll., 1946, D.C.L., 1975; J.D., U. Md., 1949; m. May Honemann, July 14, 1945; children—Richard, Douglas, Bruce, Robert. Admitted to Md. bar; practice law, Balt., 1948—; partner firm Whiteford, Taylor, Preston, Trimble & Johnston, 1953—; dir. CM Kemp Mfg. Co. Chmn. bd. trustees Western Md. Coll., 1971—. Served to capt. inf., AUS, 1943-46. Fellow Am. Bar Found., Md. Bar Found., Am. Coll. Trial Lawyers; mem. Bar Assn. Balt. City (pres. 1972-73), Md. State (pres. 1975—), Am. (ho. of dels. 1973—) bar assns., Am. Law Inst., Order of Coif. Democrat. Mem. Swedenborgian Ch. Clubs: Baltimore Country, Merchants. Home: 300 Northway Baltimore MD 21218 Office: IBM Bldg 100 E Pratt St Baltimore MD 21202

PRESTON, WILL MANIER, lawyer, banker; b. Nashville, May 27, 1904; s. Robert Hatton and Dayse (High) P.; LL.B., Vanderbilt U., 1925; m. Eunice Lannom, Dec. 29, 1926; 1 dau., Dolores Clyntelle Preston Fields. Admitted to Tenn. bar, 1925, Fla. bar, 1926; practice in Miami, 1926—; mem. Scott, McCarthy, Preston & Steel, 1943-66; cons. Scott, McCarthy, Steel, Hector & Davis, 1966-75, Steel, Hector & Davis, 1975—; gen. counsel Everglades Nat. Park Assn., 1947—. Chmn. bd., dir. Dade Nat. Bank, Miami, 1956-69. Charter member, past pres., dir. Orange Bowl Com. Mem. Am., Fla., Dade County (past pres.) bar assns. Lion (past pres. Miami), Kiwanian (past pres. Miami). Home: 710 Lake Rd Miami FL 33137 Office: SE First Nat Bank Bldg Miami FL 33131

PRESTOPINO, GREGORIO, artist; b. N.Y.C., June 21, 1907; s. Anthony and Lillian (Rando) P.; student Nat. Acad. Design, N.Y.C., 1922-28; m. Elizabeth Dauber, June 21, 1931; children—Paul, Gregory. Tchr. art New Sch., N.Y.C., dir. Edward McDowell Colony; exhibited in numerous shows, including Whitney Mus., Mus. Modern Art (both N.Y.C.), Corcoran Art Galley, Washington, Pa. Acad., St. Louis Mus., Joseph H. Hirshhorn Mus., Washington paintings in permanent collections including Mus. U. Minn., Walker Art Gallery, Mpls., Philips Meml. Gallery, Washington, Mus. Modern Art, Whitney Mus., N.Y.C., Rochester (N.Y.) Mus., U. Neb., U. Ill., U. Okla., Hawaii Mus., Butler Art Inst., State Mus., Trenton, N.J., Notre Dame U., Montclair (N.J.) Mus., Nat. Inst. Arts and Letters, Keene (N.H.) State Coll., Currier Gallery Mus., Manchester, N.H., numerous pvt. collections. Recipient 3d prize Second Ann. Portrait of Am. competition, 1946; Temple gold medal Pa. Acad. Fine Arts, 1946; Benjamin Altman prize N.A.D., 1972, Henry T. Ranger Purchase Fund, 1976; voted Nat. Academician, 1976. Nat. Inst. Arts and Letters grantee, 1961. Home: 20 Farm Ln Roosevelt NJ 08555

PRESTWOOD, ALVIN TENNYSON, lawyer; b. Roeton, Ala., June 18, 1929; s. Garret Felix and Jimmie (Payne) P.; B.S., U. Ala., 1951, LL.B., 1956, J.D., 1970; m. Sue Burleson Lee, Nov. 27, 1974; children—Ann Celeste, Alison Bennett, Cynthia Joyce Lee, William Alvin Lee, Garret Courtney. Admitted to Ala. bar, 1956; law clk. Supreme Ct. Ala., 1956-57; asst. atty. gen. Ala., 1957-59; commr. Ala. Dept. Pensions and Security, 1959-63; pvt. practice, Montgomery, Ala., 1963-65, 77—; partner Volz, Capouano, Wampold, Prestwood & Sansone, 1965-77. Chmn., Gov.'s Com. on White House Conf. on Aging, 1961; mem. adv. com. Dept. Health, Edn. and Welfare, 1962; sec. Nat. Council State Pub. Welfare Adminstrs., 1962; pres. Morningview Sch. P.T.A., 1970; chmn. Am. Nursing Home Assn. Legal Com., 1972; bd. dirs. Montgomery Bapt. Hosp., 1958-65; chmn. bd. mgmt. East Montgomery YMCA, 1969. Served to 1st lt., inf. AUS, 1951-53. Decorated Combat Inf. Badge. Recipient Sigma Delta Kappa Scholastic Achievement award U. Ala. Sch. Law, 1956, Law Day Moot Ct. award U. Ala. Sch. Law, 1956. Mem. Am., Ala. (chmn. adminstrv. law sect. 1972, 78), Montgomery County (chmn. exec. com. 1971) bar assns., Farrah Order Jurisprudence, Kappa Sigma, Phi Alpha Delta. Club: Exchange Greater Montgomery (pres. 1971). Editorial bd. Ala. Law Rev., 1955-56. Contbr. articles to profl. jours. Home: 1431 Magnolia Curve Montgomery AL 36111 Office: Suite 209 One Court Sq Montgomery AL 36101

PRETTY, DAVID W., ins. co. exec.; b. Toronto, Ont., Can., Aug. 23, 1925; s. Joseph Melville and Olive Frances (Page) P.; B.Commerce, U. Toronto, 1947, M.B.A., 1955. With N.Am. Life Assurance Co., Toronto, Ont., 1947—, v.p., 1966-71, treas., 1965-68, exec. v.p., 1971-72, pres., 1972—, dir., 1969—; chmn. Can. Life Ins. Assn.; dir. Gen. Accident Assurance Co. Can.; former nat. v.p. Royal Life Savs. Soc. Can. Past pres. bd. govs. Queen Elizabeth Hosp., Toronto; treas., bd. regents Victoria U., Toronto. Mem. United Ch. Clubs: Toronto Golf, Toronto, Granite, Board Trade Metropolitan Toronto. Home: 206 St Leonard's Ave Toronto ON M4N 1K7 Canada Office: 105 Adelaide St W Toronto ON M5H 1R1 Canada

PRETTYMAN, ELIJAH BARRETT, JR., lawyer; b. Washington, June 1, 1925; s. Elijah Barrett and Lucy Courtney (Hill) P.; grad. St. Albans Sch., Washington, 1943; B.A., Yale, 1949; LL.B., U. Va., 1953; m. Victoria Ann Keesecker, Dec. 29, 1979; children by previous marriage—Elijah Barrett III, Jill Savage. Admitted to D.C. bar, 1953, U.S. Supreme Ct. bar, 1957; practiced in Washington, 1953—; law clk. to Justices Jackson, Frankfurter and Harlan, U.S. Supreme Ct., 1953-55; asso. firm Hogan & Hartson, Washington, 1955-63, partner, 1964—; spl. asst. to Atty. Gen. U.S., 1963; spl. asst. to White House, 1963-64, also rep. to Interagy. Com. on Transport Mergers; spl. cons. subcom. to investigate problems connected with refugees and escapees U.S. Senate Judiciary Com., Vietnam, 1967-68. Trustee, Am. U., Washington, Washington Journalism Center, Center for Law and Social Policy; bd. dirs. Georgetown U. Inst. Pub. Interest Representation, Nat. Council on Crime and Delinquency; corporate mem. Children's Hosp. D.C.; mem. adv. bd. Salvation Army; mem. advisory com. on Procedures of Judicial Council, D.C. Served with AUS, 1943-45; ETO. Fellow Am. Bar Assn.; mem. Jud. Conf. D.C. Circuit, Met. Washington Bd. Trade, D.C. Bar (1st pres. 1972-73, bd. govs. 1973-74). Methodist (past dir. ch.). Clubs: Lawyers, Vinson, Alfalfa. Author: Death and the Supreme Court, 1961. Editor: (with William E. Jackson) The Supreme Court in the American System of Government (Justice Robert H. Jackson), 1955. Contbr. articles to profl. jours. Home: Apt 235 3100 Connecticut Ave NW Washington DC 20008 Office: 815 Connecticut Ave NW Washington DC 20006

PREUL, HERBERT CHARLES, educator, cons. engring.; b. Berger, Mo., Jan. 11, 1926; s. Fred C. and Hulda F. (Schake) P.; B.S., U. Iowa, 1950; M.S., U. Minn., 1955, Ph.D., 1964; m. Audrey A. Van Roekel, May 27, 1950; 1 son, Mark C. Profl. baseball player N.Y. Yankee System, 1948-49; hydraulic engr. U.S. Bur. Reclamation, Denver, also Goleta, Calif., 1950-52; hydraulic engr., C.E., U.S. Army, St. Paul and Omaha, 1952-60, chief san. engr. design, 1955-60; research fellow div. san. engring., dept. civil and environ. engring. U. Minn., Mpls., 1960-64; faculty U. Cin., 1964—, prof. civil and environ. engring., 1964—, dir. div. water resource, 1964—; cons. engring. edn., water pollution; internat. cons. World Bank, WHO, U.S. AID, NSF. Served with AUS, 1944-46. Registered profl. engr. Ohio, Iowa, Minn. Mem. Am. Waterworks Assn., Internat. Water Resources Assn., Internat. Assn. Water Pollution Research, Am. Soc. Engring. Edn., ASCE, Water Pollution Control Fedn., Ohio Water Pollution Conf., Am. Water Resources Assn. (state pres. Ohio 1972-73), Engring. Soc. Cin. (pres. 1975-76), Internat. Water Resources Assn. (co-founder, dir. 1971-79), Sigma Xi. Contbr. articles to profl. publs. Home: 760 Ludlow Ave Cincinnati OH 45220

PREUS, DAVID WALTER, clergyman; b. Madison, Wis., May 28, 1922; s. Ove Jacob Hjort and Magdalene (Forde) P.; B.A., Luther Coll., Decorah, Iowa, 1943, D.D., 1969; B.Th., Luther Sem., St. Paul, 1950; postgrad. U. Minn., 1946-47, Union Sem., 1951, Edinburgh U., 1951-52; hon. degrees: LL.D., Wagner Coll., 1973, Gettysburg Coll., 1976; D.D., Pacific Luth. Coll., 1974, St. Olaf Coll., 1974, Dana Coll., 1979; L.H.D., Macalester Coll., 1976; m. Ann Madsen, June 26, 1951; children—Martha, David, Stephen, Louise, Laura. Ordained to ministry Luth. Ch., 1950; asst. pastor First Luth. Ch., Brookings, S.D., 1950-51; pastor Trinity Luth. Ch., Vermillion, S.D., 1952-57; campus pastor U. Minn., Mpls., 1957-58; pastor Univ. Luth. Ch. of Hope, Mpls., 1958-73; v.p. Am. Luth. Ch., 1968-73, pres., 1973—. Luccock vis. pastor Yale Div. Sch., 1969; chmn. bd. youth activity Am. Luth. Ch., 1960-68; mem. exec. com. Luth. Council U.S.A.; v.p. Luth. World Fedn., 1977—; mem. central com. World Council Chs., 1973-75; Luth. del. White House Conf. on Equal Opportunity; chmn. Greater Mpls. Fair Housing Com., Mpls. Council Chs., 1960-64. Mem. Mpls. Planning Commn., 1965-67; mem. Mpls. Sch. Bd., 1965-74, chmn., 1967-69; mem. Mpls. Bd. Estimate and Taxation, 1968-73, mem. Mpls. Urban Coalition. Bd. dirs. Mpls. Inst. Art, Walker Art Center, Hennepin County United Fund, Ams. for Childrens Relief, Luth. Student Fedn., Research Council of Gt. City Schs., Urban League, NAACP; bd. regents Augsburg Coll., Mpls. Served with Signal Corps, AUS, 1943-46; PTO. Decorated comdr.'s cross Royal Norwegian Order St. Olav; recipient Regents medal Augustana Coll., Sioux Falls, S.D., 1973; Torch of Liberty award Anti-Defamation League, 1973. Home: 60 Seymour Ave SE Minneapolis MN 55414 Office: 422 S 5th St Minneapolis MN 55415

PREUS, JACOB AALL OTTESEN, sem. pres.; b. St. Paul, Jan. 8, 1920; s. J. A. O. and Idella (Haugen) P.; B.A., Luther Coll., 1941; B.D., Luther Sem., 1945; M.A., U. Minn., 1946, Ph.D., 1951; m. Delpha Holleque, June 12, 1943; children—Patricia (Mrs. Gerhard Bode), Delpha (Mrs. George Harris), Carolin (Mrs. Louis LaPrairie), Sarah (Mrs. Dennis Schwab), Idella (Mrs. Mark Moberg), Mary (Mrs. William Churchill), Jacob, Margaret (Mrs. Timothy Weible). Ordained to ministry Lutheran Ch., 1945; pastor, South St. Paul, Minn., 1945-46; prof. Bethany Coll., Mankato, Minn., 1947-50, 56-58; pastor, Luverne, Minn., 1950-56; prof. Concordia Theol. Sem., Springfield, Ill., 1958-69, pres., 1962-69; pres. Luth. Ch. Mo. Synod, 1969—. Mem. constituting com. Luth. Council in U.S.A. Mem. negotiating com. with Am. Luth. Ch. Translator Chemnitz DeDuabus Naturis in Christo, Luther's Commentary on Romans; De Coena Domini. Contbr. chpt. to The Doctrine of God, 1962. Contbr. articles to theol. jours. Home: 400 N 4th St Apt 1502 St Louis MO 63102

PREUSS, ROGER E(MIL), artist; b. Waterville, Minn., Jan. 29, 1922; s. Emil W. and Edna (Rosenau) P.; student Mankato Comml. Coll., Mpls. Sch. Art; m. MarDee Ann Germundson, Dec. 31, 1954. Painter of nature art; one man shows St. Paul Fine Art Galleries, 1959, Albert Lea Art Center, 1963, Hist. Soc. Mont., Helena, 1964, Bicentennial exhbn. Le Sueur County Hist. Soc. Mus., Elysian, Minn., 1976; exhibitions include Midwest Wildlife Conf. Exhbn., Kerr's Beverly Hills, Cal., 1947, Joslyn Meml. Mus., Omaha, 1948, Minn. Centennial, 1949, Federated Chaparral Authors, 1951, Nat. Wildlife Art, 1951, 52, N.Am. Wildlife Art, 1952, Ducks Unltd. Waterfowl exhibit, 1953, 54, St. Paul Winter Carnival, 1954, St. Paul Gallery Art Mart, 1954, Holy Land Conservation Fund, N.Y.C., 1976; represented in permanent collections Demarest Meml. Mus., Hackensack, N.J., Smithsonian Instn., N.Y. Jour. Commerce, Mont. Hist. Soc., Inland Bird Banding Assn., Minn. Capitol Bldg., Mont. State U., Wildlife Am. Collection, LeSueur Hist. Soc., Voyageurs Nat. Park Interpretive Center, Roger Preuss Art Collection, Lucky 11 VFW Post, Mpls., Nat. Wildlife Fedn. Collection, Minn. Ceremonial House, Fine Arts Center of Brigham Young U., U.S. Wildlife Service Fed. Bldg., Fort Snelling, Minn., Crater Lake Nat. Park Visitors Center, VA Hosp., Mpls., Luxton Collection, Banff, Alta., Can., Inst. Contemporary Arts London, others, numerous galleries and pvt. collections; designer Fed. Duck Stamp, U.S. Dept. Interior, 1949; instr. seminar Mpls. Coll. Art and Design. Judge ann. Goodyear Nat. Conservation Awards Program. Del. Nat. Wildlife Conf. Bd. dirs. Voyageurs Nat. Park Assn., N.Am. Conservation Hall and Mus.,

Wetlands for Wildlife U.S.A.; pres. Wildlife Am.; Minn. Conservation Fedn., 1952-54; panelist Sportsman's Roundtable, WTCN-TV, Mpls., 1953—. Served with USNR, World War II. Recipient Minn. Outdoor award, 1956; Patron of Conservation award, 1956; 1st award Am. Indsl. Devel. Council; citation of merit V.F.W.; Award of Merit, Mil. Order Cootie, 1963, Merit award Minn. Waterfowl Assn., 1976; named Wildlife Conservationist of Yr. Sears Found.-Nat. Wildlife Fedn. Program, 1966, Am. Bicentennial Wildlife Artist, Am. Heritage Assn., 1976; hon. mem. Ont. Chippewa Nation of Can., 1957; named Knight of Mark Twain for contbns. to Am. art, Mark Twain Soc., 1978. Fellow Internat. Inst. Arts (life), Soc. Animal Artists, N.Am. Mycol. Assn.; mem. Nat. Audubon Soc., Internat. Sci. Info. Service, Am. Mus. Natural History, Nat. Wildlife Fedn. (nat. wildlife week chmn. Minn.), Minn. Ducks Unltd. (dir.), Minn. Artists Assn. (v.p., dir.), Soc. Artists and Art Dirs., Outdoor Writers Am., Am. Artists Profl. League, Mpls. Soc., Fine Arts, Wildlife Soc., Zool. Soc., Nature Conservancy, Minn. Mycol. Soc. (pres. emeritus; hon. life mem.), Le Sueur County Hist. Soc. (hon. life mem.), Minn. Conservation Fedn. (hon. life). Clubs: Beaverbrook (hon. life), Minn. Press (Mpls.); Explorers (N.Y.C.). Contbr. Christmas Echos, 1955, Wing Shooting, Trap & Skeet, 1955; also illustrations and articles in Country Gentlemen, Nat. Wildlife, others. Editor: Sports and Recreation mag., Out-of-Doors mag. Compiler and artist: Outdoor Horizons, 1957; Twilight over the Wilderness, 1972; contbr. Educators Guide to Science Materials; paintings and text Minnesota Today. Creator Preuss Wildlife Calendar; inventor Wildlife Am. Calendar. Studio: 2224 Grand Ave Minneapolis MN 55405 Office: care Wildlife of America Gallery PO Box 556-A Minneapolis MN 55440. *With a modicum of natural skills in painting and writing, my basic goal throughout all my work has been to help people appreciate and understand nature. If I as a naturalist am a small voice for our world's waters, woods, and wildlife, if I have influenced many children and adults to become more environment conscious, if my art brings to others a measure of joy, then my best aspirations for my creations have been fulfilled.*

PREVES, MILTON, violist; b. Cleve. Formerly head viola sect. Chgo. Little Symphony Orch., also mem. Mischakoff String Quartet; mem. Chgo. Symphony Orch., 1934—, prin. violist, 1939—; also now condr. North Side Symphony, Chgo. and Wheaton (Ill.) Summer Symphony; appearances as soloist with Chgo. Symphony Orch. and summer concerts Ravinia (Ill.) Festival; mem. Chgo. Symphony String Quartet. Address: care Chicago Symphony Orch 220 S Michigan Ave Chicago IL 60604*

PREVIN, ANDRE, composer, condr.; b. Berlin, Germany, Apr. 6, 1929; s. Jack and Charlotte (Epstein) P.; came to U.S., 1938, naturalized, 1943; student Berlin Conservatory, Paris Conservatory, privately with Pierre Monteux, Mario Castelnuovo-Todesco; m. Mia Farrow, Sept. 10, 1970; children—Matthew and Sascha (twins), Fletcher, Lark Song, Summer, Soon-Yi. Rec. artist classical music, 1946—; composer chamber music, cello concerto, guitar concerto, piano music, music for strings, serenades for violin, brass quintet, wind quintet, also song cycle on poems by Philip Larkin, Every Good Boy Deserves Favour, others; composer film scores Metro-Goldwyn-Mayer, 1950-59; guest condr. most maj. symphony orchs., U.S., Europe; rec. artist for RCA, EMI, English Decca; condr.-in-chief Houston Symphony, 1967-69; prin. condr. London Symphony Orch., 1968—; music dir. South Bank Music Festival, London, 1972-74, Pitts. Symphony, 1976—; guest condr. Covent Garden Opera, festivals in Salzburg, Edinburgh, Flanders, Vienna, Osaka, Prague, Berlin, Bergen; mem. faculty Guildhall Sch., London, Royal Acad. Music. Served with AUS, 1950-51. Recipient 4 Acad. awards, awards Nat. Grammophone Soc. Mem. Acad. Motion Picture Arts and Scis., Dramatists Guild, Brit. Composers Guild, Nat. Composers and Condrs. League. Club: Garrick. Author: Music Face to Face, 1971. Office: care Harrison/Parrott Ltd 22 Hillgate St London W8 England

PREVIN, DORY LANGAN, author, composer, singer; b. Rahway, N.J.; d. Michael Joseph and Florence Annastasia (Shannon) Langan; student Am. Acad. Dramatic Art; m. Andre Previn (div.). Began career as jr. writer MGM Studios; writer UPA Animation Studios, 2 years; lyricist for numerous films, including song The Faraway Part of Town from Pepe, 1961, Second Chance from Two for the Seesaw, 1962, Come Saturday Morning from the Sterile Cuckoo, 1969; author Go Go Frug (satirical protest songs), 1967; author English libretto for opera The Impresario (Mozart), 1969; author, performer record albums, 1970—. Lectr. lyric writing course U. Calif. at Los Angeles. Author: On My Way to Where (collected lyrics), 1971; (autobiographies) Midnight Baby, 1976, Bog-Trotter, 1979. Address: care Robert Ginter 10889 Wilshire Blvd Los Angeles CA 90024

PREVOST, ANDRE, composer; b. Hawkesbury, Ont., Can., July 30, 1934; s. Jules Edouard and Hermine (Smith) P.; student Conservatoire de musique de Montreal, Can., 1951-60, Conservatoire nat. superieur de musique, Paris, 1960-62, Ecole normale superieure de musique, Paris, 1961-62; m. Lise Vezina, July 18, 1959; children—Christian and Yolaine (twins), Dominique, Yannik. Composer of various works for orchestra, including Pyknon, 1966, chamber music, including Sonate pour Violin et Piano, 1960-61, works for solo voice, for chorus, including Terre des Hommes, 1967, for keyboard; prof. U. Montreal, 1965—. Recipient numerous musical awards including First Prize for Chamber Music, Les Amis de l'Art, 1959; scholarships from Province of Que., 1960, Canada Arts Council, 1960, 72; Medal, Canada Music Council, 1977. Roman Catholic. Music choreographed, recorded by various conductors. Home: 227 Ave Querbes Outremont Montreal PQ H2V 3W1 Canada Office: Faculte de Musique Universite de Montreal Montreal PQ Canada

PREVOST, EDWARD JAMES, broadcasting exec.; b. Baie Comeau, Que., Can., May 26, 1941; s. Omer and Jeanne (Ouellet) P.; B.A. with honors, Loyola Coll., Montreal, Que., 1962; M.B.A., U. Western Ont., London, 1964; m. Anna Marie Murphy, June 20, 1964; children—Marc, Louise, Eric. Luc. Account exec. J. Walter Thompson Co., Montreal, 1964-66; account exec. Cockfield Brown & Co. Ltd., Montreal, 1966-69, v.p., 1968-69; gen. mgr. CJRP Radio Provinciale affiliate Radiomutuel network, Quebec City, Que., 1969-71; exec. v.p. Mut. Broadcasting Ltd., Radiomutuel, Montreal, 1971-73, pres., 1973-76, chmn. bd., 1976—; exec. v.p. Civitas Corp. Ltd., Montreal, 1973-74, pres., chief exec. officer, 1974—, also chmn. bd. many subs.; bd. dirs. BBM Bur. Measurement, 1971-77; mem. Montreal Bd. Trade. Pres. Montreal Inst. Cardiology Research; mem. Canadian Council Christians and Jews. Mem. Jeune Chambre de Montreal Inc. (gov.), Que. M.B.A. Assn. (gov.), Internat. Inst. Communications, Montreal, Province Que., Can., chambers commerce, Canadian Assn. Broadcasters (chmn. 1977-79), Inst. Canadian Advt. (cert. advt. agency practitioner). Club: St.-Denis (Montreal). Office: 1155 Dorchester Blvd W Suite 2707 Montreal PQ H3B 2K8 Canada

PREVOZNIK, STEPHEN JOSEPH, anesthesiologist; b. McAdoo, Pa., June 21, 1929; s. John George and Mary Margaret (Ficek) P.; R.N., St. Joseph Hosp. Sch. Nursing, Phila., 1951; B.S., U. Notre Dame, 1955; M.D., U. Pa., 1959; m. Rita Agnes Kellett, Aug. 20, 1955; children—Mary Therese, Stephen Joseph, John Cyril, Michael Edward, Margaret Anne, Rita Marie, Thomas William, Jean Marie. Intern, Fitzgerald Mercy Hosp., Darby, Pa., 1959-60; resident in anesthesia U. Pa., Phila., 1960-62; practice medicine specializing in anesthesiology, Phila., 1962—; mem. staff U. Pa. Hosp.; dir. clin. activities U. Pa., 1971—, prof. anesthesia, 1977—. Mem. Upper Darby (Pa.) Health Adv. Bd., 1972-74. Mem. Am. Soc. Anesthesiologists, Pa. Soc. Anesthesiologists, Phila. Soc. Anesthesiologists (pres. 1975-77), Internat. Anesthesia Research Soc., Assn. Univ. Anesthetists. Contbr. to textbooks on anesthesiology. 474 Fairfax Rd Drexel Hill PA 19026 Office: Dept Anesthesia Hosp U Pa Philadelphia PA 19104. *No one does everything by or for himself; someone is always there to provide a boost or a helping hand. As one progresses and matures, he finds many opportunities to repay what he has received. Without this repayment, the chain is broken and that life is without meaning.*

PREWITT, CARL KENNETH, JR., polit. scientist; b. Alton, Ill., Mar. 16, 1936; s. Carl Kenneth and Louise (Carpenter) P.; B.A., So. Meth. U., 1958; M.A., Washington U., 1959; Ph.D., Stanford U., 1963; m. Ann Christine Biggar, Sept. 6, 1963; children—Jennifer Ann, Geoffrey Douglas. Prof. polit. sci. U. Chgo., 1964—, chmn. dept. polit. sci., 1975-76, dir. Nat. Opinion Research Center, 1976-79; pres. Social Sci. Research Council, 1979—; vis. scholar U. Nairobi, Kenya, 1968-71; teaching and research Stanford U., 1964-68; cons. Rockefeller Found., Zaire, 1972, Thailand, 1973. Mem. governing bd. Internat. Center Insect Physiology and Ecology; trustee Nat. Opinion Research Center; bd. dirs. Internat. Research and Exchanges Bd. Fellow Am. Acad. Arts and Scis.; mem. Am. Polit. Sci. Assn., Am. Assn. for Pub. Opinion Research, AAAS. Author: Political Socialization, 1969; Ruling Elites, 1973; Labryrinths of Democracy, 1973; Introduction to American Government, 1977. Home: 30 Scenic Dr Hastings-on-Hudson NY Office: 605 3d Ave New York NY 10016

PREYER, L. RICHARDSON, congressman; b. Greensboro, N.C., Jan. 11, 1919; s. William Y. and Mary Norris (Richardson) P.; grad. Woodberry Forest Sch.; A.B., Princeton, 1941; LL.B., Harvard, 1949; LL.D., Elon Coll., U. N.C., Greensboro, Davidson Coll.; m. Emily Irving Harris, May 11, 1946; children—L. Richardson, Mary Norris, Britt Armfield, Jane Bethel, Emily Harris. Admitted to N.C. bar; mem. firm Preyer & Bynum, Greensboro, 1950-56; city judge, Greensboro, 1953-56; N.C. superior ct. judge, 1956-61; U.S. dist. judge 18th Dist. N.C., 1961-63; engaged in N.C. gubernatorial campaign, 1963-64; sr. v.p., trust officer N.C. Nat. Bank, Greensboro, 1964-66, exec., 1966-68; mem. 91st-96th congresses from 6th Dist. N.C., mem. Govt. Ops. Com., Interstate and Fgn. Commerce Com., Standards Ofcl. Conduct Com. Served with USNR, World War II. Decorated Bronze Star medal; named Greensboro's Outstanding Young Man, U.S. Jr. C. of C., 1954, Outstanding Leader, Inter-Club Council, 1968. Mem. Newcomen Soc. Democrat. Office: 2344 Rayburn House Office Bldg Washington DC 20515

PREYER, ROBERT OTTO, educator; b. Greensboro, N.C., Nov. 11, 1922; s. William Yost and Mary Norris (Richardson) P.; grad. Choate Sch. 1939; student Davidson Coll., 1939-40; A.B., Princeton, 1945; M.A., Columbia, 1948, Ph.D., 1954; m. Renee Haenel, June 14, 1947; children—Jill, Sally, Elizabeth; m. Kathryn Conway Turner, July 19, 1966. Instr., Smith Coll., 1948-54; asst. prof. Brandeis U., Waltham, Mass., 1954-55, prof., chmn. dept. English and Am. lit., 1963—, chmn. faculty senate, 1976—, dir. univ. studies program, 1979—; vis. lectr. Amherst Coll., 1952; vis. prof. Freiburg U., Germany, 1956-57; guest prof. Heidelberg U., Germany, 1973-74. Dir. Piedmont Financial Corp., Richardson Corp. Served to ensign USNR, 1940-43; PTO. Mem. Modern Lang. Assn., N.A.A.C.P. (steering com.), Am. Civil Liberties Union. Democrat. Clubs: Cottage (Princeton); St. Botolph (Boston); Princeton (N.Y.C.). Author: Bentham, Coleridge and The Science of History, 1958. Adv. editor: Victorian Studies, 1961—; editor Victorian Literature. Contbr. essays profl. jours. Home: 6 Maple Ave Cambridge MA 02139

PRIAULX, A(LLAN), editor; b. Eugene, Oreg., May 13, 1940; s. Arthur W. and Kathleen Deltry (Bean) P.; student Dartmouth Coll., 1958-60; student U. Southampton (Eng.), 1960, New Sch. for Social Research, 1961-62; m. Jacqueline Markham, Jan. 10, 1976; children—Sharmon, Elizabeth. Corr. UPI, Buffalo, 1962-63, mgr. bur., Concord, N.H., 1963-65, Honolulu, 1965-66, news mgr., Paris, 1966-68; dir. spl. projects McLendon Corp., Dallas, 1968-70; v.p. Register & Tribune Syndicate, N.Y.C., 1970-76; exec. editor King Features Syndicate, N.Y.C., 1976-79, editor, 1979—. Creative arts instr. United Cerebral Palsy of N.Y. State, 1977-79; vice chmn. nat. public relations com. United Cerebral Palsy Assns. Mem. Overseas Press Club Am., Nat. Cartoonists Soc., Newspaper Comics Council, Am. Assn. Sunday and Feature Editors. Episcopalian. Clubs: Dartmouth, Yale (N.Y.C). Author: (with S.J. Ungar) The Almost Revolution, 1969. Home: 139 E 35th St New York NY 10016 Office: 235 E 45th St New York NY 10017

PRIBRAM, KARL HARRY, physician, med. research; b. Vienna, Austria, Feb. 25, 1919; s. Ernst August and Maria Dee (Salomonson) P.; B.S., U. Chgo., 1939, M.D., 1941; m. Helen B. Finnegan, June 15, 1940 (div. 1958); children—John, Joan, Bruce; m. 2d, Amy E. Isle., June 25, 1960; children—Cynthia, Karl S. Resident neurol. surgeon Chgo. Meml. Hosp., 1942-43; asst. neurologist, neurol. surgeon U. Ill., 1943-45; resident neurologist, neurol. surgeon St. Luke's Hosp., Chgo., 1943-45; instr. neurology and surgery U. Tenn., 1945-46; individual practice neurology, neurol. surgery, Jacksonville, Fla., 1946-48; neurosurgeon neurophysiologist Yerkes Labs. Primate Biology, Orange Park, Fla., 1946-48; research asst. prof. physiology and psychology Yale Sch. Medicine, 1948-51, lectr. depts. physiology and psychology, 1951-58; chmn. dept. neurophysiology Inst. Living, Hartford, Conn., 1951-55, dir. research and labs., 1956-58; asso. prof. dept. psychiatry and psychology Stanford Med. Center, 1959-62, prof., 1962—. Recipient USPHS Career award, 1962. Diplomate Am. Bd. Neurol. Surgery. Fellow Am. Acad. Arts and Scis.; mem. A.M.A., A.A.A.S., Am. Physiol. Assn., Am. Psychol. Assn. (pres. div. comparative and physiol. psychology 1967-68), Internat. Brain Research Orgn., Psychonomic Soc., A.A.U.P., Internat. Neuropsychol. Assn. (pres. 1967-69), Sigma Xi. Author: Languages of the Brain, 1971, co-author: Plans and the Structure of Behavior, 1960; Freud's Project Re-assessed, 1976. Editor: Brain and Behavior, 4 vols., 1969; On the Biology of Learning, 1969; co-editor Biology of Memory, 1970, Perception and Its Disorders, 1970, Psychophysiology of the Frontal Lobes, 1973, The Hippocampus, 1976. Home: 346 Costello Ct W Los Altos CA 94022 Office: Dept Psychology Stanford U Stanford CA 94305

PRICE, ALVIN AUDIS, univ. adminstr.; b. Lingleville, Tex., Oct. 8, 1917; s. Sam C. and Lillie M. (Bays) P.; student Tarleton State Coll., Stephenville, Tex., 1936-38; B.S., Tex. A and M U., 1940, D.V.M., 1949, M.S., 1956; m. Helen L. Bachschmid, Mar. 17, 1943; children—Robert Alan, Mona Annette. Prodn. mgr. Lockhart Creamery (Tex.), 1940-42; mem. faculty Tex. A and M Univ., 1949—, asst. prof. vet. anatomy, 1951-57, dean Coll. Vet. Medicine, 1957-73, adminstr. biomed. sci., 1973—; asso. dir. Tex. Agrl. Expt. Sta., 1959-73. Spll. cons. to E. Pakistan, 1959. Nat. adv. com. SSS, 1967-76; adv. com. Nat. Health Resources, 1968-79; cons. U. P.R., 1977—; dir. Univ. Nat. Bank. Served with U.S. Army, 1942-46; lt. col. Res. Recipient Faculty Distinguished Achievement award Tex. A and M U., 1956, Faculty Appreciation award, 1970, Student Dedication award, 1973, Disting. Alumnus award, 1979. Mem. Am., Tex. (pres. 1956, Recognition award 1970, Service award 1979), Brazos Valley vet. med. assns., Tex. Acad. Sci., U.S. Animal Health Assn., Am. Assn. Vet. Anatomists (pres. 1957), Assn. Am. Vet. Med. Colls. (pres. 1967). Democrat. Baptist (deacon, Sunday sch. tchr.). Lion (dep. dist. gov. 1952-53). Home: 1203 Walton Dr College Station TX 77840 Office: Biomed Sci Tex A and M U College Station TX 77843

PRICE, BRUCE HAYS, clergyman; b. Scottsville, Ark., Oct. 19, 1904; s. Samuel Robert and Maggie Jones (McCracken) P.; A.B., Ouachita U. (Ark.), 1928, D.D., 1948; Th.B., Th.M., So. Bapt. Sem., 1931; postgrad. U. Louisville, 1931; LL.D. (hon.), Atlanta Law Sch., 1950; m. Eva Rankin, Nov. 16, 1931; children—Madison Rankin, Adrienne (Mrs. Joseph C. Cox, Jr.). Instr., Summer Sch., Ark. Tech., 1929, U. Richmond Extension Sch., 1952-58; ordained to ministry Bapt. Ch., 1928; pastor in Ellenton-Dunbarton, S.C., 1931-34, Timmonsville (S.C.) Bapt. Ch., 1934-38, First Bapt. Ch., Daytona Beach, Fla., 1938-41, First Bapt. Ch., Asheboro, N.C., 1941-44, Beech St. Bapt. Ch., Texarkana, Ark., 1944-48, First Bapt. Ch., Newport News, Va., 1948-70; asso. minister Orcutt Bapt. Ch., Newport News, 1970—; owner Dr. Price Tows Abroad, 1958—. Pres., So. Bapt. Conv. Pastors Conf., 1957-58; v.p. Ark. Bapt. Conv., 1947; v.p. Va. Bapt. Conv., 1955; v.p. So. Bapt. Conv., 1960, mem. home mission bd., 1946-48, radio com., 1949-52, annuity bd., 1953-58, Sunday Sch. pub. bd., 1959-65, fgn. mission bd., 1968-71, 73—; del. White House Conf. Chs. Role with Govt., 1964; mem. Lord's Day Alliance of U.S., 1972—, Bapt. Homes of Va., 1974—; preaching missions to Germany, 1961, P.R., 1962, Scotland, 1965, Alaska, 1966; hon. chmn. Va. Evangelism Conf., 1977. Owner Dr. Price Tours Abroad, 1978—. Trustee Coker Coll. S.C., 1937-38, Central Coll. Ark., 1944-48, Religious Herald, Va., 1950-65, Bluefield (Va.) Coll., 1955-65; advisory bd. Nat. Former Students Assn. Ouachita U., 1979—. Mem. So. Bapt. Sem. (Ky.) Nat. Alumni Assn. (v.p. 1946-47). Mason (32 deg., Shriner), Order Alaska Walrus. Contbr. articles to religious publs., newspapers. Address: 6400 Huntington Ave Newport News VA 23607

PRICE, C. HOYT, oil co. exec.; b. Ozark, Ark., June 7, 1918; s. Hessie and Minnie Lee (Davis) P.; student Jr. Coll., Beebe, Ark., 1935-37; B.C.S., U. Va., 1939, M.A., 1942, Ph.D., 1947; m. Rosemary Hammond, Apr. 1, 1950; children—Andrew, Carl and Roger (twins). Fgn. service officer, 1947-68; assigned Berlin, Paris, Brussels, Saigon, Bern and Washington 1947-62; counselor for common market affairs U.S. Mission European Communities, Brussels, 1962-65; dir. office Telecommunications, Bur. Econ. Affairs, Dept. State, 1965-67, country dir. Philippines, Bur. E.. Asia and Pacific Affairs, 1967-68, with Gulf Oil Corp., 1968—. Mem. Am., So. econ. assns., Am. Finance Assn., Am. Acad. Polit. and Social Scis., Ark. Hist. Assn., Beta Gamma Sigma. Author: (with C. E. Schorske) The Problem of Germany, 1947. Home: 1841 Brandywine Dr Allison Park PA 15101 Office: Gulf Oil Corp Pittsburgh PA 15219

PRICE, C. JACK, hosp. adminstr.; student Wingate Jr. Coll., 1938-39, 46-47; B.A., Catawba Coll., 1949; grad. hosp. adminstrn. course Meml. Mission Hosp., Asheville, N.C., 1951. Office mgr. Southeastern div. R.B. Tyler Constrn. Co., Monroe, N.C., until 1943; asst. adminstr. Meml. Mission Hosp., 1951-55; adminstr. Stanly County Hosp. Dist., Dallas, 1955-63, adminstr., 1963-79; exec. dir. Cypress Community Hosp., Pompano Beach, Fla., 1979—; v.p. Dallas Hosp. Council, 1966, pres., 1967; mem. hosp. adv. com. North Central Tex. Council Govts., 1968-71; clin. prof. preventive medicine and pub. health U. Tex. Southwestern Med. Sch., 1963—, mem. med. faculty council, 1968—; mem. adv. hosp. council Tex. Dept. Health, 1965-70; cons. manpower div. USPHS, 1970-71; mem. Dallas County Spl. Drug Abuse Study Com.; mem., spl. cons. neurology program-project A com. Nat. Inst. Neurol. Diseases and Stroke, NIH, 1969—; mem. membership body Dallas County Health Planning Council, 1971—. Active numerous civic orgns. Bd. dirs. Vis. Nurse Assn., Dallas Area Respiratory Health Assn., Dallas Council on Alcoholism, 1968-71. Served with AUS, 1943-46. Fellow Am. Coll. Hosp. Adminstrs.; mem. Royal Soc. Health (London), Am. (com. on rehab. 1966-68), Tex. (trustee 1968-71, v.p., 1970-71, pres.-elect 1971-72, pres. 1972-73) hosp. assns., Dallas C. of C. (pub. health com. 1968-71). Methodist (past steward). Clubs: Rotary (past treas. Dallas), Press. Office: Cypress Comm Hosp 600 SW Third St Pompano Beach FL 33060

PRICE, CHARLES COALE, educator; b. Passaic, N.J., July 13, 1913; s. Thornton Walton and Helen Marot (Farley) P.; A.B., Swarthmore Coll., 1934, hon. Sc.D., 1950; M.A., Harvard, 1935, Ph.D., 1936; m. Mary Elma White, June 29, 1936; children—Patricia, Susanne, Sarah S., Judith S., Charles C. IV. Research asst. U. Ill., 1936-37, instr., 1937-39, asso., 1939-41, asst. prof., 1941-42, asso. prof., 1942-46; prof. chemistry U. Notre Dame, 1946-54, head dept., 1946-52; Benjamin Franklin prof. chemistry U. Pa., 1965-78, emeritus, 1978—, chmn. dept., 1954-65. Chmn. adv. council on coll. chemistry NSF, 1962-66. Pres. United World Federalists, Inc., 1959-61; bd. dirs., chmn. Council for Livable World; chmn. bd. Swarthmore Coll., 1977—. Recipient Am. Chem. Soc. award Pure Chemistry, 1946; Parsons award for distinguished pub. service, 1973. Mem. Am. Chem. Soc. (pres. 1965), A.A.A.S., Phi Beta Kappa, Sigma Xi, Phi Lambda Upsilon, Phi Sigma Kappa, Alpha Chi Sigma. Author: Brief Course in Organic Chemistry, 1940; Mechanism of Reactions at the Carbon-Carbon Double Bond, 1946; Sulfur-Bonding, 1962; Geometry of Molecules, 1972; The Synthesis of Life, 1974. Editor: Jour. Polymer Sci., Organic Syntheses; asso. editor Chem. Revs.; contbr. numerous tech. papers to Jour. Am. Chem. Soc., Jour. Organic Chemistry, Jour. Polymer Sci. Home: 120 Hilldale Rd Lansdowne PA 19050

PRICE, CHARLES MORGAN, lawyer; b. Chgo., July 17, 1898; s. L. Morgan and Eva (Lapham) P.; A.B., Northwestern, 1920, J.D., 1923; m. Elinor Rew, Oct. 8, 1932; children—Henry Morgan, Rew (Mrs. Donald F. Carne), Charles Morgan. Admitted to Ill. State bar, 1923; partner firm Price, Cushman, Keck, Mahin & Cate and predecessor firms, 1923—. Mem. Am., Ill., Chgo. bar assns., Delta Upsilon, Phi Delta Phi. Republican. Episcopalian. Clubs: Chgo.; Glen View. Home: 1500 Lake Shore Dr Chicago IL 60610 Office: 8300 Sears Tower 233 S Wacker Dr Chicago IL 60606

PRICE, DALIAS ADOLPH, educator; b. Newtonville, Ind., June 28, 1913; s. Fred J. and Rose (Gillam) P.; B.A., U. Ill., 1937, M.A., 1938; Ph.D., U. Wis., 1954; m. Lillian O. Alexander, May 14, 1943; children—David, Curtis, Kent, Roger. Instr. geography U. Ill., 1938-40; acting head dept. S.W. Mo. State Coll., Springfield, 1940-45; asst. U. Wis., 1945-47; asso. prof. geography So. Ill. U., 1947-58; prof. geography, head dept. Eastern Ill. U., 1958—. Mem. Wabash Valley Interstate Commn., 1965—. Bd. suprs. Coles County, Ill., 1967, chmn. 1971-72. Bd. dirs. Charleston Community Hosp., 1966—, Inst. Urban and Regional Affairs, 1967—. Hon. fellow U. Wis., 1953. Mem. AAUP (sec.-treas. Ill. conf. 1958-62), Ill. Geog. Soc. (sec. 1950, chmn. 1951,62, distinguished geographer award 1976), Charleston C. of C. (bd. dirs. 1961-64), Assn. Am. Geographers, Gamma Theta Upsilon. Democrat. Unitarian. Rotarian (pres. Charleston 1965). Author articles in field. Home: 414 Cedar Dr Charleston IL 61920

PRICE, DAVID DEAKINS, publisher; b. Section, Ala., June 22, 1902; s. Samuel Cowan and Gertrude (Deakins) P.; student U. Okla., 1924-26; m. Bernice Ford, May 1927 (dec. May 1974); children—David Deakins Jr., LaVona Bernice (Mrs. William J. Rushton III), Ford Cowan. Founder, The Economy Co., ednl. pubs., Oklahoma City, 1929—, also chmn. bd.; dir. Eason Oil Co. Mem. adv. bd. Salvation Army, 1951-60, St. Anthony Hosp., 1962-66, St. Anthony Hosp. Found., 1963—; found. mem. Frontiers Found. Sci. Okla., 1955—; bd. dirs. Last Frontier council Boy Scouts Am., 1940-49. Mem. Phi Delta Theta. Democrat. Methodist. Rotarian. Clubs: Men's Dinner, Oklahoma City Golf and Country, Petroleum, Beacon (Oklahoma City). Home: 1435 Duffner Oklahoma City OK 73118 Office: 1901 N Walnut St Oklahoma City OK 73105

PRICE, DAVID EDGAR, educator, physician; b. San Diego, July 5, 1914; s. Charles David and Pearl Mae (McCune) P.; A.B., U. Cal. at Berkeley, 1936, M.A., 1937, M.D., 1940; M.P.H., Johns Hopkins, 1945, Dr.P.H., 1946; m. Jean Shearer, June 5, 1936; children—William David, Janet Ruth. Commd. officer USPHS, 1941, epidemiologist San Diego Health Dept., 1941-42, staff physician Venereal Disease Center, Hot Springs, Ark., 1942-44, asst. to chief of research grants div. NIH, 1946-47, chief of cancer research grants, 1947-48, chief div. research grants, 1948-50, asso. dir NIH, 1950-52, asst. surgeon gen. USPHS, Washington, 1952-57, dep. chief Bur. Med. Services, 1957-58, chief Bur. State Services, 1958-60, dep. dir. NIH, 1960-62, dep. surgeon gen. USPHS, 1962-65; program adviser family planning Ford Found., India, 1965-67; prof. pub. health adminstrn. Johns Hopkins Sch. Hygiene and Pub. Health, Balt., 1967—. Mem. Phi Beta Kappa, Alpha Omega Alpha, Phi Chi. Research in exptl. and pituitary endocrinology, family planning. Home: 5 W Melrose Ave Baltimore MD 21210

PRICE, DEREK DE SOLLA, educator, sci. historian; b. London, Eng., Jan. 22, 1922; s. Philip and Fanny Marie (de Solla) P.; B.S., U. London, 1942, Ph.D. in Physics, 1946; Ph.D. in History of Sci., Cambridge (Eng.) U., 1954; M.A., Yale, 1960; m. Ellen Hjorth, Oct. 30, 1947; children—Linda Marie, Jeffrey Phillip, Mark de Solla. Lab. asst., research asst., lectr. war research S.W. Essex Tech. Coll. U. London, 1938-46; Commonwealth Fund fellow math. physics Princeton, 1946-47; lectr. applied math. U. Malaya, Singapore, 1947-50; cons. history physics, astronomy Smithsonian Inst., Washington, 1957; Donaldson fellow Inst. Advanced Study, Princeton, 1958-59; prof., Avalon prof. history sci. Yale, 1960—, chmn. dept. history sci. and medicine, 1960-64, 74—; cons. NSF. Chmn. UNESCO Working Group Sci. Policy, 1967-70; hon. research asso. Smithsonian Instn. Guggenheim fellow, 1969, pres., Internat. Commn. for Science Policy Studies, 1971-75. Mem. Internat. Acad. History Sci., Soc. History Tech., History Sci. Soc., Soc. Social Studies Sci. (founding council mem.), Sigma Xi. Author: The Equatorie of the Planetis, 1955; (with Needham and Wang) Heavenly Clockwork, 1959; Science since Babylon, 1961, enlarged edit., 1975, Little Science, Big Science, 1963; Gears From the Greeks, 1974. Editor: (with I. Spiegel-Rösing) Science, Technology and Society—A Cross-Disciplinary Perspective, 1977. Home: 50 Trumbull St New Haven CT 06510 Office: 2036 Yale Station New Haven CT 06520

PRICE, DON K., educator; b. Middlesboro, Ky., Jan. 23, 1910; s. Don K. and Nell (Rhorer) P.; A.B., Vanderbilt U., 1931; B.A., Oxford U. (Rhodes scholar 1932), 1934, B. Litt., 1935; L.H.D., Case Inst. Tech., 1967, Coll. Wooster, 1972; Litt.D., U. Pitts., 1968; LL.D., Centre Coll. Ky.; 1961, Syracuse U., 1962, Bucknell U., Harvard U., 1970; m. Margaret Helen Gailbreath, Mar. 3, 1936 (dec. Feb. 1970); children—Don C., Linda; m. 2d, Harriet Sloane Fels, May 8, 1971. Reporter, state editor Nashville Eve. Tennessean, 1930-32: research asst. H.O.L.C., and asst. to chmn. Central Housing Com., 1935-37; staff mem., com. on pub. adminstrn. Social Sci. Research Council, 1937-39: editorial asso. Pub. Adminstrn. Clearing House, 1939-41, asst. dir., 1941-43, asso. dir., 1946-53; staff mem. U.S. Bur. Budget, 1945-46; dep. chmn. Research and Devel. Bd., U.S. Dept. Def., 1952-53; asso. dir. The Ford Found., 1953-54, v.p. 1954-58; prof. govt. Kennedy Sch. Govt. Harvard, 1958—, dean, 1958-77; trustee Twentieth Century Fund, 1965—, chmn. bd. trustees, 1977—; bd. trust Vanderbilt U., 1964—; trustee Rand Corp., 1961-71; sr. mem. Inst. Medicine of Nat. Acad. Scis., 1979—; asst. to Herbert Hoover on study of U.S. Presidency under auspices Commn. on Orgn. Exec. Br. Govt., 1947-48; cons. Exec. Office of Pres., 1961-72; dir. Social Sci. Research Council, 1949-52, 64-69; staff dir. Committee on Dept. Def. Orgn., 1953; mem. Pres.'s adv. com. on government orgn., 1959-61; adviser to the King of Nepal, Kathmandu, Nepal, 1960. Trustee Rhodes Trust, 1968-78, Weatherhead Found., 1973—. Served as lt., USCGR, 1943-45. Fellow Am. Acad. Arts and Scis.; mem. Am. Philos. Soc., AAAS (bd. dirs. 1959-64, 66-69, pres. 1967), Phi Beta Kappa. Clubs: Cosmos (Wash.); Century Assn. (N.Y.C.). Author: City Manager Government in the United States (with Harold and Kathryn Stone), 1940; U.S. Foreign Policy, Its Organization and Control (with W. Y. Elliott and others), 1952, also The Political Economy of American Foreign Policy, 1955; Government and Science, 1954; The Scientific Estate, 1965. Editor, co-author: The Secretary of State, 1960. Home: 984 Meml Dr Cambridge MA 02138 Office: 79 Boylston St Cambridge MA 02138

PRICE, DONALD ALBERT, veterinarian; b. Bridgeport, Ohio, Dec. 25, 1919; s. Arthur D. and Louise A. (Knellinger) P.; student Wheeling (W.Va.) Coll., 1937-38; D.V.M., Ohio State U., 1950; m. June Loree Fleming, 1946; children—Karen Louise, Benita Ann, Donna Jean. With Wheeling Steel Corp., 1938-41; with psychology dept. Ohio State U., 1946-48, lab. asst. parasitology Coll. Vet. Medicine, 1948-50; research faculty Tex. A&M U., 1950-55; partner San Angelo (Tex.) Vet. Hosp., 1955-58; asst. editor jours. AVMA, Chgo., 1958-59, editor-in-chief publs., 1959-72, asst. exec. v.p., 1972—. Served to capt. USAAF, 1941-46. Recipient Disting. Alumnus award Ohio State U. Coll. Vet. Medicine, 1966. Fellow Am. Med. Writers Assn.; mem. AVMA, U.S. Animal Health Assn., Am. Animal Hosp. Assn., Am. Assn. Equire Practitioners, Assn. Sheep and Goat Practitioners, Ill. Vet. Med. Assn., Phi Zeta, Phi Eta Sigma, Alpha Psi. Methodist. Club: Shriners. Home: 230 Valley Rd Cary IL 60013 Office: 930 Meacham Rd Schaumberg IL 60196

PRICE, DONALD ALBERT, assn. exec., veterinarian; b. Bridgeport, O., Dec. 25, 1919; s. Arthur D. and Louise (Knellinger) P.; student Elliott Sch. Bus., Wheeling, W.Va., 1937-39; D.V.M., Ohio State U., 1950; m. June Loree Fleming, July 19, 1945; children—Karen Louise, Benita Ann, Donna Jean. Adminstrv. asst. Wheeling Steel Corp., 1939-41; research scientist Tex. A. and M. Expt. Sta., 1950-55; practice vet. medicine, San Angelo, Tex., 1955-58; editor-in-chief Am. Vet. Med. Assn., Chgo., 1958-71; exec. v.p., 1971—. Served to capt. USAAF, 1941-46. Named Distinguished Alumnus, Ohio State U., 1966. Fellow Am. Med. Writers Assn.; mem. Am., Ill., Chgo. vet. med. assns., Am. Assn. Equine Practitioners (hon.), Am. Animal Hosp. Assn. (hon.), Am. Assn. Sheep and Goat Practitioners (hon.), Panam. Vet. Assn. (Bogota, Colombia) (dir., v.p. 1973—). Methodist. Mason (Shriner). Home: 230 Valley Rd Cary IL 60013 Office: 930 N Meacham Rd Schaumburg IL 60196

PRICE, EDGAR HILLEARY, JR., food co. exec.; b. Jacksonville, Fla., Jan. 1, 1918; s. Edgar Hilleary and Mary Williams (Phillips) P.; student U. Fla., 1937-38; m. Elise Ingram, June 24, 1947; 1 son, Jerald Steven. Mgr. comml. flower farm, 1945-49, Fla. Gladiolus Growers Assn., 1949-55; exec. v.p. Tropicana Products, Inc., Bradenton, Fla., 1955-73, dir. div. govt. and industry regulations, to 1979, dir.; exec. v.p. Indsl. Glass Co., Inc., Bradenton, 1963-73; pres., chmn. bd. Price Co., Inc., cons., Bradenton, 1973—; dir. First City Fed. Savs. and Loan Assn. Manatee County, Fla. Power and Light Co., Gen. Telephone Co. Fla. Past pres. Fla. C. of C.; past chmn. Fla. Citrus Commn., Fla. Gov.'s Freeze Damage Survey Team, Spl. Commn. for Study Abolition Death Penalty; bd. dirs. Fla. Fair Assn., Fla. Citrus Expn., Fla. Fruit and Vegetable Assn.; past chmn. Joint Citrus Legislative Com.; past mem. Fla. Plant Bd., Fla. Bd. Control, Fla. Legislative Council; exec. com. Growers and Shippers League Fla., Fla. Agrl. Council, Spl. Health Agrl. Research and Edn.; past pres., chmn. bd. Fla. Hort. Soc.; past chmn., commr. census 12th Jud. Circuit; mem. Gov. Fla. Com. Rehab. Handicapped, Fla. Commn. on Ethics; mem. Presdl. Inaugural Fin. Com., 1977, Eastern 5th Circuit U.S. Jud. Nominating Commn., 1977—. Mem. Fla. Senate from 36th Dist., 1958-66; past chmn. Manatee County Bd. Sch. Dist. Trustees, Local Housing Authority Bradenton, Bradenton Sub-Standard Housing Bd., Bradenton Charter Adv. Com.; del. Democratic Nat. Conv., 1960, dist. del., 1964. Past trustee, mem. exec. com. Stetson U. Served to 1st lt. USAAF, 1941-45. Named Boss of Yr., Nat. Secs. Assn., 1959, Man of Yr. for Fla. Agr., Progressive Farmer mag., 1961; recipient Merit award Am. Flag Assn., 1962, Gamma Sigma Delta, 1965; Leadership award Fla. Agrl. Extension Service, 1963; Outstanding Senator award Fla. Radio Broadcasters, 1965, Allen Morris award as most valuable mem. Fla. Legislature, 1965; Most Valuable Mem. Fla. Senate award St. Petersburg Times, 1965; Brotherhood award Sarasota chpt. Nat. Council Christians and Jews, 1966; Distinguished Citizen award Manatee County, 1970; Distinguished Alumnus award U. Fla., 1972; Service to Mankind award Sertoma Internat., 1976. Mem. Am. Legion, V.F.W., Mil. Order World Wars, Bradenton C. of C. (v.p. 1949-51), Fla. Hort. Soc., Fla. Flower Assn., Blue Key (hon.), Omicron Delta Kappa (hon.), Sigma Alpha Epsilon. Baptist (deacon 1953—). Kiwanian (pres. 1955). Home: 3009 Riverview Blvd Bradenton FL 33550 Office: PO Box 9270 Bradenton FL 33506. *The turning point in my life came at the age of 32 when I accepted Jesus Christ as my personal Lord and Saviour. I believe every person should live his life up to the fullest extent of his God-given talents and ability. I think we have a responsibility to "pay our dues" for the privilege of living in a free land by being actively involved in our government.*

PRICE, EDWARD WARREN, aerospace engr.; b. Detroit, Dec. 6, 1920; s. Frank E. and Elizabeth Allyne (Rattray) P.; B.A., U. Calif., Los Angeles, postgrad., 1949-51; postgrad. U. Mich., 1950-51; m. Mary Kate Howard, June 21, 1952; children—Douglas Brian, Alison Tamara, Carolyn Louise. Mem. research staff Calif. Inst. Tech., 1941-44; head aerothermo-chemistry dept. U.S. Naval Weapons Center, 1944-74; prof. aerospace engring. Ga. Inst. Tech., 1967, 74—. Served with USNR, 1944-46. Recipient Thompson award, 1960, Superior Civilian Service medal, 1975 (both U.S. Navy). Fellow Am. Inst. Aeros. and Astronautics (dir. 1966, v.p., 1967-68; Dryden Research award 1967, Pendray award 1971, Robert H. Goddard award 1976); mem. AAAS, Internat. Combustion Inst., Sigma Xi. Contbr. articles on rocket propulsion, combustion to profl. jours. Patentee in field. Home: 5058 Highpoint Rd NE Atlanta GA 30342 Office: Sch of Aerospace Engring Ga Inst Tech Atlanta GA 30332

PRICE, EDWIN FARROW, mfg. co. cons., engr.; b. Jacksonville, Fla., Jan. 3, 1922; s. Harry Calder and Alma (Farrow) P.; Met.E. in Metall. Engring., U. Cin., 1947; m. Alice Bowman, Aug. 31, 1946; children—Harry, Barbara, Richard. Metall. engr. Ironton div. Dayton Malleable Inc., 1947-48, quality control mgr., 1948-53, sales engr., 1953-64, gen. sales mgr., 1964-68, gen. mgr. GHR div., 1968-77, pres., 1977-79, cons., 1979—. Active Boy Scouts Am., 1959-72, United Fund Drive, Dayton, 1976-77. Served with U.S. Army, 1942-46. Recipient Distinguished Alumni award U. Cin., 1969. Mem. Am. Soc. Metals, Am. Foundrymen's Soc., Iron Castings Soc., Engrs. Club Dayton, Alpha Chi Sigma. Republican. Episcopalian. Author: Statistical Quality Control for Foundries, 1953. Home: 128E Dixon Ave Dayton OH 45419 Office: 3931 S Dixie Dr Dayton OH 45439

PRICE, FRANK, motion picture and TV co. exec.; b. Decatur, Ill., May 17, 1930; s. William F. and Winifred A. (Moran) P.; student Mich. State U., 1949-51; m. Katherine Huggins, May 15, 1965; children—Stephen, David, Roy, Frank. Writer, story editor CBS-TV, N.Y.C., 1951-53, Columbia Pictures, Hollywood, Calif., 1953-57, NBC-TV, 1957-58, Hollywood; producer, writer ZIV-TV, 1958; producer, writer Universal Television, Universal City, Calif., 1959-64, v.p., 1964-71, sr. v.p., 1971-73, exec. v.p. in charge of production, 1973-74, pres., 1974-78; v.p., dir. MCA, Inc., 1976-78; pres. Columbia Pictures Prodn., 1978-79, Columbia Pictures, 1979—; exec. producer The Virginian, 1961-64, Ironside, 1965, It Takes A Thief, 1966, also TV series Kojak, Six Million Dollar Man, Bionic Woman, Baretta, Rockford Files, Quincy, The Hardy Boys and Nancy Drew, Rich Man, Poor Man, 79 Park Ave., Captains and the Kings. Served with USN, 1948-49. Mem. Writers Guild Am., West. Office: Columbia Pictures Burbank CA 91505

PRICE, FRANK JAMES, educator, writer; b. Logansport, La., Mar. 1, 1917; s. William Hall and Mary Elizabeth (Loving) P.; B.A. cum laude, La. Poly. Inst., 1938; M.A., La. State U., 1940; Ph.D., State U. Ia., 1956; m. Lucile Kendrick, Nov. 16, 1940; children—Virginia, James Patrick. Reporter, Interstate Progress, Logansport, summers 1937-38; instr. journalism U. Ga., spring 1940; mem. faculty La. State U., Baton Rouge, 1940—, prof. journalism, 1956—, dir. Sch. Journalism, 1956-69. Reporter, alternate telegraph editor Baton Rouge Morning Advocate, summer, 1941, editorial writer, 1941-42; reporter Baton Rouge State-Times, summers 1942-43, editorial writer, 1943-44, 46-53; legislative reporter A.P., Baton Rouge, 1948; copy editor Fla. Times Union, Jacksonville, summer 1962; pres. Southwestern Journalism Congress, 1950; exec. dir. La. Scholastic Press Assn., 1956-70; publs. cons. Served to 2d lt. AUS, 1945-46. Named to La. State U. Sch. Journalism Hall of Fame. Mem. Assn. Edn. Journalism, Am. Assn. U. Profs., La. Press Assn., Internat. Assn. Bus. Communicators, Quill and Scroll (hon.), Soc. Profl. Journalists, Sigma Delta Chi (pres. S.E. La. chpt. 1963-64), Kappa Tau Alpha, Phi Kappa Phi. Presbyn. Author: Troy H. Middleton, A Biography, 1974, Story of the Baton Rouge Refinery, Two Minutes of Basketball. Contbr. to popular mags, also profl. jours. Home: 545 Centenary Dr Baton Rouge LA 70808

PRICE, GEORGE, cartoonist; b. Coytesville, N.J., June 9, 1901; s. George and Camille (Vidal) P.; ed high sch., Ft. Lee, N.J.; m. Florence Schwank, Dec. 3, 1927; children—George, Wilfrid, Charles, Susan. Various positions all branches of advt. art, printing, lithography, art service, agy., and free lance work, 1920-29; cartoonist, book illustrator. Author and illustrator; Good Humor Man, 1940; It's Smart to be People, 1942; Who's in Charge Here?, 1943: Is It Anyone We Know?, 1944; Geo. Price's Ice-Cold War, 1951; We Buy Old Gold, 1952; George Price's Characters, 1955; My Dear 500 Friends, 1963; The People Zoo, 1971; Browse At Your Own Risk, 1977. Contbr. to New Yorker mag., 1929—. Address: 81 Westervelt Ave Tenafly NJ 07670

PRICE, HAROLD ARCHIBALD, lawyer; b. Morristown, N.J., July 13, 1893; s. Archibald and Jane (Babbitt)P.; LL.B., N.Y.U., 1916; m. Elizabeth Reed, Apr. 5, 1926; children—Charlton R., Jane (Mrs. Frederick C. J. Willsea), Miriam (Mrs. Amory McC. Patten). Admitted to N.J. bar, 1916; practice in Morristown, 1916-56, 63—; partner firm Schenck, Price, Smith & King, and predecessors, 1963—; judge Superior Ct. N.J., 1956-63, presiding judge part B appellate div., 1957-63; apptd. by N.J. Supreme Ct. to investigate Twp. Lodi, N.J., 1930, City Newark, 1936; dep. atty. gen. N.J., 1947; vice chmn. N.J. Joint Legislative Commn. to study capital punishment, 1964. Prs. Morristown YMCA, 1948-50; trustee Morristown chpt. A.R.C., 1941-45, chmn., 1943-45; trustee Community Chest and Council Morris County, 1949-50; trustee Morristown Meml. Hosp., 1943-58, com. mgrs., 1943-58, v.p., 1958. Fellow Am. Bar Found., Am. Probate Counsel; mem. Am., N.J., Essex County, Morris County bar assns., Am. Coll. Trial Attys., Am. Judicature Soc. (dir. 1966—), Inst. Practicing Lawyers (founder, trustee 1941—), Washington Assn. N.J. (trustee 1948-66, pres. 1948-53, 63-66, N.Y.U. Law Alumni Assn. (dir. 1964-67). Presbyn. (pres. bd. trustees 1934-35, 36-38). Mason. Home: Box 84 Bailey Hollow Rd Morris Twp NJ 07960 Office: 10 Washington St Morristown NJ 07960

PRICE, HAROLD LAFLER, corp. exec., ret. air force officer; b. Potter, N.Y., July 2, 1918; s. Fred Reynolds and Clarice Amelia (Lafler) Osman; B.A., Pa. State Coll., 1941; grad. Air Corps Flying Sch., 1942, Air Command and Staff Coll., 1953, Nat. War Coll., 1963; M.A., George Washington U., 1963; m. Blanche McCord, Oct. 17, 1942; children—Harold Lafler II, Gary McCord, Kathryn. Commd. 2d lt. USAAF, 1942, advanced through grades to maj. gen. USAF, 1973; war planner Hdqrs. USAF and Joint Chiefs of Staff, 1959-62; dep. dir. ops. 9th Air Force, 1963-64; dep. chief staff operations 2d Air Div., S.Vietnam, for USAF Air Operations in S.E. Asia, 1964-65; comdr. 354th Tactical Fighter Wing, 1965-66; with Office Sec. Def., 1966-69; sr. USAF MAAG adviser to Imperial Iranian Air Force, 1969-72; dir. mil. assistance and fgn. mil. sales Hdqrs. USAF, Washington, 1972-75, ret.; v.p., mgr. Ford Aerospace and Communications Corp., Tehran, Iran, 1976—. Decorated D.S.M., Legion of Merit with 2 oak leaf clusters, D.F.C. with 2 oak leaf clusters, Soldiers medal for heroism, Bronze Star medal, Air medal with 11 oak leaf clusters, South Vietnam Air Force D.S.M., Iranian medal of merit 1st class. Mason. Home: 300 W North Park St Okeechobee FL 33472

PRICE, HARRISON ALAN, research co. exec.; b. Oregon City, Oreg., May 17, 1921; s. Harry I. and Isabel (Esson) P.; B.S., Calif. Inst. Tech., 1942; M.B.A., Stanford U., 1951; m. Anne Shaw, Apr. 29, 1944; children—Bret, David, Dana, Holly. Mgr. econ. research Stanford Research Inst., Los Angeles, 1951-55; gen. mgr. Def. Plant div. Harvey Aluminum, Torrance, Calif., 1955-58; pres. Econ. Research Assos., West Los Angeles, Calif., 1958-73; sr. v.p., chmn. planning Research Corp., Los Angeles, 1973-76, chmn., 1976-78; pres. Harrison Price Co., Los Angeles, 1978—; dir. Bekins Co. Bd. dirs. Mind Sci. Found., San Antonio; trustee Calif. Inst. of Arts. Served with inf., U.S. Army, 1944-46. Clubs: Cosmos (Washington); Los Angeles Athletic, Los Angeles, Calif. Home: 542 Lorraine Blvd Los Angeles CA 90020

PRICE, HARRY BORUM, JR., merchant; b. Norfolk, Va., Mar. 4, 1911; s. Harry B. and Bertie T. P.; student U. Va.; m. Sue Spaulding Deitrick, June 3, 1933; children—Harry Borum, Bruce D., Michael Wayne. With Price's Inc., Norfolk, 1933—, pres. 1939—; pres. Colonial Finance Corp. Past pres. community chest Norfolk, Central YMCA, Leigh Meml. Hosp., Norfolk. Trustee Norfolk Acad., Past v.p. Nat. Found. Consumer Credit. Mem. Norfolk C. of C. (past pres.), Young President's Orgn., Nat. Appliance and Radio-TV Dealers Assn. (past pres.), Alpha Kappa Psi (hon.). Club: Optimist. Home: 7106 Ocean Front Virginia Beach VA 23451 Office: 1900 Monticello Ave Norfolk VA 23517

PRICE, HARRY STEELE, JR., constrn. materials co. exec.; b. East Jordan, Mich., Oct. 11, 1910; s. Harry S. and Grace B. (Beers) P.; B.S., U. Mich., 1932; m. Janet Smith, Apr. 7, 1934; children—Pamela, Harry Steele III, Marlay B. Office and field office on heavy constrn. Price Bros. Co., 1932-36, designer, constrn. and operation of gravel plant, 1936-38, in charge concrete sewer and culvert pipe operations, sand and gravel operations, gen. sec., 1938-45, v.p. in charge of pressure pipe div., 1945-67, exec. v.p., 1953-67, chmn., pres., 1967-73, chmn, 1973—; pres., dir. Price Bros. Pipe & Constrn. Co., Price Bros., Independent Concrete Pipe Co., St. Louis, Flexicore Co., Inc.; dir. Winters Nat. Bank & Trust Co., Durinon Co., Inc. Commr. Montgomery County Park Dist. Bd. dirs., past pres. Dayton Art Inst.; adv. bd. Kettering Meml. Hosp. Mem. Am. Concrete Pipe Assn. (past pres.), Am. Soc. C.E., Nat. Soc. Profl. Engrs., Water and Wastewater Equipment Mfg. Assn. (past pres.), Am. Water Works Assn. (past trustee), N.A.M. (urban affairs com.). Clubs: Engineers, Dayton, Buz-Fuz, Moraine Country. Home: 314 Stonehaven Rd Dayton OH 45429 Office: 367 W 2d St Dayton OH 45401

PRICE, HARVEY EARL, banker; b. Johnston County, N.C., Aug. 6, 1920; s. Moses Leon and Lettie (Wall) P.; grad. Sch. Commerce, Atlantic Christian Coll., Wilson, N.C., 1941; Carolinas Sch. Banking, Chapel Hill, N.C., 1946, 58; m. Eleanor Farmer Blow, Feb. 22, 1947; children—Harvey Craig, Stephen Russ. With accounting sect. Post Ordnance Dept., U.S. Army, Ft. Bragg, 1941-42; with First-Citizens Bank & Trust Co., Smithfield, N.C., 1942—, auditor, 1950-68, v.p. 1968-71, sr. v.p., 1971—; instr. auditing and comml. law, 1955-56. Pres. Smithfield P.T.A., 1965-66; chmn. Smithfield chpt. N.C. Symphony Soc., 1968-71; dist. committeeman, financial chmn. Century Club, Boy Scouts Am., 1965-69. Bd. dirs. Johnston County Mental Health Assn., 1962-66, 66-70. Mem. Bank Adminstrn. Inst. Democrat. Baptist (sec. bd. deacons 1963-67, chmn. bd. deacons 1970-72, Sunday sch. tchr. 1962-69). Rotarian (pres. Smithfield 1964-65). Home: PO Box 1024 Smithfield NC 27577 Office: 241 E Market St Smithfield NC 27577

PRICE, J(OHN) WILLIAM, paper co. exec.; b. Quebec, Can., June 23, 1927; s. John Herbert and Lorna (Macdougall) P.; came to U.S., 1952; student U. N.B., 1945-47, Bishops U., 1947-48; m. Helen Julia Stevenson, Jan. 15, 1954; children—Diana, John, David. Asst. forestry engr. Powell River Paper Co., Vancouver, B.C., 1948-50; adminstrv. asst. Bowaters Nfld. Pulp & Paper Co., 1950-52; serviceman Bowater Paper Co., N.Y.C., 1952, service mgr., 1953-54, salesman, 1954-55, dist. sales mgr., 1956-58, v.p. N. Am. sales, 1959-64; v.p., dir. Perkins Goodwin Co., Inc., N.Y.C., 1964-74, chmn. bd., 1970-74; v.p., gen. mgr. southwoods div. St. Regis Paper Co., 1979—; exec. v.p., dir. Southland Paper Mills Inc. Clubs: Canadian (N.Y.C.), Winged Foot Golf (Mamaroneck, N.Y.); Preson Trail, Brookhollow (Dallas); River Oaks Country (Houston). Home: 5423 Meaders Ln Dallas TX 75229 Office: 1111 Fannin St Houston TX 77002

PRICE, JACKSON ERNEST, govt. ofcl.; b. Washington, Sept. 7, 1907 s. Jackson Ernest and Cornelia (Beall) P.; student Georgetown U., 1927-28, J.D., 1932; student George Washington U., 1928-29; m. Frances Powell, May 25, 1934; children—Pamela Ann Malley, Patricia Beall Frederick. Admitted to D.C. bar, 1932, Md. bar, 1955; practiced in Washington, 1932-34; asst. solicitor Dept. Interior,

1934-42, chief counsel grazing service, 1942-44, chief counsel Nat. Park Service, 1944-54, chief lands, 1954-55, asst. dir., 1955-66; dir. Southeast region Nat. Park Service, 1966-68, spl. asst. to dir., Wilderness Hearing Officer, 1968—. Recipient Distinguished Service award Dept. Interior, 1968. Mem. Am. Inst. Park Execs., Kappa Alpha. Clubs: Kenwood Golf and Country; Boca Del Mar Golf and Tennis; Coral Key Yacht. Home: 3100 NE 48 Ct Apt 102 Lighthouse Point FL 33064

PRICE, JACOB MYRON, educator, historian; b. Worcester, Mass., Nov. 8, 1925; s. Abraham Oscar and Alice (Pike) P.; A.B., Harvard U., 1947, A.M., 1948, Ph.D., 1954; postgrad. Worcester Coll., Oxford (Eng.) U., 1949-50, London Sch. Econs., 1950-51. Instr. history Smith Coll., Northampton, Mass., 1954-56; instr. history U. Mich., Ann Arbor, 1956-58, asst. prof., 1958-61, asso. prof., 1961-64, prof., 1964—, chmn. dept., 1971-72, 79—. Mem. editorial com. U. Mich. Press, 1959-65. Served to staff sgt. USAAF, 1944-46. Recipient Gilbert Chinard prize, 1974, U. Mich. Press Book award, 1974. Guggenheim fellow, 1958-59, 65-66, Social Sci. Research Council faculty research fellow, 1962-63; Am. Council Learned Socs. fellow, 1972-73; Nat. Endowment Humanities fellow, 1977-78. Fellow Royal Hist. Soc.; mem. Am. Hist. Assn. (program com. 1962, 68, 76) Econ. History Assn., Conf. Brit. Studies (exec. sec. 1978—), Midwest Conf. Brit. Hist. Studies (pres. 1976-78), Soc. Comparative Study Soc. and History (sec. 1974—). Club: Cosmos. Author: The Tobacco Adventure to Russia, 1961, France and the Chesapeake, 1973. Editor: Reading for Life, 1959, The Dimensions of the Past, 1972, Joshua Johnson's Letterbook, 1979. Editorial bd. Jour. Modern History, 1968-70; Jour. Brit. Studies, 1974—, William and Mary Quar., 1974-77, Comparative Studies in Society and History, 1974—, Papers of George Washington, 1977—. Home: 1050 Wall St Apt 4-D Ann Arbor MI 48105 Office: Dept History U Mich Ann Arbor MI 48109

PRICE, JAMES GORDON, physician; b. Brush, Colo., June 20, 1926; s. John Hoover and Rachel Laurette (Dodds) P.; B.A., U. Colo., 1948, M.D., 1951; m. Janet Alice McSween, June 19, 1949; children—James Gordon II, Richard Christian, Mary Laurette, Janet Lynn. Intern Denver Gen. Hosp., 1951-52; practice medicine specializing in family medicine, Brush, 1952-78; asso. prof. family practice U. Kans. Med. Center, 1978—; mem. staff East Morgan County Hosp. Mem. Inst. Medicine, Nat. Acad. Scis., 1973—. Trustee Family Health Found. Am. Served with USNR, 1943-46. Charter diplomate Am. Bd. Family Practice (dir., pres. 1979), Charter fellow Am. Acad. Family Physicians (pres. 1973-74); mem. Phi Beta Kappa, Alpha Omega Alpha. Mason. Editorial bd. Med. World News, 1969—; editor Am. Acad. Family Practice Home Study Self Assessment Program, 1978—. Home: 127736 St Andrew Dr Kansas City MO 64145 Office: U Kans Med Center Coll Health Scis and Hosp Rainbow Blvd at 39th St Kansas City KS 66103

PRICE, JAMES HARDY, JR., judge; b. Greenville, S.C., Oct. 3, 1914; s. James Hardy and Alyce Louise (Baker) P.; B.A., Furman U., 1936; LL.B., U. S.C., 1939; grad. Nat. Coll. State Judiciary, 1971; m. Alice Celeste Rogers, May 29, 1944; children—James Hardy, Lisa Bruce. Admitted to S.C. bar, 1939, practiced in Greenville, 1939-41, 45-61; county judge Greenville county, Greenville, 1961-72, state circuit judge, 1976—. Lectr. seminars Greenville Tech. Edn. Center, 1969-70, 72; del. from S.C. to jud. sect. Am. Bar Assn., 1970-76. Mem. Jud. Reform Com., 1970-72; mem. Regional Com. Law Enforcement Assistance Program, chmn., 1973; chmn. S.C. Jud. Discipline and Standards Commn., 1976—; mem. State Task Force on Cts., Omnibus Crime Commn., 1968-70. Served with USNR, 1941-45. Recipient Outstanding Jud. Service award Assn. Trial Lawyers Am. and S.C. Trial Lawyers Assn., 1972; award of pub. safety Appalachin Council Govts. Mem. Am., S.C. bar assns., Greenville Lawyers Club (pres. 1960), Theta Chi (pres. 1936). Baptist (tchr. Bible class 1955). Rotarian, Elk. Club: Poinsett. Home: 3 Brookside Way Greenville SC 29605 Office: 307 County Court House Greenville SC 29601

PRICE, JAMES LIGON, JR., educator; b. Chase City, Va., Sept. 11, 1915; s. James Ligon and Marguerite (Wright) P; A.B., Washington and Lee U., 1936; B.D., Union Theol. Sem. Va., 1941; Th. M., Princeton Theol. Sem., 1943; Ph.D., U. Cambridge (Eng.), 1951; m. Ruth Gordon Watts, May 19, 1943; children—James Ligon III, Linda Gordon, Elisabeth Carmichael. Ordained to ministry Prsbyn. Ch., 1941; minister edn. St. Charles Av. Presbyn. Ch. New Orleans, 1941-42; asst. prof. philosophy and religion Washington and Lee U., 1946-48; asso. prof. Bible, coll. chaplain Southwestern at Memphis, 1950-52; mem. faculty Duke, 1952—, prof. religion, 1961—, chmn. dept., 1957-65, dean Trinity Coll., 1964-69, vice provost dean undergrad. edn., 1969-72, chmn. Univ. Research Council, 1977—. Chmn. exec. com. Ednl. Instns., Presbyn. Synod N.C., 1966-68. Pres. Durham Civic Choral Soc., 1956-57. Served as chaplain USNR, 1943-46. Salem fellow, 1938. Mem. Am. Acad. Religion (pres. 1965), Soc. Bib. Lit. (pres. So. sect. 1961-62), Am. Assn. U. Profs. (pres. Duke chpt. 1963-64), Sigma Delta Chi, Delta Tau Delta. Democrat. Author: Interpreting the New Testament rev. edit., 1971; Qumran and Johannine Theology, John and Qumran, 1972; Search for the Theology of the Fourth Evangelist, New Testament Issues, 1970; 1, 2 Corinthian, Interpreters' Bible One-Volume Commentary, 1971. Editorial bd. Interpretation, A Jour. Bible and Theology, 1963-76. Home: 2330 Hilton Ave Durham NC 27707

PRICE, JOHN HERBERT, former Can. army officer; b. Quebec, Que., Can., Aug. 5, 1898; s. Sir William and Lady Amelia Blanche P.; student Bishop's Coll. Sch., Lennoxville, Que., Royal Mil. Coll.; m. Katherine Lorna MacDougall, Sept. 23, 1924; Dir., Saguenay Power Co. Ltd., J.H. Minet & Co. (1954) Can. Ltd., Robert McAlpine Ltd., Consol. Plant Airport Bldg. Holdings Ltd. Served to brig. gen. Royal F.A., World War I, Royal Rifles of Can., World War II. Decorated officer Order Can., Order Brit. Empire, M.C., knight comdr. St. Lazarus of Jerusalem. Anglican. Freemason. Clubs: Mount Royal; Garrison (Quebec); The Brook, Canadian (N.Y.C.); Montreal Racket, Farmers of Montreal; Mount Bruno Golf and Country; Hermitage; Carleton (London, Eng.). Home: 2 Westmount Sq Westmount PQ H3Z 2S4 Canada

PRICE, JOHN ROY, JR., fin. co. exec.; b. N.Y.C., Dec. 20, 1938; s. John Roy and Pauline (Milnes) P.; B.A., Grinnell Coll., 1960; B.A., Queens Coll., Oxford (Eng.) U., 1962, M.A., 1965; J.D., Harvard U., 1965; m. Victoria Scott Pohle, Dec. 19, 1970; 1 son, Matthew Roy. Asso. law firm Casey, Lane & Mittendorf, N.Y.C., 1965-67; v.p. Bedford-Stuyvesant DB& S Corp., N.Y.C., 1967-68; spl. asst. to Pres. U.S., 1968-71; asso. firm Donaldson, Lufkin & Jenrette, N.Y.C., 1971-72; v.p. Mfrs. Hanover Trust, N.Y.C., 1972-75, Mfrs. Hanover Corp., N.Y.C., 1975—; dir. Mfrs. Hanover Leasing Corp., Mfrs. Hanover Mortgage Corp., Ritter Fin. Corp., Ritter Life Ins. Co., Mchts. Indsl. Bank. Nat. chmn. Ripon Soc., 1967-68; trustee Grinnell Coll. 1970—; bd. dirs. New Communities Corp., 1976-77. Rhodes scholar. Mem. Council Fgn. Relations, Phi Beta Kappa. Club: Harvard (N.Y.C.). Office: 350 Park Ave New York NY 10022

PRICE, JOSEPH EARL, educator; b. Denver, Sept. 23, 1930; s. Joseph Elias and Gladys (Hagar) P.; B.S., Colo. Coll., 1952; M.A., Rice U., 1954, Ph.D., 1956; m. Nola Ann Iverson, Aug. 11, 1962; children—Rodney Jay, Andrea Jo. Asst. prof. physics Lamar State Coll. Tech., Beaumont, Tex., 1956-59; prof., chmn. physics dept. Idaho State U., Pocatello, 1959—; physicist Idaho Nuclear Corp., Idaho Falls, summers 1968-70. Mem. AAUP, Am. Assn. Physics Tchrs., Idaho Acad. Scis., Am. Inst. Physics, Phi Beta Kappa, Sigma Xi. Methodist. Home: 26 Davis Dr Pocatello ID 83201

PRICE, KARL RHORER, lawyer; b. Middlesboro, Ky., Jan. 10, 1914; s. Don K. and Nell (Rhorer) P.; B.A., Vanderbilt U., 1935; LL.B., Yale, 1940; B.A., Oxford (Eng.) U., 1939; m. Margaret Craighill, Feb. 1, 1947; children—Sharon, Margaret, Deborah, Carolyn. Admitted to D. C. bar, 1942; law clk. U.S. Ct. Appeals for 2d Circuit, 1940-41, U.S. Supreme Ct., 1946-47; with Bur. Internal Revenue, Treasury Dept., 1947-50, head interpretative div., 1949-50; mem. firm Alvord & Alvord, Washington, 1950-65, Ivins, Phillips & Barker, Washington, 1965—. Served to capt., inf., AUS, 1942-46; ETO. Mem. Phi Beta Kappa. Democrat. Presbyn. Clubs: Chevy Chase (Md.); Metropolitan (Washington). Home: 3121 45th St NW Washington DC 20016 Office: 1700 Pennsylvania Ave NW Washington DC 20006

PRICE, KARL S., lawyer, TV prodn. co. exec.; b. Louisville, Apr. 11, 1921; s. David and Eva (Korn) P.; B.A., Stanford, 1947, LL.D., 1950; m. Sylvia Claire Nevelson, Apr. 3, 1955; children—Howard Marshall, Elisa Joy. Admitted to Calif. bar, 1950, since practiced in Los Angeles; mem. firm Kaplan, Livingston, Goodwin, Berkowitz & Selvin, until 1975; exec. v.p. Corday Prodns., Inc., 1975—. Served with AUS, World War II. Mem. Am., Calif., Los Angeles, Beverly Hills bar assns., Los Angeles Copyright Soc., Hollywood Radio and TV Soc., Phi Beta Kappa. Home: 1649 Stradella Rd Los Angeles CA 90024 Office: Burbank Studios Burbank CA 91522

PRICE, KENNETH MARTIN, artist, printmaker, sculptor; b. Los Angeles, Feb. 16, 1935; s. Kenneth A. and Joan A. (Collins) P.; student Chounard Art Inst., Los Angeles County Art Inst.; B.F.A., U. So. Calif., 1956; M.F.A., SUNY, Alfred, 1959; m. Happy Ward, May 13, 1969; 1 son, Jackson. One-man exhbns. include Ferus Gallery, Los Angeles, 1960, 61, 64, Kasmin Gallery, London, 1968, 70, Mizuno Gallery, Los Angeles, 1969, 71, Whitney Mus. Am. Art, N.Y.C., 1969, Gemini G.E.L., Los Angeles, 1970, 72, David Whitney Gallery, N.Y.C., 1971, Galerie Neuendorf, Cologne and Hamburg, W. Ger., 1971, Hamburg, 1973, Nicholas Wilder Gallery, Los Angeles, 1973, Felicity Samuel Gallery, London, 1974, Willard Gallery, N.Y.C., 1974, Ronald Greenberg Gallery, St. Louis, 1976, James Corcoran Gallery, Los Angeles, 1976, Los Angeles County Mus. Art, 1978, Gallery Contemporary Art, Taos, N.Mex., 1978, Tex. Gallery, Houston, 1979; numerous group exhbns., 1962—, including Mus. Modern Art, N.Y.C., 1969, 70, 71, 74, Phila. Mus., 1972, Whitney Mus. Am. Art, 1967, 70, 76, 79. Guggenheim fellow, 1978; grantee Nat. Endowment Arts, 1967. Address: PO Box 1356 Taos NM 87871

PRICE, LEONTYNE, concert, opera singer; b. Laurel, Miss., Feb. 10, 1927; d. James A. and Kate (Baker) Price; B.A., Central State Coll., Wilberforce, Ohio, 1949, D.Mus., 1968; student Juilliard Sch. Music, 1949-52; pupil Florence Page Kimball; L.H.D., Dartmouth Coll., 1962, Fordham U., 1969, Yale U., 1979; Mus.D., Howard U., 1962; Dr. Humanities, Rust Coll., 1968; m. William Warfield, Aug. 31, 1952 (div.). Appeared as Bess in Porgy and Bess, Vienna, Berlin, Paris, London, under auspices U.S. State Dept., also N.Y.C. and U.S. tour, 1952-54; recitalist, soloist with symphonies, U.S., Can., Australia, Europe, 1954—; appeared concerts in India, auspices State Dept., 1956, 64; soloist Hollywood Bowl, 1955-59, 66, Berlin Festival, 1960; opera debut as Mme. Lidoine in Dialogues des Carmelites, San Francisco Opera, 1957; opera singer NBC-TV, 1955-58, 60, 62, 64, San Francisco Opera Co., 1957-59, 60-61, 63, 65, 67, 68, 71, Vienna Staatsoper, 1958, 59-60, 61, Berlin Opera, 1964, Rome Opera, 1966, Paris Opera, 1968; recital Brussels Internat. Fair, auspices State Dept., 1958, Verona Opera Arena, 1958-59, recitals Yugoslavia for State Dept., 1958; rec. artist RCA-Victor, 1958—; appeared Covent Garden, London, 1958-59, 70, Chgo. Lyric Theatre, 1959, 60, 65, soloist Salzburg Festival, 1959-63, Tetro alla Scala, Milano, 1960-61, 63, 67; appeared Met. Opera, N.Y.C., 1961-62, 63-70, 72, now resident mem.; soloist Salzburg Festival, 1950, 60; debut Teatre Dell'Opera, Rome, 1967, Teatro Colon, Buenos Aires, Argentina, 1969, Hamburg Opera, 1970. Hon. bd. dirs. Campfire Girls; hon. vice-chmn. U.S. com. UNESCO; co-chmn. Rust Coll. Upward Thrust Campaign; trustee-Internat. House. Decorated Order at Ment (Italy), recipient merit award for role of Tosca in NBC-TV Opera; Mademoiselle mag., 1955; 20 Grammy awards for classical vocal recs. Nat. Acad. Rec. Arts and Scis.; citation YWCA, 1961; Spirit of Achievement award Albert Einstein Coll. Medicine, 1962; Presdl. medal of freedom, 1964; Spingarn medal NAACP, 1965; Schwann Catalog award, 1968; named Musician of Year Mus. Am. mag., 1961; others. Fellow Am. Acad. Arts and Sci.; mem. AFTRA, Am. Guild Mus. Artists, Actors Equity Assn., Sigma Alpha Iota, Delta Sigma Theta. Address: care Columbia Artists Mgmt Inc 165 W 57th St New York NY 10019*

PRICE, MARION WOODROW, journalist; b. Elizabeth City, N.C., Oct. 13, 1914; s. James Asa and Meddie (Divers) P.; student Wake Forest Coll., 1933-34; m. Mary Dudley Pittman, Aug. 31, 1940; children—Wiley, Dudley, Mary, Catherine. Reporter, Daily Advance, Elizabeth City, 1935-39, Raleigh (N.C.) Times, 1939-41; mng. editor Kannapolis (N.C.) Ind., 1941-42; reporter AP, Raleigh, 1942-43; reporter News and Observer, Raleigh, 1946-57, mng. editor, 1957-72; outdoor editor, 1949-76. Mem. Kerr Reservoir Devel. Commn., 1950-52, Cape Hatteras Seashore Commn., 1949-50, N.C. Wildlife Resources Commn., 1977—; chmn. N.C. Outer Banks Park Commn., 1962-63, N.C. Seashore Commn., 1963-69, N.C. State Ports Authority, 1969-73. Served with USAAF, 1943-45. Mem. AP Mng. Editors Assn., Outdoor Writers Am. Baptist. Home: Old Ferry Dock Rd Gloucester NC 28528

PRICE, MAX, journalist; b. Cleve., July 2, 1927; s. Jack and Rachel (Graman) P.; B.A., Cleve. State U., 1950; postgrad. Ohio State U., 1950; m. Eileen Blecher, May 27, 1951; children—Robert, Kenneth. City editor Willoughby (O.) News-Herald, 1951-56; edn. editor Cleve. News, 1956-60; edn. editor Denver Post, 1960-64, editorial writer, 1964-79, critic-at-large, columnist, 1979—. Served with USNR, 1945-46. Recipient awards for distinguished reporting pub. affairs Am. Polit. Sci. Assn., 1964, 71; Alfred P. Sloan award for editorials on hwy. safety, 1970. Contbr. articles to profl. jours. Home: 6101 E 3d Ave Denver CO 80220 Office: 650 15th St Denver CO 80202

PRICE, MELVIN, congressman; b. East St. Louis, Ill., Jan. 1, 1905; s. Lawrence Wood and Margaret Elizabeth (Connolly) P.; ed. parochial schs., E. St. Louis; grad. St. Louis U. High Sch.; student St. Louis U., 1923-25; m. Garaldine Freelin, July 7, 1952; 1 son, William Melvin. Sports writer E. St. Louis News-Rev., 1925-27; corr. East St. Louis Jour., 1927- 33, St. Louis Globe-Democrat, 1943; sec. to Congressman Edwin M. Schaefer, 1933-43; mem. 79th and 80th congresses (1945-49) from 22d Ill. Dist., 81st to 82d congresses from 25th Ill. Dist., 83-92d Congresses from 24th Ill. Dist., 93d-95th congresses from 23d Ill. Dist., chmn. house armed service com. Mem. St. Clair County Bd. Suprs.: 1929-31. Served with AUS, 1943-44. Mem. Am. Legion, Amvets. Democrat. Roman Catholic. K.C., Moose, Eagle, Elk, Ancient Order of Hibernians. Club: Nat. Press (Washington). Home: 426 N 8th St East Saint Louis IL 62201 Office: House Office Bldg Washington DC 20515

PRICE, PAUL BUFORD, physicist, educator; b. Memphis, Nov. 8, 1932; s. Paul Buford and Eva (Dupuy) P.; B.S. summa cum laude, Davidson Coll., 1954, D.Sc., 1973; M.S., U. Va., 1956, Ph.D., 1958; m. JoAnn Margaret Baum, June 28, 1958; children—Paul Buford III, Heather Alynn, Pamela Margaret, Alison Gaynor. Fulbright scholar U. (Eng.) Bristol 1958-59; NSF postdoctoral fellow Cambridge (Eng.) U., 1959-60; physicist Gen. Elec. Research & Devel. Center, Schenectady, 1960-69; vis. prof. Tata Inst. Fundamental Research, Bombay, India, 1965-66; adj. prof. physics Rensselaer Poly. Inst., 1967-68; prof. physics U. Calif. at Berkeley, 1969—, dir. Space Scis. Lab., 1979—. Cons. for NASA on Lunar Sample Analysis Planning Team; mem. space sci. bd. Nat. Acad. Scis. Recipient Distinguished Service award Am. Nuclear Soc., 1964, Indsl. Research awards, 1964, 65, E.O. Lawrence Meml. award AEC, 1971, medal exceptional sci. achievement NASA, 1973. John Simon Guggenheim fellow, 1976-77. Fellow Am. Phys. Soc., Am. Geophys. Union; mem. Nat. Acad. Scis., Am. Astron. Soc. Author: (with others) Nuclear Tracks in Solids. Contbr. articles to profl. jours. Patentee in field; research on space and astrophysics, nuclear physics, particularly devel. solid state track detectors and their applications to geophysics, space and nuclear physics problems; discovery of fossil particle tracks and fission track method of dating; discovery of ultra-heavy cosmic rays. Home: 1056 Overlook Rd Berkeley CA 94708

PRICE, PAXTON (PATE), librarian; b. Batesville, Ark., June 18, 1913; s. John M. and Clara (Pate) P.; grad. N.Mex. Mil. Inst., 1933; B.S., George Peabody Coll., 1937, B.S. in L.S., 1941; grad. study Columbia, 1946; m. Ella Ida Tarbell, Aug. 23, 1941; children—John Scott, Peter Tarbell, Clayton Eversole, Sumner Seabury; m. 2d, June Riekhof, June 17, 1978. Instr. Roswell (N.Mex.) Sr. High Sch., 1937-40; librarian N.Mex. Mil. Inst., 1940-43, N.W. Mo. State Coll., Maryville, 1947-49; librarian Mo. State Library, 1949-64; dir. library services br. U.S. Office Edn., 1964-65, acting dir. div. library services, 1965-68; librarian St. Louis Public Library, 1969-77; exec. dir. Urban Libraries Council, 1977—. U.S. rep. to UNESCO Conf. on Nat. Library Planning for Latin Am., 1966; U.S. rep. on Internat. Team To Develop Nat. Library Plan for Colombia, 1970. Served to 1st lt. AUS, World War II; ETO; lt. col. Mo. N.G. Mem. Nat. Assn. State Librarians (pres. 1954), ALA (mem. council 1959-63, chmn. joint com. with Rural Sociol. Soc. 1953-55, v.p. library adminstrn. div. 1975, pres. div 1976), Bibliog. Soc. Am., Mo. Library Assn. (pres. 1959), Mo. Adult Edn. Assn. (sec.-treas.), Am., Mo. N.G. assns. past editor: Library Trends. Contbr. articles to profl. jours., encys. and biog. dictionary. Home: 1101 N 3d St Las Cruces NM 88001

PRICE, (NOBLE) RAY, singer; b. Perryville, Tex., Jan. 12, 1926; student N. Tex. Agrl. Coll., Arlington, 1946-49; m. Janie M. Price; 1 son, Clifton Ray. Rec. artist Bullet Records, 1949-50, Columbia Records, 1950-74, 77—, ABC/DOT Records, 1975-77, Myrrh Religious Records, 1974—, Monument Records, 1978-79; radio appearances WSM, Nashville, 1950-63, Grand Ole Opry, Nashville, 1952-63, Red Foley's Ozark Jubilee U.S.A., 1960-63; TV appearances include Johnny Carson Show, Merv Griffin Show, Dean Martin Comedy Hour, Pop Goes to Country, Marty Robbins Show, others; recorded songs include Crazy Arms (Gold Guitar award, Gold record, Billboard award, Cash Box award), Under Your Spell Again, Heartaches By The Number (Gold Guitar award, Gold record, Billboard award, Music Reporter Hit award), Release Me (Gold Guitar award, Gold record), Burning Memories, A Thing Called Sadness, A Way To Survive, Touch My Heart (Billboard award), Danny Boy (Gold Guitar award, Gold record, A.S.C.A.P. Chart Buster award), I'm Still Not Over You, Sweetheart of the Year (Gold Guitar award), She Wears My Ring, For the Good Times (Grammy award, Gold Guitar award, Gold record, Billboard awards), I Won't Mention It Again (Gold Guitar award, Gold record), others; albums include For The Good Times (Platinum album, Gold album), I Won't Mention It Again (Album of Year 1972), Faith, San Antonio Rose, Night Life, Love Life, Burning Memories, The Other Woman, Another Bridge to Burn, Touch My Heart, Talk to Your Heart, You're the Best Thing That Ever Happened To Me, Welcome To My World, Like Old Times Again, Say I Do, Rainbows and Tears, Hank N Me, Ray Price and the Cherokee Boys Reunited, This Time Lord, Precious Memories, How Great Thou Art, Born to Love Me, Feet, There's Always Me; owner Ray Price Enterprises, Ray Price Booking Agy., Ray Price Promotion Co., Ray Price Music Pub. Co., Janie Price Music Pub. Co., Ray Price Internat. Fan Club, Golden Cross Farm, Ray Price Racing Stables. Elected to Country Music Hall of Fame Walk Way of Stars, 1971; named Number One Country and Western Singer, 8 times; recipient numerous awards including Outstanding Profl. Achievement award U. Tex. at Arlington Alumni Assn., 1972; Spl. citation State of Tex., 1971; Dallastar award Press Club of Dallas, 1972. Address: care Ray Price Enterprises PO Box 30384 Dallas TX 75230. *Each time I move an audience to laugh when I laugh, cry when I cry and be moved by my innermost emotions which I project through my songs, I leave the stage totally contented with the feeling of having removed each person from the ordinary into a world of ecstasy.*

PRICE, RAYMOND ALEXANDER, geologist, educator; b. Winnipeg, Man., Can., Mar. 25, 1933; s. Alexander Frederick and Edith Olga (Arlt) P.; B.Sc. with honors, U. Man., Winnipeg, 1955; A.M., Princeton U., 1957, Ph.D., 1958; m. Mina Sofia Geurds, Sept. 15, 1956; children—Paul Raymond, Patricia Ann, Linda Marie. Research scientist Geol. Survey Can., Ottawa, Ont., 1958-68; prof. geol. scis. Queens U., Kingston, Ont., 1968—, head dept. geol. scis., 1972-77. Fellow Royal Soc. Can. Home: Box 2226 Rural Route 1 Kingston ON K7L 4V1 Canada Office: Miller Hall Queen's Univ Kingston ON K7L 3N6 Canada

PRICE, RAYMOND KISSAM, JR., author, former govt. ofcl.; b. N.Y.C., May 6, 1930; s. Raymond Kissam and Beth (Porter) P.; B.A., Yale U., 1951. With Crowell-Collier Pub. Co., 1955-57, asst. to editor Collier's mag., 1956-57, reporter Life mag., 1957; with N.Y. Herald Tribune, 1957-66, editor editorial page, 1964-66; asst. to Richard M. Nixon, N.Y.C., 1967-69; spl. asst. to Pres. Nixon, 1969-73; spl. cons. to Pres., 1973-74; vis. fellow Am. Enterprise Inst., 1977; fellow John F. Kennedy Inst. Politics, Harvard U., 1977; Nixon prof. Whittier (Calif.) Coll., 1978. Served to lt. (j.g.) USNR, 1952-55. Mem. Aurelian Honor Soc., Skull and Bones. Clubs: Yale, Overseas Press (N.Y.C.), Metropolitan, Federal City (Washington). Author: With Nixon, 1977. Home: 3234 Prospect St NW Washington DC 20007

PRICE, REYNOLDS, novelist, educator; b. Macon, N.C., Feb. 1, 1933; s. William Solomon and Elizabeth (Rodwell) P.; A.B. summa cum laude (Angier Duke scholar), Duke, 1955; B.Litt. (Rhodes scholar), Merton Coll., Oxford (Eng.) U., 1958; Litt.D., St. Andrew's Presbyn. Coll., 1978, Wake Forest U., 1979. Mem. faculty English, Duke U., 1958—; asst. prof., 1961-68, asso. prof., 1968-72, prof., 1972-77, James B. Duke prof., 1977—; writer in residence U. N.C., Chapel Hill, 1965, U. Kan., 1967, 69, U.N.C., Greensboro, 1971; Glasgow prof. Washington and Lee U., 1971; faculty Salzburg Seminar, 1977. Recipient William Faulkner Found. award notable 1st novel, 1962; Sir Walter Raleigh award, 1962, 76; award Nat. Assn. Ind. Schs., 1964; Guggenheim fellow, 1964-65; fellow Nat. Endowment for Arts, 1967-68, lit. adv. panel, 1973, chmn., 1976; Nat.

Inst. Arts and Letters award, 1971; Bellamann Found. award, 1972; Lillian Smith award, 1976; N.C. award, 1977. Mem. Phi Beta Kappa, Phi Delta Theta. Author: A Long and Happy Life, 1962; The Names and Faces of Heroes, 1963; A Generous Man, 1966; Love and Work, 1968; Permanent Errors, 1970; Things Themselves, 1972; The Surface of Earth, 1975; Early Dark, 1977; A Palpable God, 1978. Home: 4813 Duke Station Durham NC 27706 Office: care Russell and Volkening Inc 551 Fifth Ave New York NY 10017

PRICE, RICHARD, anthropologist, ednl. adminstr.; b. N.Y.C., Nov. 30, 1941; s. George and Gertrude (Swee) P.; A.B. in History and Lit. magna cum laude, Harvard, 1963, Ph.D. in Social Anthropology, 1970; m. Sally Hamlin, June 22, 1963; children—Niko, Leah. lectr. anthropology Yale U., 1969-70, asst. prof., 1970-73, asso. prof., 1973-74; prof., anthropology Johns Hopkins U., 1974—, chmn. dept., 1974-77, 79—. Social Sci. Research Council Joint Com. Latin Am. Studies fellow, 1972-73; African Studies Assn. grantee, 1972-73; Sigma Xi grantee, 1974; NSF grantee, 1976-78; Residential fellow, Netherlands Inst. Advanced Study, Wassenaar, 1977-78; Am. Council Learned Socs. fellow, 1978. Mem. Am. Anthropol. Assn., Am. Ethnol. Soc., African Studies Assn., Royal Anthropol. Inst. Great Britain, Koninklijk Instituut voor Taal-, Land-en Volkenkunde, Phi Beta Kappa, Sigma Xi. Author: Maroon Societies: Rebel Slave Communities in the Americas, 1973, rev. edit., 1979; Saramaka Social Structure, 1975; (with S.W. Mintz) An Anthropological Approach to the Afro-American Past, 1976; The Guiana Maroons, 1976; (with S. Price) Arts of the Surinam Maroons, 1980; editor Johns Hopkins Studies in Atlantic History and Culture, 1975—. Home: 215 Overhill Rd Baltimore MD 21210 Office: Dept Anthropology Johns Hopkins U Baltimore MD 21218

PRICE, RICHARD JAY, author, educator; b. N.Y.C., Oct. 12, 1949; s. Milton and Harriet (Rosenbaum) P.; B.S., Cornell U., 1971; M.F.A., Columbia U., 1976. Tchr. urban studies N.Y. U., 1973; tchr. English, Hostos Coll., Bronx, 1973, tchr. fiction writing, 1975; tchr. fiction writing SUNY at Stony Brook, 1974, at Binghamton, 1976, 77, Hofstra U., 1978, 79, Yale U., 1979. Mary Roberts Rinehart Found. grantee, 1973; Macdowell fellow, 1973, Edith Mirillees fellow Stanford U., 1973; Yaddo fellow, 1977, 78. Named Knight of Mark Twain. Mem. Authors Guild, PEN (exec. com. 1979-80). Author: The Wanderers, 1974; Bloodbrothers, 1976; Ladies' Man, 1978; (play) Murphy. Home: 10 Jones St New York NY 10014 Office: care Brandt & Brandt 101 Broadway New York NY 10036

PRICE, ROBERT, investment banker, lawyer; b. N.Y.C., Aug. 27, 1932; s. Solomon and Frances (Berger) P.; A.B., N.Y.U., 1953; LL.D., Columbia, 1958; m. Margery Beth Wiener, Dec. 18, 1955; children—Eileen Marcia, Steven. With R. H. Macy & Co., Inc., 1955-58; admitted to N.Y. bar, 1958, also U.S. Dist. Cts., U.S. Ct. Appeals, U.S. Supreme Ct., ICC, FCC, U.S. Internal Revenue Service; practiced in N.Y.C., 1958—; law clk. to judge U.S. Dist. Ct. So. Dist. N.Y., 1958-59; asst. U.S. atty. So. Dist. N.Y., 1959-60; partner Kupferman & Price, 1960-65; chmn. bd. pres. Atlantic States Ind. Inc., 1963-66; pres. WNVY, Pensacola, Fla., 1965-66, WLOB, Portland, Me., 1965-66; dep. mayor, N.Y.C., 1965-66; exec. v.p., dir. Dreyfus Corp., N.Y.C., 1966-69; v.p., investment officer Dreyfus Fund, until 1969; chmn., pres., dir. Price Capital Corp., also Price Mgmt. Corp., N.Y.C., 1969-72; gen. partner, spl. counsel Lazard, Freres & Co., 1972—; adv. com. Bankers Trust Co. N.Y.; dir. Transocean Holding Corp., Lane Bryant, Inc.; lectr. National Industrial Conf. Bd. Chmn. N.Y.C. Port Authority Negotiating Com. for World Trade Center, 1965-66; mem. N.Y.C. Policy Planning Council, 1966; spl. counsel N.Y. State Joint Legis. Com. on Ct. Reorganization, 1962-63; asst. counsel N.Y. State Joint Legis. Com. on N.Y. Banking Laws, 1961-62; chmn. govt. and civil service div. United Jewish Appeal Greater N.Y., 1966; co-chmn. Met. N.Y. Red Cross Blood Drive, 1966; mem. nat. exec. com. Columbia Law Sch. 16th Ann. Fund Drive, 1966-67. Vice pres. N.Y. Young Republican Club, 1957-58; campaign mgr. John V. Lindsay campaigns for congressman, N.Y.C., 1958, 60, 62, 64; del. N.Y. Republican State Conv., 1962, 66; campaign mgr. Nelson A. Rockefeller, Ore. Rep. presidential primary campaign, 1964; campaign mgr. Lindsay campaign for mayor, N.Y.C., 1965; lectr. Rep. Nat. Com., 1966—. Bd. dirs. Am. Friends Hebrew U.; past trustee Columbia U. Sch. Pharm. Scis., Birch Wathen Sch. Served with U.S. Army, 1953-55. Recipient Yeshiva U. Heritage award, 1966, Pub. Service award Queens Catholic War Vets., 1966, Pub. Service award Phila. 21 Jewel Sq. Club, 1967, Outstanding Young Man of Year award N.Y.C. Jr. C. of C., 1967; named One of America's Ten Outstanding Young Men U.S. Jr. C. of C., 1967. Mem. Am., Fed., N.Y.C. bar assns., N.Y. State Dist. Attys. Assn., Council Fgn. Relations, Scribes, Tau Kappa Alpha. Author articles. Home: 25 E 86th St New York NY 10028 Office: Lazard Freres Co One Rockefeller Plaza New York NY 10020

PRICE, ROBERT DALE, state senator, former congressman; b. Reading, Kans., Sept. 7, 1927; s. Ben F. and Gladys Ann (Watson) P.; B.S., Okla. State U., 1951; m. Martha Ann White, Dec. 29, 1951; children—Robert Grant, Benjamin Carl, Janice Ann. Owner-operator ranches in Tex. and Kan., 1945—, v.p., dir. Reading State Bank, 1950—; mem. 90th-93d Congress from 13th Dist. Tex., mem. agr., armed services, sci. and astronautics coms., also Republican policy com.; mem. 65th-66th Tex. Legislature from 31st dist., mem. natural resources com. Chmn. dist. orgn. and extension local Boy Scouts Am., 1964, recipient Silver Beaver award. Served with USAF, 1951-55; Korea. Decorated Air medal; recipient citation Tex. Senate, 1978. Mem. Pampa, W. Tex. chambers commerce, U.S. Air Force Assn., Am. Legion, V.F.W., Sigma Alpha Epsilon. Republican. Baptist. Mason (Shriner), Kiwanian (past pres. Top o' Tex. club). Home: Route 1 Box 61A Pampa TX 79065

PRICE, ROBERT EBEN, lawyer; b. Waco, Tex., Jan. 13, 1931; s. Robert Eben and Mary Hamilton (Barnett) P.; B.A., So. Methodist U., 1952, J.D., 1954, LL.M., 1972; Air War Coll., 1976; m. Ann Hodges, June 4, 1954; children—Eben, Mary, Ann, Emily. Admitted to Tex. bar, 1954, also U.S. Supreme Ct., U.S. Ct. Mil. Appeals, U.S. Ct. Claims, U.S. Dist. Ct. for No. Dist. Tex. bars; mem. firm Taylor, Mizell, Price, Corrigan & Smith, Dallas, 1956—; lectr. law So. Meth. U. Law Sch., 1973—; lectr. Practice Skills Program, State Bar Tex., 1974—. Trustee St. Michael and All Angels Found., Lanham Croley Found.; chmn. legis. and legal awareness subcom. Tex. Gov.'s Com. on Employment of Handicapped. Served as legal officer USAF, 1954-56; col. JAGD Res. Fellow Am. Coll. Probate Counsel: mem. Am., Dallas bar assns., State Bar Tex., Phi Alpha Delta, Phi Eta Sigma, Phi Delta Theta. Episcopalian. Home: 4300 Arcady Ave Dallas TX 75205 Office: 2700 Republic Bank Tower Dallas TX 75201

PRICE, ROBERT IRA, coast guard officer; b. N.Y.C., Sept. 22, 1921; s. Alfred and Mary Edna (Schweitzer) P.; B.B.A., CCNY, 1942; B.S., U.S. Coast Guard Acad., 1945; postgrad. M.I.T., 1950-53; m. Virginia Louise Miller, June 20, 1946; children—Andrea Jean, Keven Virginia. Commd. ensign U.S. Coast Guard, 1945, advanced through grades to vice adm., 1978; asst. chief Mcht. Marine Tech. Div., Washington, 1965-67; chief planning staff Office Mcht. Marine Safety, 1967-71; capt. Port of Phila., 1971-73; chief Office Marine Environ., Washington, 1974-76; comdr. 11th Coast Guard Dist., Long Beach, Calif., 1976-78; comdr. Atlantic Area and 3d Coast Guard Dist., N.Y.C., 1978—; prin. U.S . negotiator to tech. programs Intergovtl. Maritime Consultative Orgn., UN, 1962-71. Decorated Legion of Merit with gold star, Meritorious Service medal with gold star, Coast Guard Commendation medal. Registered profl. engr., D.C. Fellow Royal Instn. Naval Architects; mem. Soc. Naval Sigma Xi. Clubs: Propeller; Army Navy Contbg. author: Ship Design and Construction, 1980. Contbr. articles to profl. jours. Home: Quarters One Governors Island New York NY 10004 Office: Comdr Atlantic Area and Third Coast Guard Dist Governors Island New York NY 10004

PRICE, ROGER TAYLOR, publisher; b. Charleston, W.Va., Mar. 6, 1922; s. Roger Taylor and Mary (Presley) P.; student U. Mich., 1937, Am. Acad. Art, Chgo., 1938-39, Max Reinhart's Dramatic Sch., Los Angeles, 1940; div. four times; children—Roger Taylor III, Sandi Hope. Night club, tv comedian, 1950-63; appeared in Broadway revue Tickets Please, 1951; founder, v.p. Price/Stern/Sloan Pubs., Inc., Los Angeles, 1960—. Author: In One Head and Out The Other, 1951; Droodles, 1952; I'm For Me First, 1956; J.G., The Upright Ape, 1960; Mad Libs, 1968; The Decline and Fall, 1969; The Great Roob Revolution, 1970. Home: 12949 Blairwood Dr Studio City CA 91604 Office: 410 N LaCienega Blvd Los Angeles CA 90048. *During the short walk we all make across the face of the world I have acquired a few skills and a little wisdom. The skills are mostly technical and the wisdom is dubious. It consists of a belief that What Happens Happens. What Does Not Happen Did Not Happen. What Should Happen is of no importance. Happiness, on the other hand, is Not Having a Tooth Ache at 3 A.M. with no aspirin in the house.*

PRICE, ROY ARTHUR, educator; b. Chgo., Apr. 29, 1905; s. Henry T. and Jessie (Butler) P.; Ph.B., U. Chgo., 1927; Ed.M., Harvard U., 1932, Ed.D., 1938; m. Frances G. Becker, June 18, 1932 (dec. 1964); children—James Roy, David A.; m. 2d, Polly Cummins, Jan. 26, 1966. Instr. history and govt. Culver Mil. Acad., 1927-32; head dept. social studies Quincy (Mass.) High Sch., 1932-35; prof. social sci. and edn. Syracuse U., 1935-73, dir. Washington internships in edn., dir. Social Studies Curriculum Center; interim pres. Onondaga Community Coll., 1973-76; asso. on aging Maxwell Policy Center on Aging, Syracuse U., 1976—; cons. Citizenship edn. pub. sch. systems; citizenship research program Edn. Research Corp., Mass., N.Y. State Edn. Dept. (mem. regents history com). Adminstr. Danforth Found. Summer sessions; mem. exec. com. bd. trustees Joint Council Econ. Edn.; exec. sec. N.Y. State Council Econ. Edn.; mem. adv. com. Am. Viewpoints; cons. Coronet Films. Mem. Assn. Higher Edn. (dirs., past pres.), Nat. (past pres.), N.Y. State (founder) councils social studies, N.Y. State Hist. Assn. Republican. Methodist. Editor: Social Sci. textbook series John C. Winston Co., Silver Burdette Co., Macmillan Co., New Viewpoints in the Social Sciences, Needed Research on the Teaching of the Social Studies, Major Concepts for the Social Studies. Contbr. profl. articles jours. and yearbooks. Home: 213 Wellington Rd De Witt NY 13214

PRICE, SELIG HARVEY, food co. exec.; b. N.Y.C., Apr. 25, 1938; s. Julius and Beatrice (Cohen) P.; B.A., Columbia U., 1959, B.S., 1960; M.B.A., Harvard U., 1963; m. Deana Schwartz, June 5, 1960; children—Mark Andrew, Bruce Michael. With Gen. Foods Corp., White Plains, N.Y., 1959-69, product mgr. Maxwell House IMH, 1966-67, product group mgr. Maxwell House/Sanka, 1967-69, adminstrv. asst. to pres., 1969; v.p. mktg. and devel. Burger Chef Systems, Inc., Indpls., 1969-70, exec. v.p. mktg. and devel., 1970, exec. v.p. ops. and planning, 1970-74; mktg. mgr. Maxwell House div. Gen. Foods, 1974-77, v.p. devel., 1977—. Pres. Columbia U. FM/AM Radio Sta., 1958-59. Mem. Harvard Bus. Sch. Alumni Assn., Am. Mgmt. Assn., Alpha Pi Mu. Home: 56 Caiass Ln Stamford CT 06900 Office: 250 North St White Plains NY 10625

PRICE, THOMAS BENJAMIN, textile co. exec.; b. W. Jefferson, N.C., Aug. 23, 1920; s. Avery Astor and Jenny L. (Goss) P.; B.S. in Textile Engring., N.C. State U., 1941; m. Judith Ostberg, Jan 28, 1950; children—Jonathan R., Gregory W., Timothy C. With J.P. Stevens & Co., Inc., 1941—, corp. v.p., 1964—, pres. Domestics and Allied Products div., 1971—, corporate group v.p., 1974—, also dir., mem. exec. com., chmn.'s office. Served to lt. comdr. USNR, World War II, Korean Conflict. Mem. Am. Arbitration Council, Sigma Tau Sigma, Phi Psi. Clubs: Morris County Golf (Morristown); N.Y. Athletic; Pine Valley; Royal Poincianna, Naples Beach and Tennis (Naples, Fla.); Mendham Valley; Univ. (N.Y.C.). Home: Glen Alpine Rd New Vernon NJ 07976 also 3483 Gulf Shore Blvd N Naples FL Office: 1185 Ave of Americas New York NY 10036

PRICE, VINCENT, actor; b. St. Louis, May 27, 1911; s. Vincent L. and Marguerite (Wilcox) P.; B.A., Yale U., 1933; student U. London (Eng.), 1934-35; D.F.A., Calif. Coll. Arts and Crafts.; LL.D., Ohio Weselyan U., 1963; m. Edith Barrett, 1938 (div.); 1 son, Vincent B.; m. 2d, Mary Grant, Aug. 28, 1939 (div. 1972); 1 dau., Mary Victoria; m. 3d, Coral Browne, 1974. Stage appearances include Victoria Regina, 1935-37, Mercury Theatre, 1937-38, Outward Bound, 1939-40, Angel Street, 1941-42, Don Juan in Hell, 1952, Cocktail Party, 1951, The Lady's Not For Burning, 1952, Ardele, London, 1975; Diversions and Delights, one-man play as Oscar Wilde, nat. tour, 1977-79; tour in Charlie's Aunt, 1975; motion pictures include Song of Bernadette, 1943, Eve of St. Mark, 1944, Laura, 1944, Leave Her to Heaven, 1945, Shock, 1946, House of Seven Gables, 1940, The Web, 1947, His Kind of Woman, 1951, Dragonwyck, 1946, Three Musketeers, 1948, Champagne for Caesar, 1950, Baron of Arizona, 1950, The House of Wax, 1953, Ten Commandments, 1956, Story of Mankind, 1957, The Big Circus, 1959, Pit and the Pendulum, 1961, Convicts 4, 1962, The Raven, 1962, Masque of The Red Death, 1964, The Last Man in the World, 1964, Dr. Phibes, 1971, Theatre of Blood, 1974; appeared on radio in The Saint, 1947-50, on TV numerous maj. programs including $64,000 Challenge; TV series Time Express, 1979; lectr. primitive and modern art, letters of Van Gogh. Former mem. bd. Archives Am. Art.; mem. Whitney Museum Friends Am. Art.; former pres. art council U. Calif. at Los Angeles; mem. U.S. Indian Arts and Crafts Bd.; art cons. Sears Roebuck & Co.; former mem. fine arts com. The White House; bd. dirs. Center for Arts of Indian Affairs; adv. com. Friends of Art, U. So. Cal. Recipient Acad. award for documentary, 1963. Mem. Royal Soc. Art. Author: I Like What I Know, 1958; Book of Joe, 1960; (with Mary Price), Michelangelo Bible, 1964, A Treasury of Great Recipes, 1965, Come into the Kitchen Cook Book, 1969, Treasury of American Art, 1972. Editor: (with Ferdinand V. Delacroix) Drawings of Delacroix. Office: 315 S Beverly Dr Beverly Hills CA 90212

PRICE, WILLIAM JAMES, orgn. exec.; b. Alexandria, Ohio, Dec. 3, 1918; s. Lewis J. and Mary (Wright) P.; A.B., Denison U., 1940, Sc.D., 1969; M.S., Rensselaer Poly. Inst., 1941, Ph.D., 1948; m. Betty Kistler, Aug. 22, 1943; children—Mary Barbara, Sarah Margaret, Lewis Charles. Research physicist Bendix Aviation Corp., 1942-45, Battelle Meml. Inst., Columbus, Ohio, 1948-50; head dept. physics Air Force Inst. Tech., Dayton, Ohio, 1950-57; chief modern physics br. Aero. Research Lab., Dayton, 1957-59, chief scientist, 1959-63; exec. dir. Air Force Office Sci. Research, 1963-74; mgmt. cons., 1974-78; coordinator World Peacemakers, 1978—; instr. Rensselaer Poly. Inst., 1948; part-time lectr. Wright-Patterson Grad. Center, Ohio State U., 1950-57. An organizer Yokefellowship in Nation's Capital, 1964; fed. exec. fellow The Brookings Instn., 1967-68; chmn. Commn. Govt. Procurement Study Group Research and Devel., 1970-71. Mem. bd. stewardship Ohio Synod, Lutheran Ch. Am., 1952-57. Bd. dirs. Yokefellows Internat., 1967-71, Washington Lift, Inc., 1971—. Recipient Alumni citation Denison U., 1965, Outstanding Unit award citation Office Aerospace Research, 1965, Air Force Inst. Tech., 1964. Mem. Am. Phys. Soc., A.A.A.S., Phi Beta Kappa, Sigma Xi, Tau Beta Pi (hon.). Author: Nuclear Radiation Detection, rev. edit., 1964; also numerous articles. Home: 2852 Ontario NW Washington DC 20009

PRICE, WILLIAM JAMES, IV, investment banker; b. Balt., Md., Oct. 6, 1924; s. William James 3d and Frances (Robbins) P.; grad. St. Paul's Sch., 1942; B.S., Yale, 1949; m. Marjorie Beard, Dec. 6, 1952; children—Marjorie, Jonathan Robbins, William James V, Juliet Robbins. Propr., Price & Co., 1949-52; with Alex. Brown & Sons, Balt., 1952—, gen. partner, 1959—; dir. PHH Group, Chessie System, Inc., C. & O. Ry., B. & O. R.R., Eastmet Corp. Served with inf. AUS, 1943-46; ETO. Decorated Bronze Star, Purple Heart with oak leaf cluster. Mem. Nat. Assn. Securities Dealers (bd. govs. 1964-66, vice chmn. 1966). Home: 825 Hillside Rd Brooklandville MD 21022 Office: 135 E Baltimore St Baltimore MD 21202

PRICE, WILLIAM STANLEY, ins. co. exec.; b. Paris, France, Oct. 10, 1927 (parents Am. citizens); s. William Stanley and Florence (Walter) P.; student U.S. Naval Acad., 1945, San Mateo Coll., 1946-47; B.S. in Bus. Adminstrn., U. So. Calif., 1950; m. Patricia B. Schell, Feb. 9, 1951; children—Sandra Schell, William Stanley III. With St. Paul Group Ins. Co., Los Angeles, 1950; with Indsl. Indemnity Co., San Francisco, 1951-72, div. mgr., 1961-65, corp. officer, 1965-67, v.p. ops., 1967-70, sr. v.p. ops., 1970-72; pres., dir., First Ins. Co. of Hawaii, Ltd., 1972-75; v.p. Service Center, 1975-76, regional v.p., 1976-79; now exec. v.p. Crum & Forster Ins. Cos., Morristown, N.J. Active various community orgns. Served with USNR, 1944-46. Mem. Commerce Assn. U. So. Calif., U. So. Calif. Assos., Kappa Sigma. Clubs: Trojan (U. So. Calif.); Mchts. Exchange (San Francisco); Morris County Country. Address: Crum & Forster Ins Cos PO Box 2387 Morristown NJ 07960

PRICHARD, EDGAR ALLEN, lawyer; b. Brockton, Mont., Mar. 6, 1920; s. Clifford B. and Helen (Ouwersloat) P.; student U. Tulsa, 1937-39, U. Okla., 1940-41; LL.B., U. Va., 1948; m. Nancy M. McCandlish, Apr. 7, 1945; children—Helen Montague (Mrs. Thomas C. Foster), Robert Walton, Thomas Morgan. Admitted to Va. bar, 1947, since practiced in Fairfax; partner firm Boothe, Prichard, & Dudley, 1948—; dir. George Mason Bank. Mem. gen. bd. Nat. Council Chs., 1966-72; counsel Va. Councils Chs., 1955—. Councilman, Fairfax, 1953-64, mayor, 1964-68; chmn. Fairfax Democratic Com., 1962-64, 69-72; mem. Va. Bd. Elections, 1970-75. Bd. dirs. Lynch Found., Trinity Episcopal Sch. Ministry, George Mason U. Found. Served to 1st lt. AUS, 1942-45. Mem. Am., Va., Fairfax (pres. 1959) bar assns., Va. State Bar (v.p. 1969), Am. Law Inst. Episcopalian (lay reader, warden). Home: 3820 Chain Bridge Rd Fairfax VA 22030 Office: 4085 University Dr Fairfax VA 22030

PRICHER, LAWRENCE STADON, JR., oil and gas co. exec.; b. N.Y.C., Feb. 26, 1918; s. Lawrence Stadon and Maud (Robinson) P.; student Dickinson Coll.; m. Audrey Jervis, Aug. 27, 1941; children—Virginia Robinson, John Lawrence. With Foster Wheeler Corp., 1946-59, v.p. fin., 1957-59, also dir. fgn. ops.; v.p., treas., dir. N.J. Zinc Co., N.Y.C., 1959-65; v.p. fin. C. Brewer & Co., Ltd., Honolulu, 1965-69, exec. v.p., 1969-71, pres., 1971; v.p. fin. Alexander & Baldwin, Inc., Honolulu, 1972, then pres., dir., chief exec. officer until 1978; sr. v.p. Consol. Oil & Gas Co., Denver, 1979—; dir. First Hawaiian Inc. Trustee, pres. Bishop Mus. Mem. Fin. Execs. Inst. Clubs: Pacific, Oahu Country, Waialae. Home: 1010 Wilder Ave Honolulu HI 96822 Office: 225 Queen St Honolulu HI 96813

PRICKETT, WILLIAM, lawyer; b. Wilmington, Del., Nov. 13, 1925; s. William and Elisabeth Susan (DeBoeck) P.; A.B., Princeton U., 1947; J.D., Harvard U., 1954; m. Louise Loening (div.); m. 2d, Linda Rollins, July 23, 1976; children—William Loening, Priscilla DeBoeck, Ann Elizabeth DeBoeck; stepchildren—Theodore Wayne Rollins, Jeffrey William Rollins. Admitted to D.C. bar, 1955, Del. bar, 1955; partner firm Prickett, Sanders, Jones, Elliott and Kristol, Wilmington, 1954—. Sec., Brandywine River Mus., Chadds Ford, Pa., 1968-72; pres. Grand Opera House, Wilmington, 1972-75. Served with USN, 1943-46, USMC, 1952-54. Mem. Del. State Bar Assn., Am. Bar Assn., Am. Law Inst. Republican. Clubs: Wilmington, Vicmead Hunt, Racquet and Tennis. Contbr. fictions to lit. jours., articles to travel jours. Home: Campbell Rd PO Box 3663 Greenville DE 19807 Office: 1310 King St Wilmington DE 19899

PRIDDLE, WILLIAM WELMORE, physician; b. Eden, Ont. Can., Mar. 14, 1904; s. George and Lillian Blanche (Abbott) P.; B.A., U. Western Ont., London, 1922, M.D., 1926; m. Charlotte Agatha Rider, Dec. 24, 1926; children—Nancy Anne (Mrs. Carl Corcoran), Barbara Mae (Mrs. Jan van Diepen), Elizabeth Jane (Mrs. Gary McGregor), Diane (Mrs. John Savage), Susan (Mrs. Edmund Shaker). Intern, Buffalo Gen. Hosp., 1926-27; asst. resident medicine Buffalo City Hosp., 1927-28; mem. profl. unit St. Bartholomew's Hosp., London, Eng., 1934-35; mem. outpatient attending staff Toronto Western Hosp., 1929; pvt. practice, Toronto, 1929—. Cons. geriatrics, chmn. minister's adv. com. geriatric studies Province Ont., 1953—; cons. cardiovascular disease Geriatric Study Center, Toronto, 1960—; spl. research hypertension, cardiovascular diseases, geriatrics. Served to maj. Royal Canadian M.C., 1943-46. Fellow Toronto Acad. Medicine, A.C.P., Am. Geriatrics Soc. (former dir.); mem. Canadian, Ont. med. assns., Ont. Geriatric Research Soc. (hon. chmn. med. adv. bd.), Can. Assn. Gerontology, Alpha Omega Alpha. Contbr. articles to profl. jours. Home: 5608 Trafalgar Rd Hornby ON Canada Office: Medical Arts Bldg Toronto ON Canada

PRIDE, CHARLEY, singer; b. Sledge, Miss., Mar. 18, 1939; grad. high sch.; m. Rozene Pride, Dec. 28, 1956; children—Kraig, Dion, Angela. Formerly with constrn. cos., refining plants; profl. baseball player with Detroit, Memphis Red Sox, Birmingham Black Barons (all Negro Am. League), Los Angeles Angels (Am. League); appeared with WSM Grand Ole Opry, Nashville, 1967, Lawrence Welk Show, ABC-TV, Joey Bishop Show, ABC-TV, Ralph Emery Show, WSM-TV, Nashville, Syndicated Bill Anderson, Bobby Lord and Wilburn Brothers, Hee Haw, Tom Jones Show, Flip Wilson Show, Johnny Cash Show, numerous other TV shows; recorded for RCA; made record albums Country Charlie Pride, Charley Pride Sings Heart Songs, Charley, Happiness, Charley Pride—; In Person, She's Just Sunday, Happiness of Having You, Did You Think to Pray, The Best of Charley Pride; recorded songs Snakes Crawl at Night, Just Between You & Me, Let the Chips Fall, I Know One, Day You Stopped Loving Me, Someday They Will, One of These Days, Let Me Help You Work It Out, She Made Me Go, Does My Ring Hurt Your Finger, Let Me Live, I'd Rather Love You, Is Anyone Goin' to San Antone, Afraid of Losing You Again, Kiss an Angel Good Mornin'. Served with U.S. Army, 1956-58. Named Most Promising Male Artist, Country Song Roundup, 1967, Male Vocalist of Year, Country Music Assn., 1971, 72 Entertainer of Yr. in Country Music, 1971; winner Grammy awards for best scored rec., 1971, for best country vocal, 1972, Trendsetter award Billboard, 1970, Top Male Vocalist award Cashbox, Photoplay Gold Medal award, 1976. Address: care Chardon Inc 5952 Royal Ln Suite 160 Dallas TX 75230•

PRIDEAUX, THOMAS STEPHEN, banker; b. Portland, Ore., Aug. 26, 1914; s. Thomas Vivian and Bellini (Crosby) P.; B.A., Albany Coll., 1937; grad. Pacific Banking Sch., 1949, Stonier Grad. Sch. Banking, 1960; m. Alma B. Roth, Dec. 18, 1975. With U.S. Nat. Bank Oreg., Portland, 1937—, vice chmn., 1974—; v.p., dir. Commerce Mortgage Co.; vice chmn. U.S. Bancorp., 1974—; dir. Allied Bank Internat., N.Y.C. Chmn., U.S. Savs. Bond Com. Oreg., 1960—. Served to maj. AUS, 1941-46. Home: 4406 SW Council Crest Dr Portland OR 97201 Office: 321 SW 6th Ave Portland OR 97204

PRIESAND, SALLY JANE, clergywoman; b. Cleve., June 27, 1946; d. Irving Theodore and Rosetta Elizabeth (Welch) Priesand; B.A. in English, U. Cin., 1968; B.Hebrew Letters, Hebrew Union Coll.-Jewish Inst. Religion, 1971, M.A. in Hebrew Letters, 1972; D.H.L. (hon.), Fla. Internat. U., 1973. Student rabbi Sinai Temple, Champaign, Ill., 1968, Congregation B'nai Israel, Hattiesburg, Miss., 1969-70, Congregation Shalom, Milw., 1970, Temple Beth Israel, Jackson, Mich., 1970-71; rabbinic intern Isaac M. Wise Temple, Cin., 1971-72; ordained rabbi, 1972; asst. rabbi Stephen Wise Free Synagogue, N.Y.C., 1972-77, asso. rabbi, 1977-79; rabbi Temple Beth El, Elizabeth, N.J., 1979—. Active ACLU, Am. Jewish Congress, Common Cause; mem. commn. on synagogue relations Fedn. Jewish Philanthropies N.Y., 1972—, mem. com. on aged commn. synagogue relations, 1972-75; mem. task force on equality of women in Judaism pub. affairs com. N.Y. Fedn. Reform Synagogues, 1972—; mem. com. on resolutions Central Conf. Am. Rabbis, 1975-77, com. on cults, 1976-78, chmn. Task Force on women in rabbinate, 1977—, mem. exec. bd., 1977-79; mem. joint commn. on Jewish edn. Central Conf. Am. Rabbis — Union Am. Hebrew Congregations, 1974-77, mem. task force on Jewish singles Commn. Synagogue Relations, 1975-77; mem. N.Y. Bd. Rabbis, 1975—. Asso., Kirkland Coll., Clinton, N.Y., 1973—. Cited by B'nai B'rith Women, 1971; named Man of Yr., Temple Israel, Columbus, Ohio, 1972; Woman of Yr., Ladies Aux. N.Y. chpt. Jewish War Vets., 1973; Woman for All Seasons, N. L.I. region Women's Am. ORT, 1973; recipient Quality of Life award Dist. One chpt. B'nai B'rith Women, 1973; Medallion Judaic Heritage Soc., 1978; named Extraordinary Women of Achievement NCCJ, 1978. Mem. Nat. Fedn. Temple Sisterhoods, Hadassah (life), Central Conf. Am. Rabbis. Mem. B'nai B'rith Women. Author: Judaism and the New Woman, 1975. Home: 205 West End Ave New York NY 10023 Office: 1374 North Ave Elizabeth NJ

PRIESING, JOHN WASHBURN, mfg. corp. exec.; b. Bridgeport, Conn., Mar. 19, 1929; s. Carl William and Elizabeth (James) P.; B.A., Amherst Coll., 1950; M.B.A., Harvard U., 1956; m. Marilyn Wilson, June 20, 1968; 1 son, John Washburn. Regional sales mgr. Allied Chem. Corp., N.Y.C., 1956-63; con. McKinsey & Co., Inc., N.Y.C., 1963-67; gen. mgr. H.K. Porter, Inc., Pitts., 1967-69; group v.p. Phelps Dodge Industries, N.Y.C., 1969-78; exec. v.p. A. Johnson & Co., Inc., N.Y.C., 1978—, dir., 1978—; dir. Reading Industires, 1978—, Sirius Reins. Corp., 1979—. Served to lt. (j.g.) USN, 1952-55. Home: 44 Avon St Bronxville NY 10708 Office: A Johnson & Co Inc 110 E 59th St New York NY 10022

PRIEST, MELVILLE STANTON, cons. hydraulic engr.; b. Cassville, Mo., Oct. 16, 1912; s. William Tolliver and Mildred Alice (Messer) P.; B.S., U. Mo., 1935; M.S., U. Colo., 1943; Ph.D., U. Mich., 1954; m. Vivian Willingham, Mar. 22, 1941. Jr. engr. U.S. Engrs. Office, 1937-39; from jr. to asst. engr. Bur. Reclamation, 1939-41; from instr. to asso prof. civil engring. Cornell U., 1941-55; prof. hydraulics Auburn (Ala.) U., 1955-58, prof. civil engring., head dept., 1958-65; dir. Water Resources Research Inst., Miss. State U., 1965-77; UN adviser on hydraulics, Egypt, 1956, 57, 60. Mem. Ala. Bd. Registration Profl. Engrs., 1962-65. Registered profl. engr., Ala., La., Miss., Tex. Fellow ASCE (pres. Ala. 1962, exec. com., pipeline div., 1971-74); Am. Water Resources Assn. (dir. 1973-75), Internat. Assn. Hydraulic Research, Permanent Internat. Assn. Nav. Congresses, Sigma Xi, Tau Beta Pi, Chi Epsilon, Pi Mu Epsilon. Contbr. articles to profl. jours. Address: PO Box 541 Starkville MS 39759

PRIESTLEY, JAMES TAGGART, II, surgeon; b. Des Moines, Ia., Apr. 7, 1903; s. Crayke Simpson and Lillian Independence (Marquardt) P.; A.B., U. of Pa., 1923, M.D., 1926; M.S., U. of Minn., 1931, Ph.D., 1932; LL.D., U. of Alberta, 1958; m. Klea Palica, Aug. 23, 1930; children—Barbara (Mrs. Jack Garst), Martha (Mrs. Bruce Jackson), Judith (Mrs. Raymond N. Kjellberg), James Taggart III. Surg. fellow, The Mayo Grad. Sch. Medicine, 1928-33; mem. surgical staff, The Mayo Clinic, 1933-68, emeritus staff, 1968; prof. Mayo Grad. Sch. of Medicine, U. of Minn. Served as lt. col., M.C., AUS, 1943-46. Awarded bronze Star, oak leaf cluster. Diplomate Am. Bd. Surgery. Hon. fellow Royal Coll. Surgeons (England); mem. A.M.A., Am. Coll. Surgeons, Western Surgical Assn., Central Surg. Assn., Clinical Soc. Genito-Urinary Surgeons, Soc. Clin. Surgery, Am. Surg. Assn., Southern Surgical Assn., Sigma Xi, Phi Beta Kappa, Phi Gamma Delta, Alpha Mu Pi Omega. Clubs: Univ. (Rochester, Minn.); Surgeons. Author: (with Waltman Walters and H. K. Gray) Carcinoma and Other Malignant Lesions of the Stomach, 1942, rev. edit., 1964, Cancer of the Stomach, and various surgical articles. Home: 1010 SW 10th St Rochester MN 55901 Office: 200 First Street SW Rochester MN 55901

PRIESTLEY, WILLIAM TURK, architect; b. Yazoo City, Miss., Mar. 3, 1907; s. William Turk and Annola (Beamon) P.; B.S., Princeton U., 1929; student N.Y.U. Sch. Architecture, 1930-32, Bauhaus, Dessau, Berlin, Germany, 1932-33; M.F.A., Columbia, 1935; m. Christabel Wheeler, June 11, 1938; children— William Turk, Seymour Wheeler. Grad. asst. Columbia Sch. Architecture, 1934-35; tchr. art Dalton Sch., N.Y.C., 1935-37; instr. architecture Cooper Union, 1937-40; asst. prof. architecture Ill. Inst. Tech., 1940-42; prof. architecture, chmn. dept. Western Res. U., 1960-66; mem. Rodgers & Priestley, N.Y.C. and Chgo., 1935-42; with firm Skidmore Owings Merrill, architects, Chgo., 1945-52, Pace Assos., architects, Chgo., 1952-60; archtl. adviser Western Res. U., 1960-66; with firm Bertrand, Goldberg & Assos., Chgo., 1967-71; pvt. practice of architecture, Lake Forest, Ill., 1971—. Prin. works include hosps., schs., apts., residences, comml. and indsl. bldgs. Former mem. Fine Art Adv. Com. Cleve. Served to maj. USAAF, 1942-45. Fellow A.I.A. Club: Arts (Chgo.). Home: 55 Negaunee Ln Lake Forest IL 60045

PRIESTMAN, BRIAN, condr.; b. Birmingham, Eng., Feb. 10, 1927; s. Miles and Margaret (Messer) P.; B.Mus., U. Birmingham, 1950, M.A., 1952; Diplome Superieur, Conservatoire Royale de Bruxelles, Belgium, 1952; D.F.A., Regis Coll., 1972; D.H.L., U. Colo., 1977. Prof., U. Birmingham, 1957-58; music dir. Royal Shakespeare Theatre, Stratford-on-Avon, Eng., 1960-63, Edmonton (Alta., Can.) Symphony, 1964-68; acting music dir. Balt. Symphony, 1968-69; music dir. Denver Symphony Orch., 1970-77, Fla. Philharmonic, 1977—; prin. condr. New Zealand Broadcasting Corp., 1973-75. Office: Fla Philharmonic 120 SE 2d Ave Miami FL 33131

PRIGMORE, CHARLES SAMUEL, educator; b. Lodge, Tenn., Mar. 21, 1919; s. Charles H. and Mary Lou (Raulston) P.; A.B., U. Chattanooga, 1939; M.S., U. Wis., 1947, Ph.D., 1961; extension grad. Air War Coll., 1967, Indsl. Coll. Armed Forces, 1972; m. Shirley Melaine Buuck, June 7, 1947; 1 son, Philip Brand. Social caseworker Children's Service Soc., Milw., 1947-48; social worker Wis. Sch. Boys, Waukesha, 1948-51; supr. tng. Wis. Bur. Probation and Parole, Madison, 1951-56; supt. Tenn. Vocat. Tng. Sch. for Boys, Nashville, 1956-59; asso. prof. La. State U., 1959-64; ednl. cons. Council Social Work Edn., N.Y., 1962-64; exec. dir. Joint Commn. Correctional Manpower and Tng., Washington, 1964-67; prof. Sch. Social Work, U. Ala., 1967—, chmn. com. on Korean relationships; Fulbright lectr., Iran, 1972-73; vis. lectr. U. Sydney, 1976; cons. Iranian Ministry Health and Welfare, 1976-78; frequent lectr., workshop leader. Chmn., Ala. Citizens Environ. Action, 1971-72, Tuscaloosa Council Environ. Quality, 1970-72; pres. Ala. Conservancy, 1969-72; mem. Ala. State Citizens Advisory Bd. Health and Environ. Protection, 1972-73; mem. exec. com. Democratic Com. Tuscaloosa County, 1970; chmn. pub. safety com. Community Devel. Action Group, Tuscaloosa, 1974. Served to 2d lt. USAAF, 1940-45; lt. col. Res. ret. Decorated Air medal with oak leaf cluster; recipient Conservation award Woodmen of the World, 1971; Fulbright research fellow, Norway, 1979-80. Fellow Am. Sociol. Assn., Royal Soc. Health; mem. Acad. Cert. Social Workers, Nat. Council Crime and Delinquency, Tuscaloosa C. of C., Tuscaloosa Civitan Club, Alpha Kappa Delta, Beta Beta Beta. Club: Tuscaloosa Country. Author: Textbook on Social Problems, 1971; Social Work in Iran Since the White Revolution, 1976; Social Welfare Policy Analysis and Formulation, 1979. editor 2 books; contbr. articles to profl. jours. Home: 19 High Forest Tuscaloosa AL 35406 Office: Box 1935 University AL 35486. *The following principles seem most related to my success: 1) From childhood I was encouraged to formulate specific vocational goals and work toward them; 2) support of friends and relatives is secondary, though important; more significant is one's own effort and planning. 3) Objectives and plans usually can be achieved only through persistence and determination. Usually one is forced to sacrifice a measure of peer fellowship and conviviality. 4) Belief in oneself and one's own potentialities makes for a self-fulfilling prophecy.*

PRIGMORE, DONALD GENE, utility co. exec.; b. Leon, Kans., Sept. 26, 1932; s. Harry Edward and Mary Julia (Doyle) P.; B.S.C.E., Kans. State Coll., 1955; M.B.A., U. Mich., 1958; m. June Mary O'Connell, May 15, 1970; children—Marc, Elizabeth Ann, Mary Kathryn, Christine. Spl. studies engr. Gen. Telephone Co. of Mich., Muskegon, 1958-62, div. mgr., Three Rivers, 1962-69, pres., Muskegon, 1979—; plant dir., service dir. GTE Service Corp., N.Y.C., 1969-72, regional v.p. mktg. and customer services, Irving, Tex., 1978-79; v.p. ops. Gen. Telephone Co. of Ind., Ft. Wayne, 1972-76; v.p. ops. Gen. Telephone Co. S.W., San Angelo, Tex., 1976-77, v.p. mktg. and customer services, 1977-78; dir. Hackley Union Bank. Mem. adv. bd. Ft. Wayne United Way, 1972-75; gen. chmn. Tom Green County (Tex.) United Way, 1978; bd. dirs. Mfrs. and Employers, Muskegon, Mich., 1979; dir.-at-large Mich. State C. of C., 1979; trustee Greater Muskegon Indsl. Fund, 1979. Registered profl. engr., Mich., Ind., Tex. Mem. Am. Mktg. Assn. (dir. Dallas chpt. 1978), Nat. Soc. Profl. Engrs., Phi Delta Theta. Clubs: Muskegon Country, Century. Office: 455 E Ellis Rd Muskegon MI 49443

PRIGOGINE, ILYA, educator; b. Moscow, USSR, Jan. 25, 1917; s. Roman and Julie (Wichmann) P.; Ph.D., Free U. Brussels, 1942; hon. degrees U. Newcastle (Gt. Britian), U. Poitiers (France), U. Chgo., U. Bordeaux (France), numerous others; m. Marina Prokopowicz, Feb. 25, 1961; children—Yves, Pascal. Prof., U. Brussels, 1947—; dir. Internat. Insts. of Physics and Chemistry, Solvay, Belgium, 1962—; dir. center for statis. mechanics and thermodynamics U. Tex., Austin, 1967—. Recipient Prix Francqui, 1955; Prix Solvay, 1965; Nobel prize in chemistry, 1977; medal Assn. Advancement of Sci. (France), 1975; Rumford gold medal Royal Soc. London, 1976; Descartes medal U. Paris, 1979. Mem. Royal Acad. Belgium, Am. Acad. Sci., Royal Soc. Scis. of Uppsala (Sweden), Fgn. Assn. Nat. Acad. Scis. U.S.A., Soc. Royale des Scis. Liege Belgium (corr.), Acad. Gottingen Germany, Deutscher Akademie der Naturforscher Leopoldine (Medaille Cothenius 1975), Osterreichische Akademie der Wissenschaften (corr.), Chem. Soc. Poland (hon.), others. Author: (with R. Defay),Traite de Thermodynamique, conformement aux methodes de Gibbs et de De Donder, 1944, 50; Etude Thermodynamique des Phenomenes Irreversibles, 1947; Introduction to Thermodynamics of Irreversible Processes, 1962; (with A. Bellemans, V. Mathot) The Molecular Theory of Solutions, 1957; Statistical Mechanics of Irreversible Processes, 1962; (with others) Non Equilibrium Thermodynamics, Variational Techniques and Stability, 1966; (with R. Herman) Kinetic Theory of Vehicular Traffic, 1971; (with R. Glansdorff) Thermodynamic Theory of Structure, Stability and Fluctuations, 1971; (with G. Nicolis) Self-Organization in Nonequilibrium Systems, 1977; From Being to Becoming—Time and Complexity in Physical Sciences, 1979, Order Out of Chaos, 1979. Address: 67 ave Fond'Roy 1180 Brussels Belgium also Dept Physics U Tex Austin TX 78712

PRILLAMAN, RICHARD LEE, army officer; b. Sophia, W.Va., May 4, 1928; s. John Henry and Gladys Wriston (Lewis) P.; B.S. in Chemistry, Va. Mil. Inst., 1949; grad. U.S. Army War Coll., 1969; m. Jacqueline Hale, Nov. 19, 1950; children—Grant H., Robin L. Commd. 2d lt. U.S. Army, 1950, advanced through grades to maj. gen., 1976; served with inf. Korean War, 1951-52, Vietnam War, 1964-66, 69-70; ops. officer VIII Corps, Europe, 1972-74; from dep. comdr. to comdr. Ft. Jackson, S.C., 1975-77; ops. dir. UN Command, Korea, 1977-80; comdr. 2d Armored Div., Ft. Hood, Tex., 1980—. Decorated Silver Star, Legion of Merit with 2 oak leaf clusters, Bronze Star with 3 oak leaf clusters, Purple Heart. Address: ACS G-3-8th US Army APO San Francisco CA 96301

PRIM, WAYNE LAVERNE, lawyer; b. Grenora, N.D., Oct. 22, 1926; s. Frank E. and Christine (May) P.; B.S., U. Wash., 1950, LL.B., 1951; m. Loretta Jean Prim; children—Andrea Louise, Wayne LaVerne. With Ernst & Ernst, C.P.A.'s Seattle, 1950-52; admitted to Wash. bar, 1950, Cal. bar, 1953; spl. atty. Internal Revenue Service, San Francisco, 1952-54; partner firm Howard Prim, Rice, Nemerovski, Canady & Pollak, P.C., San Francisco, 1954—. Chmn. bd., dir. Butler Publns., 1965-68; dir., mem. exec. com. Arcata Corp., 1968—; partner Hambrecht & Quist, investment bankers, 1968—. Trustee, pres. San Francisco Ballet Assn., 1974-75, now chmn. exec. com.; trustee Menlo Sch. and Coll. Served to capt. USNR, and USAAF, 1944-46. C.P.A., Wash. Mem. Am., San Francisco (vice chmn. sect. taxation) bar assns., Western Assn. Venture Capitalists (speaker), Delta Upsilon, Delta Theta Phi, Phi Alpha Delta. Clubs: Menlo Circus (Atherton); Bankers, Villa Taverna (San Francisco). Home: 30 Cowell Lane Atherton CA 94025 Office: 650 California St San Francisco CA 94108

PRIMACK, JOEL ROBERT, educator; b. Santa Barbara, Calif., July 14, 1945; s. Roy and Loretta (Zabarsky) P.; A.B., Princeton U., 1966; Ph.D., Stanford U., 1970, m. Nancy Ellen Abrams, Sept. 4, 1977. Research asso. Stanford Linear Accelerator Center, 1970; jr. fellow Soc. Fellows Harvard, 1970-73; asst. prof. physics U. Calif. at Santa Cruz, 1973-77, asso. prof., 1977—. Sloan fellow, 1974-78. Mem. Am. Phys. Soc., AAAS, Fedn. Am. Scientists (nat. council 1970-74). Author: (with Frank von Hippel) Advice and Dissent: Scientists in the Political Arena, 1974. Contbr. articles on physics and tech. issues to profl. jours. Office: Physics Dept U of Calif Santa Cruz CA 95064

PRIMELO, ANTHONY MARTIN, psychiatrist, health center exec.; b. N.Y.C., Mar. 12, 1931; s. Albert and Josephine (Guerrieri) P.; B.S., Coll. City N.Y., 1952; M.D., U. Padua (Italy), 1957; m. Basso Nella, Sept. 8, 1958; children—Ralph, Claudia. Intern Queens (N.Y.) Gen. Hosp., 1957-58; resident Creedmoor State Hosp., Queens, 1964-66; dep. dir. Bklyn. State Hosp., 1969-72; dir. Harlem Valley State Hosp., Wingdale, N.Y., 1973-74; dep. dir. clin. Creedmoor Psychiat. Center, Queens Village, N.Y., 1974-75, 76—; dir. Pilgrim Psychiat. Center, West Brentwood, N.Y., 1975-76; clin. asst. prof. psychiatry State U. N.Y., N.Y.C., 1972—; adj. asso. prof. dept. community health Long Island U., N.Y.C., 1971—. Diplomate Am. Bd. Psychiatry and Neurology. Mem. Am. Psychiat. Assn. (Physicians' Recognition award 1979). Home: 11 Ingram St Forest Hills NY 11375 Office: 114-20 Queens Blvd Forest Hills NY 11375

PRIMM, BENY JENE, physician; b. Williamson, W.Va., May 21, 1928; s. George Oliver and Willie H. (Martin) P.; B.S., W.Va. State Coll., 1950; M.D., U. Geneva (Switzerland), 1959— m. Annie Delphine Evans, Jan. 1, 1952 (dec. Nov. 1975); children—Annelle Benee, Martine Armande, Jeanine Bari. Intern, Meadowbrook Hosp., Hempstead, L.I., N.Y., 1960-61, resident, 1961-63; attending anesthesiologist Harlem Hosp., 1963-64; dir. anesthesiology Oyster Bay Hosp., Bayville, L.I., 1964-67; co-dir. anesthesiology Whitestone Hosp., Queens, N.Y., 1966-68; dir. anesthesiology Interfaith Hosp., Jamaica, L.I., 1966-69, dir. profl. med. services, 1966-69; asso. anesthesiologist Harlem Hosp. Center, 1966-69, dir. narcotics control, 1968-69; cons. anesthesiologist Vets Meml. Hosp., Ellenville, N.Y., 1964-68, Hamilton Ave. Hosp., Monticello, N.Y., 1966-68; exec. dir., pres. Addiction Research & Treatment Corp., Bklyn., 1969—; co-med. dir. M.J. Lewi Coll. Podiatry, N.Y.C., 1969-71; med. cons. Dist. Atty., Queens, N.Y., 1969-73; adj. asst. prof. Hunter Coll.; vis. prof. behavioral sci. Eckerd Coll., St. Petersburg, Fla., 1977; narcotic cons. Blvd. Hosp., City U. N.Y., Sch. Dist. 4, Bd. Edn. N.Y.C., Spl. Action Office Drug Abuse Prevention. Mem. Narcotic Guidance Council, New Rochelle, N.Y.C., Urban Coalition Health Task Force; v.p. Harlem Health Council, 1968-70; cons. Social Consult, Inc., 1970—; pres. Council Community Voices on Narcotics; mem. com. problems drug dependence Nat. Acad. Scis.-NRC, 1972—; mem. Pres.'s Adv. Council Drug Abuse Prevention, 1972—; mem. controlled substances adv. com. FDA, 1978—; advisor Health Affairs Office, NAACP, 1977—; mem. health brian trust Congl. Black Caucus, 1977—; mem. adv. bd. Minority Aged Services Tng. Inst., Nat. Urban League, 1977—. Trustee W.Va. State Coll. Found.; bd. dirs. Jamaica Service Program for Older Adults, 1977—, Internat. Sickle Cell Anemia Research Inst., Washington, 1977—. Served to 1st lt. AUS, 1950-53. Fellow Am. Coll. Anesthesiology; mem. Nat. Med. Assn. Home: 86 Colonial Pl New Rochelle NY 10801 Office: Addiction Research and Treatment Corp 22 Chapel St Brooklyn NY 11201

PRIMM, JAMES NEAL, educator; b. Edina, Mo., Feb. 5, 1918; s. Frank Bryan and Grace (Rampy) P.; B.Ed., Northeast Mo. State Tchrs. Coll., 1941; A.M., U. Mo., 1949, Ph.D., 1951; m. Marian Ella Faris, May 18, 1946; 1 dau., Jacqueline Susan. Asst. dir. then dir. Western Hist. Manuscripts collection U. Mo., 1951-58, asst. prof. history, 1954-57, asso. prof., 1957-58; dean of coll. Hiram Coll., 1958-64, v.p., 1963-64, pres., 1964-65; prof., chmn. dept. history U. Mo. at St. Louis, 1966-70. Served from ensign to lt. comdr., USNR 1942-46; PTO. Mem. Am., Econ., So. hist assns., Orgn. Am. Historians. Democrat. Mem. Disciples of Christ Ch. Author: Economic Policy in Missouri, 1954; (with Abe C. Ravitz) The Haywood Case, 1963; The American Experience, 1973. Home: 7236 S Roland St St Louis MO 63121

PRINA, L(OUIS) EDGAR, journalist; b. West New York, N.J., Oct. 7, 1917; s. Louis Edgar and Marion (Duggan) P.; A.B., Syracuse U., 1938, M.A., 1940; m. Frances Lee Lorick, Feb. 14, 1947; 1 dau., Lee Lorick II. Copy editor, asst. night city editor N.Y. Sun, N.Y.C., 1946-48, Washington corr., 1948-50; nat. affairs writer Washington Star, 1950-66; mil. affairs writer/editor Copley News Service, Washington, 1966-77, bur. chief, 1977—; editor Navy Mag., Washington, 1961-68; columnist Sea Power Mag., 1968—. Served with USN, 1941-46, 51-53, capt. Res. (ret.). Recipient Disting. Public Service award USN, 1965. Mem. U.S. Naval Inst., Nat. Press Club, Explorers Club, Sigma Delta Chi (v.p. Washington chpt.). Roman Catholic. Clubs: Chevy Chase, Met. of Washington. Author: The Political Virgin, 1958; Flew to South Pole for Overnight Visit, 1966. Home: 4813 Quebec St NW Washington DC 20016 Office: Suite 1100 National Press Bldg Washington DC 20045

PRINCE, AARON ERASTUS, clergyman, educator; b. Fairfield, Ill., Jan. 1, 1887; s. Rev. Peter and Emma Jane (Young) P.; A.B., Howard Payne U.; S.T.B., LL.D., La Grange Coll.; D.D., Ewing Coll.; m. Pearl Bonner, Aug. 24, 1909; (dec. Oct. 18, 1946); children—Esther E. (Mrs. Howard L. Jackson), Ruth A. (Mrs. R. Allen Hunt), Mary L. (Mrs. Edwin F. Moore), Grace L. (Mrs. Glen Lee Greene), Dorothy E., Aaron, Jr.; m. 2d, Virginia Faye Dixon, June 9, 1949. Ordained to ministry Baptist Ch., 1904; held student pastorates in Ill., 1904-10; pastor, Casey, Ill., 1910-12, Ewing, Ill., 1912-14, Charleston, Ill., 1914-16, LaGrange, Mo., 1916-19, Eldorado, Ill., 1919-21, Marion, Ill., 1921-27, Brownwood, Texas, 1927-34, Pineville, La., 1934-39, West Monroe, La., 1939-41; pastor Fifth St. Ch., Hannibal, Mo., 1941-44, pastor emeritus, 1944—; pres. Hannibal LaGrange Coll., 1941-50; pastor First Bapt. Ch., Effingham, Ill., 1950-51; pastor Bapt. Tabernacle, Auckland, New Zealand, 1951-52; prin. Hawaiian Bapt. Acad., 1952-53; 1st pres. Honolulu Christian Coll., 1953-55; stewardship Evangelist, 1955-57; pastor 1st Bapt. Ch., Lafayette, La., 1957-58, Emmanuel chapel, Scott Field AFB, 1958-59, Maplewood Park Bapt. Ch., Cahokia, Ill., 1960-66, pastor emeritus, 1977—; pastor Water Tower Bapt. Ch., St. Louis, 1966-68, 70-74, pastor emeritus, 1974—; adminstr. chaplain Temple Retirement Home, Bridgeton, Mo., 1966-67. Dir. 4 Minute Speakers, Publicity Dept., U.S. Govt. for Northeast Mo., World War I, 1917-19. Chaplain U.S. Vets. Hosp., Alexandria, La., 1937-39, Central La. State Hosp., 1935-39, La. State Indsl. Sch. for Girls, 1937-39. Mem. edn. bd. So. Bapt. Conv., 1919-21, Bd. Fgn. Missions, 1921-27, Relief and Annuity Bd., 1937-40. Rec. sec. exec. bd. Ill. Bapt. State Assn., 1919-27; trustee Ewing Coll., 1919-25, pres. Ewing Coll., 1924-25; trustee Howard Payne Coll., 1927-34; mem. exec. bd. Bapt. Gen. Conv., Tex., 1927-34; moderator Brown County (Tex.) Bapt. Assn., 1929-34; mem. La. Bapt. Hosp. Bd., 1935-41; pres. exec. bd. La. Bapt. Conv., 1937-41. Mem. Ewing Coll. Alumni Assn. (pres. 1958—). Mason (32 deg.), Odd Fellow, Rotarian. Editor: Life's Best, 1940; Meeting Life's Reverses, 1941. Author: Christ Is All, 1940 (English edit.); Cristo E. Tudo, 1941 (Portuguese edit.); Back to Bethel, 1942; To My Friends, 1943; History of Fifth Street Baptist Church, 1944; History of Ewing College, 1961; History Maplewood Park Baptist Church, 1974. Home: PO Box 4015 St Louis MO 63136

PRINCE, ALAN THEODORE, Canadian govt. ofcl.; b. Toronto, Can., Feb. 15, 1915; s. Theodore and Sarah Helena (McMillan) P.; B.A., U. Toronto, 1937, M.A., 1938; Ph.D., U. Chgo., 1941; m. Virginia C. Lea, May 30, 1942; children—Linda Lea Prince Anderson, Mary Catherine Prince Kaschub. With div. chemistry Nat. Research Council Can., Ottawa, 1940-43, Can. Refractories Ltd., 1943-45; lectr. geology U. Man., 1945-46; with Canadian Dept. Mines and Tech. Surveys, 1946-67, dir. water research br., 1965-67; dir. inland waters br. Dept. Environment, 1967-73; asst. dep. minister planning and evaluation Dept. Energy, Mines and Resources, 1973-75; pres. Atomic Energy Control Bd., Ottawa, 1975-79. Registered profl. engr., Ont. Fellow Chem. Inst. Can., Mineral. Soc. Am., Am. Ceramic Soc.; mem. Canadian Inst. Mining and Metallurgy, Assn. Profl. Engrs. Ont. Home: 20 Riverside Dr PO Box 106 Manotick ON K0A 2N0 Canada

PRINCE, ALBERT IRVING, educator, psychologist; b. Hartford, Nov. 2, 1925; s. Albert I. and Ethel (Snow) P.; A.B., Wesleyan U., Middletown, Conn., 1948; A.M., U. N.H., 1949; Ph.D., U. Conn., 1953; m. Anna-May T. Thornhill, Aug. 15, 1952; children—Frederick C., Jason E., Martin R. Research psychologist Research Center, George Washington U., 1953-56; asst. prof. Stetson U., 1956-59; asst. prof. U. Denver, 1959-63; research psychologist McDonnell Aircraft Corp., 1963-67; chmn. psychology dept. Marietta (Ohio) Coll., 1968—. Served with AUS, 1944-46. NSF grantee, 1965-71. Mem. Am. Psychol. Assn., Sigma Xi, Psi Chi. Contbr. articles profl. jours. Home: 116 Hillcrest St Marietta OH 45750

PRINCE, CARL E., historian; b. Newark, Dec. 8, 1934; s. Phillip G. and Anne (Silver) P.; B.A. with honors, Rutgers U., 1956, M.A., 1958, Ph.D. in History, 1963; m. Sue Grill, June 14, 1959; children—Elizabeth, Jonathan. Instr. history Fairleigh Dickinson U., 1960-63; asst. prof. history Seton Hall U., 1963-66, asso. prof., 1966-68; asso. prof. N.Y. U., 1968-74, prof., 1974—, chmn. dept. history, 1978—; postdoctoral fellow Hebrew Union Coll., 1966; Fulbright scholar, Israel, 1972-73; mem. exec. bd. N.J. Catholic Hist. Records Commn.; mem. N.J. Hist. Records Commn.; mem. exec. bd. United Negro Coll. Fund Archives. Chmn. West Orange (N.J.) Citizens Against the Vietnam War, 1965-70; adv. to Democratic Party del. to N.J. Constl. Conv., 1968; county coordinator Essex County (N.J.) Citizens for McCarthy, 1968; mem. West Orange Bicentennial Com., 1976. Nat. Endowment for Humanities younger scholar fellow, 1968-69. Fellow N.J. Hist. Soc.; mem. Soc. for Historians of Early Am. Republic (exec. bd.), Inst. Early Am. History and Culture (asso.), Columbia U. Seminar in Early Am. History (asso.). Jewish. Author books, including: New Jersey's Jeffersonian Republicans, 1789-1817, 1967; The Federalists and the Origns of the U.S. Civil Service, 1977; The Papers of William Livingston, 5 vols., 1979—. Home: 35 Korwell Circle West Orange NJ 07052 Office: Dept History 19 University Pl NY U New York NY 10003

PRINCE, DAVID ALLAN, neurologist; b. Newark, July 14, 1932; B.S. cum laude, U. Vt., 1952, postgrad. Coll. Medicine, 1952-54; M.D., U. Pa., 1956. Asst. prof. medicine (neurology) Stanford (Calif.) U. Sch. Medicine, asso. prof., dir. neurol. tng. program, 1968-70, asso. prof., acting chmn. dept. neurology, 1970-71, prof. medicine (neurology), chmn. dept., 1971—. Served with M.C., AUS. Epilepsy Found. Am. grantee, 1965-66, 67-68, 71-72, USPHS research grantee, 1966-69, 69-72, 72-80, Nat. Inst. Neurol. Diseases and Stroke grantee, 1969-75; Grass Found. fellow, 1967, Guggenheim fellow, 1971-72. Mem. Am. Acad. Neurology, Assn. for Research in Nervous and Mental Disease, N.Y. Acad. Sci., Am. Epilepsy Soc. (sec. 1970-72, pres. elect 1973, Lennox award 1978), Bay Area Neurophysiol. Group, Am. EEG Soc., Soc. for Neurosci., Am. Neurol. Assn., Phi Beta Kappa, Sigma Xi, Alpha Omega Alpha. Contbr. articles to profl. jours. Office: Room C338 Dept Neurology Stanford U Med Center Stanford CA 94305

PRINCE, DAVID CHANDLER, cons. engr.; b. Springfield, Ill., Feb. 5, 1891; s. A.E. and Charlotte (Hitchcock) P.; student U. Mich., 1908-10; B.S. in E.E., U. Ill., 1912, M.S. in E.E., 1913; student Lincoln Coll. of Law, Springfield, Ill., 1915-16; Sc.D. (hon.), Union Coll., Schenectady, 1943; m. Winifred Notman, May 14, 1918; children—David Chandler, Jr., George N., Winifred (Mrs. Charles D. Hyson), Edward. Test engr. Gen. Electric Co., 1913-14; mem. engring. staff Pub. Utilities Commn. of Ill., 1914-17; employed in radio dept. Gen. Electric Co., 1919-23, research lab., 1923-31, chief engr. switchboard dept., 1931-40, mgr. comml. engring., 1940-41, vice chmn. Field Devel. div. Com. for Econ. Devel., 1941-45, v.p. charge gen. engring. and cons. lab., 1945-51, mem. corporate atomic energy commn., v.p., mem. pres.'s staff, 1951, ret., 1951; now in cons. practice. Served as 1st lt. Ordnance Dept., U.S. Army Air Service, 1917-19. Received citation for especially meritorious service in the solution of engring. problems relating to aircraft; Modern Pioneer Award, 1940; Lamme medal, 1946. Fellow IEEE (pres. 1941-42); mem. Inst. Aero. Scis., ASME, Soc. Automotive Engrs., Am. Rocket Soc., Am. Helicopter Soc., AAAS, Am. Nuclear Soc., N.Y. State Soc. Profl. Engrs., Chi Psi, Eta Kappa Nu, Tau Beta Pi, Sigma Xi. Clubs: Univ. (N.Y.); Ausable (St. Huberts, N.Y.); Ocean (Ocean Ridge, Fla.). Author two books and numerous tech. papers. Patentee in field. Address: 24 Hibiscus Way Ocean Ridge FL 33435. *The engineer views hopefully the hitherto unattainable.*

PRINCE, GREGORY SMITH, assn. exec.; b. Mobile, Jan. 26, 1910; s. Sydney Rhodes and Hattie Beverly (Smith) P.; A.B., Yale, 1931, LL.B., 1934; grad. Command and Gen. Staff Sch., 1943; m. Margaret Eastman Minor, Oct. 5, 1935 (dec. Feb. 1968); children—Edward Minor, Gregory Smith; m. 2d, Cynthia Borden Ayers, Oct. 10, 1969. Admitted to D.C. bar, 1935; atty. Assn. Am. R.R.'s, 1934-42, asst. gen. solicitor, 1945-50, asst. gen. counsel, 1950-52, gen. solicitor, 1952-57, v.p., gen. counsel, 1957-61, exec. v.p., gen. counsel, 1961-67, exec. v.p., 1967-75. Vice pres., gen. counsel Nat. Def. Transp. Assn., 1966-69. Bd. mgrs. Chevy Chase Village, 1969-72, vice chmn., 1972-74, chmn., 1974-76. Trustee Transp. Research Found., 1964-67; mem. Yale Alumni Bd., 1955-57. Served to lt. col. AUS, 1942-45; dir. Security Mil. Ry. Service. Mem. Am. Bar Assn. (chmn. council sect. pub. utility law 1966-67), Transp. Assn. Am. (dir., chmn. r.r. panel 1957-75), Phi Delta Phi, Zeta Psi. Clubs: Chevy Chase (bd. govs. 1953-59, pres. 1956-58); Metropolitan, Lawyers, Univ., Burning Tree, Alfalfa (Washington); Yale (N.Y.C.); Royal Ashdown Forest Golf (Sussex, Eng.). Home: 3512 Hamlet Pl Chevy Chase MD 20015

PRINCE, HAROLD S., theatrical producer; b. N.Y.C., Jan. 30, 1928; s. Milton A. and Blanche (Stern) P.; A.B., U. Pa., 1948, D.F.A. (hon.), 1971; Litt.D., Emerson Coll., 1971; m. Judith Chaplin, Oct. 26, 1962; children—Charles, Daisy. Co-producer Pajama Game, 1954-56 (Antoinette Perry award), Damn Yankees, 1955-57 (Antoinette Perry award), New Girl in Town, 1957-58, West Side Story, 1957-59, Fiorello, 1959-61 (Antoinette Perry award, Pulitzer prize), Tenderloin, 1960-61, A Call on Kuprin, 1961, They Might Be Giants, London, 1961, Side by Side by Sondheim, 1976; producer Take Her, She's Mine, 1961-62, A Funny Thing Happened on the Way to the Forum, 1962-64 (Antoinette Perry award), Fiddler on the Roof, 1964-72 (Antoinette Perry award), Poor Bitos, 1964, Flora the Red Menace, 1965; dir., producer She Loves Me, 1963-64 (London 1964), Superman, 1966, Cabaret, 1966-69 (Antoinette Perry award) (London 1968), Zorba, 1968-69, Company, 1970-72 (Antoinette Perry award) (London 1972), A Little Night Music, 1973-74 (Antoinette Perry award) (London 1975), Pacific Overtures, 1976, Evita (Best Mus. award 1977-78, London SWET award); co-dir., producer Follies, 1971-72; co-producer, dir. Candide, 1974-75; dir. A Family Affair, 1962, Baker Street, 1965, Great God Brown, 1972-73, The Visit, 1973-74, Love for Love, 1974-75, Ashmedai, 1976, On The Twentieth Century, 1978, Evita, London, 1978, Broadway, 1979, Sweeney Todd, 1979, The Demon Barber of Fleet Street, 1979; co-producer films The Pajama Game, 1957, Damn Yankees, 1958; dir. films Something for Everyone, 1970, A Little Night Music, 1978. Mem. council Nat. Endowment Arts. Recipient Antoinette Perry Meml. awards, Critics Circle awards, Pulitzer prize, 1961; Best Mus. award London Evening Standard, 1955-58, 72. Mem. League N.Y. Theatres (pres. 1964-66). Office: 1270 Ave of Americas New York NY 10020

PRINCE, JULIUS SAMUEL, ret. fgn. service officer, physician; b. Yonkers, N.Y., July 21, 1911; s. Julius and Clara B. (Rich) P.; B.A., Yale U., 1932; M.D., Columbia U., 1938, M.P.H., 1948; Dr.P.H., Harvard, 1957; m. Eleanora Molloy, July 6, 1943; children—Thomas Marc, Tod Ainslee. Intern Sinai Hosp., Balt., 1939-40; asst. resident medicine N.Y.U. div. Goldwater Meml. Hosp., 1941-42; dist. health officer N.Y. State Dept. Health, Jamestown, 1948-58; chief pub. health div. AID, Ethiopia, 1958-67, prin. investigator demonstration and evaluation project. 1964-67; chief Africa div. Population and Humanitarian Affairs, Population Office, AID, Washington, 1967-73, chief health, population and nutrition projects U.S. AID/Ghana, Accra, 1973-76; cons., internat. dir. health, population and nutrition program Pacific Cons., Inc. Served from lt. to maj. M.C., Royal Canadian Army, 1942-46. Recipient Superior honor award AID, 1968, Letter of Commendation, 1977. Fellow Am. Pub. Health Assn., Am. Coll. Preventive Medicine, Royal Soc. Health, Am. Soc. Applied Anthropology; mem. AMA, Pan Am. Med. Assn., Ghana Med. Soc., Internat. Union Sci. Study Population, AAAS, Internat. Health Soc. (pres.), Population Assn. Am., Soc. Internat. Devel. Home: 7103 Pinehurst Pkwy Chevy Chase MD 20015 Office: Pacific Cons 2020 K St NW Washington DC 20006

PRINCE, KENNETH C., lawyer, bus. exec.; b. Chgo., July 15, 1912; s. Charles S. and Rose (Lazarus) P.; Ph.B., U. Chgo., 1932, J.D., 1934; m. Pearl Lubin, June 16, 1935; children—Judith Marilyn, Linda Kay. Admitted to Ill. bar, 1934; mem. Ungaro & Sherwood, 1934-43; own law offices, 1946-48; pres. Prince, Schoenberg, Fisher & Newman Ltd., 1948—; gen. counsel Electronic Industry Show Corp.; sec., dir. C-L Realty Corp., Russ Diethert Co., Inc., John G. Twist Co., Reeve Electronics, Inc., George Petitt Co., Inc., Reevelec, Inc., Russell Industries, Inc., Russales, Inc., Twist Assos., Inc., G. McL. Cole Co., Aracon Electronics, Inc.; asst. sec., dir. Argos Products Co., Inc., Quam-Nichols Co.; asst. sec. G.E.D. Corp., Mid-Am. Co., Inc., R.R.J. Corp., Como Inn, Inc., Handmacher Co., Inc.; sec. Craftsman Plating & Tinning Co., Grayhill, Inc., Grayhill Moldtronics, Inc., R-V Supply Co., Go Inc., Slifer Packaging Systems, Inc., Parkview Metal Products, Inc., Execs. Tng., Inc., Realty Partners, Inc., Grayhill Moldtronics N.J., Inc.; dir. Littelfuse, Inc., Ellinger Sales Corp., Stewart-Keator-Kessberger & Lederer, Inc., Indsl. Reps., Inc., Triplett Corp. Bd. dirs. Chgo. Bar Found., Ill. Inst. Continuing Legal Edn.; bd. dirs., adv. bd. Loyola Law Sch.; mem. vis. com. U. Chgo. Law Sch. Served to lt. USNR, 1943-46. Mem. Am. Fed., Ill., Chgo. (pres. 1976-77), North Suburban bar assns., Comml. Law League, Decalogue Soc. Lawyers, Phi Beta Delta. Jewish. Mason; mem. B'nai B'rith. Club: Briarwood Country (pres. 1968-70). Home: 1045 Hillcrest Rd Glencoe IL 60022 Office: 222 S Riverside Plaza Chicago IL 60606

PRINCE, PHILIP HUNTER, bus. exec.; b. Bostic, N.C., Aug. 4, 1926; s. Walter Eugene and Mary Hunter (Palmer) P.; B.S., Clemson U., 1949; grad. exec. program U. N.C., 1968; m. Celeste Lourine Orr, Mar. 11, 1950; children—Kevin Hunter, James Bryan. Tchr., coach public schs., Bristol, Tenn., 1950; prodn. control mgr. Milliken & Co., 1951-56, v.p. personnel and mgmt. devel., 1967-78; prodn. control mgr. Burlington Industries, 1956-57; sr. v.p. Am. Express Co., N.Y.C., 1978--. Mem. S.C. Council on Econ. Edn. Served with U.S. Army, 1945-46, 50-51. Mem. Ga. Textile Mfrs. Assn. (bd. dirs.), S.C. Textile Mfrs. Assn., So. Indsl. Relations Conf. (bd. dirs.), U.S. C. of C. (mem. labor com.). Presbyterian. Clubs: Country (Spartanburg, S.C.); Ponte Vedra (Fla.). Home: Lower Waverly Pawleys Island SC 29585 Office: American Express Co American Express Plaza New York NY 10004

PRINCE, ROBERT MASON, financial exec.; b. Madison, Wis., Oct. 22, 1914; s. Robert Ellsworth and Florence Elizabeth (Mason) P.; A.B., U. Mich., 1936; J.D., Detroit Coll. Law, 1939; m. Elizabeth Harvey Sherk, 1937; children—Dana (Mrs. Bruce L. Davis), Kathy (Mrs. Conrad Schaefer); m. 2d, Sheila Anna Hoban, 1973. Accountant, Haskins & Sells, C.P.A.'s, Am. Surety Co., Detroit, 1937-41; admitted to Mich. bar, 1939, Ill. bar, 1948; mem. exec. and legal dept., atty.-mgr. ins. dept., also mgr. govt. controls Dow Chem. Co., 1941-47; engaged in ins., Chgo., 1947-49; partner firm Norman, Engelhardt, Zimmerman & Prince, and predecessor, Chgo., 1949-57; exec. v.p. Devel. Corp. Am. and subsidiary Acorn Paint & Chem. Co., 1957-58; v.p., dir. Bankers Life and Casualty Co., Chgo., 1958-61; chmn. bd. Am. Airmotive Corp., Shasta Cattle Co., Greengold Farms, Inc., 1958-61; pres. Datronics, Inc., Nat. Drilling Co., Fla. Aviation Corp., 1958-61; dir. Chgo. City Bank & Trust Co., 1959-61; vice chmn. bd. Diversa, Inc., Dallas, 1959-63; chmn. bd. Prince & Cummins, Inc., Chgo., 1962-65, Prince Roosevelt & Cummins, Miami, Fla., 1962-64; asst. to pres. Dow Chem. Internat., 1963-65; dir. Investment services exec. dept. Dow Chem. Co., 1965-69; v.p. ventures investment, finance div. Dow Chem., 1969-72; v.p., dir. Dow Chem. Financial Corp., 1966-72, Dolco Packaging Corp., North Hollywood, Calif., 1967-72; chmn. bd. Austral-Pacific Fertilizers, Ltd., Brisbane, Queensland, Australia, 1968-70; dir. Austral-Pacific Fertilizers, Ltd., 1966-72; with affiliates cos. Valley Nat. Bank Phoenix; v.p., gen. mgr., dir. Concho Investment Corp., Concho Life Ins. Co., 1972-75; mng. dir. Prince & Co., 1975—; atty., of counsel firm Martin, Craig, Chester and Sonnenschein, Chgo., 1975—. Chmn. zoning and planning com. Village Barrington Hills, 1957-58. Mem. Am., Ill., Mich. bar assns. Club: Union League (Chgo.). Home: 471-C Valley View Lake Barrington Shores Barrington IL 60010 Office: 115 S La Salle St Suite 2400 Chicago IL 60603

PRINCE, THOMAS RICHARD, educator; b. New Albany, Miss., Dec. 7, 1934; s. James Thompson and C. Florence (Howell) P.; B.S., Miss. State U., 1956, M.S., 1957; Ph.D. in Accountancy, U. Ill., 1962; m. Eleanor Carol Polkoff, July 14, 1962; children—Thomas Andrew, John Michael, Adrienne Carol. Instr., U. Ill., 1960-62; mem. faculty Northwestern U., 1962—, prof. acctg. and info. systems, 1969—, chmn. dept. accounting and info. systems Grad. Sch. Mgmt., 1968-75; cons. in field; dir. Applied Research Systems, Inc. Served to 1st lt. AUS, 1957-60. C.P.A., Ill. Mem. Am. Accounting Assn., Am. Inst. C.P.A.'s, Am. Econ. Assn., Inst. Mgmt. Scis., Fin. Execs. Inst., AAAS, Ill. Soc. C.P.A.'s, Nat. Assn. Accts., Alpha Tau Omega, Phi Kappa Phi, Omicron Delta Kappa, Delta Sigma Pi, Beta Alpha Psi. Unitarian (chmn. trustees 1964-65). Author: Extension of the Boundaries of Accounting Theory, 1962; Information Systems for Management Planning and Control, 3d edit., 1975. Home: 303 Richmond Rd Kenilworth IL 60043 Office: Leverone Hall Northwestern U Evanston IL 60201

PRINCE, WILLIAM HENRY WOOD, investments and real estate exec.; b. St. Louis, Feb. 7, 1914; grad. Princeton U., 1936; m. Eleanor Edwards, 1940; children—Alain Wood, William Norman Wood, Alexander Wood. With First Nat. Bank of Chgo., 1936-42, 45-47; sec.-treas. Sherman Hotel, Coll. Inn Food Products Co., Chgo., 1939-42; with Union Stock Yard & Transit Co., 1948-57, pres., 1949-57, dir.; dir. Armour & Co., 1950, vice chmn. 1957, pres., 1957-61, chmn. 1961-67, chmn. chief exec. officer, until 1969; pres. F.H. Prince & Co. Inc., Chgo., 1969—; chmn. USY&T Industries, Inc., Chgo.; dir. Eastern Airlines, First Nat. Bank Chgo., First Chgo. Corp., W.R. Grace and Co., Pebble Beach Corp., Commonwealth Edison Co., Baxter Travenol Labs., Inc.; trustee Central Mfg. Dist. Served as capt. F.A., 25th Inf. Div., AUS, 1942-45. Clubs: Chicago, Racquet, Saddle and Sirlion (Chgo.); Racquet and Tennis (N.Y.C.); Travelers (Paris, France). Office: FH Prince Co Inc One First National Plaza Chicago IL 60603

PRINCIPAL, VICTORIA, actress; b. Fukuoka, Japan, Jan. 3; d. Victor and Ree Veal P.; attended Miami-Dade Community Coll.; studied acting with Max Croft, Al Sacks and Estelle Harman; m. Christopher Skinner, 1979. Worked as model, including TV comml. appearances; film debut in The Life and Times of Judge Roy Bean, 1972; other movie appearances include: The Naked Ape, Earthquake; I Will, I Will... For Now; Vigilante Force; TV film appearances include: Fantasy Island, Delancey, The Night They Stole Miss Beautiful; became theatrical agt., 1975; appears on TV series Dallas, 1978—; other TV appearances include: Love Story, Love, American Style, Greatest Heroes of the Bible, Battle of the Network Stars. Office: care Lorimar Prodns 4000 Warner Blvd Burbank CA 91522*

PRINDLE, CHARLES O'BRIEN, naval officer; b. Nyack, N.Y., Nov. 20, 1931; s. Charles Henry and Marjorie Teresa (O'Brien) P.; B.A., U. Miss., 1953; M.S. in Mgmt., U.S. Naval Postgrad. Sch., 1967; grad. Nat. War Coll., 1974; m. Leota Jane Janson, Oct. 31, 1954; children—Sharon, Cheryl, Brian, Kevin, Debra. Commd. ensign U.S. Navy, 1953, advanced through grades to rear adm., 1977; served with Patrol Squadron 28, Barbers Point, Hawaii, 1955-57; flight instr. Naval Air Basic Tng. Command, Pensacola, Fla., 1957-59, Naval Air Sta. Saufley Field, Pensacola, 1960-62; CIC officer Carrier Div. 6, Mayport, Fla., 1962-64; assigned to Patrol Squadron 10, Naval Air Sta. Brunswick, Maine, 1964-66; asst. plans facilities support officer Fleet Air Wings Pacific, Naval Air Sta. Moffet Field, Calif., 1968-69, exec. officer Patrol Squadron 50, 1969-70, comdr., Western Pacific, 1970-71; assigned to strategic plans and policy div. Office Chief of Naval Ops., Washington, 1971-73; Navy asst. to chmn. Joint Chiefs of Staff, Washington, 1974-76; comdr. Patrol Wing 11, Naval Air Sta., Jacksonville, Fla., 1976-77; comdr. Patrol Wings, U.S. Pacific Fleet, Naval Air Sta. Moffett Field, 1977—. Lay minister Roman Cath. Ch. Decorated Legion of Merit, Bronze Star, Meritorious Service medal. Mem. U.S. Naval Inst., Alpha Tau Omega. Club: St. Francis Yacht (San Francisco). Home: Quarters A Naval Air Sta Moffett Field CA 94043 Office: Comdr Patrol Wings US Pacific Fleet Naval Air Sta Moffett Field CA 94035

PRINDLE, PAUL EDWIN, coll. textbook co. exec.; b. Boston, July 30, 1935; s. Harold Edwin and Agnes D. (Chenoweth) P.; A.B., Brown U., 1958; m. Susan Dwight, June 25, 1966; children—Carl Edwin, Barbara Gay. With Allyn & Bacon Co., 1960-65, sr. editor, 1963-65; founder, v.p. Prindle, Weber & Schmidt Inc., Boston, 1965-73, pres., 1973—, also dir.; group exec., v.p. Wadsworth Pub. Co., 1977—; chmn. bd. Stephen Greene Press, 1978—; dir. Visidyne Corp. Served with AUS, 1958-60. Mem. Math. Assn. Am. Club: University (Boston). Home: 140 Marlborough St Boston MA 02116 Office: 20 Newbury St Boston MA 02116

PRINE, ANDREW LOUIS, actor; b. Jennings, Fla., Feb. 14, 1936; s. Randy and Florence (Riviere) P.; student Miami U., 1954-56, Welch Workshop, N.Y.C. Stage debut in The Rainmaker, 1956; other stage appearances include: Mrs. Patterson, 1956, Look Homeward, Angel, 1957, Borak, 1960, Distant Bell, 1960, The Caine Mutiny Court-Martial, 1971; films include: The Miracle Worker, 1962, Advance to the Rear, 1964, Bandolero!, 1968, This Savage Land, 1969, Generation, 1969, Chisum, 1970, Squares, 1972, One Little Indian, 1973, The Centerfold Girls, 1974, Grizzly, 1976, Company of Cowards, 1964, The Town That Dreaded Sundown, 1977, The Evil, 1978; TV appearances include: U.S. Steel Hour, Playhouse 90, Gunsmoke, Bonanza, Ironside; regular TV series Wide Country, 1962-63; TV spl. Roughing It; TV movies Along Came a Spider, Night Slaves, The Law of the Land, Last of the Mohicans, 1977. Recipient Century Theatre award for Look Homeward, Angel, 1958. Office: care David Shapiro & Assos 9171 Wilshire Blvd Beverly Hills CA 90210*

PRINE, CHARLES W., JR., homebuilding co. exec.; b. Pitts., Apr. 23, 1926; s. Charles W. and Mabel (Kerr) P.; A.B., Princeton U., 1948; m. Elizabeth Erskine, Aug. 2, 1969; children—Linda, Janet, Karen, Roger, Barbara, Alison. Journalist, Pitts. Sun-Telegraph, 1948-56; pres. P.R. Counselors, Inc., Pitts., 1957-69; sr. v.p. Ryan Homes, Inc., Pitts., 1969—. Chmn. Mt. Lebanon Joint Recreation Commn., 1968-70; bd. dirs. Transitional Services, Inc., South Hills Child Guidance Center, Pitts. Opera; elder Bower Hill Community Presbyn. Ch.; chmn. Pres.' Roundtable Pitts. Theol. Sem. Served with USNR, 1944-46. Mem. Nat. Assn. Homebuilders. Clubs: Harvard-Yale-Princeton (Pitts.). Home: 1108 Lindendale Dr Pittsburgh PA 15243 Office: 100 Ryan Ct Pittsburgh PA 15205

PRINGLE, ANDREW, JR., air force officer; b. Seattle, Mar. 19, 1927; s. Andrew and Alice Marrow (Hollywood) P.; B.A., Central Mich. U.; m. Anne L. Bachmann, June 30, 1950. Commd. 2d lt. U.S. Air Force, 1950, advanced through grades to maj. gen., 1978; assigned to Castle AFB, Calif., 1950-54; served with 90th Strategic Reconnaissance Wing, Forbes AFB, Kans., also 100th Bombardment Wing, Pease AFB, N.H., 1954-60; pilot evaluator 1st Combat Evaluation Group, Barksdale AFB, La., 1960-63; served in various ops. positions Hdqrs. 8th Air Force, SAC, Westover AFB, Mass., 1963; served with 99th Bombardment Wing, 1969; dep. comdr. 99th Combat Support Group; plans officer Hdqrs. SAC, Offutt AFB, Nebr.; dep. comdr. for ops 97th Bombardment Wing, Blytheville AFB, Ark.; dep. comdr. for ops. 72d Strategic Wing (Provisional) on temporary duty to Andersen AFB, Guam, 1972-74, comdr. 43d Strategic Wing, 1974-75, insp. gen. for air tng. command, 1975-77; comdr. 17th Bombardment Wing, SAC, Wright-Patterson AFB, Ohio, 1974; comdr. Lowry Tech. Tng. Center, Lowry AFB, Colo., 1977-78; comdr. Hdqrs 3d Air Div., SAC, Andersen AFB, 1978—. Decorated Legion of Merit with oak leaf cluster, Bronze Star, Meritorious Service medal, Air medal with 3 oak leaf clusters. Mem. Air Force Assn. Episcopalian. Home: 1000 Rota Dr APO San Francisco CA 96334 Office: 3AD/CC APO San Francisco CA 96334*

PRINGLE, EDWARD E., former chief justice Colo. Supreme Ct., legal educator; b. Chgo., Apr. 12, 1914; s. Abraham J. and Lena (Oher) P.; LL.B., U. Colo., 1936, LL.D., 1976; LL.D., U. Denver, 1979; m. Pauline Judd, Aug. 17, 1941; children—Bruce, Eric. Admitted to Colo. bar; practiced in Denver, 1936-42, 47-57; with fed. govt. service, Washington, 1943-47; dist. judge Colo. Dist. Ct., Denver, 1957-61; justice Supreme Ct. Colo., Denver, 1961-79, chief justice, 1970-78; dir. research and writing program U. Denver Coll. Law, 1979—. Bd. dirs. Am. Med. Center, Denver; mem. Nat. Commn. for Establishment of Nat. Inst. Justice. Served with USAAF, 1942. Recipient William Lee Knovs award U. Colo. Law Sch., 1975. Mem. Am., Colo., Denver bar assns., Conf. Chief Justices (chmn. 1973-74), Am. Judicature Soc. (Herbert Lincoln Harley award 1973; chmn. bd. 1974-76), Nat. Center State Cts. (pres. 1977-79. Jewish. Club: Mason (33 deg.). Contbr. articles to profl. jours. Office: U Denver Coll Law 200 W 14 St Denver CO 80204

PRINGLE, HENRY HUDSON, steel co. exec.; b. Grand Forks, N.D., Sept. 19, 1894; s. William H. and Lois A. (Griggs) P.; student U. Wash., 1915; m. Hazel F. Antle, May 20, 1922 (dec. Oct. 1961); 1 dau., Lois A. (Mrs. Jacob J. Vander Ploeg); m. 2d, Marian V. Riegel, Jan. 26, 1963. Pres. Concrete Steel Corp., Medford, Ore., 1960-75, now chmn.; dir. emeritus Pacific Power & Light Co. Served with arty., U.S. Army, World War I; AEF in France. Clubs: University, Rogue River Country (Medford). Home: 601 N Modoc Ave Medford OR 97501 Office: PO Box 1588 Medford OR 97501

PRINGLE, KENNETH GEORGE, lawyer; b. Minot, N.D., May 13, 1914; s. Alexander Dixon and Florence (Gridley) P.; B.S., N.D. State U., 1936; student Minot State Tchrs. Coll., 1932-34; m. Jean Leone Herigstad, Sept. 1, 1937; children—Priscille Jean Pringle Wells, Roger Kenneth, Alice Fern Pringle Heitlinger, Jane Florence Pringle Hirst. Tchr., Harvey (N.D.) High Sch., 1936-37; asst. Boy Scout exec., Albert Lea, Minn., 1937-39; scout exec., Sioux Falls, S.D., 1939- 44; studying law Supreme Ct. Clerkship, Minot, 1946-49; admitted to N.D. bar, 1949, since practiced in Minot; partner firm Pringle, Herigstad, Meschke, Loder, Mahoney & Purdy, 1963-68; partner Pringle & Herigstad, 1968-70; pres. Pringle & Herigstad, P.C., 1970—. Pres. Gt. Plains Area council Boy Scouts Am., 1952-55, 68, pres. No. Lights council, 1973-75 mem. nat. council, mem. N. Central region Boy Scout com., 1974—; chmn. nat. law exploring com. Chmn. Ward County Republican Com., 1955-60. Bd. dirs. Minot Community Chest. Served from ensign to lt. USNR, 1944-46. Recipient Silver Beaver award Boy Scouts Am., 1954, Silver Antelope, 1967, Distinguished Eagle Scout award, 1975. Fellow Am. Coll. Probate Counsel (bd. regents 1971-77, exec. com. 1974—), Am. Judicature Soc.; mem. World Assn. Lawyers (founding mem.), Am. (adv. bd. editors Jour. 1964-67, ho. of dels. 1971-76, chmn. spl. com. on legal assts. 1974-75, chmn. standing com. on legal assistants 1975-78, bd. govs. 1974), N.D. (chmn. legal econs. com. 1964-66, chmn. def. of indigents and legal aid com., 1966-67, pres. elect 1967-68, pres. 1968-69), Ward County (pres. 1956), 5th Dist. bar assns., Assn. Bars Northwestern Plains and Mountains (chancellor 1970-71), Minot C. of C. (dir.; Outstanding Citizen award 1975). Presbyterian (elder, trustee). Kiwanian. (pres. 1951). Club: Minot Metropolitan Dinner (past pres., dir. 1964-77). Home: 625 3d St SE Minot ND 58701 Office: Am Bank & Trust Co Bldg Minot ND 58701

PRINGLE, ORAN ALLAN, educator; b. Lawrence, Kan., Sept. 14, 1923; s. Oran Allan and Mae (McClelland) P.; B.S. in Mech. Engring., U. Kan., 1947; M.S., U. Wis., 1948, Ph.D., 1967; m. Billie Hansen, June 25, 1947; children—Allan, Billie, James, Rebecca. Mech. engr. Black and Veatch, cons. engrs., Kansas City, Mo., 1947-48; engr. Boeing Airplane Co., Wichita, 1952—; prof. U. Mo., Columbia, 1948—. Bd. dirs. United Cerebral Palsy Boone County (Mo.) Served with AUS, 1943-45. Registered profl. engr., Mo. Ford Found. grantee. Mem. Am. Soc. M.E. (chmn. fastening and joining com., design engring. div.), Sigma Xi. Co-author: Engineering Metallurgy, 1957; contbr. articles to profl. lit. Home: 1820 University Ave Columbia MO 65201 Office: Dept Mech and Aerospace Engring U Mo Columbia MO 65201

PRINS, DAVID, speech pathologist; b. Herkimer, N.Y., Oct. 4, 1930; s. Tunis W. and Harriett Z. (Baker) P.; B.A., Central Coll. Iowa, 1952; M.A., U. Mich., 1957, Ph.D., 1961; m. Gloria B. Fleming, June 4, 1955; children—Leslie, Steven, Douglas, Michael. Tchr. Denison (Iowa) High Sch., 1953-55; instr. U. Mich., 1960-63, asst. prof., 1963-66, asso. prof., 1966-69, asst. dir. U. Mich. Speech and Hearing Camp, 1960-64, dir., 1964-69; dir. program in speech and hearing scis. U. Wash., 1974-75, asso. prof., 1969-72, prof., 1973—, chmn. dept. speech and hearing scis., 1975-79, asso. dean Coll. Arts and Scis., 1979; vis. prof. U. Va. Served with U.S. Army, 1952-54. Mem. Am., Wash., Mich. (past pres.) speech and hearing assns., Phi Beta Kappa, Phi Kappa Phi. Contbr. articles in field of stuttering and articulation disorders to profl. jours. Home: 13130 NE 31st Pl Bellevue WA 98005 Office: Dept Speech and Hearing Scis U Wash Seattle WA 98195

PRINZ, JOACHIM, clergyman; b. Burkhardsdorf, Germany, May 10, 1902; s. Joseph and Nani (Berg) P.; rabbi, Jewish Theol. Sem., Breslau, Germany, 1925; student U. Berlin (Germany), 1922-23; Ph.D., U. Giessen (Germany), 1924; m. Lucie Horovitz, Dec. 25, 1925 (dec. Jan. 1931); 1 dau., Lucie Berkowitz; m. 2d, Hilde Goldschmidt, May 24, 1932; children—Michael, Jonathan, Deborah. Came to U.S., 1937, naturalized, 1944. Rabbi, Jewish community, Berlin, 1926-37; expelled by gestapo, 1937; lectr. European and Near Eastern policies, U.S., 1937-39; rabbi Temple B'nai Abraham, Newark, 1939—. Nat. pres. Am. Jewish Congress, 1958-66, chmn. commn. internat. affairs, 1966-68; chmn. Conf. Pres.'s Maj. Am. Jewish Orgns., 1966-69, World Conf. of Jewish Orgns., 1975—; exec. bd. World Jewish Congress, 1946, chmn. gov. council, 1967-75, v.p., 1975—; dir. Conf. Jewish Materials Claims Against Germany, Inc., 1956. Chmn, United Jewish Appeal Essex County, N.J., 1945; pres. Jewish Edn. Assn. Essex County, 1944; bd. dirs. Jewish Community Council Essex County, Essex County Heart Assn. Author: Judische Geschichte, 1931; Illustrierte Judische Geschichte, 1933; Die Geschichten der Bible, 1934; Wir Juden, 1934; Die Reiche Israel and Juda, 1935; Der Freitagabend, 1935; Das Leben Im Ghetto, 1937; Relatos de la Biblia, 1941; Heroes y Principes Hebroes, 1941; Cartes Cartolor, 1946; The Great Jewish Books (edited by S. Caplan and H. U Ribalow), 1952; The Dilemma of the Modern Jew, 1962; Popes from the Ghetto, 1966; The Secret Jews, 1973. Editorial bds. Reconstruction, 1958. Judaism, 1958—. Home: 306 Elmwynd Dr Orange NJ 07050 Office: 300 E Northfield Rd Livingston NJ 07039

PRINZ, JOHN SEBASTIAN, III, dancer; b. Chgo., May 14, 1946; s. John Sebastian, Jr. and Eva Prinz; student Am. Ballet Center, Sch. Am. Ballet; m. Nanette Glushak. Debut, N.Y.C. Ballet, 1964; then prin.; mem. Am. Ballet Theatre, 1970—; roles include Don Quixote, Jewels, Pas de Deux La Source, Dances at a Gathering, Giselle, Cordelia, Jardin aux Lilas, Romeo and Juliet, Flames of Paris; choreographer, guest tchr.; guest artist for other cos., concerts. Address: 40 W 86th St New York NY 10024

PRIOR, JOHN ALAN, educator, physician; b. Columbus, Ohio, Apr. 17, 1913; s. John Clinton and Edna (Cones) P.; B.A., Ohio State U., 1935, M.D. 1938; m. Helen Eileen Zurmehly, Mar. 24, 1936; children—John Alan, Robert Lee, Richard Ray (dec.), Ann E. Intern Grant Hosp., Columbus, 1938-39; resident pulmonary diseases Dunham Hosp., Cin., 1939-43; instr. U. Cin. Med. Sch., 1942-43; asst. prof. medicine Ohio State U. Med. Coll., 1944-48, asso. prof., 1948-51, prof. medicine, 1951—, asst. dean Coll. Medicine, 1961-63, asso. dean, 1963-70, dean, 1970-72; cons. internal medicine USAF, VA, USPHS; mem. med. rev. bd. Ohio State Tchrs. Retirement and Sch. Employee Retirement Systems. Mem. Upper Arlington Sch. Bd., 1958-62; pres. Upper Arlington Booster Assn., 1956-57. Bd. dirs. Willson Childrens Center, Childrens Hosp. Research Found., Ohio State U. Research Found.; exec. com. Bremer Found. Recipient Distinguished Service Alumni award Ohio State U. Coll. Medicine, 1963, Distinguished Teaching award, Ohio State U., 1965. Diplomate Am. Bd. Internal Medicine. Mem. A.C.P., Am., Ohio (pres. 1956-57) thoracic socs., Am. Coll. Chest Physicians, Columbus Acad. Medicine, Ohio Med. Assn., Ohio State Coll. Medicine Alumni Soc. (pres. 1977-78), Alpha Omega Alpha (hon.), Phi Delta Theta. Mem. Community Ch. Rotarian. Club: Scioto Country. Author: Physical Diagnosis, 5th edit., 1973; also articles pulmonary and fungus diseases. Home: 2650 Donna Dr Columbus OH 43220

PRITCHARD, DONALD WILLIAM, oceanographer; b. Santa Ana, Calif., Oct. 20, 1922; s. Charles Lorenzo and Madeleine (Sievers) P.; B.A., UCLA, 1942; M.S., Scripps Instn. Oceanography, La Jolla, 1948, Ph.D., 1951; m. Thelma Lydia Amling, Apr. 25, 1943; children—Marian Lydia, Jo Anne, Suzanne Louise, Donald William, Albert Charles. Research asst. Scripps Instn. Oceanography, 1946-47; oceanographer USN Electronics Lab., 1947-49; asoc. dir. Chesapeake Bay Inst., Johns Hopkins, Balt., 1949-51, dir., 1951-74, chief scientist, 1974-79, prof., 1958-79, chmn. dept. oceanography, 1951-68; asso. dir. for research, prof. Marine Scis. Research Center, SUNY at Stony Brook, 1979—; cons. C.E., U.S. Army, USPHS, AEC, Internat. AEC, NSF, Adv. Panel Earth Scis.; mem. adv. bd. to Sec. Natural Resources, State of Md.; mem. adv. bd. Nat. Oceanographic Data Center. Served from 2d lt. to capt. USAAF, 1943-46. Fellow Am. Geophys. Union (past pres. oceanography sect.); mem. Am. Soc. Limnology and Oceanography (past v.p.), Am. Meteorol. Soc. A.A.A.S., Nat. Acad. Scis. (com. oceanography; past chmn. panel radioactivity in marine environment), Sigma Xi (past chpt. pres.). Bd. editors Jour. Marine Research, 1953—, Bull. Bingham oceanographic Collection, 1960—, Geophys. Monograph Bd., Am. Geophys. Union, 1959—, Johns Hopkins Oceanographic Studies, 1962—. Author articles in field. Home: 23 Harbor Hills Dr Port Jefferson NY 11777 Office: MSRC SUNY Stony Brook NY 11794

PRITCHARD, HAROLD WAYNE, conservation cons.; b. Estevan, Sask., Can., Mar. 3, 1916; s. John and Ethel Ann (Spurrier) P.; brought to U.S., 1922, naturalized, 1933; B.S., Iowa State U., 1939; m. Helen Spayde, June 30, 1940; children—Nancy Ann (Mrs. Edwin L. Miller), Mary Elizabeth (Mrs. Dean Ehling). Instr. vocat. agr. high schs., Iowa, 1939-49; exec. sec. Iowa Soil Conservation Com., 1949-52; exec. sec. Soil Conservation Soc. Am., Ankeny, Iowa, 1952-66, exec. dir., 1966-72, exec. v.p., 1973-78, editorial dir. Jour. Soil and Water Conservation, 1960-78, fellow soc., 1959; conservation cons., writer, 1978—. Mem. Central States forest adv. council U.S. Forest Service, 1960-67; steering com. Nat. Water Pollution Conf., HEW, 1960; sec. Pan Am. Soil Conservation Commn., 1966-78; mem. advisory panel Office Water Resources Research, Dept. Interior, 1971; bd. govs. Living Hisotry Farms Found., 1968—. Served with USAAF, 1943-45. Recipient Leadership Recognition award Iowa Dept. Soil Conservation, 1970; Hugh Hammond Bennett award in conservation Soil Conservation Soc. Am., 1974; named only Am. hon. mem. Soil Conservation Soc. Sri Lanka, 1974. Fellow AAAS; mem. Council Agrl. Sci. and Tech., Nat. Farm Inst. (chmn. 1966-67), Alpha Gamma Rho (Outstanding Service award Eta chpt. 1971). Mem. Christian Ch. Kiwanian (pres. 1964, past dir.). Club: Downtown (dir.) (Des Moines). Home and Office: 2724 61st St Des Moines IA 50322

PRITCHARD, JAMES BENNETT, educator, author: b. Louisville, Oct. 4, 1909; s. John Hayden and Mary (Bennett) P.; A.B., Asbury Coll., 1930; B.D., Drew U., 1935; Ph.D., U. Pa., 1942; S.T.D., Phila. Div. Sch., 1961; D.D., Ch. Div. Sch. of Pacific, 1962; L.H.D., Swarthmore Coll., 1977, D.D., U. Uppsala (Sweden), 1977; m. Anne Elizabeth Cassedy, June 30, 1937; children—Sarah Anne (Mrs. Robert F. Hayman), Mary Bennett (Mrs. Clifton Mitchell). Prof. O.T. lit. Crozer Theol. Sem., 1942-54; ann. prof. Am. Sch. Oriental Research, Jerusalem, 1950-51, archeol. dir. expdn. to Jericho, Jordan, 1951, vis. prof., 1956-57, 61-62, dir. expdns. to el-Jib, Jordan, 1956-62, to Tell es-Sa'idiyeh, Jordan, 1964-67, Sarafand, Lebanon, 1969, 1970, 1971, 1972, 74; prof. O.T. lit. Ch. Div. Sch. Pacific, 1954-62; curator Bib. archeology Univ. Mus., 1962-78, asso. dir., 1967-76, dir., 1976-77, prof. religious thought U. Pa., 1962-78; Winslow lectr. Gen. Theol. Sem., 1960; Fulbright-Hays vis. prof. archaeology Am. U. Beirut, 1966-67; mem. Inst. Advanced Study, Princeton, N.J., 1978. Sec., Am. Schs. Oriental Research, 1963-71. Trustee Am. U. Beirut, 1970—. Decorated Order of Istiqlal, 1st Class, Jordan, 1964. Mem. Am. Philos. Soc., Am. Oriental Soc., Archeol. Inst. Am. (pres. 1973, 74), Soc. Bibl. Lit. Clubs: Franklin Inn, Athenaeum. Author: Palestinian Figurines, 1943; Ancient Near Eastern Texts, 1950, 55, 69; The Ancient Near East in Pictures, 1954, 69; Archaeology and the Old Testament, 1958; The Excavation at Herodian Jericho, 1958; The Ancient Near East, 1958, vol. 2, 1975; Hebrew Inscriptions from Gibeon, 1959; The Water System at Gibeon, 1961; Gibeon, Where the Sun Stood Still, 1962; Bronze Age Cemetery at Gibeon, 1963; Winery, Defenses and Soundings at Gibeon, 1964; Sarepta, 1975; Recovering Sarepta, A Phoenician City, 1978. Asso. editor Jour. Am. Oriental Soc., 1948-52, editor, 1952-54. Home: Tunbridge Rd Haverford PA 19041 Office: Univ Mus 33rd and Spruce Sts Philadelphia PA 19104

PRITCHARD, JOEL M., congressman; b. Seattle, May 5, 1925; student John Hay Sch., 1931-39, Queen Anne High Sch., 1939-43, Marietta Coll., 1946-48; m. Joan Sue Sutton, 1948; children—Peggy, Frank, Anne, Jean. Pres. Griffin Envelope Co., Seattle; mem. 93d-95th congresses from Wash. Mem. Wash. Ho. of Reps., 1958-66; mem. Wash. Senate, 1966-70. Served with AUS, 1944-46. Republican. Office: 2349 Rayburn House Office Bldg Washington DC 20515*

PRITCHARD, ROSS JOSEPH, univ. chancellor; b. Paterson, N.J., Sept. 3, 1924; s. Ross W. and Camille (Beltramo) P.; B.A. in History and Polit. Sci., U. Ark., 1951, M.A., 1951; M.A., Fletcher Sch. Law and Diplomacy, 1952, Ph.D., 1954; m. Emily Gregg, June 2, 1948; children—Michael, Russell, Irene, Vol Walker, Ross Joseph, Mehran, Feresteh. Asst. prof. Tufts U., 1954; asst. prof. internat. studies Southwestern Coll. at Memphis, 1955-57, asso. prof., chmn. dept 1957-60, prof., chmn. dept., 1960-62; spl. asst. Peace Corps, 1962, dep. sec. gen. internat. secretariat, 1963, dir. for Turkey, 1963-65; regional dir. for East Asia and Pacific, 1965-68; v.p., project mgr. Devel. & Resources Corp., N.Y.C., 1968-71; pres. Internat. House, Phila., 1972; pres. Hood Coll., Frederick, Md., 1972-75, Ark. State U., 1975-78; chancellor U. Denver, 1978—. Dem. candidate for Congress, 1960. Served with USN, 1941-46. Recipient Silver Anniversary award Nat. Collegiate Athletic Assn., 1976. Office: U Denver Denver CO 80210

PRITCHARD, WALTER HERBERT, physician, educator; b. Hancock, N.Y., Apr. 14, 1910; s. Edson Jay and Mertie (Cady) P.; A.B., Hamilton Coll., Clinton, N.Y., 1932; M.D., Harvard, 1936; m. Marian Louise Moore, Aug. 12, 1939; children—Walter Herbert, Lawrence, Diana, Marian, Timothy, Caroline. Intern., Univ. Hosps., Cleve., 1936-38, resident, fellow medicine, 1938-40; faculty Case Western Res. U. Sch. Medicine, 1947—, prof. medicine, 1960-65, Argyl J. Beams prof. medicine, 1965—, dir. div. cardiology, 1956-76, asso. dir. medicine Univ. Hosps., 1960—, acting dir. dept. of medicine, 1970-71, chief of staff, 1971-78. Mem. Olympic Track Team, 1932. Trustee Hamilton Coll., Clinton, N.Y., 1973-77. Mem. Assn. Am. Physicians, Am. Soc. Clin. Investigation, Central Soc. Clin. Research, AMA, Am. Heart Assn. (chmn., council on clin. cardiology, 1970-72), A.C.P., Soc. Exptl. Biology and Medicine, Assn. Univ. Cardiologists (pres. 1973), Sigma Xi. Contbr. articles on cardiovascular diseases to profl. jours. Home: 2517 Wellington Rd Cleveland Heights OH 44118 Office: 2065 Adelbert Rd Cleveland OH 44106

PRITCHARD, WILLIAM ROY, univ. system adminstr.; b. Portage, Wis., Nov. 15, 1924; s. William Roy and Lillian Edith (Roberts) P.; student U. Wis., 1942-43; D.V.M., Kans. State U., 1946, D.Sc. (hon.), 1970; Ph. D., U. Minn., 1953; J.D., Ind. U., 1957; D.Sc. (hon.), Purdue U., 1977; div.; children—Rosan June, William Roy, Caryl Jean, Alyn Evan. Asst. prof. U. Wis., 1946-49; asso. prof. U. Minn., 1949-53; prof. Purdue U., 1953-57; prof., head vet. sci. U. Fla., 1957-61; asso. dir. Vet. Med. Research Inst., Ia. State U., 1961-62; dean Sch. Vet Medicine, U. Calif. at Davis, 1962—, asso. dir. Agrl. Expt. Sta., 1962-72; coordinator internat. agrl. programs U. Calif. system, 1977—, vis. fellow Woodrow Wilson Sch. Pub and Internat. Affairs, Princeton, 1968-69; John Thomson lectr. U. Queensland, 1966; spl. research hemmorrhagic diseases animals. Cons. Dept. Agr., Def. Dept., USPHS, VA, Calif. Dept. Health, 1962—; bd. cons. agr. Rockefeller Found., 1962-66; nat. med. cons. surgeon gen. USAF, 1962-64; mem. FAO/WHO Expert Panel Vet. Edn.; mem. President's Sci. Advisory Com. Panel World Food Supply, 1966-67, President's Sci. Advisory Com. Panel Biology and Med. Sci., 1969-70; mem. Joint Research Com. Bd. Internat. Food and Agr. AID, 1977—. Served with U.S. Army, 1942-44. Recipient Gov. Fla. award, 1961; Distinguished Service award Kans. State U., 1963. Mem. Am. Vet. Med. Assn., Am. Pub. Health Assn., U.S. Animal Health Assn., Nat. Assn. State Univs. and Land-Grant Colls. (internat. affairs com. 1965-70), Assn. Am. Med. Colls., Sigma Xi, Order Coif, Phi Zeta, Gamma Alpha. Home: 2409 Madrid Ct Davis CA 95616

PRITCHETT, CHARLES HERMAN, educator; b. Latham, Ill., Feb. 9, 1907; s. Charles and Anna Margaret (Nottelmann) P.; A.B., James Millikin U., 1926; Ph.D., U. Chgo., 1937; m. Marguerite A. Lentner, July 27, 1937; children—Jean Charla, Philip Lentner. Research asst. U. Chgo., 1934, asst. prof. polit. sci., 1940-46, asso. prof. 1946-52, prof., 1952-69, acting chmn. dept., 1948-49, chmn. dept., 49-55, 58-64; research asso. TVA, 1934-37; research asso. pub. adminstrn. com. Social Sci. Research Council, 1937-38, post-doctoral research fellow, 1938-39; Ford prof. govtl. affairs, 1958-59; Bacon lectr. constn. Boston U., 1957; Dillon lectr. law and govt. U. S.D., 1957; Guy Stanton Ford lectr. U. Minn., 1959; vis. prof. Stanford, 1966; prof. U. Calif. at Santa Barbara, 1965-67, 69—, faculty research lectr., 1975, dir. Nat. Endowment for Humanities summer seminar, 1975, Residential Fellowships seminar, 1977; adminstrv. analyst Dept. Labor, 1939. Staff Commn. Orgn. Exec. Branch Govt. (Hoover Commn.), 1948. Mem. Am. Polit. Sci. Assn. (pres. 1963-64), Am. Bar Assn. (com. electoral coll. reform 1966), Am. Soc. Pub. Adminstrn., Sigma Alpha Epsilon. Author: The Tennessee Valley Authority, A Study in Public Administration, 1943; The Roosevelt Court, 1948; Civil Liberties and the Vinson Court, 1954; The Political Offender and the Warren Court, 1958; The American Constitution, 3d edit., 1977; Congress Versus the Supreme Court, 1960; Courts Judges and Politics, 3d edit., 1979; American Constitutional Issues, 1962; The Third Branch of Government, 1963; The American Constitutional System, 4th edit., 1976; co-author: The Revolutionary Theme in Contemporary America, 1965; American Government in World Perspective, 4th edit., 1976; The Presidency Reappraised, 2d edit., 1977; The Federal System in Constitutional Law, 1978; Essays on the Constitution of the United States, 1978. Contbr. articles to sci. revs. Home: 430 Northridge Rd Santa Barbara CA 93105

PRITCHETT, JAMES TURNER, actor; b. Lenoir, N.C., Oct. 27, 1922; s. James Turner and Margaret Preston (Martin) P.; A.B., U. N.C., 1944, J.D., 1949; B.S., U. Chgo., 1945; m. Cynthia Doris Arnold, Mar. 8, 1958; children—Laura McNairy, Shelley Mebane, Kyle Massey. Admitted to N.C. bar, 1949; partner firm Pritchett & Pritchett, Lenoir, 1949-51; star TV drama The Doctors, 1963—. Served to 1st lt. USAAF, 1943-46. Recipient Emmy award as outstanding actor in daytime dramatic series, 1978. Mem. AFTRA, Screen Actors Guild, Actors Equity Assn., Acad. TV Arts and Scis., Phi Delta Theta, Phi Alpha Delta, Phi Beta Kappa. Democrat. Presbyterian. Club: Players (N.Y.C.). Home: 53 W 74th St New York NY 10023 Office: 1515 Broadway New York NY 10036

PRITIKIN, ROLAND I., eye surgeon; b. Chgo., Jan. 9, 1906; s. Edward and Bluma (Saval) P.; B.S., Loyola U., 1928, M.D., 1930; diploma U.S. Army Command and Gen. Staff Coll., 1964; m. Jeanne DuPre Moore, May 25, 1940; children—Gloria Anne, Karen (Mrs. Craig Howard Heiser). Eye department Loyola U. School Medicine, 1933-35; resident Ill. Eye and Ear Infirmary, 1936-38, staff, 1939-48; vis. eye surgeon, Shikarpur, Sind, Pakistan, under Sir Henry Holland, 1939, 57; cons. Rockford industries, 1946—; pvt. practice ophthalmology, Rockford, 1946—; pres. staff Winnebago County Hosp., 1950; lecture, research tour, Western Europe, Near and Middle East, 1951; vis. eye surgeon Pakistan, 1960, Pakistan, 1963, 66, 71; cons. ophthalmology 5th U.S. Army, U.S. Army Health Services Command; study med. ednl. facilities, Ethiopia, 1972; mem. research and devel. command project Office Surgeon Gen. U.S. Army, 1972, spl. mission to Africa and Europe, 1973; faculty Rockford Sch. Medicine, U. Ill., 1970—. Ofcl. del. Assn. Mil. Surgs. U.S. and Am. Assn. Indsl. Phys. and Surg., 16th Internat. Congress Ophthalmology, London, 1950, 17th Internat. Congress, Montreal and N.Y.C., 1954, 18th Internat. Congress, Brussels, 1958, 19th Internat. Congress, New Delhi, India, 20th, Munich, 21st, Mexico City, 1970, 22d, Paris, 1974, 20th Internat. Congress History Medicine, 20th Internat. Confedn., 25th Internat. Congress, 1976. Med. Res. Officers; chmn. meeting on computers in ophthalmology Internat. Symposium on Bio-Engring. in Ophthalmology, Haifa, Israel, 1975; life mem. Weizmann Inst., Sci. Served as col. M.C. AUS, 1941-45; chief eye, ear, nose and throat service Stark Gen. Hosp., 1941-45. Recipient 1st award World Medical Assn., 1964; Quetta Mission Hosp. medal, 1964; Physician's Recognition award AMA, 1972, 75, 77; decorated Army Commendation medal, 1965, Order St. John of Jerusalem. Diplomate Am. Bd. Ophthalmology. Fellow Indsl. Med. Assn., Am. Med. Writers Assn., Soc. Mil. Ophthalmologists (bd. govs.; 1st life), AMA, A.C.S., Internat. Coll. Surgeons, AAAS, Am. Geriatrics Soc., Royal Soc. Health, Am. Coll. Nuclear Medicine (distinguished, founding) Instituto Barraquer, Barcelona; asso. Royal Soc. Medicine London; mem. Internat. Assn. Secs. Ophthalmol. and Otolaryngol. Socs. (editor ophthalmology 1973—), Ill., Winnebago County med. socs., Am. Nuclear Soc., Am. Acad. Ophthalmology and Otolaryngology, Chgo. Ophthal. Soc., Assn. Mil. Surgeons U.S., Rock River Valley Ophthalmology Assn. (sec. 1978—), World Med. Assn., Pan-Am. Assn. Ophthalmology, Am. Assn. History of Medicine, Assn. Am. Phys. and Surg., Internat. Assn. Prevention of Blindness, Joseph Waring Meml. Library Assn. History of Medicine, Soc. Med. Cons. to Armed Forces, N.Y. Acad. Scis., Contact Lens Soc. of Ophthalmologists, Nat. Soc. Prevention Blindness, Henry Holland Hosps. Alumni Assn. and Fund (pres.), Internat. Assn. Against Trachoma, Assn. Research Ophthalmology, Soc. Nuclear Medicine, Pan Am. Soc. Ophthalmic Microsurgery (charter), Ophthalmol. Soc. Canary Islands (hon.), Internat. Soc. History Medicine (hon.), C. of C., 33d Div. War Vets. Assn. (surgeon 1975—), Am. Legion, Res. Officers Assn. U.S., Internat. Agy. Prevention Blindness, others. Club: Univ. (Rockford). Author: Essentials of Ophthalmology, 1950, 3d edit., 1975; World War Three Is Inevitable, 1976. Contbr. Ency. Americana supplements, 1946—, reg. vols., 1955-72. Contbr. articles on ophthalmology various med. jours. Inventor surg. and diagnostic equipment for the eye. Home: 3505 Highcrest Rd Rockford IL 61101 Office: Talcott Bldg Rockford IL 61101

PRITSKER, A.B., educator; b. Phila., Feb. 5, 1933; s. Robert and Gertrude (Leibowitz) P.; B.S. in Elec. Engring., Columbia, 1955, M.S. in Indsl. Engring., 1956; Ph.D., Ohio State U., 1961; m. Anne Gruner, Sept. 22, 1956; children—Caryl Anne, Pamela Sue, Kenneth David, Jeffrey Richard. Dir. for systems analysis Battelle Meml. Inst., Columbus, O., 1956-62; prof. Ariz. State U., Tempe, 1962-69, Va. Poly. Inst., Blacksburg, 1969-70; prof. indsl. engring. Purdue U., 1970—; pres. Pritsker & Assos., Inc., 1973—; cons. to industry and govt., 1962—. Mem. systems and mgmt. advisory council U.S. Army Computer Systems Command, 1971-74. Recipient Faculty Achievement award Ariz. State U., 1967. Registered profl. engr., Ariz. Fellow Am. Inst. Indsl. Engrs. (dir. operations research div. 1970-72, editorial bd. 1961-71; Distinguished Research award 1966; H.B. Maynard Innovation Achievement award 1978), Am. Soc. Engring. Edn., Smithsonian Instn., Operation Research Soc. Am., Inst. Mgmt. Scis., Project Mgmt. Inst., Sigma Xi (pres. Ariz. State U. chpt. 1966-67), Pi Mu Epsilon, Alpha Pi Mu, Tau Beta Pi, Phi Kappa Phi. Author: Simulation with GASP II, 1969; The GASP IV Simulation Language, 1974; Simulation with GASP-PL/I, 1975; Modeling and Analysis Using Q-GERT Networks, 1977; Introduction to Simulation and SLAM, 1978; also papers, sci. reports. Developer GASP-PL/I, GASP IV, GASP II, JASP, GERT, SLAM. Home: 1201 Wiley Dr West Lafayette IN 47906

PRITZKER, JACK NICHOLAS, lawyer; b. Chgo., Jan. 6, 1904; s. Nicholas J. and Annie (Cohen) P.; A.B., U. Mich., 1926; J.D., Northwestern U., 1927; m. Rhoda R. Goldberg, Jan. 9, 1944; 1 son, Nicholas J. Admitted to Ill. bar, 1927, since practiced in Chgo.; partner firm Pritzker & Pritzker. Dir. Hyatt Internat. Corp. Hon. dir. Jewish Children's Bur. Chgo. Served to lt. comdr. USNR, 1942-45. Mem. Ill., Chgo. bar assns. Clubs: Arts Mid-Day, Standard (Chgo.); University (Sarasota, Fla.). Home: 179 Lake Shore Dr Chicago IL 60611 Office: Two First National Plaza Chicago IL 60603

PRITZKER, JAY ARTHUR, lawyer; b. Chgo., Aug. 26, 1922; s. Abraham Nicholas and Fanny (Doppelt) P.; B.Sc., Northwestern U., 1941, J.D., 1947; m. Marian Friend, Aug. 31, 1947; children—Nancy (dec.), Thomas, John, Daniel, Jean. Asst. custodian Alien Property Adminstrn., 1947; admitted to Ill. bar, 1947, since practiced in Chgo.; partner firm Pritzker & Pritzker, 1948—; chmn. bd., pres. Hyatt Corp., Hyatt Internat.; chmn. bd. Marmon Group, Inc.; dir. Continental Air Lines; partner Chgo. Mill & Lumber Co., Mich.-Calif. Lumber Co. Trustee, U. Chgo. Served as aviator USNR, World War II. Mem. Am., Chgo. bar assns. Clubs: Standard, Comml., Lake Shore, Mid-Day, Arts, Vince (Chgo.). Office: 2 First Nat Plaza Chicago IL 60603

PRITZKER, ROBERT ALAN, mfg. co. exec.; b. Chgo., June 30, 1926; s. Abram Nicholas and Fanny (Doppelt) P.; B.S. in Indsl. Engring., Ill. Inst. Tech., 1946; postgrad. in Bus. Adminstrn., U. Ill.; m. Audrey Gilbert, Dec. 19, 1948; children—James Nicholas, Linda, Karen. Engaged in mfg., 1946—; pres., dir. The Marmon Group, GL Corp., Marmon Group Inc. (formerly Cerro-Marmon Corp.); partner Colson Co., Chgo.; dir. Peoples Gas Co., Hyatt Corp., Chgo., Salem Corp., Pitts. Vice pres., bd. dirs. Pritzker Found., Chgo.; trustee, vice chmn. Ill. Inst. Tech. Office: 39 S LaSalle St Chicago IL 60603

PRITZLAFF, JOHN CHARLES, JR., state senator; b. Milw., May 10, 1925; s. John C. and Elinor (Gallun) P.; B.A., Princeton, 1949; m. Mary Dell Olin, Feb. 10, 1951; children—Ann, John, Barbara, Richard. Pres. John Pritzlaff Hardware Co., Milw., 1957-59; v.p. Arrow Valve Co., Phoenix, 1959-60, exec. v.p. Oxford Life Ins. Co., Scottsdale, Ariz., 1960-63; v.p. Republic Properties, Scottsdale, 1961-67, chmn. bd., 1963-67; pres. Rockmount Mgmt. Corp., 1967—; partner Cudia City Investment Corp., 1967—; dir. Marshall & Ilsey Trust Co. Ariz.; U.S. ambassador to Malta, 1969-72; mem. Ariz. senate, 1975—, minority whip, 1977-78, chmn. appropriations com., 1979-80. Mem. Ariz. Ho. of Reps., 1963-69, chmn. appropriations com., 1966-69; mem. Republican Nat. Fin. Com., 1968-69. Bd. dirs. Heard Museum, Phoenix; bd. dirs. Am. Grad. Sch. Internat. Mgmt., Phoenix, St. Luke's Hosp., Phoenix; trustee Nashotah (Wis.) Sem. Served with AUS, 1943-45. Home: 4954 E Rockridge Rd Phoenix AZ 85018 Office: 4327 N Scottsdale Rd Scottsdale AZ 85251

PRIVAT, JEANNETTE MARY, librarian; b. Seattle, May 2, 1938; d. Glenn Mackenzie and Katherine (Vanderveer) Privat; B.A. in Bus. Adminstrn., U. Wash., 1960, M.L.S., 1969. Asst. librarian United Control Corp., Redmond, Wash., 1960-64, librarian, 1964-68; librarian Seattle-First Nat. Bank, 1968-75, asst. v.p., librarian, 1975-78, asst. v.p., mgr. library, 1978—. Mem. Spl. Libraries Assn. (nat. dir. 1977-79), Nat. Assn. Bank Women. Club: Wash. Athletic. Home: 162 140th Pl NE Bellevue WA 98007 Office: PO Box 3586 Seattle WA 98124

PRIVER, JULIEN, physician, former hosp. ofcl.; b. N.Y.C., Nov. 8, 1914; s. Charles and Bertha (Hirsch) P.; B.S., CCNY, 1937; M.D., U. Western Ont. (Can.), 1940. Intern, Marine Hosp., USPHS, Stapleton, Staten Island, N.Y., 1940-41; epidemiologist-in-tng. N.Y. State Health Dept., 1941-42; resident hosp. adminstrn. Hosp. for Joint Diseases, N.Y.C., 1946; practice medicine specializing in hosp. adminstrn., N.Y.C., 1946-51, Detroit, 1951-79; asst. dir. Mt. Sinai Hosp., N.Y.C., 1946-49, asso. dir., 1950-51; exec. dir. Sinai Hosp., Detroit, 1951-63, exec. v.p., 1963-79, exec. cons., 1979, ret., 1979; adj. asso. prof. dept. community and family medicine Wayne State U. Sch. Medicine, Detroit, 1972-74, clin. asso. prof. dept. community medicine, 1974—; mem. Bd. Health, City of Detroit, 1973-75. Mem. State Adv. Bd. for Wage and Price Commn., 1972-75; MD Hosps. Team chmn. United Found., 1971; bd. dirs. Tri-State Hosp. Assembly, 1970-72, Greater Detroit Area Hosp. Council, Inc., 1969—; trustee United Health Orgn., 1967—, pres., 1972-73; trustee New Detroit, Inc., 1972-73. Served to maj., Inf., U.S. Army, 1942-46; PTO. Decorated Bronze Star with oak leaf cluster. Fellow Am. Coll. Hosp. Adminstrs.; mem. Am. Hosp. Assn. (life), Internat. Hosp. Fedn., Mich. Hosp. Assn. (pres. 1970-71, Joseph R. Homminga Meml. award 1979), Am. Public Health Assn., AMA, Mich. Soc. Mental Health (dir. 1970-72), Dirs. of Jewish Hosps., Mich. State Med. Soc., Wayne County Med. Soc.

PROBERT, WALTER, educator; b. Portland, Ore., Jan. 13, 1925; s. Raymond and Mildred Marie (Pyburn) P.; student Alfred U., 1944; B.S., U. Oreg., 1948, J.D., 1951; J.S.D. (Grad. fellow), Yale, 1957; m. Barbara Louise Stevenson, Mar. 22, 1952; children—Richard Walter, James Stevenson. Admitted to Oreg. bar, 1951; practiced in Portland, 1951-52; asst. prof. Western Res. U., 1953-57, asso. prof., 1957-59; prof. U. Fla., Gainesville, 1959—; vis. prof. Northwestern U., 1960-61, U. Tex., summer 1970, U. Wash., 1972-73; vis. research prof. U. Denver, 1966-67; prof. law-medicine Health Center, U. Fla.; lectr. Balliol Coll., Oxford, 1968. Dir. law and social sci. program NSF, 1973—. Editorial cons. Gen. Semantics Bull., 1959—. Served with AUS, 1943-47. Recipient grants for law-communication research Nat. Found. for Humanities and Ednl. Testing Service, 1968, Distinguished Tchr. award U. Fla., 1970. Mem. Assn. Am. Law Schs. (mem. panel advocates), Am. Trial Lawyers Assn., Oreg. Bar Assn., Internat. Assn. for Philosophy of Law and Social Philosophy, Law and Soc. Assn., Am. Psychology-Law Soc., Am. Soc. for Polit. and Legal Philosophy, Soc. for Health and Human Values, Am. Arbitration Assn. (nat. panel arbitrators), Order of Coif, Order of St. Ives, Delta Theta Phi. Author: Law, Language, and Communication, 1972. Faculty editor: Western Res. U. Law Rev., 1953-59. Contbr. articles to profl. jours. Home: 1929 NW 14th Ave Gainesville FL 32601

PROBST, GERALD GRAHAM, computer co. exec.; b. Ogden, Utah, Sept. 11, 1923; s. Keimer Sawyer and Ruth (Graham) P.; B.S. (with high honors), U. Utah, 1951; M.S., Mass. Inst. Tech., 1956; m. Betty Ann Forbes, Oct. 16, 1943; children—Susan Stevens, Kevin Forbes, Kathleen Hess, Marcus Forbes. With Univac div. Sperry Rand, Blue Bell, Pa., 1961—, v.p., gen. mgr. data processing div., 1968-70, exec. v.p. world wide devel. and mfg., 1970-71, pres., 1971-78, v.p. Sperry Rand Corp., 1974, exec. v.p., 1975-78, group exec. v.p., 1978—. Served with USAAF, 1942-47, USAF, 1952-61. Decorated DFC., Air medal with 5 oak leaf clusters, Commendation medal; recipient Outstanding Alumni award U. Utah, 1970. Mem. IEEE, Am. Inst. Aeros. and Astronautics, Tau Beta Pi, Phi Kappa Phi. Home: 110 Law Rd Briarcliff Manor NY 10510 Office: Sperry Corp 1290 Ave of Americas New York NY 10019. *People are not excellent because they achieve great things; they achieve great things because they choose to be excellent.*

PROBST, WALTER F., wire mfg. co. exec.; b. Pigeon, Mich., Feb. 25, 1915; s. Walter F. and Theresa (Kulschar) P.; A.B., Wayne State U., 1934; J.D., U. Mich., 1937; m. Carol Ann Caverly, Nov. 5, 1977; children—Sharon (Mrs. John R. Boothe), Gary W. Admitted to Mich. bar, 1937; with firm Cook, Smith, Jacobs & Beake, Detroit, 1937-42; with Essex Wire Corp., Detroit, 1942—, exec. v.p., 1958-59, pres., 1959-66, chmn. bd., 1966—, also dir.; chmn. bd., chief exec. officer Essex Internat. Inc., Ft. Wayne, Ind., 1966-74; dir., mem. exec. com. United Technologies Corp.; dir. Lincoln Nat. Bank & Trust Co., Ft. Wayne, Am. Fletcher Corp., Indpls. Trustee Eisenhower Med. Center, Palm Desert, Cal., U. So. Calif. Mem. Order of Coif. Lutheran (council). Home: 861 Lakeshore Dr Incline Village NV 89450 Office: 12207 Illinois Rd Fort Wayne IN 46804

PROBSTEIN, RONALD FILMORE, engring. educator; b. N.Y.C., Mar. 11, 1928; s. Sidney and Sally (Rosenstein) P.; B.M.E., N.Y. U., 1948; M.S.E., Princeton U., 1950, A.M., 1951, Ph.D., 1952; A.M. (hon.), Brown U., 1957; m. Irene Weindling, July 30, 1950; 1 son, Sidney. Research asst. physics N.Y. U., 1946-48, instr. engring. mechanics, 1947-48; research asst. dept. aero. engring. Princeton U., 1948-52, research asso., 1952-53, asst. prof., 1953-54; asst. prof. divs. engring., applied math. Brown U., 1954-55, asso. prof., 1955-59, prof., 1959-62; prof. mech. engring. M.I.T., 1962—; sr. partner Water Purification Assos., Cambridge, 1974—. Guggenheim fellow, 1960-61. Fellow Am. Acad. Arts and Scis.; mem. Internat. Acad. Astronautics, Nat. Acad. Engring., ASME (Freeman award 1971), Am. Phys. Soc., AIAA, Am. Inst. Chem. Engrs., Water Pollution Control Fedn., AAAS. Democrat. Jewish. Author: Hypersonic Flow Theory, 1959; Hypersonic Flow, Inviscid Flows, 1966; Water in Synthetic Fuel Production, 1978; editor: Introduction to Hypersonic Flow, 1961; Physics of Shock Waves, 1966; contbr. articles to profl. jours. Home: 5 Seaver St Brookline MA 02146 Office: 77 Massachusetts Ave Cambridge MA 02139

PROCHASKA, FRANK J., chem. co. exec.; b. Crete, Nebr., Apr. 2, 1906; s. John J. and Frances (Cursak) P.; B.A., Doane Coll., 1926; M.Sc., U. Nebr., 1929; postgrad. Iowa State U., 1928-31; m. Ruth Elanor Fuchs, Mar. 21, 1930; children—Ann (Mrs. John Connor), Frances (Mrs. Maurice McCullen), Carol (Mrs. Joseph Saviano). Prof. chemistry Muscatine (Iowa) Jr. Coll, 1931-42; with Grain Processing Corp., Muscatine, 1943—, exec. v.p., 1955—, also dir. Served to lt. USNR, 1942-43. Home: 1452 Camino Del Monte Nogales AZ 85621 Office: 1600 Oregon St Muscatine IA 52761

PROCHNOW, HERBERT VICTOR, former govt. ofcl., banker, author; b. Wilton, Wis., May 19, 1897; s. Adolph and Alvina (Liefke) P.; B.A., U. Wis., 1921, M.A., 1922, LL.D., 1956; Ph.D., Northwestern U., 1947, LL.D., 1963; hon. Litt. D., Millikin U., 1952; LL.D., Ripon (Wis.) Coll., 1950, Lake Forest Coll., 1964, Monmouth Coll., 1965, U. N.D., 1966; D.H.L., Thiel Coll., 1965; m. Laura Virginia Stinson, June 12, 1928 (dec. Aug. 1977); 1 son, Herbert Victor. Prin. Kendall (Wis.) High Sch.; asst. prof. bus. adminstrn. Ind. U.; advt. mgr. Union Trust Co., Chgo.; officer First Nat. Bank of Chgo., pres., 1962-68, dir. 1960-68, hon. dir., 1968-73; dir. Carter H. Golembe Assos., Inc., 1972-76, Banco di Roma, Chgo., FRS Assos. Columnist Chgo. Tribune, 1968-70; sec. Fed. adv. council Fed. Res. System, 1945—; apptd. spl. asst. to sec. of state, 1955; dep. under sec. of state for econ. affairs, 1955-56; alt. gov. for U.S. Internat. Bank and Internat. Monetary Fund., 1955-56; pres. Internat. Monetary Conf., 1968, now cons., hon. mem. Chmn. U.S. delegation GATT, Geneva, 1956; del. Colombo Conf., Singapore, 1955, OECD, Paris, 1956. Former lectr. Loyola U., Ind. U., Northwestern U.; dir. grad. sch. of banking U. of Wis., 1945—; Trustee McCormick Theol. Sem., Chgo. Sunday Evening Club. Served with AEF, 1918-19. Decorated Order of Vasa (Sweden); comdrs. Cross Order of Merit (Fed. Republic of Germany). Recipient Bus. Statesmanship award Harvard Bus. Sch. Assn. Chgo., 1965; Ayres Leadership award Stonier Grad. Sch. Banking, Rutgers U., 1966; Silver Plaque NCCJ, 1967. Mem. Chgo. Council on Fgn. Relations (pres. 1966-67), Am. Econ. Assn., Am. Finance Assn., Chgo. Assn. Commerce and Industry (pres. 1964-65), Nat. Assn. Bus. Economists, Soc. Midland Authors, Beta Gamma Sigma (nat. honoree). Clubs: Commercial; Glen View; University, Mid-Day, Chicago, Rotary, Union League (Chgo.); Executives, Bankers (past pres.). Co-author: The Next Century Is America's, 1938; Practical Bank Credit, 1963; (with Herbert V. Prochnow, Jr.) A Dictionary of Wit, Wisdom and Satire, 1962, The Public Speaker's Treasure Chest, 1976; The Successful Toastmaster, 1966; A Treasury of Humorous Quotations, 1969; The Changing World of Banking, 1973; The Toastmaster's Treasure Chest, 1979; (with Everett M. Dirksen) Quotation Finder, 1971. Author: Great Stories from Great Lives (an anthology), 1944; Meditations on the Ten Commandments, 1946; The Toastmaster's Handbook, 1949; Term Loans and Theories of Bank Liquidity, 1949; Successful Speakers Handbook, 1951; 1001 Ways to Improve Your Conversations and Speeches, 1952; Meditations on the Beatitudes, 1952; The Speaker's Treasury of Stories for All Occasions, 1953; The Speaker's Handbook of Epigrams and Witticisms, 1955; Speakers Treasury for Sunday School Teachers, 1955; A Treasury of Stories, Illustrations, Epigrams and Quotations for Ministers and Teachers, 1956; The New Guide for Toastmasters, 1956; Meditations on The Lord's Prayer, 1957; The New Speaker's Treasury of Wit and Wisdom, 1958; A Family Treasury of Inspiration and Faith, 1958; The Complete Toastmaster, 1960; Speaker's Book of Illustrations, 1960; 1000 Tips and Quips for Speakers and Toastmasters, 1962; 1400 Ideas for Speakers and Toastmasters, 1964; Tree of Life, 1972; Speaker's Source Book, 1972; A Speaker's Treasury for Educators, Convocation Speakers, 1973; 1,000 Quips, Stories, and Illustrations for All Occasions, 1973. Editor: American Financial Institutions, 1951; Determining the Business Outlook, 1954; The Federal Reserve System, 1960; World Economic Problems and Policies, 1965; The Five Year Outlook for Interest Rates, 1968; The One-Bank Holding Company, 1969; The Eurodollar, 1970; The Five Year Outlook for Interest Rates in the U.S. and Abroad, 1972; Dilemmas Facing the Nation, 1979. Home: 2950 Harrison St Evanston IL 60201 Office: 1 First National Plaza Chicago IL 60670

PROCHNOW, HERBERT VICTOR, JR., banker; b. Evanston, Ill., May 26, 1931; s. Herbert V. and Laura (Stinson) P.; A.B., Harvard U., 1953, J.D., 1956; A.M., U. Chgo., 1958; m. Lucia Boyden, Aug. 6, 1966; children—Thomas Herbert, Laura. Admitted to Ill. bar, 1957; with 1st Nat. Bank Chgo., 1958—, atty., 1961-70, sr. atty., 1971-73, counsel, 1973—, adminstrv. asst. to chmn. bd., 1978—. Mem. Am., Ill. (chmn. sect. internat. law 1967-68), Chgo. (chmn. com. internat. law 1970-71) bar assns., Am. Soc. Internat. Law, Phi Beta Kappa. Clubs: Harvard (N.Y.C.); Chicago, Legal, Law, Onwentsia Economic, Executives, University (Chgo.). Author (with Herbert V. Prochnow) A Treasury of Humorous Quotations, 1969; The Changing World of Banking, 1974; The Public Speaker's Treasure Chest, 1977; The Toastmaster's Treasure Chest, 1979; also articles in legal publs. Home: 226 Ravine Forest Dr Lake Bluff IL 60044 Office: 1 First Nat Plaza Chicago IL 60670

PROCKNOW, DONALD EUGENE, communications co. exec.; b. Madison, S.D., May 27, 1923; B.S. in Elec. Engring., U. Wis., 1947; D.Eng. (hon.), S.D. Sch. Mines and Tech., 1973; m. Esther J. Ehlert, May 16, 1953; children—Eugene, Charles. With Western Electric Co., 1947—, pres., dir., mem. exec. com., 1971—; dir. Morgan Guaranty Trust Co., J.P. Morgan & Co., CPC Internat., Bell Telephone Labs., Inc., Ingersoll-Rand Co., Prudential Life Ins. Co., Teletype Corp. Chmn., trustee, exec. com. Ind. Coll. Funds Am.; trustee Clarkson Coll. Served with USNR, 1943-46. Mem. N.Y. Chamber Commerce and Industry, Tau Beta Pi. Office: Western Electric Co 222 Broadway New York NY 10038

PROCTER, ARTHUR NEVILLE, rubber co. exec.; b. St. Helens, Lancashire, Eng., Mar. 19, 1923; s. Albert and Florence (Barrett) P.; M.A. with honors, Edinburgh U., 1950; m. Mary Virginia Gill, Mar. 19, 1955; children—Iain Neville, Isabel Vanessa, Erica Virginia. Came to U.S., 1970. With Dunlop Co., Ltd., 1950—, mng. dir. Socieded de Gomas y Amiantos S.A. in Spain, 1958-61, chmn., mng. dir. Dunlop Nigerian Industries, Ltd., Lagos, 1962-68, pres. Dunlop Can., Ltd., Toronto, 1968-70, exec. v.p. Dunlop Tire & Rubber Co., Buffalo, 1970, pres., 1971—. Vice pres. Lagos C. of C. and Industry, 1965-68. Served as lt. Brit. Royal Navy, 1942-46. Home: 30 Hallam Rd Buffalo NY 14216 Office: Box 1109 Buffalo NY 14240

PROCTER, JOHN ERNEST, publishing co. exc.; b. Gainesboro, Tenn., July 23, 1918; s. Leon and Mary (Poteet) P.; student Vanderbilt U., 1940-41, U. Miami, 1943-44, also extension div., U. Tenn., 1946-50; LL.D., Ohio No. U., 1971; m. Jane Sprott, May 23, 1941; children—Mary Carol, Valere Kay. With Methodist Pub. House, Nashville, 1945—, v.p., pub., 1964-70, pres., pub., 1970—; dir. 3d Nat. Bank, Nashville. Bd. dirs. Tenn Council on Econ. Edn.; bd. dirs., exec. com. Vanderbilt U. Med. Center. Served to capt. USAAF and USAF, 1944-45, 50-52. Decorated Certificate of Valor, Air medal with 7 oak leaf clusters, D.F.C. Mem. Adminstrv. Mgmt. Soc. (past pres. Nashville; area. sec.-treas. 1967-68; Merit Key award 1961, Diamond Merit award 1967), Nashville C. of C. (past mem. bd. govs.), Assn. Am. Pubs. (past dir.). Clubs: Rotary, Belle Meade Golf & Country. Home: 6313 Noel Dr Brentwood TN 37027 Office: 201 8th Ave S Nashville TN 37203. *The modest success I have achieved is the result of an intense commitment to intellectual honesty, sensitivity to the needs of my associates, the setting of challenging and realistic goals, striving for efficiency by doing things right and being effective by doing the right things, always with faith in myself and my associates.*

PROCTER, RUSSELL, wholesale hardware exec.; b. Auburn, Ky., Dec. 3, 1903; s. Robert Emmett and Mary Holland (Mobley) P.; student pub. schs.; m. Nancy Waples Dunn, Dec. 9, 1933; 1 dau., Mary Nancy (Mrs. John W. Saltsman). With Belknap Hardware & Mfg. Co. (co. name changed to Belknap, Inc.), Louisville, 1925—, successively order clk., checker, stocktaker, splty. harness salesman, gen. hardware sales in Tex., Okla., buyer sporting goods, mng. buyer, 1925-55, pres., 1955-69, chmn. bd., 1969—, also dir.; former dir. First Nat. Bank, 1st Ky. Trust Co., Louisville, 1st Ky. Co., Louisville. Overseer Ky. So. Coll.; bd. dirs. Asso. Industries Ky.; trustee So. Bapt. Theol. Sem., Shaker Mus., South Union, Ky.; mem. Historic Homes Found., Louisville. Named Hardware Man of Yr., Philia., 1957. Mem. Ducks Unltd., Bklyn. Botanic Garden, Nat. Wildlife Fedn., Nat. Audubon Soc., Friends of Bernheim Forest, Nat. Trust, C. of C. Baptist. Clubs: Pendennis, Agricultural, Filson (Louisville). Home: 18 Westwind Rd Louisville KY 40207 Office: 111 E Main St Louisville KY 40202

PROCTOR, ALVIN HORACE, coll. adminstr.; b. South Haven, Kans., July 29, 1912; s. Joseph Wayman and Hazel (Judd) P.; student U. Kans., 1930-31; B.S., Kans. State Tchrs. Coll., Pittsburg, 1935, M.S., 1936; Ph.D., U. Wis., 1948; Ford faculty fellow, Harvard U., 1954-55; m. Mary Faye Cooper, Dec. 20, 1933; 1 dau., Margaret Mary (Mrs. John Shepherd Mahoney). Instr. high sch. Hot Springs (N.Mex.) Sr. High Sch., 1936-38; grad. asst. U. Wis., 1938-39, 47-48; journalism instr. Pittsburg (Kans.) Sr. High Sch., 1939-40; instr. history and govt. Pratt (Kans.) Jr. Coll., 1940-43; asst. prof. history Ft. Hays State Coll., 1943-44, 46-47; asso. prof. history Kans. State Coll., Pittsburg, 1948-50, chmn. dept. social sci., prof. govt. and history, 1950-59, dean grad. studies, 1959-66, exec. v.p., 1966-68, acad. v.p., 1968-78, asst. to pres., 1978—; Theodore Fink Meml. lectr. U. Melbourne (Australia), summer 1972. Mem. Kans. Bd. Regents Council Chief Acad. Officers, chmn., 1973, mem. Formula Task Force, 1973-74; cons. U.S. Office Edn., 1965-73, N.D. Bd. Higher Edn., 1978-79. Mem. Pittsburg Zoning and Planning Commn. Del. Nat. UNESCO Conf., 1949, 50, 56, Nat. Citizenship Conf., 1949, 50; mem. Gov. Commn. Revision Kans. Constn., 1958; mem. Kans. Interdepartmental Com. on Aging, 1959—; v.p. Pittsburg United Fund, 1973. Chmn. Crawford County (Kans.) Democratic Com., 1956-58. Chmn. bd. trustees Mt. Carmel Med. Center, 1972-73, 76-77. Served to lt. USNR, 1944-46. Mem. Am., Kans., Midwest polit. sci. assns., AAAS, Smithsonian Assos., AAUP, Assn. Higher Edn. of NEA, Kans. Citizenship Clearing House, Kans. History Tchrs. Assn., Kans. Tchrs. Assn., Council Grad. Schs. U.S. (chmn. com. preparation coll. tchrs., 1968-73, nat. chmn. 1969, mem. exec. com. 1965-70, chmn. 1969), Midwest Conf. Grad. Study and Research (pres. 1968-69), Omicron Delta Kappa, Phi Alpha Theta, Phi Kappa Phi, Sigma Tau Delta, Kappa Delta Pi, Scabbard and Blade. Presbyterian (elder). Kiwanian. Home: 2005 S Homer St Pittsburg KS 66762

PROCTOR, DONALD FREDERICK, educator, physician; b. Red Bank, N.J., Apr. 19, 1913; s. Frederick R. and Gertrude (Chauncey) P.; A.B., Johns Hopkins, 1933, M.D., 1937; m. Janice Carson, June 10, 1937; children—Douglas, Nan. With otol. lab. Johns Hopkins Hosp., 1937-38, mem. otolaryn. house staff, 1938-40; resident otolaryngology Balt. City Hosps., 1940-41; pvt. practice otolaryngology, Balt., 1941-56; asso. prof. otolaryngology Med. Sch., Johns Hopkins, 1946-51, 58-73, prof. anesthesiology, 1951-55, 77—, asst. prof. physiology, laryngology and otolaryngology, 1955-58, 77—, prof. laryngology and otology, 1973—, prof. environ. health sci., 1965—, chief bronchoscopic clinic, 1962-66, chief research program air hygiene, dept. environmental medicine, 1955—; with dept. physiology U. Rochester, 1946-47; fellow anesthesiology U. Pa., 1951-52. Diplomate Am. Bd. Otolaryngology. Fellow A.C.S., Am. Acad. Otolaryngology; mem. Am. Bronchoesophagol. Assn., Am. Indsl. Hygiene Assn., Air Pollution Control Assn., Am. Physiol. Soc.,

Phi Beta Pi, Sigma Xi. Club: 14 West Hamilton Street (Balt.). Author: Anesthesia and Otolaryngology, 1957; Tonsils and Adenoids in Childhood, 1960; Nose Paranasal Sinuses and Ears in Childhood, 1962. Editor: Respiratory Defense Mechanisms, 1977. Author articles, book chpts. deafness, respiration, air hygiene, air pollution, mucous membrane. Home: 1010 St George's Rd Baltimore MD 21210

PROCTOR, HARVEY ALBERT, utilities exec.; b. Denver, Mar. 25, 1916; s. Harvey Thomas and Mabel (Eustice) P.; B.S. in Mech. Engring., U. Colo., 1939; m. Virginia Ann Jacobberger, June 22, 1939; children—Michael Eustice, Harvey Christopher, James Timothy. With So. Calif. Gas Co., Los Angeles, 1939-64, 66-68, 70—, v.p., controller, dir., 1966-68, exec. v.p., dir., 1970-71, pres., 1971-72, chmn. bd., 1972—; group v.p. parent co. Pacific Lighting Corp., 1972-75, exec. v.p., dir., 1975—, also dir.; pres. Pacific Alaska LNG Co., also dir.; chmn. bd., dir. Pacific Australia LNG Pty. Ltd.; dir., pres. Pacific Indonesia LNG Co., Pacific Lighting Marine Co.; dir., chmn. bd. Pacific Lighting Service Co.; dir., exec. v.p. Hood Corp., Whittier, Calif., 1965; pres. Hoodco Farms, Inc., Boise, Idaho, 1965; sr. v.p., exec. v.p. dir. Pacific Lighting Service Co., Los Angeles, 1968-69; dir. Los Angeles br. Fed. Res. Bank San Francisco. Chmn. Future Requirements Com., 1969-71. Bd. dirs. Los Angeles chpt. AID, 1969-75, Los Angeles YMCA, 1974-79, Gas Research Inst., 1976—; founder Los Angeles Music Center. Recipient Disting. Engring. Alumnus award U. Colo., 1977. Fellow ASME; mem. Inst. Gas Tech. (chmn. bd. trustees, chmn. exec. com. 1973-75), Pacific Coast (past dir.), Am. (1st vice chmn., chmn. bd. 1977-78, dir., exec. com., chmn. research and devel. exec. com. 1973-75) gas assns., Phi Kappa Psi. Clubs: Los Angeles, Jonathan (Los Angeles); International (Washington). Office: So Calif Gas Co 810 S Flower St Los Angeles CA 90017

PROCTOR, JESSE HARRIS, JR., educator; b. Durham, N.C., Sept. 3, 1924; s. Jesse Harris and Rosa Belle (Rogers) P.; A.B., Duke, 1948; M.A., Fletcher Sch. Law and Diplomacy, 1949; Ph.D., Harvard, 1955; m. Ella Jane Callahan, Mar. 27, 1948; children—Edward Sidney, Thomas Christopher, Kenneth Stuart. Instr., asst. prof. polit. sci. Mass. Inst. Tech., 1949-56; asst. prof., asso. prof., polit. sci. Am. U., Cairo, Egypt, 1956-58; asst. prof., asso. prof., prof. polit. sci. Duke, 1958-70; Charles A. Dana prof. polit. sci. Davidson (N.C.) Coll., 1970—, chmn. dept. polit. sci., 1972—; vis. asso. prof. polit. sci. U. Coll., Nairobi, Kenya, 1964-65; vis. prof. polit. sci. U. Coll., Dar es Salaam, Tanzania, 1969-70; conducted research in W. Indies, summers 1951, 59, 61, Gambia and Senegal, summer 1966, Botswana, summer 1967, Lesotho, summer 1968, Swaziland, summer 1972, Malawi, summer 1974. Served with USAAF, 1943-46. Mem. Am., So. polit. sci. assns., African Studies Assn., Phi Beta Kappa, Pi Sigma Alpha, Omicron Delta Kappa. Democrat. Presbyn. Editor: Islam and International Relations, 1965. Contbr. chpt. to Federalism in the Commonwealth, 1963, Prospects for Constitutional Democracy, 1976. Contbr. articles to profl. jours. Home: PO Box 567 Davidson NC 28036

PROCTOR, JOHN FRANKLIN, lawyer; b. Scottsboro, Ala., May 6, 1931; s. James Moody and Lucy (May) P.; B.S., U. Ala., 1953, LL.B., 1957; m. Judith Jones, Apr. 6, 1957; children—James Moody, Laura. Admitted to Ala. bar, 1957; asst. atty. gen., 1957-59; practice in Scottsboro, 1959—; judge Jackson County Ct., 1959-63; pvt. practice, 1963-66, 68—; judge 9th Jud. Circuit, 1966-68. Vice pres., dir. First Fed. Savs. & Loan Assn. of Jackson County. Served with U.S. Army, 1953-55. Mem. Alaska Bar Assn. (commr. 1979—), Sigma Chi, Phi Alpha Delta. Methodist. Rotarian. Club: Scottsboro Golf and Country. Home: Box 726 Scottsboro AL 35768 Office: Proctor Bldg Scottsboro AL 35768

PROCTOR, PAUL DEAN, educator; b. Salt Lake City, Nov. 24, 1918; s. John and Emily I. (Triptow) P.; B.A., U. Utah, 1942; M.A., Cornell U., 1943; Ph.D., Ind. U., 1949; m. Martha Facer, Mar. 5, 1945; children—Paul F., Lane F., Kirk F., Scot F. Geologist, Kalunite, Inc., Marysvale, Utah, 1943; from jr. geologist to geologist U.S. Geol. Survey, 1944-52; asst. prof., then asso. prof. Brigham Young U., 1947-53; asso. prof. Ind. U., 1950-52; asst. supr. field exploration U.S. Steel Co., 1953-57; prof. geology, chmn. dept. Mo. Sch. Mines, 1957-64; prof., dean Sch. Sci., U. Mo. at Rolla, 1964-70, prof., research dir., 1970—. NSF vis. prof. Middle East Tech. U., 1973-74; Internat. Geol. Congresses, 1956, 60, 68; mem. Internat. Field Inst., NSF, Italy, 1964; UNESCO specialist, Ankara, Turkey, 1966-67. Bd. dirs. Rolla U.S.O., 1958-63. Registered profl. engr., Utah. Fellow Geol. Soc. Am.; mem. Am. Inst. M.E., Soc. Econ. Geologists, Assn. Mo. Geologists, Nat. Assn. Geology Tchrs., AAAS, Sigma Xi (pres. local chpt. 1962), Phi Kappa Phi (pres. local chpt. 1963), Sigma Gamma Epsilon (nat. grand historian, editor 1951-53), Gamma Alpha, Beta Sigma, Lambda Delta Sigma. Mem. Ch. of Jesus Christ of Latter-day Saints (bishop Rolla ward 1965-70, bishopric 1979—, high council Columbia stake 1970-79). Club: Rotarian (dir. Rolla 1968, 78-79, pres.-elect 1980). Co-designer single prism field stereoscope. Author: Uranium, 1954; also lab. manual, sci. articles. Home: PO Box 607 Rolla MO 65401

PROCTOR, RICHARD CULPEPPER, educator, physician; b. Raleigh, N.C., Apr. 4, 1921; s. Creasy Kinion and Mattie (Culpepper) P.; student Mars Hill Jr. Coll., 1938-40; B.S., Wake Forest Coll., 1942, M.D., 1945; m. Daisy Bethea Chamness, Jan. 1, 1948; children—Sallie Earle, Richard Culpepper. Intern U.S. Naval Hosp., Bremerton, Wash., 1945-46; instr. Wake Forest Coll., 1950-52, asst. prof. psychiatry, 1952-60, asso. prof., chmn. dept., 1960-62, prof., chmn. dept. psychiatry, 1962—; cons. indsl. psychiatry. Served with USNR, 1945-48. Fellow Am. Coll. Psychiatrists, Am., (past pres.) So. psychiat. assns.; mem. N.C. Neuropsychiat. Assn. (past pres.) Southeastern Psychiat. Assn. (past pres.), SAR, Magna Carta Barons, Jamestown Soc., Tenn. Squire. Clubs: Torch, Old Town Country, (Winston-Salem); Grandfather Golf and Country. Contbr. articles profl. jours. Home: 381 Westview Dr S Winston-Salem NC 27104. *Life is meant to be composed like a song—from the heart, with instinct and compassion—not copied in block type from a book of rules. I have tried to make my standard of conduct "others" and my professional goal modeled after Peabody's statement that "the good physician knows his patients through and through, and his knowledge is bought dearly. Time, sympathy, and understanding must be lavishly dispensed . . . One of the essential qualities of the clinician is interest in humanity where the secret of care of the patient is in caring for the patient."*

PROCTOR, SAMUEL, educator; b. Jacksonville, Fla., Mar. 29, 1919; s. Jack and Celia (Schneider) P.; B.A., U. Fla., 1941, M.A., 1942, Ph.D., 1958; postgrad. U. N.C., 1948, Emory U., 1949; m. Bessie Rubin, Sept. 8, 1948; children—Mark Julian, Alan Lowell. With U.S. Army Engrs., Miami, Fla., 1942-43; mem. faculty U. Fla., Gainesville, 1946—, prof. history and social scis., 1963-74, Disting. Service prof. history and social scis., 1974, Julien C. Yonge prof. Fla. history, 1976—, univ. historian, 1953—, dir. oral history program, 1968—; curator history Fla. State Museum; co-dir. Doris Duke Southeastern Indian Oral History Program; dir. Center for Study of Fla. History and Humanities; vis. prof. history Jacksonville U., summers 1963-66. Historian, Fla. Civil War Centennial Commn., 1960-65; historian, cons. Fla. Public Relations Hall of Fame Commn., 1961—; cons. Fla. Bd. Parks and Hist. Memls., 1965—, historian Pensacola Preservation Bd., 1968; mem. adv. commn. Fla. div. Archives History and Records Mgmt., 1970—, now chmn.; mem. Fla. Am. Revolution Bicentennial Commn.; mem. Fla. rev. com. Nat. Register Hist. Places, 1971—; mem. adv. com. Am. Assn. State and Local Hist. Bicentennial Publs.; chmn. adv. com. Naming of State Bldgs.; acad. adv. council Am. Jewish Hist. Soc. Mem. exec. com. Fla. Anti-Defamation League, 1957—; bd. dirs. Jacksonville River Garden Home for Aged. Served with U.S. Army, 1943-46. Named Fla. Historian of Year, Peace River Valley Hist. Soc., 1967; recipient Outstanding Alumnus award Tau Epsilon Phi, 1971. Mem. Fla. (dir. 1951-53, 61—) Hist. Assn., Orgn. Am. Historians, So. Hist. Assn., Am. Assn. State and Local History (council 1973-77), Nat. Oral History Assn. (council 1971—, pres. 1976), Fla. Antrop. Soc., U. Fla. Alumni Assn. (exec. bd.), Fla. Blue Key, Tau Epsilon Phi (Service award key 1953, Michael C.C. Lilienfeld Nat. Disting. Service award 1958), Phi Beta Kappa, Pi Kappa Phi, Alpha Kappa Delta, Phi Alpha Theta, Pi Gamma Mu. Democrat. Jewish. Author: Napoleon Bonaparte Broward, Florida's Fighting Democrat., 1950; Florida Commemorates the Civil War Centennial, 1962; Florida a Hundred Years Ago, 1966; Florida Historic Preservation Planning, 1971; editor, author introduction: Dickison and His Men: Reminiscences of the War in Florida, 1962; series editor Bicentennial Floridiana Facsimile Series; editor Eighteenth Century Florida and Its Borderlands, 1972; Eighteenth Century Florida and the Carribean, 1976; Eighteenth Century Florida, Life on the Frontier, 1976; Eighteenth Century Florida and the Revolutionary South, 1977; Eighteenth Century: Impact of the Revolution, 1978; Tacachale, Essays on the Indians of Florida and Southeastern Georgia during the Historic Period; editorial bd. Oral History Rev.; asso. editor Fla. Hist. Quar., 1962-64, editor, 1964—; contbr. articles to profl. jours. Home: 2235 NW 9th Pl Gainesville FL 32605 Office: Fla State Museum Museum Rd U Fla Gainesville FL 32611

PROCTOR, SAMUEL DEWITT, clergyman, educator; b. Norfolk, Va., July 13, 1921; s. Herbert Quincy and Gladys Velma (Hughes) P.; A.B., Va. Union U., 1942; grad. student U. Pa., 1944-45; B.D., Crozer Theol. Sem., 1945; student Div. Sch., Yale U., 1945-46; Th.D., Boston U., 1950; hon. degrees: Bryant Coll., Bucknell U., Davidson Coll., Ottawa U., Dillard U., Rider Coll., Stillman Coll., N.C. A&T State U., Fisk U., Howard U., U. R.I., Atlanta U., Wilberforce U., Va. Union U., St. Peters Coll., N.J., Coe Coll., Central Mich. U., U. Md.; m. Bessie Louise Tate, Sept. 23, 1944; children—Herbert, Timothy, Samuel, Steven. Ordained to ministry Bapt. Ch., 1943; pastor Pond Street Ch., Providence, 1945-49; prof. religion and ethics Va. Union U., 1949-50, dean Sch. Religion, 1949-50, v.p., 1953-55, pres., 1955-60; pres. A&T Coll. N.C., 1960-64; asso. dir. Peace Corps, 1963-64; asso. gen. sec. Nat. Council Chs., 1964-65; dir. N.E. region, later spl. asst. to nat. dir. OEO, 1965-66; pres. Inst. for Services to Edn., 1966-68; univ. dean spl. projects U. Wis., Madison, 1968-69; prof. edn. Grad. Sch. Edn., Rutgers U., New Brunswick, N.J., 1969—; sr. minister Abyssinian Bapt. Ch., N.Y.C., 1972—; vis. lectr. edn. Emory U., Atlanta, 1967-69. Trustee United Negro Coll. Fund, Meharry Med. Coll., Overseas Devel. Council, Council on Religion in Internat. Affairs, Middlesex Gen. Hosp. Recipient Outstanding Alumnus award Boston U., 1964; Distinguished Service award State U. N.Y. at Plattsburgh, 1966. Mem. N.E.A., Kappa Alpha Psi, Sigma Pi Phi. Author: The Young Negro in America, 1960-1980, 1966. Home: 63 MacAfee Somerset NJ 08873

PROCTOR, WILLIAM ZINSMASTER, lawyer; b. Des Moines, Nov. 30, 1902; s. Frank and Louise (Zinsmaster) P.; student Drake U., 1920; J.D., U. Mich., 1925; m. Alice S. Bowles, Nov. 24, 1944; children—David J. W., Mary Martha. Admitted to Iowa bar, 1925; asso. Bradshaw, Schenk & Fowler, 1925-35; partner Bradshaw, Fowler, Proctor & Fairgrave, Des Moines, 1935—. Dir., gen. counsel Employers Mut. Casualty Co., Employers Modern Life Co., Emcasco Ins. Co., Dakota Fire Ins. Co., Bismarck, N.D., Union Mut. Ins. Co. Providence; dir. emeritus Iowa-Des Moines Nat. Bank. Pres. Des Moines Community Chest, 1956, Des Moines United Community Services, 1957; mem. bd. SSS, 1942-55, Iowa appeal bd., 1955-67. Pres. Des Moines Roadside Settlement, 1950-53. Chmn. bd. trustees Hawley Welfare Found., 1968—, Preston Ednl. Trust, 1952—. Mem. Am., Iowa, Polk County (pres. 1945), Internat., Inter-Am. bar assns., Am. Judicature Soc., Assn. Bar City N.Y., Fedn. Ins. Counsel. Mason (Shriner, Jester). Clubs: Wakonda, Des Moines (pres. 1953); University (Chgo.). Home: 3401 Lincoln Pl Dr Des Moines IA 50312 Office: Des Moines Bldg Des Moines IA 50309

PROFFER, ELLENDEA CATHERINE, publisher, author; b. Phila., Nov. 24, 1944; d. Joseph and Helen (Jardine) McEnness; B.A., U. Md., 1966; M.A., Ind. U., 1968, Ph.D., 1971; m. Carl Ray Proffer, Oct. 1967. Asst. prof. Slavic, Wayne State U., Detroit, 1970-71; asso. prof. humanities U. Mich., Dearborn, 1972-73; co-founder, 1971, since pres., owner Ardis Pubs., Ann Arbor; author: Bulgakov, 1971; The Early Plays of Mikhail Bulgakov, 1971; The Silver Age of Russian Culture, 1975; editor: Ardis Anthology of Recent Russian Literature, 1975; Ardis Anthology of New American Poetry, 1977; Russian Literature Triquar., 1971—; Regency Miss (novel), 1978. NDEA fellow, 1968-69. Mem. Am. Assn. Advancement Slavis Studies, P.E.N. Home: 2901 Heatherway St Ann Arbor MI 48104 Office: Ardis Publishers Ann Arbor MI 48104

PROFFITT, NICHOLAS CHARLES, journalist; b. Sault Ste. Marie, Mich., Feb. 23, 1943; s. Stanley and Rose Angeline (Graziani) P.; B.A., U. Ariz., Tucson, 1968; m. Martha Hudson, Aug. 8, 1970; children—Timothy Stanley, Paine Hudson, Lucrezia Graziana. Reporter, AP, Los Angeles, 1968-69; with Newsweek mag., 1969—, bur. chief, Saigon, 1972, Beirut, 1973-75, London, 1976, Houston, 1977-78, Nairobi, Kenya, 1978—. Served with USAR, 1961-64. Recipient Nat. Mag. award for coverage fall of Saigon, 1975, Overseas Press Club award for coverage Arab-Israeli War, 1973. Mem. E. Africa Fgn. Corr. Assn., Hong Kong Fgn. Corr. Club, Sigma Delta Chi. Address: PO Box 30347 Nairobi Kenya

PROFFITT, ROY FRANKLIN, educator; b. Hastings, Neb., Aug. 6, 1918; s. Harry Louis Franklin and Vera (Roe) P.; B.S. in Bus. Adminstrn., U. Neb., 1940; J.D., U. Mich., 1948, LL.M., 1956; m. Jean Malott Humphrey, Mar. 25, 1944. Admitted to Colo. and Neb. bars, 1948, Mo. bar, 1955; with firm Miller, McKinnley & Walsh, Greeley, Colo., 1948; research asso. U. Neb. Coll. Law, 1948-49; from asst. prof. to prof. law U. Mo., 1949-56; Cook fellow U. Mich., 1955-56, mem. faculty Law Sch., 1956—. prof. law, 1958—, asst. dean, 1956-68, asso. dean, 1968-70, asso. dir. Inst. Continuing Legal Edn., 1970-72, dir. law sch. relations, 1972—. Tech. adviser criminal law revision com. Mo. Senate, 1951-54; member adv. com. drafting rules procedure municipal cts. Mo. Supreme Ct., 1954-55; mem. Spl. Com. Traffic Safety Mich., 1964; mem. Mich. Bail and Criminal Justice Com., 1965-70; mem., sec. Spl. Com. Revision Mich. Criminal Code, 1965-71. Served to lt. comdr. USNR, 1940-45. Mem. Maritime Law Assn. U.S., Order of Coif, Beta Gamma Sigma, Alpha Tau Omega. Mason. Editor: (with others) Statutes, Rules and Cases on Criminal Procedure, 2d edit., 1961. Home: 580 Rock Creek Dr Ann Arbor MI 48104

PROFFITT, WILLIAM LLOYD, utility exec.; b. Buckingham, Va., Mar. 3, 1929; s. William Washington and Mary Lola (Patterson) P.; B.M.E., Va. Poly. Inst., 1950; m. Barbara Ann Alexander, Aug. 1, 1953; children—Barry, Susan, Bryan. With Va. Electric & Power Co., Richmond, 1972—, v.p. power sta. engring. and constrn., 1974-76, sr. v.p. power, 1976—; dir. Carolinas Va. Nuclear Power Assos., Inc.; chmn. Southeastern Electric Reliability Council. Served with AUS, 1950-53. Baptist. Club: Stonehenge Golf and Country. Home: 2532 Devenwood Rd Richmond VA 23235 Office: One James River Plaza Richmond VA 23261

PROFUMO, LOUIS, JR., liquor co. exec.; b. Ridgewood, N.J., Sept. 21, 1915; s. Louis Angelo and Colomba Rosa (Cavagnare) P.; B.S. cum laude, Fordham U., 1936; m. Rita Carpientieri, Oct. 26, 1941; children—Peter, Alice, Louis, Anne. Partner, L. Profumo & Co., N.Y.C., 1936-41; ceramic engr. Isolantite, Inc., Belleville, N.J., 1941-47; with Galsworthy, Inc., Newark, 1947—, exec. v.p., 1967-76, pres., 1976-78, vice-chmn. parent co. Reitman Industries, 1978—. Home: 2070 Brookside Dr Scotch Plains NJ 07076 Office: 10 Patton Dr West Caldwell NJ 07006

PROGER, SAMUEL HERSCHEL, physician; b. Jan. 21, 1906; s. Louis Proger; B.S., Emory U., 1925, M.D., 1928, D.Sc., 1975; D.Sc., Tufts U., 1952; m. Evelyn Levinson, Sept. 8, 1929; children—Susan Jean, Nancy Lane. Mem. staff New England Med. Center, 1931—, physician-in-chief, 1948-71; prof. medicine, chmn. dept. Tufts U. Sch. Medicine, 1948-71. Pres. Bingham Assos. Fund. Med. cons. VA, NIH; vice chmn. bd. trustees, past pres. New Eng. Med. Center Hosp.; past chmn. adminstrv. bd. Tufts-New Eng. Med. Center. Chmn. Health and Welfare Commn., Commonwealth Mass., 1967-69. Trustee Wellesley Coll., Boston Med. Library, Med. Found., Inc. Recipient Am. Design award, 1951. Fellow Am. Coll. Cardiology, A.C.P.; mem. Assn. Am. Physicians, Am. Soc. for Clin. Investigation, Am. Acad. Arts and Scis., Am. Heart Assn., A.M.A., Mass. Heart Assn. (past pres.), New England Cardiovascular Soc. (past pres.), Phi Beta Kappa, Alpha Omega Alpha. Contbr. articles on cardio-vascular disease and medical edn. Home: 45 Willow Crescent Brookline MA 02146 Office: New England Medical Center Hosps 171 Harrison Ave Boston MA 02111. *To succeed is to learn from failures and successes, and to be unafraid of new failures in seeking new successes.*

PROHME, RUPERT, internat. orgn. exec.; b. San Francisco, Aug. 13, 1915; s. William Christian and Martha Sophei (Ellison) P.; A.B. in Econs., Stanford U., 1936, M.A. in Polit. Sci., 1937, postgrad. journalism, 1937-38; m. Eva-Maria Stange Godon, June 28, 1969; 1 dau., Cleo Martha; stepchildren—Aline Marie Antoinette, Corinne Helene. Night city editor Salinas (Calif.) Morning Post, 1938-41; commentator radio sta. KDON, Salinas, 1941; joined U.S. Fgn. Service, 1946; assigned Sydney and Canberra, Australia, 1946-47, Athens, Greece, 1947-50, Brussels, Belgium, 1950-54; pub. affairs adviser State Dept., 1955-59; assigned Alexandria, UAR, 1959-64; counselor for econ. affairs, Baghdad, Iraq, 1964-67; dep. U.S. permanent rep. to UNESCO, Paris, France, 1967-74; internat. relations officer U.S. Mission, Geneva, Switzerland, 1974-75; chief relations with internat. orgns. World Tourism Orgn., Madrid, Spain, 1976-79. Served to capt., inf. AUS, 1941-46; lt. col. Res. Decorated Silver Star, Bronze star. Mem. Stanford Alumni Assn., Phi Beta Kappa, Sigma Delta Chi, Pi Sigma Alpha. Christian Scientist. Author: The History of 30th Infantry Regiment, World War II, 1947. Home: Burlingame CA 94010 Office: Marques de Monistrol 7 Madrid Spain

PROKASY, WILLIAM FREDERICK, univ. dean.; b. Cleve., Nov. 27, 1930; s. William Frederick and Margaret Louise (Chapman) P.; B.A., Baldwin-Wallace Coll., 1952; M.A., Kent State U., 1954; Ph.D., U. Wis., 1957; children—Kathi Lynn, Cheryl Anne. Grad. asst. Kent State U., 1953-54; W.A.R.F. fellow U. Wis., 1954-55, teaching asst., 1955-57; asst. prof., then asso. prof. Pa. State U., 1957-66; prof. psychology, chmn. dept. U. Utah, 1966-69, dean social and behavioral sci., 1968-70, dean Coll. Social and Behavioral Sci., 1970-79, acting dean Grad. Sch. Social Work, 1979-80; cons. in field. Del., Utah Democratic Conv., 1968-70, 72-74; trustee Utah Planned Parenthood Assn., 1977—; Utah bd. dirs. ACLU, 1978—. NSF sr. postdoctoral fellow, 1963-64. Fellow Am. Psychol. Assn. (chmn. bd. sci. affairs 1977-78); mem. Psychonomic Soc., Soc. Psychophysiol. Research (dir. 1978—), Utah Psychol. Assn. (exec. bd. 1968-70, pres. 1971-72), A.A.A.S., Sigma Xi (pres. U. Utah chpt. 1972-73), Phi Kappa Phi. Editor: Classical Conditioning, 1965; (with A.H. Black) Classical Conditioning II, 1971; (with D. Raskin) Electrodermal Responding in Psychological Research, 1973; Psychophysiology, 1974-77; asso. editor Learning and Motivation, 1969-76; cons. editor Jour. Exptl. Psychology, 1968—; Home: 875 Donner Way Apt 805 Salt Lake City UT 84108

PROKOP, RUTH TIMBERLAKE, lawyer, govt. ofcl.; b. San Saba, Tex., May 30, 1939; d. Harry Carver and Anna Grace (Winslow) Timberlake; B.A., George Washington U., 1961, J.D., 1965; m. John Andrew Prokop, Aug. 29, 1962; 1 dau., Kristina Elizabeth. Admitted to D.C., U.S. Supreme Ct. bars; mem. staff Vice Pres. Lyndon B., Johnson, 1961-62; legis. asst. Pres.'s Commn. on Status of Women, 1962-64; legis. counsel Pres.'s Com. on Consumer Affairs, 1964-66; spl. asst. to sec. HUD, 1966-69; mem. firm Brownstein Zeidman & Schomer, 1970-72; sr. counsel Gen. Telephone & Electronics Corp., 1972-77; gen. counsel HUD, Washington, 1977-79; chmn. Merit Systems Protection Bd., 1979—; tax commr. D.C., 1976-77; mem. bd. dirs. Nat. Com. on Household Employment, 1973-77. Bd. govs. Women's Nat. Democratic Club, 1972-77. Mem. Am. (council sci. and tech. sect. 1976-77; chmn. privacy com. 1976), Fed., FCC bar assns., D.C. Integrated Bar, George Washington U. Law Sch. Alumni Assn. (pres. 1973). Democrat. Episcopalian. Home: 4854 Loughboro Rd NW Washington DC 20016 Office: 451 7th St SW Washington DC 20410

PROKOPOFF, STEPHEN S., museum exec.; b. Chgo., 1929; B.A., U. Calif., Berkeley, 1951, M.A., 1952; Ph.D., N.Y. U., 1962; m. Paula Prokopoff; 2 children. Formerly prof. art Skidmore Coll., U. Wash.; dir. Inst. Contemporary Art, Phila., 1967-71, Mus. of Contemporary Art, Chgo., 1971-77, Inst. Contemporary Art, Boston, 1978—. Author: The Nineteenth Century Architecture of Saratoga Springs, N.Y., 1970; contbr. articles to profl. jours., exhbn. catalogues. Office: 955 Boylston St Boston MA 02115

PROMISEL, NATHAN E., materials scientist, metall. engr.; b. Malden, Mass., June 20, 1908; s. Solomon and Lyna (Samwick) P.; D.Engring. (hon.), Mich. Tech. U., 1978; m. Evelyn Sarah Davidoff, May, 17, 1931; children—David Mark, Larry Jay. Asst. dir. lab. Internat. Silver Co. Meriden, Conn., 1930-40; chief materials scientist and engr. Navy Dept., Washington, 1940-66; exec. dir. nat. materials adv. bd. Nat. Acad. Scis., Washington, 1966-74; cons. on materials and policy, internationally, Washington, 1974—; mem., chmn. NATO Aerospace Panel, 1959-71; U.S. chmn. U.S./USSR Sci. Exchange Program (materials), 1973-77; dir. Value Engring. Co.; mem. Nat. Materials Adv. Bd.; adv. com. Oak Ridge Nat. Lab., Lehigh U., U. Pa., U.S. Navy Dept. Labs, U.S. Congress Office Tech. Assessment. Named Nat. Capitol Engr. of Yr., Council Engring. and Archtl. Socs., 1974; recipient Outstanding Accomplishment awards Navy Dept., 1955-64. Fellow Am. Soc. Metals (pres. 1972, Burgess award 1961, lectr. 1967), Brit. Instn. Metallurgists; mem. Nat. Acad. Engring., Fedn. Materials Socs. (pres. 1972-73), Soc. Automotive Engrs. (chmn. aerospace materials div. 1959-74), Brit. Metals Soc., Soc. Advanced Materials and Process Engring., AIME (hon.), ASTM (hon.; ann.

disting. lectr. 1964), Alpha Sigma Mu. Contbr. articles to profl. publs.; editor: Advances in Materials Research, 1963; Science and Technology of Refractory Metals, 1964; Science, Technology and Application of Titanium, 1970. inventor in electroplating, 1930-40; metall. devels., 1941-66. Home and Office: 12519 Davan Dr Silver Spring MD 20904. *Ten key words and phrases for a professional career: identified goals, long range vision, can-do attitude, integrity, objectivity, understanding and tolerance, faith and trust, loyalty, dedication and perserverance, sense of humor.*

PRONZINI, BILL (WILLIAM) JOHN, author; b. Petaluma, Calif., Apr. 13, 1943; s. Joseph and Helene (Guder) P.; coll. student, 2 years; m. Brunhilde Schier, July 28, 1972. Author 18 novels (including under pseudonymns), 1971—; first novel: The Stalker, 1971. Mem. Authors Guild, Writers Guild Am.—West, Mystery Writers Am. (Scroll award, Best First Novel 1972, v.p. chpt. 1976-78), Sci. Fiction Writers Am., Western Writers Am. Democrat. Editor 8 anthologies Contbr. numerous short stories to publs. Home: 40 San Jacinto Way San Francisco CA 94127 Office: PO Box 27368 San Francisco CA 94127

PROOST, ROBERT LEE, lawyer; b. St. Louis, July 30, 1937; s. Virgil Raymond and Anna Marie (Gaeng) P.; B.S. magna cum laude, St. Louis U., 1959; J.D., Washington U., St. Louis, 1962; m. Mary Jo McDonald, July 1, 1961; children—Timothy Robert, Mary Elizabeth, Thomas Edward, Daniel Joseph. Admitted to Mo. bar, 1962, Ill. bar, 1962; mem. firm Peper, Martin, Jensen, Maichel & Hetlage and predecessor, St. Louis, 1962—, partner, 1968—; pres., dir. Silmasco Inc., St. Louis, 1971—, Executype Inc., St. Louis, 1971-78; lectr. in field. Served with USAF, 1962-65. Mem. Am., Mo., Ill., Met. St. Louis (pres. 1978) bar assns., Washington U. Law Alumni Assn. (pres. 1972-73), St. Louis U. Arts and Scis. Alumni Assn. (v.p. 1971), Order of Coif, Alpha Sigma Nu, Phi Delta Phi. Roman Catholic. Clubs: Media, Washington U. Faculty. Author: Financing the On-Going Business, 1973, 79; contbr. articles to profl. jours. Home: 319 Claymont Dr Ballwin MO 63011 Office: Peper Martin Jensen Maichel & Hetlage 720 Olive St 24th Floor Saint Louis MO 63101

PROPHET, WILLIAM FORBES, hotel co. exec.; b. Newark, May 28, 1922; s. William and Elsie Belle (Forbes) P.; student Juilliard Sch. Music, 1939-42, Columbia Theol. Sem., 1957-58; m. Thelma I. Gilliam, Jan. 6, 1943; children—Diane Elizabeth, William David. Mgmt. trainee Oakwood Markets, Kingsport, Tenn., 1950-53, mgr. store, 1953-54; owner, operator grocery store, 1954-57; bus. missionary Presbyterian Ch. U.S., Mexico, 1957-59; ch. bus. adminstr. First Presbyn. Ch., Nashville, 1959-67; ch. adminstr. Second Presbyn. Ch., Memphis, 1967-69; with Holiday Inns Inc., 1969-74, dist. dir. Benelux Dist., Brussels, 1973-74; innkeeper Holiday Inn Downtown, Servico Corp., Raleigh, N.C., 1974-78, v.p. western region, Houston, 1978—; guest lectr. Harvard U. Bus. Sch.; bd. dirs. Nassau Paradise Island Promotion Bd. Scoutmaster Middle Tenn. council Boy Scouts Am., 1959-67; mem. Ch. Adminstr. Nat. Assn., Nashville, 1966-69. Served with USN, 1942-49. Recipient spl. citation for outstanding goodwill in tourism State of Mass., 1964, Long Rifle award Middle Tenn. council Boy Scouts Am., 1969; named Fellow in Ch. Bus. Adminstrn., Nat. Assn. Ch. Bus. Adminstrs. Mem. Am. Hotel and Motel Assn., Nat. Restaurant Assn., Tex. Restaurant Assn., Tex. Hotel and Motel Assn., Houston Hotel Assn., Greater Houston Visitor and Conv. Council. Republican. Clubs: Woodlands Country. Home and Office: 2350 South Loop W Houston TX 77054

PROPPER, GRANT EMIL, lawyer; b. Los Angeles, May 18, 1933; s. Henry and Adela Durraine (Ganz) P.; B.A. in Econs., U. Calif., Los Angeles, 1957, LL.B., J.D., 1960; m. Joyce Suzanne Berman, June 14, 1959; children—Catherine Rebecca, Matthew Richard. Admitted to Calif. bar, 1961; law clk. Calif. Ct. Appeals, 1961-62; individual practice law, Los Angeles, 1962-69; partner firm Blum, Propper & Hardacre, Inc., 1969—; arbitrator Am. Arbitrator Assn.; spl. arbitrator Calif. Superior Ct.; mediator family law Santa Monica Superior Ct. Served with AUS, 1953-55. Mem. Los Angeles County, Beverly Hills bar assns., State Bar Calif. Family law editor Calif. Trial Lawyers Assn. Forum. Office: 10960 Wilshire Blvd Los Angeles CA 90024

PROPST, JOHN LEAKE, banker; b. Winnsboro, S.C., Apr. 7, 1914; s. Floyd Ernest and Jennie (Leake) P.; A.B., Princeton, 1935; LL.B., Duquesne U., 1940, LL.D. (hon.), 1970; m. Marjorie Vilsack, Oct. 4, 1941; children—Marie T. Propst MacPhail, Pamela A. Propst Campbell, Suzanne L. Propst Honeycutt, Marjorie Louise. With The Union Trust Co., Pitts., 1935-46; with Mellon Nat. Bank & Trust Co., 1946—, successively asst. trust officer, trust officer, asst. v.p., 1946-54, v.p. trust dept., 1954-65, v.p., sr. trust officer, 1965-70, sr. v.p., 1970-77; exec. Roldiva, Inc., 1977—. Treas. Pitts. Urban Redevel. Authority, 1957-71; sponsor Allegheny Conf. on Community Devel. Trustee Edgar J. Kaufmann Found., Shadyside Hosp., Ellis Sch., 1960-74, Pitts. Found., 1970-77, Mercy Hosp.; bd. dirs. Duquesne U., Pitts. Boys Club; mem. distbn. com. Pitts. Found., 1978—. Served to lt. USNR, 1942-45. Mem. Pa. Bankers Assn. (past chmn. trust div.), Allegheny County Bar Assn. Clubs: Fox Chapel Golf; Pitts. Law, Pitts. Golf; Sewickley Heights Golf; Duquesne; Princeton (N.Y.C.). Home: 5521 Dunmoyle St Pittsburgh PA 15217 Office: 3 Gateway Center 6 North Pittsburgh PA 15222

PROSHANSKY, HAROLD MILTON, psychologist, educator; b. N.Y.C., Sept. 16, 1920; s. Samuel N. and Rose (Enteles) P.; B.S., City Coll. N.Y., 1941; M.A., Columbia U., 1942; Ph.D., N.Y. U., 1952; m. Etta Weissman, Sept. 19, 1942; children—Eric Jay, Ellen Jane. Asst. prof. psychology Bklyn. Coll., City U. N.Y., 1953-59; spl. research fellow NIMH, asso. prof. psychology U. Mich., Ann Arbor, 1959-61; asso. prof. Bklyn. Coll., 1961-66, exec. officer Ph.D. program psychology Grad. Sch. and Univ. Center, City U. N.Y., 1966-68, dean grad. sch., 1968-69, provost, 1971-72, pres. Grad. Sch. and Univ. Center, 1972—; cons. in field. Profl. adv. com. Cooper-Hewitt Mus. Bd. dirs. Catalyst. Served to sgt. AUS, 1942-46. NIMH research grantee 1960-67, 67-74; NIMH spl. research fellow Univ. Coll., London, 1969-70. Fellow Am. Psychol. Assn., AAAS, Soc. Psychol. Study Social Issues (pres. 1972-73); mem. Environ. Design Research Assos. Author, contbg. author books. Contbr. articles to profl. jours. Home: 145 Central Park W New York City NY 10023 Office: City U NY Grad Sch and Univ Center 33 W 42d St New York City NY 10036

PROSSER, ARNOLD HAROLD, mfg. co. exec.; b. Fountain City, Wis., Mar. 5, 1917; s. John Rushford and Mabel (Baertsch) P.; B.S., U. So. Cal., 1940; m. Alicemae Jensen, June 26, 1942; children—Daniel Jensen, Thomas Arnold, Rebecca Lynn. Div. gen. mgr. A.O. Smith Corp., Los Angeles, 1940-61; pres., chmn. bd. Prosser Industries, Inc., Anaheim, Calif., 1961-67; exec. v.p. Purex Corp., Lakewood, Calif., 1967—; dir. Stewart-Walker Co., San Simeon Pines. Bd. dirs. Presbyn. Intercommunity Hosp., Whittier, Calif. Served to lt. USNR, 1943-46. Recipient medal of bravery Royal Canadian Humane Soc., 1929. P.A. Calif. Mem. U. So. Calif. Assos. Republican. Presbyn. (trustee). Club: Friendly Hills Country (Whittier).

PROSSER, CLIFFORD LADD, emeritus educator, biologist; b. Avon, N.Y., May 12, 1907; s. Clifford James and Izora (Ladd) P.; A.B., U. Rochester, 1929; Ph.D., Johns Hopkins, 1932; D.Sc., Clark U., 1975; m. Hazel Blanchard, Aug. 25, 1934; children—Jane Ellen, Nancy Ladd, Loring Blanchard. Research fellow Harvard and Cambridge U., 1932-34; asst. prof. physiology Clark U., 1934-39; asst. prof. zoology U. Ill. at Urbana, 1939-43, asso. prof., 1943-49, prof. physiology, 1949-75, prof. emeritus, 1975—, head dept., 1960-69; cons. NRDC, 1942-43; asso. sect. chief, metall. lab. U. Chgo., 1943-46; Carnegie vis. prof. U. Hawaii, 1957; vis. prof. U. Mass., 1977, Ariz. State U., 1978. Trustee Marine Biol. Lab., Woods Hole, Mass. Guggenheim fellow, 1963-64; Australian-Am. Edn. Exchange fellow, 1971-72. Fellow Am. Acad. Arts and Scis.; mem. Nat. Acad. Scis., A.A.A.S. (sectional v.p. 1965), Am. Soc. Zoologists (pres. 1961-62), Am. Physiol. Soc. (pres. 1969-70), Soc. Gen. Physiologists (pres. 1958-59), Phi Beta Kappa, Sigma Xi, Phi Kappa Phi, Gamma Alpha. Author, editor: Comparative Animal Physiology, rev. edit., 1973. Contbr. articles to sci. jours. Office: Physiology Dept U Ill Urbana IL 61801

PROSSER, FRANKLIN PIERCE, computer scientist; b. Atlanta, July 4, 1935; s. Edward Theron and Eunice (McDaniel) P.; B.S., Ga. Inst. Tech., 1956, M.S., 1958; Ph.D., Pa. State U., 1961; m. Brenda Mary Lau, June 16, 1960; children—Edward, Andrea. Prof. computer sci. Ind. U., Bloomington, 1969—, asso. dir. Wrubel Computing Center, 1969—, chmn. dept. computer sci., 1971-77; cons. Lockheed Theoretical Physics Lab., Palo Alto, Calif., 1967. Mem. Assn. Computing Machinery, AAAS, IEEE. Home: 1200 Longwood Dr Bloomington IN 47401 Office: Dept Computer Science Indiana U Bloomington IN 47401

PROST, JUDE HENRY, clergyman; b. Chgo., Dec. 6, 1915; s. Mathias J. and Mary Elizabeth (Krug) P.; student St. Joseph Sem., Westmont, Ill., 1933-35; B.S. in Philosophy, Lady of the Angels Sem., Cleve., 1939, degree in Polit. Economy, 1939; D.D., St. Joseph Sem., Teutopolis, Ill., 1942. Ordained priest Roman Catholic Ch., 1942; founder Franciscan Mission on Tapajós River in Prelacy of Santarém, 1943; asst. pastor in Belterra, 1943-48; del. provincial for Franciscab Commisariate of the Sacred Heart in Brazil, 1948-54; canonical visitator Franciscan Fathers in State of Goias in Brazil, 1951; founder first residence Am. Franciscans in Santarém, Brazil, 1955, in Belém, 1956; named aux. bishop Archdiocese of Belém, 1962, consecrated aux. bishop Belém, Pará, Brazil, 1962—. Regional dir. Cath. Charities and Food for Peace Program in No. Brazil, 1962-71; pres. Central Coop. of Pará, 1964-69; built new minor sem. and opened maj. sem., 1970. Address: Caixa Postal 660 Belém Pará Brazil

PROTHRO, JAMES WARREN, educator, polit. scientist; b. Robeline, La., Apr. 15, 1922; s. Edwin Thomas and Frances (Terry) P.; B.A., N. Tex. State U., 1943; M.A., La. State U., 1948; M.A., Princeton U., 1949, Ph.D., 1952; m. Mary Frances Harris, Oct. 17, 1943 (div. Feb. 1971); children—Pamela, Barbara, Susan; m. 2d, Ana Posada Samper, Sept. 10, 1971. Asst. prof. polit. sci. Fla. State U., 1950-53, asso. prof., 1953-57, prof., 1957-61; vis. prof. U. N.C., Chapel Hill, 1960-61, prof. polit. sci., research prof. Inst. for Research in Social Sci., 1961—, Alumni Distinguished prof., 1975—, dir. Inst. for Research in Social Sci., 1967-73, dir. Louis Harris Data Center, 1965-73; vis. prof. Escuela Latino-americana de Ciencia Politica y Adminstracion Publica, Flacso, Chile, 1966-67; book rev. editor Am. Polit. Sci. Rev., 1965-68; editorial bd. Pub. Opinion Quart., 1965-69; mem. adv. bd. Jour. of Politics, 1965-75; cons. U.S. Commn. on Civil Rights, 1964-65; editor Harbrace series in Political Behavior, 1966—. Rockefeller Found. grantee, 1960-64; Social Sci. Research Council grantee, 1963-64; Ford Found. grantee, 1967-70; Fgn. Area Fellowship program, Chile, 1972. Mem. Am. (exec. council 1970-73), So. (pres. 1970-71) polit. sci. assns., AAUP. Author: Dollar Decade: Business Ideas in the 1920s, 1954; (with Richard Richardson) The Politics of American Democracy, 6th edit., 1977; (with Donald R. Matthews) Negroes and the New Southern Politics, 1966; (with David Kovenock) Explaining the Vote: Presidential Choices in the Nation and the States, 1973. Contbr. articles in field to sci. jours. Research, publs. on Negro polit. participation in the South combining aggregate data, opinion survey data, depth community studies in a single explanatory model. Home: 306 Elliott Rd Chapel Hill NC 27514

PROTTER, MURRAY HAROLD, educator, mathematician; b. N.Y.C., Feb. 13, 1918; s. Aron and Bertha (Keller) P.; B.A., U. Mich., 1937, M.A., 1938; Ph.D., Brown U., 1946; m. Ruth Rotman, June 24, 1945; children—Barbara, Philip. Instr. Brown U., 1946-47; asst. prof. Syracuse U., 1947-51; mem. faculty U. Calif. at Berkeley, 1953—, prof. math., 1958—, chmn. dept., 1962-65, dir. Center Pure and Applied Math., 1968-69, 72-77; mem. Inst. Advanced Study, Princeton, 1951-53, 59. Mem. Am. Math. Soc. (editor bull. 1967-73, asso. treas. 1973-77), Math. Assn. Am. Author: (with C. B. Morrey, Jr.) Calculus with Analytic Geometry, 1963; College Calculus, 1963; Modern Mathematical Analysis, 1964; Analytic Geometry, 1966; (with H.F. Weinberger) Maximum Principles in Differential Equations, 1967; (with H. Flanders) Loewner Theory of Continuous Groups, 1971; (with C.B. Morrey, Jr.) Calculus with Analytic Geometry, 2d course, 1971, A First Course in Real Analysis, 1977. Office: Math Dept U Calif Berkeley CA 94720

PROUD, G. O'NEIL, physician, educator; b. Oregon, Mo., Aug. 6, 1913; s. Willard C. and Alice (Kunkel) P.; A.B., U. Mo., 1935; M.D., Washington U., 1939; m. Nelle Frances Phillips, July 10, 1937; children—Jan Alicia, Wendy Green. Intern, St. Luke's Hosp., Kansas City, Mo., 1939-40; resident Barnes Hosp., St. Louis, 1940-43; instr. dept. otorhinolaryngology Washington U., 1946-48, asst. prof., 1948-50; asso. prof., chmn. otolaryngology U. Kans., Kansas City, 1950-52, prof., chmn. otolaryngology, 1950—. Served to lt. USNR, 1943-46. Diplomate Am. Bd. Otolarynology. Mem. Am. Laryngology, Rhinology Otol. Soc., Am. Otol. Soc., Am. Acad. Ophthalmology and Otolaryngology (1st v.p. 1974-75). Research, publs. in otology. Home: 3721 W 87th St Shawnee Mission KS 66206 Office: 39th and Rainbow Blvd Kansas City KS 66103. *The road to modest success is smoother when the mind is tranquil and uncomplicated.*

PROUDFOOT, ALLIN WHITFIELD, brewing co. exec.; b. Chgo., Jan. 23, 1929; s. Alfred C. and Dorothy M. (Whitfield) P.; B.S.B.A., Northwestern U., 1950, M.B.A., 1961; m. Ruth Ann Shumm, June 3, 1951; children—Alfred, Marcia Proudfoot Wolfson, Malcolm. Vice-pres. brand mgmt. R.J. Reynolds Foods, Winston-Salem, N.C., 1967-61; pres., chief exec. officer Curtiss Candy Co., N.Y.C., 1971-73; pres., chief exec. officer Coca-Cola Bottling Cos. of Chgo. and Wis., 1973-76; sr. v.p. mktg. Coca-Cola Co., Atlanta, 1976-78; exec. v.p. mktg. Joseph Schlitz Brewing Co., Milw. Bd. trustees Northwestern U.; vice chmn. United Cerebral Palsy Nat. Telethon; mem. nat. adv. bd.; dep. sheriff Fulton County, Atlanta. Republican. Methodist. Clubs: Milw. Country, Milw. Athletic, Masons. Home: 9401 N Range Line Rd River Hills WI 53217 Office: PO Box 614 Milwaukee WI 53201

PROUJAN, CARL, author, editor; b. N.Y.C., Feb. 15, 1929; s. Mathieu M. and Clara (Fish) Immerman; student Reed Coll., 1947-50; B.S., Coll. City N.Y., 1957; m. Sonia Christine Candalas, Jan. 23, 1954; children—David, Lisa, Suzanne. Research chemist Pfister Chem. Works, Ridgefield, N.J., 1957-59; chemistry editor Acad. Press, N.Y.C., 1959-61; med. text editor Harper & Row, N.Y.C., 1961-62; asso. editor Sci. World, Scholastic Mags., Inc., N.Y.C., 1962-66, mng. editor, 1967-68, editor, 1968-73, editorial dir. sci. dept., 1973-77; ind. writer/producer, 1977—; chief editor Customized Communications, Med. Econs. Co., 1979—. Served with M.C., AUS, 1951-53. Recipient gold medal V.I. Internat. Film Festival, Silver Screen award U.S. Indsl. Film Festival. Mem. N.Y. Newspaper Guild (chmn. representative assembly 1967-68). Author: Secrets of the Sea, 1971. Editorial dir. Human Issues in Science (filmstrips); creator, author (filmstrips) Adventures in Science (Cindy award Info. Film Producers Am. 1976). Home: 167 S Mountain Rd New City NY 10956

PROULX, ADOLPHE, clergyman; b. Hanmer, Ont. Can., Dec. 12, 1927; s. Augustin and Marie-Louise (Tremblay) P.; B.A., St. Augustine's Sem., Toronto, Ont.; postgrad. in canon law, Rome, Italy, 1958-60. Ordained priest Roman Catholic Ch., 1954; parish priest, North Bay and Sudbury, Ont., Can., 1954-57; chancellor Sault Ste. Marie (Ont.) Diocese, 1960-64, aux. bishop, 1965-67; bishop Alexandria (Ont.) Diocese, 1967-74; bishop Hull, Que., Canada, 1974—. Address: 119 Carillon St Hull PQ J8X 2P8 Canada

PROULX, AMEDEE WILFRID, bishop; b. Sanford, Maine, Aug. 31, 1932; s. Francis Adelard and Rose Anna (Sevigny) P.; B.A., Seminaire de St. Hyancinthe (Que.), 1954; S.T.L., St. Paul's Sem., U. Ottawa, 1958; J.C.L., Cath. U. Am., 1968. Ordained priest Roman Catholic Ch., 1958, became monsignor, 1971, consecrated bishop, 1976; asso. pastor Caribou, Maine, 1958-60, Fort Kent, Maine, 1960-64, Auburn, Maine, 1964-66; advocate Tribunal of Portland, Maine, 1968—, vicar of religious, 1970-76, vicar gen., 1975—; titular bishop of Clipia, aux. bishop of Portland, 1975—. Mem. Canon Law Soc. Am. (ad hoc com. ordination of women 1972-73). Home: 163 Danforth St Portland ME 04102 Office: 510 Ocean Ave Portland ME 04103

PROUT, CHARLES HENRY, JR., corp. exec.; b. N.Y.C., Mar. 15, 1920; s. Charles Henry and Anna (Bartosch) P.; Litt.B., Rutgers U., 1941; m. Dorothy M. Baldwin, Feb. 6, 1943; 1 son, Gerald Robert. Mktg. exec. Richardson-Merrell, Inc., 1941-54; dir. pub. relations Mead Johnson & Co., 1954-63; dir. corporate relations Cutler-Hammer, Inc., 1963-68, v.p., sec., 1969—; founder, 1st editor-pub. PR Reporter, 1958-60. Pres. Cutler-Hammer Found., 1968—; trustee Mount Mary Coll., Milw., 1973—; mem. Columbia Hosp. Corp., Milw.; vice chmn. United Way, Milw., 1973; bd. dirs. Jr. Achievement Southeastern Wis., 1969-74, United Performing Arts Fund, Milw. Served to maj. AUS, 1942-46. Decorated Bronze Star. Mem. Pub. Relations Soc. Am., Am. Soc. Corp. Secs., Beta Theta Pi. Contbr. articles to gen. mags., profl. jours. Home: 6941 N Barnett Ln Fox Point WI 53217 Office: 4201 N 27th St Milwaukee WI 53216

PROUT, GEORGE RUSSELL, JR., med. educator; b. Boston, July 23, 1924; s. George Russell and Marion (Snow) P.; student Union Coll., 1943; M.D., Albany Med. Coll., 1947; M.A. (hon.), Harvard; m. Loa Katherine Wheatley, Oct. 17, 1950; children—George Russell III, Elizabeth Louise. Resident, N.Y. Hosp., 1952-56; asst. attending Meml. Center for Cancer and Allied Disease, N.Y.C., 1956-57; asst. clinician surgery James Ewing Hosp., N.Y.C., 1956-57; asso. prof., chmn. div. urology U. Miami, 1957-60; prof., chmn. div. urology Med. Coll. Va., 1960-69; chief urol. service Mass. Gen. Hosp., Boston, also prof. surgery Harvard Med. Sch., 1969—. Chmn. Adjuvants in Surg. Treatment of Bladder Cancer; mem. advisory task force to Nat. Cancer Inst., 1968—, chmn. Nat. Bladder Coop. Group, 1973—. Served with USNR, 1950-52. Fellow A.C.S., Acad. Medicine Toronto (corr.); mem. Am., Canadian urol. assns., Am. Cancer Soc., Soc. Pelvic Surgeons, Soc. Surg. Oncology, Soc. Univ. Urologists, AAUP, AMA, Dallas So. Clin. Soc. (hon.), Am. Assn. Genitourinary Surgeons, Soc. Pediatric Urology, Alpha Omega Alpha. Bd. editors of Jour. Surg. Oncology, The Kidney, Urol. Survey, Contemporary Medicine. Home: 174 Puritan Rd Swampscott MA 01907 Office: Fruit St Boston MA 02114

PROUT, RALPH EUGENE, physician; b. Los Angeles, Feb. 27, 1933; s. Ralph Byron and Fern (Taylor) P.; B.A., La Sierra Coll., 1953; M.D., Loma Linda U., 1957; m. Darlene May Denney, June 16, 1957; 1 son, Michael. Intern, Los Angeles County Hosp., 1957-58; resdient internal medicine White Meml. Hosp., Los Angeles, 1958-60; resident psychiatry Harding Hosp., Worthington, Ohio, 1960-61; practice medicine specializing in internal medicine, Napa, Calif., 1961-63; staff internist Calif. Med. Facility, Vacaville, 1963-68, chief med. officer, 1968—; instr. Sch. Medicine, Loma Linda U., 1965-66; clin. asso. U. Calif. at Davis Sch. Medicine, 1978—. Treas., Vacaville Republican Assembly, 1972-75; del. Republican Central Com. Solano County, 1975-78. Bd. dirs. Napa-Solano County United Crusade, Vallejo, Calif., 1969-71, v.p., 1970-71; bd. dirs. Project Clinic, Vacaville, 1974-77, Home Health Com. Inter-Community Hosp., Fairfield, 1978—. Named One of Outstanding Young Men of Am., 1968. Diplomate Nat. Bd. Med. Examiners. Mem. Calif. Med. Assn., Am., Calif. socs. internal medicine, Solano County Med. Soc., Calif. Thoracic Soc., Calif. Employed Physicians Assn. (dir. 1973—, pres. 1976-78), Union Am. Physicians (dir. 1976-78), Vacaville C. of C. (dir. 1974-78), Native Sons of Golden West, Alpha Omega Alpha. Republican. Seventh-day Adventist. Club: Commonwealth of Calif. Home: 725 Linwood Dr Vacaville CA 95688 Office: Calif Med Facility Vacaville CA 95688

PROUTY, CHILTON EATON, geologist, educator; b. Tuscaloosa, Ala., Sept. 8, 1914; s. William Frederick and Lucille Winifred (Thorington) P.; B.S., U. N.C., 1936; M.S., Mo. Sch. Mines, 1938; Ph.D., Columbia, 1944; m. Norma Victoria Fruvog, Sept. 3, 1942; children—William Eaton, John Fruvog. With Va. Geol. Survey, 1939, N.Y. Geol. Survey, 1940; geologist TVA, 1942-44, U.S. Geol. Survey, 1944-46; asst. prof. geology U. Pitts., 1946-48, asso. prof., 1948-51, prof., head dept., 1951-57; prof., head dept. Mich. State U., 1957-69, prof., 1969—; cons. geologist, 1946—; cooperating geologist Pa. Topog. and Geol. Survey, 1947—; pres. Geo-Research & Indsl. Devel. Corp., 1956. Cons.-examiner commn. on colls. and univs. N. Central Assn. of Colls. and Secondary Schs., 1967—. Fellow Geol. Soc. Am.; mem. Assn. Geology Tchrs. (pres. Eastern sect. 1952, nat. pres. 1958), Pitts. Geol. Soc. (pres. 1950), Paleontological Soc. Am., A.A.A.S., Am. Assn. Petroleum Geologists, Soc. Econ. Paleontologists and Mineralogists, Assn. Profl. Geol. Scientists (editor 1977-78), Sigma Xi. Contbr. articles to profl. publs. Office: Dept Geology Mich State U East Lansing MI 48824

PROVENCHER, ROGER ARTHUR, internat. assn. exec.; b. Manchester, N.H., June 20, 1923; s. Arthur J. and Rose Albina (Briere) P.; B.A., U. N.H., 1949; postgrad. U. Paris, 1950; m. Josette Marguerite Camus, Jan. 3, 1946 (dec. 1976); children—Frances Provencher-Ryder, Carl; m. 2d, Barazandeh Samiian, Apr. 9, 1977; 1 stepdau., Mina Cullimore. Joined Dept. State, 1950; asst. commr. gen. Expo 67, Montreal, Que., Can., 1965-67; mgmt. analyst, Washington, 1968; assigned to Nat. War Coll., 1969-70; 1st sec., counselor Am. embassy, Moscow, 1970-73; counselor for administrv. affairs Am. embassy, Vientiane, Laos, 1973-74, Tehran, Iran, 1974-77; sr. counsellor Internat. Telecommunication Union, Geneva, 1977—; mng. dir. Pan African Airlines (Nigeria) Ltd., Lagos, 1962-63. Served to 1st lt. AUS, 1943-46; ETO. Recipient Meritorious Honor award Dept. State, 1958, 62, also Superior Honor award, 1975. Mem. Nat.

War Coll. Alumni Assn., Lambda Pi. Home: 3519 Leland St Chevy Chase MD 20015 Office: Internat Telecommunication Union Place des Nations 1211 Geneva 20 Switzerland

PROVENCHER, RONALD, educator; b. Springerville, Ariz., Oct. 7, 1934; s. George C. and Ada L. (Mann) P.; B.A. with distinction, U. Mo., 1959; Ph.D., U. Calif. at Berkeley, 1968; m. Barbara L. Carlson, Juen 22, 1935; children—Melodie Anne, Lori Michelle, Sherry Lynne. Asst. prof. anthropology San Diego State U., 1966-69, Rice U., Houston, 1969-74; asso. prof., chmn. anthropology No. Ill. U., DeKalb, 1974—; vis. scholar Nat. U. Malaysia, 1971-72; asso. dir. NSF Field Sch. in Urban Anthropology, 1969. Served with U.S. Army, 1954-57. Woodrow Wilson Found. fellow, 1959-60, U. Calif. fellow, 1961-62, Fgn. Area Fellowship Found. fellow, 1964-66, George William Hooper Found. postdoctoral fellow, 1971-72. Fellow Am. Anthropol. Assn.; mem. AAAS, Assn. Applied Anthropology, Assn. Med. Anthropology, Phi Beta Kappa. Democrat. Episcopalian. Author: (with Douglas Uzzell) Urban Anthropology, 1976; Mainland Southeast Asia: An Anthropological Perspective, 1975; Two Malay Worlds, 1971. Home: 714 Normal Rd DeKalb IL 60115

PROVENSEN, ALICE ROSE TWITCHELL, author, artist; b. Chgo.; d. Jay Horace and Kathryn (Zelanis) Twitchell; student Chgo. Art Inst., 1930-31; U. Calif., Los Angeles, 1939; Art Student League, N.Y., 1940-41; m. Martin Provensen, Apr. 17, 1944; 1 dau., Karen Anna. With Walter Lanz Studios, Los Angeles, 1942-43; OSS, 1944-45; exhibited (with Martin Provensen) Balt. Mus., 1954, Am. Inst. Graphic Arts, N.Y., 1959, Botolph Group, Boston, 1964; books represented in Fifty Books of Yr. Selections, Am. Inst. Graphic Arts, 1947, 48, 52. The Charge of the Light Brigade named Best Illustrated Children's Book of the Yr., N.Y. Times, 1964; co-recipient Gold medal Soc. Illustrators, 1960. Author, illustrator books including Karen's Opposites, 1963; Karen's Curiosity, 1963; What is a Color?, 1967; (with Martin Provensen) Who's In the Egg, 1970; The Provensen Book of Fairy Tales, 1971; Play on Words, 1972; My Little Hen, 1973; Roses are Red, 1973; Our Animal Friends, 1974; The Year at Maple Hill Farm, 1978; A Horse and a Hound, A Goat and a Gander, 1979; illustrator children's books including Mother Goose Book, 1976; Old Mother Hubbard, 1977; (with Martin Provensen) A Peaceable Kingdom, 1978; also textbooks. Home: Meadowbrook Ln Clinton Hollow Rd Staatsburg NY 12580

PROVENSEN, MARTIN ELIAS, author, illustrator; b. Chgo., July 10, 1916; s. Marthin C. and Berendina (Kruger) P.; ed. U. Calif., Berkeley; m. Alice Twitchell, Apr. 17, 1944; 1 dau., Karen Anna. Exhbns. (with wife) include Balt. Mus., 1954, Am. Inst. Graphic Arts, N.Y.C., 1959, Botolph Group, Boston, 1964; illustrator children's books: The Fireside Book of Folk Songs, 1949; The New Testament, 1953; The Iliad and Oddysey, 1956; Myths and Legends, 1969; Aesop's Fables, 1965; Fun and Nonsense, 1970; The Provensen Book of Fairy Tales, 1971; also Shakespeare, 10 Great Plays, 1961; and text books; author-illustrator: (with wife) The Animal Fair, 1952, Karen's Opposites, 1963, Karen's Curiosity, 1963, What Is a Color, 1967, Who's in The Egg, 1970, Play on Words, 1972, My Little Hen, 1973, Roses Are Red, 1973, Our Animal Friends, 1974, The Book of Seasons, 1976, The Year at Maple Hill Farm, 1978, A Horse and a Hound, A Goat and a Gander, 1979; books rep. Fifty Book Year selections Am. Inst. Graphic Arts, 1947, 48, 72. Served with USNR, 1941-45. Recipient Best Illustrated Book of Year award (for Charge of Light Brigade), N.Y. Times, 1964, Best of Year citation, 1952, 53, 59, 63, 64, 76, 78; co-recipient Gold medal Soc. Illustrators, 1960, Art Books for Children citation Bklyn. Mus., 1975. Address: Meadowbrook Ln Clinton Hollow RD Staatsburg NY 12580

PROVOST, DONALD EDGAR, engring. and constrn. co. exec.; b. Denver, Aug. 26, 1912; s. Charles Edgar and Beda Amanda (Rapp) P.; student U. Colo., 1932-33; m. Eldyne Herbst, Dec. 15, 1938; 1 dau., Sheila Kay Provost Meredith. With Stearns-Roger Corp., Denver, 1937—, mgr. power div., 1955-59, v.p., 1959-63, pres., 1963—, chmn. bd., 1968—; pres., chmn. bd. Stearns-Roger Inc., Stearns-Roger Architects, Ltd., Stearns-Roger Equipment Co., Stearns-Roger Export, Ltd., Stearns-Roger Elec. Contractors Inc., Stearns-Roger Fabricators, Inc., Stearns-Roger Engring. Co., Stearns-Roger Services, Inc., Stearns-Roger Engring. Corp.; dir. Stearns-Roger Can. Ltd., Rio Grande Industries, Inc., Denver and Rio Grande Western R.R., 1st Nat. Bancorp., 1st Nat. Bank of Denver, Mountain Bell Co., Gen. Iron Works Co.; dir., past pres. Rocky Mountain Elec. League. Bd. dirs. Lutheran Med. Center, 1968—; trustee U. Denver. Registered profl. engr., Colo. Republican. Congregationalist. Clubs: Cherry Hills Country, Denver Country. Office: 4500 Cherry Creek Dr Denver CO 80222

PROVOST, WALLY (WALLACE B.), journalist; b. Lincoln, Nebr., May 20, 1922; s. Orison C. and Irma (Arbogast) P.; student U. Nebr., 1940-43, Milw. State Tchrs. Coll., 1943; m. Irene Peckham, May 19, 1947. Rewrite man U.P.I., Lincoln, 1942; asst. sports editor Nebr. State Jour., Lincoln, 1942-43, Lincoln Evening Jour., 1946-51; sports and courthouse reporter Omaha World-Herald, 1951-54, sports editor, 1955-72, sports columnist, 1972—. Vice pres. Nat. Golden Gloves Assn., 1961-63; mem. nat. boxing com. Amateur Athletic Union, 1958-60. Pres. World-Herald Good Fellows Charities, 1964-70. Served with USAAF, 1943-46; CBI. Recipient citizen's award of merit Urban League, 1966; sports writing award Nebr. A.P., 1969, 70, Humanitarian award Jewish Fedn. Omaha, 1976, Communications award U. Nebr. at Omaha, 1978, Clarence F. Swanson Service award, 1979; Sportsman and Humanitarian award B'nai B'rith, 1979; mem. Omaha Met. Wrestling Hall of Fame. Mem. Football Writers Assn., Baseball Writers Assn., Nat. Assn. Sportscasters and Sportswriters (Nebr. Sports Writer of Year 1963-65, 68), Omaha Sportscasters Assn. Club: Omaha Press. Home: 5135 Parker St Omaha NE 68104 Office: 14th and Dodge Sts Omaha NE 68102

PROWN, JULES DAVID, educator; b. Freehold, N.J., Mar. 14, 1930; s. Max M. and Matilda (Casileth) P.; A.B., Lafayette Coll., 1951; A.M., U. Del., 1956; A.M., Harvard U., 1953, Ph.D., 1961; A.M. (hon.), Yale U., 1971; D.F.A. (hon.), Lafayette Coll., 1979; m. Shirley Ann Martin, June 23, 1956; children—Elizabeth Anderson, David Martin, Jonathan, Peter Casileth, Sarah Peiter. Dir. Hist. Soc. Old Newbury, Newburyport, Mass., 1957-58, Old Gaol Mus., York, Maine, 1958-59; asst. to dir. Fogg Art Mus., Harvard U., 1959-61, study higher edn. in visual arts Coll. Art Assn., 1962-64; mem. faculty Yale U., 1961, asso. prof. history art, 1967-71, prof., 1971—, curator Garvan and related collections of Am. art at univ. gallery, 1963-68, dir. Yale U. Center for Brit. Art and Brit. Studies, 1968-76; exec. bd. Nat. Humanities Inst., New Haven, 1975-78, asso. dir., 1977-78; vis. lectr. Smith Coll., 1966-67; consultative com. Art Quar., 1969-76. Bd. govs. Yale Press, 1969-76, Paul Mellon Centre for Studies in Brit. Art, London, 1970-76; trustee Historic Deerfield, Mass., 1971-75, Whitney Mus. Am. Art, N.Y.C., 1975—; mem. steering com. bicentennial exhbn. Nat. Gallery Art, 1973-76; mem. advisory com. Yale Edit. Horace Walpole Correspondence, 1971-76, Archives of Am. Art, 1972—, Inst. Early Am. History and Culture, Williamsburg, Va., 1972-75, Found. for Art Edn., 1976-78, Am. Art Jour., 1977—. Guggenheim fellow, 1964-65. Benjamin Franklin fellow Royal Soc. Arts, London; mem. New Haven Colony Hist. Soc., Colonial Soc. Mass., Am. Antiquarian Soc. (council 1977—), Am. Soc. 18th Century Studies (exec. bd. 1973-76), Coll. Art Assn. (dir. 1975-79), Am. Assn. Museums, AAUP, Author: John Singleton Copley, 2 vols., 1966; American Painting From Its Beginnings to the Armory Show, 1969; The Architecture of the Yale Center for British Art, 1977. Editorial bd. Winterthur Portfolio, 1978—. Office: PO Box 2009 Yale Sta New Haven CT 06520

PROWSE, JULIET, actress, dancer; b. Bombay, India, 1937; came to U.S., 1959; attended Royal Acad. Dance, Johannesburg, South Africa; m. Eddie James; m. 2d, John McCook; 1 son, Seth. Film debut in Can-Can, 1960; other film appearances include: G.I. Blues, The Fiercest Heart, The Right Approach, The Second Time Around, Dingaka, Who Killed Teddy Bear?, Run for Your Wife, Spree; appeared in TV film Second Chance; star TV series Mona McClusky, 1966; other TV appearances include: Adventures in Paradise, Burke's Law, Danny Thomas Show, Name of the Game, Happy Birthday, Las Vegas, Paul Lynde Comedy Hour; stage appearances include: Eddie Fisher at the Winter Garden, Sweet Charity; performs regularly in Las Vegas, Nev. Office: care William Morris Agy 151 El Camino Dr Beverly Hills CA 90212*

PROXMIRE, WILLIAM, U.S. senator; b. Lake Forest, Ill., Nov. 11, 1915; s. Theodore Stanley and Adele (Flanigan) P.; grad. Hill Sch., 1934; B.A., Yale, 1938; M.B.A., Harvard, 1940, M.P.A. in Pub. Adminstrn., 1948; m. Ellen Hodges. Pres., Artcraft Press, Waterloo, Wis., 1953-57; U.S. senator from Wis., 1957—. Nonimee gov. Wis., 1952, 54, 56; assemblyman Wis. Legislature, 1951. Democrat. Author: Can Small Business Survive?; Report from Wasteland-America's Military Industrial Complex; Uncle Sam, Last of the Big Time Spenders; You Can Do It!. Office: 5241 Dirksen Senate Office Bldg Washington DC 20510

PROYECT, MARTIN H., investment banker; b. N.Y.C., Oct. 24, 1932; s. Max and Fay (Madison) P.; B.A., Columbia U., 1954, L.D., 1956; m. Nellie R. Washington, Mar. 14, 1958; children—Christopher T., Michele F. Admitted to N.Y. bar, 1956; asso. firm Reavis & McGrath, N.Y.C., 1956-59; exec. v.p. Calvin Bullock Ltd., N.Y.C., 1959-79; chmn., pres. Venture Advisers, Inc., Santa Fe, 1968—, N.Y. Venture Fund, Inc., 1968—. Bd. dirs. The Bristol Fund; pres. bd. trustees Barnard Sch. Girls; bd. govs. Investment Co. Inst.; trustee New Lincoln Sch.; Club: River. Author: Investors Guide to the Tax Reform Act of 1976. Editor: How to Succeed in Spite of Yourself. Home: 1001 Camino Pinones Santa Fe NM 87501 Office: 231 Washington Ave Santa Fe NM 87501

PRUCHA, JOHN JAMES, ednl. adminstr., geologist; b. River Falls, Wis., Sept. 22, 1924; s. Edward Joseph and Katharine (Schladweiler) P.; student Wis. State U., River Falls, 1941-43; Ph.B., U. Wis., 1945, Ph.M., 1946; M.A., Princeton, 1948, Ph.D., 1950; m. Mary Elizabeth Helfrich, June 12, 1948; children—David, Stephen, Katharine, Carol, Mark, Barbara, Margaret, Christopher, Anne, Andrew. Asst. prof. geology Rutgers U., 1948-51; sr. geologist N.Y. State Geol. Survey, 1951-56; research geologist Shell Devel. Co., 1956-63; prof. geology, chmn. dept. Syracuse U., 1963-70, dean Coll. Arts and Scis., 1970-72, vice chancellor acad. affairs, 1972—, pres. Syracuse U. Press, 1973—. Trustee Le Moyne Coll., 1971-78; bd. dirs. Cultural Resources Council Syracuse, 1974—, pres., 1978-79; bd. dirs. Everson Mus. Art, Syracuse, 1977—. Fellow Geol. Soc. Am.; mem. Am. Assn. Petroleum Geologists, AAAS. Author: Basement Tectonics of Rocky Mountains, 1965, Structural Behavior of Salt, 1967, Stratigraphy and Structure of Southeastern New York, 1959. Home: 112 Ardsley Dr DeWitt NY 13214 Office: 303 Adminstrn Bldg Syracuse Univ Syracuse NY 13210

PRUETT, JAMES DANIEL, lawyer; b. Tuscaloosa, Ala., Feb. 4, 1938; s. James Howe-l and Sara Elizabeth (Daniel) P.; A.B., U. Ala., 1960, LL.B., 1963; m. Alice Jane Berrey, Sept. 11, 1959; children—Mary Elizabeth, Sara Ruth, Anne Leone. Admitted to Ala. bar, 1963, U.S. Supreme Ct., 1971; individual practice law, Gadsden, Ala., 1965—; mem. Ala. Securities Commn., 1974—. Served with U.S. Army, 1963-65. Mem. Am. Law Inst., Ala. Law Inst. Democrat. Methodist. Office: 610 Chestnut St Gadsden AL 35901

PRUETT, JAMES WORRELL, musicologist; b. Mt. Airy, N.C., Dec. 23, 1932; s. Samuel Richard and Gladys Dorne (Worrell) P.; B.A., U. N.C., Chapel Hill, 1955, M.A., 1957, Ph.D., 1962; m. Lilian Maria-Irene Pibernik, July 20, 1957; children—Mark, Ellen. Mem. faculty U. N.C., Chapel Hill., 1961—, prof. music, 1974—, music librarian, 1961-76, chmn. dept. music, 1976—; vis. prof. U. Toronto, 1976. Newberry Library fellow, summer 1966. Mem. Internat., Am. (chpt. chmn. 1964-66, mem. council 1974-77) musicol. socs., Music Library Assn. (pres. 1973-75, editor jour. 1974-77), Internat. Assn. Music Libraries. Editor: Studies in the History, Style and Bibliography of Music in Memory of Glen Haydon, 1969. Contbr. profl. jours., encys. Home: 343 Wesley Dr Chapel Hill NC 27514 Office: Dept Music Univ NC Chapel Hill NC 27514

PRUGH, GEORGE SHIPLEY, lawyer; b. Norfolk, Va., June 12, 1920; s. George Shipley and Florence (Hamilton) P.; A.B., U. Calif., San Francisco, 1941, J.D., 1948; postgrad. Army War Coll., 1961-62; M.A., George Washington U., 1963; m. Katherine Buchanan, Sept. 27, 1942; children—Stephanie Dean, Virginia Patton. Commd. 2d lt. U.S. Army, 1942, advanced through grades to maj. gen. Judge Adv. Gen. Corps., 1971; admitted to Calif. bar, 1949, U.S. Supreme Ct. bar, 1954; legal advisor U.S. Mil. Assistance Command, Vietnam, 1964-66; legal adviser U.S. European Command, Stuttgart, Ger., 1966-69; Judge Adv., U.S. Army Europe, Heidelberg, Ger., 1969-71; Judge Adv. Gen., Washington, 1971-75; ret., 1975; prof. law Hastings Coll. Law, U. Calif., San Francisco, 1975—; mem. Sec. of Def. Task Force on Racial Discrimination in Adminstrn. Mil. Justice, 1973; mem. U.S. del. Diplomatic Conf. on Law of War, Geneva, 1974, 75. Decorated D.S.M. with oak leaf cluster, Legion of Merit with oak leaf cluster. Mem. Am. Bar Assn. (cons. on internat. criminal law to criminal justice sect., chmn. internat. criminal law com.), Am. Law Inst., Am. Judicature Soc., Judge Adv. Assn. (hon. dir.), Am. Soc. Internat. Law, Internat. Soc. Mil. law and Law of War (v.p.), Civil Affairs Assn. (hon. dir.), Selden Soc., Calif. Bar, Order of Coif, Phi Delta Phi (hon.). Episcopalian. Clubs: Bohemian; Army and Navy (Washington). Author: (with others) Law at War, 1975; contbr. articles and law and mil. law to profl. jours. Home: 17 Cedar Ln Orinda CA 94563 Office: 198 McAllister St San Francisco CA 94563

PRUGH, JEFFERY DOUGLAS, journalist; b. Pitts., Sept. 15, 1939; s. Harold H. and Janice B. (Fryer) P.; B.Journalism, U. Mo., 1962. Reporter, Glendale (Calif.) News-Press, 1958-61; sports writer Los Angeles Times, 1962-75, nat. correspondent, bur. chief, Atlanta, 1976—. Served with U.S. Army, 1957. Recipient 1st prize sports Los Angeles Press Club, 1973. Mem. U.S. Basketball Writers Assn. (pres. 1972), So. Calif. Football Writers (pres. 1969), U. Mo. Alumni Assn., Sigma Delta Chi. Clubs: Atlanta Press (v.p.), Sporting (Atlanta). Co-author: The Wizard of Westwood, 1973. Home: 213 Skyland Dr Roswell GA 30075 Office: 233 Peachtree St Suite 708 Atlanta GA 30303

PRUIS, JOHN J, business exec.; b. Borculo, Mich., Dec. 13, 1923; s. Ties J. and Trientje (Koop) P.; B.S., Western Mich. U., 1947; M.A., Northwestern U., 1949, Ph.D., 1951; Litt.D., Yeungnam U., Taegu, Korea, Ind. State U.; m. Angeline Rosemary Zull, Sept. 14, 1944; children—David Lofton, Daniel J., Dirk Thomas. Tchr. pub. schs., Mich., 1942-43; supervising tchr. Campus Sch., Western Mich. U., 1947-48; instr. speech U. No Ia., 1951-52; from asst. prof. to asso. prof. speech So. Ill. U., 1952-55; mem. faculty Western Mich. U., 1955-68, sec. bd. trustees, 1964-68, v.p. adminstrn., 1966-68; pres. Ball State U., 1968-78; v.p. corporate relations Ball Corp., 1978—. Cons., examiner N. Central Assn., 1959—, also bd. dirs.; v.p. County drive chmn. Kalamazoo Community Chest, 1964. Bd. dirs. Kalamazoo chpt. Am. Cancer Soc., 1963-68, Delaware County United Fund, Muncie Symphony Assn., Ball Meml. Hosp., Big Bros./Big Sisters. Served with USNR, 1943-46; capt. Res. Mem. Am. Assn. Higher Edn., Speech Communication Assn., Muncie C. of C., Phi Delta Kappa, Omicron Delta Kappa, Blue Key. Presbyterian. Rotarian. Home: 305 N Brentwood Ln Muncie IN 47304

PRUITT, BASIL ARTHUR, surgeon, army officer; b. Nyack, N.Y., Aug. 21, 1930; s. Basil Arthur and Myrtle Flo (Knowles) P.; A.B., Harvard U., 1952, postgrad., 1952-53; M.D., Tufts U., 1957; m. Mary Sessions Gibson, Sept. 4, 1954; children—Scott Knowles, Laura Sessions, Jeffrey Hamilton. Intern, Boston City Hosp., 1957-58, resident in surgery, 1958-59, 61-62; commd. capt., M.C., U.S. Army, 1959, advanced thorugh grades to col., 1972; resident Brooke Gen. Hosp., Ft. Sam Houston, Tex., 1962-64; chief clin. div. Inst. Surg. Research, Ft. Sam Houston, 1965-67; chief profl. services, Vietnam, 1967-68; comdr., dir. U.S. Army Inst. Surg. Research, Brooke Army Med. Center, Ft. Sam Houston, 1968—; clin. prof. surgery U. Tex. Med. Sch., San Antonio, 1975—, Uniformed Sers. U. Health Scis., Bethesda, Md., 1978—; cons. U. Tex. Cancer Center, 1974—; mem. surgery, anaesthesiology and trauma study sect. NIH, 1978—. Decorated Bronze Star. Diplomate Am. Bd. Surgery. Fellow A.C.S. (bd. govs. 1973—); mem. Am. Burn Assn. (pres. 1975-76), Internat. Soc. Burn Injuries (nat. rep.), Smoke Burn and Fire Assn., Am. Trauma Soc. (dir.), Soc. Univ. Surgeons, Am., Tex., So. surg. assns., Halsted Soc., Am. Assn. Surgery of Trauma (recorder), Surg. Biol. Club, Internat. Soc. Surgeons, Assn. Acad. Surgery. Author med. books; contbr. chpts. to textbooks, articles to profl. jours.; asso. editor Jour. Trauma. Home: 402 Tidecrest Dr San Antonio TX 78239 Office: US Army Inst Surgical Research Fort Sam Houston TX 78234

PRUITT, DEAN GARNER, psychologist, educator; b. Phila., Dec. 26, 1930; s. Dudley McConnell and Grace Richards (Garner) P.; A.B., Oberlin Coll., 1952; M.S., Yale U., 1955, Ph.D., 1957; m. France Juliard, Dec. 27, 1959; children—Andre Juliard, Paul Dudley, Charles Alexandre. Postdoctoral fellow U. Mich., 1957-59; research asso. Northwestern U., 1959-61; asst. prof., asso. prof. U. Del., 1961-66; asso. prof., prof. State U. N.Y. at Buffalo, 1966—, dir. Grad. Program in Social Psychology, 1969-73, 76—. Grantee Office Naval Research, 1965, NIMH, 1969, NSF, 1969, 74, 76, Guggenheim Found., 1978-79. Fellow Am. Psychol. Assn., Soc. for Psychol. Study Social Issues; mem. Phi Beta Kappa, Sigma Xi. Cons. editor: Jour. Applied Social Psychology. Editor: (with R.C. Snyder) Theory and Research on the Causes of War, 1969; Problem Solving in the Department of State, 1964. Home: 9006 Friars Rd Bethesda MD 20034 Office: 4230 Ridge Lea Rd Buffalo NY 14226

PRUITT, GREGORY DONALD, football player; b. Houston, Aug. 18, 1951; s. Herman and Maggie Lee P.; B.J., U. Okla. Running back Cleve. Browns, 1973—; played in Pro Bowl, 1973, 74, 76, 77. Office: care Cleve Browns Cleve Stadium Cleveland OH 44114*

PRUITT, MALCOLM EVERETT, chem. co. exec.; b. Hamilton, Tex., Oct. 15, 1915; s. Jesse F. and Mattie Knoxie (Stone) P.; B.S., Abilene Christian U., 1941, Ph.D. (hon.), 1973; m. Cleo Obannon, Jan. 14, 1938; children—Shirley, Ronnie. Sci. tchr. Clyde (Tex.) High Sch., 1936-42; with Dow Chem. Co., Midland, Mich., 1942—, dir. research and devel. Tex. div., 1966-71, dir. research and devel., v.p., 1971-75, v.p. research and devel., 1975—; chmn. bd. Chem. Industry Inst. Toxicology. Recipient Indsl. Research medal, 1977. Mem. Am. Chem. Soc., Soc. Chem. Industry. Patentee in field. Home: 4507 Linden Dr Midland MI 48640 Office: 2020 Dow Bldg Midland MI 48640

PRUITT, RAYMOND DONALD, physician, educator; b. Wheaton, Minn., Feb. 6, 1912; s. Lyman Burton and Ada (Brandes) P.; B.S., Baker U., 1933; B.A. (Rhodes Scholar), Oxford U., 1936; M.D., U. Kans., 1939; M.S., U. Minn., 1945; D.Sc., Baker U., 1956; m. Lillian Elaine Rasmussen, July 31, 1942; children—Virginia, Kristin, David, Charles. Intern U. Kan. Hosps., 1939-40; fellow medicine Mayo Found., 1940-43, prof. medicine, asso. dir. for med. edn. Mayo Found., 1954-59; cons. physician Mayo Clinic, 1943-59; instr. medicine U. Minn., 1945-48, asst. prof., 1948-52, asso. prof., 1952-55, prof., 1955-59; prof., chmn. dept. medicine Baylor U. Coll. Medicine, 1959-68, v.p. med. affairs, chief exec. officer, 1966-68; dir. Mayo Grad. Sch. Medicine, U. Minn., 1968-75, prof. medicine, 1968-77, dean, Mayo Med. Sch., 1972-77, emeritus, 1977—, dir. for medical edn. Mayo Found., 1968-77; prof. medicine Baylor Coll. Medicine, Houston, 1977-78; cons. in residence Meth. Hosp., Houston, 1977—; prof. medicine Mayo Med. Sch., Rochester, Minn., 1978—; cons. cardiovascular disease Mayo Clinic, Rochester, 1978—; mem. Nat. Adv. Research Resources Council, 1969-73; mem. nat. adv. heart council USPHS, 1964-68; mem. Pres.'s Commn. Heart Disease, 1972; chmn. credentials com. council clin. cardiology Am. Heart Assn., 1973-75. Diplomate Am. Bd. Internal Medicine (cardiovascular diseases). Mem. Central Clin. Research, AMA, Assn. Profs. Medicine, Assn. U. Cardiologists (pres. 1967), Assn. Am. Physicians, Am. Osler Soc. (pres. 1976-77), Sigma Xi, Alpha Omega Alpha. Methodist. Home: 780 Sierra Ln NE Rochester MN 55901 Office: Mayo Clinic Rochester MN 55901

PRUITT, SAMUEL ORR, JR., lawyer; b. Anderson, S.C., Dec. 26, 1919; s. Samuel Orr and Mary Burton (Cullum) P.; A.B. magna cum laude, Washington and Lee U., 1941; LL.B. cum laude, Harvard U., 1948; m. Martha-Jane Jones, Feb. 1, 1944; children—Robert Bruce, Sheryl Ann, Debra Kay. Admitted to Calif. bar, 1948, U.S. Supreme Ct. bar, 1967; partner firm Gibson, Dunn & Crutcher, Los Angeles, 1948—, mem. exec. com., 1969—. Served to lt. comdr. USNR, 1941-45. Fellow Am. Coll. Trial Lawyers, Am. Bar Found.; mem. Am. Bar Assn., State Bar Calif. (pres. 1968-69), Los Angeles County Bar Assn. (trustee 1964-66), Chancery Club Los Angeles (pres. 1971-72), Am. Judicature Soc., Am. Law Inst., Phi Beta Kappa. Home: 470 Prospect Terr Pasadena CA 91103 Office: 515 S Flower St Los Angeles CA 90071

PRUNTY, BERT SHERMAN, JR., lawyer; b. Des Moines, Jan. 4, 1924; s. Bert Sherman and Carrie Blanch (Quiner) P.; B.A., Drake U., 1947, J.D., 1950; m. Lois Bernice Cummins, Nov. 27, 1946; children—Randall Charles, Mary Lou, Bert Sherman, III. Admitted to Iowa bar, 1950, N.Y. bar, 1972, Maine bar, 1973; asst. prof. law N.Y. U., 1951-53, asso. prof., 1953-56, prof., 1956-73, asso. dean. 1967-73; prof. U. Maine, 1973—, dean, 1973-78; vis. prof. U. Calif. Hastings Sch. Law, 1977—, Duke U., 1978-79, Hebrew U., Jerusalem, 1972—, U. Naples (Italy), 1967—; cons. to numerous legis. and jud. bodies, N.Y., Maine. Served with U.S. Army, 1943-46. Mem. Am. Law Inst. Author: Not-for-Profit Corporation Law, 3 vols., 1973; contbr. numerous articles to law jours. Home: 882 Shore Rd Cape Elizabeth ME 04107 Office: 246 Deering Ave Portland ME 04102

PRUNTY, MERLE CHARLES, educator; b. St. Joseph, Mo., Mar. 2, 1917; s. Merle Charles and Emma Mae (Holliday) P.; B.S., U. Mo., 1939, A.B., 1940, A.M., 1940; Ph.D., Clark U., 1944; m. Eugenia Wyatt, June 3, 1939; children—Mary Merle, Eugene Wyatt, Florence Holliday. Grad. asst. U. Mo., 1939-40; grad fellow Clark U., 1940-42; asst. prof. geography Miss. State Coll., 1942-43, asso. prof. (on leave), 1943-46; prof., head dept. geography and geology U. Ga., 1946-61, prof., head dept. geography, 1961-70, Alumni Found. distinguished prof., 1969—, acting v.p. acad. affairs, 1977, sr. faculty adviser to pres., 1977-79; asst. to chancellor U. System of Ga., 1951; vis. prof. Northwestern U., 1954; cons. geographer Atlantic Steel Co., 1958—, Tara Plantation, Inc., 1959-62, Jefferson Mills, Inc., 1962-63, U.S. Office Edn., 1965-67; vis. lectr. Oglethorpe U., 1956, Antioch Coll., 1959, Miss. State U., 1965, U. Utah, 1965, Western Mich. U., 1966, U. Wis., 1968, Clark U., 1967, Duke U., 1967, U. Fla., 1968, U. Tenn., 1969, 78, U. S.C. 1970, 78, Auburn U., 1971, U. Ky., 1972, U. So. Miss., 1973, 75, U. Minn., La. State U., 1975, U. N.C., 1976, U. N.C.-Charlotte, 1977, Valdosta State Coll., 1977, others. Cons. to Ednl. Testing Service, 1964-69; cons. Pres.'s Com. Equal Employment Opportunity, 1961-64. U.S. nat. del. 20th Internat. Geog. Congress, London, 1964; co-chmn. 5th Nat. Conf. Fire Ecology, Tall Timbers Found., 1965. Guggenheim Found. fellow, 1957-58; Michael Found. Research fellow, 1961-62; recipient citation meritorious research contbns. Assn. Am. Geographers, 1963, field research award, 1953. Served as lt. USNR, 1943-46. Mem. adv. bd. USAF Air U. Library, 1950-56, vice chmn., 1951, chmn., 1952. Middle Am. com., Sect. Geography and Geology, NRC, 1948-50. Mem. Am. Geog. Soc., Assn. Am. Geographers (chmn. membership and credentials com. 1953-54, chmn. adv. com. to Air Force ROTC, 1954, chmn. honors and awards com. 1959-60, exec. com. 1953-55, 67-69, nat. program com. 1958, chmn. research grants com. 1962-63; S.E. div. mem. exec. com. 1947-69, pres. 1953-55, hon. life mem.), Nat. Council Geog. Edn. (dir. 1966-69), Am. Geophys. Union, Ga. Acad., Sci. (chmn. earth scis. div. 1949-50), Tenn. Acad. Sci., Internat. Geog. Union, Phi Kappa Phi, Alpha Kappa Delta, Sigma Nu. Democrat. Author: The Central Gulf South, 1960; Festschrift: Clarence F. Jones, Northwestern University Studies in Geography, No. 6, 1962. Editorial bd. U. Ga. Press, 1969-73, Southeastern Geographer, 1971—, Ga. Rev., 1974-77; cons. editor Macmillan Co., 1968—, Coronet Films, 1972-73, Ency. Brit. Ednl. Corp., 1978. Contbr. articles to profl. jours., several textbooks. Home: 255 Terrell Dr Athens GA 30606

PRUSMACK, JOHN JACOB, psychiatrist; b. N.Y.C., Mar. 13, 1911; s. Harry and Anna (Knopf) P.; B.S., U. Louisville, 1932, M.D., 1936, M.S., 1937; m. Gertrude Mary Dake, July 19, 1939; children—John, Kathleen (Mrs. Barton Graham), Thomas, Mary. Intern, Creighton Meml.-St. Josephs Hosp., Omaha, 1937-38; resident psychiatry Iowa State Hosp., Clarinda, 1938-40, supt., 1940-41; hosp. dir. VA Hosp., Palo Alto, 1946-64, chief psychiatry research, 1964-74; med. dir. Bur. Alcoholism Services Santa Clara County (Calif.) Pub. Health Dept., 1974—; pvt. practice, 1965-69. Instr., U. Louisville, 1936-37, Creighton U., 1945-46; asso. clin. prof. emeritus Stanford U. Med. Sch., 1949—; prof. emeritus St. Patrick's Coll., Menlo Park, Calif., 1965-72. Served to lt. col. M.C., AUS, 1941-46. Diplomate Am. Bd. Psychiatry and Neurology. Fellow Am. Psychiat. Assn. (life); mem. Santa Clara County (Cal.) Psychiat. Soc. (pres. emeritus), Alpha Omega Alpha. Contbr. articles to profl. jours. Home: 1264 Sharon Park Dr Menlo Park CA 94025 Office: Santa Clara County Pub Health Dept 976 Lenzen Ave San Jose CA 95128

PRUSOFF, WILLIAM HERMAN, educator, biochem. pharmacologist; b. N.Y.C., June 25, 1920; s. Samuel and Mary (Metrick) P.; B.A., U. Miami (Fla.), 1941; M.A., Columbia, 1947, Ph.D., 1949; m. Brigitte Auerbach, June 19, 1948; children—Alvin Saul, Laura Ann. Research asso., instr. pharmacology Western Res. U., 1949-53; mem. faculty Yale Med. Sch., 1953—, prof. pharmacology, 1966—, acting chmn. dept., 1968; cons. in field, 1965—. Mem. Am. Assn. Cancer Research, Am. Chem. Soc., Am. Soc. Biol. Chemists, Am. Soc. Pharmacology and Exptl. Therapeutics, Sigma Xi. Research in virology. photochemistry, mechanism drug action, synthesis potential drugs; synthesized Idoxuridine, 1959. Home: De Forest Dr Branford CT 06471 Office: Yale Sch Medicine Yale Univ New Haven CT 06510

PRUSSING, ELLIS MOULTON, mfg. co. exec.; b. Chgo., Apr. 5, 1919; s. Delbert Irwin and Jane P.; B.A., Oberlin Coll., 1942; M.B.A., Harvard U., 1947; m. Grace I. Wolvington, June 2, 1943; children—Cynthia L., Richard M., Kenneth W., Steven C. Vice-pres., gen. mgr. Baker Truck Rental, Inc., 1947-55; v.p. Ryder Truck Rental, Inc., Denver, 1955-64; v.p. Ryder System, Inc., Miami, Fla., 1964-67; exec. v.p. Aegis Corp., Coral Gables, Fla., 1967—, also dir.; dir. Suave Shoe Corp. Served with USNR, 1942-46. Presbyterian. Home: 1131 Manati Ave Coral Gables FL 33146 Office: 250 Catalonia Ave #705 Coral Gables FL 33134

PRUTER, KARL HUGO, bishop; b. Poughkeepsie, N.Y., July 3, 1920; s. William Karl and Katherine (Rehling) P.; B.A., Northeastern U., 1943; M.Div., Lutheran Theol. Sem., Phila., 1945; M.A. in Edn., Roosevelt U., 1963; M.A. in History, Boston U., 1968; m. Nancy Lee Taylor, 1943; children—Hugo Jr., Robert, Karl, Stephen, Maurice, Katherine, Nancy Goodman. Guest lectr. Landerziehungsheim, Stein, West Germany, 1964-65; ordained priest Christ Catholic Ch., 1965; pastor Ch. of the Transfiguration, Boston, 1965-70; presiding bishop Christ Cath. Ch. Author: Neo-Congregationalism, 1951; The Theology of Congregationalism, 1953; The Teachings of the Great Mystics, 1969; A History of the Old Catholic Church, 1973; The People of God, 1975. Home: 1638 W Granville Chicago IL 60660 Office: 1744 W Devon Ave Chicago IL 60660

PRUYN, WILLIAM J., utilities exec.; b. Boston, Aug. 25, 1922; s. William J. and Ida M. (Langan) P.; student Bentley Coll., 1939-41, Harvard U., 1944-45, 64; B.B.A., Northeastern U., 1948; m. Mary Anton, May 19, 1945; children—William J., Barbara, Marilyn, Ann Marie, Stephen, Christopher. Pub. accountant Meahl, McNamara & Co., 1946-51; with Eastern Gas & Fuel Assos., 1951—, sr. v.p., 1972-76, trustee, 1973—, pres., chief adminstrv. officer, 1976-77, pres., chief exec. officer, 1977—; dir. Algonquin Gas Transmission Co., Shawmut Corp., Shawmut Bank Boston, N.A. Bd. dirs. Med. Found., Inc., Boston Municipal Research Bur.; trustee Northeastern U., Mus. Sci.; bd. visitors Sch. Social Work, Boston U.; mem. Pres.'s adv. council Bentley Coll.; bd. dirs. United Way of Mass. Bay. Served with USNR. Mem. Greater Boston C. of C. (v.p.). Clubs: Algonquin, Union (Boston); Duquesne (Pitts.); Corinthian Yacht. Home: 422 Ocean Ave Marblehead MA 01945 Office: One Beacon St Boston MA 02108

PRYDE, BASIL RICHMOND, paper mfg. co. exec.; b. Travancore, South India, Mar. 9, 1924; s. James Richmond and Katharine (McNeil) P.; student Harvard Advanced Mgmt. Program, 1964; m. Mary Elizabeth Carson, Dec. 14, 1948. Joined woodlands dept. Bowaters Nfld. Ltd. (formerly Bowater's Nfld. Pulp & Paper Mills Ltd.), Corner Brook City, 1947, personal asst., to gen. mgr., 1948-51, asst. sec., 1951-56, asst. to pres., gen. mgr., 1956-64, asst. gen. mgr., 1965, v.p., 1966-68, pres., gen. mgr., 1968-73, also dir.; pres. Bowater Sales Co., 1973—; v.p. marketing Bowater, Inc., 1973—. Mem. Corner Brook City Council, 1956-62, City Commn., 1963-64; Served with Royal Armoured Corps, 1942-47. Mason. Clubs: Winged Foot Golf (Mamaroneck, N.Y.); Blomidon Country (Corner Brook). Home: 118 Butternut Hollow Rd Greenwich CT 06830 Office: 1500 E Putnam Ave Greenwich CT 06830

PRYNE, PHILLIP DONALD, electric appliance mfg. co. exec.; b. Los Angeles, Jan. 8, 1927; s. Ralph Rhodes and Esther Isabel (Angier) P.; B.Engring. cum laude, U. So. Calif.; children—Sydney, Teresa, Kathryn, Tyler. Pres. products div. Emerson Buider Co., St. Louis, 1962-64; v.p. operations U.S. Elec. Motors Co., 1964-68; pres. Thermador div. Norris Industries Inc., Los Angeles, 1968-72, sr. v.p. Norris Industries Inc., 1972—. Pres. Pryne Found., Los Angeles. Served with USNR. Mem. Elec. Industries Assn. (pres. 1971-73), Tau Beta Pi. Clubs: Los Angeles Yacht, Los Angeles Athletic. Home: 3448 Starline Rancho Palos Verdes CA 90274 Office: 5119 District Blvd Los Angeles CA 90040

PRYOR, DAVID HAMPTON, U.S. senator; b. Camden, Ark., Aug. 29, 1934; s. Edgar and Susan (Newton) P.; B.A. in Polit. Sci., U. Ark., 1957, LL.B., 1961; m. Barbara Lunsford, Nov. 27, 1957; children—David, Mark, Scott. Admitted to Ark. bar, 1964; practiced in Camden; mem. firm Pryor and Barnes; mem. Ark. Ho. of Reps., 1961-67; mem. 89th-92d Congresses from 4th Dist. Ark.; gov. Ark., 1974-79; senator from Ark., 1979—. Address: Russell Senate Office Bldg Washington DC 20510

PRYOR, HAROLD S., coll. pres.; b. Overton County, Tenn., Oct. 3, 1920; s. Hubert S. and Ethel (Stockton) P.; B.S., Austin Peay State U., 1946; M.A., George Peabody Coll., 1947; Ed.D., U. Tenn., 1951; m. LaRue Vaughn, June 26, 1946. Instr., George Peabody Coll., 1946-47, E. Tenn. State U., 1947-49, U. Tenn., Knoxville, 1949-51; head dept. edn. Austin Peay State U., 1952, dir. tchr. edn., 1954-68; pres. Columbia (Tenn.) State Community Coll., 1968—; dir. First Farmers and Merchants Nat. Bank, Columbia, 1970—; bd. trustees Cumberland Equity Trust, Clarksville, 1973—; pres. Columbia State Found., 1971—. Served with U.S. Army, 1943-46. Grantee Dept. Labor, HEW. Mem. Tenn. Coll. Assn. (past pres.), Tenn. Edn. Assn., NEA, Am. Assn. Higher Edn., Comparative Edn. Soc., Kappa Delta Pi, Phi Delta Kappa. Democrat. Presbyterian. Clubs: Kiwanis, Graymere Country. Contbr. articles to profl. jours. Home: 1002 Hillcrest Ave Columbia TN 38401 Office: Columbia State Community Coll Hampshire Pike Columbia TN 38401

PRYOR, HUBERT, magazine editor; b. Buenos Aires, Argentina, Mar. 18, 1916; s. John W. and Hilda A. (Cowes) P.; grad. St. George's Coll., Argentina, 1932; student U. London (Eng.), 1934-36; m. Ellen M. Ach, Sept. 25, 1940; children—Alan, Gerald, David; m. 2d, Roberta J. Baughman, Apr. 11, 1959; m. 3d, Luanne Williamson Van Norden, Oct. 31, 1967. Came to U.S., 1940, derivative citizenship. Corr. in S.Am. for United Press, 1937-39; pub. relations rep. Pan Am. Airways in Buenos Aires, 1939-40; reporter N.Y. Herald Tribune, 1940-41; writer, dir. short-wave newsroom, CBS, 1941-46; asst. mng. editor Knickerbocker Weekly, 1946-47; sr. editor Look mag., 1947-62; creative supr. Wilson, Haight & Welch, advt., 1962-63; editor Science Digest, 1963-67; mng. editor Med. World News, 1967; editor Modern Maturity, NRTA Jour., 1967—; editorial dir. Dynamic Years, 1977—. Served to lt. USNR, 1943-46. Mem. Am. Soc. Mag. Editors. Home: 44 Paloma Ave Long Beach CA 90803 Office: 215 Long Beach Blvd Long Beach CA 90801

PRYOR, JOHN PAUL, athletic ofcl.; b. Woonsocket, R.I., July 10, 1927; B.A., High Point (N.C.) Coll., 1952; postgrad. U. S.D., 1957; m. Frances Carleen Hammond, Aug. 1, 1952; children—Frederick, Paula Ross (dec.), Melanie, Patrick. Umpire profl. baseball, 1950—, with Nat. League, 1961—; umpire World Series, 1967, 73, also 3 All-Star Games, 3 championship playoffs; tchr. pub. schs., N.C., 1952-61, St. Lucy's Sch., Racine, Wis., 1962-67; basketball coach Dominican Coll., Racine, 1963-66, Shorecrest Sch., St. Petersburg, Fla., 1972-73, 73-74; owner Paul Pryor Travel & Sports Bags, Clearwater, Fla. Mem. Jaycees. Lion. Clubs: Monogram. Home: 1088 45th Ave NE Saint Petersburg FL 33703 Office: 1 Rockefeller Plaza New York NY 10020

PRYOR, JOSEPH EHRMAN, coll. dean; b. Melber, Ky., Mar. 19, 1918; s. Lonnie Ernest and Queetro Desdemona (Rives) P.; B.A., B.S., Harding Coll., Searcy, Ark., 1937; M.A., La. State U., 1939, Ph.D., 1943; student U. Minn., summers 1949, 55, U. Chgo., summer 1950; m. Bessie Mae Ledbetter, Aug. 16, 1946; children—Beverly Jo, Joseph Byron, Susan Rebecca. Teaching fellow math. La. State U., 1937-39, teaching fellow chemistry, 1939-41, Charles Edward Coates research fellow chemistry, 1941-42, instr. math., 1942-44; prof. phys. sci., chmn. dept. Harding Coll., 1944-62, dean coll., 1960—, v.p. acad. affairs, 1973—, distinguished alumnus award, 1974; research chemist Lion Oil Co., El Dorado, Ark., summer 1957. Mem. com. liberal arts edn. N. Central Assn., 1952-54, coordinator, 1963-69; faculty rep. Ark. Intercollegiate Athletic Conf., 1957—, pres., 1967-68, 77-78. Bd. dirs. Camp Wyldewood, Searcy, 1948-51. Fellow AAAS; mem. Am. Chem. Soc. (chmn. central Ark. sect. 1954-55, sect. councilor 1959-65), Am. Sci. Affiliation, Ark. Acad. Sci., Nat., Ark. (2d v.p. dept. higher edn. 1964-65, pres. dept. 1965-66) edn. assns., Ark. Deans Assn. (past chmn.), Nat. Council Coll. Publs. Advisers (dist. chmn. 1973-75, distinguished yearbook adviser award 1973), Assn. Coll. Honor Socs. (exec. com. 1976-80), Searcy C. of C., Alpha Phi Gamma, Sigma Xi, Alpha Chi (nat. council 1959—, sec.-treas. region II, 1959-71, nat. sec.-treas. 1970—), Phi Kappa Phi, Alpha Psi Omega, Sigma Delta Psi, Alpha Chi Sigma, Phi Lambda Upsilon, Kappa Mu Epsilon, Pi Kappa Delta, Delta Mu Delta. Mem. Ch. of Christ (preacher, elder). Home: 924 E Center St Searcy AR 72143

PRYOR, RICHARD, actor; b. Peoria, Ill., Dec. 1, 1940; s. Leroy and Gertrude (Thomas) P.; grad. high sch.; children—Elizabeth Ann, Richard, Rain, Renee. Appeared on Ed Sullivan, Merv Griffin and Johnny Carson television shows in 1960's; appeared in motion pictures Lady Sings the Blues, 1972, Hit, 1973, Wattstax, 1973, Uptown Saturday Night, 1974, Blue Collar, 1978, California Suite, 1978, The Wiz, 1978, Richard Pryor Live in Concert, 1979; writer scripts for Sanford and Son, Flip Wilson; co-writer TV spls. for Lily Tomlin (Emmy award), 1973; co-writer movie script Blazing Saddles (Am. Writers Guild award, Am. Acad. Humor award), 1973; script writer movie Lily (Am. Acad. Humor award), 1974, Adios Amigos, 1976; The Bing Long Traveling All-Starts and Motor Kings, 1976, Car Wash, 1976, Silver Streak, 1976, Greased Lightening, 1977; Which Way is Up?, 1977, Blue Collar, 1978; recorded That Nigger's Crazy (Grammy award, certified Gold and Platinum album), 1974, Bicentennial Nigger (Grammy award), 1976; star Richard Pryor Show NBC-TV, 1977; owner Richard Pryor Enterprises, Inc., Los Angeles, 1975—. Served with U.S. Army, 1958-60. Mem. Nat. Acad. Recording Arts and Scis., Writers Guild Am. Office: care Writers Guild Am West Inc 8955 Beverly Blvd Los Angeles CA 90048*

PRYOR, WILLIAM AUSTIN, educator; b. St. Louis, Mar. 10, 1929; s. Saul Arnold and Adeline (Franzel) P.; Ph.B., U. Chgo., 1948, B.S., 1951; Ph.D., U. Calif. at Berkeley, 1954; m. Elsa Felicia Anne Yoder, Dec. 22, 1962. Chemist, Calif. Research Corp., Richmond, 1954-60; lectr. U. Calif. at Berkeley, 1956-60; asst. prof. Purdue U., Lafayette, Ind., 1960-63; asso. prof. La. State U., Baton Rouge, 1963-67, prof., 1967-72, Boyd prof. chemistry, 1972—; vis. prof. Washington U., St. Louis, 1968, UCLA, 1970, U. Calif. at Berkeley, 1971, Duke U., 1978, U. Calif., Davis, 1978, U. Calif., San Diego, 1978; cons. to chem. co., 1963—. NIH grantee, 1964—; NSF grantee, 1964—; Air Force Office Sci. Research grantee, 1964-68; AEC grantee, 1960-64; U.S. Army grantee, 1965-69; Dow Chem. Co. grantee, 1964—. Distinguished Faculty fellow La. State U. Found., 1969; NIH Spl. Postdoctoral fellow, 1970-71; John Simon Guggenheim fellow, 1970-71. Fellow Am. Inst. Chemists; mem. Am. Chem. Soc. (Southwest sect. award 1975, Petroleum Chemistry award 1980), Chem. Soc. London, AAAS, Faraday Soc., Gerontological Soc., Radiation Research Soc., Am. Aging Assn., Pan-Am. Med. Assn. (hon. life). Author books including: Free Radicals, 1966; (with Melvin Calvin) Organic Chemistry of Life, 1973; Organic Free Radicals, 1978; Free Radicals in Biology, vols. I and II, 1976, vol. III, 1977; also numerous articles. Editorial bd. internat. jours. in chemistry and gerontology. Patentee in field. Home: 3631 S Lakeshore Dr Baton Rouge LA 70808 Office: Dept Chemistry La State U Baton Rouge LA 70803

PRYSTOWSKY, HARRY, physician, educator; b. Charleston, S.C., May 18, 1925; s. Moses Manning and Raye (Karesh) P.; B.S., The Citadel, 1944, D.Sc., 1974; M.D., Med. Coll. S.C., 1948, L.H.D., 1975; m. Rhalda Betsy Bressler, Mar. 8, 1951; children—Michael Wayne, Ray Ellen, Jay Bressler. Intern Johns Hopkins Hosp. and Med. Sch., 1948-49, resident, 1950-51, 53-55, instr., 1955-56, asst. prof., 1956-58; research fellow U. Cin. Sch. Medicine, 1949; research fellow physiology Yale Med. Sch., 1955-56; prof., chmn. obstetrics and gynecology U. Fla. Coll. Medicine, 1958-73; provost Milton S. Hershey Med. Center, Pa. State U., 1973—, dean Coll. Medicine, 1973—. Cons. surgeon general USAF, Served as capt., M.C., U.S. Army, 1951-53. Named 1 of 10 outstanding young men U.S. Jr. C. of C. Diplomate Am. Bd. Obstetrics and Gynecology (dir., asso. examiner). Fellow A.C.S. (gov.); mem. AMA, Council of Deans, Assn. Am. Med. Colls., Assn. Acad. Health Centers, AAAS, A.M.A., Soc. Gynecol. Investigation, Am. Coll. Obstetrics and Gynecology, Am. Assn. Obstetricians and Gynecologists, Am. Fedn. Clin. Research, Pa. Med. Soc., Am. Gynecol. Soc., S. Atlantic Assn. Obstetricians and Gynecologists, N.Y. Acad. Scis., Assn. Profs. Gynecology and Obstetrics (pres.), U. Fla. Alumni Assn. (hon.), Alpha Omega Alpha. Contbr. articles to med. jours. Home: 1141 Cocoa Ave Hershey PA 17033

PRZEMIENIECKI, JANUSZ STANISLAW, engring. coll. dean; b. Lipno, Poland, Jan. 30, 1927; s. Leon and Maria (Sarnacka) P.; B.S., U. London, 1949, Ph.D., 1958; diploma Imperial Coll. Sci. and Tech. in Aeros., 1953; m. Stefania Rudnicka, July 17, 1954; children—Anita, Christopher. Came to U.S., 1961, naturalized, 1967. Head structural research and devel. sect. Bristol Aircraft Ltd. (Eng.), 1954-61; asso. prof. Sch. Engring Air Force Inst. Tech., Wright-Patterson AFB, Ohio, 1961-64, prof. mechanics, 1964-66, asst. dean, asso. dean research, 1966-69, dean, 1969—; cons. in field. Recipient USAF superior performance award, 1965, exceptional civilian service decoration, 1978; registered profl. engr., Ohio. Fellow Royal Aeros. Soc. (Usborne meml. prize 1959); asso. fellow Am. Inst. Aeros. and Astronautics; mem. Am. Soc. Engring. Edn., Nat. Soc. Profl. Engrs., Ohio Acad. Sci., Tau Beta Pi. Author: Theory of Matrix Structural Analysis, 1968. Asso. editor: Jour. Aircraft, 1970-71. Editorial bd. Internat. Jour. Numerical Methods in Engring., 1969-75. Contbr. articles to profl. jours. Home: 2535 Valdina Dr Xenia OH 45385 Office: Air Force Inst Tech Wright-Patterson AFB OH 45433

PSOMIADES, HARRY JOHN, educator; b. Boston, Sept. 8, 1928; s. John and Koula (Yalmanides) P.; B.A., Boston U., 1953; M.Internat. Affairs, Columbia, 1955, certificate Middle East Inst., 1956, Ph.D. (Ford Found. fellow), 1962; m. Dorothy Smith, Aug. 18, 1962; children—Kathy Alexis, Christine Anne. Lectr. govt. Columbia, 1959-65, asst. dean Grad. Sch. Internat. Affairs, 1959-65, dir. Carnegie Endowment Fellowships in Diplomacy, 1959-71; asso. prof. polit. sci. Queens Coll., City U. N.Y., 1965-69, prof., 1970—, chmn. dept. polit. sci., 1967-71, dep. exec. officer Ph.D. program in polit. sci., 1975-76, program dir. seminar on the modern Greek state, 1976—, dir. Center Byzantine and Modern Greek Studies, 1976—; cons. faculty U.S. Army Command and Gen. Staff Coll., 1968—; U.S. Dept. State Fgn. Service Inst., 1968-71; mem. screening com. Fgn. Area Fellowships Program for Asia and Middle East Joint Com., Social Sci. Research Council and Am. Council Learned Socs., 1967-69. Served with U.S. Army, 1946-50. Hon. fellow Soc. Macedonian Studies, Thessaloniki, Greece, 1970—. Fellow Middle East Studies Assn. N.Am.; mem. Am. Polit. Sci. Assn., Middle East Inst., Modern Greek Studies Assn. (mem. exec. com. 1972—), Phi Beta Kappa. Greek Orthodox. Author: Greece and Turkey: Mutual Economic Interests, 1964; (with Thomas Spelios) A Pictorial History of the Greeks, 1967; The Eastern Question: The Last Phase, 1968; Foreign Interference in Greek Politics, An Historical Perspective, 1976. Contbr. articles to profl. jours. Home: 440 Riverside Dr New York City NY 10027 Office: Dept Polit Sci Queens Coll Flushing NY 11367

PUCCETTI, ROLAND PETER, educator; b. Oak Park, Ill., Aug. 11, 1924; s. George and Marie (McKone) P.; B.A., U. Ill., 1948; M.A., U. Toronto, 1950; D.de l'U., U. Paris, 1952; m. Jeanne Marie-Rose Maroun, Nov. 7, 1959; children—Maia Clara, Peter Harry. From instr. to asso. prof. philosophy Am. U. Beirut (Lebanon), 1954-65, asst. dean faculty arts and scis., 1962-64; prof. philosophy, head dept. U. Singapore, 1965-71, pres. acad. staff assn., 1970; prof. philosophy, chmn. dept. Dalhousie U., 1971-76, pres. faculty assn., 1976-77. Fulbright lectr. U. Singapore, 1965-67; Can. Council fellow, 1977-78. Served with AUS, 1942-44. Mem. AAUP (v.p. Am. U. Beirut chpt. 1964-65), Am., Canadian philos. assns., Sigma Nu. Author: Persons: A Study of Possible Moral Agents in the Universe, 1968; (novels) The Death of the Fuehrer, 1972, The Trial of John and Henry Norton, 1973; also articles. Home: 14 Oceanview Dr Purcell's Cove Halifax NS B3P 2H3 Canada Office: Dept Philosophy Dalhousie U Halifax NS B3H 3J5 Canada

PUCCIANI, ORESTE FRANCESCO, educator; b. Cleve., Apr. 7, 1916; s. Ettore and Eugenie (Williams) P.; B.A. (Ohio fellow), Western Res. U., 1939; M.A., Harvard, 1940, Ph.D., 1943. Instr. French and Italian, Harvard, 1943-46, 47-48; mem. faculty U. Calif. at Los Angeles, 1948—, prof. French, 1960-79, prof. emeritus, 1979—, chmn. dept., 1961-66, affiliated prof. Sch. Edn., 1973-77. Decorated chevalier Légion d'Honneur. Sheldon travelling fellow, Harvard, 1946-47. Hon. bd. dirs. Lycée Francais De Los Angeles. M.B.L.S. Mem. Am. Soc. French Legion of Honor, Fedn. Internationale des Professeurs de Français, Am. Assn. Tchrs. French, Modern Lang. Assn. So. Calif., Alliance Française Los Angeles (hon.), Phi Beta Kappa. Author: The French Theatre since 1930, 1954; (with J. Hamel) Langue Et Langage, 1967, rev. edits., 1974, 79, Langue Et Langage Le Manuel Du Professeur, 1967, 74, 79; (with J. Barcia & J. Hamel) Lengua y Cultura: El Manual del instructor, 1973; Jean Paul Sartre, Histoire de la Philosophie III, Encyclopedie de la Pléiade, 1974; also articles. Editor: Le Voyeur (Alain Robbe-Grillet) 1970. Translator: (Racine) Phaedra, 1960; (Oscar Panizza) The Council of Love, 1973. Home: 2192 Beech Knoll Rd Los Angeles CA 90046

PUCHTA, CHARLES GEORGE, lawyer; b. Cin., Feb. 19, 1918; s. Charles George and Kate (Carlisle) P.; B.A., U. Cin., 1940, LL.B., J.D., 1943; m. Jean Geary, Dec. 12, 1959; children—Polly Carlisle, Charles George. Admitted to Ohio bar, 1943, since practice in Cin.; partner firm Frost & Jacobs, 1953—, chmn. ops. com., 1979—; sec., dir. Ames Travel Service, Inc., Anchor Paper Co., Barrows Corp.; dir. King Kwik Minit Market Inc. Pres. Cin. Nature Center, 1979—; trustee U. Cin. Endowment Fund, 1979—, U. Cin. Found., 1978—; mem. president's council Xavier U., Cin., 1978—; chmn. Bus. Mobilized for Xavier campaign, 1976; co-founder Father O'Connor Club, Xavier U., 1976; past trustee, sec. Cin. Country Day Sch. Mem. Am. Bar Assn., Ohio Bar Assn., Cin. Bar Assn., Cin. C. of C. (pres. 1978, pres. found. 1978). Republican. Episcopalian. Clubs: Cin. Country, Comml., Commonwealth, Queen City, Recess (past pres.). Home: 8375 Eustis Farm Ln Cincinnati OH 45263 Office: 2500 Central Trust Tower 201 E 5th St Cincinnati OH 45202

PUCINSKI, ROMAN C., city ofcl.; b. May 13, 1919; student Northwestern U., John Marshall Law Sch.; m. Aurelia Bordin, Dec. 26, 1945; children—Aurelia Marie, Christopher Bordin. Staff reporter, writer Chgo. Sun Times, 1938-58; mem. 86th, 87th, 88th-92d congresses from 11th Ill. Dist., chmn. gen. subcom. edn. of house edn. and labor com.; alderman City of Chgo., 1973—. Served to capt. USAAF, World War II. Decorated Air medal with clusters, D.F.C. Democrat. Office: 6200 N Milwaukee Ave Chicago IL 60646

PUCK, THEODORE THOMAS, educator, geneticist, biophysicist; b. Chgo., Sept. 24, 1916; s. Joseph and Bessie (Shapiro) Puckowitz; B.S., U. Chgo., 1937, Ph.D., 1940; m. Mary Hill, Apr. 17, 1946; children—Stirling, Jennifer, Laurel. Mem. commn. airborne infections Army Epidemiological Bd., Office Surgeon Gen., 1944-46; asst. prof. depts. medicine and biochemistry U. Chgo., 1945-47; sr. fellow Am. Cancer Soc., Calif. Inst. Tech., Pasadena, 1947-48; prof. biophysics U. Colo. Med. Sch., 1948—, Chmn. dept., 1948-67, dir. Eleanor Roosevelt Inst. Cancer Research, 1962—; life-time research prof. Am. Cancer Soc., 1967—. Nat. lectr. Sigma Xi, 1975-76; mem. Commn. on Physicians for the Future. Recipient Albert Lasker award, 1958; Borden award med. research, 1959; Louisa Gross Horwitz prize, 1973; Gordon Wilson medal Am. Clin. and Climatological Assn., 1977. Fellow Am. Acad. Arts and Scis.; mem. Am. Chem. Soc., Soc. Exptl. Biology and Medicine, A.A.A.S., Am. Assn. Immunologists, Radiation Research Soc., Biophys. Soc., Genetics Soc. Am., Nat. Acad. Sci., Inst. Medicine, Phi Beta Kappa, Sigma Xi. Author: The Mammalian Cell as a Microorganism: Genetic and Biochemical Studies in Vitro, 1972. Address: 10 S Albion St Denver CO 80222. *Our age is threatened by distorted emphasis on power, material wealth, and competitiveness, and by an explosive increase in population which exceeds our traditional regulative capacities. But it also holds promise for new and profound understanding of ourselves-of our basic human biological intellectual and emotional needs. There is room for hope.*

PUCKETT, ALLEN EMERSON, aero. engr.; b. Springfield, Ohio, July 25, 1919; s. Roswell C. and Catherine C. (Morrill) P.; B.S., Harvard, 1939, M.S., 1941; Ph.D., Calif. Inst. Tech., 1949; m. Betty J. Howlett; children—Allen W., Nancy L., Susan E.; m. 2d, Marilyn I. McFarland; children—Margaret A., James R. Lectr. aeros., chief wind tunnel sect. Jet Propulsion Lab., Calif. Inst. Tech., 1945-49; tech. cons. U.S. Army Ordnance, Aberdeen Proving Ground, Md., 1945—, mem. sci. adv. com. Ballistic Research Labs., 1958—; with Hughes Aircraft Co., Culver City, Calif., 1949—, exec. v.p., 1965-77, pres., 1977-78, chmn. bd., chief exec. officer, 1978—; mem. steering group OASD adv. panel on aeros.; cons. Pres.'s Sci. Adv. Com.; chmn. research adv. com. control, guidance and navigation NASA, 1959-64; vice chmn. Def. Sci. Bd., 1962-66; cons. ops. evaluation group Chief Naval Ops., 1960—; mem. Army Sci. Adv. Panel, 1965-69; mem. NASA tech. and research adv. com., 1968—, space program adv. council, 1974—. Recipient Lawrence Sperry award Inst. Aero. Scis., 1949, Lloyd V. Berkner award Am. Astronautical Soc., 1974. Fellow Am. Inst. Aeros. and Astronautics (pres. 1972); mem. Aerospace Industries Assn. (chmn. 1979), Nat. Acad. Scis., Nat. Acad. Engring., A.A.A.S., Sigma Xi, Phi Beta Kappa. Author: (with Hans W. Liepmann) Introduction to Aerodynamics of a Compressible Fluid, 1947; editor: (with Simon Ramo) Guided Missile Engineering, 1959; contbr. tech. papers on high-speed aerodynamics. Home: 935 Corsica Dr Pacific Palisades CA 90272 Office: Hughes Aircraft Co Centinela and Teale St Culver City CA 90230

PUCKETT, ROBERT HUGH, polit. scientist, educator; b. Kansas City, Mo., July 16, 1935; s. John William and Marjorie (Shirlaw) P.; B.A., De Pauw U., 1957; M.A., U. Chgo., 1958, Ph.D., 1961; m. Barbara Ann Chandley, Dec. 23, 1964; 1 dau., Sarah Anne. Asst. prof. polit. sci. Mary Washington Coll., Fredericksburg, Va., 1961-63; vis. scholar, postdoctoral fellow social sci. research council M.I.T., Cambridge, 1963-64; asst. prof. govt. and fgn. affairs U. Va., Charlottesville, 1964-66; asst. prof. social sci. Mich. State U., East Lansing, 1966-68; prof. polit. sci. Ind. State U., Terre Haute, 1968—; cons. in field. Bd. dirs. So. Ind. Health Systems Agy., 1978—. Mem. DePauw U. Alumni Assn. (pres. chpt. 1973-74), Am. Polit. Sci. Assn., Indpls. Com. Fgn. Relations, Midwest Polit. Sci. Assn., Internat. Studies Assn., So. Polit. Sci. Assn., Ind. Acad. Social Scis., Ind. Polit. Sci. Assn. (v.p. 1977-79), Phi Beta Kappa, Phi Eta Sigma. Kiwanian (dir. 1975-79). Author: America Faces the World: Isolationist Ideology in American Foreign Policy, 1972; (with Oscar H. Rechtschaffer) Reflections on Space, 1964. Contbr. articles to polit. sci. jours. Home: 122 Marigold Dr Terre Haute IN 47803

PUCKETTE, STEPHEN ELLIOTT, coll. dean; b. Ridgewood, N.J., Oct. 18, 1927; s. Charles McDonald and Elizabeth Argyle (Gettys) P.; B.S., U. of South, Sewanee, Tenn., 1949; M.S., Yale, 1950, M.A., 1951, Ph.D., 1957; postgrad. Université de Nancy, 1952-53; m. Upshur Smith, June 22, 1957; children—Robert, Miller, Emily, Charles, Charlotte. Asst. prof., asso. prof. math. U. of South, 1956-66, prof. math., dean of Coll., 1969-79; vis. asst. prof. math. U. Ga., 1962-63; asso. prof. math. U. Ky., 1966-69; Fulbright lectr. U. Ivory Coast, Abidjan, 1979-80. Served with USNR, 1945-46. NSF Sci. Faculty fellow, 1964-65. Mem. Math. Assn. Am. (Cons. Bur.), Am., London math. socs., Société Mathematique de France, Deutsche Mathematiker Vereinigung. Home: Morgan's Steep Sewanee TN 37375

PUDNEY, GARY LAURENCE, television exec.; b. Mpls., July 20, 1934; s. Lawrence D. and Agnes (Hansen) P.; B.A., UCLA, 1956. Vice-pres., ABC, Inc., N.Y.C., 1968—, v.p. spl. projects, sr. exec. in charge of talent ABC Entertainment, 1979—. Served to capt. USAF, 1957-60. Bd. dirs. Nat. Cerebral Palsy Found. Mem. Hollywood Radio and TV Soc., Acad. TV Arts and Scis. Democrat. Lutheran. Office: ABC Entertainment 2040 Ave of the Stars Century City CA

PUENTE, TITO ANTHONY, orch. leader, composer; b. N.Y.C., Apr. 20, 1923; s. Ernest Anthony and Ercilia (Ortiz) P.; student Julliard Conservatory Music, N.Y. Sch. Music, Schillinger System; m. Margaret Asencio, Oct. 19, 1963; children—Ronald, Audrey, Tito Anthony. Orch. leader appearing in numerous night clubs and ballrooms throughout U.S., 1949—; host weekly television show El Mundo de Tito Puente, 1968; grand marshal Puerto Rican Day Parade, 1968; appeared in concert at Avery Fisher Hall, N.Y.C., 1977, 78; appeared in concert at Monterey (Calif.) Jazz Festival, 1976, Radio City Music Hall, N.Y.C., 1979, Newport Jazz Festival, Symphony Hall, Boston, 1979, Bronx Community Coll. Festival, 1979; 90 recs. for RCA and Tico Rec. Co. Served with USN, 1942-45. Recipient Bronze medallion City of N.Y., 1969, Key to City Los Angeles, 1976; Grammy award, 1978; named Musician of Month on several occasions by Downbeat, Metronome, Playboy and trade mags., 1950's; King of Latin Music, La Prensa newspaper, 1955; Goodwill Ambassador for tourism of P.R., 1979; his band named Best Latin Am. Orch., New York Daily News, 1977. Composer: Para Los Rumberos, 1960; Dye Como Va, 1962; numerous others. Office: care Joe Conzo 1144 Pelham Pkwy Bronx NY 10461

PUFFER, RICHARD JUDSON, coll. pres.; b. Chgo., Aug. 20, 1931: s. Noble Judson and Lillian Katherine (Olson) P.; Ph.B., Ill. Wesleyan U., 1953; M.S. in Edn., Ill. State U., 1962; Ph.D. (Univ. scholar 1965-66, Roy Clark Meml. scholar 1966—), Northwestern U., 1967; m. Alison Foster Cope, June 28, 1952; children—Lynn, Mark, Andrew. Asst. plant supt. J.A. Olson Co., Winona, Miss., 1957-59; tchr., prin. Community United Dist. 7, Lexington, Ill., 1959-62; asst. county supt. schs. Cook County, Ill., 1962-65; dean arts and scis. Kirkwood Community Coll., Cedar Rapids, Iowa, 1967-69; v.p. Black Hawk Coll., Moline, Ill., 1969-77, pres., 1977—; dir. W. Central Ill. Ednl. TV Corp., Springfield, Ill., 1977—; cons. examiner North Central Assn., 1978—. Bd. dirs. Cedar Rapids Symphony, 1967-69, United Way of Rock Island and Scott Counties (Ill.), 1978—, Illowa council Boy Scouts Am., 1979—. Served with Supply Corps, USNR, 1953-57. Mem. Public Community Coll. Presidents Assn. (mem. Ill. council), Green Medallion, Blue Key, Pi Gamma, Phi Delta Kappa. Clubs: Rotary (pres. 1975-76) (East Moline, Ill.); Masons. Editor Cook County Ednl. Digest, 1962-65. Home: 1119 20th Ave East Moline IL 61244 Office: 6600 34th Ave Moline IL 61265

PUGH, DAVID ARTHUR, architect; b. Pitts., Aug. 10, 1926; s. George Arthur and Ellen (Burton) P.; B.Arch., Yale, 1947; m. Patricia Ann Lawton, Dec. 21, 1948; children—Ellen Burton, Margaret Lawton, David Arthur, Douglas Burton. With SOM & Gardner A. Dailey, 1948-49; designer Gardner A. Dailey & Assos., 1950-51, Skidmore, Owings & Merrill, 1952 (all San Francisco); designer Skidmore, Owings & Merrill, Portland, Oreg., 1952-55, participating asso., 1955-59, asso., 1959-63, gen. partner, 1963—. Mem. adv. com. Region 10, GSA, 1968-70; adv. panel West Front of Capitol, AIA, Washington, 1979—. Pres., Contemporary Crafts Gallery 1963-66. Bd. dirs. Pacific N.W. Ballet Assn.; finance chmn. Portland State U. Found., 1969-70, pres., 1972-73; chmn. bd. Human Resources Council Oreg., 1971-75; bd. dirs. Portland Symphony Soc., 1973-79. Portland Civic Theater, 1973—. Fellow AIA (nat. v.p. 1973, dir. Portland chpt. 1965-66, chancellor Coll. of Fellows 1978-79); mem. Oreg. Hist. Soc., Portland C. of C., Portland Art Assn. Rotarian. Prin. works include: Portland Hilton Hotel, 1961, Memorial Coliseum, Portland, 1960, Portland Center, urban renewal, 1967, Ga.-Pacific hdqrs. bldg., Portland, 1970, Pacific Nat. Bank Wash. hdqrs. bldg., Tacoma, 1970, Autzen Stadium, U. Oreg., 1968, Salishan, beach resort, Gleneden Beach, Oreg., 1965; U.S. Nat. Bank Ore. hdqrs., Portland, 1973; Portland Transit Mall, 1978. Home: 16755 SW Graef Circle Lake Oswego OR 97034 Office: Skidmore Owings & Merrill 900 SW 5th St Portland OR 97204

PUGH, EDMUND WRIGHT, JR., corp. exec.; b. Los Angeles, Jan. 15, 1920; s. Edmund Wright and Wanda Elizabeth (Holley) P.; A.B., Stanford, 1941; M.B.A., Harvard, 1943; m. Patricia Ann Padgett, Sept. 17, 1945; children—David Francis, James Richard, Elizabeth Louise. Asst. dean Grad. Sch. Bus. Adminstrn., Harvard, 1946-48; asst. to treas. The Coca-Cola Co., 1948-49, asst. treas., 1949-52, treas., 1952-59; v.p. CBS, 1959-65; adminstrv. v.p., dir. Lever Bros. Co., 1965-67; v.p. finance and corp. strategy Weyerhaeuser Co., Tacoma, 1967-69; v.p. corp. planning Avon Products, Inc., 1969-72, v.p. fin., 1972—. Trustee Burke Found., Osborn Home. Served to capt. USAAF, 1943-46. Mem. Phi Beta Kappa, Delta Chi. Republican. Episcopalian. Clubs: Apawamis, Am. Yacht (Rye); University, Links (N.Y.C.). Home: 105 Stuyvesant Ave Rye NY 10580 Office: 9 W 57th St New York NY 10019

PUGH, GEORGE WILLARD, legal educator; b. Napoleonville, La., Aug. 17, 1925; s. William Whitmell and Evelyn (Foley) P.; B.A., La. State U., 1947, J.D., 1950; J.S.D., Yale, 1952; m. Jean Earle Hemphill, Sept. 6, 1952; children—William Whitmell III, George Willard, David Nicholls, James Hemphill. Admitted to La. bar, 1950; instr. La. State U. Law Sch., 1950, mem. faculty, 1952—, prof. law, 1959—, faculty summer session abroad U. Thessaloniki, Greece, summer 1974; mem. faculty summer program U. San Diego, Paris, 1977; part-time research cons. La. State Law Inst., 1953-54; 1st jud. adminstr. Jud. Council Supreme Ct. La., 1954-56; vis. prof. U. Tex., summer 1961; vis. Doherty prof. law U. Va., 1966-67; mem. faculty orientation program in Am. law Assn. Am. Law Schs., 1968, law teaching clinic, summer 1969; cons. La. State U.S. Vietnam Legal Adminstrn. Project, 1969. Bd. dirs. Legal Aid Soc. Baton Rouge, 1965—, chmn. 1963-64; adv. bd. St. Alban's Episcopal Student Center, La. State U., 1965-68, 70-72. Served with AUS, World War II. Fellow Comparative Study Adminstrn. Justice, 1962-65. Mem. Am., La., Baton Rouge bar assns., Order of Coif, Omicron Delta Kappa, Lambda Chi Alpha. Democrat. Episcopalian. Author: Louisiana Evidence Law, 1974, supplement, 1978. Co-author: Cases and Materials on the Administration of Criminal Justice, 2d edit., 1969. Home: 167 Sunset Blvd Baton Rouge LA 70808

PUGH, HERBERT LAMONT, ret. naval officer, physician, author; b. Batesville, Va., Feb. 5, 1895; s. Samuel Eli and Mary Elizabeth (Thompson) P.; B.S., M.D., U. Va., 1923; postgrad. surgery U. Pa., 1928, thoracic surgery Barnes Hosp., St. Louis, 1940; LL.D., Wagner Coll.; m. Martha Catherine Schmidt, June 30, 1926; 1 son, Lamont. Student interne, Martha Jefferson Hosp., Charlottesville, Va., 1923; commd. lt. (j.g.) USN, 1923, advancing to rank of rear adm., 1946; dep. and assistant chief Bur. Medicine and Surgery, Navy Dept., 1946-51; surg. gen. USN, chief Bur. Medicine and Surgery, 1951-55; insp. gen., med. dept. USN, 1955; comdg. officer Nat. Naval Med. Center, Bethesda, Md., 1955-56; ret. from active duty, 1956; univ. physician George Washington U., 1956-68; med. dir. Navy-Marine Corps-Coast Guard Residence (Vinson Hall), 1969-79; profl. attendance at various med. facilities, including clinics of Vienna. Trustee Navy-Marine Corps-Coast Guard Residence Found.; past bd. govs. ARC. Served with U.S. Marine Corps during World War I. Decorated Commendation Ribbon, Marine Good Conduct and Expeditionary medals, Victory medal, 2d Nicaraguan Campaign medal, Nat. Def. Service medal, Asiatic-Pacific Area Campaign medal, World War II Victory medal, Korean Service medal, Korean Presdl. citation, UN Service medal; recip. Outstanding Alumnus award U. Va. Club of Washington; Am. Podiatry Assn.'s award for Distinguished Service; Wisdom Award Honor, Wisdom Soc. Diplomate Am. Bd. Surgery, Am. Bd. Preventive Medicine and Pub. Health, Nat. Bd. Med. Examiners (former mem.). Fellow A.C.S., Am. Surg. Assn.; hon. fellow Internat. Coll. Surgeons, Am. Assn. for Surgery of Trauma, Am. Coll. Hosp. Adminstrs., Am. Coll. Chest Physicians; mem. Med. Soc. of Va., Alexandria Med. Soc., A.M.A. (past mem. ho. of dels., past chmn. mil. med. sect.), Assn. Mil. Surgeons, Soc. Med. Cons. to Armed Forces, Med. Soc. D.C. (hon.), Washington Acad. Surgery (hon.), Acad. Medicine Washington (hon.), U. Va. Med. Alumni Assn., Soc. of Cincinnati, Alpha Omega Alpha, Phi Beta Kappa, Omicron Delta Kappa, Raven Soc. (U. Va.). Presbyn. Mason. Clubs: Cosmos (Washington); Explorer's (N.Y.C.); Farmington Country (Charlottesville, Va.). Author: History of the Medical Department of U.S. Navy, 1945-55, 1958; Navy Surgeon, 1959; also articles to sci. jours. and various lay publs. Office: Carl Vinson Hall 6251 Old Dominion Dr McLean VA 22101. *A conviction that people tend to rust out much more readily than wear out has prompted me to keep active and to hold before me a vision of the future. It is not what one obtains from life but what one contributes to life that is important.*

PUGH, OLIN SHARPE, educator; b. Prosperity, S.C., Mar. 6, 1923; s. Joseph E. and Martha (Counts) P.; student Newberry Coll., 1942-43; B.S., U. S.C., 1948; A.M., Duke U., 1949, Ph.D., 1956; m. Louise Ewell, Sept. 3, 1949; children—Catherine, Walter, Ernest. Instr., asst. prof., asso. prof., prof. econs. U. S.C., Columbia, 1949-61, prof. banking and finance, holder chair banking, 1961—, acting dean Coll. Bus. Adminstrn., 1966-67, dir. grad. studies Coll. Bus. Adminstrn., 1967-71, dir. Bur. Bus. and Econ. Research, 1971-78. Research dir. Small Bus. Finance Project and Food Products Study, 1959-61; ednl. dir. S.C. Bankers Sch., 1961—. Served with AUS, 1943-46. Mem. Am., So. (past pres.) fin. assns., Am. Econ. Assn., AAUP, (past pres. U. S.C.), Am. Bankers Assn., Phi Beta Kappa, Beta Gamma Sigma. Author: The Export-Import Bank of Washington, 1957; Financing Small Business Firms, 1961; Difficult Decades of Banking, 1964; (with C.H. Kreps) Money, Banking and Monetary Policy, 1967; Financial Services: Household Attitudes and Practices, 1977. Contbr. articles profl. jours. Home: 1502 Milford Rd Columbia SC 29206

PUGH, RICHARD CONELLEY, educator; b. Marion, Ind., Sept. 14, 1934; s. James Lewis and Cora Ann (Conelley) P.; B.S., Purdue U., 1956; M.S., Ind. U., 1960, Ed.D., 1964; m. Shirley Rae Whitledge, Nov. 22, 1956; children—Karen Ann, Gregory Eric. Tchr. sci. Horace Mann High Sch., Gary, Ind., 1958-62; research asso. U. Minn., Mpls., 1964-65; asst. prof. edn. Ind. U., 1965-67, asso. prof., 1967-70, prof., 1970—, asso. dean research Sch. Edn., 1978—. Served as officer USN, 1956-58. Mem. Am. Psychol. Assn., Am. Ednl. Research Assn., Nat. Council Measurement in Edn., Phi Delta Kappa. Author profl. monographs; contbr. numerous articles to profl. publs.; producer film: (with David Gliessman) Categorizing Teacher Behavior, 1974. Home: 2513 Buttonwood Ln Bloomington IN 47401 Office: Sch Edn Ind U Bloomington IN 47401

PUGH, RICHARD CRAWFORD, lawyer; b. Phila., Apr. 28, 1929; s. William and Myrtle (Crawford) P.; A.B. summa cum laude, Dartmouth Coll., 1951; B.A. in Jurisprudence (Rhodes scholar), Oxford (Eng.) U., 1953; LL.B., Columbia U., 1958; m. Nanette Bannen, Feb. 27, 1954; children—Richard Crawford, Andrew Lembert, Catherine Elizabeth. Admitted to N.Y. bar, 1958; asso. firm Cleary, Gottlieb, Steen & Hamilton, N.Y.C., 1958-61, partner, 1969—; mem. faculty Law Sch. Columbia, 1961—, prof., 1964-69, adj. prof., 1969—; lectr. Columbia-Amsterdam-Leyden (Netherlands) summer program Am. law, 1963, 79; dep. asst. atty. gen. tax div. U.S. Dept. Justice, 1966-68. Cons. fiscal and financial br. UN Secretariat, 1962, 64. Served with USNR, 1954-56. Mem. Am. Law Inst., Am., N.Y. State bar assns., Bar Assn. City N.Y., Am. Soc. Internat. Law, Council Fgn. Relations, Internat. Fiscal Assn. (pres. U.S. br. 1978-79). Editor Columbia Law Rev., 1957-58; editor: (with W. Friedmann) Legal Aspects of Foreign Investment, 1959; (with W. Friedmann and O. Lissityzn) International Law, 1969; (with others) The Study of Federal Tax Law, 1979. Home: 68 Otter Rock Dr Greenwich CT 06830 Office: 1 State St Plaza New York NY 10004

PUGH, RODERICK WELLINGTON, psychologist, educator; b. Richmond, Ky., June 1, 1919; s. George Wilmer and Lena Bernetta (White) P.; B.A., Fisk U., 1940; M.A., Ohio State U., 1941; Ph.D., U. Chgo., 1949; m. Harriet Elizabeth Rogers, Aug. 29, 1953 (div. 1955). Instr., Albany (Ga.) State Coll., 1941-43; psychology trainee VA, Chgo., 1947-49; lectr. Roosevelt U., Chgo., 1951-54; staff clin. psychologist VA Hosp., Hines, Ill., 1950-54, asst. chief psychologist for psychotherapy, 1954-58, chief, clin. psychology sect., 1958-60, supervising psychologist, coordinator psychol. internship tng., 1960-66; asso. prof. psychology Loyola U., Chgo., 1966-73, prof., 1973—; pvt. practice clin. psychology, 1958—. Cons., St. Mary of the Lake Sem., Niles, Ill., 1965-66, Ill. Div. Vocational Rehab., 1965—, Center for Inner City Studies, Northeastern State U., Chgo., 1966-67, VA Psychology Tng. Program, 1966—, Am. Psychol. Assn. and Nat. Inst. Mental Health Vis. Psychologists Program, 1966—, juvenile problems research rev. com. NIMH, 1970-74, cons. Center for Minority Group Mental Health Programs, 1975-77, cons. psychology edn. br., 1978—; lectr. U. Ibadan (Nigeria), 1979. Mem. policy bd. Chgo. Quality of Life Center, Model Cities Com. on Urban Opportunities, 1975-76. Sec. bd. trustees Fisk U., 1968-78. Served to 2d lt. AUS, 1943-46; ETO. Vis. scholar Fisk U., 1966. Diplomate Am. Bd. Profl. Psychology. Fellow Am. Psychol. Assn.; mem. Midwestern, Ill. (chmn. legis. com. 1961, council mem. 1960-62) psychol. assns., Soc. for Psychol. Study Social Issues, Midwestern Assn. Behavior Analysis, AAUP, Sigma Xi, Alpha Phi Alpha, Psi Chi. Author: Psychology and the Black Experience, 1972. Contbr. chpt. in Black Psychology, 1972. Cons. editor Contemporary Psychology, 1975—. Contbr. articles to profl. jours. Home: 5201 S Cornell Ave Chicago IL 60615 Office: 30 N Michigan Ave Chicago IL 60602 also Loyola U of Chgo 6525 N Sheridan Rd Chicago IL 60626

PUHVEL, JAAN, educator, philologist; b. Tallinn, Estonia, Jan. 24, 1932; s. Karl and Meta Elisabeth (Pärn) P.; came to U.S., 1952, naturalized, 1962; B.A., McGill U., 1951, M.A., 1952; Ph.D. (Jr. fellow 1953-57), Harvard, 1959; m. Sirje Madli Hansen, June 4, 1960; children—Peter Jaan, Andres Jaak, Markus Jüri. Lectr., McGill U., 1955-56; instr. U. Tex., 1957-58, vis. prof., 1960; mem. faculty U. Calif. at Los Angeles, 1958—, prof. classics and Indo-European studies, 1964—, dir. Center Research Langs. and Linguistics, 1962-67, vice chmn. charge sect. Indo-European studies, 1964-68, chmn. dept. classics, 1968-75; Collitz prof. Indo-European comparative philology State U. N.Y. at Buffalo, 1971. Recipient Gold medal Gov. Gen. Can., 1951; officer 1st class Order White Rose (Finland), 1967. Moyse travelling fellow, 1952; fellow Am. Council Learned Socs., 1961-62, 75-76; Guggenheim fellow, 1968-69. Mem. Linguistic Soc. Am., Am. Oriental Soc., Am. Philol. Assn., Estonian Learned Soc. Am., Assn. Advancement Baltic Studies (pres. 1971-72). Author and editor: Laryngeals and the Indo-European Verb, 1960; Ancient Indo-European Dialects, 1966; Substance and Structure of Language, 1969; Myth and Law among the Indo-Europeans, 1970. Home: 15739 High Knoll Rd Encino CA 91436 Office: Dept Classics Univ Calif Los Angeles CA 90024

PULFORD, ROBERT JESSE (BOB), profl. hockey team exec.; b. Newton Robinson, Ont., Can., Mar. 31, 1936. Formerly center Toronto Maple Leafs; past center, capt. Los Angeles Kings, also formerly coach; was coach, now gen. mgr. Chgo. Black Hawks. Office: care Chgo Black Hawks 1800 W Madison St Chicago IL 60612*

PULITZER, EMILY S. RAUH (MRS. JOSEPH PULITZER, JR.), former museum curator; b. Cin., July 23, 1933; d. Frederick and Harriet (Frank) Rauh; A.B., Bryn Mawr Coll., 1955; student Ecole du Louvre, Paris, France, 1955-56; M.A., Harvard, 1963. Mem. staff Cin. Art Mus., 1956-57; asst. curator drawings Fogg Art Mus., Harvard, 1957-64, asst. to dir., 1962-63; curator City Art Mus., St. Louis, 1964-73; mem. painting and sculpture com. Mus. Modern Art, 1975; chmn. visual arts com. Mo. Arts Council, 1976—; co-chmn. fellows

Fogg Art Mus.; mem. bd. Inst. Mus. Services, 1979—. Vice pres. Mark Rothko Found., 1976—. Mem. Am. Fedn. Arts (dir. 1976—). Home: 4903 Pershing Pl Saint Louis MO 63108

PULITZER, JOSEPH, JR., newspaper editor; b. St. Louis, May 13, 1913; s. Joseph and Elinor (Wickham) P.; student St. Mark's Sch., Southborough, Mass.; A.B., Harvard, 1936; m. Louise Vauclain, June 2, 1939 (dec. Dec. 1968); 1 son, Joseph IV; m. 2d, Emily S. Rauh, June 30, 1973. Reporter San Francisco News, 1935; mem. staff St. Louis Post-Dispatch, 1936-48, asso. editor, 1948-55, editor and pub., 1955—. Served ensign to lt. USNR, 1942-45. Home: 4903 Pershing Pl St Louis MO 63108 Office: Post Dispatch St Louis MO 63101

PULITZER, MICHAEL EDGAR, newspaper editor; b. St. Louis, Feb. 23, 1930; s. Joseph and Elizabeth (Edgar) P.; grad. St. Mark's Sch., Southborough, Mass., 1947; A.B., Harvard, 1951, LL.B., 1954; m. Cecille Stell Eisenbeis, Apr. 28, 1970; children—Michael Edgar, Elizabeth E., Frederick D., Catherine D. Eisenbeis, Christina H. Eisenbeis, Robert S., Mark C. Eisenbeis, William H. Eisenbeis. Admitted to Mass. bar, 1954; asso. firm Warner, Stackpole, Stetson & Bradlee, Boston, 1954-56; reporter Louisville Courier Jour., 1956-60; reporter, news editor, asst. mng. editor St. Louis Post-Dispatch, 1960-71, asso. editor, 1978—; editor, pub. Ariz. Daily Star, Tucson, 1971—; pres., chief operating officer Pulitzer Pub. Co. and subs., 1979—, also dir. Mem. Nat. News Council, 1976—; bd. dirs. St. Louis Post-Dispatch Found. Clubs: St. Louis Country; Tucson Country; Balboa (Mazatlan, Mexico). Home: 625 S Skinker Blvd Saint Louis MO 63105 Office: 900 N 12th Blvd Saint Louis MO 63101

PULKRABEK, LARRY ALSTER, lawyer, mfg. co. exec.; b. Freeport, Ill., Sept. 18, 1939; s. George Mathias and Helen Francis (Ross) P.; B.A., Beloit Coll., 1961; J.D., U. Mich., 1964; m. Mary Kaye Baughman, July 18, 1968; 1 son, Ross Whiting. Admitted to Wis. bar, 1963, Pa. bar, 1969; law clk. firm Stroud, Stebbins & Stroud, Madison, Wis., 1964; dir. legal dept. Keco Industries, Inc., Cin., 1964-68; atty. Armstrong Cork Co., Lancaster, Pa., 1968-74, mgr. legal dept., 1974-77, v.p., sec., gen. counsel, 1977—. Chmn. Lancaster County chpt. Pa. Economy League, 1976-77. Mem. Am., Pa., Wis., Lancaster County bar assns. Home: 1287 Wheatland Ave Lancaster PA 17603 Office: Armstrong Cork Co Lancaster PA 17601

PULLEN, ROBERT WHITE, ednl. adminstr.; b. Danforth, Me., July 7, 1919; s. Horace M. and Marjorie (White) P.; A.B., Colby Coll., 1941; Ph.D., Mass. Inst. Tech., 1949; m. Mary E. Varney, Oct. 30, 1943 (dec.); children—Susan, Deborah; m. 2d, Paula M. Cyr, Aug. 1, 1964 (dec.); m. 3d, Marjorie M. Downie, Feb. 25, 1970. Teaching fellow Mass. Inst. Tech., 1942-44; Social Sci. Research Council fellow, 1944-45; mem. faculty Colby Coll., 1945—, prof. econs., 1956—, chmn. dept. econs., 1964-72, treas., 1972-73, adminstrv. v.p., sec., 1970-71, 73—; summer instr. Bowdoin Coll., 1951, Tufts U., 1956, U. Me., 1959; mem. Econs. in Action Program, Case Inst. Tech., summer 1952. Dir. Depositors Trust Co., WCBB Broadcasting Co; incorporator Waterville Savs. Bank. Pub. mem. adv. council Me. Employment Security Commn., 1960-71; mem. pub. adv. com. truth-in-lending Fed. Res. Bd., 1970-76. Bd. dirs. Thayer Hosp., New Eng. Council; bd. dirs., treas. Hinckley Sch. Research grantee Fed. Res. Bank, Boston, 1966. Mem. Am. Econ. Assn., Indsl. Relations Research Assn., Phi Beta Kappa, Pi Gamma Mu. Methodist (bd. dirs.). Kiwanian (bd. dirs.). Home: 4 Newland Ave Waterville ME 04901

PULLEN, THOMAS GRANVILLE, JR., ret. univ. pres.; b. Madison Court House, Va., Feb. 4, 1898; s. Thomas Granville and Annie Brown (Hilldrup) P.; A.B., Coll. William and Mary, 1917; A.M., Columbia, 1925, Ed.D., 1940; LL.D., Loyola Coll., 1947, Morgan State Coll., 1954, St. Marys Coll. Md., 1975; D.H.L., U. Md., 1950, Coll. William and Mary, 1974, U. Balt., 1974; Ped.D., Western Md. Coll., 1951; m. Margaret Louise Rowe, July 10, 1922. Prin., tchr. Dinwiddie (Va.) High Sch., 1917-18; asst. prin., tchr. Latin, Martinsville (Va.) High Sch., 1919-20; prin. Hampton (Va.) High Sch., 1920-23; head English dept. Newport News (Va.) High Sch., 1923-26; prin. Catonsville (Md.) High Sch., 1926-32; supt. Talbot County Sch., Easton, Md., 1932-34; high sch. supr. Md. Dept. Edn., 1934-36, asst. supt. schs., 1936-42, supt., 1942-64; pres. U. Balt., 1969, pres. emeritus, 1969-79; chmn. Com. Internat. Ednl. Reconstrn., 1945. Chmn. sch. com. Nat. Conf. for Prevention and Control Juvenile Delinquency, 1946; mem. Md. Com. Prevention and Treatment Juvenile Delinquency, 1959-64; mem. Md. Constl. Conv., 1967-68; mem. exec. com. devel. program for William and Mary Coll., 1959-79; chmn. Md. Permanent Adv. Com. on Higher Edn., 1956-63; trustee, treas. Council Advancement Secondary Edn., 1954-79; Md. chmn. White House Conf. Edn., 1950, 55; chmn. Commn. to Study Needs Higher Edn. in Md., 1953-55; mem. Com. Expansion Pub. Higher Edn. in Md., 1961-79; chmn. Md. Com. on Fulbright Scholarships; trustee Md. Tchrs. Retirement System, 1942-64, vice chmn., then chmn., 1963-64; cons. Center Study Instrn., NEA, 1964-79; mem. So. Regional Edn. Bd., 1948-55; tchr. U. N.C. summer schs., 1927-28. Pres. bd. trustees Catonsville Pub. Library Assn., 1941-47; bd. govs. Westminster Theol. Sem. Served from pvt. to 2d lt., USMC, 1918-19. Mem. Nat. Council Chief State Sch. Officers (pres. 1945, 46), Am. Vocat. Assn., NEA, Am. Assn. Sch. Adminstrs., State Tchrs. Assn., Md., Catonville (pres. 1973-79) hist. socs., Phi Beta Kappa, Theta Delta Chi, Phi Delta Kappa, Kappa Phi Kappa. Methodist. Mason, Rotarian. Clubs: Merchants, Maryland. Author: A High School Reading Program, 1941. Contbr. articles to profl. mags. and bulls. Md. Dept. Edn. . *Died Nov. 17, 1979.*

PULLEN, WINSTON EUGENE, educator, economist; b. Monson, Me., Mar. 12, 1916; s. Winfred Wentworth and Agrandece (Record) P.; B.S., U. Me., 1941; M.S., Cornell U., 1942, Ph.D., 1950; m. Mary Nardi, June 17, 1943; children—Michael, Janet, Rita, Ann, Richard. Tchr. agrl. econs. U. Me., 1947-49, research, tchr., 1950-62, prof. agrl. econs., also head dept. agrl. bus. and econs., asso. dean instrn., 1963-71, acting dean Coll. Life Scis. and Agr., i971-72, asso. dean instrn., 1972-75, acting dean, 1975-76, asso. dean instrn., 1976—. Served with USNR, 1943- 46. Mem. Am. Farm Econ. Assn., N.E. Farm Mgmt. Research Com., Alpha Zeta, Phi Kappa Phi. Author numerous articles in field. Home 80 N Main St Orono ME 04473

PULLEY, CHARLES HENSON, mfg. co. exec.; b. Cambridge, Ohio, Apr. 22, 1918; s. John Wesley and Bess Idle (Bay) P.; B.A., Ohio Wesleyan U., 1940; postgrad. U. Iowa, 1940-41; m. Martha Jeanne Law, July 3, 1942; children—Lee (Mrs. Chase D. Knight), Jill (Mrs. James Harris), Robyn (Mrs. Thompson Roach), Bruce, Laurel. With Irvin Industries, Inc. (formerly Irving Air Chute Co., Inc.), Lexington, Ky., 1950—, exec. v.p., 1956-60, pres., 1960-71, vice chmn. bd., 1971-78, also dir.; pres. Quinton Hazell Inc., 1978—; dir. Irving Air Chute Ltd. Can., Parachutes (Pty.) Ltd. Australia, Irving Air Chute South Africa (Pty.) Ltd., K-F Products, Inc. Mem. Pres.'s Com. Aeros., 1957-60, Ky. Indsl. Devel. Com., 1958-61. Served to comdr. USNR, World War II. Mem. A.I.M. (pres.'s council), Am. Inst. Aeros. and Astronautics, Inst. Aero. Scis., Soc. Automotive Engrs., Am. Seat Belt Council (1st pres. 1962-79), Navy League. Episcopalian. Rotarian. Club: Lexington Country. Home: Route 1 Midway KY 40347 Office: 152 E Reynolds Rd Lexington KY 40503 also 1730 Pennsylvania Ave NW Washington DC 20006

PULLEYBLANK, EDWIN GEORGE, educator; b. Calgary, Alta., Can., Aug. 7, 1922; s. W. George E. and Ruth Elizabeth (Willoughby) P.; B.A., U. Alta., 1942; Ph.D., U. London, 1951; m. Winona Ruth Relyea, July 17, 1945 (dec. Jan. 1978); children—David Edwin, Barbara Jill Pulleyblank Camp, Marcia Ruth. Research officer Nat. Research Council, Ottawa, 1943-46; lectr. Sch. Oriental and African studies U. London, 1948-53; prof. Chinese, U. Cambridge, 1953-66; prof. Asian studies U. B.C., 1966—, head dept., 1968-75; editorial adviser Ency. Brit. Mem. Royal Asiatic Soc. (council 1956-59), Philol. Soc. London (council 1961-66), Assn. Asian Studies (dir. 1969-73), Linguistic Soc. Am., Canadian Soc. Asian Studies (pres. 1971-74). Author: The Background of the Rebellion of An Lu-shan, 1954. Editor: (with W.G. Beasley), Historians of China and Japan, 1961. Contbr. articles to profl. jours. Office: University of British Columbia Vancouver 8 BC Canada

PULLIAM, EUGENE SMITH, publisher; b. Kans., 1914; s. Eugene C. and Myrta (Smith) P.; A.B., DePauw U., 1935, LL.D., 1973; m. Jane Bleecker, 1943; children—Myrta, Russell, Deborah. Reporter, United Press, Chgo., Detroit and Buffalo burs., 1935-36; news editor radio sta. WIRE, Indpls., 1936-41; city editor Indpls. Star, 1947-48; mng. editor Indpls. News, 1948-62; now pub. Indpls. Star and Indpls. News; exec. v.p. Central Newspapers, Inc.; pres. Phoenix Newspapers Inc. Vice pres. U.S. Golf Assn. Co-founder St. Richard's Sch. Served as lt. USNR, 1942-46. Mem. Am. Soc. Newspaper Editors, Am. Press Inst. (dir.), Am. Newspaper Pubs. Assn. (past pres. found.), Hoosier State Press Assn. (treas.), Ind. Acad., Delta Kappa Epsilon, Sigma Delta Chi. Episcopalian. Rotarian. Clubs: University (Indpls.); Crooked Stick (Carmel, Ind.); Woodstock; Links (N.Y.C.); Pine Valley Golf; Royal and Ancient Golf. Co-author textbook. Home: 8830 Pickwick Dr Indianapolis IN 46260 Office: Indianapolis News Indianapolis IN 46206

PULLIAM, NINA MASON (MRS. EUGENE C. PULLIAM), pub.; b. Martinsville, Ind., Sept. 19, 1906; d. Benjamin F. and Laura (Gesaman) Mason; student Ind. U., 1927-28, Franklin Coll., 1925-26, U. N.Mex., 1928-29; Litt. D., U. Ariz., 1963; L.H.D., Ind. U., 1967; LL.D., Franklin Coll., 1970; m. Eugene C. Pulliam, 1941 (dec. 1975). Sec.-treas., dir. Central Newspapers, Inc., Indpls., 1932-75, pres., 1975—; sec.-treas. Indpls. Newspapers, Inc., 1944-75, v.p., 1975—; sec.-treas. Phoenix Newspapers, Inc., 1944-75, pres., 1975—; v.p., dir. Muncie (Ind.) Newspapers, Inc., 1942—; pub. Ariz. Republic, Phoenix Gazette, 1975—. Mem. civilian adv. com. WAC Fifth Corps, World War II. Bd. dirs. Nat. Soc. Prevention Blindness; v.p., dir. Franklin Coll. Alumni Council, 1952-55; trustee Franklin Coll., 1962-72. Mem. Nat. Fedn. Press Women, Bus. and Profl. Women's Club, Theta Sigma Phi (Nat. Headliner award 1954), Sigma Delta Chi. Club: Women's Press. Author: I Traveled A Lonely Land, 1955. Office: Star-News Bldg Indianapolis IN 46206 also Phoenix Newspapers Inc 1201 E Van Buren St Phoenix AZ 85001*

PULLIAS, EARL VIVON, educator; b. Castalian Springs, Tenn., Mar. 12, 1907; s. John Grey and Margaret (Leath) P.; student David Lipscomb Coll.; A.B., Cumberland U., 1928; A.M., U. Chgo., 1931; Ph.D., Duke, 1936; student U. London, Inst. Med. Psychology, Oxford U., 1937-38; m. Pauline Boyce, Dec. 21, 1929; children—Calvin Moffatt, John Malcolm. Tchr. jr. high sch., 1928-30; research asst. Pres.'s Commn. on Social Trends, summer 1931; teaching fellow Duke U., 1931-36, instr., 1936-37; prof. psychology Pepperdine Coll., 1937-57, dean, 1940-57; prof. higher edn. U. So. Calif., 1958-77, emeritus, 1977—. Mem. Los Angeles County Bd. Edn., 1954—, pres., 1956-57, 62-63, 67-68; chmn. Commn. Higher Edn. Calif. Tchrs. Assn., 1963-66. Mem. Am. Assn. Higher Edn., Am. Assn. Ednl. Research, Am. Psychol. Assn., Phi Beta Kappa, Kappa Delta Pi, Pi Gamma Mu. Author: Variability in Results from New Type Achievement Tests, 1937; (with others) Toward Excellence in College Teaching, 1963; A Search for Understanding, 1965; (with James D. Young) A Teacher Is Many Things, 1968, rev. edit., 1977; A Common Sense Philosophy for Modern Man, 1975. Editor: Christian Courtship and Marriage, 1946; contbr. articles to edn. and psychol. jours. Home: 7422 Brighton Ave Los Angeles CA 90047

PULLMAN, MAYNARD EDWARD, biochemist; b. Chgo., Oct. 26, 1927; s. Harry and Gertrude (Atlas) P.; B.S., U. Ill., 1948, M.S., 1950; Ph.D. (NIH fellow), Johns Hopkins U., 1953; m. E. Phyllis Light, Sept. 12, 1948; children—H. Cydney, B. Valerie, Jacky Leigh. Fellow in pediatrics Johns Hopkins Hosp., 1953-54; asst. Pub. Health Research Inst. City N.Y., 1954-56, asso., 1956-61, asso. mem., 1961-65, mem., 1965—, chief, 1973—, vis. prof. biochemistry U. Sao Paulo (Brazil) Sch. Medicine, 1963-64; research asso. prof. biochemistry Sch. Medicine N.Y. U., 1966-76, research prof., 1976—. NIH grantee, 1956—; Shubert Found. grantee, 1972-74. Mem. Am. Soc. Biol. Chemists, AAAS, Brit. Biochem. Soc., Am. Chem. Soc. Editorial bd. Jour. Biol. Chemistry, 1967-71, 78—. Home: 338 Archer St Freeport NY 11520 Office: 455 1st Ave New York NY 10016

PULOS, ARTHUR JON, indsl. design exec.; b. Vandergrift, Pa., Feb. 3, 1917; s. John and Argyro (Tsakalos) Palukakos; B.F.A., Carnegie Inst. Tech., 1939; M.F.A., U. Oreg., 1943; m. Elizabeth Jane McQueen, Jan. 28, 1944; children—Cristofer, Maria, Demetra. Teaching asst. design and crafts U. Oreg. at Eugene, 1939-41; asso. prof. design U. Ill., 1946-55; prof., chmn. dept. design Syracuse (N.Y.) U., 1955—; pres. Pulos Design Assos., Syracuse, 1958—. Mem. planning council Expo 67, Montreal, Can., Fed. Design Assembly, 1974, Am. Design Bicentennial, 1974-75; mem. policy panel for architecture, planning and design Nat. Endowment for Arts, 1978—; cons. Colonial Williamsburg; lectr. in USSR, Romania, Pakistan, others for UNESCO, USIA. Served to 1st lt. USAF, 1944-46. Ford Found. fellow. Fellow Indsl. Design Soc. Am. (chmn. bd. 1975-76); mem. Internat. Council Socs. (v.p. 1978-79), Am. Steel Inst. (juror, cons.), AAUP, Alpha Rho Chi, Alpha Zi Alpha. Unitarian. Author: Careers in Industrial Design, 1970; Contact-Selling Design Services, 1975; American Design Ethic; contbr. articles in design and design edn. to profl. jours. Home: 201 Churchill Ln Fayetteville NY 13066 Office: 1939 E Genesee St Syracuse NY 13210

PULS, FRITZ L., lawyer; b. Wis., July 31, 1921; s. Fritz L. and Marjorie A. P.; J.D., U. Wis., 1947; m. Ethel Kelleher, July 31, 1947; children—Elizabeth, Robert, Teresa. Jr. atty. Dept. Commerce; enforcement atty. CAA, 1949-54, dep. regional counsel, Kansas City, Mo., 1955-60; asso. gen. counsel FAA, Washington, 1962-67; gen. counsel Nat. Transp. Safety Bd., Washington, 1967—. Served with U.S. Army, 1942-44. Decorated Bronze Star, Purple Heart. Mem. Wis. Bar Assn. Roman Catholic. Office: 800 Independence Ave SW Washington DC 20594*

PULTE, WILLIAM JOHN, constrn. co. exec.; b. Detroit, May 16, 1932; s. William John and Marguerite Hanna (Lynch) P.; grad. high sch.; m. Joan Marie Baker, June 23, 1973, children—Bryan, Mary Jo, Nancy, Thomas, T.Albert, Kathy, Sharon, Bob, Patrick, Mark, Suzanne, Mary Jane, Carolyn. Owner, William J. Pulte builder, Birmingham, 1950-56; pres. William J. Pulte, Inc., 1956-68; chmn. bd., chief exec. officer Pulte Home Corp., West Bloomfield, Mich., 1968-74, chmn. exec. com., 1974—. Trustee Kensington Acad., Bloomfield Hills, Mich. Served with AUS, 1952-54. Mem. Builders Assn. Met. Detroit (dir. 1967-70). Roman Catholic. Clubs: Birmingham Athletic. Home: 1505 Kirkway Rd Bloomfield Hills MI 48013 Office: 6400 Farmington Rd West Bloomfield MI 48033

PUNDSACK, FRED LEIGH, mfg. co. exec.; b. Pinckneyville, Ill.; s. Fred and Ruby (Harriss) P.; B.S., U. Ill., 1949, Ph.D., 1952; m. Barbara Keene, 1948; 5 children. With Johns-Manville Corp., Denver, 1952—, sr. v.p., 1973-76, exec. v.p. ops., 1976-79, pres., chief operating officer, 1979—, also dir.; dir. Colo. Nat. Bank. Served with inf. U.S. Army, 1943-46. Decorated Bronze Star, Purple Heart. Mem. Indsl. Research Inst., Midwest Research Inst., Am. Chem. Soc., AAAS. Clubs: Cherry Hills Country, Denver Country. Contbr. articles to tech. jours.; patentee in field. Office: PO Box 5108 Denver CO 80217

PUNZO, VINCENT CHRISTOPHER, educator, philosopher; b. Chgo., Apr. 29, 1934; s. Anthony J. and Rose (Tortorello) P.; B.A., John Carroll U., 1956; M.A., St. Louis U., 1961, Ph.D., 1963; m. Nelia M. Cunnea, Dec. 28, 1957; children—Margaret, Mary, Joseph, Vincent, Christine, Anthony. Instr., Loyola U., Chgo., 1961-62; faculty St. Louis U., 1962—, prof. phiosophy, 1967—, dir. honors program, 1969-74, exec. dir. Inst. Communism and Freedom, 1962-64. Mem. Nat. Collegiate Honors Council, 1969-74, exec. com., 1971-73. Chmn., Jefferson Twp. (Mo.) Democratic Club, 1968-69. Served as 2d lt. U.S. Army, 1957. Mem. Am. Cath. Philos. Assn. (program chmn. 1975-76, exec. bd.), Metaphys. Soc., Mo. Philos. Assn. (pres. 1973), Phi Beta Kappa. Author: Reflective Naturalism: An Introduction to Moral Philosophy, 1969. Contbr. articles to profl. pubis. Home: 8714 Litzsinger Saint Louis MO 63144

PURCELL, ARTHUR HENRY, engr., educator; b. Evanston, Ill., Aug. 11, 1944; s. Edward and Ethel (Lohman) P.; B.S., Cornell U., 1966; M.S., Northwestern U., 1971, Ph.D., 1972; m. Deborah Ross Purcell, Feb. 2, 1973. Environmentalist U.S. Army Environ. Office, 1971; asso. dir., Congl. Sci. fellow program, staff officer AAAS, Office of Sci. and Govt., 1973-74; co-founder, dir. Tech. Info. Project, Inc., Washington, 1975—; adj. asso. prof. dept. civil, mech. and environ. engring. George Washington U., 1975—; cons. engr., 1974—; staff prin. Pres.'s Commn. on Accident at Three Mile Island, 1979. Chmn., Scientist and Engrs. for Carter, 1976-77; mem. Jimmy Carter Sci. Policy Task Force, 1976, Pres.'s Commn. on Scholars, 1978. Mem. Am. Inst. Mining, Metall. and Petroleum Engrs., AAAS, Fedn. Materials Socs., Sigma Xi. Democrat. Contbr. publs. and lectrs. on resource policy, materials research and sci. and tech. policy to popular and profl. publs.; author: Trimming the Nation's Waste, 1979. Home: 3014 Q St NW Washington DC 20007 Office: Suite 217 1346 Connecticut Ave NW Washington DC 20036. *Love among all creatures, a sound environment, and respect for our limited resources. We need all of them, and I dedicate my life to meeting this need.*

PURCELL, DALE, cons. non-profit orgns.; b. Baxley, Ga., Oct. 20, 1919; s. John Groce and Agnes (Moody) P.; B.A., U. Redlands, 1948, M.A., 1949; postgrad. Northwestern U., 1951-52; LL.D., Lindenwood Colls., 1974; m. Edna Jean Rowell, Aug. 2, 1944; children—David Scott, Steven Dale, Pamela Jean; m. 2d, Mary Louise G. Kuyawski, Aug. 26, 1962; stepchildren—Amelia Allerton, Jon Allerton. Topographer, U.S. E.D., 1939; U.S. counter-intelligence agt., 1940-42; asso. prof. Ottawa U., 1953-54, asst. to pres., 1954-58; gen. sec. Earlham Coll., 1958-61; dir. devel. U. So. Fla., 1961-63; exec. dir. Cancer Research Center, Columbia, Mo., 1963-65; pres. Dale Purcell Assos., Inc., Columbia, 1965-73; pres. Westminster Coll., Fulton, Mo., 1973-76; cons. to colls., univs., research hosps., 1965-73, non-profit orgns., 1976—. Mem. Mo. Com. for Humanities, 1974-76. Served to capt. USMCR, 1942-46, 52-53. Decorated D.F.C., Air medal with 4 gold stars, Bronze Star, Purple Heart; recipient Distinguished Achievement award Berry Coll., 1974. Mem. Pi Kappa Delta. Presbyn. (elder 1964—). Clubs: Country, Saugahatchee (Auburn); St. Louis (St. Louis). Address: 2405 Heritage Dr Opelika AL 36801. *My father and other mentors taught me how to encourage voluntary support of good causes by resourceful people. Many such people work very hard to create wealth in a free society. Some of them need dependable help in identifying, validating, and gaining confidence in projects to support with their funds and by their wills. As their advocate, I find satisfaction in helping them determine a few which they can undertake, enjoy, and support significantly. Thus their financial success provides them fulfillment and their creative giving makes a greater difference.*

PURCELL, EDWARD MILLS, physicist; b. Taylorville, Ill., Aug. 30, 1912; s. Edward A. and Mary Elizabeth (Mills) P.; B.S. in Elec. Engring., Purdue U., 1933, D. Engring. (hon.), 1953; Internat. Exchange student Technische Hochschule, Karlsruhe, Germany, 1933-34; A.M., Harvard U., 1935, Ph.D., 1938; m. Beth C. Busser, Jan. 22, 1937; children—Dennis W., Frank B. Instr. physics Harvard U., 1938-40, asso. prof., 1946-49, prof. physics, 1949-58, Donner prof. sci., 1958-60, Gerhard Gade Univ. prof., 1960—; sr. fellow Soc. of Fellows, 1949-71; group leader Radiation Lab., Mass. Inst. Tech., 1941-45. Mem. Pres.'s Sci. Advisory Com., 1957-60, 62-65. Co-winner Nobel prize in Physics, 1952; Oersted medal Am. Assn. Physics Tchrs., 1968. Mem. Am. Philos. Soc., Nat. Acad. Sci., Phys. Soc., Am. Acad. Arts and Scis., Contbg. author: Radiation Lab. series, 1949; Berkeley Physics Course, 1965. contbr. sci. papers on nuclear magnetism, radio astronomy, astrophysics, biophysics. Home: 5 Wright St Cambridge MA 02138

PURCELL, FRANCIS EUGENE, bldg. materials co. exec.; b. Las Vegas, N.Mex., Apr. 6, 1931; s. Charles Albert and Mary Florence (Elliott) P.; B.S., N.Mex. Highland U., 1956, M.S., 1958; J.D., U. Balt., 1964; postgrad. Northeastern Advancement Mgmt. Sch., 1971; m. Carol Marie Burke, Sept. 4, 1961; children—Francis Eugene, Suzanne Burke, David Elliott. Asst. to v.p. sales, mktg. advance planning and public affairs Martin Marietta Corp., then mgr. Washington office, 1959-67; v.p. public affairs Portland Cement Assn., 1967-71; with Lone Star Industries, Inc., 1971—, v.p. adminstrn., Greenwich, Conn., to 1978, sr. v.p. public affairs, Washington, 1978—; bd. dirs. Public Affairs Council; trustee Conn. Public Expenditure Council. Served to capt. USAF, 1951-54; Korea, Japan. Mem. Portland Cement Assn. Democrat. Roman Catholic. Clubs: Univ. (Washington); Bethesda (Md.) Country. Home: 7201 Dulany Dr McLean VA 22101 Office: Lone Star Industries Suite 300 1919 Pennsylvania Ave NW Washington DC 20006

PURCELL, JAMES FRANCIS, utility exec.; b. Miles City, Mont., May 13, 1920; s. Robert E. and Mary A. (Hickey) P.; A.B. magna cum laude, U. Notre Dame, 1942; Indsl. Adminstr., Harvard U., 1943; m. Dorothy Marie Abel, Nov. 4, 1944; children—Angela, Ann, Alicia, Anita, Alanna, James Francis, Andrea, Adria, Michael, Gregory, Amara. With McGraw-Hill Pub. Co., N.Y.C., 1946-48; dir. public relations Am. Maize Products Co., N.Y.C., 1948-51; public relations cons. Selvage & Lee, Chgo., 1951-53; with No. Ind. Public Service Co., Hammond, 1953—, v.p. public relations, 1961-75, sr. v.p., 1975—, also dir., chmn. environ. and consumer affairs com.; dir. Money Mgmt. Corp., Bank of Ind. Chmn. bd. govs. Our Lady of Mercy Hosp., Dyer, Ind., 1979—; past chmn. Hammond Community Chest drive; past mem. nat. president's council St. Mary's (Ind.) Coll.; bd. dirs. Catholic Charities, 1965—. Served to lt. USNR, 1943-46. Named Man of Year, Notre Dame U., 1967. Mem. Public Relations Soc. Am. (past pres. Hoosier chpt.), N.W. Ind. Assn. Commerce and

Industry (v.p., dir. 1979—), Newcomen Soc. N. Am. Clubs: Woodmar Country (Hammond); Serra (past pres. Calumet region); Notre Dame, Harvard U. Bus. Sch. Office: 5265 Hohman Ave Hammond IN 46325

PURCELL, JOE EDWARD, lt. gov. Ark.; b. Warren, Ark., July 29, 1923; s. Edward L. and Lynelle M. (Cunningham) P.; certificate Little Rock Jr. Coll., 1949; J.D., U. Ark., 1952; m. Helen C. Hale, Oct. 14, 1948; children—Lynelle Purcell Lehman, Ede Parr. Admitted to Ark. bar, 1952, since practiced in Benton; city atty. City of Benton, 1955-59; municipal judge Benton and Saline County Municipal Ct., 1959-66; atty. gen. State of Ark., 1967-71, lt. gov., 1975—. Chmn. Ark. Democratic Com., 1970-72; mem. Nat. Dem. Com., 1972; chmn. Ark. March of Dimes, 1975. Served with AUS, 1943-45. Mem. Ark Bar Assn. (chmn. membership com. 1971-72), Delta Theta Phi (dist. chancellor 1971—). Club: Lions. Office: Office Lt Gov State Capitol Little Rock AR 72203*

PURCELL, JOHN ROPER, communications co. exec.; b. Petersburg, Va., Nov. 17, 1931; s. John and Emily (Roper) P.; student Bucknell U., 1949-50; J.D., U. Va., 1959; m. Ann L. Sundberg, July 24, 1954; children—Kathleen A., John R., Wendy L., Michael B. Admitted to Va. bar, 1959, D.C. bar, 1959; with firm Covington & Burling, Washington, 1959-62; asst. controller United Aircraft Corp., 1962-68; sr. v.p. finance and bus. ops., dir. Gannett Co. Inc., Rochester, N.Y., 1968-77; exec. v.p., dir. CBS, Inc., 1977—; dir. Bausch & Lomb, Inc., Rochester. Trustee, Bucknell U., Lewisburg, Pa., St. John Fisher Coll., Rochester, Com. for Econ. Devel. Served with USN, 1950-54. Decorated Purple Heart. Mem. Order of Coif. Clubs: Country of Rochester, Winged Foot, N.Y. Athletic. Home: 7 South Trail Darien CT 06820 Office: 51 W 52d St New York NY 10019

PURCELL, KENNETH, univ. dean; b. N.Y.C., Oct. 21, 1928; s. Herman and Ann (Bulkin) P.; B.A., Ph.D., U. Nebr.; m. Claire Dickson Kepler, Dec. 17, 1949; children—Kathleen Ann, Andrew Kepler. Asst. prof. U. Ky., 1956-58; dir. behavior sci. div. Children's Asthma Research Inst., asst. prof. U. Colo. Med. Center, 1958-68; prof., dir. clin. tng. psychology U. Mass., 1968-69, chmn. dept. psychology, 1969-70; prof. psychology, chmn. dept. U. Denver, 1970—, dean Coll. Arts and Scis., 1976—. Served to 2d lt. AUS, 1953-56. Fellow Am. Psychol. Assn., Soc. Research Child Devel.; mem. Colo. Psychol. Assn. (bd. dirs. 1962-64). Author papers in field. Home: 2305 S Jackson St Denver CO 80210 Office: Coll Arts and Scis Univ Denver Denver CO 80208

PURCELL, MARTIN JAMES, lawyer; b. Clinton, Iowa, Dec. 24, 1918; s. Martin W. and Evelyn L. P.; student Cornell Coll., Mt. Vernon, Iowa, 1936-38; LL.B. cum laude, U. Iowa, 1948; m. Elizabeth Anne McCambridge, Apr. 20, 1946; children—Jane, Mary Dey, Anne, Martha. Admitted to Iowa bar, 1948, Mo. bar, 1948, U.S. Supreme Ct. bar, 1960, other fed. bars; asso. firm Morrison, Hecker, Curtis, Kuder & Parrish, Kansas City, Mo., 1948-53, partner, 1953—. Served lt. col. U.S. Army, 1941-46. Fellow Am. Bar Found., Am. Law Inst., Am. Coll. Trial Lawyers; mem. Am. Bar Assn., Lawyers Assn. Kansas City (pres. jr. sect. 1951, sec. sr. sect. 1958), Kansas City Bar Assn., Iowa Bar Assn., Am. Judicature Soc., Nat. Assn. R.R. Trial Counsel, Mo. Bar Found. (pres. 1973-75), Mo. Bar (exec. com. 1964-69, v.p., 1966-67, pres., 1968-69, Pres.'s award 1970). Clubs: Univ., Milburn Country (pres. 1960). Home: 8721 Riggs Dr Overland Park KS 66212 Office: Morrison Hecker Curtis Kuder & Parrish 1700 Bryant Bldg 1102 Grand Ave Kansas City MO 64106

PURCELL, PHILIP JAMES, retail chain exec.; b. Salt Lake City, Sept. 5, 1943; s. Philip James and Shirley (Sorensen) P.; B.B.A., U. Notre Dame, 1965; M.Sc., U. London, 1967; M.B.A., U. Chgo., 1967; m. Anne Marie McNamara, Apr. 2, 1964; children—David Philip, Peter Andrew, Mark Edward, Michael James, Paul Martin, Philip Patrick. Dir., mng. dir. Chgo. office McKinsey & Co., Inc., 1967-78; v.p. corp. planning Sears, Roebuck and Co., Chgo., 1978—; dir. Homart Devel. Co. Clubs: Econ., Chgo., Mid-Am., North Shore Country (Chgo.). Office: Sears Tower Chicago IL 60684

PURCELL, ROBERT BAKER, business exec.; b. Payette, Idaho, Dec. 3, 1928; s. Leslie Irvin and Hazel (Cooper) P.; student U. Idaho, 1948-49; B.A., Coll. Idaho, 1952; m. Mary Edith Maxwell, June 7, 1953; children—Debra, Teresa (Mrs. Arthur Meushaw III), Robin, Leslie. Tchr. pub. schs., New Meadows, Idaho, 1952-55, Fruitland, Idaho, 1955-57; field asst. Equitable Life, Caldwell, Idaho, 1957-60; mgr. Caldwell C. of C., 1960-64, Lewiston (Idaho) C. of C., 1964-68; pres. Component Therapy Inst., Washington, 1968-73; v.p. Goddard, Purcell & People, Boulder, Colo., 1972-73, pres., 1973-78; exec. v.p. Prescott Purcell Karsh & Hagan, Inc., Englewood, Colo., 1978—; cons. J.C. Penney Co., Washington, 1969—, now sr. govtl. relations rep., Boston. Chmn. Nez Perce County (Idaho) Republican Com., 1966; state sec. Young Reps. Idaho, 1962. Cons. Am. Hemophilia Fedn., 1972; adv. Nat. Insts. Health Blood Resources Program, 1972; commr. from Idaho, Columbia Interstate Compact Commn., 1964-68. Bd. dirs. Boys Clubs of Denver, Denver Advt. Fedn.; trustee Pacific N.W. Ballet Assn., 1966-68 chmn. bd. Denver Opera Co., 1978. Named Man of Year, Idaho, Nev., Oreg. dist. Equitable Life, 1958. Episcopalian (Bishops council diocese of Idaho 1962-64, sr. warden 1968). Mason. Author: (with others) An Evaluation of the Utilization of Human Blood Resources in United States, 1970. Home: 11 Morse Dr Medfield MA 02052

PURCELL, ROBERT LAUGHLIN, mfg. co. exec.; b. Norway, Mich., June 21, 1910; s. Robert L. and Hannah M. (Peterson) P.; Ph.B., U. Chgo., 1931; m. Marion Cook, Apr. 21, 1934; children—Jean E., Mary Ellen. With Swift & Co., 1934-36, Ernst & Ernst, C.P.A.'s, Chgo., 1936-46; controller Internat. Detrola Corp., 1946-47; treas., controller Ekco Products Co., 1947-52; v.p., treas. Am. Bosch Co., 1952; exec. v.p., dir. N.Y. Shipbldg. Corp., and predecessors, 1952-55; exec. v.p., dir. Lear Siegler, Inc., Santa Monica, Calif., 1955-71, chmn. bd., 1971-74; dir. Lear Siegler Western Progress, Inc., Angeles Corp., Acme Gen. Corp. Served to maj. AUS, 1941-46. C.P.A., Ill. Named to U. Chgo. Pres.'s Fund Honor Roll. Mem. Fin. Execs. Inst., U. So. Calif. Assos., Delta Upsilon. Clubs: Bel Air Country, Jonathan (Los Angeles). Home: 14901 Ramos Pl Pacific Palisades Los Angeles CA 90272 Office: 3171 S Bundy Dr Santa Monica CA 90405

PURCELL, ROBERT W., corp. exec.; b. Watertown, N.Y., Oct. 24, 1911; s. Francis and Ella (Conger) P.; A.B., Cornell U., 1932, LL.B., 1935; m. Hazel Becker, Oct. 14, 1939 (dec. Nov. 1978). Asso. White & Case, N.Y.C., 1935-38; practice law, Cleve., 1938-40; office counsel Alleghany Corp., 1940-53, v.p., 1945-53, dir., 1946-53, vice chmn., 1947-53; gen. counsel C. & O. Ry., 1943-53, v.p., gen. counsel, 1945-53, v.p. charge law, dir., mem. retirement, finance com., 1946-53, vice chmn., 1947-53; chmn. bd. Pathe Industries, Inc., 1945-50, dir., 1941-53; v.p., dir. White Sulphur Springs Co., 1946-53; dir. Cleve. Cliffs Iron Co., 1946-53; chmn. bd. Investors Diversified Services, Inc., Mpls., 1953-57; bus. cons. Rockefeller Family & Assos., 1955—; dir. Internat. Basic Economy Corp., chmn. bd., 1958-68; chmn. bd., dir. Basic Resources Internat. S.A.; dir. C.I.T. Financial Corp., Internat. Minerals & Chem. Corp., Investors Group, Pittston Co., Bendix Corp., Caneel Bay, Inc., Rockefeller Center, Inc., Seaboard World Airlines, Inc., K Mart Corp. Bd. govs. N.Y. Hosp.; trustee emeritus Cornell U., chmn. bd. trustees, 1968-78; trustee Internat. House. Mem. Psi Upsilon. Clubs: New York Yacht, Cornell, University (N.Y.C.). Home: 765 Park Ave New York NY 10021 Office: 30 Rockefeller Plaza New York NY 10020

PURCELL, WILLIAM PAUL, educator; b. Tulsa, Dec. 11, 1935; s. William Whitaker and Amolia (Anderson) P.; A.B., Ind. U., 1957; A.M., Princeton, 1959, Ph.D., 1960; postgrad. Poly. Inst. Bklyn., 1961; m. Eleanor J. Black, Aug. 31, 1957 (div. Aug. 1972); children—Lisa Jeanne, Jennifer Lee, Paul Barclay; m. 2d, Jeanne Louise Williams, Nov. 11, 1972 (div. June 1979). Chemist Buckeye Cellulose Corp., Memphis, 1955-56; with Buckman Labs., Inc., Memphis, 1957-63, research chemist, 1958-59, chief inorganic chemist, 1960-63; asso. prof. medicinal chemistry Med. Units, U. Tenn. at Memphis, 1963-67, prof., 1967-69, chmn. dept. molecular and quantum biology, 1969-74, dir. drug design div. Center for Health Scis., 1974—, prof. pharmacology, 1975—; cons. Diamond Shamrock Chem. Co., Diamond Shamrock Corp., FMC Corp., Ciba-Geigy, Miles Labs. Inc., Molecular Design Inc., Wyeth Labs., Searle Labs.; vis. prof. U. Lausanne, Switzerland, 1975-77. Mem. Memphis Water Pollution Adv. Com., 1971—. Allied Chem. Co. fellow, 1959-60. Fellow The Chem. Soc., Am. Pharm. Assn., Acad. Pharm. Scis.; mem. Am. Chem. Soc., Internat. Soc. Quantum Biology, (founder, sec.), Sigma Xi, Alpha Chi Sigma, Rho Chi (adv. 1964-67). Episcopalian. Mem. editorial bd. Jour. Medicinal Chemistry, 1969-73; contbr. numerous articles to profl. jours. Home: PO Box 41151 Memphis TN 38104 Office: 874 Union Ave Memphis TN 38163

PURCIFULL, ROBERT OTIS, ins. co. exec.; b. Grinnell, Iowa, July 1, 1932; s. Chauncey O. and Mildred E. (Clendenen) P.; B.A., Grinnell Coll., 1954; m. Mary G. White, Sept. 12, 1953; children—Jane, Robert Otis, Patricia, Elizabeth. With Occidental Life Ins. Co. Calif., 1960-78, 1st. v.p. charge agys., Los Angeles, 1968-71, exec. v.p. sales, 1971-76; pres., chief exec. officer Transmerica Ins. Mgmt., Inc., Los Angeles, 1972-78; pres., chief exec. officer Countrywide Life Ins. Co., Los Angeles, 1973-76, dir., 1973-78; chmn. bd., pres. Plaza Ins. Sales Inc., San Francisco; pres. Canadian div. Occidental Life Ins. Co., 1977-78; pres., chief exec. officer Occidental Life of Can., 1977-78; pres., chief operating officer, trustee Penn Mut. Life Ins. Co., Phila., 1979—. Past pres. Vols. of Am., Los Angeles, 1971-73. Councilman, City of Upper Arlington, Ohio, 1962-66. Trustee, Life Underwriters Tng. Council, Washington, 1975-78. Served to 1st lt. USAF, 1955-57. C.L.U. Clubs: Union League, Phila. Country (Phila.). Home: 118 Woods Ln Radnor PA 19087 Office: Penn Mut Life Ins Co Independence Sq Philadelphia PA 19172

PURDOM, PAUL WALTON, civil engr., educator; b. Sparta, Ga., July 23, 1917; s. Izaac Walton and Seaton (Taylor) P.; B.S. in Civil Engring., Ga. Inst. Tech., 1973; postgrad. in pub. health Vanderbilt U., 1940; M.S. in San. Engring., U. Mich., 1951; M.Govtl. Adminstrn., U. Pa., 1958, Ph.D. in Polit. Sci., 1963; m. Bettie Mahala Miller, Apr. 12, 1939; children—Paul Walton, Anne Elizabeth Purdom Cross, Wayne Miller. Materials insp. Ga. Hwy. Dept., 1938-39, supervising insp., 1939-40; trainee Ga. Dept. Pub. Health, Atlanta, 1940, pub. health engr., Macon, 1943; pub. health engr. Colquitt County Health Dept., Moultrie, Ga., 1940-41; jr. hydraulic engr. Little Rock dist. U.S. Engrs. Dept., 1941-42, asso. civil engr. Louisville dist., Indpls., 1942-43; structural engr. Union Bag and Paper Co., Savannah, Ga., 1942; sr. san. engr. Tenn. Dept. Pub. Health, 1943-47; dir. sanitation div. Bur. Health, Knoxville, Tenn., 1947-52; dir. div. environ. health Phila. Dept. Pub. Health, 1953-63; asso. prof., asso. dir. environ. engring. and sci. Drexel U., Phila., 1963-64, prof., dir. environ. engring. and sci., 1964-70, prof. environ. engring., 1970—, dir. Center for Urban Research and Environ. Studies, 1970-73, chmn., dept. civil engring., 1973-75, dir. Environ. Studies Inst., 1975—. Mem. subcom. tng. and utilization san. engrs. NRC, 1957; mem. ad hoc study group community solid waste disposal USPHS, 1957, cons., mem. subcom. environ. engring. Com. on Environ. Health Problems, 1961, mem. urban and environ. study sect., 1967-71; mem. steering com. 1st Nat. Conf. Air Pollution, 1958; gen. chmn. 3d Nat. Conf. Environ. Engring. Edn., 1973; mem. task force on environ. health Nat. Commn. Community Health Services, 1963-65; staff dir. spl. adv. com. on realtionships with state health agys. HEW, 1966; mem. subcom. on new housing Delaware Valley (Phila.) Housing Assn., 1964-66, chmn. interagy. com. low income housing, 1967, mem. exec. bd., 1967-69; mem. subcom. regional planning Citizens Council on City Planning, Phila., 1968; mem. civilian adv. com. radiation hazards and safety City of Phila., 1967-71; co-chmn. workshop on planning a healthful residential environment 1st Nat. Conf. Health Research in Housing and its Environment, 1970; mem. ad hoc vis. com. for accreditation Engrs. Council Profl. Devel., 1969-75; mem. Mid-Atlantic Consortortium on Air Pollution, 1971, chmn., 1971-72; mem. atomic safety and licensing bd. panel U.S. Nuclear Regulatory Commn. (formerly AEC), 1972—; mem. Southeastern Pa. Comprehensive Health Planning Council, 1967-70, mem. environ. health subcom., 1971, mem. steering com. Montgomery County, 1972-73; mem. Pa. Comprehensive Health Planning Council, 1968-71, chmn. projects rev. com., 1969-71, mem. task force on environmental health, 1969; mem. Gov.'s Sci. Adv. Com., 1969-71, mem. panel on health delivery systems, 1969-71; chmn. environ. health div. Mayor's Sci. and Tech. Adv. Com., Phila., 1972-73; mem. citizens adv. council Pa. Dept. Environ. Resources, 1972—, chmn. joint com. environ. health, 1974-76; mem. tech. assessment and polution control adv. com., mem. sci. adv. bd. EPA, 1976—. Trustee Pa. Health Research Inst., 1964-69, pres., 1968-69; organizer, 1st pres. Delaware Valley Citizens Council for Clean Air, 1967, trustee, 1967-75, chmn. program council, 1974-76. Served as san. engr. USPHS, 1952-53. Recipient citation Knoxville Jr. C. of C., 1949; Crumbine award for outstanding environ. health program in U.S., 1961; citation City Council, Phila., 1961; named Outstanding Employee, Phila. Dept. Pub. Health, 1961; Pub. Service award Phila. and Montgomery Tb and Respiratory Disease Assn., 1970; citation Conf. Local Environmental Health Adminstrs., 1972; Achievement award Drexel U., 1976. Registered profl. engr., Pa., Ga. Diplomate Am. Acad. Environ. Engrs. (past chmn. citation 1970). Fellow Am. Pub. Health Assn. (chmn. nominating com. 1962, mem. program area com. air pollution 1965-66, chmn. ad hoc com. nat. water policy 1964, mem. governing council 1958-61, 64-66, 67-72, 76—, mem. exec. bd. 1967-69, 70-72, pres. 1971, mem. tech. devel. bd. 1973; numerous other offices), ASCE (air pollution com. 1964-70, chmn. air pollution com. 1969-70, mem. solid wastes com. 1964-70, mem. san. engring. manpower com. 1969-75, chmn., 1974-75), Royal Soc. Health (hon.); mem. Am. Acad. Environ. Engrs. (trustee 1960-65, 77—, chmn. 1963-64, chmn. com. publicity and pub. relations 1962, chmn. com. reorgn. 1965, mem. edn. com. 1970-76, chmn. 1973-76, rep. ad hoc com. on accreditation 1978-79), Conf. Local Environ. Health Adminstrs. (sec. 1950-52, news editor 1950, vice chmn. 1953, chmn. 1954, chmn. air pollution control com. 1958, chmn. com. local control ionizing radiation 1962), Pa. Pub. Health Assn. (v.p. 1958, pres. 1959, rep. to nat. assn. 1958-59, chmn. nominating com. 1973), Am. Soc. Pub. Adminstrn. (mem. exec. com. Phila. sect. 1966-67), Air Pollution Control Assn. (mem. exec. com. Middle Atlantic States sect. 1964-65, 76-79), Am. Acad. Polit. and Social Sci., Am. Indsl. Hygiene Assn., Water Pollution Control Fedn., Am. Assn. Environ. Engring. Profs. (edn. com. 1970, rep. to Am. Acad. Environ. Engrs. bd. trustees 1977—), AAAS (mem. engring. com. 1976), Sigma Xi, Delta Omega. Editor: Environmental Health. Home: 245 Gulph Hills Rd Radnor PA 19087 Office: 32d and Chestnut Sts Philadelphia PA 19104

PURDOM, THOMAS JAMES, lawyer; b. Seymour, Tex., Apr. 7, 1937; s. Thomas Exer and Juanita Florida (Kuykendall) P.; student U. Syracuse, 1956-57, U. Md., 1958-59; B.A., Tex. Tech. Coll., 1962; J.D., Georgetown U., 1966; m. Betty Marie Shoemaker, May 31, 1969; 1 son, James Robert. Admitted to Tex. bar, 1966; partner Griffith & Purdom, 1966-67; asst. dist. atty. 72d Jud. Dist., 1967-68; county atty. Lubbock County, Tex., 1968-72; partner firm Vickers Purdom & Nelson, and predecessors, Lubbock, Tex., 1972—. Served with USAF, 1956-59. Mem. Am., Lubbock County bar assns., State Bar Tex. mem. and past chmn. family law council), Delta Theta Phi. Democrat. Baptist (deacon). Lions (dir.). Home: 3619 55th St Lubbock TX 79413 Office: 1801 Ave Q Lubbock TX 79401

PURDY, CHARLES ROBERT, corp. exec.; b. St. Louis, Oct. 2, 1937; s. Wilbur Charles and Myrtle (Baker) P.; B.S.C., DePaul U., 1959; m. Carolyn Joan Leppa, Aug. 29, 1959; children—Maureen Carol, Kelly Ann, Jeffrey Scott, Mark Edward. Jr. accountant Price Waterhouse & Co., Chgo., 1958-61, sr. accountant, 1961-62; asst. controller Scot Lad Foods, Inc., Chgo., 1962-64, adminstrv. v.p., 1964-66, exec. v.p., dir., 1966-69, pres., dir., 1969-71; prin. Purdy Enterprises, Chgo., 1971-77; vice-chmn., chief exec. officer, dir. Scot Lad Foods, Inc., Lansing, Ill., 1977-78; prin. Purdy Enterprises, Chgo., 1978—. Recipient DePaul U. Alumni Assn. Achievement award, 1971-72. Mem. Delta Sigma Pi, Beta Gamma Sigma, Beta Alpha Psi. Club: Olympia Fields (Ill.) Country. Home: 792 Brookwood Terr Six Olympia Fields IL 60461 Office: One Scot Lad Ln Lansing IL 60438

PURDY, FRAZIER RODNEY, advt. agy. exec.; b. N.Y.C., Oct. 31, 1929; s. Harris Levitt and Mary Irene (Long) P.; student public schs., Westport, Conn.; m. Joan W. Smith, Apr. 11, 1953; children—Mark Cranston, Kevin Barr, Christopher Paul. Apprentice, Lennen and Newell Advt., N.Y.C., 1950-52, asst. art dir., 1952-54; with Young & Rubicam Inc., N.Y.C., 1954—, mgr. copy dept., 1973-75, creative dir., 1975—, sr. v.p., 1975-79, exec. v.p., 1979—, mem. N.Y. exec. com., 1975—, dir. Young & Rubicam, U.S.A. Served with U.S. Army, 1948-49. Recipient numerous awards including Clio award for art direction from various orgns., including Internat. Broadcasting-Hollywood Radio and TV Soc., N.Y. Art Dirs. Club, Advt. Club N.Y., Internat. Advt. Film Festival, Cannes. Mem. N.Y. Art Dirs. Club. Office: 285 Madison Ave New York NY 10017

PURDY, FREDERICK DUNBAR, fgn. service officer; b. Pitts., Feb. 9, 1928; s. Carroll Foster and Mary Margaret (Dunbar) P.; A.B., U. Pitts., 1950; m. Gisela Wilma Mohn, Feb. 28, 1972; 1 dau., Caterina Luisa Mohn. Geographer, Army Map Service, 1951-52; geographer Dept. Navy, 1952-53; commd. fgn. service officer, Dept. State, 1956; vice consul, Ciudad Juarez, Mex., 1958-59; vice consul, Kingston, Jamaica, 1962-64; consul, Ponta Delgada, Azores, 1964-66; 2d sec., Brasilia, Brazil, 1966-68; consul, Santiago, Chile, 1970-75; dep. consul gen., Manila, Philippines, 1975-78; consul gen., Seville, Spain, 1978—. Served with U.S. Army, 1946-47, USN, 1953-55. Mem. Omicron Delta Kappa. Home: Ave Maria Luisa s/n Sevilla Spain Office: American Consulate General Sevilla APO NY 09282

PURDY, HAROLD WAYNE, telephone co. exec.; b. Star City, Ind., Aug. 15, 1920; s. Chester Elroy and Lena Gladys (King) P.; B.S. in Fin., Ind. U., 1948; m. Virginia L. Bender, Jan. 13, 1945; children—Harold Wayne, Barbara Lynn. Internal auditor Gen. Telephone Co. of Ind., Inc., Ft. Wayne, 1948-52, personnel asst., 1953, asst. sec., asst. treas., 1959-72, sec., treas., 1972—, pension chmn., 1952—. Mem. personnel com. United Fund, Ft. Wayne. Served to maj. USAAF, 1941-45; ETO. Decorated D.F.C. with oak leaf cluster, Air medal with four oak leaf clusters. Mem. U.S., Ind., Ft. Wayne chambers commerce. Methodist (fin. sec. 1964-70, trustee 1966-72, mem. pastor parish relations com. 1972-76). Club: Kiwanis (v.p., dir.). Home: 2000 Garden Park Dr Fort Wayne IN 46825 Office: 8001 US 24 W PO Box 1201 Fort Wayne IN 46801

PURDY, JAMES, writer; b. 1923; ed. Chgo., Spain. Interpreter, editor, other positions, Cuba, Mexico, also Washington. Author: Don't Call Me by My Right Name, 1956; 63 Dream Palace, 1956, reissued, 1980; Color of Darkness, 1957; Malcolm, 1959, reissued, 1980; The Nephew, 1960, reissued, 1980; (play) Children is All, 1962; Cabot Wright Begins, 1964; Eustance Chisholm and The Works, 1967; An Oyster is A Wealthy Beast, 1967; Mr. Evening, 1968; Jeremy's Version, 1970; On the Rebound, 1970; (poems) The Running Sun, 1971; I am Elijah Thrush, 1971; (poems) Sunshine is an Only Child, 1973; Sleepers in Moon Crowned Valleys, The House of the Solitary Maggot, 1974; (novel) In a Shallow Grave, 1976; (plays and stories) A Day After the Fair, 1977; recordings Eventide, 63; Dream Palace, 1968, reissued, 1980; (novel) Narrow Rooms, 1978; (poetry) I Will Arrest the Bird that has No Light, 1978; Lessons and Complaints, 1978; (short fiction) Sleep Tight, 1978; Out of a Clear Blue Sky, 9 short plays, 1980; subject of book James Purdy (Stephen D. Adams), 1976. Address: 236 Henry St Brooklyn NY 11201

PURDY, JAMES ARTHUR, corp. exec.; b. Chgo., May 11, 1922; B.S. in Adminstrv. Mech. Engring., Cornell U., 1943; m. Janet LaMarr, Jan. 13, 1945; children—James Arthur, Stephen L., Jeffrey A., John A. Div. mgr. Fisher & Porter Co., Hatboro, Pa., 1946-53; gen. mgr. Horberg Grinding Industries, Bridgport, Conn., 1953-55; asso. Robert Heller & Assos., Cleve., 1955-63; dir. orgn. and planning ITT, Standard Telephones & Cables, Ltd., London, 1964-65, dir. adminstrn., 1965-67, dep. group exec. Far East and Pacific group, 1967-68, group gen. mgr., 1968-77, group exec., 1977—, v.p. ITT, N.Y.C., 1969—. Served with USN, 1943-46. Office: ITT 320 Park Ave New York NY 10022

PURDY, LAURENCE HENRY, educator; b. Miami, Ariz., Sept. 28, 1926; s. Laurence Henry and Winnie Estella (Gibson) P.; student Mont. U., 1944, 46-47; B.S., San Diego State Coll., 1949; Ph.D., U. Calif. at Davis, 1954; m. Barbara Ann Pershal, Feb. 14, 1948; children—Cynthia D., L. Jeffrey, Timothy C., Paula E. Asst. prof. plant pathology Wash. State U., 1960, asso. prof., 1961-66, prof., 1966; research plant pathologist regional cereal disease research lab. U.S. Dept. Agr. Agrl. Research Service, Pullman, Wash., 1953-67; chmn. plant pathology dept. U. Fla., Gainesville, 1967-79, prof., 1967—. Served with USAAF, 1945. Recipient Unit award for superior service Dept. Agr., 1960. Mem. Am. Phytopathol. Soc. (treas. 1971-76, v.p. 1977-78, pres. 1979-80), AAAS, Fla. Hort. Soc., Sigma Xi. Contbr. articles to profl. jours. Home: 1519 NW 25th Terr Gainesville FL 32605

PURDY, ROB ROY, univ. adminstr.; b. Pensacola, Fla., Feb. 11, 1914; s. William Wallace and Margaret (McLellan) P.; A.B., Davidson U., 1937; M.A., Vanderbilt U., 1938, Ph.D., 1946; postgrad. U. Grenoble, 1939; m. Frances Norine Edwards, June 15, 1939; children—Alan M., Rob, Frank C. Asst. prof. English, Florence (Ala.) State Coll., 1941-42; with Vanderbilt U., 1942—, prof. English, 1955—, vice chancellor univ., 1959-66, sr. vice chancellor, 1966-77, sr. v.p., 1977-79, sr. vice chancellor emeritus, 1979—; dir. Vanderbilt U. Press, 1957-59. Sec., Southeastern Conf., 1971-79. Served from ensign to lt. (j.g.) USNR, 1944-46. Am. Field Service fellow Inst.

Internat. Edn., 1939-40. Mem. Modern Lang. Assn., Omicron Delta Kappa. Presbyn. Rotarian (dir.) Editor: Fugitives Reunion, 1958. Contbr. articles to profl. publs. Home: 4305 Esteswood Dr Nashville TN 37215

PURDY, WILLIAM CROSSLEY, educator, chemist; b. Bklyn., Sept. 14, 1930; s. John Earl and Virginia (Clark) P.; B.A., Amherst Coll., 1951; Ph.D., Mass. Inst. Tech., 1955; m. Myrna Mae Moman, June 17, 1953; children—Richard Bruce (dec.), Richard Scott, Lisa Patrice, Diana Lori. Instr., U. Conn., Storrs, 1955-58; faculty U. Md., College Park, 1958-76, prof. chemistry, 1964-76, head div. analytical chemistry, 1968-76; prof. chemistry, asso. in medicine McGill U., 1976—; vis. prof. Institut für Ernahrungswissenschaft, Justus Liebig-Universitat, Giessen, Germany, 1965-66; Nat. lectr. AM. Assn. Clin. Chemistry, 1971; cons. Surg. Gen., U.S. Army, 1959-75; sci. adviser Balt. dist. FDA. Fellow Nat. Acad. Clin. Biochemistry; mem. Am. Chem. Soc., Am. Assn. Clin. Chemistry, The Chem. Soc. (London), Chem. Inst. Can., Can. Soc. Clin. Chemists, Sigma Xi. Author: Electro-analytical Methods in Biochemistry, 1965; also numerous articles. Bd. editors Clin. Chemistry, 1971—, Anal. Letters, 1979—, Anal. Chim. Acta, 1979—; adv. bd. editors Analytical Chemistry, 1971-73. Research on application of modern analytical methods to biochem. and clin. systems, separation sci., trace metal analysis. Home: 1321 Sherbrooke St W C-40 Montreal PQ H3G 1J4 Canada Office: McGill U 801 Sherbrooke St W Montreal PQ H3A 2K6 Canada

PURI, MADAN LAL, educator; b. Sialkot, Feb. 20, 1929; s. Ganesh Das and S. V. Puri; B.A., Punjab U., India, 1948, M.A., 1950, D.Sc., 1975; Ph.D., U. Calif. at Berkeley, 1962; m. Uma Kapur, Aug. 24, 1962; 3 children. Came to U.S., 1957, naturalized, 1973. Head dept. math. D.A.V. Coll., Punjab U., 1955-57; instr. U. Colo., 1957-58; teaching asst., research asst., jr. research statistician U. Calif. at Berkeley, 1958-62; asst. prof., asso. prof. math. Courant Inst., N.Y. U., 1962-68; vis. asso. prof. U. N.C., summers 1966-67; prof. math. Ind. U., Bloomington, 1968—. Guest prof. statistics U. Gottingen (West Germany), 1972, Alexander von Humboldt guest prof., 1974-75; guest prof. U. Dortmund (West Germany), 1972, Technische Hochschule Aachen (West Germany), 1973, U. Goteborg, Chalmers U. Tech. (both Sweden), 1974; vis. prof. U. Auckland (N.Z.), 1977, U. Wash., Seattle, 1978-79. Recipient Sr. U.S. Scientist award, 1974-75. Fellow Royal Statis. Soc., Inst. Math. Statistics, Am. Statis. Assn.; mem. Math. Assn. Am., Internat. Statis. Inst., Am. Math. Soc., Bernoulli Soc. Math. Stats. and Probability. Author: Non Parametric Methods in Multivariate Analysis, 1971; Statochastic Process and Related Topics, 1975; Statistical Inference and Related Topics, 1975. Editor: Non Parametric Techniques in Statistical Inference, 1970. Office: Dept Math Ind U Bloomington IN 47401

PURIM, FLORA, singer; b. Rio de Janeiro, Brazil, Mar. 6, 1942; d. Naum and Rachel (Vaisberg) Purim; came to U.S., 1967; student U. Cal. at Long Beach; 1 dau. by previous marriage, Niura Band; m. Airto Moreira, Mar. 19, 1972; 1 dau., Diana. With RCA Records, Rio de Janeiro, Brazil, 1965-67; with Buddah Records, N.Y.C., 1969-71, CTI Records, N.Y.C., 1971-73, Warner Bros. Records; composer-lyricist: (with Airto Moreira) Seeds on the Ground, 1970, Natural Feelings, 1969, Free, 1971, Fingers, 1972, Identity, 1975, Promises of the Sun, 1976; solo albums: Butterfly Dreams, 1973, Stories to Tell, 1974, Open Your Eyes You Can Fly, 1976, 500 Miles High in Montreaux, 1976, Encounter, 1977, Nothing Will Be As It Was Tomorrow, 1977; album (with Airto Moreira) Virgin Land, 1972; albums (with Chick Corea) Return to Forever, 1972, Light as a Feather, 1973; album (with Carlos Santana) Welcome, 1973, Borboletta, 1974; composer/lyricist: (with Stanley Clarke) Light as a Feather, 1972, (with Airto Moreira, Neville Potter) San Francisco River, 1972, (with McCoy Tyner) Search for Peace, 1974, (with George Duke) Love Reborn, 1973, Feel, 1974, (with Airto Moreira) Alue, 1969, (with Hermeto Paschoal) We Love, 1970, (with Ernie Hood) Mountain Train, 1974, (with Duke Pearson) How Insensitive, 1969, It Could Only Happen with You, 1970; (with Airto and Deodato) Deodata/Airto in Concert, 1973; producer (with Moreira) I'm Fine, How Are You, 1977. Named Number 1 Female Singer Deserving Wider Recognition, Down Beat Critics Poll, 1974, Number 1 Established Female Singer, Down Beat Readers' Poll, 1974, 75, 76, 77, 78 Top Female Jazz Artist, Record World, 1974, 76, Top New Female Jazz Artist Cash Box, 1974. Office: care William I Hoyt CPA 9034 Sunset Blvd Suite 200 Los Angeles CA 90069

PURINTUN, ORIN, lawyer; b. DeSmet, S.D., Mar. 6, 1923; s. Joseph O. and Florette (Wheat) P.; B.A., Yale, 1944, LL.B., 1948; m. Elizabeth K. Thorson, June 19, 1943; children—James, Ann-Elizabeth, Sally Jean, Teresa, Alan. Admitted to Wis. bar, 1948, since practiced in Milw.; partner firm Foley & Lardner, 1948—. Sec., Sola Basic Industries, Inc. Served with USNR, 1943-46. Home: 3601 N Lake Dr Milwaukee WI 53211 Office: 777 E Wisconsin Ave Milwaukee WI 53202

PURKISER, WESTLAKE TAYLOR, educator, editor; b. Oakland, Calif., Apr. 28, 1910; s. Jacob W. and May F. (Naismith) P.; A.B., Pasadena Coll., 1930; A.M., U. So. Calif., 1939, Ph.D., 1948; m. Arvilla M. Butler, July 24, 1930; children—Joyce Mae (dec.), Joanne Lois, Sharon Lee. Ordained to ministry Ch. of the Nazarene, 1932; pastor, Riverside, Calif., 1930-34, Bellflower, 1934-35, Corning, 1935-37; prof. philosophy Pasadena Coll., 1937-43, dean, 1943-45, v.p., 1945-49, pres., 1949-57; prof. English Bible, Nazarene Theol. Sem., 1957-60; editor Herald of Holiness, 1960-75; prof. Bibl. theology Point Loma Coll., San Diego, 1975-77, emeritus, 1977—. Mem. Phi Beta Kappa, Pi Epsilon Theta, Phi Delta Lambda, Kappa Phi Kappa. Author: Know Your Old Testament, 1947; Some Concepts of the Datum in American Realism (abstract), 1948; Conflicting Concepts of Holiness, 1953. Editor: Exploring the Old Testament, 1956; Security: The False and the True, 1956; Beliefs that Matter Most, 1959; Adventures in Truth, 1960; Exploring Our Christian Faith, 1960; Sanctification and Its Synonyms, 1961; The Message of Evangelism, 1963; Spiritual Gifts: The Charismatic Revival, 1964; Search the Scriptures: First and Second Samuel, 1965; Give Me an Answer, 1968; The New Testament Image of the Ministry, 1969; When You Get to the End of Yourself, 1970; Search the Scriptures: Genesis, 1970; Search the Scriptures: Psalms, 1970; Interpreting Christian Holiness, 1971; Adventures in Bible Doctrine, 1971; The Paradox of Prayer, 1974; Our Wonderful World, 1974; Beacon Bible Expositions: Hebrews, James and Peter, 1974; God's Spirit in Today's World, 1974; Gifts of the Spirit, 1975; God, Man, and Salvation, 1977. Address: 604 Auburn Ave Sierra Madre CA 91024

PURNELL, MAURICE EUGENE, JR., lawyer; b. Dallas, Feb. 17, 1940; s. Maurice Eugene and Marjorie (Maillot) P.; B.A., Washington and Lee U., 1961; M.B.A., Wharton Grad. SCh. Bus. U. Pa., 1963; LL.B., So. Meth. U., 1966; m. Diane Blake, Aug. 19, 1966; children—Maurice Eugene III, Blake Maillot. Admitted to Tex. bar, 1966; mem. firm Locke, Purnell, Boren, Laney & Neely, Dallas, 1972—; dir. Pioneer Corp. Mem. Am., Tex., Dallas bar assns., Am. Judicature Soc. Clubs: Brook Hollow Golf, Koon Kreek Klub, Dallas. Home: 4409 S Versailles Dallas TX 75205 Office: 3600 Republic Bank Tower Dallas TX 75201

PURNELL, RICHARD INGRAM, ins. co. exec.; b. Balt., July 25, 1918; s. Lyttleton Bowen and Mary D. (Ingram) P.; A.B. with honors, Princeton, 1940; m. Marguerite Wright Hillman, July 9, 1958; children—Marguerite, Peter. With Johnson & Higgins, 1946—, pres. Johnson & Higgins Pa. Inc., 1962-70, dir. Johnson & Higgins, N.Y.C., 1963—, pres., 1970—, chmn., 1974—. Mem. Phila. Hosp. Survey Com., 1968-70. Trustee, United Fund Greater Phila., 1966-70, Kent Sch., 1971-77, Coll. of Ins., 1975—, Protestant Theol. Sem., Alexandria, Va., 1976—, Presbyn. Hosp., N.Y.C., 1977—, Cardigan Mountain Sch., 1977—; bd. mgrs. Children's Hosp., Phila., 1966-70; bd. dirs. Shipley Sch., Bryn Mawr, Pa., 1966-72, Downtown-Lower Manhattan Assn., 1971—; pres. Anglo-Am. Ins. Scholarship Found.; vice-chmn. council univ. resources Princeton U. Served with USAAF, 1941-46. Decorated Silver Star, Purple Heart, Air medal with 2 oak leaf clusters. Episcopalian (vestry). Clubs: Augusta (Ga.) Nat. Golf; Down Town Assn., India House, Links (N.Y.C.); Piping Rock (Locust Valley). Home: Piping Rock Rd Locust Valley NY 11560 Office: Johnson & Higgins 95 Wall St New York NY 10005

PURPURA, DOMINICK PAUL, educator, med. scientist; b. N.Y.C., Apr. 2, 1927; s. John R. and Rose (Ruffino) P.; A.B., Columbia U., 1949; M.D., Harvard, 1953; m. Florence M. Williams, May 31, 1948; children—Craig, Kent, Keith, Allyson. Intern, Columbia Presbyn. Med. Center, N.Y.C., 1953-54; resident Neurol. Inst. N.Y.C., 1954-55; asso. prof. neurosurgery, neurology and anatomy Columbia Coll. Physicians and Surgeons, 1958-66; prof., chmn. dept. anatomy Albert Einstein Coll. Medicine, 1967-74; chmn. dept. neurosci. Albert Einstein Coll. Medicine, 1974—; sci. dir. Rose F. Kennedy Center for Research in Mental Retardation N.Y.C., 1969-72, dir., 1972—; NIH adv. com. on epilepsies USPHS; councillor Soc. Neurosci.; chief editor Brain Research. Served with USAAF, 1945-47. Mem. Am. Physiol. Soc., Am. Neurol. Assn., Am. Epilepsy Assn., AAAS. Research on the structure and function of the mature and immature brain; origin of brain waves; developmental neurobiology; mechanisms of epilepsy. Home: 119 E 35th St New York City NY 10016 Office: 1410 Pelham Pkwy S Bronx NY 10461

PURSE, JAMES NATHANIEL, bus. exec.; b. Detroit, Aug. 19, 1923; s. Gilbert R. and Eleanor F. (Leitert) P.; student Mich. Coll. Mining and Tech., 1943; B.S. in Metall. Engring., U. Wis., 1947; m. Rolonde M. L. Redon, Aug. 24, 1946; children—John R., Charles R. With Gt. Lakes Steel Co., Detroit, 1947-55; with Hanna Mining Co., Cleve., 1955-79, mgr. fgn. sales, then v.p. sales, 1960-69, exec. v.p., 1969-74, pres., chief exec. officer, dir., 1974-78, vice chmn., 1978-79, also dir.; dir. B.F. Goodrich Co., Lubrizol Corp., St. John d'el Rey Mining Co., Ltd., Nat. City Corp. Mem. exec. bd. Greater Cleve. council Boy Scouts Am., 1975—; bd. dirs. Greater Cleve. Growth Assn., 1971-76, 78—. Served with USNR, 1942-46. Mem. Am. Iron Ore Assn. (dir. 1970-79, chmn. bd. dirs. 1975-77), Am. Iron and Steel Inst. (dir. 1975-79), Am. Mining Congress (dir. 1977-79). Clubs: Union, Cleve. Athletic, Clevelander, Pepper Pike (Cleve.); Laurel Valley (Ligonier, Pa.). Home: 15 High St Hudson OH 44236 Office: 100 Erieview Plaza Cleveland OH 44114

PURSELL, CARL DUANE, congressman; b. Imlay City, Mich., Dec. 19, 1932; s. Roy and Doris (Perkins) P.; B.A., Eastern Mich. U., 1957, M.A., 1962; LL.D., Madonna Coll., 1977; m. Peggy Jean Brown, 1956; children—Philip, Mark, Kathleen. Former educator, small bus. owner; mem. Wayne County Bd. Commnrs., 1969-70; mem. Mich. Senate, 1971-76; mem. 95th Congress from 2d Mich. Dist. Past mem. Mich. Crime Commn. Served in U.S. Army, 1957-59. Recipient award EPA, 1976. Republican. Address: US House of Representatives 1414 Longworth House Office Bldg Washington DC 20515

PURSELL, CARROLL WIRTH, educator; b. Visalia, Calif., Sept. 4, 1932; s. Carroll Wirth and Ruth Irene (Crowell) P.; B.A., U. Calif., Berkeley, 1956, Ph.D., 1962; M.A., U. Del., 1958; m. Joan Young, Jan. 28, 1956; children—Rebecca Elizabeth, Matthew Carroll. Asst. prof. history Case Inst. Tech., Cleve., 1963-65; asst. prof. U. Calif., Santa Barbara, 1965-69, asso. prof., 1969-76, prof., 1976—; Mellon prof. Lehigh U., Bethlehem, Pa., 1974-76; vis. research scholar Smithsonian Instn., 1970. Mem. Soc. History of Tech. (sec.), History of Sci. Soc., Orgn. Am. Historians, Am. Hist. Assn., AAAS, Phi Beta Kappa. Democrat. Author: Early Stationary Steam Engines in America, 1969; The Military Industrial Complex, 1972; From Conservation to Ecology. Home: 624 Chelham Way Santa Barbara CA 93108 Office: Dept History U Calif Santa Barbara CA 93106

PURVES, ALAN CARROLL, educator; b. Phila., Dec. 14, 1931; s. Edmund Randolph and Mary Carroll (Spencer) P.; A.B., Harvard U., 1953; M.A., Columbia, 1956, Ph.D., 1960; m. Anita Woodruff Parker, June 18, 1960 (dec. 1975); children—William Carroll, Theodore Rehn; m. 2d, Anne Hathaway Nesbitt, July 14, 1976. Lectr. Hofstra Coll., 1956-58; instr. Columbia, 1958-61; asst. prof. English, Barnard Coll., N.Y.C., 1961-65; examiner in humanities Ednl. Testing Service, 1965-68; asso. prof. English, U. Ill., Urbana, 1968-70, prof., 1970-73, prof. English edn., 1973, dir. Curriculum Lab., 1976—; staff asso. Central Midwest Regional Ednl. Lab., St. Ann, Mo., 1968-70. Pres. Wonalancet (N.H.) Corp., 1967-70, 75-77. Served with AUS, 1953-55. Recipient Internat. Assn. Evaluation Edn. Achievement Internat. Fellowship, 1971, Fulbright Hayes award, 1977. Mem. Nat. Council Tchrs. English (trustee research found. 1969-72, mem. com. research 1968-77, v.p. 1977-78, pres. 1979-80), Newcomen Soc. (hon.), Ill. Assn. Tchrs. English, Nat. Conf. Research English, Ill. Conf. English Edn., Am. Ednl. Research Assn. Episcopalian (mem. vestry 1970-73, 77-79). Clubs: Wonalancet Outdoor (pres. 1965-69), Appalachian Mountain. Author: The Essays of Theodore Spencer, 1968; The Elements of Writing about a Literary Work, 1968; Testing in Literature, 1971; How Porcupines Make Love, 1972; Literature and the Reader, 1972; Responding, 1973; Literature Education in Ten Counties, 1973; Educational Policy and International Assessment, 1975; Common Sense and Testing in English, 1975; Evaluation in English, 1976; Achievement in Reading and Literature: New Zealand in International Perspective, 1979; editor: Research in the Teaching of English, 1971-77. Home: Main St Fithian IL 61844 Office: Curriculum Lab Univ Ill Urbana IL 61801

PURVES, CECIL JOHN, mayor; b. Edmonton, Alta., Can., Oct. 18, 1933; s. Cecil S. and Elsie Jean (Meakins) P.; student public schs.: m. Clare Heller, Dec. 29, 1956; children—Cindy, Corinne, Caroline, Catherine. Gen. mgr. Apex Auto Upholstery Co., Edmonton, after 1950; alderman City of Edmonton, 1966-74, mayor, 1977—. Bishop, Mormon Ch., 1974-77; mem. Edmonton Exhbn. Assn.; bd. mgmt. St. Joseph's Hosp. Mem. Edmonton C. of C., Can. Progress Club. Address: Office Mayor City Hall Edmonton AB T5J 0G4 Canada

PURVIN, ROBERT LEMAN, chem. engr.; b. Farmersville, Tex., June 5, 1917; s. Julius L. and Adelaide F. (Mittenthal) P.; B.A. with highest honors, U. Tex., 1937, B.S. with highest honors, 1938; D.Sc. in Chem. Engring., Mass. Inst. Tech., 1941; m. Maria Czartoryski Chajecki, Feb. 1972; children—James Kenneth, Laura Jill Purvin Wynner, Duane Emory, Robert Leman, Jeffrey Leon, Lisa Purvin Oliner. Engr. refinery tech. service Humble Oil & Refining Co., 1941-46; cons., 1946-50; cons. sr. partner Purvin & Gertz, Inc., 1946-57; pres., dir. Purmil Corp., 1953—; exec. v.p., dir. Foster Grant Co., Inc., 1957-62; v.p., dir. TransAtlantic Trading Ltd., 1965-66; mgr. TransAtlantic Gas Assos., 1963-69; sub. dir. gen. Fertilizantes Fosfatados Mexicanos, S.A. de C.V., 1965-67, cons., 1962-70; exec. v.p., dir. Distrigas Corp., 1969-70; chmn. bd. Purvin & Lee, Inc., 1970-75; pres., chief exec. officer Barber Oil, 1975-78; cons., 1978—. Consultor Manhattan Coll., 1967—. Recipient Distinguished Engring. Grad. award U. Tex., 1969. Fellow Am. Inst. Chem. Engrs.; mem. Am. Chem. Soc., Nat. Soc. Profl. Engrs., Soc. Gas Operators, Ind. Petroleum Assn. Am., Phi Beta Kappa, Sigma Xi, Phi Lambda Upsilon, Tau Beta Pi. Mason (Shriner). Clubs: Sky, Chemists, N.Y. Athletic (N.Y.C.). Home: 770 Taylors Ln Mamaroneck NY 10543 Office: 641 Fifth Ave New York City NY 10017

PURVIS, GEORGE FRANK, JR., life ins. co. exec.; b. Rayville, La., Nov. 22, 1914; s. George Frank and Ann Mamie (Womble) P.; A.A., Kemper Mil. Sch., 1932; LL.B., La. State U., 1935; m. Virginia Winston Wendt, May 16, 1942; children—Virginia Reese (Mrs. William H. Freshwater), Winston Wendt, George Frank III. Admitted to La. bar, 1935; individual practice, Rayville, 1935-37; atty. for sec. state La., La. Ins. Dept., also spl. asst. to atty. gen. La., 1937-41; atty. for sec. state La., also dep. ins. commr., 1945-49; with Pan-Am. Life Ins. Co., New Orleans, 1949—, exec. v.p., 1962-64, pres., chief exec. officer, 1964—, chmn. bd., 1969—, also dir.; pres., dir. Compania de Seguros Panamericana, S.Am., Pan-Am. Venezuela Compania de Seguros, C.A.; pres. Pan-Am. de Colombia Compania de Seguros de Vida, S.A.; chmn., dir. Internat. Reins. Co.; dir. First Nat. Bank Commerce in New Orleans, So. Airways, Inc., Pan-Am de Mexico Compania de Seguros Sobre la Vida, S.A., South Central Bell Telephone Co., First Commerce Corp. Lectr. ins. law Tulane U., 1949-56. Big donors chmn. New Orleans Christmas Seal Campaign, 1961, gen. campaign chmn., 1962, chmn. profl. group VIII, 1963; vice chmn. New Orleans United Fund campaign, 1965, gen. chmn., 1967, pres. Tb Assn. Greater New Orleans, 1967, La. State U. Found., 1967, YMCA, New Orleans, 1968—; Geog. chmn. U.S. Savs. Bond campaign, Greater New Orleans, 1971. Mem. Bd. City Park Commrs., 1965—; pres. Met. Area Com., 1979. Pres. Internat. House, 1977; bd. dirs. Family Service Soc. New Orleans, Council for a Better La., New Orleans Philharmonic Symphony Soc., Summer Pop Concerts, Bur. Govt. Research New Orleans; chmn. S.S. Huebner Found. Ins. Edn., 1977—. Served as officer USNR, 1941-45. Recipient award Inst. for Human Understanding, 1975; Weiss Meml. award, 1976; Vol. Activist award, 1978; named alumnus of yr. La. State U., 1975. Mem Am., La. bar assns., La. Law Inst., Am. Judicature Soc., Assn. Life Ins. Counsel, Am. Life Conv. (past chmn. legal sect., exec. com., v.p. La., chmn. 1972), Health Ins. Assn. Am. (dir., chmn. 1970), La. Assn. Legal Res. Life Ins. Cos. (pres. 1963-68), C. of C. Greater New Orleans Area (dir., pres. 1970), Phi Delta Phi, Omicron Delta Kappa, Delta Kappa Epsilon. Episcopalian. Compiler, author: Louisiana Insurance Code, 1948. Contbr. articles to profl. jours. Office: 2400 Canal St New Orleans LA 70119

PURVIS, HUGH FRANK, ret. accountant; b. Moultrie, Ga., Feb. 7, 1904; s. Elias Frank and Eva (Dodd) P.; student Pace Inst., 1922, Eastman Coll., Poughkeepsie, N.Y., 1924; m. Rachel Elizabeth Bowen, Oct. 12, 1963; children by previous marriage—Lorraine (Mrs. John E. Morris), Constance (Mrs. William F. Field); stepchildren—Joan (Mrs. Joseph S. Gratton), Barbara (Mrs. Eugene Patterson). Partner firm Pentland, Purvis, Keller & Co., C,P.A.'s, Miami, Fla., 1933-61; partner, charge Fla. offices Haskins & Sells, C.P.A.'s, Miami, 1961-69. Past pres. Miami Jr. C. of C., Dade County Com. 21. C.P.A., 1929. Mem. Am., Fla. (past pres.) inst. C.P.A.'s Beta Alpha Psi. (hon.). Clubs: Miami; Riveria Country (Coral Gables); Bath (Miami Beach). Home 1212 S Greenway Dr Coral Gables FL 33134 also 415 Longview Dr Waynesville NC 28786

PURYEAR, ALVIN NELSON, educator; b. Fayetteville, N.C., Apr. 6, 1937; s. Byron Nelson and Gladys (Bizzell) P.; B.A., Yale, 1960; M.B.A., Columbia, 1962, Ph.D., 1966; m. Catherine Paulette Wiggins, Aug. 30, 1962; children—Pamela Susan, Susan Catherine, Karen Paulette. Employee relations adviser Mobil Oil Corp., N.Y.C., 1965-66, financial analyst, 1966-67; specialist computational systems Allied Chem. Corp., 1967-68; asso. prof. Rutgers U., Newark, 1968-69; asso. prof. mgmt. Bernard M. Baruch Coll., N.Y.C., 1970-72, prof. mgmt., 1972—, chmn. dept., 1978—, dean coll., 1972-75, dir. Baruch/Cornell M.S. program in Indsl. and Labor Relations; pres. Bentley Clark Assos., Inc., N.Y.C., 1978—; dir. Dollar Savs. Bank N.Y. Trustee, Barber-Scotia Coll., Loyola Coll. (Balt.); bd. dirs. Jarvie Common Weal Service; bd. dirs., treas. Presbyn. Found. N.Y.C.; bd. dirs. Yale Alumni Fund. John Hay Whitney fellow, 1960-61, Samuel Bronfman fellow, 1960-62. Mem. Acad. Mgmt., Am. Mgmt. Assn., Nat. Council Small Bus. Mgmt. Devel. Presbyn. (elder). Co-author: Black Enterprise, Inc., 1973; also articles. Home: 4580 Delafield Ave Bronx NY 10471

PUSEY, WILLIAM WEBB, III, educator; b. Wilmington, Del., Nov. 16, 1910; s. William Webb, II, and Edith White (Lobdell) P.; B.S., Haverford Coll., 1932; A.M., Harvard, 1933; Ph.D., Columbia, 1939; m. Mary Hope Smith, June 18, 1940; children—Mary Faith Pankin, Diana Pickral. Exchange scholar, Bonn, Germany, 1934-35; asst. in German, Columbia U., 1935-37, instr. German and humanities, 1937-39; asso. prof., head German dept. Washington and Lee U., 1939-47, prof., head German dept., 1947-76, prof. German on Thomas Ball Found., 1956-60, S. Blount Mason, Jr. prof. German, 1974—, dean coll., 1960-71, acting pres., 1967. Recipient Am. Council Learned Socs. faculty study fellowship, 1952-53. Served as lt. (j.g.), lt., lt. comdr. USNR, Washington, London, Berlin, 1942-45. Mem. Modern Lang. Assn., Phi Beta Kappa. Author: Louis Sebastien Mercier in Germany, 1939; The Interrupted Dream, 1976. Editor: (with A.G. Steer and B.Q. Morgan) Readings in Military German, 1943. Contbr. articles and revs. to profl. jours. Home: 618 Marshall St Lexington VA 24450

PUSTAY, JOHN STEPHEN, air force officer; b. Roebling, N.J., July 7, 1931; s. Stephen and Mary (Sencak) P.; student Rutgers U., 1949-50; B.S., U.S. Naval Acad., 1954; M.A., San Francisco State Coll., 1960; Ph.D., U. Denver, 1963; grad. Indsl. Coll. Armed Forces, 1970; m. Lorraine Bago, June 4, 1954; children—Tanya M., Melanie A., Jean S., John Stephen. Commd. 2d lt. U.S. Air Force, 1954, advanced through grades to lt. gen., 1976; served in intelligence assignments, Stewart AFB, N.Y., Korea, Japan, 1954-58; instr. USAF Acad., 1960-61, asso. prof. polit. sci., asst. dean faculty, 1963-66; exec. asst. to Sec. State, Washington, 1966-67; dir. doctrine Concepts and Objectives, Hdqrs, USAF, Washington, 1967-69; exec. officer to Chief of Staff, Hdqrs. SHAPE, Belgium, 1970-73; exec. asst. to sec. USAF, Washington, 1973-74; dep. asst. chief of staff Intelligence, Hdqrs. USAF, 1974-76; dir. Concepts, Hdqrs. USAF, 1976-77; comdr. Keesler Tech. Tng. Center, Keesler AFB, Miss., 1977-79; asst. to chmn., joint chiefs staff, Washington, 1979—. Bd. dirs. United Services Automobile Assn. Decorated D.S.M., Legion of Merit with 2 oak leaf clusters, Meritorious Service medal, Air Force Commendation medal with oak leaf cluster; recipient Distinguished Service award Am. Newspaper Women's Club, 1967; White House fellow, 1967. Mem. White House Fellows Assn., Am. Polit. Sci. Assn., Internat. Studies Assn., Council Fgn. Relations, Pi Sigma Alpha, Delta Sigma Phi. Author: Counterinsurgency Warfare, 1965; contbr. articles to mil. publs. Home and Office: 29 Westover Ave SW Bolling AFB Washington DC 20336

PUTKA, ANDREW CHARLES, lawyer; b. Cleve., Nov. 14, 1926; s. Andrew George and Lillian M. (Koryta) P.; student John Carroll U., 1944, U.S. Naval Acad., 1945-46; A.B., Adelbert Coll., Western Res. U., 1949, LL.B., 1952. Admitted to Ohio bar, 1952, since practiced in Cleve.; instr. govt. Notre Dame Coll. for Women, South Euclid, Ohio; v.p. Koryta Bros. Coal Co., Cleve., 1952-56; supt. div. bldg. and loan assns. Ohio Dept. Commerce, 1959-63; pres., chmn. bd., chief exec. officer Am. Nat. Bank, Parma, Ohio, 1963-69; dir. fin. City of Cleve., 1971-74, dir. port control, 1974-78; dir. Cleve. Hopkins Internat. Airport, 1974-78. Mem. Ohio Ho. of Reps., 1953-56, Ohio Senate, 1957-58; dep. auditor, acting sec. Cuyahoga County Bd. Revision, 1970-71; mem. exec. com. Cuyahoga County Democratic Com., 1973—; bd. govs. Sch. Law, Western Res. U., 1953-56; mem. exec. com. World Service Student Fund, 1950-52; U.S. rep. Internat. Pax Romana Congress, Amsterdam, 1950, Toronto, 1952; mem. lay advisory bd. Notre Dame Coll., 1968—; trustee Case-Western Res. U. Voted an outstanding legislator Ohio Press Corrs., 1953; named to All-Star Legislative team Ohio Newspaper Corrs., 1955; named one of Fabulous Clevelanders. Mem. Am., Ohio, Cuyahoga County, Cleve. bar assns., Nat. Assn. State Savs. and Loan Suprs. (past nat. pres.), U.S. Savs. and Loan League (mem. legis. com. 1960-63), Am. Legion, Ohio Municipal League (bd. trustees 1973), Parma C. of C. (bd. dirs., treas. 1965-67), Newman Fedn. (past nat. pres.), Nat. Assn. Christians and Jews, Catholic Lawyers Guild (treas.), Am., Ohio bankers assns., Am. Inst. Banking, Adelbert Alumni Assn. (exec. com.), Internat. Order of Alhambra (internat. parliamentarian 1971—, past grand comdr., supreme advocate 1973), Pi Kappa Alpha, Delta Theta Phi (past pres. Cleve. alumni senate, master inspector 1975). Club: K.C. Home: 17013 Scottsdale Blvd Shaker Heights OH 44120 Office: 10301 Lake Ave Cleveland OH 44102

PUTMAN, DALE CORNELIUS, bus. exec.; b. Ponca, Nebr., Apr. 29, 1927; s. Merle H. and Catherine V. (Sheahan) P.; B.S., U. Nebr., 1949, LL.B., 1951; m. Alice Anselmi, Sept. 8, 1951; children—Mark, Lee, Neil, Bruce, Kirk, Nancy, Wendy. Admitted to Nebr. bar, 1951, Iowa bar, 1951, Mo. bar, 1977; mgr. Interstate Assn. Credit Mgmt., Sioux City, Iowa, 1951-52; sec., legal counsel Metz Baking Co., Sioux City, 1953-66, v.p., 1966-69, exec. v.p., 1969-72, pres., 1972-76; chief operating officer Interstate Brands Corp., Kansas City, Mo., 1976-77, pres., dir., 1977—. Served with U.S. Army, 1945-46. Mem. Am. Bakers Assn. (bd. govs.), Am. Inst. Baking (bd. trustees), Am., Iowa, Nebr., Mo., bar assns., Delta Theta Phi. Republican. Roman Catholic. Home: 8405 Reinhardt Ln Leawood KS 66206 Office: 12 E Armour Blvd Kansas City MO 64141

PUTMAN, PAUL, mfg. co. exec.; b. 1929; grad. Northwestern U., 1950. Pres., chief exec. officer, dir. A P Parts Corp. (merged with Questor Corp. 1967), 1950-67, chmn. bd. Questor Corp., Toledo, 1967—, dir., 1967—. Office: One John Goerlich Sq Toledo OH 43691

PUTNAM, ALFRED WYNNE, lawyer; b. Phila., May 27, 1919; s. Alfred and Nancy Wynne (Cook) P.; A.B., Harvard U., 1940; LL.B., U. Pa., 1947; m. Anne Beale, June 25, 1948; children—Anne Leonard, Alfred Wynne, Edward Beale. Admitted to Pa. bar, 1947; asso. firm Hepburn Ross Willcox & Putnam, and predecessors, Phila., 1947—, partner firm, 1953—. Sec., dir. Pa. Warehousing & Safe Deposit Co.; dir. South Chester Tube Co., Mut. Assurance Co., Tacony Indsl. Park, Inc. Mem. standing com. Episcopal Diocese of Pa.; pres. Family Service of Phila., 1956-59; sec. Library Co. of Phila.; past pres. Chestnut Hill Acad. Bd. dirs. Spring Garden Coll., Am. Oncologic Hosp. Served to lt. comdr. USNR, 1941-45. Mem. Am., Pa., Phila. bar assns., Am. Judicature Soc., Juristic Soc., Chevaliers des Tastevin (grand officier), Delta Psi. Republican. Episcopalian. Clubs: Philadelphia (pres.), Sharswood Law, Racquet, Penn., St. Anthony (Phila.); Delphic (Cambridge, Mass.); State-in-Schuylkill; Rabbit. Home: 8500 Seminole Ave Philadelphia PA 19118 Office: Two Penn Center Plaza Philadelphia PA 19102

PUTNAM, ALLAN RAY, assn. exec.; b. Melrose, Mass., July 16, 1920; s. Carl Eugene and Alice (Atwood); B.S. in Econs., Wharton Sch. of U. Pa., 1942; m. Marion S. Witmer, Aug. 8, 1942; children—Judith H. (Mrs. Martin Kaliski), Robert W., Victoria, Christian. Mem. exec. staff Am. Electroplaters Soc., 1946-49; asst. exec. sec., pub. mag. Tool Engr., Am. Soc. Tool and Mfg. Engrs., 1949-59; mng. dir. Am. Soc. Metals, Metals Park, Ohio, 1959—; pres. Nat. Assn. Exhibit Mgrs., 1955, Council Engring. and Sci. Soc. Execs., 1958; mgr. Am. Soc. Metals Found. Edn. and Research, 1963—. Served to capt. USAAF, 1942-46. Mem. Am. Soc. Assn. Execs. (past dir.), Cleve. Conv. and Visitors Bur. (dir.), Pres.'s Assn., Am. Mgmt. Assn., Metal Properties Council (dir.), Franklin Inst., Internat., Am., S.E. Asia iron and steel insts., Metals Soc. (London), ASTM, Am. Assn. Cost Engrs., Associacao Brasileira de Metais, Italian Soc. of Metallurgy, Chinese Soc. Metals, German Soc. Metals, Australasian Inst. Metals, Am. Nuclear Soc., Cleve. Soc. Assn. Execs., Soc. Automotive Engrs., Soc. Mfg. Engrs., AAAS, Cyrogenic Soc., Soc. for Advancement Materials and Process Engring., Am. Soc. for Engring. Edn., Iron and Steel Inst. Japan (hon.), Nat. Sci. Tchrs. Assn. (life), Metall. Soc., Greater Cleve. Growth Assn., Buckeye Trail Assn. Clubs: Country (Pepper Pike, Ohio); Cleve. Athletic; Appalachian Mountain; Horseshoe Trail; University (Washington). Home: 60 N Strawberry Ln Chagrin Falls OH 44022 Office: Am Soc for Metals Metals Park OH 44073

PUTNAM, CALVIN RICHARD, mathematician, educator; b. Balt., May 25, 1924; s. Calvin Sibley and Miriam May (Kolbe) P.; A.B., Johns Hopkins, 1944, M.A., 1946, Ph.D., 1948; m. Emogene Mae Ferrell, June 14, 1952; children—Bryan Ferrell, James Edward, Vicky Lynn. Instr., Johns Hopkins, 1948-50; mem. Inst. for Advanced Study, 1950-51; asst. prof. Purdue U., West Lafayette, Ind., 1951-54, asso. prof., 1954-59, prof. math., 1959—. Mem. Am. Math. Soc., Math. Assn. Am., Phi Beta Kappa, Sigma Xi. Author: Commutation Properties of Hilbert Space Operators and Related Topics, Ergebnisse der Mathematik, Vol. 36, 1967. Home: 1715 Klondike Rd West Lafayette IN 47906

PUTNAM, CARLETON, author, former air lines exec.; b. N.Y.C., Dec. 19, 1901; s. Israel and Louise (Carleton) P.; B.S., Princeton, 1924; LL.B., Columbia U., 1932; m. 2d, Lucy A. Chapman, Sept. 12, 1944 (div. 1956); m. 3d, Esther Willcox, 1956; 1 dau., Esther Louise. Founder, pres. Chgo. and So. Air Lines, 1933-48, chmn. bd., 1948-53; chmn. bd. Delta C & S Air Lines, 1953-54; dir. Delta Air Lines; mem. nat. labor-mgmt. manpower policy com. ODM, 1953-61; mem. U.S. delegation Internat. Civil Aviation Conf., Chgo., 1944 (adviser); past gov. Nat. Aeronautic Assn. for Mo.; past dir. Air Transport Assn. Am. Trustee Theodore Roosevelt Assn. Republican. Presbyn. Clubs: Cosmos, Chevy Chase (Washington); Princeton (N.Y.C.). Author: High Journey—A Decade in the Pilgrimage of an Airline Pioneer, 1945; Theodore Roosevelt, Vol. I The Formative Years, 1958; Race and Reason: A Yankee View, 1961; Race and Reality: A Search for Solutions, 1967; also numerous papers. Address: 1465 Kirby Rd McLean VA 22101

PUTNAM, DONALD HARDING, electronics mfr.; b. Washington, Apr. 19, 1925; s. Borden R. and Mable (Ernst) P.; B.S.E., Princeton U., 1947, M.S.E., 1948; student corp. finance, Columbia U., 1948-49; m. Eileen Mintz, July 29, 1950; children—Donald Harding, Charles Lawrence, Elizabeth Mary. With Sherman Fairchild Assos., 1948-50, Applied Physics Lab., Johns Hopkins, 1950-51; with Conrac Corp., 1951—, pres., dir., 1958—; dir. Western Union Corp., Nat. Aviation Corp. Sec., dir. Deer Park Assn.; mem. joint commn. Nat. Episcopal Ch. Served with USNR, 1944-46. Mem. Instrument Soc. Am., Inst. Aero. Scis., Sigma Xi. Clubs: Princeton, Sky, University (N.Y.C.); Indian Harbor Yacht (Greenwich). Home: Deer Park Greenwich CT 06830 Office: Three Landmark Sq Stamford CT 06901

PUTNAM, FRANK WILLIAM, educator; b. New Britain, Conn., Aug. 3, 1917; s. Frank and Henrietta (Holzmann) P.; B.A., Wesleyan U., Middletown, Conn., 1939, M.A., 1940; Ph.D., U. Minn., 1942; M.A. (hon.), Cambridge (Eng.) U., 1973; m. Dorothy Alice Linder, Nov. 18, 1942; children—Frank William, Beverly Susan. Instr., research asso. Duke U. Med. Sch., 1942-46; biochemist CWS, Camp Detrick, Md., 1946; asst. prof. U. Chgo., then asso. prof. biochemistry, 1947-55; Lasdon research fellow Cambridge U., 1952-53; prof. biochemistry, head dept. U. Fla., 1955-65; prof. biology, dir. div. biol. scis. Ind. U., Bloomington, 1965-69, prof. molecular biology and zoology, 1972-74, distinguished prof. molecular biology and biochemistry, 1974—; bd. visitors Duke U. Med. Center, 1970-75; chmn. com. nomenclature of human immunoglobulins Internat. Union Immunol. Socs., 1971-76; chmn. basic sci. rev. bd. VA, 1972-76; chmn. cancer cause and prevention adv. com. Nat. Cancer Inst., 1974-75; sci. adv. com. Papanicolaou Cancer Research Inst., 1976—; research rev. com. ARC, 1973-77; sci. com. Brussels Colloquium on Protides of Biol. Fluids, 1970—; chmn. virus cancer program adv. com. Nat. Cancer Inst., 1975-77; sr. med. adv. group VA, 1976—; council div. biol. scis. and Pritzker Med. Sch., U. Chgo., 1977—; chmn. Assembly Life Scis. Nat. Acad. Scis., 1977—; mem. U.S. Nat. Com. Biochemistry, 1973—. Markle scholar med. scis., 1950-56; Guggenheim fellow, 1970; fellow Churchill Coll., Cambridge U., 1973—; recipient Distinguished award teaching and research Wesleyan U., 1964, Distinguished Service award in medicine U. Chgo., 1968; Outstanding Achievement award U. Minn., 1974. Fellow AAAS; mem. Nat. Acad. Scis., Am. Acad. Arts and Scis. (Midwest council 1975—), Pan-Am. Assn. Biomed. Scis. (sec.-gen. 1975-78), Japan Electrophoresis Soc. (hon.), Am. Inst. Biol. Scis. (life), N.Y. Acad. Scis. (life), Am. Soc. Biol. Chemists (sec. 1958-63), Soc. Exptl. Biology and Medicine, Am. Assn. Immunologists, Am. Chem. Soc. (chmn. div. biol. chemistry 1966-67), Soc. Peruana de Patologia (hon.), Fedn. Socs. Exptl. Biology (chmn. secs. com. 1958-63), Phi Beta Kappa, Sigma Xi, Phi Lambda Upsilon, Delta Sigma Rho. Club: Cosmos. Co-author, editor: The Plasma Proteins, vol. 1, Isolation, Characterization and Function, 1960, vol. 2, Biosynthesis, Metabolism, Alterations in Disease, 1960; The Plasma Proteins, 2d edit., Structure, Function, and Genetic Control, Vol. 1, 1975. Vol. 2, 1975, Vol. 3, 1977. Editorial bd. Archives of Biochemistry and Biophysics, 1954-59, Science, 1968—, Immunochemistry, 1972-75, Biomed. News, 1969-73, Fedn. Proc., 1958-63. Author numerous research papers. Address: 5025 E Heritage Woods Rd Bloomington IN 47401

PUTNAM, FREDERICK A(SAHEL), chem. engr.; b. Keene, N.H., July 4, 1947; s. David F. and Rosamond P. (Page) P.; B.A., Dartmouth Coll., 1969; M.S., Case Western Res. U., 1974; Ph.D., Carnegie-Mellon U., 1976. DuPont asst. prof. chem. engring. M.I.T., 1976-78, Joseph R. Mares asst. prof., 1978—. Mem. Am. Phys. Soc., Am. Chem. Soc. (Victor K. La Mer award in colloid and surface chemistry 1977), Am. Inst. Chem. Engrs., Am. Vacuum Soc., Sigma Xi. Research, publs. in applied surface chemistry. Office: MIT Bldg 66-454 Cambridge MA 02139

PUTNAM, FREDERICK WARREN, JR., bishop; b. Red Wing, Minn., June 17, 1917; s. Frederick W. and Margaret (Bunting) P.; B.A., U. Minn., 1939; B.D., Seabury-Western Theol. Sem., 1942, D.D., 1963; postgrad. State U. Iowa, 1946-47; m. Helen Kathryn Prouse, Sept. 24, 1942; children—James Douglas, John Frederick, Andrew Warren. Ordained deacon, priest Episcopal Ch., 1942; pastor in Windom and Worthington, Minn., 1942-43, Iowa City, 1943-47, Evanston, Ill., 1947-59, Wichita, Kans., 1960-63; Episcopalian chaplain State U. Iowa, 1943-47; suffragan bishop Episcopal Diocese Okla., 1963-79; bishop Episc. Ch. in Navajoland, 1979—; cons. Oklahoma City Community Relation Commn., 1966-70. Pres. Okla. Conf. Religion and Race, 1963-67; v.p. Greater Oklahoma City Council Chs., 1966-67; nat. chaplain Brotherhood of St. Andrew, 1967-79, mem. brotherhood legion, 1972—; priest asso. Order Holy Cross, 1942—; exec. com. Conf. Diocesan Execs., 1969—, pres., 1972-74; mem. Okla. Commn. United Ministries in Higher Edn., 1970-79, pres., 1973—; mem. com. on canons, chmn. com. on lay ministry Ho. of Bishops Episc. Ch.; chaplain Okla. Assn. Alcoholism and Alcohol Abuse, 1974-78; founder, pres. Oklahoma City Met. Alliance for Safer City, 1971-78; patron Oklahoma City Ballet Soc. Trustee Seabury-Western Theol. Sem., 1959-65, Episcopal Theol. Sem. Southwest, 1966-69, St. Simeon's Episcopal Home, 1963-79, St. Crispins Episcopal Conf. Center, 1963-79, Casady Sch., 1963-79, Holland Hall Sch., 1963-79, Episcopal Soc. Cultural and Racial Unity, 1967-70; trustee Neighborhood Services Orgn., treas., 1969; founder, 1st pres. Friends of Wichita Pub. Library, 1962. Recipient Distinguished Service award Evanston Jr. C. of C., 1952; Merit award Photog. Soc. Am. Fellow Coll. Preachers; mem. Inst. Pastoral Care, Acad. Religion and Mental Health, ACLU, Asso. Parishes (pres. 1960-64), Overseas Mission Soc., Assn. Am. Indian Affairs, Photog. Soc. Am., Am. Com. for KEEP (v.p. 1961-70), Assn. Clin. Pastoral Edn., Religious Pub. Relations Council, Ch. Soc. Coll. Work, Okla. Camera Club, Center Study Dem. Instns., Nat. Citizens Com. for Broadcasting, Am. Acad. Polit. and Social Sci., World Future Soc., Clergy Assn. Diocese Okla., U. Minn. Alumni Assn., Phi Kappa Psi. Club: Explorers. Author articles. Editor, pub. Shareres mag., 1957-63. Home: 4201 Wilshire Dr Farmington MN 87401 Office: Box 720 Farmington NM 87401

PUTNAM, GEORGE, investment co. exec.; b. Manchester, Mass., Aug. 30, 1926; s. George and Katharine (Harte) P.; A.B. magna cum laude, Harvard, 1949, M.B.A. with distinction, 1951; m. Barbara Weld, June 23, 1949; children—George III, Barbara, Susan Weld. With Putnam Mgmt. Co., Boston, trustee Putnam Growth Fund, 1957—, chmn., 1969—; trustee George Putnam Fund of Boston, 1959—, chmn., 1969—, pres., 1961-70, chief exec. officer, 1961—; pres. Putnam Income Fund Inc., 1968—; pres. Putnam Equities Fund Inc., Putnam Investors Fund, Putnam Convertible Fund, Putnam Vista Fund Inc., Putnam Voyager Fund Inc., Putnam Duofund Inc., Putnam Daily Dividend Trust, Putnam Tax Exempt Income Fund, Putnam Option Income Trust; dir. Freeport Minerals Co., Am. Mut. Ins. Co., Boston Safe Deposit & Trust Co., Boston Co., Inc., Combustion Engring. Inc., Mallinckrodt Inc. Mem. Nat. Market Adv. Bd. Chmn. Manchester Finance Com.; chmn. Gov. Mass. ad hoc Com. to Select Judges; mem. Twentieth Century Fund Task Force on Univ. Endowment. Former trustee, treas. Boston Mus. Sci., St. Mark's Sch.; chmn. com. to visit Arnold Arboretum, 1969-73; trustee New Eng. Aquarium, Bradford Jr. Coll., Shore Country Day Sch., Brookwood Sch., Animal Rescue League of Boston, Com. on Econ. Devel., Mass. Gen. Hosp., Wellesley Coll., Vincent Meml. Hosp., Colonial Williamsburg Found., Harvard Black Rock Corp.; pres. Pub. Health Found. Cancer and Blood Pressure Research, Pub. Health Properties Corp.; bd. govs. Investment Co. Inst., chmn., 1972-74; treas. Harvard-Yenching Inst.; treas., trustee Harvard U.-Dunbarton Oaks Research Library and Collection Center for Hellenic Studies; bd. overseers Harvard U., 1967—, treas., mem. corp., 1973—. Served with USAAF, 1944-45. Clubs: Essex County (Mass.), Somerset, Downtown, Manchester Yacht, Harvard of Boston, Union League; Links (N.Y.C.). Home: Proctor St Manchester MA 01944 Office: 265 Franklin St Boston MA 02110

PUTNAM, GEORGE W., JR., army officer; b. Ft. Fairfield, Maine, May 5, 1920; s. George W. and Rae B. (Merrithew) P.; married; children—James M., J. Glenn. Served as enlisted man U.S. Army, 1941-42, commd. 2d lt., 1942, advanced through grades to maj. gen., 1970; comdg. gen. 1st Cavalry Div., Vietnam, 1970-71; dir. Mil. Personnel Mgmt., Hdqrs. Dept. Army, Washington, 1971-75; comdg. gen. U.S. Army So. European Task Force, Vicenza, Italy, 1975-77; comdg. gen. U.S. Army Phys. Disability Agy., Washington, 1977—; dir. Army Council Rev. Bds. Office: US Army Phys Disability Agency WRAMC Washington DC 20012

PUTNAM, HOWARD DEAN, airline exec.; b. Bedford, Iowa, Aug. 21, 1937; s. Virgil Glen and Mary Nancy (Livingston) P.; M.B.A. in Mktg., U. Chgo., 1966; grad. Advanced Mgmt. Program Harvard U., 1978; m. Krista Delight Moser, Oct. 20, 1957; children—Michael Dean, Susan Delight. With Capital Airlines, Chgo., 1955-61, passenger service mgr., 1957-59, sales rep., 1959-61; with United Airlines, Chgo., 1961-78, regional v.p., San Francisco, 1971-74, group v.p. mktg., Chgo., 1974-78; pres., chief exec. officer S.W. Airlines, Dallas, 1978—, also dir.; dir. Mercantile Bank, Dallas. Mem. Am. Soc. Travel Agts. (allied asso.). Presbyterian. Club: Bohemian (San Francisco). Office: Box 37611 Love Field Dallas TX 75235

PUTNAM, JOHN BRUCE, assn. exec.; b. Somerville, Mass., July 2, 1936; s. Philip Austin and Thelma Madeleine (Arthur) P.; A.B., Harvard, 1958; m. Dianne Maxwell Coyle, Sept. 13, 1958; children—Sara Lynn, Jennifer Restieaux, Nathaniel Stephen. Social scis. editor Princeton Univ. Press, 1960-63; editor East West Center Press, Honolulu, 1963-64; mng. editor Northwestern U. Press, Evanston, Ill., 1964-67, sr. editor, 1967-71, asst. dir., 1969-71; asso. exec. dir. Assn. Am. Univ. Presses, N.Y.C., 1971, exec. dir., 1971—; pres. Am. Univ. Press Services, 1971—; observer Govt. Advisory Com. Internat. Book and Library Programs Dept. State, 1971-77; lectr., cons. in field. Mem. U.S. com. Internat. Book Year, 1971; mem. Heritage '76 Publs. and Research Advisory Panel, Am. Revolution Bicentennial Commn., 1972. Bd. dirs. Centro Interamericano de Libros Academicos, Mexico City, 1971-76. Served with USNR, 1958-60. Mem. ALA, Am. Printing History Assn., Aircraft Owners and Pilots Assn., Exptl. Aircraft Assn. Episcopalian (lay reader). Author: (with Robert Gesteland) Project Survival, 1969. Contbr. articles to profl. jours. Office: Assn Am Univ Presses One Park Ave New York NY 10016*

PUTNAM, LEON JOSEPH, educator; b. Kalamazoo, Dec. 7, 1928; s. Forrest Elmer and Hazel Effie (Dresselhouse) P.; A.A. (Tompkins scholar), 1948; A.B., U. Mich., 1950, A.M., 1951; B.D. (fellow), Colgate Rochester Div. Sch., 1955; Ph.D. (fellow), Harvard, 1962; m. Phyllis Irene Millspaugh, May 17, 1955; children—Mark, Lee. Ordained to ministry Baptist Ch., 1955; asst. prof. Heidelberg Coll., Tiffin, Ohio, 1959-62, asso. prof., 1962-66, prof. philosophy and religion, 1966—; instr. Winebrenner Theol. Sem., Findlay, Ohio, part time 1970-71. Recipient Swedenborg Essay award, 1958. Mem. Am. Philos. Assn., Am. Acad. Religion, Soc. For Sci. Study Religion, AAUP. Author: The Future of Faith, 1967. Home: 16 Park Pl Tiffin OH 44883

PUTNAM, MICHAEL COURTNEY JENKINS, educator; b. Springfield, Mass., Sept. 20, 1933; s. Roger Lowell and Caroline (Jenkins) P.; A.B., Harvard U., 1954, A.M., 1956, Ph.D., 1959. Instr. classics Smith Coll., 1959-60; faculty classics Brown U., Providence, 1960—, prof., 1967—, chmn., 1968, 70-72, 77-78, acting dir. Center for Hellenic Studies, 1961-62, sr. fellow Center for Hellenic Studies, 1971—. Scholar in residence Am. Acad. in Rome, 1969-70; asso., univ. seminar on classical civilization Columbia U., 1972—. Mem. Cath. Commn. on Intellectual and Cultural Affairs, 1969—. Sole trustee Lowell Obs., Flagstaff, Ariz., 1967—; trustee Bay Chamber Concerts, Camden, Maine, 1972—. Recipient Charles J. Goodwin award of merit Am. Philol. Assn., 1971. Rome Prize fellow Am. Acad. in Rome, 1963-64; Guggenheim Meml. fellow, 1966-67; sr. fellow Nat. Endowment for Humanities, 1973-74, cons., 1974—. Mem. Am. Philol. Assn. (dir. 1972-75, mem. com. on award of merit 1975-78, chmn. 1978—), Archeol. Inst. Am., Classical Assn. New Eng., Mediaeval Acad. Am., Vergilian Soc. Am. (trustee 1969-73, v.p. 1974-76). Democrat. Roman Catholic. Club: Art (Providence). Author: The Poetry of the Aeneid, 1965; Virgil's Pastoral Art, 1970; Tibullus: A Commentary, 1973; Virgil's Poem of the Earth, 1979; contbr. articles to profl. jours. Home: 77 Williams St Providence RI 02906

PUTNAM, PETER BROCK, author, lectr.; b. Georgia, June 11, 1920; s. Brock and Margaret (Faber) P.; grad. Hill Sch., 1938; B.A., Princeton, 1942, Ph.D., 1950; m. Durinda Dobbins, Aug. 12, 1944; children—Brock, Barbara Durinda, John Gerry. Lectr. history Princeton, 1950-55; v.p. Unitarian Universalist Assn., 1965-67. Pres., Chapin Sch., 1961-63; exec. com. Princeton Alumni Council, 1972-76, Bd. dirs. Recording for Blind, 1955—, pres., 1976—; bd. dirs. Mass. Assn. Blind, 1967-71, Star Island Corp.; pres. Unitarian Ch., 1954-57; bd. dirs. Lucerna Fund, 1976—. Mem. Author's League, Princeton Meml. Assn. (dir. 1954), P.E.N. Clubs: Cottage, Princeton Triangle (trustee 1962—). Author: Keep Your Head Up, Mr. Putnam, 1952; Seven Britons in Imperial Russia, 1952; Cast off the Darkness, 1957; Triumph of the Seeing Eye, 1962; Peter, the Revolutionary Tsar, 1973; Love in the Lead, 1979. Translator: (Marc Bloch) Apologie Pour l'Histoire, 1953. Home: 48 Roper Rd Princeton NJ 08540

PUTNAM, RICHARD JOHNSON, SR., U.S. judge; b. Abbeville, La., Sept. 27, 1913; s. Robert Emmett and Mathilde (Young) P.; B.S. cum laude, Springhill Coll., Mobile, 1934; LL.B., Loyola U., New Orleans, 1937; m. Dorethea Gooch, Jan. 27, 1940; children—Richard Johnson, Claude Robert, Mary Stacy, Cynthia Anne. Admitted to La. bar, 1937; pvt. practice, Abbeville, 1937-54; dist. atty. 15th Jud. Dist., 1948-54; judge 15th Jud. Dist. Ct. La., 1954-61; U.S. dist. judge West Dist. La., 1961—, sr. U.S. dist. judge, 1975—; rep. of fed. cts. La. Law Inst., 1976—. Served from ensign to lt. (s.g.) USNR, 1942-45. Mem. Dist. Judges Assn., Am., La. bar assns., Am. Legion, V.F.W., C. of C., St. Thomas Moore Soc. (Service award 1937), Delta Theta Phi. K.C. (4 deg.). Home: Windover Old LaFitte Rd Abbeville LA 70510 Office: US District Court Lafayette LA 70502

PUTNAM, ROBERT E., editor; b. Mt. Sterling, Ill., Sept. 13, 1933; s. John Harold and Florence Pauline (Curran) P.; B.A., U. Ill., 1959; M.A., Roosevelt U., 1969; m. Linda J. Wiant, Aug. 30, 1960; children—Justine, Robbie, Dylan. Asso. engr. Western Electric Co., Chgo., 1960-62; with Am. Tech. Soc., Chgo., 1964—, editor-in-chief, 1973—. Served with AUS, 1953-55. Mem. Am. Vocat. Assn. Author: Fundamentals of Carpentry, 1967; Concrete Block Construction, 3d edit., 1973; Bricklaying Skill and Practice, 3d edit., 1974; Architectural and Building Trades Dictionary, 3d edit., 1974; Fundamentals of Carpentry: Tools, Materials and Practices, 5th edit., 1977; Basic Blueprint Reading: Residential, 1980. Home: 84

Dogwood St Park Forest IL 60466 Office: 5608 S Stony Island Ave Chicago IL 60637

PUTTER, IRVING, educator; b. N.Y.C., Dec. 3, 1917; s. Joseph and Anna (Schrank) P.; B.A., Coll. City N.Y., 1938; M.A., State U. Iowa, 1941; Ph.D., Yale U., 1949; children—Paul Stephen, Candace Anne Putter Newlin. Mem. faculty U. Calif. at Berkeley, 1947—, prof. French, 1961—, chmn. dept., 1968-71, humanities research fellow, 1971-72, 78-79. Guggenheim fellow, 1955-56; Fulbright fellow, 1955-56. Author: Leconte de Lisle and His Contemporaries, 1951; The Pessimism of Leconte de Lisle: Sources and Evolution, 1954; The Pessimism of Leconte de Lisle: The Work and The Time, 1961; La Dernière Illusion de Leconte de Lisle: Lettres Inédites a Emilie Leforestier, 1968; also numerous articles. Editor, translator: Chateaubriand: Atala, René, 1952. Home: 115 St James Dr Piedmont CA 94611 Office: Dept French Univ Calif Berkeley CA 94720

PUTZE, LOUIS, corp. ofcl.; b. Woodriver, Ill., Sept. 13, 1916; s. Edward and Tillie (Fisher) P.; B.S., Purdue U., 1938, D. Indsl. Mgmt. (hon.), 1974; grad. Am. Inst. Banking, 1941; m. Mary Louise Bonucci, July 6, 1949; children—Sally, William, Thomas, John. Engr., trainee Harris Trust & Savs. Bank, Chgo., 1938-40; pres., dir. Sampsel Time Control, Inc., wholly-owned subs. Sears, Roebuck & Co., Spring Valley, Ill., 1947-53; cons. to dir. sci. and tech. equipment div. NPA, Dept. Commerce, Washington, 1952-53; pres., dir. Soreng Products Corp., 1953-56, Controls Co. Am., 1956-66; exec. v.p., dir. Gen. Precision Equipment Corp., Tarrytown, N.Y., 1966-68; group v.p., dir. Singer Co., N.Y.C., 1968-71; pres., chief exec. officer Rockwell Mfg. Co., Pitts., 1971-73; v.p., mem. exec. com., dir. Rockwell Internat., Pitts., 1973-79, pres. utility and indsl. ops., 1973-79, cons., 1979—; dir. Interlake Inc., Chgo., McGraw-Hill, Inc., N.Y.C., Cordes Corp., Miami, Fla., Thomas & Betts Corp., Raritan, N.J. Mem. Corp. Babson Coll. Corp.; mem. pres.'s council Purdue U. Served to maj. AUS, 1940-45; procurement arty. equipment and fire control instruments Chgo. Ordnance Dist., and ETO, 1945-46. Mem. Chief Execs. Forum, Inc., Elec. Mfrs. Club, Internat. C. of C. (trustee U.S. Council internat. orgn., mem. exec. com.), Newcomen Soc. N.Am., Sigma Chi. Episcopalian. Clubs: Chicago; Economic, University (N.Y.C., Chgo.); Rolling Rock (Liqonier, Pa.); Duquesne, Pitts. Golf, Allegheny (Pitts.). Home: Farfields McDowell Rd Ligonier PA 15658 Office: 600 Grant St Pittsburgh PA 15219

PUTZEL, CONSTANCE KELLNER, lawyer; b. Balt., Sept. 5, 1922; d. William Stummer and Corinne (Strauss) Kellner; A.B., Goucher Coll., 1942; LL.B., U. Md., 1945, J.D., 1969; m. William L. Putzel, Aug. 28, 1945; 1 son, Arthur William. Social worker Balt. Dept. Pub. Welfare, 1945-46; admitted to Md. bar, 1945; atty. New Amsterdam Casualty Co., Balt., 1947; staff atty. Legal Aid Bur., Balt., 1947-49; asso. firm Putzel, Putzel & Danoff, Balt., 1950—, sr. partner, 1967—; instr. U. Balt. Sch. Law, 1975-77, Goucher Coll., 1976-77. Mem. character com. Ct. Appeals of Md., 1976—; mem. Md. Com. on Status of Women, 1972-76, Com. to Implement ERA, 1973-76; Pres. U. Md. Law Alumni Assn., 1978; bd. dirs. Legal Aid Bur., 1951-52, 71-73. Mem. Am., Md. (bd. govs. 1972-73, chmn. family law sect. 1978-79) bar assns., Bar Assn. Balt. City (exec. com. 1970-71), Women's Bar Assn. Balt. (pres. 1951-52), United World Fedn. (vice chmn. nat. exec. council 1968, chmn. Balt. 1967-69). Home: 8207 Spring Bottom Way Pikesville MD 21208 Office: 600 Reisterstown Rd Pikesville MD 21208

PUTZEL, WILLIAM L., lawyer; b. Newark, Dec. 4, 1918; s. Arthur B. and Jeanette (Meyers) P.; J.D., U. Md., 1951; m. Constance B. Kellner, Aug. 28, 1945; 1 son, Arthur W. Claim supr. Md. Casualty Co., 1945-50; partner firm Putzel, Putzel & Danoff, Attys., Balt., 1950—. Bd. dirs. Balt. Poly. Inst. PTA, 1967-71, pres., 1969-70; trustee Oheb Shalom Congregation, 1966-77, pres., 1973-75. Served with USAAF, 1941-45. Mem. Am., Md., Balt. County bar assns., Balt. Estate Planning Council, Comml. Law League, Am. Judicature Soc. Home: 8207 Springbottom Way Pikesville MD 21208 Office; Pikesville Plaza Bldg 600 Reisterstown Rd Baltimore MD 21208

PUTZELL, EDWIN JOSEPH, JR., lawyer; b. Birmingham, Ala., Sept. 29, 1913; s. Edwin Joseph and Celeste (Joseph) P.; A.B., Tulane U., 1935; LL.B., Harvard U., 1938; children—Cynthia Putzell Reidy, Edwin Joseph III; m. 2d, Dorothy Corcoran Waters, Aug. 5, 1967. Admitted to N.Y. bar, 1939, U.S. Supreme Ct., 1945, Mo. bar, 1946; atty. Donovan, Leisure, Newton & Lumbard, N.Y.C. and Washington, 1937-42; asst. treas. Monsanto Co., St. Louis, 1945-46, asst. sec., atty., 1946-51, sec., 1951-77, dir. law dept., 1953-68, v.p., gen. counsel, 1963-77; partner Coburn, Croft, Shepherd, Herzog & Putzell, St. Louis, 1977-79, of counsel, 1979—; dir. Mfrs. Bank & Trust Co., St. Louis. Vice chmn. St. Louis County Bd. Police Commrs., 1964-72; pres. Social Planning Council St. Louis, 1954-57; mem. Naples (Fla.) Airport Authority, 1979—; vice chmn. Westminster Coll., 1976-79; chmn. St. Louis ednl. TV sta. KETC, 1977-79; trustee St. Lukes Hosp., 1973-79. Served to lt. USNR, 1942-45; exec. officer, asst. to dir. OSS. Mem. Am., Mo., St. Louis bar assns., St. Louis Symphony Soc. (dir. 1955-69), Am. Law Inst., Am. Soc. Corporate Secs. (pres. 1968-69), Assn. Gen. Counsel, Phi Beta Kappa, Delta Sigma Phi. Episcopalian. Clubs: Bogey; Noonday, Bellerive Country (St. Louis); F St. (Washington); Port Royal Beach (Naples, Fla.). Home: 3033 Rum Row Naples FL 33940 Office: #1 Mercantile Center Saint Louis MO 63101

PUZO, MARIO, author; b. N.Y.C., Oct. 15, 1920; ed. Columbia, New Sch. for Social Research; children—Anthony, Joey, Dorothy, Virginia, Eugene, Anthony. Lit. reviewer various mags.; former civil service employee; former editor Stag mag., Male mag. Recipient Acad. awards for The Godfather, 1972, The Godfather, Part II, 1974. Author: Dark Arena, 1955; The Fortunate Pilgrim, 1965; The Runaway Summer of Davie Shaw, 1966; The Godfather, 1969; The Godfather Papers and Other Confessions, 1972; Inside Las Vegas, 1977; Fools Die, 1979; (film screenplays) The Godfather, 1972, The Godfather, Part II, 1974, Earthquake, 1974, Superman, 1979, Superman II, 1980. Address: care Russell Snyder Dir Advt and Promotion Adult Trade Dept GP Putnam's Sons 200 Madison Ave New York City NY 10016

PUZZO, CHARLES JOSEPH, public relations co. exec.; b. Enfield, Conn., Sept. 1, 1921; s. Dominick and Anna (Chianta) P.; student in bus. adminstrn. and acctg. Packard Jr. Coll., 1951, Columbia U., 1951-53; m. Mary A. Fiore, June 3, 1944; children—Marilyn Ann Puzzo Sacco, Marie Rachelle Puzzo Garin. Acct., Panagra Co., N.Y.C., 1948-51; with Hill and Knowlton, Inc., N.Y.C., 1951—, sr. v.p., 1972-73, exec. v.p., fin., treas., mem. office chief exec., 1973—, also dir. Served to capt. USAAF, 1942-46. Mem. Fin Execs. Inst., Nat. Assn. Accountants, Homefield Assn. Republican. Roman Catholic. Club: Am. Legion. Home: 127 Hoover Rd Yonkers NY 10710 Office: 633 Third Ave New York NY 10017. *My principles: respect of life, property and law; highest integrity in decision making.*

PYATT, EVERETT ARNO, govt. ofcl.; b. Kansas City, Mo., July 22, 1939; s. Arno Doyne and Myrl Elizabeth (Osborn) P.; B.E., B.S., Yale U., 1962; M.B.A., U. Pa., 1977; m. Susan Evelyn Kristal, Sept. 28, 1968; children—Jennifer, Laura. Staff engr. office dir. def. research and devel. Office Sec. Def., Dept. Def., Washington, 1962-72, dir. acquisition planning Office Asst. Sec. Def. for Program Analysis and Evaluation, 1972-75, dir. logistics resources Office Asst. Sec. Def. for Installations and Logistics, 1975-77; prin. dep. asst. sec. of navy for logistics Dept. Navy, Washington, 1977-79; dep. chief fin. officer Dept. Energy, Washington, 1979—. Office of Sec. of Def. fellow, 1975-77. Mem. IEEE. Club: Yale. Home: 4560 N 25th Rd Arlington VA 22207 Office: 266 Crystal Plaza Suite 5 Arlington VA 22222

PYDEE, ERNEST SAMUEL, electric co. exec.; b. Winnipeg, Man., Can., Mar. 27, 1926; s. Ernest William and Jean Elizabeth (Cameron) P.; student Banff Sch. Advanced Mgmt., 1973; m. Geraldine Patricia Brady, Apr. 14, 1949; children—Susan Patricia, Bruce Ernest, Ronald Dale. Securities officer Man. Hydro, Winnipeg, 1956-63, asst. treas., 1963-71, treas., 1971—. Served in Candian Navy, 1943-46. Mem. Canadian Elec. Assn., Navy League Can. (past sec. Winnipeg br.). Home: 1095 Mulvey Ave Winnipeg MB R3M 1H2 Canada Office: PO Box 815 Winnipeg MB R3C 2P4 Canada

PYE, AUGUST KENNETH, univ. chancellor; b. N.Y.C., Aug. 21, 1931; s. Cyril and Hazel (Forrest) P.; B.A., U. Buffalo, 1951; J.D., Georgetown U., 1953, LL.M., 1955, LL.D., 1978; L.H.D., Belmont Abbey Coll., 1979; m. Judith Hope King, Feb. 6, 1965; 1 son, Henry Williams. Admitted to D.C. bar, 1953, N.C. bar, 1970; prof. law Georgetown U. Law Center, 1955-66, asso. dean, 1961-66; prof. law Duke, 1966—, dean Law Sch., 1968-70, 73-76, chancellor, 1970-71, 76—, univ. counsel, 1971-73. Program specialist legal edn. Ford Found., India, 1966-67. Served with AUS, 1953-55. Mem. Am. Law Inst., Assn. Am. Law Schs. (pres. 1976-77), Phi Beta Kappa. Club: Army-Navy. Home: 2802 Chelsea Circle Durham NC 27707

PYE, LUCIAN WILMOT, educator, polit. scientist; b. Shansi, China, Oct. 21, 1921 (parents Am. citizens); s. Watts Orson and Gertrude (Chaney) P.; B.A., Carleton Coll., 1943; M.A., Yale, 1949, Ph.D., 1951; m. Mary Toombs Waddill, Dec. 24, 1944; children—Evelyn, Lucian, Virginia. Instr., then asst. prof. polit. sci. Washington U., St. Louis, 1949-52; research asso. Yale, 1951-52, Princeton, 1952-56; vis. lectr. Columbia, 1956; mem. faculty Mass. Inst. Tech., 1956—, prof. polit. sci., 1960—, Ford prof., 1972—, chmn. sect., 1961-63, sr. staff mem. Center Internat. Studies, 1956—; vis. asso. prof. Yale, 1959-61. Chmn. com. comparative politcs Social Sci. Research Council, 1963-73; mem. adv. com. adminstr. AID, 1961-68; cons. Dept. State, 1962-68, Nat. Security Council, 1968—. Trustee Asia Found., 1963—; gov. East-West Center, Honolulu, 1976—; bd. dirs. Nat. Com. U.S.-China Relations. Served as 1st lt. USMCR, 1945-46. Fellow Center Advanced Study Behavioral Scis., 1963. Fellow Am. Acad. Arts and Scis., Am. Philos. Soc.; mem. Assn. Asian Studies (dir.), Am. Polit. Sci. Assn. (dir.), Council Fgn. Relations (dir.), Asia Soc. (dir.), Pilgrim Soc., Phi Beta Kappa. Unitarian. Club: Cosmos. Author: Guerrilla Communism in Malaya, 1956; Politics, Personality and Nation Building, 1961; Aspects of Political Developments, 1966; Southeast Asia's Political Systems, 1967; The Spirit of Chinese Politics, 1968; Warlord Politics, 1971; China: An Introduction, 1972; Mao Tse-tung: The Man in The Leader, 1976. Co-author: The Politics of the Developing Areas, 1960; The Emerging Nations, 1961. Editor: Communications and Political Development, 1963; Political Culture and Political Development, 1965, Political Science and Area Studies, 1975. Home: 72 Fletcher Rd Belmont MA 02178 Office: Mass Inst Tech Dept Polit Sci Cambridge MA 02139

PYE, MORT, newspaper editor; b. Rochester, N.Y., May 28, 1918; s. Arthur and Lillian (Palley) P., student U. Ill., 1936-38; B.S., Coll. City N.Y., 1940; L.H.D., Seton Hall U., 1975; m. Florence M. Newhouse, Oct. 31, 1942; 1 son, Richard. Various editorial positions L.I. Daily Press, 1941-57; asso. editor Newark Star-Ledger, 1957-63, editor, 1963—. Served with VIII Corps, AUS, 1944-45. Decorated Bronze Star; Croix de Guerre (France). Home: South Orange NJ 07079 Office: Star-Ledger Plaza Newark NJ

PYLE, EVERETT GUSTAV, educator; b. Kewanee, Ill., Aug. 5, 1913; s. John Cronau and Amanda (Rathnow) P.; B.E., Western Ill. U., 1931; M.A., U. Ia., 1939, Ph.D., 1961; m. Opal Freda Hatfield, May 10, 1941; children—John Burton, Lola Anne. Tchr. English, Mitchell (Ia.) Consol. Schs., 1936-38, Unionville (Mo.) Pub. Schs., 1938-42; instr. Nat. Sch. Aeros., Kansas City, Mo., 1942-43; USAAF procurement insp. Glenn L. Martin Co., Omaha, 1943-45; instr. English, S.D. State U., 1945-46; mem. faculty Wis. State U., Oshkosh, 1946—, prof. English, 1961—, dean Grad. Sch., 1963-74. Mem. exec. bd., commr. council Twin Lakes council Boy Scouts Am., 1962-63, mem. nat. council, 1966-74. Recipient Silver Beaver award Boy Scouts Am., 1964. Mem. Nat. Council Tchrs. English, Am. Assn. Higher Edn., Kappa Delta Pi (Honor Key award 1961), Alpha Phi Omega. Presbyn. (elder 1964-66). Odd Fellow. Club: Candlelight (Oshkosh). Home: 1278 Elmwood Ave Oshkosh WI 54901

PYLE, FRANCIS JOHNSON, educator; b. South Bend, Ind., Sept. 13, 1901; s. Dan and Zoula Angie (Johnson) P.; B.A., Oberlin Coll., 1923; M.A., U. Wash., 1932; Ph.D., U. Rochester, 1945; m. Eleanor Meneghel, Apr. 14, 1927; 1 dau., Zoula Pauline (Mrs. Ahmed Zein-Eldin). Dir. instrumental music Wash. pub. schs., 1927-29; dir. instrumental music, asst. prof. music theory Central State Coll., 1929-37; prof. theory and musicology, head dept. Drake U., 1937—; vis. prof. theory U. Calif. at Los Angeles, summer 1955; Bicentennial composer in residence St. Cloud (Minn.) State U., 1976; vis. prof., orch. dir. Central Coll., Pella, Iowa; composer, editor, lectr., guest condr. program annotator Des Moines Symphony Orch.; music advisor Iowa Fine Arts Council. Recipient Distinguished Service award to music educators, 1970; Robert M. McCowan meml. award outstanding contbrn. choral music, 1970. Mem. Music Tchrs. Nat. Assn. (nat. exec. bd.), Music Educators Nat. Conf. (Iowa exec. bd.), Nat. Fedn. Music Clubs (exec. com. Iowa Bicentennial 1976), Am. Musicol. Soc., ASCAP, Phi Mu Alpha, Pi Kappa Lambda. Presbyn. Mason. Composer: Pictures for Suzanne, 1958; Woodwind Quintet, 1959; Sonata for Clarinet and Piano, 1959; Sonata for Three, 1964; Violin Piano Sonata, 1964; Far Dominion, 1966; TeDeum, 1962; Concerto for Trumpet and Wind Ensemble, 1966; Symphony in One Movement for Accordion Orchestra, 1966; Concerto Giubilante for Organ, 19 Winds and Percussion, 1967; Mountain Tarn, Henry Was a Worthy King, Elkan-Vogel, 1967; Four Dialogues for Harp and Orchestra, 1969; Sonata for Piano, 1968; Full Stature, 1968; Sonata Nos. 1 and 2 for Free Bass Accordion, 1968, 69; Overture for Accordion Orchestra, 1969; I Have Chosen Thee, 1968; Canticle of the Sun (brass sextet or piano), 1970; Three Psalms (orch., chorus and brass choir), 1971; Studies in 20th Century Idioms (8 etudes for free bass accordion), 1971; Sonata for Flute and Piano, 1970; Sinfonietta No. 1 for Chamber Orchestra, 1971; Overture Pasadena for Concert Band, 1971; Psalm 133 for Male Chorus and Keyboard, 1972; For Those Who Seek (trumpet solo, double brass sexette, percussion), 1972; Symphony No. 1 for Concert Band, 1973; Sonata for Bassoon and Piano, 1973; 2d Sonata for Bassoon and Piano, 1973; Dialogues for Piano Duet, 1974; Quartet for Saxaphones, 1974; Sonata No. 3 for Piano, 1975; Memorial Chorus, 1975; Sinfonietta No. 2 for Chamber Orch., 1976; Eight Duos for 2 Clarinets, 1976; Festival Prelude, Multiple Pianos, 1976; Eight Duos for Advanced Clarinet, 1977; Sinfonietta No. 3 for Orch. (joint commn. Ft. Dodge Symphony-Iowa Arts Council), 1977. Home: 1535 41st St Des Moines IA 50311

PYLE, KENNETH BIRGER, historian; b. Bellefonte, Pa., Apr. 20, 1936; s. Hugh Gillespie and Blanche Ingeborg (Petterson) P.; A.B. magna cum laude, Harvard Coll., 1958; Ph.D., Johns Hopkins U., 1965; m. Anne Hamilton Henszey, Dec. 22, 1960; children—William Henszey, Anne Hamilton. Asst. prof. U. Wash., 1965-69, asso. prof., 1969-75, prof. history and Asian studies, 1975—, dir. Sch. Internat. Studies, 1978—; vis. lectr. in history Stanford U., 1964-65; vis. asso. prof. history Yale U., 1969-70. Ford Found. fellow, 1961-64; Fulbright-Hays fellow, 1970-71; Social Sci. Research Council-Am. Council Learned Socs. fellow, 1970-73, 77. Mem. Assn. Asian Studies, Am. Hist. Assn. Presbyterian. Author: The New Generation in Meiji Japan, 1969; The Making of Modern Japan, 1978; editor Jour. Japanese Studies, 1974—. Home: 8416 Midland Rd Bellevue WA 98004 Office: Sch Internat Studies U Wash Seattle WA 98195

PYLE, ROBERT MILNER, JR., profl. assn. exec.; b. Orange, N.J., Oct. 24, 1938; s. Robert M. and Dorothy (Collings) P.; B.A., Williams Coll., 1960; J.D., U. Va., 1963; m. C. Page Neville, May 31, 1969; children—Cynthia Neville, Laura Collings. Admitted to N.Y. bar, 1964; asso. firm Mudge Rose Guthrie & Alexander, N.Y.C., 1963-68; with Studebaker-Worthington, Inc., N.Y.C., 1968-77, sec., 1972-76, asso. gen. counsel, 1974-77, sr. corp. counsel, asst. to sec., 1979; corp. counsel, asst. to sec. Singer Co., N.Y.C., 1977-79; v.p., counsel Am. Soc. Corp. Secs., Inc., N.Y.C., 1979—. Trustee, Pingry Sch., Elizabeth, N.J., 1972-74; bd. govs. Colonial Dances, Ltd., N.Y.C., 1970-74. Mem. Am. Bar Assn., Assn. Bar City N.Y., Met. Squash Racquets Assn. (past treas.), Pingry Sch. Alumni Assn. (pres. 1972-74, dir. 1966-78, certificate of merit 1968), Sigma Phi, Delta Theta Phi, Pi Delta Epsilon. Republican. Episcopalian. Clubs: Racquet and Tennis (N.Y.C.); Bay Head (N.J.) Yacht; Short Hills. Office: One Rockefeller Plaza New York NY 10020

PYLES, THOMAS, philologist; b. Frederick, Md., June 5, 1905; s. Joseph Thomas and Charlotte (Bowers) P.; B.A., U. Md., 1926, M.A., 1927; Ph.D., Johns Hopkins, 1938; m. Bessie Alice Yort, Dec. 21, 1929; 1 son, Thomas. With dept. English, U. Md., 1927-44; instr. English, Johns Hopkins, 1938-44; prof. English, U. Okla., 1944-48; prof. English, U. Fla., 1948-66, prof. emeritus, 1972—; prof. English and linguistics Northwestern U., 1966-71, prof. emeritus, 1971—; guest prof. English philology U. Göttingen (Germany), 1956-57; vis. prof. N.Y. U., summer 1965, Northwestern U., 1965-66. Mem. editorial adv. bd. Funk and Wagnalls Standard Dictionary, 1963; mem. internat. editorial adv. com. World Book Dictionary, 1963, 76; editorial adv. com. Thorndike-Barnhart Coll. Dictionary, 1965—. Mem. Am. Dialect Soc. (sec. 1952-56, v.p. 1958-60, pres. 1960-62), Linguistic Soc. Am., Modern Lang. Assn., Modern Humanities Research Assn., Am. Name Soc. (bd. mgrs. 1960-63), Internat. Assn. U. Profs. English, Phi Beta Kappa. Episcopalian. Author: Words and Ways of American English, 1952; The Origins and Development of the English Language, 3d rev. edit., 1980; The English Language: A Brief History, 1968; (with John Algeo) English: An Introduction to Language, 1970; Thomas Pyles: Selected Essays on English Usage (edited by John Algeo), 1979; also articles, revs.; editorial adv. bd. Dictionary Am. Regional English; adviser to editors Ency. Brit., 1968-76; editorial adv. com. Am. Speech, 1966-67, 70-71; editor: (with S.V. Larkey) An Herbal, 1941; Home: 629 NE Boulevard Gainesville FL 32601

PYNCHON, DAVID MELVILLE, headmaster; b. Boston, June 24, 1927; s. Joseph Henry and Susan (Peckham) P.; B.A., Williams Coll., 1950, LL.D. (hon.), 1977; postgrad. Harvard U., 1953-54; LL.D. (hon.), Bowdoin Coll., 1978; m. Janet Hunter Munroe, June 18, 1960; children—Mary Hunter, Janet Munroe, Sarah Melville, Elizabeth Brewster. Asst. dir. admissions Williams Coll., 1950-53, 54-56, instr. English, 1954-56; instr. English, Phillips Acad., Andover, Mass., 1956-63; headmaster St. Louis (Mo.) Country Day Sch., 1963-68, Deerfield (Mass.) Acad., 1968—. Dir. Franklin County Trust Co. Trustee Ednl. Records Bur., Coll. Retirement Equities Fund, Deerfield Acad., Williams Coll., Historic Deerfield Found.; corporator Franklin County Pub. Hosp., Farran Meml. Hosp. Served with USNR, 1945-47. Mem. Headmasters Assn., Country Day Headmasters Assn., Ind. Sch. Assn. Mass. Home: Deerfield MA 01342

PYNCHON, THOMAS, novelist; b. Glen Cove, N.Y., May 8, 1937; s. Thomas R. Pynchon; B.A., Cornell U., 1958. Former editorial writer Boeing Co., Seattle. Served with USNR. Author: V. (Faulkner prize as best 1st novel of 1963, 1964); The Crying of Lot 49 (Rosenthal Found. award Nat. Inst. Arts and Letters 1967), 1966; Gravity's Rainbow, 1973; also short stories in publs. including Kenyon Rev., New World Writing 16, Sat. Eve. Post. Address: care JB Lippincott Inc E Washington Sq Philadelphia PA 19105*

PYNE, EBEN WRIGHT, banker; b. N.Y.C., June 14, 1917; s. Grafton H. and Leta Constance (Wright) P.; grad. Groton Sch., 1935; A.B., Princeton U., 1939; M. Hilda Holloway, Dec. 16, 1941; children—Lillian Pyne-Corbin, Mary Alison. Clk., First Nat. City Trust Co., 1939, v.p., asst. to pres., 1952-56, exec. v.p., 1956, pres., dir., 1957-61; asst. cashier Citibank, N.A., 1946-50, asst. v.p., 1950-52, v.p., 1952-53, sr. v.p., 1960—; dir. U.S. Life Ins. Co. City of N.Y., City Home Corp., Gen. Devel. Corp., GOV, Inc., City Investing Co., Home Ins. Co., L.I. Lighting Co., W.R. Grace and Co. Bd. dirs. Met. Transp. Authority, 1965-75, Triborough Bridge and Tunnel Authority, 1965-75, N.Y.C. Transit Authority, 1965-75, Manhattan and Bronx Surface Transit Operating Authority, 1965-75, Steward Airport, 1965-75, S.I. Rapid Transit Operating Authority, 1965-75, Winifred Masterson Burke Relief Found., 1958-70, Downtown Bklyn. Devel. Assn., 1965-74; mem. adv. bd. Nassau County council Boy Scouts Am.; bd. dirs. Nassau Hosp.; trustee St. Lukes-Roosevelt Hosp., Grace Inst., Bklyn. Inst. Arts and Scis., Juilliard Sch., Dowling Coll., Hall of Sci. City N.Y., Inc., United Fund L.I., Groton Sch., 1957-62; mem. governing com. Bklyn. Mus. Served as maj. AUS, 1940-46. Mem. Pilgrims of U.S. (mem. exec. com.), N.Y. Zool. Soc. (trustee). Clubs: Piping Rock (Locust Valley, N.Y.); Bond, Links (gov.), Racquet and Tennis, River (N.Y.C.); Ivy (Princeton, N.J.); Links Golf (North Hills, N.Y.); Nat. Golf Links Am. (Southampton, N.Y.). Home: Old Westbury NY 11568 Office: One Citicorp Center New York NY 10043

PYRON, JOHN ROLAND, transp. co. exec.; b. Charlotte, N.C., July 9, 1926; s. Clifford Wesley and Agnes (McCachren) P.; A.B., U. N.C., 1950; m. Suzanne Reagan, June 18, 1955; children—John R., Clifford R., William C., Judson. With McLean Trucking Co., 1954-63; with Sea Land Service, Inc., Edison, N.J., 1963—, exec. v.p., 1979—. Dep. mayor, Colts Neck, N.J., 1970-73. Served with AUS, 1944-46. Office: PO Box 900 Edison NJ 08817

PYTELL, ROBERT HENRY, judge; b. Detroit, Sept. 27, 1926; s. Henry Carl and Helen (Zielinski) P.; J.D., U. Detroit, 1951; m. Laurie Mazur, June 2, 1956; children—Mary Beth, Mark Henry, Robert Michael. Admitted to Mich. bar, 1952; individual practice law, Detroit, 1952—; asst. U.S. atty. Eastern Dist. Mich., 1962-65; judge Municipal Ct., Grosse Pointe Farms, Mich., 1967—. Served with USNR, 1945-46. Mem. Am. Bar Assn., Am. Judicature Soc., Delta Theta Phi. Roman Catholic. Club: Crescent Sail Yacht (Grosse Pointe). Home: Grosse Pointe Farms MI 48236 Office: 90 Kerby Rd Grosse Pointe Farms MI 48236 also 18580 Mack Ave Grosse Pointe Farms MI 48236

PYTTE, AGNAR, theoretical physicist; b. Kongsberg, Norway, Dec. 23, 1932; s. Ole and Edith (Christiansen) P.; came to U.S., 1949, naturalized, 1965; A.B., Princeton, 1953; A.M., Harvard, 1954, Ph.D., 1958; m. Anah Currie Loeb, June 18, 1955; children—Anders H., Anthony M., Alyson C. Mem. faculty Dartmouth Coll., 1958—, prof. physics, 1967—, chmn. dept. physics and astronomy, 1971-75, asso. dean faculty, 1975-78, dean grad. studies, 1975-78; mem. Project Matterhorn, Princeton, 1959-60. NSF faculty fellow U. Brussels, 1966-67, Plasma Physics Lab., Princeton, 1978-79. Mem. Am. Phys. Soc., Phi Beta Kappa, Sigma Xi. Author: (with R.W. Christy) Structure of Matter, 1965. Research in plasma physics. Office: Dept Physics and Astronomy Dartmouth Coll Hanover NH 03755

QUAAL, WARD LOUIS, broadcasting exec.; b. Ishpeming, Mich., Apr. 7, 1919; s. Sigfred Emil and Alma Charlotte (Larson) Q.; A.B., U. Mich., 1941; LL.D., Mundelein Coll., 1962, No. Mich. U., 1967; D. Pub. Service, Elmhurst Coll., 1967; D.H.L., Lincoln Coll., 1968; m. Dorothy G. Graham, Mar. 9, 1944; children—Graham Ward, Jennifer Anne. Announcer-writer radio sta. WBEO, now sta. WDMJ, Marquette, Mich., 1936-37; announcer, writer, producer WJR, Detroit, 1937-41; spl. events announcer-producer WGN, Chgo., 1941-42, asst. to gen. mgr., 1945-49; dir. Clear Channel Broadcasting Service, Washington, 1949-52, pres., chief exec. officer; asst. gen. mgr. Crosley Broadcasting Corp., Cin., 1952, v.p., asst. gen. mgr., 1953-56; v.p., gen. mgr., mem. bd. WGN, Inc., Chgo., 1956-61, exec. v.p., then pres., 1961-74, now ret.; pres. Ward Quall Co.; chmn. bd. United Telecom Corp.; chmn. exec. com. Queen City Communication, Inc., Cin.; past dir. Tribune Co. Chmn. bd., chmn. com. Council for TV Devel., Broadcasters Found; Inc.; bd. dirs. Internat. Radio and TV Found., Sears Roebuck Found. Served as lt. USNR, 1942-45. Recipient Distinguished Alumnus award U. Mich., 1967, Advt. Man of Year Gold medallion Chgo. Advt. Club, 1969, Distinguished service award Nat. Assn. Broadcasters, 1973, others; named Communicator of Year Jewish United Fund, 1969, Ill. Broadcaster of Year, 1973. Mem. Assn. Better Bus. Burs. (gov. 1966-70, chmn.), Better Bus. Bur. Met. Chgo. (dir., named to Hall of Fame 1973), Broadcast Pioneers (pres., dir. 1962-63), Am. Advt. Fedn. (mem. ethics com.), Delta Tau. Delta. Clubs: Chicago (Chgo.); Exmoor Country; Kenwood Golf and Country (Washington); Lakeside Golf (North Hollywood, Cal.); Mid-America, Commonwealth; El Niguel Country (Laguna Beach, Cal.). Author: (with Leo A. Martin) Broadcast Management, 1968, rev. edit. (with James A. Brown), 1975. Home: 1706-D Northfield Sq Northbrook IL 60062 Office: Suite 370 O'Hare Plaza 5725 River Rd Chicago IL 60631

QUACKENBUSH, AUSTIN JOSEPH, JR., aerospace co. exec.; b. Norwood, Mass., Sept. 6, 1924; s. Austin Joseph and Catherine Mary (Kane) Q.; B.S.A.E., U. Mich., 1946; grad. exec. devel. program UCLA, 1964; m. Margaret Mary Davey, Aug. 9, 1947; children—Diane, Karen, Nancy, Susan, Katherine, Teresa. With Douglas Aircraft Co., 1946-68, dir. corp. planning, Santa Monica, Calif., 1962-66, v.p. corp. planning, 1966-68; staff v.p. corp. planning McDonnell Douglas Corp., St. Louis, 1968-70, exec. v.p. McDonnell Douglas Automation Co., St. Louis, 1970-75, corp. v.p., 1975—. Served with USNR, 1942-46; ATO. Fellow AIAA. Club: Bellerive Country (St. Louis). Home: 1447 Meadowside Dr Creve Coeur MO 63141 Office: PO Box 516 Saint Louis MO 63166

QUADE, QUENTIN LON, educator; b. Ft. Dodge, Ia., Jan. 28, 1933; s. Louis Anton and Vera (Chrisman) Q.; B.S., Creighton U., 1957; M.A., Notre Dame U., 1958, Ph.D., 1965; m. Phyllis F. Fleskes, Jan. 2, 1954; children—Zachary, Christopher, Matthew, Stephanie, Leslie. Instr. polit. sci. St. Louis U., 1959-61; faculty polit. sci. Marquette U., Milw., 1961—, prof., 1968—, dean Grad. Sch., 1968, asso. acad. v.p., grad. dean, 1970-72, acad. v.p., 1972-74, exec. v.p., 1974—. Bd. dirs. Wis. region NCCJ. Served with USAF, 1950-53. Roman Catholic. Author: (with T.J. Bennett) American Politics: Responsible and Effective?, 1969; U.S. and Wars of National Liberation, 1966. Contbr. articles to profl. jours. Home: 7326 Maple Terr Wauwatosa WI 53213 Office: 615 N 11th St Milwaukee WI 53233

QUADT, RAYMOND ADOLPH, metallurgist, cement co. exec.; b. Perth Amboy, N.J., Apr. 16, 1916; s. Adolph and Florence (MacCracken) Q.; B.S., Rutgers U., 1939; M.A., Columbia U., 1943; M.S., Stevens Inst. Tech., 1948; m. Jean Patton, Mar. 18, 1975; 1 son by previous marriage, Brian. Tchr. high sch., Plainfield, N.J., 1939-42; research metallurgist Am. Smelting & Refining Co., Barber, N.J., 1942-48, dir. aluminum devel. 1948-50; v.p. Hunter Douglas Corp., Riverside, Calif., 1950-57; v.p. research and devel. Bridgeport Brass Co., 1958-60, v.p. spl. metals, 1962-63; v.p. Nat. Distillers and Chem. Corp., N.Y.C., 1963—; chmn. bd. Loud Co., Pomona, Calif., 1963—; pres., gen. mgr. Reactive Metals Inc., 1960-62; v.p., gen. mgr. Pascoe Steel Corp., Pomona, 1965-73; pres. Phoenix Cement Co., 1973—. Mem. Am. Soc. Metals, Pomona C. of C. (pres. 1970), Phi Beta Kappa. Home: 15 E San Miguel Phoenix AZ 85012 Office: 3550 N Central Ave Phoenix AZ 85012

QUAGLIA, LOUIS ANTHONY, hosp. adminstr.; b. Trail, B.C., Can., Oct. 18, 1930; s. Frank and Olga (Valca) Q.; B.A. in Math. and Chemistry, U. B.C., 1952, B. Commerce, 1954; diploma in hosp. adminstrn. U. Toronto, 1956; m. Beatrice Jeannette Farrell, Oct. 31, 1959; children—Michelle Marie, Francis Anthony, Jonathan Mario, Mona Eoldie. Asst. adminstr. Hilltop Acres, Municipality of Met. Toronto (Ont.), 1956-57, adminstr., 1957-58; adminstr. Kipling Acres, 1958-60; asst. exec. dir. Asso. Hosp. of Alta., Edmonton, 1960-62; adminstr. Victoria Gen. Hosp., Winnipeg, Man., 1962-69; pres. St. Boniface Gen Hosp., Winnipeg, 1969—; asso. prof. social and preventive medicine U. Man.; past pres., mem. adv. council bd. Man. Health Orgns. Bd. dirs. Youville Found.; past pres. Family Bur. Greater Winnipeg. Mem. Cath. Health Assn. Can. (past pres.), Can. Health Conf. of Man. (past pres.), Can. Coll. Health Service Execs. Roman Catholic. Home: 7 Windermere Bay Winnipeg MB R3T 1B1 Canada*

QUAGLIANO, JAMES VINCENT, educator, chemist; b. Bklyn., Nov. 9, 1915; s. John and Christina (Quagliano) Q.; B.S., Poly. Inst. Bklyn., 1938, M.S., 1940; Ph.D., U. Ill., 1946; m. Lidia Marisa Vallarino, July 3, 1961; children—John, Peter, Mary. Asst. prof. chemistry U. Md., 1946-48; asso. prof. chemistry U. Notre Dame, 1948-58; sci. adminstr. Office Naval Research, Chgo., 1954-55; prof. chemistry Fla. State U., Tallahassee, 1958-75; Hudson prof. Auburn (Ala.) U., 1975—. Mem. Am. Chem. Soc. (chmn. St. Joseph Valley sect. 1953-54, councilor 1965-66), Am. Inst. Chemists, AAAS, N.Y. Acad. Scis., Sigma Xi, Phi Lambda Upsilon. Author: Chemistry, 3d edit., 1969; Coordination Chemistry, 1969; also numerous articles. Asso. editor Chem. Revs., 1965-67. Research on amino acids and related compounds with metals, fundamental work on basic problems of chemistry; determination of structure, properties and uses of newly synthesized complexes. Home: 365 Gardner Dr Auburn AL 36830

QUAINTON, ANTHONY CECIL EDEN, ambassador; b. Seattle, Apr. 4, 1934; s. Cecil Eden and Marjorie Josephine (Oates) Q.; B.A., Princeton, 1955; B.Litt., Oxford (Eng.) U., 1958; m. Susan Long, Aug. 7, 1958; children—Katherine, Eden, Elizabeth. Research fellow St. Anthony's Coll., Oxford, 1958-59; with Fgn. Service, State Dept., 1959—; vice consul, Sydney, Australia, 1960-62; Urdu lang. trainee, 1962-63; 2d sec., econ. officer Am. embassy, Karachi, Pakistan, 1963-64, Rawalpindi, Pakistan, 1964-66; 2d sec., polit. officer mem. sr. polit. officer for India, 1969-72; 1st sec. Am. embassy, Paris, 1972-73; counselor dep. chief mission Am. embassy, Kathmandu, Nepal, 1973-77; ambassador to Central African Empire, Bangui, 1977-78; dir. Office for Combatting Terrorism, Dept. State, Washington, 1978—, apptd. rank of ambassador, 1979. English Speaking Union fellow, 1951-52; Marshall scholar, 1955-58. Recipient Rivkin award, 1972. Office: care US Dept State 2201 C St NW Washington DC 20520

QUALEY, CARLTON CHESTER, historian, educator; b. Spring Grove, Minn., Dec. 17, 1904; s. Ole O. and Clara (Knatterud) Q.; B.A., St. Olaf Coll., 1929; M.A., U. Minn., 1930; Ph.D., Columbia U., 1938; m. Elizabeth Frances Cummings, Apr. 29, 1933; children—John, Mary. From lectr. to asso. prof. history Bard Coll. of Columbia, 1936-44, asso. prof. at univ., 1945-46, vis. summer prof., 1938-46; asso prof. Swarthmore Coll., 1944-45; prof. Am. history Carleton Coll., 1946-67, Laird Bell prof. history, 1967-70, chmn. dept., 1960-67, vis. prof., fall 1972; part-time dir. Minn. Hist. Soc., 1947-48, research fellow, 1970—; dir. Minn. Ethnic History Project, 1973-78; vis. prof. Northwestern U., summer 1951, Cleve. State U., 1971-72, Augsburg Coll., fall 1976; vis. Coe prof. Am. history Stanford U., summer 1966. Participant Minn. Russian Seminar, USSR, 1958, Internat. Congress Hist. Scis., Stockholm, 1960, San Francisco, 1975. Shevlin fellow U. Minn., 1931-32; Univ. fellow Columbia U., 1932-33; travel grantee Social Sci. Research Council, 1960; research grantee Hill Found., St. Paul, 1954-55, Am. Council Learned Socs., 1962-63, Huntington Library, 1968, Bush Found., 1973-75, Nat. Endowment for Humanities, 1975-77. Mem. Orgn. Am. Historians (mem. nominating com. 1966-68), Am., Norwegian-Am. (bd. editors), Western hist. assns., Minn., Immigration (editor newsletter) hist. socs., AAUP. Unitarian. Author: Norwegian Settlement in the United States, 1938, 70, Thorstein Veblen, 1968; On Being an Ethnic Historian, 1972; also articles on immigration, book revs. Home: 2110 Carter Ave Saint Paul MN 55108

QUALL, ALVIN BERTRAND, coll. dean; b. Acme, Wash., Apr. 11, 1913; s. Arnt Olson and Florence Lillian (Reed) Q.; A.B., Seattle Pacific Coll., 1934; A.M., U. Wash., 1934; Ed.D., 1946; m. Alice Warren, June 12, 1936; children—Joan Elaine, Robert Dean. Asst., physics Seattle Pacific Coll., 1933-34; instr., coach Selah (Wash.) High Sch., 1935-40; dir. phys. edn., asso. prof. edn. Greenville (Ill.) Coll., 1940-42, registrar, dean men, 1942-44, dean, prof. edn., 1944-53; dean men, prof. edn. and psychology Whitworth Coll., Spokane, 1953-54, prof. edn. and psychology, dean coll., 1954-64, dir. grad. studies, 1964—. Mem. N.E.A., Wash. Edn. Assn., Nat. Soc. Study Edn., Alpha Kappa Sigma, Kappa Delta Pi, Phi Delta Kappa. Home: W 322 Holland Rd Spokane WA 99218

QUALLEY, CHARLES ALBERT, educator; b. Creston, Ia., Mar. 19, 1930; s. Albert Olaf and Cleora (Dietrick) Q.; B.F.A., Drake U., 1952; M.A., U. Iowa, 1956, M.F.A., 1958; Ed.D., Ill. State U., 1967; m. Betty Jean Griffith, Nov. 26, 1954; children—Janet Lynn, John Stuart. Art tchr. Des Moines Pub. Schs., 1952,, 54-55; critic art tchr. U. Iowa, 1955-57; prof. fine arts U. Colo., Boulder, 1958—, chmn. dept. fine arts, 1968-71. Served with AUS, 1952-54; Korea. Mem. Nat. (v.p. 1978—), Colo. (editor 1965-67, 75, pres. 1976-78) art edn. assns., Delta Phi Delta, Omicron Delta Kappa, Pi Kappa Delta. Contbg. editor Sch. Arts, 1978—. Home: 4285 Milliken Ct Boulder CO 80303

QUALLS, GEORGE WYCKOFF, architect; b. Osweo, Kans., July 3, 1923; s. George Worsdall and Leondine (Wyckoff) Q.; student U. Okla., 1941-43, 46-49; B. Arch., N.C. State U., 1950; M.Arch., Harvard U., 1952; m. Sarah H. Thompson, Mar. 25, 1967. With John Erwin Ramsey, Salisbury, N.C., 1950, Thalheimer & Weitz, Phila., 1952-53, Vincent G. Kling, Phila., 1953-56; partner Geddes Brecher Qualls Cunningham, Phila., 1956—; instr. architecture N.C. State U., 1950-51; prof. architecture U. Pa. Grad. Sch. Fine Arts, 1952—. Mem. jury honor awards Tex. Soc. Architects, 1964, So. Calif. AIA, 1966; mem. jury Louisville Urban Renewal Competition, 1965, Ball State Archtl. Competition, 1967, Supreme Ct. Competition, Salem, Ore., 1968; mem. design rev. bd. Balt. Housing and Community Devel., 1964—; mem. regional design com. Pa., N.J., Md., Va. of HUD, 1967; mem. Charles Center Archtl. Rev. Bd., Balt. Served with AUS, 1943-46. Recipient Second prize Alcoa Archtl. Competition, 1956; Second prize Internat. Competition, Sydney (Australia) Opera House, 1957; First Design award Progressive Arch., 1958; Urban Design award, Phila., 1960; First prize Nat. Competition, Birmingham, Ala., 1967; First prize Internat. Town Planning Competition, Vienna, Austria, 1971. Fellow A.I.A. Prin. works include Phila. Police Hdqrs., 1962; Northwest Regional Library, Phila., 1963; U.S. Embassy Compound, Islamabad, West Pakistan, 1971; Birmingham-Jefferson Civic Center, Ala., 1971; Social Security Computer Center, Woodlawn, Md. Home: 2101 Delancey Pl Philadelphia PA 19103 Office: Geddes Brecher Qualls Cunningham 2410 Pine St Philadelphia PA 19103

QUALLS, ROBERT L., mem. staff gov. Ark.; b. Burnsville, Miss., Nov. 6, 1933; s. Wes E. and Letha (Parker) Q.; B.S., Miss. State U., 1954, M.S., 1958; postgrad. La. State U., 1959-61; LL.D., Whitworth Coll., 1974; m. Carolyn Morgan, Feb. 10, 1979. Prof., chmn. div. econs. and bus. Belhaven Coll., Jackson, Miss., 1962-66, asst. to pres., 1965-66; asst. prof. finance Miss. State U., State College, 1967-69, adj. prof., 1969-73; sr. v.p., chmn. venture com. Bank of Miss., Tupelo, 1969-74; v.p. Wesleyan Coll., Macon, Ga., 1974; pres. Coll. of the Ozarks, Clarksville, Ark., 1974-79; mem. cabinet Gov. Bill Clinton of Ark., 1979—; cons. Unifirst Savs. & Loan Assn., Jackson, 1963-68, dir. mktg., 1968-69; mktg. cons. Ill. Central Industries, Chgo., 1964. Mem. faculty, thesis examiner Stonier Grad. Sch. Banking, Rutgers U., 1973—; mem. faculty Miss. Sch. Banking, U. Miss., 1973-78; course coordinator Grad. Banking Sch. of South, La. State U., 1978—, Essentials of Banking Sch., Duke Johnson County, 1977. U., 1978-79. Chmn. community service and continuing edn. com. Tupelo Community Devel. Found., 1972-73; mem. Miss. 4-H adv. council, 1969; active Boy Scouts Am.; mem. Lee County Democratic Exec. Com., 1973-74; trustee Wal-Mart Found., 1975—. Served to lt. AUS, 1954-56. Found. for Econ. Edn. fellow, 1964; Ford Found. faculty research fellow Vanderbilt U., 1963-64; recipient Pillar of Progress award Johnson County, 1977. Mem. Am. Bankers Assn. (mktg. planning and research com. 1972-73), Am. Mgmt. Assn. (pres.'s assn.), Bus. and Profl. Group of Am. (dir. 1969), Ark. Council Ind. Colls. and Univs. (chmn. 1978-79), Newcomen Soc., Johnson County C. of C. (pres. 1977), Blue Key, Omicron Delta Kappa, Delta Sigma Pi, Sigma Phi Epsilon (citation 1977). Presbyn. Clubs: Masons (32 deg.), Clarksville Rotary (pres. 1979). Co-author: Strategic Planning for Colleges and Universities: A Systems Approach to Planning and Resource Allocation, 1979; Corporate Planning: A Guide for Savings and Loan Associations, 1979. Home: 308 College Ave Clarksville AR 72830 Office: State Capitol Little Rock AR 72201

QUALLS, YOURA THELMA, ret. educator; b. Clarksville, Tex., Oct. 1913; d. Thomas Hugh and Leola Mae (Smith) Qualls; B.A., Fisk U., 1937; M.A., Radcliffe Coll., 1943, Ph.D. (Anne Radcliffe fellow), 1956. Prof. English, Langston (Okla.) U., 1943-53; prof. English, chmn. dept. English and langs. U. Md. Eastern Shore, Princess Anne, 1957-64; prof., chmn. dept. communications Tuskegee Inst. (Ala.), 1964-67, chmn. dept. English, 1967-71, chmn. div. humanities, prof. English, 1971-79, ret., 1979. Kent fellow Nat. Soc. for Religion, 1951. Mem. Am. Assn. Colls. for Tchr. Edn. (com. on performance based tchr. edn.), Nat. Council Tchrs. English (state judge Md., Ala. nat. achievement awards high sch. jrs., commn. on lit. 1972-75), Conf. on Coll. Composition and Communication (exec. com. 1973-76), Alpha Kappa Alpha. Editor: Southwestern Jour., 1945-55. Home: 306 S Elm St Tuskegee AL 36083

QUALTER, TERENCE HALL, educator; b. Eltham, New Zealand, Apr. 15, 1925; s. Michael Frederick and Mary (Hall) Q.; B.A., U. New Zealand, 1951; Ph.D., U. London-London Sch. Econs., 1956; m. Shirley Anne Card, May 19, 1951; children—Karen Anne, Matthew John, Paul Michael, Adam James. Came to Can., 1957. Newscaster, New Zealand Broadcasting Service, Wellington, 1948-51; various positions, London, 1951-57; lectr. United Coll. Winnipeg, Man., Can., 1957-58; spl. lectr. U. Sask., Can., 1958-60; lectr. polit. sci. U. Waterloo, Ont., Can., 1960-61, asst. prof. polit. sci., 1961-64, asso. prof., 1964-67, prof. polit. sci., 1967—, chmn. dept. polit. sci., 1965-67, 70-73. Exec. mem. Kitchener New Democratic party, 1962-72, pres., 1962-63, 72-73. Served with Royal New Zealand Air Force, 1944-47. Grantee Can. Council, NRC Can. Mem. Canadian Polit. Sci. Assn. Roman Catholic. Author: Propaganda and Psychological Warfare, 1962; The Election Process in Canada, 1970; Graham Wallas and the Great Society, 1979. Home: 249 Stonybrook Dr Kitchener ON Canada Office: U Waterloo Dept Polit Sci Waterloo ON Canada

QUAMME, JACK O., rubber mfg. co. exec.; b. Colorado Springs, Colo., Oct. 31, 1927; s. Clarence N. and Nora C. Q.; B.A., Colo. Coll., 1950; m. Virginia Anne, Sept. 6, 1959; children—Steven J., Julie Anne. Sales engr. Goodyear Tire & Rubber Co., Denver, 1950-52, Boise, Idaho, 1952-54, Los Angeles, 1954-59; with Dayco Corp., 1959—, regional mgr., Dallas/Atlanta, 1960-64, distbn. sales mgr., 1964-66, v.p. mktg., 1966-70, div. group v.p., Dayton, Ohio, 1970-74, pres. Dayco Rubber Products Co. div., 1975—, corp. group v.p., 1979—. Office: 333 W First St Dayton OH 45402

QUANDT, RICHARD EMERIC, educator; b. Budapest, Hungary, June 1, 1930; s. Richard F. and Elisabeth (Toth) Q.; came to U.S., 1949, naturalized, 1954; B.A., Princeton, 1952; M.A., Harvard, 1955, Ph.D., 1957; m. Jean H. Briggs, Aug. 6, 1955; 1 son, Stephen. Mem. faculty Princeton, 1956—, prof. econs., 1964—, Hughes-Rogers prof. econs., 1976—, chmn. dept., 1968-71, Ford Found. research prof., 1967-68; cons. Alderson Assos., 1959-61; sr. cons. Mathematica, Inc., 1961-67; cons. Internat. Air Transport Assn., 1974-75, N.Y. Stock Exchange, 1976-77, N.Y. State Dept. Edn., 1978; adviser Am.-Hungarian Found., 1977—; editorial adviser Holt, Rinehart & Winston, 1968-72. Guggenheim fellow, 1958-59; McCosh fellow, 1964; NSF Sr. Postdoctoral fellow, 1971-72. Fellow Am. Statis. Assn., Econometric Soc.; mem. Am. Econ. Assn., Regional Sci. Assn., Math. Programming Soc. Author: (with J. M. Henderson) Microeconomic Theory: A Mathematical Approach, 1958, 2d edit., 1971; (with W.L. Thorp) The New Inflation, 1959; (with B.G. Malkiel) Strategies and Rational Decisions in the Securities Option Market, 1969; editor: The Demand for Travel: Theory and Measurement, 1970; (with S.M. Goldfeld) Nonlinear Methods in Econometrics, 1972, Studies in Nonlinear Estimation, 1976; also numerous articles; editorial bd. Environment and Planning, Transp. Research, Applied Econs.; asso. editor Rev. Economics and Statistics, Econometrica, Jour. Am. Statis. Assn., Bell Jour. Econs. Home: 162 Springdale Rd Princeton NJ 08540

QUARESMA, EDWARD ANTHONY, lawyer; b. Oceano, Calif., Jan. 20, 1907; s. Manuel S. and Maria (Brum) Q.; A.A., Santa Clara U., 1927; B.S. cum laude, Loyola U., 1929, J.D. cum laude, 1931; m. Emma Savio, June 16, 1939; children—Ronald, Madeline, Thomas, Lynn Quaresma Weber, Steven. Admitted to Calif. bar, 1931; city atty., Arroyo Grande, Calif., 1934-38; asst. dist. atty. San Luis Obispo County, Calif., 1935-39; individual practice law, Fremont, Calif., 1939-42, 46-59, 67—; asst. spl. rep. Fgn. Econ. Adminstrn., Rio de Janeiro, Brazil, 1942-45; judge Justice Ct., 1946-59; municipal ct. judge, Fremont, Newark and Union City Jud. Dist., 1959-67; pres. Bank of Fremont, 1964-67, dir., 1964—; dir. Kraft Tile Inc., Fremont; atty. Alameda County Water Dist., Washington Hosp. Dist. Trustee, Washington Union High Sch. Dist., Fremont, 1947-54, chmn. bd., 1952-54; mem. advisory bd. Calif. State U., Hayward, 1967-73. Recipient Distinguished Service award Ohlone Coll., 1975. Mem. State Bar Calif., Alameda County Bar Assn., I.D.E.S. (state pres. 1935-36), Fremont C. of C. (hon. life). Democrat. Roman Catholic. Clubs: K.C., Elks, Rotary (past pres.). Office: 37323 Fremont Blvd at Peralta Blvd Fremont CA 94536

QUARLES, ALBERT MEROLD, hotel exec.; b. Mound City, Ill., Mar. 24, 1910; s. James David and Grace (Durning) Q.; student Cornell U.; m. Lois Patterson Gibson; children—Beverly (Mrs. Paul E. Hardy), David Wayland. Various positions Stevens Hotel, Chgo., 1926-36, gen. purchasing agt., 1936-42; resident mgr. Hotels Windermere, Chgo., 1942-45; asst. to pres. LaSalle Hotel, Chgo., 1945-49, v.p., gen. mgr., 1949-58; gen. mgr. Executive House, Chgo., 1958-67; v.p. College Inns of Am., 1967-68; v.p., gen. mgr. Pheasant Run, 1968-70; exec. v.p., treas. Greater Chgo. Hotel & Motel Assn., 1970—. Bd. dirs. Met. Fair and Expdn. Auth. Mem. Chgo. Restaurant Assn. (mem. bd.), Am (dir.), Ill. (dir.), Greater Chgo. (past pres., dir.) hotel assns., Chgo. Conv. Bur. (dir.), Hotel Greeters Am. Address: 1340 Astor St Chicago IL 60610

QUARLES, CARROLL ADAIR, JR., educator, physicist; b. Abilene, Tex., Nov. 24, 1938; s. Carroll Adair and Marguerite Marie (Vollmers) Q.; B.A., Tex. Christian U., 1960; Ph.D., Princeton, 1964; m. Sonja Gale Bandy, May 14, 1971; 1 dau., Jennifer Anne. Research physicist Brookhaven Nat. Lab., Upton, N.Y., 1964-67; mem. faculty Tex. Christian U., 1967—, asso. prof. physics, 1970-76, prof., 1976—, chmn. dept., 1978—, asso. dean Coll. Arts and Scis., 1974-78. Mem. Am. Phys. Soc., Am. Assn. Physics Tchrs., A.A.A.S., Fedn. Am. Scientists, Sigma Xi, Alpha Chi, Pi Mu Epsilon. Roman Catholic. Contbr. articles to profl. jours. Office: Dept Physics Tex Christian U Fort Worth TX 76129

QUARLES, JAMES CLIV, educator; b. Charlottesville, Va., Mar. 18, 1921; s. James Cliv and Lucy (Sinclair) Q.; B.A., U. Va., 1942, LL.B., 1945; m. Prudence White, Sept. 1, 1944; children—Rebecca Wayne (Mrs. Douglas S. McLeod), James Peyton, Christopher Sinclair. Admitted to Va. bar, 1944, Ga. bar, 1955; law clk. U.S. circuit judge, 1945-47; instr. law Walter F. George Sch. Law, Mercer U., 1947-48, asst. prof., 1948-49, asso. prof., 1949-52, prof., 1952-69, acting dean, 1950-51, 56-58, dean, 1958-69; prof. law U. Fla., Gainesville, 1969—. Exec. dir. Fla. Law Revision Commn., 1969-71; chmn. research group Ga. Criminal Law Study Com., 1961-66. Mem. Gainesville Human Relations Adv. Bd., 1972—, chmn., 1975-77. Bd. dirs. Macon Legal Aid Soc., 1956-60. Mem. Am., Ga., Macon bar assns., Am. Law Inst., State U. System Faculty Assn. (pres. 1975—), Order Coif, Raven Soc., Pi Delta Epsilon. Democrat. Presbyn. Kiwanian. Editor: Cases and Materials on Florida Constitutional Law, 1977. Contbr. articles to legal publs. Home: 2076 NW 20th Ln Gainesville FL 32605

QUARLES, JOSEPH VERY, III, home furnishings co. exec.; b. Evanston, Ill., Oct. 24, 1933; s. Joseph Very and Mary Louise (Fronheiser) Q.; B.A., Princeton U., 1955; m. Virginia Cornelia Schwab, June 6, 1959; children—Cornelia, Catherine, Caroline. With Simmons Co., 1959-69, 72—, gen. mgr. Atlantic div., 1972-75, exec. v.p. corp. devel. and affiliates, Atlanta, 1977—, also dir.; pres. Thonet Industries, N.Y.C., 1969-72. Served with AUS, 1955-58. Presbyterian. Address: Simmons Co PO Box 49000 Atlanta GA 30362

QUARTON, WILLIAM BARLOW, broadcasting co. exec.; b. Algona, Iowa, Mar. 27, 1903; s. William B. and Ella B. (Reaser) Q.; student U. Iowa, 1921-22, George Washington U., 1923-25. m. Elnora Bierkamp, Aug. 24, 1935; 1 dau., Diane (Mrs. Waldo F. Geiger). Joined radio sta. KWCR, Cedar Rapids, Iowa, 1931; comml. mgr. radio sta. WMT, 1936, gen. mgr., 1943; exec. v.p. Am. Broadcasting Stas., Inc., 1959-68, chmn., 1968-70; chmn. bd. KWMT Inc., Ft. Dodge, Iowa, 1968—, Cable Communications Iowa, Inc., 1971—; pres. WMT-TV, Inc., 1959-68; chmn. adv. bd. CBS-TV Affiliates, 1960. Mem. bd. Iowa Ednl. Broadcasting Network, 1967-77; bd. govs. Pub. Broadcasting Service, 1973-78, vice chmn., 1975; trustee Coe Coll., Herbert Hoover Presdl. Library; bd. regents State Iowa, 1965-71. Mem. Cedar Rapids C. of C. (pres. 1944), Nat. Assn. Broadcasters (chmn. TV bd. 1962-63, chmn. joint bd. 1963-64). Elk, Mason, Rotarian. Clubs: Pickwick (past pres.); Ft. Lauderdale Country, Coral Ridge Yacht (Ft. Lauderdale, Fla.); Cedar Rapids Country. Home: 134 Kyrie Dr SE Cedar Rapids IA 52403 Office: 1810 I E Tower Cedar Rapids IA 52401

QUAY, HERBERT CALLISTER, educator; b. Portland, Me., Aug. 27, 1927; s. George J. and Susannah Fay (Bankerd) Q.; B.S., Fla. State U., 1951, M.S., 1952; Ph.D., U. Ill. at Urbana, 1958; m. E. Lorene Childs, June 13, 1953 (div. 1974); children—Jonathan, Jennifer. Asst. prof. psychology Vanderbilt U., 1958-61; asso. prof. psychology Northwestern U., 1961-63; mem. faculty, dir. Children's Research Center, U. Ill. at Urbana, 1963-68; prof., chmn. div. edn. psychology Temple U., Phila., 1968-74; dir. program in applied social scis., prof. psychology and pediatrics U. Miami (Fla.), 1974—. Mem. adv. com. Nat. Program Early Childhood Edn., 1970-73; cons. Fed. Bur. Prisons, 1967-77, adv. com., 1970-73. Served with AUS, 1946-48. Mem. Am. Psychol. Assn., Am. Assn. Correctional Psychologists (Distinguished Contbn. award 1974), A.A.A.S., Council Exceptional Children (chmn. research com. 1960-65), Sigma Xi. Editor: Research in Psychopathology, 1963; Juvenile Delinquency Theory and Research, 1965; Childrens Behavior Disorders, 1968; Psychopathological Disorders of Childhood, 1972, 2d edit., 1979; asso. editor Exceptional Children, 1965-75; editorial bd. Psychology in the Sch., 1968-70, Criminal Justice and Behavior, 1975—; editor Jour. Abnormal Child Psychology, 1972—; editorial cons. Jour. Abnormal Psychology, 1972, Jour. Clin. and Cons. Psychology, 1972—. Home: 550 Ocean Dr Key Biscayne FL 33149 Office: U Miami Coral Gables FL 33124

QUAY, THOMAS EMERY, pharm. co. exec., lawyer; b. Cleve., Apr. 3, 1934; s. Harold Emery and Esther Ann (Thomas) Q.; A.B. in Humanities magna cum laude (Univ. scholar), Princeton U., 1956; LL.B. (Univ. scholar), U. Pa., 1963; m. Martha Beckham Graham, June 9, 1961; children—Martha Wyndham, Glynis Cobb, Eliza Emery. Admitted to Pa. bar, 1964; asso. firm Pepper, Hamilton & Scheetz, Phila.,1963-65; with William H. Rorer, Inc., Ft. Washington, Pa., 1965—, sec., counsel, 1974-79, v.p., gen. counsel, sec., 1979—, also dir.; dir. Rorer subs.'s: Dermik Labs., Dooner Labs. Inc., Barcroft Co. Bd. dirs. Main Line YMCA, Ardmore, Pa., 1971-73, chmn. bd., 1972-73; editor 10th Reunion Book, Princeton Class of 1956, 1966, class sec., 1966-71, class v.p., 1971—, editor 25th Reunion Book, 1981—. Served to lt. (j.g.) USNR, 1957-60. Recipient service commendation Main Line YMCA, 1973. Mem. Am. Bar Assn., Pa. Bar Assn., Phila. Bar Assn., Pharm. Mfrs. Assn., Phila. Drug Exchange (chmn. legis. com. 1975-78), Juristic Soc. Democrat. Unitarian. Clubs: Cannon of Princeton U., Sharswood Law of U. Pa., Martin's Dam. Office: 500 Virginia Dr Fort Washington PA 19034

QUAYLE, CALVIN KING, educator; b. Logan, Utah, July 22, 1927; s. Joseph Larson and Addie Mabel (Hillman) Q.; B.S., Utah State U., 1950, M.S., 1954; Ph.D., U. Minn., 1958; m. Ruth Virginia Winget, Aug. 4, 1949; children—Susanne, Pamela, Gordon Calvin. Instr. speech and English, Preston (Ida.) High Sch., 1951-53; part-time instr. U. Minn., 1953-56; instr., asst. prof., asso. prof. speech and theatre Chico (Cal.) State Coll., 1956-63; asst. prof. U. Mich., 1963-65; prof., chmn. dept. speech U. Wis.-Eau Claire, 1965—. Served with inf., AUS, 1945-47. Ford Found. intern for coll. teaching, 1955-56. Mem. Am. Ednl. Theatre Assn. (project chmn. 1965-69), Speech Assn. Am., Wis. Communication Assn. (1st v.p. 1976-77, pres. 1977-78). Mem. Ch. of Jesus Christ of Latter-day Saints (bishop Eau Claire). Home: 3756 Halsey St Eau Claire WI 54701

QUAYLE, DAN, congressman; b. Indpls., Feb. 4, 1947; s. James C. and Corinne (Pulliam) Q.; B.S. in Polit. Sci., DePauw U., Greencastle, Ind., 1966; LL.B., Ind. U., 1974; m. Marilyn Tucker, Nov. 18, 1972; children—Tucker Danforth, Benjamin Eugene, Mary Corinne. Ct. reporter, pressman Huntington (Ind.) Herald-Press, 1965-69, asso. pub., gen. mgr., 1974-76; mem. consumer protection div. Office Atty. Gen., State of Ind., 1970-71; adminstrv. asst. to gov. Ind., 1971-73; dir. Ind. Inheritance Tax Div., 1973-74; admitted to Ind. bar, 1974; mem. 95th Congress, 4th Dist. Ind.; tchr. bus. law Huntington Coll., 1975. Mem. Ind., Huntington bar assns., Hoosier State Press Assn., Huntington C. of C. Republican. Clubs: Ft. Wayne (Ind.) Press; Elks, Rotary. Home: 7 N Jefferson St Huntington IN 46750 Office: 1407 Longworth House Office Bldg Washington DC 20515

QUAYLE, ROBERT HARWOOD, JR., mfg. co. exec.; b. Oak Park, Ill., Sept. 23, 1914; s. Robert Harwood and Marie Pauline (Cline) Q.; B.A., U. Ill., 1936; m. Ruth Hackley, Jan. 14, 1939; children—Robert Harwood III, Mary Jon, Thomas Cline. With Sears, Roebuck & Co., 1938-52; mdse. mgr. hard line and big ticket dept. Simpsons-Sears, Ltd., Toronto, Ont., Can., 1952-56; heavy line mdse. mgr. Montgomery Ward & Co., Chgo., 1956-58; exec. v.p. Norge div. Borg-Warner Corp., 1958-60, pres., 1960-62; exec. v.p. Franklin div. Studebaker Corp., 1962-64, pres. Franklin div., 1964-66; v.p. corporate planning The Carborundum Co., 1966-67, v.p., gen. mgr., comml. filters div., 1967-69, v.p. mktg., 1969—. Served to lt. (j.g.) USNR, 1943-46. Mem. Alpha Delta Phi. Unitarian. Home: 699 Mountain View Dr Lewiston NY 14092 Office: The Carborundum Co Carborundum Center Niagara Falls NY 14302

QUAYTMAN, HARVEY, artist; b. Far Rockaway, N.Y., Apr. 20, 1937; s. Marcus and Rose Naomi (Press) Q.; student Syracuse U., 1955-57; Boston Mus. Sch., 1957-61; B.F.A., Tufts U., 1961; m. Frances Barth, Apr. 1, 1972; 1 dau., Rebecca. One-man exhbns. include: AIA Gallery, London, 1962, Contemporary Arts Mus., Houston, 1967, 73, Paula Cooper Gallery, N.Y.C., 1969, 71, Onnasch Galerie, Cologne, 1971, Mikro Galerie, Berlin, 1972, David McKee Gallery, N.Y.C., 1975, 77, 78, Nina Nielsen Gallery, Boston, 1976, 78; group exhbns. include: Whitney Annuals-Painting, Whitney Mus., N.Y.C., 1969, 72, 73, Akron Art Inst., 1970, Young Am. Artists, Poindexter Gallery, N.Y.C., 1973, Curator's Choice Balt. Mus. Art, 1974, U. Calif. Art Gallery, Los Angeles, 1975, Drawing Today Rice U., Houston, 1976; represented in permanent collections: Corcoran Mus., Washington, Fogg Art Mus., Houston Mus. Fine Arts, Herbert F. Johnson Mus., Ithaca, N.Y., Carnegie Inst. Mus. Art, Pitts., Whitney Mus., Mus. Modern Art, N.Y.C., High Mus. Art, Atlanta; mem. faculty Sch. Visual Arts, N.Y.C., 1969-72, Cooper Union, N.Y.C., 1972-77; mem. faculty Parsons Sch. Design, N.Y.C., 1978-79. Guggenheim fellow, 1979. Jewish. Address: 231 Bowery New York NY 10002

QUEALY, WILLIAM HARRISON, judge; b. New Orleans, Mar. 11, 1913; s. William Ignatius and Elizabeth (Harrison) Q.; A.B. cum laude, Georgetown U., 1933, LL.B., 1937; m. Betty Alice Shallberg, June 29, 1940; children—Kathleen A. Quealy Brady, Margaret M. Quealy Charles, William Harrison, Patricia A. Admitted to D.C. bar, 1936, Ill. bar, 1942; practice law, Washington, 1936-41, 57-61, Chgo., 1946-56; exec. asst. to pres. W.R. Grace & Co., 1956-57; minority counsel ways and means com. U.S. Ho. of Reps., 1962- 69; judge U.S. Tax Ct., Washington, 1969—. Served to capt. AUS, 1942-45; PTO. Roman Catholic. Home: 2008 SE 26th Terr Fort Lauderdale FL 33316 Office: 400 2d St NW Room 432 Washington DC 20217

QUEENAN, JOHN THOMAS, obstetrician, gynecologist; b. Aurora, Ill., June 4, 1933; s. John William and Alice Margaret (Thomas) Q.; B.C. cum laude, U. Notre Dame, 1954; M.D., Cornell U., 1958; m. Carrie Ethel Neher, June 15, 1957; children—John Thomas, Carrie Lynne. Intern, Bellevue Hosp., N.Y.C., 1958-59; resident N.Y. Hosp., 1959-62; instr. Cornell U., 1962-65, clin. asst. prof. ob-gyn. 1965-70, asso. prof., 1970-72; prof. ob-gyn, chmn. dept. ob-gyn U. Louisville, 1972-80; prof., chmn. dept. ob-gyn Georgetown U., 1980—; chief ob-gyn Norton-Children's Hosps., Louisville, Louisville Gen. Hosp.; spl. adv. ob-gyn devices panel FDA, 1978—. Bd. dirs. ARC, Greenwich, Conn., 1970-72. Diplomate Am. Bd. Ob-Gyn. Fellow Am. Assn. Obstetricians and Gynecologists, Am. Gynecol. Soc.; mem. Am. Coll. Obstetricians and Gynecologists, A.C.S., Am. Fertility Soc., Nat. Perinatal Assn. (pres. 1976-78), So. Perinatal Assn. (pres. 1975), Royal Soc. Medicine, Alpha Omega Alpha. Clubs: Round Hill (Greenwich); River Valley (Louisville). Author: Modern Management of the Rh Problem, 1977; High Risk Pregnancy, 1980; editor-in-chief Contemporary Ob-Gyn, 19—. Office: Georgetown U Dept Ob-Gyn 3800 Reservoir Dr NW Washington DC 20007

QUEHL, GARY HOWARD, assn. exec.; b. Green Bay, Wis., Mar. 25, 1938; s. Howard and Virginia Babcock (Dunning) Q.; B.A., Carroll Coll., 1960; M.S., Ind. U., 1962, Ed.D., 1965; L.H.D., Buena Vista Coll., 1977; LL.D., Davis and Elkins Coll., 1979; m. Marion L. Bordick, Dec. 16, 1977; children—Scott Boyer, Catherine Mary. Asst. dean students Wis. State U., 1962; asst. dean of coll. Wittenberg U., 1965-76; v.p., dean coll. Lindenwood Colls., St. Charles, Mo., 1967-70; exec. dir. Coll. Center of the Finger Lakes, Corning, N.Y., 1970-74; pres. Council for the Advancement Small Colls., Washington, 1974—; cons. in field. Mem. secretariat Nat. Center for Higher Edn.; bd. dirs. Carroll Coll., Muskingum Coll. Mem. Nat. Assn. Ind. Colls. and Univs., Am. Council Edn., Am. Conf. Acad. Deans, Nat. Panel for Women in Higher Edn., North Central Assn. Acad. Deans (past pres.). Presbyterian. Editor, author books in field. Home: 2315 N Upton St Arlington VA 22207 Office: Suite 320 1 Dupont Circle NW Washington DC 20036

QUELLER, DONALD EDWARD, historian; b. St. Louis, Jan. 14, 1925; s. A.J. and Lee (Straub) Q.; A.B., U. Mich., 1949, M.A., 1951; postgrad. Stanford Law Sch., 1949-50; Ph.D., U. Wis. 1954; m. Marilyn Lucille Johnson, June 12, 1949; children—Kurt, David, Susan, Katherine, Sarah. With Beloit Coll., 1955-56; faculty U. So. Cal., 1956-68; prof. medieval history U. Ill., Urbana, 1968—. Chmn., South Pasadena Human Relations Council, 1964-65; chmn. C-U Day Care Center. Served with AUS, 1943-46. Fulbright fellow, Belgium, 1954-55; Fulbright research fellow, Italy, 1962-63; Rockefeller Internat. Relations fellow, 1962-63, 64-65; Guggenheim fellow, 1972-73; Am. Council Learned Socs. grant-in-aid, 1973. Mem. Am. Hist. Assn., Inst. Advanced Study, Mediaeval Acad. Am. Author: Early Venetian Legislation on Ambassadors, 1966; The Office of the Ambassador in the Middle Ages, 1967; The Fourth Crusade, 1977; Two Studies on Venetian Government; 1977. Editor: The Latin Conquest of Constantinople, 1971; co-editor Post Scripta, Essays in Honor of Gaines Post. Home: 2406 S Prospect Champaign IL 61820 Office: Gregory Hall U Ill Urbana IL 61801

QUELLMALZ, FREDERICK, assn. exec., editor, photographer; b. N.Y.C., May 24, 1912; s. Frederick and Edith (Shaw) Q.; A.B., Princeton U., 1934; grad. Woodrow Wilson Sch. of Pub. and Internat. Affairs, 1934; B.Profl. Arts, Brooks Inst., 1968; m. Jayne Elysabeth Osten, May 29, 1942; children—Barbara Jayne, Carol Grant, Patricia Ellen, Sandra Lee, Tracy Louise. Spl. asst. Pepperell Mfg. Co., N.Y.C., 1934-40; dir. photo activities N.Y. World's Fair, 1940; asst. to chief engr. Naval Ordnance Plant, York, Pa., 1942-45; exec. sec. Photog. Soc. Am., Phila., 1940-42, editor soc.'s jour., 1939-52; exec. v.p. Profl. Photographers Am., Des Plaines, Ill., 1953-74, hon. exec. v.p. emeritus, 1974—, editor, pub. Profl. Photographer mag., 1953-74; exec. dir. Photo Art & Sci. Found., Inc., Des Plaines, 1972—, sec., 1965—, accredidation commn., 1976—. Trustee, sec. Winona Sch. Photography, 1953-75. Named hon. Master of Photography and Photog. Craftsman, Profl. Photographers Am.; hon. Ky. Col. Fellow Royal Soc. Arts (Eng.); mem. Am. (dir. 1963-66, certified assn. exec.), Wis. (pres. 1965), Chgo. socs. assn. execs. (dir. found. 1962-67, 76-78, pres. 1966), C. of C. U.S. (mem. assns. com. 1964—), Am. Soc. Photographers, Photographic Soc. Am. (hon. and asso.), Nat. Press Photographers Assn., Oval Table Soc., Nat. Assn. Exhbn. Mgrs. (certified exhibit mgr., dir. 1960-62), Royal Photog. Soc. Gt. Britain, Europhot, Am. Soc. Medalists, Soc. Photo Edn., Tex. Profl. Photog. Assn. (hon. life), Kappa Alpha Mu. Republican. Lutheran. Elk. Clubs: Princeton (Chgo.); York Camera (hon.). Home and office: 111 Stratford Rd Des Plaines IL 60016. *I have tried to live by the Golden Rule, believing in an ideal and willing to devote time, energy and hard work to accomplish a goal. An essential has been unlimited patience, ability to express oneself and to anticipate the needs of publics with which I have come into contact, and to fulfill those needs. Plus a firm belief the American way of life is the best in the world and that "profit" is not a dirty word.*

QUENEAU, PAUL ETIENNE, engr., educator; b. Phila., Mar. 20, 1911; s. Augustin L. and Jean (Blaisdell) Q.; B.A., Columbia, 1931, B.Sc., 1932, E.M., 1933; postgrad. (Evans fellow) Cambridge (Eng.) U., 1934; D.Sc., Delft (Netherlands) U. Tech., 1971; m. Joan Osgood Hodges, May 20, 1939; children—Paul Blaisdell, Josephine Downs (Mrs. George Stanley Patrick). With Internat. Nickel Co., 1934-69, dir. research, 1940-41, 46-48, v.p., 1958-69, tech. asst. to pres., 1960-66, asst. to chmn., 1967-69; vis. scientist Delft U. Tech., 1970-71; prof. engring. Dartmouth Coll., 1971—; cons. engr., 1972—; vis. prof. U. Minn., 1974-75. Geographer Perry River Arctic Expdn., 1949; chmn. U.S. Navy Arctic Research Adv. Com., 1957; gov. Arctic Inst. N.Am., 1957-62; mem. engring. council Columbia, 1965-70; mem. vis. com. Mass. Inst. Tech., 1967-70. Bd. dirs. Engring. Found., 1966-76, chmn., 1973-75. Served with U.S. Army, World War II; ETO; col. C.E. (ret.). Recipient Egleston medal Columbia U., 1965. Fellow Metall. Soc. of Am. Inst. M.E. (dir. 1964, 68-71, pres. 1969, Extractive Metallurgy Lecture award 1977); mem. Am. Inst. Mining, Metall. and Petroleum Engrs. (Douglas Gold medal 1968; v.p. 1970, dir. 1968-71), Nat. Soc. Profl. Engrs., Canadian Inst. Mining and Metallurgy, Inst. Mining and Metallurgy U.K. (overseas mem. council 1970—), Australasian Inst. Mining and Metallurgy, Sigma Xi, Tau Beta Pi. Author: (with Hanson) Geography, Birds and Mammals of the Perry River Region, 1956; Cobalt and the Nickeliferous Limonites, 1971. Editor: Extractive Metallurgy of Copper, Nickel and Cobalt, 1961; (with Anderson) Pyrometallurgical Processes in Nonferrous Metallurgy, 1967; The Winning of Nickel, 1967. Contbr. articles to profl. jours. Patentee in field. Home: Cornish NH 03746 Office: Thayer Sch Engring Dartmouth Coll Hanover NH 03755

QUENON, ROBERT HAGERTY, coal co. exec.; b. Clarksburg, W.Va., Aug. 2, 1928; s. Ernest Leonard and Josephine (Hagerty) Q.; B.S. in Mining Engring., W.Va. U., 1951; LL.B., George Washington U., 1964; m. Jean Bowling, Aug. 8, 1953; children—Evan, Ann, Richard. Mine supt. Consol. Coal Co., Fairmont, W.Va., 1956-61; mgr. deep mines Pittston Co., Dante, Va., 1964-66; gen. mgr. Riverton Coal Co., Crown Hill, W.Va., 1966-67; mgr. ops. coal and shale oil dept. Exxon Co., Houston, 1967; pres. Monterey Coal Co., Houston, 1969-76; sr. v.p. Carter Oil Co., Houston, 1976-77; exec. v.p. Peabody Coal Co., St. Louis, 1977-78, pres., chief exec. officer, 1978—; dir. First Union Bancorp., St. Louis. Trustee Blackburn Coll., Carlinville, Ill., 1975—. Served with AUS, 1946-47. Mem. Nat. Coal Assn. (chmn. bd. 1978-80). Office: 301 N Memorial Dr St Louis MO 63102

QUERY, JOY MARVES NEALE, educator; b. Worcestershire, Eng., June 18, 1926; d. Samuel and Dorree (Oakley) Neale; came to U.S., 1952; A.B., Drake U., 1954, M.A., 1955; postgrad. U. Syracuse, 1955-56; Ph.D., U. Ky., 1960; children—Jonathan, Margo, Evan. Tchr. secondary schs., Staffordshire, Eng., 1947-52; dep. prin. Smethwich Hall Girls' Sch., Staffordshire, 1948-52; instr. U. Ky., 1956-57, asst. prof., 1960; asso. prof. sociology and psychology Transylvania Coll., Lexington, Ky., 1961-66; asso. prof. N.D. State U., Fargo, 1966-68, prof. sociology and psychology, 1969-75, also chmn. sociology and psychology depts., 1969-70; chmn. sociology and anthropology dept., 1968-73; prof. behavioral sci. dept. neurosci. and psychiatry U. N.D. Med. Sch., Fargo, 1975—; on sabbatical leave Yale U., 1974-75. Field dir. Girl Scouts U.S.A., 1953-55; mem. Lexington Civil Rights Commn., 1960-66; bd. dirs. Fargo-Moorhead Family Service Agy., 1967-70; mem. Mayor's Coordinating Council for Youth, Fargo-Moorhead, 1976—. Fellow Internat. Assn. Social Psychiatry; mem. Am. Sociol. Assn., Am. Psychol. Assn., N.D. Psychol. Assn., AAUP, Midwest Sociol. Soc. (dir. 1970-73, 75-78), Alpha Kappa Delta. Unitarian. Contbr. articles and papers to profl. jours. Home: 1202 Oak St N Fargo ND 58102

QUEST, CHARLES FRANCIS, artist, educator, lectr.; b. Troy, N.Y., June 6, 1904; s. Charles F. and Ann (Hogan) Q.; student Washington U. Sch. Fine Arts, 1924-29, courses edn., 1938-39, Paris, 1929; m. Dorothy Johnson, Sept. 7, 1928. Executed murals pub. bldgs. libraries, and several large chs., 1930-45; instr. drawing and art analysis Washington U. Sch. Fine Arts, St. Louis, 1945, now prof. emeritus. Print maker wood engravings, wood cuts, etchings, copper engraving; painter oil, watercolor, tempera; sculptor; crafts stainglass, mosaic. Works purchased by Met. Mus. N.Y., Mus. Modern Art N.Y., Chgo. Art Inst., Phila. Art Mus., Library of Congress, St. Louis Art Mus., Bklyn. Mus., Brit. Mus., Victoria and Albert Mus., London, Bibliotheque Nationale, Paris, Nat. Mus. Stockholm, Nat. Mus. Jerusalem, Nat. Gallery Australia, Toledo Mus., Greenville County (S.C.) Mus. Art, and others; exhibited in 90 mus. and galleries in U.S., France, Germany, Italy; represented in permanent collections 40 mus., also oil painting at U.S. State Dept. Art in the Embassies Program. Exhibit color woodcuts Am. embassy, Paris, followed by year's tour of France, 1951; one-man show Smithsonian Inst., U.S. Nat. Mus., 1951, Maryville Coll. Mus., 1966, Am. Fedn. Arts, 1966, Mint Mus., Charlotte, N.C.; exhibited at Boston Mus. Art, Detroit Inst. Art, Cleve. Mus. Art, Fogg Mus. Harvard; two-man show Phila. Print Club (wood engravings and woodcuts), 1951; altar painting for Old Cathedral St. Louis, 1960. Recipient 53 prizes, 1923-72. Mem. Soc. Am. Graphic Artists N.Y., Phila. Color Print Soc., So. Vt. Artists, Painters Gallery, Hampton III Gallery (Greenville, S.C.). Club: St. Louis (life). Home: 200 Hillswick Rd Tryon NC 28782

QUESTEL, MAE, actress; b. Bronx, N.Y., Sept. 13, 1908; d. Simon and Frieda (Glauberman) Q.; student in drama J.G. Geiger, N.Y.C., 1916-24, (scholar) Theatre Guild, N.Y.C., 1923, Columbia U., 1949, Theatre Wing, 1951; m. Leo Balkin, Dec. 22, 1930; children—Robert (dec.), Richard; m. 2d, Jack E. Shelby, Nov. 19, 1970. Appeared in vaudeville at Palace Theatre, 1930, on RKO theater circuit, 1931-38; radio shows include: Betty Boops Frolics, NBC, 1932; cartoon voices: Betty Boop, 1931—, Olive Oyl, 1933—, Mr. Bugs Goes to Town, 1934, Little Audrey, 1946; TV cartoon: Winky Dink and You, 1956-60; stage appearances include: Dr. Social, 1948, A Majority of One, 1959-61, Come Blow Your Horn, 1963, Enter Laughing, 1963, Bajour, 1964, The Warm Peninsula, 1966, Walk Like A Lion, 1969, Barrel Full of Pennies, 1970, Where Have You Been, Billy Boy, 1969; films: A Majority of One, 1961, It's Only Money, 1962, Funny Girl, 1967, Move, 1969; TV spokeswoman for Scott Paper Co. as Aunt Bluebell, 1971-78; other commls. include: Playtex, 1970-72, Romilar, 1970-72, Folger's Coffee, 1970-72; soap opera: Somerset, 1976-77; also numerous recs. including Good Ship Lollipop. Mae Questel Day named by City of Indpls., 1968; named Living Legend, N.Y. U. Sch. Social Work, 1979; Troupers award for outstanding contbn. to entertainment, 1979; Annie award Internat. Animated Film Soc., 1979. Mem. Screen Actors Guild, AFTRA, Actors Equity Assn., Nat. Acad. TV Arts and Scis. (award 1978), Hadassah. Clubs: Troupers (award 1963), Variety. Office: care Fred Amsel & Assos 215 S LaCienega Blvd Suite 200 Beverly Hills CA 90211 also care Michael Thomas Agy 22 E 60th St New York NY 10022

QUESTER, GEORGE HERMAN, polit. scientist; b. Bklyn., July 14, 1936; s. Jacob George and Elizabeth (Mattern) Q.; A.B., Columbia U., 1958; M.A., Harvard U., 1964, Ph.D., 1965; m. Aline Marie Olson, June 20, 1964; children—Theodore, Amanda. Instr., then asst. prof. govt. Harvard U., 1965-70; asso. prof. govt. Cornell U., 1970-73, prof., 1973—. Served with USAF, 1958-61. Fellow Center Advanced Study Behavioral Scis., 1974-75. Mem. Council Fgn. Relations, Inst. Strategic Studies, Am. Polit. Sci. Assn. Author: Deterrence Before Hiroshima, 1966; Nuclear Diplomacy, 1970; The Politics of Nuclear Proliferation, 1973; The Continuing Problem of International Relations, 1974; Offense and Defense in the International System, 1977. Home: 316 Eastwood Ave Ithaca NY 14850 Office: McGraw 140 Cornell U Ithaca NY 14853

QUIAT, GERALD M., lawyer; b. Denver, Jan. 9, 1924; s. Ira L. and Esther (Greenblatt) Q.; A.A., U. Calif., Berkeley, 1942; A.B. and LL.B., U. Denver, 1948, J.D., 1972; m. Roberta M. Nicholson, Sept. 26, 1962; children—James M., Audrey L., Melinda, Daniel P., Ilana L., Leonard E. Admitted to Colo. and Fed. bars, 1948; dep. dist. atty. County of Denver (Colo.), 1949-52; partner firm Quiat, Seeman & Quiat, Denver, 1952-68, later Quiat & Quiat then changed to Quiat, Bucholtz & Bull, P.C., 1968; pres. firm Quiat Bucholtz Bull & Laff, P.C., and predecessors, Denver, 1968—; post comdr. Am. Legion, 1955-56, past judge adv. Colo. dept.; dir. Guaranty Bank & Trust Co., Denver, Guaranty Bank of Stapleton. Active Rose Med. Center, Denver, 1967—, pres., 1976-79; mem. Colo. Civil Rights Com.,

1963-71, chmn., 1966-67, 1969-70, chief hearing officer, 1963-71; bd. dirs. Am. Med. Center, Denver, Denver Central YMCA; vice chmn. Latin Am. desk, mem. nat. civil rights com., nat. commr. Anti-Defamation League, B'nai B'rith. Served with U.S. Army Inf., 1942-45. Decorated Bronze Star. Mem. Denver, Colo., Am. bar assns., Am., Denver, Colo. (pres. 1970-71) trial lawyers assns. Home: 6600 E Colorado Dr Denver CO 80224 Office: 621 17th St 1776 Denver CO 80293

QUIE, PAUL GERHARDT, educator, physician; b. Dennison, Minn., Feb. 3, 1925; s. Albert Knute and Nettie Marie (Jacobson) Q.; B.A., St. Olaf Coll., 1949; M.D., Yale U., 1953; m. Elizabeth Holmes, Aug. 10, 1951; children—Katie, Bill, Paul, David. Intern Hennipen County Hosp., 1953-54; pediatric resident U. Minn. Hosps., 1957-59; mem. faculty U. Minn. Med. Sch., 1959—, prof. pediatrics, 1968—, prof. microbiology, 1974—, Am. Legion meml. heart research prof., 1974—; attending physician Hennipen County Hosp., 1959—. Cons. Armed Forces Epidemiology Bd., 1969—, NIH, 1971—, U. Minn. Nursery Sch., 1959—; chief of staff U. Minn. Hosp., 1979; vis. physician Radcliffe Infirmary, Oxford, Eng., 1971-72; mem. Nat. Advisory Allergy and Infectious Disease Council, 1976—; mem. pediatric com. NRC, 1978. Bd. govs. U. Minn. Hosp., 1977—. Served with USNR, 1954-57; med. officer. Recipient E. Mead-Johnson award Am. Acad. Pediatrics, 1971; Guggenheim fellow, 1971-72; John and Mary R. Markle scholar, 1960-65. Diplomate Am. Bd. Pediatrics, Nat. Bd. Med. Examiners (mem.). Mem. N.Y. Acad. Scis., N.W. Pediatrics Soc., AAAS, Minn. Med. Found., Midwest Soc. Pediatric Research, Am. Fedn. Clin. Research, Am. Soc. Microbiology, AAUP, Harvey Soc., Am. Assn. Immunologists, Central Soc. for Clin. Research, Infectious Diseases Soc. Am. (council 1977—), Soc. Pediatric Research, Am. Pediatric Soc. (council 1976—), Am. Soc. Clin. Investigation, Soc. Exptl. Biology and Medicine (editorial bd. procs.), Minn. Acad. Pediatrics Am. Acad. Pediatrics Am. Assn. Physicians, Sons Norway, Sigma Xi. Editorial bd. Pediatrics, 1970—, Advances in Internal Medicine, 1977—, Antimicrobial Agts. and Chemotherapy, Jour. Infectious Diseases, 1979—. Research in function human leukocytes. Home: 2154 Commonwealth Ave Saint Paul MN 55108 Office: PO Box 483 U Minn Hosp Minneapolis MN 55455

QUIGG, CHRIS, physicist; b. Bainbridge, Md., Dec. 15, 1944; s. John Mitchell and Geneva Anne (Zimny) Q.; B.S. in Physics, Yale U., 1966; Ph.D. in Physics, U. Calif., Berkeley, 1970; m. Elizabeth Kelley, Sept. 2, 1967; children—David Michael, Katherine Kelley. Research asso. SUNY, Stony Brook, 1970-71, asst. prof. physics, 1971-74, asso. prof., 1974; physicist Fermi Nat. Accelerator Lab., Batavia, Ill., 1974—, head dept. theoretical physics, 1977—; mem. program advisory com. Stanford Linear Accelerator Center, 1974-77; vis. scholar Enrico Fermi Inst., 1974-78; mem. high energy adv. com. Brookhaven Nat. Lab., 1977-79; mem. high energy physics rev. com. Lawrence Berkeley Lab., 1978—; professorial lectr. U. Chgo., 1978—. Alfred P. Sloan Found. fellow, 1974-78. Mem. Am. Phys. Soc., AAAS. Home: 1218 Howard Circle Wheaton IL 60187 Office: Fermi Nat Accelerator Lab PO Box 500 Batavia IL 60510

QUIGG, HORACE DASHER, newspaperman; b. Marshall, Mo., Nov. 22, 1911; s. Horace Dasher and Elizabeth (Craig) Q.; A.B., U. Mo., 1934, B.J. (John W. Jewell scholar), 1934; m. Mary Pauline Hollomon, Aug. 9, 1937 (dec. Oct. 1965); 1 dau., Susan Elizabeth. Reporter, editor Boonville (Mo.) Daily News, Cooper County (Mo.) Record, 1929-33; news., sports editor Boonville Daily News, 1934-36; staff corr. U.P.I., Cleve., 1936-37, N.Y.C., 1937-67, sr. editor, N.Y.C. 1967—; war corr. PTO, 1943-45; corr. Byrd South Polar Expdn., 1946-47; columnist Korean War, 1950-51. Mem. N.Y. Press Club, Overseas Press Club, Phi Delta Theta, Kappa Tau Alpha. Club: Silurians. Author: (with others) Four Days, 1964, Gemini-America's Historic Walk in Space, 1965. Home: 41 W 8th St New York City NY 10011 Office: 220 E 42d St New York City NY 10017

QUIGLEY, JACK ALLEN, service co. exec.; b. Bloomington, Ill., Apr. 11, 1914; s. Thomas M. and Margaret (Brown) Q.; B.S., Northwestern U., 1935; m. Eleanor T. Steen, Nov. 17, 1946; children—James T., J. William, Margaret N., Richard A. With Means Services, Inc., 1935—, personnel dir., 1935-37, div. mgr., 1937-41, gen. mgr., 1946-48, v.p., dir., 1948-50, pres., dir., 1950-72, chmn. bd., chief exec. officer, 1972—. Co-chmn. First and Second Internat. linen supply congresses, 1959, 62; founder, chmn. Chgo. Pres.'s Orgn., 1966-68. Served with USAF World War II. Mem. Linen Supply Assn. Am. (pres. 1955-57, founder chmn. research group 1957-60), Chief Execs. Forum, Beta Theta Pi. Clubs: Butler Nat. (Oak Brook, Ill.); Royal Poinciana Country (Naples, Fla.); Mid Am. (Chgo.); Exmoor Country (Highland Park, Ill.). Home: 640 Winnetka Mews Apt 104 Winnetka IL 60093 Office: 35 E Wacker Dr Chicago IL 60601

QUIGLEY, JOSEPH MILTON, energy holding co. exec.; b. Belle Plaine, Iowa, Dec. 2, 1922; s. Lee L. and Emma (Polichek) Q.; student Loras Coll., Dubuque, Iowa, 1940-42, DePaul U., 1943; B.S.C., State U. Iowa, 1950, M.A., 1951; m. Margaret M. Scriven, Feb. 26, 1946; children—Joseph B., Mark W., Lisa Ann, Susan. Audit mgr. Arthur Andersen & Co., 1951-59; auditor State U. Iowa, 1959-61; with No. Ill. Gas Co., 1961—, treas, 1964-70, v.p., sec.-treas., 1970-73, financial v.p., sec., 1973—; financial v.p., sec. NICOR Inc., 1976—; dir. Nat. Marine Service Inc., Ni-Gas Exploration, Inc., NI-Gas Supply, Inc., Bank of Naperville, Mid-Continent Gasification Co., Mid-Continent Gas Storage Co., First Security Bank of Fox Valley; dir., sec. NICOR Exploration Co., NICOR Resources Ltd., NICOR Belize Inc., NICOR Minerals Inc., NICOR Mining Inc., NICOR Australia Inc. Treas., No. Ill. Gas Retirement Trust, No. Ill. Gas Employee Benefit Assn. Mem. adv. com. Coll. DuPage, U. Ill. Coll. Commerce and Bus. Adminstrn., Inst. Pub. Utilities, Mich. State U. Trustee, regional v.p. Taxpayers' Fedn. Ill.; bd. dirs. Iowa State Regulatory Conf. Bd. Served with AUS, 1943-46. Decorated Bronze Star medal. Mem. Ill. C. of C., Am. Mgmt. Assn. (fin. council), So. Gas Assn., Chgo. Tax Club, Am. Gas Assn., Am. Soc. Corp. Secs., Financial Execs. Inst. Clubs: Economic, Public Utility Securities, Executives (Chgo.); Naperville Country. Home: 312 W Tamarack Dr Naperville IL 60540 Office: P O Box 200 1700 W Ferry Rd Naperville IL 60540

QUIGLEY, LEO BERNARD, editor; b. Winnipeg, Man., Can., Oct. 4, 1941; s. Leo Dennis and Margurite Marie (Russell) Q.; asso. diploma journalism, Mt. Royal Coll., Calgary, Alta., 1965; m. Linda Ann Reid, May 3, 1974; children—Jodie Lynn, Jacqueline Joy, Kathleen Marie, Thomas Russell. Info. officer Govt. Sask., Regina, 1965-68; communications specialist Govt. Man., Winnipeg, 1968-72; info. officer Govt. Yukon Ter., White Horse, 1972-73; columnist, reporter Regina Leader Post, 1973-76; mng. editor Report on Farming, Winnipeg, 1976—. Mem. Canadian Farm Writers Fedn. (award Merit for editorial 1976, honorable mention 1977, 79), Newspaper Farm Editors Am., Am. Agrl. Editors Assn., Man. Farm Writers and Broadcasters Assn., Winnipeg C. of C. Roman Catholic. Home: 202 3915 Grant Ave Winnipeg MB R3N 1T1 Canada Office: 300 Carlton St Winnipeg MB R3C 3C1 Canada

QUIGLEY, MARTIN SCHOFIELD, educator, publishing co. exec.; b. Chgo., Nov. 24, 1917; s. Martin Joseph and Gertrude Margaret (Schofield) Q.; A.B. magna cum laude, Georgetown U., 1939; M.A., Columbia, 1973, Ed.D., 1975; m. Katherine J. Dunphy, July 2, 1946; children—Martin, Elin, William, Kevin, Karen, Patricia, John, Mary Katherine, Peter. Reporter, Motion Picture Herald, N.Y.C. and Hollywood, Calif., 1939-41; with overseas br. OWI, 1942; secret war work U.S. Govt., 1943-45; various editorial and mgmt. posts Quigley Pub. Co., Inc., N.Y.C., 1946—, pres., 1964—; staff, dept. higher and adult edn. Tchrs. Coll., 1974-75; prof. higher edn. grad. courses Baruch Coll., City U. N.Y., 1977—, Tchrs. Coll., Columbia U., summer 1979; pres. QWS, Inc. ednl. cons.; cons. supt. schs. N.Y. Archdiocese, 1962-70. Pres. New York Christian Family Movement, 1960-62, mem. nat. exec. com., 1960-65; founder, chmn. N.Y. Ind. Schs. Opportunity Project, 1965-77. Pres., Found. Internat. Coop., 1960-65; bd. dirs. Will Rogers Inst., Motion Picture Pioneers; treas. Religious Edn. Assn. U.S. and Can., 1975—; trustee Village of Larchmont (N.Y.), 1977-79. Roman Catholic. Club: Larchmont Yacht. Author: Great Gaels, 1944; Roman Notes, 1946; Magic Shadows-the story of the origin of motion pictures, 1948; Government Relations of Five Universities in Washington, D.C., 1975; co-author: Catholic Action in Practice, 1962; Films in America, 1969. Editor: New Screen Techniques, 1953. Home: 1 Locust Ave Larchmont NY 10538 Office: 159 W 53d St New York NY 10019

QUIGLEY, ROBERT ALAN, publisher; b. Rochester, N.Y., Dec. 27, 1943; s. J. Leslie and Mary Elizabeth (Thomas) Q.; B.A., Wesleyan U., Middletown, Conn., 1965; m. Carolyn A. Stanton, June 28, 1969; children—Kristina Louise, Benjamin Leslie. Loan officer trainee Hanover Trust Co., N.Y.C., 1965-66; asst. circulation dir. Life mag. Time, Inc., N.Y.C., 1966-70; mgr. paperback book club Xerox Edn. Publs., Middletown, Conn., 1970-73, v.p., pub. periodicals div., 1973—. Mem. Community Scholarship Evaluation Com., 1976-79; pres. PTA, Killingworth, Conn., 1979. Served with U.S. Army, 1967. Mem. Assn. Am. Pubs., Direct Mail/Mktg. Assn. Democrat. Home: Schnoor Rd Killingworth CT 06417 Office: Xerox Edn Publs 245 Long Hill Rd Middletown CT 06457

QUILICO, LOUIS, dramatic baritone; b. Montreal, Que., Can., Jan. 14, 1931; s. Louis and Jeanne (Gravel) Q.; studied Conservatoire de la Province de Que., Ont., Can.; Mannes Coll. Music, N.Y.C.; m. Oct. 30, 1949; children—Donna Maria, Gino. Debut in opera in La Traviatta, N.Y.C., Opera, 1956; with Major Opera cos. including Royal Opera (Covent Garden) Staatsopher, Opera National de Belgique, L'Opera de Quebec, Canadian Opera Co., Bolshoi Opera, Opera Co. of Phila., San Francisco Opera, Seattle Opera, San Diego Opera, Opera Soc. of Washington (D.C.) many others; resident mem. Metropolitan Opera; prof. U. Toronto (Ont.). Winner Nos Futurs Etacles, Montreal, 1953, Met. Opera Audition of the Air, 1955; named Esquire, Montreal Expo, 1967; decorated companion Order of Can. Roman Catholic. Office: care Shaw Concerts Inc 1995 Broadway New York NY 10023*

QUILLEN, JAMES HENRY, congressman; b. Wayland, Va., Jan. 11, 1916; s. John A. and Hannah (Chapman) Q.; ed. high sch.; LL.D. (hon.), Steed Coll., Johnson City, Tenn., 1963, Milligan Coll., Tenn., 1978; m. Cecile Cox, Aug. 9, 1952. With Kingsport Press, 1934-35, Kingsport Times, 1935-36; founder newspaper Kingsport Mirror, semi-weekly, 1936, pub., 1936-39; founder Johnson City (Tenn.) Times, 1939, pub., 1939-44, converted to daily, 1940; mem. Tenn. Ho. of Reps., 1954-62, minority leader, 1959-60, mem. legislative council, 1957, 59, 61; mem. 88th-96th congresses from 1st Dist. Tenn., ranking minority mem. Rules com. Served to lt. USNR, 1942-46. Mem. Am. Legion, VFW, C. of C. Republican. Methodist. Clubs: Lions; Ridgefields Country (Kingsport); Capitol Hill (Washington). Home: 1601 Fairidge Pl Kingsport TN 37664 Offfice: Cannon House Office Bldg Washington DC 20515

QUILLEN, WILLIAM TATEM, state supreme ct. justice; b. Camden, N.J., Jan. 15, 1935; s. Robert James and Gladys Collings (Tatem) Q.; B.A., Williams Coll., 1956; LL.B., Harvard U., 1959; m. Marcia Everhart Stirling, June 27, 1959; children—Carol Everhart, Tracey Tatem. Admitted to Del. bar, 1959; asso. firm Richards, Layton & Finger, Wilmington, Del., 1963-64; adminstrv. asst. to Gov. of Del., 1965; asso. judge Superior Ct. of Del., 1966-73; chancellor State of Del., 1973-76; sr. v.p. Wilmington Trust Co., 1976-78; justice Supreme Ct. of Del., 1978—; adj. faculty mem. Del. Law Sch., Widener U., 1976—. Trustee Widener U., 1979—. Served with Judge Adv. Corps, USAF, 1959-62. Mem. Am. Bar Assn., Del. State Bar Assn. Democrat. Presbyterian. Club: Wilmington. Office: State Office Bldg 820 N French St Wilmington DE 19801

QUILLIAN, WILLIAM FLETCHER, JR., banker, former coll. pres.; b. Nashville, April 13, 1913; s. William Fletcher and Nonie (Acree) Q.; A.B., Emory U., 1935, Litt.D. (hon.), 1959; B.D., Yale, 1938, Ph.D., 1943; postgrad., U. Edinburgh, 1938-39, U. Basel, 1939; Day fellow from Yale, 1938-39; Rosenwald fellow, 1940-41; LL.D., Ohio Wesleyan U., 1952, Hampden-Sydney Coll., 1978; LL.D., Randolph-Macon Coll., 1967, D.H.L., Woman's Coll., 1978; m. Margaret Hannah Weigle, June 15, 1940; children—William Fletcher III, Anne Acree, Katherine, Robert. Student asst. Stamford (Conn.) Presbyn Ch., 1936-38; del. Gen. Com. of World Student Christian Fedn., Bievres, France, 1938; discussion leader World Conf. Christian Youth, Amsterdam, Holland, 1939; pastor Clarendon (Vt.) Community Ch., summer 1940; ordained to ministry Meth. Ch., 1942; asst. prof. philosophy Gettysburg Coll., 1941-43, prof., 1943-45; prof. philosophy Ohio Wesleyan U., 1945-52; pres. Randolph Macon Woman's Coll., 1952-78, pres. emeritus, 1978—; sr. v.p. Fidelity Am. Bank, 1978—; tchr. Garrett Biblical Inst., summer 1951. Bd. dirs. Alpha Tau Omega Found.; Lynchburg Gen. Hosp.; hon. life trustee Va. Found. Ind. Colls., pres., 1958-61). Mem. Assn. Va. Colls. (past pres.), So. U. Conf. (pres. 1967-68), So. Assn. Colls. for Women (pres. 1956), Nat. Assn. United Methodist Colls. and Univs. (pres. 1973), Am. Philos. Assn., Soc. for Values in Higher Edn. (mem. central com. 1945-48; chmn. 1947-48), Nat. Assn. Bibl. Instrs., AAUP, Greater Lynchburg C. of C. (dir., pres. 1979-80), Phi Beta Kappa. Omicron Delta Kappa, Alpha Tau Omega (dir. found.). Author: The Moral Theory of Evolutionary Naturalism, 1945, Evolution and Moral Theory in America, Evolutionary Thought in America, 1950. Contbr. articles to philos. and religious jours. Home: 1407 Club Dr Lynchburg VA 24503 Office: Fidelity Am Bank Lynchburg VA 24505

QUILLIGAN, EDWARD JAMES, educator; b. Cleve., June 18, 1925; s. James Joseph and Maude Elvira (Ryan) Q.; B.A., Ohio State U., 1951, M.D., 1951; M.A. (hon.), Yale, 1967; m. Betty Jane Cleaton, Dec. 14, 1946; children—Bruce, Jay, Carol, Christopher, Linda, Ted. Intern, Ohio State U. Hosp., 1951-52, resident, 1952-54; resident Western Res. U. Hosps., 1954-56; asst. prof. obstetrics and gynecology Western Res. U., 1957-63, prof., 1963-65; prof. obstetrics and gynecology U. Calif. at Los Angeles, 1965-66; prof., chmn. dept. Ob-Gyn, Yale U., 1966-69; prof., chmn. dept. Ob-Gyn, U. So. Calif., 1969-78, asso. v.p. med. affairs, 1978-79; prof. Ob-Gyn., U. Calif., Irvine, 1980—. Served to 2d lt. AUS, 1944-46. Recipient Centennial award Ohio State U., 1970. Mem. Soc. Gynecologic Investigation, Am. Gynecol. Soc., Am. Coll. Obstetics and Gynecology, Sigma Xi. Contbr. articles to med. jours. Editor: Am. Jour. Obstetrics and Gynecology. Home: 86 Monarch Bay South Laguna CA 92677 Office: 1240 N Mission St Los Angeles CA 90033

QUIMBY, GEORGE IRVING, mus. dir.; b. Grand Rapids, Mich., May 4, 1913; s. George Irving and Ethelwyn (Sweet) Q.; B.A., U. Mich., 1936, M.A., 1937, grad. fellow, 1937-38; postgrad. U. Chgo., 1938-39; m. Helen M. Ziehm, Oct. 13, 1940; children—Sedna H., G. Edward, John E., Robert W. State supr. Fed. Archaeol. Project in La., 1939-41; dir. Muskegon (Mich.) Mus., 1941-42; asst. curator N.Am. archaeology and ethnology Field Mus. Natural History, 1942-43, curator exhibits, anthropology, 1943-54, curator N.Am. archeology and ethnology, 1954-65, research asso. in N. Am. archaeology and ethnology, 1965—; curator anthropology Thomas Burke Meml. Wash. State Mus., prof. anthropology U. Wash., 1965—, mus. dir., 1968—; lectr. U. Chgo., 1947-65, Northwestern U., 1949-53; Fulbright vis. prof. U. Oslo, Norway, 1952; archaeol. expdns. and field work, Mich., 1935, 37, 42, 56-63. Wis., 1936, Hudson's Bay, 1939, La., 1940-41, N.M., 1947, Lake Superior, 1956-61. Fellow A.A.A.S., Am. Anthrop. Assn.; mem. Soc. Am. Archaeology (pres. 1958), Am. Soc. Ethnohistory, Wis. Archeol. Soc., Soc. Historical Archeology (council 1971-74, 75-78), Assn. Sci. Mus. Dirs. (pres. 1973—), Norwegian Totemic Soc., Arctic Inst. N.Am., Am. Assn. Museums (council 1971-74), Sigma Xi, Phi Sigma, Chi Gamma Phi, Zeta Psi. Author: The Goodall Focus, 1941, Aleutian Islanders, 1944; (with J. A. Ford) The Tchefuncte Culture, an Early Occupation of the Lower Mississippi Valley, 1945; (with P. S. Martin, D. Collier) Indians Before Columbus, 1947; Indian Life in the Upper Great Lakes, 1960; Indian Culture and European Grade Goods, 1966. Editor: (with others) 1914 documentary film In the Land of the War Canoes, 1973; co-editor Maritime Adaptations of The Pacific, 1975. Contbr. articles to profl. jours. Home: 6001 52d Ave NE Seattle WA 98115 Office: Thomas Burke Meml Wash State Museum U Wash Seattle WA 98195

QUINBY, CHARLES EDWARD, JR., mfg. co. exec.; b. Passaic, N.J., Jan. 12, 1943; s. Charles Edward and Josephine (Smolak) Q.; B.S., Fairleigh Dickinson U., Rutherford, N.J., 1968; m. Brenda Hoffman, Dec. 7, 1963; children—Charles, Tammy. Various adminstrn. and accounting positions Becton Dickinson & Co., East Rutherford, N.J., 1964-68; corporate controller Athlone Industries, Inc., Parsippany, N.J., 1973-78, v.p., controller, 1978—. Mem. Am. Assn. Corporate Controllers. Home: Old Rifle Camp Rd West Paterson NJ 07424 Office: 200 Webro Rd Parsippany NJ 07054

QUINLAN, JOSEPH EDWARD, meat processing co. exec.; b. Monroeville, Ind., Apr. 8, 1917; s. Walter E. and Kathryn (Brooks) Q.; ed. pub. schs.; m. Virginia Oetting, Oct. 23, 1937; children—Janice M. Quinlan Smink, Joyce M. Quinland Bellner, Beverly Quinlan Weinraub, Terrence E. Apprentice tool and die-maker, then model maker Gen. Electric Co., Ft. Wayne, Ind., 1937-50; sales agt. Western & So. Life Ins. Co., Ft. Wayne, 1950-51; with Peter Eckrich & Sons, Inc., Ft. Wayne, 1951—, asst. div. mgr., 1961-65, div. mgr., 1965-68, group v.p. mktg., 1969-73, exec. v.p., 1973-74, pres., 1974—, chmn. bd., chief exec. officer, 1975—; pres. splty. meat div. Beatrice Foods Co., 1976—, v.p. Beatrice Foods Co., 1977—. Roman Catholic. Home: 6417 Centerton Dr Fort Wayne IN 46815 Office: PO Box 388 Fort Wayne IN 46801

QUINLAN, MICHAEL ROBERT, fast food chain exec.; b. Chgo., Dec. 9, 1944; s. Robert Joseph and Kathryn Janith (Koerner) Q.; B.S., Loyola U., Chgo., 1967, M.B.A. in Fin., 1970; m. Marilyn Decashmutt, Apr. 23, 1966; children—Kevin, Michael. With McDonald's Corp., 1972—, sr. v.p., Chgo., 1976-78, exec. v.p., from 1978, now sr. exec. v.p., chief ops. officer, Oak Brook, Ill., adv. dir., 1977-78, also dir. Republican. Roman Catholic. Clubs: Butterfield Country, Oakbrook Handball-Racquetball. Home: 3800 Belle Aire Downers Grove IL 60515 Office: #1 McDonald's Plaza Oak Brook IL 60521

QUINLAN, STERLING CARROLL, television exec.; b. Maquoketa, Ia., Oct. 23, 1916; s. Carroll and Lillian (Sterling) Q.; student Cleve. Coll., 1936-37, N.Y. U., 1945-46; m. Mary Janda, Feb. 23, 1963; 1 son, Thomas; 1 son (by previous marriage) Terry. With Sta. WIND, Gary, Ind., 1930-35; writer, lead player NBC documentary series on transient life in Am., 1936; staff writer NBC, Cleve., 1936-37; free-lance actor, writer, Chgo. and Hollywood, Calif., 1937-40; with WBKB, Chgo., 1947-67, v.p., 1953-67; v.p. ABC, 1953-64; pres. Field Communications Corp., Chgo., until 1967; now v.p. broadcast services div. IDC Services, Inc., Chgo. Bd. dirs. Better Bus. Bur., Chgo. Mem. Def. Orientation Conf. Assn., Navy League, Broadcast Advt. Club (dir., past pres.), Chgo. Advt. Club (dir., past pres.). Clubs: Tavern, M and M, Economics (Chgo.). Author: The Merger, Jugger, Muldoon Was Here, The Hundred Million Dollar Lunch, Inside ABC, Day the Sun Caught Cold (play). Home: 5121 S Harvey Western Springs IL 60558 Office: 303 E Ohio St Chicago IL 60611

QUINLAN, THOMAS E., JR., ins. co. exec., lawyer; b. N.Y.C., Jan. 20, 1922; B.A., LL.B., Columbia U.; m. Florence Butler, June 5, 1946; children—Carol, Joan, Christopher. Counsel Home Life Ins. Co., N.Y.C., 1948-71; v.p., gen. counsel Penn Mut. Life Ins. Co., Phila., 1971—. Served to 1st lt. AC, U.S. Army, World War II. Mem. Assn. Life Ins. Counsel (past pres.), Am., Phila. bar assns., Assn. Bar City N.Y. Office: Penn Mut Life Ins Co Independence Sq Philadelphia PA 19172

QUINN, ALFRED O(TTO), engr.; b. Syracuse, N.Y., Apr. 2, 1915; s. Otto A. and Daisy (Fortin) Q.; B.S. in Civil Engring., Syracuse U., 1936; LL.B., Chattanooga Coll. Law, 1940; m. Doris Harriman, June 5, 1937; children—Nancy Jean, Janet Anne, Pamela Sue, John Alfred. Photogrammetric engr. T.V.A., 1936-43; admitted to Tenn. bar, 1940; asso. prof. photogrammetry Syracuse U., 1946-50; chief engring. and field surveys Aero Service Corp., Phila., 1950-56, formerly chief engr. and dir. photogrammetric engring. div.; pres. Quinn and Assos., Photogrammetric Engrs., Horsham, Pa., 1965—. Mem. OAS Mission to Chile, 1960. Mem. tech. adv. com. Pa. State U. Served to lt., Photo Intelligence, Amphibious ops., USNR, Philippines, Iwo Jima, Ckinawa, Japan, 1943-46, Bikini atom bomb tests, 1946. Recipient Navy commendation. Registered profl. engr.-surveyor, Utah, Pa., N.Y., Alaska, Va., Conn., Tenn., N.J., Fla. Fellow Am. Soc. C.E. (v.p. Phila. sect. 1972-73, pres. sect. 1974-75); mem. Am. Soc. Photogrammetry (dir. 1949-52, v.p. 1952, pres. 1953, hon. mem. 1975), Am. Congress Surveying and Mapping (dir. 1960-61), Am. Geophys. Union, Asso. Profl. Photogrammetrists (chmn. 1958-60), Nat. Soc. Profl. Engrs., Sigma Xi, Delta Kappa Epsilon. Episcopalian (vestryman). Club: Varsity (Syracuse U.). Author: Elements of Photogrammetry (with Earl Church), 1948. Home: 1106 Country Club Dr Oreland PA 19075 Office: 460 Caredean Dr Horsham PA 19044

QUINN, ANDREW PETER, JR., lawyer; b. Providence, Oct. 22, 1923; s. Andrew Peter and Margaret (Canning) Q.; A.B., Brown U., 1945; LL.B., Yale, 1950; m. Sara G. Bullard, May 30, 1952; 1 dau., Emily H. Admitted to R.I. bar, 1949, Mass. bar, 1960, also U.S. Tax Ct.; practice in Providence, 1950-59, Springfield, Mass., 1959—; partner Letts & Quinn, 1950-59; with Mass. Mut. Life Ins. Co., 1959—, exec. v.p., gen. counsel, 1971—. Trustee, chmn. bd. MacDuffie Sch.; trustee Baystate Med. Center, Springfield. Served from ensign to lt. (j.g.), USNR, 1944-46. Mem. Am. (co-chmn. nat. conf. lawyers and life ins. cos. 1973), Hampden County (Mass.) bar assns., Assn. Life Ins. Counsel (bd. govs.), Am. Council Life Ins.

(chmn. legal sect. 1971), Life Ins. Assn. Mass. (chmn. exec. com. 1975-77), Asso. Alumni Brown U. (dir. 1969-72). Clubs: New York Yacht; Longmeadow Country; Connecticut Valley Brown University (past pres.) (Springfield). Home: 306 Ellington Rd Longmeadow MA 01106 Office: 1295 State St Springfield MA 01101

QUINN, ANTHONY RUDOLPH OAXACA, actor, writer; b. Chihuahua, Mexico, Apr. 21, 1915; s. Frank and Nellie (Oaxaca) Q.; student pub. schs.; m. Katherine de Mille, Oct. 2, 1937 (div.); children—Christina, Kathleen, Duncan, Valentina; m. 2d, Iolanda Addolori, Jan. 1966; children—Francesco, Daniele, Lorenzo. Naturalized Am. citizen, 1947. Actor in plays including Clean Beds, 1936, Gentleman from Athens, 1947, Street Car Named Desire, Let Me Hear the Melody, Beckett, 1961, Tchin-Tchin, 1963; has appeared in many motion pictures including Buccaneer, Viva Zapata (Acad. award 1952), Lust for Life (Acad. award best supporting actor 1956), La Strada, 1954, Man from Del Rio, 1956, The Black Orchid, 1958, Last Train From Gun Hill, 1958, Warlock, 1959, Heller in Pink Tights, 1960, Portrait in Black, 1960, Guns of Navarrone, 1961, Barabbas, 1962, Lawrence of Arabia, 1962, Requiem for a Heavyweight, 1963, The Visit, 1963, Behold a Pale Horse, 1964, Zorba the Greek, 1964, The Shoes of the Fisherman, 1968, The Secret of Santa Vittoria, 1969, Across 110th Street, 1972, Arruza (narrator), Deaf Smith and Johnny Ears, 1973, The Don Is Dead, 1973, Mohammed Messenger of God, 1977, Caravans, 1978, The Children of Sanchez, 1978, The Greek Tycoon, 1978, The Inheritance, 1978, The Passage, 1979; appeared in TV prodn. of The Life of Christ; script writer Metro-Goldwyn-Mayer prodn. The Farm. Author: The Original Sin, 1972. Address: 333 Las Casa Ave Pacific Palisades CA 90272*

QUINN, BAYARD ELMER, educator; b. Phila., May 10, 1915; s. Bayard Elmer and Martha (Engle) Q.; B.S., Drexel Inst. Tech., 1937; M.S., Cornell U., 1942, Ph.D., 1945; m. Charlotte Louise Benedict, June 30, 1945; children—Bayard Paul, James Benedict. Draftsman, RCA Mfg. Co., Camden, N.J., 1934-37; engr. Gen. Electric Co., Schenectady, 1937-40; asst. prof. Cornell U., 1940-46; prof. Purdue U., Lafayette, Ind., 1946—; mem. pavement condition evaluation com. Transp. Research Bd., NRC, 1968—, mem. surface properties-vehicle interaction com., 1973—; cons. Boeing Airplane Co., Gen. Motors Corp., AEC, NSF, Hwy. Research Bd., Am. Assn. State Hwy. Ofcls. Road Test. Dist. commr. Boy Scouts Am., 1965—. Registered profl. engr., Ind., Pa. Mem. Am. Soc. Mech. Engrs., Am. Soc. Engring. Edn., Sigma Xi, Pi Tau Sigma, Tau Beta Pi. Presbyn. (elder). Clubs: University, Sailing, Wabash Valley Torch (pres. 1966) (Lafayette). Patentee in field. Home: 1007 Hillcrest Rd West Lafayette IN 47906 Office: Mech Engring Sch Purdue U Lafayette IN 47907

QUINN, CHARLES NICHOLAS, journalist; b. Utica, N.Y., July 28, 1930; s. Charles Dunaway and Elsa (Zarth) Q.; B.A., Cornell U., 1951; M.S., Columbia U. Sch. Journalism, 1954; children—Diana David, Ben, Jane. Reporter, Providence Jour., 1954-56, N.Y. Herald Tribune, 1956-62; corr. NBC News, N.Y.C., 1962-66, Washington, 1966-71, 74—, Rome, 1971-74; mng. editor, chief corr. NBC Radio News, Washington, 1978—. Served with arty. U.S. Army, 1951-53. Reported on hunger in U.S. on Huntley-Brinkley Report (co-recipient Emmy 1969). Office: 498 Nat Press Bldg Washington DC 20045

QUINN, EDWARD JAMES, banker; b. N.Y.C., Apr. 2, 1911; s. Edward M. and Mary M. (Schneider) Q.; student Hofstra Coll., 1946-52; grad. Am. Inst. Banking, 1932-39, Grad. Sch. Banking at Rutgers, 1955-57; m. Marie A. Stafford, Apr. 22, 1939; children—Mary Ann Brown, James E., Patrick M., Sheila G. Messenger, J.S. Bache & Co., N.Y.C., 1926-27; bookkeeper Nassau-Suffolk Bond & Mortgage Guaranty Co., Mineola, N.Y., 1928; sr. v.p. European-Am. Bank & Trust Co., 1928—. Chmn. investment com. United Fund L.I., 1968-71; treas. Nassau County Boy Scouts Am., 1936-39, Nassau County March Dimes, 1947-48, Nassau County Easter Seal Appeal, 1948-55, Suffolk County Cancer Soc., 1955-57, Union Free Sch. Dist. 22, Farmingdale, 1948-57; mem. U.S. Savs. Bond Com., Nassau County, 1952-65; bd. regents Royal Arcanum, 1938-39, grand committeeman, 1940-41. Mem. Bd. Appeals Village Farmingdale, 1941-56. Served with Med. Detachment AUS, 1943-46. Mem. Municipal Forum N.Y., Municipal Finance Officers Assn. U.S., L.I. Bankers Assn. (chmn. check clearing com. 1955, legislative com. 1965-71), Nat. Assn. Accountants, Am. Legion. Rotarian. Clubs: Brentwood (N.Y.) Country; Gull Haven Golf (Central Islip, N.Y.); Harbor Hills Country (Belle Terre, N.Y.). Home: 383 West Hills Rd Huntington NY 11743 Office: 730 Veterans Meml Hwy Hauppauge NY 11787

QUINN, JAMES BRIAN, educator; b. Memphis, Mar. 18, 1928; s. Clarence A. and Henriette (Rein) Q.; B.S. in Engring., Yale, 1949; M.B.A., Harvard, 1951; Ph.D., Columbia, 1958; M.A. (hon.), Dartmouth, 1964; m. Allie Brady James, Feb. 9, 1950; children—James Franklin, John Brady, Virginia Anne. With research div. Allen B. DuMont Labs., Inc., 1951-54; faculty marketing dept. U. Conn. 1954-57; faculty Amos Tuck Sch. Bus. Adminstrn., Dartmouth, 1957—, asst. dean, 1957-58, prof., 1964—. Cons. in field, 1958—; pres. James Brian Quinn & Assos., cons. research and devel., Hanover, N.H., 1961—; cons. govt. depts., Norwegian govt., corps., 1961—; mem. tech. adv. bd. U.S. Dept. Commerce, 1968-72. Recipient McKinsey Found. award, 1963. Ford Found. fellow, 1963-64; Sloan Found. fellow, 1967-68; Fulbright fellow, 1973. Mem. A.A.A.S. Author: Yardsticks for Industrial Research, 1959. Contbr. articles to profl. jours. Home: 22 Rayton Rd Hanover NH 03755

QUINN, JAMES HOCKLEY MCKEE, hosp. adminstr.; b. Cynwyd, Pa., Feb. 12, 1916; s. Arthur Hobson and Helen (McKee) W.; A.B., U. Pa., 1937; LL.D., Widener Coll., 1970; m. Frances Wharton Lucas, Dec. 27, 1943; children—James McKee, Frances Wharton Quinn Campbell, Kathleen McDonough Quinn Slaton, Sara Cloyd Quinn Byecroft, Peter Arrison, John Carberry. Master, St. Albans Sch., Washington, 1940-43; master Episcopal Acad., Phila., 1943-53, asst. headmaster, 1953-57, headmaster, 1957-73, pres., 1973-75; headmaster Barstow Sch., Kansas City, Mo., 1975-79; asst. dir. Inglis House, Phila., 1979—; sec. Secondary Edn. Bd., 1955-61; chmn. Ind. Schs. Fund Phila., 1955-57. Pres. Pa. Assn. Ind. Schs., 1968-70. Chmn. trustees Ednl. Records Bur., 1969-71. Mem. Headmasters Assn., Country Day Headmasters Assn., Pvt. Sch. Tchrs. Assn. Phila. and Vicinity (pres. 1947-49). Home: 102 Ashton Way West Chester PA 19380 Office: 2600 Belmont Ave Philadelphia PA 19131

QUINN, JAMES LELAND, III, physician, educator; b. Pitts., July 12, 1933; s. James Leland, Jr. and Mary (Dunn) Q.; B.S., Belmont Abbey Coll., 1955, LL.D., 1973; M.D., Bowman Gray Sch. Medicine, 1959; m. Marie Magdalene Boschman, Aug. 26, 1973; children by previous marriage—Megan, Michelle Diane, James Leland IV, Michael Dennis. Intern, Pa. Hosp., Phila., 1959-60; resident radiology N.C. Baptist Hosp., Winston-Salem, 1960-63, dir. nuclear medicine, 1963-64; instr. radiology Bowman Gray Sch. Medicine, 1963-64; practice medicine, specializing in radiology, Chgo., 1964—; dir. nuclear medicine Northwestern Meml. Hosp., 1964-79; asst. prof. radiology Northwestern U., 1964-66, asso. prof., 1966-68, prof., 1968—, asso. chmn., 1973-79, prof. pathology, 1975—; cons. Western Med. Bd. Ireland, WHO expert Com. on radiation, 1975—. Named Outstanding Young Man of Am., 1966. Fellow Am. Coll. Radiology, Royal Coll. Surgeons Ireland (hon.); mem. A.M.A., Assn. U. Radiologists, Soc. Nuclear Medicine (pres. 1971-72, Disting. Service award 1979), Radiol. Soc. N.Am., Soc. Clin. Research, Alpha Omega Alpha. Democrat. Roman Catholic. Editor: Scintillation Scanning in Clinical Diagnosis, 1964; Yearbook of Nuclear Medicine, 1966—. Contbr. articles to tech. jours. Home: 1448 N Lake Shore Dr Chicago IL 60610 Office: 5700 N Ashland Ave Chicago IL 60660

QUINN, JANE BRYANT, journalist; b. Niagara Falls, N.Y., Feb. 5, 1939; d. Frank Leonard and Ada (Laurie) Bryant; B.A. magna cum laude, Middlebury Coll., 1960; m. David Conrad Quinn, June 10, 1967; children—Matthew Alexander, Justin Bryant. Asso. editor Insiders Newsletter, N.Y.C., 1962-65, co-editor, 1966-67; sr. editor Cowles Book Co., N.Y.C., 1968; editor-in-chief Bus. Week Letter, N.Y.C., 1969-73, gen. mgr., 1973-74; syndicated financial columnist Washington Post Writers Group, 1974—; contbr. fin. column to Women's Day mag., 1974—; contbr. NBC News and Info. Service, 1976-77; bus. corr. WCBS-TV, N.Y.C., 1979, CBS-TV News, 1980—; contbg. editor Newsweek mag., 1978—; author: Everybody's Money Book, 1979. Mem. Phi Beta Kappa. Home: 7 Berrybrook Circle Chappaqua NY 10514 Office: Newsweek 444 Madison Ave New York City NY 10022

QUINN, JARUS WILLIAM, physicist, assn. exec.; b. West Grove, Pa., Aug. 25, 1930; s. William G. and Ellen C. (DuRoss) Q.; B.S., St. Joseph's Coll., 1952; postgrad. Johns Hopkins U., 1952-55; Ph.D., Cath. U. Am., 1964; m. Margaret M. McNerney, June 27, 1953; children—J. Kevin, Megan, Jennifer, Colin, Kristin. Research asso. physics Johns Hopkins U., 1954-55; staff scientist Research Inst. Advanced Study, 1956-57; research asso. physics Cath. U. Am., 1958-60, instr., 1961-64, asst. prof., 1965-69; exec. dir. Optical Soc. Am., Washington, 1969—; governing bd. Am. Inst. Physics, 1973—. Fellow Optical Soc. Am.; Mem. Am. Phys. Soc., Am. Soc. Assn. Execs., Council Engring. and Sci. Soc. Execs., Sigma Xi. Office: 1816 Jefferson Pl NW Washington DC 20036

QUINN, JOHN COLLINS, editor; b. Providence, Oct. 24, 1925; s. John A. and Kathryn H. (Collins) Q.; A.B., Providence Coll., 1945; M.S., Columbia U. Sch. Journalism, 1946; m. Lois R. Richardson, June 20, 1953; children—John Collins, Lo-anne, Richard B., Christopher A. Successively copy boy, reporter, asst. city editor, Washington corr., asst. mng. editor, day mng. editor Providence Jour.-Bull., 1943-66; with Gannett Co. Inc., Rochester, N.Y., 1966—, exec. editor Rochester Democrat & Chronicle, Times-Union, 1966-71, gen. mgr. Gannett News Service, 1967-74, v.p. parent co., 1971-75, sr. v.p. news and info., 1975—. Named to R.I. Hall of Fame, 1975. Mem. AP Mng. Editors (past dir., nat. pres. 1973-74), Am. Soc. Newspaper Editors (dir., chmn. editorial bd., chmn. conv. program). Roman Catholic. Home: 2755 East Ave Rochester NY 14610 Office: Lincoln Tower Rochester NY 14604

QUINN, JOHN FENTON, auditor; b. Phila., Sept. 21, 1933; s. John F. and Mary K. (Bunce) Q.; B.S., St. Joseph's U., Phila., 1955; m. Eileen K. O'Brien, Nov. 30, 1957; children—Michael, Andrea, Kathleen, Kevin. Sr. accountant Peat, Marwick, Mitchell & Co., Phila., 1958-62; auditor Stroud & Co., Inc., Phila., 1962-66; asst. treas. Fidelity Bank, Phila., 1966-71; gen. auditor Equitable Trust Bank, Balt., 1971—; gen. auditor Equitable Bancorporation, Balt., 1972—. Pres. Confraternity of Christian Doctrine, St. James Parish, Elkins Park, Pa., 1968-70, pres. parish council, 1970; v.p. Glenwood (Md.) Middle Sch. P.T.A., 1972—; chmn. total edn. com. St. Pauls Parish, Ellicott City, Md., 1973—; chmn. fin. com. Resurrection Parish, Ellicott City, Md., 1977—; mem. alumni bd. govs. St. Joseph's U. Served with AUS, 1956-58. C.P.A., Pa. Mem. Pa. Inst. C.P.A.'s, Inst. Internal Auditors (v.p. 1979), Bank Adminstrn. Inst., Alumni Acctg. Assn. St. Joseph's U. (pres. 1966, Ann. Achievement award 1968). Republican. Roman Catholic. Club: Turf Valley Country (Ellicott City). Home: 3264 Old Fence Rd Ellicott City MD 21043 Office: PO Box 1556 Baltimore MD 21203

QUINN, JOHN JOSEPH, physicist; b. N.Y.C., Sept. 25, 1933; s. Daniel and Anne (Reid) Q.; B.S., St. John's U., 1954; Ph.D., U. Md., 1958; m. Betsy Rose Vincent, Aug. 30, 1958; children—Daniel, Elizabeth, Heather, Jennifer. Mem. tech. staff RCA Labs., Princeton, N.J., 1959-64; vis. prof. physics Purdue U., Lafayette, Ind., 1964-65; prof. physics Brown U., Providence, R.I., 1965—; vis. prof. State U. N.Y. at Stony Brook, 1968, U. Roma (Italy), 1971, U. Calif. at Irvine, 1977. Recipient outstanding achievement award RCA, 1963, Outstanding Publication award Naval Research Lab., 1972. NATO fellow, 1971-72. Fellow Am. Phys. Soc. (vice chmn. elect div. condensed matter physics 1979). Home: Rural Route 1 Box 544 North Scituate RI 02857 Office: Dept Physics Brown U Providence RI 02912

QUINN, JOHN R., archbishop; b. Riverside, Calif., Mar. 28, 1929; s. Ralph J. and Elizabeth (Carroll) Q.; Ph.B., Gregorian U., Rome, 1950, S.T.B., 1952, S.T.L., 1954. Ordained priest Roman Catholic Ch., 1953; asst. priest St. George Ch., Ontario, Calif., 1954-55; prof. theology Immaculate Heart Sem., San Diego, 1955-62, vice rector, 1960-62; rector St. Francis Coll. Sem., El Cajon, Calif., 1962-64, Immaculate Heart Sem., 1964-68; aux. bishop, vicar gen., San Diego, 1967-72; bishop, Oklahoma City, 1972-73; archbishop Oklahoma City, 1973-77, San Francisco, 1977—; provost U. San Diego, 1968-72; pres. Nat. Conf. Cath. Bishops, 1977—. Mem. Cath. Theol. Soc. Am., Canon Law Soc. Am., Am. Cath. Hist. Soc. Address: 445 Church St San Francisco CA 94114

QUINN, JOSEPH FELIX, ins. co. exec.; b. N.Y.C., Mar. 6, 1931; s. Felix A. and Estelle K. (Donohue) Q.; A.B., Fordham Coll., 1952, LL.B., 1957; LL.M. in Taxation, N.Y. U., 1963; m. Anne J. Broccoli (dec. Aug. 1975); children—Andrew J., Stephanie A.; m. Susan Young, Sept., 1977. Admitted to N.Y. bar, 1957; atty. Mut. Life Ins. Co., N.Y.C., 1957-61; atty., gen. counsel Comml. Union Ins. Co., N.Y.C., 1961-68; v.p. Home Ins. Co., N.Y.C., 1968-72, sr. v.p., 1972-79; sr. v.p. Royal-Globe Ins. Cos., N.Y.C., 1979—; dir. Am. and fgn. Globe Indemnity, Newark, Royal Indemnity Safeguard, Royal Globe Ins. Co., Royal Globe Life Ins. Co., Royal Globe Life Ins. Co. N.Y., Brit. Engine Ins. Services, Inc. Served with U.S. Army, 1952-54. Mem. Am. Bar Assn., Assn. Bar City N.Y., N.Y. C. of C. and Industry. Club: N.Y. Athletic. Home: 5001 Goodridge Ave Bronx NY 10471 Office: 150 William St New York NY 10038

QUINN, PATRICK JAMES, architect; b. Dublin, Ireland, Jan. 15, 1931; s. Patrick Brian and Anne Mary (Toner) Q.; came to U.S., 1958; B.Arch., Univ. Coll., Dublin, 1954; M.Arch., U. Pa., 1959; m. Maureen Kennedy, June 25, 1958; children—Ciaran, Paul, Diarmuid, Aidan, Aoife, Siobhan. Asst. architect Michael Scott Friai, Dublin, Ireland, 1956-57, Dublin Corp., 1957-58; sr. designer FCWP Architects, Phila., 1958-59; designer McCue Assos., Berkeley, Calif., 1960-61; partner Shanagher Quinn Assos., San Francisco, 1964-67, Quinn Oda Architects, Berkeley, 1968-71, Quinn Williams Architects, Troy, N.Y., 1973—; asst. prof. architecture U. Calif., Berkeley, 1962-66, asso. prof., 1966-71, vice chmn. dept., 1969-71; dean Sch. Architecture Rensselaer Poly. Inst., Troy, 1971—; vis. lectr. numerous U.S. and European univs.; mem. environ. com. San Francisco Urban Renewal Assn., 1964-67, Troy Landmarks Commn., 1976—; v.p. Hudson-Mohawk Indsl. Gateway; mem. Nat. Advisory Council on Energy Conservation Research, 1975—. Danforth Found. fellow, 1968; Am. Council Learned Socs. fellow, 1971; NEA grantee, 1974; recipient Liturgical Conf. awards, 1968-70, Bartlett award for barrier-free design, 1971, Outstanding Irish Immigrant award Internat. Soc. East Bay, 1970. Fellow Am. Acad. at Rome; mem. AIA (pres. Eastern N.Y. chpt. 1975, mem. nat. environ. edn. com. 1975—, recipient Nat. Honor award 1971), N.Y. State Assn. Architects, Royal Inst. Brit. Architects, Royal Inst. Architects of Ireland, Soc. Archtl. Historians, Calif. Council Architects, Assn. Collegiate Schs. Architecture. Roman Catholic. Club: Frear Park Golf. Contbg. author: Roots of Ritual, 1972; prin. bldgs. include: Ch. of St. Jude, Marina, Calif., 1966, Rice house, Tiburon, Calif., 1968, Ch. of Divine Savior, Chico, Calif., 1970. Home: 12 Whitman Ct Troy NY 12180 Office: Sch Architecture Greene Bldg Rensselaer Poly Inst Troy NY 12181. *I backed into reading because I was sick and could not run. I backed into architecture though wanting to be a painter. I backed into teaching through wanting more time for research. I backed into deaning because I thought schools could be better. God knows what I will back into next, probably a truck. But there is a poetic irony in backing into things that you did not know you were looking for.*

QUINN, ROBERT KEVIN, lawyer; b. Buffalo, July 29, 1934; s. John Joseph and Margaret Mary (Bresnahan) Q.; B.B.A., St. Bonaventure (N.Y.) U., 1956; J.D., Chgo. Kent Coll. Law, 1966; m. Jean Mary Davis, May 18, 1974; children—Kelly M., Kerry S. Admitted to Ill. bar, 1966; with La Salle Nat. Bank, Chgo., 1959—, v.p., 1969-79, counsel, sec., 1972—, sr. v.p., 1979—. Served with AUS, 1957-59. Mem. Ill. Bar Assn., Chgo. Bar Assn. Roman Catholic. Club: Chgo. Athletic. Home: 2543 N Burling St Chicago IL 60614 Office: 135 S LaSalle St Chicago IL 60690

QUINN, ROBERT WILLIAM, physician, educator; b. Eureka, Calif., July 22, 1912; s. William James and Norma Irene (McLean) Q.; student Stanford, 1930-33; M.D., C.M., McGill U., 1938; m. Julia Rebecca Province, Jan. 21, 1942; children—Robert Sean Province, Judith D. Rotating intern Alameda County Hosp., Oakland, Calif., 1938-39; postgrad. tng. internal medicine U. Calif. Hosp., San Francisco, 1939-41, research fellow internal medicine, 1940-41; postgrad. tng. internal medicine Presbyn. Hosp., N.Y.C., 1941-42; research fellow Yale, 1946-47, instr. preventive medicine, 1947-49; asso. prof. preventive medicine and student health U. Wis., 1949-52; prof., head dept. preventive medicine and pub. health Vanderbilt U., 1952—; dir. venereal disease and Tb control Met. Health Dept. Bd. dirs., med. adv. com. Planned Parenthood Assn. of Nashville. Served with M.C., USNR, 1942-46. Diplomate Am. Bd. Preventive Medicine. Mem. Am. Acad. Preventive Medicine, Infectious Diseases Soc. Am., Am., Middle Tenn. (pres. 1957) heart assns., Assn. Am. Med. Coll., Nashville Acad. Medicine, Assn. Tchrs. Preventive Medicine, Am. Pub. Health Assn., Am. Epidemiol. Soc., Am. Venereal Disease Assn. Club: Belle Meade Country. Contbr. articles to med. jours. Home: 508 Park Center Dr Nashville TN 37205

QUINN, RODNEY SHARON, state ofcl.; b. Portland, Maine, May 27, 1923; s. John Francis and Edith M. (Sharon) Q.; B.A., Sacramento State Coll., 1953; M.A., Stanford U., 1956; postgrad. George Washington U., 1966-69; m. Melba Robbins, Apr. 15, 1947; children—Roy, Sharon, Kathleen, Kelly. Joined U.S. Air Force, 1942, advanced through grades to lt. col.; ret., 1968; sec. of State, Maine, Augusta, 1979—; mem. faculty U. Md., 1958-60, George Washington U., 1962-64, U. Maine, 1972—. Mem. Maine State Legislature, 1974-78, House Democratic floor whip, 1976-77. Home: 15 Green St Gorham ME 04038 Office: State House Augusta ME 04333

QUINN, SALLY, journalist; b. Savannah, Ga.; July 1, 1941; d. Lt. Gen. and Mrs. William Wilson Quinn; grad. Smith Coll.; m. Benjamin Crowninshield Bradlee, Oct. 20, 1978. Reporter, Washington Post, 1969-73, 74—; co-anchorperson CBS Morning News, N.Y.C., 1973-74. Author: We're Going to Make You a Star, 1975. Address: Washington Post 1150 15th St NW Washington DC 20071

QUINN, THOMAS HOWARD, banker; b. N.Y.C., Aug. 4, 1902; s. Thomas Charles and Frances (Quinn) Q.; ed. law N.Y. U., 1927; m. Adele G. Pearl, Aug. 28, 1948 (dec.). Founder, pres. US LIFE Title Ins. Co. (formerly Inter-County Title Guaranty & Mortgage Co.), N.Y.C., 1937-74; founder, chmn. First Gen. Resources Co., N.Y.C., 1962—; pres., dir. Park Electro Chem. Co., Gt. Neck, N.Y., 1961—; chmn. bd. Refinery Corp., Denver, 1969—, Crystal River Devel. Corp. (Fla.), 1975—, Pilgrims Devel. Corp., Plymouth, 1974—; dir., mem. mortgage com. Westside Fed. Savs. & Loan, N.Y.C.; dir. Fiduciary Ins. Co. Am., N.Y.C.; regional dir. Bank of N.Y., Valley Bank region, Valley Stream, L.I., County Trust region, White Plains; mem. regional bd. So. dist. Nat. Comml. of Albany (N.Y.). Bd. dirs. Columbia Meml. Hosp., Hudson, 1970—, N.Y.C. Pub. Devel. Corp., 1973—; pres. Cath. Community Welfare Assn., Columbia County, 1977—; trustee, pres. Caldwell B. Esseltyn Found. Mem. N.Y. State Land Title Assn. (pres. 1937-38, 53-54), N.Y. State Mortgage Bankers Assn., Columbia Driving Soc. (pres. 1977—), Olana Hist. Soc. (pres., trustee). Club: Old Chatham Hunt (dir.). Home: 37 E 64th St New York NY 10021 Office: First Gen Resources 505 Park Ave New York NY 10021

QUINN, BROTHER THOMAS MICHAEL (THOMAS LEO QUINN, JR.), educator; b. Oakland, Calif., Aug. 9, 1922; s. Thomas and Ellen (Buckley) Quinn; B.A., St. Mary's Coll. Calif., 1947; M.A., Loyola U., Chgo., 1959, Ph.D., 1963; LL.D., U. Santa Clara, 1963. Joined Brothers of Christian Schs., 1942; instr. Cathedral High Sch., Los Angeles, 1945-48; prin. Mont La Salle High Sch., Napa, Calif., 1949-54; instr. psychology St. Mary's Coll. Calif., 1960-62, pres., 1962-69, chmn. psychology dept., 1973—, dir. masters program in psychology, 1976—. Author: Differences in Motivational Patterns of College Student Brothers as Revealed in the Thematic Apperception Test, 1962. Address: St Mary's College CA 94575

QUINN, WESLEY MARION, lawyer; b. nr. Wellington, Kans., Feb. 21, 1907; s. Thaddeus and Rebecca Alice (Bledsoe) Q.; student U. N.Mex., 1927-29; m. Jeanne E. Knowles, Nov. 26, 1936; 1 son, Stephen Knowles. Admitted to N.Mex. bar, 1934, since practiced in Clovis; mem. firm Quinn & Quinn; dir. Western Nat. Bank, Amarillo, Tex. Candidate for nomination U.S. Senate from N.Mex., 1952. Chmn. N.Mex. Comprehensive Health Planning Commn.; chmn. bd. govs. Health Planning Program for State of N.Mex., 1967-71; mem. govs. com. Cancer Control Bd. Bd. dirs. Retirement Ranches; bd. regents U. N.Mex., 1951-59. Served with USNR, 1942-45. Mem. N.Mex. Bar (pres. 1965-66), Pi Kappa Alpha. Home: Star Route Clovis NM 88101 Office: PO Box 490 Clovis NM 88101

QUINN, WILLIAM FRANCIS, lawyer; b. Rochester, N.Y., July 13, 1919; s. Charles Alvin and Elizabeth (Dorrity) Q.; B.S. summa cum laude, St. Louis U., 194O; LL.B. cum laude, Harvard, 1947; m. Nancy Ellen Witbeck, July 11, 1942; children—William Francis, Stephen Desford, Timothy Charles, Christopher Thomas, Ann Cecily, Mary Kaiulani, Gregory Anthony. Admitted to Hawaii bar, 1948; atty., partner firm Robertson, Castle & Anthony, Honolulu, 1947-57; gov. T.H., 1957-59, state Hawaii, 1959-62; partner firm Quinn & Moore, Honolulu, 1962-64; exec. v.p. Dole Co., Honolulu. 1964-65, pres., 1965-72, partner firm Jenks, Kidwell, Goodsill, and Anderson,

Honolulu, 1972-73, Goodsill, Anderson & Quinn, 1973—; dir. 1st Ins. Co. Hawaii, Ltd. bd. dirs. Oahu Devel. Conf., Honolulu; v.p. Nat. Municipal League N.Y. Served with USNR, 1942-46. Republican. Roman Catholic. Clubs: Bohemian (San Francisco); Waialae Country, Pacific (Honolulu). Home: 1365 Laukahi St Honolulu HI 96821 Office: 1600 Castle and Cook Bldg Financial Plaza Pacific Honolulu HI 96813

QUINN, WILLIAM GEORGE, hotel exec.; b. Harlan, Iowa, July 11, 1928; s. Daniel William and Hazel (Brown) Q.; student U. Iowa, 1948-50; B.S. in Hotel and Restaurant Mgmt., U. Denver, 1951; m. Judith Ann Secunda, Sept. 16, 1967; children—William Patrick, Sherry Ann. With Western Internat. Hotels, 1954—, gen. mgr. St. Francis Hotel, San Francisco., 1966-76, v.p. corp., 1970-75; v.p., mng. dir. Los Angeles Bonaventure Hotel, 1975—, Century Plaza Hotel, Century City, Los Angeles, 1978—. Bd. dirs. San Francisco Conv. and Visitors Bur. Served with USNR, 1946-48. Mem. Calif. Hotel and Motel Assn. (1st v.p. 1971, pres. 1972, chmn. bd. 1973), Calif. No. Hotel Assn. (pres. 1968), Hotel Employers Assn. San Francisco (pres. 1969-70), Greater San Francisco C. of C. (dir. 1974—). Rotarian. Clubs: Olympic (San Francisco); Los Angeles; California; Wilshire Country, Bel Air Country. Home: 2815 Club Dr Los Angeles CA 90064

QUINN, WILLIAM JOHN, lawyer, ry. exec.; b. St. Paul, May 8, 1911; s. William J. and Celina (LaRocque) Q.; A.B., St. Thomas Coll., St. Paul, 1933, LL.D. (hon.), 1949; LL.B., U. Minn., 1935; m. Floy I. Heinen, July 2, 1942; children—William John III, George Michael, Patrick Joseph, Richard T., Floy I., Maureen L., Michaele P., Shannon M. Admitted to Minn. bar, 1935, practiced in St. Paul, 1935-37; asst. U.S. atty. Dist. Minn., 1937-40; atty. Soo Line R.R., Mpls., 1940-42, asst. commerce counsel, 1945, commerce counsel, 1945-52, asst. gen. counsel, 1952, gen. counsel, 1952-54, v.p., 1953-54; gen. solicitor C., M., St. P. & P. RR Co., 1954-55, v.p., gen. counsel, 1955-58, pres., 1958-66; pres., chief exec. officer Chgo., Burlington and Quincy R.R., 1966-70; vice chmn. Burlington No. Inc., 1970—; chmn., chief exec. officer C.M. P. & P. R.R. Co., 1970-78; pres., chmn. Chgo. Milw. Corp., 1972-78; dir. Clow Corp., Peavey Co., Nat. R.R. Passenger Corp. (AMTRAK); spl. agt. FBI, 1942-45. Bd. dirs., exec. com. St. Francis Hosp., Evanston, Ill.; chmn. bd. trustees Loyola U., Chgo.; trustee Coll. St. Thomas, St. Paul; trustee emeritus Nat. Jewish Hosp.; mem. adv. council Coll. Bus. Adminstrn., U. Notre Dame; bd. dirs., mem. exec. com. Catholic Charities Chgo.; exec. bd. Chgo. council Boy Scouts Am.; bd. dirs. Comprehensive Community Services Met. Chgo. Mem. Am., Minn., Hennepin County, Ill., Chgo. bar assns., Newcomen Soc. N.Am., Chgo. Assn. Commerce and Industry (sr. council), Phi Delta Phi. K.C. Clubs: Economic, Executives, Commercial, Chgo., Mid-Am. (Chgo.); Skokie (Ill.) Country. Home: 1420 Sheridan Rd #4D Wilmette IL 60091 Office: 111 W Washington St Room 1432 Chicago IL 60602

QUINN, WILLIAM WILSON, corp. exec.; b. Crisfield, Md., Nov. 1, 1907; s. William Samuel and Alice (Wilson) Q.; student St. John's Coll., Annapolis, Md., 1927-29; B.S., U.S. Mil. Acad., 1933; postgrad. Inf. Sch., Ft. Benning, Ga., 1938-39, Command and Staff Sch., Ft. Leavenworth, Kans., 1941, Nat. War Coll., Washington, 1948-49; m. Bette Williams, Dec. 16, 1939; children—Sally, Donna, William Wilson. Commd. 2d lt. inf. U.S. Army, 1933, advanced through grades to lt. gen., 1961; co. comdr. inf., 1933-36; provost marshal city of Manila, 1937-38; assigned G-2 IV Corps, 1943-44, 7th Army, 1944-45; dir. Strategic Service Unit, 1946-47, with G-2 X Corps, Inchon Landing, Korea, 1950; comdg. officer 17th Inf. Regt., 7th Inf. Div., Korea, 1951; office Chief of Staff U.S. Army, 1952; asst. div. comdr. 47th Inf. Div., 1953; chief Army sect. Joint U.S. Mil. Adv. Group to Greece, 1953-55; asst. div. comdr. 9th Inf. Div., Germany, 1955-56; comdg. gen., Ft. Carson, Colo., 1956; comdg. gen. 4th Inf. Div., Ft. Lewis, Washington, 1957; chief pub. info. Dept. Army, 1960-61; dep. dir. Def. Intelligence Agy., 1961-64; comdg. gen. 7th U.S. Army Germany, 1964-66; ret., 1966; v.p. Martin Marietta Corp., Washington, 1966-72; pres. Quinn Assos., Washington, 1972—. Decorated D.S.M., Silver Star, Legion of Merit with cluster, Air medal with clusters, Purple Heart (U.S.); Legion of Honor, Croix de Guerre (France); Presdl. Unit Citation (Korea); Das Grosse Verdienstkreuz mit Stern (Germany). Mem. Kappa Alpha. Episcopalian. Clubs: Explorers, Pisces, Army Navy, Les Chevaliers du Tastevin (Washington); Chevy Chase (Md.). Home and Office: 2101 Connecticut Ave Washington DC 20008

QUINSLER, WILLIAM THOMSON, utility co. exec.; b. Watertown, Mass., June 21, 1924; S. Phillips Brooks and Eleanor (Macurdy) Q.; B.S. in Elec. Engring., U. Ariz., 1950; m. Barbara Jean Faust, June 15, 1957; children—William Thomson, Harry Faust, Catharine Marten. Jr. engr. Ariz. Pub. Service Co., Phoenix, 1950-53, staff cons. treasury dept., 1953, supr. treasury dept., 1954, mgr. fin. services, 1955-62, asst. treas., 1962-69, sec., asst. treas., 1969—; dir., mem. exec. com., investment com. Utility Services Ins. Co., Ltd., Hamilton, Bermuda. Mem. adv. bd. Apache Nat. Forest Service; mem. Phoenix Symphony Assn. Served with USAAF, 1943-46. Registered profl. engr., Ariz. Mem. Am., Pacific Coast gas assns., Am. Soc. Corp. Secs., Pacific Coast Electric Assn., C. of C., Ariz., Greenlee County cattle growers assns., Ariz., Nat. socs. profl. engrs., IEEE, Phoenix Soc. Financial Analysts. Home: 5428 E Calle del Medio Phoenix AZ 85018 Office: PO Box 21666 Phoenix AZ 85036

QUINSON, BRUNO ANDRE, pub. co. exec.; b. Norwich, Conn., Jan. 1, 1938; s. Louis Jean and Suzanne Marie (Richard) Q.; B.A., Williams Coll., 1958; postgrad. N.Y. U. Grad. Bus. Sch., 1960-61; children—Timothy Bruno, Marc Albert (dec.), Christopher Louis. Product mgr. Simon & Schuster, N.Y.C., 1960-65; pub., gen. mgr. Golden Press, div. Western Pub. Co., Inc., 1965-70; pres. Larousse & Co., Inc., N.Y.C., 1970—, also dir.; v.p. Librairie Larousse U.S.A. Inc.; dir. One-Strawberry, Inc. Bd. dirs. Rye Art Center (N.Y.), treas., 1973-74. Mem. French-Am. C. of C. (counselor). Home: 1115 Fifth Ave New York NY 10028 Office: 572 Fifth Ave New York NY 10036

QUINTANA, RICARDO BECKWITH, educator; b. Albany, N.Y., Oct. 6, 1898; s. Manuel Perez and Harriet Meade (Beckwith) Q.; A.B., Harvard, 1920, A.M., 1921, Ph.D., 1927; m. Janet Garland MacQueary, Apr. 7, 1928; 1 son, Ricardo Beckwith. Instr. English, Washington U., 1921-24; instr. English, tutor div. modern langs. Harvard, 1924-26, Austin resident fellow Grad. Sch., 1926-27; asst. prof. English, U. Wis., 1927-30, asso. prof., 1930-36, prof., 1936-69, prof. emeritus, 1969—; research fellow Huntington Library, San Marino, Calif., 1937-38, 1969; Distinguished vis. prof. English, U. Del., 1963, 1970; vis. prof. Fla. State U., 1970-71; vis. mem. Wis. Inst. Research in Humanities, 1963-64. Served as 2d lt., inf., U.S. Army, 1918. Mem. Modern Lang. Assn. Am. Author: The Mind and Art of Jonathan Swift, 1936; Swift: An Introduction, 1955; Oliver Goldsmith: A Georgian Study, 1967; Two Augustans: John Locke, Jonathan Swift, 1978; editor: Two Hundred Poems, 1947; Eighteenth Century Plays, 1952; Jonathan Swift: Gulliver's Travels, and Other Writings, 1958; co-editor: Seventeenth Century Verse and Prose: 1600-1660, 1951; Seventeenth Century Verse and Prose: 166O-17OO, 1952; English Poetry of the Mid and Late Eighteenth Century, 1963; fgn. asso. Etudes Anglaises. Home: 2100 Commonwealth Ave Madison WI 53705

QUINTANA, RONALD PRESTON, educator; b. New Orleans, Feb. 23, 1936; s. Robert Roig and Clara (Schneider) Q.; B.S., Loyola U., New Orleans, 1956; M.S., U. Wis., Madison, 1958, Ph.D., in Pharm. Chemistry, 1961; m. Alma Marie Fuxan, Sept. 7, 1957; children—Ronald Preston, Mary Catherine. Instr. dept. medicinal chemistry Coll. Pharmacy U. Tenn. Center for Health Scis., 1960-61, asst. prof., 1961-65, asso. prof., vice chmn. dept., 1965-67, prof., vice chmn., 1967-71, dist. service prof., vice chmn., 1971—, prof. dept. periodontics Coll. Dentistry, 1972-74; del. U.S. Pharmacopeial Conv., 1970—. Mem. Acad. Pharm. Scis., Am. Chem. Soc., Am. Pharm. Assn., The Chem. Soc., Sigma Xi, Alpha Sigma Nu, Phi Lambda Upsilon, Rho Chi. Roman Catholic. Co-editor, contbr. Surface Chemistry and Dental Integuments, 1973; contbr. articles to profl. jours. Home: 1591 Old Mill Rd Germantown TN 38138 Office: 26 S Dunlap St Memphis TN 38163

QUINTERO, CARLOS ARCE, archbishop; b. Etzatlan, Jalisco, Mexico, Feb. 13, 1920; s. Silverio Real and Lucrecia Meza (Arce) Q.; S.T.D., Gregorian U., Rome, Italy, 1946. Ordained priest, Roman Cath. Ch., 1944; mem. faculty Guadalajara Sem., 1947-54, prefecto of studies, 1954-61; bishop of Ciudad Valles, 1961-66; titular archbishop Tysdro, Mexico, 1966-68; archbishop, Hermosillo, Mexico, 1968—; mem. Conf. Latin Am. Bishops, Medellin, 1968, Puebla, 1979; pres. Commn. on Edn. and Culture in Mexico, 1969-72; mem. Synod Rome; pres. Dept. Edn., Consejo Episcopal Latino Americano, 1976-78. Mem. Mexican Bishop's Conf. Office: 1 Apartado P Hermosillo Sonora Mexico. *Mi ideal fué anunciar el Misterio de Jesús de Nazareth Hijo de Dios porque 'en sus palabras hay Vida eterna' (Jn, 61 6.68). Del conocimiento de Jesés nace el vigor de la Fe y la fuerte adhesión a la Iglesia y por consiguiente la presencia activa en la sociedad para formar una humanidad nueva. La Educación humaniza y personaliza al hombre, lo acerca a Cristo y lo integra al proceso social latino americano para lograr los cambios necesarios en America.*

QUINTERO, JOSE BENJAMIN, theatrical dir.; b. Panama City, Panama, Oct. 15, 1924; s. Carlos Rivira and Consuelo (Palmerola) de Q.; B.A., U. So. Calif., 1948; student Goodman Theater, Chgo., 1934-35. Producer, dir. Circle in the Square Theatre (off-Broadway), 1951—, prodns. include: The Girl on the Via Flaminia, Cradle Song, The Iceman Cometh, La Ronde, Summer and Smoke, The King and the Duke, Burning Bright, Yerma, Dark of the Moon, Our Town, Plays for Bleecker Street, Desire Under the Elms; Broadway prodns. include: The Innkeepers, Portrait of a Lady, In the Summer House, Girl on the Via Flaminia, Long Day's Journey into Night, Look, We've Come Through, Great Day in the Morning, Strange Interlude, Diamond Orchid, A Moon for the Misbegotten (Tony award), Gabrielle, The Skin of Our Teeth, A Touch of the Poet, Anna Christie, others. Decorated Cabellero de la Order de Vasco Nunez de Balboa; recipient spl. citation La Asamblea Nacional de Panama; Drama Desk award, Page One award. Office: care Soc Stage Directors and Choreographers 1501 Broadway New York City NY 10022*

QUINTON, ARTHUR ROBERT, educator; b. Lowestoft, Eng., July 1, 1924; s. Richard John and Lilian (Hood) Q.; B.Sc., U. London, 1945; M.Sc., Western Ont. U., 1951; Ph.D., Yale, 1954; m. Trebilcock, Nov. 16, 1946; children—Hebe, Keith, Tracy. Came to U.S., 1951, naturalized, 1960. Vacuum physicist Mullard Radio Valve Co., 1946-48; instr. Yale, 1954-57, asst. prof., 1957-63; asso. prof. U. Fla., 1963-66; prof. U. Mass., Amherst, 1966—; vis. fellow Australian Nat. U., 1961-62, 72-73. Served to sub-lt. Royal Navy, 1944-46. Mem. Am. Assn. Physics Tchrs. Author: (with H.S.W. Massey) Basic Properties of Matter, 1961. Home: 75 Red Gate Ln Amherst MA 01002

QUINTRELL, THOMAS ARMSTRONG, lawyer; b. Cleve., May 15, 1920; s. Clayton A. and Margaret C. (Armstrong) Q.; A.B., Princeton U., 1942; LL.B., Harvard U., 1948; m. Ella H. Hornickel, July 7, 1950; children—Lute A., Margaret S., Ella S., Edith P. Partner firm Arter & Hadden, Cleve.; dir. Centran Corp., Central Nat. Bank Cleve. Trustee, v.p. Univ. Sch., Cleve.; trustee United Way, Cleve.; v.p. Diabetes Assn. Greater Cleve.; trustee Cleve. Council Ind. Schs.; trustee, v.p. Cleve. Law Library. Decorated Bronze Star. Mem. Am. Law Inst., Am. Bar Assn. (sec. subcom. of sect. of corp., banking and bus. law), Ohio State Bar Assn., Cleve. Bar Assn. (dir.). Republican. Presbyterian. Clubs: Union, The Tavern, Kirtland Country. Home: PO Box 415 County Line Rd Gates Mills OH 44040 Office: 1144 Union Commerce Bldg Cleveland OH 44115

QUIRARTE, JACINTO, art historian; b. Jerome, Ariz., Aug. 17, 1931; s. Francisco and Fructuosa (Jimenez) Q.; B.A., San Francisco State U., 1954, M.A., 1957; Ph.D., Nat. U. Mex., 1964; m. Sara Farmer, Dec. 18, 1954; 1 dau., Sabrina Pilar. Art tchr. AM. Coll., Mexico City, 1959-61; asst. Nat. U. Mex., 1961-62; dean men, prof. history art U. of Ams., 1962-64; dir. cultural affairs Centro Venezolano Americano, Caracas, Venezuela, 1964-66; vis. prof. Central U., Caracas, 1966, Yale U., 1967; prof. history of art U. Tex., Austin, 1967-72; dean Coll. Fine and Applied Arts, prof. history of art U. Tex., San Antonio, 1972—, dir. Research Center for Arts; vis. prof. U. N.Mex., 1971; cons.-panelist Nat. Found. on Arts and Humanities; cons.-panelist Nat. Endowment for Arts, spl. projects, 1974-76; cons.-panelist edn. dept., research grants dept. Nat. Endowment for Humanities, 1975—, div. spl. projects, fellowships dept., 1976—, nat. bd. consultants, 1977-78, mem. adv. com. on affirmative action in instns. of higher edn. HEW/Labor Dept., 1976-77; mem. task force on edn., tng. and devel. profl. artists and arts educators Nat. Council on Arts, 1977-78, chmn. task force on Hispanic Am. Arts, 1978-79; mem. visual arts and humanities panel Tex. Commn. on Arts and Humanities, 1976—; cons. Tex. Edn. Agy. Adv. com. Am. Revolution Bicentennial Adminstrn., 1974-76; mem. adv. com. Trustees for Harvard U., 1978; lectr. in field, U.S., abroad; adv. bd. Festival Ballet, San Antonio, Mexican Mus., San Francisco, La Luz, Denver; bd. dirs., v.p. San Antonio Arts Council, 1973-77; bd. dirs., mem. exec. com. San Antonio Symphony, 1976—. Served with SAC, USAF, 1954-57. Mem. Mid-Am. Coll. Art Assn., Soc. for Am. Archaeology, Internat. Congress Americanists, Internat. Congress History of Art, Internat. Congress Ethnology and Anthropology, Latin Am. Studies Assn., Internat. Council Fine Arts Deans, Tex. Council on Arts in Edn., Assn. for Latin Am. Arts (chmn. interim exec. com.), Nat. Chicano Council on Higher Edn., Am. Research Inst. for Arts, Tex. Alliance for Arts. Transl.: El Codice Selden (Alfonso Caso), 1964. Author book preface, catalogue; contbr. transls., numerous articles, revs. to profl. jours. Home: 10902 Bar X Trail Helotes TX 78023 Office: Research Center for Arts Coll Fine and Applied Arts U Tex San Antonio TX 78285

QUIRICO, FRANCIS JOSEPH, state justice; b. Pittsfield, Mass., Feb. 18, 1911; s. Luigi and Lucia (Giovanetti) Q.; LL.B., Northeastern U., 1932, LL.D., 1970; J.D. (hon.), Suffolk U., 1971; LL.D., Am. Internat. U., 1974, New Eng. Sch. Law, 1975. Admitted to Mass. bar, 1932; pvt. practice law, Pittsfield, 1932-56; city solicitor, Pittsfield, 1948-52; justice Superior Ct. Mass., 1956-69; justice Supreme Jud. Ct. Mass., 1969—. Served with USAAF, 1942-46. Mem. Am., Berkshire County bar assns., Am. Law Inst., Am. Legion. Roman Catholic. Home: 1282 East St Pittsfield MA 01201 Office: 1300 Pemberton Sq Court House Boston MA 02108

QUIRK, JAMES PATRICK, economist; b. St. Paul, Nov. 27, 1926; s. William Martin and Teresa Elizabeth (McMahon) Q.; B.B.A., U. Minn., 1948, M.A., 1949, Ph.D., 1959; m. Shirley Mae Krois, June 25, 1948; children—Gail, James, Janice, Jill, Colleen, Thomas. Faculty, St. Mary's U., San Antonio, 1949-51; with Bur. of Census, Washington, 1951-53, G.H. Tennant Co., Mpls., 1953-56; faculty U. Minn., Mpls., 1956-58, Purdue U., Lafayette, Ind., 1959-65, U. Kans., Lawrence, 1966-70; faculty Calif. Inst. Tech., Pasadena, 1971—. Served with USNR, 1944-46. NSF grantee, 1966-68, 73-76, 78, Ford Found. grantee, 1963. Author: (with R. Saposuite) Introduction to General Equilibrium Theory, 1968, Intermediate Microeconomics, 1976. Editor: (with A. Zauley) Papers in Quantitative Economics, 1969. Home: 911 S Oakland Ave Pasadena CA 91106 Office: Dept Humanities and Social Scis Calif Inst Tech Pasadena CA 91125

QUIRK, JOHN JAMES, business exec.; b. N.Y.C., July 10, 1943; s. Francis J. and Madeline A. (Meizinger) Q.; B.A., Georgetown U., 1965; M.B.A., U. Va., 1967; m. Kathryn Anne O'Brien, Mar. 21, 1963; children—John James, Ashlin Carter. Asst. treas., mgr. corp. fin. dept. W.R. Grace & Co., N.Y.C., 1967-74; asst. v.p., asst. treas. City Investing Co., N.Y.C., 1974-77, v.p., treas., 1978—; dir. Global Union Bank, N.Y.C. Mem. Soc. Internat. Treas.'s. Home: Brush Island Rd Darien CT 06820 Office: 767 Fifth Ave New York NY 10022

QUITTMEYER, CHARLES LOREAUX, coll. dean; b. Peekskill, N.Y., Dec. 23, 1917; s. Ernest Martin and Edith Grace (Loreaux) Q.; A.B., Coll. William and Mary, 1940; M.B.A., Harvard U., 1947; Ph.D. (fellow), Columbia U., 1955; m. Maureen J. Rankin, June 2, 1956; children—Peter Charles, David Rankin, Andrew Robert, Jane Loreaux. Bus. and govt. positions, 1941-42, 47-48; asst. prof. bus. adminstrn. Coll. William and Mary, Williamsburg, Va., 1948-54, prof., head dept., 1962-68, dean Sch. Bus. Adminstrn., 1968—; lectr., asst. prof. marketing U. Buffalo, 1954-57; research asso., asso. prof. commerce U. Va., 1957-61; sr. scientist Tech. Operations, Inc., 1961-62; dir., adv. bd. First & Mchts. Nat. Bank (Peninsula). Bd. suprs. James City County, 1969-71, chmn., 1971. Mem. Peninsula Airport Commn., 1971—, sec., 1973—. Served to capt., F.A. and M.I., AUS, 1942-46. Recipient William and Mary Alumni medallion, 1976. Mem. Acad. Mgmt., Am. Assembly Coll. Schs. Bus. (visitation panel 1976-79), So. Bus. Adminstrn. Assn. (exec. com. 1973—, pres. 1976-77), Newcomen Soc. N.Am., Phi Beta Kappa, Beta Gamma Sigma. Episcopalian. Club: Harvard of Virginia. Contbr. to Ency. Brit.; also monographs papers in field. Home: 210 Kingswood Dr Williamsburg VA 23185

QUITTMEYER, ROBERT THEODORE, food and indsl. equipment co. exec.; b. Peekskill, N.Y., Sept. 12, 1920; s. Ernest Martin and Edith Grace (Loreaux) Q.; A.B., Columbia U., 1941, J.D., 1946; postgrad. Exec. Program in Bus. Adminstrn., 1966; m. Marilyn Louise Prehm, Mar. 20, 1948; children—Richard Charles, Susan Louise, James Prehm. Admitted to N.Y. bar, 1946, since practiced in N.Y.C.; asso. firm Sullivan & Cromwell, 1946-56; mem. law dept. Amstar Corp., N.Y.C., 1956-59, asst. sec., 1959-61, asst. gen. counsel, 1961-66, v.p., 1966-71, exec. v.p., 1971, pres. and chief exec. officer, 1971—; dir. Bank of N.Y.; trustee Dry Dock Savs. Bank. Chmn., Village of Baxter Estates (N.Y.) Bd. Appeals, 1958—; bd. dirs. Consumers Research Inst.; trustee Nutrition Found. Served with inf. AUS, 1942-45. Decorated Combat Inf. Badge. Mem. Grocery Mfrs. Am. (dir.), Phi Gamma Delta. Episcopalian. Clubs: Port Washington (N.Y.) Yacht; Economic (N.Y.C.). Home: Port Washington NY 11050 Office: 1251 Ave of Americas New York NY 10020

QUITUGUA, FRANKLIN JOSEPH, govt. ofcl. Guam; b. Asan, Guam, Nov. 6, 1933; s. Ignacio Perez and Rosa (Arceo) Q.; B.S.Ed., No. Ariz. U., 1956, M.A.Ed., 1962; Ph.D. in Edn. Adminstrn., U. Oreg., 1975; m. Julia Jane Siguenza, July 27, 1957; children—Clare Jane, Franklin Joseph, Evangeline Rose, Mark Anthony, Jacqueline Ann. Dir. edn. Guam Dept. Edn., Agana, 1969-72, 75-76; asst. prof. U. Guam, Mangilao, 1972-75; mem. Guam Senate, 1977—, vice chmn. com. edn., com. ethics and standards, 1977-78. Mem. Nat. Assn. Secondary Sch. Prins., Kappa Delta Pi, Phi Delta Kappa. Democrat. Roman Catholic. Home: Chalan Pago GU 96910 Office: PO Box 373 Agana GU 96910

QUON, JIMMIE EARL, civil engr.; b. Canton, China, Apr. 13, 1934; s. Lester and Sau (Tse) Q.; came to U.S., 1939; B.S. in Civil Engring. with highest honors, U. Calif., Berkeley, 1955; M.S. in San. Engring. (NSF grad. fellow), 1956, Ph.D., 1961; m. Helen Tang, Aug. 4, 1956; children—Michael J., Mary A. Successively teaching asst., asso. in public health, grad. research engr. U. Calif., Berkeley, 1955-60; san. chemist Oro Loma San. Dist., San Lorenzo, Calif., 1956-58; mem. faculty Northwestern U., 1960—, prof. civil engring., 1967—, chmn. dept., 1976—; cons. to govt. and industry. Recipient Legge award Am. Indsl. Hygiene Assn., 1960; diplomate Am. Acad. Environ. Engrs.; registered profl. engr., Ill. Fellow ASCE (Huber research prize 1968); mem. Air Pollution Control Assn., Water Pollution Control Fedn., Phi Beta Kappa, Sigma Xi, Tau Beta Pi, Chi Epsilon, Delta Omega. Author papers in field. Home: 3004 Central Ave Wilmette IL 60091 Office: Dept Civil Engring Northwestern Univ Evanston IL 60201. *An attempt to learn something from each situation which will increase your capacity to deal with future problems and issues is a basic principle.*

RAAB, SELWYN, journalist; b. N.Y.C., June 26, 1934; s. William and Berdie (Glantz) R.; B.A., Coll. City N.Y., 1956; m. Helene Lurie, Dec. 25, 1963; 1 dau., Marian. Reporter, N.Y. World-Telegram and Sun, N.Y.C., 1960-66; producer, news editor NBC-TV News, N.Y.C., 1966-71; exec. producer WNET-News, N.Y.C., 1971-74; reporter New York Times, 1974—. Recipient award for best mag. consumer protection article U. Mo. Sch. Journalism, 1969, Deadline awards for excellence in television reporting Sigma Delta Chi, 1971, 73, 1st prize for excellence in television reporting N.Y. State A.P., 1973, Best Television Reporting award N.Y. Press Club, 1973, Heywood Broun Meml. award, 1974, Page One award Newspaper Guild of New York, 1975. Author: Justice In The Back Room, 1967. Office: NY Times 229 W 43d St New York NY 10036

RAAB, WALTER F., corp. exec.; b. 1924; B.S. in Econs., Wharton Sch., U. Pa., 1945; married. With Coopers & Lybrand, 1945-53; with AMP Inc., 1953—, treas., 1968-71, v.p., treas., 1971-75, v.p., treas., dir., 1975-79, v.p., chief fin. officer, 1979—; dir. West Co., Dauphin Deposit Trust Co., Harrisburg, Pa. Chmn. bd. dirs. Harrisburg Area YMCA; treas. bd. dirs. Holy Spirit Hosp., Harrisburg. C.P.A., Pa. Mem. Am. Inst. C.P.A.'s, Financial Execs. Inst., N.A.M., Machinery and Allied Products Inst. (financial council). Address: AMP Inc Eisenhower Blvd Harrisburg PA 17111

RAACH, FREDERICK RAYMOND, business exec.; b. Kokomo, Ind., Sept. 12, 1914; s. Elery Earl and Sadie C. (Carney) R.; student Case Inst. Tech., 1937-38; B.A., Western Reserve U., 1940; postgrad. N.Y. U., 1941; Ph.D., Bloomfield Coll., 1972; m. Ruth Mildred Aurada, Sept. 7, 1940; children—Frederick Ellward, Sally Ruth. Engr., plant controller, plant asst. gen. mgr. lamp dept. Gen. Electric Co., 1938-42; exec. Cleve. Pneumatic Tool Co., 1942-44; partner Robert Heller & Assos., Inc., mgmt. cons., Cleve., 1945-59; v.p. RCA, N.Y.C., 1960-61; v.p., dir. Robert Heller & Assos., Inc., Cleve., 1961-63; v.p. finance and adminstrn. UNIVAC-Sperry Rand Corp.,

N.Y.C., 1963, v.p., gen. mgr., 1964-66; sr. v.p. Wallace-Murray Corp., N.Y.C., 1966-68, exec. v.p., dir., 1968-69, pres., chief exec. officer, 1969-73; pres. Fred R. Raach Assos., Inc., 1973—; dir. Interstate Brands Corp., Kansas City. Trustee Council for Technol. Devel.-Machinery and Allied Products Inst., 1969-74; bd. dirs. Nat. Council on Crime and Delinquency, 1970-75. Mem. A.I.M., Am. Mgmt. Assn., Bus. Equipment Mfrs. Assn. (chmn., dir. 1966), Mfrs. Assn. Greater Phila. (dir.), Newcomen Soc., Beta Alpha Psi. Republican. Presbyn. Clubs: University (New York City), Turtle Creek Country (Tequesta, Fla.), Yacht of Stone Harbor (N.J.); Wildwood Country (Wildwood, N.J.). Home: 58 Turtle Creek Dr Tequesta FL 33458 Office: 304 Tequesta Dr Tequesta FL 33458. *In reviewing my life, two thoughts stand out clearly: (1) that most goals, reasonable or even far out are attainable if one is willing to plan carefully, work diligently, and accept gracefully temporary setbacks and (2) that the ability to appreciate, understand, and work well with others could well be man's (or woman's) greatest personal asset.*

RAAD, VIRGINIA, pianist, lectr.; b. Salem, W.Va., Aug. 13, 1925; d. Joseph M. and Martha (Joseph) Raad; B.A., Wellesley Coll., 1947; spl. student New Eng. Conservatory Music, 1947-48; diplome Ecole Normale de Musique, Paris, 1950; Doctorat de l'Universite (French Govt. grantee 1950-52, 54-55), U. Paris, 1955; student Alfred Cortot, Jeanne Blancard, Berthe Bert. Artist-in-residence Salem Coll., 1959-70; musician-in-residence N.C. Arts Council, 1971-72; concerts, lectures, master classes at Carleton Coll., Northfield, Minn., Viterbo Coll., Portland State U., Notre Dame U., Mt. Mary Coll., Mundelein Coll., Trinity Coll., Washington, Phillips Gallery, Washington, Norton Gallery, Rollins Coll., Marietta (Ohio) Coll., Huntington (W.Va.) Galleries, W.Va. U., Coll. William and Mary, Channel 13 (WQED), Pitts., Channel 24 (WWVU), Morgantown, W.Va., Lincoln (Pa.) U., U. Pitts., U. Mich., Dearborn, Fordham U., N.Y. Piano Tchrs. Congress, So. Conn. State Coll., Wellesley (Mass.) Coll., Middlebury (Vt.) Coll., Manhattanville (N.Y.) Coll., Elmira (N.Y.) Coll., Ladycliff (N.Y.) Coll., numerous others; adjudicator Nat. Guild Piano Tchrs., Nat. Fedn. Music Clubs; panelist Nat. Endowment for Humanities; Am. rep. Debussy Colloque, Paris, 1962. Named Outstanding W.Va. Woman Educator, Delta Kappa Gamma, 1965; included in Schlesinger Library on History of Women in Am., Radcliffe Coll., 1967; Am. Council Learned Socs. grantee, 1962. Mem. Soc. Française de Musicologie, Am. Musicol. Soc. (regional officer 1960-65), Am. Soc. for Aesthetics, Internat. Musicol. Soc., Music Tchrs. Nat. Assn. (adjudicator). Contbg. author Debussy et l'Evolution de la Musique au XX siècle, 1965; also articles in profl. jours. Address: 60 Terrace Ave Salem WV 26426

RAAEN, JOHN CARPENTER, JR., army officer; b. Ft. Benning, Ga., Apr. 22, 1922; s. John Carpenter and Alexandra (Hoffman) R.; B.S., U.S. Mil. Acad., 1943; M.A., Johns Hopkins U., 1951; grad. U.S. Army Command and Staff Coll., 1955, Indsl. Coll. Armed Forces, 1963; m. Emily Caroline Berry, June 15, 1945; children—Caroline E., Lindsay W., Sandra. Commd. 2d lt. U.S. Army, 1943, advanced through grades to maj. gen., 1972; Ranger Co. comdr., 1943-44; comdr. 83d Ordnance Bn., Korea, 1955, Army Research Office, Durham, N.C., 1965-67, Ballistics Research Labs., Aberdeen Proving Ground, Md., 1967-69; served in Vietnam, 1969; comdr. Army Mobility Equipment Command. St. Louis, 1971-72, Army Weapons Command, 1972-73, Army Armament Command, 1973-75, Def. Fuel Supply Center, Washington. 1976—. Decorated Legion of Merit (4). Silver Star, Bronze Star (3). Army Commendation medal. Mem. Am. Def. Preparedness Assn., Assn. U.S. Army. Episcopalian. Office: Commander Def Fuel Supply Center Cameron Sta Alexandria VA 22314

RAAF, JOHN ELBERT, neurosurgeon; b. Hailey, Idaho, Nov. 12, 1905; s. John J. and Madge (Hart) R.; A.B., Stanford, 1926, M.D., 1930; M.S., U. Minn., 1935, Ph.D., 1941; m. Lorene Rardin, Oct. 26, 1938; children—John Hart, Jean Raaf Binnewies. Intern, asst. resident Strong Meml. Hosp., also Rochester Municipal Hosp., Rochester, N.Y., 1929-31; fellow gen. surgery and neurosurgery Mayo Clinic, Rochester, Minn., 1931-36; practice of neurosurgery, Portland, Oreg., 1936—; asso. clin. prof. surgery U. Oreg., 1946-57, clin. prof., 1957—; chief neurol. surgery, Good Samaritan Hosp., 1947—; spl. med. adviser VA, Washington, 1953-58. Bd. dirs. Library Assn. of Portland, 1953—. Trustee Med. Research Found., Oreg., 1950—, pres., 1951-56. Diplomate Am. Bd. Neurol. Surgery (bd. dirs., 1956-62); Fellow A.C.S. (v.p. 1964); mem. Soc. Neurol. Surgery, Am. Trauma Soc. (bd. dirs. 1972), Neurol. Scis. Found. (pres. 1971—), Western Neurosurg. Assn., A.M.A., No. Pacific Soc. Neurology and Psychiatry (pres. 1945-46), Am., North Pacific, Pacific Coast, Western surg. assns., Am. Assn. Surgery Trauma (pres. 1968-69), Am. Acad. Neurosurgery (pres. 1948-49), Am. Assn. Neurol. Surgeons, Harvey Cushing Soc., Phi Beta Kappa Assos., mem. Phi Beta Kappa, Sigma Xi, Alpha Omega Alpha. Republican. Episcopalian. Clubs: Waverley Country, University, Arlington (Portland); Army and Navy (Washington); Bohemian (San Francisco). Editorial bd. Western Jour. Surgery, Obstetrics and Gynecology, 1946-68; Jour. of Trauma, 1961—. Author articles med. subjects. Home: 390 SW Edgecliff Rd Portland OR 97219 Office: 1120 NW 20th Ave Portland OR 97209

RAASCH, ERNEST MARTIN, business exec.; b. Norfolk, Nebr., May 15, 1929; s. Ernest Carl and Esther Eleanor (Martin) R.; B.S. B.A., Babson Inst., 1953; postgrad. Columbia U., 1956-57, N.Y. U., 1957-58; m. Helen V. Gillespie, Dec. 22, 1973. Pres., Dixon Ltd., Toronto, Ont., Can., 1967-69; v.p. mktg. Borden Chem. Co. div. Borden, Inc., 1969-71; exec. v.p. Swingline Co., L.I., N.Y., 1971-77, exec. v.p., chief oper. officer, 1977-78, pres., chief exec. officer, 1979—. Served with USAF, 1945-47. Mem. Nat. Office Products Assn., Am. Mktg. Assn., Am. Mgmt. Assn., Wholesale Stationery Assn. Patentee in field. Office: Swingline Inc 32-00 Skillman Ave Long Island NY 11101

RABA, ERNEST ALOYSIUS, lawyer; b. San Antonio, Dec. 1, 1912; s. Ernest Wilhelm and Maria Margaret (Fuhrwerk) R.; B.A., St. Mary's U., San Antonio, 1934, J.D., 1937, LL.D. (hon.), 1977; grad. JAGC Sch. at U. Mich., 1943; m. Betty Vivian Myers, Mar. 10, 1945; children—Ernest Aloysius, Cindy A. Raba Malone, Paul A., John T. Admitted to Tex. bar, 1937; practiced law, San Antonio, 1937-42; instr. St. Mary's U. Law Sch., 1938-42, prof. constl. law, 1946—, dean Sch. Law, 1946-77, v.p. St. Mary's U., 1963-65. Chmn., San Antonio Firemen and Policemen's CSC, 1957-63. Served with U.S. Army, 1942-46, JAGC, 1943-46. Recipient Outstanding Alumnus award St. Mary's U., 1977. Mem. San Antonio Bar Assn., Tex. Bar Assn., Tex. Bar Found. (charter), Harlan Soc., Phi Delta Phi. Roman Catholic. Home: 2511 Old Orchard San Antonio TX 78230 Office: Saint Mary's U One Camino Santa Maria San Antonio TX 78284

RABAHY, DONALD LIAN, mfg. co. exec.; b. Bklyn., Mar. 3, 1936; s. George and Rose Rabahy; B.B.A., U. Detroit, 1963; postgrad. in bus. adminstrn. Western Mich. U., 1965-66; m. Rosemary Anne Fitzpatrick, July 6, 1957; children—David, Susan, Linda, Daniel. Controller, ops. mgr. Cadillac Plastic & Chem. Co., Kalamazoo, 1964-66; mgr. cost dept. Woodall Industries, Detroit, 1966-67; with Masco Corp., Taylor, Mich., 1967-78, controller, v.p., 1970-73, group v.p., 1973-78; pres., chief exec. officer Flint & Walling, Inc., Livonia, Mich., 1978—; cons. Masco Corp. Served with U.S. Army, 1955-57. Republican. Roman Catholic. Home: 27605 Morningside Lathrop Village MI 48076 Office: 32490 Schoolcraft Rd Livonia MI 48150

RABB, BRUCE, lawyer; b. Cambridge, Mass., Oct. 4, 1941; s. Maxwell M. and Ruth (Cryden) R.; A.B., Harvard U., 1962; C.E.P., Institut d'Etudes Politiques, Paris, 1963; LL.B., Columbia U., 1966; m. Harriet Rachel Schaffer, Jan. 4, 1970; children—Alexander Charles, Katherine Anne. Admitted to N.Y. State bar, 1966; clk. to Judge John Minor Wisdom, 5th Circuit Ct. Appeals, 1966-67; asso. firm Stroock & Stroock & Lavan, N.Y.C., 1967-68; 71-75, partner, 1976—; staff asst. to Pres. U.S., 1969-70; bd. dirs. Internat. League Human Rights, 1971—, gen. counsel, 1977—; sec., bd. dirs. Lawyers Com. Internat. Human Rights, 1977—; sec. Lehrman Inst., 1978—. Mem. Assn. Bar City N.Y., Am. Bar Assn., Am. Law Inst. Clubs: Harvard, Recess (N.Y.C.); Met. (Washington). Home: 580 West End Ave New York NY 10024 Office: 61 Broadway New York NY 10006

RABB, ELLIS, actor, dir., writer; b. Memphis, June 20, 1930; s. Clark Williamson and Mary Carolyn (Ellis) R.; student U. Ariz., 1949-50; B.F.A. with honors, Carnegie Inst. Tech., 1953; hon. degree Southwestern at Memphis, 1977; m. Rosemary Harris, Dec. 4, 1959 (div. June 1967). Actor-dir. Antioch Shakespeare Festival, Yellow Springs, Ohio, summers 1952-57, Group 20, Wellesley, Mass., 1959; Broadway appearances in Jolly's Progress, 1960, Look After Lulu, 1958; Macbeth and others at Old Globe, summers 1963-69; actor-dir. Am. Shakespeare Festival, Stratford, Conn., 1958—; dir. The Grass Harp, 1971, Twelfth Night, 1972, Enemies, 1972, Merchant of Venice, A Streetcar Named Desire, Veronica's Room, 1973, Who's Who in Hell, 1974, Edward II, The Royal Family, 1975, Caesar and Cleopatra, 1977; actor The Royal Family, 1976; staged Dido and Aneas, Orpheus in the Underworld, Kansas City (Mo.) Center of the Performing Arts, 1966, Aida, Dallas Civic Opera, 1969; created Love In for Kansas City Center Performing Arts, 1968; founder, 1959, since pres., artistic dir. APA Repertory Co.; actor, dir. A.C.T., San Francisco, 1970, 71; dir. for Beaumont Theatre, Lincoln Center, N.Y.C., 1972-73; dir., appeared in lead part Enemies, The Royal Family, NET TV; dir. Mid Summer Night's Dream for Theatre Memphis, 1976; appeared as Robert in A Life in the Theatre, 1977-78; actor TV movie The Dain Curse, 1978. Recipient Clarence Derwent award, 1957, OBIE award, 1962, Outer Circle award, 1965, Lola D'Annunzio award, Tony award for direction, 1976. Office: RABCO 2784 Lombardy Rd Memphis TN 38111

RABB, GEORGE B., zoologist; b. Charleston, S.C., Jan. 2. 1930; s. Joseph and Teresa C. (Redmond) R.; B.S., Coll. Charleston. 1951; M.A., U. Mich.. 1952, Ph.D.. 1957; m. Mary Sughrue, June 10, 1953. Teaching fellow zoology U. Mich.. 1954-56; curator. coordinator research Chgo. Zool. Park, Brookfield. Ill., 1956-64, asso. dir. research and edn.. 1964-75, dep. dir., 1969-75, dir., 1976—; research asso. dept. psychology U. Chgo., 1960—; research asso. Field Mus. Natural History, 1965—; lectr. dept. zoology U. Chgo., 1965—, mem. Com. on Evolution Biology, 1969—. Pres. Chgo. Zool. Soc., 1976—. Fellow AAAS; mem. Am. Soc. Ichthyologists and Herpetologists (pres. 1978), Herpetologists League, Soc. Systematic Zoology, Soc. Mammalogists, Soc. Study Evolution, Ecol. Soc. Am., Am. Soc. Zoologists, Soc. Study Animal Behavior, Am. Assn. Museums, Am. Soc. Naturalists, Am. Assn. Zool. Parks and Aquariums (dir. 1979—), Internat. Union Dirs. Zool. Gardens, Sigma Xi. Office: Chgo Zool Park Brookfield IL 60513

RABB, HARRIET SCHAFFER, lawyer, univ. adminstr.; b. Houston, Tex., Sept. 12, 1941; d. Samuel S. and Helen G. Schaffer; B.A. in Govt., Barnard Coll., 1963; J.D., Columbia U., 1966; m. Bruce Rabb, Jan. 4, 1970; children—Alexander, Katherine. Admitted to N.Y. bar, 1966, U.S. Supreme Ct. bar, 1969, D.C. bar, 1970; instr. seminar on constl. litigation Rutgers Law Sch., 1966-67; staff atty. Center for Constl. Rights, 1966-69; spl. counsel to commr. consumer affairs N.Y.C. Dept. Consumer Affairs, 1969-70; sr. staff atty. Stern Community Law Firm, Washington, 1970-71; asst. dean urban affairs Columbia U. Law Sch., N.Y.C., 1971—, co-dir. employment rights project, 1971—; mem. faculty employment and tng. policy Harvard Summer Inst., Cambridge, Mass., 1975-79. Bd. dirs. Ford Found., 1977—, N.Y. Civil Liberties Union, 1972—, Lawyers Com. for Civil Rights Under Law, 1978—, NAACP Legal Def. Fund, 1978—. Author: (with Agid, Cooper and Rubin) Fair Employment Litigation Manual, 1975; (with Cooper and Rubin) Fair Employment Litigation, 1975. Office: 435 West 116th St New York NY 10027

RABB, IRVING WILLIAM, chain store exec.; b. Boston, Feb. 4, 1913; s. Joseph and Lottie (Wolf) Rabinovitz; A.B. cum laude, Harvard U., 1934, postgrad. Bus. Sch., 1935; m. Charlotte Frank, June 23, 1938; children—Betty Ann Rabb Schafer, James Mark. With Stop & Shop, Boston, 1935—, v.p. retailing, exec. v.p., 1957-61, gen. mgr., v.p., 1961-64, pres., 1964-66, vice chmn. bd., dir., 1966—, also chmn. exec. com.; dir. Plymouth Rubber Co., Canton, Mass.; mem. corp. Provident Instn. for Savs. Bd. dirs. Harvard Community Health Plan; trustee Beth Israel Hosp., past pres.; past pres., trustee Combined Jewish Philanthropies Boston; trustee Boston Symphony Orch., Mus. Fine Arts, Council Jewish Fedns. and Welfare Funds. Fellow Am. Acad. Arts and Scis.; mem. Super Market Inst. (past pres.), Food Mktg. Inst. (chmn. 1977). Office: PO Box 369 Boston MA 02101

RABB, MAXWELL M., lawyer; b. Boston, Sept. 28, 1910; s. Solomon and Rose (Kostick) R.; A.B., Harvard, 1932, LL.B., 1935; LL.D., Wilberforce U., 1957; m. Ruth Cryden, Nov. 2, 1939; children—Bruce, Sheila (Mrs. Edward L. Weidenfeld), Emily (Mrs. Howard F. Maltby), Priscilla (Mrs. John W. Haskins). Admitted to Mass. bar, 1935; mem. firm Rabb & Rabb, Boston, 1935-37; adminstrv. asst. to U.S. Senator H.C. Lodge, Mass., 1937-43; adminstrv. asst. U.S. Senator Sinclair Weeks, Mass., 1944; legal, legis. cons. Sec. Navy Forestal, 1946; practice of law, Boston, 1946-51; cons. U.S. Senate Rules Com., 1952; presdl. asst., Sec. to Cabinet, 1953-58; partner law firm Stroock, Stroock & Lavan, N.Y.C., 1958—; admitted to N.Y. bar, 1958; dir. Rite Aid Corp., Sterling Nat. Bank and Trust Co. N.Y., Westons Shoppers City, Inc. Exec. asst. campaign mgr. Eisenhower presdl. campaign, 1951-52; del. Republican Nat. Conv., 1952, 56, 76; chmn. N.Y. Rep. Congl. Campaign Com. Mem. exec. com. U.S. Commn. for UNESCO, 1959-60, Council on Fgn. Relations, 1978—; chmn. U.S. delegation to UNESCO conf., Paris, 1958. Bd. dirs. U.S. Com. for Refugees, N.A.A.C.P. Legal Def. and Ednl. Fund, Inc.; chmn. govt. div. United Jewish Appeal, 1953-58; mem. exec. bd. Mass. Com. Catholics, Protestants, Jews; pres. Congregation Emanu-El, N.Y.C.; mem. nat. adv. bd. AJC-Wiener Oral Hist. Library; bd. dirs. United Cerebral Palsy Research and Ednl. Found., Alliance Israelite Universelle (N.Y.), NCCJ; mem. overseers com. to Harvard U. Sch. Public Health; trustee Eisenhower Coll., NCCJ, Champlin Founds. R.I., N.Y. Med. Coll., Nat. Jewish Hosp., Denver, Cardinal's Inner City Scholarship Fund; mem. presdl. adv. panel on South Asian Relief assistance, 1971; mem. panel conciliations World Bank Internat. Centre for Settlement of Investment Disputes, 1967-73, U.S. rep., 1974-77; mem. Presdl. Commn. on Income Maintenance Programs, 1968-69. Served as lt. amphibious corps., USNR, 1944-46. Decorated Commendation Ribbon (Navy), commendatore Order of Merit of Republic of Italy, 1958. Mem. Assn. Bar City of New York, Pilgrims of the U.S., Am. Bar Assn., Am. Law Inst. Clubs: Harvard, Recess, Harmonie (N.Y.C.); Greenfield (Mass.) Country; Army and Navy, Federal City, Metropolitan (Washington). Home: 1025 Fifth Ave New York NY 10028 also Wilson Hill Rd Colrain MA 01340 Office: 61 Broadway New York NY 10006

RABB, SIDNEY R., retail food and merc. exec.; b. Boston, Oct. 20, 1900; s. Joseph and Lottie Rebeca (Wolf) R.; M.A. (hon.), Harvard, 1962; LL.D., Tufts U., 1961; D.C.S., Suffolk U., 1966; L.H.D., Boston Coll., 1964; D.H., Northeastern U., 1976; D.H.L., Brandeis U., 1977; m. Esther Vera Cohn, Feb. 29, 1920; children—Helene J. (Mrs. Norman Cahners), Carol P. (Mrs. Avram Goldberg). chmn. bd. The Stop & Shop Cos., Inc., 1930—; v.p., dir. Nathan H. Gordon Corp.; dir. Ritz-Carlton Hotel Co. Boston; hon. dir. Boston Safe Deposit & Trust Co. Hon. life trustee, exec. com., past pres. Beth Israel Hosp.; hon. life trustee Combined Jewish Philanthropies; hon. trustee Mass. Gen. Hosp., mem. trustee com. McLean Hosp.; bd. overseers Boys Clubs Boston; bd. dirs. Civic Edn. Found., Inc. Hebrew Rehab. Center for Aged; hon. trustee Boston Mus. Fine Arts, Recuperative Center; trustee, past pres. Boston Pub. Library; vice chmn., mem. exec. com. Mass. Com. Catholics, Protestants and Jews; bd. overseers Florence Heller Grad. Sch. Advanced Study Social Welfare, fellow Brandeis U.; hon. trustee, vis. com. Harvard Bus. Sch.; com. univ. resources bd. overseers Harvard U.; mem. corp. Mus. of Sci., Boston; incorporator Neuroscis. Research Found.; mem. nat. bd. govs. Israel Bond Orgn.; mem. at large Nat. Council Boy Scouts Am.; hon. bd. dirs. Food Mktg. Inst. Served with USMC, World War I. Fellow Am. Acad. Arts and Scis.; mem. Super Market Ins. (exec. com., past pres.) Jewish religion (dir. synagogue, hon. life trustee temple), Mason. Clubs: Harvard, Belmont Country, Commercial (Boston); Palm Beach Country. Home: 65 Commonwealth Ave Boston MA 02116 Office: PO Box 369 Boston MA 02101

RABB, THEODORE K., historian; b. Teplice-Sanov, Czechoslovakia, Mar. 5, 1937; s. Oskar Kwasnik and Rose (Oliner) Rabinowicz; came to U.S., 1956, naturalized, 1978; B.A., Queen's Coll. Oxford (Eng.) U., 1958, M.A., 1962; M.A., Princeton U., 1960, Ph.D., 1961; m. Tamar Miriam Janowsky, June 7, 1959; children—Susannah Lynette, Jonathan Richard, Jeremy David. Instr., Stanford U., 1961-62, Northwestern U., 1962-63; asst. prof. Harvard U., 1963-67; mem. faculty Princeton U., 1967—, prof. history, 1976—; vis. asso. prof. Johns Hopkins U., 1969, State U. N.Y., Binghamton, 1973-74; visitor Inst. Advanced Studies, Princeton, 1973; mem. nat. bd. cons. Nat. Endowment Humanities; cons. in field. Fellow and/or grantee Folger Shakespeare Library, Am. Philos. Soc., Social Sci. Research Council, Am. Council Learned Socs., Guggenheim Found., Nat. Endowment Humanities. Mem. Am. Hist. Assn. (chmn. com. quantitative research history), Social Sci. History Assn. (exec. com., treas.), Am. Assn. Advancement Humanities (dir., sec.-treas.), Royal Hist. Soc., Internat. Commn. History Parliamentary and Rep. Instns., Renaissance Soc. Am., Hakluyt Soc., Historians Early Modern Europe, Past and Present Soc. Author: The Thirty Years War, 2d edit., 1972; Enterprise and Empire, 1967; The Struggle for Stability in Early Modern Europe, 1975; co-author: The Western Experience, 1974; editor: Jour. Interdisciplinary History, 1970—; co-editor: Action and Conviction in Early Modern Europe, 1969. Office: History Dept Princeton Univ Princeton NJ 08544

RABBITT, EDWARD THOMAS, singer, songwriter; b. Bklyn., Nov. 27, 1941; married. Previously worked as truck driver, soda jerk, fruitpicker; nightclub and concert singer, 1962—; composer more than 300 songs, including Kentucky Rain, Pure Love; worked on WRGB, Albany, 1967-68, WWVA, Wheeling, 1968; recs. for 20th Century Fox, Columbia, now with Elektra Records; recs. of own compositions include: Forgive and Forget, Rocky Mountain Music, Drinkin' My Baby Off My Mind, Two Dollars in the Jukebox. Office: care Stan Moress-Scotti Bros Entertainment 9229 Sunset Blvd Los Angeles CA 90069*

RABE, DAVID WILLIAM, playwright; b. Dubuque, Iowa, Mar. 10, 1940; s. William and Ruth (McCormick) R.; B.A. in English, Loras Coll. Formerly bellhop, parking lot attendant, tchr., reporter. Recipient Obie award, Drama Desk award, Variety Poll award, all 1971; Tony award, Outer Critics Circle award, N.Y. Drama Critics Circle citation, all 1972; Am. Acad. Arts and Letters award, 1974: N.Y. Drama Critics Circle award, 1976. Author: The Basic Training of Pavlo Hummel, 1971; Sticks and Bones, 1972, The Orphan, 1972; In the Boom Boom Room, 1973; Streamers, 1976. Address: care Alfred A Knopf 201 E 50th St New York NY 10022*

RABI, ISIDOR ISAAC, physicist; b. Austria, July 29, 1898; s. David and Jennie (Teig) R.; brought to U.S. in infancy; B.Chem., Cornell U., 1919; Ph.D., Columbia U., 1927, Sc.D., 1968; grad. study in Munich, Copenhagen, Hamburg, Leipzig, Zurich, 1927-29; D. Sc. (hon.), Princeton, 1947, Harvard, 1955, Williams Coll., 1958, U. Birmingham, 1960, Clark U., 1962, Adelphi Coll., 1962, Technion, 1963, Franklin Marshall Coll., 1964, Brandeis U., 1965, U. Coimbra, Portugal, 1966, Hebrew U., Jerusalem, 1972, Coll. City N.Y., 1977, Bates Coll., 1977, L.I. U., 1977; L.H.D., Hebrew Union Coll., Cin., 1958, Oklahoma City U., 1960; LL.D., Dropsie Coll., 1956; D.H.L., Yeshiva U., 1964; Litt. D., Jewish Theol. Sem., 1966; m. Helen Newmar, 1926; children—Nancy Elizabeth, Margaret Joella. Tutor in physics, Coll. City N.Y., 1924-27; lectr. Columbia U., 1929-30, asst. prof., 1930-35, asso. prof., 1935-37, prof., 1937-64, Higgins prof., 1950-64, U. prof., 1964-67, U. prof. emeritus, 1967—, also exec. officer, dept. physics, 1945-49; Karl Taylor Compton vis. prof. physics, 1968-71; lectr. U. Mich., summer 1936. Stanford U., summer 1938; cons. sci. adv. com. Ballistic Research Lab., Aberdeen, 1939-65; mem. sci. bd. Itek Corp. Staff mem. and asso. dir., Radiation Lab., M.I.T., 1940-45; mem. gen. adv. com. AEC, 1946—, chmn., 1952-56, cons., 1956—; chmn. sci. adv. Com. ODM, 1953-57; cons. Dept. State, 1958—; mem. Naval Research Adv. Com., 1952—, cons., sci. adv. com., v.p. Internat. Conf. on Peaceful Uses Atomic Energy, Geneva, 1955, 58, 64; v.p. UN Conf. on Peaceful Uses Atomic Energy, 1971—; U.S. rep. adv. com. to sec. gen. UN, 1955—; mem. President's Sci. Adv. Com., 1957-68, chmn., 1957; cons. Los Alamos Sci. Lab., 1943-45, 56—; mem. NATO Sci. Com., 1958—; cons. Research and Devel. Bd., 1946-49; U.S. del. UNESCO Conf., Florence, Italy, 1950; mem. U.S. Nat. Commn. UNESCO, 1950-53, 58; mem. UN Sci. Com., 1954—; mem. IAEA Sci. Com., 1958-72; vis. prof. Rockefeller U. (formerly Inst.), 1957-79; Shreve fellow Princeton, 1961-62; Karl Taylor Compton lectr. Mass. Inst. Tech., 1962; gen. adv. com. ACDA, 1962—. Served in S.A.T.C., 1918. Decorated Officer French Legion of Honor, 1956; comdr., 1968. Barnard fellow, 1927-28; Internat. Ednl. Bd. fellow, 1928-29; Ernest Kempton Adams fellow, 1935; Sigma Xi Semicentennial prize for physical scis., 1936; Henrietta Szold award, 1956; $1,000 prize from A.A.A.S., for study of radio frequency spectra of atoms and molecules, 1939; Elliot Cresson medal of Franklin Inst., 1942; Nobel Prize in Physics, 1944; Barnard medal, 1960; U.S. Medal for Merit, 1948; King's Medal (British, 1948); Comdr., Order So. Cross, Brazil, 1952; Priestley Meml. award Dickenson Coll., 1964; Niels Bohr Internat. Gold Medal, 1967; co-recipient, Atoms for Peace award, 1967. Trustee Assoc. Univs., Inc., 1946—, pres., 1961-62, chmn. bd., 1962-63; bd. govs. Weizmann Inst. Sci., Rehovoth, Israel, 1949—; trustee Mt. Sinai Hosp., 1960—. Fellow Am. Phys. Soc. (pres. 1950-51); mem. Council on Fgn. Relations, Am. Philos. Soc., Japan Acad. Sci. (fgn. mem.), Nat. Acad. Scis., N.Y. Acad. Scis., Sigma Xi. Clubs: Cosmos (Washington); Faculty (Columbia U.); Athenaeum

(London). Author: My Life and Times as a Physicist, 1960; Science: The Center of Culture, 1970. Asso. editor Physical Review, 1935-38, 1941-44. Contbr. to sci. jours. in field. Home: New York City NY 10027

RABIN, EDWARD WILLIAM, JR., hotel exec.; b. Grand Rapids, Mich., Mar. 21, 1947; s. Edward W. and Mary Louise R. Gen. mgr. Mills Hyatt Hotel, Charleston, S.C., 1971-73, Water Tower Hyatt Hotel, Chgo., 1973-75, Hyatt on Union Sq., San Francisco, 1975-78, Hyatt Regency Atlanta, 1978-79; v.p. Hyatt Hotels Corp., Atlanta, 1979—. Bd. dirs. Downtown Council, Charleston, 1970-73, San Francisco Parking Corp., 1975-78, Central Atlanta Progress, 1979—, Atlanta Conv. Bur., 1979—. Served with U.S. Army, 1967-69. Named Gen. Mgr. of Yr., Hyatt Corp., 1977. Mem. Am. Hotel and Motel Assn., Am. Sales Assn. Execs. Club: Rotary. Home and Office: Hyatt Regency Atlanta 265 Peachtree St Atlanta GA 30303

RABIN, HERBERT, physicist; b. Milw., Nov. 14, 1928; B.S., U. Wis., 1950; M.S., U. Ill., 1951; in Physics, U. Md., 1959; married; 2 children. Physicist elec. div. U.S. Naval Research Lab., 1952-54, physicist solid state physics div., 1954-62, head radiation effects sect. optical materials br., 1962-67, head quantum optics sect., applied optics br., 1967-68, head quantum optics br., 1968-71, asso. dir. research for space sci. and tech., 1971-77, asso. dir. research for space and communication sci. and tech., 1977-79; dep. asst. sec. of Navy for research, applied and space tech. Office of Navy Secretariat, Washington, 1979—; vis. scientist Technisch Hochschule, Stuttgart, Germany, 1960-61; mem. staff physics dept. George Washington U., 1955-73; cons. Sch. Engring. of Sao Carlos, U. Sao Paulo (Brazil), 1964, 70. Recipient Meritorious Civilian Service award U.S. Navy, 1969, Disting. Civilian Service award, 1976, E.O. Hulburt Sci. award, 1970. Fellow Am. Phys. Soc.; mem. AAAS, Optical Soc. Am., Philos. Soc. Am., Philos. Soc. Washington, AIAA, Brazilian Acad. Scis. (corr.). Contbr. articles to tech. jours.; patentee in field. Home: 7109 Radnor Rd Bethesda MD 20034 Office: US Naval Research Lab Code 7000 4555 Overlook Ave SW Washington DC 20375

RABINEAU, LOUIS, state edn. ofcl.; b. Albany, N.Y., Apr. 30, 1924; s. Nathan and Ada (Mosher) R.; student Yale U., 1943-44, Biarritz (France) Am. U., 1945; B.A., State U. N.Y. at Albany, 1947, M.A., 1950; Ed.D., Harvard U., 1954; D.H.L. (hon.), Yeshiva U., 1975; m. Mona Lipofsky, Aug. 17, 1961; 1 dau., Elizabeth. Supr. profl. edn. N.Y. State Edn. Dept., 1947-54; dir. admissions, registrar Pratt Inst., Bklyn., 1955-59, lectr., 1955-57, dir. student personnel, 1958-59, v.p. student affairs, 1959-65; spl. asst. to pres., prof. social sci. N.Y. Inst. Tech., Old Westbury, 1965-66; asso. dir. higher edn. Conn. Commn. for Higher Edn., Hartford, 1966-69, dep. dir. and vice chancellor higher edn., 1969-74, chancellor for higher edn., 1974-76; dir. inservice edn. program Edn. Commn. States, Denver, 1976—; vis. lectr. N.Y. U., 1964-65, Tchrs. Coll. Columbia, summer, 1964; mem. Conn. Bd. Edn., Conn. Scholarship Commn., Conn. Student Loan Found., steering com. Edn. Commn. of the States, New Eng. Bd. Higher Edn., Conn. Adv. Council on Vocat. Edn.; bd. dirs. Conn. Ednl. TV Corp.; trustee Conn. Regional Med. Program, Ednl. Commn. for Fgn. Med. Grads.; chmn. bd. govs. Higher Edn. Centers Conn. Served with AUS, 1943-46. Decorated Bronze Star medal; recipient Distinguished Alumni award State U. N.Y. at Albany. Mem. N.Y. State Personnel and Guidance Assn. (pres. 1964, life), Kappa Phi Kappa, Phi Delta Kappa. Contbr. articles to profl. jours. Home: 109 Krameria St Denver CO 80220 Office: 1860 Lincoln St Suite 300 Denver CO 80295

RABINER, SAUL FREDERICK, educator, physician; b. Bklyn., Aug. 11, 1926; s. Abraham M. and Ella (Feldman) R.; B.S., Tulane U., 1949; M.D., State U. N.Y. at Bklyn., 1952; m. Marion Evans, Apr. 2, 1949; children—Mark, Elizabeth, David. Intern Maimonides Hosp., Bklyn., 1952, resident 1953; resident Montefiore Hosp., Bronx, 1956; attending dept. medicine VA Research Hosp., Chgo., 1960-68; asso. medicine Northwestern U. Med. Sch., 1960-65, asst. prof. medicine, 1960-69; asso. prof. medicine Pritzker Med. Sch., U. Chgo., 1970-71; asso. dir. clin. hematology Michael Reese Hosp., Chgo., 1962-63, dir., 1964-71; asso. prof. medicine U. Oreg. Med. Sch., 1971-74, prof. medicine, 1974—; chief of medicine Good Samaritan Hosp. and Med. Center, 1971—. Served with USAAF, 1943-45. Home: 614 NW Macleay Blvd Portland OR 97210 Office: 2222 NW Lovejoy St 350 Portland OR 97210

RABINOVITCH, BENTON SEYMOUR, educator, chemist: b. Montreal, Que., Can., Feb. 19, 1919; s. Samuel and Rachel (Schachter) R.; B.Sc., McGill U., 1939, Ph.D., 1942; m. Marilyn Werby, Sept. 18, 1949; children—Peter Samuel, Ruth Anne, Judith Nancy, Frank Benjamin. Came to U.S., 1946. Postdoctoral fellow Harvard, 1946-48; mem. faculty U. Wash., 1948—, prof. chemistry, 1957—. Cons. and/or mem. sci. adv. panels, coms. NSF, Nat. Acad. Scis.-NRC; adv. com. phys. chemistry Nat. Bur. Standards. Served to capt. Canadian Army, 1942-46; ETO. Nat. Research Council Can. fellow, 1940-42; Royal Soc. Can. Research fellow, 1946-47; Milton Research fellow Harvard, 1948; Guggenheim fellow, 1961; vis. fellow Trinity Coll., Oxford, 1971. Fellow Am. Phys. Soc.; mem. Am. Chem. Soc. (past chmn. Puget Sound sect., past chmn. phys. chemistry div., editor jour.), Faraday Soc., AAUP. Editor: Ann. Rev. Phys. Chemistry; editorial bd. Jour. Phys. Chemistry, Internat. Jour. Chem. Kinetics. Spl. research Unimolecular gas phase reaction. Home: 12530-42 Ave NE Seattle WA 98125

RABINOVITSJ, MAX, violinist; b. Brussels, Belgium, May 7, 1934; s. Isaac and Sara (Korzuszek) R.; came to U.S., 1949, naturalized, 1960; student Brussels Royal Conservatory Music, 1945-49, Curtis Inst. Music, 1955-59; m. Gita Keiserman, Oct. 10, 1959; children—Finette Rachel, Daniel Aaron, Tova Michele. Concertmaster, Ottawa (Can.) Philharmonic, 1959-60; asst. concertmaster New Orleans Philharmonic, 1960-61, Cin. Symphony Orch., 1961-65; concertmaster Santa Fe Opera Co., 1961-63, St. Louis Symphony, 1965-77, Casals Festival, 1975, Marlboro Music Festival, 1963-66, St. Louis String Quartet, 1966-76; dir. St. Louis Conservatory Music, from 1977; now mem. faculty U. Tex., Austin; bd. dirs. C.A.S.A. Recordings for VOX and Columbia; soloist numerous cities throughout world; faculty Washington U., 1966-75. Recipient Grand Prix award in solfege and violin Royal Conservatory Music, Brussels, 1949. Jewish. Office: Dept Music U Tex Austin TX 78712. *Never look back, always look to the future. Learn from mistakes; never dwell on them. By keeping myself receptive to new ideas, I find I feel always fresh and young.*

RABINOVITZ, JASON, motion picture co. exec.; b. Boston, Aug. 17, 1921; s. Morris J. and Martha (Leavitt) R.; B.A. magna cum laude, Harvard, 1943, M.B.A. with distinction, 1948; m. Frieda Pearlson, July 18, 1948; children—Abby, Judith, Daniel, Jonathan. With Chase Nat. Bank, N.Y.C., 1948-49; asst. to sec.-treas. United Paramount Theatres, Inc., N.Y.C., 1949-53; asst. controller ABC, N.Y.C., 1953-56; adminstrv. v.p. ABC-TV Network, N.Y.C., 1956-57; with Metro-Goldwyn-Mayer, Inc., N.Y.C., 1957-69, treas., 1963, financial v.p., 1967-69; exec. v.p., gen. mgr. Ency. Brit. Ednl. Corp., Chgo., 1971-73; sr. v.p., gen. mgr. Am. Film Theatre, N.Y.C., 1974-75; v.p., asst. to pres. Metro-Goldwyn-Mayer, Inc., Culver City, Calif., 1976-79, v.p. fin., 1979—. Served to capt., parachutist, AUS, 1942-46. Decorated Bronze Star. Mem. Phi Beta Kappa, Phi Eta Sigma. Home: 1675 Stone Canyon Rd Los Angeles CA 90024 Office: MGM Inc 10202 W Washington Blvd Culver City CA 90230

RABINOW, JACOB, elec. engr.; b. Kharkov, Russia, Jan. 8, 1910; s. Aaron and Helen (Fleisher) Rabinovich; came to U.S., 1921, naturalized, 1930; B.S. in Elec. Engring. Coll. City N.Y., 1933, E.E., 1934; m. Gladys Lieder, Sept. 26, 1943; children—Jean Ellen, Clare Lynn. Radio serviceman, N.Y.C., 1934-38; mech. engr. Nat. Bur. Standards, Washington, 1938-54; pres. Rabinow Engring. Co., Washington, 1954-64; v.p. Control Data Corp., Washington, 1964-72; research engr. Nat. Bur. Standards, 1972—; Regent's lectr. U. Calif., Berkeley, 1972; lectr., cons. in field. Recipient Pres.'s Certificate of Merit, 1948; certificate appreciation War Dept., 1949; Exceptional Service award Dept. Commerce, 1949; Edward Longstreth medal Franklin Inst., 1959; Jeffersom medal N.J. Patent Law Assn., 1973. Fellow IEEE (Harry Diamond award 1977); mem. Nat. Acad. Engring., AAAS, Philos. Soc. Washington, Audio Engring. Soc., Sigma Xi. Club: Cosmos (Washington). Author, patentee in field. Home: 6920 Selkirk Dr Bethesada MD 20034 Office: Nat Bur Standards Washington DC 20234

RABINOWICZ, ERNEST, educator; b. Berlin, Germany, Apr. 22, 1926; s. Leo and Fanny (Bochner) R.; B.A., Cambridge U., Eng., 1947, Ph.D., 1950; m. Ina Lee Feldman, Aug. 23, 1953; children—Deena P., Judith R., Laura A. Came to U.S., 1950, naturalized, 1963. Research staff Mass. Inst. Tech., 1950-54, asst. prof. mech. engring., 1954-61, asso. prof., 1961-67, prof., 1967—; vis. prof. Haifa Technion, 1969. Mem. Am. Phys. Soc., ASME, Am. Soc. Lubrication Engrs. (Hodson award 1957), Phys. Soc. London. Author: (with N.H. Cook) Physical Measurement and Analysis, 1963; Friction and Wear of Materials, 1965; An Introduction to Experimentation, 1970; (videotaped lecture series) An Introduction to Experimentation, 1972, Friction, Wear and Lubrication, 1974. Home: 14 Exmoor Rd Newton MA 02159 Office: Room 35-010 Mass Inst Tech Cambridge MA 02139

RABINOWITCH, VICTOR, scientist; b. London, Eng., Aug. 30, 1934; s. Eugene I. and Anna D. (Morosoff) R.; came to U.S., naturalized; B.S., U. Ill., 1956; M.S., U. Wis., 1961, Ph.D. in Zoology and Internat. Relations, 1965; m. Ann Elizabeth Collins, Aug. 30, 1958; children—Nikolai, Peter, Alexander. Research asst. zoology U. Wis.-Madison, 1961-65; staff dir. sci. orgn. devel. bd. Nat. Acad. Scis., Washington, 1965-69, staff dir. bd. sci. and tech. internat. devel. Office Fgn. Sec., 1970—; asso. prof. State U. N.Y. at Albany, 1969-70. Vice pres. Inst. Man and Sci., Rennselareville, N.Y., 1969-75; mem. Pugwash Confs. Sci. and World Affairs, 1960—, chmn. Pugwash Study Group Developing Countries, 1970-73; mem. Am. Acad. Com. Devel., 1965-70. Mem. governing bd. Internat. Center Insect Physiology and Ecology, Nairobi, Kenya, 1970-71; mem. vis. team Lehigh U., 1975—. Served with AUS, 1957-59. Mem. Assn. Advancement Agrl. Scis. Africa, AAAS (com. sci. and pub. policy 1972-76), Fedn. Am. Scientists, (mem. council 1975-79), Soc. Internat. Devel., Wis. Acad. Scis., Internat. Center Insect Physiology and Ecology, Council on Fgn. Relations, Sigma Xi, Phi Sigma. Dir. Bull. Atomic Scientists, 1970—; sci. editor World Devel., 1973—. Author: (with Eugene I. Rabinowitch) Views on Science, Technology and Development), 1975. Editorial bd. Sci. Studies, Pub. Sci., 1973-75, Tech. and Society, 1979—. Contbr. articles to profl. jours. Home: 8606 Battailles Ct Annandale VA 22003 Office: 2101 Constitution Ave NW Washington DC 20418

RABINOWITZ, ALAN, urban planner, educator; b. N.Y.C., Jan. 18, 1927; s. Aaron and Clara (Greenhut) R.; A.B., Yale U., 1948; M.B.A., Harvard U., 1950; Ph.D., M.I.T., 1969; m. Andrea Wolf, Dec. 2, 1951; children—Eric, Peter, Martha, Katherine. With Fred F. French Investing Co., Inc., 1950-59; mem. staff Regional Plan Assn., N.Y.C., 1956-57; cons. Arthur D. Little, Inc., Cambridge, Mass., 1959-63; cons. Urban Survey Corp., Cambridge, 1963-68; adminstr. for program planning and fin. Boston Redevel. Authority, 1969-71; prof. urban planning U. Wash., Seattle, 1971—. Served with USNR, 1945-46, 51-53. Mem. Am. Inst. Certified Planners. Author: Municipal Bond Finance and Administration, 1969. Home: 3400 E Laurelhurst Dr Seattle WA 98105 Office: Univ of Washington Seattle WA 98195

RABINOWITZ, JAY ANDREW, justice Alaska Supreme Ct.; b. Phila., Feb. 25, 1927; s. Milton and Rose (Rittenberg) R.; B.A., Syracuse U., 1949; LL.B., Harvard, 1952; m. Anne Marie Nesbit, June 14, 1957; children—Judith, Mara, Max, Sara. Admitted to N.Y. State bar, 1952, Alaska bar, 1958; practiced in N.Y.C., 1952-57; law clk. U.S. Dist. Ct. judge, Fairbanks, Alaska, 1957-58; asst. U.S. atty., Fairbanks, 1958-59; dep. atty. gen., chief civil div. State of Alaska, 1959-60; judge Superior Ct. Alaska, 1960-65; justice Alaska Supreme Ct., Juneau, 1965—, chief justice, after 1972; lectr. U. Alaska. Served with AUS, 1945-46. Mem. N.Y., Alaska bar assns. Club: Harvard (N.Y.C.). Office: Box 850 Supreme Court Alaska Juneau AK 99801*

RABINOWITZ, PAUL H., mathematician; b. Newark, Nov. 15, 1939; s. Harry and Fay Rabinowitz; B.A., N.Y. U., 1961, Ph.D., 1966; m. Birgit Christensen, Sept. 24, 1971. Asst. prof. math. Stanford U., 1966-69; asso. prof. math. U. Wis., Madison, 1969-71, prof., 1971—. J.S. Guggenheim fellow, 1978-79. Mem. Am. Math. Soc., Soc. Indsl. and Applied Math. Office: Dept Math U Wis Madison WI 53706

RABINOWITZ, STANLEY SAMUEL, rabbi; b. Duluth, Minn., June 8, 1917; s. Jacob Mier and Rose (Zeichik) R.; B.A., State U. Iowa, 1939; M.A., Yale U., 1950; M. Hebrew Lit., Jewish Theol. Sem., 1944, Doctor Hebrew Lit., 1971; m. Anita Bryna Lifson, June 24, 1945; children—Nathaniel Herz, Sharon Deborah, Judith Leah. Ordained rabbi, 1943; dir. United Synagogue, N.Y.C., 1943-46; rabbi B'nai Jacob Synagogue, New Haven, Conn., 1946-53, Adath Jeshurun Synagogue, Mpls., 1953-60, Adas Israel Synagogue, Washington, 1960—; v.p. Rabinical Assembly, N.Y.C., 1974-76, pres., 1976-78; vice chmn. B'nai B'rith Youth Commn., 1965-76; pres. Mercaz, 1978—. Club: Cosmos (Washington). Home: 3115 Normanstone Terr NW Washington DC 20008 Office: 2850 Quebec St NW Washington DC 20008

RABINOWITZ, WILLIAM, educator; b. N.Y.C., June 24, 1925; s. Joseph and Sophie (Spitzer) R.; B.S., Coll. City N.Y., 1947; M.A., Columbia, 1949, Ph.D., 1955; m. Martha Ferber, June 25, 1950; children—Joseph E., David A. Lectr. div. tchr. edn. City U. N.Y., 1950-53, mem. faculty, 1956-64; research asso. Bank Street Coll. Edn., N.Y.C., 1953-56; prof. ednl. psychology Pa. State U. at University Park, 1964—, head dept., 1964-74. Vis. prof. psychology, edn. Bar-Ilan U., Israel, 1970-71. Served to lt. (j.g.), USNR, 1943-46. Recipient Distinguished Tchr. award Pa. State U. chpt. Iota Alpha Delta, 1966. Fulbright research scholar Inst. Ednl. Research, U. Oslo, Norway, 1962-63. Fellow Am. Psychol. Assn., A.A.A.S.; mem. Am. Ednl. Research Assn., A.A.U.P. (v.p. Pa. State U. chpt. 1973), Sigma Xi. Contbr. articles profl. jours. Home: 1245 S Garner St State College PA 16801

RABJOHN, NORMAN, educator; b. Rochester, N.Y., May 1, 1915; s. Alfred Augustus and Elizabeth Mary (Hooper) R.; B.S., U. Rochester, 1937; M.S., U. Ill., 1939, Ph.D., 1942; m. Dora I. Taylor, Sept. 9, 1943; 1 son, James Norman. Instr. chemistry U. Ill., Champaign-Urbana, 1942-44; researcher Goodyear Tire, Akron, O., 1944-48; from asso. prof. to prof. chemistry U. Mo., Columbia, 1948—. Fellow A.A.A.S.; mem. Am. Chem. Soc. (chmn. council com. publs. 1970-71), Phi Beta Kappa, Sigma Xi, Phi Lambda Upsilon, Alpha Chi Sigma. Edit. bd. Organic Syntheses, 1960—. Asso. editor Chem. Reviews, 1965-67. Home: 100 E Ridgeley Rd Columbia MO 65201

RABKIN, LEO, artist; b. Cin., July 21, 1919; s. David and Bessie Rabkin; B.A., U. Cin., 1940, B.Ed., 1941; M.A., N.Y. U., 1946; m. Dorothy Herz, May 9, 1958. Vocat. counsellor N.Y. U., 1946-49; artist, N.Y.C., 1950—; tchr., spl. schs. for emotionally disturbed adolescents N.Y.C. Bd. Edn., 1952-72; one-man shows: Fairleigh-Dickinson U., 1971, Truman Gallery, N.Y.C., 1978, 79, Allentown (Pa.) Art Mus., 1978; exhibited group shows Mus. Modern Art, N.Y.C., 1959, 60, 65, 66, Whitney Mus., Am. Art, N.Y.C., intermittently, 1959-75, Guggenheim Mus., N.Y.C., 1962, 65, 77, N.C. Mus. Art, Raleigh, 1969, 70, Neuberger Mus., N.Y.C., 1975, San Francisco Mus. Art, Milw. Art Center, Jewish Mus., N.Y.C., 1970, Albright Coll., Redding, Pa., 1979, numerous others; works included in permanent collections Chase Manhattan Bank, N.Y.C., Guggenheim Mus., Mus. Modern Art, Phila. Mus. Art, Whitney Mus. Am. Art, Woodward Found., Washington, others; retrospective exhbn. Stormking Art Center, Mountainville, N.Y., 1979. Served with AUS, 1942-45. Recipient Ford Found. award for watercolor, 1961, 1st prize for watercolor Silvermine Guild Artists, 1961. Mem. Am. Abstract Artists (pres. 1964-78), Fine Arts Fedn. N.Y. (dir. 1970-75, v.p. 1975-80), U.S. Com. Internat. Assn. Art (del. 1964, sec. 1968-70). Editor: American Abstract Artists, 1936-66, 1966. Gallery: Parsons-Dreyfuss 24 W 57th St New York NY 10019

RABORN, WILLIAM FRANCIS, JR., ret. naval officer, corp. exec.; b. Decatur, Tex., June 8, 1905; s. William Francis and Cornelia Victoria (Moore) R.; B.S., U.S. Naval Acad., 1928; student Naval War Coll., 1951-52; m. Mildred T. Terrell, Apr. 5, 1955; children—Barbara Raborn Richardson, William Francis III. Commd. ensign USN, 1928, advanced through grades to vice adm., 1960; designated naval aviator, 1934; assigned battleships, destroyers, aircraft carriers, 1928-40; established Aviation Gunnery Sch., Barbers Point, Pearl Harbor, T.H., 1940-42; exec. officer U.S.S. Hancock, Fast Carrier Task Forces Pacific, 1943-45; chief staff Comdr. Task Force 77, Comdr. Carrier Div. 2, Western Pacific, 1945-47; operations officer Comdr. for Naval Air West Coast, 1947-49; research and development guided missiles Bur. Ordnance, 1949-50; dep. dir. guided missile div. Office Chief Naval Operations, 1952-54; comdg. officer U.S.S. Bennington, 1954-55; asst. chief staff (ops.) Comdr. Atlantic Fleet, 1955; 1st dir. Navy's Fleet Ballistic Missile Program; dir. Office of Spl. Projects, Polaris Program; then dep. chief naval operations (devel.), ret. USN, 1963; v.p. program mgmt. Aerojet-Gen. Corp., Azusa, Calif., 1961-63, v.p., gen. rep., 1966—; pres. W.F. Raborn, Co., Inc.; dir. CIA, 1965-66. Decorated D.S.M.; recipient Robert J. Collier Trophy, Nat. Aero. Assn., 1961, Presdl. Nat. Secuity medal, 1966, James V. Forrestal award Nat. Security Indsl. Assn., 1966. Baptist. Mason (33 deg.). Office: 1606 Crestwood Ln McLean VA 22101

RABSON, ALAN SAUL, physician; b. N.Y.C., July 1, 1926; s. Abraham and Florence (Shulman) R.; B.A., U. Rochester (N.Y.), 1948; M.D., State U. N.Y. Downstate, 1950; m. Ruth L. Kirschstein, June 11, 1950; 1 son, Arnold B. Intern, Mass. Meml. Hosp., Boston, 1951-52; resident in pathology N.Y. U. Hosp., 1952-54, USPHS Hosp., New Orleans, 1954-55; pathologist Nat. Cancer Inst., Bethesda, Md., 1955—; prof. pathology Georgetown U. Med. Sch., 1974—. Mem. Am. Assn. Pathologists, Phi Beta Kappa, Sigma Xi, Alpha Omega Alpha. Asso. editor Jour. Nat. Cancer Inst., Am. Jour. Pathology. Contbr. articles to med. jours. Address: Room 3A03 Bldg 31 NIH Bethesda MD 20014

RABY, WILLIAM LOUIS, accountant; b. Chgo., July 16, 1927; s. Gustave E. and Helen (Burgess) R.; student U. Ill., 1945-47; B.S. in Bus. Adminstrn., Northwestern U., 1949; M.B.A., U. Ariz., 1961, Ph.D., 1971; m. Norma Claire Schreiner, Sept. 8, 1956; children—B.J., Marianne, Marlene. Partner, Laventhol & Horwath and predecessor firms, 1961-76, Touche Ross & Co., N.Y.C., 1977—. Served with USN, 1942-45. C.P.A., Ill., Nebr., Ariz. Mem. Am. Inst. C.P.A.'s (past chmn. com. on tax determination), Am. Acctg. Assn., Am. Taxation Assn. (pres.-elect 1979-80), Tax Ct. Bar, Beta Gamma Sigma (past pres. Ariz. alumni chpt.), Delta Mu Delta, Beta Alpha Psi, Alpha Kappa Psi. Presbyn. (elder; chmn. adv. council on ch. and soc.). Club: N.Y. Athletic. Author: The Income Tax and Business Decisions, 4th edit., 1978; Building and Maintaining a Successful Tax Practice, 1964; The Reluctant Taxpayer, 1970; Tax Practice Management, 1974; editorial adv. bd. Taxation for Accountants, The Tax Adviser; tax columnist Nat. Law Jour.; contbr. articles profl. jours. Office: Touche Ross & Co 1633 Broadway New York NY 10019

RACE, GEORGE JUSTICE, physician, educator; b. Everman, Tex., Mar. 2, 1926; s. Claude Ernest and Lila Eunice (Bunch) R.; M.D., U. Tex., Southwestern Med. Sch., 1947; M.S. in P.H., U. N.C., 1953; Ph.D. in Ultrastructural Anatomy and Microbiology, Baylor U., 1969; m. Annette Isabelle Rinker, Dec. 21, 1946; children—George William Daryl, Jonathan Clark, Mark Christopher, Jennifer Anne (dec.), Elizabeth Margaret Rinker. Intern Duke Hosp., 1947-48, asst. resident pathology, 1951-53; intern Boston City Hosp., 1948-49; asst. pathologist Peter Bent Brigham Hosp., Boston, 1953-54; pathologist St. Anthony's Hosp., St. Petersburg, Fla., 1954-55; staff pathologist Tex. Children's Hosp., Dallas, 1955-59; dir. labs. Baylor U. Med. Center, Dallas, 1959—, chief dept. pathology, 1959—, vice chmn. exec. com. med. bd., 1970—; cons. pathologist VA Hosp., Dallas, 1955—; adj. prof. anthropology and biology So. Meth. U., Dallas, 1969; instr. pathology Duke, 1951-53, Harvard Med. Sch., 1953-54; asst. prof. pathology U. Tex. Southwestern Med. Sch., 1955-58, clin. asso. prof., 1958-64, clin. prof., 1964-73, prof., 1973—, dir. Cancer Center, 1973-76, asso. dean for continuing edn., 1973—; pathologist-in-chief Baylor U. Med. Center, 1959—, prof. microbiology, 1962-68, prof. pathology, 1964-68, prof., chmn. dept. pathology, 1969-73; dean A. Webb Roberts Continuing Edn. Center, 1973—; spl. adv. on human and animal diseases Gov. Tex., 1979—. Pres., Tex. div. Am. Cancer Soc., 1970. Served with AUS, 1944-46; from 1st lt. to maj. USAF, 1948-51. Decorated Air medal. Fellow Coll. Am. Pathologists, Am. Soc. Clin. Pathologists, A.A.A.S., Am. Coll. Legal Medicine; mem. A.M.A. (chmn. multiple discipline research forum 1969), Am. Assn. Pathologists, Internat. Acad. Pathology, N.Y. Acad. Sci., Am. Soc. Tropical Medicine and Hygiene, Am. Soc. Parasitologists, Am. Assn. Med. Colls., Am. Assn. Cancer Research, Am. Assn. Phys. Anthropologists, Am. Med. Writers Assn., Sigma Xi. Editor: Laboratory Medicine (4 vols.), 1973, 6th edit., 1979. Contbr. articles to profl. jours., chpts. to textbooks. Home: 3429 Beverly Dr Dallas TX 75205

RACHIE, CYRUS, lawyer; b. Willmar, Minn., Sept. 5, 1908; s. Elias and Amanda (Lien) R.; student U. Minn., 1927-28; J.D., George Washington U., 1932; m. Helen Evelyn Duncanson, Nov. 25, 1936; children—John Burton, Janice Carolyn, Elisabeth Dorthea. Admitted to Minn. bar, 1934; atty. Minn. Hwy. Dept., 1934-43; spl. asst. atty. gen. Minn., 1946-50; counsel Luth. Brotherhood, fraternal life ins. co., 1950-61; pvt. practice law, Mpls., 1961-62; v.p., counsel Gamble-Skogmo, Inc., Mpls., 1962-64; v.p., gen. counsel Aid Assn. Lutherans, Appleton, Wis., 1964-70, sr. v.p., gen. counsel, 1970-73;

mem. firm Rachie & Rachie, Mpls., 1973—. Lutheran Ch. in Am. del. to 4th Assembly Luth. World Fedn., Helsinki, 1963; past pres. Luth. Welfare Soc. Minn. Past chmn. Mpls. Mayor's Council on Human Relations; chmn. finance United Fund drive, 1967-68. Trustee William Mitchell Coll. Law. Served with USNR, 1943-46. Mem. Am., Minn., Wis. bar assns., Am. Legion, Minn. Fraternal Congress (past pres.). Lutheran. Rotarian. Home: 5510 W Highwood Dr Edina MN 55436 Office: 1216 Foshay Tower Minneapolis MN 55402. *I always try to keep in mind that the Christian Cross consists of both vertical and horizontal lines. The vertical is the longest line and represents a direct line from all of us on the bottom to God on the top and we must commune with Him. The horizontal represents an encompassing line that takes in all of mankind. If my life activities do not include the implementation of both lines of the cross, I will not have a balanced and Christian life.*

RACHLEFF, OWEN SPENCER, author, actor, educator; b. N.Y.C., July 16, 1934; s. Harold Kirman and Theresa (Friedman) R.; B.F.A., Columbia, 1956; M.A., London U., 1958. Staff writer Harry N. Abrams, Inc., N.Y.C., 1962-67, Am. Heritage Co., N.Y.C., 1967-68; asst. prof. humanities N.Y. U., N.Y.C., 1969—; lectr. Program Corp. Am., 1973—; culture reviewer Midstream mag., 1974—; profl. actor on Broadway in Catsplay, 1978, The Lesson, 1978; appeared in films The Dain Curse, 1977, Night Flowers, 1979. Dir. European affairs Anti-Defamation League, N.Y.C., 1970-74. MacDowell Colony fellow, 1965. Author: Rembrandt's Life of Christ, 1969; Young Israel, 1969; Great Bible Stories and Master Paintings, 1970; The Occult Conceit, 1971; Sky Diamonds, 1973; Secrets of Superstitions, 1976; Exploring the Bible, 1979. Home: 135 E 71st St New York NY 10021

RACHMELER, LOUIS, army officer; b. Kings County, N.Y., Feb. 16, 1923; s. Jack Nathan and Sophie (Schneider) R.; B.S., U.S. Mil. Acad., 1947; M.S., Stanford U., 1954; grad. various army schs.; m. Mary Lou Johnson, June 23, 1950; children—Dale Nelson, Catherine Lynn, Richard Forrest, Kimberly Ann. Commd. 2d lt. U.S. Army, 1947, advanced through grades to maj. gen., 1973; service in Ger., France, Marshall Islands and Vietnam; dir. indsl. preparedness and munitions prodn. Office Asst. Sec. Def., Washington, 1973-74; dep. materiel acquisition Office Asst. Sec. Army, 1974-76; coordinator army security assistance Office Chief Staff Dept. Army, 1976-77; comdg. gen. Army Missile Materiel Readiness Command, Redstone Arsenal, Ala., 1977—. Decorated Legion of Merit with 3 oak leaf clusters, Air medal, Army Commendation with 2 oak leaf clusters. Mem. Assn. U.S. Army, Am. Def. Preparedness Assn., Stanford U. Alumni Assn. Presbyn. Club: Army-Navy Country (Arlington). Home: 1 Wadsworth Dr Redstone Arsenal AL 35808 Office: Comdg Gen US Army Missile Command Redstone Arsenal AL 35809

RACICH, JOHN, mining co. exec.; b. Vancouver, B.C., Can., Feb. 28, 1936; s. John and Manda (Sulentic) R.; B.Commerce, U. B.C., 1958; chartered accountant, 1961; m. Ann Lowell Fox, Dec. 29, 1960; children—Theresa, John, Elizabeth. Accountant, Price Waterhouse & Co., C.P.A.'s, Vancouver, 1958-64, Can. Nat. Ry., Edmonton, Alta., 1964-67; with Placer Devel. Ltd., Vancouver, 1967-69, 70—, treas., 1975—; systems accountant Marcopper Mining Corp., Manila, 1969-70; treas. Gibraltar Mining Corp., 1975, Equity Silver Mine Ltd., 1975, Craigmont Mines Ltd., 1975; dir. Minera Real de Angeles. Mem. Fin. Execs. Inst., Inst. Chartered Accountants B.C. Clubs: University (Vancouver); Men's Canadian. Office: 700 Burrard Bldg 1030 W Georgia St Vancouver BC V6E 3A8 Canada

RACKER, EFRAIM, biochemist; b. Neu Sandez, Poland, June 28, 1913; came to U.S., 1941, naturalized, 1947; M.D., U. Vienna (Austria), 1938; D.S. (hon.), U. Chgo., 1968; m. Franziska Weiss, Aug. 25, 1945; 1 dau., Ann Racker Costello. Research asst. in biochemistry Cardiff (South Wales) Mental Hosp., 1938-40; research asso. dept. physiology U. Minn., 1941-42; intern, then resident Harlem Hosp., N.Y.C., 1942-44; asst. prof. microbiology N.Y. U. Sch. Medicine, 1944-52; asso. prof. biochemistry Yale U., 1952-54; chief div. nutrition and physiology Public Health Research Inst. City N.Y., 1954-66; Albert Einstein prof. biochemistry Cornell U., 1966—; mem. biochemistry study sect., div. research grants NIH, 1957-70; chmn. bd. sci. counselors Cancer Inst., 1975-76; 73d Christian A. Herter lectr., 1975; 10th Sir Frederick Gowland Hopkins Meml. lectr., 1975; Walker-Ames lectr., 1977. Recipient Warren Triennial prize Mass. Gen. Hosp., 1974, Nat. Medal Sci., 1976. Mem. Am. Soc. Biol. Chemists, Harvey Soc., Brit. Biochem. Soc., Nat. Acad. Scis., Am. Acad. Arts and Scis., AAAS. Author: Mechanism in Bioenergetics, 1965: A New Look at Mechanisms in Bioenergetics, 1976; editor: Membranes of Mitochondria and Chloroplasts, 1970; Energy Transducing Mechanisms, 1975; editorial bd. Jour. Biol. Chemistry, 1959-72. Home: 305 Brookfield Rd Ithaca NY 14850 Office: Sect Biochemistry Wing Hall Cornell U Ithaca NY 14853

RACKLEY, AUDIE NEAL, editor; b. Oney, Okla., Oct. 11, 1934; s. Emmet Irvin and Jesse Lela (Morrison) R.; B.S. in Animal Sci., Okla. State U., 1957; m. Willie Mae Holsted, Aug. 26, 1956; children—Leicia Leann, Renee, Audette Marshelle. Mgr. Hissom A. and M. Farm, Okla. State U., Sand Springs, 1957; swine herdsman Okla. State U., 1959-61; field rep., advt. salesman Cattleman Mag., Ft. Worth, 1961-67; pub. relations and field rep. Am. Angus Assn., St. Joseph, Mo., 1967-70; dir. advt. Quarter Horse Jour., Amarillo, Tex., 1970-72, editor, mgr., 1972—; pres. Am. Horse Publs., 1976—. Served with AUS, 1957-59. Mem. Am. Horse Publs. (1st v.p. 1974—), Soc. Nat. Assn. Publs. (dir. 1978—, sec. 1979). Home: Rt 4 Box 58 Amarillo TX 79119 Office: PO Box 9105 Amarillo TX 79105

RACKLEY, CLIFFORD WALKER, oil co. exec.; b. Tifton, Ga., Sept. 19, 1923; s. Thomas B. and Datie (Ross) R.; B.Ch.E., Ga. Inst. Tech., 1949; m. Julia Susan Old, Feb. 6, 1945; children—Jennifer Rackley Sullivan, Clara Anne Rackley Eller, Sherrie Gail Rackley Webb. Supervisory process engr. Mobil Oil, Beaumont, Tex., 1949-56; sr. process engr. Tenneco Oil Co., New Orleans, 1956-60; sr. v.p. marketing Tenneco Oil Co., Houston, 1960-72; exec. v.p., refining and mktg., 1972-74, pres., 1974—, chmn. bd., 1978—. Served to 1st lt., USAAF, 1943-45. Decorated D.F.C., Air Medal. Mem. Am. Inst. Chem. Engrs., Am. Petroleum Inst., Profl. Engrs. La., Alumni Assn. Ga. Inst. Tech. Presbyterian. Office: PO Box 2511 1010 Milam St Houston TX 77001

RACKMAN, EMANUEL, rabbi, univ. pres.; b. Albany, N.Y., June 24, 1910; s. David and Anna (Mannesovitch) R.; B.A., Columbia, 1931, LL.B., 1933, Ph.D., 1953; rabbi, Yeshiva U., 1934, D.D., 1961; m. Ruth Sylvia Fischman, Dec. 28, 1930; children—Michael I., Bennett M., Joseph R. Rabbi, Congregation Shaaray Tefilia and Jewish Center, Far Rockaway, N.Y., 1946-67, Fifth Avenue Synagogue, N.Y.C., 1967-77; past univ. prof. polit. philosophy and jurisprudence Yeshiva U., also asst. to pres. and provost; prof. Judaic studies, cons. to chancellor on Judaic studies City U. N.Y., 1971-77; adj. prof. Jewish law N.Y. Law Sch., 1976-77; pres. Bar-Ilan U., Ramat-Gan, Israel, 1977—; pres. N.Y. Bd. Rabbis, 1955-57, Rabbinical Ct. Am., 1960-77; pres. Rabbinical Council Am., 1958-60, hon. pres., 1960-61; v.p. Religious Zionist America, 1959-61; chmn. commn. Jewish chaplaincy Nat. Jewish Welfare Bd., 1972-75; mem. exec. Jewish Agy. Israel. Served as chaplain AUS, World War II; col. USAF Res. Decorated Commendation ribbon with oak leaf cluster. Mem. Assn. Jewish Chaplains Armed Forces U.S. (past pres.) Author: Israel's Emerging Constitution, 1955; One Man's Judaism, 1970. Asso. editor Tradition, 1959—. Office: Bar-Ilan U Ramat-Gan Israel. *All my life I have striven to be preponderantly occupied professionally and avocationally with activities that are ends in themselves and not simply means.**

RACKOW, LEON LIONEL, psychiatrist; b. N.Y.C., Dec. 28, 1910; s. Hyman and Bertha (Barandes) R.; B.S., Pa. State Coll., 1932; M.D., U. Edinburgh, Scotland, 1936; m. Doris Starkman, Feb. 11, 1945; children—Eric Charles, Kenneth Mark. Intern, Kings County Hosp., Jewish Hosp., Bklyn., St. Peters Hosp., New Brunswick, N.J., 1936-38; practice medicine, specializing in psychiatry, Roanoke, Va., 1941-42, Coatsville, Pa., 1942-43, Northport, N.Y., 1943-44, Tuscaloosa, Ala., 1944-50, Montrose, N.Y., 1950—; staff physician VA Hosps., Roanoke, 1941-42, Coatesville, 1942-43, Northport, 1943-44; chief continued treatment service and acute intensive treatment service VA Hosp., Tuscaloosa, 1944-50; chief continued treatment service, asst. dir. profl. services, dir. profl. services and mgr. VA Hosp., Montrose, 1950-61, hosp. dir., 1961-74; dir. North Westchester Mental Health Clinic, also dir. trans. and geriatric service Westchester Community Mental Health Bd., 1974-77; instr. dept. psychiatry Med. Coll. Cornell U., 1951-56, asst. prof. clin. psychiatry, 1956-62, clin. asso. prof., 1962-70; prof. clin. psychiatry N.Y. Med. Coll., 1970—; dir. Sci. Seminar Henrik Hudson High Sch., Montrose. Served as maj., M.C., AUS, 1942-46. Diplomate Am. Bd. Psychiatry and Neurology. Fellow Am. Coll. Psychiatry, A.C.P.; mem. Westchester Country (dir.), Peekskill (dir.) mental health assns., Am. Hosp. Assn. (bd. govs. psychiat. hosp. sect.). Contbr. articles to sci. jours. Home: 3930 Oaks Clubhouse Dr Pompano Beach FL 33060

RACLIN, ERNESTINE MORRIS, banker; b. South Bend, Ind., Oct. 25, 1927; d. Ernest M. and Ella L. Morris; student St. Mary's Coll., South Bend, 1947; LL.D. (hon.), U. Notre Dame, 1978; L.H.D. (hon.), Converse Coll., 1974; m. O.C. Carmichael, Jr., Sept. 28, 1946; children—Carmen Carmichael Murphy, O.C., III, Ernestine Carmichael Nickle, Stanley Clark; m. 2d, Robert L. Raclin, July 22, 1977. Chmn., Marshall County Bank & Trust Co., Plymouth, Ind., 1976—, Bremen State Bank, 1976—, FBT Bancorp., Inc., South Bend, 1976—; dir. First Chgo. Corp., Peoples Gas Co. Trustee U. Notre Dame, 1973—, Converse Coll., 1976—, Housing Allowance Office, South Bend, 1978—; bd. govs. United Way Am., UWA Internat., 1973—; bd. dirs. Mich. Public Broadcasting, South Bend Jr. Achievement, 1978—. Recipient E.M. Morris Meml. award Ind. Acad. Mem. South Bend C. of C. (dir. 1977—; Woman of Yr. award 1970). Republican. Presbyterian. Clubs: Summit (South Bend); Ocean (Delray Beach, Fla.). Office: Suite 415 First Bank Bldg South Bend IN 46601

RACZ, ANDRE, painter, engraver, educator; b. Cluj, Rumania, Nov. 21, 1916; s. Simion and Ana (Rosenmann) R.; B.A., U. Bucharest, 1935; m. Claire Enge, May 25, 1962; children (by a previous marriage)—Juan Andres, Maria Simone, Ana Constanza. Came to U.S., 1939, naturalized, 1948. Teaching asst. Atelier 17, N.Y.C., 1944; dir. Academia Villavicencio, Santiago, Chile, 1950; lectr. Columbia, 1951-54, instr., 1954-56, asst. prof., 1956-61, asso. prof., 1961-67, prof., 1967—, chmn. dept. painting and sculpture, 1964-73, 75-77; vis. prof. U. Ky., 1960; one man shows N.Y.C., 1942-44, 46, 48, 49, 51, 53, 56, 57, 59, 61, 77, Phila., 1945, Washington, 1947, U. Tenn., U. Iowa, 1948, Green Lake, Wis., 1951, Rio de Janeiro, Brazil, 1946, Santiago, 1947-50, Buenos Aires, Argentina, 1949, Cordoba, Argentina, 1949, Valdivia, Valparaiso, Vina, Chile, 1957; one man show circulated by Am. Fedn. Art, 1948-51; retrospective show graphic work N.Y. Pub. Library, 1954-55, Museo de Bellas Artes, Santiago, 1957, U. Ky., Lexington, 1960; exhibited group shows Mus. Modern Art, Whitney Mus., Bklyn. Mus., Carnegie Inst., Phila. Mus., Library Congress San Francisco Mus., N.Y. Pub. Library, also internat. shows. France, Eng., Itlay, Spain, Germany, Austria, Norway, Poland, Yugoslavia, Switzerland, Argentina, Peru, Bolivia, Chile, Mexico, Venezuela, Australia; exhibited Fifty Years of Am. Art, Mus. Modern Arts show, Paris, London, Barcelona and Belgrade, 1955, 1st Inter-Am. Biennial in Mexico, 1958, 1st Biennial of Religious Art, Salzburg, Austria, 1958, Internat. Watercolor Biennial, Bklyn. Mus. Art, 1961, Nat. Inst. Arts and Letters, 1968, 25th Anniversary Rockefeller Print Room, Mus. Modern Art, 1975, Surrealism in Am. Art, Rutgers U., 1977, 50th Anniversary Atelier 17, U. Wis., 1978, Mus. Modern Art, Bklyn. Mus., Whitney Mus., N.Y. Pub. Library, Butler Inst., Smithsonian Instn., Library Congress, San Francisco Mus., Rosenwald Collection, Dept. State, Hartford Cath. Library, U. Ky., Albion Coll., Downer Coll., Columbia, Smith Coll., U. St. Louis, U. Minn., New Sch. for Social Research, N.Y.C., Phila. Mus., Tulsa Mus., Museum of Oslo (Norway), Museo de Cordoba, Argentina, Salzburg Mus., Austria, Nat. Gallery, Melbourne, Australia, Bibilotheque Nationale, Paris, U. P.R., Rio Piedras, others. Recipient Erickson prize for intaglio, 1953. Noyes prize, 1st prize for intaglio Soc. Graphic Artists, 1955, 1st prize Motive mag., 1957, purchase prize U. Ky., 1959; Guggenheim fellow for printmaking, 1956; Fulbright research scholar, Chile, 1957; Ford Found. Award, 1962. Mem. Am. Soc. Graphic Artists (past v.p.), Am. Assn. U. Profs. Author: The Flowering Rock, 1943; The Battle of the Starfish, 1944; The Reign of Claws, 1945; XII Prophets of Aleijandinho, 1947; Via Crucis, 1948; Mother and Child, 1949; Voz de Luna, 1951; Sal de Dunas,, 1953; Canciones Negras, 1953; Salmos y Piedras, 1955; Editor: Poemas de las Madres by Gabriela Mistral (Nobel prize 1945), pub. in 1950 with 63 of his drawings. Home: PO Box 43 Demarest NJ 07627 Office: 305 Dodge Columbia U New York City NY 10027

RADAKER, BYRON CLAIRE, mfg. co. exec.; b. West Freedom, Pa., Mar. 19, 1934; s. Ralph Jacob and Mary Grace (Kilgore) R.; B.S., Kent State U., 1959; m. Shirley Ann Hotchkiss, Nov. 28, 1953; children—Keith, Kelly, Kirsten, Kyle. Prodn. worker Gen. Tire and Rubber Co., Akron, Ohio, until 1959; with Gillette Safety Razor Co., from 1960; then with Allied Chem. Corp., until 1966; corporate v.p. Certain-Teed Products Corp., Valley Forge, Pa., 1966-70, exec. v.p., chief operating officer, 1971-72, pres., chief operating officer, 1972-74; v.p. planning Congoleum Corp., Milw., 1975-76, dep. chmn., 1976-77; pres., chief exec. officer, 1977-79, chmn., pres., chief exec. officer, 1979—, also dir.; dir. Curtis Noll Corp., Bath Iron Works Corp. Served with C.E., U.S. Army, 1954-56. Clubs: Union League of Phila.; Milw., Milw. Country. Home: 718 E Daisy Ln Fox Point WI 53217 Office: PO Box 1232 Milwaukee WI 53201

RADCLIFFE, GEORGE GROVE, life ins. co. exec.; b. Balt., Nov. 12, 1924; s. George G. and Elsie (Winter) R.; B.A., Johns Hopkins, 1947; grad. Advanced Mgmt. Program, Harvard Grad. Sch. Bus. Adminstrn., 1962; m. Bettie Howell, Feb. 10, 1951; 1 dau., Cynthia. With Balt. Life Ins. Co., 1947—, v.p. treas., 1963-69, exec. v.p., 1969-72, pres., 1972—, chief exec. officer, 1974—; dir. Md. Nat. Bank, Hutzler Bros. Co., Md. Nat. Corp.; trustee Md. Realty Trust. Mem. Greater Balt. Commn. Trustee Johns Hopkins U. Served with AUS, 1943-46. Mem. Am. Council Life Ins. (dir.), Delta Upsilon. Methodist. Clubs: Maryland, Harvard Business School, Center, Johns Hopkins (Balt.); Gibson Island (Md.). Home: 305 Weatherbee Rd Baltimore MD 21204 Office: Mt Royal Plaza Baltimore MD 21201

RADCLIFFE, REDONIA WHEELER, journalist; b. Republican City, Nebr.; d. Donnel F. and Lois (Woolman) Wheeler; B.A., San Jose (Calif.) State Coll., 1951; m. Melvyn J. Nunes, 1947 (div. 1949); 1 son, Melvyn D.; m. 2d, Robert C. Radcliffe, 1957. Reporter, women's editor, county editor The Salinas Californian, 1951-59; free-lance writer, Europe, 1959-66; reporter Washington Star, 1967-72; social editor, reporter Washington Post, 1972—. Mem. White House Corr. Assn., Sigma Delta Chi, Washington Press Club. Address: 1920 Valley Wood Rd McLean VA 22101

RADCLIFFE, ROBERT LANE, financial devel. exec.; b. Oak Park, Ill., Nov. 10, 1925; s. Barney S. and Virginia (Prather) R.; B.S., Bradley U., 1950; m. Nancy Reese, June 5, 1954; children—Kristy, Robin, Thomas. Owner, R.L. Radcliffe Co., Chgo., 1950-58; v.p., nat. field dir. Radio Free Europe Fund, N.Y.C., 1958-70; asso. Browning Assos. Inc., financial devel. cons. for instns., Newark, 1970-74; exec. dir. Overlook Hosp. Found., Summit, N.J., 1974-77, St. Luke's Founds., Milw., 1977—. Served with USNR, 1943-46; PTO. Mem. Tau Kappa Epsilon. Republican. Presbyn. Home: 1950 Limerick Ln Brookfield WI 53005 Office: St Luke's Founds 2900 W Oklahoma Ave Milwaukee WI 53215

RADCLIFFE, S. VICTOR, educator, business exec.; b. Cheshire, Eng., July 28, 1927; s. Andrew Hunter and Ellen (Waring) R.; B. Engring., U. Liverpool (Eng.), 1948, Ph.D. (Univ. fellow 1953-56), 1956; m. Wanda (Reid) Koskinen, June 4, 1977. Came to U.S., 1956. Research metallurgist Rylands Bros., Ltd., also Lancashire Steel Corp., 1948-53; research asso. Mass. Inst. Tech., 1958-62; research mgr. Man Labs., Inc., Cambridge, Mass., 1961-63; mem. faculty Case Western Res. U., 1963-75, prof. metallurgy, 1966-75, head div. metallurgy and materials sci., 1969-75; sr. policy analyst Office Sci. Adviser to Pres., Washington, 1974-75; sr. fellow Resources for the Future, Washington, 1976-79; v.p. Nat. Forge Co., N.Y.C., 1979—; dir. IMT Inc., Boston; cons. to industry and internat. orgns., 1959—. Mem. study group sci. and engring. edn. in Mexico, Ford Found, 1966; dir., survey of material, sci. and engring., Nat. Acad. Sci., 1971-74; mem. adv. bd., polymer engring. and sci., Apollo Lunar Sci. Program. Recipient Waverly Gold medal award, 1961; chartered engr. Fellow Instn. Metallurgists; mem. Am. Chem. Soc., Am. Phys. Soc., Am. Inst. Mining, Metall. and Petrolrum Engrs., Nat. Assn. Bus. Economists. Club: Cosmos. Author research papers and articles. Home: 2101 Connecticut Ave NW Washington DC 20008 Office: Resources for Future 1755 Massachusetts Ave NW Washington DC 20036

RADDALL, THOMAS HEAD, SR., author; b. Kythe, Kent, Eng., Nov. 13, 1903; s. Thomas Head and Ellen (Gifford) R.; student public and pvt. schs., Eng., N.S., Can.; LL.D. (hon.), Dalhousie U., Halifax, N.S., 1949, St. Francis Xavier U., Antigonish, N.S., 1973; Litt.D. (hon.), St. Mary's U., Halifax, 1969; D.C.L. (hon.), U. King's Coll., Halifax, 1972; m. Edith Margaret Freeman, June 9, 1927; children—Thomas Head, Frances Raddall Dennis. Wireless officer Can. Merchant Marine, 1918-22; accountant Mersey Paper Co., Liverpool, N.S., Can., 1923-38; novels: His Majesty's Yankees, 1942, Roger Sudden, 1945, Pride's Fancy, 1946, The Nymph and The Lamp, 1953, The Wings of Night, 1957, The Governor's Lady, 1960, Hangman's Beach, 1960; short story collections: Pied Piper of Dipper Creek, 1939, Tambour and Other Stories, 1945, The Wedding Gift and Other Stories, 1947, A Muster of Arms and Other Stories, 1954, Footsteps on Old Floors, 1968; history books: West Novas, 1948, Halifax, Warden of the North, 1950, The Path of Destiny, 1957, The Rover, 1958. Served with West N.S. Regit., 1942-43. Decorated officer Order Can. Fellow Royal Soc. Can. Mem. United Ch. of Canada. Club: Royal Can. Legion. Home and Office: 44 Park St Liverpool NS B0T 1K0 Canada

RADELL, NICHOLAS JOHN, mgmt. cons.; b. South Range, Mich., Sept. 2, 1930; s. Nicholas and Anna (Pekkala) R.; B.S., U. Mich., 1952, M.B.A., 1956; m. Patricia A. Seibert, June 21, 1952; children—Susan Diane, Sally Anne, Nicholas Steven. Application engr. Square D Co., Detroit, 1954-55; mem. firm Touche, Ross, Bailey & Smart, C.P.A.'s, Detroit, 1956-61; with Cresap, McCormick & Paget Inc., N.Y.C., Chgo., 1961—, partner, Chgo., 1967-69, v.p., 1969—, region mgr., 1971-75, mgr. internat. ops., 1975—; v.p. Engrs. Joint Council, 1979. Served to 1st lt. USAF, 1952-54. C.P.A., Mich.; registered profl. engr., Mich. Mem. Soc. Mfg. Engrs. (bd. dirs., nat. v.p. 1971, pres. 1973) Am. Inst. Indsl. Engrs., Am. Inst. C.P.A.'s, Phi Gamma Delta. Presbyn. Clubs: Chicago, Mid-Day, Metropolitan, Indian Hill. Contbg. author: Handbook of Process Planning and Estimating, 1962; Scientific Inventory Management, 1963; Introduction to Manufacturing Management, 1969. Home: 328 Linden St Winnetka IL 60093 Office: 30 N La Salle St Chicago IL 60602

RADER, DAVID MARTIN, athlete; b. Claremore, Okla., Dec. 26, 1948; s. Porter Martin and Delvia May (Sellers) R.; student Bakersfield Coll.; children—Shelley Lynnette, David Lance. Formerly catcher Salt Lake City Baseball Club, Fresno Baseball Club, Amarillo Giants, Phoenix Giants; catcher San Francisco Giants, St. Louis Cardinals, 1976-77, Chgo. Cubs, 1978-79, Phila. Phillies, 1979—; pres. Con Cast Co., Inc., realtor. Served with AUS. Named Outstanding Athlete, All-League Football-Baseball; Sporting News Rookie of Yr., Nat. League, 1972. Mem. Ch. Christ. Office: care Phila Phillies PO Box 7575 Philadelphia PA 19101*

RADER, DOTSON CARLYLE, author, journalist; b. Evanston, Ill., July 25, 1942; s. Paul Carlyle and Lois (Schacht) R.; student Columbia, 1962-68. Editor, Defiance: A Radical Rev. (Warner Communications, Inc.), 1969-71; contbg. editor Evergreen Rev., 1969-73, Esquire, N.Y.C., 1973—, N.Y. mag., 1977—. Mem. sponsoring bd. New Politics, 1972—; host Free Time Show, WNET-TV, N.Y.C., 1972-73. Mem. Student Peace Union, 1961-63, Students for a Democratic Soc., 1964-69, War Resisters League, 1970—; pres. Humanitas, Columbia, 1963-67; vice chmn. Peoples Coalition for Peace and Justice, 1972. Mem. PEN. Author: I Ain't Marchin' Anymore!, 1969; Government Inspected Meat and Other Fun Summer Things, 1971; Blood Dues, 1973; (screenplay) The Bronze Lily, 1974; The Dream's on Me: A Love Story, 1976; Miracle, 1978.

RADER, LLOYD EDWIN, state govt. ofcl.; b. Bridgeport, Okla., Aug. 30, 1906; s. Otis Zimmerman and Bedia Sarah (Boston) R.; student Southwestern State Coll., Weatherford, Okla., 1924-26; LL.B., Oklahoma City U., 1956; m. Ruth Schreiner, Sept. 9, 1930; 1 son, Lloyd Edwin. Asst. sec. Weatherford Bldg. and Loan Assn., 1925-31; relief dir. Custer County, Okla., 1932-33; chief auditor sales tax div. Okla. Tax Commn. 1933-35, dir. gen. enforcement, 1935-39; engaged in gen. mercantile, hardware, lumber, implement and constrn. bus., also rancher, 1939-51; dir. pub. welfare Okla., 1951—. Treas. Okla. Capitol Improvement Authority, 1959—. Mem. Adv. bd. Children's Convalescent Hosp., Bethany, Okla., 1959—; mem. Okla. Mental Health Planning Com., 1965—; mem. President's Com. on Mental Retardation, 1966-76. Named to Okla. Hall of Fame, 1966; recipient 1st ann. award for distinguished service to state govt. Nat. Govs.' Conf., 1977. Mem. Am. Pub. Welfare Assn. (treas. 1965—), Okla. Health and Welfare Assn., Nat. Assn. Tng. Schs. Assn. State Welfare Dirs. and Adminstrs. (exec. council 1953-76, Exec. Dir.'s award 1975), Democrat. Mem. Disciples of Christ Ch. Mason. Home: 6413 N Harvard Ave Oklahoma City OK 73132 Office: Sequoyah Mel Office Bldg Oklahoma City OK 73125

RADER, LOUIS T., corp. exec., educator; b. Frank, Can., Aug. 24, 1911; s. Italo and Louise (Bonamico) R.; B.S., U. B.C., 1933; Ph.D. in Elec. Engring., Calif. Inst. Tech., 1938; m. Constance Wayland, Sept. 10, 1938; children—Louis Albert, John Newton. Came to U.S., 1934, naturalized, 1940. Engr. Gen. Electric Co., 1937-45; prof., head dept. elec. engring. Ill. Inst. Tech., 1945-47; with Gen. Electric Co., 1947-59, gen. mgr. splty. control div., 1951-59; v.p., dir. ITT, N.Y.C., 1959-61; group v.p. U.S. Commercial, 1961—; pres. Univac div. Sperry Rand Corp., N.Y.C., 1962-64; v.p., gen. mgr. Indsl. Process Control div. Gen. Electric Co., N.Y.C., 1964-69; prof. elec. engring. U. Va., 1969—, prof., grad. sch. business, 1969—; vis. com. div. engring. and applied sci. Calif. Inst. Tech., 1968-75; dir. Smith's Transfer Corp., Verona, Va. Trustee, Taft Inst. Govt., N.Y., 1969—, Human Resources Research Orgn., Alexandria, Va., 1969-79; mem. adv. com. Presdl. Adminstrn. Services Reorgn. Project, 1978. Recipient Alumni distinguished service award Calif. Inst. Tech., 1966. Fellow IEEE; mem. Am. Soc. Engring. Edn., Nat. Acad. Engring., Newcomen Soc., Sigma Xi, Tau Beta Pi, Beta Gamma Sigma, Eta Kappa Nu. Club: University (N.Y.C.). Home: 1200 Boxwood Circle Waynesboro VA 22980 Office: Darden Grad Sch Bus Box 6550 U Va Charlottesville VA 22906

RADEST, HOWARD BERNARD, educator, clergyman; b. N.Y.C., June 29, 1928; s. Louis and Gussie (Permison) R.; A.B., Columbia, 1949, Ph.D., 1971; M.A. (Hillman fellow 1950), New Sch. Social Research, 1951; m. Rita Stollman, Dec. 22, 1951; children—Robert, Michael. Dir. youth activities N.Y. Soc. Ethical Culture, 1955-56; leader Ethical Culture Soc. Bergen County, Teaneck, N.J., 1956-64; leader Ethical Culture Movement, 1956—; mem. Frat. Ethical Leaders, 1958—; exec. dir. Am. Ethical Union, N.Y.C., 1964-70; asso. prof. philosophy Ramapo Coll., N.J., 1971-73, prof., 1973-79; dir. Ethical Culture Schs., 1979—; co-chmn., sec. gen. Internat. Humanist and Ethical Union, 1970—; asso. Am. Civilization seminar, Columbia U.; dir. Camp Elliott, Jeffersonville, N.Y., 1963, 64; cons. state based programs Nat. Endowment Humanities. Mem. bd. Encampment for Citizenship, 1963-71, Mental Health Assn. Bergen County, Bergen Co. Mental Health Bd., 1964-67; mem. bd. past treas., v.p. N.J. Welfare Conf., 1958-64; mem. bd., past pres. Health and Welfare Council Bergen County, 1956-64; bd. mgrs. Bergen Pines County Hosp., 1966-70. Bergen County (N.J.) Mem.. Democratic Com., 1970-71. Served with AUS, 1953-55. Mem. Com. Sane Nuclear Policy (sponsor N.J.) Am. Assn. UN, Am. Philos. Assn., AAUP (treas. N.J. council 1973-74), Soc. Advancement Am. Philosophy, Phi Beta Kappa. Author: Understanding Ethical Religion, 1958; On Life and Meaning, 1963; Toward Common Ground, 1969; To Seek a Humane World, 1971; also articles; editor: Ramapo Papers, 1976-79; International Humanism; editorial bd. Religious Humanism. Home: 2-10 32d St Fair Lawn NJ 07410

RADEWAGEN, FRED, orgn. exec.; b. Louisville, Mar. 20, 1944; s. Hobart Fred and Mildred Lillian (Carlsen) R.; B.A., Northwestern U., 1966; M.S., Georgetown U., 1968; m. Amata Catherine Coleman, Dec. 4, 1971; children—Erika Catherine, Mark Peter. Research asst. Republican Nat. Com., Washington, 1967-68; dir. mgmt. services Republican Presdl. Campaign and Inaugural Com., Washington, 1968-69; liaison officer Trust Terr. Washington, 1969-71; staff coordinator for territorial affairs Dept. Interior, Washington, 1971-75; asso. dir. govtl. and polit. participation programs C. of C. U.S., 1975-76, dir., 1976-79; dir. resource devel. Rep. Govs. Assn., Washington, 1979—; pres. Washington and Pacific Assos., 1975—; staff exec. Bus. Alliance for Congl. Action, 1975-77; lectr. Insts. for Orgn. Mgmt., 1977-79; exec. dir. Nat. Chamber Alliance for Politics, 1977-79; mem. U.S. del. UN Trusteeship Council, 1972. Mem. D.C. Young Republicans, 1968-69, 71, Everett McKinley Dirksen Rep. Forum, 1970-71; mem. Alexandria Rep. City Com., 1979—. Mem. Northwestern U. Alumni Assn. (bd. govs.), Nat. Capital Interfrat. Forum (past pres.), Delta Tau Delta (past pres. Washington alumni). Presbyn. Clubs: Ill. State Soc. (v.p.); Capitol Hill (life). Home: 103 E Luray Ave Alexandria VA 22301 also 1245 Taft Ave Berkeley IL 60163 also 1019 3d St Bay Vista DE 19971 Office: 310 1st St SE Washington DC 20003

RADFORD, EDWARD PARISH, JR., med. educator; b. Springfield, Mass., Feb. 21, 1922; s. Edward Parish and Irene (McBride) R.; grad. Phillips Exeter Acad., 1940; student Mass. Inst. Tech., 1940-43; M.D., Harvard, 1946; m. Nettie A. Garrison, Mar. 9, 1945; (div. June 1968); children—Martha, George, Donna, Catherine; m. 2d, Olivia Kolar, Aug. 10, 1968; 1 dau., Lilith. Intern, Geisinger Meml. Hosp., Danville, Pa., 1946-47; instr. physiology Harvard Med. Sch., Boston, 1949-52; asso. in physiology Harvard Sch. Pub. Health, 1952-55, asso. prof. physiology, 1959-65; physiologist E.I. du Pont de Nemours & Co., Inc., Newark, Del., 1955-59; prof. environmental health, physiology, head dept. environmental health U. Cin., 1965-68; prof. environmental medicine Johns Hopkins Sch. Hygiene and Pub. Health, Balt., 1968-77; prof. environ. epidemiology U. Pitts. Grad. Sch. Pub. Health, 1977—; cons. dept. anesthesiology Mass. Gen. Hosp., Boston, 1962-76. Mem. vis. com. to med. dept. Mass. Inst. Tech., 1968-70. Served with AUS, 1943-46, USAF, 1947-49. Mem. Am. Pub. Health Assn., Am. Physiol. Soc., Radiation Research Soc., Soc. Occupational and Environ. Health. Research in pulmonary and renal physiology, 1952-68; polonium and lung cancer from cigarettes, health aspects of environmental agts., 1963—. Home: 716 Delafield Rd Fox Chapel PA 15215

RADFORD, GENE ALLEN, photog. co. exec.; b. Jasper, Mo., Apr. 2, 1918; s. Arthur Webster and Merta Dell (Peterson) R.; A.B., Drury Coll., 1939; M.C.S., Dartmouth, 1941; postgrad. Mass. Inst. Tech., 1969; m. Betty Macdonald, Oct. 3, 1942; children—Sharon Radford Dorminey, Larry D. With Eastman Kodak Co., Rochester, N.Y., 1941—, mem. statis. dept., 1941-43, 46; treas. staff, 1947-59, asst. to treas., 1959-67, asst. treas., 1968-73, treas., 1973—; dir. Eastman Savs. and Loan Assn., Rochester, 1970—, chmn. bd., 1973—. Bd. dirs. YMCA, Rochester and Monroe County, 1969—, vice-chmn. bd., 1975-77; bd. dirs., finance com. Rochester Hosp. Service Corp. (Blue Cross), 1974—; trustee Drury Coll., 1968-72. Served with USNR, 1943-45. Mem. Am. Finance Assn., Financial Mgmt. Assn., Rochester Soc. Investment Analysts, Rochester C. of C., Pi Gamma Mu. Presbyn. (elder). Home: 30 Indian Spring Ln Rochester NY 14618 Office: 343 State St Rochester NY 14650

RADFORD, WESLEY E., utilities exec.; b. Portland, Oreg., Jan. 9, 1926; s. Ervin F. and Mildred Rose (Hollingberry) R.; student Occidental Coll., 1944, U. Redlands, 1945; B.S., Oreg. State U., 1949; m. Janet Hickox, Sept. 2, 1947; children—Juliane Radford Cross, Catherine Radford Warr. With N.W. Natural Gas Co., Portland, Oreg., 1949—, asst. treas., 1965-69, corp. sec., asst. treas., 1969—. Served with USNR, 1943-46, 51-53. Mem. Am. Soc. Corp. Secs. (pres. Pacific N.W. regional group 1971-72), Tax Execs. Inst. (past pres. Portland chpt.), Inst. Internal Auditors, Am. Gas Assn., Pacific Coast Gas Assn., Western States Assn. Tax Reps., Portland C. of C. Republican. Lutheran. Clubs: Aero, Internat. Home: 7358 SW Arranmore Way Portland OR 97223 Office: 123 NW Flanders St Portland OR 97209

RADIN, NORMAN SAMUEL, biochemist; b. N.Y.C., July 20, 1920; s. Joseph and Bertha (Sherson) R.; B.A., Columbia U., 1941, Ph.D., 1949; m. Norma Levinson, Dec. 23, 1947; children—Lon, Laurie. Asst. research chemist Nat. Def. Research Com., Carnegie Inst. Tech., 1942-45; research chemist Biochem. Inst., U. Tex., Austin, 1950-52; prin. scientist Hines Hosp., VA, Maywood, Ill., 1952-54, VA Research Hosp., Chgo., 1954-57; mem. faculty dept. biochemistry Northwestern U. Med. Sch., Chgo., 1952-60, asso. prof., 1957-60; research scientist Mental Health Research Inst., U. Mich., 1960—, prof. biol. chemistry, 1973—. NIH fellow, 1946-48; AEC fellow, 1949-50. Mem. Am. Soc. Biol. Chemists, Am. Soc. Neurochemistry, Internat. Soc. Neurochemistry, AAAS. Editor book in field. Office: 1103 E Huron Ann Arbor MI 48109

RADLER, WARREN S., lawyer; b. Mt. Kisco, N.Y., July 6, 1936; s. Hyman Joel and Freda R.; B.A., Cornell U., 1957, J.D., 1960; m. Leontine Van Lent, Sept. 1, 1973; children—Jennifer, James. Admitted to N.Y. bar, 1960, Ill. bar, 1979; trial atty. Dept. Justice, 1960-61; asso. firm Saperston, McNaughtan & Saperston, Buffalo, 1961-64; partner firm Saperston, Day & Radler, Buffalo, 1964-79, Reuben & Proctor, Chgo., 1979—. Bd. dirs. Buffalo Council on World Affairs, 1962-64, Buffalo Children's Aid Soc., 1962-64. Fellow Am. Coll. Trial Lawyers; mem. Am. Bar Assn., Erie County (N.Y.) Bar Assn., Erie County Trial Lawyers (bd. govs. 1974-76). Clubs: Mid-Day (Chgo.); Exec. Suite (Buffalo). Office: 11 S LaSalle St Chicago IL 60603

RADLEY, VIRGINIA LOUISE, ednl. adminstr.; b. Marion, N.Y., Aug. 12, 1927; d. Howard James and Lula (Ferris) Radley; B.A., Russell Sage Coll., 1949; M.A., U. Rochester, 1952; M.S., Syracuse U., 1957, Ph.D., 1958. Instr. English, Chatham (Va.) Hall, 1952-55; asst. dean students, asst. prof. English, Goucher Coll., 1957-59; dean freshmen, asst. prof. English, Russell Sage Coll., 1959-60, asso. dean, asso. prof. English, 1961-62, prof. chmn. dept., 1963-69; dean coll., prof. English, Nazareth Coll., Rochester, N.Y., 1969-73, provost for undergrad. edn., central adminstrn. State U. N.Y., Albany, 1973-74; exec. v.p., provost Coll. Arts and Scis., State U. N.Y., Oswego, 1974-77, acting pres., 1977-78, pres., 1978—; vis. prof. Syracuse U., summer 1957-58, Nazareth Coll., summer 1966; cons. N.Y. State Dept. Edn. Mem. Modern Lang. Assn. (chmn. regional sect. Romanticism 1968), English Inst., Pi Lambda Theta. Republican. Author: Samuel Taylor Coleridge, 1967; Elizabeth Barrett Browning, 1972; also articles. Home: Shady Shore Oswego NY 13126

RADNER, EPHRAIM, mfg. co. exec.; b. Springfield, Mass., Oct. 23, 1921; s. Max and Stella (Gottlieb) R.; B.A. summa cum laude, U. Mass., 1943; M.S., Mass. Inst. Tech., 1945; M.B.A. with distinction, Harvard, 1948; m. Babette Solomon, June 4, 1950; children—Judith May, James Mark, Wendy Herman, Nancy Lee. Small bus. adviser to investment group, 1948-49; mgmt. adminstrv. position Geophysics Research Directorate, Air Force Cambridge Research Center, Bedford, Mass. 1949-58; v.p., treas. GCA Corp., Boston, 1958-67, 58; sr. v.p. finance, 1967—, dir., 1970—. Trustee, chmn. audit com., vol. treas. Children's Hosp. Med. Center, Boston; past mem. parents' com. Harvard Coll.; bd. dirs. Associated Harvard Alumni, 1976-78. Served with USAAF, 1943-46. Mem. Am. Mgmt. Assn. (finance planning council), Am. Arbitration Assn. (panel arbitrators), Harvard Bus. Sch. Assn. (bd. govs. Boston 1974-75, N.E. area chmn., exec. council), Financial Execs. Inst., Greater Boston C. of C. (execs. club), Newcomen Soc. N.Am., Phi Beta Kappa. Clubs: Harvard, Treasurers' (Boston) (pres. 1973-74); Bankers, Harvard (N.Y.C.). Home: 116 Douglas Rd Belmont MA 02178 Office: GCA Corp Burlington Rd Bedford MA 07130

RADNER, GILDA, comedienne; b. Detroit, June 28; ed. U. Mich. Formerly with Second City company, Toronto, Ont., Can.; appeared in Can. performance of Godspell, also various CBC prodns.; wrote and performed Nat. Lampoon Radio Hour, appeared Nat. Lampoon Show, off-Broadway; regular on NBC's Saturday Night Live, 1975—; Broadway debut in Live from New York, 1979. Mem. AFTRA. Jewish.

RADO, LADISLAV LELAND, architect; b. Cadca, Czechoslovakia, Feb. 16, 1909; s. Hugo and Gertrude (Winter) R.; Architect-Engr. degree, Tech. U. Prague (Czechoslovakia), 1932; M.A. in Architecture, Harvard, 1940; m. Emilie Muller, June 16, 1952. Came to U.S., 1939, naturalized, 1946. Practice architecture in Brno, Czechoslovakia, 1932-39, Boston, 1939-44; partner firm Raymond, Rado, Caddy & Bonington, N.Y.C. and Tokyo, Japan, 1946—; prin. works include recreation and indsl. bldgs. Electrolux Corp., 1950, Reader's Digest bldg., 1951, apt. bldgs. for Am. embassy, Tokyo, 1953, Am. embassy, Djakarta, Indonesia, 1958, U.S. hdqrs. KLM Royal Dutch Airlines, N.Y.C., 1961, Municipal Water Works, Saigon, Vietnam, 1963, campus Cath. U. Nagoya, Japan, 1963, high sch. for Bd. Edn., N.Y.C., 1963, also chs. in Philippines and Bennington, Vt., works for U.S. armed forces in U.S. and overseas, cargo bldg. Brit. Overseas Airlines, Kennedy Internat. Airport, 1964, indoor Olympic swimming pool bldg. U.S. Mil. Acad., 1964, IBM Bldg., Poughkeepsie, N.Y., 1966, Seaboard World Airlines Cargo Terminal, J.F. Kennedy Airport, 1966, IBM Bldg., Rochester, N.Y., 1968, Fed. Office Bldg., Albany, N.Y., 1968, Greek Orthodox Ch., Flushing, N.Y., 1969, Hammarskjold Plaza Office Bldg., N.Y.C., 1969, engring. campus State U. N.Y. at Stony Brook, U.S. Embassy, Belgrade, Yugoslavia, Corporate Hdqrs. for Panasonic, Secaucus, N.J.; U.S. hdqrs. for Brit. Airways, N.Y.C., also ticket offices in N.Y.C., Washington, Boston; critic archtl. design, Yale, 1955-59. Recipient Progressive Architecture Design award, 1958. Fellow A.I.A. (First Honor award 1957); mem. Archtl. League N.Y. (Silver medal 1953). Club: Whippoorwill Country (Westchester, N.Y.) Home: 55 The Crossing Armonk NY 10504 Office: 201 E 42d St New York City NY 10017

RADOCK, MICHAEL, univ. adminstr., pub. relations exec.; b. Belle Vernon, Pa., July 17, 1917; s. Nicholas M. and Pauline (Radish) R.; A.B. magna cum laude, Westminster Coll., New Wilmington, Pa., 1942, Litt.D., 1965; M.S. in Journalism, Northwestern U., 1946; post-grad. Western Res. U., 1950-52; m. Helen A. Hower, Sept. 2, 1944; children—Robert Hower, William Michael. Reporter, Fayette City (Pa.) Jour., 1937-39; corr. for Pa. newspapers, 1937-39; reporter, sports editor Charleroi (Pa.) Daily Mail, 1942; dir. news bur., mem. journalism faculty Westminster Coll., 1942-45; dir. news bur., asst. prof. journalism Kent State U., 1945, asso. prof., dir. pub. relations, 1947-52, prof. journalism, 1952-53; ednl. relations rep. Ford Motor Co., 1953-55, mgr. pub. relations publs. dept., 1955-56, mgr. graphic and info. services, 1956-58, mgr. ednl. affairs, 1958-61; dir. univ. relations, prof. journalism U. Mich, 1961—, v.p. univ. relations, prof. journalism, 1963, v.p. univ. relations and devel., prof. journalism, 1969—; vis. prof. journalism U. Wyo., summer 1951; spl. radio-TV reporter covering nat. polit. convs., July 1952; newsman radio sta. WHBC, Canton, Ohio, summer 1946; cons. Ford Found., NSF, USIA. Pres. Kent Research Group, 1952; established Inst. Pub. Relations, 1947, exec. sec., 1947-49, Office Advancement Pub. Negro Colls. Bd. dirs. Detroit Press Club Found., R.R. Moton Meml. Inst., 1976—; trustee Green Hills Sch., 1967-71, Westminster (Pa.) Coll., 1970-72, 74—; steering com. Office of Inst. Research; Council U. Relations. exec. com. Nat. Assn. State Univs. and Land Grant Colls., 1968-73; Recipient Distinguished Service award Kent State U., 1965; Frank Ashmore award for distinguished service to edn., 1974. Mem. Pub. Relations Soc. Am. (accredited), Am. Coll. Pub. Relations Assn. (pres. 1968-69, trustee Council Advancement and Support Edn. 1973-74), Am. Alumni Council, Sigma Delta Chi, Sigma Nu. Presbyn. Rotarian. Clubs: Detroit Press; Grizzly Riders Internat. Editor The Coll. Pub., 1955-60. Contbr. to profl. and ednl. publs. Office: Univ Mich Ann Arbor MI 48109

RADOCK, MICHAEL, univ. adminstr., pub. relations exec.; b. Belle Vernon, Pa., July 17, 1917; s. Nicholas M. and Pauline (Radish) R.; A.B. magna cum laude, Westminster Coll., New Wilmington, Pa., 1942, Litt.D., 1965; M.S. in Journalism, Northwestern U., 1946; postgrad. Western Res. U., 1950-52; m. Helen A. Hower, Sept. 2, 1944; children—Robert Hower, William Michael. Reporter, Fayette City (Pa.) Jour., 1937-39; corr. for Pa. newspapers, 1937-39; reporter, sports editor Charleroi (Pa.) Daily Mail, 1942; dir. news bur., mem. journalism faculty Westminster Coll., 1942-45; dir. news bur., asst. prof. journalism Kent State U., 1945, asso. prof., dir. pub. relations, 1947-52, prof. journalism, 1952-53; ednl. relations rep. Ford Motor Co., 1953-55, mgr. pub. relations publs. dept., 1955-56, mgr. graphic and info. services, 1956-58, mgr. ednl. affairs, 1958-61; dir. univ. relations, prof. journalism U. Mich, 1961—, v.p. univ. relations, prof. journalism, 1963, v.p. univ. relations and devel., prof. journalism, 1969—; vis. prof. journalism U. Wyo., summer 1951; spl. radio-TV reporter covering nat. polit. convs., July 1952; newsman radio sta. WHBC, Canton, Ohio, summer 1946; ednl. cons.; cons. Ford Found., NSF, USIA. Pres. Kent Research Group, 1952; established Inst. Pub. Relations, 1947, exec. sec., 1947-49, Office Advancement Pub. Negro Colls. Bd. dirs. Detroit Press Club Found., R.R. Moton Meml. Inst., 1976-79; trustee Green Hills Sch., 1967-71, Westminster (Pa.) Coll., 1970-72, 74—, Ann Arbor Summer Festival, Inc., 1978—, Found. for Public Relations Research and Edn., Inc., 1978—; mem. exec. bd. Univ. Hosp., 1979—; steering com. Office of Inst. Research; Council U. Relations; exec. com. Nat. Assn. State Univs. and Land Grant Colls., 1968-73; mem. Bd. Fgn. Scholarships, 1975-79; mem. community adv. bd. St. Joseph's Mercy Hosp., 1977—; mem. fund raising mgmt. adv. com. New Sch. Social Research, 1978—. Recipient Distinguished Service award Kent State U., 1965; Frank Ashmore award for distinguished service to edn., 1974. Mem. Pub. Relations Soc. Am. (accredited; chmn. ednl. instns. sect. 1978-79), Am. Coll. Pub. Relations Assn. (pres. 1968-69, trustee Council Advancement and Support Edn. 1973-74), Nat. Soc. Fund Raising Execs., Sigma Delta Chi, Sigma Nu. Presbyn. Rotarian. Clubs: Travis Pointe Country, Ann Arbor, Detroit Press; University; Grizzly Riders Internat. Editor The Coll. Pub., 1955-60. Contbr. to profl. and ednl. publs. Home: 384 Orchard Hills Dr Ann Arbor MI 48104

RADOMSKI, JACK LONDON, scientist; b. Milw., Dec. 10, 1920; s. Joseph Elwood and Evelyn (Hansen) R.; B.S., U. Wis., 1942; Ph.D., George Washington U., 1950; m. Teresa Pascual, Feb. 19, 1971; children—Mark, Linda, Eric, Janet, Maria. Chemist, Gen. Aniline & Film Corp., Binghamton, N.Y., 1942-44; pharmacologist FDA, Washington, 1944-52, acting chief acute toxicity br., 1952-53; prof. pharmacology U. Miami, Coral Gables, Fla., 1953—; cons. WHO, Gen. Acctg. Office, EPA, HEW. Recipient Spl. award Commr. FDA, 1952. Mem. Am. Soc. Pharmacology and Exptl. Therapeutics, Soc. Toxicology, Am. Assn. Cancer Research, Internat. Assn. Biochem. Pharmacology. Contbr. articles to profl. jours. Home: Route 3 Box 311-D Andalusia AL 36420 Office: Dept Pharmacology U Miami Med Sch Miami FL 33101. *The single most important thing in life is to make a continuous, intensive effort to comprehend things as they really are, as distinct from as we wish them to be. Failure to perceive the world and everything in it accurately and objectively, admittedly a difficult and frequently fearful task, causes untold misery and misfortune to individuals, organizations and nations. Success in all endeavors is in direct proportion to the degree we achieve this goal.*

RADOMSKY, WILLIAM, corp. exec.; b. Osceola Mills, Pa., Sept. 9, 1933; s. Joseph and Elizabeth R.; B.A., Harvard U., 1956; M.B.A., U. Pa., 1964; children—Eric Olney, Charles Shaw. With Container Corp. Am., Oaks, Pa., 1958-62; fin. exec. Chrysler Corp., Highland Park, Mich., 1964-69; sr. v.p., chief fin. officer Comml. Credit Co., Balt., 1969—. Served with U.S. Army, 1956-58. Home: 5006 Hydes Rd Hydes MD 21082 Office: 300 St Paul Pl Baltimore MD 21202

RADOW, RAY SAUL, stock broker; b. Phila., Jan. 14, 1904; s. Bernard and Ray R. (White) R.; student N.Y.U., 1926-27; m. Evelyn Bernstein, Nov. 3, 1935; children—Marilyn J. (Mrs. Michael Stern), Roy Bernard. With Radow & McGuire, 1922-26, Townsend, Graff & Co., mems. N.Y. Stock Exchange, 1932-41, Eisle, King, Libaire & Stout, mems. N.Y. Stock Exchange, 1941-43; sr. partner Bruns, Nordeman, Rea & Co., mems. N.Y. Stock Exchange, N.Y.C., 1943-78, v.p., ltd. partner, 1978—. Pres. Radow Found.; mem. N.Y. Produce Exchange; mem. hearing bd. N.Y. Stock Exchange, 1972—; past pres., mem. fin. com. Civic Center Synogogue; mem. endowment fund com. Hill Crest Jewish Center; chmn. parents com. U. Pa., Queens County; financial adviser ZRW Cancer Fund. Clubs: Woodcrest Country (vice chmn. admission and membership bd., mem. admission bd., grievance bd.) (Syosset, N.Y.); Redman Club of St. Johns U. (dir. emeritus) (Jamaica, N.Y.); Aventura Country (North Miami, Fla.). Home: 3375 N Country Club Dr North Miami FL 33180 Office: 90 Worth St New York City NY 10013

RADUTA, HENRY EUGENE, writer; b. Maspeth, N.Y., Mar. 14, 1928; s. Walter and Elizabeth (Krupski) R.; B.S., N.Y. U., 1954. Freelance writer, 1947-52; mem. editorial dept. N.Y. News, 1952-54; with Chgo. Tribune-N.Y. News Syndicate, Inc., 1954-72, mgr. 1967-72; continuity writer comic strip Winnie Winkle, 1958—. Served with AUS, 1946-47. Home. Gray Gables Glen Gardner NJ 08826 Office: 220 E 42d St New York NY 10017

RADWAY, DONALD GUY, architect; b. New London, Conn., July 26, 1915; s. Guy Frank and Maude Esther (Greenwood) R.; B.Arch., Rensselaer Poly. Inst., Troy, N.Y., 1937; m. Margaret Isabella Greene, Apr. 27, 1940; children—Anne Hutton Radway Atchley, Stephen Woodruff. Archtl. designer Detroit Edison Co., 1937-43; structural test engr. Curtiss Wright Research Labs., Buffalo, 1943-45; with Lockwood Greene Engrs., Inc., N.Y.C., 1945—, dir., 1964—, v.p., 1968-74, sr. v.p., 1974—. Certified Nat. Council Archtl. Registration Bds. and Nat. Bur. Engring. Registration Bds. Fellow Am. Cons. Engrs. Council; mem. N.Y. State Soc. Architects, Constrn. Specifications Inst., ASTM, Theta Chi. Republican. Club: Union League (N.Y.C.). Home: 19 Magonk Point Rd Waterford CT 06385 Office: care Lockwood Greene Engrs 200 Park Ave New York City NY 10017

RADWAY, LAURENCE INGRAM, educator; b. Staten Island, N.Y., Feb. 2, 1919; s. Frederick and Dorothy (Segall) R.; B.S., Harvard, 1940, M.A., 1948, Ph.D., 1950; M.P.A., U. Minn., 1943; M.A. (hon.), Dartmouth, 1959; m. Patricia Ann Headland, Aug. 20, 1949; children—Robert Russell, Carol Sinclair, Michael Porter, Deborah Brooke. Jr. economist OPA, 1941; intern U.S. Bur. Budget, 1941-42, Nat. Inst. Pub. Affairs, 1941-42; teaching fellow govt. dept. Harvard, 1946-50; instr. govt. dept. Dartmouth, 1950-52, asst. prof. 1952-57, asso. prof. 1957-58, prof., 1958—, chmn. dept., 1959-62, 70-72, 77—, dir. Comparative Studies Center, 1963-68; cons. ODM, 1952; prof. Nat. War Coll., 1962-63; civilian aide to sec. army, 1962-70; mem. N.H. Hou. Reps., 1968-72. Chmn. Hanover Democratic Com., 1954-56; mem. N.H. Dem. Com., 1958-60, chmn. Platform Conf., 1959, 60, chmn., 1975-77; chmn. Grafton County Dem. Com. 1956-58; mem. Dem. Nat. Com., 1975-77. Bd. dirs. N.H.

World Affairs Council, 1955-57; bd. advisers Indsl. Coll. Armed Forces, 1958-62. Served from pvt. to capt., Transp. Corps, AUS, 1943-46. Pub. Adminstrn. fellow U. Minn., 1940-42, Social Sci. Research Council fellow, 1957. Mem. Council Fgn. Relations, Am. Polit. Sci. Assn. (nat. council 1965-67), Am. Soc. Pub. Adminstrn., Am. Assn. U. Profs., New Eng. Polit. Sci. Assn. (mem. com. 1959-60, pres. 1964-65), Phi Beta Kappa. Presbyn. Author: (with John W. Masland) Soldiers and Scholars, 1957; Military Behavior in International Organizations, 1962; Foreign Policy and National Defense, 1969. Home: 22 Occom Ridge Hanover NH 03755

RADY, JOSEPH JAMES, engring. co. exec.; b. N.Y.C., Oct. 4, 1899; s. Jacob J. and Rose (Swarz) R.; C.E., Cornell U., 1921; m. Bettye M. Clark, June 9, 1928. Owner, Joe J. Rady & Co. (now Rady & Assos. Inc.), Fort Worth, 1924—, pres., 1964-78, chmn. bd., 1964—. Bd. dirs. Panther Boys Club. Served with AUS, World War I. Named Engr. of Yr., Fort Worth Soc. Profl. Engrs., 1957. Fellow ASCE (hon. mem., pres. Tex. sect. 1964), Am. Cons. Engrs. Council; mem. Nat. Soc. Profl. Engrs., Chi Epsilon, Tau Beta Pi. Clubs: Rotary, Fort Worth, Colonial Country (dir.). Home: 2626 Simondale Dr Fort Worth TX 76109 Office: 400 Continental Life Bldg Fort Worth TX 76102

RADZIWILL, LEE BOUVIER, b. N.Y.C., Mar. 3, 1933; d. John Vernou and Janet (Lee) Bouvier; m. Stanislas Albert Radziwill, Mar. 19, 1959 (div. 1974); children—Antony Stanislas, Anna Christina. Office: 745 Fifth Ave New York NY 10022

RAE, CHARLOTTE, actress; b. Milw., Apr. 22, 1926; d. Meyer and Esther Lubotsky; B.S., Northwestern U.; m. John Strauss, Nov. 4, 1951 (div.); 2 sons. Broadway debut in Three Wishes for Jamie, 1952; other stage appearances include: The Threepenny Opera, The Golden Apple, The Littlest Revue, L'il Abner, The Beggars Opera, The Beauty Part, The New Tenant, Victims of Duty, Pickwick Papers, Henry IV (parts 1 and 2), Romeo and Juliet, Morning; Noon; Night, The Chinese and Dr. Fish, Come Back Little Sheba, Prettybelle, Whiskey, Boom Boom Room, The Time of the Cuckoo; film appearances include: Sidewinder 1, 1977, Rabbit Test, 1978, Hair, 1979; regular on NBC-TV series Diff'rent Strokes, 1978—; other TV appearances include: The World of Sholom Aleichem; Car 54, Where Are You?; The Immovable Gordons, Apple Pie, Sesame Street, The Rich Little Show, Hot L Baltimore, Queen of the Stardust Ballroom, The Triangle Factory Fire Scandal. Office: care Creative Artists Agy Inc 1888 Century Park E Suite 1400 Los Angeles CA 90067*

RAE, MATTHEW SANDERSON, JR., lawyer; b. Pitts., Sept. 12, 1922; s. Matthew Sanderson and Olive (Waite) R.; A.B., Duke, 1946, LL.B., 1947; postgrad. Stanford, 1951; m. Janet Hettman, May 2, 1953; children—Mary-Anna, Margaret, and Janet. Asst. to dean Duke Sch. Law, Durham, N.C., 1947-48; admitted to Md. bar, 1948, Calif. bar, 1951; asso. firm Karl F. Steinmann, Balt., 1948-49, Guthrie, Darling & Shattuck, Los Angeles, 1953-54; nat. field rep. Phi Alpha Delta Frat., Los Angeles, 1949-51; research atty. Calif. Supreme Ct., San Francisco, 1951-52; partner firm Darling, Hall, Rae & Gute, Los Angeles, 1955—. Vice pres. Los Angeles County Republican Assembly, 1959-64; mem. Los Angeles County Rep. Central Com., 1960-64, 77—, exec. com., 1977—, vice chmn. 17th Congl. Dist., 1960-62, 28th Congl. Dist., 1962-64; chmn. 46th Assembly Dist., 1962-64, 27th Senatorial Dist., 1977—; mem. Calif. Rep. State Central Com., 1966—, exec. com., 1966-67; pres. Calif. Rep. League, 1966-67. Served to 2d lt., USAAF, World War II. Fellow Am. Coll. Probate Counsel; academician Internat. Acad. Estate and Trust Law (exec. council 1974-78); mem. Am., Los Angeles County (chmn. probate and trust law com. 1964-66), South Bay bar assns., State Bar Calif. (chmn. state bar jour. com. 1970-71, chmn. probate com. 1974-75, exec. com. estate planning trust and probate law sect. 1977—, probate law cons. group Calif. Bd. Legal Splzn. 1977—), Lawyers Club of Los Angeles, Am. Legion (comdr. Allied post 1969-70), Legion Lex (dir. 1964—, pres. 1969-71) Air Force Assn., Aircraft Owners and Pilots Assn., Town Hall (gov. 1970-78, pres. 1975), World Affairs Council, Rotary Internat., Internat. Platform Assn., Phi Beta Kappa, Omicron Delta Kappa, Phi Alpha Delta (supreme justice 1972-74, elected to Disting. Service chpt. 1978), Sigma Nu. Presbyn. Clubs: Commonwealth, Chancery. Home: 600 John St Manhattan Beach CA 90266 Office: 523 W 6th St Los Angeles CA 90014

RAE, WESLEY DENNIS, educator; b. Minnewaukan, N.D., Aug. 12, 1932; s. Jesse Vernon and Agnes Bertha Johanna (Olson) R.; B.S., N.D. State U., 1954; M.S., U. Wis., 1957, Ph.D., 1961; m. Bette Jane Johnson, Oct. 17, 1958; children—Amy Irene, Jonathan Goodfellow. Asst. prof. English, Utica (N.Y.) Coll., Syracuse (N.Y.) U., 1961-65, asso. prof., 1965-69; asso. prof. English, chmn. dept. U. Mich., Flint, 1969-74, dean Coll. Arts and Scis., 1974-79, prof. English, 1979—. Author: Thomas Lodge, 1967. Home: 1500 Apple Ridge Trail Flint MI 48507 Office: U Mich-Flint Flint MI 48507

RAEBURN, ANDREW HARVEY, musical adminstr., record producer; b. London, July 22, 1933; came to U.S., 1964; s. Walter Augustus Leopold and Dora Adelaide Harvey (Williams) R.; M.A. in History, King's Coll., Cambridge (Eng.) U., 1958. Mus. dir. Argo Records Co., London, 1959-64; asst. to music dir., program editor Boston Symphony Orch., 1964-73; dir. artists and repertory New World Records, N.Y.C.,1975-79; artistic adminstr. Detroit Symphony Orch., 1979—; cons. music; radio and TV commentator; mem. faculty Boston U., 1966-67; condr. New World String Orch., 1978. Served with Royal Arty., Brit. Army, 1952-55. Author record liner notes Argo, RCA, Time-Life records, 1960-79, program notes Boston Symphony Orch., 1968-73. Home: 201 E Kirby Ave Detroit MI 48202 Office: Ford Auditorium Detroit MI 48226

RAEFF, MARC, educator, historian; b. Moscow, USSR, July 28, 1923; s. Isaak and Victoria (Bychowsky) R.; came to U.S., 1941, naturalized, 1943; Baccalaureat, Lycée, 1942; M.A., Harvard, 1947, Ph.D., 1950; m. Lillian Gottesman, Sept. 24, 1951; children—Anne, Catherine. From instr. to asso. prof. history Clark U., 1949-61; mem. faculty Columbia, 1961—, prof. Russian history, 1965—, Bakhmeteff prof. Russian studies, 1973—; vis. prof. or scholar U. Wash., 1952-53, Free U. Berlin, 1966, Sorbonne, Paris, 1960-61, Acad. Scis. USSR, 1965, 68, 72, Max Planck Inst. Für Geschichte, Göttingen, Germany, 1972, 74, All Souls Coll., Oxford, Eng., 1976. Served with AUS, 1943-46. Guggenheim fellow, 1957-58; Fulbright lectr. U. Paris, 1960-61; sr. research fellow Nat. Endowment Humanities, 1967-68, fellow, 1975-76. Author: M.M. Speransky-Statesman of Imperial Russia, 1957; Siberia and the Reforms of 1822, 1956; Origins of the Russian Intelligentsia, 1966; Imperial Russia-The Coming of Age of Modern Russia 1682-1825, 1971; contributor to Am. and European jours. Home: 479 Knickerbocker Rd Tenafly NJ 07670

RAEMER, HAROLD ROY, engring. educator; b. Chgo., Apr. 26, 1924; s. Leo and Fannie (Marx) R.; B.S., Northwestern U., 1948, M.S., 1949, Ph.D., 1959; m. Paulyne Barkin, Dec. 21, 1947; children—Daniel, Liane, Diane. Physicist, Bendix Research Labs., 1952-55; staff engr. Cook Research Labs., Chgo., 1955-60; sr. engring. specialist Sylvania Electronic Systems, Waltham, Mass., 1960-63, cons., 1963-70; mem. faculty Northeastern U., 1963—, prof. elec. engring., 1965—, chmn. dept., 1967-77; vis. lectr. Harvard, 1962, hon. research asso., 1972-73. Served with USAAF, 1943-46. Mem. I.E.E.E. (sr.), Am. Phys. Soc., A.A.A.S., Am. Soc. Engring. Edn., Sigma Xi, Pi Mu Epsilon, Eta Kappa Nu, Tau Beta Pi. Author: Statistical Communication Theory and Applications, 1968. Contbr. articles profl. jours. Home: 120 Noanett Rd Needham MA 02194 Office: Northeastern Univ Boston MA 02115

RAETHER, HOWARD CHARLES, assn. exec.; b. Milw., June 12, 1916; s. William Charles and Clara (Dix) R.; Ph.B., Marquette U., 1937, J.D., 1939; m. Sylvia Ulatowski, Nov. 8, 1941; 1 dau., Carol Ann Raether Wilker. Admitted to Wis. bar, 1939; individual practice law, 1939-43, 46-48; exec. sec., counsel Wis. Funeral Dirs. Assn., 1940-43, 46-48; exec. sec. Nat. Funeral Dirs. Assn., Milw., 1948-71, exec. dir., 1971—. Bd. dirs. Urban Day Sch., 1967-71. Served with USNR, 1943-46. Recipient Distinguished Civilian Service award Dept. of Army, 1970; Roblot award for internat. excellence. Mem. Am., Wis. bar assns., Am. Soc. Assn. Execs., Wis. Soc. Assn. Execs., Am. Pub. Health Assn., Wis. Pub. Health Assn., Marquette U. Alumni Assn., Am. Legion. Lutheran. Editor: Successful Funeral Service Practice, 1971. Author, editor numerous books in field. Home: 2614 LeFeber Ave Wauwatosa WI 53213 Office: 135 W Wells St Milwaukee WI 53203. *I believe in what I am doing or I do not do it.*

RAFELSON, BOB, film dir.; b. N.Y.C., 1933. Dir. films Head, 1968, Five Easy Pieces (Acad. award nominee for best picture), 1970, The King of Marvin Gardens, 1972, Stay Hungry, 1976; author for TV series Play of the Week; creator TV series The Monkees. Recipient N.Y. Film Critics award for Five Easy Pieces, 1970. Office: care Wolff 1400 N Fuller Ave Hollywood CA 90046

RAFELSON, MAX EMANUEL, JR., coll. dean, biochemist; b. Detroit, June 17, 1921; s. Max Emanuel and Lillian (Kay) R.; B.S., U. Mich., 1943; Ph.D., U. So. Cal., 1951; m. Trudy Diane Hellem, Mar. 31, 1973; children—Mark Thomas, Anne Elizabeth. Postdoctoral research fellow U. Stockholm (Sweden), 1951-52; asst. prof. biol. chemistry U. Ill. Coll. Medicine, Chgo., 1953-55, asso. prof., 1955-60, prof., 1961-70; v.p., asso. dean biol. and behavioral scis. Rush Med. Coll., Rush-Presbyn.-St. Luke's Med. Center, 1970-72, v.p., 1972—; John W. and Helen H. Watzek meml. chmn. biochemistry Prsbyn.-St. Lukes Hosp., Chgo., 1961—; vis. prof. U. Paris (France), 1960. Asso. mem. commn. influenza Dept. Def., 1961—. Served with USNR, 1943-46. Mem. Am. Soc. Biol. Chemists, Biochem. Soc. (London), Am. Chem. Soc., A.A.A.S., Société Chemie biologique, Sigma Xi. Author: Basic Biochemistry, 1965, 68, 71. Contbr. articles biochemistry, blood platelets, viruses, protein structure and metabolism to profl. publs. Home: 2246 N Seminary Chicago IL 60614 Office: 1725 W Harrison Pkwy Chicago IL 60612

RAFF, GILBERT, pub. co. exec.; b. Newark, May 7, 1928; s. Nathan and Rose (Silberstein) R.; B.S., N.Y. U., 1949, M.B.A., 1959; m. Cynthia Rae Freedman, June 7, 1953; children—Hilary, Merritt, David. Individual practice pub. accounting, Newark, 1954-55; partner Kosson, Ruby & Raff, Passaic, N.J., 1955-60, W.C. Heaton & Co., N.Y.C., 1961-63, Raff, Kuzmiak & Metsky, East Orange, N.J., 1963-72; exec. v.p. Littlefield, Adams & Co., Totowa, N.J., 1963-69, pres., chief exec. officer, dir., 1969—; dir. Berkeley Fed. Savs. & Loan Assn., Keats Pub. Co., New Canaan, Conn., Irish Acad. Press, Dublin, Ireland. Lectr. Pace U., 1955-59; instr. Fairleigh Dickinson U., 1959-60. Chmn. bd. trustees Pub. Industry Group Ins. Fund. Served with USAF, 1950-52. C.P.A., N.J., N.Y., Ill. Mem. Am. Inst. C.P.A.'s, N.J. Soc. C.P.A.'s. Clubs: East Orange Tennis; Manhattan. Home: 15 Canterbury Rd Livingston NJ 07039 Office: 81 Adams Dr Totowa NJ 07512

RAFF, JOSEPH ALLEN, pub. co. exec.; b. N.Y.C., Sept. 28, 1933; s. Bertram and Billie (Martin) R.; B.A., U. N.C. at Chapel Hill, 1955, postgrad., 1956-57; postgrad. Harvard, Ind. U., Ohio U.; m. Judy Ann Oberfelder, Aug. 5, 1959. Wire editor A.P., Charlotte, N.C., 1958; staff writer Burlington (N.C.) Times News, then Raleigh (N.C.) Times, Sports Illus., N.Y.C., 1958-61; editor Rome Daily Am., 1961; pres. Fielding Publs., Mallorca, Spain, 1961—; cons. internat. pub. relations. Decorated chevalier Ordre de Couteaux (France). Mem. Soc. Am. Travel Writers. Clubs: Overseas Press; Nautico de Puerto de Pollensa. Contbr. numerous articles to mags., newspapers. Home: PO Box 50 Pollensa Mallorca Spain Office: care Fielding Publs 105 Madison Ave New York City NY 10016

RAFFAEL, JOSEPH, artist; b. Bklyn., Feb. 22, 1933; student Cooper Union Sch. Art and Architecture, 1951-54; B.F.A., Yale, 1955; studied with Joset Albers; married; children—Matthew, Robert, Rachel, Reuben. One-man shows: Stable Gallery, N.Y.C., 1965, 66, 68, Reese Palley Gallery, San Francisco, 1970, Reese Palley Gallery, N.Y., 1972, Nancy Hoffman Gallery, N.Y., 1972, 73, 74, 76, 79, Mus. Contemporary Art, Chgo., 1973, Wichita Art Mus. (Kans.), 1970, U. Calif. at San Diego Art Gallery, 1971, U. Calif. at Berkeley Art Mus., 1973, John Berggruen Gallery, San Francisco, 1978, Barbara Fendrick Gallery, Washington, 1978; retrospective exhbn. San Francisco Mus. Modern Art, 1978, traveled to Des Moines Art Center, Joslin Art Mus., Omaha, Newport Harbor Art Mus., Denver Art Mus.; exhibited in group shows at Bklyn. Mus., Art Inst. Chgo., Guggenheim Mus., N.Y.C., Mus. Modern Art, Kent U., Corcoran Gallery Art, Washington, U. Ill., Champaign, Newport Harbor Mus. (Calif.), Whitney Mus. Am. Art, N.Y.C., Los Angeles Municipal Art Gallery, DeCordova Mus., Lincoln, Mass., Worcester Art Mus. (Mass.), others; represented in private collections and Metropolitan Mus., N.Y.C. Brooklyn Mus., Hirshhorn Mus., Washington, U. Calif. Berkeley Mus., Los Angeles County Mus. of Art, Long Beach Mus. (Calif.), Everson Mus., Syracuse, N.Y., Library of Congress, San Francisco Mus. Modern Art, Wichita Mus., Joslin Mus., Krannert Mus., Lowe Mus. U. Miami, Coral Gables, Calif. Coll. Arts and Crafts, Oakland, Chgo. Art Inst., Des Moines Art Center, Jacksonville Art Mus., Mus. Contemporary Art, Chgo., Mus. Fine Arts, St. Petersburg, Fla., Oakland Mus. Art, Phila. Mus. Art, Santa Barbara Mus., Toledo Mus. Art, Utah Mus. Fine Art, Va. Mus. Fine Arts, Richmond, Washington County (Md.) Mus. Fine Art, Whitney Mus. Am. Art, N.Y.C.; instr. U. Calif., Davis, 1966; instr. Visual Arts, N.Y.C., U. Calif. at Berkeley, summer 1969; prof. Calif. State U. at Sacramento, 1969-73. Fulbright fellow, Florence, Rome, 1958-60; Tiffany Found. fellow, 1961. Address: San Geronimo CA 94963

RAFFEL, LEROY B., real estate devel. co. exec.; b. Zanesville, Ohio, Mar. 13, 1927; s. Jacob E. and Anne M. (Oliker) R.; B.S., U. Pa., 1949; m. Shirley Balbot, Sept. 27, 1949; children—Kenneth, Janet, James, Nancy. Pres. Raffel Bros., Inc., Youngstown, Ohio, 1949-78; ret., 1978; pres. York Mahoning Co., Youngstown, 1950-64; pres. Arby's, Inc., Youngstown, 1964-70, chmn. bd., 1971-78; ret., 1978; pres. Brom Equity Devel., Inc., Youngstown, 1979—. Served with USNR, 1945-46. Home: 3511 5th Ave Youngstown OH 44505 Office: 3511 5th Ave Youngstown OH 44505

RAFFEL, SIDNEY, med. educator; b. Balt., Aug. 24, 1911; s. Saul and Leah (Katlan) R.; A.B., Johns Hopkins, 1930, Sc.D., 1933; M.D., Stanford, 1943; m. Yvonne Fay, Apr. 15, 1938; children—Linda, Gail, Polly, Cynthia, Emily. Staff dept. med. microbiology Stanford Sch. Medicine, 1935—, successively research asst., intr. asst. prof., asso. prof., 1947—, exec. head dept., 1953—, acting dean, 1964—; staff labs. Basel, Copenhagen, Stockholm; cons. VA Hosps., Palo Alto, Calif., City and County San Francisco Tb Sanatorium, Redwood City, Calif. Chmn. allergy and immunology study NIH, Guggenheim fellow, 1949-50; spl. NIH fellow U. Edinburgh, 1961-62. Mem. Am. Assn. Immunologists, Soc. Am. Bacteriologists, Soc. Exptl. Biol. and Medicine, Am. Trudeau Soc., Sigma Xi, Alpha Omega Alpha, Delta Omega. Author: Immunity, Hypersensitivity, Serology, 1953; Editor Ann. Revs. Microbiology, Am. Rev. Respiratory Diseases (until 1962), Proc. Soc. Exptl. Biology and Medicine (until 1957), Stanford Med. Bull., Bacteriological Revs. Home: 770 Santa Ynez St Stanford Univ CA 94305

RAFFERTY, MAX, univ. dean; b. New Orleans, May 7, 1917; s. Maxwell L. and DeEtta (Cox) R.; B.A., U. Calif. at Los Angeles, 1938, M.A., 1949; Ed.D., U. So. Calif., 1955; m. Frances Longman, June 4, 1944; children—Kathleen, Dennis, Eileen. Tchr., Trona (Calif.) Sch. Dist., 1940-48; prin. Big Bear High Sch., Big Bear Lake, Calif., 1948-51; dist. supt. schs. Saticoy (Calif.) Sch. Dist., 1951-55, Needles (Calif.) Sch. Dist., 1955-61, La Canada (Calif.) Sch. Dist., 1961-62; supt. pub. instrn. State of Calif. 1963-71; dean Sch. Edn., Troy (Ala.) State U., 1971—. Mem. Am. (Shankland Meml. Research award 1955), Calif. assns. sch. adminstrs., N.E.A., Calif. Tchrs. Assn. Lion, Rotarian. Author: Suffer, Little Children, 1962; Practices and Trends in School Administration, 1961; What They are Doing to Your Children, 1964; Max Rafferty on Education, 1968; Classroom Countdown, 1970; A Handbook of Educational Administration, 1975. Office: Troy State Univ Troy AL 36081

RAFFETY, THOMAS ALVA, JR., airport mgr.; b. Roseburg, Oreg., Dec. 13, 1916; s. Thomas Alva and Cora Etta (Bell) R.; student Willamette U., 1939-40, U. So. Calif., 1952-56, Inst. Govt., U. N.C., 1963; m. Dorothy Maxine Harris, Nov. 22, 1944. Spl. projects engr. City of Long Beach (Calif.), 1946-57, dir. aeros., 1958-61; airport mgr., Charlotte, N.C., 1962-66; dir. aviation San Antonio, 1967—, city mgr., 1977; 2d v.p. Airport Operators Council Internat., 1978-79; cons. Airport Security Procedures, Expo '74; instr. airport econs. Tex. A. and M. U. Bd. dirs. Charlotte Travelers Aid Soc., 1962-66, San Antonio Travelers Aid Soc., 1967-72. Served with C.E., U.S. Army, 1940-45; PTO, ETO. Named Airport Mgr. of Year, Calif. Assn. Airport Execs., 1962; recipient Franklin Achievement award Inst. Govt., U. N.C., 1963; registered profl. engr., Calif.; accredited airport exec. Mem. Am. Assn. Airport Execs., Airport Operators Council Internat., Nat. Fire Protection Assn. Office: San Antonio Internat Airport 9700 Airport Blvd San Antonio TX 78216

RAFFIN, BENNETT LYON, gen. contractor; b. Terre Haute, Ind., Jan. 3, 1918; s. Isidor D. and Florence L. (Levy) R.; A.B. in Engring., Stanford U., 1938, M.C.E., 1964; m. Caroline Louise Meyer, Dec. 14, 1939; children—Steven B., Thomas A. With Stone & Webster Engring. Corp., Boston, 1940-41. Barret & Hilp. gen. contractors, San Francisco, 1941-42, 46-51; exec. v.p. Rothschild & Raffin. Inc.. San Francisco, 1951-72, pres., 1972—; exec. v.p. Swinerton & Walberg Co., gen. contractors, 1973—; lectr. Stanford U. Bd. dirs. Children's Hosp.. Stanford, Hearing Soc. San Francisco. Served as lt. USNR, 1942-46. Fellow ASCE; mem. Assn. Gen. Contractors Am., Structural Engrs. Assn. No. Calif., Tau Beta Pi. Clubs: Family. Laked Merced Golf and Country, Spyglass Hill Golf. Office: 100 Pine St San Francisco CA 94111

RAFFMAN, RELLY, educator, composer; b. New Bedford, Mass., Sept. 4, 1921; s. Joseph and Mary Alice (Worswick) R.; B.A., Dartmouth, 1947; M.A., Columbia, 1949; postgrad. Ind. U., 1950-51; m. Rita LaPlante, Feb. 14, 1951; children—Diana, Nancy. Instr. music S.W. Mo. State Coll., 1949-50; prof. music Clark U., Worcester, Mass., 1954—, now George N. and Selma Jeppson prof. music. Served to comdr. USNR, 1942-45, 51-54. Decorated D.F.C. with oak leaf cluster, Air medal with 6 oak leaf clusters; recipient Ernest Bloch award, 1959. Composer: The Friendly Beasts, 1956; Triptich, 1957; Fye on Sinful Fantasy, 1959; Sonnet XXX, 1959; Come be my Love, 1959; In the Beginning, 1960; Shall I Compare Thee?, 1961; The Passionate Pilgrim, 1962; Farewell, Thou Art Too Dear, 1964; Jubilate Deo (Psalm 100), 1966; Matins, 1970; Sweet Was The Song, 1970; Virtue, 1975; The Three Ravens, 1975. Home: 209 Lovell St Worcester MA 01603

RAFKIN, ALAN, TV dir.; b. N.Y.C., July 23, 1928; s. Victor and Til (Bernstein) R.; B.S., Syracuse U., 1950; children—Dru, Leigh Ann. Actor, Robert Q. Lewis TV Show, 1955, daytime shows CBS-TV; dir. Verdict is Yours, 1960, Mary Tyler Moore Show, 1970-71, Sanford and Son, 1972, Bob Newhart Show, 1972-73, Rhoda, 1973, Mash, 1976-77, Love, American Style, 1970-71, Laverne & Shirley, 1977—; guest lectr. Bowling Green State U., 1975. Served with U.S. Army, 1950-52. Democrat. Jewish. Address: care Contemporary-Korman 132 Lasky Dr Beverly Hills CA 90212*

RAFSHOON, GERALD MONROE, mem. presdl. staff; b. N.Y.C., Jan. 11, 1934; s. Jack and Helen (Goodman) R.; B.J., U. Tex., 1955; m. Eden White Donohue, Mar. 3,1978; children by previous marriage—Susan, Patricia, Janet, Scott. Copywriter, Rich's Dept. Store, Atlanta, 1959; Southeastern advt. and publicity mgr. 20th Century Fox Film Corp., Atlanta, 1959-62; nat. advt. mgr. 20th Century Fox, N.Y.C., 1962-63; pres. Gerald Rafshoon Advt., Inc., Atlanta, 1963-77, chmn. bd., 1977-78; asst. to pres. U.S. for communications White House, Washington, 1978—; exec. producer NBC-TV Spl., 1978. Served to lt. (j.g.) USN, 1955-58. Democrat. Jewish. Office: The White House Washington DC 20500

RAFTERY, SYLVESTER FRANK, labor union ofcl.; b. St. Louis, Nov. 30, 1918; s. Lawrence Michael and Enid Vale (King) R.; student St. Louis U., 1950-53; m. Marjorie Jane Belt, May 24, 1941; children—Elizabeth Kathleen, Marjorie Jo, Barbara Sue, Mary Ann, Virginia Louise, James Patrick, Jane Marie. Affiliated with labor movement, 1935—; succesively bus. agt., fin. sec. Painters Local, St. Louis; mem. local apprenticeship com., del. confs., v.p. Glaziers Nat. Conf., gen. organizer, nat. coordinator apprenticeship and tng. for painters, sign painters, glaziers, auto glass workers, stained glass workers and carpet and linoleum layers, mem. nat. joint trade adv. com. Glass and Glazing Industry, labor mem. Nat. Joint Bd. for Settlement Jurisdictional Disputes, mem. screening com. internal disputes Bldg. Trades Dept. AFL-CIO; mem. joint jurisdictional com. Stained Glass Industry; lectr. ILO; mem. nat. apprenticeship com. metal trades dept. AFL-CIO; chmn. joint jurisdictional com. Gypsum Drywall Contractors Internat.; chmn. painting and decoration Nat. Joint Industry Promotion Program; gen. pres. Internat. Brotherhood of Painters and Allied Trades, Washington, 1965—; acting gen. sec.-treas. Brotherhood Painters; mem. exec. council AFL-CIO. Mem. steering com. Bldg. Research Inst.; rep. AFL-CIO at Canadian Labor Congress, Canadian Nat. Expn.; vice chmn. Histradut, Am. Trade Union Council of Nat. Com. for Labor Israel; sec. navy's rep. goodwill ambassador maritime trades dept., AFL-CIO to Latin Am. Trade Unions; mem. exec. bd. indsl. trades dept. AFL-CIO, v.p. bldg., constrn. trades dept., metal trades dept.; nat. appeals bd. Bldg. and Constrn. Industry, Dir. Union Labor Life Ins. Co. Mem. nat. adv. council Peace Corps; citizens adv. council White House Conf. Children and Youth. Democratic judge elections, Montgomery County, Md. Trustee George Meany Found.; bd. dirs. Am. Inst. Human Engring. Served with USNR, World War II. Mem. Nat. Planning Assn., Holy Name Soc. K.C. Office: Internat Brotherhood

Painters and Allied Trades 1750 New York Ave NW Washington DC 20006*

RAFTON, MICHAEL GEORGE, banker; b. Wilmington, Del., Mar. 30, 1924; s. George Zografos and Aspasia R.; A.B., Dickinson Coll., 1947; LL.B. with honors (Univ. scholar), U. Calif., 1950; m. Jennie Tripli, May 18, 1946; children—Philip, Aleta, Karen, James. Admitted to Calif. bar, 1951; research atty. to Justice Roger Traynor, Calif. Supreme Ct., 1950-51; practiced in Oakland, Calif., 1951-58; owner, operator investment counseling co., Oakland, 1958-61; mgr., partner, then pres. Calif. Cargo Containers, from 1961; dir., chmn. bd. Central Bank, N.A., Oakland, 1965—, pres., 1966—. Trustee, Philos. Research Soc.; bd. regents CBN U., Virginia Beach, Va. Served with USAAF, 1943-46. Mem. Calif., Am. bankers assns., World Bus. Council, Order Coif, Phi Beta Kappa. Author: Homeowner's Property Tax Guide. Office: 301 20th St Oakland CA 94612

RAGAN, DAVID, pub. co. exec.; b. Jackson, Tenn., Aug. 26, 1925; s. Amos and Esther Lee (Tacker) R.; B.A. in English, Union U., Jackson, 1947; M. Theatre Arts, Calif. Sch. Theatre, 1950; m. Violet Claire Sills, Dec. 27, 1948; children—David Nathaniel, Sarah Sills, Jennifer Leigh. Radio writer Grand Central Sta., 1950; syndicated columnist Hollywood South Side, 1951; mng. editor Tele-Views mag., 1952; free lance writer, 1952-57, 74-77; editor TV and Movie Screen, Sterling Group, Inc., N.Y.C., 1957-61; mng. editor Motion Picture mag. Fawcett Pub. Co., N.Y.C., 1961-64; editor TV Radio Mirror, Macfadden-Bartell Pub. Co., N.Y.C., 1964-71; pub., editorial dir. Movie Digest, Words and Music, Planet mags. Nat. Periodical Publs., Warner Communications, N.Y.C., 1971-74; editorial dir. Photoplay, Motion Picture, TV Mirror mags. Macfadden Women's Group, N.Y.C., 1977-79; entertainment editor Globe Nat. Weekly, Greenwich, Conn., 1979—. Served with U.S. Army, 1952-54. Mem. Screen Actors Guild, TV Acad., Alpha Tau Omega, Tau Kappa Alpha. Republican. Presbyterian. Author: Who's Who in Hollywood 1900-1976, 1977. Contbr. articles to profl. jours. Home: 1230 Park Ave New York NY 10028

RAGAN, KEITH WESLEY, lawyer; b. Atlanta, Ill., Jan. 15, 1924; s. Raye and Edith (Branan) R.; A.B., DePauw U., 1948; J.D., Northwestern U., 1951; m. Lorraine Ann Gutz, Sept. 20, 1958; children—David W., Peter J., John Raye, Susan Lorraine. Admitted to Ill. bar, 1951, Ariz. bar, 1953; individual practice, Springfield, Ill., Phoenix, 1951-54; partner Ragan & Rehnquist, Phoenix, 1955-56, Carson, Messinger, Elliott, Laughlin & Ragan, Phoenix, 1957—. Served with AUS, 1943-46. Mem. State Bar Ariz., Ill., Am. bar assns. Democrat. Methodist. Home: 6638 N 40th St Phoenix AZ 85018 Office: 3550 N Central St Phoenix AZ 85012

RAGAN, ROY ALLEN, editor; b. Indpls., Sept. 9, 1929; s. Paul Elden and Nora Elvira (Merritt) R.; B.A. in Sociology, Ind. U., 1956; m. Frankie M. Jones, Dec. 11, 1974; children—Paul Allen, Kevin Linder, Sheryl Ann, Mark Ray, Gregory Reese. Agt., Lincoln Nat. Life Ins. Co., Indpls., 1957-60; asst. editor Rough Notes Publishing Co., Indpls., 1960-64; tchr. 6th grade pub. schs., Indpls., 1964-67; mng. editor Rough Notes Pub. Co., 1967-70, editor, 1970—; freelance copywriter, editor. Active local Boy Scouts Am., 1968—. Vice pres., bd. dirs. PSI, Indpls., extrasensory perception and other parapsychol. phenomena. Served with AUS, 1948-52. Mem. Nat. Assn. Life Underwriters, Gen. Agts. and Mgrs. Assn., Internat. Assn. Health Underwriters, Nat. Writers Club. Republican. Presbyn. Mason. Club: Toastmasters. Home: 5669 Whitcomb Terr Indianapolis IN 46224 Office: 1200 N Meridian St Indianapolis IN 46204

RAGAN, SAMUEL TALMADGE, newspaper editor; b. Berea, N.C., Dec. 31, 1915; s. William Samuel and Emma Clare (Long) R.; A.B., Atlantic Christian Coll., 1936, Litt.D., 1972; m. Marjorie Usher, Aug. 19, 1939; children—Nancy, Ann Talmadge. Newspaperman in N.C. and Tex., 1936—; mng. editor, author column Southern Accent in Raleigh (N.C.) News and Observer, 1948-69; exec. editor Raleigh News and Observer, also Raleigh Times, 1957-69; editor, pub. The Pilot, Southern Pines, N.C., 1969—; sec. N.C. Dept. Arts, Culture and History, 1972-73; conductor program, commentator sta. WTVD, Durham, 1969—; spl. lectr. contemporary issues N.C. State U., 1959-68, dir. Writer's Workshop, 1963—; instr. creative writing St. Andrews Coll., 1970—, Sandhills Coll.; 1969—; cons. editor St. Andrews Rev., Pembroke Mag. Pres. Friends Coll., Inc., N.C. State, 1961-62; mem. N.C. Library Resources Com.; mem. N.C. Govt. Reorgn. Commn., 1970—; moderator N.C. Writers Forum of Charlotte, 1963—. Trustee N.C. Sch. Arts, 1963-72; mem. N.C. Adminstrn. of Justice Council, 1964—; bd. dirs. N.C. Symphony Soc. Served with AUS, 1943-46; PTO. Recipient N.C. Tercentenary Poetry award, 1963, spl. citation for contbns. to journalism Atlantic Christian Coll.; Distinguished Service medal DAR, 1974; Morrison award for contbns. to arts in N.C., 1976; N.C. award for achievements in arts, 1979. Mem. N.C. Lit. Forum (moderator 1956—), N.C. Writers Conf. (chmn. 1962-63), Eastern N.C. (past pres.), N.C. (pres. 1973-74) press assns., Asso. Press Mng. Editors Assn. (dir. gen. chmn. continuing studies 1961, sec. 1962, v.p. 1963, pres. 1964), Am. Soc. Newspaper Editors (dir., chmn. freedom of info. com. 1968), Roanoke Island Hist. Soc. (dir.), N.C. News Council (past pres.), N.C. Arts Council (chmn. 1967-72), Am. Newspaper Pubs. Assn., N.C. Lit. and Hist. Assn. (pres. 1977), Sigma Delta Chi. Democrat. Presbyn. Clubs: Sandhills Kiwanis (Southern Pines). Author: (collected poems) The Tree in the Far Pasture, 1964; To the Water's Edge, 1971; The Democratic Party: Its Aims and Purposes, 1961; The New Day, 1964; Free Press and Fair Trial, 1967; (with Elizabeth S. Ives) Back to Beginnings, 1969. Contbg. editor World Book Ency., 1964—. Author articles, poems. Home: 255 Hill Rd Southern Pines NC 28387 Office: 145 W Pennsylvania Ave Southern Pines NC 28387

RAGANO, FRANK PAUL, army officer; b. Pitts., Sept. 7, 1928; s. Joseph James and Genevieve Theresa R.; B.S.E., Duquesne U., 1950; M.B.A., Syracuse U., 1964; grad. Command and Gen. Staff Coll., U.S. Army War Coll.; m. Elizabeth Emma Armstrong, July 3, 1954; children—Joseph, Christina, David, John. Enlisted U.S. Army, 1950, advanced through grades to maj. gen.; mem. faculty Indsl. Coll. Armed Forces, 1969-70, U.S. Army War Coll., 1970-72; project mgr. 2.75 rocket system, Picatinny Arsenal, N.J. and Redstone Arsenal, Ala., 1972-74, mgr. copperhead laser projectile project, Rock Island Arsenal, Ill., 1974-76, project mgr. U.S. Roland missile system, Redstone Arsenal, 1976-78, comdg. gen. U.S. Army Missile Research and Devel. Command, 1978-79; dep. insp. gen. U.S. Army, Falls Church, Va., 1979—; asst. lectr. George Washington U. Pres. Ravensworth Civic Assn., Springfield, Va., 1969-70. Decorated Legion of Merit with 2 oak leaf clusters, Meritorious Service medal, Joint Staff Service medal, Army Commendation medal with oak leaf cluster, Air medal with 4 oak leaf clusters. Mem. Am. Def. Preparedness Assn., Assn. U.S. Army, Soc. Logistics Engrs., U.S. Army Comptrollers. Republican. Roman Catholic. Club: K.C. Author articles on rocketry. Home: 10025 Nadina Circle Huntsville AL 35803 Office: 5611 Columbia Pike NASSIF Bldg Room 332 Falls Church VA 22041. *The impact of fire on darkness is of small note compared to the visibility and vision man enjoys by working together.*

RAGG, THEODORE DAVID BUTLER, bishop; b. Trail, B.C., Can., Nov. 23, 1919; s. Harry Richard and Winnifred Mary (Groves) R.; B.A., U. Toronto, 1947; L.Th., Trinity Coll., Toronto, 1950, B.D., 1951, D.D. (hon.), 1975; D.D. (hon.) Huron Coll., London, Ont., 1975; m. Dorothy Mary Lee, Jan. 24, 1945; children—Margaret Lee, David Mark, Maxine Elizabeth. Ordained deacon Anglican Ch. Can., 1949, priest, 1950; asst., then vicar chs. in Ont., Sask. and B.C., 1951-66; archdeacon of Saugeen, rector St. George's, Owen Sound, Ont., 1967-73; suffragan bishop of Huron, London, 1974, bishop, 1974—. Served with RCAF, 1941-45. Home: 25 Cherokee Rd London ON N6G 2N7 Canada Office: 4th Floor 220 Dundas St London ON N6A 1H3 Canada

RAGGIO, LOUISE BALLERSTEDT (MRS. GRIER H. RAGGIO), lawyer; b. Austin, Tex., June 15, 1919; d. Louis F. and Hilma (Lindgren) Ballerstedt; B.A., U. Tex., 1939; student Am. U. Washington, 1939-40; J.D., So. Methodist U., 1952; m. Grier H. Raggio, Apr. 19, 1941; children—Grier, Thomas, Kenneth. Intern, Nat. Inst. Pub. Affairs, Washington, 1939-40; asst. dist. atty. Dallas County, Tex., 1954-56; partner Raggio and Raggio, 1956—. Sec., Gov.'s Commn. on Status Women, 1970-71. Recipient citation for law reform State Bar Tex., 1967, Zonta award, Bus. and Profl. Womens Club award, So. Meth. U. Alumni award. Mem. Am. Bar Assn. (chmn. family sect. 1975-76), State Bar Tex. (chmn. family law sect. 1965-67, dir. 1979—), Am. Acad. Matrimonial Lawyers (gov. 1973—), Bus. and Profl. Women's Club (pres. Town North 1958-59), League Women Voters (pres. Austin 1945-46), Phi Beta Kappa (pres. Dallas chpt. 1970-71). Unitarian. Mem. editorial adv. bd. Shepard's, 1978—. Home: 3561 Colgate St Dallas TX 75225 Office: 516 United Fidelity Bldg 1025 Elm St Dallas TX 75202. *All things are possible in our expanding universe if we can tune in to the infinite power available to all of us. Our ancestors concentrated on the problems—let us be a part of the solutions so desperately needed in our complex and troubled world.*

RAGGIO, OLGA, mus. curator, educator; b. Rome, Italy, Feb. 5, 1926; d. Enrico and Renee (Levine) R.; Diploma, Internat. Library Sch., Vatican, 1947; Ph.D., U. Rome, 1949; postgrad. N.Y. U., 1951-52. With Met. Mus. Art, N.Y.C., 1952—, asso. research curator, 1966-68, curator Western European arts, 1968-71, chmn. dept. European sculpture and decorative arts, 1971—; adj. asso. prof. Inst. Fine Arts, N.Y. U., 1964-68, adj. prof., 1968—. Am. Council Learned Socs. fellow, 1962-63. Mem. Coll. Art Assn. Am., Renaissance Soc. Am., Am. Assn. Museums, Internat. Com. Mus. Orgn. Roman Catholic. Author works in field. Office: Met Mus of Art Fifth Ave and 82d St New York NY 10028

RAGGIO, THOMAS LOUIS, lawyer; b. Dallas, Sept. 11, 1946; s. Grier Henry and Louise Hilma (Ballerstedt) R.; B.A., U. Tex. at Austin, 1968; J.D., So. Meth. U., 1971; m. Janice Beth Savage, May 23, 1970. Exec. v.p. firm Raggio & Raggio Inc., Dallas, 1971—. Cert. in family law, Tex. Mem. Dallas Bar Assn. (chmn. sect. family law 1976). Home: 9322 Moss Trail Dallas TX 75231 Office: 516 United Fidelity Bldg Dallas TX 75202

RAGIN, JOHN S., actor; b. Newark, May 5; student Rutgers U., Carnegie Inst. Tech.; studied acting in London, also with Sanford Heisner, Lee Strasberg. Appeared in Macbeth and Winter's Tale at N.Y. Shakespeare Theatre, in Antony and Cleopatra, The Tempest, All's Well That Ends Well and A Midsummer Night's Dream at Shakespeare Festival, Stratford, Conn.; appeared in films including: Bob and Carol and Ted and Alice, 1969, I Love You, Alice B. Toklas, 1969, Marooned, 1969, Doctors' Wives, 1971, Earthquake, 1974, The Parallax View, 1974, Moving Violation, 1976; regular on NBCTV series Quincy, 1976—; other TV appearances include: Sons and Daughters, McCloud, Switch. Fulbright grantee. Office: care Internat Creative Mgmt 8899 Beverly Blvd Los Angeles CA 90048*

RAGLAND, JACK WHITNEY, artist; b. El Monte, Calif., Feb. 25, 1938; s. Jack Rider and Dorsey (Whitney) R.; B.A., Ariz. State U., 1960, M.A., 1964; postgrad. U. Calif. at Los Angeles, 1961-64; m. Marilee J. Weaver, July 31, 1969; children—Roxanne, Natasha. Grad. asst. tchr. Ariz. State U., 1960-61; grad. teaching asst. U. Calif. at Los Angeles, 1961-64; head art dept. Simpson Coll., Indianola, Iowa, 1964-76; one-man shows Kleine Gallery, Vienna, Austria, Billy Son Gallery, Coralville, Iowa, Tamarack Gallery, Stillwater, Minn., Percival Galleries, Des Moines, Simpson Coll., Art and Design Shop, Bonsall, Calif., Lakes Art Center, Okoboji, Iowa, Mary Knowles Gallery, LaJolla, Calif.; exhibited in group shows Lyn Kottler Gallery, N.Y.C., Phoenix Art Mus., Tucson Festival Art, Talisman Gallery, Bartlesville, Okla., Exhibiting Artists Fedn., Poultney, Vt., Des Moines Art Center, Mary Knowles Gallery, Poulson Galleries, Pasadena, Calif., Joslyn Mus. Art, Omaha, Haymarket Gallery, Lincoln, Nebr.; represented in permanent collections Albertina Museum, Vienna, Kunsthaus, Basel, Switzerland, Los Angeles County Mus., Simpson Coll., Phoenix Art Mus., Ariz. State collection, Graphische Bundes Versuchsanstalt, Vienna, Austria, also pvt. collections; works include stained glass windows Meth. Ch., Perry, Iowa. Recipient grand purchase prize Ariz. Ann. Art Show, 1961; 1st prize Iowa State Fair, 1974. Works reproduced Applause mag., 1971, New Woman mag., 1974. Home: 5490 Rainbow Heights Rd Fallbrook CA 92028

RAGLE, THOMAS BRAMBLE, coll. pres.; b. Boston, Nov. 25, 1927; s. Benjamin Harrison and Marguerite (Williams) R.; grad. Phillips Exeter Acad., 1945; A.B. magna cum laude, Harvard, 1949; B.A., Wadham Coll., Oxford U., 1951, M.A., 1955; L.H.D., Windham Coll., Vt., 1974; m. Euphemia Hunter, June 13, 1953 (div. 1963); children—Robin Lee, Timothy Hunter; m. 2d, Nancy Morrill Koch, Nov. 6, 1965; stepchildren—William Conrad Koch, Melendy Fairfield Koch, Fritz Karel Koch, Elizabeth Anne Koch. Instr., Phillips Exeter Acad., 1951-52, 54-58; pres. Marlboro (Vt.) Coll., 1958—. Pres., Brattleboro Adult Edn. Program, Vt. Found. Ind. Colls., 1968-69, Vt. Higher Edn. Council, 1967-68; mem. Vt. Higher Edn. Planning Commn., 1974-76. Vice chmn. Vt. Student Assistance Corp.; bd. dirs. Stowe Sch., 1966-74, Brattleboro Music Center, Crosby Found., Council on Postsecondary Accreditation. Served with USNR, 1946; with U.S. Army, 1952-54. Mem. New Eng. Assn. Schs. and Colls. (mem. commn. instns. higher edn. 1972-76, exec. com. 1976—), Vt. Hist. Soc., Phi Beta Kappa. Mem. United Ch. of Christ. Club: Harvard (N.Y.C.). Home: Melendy Farm RFD 3 Guilford VT 05301 Office: Marlboro Coll Marlboro VT 05344

RAGONE, DAVID VINCENT, univ. dean; b. N.Y.C., May 16, 1930; s. Armando Frederick and Mary (Napier) R.; S.B., Mass. Inst. Tech., 1951, S.M., 1952, Sc.D., 1953; m. Katherine H. Spaulding, Dec. 18, 1954; children—Christine M., Peter V. Asst. prof. chem. and metall. engring. U. Mich., Ann Arbor, 1953-57, asso. prof., 1957-61, prof., 1961-62, dean Coll. Engring., 1972—; asst. dir. John J. Hopkins Lab for Pure and Applied Sci., also chmn. metallurgy dept. Gen. Atomic div. Gen. Dynamics, La Jolla, 1962-67; Alcoa prof. metallurgy Carnegie-Mellon U., Pitts., 1967-69, asso. dean Sch. Urban and Pub. Affairs, 1969-70; dean Thayer Sch. of Engring., Dartmouth, 1970-72. Trustee Mitre Corp.; dir. McLouth Steel Corp., Ann Arbor Trust Co. Mem. Nat. Sci. Bd.; mem. tech adv. bd. U.S. Dept. Commerce, 1967-75; chmn. adv. com. advanced auto power systems Council on Environmental Quality, 1971-75. Trustee C.F. Kettering Found. Named Outstanding Young Engr., Engring. Soc. Detroit, 1957. Mem. Sigma Xi, Tau Beta Pi. Club: Cosmos (Washington). Home: 3951 Waldenwood Ann Arbor MI 48105

RAGONE, STANLEY, utility co. exec.; b. Norfolk, Va., May 7, 1925; s. Vincent George and Jennie (Gross) R.; B.S., Va. Poly. Inst., 1947, M.S., 1948; m. Bertha Perlin, Sept. 5, 1954; children—Vernon George, Mitchell Floyd, Sharon. With Va. Electric & Power Co., various locations, 1948—, v.p. power, Richmond, 1967-73, sr. v.p. power group, 1973-76, exec. v.p., 1976-78, pres., chief operating officer, dir., 1978—; dir. United Va. Bank, Richmond, Dana Corp.; instr. physics William and Mary Coll./Va. Poly. Inst. extension at Norfolk, 1948-53. Served with USNR, 1944-46; PTO. Registered profl. engr., Va. Fellow ASME, Va. Acad. Sci. (pres. 1973-74). Jewish. Clubs: Masons, Shriners. Home: 402 Lakeway Ct Richmond VA 23229 Office: One James River Plaza Richmond VA 23261

RAGSDALE, CARL VANDYKE, motion picture producer; b. Illmo, Mo., May 16, 1925; s. Vandyke and Iona Lee (Bledsoe) R.; B.A., Denison U., 1950; m. Diane E. Ringrose, Sept. 18, 1976; children—John Sheldon, Susan Lee. Commd. ensign U.S. Navy, 1944, advanced through grades to capt., 1944-54; ops. officer on staff comdr. in-chief Pacific, 1945; officer-in-charge Western Pacific Fleet Camera Party, 1946-47; capt. Res., 1973—; comdg. officer Naval Res. Combat Camera Group, 1972-74, Naval Res. Office Info. Units 102 and 310, 1975-79; v.p. Depicto Films Inc., N.Y.C., 1954-62; pres. Carl Ragsdale Assos. Inc., Houston and N.Y.C., 1962—; producer films, including: A Year Towards Tomorrow, 1966; While I Run This Race, 1967. Decorated Navy Commendation medal; recipient Academy award for Best Documentary Short, 1966. Mem. Dirs. Guild Am., Naval Res. Assn., Res. Officers Assn., Am. Legion, DAV, Naval Aviation Commandery, Navy League, Inst. Diving, Underwater Photog. Soc. Republican. Congregationalist. Clubs: Briar, Willowisp Country, Masons, Shriners (Houston); N.Y. Athletic. Home and Office: 4725 Stillbrooke Houston TX 77035

RAGSDALE, DUANE WILLIAM, advt. agy. exec.; b. Baker, Oreg., Sept. 3, 1924; s. Lee A. and Mabel C. (Hall) R.; B.S., U. Colo., 1945; postgrad. U. Wash., 1947-49; M.B.A., Harvard U., 1951; m. Miriam W. Coffin, June 28, 1952; 1 dau., Martha W. Adminstrv. asst. Paramount Pictures Co., N.Y.C., 1951-56; clinet contact Compton Advt. Co., N.Y.C., 1956-68, v.p., 1958-65, sr. v.p., 1965-68; sr. v.p. William Esty Co., N.Y.C., 1968-73, mgmt. supr., 1968-73; vice chmn. bd. Ted Bates & Co. Inc., N.Y.C., 1973—. Served with USNR, 1943-46. Home: 1112 Park Ave New York NY 10028 Office: 1515 Broadway New York NY 10036

RAGSDALE, WILMOTT, journalist, educator; b. Aberdeen, Wash., Aug. 19, 1911; s. Wilmott P. and Amy M. R.; student Sorbonne, 1933; B.A., U. Wash., 1949; M.A., Johns Hopkins U., 1950; m. Eleanor Murray Jones, June 10, 1938 (div. 1957); children—Noel, Dana; m. 2d, Jane Slichter, Apr. 4, 1957; 1 dau., Amy. Reporter, Trandradio Press, Phoenix, Chgo., Hartford and Washington, 1937-39; White House corr. Wall Street Jour., 1940-41; diplomatic corr. Time mag., Washington, 1942-43, contbg. editor, N.Y.C. and London, 1943-47; lectr. New Sch. for Social Research, N.Y.C., 1951-52; asso. prof. English, Grinnell (Iowa) Coll., 1953-57; writer Newsweek mag., N.Y.C., 1957-58, corr., Bangkok, Thailand, 1959-60; asso. prof. journalism U. Wis., Madison, 1960, prof., 1962—; vis. prof. U. Wash., 1963; UNESCO expert, Manila, 1964; prof. U. Philippines, 1965; cons., prof. Am. U. In Cairo, 1969-71; cons. UNESCO, Paris, 1979. Recipient Disting. Teaching award U. Wis., 1978. Mem. Psi Upsilon. Club: Overseas Press (N.Y.C.). Office: Journalism Sch U Wis Madison WI 53706

RAHALL, NICK, II, congressman; b. Beckley, W.Va., May 20, 1949; s. Joe and Alice Rahall; A.B., Duke U., 1971; m. Helen McDaniel, Aug. 19, 1972; children—Rebecca Ashley, Nick Joe III. Staff asst. to U.S. Senator Robert C. Byrd, 1971-74; sales rep. Sta. WWNR, Beckley, 1974; pres. Mountaineer Travel Co., Beckley, 1975-77; dir. Rahall Communications Corp., 1975—; mem. 95th-96th Congresses from 4th Dist. W.Va. mem. Public Works and Transp. Com., Interior and Insular Affairs Com.; mem. steel caucus, rural caucus Dem. Study Group, chmn. Coal Group; del. Dem. Nat. Conv., 1972, 74, 78. Named Young Man of Year, Beckley Jaycees, 1972, Outstanding Young Man in W.Va., W.Va. Jaycees, 1977; recipient Achievement award Logan Crippled Children Soc., 1978; Citizenship award K.C., 1978. Mem. NAACP. Presbyterian. Clubs: Rotary, Elks, Moose, Eagles, Shriners. Address: 408 Cannon House Office Bldg Washington DC 20515

RAHIMTOOLA, SHAHBUDIN HOOSEINALLY, physician, educator; b. Oct. 17, 1931; student Dow Med. Coll., Karachi, Pakistan, 1949-54; M.B., B.S., U. Karachi, 1956; m.; 2 children. Intern, Civil Hosp., Jinnah Central Hosp., Karachi, 1954-56; sr. house officer Barrowmore Chest Hosp., Chester, Eng., 1956-57; sr. house officer Whittington Hosp., London, 1958-59, locum med. registrar, 1960; house physician, cardiac unit London Chest Hosp., 1959-60; registrar to cardiac unit Wessex Regional Hosp. Bd., Chest Hosp., Southampton, Eng., 1960-63; Fulbright scholar, Mayo fellow cardiovascular lab. St. Marys Hosp., Mayo Clinic, Rochester, Minn., 1963-64, Minn. Heart Assn. research fellow, research asst. cardiac lab. Mayo Clinic and Mayo Grad. Sch. Medicine, 1964-65, co-dir. cardiac lab., 1965-66; sr. registrar cardiopulmonary diseases, dept. medicine Queen Elizabeth Hosp., Birmingham, research fellow dept. medicine U. Birmingham, 1966-67; research asst., hon. sr. registrar, dept. medicine Royal Postgrad. Med. Sch. and Hammersmith Hosp., London, 1967-68, sr. registrar dept. medicine, 1969; co-dir. dept. adult cardiology Cook County Hosp., Chgo., 1969-70, dir., 1970-72, chmn. search com. for chief of pulmonary medicine, 1971; cons. cardiology Madigan Gen. Army Hosp., Ft. Lewis, Wash., 1972—; dir. research div. cardiology U. Oreg. Med. Sch., Portland, 1972—, dir. cardiac catheterization labs., 1973-78; cons. Nat. Coop. Study on Valvular Heart Disease, VA Central Office, Washington, 1976-77, mem. exec. com., 1977—; chmn. circulatory system devices panel FDA, HEW, 1977—; asso. prof. medicine Abraham Lincoln Sch. Medicine, U. Ill. Coll. Medicine, Chgo., 1969-72, mem. adv. com., 1970-72; prof. medicine U. Oreg. Med. Sch., 1972—; senator faculty U. Oreg. Health Sci. Center, 1978—, chmn. autopsy service med. bd. Univ. Hosps., 1975-76; vis. prof. medicine, vis. scientist Cardiovascular Research Inst. U. Calif., San Francisco, 1978-79; Am. Heart Assn. internat. vis. teacher, Thailand, 1979. Fellow Am. Coll. Cardiology (asst. sec. 1978—; trustee 1978—), A.C.P., Am. Heart Assn. (exec. com. Council Clin. Cardiology 1977—), Am. Coll. Chest Physicians (program chmn. Ill. chpt. 1971-72), Royal Soc. Medicine (London); mem. Assn. U. Cardiologists, Central, Western socs. for clin. research, Brit. Cardiac Soc., Western Assn. Physicians, Internat. Soc. for Heart Research, Am. Fedn. for Clin. Research, Brit., Pakistan med. assns., AAAS, AAUP, Oreg. Soc. for Critical Care Medicine, Oreg. Heart Assn. (sec. session program com. 1978—), Alpha Omega Alpha. Author: (with R.M. Gunnar and H.S. Loeb) Shock in Myocardial Infarction, 1974; Coronary ByPass Surgery, 1977; Infective Endocarditis, 1978. Mem. editorial bd. Cardiology Digest, 1975—, Circulation, 1977—, Chest, 1978—; guest editor Am. Jour. of Cardiology, 1975, Newsletter of Council on Clin. Cardiology, 1979—, Clin. Cardiology series in Jour. AMA, 1980—. Contbr. chpts. to books and articles to med. jours. Office: U Oreg Health Scis Center Portland OR 97201. *In life, one has to do what one thinks is important.*

RAHL, JAMES ANDREW, lawyer, educator; b. Wooster, Ohio, Oct. 8, 1917; s. James Blaine and Harriet (Munson) R.; B.S., Northwestern U., 1939, J.D., 1942; m. Jean Mayberry, Sept. 5, 1942; 1 son, James Andrew. Admitted to Ohio bar, 1942, Ill. bar, 1950, also U.S. Supreme Ct.; atty. OPA, 1942-43; mem. faculty Northwestern U. Law Sch., 1946—, prof. law, 1953—, Owen L. Coon prof., 1974—, dir. research, 1966-72, dean, 1972-77; counsel Chadwell, Kayser, Ruggles, McGee & Hastings, Chgo., 1952—, resident partner firm, Brussels, Belgium, 1963-64; mem. faculty Salzburg Seminar Am. Studies, 1967, 72. Mem. Atty. Gen.'s Nat. Com. to Study Antitrust Laws, 1953-55; mem. White House Task Force Antitrust Policy, 1967-68, UNCTAD Group Experts on Internat. Restrictive Trade Practices, 1973; mem. adv. com. on internat. investment, tech. and devel. Dept. State, 1979—. Served to 2d lt. AUS, 1943-46. Mem. Am. (council anti trust sect. 1965-67), Ill., Chgo. bar assns., Chgo. Council Lawyers, Am. Law Inst., Am. Soc. Internat. Law, AAUP, Law Club Chgo. (pres. 1976-77). Methodist. Author: (with others) Cases on Torts, 1968, 2d edit., 1977; (with others) Advanced Torts, 1977; (with Schwerin) Northwestern University School of Law: A Short History, 1960; Common Market and American Antitrust: Overlap and Conflict, 1970; also articles. Editor-in-chief Ill. Law Rev., 1941-42. Home: 2426 Marcy Ave Evanston IL 60201 Office: 357 E Chicago Ave Chicago IL 60611

RAHMAN, ANEESUR, physicist; b. Hyderabad, India, Aug. 24, 1927; s. Habibur and Aisha (Abdullah) R.: came to U.S., 1960; B.Sc., Osmania (India) U., 1946: M.A., Cambridge (Eng.) U., 1948; D.Sc., Louvain (Belgium) U., 1953: m. Yueh-Erh Li, Nov. 3, 1956; 1 child, Aneesa. Lectr., Osmania U., Hyderabad, 1949-57; scientist Tata Inst. of Fundamental Research, Bombay, India, 1957-60; sr. scientist, theoretical physicist Argonne (Ill.) Nat. Lab., 1960—. Mem. Am. Phys. Soc. (Langmuir Award 1977). Home: 1409 Burr Oak Rd Hinsdale IL 60521 Office: Argonne Lab 9700 S Cass Ave Argonne IL 60439

RAHMAN, YUEH-ERH, biologist; b. Kwangtung, China, June 10, 1928; d. Khon and Kwei-Phan (Chan) Li; came to U.S., 1960; B.S., U. Paris, 1950; M.D. magna cum laude, U. Louvain (Belgium), 1956; m. Aneesur Rahman, Nov. 3, 1956; 1 dau., Aneesa. Clin. and postdoctoral research fellow Louvain U., 1956-60; mem. staff Argonne (Ill.) Nat. Lab., 1960—, biologist, 1972—; vis. scientist State U. Utrecht (Netherlands), 1968-69; adj. asso. prof. No. Ill. U., DeKalb, 1971—. Recipient IR-100 award, 1976; grantee Nat. Cancer Inst., Nat. Inst. Arthritis, Metabolic and Digestive Diseases. Mem. Am. Soc. Cell Biology, N.Y. Acad. Scis., Radiation Research Soc., Gerontol. Soc., AAAS, Assn. for Women in Sci. (pres. Chgo. area chpt.), Am. Inst. Biol. Scis. Unitarian. Author, patentee in field. Home: 1409 Burr Oak Rd Hinsdale IL 60521 Office: Argonne Nat Lab 9700 S Cass Ave Argonne IL 60439

RAHMIG, WILLIAM CONRAD, investment co. exec.; b. Newark, Jan. 15, 1936; s. Conrad and Else Marie Elizabeth (Ollemar) R.; B. in Chem. Engring., U. Va., 1957; M.S., U. N.Mex., 1960; m. Katharine Gertraud Meier, July 9, 1960; children—Barbara, Kenneth, Clinton. Analyst. Dreyfus Fund, N.Y.C., 1961-63; with Madison Fund, Inc., N.Y.C., 1963-77, exec. v.p., 1973-77; investment adviser, sr. portfolio mgr., investment banker Stephenson & Co., Denver, 1977—. Served with USN, 1958-61. Mem. Denver Soc. Security Analysts, Fin. Analysts Assn., N.Y. Soc. Security Analysts (sr. securities analyst). Club: Toastmasters (pres. 1974-75) (N.Y.C.). Editorial adv. Denver Bus. World. Home: Route 6 Box 7 Golden CO 80401 Office: 899 Logan St Denver CO 80203

RAHN, HERMANN, physiologist; b. East Lansing, Mich., July 5, 1912; s. Otto and Bell S. (Farrand) R.; A.B., Cornell U., 1933; student U. Kiel, 1933-34; Ph.D., U. Rochester, 1938, D.Sc. (hon.), 1973; Docteur Honoris Causa, U. Paris, 1964; LL.D. (hon.), Yonsei U., Korea, 1965; m. Katharine F. Wilson, Aug. 29, 1939; children—Robert F., Katharine B. NRC fellow Harvard, 1938-39; instr. physiology U. Wyo., 1939-41; asst. physiology Sch. Medicine, U. Rochester, 1941-42, instr., 1942-46, asst. prof., 1946-50, asso. prof., vice chmn. dept., 1950-56; Lawrence D. Bell prof. physiology, chmn. dept. Sch. Medicine, U. Buffalo (now State U. N.Y. at Buffalo), 1956-73, distinguished prof. physiology, 1973—; vis. prof. Med. Faculty San Marcos U., Lima, Peru, 1955, Dartmouth Med. Sch., 1962, Lab. de Physiologie Respiratoire, CNRS, Strasbourg, France, 1971, Max-Planck-Inst. für experimentelle Medizin, Göttingen, W.Ger., 1977. Mem. adv. com. biol. sci. Air Force Office Sci. Research and Devel., 1958-64; physiol. study sect. NIH, 1958-62; mem. working committee space sci. bd. Nat. Acad. Sci.-NRC, 1962-65; mem. gen. med. research program project com. NIH, 1964-67; mem. research career award com. Nat. Inst. Gen. Med. Scis., 1968-72; cardiopulmonary adv. com. Nat. Heart Inst., 1968-71; mem. nat. adv. bd. R/V Alpha Helix, 1968-71; chmn. com. on underwater physiology and medicine NRC, 1972-74. Recipient Sr. U.S. Scientist award Alexander von Humboldt Found., 1976. Mem. Am. Inst. Biol. Sci. (adv. com. physiol. 1957-64, adv. panel 1967-71), Am. Physiol. Soc. (council 1960-65, pres. 1963-64), Nat. Acad. Scis., Inst. Medicine, Nat. Acad. Sci., Harvey Soc. (hon.), Soc. Exptl. Biology and Medicine, Internat. Union Physiol. Scis. (council 1965-74, U.S. nat. com. 1966-74, v.p. 1971-74, exec. com. 1971-74), Am. Soc. Zoologists, Am. Acad. Arts and Sci., Sigma Xi. Author: (with W.O. Fenn) A Graphical Analysis of the Respiratory Gas Exchange, 1955; (with others) Blood Gases: Hemoglobin, Base Excess and Maldistribution, 1973. Editorial bd. Am. Jour. Physiology, Jour. Applied Physiology, 1953-62, sect. editor for respiration, 1962, bd. publ. trustees, 1959-62; co-editor (with W.O. Fenn) Handbook of Physiology-Respiration, Vols. I, II, 1964-65; editor: Physiology of Breath-Hold Diving and the Ama of Japan, 1965. Research in pulmonary physiology, gas exchange, environmental physiology. Home: 75 Windsor Ave Buffalo NY 14209

RAHN, RICHARD WILLIAM, economist, assn. exec.; b. Rochester, N.Y., Jan. 9, 1942; s. William Fred and Evelyn Janet (Chapman) R.; B.A., U. South Fla., 1963; M.B.A., Fla. State U., 1964; Ph.D., Columbia U., 1972; m. Joy Virginia Moore, May, 1961; 1 dau., Margie Lynn; m. 2d, Ann Clarke Sherman, Jan. 20, 1971. Instr., Fla. State U., Tallahassee, 1964-66; mem. grad. faculty dept. mgmt. Poly. Inst. N.Y., 1964-72, asso. prof., 1973, adminstrv. officer, 1970-72; head dept., 1972-73; mng. dir. Ripon Soc., Cambridge, Mass., Washington, 1973-74; pres. Richard W. Rahn & Assos., Managerial Economists, Washington, 1974-76; econ. cons. N.Y. Merc. Exchange, 1974—; exec. dir., bd. dirs. Am. Council for Capital Formation, Washington, 1976—; bd. dirs. Center for Policy Research; adj. prof. George Mason U., Fairfax, Va., 1974—. Mem. N.Y. County Republican Com., 1973. Mem. Nat. Assn. Bus. Economists (v.p. Washington chpt. 1978), Nat. Economists Clubs, Am. Econ. Assn., Ripon Soc. (chmn. N.Y. 1972-73, pres. Washington 1974-76, mem. nat. governing bd. 1971-77, nat. fin. chmn. 1974-75). Republican. Club: Internat. Contbr. articles to profl. jours. Home: 2939 Rosemoore Ln Fairfax VA 22030 Office: 1919 Pennsylvania Ave NW Washington DC 20006

RAICEVIC, DUSAN, research scientist; b. Golubovci, Yugoslavia, May 26, 1916; s. Jovan and Danica (Slavkovic) R.; came to Can., 1948, naturalized, 1955; B.S. with honors, U. Beograd, Yugoslavia, 1940; m. Darinka Raicevic, Mar. 13, 1945; children—Mickey, Helen, Eddie. Various positions in mineral dressing, extraction metallurgy and chem. fields with Hudson Bay Mining & Smelting Co. Ltd., Flin Flon, Man., 1948-56, Kerr Addison Gold Mines Ltd., Virginia-Town, Ont., 1956-57, Stanleigh Uranium Mining Corp., Elliot Lake, Ont., 1957-60; Canadian Industries Ltd., McMasterville, Que., 1960-64, Que. Iron and Titanium Corp., Sorel, Que., 1964-65, Ore Processing Lab., Can. Centre for Mineral and Energy Tech. Dept. Energy, Mines and Resources, Ottawa, Ont., 1966—. Served in Brit. 8th Army, World War II. Mem. Canadian Inst. Mining and Metallurgy. Contbr. to various publs. Patentee in metall. field. Home: 11 Attwood Crescent Ottawa ON K2E 5B1 Canada Office: 555 Booth St Ottawa ON K1A 0G1 Canada

RAIKES, CHARLES FITZGERALD, lawyer; b. Mpls., Oct. 6, 1930; s. Arthur FitzGerald and Margaret (Hawthorne) R.; B.A., Washington U., 1952; M.A., Harvard, 1955, LL.B., 1958; m. Antonia Raikes, Dec. 20, 1969; children—Jennifer Catherine, Victoria Samantha. Admitted to N.Y. State bar, 1959; asso. firm White & Case, N.Y.C., 1958-69; asso. gen. counsel Dun & Bradstreet, Inc., N.Y.C., 1969-72, v.p., gen. counsel, 1972-73, v.p., gen. counsel The Dun & Bradstreet Corp., Inc., N.Y.C., 1973-76, sr. v.p., gen. counsel, 1976—; cons. Bd. Govs. Fed. Reserve System, 1958—. Served with U.S. Army, 1952-54. Woodrow Wilson fellow, 1952. Mem. Assn. Bar City N.Y., Phi Beta Kappa. Clubs: Down Town Assn., Harvard, Manhattan. Home: 126 The Common Old Greenwich CT 06870 Office: 299 Park Ave New York NY 10017

RAILSBACK, THOMAS F., congressman; b. Moline, Ill., Jan. 22, 1932; B.A. in English, Grinnell (Iowa) Coll., also LL.D.; J.D., Northwestern U.; LL.D., Monmouth Coll.; m. Patricia Sloan; children—Kathryn, Julia, Margaret Ann, Lisa. Admitted to Ill. bar, 1957, D.C. Ct. Appeals bar; partner Fred Railsback, 1957-63; former asso. firm Graham, Califf, Harper, Benson & Railsback; mem. 90th-96th Congresses, 19th Ill. Dist., mem. House judiciary com., select com. on narcotics abuse and control, chmn. Ill. Republican del. to Congress. Mem. Ill. Ho. Reps., 1962-66, chmn. House-Senate Legislative Flood Commn., House Republican Human Relations Task Force. Served with U.S. Army, 1957-59. Recipient Outstanding Young Man of Year award Moline, 1964, Jaycees Distinguished Service award, 1964, Alumni award Grinnell Coll., 1973; Flandrau award Nat. Council Crime and Delinquency, 1974; certificate of appreciation Safer Found., 1977; Spl. Service award Nat. Clients Council, 1977; named One of 200 Future Am. Leaders, Time mag., 1974. Mem. Am. Bar Assn., Ill. Bar Assn. (past chmn. Younger Mems. Conf.), Rock Island County Bar Assn., Grinnell Coll. Alumni Assn. (past pres. bd. dirs.), Blue Key, Phi Gamma Delta. Conglist. Home: 2800 12th St Moline IL 61265 Office: 2104 Rayburn House Office Bldg Washington DC 20515

RAILTON, WILLIAM SCOTT, lawyer; b. Newark, July 30, 1935; s. William Scott and Carolyn Elizabeth (Guiberson) R.; B.S. in Elec. Engring., U. Wash., 1962; J.D. with honors, George Washington U., 1965; m. Karen Elizabeth Walsh, Mar. 31, 1979; children by previous marriage—William Scott, III, Anne Greenwood. Admitted to D.C. bar, 1966; asso., then partner firm Kemon, Palmer & Estabrook, Washington, 1966-70; sr. trial atty. Dept. Labor, 1970-71; asst. counsel OSHA, 1971-72, chief counsel, 1972-77, acting gen. counsel rev. commn., 1975-77; partner firm Reed, Smith, Shaw & McClay, Washington, 1977—; lectr. George Washington U. Law Sch., 1977—, Georgetown U. Law Sch., 1979—. Chmn. Montgomery County (Md.) Republican Party, 1968-70; pres. Montgomery Sq. Citizens Assn., 1970-71; bd. dirs. Foxvale Farms Homeowners Assn., 1979—. Served with USMC, 1953-58. Recipient Meritorious Achievement medal Dept. Labor, 1972, Outstanding Service award OSHA rev. commn., 1977. Mem. Am. Bar Assn., Md. Bar Assn., Bar Assn. D.C. (vice chmn. young lawyers sect. 1971), Order of Coif, Sigma Phi Epsilon, Phi Delta Phi. Clubs: Oval (U. Wash.); River Bend Country (Gt. Falls). Author legal handbooks. Home: 890 Van Dusen Ct Great Falls VA 22066 Office: 1150 Connecticut Ave NW Washington DC 20036. *Lawsuits are won by hard work during pre-trial preparation. A litigator should be candid with his clients and honest in his dealings with associates, opponents and the courts.*

RAIMI, RALPH ALEXIS, educator; b. Detroit, July 25, 1924; s. Jacob and Sylvia (Krusner) R.; B.S. in Physics, U. Mich., 1947, M.S. in Math., 1948, Ph.D., 1954; m. Sonya Lenore Drews, June 29, 1947; children—Jessica, Diana. Faculty, U. Rochester (N.Y.), 1952—, prof., 1966—, asso. dean for grad. studies Coll. Arts and Sci., 1967-75. Served to 1st lt. USAAF, 1943-46. Fulbright Grad. fellow, Paris, 1949-50; Lloyd postdoctoral fellow U. Mich., 1955-56. Mem. Am. Math. Soc., Math. Assn. Am. Contbr. articles to mags., jours. Home: 46 Glen Ellyn Way Rochester NY 14618

RAIMONDI, ALBERT ANTHONY, mech. engr.; b. Plymouth, Mass., Mar. 29, 1925; s. William and Amelia (Taddia) R.; B.S., Tufts U., 1945; M.S., U. Pitts., 1963, Ph.D. in Mech. Engring., 1968. Research engr. Westinghouse Research Labs., Pitts., 1945-68, mgr. lubrication mechanics, 1966-78, mgr. mech. tribology and exptl. structural mechanics, 1978—. Fellow Am. Soc. Lubrication Engrs. (Hunt award 1959, nat. award 1968); mem. Am. Soc. M.E. Contbr. Am. Soc. Lubrication Engr. Handbook, 1968; editor jours. Am. Soc. Lubrication Engrs., 1971-76; asso. editor Am. Soc. Lubrication Engrs. trans., 1960-71. Contbr. articles profl. jours. Home: 140 LaVale Dr Monroeville PA 15146 Office: Westinghouse Research and Devel Center 1310 Beulah Rd Pittsburgh PA 15235

RAIN, ROBERT ELEY, JR., lawyer; b. Atlanta, Nov. 11, 1918; s. Robert Eley and Cornie (Talbot) R.; student Va. Mil. Inst., 1936-37; B.A., U. Tex., 1941, LL.B., 1946; m. Eugenia Gano Wharton, June 7, 1947; children—John Wharton, Martha Talbot (Mrs. William E. Black), James Talbot. Admitted to Tex. bar, 1946; since practiced in Dallas; asso. firm Thompson, Knight, Simmons & Bullion, 1946-54, partner, 1954-65; co-founder, partner firm Rain, Harrell, Emery, Young & Doke, 1965—; dir. J-W Operating Co., Carlson Petroleum Co., Gatogordo Oil Co. (all Dallas). Pres. Child Guidance Clinic, Dallas, 1968-69. Bd. dirs. Dallas Day Nursery Assn., 1958-64; bd. dirs. YMCA Camp Grady Spruce; trustee Dallas Hist. Soc., Dallas Zool. Soc., 1978—. Served to capt. USMC, 1941-46; Decorated Purple Heart, Bronze Star. S.W. Legal Found. Research fellow, 1965—. Mem. Dallas, Am. bar assns., State Bar Tex. (chmn. natural resources law sect. 1976-77), Tex. Bar Found. (charter), Salesmanship Club of Dallas, Kappa Sigma, Phi Delta Phi. Presbyn. (ruling elder). Clubs: Dallas Country (dir. 1975—), Idlewild, Terpsichorean (Dallas). Home: 4404 Lorraine Ave Dallas TX 75205 Office: 4200 Republic Bank Tower Dallas TX 75201

RAINER, REX KELLY, educator, civil engr.; b. Montgomery, Ala., July 17, 1924; s. Kelly Kenyon and Pearl (Jones) R.; B.S., Auburn (Ala.) U., 1944, M.S., 1946; Ph.D., Okla. State U., 1967; m. Betty Ann Page, Aug. 28, 1945; children—Rex Kelly, John Kenyon. Asst. engr. L. & N. R.R. Co., Cin., 1944-45; design engr. Polglaze & Basenberg, cons. engrs., Birmingham, Ala., 1945-51; pres., chmn. Rainer Co., Inc., Orlando, Fla., 1951-62; prof. Auburn U., 1962-67, prof., head civil engring. dept., 1967— (on leave); hwy. dir. State of Ala., 1979—; cons. to ins. cos., constrn. engring. firms; mem. Ala. Bd. Registration Profl. Engrs. and Land Surveyors, 1977—. Mem. Municipal Planning Bd., 1963-65, Indsl. Park Devel. Bd., 1969-71. Served with AUS, 1943. Fellow Am. Soc. C.E. (sec.-treas. 1970, pres. Ala. sect. 1976-77, chmn. Constrn. Research Council, chmn. hwy. div. publs. com.); mem. Asso. Gen. Contractors Am. (dir. 1955), Am. Soc. for Engring. Edn. (chmn. constrn. engring. com.), Am. Pub. Works Assn., Asso. Gen. Contractors Am., Phi Kappa Phi, Tau Beta Pi, Chi Epsilon. Contbr. articles profl. jours. Home: Rt 3 Box 306 Opelika AL 36801

RAINEY, CHARLES PETER, JR., bus. exec.; b. Greenwich, Conn., Apr. 29, 1941; s. Charles Peter and Cherilla Katherine (Buckout) R.; A.B., Duke U., 1962: M.B.A., U. N.C., 1963; J.D., U. Mo., 1970; m. Kathleen Marie Sshliebner, May 6, 1960; children—Sherry Lucille, Charles Peter, III, Mark Kevin. Supr. fed. taxes, taxes and fin. planning E.I. DuPont de Nemours & Co., 1962-69: dir. taxes, treas. Castle & Cooke, Inc., San Francisco, 1969-79; v.p. fin., treas. PVO Internat., Inc., San Francisco, 1979—; admitted to Calif. bar, also D.C. bar. Mem. Calif., D.C. bar assns. Home: 282 Birchwood Dr Moraga CA 94556 Office: World Trade Center San Francisco CA 94111

RAINEY, EDWARD CARR, banker; b. Covington, Ga., Apr. 22, 1913; s. William Nathaniel and Ann Cureton (Carr) R.; certificate radio engring., Ga. Inst. Tech., 1938; grad. Rutgers U. Grad. Sch. Banking, 1950, Advanced Mgmt. Program, Harvard, 1958; m. Lillian B. Sams, Nov. 30, 1938; children—Edward Carr, Linda Diane. With Fed. Res. Bank Atlanta, 1932-78, v.p., mgr. Birmingham (Ala.) br., 1963-68, sr. v.p. Jacksonville (Fla.) br., 1969-78; instr. Am. Inst. Banking, 1957, 60, 61. Mem. adv. bd. Salvation Army, 1972—. Bd. dirs. Indsl. Health Council Birmingham, 1963-68. Clubs: Timuquana Country, Fla. Yacht, Rotary (Jacksonville). Home: 3800 Ortega Blvd Jacksonville FL 32210

RAINIE, HARRISON MCKINLEY, JR., marketing cons.; b. Billerica, Mass., May 30, 1919; s. Harrison McKinley and Alice (Bateson) R.; A.B., Harvard, 1940. A.M., 1941, M.B.A., 1947; m. Priscilla Loomis Damon, Feb. 18, 1950; children—Harrison, McKinley III, Shepard Damon, Priscilla Alden. With Pratt & Whitney Aircraft, 1941-42; with Stewart, Dougall Assoc., N.Y.C., 1947—, v.p., 1956-65, pres., 1965-69, also dir.; dir./owner merged company Drake Sheahan/Stewart Dougall, 1969-70; ind. marketing mgmt. cons., 1970-73; dir. eastern region Robert H. Hayes & Assos., Inc., 1973-75; prin. Frank B. Manley & Assos., Greenwich, Conn., 1975—. Served as tech.-sgt., ordnance dept., AUS, 1942-45. Decortated Medalha de Campagna, Medalha de Guerra (Brazil). Mem. Inst. Mgmt. Cons. (founding mem.), Assn. Cons. Mgmt. Engrs., Market Research Council, Newcomen Soc. N.Am. Clubs: Sales Executives, Harvard (N.Y.C.). Home: 91 10th St Garden City NY 11530 Office: 1 Pickwick Plaza Greenwich CT 06830

RAINSFORD, GEORGE NICHOLS, coll. pres.; b. N.Y.C., June 27, 1928; s. Kerr and Christine (Nichols) R.; grad. Deefield Acad., 1946; student Williams Coll., 1946-47; B.A. cum laude, U. Colo., 1950; postgrad. London Sch. Econs., 1950-51; LL.B., Yale U., 1954; M.A., U. Denver, 1963; Ph.D., Stanford U., 1967; m. Jean Wedmore, Sept. 12, 1954; children—Guy, Amy, Anne, Angela, Emily. Admitted to Colo. bar, 1954; asso. mem. firm Holme, Roberts, More & Owen, Denver, 1954-56; dir. devel. U. Denver, 1956-63; intern Ellis L. Phillips Found., U. Wash., 1963-64; asso. dean Coll. Arts and Scis., asst. prof. history and law U. Denver, 1967-69; asst. to pres. U. Colo., 1969-71, also asso. prof. history; pres. Kalamazoo Coll., 1972—, also prof. history; ednl. cons. Robert Johnson Co. Trustee Colo. Outward Bound Sch., Denver, 1961—, Grad. Theol. Union, Berkeley, Calif., 1965—. Mem. Kalamazoo Council Coll. Pres.'s (chmn. 1973—), Great Lakes Colls. Assn. (sec.-treas. 1972—), Detroit Econ. Club, Phi Gamma Mu, Phi Alpha Theta, Phi Delta Phi. Clubs: Park, Kalamazoo Country; University (Denver and N.Y.C.). Author: Congress and Higher Education in the 19th Century, 1972. Office: 1200 Academy St Kalamazoo MI 49007*

RAINWATER, CRAWFORD VEAZEY, bottling co. exec.; b. Atlanta, Apr. 23, 1916; s. Charles Veazey and Blanche (Edmondson) R.; B.B.A., Emory U., 1937; m. Betty Gregg, Oct. 29, 1938; children—Elizabeth Adair (Mrs. Kenneth H. Woolf), Crawford Veazey Jr., Nancy Gregg. With Hygeia Coca-Cola Bottling Co., Pensacola, Fla., 1937—, pres., 1961-77, chmn. bd., 1977—, also dir.; dir. Gulf Power Co., Pensacola, So. Co., Atlanta. Pres. Gulf Coast council Boy Scouts, 1958-60, mem. nat. exec. bd., 1962-69; pres. Pensacola United Fund, 1963-64. Trustee Escambia County 4-H Timber Grazing and Game Project, 1941—; trustee, past pres. Pensacola Jr. Coll. Found., Inc., U. West Florida Found., Inc., 1966-73; exec. bd. Bapt. Hosp., Pensacola, 1969-75. Served with USNR, 1943-46. Recipient Silver Beaver, Silver Antelope, Silver Buffalo awards Boy Scouts Am.; Outstanding Citizens award Pensacola Kiwanis Club, 1956; named Beverage Industry Man of Year, 1975. Mem. So. Golf Assn. (dir. 1966—), Nat. Soft Drink Assn. (pres. 1970-72), Chi Phi. Episcopalian (vestry). Clubs: Pensacola Country, Rotary (pres. 1956), Scenic Hills Country (Pensacola); Royal and Ancient (St. Andrews, Scotland). Home: 3231 Seville Dr Pensacola FL 32503 Office: 7330 N Davis Hwy Pensacola FL 32504

RAINWATER, JAMES, educator; b. Council, Idaho, Dec. 9, 1917; s. Leo J. and Edna E. (Teague) R.; B.S., Calif. Inst. Tech., 1939: Ph.D., Columbia, 1946; m. Emma Louise Smith, Mar. 7, 1942; children—James Carlton, Robert Stephen, Elizabeth (dec.), William George. Asst. physics Columbia. 1939-42, scientist OSRD and Manhattan dist., 1942-46, instr., 1946-47, asst. prof. physics, 1947-49, asso. prof. physics, 1949-52, prof. physics, 1952—; dir. Nevis Cyclotron Lab., 1951-53, 56-61, research scientist AEC, ERDA, NSF and Office Naval Research projects, 1947—. Mem. adv. com. physics and electronuclear divs. Oak Ridge Nat. Lab., 1962-65; mem. physics rev. panel Argonne Nat. Lab., 1967-70. Recipient Ernest Orlando Lawrence award AEC, 1963, Nobel prize in physics, 1975. Fellow A.A.A.S., Am. Phys. Soc., I.E.E.E., N.Y. Acad. Scis.; mem. Am. Inst. Physics, Am. Assn. Physics Tchrs., Optical Soc. Am., Nat. Acad. Scis. Contbr. articles to profl. jours.

RAINWATER, LEE, sociologist, educator; b. Oxford, Miss., Jan. 7, 1928; s. Percy Lee and J. Tennis (McDowell) R.; student George Washington U., 1944-45, U. So. Calif., 1945-46; M.A., U. Chgo., 1950, Ph.D., 1954; m. Carol Lois Kampel, July 16, 1959; children—Jonathan Lee, Katherine Anne. Asso. dir. Social Research, Inc., Chgo., 1950-63; asso. prof. sociology, anthropology Washington U., St. Louis, 1963-65, prof., 1965-68; exec. dir. Pruitt-Igoe Research, Social Sci. Inst., 1963-68; sr. editor Transaction mag., 1963-71; prof. sociology Harvard U., 1968—. Mem. Soc. Study Social Problems (mem. exec. com. 1966-70, v.p. 1970-71), Am. Sociol. Assn. (chmn. family sect. 1967-68). Author: (with Richard Coleman, Gerald Handel) Workingman's Wife: Her Personality, World and Life Style, 1959; And the Poor Get Children: Sex, Contraception and Family Planning in the Working Class, 1961: Family Design: Marital Sexuality, Family Size and Contraception, 1965: (with William Yancey) The Moynihan Report and the Politics of Controversy, 1967; Behind Ghetto Walls, 1970; Social Problems and Public Policy, 2 vols., 1974; What Money Buys: Inequality and the Social Meaning of Income, 1974; (with Richard Coleman and Kent McClelland) Social Standing in America: New Dimensions of Class, 1978; contbr. articles to profl. jours. Office: 530 William James Hall Harvard U Cambridge MA 02138

RAITT, BONNIE, singer, musician; b. Burbank, Calif., Nov. 8, 1949; student Radcliffe Coll. Performer blues clubs East coast; concert performer; concert tour Britain, 1976, 77; albums include: Bonnie Raitt, 1971, Give It Up, 1972, Takin' My Time, 1973, Streetlights, 1974, Home Plate, 1975, Sweet Forgiveness, 1977, The Glow, 1979. Address: care Avalon Productions 1588 Crossroads of the World Hollywood CA 90028

RAITT, CECIL GERALD, lawyer; b. Detroit, Aug. 3, 1939; s. Abraham H. and Beatrice (Oppenheim) R.; A.B., U. Mich., 1961; J.D. with distinction, Wayne State U., 1964; m. Nancy B. Schulman, July 8, 1962; children—Karen Gail, Sandra Ellen. Admitted to Mich. bar, 1965; law clk. to fed. dist. judge So. div. Eastern dist. Mich., 1965; instr. Law Sch., Wayne State U., 1966-67; practiced in Detroit, 1966—; asso. firm Levin, Levin, Garvett and Dill, 1966-68; mem. firm Jaffe, Snider, Raitt, Garratt & Heuer, profl. corp., 1968—. Mem. Am. Bar Assn., State Bar Mich. (corp., finance and bus. law sect., real property law sect.), Detroit Bar Assn. Editor-in-chief Wayne Law Rev., 1963-64. Home: 28470 S Harwich St Farmington Hills MI 48018 Office: 1800 1st Nat Bldg Detroit MI 48226

RAITT, DAVID HARRIS, lawyer; b. Detroit, Sept. 26, 1942; s. Abe H. and Beatrice (Oppenhiem) R.; B.A. with distinction, U. Mich., 1964, J.D. cum laude, 1967; m. Lois Beth Teache, Aug. 7, 1966. Admitted to Mich. bar, 1968; asso. Milton Y. Zussman, 1967-69; asso. firm Jaffe, Snider, Raitt, Garratt & Heuer, 1969-70, mem. firm, 1971—. Mem. Am., Detroit, Mich. (franchise investment law rules and regulations com., franchise adv. com.) bar assns., Order of Coif. Home: 4897 Faircourt West Bloomfield MI 48033 Office: 1800 1st Nat Bldg Detroit MI 48226

RAITT, JOHN EMMET, actor-singer, producer, dir.; b. Santa Ana, Calif., Jan. 29, 1917; s. Archie John and Stella (Walton) R.; student U. So. Calif., 1935-36; A.B., U. Redlands, Calif., 1939; Dr. of Music (hon.), 1958; m. Marjorie Geraldine Haydock, Dec. 28, 1942 (div. 1971); children—Steven James, Bonnie Lynn, David John; m. 2d, Kathleen Smith-Landry, June 25, 1972. With Riverside Opera Co., 1939; sec. YMCA, Los Angeles, 1940; appeared in light operas; Rose Marie, Vagabond King, Die Fliedermaus, also singer Los Angeles Civic Light Opera Co., 1940; appeared motion pictures: Flight Command, Billy the Kid, Ziegfeld Girl, Metro-Goldwyn Mayer, 1940; appeared Am. Music Theatre operas, Barber of Seville, Carmen, Marriage of Figaro, 1941-44; soloist Los Angeles Symphonic Band, 1941-42; appeared concert artist series Occidental Coll., 1943, U. Redlands, 1943, U. Calif., Los Angeles, 1944; soloist Los Angeles Philharmonic Orchestra, 1943, radio show Shaeffer Pen World Parade, WMAQ, 1943; appeared as Curley, stage show Oklahoma, 1944; featured in Carousel, 1945-47 (Drama Critics and Donaldson awards); starred in Magdalena, 1948, Three Wishes for Jamie, 1950-51, The Buick Circus Hour, NBC-TV, 1952-53, Carnival in Flanders, 1953; starred in Pajama Game, 1954-56, and Pajama Game picture for Warner Bros., Annie Get Your Gun, 1957, A Joyful Noise, Hellinger Theatre, N.Y.C., 1966, Many Happy Returns, Desert Inn Hotel, Las Vegas, 1969, Nat. Co. of Zorba, 1970; with tour On A Clear Day, 1968; at Drake Hotel, Chgo., 1967; prod. tours of Carousel, Kiss Me Kate, Camelot; guest appearances on TV; summer Chevy Show, 1959, 60; starred on Bell Telephone Hour; Australian TV appearance, 1960, London Palladium, 1959, 60, summer stock, 1960-63; producer, star shows San Francisco Dinner Theatre, 1974—; producer, star 2d nat. co. of Seesaw, 1974-75; star Sing, America, Sing, Kennedy Center, An Evening with Sigmund Romberg, A Musical Jubilee, St. James Theatre, N.Y.C., 1975 star spl. Sing, America, Sing, Pub. Broadcasting System, 1976; star nat. co. Shenandoah, 1976-78, An Evening with John Raitt, 1979—. Office: James Fitzgerald Enterprises Inc 1061 Ravoli Dr Pacific Palisades CA 90272. *My voice is a gift, and I have always felt that I must share it with the world. I have been extremely fortunate in that my avocation became my vocation . . . success is incidental to my love for my work.*

RAIZES, MAURICE PHILIP, lawyer; b. Newton, Iowa, Oct. 3, 1929; s. Louis and Rose (Heend) R.; student LaSalle-Peru Oglesby Jr. Coll., 1947-49; B.S., U. Ill., 1951, J.D., 1953; m. Sandra Faye Cohon, June 16, 1953; children—Sheryl Jo, Elliot Gene, Lorri Beth. Admitted to Ill. bar, 1953; mem. firm Cohon, Raizes & Regal, Chgo., 1956—. Served with U.S. Army, 1953-56. Mem. Am., Fed., Ill., Chgo. bar assns., Am. Judicature Soc., Decalogue Soc., Men's ORT (officer), U. Ill. Alumni Assn. (dir.). Jewish religion. Mason; mem. B'nai B'rith (officer). Club: Illinois (past pres.) (Chgo.). Home: 272 Sheridan Rd Highland Park IL 60035 Office: 208 S La Salle St Chicago IL 60604

RAJAN, BALACHANDRA, educator; b. Toungoo, Burma, Mar. 24, 1920; s. Arunachala and Visalam Tyagurajan; B.A., U. Cambridge (Eng.), 1941, M.A., 1944, Ph.D., 1946; m. Chandra Sarma, Aug. 29, 1946; 1 dau., Tilottoma. Came to Can., 1965. Fellow Trinity Coll. Cambridge, 1944-48, dir. studies in English, 1945-48; mem. Indian Fgn. Service, 1948-61; head English dept. Delhi (India) U., 1961-64; vis. prof. U. Wis., 1964-65; prof. U. Windsor (Ont., Can.), 1965-66; sr. prof. English, U. Western Ont., London, 1965—. Chmn. adminstrv. and legal com., 2d gen. conf. Internat. Atomic Energy Agy., 1959. Chmn. exec. bd. UN Children's Fund, 1955-57. Fellow Royal Soc. Can.; mem. Milton Soc. Am. (pres. 1972). Author: Paradise Lost and the Seventeenth Century Reader, 1947; The Lofty Rhyme A Study of Milton's Major Poetry, 1970; William B. Yeats A Critical Introduction, 1965; The Dark Dancer, 1958, Too Long in the West, 1961 (novels); The Overwhelming Question: a Study of the Poetry of T.S. Eliot, 1976. Home: 478 Regent St London ON Canada

RAJCHMAN, JAN ALEKSANDER, elecronics engr.; b. London, Aug. 10, 1911; s. Ludwik Witold and Marjia Clotylda (Bojanczyk) R.; came to U.S., 1935, naturalized, 1940; grad. Coll. Geneva, 1930; E.E. Master, Swiss Fed. Inst. Tech., 1935, Dr.Sc., 1938; m. Ruth Vi Teitrick, June 30, 1944; children—Alice Rajchman Hammond, John A. Engr., RCA Mfg. Co., 1935-36; with RCA Labs., 1936-76, dir. computer research lab., 1961-67, staff v.p. data processing, 1967-71, staff v.p. info. scis., 1971-76; vis. Mackay prof. U. Calif., Berkeley, winter 1977; mem. user grantee group in optical communication NSF, 1969—; mem. advanced memory adv. com. Advanced Research Project Agy., 1975, cons., 1977—; mem. peer rev. com. Nat. Acad. Eng., 1975-77; chmn. editorial adv. bd. RCA Rev., 1969-76. Co-recipient Levy medal Franklin Inst., 1947; recipient Harold Pender award U. Pa., 1977. Fellow IEEE (chmn. Liebman award com. 1970, chmn. awards fields com. 1971-73; Liebman Meml. award 1960, Edison medal 1974), Am. Phys. Soc.; mem. AAAS, Nat. Acad. Engring., Am. Optical Soc., N.Y. Acad. Scis., Sigma Xi (chpt. pres.). Author, patentee in field. Address: 268 Edgerstoune Rd Princeton NJ 08540

RAJKI, WALTER ALBERT, mfg. co. exec.; b. Cleve., Sept. 24, 1925; s. Stephen and Julia (Zajac) R.; B.S., M.I.T., 1951; J.D., Cleve. State U., 1958; m. Mary Elizabeth Koch, July 12, 1952; children—William, Carl, Joan. Engr., Chain Belt Co., Milw., 1951-53; admitted to Ohio bar, 1958; plant mgr., pres. Adalet Mfg. Co., Cleve., 1953-72; group v.p. Scott & Fetzer Co., Cleve., 1972-78, sr. v.p., 1978—; dir. Highland Farms Inc., 1960—, Brost Foundry Co., 1979—. Mem. IEEE, Cleve. Engring. Soc. Ohio Bar Assn., Cleve. Bar Assn. Club: Cleve. Yachting. Office: Scott & Fetzer Co 14600 Detroit Ave Lakewood OH 44107

RAKEL, ROBERT EDWIN, physician, educator; b. Cin., July 13, 1932; s. Edwin J. and Elsie (Machino) R.; B.S., U. Cin., 1954, M.D., 1958; m. Peggy Klare; children—Barbara, Cindy, Linda, David. Intern, St. Mary's Hosp., Cin., 1958-59; resident in internal medicine USPHS Hosp., Seattle, 1959-61; resident in gen. practice Monterey County Hosp., Salinas, Calif., 1961-62; practice medicine, Newport Beach, Calif., 1962-69; chmn. family practice program U. Calif., Irvine, 1969-71; prof., head dept. family practice U. Iowa, 1971—. Served with USPHS, 1959-61. Charter diplomate Am. Bd. Family Practice (v.p., dir.). Fellow Am. Acad. Family Physicians; mem. AMA, Nat. Bd. Med. Examiners, Soc. Tchrs. Family Medicine (dir., sec. 1971-73). Author, editor books. Mem. editorial bds. med. jours. Contbr. articles to med. jours. Home: 1950 Calvin St Iowa City IA 52240 Office: U of Iowa Hosps and Clinics Iowa City IA 52242

RAKER, JOHN PETER, judge; b. Shamokin, Pa., Feb. 27, 1914; s. Edward and Bertha Edith (Graeber) R.; A.B., Muhlenberg Coll., 1936; J.D., George Washington U., 1940: m. Rita Quitugua, Apr. 15, 1953; 1 son, Frank. Admitted to D.C. bar, 1940, Ter. of Guam bar, 1950: individual practice law Washington, 1940-41; atty. Dept. Army, 1945-47, Govt. Guam, 1948-51, 62-75, OPA., 1952; U.S. atty. Ter. Guam, 1952-54; atty. Dept. Navy, 1954-62: judge Guam Superior Ct., Agana, 1975—. Served with U.S. Army, 1942-45. Mem. Am., Fed. bar assns., Phi Alpha Delta. Lutheran. Club: Windward Hills Golf and Country, Elks. Home: pO Box 875 Agana GU 96910 Office: PO Box CT Agana GU 96910*

RAKESTRAW, WARREN VINCENT, lawyer; b. Dayton, Ohio, July 6, 1940; s. David Warren and Lou Ann (Hobbs) R.; B.S., Ohio U., 1963; J.D., Capital U., 1968; m. Penny Lynn Blackford, June 23, 1963. Admitted to Ohio bar, 1968; asst. atty. gen. State of Ohio, Columbus, 1968; legis. dir. to U.S. Senator William B. Saxbe, Washington, 1969-74; asst. atty. gen. U.S. Dept. Justice, Washington, 1974-75; counsel to ambassador, New Delhi, India, 1975-77; partner firm Chester, Saxbe, Hoffman & Willcox, Columbus, 1977—. Mem. Am., Ohio, Fla., D.C. bar assns., Sigma Chi. Club: Belmont Hills Country (Ohio). Home: 7179 Avery Rd Dublin OH 43017 Office: 8 E Broad St Columbus OH 43215

RAKITA, LOUIS, cardiologist, educator; b. Montreal, Que., Can., July 2, 1922; s. S. and Rose (Weinman) R.; came to U.S., 1951, naturalized, 1962; B.A., Sir George Williams Coll., Montreal, 1942; M.D., C.M., McGill U., 1949; m. G. Blanche Michlin, Dec. 4, 1945; 1 son, Robert M. Intern Montreal Gen. Hosp., 1949-50; resident in medicine Jewish Gen. Hosp., Montreal, 1950-51; fellow in medicine Alton Ochsner Med. Found., New Orleans, 1951-52; chief resident in medicine Cleve. City Hosp., 1952-53, Am. Heart Assn. fellow, 1954-55; Am. Heart Assn. fellow Inst. for Med. Research, Cedars of Lebanon Hosp., Los Angeles, 1953-54; practice medicine specializing in internal medicine and cardiology, Cleve., 1954—; instr. medicine Western Res. U., Cleve., 1954-55, sr. instr., 1955-57, asst. prof., 1957-61, asso. prof., 1961-71; asst. vis. physician Cleve. City Hosp., 1954-57, vis. physician, 1957—; advanced fellow Cleve. Met. Gen. Hosp., 1959-61, dir. cardiology, 1966—; asso. div. of research in med. edn. Case Western Res. U., Cleve., 1969-75, prof. medicine, 1971—; cons. in cardiology Lutheran Med. Center, Cleve., 1970—, Crile VA Hosp., Cleve., 1969—; vis. cardiologist Sunny Acres Hosp., Cleve., 1973—; cardiologist rep. of del. to USSR, 1973. Served with RCAF, 1942-45. Recipient Research Career Devel. award USPHS, 1962-69. Diplomate Am. Bd. Internal Medicine. Fellow Am. Heart Assn. (mem. exec. com. N.E. Ohio chpt. 1972—, trustee 1969—, pres. N.E. Ohio chpt. 1972-74, council on clin. cardiology 1972—), A.C.P., Am. Coll. of Cardiology, Royal Coll. Physicians and Surgeons (Can.); mem. Ohio State Heart Assn. (mem. research study sect. 1969-70), Am. Fedn. Clin. Research, Central Soc. Clin. Research, Soc. Exptl. Biology and Medicine, AAUP, Cleve. Med. Library Assn. (trustee 1972—), Sigma Xi, Alpha Omega Alpha. Author: (with M. Broder) Cardiac Arrhythmias, 1970; (with M. Kaplan) Immunological Diseases, 1972. Contbr. articles on cardiovascular diseases to profl. publs. Home: 24151 S Woodland Rd Shaker Heights OH 44122 Office: 3395 Scranton Cleveland OH 44109

RALEIGH, CECIL BARING, geophysicist; b. Little Rock, Aug. 11, 1934; s. Cecil Baring and Lucile Nell (Stewart) R.; B.A., Pomona (Calif.) Coll., 1956; M.A., Claremont (Calif.) Grad. Sch., 1958; Ph.D., U. Calif., Los Angeles, 1963; m. Gail Wright Lohman, July 4, 1976; children—Alison, Marianne, Lawrence, David. Fellow, Research Sch. Phys. Sci., Australian Nat. U., Canberra, 1963-66; geophysicist U.S. Geol. Survey, Menlo Park, Calif., 1966—; Richard M. Nixon prof. geology Whittier (Calif.) Coll., 1977. Recipient Interdisciplinary award U.S. Nat. Com. Rock Mechanics, 1969, 74; Meritorious Service award Dept. Interior, 1974. Fellow Am. Geophys. Union, Geol. Soc. Am. Democrat. Inventor formation fracturing method. Author papers control earthquakes, rheology of the mantle, mechanics of faulting, crystal plasticity. Home: 44 Mesa Ct Atherton CA 94025 Office: 345 Middlefield Rd Menlo Park CA 94025

RALEIGH, HENRY PATRICK, educator, artist; b. N.Y.C., Feb. 5, 1931; s. Henry Patrick and Holly (Wilcox) R.; B.S., Pratt Inst., 1956, M.S., 1959; Ph.D., N.Y. U., 1963; m. Barbara Verne Epstein, Aug. 15, 1970; 1 dau., Alison; children by previous marriage—Stephen, Nora, Anne. Dir. evening art and architecture Pratt Inst., 1959-65, chmn. dept. art edn., 1965-68; chmn. dept. studio art State U. Coll., New Paltz, N.Y., 1968—, prof. film history and art criticism, 1968—, dean Faculty Fine and Performing Arts, 1971-73, chmn. dept. art history, 1971—. Exhibited paintings at March Gallery, N.Y.C., 1957-58, Roko Gallery, N.Y.C., 1958-59, Tanager Gallery, N.Y.C., 1961, Riverside Mus., N.Y.C., 1965, Albany Inst. Art, 1971, 72, 73, 75; editorial cons. Jour. Aesthetic Edn.; mem. ednl. bd. Internat. Inst. Packaging. Served with AUS, 1950-52. Mem. Am., Brit. socs. aesthetics, Coll. Art Assn. Contbr. articles profl. jours. Home: 304 Springtown Rd New Paltz NY 12561. *I attribute my success to an unswerving faith in the principle that everyone else is as incompetent as I.*

RALEIGH, JOHN HENRY, educator; b. Springfield, Mass., Aug. 30, 1920; s. John Joseph and Theresa A. (King) R.; B.A., Wesleyan U., Middletown, Conn., 1943; Ph.D., Princeton, 1948; m. Jo Dodson Shaw, Aug. 1, 1949; children—Kingsley D., John Locke, Lydia King. Lectr., U. Calif., Berkeley, 1947-49, asst. prof. English, 1949-54, asso. prof., 1954-60, prof., 1960—, chmn. dept., 1969, vice-chancellor for acad. affairs, 1969-72. Recipient citation outstanding achievement as tchr. and scholar Wesleyan U., 1963; Guggenheim fellow, 1962. Mem. MLA. Author: Matthew Arnold and American Culture, 1957; The Plays of Eugene O'Neill, 1965; Time, Place, and Idea: Essays on the Novel, 1968; The Chronicle of Leopold and Molly Bloom: "Ulysses" as Narrative, 1977. Home: 1020 Keeler Ave Berkeley CA 94708

RALEY, DONALD WILLIAM, lawyer; b. Hanoverton, Ohio, Mar. 30, 1905; s. Austin Robert and Blanche (Ray) R.; A.B. cum laude, Coll. of Wooster, 1927; J.D., Harvard 1931; m. Helen Reardon, June 8, 1935 (dec.); children—David (dec.), Mary C., Helen, Gertrude; m. 2d, Edythe F. Fitzgerald, Aug. 11, 1979. Admitted to Ohio bar, 1931, since practiced in Canton; partner firm Day, Ketterer, Raley, Wright & Rybolt, and predecessors, 1937—. Pres. Mahoning Presbyn. Men; trustee, Canton Welfare Fedn.; trustee, pres. Canton Dist. YMCA. Mem. Am., Ohio (chmn. uniform state laws com.), Stark County (exec. com., chmn. cts. com., unauthorized practice com.) bar assns., Internat. Assn. Ins. Counsel, Fedn. Ins. Counsel, Nat. Assn. R.R. Trial Counsel, Phi Beta Kappa, Phi Sigma Iota. Republican. Presbyn. (elder). Clubs: Canton, Rotary (pres.), Oakwood Country (Canton). Home: 3305 Enfield Rd NW Canton OH 44708 Office: Cleve-Tusc Building Canton OH 44702

RALEY, THOMAS PORTER, supermarket and drug chain exec.; b. Lead Hill, Ark., Apr. 8, 1903; s. Reglus and Nancy (Parrish) R.; 1 dau., Joyce Nadine Raley Teel. Owner, chmn. bd. Raley's Supermarketsand Drug Centers, Sacramento, 1935—; chmn. United Grocers, Ltd., 1974—, dir., 1950—; pres., dir. Ins. Buyers, Inc. Clubs: Rotary (Paul Harris fellow), World Trade, St. Francis Yacht, Masons, Del Paso Country, Shriners. Home: Sacramento CA 95819 Office: 1515 20th St Sacramento CA 95814

RALL, DAVID PLATT, ofcl. NIH; b. Aurora, Ill., Aug. 3, 1926; s. Edward Everett and Nell (Platt) R.; B.A., North Central Coll., Naperville, Ill., 1946; M.S., Northwestern U., 1948, M.D., Ph.D., 1951; m. Edith Levy, July 17, 1954; children—Jonathan D., Catharyn E. Intern, Bellevue Hosp., N.Y.C., 1952-53; commd. officer USPHS, 1953—, asst. surgeon gen., 1971—; sr. investigator Lab. Chem. Pharmacology, Nat. Cancer Inst., NIH, Bethesda, Md., 1953-55, Clin. Pharmacology and Exptl. Therapeutics Service, 1956-58, head service, 1958-63, chief Lab. Chem. Pharmacology, 1963-69, asso. sci. dir. for exptl. therapeutics Nat. Cancer Inst., 1966-71, dir. Nat. Inst. Environ. Health Scis., 1971—, dir. Nat. Toxicology Program, 1978—; adj. prof. pharmacology U. N.C., Chapel Hill, 1971—. Mem. AAAS, Am. Assn. Cancer Research, Am. Soc. Clin. Investigation, Am. Soc. Clin. Pharmacology and Therapeutics, Am. Soc. Pharmacology and Exptl. Therapeutics, Soc. Exptl. Biology and Medicine, Soc. Occupational and Environ. Health, Soc. Toxicology, Fedn. Am. Socs. for Exptl. Biology. Office: Nat Inst of Environ Health Scis NIH Research Triangle Park NC 27709

RALL, JOSEPH EDWARD, physician; b. Naperville, Ill., Feb. 3, 1920; s. Edward Everett and Nell (Platt) R.; B.A., N. Central Coll., 1940; M.S., Northwestern U., 1944, M.D., 1945; Ph.D., U. Minn., 1952; D.Sc. (hon.), N. Central Coll., 1966; Dr.h.c., Faculty of Medicine, Free U. Brussels (Belgium), 1975; m. Caroline Domm, Sept. 28, 1944 (dec. Apr. 1976); children—Priscilla, Edward Christian; m. 2d, Nancy Lamontagne, Apr. 15, 1978. Asso. mem. Sloan Kettering Inst., N.Y.C., 1950-55; chief clin. endocrinology br. Nat. Inst. Arthritis, Metabolism and Digestive Diseases, NIH, 1955-62, dir. intramural research, 1962—. Mem. NRC, 1960-65. Served to capt. M.C., AUS, 1946-48. Recipient Van Meter prize Am. Goiter Assn., 1950, Fleming award, 1959, Outstanding Achievement award Mayo Clinic and U. Minn., 1964; Distinguished Service award Am. Thyroid Assn., 1967, HEW, 1968; named Outstanding Alumnus N. Central Coll., 1966. Mem. A.A.A.S., Am. Soc. Clin. Investigation, Am. Phys. Soc., Endocrine Soc., Assn. Am. Physicians, Societe de Biologie (France), Royal Acad. Medicine (Brussels). Author numerous articles, chpts. in books on thyroid gland and radiation. Home: 3947 Baltimore St Kensington MD 20795 Office: National Institutes Health Bldg 10 Room 9N222 Bethesda MD 20205

RALL, OWEN, lawyer; b. Cedar Rapids, Iowa, Dec. 1, 1901; s. Julius Frederick and Flora Ellen (Ashby) R.; A.B. magna cum laude, Coe Coll., 1921; J.D., Northwestern U., 1924; m. Bertha L. Biedermann, Mar. 19, 1923 (dec. Apr. 1976); 1 dau., Kathryn Rall Jacky. Admitted to Ill. Bar, 1924, since practiced in Chgo.; of counsel firm Peterson, Ross, Schloerb & Seidel, 1933—. Mem. com. character and fitness Ill. Supreme Ct., 1937-42, chmn., 1942; adv. council U. Ill. Law Forum, 1950-52; chmn. joint com. Ill. civil procedure which revised procedural statutes and Ill. Supreme Ct. and Appellate Ct. rules, 1950-55; mem. Jud. Adv. Council Ill., 1957-61; active constl. revision Ill., legis. reapportionment, jud. reorgn.; chmn. Ill. Supreme Ct. Rules Com., 1963-67. Fellow Am. Coll. Trial Lawyers; mem. Am., Ill. (pres. 1961-62, award of Merit 1972), Chgo. (librarian, bd. mgrs. 1942-43, 46-49) bar assns., Bar Assn. Seventh Fed. Circuit (pres. 1966-67), Am. Judicature Soc. (Herbert Lincoln Harley award 1973), ADA (hon.), Scabbard and Blade (nat. v.p. 1924-26), Delta Theta Phi (nat. sec., editor 1927-29). Republican. Presbyn. Clubs: Union League (chmn. modern cts. com. 1958), Plaza (Chgo.). Author articles legal jours. Home: 721 Foster St Evanston IL 60201 Office: 200 E Randolph Dr Chicago IL 60601

RALLS, CHARLES C., lawyer; b. Missoula, Mont., Mar. 29, 1904; s. Claude and Frances (Kasper) R.; LL.B., Gonzaga U., 1930; m. Alice O'Leary, Oct. 14, 1935; children—Richard Charles, Charles Patrick. Admitted to Wash. bar, and since practiced in Seattle; spl. asst. atty. gen. State of Wash.; chief dep. pros. atty. King County, 1936-42; chmn. Wash. State Census Bur.; dir. Civil Def., State of Wash., 1957-62; dir. Region 8 (Alaska, Mont., Idaho, Wash., Oreg.) Office of Civil Def., Dept. of Def., 1962-71; judge N.E. Dist. Ct., Redmond, Wash., 1971—. Mem. V.F.W., successively comdr., Seattle post, mem. nat. finance com., chmn. nat. security com., 1947, encampment at Cleve.; sr. vice comdr. Dept. of Wash., 1946-47, dept. comdr., 1947-48, jr. vice comdr., 1948, sr. vice comdr., 1949, comdr. in chief, 1950. Served from pvt. to maj., U.S.M.C.; overseas with Fifth Amphibious Corps, P.T.O. Mem. Wash., Seattle (past sec.) bar assns. Home: 12625 Avondale Rd Redmond WA 98052 Office: 7425 170th NE Redmond WA 98052

RALLS, KATHERINE, biologist; b. Oakland, Calif., Mar. 21, 1939; d. Alvin Wallingsford and Ruth (McQueen) Smith; A.B., Stanford, 1960; M.A., Radcliffe Coll., 1962; Ph.D., Harvard, 1965; m. Kenneth M. Ralls, June 1958 (div. Sept. 1968); children—Robin, Tamsen, Kristin. Guest investigator Rockefeller U., N.Y.C., 1968-70, adj. asst. prof., 1970—; asst. prof. biology Sarah Lawrence Coll., Bronxville, N.Y., 1970-73; research zoologist Inst. for Research in Animal Behavior, N.Y. Zool. Soc., 1970-73; zoologist Nat. Zool. Park, Smithsonian Instn., 1976—; fellow Radcliffe Inst., 1973-74, Smithsonian Instn., 1973-76, AAUW, 1975-76. Contbr. articles to profl. jours. Home: 2710 Cortland Pl Washington DC 20008

RALSON, LESLEY LLOYD, ins. co. exec.; b. Rusk, Tex., Oct. 12, 1929; s. James Herbert and Virginia Mae (Sword) R.; B.B.A. in Bus., U. Houston, 1952; children—Leslie Ann, Sylvia Simona, Stephanie Jean. With Prudential Ins. Co., 1957—, mgr. Milw. office, 1964-66, dir. group sales, eastern office, Newark, 1966-68, v.p., Houston, 1968-73, sr. v.p. group ins., corp. office, Newark, 1973—; chmn. bd. Kaiser-Prudential Health Plan, Dallas, Prudential Health Plan of Okla.; dir. Prudential Reins. Co., Bd. dirs. Clara Maass Hosp., Essex County (N.J.) United Way. Served to 1st lt. USMC, 1952-57. Home: One Scenic Dr Highlands NJ 07732 Office: Prudential Ins Co Am Prudential Plaza Newark NJ 07101

RALSTON, ANTHONY, educator, computer scientist; b. N.Y.C., Dec. 24, 1930; s. Alfred Joseph and Ruth (Bien) R.; B.S., Mass. Inst. Tech., 1952, Ph.D., 1956; m. Jayne Madeleine Rosenthal, Feb. 14, 1958; children—Jonathan, Geoffrey, Steven, Elizabeth. Mem. Tech. staff Bell Telephone Labs., 1956-59; lectr. U. Leeds, 1959-60; mgr. tech. computing Am. Cyanamid Co., 1960-61; asso. prof. math. Stevens Inst. Tech., 1961-64, prof., 1964-65; dir. computer services State U. N.Y., Buffalo, 1965-70, prof., chmn. dept. computer sci., 1967—; dir. Genesee Computer Center; bd. examiners Grad. Record

Exam in Computer Sci., 1976—; mem. computer sci. and tech. bd. NRC; Served as 2d lt. U.S. Army, 1957. Mem. Assn. Computing Machinery (pres. 1972-74, mem. council 1968-76), Am. Fedn. Info. Processing Socs. (pres. 1975-76). Author: A First Course in Numerical Analysis, 1965, 2d edit., 1978; Introduction to Programming and Computer Science, 1971. Editor: Ency. of Computer Science, 1976; co-editor: Mathematical Methods for Digital Computers, Vol. 1, 1960, Vol. 2, 1967, Vol. 3, 1977. Home: 475 N Forest Rd Williamsville NY 14221 Office: 4226 Ridge Lea Rd Amherst NY 14226

RALSTON, HENRY JAMES, III, neurobiologist: b. Berkeley, Calif., Mar. 12, 1935; s. Henry James and Sue Harris (Mahnke) R.; B.A., U. Calif., Berkeley, 1956, M.D., San Francisco, 1959; m. Diane Cornelia Daly, Oct. 29, 1960; children—Rachel Anne, Amy Sue. Intern, Mt. Sinai Hosp., N.Y.C., 1959-60; resident in medicine U. Calif., San Francisco, 1960-61; spl. post-doctoral fellow Univ. Coll., London, 1963-65; asst. prof. anatomy Stanford (Calif.) U., 1965-69, asso. prof. U. Wis., Madison, 1969-73; prof., chmn. dept. anatomy U. Calif., San Francisco, 1973—; cons. NIH; mem. Macy Found. com. for future of anat. scis., 1977-80. Served with M.C., U.S. Army, 1961-63. Recipient Borden award for undergrad. med. research, 1959; Henry J. Kaiser award for excellence in teaching, 1978; USPHS grantee, 1966—. Mem. AAAS, Am. Soc. Cell Biology, Soc. Neurosci., Soc. Study Pain, Am. Assn. Anatomists, Am. Acad. Neurology, Anat. Assn. Gt. Britain, Phi Beta Kappa. Contbr. articles in field of organization of mammalian nervous system studied by electron microscopy, mechanisms subserving pain in animals and man. Office: Dept Anatomy Univ Calif Sch Medicine San Francisco CA 94143

RALSTON, LLOYD STANLEY, physician; b. Crystal, N.D., Oct. 13, 1919; s. Frank Stanley and Ruth Jane (Coker) R.; B.A., Mayville State Coll., 1939; B.S., U. N.D., 1943; M.D., U. Ill., 1944. Intern, Garfield Park Community Hosp., Chgo., 1944-45; resident in internal medicine Wadsworth Gen. Hosp., UCLA, 1950-52; practice medicine specializing in internal medicine Grand Forks, N.D., 1953—; asst. prof. bacteriology and pathology U. N.D., Grand Forks, 1947-48, prof. medicine U. N.D. Sch. Medicine, 1966—; chief of staff Deaconess Hosp., 1957-60; chief of medicine United Hosp., 1970—, dir. med. edn., 1970—; chief of medicine U. N.D. Rehab. Hosp., Grand Forks, 1966—, v.p., 1976—; mem. N.D. State Bd. Med. Examiners, 1970—, pres., 1975-76; guest lectr. various med. centers in U.S., 1953—. Served to capt. M.C., U.S. Army, 1945-47. Recipient Distinguished Grad. award Mayville State Coll., 1976, Fedn. Women's Clubs award, 1974; diplomate Am. Bd. Internal Medicine. Fellow A.C.P., Am. Coll. Chest Physicians, Am. Acad. Dirs. of Med. Edn.; mem. AMA (Physicians Recognition award 1969, 72, 76), Sigma Xi, Alpha Omega Alpha. Contbr. numerous articles in field of internal medicine to profl. jours.; established regional med. edn. program for rural area hosps. in Minn. and N.D.; upper Midwestern states champion in equestrian events, 1960-79. Home: 1000 S Columbia Rd Grand Forks ND 58201 Office: University of North Dakota School of Medicine Grand Forks ND 58201 also United Hosp and Grand Forks Clinic 1000 S Columbia Rd Grand Forks ND 58201

RALSTON, NOEL PRINTISS, govt. ofcl.; b. Carthage, Mo., Nov. 24, 1915; s. Ralph N. and Dollye O. (Patterson) R.; B.S., U. Mo., 1937, M.A., 1939; Ph.D., Cornell U., 1942; m. Marie E. Olmsted, May 31, 1942; children—Judith Ann (Mrs. Richard Burr), Gary O. (dec.), Susan P. (Mrs. John Coon), Peter N. Staff animal husbandry dept. U. Calif., Davis, 1942-49; from asst. to prof. Mich. State U., 1949-54, head dairy dept., 1954-59, dir. coop. extension serive, asst. dean Coll. Agr., 1959-66; dep. adminstr. Fed. Extension Service, Dept. Agr., Washington, 1966-68, dep. dir. Office Sci. and Edn., 1968-70, asso. dir., 1970-73, program leader, dairy prodn. Sci. and Edn. Adminstrn. Extension, 1973-79; ret., 1979. Mem. Gov.'s Coordinating Com. Area Redevel. Program. Served to capt. AUS, 1942-45. Cert. animal scientist (dairy). Fellow AAAS; mem. Adult Edn. Assn. Am., Inst. Biol. Scis., Am. Dairy Sci. Assn., Am. Soc. Animal Sci., Am. Soc. Pub. Adminstrn., Sigma Xi, Phi Kappa Phi, Alpha Zeta, Gamma Sigma Delta, Alpha Gamma Rho, Gamma Alpha. Contbr. articles profl. jours. Home: 1784 Hamilton Rd Okemos MI 48864

RAMADAN, PAUL RAFIQ, meat co. exec.; b. Haifa, Palestine, June 21, 1931; s. Richard A. and Rose (de Monde) R.; B.A., B.S., U. No. Colo., 1953; M.B.A., U. Denver, 1960; m. Lorraine Shirley Cyriacks, Apr. 10, 1951; children—Roland, Linda, Rafiq. Corp. controller Capitol Packing Co., Denver, 1954-67; internat. controller Gates Rubber Co., Denver, 1968; div. controller Pet Inc., St. Louis, 1968-70; v.p. Fenton Sports Inc., Denver, 1970-71, pres., 1971-72; exec. v.p. Litvak Meat Co., Denver, 1972—, also dir.; dir. Litvak Internat., York Cattle Co. Mem. Nat. Assn. Accountants, Am. Mgmt. Assn., M.B.A. Execs. Club, Nat. Ind. Meat Packers Assn., Nat. Assn. Arab-Ams., Nat. Hide Assn., Colo. Meat Dealers Assn., Denver Grad. Sch. Alumni, Denver C. of C., Adams County C. of C. Club: Pinehurst Country. Home: 9369 W Baltic Dr Lakewood CO 80227 Office: 5900 York St Denver CO 80216

RAMAGE, COLIN STOKES, educator, meteorologist; b. Napier, New Zealand, Mar. 3, 1921; s. James Gorman and Margaret (Stokes) R.; B.Sc., Victoria Coll., Wellington, New Zealand, 1940; D.Sc., U. New Zealand, 1961; Commonwealth Fund fellow, U. Chgo., 1953-54; m. Mary Louis Clements, Dec. 23, 1964. Came to U.S., 1956, naturalized, 1962. With New Zealand Meteorol. Service, 1940-41; successively sci. officer, dep. dir., acting dir. Royal Obs., Hong Kong, 1946-56; mem. faculty U. Hawaii, 1956—, prof. meteorology, 1958—, chmn. dept. meteorology and oceanography, 1960-61, chmn. dept. geosci., 1964-69, chmn. dept. meteorology, 1971—; asso. dir. Hawaii Inst. Geophys., 1964-71; cons. USAF; meteorology dir. Internat. Indian Ocean Expdn., 1961-72. Served with Royal New Zealand Air Force, 1942-46. Fellow Am. Meteorol. Soc.; mem. Am. Geophys. Union, Univ. Corp. Atmospheric Research, A.A.U.P., Sigma Xi. Club: Cosmos. Author: Monsoon Meteorology, 1971; also articles tropical and monsoon meteorology. Home: 4959 Mana Pl Honolulu HI 96816

RAMAGE, EDWIN STEPHEN, educator; b. Vancouver, B.C., Can., July 19, 1929; s. Edwin Havelock and Mary (Cardinell) R.; B.A., U. B.C. (Vancouver), 1951, M.A., 1952; Ph.D., U. Cin., 1957; m. Shirley Sue LaRue, June 16, 1956; children—Bruce Edwin, Victoria Sue. Came to U.S., 1953. Mem. faculty dept. classical studies Ind. U., Bloomington, 1957—, asso. prof., 1964-68, prof., 1968—, chmn. dept., 1971-75. Mem. Am. Philol. Assn., Classical Assn. Can. Author: Urbanitas: Ancient Sophistication and Refinement, 1973; (with D.L. Sigsbee, S.C. Fredericks) Roman Satirists and Their Satire, 1974; translator: Roman Satire (U. Knoche), 1975; editor: Atlantis: Fact or Fiction?, 1978; contbr. profl. jours. Home: 1935 Montclair Ave Bloomington IN 47401

RAMALEY, JUDITH AITKEN, neuroendocrinologist; b. Vincennes, Ind., Jan. 11, 1941; d. Robert H. and Mary Crebs (McCullough) Aitken; B.A. in Zoology, Swarthmore Coll., 1963; Ph.D. in Anatomy, UCLA, 1966; m. Robert F. Ramaley, Mar. 6, 1966; children—Alan, Andrew. Summer fellow U. Pa., 1962; NSF summer fellow Rocky Mountain Biol. Lab., 1963; teaching asst. neuroanatomy and histology U. Calif., Los Angeles, 1963-66; NIH postdoctoral fellow Center Neurol. Scis., dept. chemistry Ind. U., 1967-69, lectr. dept. zoology, summer 1967, research asso., lectr. Biomedical Scis. Program, 1967-68, asst. prof. dept. anatomy and physiology, div. biol. scis., 1969-71; asst. prof. dept. physiology and biophysics U. Nebr. Med. Center, Omaha, 1972-74, asso. prof., 1974-78, prof., 1978—, asso. dean research and devel., 1979—, mem. exec. grad. council, com. II, 1973-78, exec. faculty Med. Sch., 1974-75, chmn. departmental grad. com., 1974-76; producer film for Nebr. Ednl. TV; mem. NSF regulatory biology panel, 1978-81. NSF grantee, 1969—, NIH grantee, 1975—; Am. Council on Edn. fellow in acad. adminstrn., 1978-79. Mem. Endocrine Soc. (pres. Women's Caucus, chmn. edn. com.), Am. Physiol. Soc., Am. Assn. Anatomists, Soc. for Study Reproduction (chmn. edn. com. 1976-78, chmn. nominating com. 1978), Soc. for Neuroscis., Assn. Women in Sci. (pres. 1977-79, chmn. nominating com. 1974-75), Sigma Xi. Quaker. Author: Progesterone Function: Molecular and Biochemical Aspects, 1972; (with G. Bevelander), Essentials in Histology, 1974, 8th edit., 1979; mem. editorial bd. Signs, 1975—, Proc. Exptl. Biol. Medicine, 1978—, Biology of Reprodn., 1978—; contbr. articles to profl. jours. Home: 1702 N 52 St Omaha NE 68104 Office: Dept Physiology U Nebr Med Center Omaha NE 68105

RAMAZANI, ROUHOLLAH KAREGAR, educator; b. Tehran, Iran, Mar. 21, 1928; s. Ali Karegar and Khadijeh (Sultani) R.; LL.M., U. Tehran, 1951; postgrad. U. Ga., 1952; S.J.D., U. Va., 1954; m. Nesta Shahrokh, Feb. 22, 1952; children—Vaheed, David, Jahan, Sima. Came to U.S., 1952, naturalized, 1961. Lectr. fgn. affairs U. Va., Charlottesville, 1954-57, research asso. Soviet Fgn. Econ. Relations Project, 1956-59, asst. prof. fgn. affairs, 1957-60, asso. prof., 1960-64, prof. govt. and fgn. affairs, 1964—, Edward R. Stettinius Jr. prof. govt. and fgn. affairs, 1972; Aga Khan vis. prof. Islamic studies Am. U., Beirut, 1967-68; vis. prof. Middle East studies Sch. Advanced Internat. Studies, Johns Hopkins, 1967, 70-71, 72-73, 75, 77, 79; vis. prof. Cambridge (Eng.) U., spring 1975; cons. internat. relations Rockefeller Found.; cons. Inst. Fgn. Policy Analysis. Vice pres., trustee Am. Inst. Iranian Studies; cons. Pan Am. Internat. Oil Co., Research Analysis Corp. Mem. exec. com. Council on Fgn. Relations, Charlottesville, 1965-67; mem. Citizens for Albemarle, 1972—. Recipient prize for distinguished contbn. Am. Assn. Middle East Studies, 1964; Social Sci. Research Council grantee, 1967, Fulbright research grantee, 1968. Fellow Middle East Studies Assn. N.Am.; mem. Am. Soc. Internat. Law, Am., So. polit. sci. assns., Middle East Inst., Shaybani Soc. Internat. Law (exec. officer), Phi Beta Kappa. Author: The Middle East and the European Common Market, 1964; The Northern Tier: Iran, Afghanistan and Turkey, 1966; The Foreign Policy of Iran, 1500-1941: A Developing Nation in World Affairs, 1966; The Persian Gulf: Iran's Role, 1972; Iran's Foreign Policy, 1941-1973: A Study of Foreign Policy in Modernizing Nations, 1975; Beyond the Arab-Israeli Settlement: New Directions for U.S. Policy in the Middle East, 1977; The Persian Gulf and the Strait of Hormuz, 1979; asso. editor Jour. South Asian and Middle Eastern Studies; adv. editor Middle East Jour., Fgn. Policy Report; contbr. to Soviet Foreign Relations and World Communism, 1965; The Search for World Order, 1971; Concise Ency. of the Middle East, 1973; The Anatomy of Communist Takeovers, 1975; Energy and World Politics, 1975; Iran: Past, Present, and Future; From June to October: The Middle East Between 1967 and 1973, 1978; Iran in the 1980's, 1978; The Middle East Contemporary Survey, 1967-77; The Middle East Contemporary Survey, 1977-78; World Politics and the Arab-Israeli Conflict, 1979; The Impact of the Iranian Events upon Persian Gulf and United States Security, 1979; The Revolution in Iran: Its Character and Political-Economic Complications, 1979; mem. editorial adv. bd. Fgn. Policy Analysis. Home: RFD 3 Glenaire Charlottesville VA 22901

RAMBECK, LEROY (ROY) STANLEY, hosp. adminstr.; b. Parshall, N.D., Oct. 13, 1919; s. Adolph Olson and Maren Anna (Oksness) R.; B.A., U. Wash., 1951; m. Beth Eleanor Haugen, Oct. 11, 1941; children—Todd Oscar, Richard John. Adminstr., Univ. Hosp., Seattle, 1954-68, exec. dir. U. Wash. Hosps., Seattle, 1968—, clin. prof. Sch. Pub. Health, 1974—; cons. NIH; chmn. health panel United Way King County (Wash.), 1976. Fellow Am. Coll. Hosp. Adminstrs.; mem. Am. Hosp. Assn. (trustee), Nat. Bd. Med. Examiners, Wash. Hosp. Assn. (pres. 1975-76), Fed. Hosp. Council. Presbyterian. Home: 7347 51st St NE Seattle WA 98115 Office: U Wash Seattle WA 98195

RAMBERG, WALTER DODD, architect; b. Charlotte, N.C., Feb. 17, 1932; s. Walter Gustav Charles and Julia Elisabeth (Lineberger) R.; B.A., Yale U., 1953, M.Arch., 1956; m. Lucinda Jenifer Ballard, Nov. 25, 1961; children—Lucinda E.G., Jenny S.F., Julia E.L. Fulbright fellow Kyoto (Japan) U., 1956-58; apprentice architect Paul Rudolph, New Haven, 1958-61; project designer Meyer & Ayers, Balt., 1961-63; partner Howe & Ramberg, Washington, 1963-65; prin. Walter Dodd Ramberg, Architect, Washington, 1965—; prof. architecture Cath. U. Am., 1977—; mem. design advisory panel Balt. Dept. Housing and Community, 1973—. Served to lt. USCGR, 1958-59. Mem. AIA (corp.), AAUP, Soc. Archtl. Historians. Episcopalian. Club: Met. (Washington). Designer: N.W. Balt. High Sch., 1963 (P.A. Excellence in Design award); architect: Bridge for Washington Cathedral, 1965 Excellence in Design award Washington Bd. Trade, AIA); Kidder Guest House, 1965 1st Honor award Balt. AIA); Azrael House, 1969 (Honor award Balt. AIA); Cutts House, 1973 (Honor award Balt. AIA); Woody House, 1975 (Merit award Balt. AIA); Lineberger Meml. Library, 1976 (Merit award Nat. AIA, ALA); contbr. articles to profl. publs. Home: Box 77 Belfast Rd Sparks MD 21152 Office: 1830 T St NW Washington DC 20009

RAMBERG, WOLFGANG PETER, banker; b. Copenhagen, Denmark, May 10, 1921; s. Karl Peter and Elfriede Antonie (Milbitz) Hansen-Ramberg; came to U.S., 1928, naturalized, 1939; B.S., Drexel U., 1949; children—Marilyn Esther, Elizabeth Anne; m. Joan Morgan Young, Dec. 27, 1973. Anne. With Chase Manhattan Bank, N.Y.C., 1949-57, asst. treas., 1956-57; with United Calif. Bank, Los Angeles, 1957-76, v.p. 1959-68, sr. v.p. Fresno Regional Hdqrs., 1968-71, European Regional Hdqrs., London, 1971-73, Los Angeles hdqrs., 1973-74, San Francisco hdqrs., 1974-76; sr. v.p., sr. banking officer The Hibernia Bank, San Francisco, 1976—, also dir. Served with AUS, 1940-45. Mem. Inst. Dirs. Phi Kappa Phi. Clubs: Number 10, Les Ambassadeurs (London); University (San Francisco). Home: 221 Evergreen Dr Kentfield CA 94904 Office: Hibernia Bank 1 Jones St San Francisco CA 94102

RAMBO, JAMES EDMONDSON, mfg. co. exec.; b. Dayton, Ohio, July 26, 1923; s. Thomas B. and Anna (Dopf) R.; A.B., Ohio U., 1947; LL.B., U. Cin., 1949; m. Sylvia Yvonne Lower, Nov. 2,1957; children—Eric, Todd, Bradley. Admitted to Ohio bar, 1949; asso. firm Coolidge, Wall & Wood, Dayton, 1949-54; asst. U.S. atty., Dayton, 1954-57; asst. gen. counsel NCR Corp., Dayton, 1957-65, sec., gen. counsel, 1965-66, v.p., sec., gen. counsel, 1966-77, v.p., gen. counsel, 1978—, dir., 1971—. Trustee Good Samaritan Hosp. Served to 1st lt. C.E., AUS, 1943-46. Mem. Am., Ohio, Dayton bar assns., Assn. Gen. Counsel, Lawyers Club Dayton, Order of Coif, Beta Theta Pi, Phi Delta Phi. Republican. Methodist. Clubs: Dayton Country, N.Y. Athletic. Home: 1111 Oakwood Ave Dayton OH 45419 Office: NCR Corp World Hdqrs Dayton OH 45479

RAMBO, VICTOR CLOUGH, ophthalmologist, missionary; b. Landour, Mussoorie, United Provinces, India. July 6, 1894; s. William Eagle and Kate (Clough) R.; student Fairmount Coll., Wichita, Kans., 1915-17; B.A., Wichita State U., 1970; M.D., U. Pa., 1921; m. Louise Steinmetz Birch, Oct. 8, 1923; children—Helen Elisabeth, Victor Birch, William Milton, Barbara Louise, Thomas Clough. Intern, Pa. Hosp., Phila., 1921-23; surgeon, ophthalmologist Christian Hosp., Mungeli, India, 1923-47; prof. ophthalmology Christian Med. Coll., Vellore, S. India, 1947-57; inaugurator mobile eye hosps., Vellore, 1947; prof. ophthalmology Christian Med. Coll., Ludhiana, N. India, 1957-67, prof. emeritus, 1967—; affiliated with research demonstration project for mobile ophthal. units, Center NSEW, 1930—; served with United Christian Missionary Soc., 1923-73; pres. Rambo Com., Inc., Sight for Curable Blind, Phila., 1973—; ophthalmologist numerous sight-restoring operations for blind. Recipient Kaisar I Hind Gold medal Pub. Service India, King George VI, 1947; Ehrenzeller award Pa. Hosp., 1972; certificate of appreciation World Conv. Chs. Christ, 1974 Pranam Patra award Punjab Govt. Diplomate Am. Bd. Ophthalmology, Nat. Bd. Med. Examiners. Fellow A.C.S., Royal Coll. Surgeons Edinburgh (Scotland); mem. All-India Ophthal. Soc. (pres. 1957), AMA, Pa. Med. Soc., Phila. County Med. Soc., Internat. Congress Ophthalmology, Oxford Ophthalmic Congress, Sigma Xi. Mem. Disciples of Christ, also mem. Ch. of Christ. Author: (with Arin Chatterjee) The Curable Blind—A Guide for Establishing and Maintaining Mobile Eye Hospitals, 1974; contbr. numerous articles in field. Home: 6101 N Morris St Apt 712 Philadelphia PA 19144 Office: RAMBO Com PO Box 4288 6100 Greene St Philadelphia PA 19144

RAMER, LAWRENCE JEROME, corp. exec.; b. Bayonne, N.J., July 29, 1928; s. Sidney and Anne (Strassman) R.; B.A. in Econs., Lafayette Coll., 1950; M.B.A., Harvard, 1957; m. Ina Lee Brown, June 30, 1957; children—Stephanie Beryl, Susan, Meredith, Douglas Strassman. Sales rep., then v.p. United Sheet Metal Co., Bayonne, 1953-55; with Am. Cement Corp., 1957-64, v.p. mktg. div. Riverside Cement Co., 1960-62, v.p. mktg. parent co., 1962-64; vice chmn. bd., chief exec. officer Clavier Corp., N.Y.C., 1965-66; chmn. exec. com., v.p., treas. Roddy Recreation Products, Inc., Los Angeles, 1965-66; exec. v.p., vice chmn. bd. Pacific Western Industries, Los Angeles, 1966-70; chmn., pres., chief exec. officer Nat. Portland Cement Co. Fla., 1975—; chmn. bd. Sutro Partners, Inc., Los Angeles, 1977—, Somerset Mgmt. Group, 1975—, Luminall Paints Inc., Los Angeles, 1972—, Bruning Paint Co., Balt.; chmn. bd., chief exec. officer Pacific Coast Cement Co., Los Angeles, 1979—. Trustee Lafayette Coll., Easton, Pa.; exec. bd. Am. Jewish Com., Los Angeles. Office: 1800 Century Park E Los Angeles CA 90067

RAMER, MARVIN MAXWELL, engring. and constrn. co. exec.; b. Phila., Aug. 11, 1919; s. Edward James and Julia (Hoffmann) R.; B. Chem. Engring., Rensselaer Polytech. Inst., 1940; postgrad. Columbia U., 1948-49; m. A. Stella Hornstein, May 20, 1945; children—Joan E., Karen J. Ramer Sinnreich, Frances M. Project mgr. Allied Chem. Co., 1940-47; co-mgr. Arlin Chem. Co., Elizabeth, N.J., 1947-50; dist. sales mgr. Blaw Knox Co., Pitts., 1950-61; exec. v.p. Lummus Co. subs. Combustion Engring. Inc., Bloomfield, N.J., 1961—, also dir.; pres. Resource Devel. Services, Bloomfield, N.J., 1976—, also dir. Registered profl. engr., N.J., Okla. Mem. Am. Inst. Chem. Engrs., Am. Inst. Mining, Metall. and Petroleum Engrs., Petroleum Engrs. Soc. Clubs: Crestmont Country (West Orange, N.J.); Chemists, Union League, Marco Polo (N.Y.C.). Home: 24 Pine Rd Roseland NJ 07068 Office: Lummus Co 1515 Broad St Bloomfield NJ 07003

RAMEY, CECIL EDWARD, JR., lawyer; b. Shreveport, La., Nov. 9, 1923; s. Cecil Edward and Blanche (Gwin) R.; B.S. summa cum laude, Centenary Coll. La., 1943; postgrad. Tulane U., 1946-47, 50-51; LL.B., Yale, 1949; m. Betty Loper, June 15, 1945; children—Martha Lynn, Linda Christine, Stephen Edward. Admitted to Wis. bar, 1949, La. bar, 1951; practice in Milw., 1949-50, Shreveport, 1954—; asso. Miller, Mack & Fairchild, 1949-50; asso. Hargrove, Guyton, Van Hook & Hargrove, 1954-56, partner, 1956-63; partner Hargrove, Guyton, Ramey and Barlow, and predecessor firms, 1963—. Faculty, Tulane U. Sch. Law, 1950-54, dir. Program of Continuing Profl. Edn., 1953-54, also mem. bd. advisers; faculty Centenary Coll., 1958—; lectr. com. on continuing legal edn. La Bar Assn., 1965-69. Chmn., Citizens Capital Improvement Com. City of Shreveport, 1969; v.p. Norwela council Boy Scouts Am., 1968-69; mem. met. bd. Shreveport YMCA; trustee Centenary Coll. Served with USAAF, 1943-46. Recipient Colby Townsend Meml. award, 1948, Francis Weyland award Yale Law Sch., 1949; named Shreveport's Outstanding Young Man of Year, 1956, Mr. Shreveport, 1968, to Alumni Hall of Fame Centenary Coll., 1970. Fellow Am. Coll. Probate Counsel; mem. Am. Law Inst., Am., La. (past bd. govs.), Shreveport (exec. com., pres.) bar assns., Shreveport C. of C. (com. chmn., pres.), Centenary Alumni Assn. (past pres.), Order of Coif, Phi Delta Phi, Kappa Sigma. Methodist (trustee). Mason. Home: 405 Albany Ave Shreveport LA 71105 Office: Mid South Towers Bldg Shreveport LA 71101

RAMEY, ESTELLE R., physiologist, educator; b. Detroit, Aug. 23, 1917; B.A., Bklyn. Coll.; M.A., Columbia, 1940; Ph.D. in Physiology (Mergler scholar, USPHS fellow), U. Chgo., 1950; Sc.D. (hon.), Georgetown U., 1977, Hood Coll., 1978; m. James T. Ramey, 1941; children—James N., Drucilla. Lectr., U. Tenn., 1942-47; instr. physiology U. Chgo., 1951-54, asst. prof., 1954-56; asst. prof. physiology Georgetown U. Sch. Medicine, Washington, 1956-60, asso. prof., 1960-66, prof., 1966—. Active in feminist movement. Mem. Am. Physiol. Soc., Soc. Exptl. Biology and Medicine, Endocrine Soc., Am. Diabetes Assn., Am. Acad. Neurology, Assn. Women in Sci. Found. (pres.). Research on stress responses and insulin action. Home: 6817 Hillmead Rd Bethesda MD 20034 Office: Georgetown University Sch Medicine Washington DC 20007

RAMEY, MADISON LOUIE, aircraft co. exec.; b. Gladewater, Tex., Sept. 3, 1919; s. William A. and Ila Olive (Smith) R.; C.E., U. Tex., 1941; m. Margaret Mary McGown, Oct. 16, 1948; children—Peter M., Michael P., Patricia M., David A. Engr., McDonnell Douglas Corp., 1941-45, project stress engr., 1945-55, chief structural research engr., 1955-59, mgr. structures, 1959-68; div. v.p. engring. tech. McDonnell Aircraft Co., St. Louis, 1969-73, divisional v.p. engring., 1973—. Asso. fellow Am. Inst. Aeros. and Astronautics; mem. McDonnell Mgmt. Club, Tau Beta Pi, Chi Epsilon. Home: 24 Forsythia Ln Saint Louis MO 63132 Office: McDonnell Aircraft Co D200 Bl PO Box 516 Saint Louis MO 63166

RAMIREZ, MARIO EFRAIN, physician; b. Roma, Tex., Apr. 3, 1926; s. Efren M. and Carmen (Hinoiosa) R.; student U. Tex., 1942-45; M.D., U. Tenn., 1948; m. Sarah B. Aycock, Nov. 25, 1949; children—Mario, Patricia Ann, Norman Michael, Jaime Eduardo, Roberto Luis. Intern, Shreveport (La.) Charity Hosp., 1949, resident; practice medicine specializing in family practice, Roma, 1950-75, Rio Grande City, Tex., 1975—; owner, adminstr. Ramirez Meml. Hosp., Roma, 1958-75; county judge Starr County, Rio Grande City, 1969-78. Chmn. South Tex. Devel. Council, 1975-76; chmn. Tri-County Community Action Council, 1971—; mem. coordinated bd. Tex. Colls. and Univs., 1979—. Served to capt. USAF, 1955-57. Recipient Spl. citation Surgeon Gen., 1967; Distinguished Alumnus award U. Tex., 1975; Achievement award Lab World, 1978; named Family Dr. of Yr. Good Housekeeping mag. and Am. Acad. Family

Physicians, 1978. Diplomate Am. Bd. Family Physicians. Fellow Am. Acad. Family Physicians; mem. AMA (vice chmn. com. health care of poor 1971-75, Benjamin Rush Bicentennial award 1976), Tex. Med. Assn. (chmn. com. health care of poor 1971, Disting. Service award 1972, pres. 1979-80), Tex. Acad. Family Physicians (v.p. 1973, pres. 1975, Distinguished Service award 1967, Outstanding Leadership award 1975-76; v.p. Valley chpt. 1960-61, pres. 1961-62), Hidalgo-Starr Counties Med. Soc. (pres. 1964). Clubs: Lions, K.C., Rotary, Alhambra. Home: PO Box 188 Roma TX 78584 Office: Route 1 Box 10 Rio Grande City TX 78582

RAMIREZ, RAUL, tennis player; b. Ensenada, Mex., June 20, 1953; student U. So. Calif. Profl. tennis player; winner Italian Men's Singles, 1975; (with Brian Gottfried) Italian Men's Doubles, 1974, 76, French Men's Doubles, 1974, 75, Wimbledon Men's Doubles, 1976, World Championship Tennis Men's Doubles, 1975, Swiss Open, 1976, Dewar Cup, 1976. Home: Avenida Ruiz No 65 Sur Ensenada Baha California Mexico*

RAMLOW, DONALD ERIC, mgmt. cons. co. exec.; b. Toledo, Apr. 13, 1919; s. Albert G. and Anna M. (Bullerdick) R.; student Wittenberg U., 1936-38, U. Toledo, 1938, U. W.Va., 1943-44; m. Helen Cousineau, Aug. 16, 1941; children—Patricia Ann, Donald Gilbert, Linna Dell. Mgr., Owens Corning Fiberglas, Newark, Ohio, 1946-57; asso. A.T. Kearney, Inc., Chgo., 1957-60, prin., 1960-64, v.p., 1964-74, pres., 1974—. dir., 1964—; dir., chmn. exec. com. RTE Corp., Koehring Co.; dir., chmn. nominating co. Koehring Co.; dir. A.T. Kearney Internat. Bd. dirs. Ill. Child and Family Services; chmn. suburban campaigns Chgo. Crusade Mercy, 1975. Served to capt. AUS, 1942-46. Certified mgmt. cons. Mem. Assn. Cons. Mgmt. Engrs. (past dir.), Inst. Mgmt. Consultants, Ill. C. of C. (chmn. bd.), Chgo. Assn. Commerce and Industry. Lutheran. Author: Production Planning and Control, 1967. Home: 931 S Broadway Park Ridge IL 60068 Office: AT Kearney Inc 100 S Wacker Dr Chicago IL 60606

RAMM, HANS HENRY, lawyer, former assn. exec.; b. Chgo., Dec. 2, 1905; s. Ernst Ludwig and Elisa Magdalen (Fornebo) R.; A.B. magna cum laude, U. Minn., 1926; LL.B., Harvard, 1929; m. Katherine Shelor Gravely, Oct. 27, 1934; children—Peter Henry, Katherine Elizabeth. Admitted to N.Y. State bar, 1931, N.C. bar, 1947; practiced law, N.Y.C., 1931-46; dir., solicitor and asst. to chmn. bd. R.J. Reynolds Tobacco Co., 1946-55, gen. counsel, 1955-69, v.p., 1957-69; dir., chmn. exec. com., sr. v.p. and gen. counsel R.J. Reynolds Industries, Inc., 1970; chmn. bd., pres. Council for Tobacco Research-U.S.A., Inc., 1971-75. Mem. Am. Bar Assn., Phi Beta Kappa. Episcopalian. Club: Old Town Country. Home: 714 Oaklawn Ave Winston-Salem NC 27104

RAMMELKAMP, CHARLES HENRY, JR., physician, educator; b. Jacksonville, Ill., May 24, 1911; s. Charles Henry and Jeanette (Capps) R.; A.B., Ill. Coll., Jacksonville, 1933, D.Sc., 1958; M.D., U. Chgo., 1937; D.Sc., Northwestern U., 1975; m. Helen Chisholm, Dec. 20, 1941; children—Charles Henry, Colin Chisholm, Anne Capps. Asst. medicine Washington U., 1939; research fellow medicine Harvard, 1939-40; instr. medicine Boston U., 1940-46; asst. prof. medicine and preventive medicine Case Western Res. U., 1946-47, asso. prof. preventive medicine, 1947-60, prof. medicine, 1950—, prof. preventive medicine, 1960—; dir. research Cleve. City Hosp., 1950—; dir. medicine Cleve. Met. Gen. Hosp., 1958—. Cons. sec. of war, mem. Commn. on Acute Respiratory Diseases, Ft. Bragg, N.C., 1943-46; dir. streptococcal disease lab. Francis E. Warren AFB, Wyo., 1949-55; dir. Com. Streptcoccal Disease 1955-57; dir. Commn. on Streptococcal and Staphylococcal Diseases, 1959-67. Recipient Lasker award, 1954, Am. Heart Assn. Research Achievement award, 1961, James Bruce Meml. award, 1963. Mem. Am. Epidemiol. Soc. (v.p. 1964-65), Central Soc. Clin. Research (pres. 1961-62), Am. Heart Assn. (v.p. 1960-63), Am. Soc. Clin. Investigation (v.p. 1956), Am. Fedn. Clin. Research, (pres. 1951), Infectious Disease Soc. Am. (pres. 1966-67), Am. Assn. Physicians, A.C.P. (gov. 1969-72, regent 1972-77), Armed Forces Epidemiol. Bd., Inst. Medicine Nat. Acad. Scis. Contbr. articles profl. periodicals. Home: 3034 Berkshire Rd Cleveland Heights OH 44118 Office: Met Gen Hospital Cleveland OH

RAMO, SIMON, engring. exec.; b. Salt Lake City, May 7, 1913; s. Benjamin and Clara (Trestman) R.; B.S., U. Utah, 1933, D.Sc. (hon.), 1961; Ph.D., Calif. Inst. Tech., 1936; D.Eng. (hon.), Case Inst. Tech., 1960, U. Mich., 1966, Poly. Inst. N.Y., 1971; D.Sc. (hon.), Union Coll., 1963, Worcester Poly. Inst., 1968, U. Akron, 1969, Cleve. State U., 1976; LL.D. (hon.), Carnegie-Mellon U., 1970, U. So. Calif., 1972; m. Virginia Smith, July 25, 1937; children—James Brian, Alan Martin. With Gen. Electric Co., 1936-46, Hughes Aircraft Co., 1946-53, Ramo-Woolridge Corp., 1953-58; pres. Space Tech. Labs., 1957-58; sci. dir. U.S. intercontinental guided missile program, 1954-58; dir. TRW Inc., 1954—, exec. v.p., 1958-61, vice chmn. bd., 1961-78, chmn. exec. com., 1969-78, chmn. sci. and tech. com., 1978—; pres., dir. The Bunker-Ramo Corp., 1964-66; vis. prof. mgmt. sci. Calif. Inst. Tech., 1978—; chmn. Center for Study Am. Experience, U. So. Calif., 1978—; dir. Union Bank, Times Mirror Co. Mem. White House Energy Research and Devel. Adv. Council, 1973-75; mem. adv. com. on sci. and fgn. affairs U.S. State Dept., 1973-75; chmn. Pres.'s Com. on Sci. and Tech., 1976-77; mem. adv. council to Sec. Commerce, 1976-77; mem. roster consultants to adminstr. ERDA, 1976-77; bd. dirs. Los Angeles World Affairs Council, Music Center Found., Los Angeles; bd. govs. Performing Arts Council of Music Center of Los Angeles; trustee Calif. Inst. Tech., Nat. Symphony Orch. Assn.; trustee emeritus Calif. State Univs. Recipient Turnbull award IAS, 1956; Steinmetz award Am. Inst. Elec. Engrs., 1959; Paul T. Johns award Arnold Air Soc., 1960; Am. Acad. Achievement award, 1964; Charles M. Schwab award Am. Iron and Steel Inst., 1968; Distinguished Service gold medal Armed Forces Communication and Electronics Assn., 1970; medal of achievement WEMA, 1970; outstanding achievement in bus. mgmt. citation U. So. Calif., 1971; Kayan medal Columbia U., 1972; Merit award Am. Cons. Engrs. Council, 1974; Delmer S. Fahrney medal Franklin Inst., 1978. Fellow IEEE (Electronic Achievement award 1953, Golden Omega award 1975), Am. Phys. Soc., Am. Inst. Aeronatics and Astronautics, Am. Acad. Arts and Scis., Am. Astronautical Soc., Inst. Advancement Engring., AAAS; mem. Nat. Acad. Engring. (founder, council mem.), Nat. Acad. Scis., Internat. Acad. Astronautics, Am. Philos. Soc., Eta Kappa Nu (eminent mem. award 1966). Author engring. and mgmt. books. Home: Beverly Hills CA Office: One Space Park Redondo Beach CA 90278

RAMOND, CHARLES KNIGHT, II, mgmt. services co. exec.; b. New Orleans, Oct. 9, 1930; s. Charles Knight and Ethel Chamberlain (Bauer) R.; B.S. with honors, Tulane U., 1950; M.S., State U. Iowa, 1952, Ph.D., 1953; m. Mary Minter Patterson, June 13, 1959; 1 son, Nicholas Bauer. Research asso. Human Resources Research Office, Washington, 1953-54; mgr. advt. research E.I. duPont de Nemours & Co., Inc., Wilmington, Del., 1956-59; tech. dir. Advt. Research Found., N.Y.C., 1959-65, asso. prof. bus. Columbia, 1965-68, adj. prof., 1968-71; pres. Mktg. Control, Inc., N.Y.C., 1968-79, Predex Corp., N.Y.C., 1974—; adj. prof. bus. N.Y. U., 1971-76; chmn. dept. mktg. Rutgers U., 1977-78. Served to 1st lt. AUS, 1954-56. Recipient Marcel Dassault medal for media research, 1970. Fellow Am. Psychol. Assn.; mem. Am. Mktg. Assn., Inst. Mgmt. Scis., Ops. Research Soc. Am., Acad. Internat. Bus., Market Research Council (pres. 1973-74), N.Y. Acad. Scis., Phi Beta Kappa, Omicron Delta Kappa, Kappa Delta Phi, Delta Tau Delta. Clubs: University, Coffee House (N.Y.C.); Rockaway Hunting (Cedarhurst, N.Y.). Author: The Art of Using Science in Marketing, 1974; Advertising Research: The State of the Art, 1976. Founder, editor Jour. Advt. Research, 1960—. Home: 1170 Fifth Ave New York City NY 10029 Office: 680 Fifth Ave New York City NY 10019

RAMPAL, JEAN-PIERRE LOUIS, flutist; b. Marseilles, France, Jan. 7, 1922; s. Joseph and Andrée (Roggero) R.; student U. Marseilles; m. Françoise-Anne Bacqueyrisse, June 6, 1947; children—Isabelle Rampal Dufour, Jean-Jacques. Flutist throughout world, 1945—, including appearances at maj. internat. festivals; prof. Nat. Conservatory of Music, France; editor Internat. Music Co., N.Y.C., 1958—. Mem. French Musicol. Soc., Assn. Music and Musicians (pres. 1974—). Decorated officier Legion d'Honneur, chevalier de l'Ordre des Arts et Lettres; recipient Grand Prix du Disque (8), 1954-78; Oscar du Premier Virtuose Français, 1956; Prix Edison, 1969; Prix Leonie Sonning, 1978. Author: (children's book) La flûte, 1978. Home: Paris France Office: care Colbert Artists Mgmt Inc 111 W 57 St New York NY 10019

RAMPEY, DENVER LEE, JR., U.S. atty.; b. Elberton, Ga., Apr. 4, 1941; s. Denver Lee and Sarah Ruby (Blackmon) R.; B.A. in History, Emory U., 1962; LL.B. cum laude, Mercer U., 1968; m. Judith Mary Sinnott, Aug. 20, 1965; children—Jennifer, Melissa, Melaine. Admitted to Ga. bar, 1967, Fla. bar, 1974; asst. U.S. atty. for Middle Dist. of Ga., Macon, 1968-71 (Honor Law Grad. appointment); mem. firm Nunn, Geiger, & Rampey, Warner Robins and Perry, Ga., 1971-73, Nunn, Geiger, Rampey, Buice & Harrington, Warner Robins and Perry, 1973-76, Hawes & Rampey, Elberton, Ga., 1976-77; U.S. atty. for Middle Dist. of Ga., 1977—. Recipient Meritorious Service award Dept. Justice, 1970. Mem. Fed. (pres. Middle Ga. chpt. 1975-76), Macon, Houston County (sec.-treas. 1973-74) bar assns., Blue Key Honor Soc., Delta Theta Phi. Adminstrv. editor, contbr. Mercer Law Rev., 1967, 69, 70. Home: 508 Kimberly Rd Warner Robins GA 31093 Office: PO Box U Mulberry and 3d Sts Macon GA 31202

RAMSAY, DONALD ALLAN, phys. chemist; b. London, July 11, 1922; s. Norman and Thirza Elizabeth (Beckley) R.; B.A., St. Catharine's Coll., Cambridge (Eng.) U., 1943, M.A., 1947, Ph.D., 1947, Sc.D., 1976; D.honoris causa, U. Reims (France), 1969; m. Nancy Brayshaw, June 8, 1946; children—Shirley Margaret, Wendy Kathleen, Catharine Jean, Linda Mary. With div. chemistry Nat. Research Council Can., Ottawa, Ont., 1947-49, div. physics, 1949-75, Herzberg Inst. Astrophysics, 1975—, sr. research officer, 1961-68, prin. research officer, 1968—; vis. prof. U. Minn., 1964, U. Orsay, 1966, U. Stockholm, 1967, 71, 74, U. Calif., Irvine, 1970, U. Sao Paulo, 1972, 78, U. Bologna, 1973, U. Western Australia, 1976, Australian Nat. U., 1976. Decorated Queen Elizabeth Silver Jubilee medal. Fellow Royal Soc. London, Royal Soc. Can., Am. Phys. Soc., Chem. Inst. Can.; mem. Can. Assn. Physicists. Mem. United Ch. of Canada (organist 1954—). Club: Leander (Henley-on-Thames, Eng.). Editor: (with J. Hinze) Selected Works of Robert S. Mulliken, 1975; contbr. numerous articles on molecular spectra and molecular structure to profl. jours. Home: 1578 Drake Ave Ottawa ON K1G 0L8 Canada Office: 100 Sussex Dr Ottawa ON K1A 0R6 Canada

RAMSAY, JOHN ERWIN, architect; b. Salisbury, N.C., Sept. 23, 1915; s. John Ernest and Elizabeth (Craige) R.; B.A., U. N.C., 1938; B.F.A., M.A., Yale, 1941; m. Jean Anne Ferrier, Oct. 1, 1945; children—Anne Ferrier (Mrs. Frank L. Saunders, Jr.), John Erwin, Kerr Craige II, George Bard Ferrier. Pvt. practice, Salisbury, 1946—; pres. Ramsay Assos.; pres. N.C. Bd. Architecture, 1958-64; N.C. rep. Nat. Council Archtl. Registration Bds., sec., 1964-65, 2d v.p., 1965-66. Pres. N.C. Symphony Soc., 1967-68, Rowan Civic Music Assn., 1950; chmn. troop com. Uwharrie council Boy Scouts Am., 1949. Served to lt. USNR, 1942-46. Recipient 3 Merit awards N.C. chpt. AIA, 1955, 60; certicicate of recognition United Methodist Ch., 1963; Modern Office Procedures award, 1961. Registered architect, N.C., S.C., Va. Fellow AIA (past pres. N.C. chpt.); mem. Guild Religious Architecture, Am. Assn. Sch. Adminstrs., Am. Theatre Assn., Soc. Coll. and Univ. Planning, N.C. Assn. Professions, Sigma Nu. Presbyn. (ruling elder). Home: 119 Pine Tree Rd Salisbury NC 28144 Office: 625 W Innes St Salisbury NC 28144

RAMSAY, REX CARLYLE, JR., physician, state ofcl.; b. Nashville, Ark., Oct. 6, 1927; s. Rex C. and Evelyn (Hill) R.; B.S., U. Ark., 1949; M.D., Tulane U., 1953; m. Glenna Patrick, Dec. 17, 1953; children—Cheryl, Pat, Larry, Wendy, Rebecca, Christy. Intern, Colo. Gen. Hosp., Denver, 1953-54; resident in pediatrics Variety Childrens Hosp., Miami, Fla., 1959-61; gen. practice medicine, Raiford, Fla., 1957-59; practice medicine specializing in pediatrics, Pahokee, Fla., 1961-62; dir. child devel. center Ark. Dept. Health, Little Rock, 1962-63, dir. div. maternal and child health, 1963-73, dir. bur. med. care services, 1973-74, acting dir. Ark. Dept. Health, 1974-75, dir., 1975-79; prof. pediatrics U. Ark. Sch. Medicine; med. dir. Alcoa Ark. Ops., 1979—. Charter mem. Francis Allen Sch. for Exceptional Children, Little Rock; mem. Nat. Council on Child Health. Served as capt. M.C., USAF, 1954-56. Named Man of Yr., Golden chpt. Ark. Bus. Women's Assn., 1968; recipient Ross award for contributions in maternal and child health So. br. Am. Pub. Health Assn., 1977; Outstanding Achievement award Ark. Hosp. Assn. Mem. Am. (chmn. public communication com.), Ark. acads. pediatrics, Ark. Pub. Health Assn. (past pres.), Central Ark. Pediatric Soc. (pres.), Ark., Pulaski County med. socs., Ark. Assn. Pub. Health Physicians (pres.), Ark. Conf. Social Workers (past v.p.), Am. Acad. Gen. Practice, Phi Beta Kappa. Baptist. Club: Rotary. Home: 1907 Durwood Rd Benton AR 72015 Office: 4815 W Markham St Little Rock AR 72201

RAMSDELL, VITTZ-JAMES, motor truck sales co. exec., orgn. ofcl.; b. Portland, Oreg., Sept. 20, 1921; s. George Vittz-James and Ruth (Kelly) R.; B.S., Oreg. State U., 1942; m. Elaine Roberts, Sept. 25, 1943; children—Lynn, Vittz-James L., Howard Scott. Vice pres., gen. mgr. Roberts Motor Co., Portland, 1956-64, pres., gen. mgr., 1964—; pres. Truck and Indsl. Equipment Co., Portland, 1952—, Trent, Inc., Portland, 1957—, Roberts Motor Inc. Oreg., Medford, 1957—, Redding Kenworth Co. (Calif.), 1966—, Redwood Kenworth Co., Eureka, 1966—. Mem. region XI exec. com. Boy Scouts Am., 1955—, pres. Portland Area Council, 1956-58, mem. nat. exec. bd., 1962—. Served with AUS, 1942-46. Recipient Silver Beaver, Silver Antelope, Buffalo awards Boy Scouts Am. Mem. Metal Trades Assn. (dir. Portland 1961—), Truck Assn. (dir. Portland 1960—). Republican. Presbyn. (trustee, elder). Rotarian (dir.). Home: 3011 SE Bybee Blvd Portland OR 97202 Office: 123 NE Pacific St Portland OR 97232

RAMSEUR, FRED H., JR., petroleum co. exec.; b. Lincolnton, N.C., Oct. 27, 1915; s. Fred H. and Mary (McMillan) R.; B.S. in Chem. Engring., N.C. State U., 1936; m. Beatrice F. Robeson, Oct. 12, 1946; children—Richard McMillan, Lillian Robeson. With Cities Service Co., 1936—, now exec. v.p., dir.; pres. Energy Resources Group; pres., dir. Cities Service Internat., Inc. Served to lt. USNR, 1943-46. Mem. Am. Petroleum Inst. (dir.). Office: Cities Service Bldg Box 300 Tulsa OK 74102

RAMSEY, CHARLES EUGENE, educator, sociologist; b. Paragon, Ind., Apr. 24, 1923; s. Sarcefield Dodson and Stella (Goss) R.; B.S., Ind. State Tchrs. Coll., 1947; M.S., U. Wis., 1950, Ph.D., 1952; m. Alberta Mae Jordan, July 19, 1943; children—James D., Charles W., Jane E., Suzanne. Faculty, U. Wis., 1951-52, U. Minn., 1952-54, Cornell U., 1954-62, Colo. State U., 1962-65; prof. sociology U. Minn., Mpls., 1965-77; chmn. dept. sociology U. Tex., Arlington, 1977—; vis. prof. Inter-Am. Instn. Agrl. Sci., Costa Rica, 1961, Exptl. Sta., U. P.R., 1961-62; research cons. to various univs., agys. Mem. Am. Sociol. Assn., Rural Sociol. Soc., Sigma Xi. Author: (with Lowry Nelson and Cooley Verner) Community Structure and Change, 1960; (with David Gottlieb) The American Adolescent, 1965, Understanding the Deprived Child, S.R.A., 1967; Problems of Youth, 1967; (with D.J. McCarty) The School Managers: Power and Conflict in American Public Education, 1971; also articles. Developed and tested theory of variations in community power structure, types of sch. bds., and roles of sch. supt., developed method of comparative measurement of level of living for different countries. Home: 1102 Depauw Dr Arlington TX 76012 Office: Dept Sociology U Tex Arlington TX

RAMSEY, CHARLES FREDERIC, JR., author; b. Pitts., Jan. 29, 1915; s. Charles Frederic and Ethel (Runnette) R.; B.A. cum laude, Princeton, 1936; m. Amelia Johnston, Apr. 16, 1948 (dec. Jan. 1979); children—Loch, Martha, Alida. Editorial, book design Harcourt, Brace & Co., N.Y.C., 1936-39; writer information service Dept. Agr., 1941-42; free-lance writer Voice Am., Dept State, 1942—; music editor Charm mag., N.Y.C., 1946-52, Sat. Rev., 1950—; recordist, anthologist Folkways Records; TV writer, producer CBS, NBC, ABC, Tulane U.; seminars in history Am. informal music Solebury Sch., New Hope, Pa., 1962—; Inst. Jazz Studies, ednl. programming cons. Rutgers U.; biog. writer Time-Life Records; cons. Time-Life Books; councillor Soc. Ethnomusicology, 1961-63. Recipient Prix France-Amérique Princeton, 1936, Best Textbook Design award Am. Inst. Graphic Arts, 1939, Jour. Fund Silver Pen award, 1960, Peabody award to co-producers NBC-TV, 1964; Nat. Brotherhood award to co-producers, writers NBC news documentary, 1967; Guggenheim fellow, 1953, 55; Nat. Endowment for Humanities fellow, 1974-75; Ford Found. fellow, 1975-76. Author: Jazzmen, 1939; A Guide to Longplay Jazz Records, 1954; Been Here and Gone, 1960; Where The Music Started, 1970. Recordings include: Leadbelly's Last Sessions, Music From the South, Anthology of Jazz; Prose du Transsiberien et de la Petite Jeanne de France, 1967, Fasola, 53 Shape-Note Folk Hymns, 1970; 16 Poems by Sterling A. Brown Read by Sterling A. Brown. Film documentaries include: Music of the South, 1957; The Evangelists, 1957; The American Revolution of '63; Anatomy of Pop, 1966; Mississippi: A Self Portrait, 1966; The Songmakers, 1967; Image of America, 1967. Contbr. photographs La Musique, 1967, Histoire du Jazz, 1967, Le Sud au Temps de Scarlette, Focus Internat. Ency., The Story of the Blues, 1969; others. Address: The Federal Twist RD 2 Stockton NJ 08559

RAMSEY, CLAUDE SWANSON, JR., indsl. exec.; b. Asheville, N.C., Feb. 6, 1925; s. Claude Swanson and Nell Grace (Hendon) R.; B.S. in Textiles, N.C. State U. at Raleigh, 1949; M.S. in Retailing, N.Y. U., 1950; m. Kay Kemp; children—Kay (Mrs. George Saenger), Scott, Steven. With Am. Enka Corp. (N.C.), 1950-70, v.p., 1962-65, exec. v.p., 1965-67, pres., chief exec. officer, 1967-70, also dir., chmn. exec. com.; pres., chief exec. officer, chmn. exec. com. Akzona Inc. (formerly Am. Enka Corp.), 1970—, chmn. bd., 1972—; dir. Wachovia Corp. Trustee U. N.C.-Asheville (formerly Asheville-Biltmore Coll.), 1964-69, N.C. Engring. Found., 1965-69, N.C. Textile Found., 1965-69, Rockefeller U. Council, 1973—. Served to 1st lt. USAAF, 1943-46. Mem. Man-Made Fibers Assn. (chmn. 1970). Clubs: Union League, Sky, Econ. (N.Y.C.); Biltmore Forest Country, Asheville Country, Asheville Downtown City, Mountain City (Asheville); Hound Ears Country, Grandfather Country, Country of N.C.; Lyford Cay (Nassau). Home: 9 Fairway Pl Biltmore Forest Asheville NC 28802 Office: Akzona Inc Asheville NC 28802

RAMSEY, FRANK KENNETH, vet. pathologist; b. Princeton, Mo., June 5, 1910; s. Carl L. and Bertha E. (Powell) R.; B.S. North State Tchrs. Coll., Aberdeen, S.D., 1936; M.A. in Zoology, U. Mont., 1940; D.V.M., Iowa State U., 1946, Ph.D., 1955; m. Joyce B. Woodford, Aug. 4, 1936; children—Gerald F., Richard A., Homer L., Janet J. Ramsay Durlam. Instr., asst. prof. vet. anatomy Iowa State U., Ames, 1946-49, asso. prof. vet. pathology, 1957-75 disting. prof., 1975-80, prof. emeritus, 1980—. Mem. AVMA, Iowa Vet. Med. Assn., Am. Coll. Vet. Pathologists, Am. Assn. Avian Pathologists, Iowa Public Health Assn., Osborn Research Club, Phi Kappa Phi, Phi Zeta, Gamma Sigma Delta, Alpha Zeta. Methodist. Contbr. chpts. to textbooks, articles to profl. jours. Home: Route 3 Ames IA 50010 Office: Dept Vet Pathology Iowa State U Ames IA 50010

RAMSEY, HENRY BASSETTE, JR., life ins. co. exec.; b. Omaha, July 18, 1924; s. Henry B. and Blanche (Farmer) R.; B.S., Iowa State U., 1949; M.A., U. Mich., 1950; m. Dorothy Shields, Sept. 17, 1949; children—Craig C., Matthew J., Henry Bassette III, Anne E. With Penn Mut. Life Ins. Co., Phila., 1950—, comptroller, 1962-69, v.p., 1968—. Served to 1st lt. USAAF, 1943-46. Fellow Soc. Actuaries; mem. Acad. Actuaries, Financial Execs. Inst. (past pres. Phila.), Life Office Mgmt. Assn. (chmn. financial planning and control council, mem. bd. 1972-74), Actuaries Club Phila. (pres. 1966-67). Republican. Episcopalian. Club: Phila. Cricket. Home: 808 S Fairway Rd Glenside PA 19038 Office: 530 Walnut St Philadelphia PA 19172

RAMSEY, IRA CLAYTON, pipeline co. exec.; b. Quitman, Ga., May 13, 1931; s. James Redding and Ruth (Treadaway) R.; B.B.A., U. Ga. at Atlanta, 1954; LL.B., Atlanta Law Sch., 1950; m. Marianne Vinzant, Dec. 23, 1962; children—Clayton Hamilton, Robin Leigh. With Plantation Pipe Line Co., Atlanta, 1948—, asst. sec., 1967-70, treas., 1970—. Served with AUS, 1954-56. Baptist. Home: 780 Wesley Oak Rd NW Atlanta GA 30328 Office: 3390 Peachtree Rd NE Atlanta GA 30326

RAMSEY, JACK AUSTIN, librarian; b. Kansas City, Kans., June 12, 1922; s. Clay I. and Floy (Smith) R.; B.A., U. Kans., 1945; B.S., U. Ill., 1946, M.S., 1947; m. Sue Worsley, Apr. 4, 1946. Librarian, N.Y. Pub. Library, N.Y.C., 1947-48; adminstrv. asst. Pub. Library Stockton and San Joaquin County (Calif.), 1948-49; librarian Solano (Calif.) County Library, 1949-52; chief librarian City Glendale, Calif., 1952-59, 66—; chief customer relations H.W. Wilson Co., pubs., N.Y.C., 1959-65. Pres. So. Calif. Library Film Circuit Com., 1958-59; mem. U. So. Calif. Library Sch. Adv. Bd., 1967-70; chmn. U. Calif. Adv. Com. Edn. for Librarianship, 1968-75. Pres., bd. dirs. Glendale Welfare Council; bd. dirs. Glendale Coordinating Council. Served with AUS, 1942-43. Mem. A.L.A. (past dir. Exhibitors Round Table), Spl. Libraries Assn., N.Y. Library Club (past pres.), Pub. Libraries Exec. Assn. So. Calif. (past v.p.), So. Calif. Recorder Soc. (past pres., dir.), Phi Kappa Psi, Beta Phi Mu (past pres.). Home: 548 Mesa Lila Rd Glendale CA 91208 Office: 222 E Harvard St Glendale CA 91205

RAMSEY, JAMES BERNARD, econometrician, educator; b. Daytona Beach, Fla., Sept. 9, 1937; s. Geoffrey A. W. and Earlie Mae (Chew) R.; B.S. in Math. and Econs., U. B.C. (Can.), Vancouver, 1963; M.A. in Econs., U. Wis.-Madison, 1964, Ph.D. in Econs., 1968;

m. Grace Diana O'Malley, Dec. 26, 1958; children—Geoffrey, Shannon, Christopher. Prof. econs. Mich. State U., 1966-71, 73—; prof.-chair econometrics and social statistics U. Birmingham (Eng.), 1972-73; research fellow Hoover Instn., Stanford, 1976-77; prof., chmn. dept. econs. N.Y. U., 1976—; econ. cons. Can. Dept. No. Affairs and Natural Resources, 1963-66. Mem. Mich. Civil Service Exec. Bd.; founder ISA (Birmingham) Ltd., 1971. Bd. dirs. Mich. Pub. Theater Inc. Served to 2d lt., Royal Signals, Brit. Army. NSF grantee, 1969-74; Social Sci. Research Council-U.K. grantee, 1972-73. Mem. Am. Econ. Assn., Econometric Soc., Royal, Am. statis. socs., Inst. Math. Statistics. Author: Bidding and Oil Leases, 1976. Contbg. author: Frontiers in Econometrics, 1973. Contbr. articles to profl. jours. Home: 1601 Ditmas Ave Brooklyn NY 11226 Office: Dept of Econs New York U 15-19 W 4th St New York NY 10003

RAMSEY, JOSEPH ROBERT, lawyer; b. Dothan, Ala., July 26, 1906; s. Richard Hawthorne and Cora (Dowling) R.; LL.B., U. Ala., 1929; m. Hilda Hawkins, May 3, 1936; children—Philip H., Edward L., Joel W., William A. Admitted to Ala. bar, 1929, also U.S. Supreme Ct.; practice in Dothan, 1929—; mem. firm Ramsey & Baxley. Pres. Houston Hotel Corp., 1959—, City Realty Co., 1956—; v.p. City Nat. Bank, Dothan, 1952—. Active local Boys Club, The Haven. Pres. Ramsey Found. Mem. Am., Ala., Houston County bar assns., Def. Research Inst., Ala. Def. Lawyers Assn., Am. Judicature Soc., Phi Alpha Delta, Pi Kappa Phi. Baptist (past chmn. deacons). Home: 3 Danmor Pl Dothan AL 36303 Office: 207 W Troy St Dothan AL 36301

RAMSEY, LLOYD BRINKLEY, savs. and loan exec., ret. army officer; b. Somerset, Ky., May 29, 1918; s. William Harold and Mary Ella (Barnett) R.; A.B., U. Ky., 1940; postgrad. Yale, 1946, Command and Gen. Staff Coll., Ft. Leavenworth, Kans., 1949-50, U.S. Army War Coll., Carlisle Barracks, Pa., 1953-54, Harvard, 1961; m. Glenda Burton, Feb. 22, 1941; children—Lloyd Ann (Mrs. Kyle D. Wallace), Larry Burton, Judi Carol (Mrs. David E. Derr), Commd. 2d lt. U.S. Army, 1940, advanced through grades to maj. gen., 1968; bn. comdr. 7th Inf., 3d Inf. Div., 1944-45; instr. Inf. Sch., Ft. Benning, Ga., 1946-49; assigned Office G-2 Dept. Army Gen. Staff, 1950-53; sec. joint staff UN Command and Far East Command, 1954-57; comdg. officer 1st Inf. Brigade, 1957-58; with Office Chief Legis. Liaison, Dept. Army Gen. Staff, 1960-63, Office Asst. Chief Staff Force Devel., 1963-64; dep. chief information, 1966-67; div. comdr. Am. 23d Div., Vietnam, 1969-70; provost marshall gen. Army, Washington, 1970-74, ret., 1974; chmn. bd. McLean Savs. & Loan Assn. (Va.), 1974—. Decorated D.S.M. with oak leaf cluster, Silver Star medal with two oak leaf clusters, Legion of Merit with oak leaf cluster, D.F.C., Bronze Star medal with three oak leaf clusters, Air medal with 17 oak leaf clusters, Army Commendation medal with oak leaf cluster, Purple Heart with four oak leaf clusters, Combat Inf. badge; mem. Order Brit. Empire; Croix de Guerre (France); Vietnamese Nat. Order, Vietnamese Armed Forces Honor medal, Vietnamese Gallantry Cross with palm. Mem. Sigma Chi, Omicron Delta Kappa. Baptist. Home: 6451 Dryden Dr McLean VA 22101 Office: McLean Savings & Loan Assn 1307 Dolley Madison Blvd McLean VA 22101. *Accept a man for what he is, not for what you want him to be.*

RAMSEY, MARJORIE ELIZABETH, educator; b. Kimball, Minn., May 25, 1921; d. William Emil and Emma Edith (Ryti) Leppa; B.S., St. Cloud State Coll., 1955, M.S., 1957; Ed.D. (Ford Found. fellow), George Peabody Coll., 1961; children—Rebecca, Cynthia. Tchr., prin., vis. lectr., Minn., 1940-57; asst. prof. St. Cloud State Coll., Minn., 1957-59; supr. edn. Montgomery County, Md., 1961-64; research asso. George Peabody Coll., Nashville, 1964-68; supr. Vanderbilt U., Nashville, 1964-69; asso. prof. early childhood edn. Kent (Ohio) State U., 1969-73, prof., 1973—, dean student personnel Coll. Edn., 1973-79; head div. edn., dir. tchr. edn. Ga. Southwestern Coll., Americus, 1979—. Mem. Assn. Supervision and Curriculum Devel., Nat. Assn. Edn. Young Children, Internat. Reading Assn., Assn. Childhood Edn. Internat., Delta Kappa Gamma, Kappa Delta Pi, Phi Delta Kappa. Author: Music: A Way of Life for the Young Child, 1978; contbr. articles to profl. jours. Home: 205 17th Green Americus GA 31709

RAMSEY, NORMAN, physicist; b. Washington, Aug. 27, 1915; s. Norman F. and Minna (Bauer) R.; A.B., Columbia, 1935; B.A., Cambridge (Eng.) U., 1937, M.A., 1941, D.Sc., 1954; Ph.D., Columbia U., 1940; M.A. (hon.), Harvard, 1947; D.Sc. (hon.), Case Western Res. U., 1968, Middlebury Coll., 1969, Oxford (Eng.) U., 1973; m. Elinor Jameson, June 3, 1940; children—Margaret, Patricia, Janet, Winifred. Kellett fellow Columbia, 1935-37, Tyndall fellow, 1938-39; Carnegie fellow Carnegie Inst. Washington, 1939-40; asso. U. Ill., 1940-42; asst. prof. Columbia, 1942-46; asso. Mass. Inst. Tech. Radiation Lab., 1940-43; cons. Nat. Def. Research Com., 1940-45; expert cons. sec. of war, 1942-45; group leader, asso. div. head Los Alamos Lab., 1943-45; asso. prof. Columbia, 1945-47; head physics dept. Brookhaven Nat. Lab. of AEC, 1946-47; asso. prof. physics Harvard, 1947-50, prof. physics, 1950-66, Higgins prof. physics, 1966—; Eastman prof. Oxford U., 1973-74; dir. Harvard Nuclear Lab., 1948-50, 52-53. Dir. Varlan Assos., 1963-66. Mem. Air Forces Sci. Adv. Com., 1947-54; sci. adviser NATO, 1958-59; mem. Dept. Def. Panel Atomic Energy; exec. com. Cambridge Electron Accelerator and gen. adv. com. AEC. Trustee Assos. Univs., Inc., Brookhaven Nat. Lab., Carnegie Endowment Internat. Peace, 1962—; pres. Univs. Research Assos., Inc., 1966-72, 73—. Recipient Presdl. Order of Merit for radar devel. work, 1947, E.O. Lawrence award AEC, 1960; Guggenheim fellow Oxford U., 1954-55. Fellow Am. Acad. Sci., Am. Phys. Soc. (council 1956-60, pres. 1978-79, Davisson-Germer prize 1974); mem. N.Y., Nat. acads. sci., Am. Philos. Assn., AAAS (chmn. physics sect. 1977), Phi Beta Kappa, Sigma Xi. Author: Nuclear Moments and Statistics, 1953; Nuclear Two Body Problems, 1953; Molecular Beams, 1956; Quick Calculus, 1965. Contbr. articles Phys. Rev., other sci. jours. on nuclear physics, molecular beam experiments, radar, nuclear magnetic moments, radiofrequency spectroscopy, masers, nucleon scattering. Home: 55 Scott Rd Belmont MA 02178 Office: Lyman Lab Harvard Univ Cambridge MA 02138

RAMSEY, NORMAN PARK, lawyer; b. Fairchance, Pa., Sept. 1, 1922; s. Joseph L. and Florence (Bennett) R.; student Loyola Coll., Balt., 1939-41; LL.B., U. Md., 1947; m. Margaret Quarngesser, Apr. 15, 1944; children—Margaret S., Mary S. Christine M., Ann L. Admitted to Md. bar, 1946; law clk. U.S. dist. ct. Judge Chesnut, 1947-48; asst. U.S. atty., 1948-50; asso. firm Semmes, Bowen & Semmes, Balt., 1951-54, partner, 1957—; asst. atty. gen. Md., 1955, dep. atty. gen., 1955-57; lectr. U. Md. Law Sch., 1951-71. Pres. Balt. Civil Service Commn., 1963-70; pres. Bd. Sch. Commrs., 1975. Served to 1st lt. USMCR, 1943-46. Mem. Bar Assn. Balt. City, Am. (ho. of dels. 1961—, bd. govs. 1975-78), Md. (bd. govs. 1965-75, pres. 1973) bar assns., Order of Coif, Phi Kappa Sigma. Home: 304 Wendover Rd Baltimore MD 21218 Office: 10 Light St Baltimore MD 21202

RAMSEY, PAUL WILLARD, metall. engr.; b. Wilkinsburg, Pa., Feb. 17, 1919; s. Harry Floyd and Edna Clara (Renfrew) R.; B.S., Carnegie-Mellon U., 1940; M.S., U. Wis., 1956; m. Shirley Rae Karper, June 27, 1942; children—Paul, Jr., Susan, Roger. Metall. engr. N.J. Zinc Co., Palmerton, Pa., 1940-51; metall. researcher A.O. Smith Corp., Milw., 1951-56, welding researcher, 1956-65, mgr. welding research and devel., 1965—. Troup com. chmn. Boy Scouts Am., 1957-59; group chmn. United Fund, 1973, div. chmn., 1974; alderman City of Wauwatosa, Wis., 1956-72, pres. Common Council, 1968-70; plan commr., chmn. Comprehensive Plan Commn., 1972—. Mem. indsl. adv. council U. Wis.-Milw., 1968—; bd. visitors Coll. Engring. U. Wis.-Madison, 1973—. Served with USNR, 1944-46. Recipient Distinguished Service citation Coll. Engring. U. Wis., 1973. Mem. Am. Welding Soc. (bd. dirs. 1966-78, v.p. 1972-75, pres. 1975-76), Am. Inst. M.E., Am. Soc. Metals, Welding Research Council, Beta Theta Pi, Theta Tau. Contbr. articles to profl. jours. Patentee in field. Home: 3125 N Menomonee River Pkwy Wauwatosa WI 53222 Office: 3533 N 27th St Milwaukee WI 53201

RAMSEY, ROBERT PAUL, educator; b. Mendenhall, Miss., Dec. 10, 1913; s. John William and Mamie (McCay) R.; B.S., Millsaps Coll., Jackson, Miss., 1935; B.D., Yale, 1940, Ph.D., 1943; Litt.D. (hon.), Marquette U., 1968; Sc.D., Worcester Poly. Inst., 1972; H.L.D., Rockford Coll., 1973, Millsaps Coll., 1974, Fairfield U.; D.D. (hon.), St. Anselm's Coll., 1978; m. Effie Register, June 23, 1937; children—Marcia Neal, Janet and Jenifer. Instr. history and social sci. Millsaps Coll., 1937-39; asst. to instr. social philosophy Yale, 1941-42; asst. prof. Christian ethics Garrett Bibl. Inst., Evanston, Ill., 1942-44, vis. prof., summer 1950; asst. prof. religion Princeton, 1944-47, asso. prof., 1947-54, prof., 1954—, Harrington Spear Paine prof. religion, 1957—, chmn. dept., 1959-63, acting chmn., 1973, 76, sr. fellow Council Humanities, 1958-59, McCosh faculty fellow, 1965-66; vis. prof. Colgate U., 1945, Div. Sch., U. Chgo., 1949, Pacific Sch., 1952, Perkins Sch. Theology, 1953, Yale Div. Sch., 1963; Joseph P. Kennedy, Jr. Found. vis. prof. genetic ethics Georgetown U. Med. Sch., 1968-69; Ashley Meml. lectr. N.Y. U. Law Sch., 1958; Thomas White Curry lectr. Austin Presbyn. Sem., 1967; Gray M. Blandy lectr. Episcopal Theol. Sem. of Southwest, 1968; Lyman Beecher lectr. Yale, 1969; Christian A. Herter lectr. Johns Hopkins; Gray lectr. Duke, 1974; Bampton lectr. Columbia, 1975; Whidden lectr. McMaster U., 1978; T.V. Moore lectr. St. Anselm's Abbey, Catholic U., 1979. Trustee, Council Religion in Internat. Affairs, 1968-75, Drew U., 1968-75; mem. adv. council Kennedy Center Bioethics, Georgetown U. Nat. Endowment Humanities sr. fellow, 1973-74; Guggenheim fellow, 1978. Mem. Inst. Soc., Ethics and Life Scis. (dir.), Am. Theol. Soc. (v.p. Eastern div. 1959-60, pres. 1964-65), Am. Soc. Christian Ethics (pres. 1962-63), Inst. Medicine, Nat. Acad. Scis. Author: Basic Christian Ethics, 1950; War and the Christian Conscience, 1961; Christian Ethics and the Sit-In, 1961; Nine Modern Moralists, 1962; Deeds and Rules in Christian Ethics, 1967; Who Speaks for the Church, 1967; The Just War: Force and Political Responsibility, 1968; Fabricated Man: The Ethics of Genetic Control, 1970; The Patient as Person: Explorations of Medical Ethics, 1971; The Ethics of Fetal Research, 1975; Ethics at the Edges of Life: Medical and Legal Intersections, 1978. Editor: Freedom of the Will (Jonathan Edwards), 1957; Faith and Ethics: The Theology of H. Richard Niebuhr, 1957; Religion, 1965; co-editor: Norm and Context in Christian Ethics, 1968; The Study of Religion in Colleges and Universities, 1970; Doing Evil to Achieve Good, 1978. Editorial bd. Works of Jonathan Edwards; Theology Today; Worldview; Jour. Religious Ethics; Linacre Quar. Contbr. articles to religious philos. jours. Home: 152 Cedar Ln Princeton NJ 08540

RAMSEY, WILLIAM LEE, ednl. adminstr.; b. Loveland, Ohio, Jan. 1, 1927; s. Gerald Waldo and Adeline (Boothby) R.; B.S., A.B., Wilmington Coll., 1948; M.A., Xavier U., 1956; Ph.D., U. No. Colo., 1960; m. Dorothy Louise White, July 10, 1948; children—Stephanie Lee, William Christopher, Sheila Lou. Tchr. jr. and sr. high schs. Clarksville Schs., Clinton, Ohio, 1946-47, elementary and jr. high schs. Lemon Twp. Schs., Middletown, Ohio, 1948-49, jr. and sr. high schs. Glendale Schs., Cin., 1949-51; designer, supr. purchasing services Gen. Electric Co., 1951-54; supt., tchr. Belfast Schs., Highland County, Ohio, 1954-55; prin. Middletown City Schs., 1955-61; supt. Rossford City Schs., 1961-65; pres. Penta-County Vocat. Sch. and Owens Tech. Coll., Perrysburg, Ohio, 1965-68; pres. Milw. Area Tech. Coll., 1968—; exec. dir. Milw. Pub. TV stas., 1968—; prof. Miami U., Xavier U., Colo. State Coll., U. Toledo, Bowling Green State U., 1957-68; ednl. cons. Ford Found. Ednl. Facilities Lab., 1959—, also to numerous ednl. instns., state govts., profl. socs. Mem. mayor's com. Milw. Model Cities Project, 1968—, Milw. Mental Health Assn., 1968—, Milw. Soc., 1968—, Milw. YMCA Bus. and Profl. Men's Club, 1968—, Research Clearing House Met. Milw., 1968—, Milw. Area Com. Employment of Handicapped, 1969—; adv. bd. Ednl. Testing Service, Ohio Little Hoover Commn., 1965, Ohio Sch. Survey Com.; mem. adv. council Citizens Opportunities Industrialization Center, 1969—; bd. dirs. Milw. Council for Adult Learning, 1969—, Greater Milw. Survey Social Welfare and Health Services, 1971—, Student Leadership Services State Wis., 1973—, Sch. Mgmt. Inst., 1965—; trustee Aerospace Edn. Found., 1970—, pres., 1975—; trustee Midwestern Ednl. Television, 1971—. Served with USNR, 1951-55. Recipient numerous awards including Distinguished Service award Ohio Assn. Sch. Adminstrs., 1965, Service Above Self award Rotary Internat., 1966, Distinguished Service award U.S. Jr. C. of C., 1966. Mem. NEA (life), Am. Assn. Sch. Adminstrs., Am. Vocat. Assn. (nat. com. for vocat. edn. 1969—, task force on vocat. edn. in urban areas 1972—), Am. Assn. Community and Jr. Colls. (post secondary adv. council career edn. 1973—, pres. council occupational edn. 1976, dir. 1976—), Nat. Aerospace Edn. Council, Am. Assn. Higher Edn., N. Central Assn. Colls. and Schs. (exec. bd. 1974—), Nat. Council on Schoolhouse Constrn., Schoolmasters Club Milw. (exec. com. 1968—), Wis. Assn. Vocat. Tech. and Adult Edn. Adminstrs. (pres. 1973-74), Wis. Assn. Vocat. and Adult Edn., Ohio Edn. Assn. (life), Sigma Xi, Alpha Psi Omega, Phi Delta Kappa, Phi Theta Kappa. Methodist (trustee). Mason, Rotarian. Contbr. articles profl. jours.; speaker in field. Mem. editorial adv. bd. Sch. Shop mag., 1972-76. Home: 21810 Locksley Ln Brookfield WI 53005 Office: 1015 N 6th St Milwaukee WI 53203

RAMSEY, WILLIAM MCCREERY, III, singer, actor, composer-lyricist, TV exec.; b. Cin., Apr. 17, 1931; s. William McCreery II and Olivia (James) R.; student Yale, 1949-51, Goethe U., Frankfurt/Main, Germany, 1955, 57, U. Cin., 1956-57; m. Erica Moeckli, Dec. 14, 1962; 1 son, Joachim. Partime profl. singer, 1949; appeared on Horace Heidt show, Hollywood, Calif., 1951; Eddie Fisher tour, Europe, 1953, Raymond Burr tour, Europe and North Africa, 1954, series jazz concerts Germany and Am., 1953-55; jazz concerts, 1955; 1st Am. to appear at German Jazz Festival, 1955, 1st Am. jazz vocalist after war to tour Yugoslavia, 1955; 1st TV portrait, Frankfurt/Main, 1955; 1st films in Baden-Baden, Munich and Hamburg, 1955; full-time profl. jazz and pop vocalist, 1957—, numerous recordings; actor numerous films, TV shows; songwriting, disc jockey work with Radio Luxembourg, Europawelle Saar, Radio Salzburg; 1st Am. jazz singer to tour Poland after war, also appearances Polish Jazz Festival, 1957, 67; Czek Jazz Festival, 1966; 1st pop record hit German version of Purple People Eater, 1958; program dir. Televico AG, Zurich/Gockhausen, Swiss TV and Film Prodn. Co., 1968-72. Active Czechoslovakian refugees in Switzerland, orphan villages in Germany and Austria. Served with USAF, 1951-55. Recipient top positions in various jazz polls. Mem. Swiss Cancer Soc., World Wildlife Fund, German Authors and Composers Soc., Internat. Jazz Fedn., Swiss Theater Assn., German Performing Artists Lodge. Rec. artist for Polydor, Electrola, Columbia, Cornet, Warner Bros. Address: Biebricher Allee 37 62 Wiesbaden West Germany

RAMSEY, WILLIAM RAY, assn. dir.; b. Minerva, Ohio, Aug. 25, 1926; s. Carl Andrew and Alwilda Pauline (Foss) R.; B.S., Mt. Union Coll., 1948; postgrad. Kent State U., 1948; M.H.A., Washington U., St. Louis, 1950; m. Betty Jane Hawkins, Dec. 2, 1950 (dec. Dec. 1975); children—Thomas, Kevin, Mary Joanne, Robert, Matthew; m. 2d, Linda Rae Foss, May 14, 1977. Exec. sec. King County Med. Soc., Seattle, 1953-61; field rep. AMA, Chgo., 1961-64, asst. dir. div. field service, 1964-68; exec. dir. Am. Soc. Internal Medicine, San Francisco, 1968-78, exec. v.p., Washington, 1978—. Served with USAAF, 1944, with USAF, 1950-53. Mem. Am. Assn. Med. Soc. Execs. (dir. 1978-80). Republican. Roman Catholic. Home: 3817 N Oakland St Arlington VA 22207 Office: 2550 M St NW Washington DC 20037

RAMSTAD, PAUL ELLERTSON, cons.; b. Mpls., Jan. 30, 1918; s. Otto and Otilia (Ellertson) R.; B.S., U. Minn., 1939, Ph.D., 1942; m. Jean Heffron, Mar. 21, 1941; children—John Richard, Julie Carolin, William Edward, Polly Ellen. Research chemist Gen. Mills, Inc., 1942-48; asso. prof. Cornell U., Ithaca, N.Y., 1948-53; asst. dir. research Oscar Mayer & Co., Madison, Wis., 1953-55; quality control exec. Gen. Mills, Inc., Mpls., 1955-65; v.p., dir. Am. Maize-Products Co., Hammond, Ind., also N.Y.C., 1965-78, pres. Corn processing div., 1968-75, pres., chief operating officer, 1976-78; cons., 1978—; dir. Money Mgmt. Corp. Trustee Nutrition Found., 1976-78. Fellow AAAS; mem. Am. Asso. Cereal Chemists (past pres.), Inst. Food Technologists, Am. Chem. Soc., Corn Refiners Assn. (chmn. 1977), Sigma Xi, Phi Lambda Upsilon. Club: Ithaca Yacht. Editor: Cereal Science Today, 1957-62; sci. editor Cereal Chemistry, 1978—. Patentee in field. Address: PO Box 841 Ithaca NY 14850

RAMWELL, PETER WILLIAM, physiologist, pharmacologist; b. Bradford, Eng., Apr. 3, 1930; s. Joseph E. and Louisa M. (Mayer) R.; came to U.S., 1964, naturalized, 1969; B.Sc. with honors, Sheffield (Eng.) U., 1951; Ph.D., Leeds (Eng.) U., 1958; m. Heather P. Dutton, Oct. 11, 1952; children—Mark A., Joanna H., Carolyn B. Mem. sci. staff Med. Research Council U. Leeds, 1955-58, U. Oxford (Eng.), 1960-61, U. Birmingham (Eng.), 1961-64; sr. lectr. pharmacology U. Bradford, 1958-60; dir. NIMH postdoctoral tng. program, sr. scientist Worcester (Mass.) Found., 1964-69; asso. prof. physiology Stanford U., 1969-72; prof. physiology and biophysics Georgetown U., 1973—; prin. scientist Alza Corp., Palo Alto, Calif., 1969-72; scholar Kennedy Inst. for Study Human Reproduction and Bioethics, Georgetown U., 1973—. Mem. U.S., U.K. physiol. and pharmacol. socs. Author: The Prostaglandins, 1973, 74, 77, also 3 other books; editor Prostaglandin Jour., 1975—; contbr. articles to profl. jours.; inventor erodible intrauterine device, viable platelet concentrate preparation method, prostaglandin device and preparation. Home: 1356 Kirby Rd McLean VA 22101 Office: Dept Physiology Biophysics Georgetown U 3900 Reservoir Rd Washington DC 20007

RAND, AYN, writer, lectr.; b. St. Petersburg (now Leningrad), Russia, 1905; grad. U. Leningrad, 1924; D.H.L. (hon.), Lewis and Clark Coll., 1963; m. Frank O'Connor, 1929. Came to U.S., 1926, naturalized, 1931. Screen writer, 1932-34, 44-49; vis. lectr. Yale, 1960, Princeton, 1960, Columbia, 1960, 62, U. Wis., 1961, Johns Hopkins, 1961. Ford Hall Forum, Boston, 1961—, Harvard, 1962, Mass. Inst. Tech., 1962, U.S. Mil. Acad. at West Point, 1974, other univs. Author: Night of January 16th (play, revived as Penthouse Legend 1973), 1935; We the Living, 1936; Anthem, 1938; The Unconquered (play), 1940; The Fountainhead (also screenplay), 1943; Atlas Shrugged, 1957; For the New Intellectual, 1961; The Virtue of Selfishness, 1965; Capitalism; The Unknown Ideal, 1966; Introduction to Objectivist Epistemology, 1967; The Romantic Manifesto: A Philosophy of Literature, 1969; The New Left: The Anti-Industrial Revolution, 1971. Editor: The Objectivist, 1962-71, The Ayn Rand Letter, 1971-76. Address: PO Box 177 Murray Hill Station New York City NY 10016

RAND, DUNCAN D., librarian; b. Biggar, Sask., Can., Oct. 28, 1940; s. Dawson Ellis and Elizabeth Edna (Gabie) R.; B.A., U. Sask., 1963; B.L.S., McGill U., 1964; m. Nancy Jean Daugherty, Sept. 7, 1963; children—Duncan Dawson, Thomas Nelson, Jennifer Nancy, John David. Young adult librarian Regina (Sask.) Pub. Library, 1964-65; coordinator library services Regina Separate Sch. Bd., 1965-68; asst. chief librarian Regina Pub. Library, 1968-71; dep. dir. London Pub. Library and Art Mus., 1971-73, acting dir., 1973-74; chief librarian Lethbridge (Alta.) Pub. Library, 1974—. Vice pres. Alta. council Boy Scouts. Mem. Library Assn. Alta. (dir.), Can. Assn. Pub. Librarians (pres.), Can. Library Assn. (dir.), Sask. Geneal. Soc. (pres.). Mem. United Ch. Can. Club: Rotary Internat. Editor: Sask. Geneaol. Soc. Bull., 1968-71. Office: 810-5 Ave S Lethbridge AB T1J 4C4 Canada

RAND, JAMES HENRY, shipping co. exec.; b. N.Y.C., July 9, 1943; s. Marcell Nelson and Jane Ann (Edwards) R.; B.A., Colgate U., 1966; M.B.A., Columbia U., 1969; m. Gail Patricia Sullivan, Sept. 10, 1979; children—Kimberly, Marcella, Jane. Asso., Hornblower & Weeks-Hemphill, Noyes Inc., N.Y.C., 1970-73; v.p. Universal Gas & Oil Co., Inc., N.Y.C., 1973-76; partner Dowling & Co., Stamford, Conn., 1976-77; mgr. bus. devel. Burmah Oil Tankers Ltd., N.Y.C. 1977-78; pres. Marine Transport Lines, Inc., N.Y.C., 1978—. Bd. dirs. Deafness Research Found., N.Y.C., Colonial Research Inst., Nassau, Bahamas, Rockledge Inst., Darien, Conn. Served with USNR, 1966-69. Mem. Am. Inst. Mcht. Shipping (exec. com.). Home: 31 Ox Ridge Ln Darien CT 06820 Office: 5 Hanover Sq New York NY 10004

RAND, JOHN B., advt. agy. exec.; b. Chgo., May 21, 1921; s. Edwin S. and Adelaide R. (Born) R.; B.A., Harvard U., 1943: m. Judith Lane, Oct. 2, 1954; children—Hilary B., Eliza L. With Foote, Cone and Belding, Chgo., 1947-67, asso. creative dir., until 1967; creative dir., sr. v.p., dir. Ogilvy and Mather Inc., N.Y.C., 1967-78, exec. creative dir., 1978—; artist-in-residence various colls.; lectr. at univs., seminars, ad clubs. Served to capt. U.S. Army, 1943-47. Named Young Man of Yr., Chgo., 1951; recipient David Ogilvy Advt. award, 1975, 77, also Clio awards. Author, producer actor Quick Changes, musical revue, Chgo. Home: 10 East End Ave New York NY 10021 also Ocean Rd Bridgehampton LI NY Office: Ogilvy and Mather 2 E 48th St New York NY 10017

RAND, LEON, educator; b. Boston, Oct. 8, 1930; s. Max B. and Ricka (Muscanto) Rakisky; B.S., Northeastern U., 1953; M.A., U. Tex., 1956, Ph.D., 1958; m. Marian L. Newton, Aug. 29, 1959; children—Debra Ruth, Paul Martin, Marta Leah. Postdoctoral fellow Purdue U., 1958-59; asst. prof. to prof. U. Detroit, 1959-68; prof., chmn. dept. chemistry Youngstown (Ohio) State U., 1968-74, dean grad. studies and research, 1974—; dir. Autosonics, Inc., Norristown, Pa. Mem. Am. Chem. Soc., Am. Inst. Chemists, Electrochem. Soc., A.A.U.P., Sigma Xi, Phi Kappa Phi. Home: 19 Centennial Dr Poland OH 44514 Office: 410 Wick Ave Youngstown OH 44503

RAND, NORFLEET HALE, shoe mfr.; b. St. Louis, Dec. 8, 1913; s. Frank Chambless and Nettie Lumpkin (Hale) R.; B.A., Vanderbilt U., 1934; m. Eloise Alice Stephens, Oct. 13, 1948 children—Miriam McLeod, Helen Norfleet, Norfleet Hale, Edgar Stephens. With Internat. Shoe Co., St. Louis, 1935-65, mgr. upper leather procurement and supply, 1950-57, dir. charge merchandising and mfg., 1956-65, v.p., 1957-65, also treas.; vice chmn. bd., treas. Interco,

Inc., 1965-74, dir., mem. exec. com., 1974—; dir. Mercantile Commerce Nat. Bank, Am. Investment Co. Exec. bd. St. Louis council Boy Scouts Am.; dir. Big Bros. of Am. Inc., Big Bro. Orgn. of St. Louis, Inc., Thomas Dunn Meml.; pres. Barnard Free Skin and Cancer Hosp., 1967-72. Recipient Bro. of the Year award, St. Louis, 1959. Mem. Delta Kappa Epsilon. Clubs: St. Louis Country, University, Log Cabin (St. Louis). Home: 46 Glen Eagles Dr Clayton MO 63105 Office: 7811 Carondelet Ave Clayton MO 63105

RAND, PAUL, typographer, designer, educator; b. N.Y.C., Aug. 15, 1914; grad. Pratt Inst., 1932; student Parson's Sch. Design, 1932, Art Students League, 1934; 1 dau., Catherine; m. 2d, Marion Swannie Hall, Aug. 20, 1975. Apprentice in studio of George Switzer, 1932-35; art dir. Esquire-Coronet, Apparel Arts, 1936-41; tchr. graphic design Lab. Sch. Design, Cooper Union, 1938-42; instr. post grad. course Pratt Inst., 1946; prof. graphic design Yale, 1956—; graphic cons. IBM Corp., Westinghouse Elec. Corp.; cons. and design various corps. Mem. Fulbright Scholarship Jury; mem. art edn. adv. bd. N.Y.U.; visitor Mus. Fine Arts, Boston, Carnegie Mellon U.; hon. prof. Tama U., Tokyo, Japan. Recipient awards N.Y. Arts Dirs. Club, Am. Inst. Graphic Arts, Mus. Modern Art, N.Y. Times Jury, numerous others; citation for outstanding achievement in arts Phila. Coll. Art, 1962; Gold medal Am. Inst. Graphic Arts, 1966; named to N.Y. Art Dirs. Hall of Fame, 1972; named Royal Designer for Industry, London, 1973. Benjamin Franklin fellow Royal Soc. Arts. Author: Thoughts on Design, 1946, rev. paperback, 1970; The Trademarks of Paul Rand, 1960; (illustrator) Little 1, I Know a Lot of Things, Sparkle and Spin; Listen, Listen. Contbr. numerous articles on art, design, typography, advt. Address: 87 Goodhill Rd Weston CT 06883

RAND, SIDNEY ANDERS, ambassador; b. Eldred, Minn., May 9, 1916; s. Charles William and Ida Alice (Pedersen) R.; B.A., Concordia Coll., Moorhead, Minn., 1938, D.D. (hon.), 1956; C.T., Luther Theol. Sem., St. Paul, 1943; LL.D., Colo. Coll., 1976; student U. Chgo., 1947-48, 49, 50; m. Dorothy Alice Holm, Sept. 1, 1942 (dec. Jan. 1974); children—Peter Anders, Mary Alice; m. 2d, Lois M. Ekeren, Nov. 23, 1974. Ordained to ministry Lutheran Ch., 1943; pastor in Nashwauk, Minn., 1943-45; asst., then asso. prof. religion Concordia Coll., 1945-51; pres. Waldorf Coll., Forest City, Iowa, 1951-56; exec. dir. bd. Christian edn. Evang. Luth. Ch., 1956-61; exec. dir. bd. coll. edn. Am. Luth. Ch., 1961-63; pres. St. Olaf Coll., Northfield, Minn., 1963-80; U.S. ambassador to Norway, 1978—. Decorated knight 1st class Order St. Olav (Norway). Mem. Phi Beta Kappa. Rotarian. Co-author: Christian Faith and the Liberal Arts, 1960. Home: 1215 St Olaf Ave Northfield MN 55057 Office: US Embassy Norway APO New York 09085

RANDALL, CLARENCE A., dept. store exec.; b. Ravenna, Ohio, Aug. 29, 1918; s. Roscoe C. and Ethel M. Randall; student public schs., Ravenna; m. Emma Elizabeth Fisher, Jan. 2, 1940; children—Jon P., Nancy Randall Pala, Judith Randall Conley, Kathleen Randall Whittaker. With M. O'Neil Co., Akron, Ohio, 1943—, v.p. ops., 1968-74, exec. v.p. ops., personnel, control, 1974-75, chmn. bd., 1975—. Bd. dirs. Salvation Army, Akron, East Akron Community Center; chmn. Akron Action Com.; pres. Downtown Assn., Akron. Lutheran. Clubs: Akron City, Portage Country. Home: 2418 Stockbridge Rd Akron OH 44313 Office: 226 S Main St Akron OH 44308

RANDALL, FRANCIS BALLARD, educator, historian; b. N.Y.C., Dec. 17, 1931; s. John Herman, Jr. and Mercedes (Moritz) R.; B.A., Amherst Coll., 1952; M.A., Columbia, 1954, Ph.D., 1960; m. Laura Regina Rosenbaum, June 11, 1957; children—David R., Ariane R. Instr. history Amherst Coll., 1956-59; instr., asst. prof. history Columbia, 1959-61, vis. prof., 1967-68; mem. social sci. and humanities faculties Sarah Lawrence Coll., Bronxville, N.Y., 1961—, trustee, 1971-76. Freedom rider civil disobedience to racism, 1961, war draft resistance arrests, 1967, 70. Fulbright fellow for study in India, 1965. Mem. Am. Hist. Assn., Am. Assn. for Advancement Slavic Studies, Am. Assn. U. Profs. (chpt. chmn. 1966-69), Phi Beta Kappa, Sigma Xi. Author: (with others) Essays in Russian and Soviet History, 1963; Stalin's Russia, an Historical Reconsideration, 1965; N.G. Chernyshevskii, 1967. Home: 425 Riverside Dr New York City NY 10025 Office: Sarah Lawrence Coll Bronxville NY 10708

RANDALL, FRANK LESLIE, JR., electronics co. exec.; b. San Pedro., Calif., Oct. 23, 1917; s. Francis Leslie and Helen (Brannen) R.; B.S. in Bus. Administrn., U. Calif. at Los Angeles, 1940; m. Rosemary Pennington, Sept. 12, 1942; children—Frank Leslie III, Teresa Ann. Exec. v.p. N.Am. Philips Corp., 1968-77, vice chmn., 1978—; chmn. bd. Signetics Corp., Sunnyvale, Calif., 1975—. Mem. Electronics Industries Assn. (v.p., dir.), Phi Delta Theta. Clubs: Creek; Union League (N.Y.C.). Home: 14 Locust Ln Upper Brookville Glen Head NY 11545 Office: 100 E 42d St New York City NY 10017

RANDALL, HENRY THOMAS, surgeon; b. N.Y.C., Aug. 29, 1914; s. Henry Thomas and Helen (Nixon) R.; A.B., Princeton, 1937; M.D., Columbia, 1941, M.Sc.D., 1950; M.A., Brown U., 1968; m. Louise Elinor Harman, June 5, 1940; children—Martha Emily, Deborah Ann, Henry Thomas III. Surg. intern Presbyn. Hosp., N.Y.C., 1941-42, jr. asst. resident surgery, 1942, asst. resident surgery, 1945-48, resident surgery, 1949, asst. attending surgeon, 1950-51; instr. surgery Columbia Coll. Phys. and Surg., 1950, asst. prof., 1950-51; asst. vis. surgeon Francis Delafield Hosp., 1950-51; clin. dir. Meml. Hosp., N.Y.C., 1951-61, med. dir., v.p. med. affairs, 1961-65, chmn. dept. surgery, 1951-66, attending surgeon, dir. surg. research, 1966-67; surgeon in charge div. surg. research dept. surgery R.I. Hosp., 1967-70, surgeon-in-chief dept. surgery, 1970-79, cons., 1980—; vis. surgeon James Ewing Hosp., 1951-67; asso. prof. surgery Cornell U. Med. Coll., 1951-54; prof. surgery Cornell U. Med. Coll., 1955-67; prof. med. sci. div. biol. and med. scis. Brown U., 1967-79, prof. med. sci. emeritus, 1979—; mem. Sloan-Kettering Inst., 1951-67, v.p. clin. affairs, 1961-65. Served from 1st lt. to maj. M.C., AUS, 1942-45. Diplomate Am. Bd. Surgery, 1951. Fellow N.Y. Acad. Med., Am. Surg. Assn., A.C.S. (vice chmn. com. pre and postoperative care 1963-65, chmn. 1966-69, com. on continuing edn. 1972—, pres. R.I. chpt. 1976-78, Disting. Service award 1977); mem. AMA, AAAS, James Ewing Soc., R.I. (com. publs.), Providence med. socs., Am. Cancer Soc. (pres. N.Y.C. div. 1966-67, now hon. life mem.; mem. bd., exec. com. R.I. div., pres. elect R.I. div. 1977, pres. 1978-80), Soc. Univ. Surgeons (pres. 1959-60), Soc. Clin. Surgery, Harvey Soc., Halstead Soc. (pres. 1963-65), N.Y. (pres. 1967), Boston, New Eng. surg. socs., N.Y. Acad. Sci., N.Y. Clin. Soc., N.Y. (pres. 1961-62), New Eng. cancer socs., Assn. Am. Med. Colls., Sigma Xi. Club: Univ. (Providence). Editor: Manual of Preoperative and Postoperative Care, 1967. Contbr. to textbooks and profl. jours. Home: 100 Angell St Providence RI 02906 Office: RI Hosp 593 Eddy St Providence RI 02903

RANDALL, JAMES EDWIN, educator; b. Bloomington, Ind., July 23, 1924; s. Thomas Edwin and Blanche (Helfrich) R.; B.S. in Elec. Engring., Purdue U., 1947; M.S., State U. Iowa, 1952; Ph.D., Ohio State U., 1955; m. Barbara L. Feucht, Nov. 23, 1949; children—David, Christopher, Karen, Sara. Engr., Collins Radio Co., Cedar Rapids, Iowa, 1947-49; research asst. State U. Iowa, 1949-52, Ohio State U., 1952-55; asst. prof., then asso. prof. physiology U. Mo. Med. Sch., 1955-63; prof. physiology Northwestern U. Med. Sch., 1963-68; prof. physiology and biophysics Ind. U., 1968—. Served with USNR, 1944-46. Mem. Am. Physiol. Soc., Biophys Soc., I.E.E.E., A.A.A.S., Sigma Xi. Author: Elements of Biophysics, 2d edit., 1962. Spl. research statis. properties physiol. signals. Home: 609 S Jordan Ave Bloomington IN 47401

RANDALL, JOHN, educator; b. Mar. 23, 1905; s. Sidney and Hannah (Cawley) R.; M.S., U. Manchester, 1926, D.Sc., 1938; m. Doris Duckworth, 1928; 1 son, Christopher John. Research physicist Research Labs., Gen. Electric Co., Ltd., 1926-37; Warren research fellow Royal Soc., U. Birmingham, 1937-43, hon. mem. staff, 1940-43; temporary lectr. Cavendish Lab., Cambridge, 1943-44; prof. natural philosophy United Coll. St. Salvator and St. Leonard, U. St. Andrews, 1944-46; Wheatstone prof. physics, King's Coll., U. London, 1946-61, prof. biophysics, 1961-70, prof. emeritus, 1970—, hon. dir. med. research council Biophysics Research Unit, 1947-70, chmn. Sch. Biol. Scis., 1964-68; lectr. Rockefeller Inst. Med. Research, N.Y.C., 1956-57; Greg Y Nog lectr. U. Coll. Wales, Aberystwyth, 1958; vis. prof. biophysics Yale, 1960; hon. prof. U. Edinburgh, 1970—. Created knight, 1962; recipient Thomas Gray Meml. prize for discovery cavity magetron Royal Soc. Arts, 1943; Duddell medallist Phys. Soc. London, 1945; Hughes medallist Royal Soc., 1946; John Price Wetherill medal Franklin Inst., 1958; John Scott award City of Phila., 1959; fellow of King's College, London, Eng., 1960. Fellow Royal Soc. Club: Athenaeum (London). Research on luminescence of solids, neutron and x-ray scattering by biol. systems. Joint inventor cavity magnetron. Home: 16 Kevock Rd Lasswade Midlothian Scotland Office: Univ Edinburgh West Mains Rd Edinburgh EH93JT Scotland

RANDALL, JOHN ERNEST, JR., marine biologist; b. Los Angeles, May 22, 1924; s. John Ernest and Mildred (McKibben) R.; B.A., U. Calif. at Los Angeles, 1950; Ph.D. in Marine Zoology, U. Hawaii, 1955; m. Helen Lai Sinn Au, Nov. 9, 1951; children—Loreen Ann, Rodney Dean. Yale research fellow Bernice P. Bishop Mus., Honolulu, 1955-57, ichthyologist, 1965—; asst. prof. Marine Lab., U. Miami, Coral Gables, Fla., 1957-61; prof. biology, dir. Inst. Marine Biology, U. P.R., Mayaguez, 1961-65; dir. Oceanic Inst., Waimanalo, Hawaii, 1965-66; marine biologist U. Hawaii, 1967-69; mem. Hawaii Adv. Com. on Invertebrates and Aquatic Vertebrates, Gt. Barrier Reef Com.; mem. marine steering com. and Survival Service Commn., Internat. Union for Conservation Nature. Served to 2d lt. AUS, 1943-46. Mem. Am. Soc. Ichthyologists and Herpetologists, Hawaiian Acad. Sci., Pacific Sci. Assn. (sci. com. on coral reefs), Indian Soc. Ichthyologists, Phi Beta Kappa, Sigma Xi, Phi Sigma Kappa. Author: Caribbean Reef Fishes. Bd. editors Caribbean Jour. Sci., Micronesica; Contbr. numerous articles on marine fish to sci. publs. Dir. marine biol. survey V.I., 1958-61. Office: Bishop Mus PO Box 19000-A Honolulu HI 96819

RANDALL, JOHN HERMAN, JR., author, educator; b. Grand Rapids, Mich., Feb. 14, 1899; s. John Herman and Minerva I. (Ballard) R.; A.B., Columbia, 1918, A.M., 1919, Ph.D., 1922, L.H.D., 1968; Litt. D., Ohio Wesleyan U., 1961; Ph.D. (hon.), U. Padua (Italy), 1967; LL.D., Temple U., 1968; L.H.D., Bard Coll., 1972; m. Mercedes Irene Moritz; Dec. 23, 1922; children—John Herman III, Francis Ballard. Asst. prof. philosophy Columbia, 1925-31, asso. prof., 1931-35, prof., 1935-51, F.J.E. Woodbridge prof. philosophy, 1951-67, Woodbridge prof. emeritus, 1967—. Fellow Am. Acad. Arts and Scis.; mem. Renaissance Soc. Am. (pres. 1953-57), Am. Philos. Assn. (pres. 1956), Metaphys. Soc. Am. (pres. 1966-67), Phi Beta Kappa, Alpha Delta Phi. Mem. Ethical Culture Soc. Club: Columbia Faculty. Author: The Problem of Group Responsibility, 1922; The Making of the Modern Mind, 1926, 50th Anniv. Edit., 1976; Our Changing Civilization, 1929; The Role of Knowledge in Western Religion, 1958; Nature and Historical Experience, 1958; Aristotle, 1960; The School of Padua and the Emergence of Modern Science, 1961; The Career of Philosophy in Modern Times, Vol. I, 1962, Vol. II, 1965; How Philosophy Uses Its Past, 1963; The Meaning of Religion for Man, 1968; Plato: Dramatist of the Life of Reason, 1970; Hellenistic Ways of Deliverance and the Making of the Christian Synthesis, 1970; Philosophy After Darwin, 1977. Co-author: Introduction to Contemporary Civilization (syllabus), 1920-26; Introduction to Reflective Thinking, 1923; Studies in the History of Ideas (Vol. II), 1925; Religion and the Modern World, 1929; American Philosophy Today and Tomorrow, 1935; The Philosophy of John Dewey, 1939; The Philosopher of the Common Man, 1940; Philosophy: An Introduction, 1942; Naturalism and the Human Spirit, 1944; Preface to Philosophy, 1946; Theory and Practice in Historical Study, 1946; Freedom and Experience, 1947; Wellsprings of the American Spirit, 1948; Organized Religion in the U.S., 1948; Renaissance Philosophy of Man, 1948; The Philosophy of Ernest Cassier 1949; Freedom and Reason, 1951; Philosophy of Paul Tillich, 1952; Contemporary American Philosophy, 1970. editor Jour. History of Ideas; joint editor Jour. Philosophy. Editor: Aristotle's Vision of Nature (Frederick J. E. Woodbridge), 1965. Home: 15 Claremont Ave New York City NY 10027 also Peacham VT 05862

RANDALL, KENNETH ALFRED, orgn. exec.; b. Ogden, Utah, June 22, 1927; s. J. William and Beatrice (Pingree) R.; student Weber Coll., 1945-47; B.S., Brigham Young U., 1949, M.S., 1958; m. Jeraldine Daynes Smith, Aug. 20, 1952; children—Shelly Marie Randall Millard, Nancy Kay, Tami Lee. Asst. cashier State Bank Provo (Utah), 1949-52, cashier, 1953-59, dir., 1954-64, v.p., cashier, 1959-63, pres., 1963-64; with Citizens Nat. Bank, Los Angeles, 1952-53; dir. Fed. Deposit Ins. Corp., Washington, 1964-65, chmn., 1965-70; vice chmn. bd. United Va. Bankshares Inc., 1970-71, dir., 1970-78, pres., chief exec. officer, 1971-75, chmn., chief exec. officer, 1975-76; pres. The Conf. Bd. Inc., 1976—; dir. Va. Electric & Power Co., Consol.-Bathurst Ltd. (Montreal, Que., (Can.), Bathurst Paper Ltd., Domglas Ltd., Jaguar Rover Triumph Inc., N.E. Bancorp, Inc., Union Trust Co. Mem. Adv. Council Japan-U.S. Econ. Relations, U.S. sect. European Community-U.S. Businessmen's Council, Nat. Adv. Council Minorities in Engring.; mem. adv. council Electric Power Research Inst., Grad. Sch. Mgmt., Northwestern U.; mem. Pres.'s Commn. Financial Structure and Regulation, 1970-71; mem.-at-large U.S. bus. and industry adv. com. OECD. Trustee-at-large, mem. exec. com. Ind. Coll. Funds Am.; trustee Mary Baldwin Coll.; asso. trustee Council of Ams. Republican. Mem. Ch. of Jesus Christ of Latter-day Saints. Home: 13 Valley Rd New Canaan CT 06840 Office: 845 3d Ave New York NY 10022

RANDALL, THEODORE AMASA, educator; b. Indpls., Oct. 18, 1914; s. James E. and Helen (Darling) R.; B.F.A., Yale, 1938; M.F.A., Alfred U., 1949; m. Catherine Steckel, Feb. 26, 1938; children—Theodore Amasa III, Thomas Edward. Sculptor, N.Y.C., 1938-40; with Randall Oil Co., 1940-42, 45-48; pres. Randall Pottery Inc., Wellsville and Alfred, N.Y., 1949-69; instr. Alfred (N.Y.) U., 1952-53, asst. prof., 1953-56, prof. ceramics, 1960—, head div. art and design, 1956-73. Represented in permanent collections Everson Mus., Krannert Mus., Smithsonian Instn., Met. Mus. Art, Mus. Contemporary Craft, others. Ednl. cons. N.Y. State Edn. Dept., Middle Atlantic Assn. Schs. and Colls., Nat. Assn. Schs. Art. Served with Signal Corps AUS, 1942-45. Decorated Bronze Star. Fellow Nat. Assn. Schs. Art (dir.), Nat. Council Edn. for Ceramic Arts (dir.), Am. Ceramic Soc. (div. sec.); mem. Council Art Dept. Chmn. (chmn.), Academie Internacional de la Ceramique (hon.). Home: Jericho Hill Rd Alfred NY 14802

RANDALL, TONY, actor; b. Tulsa, Feb. 26, 1920; student Northwestern U., Columbia; studies Neighborhood Playhouse Sch. of Theater, N.Y.C.; m. Florence Mitchell. Actor, Circle of Chalk, 1941, Candida, 1941, Corn is Corn, 1942, Barretts of Wimpole St., 1947, Antony and Cleopatra, 1948, Caesar and Cleopatra, 1950, O Men, O Women, 1954, Inherit the Wind, 1955-56; motion picture, O Men, O Women, 1957; on TV in Mr. Peepers, 1952-55, also Max Liebman Spectaculars, Tonight Show, 1956, the Odd Couple, 1970—, The Tony Randall Show, 1976—; (play) Oh Captain, 1958; (motion pictures) Will Success Spoil Rock Hunter, No Down Payment, The Mating Game, Pillow Talk, Huckleberry Finn, Lover Come Back, Let's Make Love, Boy's Night Out, Send Me No Flowers, 1964, Fluffy, The Alphabet Murders, Bang: You're Dead, Everything You Always Wanted to Know About Sex But Were Afraid to Ask, Hell Down There, Scavenger Hunt, 1979; appeared in TV movie Kate Bliss and the Ticker Tape Kid, 1978; (play) UTBU, 1966. Served from pvt. to 1st lt., Signal Corps, AUS, 1942-46.*

RANDALL, WALTER CLARK, educator; b. Akeley, Pa., Dec. 12, 1916; s. Harry Warren and Ruth Nancy (Wiggins) R.; A.B., Taylor U., 1938; M.S. in Physiology, Purdue U., 1940, Ph.D. in Physiology, 1942; postdoctoral fellow physiology, Western Res. U., 1942-43; m. Gwendolyn R. Niebel, Aug. 1, 1943; children—David Clark, Marilyn Ruth, Douglas Warren, Craig Mathias. Grad. asst. biology Purdue U., 1938-42; mem. faculty St. Louis U., 1943-54, asso. prof. physiology, 1949-54; prof. physiology, chmn. dept. Stritch Sch. Medicine, Loyola U., 1954—; spl. research nervous control heart and blood vessels, regulation sweating and body temperature. Active local Boy Scouts Am. Trustee W. Side Med. Center-Wesley Found., Chgo. Recipient Stritch medal, 1971; named Alumnus of Yr., Taylor U., 1962. Fellow A.A.A.S.: mem. Am. (sci. council), Chgo. heart assns., Am. Physiol. Soc., Soc. Exptl. Biology and Medicine (nat. membership com. 1960—, pres. Ill. 1959-60), Am. Assn. Higher Edn., Am. Inst. Biol. Scis., Sigma Xi (pres. Loyola 1959-60), Chi Alpha Omega. Methodist. Bd. editors Circulation Research, 1964-68, Am. Jour. Physiology, 1968-72, Jour. Applied Physiology, 1968-72. Author numerous articles in field. Home: 624 N Hamlin Ave Park Ridge IL 60688 Office: 2160 S 1st Ave Maywood IL 60153

RANDALL, WILLIAM B., mfg. co. exec.; b. Phila., Jan. 8, 1921; s. Albert and Ann (Fine) R.; student Rider Coll., Trenton, N.J., 1940-41; m. Geraldine Kempson, Aug. 10, 1943; children—Robert, Erica Lynn, Lisa. Gen. Sales mgr. Lowres Optical Mfg. Co., Newark, 1946-49; pres., founder Rand Sales Co., N.Y.C., 1949-58; gen. mgr. Sea & Ski Co. div. Botany Industries, Inc., Millbrae, Calif., 1958-61, pres., dir., 1961-66; v.p. Botany Industries, Inc., 1961-65; pres. Renauld of France, Reno, 1967-68; chmn. bd. Renauld Internat., Reading Pa., 1963-65; pres., chief operating officer Renauld Internat., Ltd., Burlingame and Reno, 1966-67; pres., chmn. bd. Randall Internat., Ltd., 1967-68; sr. exec. v.p. Forty-two Prods. Ltd., 1969-71; pres. Exec. Products Internat. Ltd., 1969-71, New Product Devel. Center, Irvine, 1971—, Internat. Concept Center, Irvine, 1971—, Sun Research Center, Irvine, 1974—, La Costa Products Internat., 1975—. Served to 1st lt., navigator, USAAF, 1942-45. Mem. Am. Mgmt. Assn., Nat. Wholesale Druggists Assn., Nat. Assn. Chain Drug Stores, Hon. Order Ky. Cols. Home: 7150 Arenal Ln Carlsbad CA 92008 Office: 6211 Yarrow Dr Carlsbad CA 92008. *I play to win. I like to win. And I don't understand good losers.*

RANDALL, WILLIAM MADISON, educator; b. Belleville, Mich., Aug. 16, 1899; s. Will M. and Emma Adele (Henry) R.; A.B., U. Mich., 1921, A.M., 1924; Ph.D. summa cum laude, Hartford Theol. Sem., 1929; travelling fellow Gen. Edn. Bd., 1935, Am. Assn. Learned Socs. (Middle East), 1938; Litt.D., U. N.C. at Wilmington, 1970; m. Myldred Randolph Cady, June 21, 1924 (dec.); children—William D., Duncan P.; m. 2d. Mary Johnson McGee, May 1, 1954; 1 step-son, Robert McGee. Asso. prof. library sci. U. Chgo., 1929, prof., 1931, asst. dean students, 1938; v.p. Snead and Co., Orange, Va., 1946; dir. libraries, student affairs U. Ga., 1947; capt. U.S. Maritime Service; acad. dean U.S. Mcht. Marine Acad., 1948-51; dean Wilmington Coll. (now U. N.C. at Wilmington), 1951-58, pres., 1958-68, pres. emeritus, prof. modern langs., 1968-77; ret., 1977; mng. editor Library Quar., 1931-42; cons. Carnegie Corp. of N.Y. 1929-32; active in ednl. survey work Gen. Edn. Bd., Meth. Bd. of Edn., N. Central Assn., 1929-49. Mem. commn. sent to reorganize Vatican library, Carnegie Endowment for Internat. Peace, 1928. Served as maj., lt. col., USAAF, 1942-45; with War Dept. Intelligence, stationed in Cairo, Egypt, Casablanca, Morocco. Mem. Library Assn., Nat. Ednl. Assn., Phi Sigma. Democrat. Clubs: Rotary (pres. 1956-57). Episcopalian. Author: The College Library 1932; (with F.L.D. Goodrich) Principles of College Library Administration, 1935; (one-act play) Tobacco Alley, 1937; Acquisition and Cataloging of Library Materials 1941. Address: 4622 Mockingbird Ln Wilmington NC 28403

RANDALL, WILLIAM SEYMOUR, mfg. co. exec.; b. Champaign, Ill., July 5, 1933; s. Glenn S. and Audrey H. (Honnold) R.; B.S., Ind. State U., 1959; m. Carol Mischler, Aug. 23, 1958; children—Steve, Cathy, Mike, Jennifer. Controller, Amana Refrigeration Co. (Iowa), 1966-70; div. controller Trane Co., Clarksville, Tenn., 1970-74, corporate controller, La Crosse, Wis., 1974-79; v.p., chief fin. officer Sta-Rite Industries, Milw., 1979—. Pres., bd. dirs. Jr. Achievement. Served with AUS, 1953-55. Mem. Financial Execs. Inst. Kiwanian. Home: 2250 Hickory Ln La Crosse WI 54601 Office: 777 E Wisconsin St Milwaukee WI 53202

RANDAZZO, ARLENE, soprano; b. Chgo., June 17, 1943; d. Alfredo and Herminia (Melendez) Hampe; student Henry St. Music Settlement, N.Y.C., (Festival scholar) Aspen Music Festival, student with Felix Popper, Lola Urbach, Otto Guth, Kurt Adler and Carlo Moresco; m. Salvatore Randazzo; 1 dau., Maria. Appearances include: Festival of Two Worlds, Spoleto, Italy, Opera Internacional, Caracas, Venezuela, Conn. Opera Assn., Hartford, Phila. Opera Co., Tulsa Opera, N.J. State Opera, Buffalo Symphony, Syracuse Symphony, P.R. Symphony, and Art Park, Aspen, and Kennedy Center festivals; mem. N.Y.C. Opera and N.Y.C. Opera Theater, 1968-79; debut with operas of P.R. and Santo Domingo, 1979; roles include Elvira in I Puritani. Recipient Scholarship award Liederkranz Found., 1964; named Singer of Yr., Inst. P.R., 1977. Mem. Am. Guild Musical Artists (bd. govs., dir.). Office: NYC Opera State Theater Lincoln Center New York NY 10023

RANDAZZO, CHARLES LOUIS, fin. co. exec.; b. Bklyn., Mar. 17, 1927; s. Charles Michael and Leonarda (Alesi) R.; B.B.A., Pace U., 1950; m. Aurelie Catherine Pelton, June 28, 1952; children—Carla Jeanne, Donna Marie. Staff accountant, supr., sr. auditor S.D. Leidesdorf & Co., C.P.A.'s, 1955-60; with Belding Heminway Co. Inc., N.Y.C., 1960—, v.p., sec., treas., 1972—. Mem. Am. Inst. C.P.A.'s, Am. Soc. Corp. Secs., L.I. Accounting Soc. Club: Commack Heights Country. Home: 31 Franklin Ct W Garden City NY 11530 Office: 1430 Broadway New York NY 10018

RANDEL, DON MICHAEL, musicologist, univ. adminstr.; b. Edinburg, Tex., Dec. 9, 1940; s. Clay Don and DeLila May (Norman) R.; A.B. magna cum laude, Princeton U., 1962, M.F.A. (Danforth fellow), 1964, Ph.D. (Danforth fellow), 1967; m. Mary Malcolm Gaylord, June 18, 1966; children—Julia Phillips, Sally Katherine. Asst. prof. dept. fine arts Syracuse U., 1966-68; asst. prof. music

Cornell U., 1968-71, asso. prof., 1971-75, prof., 1975—, chmn. dept. music, 1971-76, vice provost, 1978-79; Fulbright grantee, Spain, 1964-66. Hon. Woodrow Wilson fellow, 1962; Nat. Endowment for Humanities fellow, 1976-77. Mem. Am. Musicological Soc. (sec.-treas. N.Y. State chpt. 1970-72, mem. nat. council 1971-73, editor-in-chief Jour. 1972-74, v.p. 1977-78), Music Library Assn. (book rev. editor Notes 1968-70), Phi Beta Kappa. Democrat. Author: The Responsorial Psalm Tones for the Mozarabic Office, 1969; An Index to the Chant of the Mozarabic Rite, 1973; Harvard Concise Dictionary of Music, 1978; contbr. articles to profl. jours. Home: 250 Burns Rd Ithaca NY 14850 Office: 211 Lincoln Hall Cornell U Ithaca NY 14853

RANDEL, JAMES BUFORD, JR., utility exec.; b. Okla., June 5, 1925; s. James Buford and Clara Marie (Richards) R.; B.S., U. Okla., 1950; m. Emma Elizabeth French, Apr. 28, 1951; children—James Buford, III, Ellen, Carrie, Sally, Nathan. Engr., FPC, Washington, 1950-53; with Public Service Electric & Gas Co., Newark, 1953—, sr. v.p. engrng. and prodn., then sr. v.p. cons., 1974-77, sr. v.p. corp., pres. Energy Devel. Corp., 1977—. Served with USNR, 1943-45. Mem. Soc. Gas Lighting, Soc. Petroleum Engrs., Am. Gas Assn. Methodist. Address: Public Service Electric & Gas Co 80 Park Pl Newark NJ 07101

RANDLE, MARVIN HERBERT, mayor; b. Irving, Tex., Sept. 10, 1936; s. Alfred Ernest and Adina (Herbert) R.; student pub. schs., Irving; m. Cecilia Aline Ingram, June 17, 1955; children—Randy Ray, Marvin DeWayne, Marvis Elaine, John Edward. With Dixie Chrome Co., 1952-55, Fully Formed Top Co., 1955-62; owner, mgr. Irving Countertop Co., 1962—; mayor City of Irving, 1977—. Mem. Irving City Council, 1970-77; mem. Irving Bicentennial Com.; trustee Buckner Bapt. Benevolences. Mem. Irving Homebuilders, Nat. Homebuilders, Irving C. of C. Baptist. Club: Rotary. Home: 639 W Arawe Circle Irving TX 75060 Office: 1801 E Pioneer Dr Irving TX 75061

RANDOLPH, ARTHUR RAYMOND, JR., lawyer; b. Riverside, N.J., Nov. 1, 1943; B.S., Drexel U., 1966; J.D., summa cum laude, U. Pa., 1969. Admitted to Calif. bar, 1970, U.S. Supreme Ct. bar, 1973, D.C. bar, 1973; law clk. to Judge Henry J. Friendly, U.S. Ct. Appeals, 2d Circuit, N.Y.C., 1969-70; asst. to solicitor gen. U.S. Dept. Justice, Washington, 1970-73; asso. firm Miller, Cassidy, Larroca & Lewin, Washington, 1973-75; dep. solicitor gen. U.S. Dept. Justice, Washington, 1975-77; partner firm Sharp, Randolph & Green, Washington, 1977—; spl. counsel Com. on Standards of Ofcl. Conduct, U.S. Ho. of Reps., 1979—; adj. prof. law Georgetown Law Center, 1974-78; dir. Atty. Gen.'s Com. on Reform of Fed. Jud. System, 1975-77; mem. com. on Fed. Rules of Evidence U.S. Justice Dept., 1972. Chmn. Com. on Govtl. Structures, McLean, Va., 1973-74. Recipient Spl. Achievement award U.S. Dept. Justice, 1971. Mem. Am., Calif., D.C. bar assns., Am. Law Inst., Supreme Ct. Hist. Soc., Order of Coif. Home: 6901 Oakridge Ave Chevy Chase MD 20015 Office: 1800 Massachusetts Ave NW Washington DC 20036

RANDOLPH, CARL LOWELL, corp. exec.; b. Pasadena, Calif., May 30, 1922; s. Carl L. and Lulu (McBride) R.; B.A., Whittier Coll., 1943; M.S., U. So. Calif., 1947, Ph.D., 1949; m. Jane Taber, June 25, 1943; children—Margaret, Stephen. Prin. chemist Aerojet-Gen. Corp., 1949-57; v.p. U.S. Borax Research Corp., Anaheim, Calif., 1957-63; asst. to pres. U.S. Borax & Chem. Corp., Los Angeles, 1963-66, v.p., 1966-68, exec. v.p., 1968-69, pres, 1969—, also dir. Trustee, chmn. bd. Whittier Coll. Served from ensign to lt. (j.g.), USNR, 1944-46. Licensed shipmaster. Mem. Am. Chem. Soc., Phi Beta Kappa, Sigma Xi. Contbr. articles to profl. jours. Patentee in field. Home: 16812 Baruna Ln Huntington Beach CA 92649 Office: 3075 Wilshire Blvd Los Angeles CA 90005

RANDOLPH, CHARLES CLIFFORD, III, publishing co. exec.; b. Point Pleasant, N.J., July 8, 1926; s. Charles Clifford Jr. and Mildred (Biddle) R.; A.B., Dartmouth, 1948; m. Donna Gibson, Apr. 24, 1973; children by previous marriage—Katherine, John. Classified advt. salesman McGraw-Hill Pub. Co., N.Y.C., 1948-49, dist. mgr. Food Engrng., 1949-54, dist. mgr. Business Week, 1954-58, Eastern advt. sales mgr., 1958-60, advt. dir., 1960-63, pub., 1966-74, group publisher v.p. McGraw Hill, 1974-76, group v.p., 1976-77; pub. Electronics, 1963-66; pres. Gruner & Jahr, USA Inc., pub. GEO mag.; chmn., chief exec. officer Parents Mag. Enterprises, 1978-79. Trustee, Outward Bound Inc. Served with USNR, 1943-46. Mem. Econ. Club N.Y. Clubs: Winged Foot Golf (Mamaroneck, N.Y.); Racquet and Tennis (N.Y.C.). Home: 75 East End Ave New York NY 10028

RANDOLPH, DAVID, conductor; b. N.Y.C., Dec. 21, 1914; s. Morris and Elsie (Goodman) R.; B.S., Coll. City N.Y., 1936; M.A., Tchrs. Coll., Columbia, 1941; m. Mildred Greenberg, July 18, 1948. Music specialist OWI, N.Y.C., 1943-47; condr. Randolph Singers, 1944-62, United Choral Soc., 1961—, St. Cecilia Chorus, N.Y.C., 1965—; music annotator CBS, N.Y.C., 1947-48; music dir., condr. Masterwork Chorus and Orch., 1955—; adj. prof. music N.Y.U., 1948—; lectr. Columbia, 1957; pre-Philharmonic lectr. Philharmonic Hall, 1964-72; tchr. conducting Dalcroze Sch., 1948-49; music commentator Little Orch. Soc. Concerts and Broadcasts, 1950-62; broadcaster Music for the Connoisseur, David Randolph Concerts, WNYC and numerous radio stas. of Nat. Assn. Ednl. Broadcasters, 1946—, Young Audience telecasts CBS-TV, 1958-59; host Lincoln Center Spotlight, weekly broadcasts radio station WQXR, N.Y.C., 1966-67; vis. prof. music State U. N.Y. at New Paltz, 1970-72, Fordham U., 1972-73; lectr. New Sch., 1973—; prof. music Montclair State Coll., Upper Montclair, N.J., 1973—; guest condr. Rockland County (N.Y.) Ann. Choral Festival, 1972, 73; adviser film Music to Live By. Mem. N.J. Arts Council, 1967-70; mem. music com. Gov. N.J.'s Commn. to Study Arts, 1965. Recipient first award for edn. by radio Ohio State Inst., 1948, 50, 51, Sylvania TV award, 1959. Author: This Is Music, 1964. Editor: David Randolph Choral Series. Writer, narrator Instruments of the Orchestra, 1958; Stereo Review's Guide to Understanding Music, 1973. Composer: A Song for Humanity, 1968. Contbg. author: The N.Y. Times Guide to Listening Pleasure, 1968. Recs. for Columbia, Vanguard, Westminster, Composers Recs. Inc., Esoteric. Address: 420 E 86th St New York City NY 10028

RANDOLPH, JENNINGS, U.S. senator; b. Salem, W.Va., Mar. 8, 1902; s. Ernest and Idell (Bingman) R.; A.B. magna cum laude, Salem Coll., 1924, D. Aero. Sci., 1943; LL.D., Davis and Elkins Coll., 1939, U. Pitts., 1965, Alderson Broaddus Coll., 1966, W.Va. U., W.Va. Wesleyan, Milton, Waynesburg, 1967, Oral Roberts U., 1972, Pikeville Coll., 1973, Morris Harvey Coll., 1973, Gallaudet Coll., 1976, Marshall U., 1977, Coll. Steubenville, 1978; Litt.D., Southeastern U., 1940; H.H.D., W.Va. State Coll., 1964, Wheeling Coll., 1976; L.H.D., Maryville Coll., 1966, West Liberty State Coll., 1978; D.Pub. Service, Bethany Coll., 1970; m. Mary Katherine Babb, Feb. 18, 1933; children—Jennings, Frank. Mem. editorial staff Clarksburg (W.Va.) Daily Telegram, 1924; asso. editor W.Va. Rev., Charleston, 1925; head dept. pub. speaking and journalism, dir. athletics Davis and Elkins Coll., 1926-32; prof. pub. speaking Southeastern U., Washington, 1935-53, dean Coll. Bus. Adminstrn., 1952-58; instr. Leadership Tng. Inst., Washington, 1948-58; mem. 73d-79th Congresses from 2d W.Va. Dist.; U.S. senator from W.Va., 1958—, chmn. pub. works com., 1966—; lectr.; former asst. to pres., dir. pub. relations Capital Airlines; chmn. W.Va. Planning Bd. Aviation Com., 1940-45, Washington Aviation Planning Commn., 1947-49; chmn. airport panel Transp. Council Commerce, 1953; mem. U.S. del. to spring meeting Interparliamentary Union, Rome, 1962, NATO Parliamentarian's Conf., 1962, Mexico-U.S. Interparliamentary confs., 1970, 73, 75, N. Atlantic Assembly Plenary Session, Ankara, Turkey, 1973, Brit.-Am. Parliamentary Conf., Hamilton, Bermuda, 1977, Interparliamentary Union, Prague, Czechoslovakia, 1979; past asso. editor, co-owner Randolph Enterprise-Rev. Trustee emeritus Salem Coll.; bd. dirs. Claude Worthington Benedum Found.; adv. com. Nat. Blinded Vets. Assn.; nat. adv. com. United Bus. Sch. Assn.; past gov. Nat. USO; trustee, chmn. adv. cabinet Southeastern U.; hon. trustee Davis and Elkins Coll.; mem. James Madison Meml. Com., Nat. Com. on Water Quality, Hwy. Beautification Com.; mem. Pres. U.S. and Gov.'s W.Va. Com. Employment Handicapped; mem. nat. adv. bd. Council Advancement Small Colls.; pres. airport div. Am. Road Builders Assn., 1948-50, past treas.; past dir. Washington Bd. Trade, chmn. world trade com., 1947-50); mem. Elkins Indsl. Devel. Corp.; past vice chmn. N.Am. fellowship Bapt. World Alliance. Named West Virginian of Year, Gazette-Mail, 1964; named W.Va. Speaker of Year, W.Va. U. chpt. Delta Sigma Rho, 1968; B'nai B'rith award, 1961; gold medal of merit VFW, 1969; City of Hope award, 1971; Man of Year, Nat. Fedn. Ind. Businessmen, 1971, Nat. Center Resource Recovery, 1976; Humanitarian of Year, D.C. Dental Soc., 1978; Pres.'s award Nat. Rehab. Assn., 1971; Elder Statesman of Aviation, Nat. Aero. Assn., 1972; Migel medal Am. Found. for Blind, 1972; Nat. Service Recognition award Izaac Walton League, 1974; Neil J. Curry Meml. award Hwy. Users Fedn., 1974; Bell Greve award Nat. Rehab. Assn., 1975; Service to Blind award Lions Internat., 1975; award Nat. Easter Seal Soc. for Crippled Children and Adults, 1976, K.C., 1976, USO, 1976, Nat. Environ. Developmental Assn., 1976; Environmental award Pollution Engrng. Mag., 1977; Conservation Leadership award W.Va. Wildlife Fedn., 1977; President's Medallion, Industry-Labor Council, White House Conf. on Handicapped, 1978; Legis. award Am. Legion, 1978; Wright Bros. Meml. trophy Nat. Aero. Assn., 1978. Mem. Elkins (dir.), W.Va. (dir.) chambers commerce, W.Va., Randolph County hist. socs., W.Va. Press Assn., Nat. Aero. Assn (past v.p.), Nat. Assn. Physically Handicapped, People to People, U.S. Capitol Hist. Soc., W.Va. Acad. Sci., Lions Clubs W. Va. (dist. gov. 1931-32, now internat. counsellor), Tau Kappa Alpha, Southeastern U. Honor Frat. Democrat. Seventh Day Baptist. Clubs: Nat. Press, Univ. (Washington). Co-author: Speaking That Wins; Mr. Chairman, Ladies and Gentlemen; author: Going to Make a Speech; contbr. articles to mags. Office: Dirksen Senate Office Bldg Washington DC 20510

RANDOLPH, JOHN HAGER, JR., savs. and loan assn. exec.; b. Fredericksburg, Va., July 27, 1921; s. John Hager and Grace (Lee) R.; B.C.E., Va. Mil. Inst., 1942; div.; children—Beverly Langhorne, Rebecca Hutter. Mgr. appraisal dept. Va. Fed. Savs. & Loan Assn., Richmond, 1948, v.p., 1948-54, exec. v.p., 1954-55, pres., 1955—, also dir.; dir. Home Guaranty Ins. Corp., Germantown Ins. Co., Va. Indsl. Devel. Corp., Cecil, Waller & Sterling, Inc., So. Service Corp., So. Homes of Va., Inc., Fed. Home Loan Bank of Greensboro, So. Title Ins. Corp. Pres., Better Bus. Bur. Richmond; Va. chmn. U.S. Savs. Bond Program; bd. dirs., fin. chmn. Commonwealth council Girl Scouts U.S.A.; pres. adult Bible class St. Stephen's Episcopal Ch. Served with USAAF, 1942-45. Decorated D.F.C., Air medal with five oak leaf clusters. Mem. Soc. Residential Appraisers (charter pres. Richmond chpt.), Am. Savs. and Loan Inst. (pres. Richmond chpt.), U.S. (pres., dir.), Va. savs. and loan leagues, Richmond C. of C., Central Richmond Assn., U.S. Navy League (Richmond council). Democrat. Clubs: Country of Va., Commonwealth, Bull and Bear. Home: Topping VA 23169 Office: 224 E Broad St Richmond VA 23219

RANDOLPH, JOHN MAURICE, leasing co. exec.; b. London, Eng., Mar. 28, 1926; s. Simon and Fira (Rouff) R.; came to U.S., 1940, naturalized, 1945; student Phillips Andover Acad., 1940-43; B.S., Mass. Inst. Tech., 1948; m. Kathleen MacGregor, Nov. 26, 1955; children—John Whitney, Emily MacGregor. Financial analyst Johns-Manville Corp., 1948-52; operations analyst C. & O. Ry., 1952-55; asst. to pres. Textron Inc., 1955-60; v.p. Boothe Leasing Corp., 1960-65; chmn. bd. Randolph Computer Corp., Greenwich, Conn., 1965-73; pres. J.M. Randolph & Assos., Inc., Greenwich, 1973-77, States Rail Service div. States Marine Corp., Greenwich, Conn., 1978-79; exec. v.p. Boothe Fin. Corp., Greenwich, 1979—. Served with AUS, 1944-45. Mem. Theta Xi. Home: West Old Mill Rd Greenwich CT 06830 Office: 2 Sound View Dr Greenwich CT 06830

RANDOLPH, JOHN WILSON, educator; b. Corydon, Ky., Sept. 17, 1911; s. Joe Drane and Nannie Elam (Wilson) R.; B.A., Central Coll., 1932; M.A., Vanderbilt U., 1934, Ph.D., 1939; LL.D., Drury Coll., 1960; m. Esther Margrethe Laursen, June 27, 1935; children—Karen (Mrs. Willis Baker), Lance, John. Instr. English, Central Methodist Coll., 1936-43; instr. English, Westminster Coll., Fulton, Mo., 1943-44, prof., chmn. dept. English, 1946-67, Distinguished Service prof. and A.P. Green prof. English, 1963-77, prof. emeritus, 1977—, dean, 1966-67, chmn. div. fine arts, 1969-77. Bd. dirs. Fulton Art League. Served as lt. (j.g.) USNR, 1944-46. Recipient Distinguished Alumnus award Central Meth. Coll., 1958. Mem. Modern Lang. Assn., Assn. Contemporary Greek Studies, Mo. Assn. Coll. Debate Dirs. (pres. 1940-42), Pi Kappa Delta (nat. pres. 1953-55). Author: The Devil's Apostle: A Biography of William Cowper Brann, 1939. Editor: The Forensic, 1959-63. Home: 1304 Wood St Fulton MO 65251

RANDOLPH, KENNETH VINCENT, univ. ofcl.; b. Masontown, W.Va., Apr. 14, 1915; s. Russell Burton and Maude Gay (Vincent) R.; student W.Va. U., 1933-35; D.D.S., U. Md., 1939, B.S. in Edn., 1951; m. Elizabeth Virginia Bachman; Aug. 3, 1940; children—Janice Lee, Kenneth Vincent. Fellow operative dentistry U. Md., 1939-40, instr., then asst. and asso. prof. operative dentistry, 1940- 46, prof., head dept., 1946-57; asso. dean, head dept. operative dentistry W.Va. U., 1957-58, dean, prof., 1958-68; prof., dean Baylor Coll. Dentistry, 1968-71, pres., dean, 1971—; cons. VA Hosp. Dallas. Mem. council Nat. Bd. Dental Examiners, 1965-71, chmn., 1969-71; bd. dirs. Tex. Area 5 Health Systems Agy.; trustee Am. Fund Dental Edn. Mem. Am. Coll. Dentists, Am. Dental Assn. (ho. dels. 1965-68), Tex., Dallas County dental socs., Am. Acad. Gold Foil Operators, So. Conf. Dental Deans and Examiners (pres. 1976), Am. Acad. History of Dentistry (pres. 1977-78), Phi Kappa Psi, Xi Psi Phi, Phi Delta Kappa, Omicron Kappa Upsilon. Democrat. Methodist. Home: 9533 Fieldcrest Ct Dallas TX 75238

RANDOLPH, ROBERT LEE, economist, educator; b. East St. Louis, Ill., Jan. 2, 1926; s. John Andrew and Willye (Smith) R.; A.B., DePauw U., Greencastle, Ind., 1948; M.S., U. Ill., Urbana, 1954, Ph.D., 1958; postdoctoral student Case Western Res. U., 1960, U. Mich., 1962; m. Patricia Smith, June 13, 1954; 1 dau., Heather Elizabeth. From instr. to asso. prof. econs. Springfield (Mass.) Coll., 1958-65, chmn. dept., 1960-63, dir. eve. and summer schs., 1960-64; dep. exec. dir. Equal Employment Opportunity Commn., Washington, 1967-68; dep. asso. dir. Job Corps, 1965-67; exec. v.p. Chgo. State U., 1969-73; pres. Westfield (Mass.) Coll., 1973-79; vice-chancellor Mass. State Coll. System, 1979—; cons. to industry. Vice pres. Springfield Urban League, 1962-66. Bd. dirs. Wesson Hosp., Springfield, Holyoke (Mass.) Hosp., Sickle-Cell Anemia Found. Served to lt. (j.g.) USNR, 1943-45, 50-51. Decorated Bronze Star; Navy V-12 scholar, 1943-45; State of Ill. scholar, 1952-56; Bailey fellow, 1957-58; Carnegie fellow, 1962; recipient Danforth Found. award, 1943; Republic Steel Found. award, 1961; Vice Pres.'s award excellence pub. service U.S. Govt., 1967; Outstanding Alumni award Lincoln High Sch., E. St. Louis, 1973. Mem. Am. Assn. State Colls. and Univs. (chmn. personnel com. 1974—), Am. Assn. Polit. and Social Scis., Am. Econ. Assn., Phi Delta Kappa, Alpha Phi Omega, Kappa Alpha Psi. Democrat. Unitarian-Universalist. Clubs: Quandrangle (Chgo.); Internat. (Washington). Author articles, monographs.

RANDOLPH, WILLIAM DEVINE, lawyer; b. Belleville, Ill., July 9, 1922; s. Claudius. L. and Gladys (Devine) R.; B.S. with honors, U. Ill., 1948, J.D. with honors, 1950; m. Evelyn Zipprodt, Aug. 10, 1946; children—Karen R. Friden, Susan, Jane, Anne R. Bacon, David. Admitted to Ill. bar, 1950, Cal. bar, 1961; with Johnston, Thompson, Raymond, Mayer & Jenner, Chgo., 1950-56; counsel Fairbanks, Morse & Co., 1956-57, gen. atty., 1957-60; gen. counsel Hunt Foods Industries, Inc., 1960-66, v.p., 1961-68; sec., gen. counsel Norton Simon, Inc., 1968-72, v.p., 1968-73; partner firm Duryea, Randolph, Malcolm & Daly, Newport Beach, Calif., 1973-76; prof. law U. Oreg., Eugene, 1976—. Served as capt., inf., AUS, World War II, capt., intelligence, Korean War. Mem. Am., Ill., Calif., Chgo., Los Angeles bar assns., Am. Soc. Corp. Secs., Order of Coif, Beta Gamma Sigma, Beta Alpha Psi, Phi Delta Phi. Home: 2245 S Lawrence St Eugene OR 97405 Office: Sch of Law Univ of Oreg Eugene OR 97403

RANDT, CLARK THORP, educator, physician; b. Lakewood, Ohio, Nov. 18, 1917; s. Herbert W. and Bessie (Thorp) R.; A.B., Colgate U., 1940; M.D., Western Res. U., 1943; m. Mary-Louise Paull Mitchell, Jan. 15, 1944; children—Clark Thorp, Dana M., Thomas P. Intern Univ. Hosps., Cleve. 1943-45; resident Neurol. Inst. N.Y. 1947-50; practice medicine, specializing in neurology, N.Y.C., 1962—; asst. in neurology Coll. Phys. and Surgs., Columbia, 1949-50; asso. prof. neurology Sch. Medicine, Western Res. U., 1950-59; dir. life sci. NASA, Washington, 1959-61; prof. neurology Sch. Medicine, N.Y. U., 1962-70, prof., chmn. dept. neurology, 1970—; dir. Neurology Service, N.Y. U.-Bellevue Med. Center, also N.Y. U. Hosp.; cons. in neurology N.Y. VA Hosp.; med. cons. NASA Project Mercury; established NASA Ames Research Center, Life Sci. Lab., Calif., 1959-61; mem. med. adv. bd. Nat. Multiple Sclerosis Soc.; chief neurology sect. U.S. Army Psychiat. Center, Mason Gen. Hosp., Brentwood, N.Y.; co-chmn. bioastronautics com. NRC, 1959-60, NASA-DOD bioastronautics coordinating com., Washington, 1960-61. Served to capt., M.C., AUS, 1945-47. Fellow Am. Acad. Neurology; mem. Am. Neurol. Assn., N.Y. Neurol. Soc. (pres. 1967-68), Aerospace Med. Assn. (v.p. 1961-62), Assn. for Research in Nervous and Mental Disease chmn. bd. trustees 1972-73). Home: 59 Husted Ln Greenwich CT 06830 Office: 550 1st Ave New York City NY 10016. *Dreams are a prelude to accomplishment. Great challenges lead to adversity which, in turn, brings forth the qualities of perseverance and a sense of humor. The determining influence of self-fulfilling prophecy cannot be overestimated.*

RANEY, EDWARD THOMAS, educator; b. East St. Louis, Ill., Mar. 7, 1906; s. John Thomas and Lydia (Perryman) R.; A.B., Maryville Coll., 1931; M.A., Brown U., 1933, Ph.D., 1938; m. Margaret Melody, July 26, 1932, (dec. Oct. 1966); children—Cynthia Ann (Mrs. Lanny Hatman), James E.; m. 2d, Helen Albert Jesse, Mar. 1969. Clin. psychologist State R.I., 1936-38; instr. U. Mich., 1938-39; supr. Occupational Research Center, Mich. Employment Service, 1940-42, chief staff services, 1942-43; asst. dir. War Manpower Commn. for Mich., 1944-46; asso. prof. Mgmt. Sch. Bus. Adminstrn., Wayne State U., Detroit, 1946-50, prof. mgmt., 1950—, chmn. dept. mgmt., 1960—. Dir. Chatham Super Markets. Mem. bd. edn., Ferndale, Mich., 1946. Pres. Oakland County Mental Health Soc. Diplomate Am. Psychol. Assn. Mem. Indsl. Relations Research Assn., Inst. Mgmt. Sci., Mich. Psychol. Assn. (pres. 1947), Acad. Mgmt., Sigma Xi, Sigma Iota Epsilon. Home: 310 Greenwood St Birmingham MI 48009 Office: Wayne State U Detroit MI 48202

RANEY, GEORGE NEAL, educator; b. Portland, Oreg., Oct. 14, 1922; s. George William and Helen Louise (Smith) R.; B.S. in Math., Queens Coll., 1943; postgrad. Mass. Inst. Tech., 1943-44; Ph.D. in Math., Columbia, 1953; m. Barbara Louise Robinson, Sept. 4, 1952; children—Rebecca, Patricia. Math. instr. Mass. Inst. Tech., Cambridge, 1943-44; instr. Columbia, N.Y.C., 1946-53, Bklyn. Coll., 1953-55; asst. prof. Pa. State U., State Coll., 1955-61; vis. asso. prof. Wesleyan U., Middletown, Conn., 1961-63; asso. prof. U. Conn., Storrs, 1963-66, prof., 1966—, acting head dept. math., 1966-67, acting dir. honors programs, 1970-71; vis. research asso. prof. NSF automata theory project Wesleyan U., Middletown, 1964-66. Served with USNR, 1944-46. Mem. Am. Math. Soc., Assn. Symbolic Logic, Assn. for Computing Machinery, Math. Assn. Am. Contbr. articles math. jours; author numerous book and article revs. Asso. editor Am. Math. Monthly, 1967-68. Home: 399 Middle Turnpike Storrs CT 06268 Office: Dept Math U Conn Storrs CT 06268

RANGEL, CHARLES BERNARD, congressman; b. Harlem, N.Y., June 11, 1930; s. Ralph and Blanche (Wharton) R.; B.S., N.Y. U., 1957; J.D., St. John's U. Sch. Law, 1960; m. Alma Carter, July 26, 1964; children—Steven, Alicia. Admitted to N.Y. bar, 1960; asst. U.S. atty. So. Dist. N.Y., 1961-62; mem. N.Y. State Assembly, 1966-70; mem. 92d-96th Congresses, 19th N.Y. Dist., mem. Ways and Means Com., Select Com. Narcotics Abuse and Control; mem. Adv. Commn. Intergovtl. Relations. Served with AUS, 1948-52; Korea. Decorated Bronze Star, Purple Heart, U.S., Korean presdl. citations. Office: House Office Bldg Washington DC 20515

RANGELL, LEO, psychoanalyst, psychiatrist; b. N.Y.C., Oct. 1, 1913; s. Morris and Pauline (Kaiser) R.; A.B., Columbia, 1933: M.D., U. Chgo., 1937; m. Anita J. Buchwald, Feb. 22, 1939; children—Judith Ellen, Susan Roberta, Richard Neal, Paul Charles. Intern Bklyn. Jewish Hosp., 1937-39; resident neurology Montefiore Hosp., N.Y.C., 1939; resident psychiatry Grasslands Hosp., Valhalla, N.Y., 1940, N.Y. State Psychiat. Inst. and Hosp., N.Y.C., 1941; pvt. practice neurology and psychiatry, N.Y.C., 1942-43; instr. neurology Columbia U. Coll. Physicians and Surgeons, 1942-46; research fellow neuropsychiatry Montefiore Hosp., 1942-43; psychoanalytic tng. N.Y. Psychoanalytic Inst., later Los Angeles Psychoanalytic Inst., 1941-49; pvt. practice psychoanalysis and neuropsychiatry, Beverly Hills and Los Angeles, 1946—; tng. analyst Los Angeles Psychoanalytic Inst., 1956—, dir. extension div., 1956-57, bd. trustees, 1958—; pres. bd. dirs. Westwood Hosp., Los Angeles, 1959-60; cons. Reiss-Davis Clinic Child Guidance, Los Angeles, 1953-65; clin. prof. psychiatry U. Calif. at Los Angeles Sch. Medicine, 1953—, U. Calif., San Francisco, 1976—; fellow Center Advanced Study Behavioral Scis., Stanford, 1962-63; John B. Turner vis. prof. psychiatry Columbia U. Psychoanalytic Clinic for Tng. and Research, N.Y.C., 1971-72. Served to maj. M.C., USAAF, 1943-46. Guggenheim fellow, 1971-72. Recipient Internat. Clin. Essay prize Brit. Inst. Psychoanalysis, 1951, 53. Diplomate Am. Bd. Neurology and Psychiatry. Mem. Am. Psychoanalytic Assn. (pres. 1961-62, 66-67, bd. editors 1956-60, 62-66, 76-79, cons. 1979—), Los Angeles psychoanalytic Soc. (pres. 1956-58, 64-65), Internat. Psychoanalytic Assn. (v.p. 1967-69, pres. 1969-71, 71-73), Am., So. Calif. (pres. 1955-56) psychiat. assns. Editorial bd. Jour. Phila. Assn. Psychoanalysis, Imago, Israel Annals Psychiatry and Related Disciplines, 1973—, Hillside Jour. Clin. Psychiatry, 1978—. Contbr. numerous articles to profl. jours. Address: 456 N Carmelina Ave Los Angeles CA 90049

RANKIN, ALAN CARSON, educator; b. Hoisington, Kans., Dec. 19, 1914; s. Roy and Laura (Lanning) R.; A.B., B.S., Ft. Hays (Kans.) State U., 1937; M.A., Syracuse U., 1939, D.Social Sci., 1955; Litt.D. (hon.), Rose Hulman Inst., 1967, Ind. State U., 1975; LL.D., Vincennes U., 1970, Oakland City Coll., 1971; H.H.D. (hon.), Ind. State U., Evansville, 1975; m. Frances Goodnough Atkins, Oct. 17, 1958; 1 dau., Lynn. Student personnel asst., chief research and service bur. Panama Canal, 1940-44; asst. prof. govt. Miami U., Oxford, Ohio, 1946-48, 52-54; personnel cons. Nat. Personnel Authority, GHQ-SCAP, Tokyo, Japan, 1948-50; asst. prof., dir. student affairs Grad. Sch. Pub. and Bus. Adminstrn., Cornell U., 1954-56; exec. asst. to chancellor, prof. polit. sci., also asst. sec. bd. trustees U. Pitts., 1956-65, asst. chancellor for gen. affairs, 1958-61, for student and gen. affairs, 1961-64, vice chancellor for student and gen. affairs, 1964-65; pres. Ind. State U., 1965-75, spl. asst. to pres., 1975—; dir. Govt. Affairs Inst., Washington, 1965-74; exec. dir. Leadership Terre Haute, 1978—. Pres. Terre Haute Com. Area Progress, 1965-73, Ind. Conf. Higher Edn., 1968-69; v.p. World Affairs Council Pitts., 1959-65. Trustee Winchester-Thurston Sch., Pitts., 1963-65; bd. dirs. Pitts. Chamber Music Soc., 1961-65, Pitts. Playhouse, 1963-65; bd. dirs. Swope Art Gallery, Terre Haute, 1965—, pres., 1979—; bd. dirs. Midwest Devel. Found., 1965-73; hon. trustee St. Mary-of-the-Woods Coll., 1977—. Served to capt. AUS, World War II. Mem. Am. Polit. Sci. Assn., Phi Delta Phi, Omicron Delta Kappa, Phi Mu Alpha, Pi Gamma Mu, Sigma Chi. Presbyn. Rotarian. Author: City Manager Government in Wichita, Kansas, 1939; The Administration of Federal Contract and Grant Research, 1955; (with E. H. Litchfield) Public Administration in Indonesia, 1954. Home: 78 Allendale St Terre Haute IN 47802 Office: 103 Alumni Center Ind State U Terre Haute IN 47809

RANKIN, GEORGE CARLSON, banker; b. Headrick, Okla., Feb. 8, 1915; s. Walter W. and Blanche (Carlson) R.; B.S., Kans. State U., 1938; grad. Stonier Grad. Sch. Banking, Rutgers U., 1962; m. Jane M. Reynolds, Apr. 19, 1941; children—Donna Kay, Jane Carolyn. With Penn Mut. Life Ins. Co., 1938-40, Universal CIT Corp., 1940-41; dir. for Kans., U.S. Savs. Bonds, 1948-56; asst. cashier Fed. Res. Bank Kansas City, 1956-60, cashier Omaha br., 1960-62, v.p. charge Omaha br., 1963-71, v.p. in charge Denver br., 1971-73, sr. v.p. in charge Denver br., 1973-74; 1st v.p. Fed. Res. Bank Richmond, 1974—. Active Denver United Way campaign, 1973. Served to lt. col. USAAF, 1941-46, USAF, 1951-53; PTO. Mem. Robert Morris Assos., Omaha C. of C., Kappa Sigma. Club: Rotary. Home: 11330 Edenberry Dr Richmond VA 23235 Office: Fed Res Bank 701 E Byrd St Richmond VA 23261

RANKIN, JAMES, journalist; b. Lakeworth, Fla., Sept. 26, 1923; s. John Munro and Grace (Crews) R.; A.B., U. N.C., 1949; m. Sallie Lynwood Baber, June 6, 1953; 1 son, William Lynn. Reporter, News & Observer, Raleigh, N.C., 1949-51; city editor Raleigh Times, 1953-56; copy editor, reporter Louisville Times, 1956-60; night city editor Atlanta Constn., 1960-66, editorial writer, columnist, 1966-68, city editor, 1968-71, asst. mng. editor, 1971—. Served with USNR, 1943-46, 51-53. Recipient Pub. Service award Ga. AP, 1974. Mem. Atlanta Press Club, Sigma Nu. Democrat. Episcopalian. Home: 391 Golfview Rd NW Atlanta GA 30309 Office: 52 Marietta St Atlanta GA 30302

RANKIN, JAMES A., mfg. co. exec.; b. Covington, Ky., July 25, 1928; s. Grover C. and Alice Mae R.; B.A., Eastern Ky. U.; m. Mary Jane Butsch, July 26, 1951; children—Nancy, Peggy Ann. With NuTone div. Scovill Mfg. Co., 1954—, gen. mgr. NuTone, 1967-78, group v.p. Scovill Mfg. Co., Cin., 1975-78, exec. v.p., 1978—. Served with U.S. Army, 1945-47. Home: 832 Rosewood Covington KY 41011 Office: Scovill Mfg Co Madison and Red Bank Rds Cincinnati OH 45227*

RANKIN, JUDITH TORLUEMKE, profl. golfer; b. St. Louis, Feb. 18, 1945; d. Paul W. and Waneta (Clifton) Torluemke; student pub. schs., Eureka, Mo.; m. Walter Rankin, June 12, 1967; 1 son, Walter. Profl. golfer; pres. Ladies Profl. Golfers Assn., 1976-77. Recipient Vare trophy for lowest scoring average, 1973-77; Victor award for Female golfer, 1976; leading money winner, 1977. Author: Natural Way to Golf Power. Address: 1609 W Pine St Midland TX 79701

RANKIN, KARL LOTT, ret. fgn. service officer; b. Manitowoc, Wis., Sept. 4, 1898; s. Emmet Woollen and Alberta (Lott) R.; grad. Mercerburg Acad., 1916; student Calif. Inst. Tech., 1917-19, Fed. Polytechnic, Zürich, 1920-21; C.E., Princeton, 1922; LL.D., Bowdoin Coll., Bates Coll.; m. Pauline Jordan, Oct. 3, 1925 (dec.); m. 2d, Ruth Thompson, Mar. 6, 1978. Constrn. supt. Nr. East Relief, Caucasus, 1922-25; mgr. of real estate devel. co., Linden, N.J., 1925-27; entered U.S. Govt. service, 1927, assigned as asst. trade commr., Prague, Czechoslovakia, comml. attaché, Prague, 1929, Athens and Tirana, 1932, Brussels and Luxembourg, 1939; comml. attaché, consul, Belgrade, 1940; comml. attaché, Cairo, 1941, interned by Japanese in Manila before reaching Egypt, 1942-43; comml. attaché, Cairo, 1944; counselor of embassy for econ. affairs, Athens and Belgrade, 1944; chargé d'affaires a.i., Athens, 1946; counselor of legation, Vienna, 1946-47; counselor of embassy, Athens, 1947, chargé d'affaires a.i., 1947-48; apptd. career minister, 1948; consul gen., Canton, 1949, Hong Kong and Macau, 1949; minister and chargé d'affairs, Taipei, 1950-53; ambassador to China, 1953-57, to Yugoslavia, 1958-61; ret., 1961. Hon. trustee Deree-Pierce Colls., Athens, Greece. Served on active duty USN, 1918; lt. comdr. Res., 1937. Decorated Grand Cordon Order Brilliant Star (China). Mem. Am. Soc. C.E. (life). Am.-Hellenic C. of C. (hon. pres.), Phi Kappa Sigma, Dial Lodge (Princeton). Conglist. Clubs: Cosmos (Washington); Princeton (N.Y.C.). Author: China Assignment, 1964. Home: 1 Colony Point Dr Punta Gorda FL 33950 also Kings Hwy Kennebunkport ME 04046

RANKIN, MARJORIE EUNICE, coll. dean; b. Troy, N.Y., Mar. 15, 1918; d. Alexander and Melissa (Speidel) Rankin; B.S. in Home Econs., Russell Sage Coll., 1939; M.S., Cornell U., 1945. Tchr. home econs. pub. schs., Argyle, N.Y., 1939-41, Batavia, N.Y., 1941-44; with Nesbitt Coll., Drexel U., Phila., 1945—, asso. prof., 1950-55, prof., asst. dean, 1955-62, asso. prof., 1962-63, dean 1963—. Mem. ednl. adv. com. Wool Bur., Inc., 1954-57. Trustee, Russell Sage Coll., 1976—. Mem. Am., Pa., (treas. 1959-61, 64-65, pres. 1970-71), Phila. (pres. 1955-56) home econs. assns., Nat. Council Adminstrs. Home Econs. (exec. bd. 1976-78, pres. elect 1978, pres. 1979), AAUW, (pres. Phila. 1966-68), League Women Voters, Omicron Nu (treas. 1977-79), Phi Kappa Phi. Democrat. Christian Scientist. Home: 2136 Locust St Philadelphia PA 19103 Office: Nesbitt Coll Drexel U Philadelphia PA 19104

RANKIN, NELL, opera singer; b. Montgomery, Ala., Jan. 3, 1926; d. Allen and Eugenia (Knabe) Rankin; student Birmingham Conservatory of Music, 1940-43; vocal study with Madame Jeanne Lorraine, 1940-43, also Coenraad V. Bos, 1943-49, Karin Branzell, 1945-49; m. Dr. Hugh Clark Davidson, Apr. 6, 1951. First Town Hall recital, N.Y.C., 1947; operatic debut as Ortrud in Lohengrin, Stadttheater, Zûrich, Switzerland, 1949, resident mezzo soprano, 1949-50; numerous guest appearances concert and opera in Europe, including Vienna State Opera, Vienna Symphony, 1949-51; resident mezzo soprano Basel Stadttheater, Switzerland, 1950-51; debut La Scala, Milan, Italy, 1951; debut in Aida, Met. Opera, N.Y.C., 1951, since leading mezzo soprano; Met. roles include Carmen, Amneris in Aida, Eboli in Don Carlo, Marina in Boris Godunov, Azucena in Il Trovatore, Laura in La Gioconda, Ortrud in Lohengrin, Santuzza in Cavalleria Rusticana; in recital at Town Hall, 1953; appeared as Carmen, Covent Garden Royal Opera, London, 1953-54; debut as Carmen, San Francisco Opera Co., 1955; debut Chicago Lyric Theater As Eboli in Don Carlo; debut Mexico City as Amneris in Aida, 1957, as Amneris in Mexico City as Amneris in Aida, 1957, as Amneris in Aida, Teatro Colon, Buenos Aires, 1958; recordings, Capital Records. London FFRR. Recipient 1st prize, Internat. Concours de Musique, Geneva, Switzerland, 1950; Critics Circle award, 1968; named to Am. Hall of Fame, 1972. Home: 1040 Park Ave New York NY 10028 Office: care Met Opera New York NY

RANKIN, ROBERT, ednl. found. exec.; b. Des Moines, Sept. 14, 1915; s. Wiley Strange and Estelle Blanche (Renne) R.; B.A., State U. Iowa, 1937; B.D., Yale, 1940, M.A., 1942; D.D. (hon.), Lindenwood Coll., St. Charles, Mo., 1964; D.H.L. (hon.), U. So. Calif., 1967; m. Martha Jean Roberts, Sept. 7, 194O; children—Mary Renne (Mrs. Robert M. Dawson), Margaret Lloyd, Wiley Robert, William Roberts. Ordained to ministry Methodist Ch., 1944, United Ch. Christ, 1960; minister, Sunnyvale, Calif., 1942-44; campus minister, lectr. religion Oberlin Coll., 1946-51; chaplain, asso. prof. religion Claremont Colls., 1951-58; exec. dir. Rockefeller Bros. Theol. Fellowship Program, Princeton, N.J., 1954-55; asso. dir. Danforth Found., St. Louis, 1958-66, v.p., 1966—, dir. programs campus ministry, 1958, asso. program, 1958-75; cons. Fund Theol. Edn., Lilly Endowment Inc., Pres.'s Commn. on Campus Unrest, Denison U., Oberlin Coll., Stephens Coll.; bd. dirs. White House Conf. Edn. of St. Louis, 1959-65; chmn. St. Louis Met. Conf. Edn. Culturally Disadvantaged, 1962; cons. to bd. dirs. Nat. Inst. for Campus Ministry, 1974—; mem. selection panel White House fellows, 1975, 77, chmn., 1978; mem. Commn. Religion Assn. Am. Colls., 1974-76; mem. Nat. Commn. Higher Edn., United Meth. Ch., 1975-77. Trustee Sch. Theology at Claremont, 1955-59; bd. dirs., v.p. Am. Friends of Wilton Park; bd. dirs. Loretto Hilton Repertory Theatre St. Louis, 1971-73, St. Louis UN Conf. on Food and Population, 1975, Healing Community St. Louis, 1976—, Therapy Cons. Assos., St. Louis, 1976—; Radio Info. Service, 1978—, Nat. Task Force for Disability and the Arts, 1978—. Recipient E. Harris Harbison award for gifted teaching, 1970. Fellow Wilton Park Conf., Sussex, Eng., Soc. Values Higher Edn. Served as chaplain, capt. USAAF, 1944-46. Mem. Nat. Assn. Coll. and Univ. Chaplains, Am. Friends Service Comm., Assn. Coordination Univ. Religious Affairs, ACLU, Am. Assn. UN, Friends St. Louis City Mus., NAACP, Am. Acad. Religion, Ch. Soc. for Coll. Work (dir. 1970-75), Am. Assn. for Higher Edn., Common Cause, Sigma Chi. Author articles, chpts. in books. Home: 330 S Maple St St Louis MO 63119 Office: 222 S Central Ave Saint Louis MO 63105

RANNELLS, WILL, artist; b. Caldwell, Ohio, July 21, 1892: S. James Falls and Sarah (Allison) R.; ed. Art Acad. of Cincinnati, 1913-16; unmarried. Magazine and book illustrator, specializing in dog portrature, 1916—; instr. in fine arts Ohio State U., 1926-32, asso. prof. 1932-64, asso. prof. emeritus, 1964—. Pres. Columbus Humane Soc., 1936-39. Recipient awards Am. Humane Assn., 1972, Capital Area Humane Soc., 1974, Humane Soc. U.S., 1976, Pilot Dogs, 1977. Mem. The Artists' Guild, Ohio Water Color Soc., Am. Water Color Soc. Club: Faculty. Contbr. of cover designs and illustrations to McCall's Magazine, Life, Judge, Country Gentleman, Farm and Fireside, Outing, etc. Illustrator Dog Stars, 1916; collaborator and illustrator Waif, The Story of Spe, 1937; illustrator Animals Baby Knows, 1938, Jack, Jock and Funny, 1938, Farmyard Play Book, 1940, Timmy, 1941, Just a Mutt, 1947, Animal Play Book, 1947; illustrator and author Animal Picture Story Book, 1938; illustrator ann. Buckeye Union Dog Calendar. Address: 4345 Central College Rd Westerville OH 43081. *Hurt no living thing.*

RANNEY, GEORGE ALFRED, ret. steel co. exec., lawyer; b. Chgo., May 30, 1912; s. George Alfred and Cornelia (Williams) R.; A.B., Yale, 1934, LL.B., 1939; m. Nora Ryerson, June 18, 1938; children—George Alfred, Edward R., David M., Nancy R. (Mrs. David F. Levi). Admitted to Ill. bar, 1939; mem. firm Sidley, Austin, Burgess & Smith, Chgo., 1939-62; v.p., gen. counsel Inland Steel Co., Chgo., 62-68, sr. v.p., 1968-71, vice chmn., 1971-77, also dir. Trustee, U. Chgo. Served as 1st lt. AUS, 1942-45. Mem. Am., Chgo. bar assns. Episcopalian. Home: Casey Rd Libertyville IL 60048 Office: 115 S La Salle St Room 2270 Chicago IL 60603

RANNEY, HELEN MARGARET, physician, educator; b. Summer Hill, N.Y., Apr. 12, 1920; d. Arthur C. and Alesia (Toolan) Ranney; A.B., Barnard Coll., 1941; M.D., Columbia, 1947. Intern Presbyn. Hosp., N.Y.C., 1947-48, resident, 1948-50; practice medicine specializing in internal medicine, hematology, N.Y.C., 1954-70; asst. physician Presbyn. Hosp., 1954-60; instr. Coll. Phys. and Surg. Columbia, 1954-60; asso. prof. medicine Albert Einstein Coll. Medicine, 1960-64, prof. medicine, 1965-70; prof. medicine State U. N.Y. at Buffalo, 1970-73; prof. medicine, chmn. dept. medicine U. Calif. at San Diego, 1973—. Diplomate Am. Bd. Internal Medicine. Mem. Am. Soc. for Clin. Investigation, Am. Soc. Hematology, Harvey Soc., Am. Assn. Physicians, Nat. Acad. Sci., Inst. Medicine, Am. Acad. Arts and Scis., Phi Beta Kappa, Sigma Xi, Alpha Omega Alpha. Home: 6229 La Jolla Mesa Dr La Jolla CA 92037 Office: Hosp Dept Medicine 8110 225 W Dickinson St San Diego CA 92103

RANSOHOFF, JOSEPH, neurosurgeon; b. Cin., July 1, 1915; s. Joseph and Doris (Kaufmann) R.; B.S., Harvard U., 1938; M.D., U. Chgo., 1941; m. Rita Mayer, Sept. 17, 1937; children—Joan, Joseph. Intern, Cin. Gen. Hosp., 1941-42, resident in surgery, 1942-44; practice medicine specializing in neurosurgery, N.Y.C., 1961—; prof., chmn. dept. neurosurgery N.Y. U.-Bellevue Med. Center, N.Y.C., 1961—; cons. in neurosurgery St. Vincent's Hosp., Lenox Hill Hosp., Beekman-Downtown Hosp., Manhattan VA Hosp. Served with AUS, 1944-46. Fellow A.C.S., N.Y. Acad. Scis.; mem. Am. Acad. Neurol. Surgeons, Am. Acad. Neurology, Am. Congress of Phys. Medicine and Rehab., AMA, Assn. Research in Nervous and Mental Disease, Am. Neurol. Assn., Am. Assn. Neurol. Surgeons, N.Y. Neurosurg. Soc., Pan Am. Med. Assn., Internat. Soc. Pediatric Neurosurgeons. Office: 560 1st Ave New York NY 10016

RANSOHOFF, MARTIN, motion picture producer; b. New Orleans, 1927; grad. Colgate U., 1949. Founder Filmways, Inc., N.Y.C., early 1950's, chmn. bd., pres., until 1972; pres. Martin Ransohoff Prodns., Inc., 1972—. Office: Columbia Pictures 300 Colgems Sq Burbank CA 91505

RANSOM, EDWARD DUANE, lawyer; b. Minot, N.D., Jan. 3, 1914; s. Edward M. and Gladys (Root) R.; student Minot State Tchrs. Coll., 1932-34; A.B., U. Mich., 1936, J.D., 1938; m. Margaret E. Phelps, Oct. 6, 1940; children—Edward P., Susan M., Richard M., Mary A. Admitted to Cal. bar, 1939, also U.S. Supreme Ct., Circuit Ct. Appeals for D.C. and 1st, 2d, 5th and 9th Circuits, ICC, Fed Maritime Commn.; asso. admiralty law firm Lillick, McHose, Wheat, Adams & Charles, San Francisco, 1938-41, 45—, partner, 1950-55, 57—; gen. counsel Fed. Maritime Bd. and Maritime Administrn., 1955-57. U.S. del. Internat. Maritime Law Conf., 1959, 65, 74, 77. Served as lt. comdr. USN, 1941-45. Mem. Am. (chmn. com. on maritime transp. 1964), Calif., San Francisco, bar assns., Maritime Law Assn. (exec. com. 1957-60, com. on maritime legislation), San Francisco Legal Aid Soc. (dir. 1966-72), Marine Exchange of San Francisco (pres. 1971-73). Clubs: Propeller of U.S. (pres. chpt. 1975-76), Comml., San Francisco, World Trade (San Francisco); Whitehall (N.Y.C.); Claremont Country (Oakland). Home: 190 Estates Dr Piedmont CA 94611 Office: 2 Embarcadero Center San Francisco CA 94111

RANSOM, GRAYCE ANNABLE, educator; b. La Porte, Ind.; d. Irving H. and Louisa Sabra (Sawin) Annable; B.R.E., McCormick Theol. Sem., 1937; M.A., Lewis and Clark Coll., 1954; B.A., Kalamazoo Coll., 1965; Ph.D., U. So. Calif., 1967; m. John T. Seeley, Mar. 20, 1970; children—Judith Ransom Lodhie, Kenneth C., Janet. Asst. camp dir., Portland, Oreg., 1947-55; tchr. religious edn., tchr. tng. Portland Council Chs., 1949-54; tchr. elementary schs., Portland, Oreg., 1955-58, Los Angeles, 1959-62; asst. prof. Calif. State U., Long Beach, 1963-65; mem. faculty U. So. Calif., Los Angeles, 1965—, prof. curriculum and reading instrn., 1974—, dir. campus and Nat. Charity League reading centers, 1967—; cons. various Calif. schs. dists., also Calif. Dept. Edn. Bd. dirs. Footlighters Child Guidance Clinic. Mem. Internat. (dir.), Calif. (pres. 1976-77), Los Angeles (pres. 1973-74) reading assns., AAUP, Am. Ednl. Research Assn., NEA, Nat. Council Tchrs. English, League Women Voters (pres. Portland 1947-48), Pi Lambda Theta, Phi Delta Kappa. Presbyterian. Author: Crackerjacks, 1969; Evaluating Teacher Education Programs in Reading, 1972; Teacher's Guide for Electronic Card-Reading Machines, 1974; The Ransom Reading Program, 1974; Multi Media Kits—Reading, Researching, Reporting in Social Studies, 1975; Preparing to Teach Reading, 1978; research in diagnostic-prescriptive teaching. Home: 4830 Maytime Ln Culver City CA 90230 Office: U So Calif Campus Reading Centers Waite Phillips Hall University Park Los Angeles CA 90007. *In my ongoing work with teachers and students I am continuously impressed with the fact that children and youth are America's greatest resources. There is immense challenge to nurture all young people not only to effective literacy but also to worthwhile life goals and self-actualizing work and citizenship commitments. As we help children grow in thinking, creative and moral powers we participate in building an enduring bank of resources which become national and international bulwarks against decay and death. The task is endless—but endlessly exciting!*

RANSOM, HARRY HOWE, polit. scientist, educator; b. Nashville, May 14, 1922; s. John Bostick, Jr., and Marie Litton (Howe) R.; B.A., Vanderbilt U., 1943; M.A., Princeton, 1949, Ph.D., 1954; m. Nancy Anne Alderman, July 6, 1951; children—Jenny Alderman, Katherine Marie, William Henry Howe. Instr. Princeton, 1947-48; instr. polit. sci. Vassar, 1948-52; research dir. Democratic Com. N.J., 1954; asst. prof. polit. sci. Mich. State U., 1955; research asso. def. studies program Harvard, 1955-61; asso. prof. polit. sci. Vanderbilt U., 1961-63, prof., 1964—, chmn. dept., 1969-74; vis. prof. Sch. History, U. Leeds (Eng.), 1977-78. Served with AUS, 1943-45. Fellow Woodrow Wilson Internat. Center for Scholars, 1974-75. Congl. fellow, Am. Polit. Sci. Assn., 1953-54; recipient research award, Rockefeller Found., 1964-65. Mem. Am., So. polit. sci. assns., Internat. Studies Assn., Internat. Inst. Strategic Studies (London), A.A.U.P. Author: Central Intelligence and National Security, 1958; Can American Democracy Survive Cold War?, 1953; An American Foreign Policy Reader, 1965; The Intelligence Establishment, 1970. Home: 511 Belle Meade Blvd Nashville TN 37205

RANSOM, WILLIAM MICHAEL, author; b. Puyallup, Wash., June 6, 1945; s. Bert and LaVerne (Marcoe) R.; student Wash. State U., 1963-65, U. Puget Sound, 1965-67; B.A. in Edn., U. Wash., 1970; postgrad. U. Nev., 1970-72; m. Kathy Ann Potocki, June 17, 1967; 1 dau., Hali Kalae. Nat. Endowment for Arts and Wash. State Arts Commn. poet-in-residence, Tacoma and Port Townsend, Wash., 1972-75; Manpower Tng. Act master poet for Wash. and Colo., 1974. Dir. Fort Worden Writers' Symposium, 1973-77. Mem. Internat. Assn. Machinists, Aerospace Workers. Author: Finding True North, 1974 (Nat. Book award and Pulitzer prize nominee 1974); Last Rites, 1978; author chapbook: Waving Arms At The Blind, 1975; author: (with Frank Herbert) The Jesus Incident, 1979; author film: Look: Listen, documentary of Artists-in-Schs. Program, 1975. Home: PO Box 420 Port Townsend WA 98368 Office: Fort Worden State Park Port Townsend WA 98368

RANSON, CHARLES WESLEY, clergyman; b. Ballyclare, No. Ireland, June 15, 1903; s. The Rev. Henry John Frederick and Elizabeth (Clarke) R.; B.Litt. (Oxon), Methodist Coll., Belfast; Queens U., Belfast; Oriel Coll., Oxford; Dr. Theology, U. Kiel; S.T.D. (hon.), Dickinson Coll.; m. Jessie Grace Margaret Gibb, 1932 (died 1957); children—Mary Elizabeth, John Hugh, Kathleen Anne; m. 2d, Barbara Buttenheim Hicks, Aug. 22, 1962. Came to U.S., 1948. Ordained to ministry of the Methodist Ch., at Cork, Ireland, 1929; missionary, Madras, South India, 1929-43; sec. Nat. Christian Council of India, Burma and Ceylon, 1943-45; research sec., Internat. Missionary Council, London, 1946-47, gen. sec., 1948-58, dir. theol. edn. fund, 1958-64; prof. ecumenical theology Drew U. Theol. Sch., Madison, N.J., dean, 1964-68; prof. Hartford Sem. Found., 1968-72; minister Salisbury Congl. Ch., 1971—; vis. lectr. Princeton Theol. Sem., Episcopal Theol. Sch., Cambridge, Mass.; Otts lectr. Davidson Coll.; Earl lectr. Pacific Sch. Religion; Fondren lectr. So. Meth. U., 1964. Pres. Meth. Church in Ireland, 1961-62. Fellow Royal Econ. Soc.; mem. Royal Inst. Internat. Affairs, Chatham House London, Eng. Clubs: Athenaeum (London); University (Dublin). Author: A City in Transition, 1937; The Things that Abide, 1940; The Christian Minister in India, 1946; Renewal and Advance (editor), 1948; That the World May Know, 1953. Home: Lakeville CT 06039

RANSON, GUY HARVEY, clergyman, educator; b. Godley, Tex., Nov. 26, 1916; s. Jake Mincer and Willie Ann (Hardesty) R.; B.A., Hardin-Simmons U., 1939; M.A., U. Ky., 1944; postgrad. U. Cambridge (Eng.), 1947-48; Ph.D., Yale, 1956; m. Rose Ellen Clark, May 24, 1949; children—Kenneth Clark, Kelly Maurice, Diana Louise. Ordained minister Presbyn. Ch., 1961; asst. prof. philosophy William Jewell Coll., Liberty, Mo., 1948-49, prof., chmn. dept., 1949-52; asst. prof. ethics So. Bapt. Theol. Sem., Louisville, 1952-53, asso. prof., 1953-58; asso. prof. ethics Divinity Sch., Duke, Durham, N.C., 1959-60, Princeton Theol. Sem., 1960-61; prof. religion Trinity U., San Antonio, 1961—, chmn. dept., 1961-77, mem. curriculum council, 1961-77, chmn., 1967-68, mem. faculty senate, 1964-69, chmn., 1968-69; mem. gen. council Alamo Presbytery, 1967-73, vice moderator, 1973—, chmn. ministerial relations com., 1973—; mem. com. ecumenical relations Alamo Presbytery and Synod of Tex., 1967-70. Chmn. social action com. San Antonio Council Chs., 1968-70; mem. central priorities com. Community Welfare Council, San Antonio, 1968-69, Com. to Study San Antonio Sch. Dist., 1966-67. Bd. dirs. Inman Christian Center, 1964-70, chmn. bd., 1969, 70. Recipient research grant Trinity U. for archeol. excavation

Hebron, Jordan, summer 1966. Mem. AAUP (chpt. pres. 1962-63), Am. Soc. Ch. History, Am. Philos. Assn., Am. Soc. Christian Ethics, Am. Acad. Religion, Am. Inst. Archaeology, Southwestern Philos. Soc. Club: So. Tex. Yale (pres. 1977). Author: F.D. Maurice's Theology of Society, 1956. Mng. editor Rev. and Expositer, 1957, 58. Contbr. articles to profl. jours. Home: 116 Bushnell Ave San Antonio TX 78212

RANSON, NANCY SUSSMAN, artist; b. N.Y.C., Sept. 13, 1905; d. Bernard and Ida (Jablonsky) Sussman; grad. Pratt Inst. Art Sch., 1926, B.F.A., 1974; student Art Students League, Bklyn. Mus. Art Sch.; m. Jo Ranson, Jan. 1927 (dec. 1965); children—Justine Ranson Schachter, Ellen Toby Ranson Adams. One-woman exhbns. include: George Binet Gallery, N.Y.C., 1948, 50, main br. Bklyn. Pub. Library, 1951, Mexican Govt. Tourist Commn., N.Y.C., 1952, U. Maine, 1964, 78; group exhbns. include: Am. Water Color Soc., 1940, 42, 43, Nat. Assn. Women Artists, 1943—, Bklyn. Soc. Artists, 1941-62, Am. Soc. Contemporary Artists, 1963—, Tomorrow's Masterpieces, 1943, Artists for Victory, 1944, Critics Choice show Grand Central Galleries, N.Y.C., 1947, Prize Winners show, 1947, Butler Inst. Am. Art, Youngstown, Ohio, 1950, Audubon Artists, 1950—, Bklyn. Artists Biennial, Bklyn. Mus., 1950, 54, 56, N.W. Printmakers Internat., 1952, 55, 56, Silvermine Guild Ann., 1956, Nat. Art Gallery N.S.W., Sydney, Australia, 1956, Nat. Exhbn. Contemporary Arts U.S., Pomona, Calif., 1956, N.Y. Soc. Women Artists, 1952—, Am. Color Print Soc., 1952—, Pa. Acad. Fine Art, 1957, Whitney Mus. Artists Equity, N.Y.C., 1951, Nat. Soc. Painters in Casein and Acrylic, 1958—, Color Prints Americas, N.J. State Mus., 1970, other museums and galleries in U.S., Can., France, Switzerland, India, Japan, Scotland, Eng.; rep. permanent collections Fogg Mus. Art (Harvard U.), Norfolk Art Mus., Brandeis U., U. Maine, Mexican Govt. Tourist Commn., Mus. City N.Y., Key West (Fla.) Art Hist. Soc., Reading (Pa.) Public Mus., Free Library, Phila., Slater Meml. Mus., Norwich, Conn., Butler Inst. Am. Art, Smithsonian Instn. Archives of Am. Art, Washington, also nat. museums of Jerusalem, New Delhi, Tokyo, Sydney, Australia, Arts and Crafts Inst., Peking, China. Recipient hon. mention in oil Bklyn. Mus., 1946, Eve Clendenin prize, 1953; Nat. Serigraph Soc. award, 1953; Medal of Honor in Graphics, Nat. Assn. Women Artists Ann., 1956; popular painting prize Critics Choice show Grand Central Galleries, 1947; Grumbacher award Bklyn. Soc. Artists, 1954, 1st prize graphics, 1955, 58; Presentation print Bklyn. Soc. Artists, 1962; Joseph Torch award, 1955, Francesca Wood award, 1955; Presentation print Am. Color Print Soc., 1955; 1st prize graphics Nat. Assn. Women Artists, 1958, prize print and drawing exhbn., 1962; Harold Kovner prize Audubon Artists Ann., 1958, Audubon Artists award, 1961; Gramercy prize Nat. Soc. Painters in Casein, 1963; Andrews-Nelson-Whitehead award Am. Soc. Contemporary Artists, 1964; 1st prize graphics, 1970; Barbara Kulicke award acrylics, 1975; Internat. Women's Yr. award for cultural contbns., 1975-76; MacDowell Found. fellow, 1964. Mem. N.Y. Soc. Women Artists (v.p. 1967-69), Nat. Assn. Women Artists (chmn. fgn. exhbns. 1964-67, chmn. admissions, 1969-71, chmn. oil jury, 1973-75, chmn. nominations 1975-77, adv. bd. 1977-80), Bklyn. Soc. Artists (corr. sec. 1948-53, pres. 1954-56), Am. Color Print Soc., Hunterdon County Art Center, Audubon Artists (chmn. awards com. 1958, dir. graphics 1970-73, 75-78), Nat. Soc. Painters in Casein and Acrylics, Artists Equity Assn., Am. Soc. Contemporary Artists (chmn. constn. 1963-78, pres. 1969-71, permanent dir.), Internat. Assn. Art (del. U.S. com. 1964—, rec. sec. 1977—). Slide lectures on art and archaeology around the world; India, Indonesia, Africa, China. Address: 1299 Ocean Ave Brooklyn NY 11230

RANSONE, COLEMAN BERNARD, JR., polit. scientist, educator; b. Norfolk, Va., Jan. 27, 1920; s. Coleman Bernard and Natalie (Neblett) R.; A.B., Coll. William and Mary, 1941; M. Public Adminstrn., Harvard U., 1947; Ph.D., 1950; m. Katherine May, Dec. 19, 1949; children—Natalie Gray, Kathleen Susan, Katherine Neblett. Instr. to asso. prof. polit. sci. U. Ala., 1947-57; prof. govt. Coll. William and Mary, 1957-58; prof. polit. sci. U. Ala., University, 1958—, dir. So. regional tng. program in pub. adminstrn., 1958—. Served to 1st lt. USAAF, 1943-46. Fund for Advancement Edn. faculty fellow, 1953-54. Mem. Am. Polit. Sci. Assn., So. Polit. Sci. Assn. (v.p. 1963), Ala. Polit. Sci. Assn. (pres. 1979-80), Am. Soc. Pub. Adminstrn. (sr.), Nat. Assn. Schs. for Pub. Affairs and Adminstrn. (exec. com. 1962-65), Phi Beta Kappa (pres. Alpha of Ala. chpt. 1961-62, 74-75), Pi Sigma Alpha. Episcopalian (lay reader). Author: The Office of Governor in the South, 1951; The Office of Governor in the United States, 1956; Ethics in Alabama State Government, 1972; The Alabama Government Manual, 1977. Mem. editorial bd. Pub. Adminstr. Rev., 1967-70. Home: 34 Ridgeland Tuscaloosa AL 35406 Office: Drawer I University AL 35486

RANTA, HUGO ARMAS, govt. ofcl., lawyer; b. Maple, Wis., Mar. 20, 1914; s. John and Aurora (Aho) R.; Ed.B., Superior (Wis.) State Tchrs. Coll., 1934; LL.B., U. Wis., 1940; m. Mary Naomi Hayden, Apr. 24, 1948; 1 son, Jeffrey Alan. Admitted to Wis. bar, 1941; tchr. schs. Douglas County, Wis. 1934-36, 37- 38; atty. Treasury Dept., 1941-48, asst. to gen. counsel, 1949-62, asst. gen. counsel 1962-79. Home: 12031 Remington Dr Silver Spring MD 20902 Office: Treasury Dept Washington DC 20220

RANTA, HUGO ARMAS, govt. ofcl., lawyer; b. Maple, Wis., Mar. 20, 1914; s. John and Aurora (Aho) R.; Ed.B., Superior (Wis.) State Tchrs. Coll., 1934; LL.B., U. Wis., 1940; m. Mary Naomi Hayden, Apr. 24, 1948; 1 son, Jeffrey Alan. Admitted to Wis. bar, 1941; tchr. schs. Douglas County, Wis. 1934-36, 37-38; atty. Treasury Dept., 1941-48, asst. to gen. counsel, 1949-62, asst. gen. counsel 1962—. Home: 12031 Remington Dr Silver Spring MD 20902 Office: Treasury Dept Washington DC 20220

RANZ, JOHN HAYNES, lawyer; b. Youngstown, Ohio, Aug. 25, 1905; s. William E. and Elizabeth (Brady) R.; A.B., Capital U., 1928; LL.B., Ohio State U., 1930; m. Mary Eversole, June 19, 1948; 1 dau., Carol L. (Mrs. Robert C. Krause). Admitted to Ohio bar, 1930, since practiced in Youngstown; mem. firm Manchester, Bennett, Powers & Ullman. Mem. Am., Ohio bar assns., Am. Coll. Trial Lawyers, Internat. Assn. Ins. Counsel, Nat. Assn. R.R. Trial Counsel. Home: 4200 Hillman Way Youngstown OH 44512 Office: Union Nat Bank Bldg Youngstown OH 44503

RANZ, WILLIAM EDWIN, educator; b. Cin., June 3, 1922; s. William R. and Alvina (Aldinger) R.; Chem. Engr., U. Cin., 1947; M.S., U. Wis., 1947, Ph.D., 1950; student Cambridge (Eng.) U., 1952-53; m. Lucile Adams, Aug. 29, 1952; children—Beth, Christina, Roger Adams, Jennifer; m. 2d, Virginia Lee Horrocks, July 14, 1974. Research asso., then asst. prof. U. Ill., 1950-53; asso. prof., then prof. engring. research Pa. State U., 1953-58; mem. faculty U. Minn., 1958—, prof. chem. engring., 1958—; cons. in field, 1953—. Served with AUS, 1943-46. Mem. Am. Chem. Soc., A.A.A.S., Am. Inst. Chem. Engrs., Sigma Xi, Phi Lambda Upsilon, Tau Beta Pi, Alpha Chi Sigma. Contbr. profl. jours. Home: 4817 Emerson Ave S Minneapolis MN 55409

RAO, DESIRAJU BHAVANARAYANA, meteorologist, oceanographer, educator; b. Visakhapatnam, India, Dec. 8, 1936; s. Desiraju Sreeramulu and Desiraju Hanumayamma Adavikolanu; came to U.S., 1960, naturalized, 1974; B.Sc., Andhra U., Waltair, India, 1956, M.Sc., 1959; M.S., U. Chgo., 1962, Ph.D., 1965; m. Vundavalli Uma Devi, Oct. 3, 1965; children—Desiraju Pramila, Desiraju Kavitha. Research scholar Indian Naval Phys. Labs., Cochin, 1959-60; postdoctoral fellow Nat. Center Atmospheric Research, Boulder, Colo., 1965-67; research scientist marine scis. br. Can. Dept. Energy, Mines and Resources, Ottawa, Ont., 1967-68; asst. prof. atmospheric sci. Colo. State U., Ft. Collins, 1968-71; asso. prof. energetics, also Center Gt. Lakes Studies, U. Wis.-Milw., 1971-74, prof., 1974-76; head phys. limnology and meteorology group Gt. Lakes Environ. Research Lab., NOAA, Ann Arbor, Mich., 1975—; adj. prof. limnology and meteorology U. Mich., Ann Arbor, 1977—; cons. in field. Mem. Am. Meteorol. Soc. (v.p. Denver chpt. 1969-70), Am. Soc. Limnology and Oceanography, AAAS, Internat. Water Resources Assn. (charter). Am. Geophys. Union, Internat. Assn. for Gt. Lakes Research, Sigma Xi. Contbr. articles on atmospheric, oceanic and lake dynamics to sci. jours. Home: 3520 Charter Pl Ann Arbor MI 48105 Office: Gt Lakes Environ Research Lab 2300 Washtenaw Ave Ann Arbor MI 48104

RAO, NANNAPANENI NARAYANA, elec. engr.; b. Kakumanu, Andhra Pradesh, India; B.Sc. in Physics, Presidency Coll., Madras, India, 1952; D.M.I.T. in Electronics, Madras Inst. Tech., 1955; M.S.E.E., U. Wash., 1960, Ph.D. in Elec. Engring., 1965; m. Sarojini Jonnalagadda, June 10, 1955; children—Vanaja, Durgaprasad, Hariprasad. Acting instr. elec. engring. U. Wash., 1960-64, acting asst. prof., 1965; asst. prof. elec. engring. U. Ill., Urbana, 1965-69, asso. prof., 1969-75, prof., 1975—. Mem. Am. Soc. Engring. Edn., Internat. Union Radio Sci. Author: Basic Electromagnetics With Applications, 1972; Elements of Engineerig Electromagnetics, 1977; contbr. numerous articles to profl. jours. Office: Dept Elec Engring U Ill Urbana IL 61801

RAO, NARAHARI KANDARPA, educator; b. Kovvur, India, Sept. 5, 1921; s. Ramakrishna Moorty and Venkatasubbamma (Neti) Kandarpa; M.Sc., Andhra (India) U., 1942; Ph.D., U. Chgo., 1949; m. Syamala Mahankali, Aug. 15, 1952; 1 son, Mohan Kandarpa. Research asso. Duke, 1952-53, U. Tenn., 1953-54, Ohio State U., 1954-60; asso. prof. dept. physics Ohio State U., 1960-63, prof., 1963—. Mem. com. basic research Nat. Acad. Scis.-NRC, 1970-72. Fellow Optical Soc. Am., Am. Phys. Soc.; mem. Am. Astron. Soc. Club: Cosmos (Washington). Author: (with C.J. Humphreys, D.H. Rank) (monograph) Wavelength Standards in the Infrared, 1966; also numerous articles. Asso. editor Jour. Molecular Spectroscopy, 1957-68, editor, 1968—; editor (with C.W. Mathews) Molecular Spectroscopy: Modern Research, 1972, Vol. 2, 1976. Home: 1000 Urlin Ave Columbus OH 43212 Office: 174 W 18th Ave Columbus OH 43210

RAO, PAUL PETER, judge; b. Prizzi, Italy, June 15, 1899; s. Vincent and Anna (Fugarini) R.; LL.B., Fordham U. Law Sch., 1923; H.H.D., Philathea Coll., London, Ont., Can., 1958; LL.D., Manhattan Coll., 1971, Pace Coll., 1972; m. Grace Malatino, June 22, 1922 (dec.); children—Nina Rao Cameron, Grayce Rao Visconti, Paul Peter; m. 2d, Catherine Marolla, 1973. Admitted to N.Y. bar, 1924; admitted to practice U.S. Supreme Ct., U.S. Ct. Appeals, U.S. Ct. Customs and Patent Appeals, other fed. cts.; asst. dist. atty. New York County, 1925-27; pvt. practice, 1927-41; asst. atty. gen. U.S. in charge of customs, 1941-48; judge U.S. Customs Ct., 1948—, chief judge, 1965-71, asso. judge, 1971—. Trustee, Ch. of Our Lady of Peace; bd. dirs. Nat. Cath. Community Service, Fordham Law Alumni Assn., Sons of Union Vets. of Civil War (hon. asso. N.Y. dept.). Served in U.S. Navy, 1917-19; ofcl. French interpreter with French Cruiser Div. Decorated knight Order of St. Hubert, Knight of Lateran, Italian Star of Solidarity, Grand Cross Eloy Alfaro Internat. Found., Republic Panama, 1959; Knight of Malta of Am. chpt., 1962, Mil. Order of Lafayette, 1963; comdr. Order of Merit Italian Republic, 1968; commendatore Republic of San Marino; recipient Charles A. Rapallo award, 1970; Gold medal Nat. Acad. Sci. in Rome, 1973; Pub. Service award Italian Hist. Soc. Am., 1974. Mem. Am. Bar Assn., Fed. Bar Assn. N.Y., N.J. and Conn., Fed. Bus. Assn. N.Y. (exec. com.; citation 1962), Am. Legion (past post comdr., life mem.), VFW (hon. comdr. N.Y. County council 1951-56, 57-62), Am. Internat. Acad. U.S.A. (awarded star and cross, hon. life mem. 1958), DAV (citation 1957), Cath. War Vets. (Americanism award 1949), Am. Justinian Soc. Jurists (founder, 1st pres.), Cath. Ct. Attaches Guild N.Y.C. (hon.), Bklyn.-Manhattan Trial Counsel Assn. (hon.), Phi Alpha Delta (hon.). Democrat. Catholic. Home: 210 E 61st New York City NY 10021 Office: One Federal Plaza New York City NY 10007

RAPAPORT, ELLIOT, cardiologist; b. Los Angeles, Nov. 22, 1924; s. Hyman and Bertha (Krupnick) R.; A.B., U. Calif. at Berkeley, 1944; M.D., U. Cal. at San Francisco, 1946; m. Vivian Wrobel, Dec. 23, 1943; children—Daniel, Diane, David. Intern San Francisco Gen. Hosp., 1946-47; asst. resident U. Calif. Hosp., San Francisco, 1948-50; resident fellow, 1950-51, asst. clin. prof., 1957-60, asso. prof., 1960-66, prof., 1966—, William Watt Kerr prof. clin. medicine, 1970—; research fellow Harvard Med. Sch., 1953-55, Peter Bent Brigham Hosp., Boston, 1953-55; asst. dir. profl. services for research VA Hosp., Albany, N.Y., 1955-57; dir. Cardiopulmonary Lab. Mt. Zion Hosp., San Francisco, 1957-60; active staff San Francisco Gen. Hosp., 1960—, dir. cardiopulmonary unit, chief cardiology service, 1961—, chief Gold med. service, 1961-67, dir. coronary care unit, 1967-71, acting chief med. service, 1967-70; cons. USPHS Hosp., San Francisco, 1958—, U.S. Army Letterman Gen. Hosp., San Francisco, 1959—, USAF Hosp., Travis AFB, Calif., 1962—, VA Hosp., Martinez, Calif., 1963—, others. Served with U.S. Army. Mem. Am. Fedn. Clin. Research (chmn. Western sect. 1963-64), Am. Heart Assn. (pres. 1974-75, Gold Heart award 1977), AMA, Am. Physiol. Soc., Am. Soc. Clin. Investigation, Assn. Univ. Cardiologists, Calif. Acad. Medicine, Calif. Heart Assn. (pres. 1972-73) Silver Service medallion 1967, Silver Distinguished Service medallion 1973, Distinguished Achievement award 1977), San Francisco Heart Assn. (pres. 1972-73; Silver Distinguished Service medallion 1973), Interam. Soc. Cardiology (v.p. 1976—), Internat. Soc. and Fedn. Cardiology (exec. bd. 1978—), San Francisco Med. Soc., Soc. Exptl. Biology and Medicine, Western Assn. Physicians, Western Soc. Clin. Research, Assn. Am. Physicians, Alpha Omega Alpha. Editor supplements Circulation, Circulation Research and Stroke, 1971-74; editorial bd. Clin. Research, 1963-66, Circulation Research, 1966-70; editorial bd. Circulation, 1970-73, editor, 1978—. Contbr. numerous articles to profl. jours. Home: 2186 9th Ave San Francisco CA 94116 Office: 1001 Potrero St San Francisco CA 94110

RAPAPORT, ROBERT M., fin. exec.; b. Vienna, Austria, July 12, 1931; s. Gustav H. and Rose (Katz) R.; came to U.S., 1940, naturalized, 1944; B.S., U. Mo., 1952; m. Annette Kohn, Aug. 2, 1953; children—Gary Michael, Steven Mark, Gail Ann, Amy Sue. Mgr., Breddo Food Products, Midland Labs., Kansas City, Mo., 1953-60, pres., 1960-67; v.p. Sucrest Corp., N.Y.C., 1967-74, pres., chief exec. officer, 1974-77, also dir.; internat. commodity exec. E.F. Hutton & Co., N.Y.C., 1977-78; sr. partner, chmn. bd. Lamborn & Co., N.Y.C., 1978—; dir. Bestex Corp., Kansas City, Mo. Mem. Am. Soc. Bakery Engrs. and Food Technicians, Am. Soc. Cereal Chemists. Patentee in field. Home: 50 E 72d St New York NY 10021 Office: 60 E 42d St New York NY 10017

RAPAPORT, SAMUEL I., educator, physician; b. Los Angeles, Nov. 19, 1921; s. Hyman and Bertha (Krupnick) R.; student U. Calif. at Los Angeles; M.D., U. So. Calif., 1945; m. Joyce Mildred Cooperman, Oct. 3, 1950; children—Susan (Mrs. Jack Braunwald), Sally (Mrs. Albert Hartinian), Mark Hyman, Bruce Allen. Intern, Los Angeles County Hosp., 1945; resident medicine VA Hosp., Long Beach, Calif., 1948-50, chief hematology sect., 1950-57; asso. prof. medicine U. Calif. at Los Angeles Med. Center, 1957-58; mem. faculty U. So. Calif. Sch. Medicine, 1958-74, head hematology div. dept. medicine, 1958-74, prof. medicine, 1964-74, head hematology div. Los Angeles County-U. So. Calif. Med. Center, 1958-74; chief med. service San Diego VA Hosp., 1974-78; prof. medicine, U. Calif., San Diego, 1974—, vice chmn. dept. medicine, 1974-78, head hematology-oncology div., 1978—; cons. hematology tng. grants study sect. Nat. Inst. Arthritis and Metabolic Diseases, 1968-71; mem. med. adv. council Nat. Hemophilia Found., 1970, 77—. Served with USAAF, 1946-48. Spl. fellow Nat. Heart Inst., U. Oslo, 1964-65; Fulbright research scholar U. Oslo, 1953-54. Diplomate Am. Bd. Internal Medicine (mem. bd. 1973—, bd. govs. 1976—, sec.-treas., chmn. hematology subcom. 1978—). Fellow A.C.P.; mem. Assn. Am. Physicians, Am. Soc. Hematology (pres. 1977), Western Soc. Clin. Research (pres. 1966), Am. Fedn. Clin. Research (chmn. Western sect. 1960), Am. Soc. Clin. Investigation, Soc. Exptl. Biology and Medicine, Western Assn. Physicians (pres. 1973). Author: Introduction to Hematology, 1971; also papers in field. Home: 7887 Lookout Dr LaJolla CA 92037 Office: Univ Hospital H 811 K 225 Dickinson St San Diego CA 92103

RAPAPORT, WALTER, hosp. adminstr.; b. nr. Carmel, N.J., Aug. 8, 1895; s. Charles and Reba (Sverlof) R.; B.S., Georgetown U., 1917, M.D., 1919; LL.D., U. Santa Clara, 1970; m. Sadye Robin, Aug. 2, 1919 (dec. Sept. 1966); children—Janet (Mrs. George Einstoss), Robert, Shirley (Mrs. Thomas Donovan); m. 2d, Leonie Mae Rannie, May 6, 1974. Intern Washington Asylum, 1919-21; practice medicine, specializing in psychiatry, Washington, 1921-22, Oakland, Calif., 1929-34; med. dir., supt. Mendocino State Hosp., Talmage, Calif., 1939-47, Agnews State Hosp., San Jose, Calif., 1947-53, 57—; dir. mental hygiene State Cal., 1953-57. Bd. regents U. Santa Clara. Served to capt. M.C., USNR, 1941-46. Fellow Am. Psychiat. Assn.; mem. A.M.A., Calif. Med. Soc. Mason (Shriner). Club: Commonwealth of Calif. Home: 460 34th St Oakland CA 94609 Office: 460 34th St Oakland CA 94609

RAPER, CHARLES ALBERT, foot care co. exec.; b. Charleston, W.Va., Aug. 18, 1926; s. Kenneth B. and Louise (Williams) R.; student Okla. State U., 1945; B.S., U. Ill., 1949; m. Margaret Ann Weers, Dec. 26, 1947; children—Kathleen, Josephine, Charles. Sales mgr. Meyer Furnace Co., Peoria, Ill., 1949-54; v.p. mktg. Master Consol., Inc., Dayton, Ohio, 1954-61; mgmt. cons. McKinsey & Co., Inc., Chgo., 1961-67; v.p. mktg. Gen. Portland Inc., Dallas, 1967-69, pres., 1969-75 also dir.; v.p., gen. mgr. Scholl Inc., Chgo., 1975—. Vice chmn. devel. bd. U. Tex. at Dallas; exec. bd. Circle 10 council Boy Scouts Am. Served with USNR, 1944-46. Mem. Dallas C. of C. (chmn. bd. dirs. 1974—), Sales Execs. Club, Phi Gamma Delta. Methodist. Club: Saddle & Cycle (Chgo.). Home: 175 E Delaware St #8908 Chicago IL 60511

RAPER, JOHN F., JR., chief justice Wyo. Supreme Ct.; b. Mapleton, Iowa, June 13, 1913; s. John F. and Anna S. (Peterson) R.; student Drake U., Des Moines, 1934-35; LL.B., U. Wyo., 1936; m. Nell M. Chesler, Aug. 4, 1939; children—Thomas J., Larry Harlan, Robert Bruce, Charles Ross. Admitted to Wyo. bar, 1936; practice in Sheridan, 1936-40, 45-50, 51-53; city atty., Sheridan, 1949-50, 51-53; U.S. atty., 1953-61; atty. gen. Wyo., 1963-66; dist. judge 1st Jud. Dist. Wyo., Cheyenne, 1966-74; justice Wyo. Supreme Ct., Cheyenne, 1974—, chief justice, 1979—. Served with AUS, 1941-45, 50-51; ret. col. Wyo. N.G. Decorated Distinguished Unit citation, Silver Star. Mem. Am. Legion, VFW, Sigma Nu. Clubs: Masons (knight comdr. ct. of honor), Shriners, Rotary. Home: 3733 Dover Rd Cheyenne WY 82001 Office: Supreme Court Bldg Cheyenne WY 82001

RAPER, KENNETH BRYAN, microbiologist, botanist; b. Welcome, N.C., July 11, 1908; s. William Franklin and Julia Selina (Crouse) R.; A.B., U. N.C., 1929, D.Sc. (hon.), 1961; A.M., George Washington U., 1931; A.M., Harvard, 1935, Ph.D. (Austin fellow 1935-36), 1936; m. Louise Montgomery Williams; 1 son, Charles Albert. With Dept. Agr. 1929-53, jr. mycologist Bur. Chemistry and Soils, 1929-36, asst. mycologist Bur. Plant Industry, Washington, 1936-40; microbiologist, sr. microbiologist and prin. microbiologist No. Regional Research Lab., Peoria, Ill., 1941-53; vis. prof. botany U. Ill., 1946-53; prof. bacteriology and botany U. Wis., 1953-79, emeritus, 1979—, William Trelease prof., 1966-79; Chmn. Am. delegation 13th gen. assembly Internat. Union Biol. Scis., London, 1958, chmn. U.S. nat. com.; mem. exec. com. div. biology and agr. NRC, 1956-61; chmn. U.S. nat. com. v.p. 11th Internat. Bot. Congress, Seattle, 1969. Trustee Biol. Abstracts, Inc., 1964-69, exec. com., 1966-69, v.p., 1969. Fellow A.A.A.S. (mem. council 1971-73); mem. Nat. Acad. Scis. (council 1961-64, com. sci. and pub. policy 1966-69), Am. Acad. Microbiology, Am. Soc. Naturalists, Am. Philos. Soc., Soc. Gen. Microbiology, Am. Acad. Arts and Scis., Bot. Soc. Am. (chmn. microbiol. sect. 1949; award of merit 1961), Mycol. Soc. Am. (pres. 1951), Soc. Am. Bacteriologists (councilor 1954-58), Soc. Indsl. Microbiologists (past pres.; Charles Thom award 1967), Phi Beta Kappa (pres. U. Wis. chpt. 1974-75, del. 31st triennial council 1976), Sigma Xi (pres. U. Wis. chpt. 1970-71). Author: (with Charles Thom) A Manual of the Aspergilli, 1945; (with Charles Thom) A Manual of the Penicillia, 1949; (with Dorothy I. Fennell) The Genus Aspergillus, 1965; also research papers.

RAPER, WILLIAM BURKETTE, coll. pres.; b. nr. Wilson, N.C., Sept. 10, 1927; s. William Cecil and Beulah Maybelle (Davis) R.; A.B., Duke, 1947, M.Div., 1951; M.S. (Kellogg fellow), Fla. State U., 1962; LL.D., Atlantic Christian Coll., 1960; m. Rose Mallard, Aug. 19, 1951; children—Olivia, Kristie, Burkette, Elizabeth, Stephen, Laura. Ordained to ministry Free Will Baptist Ch., 1946; pastor Hull Rd. Free Will Bapt. Ch., Snow Hill, N.C., 1951-55; pres. Mt. Olive (N.C.) Coll., 1954—; dir. Wachovia Bank and Trust Co., Mt. Olive. Promotional dir. Free Will Bapt. State Conv. N.C., 1953-54; pres. council Ch.-Related Colls. N.C., 1966-67; mem. N.C. Edn. Assistance Authority, 1972-76; sec. Ind. Coll. Fund of N.C., 1976-78. Mem. N.C. Gov.'s Com. on Hwy. Traffic Safety, 1968; regional coordinator U.S. Office Edn. Program with Developing Instns., 1968-70. Dir. Edn. Professions Devel. Act Grant for Strengthening Devel. in Pvt. Two-Year Colls., 1970-72. Trustee N.C. Coll. Found., 1977—. Recipient Distinguished Service award Mt. Olive Jr. C. of C., 1961; named N.C. Young Man of Year, 1961. Mem. Am. Assn. Community and Jr. Colls. (commn. on legislation 1963-66, cons. 1968-71, chmn. commn. on student personnel 1970-71), N.C. Assn. Ind. Colls. and Univs. (exec. com. 1967-70, 76-77), N.C. Assn. Colls. and Univs. (pres. 1969-70). Democrat. Mason, Rotarian (v.p. Mt. Olive). Home: 619 W Main St Mount Olive NC 28365 Office: Mt Olive College Mount Olive NC 28365

RAPF, MATTHEW WALLACE, TV producer; b. N.Y.C., Oct. 22, 1920; s. Harry and Clementine (Uhlfelder) R.; B.A., Dartmouth, 1942; m. Carol Tannenbaum, June 28, 1958; children—James, Steven, H. John, Matthew. Exec. producer TV series Ben Casey, 1961-65,

Slattery's People, 1964-65, Marcus Nelson Murders, 1973, Kojak, 1973-78, Switch, 1976-78; producer A Letter to Loretta, 1953-54; producer films Desperate Search, Big Leagues, Half a Hero. Served as lt. USNR, 1942-46. Mem. Producers Guild Am. (dir.), Writers Guild Am., Caucus Producers, Writers and Dirs. Home: 120 Malibu Colony Rd Malibu CA 90265 Office: 100 Universal Plaza Universal City CA 91608*

RAPHAEL, ALBERT ASH, JR., lawyer; b. N.Y.C., June 4, 1925; s. Albert Ash and Clare (Schindler) R.; A.B., Yale, 1947; LL.D., Harvard, 1950; m. Dorothy Buck, Oct. 7, 1960; 1 son, Bruce William. Admitted to N.Y. State bar, 1950, Vt. bar, 1972; mem. firm Gallert, Hilborn & Raphael, N.Y.C., 1950-60, Alter, Lefevre, Raphael, Lowry, and Gould, N.Y.C., 1960; individual practice, Waitsfield, Vt., 1972—. Dir. various real estate cos. Mem. bd. zoning appeals, Waitsfield, 1974—, selectman, 1976—. Served with F.A., AUS, 1943-46. Mem. Assn. Bar City N.Y., Vt. Bar Assn. Home: RFD 1-148 C Waitsfield VT 05673 Office: 530 Fifth Ave New York NY 10036

RAPHAEL, FREDERIC MICHAEL, author; b. Chgo., Aug. 14, 1931; s. Cedric Michael and Irene (Mauser) R.; M.A. (Major Open scholar), St. John's Coll., Cambridge (Eng.) U., 1954; m. Sylvia Betty Glatt, Jan. 17, 1955; children—Paul Simon, Sarah Natasha, Stephen Matthew Joshua. Recipient Oscar award for original screen-play Darling, 1966; named Writer of Year, Royal TV Soc., 1976. Fellow Royal Soc. Lit. Author: (novels) Obbligato, 1956, The Earlsdon Way, 1958, The Limits of Love, 1960, A Wild Surmise, 1961, The Graduate Wife and The Trouble with England, 1962, Lindmann, 1963, Orchestra and Beginners, 1967, Like Men Betrayed, 1970, Who Were You With Last Night?, 1971, April, June and November, 1972, Richard's Things, 1973, California Time, 1975, The Glittering Prizes, 1976, (short stories) Sleeps Six, 1979, Oxbridge Blues, 1980, (screenplays) Nothing But the Best, 1964, Darling, 1965, Two For the Road, 1967, Far From the Madding Crowd, 1967, A Severed Head, 1971, Daisy Miller, 1973, The Glittering Prizes, 1976, Rogue Male, 1976, Something's Wrong, 1978, Oresteia of Aeschylus, 1978; A New Wife, 1980; Richard's Things, 1980; (criticism) Somerset Maugham and His World, 1977; also books revs. in New Statesman, London Sunday Times, other publs.; translator: (with Kenneth McLeish) The Poems of Catullus, 1978, The Oresteia of Aeschylus, 1979; editor: (essays) Bookmarks, 1975; A List of Books, 1980.

RAPHAEL, JOHN JOSEPH, banker; b. N.Y.C., Apr. 10, 1928; s. John Joseph and Genevieve (Coniker) R.; B.A., Fordham U., 1950; m. Lucille V. Gallagher, Feb. 14, 1953; children—John J., Kevin E., Gregory J., James J., Marylou. Exec. v.p., pres. Eastern region Marine Midland Bank, N.Y.C., 1976—; dir. Dominion Ins. Co. Am., West Side Assn. Am., Hollenbach, Inc. Served with USN, 1946, to lt., 1953-56. Mem. N.Y. State Bankers Assn. (vice chmn. group VIII), Robert Morris Assos. Clubs: City Midday, Wheatley Hills Golf, N.Y. Economic. Home: 269 Beach 140th St Belle Harbor NY 11694 Office: Marine Midland Bank 140 Broadway New York NY 10015

RAPHAELSON, JOEL, advt. agy. exec.; b. N.Y.C., Sept. 27, 1928; s. Samson and Dorothy (Wegman) R.; B.A., Harvard, 1949; m. Mary Kathryn Hartigan, Aug. 20, 1960; children—Matthew, Katherine, Paul. Copywriter Macy's, N.Y.C., 1950-51, BBDO, N.Y.C., 1953-58; copywriter Ogilvy & Mather, Inc., N.Y.C., 1958-60, copy supr., 1960-64, v.p., joint copy chief, 1964-66, sr. v.p., creative dir., 1966—, dir., 1968—, mem. exec. com., 1970—, creative cons., Europe, 1975-76, exec. creative dir., Chgo., 1976-79, creative head, 1979—. Served with AUS, 1951-53. Author: (with Ken Roman) How To Write Better, 1978. Home: 20 E Cedar St Chicago IL 60611 Office: 200 E Randolph Chicago IL 60601

RAPHAELSON, SAMSON, author; b. N.Y.C., Mar. 30, 1896; s. Ralph and Anna (Marks) R.; A.B., U. Ill., 1917; m. Dorothy Wegman, Dec. 24, 1927; children—Joel, Naomi. Reporter, City News Service, 1917-18; with Chgo. advt. agys., 1918-20; instr. English, U. Ill., 1920-21, vis. prof. creative writing, 1948; short story writer, 1915—, playwright, 1925—; screen writer, 1929—, dir., 1933—; contbg. writer films and TV, Am. Film and Film Comment, 1975—; adj. prof. film div. Columbia, 1976—. Mem. Dramatists' Guild, Screen Writers' Guild (Laurel award 1977), Authors' Guild. Author: The Human Nature of Playwriting, 1949; (plays) Jazz Singer, 1925; The Store, 1926; Young Love, 1928; The Magnificent Heel, 1930; The Wooden Slipper, 1933; Accent on Youth, 1935, Skylark, 1939, Jason, 1942; The Perfect Marriage, 1944; Hilda Crane, 1950; The Peanut Bag, 1967; Two Acts in October, 1974; (screen plays) That Lady in Ermine, Green Dolphin Street, Heaven Can Wait, Suspicion, The Shop Around the Corner, Trouble in Paradise, The Smiling Lieutenant, Broken Lullaby, One Hour With You, Angel, The Crazy Americans, others; (radio play) General Armchair (in book Free World Theatre), 1944. Contbr. fiction to Sat. Eve. Post, Esquire, Good Housekeeping, others. Dir.: (plays) Jason, Skylark, Accent on Youth, The Wooden Slipper, The Perfect Marriage. Stories included in Martha Foley's Best American Stories, 1947 and in Editor's Choice, 1948, Sat. Eve. Post Best Stories, 1957, other collections; entered photog. field, 1951.

RAPHEL, ARNOLD LEWIS, fgn. service officer; b. Troy, N.Y., Mar. 16, 1943; s. Harry and Sara (Rosen) R.; A.B., Hamilton Coll., 1964; M.A., Syracuse U., 1966; m. Robin Lynn Johnson, June 9, 1972; 1 dau., Stephanie Joyce. Commd. fgn. service officer Dept. State, 1967; vice consul, Isafahan, Iran, 1967-69; polit. officer Tehran, Iran, 1969-71; spl. asst. to under sec. state, Washington, 1971-75; polit. officer, Islamabad, Pakistan, 1975-78; spl. asst. to sec. state, Washington, 1978—. Home: 1365 A St NE Washington DC 20002 Office: Dept State Washington DC 20520

RAPKIN, CHESTER, urban planner; b. N.Y.C., Feb. 19, 1918; s. Robert and Minnie (Bogan) R.; B.S., CCNY, 1939; Ph.D., Columbia U., 1953; m. Eva Samuel, Aug. 3, 1942; children—David Samuel, Naomi Ruth (dec.). Economist, statistician Fed. Home Loan Bank Bd., 1941-46; credit, fin. specialist Nat. Housing Agy., 1946-47; research economist Nat. Bur. Econ. Research, 1947-49; research asso. Inst. for Land Urban Use and Housing Studies, Columbia U., N.Y.C., 1949-54, prof. urban planning Grad. Sch. Architecture, dir. Inst. Urban Environment, 1966-73; prof. city, regional planning, chmn. urban studies group, prof. fin. Wharton Sch. Fin. and Commerce, U. Pa., Phila., 1954-66; commr. N.Y.C. Planning Commn., 1969-76; prof. urban planning Sch. Architecture and Urban Planning, Princeton (N.J.) U., 1976—; cons. mcpl., state, U.S., fgn. govts., planning commns., civic assns., banking instns., developers and architects, 1955—; vis. prof. U. P.R., 1967, Technion in Israel, 1970, 77, 79; mem. Urban Design Council of City N.Y., 1967-69. Bd. dirs. Citizens Housing and Planning Council, 1959-69; bd. visitors CCNY, 1973—. Recipient Disting. Alumni medal 125th Anniversary, CCNY, 1973. Mem. AAUP, Am. Econ. Assn., Am. Fin. Assn., Am. Planning Assn., Am. Econs. and Urban Econs. Assn., Am. Statis. Assn., Am. Sociol. Soc., Internat. Fedn. for Housing and Planning, Nat. Assn. Housing and Redevel. Ofcls., Regional Sci. Assn., Beta Gamma Sigma. Democrat. Jewish. Author: (with L. Winnick, D. Blank), Housing Market Analysis, 1953, (with R.B. Mitchell) Urban Traffic, 1954, (with E.M. Fisher) The Mutual Mortgage Finance Fund, 1956, Real Estate Market in an Urban Renewal Area, 1959, Residential Renewal in the Urban Area, 1959, (with W.G. Grigsby) The Demand for Housing in Racially Mixed Areas, 1960, Rental Housing Market in New York City—Two Decades of Rent Control, 1967. Contbr. numerous articles, tech. papers to profl. lit. Home: 11 MacLean Circle Princeton NJ 08540 also 473 W End Ave New York NY 10024 Office: Sch Architecture and Urban Planning Princeton U Princeton NJ 08544

RAPMUND, GARRISON, army officer, physician; b. Buenos Aires, Argentina, Aug. 11, 1927; s. Joseph L. and Kathleen (Henry) R.; A.B., Harvard U., 1949; M.D., Columbia U., 1953; m. Janet Campbell, May 10, 1957; children—Neil Bruce, Elizabeth Campbell. Intern, Bellevue Hosp., N.Y.C., 1953-54; resident Babies Hosp., N.Y.C., 1954-57; commd. M.C., U.S. Army, 1957, advanced through grades to brig. gen., 1979; mem. staff Walter Reed Army Inst. Research, Washington, 1957-58, 61-64, 74-76, dep. dir. 1975, dir., 1976-79; mem. staff Inst. Med. Research, Kuala Lumpur, Malaysia, 1958-60, 64-69; comdr. U.S. Army Med. Research Unit, Hdqrs. Dept. Army, 1969-74; asst. surgeon gen. research and devel. U.S. Army, Washington, 1979—. Decorated Legion of Merit with oak leaf cluster and others. Fellow Am. Acad. Pediatrics, Royal Soc. Tropical Medicine and Hygiene; mem. Am. Soc. Tropical Medicine and Hygiene, Malaysian Soc. Parasitology and Tropical Medicine (past pres.). Contbr. articles to profl. jours. Office: Asst Surgeon Gen Dept Army Washington DC 20310

RAPOPORT, ANATOL, educator, math. biologist; b. Lozovaya, Russia, May 22, 1911; s. Boris and Adel (Rapoport) R.; came to U.S., 1922, naturalized, 1928; Ph.D., U. Chgo., 1941; D.H.L., U. Western Mich., 1971; m. Gwen Goodrich, Jan. 29, 1949; children—Anya, Alexander, Charles Anthony. Faculty dept. math. Ill. Inst. Tech., 1946-47; com. math. biology U. Chgo., 1947-54; asst. prof. Center Advanced Study Behaviorial Scis., Stanford, 1954-55; asso. prof. Mental Health Research Inst., prof. math. biology U. Mich., 1955-70; prof. psychology and math. U. Toronto, 1970—. Served to capt. USAAF, 1942-46. Fellow Am. Acad. Arts and Scis.; mem. Am. Math. Soc., Internat. Soc. Gen. Semantics (pres. 1953-55), Canadian Peace Research and Edn. Assn. (pres. 1972-75), Soc. for Gen. Systems Research (pres. 1965-66). Author: Science and the Goals of Man, 1950; Operational Philosophy, 1953; Fights, Games, and Debates, 1960; Strategy and Conscience, 1964; Prisoner's Dilemma, 1965; Two-Person Game Theory, 1966; N Person Game Theory, 1970; The Big Two, 1971; Conflict in Man Made Environment, 1974; Semantics, 1975; The 2 x 2 Game, 1976. Editor General Systems, 1956-77. Home: 38 Wychwood Park Toronto ON Canada

RAPOPORT, BERNARD ROBERT, lawyer; b. N.Y., Jan. 18, 1919; s. Max and Rose (Gerard) R.; A.B., Cornell U., 1939, LL.B., 1941; m. Robyrta Wechter, May 31, 1959; 1 son, Michael Robert. Admitted to N.Y. bar, 1941; with firm Proskauer, Rose, Goetz & Mendelsohn, N.Y.C., 1941-50; gen. counsel M. Lowenstein & Sons, Inc., N.Y.C., 1950—, also sec. and dir., 1961—, treas., 1975—. Bd. dirs. Leon Lowenstein Found. Served to capt., Signal Corps, AUS, 1942-45. Mem. Am. Bar Assn., Assn. Bar City N.Y. Editor Cornell Law Rev., 1940-41. Home: 910 Fifth Ave New York NY 10021 Office: 1430 Broadway New York NY 10018

RAPOPORT, DANIEL, writer; b. N.Y.C., Jan. 19, 1933; s. David and Ida (Bernstein) R.; B.A., U. Ill., 1954; m. Maxine Barczak; children—Victoria, Andrew, Adam. With U.P.I., Washington, 1958-72; free lance writer, 1972—. Served with USN, 1955-58. Nieman fellow, 1970-71. Author: Inside the House: An Irreverant Guided Tour through the House of Representatives from the days of Adam Clayton Powell to those of Peter Rodino; also mag. and newspaper articles. Home: 3804 Jenifer St NW Washington DC 20015

RAPOPORT, RONALD JON, journalist; b. Detroit, Aug. 14, 1940; s. Daniel B. and Shirley G.; B.A., Stanford U., 1962; M.S., Columbia U., 1963; m. Joan Zucker, Sept. 2, 1968; children—Rebecca, Julie. Reporter, Mpls. Star, 1963-65; asso. editor Sport mag., 1965-66; sports reporter AP, N.Y.C., San Francisco, 1966-70; sports reporter Los Angeles Times, 1970-77; sports columnist Chgo. Sun-Times, 1977—. Served with U.S. Army Res., 1963. Author: (with Chip Oliver) High for the Game, 1971; (with Stan Love) Love in the NBA, 1975; (with Jim McGregor) Called for Travelling, 1979. Office: Chgo Sun-Times 401 N Wabash Chicago IL 60611

RAPORTE, ARTHUR JAMES, corporate exec.; b. N.Y.C., May 31, 1917; s. Samuel and Florence (Aronson) R.; A.B., U. Mich., 1938; LL.B., Harvard, 1941; m. Bernice Mary Olcott, Feb. 21, 1945; children—Stephenie Ina Lindquist, Arthur James. Admitted to N.Y. bar, 1941; with firm Van Vorst, Siegel & Smith, 1942, Harris Berlack, 1944-48; counsel, dir. Welch Grape Juice Co., 1948-58; atty. firm Wien, Lane, Klein & Purcell, N.Y.C., 1958-60; dir. real estate Loews Corp., N.Y.C., 1960—, v.p., 1962—. Mem. 3d Assembly Dist. Democratic Orgn. Bd. dirs., exec. com. Asthma and Allergy Found. Am., 1972—. Served to 2d lt. AUS, 1942-44. Mem. N.Y. County Lawyers Assn., Real Estate Bd. N.Y.C., Phi Beta Kappa, Phi Kappa Phi. Club: Harvard (N.Y.C.). Contbr. profl. jours. Home: 1 Harding Dr Rye NY 10580 Office: 666 Fifth Ave New York City NY 10019

RAPOSO, JOSEPH GUILHERME, publisher, composer, author; b. Fall River, Mass., Feb. 8, 1938; s. Jose Soares and Maria Ascencao (Victorine) R.; A.B., Harvard Coll., 1958; diplome, Ecole Normale de Musique, Paris, 1960; Ph.D. (hon.), U. Mass., 1973; m. Patricia G. Collins, Jan. 26, 1976; 1 dau., Elizabeth C.; children by previous marriage—Joseph R., Nicolas A. Mus. dir. Loeb Drama Center, Harvard U., 1960-61, Boston Conservatory, 1961-64, Exptl. Theatre, 1961-64, Lincoln Center, N.Y.C., 1965-66, New Theatre, 1965-67, Am. Theatre Lab., N.Y.C., 1967, Metromedia Television, 1967-69, ABC-CBS-NBC Networks, 1967-69, numerous motion pictures, television programs, stage plays; mus. dir., composer, lyricist Childrens Television Workshop, 1969-74; created Sesame St. and Electric Co. for pub. TV; animated mus. Raggedy Ann, 1977; popular song writer, author, lectr.; now producer entertainment projects with major film studios and TV networks; guest lectr. Harvard U., Yale U., So. Mass. U.; pres. Jonico Music, Inc.; guest condr. Boston Pops and other maj. symphonies. Mem. vis. com., bd. overseers Harvard U. Recipient Television Acad. awards and nominations for music, lyrics, mus. direction, 4 Recording Industry Acad. awards as producer, composer and mus. dir., numerous citations from schs., charities, civic groups for Sesame St. Mem. ASCAP (numerous citations for hit songs), Nat. Acad. Recording Arts and Scis. (bd. govs., numerous Gold Records), Am. Fedn. Musicians, Screen Actors Guild, AFTRA. Roman Catholic. Clubs: Harvard (N.Y.C.), Hasty Pudding Inst., Signet Soc. Harvard Coll. Author: Sesame Street Songbook, 1971; It's Not Easy Being Green, 1972. Composer: Sing, 1971; Sesame Street, 1969; Being Green, 1970; You Will Be My Music, 1974. Home: 2 E 88th St New York City NY 10024 Office: 881 7th Ave New York City NY 10019

RAPP, DENNIS ARTHUR, govt. ofcl.; b. Chgo., Aug. 24, 1929; s. George Frederick and Elsie Minnie R.; B.S., U. Minn., 1952; M.P.A., Harvard U., 1958; children—Dennis E., Amy J. Budget examiner Bur. of the Budget, Exec. Office of the Pres., Washington, 1960-65; chief resources and policy evaluation group Public Land Law Review Commn., 1965-70; dir. Office of Environ. Planning, N.Y. Public Service Commn., 1970-77; mng. dir. CAB, Washington, 1977-79; chief of staff Office of Advisor to Pres. on Inflation, White House, 1979—. Served with USAF, 1952-55. Ford Found. fellow, 1957. Office: White House Old Exec Office Bldg Washington DC 20500

RAPP, FRED, virologist; b. Fulda, Germany, Mar. 13, 1929; s. Albert and Rita (Hain) R.; brought to U.S., 1936, naturalized, 1945; B.S., Bklyn. Coll., 1951; M.S., Albany Med. Coll., Union U., 1956; Ph.D., U. So. Calif., 1958; m. Barbara A. McCarthy, Sept. 3, 1974; children by previous marriage—Stanley I., Richard J., Kenneth A. Jr. bacteriologist, bacteriologist div. labs. and research N.Y. State Dept. Health, 1952-55; from teaching asst. to instr. dept. med. microbiology Sch. Medicine, U. So. Calif., 1956-59; cons. supervisory microbiologist Hosp. Spl. Surgery, N.Y.C., 1959-62, also virologist div. pathology Philip D. Wilson Research Found., N.Y.C.; asst. prof. microbiology and immunology Med. Coll. Cornell U., 1961-62; asso. prof. virology and epidemiology Coll. Medicine Baylor U., 1962-66, prof., 1966-69; prof., chmn. dept. microbiology Coll. Medicine Pa. State U., 1969—, Evan Pugh prof. microbiology, 1978—, asso. provost, dean for health affairs, 1973—, dir. Specialized Cancer Research Center, 1973—, also sr. mem. grad. Sch. Mem. research reference reagents com. Nat. Inst. Allergy and Infectious Diseases, NIH, 1967-71, mem. virology study sect., 1972-76, mem. virology task force, 1976—; also chmn. Atlantic Coast Tumor Virology Group, NIH, 1971—; cons. virus cancer program Nat. Cancer Inst., mem. working cadre Nat. Bladder Cancer Project, 1973-76; mem. delegation viral oncology U.S.-USSR Joint Com. on Health Cooperation; chmn. Gordon Research Conf. on Cancer, 1975; mem. council projection and analysis Am. Cancer Soc., 1976—; mem. delegation viral oncology U.S.-France Joint Com. Health Cooperation, 1976—; mem. adv. bd. Cancer Info. Dissemination and Analysis Center, 1976—. Bd. dirs. WITF Ednl. TV and Radio; trustee, mem. med. sci. adv. com. Leukemia Soc. Am., 1972-77. Research Career prof. virology Am. Cancer Soc., 1966-69, prof. virology, 1977—. Recipient 1st Ciba-Geigy Drew award for biomed. research, 1977. Diplomate fellow Am. Acad. Microbiology; mem. Am. Soc. Microbiology, A.A.A.S., Am. Assn. Immunologists, Harvey Soc., Soc. Exptl. Biology and Medicine, Am. Assn. Cancer Research (chmn. membership com. 1975-76, dir. 1975-78), Soc. Gen. Microbiology, A.A.U.P., Assn. Med. Sch. Microbiology Chmn., Royal Soc. Medicine (affiliate), Sigma Xi (nat. lectr. 1977-79). Editorial bd. Jour. Immunology, 1966-73, asso. editor, 1971-73; editorial bd. Jour. Virology, 1968—; asso. editor Cancer Research, 1972—; sect. editor on oncology Intervirology, 1972—. Contbr. articles profl. jours., chpts. in books. Home: 2 Laurel Ridge Rd Hershey PA 17033

RAPP, GERALD DUANE, lawyer, mfg. co. exec.; b. Berwyn, Nebr., July 19, 1933; s. Kenneth P. and Mildred (Price) R.; B.S., U. Mo., 1955; J.D., U. Mich., 1958; m. Jane Carol Thomas, Aug. 14, 1954; children—Gerald Duane, Gregory T., Amy Frances. Admitted to Ohio bar, 1959; practice in Dayton, 1960—; partner Smith & Schnacke, 1963-70; legal counsel Mead Corp., 1970—, v.p., 1973—, gen. counsel, sec., 1975—. Past chmn. Oakwood Youth Commn. Past v.p., bd. dirs. Big Bros. Greater Dayton; mem. president's visitors com. U. Mich. Law Sch.; trustee Urbana Coll., 1975, Center Internat. Mgmt. Studies, Internat. YMCA, N.Y.C., 1975, Ohio Center Leadership Studies, Center for Applied Studies, Cambridge, Mass. Served to 1st lt. U.S. Army, 1958-60. Mem. Am., Ohio, Dayton bar assns., Phi Kappa Psi, Phi Delta Phi, Beta Gamma Sigma. Presbyn. (trustee). Clubs: Rod and Reel, Moraine Country, Dayton Racquet, Dayton Bicycle. Sr. editor: U. Mich. Law Review, 1957-58. Home: 309 Hathaway Rd Dayton OH 45419 Office: Courthouse Plaza NE Dayton OH 45463

RAPP, JOHN CYRIL, food co. exec.; b. Altantic, Iowa, Apr. 25, 1901; s. John Joseph and Ethel G. (Sutton) R.; student elec. engring. Des Moines U., 1923; m. Mabel Ellen Azeltine, Nov. 8, 1926; 1 son, Alan Dean. Engaged in radio engring., 1923-27; mgr. radio sta. KMA, Shenandoah, Iowa, 1927-40; a founder Tidy House Products Co., Shenandoah, 1940, v.p., 1945-47, pres., 1947-60; v.p., mgr. non-foods div. Pillsbury Co., 1960-63, also dir.; pres. Shenandoah Industries, Inc., 1954-62, Shenandoah Airways, Inc., 1948-62, Tidy House Products Co., Omaha, 1963-70; now pres. Silver Creek Lakes Inc., Colorado Springs, Colo. Mem. 7th Republican Congl. Dist. Iowa Com., 1960-62; mem. Iowa Rep. Central Com., 1960-62. Bd. assos. Chgo. Theol. Sem.; trustee Doane Coll. Mem. Am. Trapshooting Assn. Mason (Shriner), Elk, Kiwanian. Clubs: Omaha; Garden of Gods (Colorado Springs). Home: 16 Applewood Dr Shenandoah IA 51601. *Never work for a man from whom you cannot learn.*

RAPP, RICHARD, ballet dancer; b. Milw.; studied dance with Adele Artinian, Ann Barzel, Sch. Am. Ballet, N.Y. Joined N.Y.C. Ballet, 1956, promoted soloist, 1961; dances repertoire, including roles in Agon, Arcade, Donizetti Variations; created title role George Balanchine's prodn. of Don Quixote, 1965; appeared in Mid-Summer Night's Dream, N.Y. City Ballet; instr. Sch. Am. Ballet, N.Y.C., 1972—. Address: care NYC Ballet NY State Theatre Lincoln Center Plaza New York NY 10023*

RAPPAPORT, BERNARD ALVIN, educator, physician; b. Paterson, N.J., Jan. 4, 1934; s. Joseph and Ida (Licker) R.; B.A. magna cum laude, Rutgers U., 1956; M.D., Western Res. U., 1960; m. Linda Mau, Aug. 11, 1964. Intern Balt. City Hosp., 1960-61; resident Menninger Sch. Psychiatry, 1961-62; resident psychiatry U. Chgo., 1963-64; fellow Columbia-Presbyn. Med. Center, 1966-68; clin. dir. Wichita Falls (Tex.) State Hosp., 1968, supt., 1968-71; asst. prof. medicine Abraham Lincoln Sch. Medicine, Chgo., 1971-75; asst. clin. prof. psychiatry U. Calif. at Irvine, 1975—; dir. psychiatry and neurology Westside VA Hosp., Chgo., 1971-75; dep. dir. children and youth mental health services Orange County (Calif.) Human Service Agy., 1975—. Served with USAF, 1964-66. Mem. Am. Psychiat. Assn., Phi Beta Kappa. Rotarian. Home: 23141 Somerset Circle Laguna Niguel CA 92677 Office: 515 N Sycamore Santa Ana CA 92701

RAPPAPORT, EARLE SAMUEL, JR., lawyer; b. Chgo., Jan. 24, 1935; s. Earle Samuel and Marion I. (Hendry) R.; student U. Ill., 1952-53, Roosevelt U.; B.S. in Law, Northwestern U., 1956, J.D., 1958; m. Nancy Kay Karzen, Aug. 4, 1957; children—Tracey, Bret, Leigh, Adam, Kent. Admitted to Ill. bar, 1958; law clk. to U.S. dist. judge, 1958-59; asso. firm Edelman, Edelman & Rappaport, Chgo., 1959-64, mem. firm, 1965-72, officer, dir. profl. corp., 1972—. Law lectr. John Marshall Law Sch., 1959-64. Pres. Wilmot Parent Tchr. Orgn., Deerfield, Ill., 1972-74; pres. Niles Jaycees, 1965-66; v.p. Deerfield High Sch. Parent Tchr. Orgn., 1975. Trustee, treas., pres. Deerfield-Bannockburn Fire Dist., 1974-78. Mem. Am., Ill. State, Chgo. bar assns., Am. Judicature Soc., Order of Coif. Editor: Northwestern Law Rev., 1957-58. Contbr. articles to profl. publs. Home: 1247 Deerfield Rd Deerfield IL 60015 Office: 1 N LaSalle St Chicago IL 60602

RAPPAPORT, HENRY, pathologist, educator; b. Lemberg, Austria, Mar. 12, 1913; s. Leo and Amelia (Bak) R.; M.D., U. Vienna (Austria), 1937; m. Dina Braude, May 24, 1939; children—Elizabeth, Edward, Katherine, Stephen. Came to U.S., 1940, naturalized, 1943. Asst. prof. pathology George Washington U., 1946-47; pathologist VA Hosp., Washington, 1947-49; lectr. pathology George Washington U.,

1947-54; sr. pathologist, chief sect. reticuloendothelial pathology and hematology Armed Forces Inst. Pathology, 1949-54; asso. prof. pathology to prof. oncology Chgo. Med. Sch., 1954-65; prof. pathology U. Chgo. Sch. Med., 1965-75, prof. emeritus, 1975—; chmn. dept. anatomic pathology City of Hope Nat. Med. Center, Duarte, Calif., 1975—. cons. Nat. Cancer Inst., Walter Reed Army Inst. Research; mem. WHO Internat. Reference Center for Nomenclature and Histopathologic Classification of Leukemias and other Neoplastic Diseases of Hematopoietic system. Served to maj. AUS, 1943-46. Mem. A.C.P., Am. Soc. Cancer Research, Am. Soc. Cell Biology, Am., Internat. hematology Socs., Am. Soc. Exptl. Pathology, Am. Assn. Pathologists and Bacteriologists. Author: Tumors of the Hematopoietic System; also articles in field. Spl. research tumors of hematopoietic system. Home: 230 W Orange Grove Ave Arcadia CA 91006 Office: City of Hope Nat Med Center Duarte CA 91010

RAPPAPORT, ROY ABRAHAM, anthropologist, educator; b. N.Y.C., Mar. 25, 1926; s. Murray and Judith (Israelson) R.; B.S., Cornell U., 1949; Ph.D. (Burgess hon. fellow), Columbia U., 1966; m. Ann Allison Hart, Aug. 15, 1959; children—Amelia, Georgiana. Owner, operator Avaloch Inn, Lenox, Mass., 1951-59; mem. faculty, dept. anthropology U. Mich., Ann Arbor, 1965—, chmn., 1974—; participant archaeol. fieldwork, Society Islands, 1960, ethnol. fieldwork, New Guinea, 1962-64; sr. scholar East-West Center, 1968-69; cons. ERDA, 1976. Guggenheim fellow, 1969; Am. Council Learned Socs. fellow, 1972-73. Mem. Am. Anthrop. Assn., Am. Ethnol. Soc. Jewish. Author: (with others) Archaeology on Moorea, French Polynesia, 1967; Pigs for the Ancestors, 1968; The Sacred in Human Evolution, 1971; The Flow of Energy in an Agricultural Society, 1971; Liturgies and Lies, 1976; Ecology, Meaning and Religion, 1979; contbr. articles to anthrop. jours. Home: 2360 E Delhi Rd Ann Arbor MI 48103

RAPPAPORT, SYDNEY CHARLES, dentist, educator; b. N.Y.C., Nov. 16, 1919; s. Louis and Helen (Mermelstein) R.; B.S., Coll. City N.Y., 1964; D.D.S., U. Pa., 1942; m. Rosalind Appel, July 31, 1949; children—Elizabeth Appel, Suzanne Helen. Practice dentistry, N.Y.C., 1947—; research asso. Columbia Sch. Dentistry, 1950-58; mem. faculty N.Y. Med. Coll., 1969—, prof., chmn. dept. dentistry, 1972—; dir. dept. dentistry Met. Hosp., N.Y.C., 1967—, Bird S. Coler Hosp., Roosevelt Island, N.Y., 1967—; dir. dentistry Mental Retardation Inst., N.Y. Med. Coll., Valhalla. Served to capt. AUS, 1943-46. Fellow Am. Coll. Dentists, N.Y. Acad. Dentistry; mem. Am. Dental Assn., AAAS, Am. Assn. Hosp. Dentists (pres. 1978), Am. Bd. Oral Medicine, N.Y. Bd. Oral Surgery. Office: 123 E 37th St New York City NY 10016

RAPPORT, MAURICE M., educator, biochemist; b. N.Y.C., Sept. 23, 1919; s. Daniel and Sarah (Conjorsky) R.; B.S., Coll. City N.Y., 1940; Ph.D., Calif. Inst. Tech., 1946; m. Edith Radin, July 15, 1942; children—Erica, Ezra. Chief div. neurosci. N.Y. State Psychiat. Inst., 1969—; prof. biochemistry Columbia Coll. Phys. and Surg., 1967—. Recipient Ketcham prize in econs. Coll. City N.Y., 1938; Fulbright research scholar, 1952. Mem. Am. Soc. Biol. Chemists, Soc. Neurosci., Harvey Soc., Am. Soc. Neurochemistry, Internat. Soc. Neurochemistry. Author papers immunochemistry lipids and proteins, isolation and chem. structure aldehydogenic phosphatides and other complex lipids, structure and metabolism of serotonin, immunoneurological approaches to brain function. Home: 3967F Sedgwick Ave New York NY 10463. *Most of the more substantial goals in science are only attainable through the persevering efforts of a group of individuals. I believe the chances for success are greatly enhanced when the many individual and group frustrations encountered during such sustained effort are short-lived. I think that two very important characteristics of the group members, aside from talent and luck, are the ability to develop an effective system of internal reward and a willingness to accept a restricted role.*

RAPSON, DONALD JAY, lawyer; b. N.Y.C., July 12, 1930; s. Louis and Grace Lillian (Levinkind) R.; A.B., Columbia U., 1951, J.D., 1954; m. Ellen Lautman, Mar. 1, 1956; children—David, Jeffrey. Admitted to N.Y. bar, 1955, U.S. Supreme Ct. bar, 1958, N.J. bar, 1960; asso. in law with faculty Columbia Law Sch., 1954-55; asso. firm Nordlinger, Riegelman, Benetar & Charney, N.Y.C., 1958-60; mem. firm Lautman, Rapson & Henderson, Asbury Park, N.J. and Manasquan, N.J., 1960—; adj. asso. prof. law N.Y. U. Sch. Law, 1979—; cons. N.Y. State Law Revision Commn. on Uniform Comml. Code, 1954-55, 59; chmn. N.J. Bd. Bar Examiners, 1970-75; bd. mgrs. Nat. Conf. Bar Examiners, 1974-76; mem. Multi-State Bar Exam. Com., 1974—; lectr., panelist various law, bank insts., assns. Mem. Deal (N.J.) Bd. Edn., 1970-76, pres., 1973-74. Served to lt. col. Judge Adv. Gen. Corps, AUS, 1956-72. Mem. Fed. Bar Assn., Am. Bar Assn., Assn. Bar of City N.Y. (spl. com. on mil. justice 1959-66, com. on uniform state laws 1966-69, 72-75), N.J. State Bar Assn., Monmouth County Bar Assn. Contbr. articles to profl. jours. Home: 74 Runyan Ave Deal NJ 07723 Office: Lautman Rapson & Henderson 501 Grand Ave Asbury Park NJ 07712

RAPSON, WILLIAM HOWARD, educator; b. Toronto, Ont., Can., Sept. 15, 1912; s. Alfred Ernest and Lillian Jane (Cannicott) R.; B.A.Sc., U. Toronto, 1934, M.A.Sc., 1935, Ph.D., 1941; D. Eng., U. Waterloo, 1976; m. Mary Margaret Campbell, Jan. 29, 1937; children—Margaret (Mrs. Brian A. Fox), Linda (Mrs. Morris Manning), Lorna (Mrs. John A. Ferguson), William Howard II. Demonstrator chem. engring. U. Toronto, 1934-40, instr., 1940, prof., 1953—, Univ. prof., 1976—; with research dept. Canadian Internat. Paper Co., 1940-42, head pioneering research, 1942-53; cons. in field, 1953—; v.p. Chem. Engring. Research Cons., Ltd., 1962-70, pres., 1970—; pres. W.H. Rapson Ltd., 1964—, chmn. bd., 1977—; chmn. bd. Rapson Farms Ltd., 1971-78. Trustee Hawkesbury (Ont.) Pub. Sch. Bd., 1947-52, chmn., 1949-52. Bd. govs. Ont. Inst. Studies in Edn., 1971-77. Recipient Weldon medal, 1954; R.S. Jane Meml. award, 1965; McCharles prize, 1966; Canadian Centennial medal, 1967; Brazilian Pulp and Paper Assn. medal, 1974; Shalimar Gold medal Indian Pulp and Paper Assn., 1976; Forest Products award Am. Inst. Chem. Engrs., 1976; Anselme Payen award Am. Chem. Soc., 1978; Can. medal Soc. Chem. Industry, 1978; named to Engring. Hall of Distinction, U. Toronto, 1979. Fellow Royal Soc. Can., Chem. Inst. Can., T.A.P.P.I. (Mfg. Div. award 1967, Gold medal 1976; hon. life mem.); mem. tech. sect. Can. Pulp and Paper Assn. (sr., hon. life mem.; chmn. 1970-71), Canadian Soc. Chem. Engring. (dir. 1966-68), Assn. Profl. Engrs. Province Ont. (Gold medal 1975), Royal Swedish Acad. Engring. Scis. (fgn.). Club: Faculty (U. Toronto). Author, editor: The Bleaching of Pulp, 1963. Patentee in field; pioneer use chlorine dioxide for pulp bleaching. Home: 3 Fallingbrook Crescent Scarborough ON M1N 1B1 Canada Office: Univ Toronto Toronto ON Canada

RAPUANO, ALBERT JOHN, conv. bur. exec.; b. New Haven, Jan. 20, 1942; s. Albert and Louise R.; B.S., Fordham U., 1963; m. Elizabeth Bolin, May 27, 1967; children—Richard, Danielle. Conv. service mgr. Palmer House Hotel, Chgo., 1963-67; with Pick Hotels, Chgo., 1967-70; regional dir. sales Fairmont Hotel Co., Chgo., 1970-72; dir. sales Fairmont Hotel, Dallas, 1972-75; gen. mgr. Fairmont Colony Sq. Hotel, Atlanta, 1975-79; exec. v.p. Atlanta Conv. and Visitors Bur., 1979—; dir. Bancroft Group. Mem. mayors adv. com. U.S. Conf. Mayors, 1978; bd. dirs. Colony Sq. Bus. Assn.; mem. Atlanta Taxicab Commn. Mem. Am. Soc. Assn. Execs., Ga. Soc. Assn. Execs., Am. Mgmt. Assn., Atlanta Hotel Motel Assn. (bd. dirs.), Ga. Hotel Motel Assn. (mem. conv. com.). Roman Catholic. Home: 5270 Lake Springs Dr Atlanta GA 30338 Office: 233 Peachtree St NE 200 Atlanta GA 30303

RARICK, JOSEPH FRANCIS, SR., lawyer; b. Bartonville, Ill., July 6, 1921; s. Orville Rufus and Jessie Sally (Boman) R.; B.A. with highest honors, U. Ill., 1943, J.D., 1948; LL.M. (Regent fellow), 1949, J.S.D., 1956; m. Louise Lucille Strickfaden, Aug. 12, 1946; 1 son, Joseph Francis. Admitted to Ill. bar, 1948, Okla. bar, 1956; asst. prof. law U. Minn., 1949-53; asso. prof. U. Okla., 1953-57, prof., 1957-67, David Ross Boyd prof. law, 1967—; cons. in field; adv., mem. legis. coms. Okla. Water Resources Bd. Served to capt. U.S. Army, 1943-46. Recipient cert. meritorious service Okla. Water Users Assn., 1970, Okla. Water Resources Bd., 1971, Okla. Water Pollution Control Bd., 1979; Kerr Found. grantee, 1968, 70, 72; Rocky Mountain Mineral Law Found. grantee, 1977. Mem. Okla. Bar Assn., Order of Coif, Phi Beta Kappa, Phi Kappa Phi, Omicron Delta Kappa, Phi Delta Phi. Democrat. Anglican. Author: The Right to Use Water in Oklahoma, 1975; Problems in Lands Allotted to American Indians, 1978; contbr. articles to law revs. and jours. Home: 608 E Boyd St Norman OK 73071 Office: 300 Timberdell Rd Norman OK 73019

RARIDON, RICHARD JAY, chemist; b. Newton, Iowa, Oct. 25, 1931; s. Jack Allison and Letha Helen (Woods) R.; B.A., Grinnell Coll., 1953; M.A., Vanderbilt U., 1955, Ph.D., 1959; m. Mona Marie Herndon, May 28, 1956; children—Susan Gayle, Ann Chaney. Asso. prof. phys. sci. Memphis State U., 1958-62; research chemist Oak Ridge Nat. Lab., 1962—; environmental specialist Coop. Sci. Edn. Center, Oak Ridge, 1971-72. Radiol. Physics fellow AEC, 1953-55. Fellow AAAS, Tenn. Acad. Sci. (pres. 1971); mem. Assn. Acads. Sci. (sec.-treas. 1972-76, pres. 1977), Am. Chem. Soc., Sigma Xi. Contbr. articles to profl. jours. Home: 111 Columbia Dr Oak Ridge TN 37830 Office: ORNL Oak Ridge TN 37830

RARIG, FREDERICK JOHN, lawyer; b. Mpls. July 3, 1915; s. Frank Miller and Eta C. (Galbreath) R.; B.A. cum laude, U. Minn., 1935; LL.B., Cornell U., 1939; m. Reva M. Schoenberg, June 26, 1938; children—Elizabeth Ann (Mrs. Chester J. Tyson III), Alice Jane (Mrs. Peter C. Westover), Susan Jonna (Mrs. Paul Todd Makler, Jr.), Frederick John. Admitted to Minn. bar, 1940; spl. asst. to atty. gen. Dept. Justice, 1940-46, chief Los Angeles office Anti-Trust div., 1944-46; v.p., legal counsel Rohm and Haas Co., Phila., also asso. firms; dir. Rohm & Haas Co. of Can., Ltd.; mem. Industry Adv. Com. on U.S. Technol. Innovation Policy. Trustee Honey Hollow Watershed Assn. Mem. Am., Fed. bar assns., Isaac Walton League, Am. Soc. for Testing and Materials (dir.), Am. Nat. Standards Inst., Gt. Books Found., Devon Breeders Assn. N.Am. Democrat. Mem. Soc. of Friends Internat. House. Home: Point Pleasant Pike Doylestown PA 18901 Office: Independence Mall W Philadelphia PA 19105. *I view life as an opportunity to contribute to the enrichment and preservation of the human tradition through the fullest possible development of my creative power and the creative power of others whom I may influence. Civilization hangs by the thread of recorded history; I would strive by deed and word to make that thread a little stronger. If we are to have a history, we must learn to live with the other forms of life on this beautiful planet Earth.*

RARIG, HOWARD R., univ. adminstr., musicologist, conductor; b. Au Sable Forks, N.Y., Nov. 27, 1915; s. Howard R. and Isadora M. (Corneal) R.; student Temple U., 1941-42; B.Mus. cum laude, Ithaca (N.Y.) Coll., 1949, M.Mus., 1952; postgrad. Cornell U., 1951; Ph.D., U. Mich., 1958; m. Jean Clark Evans, June 1, 1946; children—Jonathan, Kim, Jan Ingrid. Asst. prof. Ithaca Coll., 1950-53; instr. U. Mich., Ann Arbor, 1954-58; asso. prof. Grinnell (Iowa) Coll., 1958-65, chmn. div. fine arts, 1961-64; prof. Eastern Mich. U., 1965-71, also head dept. music; prof. U. So. Calif., Los Angeles, 1971—, dir. Sch. Music, 1971—, asso. dean Sch. Performing Arts, 1971—. Bd. dirs. Ford Found. Contemporary Music Project, Midwest region, 1966-70, project head Eastern Mich. U., 1966-70. Danforth Found. Research grantee, 1963, Grinnell Coll. grantee, 1964, Contemporary Music Project grantee, 1970; Tanglewood Scholar Berkshire (Mass.) Music Center, 1964; recipient Composition award Kappa Gamma Psi, 1950. Mem. Calif. Music Execs. Assn. (past pres.), Coll. Music Soc., AAUP, Music Educators Nat. Conf., Nat. Assn. Composers U.S.A., Am. Musicol. Soc., Nat. Assn. Schs. Music (regional Midwest dir. 1970-72, mem. commn. grad. studies 1970-76, 77—), U. So. Calif. Sch. Music Alumni Assn. (pres. 1976—), Skull and Dagger, Music Library Assn., Pi Kappa Lambda (pres. Eta chpt.), Phi Mu Alpha. Author: The 2d String Quartet of Charles Ives, 1952; The Instrumental Sonatas of Antonio Vivaldi, 1958. Conductor contemporary music ensembles, music for theater and dance, Chinese opera, collegium musicum and various choral, brass and orchestral ensembles. Composer songs, piano works, chamber music. Home: 8332 Loyola Blvd Los Angeles CA 90045 Office: Sch Music U So Calif Los Angeles CA 90007

RASCHKE, KENNETH EDWARD, educator; b. Watertown, S.D., Oct. 7, 1918; s. Edward and Anna Marie (Jacobsen) R.; B.A. cum laude, Augustana Coll., 1941; LL.B., summa cum laude, U. S.D., 1948, J.D. summa cum laude, 1969; LL.D., Jamestown Coll., 1972; m. Avis Ione Bekke, Mar. 7, 1943; children—Kenneth Edward, Beverly Raschke Nielson, Steven. Instr. govt., psychology Worthington (Minn.) High Sch., 1941-42; coordinator instrn. USAAF Tech. Schs., 1942-43; spl. cons. S.D. Natural Resources Commn., 1949-52; admitted to S.D. bar, 1948; prof. bus. law U. S.D., 1948-56, exec. asst. to pres., 1956-64; prof. law U. Fla., 1950; commr. high edn. N.D. Bd. Higher Edn., Bismarck, 1964-78; asst. to pres, prof. bus. law N.D. State U., Fargo, 1978—. Chmn., State Bd. Indian Scholarships, 1964-78; mem. State Licensure Bd. for Nursing Home Adminstrs., 1969—, Gov.'s Com. on Safety, 1965-78; exec. officer Higher Edn. Facilities Commn., 1964-78; mem. State Planning Adv. Council, 1971-78, Health Manpower Com., 1969-78, State Health Planning Council, 1969-78, State Alcohol Commn., 1964-71, State Ednl. TV Council, 1969-78, State Library Commn., 1964-71; mem. adv. com. on higher edn. Midwest Council State Govts., 1964; v.p. Mo. Valley council Boy Scouts Am., 1967-70, advancement chmn., 1971—. Bd. dirs. United Fund, Bismarck, Dakota Hosp., Vermillion, S.D. Served with USAAF, 1943-46. Mem. S.D. Bar Assn., Higher Edn. Exec. Officers Assn., North Central Assn. Colls. and Univs., Order of Coif, Phi Delta Phi, Delta Sigma Pi, Beta Gamma Sigma. Lutheran (pres. ch. council 1972). Clubs: Masons, Shriners, Lions, Elks. Home: 152d St Fargo ND 58103 Office: Minard Hall ND State U Fargo ND 58102

RASH, BRYSON BRENNAN, television journalist; b. Los Angeles, Aug. 18, 1913; s. Wootson Elmer and Naomi Catherine (Crain) R.; J.D., American U., 1941; m. Esther Julie Jenkins, June 8, 1940; children—Brennan, Julianne. White House corr. NBC, ABC, 1940-54, including coverage nat. polit. convs., Japanese Peace Conf., San Francisco, 1951, Kefauver Crime Investigation, 1951-52, Army-McCarthy hearings, 1954; pool corr. radio networks H-Bomb Tests, Bikini Atoll, 1956; now contbg. editor P.M. mag., WDVM, Washington. Bd. dirs. Washington chpt. ARC; trustee Holton Arms Sch., Washington. Recipient alumni recognition award Am. U., 1957; Preceptor award San Francisco State U., 1972; Peabody award for meritorious service to broadcasting, 1973; Gov.'s award Washington chpt. Nat. Acad. TV Arts and Scis., 1974, Community Service award, 1974. Mem. Radio and TV Corr. Assn. (sec. 1956), Nat. Broadcast Editorial Assn. (pres. 1973). Clubs: Chevy Chase, Nat. Press (pres. 1963) (Washington); Federal City. Home: 4000 Cathedral Ave NW Washington DC 20016 Office: 4001 Brandywine St Washington DC 20016

RASH, W(ILLIAM) DUANE, constrn. co. exec.; b. Santa Ana, Calif., May 5, 1923; s. Stewart and Stella (Barton) Taylor; B.S., U. So. Calif., 1949; m. Elsie Amelia Damon, Aug. 7, 1948; children—William Duane, Robert Allen, Patricia Lynn. With Sully-Miller Contracting Co., Long Beach, Calif., 1949—, treas., 1954-65, v.p. fin., 1965-74, sr. v.p., sec.-treas., 1974—, Mem. adv. bd. ARC, 1970, 71, Salvation Army, 1970, 71; trustee Meml. Hosp. Long Beach, 1970—; mem. bd. Meml. and Children's Med. Center Found., Long Beach, 1976—. Served with AAC, 1942-45. Mem. Fin. Execs. Inst. Clubs: Old Ranch Country, Rotary. Home: 321 Linares Ave Long Beach CA 90803 Office: 3000 E South St Long Beach CA 90805

RASHAD, AHMAD (BOBBY MOORE), profl. football player; b. Portland, Oreg., Nov. 19, 1942; student U. Oreg. With St. Louis Cardinals (Nat. Football League), 1972-73, Buffalo Bills (Nat. Football League), 1973-74, Minn. Vikings (Nat. Football League), 1974—; played in Pro Bowl (Nat. Football League All-Star Game), 1979. Office: care Minn Vikings 7110 France Ave S Edina MN 55435*

RASHKIND, WILLIAM JACOBSON, pediatric cardiologist; b. Patterson, N.J., Feb. 12, 1922; s. Jacob Louis and Charlotte Florence (Jacobson) R.; A.B., U. Louisville, 1943, M.D., 1946; m. Rita Shirley Leisten, Dec. 17, 1949; children—Marilyn, Jean, Charles. Intern, Michael Reese Hosp., Chgo., 1946-47; resident in pediatrics U. Pa. Hosp., Phila., 1953-55; asst. prof. physiology U. Pa. Sch. Medicine, Phila., 1950-53, asst. prof. pediatrics, 1959-63, asso. prof., 1963-71, prof., 1971—; dir. cardiovascular labs. Children's Hosp. Phila., 1955—; mem. internat. com. coding congenital heart disease, 1969-72; mem. intersoc. commn. heart disease resources, 1971-74; mem. exec. com., congenital heart disease com. Am. Heart Assn., 1970-74. Served with USN, 1943-49. Nat. Heart and Lung Inst. fellow, 1949-50; NIH grantee, 1952—; diplomate Am. Bd. Pediatrics, Mem. Am. Pediatric Soc., Soc. Pediatrics Research, Am. Physiol. Soc., Am. Acad. Pediatrics, Am. Soc. Artificial Internal Organs, Assn. European Pediatric Cardiologists. Inventor balloon atrioseptostomy cardiac catheter, transatrial septal defect closure system; contbr. articles to med. jours. Home: 121 Merion Rd Merion PA 19066 Office: One Children's Center 34th St and Civic Center Blvd Philadelphia PA 19104

RASI, HUMBERO MARIO, editor; b. Buenos Aires, Argentina, Mar. 23, 1935; came to U.S., 1962, naturalized, 1968; s. Mario and Gertrudis Frida (Heyde) R.; B.A., Instituto Superior del Profesorado, Buenos Aires, 1960; M.A., San Jose State U., 1966; Ph.D., Stanford U., 1971; m. Julia Cuchma, Mar. 28, 1957; children—Leroy Mario, Sylvia Beatrice. Mem. faculty Instituto Florida, Buenos Aires, 1957-61; asst. editor Spanish dept. Pacific Press Publ. Assn., Mountain View, Calif., 1962-66, chief editor internat. publs., 1978—; asst. prof. modern langs. Andrews U., 1969-73, asso. prof., 1973-76, prof., 1976-78, dean Sch. Grad. Studies, 1976-78; contbg. editor Handbook of Latin Am. Studies, Library of Congress, 1972—; ordained to ministry Seventh-day Adventist Ch., 1980. Nat. Endowment for Humanities postdoctoral fellow Johns Hopkins U., 1975-76. Mem. MLA, Am. Assn. Tchrs. Spanish and Portuguese, Instituto Internacional de Literatura Iberoamericana. Contbr. articles on modern Hispanic lit., current events and religious trends to profl. jours.; pres. editorial council El Centinela, 1978—, Viva Mejor, 1978—. Home: 1492 Revelstoke Way Sunnyvale CA 94087 Office: 1350 Villa St Mountain View CA 94042

RASIN, RUDOLPH STEPHEN, investment banker; b. Newark, July 5, 1930; s. Simon Walter and Anna (Sinovc) R.; B.A., Rutgers Coll., 1953; postgrad. Columbia, 1958-59; m. Joy Kennedy Peterkin, Apr. 11, 1959; children—Rudolph Stephen, James Stenning, Jennifer Shaw. Mgr., Miles Labs., Inc., 1959-61; devel. mgr. Gen. Foods Corp., White Plains, N.Y., 1961-62; asst. to pres., chmn. Morton-Norwich Products, Inc., Chgo., 1962-71; pres. Rasin Corp., Chgo., 1971—; dir. several corps. Bd. dirs. Center for Def. Info., Bus. and Profl. People for Pub. Interest, 1972—; mem. Chgo. Crime Commn., 1974—; bd. dirs. Internat. Inst. for Rural Reconstrn.; bd. govs. Chgo. Zool. Soc. Served with USAF, 1954-56. Mem. Assn. for Corp. Growth. Republican. Mem. United Ch. of Christ. Clubs: Hinsdale Golf; Mid America; Lake Geneva Country, Lake Geneva Yacht. Home: 328 E 8th St Hinsdale IL 60521 Office: 120 S La Salle St Chicago IL 60603

RASKIN, ABRAHAM HENRY, editor; b. Edmonton, Alta., Can., Apr. 26, 1911; s. Henry and Mary (Slatkin) R.; came to U.S., 1913, naturalized, 1920; B.A., City Coll. N.Y., 1931; m. Rose Samrock, Sept. 27, 1933; children—Jane, Donald. Mem. staff N.Y. Times, 1931-77, mem. editorial bd., 1961-64, asst. editor editorial page, 1964-76, labor columnist, 1976-77; asso. dir. Nat. News Council, 1978—; lectr. N.Y. Sch. Social Work, 1947-52; adj. prof. Grad. Sch. Bus. Columbia, 1976; cons. President's Com. Universal Tng., 1947. Bd. dirs. Jewish Family Service N.Y., 1950-62, Legal Aid Soc., N.Y.C., 1967-74; trustee Lowell Mellett Fund, 1968—, James Gordon Bennett Found., 1971—. Served to lt. col. AUS, 1942-45. Decorated D.S.M.; recipient George Polk Meml. award, 1953, 64, Sidney Hillman Meml. award, 1951, Page One award N.Y. Newspaper Guild, 1961, 64, Soc. Silurians award, 1964, 70, Heywood Broun Meml. citation, 1964, Journalism award Columbia U., 1976. Mem. N.Y. Guild (vice chmn. 1948-62), Indsl. Relations Research Assn. (nat. exec. bd.), Internat. Press Inst., Am. Acad. Polit. Sci., Phi Beta Kappa. Mem. Liberal Party. Jewish. Co-author: David Dubinsky: A Life with Labor, 1977. Home: 136 E 64th St New York NY 10021 Office: 1 Lincoln Plaza New York NY 10023

RASKIN, ELLEN, writer, illustrator; b. Milw., Mar. 13, 1928; d. Sol and Margaret (Goldfisch) R.; student U. Wis., Madison, 1945-48; m. Dennis Flanagan, Oct. 17, 1966; 1 dau., Susan Kuhlman Metcalfe. Free-lance illustrator, N.Y.C., 1955-68; writer, illustrator children's books: Nothing Ever Happens on My Block, 1966, Silly Songs and Sad, 1967, Ghost in a Four-Room Apartment, 1969, And It Rained, 1969, A & The, 1970, The World's Greatest Freak Show, 1971, The Mysterious Disappearance of Leon (I Mean Noel), 1971, Franklin Stein, 1972, Who, Said Sue, Said Whoo?, 1973, Figgs & Phantoms, 1974, Moose, Goose and Little Nobody, 1974, The Tattooed Potato and Other Clues, 1975, Twenty-two, Twenty-three, 1976, The Westing Game, 1978; instr. in illustration Pratt Inst., 1963, Syracuse U., 1976; guest lectr. U. Berkeley, 1969, 72, 77; exhibited illustrations in group shows: AIGA 50 Years of Graphic Arts in America, 1966, Biennale of Illustrations, Bratislava, Czechoslovakia, 1969, Biennale of Applied Graphic Art, Brno, Czechoslovakia, 1972, Contemporary Am. Illustrators of Children's Books, 1974-75. Recipient Distinctive Merit award Art Dirs. Clubs, 1958, Silver medal, 1959; citation of merit Soc. Illustrators, 1966, 70, 71, Best Picture Book award World-Jour.-Tribune, 1966, Honor Book award Boston Globe-Horn Book, 1973, citation Bklyn. Mus. Art, 1973, 74, Edgar Allan Poe Spl. award Mystery Writers Am., 1975, Newbery Honor Book award

ALA, 1975, Best Fiction award Boston Globe-Horn Book, 1978, John Newbery medal for The Westing Game, 1979; book named to Am. Inst. Graphic Arts 50 Books of Yr., 1966, 68, N.Y. Times 10 Best Books, 1966, 68. Mem. Authors Guild, Graphic Artists Guild. Home and Office: 12 Gay St New York NY 10014

RASKIN, JUDITH, soprano; b. N.Y.C., June 21, 1928; d. Harry A. and Lillian (Mendelson) Raskin; B.A., Smith Coll., 1949, M.A. (hon.), 1963; D.Music (hon.), Ithaca Coll., 1979. Debut in NBC-TV opera Dialogues of the Carmelites, 1957; debut N.Y.C. Opera in Cosi Fan Tutte, 1959, Met. Opera Co. in Nozze di Figaro, 1962; recital debut in N.Y.C. as Ford Found. winner, 1964; appearances with symphony orchs. in Mpls., Phila, N.Y.C.; European debut, Glyndebourne, Eng., 1963; Lieder recital N.Y. Town Hall, 1965; Lincoln Center Festival, 1967; instr. voice Manhattan Sch., Mannes Coll. Music, N.Y.C.; rec. artist Columbia, London, Decca, RCA Victor, C.R.I. records; mem. adv. bd. Young Concert Artists, 1978—; panelist Nat. Opera Inst., 1978—, chief judge, 1978; chmn. opera panel, co-chmn. music panel Nat. Endowment Arts, 1972-76, co-chmn. chamber music panel, 1979. Trustee, Martha Baird Rockefeller Fund for Music, 1976—, Beth Israel Hosp., 1976—. Office: care Melvin Kaplan Inc 1860 Broadway New York NY 10023

RASKIN, MICHAEL A., retail co. exec.; b. N.J., Feb. 26, 1925; s. Harry and Elizabeth Rose (Furstenburg) R.; A.B., Pa. State Coll., 1947; M.B.A., Columbia, 1948; m. Mary Bonetta Whalen, June 12, 1948; children—Robin Suzanne, Hillary Whalen, Mary Allison. With Abraham & Straus, 1949-65; successively mdse. v.p., dir. stores, sr. v.p. Abercrombie & Fitch, N.Y.C., 1966-68; exec. v.p. Dayton's div. Dayton Hudson Corp.; pres. Jos. Magnin Co., San Francisco, 1978—; dir. Buttery's Inc., Stein Industries, Northwestern Bank St. Paul, Knox Lumber Co., Great Luggage Inc. Mem. adv. bd. Downtown Council, U. Minn. Exec. Program. Bd. dirs. Minn. Dance Theatre, Urban Coalition. Served to lt. USNR, 1942-46. Mem. Mpls. C. of C.

RASKIND, LEO JOSEPH, educator; b. Newark, Nov. 2, 1919; s. Isaac and Fannie (Michelson) R.; A.B., U. Calif., Los Angeles, 1942; M.A., U. Wash., 1949; Ph.D. (Fulbright fellow), London Sch. Econs., 1952; LL.B., Yale, 1955; m. Mollie Gordon, June 14, 1948; children—Carol Inge, John Richard. Faculty, Stanford Law Sch., 1955-56; lectr., research asso. Yale Law Sch., 1956-58; faculty Vanderbilt Law Sch., 1958-64, Ohio State U. Coll. of Law, 1964-70; prof. law U. Minn. Law Sch., Mpls., 1970—; summer teaching N.Y. U., 1964, U. Tex., 1964, U. Utah, 1967, So. Meth. U., 1973, U. N.C., 1978. Served to capt. AUS, 1942-46. Co-author: Casebook Corporate Taxation, 1978. Home: 3 Orchard Ln Edina MN 55436 Office: Law Bldg U Minn Minneapolis MN 55455

RASKOSKY, EDWARD J., mayor; b. East Chicago, Ind., Feb. 8, 1922; LL.B., Ind. U., 1949; m. Dorothea E. Smith, Apr. 8, 1949; children—Phillip E., Roger A. Admitted to Ind. bar; rep. Ind. Ho. of Reps., Indpls., 1965-67; judge City of Hammond (Ind.), 1967-76; mayor City of Hammond, 1977—. Served to lt. (j.g.), USN. Mem. Am. Trial Lawyers Assn., Ind. Bar Assn., VFW, Am. Legion. Democrat. Roman Catholic. Club: Moose. Office: 5925 Calumet Ave Hammond IN 46320*

RASKY, HARRY, producer, dir., writer; b. Toronto, Ont., Can., May 9, 1928; s. Louis and Pearl (Krazner) R.; came to U.S., 1955; B.A., U. Toronto, 1949; m. Arlene Ruth Werkhoven, Mar. 21, 1965; children—Holly Laura, Adam Louis. Reporter, No. Daily News, Kirkland Lake, Ont., 1949; news editor-producer Sta. CHUM, Toronto, 1950; news editor-producer Sta. CKEY, 1951-52; co-founder new documentary dept. CBC, 1952-55; asso. editor Saturday Night Mag., 1955; producer-dir-writer Columbia Broadcasting Corp., 1955-60; NBC-TV, N.Y.C., 1960-61, ABC-TV, N.Y.C., 1963-69, CBC-TV, Toronto, 1971-78; pres. Harry Rasky Prodns., N.Y.C. and Toronto, 1971—, Maragall Prodns., Toronto, 1978—; guest lectr. film and TV at various univs., colls., creator Raskymentary. Recipient numerous awards, including Emmy award; 1978, San Francisco Film Festival award, 1978, Grand prize N.Y. TV-Film Festival, 1978, Jerusalem medal, 1975; honors City of Venice (Italy), 1970, Mayor N.Y.C., 1977, City of Toronto, 1979. Mem. Writers Guild Am., Dirs. Guild Am., Overseas Press Club Am., Acad. TV Arts and Scis., Assn. Can. TV and Radio Artists, Producers Assn. Can. Jewish. Clubs: YMCA, Club of Gnu, U. Toronto. Numerous films include: Travels Through Life with Leacock, 1976, The Peking Man Mystery, 1978, Arthur Miller on Home Ground, 1979 (producer, dir., writer); Next Year in Jerusalem, 1973, The Wit and World of G. Bernard Shaw, 1974, Tennessee Williams South, 1975, Homage to Chagall-The Colours of Love, 1977 (15 internat. prizes including Oscar nomination); (play) Tiger Tale, 1978 (dir.); author: (memoirs) Nobody Swings on Sunday—The Many Lives of Harry Rasky, 1980. Office: care CBC Box 500 Terminal A Toronto ON M5W 1E6 Canada. *I have tried to find the positive forces in life and out of them create works of art of a lasting nature with the idea of improving the lives of others. This, plus the adventure of passing on the tradition of my father and his, is my life.*

RASMUS, HENRY IRVING, JR., clergyman; b. Spokane, Wash., Mar. 30, 1894; s. Henry Irving and Anna Margaret (Sniff) R.; A.B., U. So. Calif., 1917, B.D., 1925, D.D. (hon.), 1938; student Boston U. Sch. Theology, 1917-18; m. Beulah Mae Byrum, Feb. 20, 1919. Pastor, La Mesa, Calif., 1919-22, asso. minister First Church, Glendale, Calif., 1922-26, El Monte, 1926-28, Mount Olive, Hollywood, 1928-32, First Church, Pomona, 1932-35, Univ. Ch., Los Angeles, 1935-36, First Ch., Pasadena, 1936-37, Central Park Ch., Buffalo, 1938-56; sabbatical leave, 1956-57; minister Community Methodist Ch., Balboa Island, Calif.; interim minister 1st Meth. Ch., Fullerton, Calif., 1959. Pres. Gen. Ministerium Buffalo and Erie County, 1951-52. Mem. Commn. World Service and Finance, Genesee Conf., 1948-56; pres. Buffalo Meth. Ministerium, 1948-49. Member Bds. Ministerial Tng., Conf. Relations, Genesee Conf., 1938-56; trustee Buffalo Council Chs., 1946-48. Served in O.T.C., 1918. Mem. Kappa Alpha, Phi Kappa Phi. Mason. Club: Rotary (Buffalo, N.Y.). Author: Ministry of Symbolism. Contbr. to books of sermons and devotion. Spl. lectr. on Abraham Lincoln to clubs, schs., chs. Home: 325 Kempton St Spring Valley CA 92077

RASMUS, ROBERT NELSON, bldg. materials mfg. co. exec.; b. Chgo., Sept. 17, 1925; s. Walter E. and Edith C. (Nelson) R.; B.S. in Gen. Engring., U. Ill., 1948; M.M.E., Cornell U., 1949; m. Annette E. Avery, Dec. 28, 1951; children—John, Richard. Vice pres. mfg. Masonite Corp., Chgo., 1965-70, v.p., gen. mgr. Bldg. Products div., 1970-71, group v.p. board products group, 1971-74, exec. v.p., 1975-76, pres., 1976—, chief exec. officer, 1977—, also dir.; dir. Employers Ins. of Wausau. Served with AUS, 1943-46. Decorated Bronze Star with oak leaf cluster. Conglist. Clubs: Econ., Met., Tower (Chgo.). Home: 59 Lakewood Dr Glencoe IL 60022 Office: 29 N Wacker Dr Chicago IL 60606

RASMUSEN, ROGER WARD, agribus. exec.; b. DeKalb, Ill., May 6, 1934; s. Russel Nelferd and Mary Edna (McAllister) R.; B.A., Monmouth Coll., 1956; M.B.A., Harvard U., 1958; m. Dorothy Jane Stokes, Aug. 27, 1957; children—Mark Russel, Karen Denise. Trainee to asst. controller Internat. Harvester Co., 1962-66; dir. internat. seed operations DeKalb AgResearch, Inc. (Ill.), 1966-72, mgr. investment planning, 1969-72, financial v.p., 1972—, treas., 1973—; dir. Depco, Inc., DeKalb Petroleum Corp., DeKalb Italiana SpA, Marchetto & Co. SpA, Semillas Agricolas, Nuclear Assurance Corp. Bd. trustees, exec. com. Monmouth Coll. Served to 1st lt. Finance Corps, AUS, 1958-62. Named outstanding young alumnus Monmouth Coll., 1973. Mem. Am. Inst. C.P.A.'s, Financial Execs. Inst. Congregationalist. Home: 135 Thornbrook Rd DeKalb IL 60115 Office: DeKalb AgResearch Inc Sycamore Rd DeKalb IL 60115

RASMUSON, ELMER EDWIN, banker, mayor Anchorage; b. Yakutat, Alaska, Feb. 15, 1909; s. Edward Anton and Jenny (Olson) R.; B.S. magna cum laude, Harvard U., 1930, A.M., 1935; student U. Grenoble, 1930; LL.D., U. Alaska, 1970; m. Lile Vivian Bernard, Oct. 27, 1939 (dec. 1960); children—Edward Bernard, Lile Muchmore (Mrs. John Gibbons, Jr.), Judy Ann; m. 2d, Col. Mary Louise Milligan, Nov. 4, 1961. Chief accountant Nat. Investors Corp., N.Y.C., 1933-35; prin. Arthur Andersen & Co., N.Y.C., 1935-43; pres. Nat. Bank of Alaska, 1943-65, chmn. bd., 1966-74, chmn. exec. com., 1975—; mayor City of Anchorage, 1964-67, Civilian aide from Alaska to sec. army, 1959-67; Swedish consul Alaska, 1955-77. Chmn. Rasmuson Found. Rep. nominee U.S. Senate from Alaska, 1968. U.S. commr. Internat. N. Pacific Fisheries Commn., 1969—; mem. Nat. Marine Fisheries Adv. Com., 1974-77; mem. North Pacific Fishery Mgmt. Council, 1976-77. Mem. city council, Anchorage, 1945, chmn. city planning commn., 1950-53. Pres. Alaska council Boy Scouts Am., 1953. Sec.-treas. Loussac Found.; regent U. Alaska, 1950-69; trustee King's Lake Camp, Inc., 1944—; bd. dirs. Coast Guard Acad. Found. Decorated knight first class Order of Vasa, comdr. Order No. Star (Sweden); recipient Silver Antelope award Boy Scouts Am., outstanding civilian service medal U.S. Army, Alaskan of Year award, 1976. C.P.A., N.Y., Tex., Alaska. Mem. Pioneers Alaska, Alaska Bankers Assn. (past pres.), Defense Orientation Conference Assn., N.A.A.C.P., Alaska Native Brotherhood, Phi Beta Kappa. Republican. Presbyn. Mason, Elk. Clubs: Explorers, Bohemian, Anchorage Rotary (past pres.); Harvard (N.Y.C.; Boston); Wash. Athletic, Seattle Yacht, Rainier (Seattle); Thunderbird Country (Palm Desert, Calif.). Address: PO Box 600 Anchorage AK 99501

RASMUSSEN, AARON FREDERICK, physician, educator; b. St. Anthony, Idaho, May 27, 1915; s. Aaron Frederick and Nancy Blanche (Costley) R.; B.S., U. Idaho, 1937; M.S., U. Wis., 1940, Ph.D., 1941, M.D., 1943; m. Besse Carol Tatum, June 12, 1941; children—Frederick Tatum, Nancy Mabel, Carol Irene. Research asso. U. Wis. Sch. Medicine, 1941-42; chief chemotherapy research sect., dept. viral and rickettsial diseases Army Med. Center, 1947-48; asso. prof. microbiology and preventive medicine U. of Wis., 1948-51, prof., 1951-52; prof. and chmn. med. mircrobiology and immunology, 1962-69, asso. dean U. Calif. at Los Angeles Sch. of Medicine; vis. scientist at the U.S. Naval Medical Research Unit 2, Taipei, Taiwan, 1960-61. Cons. microbiology br. Office Naval Research; asso. Armed Forces Commn. Influenza; cons. div. gen. med. scis. Nat. Insts. Health. Served with M.C., AUS, 1943-47. Diplomate Am. Bd. Pathology. Mem. Am. Bd. Microbiology, Am. Soc. Microbiology (v.p. 1976-77, pres. 1977-78), Am. Acad. Microbiology, Assn. Immunologists, Soc. Clin. Investigation, Western Assn. Physicians. Home: 1015 Franklin St Santa Monica CA 90403 Office: 405 Hilgard Ave Los Angeles CA 90024

RASMUSSEN, JOHN OSCAR, JR., educator; b. St. Petersburg, Fla., Aug. 8, 1926; s. John Oscar and Hazel (Ormsby) R.; B.S., Calif. Inst. Tech., 1948; Ph.D., U. Calif. at Berkeley, 1952; M.A. (hon.), Yale, 1969; m. Louise Brooks, Aug. 27, 1950; children—Nancy Louise, Jane Elizabeth, David Brooks, Stephen John. Mem. chemistry faculty U. Calif. at Berkeley, 1952-68, 73—, prof. chemistry, 1973—, mem. research staff Radiation Lab., 1952-68, sr. research asso. Lawrence Berkeley Lab., 1972—; prof. chemistry Yale, 1969-73, asso. dir. Yale Heavy Ion Accelerator Lab., 1970-73; vis. research prof. Nobel Inst. Physics, Stockholm, Sweden, 1953; vis. prof. Japan Soc. Promotion Sci., 1974. Served with USN, 1944-46. NSF sr. post-doctoral fellow Niels Bohr Inst., Copenhagen, Denmark, 1961-62; recipient E.O. Lawrence Meml. award AEC, 1967. J.S. Guggenheim Meml. fellow, 1973. Fellow Am. Phys. Soc.; mem. Am. Chem. Soc. (Nuclear Applications in Chemistry award 1976), Fedn. Am. Scientists (chmn. 1969, mem. council 1967-73), AAAS, Am. Radio Relay League, ACLU, Sierra Club. Democrat. Unitarian (trustee 1963-66). Author: Alpha Radioactivity, 1958; Models of Heavy Nuclei, 1974; also articles. Home: 817 Oxford St Berkeley CA 94707

RASMUSSEN, L.V., educator; b. Ladysmith, Wis., May 4, 1927; s. H.B. Rasmussen; B.S., U. Minn., 1950, M.A., 1952; Ph.D. (Noyes scholar), U. Chgo., 1961; m. Jean Luckman; children—Jay, Andrew. Asst. supt. schs., Marietta, Ohio, 1956-58; supt. schs., Wooster, Ohio, 1959-62, Duluth, Minn., 1962-69; prof., head dept. ednl. adminstrn. Fla. State U., Tallahassee, 1969—. Mem. evaluation adv. com. U.S. Office Edn., 1970. Pres. Aerospace Edn. Found., 1968-70. Served with U.S. Maritime Service, 1945-47. Mem. Nat. Soc. Study Edn., Phi Delta Kappa. Office: Dept Educational Administration Fla State U Tallahassee FL 32306

RASMUSSEN, LEONARD ELTON, mgmt. cons.; b. Bayonne, N.J., May 27, 1920; s. Harold Joncke and Anna (Milkowski) R.; A.B., Columbia, 1941, B.S. in Chem. Engring., 1943; m. Gertrude Margaret Hay, Apr. 25, 1942; children—Geoffrey, Gregory, Gordon. Mech. engr. Electric Boat Co., 1941-43; chem. engr. Celanese Corp., 1943-44; asst. to med. dir. Manhattan Engr. Dist., Oak Ridge, 1946; chief radiation instruments br. AEC, 1946-47; v.p. Keleket Mfg. Co., Covington, Ky., 1947-51; gen. mgr. Bendix Corp., 1951-64. v.p., group exec., 1964-67, v.p. Bendix Internat., 1967-68; exec. v.p., chief operating officer Packard Instrument Co., Inc., Downers Grove, Ill., 1968-69, pres., chief exec. officer, 1969-71; group v.p. Ambac Industries, Inc., Carle Place, N.Y., 1971-72, v.p. corporate devel., 1972; exec. v.p., chief operating officer NRG Tech., Inc., Newport Beach, Calif., 1973-74; exec. v.p., dir. RDM Electronics, Inc., Anaheim, Calif., 1974-75; mgmt. cons. Oasis Drinking Waters Inc., Garden Grove, Calif., 1975-76, TRC Assos., Irvine, Calif., 1976, Newport Energy Resources, 1976—; gen. mgr. Advanced Solar Power Co., Newport Beach, Calif., 1978—. Sr. mem. Instrument Soc. Am., I.E.E.E.; mem. Am. Inst. Chem. Engrs. (past pres. N.Y.C.), Cin. Radiation Soc. (past pres.), Am. Mgmt. Assn., Assn. Nuclear Instrument Mfrs. Inc., Beta Theta Pi (past treas.). Home: 5012 Paseo de Vega Irvine CA 92715

RASMUSSEN, LYMAN MERRILL, petroleum co. exec.; b. Cardston, Alta., Can., Apr. 17, 1920; s. Lyman Merrill and Annie (Woolf) R.; attended Mt. Royal Coll.; B.Sc. in Petroleum Engring., U. Okla.; m. Enid Atkins, June 3, 1943; children—Ronald, Karen. With Gulf Oil Corp. and British American Oil Co., 1949-59; mgr. production Pacific Petroleums Ltd., 1959-64, v.p. exploration and production, 1964-67, sr. v.p., 1967-69, exec. v.p., 1969-70, pres., 1970—, chief exec. officer, 1974-79; pres., chief exec. officer Husky Oil Co., Cody, Wyo., 1979—; dir. Husky Oil Ltd., Westcoast Transmission Co. Ltd., Foothills Pipe Lines (Yukon) Ltd., Foothills Oil Pipe Line Ltd., Energy Equipment & Systems, Inc., Royal Bank Can., Grove Valve & Regulator Co., Oakland, Wagi Internat., Rome. Served to lt., Royal Can. Arty., 1942-46. Mem. Assn. Profl. Engrs. Alta., Canadian Gas Assn. (past chmn.; dir.), Canadian Petroleum Assn. (past chmn. bd. govs.), Calgary C. of C. (v.p., dir.). Clubs: Calgary Petroleum, Glencoe, Calgary Golf and Country, Ranchmen's, Desert Island Country (Rancho Mirage, Calif.); Olive-Glenn Country (Cody). Home: 900 Skyline Dr Cody WY 82414 Office: Husky Oil Co PO Box 380 Cody WY 82414

RASMUSSEN, NORMAN CARL, nuclear engr.; b. Harrisburg, Pa., Nov. 12, 1927; s. Frederick and Faith (Elliott) R.; B.A., Gettysburg (Pa.) Coll., 1950, Sc.D. (hon.), 1968; Ph.D., Mass. Inst. Tech., 1956; m. Thalia Tichenor, Aug. 23, 1952; children—Neil, Arlene. Mem. faculty Mass. Inst. Tech., 1958—, prof. nuclear engring., 1965-75, head dept., 1975—; dir. reactor safety study AEC, 1972-75; mem. Def. Sci. Bd., 1974-78, Presdl. Adv. Group on Contbns. Tech. to Econs. Strength, 1975; dir. Bedford Engring. Corp.; adv. com. components tech. div. Argonne Univs. Assn., 1977—; chmn. sci. rev. com. Idaho Nat. Engring. Lab., 1977—; trustee N.E. Utilities, 1977—. Chmn. Lincoln-Sudbury Sch. Com., 1971-72. Served with USNR, 1945-46. Recipient Distinguished Achievement award Health Physics Soc., 1976; Distinguished Service award NRC, 1976. Fellow Am. Nuclear Soc. (spl. award nuclear power reactor safety 1976); mem. Inst. Nuclear Materials Mgmt., AAAS, Nat. Acad. Engring., Nat. Acad. Sci. Co-author: Modern Physics for Engineers, 1966; contbr. articles to profl. jours. Home: 80 Winsor Rd Sudbury MA 01776 Office: 77 Massachusetts Ave Cambridge MA 02139

RASMUSSEN, PHIPPS LOUIS, advt. exec.; b. San Francisco, June 12, 1912; s. Louis and Lillian (Phipps) R.; B.S., St. Mary's Coll., Moraga, Calif., 1935; m. Shirley Frick, Aug. 22, 1939; children—Sherryl Frick (now Mrs. William Hosie), and Mark Phipps. With McCann-Erickson, Inc., 1939—, v.p., 1954—, gen. mgr. San Francisco office, 1956-58, exec. v.p. and Western regional mgr., 1958-62; exec. v.p. McCann-Erickson (Corp.) Internat., 1959-63, pres., 1964-66, dir. various foreign subsidiaries; sr. cons. Interpublic, Inc., N.Y.C., 1966—; cons. fgn. service div. U.S. Dept. Agr. Served as lt. commdr. USNR. World War II; mem. U.S. Joint Purchasing Bd., New Zealand, Australia. Mem. Am. Assn. Advt. Agencies (gov. No. Calif. council), Am. Legion (mem. nat. security council 1947), Am. Marketing Assn., San Francisco Mus. Art, C. of C. Clubs: San Francisco Stock Exchange, San Francisco Advertising; Commonwealth, Press and Union League, Orinda Country; American (Switzerland). Home: Ridge Rd Sutter Creek CA 95685 Office: 15 Passage Malbisson Geneva Switzerland

RASMUSSEN, WALLACE N., food co. exec.; b. 1914; married. With Beatrice Foods Co., 1934—, dist. mgr.-so. dist. diary div., 1957-65, sr. v.p.-eastern dairy area, 1965-72, sr. v.p.-eastern, eastern Can., European dairy areas and wholesale div., 1972-74, exec. v.p. and pres.-food ops., 1974-76, chmn. bd. and chief exec. officer, 1976-79, chmn. exec. com., 1979—. Office: Beatrice Foods Co 120 S LaSalle St Chicago IL 60603*

RASOR, RICHARD DAVID, resort exec.; b. N.Y.C., Jan. 2, 1939; s. William Barmore and Lucille Evelyn (Sist) R.; B.A. in English Lit., Colgate U., 1961; children—Richard David, Kathryn Ellen, Mary Elizabeth. Acct. supr. J. Walter Thompson, N.Y.C., 1964-69, mgmt. supr., 1971-77, exec. v.p., gen. mgr., Detroit, 1977-79; advt. dir. P. Ballantine, Newark, 1969; pres. Promotivation, Inc., N.Y.C., 1970; chmn., pres. Bethel (Maine) Commodore Corp., 1979—; active in area devel. and seminars relating to resort industry. Com. chmn. United Fund, Detroit, 1978. Served to lt. USAF, 1961-64. Mem. Delta Kappa Epsilon. Club: Yale (N.Y.C.). Home and Office: Bethel Inn PO Box 26 Bethel ME 04217

RASOR, ROBERT WILLIAM, physician; b. Santa Cruz, Calif., July 9, 1911; s. Frank and Hattie (Bryson) R.; B.A., Colo. Coll., 1935; M.D., U. Colo., 1941; m. Annette Mathers, Sept. 17, 1942; children—Amy Cone, Robert William, Susan Anne, Sally Lou; m. 2d, Celia K. Zyzniewski, Feb. 7, 1970. Intern U.S. Marine Hosp., Balt., 1941-42; resident USPHS Hosps., New Orleans, N.Y.C., 1942-45; chief med. officer Nat. Tng. Sch. For Boys, Washington, 1945-47; resident psychiatry USPHS Hosp., Ft. Worth, 1947-48, dep. med officer in charge, 1957-61, med. officer in charge, 1961-62; psychiat. tng. U. Chgo. Clinics, Chgo. Psychoanalytic Inst., 1948-51; practice medicine, specializing in psychiatry, Ft. Worth, 1947-48, 57-61, Lexington, Ky., 1951-57, 62—; asst. chief Psychiat. Service USPHS Hosp., Lexington, 1951-57, med. officer in charge, 1962-70; ret.; psychiat. cons. Pikes Peak Family Counseling and Mental Health Center, Colorado Springs, 1970—; clin. prof. U. Colo. Med. Sch.; lectr. psychology U. Ky., asso. prof. dept. psychiatry Coll. Medicine. Mem. adv. bd., survey adv. com. to planning com. Mental Health Assn. Ky., 1964—; govt. rep. Lexington Commn. Human Rights, 1965—. Diplomate Am. Bd. Psychiatry and Neurology. Fellow Am. Psychiat. Assn., A.A.A.S.; mem. A.M.A., Am. Pub. Health Assn., Nat. Acad. Religion and Mental Health, Ky. Psychiat. Assn., Ky. Mental Health Assn., Assn. Med. Supts. Mental Hosps. Rotarian. Address: 411 Lakewood Circle Colorado Springs CO 80910

RASPBERRY, WILLIAM JAMES, journalist; b. Okolona, Miss., Oct. 12, 1935; s. James Lee and Willie Mae (Tucker) R.; B.S. in History, Ind. Central Coll., 1958, L.H.D., 1973; m. Sondra Patricia Dodson, Nov. 12, 1966; children—Patricia D., Angela D., Mark J. Reporter-editor Indpls. Recorder, 1956-60; reporter-editor Washington Post, 1962-65, urban affairs columnist, 1965—. Instr. journalism Howard U., 1971—; TV commentator sta. WTTG, Washington, 1973—; TV discussion panelist sta. WRC-TV, Washington, 1974—; lectr. on race relations and pub. edn. Juror for Robert F. Kennedy and Pulitzer awards, 1975. Served with AUS, 1960-62. Mem. Capital Press Club, Kappa Alpha Psi. Club: Gridiron. Contbr. articles on race relations and pub. edn. to popular mags. Home: 1301 Iris St NW Washington DC 20012 Office: 1150 15th St NW Washington DC 20071

RASSMAN, EMIL CHARLES, lawyer; b. Indpls., July 27, 1919; s. Fred Wolf and Helen (Leming) R.; B.A., Washington and Lee U., 1941; LL.B., U. Tex., 1947; LL.D., Baylor U., 1977; m. Annie de Montel, Jan. 31, 1943; children—Laura Helen (Mrs. Edward E. Bates, Jr.), James Neal. Admitted to Tex. bar, 1947, U.S. Supreme Ct., 1951; mem. firm Rassman, Gunter & Boldrick, Midland, Tex. Dir. Comml. Bank & Trust Co., Midland. Mem. Tex. Jud. Council, 1958-61. Campaign chmn., pres. Midland County United Fund, 1956-57; chmn. Midland County chpt. A.R.C., 1971-73. Trustee Midland Ind. Sch. Dist., 1958-61; bd. regents Tex. State Univ. System, 1961-79, chmn. bd., 1967-69; chmn. bd. executors Permian Basin Petroleum Mus., Library and Hall of Fame, 1973-78. Served to capt. AUS, 1941-46. Fellow Am. Coll. Trial Lawyers, Am., Tex. bar founds., Internat. Acad. Trial Lawyers, Am. Coll. Probate Counsel; mem. Internat. Assn. Ins. Counsel, Fedn. Ins. Counsel, Midland County Bar Assn. (pres. 1960), State Bar Tex. (dir. 1972-75, chmn. bd. 1974-75), West Tex. (pres. 1973-74), Tex. State (pres. 1973-74) chambers commerce, Philos. Soc. Tex., Phi Delta Phi, Delta Tau Delta. Episcopalian. Mason. Address: 400 Midland Tower Bldg Midland TX 79701

RAST, LOY EDMUND, telephone co. exec.; b. Athens, Ga., Mar. 17, 1916; s. Loy E. and Clara Louise (Rentz) R.; student Mich. State U., 1933-34; B.S. in Commerce, U. Ga., 1937; m. Evelyn Page, Feb. 23, 1941; children—T. Edmund, Philip R. With So. Bell Tel. and Tel.

Co., 1937-59, v.p., comptroller, 1961-64, v.p., gen. mgr., Fla., 1965-67, exec. v.p., dir., 1969-70, pres., dir., Atlanta, 1970—; asst. comptroller AT&T, 1959-61; v.p. ops., dir. S. Central Bell Telephone Co., 1968-69; dir. 1st Nat. Bank Atlanta, 1st Atlanta Corp., Met. Life Ins. Co., N.Y.C. Chmn. Central Atlanta Progress, Inc., 1979—; pres. United Way Met. Atlanta, 1976; bd. dirs. Met. Atlanta chpt. ARC, 1970—, vice chmn., 1971-76; mem. regional exec. com. Boy Scouts Am., 1970—, exec. bd. Atlanta Area council, 1970—, pres., 1971-73; mem. vestry St. Philip's Episcopal Cathedral, Atlanta, 1975-79. Mem. Telephone Pioneers Am. (pres. 1977). Clubs: Capital City (bd. govs. 1973-77), Piedmont Driving, Rotary (v.p. 1977-78), Commerce (dir. 1970—). Office: 67 Edgewood Ave SE Atlanta GA 30303

RAST, MENDEL WALKER, consumer products mfg. co. exec.; b. Florence, S.C., Sept. 9, 1935; s. Mendel B. and Sue (Herring) R.; B.S. in Mech. Engring., U. S.C., 1958; M.B.A. in Labor Law, Seton Hall U., East Orange, N.J., 1965; m. Alva Gonder, Aug. 18, 1973; children—Martha Sue, Edie. With U.S. Gypsum Co., 1958-70, tech. mgr. paper, 1967-70; with Arcata Corp., 1970—, v.p. corp. devel., 1978-79, v.p., group exec., Montvale, N.J., 1979—; pres. div. Keyes Fibre Co., 1979—; mem. faculty U. Pitts., eves. 1966; mem. Gov. Maine Adv. Com. World Trade, 1979—. Mem. TAPPI. Republican. Methodist. Clubs: Commonwealth (San Francisco); Union League (N.Y.C.); Rotary. Office: 160 Summit Ave Montvale NJ 07645

RATCHFORD, WILLIAM RICHARD, congressman; b. Danbury, Conn., May 24, 1934; s. Harold and Susie (Klinzing) R.; A.B., U. Conn., 1956; postgrad. Georgetown U. Law Sch., 1956-59; m. Barbara Jean Carpenter, June 22, 1957; childrenl—Shaun, Scott, Brian. Admitted to Conn. bar, 1959, since practiced in Danbury; mem. Conn. Ho. of Reps., after 1963, asst. majority leader, 1967-68, house speaker, 1969-72, minority leader at large, 1972; mem. 96th Congress from 5th Dist. Conn.; instr. polit. sci. Western Conn. State Coll., 1976. Adviser Danbury Assn. to Advance Retarded; vice chmn. Regional Legal Aid Program; mem. clean air com. Conn. Tb Assn.; chmn. Community Action Com.; v.p. U. Conn. Alumni Council. Chmn., Democratic State Conv., 1970-71; co-chmn. platform com., 1970, 72: pres. Nat. Legis. Conf., 1972-73. Chmn. bd. dirs. Camp Fire Girls, 1963-64; mem. Presdl. Adv. Commn. on Intergovernmental Relations; chmn. Gov.'s Blue Ribbon Com. to Investigate Nursing Homes, 1976. Served with Conn. N.G., 1965. Recipient State Vocational Edn. award, 1969, Outstanding Legis. Leadership award Nat. Citizens Conf., 1971, award for contbn. to vocat. edn., 1975. Mem. U. Conn. Nat. Alumni Assn. (past 1st v.p., mem. council), Phi Beta Kappa. Universalist Unitarian (past chmn. bd.). Home: 2 Johnson Dr Danbury CT 06810 Office: care Postmaster of House B-227 Longworth House Office Bldg Washington DC 20515

RATCLIFF, PERRY ALBERT, educator; b. Marion County, Ind., Aug. 25, 1915; s. Thomas Roscoe and Marie (Boardman) R.; D.D.S., Ind. U., 1939; m. Viola Hall, Aug. 20, 1939; 1 son, James Ratcliff; m. 2d, Roberta AmStein, Dec. 26, 1972. Pvt. practice dentistry, Dunkirk, Ind., 1940-43, San Bernardino, Calif., 1948-50; from instr. to asso. prof. U. So. Calif. Sch. Dentistry, 1950-59; mem. faculty U. Calif. at San Francisco Dental Sch., 1959—, prof. periodontology, 1959-70, emeritus, 1971—; vis. lectr. grad. dept. U. Nebr., 1965-69; prof. oral medicine Loma Linda U. Dental Sch., 1961-79; prof. dental hygiene and periodontics No. Ariz. U., 1974-79. Cons. Letterman Gen. Hosp., San Francisco, 1962-69, U.S. Naval Base, Treasure Island, Calif., 1967-70, Nat. Inst. Dental Research, 1967-70, edn. periodontics USPHS, 1965-70, Universidad de Nacionale de Mex. Pres. Nat. Found. for Prevention Oral Disease, 1971-76. Served with USNR, 1941-43. Diplomate Am. Bd. Periodontology. Fellow AAAS, Am. Coll. Dentists, Internat. Coll. Dentists, Am. Acad. Periodontology (chmn. specialists sect. 1966, pres. 1970); mem. Western Soc. Periodontology (pres. 1953), Internat. Assn. Dental Research, Am. Dental Assn., Omicron Kappa Upsilon, Kappa Tau Alpha. Author: Workshop for Teachers in Graduate and Postgraduate Periodontics, 1962; (with Dr. R. John) Gingivectomy/Gingivoplasty, 1966; (with Raust, Pipe) For 9 Out of 10 Adults Only, 1969; (with Pipe) Developing a Plaque Control Program, 1973; (with Pipe) Examination and Diagnosis of Periodontial Disease, 1974; (with Pipe) Tooth Preparation, 1974; also articles. Home: 7439 E Lincoln Dr Scottsdale AZ 85253. *A helping hand is found, most frequently, at the end of your own arm.*

RATCLIFFE, GEORGE JACKSON, JR., corp. exec.; b. Charleston, W.Va., Mar. 22, 1936; s. George Jackson and Dorothy (Ward) R.; A.B., Duke, 1958; LL.B., U. Va., 1961; m. Nancy Lenhardt, Oct. 5, 1963; children—George Jackson III, Dorothy Margaret. Admitted to N.Y. bar, 1964, Ohio bar, 1962; with firm Taft, Stettinius & Hollister, Cin., 1961-63; lawyer IBM Corp., 1963-65; mem. firm Perkins, Daniels & McCormack, N.Y.C., 1965-70, partner, 1970; v.p., sec., gen. counsel Helme Products, Inc., N.Y.C., 1970-71, exec. v.p., 1972-75, also dir.; v.p., sec., gen. counsel Harvey Hubbell, Inc., Orange, Conn., 1975—. Mem. Am. Bar Assn., Assn. Bar City N.Y. Clubs: N.Y. Athletic; Brooklawn, Country (Fairfield, Conn.); Galen Hall Country (Reading, Pa.). Home: 278 Sherwood Dr Southport CT 06490 Office: Orange CT 06477

RATCLIFFE, MYRON FENWICK, investment mgmt. exec., banker; b. Evanston, Ill., June 5, 1902; s. James Lewis and Jean (Gardner) R.; B.S., U. Ill., 1925; m. Margaret Archibald, May 5, 1945; 1 dau., Elizabeth Robertson (Mrs. Robert W. Heinze). With firm Goldman, Sachs & Co., N.Y.C., 1925-33; adminstr. financial codes NRA, 1934-35; syndicate mgr. Lehman Bros., N.Y.C., 1936-49; partner Bache & Co., Chgo., 1949-56; pres. Miami Corp., Chgo., 1956-77, dir., 1956—; pres. Cutler Oil & Gas Corp., Chgo., 1956-77, dir., 1956—; chmn. bd., dir. Nat. Blvd. Bank, Chgo., 1956—; dir. Nat.-Standard Co. (Niles, Mich.). Bd. govs. Midwest Stock Exchange, 1949-56. Trustee Ill. Children's Home and Aid Soc. Served as lt. col. AUS, 1942-46. Decorated Legion of Merit. Mason. Clubs: Bond, Casino, Chicago, Mid-Am. (Chgo.); Indian Hill Country (Winnetka, Ill.); Old Elm Country (Ft. Sheridan, Ill.); Birnam Wood Golf (Santa Barbara, (Calif.). Office: 410 N Michigan Ave Chicago IL 60611*

RATCLIFFE, ROBERT EDWARD, govt. ofcl.; b. Portland, Oreg., Nov. 20, 1923; s. George and Genevieve (Smith) R.; J.D., Willamette U., 1949; m. Bettie Woodhouse, Jan. 26, 1946; children—Rebecca L., Robert C. Admitted to Oreg. bar, 1949; pvt. practice law, Portland, 1949-59; atty. Office of Portland Regional Solicitor, 1959-66, asst. regional solicitor, 1966-67; asst. to under sec., Dept. of Interior, Washington, 1967-68, Portland regional solicitor, 1968-77; gen. counsel Bonneville Power Assn., 1977—. Bd. dirs. Boys Club Am. Served with USNR, 1943-46. Deorated Bronze Star; recipient Meritorious Service award, Spl. Achievement award Dept. Interior, 1974. Club: Optimists (pres. 1960-61). Home: 14328 NE Rose Pkwy Portland OR 97230 Office: 1002 NE Holladay St Portland OR 97232

RATH, GEORGE EDWARD, bishop; b. Buffalo, Mar. 29, 1913; s. Edward F. and Eudora Pearl (Chadderdon) R.; A.B., Harvard, 1933; B.D., Union Theol. Sem., 1936; S.T.D., Gen. Theol. Sem., 1964; m. Margaret Webber, Apr. 7, 1934; children—Peter F. (dec.), Gail (Mrs. Richard M. Sherk). Ordained deacon Episcopal Ch., 1938, priest, 1939; asst. to chaplain Columbia, 1936-39, asst. chaplain, 1939-41; vicar All Saints' Ch., Millington, N.J., 1941-49, rector, 1949-64; suffragan bishop Episcopal Diocese Newark, 1964-70; bishop coadjutor, 1970-73, bishop, 1974-78; ret., 1978; archdeacon Morris County, 1959-64. Chmn. bd. trustees Christ Hosp. Jersey City, 1966-79. Mem. Wilderness Soc., Sierra Club, Appalachian Trail Conf. Clubs: Cape Cod; Brookline (Mass.). Home: 2 Cedar Land Rd PO Box 996 East Orleans MA 02643

RATH, GUSTAVE JOSEPH, educator; b. N.Y.C., May 19, 1929; s. Gustavo Jules and Margaret R. (Payor) R.; B.S., Mass. Inst. Tech., 1952; M.S., Ohio State U., 1955, Ph.D., 1957; m. Karen S. Stoyanoff; m. Karen Stoyanoff; children—Gustave Alexander, Christopher Kent. Research psychologist IBM Corp. Research Center, Yorktown Heights, N.Y., 1957-59; mgr. ops. research group Admiral Corp., Chgo., 1959-60; mgr. mil. financial analysis Raytheon Corp., Lexington, Mass., 1960-61, mgr. systems research group, 1962-63; mem. faculty Northwestern U., 1963—, prof. indsl. engring. and mgmt. sci., 1969—, prof. ednl. organizational devel., 1975—, chmn. Design and Devel. Center, 1968—; pres. Cassell, Rath, Stoyanoff, Ltd., Evanston, Ill.; cons. electronics, aerospace corps.; chmn. bd. Fundamental Systems, Inc., Evanston, Ill., 1968-72. Cons. Ill. Council on Continuing Med. Edn., 1975—, Am. Acad. Pediatrics, 1974—, Health and Hosps. Governing Commn. Cook County, 1974, Downey VA Hosp., 1973—. Project planner Midwest Spinal Injury and Health Services/Developmentally Disabled Adults, Chgo. Rehab. Center; mem. NRC panel, tech. analysis div. Nat. Bur. Standards, 1963—, pres., 1967-70. Chmn. Evanston Child and Family Health Care Bd., 1973-75, Child and Family Advs. Evanston, 1975—. Served to 1st lt. USAF, 1952-54. Fellow A.A.A.S., Am. Psychol. Assn., Soc. Advanced Med. Systems; mem. I.E.E.E., Northeastern Research and Engring. Meeting (treas. 1961-62, bus. mgr. Scanfax 1964—), Inst. Mgmt. Sci. (chmn. coll. programs 1967), Ops. Research Soc. Am., Am. Soc. Engring. Edn. Home: 732 Colfax Ave Evanston IL 60201

RATH, HILDEGARD, artist, author, lectr.; b. Freudenstadt, Ger., Mar. 22, 1909; d. Ernst Adolf and Emma (Katz) R.; came to U.S., 1948; pvt. instrn., 1925, Kunstgewerbeschule, Stuttgart, 1926-27; student Rustinsches Lehrinstitut, Potsdam, 1928-30, Akademie Der Bildenden Kunste, Berlin, 1933-37; spl. study with Lotte Laserstein, Berlin, Otto Manigk, Berlin; m. Hermann Gross, June 14, 1946. One-woman shows: Ausstellung Weissenhof Stuttgart, 1927, Kunsthaus Schaller, Stuttgart, 1941, 46, 59, I.F.A. Gallery, Washington, 1957, Avante Garde Gallery, N.Y.C., 1961, Ligoa Duncan Gallery, N.Y.C., 1963, 65, Raymond Duncan, Paris, 1963, Galerie Internationale, N.Y.C., 1972, Nat. Soc. Mural Painters Travelling Exhbn., 1977—; group shows throughout U.S., fgn. countries; represented in numerous museums U.S. and Europe including Library of Congress, Met. Mus., N.Y.C., Whitney Mus., Bklyn. Mus., others, also pvt. collections; owner, dir. European Sch. Fine Arts, N.Y.C., 1949-54; lectr. art and artists from prehistoric times to present, art socs. and museums, 1960-62; tchr. history of art Great Neck (N.Y.) Pub. Schs. Adult Edn. Program, 1960-62, North Shore Art Assn., Roslyn, N.Y., 1960-61; World field research corr. for movies, children's books, 1967. Recipient Grumbacher award of merit Fla. Internat., 1952, Salon of the Fifty States, N.Y., i962, Prix de Paris, 1963. Mem. Wurttembergisher Kunstverein Stuttgart, Landesverband Wurttembergischer Kunstler Tubingen (Ger.), So. Vt., N. Shore art assns., Artists Equity N.Y., Knickerbocker Artists N.Y., Nat. Assn. Pub. Sch. Adult Educators, Internat. Platform Assn., Nat. Soc. Mural Painters. Episcopalian. Address: Nottingham Park PO Box 298 Manchester Center VT 05255

RATH, R. JOHN, historian, educator; b. St. Francis, Kans., Dec. 12, 1910; s. John and Barbara (Schauer) R.; A.B., U. Kans., 1932; A.M., U. Calif., Berkeley, 1934; Ph.D., Columbia, 1941; m. Isabel Jones, June 26, 1937; children—Laurens John (dec.), Donald (dec.), Isabel Ferguson. Instr. history U. Ark., 1936-37, vis. prof. summer 1947; pre-doctoral field fellow Social Sci. Research Council in Austria and Italy, 1937-38; head dept. history and polit. sci. Lindenwood Coll., St. Charles, Mo., 1939- 41; asso. prof. history Miss. State Coll. for Women, 1941-43; chief bur. documentary evidence UNRRA Bur. Documents and Tracing, U.S. Zone of Germany, 1945-46; asst. prof. history U. Ga., 1946-47; asso. prof. history, asso. editor Jour. Central European Affairs, U. Colo., 1947-51, vis. prof. summer 1958; prof. history U. Tex., Austin, 1951-63; prof. history, chmn. dept. history and polit. sci. Rice U., 1963-68, named Mary Gibbs Jones prof., 1968-80; prof. Center Austrian Studies, U. Minn., Mpls., 1980—; vis. prof. U. Wis., 1955, Duke U., 1963; Guggenheim fellow in Italy, 1956-57; U.S. dep. to Study Center for Central and E. European Cultures in Vienna, 1970, 72; mem. sci. commn. Theodor Körner Found., Vienna, 1971—. Mem. Houston Com. on Fgn. Relations. Served to sgt. AUS, 1943-45. Recipient 1st class Austrian Cross of Honor in arts and scis., 1963. Mem. Am. (com. internat. activities 1960-66, exec. com. modern European history sect. 1963-66), So. (chmn. European sect. 1961-62, mem. exec. council 1965-68) hist. assns., A.A.U.P., Soc. Italian Hist. Studies, Conf. Central European History (mem. nat. exec. bd. 1959-61, vice chmn. 1969, chmn. 1970, mem. com. on Austrian history 1957-68, 70—, exec. sec. 1957-68), Am. Assn. for Study of Hungarian History (chmn. 1978), Southwestern Social Sci. Assn. (pres. 1976-77), Austrian Acad. Sci. (corr.), Deputazione di Storia Patria per le Venezie (corr.), Phi Beta Kappa. Author: The Fall of the Napoleonic Kingdom of Italy, 1941; The Viennese Revolution of 1948, 1957; L'amministrazione austriaca nel Lombardo Veneto, 1814-21, 1959; The Austrian Provisional Regime in Lombardy Venetia, 1969; contbg. author East Central Europe and the World (edited Stephen Kertesz), 1962; also Ency. Americana. Editor: Austrian History Newsletter, 1960-63, Austrian History Yearbook, 1965—. Contbr. to Die Auflösung des Habsburgerreiches, 1970, Native Fascism in the Successor States, 1971, Beiträge zur Zeitgeschichte, 1976. Office: Dept History U Minn Minneapolis MN 55455

RATH, RICHARD LAVERNE, JR., editor; b. Akron, Ohio, Dec. 16, 1928; s. Richard LaVerne and Fern Elsie (Carroll) R.; B.A., Allegheny Coll., 1953; m. Bonnie Lee Reisman, Nov. 23, 1963; children—Kitt, Rima. Report writer Parsons, Brinckerhoff, Quade & Douglas, engrs., N.Y.C., 1956-61; capt. Inter-Island Shipping Co., San Juan, P.R., 1962-65; asso. editor, then editor Boating Mag., N.Y.C., 1966-79; editorial dir. Boating mag. and Yachting mag., 1979—. Founder, chmn. Pioneer Marine Sch., South St. Seaport Mus., N.Y.C., 1971—, trustee mus., 1974—; bd. dirs. Am. Boat and Yacht Council, 1978—. Mem. Am. Schooner Assn. Club: N.Y. Yacht. Home: 50-14 217 St Bayside NY 11364 Office: 1 Park Ave New York NY 10016

RATH, THOMAS DAVID, lawyer, state atty. gen.; b. East Orange, N.J., June 1, 1945; s. Harvey and Helen R.; A.B., Dartmouth Coll., 1967; J.D., Georgetown U., 1971; m. Christine Casey, Dec. 18, 1971; children— Erin, Timothy. Admitted to N.J. bar, 1971, N.H. bar, 1972, U.S. Supreme Ct. bar, 1978; law clk. Judge Clarkson Fisher, U.S. Dist. Ct., N.J., 1971-72; atty. criminal div. Office of Atty. Gen., State of N.H., 1972-73, asst. atty. gen., 1973-76, dep. atty. gen., 1976-78, atty. gen., 1978—; mem. N.H. Crime Commn., N.H. Jud. Council, N.H. Police Standards and Tng. Council; mem. jud. planning com., character and fitness com. N.H. Supreme Ct. Bd. dirs. Friends Program; mem. N.H. Sudden Infant Death Syndrome Adv. Council; state employee participation chmn. United Way, 1978, 79. Mem. Nat. Assn. Attys. Gen. (vice-chmn. Eastern region, vice chmn. standing com. on energy), N.H. Bar Assn. Club: Dartmouth Coll. (v.p. Merrimack County). Roman Catholic. Office: 208 State House Annex Concord NH 03301

RATHBONE, PERRY TOWNSEND, art museum dir.; b. Germantown, Pa., July 3, 1911; s. Howard Betts and Beatrice (Connely) R.; A.B., Harvard, 1933, postgrad., 1933-34; Arts D., Washington U., St. Louis, 1958; L.H.D., Northeastern U., 1960, Suffolk U., Williams Coll., 1970; A.F.D., Bates Coll., 1964, Boston Coll., 1970; m. Euretta de Cosson, Feb. 10, 1945; children—Peter Betts, Eliza, Belinda. Co-dir. Harvard Soc. Contemporary Art, 1931-33; ednl. asst. Detroit Inst. Arts, 1934-36; instr. fine arts Wayne U., Detroit; curator Alger House (suburban br. Detroit Inst. Arts) and gen. research asst. to Dir. Valentiner, 1936-39; asst. to Dir. Valentiner (dir. gen. masterpieces of art), N.Y. World's Fair (later dir.); dir. City Art Mus., St. Louis, 1940-55; trustee Mus. Fine Arts, Boston, 1954-72, dir., 1955-72, dir. emeritus, cons., 1972—; dir. Christie's USA, 1973—, Christie's Internat., 1977—. Pres., St. Louis Art Commn., 1940-55, St. Louis Little Symphony, 1950-55; adviser council Harvard Found. for Advanced Study and Research, 1953-58; mem. vis. com. Fogg Art Mus., Harvard, 1955-66; mem. U.S. nat. commn. Internat. Council of Museums; adviser program for humanities Ford Found., 1957-73; adviser art com. Chase Manhattan Bank, 1958-76; pres. Met. Boston Arts Center, Inc., 1958-61, chmn. bd., 1961—; adviser Rockefeller Panel on Performing Arts, 1963-64, Skowhegan Sch. Painting and Sculpture, 1965—; fine arts vis. com. R.I. Sch. Design, 1966-68, trustee, 1969-74; adviser Urasenke Found., Kyoto, Japan, 1974—; vice chmn. Mass. Art Commn.; v.p. Cosmopolitan Art Found., 1974—; mem. Cambridge Arts Council, 1978-79. Mem. bd. overseers Brandeis U., Strawbery Banke, Inc.; trustee Am. Fedn. Arts, 1959—, New Eng. Conservatory of Music, 1960—, Boston Arts Festival, Cape Cod Art Assn., Internat. Exhbns. Found., 1965—, Royal Oak Found., 1974—, Opera Co. Boston, 1976—. Served with USNR, 1942-45, PTO, lt. comdr., 1945. Decorated chevalier Legion d'Honneur; Benjamin Franklin fellow Royal Soc. Art. Mem. Am. Assn. Museums (v.p. 1960—, council), St. Louis Round Table, Mass. Hist. Soc., Colonial Soc. Mass., Assn. Art Museum Dirs. (pres. 1959-60, 69-70, trustee 1969-72), Am. Acad. Arts and Scis., Royal Art Soc. London, Phi Beta Kappa (hon. Harvard chpt.). Episcopalian (vestryman). Clubs: Century (N.Y.C.); Tavern, Odd Volumes, Somerset, Harvard (Boston). Author: Charles Wimar, 1946; Max Beckmann, 1948; Mississippi Panorama, 1950; Westward the Way, 1954; Lee Gatch, 1960; (with Peter Selz) Max Beckmann, 1964; Handbook of the Forsyth Wickes Collection, 1968; Museum of Fine Arts, Boston, Western Art, 1971; Andrew Wyeth (in Japanese), 1974; also numerous articles in mus. bulls. and art jours. Contbr. to Greatest Drawings of All Times, 1962. Home: 151 Coolidge Hill Cambridge MA 02138 Office: Christie's Internat 502 Park Ave New York NY 10022

RATHBURN, ELDON DAVIS, film composer; b. Queenstown, N.B., Can., Apr. 21, 1916; s. Caleb Davis and Blanche Vera (Puddington) R.; Licentiate Music, McGill U., Toronto Conservatory Music, 1938-39; m. Marguerite Payette, Apr. 7, 1969. Freelance musician St. John, N.B., 1933-47; staff composer Nat. Film Bd. Can., Montreal, Que., 1947-76; lectr. in field. Recipient Los Angeles Young Artists Competition award composers div., 1944. Can. Performing Rights Soc. scholar, 1938-39. Mem. Can. League Composers, Soc. Film Makers, Am. Fedn. Musicians. Composer music score Labyrinthe (Expo 67), Suite City of Gold, 1967, Aspects of Railroads, 1970, The Metamorphic Ten, 1971. Home: 760 Tasse St Montreal PQ H4L 1N7 Canada

RATHE, ALEX WERNER, educator, cons. mgmt. counsel; b. Berlin, Germany, Jan. 21, 1912; s. Alex and Anna (Mathias) R.; B.S. in Elec. Engring., Charlottenburg Inst. Tech., Berlin, 1933, M.S., 1935, D.Eng., 1936; m. Kathleen Marjory Jones, Nov. 1, 1947; 1 son, Arthur Alan. Came to U.S., 1937, naturalized, 1942. Indsl. engr. Display Lighting Corp., N.Y.C., 1937-41; sr. engr. Jackson & Moreland, Boston, 1941-43; chief prodn. engr. Gen. Instrument Corp., Elizabeth, N.J., 1943-44; chief indsl. engr., asst. to v.p. Hudson Am. Corp., N.Y.C., 1944-46; cons. engring. practice in mgmt., 1946—, now Mount Kisco, N.Y.; asso. prof. mgmt. engring, N.Y.U., 1949-62, prof. mgmt. Grad. Sch. Bus. Adminstrn., N.Y.U., 1962-77, prof. emeritus, 1977—; prof. mgmt. Grad. Sch. Bus., Pace U., 1977—; prin. lectr. Am. Mgmt. Assn., 1952-67; vis. prof. Grad. Sch. Bus., Columbia, 1961-62, U. Buenos Aires (Argentina), summer 1962; hon. mem. Def. Dept. Logistics Mgmt. Sch., 1962, Mgmt. Sch., 1965; distinguished lectr. U. So. Calif., 1971. Coll. rep. Citizens Com. for Hoover Report, 1950; U.S. del. Pan Am. Conf. on Mgmt., 1958; U.S. del. to Internat. Mgmt. Congress, 1963; mem. adv. bd. Internat. Centre Advanced Edn., ILO, 1970-72. Recipient certificates outstanding achievements Am. Inst. Indsl. Engrs., 1953, 59, 61, 62, presdl. plaque outstanding achievements, 1965; distinguished service certificates U.S. Army Command Mgmt. Sch., 1957; Oakleaf Cluster citation for meritorious service U.S. Army Logistics Mgmt. Center, 1959, Gantt Medal Bd. citation, 1962. Registered profl. engr., N.J., N.Y. Fellow Am. Inst. Indsl. Engrs. (pres. 1960-61), Am. Mgmt. Assn.; mem. Council for Internat. Progress in Mgmt. (dir. 1963-70, mem. exec. com. 1963-66, v.p. 1966-68, pres. 1969-70), Engrs. Joint Council (dir. 1956-60), Soc. Advancement Mgmt., Am. Soc. M.E., Argentine Engring. Council (hon.), Assn. Bolivian Execs. (hon.), Thai Mgmt. Assn. (hon.), Instituto para el Desarollo de la Direccion de Empressa (hon.), Korean Fedn. Execs. (hon.), Alpha Pi Mu. Author: How to Set Up Mgmt. Controls, 1948; (with Norbert Weiner, Luther Gulick) Cybernetics and Society, 1951; Lectures in Management, Planning and Controlling, 1954; Gantt on Management-Guidelines for Today's Executive, 1961; (with Dhun Irani) Scientists, Engineers, and Managers-Partners in Space, 1968; (with Frank M. Gryna) Applying Industrial Engineering to Management Problems, 1969; co-author: Management Control Systems, 1960. Home: Bittersweet Ln Mount Kisco NY 10549 Office: Grad Sch Bus Pace U Bedford Rd Pleasantville NY 10570

RATHER, DAN, broadcast journalist; b. Wharton, Tex., Oct., 1931; B.A. in Journalism, Sam Houston State Coll., Huntsville, Tex., 1953; student U. Houston, South Tex. Sch. Law; m. Jean Goebel; children—Dawn Robin, Daniel Martin. Writer, sportscaster KSAM-TV; instr. journalism Sam Houston State Coll., for 1 year; later worked for U.P.I. and Houston Chronicle; with CBS; joined staff of radio sta. KTRH, CBS affiliate, Houston, staying about 4 years as news writer, reporter, and later, as news dir.; became dir. news and pub. affairs with CBS Houston TV affiliate KHOU-TV in the late 1950's; became White House Corp., 1964, and then transferred to overseas burs., including chief of London bur., 1965-66; then worked in Vietnam; returned to White House position in fall of 1966, appearing nightly on segments of CBS Evening News; became anchorman-corr. for CBS Reports, 1974-75; co-anchorman 60 Minutes, CBS-TV, 1975—; anchorman Dan Rather Reporting, CBS Radio Network, 1977—; co-editor show Who's Who, CBS-TV, 1977; anchorman Midwest desk CBS news coverage of nat. election night returns, 1972—; mem. CBS news team nat. polit. convs., 1964—. Recipient 5 Emmy awards; Disting. Achievement for Broadcasting award U. So. Calif. Journalism Alumni Assn. Author: (with Gary Gates) The Palace Guard, 1974; (with Mickey Herskowitz) The Camera Never Blinks, 1977. Anchored numerous CBS News spl. programs; as White House corr. accompanied Pres. on numerous travels, including visits to

Mideast, USSR, People's Republic of China. Office: CBS News 555 W 57th St New York NY 10019

RATHER, HENRY LEE, hotel exec.; b. Lansing, Mich., Mar. 23, 1929; s. Howard Christian and Hazel (Cobb) R.; B.S., Cornell U. Sch. Hotel Adminstrn., 1952; m. Lavon Hallmark, June 23, 1956; children—Christine Lavon, Henry Lee. Personnel dir. Sheraton-Belveder Hotel, Balt., 1952-54; staff planning and personnel dir. Sheraton Palace Hotel, San Francisco and West Coast region, 1954-59; asst. to v.p. and gen. mgr. Sheraton Hotels in Hawaii, 1959-61; resident mgr. Sheraton-Dallas Hotel, 1961-63, acting gen. mgr., 1963-65, gen. mgr., 1970-79, v.p. and gen. mgr., 1979—, also v.p. and area mgr. N.Am. div. Sheraton Corp.; gen. mgr. Sheraton Balt. Inn., 1963, Sheraton Columbus (Ohio) Hotel, 1965-67, Sheraton Blackstone, Chgo., 1967-70; instr. hotel short course U. Houston, 1973-79. Mem. Dallas County Hotel and Motel Assn. (pres. 1964, 72), Tex. Hotel and Motel Assn. (pres. 1977-78), Am. Hotel and Motel Assn. (pres. Ednl. Inst. 1978-79), Dallas C. of C. (dir. 1973-75), Dallas Retail Mchts. Assn. (dir.), Dallas Central Bus. Dist. Assn. (dir.), Phi Sigma Kappa. Club: Dallas/Ft. Worth Skal (pres. 1974). Office: Sheraton Dallas Hotel Southland Center Dallas TX 75201

RATHER, LELLAND JOSEPH, educator, pathologist; b. College Station, Tex., Dec. 22, 1913; s. James Burness and Corinne (Carson) R.; A.B., Johns Hopkins, 1934, M.D., 1939; M.S., U. Chgo., 1936; m. Eleanor Edith Knight, June 20, 1940 (div. June 1958); children—Patricia, Leland, Noël; m. 2d, Ingeborg Gabrielle Arnold, June 19, 1959 (dec. 1965). Intern, Children's Hosp. Phila., 1939-40; resident Duke U. Hosp., 1940-41, Henry Ford Hosp., Detroit, 1941-42; practice medicine, specializing in pathology, San Francisco and Palo Alto, Calif., 1946—; faculty dept. pathology Stanford Sch. Medicine, Palo Alto, 1946—, prof., 1957—; cons. Surgeon Gen.'s Office, U.S. Dept. Agr., 1948-53. Mem. study sect. NIH, 1961-65. Diplomate Am. Bd. pathology. Mem. Soc. for Exptl. Biology and Medicine, Am. Soc. Exptl. Pathology, Am. Assn. History of Medicine (Welch medal 1976), Internat. Acad. History Medicine, Hist. Sci. Soc. Author: Disease, Life and Man, 1958; Mind and Body in 18th Century Medicine, 1965; Addison and the White Corpuscles: An Aspect of Nineteenth Century Biology, 1972; The Genesis of Cancer: A Study in the History of Ideas, 1978; The Dream of Self-Destruction: Wagner's Ring and the Modern World, 1979; editor, translator: (with J.M. Sharp) Therapy of the Word in Classical Antiquity, 1970. Contbr. articles profl. jours. Home: 22 Pearce Mitchell Pl Stanford CA 94305 Office: Stanford U Med Sch Med Center Stanford CA 94305

RATHGEB, PETER KARL, hotel exec.; b. Badgastein, Austraia, Aug. 14, 1935; s. Peter and Theresa (Frankenhauser) R.; m. Erica Walch, May 16, 1963; children—Nicol, Paul. Asst. mgr. Elbow Beach Hotel, Bermuda, 1960-64: mgr. Treasure Cay Hotel, Great Abaco, 1964-65; exec. asst. mgr. Kauai Surf Hotel, Hawaii, 1965-70; gen. mgr. Maui Surf Hotel, Lahaina, Hawaii, 1970—. Mem. Maui C. of C. (dir.), Hawaii Hotel Assn. (pres. Maui chpt. 1975), Kaanapali Beach Operators Assn. (pres. 1974). Office: Maui Surf Hotel Kaanapali Beach Lahaina HI 96761

RATHGEBER, ADAM JOHN, former mfg. co. exec.; b. N.Y.C., May 6, 1911; s. Adam and Caroline (Gackenheimer) R.; B.S., N.Y. U., 1935; m. Helene Reed, Mar. 11, 1943; children—Carol Ann (Mrs. Stephen Kelly), John Reed, Marilyn Sue. Accountant, Leslie Banks & Co., N.Y.C., 1936-42; pub. accountant Haskins & Sells, N.Y.C., 1946-52; v.p. finance Am. Hardware Corp., New Britain, Conn., 1952-64; sr. v.p. Emhart Corp., Farmington, Conn., 1964-77, dir., 1964-78; dir. New Britain Bank & Trust Co., Conn. Natural Gas Corp. Mem. Long Rivers council Boy Scouts Am., 1962—. Bd. dirs. Central Conn. State Coll. Found., Inc., New Britain Gen. Hosp. Served to lt. comdr. USNR, 1942-46. C.P.A., N.Y. Mem. Am. Inst. C.P.A.'s, N.Y. State Soc. C.P.A.'s, Financial Execs. Inst., Nat. Assn. Accountants, Am. Legion, Soc. Am. Wars. Clubs: Shuttle Meadow Country; New Britain; New York U. (N.Y.C.); Hartford. Home: 8 Roslyn Dr New Britain CT 06052

RATHJENS, GEORGE WILLIAM, scientist, educator; b. Fairbanks, Alaska, June 28, 1925; s. George William and Jennie (Hansen) R.; B.S., Yale, 1946; Ph.D., U. Calif., Berkeley, 1951; m. Lucy van Buttingha Wichers, Apr. 5, 1950; children—Jacqueline, Leslie, Peter. Instr. chemistry Columbia, 1950-53; staff weapons systems evaluation group Dept. Def., 1953-58; research fellow Harvard, 1958-59; staff spl. asst. to Pres. U.S. for sci. and tech., 1959-60; chief scientist Advanced Research Projects Agy., Dept. Def., 1961, dep. dir., 1961-62, dep. asst. dir. U.S. ACDA, 1962-64, spl. asst. to dir., 1964-65; dir. weapons systems evaluation div. Inst. Def. Analyses, 1965-68; prof. dept. polit. sci. Mass. Inst. Tech., 1968—. Fellow Am. Acad. Arts and Scis.; mem. A.A.A.S., Council for a Livable World (dir.), Fedn. Am. Scientists, Council on Fgn. Relations, Inst. for Strategic Studies, Sigma Xi. Office: Mass Inst Tech Cambridge MA 02139

RATHMANN, FRANZ HEINRICH, chemist, scientist, educator; b. Gotha, Fla., Apr. 8, 1904; s. Franz Karl Robert and Lina Albrecht (Mueller) R.; B.A., U. Minn., 1924, M.A., 1927, postdoctoral studies (Rockefeller fellow), 1942; postgrad. U. Ill., 1927-29; research fellow, U. Paris, 1938, U. Florence, Italy, 1938; Diplom Chemiker (Humboldt fellow), U. Goettingen, 1940, D.Natural Sci., 1941; m. Hildegard Adelheid Elfriede Friede Gerber, Jan. 25, 1949; children—Klaus Guenther John, Peter Walden Franz. Asst. prof. chemistry James Millikin U., Decatur, Ill., 1929-31; sr. sci. worker Inst. Chem. Physics, Leningrad, USSR, 1931-35, All-Union Food Research Inst. and All-Union Pharm. Research Inst., Leningrad and Moscow, USSR, 1935-37; research asso. (Naval Ordnance), U. Minn., 1947-51; asso. prof. phys. and organic chemistry U. Omaha, 1951-54, Detroit Inst. Tech., 1954-55; asso. prof. phys. and organic chemistry N.D. State U., 1955-59, prof., 1959-74, prof. emeritus, 1974—; vis. prof. phys. chemistry Mich. State U., summer 1959; vis. grad. prof. organic chemistry (Smith-Mundt fellow) U. Saigon, Viet Nam, 1962-63; adj. prof. astronomy Moorhead State U., 1974—. Del., N.D. Democratic Convs., 1960, 64, 68, 72, 76, 78. Served as lt. comdr. USNR, 1942-47. Mem. Am. Chem. Soc. (council), Ill., Minn., N.Y., Nebr., N.D., S.D. acads. sci., AAAS (del. N.D. Acad. Sci. to sect. X, mem. council 1958-76), AAUP (nat. del.), Am. Acad. Polit. and Social Sci., Philos. Soc. Washington, Deutsche Chemische Gesellshaft, Mineral. Soc. Gt. Britain, Chem. Soc. Viet Nam, Assn. Acads. Sci. (pres. 1973-76, dir.), Omaha, Fargo-Moorhead community theaters, Phi Beta Kappa, Sigma Xi (nat. del.), Phi Lambda Upsilon, Phi Kappa Phi. Unitarian (pres. Fellowship). Research in vitamin syntheses of B1 and E, arylhydroxanic acid bromides, isoxazoles, kinetics of adsorption, purine halogenation, polyhalo phenolsalts. Contbr. articles to profl. jours.; translator sci. books. Home: 1530 12th St N Fargo ND 58102

RATIGAN, WILLIAM, author, historian; b. Detroit, Nov. 7; s. Bernard Joseph and Bertie (Laing) R.; student U. Detroit, 1931, 33; A.B., U. Tenn. at Chattanooga, 1935; M.A., Mich. State U., 1961, Ph.D., 1963; m. Eleanor Dee Eldridge, Sept. 12, 1935; children—Patricia Lee (Mrs. Arthur A. Ranger), Anesta Colleen (Mrs. Arthur J. Pelton), Bobbie Laing (dec.), Shannon Leitrim. Continuity dir., producer NBC, Denver, 1937-40, pioneered news dept., 1939, supr. Far East listening post, 1940-42, mng. news editor Western div., supr. commentators and war corrs. PTO, 1942-45, news editor, scriptwriter UN Conf., 1945; short story, serial writer Curtis Pub. Co., other mags., 1946—; staff mem. NDEA Counseling and Guidance Inst. of Mich. State U., 1962; sr. extension lectr. Mich. State U., 1962—; vis. lectr. Fla. State U., 1965, U. Wis. 1966, 68, U. Miami, 1967; founder The Dockside Press, 1953. Mem.-at-large Adv. Council Naval Affairs, 1957—; cons. Smithsonian Instn., tech. devel. Great Lakes craft, 1959—. Recipient inter-collegiate Odes of Horace award, 1935; Calif. Chaparral poetry prize, 1944; named chief Ottawa tribe, Opwanan iian Kanotong, Interpreter of Dreams, 1957; recipient Distinguished Alumni award U. Tenn. at Chattanooga, 1963, Dean Jr. Coll., 1966. Mem. Am. Psychol. Assn., Blue Key (pres. 1935, Distinguished mem. 1967). Clubs: Authors (Hollywood, Calif.); Press (San Francisco); Camp Lucas Officers Open Mess (Sault Ste. Marie). Author: (poems) NBC War Poems, 1945; Great Lakes Chanteys, 1948-56; (books) Soo Canal. (foreward by Gen. Douglas MacArthur), 1954, 68; Young Mr. Big, 1955; Hiawatha and America's Mightiest Mile, 1955 (editor Song of Hiawatha, centennial facsimile edit.); The Adventures of Capt. McCargo, 1956; Straits of Mackinac, 1957; The Blue Snow, 1958; Tiny Tim Pine, 1958; Adventures of Paul Bunyan and Babe, 1958; The Long Crossing, 1959; Highways Over Broad Waters, 1959; Great Lakes Shipwrecks & Survivals, Carl D. Bradley book, 1960, Daniel J. Morrell book, 1969; Conflicts Within Counseling and Guidance, 1964; co-author Theories of Counseling, 1965, 72; School Counseling: View from Within, American School Counselors Association's First Yearbook, 1967; Great Lakes History: Steamer Edmund Fitzgerald Edition: Great Lakes Shipwrecks & Survivals, 1977. Contbr. to Great Lakes Reader, 1966, 78 Ency. Americana, 1968—. Home: 223 Park Ave Charlevoix MI 49720 Office: The Dockside Press 1 Shipyard Row Charlevoix MI 49720

RATLIFF, CHARLES EDWARD, JR., educator; b. Morven, N.C., Oct. 13, 1926; s. Charles Edward and Mary Katherine (Liles) R.; B.S., Davidson Coll., 1947; A.M., Duke, 1951, Ph.D., 1955; m. Mary Virginia Heilig, Dec. 8, 1945; children—Alice Ann, Katherine Virginia, John Charles. Instr. econs. and bus. Davidson Coll., 1947-48, asst. prof., 1948-49; scholar econs. Duke, 1949-51; mem. faculty Davidson (N.C.) Coll., 1951—, prof., 1960—, Charles A. Dana prof., 1967-77, William R. Kenan prof., 1977—; chmn. dept. econs., 1966—; prof. econs. Forman Christian Coll., Lahore, Pakistan, 1963-66, 69-70. Summer vis. prof. U. N.C. at Charlotte, 1958, 60, Appalachian State U., 1962, U. Punjab (Pakistan), 1963-64, Kinnaird Coll., Pakistan, 1965, Finance Services Acad., Pakistan, 1966; lectr. U.S. Cultural Affairs Office, East and West Pakistan, 1969-70; dir. Fulbright-Hays Group Project Abroad, Pakistan, summer 1973. Mem. Mayor's Com. on Community Relations, Davidson, 1973—, chmn., 1973-78; mem. Mecklenburg County Housing and Econ. Devel. Commn., 1975—; mem. exec. com. Mecklenburg Democratic Party, 1967-69, precinct com., 1967-69, 72-74, issues com., 1979—; nat. bd. dirs. Rural Advancement Fund of Nat. Sharecroppers Fund, Inc., 1978—. Served with USNR, 1944-46. Research fellow Inter-Univ. Com. Econ. Research on South, 1960-61. Mem. So. (exec. com. 1961-63, v.p. 1975-76), Am. econ. assns., So. Finance Assn. (exec. com. 1966-68), Nat. Tax Assn. (chmn. interstate allocation and apportionment of bus. income com. 1972-74), Assn. Asian Studies, A.A.U.P., Old Catawba Soc., Phi Beta Kappa, Omicron Delta Kappa. United Methodist (mem. conf. bd. missions 1968-72, conf. priorities com. 1972-74, commn. on planning and research 1974—, lay speaker). Author: Interstate Apportionment of Business Income for State Income Tax Purposes, 1962; co-author textbooks and monographs; contbr. to A Dictionary of the Social Sciences; also articles. Home: 301 Pinecrest St Davidson NC 28036

RATLIFF, EUGENE FIELD, corp. exec.; b. Jasper, Fla., May 8, 1919; s. Oscar Clarence and Julia (Parrish) R.; B.S. in Bus. Adminstrn., magna cum laude, U. Fla., 1941; m. Anne Tannenbaum, Mar. 9, 1946; children—Elizabeth Anne, Christine Julia, Richard Eugene. Accountant, Haskins & Sells, N.Y.C., 1941-42; with Eli Lilly & Co., Indpls., 1947—, successively mgr. internal auditing, asst. dir. accounting, asst. dir. control div., adminstrv. asst. to gen. mgr. of ops., asst. treas., 1947-56, controller, 1956-61, exec. dir. corp. devel., 1961—, treas., 1968-70, v.p. finance, dir., 1970—, v.p. Elanco Products Co. div., 1965-68; v.p. Eli Lilly Internat., dir. Lilly Industries Ltd., London, Eng., 1962-64; dir. Diamond Plastics Industries, Inc., Creative Packaging, Inc., Corn States Labs., Inc., Elizabeth Arden, Inc., IVAC Corp., Cardiac Pacemakers, Inc., Mchts. Nat. Bank & Trust Co., Inland Container Corp., Citizens Coke & Gas Utility, State Life Ins. Co. Adv. com. naval affairs 9th Naval Dist., 1957-59. Bd. dirs. Lilly Endowment, Community Hosp. of Indpls., Indpls. area chpt. ARC; trustee Butler U. Served as lt. USN, 1942-47. C.P.A., Ind. Mem. Inst. Internal Auditors (Internat. pres. 1956-57), Armed Forces Chem. Soc., Controllers, Am. Inst. C.P.A.'s, Pharm. Mfrs. Assn., Am. Accounting Assn., Financial Execs. Inst., Ind. C. of C. ((dir.). Contbr. articles profl. publs. Home: 8412 Swan's Way Indianapolis IN 46260 Office: 307 E McCarty St Indianapolis IN 46206

RATLIFF, FLOYD, scientist, educator; b. La Junta, Colo., May 1, 1919; s. Charles Frederick and Alice (Hubbard) R.; B.A. magna cum laude, Colo. Coll., 1947, D.Sc. honoris causa, 1975; M.Sc., Brown U., 1949, Ph.D., 1950; NRC postdoctoral fellow Johns Hopkins, 1950-51; m. Orma Vernon Priddy, June 10, 1942; 1 dau. Merry Alice. Instr., then asst. prof. Harvard, 1951-54; asso. Rockefeller Inst., 1954-58; mem. faculty Rockefeller U., 1958—, prof. biophysics and physiol. psychology, 1966—; cons. to govt., 1957—. Served to 1st lt. AUS, 1941-45; ETO. Decorated Bronze Star; recipient Howard Crosby Warren medal Soc. Exptl. Psychologists, 1966; Edgar D. Tillyer medal Optical Soc. Am., 1976. Fellow Am. Acad. Arts and Scis.; mem. Nat. Acad. Scis., Am. Inst. Physics, A.A.A.S., Am. Psychol. Assn., Manhattan Philos. Soc., Internat. Brain Research Orgn., Am. Philos. Soc., China Inst. Am., Oriental Ceramic Soc. (London), Oriental Ceramic Soc. (Hong Kong), Asia Soc., Japan Soc., Phi Beta Kappa, Sigma Xi. Author: Mach Bands: Quantitative Studies on Neural Networks in the Retina, 1965; also articles. Editor: Studies on Excitation and Inhibition in the Retina, 1974; editorial bd. Jour. Gen. Physiology, 1969—. Home: 500 E 63d St New York NY 10021 Office: Rockefeller U 1230 York Ave New York NY 10021

RATLIFF, LOUIS JACKSON, JR., educator; b. Cedar Rapids, Iowa, Sept. 1, 1931; s. Louis Jackson and Ruth Sarah (Sidlinger) R.; B.A., State U. Iowa, 1953; postgrad. U. Chgo., 1953-54; M.A., State U. Iowa, 1958, Ph.D. (Nat. Sci. Grad. fellow), 1961. Lectr., Ind. U., 1961-63; faculty U. Calif. at Riverside, 1963—, prof., 1969—. Served with USAF, 1953-57. NSF grantee in math. research, 1965-68, 71—. Mem. Am. Math. Soc., Phi Beta Kappa. Democrat. Seventh-Day Adventist. Home: 3139 Newell Dr Riverside CA 92507

RATLIFF, WILLIAM DURRAH, lawyer; b. Gainesville, Tex., Nov. 17, 1921; s. William Durrah and Fay (Tippit) R.; B.B.A., U. Tex., 1943, LL.B., 1948; m. Barbara Warner, June 20, 1947; children—William Durrah III, Robert Warner, Bryan Prichard, Barbara Louise, Edwin Brent, Dorothy Jeanne. Admitted to Tex. bar, 1948, since practiced in Ft. Worth; partner firm Shannon, Gracey, Ratliff & Miller, and predecessors, 1968—. Dir. Aztec Mfg. Co., Millers Ins. Group. Bd. dirs. Southwestern Expn. and Fat Stock Show. Certified in estate planning and probate law Tex. Bd. Legal Splzn. Fellow Tex. Bar Found., Am. Coll. Probate Counsel. Clubs: River Crest Country, Fort Worth. Home: 5820 El Campo Fort Worth TX 76107 Office: Continental Nat Bank Bldg Fort Worth TX 76102

RATNER, GERALD, lawyer; b. Chgo., Dec. 17, 1913; s. Peter I. and Sarah (Soreson) R.; Ph.B., U. Chgo., 1935, J.D. cum laude, 1937; m. Eunice Payton, June 18, 1948. Admitted to Ill. bar, 1937, since practiced in Chgo.; partner firm Gould & Ratner and predecessor firm, 1949—; officer, dir. Henry Crown & Co., Hoffman Group, Inc., Material Service Corp., Lindrick Corp., Univ. Exchange Corp., Pavilion Corp., Colonnade Corp., SCNO Barge Lines, Inc.; lectr., writer on real estate law. Mem. citizens bd. U. Chgo. Served to capt. AUS, 1942-46. Mem. Am., Ill., Chgo. bar assns., Order of Coif, Phi Beta Kappa. Home: 900 Lake Shore Dr Chicago IL 60611 Office: 300 W Washington St Chicago IL 60606

RATNER, LAZARUS GERSHON, physicist; b. Chgo., Sept. 14, 1923; s. Bernard Berl and Esther (Pearlsweig) R.; student U. Chgo., 1941-42; A.B., U. Cal. at Berkeley, 1948, M.A., 1950; m. Joyce Sylvia Rosenberg, Mar. 1, 1953; children—Toni Gale, Daniel Scott, Joseph Elliot. Physicist, Lawrence Radiation Lab., Berkeley, Calif., 1950-60; physicist Argonne Nat. Lab., 1960—, asso. group leader physics group particle accelerator div., 1966—; cons. to industry, 1954—; vis. Scientist CERN, Geneva, Switzerland, 1971-72. Served with AUS, 1943-46. Recipient medal for distinguished performance at Argonne Nat. Lab., U. Chgo., 1976. Jewish (pres. congregation 1966-67). Mem. B'nai B'rith (pres. lodge 1965). Discoverer heavy resonance particle N 3245, 1965, evidence for internal structure within the proton, 1966; pub. evidence for fireball model for particle prodn., 1967. Home: 22 W 280 Glen Valley Rd Glen Ellyn IL 60137 Office: 9700 S Cass St Argonne IL 60439. *It seems to me that mankind has set up ideals and in striving to reach these ideals, we consciously or subconsciously give purpose to our exestence. I think these ideals or goals for which we strive are those attributes which we have clothed in a concept of God.*

RATNER, MILTON DUNNE, transp. co. exec.; b. Oak Park, Ill., Mar. 1, 1918; s. Harry and Sadie (Kane) R.; B.S., Northwestern U., 1939, M.D., 1943; children—John, Gary, Francine. Chmn. bd. Midwest Emery Freight System, Inc., Chgo., Rentar Industries, Inc.; dir. Rentar Trailer and Container Leasing Co., Ford City Bank. Bd. overseers Jewish Theol. Sem. Am.; bd. dirs. Am. Israel Cultural Found., N.Y.C., Spertus Coll. of Judaica, Chgo., Chgo. Med. Sch., Joslyn Art Museum, Omaha, Indpls. Mus. Art; Mus. Contemporary Art, Chgo.; trustee Roosevelt U., N.Y.C. Opera; mem. governing bd. Art Inst. of Chgo. Served to capt. M.C. U.S. Army, 1942-45. Mem. Am. Trucking Assn. (com. chmn.), Irregular Common and Contract Carriers Assn. (pres. 1959-65), Internat. Inst. Refrigeration, Alpha Omega Alpha. Jewish. Home: 2209 Casey Key Rd Nokomis FL 33555 Office: Essex House Suite 4001 160 Central Park S New York NY 10019

RATNOFF, OSCAR DAVIS, physician, educator; b. N.Y.C., Aug. 23, 1916; s. Hyman L. and Ethel (Davis) R.; A.B., Columbia, 1936, M.D., 1939; m. Marian Foreman, Mar. 31, 1945; children—William Davis, Martha. Intern, Johns Hopkins Hosp., Balt., 1939-40; Austin fellow in physiology Harvard Med. Sch., Boston, 1940-41; asst. resident Montefiore Hosp., N.Y.C., 1942; resident Goldwater Meml. Hosp., N.Y.C., 1942-43; asst. in medicine Columbia Coll. Phys. and Surg., N.Y.C., 1942-46; fellow in medicine Johns Hopkins, 1946-48, instr. medicine, 1948-50, instr. bacteriology, 1949-50; asst. prof. medicine Case Western Res. U., Cleve., 1950-56, asso. prof., 1956-61, prof., 1961—; asst. physician Univ. Hosp., Cleve., 1952-56, asso. physician, 1956-67, physician, 1967—. Career investigator Am. Heart Assn., 1960—. Served to maj. M.C., Ind. 1943-46. Recipient Henry Moses award Montefiore Hosp., 1949, Distinguished Achievement award Modern Medicine, 1967; James F. Mitchell award, 1971; Murray Thelin award Nat. Hemophilia Found., 1971; H.P. Smith award Am. Soc. Clin. Pathology, 1975; Joseph Mather Smith prize Columbia Coll. Phys. and Surg., 1976. Fellow A.C.P. (John Phillips award 1974); mem. A.M.A., Am. Fedn. Clin. Research (emeritus), Nat. Acad. Scis., Soc. Scholars of Johns Hopkins U., Am. Soc. Clin. Investigation (emeritus), Central Soc. Clin. Research, Assn. Am. Physicians, Am. Soc. Hematology (Dameshek award 1972), Internat. Soc. Hematology, Internat. Soc. Thrombosis, Am. Physiol. Soc., Am. Soc. Biol. Chemists, Sigma Xi, Alpha Omega Alpha. Author: Bleeding Syndromes, 1960. Mem. editorial bd. Jour. Lab. Clin. Medicine, 1956-62, Circulation, 1961-65, Blood, 1963-69, 78—, Am. Jour. Physiology, 1966-72, Jour. Applied Physiology, 1966-72, Jour. Lipid Research, 1967-69, Jour. Clin. Investigation, 1969-71, Circulation Research, 1970-75, Annals Internal Medicine, 1973-76, Perspectives in Biology and Medicine, 1974—. Contbr. articles to med. jours. Home: 2916 Sedgewick Rd Shaker Heights OH 44120 Office: University Hospitals of Cleve Cleveland OH 44106

RATTNER, ABRAHAM, artist; b. Poughkeepsie, N.Y., July 9, 1895; s. Herman M. and Sarah (Zukerman) R.; student Corcoran Sch. Art, 1913-15, George Washington U., 1913-14, Pa. Acad. Fine Arts, 1915-17, Ecole des Beaux Arts, Paris, 1921-23, Ransom Acad., Paris, 1923-24, Acad. de la Grande Chaumiere, 1924-25, Sorbonne, Paris, 1925-26; m. Bettina Bedwell (dec. Apr. 1947); m. 2d, Esther Gentle, 1949. European traveling scholar Pa. Acad. Fine Arts, 1920, Italy, 1920, France, 1920-40; one-man shows Paris, Brussels, U.S.; exhibited Salon d' Autumn. Salon des Independants, des Surr-Independants, Paris, Julien Levy Gallery, N.Y.C., 1936-41; group shows include Miniature groups; mem. staff New Sch. for Social Research, Art Students League, N.Y.C., 1948-52; artist-in-residence, prof. painting U. Ill., 1952-54; vis. artist Yale, Pa. Acad. Fine Arts, Bklyn. Mus.; artist-in-residence Mich. State U., 1954-60; commd., executed in Paris stained glass window design for Chgo. New Loop Synagogue, 1959. Recipient Temple gold medal Nat. Exhbn. Am. Painting, Pa. Acad. Fine Arts, 1945; 1st prize Tecla Pearls exhbn. Am. Painting, 1946; purchase prize U. Ill., Nat. Exhbn. Am. Painting, 1948; 1st prize, Corcoran gold medal Corcoran Gallery Art, nat. biennial show, 1953; Citation of Honor and retrospective exhbn. Temple U., 1954. Mem. Societe des Arts Decoratif Paris; represented in permanent collections Met. Mus. Art, N.Y.C., Mus. Modern Art, Whitney Mus., N.Y.C., Pa. Acad. Fine Arts, Chgo. Art Inst., Phila. Mus. Art, Mus. Art Balt., Des Moines Inst. Art, Albright Galleries. Buffalo, univ. and pvt. collections. Home: 8 W 13th St New York City NY 10011 also 7 Rue Antoine Chantin Paris 14e France Office: Kennedy Galleries Inc 20 E 56th St New York City NY 10022

RATTRAY, MAURICE, JR., educator; b. Seattle, Sept. 16, 1922; s. Maurice and Margaret (Rae) R.; B.S., Calif. Inst. Tech., 1944, M.S., 1947, Ph.D., 1951; m. Mary Louise Wolsey, June 9, 1951; children—Julia Westwood, Maurice III, Gordon Winfield. Mem. faculty U. Wash., Seattle, 1950—, prof. oceanography, 1962—, chmn. dept., 1968-78; cons. U.S. Naval Oceanographic Office, 1968-76; mem. sci. adv. com. Nat. Acad. Scis., 1969-72, ocean sci. com., 1971-74; mem. exec. com. Joint Oceanographic Instns. Deep Earth Sampling, 1968-78, chmn., 1969, 76-78; mem. environ. pollutant movement and transformation adv. com. Sci. Adv. Bd., U.S. EPA, 1976-78. Rossby fellow Woods Hole Oceanographic Instn., 1966-67. Mem. Am. Soc. Limnology and Oceanography (pres. 1965-66), Am. Geophys. Union, Sigma Xi. Editorial bd. Jour. Marine Research, 1966-73; cons. editor Oceanography, McGraw-Hill Ency. Sci. and Tech., 1975—; mem. editorial bd. Estuarine and Coastal Marine Sci., 1971—. Developed theory of ocean internal tide generation by bathymetric coupling with surface tide at the continental shelf break; theoretical models and classification systems for estuary currents and salinity distbns.; unified theory for long period wave motions in oceans; baroclinic ocean circulation. Home: 1315 Lexington Way E Seattle WA 98112 Office: Dept Oceanography WB-10 U Wash Seattle WA 98195

RATZLAFF, JAMES WILLIAM, mut. fund exec.; b. Wichita, Kans., May 21, 1936; s. William McKinley and Lois (Stratton) R.; B.S. in Geology, U. Kans., 1958; J.D. with honors, George Washington U., 1968; m. Jane Penington, Apr. 11, 1964; children—James William, Susan. Dir. investment cos. Nat. Assn. Securities Dealers, Washington, 1962-69; admitted to Va. bar, 1968, D.C. bar, 1969; v.p. Capital Research and Mgmt. Co., Los Angeles, 1969—; exec. v.p. AMCAP Fund, Inc.; v.p., sec. Am. Mut. Fund, Inc.; v.p., dir. New Perspective Fund, Inc.; vice chmn., dir. Bond Fund Am., Inc.; vice chmn., trustee Cash Mgmt. Trust Am.; sec. Capital Research Co.; v.p. Investment Co. Am.; chmn. state liaison com. Investment Co. Inst., 1972-73; mem. investment cos. com. Nat. Assn. Securities Dealers. Served to 1st lt. USMC, 1958-62. U.S. Navy ROTC scholar, 1954-58. Mem. Fed. Bar Assn., Sierra Club, Delta Upsilon. Republican. Clubs: Nat. Lawyers (Washington); Los Angeles Athletic. Address: 333 S Hope St Los Angeles CA 90071

RAU, RALPH RONALD, physicist; b. Tacoma, Sept. 1, 1920; s. Ralph Campbell Rau and Ida (Montgall) Rau May; B.S. in Physics, Coll. Puget Sound, 1941; M.S. in Physics, Calif. Inst. Tech., 1943, Ph.D. in Physics, 1948; m. Maryjane Uhrlaub, June 2, 1944; children—Whitney Leslie, Littie Elise. Asst. prof. physics Princeton U., 1947-56; Fulbright research prof. physics Ecole Polytechnique, Paris, France, 1954-55; physicist Brookhaven Nat. Lab., Upton, N.Y., 1956-66, chmn. dept. physics, 1966-70, asso. dir. for Physics, 1970—; adj. prof. U. Wyo. Trustee U. Puget Sound, 1978—. Named Alumnus Cum laude, U. Puget Sound, 1968. Mem. Am. Phys. Soc., AAAS. Office: Brookhaven Nat Lab Upton NY 11973

RAUB, STUART HAMILTON, distbg. co. exec.; b. Lancaster, Pa., Dec. 20, 1910; s. Stuart Hamilton and Beulah (Groff) R.; grad. Widener Coll., 1930; m. Marie Thomson, Nov. 14, 1931; children—Stuart Hamilton, Peter Thomson, Marie Thomson. With Raub Supply Co., Lancaster, 1931—, sec., 1936-46, treas., 1946-58, pres., 1958-72, chmn. bd., 1972-76; pres. Raub Credit Corp., 1957—; dir. Fulton Bank, First Fed. Savs. & Loan Assn. Trustee Lancaster Country Day Sch., Widener Coll. Served to lt. USNR, 1943-46. Episcopalian. Clubs: Lancaster Country; Quentin (Pa.) Riding; Hamilton. Home: RD 3 Lititz PA 17543 Office: James and Mulberry Sts Lancaster PA 17506

RAUBITSCHEK, ANTONY ERICH, educator; b. Vienna, Austria, Dec. 4, 1912; s. Hugo Victor and Gertrude Raubitschek; Ph.D., U. Vienna, 1935; postdoctoral Austrian Archaeol. Inst., Athens, Greece, 1936-38; m. Isabelle R. Kelly, July 12, 1941; children—John, Agathokleia (Mrs. K. Luckner), Marita (Mrs. P.T. Hopmann), Andrew. Came to U.S., 1938, naturalized, 1943. Instr. classics Yale, 1942-44, asst. prof., 1945-47; asso. prof. Princeton U., 1947-63; prof. Stanford U., 1963— prof. emeritus, 1978—, Sadie Deenham Patek prof. humanities, 1974-78; mem. Inst. Advanced Study, Princeton, 1938-42, 44-45, 54-55; vis. prof. Merton Coll., Oxford (Eng.) U., 1960-61, also univs. Bonn (Germany), Heidelberg (Germany), Cologne (Germany), Athens; mem. mag. com. Am. Sch. Classical Studies, Athens, vis. prof., 1976-77. Mem. Archaeol. Inst. Am., Am. Philol. Assn., Philol. Assn. Pacific Coast, Deutsches Archäeologisches Institut, Oesterreichisches Archaeologisches Institut. Democrat. Author: Early Christian Epitaphs from Athens, 1945; Dedications from the Athenian Akropolis, 1949; Early Cretan Armor, 1972. Contbr. profl. jours. Home: 475 Embarcadero Rd Palo Alto CA 94301 Office: Dept Classics Stanford U Stanford CA 94305

RAUCH, BASIL, historian; b. Dubuque, Iowa, Sept. 6, 1908; s. William H. and Elizabeth (Wordehoff) R.; A.B., U. Notre Dame, 1929; postgrad. drama and English, Yale, 1929-33; Ph.D. in History, Columbia, 1946; m. Roberta Bruce Brown, 1936 (div. 1963); m. 2d, Elizabeth Flower Hird, 1964. Tchr. various pvt. schs., 1931-40; lectr. history Columbia U. extension, 1940-41; instr. in history Barnard Coll., Columbia U., 1941-43, asst. prof., 1946-49, asso. prof., exec. officer dept. history, 1949-52, prof. history, 1952—, chmn. Am. studies program, 1952-66, chmn. dept. history, 1966-70; faculty Seminar in Am. Studies, Salzburg, 1955, 79; Walter Prescott Webb lectr. U. Tex., 1971. Chmn. acad. adv. council Marlboro Coll., 1956-63. Served as lt. USNR, on faculty U.S. Naval Acad., Annapolis, Md., 1943-46. Recipient Edmund Campion award for service to soc. Campion Sch., 1972. Mem. Am. Hist. Assn., Nat. Archives Assos., Thimble Islands Assn. (gov.), Phi Beta Kappa (hon.). Clubs: Century, Yale, New York; Lawn, New Haven. Author: The History of the New Deal, 1933-38, 1944, 63, 75; American Interest in Cuba: 1848-1855, 1947, 73; Roosevelt: From Munich to Pearl Harbor, 1950, rev. edit., 1967, 75; Empire for Liberty: The Genesis and Growth of the U.S. of America, 2 vols. (with Dumas Malone), 1960, 6 vols., 1965; also hist. articles. Editor: Franklin D. Roosevelt: Selected Speeches, Messages, Press Conferences and Letters, 1957. Home: Route 3 Box 44 Killingworth CT 06417 Office: Dept of History Barnard Coll Columbia U New York City NY 10027

RAUCH, CHARLES E., banker; b. Lebanon, Pa., Jan. 26, 1907; s. Charles Ellwood and Elizabeth Augusta (Thompson) R.; grad. Mercersburg (Pa.) Acad., 1926; A.B., Dartmouth, 1930; spl. course Harvard Grad. Sch. Bus. Adminstrn., 1944; postgrad. Grad. Sch. Bus. Adminstrn. N.Y. U., 1947-51; m. Mildred Nicoil, Dec. 28, 1940; children—Katrina (Mrs. Alexander Finley), Charles E. With Wood, Struthers & Co., investment bankers, N.Y.C., 1930-41, New Eng. rep., 1936-41; asst. treas. New Haven Savs. Bank, 1941-46; New Eng. rep. Drexel & Co., investment bankers, Phila., N.Y.C., 1947-52; treas., v.p. Conn. Savs. Bank, New Haven, 1952-67, pres., treas., 1967—, chmn., 1970-72, also trustee; investment com.; past pres. Mut. Investment Fund Conn., Inc. Instr., Brown U. Grad. Sch. Savs. Banking, 1961-64, 68. Mem. Citizens Action Com., New Haven; dir. Taxpayers Research Council New Haven. Bd. dirs. Family Service New Haven; trustee Keene Valley (N.Y.) Hosp. Served to 1st lt. USAAF, 1942-46; maj. Res. ret. Mem. financial Analysts Fedn., Am. Finance Assn., Savs. Bank Assn. Conn., Nat. Assn. Mut. Savs. Banks, (past chmn. com. on corporate securities and portfolio mgmt.), Ex-mems. Assn. Squadron A., S.R., Pa. Soc., Huegenot Soc. Pa., Alpha Delta Phi. Episcopalian (sr. warden). Kiwanian. Clubs: Graduates Assn. (New Haven); Dartmouth (Hartford and New Haven); Ausable (St. Huberts, N.Y.). Co-author: Trusteeship of American Endowments, 1936. Home: 171 Main St Farmington CT 06032 Office: 900 Chapel St New Haven CT 06510

RAUCH, GEORGE WASHINGTON, lawyer; b. Marion, Ind., July 18, 1919; s. George W. and Emma Asenath (Nolen) R.; B.S., Ind. U., 1941; LL.B., U. Va., 1947; m. Audrey M. Cranfield; Feb. 28, 1943 (div.); children—George Washington III, Nancy Lynn, Jane Nolen; m. 2d, Dorothy D. Farlow, June 26, 1970. Admitted to Ind. bar, 1948, Ill. bar, 1957, Mass. and Fla. bars, 1972; practice law Batton, Harker and Rauch and predecessor firms, Marion, Ind., 1948-57; v.p., gen. counsel The Greyhound Corp., Chgo., 1957-61; mem. firm Hubachek, Kelly, Rauch, & Kirby, and predecessor firms, Chgo., 1961—, pres., 1972—; gen. counsel Household Finance Corp., 1967-78, dir., 1967—, mem. fin. com., 1969—, exec. com., 1972—; dir. Edwards Engring. Corp., Constrn. Materials Co., Downtown United Furniture Co.; dir. Burch Co., 1972—, pres., 1975—; dir. 1242 Lake Shore Dr. Corp., 1971—, pres., 1973-74. Mem. Nat. Conf. Commrs. on Uniform Laws, 1955-57. Served as aviator USNR, 1941-45, lt. comdr. Fellow Am. Bar Found.; mem. Am., Ill., Ind., Chgo., Mass., Fla., 7th Fed. Circuit bar assns., Raven Soc., Am. Judicature Soc., Phi Delta Phi, Delta Tau Delta. Mason (Shriner). Clubs: University, Saddle and Cycle, Racquet, Mid-Am. (dir. 1976—, v.p. 1979—), Plaza (Chgo.) (dir. 1976—); Sankaty Head Golf, Casino (Nantucket, Mass.). Home: 1242 Lake Shore Dr Chicago IL 60610 also PO Box 149 Siasconset MA 02564 also 455 Australian Ave Palm Beach FL 33480 Office: 3100 Prudential Plaza Chicago IL 60601

RAUCH, HARRY ERNEST, educator; b. Trenton, N.J., Nov. 9, 1925; s. James and Sara Edna (Litt) R.; student Calif. Inst. Tech., 1943-44; A.B., Princeton U., 1946, M.A., Ph.D., 1947; m. Helen Farber; children—Marc, James, Ann, Eve. Mem. Inst. Advanced Study, Princeton, N.J., 1949-51; asst. prof. math. U. Pa., 1952-56; asso. prof. Yeshiva U., N.Y.C., 1958-60, prof., 1960-68, asso. dean, 1964-67, faculty prof. math., 1969-71; prof. math. grad. div. City U. N.Y., 1971, disting. prof., 1972-79; prof. math. Coll. City N.Y., 1968-69. Served with AUS, 1944. NSF sr. postdoctoral fellow, 1958-59. Mem. Phi Beta Kappa, Sigma Xi. Author: Geodesics and Curvature in Differential Geometry in the Large, 1959; Elliptic Functions, Theta Functions, and Riemann Surfaces, 1973; Theta Functions with Applications to Riemann Surfaces, 1974. Contbr. articles to math. jours. Home: 77 Hillcrest Ave White Plains NY 10607 Office: Grad Sch City U NY 33 W 42d St New York NY 10036 Died June 18, 1979

RAUCH, IRMENGARD, linguist, educator; b. Dayton, Ohio, Apr. 17, 1933; d. Konrad and Elsa (Knott) R.; student Nat. U. Mex., summer 1954; B.S. with honors, U. Dayton, 1955; M.A., Ohio State U., 1957; postgrad. (Fulbright fellow) U. Munich, W. Ger., 1957-58; Ph.D., U. Mich., 1962; m. Gerald F. Carr, June 12, 1965; children—Christopher, Gregory. Instr., German and linguistics U. Wis., Madison, 1962-63, asst. prof., 1963-66; asso. prof. German, U. Pitts., 1966-68; asso. prof. German and linguistics U. Ill., Urbana, 1968-72, prof., 1972-79; prof. U. Calif., Berkeley, 1979—. Named outstanding woman on campus U. Ill. sta. WILL, 1975; research grantee U. Wis., summer 1966, U. Ill., 1975-79, Eastern Ill. U., 1976, Nat. Endowment Humanities, 1978; travel grantee NSF, Linguistics Soc. Am., 1972. Mem. Linguistics Soc. Am., MLA, Am. Assn. Tchrs. German, Societas Linguistica Europaea, Internat. Linguistic Assn., AAAS, AAUP, Phonetics Assn., Semiotic Soc. Am., Alpha Sigma Tau, Delta Phi Alpha. Author: The Old High German Diphthongization: A Description of a Phonemic Change, 1967. Editor: (with others): Approaches in Linguistic Methodology, 1967, Spanish edit., 1974; Der Heliand, 1974; Linguistic Method: Essays in Honor of Herbert Penzl, 1979. Contbr. articles to profl. jours. Home: 200 Cherry Ln Villa Grove IL 61956 Office: Dept German U Calif Berkeley CA 94720

RAUCH, JOHN HAROLD, banker, economist, real estate developer; b. Vienna, Austria, Oct. 23, 1930; s. Carl Leon and Julia (Buchwald) R.; brought to U.S., 1940, naturalized, 1945; B.A. in Econs., U. Calif. at Los Angeles, 1954; LL.D., U. So. Calif., 1961; m. Ruth Shuster, June 20, 1954; children—Daniel, Mark. With Bank of Am. in Los Angeles and Berkeley, 1948-53; with Union Bank, Los Angeles, 1957-68, v.p., 1968-74; vice chmn. bd. Beverly Hills Nat. Bank (Calif.), 1970-74; pres. Beverly Hills Bancorp.; vice chmn. bd. Western Diversified Equities, Los Angeles, 1968-74; cons. economist, real estate developer, 1975—. Mem. Am. Jewish Com., 1965—; mem. exec. bd. Calif. Job Devel., 1967-72; mem. community relations com. Los Angeles Jewish Fedn., 1966-71; bd. dirs. Herzl Schs., Los Angeles, 1975—; bd. visitors U. Judaism, Los Angeles, 1979—; del. Prime Minister's Econ. Conf., Jerusalem, 1968, 73. Served to 1st lt. AUS, 1954. Mem. Calif. Israel C. of C. (pres. 1962-67), Zionist Orgn. Am., Phi Alpha Delta. Republican. Jewish. Home: 423 N Palm Dr Beverly Hills CA 90210 Office: 8200 Wilshire Blvd Beverly Hills CA 90210

RAUCH, JOHN KEISER, JR., architect; b. Phila., Oct. 23, 1930; s. John Keiser and Marjorie (Gretz) R.; student Wesleyan U., Middletown, Conn., 1948-51; B.Arch., U. Pa., 1957; m. Carol Pfaff, Mar. 11, 1953; children—John David, Charles Daniel, Kathryn Mari, Peter, Carol Anne. Draftsman, Cope & Lippincott, Phila., 1957-60; architect Venturi and Short, Phila., 1960-64; partner Venturi and Rauch, Architects and Planners, Phila., 1964—; instr. U. Pa. Grad. Sch. Fine Arts, 1969-70. Served to 1st lt. USAR, 1951-53. Fellow AIA, mem. Pa. Soc. Architects, Constrn. Specifications Inst. Democrat. Home: 2067 Harts Ln Conshohocken PA 19428 Office: 333 S 16th St Philadelphia PA 19102

RAUCH, LAWRENCE LEE, educator, engr.; b. Los Angeles, May 1, 1919; s. James Lee and Mabel (Thompson) R.; A.B., U. So. Calif., 1941; student Cornell U., 1941; A.M., Princeton, 1948, Ph.D., 1949; m. Norma Ruth Cable, Dec. 15, 1961; children—Lauren, Maury Rauch. Instr. math. Princeton, 1943- 49; faculty U. Mich., 1949—, prof. aerospace engring., 1953—, chmn. Instrumentation Engring. Program, 1952-63, Computer, Info. and Control Engring. Program, 1971-76, asso. chmn. dept. elec. and computer engring., 1972-75; vis. prof. Ecole Nationale Supérieure de l'Aéronautique, Toulouse, France, 1970, Jet Propulsion Lab. and Calif. Inst. Tech., Pasadena, 1977—, U. Tokyo, 1978. Cons. govt. and industry, 1946—; chmn. telemetering working group, panel test range instrumentation, Research and Devel. Bd. Dept. Def., 1952-53; mem. exec. com. Nat. Telemetering Conf., 1959-64; Western Hemisphere program chmn. 1st Internat. Telemetering Conf., London, Eng., 1963, Internat. Telemetering Conf., U.S.A., 1967; supr. air blast telemetering, Bikini, 1946; mem. project non-linear differential equations Office Naval Research, 1947-49; mem. research adv. com. on communications, instrumentation and data processing NASA, 1963-68. Recipient award for outstanding contbn. Army and Navy, 1947, annual award Nat. Telemetering Conf., 1960; Donald P. Eckman award for distinguished achievement in edn. Instrument Soc. Am., 1966. Fellow IEEE (spl. award contbns. radio telemetry 1957; adminstrv. com. profl. group space electronics and telemetry 1958-64), AAAS, Explorers Club; mem. Am. Math. Soc., Soc. Engring. Edn., Am. Inst. Aeros. and Astronautics, Soc. for Indsl. and Applied Math., A.A.U.P., U. Mich. Research Club, Phi Beta Kappa, Sigma Xi, Phi Eta Sigma, Phi Kappa Phi. Author: Radio Telemetry, 1956; also numerous sci. articles and papers. Developed electronic commutation telemeter, 1943-46. Address: 759 N Citrus Ave Los Angeles CA 90038

RAUCH, PAUL DAVID, advt. exec., TV producer; b. Jersey City, Dec. 23, 1933; s. Harry and Ruth (Reyman) R.; B.A., U. Calif., Los Angeles, 1954; M.B.A., Harvard U., 1956; m. Marie Burda, Oct. 1, 1975; children—Stacie Jennifer, Tyler Meade. Staff dir. live TV programs CBS-TV, 1956-59; supr. TV programs Procter & Gamble Co., 1960-70; v.p. in charge E. Coast programming CBS-TV, 1970-72; exec. TV producer Young & Rubicam Inc., N.Y.C., 1972—. Served with AUS, 1955-56. Recipient Emmy award Nat. Acad. TV Arts and Scis., 1975, 76; Emmy award nomination for show Another World, NBC-TV, 1976-77 and NBC Bicentennial Spl. Rachel Jackson, 1976. Office: Young and Rubicam 285 Madison Ave New York NY 10016

RAUCH, PHILIP, mfg. co. exec.; b. N.Y.C., Sept. 25, 1911; s. Philip and Frances (Zahn) R.; student Lehigh U., 1929-32; B.S. in Bus. Adminstrn., N.Y. U., 1935; m. Louise Fairchild, June 15, 1949; 1 dau., Patricia. Pres., Ideal Corp., Bklyn., 1932-71; dir. Parker Hannifin Corp., Cleve., 1972—, chmn. exec. com., 1974-75, 77—, chmn. bd., 1975-77; dir. Citizens Bank of Bklyn., Fairchild Publs. Mem. vis. com. Lehigh U. Bus. Sch., N.Y. U. Bus. Sch. Recipient L-in-Life award Lehigh U., 1976. Mem. Am. Mgmt. Assn., Young Pres's. Orgn. (founding; chmn. N.Y.C. chpt. 1951-52), Chief Execs. Forum Adult Edn. Center. Republican. Clubs: Met. (N.Y.C.); Meadow Brook (Jericho, N.Y.); Pine Tree (Delray Beach, Fla.). Home: 347 Wheatley Rd Old Westbury NY 11568 Office: 1000 Pennsylvania Ave Brooklyn NY 11207

RAUCH, R. STEWART, JR., ins. exec.; b. Villanova, Pa., July 15, 1914; A.B., Princeton U., 1936; LL.B., U. Pa., 1941; LL.D. (hon.), Swarthmore Coll., 1970; D.P.S. (hon.), Temple U., 1979; m. Frances S. Brewster, June 7, 1941; 5 children. Intern on assignment to research div. Social Security Bd., and to office Senator Carter Glass, Nat. Inst. Pub. Affairs, Washington, 1936-37; asst. to factory supt. Campbell Soup Co., Camden, N.J., 1937-38; asso. firm Barnes, Dechert, Price, Myers & Clark, 1941-42, 45-49; v.p. Phila. Sav. Fund Soc., 1949-53, exec. v.p., 1953-55, pres., 1955-71, chmn., 1971-79, bd. mgrs., also trustee; chmn. exec. com. Gen. Accident Group of Ins. Cos., Phila., 1979—; dir., chmn. audit com. Bell Telephone Co. of Pa., Penjerdel Corp., Phila. Contributionship for Ins. of Houses from Loss by Fire, Phila. Contributionship Ins. Co., Penn Central Co., 1969-71, Hosp. Council Phila., 1953-55, Hosp. Survey Com., 1960-73; chmn. exec. com., dir. Camden Fire Ins. Assn., Pa. Gen. Ins. Co., Potomac Ins. Co.; trustee Com. for Econ. Devel.; chmn. exec. com. of U.S. br. Gen. Accident Fire & Life Assurance Corp., Ltd.; trustee, chmn. exec. com., mem. mktg. com., vice chmn. nominating com., chmn. gen. com. of bd. Penn Mut. Life Ins. Co. Trustee, Acad. Natural Scis., 1949-55, Acad. Music Phila., Inc., Bur. Mcpl. Research, 1950-53; chmn. bd., dir., chmn. exec. com. Food Distbn. Center; commr. Delaware River Port Authority, 1966-71, vice-chmn., 1969-71; mem. exec. com., dir. Greater Phila. Partnership; mem. City Planning Commn., 1952-55; bd. dirs. Phila. Orch. Assn. Served with USN, 1942-45; MTO, PTO. Mem. Am. Philos. Soc., Greater Phila. C. of C. (gen. chmn. 1973-74, mem. exec. com., dir.), Mut. Savs. Banks Assn. of Pa. (pres. 1971-73), Nat. Assn. Mut. Savs. Banks (pres. 1963-64, dir.), Phila. Com. on Fgn. Relations, Phi Beta Kappa. Home: 835 Mount Moro Rd Villanova PA 19085 Office: 1212 Market St Philadelphia PA 19107

RAUCH, RUDOLPH STEWART, III, journalist; b. Bryn Mawr, Pa., July 5, 1943; s. Rudolph Stewart and Frances (Brewster) R.; B.A., Princeton U., 1965; m. Sheila Prentice, Oct. 31, 1972; 1 son, Edward Prentice. Corr., Time mag., N.Y.C., 1969-70, Bonn, W. Ger., 1970-71, Saigon, Vietnam, 1971-72, Rio De Janeiro, Brazil, 1972-74, Buenos Aires, Argentina, 1974-76, Atlanta, 1976-79, dep. chief of corrs., N.Y.C., 1979—. Club: Phila. Office: Time-Life Bldg New York NY 10020

RAUCHER, HERMAN, novelist, screen writer; b. Bklyn., Apr. 13, 1928; s. Benjamin Brooks and Sophie (Weinshank) R.; B.S., N.Y. U., 1949; m. Mary Kathryn Martinet, Apr. 20, 1960; children—Jacqueline Leigh, Jennifer Brooke. Asst. trade ad mgr. 20th Century Fox Films, N.Y.C., 1950-54; copy dir. Walt Disney Studios, N.Y.C.; copy supr. Calkins & Holden Advt., N.Y.C., 1955-57; copy dir., v.p., dir. Reach McClinton Advt., N.Y.C., 1957-63; v.p., creative dir. Maxon Advt., N.Y.C., 1963-64; creative supr. Gardner Advt., N.Y.C., 1963-65; v.p. advt., cons. Benton & Bowles Advt., N.Y.C., 1965-67; author: Summer of 42 (novel and screenplay), Watermelon Man (novel and screenplay), Ode to Billy Joe (novel and screenplay), A Glimpse of Tiger (novel), Sweet November (screenplay), The Other Side of Midnight (screenplay), Class of 44 (screenplay), Hieronymus Merkin (screenplay), There Should Have Been Castles (novel), 1979; writer of various dramas appearing on TV in Studio One, Alcoa Hour and Goodyear Playhouse; pres. Bearfilm Prodns., 1971-76. Served with U.S. Army, 1950-52. Mem. Writers Build Am., Authors League Am., Am. Film Inst., Dramatists Build, Acad. of Motion Picture Arts and Scis.

RAUEN, ARNOLD JOHN, banker; b. Spring Grove, Ill., Feb. 24, 1907; s. Matthias J. and Catherine J. (Freund) R.; B.S., Jasper Coll., 1928; m. Leona Regner, Aug. 29, 1931; 1 dau., Barbara Rauen Hettermann. Supt., St. Charles Sch. for Boys, 1935-41; adminstr. war fin. com. U.S. Treasury Dept., 1941-46, dir. savs. bond div. for Ill., 1946-68; chmn., pres., chief exec. officer, dir. Bank for Savs. and Loan Assns., Chgo., 1968—; pres. McHenry Personal Loan Corp., 1955—; founder, dir. emeritus McHenry Savs. and Loan Assn.; dir. Liberty Savs. & Loan Assn., Chgo. Mem. McHenry Twp. Bd., 1932; chmn. McHenry Fire and Police Pension Bd., 1968-76; justice of peace, 1932—; mem. president's council Marmion Mil. Acad.; bd. dirs. Newman Found., No. Ill. U.; pres. McHenry County Theater Guild, 1956; chmn. Chgo. Fed. Exec. Bd., 1965-68, chmn. pub. relations com., 1963-65. Recipient Albert Gallatin award U.S. Treasury Dept., 1968; award CSC, 1968; State Dir. award U.S. Treasury Dept., 1968; award Chgo. Fed. Exec. Bd., 1969. Mem. COF. Democrat. Roman Catholic. Clubs: Union League (Chgo.); Pistakee Yacht (past commodore), Monroe, Skyline, Johnsburg Community, McHenry Country, K.C., Elks. Home: 2721 Regner Rd McHenry IL 60050 Office: 39 S La Salle St Chicago IL 60603

RAUH, CARL STEPHEN, lawyer; b. Washington, Dec. 14, 1940; s. Joseph L. and Olie (Westheimer) R.; A.B., Columbia Coll., 1962; LL.B., U. Pa., 1965; LL.M., Georgetown U., 1968. Admitted to D.C. bar, 1966, U.S. Supreme Ct. bar, 1969; asst. U.S. atty. for D.C., Dept. Justice, 1966-69, atty. Dep. Atty. Gen.'s Office, Washington, 1969-71, 1st asst. atty. gen. U.S. V.I. Dept. Law, 1971-73, prin. asst. U.S. atty. for D.C., 1974-79, 80, U.S. atty. for D.C., 1979. Recipient Dir.'s award Dept. Justice, 1976. Mem. Am. Bar Assn., D.C. Bar Assn., Asst. U.S. Attys. Assn. Office: Room 2800 US Courthouse 3d and Constitution Ave NW Washington DC 20001

RAUH, JOHN DAVID, mfg. co. exec.; b. Cin., May 28, 1932; s. Carl J. and Grace (Stix) R.; A.B., Harvard, 1954, M.B.A., 1956; m. Elizabeth Gibbons, June 19, 1954; children—Carol Miller, Daniel Gibbons. Gen. mgr. Rauh Shirt Co., Cin., 1959-61; v.p. Clopay Corp., Cin., 1961-71, exec. v.p., 1971-72, pres., 1972-75, pres., chief exec. officer, 1975—, also dir. Bd. dirs. Charter Com. Greater Cin., pres., 1969-76; bd. dirs. Childrens Hosp. Med. Center, Cin., Jewish Hosp., Cin. Served to 1st lt. Finance Corps, AUS, 1956-59. Home: 5 Stanley Ln Cincinnati OH 45226 Office: Clopay Corp Clopay Sq Cincinnati OH 45214

RAUH, JOSEPH L., JR., lawyer; b. Cin., Jan. 3, 1911; s. Joseph L. and Sara (Weiler) R.; B.S., Harvard, 1932, LL.B., 1935; L.H.D. (hon.), Hebrew Union Coll., 1978; m. Olie Westheimer, Sept. 1, 1935; children—B. Michael, Carl S. Law sec. supreme ct. justices Cardozo and Frankfurter, 1936-39; counsel various govt. agys., 1935-42; admitted to D.C. bar, 1946, since practiced in Washington; gen. dep. housing expediter Vets. Emergency Housing Program, 1946-47; mem. Rauh & Levy, Washington, 1947-61, Rauh & Silard, 1961—; Washington counsel United Automobile Workers, 1951-63, 66—; gen. counsel, 1963-66; gen. counsel Leadership Conf. on Civil Rights,

1964—, counsel Miners for Democracy, 1970-72. Del. Democratic Nat. Conv., 1948, 52, 60, 64; vice chmn. D.C. Dem. Com., 1952-64, chmn., 1964-67. Trustee Antioch Coll.; nat. bd. dirs. N.A.A.C.P. Served as lt. col. AUS, 1942-45. Decorated Legion of Merit; Distinguished Service Star (P.I.). Fellow Brandeis U., 1969—; hon. fellow U. Pa. Law Sch., 1970; John F. Kennedy Meml. fellow, New Zealand, 1974. Mem. Ams. for Dem. Action (chmn. exec. com. 1947-52, vice chmn. 1952-55, 57—, nat. chmn. 1955-57). Author articles civil rights and liberties. Home: 3625 Appleton St Washington DC 20008 Office: 1001 Connecticut Ave NW Washington DC 20036. *Do your best and don't take yourself too seriously.*

RAULINAITIS, PRANAS ALGIS, electronics co. exec.; b. Kaunas, Lithuania, May 13, 1927; s. Pranas Viktoras and Paulina (Gervaite) R.; came to U.S., 1954, naturalized, 1960; m. Angele Staugaityte, Oct. 4, 1952; 1 son, Pranas Darius. Sr. v.p. finance, sec. Commonwealth Rys. of Australia, Melbourne, 1949-53, asst. to fin. accountant Kitchen & Sons, Pty. Ltd., Melbourne, 1953-54; v.p. Photo div. Interphoto Corp., Los Angeles, 1954-71; now sr. v.p., sec. Craig Corp., Los Angeles. Former pres. Lithuanian Am. Council, Inc. of Calif.; bd. dirs. Lithuanian-Am. assns. Mem. Am. Soc. Internat. Law. Home: 1501 Riverside Dr Burbank CA 91506 Office: 921 W Artesia Blvd Compton CA 90220

RAULLERSON, CALVIN HENRY, govt. ofcl.; b. Utica, N.Y., Dec. 18, 1920; s. Calvin Thomas and Cora (White) R.; A.B., Lincoln (Pa.) U., 1943; M.P.A., N.Y. U., 1949; postgrad. Harvard, 1947; m. 2d, Olive Lewis, Dec. 1, 1956; children—Kevin Greer, Cheryl Raullerson Pellaton, Earl Henry. Instr. polit. sci. Lincoln U., 1946, 49; editor, dir. research Christian E. Burckell Assos., pubs., Yonkers, N.Y., 1950-52; asst. to exec. dir. United Negro Coll. Fund, 1952-57, dir. edni. services, 1957-61; dir. African programs Am. Soc. African Culture, Lagos, Nigeria, 1961-64, exec. dir., N.Y.C., 1964-66; chief Peace Corps, East and So. Africa, 1966-69, dir. Kenya, 1969-71, Africa regional dir., 1971-73; exec. asst. to dean Sch. Medicine, spl. asst. to pres. for internat. programs, spl. cons. research and devel., exec. dir. Internat. Center for Arid and Semi-Arid Lands, Tex. Tech. U., 1973-78; asst. adminstr., Bur. Pvt. Devel. Cooperation, AID, 1978—. mgmt. cons. Mgmt. Devel. Consortium, Phelps Stokes Fund, 1973—. Mem. information resources com. group on bus. affairs Assn. Am. Med. Colls.; mem. adv. com. on desertification AAAS, 1976-78; U.S. delegation U.N. Conf. Desertification Nairobi, 1977. research analyst Pres.'s Com. on Fair Employment Practices, 1944; treas. U.S. planning com. 1st World Festival Negro Art, Dakar, 1965-66; del. Internat. Conf. on African History, U. Ibadan (Nigeria), 1962, Internat. Conf. on African Affairs, U. Ghana, 1963. Served with AUS, 1942-44. Rockefeller travel grantee East and Central Africa, 1960, Woodrow Wilson scholar, 1978-79. Club: Monroe, Plaza (Chgo.). Asso. editor Who's Who in the United Nations, 1952. Contbr. to Negro Yearbook, 1952. Home: 5823 Bradley Blvd Bethesda MD 20014

RAUM, ARNOLD, judge; b. Lynn. Mass., Oct. 27, 1908; s. Isaac and Ida (Ross) R.; A.B. summa cum laude, Harvard, 1929; LL.B., magna cum laude, Harvard, 1932; m. Muriel Leidner Slaff, Jan. 26, 1944 (div.); m. 2d, Violet Gang Kopp, Apr. 26, 1957; stepchildren—Robert E., Elizabeth A., Katherine F. Editor, Harvard Law Rev., 1930-32; Sheldon fellow Cambridge U., Eng., 1932; admitted to Mass. bar, 1932, U.S. Supreme Ct. bar, 1935, also D.C. bar, bars of various other fed. cts.; atty for RFC, 1932-34; spl. asst. to atty. gen. U.S., 1934-50; spl. asst. to U.S. atty., Eastern Dist. of La., in connection with grand jury investigation of La., scandals, 1939; dep. solicitor gen. U.S., and from time to time acting solicitor gen., 1939-1950; directed Litigation of all Fed. tax cases as well as other types of cases in U.S. Supreme Court, 1939-1950; made arguments in numerous Supreme Ct. cases, including Calif. Tidelands case; judge U.S. Tax Ct., Washington, 1950—; lectr. on taxation Yale Law Sch., 1937-38; mem. faculty Harvard Law Sch., 1947. Served as lt. comdr. USCGR, World War II. Hon. mem. D.C. Bar Assn., Fed. Bar Assn.; mem. Am. Law Inst., Phi Beta Kappa. Club: Cosmos (Washington). Home: 2622 31st St NW Washington DC 20008 Office: US Tax Court 400 2d St NW Washington DC 20217

RAUNBORG, JOHN DEE, oil co. exec.; b. Waco, Tex., Dec. 16, 1926; s. John Oscar and Grace (Duckworth) R.; student Rutgers U., 1945; B.S. in Commerce, La. State U., 1949; postgrad. U. Tex., 1949-50; m. Betty L. Daffron, July 28, 1973; children (by previous marriage)—Sharon Lynn, Ronald Ryan, Rhonda Ruth, Randell Ralph. Staff auditor Arthur Andersen & Co., Houston, 1950-57; mgr. internal auditing Kerr-McGee Corp., Oklahoma City, 1957-59, asst. to controller, 1960-62, controller oil, gas div., 1962-67, asst. controller, 1968, controller, 1969—. Served with AUS, 1944-47. C.P.A., Tex. Mem. Am. Petroleum Inst., Am. Inst. C.P.A.'s, Independent Petroleum Assn. Am., Oklahoma City C. of C., Financial Execs. Inst. Methodist. Home: 6213 Commodore Ln Oklahoma City OK 73132 Office: McGee Tower Oklahoma City OK 73102

RAUNIO, ELMER K., univ. dean; b. Columbia City, Oreg., Dec. 29, 1918; s. John E. and Olga M. (Lehto) R.; B.A., U. Wyo., 1940; M.S., N.D. State U., 1942; Ph.D., U. Mich., 1950; m. Margaret Ruth Kelly, June 12, 1949; children—Anne Marie Raunio Gilbert, Peggy Ruth Raunio Kupper. Chemist, Hercules Powder Co., Wilmington, Del., 1942-45; asst. prof., asso. prof., prof., asso. dean, dean U. Idaho, Moscow, 1949—. NSF sci. faculty teaching fellow Stanford, 1962-63. Mem. AAUP (past pres. Idaho chpt.), Am. Chem. Soc., A.A.A.S., Idaho Acad. Sci., Sigma Xi, Phi Kappa Phi. Contbr. articles profl. jours. Home: 708 Ridge Rd Moscow ID 83843

RAUP, DAVID MALCOLM, paleontologist; b. Boston, Apr. 24, 1933; s. Hugh Miller and Lucy (Gibson) R.; B.S., U. Chgo., 1953; M.A., Harvard, 1955, Ph.D., 1957; m. Susan Creer Shepard, Aug. 25, 1956; 1 son, Mitchell D. Instr., Calif. Inst. Tech., 1956-57; faculty Johns Hopkins, 1957-65, asso. prof., 1963-65; mem. faculty U. Rochester, 1965-78, prof. geology, 1966-78, chmn. dept. geol. scis., 1968-71, dir. Center for Evolution and Paleobiology, 1977-78; curator geology, chmn. dept. geology Field Mus. Natural History, Chgo., 1978—; geologist U.S. Geol. Survey, part-time, 1959-77; vis. prof. U. Tubingen (Germany), 1965, 72. Recipient Best Paper award Jour. Paleontology, 1966; Schuchert award Paleontol. Soc., 1973. Calif. Research Corp. grantee, 1955-56; Am. Assn. Petroleum Geologists grantee, 1957; Am. Philos. Soc. grantee, 1957; NSF grantee, 1960-66, 75—; Chem. Soc. grantee, 1965-71. Fellow Geol. Soc. Am.; mem. Nat. Acad. Sci., Paleontol. Soc. (pres. 1976-77), Soc. Econ. Paleontology and Mineralogy, Soc. for Systematic Zoology, Soc. for Study Evolution, A.A.A.S., Sigma Xi. Author: (with S. Stanley) Principles of Paleontology, 1971, 78; editor: (with B. Kummel) Handbook of Paleontological Techniques, 1965. Contbr. articles profl. jours. Home: 5801 S Dorchester Ave Chicago IL 60637 Office: Dept Geology Field Museum Natural History Chicago IL 60605

RAUSCH, HOWARD, editor; b. N.Y.C., June 29, 1928; s. Sol and Helen (Kartiganer) R.; A.B., Syracuse U., 1950; m. Sidra Cohn, Apr. 22, 1979. Reporter, Phila. Bull., 1961; copy editor Wall St. Jour., 1961-63, N.Y. Times, 1963-64; editor, fgn. corr. McGraw-Hill, N.Y.C. and Moscow, 1964-68; pres. Advanced Tech. Publs., Inc., Newton, Mass., 1968—, editor Laser Focus mag., 1968—, editor, founder Energy Research, 1975—. Home: 187 Reservoir Rd Chestnut Hill MA 02167 Office: 100 Watertown St Newton MA 02165

RAUSCH, JAMES STEVEN, clergyman; b. Albany, Minn., Sept. 4, 1928; s. James and Anna (Ohmann) R.; student Crosier Sem., 1946-49, Sacred Heart Sem., 1950-52; S.T.B., St. John's Sem., 1956; M.Ed., St. Thomas Coll., St. Paul., 1961; Ph.D. cum laude, Gregorian U., Rome, 1969, also L.H.D.; LL.D. (hon.), St. John's U., 1977; Ordained priest Roman Catholic Ch., 1956; asst. pastor St. Mary's Cathedral, St. Cloud, Minn., 1956-57; instr. govt. and econs. Cathedral High Sch., St. Cloud, 1957-67; instr. econs. St. Thomas Coll., 1965-69; spl. lectr. Clergy Conf. Econ. Edn., U. Minn. Center Contination Studies, 1966-67; aux. bishop Diocese St. Cloud, 1973-77; bishop of Phoenix, 1977—. Chmn. Bishops' Com. on Farm Labor, 1977—; nat. adv. council St. John's U., Collegeville, Minn. Recipient Pax Christi award St. John's U. (Minn.), 1978. Editor: Family of Nations, 1970; contbr. articles to profl. jours. Office: 400 E Monroe St Phoenix AZ 85004

RAUSCHENBERG, ROBERT, artist; b. Port Arthur, Tex., 1925; student U. Tex., Austin, Kansas City Art Inst., Academie Julian, Paris, France, Black Mountain Coll., N.C., Art Students League, N.Y.C.; m. Sue Weil, 1950 (div. 1952); 1 son, Christopher. One man shows: Parsons Gallery, N.Y.C., 1951, Stable Gallery, N.Y.C., 1953, White Chapel Art Gallery, London, 1964, Leo Castelli Gallery, 1972, 73, Galerie Ileana Sonnabend, Paris, 1971, 72, 73, Ace Gallery, Los Angeles, 1973, Vancouver Art Gallery, 1978; exhbt. art constrns., Rome and Florence Italy, 1953, Leo Castelli Gallery, N.Y.C., 1957—; rep. internat. art festivals, Carnegie Inst. Internat. exhbns., Sao Paulo Biennial, 1959, Exposition Internat. du Surrealisme, Paris, 1959-60, Amsterdam, others; group shows Sixteen Americans at Mus. Modern Art, 1959, Art of Assemblage at Guggengeim Mus., 1961, N.Y. Collection in Stockholm, 1972, Whitney Ann., N.Y.C., 1972, 73, Garage Show, Rome, 1973, Automme Festival d'Artes, Paris, 1973, Mus. South Tex., Corpus Christi, 1974, N.Y. Cultural Center, 1973; retrospective exhbn. Nat. Collection Fine Arts, Smithsonian Inst., Washington, 1976, Mus. Modern Art, N.Y.C., 1977, Albright Knox Gallery, 1977, San Francisco Mus. Modern Art, 1977, Art Inst. Chgo., 1977; reprodn. photographs by silk screen stenciling technique to allow change in scale; on tour as set and costume designer, lighting expert, stage mgr. Merce Cunningham Dance Co., 1964; choreographer dance, Pelican, others; works include electronic sculpture Oracle, Mud Muse, Soundings, paintings, Bed, Curfew, Resevoir, Canyon, Third Time Painting, Monogram, Barge, Tut-Scape. Served with USNR, World War II; neuropsychiat. tech. Calif. Naval Hosps. Recipient 1st prize Internat. Exbn. Prints, Gallery Modern Art, Ljubljana, Yugoslavia, 1963, 1st prize Venice Biennelle, 1964, 1st prize Corcoran Biennial Contemporary Am. Painters, 1965. Mem. Am. Acad. and Inst. Arts and Letters. Address: care Leo Castelli Gallery 420 W Broadway New York NY 10012

RAUSCHER, JOHN HOWARD, JR., investment banker; b. Long Beach, Calif., Dec. 18, 1924; s. John Howard and Eleanor Ruth (Brasher) R.; B.B.A., U. Tex., 1950; m. Mary Josephine McCorkle, Feb. 10, 1979; 1 son, John Howard, III. With Rauscher Pierce Refsnes, Inc. and predecessors, Dallas, 1949—, pres., 1969-74, chmn. bd., 1974—, also chmn. exec. com.; dir. Southwestern Electric Service Co. Pres. Episcopal Found. of Diocese of Dallas. Served with AUS, 1943-46; ETO. Mem. Securities Industry Assn. (gov. 1970-73, dist. chmn. 1970-71), Kappa Sigma. Clubs: Dallas Country, Brook Hollow Golf, City (Dallas). Office: 1200 Mercantile Dallas Bldg Dallas TX 75201

RAUSHENBUSH, WALTER BRANDEIS, educator; b. Madison, Wis., June 13, 1928; s. Paul A. and Elizabeth (Brandeis) R.; A.B. magna cum laude in Govt., Harvard, 1950; J.D. with high honors, U. Wis., 1953; m. Marylu de Watteville, May 3, 1956; children—Lorraine Elizabeth, Richard Walter, Carla, Paul Brandeis. Admitted to Wis. bar, 1953; partner firm LaFollette, Sinykin & Doyle, Madison, 1956-58; mem. faculty U. Wis. at Madison, 1958—, prof. law, 1966—. Project dir. real estate transfer study Am. Bar Found., 1967-72; trustee Nat. Law Sch. Admission Council, 1968-70, 72—, chmn. pre-law com., 1970-74, chmn. services com., 1976-78, pres., 1979—; legal adviser Madison Citizens Fair Housing, 1961-63, Wis. Citizens Family Planning, 1966—. Served with USAF, 1953-56; col. Res. Mem. Am., Dane County bar assns., State Bar Wis., Judge Advs. Assn., A.A.U.P., Order of Coif, Phi Beta Kappa, Phi Delta Phi (province pres. 1963-75). Presbyn. (elder). Clubs: Blackhawk Country, Madison Racquet, Madison Tennis (Madison); Stage Harbor Yacht (Chatham, Mass.). Author: Wisconsin Construction Lien Law, 1974; (with others) Wisconsin Real Estate Law, 1976; Brown on Personal Property, 3d edit., 1975; Real Estate Transactions Cases and Materials, 1979. Home: 3942 Plymouth Circle Madison WI 53705

RAUTENSTRAUS, ROLAND CURT, educator; b. Gothenburg, Neb., Feb. 27, 1924; s. Christian and Emma (Steine) R.; student Colo. State Coll., 1941-43; B.S. in Civil Engring., U. Colo., 1947, M.S., 1950; m. Willie Dean Atler, June 30, 1946; 1 son, Curt Dean. With McNeil Engrs., San Diego, 1941-42; mem. faculty U. Colo., 1946—, prof. civil engring., 1956—, chmn. dept., 1958-64, asso. dean of the faculties, 1964-68, v.p. edni. and student relations 1968—, v.p. for univ. relations, 1970-75, exec. v.p., 1973-75, pres., 1975—. Cons., 1949—. Served to lt. USNR, 1943-46. Recipient Gold Medal award Am. Lincoln Arc Welding Soc., 1950; Robert L. Stearns medal of distinguished service, 1965, Alumni Recognition award 1970; Norlin medal, 1974, Columbine award, 1975. Registered profl. engr., Colo. Fellow Am. Soc. C.E.; mem. Am. Soc. Engring. Edn. Am. Soc. Photogrammetry, Tau Beta Pi, Chi Epsilon. Author: Field Problems for Plane Surveying, 1954; Surveying and Mapping, 1958; also articles. Home: 5480 White Pl Boulder CO 80303

RAUTH, J. DONALD, business exec.; b. Pitman, N.J., Jan. 7, 1918; s. Harry J. and H. Virginia (Kline) R.; B.S. in Mech. Engring., Drexel U., 1940, Ph.D. (hon.), 1964 m. Catherine A. Burns, May 1, 1943; children—John Donald, Kathryn Virginia. With Martin Co. (now Martin Marietta Corp., merged with Am. Marietta Corp. 1961), Balt., 1940—, v.p., gen. mgr. Denver div., 1961-67, pres. aerospace group, 1967-69; pres., chief exec. officer, dir. Martin Marietta Aluminum, Inc., 1969-72; pres. Martin Marietta Corp., Bethesda, Md., 1972-77, chmn., chief exec. officer, 1977—, also dir.; chmn. Martin Marietta Aluminum Inc.; dir. Am. Security and Trust Co., Brunswick Corp. Trustee, Drexel U. Office: Martin Marietta Corp 6801 Rockledge Dr Bethesda MD 20034

RAVAGE, MAURICE, corp. exec., lawyer; b. Mpls., July 14, 1908; s. David and Bessie (Kantar) R.; B.A., U. Minn., 1928; LL.B., 1930; J.S.D., Yale, 1931; m. Anita R. Averbook, July 26, 1931; children—Margot L. (Mrs. Richard W. Marek), Alan J., Susan L. Yaw. Admitted to Minn. bar, 1930, N.Y. bar, 1933; research asst. Yale Law Sch., 1931-32; pvt. practice, N.Y.C., 1932-39; research asst. N.Y. State Law Revision Commn., 1934-37; tax counsel N.Y.C. Corp. Counsel's Office, 1940-42; with Office Alien Property Custodian, 1942-45, chief patent, copyright and trademark sect., N.Y.C. office, 1945; mem. legal dept. C.I.T. Financial Corp., 1945-70, asst. gen. counsel, 1957-70; pres., dir. Boron Technics, Inc. Mem. Am., N.Y. State bar assns., Assn. Bar City N.y., Phi Beta Kappa, Order of Coif. Contbr. profl. jours. Editor Minn. Law Rev., 1929-30. Home and office: 350 Central Park West New York City NY 10025

RAVASZ, LASZLO ANTAL, hotel exec.; b. Hungary, Feb. 13, 1936; s. Antal Ferenc and Julianna (Heitz) R.; came to U.S., 1956, naturalized, 1963; student Pharmacy U., Budapest, Hungary, 1954-56, U. Colo., 1957-59; B.B.A. in Travel Industry Mgmt., U. Hawaii, 1968; m. Charlynne Lum, July 28, 1977; children—Loren, Lanet. With Hilton Internat. Hotels, 1963-69, asst. food and beverage mgr. Kahala Hilton, Honolulu, 1968, U.S. Virgin Islands, 1969; food and beverage mgr. Pick Congress Hotel, Chgo., 1969-71; dir. food and beverage Marriott Hotel, Cleve., 1971-72, Berkeley, Calif., 1972-73, asst. gen. mgr., Cleve., 1973-75; gen. mgr. Sheraton Cleve. Hotel, 1975-77; v.p., gen. mgr. Lord Balt. Hotel, 1977—; mem. gov.'s adv. bd. Md. Travel and Tourism Devel., 1978; mem. Balt. mayor's adv. bd. Culinary Arts Inst., 1978-79. Mem. Md. Hotel and Motel Assn. (dir.), Am. Hotel and Motel Assn. (internat. travel com.), Food Service Execs. Assn. (v.p. 1974-75, dir. 1977—), Confrerie de la Chaine des Rotisseurs, Travel Industry Mgmt. Internat. Home and Office: 20 W Baltimore St Baltimore MD 21201

RAVEL, JOANNE MACOW, biochemist; b. Austin, Tex., July 28, 1924; d. Joseph Benjamin and Sarah (Cwyan) Macow; B.S., U. Tex., Austin, 1946, Ph.D., 1954; m. Jerome O. Ravel, Mar. 23, 1946; children—Margaret, Stephen. Research scientist Clayton Found. Biochem. Inst., U. Tex., Austin, 1956—, asso. prof. chemistry, then prof., 1972-79, Ashbell Smith prof., 1979—. Mem. Am. Soc. Biol. Chemistry, Am. Chem. Soc., Am. Soc. Microbiologists, Phi Beta Kappa, Sigma Xi. Author, editor in field. Home: 4024 Tealwood St Austin TX 78731 Office: Dept Chemistry Univ Tex Austin TX 78712

RAVEN, PETER HAMILTON, bot. garden exec.; b. Shanghai, China, June 13, 1936; s. Walter Francis and Isabelle Marion (Breen) R.; A.B., U. Calif., Berkeley, 1957; Ph.D., U. Los Angeles, 1960; m. Tamra Engelhorn, Nov. 29, 1968; children—Alice Catherine, Elizabeth Marie, Francis Clark. Taxonomist, Rancho Santa Ana Bot. Garden, Claremont, Calif., 1961-62; asst. prof., asso. prof. biol. scis. Stanford, 1962-71; dir. Mo. Bot. Garden, Engelmann prof. biology Washington U., St. Louis, 1971—; mem. Nat. Mus. Services Bd. Mem. Bd. Commrs., Tower Grove Park, 1971—. Fellow Am. Acad. Arts and Scis., Calif. Acad. Scis.; mem. Nat. Acad. Scis. Bot. Soc. Am. (past pres.), Soc. for Study Evolution (past pres.), Am. Soc. Plant Taxonomists (past pres.), Am. Assn. Bot. Gardens and Arboreta, Assn. Systematics Collections, Orgn. Tropical Studies (dir.), Japan Am. Soc. (pres. St. Louis), Phi Beta Kappa, Sigma Xi. Clubs: University, Noonday (St. Louis). Author: Biology of Plants, 1971, 2d edit., 1976; Principles of Tzeltal Folk Taxonomy, 1974; others. Contbr. articles to profl. jours. Home: 2361 Tower Grove Ave Saint Louis MO 63110 Office: PO Box 299 Saint Louis MO 63166

RAVEN, ROBERT DUNBAR, lawyer; b. Cadillac, Mich., Sept. 26, 1923; s. Christian and Gladys L. (Dunbar) R.; A.B. with honors, Mich. State U., 1949; LL.B., U. Calif., Berkeley, 1952; m. Leslie Kay Erickson, June 21, 1947; children—Marta Ellen, Matt Robert, Brett Lincoln. Admitted to Calif. bar, 1953; asso. firm Morrison & Foerster and predecessor, San Francisco, 1952-56, partner, 1956—, chmn. of firm, 1979—; instr. in trade regulations U. Calif., Berkeley, spring, 1964; lectr. continuing edn. programs. Bd. dirs. Bay Area USO, 1964-71, pres., 1969-70; mem. San Francisco Mayor's Criminal Justice Council, 1971-72; co-chmn. San Francisco Lawyer's Com. for Urban Affairs, 1976-78; mem. exec. com. Lawyers Com. for Civil Rights Under Law, N.Y.C., 1976—. Served with USAAF, 1942-45. Decorated Air medal with oak leaf cluster. Mem. Bar Assn. San Francisco (pres. 1971), State Bar Calif. (gov. 1978—), Am. Bar Assn. (mem. standing com. on fed. judiciary 1976-78, chmn., 1978—), Fed. Bar Assn., Am. Law Inst., Am. Coll. Trial Lawyers, Am. Bar Found., Am. Judicature Soc., Queen's Bench, Boalt Hall Alumni Assn. (pres. 1972-73), Order of Coif. Democrat. Clubs: Bankers of San Francisco, World Trade (San Francisco). Home: 1064 Via Alta Lafayette CA 94549 Office: One Market Plaza 4200 Spear St Tower San Francisco CA 94105

RAVENHOLT, REIMERT THOROLF, govt. ofcl.; b. Milltown, Wis., Mar. 9, 1925; s. Ansgar Benjamin and Kristine Henrietta (Petersen) R.; B.S., U. Minn., 1948, M.B., 1951, M.D., 1952; M.P.H., U. Calif., Berkeley, 1956; divorced; children—Janna, Mark, Lisa, Dane. Intern USPHS Hosp., San Francisco, 1951-52; epidemic intelligence service officer USPHS Communicable Disease Center, Atlanta, 1952-54; dir. epidemiology and communicable disease div. Seattle-King County (Wash.) Health Dept., 1954-61; epidemiology cons. European area USPHS, Paris, 1961-63; asso. prof. preventive medicine U. Wash. Med. Sch., Seattle, 1963-66; dir. Office of Population, AID, Washington, 1966—. Served with USPHS, 1951-54, 61-63. Recipient Distinguished Honor award AID, 1973; John J. Sippy Meml. award Western br. Am. Pub. Health Assn., 1961; Hugh Moore Meml. award Population Crisis Com., 1974. Mem. Am. Pub. Health Assn., Population Assn. Am., Internat. Epidemiol. Assn. Democrat. Club: Cosmos (Washington). Contbr. articles to profl. publns. Home: 4940 Sentinel Dr Sumner MD 20016 Office: 1621 N Kent St Rosslyn VA 20523

RAVENTOS, ANTOLIN, med. educator; b. Wilmette, Ill., June 3, 1925; s. Enrique Antolin and Juanita (Gillespie) R.; student Northwestern U., 1941-44; S.B., U. Chgo., 1945, M.D., 1947; M.Sc., U. Pa., 1954. From instr. to prof. medicine U. Pa., Phila., 1950-70; prof., chmn. dept. radiology Sch. Medicine U. Calif. at Davis, 1970—. Served with AUS, 1944-46, 52-54. Fellow Am. Coll. Radiology (chancellor 1964-70), Am. Radium Soc. (pres. 1972-73). Asso. editor Cancer, 1964—. Home: 3216 Country Club Dr El Macero CA 95618 Office: Dept Radiology Sch Medicine U Calif Davis CA 95616

RAVESIES, PAUL, oil co. exec.; b. Tupelo, Miss., Feb. 20, 1924; s. Paul and Catherine Stuart (Best) R.; B.S., Tex. A&M U., 1949; m. Sarah Lou Ragland, Feb. 24, 1951; children—Paul, Haywood Ragland. With Seaboard Oil Co., before 1958—; with Atlantic Richfield Co., 1958—, now sr. v.p.; pres. ARCO Internat. Oil and Gas Co., also dir. numerous subsidiaries; dir. Iricon Agy. Ltd. Dir. Meth. Hosp. of So. Calif. Served with U.S. Army. Decorated Purple Heart. Mem. AIME, Am. Petroleum Inst. Clubs: California, Petroleum, Annandale Golf, Pauma Valley Country. Home: 1310 Rodeo Rd Arcadia CA 91006 Office: 515 S Flower St Los Angeles CA 90071

RAVICH, ABRAHAM, urologist; b. near Slonim, Poland, June 10, 1889; s. Isadore and Ida (Karelitz) R.; came to U.S., 1893, citizen through father, 1898; A.B., Coll. City N.Y., 1908; A.M., Columbia, 1912, M.D., 1912; m. Martha L. Zuckert, Sept. 3, 1918 (dec. Sept. 22, 1971); 1 son, Robert Alan; m. 2d, Charlotte Nathan, Mar. 22, 1973. Interne Jewish Hosp., Brooklyn, 1912-14, asst., 1914-18, asso., 1918-25, attending (chief) urologist, 1925-34; asso. urologist, Beth Moses Hosp., 1920-23; attending Beth El Hosp., 1920-24, chief urologist, 1936-39; chief urologist Brooklyn Hebrew Home and Hosp. for Aged, 1925-28, dir. urology, 1938-48; cons. urologist Menorah Home for Aged, 1930—; attending urologist Israel Zion Hosp., 1922-34, Adelphi Hosp., 1940-49, cons., 1950—; dir. Ravich Urol. Inst., 1934-40; asst. clin. prof. urology, Long Island Coll. Med., 1934; founder Trafalgar Hosp., N.Y.C., 1956. 1st lt. M.C., U.S. Army, 1918-19. Exec. dir. Cancer Research and Hospital Found., 1947-58, sec., treas., 1958—; pres. and exec. dir. Inst. Applied Biology, 1947-57. Mem. bd. visitors Creedmoor State Hosp., 1946-57. Hon. surgeon Honor Legion N.Y. City Police Dept. Fellow A.C.S., A.M.A.; mem. Am. Urol. Assn. Mason (32 deg., Shriner). Clubs: Physicians Square of Long Island, New York (past pres.). Author: Preventing VD and Cancer by Circumcision, 1973. Mem. editorial bd. Clinical Abstracts, 1934-37. Contbr. articles in med. jours. Devised Ravich cystoscope, visualized cautery prostatic punch, lithotriptoscope, etc. Awarded Townsend Harris Medal for achievement by Associated Alumni of C.C.N.Y., 1950. First to report on transmissible virus in prostate cervix and bladder cancer as venereal infection, and circumcision of new born males to prevent such cancers, also on significant role of renal vein compression by intra-renal pelvis in prodn. of essential hypertension. Home: 1135-103d St Bay Harbor Island Miami Beach FL 33154 also 1200 Midland Ave Bronxville NY 10708

RAVIN, ARNOLD WARREN, geneticist, educator; b. N.Y.C., Aug. 15, 1921; s. Max and Rae (Levinson) R.; B.S., Coll. City N.Y., 1942; M.A., Columbia, 1948, Ph.D., 1951; m. Sophie Brody, June 11, 1956; children—Sonia, Andrea. Postdoctoral fellow Laboratoire de genetique, U. Paris (France), 1951-53; mem. faculty U. Rochester, 1952-68, prof. biology, 1962-68, chmn. dept., 1957-60, asso. dean Coll. Arts and Sci., 1960-61, dean, 1961-63; prof. biology U. Chgo., 1968—, master collegiate div. biology, asso. dean div. biol. scis., 1968-73, chmn. com. on conceptual founds. of sci., 1973-77, Addie Clark Harding prof. biology, 1976—, dir. Morris Fishbein Center for Study History Sci. and Medicine, 1978—; mem. genetics tng. com. NIH, 1967-70; mem. com. biology Coll. Entrance Exam. Bd., 1956-60; mem. biology com. coll. proficiency exams. N.Y. State Edn. Dept., 1964-66; vis. prof. genetics U. Calif. at Berkeley, 1963; Sigma Xi Bicentennial lectr., 1974-76; mem. Nat. Humanities Faculty, 1972—. Trustee Bergey's Manual Trust, 1961, Am. Type Culture Collection, 1967-72. Recipient Edward Peck Curtis award for excellence in undergrad. teaching, 1966. Predoctoral fellow Nat. Cancer Inst., USPHS, 1949-50, post-doctoral fellow, 1951-53, spl. research fellow, 1960-61; NSF Faculty fellow, 1975. Served to 1st lt. USAAF, 1942-46. Fellow AAAS; mem. Genetics Soc. Am., Soc. Gen. Microbiology (Great Britain), Am. Soc. Microbiology, Am. Soc. Cell Biology, Am. Soc. Naturalists, Philosophy of Sci. Assn., History of Sci. Assn., AAUP, Sigma Xi. Author: Evolution of Genetics, 1965. Mem. editorial bd. Am. Naturalist, 1968-70; co-editor Genetic Orgn., 1969. Contbr. numerous articles to profl. jours. Home: 2626 N Lakeview Ave Chicago IL 60614

RAVIOLA, ELIO, anatomist, cell biologist; b. Asti, Italy, June 15, 1932; s. Giuseppe and Luigina (Carbone) R.; came to U.S., 1970; M.D. summa cum laude, U. Pavia (Italy), 1957, Ph.D. in Anatomy, 1963; m. Giuseppina d'Elia, Mar. 24, 1960; 1 son, Giuseppe. Resident in neurology and psychiatry U. Pavia, asst. prof., 1958-70; asso. prof. anatomy Harvard U. Med. Sch., Boston, 1970-74, prof. human anatomy, 1974—. Mem. Am. Soc. Cell Biology, Am. Assn. Anatomists. Club: Harvard (Boston). Editorial bd. Jour. Cell Biology, 1978—; asso. editor Anat. Record, 1972—; research on mechanism of vision. Office: Dept Anatomy Harvard Med Sch 25 Shattuck St Boston MA 02115

RAVIOLO, VICTOR GINO, cons. engr.; b. N.Y.C., June 20, 1914; s. John B. and Armida (Petrini) R.; student Wayne U., 1933-36; m. Janet Holcomb, 1932 (div. 1946); children—Judith Ann (Mrs. A.D. Ericsson), Caren Jane and John Bruce (twins), Victor Gino; m. 2d, Eleanor Loretta Schettler, Oct. 21, 1954. Design engr. Chrysler Corp., 1932-36, Packard Motor, 1936-37; chief engr. Van Ranst Co., Detroit, 1937-40; project engr. Ford Motor Co., 1940-42, head engine research 1945-50, chief engr. engines, 1950-54, dir. Lincoln-Mercury Engring. Office, 1954-55, dir. Advanced Product Study and Engring. Research Office, 1955-56, exec. dir. engring. staff, 1957-61, dir. Ford Motor Co., Ltd., 1961-63; cons. engr. Detroit, 1963—; group v.p. Am. Motors., Detroit, 1966-68, mgmt. cons., 1968—. Instr. Edison Inst. Tech., Dearborn, Mich., 1941; head power plant research Consol. Vultee Aircraft Corp., 1942-45; dir., v.p. Great Lakes Airmotive, Inc., Willow Run, 1958—. Mem. Soc. Automotive Engrs. (dir.), Coordinating Research Council (dir.), Instrument Soc. Am. (pres. Detroit 1948), Soc. Exptl. Stress Analysis, A.A.A.S., Mich. Aero. and Space Assn., Engring. Soc. Detroit, Am. Ordnance Assn., Assn. U.S. Army, Air Force Assn., Aircraft Owners and Pilots Assn., Inst. Mech. Engrs. (U.K.), Amateur Yacht Research Soc., Detroit Mus. Art Founders Soc., Sigma Xi, Tau Beta Pi. Clubs: Detroit Athletic, Detroit Yacht; Ford Yacht (dir. 1947-49) (Grosse Ile, Mich.); Grosse Pointe (Mich.) Yacht. Home: Angler's Cove 12-202 1456 NE Ocean Blvd Stuart FL 33494

RAVIS, HOWARD SHEPARD, conf. mgmt. co. exec.; b. Waterbury, Conn., Mar. 3, 1934; s. Paul Morton and Ida Ruth (Levin) R.; B.S. in Journalism, Boston U., 1959; m. Sophie G. Simons, Nov. 1, 1959; 1 dau., Heidi. Sports editor Milford (Conn.) Citizen, 1959-60; editor Stratford (Conn.) News, 1960-61; news editor Wallingford (Conn.) Post, 1961-62; editor Needham (Mass.) Chronicle, 1962-66; reunion coordinator Boston U. Alumni Assn., 1966; copy desk man, writer Boston Globe, 1966; news editor Scholastic Tchr. mag., 1966-67; mgmt. and careers editor Electronic Design mag., 1967-68; mng. editor Teacher mag., 1968-74; editor, asso. pub. Folio: The Magazine for Mag. Mgmt., New Canaan, Conn., 1974—; v.p. seminar programming Conf. Mgmt. Corp., Stamford, Conn., 1978—; speaker, cons. in field. Bd. dirs. Ossining (N.Y.) Open Door Med. Assos., 1973-77; chmn. United Ossining Party, 1973, Ossining Citizens Com. Edn., 1972-73; treas., bd. dirs. Ossining Interfaith Council for Action, 1970-73; rep. Town Meeting, Needham, 1966; mem. nat. alumni council Boston U., 1977—. Served with AUS, 1956-58. Recipient Jesse H. Neal Editorial Achievement award Am. Bus. Press, 1976; Top News Writing award New Eng. Press Assn., 1962. Mem. Am. Soc. Mag. Editors, Am. Soc. Bus. Press Editors, Boston U. Alumni Assn. (chmn. Westchester County 1972—). Democrat. Editor: Magazine Publishing Management, 1976. Home: 5 Amawalk Ct Ossining NY 10562 Office: 500 Summer St Stamford CT 06901

RAVITCH, MARK MITCHELL, surgeon; b. N.Y.C., Sept. 12, 1910; s. Mitchell M. and Annette (Manevitch) R.; A.B., U. Okla., 1930; M.D., Johns Hopkins, 1934; m. Irene Ravitch, Feb. 27, 1932; children—Nancy (Mrs. E.P. Schwentker), Michael Mark, Mary Robin. Resident, Johns Hopkins Hosp., 1934-43, dir. blood bank, 1939-52; from instr. to asso. prof. surgery Johns Hopkins Med. Sch., 1941-52, asso. prof., then prof. surgery, 1956-66; clin. prof. surgery Columbia Coll. Phys. and Surg., 1952-56; dir. dept. surgery Mt. Sinai Hosp., N.Y.C., 1952-56; surgeon in chief Balt. city hosps., 1956-66; prof. surgery U. Chgo. Med. Sch., 1966-69, prof. pediatric surgery, head div., 1966-69; surgeon in chief Montefiore Hosp., Pitts., 1969—; prof. surgery U. Pitts. Med. Sch., 1969—. Hon. asso., cons. surgeon Guy's Hosp., London, Eng., 1949; Felton Bequest vis. prof. surgery Royal Children's Hosp., Melbourne, Australia, 1968. Served to maj. M.C., AUS, 1943-46. Recipient medal Vishnevskii Inst. Surgery, Moscow, 1960. Diplomate Am. Bd. Surgery, Am. Bd. Thoracic Surgery. Fellow N.Y. Acad. Medicine, Royal Coll. Physicians and Surgeons (hon.) (Glasgow), Royal Australasian Coll. Surgeons (Melbourne) (hon.); mem. Am. Assn. Thoracic Surgery, Soc. Univ. Surgeons, Internat. Cardiovascular Soc., A.C.S. (1st v.p. 1977—, pres. S.W. Pa. chpt. 1977-78), Brit. Assn. Pediatric Surgeons, Soc. Vascular Surgery, Am. (1st v.p. 1973-74), So., Western, Central surg. assns., Am. Acad. Pediatrics (pres. surg. sect. 1967-69, Ladd medal 1972), Am. Assn. Pediatric Surgery, Internat. Soc. Surgery, Johns Hopkins Soc. Scholars, Phi Beta Kappa, Alpha Omega Alpha; hon. mem. Halsted Soc., Korea Surg. Soc., Surg. Research Soc. Australia. Author: Intussusception, 1959; Alfred Blalock-1899-1964, 1966; Repair of Hernias, 1969; Congenital Deformities of the Chest Wall and Their Operative Correction, 1977; also monographs, articles; editor: The Papers of Alfred Blalock, 2 vols., 1966; (with others) Pediatric Surgery, 2 vols., 3d edit., 1978; editor-in-chief Current Problems in Surgery, 1964—, Surg. Rounds, 1977—. Home: 1190 Beechwood Blvd Pittsburgh PA 15206 Office: 3459 5th Ave Pittsburgh PA 15213

RAVITZ, ROBERT ALLAN, advt. agy. exec.; b. Omaha, May 26, 1938; s. Ben and Frances (Cooper) R.; B.S., Northwestern U., 1960; m. 2d, Muriel Strickler, May 12, 1977; 1 dau. by previous marriage, Anne Cooper. Trainee/account exec. Edward H. Weiss Advt., Chgo., 1962-65; account exec. Tatham-Laird & Kudner Advt., Chgo., 1965-68; v.p., account supr. Stern, Walters & Simmons Advt., Chgo., 1968-72; sr. v.p., mgmt. rep. McCann-Erickson Inc., Chgo., 1972-77, N.Y.C., 1977—; guest lectr. Am. Mgmt. Assn.; mem. Dept. Navy Mktg. Rev. Group. Comdr., USNR. Mem. Naval Res. Assn., Navy League U.S., Chgo. Advt. Club (dir.), Am. Assn. Advt. Agys., Am. Mgmt. Assn. Jewish. Club: Rotan Point Yacht. Home: 5 Westview Ln South Norwalk CT 06854 Office: 485 Lexington Ave New York NY 10017

RAWALT, MARGUERITE, lawyer; b. Prairie City, Ill., Oct. 16; d. Charles T. and Viola Bell (Flake) Rawalt; A.B., LL.B., George Washington U., 1933, LL.M., 1936; LL.D., Baylor U. 1945; m. Harry Secord, May 1, 1937 (dec. July 1963). Admitted to D.C. bar, 1932, Tex. bar, 1935, U.S. Supreme Ct. bar, 1938; tax atty. Office Chief Counsel, Internal Revnue Service, 1933-65, successively spl. and trial atty., chief brief rev. sect., 1933-49, asst. head appeals and civil divs., 1949-59, staff asst., 1959-60, br. chief, 1961-62, asst. dir. refund litigation div., 1963-65; pvt. practice of law, 1965—; professorial lectr. grad. sch. George Washington U., 1973-74. Mem. nat. bd. Woman's Med. Coll.; dir. Found. Fed. Bar Assn. Mem. Pres.'s Commn. on Status of Women, 1961-63; mem. Adv. Council on Status of Women, 1963-69; mem. D.C. Commn. on Status of Women, 1967-69; organizing chmn. Equal Rights Amendment Ratification Council, 1972, vice-chmn., 1973-76, chmn., 1977—. Recipient centennial award Berea Coll. 1955; award of merit, D.A.R., 1956; named Ky. col., 1955. Mem. Am. (ho. dels. 1943-44, 45-46, chmn. com. on facilities Law Library of Congress 1947-48), Fed. (nat. pres. 1943-44, nat. council 1944—, asso. editor jour. 1944-47), D.C. bar assns., State Bar Tex., Women's Bar Assn. D.C., UN League Lawyers (registrar 1946-47), Nat. Assn. Women Lawyers (nat. pres. 1942-43, mem. ho. dels.), Nat. Fedn. Bus. and Profl. Women's Clubs (nat. pres. 1954-56, nat. legal adviser, v.p. 1946-54, historian 1958-69, founding pres. Bus. and Profl. Women's Found. 1956), Gen. Fedn. Women's Clubs (nat. bd. 1968-75), D.C. Fedn. Womens Clubs (pres. 1966-68), NOW Legal Def. Fund (charter), A.A.U.W., Am. Judicature Soc., Am. Acad. Polit. Sci., D.A.R., Internat Fedn. Bus. and Profl. Women (dir. 1954-56), Internat. Fedn. Women Lawyers, Order of Coif, Kappa Beta Pi, Zeta Tau Alpha. Club: Zonta. Address: 1600 S Joyce St Arlington VA 22202

RAWITSCHER, JACK JOSEPH, lawyer; b. Williston, N.D., May 11, 1932; s. Alec and Minnie (Cersonsky) R.; B.A., U. Wis., 1955; LL.B., U. Tex., 1957; children—Karey Lea, Michael Steven. Admitted to Tex. bar, 1957; asst. dist. atty. Harris County (Tex.), 1957-60; asso. atty. firm Dixie & Schulman, Houston, 1960-68; partner firm Smith, Schulman, Rawitscher & Carmahan, Houston, 1968—. Mem. faculty Nat. Coll. Criminal Def. Lawyers and Pub. Defenders, 1973—; clin. prof. law Bates Coll. Law, U. Houston, 1972—; guest participant in law programs television and radio stas. KTRH, KILT, KENR. Served with AUS, 1957-63. Recipient Outstanding Service award Midtown Kiwanis of Houston, 1971. Mem. Harris County Criminal Lawyers Assn. (dir.), Tex. Criminal Def. Lawyers Assn. (dir., recipient commendation 1972-73), Bill of Rights Found., Anti-Defamation League (dir.), State Bar Tex. (past chmn. grievance com. sect. 8, chmn. elect criminal law and procedure sect.), Tex., Houston (past chmn. criminal law sect.) bar assns. Jewish (bd. trustees temple 1971-73). Kiwanian (pres. 1973-74). Home: 7655 S Braeswood Apt 41 Houston TX 77071 Office: 806 Main St Houston TX 77002

RAWLEY, JAMES ALBERT, educator; b. Terre Haute, Ind., Nov. 9, 1916; s. Frank S. and Annie B. (Vanes) R.; A.B., U. Mich., 1938, A.M., 1939; Ph.D., Columbia, 1949; m. Ann F. Keyser, Apr. 7, 1945; children—John Franklin, James Albert. Instr. Columbia, 1946-48, N.Y. U., 1946-51, Hunter Coll., 1951-53; asso. prof. to prof. Sweet Briar Coll., 1953-64, chmn. history dept., 1953-57, chmn. div. social studies, 1962-64; prof. U. Nebr., 1964—, chmn. history dept., 1966-67, 73—; resident scholar Rockefeller Study and Conf. Center, Italy, 1977; Nat. Endowment for Humanities fellow Huntington Library, 1979. Served to 1st lt. AUS, 1942-46. Fellow Royal Hist. Soc.; mem. AAUP, Am., So. hist. assns., Nebr. State Hist. Soc. (pres.), Orgn. Am. Historians, Phi Beta Kappa. Democrat. Episcopalian. Clubs: Lincoln Country; Univ. (Lincoln, Nebr.). Author: Edwin D. Morgan: Merchant in Politics, 1811-1883, 1955; Turning Points of the Civil War, 1966; Race and Politics, 1969; The Politics of Union, 1974. Editor: The American Civil War: An English View, 1964; Lincoln and Civil War Politics, 1969. Contbr. to Essays in American Historiography, 1960. Home: 2300 Bretigne Dr Lincoln NE 68512

RAWLINGS, PAUL C., govt. ofcl.; b. Cave City, Ark., June 21, 1928; s. Otha A. and Leona (King) R.; grad. Little Rock Jr. Coll.; LL.B., Ark. Law Sch., 1950; m. Catherine Terral, 1951 (div. 1970); children—William A., Rebecca, Neal; m. 2d, Erma Martin, June 20, 1971. Admitted to Ark. bar, 1950, practiced in Little Rock, 1950, 52-73; adminstrv. law judge Office Hearings and Appeals, Social Security Adminstrn., HEW, Hattiesburg, Miss., 1973—; partner firm Terral, Rawlings, Matthews & Purtle, until 1973; asst. atty. gen. Ark., 1955-56. Bd. dirs. Ark. Enterprises for Blind, 1964-67. Served with AUS, 1950-52. Mem. Am., Ark. bar assns., Law Sci. Acad. Methodist (past chmn. bd. adminstrn., trustee). Lion (past pres.). Home: 3002 Navajo Circle Hattiesburg MS 39401 Office: Humble Bldg Hattiesburg MS 39401

RAWLINGS, WILLIAM EDWIN, diversified mfg. co. exec.; b. Newport, Ky., Oct. 5, 1931; s. John Thomas and Margaret Rose (Widrig) R.; B.A. cum laude, Washington and Lee U., Lexington, Va., 1953; M.B.A., Harvard U., 1955; m. Arlene Hunt, June 3, 1961; children—John Thomas, Christopher Hunt, Susan Avery, Lesley Ann. With Gen. Foods Corp., 1958-74, gen. mgr. pet foods div., 1970-72, pres. pet foods div., corp. v.p., 1972-74; group v.p. Gillette Corp., 1974-78; pres., chief operating officer, dir. Am. Maize Products Co., N.Y.C., 1978—; dir. John H. Swisher & Son, Inc., Boyer Bros. Lundy-Briggs Co., Inc., S.A. Schonbrunn & Co. Served to lt. USNR, 1955-58. Clubs: Harvard (N.Y.C.); Essex Country (Manchester, Mass.). Office: Am Maize Products Co 250 Park Ave New York NY 10017

RAWLINS, LESTER, actor, prodn. co. exec.; b. Sharon, Pa., Sept. 24, 1924; s. Ben and Leona (Verier) Rosenberg; B.F.A. in Drama, Carnegie-Mellon U., 1950. Charter mem. Arena Stage, Washington, 1950; N.Y.C. debut in Othello, 1956; appeared on Broadway, including: Nightride, 1971-72 (Drama Desk award 1972), as Mr. Drumm in Da, 1978-79 (Tony award 1978); appeared in off-Broadway plays, including: The Quare fellow, 1958-59 (Obie award 1959, Hedda Gabler, 1960-61 (Obie award 1961), Benito Cereno, 1964-65 (Obie award 1965); movies include: Dairy of a Mad Housewife, 1974, They Might Be Giants, 1976; guest appearances on numerous TV shows, including: Edge of Night, Kojak, Banacek, Starsky and Hutch; TV and radio comml. voice-over announcer; pres. Addison Prodns., Inc., N.Y.C., 1975—. Served to 1st sgt. USAAF, 1943-46. Mem. Actors Equity Assn., Screen Actors Guild, AFTRA, Assn. Can. TV and Radio Artists. Club: Players. Office: Addison Prodns Inc care Becker & London 15 Columbus Circle New York NY 10023

RAWLS, EUGENIA, actress; b. Macon, Ga.; d. Hubert Fields and Louise (Roberts) R.; grad. Wesleyan Conservatory, Macon, 1932; student U. N.C., 1933; L.D.H., U. No. Colo., Greeley, 1978; m. Donald Ray Seawell, Apr. 5, 1941; children—Eugenia Ashley Brook Seawell Speidel, Donald Brockman. Broadway prodns. appearances include The Children's Hour, 1934, Pride and Prejudice, 1936, The Little Foxes, 1939, 41, Guest in the House, 1942, Rebecca, 1945, The Second Mrs. Tanqueray, 1940, The Shrike, 1952, Private Lives, 1949, The Great Sebastians, 1956, First Love, 1961, The Glass Menagerie, 1964, 67, Our Town, 1967, Tallulah, A Memory, Lincoln Center, 1971, London, 1974, U.S. tour, 1979, Affectionately Yours Fanny Kemble, London, 1974, U.S. tour, 1979, The Enchanted, 1973, Sweet Bird of Youth, 1975, 76, Daughter of the Regiment, 1978, Just the Immediate Family, 1978, Women of the West, U.S. tour, 1979; one-woman show Fanny Kemble, Arts Theatre, London, 1969; appeared as Emily, Denver, 1976, with Abbey Theatre, Dublin, Ireland, 1972; one-woman show tour of Europe, 1972; appeared as Fanny Kemble, Shakespeare World Congress, Washington, 1976; Kennedy Center appearances in Tallulah, Woman of the West, Fanny Kemble; TV appearances on U.S. Steel Hour, Love of Life, also Women of the West for ednl. TV; Tallulah: A Memory performed for presdl. inauguration, 1977; appeared Memory of a Large Christmas, Folger Shakespeare Library, 1977; mem. Sarah Caldwell Opera Co., Boston, 1978; rec. talking books for blind; mem. com. Plays for Living, 1964-67; Rockefeller Found. artist-in-residence Denver U., 1967, 68, U. Tampa (Fla.), 1970; artist-in-residence U. No. Colo., 1971, 72, 73. Recipient Alumna award U. N.C., 1969; Distinguished Achievement award Wesleyan Coll., 1969; Gold Chair award Central City (Colo.) Opera House Assn., 1973; (with husband) Frederick H. Koch Drama award U. N.C., 1974; citation Smithsonian, 1977. Author: Tallulah—A Memory, 1979. Address: 510 E 84th St New York NY 10028

RAWLS, JOHN, educator, philosopher; b. Balt. Feb. 21, 1921; s. William Lee and Anna Abel (Stump) R.; grad. Kent Sch., 1939; A.B., Princeton 1943, Ph.D., 1950; postgrad. Cornell U., 1947-48; m. Margaret Warfield Fox, June 28, 1949; children—Anne Warfield, Robert Lee, Alexander Emory, Elizabeth Fox. Instr., Princeton, 1950-52; asst., then asso. prof. Cornell U., 1953-59; prof. Mass. Inst. Tech., 1960-62; vis. prof. Harvard, 1959-60, prof., 1962—, James Bryant Conant Univ. prof., 1979—. Fulbright fellow Oxford (Eng.) U., 1952-53. Served with AUS. 1943-46; PTO. Mem. Am. Philos. Assn. (exec. com. Eastern div. 1959-62, v.p. 1973, pres. 1974), Am. Acad. Arts and Scis., Am. Assn. Polit. and Legal Philosophy (pres. 1970-72), Am. Philos. Soc. Author: A Theory of Justice, 1971. Contbr. articles in field to profl. jours. Co-editor Philos. Rev., 1956-59. Home: 9 Winthrop Rd Lexington MA 02173 Office: Dept Philosophy Harvard Univ Cambridge MA 02138

RAWLS, JOHN SAMUEL, former judge; b. Greenwood, Fla., Jan. 1, 1921; s. David Gray and Ruth (Miller) R.; student U. Fla., 1938-41, J.D., 1948; m. Helen Barfield, Sept. 18, 1946; 1 dau., JoLen; 1 foster dau., Judy Rawls Connell Campbell. Admitted to Fla. bar, 1948; mem. firm Rawls & Moore, Marianna, 1948-61; judge 1st Dist. Ct. of Appeal, Tallahassee, 1961-78. Mem. Fla. Judicial Qualifications Commn., 1967—, chmn., 1967-72. Mem. Fla. Senate, 1954-61, pres. pro tem, 1959-61. Trustee Holland Law Center, U. Fla., 1971-73; bd. visitors Fla. State U. Coll. Law, 1972—. Served with USAAF, 1942-45; maj. Res. ret. Mem. Am. Judicature Soc. (dir. 1971-73). Home: 1890 Oxbottom Rd Tallahassee FL 32312 Office: 1890 Oxbottom Rd Tallahassee FL 32312

RAWLS, JOSEPH LEONARD, JR., food co. exec.; b. Rocky Mount, N.C., June 14, 1931; s. Joseph Leonard and Lallah (Mizzel) R.; student U. N.C., 1949-51; B.C.S., Benjamin Franklin U., 1953; postgrad. U. E. Carolina, 1953-54; m. Nancy Lee Williams, Dec. 21, 1951; children—Vivian Lee, Joseph Leonard III. Partner Luper & Rawls, C.P.A.'s, 1958-61; pres., chmn. Hardee's Food Systems, Inc., Rocky Mount, 1961-75, chmn. bd., 1975—; pres. Canton Sta., Ltd., Rocky Mount, 1975—; dir. Planter's Nat. Bank & Trust Co., Rocky Mount. Bd. dirs. N.C. Med. Found., 1970—; campaign chmn., pres. United Fund, 1977-78; trustee N.C. Wesleyan Coll., bd. dirs. Bus. Found. N.C. Served with AUS, 1954-56. Recipient Golden Plate award as Foodservice Operator of Year, Nat. Restaurant Assn. and Internat. Mfrs. Assn. C.P.A., N.C. Mem. Am. Inst. C.P.A.'s, Am. Mgmt. Assn., Young President's Orgn., Phi Gamma Delta. Republican. Episcopalian (vestryman, sr. warden). Clubs: Rotary, Order of Tar Heel 100. Home: 508 Wildwood Ave Rocky Mount NC 27801 Office: 820 Harbour West Dr Rocky Mount NC 27801

RAWLS, LOU, singer; b. Chgo., Dec. 1, 1936. Former mem. musical group Pilgrim Travelers; solo rec. artist, 1962— (1 platinum, 6 gold albums); appeared in motion pictures Angel Angel Down We Go, 1969, Believe in Me, 1971; star TV spls. Soul, 1968, Lou Rawls and the Golddiggers, 1969, also numerous guest TV appearances; nat. spokesman for Budweiser, 1976—. Hon. chmn. United Negro Coll. Fund, 1979. Served with U.S. Army, 1956-58. Recipient Grammy awards for recs. Dead End Street, 1967, A Natural Man, 1971, Unmistakably Lou, 1977. 1978. Address: care The Brokaw Co 9255 Sunset Blvd Suite 411 Los Angeles CA 90069

RAWLS, WENDELL LEE, JR., journalist; b. Goodlettsville, Tenn., Aug. 18, 1941; s. Wendell Lee and Madolyn (Murphy) P.; B.A., Vanderbilt U., 1970; m. Kathryn Coston Stark, June 19, 1971; children—Amanda Coston, Matthew Bradley. Sportswriter, then reporter Nashville Tennessean, 1967-72; reporter Phila. Inquirer, 1972-77, nat. corr., 1974-77; investigative reporter N.Y. Times, Washington, 1977-79, Atlanta, 1979—. Served with AUS, 1965. Recipient Pulitzer prize for reporting, 1977; Robert F. Kennedy Journalism award, 1977; Nat. Headliner award, 1977; Heywood Broun award, 1977; Clarion award, 1977; Keystone Press award, 1975; Thomas L. Stokes spl. citation, 1975; AP Mng. Editors award, 1977; Sigma Delta Chi Regional award, 1977; Pa. Prison Soc. award, 1977; Media award Nat. Mental Health Assn., 1977; John Peter Zenger award Phila. Party, 1977; Writers award Phila. Afro-Am. Hist. and Cultural Mus., 1977. Mem. Alpha Tau Omega. Methodist. Author: Cold Storage, 1980. Office: 225 Peachtree St NE Atlanta GA 30303

RAWNSLEY, HOWARD MELODY, physician, educator; b. Long Branch, N.J., Nov. 20, 1925; s. Walter A. and Elizabeth (Melody) R.; A.B., Haverford Coll., 1949; M.D., U. Pa., 1952; m. B. Eileen Fiddes, Sept. 5, 1967; children—Virgilia Ingram, Elizabeth Sue. Intern, Hosp. U. Pa., 1952-53, resident, 1953-57; practice medicine, specializing in pathology, Phila., 1957-75; mem. Wm. Pepper Lab., U. Pa., 1957-75, asst. dir., 1960-68, dir., 1968-75, asso. dir. Clin. Research Center, 1962-67, acting dir., 1969—70, asst. prof. pathology and medicine, 1960-65, asso. prof., 1965-69, prof., 1969-75; prof. pathology Dartmouth Med. Sch., Hanover, N.H., 1975—; cons. U.S. Naval Hosp. Phila., VA Hosp., U.S. Naval Hosp., Portsmouth, Va. Served with AUS, 1944-46. Woodward fellow in chemistry, 1953-55. Mem. AMA, Pathology Soc. Phila. (pres.), Coll. Am. Pathologists, Am. Soc. Clin. Pathology. Home: 7 Haskins Rd Hanover NH 03755

RAWSON, CATHARINE GROTE, interior designer; b. Chgo., June 10, 1903; d. Vance and Carrie (Clawson) R.; Ph.B., U. Chgo., 1925. Asst. interior designer Margery Sill Wickware, N.Y.C., 1927-33; interior designer antique English furniture dept. Marshall Field & Co., Chgo., 1933-35; asst. interior designer Ann Forester, Inc., Chgo., 1936-37; prin. Catharine G. Rawson-Interiors, Chgo., 1937—. Fellow Am. Soc. Interior Designers; mem. World Federalists Assn. Office: 33 E Cedar St Chicago IL 60611

RAWSON, ELEANOR S., book publisher; m. Kennett Longley Rawson; children—Linda, Kennett Longley. Former editorial staff, writer Am. mag.; free-lance writer radio, mags., newspaper syndicates, fiction editor Today's Woman mag., Collier's mag.; v.p., exec. editor David McKay Co.; now exec. v.p. Rawson, Wade Publishers, Inc.; teaching Staff Columbia U., 1956-57; lectr. N.Y. U., New Sch., N.Y. Trustee, v.p., chmn. nominating com. Museums at Stony Brook. Mem. Assn. Am. Pubs. (exec. council), Women's Nat. Book Assn., N.Y. Infirmary Aux., Soc. Meml. Hosp. Women's Aux. Mather Meml. Hosp., P.E.N., Overseas Press Club Am., Women's Forum, Women in Media. Clubs: Old Field (Stony Brook); Nissequoqe (St. James); Women's City (N.Y.). Home: Blueberry Bay Farm 23 Brewster Ln Setauket NY 11733 Office: 630 3d Ave New York NY 10017

RAWSON, KENNETT LONGLEY, publishing co. exec., b. Chgo., June 1, 1911; s. Frederick Holbrook and Edith (Kennett) R.; student Phillips Acad., Andover, Mass., 1926-29; A.B., Yale, 1933; m. Eleanor Stierhem, 1954; children—Linda Cynthia, Kennett Longley. Mem. Arctic expdns. led by Comdr. Donald MacMillan, 1925, 26, 27, 29; navigator 2d Byrd Antarctic Expdn., 1933-35; editorial dept. G.P. Putman's Sons, 1936, editor firm, 1938-41, editor, 1945, v.p., editor in chief, dir., 1947-50; pres. David McKay Co., Inc., N.Y.C., 1950-74, Rawson, Wade Pubs., Inc., N.Y.C., 1974—. Pres. Greenwich (N.Y.) House; 2d v.p., v.p., bd. dirs. Mather Hosp., Port Jefferson, N.Y. Served as lt. comdr. USNR, 1941-45, communications, navigating officer, comdg. officer. Decorated Navy Cross. Mem. Century Assn. Clubs: Yale (N.Y.C.); Oldfield; Nissequoque; Shenorock; Setauket Yacht. Author: A Boy's Eye View of the Arctic, 1926. Home: Blueberry Bay Farm 23 Brewster Ln E Setauket NY 11733 Office: 150 E 69th St New York NY 10021

RAWSON, MERLE R., mfg. co. exec.; b. Chgo., June 9, 1924; s. Richard W. and Flora R.; student U. Ill., 1946-48; B.S. in Accounting, Northwestern U., 1949; m. Jane Armstrong, July 5, 1947; children—David M., Jeffrey M., Laurel J. Asst. to plant controller John Wood Co., 1949-58; asst. controller Easy Laudry Appliances, 1958-61; controller O'Bryan Bros., 1961; with Hoover Co., North Canton, Ohio, 1961—, controller, 1962-64, v.p., treas., 1964-69, sr. v.p., treas., 1969-75, chmn. bd., chief exec. officer, 1975—, also dir.; exec. v.p. Hoover Worldwide Corp., 1971-75, chmn. bd., chief exec. officer, 1975—, also dir.; chmn. Hoover Ltd. (U.K.), 1978—; dir. Hoover Co. Ltd. (Can.), Hoover Mexicana, Hoover Holland, S.A. Hoover (France), Hoover Adminstrv. Services, S.A. (Belgium), Chemko Comml. Products Inc., Soc. Corp., Cleve., Hoover Industrial y Comercial S.A. (Colombia), Harter Bank & Trust Co. Trustee, Ohio Found. Ind. Colls., Eisenhower Exchange Fellowship, Citizens Council for Ohio Schs.; mem. adv. council Pace U.; mem. Aultman Hosp. Assn., Aultman Hosp. Devel. Found. Served with F.A., AUS, 1943-46. Mem. Stark County Bluecoats. Clubs: Capitol Hill; Union League (N.Y.C.); Congress Lake Country; Canton. Office: 101 E Maple St North Canton OH 44720

RAWSON, RALPH WILLIAM, city mgr., ret. mfg. co. exec.; b. Cass City, Mich., May 21, 1916; s. William Audley and Mary Lena (Day) R.; B.S. in Elec. Engring., U.S. Naval Acad., 1939; M.S. in Aero., Mass. Inst. Tech., 1946; grad. Advanced Mgmt. Program, Harvard, 1963; m. Julie Cabanne Parker, June 1, 1941; children—William A., Julie M., Richard L., Nancy A. Commd. ensign U.S. Navy, 1939, advanced through grades to rear adm. USNR, 1959; designated naval aviator, 1942; prin. assignments as aero. engring. duty officer, 1946-55; ret., 1959; with Fansteel Metall. Corp., 1955-64, v.p., gen. mgr. chem. and metall. div., 1962-64; pres. Fifth Sterling, Inc., Pitts., 1964-67, chmn., chief exec., 1967-68; pres. Vasco, A Teledyne Co., Latrobe, Pa., 1968-70; pres. Am. Gage and Machine Co., Elgin, Ill., 1970-72; city mgr., Madeira Beach, Fla., 1973—. Decorated D.F.C. Mem. Suncoast Municipal Employees Assn. Clubs: Harvard Bus. Sch. Central Fla.; Gulf Beaches Rotary. Home: 15330 Harbor Dr Madeira Beach FL 33708 Office: City Hall Madeira Beach FL 33708

RAWSON, RULON WELLS, physician, educator; b. Idaho Falls, Idaho, Sept. 28, 1908; s. Wilford Woodruff and Eugenia (Lefgren) R.; student Weber Coll., 1926-27, U. Utah, 1930-32; M.B., Northwestern U., 1937, M.D., 1938; m. Jane Young, Aug. 21, 1940; children—James R.Y., Elizabeth Jane, Daniel Y. Research fellow Harvard U. Med. Sch., 1938-42, instr. and Henry P. Walcott fellow clin. medicine, 1942-45, asso. medicine, 1945-47, asst. prof. medicine, 1947-48; asst. physician Mass. Gen. Hosp., 1946-47, asso. physician medicine, 1947-48; asso. prof. medicine Cornell U. Med. Coll., 1948-51, prof., 1951-67; attending physician Meml. Hosp., N.Y.C., 1948-68, chmn. dept. medicine, 1958-68; chief dept. clin. research Sloan-Kettering Inst., 1948-67; prof. medicine, dean, v.p. N.J. Coll. Medicine and Dentistry, 1967-72; prof. medicine, v.p. for edn. and program devel. U. Tex. M.D. Anderson Hosp. and Tumor Inst., 1972-73, dir. extramural programs U. Tex. System Cancer Center, 1972-75, dir. program planning, 1975-77; asso. dir. for sci. operations, chmn. working cadre Nat. Large Bowel Cancer Project, 1972-77; dir. Bonneville Center for Research on Cancer Cause and Prevention, 1977—. Mem. adv. com. med. uses of isotopes AEC, 1959-69; mem. com. on personnel for research Am. Cancer Soc., 1958-63, chmn. 1959-63; mem. adv. com. sr. clin. traineeship program HEW, 1962-67, mem. adv. council on health manpower, 1967-70. Mem. exec. bd. Hutchinson River council Boy Scouts Am., 1961-72, v.p., 1963-72, chmn. Pelham dist., 1961-63, also mem. Nat. council. Recipient award Am. Goiter Assn., 1959, Centennial award Northwestern U., 1959, Disting. Golden Eagle Scout award Boy Scouts Am., 1969, Disting. Physician award N.J. Acad. Medicine, 1972, Disting. Alumnus award U. Utah, 1977. Fellow N.Y. Acad. Medicine; mem. A.C.P., A.M.A., Am. Physiol. Soc., A.A.A.S., Am. Goiter Assn. (council 1950-53, pres. 1955-56), Endocrine Soc. (pres. 1966-67); (chmn. publs. com. 1957-63), Am. Assn. Cancer Research, Am. Soc. Clin. Investigation, N.Y. State Med. Soc., Harvey Soc. (sec. 1955-58), Assn. Am. Physicians. Clubs: Harvard (N.Y.C.). Author sci. papers, chpts. in texts on physiology and diseases of the thyroid and endocrinology of cancer. Home: 875 Donner Way 1102 Salt Lake City UT 84108 Office: Bonneville Center for Research on Cancer 520 Wakara Way Salt Lake City UT 84108. *My greatest satisfactions have come from the opportunities I have had to acquire new knowledge, to share it with my students and colleagues and then to see that knowledge applied in the treatment and control of certain human diseases. The principles, ideals, goals, and standards of conduct which have had the greatest influence on my life can be traced to the teaching of my church (Mormon) and my parents—the importance of acquiring new knowledge which will be eternal—and to several of my teachers and academic associates.*

RAWSON, WILLIAM ROBERT, lawyer, mfg. co. exec.; b. Montclair, N.J., Mar. 14, 1925; s. William Howard and Maude Elizabeth (Wheeler) R.; A.B., Brown U., 1947; LL.B., N.Y. U., 1950; m. Elizabeth S. Crandall, Sept. 30, 1949; children—Shirley, Jean, Elizabeth. Admitted to N.J. bar, 1950, Ill. bar, 1974; practice of law, Bloomfield, N.J., 1950-52; legal asst. Thomas A. Edison Industries, West Orange, N.J., 1952-57; asst. counsel T.A. Edison div. McGraw-Edison Co., Elgin, Ill., 1957-67, v.p. adminstrn., div., 1967-72, asst. gen. counsel, 1972-77, corp. v.p. adminstrn., 1977—; dir. Chgo. Econ. Devel. Corp. Chmn. Millburn (N.J.) Planning Bd. and Bd. Adjustment, 1962-70, Millburn Red Cross, 1969-70; mem. twp. council, dep. mayor Twp. of Millburn, 1970-72; v.p. Elgin (Ill.) United Way, 1978-79. Served to lt. (j.g.) USN, 1943-46. Mem. Am. Bar Assn., Ill. State Bar Assn., Elgin C. of C. (v.p. 1978-79). Republican. Episcopalian. Home: 6N 564 Fair Oaks Dr Saint Charles IL 60174 Office: 333 W River Rd Elgin IL 60120

RAWSTHORNE, RALPH, assn. exec.; b. Ormskirk, Lancashire, Eng., June 15, 1915; s. Ralph and Mary Alice (Baldwin) R.; came to Can., 1920; A.R.C.T., Royal Conservatory Music, U. Toronto (Ont., Can.), 1972; m. Dorothy Aileen Davis, July 2, 1949; children—Jeffery Arthur, Suzanne Emily Alice (dec.). Salesman, Toronto-St. Catarines Truck Lines, 1946-48; field service rep. Can. C. of C., Montreal, Que., 1948-50; mgr. Porcupine C. of C., Timmins, Ont., 1950-51; gen. mgr. St. Catharines (Ont.) Dist. C. of C., 1951—. Served with RCAF, 1940-46. Mentioned in dispatches. Mem. C. of C. Execs. Can. (pres. 1968), Can. Speech Assn., Can. Music Festival Adjudicators Assn. Mem. United Ch. of Canada. Clubs: St. Catharines Golf and Country, Masons. *

RAY, BRONSON SANDS, surgeon, educator; b. New Albany, Ind., Jan. 4, 1904; s. Herbert A. and Nellie (Sands) R.; B.S., Franklin Coll., 1924, D.Sc. (hon.), 1950; M.D., Northwestern U., 1928; m. Muriel Weeks, July 29, 1933; children—Susan (Mrs. George H. Bright, Jr.), Phoebe (Mrs. Michael Sierstorpff). Instr. surgery Harvard Med. Sch., 1931-32; asst. surgery Cornell Med. Coll., 1932-35, instr. surgery, 1935-36, surgery, 1936-39, asst. prof. surgery, 1939-41, asso. prof. surgery, 1941-45, asso. prof. clin surgery, 1945-48, prof. surgery, 1948-76, prof. emeritus, 1976—; asst. attending surgeon N.Y. Hosp., N.Y.C., 1936-39, asso. attending surgeon, 1939-43, attending surgeon, 1943-78, hon. staff, 1978—, cons. neurosurgery Westchester div. 1948-78; attending surgeon St. Luke's Hosp., N.Y.C., 1942—, cons. surgeon, 1970-78; vis. cons. neurosurgery Roosevelt Hosp., 1946-78; cons. neurosurgeon Meml. Hsop., N.Y.C., 1946-78; attending neurosurgeon Meml., Greenwich hosps.; vis. neurosurgeon Bellevue Hosp. 1955—. Sec.-gen. 2d Internat. Congress Neurosurgery, 1961; spl. cons. Neurol. Sci. Research Tng. Com., 1962-66; mem. adv. council NIH, 1969-73. Diplomate Am. Bd. Surgery, Am. Bd. Neurosurgery (bd.). Fellow A.C.S.; mem. Am. Surg. Assn., Soc. Neurol. Surgeons (pres. 1963-64, chmn. com. edn., dir. audiovisual edn. 1971—), N.Y. Neurol. Soc. (pres. 1965-66), Am. Neurol. Assn., Assn. Research in Nervous and Mental Diseases, Soc. U. Surgeons, N.Y. Surg. Soc., N.Y. Acad. Medicine, A.M.A., Clin. Surg. Soc., Am. Assn. Neurol. Surg. (pres. 1958-59), Med. and Surg. Soc. N.Y.C., Sigma Alpha Epsilon, Nu Sigma Nu, Alpha Omega Alpha. Clubs: Century Assn., Au Sable; University (N.Y.C.) Contbr. articles profl., sci. jours. Home: 178 E 70th St New York City NY 10021 also Three Pines Keene NY 12942

RAY, C(LARENCE) THORPE, internist, cardiologist; b. Hutto, Tex., July 17, 1916; B.A., U. Tex., 1937, M.D., Galveston, 1941; m. Lillian Russell; 1 dau., Marilyn Claire. Rotating intern Scott and White Hosp., Temple, Tex., 1941-42; resident in medicine Parkland Hosp., Dallas, 1942-44, dir. out-patient dispensary, 1943-44; instr. in medicine Southwestern Med. Found., Dallas, 1943-44; instr. Tulane U., 1945-47, asst. prof. medicine, 1947-52, asso. prof., 1952-58, clin. prof., 1967-75, prof., chmn. dept. medicine, 1975—, dir. Heart Sta., 1947-58; prof., chmn. dept. medicine U. Mo., 1958-67; dir. edn. and research Alton Ochsner Med. Found., New Orleans, 1967-75, head sect. cardiology, 1968-75, trustee, v.p., 1970-75; mem. cons. staff Tour Infirmary, New Orleans, 1978—; cons. to hosps. Diplomate Am. Bd. Internal Medicine (exam. bd. cardiovascular disease 1964-67, bd. examiners 1967-73). Fellow Am. Coll. Cardiology; mem. Orleans Parish Med. Soc., La. State Med. Soc., AMA, New Orleans Acad. Internal Medicine, New Orleans Grad. Med. Assembly, So. Med. Assn., Am. Soc. Clin. Investigation, Central Soc. Clin. Research, So. Soc. Clin. Research, La. Heart Assn., Am. Heart Assn. (adv. bd. sect. circulation), Am. Fedn. Clin. Research, A.C.P., Phi Beta Kappa, Sigma Xi, Phi Beta Pi, Phi Eta Sigma, Alpha Epsilon Delta, Alpha Omega Alpha. Contbr. numerous articles to profl. publs. Home: 473 Woodvine Ave Metairie LA 70005 Office: 1430 Tulane Ave New Orleans LA 70112

RAY, CHARLES DEAN, neurosurgeon; b. Americus, Ga., Aug. 1, 1927; s. Oliver Tinsley and Katherine (Broadfield) R.; A.B., Emory U., 1950; M.S., U. Miami (Fla.), 1952; M.D., Med. Coll. Ga., 1956; m. Roberta L. Mann, Dec. 17, 1978; children—Bruce, Kathy, C. Marlene, Thomas, John Blythe. Intern, Baptist Meml. Hosp., Memphis, 1956-57; resident, research asso. neurosurgery U. Tenn. Hosp., Memphis, 1957-62; fellow, research asst. Mayo Clinic and Found., Rochester, Minn., 1962-64; asst. prof. neurosurgery, lectr. bioengring. Johns Hopkins Med. Sch., Balt., 1964-68; chief dept. med. engring. F. Hoffmann-LaRoche, Basel, Switzerland, also lectr. U. Basel, 1968-73; practice medicine, specializing in neurosurgery, Mpls., 1973—; staff Sister Kenney Inst., Children's, Abbott-Northwestern hosps., Mpls., clin. asso. prof. medicine U. Minn., Mpls., 1973—; v.p. med research Medtronic Inc., Mpls., 1972—; cons. in field. Chmn. com. materials and devices World Fedn. Neurosurg. Socs., 1977—; vestry St. Martin's Episcopal Ch., Wayzata, Minn., 1976—. Served with USN, 1945-49. Diplomate Am. Bd. Neurol. Surgery. Fellow A.C.S., Royal Soc. Health; mem. Pan-Am. Med. Assns., AMA, Am. Assn. Neurol. Surgeons, Congress Neurol. Surgeons, W. Ger. Armed Forces Med. Soc., IEEE, Internat. Fedn. Med. Biol. Engring., Internat. Soc. Stereotaxic and Functional Neurosurgery, ASTM, Internat. Orgn. Standardization, Sigma Xi, others. Clubs: Cosmos, Lafayette, Minneapolis. Author: Principles of Engineering Applied to Medicine, 1964; Medical Engineering, 1974. Contbr. articles to profl. publs. Home: 19550 Cedarhurst Wayzata MN 55391 Office: Medtronic Inc Box 1453 Minneapolis MN 55440 also Sister Kenny Inst 2545 Chicago Ave Minneapolis MN 55404. *It is no worse to live forever in the past than to have none at all. It is no worse to live forever in the future than to have no prospect for one.*

RAY, CHARLES KENDALL, univ. dean; b. Boise City, Okla., Mar. 15, 1928; s. Volney Holt and Mamie (Burton) R.; B.A., U. Colo., 1951; M.A., Columbia, 1955, Ed.D., 1959; m. Doris Derby, Aug. 26, 1951. Teaching prin. Bur. Indian Affairs, Savoonga, Alaska, 1951-54; mem. faculty U. Alaska, 1957—, prof. edn., 1960—, dean Sch. Edn., 1961—. Mem. N.E.A., Am. Assn. Sch. Adminstrs., Am. Assn. U. Profs., Am. Assn. Colls. Tchr. Edn. (state liaison officer), Phi Delta Kappa. Author: A Program of Education for Alaska Natives; Alaskan Native Secondary School Dropouts, Home: 1209 10th Ave Fairbanks AK 99701

RAY, DAVID EUGENE, educator; b. Sapulpa, Okla., May 20, 1932; s. Dowell Adolphus and Catherine (Jennings) R.; B.A., U. Chgo., 1952, M.A., 1957; m. Suzanne Judy Morrish, Feb. 21, 1970; children—Winifred, Wesley, Samuel, Sapphina. Instr., Cornell U., Ithaca, N.Y., 1960-64; instr. Reed Coll., Portland, Oreg., 1964-66; lectr. U. Iowa, Iowa City, 1969-70; asso. prof. Bowling Green (Ohio) State U., 1970-71; prof. English U. Mo.-Kansas City, 1971—; vis. prof. English, Syracuse (N.Y.) U., 1978-79; lectures, poetry readings. Recipient Young Writers award New Republic, 1958; William Carlos Williams award, 1979; Woursell Found., U. Vienna (Austria) fellow, 1966-71. Author: X-Rays, 1965; Dragging the Main, 1968; A Hill In Oklahoma, 1972; Gathering Firewood, 1974; Enough of Flying, poems inspired by the Ghazals of Ghalib, 1977; The Mulberries of Mingo, 1978; The Tramp's Cup (William Carlos Williams award Poetry Soc. Am.), 1978; editor Chgo. Rev., 1956-57, The Chgo. Rev. Anthology, 1959, Epoch, 1960-64, From the Hungarian Revolution, 1966; New Letters, 1971—; (with Robert Bly) A Poetry Reading Against the Vietnam War, 1966; (with Robert Farnsworth) Richard Wright: Impressions and Perspectives, 1973; (with Jack Salzman) A Jack Conroy Reader, 1979. Home: 5517 Crestwood Dr Kansas City MO 64110. *About our future I am pessimistic, since those who seek power seem the least capable of using it wisely, and though I have been involved in ecology and anti-war efforts, I know the balance of good and evil remains constant. Nevertheless, we must keep working as if this were not the case. My joy in love and family life and in the small pleasures that make my poetry are denied, I know, to those who are more busy in their pursuit of power and its psychotic ideals—ideals which provide symbols and metaphors that make their lives poetic (irrational) too, but in a most unfortunately colorful and destructive way. I have fought depression in order to survive and enjoy, have sought humility in order to see clearly. It is not a fashionable position, yet I accept as basic Epictetus' words, We cannot make others admire us, we must look to the curing of ourselves.*

RAY, DAVID SCOTT, educator; b. New Haven, Oct. 5, 1930; s. Wilbert Scott and Dorothy Philips (Clark) R.; A.B., Washington and Jefferson Coll., 1952; M.A., U. Mich., 1956; Ph.D., U. Tenn., 1964; m. Leslie Ann Mason, Sept. 8, 1956; children—Susan Elizabeth, Jennifer Lynn, Alison Diana, Bethany Carolyn. Teaching asst. U. Mich., 1956-58; instr. U. Tenn., 1958-64; asso. prof. Bucknell U., 1964-71, prof., 1971—, chmn. dept. math., 1970—, coordinator grad. studies, 1966-71, dir. January program, 1977—. Served with USNR, 1952-55. Recipient Lindback award for distinguished teaching Bucknell U., 1970; NSF Sci. Faculty fellow, 1962-63. Mem. Math. Assn. Am., Am. Math. Soc., Am. Assn. Univ. Profs., A.A.A.S., Sigma Xi. Home: 2 Brown St Lewisburg PA 17837

RAY, DENNIS FRED, educator; b. Crestview, Fla., Nov. 29, 1930; s. Neal Flemings and Lela Mae (Sellars) R.; B.S. in Bus. Adminstrn., U. Fla., 1957, M.B.A., 1958, Ph.D., 1966; m. Brenda Gail Cox, Aug. 16, 1969. Tchr., U. Ala. Center, Dothan, 1958-63, dir. center, 1962-63; instr. U. Fla., 1964-66; mem. faculty Miss. State U., 1966—, prof., head mgmt. dept., 1968—; mgmt. cons. to govt. and industry, also mgmt. tng. cons. Served with USN, 1951-54. Mem. So. Mgmt. Assn. (v.p., program chmn., editor Proc.), Acad. Mgmt. (chmn. mgmt. cons. div., sec.-treas. 1976—, bus. mgr. publs.), Soc. Advancement Mgmt., Delta Sigma Pi, Beta Gamma Sigma. Editor: Jour. of Mgmt. Home: PO Box 5221 Mississippi State MS 39762

RAY, DIXY LEE, gov. State of Wash.; b. Tacoma, Sept. 3, 1914; d. Alvis Marion and Frances (Adams) Ray; B.A., Mills Coll., 1937, M.A., 1938, LL.D., 1967; Ph.D. (Van Sicklen fellow), Stanford, 1945; hon. degrees St. Martins Coll., 1972, Hood Coll., 1973, Seattle U., 1972, Ripon Coll., 1974, St. Mary's Coll., 1974, U. Puget Sound, 1974, Mich. State U., 1974, Union Coll., 1974, No. Mich. U., 1974, Smith Coll., L.I. U. Tchr. pub. schs., Oakland, Calif., 1938-42; John Switzer fellow Stanford, 1942-43; asso. prof. zoology U. Wash., 1945-76; mem. AEC, Washington, 1972-73, chmn., 1973-75; asst. sec. state, 1975; gov. State of Wash., 1977—. Mem. exec. com. Friday Harbor Labs., 1945-60; spl. cons. biol. oceanography NSF, 1960-62; dir. Pacific Sci. Center, Seattle, 1963-72; chief scientist, vis. prof. Stanford Research Vessel TE VEGA, Internat. Indian Ocean Expdn., 1964; mem. Presdl. Task Force on Oceanography, 1969. Recipient William Clapp award in marine biology Nat. Assn. Corrosion Engrs., 1959, Seattle Maritime award, 1967, Frances K. Hutchinson medal in conservation Garden Club Am., 1973; Am. Exemplar medal Freedoms Found., 1978; Guggenheim fellow, 1952-53. Mem. Danish Royal Soc. Natural History (fgn. mem.), Phi Beta Kappa, Sigma Xi. Author: Marine Boring and Fouling Organisms, 1959; also articles. Home: 600 3d Ave Fox Island WA 98333 Office: Office of Gov Legislative Bldg Olympia WA 98501

RAY, DONALD GORDON, church exec.; b. Toronto, Ont., Can., Jan. 24, 1918; s. Colin Archibald and Eva (Collett) R.; B.A., Victoria U., 1940; postgrad. Emmanuel Coll., 1940-43, 45-46, D.D. (hon.), U. Winnipeg, 1968; m. Mary Georgina Clark, May 12, 1943; children—Judith, Ian, Duncan. Ordained to ministry United Ch. of Can., 1946; pastor, Berwyn, Alta., 1946-49, Kettleby, Ont., 1949-51, Dauphin, Man., 1951-59, Ft. Garry, Man., 1960-70; asso. and dep. sec. Gen. Council, United Ch. of Can., Toronto, 1970-75, sec. Gen. Council, 1975—. Served with RCAF, 1942-45. Decorated D.F.C. Home: 1 Ternhill Crescent Don Mills ON M3C 2E4 Canada Office: 85 St Clair Ave E Toronto ON M4T 1M8 Canada

RAY, DONALD P., polit. economist, assn. exec., editor; b. Mpls., May 22, 1916; s. Moses and Effie (Page) R.; A.B., U. Colo., 1941; Am. Council Learned Socs. scholar Cornell U., summer 1941, Harvard, 1941-42; M.A., George Washington U., 1947, grad. student, 1949-52. Regional analyst Far Eastern div., overseas br. office of dir. OWI, 1944-45; asst. dept. econs. George Washington U., 1945-47; exec. dir. Nat. Acad. Econs. and Polit. Sci., 1947-59; dir. Nat. Inst. Social and Behavioral Sci., 1959—, also editor Symposia Studies Series, 1959—. Asso. editor Social Sci., 1950-55; editor Spl. Pubs. Series Nat. Acad. Econs. and Polit. Sci., 1953-59. Fellow A.A.A.S. (mem. council 1954-62; sec. sect. social econ. scis. 1954-62); mem. Am. Polit. Sci. Assn., Assn. Asian Studies, Am. Econ. Assn., Internat. Conf. Asian Problems, Delta Phi Epsilon, Pi Gamma Mu, Omicron Delta Gamma. Presbyn. Club: Harvard (Washington). Editor: Trends in Social Science, 1961. Contbr. articles and revs. to profl. jours. Home: 1505 28th St S Arlington VA 22206 Office: George Washington U Washington DC 20006

RAY, EDGAR WAYNE, ret. newspaper editor; b. Macon, Ga., Apr. 9, 1911; s. Edgar Leonard and Ada Wayne (Massey) R.; student Mercer U., 1929-31; m. Mary Dee Smith, Mar. 9, 1931; children—Elizabeth Lynn, Edgar Wayne. Mem. sports dept. Macon

Telegraph, 1925-31, sports editor, 1931-33; sports editor Tampa (Fla.) Times, 1933-35, mng. editor, 1935-49; exec. editor Orlando (Fla.) Sentinel-Star, 1949-53, Johnson City (Tenn.) Press-Chronicle, 1953; exec. editor San Antonio Express and News, 1953-58, editor, 1958-60; mng. editor Houston Press, 1960-64; mng. editor Memphis Press-Scimitar, 1964-74, asso. editor, 1976-77. Former pres. Tampa Urban League; speaker racial amity. Active A.R.C., Community Chest, U.S.O. Bd. dirs. Salvation Army, United Fund; past vice chmn., gov. Orange County (Fla.) Meml. Hosp. Named Outstanding Young Tampan, 1943, Jr. C. of C. Mem. San Antonio C. of C. (bd. dirs.), A.P. Mng. Editor's Assn., Fla. Asso. Press Assn. (past pres.), Tex. Asso. Press Mng. Editors, Fla. Daily Newspaper Assn. (past dir.), Tenn. Press Assn. (pres. 1976-77), Tex. (past pres.), Tenn. U.P. internat. assns., Tenn. A.P. Assn. Sigma Delta Chi. Presbyn. (elder). Home: 212 Condict Dr New Smyrna Beach FL 32069

RAY, EDGAR WAYNE, JR., food co. exec.; b. Tampa, Fla., Feb. 25, 1941; s. Edgar Wayne and Mary Dee (Smith) R.; B.B.A. with honors, U. Tex., Austin, 1963, M.B.A., 1964. Mgmt. trainee T. J. Bettes Co., Houston, 1964-66; fin. analyst Riviana Foods Inc., Houston, 1966-68, asst. treas., 1968-75, treas., 1975—. C.P.A., Tex. Mem. Am. Inst. C.P.A.'s, Tex. Soc. C.P.A.'s, Beta Gamma Sigma. Presbyterian. Home: 2326 Sunset Blvd Houston TX 77005 Office: 2777 Allen Pkwy Houston TX 77019

RAY, GEORGE EINAR, lawyer; b. Gloucester, Mass., Apr. 23, 1910; s. Matti and Sandra Sofia (Kujala) R.; A.B., Harvard, 1932, J.D. 1935; m. Mary Lee Osborne, Sept. 7, 1940; children—Mary Danforth White, Priscilla, Elizabeth Ray Hulett, George Einar, Jr., Clifford Osborne, Michael Gritton (dec.). Admitted to Mass. bar, 1935, practiced in N.Y.C., 1936-38, Boston, 1942-44; mem. firm Ray, Anderson, Shields, Trotti & Hemphill, and predecessor firms, Dallas, 1946—; faculty asso. Columbia Law Sch. 1935-36; atty. U.S. Bd. Tax Appeals, Washington, 1938-41; spl. asst. to atty. gen. U.S., tax div. Dept. Justice, 1941; prin. atty. Office Tax Legis. Counsel, U.S. Treasury Dept., 1941-42; adj. prof. So. Meth. U. Law Sch., N.Y.U. Tax Inst., Practicing Law Inst. Served as lt. comdr. USNR, World War II; attended Sch. Mil Govt., Columbia, 1944; head dept. internat. law Naval Sch. Mil. Govt., Princeton, 1944-45; chief counsel Office Army-Navy Liquidation Commr., M.T.O., 1945; dep. exec. dir. Office Fgn. Liquidation Commr., State Dept., 1946. Mem. Am., Tex., Dallas County bar assns., Tex. Bar, Tex. Bar Found., Southwestern Legal Found., Harvard Law Sch. Assn. Tex. (ex-pres.), Dallas Estate Council (pres. 1949-50). Baptist (deacon). Clubs: City, Northwood Country, Harvard (pres. 1950-51), Salesmanship; Dallas Knife and Fork (pres. 1967-68). Author: Incorporating the Professional Practice; (with Harry V. Lamon, Jr.) Fiduciary Responsibilities under the New Pension Reform Act; (with William N. Bret, Jr.) Financial Incentives for Executives: Wealth-Building Programs and Techniques. also articles in legal publs. Home: 12615 Breckenridge Dallas TX 75230 Office: 1300 Fidelity Union Tower Dallas TX 75201

RAY, GORDON NORTON, educator, found. exec.; b. N.Y.C., Sept. 8, 1915; s. Jess Gordon and Jessie (Norton) R.; A.B., Ind. U., 1936, A.M., 1936, L.H.D. (hon.), 1964; A.M., Harvard, 1938, Ph.D., 1940, Dexter fellow, 1940-41, Guggenheim fellow, 1941-42, 46, 56-57; Rockefeller fellow, 1948-49; Litt.D., Monmouth Coll., 1959, Syracuse U., 1961, Duke, 1965, U. Ill., 1968, Northwestern U., 1974; LL.D., N.Y. U., 1961, Tulane U., 1963, U. Calif., 1968, Columbia U., 1969, U. So. Calif., 1974; L.H.D., U. Pa., 1978. Instr. English, Harvard, 1940-42; prof. English, U. Ill., 1946-60, head dept., 1950-57, v.p., provost, 1957-60; vis. prof. U. Oreg., summer 1948; Berg prof. N.Y. U., 1952-53, prof. English, 1962—; Lowell lectr., Boston, 1950; adviser in lit. Houghton, Mifflin Co., 1954-71; mem. adv. bd. Soho Bibliographies, 1968-79; asso. sec. gen. John Simon Guggenheim Meml. Found, 1960-61, sec. gen., 1961-63, pres., trustee, 1963—; mem. adv. council Smithsonian Instn., 1967—, chmn., 1970—; treas., dir. Am. Council Learned Socs., 1973—; trustee Found. Library Center, 1962-68, chmn. bd., 1965-68; trustee Pierpont Morgan Library, Rosenbach Found., N.Y. Pub. Library, Columbia U. Press, Winterthur Mus. Served to lt. USNR, 1942-46. Fellow Am. Acad. Arts and Scis., Royal Soc. Lit.; mem. Am. Philos. Soc., Modern Lang. Assn. (mng. trustee), Phi Beta Kappa. Clubs: Harvard, Grolier (past pres.), Century Assn. (N.Y.C.); Athenaeum (London). Author: Letters and Private Papers of William Makepeace Thackeray, 4 vols., 1945-46; The Buried Life, 1952; Thackeray: The Uses of Adversity, 1811-1846, 1955; Thackeray: The Age of Wisdom, 1847-1863, 1958; Henry James and H.G. Wells (with Leon Edel), 1958; H.G. Wells and Rebecca West, 1974; The Illustrator and the Book in England from 1790 to 1914, 1976. Editorial bd. Manuscripta, English Language Notes. Contbr. articles and revs., mags. Home: 25 Sutton Pl S New York City NY 10022 Office: 90 Park Ave New York NY 10016

RAY, H. M., lawyer, govt. ofcl.; b. Rienzi, Miss., Aug. 9, 1924; s. Thomas Henry and Isabelle (Dunlap) R.; J.D., U. Miss., 1949; m. Merle Burt, Nov. 28, 1953; children—Howard Manfred, Mark Andrew. Admitted to Miss. bar, 1949; practice law, 1949-61; U.S. atty. No. Dist. Miss., Oxford, 1961—; mem. Atty. Gen's Adv. Com. of U.S. Attys., 1973-78, chmn., 1976; vis. lectr. UN, Asia and Far East, Inst. for Prevention of Crime and Treatment of Offenders, Tokyo, 1977; pros. atty. Alcorn County (Miss.), 1956-57, 58-61; mem. Miss. Ho. of Reps., 1948-51. Chmn., Corinth-Alcorn County Airport Bd., 1959-61; trustee Alcorn County Public Library, 1959-62. Served with USAAC, 1943-45, USAF, 1951-53. Recipient Corinth's Young Man of Yr. award, 1958. Fellow Miss. Bar Found. (dir.); mem. Am., Fed. (pres. Miss. chpt., Disting. Service award Miss. chpt. 1976, nat. chmn. council on adminstrn. justice 1979-80), Miss., Lafayette County bar assns. Co-author Miss. Workmens' Compensation Act, 1948. Office: PO Drawer 886 Oxford MS 38655

RAY, JAMES DAVIS, JR., biologist, univ. adminstr.; b. Starkville, Miss., May 5, 1918; s. James Davis and Frank Tipton (Turner) R.; B.S., Miss. State U., 1939, M.S., 1947; Ph.D., U. Ill., 1951; m. Dorothy E. Burkett, Nov. 21, 1946; children—Dorothy, Katharine, Susan, Carolyn. Asso. prof. botany, dir. herbarium Miss. State U., 1955-59; asso. prof. botany, dir. herbarium U. South Fla., Tampa, 1959-62, prof., chmn. biol. scis., 1962-71, prof., acting chmn. dept. biology, 1972-73, dean Coll. Natural Scis., 1973—; dir. Landmark Bank Tampa. Served with USNR, 1941-45. Mem. Miss., Fla. acads. scis., Assn. So. Biologists, AAAS, Internat. Assn. Plant Taxonomists, Am. Inst. Biol. Scis., Sigma Xi, Sigma Alpha Epsilon, Beta Beta Beta, Phi Kappa Phi, Omicron Delta Kappa, Phi Sigma, Alpha Epsilon Delta. Methodist. Author: The Genus Lysimachia in the New World, 1956; (with Gid E. Nelson) What a Piece of Work Is Man, 1971, Biologic Readings for Today's Students, 1971, Contemporary Readings in Biology. Home: 417 Druid Hills Rd Temple Terrace FL 33617 Office: 4202 Fowler Ave Tampa FL 33620

RAY, JETER SEEHORN, lawyer; b. Newport, Tenn., Oct. 1, 1908; s. Flint Moore and Millie Jane (McMahan) R.; student Tenn. Wesleyan, 1926-28; A.B., U. Tenn., 1930; LL.B., Duke, 1932; m. Reva Juanita Proffitt, Oct. 1, 1938; children—Richard, Donald, Pamela Elaine. Admitted to Tenn. bar, 1932, U.S. Supreme Court, 1944; gen. practice of law with firms Parrott and Ray, Allen and Ray, 1932-40; atty. U.S. Dept. Labor, 1940—, regional atty., 1941-45, asst. solicitor in charge of litigation, 1945-46, asso. solicitor, 1946, regional atty. until 1969, dep. solicitor, Washington, 1969—, mem. benefits rev. bd., 1973—, chief counsel Office Salary Stblzn., 1952; mem. Tenn. House of Reps., 1935; city atty. Newport, Tenn., 1935-37; adviser U.S. del., 32d session ILO, Geneva, 1949; mem. U.S. del. for negotiation Migrant Labor Agreement, Mexico City, 1951; chmn. Tenn. Occupational Safety and Health Rev. Commn., 1977—. Recipient Willis Smith Award for maintanining the highest average in class of 1932 at Duke U. Law Sch. Mem. Am., Tenn. bar assns., Order of the Coif, Phi Alpha Delta. Democrat. Methodist. Mason, Elk, Moose. Club: Deltona Country. Home: Manor 129 4400 Belmont Park Terr Nashville TN 37215

RAY, JOHN EDWIN, 3D, mfg. co. exec.; b. Franklin, Va., May 5, 1919; s. Burton Justice and Sallie Shepherd (Camp) R.; grad. Woodberry Forest Sch., 1938; student Cornell U., 1941; m. Margaret Ellis Smith, Aug. 15, 1942; children—Margaret Ray Gibbs, John Burton, Caroline Ray Brown. Vice pres. Camp Mfg. Co. Franklin, 1956; resident mgr. Camp div. Union Bag-Camp Paper Corp. (co. name changed to Union Camp Corp.), Franklin, 1956-62, v.p., gen. mgr. bleached products div., 1962-69, exec. v.p., 1969—. Bd. dirs. Camp Found. Dir. Am. Paper Inst.; bd. govs. Nat. Council Paper Industry for Air and Stream Improvement; trustee emeritus Va. Grad. Sch. Sponsors. Served to maj. USAAF, 1941-45. Mem. Phi Delta Theta. Baptist. Clubs: Cypress Cove Country (Franklin); Princess Anne Country (Virginia Beach, Va.); North Jersey Country; Montclair Golf. Office: 1600 Valley Rd Wayne NJ 07470

RAY, LINTON GRIER, JR., textile co. exec.; b. Washington, Ga., Jan. 23, 1917; s. Linton Grier and Eura (Combs) R.; A.B., Emory U., 1938, M.S., 1939; Ph.D., Columbia, 1943; m. Beatrice Dreyfuss, Feb. 21, 1942; children—Linton Grier III, Georgia, Sara Lee; m. 2d, Doris Pfennig, Jan. 10, 1964. With E.I. duPont de Nemours & Co., Inc., 1943-60, marketing mgr., 1960; v.p. Deering Milliken, Inc., 1960-61; pres. Deering Milliken Research Corp., 1961-63; v.p., tech. dir. Indian Head, Inc., 1964-74; pres. Joseph Bancroft & Sons, Co., 1965-74; v.p. Borg Textiles, 1975—. Mem. tech. adv. bd. Dept. Commerce, 1962-64; trustee Textile Research Inst., 1962—, chmn., 1965—. Mem. Fiber Soc. Club: Union League (N.Y.C.). Home: 420 E 51st St New York City NY 10022 Office: 104 W 40th St New York City NY 10018

RAY, REID HACKETT, motion picture producer; b. Greenville, Ill., Oct. 21, 1901; s. Joseph Gordon and Frances (Reid) R.; B.S.C., U. Iowa, 1923; m. Roxanne O'Malley, Dec. 30, 1944; children by previous marriage—Gordon Reid, James Christian. Film writer, dir., cameraman comml. films Mills & Bell Motion Picutres, Inc., St. Paul, 1924-25; reorganized company as Ray-Bell Films, Inc., 1926, pres., dir., producer films, 1926-47; pres., dir., producer films successor orgn. Reid H. Ray Film Industries, Inc., 1947-69; prof. Rochester Inst. Tech. Coll. Photographic Arts and Scis., Rochester, N.Y., 1969—. Fellow Soc. Motion Picture and Television Engrs. (exec. v.p. 1961-62, pres. 1963-64). Dirs. Guild Am., Univ. Film Assn., CINE (pres. 1968-70), Alpha Sigma Phi. Home: 8700 N Oracle Rd Tucson AZ 85704

RAY, RICHARD ARCHIBALD, editor; b. New Orleans, Jan. 22, 1936; s. Archibald Cole and Eliza Owen (Britt) R.; A.B., Dartmouth Coll., 1958; postgrad. Princeton Theol. Sem., 1958-59; B.D., Union Theol. Sem. in Va., 1961; Ph.D., U. St. Andrews (Scotland), 1964; m. Lila Frances McGeachy, Aug. 26, 1959; children—Lila English, Roderick Archibald, Alison Britt. Ordained to ministry Presbyn. Ch.; minister Presbyn. Ch., Crossett, Ark., 1963-66, Tyler Meml. Presbyn. Ch., Radford, Va., 1966-68; prof. Stephens Coll., Columbia, Mo., 1968-71; editor, mng. dir. John Knox Press, Atlanta, 1971—. Rockefeller Brothers fellow. Mem. Am. Acad. Religion, Am. Philos. Assn. Co-pub., editor Jour. of Social Philosophy. Home: 3916 Menlo Dr Atlanta GA 30340 Office: 341 Ponce de Leon Ave NE Atlanta GA 30308

RAY, RICHARD GRAYSON, mfg. co. exec.; b. San Francisco, July 6, 1919; s. William Ruth and Vida Margaret (Young) R.; B.S. in Mech. Engrng., Stanford U., 1942; m. Marcia Ellen Hollister, June 16, 1944; children—Marcia Ellen, Hollister Ann, Richard Grayson. Vice pres. mfg. Gen. Controls, Glendale, Calif., 1946-63; pres. Gen. Controls div. ITT, Glendale, 1966-73, group pres. ITT-Controls and Instruments div., Glendale, 1973—; dir. Glendale Fed. Savs. & Loan Assn., New World Mut. Fund. Served with USNR, 1942-46. Mem. Ancient Order of Supplers, Gas Appliance Mfrs. Assn., Nat. Elec. Mfrs. Assn. (chmn. controls sect. 1977-78). Republican. Presbyterian. Club: Oakmont Country. Office: ITT Controls & Instruments 801 Allen Ave Glendale CA 91201*

RAY, ROBERT D., physician, educator; b. Cleve., Sept. 21, 1914; s. Clifford A. and Edna (Durant) R.; B.A. cum laude, U. Calif., 1936, M.A., 1938, Ph.D., 1948; M.D., Harvard, 1943; Hon. H.D. (Docent), Umeö, Sweden; m. Genevieve Triau, Dec. 19, 1953; children—Frances Carol, Robert Triau, Esten Bernard, Gisele Antoinette, Charles Alexander. Teaching asst. in anatomy U. Calif. Med. Sch., 1937-38, Carnegie research fellow, 1938-40, instr. anatomy, 1947-48, postgrad. tng. U. Calif. Hosp., San Francisco, 1949; intern Peter Bent Brigham Hosp., Boston, 1943; resident orthopaedic surgery Children's Hosp., Boston, 1944-45; asst. orthopaedic surgery Harvard Med. Sch., 1944-45; asst. prof. surgery, head orthopaedic surgery U. Wash. Sch. Medicine, 1948-51, asso. prof. surgery, 1954-56; prof., chmn. dept. orthopaedic surgery Presbyn.-St. Luke's Hosp., 1956-70, also U. Ill. Med. Sch., Chgo., 1956—. Chief surgery 61st Sta. Hosp., theatre cons. orthopaedic surgery MTOUSA, 1945-47. Recipient ann. award for outstanding orthopaedic research Kappa Delta, Chgo., 1954. Diplomate Am. Bd. Surgery. Mem. Am. Orthopaedic Assn., Orthopaedic Research Soc., Soc. Nuclear Medicine, Internat. Assn. Orthopaedics and Traumatology, AAAS, Am. Assn. Anatomists, Am. Acad. Orthopaedic Surgery, A.C.S., Sigma Xi, Phi Sigma. Contbr. articles to profl. publs. Home: 227 Dempster St Evanston IL 60201 Office: Dept Orthopaedics 840 S Wood St Chicago IL 60612

RAY, ROBERT D., gov. of Iowa; b. Des Moines, Sept. 26, 1928; s. Clark A. and Mildred (Dolph) R.; B.A. in Bus. Adminstrn., Drake U., 1952, J.D., 1954; hon. degrees, Central Coll., Luther Coll., Westmar Coll., Cornell Coll., Grinell Coll., Iowa Wesleyan Coll., others; m. Billie Lee Hornberger, Dec. 21, 1951; children—Randi Sue, Lu Ann, Vicki Jo. Admitted to Iowa bar, 1954; partner firm Lawyer, Lawyer & Ray, Des Moines; gov. of Iowa, 1969—. Mem. Adv. Commn. on Intergovt. Relations; v.p. exec. com. Council State Govts.; chmn. Midwest Govs. Conf., 1972; chmn. Nat. Govs. Conf., 1975-76, also mem. exec. com.; chmn. Geol. Bd. Iowa, Iowa Exec. Council; mem. Pres.'s Nat. Reading Council; state chmn. March of Dimes, 1960-62. Del. Republican Nat. Conv., 1964, 72; chmn. Iowa Rep. Party, 1963-68, Midwest Assn. Rep. State Chmn., 1965-68; chmn. Nat. Rep. State Chmns. Assn., 1967-68. Bd. dirs. Practicing Law Inst., Family Service Des Moines. Served with AUS, 1946-48. Recipient several awards. Mem. Iowa Acad. Trial Lawyers, Am. Trial Lawyers Assn., Iowa State, Polk County, Am. bar assns., Order of Coif, Delta Theta Phi, Alpha Kappa Psi, Omicron Delta Kappa, Sigma Alpha Epsilon. Mem. Disciples of Christ Ch. Office: Office of Governor State Capitol Bldg Des Moines IA 50319*

RAY, ROBERT FREDERICK, educator; b. Davenport, Iowa, Mar. 29, 1922; s. William R. and Margaret (Ehlers) R.; B.A., Coe Coll., 1944; M.A., State U. Iowa, 1945, Ph.D., 1947; student U. Mex., summer 1943; m. Dorothy Frances Klein, Oct. 19, 1947; children—Jennifer Louise, Amelia Jo. Sr. research analyst N.Y. State Div. Budget, Albany, 1947-49; research cons. Thomas E. Dewey, 1946, 47-49; asso. prof., dir. Inst. Pub. Affairs, State U. Iowa, Iowa City, 1949-54, prof., dir. Inst. Pub. Affairs, 1954-61, prof., dean div. spl. services, 1961-63, prof., dean div. extension and univ. services, 1963-76, dean div. continuing edn., 1976—; dir. Iowa Center for Edn. in Politics, 1954-63, chmn. bd. dirs., 1963-69. Dir. Iowa City Bldg. & Loan Assn. Mem. Midwest Regional adv. com. on Higher Edn. of Council of State Govts., 1962-75; mem. Iowa Ednl. Television Bd., chmn., 1967-75; mem. U.S. Nat. Commn. for UNESCO, 1971-77; chmn. council on extension Nat. Assn. State Univs. and Land Grant Colls., 1974-75, mem. senate and exec. com., 1975-78; bd. dirs. Council on Postsecondary Accreditation, 1977—. Bd. dirs. Iowa City Community Chest, 1955-58, chmn., 1958; bd. dirs. United Fund of Iowa, 1955-56; pres. Iowa Council for Community Improvement, 1956-58; bd. dirs. Nat. Football Found. and Hall of Fame, 1963-65; bd. govs. Quad-Cities Grad. Study Center, 1969—, chmn. council mem. instns., 1975—; mem. adv. council Iowa chpt. Am. Phys. Therapy Assn., 1960-63; chmn. Iowa Bd. for Pub. Programs in Humanities, 1971-76. Recipient Disting. Alumnus award Coe Coll., 1979. Mem. Nat. Collegiate Athletic Assn. (v.p. 1959-63, pres. 1963-65, exec. com. 1965-71), North Central Assn. Colls. and Secondary Schs. (examiner-cons. 1961—, exec. bd. commn. on instns. of higher edn. 1971—, chmn. 1977—), Am., Iowa adult edn. assns., Am. Polit. Sci. Assn., Midwest Conf. Polit. Scientists, Iowa City C. of C. (dir. 1957-60, 63-65, v.p. 1964), Nat. U. Extension Assn. (treas. 1967-68, pres. 1970-71), Nat. Adv. Council on Extension and Continuing Edn. (chmn. 1970-72, 74-75), Phi Beta Kappa, Omicron Delta Kappa, Phi Kappa Phi, Delta Sigma Rho, Pi Kappa Delta, Phi Gamma Mu. Presbyterian (elder). Clubs: Rotary, Outing, Triangle, The Club. Asso. editor Quar. Jour. of Speech, 1947-49. Home: 305 Golfview Ave Iowa City IA 52241

RAY, ROYAL HENDERSON, educator; b. Scottsburg, Ind., July 27, 1905; s. John William and Eva Jane (Henderson) R.; A.B., DePauw U., 1927; A.M., U. Wis., 1935; Ph.D., Columbia, 1950; m. Esther Shirk, June 13, 1937 (dec. 1971); 1 son, John Shirk; m. 2d, Rita Gilleylen, Aug. 13, 1972. Various positions to bus. mgr. Kokomo (Ind.) Dispatch, 1922-30; advt. rep. St. Petersburg (Fla.) Times, 1930-31; instr. Ohio U., 1931-37; instr. advt. and journalism, 1940-41; chmn. advt. dept. Syracuse U., 1945-52; prof., chmn. advt. and pub. relations Fla. State U., 1952-75, prof. emeritus, 1975—. Active Leon County United Fund, 1961-70; dir. pub. relations Suwanee River area Boy Scouts Am., 1962-65. Served with USAAF, 1942-45; USAF Res., 1945-65, lt. col. ret. Faculty fellow Assn. Am. R.R.'s, 1965; fellow Fla. Power Corp., 1966. Fellow Am. Acad. Advt.; mem. Pub. Relations Soc. Am., Advt. Fedn. Am. (nat. v.p. 1957-58), Am. Acad. Advt. (nat. pres. 1962-63), Beta Gamma Sigma, Sigma Delta Chi, Delta Upsilon. Club: Capitol City Country (Tallahassee). Author: Concentration of Ownership and Control, American Daily Newspaper Industry, 1951. Home: 2230 Amelia Circle Tallahassee FL 32304

RAY, WILLIAM F., banker; b. Cin., Sept. 17, 1915; s. William F. and Adele (Daller) R.; A.B., U. Cin., 1935; M.B.A., Harvard, 1937; m. Helen Payne, 1939; children—Katharine (Mrs. Robert Sturgis), Barbara (Mrs. Jerald Stevens), Mary (Mrs. Harvey Struthers, Jr.), Margaret (Mrs. Thomas Gilbert), Deborah, William F. III, Susan. With Brown Bros. Harriman & Co., 1937—, asst. mgr., 1944-49, mgr., Boston, 1950-67, partner, N.Y.C., 1968—; dir. Centennial Ins. Co., N.Y.C.; trustee Atlantic Mut. Ins. Co., N.Y.C. Bd. dirs., v.p. Robert Brunner Found.; bd. dirs. Downtown-Lower Manhattan Assn., Inc. Mem. Bankers Assn. for Fgn. Trade (pres. 1966-67), Harvard Bus. Sch. Assn. (pres. 1963-64, exec. council), Robert Morris Assos. (pres. N.E. 1962-63), Pan Am. Soc. U.S., Pilgrims U.S., Am. Australian Assn. (dir., v.p.), Phi Beta Kappa. Republican. Clubs: Skating (pres. 1956-58) (Boston); Country (Brookline, Mass.); Harvard, Union, Links Golf, India House (N.Y.C.); Apawamis (Rye, N.Y.); Woods Hole (Mass.) Golf; Ardsley (N.Y.) Curling. Home: 1 East End Ave New York City NY 10021 Office: 59 Wall St New York City NY 10005

RAY, WILLIAM JACKSON, psychologist; b. Birmingham, Ala., Sept. 3, 1945; s. Norman M. and Mary K. Agnew; B.A., Eckert Coll., 1967; M.A., Vanderbilt U., 1969, Ph.D., 1971; m. Susan Poole, Jan. 1, 1972; children—Adam, Lauren. Fellow in med. psychology Langley Porter Neuropsychiat. Inst., U. Calif. Med. Center, San Francisco, 1971-72; faculty Pa. State U., 1972—. Recipient Nat. Media award Am. Psychol. Found., 1976, 78. Mem. AAAS, Internat. Neuropsychol. Soc., Soc. Psychophysiol. Research, Am. Psychol. Assn. Author: (with R. M. Stern) Biofeedback, 1977; (with others) Evaluation of Clinical Biofeedback, 1979; (with R.M. Stern and C.M. Davis) Psychophysiological Recording, 1980. Office: Dept Psychology Pa State U University Park PA 16802

RAYBURN, CLYDE, elec. machinery co. exec.; b. Newell, W.Va., May 18, 1923; s. Clyde Glesner and Cora Lee (Johnson) R.; B.S., W.Va. U., 1949; m. Priscilla Carol Allen, June 2, 1956; children—Thomas Jeffrey, Carol Elizabeth. Auditor, Arthur Andersen & Co., Phila., 1949-55; with AMP Inc., Harrisburg, Pa., 1955—, controller, 1969-79, v.p. adminstrv. services and controls, 1979—. Served with AUS, 1943-46. C.P.A., Pa. Mem. Pa., Am. insts. C.P.A.'s, Nat. Assn. Accountants, Phi Beta Kappa, Sigma Nu. Republican. Home: 18 Beaver Rd Camp Hill PA 17011 Office: AMP Inc Eisenhower Blvd Harrisburg PA 17111

RAYBURN, GENE, TV performer and actor; b. Christopher, Ill., Dec. 22; s. Milan and Mary (Hikec) Rubessa; student Knox Coll., Galesburg, Ill.; m. Helen Ticknor, Jan. 1, 1940; 1 dau., Lynn. On radio in Rayburn and Finch show, 1946-53; Steve Allen TV Tonight show, 1954-59, Robert Montgomery Presents, 1956, Dough-Re, Mi, 1958-61, Match Game, 1962—, others; Broadway appearances in Bye Bye Birdie, 1961, Come Blow Your Horn, 1962; host radio Monitor show, 1961-73. Served to 2d lt. USAAF, 1943-45. Mem. A.F.T.R.A. (bd. dirs., past pres. N.Y.C. local, trustee pension and welfare fund). Clubs: Wianno (Mass.); Canadian (N.Y.C.); Centerville (Mass.) Beach. *

RAYBURN, GEORGE MARVIN, business exec.; b. Cape Girardeau, Mo., Jan. 30, 1920; s. Walter Marvin and Alma Fay (McBride) R.; student Central Coll., Fayette, Mo., 1937-39; B.S. in Bus. Adminstrn., Washington U., St. Louis, 1941, M.S. in Bus. Adminstrn., 1947; m. Jane Ellen Ernst, Sept. 25, 1943; 1 son, George Marvin. Auditor, Internat. Harvester Co., 1941-45; accountant Tallman Co., 1946-47; asst. prof. U. Omaha, 1947-49; asso. prof. Millikin U., 1949-52; pvt. practice as George M. Rayburn, C.P.A., 1948-52; regional internal auditor Olin-Mathieson Chem. Corp., 1952-55; comptroller Orchard Paper Co., 1955-56; asst. controller St. L.S.F. Ry., St. Louis, 1956-62, sec., treas., 1963-69, v.p., 1969-72; pres., dir. N.M. & Ariz. Land Co., 1966—. Served to capt. AUS, 1942-45, 51-52. Mem. Am. Inst. C.P.A.'s, Am. Accounting Assn., Financial Execs. Inst., Planning Execs. Inst., Delta Sigma Pi, Phi Sigma Phi, Phi Kappa Delta. Methodist. Mason. Clubs: Arizona, Noonday, Paradise Valley Country. Author: Standard Costs Applied to Distribution Costs, 1947; BudgetsBewitched or Bewildered, 1960. Home: 7 Casa Blanca Estates Scottsdale AZ 85253 Office: Camel Sq 4350 E Camelback Rd Phoenix AZ 85018

RAYBURN, WILLIAM BUSBY, tool co. exec.; b. Canandaigua, N.Y., Mar. 31, 1925; s. Earl Reed and Elizebeth Irene (Busby) R.; student public and pvt. schs., Canandaigua; m. Margaret Mary Redfern, Aug. 24, 1946; children—John W., William D., Kathleen M. James F. Self-employed, 1946-53; with Snap-On Tools Corp., 1953—, gen. sales mgr., 1974-76, v.p., gen. sales mgr., 1976, sr. v.p., Kenosha, Wis., from 1976, now exec. v.p., also dir.; dir. Canada Ltd., Fed. Savs. & Loan, Milw. Served with AC, USN, 1943-46. Mem. Sales and Mgmt. Execs. Internat., Hand Tool Inst. (dir.), Equipment Tool Inst. Republican. Roman Catholic. Club: Kenosha Country (dir.). Home: 4802 67th Pl Kenosha WI 53142 Office: Snap on Tools Corp 80th St Kenosha WI 53140

RAYE, MARTHA (MAGGIE YVONNE O'REED), actress; b. Butte, Mont., Aug. 27, 1916; d. Pete and Mabel (Hooper) Reed; ed. pub. schs., Mont., Cath. schs., Chgo., Profl. Children's School, N.Y.C. Appeared in vaudeville act with her parents at ages 3-13; then mem. Benny Davis Revue and later with Ben Blue Co.; appeared in Calling All Stars, musical comedy and then returned to clubs and vaudeville; began in motion pictures, Mar. 1936; made personal appearances, 1937, 38, 39, 40; played in pictures Boys from Syracuse, 1940; Navy Blues, Keep 'Em Flying, Helzapoppin, 1942, Double or Nothing, Artists and Models, Pin Up Girl, Four Jills and a Jeep, Monsieur Verdoux, 1947; appeared in numerous stage plays including Hold on to Your Hat, 1940, Annie Get Your Gun, 1952, The Solid Gold Cadillac, 1960, Personal Appearance, 1961, Separate Rooms, 1961, Calamity Jane, 1961, Wildcat, 1962, Call Me Madam, 1963, Everybody Loves Opal, 1965, 77, Hello Dolly, 1967, No, No, Nanette, 1972; radio artist; TV appearances include All Star Revue, Milton Berle shows, Martha Raye Show, 1954-56, Carol Burnett Show, 1968-75, The Bugaloos series, 1970-72, McMillan series, 1976. Recipient Jean Hersholt Humanitarian award Acad. Motion Picture Arts and Sci., 1968. Mem. Screen Actors Guild, Actors Equity Assn., Am. Fedn. Radio Actors. *

RAYMAN, WARREN SAMUEL, hosp. cons., lawyer; b. Toledo, Dec. 18, 1916; s. Jacob Mendel and Jeanette (Friedman) R.; B.B.A., U. Toledo, 1937, LL.B., 1962; m. Adeline Brooks, Oct. 5, 1940 (dec. Mar. 1974); children—Mark Brooks, Steven Lee. Sec., Zanville Packers, Inc., Toledo, 1948-59; admitted to Ohio bar, 1962; asst. adminstr., comptroller Maumee Valley Hosp., Toledo, 1959-65, adminstr., 1965-71; cons. hosp. affairs Lucas County (Ohio), 1971—; pvt. practice law, Toledo, 1971—; referee Toledo Municipal Ct., 1977—. Trustee Kidney Found. Northwestern Ohio, 1966-74; trustee Zucker Diagnostic Center Retarded Children, 1972-77, pres., 1975-76; pres., trustee Toledo Hearing and Speech Center, 1966-72; treas., trustee Greater Toledo Ednl. Television Found. WGTE-TV, 1969-72; bd. dirs. Vol. program Lucas County (Ohio) Juvenile Ct., 1975-79. Served to lt. USNR, 1942-46; PTO. Mem. Ohio Hosp. Assn., Ohio, Toledo, Lucas County bar assns., Phi Alpha Delta. Jewish. Home: 6855 Queen Annes Ct Toledo OH 43615

RAYMER, STEVEN LAURENCE, photographer; b. Beloit, Wis., Nov. 25, 1945; s. Laurence Arthur and Clara June (Simeral) R.; B.S., U. Wis., 1967, M.A., 1971; m. Holly Reckord, 1977; 1 dau., Katelynn. Tchr. photojournalism U. Wis., Madison, 1969-71; staff photographer Wis. State Jour., Madison, 1971-72; staff photographer Nat. Geographic Mag., Washington, 1972—. Served as 1st. lt. AUS, 1967-69. Named Wis. Photographer of Year, Wis. News Photographers Assn., 1972; recipient Ralph O. Nafziger award for disting. achievement U. Wis. Sch. Journalism and Mass Communication, 1978. Mem. Nat. Press Photographers Assn. (1st place prize 1973, 74, Mag. Photographer of Year 1975), White House News Photographers Assn. (1st place prize 1974). Home: 5124 44th St NW Washington DC 20016 Office: 1145 17th St NW Washington DC 20036

RAYMO, ROBERT ROWLAND, English scholar; b. Pelham Manor, N.Y., Jan. 23, 1925; s. Albert Anthony and Susette (Barbagli) R.; B.A. cum laude (Coll. scholar), Fordham Coll., 1945; M.A., Columbia U., 1947; Ph.D., Cambridge (Eng.) U., 1953; m. Joyce Cynthia Hume, Mar. 31, 1953 (dec.). Instr. in English, U. Calif., Los Angeles, 1953-55, asst. prof. English, 1955-57; asst. prof. Rutgers U., 1957-59, asso. prof., 1959-60, prof., 1960-64; prof. N.Y. U., 1964—, chmn. dept. English, Washington Square Coll., 1969-72, chmn. dramatic lit. Washington Square Coll., 1969-74, head of all univ. English, 1972-74, dean Grad. Sch. Arts scis., 1974-79; mem. doctor of arts adv. council N.Y. State Edn. Dept.; mem. Middle States Assn. Evaluation Team; Fulbright fellow Cambridge U., 1949-51. Recipient award for excellence and distinguished teaching Lendback Found., 1964; Distinguished Tchr. award Rutgers U. Alumni Assn., 1964; Alumni Assn. award N.Y. U., 1976; Am. Acad. Classical Studies in Rome scholar, 1945-46; U. Calif. Presidential fellow, 1955-56; Am. Philos. Soc. grantee, 1960-61. Mem. Modern Lang. Assn., Medieval Acad. Am., Internat. Assn. Univ. Profs. English, Early English Text Soc., Northeastern Assn. Grad. Schs., Council Grad. Schs., Am. Assn. Higher Edn. Contbr. articles on Middle English and medieval Latin lit. to lit. publs. Home: 37 Washington Sq W New York NY 10011

RAYMOND, DANA MERRIAM, lawyer; b. Flushing, N.Y., July 28, 1914; s. Charles Merriam and June (Leonard) R.; A.B., U. Cal., 1935; LL.B., Columbia, 1939; m. Josephine Sheehan, June 25, 1949; children—Catherine, Peter Dana, John Dana. Admitted to N.Y. State bar, 1939, since practiced in N.Y.C.; asso. firm Cravath, Swaine & Moore, 1939-54; mem. firm Brumbaugh, Graves, Donohue & Raymond, 1954—. Bd. dirs. Armstrong Meml. Research Found. Served with AUS, 1940-45. Mem. Am., N.Y.C. bar assns., N.Y. Patent Law Assn., Am. Coll. Trial Lawyers. Clubs: University (N.Y.C.): Maidstone (East Hampton, N.Y.). Home: 14 E 90th St New York City NY 10028 also Jeffreys Ln East Hampton NY 11937 Office: 30 Rockefeller Plaza New York City NY 10020

RAYMOND, GENE, actor, producer, dir.; b. N.Y.C., Aug. 13, 1908; s. LeRoy D. and Mary (Smith) Guion; student Profl. Children's Sch., N.Y.C.; m. Jeanette MacDonald, June 16, 1937 (dec. Jan. 14, 1965); m. former Mrs. Nelson Bentley Hees, Sept. 8, 1974. Broadway debut in The Piper, 1920; actor plays, N.Y.C., including The Potters, 1923, Cradle Snatchers, 1925, Young Sinners, 1929; actor motion pictures including Personal Maid, 1932, Zoo in Budapest, 1933, Sadie McKee, 1934, Mr. and Mrs. Smith, Smilin' Thru, Cross Country Romance, Hooray for Love, That Girl from Paris, The Bride Walks Out, numerous others; pres. Masque Prodns. Inc., Los Angeles. Trustee, Motion Picture and TV Relief Fund, pres., 1978—; v.p. So. Calif. chpt. Arthritis Found., 1971-72. Served to col. USAAF, 1942-45; ETO; command pilot USAF. Decorated Legion of Merit; recipient Disting. Service award Arthritis Found. Mem. Nat. Acad. TV Arts and Scis. (gov.), Screen Actors Guild (dir.), Air Force Assn. (pres. Los Angeles chpt.; Humanitarian award), Order of Daedalians. Clubs: Bel Air Country (Los Angeles); Players', N.Y. Athletic (N.Y.C.); Army-Navy (Washington). Composer songs Will You, 1937; Let Me Always Sing, 1939; Release, 1946. Home: 250 Trino Way Pacific Palisades CA 90272 Office: 9570 Wilshire Blvd Beverly Hills CA 90212

RAYMOND, GEORGE GAMBLE, JR., material handling equipment co. exec.; b. Bklyn., Nov. 29, 1921; s. George Gamble and Madeleine (Crombie) R.; student Cornell U., 1939-42; m. Cynthia Spencer, June 27, 1942 (dec. June 1977); children—George Gamble III, Stephen Spencer, Jean Crombie; m. 2d, Ellen Robinson, Oct. 14, 1978. With Raymond Corp., Greene, N.Y., 1942—, sales mgr., 1942-43, 47-49, adminstrv. asst. to pres., 1946-47, v.p. in-charge sales, 1949-51, exec. v.p., 1951-55, pres., 1955—, chief exec. officer, 1959—, chmn., 1972—; dir. Universal Instrument Corp., 1st Nat. Bank of Greene, Security Mut. Life Ins. of N.Y., Handling Service of Central N.Y., Mobility Systems, Inc., Raymond Lease, Inc., G.N. Johnston Equipment, Ltd., Raymond Handling Equipment, Ltd., Raymond Indsl. Equipment, Ltd. Mem. adv. council Susquenago council Boy Scouts Am., 1947—. Pres. Greene Central Sch. Bd. Edn., 1955-71. Trustee Raymond Found.; chmn. bd. trustees Alfred U., 1977—. Served with inf. AUS, 1943-46. Recipient Mgr. of Year award Soc. Advancement Mgmt., Binghamton, N.Y., 1970. Mem. Am. Mgmt. Assn. (editor gen. mgmt. sect. handbook 1971—), Material Handling Inst. (past pres.), Assn. Lift Truck (past pres.), Indsl. Truck Assn. (past pres.), Assn. Lift Truck and Portable Elevator Mfrs. (past pres.), Young Presidents Orgn. (past v.p. N.E. area, past chmn. Empire chpt.), Broome County C. of C. Republican. Episcopalian. Mason, Rotarian (past pres. Greene). Club: Governor's (Albany, N.Y.). Home: Hemlock Hill Farm Greene NY 13778 Office: Raymond Corp Greene NY 13778

RAYMOND, GEORGE MARC, educator, city planner; b. Odessa, Russia, Jan. 1, 1919; s. Mark J. and Rachelle (Schneiderman) R.; came to U.S., 1937, naturalized, 1942; B. Arch., Columbia, 1946; m. Kathleen E. Waid, Oct. 3, 1942 (div. Mar. 1978); 1 dau., Valerie M.; m. 2d, Lois Jean Gainsboro, Mar. 26, 1979. Planning dir. Harrison, Ballard & Allen, Inc., N.Y.C., 1952-54; founder, pres. Raymond, Parish, Pine & Weiner, Inc., 1954—; prof. planning Pratt Inst., Bklyn., chmn. dept. city and regional planning 1959-75; founder, dir. Pratt Center for Community Improvement, 1963-70; lectr. planning Columbia, 1955-58; lectr. planning and urban renewal New Sch. Social Research, 1967-72; pres. Assn. Collegiate Sch. Planning, 1968-69. Vice pres. Citizens Housing and Planning Council N.Y.C., 1967—; 1st v.p. Federated Conservationists Westchester County, 1971—; pres. Westchester Citizens Housing Council, 1964-66; pres. Met. Com. on Planning, 1950-51. Founder, pres. Friends of Music Concerts, 1954-57. Spoken Arts Soc., 1966-67. Bd. dirs. Nat. Housing Conf., Phipps Houses, Wave Hill, Westchester Council for Arts, Community Housing Mgmt. Corp. Served with AUS, 1941-45. Mem. Am. Soc. Cons. Planners (pres. 1968-70, dir.), N.Y. Assn. Environ. Profls. (v.p. 1977—, dir.), Am. Inst. Cert. Planners, Am. Soc. Planning Ofcls., Nat. Assn. Housing and Redevel. Ofcls., Municipal Art Soc. N.Y.C., Regional Plan Assn. N.Y.C. Editor: Pratt Planning Papers, 1963-73; (with Astrid Monson) Pratt Guide to Housing, Planning and Urban Renewal for New Yorkers, 1965. Home: 969 Park Ave New York NY 10028 Office: 555 White Plains Rd Tarrytown NY 10591

RAYMOND, HARVEY FRANCIS, textile cons.; b. Yonkers, N.Y., July 13, 1915; s. Steven I. and Martha M. (Kar) R.; B.S., Trinity Coll., Hartford, Conn., 1938; m. Annette Farrington, May 1938; children—Barbara (Mrs. Lawrence Pleasants III), Anne (Mrs. A. Raymond Stewart). With Cone Mills, Inc., 1950-74, asst. v.p., 1955-56, v.p., 1956-74; ret., 1974; dir. Cone Mills Corp., 1963-74; cons. Internat. Exec. Service Corps, 1974—. Dir. Am. Printed Fabrics Council, pres., 1972-74; chmn. Corduroy Council Am., 1955-56, 59-60, 67-69, dir., 1952-63; mem. adv. com. textile sect. Japanese Reciprocal Trade Treaty, 1956. Vice chmn. YMCA Neighborhood House; mem. spl. gifts com. Glen Cove (N.Y.) Com. Hosp., 1955-56, Friends Acad., Locust Valley, N.Y., 1957-58; mem. com. for Friends World Coll., Brookville, L.I., 1961—; mem. exec. com. Am. Friends Service Com., 1962-72. Bd. dirs. Fathers Day Council. Mem. A.I.M., Am. Assn. Textile Chemists and Colorists, Am. Chem. Soc., Textile Distbrs. Assn. (dir. 1973-75), N.Y.C. C. of C., Bugatti Car Club, Delta Phi. Republican. Club: Princeton (N.Y.C.). Home: 178-2 Penny Ln Naples FL 33942 also Hopewell Farm Penrose NC 28766 Office: Internat Exec Service Corps 622 3d Ave New York NY 10017. *Creativity through self-discipline and hard work and the use of all the endowments given to me by a benevolent creator have been responsible for whatever constructive use I may have been.*

RAYMOND, JACK, pub. relations exec.; b. Lodz, Poland, Oct. 6, 1918; s. Harry and Anna (Lange) R.; student City Coll. N.Y., 1939; m. Gertrude Silverman, Oct. 6, 1946; children—David Alan, Judith. Corr., N.Y. Times, 1940-66, Berlin, 1946-47, Frankfurt, 1947-49, Bonn, 1949-52, corr. for Balkans, Belgrade, 1952-56, Moscow, 1956, Pentagon corr., Washington, 1956-66; pub. relations exec., pres. Thomas J. Deegan Co., Washington and N.Y.C., 1966-70; v.p. Bryan Publs., N.Y.C., 1970-74; pres. Dialog div. J. Walter Thompson Co., 1973-75; pres. Jack Raymond and Co., Inc., N.Y.C., 1975—. Book reviewer The Villager, N.Y.C., 1970-74; cons. UN Conf. on Human Environment, 1972—, also Aspen Inst. Humanistic Studies, HABITAT, UN Conf. Human Settlements; adv. com. Center for Environ. Info. UN Assn./U.S., 1975-78; mem. Rumanian-U.S. econ. council U.S. C. of C., 1973-75. Trustee N.Y. Urban League, 1969-72; bd. dirs. Internat. Inst. Environ. Affairs, N.Y.C., 1970-74, pres., 1970-73; bd. dirs. Internat. Inst. Environment and Devel., London, 1974-78, mem. adv. council, 1978—; bd. dirs. Epoch B Found., La Jolla, Calif., acting pres., 1977—. Served with AUS, 1942-45. Decorated Bronze Star, Purple Heart. Mem. Council on Fgn. Relations. Clubs: Overseas Press Am. (pres. 1972-76), Century Assn., Friars (N.Y.C.); Nat. Press, Internat. (Washington). Author: Power at Pentagon, 1964; Your Military Obligations and Opportunities, 1963; co-author: This is Germany, 1950; also articles. Home: Flintlock Ridge Rd RFD 3 Katonah NY 10536 Office: Look Bldg 488 Madison Ave New York NY 10022

RAYMOND, ROBERT HUGH, educator; b. Norfolk, Nebr., Apr. 12, 1923; s. Hugh P. and Myrtle (Nightingale) R.; B.S., U. Nebr., 1946, M.A., 1959; Ph.D., Mich. State U., 1964; m. Agnes V. Abraham, June 26, 1945; children—Gary R., Karen Ann, Linda Kay. With Philip G. Johnson & Co., 1946-48; C.P.A. in pvt. practice, Rapid City, S.D., 1948-52; dist. accounting dir. OPS, S.D., 1951-52; with Hansen Co., Fremont, Nebr., 1952-55; faculty Dana Coll., Blair, Nebr., 1955-57, Midland Lutheran Coll., Fremont, 1957-58; instr., asst. prof., asso. prof., prof. accounting U. Nebr., 1958—, chmn. dept. accounting, 1958-76. Served with AUS, 1943-45; ETO. Decorated Purple Heart. C.P.A., Nebr. Mem. Am. Inst. C.P.A.'s, Nebr. Soc. C.P.A.'s, Am. Accounting Assn., Nat. Assn. Accountants, Am. Risk and Ins. Assn. Presbyn. Author articles. Chmn. editorial bd. Nebraska CPA mag., 1966-74. Home: 1940 S 53d St Lincoln NE 68506

RAYMOND, THOMAS JOSEPH CICCHINO, educator; b. Newark, June 19, 1917; s. Charles Cicchino and Lillian Raymond; A.B., N.J. State Coll., Montclair, 1942; M.B.A., Harvard, 1947, Ed.D., 1956; m. Alicia Gutierrez Clark, Nov. 3, 1963; 1 son, Geoffrey Burton Clark. Instr. finance Boston Coll., 1946-49; Charles Swain Thomas fellow Harvard Grad. Sch. Edn., 1949-50; faculty Harvard Grad. Sch. Bus. Adminstrn., 1950—, prof. bus. adminstrn., 1960—; vis. prof. theatre arts dept. U. Calif. at Los Angeles, summer 1960; cons. Office Intelligence Research, State Dept., 1951-52, Nat. Credit Research Found., 1952, N.J. Bell Telephone Co., 1955, Dominion Tar & Chem. Co., Ltd., 1956-61, Am. Tel. & Tel. Co., 1960; adviser Repertory Boston, theatre group, 1959; participant Cambridge Drama Festival Producers Workshop, summer 1959; adviser Spanish Ministry Edn., ICA, 1958-60; appointed expert, arts and humanities br. HEW, 1965; research coordinator Inst. Coll. and Univ. Adminstrs., Boston, 1955—; cons. dir. Sch. Commerce, Laval U., Que., Can., 1953-57, mem. bd. govs., 1958—; v.p., treas. United Biologics Corp., San Francisco, 1964-68; pres. Social Adminstrn. Inst., Boston, 1966—; edn. dir. Harvard Instns. in Arts Adminstrs., 1970—. Trustee Inst. Arts Adminstrn., Cambridge. Served as capt. USAAF, 1942-46; PTO. Mem. Kappa Delta Pi, Phi Delta Kappa. Author: Problems in Business Adminstration, 1955; Cases in Arts Administration. Home: Quincy House 58 Plympton St Cambridge MA 02138 Office: Grad Sch Bus Adminstrn Harvard Univ Soldiers Field Boston MA 02163

RAYMONDA, JAMES EARL, banker; b. Piseco, N.Y., Feb. 20, 1933; s. Floyd E. and Bertha (Kramer) R.; B.S. magna cum laude, Syracuse U., 1955; m. Marie A. Countryman, Aug. 18, 1956; children—David J., Diane J., Daniel J. With Oneida Nat. Bank & Trust Co. Central N.Y., Utica, 1957—, v.p., comptroller, 1968—, adminstrv. v.p., until 1973, exec. v.p., 1973—; instr. Utica chpt. Am. Inst. Banking, Mohawk Valley Community Coll. Treas. Oneida County chpt. Nat. Found.; pres. Whitestown Jaycees, 1964; adv. com., sec. Whitestown Sr. Center, 1965—; mem. adv. com. St. Elizabeth Hosp., Utica, N.Y.; gen. chmn. campaign Greater Utica United Way, 1977. Mem. Nat. Assn. Accountants, C. of C. of Greater Utica Area (v.p. adminstrn.). Club: K.C., Fort Schuyler (Utica); Yahnundasis Golf (New Hartford, N.Y.). Home: 35 Chateau Drive Whitesboro NY 13492 Office: 268 Genesee St Utica NY 13503

RAYNAULD, ANDRE, Canadian provincial ofcl.; b. Quebec, Que., Can., Oct. 20, 1927; s. Léopold and Blanche (Gauthier) R.; B.A. cum laude, U. Montreal, 1948, M.A. in Indsl. Relations magna cum laude, 1951; D.Econs., U. Paris, 1954; D.Econs. (hon.), U. Ottawa, 1976, U. Sherbrooke, 1976; m. Michelle Nolin, Oct. 15, 1951; children—Francoy, Olivier, Dominique, Isabelle. Mem. faculty U. Montreal, 1954-71; vis. prof. U. Toronto, 1962-63; chmn. Economic Council Can., Ottawa, 1972-76; mem. Parliament for Que. Province, 1977—; exec. com. Canadian Social Sci. Research Council, 1961-63, 64-65; pres. Inst. Canadien Affaires Publiques, 1961-62; bd. govs. Canadian Labour Coll., 1962-66; bd. dirs. African Students Found., Toronto, 1962; dir., exec. com. CBC, 1964-67; trustee CBC Pension Fund, 1967-70; pres. Soc. Canadienne de Sci. Economique, 1967-69; mem. Royal Commn. Bilingualism and Biculturalism, 1969-70; mem. Canadian Council Urban and Regional Research, 1971, Quebech Council Planning and Devel., 1971; chmn. com. inquiry French-lang. tchr.-tng. Western provinces Dept. Sec. State, 1971; council trustees Inst. Research Pub. Policy, 1976—. Grantee Royal Soc. Can., 1952, Govt. Province Que., 1953, Can. Council, 1962-64, 66-67, Urban and Regional Research Council, 1965-66, 70; recipient ann. award des Diplomes de l'U. de Montreal, 1974. Mem. Canadian Assn. of Club de Rome, Canadian, Am. econs. assns., Royal Soc. Can. Liberal. Roman Catholic. Author books, 1961—, latest being le financement des caisses de retraite, 1970; La propriete des entreprises au Quebec, 1974; Institutions Economiques Canadiennes, 2nd edition, 1977; Le financement des exportations, 1979; also numerous articles; editor govt. reports, publns. Home: 4820 Roslyn St Montreal PQ H3W 2L2 Canada Office: National Assembly Quebec PQ Canada

RAYNER, DECOURCY HAMILTON, clergyman, editor; b. Hamilton, Ont., Can., Nov. 14, 1909; s. Thomas DeCourcy and Pearl Evelyn (McVittie) R.; B.A., U. Toronto, 1934; diploma Knox Coll., Toronto, 1937, D.D., 1966; m. Marion Eunice White, Nov. 25, 1933; children—Sally Rayner Schiller, Suzanne Rayner McBrien, Diana Rayner Tordjman. Ordained to ministry Presbyterian Ch., 1937; missionary Brit. Guiana, 1937-41; minister Outremont Presbyn. Ch., Montreal, Que., Can., 1941-43; dist. sect. Canadian Bible Soc., Montreal, 1946-58; editor Presbyn. Record, Don Mills, Ont., 1958-77; moderator gen. assembly Presbyn. Ch. in Can., 1977-78. Served to maj., chaplain, RCAF, 1943-46. Mem. Associated Ch. Press (pres. 1971-73), Canadian Ch. Press (pres. 1968). Author feature articles. Home: 153 Ridley Blvd Toronto ON M5M 3M3 Canada

RAYNOR, JOHN PATRICK, univ. pres.; b. Omaha, Oct. 1, 1923; s. Walter V. and Mary Clare (May) R.; A.B., St. Louis U., 1947, M.A., 1948, Licentiate in Philosophy, 1949, Licentiate in Theology, 1956; Ph.D., U. Chgo., 1959. Joined Soc. of Jesus, 1941, ordained priest Roman Catholic Ch., 1954; instr. St. Louis U. High Sch., 1948-51, asst. prin., 1951; asst. to dean. Coll. Liberal Arts, Marquette U., 1961, asst. to v.p. acad. affairs, 1961-62, v.p. acad. affairs, 1962-65, pres., 1965—; dir. Kimberly-Clark Corp.; mem. Wis. Gov.'s Adv. Com. Higher Edn. Act, Greater Milw. Com., Citizens Govtl. Research Bur., Wis. Higher Ednl. Aids Bd. Corp. mem. United Community Services Greater Milw.; hon. dir. Goethe House; sponsor United Negro Coll. Fund. Recipient Distinguished Service award Edn. Commn. of States, 1977. Mem. Nat. Cath. Edn. Assn. (bishops and president's com.), North Central Assn. (examiner, cons.), Am. Council Edn., Wis. Assn. Ind. Colls. and Univs. (past pres.), Wis. Found. Ind. Colls. (past pres.), Assn. Jesuit Colls. and Univs. (past chmn., dir., mem. exec. com.), Internat. Fedn. Cath. Colls. and Univs., Newcomen Soc. N.Am., Phi Beta Kappa, Phi Delta Kappa, Alpha Sigma Nu. Address: Marquette U 615 N 11th St Milwaukee WI 53233

RAYSON, EDWIN HOPE, lawyer; b. Earlville, Ill., Jan. 13, 1923; s. Edwin H. and Lillian (Astley) R.; A.B., U. Tenn., 1944, LL.B., 1948; m. Bette VanDyke Daugherty, July 25, 1944; children—Jane Gilman, Edwin Hope III, G. Scott. Admitted to Tenn. bar, 1948, since practiced in Knoxville; partner firm Kramer, Johnson, Rayson, McVeigh and Leake, 1949—; lectr. labor law U. Tenn. Coll. Law, 1951-71; dir. Genesco, Inc. Served to lt. (j.g.) USNR, 1944-46. Mem. Order of Coif, Sigma Chi, Omicron Delta Kappa. Home: 1119 Scenic Dr Knoxville TN 37919 Office: United Am Bank Plaza Knoxville TN 37901

RAYWID, ALAN, lawyer; b. Washington, Aug. 9, 1930; s. Leo and Vivian (Thrift) R.; A.B., Duke U., 1952; LL.B., U. Mich., 1957. Admitted to D.C. bar, 1957; with admiralty and shipping sect. civil div. Dept. Justice, 1957-66, spl. asst. to asst. atty. gen. charge civil div., 1963-66; asso. firm Nixon, Midge, Rose, Guthrie, Alexander & Mitchell, Washington, 1966-67; partner firm Cole, Raywid & Braverman, Washington, 1967—. Pres. 1966-67; partner firm Cole, Zylstra & Raywid, Washington, 1967—. Pres. Community Assistance, Washington, 1967-70; chmn. Duke Alumni Adv. Admissions Com., 1964-75; nat. chmn. cable TV campaign Humphrey/Muskie, 1968; trustee Mt. Zion Cemetery, Washington, 1975—. Served with USNR, 1952-54. Mem. Am., D.C. bar assns., Am. Maritime Law Assn., Fed. Communications Bar Assn. Democrat. Unitarian. Home: 1227 15th St NW Washington DC 20005 Office: 1919 Pennsylvania Ave NW Washington DC 20006

RAZAK, CHARLES KENNETH, engr., educator; b. Collyer, Kans., Sept. 5, 1918; s. Charles and Dorothy (Brown) R.; B.S., U. Kans., 1939, M.S., 1942; m. Lillian Blanche McCall, July 4, 1940; children—Nancy Louise, Jeanne Marie. Successively instr., asst., asst. prof. aero. engring., coordinator civilian pilot tng. program U. Kans., 1939-43; asso. prof. aero. engring. U. Wichita, 1943-45, prof., head dept. aero. engring., 1945-47, prof., dir. sch. engring., 1947-50, dean sch. engring., 1954-64, prof., 1950-66, research prof. in aero. engring., acting dean coll. bus. and industry 1950-54, responsible for orgn. and adminstrn. sch. engring., design, constrn. 7x10 wind tunnel, direction aero. research program; dir. Indsl. Extension for State Kans., also prof. engring. Kans. State U., Manhattan, 1966—; engring. cons. on accident analysis, expert witness in ct. cases, 1970—; cons. to NASA on agrl. airplane research, 1977—, on aerodynamics and airplane design, 1978, 79; cons. local aircraft cos.; guest lectr. agrl. airplane design Cranfield (Eng.) Inst. Tech., 1977; dir. Kans. Investment Co., KARD-TV (both Wichita); one of 3 dels. to work on problem of shortage of engring. and tech. manpower Engring. Manpower Commn. of Kans., 1951; adviser pest control div. U.S. Dept. Agr. on operation analysis, U. Calif. at Davis on agrl. aviation; tech. dir. research contract held by U. Wichita under Office of Naval Research to investigate problem of low speed flight; mem. subcom. low speed aerodynamics, NASA, also mem. com. on aircraft aerodynamics, also cons. agrl. airplanes, 1977—. Registerd profl. engr., Kans. Fellow Inst. Aero. Scis. (asso.); mem. A.A.A.S., Soc. Automotive Engrs., Am. Soc. Engring. Edn. (mem. gen. council 1961-62), Am. Assn. for Automotive Medicine, Tau Beta Pi, Pi Tau Sigma, Sigma Gamma Tau. Club: Rotary. Author articles on agrl. aviation engring. report. Home: 7717 Killarney Ct Wichita KS 67206 Office: 310 Laura St Wichita KS 67211

RE, EDWARD D., fed. judge; b. Santa Marina, Italy, Oct. 14, 1920; s. Anthony and Marina (Maetta) R.; B.S. cum laude, St. John's U., 1941, LL.B. summa cum laude, 1943, LL.D. (hon.), 1968; J.S.D., N.Y. U., 1950; Pd.D. (hon.) Aquila, Italy, 1960; LL.D. (hon.), St. Mary's Coll., Notre Dame, Ind., 1968, Maryville Coll., St. Louis, 1969, N.Y. Law Sch., 1976, Bklyn. Coll., CCNY, 1978; m. Margaret A. Corcoran, June 3, 1950; children—Mary Ann, Anthony John, Marina, Edward, Victor, Margaret, Matthew, Joseph, Mary Elizabeth, Mary Joan, Mary Ellen, Nancy Madeleine. Admitted to N.Y. bar, 1943; appointed faculty St. John's U., N.Y., 1947, prof. law, 1951-61 adj. prof. law, 1969—; vis. prof. Georgetown U. Sch. Law, 1962-67; adj. prof. law N.Y. Law Sch., 1972—; spl. hearing officer U.S. Dept. Justice, 1956-61; chmn. Fgn. Claims Settlement Commn. of U.S., 1961-68; asst. sec. state ednl. and cultural affairs, 1968-69; judge U.S. Customs Ct., N.Y.C., 1969—, chief judge, 1977—. Mem. adv. com. on appellate rules Jud. Conf. U.S., 1976—; mem. planning com., mem. jud. faculty Fed. Appellate Judges Conf., Fed. Jud. Center, 1974—, chmn. adv. com. on experimentation in the law Fed. Jud. Center, 1978—. Mem. bd. higher edn., N.Y.C., 1958-69; mem. emeritus, 1969—; Jackson lectr. Nat. Coll. State Trial Judges, U. Nev., 1970. Served with USAAF, 1943-47, col. Judge Adv. Gen.'s Dept. Res., ret. Decorated Order of Merit (Italy); recipient Am. Bill of Rights citation; Morgenstern Found. Interfaith award; USAF commendation medal; Distinguished service award Bklyn. Jr. C. of C., 1956. Mem. Am. (ho. of dels. 1976-78, chmn. sect. internat. and comparative law 1965-67), Bklyn. bar assns., Assn. Bar City N.Y., Am. Soc. Internat. Law, Am. Fgn. Law Assn. (pres. 1971-73), Am. Law Inst., Fed. Bar Council (pres. 1973-74), Am. Assn. Comparative Study Law (pres.) Am. Justinian Soc. Jurists (pres. 1974-76), Scribes Am. Soc. Writers on Legal Subjects (pres. 1978). Author: Foreign Confiscations in Anglo-American Law, 1951; (with Lester B. Orfield) Cases and Materials on International Law, rev. edit., 1965; Selected Essays on Equity, 1955; Brief Writing and Oral Argument, 4th rev. edit., 1977; (with Zechariah Chafee, Jr.) Cases and Materials on Equity, 1967; Cases and Materials on Equity and Equitable Remedies, 1975; chpt., freedom in internat. soc. Concept of Freedom (edited Rev. Carl W. Grindel), 1955. Contbr. articles legal periodicals. Office: US Customs Ct One Federal Plaza New York NY 10007

REA, BRYCE, JR., lawyer; b. N.Y.C., Jan. 22, 1918; s. Bryce and Jane (MacGregor) R.; student Queens U., Kingston, Ont., Can., 1936-37; A.B., Washington and Lee U., 1940, LL.B., 1942; m. Isabel McClintoc, Aug. 28, 1936; 1 son, Charles. Admitted to D.C. bar, Va. bar; law clk. to chief judge U.S. Ct. Appeals, D.C. Circuit; asst. gen. counsel Nat. Assn. Broadcasters; asst. prof. law Mercer U.; asso. prof. Am. U.; counsel for transp. public utilities and fuel brs. Office Price Stabilization, Washington; gen. counsel for Middle Atlantic Conf., Nat. Motor Freight Traffic Assn.; partner firm Rea, Cross & Auchincloss, Washington. Served with USNR, 1944-46. Mem. Am. Bar Assn., Am. Judicature Soc., Am. Law Inst., Bar Assn. D.C. Presbyterian. Clubs: Army/Navy, Nat. Press, Univ. Home: 8900 Old Courthouse Rd Vienna VA 22180 Office: 918 16th St NW Washington DC 20006*

REA, JOHN, architect; b. Chgo., Dec. 25, 1916; s. John W.C. and Stephanie (Hacker) R.; B.S., Armour Inst. Tech., 1939; m. Madeline Weldon, June 27, 1943; children—John, Robert, William, James, Timothy, Barbara. With Rea, Hayes, Large & Suckling, Altoona, Pa., 1949—, sr. partner, 1956—. Pres., Blair Bedford council Boy Scouts Am., 1966; mem. So. Alleghenies Comprehensive Health Planning Bd., Home Nursing Bd. Blair County. Served to lt. USNR, 1943-45. Recipient Silver Beaver award Boy Scouts Am. Fellow A.I.A. (chmn. com. on architecture for health); mem. Pa. Soc. Architects (pres., 1966). Rotary Internat. Paul Harris fellow. Author: Building a Hospital—A Primer for Administrators. Home and office: 33 Sylvan Dr Hollidaysburg PA 16648

REA, PAUL V., fruit and vegetable canning co. exec.; b. San Jose, Calif., Mar. 23, 1913; s. Paul V. and Mary M. (Moss) R.; student San Jose State Coll., 1931-35; m. Dorothy Dechman, Apr. 26, 1935; children—Judith Hert, Meredith Pratt. With Drew Canning Co., Santa Clara, Calif., 1935-53, exec. v.p., 1949-53; exec. v.p. U.S. Products Corp., San Jose, 1953-61, pres., 1961-71; pres. Pacific Coast Producers, Santa Clara, 1971—. Chmn. Santa Clara County Republican Fin. Com., 1958-72; bd. dirs. United Taxpayers Assn. Mem. Nat. Food Processors, Nat. Council Coops., Nat. Soc. Coop. Accountants, Canners League Calif. (pres. 1959), Santa Clara Canners (pres. 1957-67). Presbyterian. Clubs: San Jose Country, Sainte Claire, Masons, Rotary Kiwanis. Home: 10251 Kenny Ln San Jose CA 95127 Office: PO Box 218 Santa Clara CA 95054

READ, ALEXANDER LOUIS, investment and real estate exec., broadcasting exec.; b. New Orleans, Oct. 12, 1914; s. Elmore H. and Laurette (Landry) R.; A.B., Loyola U., 1937; m. Nathalie Doris Owings, Feb. 22, 1943; children—Michael Owings, Susan Louise (Mrs. E. Douglas Johnson, Jr.), Carolyn Mary (Mrs. Edward F. Simmons), Stephen Louis. Mem. sales staff Blue Plate Foods, New Orleans, 1938-39; comml. mgr. Radio Sta. WWL, New Orleans, 1939-41, 45-47; advt. dir. Wembley, Inc., New Orleans, 1947-48; gen. mgr. Radio Sta. WABB, Mobile, Ala., 1948-49; comml. mgr. WDSU Radio and WDSU-TV, New Orleans, 1949-50, v.p., comml. mgr. WDSU Broadcasting Corp., 1950-59, exec. v.p., gen. mgr., 1959-62, exec. v.p. Royal Street Corp. (owner of WDSU-AM-FM), also pres. WDSU-TV, Inc., 1960-72; pres. Cosmos Broadcasting La., Inc., 1973-74, chmn., 1975-78; vice chmn., dir. Royal Street Corp.; dir. Bank of New Orleans & Trust Co.; v.p., treas. Interchange Realty Co.; v.p., dir. Royal Street Investment Corp.; exec. v.p., dir. Starwood Land Corp., Aspen, Colo. Mem. Pres.'s Adv. Council Jesuit High Sch., 1969-72. Bd. dirs. New Orleans Internat. Trade Mart, Am. Automobile Assn., 1965-70, Better Bus. Bur., New Orleans chpt. ARC; bd. govs. Tulane Med. Sch. Served to lt. comdr. USNR, 1941-45. Mem. Nat. Assn. Broadcasters (chmn. TV bd. 1971), Assn. Maximum Service Telecasters, Radio Advt. Bur. (chmn. 1971, dir.), TV Bur. Advt. (chmn. 1961), NBC Affiliates (chmn. 1962-67), TV Pioneers, Internat. Radio and TV Soc., Blue Key. Roman Catholic. Clubs: New Orleans Country, Plimsoll of Internat. Trade Mart (New Orleans). Home: 326 Audubon Blvd New Orleans LA 70125 Office: Royal St Corp 4646 One Shell Sq New Orleans LA 70139

READ, ARTHUR WILLIAM, accountant; b. London, Ont., Can., Nov. 30, 1930; s. Arthur John and Kathleen (Hyatt) R.; C.P.A., U. Toronto (Ont.), 1953, Chartered Accountant, 1962; diploma hosp. orgn. and mgmt., 1960; m. Nancy Ella Foxworthy, Sept. 1, 1951; children—Susan Read Baker, Patricia Read Ciufo, A. Thomas, Christopher, Nancy, Mary. With H.J. Cornish & Co., 1948-53; assessor revenue Can.-Taxation 1953-55; chief accountant Sarnia (Ont.) Gen. Hosp., 1955-57, treas., 1957-62, asst. adminstr., 1962-66; adminstr. Queen Elizabeth Hosp., Toronto, 1966-72; sr. cons., v.p. Cunningham Mgmt. Services Ltd., Scarborough, Ont., 1972-73; resident partner Banghart, Kelly, Doig & Co., chartered accts., Exeter, Ont., 1973-77; partner G.H. Ward & Partners, chartered accts., Exeter, 1978—; owner Read Photog. Studio, Grand Bend. Mem. Hosp. Council Met. Toronto, 1966-72; sec., treas. Hosp. Personnel Relations Bur., 1970-72; sec. Grand Bend Area Med. Center, 1977—. Bd. dirs. Childrens Aid Soc. Sarnia and Lambton County, 1965-66; trustee Sarnia Bd. Edn., 1965-66, mem. vocat. adv. com., 1966; pres. Southcott Pines Park Assn., 1978—. Mem. Inst. Chartered Accountants Ont., Am. Coll. Hosp. Adminstrs., Can. Coll. Health Service Execs. Clubs: Grand Bend Cruising (treas. 1978—), Grand Bend Lions. Home: PO Box 245 Grand Bend ON Canada Office: GH Ward and Partners 486 Main St Exeter ON Canada

READ, BENJAMIN HUGER, govt. ofcl.; b. Phila., Sept. 14, 1925; s. William Bond and Rachel Biddle (Wood) R.; grad. Episcopal Acad., Overbrook, Pa., 1943; B.A., Williams Coll., 1949; LL.B., U. Pa., 1952; m. Anne Lowell Keezer, Aug. 12, 1950; children—Benjamin Huger, Dexter K., Anne L., Mary B. Admitted to Pa. bar, 1952; with firm Duane, Morris & Heckscher, Phila., 1952-55; asso. defender Vol. Defender Assn., Phila., 1955-56; atty. adviser Legal Adviser's Office, State Dept., 1957-58; legislative asst. to Senator Clark of Pa., 1958-63; spl. asst. to sec. state, also exec. sec. Dept. State, 1963-69; acting dir. Woodrow Wilson Internat. Center for Scholars, Smithsonian Instn., 1969, dir., 1969-73; pres. German Marshall Fund of U.S., 1973-77; dep. under-sec. of state for mgmt., 1977-78, under sec. of state for mgmt., 1978—. Served with USMCR, 1943-46. Mem. Phila. Bar Assn., Council Fgn. Relations, Phi Beta Kappa. Clubs: Federal City, Cosmos. Home: 1739 Crestwood Dr NW Washington DC 20011 Office: Dept State Washington DC

READ, DAVID HAXTON CARSWELL, clergyman; b. Cupar, Fife, Scotland, Jan. 2, 1910; s. John Alexander and Catherine Haxton (Carswell) R.; student Daniel Stewart's Coll., Edinburgh, 1927; M.A. summa cum laude, U. Edinburgh, 1932, D.D., 1956; student Montpelier, Strasbourg, Paris, 1932-33, Marburg, 1934; B.D., New Coll., Edinburgh, Scotland, 1936; D.D., Yale, 1959, Lafayette Coll., 1965, Hope Coll., 1969; Litt.D., Coll. Wooster, 1966; L.H.D., Trinity U., 1972, Hobart Coll., 1972, Knox Coll., 1979; m. Dorothy Florence Patricia Gilbert, 1936; 1 son, Rory David Gilbert. Came to U.S., 1956. Ordained to ministry Ch. Scotland, 1936; minister Greenbank Ch., Edinburgh, 1939-49; chaplain U. Edinburgh, 1949-55; chaplain to Her Majesty the Queen, Scotland, 1952-56; minister Madison Ave. Presbyn. Ch., 1956—; preacher Nat. Radio Pulpit; host minister TV program Pulpit and People. Served as chaplain Brit. Army, 1939-45; prisoner of war, 1940-45. Clubs: Century Assn. (N.Y.C.); Pilgrims. Author: The Spirit of Life, 1939; Prisoners' Quest, 1944; The Communication of the Gospel, 1952; The Christian Faith, 1956; I Am Persuaded, 1962; Sons of Anak, 1964; God's Mobile Family, 1966; Whose God is Dead?, 1966; The Pattern of Christ, 1967; Holy Common Sense, 1966; The Presence of Christ, 1968; Christian Ethics, 1968; Virgina Woolf Meets Charlie Brown, 1968; Religion without Wrappings, 1970; Overheard, 1971; Curious Christians, 1972; An Expanding Faith, 1973; Sent from God, 1974; Good News in the Letters of Paul, 1976; Go . . . And Make Disciples, 1978; Unfinished Easter, 1978. Translator (from German): The Church to Come, 1939. Contbr. articles religious jours., periodicals U.S. and Eng. Home: 1165 Fifth Ave New York NY 10029 Office: 921 Madison Ave New York NY 10021

READ, DONALD BURNS, physician; b. Cleve., Feb. 18, 1912; s. John Burns and Gratia Augusta (Jones) R.; student (scholar) Deep Springs (Calif.) Sch. 1928-30; A.B., Cornell, 1933, M.D. (Telluride Assn. scholar 1930-37), 1937; postgrad. in indsl. medicine L.I. Med. Coll., 1942, Post Grad. Med. Coll., 1944; m. Dorothy Elinor Kramm, June 27, 1936 (dec. June 1969); children—Patricia, Donald, Sarah Ann, Richard; m. 2d, Janice T. McGuckin, May 5, 1970; step-children—Linda McGuckin, Joan McGuckin, Susan McGuckin. Recipient Knickerbacker Bursary, Cornell Med. Coll., 1933- 37; intern Lenox Hill Hosp., 1937-39, chief staff, 1939—; med. dir. Colgate-Palmolive Co., Jersey City, 1939-74, cons., 1974—; hon. mem. med. and anesthesia staff Valley Hosp., Ridgewood. Former chmn. health and safety Ridgewood-Glen Rock council Boy Scouts Am. Mem. AMA, Am., N.J. assns. indsl. phys. and surgs., N.J., Hudson County med. assns., Alumnus Telluride Assn., Ridgewood Med. Soc. (ex-pres.). Home and office: 165 Melrose Pl Ridgewood NJ 07450

READ, EDWIN ALBERT, educator; b. Empress, Alta., Can., Oct. 8, 1922; s. S.J. Stanley and Annie (Cruttenden) R.; B.Ed., U. Alta., 1948, M.Ed., 1949; Ed.D., U. Ore., 1956; m. Joy Elizabeth Myler, Sept. 23, 1940; children—Sondra Lynn, Leslie Kathleen, Alan E., Craig S., Lance B. Elementary sch. tchr., Roselynn, Alta., 1943; high sch. tchr., Macleod, S.D., Clareholm, Alta., 1945-46; sch. prin., Lacombe, S.D, Bentley, Alta., 1949-51; supt. schs. Alta., 1951-54; instr. U. Oreg., 1954-56; dir., asso. prof., Coll. Elementary Sch., Central Wash. Coll., Ellensburg, 1956-59; dir., prof. U. Lab. Schs., Brigham Young U., Provo, Utah, 1959-64; dir., prof. Stewart Lab. Sch., U. Utah, Salt Lake City, 1964-65, asso. dean, prof. edn. adminstrn. Grad. Sch. Edn., 1965-74, dept. chmn., prof. ednl. adminstrn., 1974-76; dir. edn. Arabian Am. Oil Co., 1977—; vis. prof. U. Alta., summer 1956, Stanford, summer 1964. Served with RCAF, 1943-45. Recipient Strathcona Trust medal for teaching Calgary Normal Sch., 1943. Mem. Nat. Elementary Sch. Prins. Assn., AAUP, Phi Delta Kappa. Author: Continuous Progress in Spelling, 1977. Home: care Aramco Box 5659 Dhahran Saudi Arabia

READ, FRANK THOMPSON, lawyer, univ. adminstr.; b. Ogden, Utah, July 16, 1938; s. Frank Archie and Fay Melrose (Thompson) R.; B.S., Brigham Young U., 1960; J.D., Duke U., 1963. Admitted to Minn. bar, 1963, Mo. bar, 1966, N.Y. bar, 1968, Okla. bar, 1975; asso. firm Erickson, Popham, Haik & Schnobrich, Mpls., 1964; partner firm Hansen & Hazen, St. Paul, 1964-65; atty. AT&T, Kansas City, Mo., and N.Y.C., 1965-68; asst. prof. law, asst. dean Law Sch., Duke U., asso. prof., asst. dean, 1970-72, prof., asso. dean, 1972-73, prof., 1973-74; prof. U. Tulsa, 1974-79, dean Law Sch., 1974-79; prof., dean Law Sch., Ind. U.-Indpls., 1979—. Mem. Am. Bar Assn., Am. Law Inst., Law Sch. Admissions Council (trustee 1976—), Okla. Jud. Council (chmn. 1976—). Contbr. articles to profl. jours. Home: 3735 Briarwood Dr Indianapolis IN 46240 Office: Ind U-Indpls Sch Law 735 W New York Indianapolis IN 46202

READ, FREDERICK WILSON, JR., lawyer; b. Providence, July 30, 1908; s. Frederick Wilson and Araminta Rowena (Briggs) R.; student Trinity Coll., 1925-26; A.B., Columbia, 1930, LL.B., 1932; m. Evelyn Elaine Avery, Feb. 21, 1942; children—Frederick Wilson III, Cynthia Avery. Admitted to N.Y. bar, 1933, Mass. bar, 1939; asso. law firm Hervey, Barber & McKee, N.Y.C., 1932-35, Menken, Ferguson & Idler, 1937-39; atty. legal dept. Nat. Realty Mgmt. Co., N.Y.C., 1935-37, French Air Commn., 1939-40; mem. legal and contracts depts., Brit. Purchasing Commn., Brit. Air Commn., N.Y.C., Washington, 1940-41; atty. Glenn L. Martin Co., 1941-42; with Home Life Ins. Co., N.Y.C., 1945-73, atty., 1945-47, asst. counsel, 1947-54, counsel, 1954-64, gen. counsel, 1964-71, v.p., gen. counsel, 1971-73; counsel Daiker, D'Elia, Turtletaub & Cantino, Port Washington N.Y., 1973-77, D'Elia, Turtletaub & Cantino, 1977—; counsel Life Underwriters Assn. City N.Y., 1973—. Prof., Coll. Ins., 1974—, N.Y. Law Sch., 1974—. Mem. Bd. Edn., Port Washington, 1949-52, 59-66, pres., 1950-52, v.p., 1962-66. Trustee McAuley Water St. Mission, 1970—. Served to capt. USNR, 1942-45. Fellow Am. Bar Found.; mem. Am. (rep. ho. dels. 1969-77), N.Y. State, Nassau County (dir. 1977—) bar assns., Assn. Bar City N.Y., Assn. Life Ins. Counsel (sec.-treas. 1960-63, v.p. 1965-66, pres. 1967-68), Am. Life Ins. Assn., Health Ins. Assn. Am., Am. Soc. C.L.U.'s, Cow Neck Peninsula Hist. Soc. (trustee, 3d v.p.-legal 1974—), Alpha Delta Phi. Episcopalian. Home: 2 Lynn Rd Port Washington NY 11050 Office: 14 Vanderventer Ave Port Washington NY 11050

READ, JAMES MORGAN, educator; b. Camden, N.J., Aug. 22, 1908; s. James Morgan and Lucia Vail (Foulks) R.; A.B., Dickinson Coll., 1929, LL.D., 1962; Dr.Phil., U. Marburg (Germany), 1932; Ph.D., U. Chgo., 1940; D.Human Reconstrn., Wilmington Coll., 1973; m. Henrietta Morton, Dec. 21, 1940 (dec. 1976); children—Austine Read Wood, James Morgan, Edward Morton; m. 2d, Theresa Kline Dintenfass, 1977. Asso. prof. history U. Louisville, 1935-43; civilian pub. service, 1943-45; asso. sec. Friends Com. on Nat. Legislation, 1945-47; sec. fgn. service sect. Am. Friends Service Com., 1947-49; chief div. edn. and cultural relations Office U.S. High Commr. for Germany, 1950-51; UN dep. high commr. for refugees, 1951-60; pres. Wilmington Coll., 1960-69; v.p. for program mgmt. Charles F. Kettering Found., 1969-74, cons., 1975—. Mem. Phi Beta Kappa, Tau Kappa Alpha. Mem. Soc. of Friends. Author: Atrocity Propaganda 1914-19, 1941; Magna Carta for Refugees, 1951; The Responsibility of a Quaker College to Train for World Leadership, 1960; The United Nations and Refugees-Changing Concepts, 1962. Home: 130 E 67th St New York NY 10021

READ, JOHN CONYERS, engine co. exec.; b. N.Y.C., May 21, 1947; s. Edward Cameron Kirk and Louise (Geary) R.; A.B., Harvard, 1969, M.B.A., 1971; m. Alexandra Gould, Mar. 30, 1968; children—Cameron Kirk, Trevor Conyers, Alexandra. Ops. research analyst HEW, Washington, 1971-72; exec. asst. to dir. Cost of Living Council, Washington, 1973; chief econ. adviser to Gov. Mass., 1974; exec. asst., counselor to sec. labor, Washington, 1975, asst. sec. labor for employment standards, 1976-77; dir. corporate employee relations Cummins Engine Co., Columbus, Ind., 1977—; cons. nat. productivity and energy policies; chmn. NAM Task Force on Wage and Price Policies, 1978—. Author Ford Found. monograph on occupational disease and workers' compensation; contbr. articles to newspapers and mags. Home: 3517 Deerfield Columbus IN 47201 Office: 1000 5th St Columbus IN 47201

READ, LEONARD EDWARD, orgn. exec.; b. Hubbardston, Mich., Sept. 26, 1898; s. Orville Baker and Ada Melvina (Sturgis) R.; student Hubbardston High Sch., 1913-16; grad. Ferris Inst., Big Rapids, Mich., 1917; Litt.D., Grove City Coll.; D.Sc.S., Univesidad Francisco Marroquin; m. Gladys Emily Cobb, July 15, 1920; children—Leonard Edward, James Baker. Pres. Ann Arbor Produce Co., 1919-25; sec. Burlingame (Calif.) C. of C., 1927; mgr. Palo Alto (Calif.) C. of C., 1928; asst. mgr. western div. U.S. C. of C., 1929-32, mgr., 1932-39; gen. mgr., Los Angeles C. of C., 1939-45; dir. and mgr., Western Conf. for Comml. and Trade Execs., Stanford U., 1929-40. Dir. Nat. Assn. Comml. Orgn. Secs., 1942-44; exec. v.p. Nat. Indsl. Conf. Bd., N.Y., 1945-46; pres. Found. for Econ. Edn., N.Y., 1946—. Served in Air Service, U.S. Army, with A.E.F., 1917-19; survivor of torpedoed Tuscania. Mem. Am. Econ. Assn. Republican. Conglist. Clubs: Canadian (N.Y.); St. Andrew Golf. Author: Romance of Reality, 1937; Pattern for Revolt, 1945; Students of Liberty, 1950; Outlook for Freedom, 1951; Government-An Ideal Concept, 1954; Why Not Try Freedom, 1958; Elements of Libertarian Leadership, 1962; Anything That's Peaceful, 1964; The Free Market and Its Enemy, 1965; Deeper Than You Think, 1967; Accent on the Right, 1968; Let Freedom Reign, 1969; Talking to Myself, 1970; Then Truth Will Out, 1971; To Free or Freeze, 1972; Who's Listening, 1973; Having My Way, 1974; Castles in the Air, 1975; The Love of Liberty, 1975; Comes the Dawn, 1976; Awake for Freedom's Sake, 1977; Vision, 1978; Liberty: Legacy of Truth, 1978; The Freedom Freeway, 1979; contbr. to trade and comml. periodicals. Home: Hillside Irvington NY 10533 Office: 30 S Broadway Irvington-on-Hudson NY 10533

READ, RONALD CEDRIC, educator; b. London, Eng., Dec. 19, 1924; s. Frederick William and Hilda (Meeks) R.: B.A., Cambridge (Eng.) U., 1948; Ph.D., London U., 1958; m. Eileen Vera Propert, June 25, 1949; children—Helen Fay, Colin Richard. Mem. faculty U. West Indies, Kingston, Jamaica, 1950-70, sr. lectr., 1960—66, reader, 1966—67, prof., 1967-70; prof. U. Waterloo (Ont., Can.), 1970—. Served with Royal Navy, 1943-46. Mem. Assn. Computing Machinery. Author: Tangrams, 1965; A Mathematical Background for Economists and Social Scientists, 1972. Editor: Graph Theory and Computing, 1972. Editor combinatorics and graphy theory Jour. Assn. Computing Machinery, 1971-75; editorial bd. Discrete Applied Math. Home: 476 Parkwood Ct Waterloo ON N2L 4A8 Canada

READ, RUSSELL BURCHIEL, elec. mfg. co. exec.; b. Pinckney, Mich., Apr. 23, 1914; s. Ross T. and Sadie M. (Burchiel) R.; A.B., U. Mich., 1935, M.B.A., 1936; grad. Advanced Mgmt. Program, Harvard, 1950; m. Marjorie Stewart, Nov. 27, 1941; children—John Stewart, Linda Ruth (Mrs. Robert H. Arnold), Marianna (Mrs. James N. Nielsen), James Allan. With Westinghouse Electric Corp., 1936—, asst. treas., 1958-59, treas., 1959-64, v.p., treas., 1964—; treas. Westinghouse Broadcasting Co., Inc.; dir. Westinghouse Credit Corp. Mem., fin. exec. Conf. Bd. Bd. dirs. Home Capital Funds, St. Clair Meml. Hosp. Mem. Am. Mgmt. Assn. (dir., fin. council), Sigma Chi. Clubs: Chartiers Country. Duquesne (Pitts.). Home: 880 Osage Rd Pittsburgh PA 15243 Office: Westinghouse Bldg Gateway Center Pittsburgh PA 15222

READ, WILLARD OLIVER, educator, physiologist; b. Clay Center, Kans., Nov. 1, 1916; s. Robert Randolph and Elizabeth (Wilson) R.; B.A., U. Mo., 1941, M.A., 1947, Ph.D., 1949; m. Virginia Ann Root, Aug. 18, 1947; children—John R., Catherine A., James M., Melinda C., Sandra C., Jennifer. Instr., U. Mo., 1947-49; asso. physiology U. S.D., Vermillion, 1949-53, mem. faculty, 1953—, prof. dept. physiology, 1960—. Mem. Am. Physiol. Soc., Soc. Exptl. Biology and Medicine, S.D. Acad. Sci., Sigma Xi. Research, publs. on cause of cardiac arrhythmias. Home: 306 Lewis St Vermillion SD 57069

READ, WILLIAM EDGAR, army officer; b. Charlotte, S.C., May 17, 1927; s. William Edgar and Virginia Clark R.; B.S., U.S. Military Acad., 1950; M.S., U. Ill., 1955; M.A., Webster Coll., 1974; m. Mary Ann Gregory, Dec. 19, 1953; children—Mary V., Ann K., Sarah C. Commd. 2d lt., C.E., U.S. Army, 1950, advanced through grades to maj. gen., 1979; comdr. 4th Infantry div. Support Command and Task Force Ivy, Vietnam, 1970-71; dist. engr. Tulsa Dist., 1971-72; dir. procurement and prodn. U.S. Army Aviation Systems Command, St. Louis, 1972-75, dep. comdg. gen., 1975-76; div. engr. U.S. Army Engr. Div., Missouri River, Omaha, 1976-78; asst. chief engrs. Office Chief of Engrs., U.S. Army, Washington, 1978—; instr., asst. prof. engrng. mechanics U.S. Mil. Acad., 1959-62. Mem. Mo. River Basin Commn., 1975-78; mem. Miss. River Commn., 1977-78. Decorated Legion of Merit, Bronze star, air medal with 6 oak leaf clusters. Registered profl. engr., N.Y. Mem. Soc. Am. Mil. Engrs. (pres. Omaha post 1977-78), Assn. U.S. Army. Home: Fort Belvoir WA 22060 Office: Pentagon Washington DC 20310

READ, WILLIAM LAWRENCE, naval officer; b. Bklyn., July 8, 1926; s. Reginald A. and Martha (Bedell) R.; B.S., U.S. Naval Acad., 1949; M.S., George Washington U., 1970; m. Martha Miller, Nov. 25, 1950; children—Allison, William Lawrence, John Alexander. Commd. ensign U.S. Navy, 1949, advanced through grades to vice adm., 1977; comdr. U.S.S. Van Voorhis, 1961-63, U.S.S. King, 1966-68, Escort Squadron Ten, 1968-69, Cruiser-Destroyer Flotilla Three, 1972-73; sr. aide to SACEUR, 1970-72; mil. asst. to sec. Def., 1963-66; asst. chief Navy Personnel for officer devel. and distbn., 1973-74; dir. Ship Acquisition Div., Office Chief Naval Ops., 1974-77; comdr. Naval Surface Force, U.S. Atlantic Fleet, 1977—. Decorated Legion of Merit, Navy Commendation medal with combat V, Navy Distinguished Service Order 2d class (Republic of Vietnam). Mem. U.S. Naval Inst., U.S. Naval Acad. Alumni Assn. Episcopalian. Home: Quarters A Naval Amphibious Base Little Creek Norfolk VA 23521 Office: Comdr Naval Surface Force US Atlantic Fleet Norfolk VA 23511

READ, WILLIAM MERRITT, educator; b. Dupont, Ind., June 24, 1901; s. Parley Garfield and Ella Josephine (Smith) R.; B.A. (Rector scholar), DePauw U., 1923; M.A. (Pendleton fellow), U. Mich., 1924, Ph.D., 1927; m. Arletta Otis, Dec. 19, 1924 (dec. 1947); children—Virginia (Mrs. Stephen Dunthorne), William Merritt; m. 2d, Betty Jorgensen DeLacy, Apr. 30, 1948; children—Elaine Marie, James Garfield. Instr. Western Res. U., 1926-27; mem. faculty U. Wash., Seattle, 1927—, dir. U. Wash. Press, 1943-63, prof. classical langs., 1945—. Mem. Am. Philol. Assn., Classical Assn. Pacific N.W. (sec.-treas. 1972-75), Archeol. Inst. Am., Pacific N.W. Conf. Fgn. Langs., Wash. Assn. Fgn. Lang. Tchrs. (First Pro Lingua award 1973), Phi Beta Kappa. Democrat. Methodist. Author: Michigan Manuscript 18 of the Gospels, 1943; A Guide to Hans H. Oerberg, Lingua Latina Secundum Naturae Rationem Explicata, vol. 1, 1971, vol. II, 1973; A Manual for Teachers of Hans H. Oerberg, Lingua Latina Secundum Naturae Rationem Explicata, vols. I and II, 1973. Home: 3611 I St NE Apt 246 Auburn WA 98022 Office: Denny Hall U Wash Seattle WA 98195

READE, RICHARD SILL, mfg. co. exec.; b. Romeo, Mich., Oct. 11, 1913; s. Richard Sill and Ella (Van de Car) R.; B.S. in Mech. Engring., U. Mich., 1934; m. Arlyne Alice Conger, Apr. 7, 1938; children—William Kent, Todd Conger. Mgr., F & B div. Am. Blower Co., Detroit, 1946-51; dir. purchasing Am.-Standard Corp., N.Y.C., 1951-55; pres. Ross Heater Corp., Buffalo, 1955-60; v.p. mfg. Am.-Standard indsl. div., Detroit, 1960-64; pres. Crane Can., Ltd., Montreal, Que., 1964-76; pres. Transcar Industries, Inc., Clover, S.C., 1977—; dir. James Robertson Co., Ltd., Montreal, Kranko Holdings, Ltd., Montreal. Bd. govs. Chi Phi Ednl. Trust. Mem. Newcomen Soc., Canadian Inst. Plumbing and Heating (pres. 1971-72), Chi Phi. Clubs: River Hills Country; Seigniory. Home: 56 Fairway Ridge Route 4 Clover SC 29710 Office: PO Box 501 Clover SC 29710

READER, GEORGE GORDON, physician; b. Bklyn., Feb. 8, 1919; s. Houston Parker and Marion J. (Payne) R.; B.A., Cornell U., 1940, M.D., 1943; m. Helen C. Brown, May 23, 1942; children—Jonathan, David, Mark, Peter. Intern, N.Y. Hosp., N.Y.C., 1944, resident, 1947-49, attending physician, 1962—, dir. comprehensive care and teaching program, 1952-68, chief med. clinic, 1952-72; practice medicine specializing in internal medicine, N.Y.C., 1949—; chief div. ambulatory and community medicine N.Y. Hosp.-Cornell Med. Center, N.Y.C., 1969-72; prof. medicine Cornell U. Med. Sch., 1957—, Livingston Farrand prof., chmn. dept. pub. health, 1972—. Chmn. human ecology study sect. NIH, 1961-65; chmn. med. adv. bd. Union Family Med. Fund of Hotel Industry of N.Y.C., 1964—; chmn. med. adv. com. Vis. Nurse Service N.Y., 1963—; mem. med. control bd. Health Ins. Plan Greater N.Y., 1964—. Bd. dirs. Winifred Masterson Burke Found., N.Y.C. Vis. Nurse Service, Westchester Community Health Plan, Osborne Meml. Home. Served as lt. USNR, 1944-46; PTO. Diplomate Am. Bd. Internal Medicine. Fellow A.C.P., Am. Coll. Preventive Medicine, Am. Public Health Assn. (governing council 1968-69); fellow N.Y. Acad. Medicine (chmn. com. med. edn. 1968-71, v.p. 1978—), Am. Sociol. Assn., AAAS, AMA, Assn. Am. Med. Colls., Harvey Soc., Internat. Sociol. Assn., Internat. Epidemiological Assn., N.Y.C. Pub. Health Assn. (pres. 1956), Sigma Xi, Alpha Omega Alpha. Author: (with R. Merton, P. Kendall) The Student Physician, 1957; (with Goss) Comprehensive Medical Care and Teaching, 1967; (with Goodrich and Olendzki) Welfare Medical Care: An Experiment, 1969. Mem. editorial bd. Medical Care, 1969-70, Jour. Med. Edn., 1975—; editor-in-chief Milbank Meml. Fund Quar.: Health and Society, 1972-76. Home: 155 Stuyvesant Ave Rye NY 10580 Office: 1300 York Ave New York NY 10021

READING, JAMES EDWARD, urban transp. exec.; b. Milw., June 26, 1924; s. James Edward and Helen Marie (Boehm) R.; student San Diego State U., 1942, Ga. Inst. Tech., 1944; m. Ada Irene Kelly, May 24, 1944; children—Wendy Irene, James David, Christopher Kelly, Mary Katherine, Kevin Sinclair. With Union-Tribune Pub. Co., San Diego, 1942-59, dist. mgr., 1953-58, circulation promotion mgr., 1958-59; adminstrv. asst. to v.p. Copley Newspapers, La Jolla, Calif., 1959-60; dir. advt. and public relations San Diego Transit System, 1960-67; dir. mktg. Calif. Motor Express, 1967-68; asst. to exec. v.p. Am. Transit Assn., Washington, 1968; v.p., resident mgr. Nat. City Mgmt. Co., Rochester, N.Y., 1968-74; asst. gen. mgr. ops. regional transit dist. Regional Transit Service, Denver, 1974-77; gen. mgr. Central Ohio Transit Authority, Columbus, 1977—; guest lectr. numerous univs.; mem. Columbus Transp. and Traffic Commn., 1977—. Bd. dirs. Columbus Conv. and Vis.'s Bur., 1978—. Served with U.S. Army, 1943-46; ETO. Named Public Relations Man of Yr., Public Relations Club, San Diego, 1962. Mem. Public Relations Soc. Am., Am. Public Transit Assn., Transp. Research Bd. Republican. Roman Catholic. Clubs: Rotary, Am. Legion. Home: 84 Glen Dr Worthington OH 43085 Office: 1600 McKinley Ave Columbus OH 43222

READING, JAMES EDWARD, urban transp. exec.; b. Milw., June 26, 1924; s. James Edward and Helen Marie (Boehm) R.; student San Diego State U., 1942; Ga. Inst. Tech., 1944; m. Ada Irene Kelly, May 24, 1944; children—Wendy Irene, James David, Christopher Kelly, Mary Katherine, Kevin Sinclair. With Union-Tribune Pub. Co., San Diego, 1942-59, dist. mgr., 1953-58, circulation promotion mgr., 1958-59; adminstrv. asst. to v.p. Copley Newspapers, La Jolla, Calif., 1959-60; dir. advt. and public relations San Diego Transit System, 1960-67; dir. mktg. Calif. Motor Express, 1967-68; asst. to exec. v.p. Am. Transit Assn., Washington, 1968; v.p., resident mgr. Nat. City Mgmt. Co., Rochester, N.Y., 1968-74; asst. gen. mgr. ops. regional transit dist. Regional Transit Service, Denver, 1974-77; gen. mgr. Central Ohio Transit Authority, Columbus, 1977—; guest lectr. numerous univs.; mem. Columbus Transp. and Traffic Commn., 1977—. Bd. dirs. Columbus Conv. and Vis.'s Bur., 1978—. Served with U.S. Army, 1943-46; ETO. Named Public Relations Man of Yr., Public Relations Club, San Diego, 1962. Mem. Public Relations Soc. Am., Am. Public Transit Assn., Transp. Research Bd. Republican. Roman Catholic. Clubs: Rotary, Am. Legion. Home: 84 Glen Dr Worthington OH 43085 Office: 1600 McKinley Ave Columbus OH 43222

READY, WILLIAM BERNARD, librarian; b. Cardiff, Wales, Sept. 16, 1914; s. John and Nora (Hart) R.; m. Bessie Dyer, Apr. 24, 1945; M.A.; M.L.S.; D.Litt.; children— Patrick, Vincent, Liam, Thomas, Mary, Nora. Dir. Cromlech Press; prof. of bibliography. Served with Brit. Army, 1939-45. Decorated Queen's Can. medal. Fellow Royal Soc. Can. Author: Great Disciple, 1951; The Poor Hater, 1958; The Tolkien Relation, 1968; Necessary Russell, 1969; Notes on The Hobbitt and Lord of the Rings, 1971; Losers Keepers, 1979; also articles, short stories, plays. Home: 25 Paradise Rd N Hamilton ON Canada Office: McMaster U Hamilton ON Canada

REAGAN, BILLY REECE, supt. schs.; b. Brownsboro, Tex., Nov. 24, 1930; s. Oscar Samuel and Margie Elsie (Lutrick) R.; m. Mary Ann Turman, June 29, 1954; children—Reecia, Marilyn. Elementary sch. tchr. Austin (Tex.) Ind. Sch. Dist., 1957-59; successively dir. curriculum, asst. supt. schs., supt. schs. North East Ind. Sch. Dist., San Antonio, 1959-70; regional commr. U.S. Office Edn., Kansas City, Mo., 1970-71; exec. v.p. Mgmt. Services Assos., Austin, 1971-73; dep. dir. charge instructional services region IV Edn. Service Center, 1973-74; gen. supt. Houston Ind. Sch. Dist., 1974—. Bd. dirs. Houston Symphony, Sam Houston area council Boy Scouts Am., Houston YMCA, Houston Pub. Library, Houston Livestock Show and Rodeo. Served with USN, 1951-54. Recipient Carl Bredt award U. Tex., 1969; Outstanding Civilian Service medal U.S. Army, 1976; Outstanding Ex-Student award Henderson County (Tex.) Jr. Coll.; also various community and recognition awards. Mem. Am., Tex. assns. sch. adminstrs., Tex. Council Maj. Sch. Dists., Houston Prins. Assn., Houston Council Edn., Center Applied Linguistics, Tex. Arts Alliance, Nat. PTA, League United Latin Am. Citizens, Phi Delta Kappa. Baptist. Club: Rotary. Home: 11006 Tupper Lake St Houston TX 77042 Office: 3830 Richmond Ave Houston TX 77027

REAGAN, JAMES WILLIAM, pathologist, reproductive biologist; b. Oakmont, Pa., Aug. 6, 1918; s. William James and Lulu M. (Thompson) R.; B.S., U. Pitts., 1942, M.D., 1943; m. Angelyn B. Boezeman, June 1, 1944; children—Patricia, Kathryn, James, Michael, William. Rotating intern Mercy Hosp., Pitts., 1943; fellow in pathology Univ. Hosps. Cleve., 1946-49, asso. pathologist, 1949, pathologist in charge surg. pathology, 1957—, pathologist in charge cytology lab., 1949—; demonstrator in pathology Case Western Res. U., 1946-50, instr. in pathology, 1950-51, sr. instr. in pathology, 1951-52, asst. prof. pathology, 1952-53, asso. prof. pathology, 1953-58, prof. pathology, 1958—, prof. reproductive biology, 1975—; co-dir. tutorials cytology; moderator workshops; panelist. Served with U.S. Army, 1944-46. Recipient Maurice Goldblatt Cytology award Internat. Acad. Cytology, Paris, 1965, award for Dist. service Acad. Medicine and Cuyahoga County (Ohio) Med. Soc., 1968. Fellow Coll. Am. Pathologists, Am. Coll. Obstetricians and Gynecologists (asso.); mem. Am. Soc. Clin. Pathologists (Ward Burdick award 1973), AMA, Am. Soc. Cytology (pres. 1964, Papanicolaou award 1968), Ohio State Soc. Pathologists, Cleve. Soc. Pathologists, Acad. Medicine Cleve., Internat. Acad. Cytology, Soc. Gynecologic Oncologists. Author (with others): Atlas of Cytology, 1966; Manual of Cytotechnology, 1976; contbr. numerous articles to profl. publs. Office: Inst Pathology 2085 Adelbert Rd Cleveland OH 44106

REAGAN, MICHAEL DANIEL, educator, univ. ofcl.; b. N.Y.C., Mar. 12, 1927; s. Oliver Edward and Katherine (Wagner) R.; A.B., Coll. Holy Cross, 1948; M.A., Princeton, 1956, Ph.D., 1959; m. Celeste M. Schleeh, Mar. 21, 1970; children (by previous marriage)—Deborah S., Kevin M., Timothy A. Editorial and sales adminstrn. positions book pub. firms, 1948-53; instr. Princeton, 1955-56, Williams Coll., 1956-60; vis. asst. prof. Princeton, 1960-61; asst. prof. Syracuse U., 1961-63, asso. prof., 1963-64; prof. U. Calif. at Riverside, 1964—, chmn. dept. polit. sci., 1971-73, dean Coll. Social and Behavioral Scis., 1973-75, Coll. Humanities and Social Scis., 1975-77, vice chancellor, 1978—; cons. Nat. Commn. on Money and Credit, 1960, NSF, 1966-70. Mem. adv. com. on mgmt. social sci. research in Dept. Def., NRC, 1970-71; mem. adv. com. on social research and devel. NRC, 1974-77. Served with USMCR, 1945-46, 50-51. Social Sci. Research Council Research fellow, 1967-68. Mem. Am., Western polit. sci. assns. Author: The Managed Economy, 1963; Science and the Federal Patron, 1969; The New Federalism, 1972; also articles. Editor: Politics, Economics and the General Welfare, 1965; The Adminstration of Public Policy, 1969.

REAGAN, RONALD, businessman, rancher; b. Tampico, Ill., Feb. 6, 1911; s. John Edward and Nellie (Wilson) R.; A.B., Eureka (Ill.) Coll., 1932; m. Jane Wyman, Jan. 25, 1940 (div. 1948); children—Maureen E., Michael E.; m. 2d, Nancy Davis, Mar. 4, 1952; children—Patricia, Ronald. Sports announcer WHO, Des Moines, 1932-37, motion picture and TV actor, 1937-66; Gov., State of Calif., 1967-74; former program supr. Gen. Electric Theater. Served as capt. USAAF, 1942-45. Mem. Screen Actors Guild (pres. 1947-52, 59), Tau Kappa Epsilon. Address: 10960 Wilshire Blvd Los Angeles CA 90024

REAGAN, SYDNEY CHANDLER, educator; b. Ft. Smith, Ark., Jan. 7, 1916; s. Sydney Chandler and Ollie (Wood) R.; B.B.A., U. Tex., Austin, 1937, J.D., 1941; M.Pub. Adminstrn., Harvard, 1949, Ph.D. in Econs., 1954; m. Barbara Ruth Benton, June 8, 1940; children—Patricia Benton, Sydney Chandler III. Economist, U.S. Govt., Washington, 1941-55; prof. real estate and regional sci. Sch. Bus. Adminstrn., So. Meth. U., Dallas, 1955—, chmn. dept., 1955-76, dir. Inst. Urban and Environ. Studies, 1968-73, chmn. faculty senate, 1968-70, chmn. Univ. Planning Council, 1967-69; bus. cons. Bd. dirs. Dallas Urban League. Recipient award as one of ten outstanding profs. in Tex., Piper Found., 1969. Hon. mem. Dallas Bd. Realtors. Mem. Am. Econ. Assn., Am. Real Estate and Urban Econs. Assn. (dir. 1969-72), Dallas Economists Club (pres. 1969), Tex. Bar Assn. Author: The Economy of the Central Business District in Dallas, 1961; Economic Feasibility of Proposed Lake Shore Road in Malawi, 1965; Plan to Stablilize Economy and to Manager Resources in Texas in Event of an Enemy Nuclear Attack, 1965; Crossroads Community Study for Dallas, 1970; also numerous cases and teaching note in real estate, urban problems, minority bus. enterprises, 1962—. Home: 10 Duncannon Ct Glen Lakes Dallas TX 75225. *I have become more and more convinced that a person must first be true to himself. This means that he has values, standards and goals that he believes in and that he strives for. To the extent that he compromises and is false to himself, he is destroying his belief and credibility in himself. Unless a person has respect for himself, he is nothing.*

REAL, MANUEL LAWRENCE, dist. judge; b. San Pedro, Calif., Jan. 27, 1924; s. Francisco Jose and Maria (Mansano) R.; B.S., U. So. Calif., 1944, student fgn. trade, 1946-48; LL.B., Loyola Sch. Law, Los Angeles, 1951; m. Stella Emilia Michalik, Oct. 15, 1955; children—Michael, Melanie Marie, Timothy, John Robert. Admitted to Calif. bar, 1952; asst. U.S. Atty.'s Office, Los Angeles, 1952-55; pvt. practice law, San Pedro, Calif., 1955-64; U.S. atty. So. Dist. Calif., 1964-66; U.S. dist. judge, 1966—. Served to ensign USNR, 1943-46. Mem. Am., Fed., Los Angeles County bar assns., State Bar Calif., Am. Judicature Soc., Chief Spl. Agts. Assn., Phi Delta Phi, Sigma Chi. Democrat. Roman Catholic. Club: Anchor (Los Angeles). Office: 312 N Spring St Los Angeles CA 90012

REALE, MARCELLA, soprano; b. Calif.; student Music Acad. West, Santa Barbara, Calif., 1957-58, Musik Hochschule, Munich, W. Ger., 1958-60. Debut in world premiere of Sonzogno's Passageri, Trieste, Italy, 1961; appearances in Europe, U.S., Asia, Africa and Australia; debut Royal Opera-Covent Garden, London, 1975; prin. roles include Maddalena in Giordano's Andrea Chènier, Marguerite in Gounod's Faust, Mimi in Puccinis La Bohème, Violetta in Verdi's La Traviata; rec. artist Bayrisches Rundfunk, EMI. Recipient Puccini D'Oro for interpretations of Puccini heroines, Italy, 1970; Fulbright grantee; Rockefeller fellow.

REAM, NORMAN JACOB, mgmt. cons.; b. Aurora, Ill., June 20, 1912; s. Edward Franklin and Margaret E. (Colbert) R.; B.S. in Accountancy, U. Ill., 1934; postgrad. Northwestern U., 1940-41; m. Eileen Margaret Bouvia, May 24, 1952; children—Judith Ellen (Mrs. William B. Miles), Patricia Margaret (Mrs. Paul W. Michel), Norma Jane (Mrs. Robert Yamaguchi), John Patrick. Mem. controllers staff Pure Oil Co., 1934-41; accountant Touche, Niven & Co., C.P.A.'s, Chgo., 1941-42; sr. cons. George Fry & Assos., Chgo., 1942-47; dir. accounting research IBM Corp., 1947-50; asst. treas. Lever Bros., 1950-53; corp. dir. systems planning Lockheed Aircraft Corp., 1953-65; dir. Inst. Computer Scis. and Tech., Nat. Bur. Standards, 1965-66; spl. asst. to sec. navy, also mem. navy secretariat, 1966-69; prin. S.D. Leidesdorf & Co., 1969-71; chmn. Jamerica Cons. Group, 1971—; guest lectr. Japan Mgmt. Assn., Japan Productivity Center, 1963-67, Japan Acad. Sci., Hiroshima, 1965. Mem. U.S. del. UN Conf. Application Sci. and Tech. for Benefit Less Devel. Areas, Geneva, Switzerland, 1963; speaker Internat. Mgmt. Congress CIOS XV, Tokyo, Japan, 1969, Constl. Assembly of Inter-Am. Center Tax Adminstrn., 1967, 1st Internat. Conf. on Communications, Tokyo, 1972. Gen. chmn. Incorporation City of Downey, Calif., 1954-56. Decorated Distinguished Civilian Service medal USN. C.P.A., Calif., Ill., N.Y. Mem. Am. Inst. C.P.A.'s, Calif. Soc. C.P.A.'s, N.Y. Soc. C.P.A.'s, Am. Accounting Assn., IEEE, Inst. Mgmt. Scis., Am. Mgmt. Assn. (sr. planning council 1962—). Contbr. articles to profl. jours. Home: 511 Avenida San Juan San Clemente CA 92672 Office: San Clemente CA 92672

REAMES, TIMOTHY PAUL, ins. co. exec.; b. Dallas, Jan. 24, 1935; s. Phillip B. and Grace A. (Plauche) R.; B.B.A., So. Methodist U., 1957, LL.B., 1961; m. Ann Semmes, Nov. 7, 1959; children—Timothy, Peter, Jennifer. Admitted to Tex. bar, 1961, Calif. bar, 1962, N.Y. bar, 1971; atty. Union Oil Co. Calif., 1961-64, Litton Industries, Inc., 1964-68, City Investing Co., 1968-78; v.p., gen. counsel Home Ins. Co., N.Y.C., 1978—; dir. Home Indemnity Co., City Ins. Co., So. Calif. Fin. Corp., Franklin Fin. Corp. Mem. Am. Bar Assn., N.Y. Bar Assn., Calif. Bar Assn., Tex. Bar Assn. Roman Catholic. Home: 50 Twin Oak Rd Short Hills NJ 07078 Office: 59 Maiden Ln New York NY 10038

REANEY, GILBERT, musician, educator; b. Sheffield, Eng., Jan. 11, 1924; s. Lawrence and Mabel (Crookes) R.; B.A. with honors, Sheffield U., 1948, B.Mus., 1950, M.A., 1951; postgrad. U. Paris, 1950-52. Came to U.S., 1960. Researcher, tchr. Reading (Eng.) U., 1953-56, Birmingham (Eng.) U., 1956-59; prof. musicology U. Hamburg, 1960; asso. prof. music dept. U. Calif. at Los Angeles, 1960-62, prof., 1963—. Founder, artistic dir. London Medieval Group, 1958—; cons. panel BBC, 1958-60; guest lectr., Eng., Germany, U.S. Served with Brit. Army, 1943-46. Guggenheim fellow, 1964-65; Nat. Humanities Found. sr. fellow, 1967-68. Mem. Am., Internat. (Dent medal 1951) musicological socs., Royal Mus. Assn. Author: Early 15th Century Music, 6 vols., 1955-77; (with A. Gilles and J. Maillard) Philippe de Vitry, Ars Nova, 1964; International Inventory of Musical Source, 2 vols., 1966-69; Machaut, 1971; (with A. Gilles) Franconis de Colonia Ars Cantus mensurabilis, 1974. Gen. editor: Corpus Scriptorum de Musica; asst. editor Musica Disciplina, 1956-76. Home: 1001 3d St Santa Monica CA 90403 Office: Music Dept University of Calif Los Angeles CA 90024

REANEY, JAMES CRERAR, educator, dramatist, poet; b. South Easthope, Ont., Can., Sept. 1, 1926; s. James Nesbitt and Elizabeth Henrietta (Crerar) R.; B.A., U. Toronto, 1948, M.A., 1949, Ph.D., 1957; D.Litt., Carleton U., 1975; m. Colleen Thibaudeau, Dec. 29, 1951; children—James Stewart, Susan Alice. Asst. prof. English, U. Man., 1949-60; prof. English, U. Western Ont., London, 1960—. Recipient Massey award for the Killdeer, 1960; Chalmers award for best Can. play Sticks and Stone, 1974, The St. Nicholas Hotel, 1975, Handcuffs, 1976; decorated Order of Can. Fellow Royal Soc. Can.; mem. Can. Theatre Drama Soc., Can. Poetry League. Author: Poems, 1972; Colours in the Dark, 1969; Masks of Childhood, 1972; Listen to the Wind, 1972; Apple Butter and Other Plays for Children, 1973; plays include: Sticks and Stones: The Donnellys Part I, 1975; The St. Nicholas Hotel: The Donnellys Part II, 1976; Handcuffs: The Donnellys Part III, 1977; 14 Barrels from Seatto Sea, 1977; The Dismissal, 1978; editor, pub. Alphabet, 1960-70; contbr. articles to profl. jours. Mem. New Democratic Party. Home: 276 Huron St London ON Canada Office: Dept English Univ of Western Ont London ON N6A 3K7 Canada

REAP, ELIZABETH, ins. co. exec.; b. Little Rock, Sept. 17, 1923; d. Alvin and Lola (Reaves) Reap; B.A. with honors, George Washington U., 1945. With RFC, Washington and Little Rock, 1945-47; buyer ready-to-wear Foley's, Houston, 1947-52; office mgr. Townsend, Major, Carrigan & Blatchford, attys., Houston, 1952-54; with Am. Gen. Cos., 1954—, exec. asst., dir. pub. relations, then asst. corporate sec. Am. Gen. Ins. Co., parent co., Houston, 1972-74, corporate sec., 1974—, v.p., 1979—. Past mem. agy. allocations com. United Fund Houston and Harris County; C.L.U., 1971. Fellow Life Mgmt. Inst.; mem. Am. Soc. Corporate Secs. (regional treas.), Am. Soc. C.L.U.'s, Forum Club of Houston (founding mem.), Houston C. of C., Phi Beta Kappa (past alumni chpt. dir., v.p.). Baptist. Home: 5435 Chevy Chase Dr Houston TX 77056 Office: 2727 Allen Pkwy Houston TX 77019

REARDON, JOHN, baritone, actor; b. Apr. 8, 1930; grad. Rollins Coll., 1952, Mus.D. (hon.), 1976; studied voice with Martial Singher and Margaret Harshaw. Baritone with Met. Opera, Washington Opera Soc., Dallas Opera Co., Santa Fe Opera, San Francisco Opera, Teatro La Venice (Italy), N.Y. City Opera Co.; roles include Guglielmo in Cosi Fan Tutte, title role in Gianni Schicchi, Pelleas in Pelleas et Melisande, Doctor in Vanessa, title role in Don Giovanni, Valentine in Faust, Eisenstein in Die Fledermaus, Belaev in Natalie Petrovna, Miles Dunster in Wings of the Dove, Scarpia in Tosca, Nick Shadow in The Rake's Progress, Escamilio in Carmen, Count Almaviva in The

Marriage of Figaro, Abdul in The Last Savage, Marcello in La Boheme, Prince Danilo in The Merry Widow, Dandini in La Cenerentola, Sharpless in Madame Butterfly; Nat. Ednl. TV prodns. Queen of Spades, From the House of the Dead; made Broadway debut in The Saint of Bleecker Street, 1954; appeared in New Faces of 1956, The Song of Norway, Do Re Mi, Kismet in San Francisco and London; appeared world premiere Summer and Smoke, Mourning Becomes Electra, The Sea Gull, Am. premieres Devils of Loudon, Bassarids, The Nose; also other TV appearances including children's show Mister Roger's Neighborhood. Chmn. bd. Sunstone Corp., Santa Fe. Recs. include: The Old Maid and the Thief, The Rake's Progress, The Creation, La Boheme, The Merry Widow, Bernstein's Songfest, Lady in the Dark, also solo album contemporary art songs. Address: PO Box 2424 Santa Fe NM 87501 I suppose the word integrity comes to mind when I think of one guiding principle I have tried to have rule my life and career I have been engaged in almost all forms of musical entertainment from Las Vegas to the Metropolitan Opera and have simply tried to do my best wherever and whatever I was doing I have the feeling that if we reserve our best efforts for that long awaited "goal" we fall far short of the mark when the time comes if under those circumstances it ever does come

REARDON, JOHN EDWARD, mayor; b. Kansas City, Kans., Aug. 23, 1943; s. Joseph E. and Helen (Cahill) R.; B.S. in History and Govt., Rockhurst Coll., Kansas City, Mo., 1965; m. Helen Kasick, June 18, 1966; children—Joseph, Kathleen. Tchr., head social studies dept. Arrowhead Jr. High Sch., Kansas City, Kans., 1966-72; register of deeds Wyandotte County/Kansas City, Kans., 1972-75; mayor of Kansas City (Kans.), 1975—; mem. Kansas City Devel. Corp. Bd. dirs. Kansas City United Way. Recipient Loyalty Day award VFW; named Outstanding Young Kansan, Jaycees, 1978, also numerous certificates of appreciation. Mem. U.S. Conf. Mayors, Kans. League Municipalities (v.p.), Kansas City C. of C. Democrat. Roman Catholic. Club: Central Ave. Optimists. Home: 1513 Tauromee St Kansas City KS 66102 Office: 701 N 7th St Kansas City KS 66101

REARDON, LEONARD WOOD, mobile home components mfg. co. exec.; b. Effingham, Ill., Aug. 4, 1940; s. Leonard and Betty J. Reardon; B.S. in Acctg., Eastern Ill. U., 1965; grad. corp. fin. mgmt. tng. program Harvard U., 1979; m. Carol Lynn Kessler, July 19, 1969; children—Jeffrey, Christine, Kerri. Sr. auditor Peat Marwick & Mitchell, Kansas City, Mo., 1965-68; acctg. mgr. Fedders Corp., Effingham, 1968-70; acctg. mgr. A.E. Staley Mfg. Co., Decatur, Ill., 1970-73; v.p. fin. Philips Industries Inc., Dayton, Ohio, 1973—. Served with U.S. Army, 1958-61. C.P.A., Kans. Home: 1267 Timberwyck Ct Spring Valley OH 45370 Office: 4801 Springfield St Dayton OH 45401

REARDON, TIMOTHY JAMES, JR., former govt. ofcl.; b. Somerville, Mass., May 18, 1915; s. Timothy James and Mary Ellen (Keefe) R.; A.B., Harvard, 1938; m. Betty Jane Paden; 1 son, Timothy James III. Engaged in advt. bus., Boston, 1938-42; participated John F. Kennedy congl. campaign, 1946; adminstrv. asst. to John F. Kennedy as mem. Ho. of Reps., 1947-52, mem. Senate, 1953-60, as President U.S., 1961-63; spl. asst. to Pres. for cabinet affairs, 1961-64; asst. to chmn. FDIC, 1964-65, exec. asst. to bd. dirs., 1965-68; ret., 1968. Served to capt. USAAF, 1942-46; lt. col. Res. (ret.). Home: 3134 Dumbarton Ave NW Washington DC 20007

REASER, JAMES G., bus. exec.; b. York, Pa., May 10, 1916; s. B. Frank and L. Kathryn (Eisenhart) R.; B.S. in Econs., Franklin and Marshall Coll., Lancaster, Pa., 1939; m. D. Jane Rose, Aug. 31, 1940. Treas. Albany Internat. Corp. (N.Y.). Mem. Fin. Execs. Inst. Episcopalian. Clubs: University, Masons (Albany). Home: 19 Patroon Pl Loudonville NY 12211 Office: PO Box 1907 Albany NY 12201

REASONER, HARRY, TV news reporter; b. Dakota City, Iowa, Apr. 17, 1923; s. Harry Ray and Eunice (Nicholl) R.; m. Kathleen Ann Carroll, Sept. 7, 1946; children—Stuart, Ann, Elizabeth, Jane, Mary Ray, Ellen, Jonathan. Reporter, drama critic Mpls. Times, 1942-43, 46-48; asst. dir. publicity Northwest Airlines, 1948-50; newswriter radio sta. WCCO, Mpls., 1950-51; editor regional prodn. center USIA, Manila, Philippines, 1951-54; news dir. sta. KEYD-TV, Mpls., 1954-56; reporter, corr. CBS News, 1956-70, ABC News, 1970-78, CBS News, 1978—. Served with AUS, 1943-46. Recipient Emmy for news documentary, 1967-68; Peabody award, 1967; U. Mo. honor medal, 1970; Emmy for outstanding news broadcasting, 1974. Author: (novel) Tell Me About Women, 2d edit., 1964; (collected essays) The Reasoner Report, 1966. Office: CBS News 524 W 57th St New York NY 10019

REASONER, HARRY MAX, lawyer; b. San Marcos, Tex., July 15, 1939; s. Harry Edward and Joyce Majorie (Barrett) R.; B.A. summa cum laude, Rice U., 1960; J.D. with highest honors, U. Tex., 1962; postgrad. U. London, 1962-63; m. Elizabeth Macey Hodges, Apr. 15,1963; children—Barrett Hodges, Elizabeth Macey. Admitted to Tex. bar, 1962, D.C. bar, 1974; law clk. U.S. Ct. Appeals, 2d Circuit, 1963-64; asso. firm Vinson & Elkins, Houston, 1964-69, partner, 1970—, mem. exec. com., 1976—; dir. Fla. Gas Co.; vis. prof. U. Tex. Sch. Law, 1971, Rice U., 1976, U. Houston Sch. Law, 1977. Rotary Found. fellow, 1962-63; Nat. Merit scholar, 1956-60. Fellow Tex. Bar Found.; mem. State Bar Tex., Assn. Bar City N.Y., Am. Bar Assn., Am. Judicature Soc., Am. Law Inst., Chancellors, Order of Coif, Phi Beta Kappa, Delta Phi Alpha, Phi Delta Phi. Democrat. Baptist. Clubs: Houston Country, Rotary, Ramada. Author: (with Charles Alan Wright) Procedure: The Handmaid of Justice, 1965. Home: 2312 Rice Blvd Houston TX 77005 Office: 2100 First City Nat Bank Bldg Houston TX 77002

REASONS, GEORGE HUBERT, journalist; b. Memphis, Aug. 8, 1923; s. George Effie and Mildred Lee (Rowe) R.; B.A., UCLA, 1954, M.A., 1955; m. Ramona H. Phillips, Jan. 2, 1950; children—Frances Annette, George Hubert II, Rebecca Lee, Richard John. Reporter, edn. editor, asst. city editor Los Angeles Mirror News, 1955-62; reporter Los Angeles Times, from 1962, later asst. city editor, now investigative reporter, syndicated columnist Los Angeles Times News Syndicate, 1969-77; asso. prof. journalism Calif. State U., Northridge, 1968. Served with USAAF, 1942-45. Recipient Calif. State Bar award for Outstanding Achievement, 1965; Alumnus of Year award UCLA Journalism Dept., 1967; Newsman of Year award Valley Press Club, 1967; Greater Los Angeles Press Club awards, 1968, 72, 73; Brotherhood award NCCJ, 1972; Bronze medallion Sigma Delta Chi, 1976. Mem. Kappa Tau Alpha. Author: They Had A Dream, 1971. Office: Los Angeles Times Times Mirror Sq Los Angeles CA 90053

REATH, RICHARD FROST, educator; b. Milton, Oreg., June 14, 1916; s. William King and Mabel (Frost) R.; A.B., Pacific U., 1938; student U. Wash., 1938-39; Ph.D., U. Wis., 1944. Instr. polit. sci. U. Idaho, 1946-47; mem. faculty Occidental Coll., 1947—, Cecil H. and Louise Gamble prof. Am. instns., 1965—, chmn. div. social scis., 1963—, chmn. dept. polit. sci., 1968—. Trustee Beverly Coll. Law, 1973—. Served to lt. USNR, 1943-46; PTO. Fellow Fund Advancement Edn., 1953-54. Mem. Am., Western, Calif. polit. sci. assns., Am. Soc. Internat. Law. Mason. Home: 3744 San Rafael Ave Los Angeles CA 90065

REAVES, CHARLES DURHAM, leasing co. exec.; b. Florence, S.C., June 1, 1935; s. Howard Meacham and Kathleen (Durham) R.; B.A. magna cum laude, Furman U., 1956; LL.B., U. Ala., 1961; LL.M., Georgetown U., 1966; m. Gretchen Wuerdeman, May 4, 1963; 1 son, Mark Charles. Admitted to Ala. bar, 1961, Mass. bar, 1967, D.C. bar, 1970; legal adv. to chmn. FTC, Washington, 1963-67; sec., asso. counsel Paul Revere Life Ins. Co., Worcester, Mass., 1967-70; v.p., sec., gen. counsel Steadman Security Corp., Washington, 1970-74, Saunders Leasing System, Inc., Birmingham, Ala., 1974—. Mem. Holden (Mass.) Town Planning Bd., 1968-70; bd. dirs. Worcester Mental Health Assn., 1969-70. Served to capt. USAR, 1961-63. Decorated Army Commendation medal. Mem. Am. Bar Assn., Fed. Bar Assn., Assn. ICC Practitioners, Ala. Bar Assn., D.C. Bar Assn. Clubs: The Club (Birmingham); Inverness Country. Home: 3028 Westmoreland Dr Birmingham AL 35223 Office: 201 Office Park Dr Birmingham AL 35223

REAVES, GIBSON, astronomer, educator; b. Chgo., Dec. 26, 1923; s. Hart Walker and Helen (Gibson) R.; B.A. in Astronomy, U. Calif. at Los Angeles, 1947, Ph.D., at Berkeley, 1952; m. Mary Craig Kerr, Apr. 2, 1955; 1 son, Benjamin Kerr. Mem. faculty U. So. Calif., Los Angeles, 1952—, prof. astronomy, 1965—, chmn. dept., 1969-74. Served with AUS, 1942-46. Recipient Asso. award for teaching excellence U. So. Calif., 1974. Danforth asso., 1966—. Fellow Royal Astron. Soc.; mem. Astron. Soc. Pacific, Am. Astron. Soc., AAAS, Internat. Astron. Union, Sigma Xi. Home: 27125 Whitestone Rd Rancho Palos Verdes CA 90274 Office: Dept Astronomy Univ So Calif Los Angeles CA 90007

REAVES, KELSIE LOOMIS, ret. army officer; b. Banks, Ark., Nov. 24, 1911; s. Henry Jefferson and Elizabeth (Loomis) R.; student U. Fla., 1931-33; B.S., U.S. Mil. Acad., 1937; m. Mary Louise Moore, Oct. 23, 1937; children—Elizabeth Tirrill (Mrs. Thomas William Wanous), Mary Joanne (Mrs. Gregory Sutton Ewell). Commd. 2d lt. U.S. Army, 1937, advanced through grades to maj. gen., 1965; dir. plans, policy div. Office Def. Adviser, U.S. delegation to NATO, Paris, France, 1959-62; asst. div. comdr. 3d Armored Div., Germany, 1962-63; dep. dir. for operations, joint staff Joint Chiefs Staff, Washington, 1963-65; comdg. gen., Ft. Polk, La., 1965-66; dep. chief staff for individual tng. Hdqrs. U.S. Continental Army Command, Ft. Monroe, Va., 1966-67; comdg. gen. 6th Inf. Div., 1967-68; vice dir. joint staff Joint Chiefs Staff, 1968-69, ret., 1969; v.p. Sun State Builders, Inc., Tampa, Fla., 1969—. Decorated D.S.M. with oak leaf cluster, Silver Star medal, Legion of Merit with three oak leaf clusters; Croix de Guerre (France). Mem. Alpha Tau Omega. Home: 100 Pierce St Apt 503 Clearwater FL 33516

REAVIS, JOHN WALLACE, lawyer; b. Falls City, Nebr., Nov. 13, 1899; s. Charles Frank and Myrta A. Reavis; LL.B., Cornell U., 1921; m. Helen Lincoln, May 3, 1924 (dec.); children—John W., Lincoln. Began as asso., Tolles, Hogsett, Ginn & Morley, Cleve., now sr. partner successor firm Jones, Day, Reavis & Pogue. Dir. Gray Drug Stores, Inc., Lehman Corp. Served with USN, Flying Corps, World War I. Home: 2733 Ashley Rd Shaker Heights OH 44122 Office: Union Commerce Bldg Cleveland OH 44115

REAVLEY, THOMAS MORROW, lawyer, judge; b. Quitman, Tex., June 21, 1921; s. Thomas Mark and Mattie (Morrow) R.; B.A., U. Tex., 1942; J.D., Harvard, 1948; LL.D., Austin Coll., 1974, Southwestern U., 1977; m. Florence Montgomery Wilson, July 24, 1943; children—Thomas Wilson, Marian, Paul Stuart, Margaret. Admitted to Tex. bar, 1948; asst. dist. atty., Dallas, 1948-49; mem. firm Bell & Reavley, Nacogdoches, Tex., 1949-51; county atty., Nacogdoches, 1951; mem. firm Fisher, Tonahill & Reavley, Jasper, Tex., 1952-55; sec. state Tex., 1955-57; mem. firm Powell, Rauhut, McGinnis & Reavley, Austin, Tex., 1957-64; dist. judge, Austin, 1964-68; justice Supreme Ct. Tex., 1968-77; judge U.S. Ct. Appeals, 5th Circuit, Austin, 1979—; pres. Tex. Jud. Council, 1971-76; lectr. Baylor U. Law Sch., 1976—; adj. prof. U. Tex. Law Sch., 1958-59, 78—. Chancellor S.W. Tex. conf. United Methodist Ch., 1972—. Bd. dirs. Southwestern U., Georgetown, Tex., Huston-Tillotson Coll., Austin; pres. Meth. Home, Waco, Tex. Served to lt. USNR, 1943-45. Mason (33 deg.). Home: 1312 Meriden Ln Austin TX 78703 Office: Am Bank Tower Austin TX 78701

REBEIZ, CONSTANTIN ANIS, educator; b. Beirut, July 11, 1936; s. Anis C. and Valentine A. (Choueyri) R.; came to U.S., 1969, naturalized, 1975; B.S., Am. U., Beirut, 1959; M.S., U. Calif. at Davis, 1960, Ph.D., 1965; m. Carole Louise Conness, Aug. 18, 1962; children—Paul A., Natalie, Mark J. Dir. dept. biol. scis. Agrl. Research Inst., Beirut, 1965-69; research asso. biology U. Calif. at Davis, 1969-71; asso. prof. plant physiology U. Ill., Urbana-Champaign, 1972-76, prof., 1976—. Mem. Am. Soc. Plant Physiologists, Comite Internat. de Photobiologie, AAAS, Lebanese Assn. Advancement Scis. (exec. com. 1967-69), Sigma Xi. Greek Orthodox. Contbr. articles to sci. publs. plant physiology. Home: 301 W Pennsylvania Ave Urbana IL 61801 Office: Vegetable Crops Bldg U Ill Urbana-Champaign IL 61801

REBELSKY, FREDA ETHEL GOULD, psychologist; b. N.Y.C., Mar. 11, 1931; d. William and Sarah (Kaplan) Gould; B.A., U. Chgo., 1950, M.A., 1954; Ph.D., Radcliffe Coll., 1961; m. William Rebelsky, Jan. 1, 1956 (dec. 1979); 1 son, Samuel. Counselor, U. Chgo. Orthogenic Sch., 1952-55; research asst. Kenyon & Eckhart, Inc., 1956-58; research asst. lab. human devel. Harvard U., 1959-60, teaching asst. psychology, then instr. edn., 1960-61; research asso. Speech research lab. Children's Hosp., Boston, 1960-61, Mass. Inst. Tech., 1961-62; mem. faculty Boston U., 1962—, prof. psychology, 1972—, dir. doctoral program in devel. psychology, 1969-74; vis. lectr. U. Utrecht (Netherlands), 1965-67; Froman prof. Russell Sage Coll., Troy, N.Y., 1972. Grantee U.S. Office Edn., 1964-65, Boston U. Grad. Sch., 1967-70, OEO, 1967—, NIMH, 1974-76; recipient Distinguished Tchr. Psychology award Am. Psychol. Found., 1970; Harbison award excellence teaching Danforth Found., 1971; Metcalf award Boston U., 1978. Mem. AAAS, Soc. Research Child Devel. (sec. Boston 1963-65), AAUP (sec. Boston U. 1964-65), Am., Eastern, Mass. (chmn. program com. 1962-64) psychol. assns., Mass. Children's Lobby (pres. 1977—), Sigma Xi, Psi Chi. Author: Child Behavior and Development: A Reader, 1969; Child Behavior and Development, 2d edit., 1973: Life: The Continuous Process, 1975; Growing Children, 1976. Address: 1 Billings Park Newton MA 02158 Office: 64 Cummington St Boston MA 02215

REBENACK, JOHN HENRY, librarian; b. Wilkinsburg, Pa., Feb. 10, 1918; s. Charles Lewis and Carrie (Fielding) R.; A.B., U. Pitts., 1942; B.S. in L.S., Carnegie Library Sch., 1947; m. Dorothy Merle Treat, Oct. 31, 1942 (dec. Apr. 1971); children—Charles Edwin, Christine (Mrs. Clair N. Hayes III); m. 2d, Frances Strabley Krieger, May 6, 1972. Reference asst. Carnegie Library, Pitts., 1947-50; librarian Salem (Ohio) Pub. Library, 1950-53, Elyria (Ohio) Library, 1953-57; asst. librarian Akron (Ohio) Public Library, 1957-65, asso. librarian, 1965-67, librarian-dir., 1967—; dir. U.S. Book Exchange, Inc., 1972. Mem. United Community Council, Citizens' Com. Pub. Welfare, 1965-66, chmn. group work and recreation div., 1963-66, v.p., 1967-68, pres. conf. of execs., 1975-76; mem. steering com., planning div. United Way; mem. Akron Mayor's Task Force on Human Relations, 1962; mem. library com. President's Com. on Employment of Handicapped, 1967—, chmn., 1973—, mem. sch. library manpower adv. com., 1967-73; mem. coll. adv. com. U. Akron, 1972—; mem. adv. council on fed. programs State Library of Ohio, 1975-79. Bd. visitors Grad. Sch. Library and Info. Sci., U. Pitts., 1968-74; mem. exec. bd. Gt. Trail council Boy Scouts Am., 1977—; bd. dirs. Summit County unit Am. Cancer Soc., 1979—. Served with AUS, 1942-45. Recipient Newton D. Baker citation, 1968. Mem. Am. (chmn. personnel adminstrv. sect. 1966-67, chmn. bldgs. and equipment sect. 1971-73, chmn. legislation assembly 1976-77), Ohio (exec. bd. 1957-60, chmn. adult edn. round table 1963, chmn. legis. com. 1965-66, 70-72, 76-80, pres. 1966-67, Librarian of Year 1979) library assns., Carnegie Library Sch. Assn. (pres. 1961-63), U. Pitts. Grad. Sch. Library and Info. Sci. Alumni Assn. (exec. com. 1978-79), Am. Assn. UN (v.p. Akron chpt. 1960), Beta Phi Mu. Congregationalist. Clubs: Torch (pres. 1968-69), Kiwanis (pres. Akron 1978-79). Home: 2095 Brookshire Rd Akron OH 44313 Office: 55 S Main St Akron OH 44326

REBENFELD, LUDWIG, chemist; b. Prague, Czechoslovakia, July 10, 1928; s. Carl and Martha (Scheib) R.; came to U.S., 1939, naturalized, 1946; B.S., Lowell Tech. Inst., 1951; M.A., Princeton, 1954, Ph.D., 1955; m. Ellen Vogel, July 27, 1956. Research fellow, sr. scientist Textile Research Inst., Princeton, N.J., 1951-59, asso. research dir., also edn. program dir., 1960-66, v.p. edn. and research, 1966-70, pres., 1971—; vis. lectr., asso. prof., prof. chem. engring. Princeton, 1964—. Mem. gov. council, sec.-treas. Fiber Soc.; mem. Nat. Council Textile Edn. Trustee Phila. College Textiles and Sci. Recipient Distinguished Achievement award Fiber Soc., Harold DeWitt Smith Meml. medal ASTM. Fellow Am. Inst. Chemists, Brit. Textile Inst., Inst. Textile Sci. Can.; mem. Am. Chem. Soc., Am. Textile Chemists and Colorists, AAAS, Sigma Xi, Phi Psi. Home: 49 Pardoe Rd Princeton NJ 08540 Office: PO Box 625 Princeton NJ 08540

REBENNACK, MALCOM JOHN MICHAEL CREAUX, JR. (DR. JOHN), musician; b. New Orleans, Nov. 21, 1940. Plays keyboards, guitar, bass; session musician, producer, New Orleans, from 1955, playing with Joe Tex, Frankie Ford and Professor Longhair; later moved to Los Angeles, performing with Phil Spector, Sam Cooke, Sonny and Cher; songwriter, singer, instrumentalist thereafter; performing in extensive concert tours and TV programs; albums include: Gris-Gris, 1968, Babylon, 1969, Sun, Moon and Herbs, 1971, Gumbo, 1972, In the Right Place, 1973; songs include Iko iko; Right Place, Wrong Time; Such a Night; appeared in film The Last Waltz, 1978. Office: care Weisner-Demann Entertainment 9200 Sunset Blvd Los Angeles CA 90069*

REBER, NORMAN FRANKLIN, ret. editor; b. Centreport, Pa., Nov. 6, 1909; s. Jonathan Gicker and Clara Kramer (Snyder) R.; A.B., Elizabethtown (Pa.) Coll., 1930; M.A., U. Pa., 1935, Ph.D., 1960; m. Elsie Markey, June 26, 1938; children—Dean Howell, Barbara Reber Deardorff, Patricia Reber Belida. Tchr., prin. Weissport (Pa.) Pub. Sch., 1930-34; tchr. social studies and math. Ridgewood (N.J.) Schs., 1934-36; tchr. social studies and scis. Freehold (N.J.) Pub. Schs., 1936-43; tchr. Am. history and world history Springfield Twp. High Sch., Chestnut Hill, Pa., 1943-45; rate setter Budd Mfg. Co., 1945-46; field editor Pa. Farmer mag., Harrisburg, 1946-56, mng. editor, 1956-58, editor, 1958-74. Mem. Sch. Bd., York Imperial Sch. Dist., 1950-62; mem. Gov.'s Com. Preservation Agrl. Land, 1967-69; chmn. Keystone Expn. Center Com., 1973—. Recipient Hon. Keystone Farmer award Pa. Future Farmers Assn., 1959; hon. county agt. award Pa. County Agts. Assn., 1961; Distinguished Service to Pa. Agr. award New Holland div. Sperry Rand Corp., 1969, Distinguished Service to Agr. award Pa. Farmers Assn., 1970, Marketing award Hort. Assn. Pa., 1971, citation Pa. Forest Industries Com. and Am. Forest Products Industries, 1965; Golden Anniversary medallion Fed. Land Bank System, 1967; Disting. Service to Agr., Pa. Grange, 1974; honored at testimonial dinner, 1974, by individuals and groups including U.S. Dept. Agr., agrl. adv. council Pa. State U., Pa. Grassland Council, Pa. Gov. and House of Reps., and numerous agrl. orgns.; scholarship established in his name at Pa. State U., 1974. Mem. Pa. Master Farmers Assn. (hon.), Am. Agrl. Editors Assn. (sec.-treas. 1964-67), Pa. Flying Farmers Assn. (hon.), Pa. Farm Equipment Mfrs. Assn. (hon. life), Pa. Young Farmers Assn. (hon.), Pa. Vegetable Growers Assn. (hon. life), Acad. Polit. Sci., Phila. Soc. for Promoting Agr. (Gold medallion 1976). Republican. Mem. Ch. Brethren (minister, service vol. nat. hdqrs. 1976-77, moderator So. Pa. dist. 1979). Home: 2432 S George St York PA 17403

REBMANN, GODFREY RUHLAND, JR., lawyer; b. Phila., Feb. 6, 1898; s. Godfrey R. and Pauline (Cooper) R.; M.E., Cornell, 1919; LL.B., U. Pa., 1922; m. Mary H. Bull, Jan. 3, 1925 (dec. Apr. 1961); children—Ann (Mrs. M. Daniel Daudon), Beverly Mary (Mrs. William J. Bingham); m. 2d, Mary H. VanDoren, Nov. 27, 1970. Admitted to Pa. bar, 1922, practiced in Phila.; former partner, now counsel firm Obermayer, Rebmann, Maxwell & Hippel; asst. gen. counsel Lend Lease Adminstrn., 1942, asst. adminstr., 1942-43. Former chmn., dir. Big Brother Assn. Phila.; former dir., now hon. dir. Big Bros./Big Sisters Am., Inc.; former dir., sec. Phila. Orch. Assn. and Acad. Music Phila., Inc., now emeritus dir.; pres. community fund, Phila., 1941-42; chmn. war finance com. Pa., 1943-45; pres. Health and Welfare Council, Phila., 1950-53; asso. trustee U. Pa., until 1971; emeritus mem. council Cornell U., presdl. counsellor, 1971—; mem., past chmn. bd. govs. Eastern div. Pa. Economy League; past mem. exec. com. bd. dirs. Phila. United Fund. Mem. Am. Law Inst., Am., Pa., Phila. bar assns. Clubs: Philadelphia, Union League, Merion Cricket. Home: 10 W Old Gulph Rd Gladwyne PA 19035 Office: Packard Bldg Philadelphia PA 19102

REBOZO, CHARLES GREGORY, banker; b. Tampa, Fla., Nov. 17, 1912; s. Francisco M. and Carmen (Sarmiento) R. Pres., chmn. Key Biscayne (Fla.) Bank, 1964—. Pres. Jr. Achievement, 1959-60. Recipient Pop Warner award, 1960, Man and Boy award Boys Clubs Am., 1956. Mem. Key Biscayne C. of C. (pres. 1976-77). Clubs: Kiwanis (past club pres.), Key Biscayne Yacht (past commodore). Home: 490 Bay Ln Key Biscayne FL 33149 Office: 95 W McIntire St Key Biscayne FL 33149

RECANATI, RAPHAEL, shipping and banking exec.; b. Salonique, Greece, Feb. 12, 1924; s. Leon and Mathilde (Saporta) R.; student Israel and Eng.; m. Diane Hettena, Oct. 8, 1946; children—Yehuda, Michael. Chmn. Cargo Ships El-Yam Ltd., 1953—; pres. Overseas Discount Corp., Inc., N.Y.C., 1953—; chmn. Discount Bank (Overseas) Ltd., Geneva, Switzerland, 1970—; chmn. exec. com., mng. dir. IDB Bankholding Ltd., 1970—. Home: 944 Fifth Ave New York City NY 10021 Office: 511 Fifth Ave New York City NY 10017

RECER, PAUL HERBERT, journalist; b. Midland, Tex., Oct. 16, 1938; s. B.W. and Lennie Janet R.; attended N. Tex. State U., 1957-61; m. Donelda Louise Guthrie, Feb. 9, 1962; children—Dana Lynn, Jennifer Jaclyn. Reporter, Dallas Times Herald, 1961-63; with AP, 1963-76, night editor, Tulsa, 1963-65, Dallas, 1965, corr., San Antonio, 1965-68, aerospace writer, 1968-76; SW regional editor U.S. News & World Report, Houston, 1976—; guest lectr. N. Tex. State U., Denton, U. Tex., Arlington, Trinity U., San Antonio. Mem. Sigma Delta Chi. Club: Houston Press. Office: 801 Texas Suite 910 Houston TX 77002

RECHARD, OTTIS WILLIAM, educator; b. Laramie, Wyo., Nov. 13, 1924; s. Ottis H. and Mary (Bird) R.; B.A., U. Wyo., 1943; postgrad. U. Calif., Los Angeles, 1943; M.A., U. Wis., 1946, Ph.D., 1948; m. Dorothy Lee Duble, Nov. 19, 1943; children—Katherine L. (Mrs. Larry V. Baxter), Carol G. (Mrs. David P. Reiter), Nancy L. (Mrs. William Moore), Elizabeth A. Instr., U. Wis., 1948; instr., asst. prof. Ohio State U., 1948-51; staff mem. Los Alamos Sci. Lab., U. Calif., 1951-56; dir. Computing Center, prof. Wash. State U., Pullman, 1956-68, dir. systems and computing, 1968-70, chmn. dept. computer sci., 1963-76; prof. math., dir. computing services U. Denver, 1976—. program dir. computer sci. program NSF, 1964-65; chmn. NSF adv. panel on instl. computing facilities, 1969-70; cons. NSF, Idaho Nuclear Corp., Los Alamos Sci. Lab. Mem. Los Alamos Sch. Bd., 1954-56; mem. Pullman Sch. Bd., 1967-74. Trustee, past pres. Westminster Found., Synod Wash.-Alaska. Served to 1st lt. USAAF, 1943-45. Decorated Order of Leopold II (Belgium). Fellow AAAS; mem. Assn. for Computing Machinery, Am. Math. Soc., Math. Assn. Am., Soc. Indsl. and Applied Math., AAUP, Phi Beta Kappa, Sigma Xi, Phi Kappa Phi. Presbyn. (elder) Rotarian. Home: 3035 S Clayton St Denver CO 80210

RECHCIGL, MILOSLAV, JR., govt. ofcl.; b. Mlada Boleslav, Czechoslovakia, July 30, 1930; s. Miloslav and Marie (Rajtrova) R.; came to U.S., 1950, naturalized, 1955; B.S., Cornell U., 1954, M. Nutrition Sci., 1955, Ph.D., 1958; m. Eva Marie Edwards, Aug. 29, 1953; children—John Edward, Karen Marie. Teaching asst. Cornell U., 1953-57, grad. research asst., 1957-58, research asso., 1958; USPHS research fellow Nat. Cancer Inst., 1958-60, chemist enzymes and metabolism sect., 1960-61, research biochemist, tumor host relations sect., 1962-64, sr. investigator, 1964-68; grants asso. program NIH, 1968-69; spl. asst. for nutrition and health to dir. Regional Med. Programs Service, Health Services and Mental Health Adminstrn., HEW, 1969-70, exec. sec. nutrition program adv. com. Health Services and Mental Health Adminstrn., 1969-70; nutrition adviser AID, Dept. State, Washington, 1970—, chief Research and Instl. Grants div., 1970-73, exec. sec. research and instl. grants council, 1970-74, exec. sec. AID research adv. com., 1971—, AID rep. USC/FAR com., 1972—, asst. dir. Office Research and Instl. Grants, 1973-74, acting dir., 1974-75, dir. interregional research staff, 1975—, dir. devel. studies program, 1978; del. White House Conf. on Food, Nutrition and Health, 1969; cons. Office Sec. Agr., 1969-70, Dept. Treasury, 1973, Office Technol. Assessment, 1977—, FDA, 1979—; del. Agrl. Research Policy Adv. Com. Conf. on Research to Meet U.S. and World Food Needs, 1975. Organizer, mem. council Montrose Civic Assn., Rockville, Md.; active PTA, Boy Scouts Am., Rockville Alliance for Better Environment, Program Com. Earth Day. Nat. Acad. Scis. grantee, 1962, USPHS grantee, 1968. Fellow AAAS, Am. Inst. Chemists (councilor 1972-74, program chmn. 1974 ann. meeting, mem. program com. 1980 meeting), Internat. Coll. Applied Nutrition, Intercontinental Biog. Assn.. Washington Acad. Scis. (del. 1972—); mem. Am. Inst. Nutrition (com. Western Hemisphere Nutrition Congress 1971, 74, program com. 1979—), Am. Soc. Biol. Chemists, Am. Chem. Soc. (joint bd.-council com. on internat. activities 1975-76), D.C. Inst. Chemists (pres. 1972-74, councilor 1974—), Am. Inst. Biol. Scis., Soc. for Exptl. Biology and Medicine, Am. Soc. Animal Sci., Internat., Am. socs. cell biology, Soc. for Developmental Biology, Am. Assn. for Cancer Research, Soc. for Biol. Rhythm, Am. Pub. Health Assn., N.Y. Acad. Scis., Chem. Soc. Washington (symposium com. 1970, 71), Internat. Coll. Applied Nutrition, Internat. Soc. for Research on Civilization Diseases and Vital Substances, Soc. for Geochemistry and Health, Soc. for Internat. Devel., Internat. Platform Assn., Am. Assn. for Advancement Slavic Studies, Czechoslovak Soc. Arts and Scis. in Am. (hon., dir.-at-large 1962—, dir. publs. 1962-68, 70-74, v.p. 1968-74, pres. 1974-78, pres. collegium 1978—), History of Sci. Soc., Soc. Research Adminstrs., Sigma Xi, Phi Kappa Phi, Delta Tau Kappa (hon.). Clubs: Cosmos, Cornell (Washington). Author: (with Z. Hruban) Microbodies and Related Particles: Morphology, Biochemistry and Physiology, 1969, also Russian edit., 1972; Enzyme Synthesis and Degradation in Mammalian Systems, 1971; Food, Nutrition and Health: A Multidisciplinary Treatise Addressed to the Major Nutrition Problems from a World Wide Perspective, 1973; Man, Food and Nutrition: Strategies and Technological Measures for Alleviating the World Food Problem. 1973; World Food Problem: A Selective Bibliography of Reviews, 1975; Carbohydrates, Lipids, and Accessory Growth Factors, 1976; Nutrient Elements and Toxicants, 1977; Nitrogen, Electrolytes, Water and Energy Metabolism, 1979; Nutrition and the World Food Problem, 1979; (with Eva Rechcigl) Biographical Directory of the Members of the Czechoslovak Society of Arts and Sciences in America, 1972, 78; The Czechoslovak Contribution to World Culture, 1964; Czechoslovakia Past and Present, 1968; others. Co-editor: Internat. Jour. of Cycle Research, 1969-74, Jour. of Applied Nutrition, 1970—; series editor, Comparative Animal Nutrition, 1976—; editor-in-chief Handbook Series in Nutrition and Food, 1977—; mem. editorial bd. Nutrition Reports Internat., 1977—; translator, abstractor: Chemical Abstracts, 1959—. Contbr. sci. articles to profl. jours. Home: 1703 Mark Ln Rockville MD 20852 Office: Interregional Research Staff AID Dept State Washington DC 20523

RECHNITZ, GARRY ARTHUR, educator; b. Berlin, Germany, Jan. 1, 1936; s. Waldemar Walter and Margarete Marie (Grunow) R.; B.S. with honors, U. Mich. 1958; M.S., U. Ill., 1959, Ph.D., 1961; m. Harriet Louise Jones, June 14, 1958. Asst. prof. chemistry U. Pa., 1961-66; asso. prof. chemistry State U. N.Y., Buffalo, 1966-68, asso. provost, 1967-69, prof. chemistry, 1968-77; Unidel prof. U. Del., 1978—; indsl. cons. Recipient Regents-Alumni Honor award U. Mich., 1956; Gomberg prize in Chemistry, 1957; Van Slyke award in clin. chemistry, 1978; Alfred P. Sloan Found. fellow, 1966—; USPHS Research fellow, 1958-61. Mem. Am. Chem. Soc., AAAS, AAUP, Sigma Xi, Phi Lambda Upsilon, Alpha Chi Sigma. Home: 1014 Baylor Dr Newark DE 19711 Office: Chemistry Dept U Del Newark DE 19711

RECHTIN, EBERHARDT, aerospace systems co. exec.; b. East Orange, N.J., Jan. 16, 1926; s. Eberhardt Carl and Ida H. (Pfarrer) R.; B.S., Calif. Inst. Tech., 1946, Ph.D. cum laude, 1950; m. Dorothy Diane Denebrink, June 10, 1951; children—Andrea C., Nina, Julie Anne, Erica, Mark. Asst. dir., dir. Deep Space Network, Calif. Inst. Tech. Jet Propulsion Lab., 1949-67; dir. Advanced Research Projects Agy., Dept. Def., 1967-70, prin. dep. dir. def. research and engring., 1970-71, asst. sec. def. for telecommunications, 1972-73; chief engr. Hewlett-Packard Co., Palo Alto, Calif., 1973-77; pres. Aerospace Corp., El Segundo, Calif., 1977—. Served to lt. USNR, 1943-56. Recipient major awards NASA, Dept. Def., Fellow Am. Inst. Aeros. and Astronautics (major awards), IEEE (major awards); mem. Nat. Acad. Engring., Tau Beta Pi. Home: 1665 Cataluna Pl Palos Verdes Estates CA 90274 Office: 2350 E El Segundo Blvd El Segundo CA

RECHTSCHAFFEN, ALLAN, educator; b. N.Y.C., Dec. 8, 1927; s. Philip and Sylvia (Yaeger) R.; B.S., Coll. City N.Y., 1949, M.A., 1951; Ph.D., Northwestern U., 1956. Psychologist, Fergus Falls (Minn.) State Hosp., 1951-53; research psychologist VA, Chgo., 1956-57; instr. U. Chgo., 1957-58, asst. prof., 1958-63, asso. prof., 1963-68, prof. psychology, 1968—; lectr., cons. on sleep and dreams. Recipient Research Scientist award NIMH. Mem. Assn. Psychophysiol. Study Sleep (coordinating sec. 1978-81). Contbr. numerous articles profl. jours. Home: 1157 E 56th St Chicago IL 60637

RECHTSCHAFFEN, BERNARD, educator; b. Austria, Feb. 12, 1922; s. Sigmund and Yetta (Rechtschaffen) R.; came to U.S., 1937, naturalized, 1943; B.S., N.Y. U., 1945, M.A., 1949, Ph.D., 1954; m. Florence Fishman, Dec. 23, 1951; children—Joyce, Clifford. Grad. asst. German, then instr. N.Y. U., 1945-47; mem. faculty Bklyn. Poly. Inst., 1947—, prof. German, chmn. dept. modern langs., 1958—, chmn. dept. humanities, 1973-76, prof. humanities, 1976—; chmn. Germanistentag symposium on German lit., 1965. Adv. council Vienna Study Council, 1964—. Served with AUS, 1943-45. Recipient Founder's award N.Y. U., 1954. Mem. Am. Assn. Tchrs. German (pres. met. chpt. 1963-66), Modern Lang. Assn. (chmn. nat. conf. teaching and testing doctoral condidates in their lang. ability 1964), AAUP. Author: Kurze Deutsche Grammatik, 1965; Literatur für den Deutschunterricht, Erste Stufe, 1964; Zweite Stufe, 1964; Dritte Stufe, 1966; German-English, English-German Phonetic Dictionary, 1967; German for Research: Biological and Physical Sciences, 1971; German for Research: Humanities and Social Sciences, 1973. Mem. adminstrv. bd. German Quar., 1964-67. Home: 1015 E 24th St Brooklyn NY 11210

RECHY, JOHN FRANCISCO, author; b. El Paso, Tex.; s. Roberto Sixto and Guadalupe (Flores) R.; B.A., Tex. Western Coll.; student New Sch. Social Research. Instr. creative writing U. Calif. at Los Angeles, Occidental Coll. Served with AUS. Recipient Longview Found. award for short story The Fabulous Wedding of Miss Destiny; Nat. Endowment for Arts grantee, 1976. Mem. Authors Guild, Tex. Inst. Letters, P.E.N. Author: City of Night, 1963; Numbers, 1967; This Day's Death, 1969; Vampires, 1971; The Fourth Angel, 1973; The Sexual Outlaw, 1977; Rushes, 1979; contbr. short stories and articles to Evergreen Rev., The Nation, Big Table, Nugget, The London mag., Notes from Underground, Saturday Rev., N.Y. Times Books, Los Angeles Times, Forum, Viva, also anthologies The Moderns, Collision Course (U.S.), New Am. Writing, Voices (Eng.), Scripts, Literatura Chicana, Passing Through, Urban Reader, Black Humor, Chicano Voices; trans. stories and articles from Spanish in Evergreen Rev., Tex. Quar. Office: care Grove Press Inc 196 W Houston St New York NY 10014

RECK, ANDREW JOSEPH, educator; b. New Orleans, Oct. 29, 1927; s. Andrew Gervais and Katie (Mangiaracina) R.; B.A., Tulane U., 1947, M.A., 1949; Ph.D., Yale, 1954; student U. St. Andrews (Scotland), 1952-53, U. Paris, summers 1962, 64; m. Rima Drell, Aug. 30, 1956 (div. May 1970). Instr. English, U. Conn., 1949-50; instr. philosophy Yale, 1951-52, 55-58; mem. faculty Tulane U., 1958—, prof. philosophy, 1964—, chmn. dept., 1969—; Thomasfest lectr. Xavier U., Cin., 1970; Suarez Lectr. Spring Hill Coll., 1971; Niebuhr lectr. Elmhurst (Ill.) Coll., 1976; vis. prof. Fordham U., 1979. Served with AUS 1953-55. Fulbright scholar, 1952-53; Am. Council Learned Socs. grantee, 1961-62; Howard fellow, 1962-63; Am. Philos. Soc. grantee, 1972; Huntington Library fellow, 1973. Mem. Am. Philos. Assn. (nominating com. western div. 1975-76), Southwestern Philos. Soc. (exec. com. 1965-69, v.p. 1971-72, pres. 1972-73), So. Soc. Philosophy and Psychology (treas. 1968-71, pres. 1976-77), Am. Council Learned Socs. (Am. studies adv. com. 1972-76), Council for Internat. Exchange Scholars (philosophy screening com. 1974-77), Metaphys. Soc. Am. (councillor 1971-75, pres. 1977-78), Phi Beta Kappa (pres. Alpha of La. 1966-67). Author: Recent American Philosophy, 1964; Introduction to William James, 1967; New American Philosophers, 1968; Speculative Philosophy, 1972. Editor: George Herbert Mead, Selected Writings, 1964; Knowledge and Value, 1972; mem. adv. editorial bd. Tulane Studies in Philosophy, Southwestern Jour. Philosophy, So. Jour. Philosophy. Home: 732 Cherokee St New Orleans LA 70118 Office: Dept Philosophy Tulane U New Orleans LA 70118

RECK, W(ALDO) EMERSON, pub. relations cons., writer; b. Gettysburg, Ohio, Dec. 28, 1903; s. Samuel Harvey and Effie D. (Arnett) R.; A.B., Wittenberg U., 1926; A.M., U. Iowa, 1946; LL.D., Midland Coll., 1949; m. Hazel Winifred January, Sept. 7, 1926; children—Phyllis (Mrs. Louis E. Welch, Jr.), Elizabeth Ann (Mrs. Gabriel J. Lada). Reporter, Springfield (Ohio) News, 1922-26; publicity dir. Midland Coll., Fremont, Nebr., 1926-28, dir. pub. relations, prof. journalism, 1928-40; dir. pub. relations Colgate U., 1940-48; v.p. Wittenberg U., Springfield, Ohio, 1948-70, mem. adminstrv. com., 1968-69, v.p. emeritus, 1970—; pub. relations specialist Cumerford Corp., 1970-78; hist. columnist Springfield Sun, 1973—; spl. corr. Asso. Press, 1928-38; mng. editor Fremont Morning Guide, 1939; vis. lectr. pub. relations State U. Iowa, summers 1941, 42, U. Wyo., summer 1948; lectr. pub. relations and hist. subjects. Co-dir. Seminar on Pub. Relations for High Edn., Syracuse U., summers 1944, 45, 46. Mem. commn. on ch. papers, 1951-62, cons. com. dept. of press, radio and TV, United Luth. Ch., 1955-60; mem. commn. on ch. papers Luth Ch. in Am., 1962-64, 70-72, mem. exec. com., also chmn. com. periodicals of bd. publs., 1962-72, mem. mgmt. com. Office of Communications 1972-76; chmn. pub. relations com. Council Protestant Colls. and Univs., 1961-65. Recipient award Am. Coll. Pub. Relations Assn. for distinguished service, 1942, for outstanding achievement in interpretation of higher edn., 1944, 47; award Council for Advancement and Support of Edn., 1977. Mem. Am. Coll. Pub. Relations Assn. (v.p. in charge research 1936-38, editor assn. mag. 1938-40, pres. 1940-41, chmn. plans and policies com. 1944-50, dir. 1956, historian 1966-76), Luth. Coll. Pub. Relations Assn. (pres. 1951-53), Pub. Relations Soc. Am. (nat. jud. council 1952), Sch. Pub. Relations Assn., Assn. Am. Colls. (mem. com. on pub. relations 1945-48), AAUP, Springfield C. of C. (dir. 1958-60), Nat. Luth. Ednl. Conf. (chmn. com. pub. relations 1949-50), Ohio Coll. Pub. Relations Officers (pres. 1954-55), Nat. Trust for Hist. Preservation, Smithsonian Assos., Archives Assos., Nat. Hist. Soc. (founding asso.), Sigma Delta Chi, Pi Delta Epsilon, Delta Sigma Phi, Omicron Delta Kappa, Blue Key. Author: Public Relations: a Program for Colleges and Universities, 1946; The American College (with others), 1949; Public Relations Handbook (with others), 1950, 62, 67; The Changing World of College Relations, 1976; Father Can't Forget, 1980; editor: Publicity Problems, 1939; College Publicity Manual, 1948. Contbr. hist. and pub. relations articles to gen. ednl., profl. mags. Home: 61 Hedgely Rd Springfield OH 45506

RECKARD, EDGAR CARPENTER, JR., coll. provost; b. Huntington, W.Va., Dec. 20, 1919; s. Edgar Carpenter and Nanny Lois (Musselwhite) R.; B.A., Yale, 1942, M.Div., 1948; M.A. (ad eundem), Brown U., 1958; D.H.L., Westminster Coll. (Mo.), 1978; postgrad. U. Cambridge (Eng.), U. Edinburgh (Scotland), 1948-50; m. Susanna Laing McWhorter, June 26, 1948; children—Edgar Scott, Francis Laing, Matthew Kinsley, Charles William, Mark Alan. Ordained to ministry Presbyn. Ch., 1948; chaplain, adviser to overseas students U. Edinburgh, 1948-50; chaplain, prof. Westminster Coll., Mo., 1950-52, Brown U., 1952-58; chaplain, prof.-at-large, gen. sec. Claremont Coll., Calif., 1958-72; v.p., dean of coll., prof. Centre Coll. of Ky., Danville, 1972—, provost, 1976—; vis. mem. Sr. Common Room, Mansfield Coll., Oxford, 1964-65; Underwood fellow, 1971-72; ednl. cons., India, 1971-72. Officer local and state Councils of Chs. Bd. dirs. United Way of Claremont, Pomona Valley and Los Angeles County. Recipient Golden Goblet award Los Angeles County Youth and Recreation Commn., 1969, Human Rights award Pomona Valley UN Assn., 1969; named Citizen of Year, Claremont, 1968. Mem. Nat. Assn. Coll. and Univ. Chaplains (pres. 1957-58), AAUP, Am. Acad. of Religion, Am. Inst. Archeology, Am. Soc. Ch. History, Phi Beta Kappa, Omicron Delta Kappa. Home: 761 W Main St Danville KY 40422

RECKNAGEL, RICHARD OTTO, physiologist; b. Springfield, Mo., Jan. 11, 1916; s. Emil and Ella (Moench) R.; B.S., Wayne U., 1939; Ph.D., U. Pa., 1949; m. June 19, 1943; children—Frank Otto, Judith Susan. Asst. prof. physiology Sch. Medicine, Case Western Res. U., 1956-60, asso. prof., 1960-65, prof., 1965, dir. dept. physiology, 1978—. Served to 2d lt. USAAF, World War II. Recipient Kaiser-Permanente Teaching award, 1977; NIH grantee, 57-79. Office: Case Western Res U Sch Medicine Dept Physiology Cleveland OH 44106

RECTOR, FLOYD CLINTON, JR., physiologist, physician; b. Slaton, Tex., Jan. 28, 1929; s. Floyd Clinton and Faye Elizabeth (Tucker) R.; B.S., Tex. Tech. Coll., 1950; M.D., U. Tex. Southwestern Med. Sch., 954; m. Marjory L. Bullen, May 27, 1950; children—Lynn, Ruth, Janet. Instr., U. Tex. Southwestern Med. Sch., Dallas, 1958-59, asst. prof. medicine, 1959-63, asso. prof., 1963-66, prof., 1966-73; prof. medicine and physiology, sr. scientist Cardiovascular Research Inst., dir. div. nephrology U. Calif., San Francisco, 1973—. Served with USPHS, 1956-58. NIH grantee, 1973—. Mem. Am. Soc. Nephrology, Am. Soc. Clin. Investigation, Am. Assn. Physicians, Am. Physiol. Soc. Editor: (with Barry M. Brenner) The Kidney, 1976. Office: U Calif 1065 HSE San Francisco CA 94143

RECTOR, GAIL WESLEY, assn. exec.; b. North Platte, Nebr., Feb. 14, 1918; s. Homer Grover and Lillian Maude (Ritner) R.; B.Mus., U. Mich., 1940, postgrad., 1940-41; m. Kathryn Reich Swain, Aug. 31, 1944; children—Richard William, Ellen (Mrs. Alan Stickney), Patricia Ann. Asst. to pres. U. Mich. Univ. Mus. Soc., Ann Arbor, 1945-54, exec. dir., 1957-68, pres., 1968—; asst. mgr. Boston Symphony Orch., 1954-57. Exec. sec. Berkshire Music Center at Tanglewood, Lenox, Mass.; mem. adv. com. Nat. Music Camp, Interlochen, Mich., Mem. renovation com. Detroit Orch. Hall. Served with AUS, 1941-45; PTO. Mem. Internat. Soc. Performing Arts Adminstrs. (pres. 1969-71), Assn. Coll. and Univ. Concert Mgrs. (v.p. 1963). Rotarian (pres. Ann Arbor chpt. 1966-67). Home: 2600 Essex Rd Ann Arbor MI 48104 Office: University Musical Society Burton Memorial Tower Ann Arbor MI 48109

RECTOR, JOHN MICHAEL, lawyer govt. ofcl.; b. Seattle, Aug. 15, 1943; s. Michael Robert and Bernice Jane (Allison) R.; B.A., U. Calif., Berkeley, 1966, J.D., Hastings Coll. Law, U. Calif., San Francisco, 1969; m. Mary Kaaren Sueta Jolly, Feb. 8, 1977. Trial atty. civil rights div. Dept. Justice, 1969-71; dep. chief counsel judiciary com. U.S. Senate, 1971-73, chief counsel, staff dir., 1973-77; adminstr. Office Juvenile Justice, Dept. Justice, 1977-79, spl. counsel to U.S. atty. gen. 1979, sr. atty. Office of Govt. Ethics, 1980—; chmn. adv. bd. Nat. Juvenile Law Center, 1973-77; mem. bd. Nat. Inst. Corrections, 1977-79; chmn. U.S. Interdepartmental Council Juvenile Justice, 1977-79; mem. bd. com. civil rights and liberties Am. Democratic Action, 1976—, Pres.'s Com. Mental Health-Justice Group, 1978, com. youth citizenship Am. Bar Assn., 1978—. Perry E. Towne scholar, 1966-67. Mem. Calif. Bar Assn., ACLU, Washington Council Lawyers, Vinifera Wine Growers Assn. Va. (life), Theta Chi. Democrat. Contbr. articles to profl. jours. Home: 203 Yoakum Pkwy Alexandria VA 22304

RECTOR, MILTON GAGE, assn. exec.; b. Fallon, Nev., Jan. 3, 1918; s. William L. and Virginia E. (Renfro) R.; B.A., U. So. Calif., 1940; postgrad. U. Calif. at Berkeley, Columbia; m. Harriet Louise Phibbs, Aug. 1, 1940; children—Brian Eugene (dec.), Barbara Elaine, Dianne Eileen, Bruce Alan. With Los Angeles County Probation Dept., 1940-46, probation officer charge forestry camp for delinquent boys, 1943-46; with Nat. Council Crime and Delinquency, 1946—, cons. Western region, 1946-52, dir. parole services, 1952-55, asst. exec. dir., 1955-59, exec. dir., 1959—, pres., 1972—. Mem. President's Adv. Com. on Delinquency and Youth Crime, 1960-66. Cons. to U.S. Senate subcom. investigation delinquency, 1953; organized Nat. Conf. Parole, 1956; bd. dirs. Am. Correctional Assn., 1959-73, Osborne Assn., 1960-75, Nat. Study Service, 1960-76, U. Md. Inst. Criminal Justice, 1972-78, Center for Correctional Justice, 1972-78, SUNY-Albany Criminal Justice Inst., Acad. Jud. Edn., 1970-75, Law in Am. Society Found.; chmn. bd. dirs. Joint Commn. Correctional Manpower and Tng., 1965-70; cons. Pres.'s Crime Commn., 1965-68; U.S. rep. UN Social Def. Sect., 1965-75; U.S. del. UN World Congress on Crime and Delinquency, Stockholm, 1965, Kyoto, Japan, 1970; mem. Nat. Commn. on Reform Fed. Criminal Laws, 1969-70, N.Y.C. Criminal Justice Coordinating Council, 1967-73, Nat. Commn. on Criminal Justice Standards and Goals, 1971-73, Inst. on Jud. Adminstrn.-Am. Bar Assn. Commn. on Juvenile Justice Standards, 1973-76; mem. adv. com. on correctional edn. Edn. Commn. of States, 1975-77. Served to lt. (j.g.) USNR, 1944-46; comdr. Res. Recipient August Volmer award Am. Criminological Soc., 1971. Club: Hackensack (N.J.) Country. Contbr. numerous articles profl. jours., procs. Nat. Council Crime and Delinquency; syndicated columnist Of Crime and Punishment. Home: 288 Monroe Ave River Edge NJ 07661 Office: NCCD Center 411 Hackensack Ave Hackensack NJ 07601. *My life work in the field of juvenile and criminal justice and its insights into the depths of man's inhumanity to man have enabled me to serve in a ministry for the reform of a system which at times seems impervious to reform, and thus continues to deny the attainment of social justice in my country.*

RECTOR, RICHARD ROBERT, television exec. and producer; b. Sioux Falls, S.D., Oct. 10, 1925; s. Harry David and Naomi Leone (Wilson) R.; B.S., Northwestern U., 1950; m. Marjorie M. Gust, Apr. 12, 1957; children—Christopher, Steven, Tracey. Mgr. CBS Network ops., dir. ops. for CBS News, program sercice coordinator, unit mgr., producer CBS TV Network, N.Y.C., 1952-61; v.p. VHF, Inc., div. Reeves Broadcasting Corp., 1961-64; pres. Richard R. Rector Prodns., N.Y.C., 1964-65; asst. dir. programming WCBS-TV, N.Y.C., 1966-69; dir. CBS Network Studios, N.Y.C., 1969-70; v.p. programs and sales planning Viacom, Inc., 1970-71; dir. prodn. planning and sta. liaison Bilingual Children's Television, Oakland, Calif., 1972-75; project dir., exec. producer Over Easy Project Sta. KQED-TV, San Francisco, 1975—. Pres. Port Washington (N.Y.) Civic Assn., 1960-61; mem. bd. adult edn., Port Washington, 1963-64. Served with USNR, 1943-46. Mem. Nat. Acad. Television Arts and Scis. (bd. govs. N.Y. 1965-70, treas. 1965-67, trustee 1967-70; pres. San Francisco chpt. 1971-74, trustee 1973-77, nat. vice chmn. 1974-76, chmn. 1976—, coordinator chpt. pres. 1974-77). Presbyterian. Office: 500 8th St San Francisco CA 94301. *People are direct reflections of ourselves. Whatever is wrong with the world can only be changed if we recognize that each of us has an opportunity to change it.*

RECTOR, ROBERT WAYMAN, assn. exec.; b. San Jose, Calif., Jan. 28, 1916; s. Joseph Jones and Eva (Hembree) R.; B.A., San Jose State Coll., 1937; M.A., Stanford U., 1939; Ph.D., U. Md., 1956; m. Margaret Eileen Hayden, Aug. 25, 1940; children—Cleone Rector Grabowski, Robin Rector Krupp, Bruce Hayden. Instr., Compton (Calif.) Coll., 1939-42; asso. prof. math. U.S. Naval Acad., 1946-56;

staff mathematician Space Tech. Labs., Los Angeles, 1956-61; asso. dir. computation center Aerospace Corp., El Segundo, Calif., 1961-65; v.p. Informatics, Inc., Van Nuys, Calif., 1965-70; v.p. Cognitive Systems, Inc., Beverly Hills, Calif., 1970-71; asso. dir. continuing edn. engring. and sci. U. Calif., Los Angeles, 1971-73; exec. dir. Am. Fedn. Info. Processing Socs., Montvale, N.J., 1973-79; spl. asst. White House Conf. Library and Info. Services, 1979—; mem. Los Angeles Mayor's Space Adv. Com., 1964-73. Served with USNR, 1942-46. Mem. Math. Assn. Am., Assn. Computing Machinery, AAAS. Sec. bd. govs. Pacific Jour. Math., 1957—. Home: 10700 Stradella Ct Los Angeles CA 90024

REDCAY, EDWARD E., coll. dean; b. Germantown, Pa., Oct. 13, 1902; s. Davis Jefferson and Catherine (Angstadt) R.; B.S., Dartmouth, 1927, M.S., 1931, Yale U. fellow, 1932; Ph.D., Columbia, 1935; m. Lillian Bilkey, Dec. 19, 1959. Head dept. sci. Roxbury Sch., Cheshire, Conn., 1927-30; asso. prof. psychology Dartmouth, 1930-32; dir. research Anna T. Jeans and John F. Slater Founds., Washington, 1932-35; dean men, prof. edn. State U. N.Y. Coll. Edn., 1936-52, acting pres., 1952-54, dean of coll., 1948-70, part-time counselor Continuing Edn. dir. Coll. Arts and Sci., 1970—. Dir., sec. Econ. Council of No. N.Y.; pres. North Country Chinchilla Breeders, Inc.; dir., treas. P.S.T.C. Ednl. and Benevolent Assn., Inc.; mem., v.p. Conway College Scholarship Board; bd. dirs. N.Y. State div. Am. Cancer Soc.; trustee YMCA, Plattsburgh, N.Y. Mem. Eastern States Assn. Profl. Schs. for Tchrs. (past exec. sec., v.p., pres., mem. bd. control, com. chmn.), Am. Acad. Polit. Sci., Am. Personnel and Guidance Assn., Am. Psychol. Assn., NEA, Am. Assn. Sch. Adminstrs., N.Y. State Tchrs. Assn. (pres. Northeastern Zone), Nat. Council Family Relations, Lambda Sigma, Kappa Phi Kappa, Kappa Delta Pi, Beta Theta Pi. Presbyterian. Contbr. articles to jours. and mags. Home: Cumberland Head Plattsburgh NY 12901 Office: State Univ Coll Arts and Sci Plattsburgh NY 12901

REDD, GEORGE NATHANIEL, ret. coll. dean; b. Balt., Apr. 4, 1903; s. James Henry and Bettie Catherine (Carter) R.; B.S., Columbia U., 1927, M.A., 1930, Ed.D. (Gen. Edn. Bd. fellow), 1939; m. Ruth Dryscoll, Aug. 24, 1938. Tchr. pub. schs., N.Y.C., 1927; dean, head dept. edn. Tex. Coll., Tyler, 1930-38; supr. schs. Smith County (Tex.), 1937-38; head dept. edn., dir. summer session Fisk U., 1939-51, dean of coll., head dept. edn., 1951-70, dean emeritus, 1970—; Distinguished vis. prof. Dillard U., 1970-71; exec. com. So. Rural Life Council, 1943-45; staff survey rural elementary schs. of South (Rosenwald Fund), 1939-40, survey Negro colls. related to Meth. Ch., 1944, Episcopal Ch., 1946, survey pvt. Negro colls. and schs. of S.C., 1947; cons. survey pub. schs., Owensboro, Ky., 1953; survey staff on higher edn. in Miss., 1953-54; cons. Citizens Com. on Pub. Schs. in Nashville, 1955-57, Nashville Human Relations Conf., 1956-58, So. Assn. Colls. and Secondary Schs.; dir. Southern Edn. Reporting Service, Nashville, 1956-62, Vis. Nurse Service, Nashville; mem. exec. com. Council Grad. Schs. in U.S., 1962-68; cons. grad. acad. programs br. U.S. Office Edn., 1965-67; com. grad. deans African-Am. Inst., 1964-66; cons. research com. Nashville Council of Social Agys., 1958-60. Carnegie Found. Improvement Teaching grantee, 1948-49. Mem. AAUP, Tenn. Council Human Relations, Am. Assn. UN, Am. Edn. Research Assn., Assn. Higher Edn., Conf. So. Grad. Deans, Conf. Acad. Deans, NEA, Sigma Pi Phi (nat. sec.), Kappa Delta Pi, Kappa Alpha Psi. Republican. Baptist. Author: (with others) Private Negro Colleges and Schools of South Carolina, 1947; co-editor Arts in Childhood mag., 1947-48; editor Boule Jour., 1963-64; contbr. articles to profl. publs., gen. periodicals. Home: 3512 Geneva Circle N Nashville TN 37209

REDDALL, H(ENRY) HASTINGS, former business exec.; b. Bloomfield, N.J., Nov. 8, 1893; s. John William and May Eloise (Smith) R.; B.S., Colgate U., 1918; postgrad. U.S. Naval War Coll., 1932, 33, Rutgers U., 1955; m. Janet Ewing, Oct. 15, 1925. Joined Western Electric Co., N.Y.C., 1913 (on leave 1915-19), auditor assigned No. Electric Co., Montreal, Que., Can., 1919-22, asst. cashier Western Electric, 1922, asst. treas., 1922-31, 32-41, 46, treas. subsidiary Nassau Smelting & Refining Co., Inc., Tottenville, N.Y., 1931-32, chief corp. accountant parent co., 1941-43, chief factory auditor, 1943-45, chief field auditor, 1945-46, treas. 1946-58; treas. Weco Corp., 1946-58, dir., 1947-58. Chmn. fin. com., treas. St. James Episcopal Ch., Brookhaven, also del. diocesan convs., bd. dirs. Colgate Alumni Corp., 1937-40, 43-46; trustee Dodge Fund Colgate U., 1950-60; past pres. sr. mem. bd. trustees Brookhaven Free Library. Served to lt. (j.g.) USNR, 1917-36. Recipient Alumni award for distinguished service to Colgate U., 1945; Commodore's Meml. Sailing award, 1965; Bishop's Cross, Episcopal Diocese L.I., 1971. Mem. Mil. Order Fgn. Wars, S.R., Bellport-Brookhaven Hist. Soc. (trustee, treas., chmn. bldg. com. 1966—, trustee meml. fund), Stamford Geneal. Soc., Soc. Colonial Wars, Loyal Legion, Vets. Corps Arty. State N.Y., Soc. for Preservation L.I. Antiquities, South Country Antique Soc., Suffolk Marine Mus. N.Y., U.S. Yacht Racing Union, Great South Bay Yacht Racing Assn., U.S. Power Squadron, Telephone Pioneers Am., Conn. Hist. Soc., Mil. Soc. War of 1812, Descs. Washington Army at Valley Forge, Phi Beta Kappa, Phi Kappa Psi. Republican. Clubs: Bellport Bay (N.Y.) Yacht (comdr. 1946-47, 59-60, hon. trustee 1960—); Key Largo Anglers; Quantuck Beach (Quoque, N.Y.). Contbr. crossword puzzles to N.Y. Times, Chgo. Tribune, others. Home: Bay Rd Brookhaven NY 11719

REDDAN, HAROLD JEROME, educator, sociologist; b. N.Y.C., Dec. 4, 1926; s. Harold B. and Catherine G. (Kelly) R.; B.A., St. Francis Coll., 1950; M.S., St. Johns U., 1957, Ph.D., 1961; m. Margaret M. Byrne, Oct. 11, 1952; children—Harold James, Patricia Anne, James Joseph, Kathleen Mary. Social investigator N.Y.C. Dept. Welfare, 1950-58; asso. prof. sociology St. Johns U., 1958-68; lectr. sociology Kings County Hosp. Center Sch. of Nursing, N.Y.C., 1961-66; family counselor, 1961—; adj. asso. prof. Manhattan Coll., 1968-69, prof. sociology, head dept. managerial scis., 1969-73; adj. sociology faculty Nassau Community Coll., 1971—; adminstrv. cons. Molloy Coll., 1973-74; adj. prof. sociology and bus. adminstrn. C.W. Post Coll., 1974—; mem. behavioral scis. faculty, police sci. program N.Y. Inst. Tech., 1974-75; adj. prof. sociology SUNY, Farmingdale; provost Molloy Coll., 1975-78, v.p. for planning and spl. programs, 1978-79; ednl. cons., 1979—. Dir. Jamaica VI Peace Corps Tng. Program, 1965. Coordinator, New Hyde Park Citizens for Kennedy, 1960; campaign mgr. 1st Assembly Dist., 1962-64. Served with AUS, 1945-46. Mem. Am. Sociol. Assn., Am. Acad. Polit. and Social Sci., Am. Acad. Mgmt., Assn. Psychiat. Treatment Offenders, VFW, Garden City Park Hist. Soc. (pres. 1960-63), Delta Mu Delta, Delta Sigma Pi, Zeta Sigma Pi, Alpha Kappa Delta. Democrat. Author: Sociology, 1971. Home: 96 5th St Garden City Park NY 11040

REDDELL, WILLIAM JENNINGS, newspaper editor; b. Rule, Tex., Oct. 24, 1915; s. William C. and Bess (Roberts) R.; student Kan. City Art Inst., 1935, Baylor U., 1936-40; m. Martha Peay, Dec. 25, 1940 (dec. Aug. 1947); children—Jean, Judy; m. 2d, Cynthia Wiggins, Aug. 20, 1950; 1 dau., Molly. Reporter San Antonio (Tex.) Express, 1941-43, asst. city editor, 1943-47, Rio Grande Valley news bur. chief, 1947-51, city editor, 1951-52, columnist, 1952-55, asso. editor, 1955-56, editor editorial page, 1956—. Trustee Baylor U., 1954-64, Baptist Meml. Hosp. System, San Antonio, 1973—. Mem. Sigma Delta Chi. Home: 134 Knibbe Rd San Antonio TX 78209 Office: Ave E and 3d St San Antonio TX 78209

REDDEN, JACK ALLISON, educator; b. Rossville, Ill., Sept. 24, 1926; s. Guy C. and Edith Cornelia (Allison) R.; A.B., Dartmouth, 1948; M.S., Harvard, 1950, Ph.D., 1955; m. Harriet S. Hartmann, Oct. 6, 1951; children—Rebecca, Alison, Jill. With U.S. Geol. Survey, Custer, S.D., 1948-54, Denver, 1954-58; asso. prof. geology Va. Poly. Inst., 1958-64; dir. sci. and engring., asso. dean, prof. geology Wright State U., 1964-69; dir. Engring. and Mining Expt. Sta., prof. geology S.D. Sch. Mines and Tech., Rapid City, 1969—, acting grad. dean and dir. research, 1976—. S.D. Gov.'s rep. Nat. Govt. Council Scis. and Tech., 1971—. Served with USMCR, 1944-46. Fellow Geol. Soc. Am., Mineral. Soc. Am.; mem. Phi Beta Kappa. Editor: Mineral Indsl. Jour., Va. Poly. Inst., 1961-64. Home: 1214 West Blvd Rapid City SD 57701 Office: S D Sch Mines and Tech Rapid City SD 57701

REDDEN, JAMES ANTHONY, state ofcl.; b. Springfield, Mass., Mar. 13, 1929; s. James A. and Alma (Cheek) R.; student Boston U., 1951; LL.B., Boston Coll., 1954; m. Joan Ida Johnson, July 13, 1950; children—James A., William F. Admitted to Oreg. bar, 1955, since practiced in Medford; mem. firm Collins, Redden, Ferris & Velure, 1957-73; dist. judge pro-tem, 1958; treas. State of Oreg., 1973-77, atty. gen., 1977—. Chmn. Oreg. Pub. Employee Relations Bd.; mem. Oreg. Automobile Ins. Adv. Com. Mem. Oreg. Ho. of Reps., 1963-69, minority leader, 1967-69. Served with AUS, 1946-48. Mem. Am., Mass. bar assns., Oreg. State Bar, Oreg. Assn. Def. Counsel. Democrat. K.C. Home: 546 Welcome Way S Salem OR 97302 Office: 100 State Office Bldg Salem OR 97310

REDDEN, KENNETH ROBERT, lawyer, author, educator; b. N.Y.C., July 15, 1917; s. Vincent and Anna (Pulanska) R.; LL.B., U. Va., 1940; m. Hebe Mary Ruggieri, Sept. 11, 1943; children—Louis Rowen, Bianca Maria, George Jonas, Francesca Blakely. Admitted to N.Y. bar, 1941; asso. firm Burlingame, Norse & Pettit, N.Y.C., 1940-42; law clk. U.S. Circuit Judge, 1942-44; prof. law U. Va., 1944—, lectr. legal medicine U. Va. Med. Sch., Med. Coll. of Va., 1944-58; summer faculty George Washington U., Ind. U.; mem. U.S.-Internat. Coop. Adminstrn., Team, Turkey, 1955-57; prof. law Haile Selassie U., Addis Ababa, Ethiopia, 1964-66, U. Saigon (Vietnam), 1969-71; regional legal adviser, Indochina, 1969-71. Mem. U.S. Nat. Def. Exec. Res., 1959—; mem. Fed. Mediation and Conciliation Service. Author: Law in Our Civilization, 1946; Cases on Equity, 1946; Virginia and West Virginia Jurisprudence, 1948; So You Want to be a Lawyer, 1950; Career Planning in the Law, 1950; Law Student's Form Book, 1950; Lawyer's Investment Manual, 1952; The Mining Law of Turkey, 1955; The Petroleum Law of Turkey, 1956; Legal Education in Turkey, 1957; Bar Association Activities in Turkey and the U.S., 1958. Editor: Lawyer's Medical Cyclopedia (6 vols.), 1959. Editor of Virginia Law Review, 1942-45, Va. Bar News, 1954-55; coordinating editor An Introduction to The Uniform Commercial Code, 1964; Journal of Ethiopian Law, 1965; Ethiopian Legal Formbook, 1966; The Law Making Process in Ethiopia, 1966; The Legal System of Ethiopia, 1968; Judicial Administration of Criminal Justice in Virginia, 1974; Federal Rules of Evidence Manual, 1975, 2d edit., 1977; Federal Judicial Center Handbook, 1975; Legal Malpractice Reporter, 1976; Federal Trial Judges Seminars, 1976; Model Jury Instructions in Virginia, 1977; Model Legal Glossary, 1978; Punitive Damages, 1979; contbr. articles to legal and med. publs., Ency. Brit. Home: West Lawn U Va Charlottesville VA 22904 Office: U Va Law Sch Charlottesville VA 22204

REDDEN, LAWRENCE DREW, lawyer; b. Tallassee, Ala., Dec. 16, 1922; s. A. Drew and Berta (Baker) R.; A.B., U. Ala., 1943, LL.B., 1949; m. Christine U. Cunningham, Dec. 20, 1943. Admitted to Ala. bar, 1949, since practiced in Birmingham; asst. U.S. atty. No. Dist. Ala., 1949-52; partner firm Rogers, Howard, Redden & Mills, 1952-79, Redden, Mills & Clark, 1979—. Civilian aide for Ala. to sec. army, 1965-69. Mem. Ala. Democratic Exec. Com., 1966-74. Trustee Ala. Law Sch. Found.; adv. council Cumberland Law Sch. Served with AUS, 1943-46; maj. gen. Res. Decorated D.S.M.; recipient Outstanding Civilian Service medal Dept. Army, 1970. Fellow Am. Coll. Trial Lawyers; mem. Internat. Soc. Barristers, Am. Judicature Soc., Am., Ala. (pres. 1972-73), Birmingham (past pres.) bar assns., Ala. Law Inst. (mem. council), U. Ala. Law Sch. Alumni Assn. (past pres.), Phi Beta Kappa, Alpha Tau Omega, Omicron Delta Kappa. Baptist. Editor-in-chief Ala. Law Rev., 1948. Home: 2513 Beaumont Circle Birmingham AL 35216 Office: 940 1st Ala Bank Bldg Birmingham AL 35203

REDDICK, DEWITT CARTER, educator; b. Savannah, Ga., July 30, 1904; s. Walter Newton and Frances (Westerman) R.; student Tex. A. and M. Coll., 1921-22; B. Journalism, Tex., 1925, A.M., 1928; Ph.D., U. Mo., 1939; m. Marjorie Bryan, June 20, 1934; children—Bryan DeWitt, Frances Alicia. Reporter, Ft. Worth Star-Telegram, Austin American, 1924-26; part-time corr. Christian Sci. Monitor, 1927-31; instr. journalism U. Tex., 1927—, acting dir. Sch. Journalism, 1955-56, asso. dean Coll. Arts and Scis., 1956-59, dir. Sch. Journalism, 1959-64, dir. Sch. Communication, 1965-67, dean Sch. Communication, 1967-69, prof. journalism, 1970-75, emeritus, 1975—; asso. prof. Columbia Grad. Sch., 1941; dean Coll. Communications, U. Tenn., 1969-70. Dir. Interscholastic League Press Conf., 1927-50; adv. edn. council Nat. Bus. Publs., 1956—; chmn. accrediting com. Am. Council on Edn. for Journalism, 1962-64. Recipient Scarbrough award, 1955; award of honor U. Mo., 1964; award So. Ill. U., 1967; Distinguished Alumnus award U. Tex., 1972; Golden Crown award Columbia Scholastic Press Assn., 1975. Mem. AAUP, Assn. Edn. Journalism (v.p. 1954, 60-61, chmn. mag. journalism com. 1955-57, pres.-elect 1964-65, pres. 1965-66), Internat. Council Indsl. Editors (chmn. bibliog. com. 1958-63), Am. Assn. Schs. and Depts. Journalism (pres. 1961-62), Soc. Asso. Indsl. Editors, Am. Assn. Tchrs. Journalism, Sigma Delta Chi. Author: High School Newspaper Handbook, 1933; Journalism and the School Paper, rev. edit., 1964; Modern Feature Writing, 1949; (with Alfred A. Crowell) Industrial Editing, 1962; High School Journalism Work Book, 1964; Mass Media and the School Newspaper, 1975. Editor: Campus and Church, 1955. Adv. editor Tex. Presbyn.; chmn. editorial bd. Presbyn Survey, 1965-69. Contbr. articles numerous mags. Home: 1511 Preston Ave Austin TX 78703

REDDIG, EDWARD STERLING, mfg. exec.; b. Centerville, Iowa, Aug. 29, 1904; s. Harry F. and Jessie (Shurr) R.; student Northwestern, 1926-30; C.P.A., Ohio U., 1943; m. Elizabeth Irene Gay, July 4, 1932 (dec.); children—Gay, Sally; m. 2d, Virginia Clark Ellingen, Jan. 17, 1973; children—Steven, Lisa, Gina, Mary, Edward. Certified pub. accountant Arthur Anderson & Co., Chgo., 1931-35; spl. auditor Pub. Service Co. No. Ill., 1935-36; asst. auditor Chgo. Surface Lines, 1936-37; asst. to v.p. and controller The White Motor Co., Cleve., 1937-44, controller, 1944-47, v.p., controller, 1947-50, v.p. finance, 1950-56; chmn. bd. Mpls.-Moline Co., 1955-58; pres. White Sewing Machine Co. (name changed to White Consol. Industries, Inc 1964), Cleve., 1956-69, chmn. bd., 1969—, also chief exec. officer; chmn. bd. White Engines Inc., R.L. Consol. Inc., Canton, Ohio, 1976—; dir. Torcon Corp., Ashtabula, Ohio. Trustee Massanutten Mill. Acad., Woodstock, Va., Gilmore Acad., Gates Mills, Ohio. Mem. Am. Inst. C.P.A.'s, Ohio Soc. C.P.A.'s C. of C. Clubs: Mid-Day, Union, Mayfield Country, Cleve. Skating, Cleve. Athletic. Home: Fox Run Gates Mills OH 44040 Office: 101 11th St SE Canton OH 44707

REDDING, JAY SAUNDERS, educator, author; b. Wilmington, Del.; s. Lewis Alfred and Mary Ann (Holmes) R.; student Howard Sch., Wilmington, 1912-23, Lincoln U., Pa., 1923-24; Ph.B., Brown U., 1928, A.M., 1932, U. Scholar, 1932-33, D.Litt., 1963; student Columbia, 1933-34; hon. degrees Va. State Coll., 1963, Hobart Coll., 1964, Dickinson Coll., U. Del., U. Portland, 1970, Wittinberg U., 1977; m. Esther Elizabeth James, Aug. 19, 1929; children—Conway Holmes, Lewis Alfred. Tchr. Morehouse Coll., Atlanta, 1928-31, Louisville Municipal Coll., 1934-36, So. U., 1936-38; Rockefeller Found. fellow, 1940-41; prof. English, Hampton Inst., 1943-66, Johnson prof. creative lit. until 1966; dir. div. research and publ. Nat. Endowment for Humanities, Washington, 1966-70, cons., 1970—; Ernest I. White prof. Am. studies and humane letters Cornell U., 1970-75, emeritus, 1975—; Guggenheim fellow, 1944-45, 59-60; vis. prof. English, Brown U., 1949-50; fellow in humanities Duke U., 1964-65. Bd. fellows Brown U., 1969—; hon. cons. in Am. culture Library of Congress, 1973-76. Exchange lectr. (Dept. of State) to India, 1952; Am. Soc. African Culture exchange lectr. to Africa, 1962. Bd. dirs. Am. Council Learned Socs., 1975—, Center for Advanced Studies, 1976—. Recipient Mayflower award N.C. Hist. Soc., 1944; cited by N.Y. Amsterdam News for distinction 1944, by N.Y. Pub. Library for outstanding contbn. to interracial understanding, 1945, 46, by Nat. Urban League for outstanding achievement, 1949. Mem. fiction award com. Nat. Book Award, 1955, life mem. Nat. Book Com. Mem. Assn. for Study of Negro Life and History, Am. Folklore Soc., Modern Lang. Assn., Phi Beta Kappa. Club: Cosmos (Washington). Author: To Make A Poet Black, 1939; No Day of Triumph (winner of Mayflower award), 1942; Stranger and Alone, 1950; They Came in Chains, 1950; On Being Negro in America, 1951; Reading for Writing (coll. textbook, with Ivan E. Taylor), 1951; An Am. in India, 1954; The Lonesome Road, 1958; The Negro, 1967. Editor (with A.P. Davis) Cavalcade, 1971. Contbr. articles, essays and reviews in nat. mags. Researcher on Am. Negro life from 1950; early Am. Negro writers; collector So. folk material. Editorial bd. American Scholar, 1954-62, 70—. Home: 310 Winthrop Dr Ithaca NY 14850. *From my parents, most of my teachers in high school and college, I think I absorbed a system of values that can only be defined as humane: respect for humankind; respect for learning, respect for one's self, and personal integrity. I have tried to make this system of values operative in my life and work.*

REDDOCH, JAMES WILSON, univ. adminstr.; b. Ellisville, Miss., Oct. 15, 1924; s. Longino and Mary (Wilson) R.; B.S., Miss. State U., 1949, M.S., 1950; Ph.D., La State U., 1955; postgrad. Harvard Bus. Sch., 1957; m. Maxine Huff, Dec. 22, 1946; 1 dau., Mary Stephanie. Asst. prof. bus. adminstrn. La. State U., 1955-57, asst. to dean, 1953-57, asst. to pres., asso. prof., 1957-62, dean student affairs, prof. marketing and mgmt., 1962-70, vice-chancellor student affairs, prof., 1970—; cons. in field. Bd. dirs. A.R.C., Baton Rouge, chmn. personnel policies com., 1960-71, chmn. disaster com., 1964-66. Served with USAAF, 1944-46. Mem. Am. Marketing Assn., Nat. Assn. Student Personnel Adminstrn., Am. Personnel and Guidance Assn., Am. Legion, Delta Tau Delta, Delta Sigma Pi, Phi Kappa Phi, Beta Gamma Sigma, Omicron Delta Kappa. Pi Gamma Mu. Baptist (deacon, chmn. 1973). Lion (pres. 1961). Club: Intercivic (pres. 1959) (Baton Rouge). Contbr. articles profl. jours. Home: 856 Magnolia Wood Dr Baton Rouge LA 70808

REDDY, HELEN, vocalist; b. Melbourne, Australia, Oct. 25, 1941; d. Max and Stella (Lamond) R.; ed. pub. schs.; m. Jeff Wald, Nov. 1, 1966; children—Traci, Jordan. Vocal recs. include Crazy Love, I Don't Know How to Love Him, Peaceful, I Am Woman, Delta Dawn, 1978, Keep on Singing, You and Me Against the World, Angie Baby, 1978, Leave Me Alone, 1978; star NBC Summer Show, 1973; permanent host Midnight Special; starring role Pete's Dragon, Walt Disney Prodns.; made motion picture debut in Airport, 1975. Active Nat. Women's Polit. Caucus, NOW, Women's Center, Alliance for Women in Prison; commr. Calif. Dept. Parks and Recreation. Recipient Grammy award for writing and rec. I Am Woman, 1973; Image award NAACP, 1974; Humanitarian award B'nai B'rith, N.Y., 1975; Maggie award People Helping People, Los Angeles, 1976; named Woman of Year, Los Angeles Times, 1975; 9 gold albums, 3 platinum albums, 4 gold singles. Address: care William Morris Agency Inc 151 El Camino Dr Beverly Hills CA 90212*

REDDY, WILLIAM JOHN, educator; b. Boston, Aug. 10, 1926; s. Neil and Margaret (Doherty) R.; A.B., Harvard, 1949, M.S., 1957, Sc.D., 1960; m. Elizabeth A. Enaire, Jan. 1, 1955; children—Margaret, Elizabeth, Ann, W. John. Chemist Peter Bent Brigham Hosp., Boston, 1949-60, asso. staff, 1960-64, asso., 1964-68; dir. chemistry dept. St. Vincent Hosp., Worcester, Mass., 1968-70; prof. U. Ala. Sch. Medicine 1970—; cons. in field. Pres. Boston chpt. Muscular Dystrophy Assn., 1965, 68; mem. exec. com. Ala. Diabetes Assn., 1971. Bd. dirs. St. Vincent Research Found., Worcester, 1967-73. Boston Med. Soc. grantee, 1966-67, Am. Heart Assn., 1967-71, NIH, 1961-73. Fellow Am. Inst. Chemistry; mem. Am. Soc. Biol. Chemistry, Am. Physiol. Soc., Am. Chem. Soc., Endocrine Soc., A.A.A.S., N.Y. Acad. Sci., Am. Assn. Clin. Chemistry, Am. Assn. U. Profs. Contrb. articles profl. jours. Home: 4147 Stone River Rd Mountain Brook AL 35213 Office: Box 75 Dental Bldg U Ala Birmingham AL 35294

REDER, MELVIN W., economist; b. San Francisco, May 25, 1919; s. Frank and Ann (Liphsitz) R.; A.B., U. Calif., Berkeley, 1939; postgrad. U. Chgo., 1939-41; Ph.D., Columbia U., 1946; m. Edna B. Oliker, Dec. 20, 1942; children—Stephen, Lynne. Instr., Bryn Mawr Coll., 1942-43, Bklyn. Coll., 1943-45; asst. prof. econs. Carnegie Inst. Tech., 1946-48, U. Pa., 1948-49; asso. prof. Stanford U., 1949-53, prof., 1953-71; research asso. Nat. Bur. Econ. Research, 1971; Disting. prof. econs. U. City N.Y. Grad. Center, 1971-74; Isadore Brown and Gladys J. Brown prof. urban and labor econs. U. Chgo. Grad. Sch. Bus., 1975—; vis. prof. London Sch. Econs., 1967; fellow Center Advanced Study in Behavioral Scis., 1957. Guggenheim fellow, 1955-56; Ford faculty fellow, 1961-62. Author: Studies in the Theory of Welfare Economics, 1947; Labor in a Growing Economy, 1957. Home: 4800 S Lake Shore Dr Chicago IL 60615 Office: 1101 E 58th St Chicago IL 60637

REDER, ROBERT PAUL, shoe co. exec.; b. Cin., Sept. 26, 1927; s. Joseph Bernard and Emma (Tellmann) R.; B.S. cum laude, Xavier U., 1948; m. Patricia Ann Christian, Nov. 27, 1948; children—Thomas J., Karen Ann, Mary Sharen, Robert Paul. Plant controller Electric Auto-Life Co., Cin., 1949-58; controller, asst. gen. mgr. OKT Inc., Cin., 1958-63; controller Trailmobile div. Pullman, Inc., Cin., 1963-65; v.p., group controller U.S. Shoe Corp., Cin., 1965—; dir. Western Star Loan & Bldg. Assn., Cin. Served to lt. AUS, 1948-49. Mem. Financial Execs. Inst., Nat. Assn. Accountants, Pi Alpha Phi. Roman Catholic (lay deacon 1970—). Home: 7236 Green Farms Dr Cincinnati OH 45224 Office: 1658 Herald Ave Cincinnati OH 45212

REDETZKI, HELMUT MAX, physician, educator; b. Memel, Lithuania, Sept. 23, 1921; s. Emil and Hedwig (Preising) R.; student U. Freiburg (Germany) Med. Sch., 1941-43, U. Koenigsberg (Germany) Med. Sch., 1943-44, U. Graz (Austria) Med. Sch., 1944; M.D., U. Hamburg (Germany), 1948; m. Joyce Ehman, Mar. 15, 1957. Came to U.S., 1956, naturalized, 1961. Intern. U. Hamburg, 1947-48, research asso. in biochemistry, 1948-52; resident St. Georg

Hosp., Hamburg, 1952-56; McLaughlin Found. postdoctoral research fellow U. Tex., Galveston, 1956-59, instr. dept. pharmacology, 1959-60, asst. prof., 1960-61; asso. prof. La. State U. Med. Sch., New Orleans 1961-66, prof., 1966-68, prof., head dept. pharmacology and therapeutics, Shreveport, 1968—, dir. La. State U. Poison Control Center, 1977—; cons. clin. pharmacology VA Hosp., Shreveport, 1969—, acting asso. chief staff for research and edn., 1970-72; vis. physician Confederate Meml. Hosp., Shreveport, 1968—; cons. FDA, 1979—. Recipient Deneke medal City of Hamburg, 1955, H.M. Hub Cotton Faculty Excellence award La. State U. Found., 1975; NIH grantee in cancer research and alcoholism, 1960-69; diplomate Am. Bd. Med. Toxicology (chmn. 1975-78, mem. exam. bd. 1978—). Fellow A.C.P., Am. Acad. Clin. Toxicology (chmn. alcohol studies com. 1971, trustee 1975—, chmn. fellowship com. 1978—); mem. Am. Soc. Pharmacology and Exptl. Therapeutics, Soc. Exptl. Biology and Medicine, Am. Heart Assn., La. Med. Soc., Am. Soc. Clin. Pharmacology and Therapeutics, Sigma Xi. Contbr. chpts. to books, articles to profl. jours. Home: 643 Monrovia St Shreveport LA 71106 Office: Dept Pharmacology and Therapeutics PO Box 3932 Shreveport LA 71130

REDFERN, FRANK JAMES, banker, hosp. adminstr.; b. Jersey City, July 1, 1910; s. John Joseph and Margaret Agatha (Barry) R.; grad. St. Peter's Prep. Sch., 1932; m. Gene Marie Crosby, Nov. 16, 1935; children—Peter J., James F. With Peter F. Redfern & Sons Co., constrn., Jersey City, 1932-65, pres., 1941-65; v.p., dir. Fifth Ward Savs. Bank Jersey City, 1948-66; chmn. bd., pres. Peoples Nat. Bank Sussex County (N.J.), 1964-70; sr. v.p. N.J. Bank, 1970—; pres. Barn Hill Convalescent Center, Newton, N.J., 1972—. Mem. Sparta (N.J.) Indsl. Commn., 1965—. Clubs: Lake Mohawk Country (pres. 1971-72), Lake Mohawk Golf (Sparta); Carteret (Jersey City); PGA Golf (Palm Beach, Fla.). Home: 514 W Shore Trail Sparta NJ 07871 Office: 48 Sparta Ave Sparta NJ 07871

REDFERN, JOHN DOUGLAS, cement co. exec.; b. Ottawa, Ont., Can., May 9, 1935; s. Harry Clare and Mary Margaret (Evelyn) R.; B.S. in Civil Engring., Queen's U., 1958; m. Mary Ann Findlay Watson, June 29, 1957; children—John Stephen, Bruce Douglas, David Scott, Christine Evelyn. With Ont. Dept. Hwys., 1958; engr. Can. Cement Co., Ottawa, Ont., 1958-62, sales mgr., Moncton, Ottawa and Toronto, Ont., Can., 1962-69, v.p., Halifax, N.S., 1969-70; v.p. mktg. Can. Cement Lafarge Ltd., Halifax, 1970-71, v.p., gen. mgr. Western region, Calgary, Alta., 1971-74, v.p. ops., Montreal, Que., 1974-76, exec. v.p., gen. mgr., 1976-77, pres., chief exec. officer, 1977—, also dir.; chmn. bd., chief exec. officer, dir. Canfarge Ltd.; dir. Standard Industries Ltd., Citadel Cement Corp., Atlanta, Lafarge Conseils et Etudes (Paris). Bd. govs. Conseildu Patronat du Que. Served with Royal Canadian Navy. Mem. Portland Cement Assn., Assn. Profl. Engrs. Ont., Canadian Mfrs. Assn., Canadian C. of C., Canadian Constrn. Assn., Conf. Bd. Can. (Can. Council). Mem. United Ch. of Canada. Clubs: Mt. Royal, Royal Montreal Golf, St. James, MAAA (Montreal); Glencoe (Calgary). Office: 606 Cathcart St Montreal PQ H3B 1L7 Canada

REDFERN, JOHN JOSEPH, JR., oil and gas producer; b. Jersey City, Oct. 4, 1912; s. John Joseph and Margaret A. (Barry) R.; C.E., Rensselaer Poly. Inst., 1934; postgrad. U. Okla., 1938-39; m. Rosalind Kapps, June 26, 1936; children—John Joseph III, Rosalind, Roberta. Engr., Hoy & Co., Inc., Albany, N.Y., 1934-36; independent oil operator, Oklahoma City, 1937-39, Midland, Tex., 1939—; pres. Flag-Redfern Oil Co., 1960—, Pennant Oils Ltd., Calgary, Can., 1966-73; chmn. bd. Pennant-Puma Oils Ltd., 1973-76; chmn. Midland Map Co., 1950—. Trustee Rensselaer Poly. Inst., 1958—, sec. bd., 1965-70, vice chmn., 1970—; chmn. Midland Meml. Found., 1977—. Mem. Ind. Petroleum Assn. Am. (dir.), Tex. Ind. Petroleum and Royalty Owners (dir.), Ind. Petroleum Assn. N.Mex. (dir.). Clubs: Houston; Midland Country, Midland Petroleum. Home: 1214 Country Club Dr Midland TX 79701 Office: PO Box 2280 Wall Towers W Midland TX 79701

REDFERN, LEO F., coll. pres.; b. Berlin, N.H., June 3, 1923; s. Frank C. and Julia M. (McHale) R.; B.A., U. N.H., 1950, M.A., 1951; M.P.A., Harvard, 1952, Ph.D., 1958; m. Edmonde Olive St. Laurent, Sept. 9, 1950; children—Laurie Ellen, Charles Henry. Teaching fellow, tutor in govt. Harvard, 1954-56, Sheldon traveling fellow, 1956-57; dir. pub. adminstrn. service U. N.H., 1957-59; staff com. on govt. and higher edn. Ford Found., 1958-59; asso. prof. polit. sci., asst. dir. Bur. Govt., U. Wis., 1959-61; dir. instl. research U. Mass., 1961-64, dean adminstrn., 1964-69, acting dir. Labor Relations and Research Center, 1963-65, acting univ. sec., 1963-64; pres. Keene (N.H.) State Coll., 1969—. Bd. incorporators Keene Savs. Bank. Trustee Cheshire Hosp. Served with USAAF, 1943-46. Mem. AAUP, Assn. for Instl. Research, Am. Polit. Sci. Assn., Am. Pub. Adminstrn. Soc. Author: The Calculating Administrators: Computers, 1963; contbg. author: The Campus and the State, 1958. Home: 251 Main St Keene NH 03431 Office: 229 Main St Keene NH 03431*

REDFIELD, ALFRED CLARENCE, oceanographer; b. Phila., Nov. 15, 1890; s. Robert Stuart and Mary Thibault (Guillou) R.; student Haverford (Pa.) Sch., 1906-09, Haverford Coll., 1909-10; B.S., Harvard U., 1913, Ph.D., 1917; postgrad. Cambridge U. (Eng.), 1920, U. Munich (Germany), 1931; Ph.D. (hon.), U. Oslo, 1956; D.Sc. (hon.), Lehigh U., 1965, Meml. U. Nfld., 1967, U. Alaska, 1971; Martha Putnam, June 7, 1921; children—Elizabeth (Mrs. Charles R. Marsh), Martha Washburn Koch, Alfred Guillou. Instr. physiology Harvard, 1918-19; asst. prof. physiology, 1921-30, asso. prof., 1930-31, prof., 1931-56, prof. emeritus, 1956—; mng. editor Biol. Bull., 1930-41; asso. dir. Woods Hole Oceanographic Instn., 1942-56, sr. oceanographer, emeritus, 1956; asst. prof. physiology U. Toronto, 1919-20. Mem. Nat. Acad. Scis., Marine Biol. Assn. U.K., Am. Acad. Arts and Sci., Am. Physiol. Soc., Am. Soc. Zoölogists, Ecol. Soc. Am., Am. Soc. Limnology and Oceanography, Phi Beta Kappa. Home: 14 Maury Ln Woods Hole MA 02543

REDFIELD, ALFRED GUILLOU, phys. biochemist, educator; b. Boston, Mar. 11, 1929; s. Alfred Clarence and Martha (Putnam) R.; B.A., Harvard, 1950; Ph.D., U. Ill., 1953; m. Sarah Cossum, July 15, 1970; children—Rebecca, Samuel Duthie, Wendy. Fellow Harvard, 1953-55; prof. physics IBM Watson Lab. Columbia, 1955-70; research asso. biochemistry U. Calif. at Berkeley, 1970-72; prof. physics and biochemistry Rosenstiel Center, Brandeis U., 1972—. Mem. Nat. Acad. Scis. Office: Brandeis U Waltham MA 02154

REDFIELD, EMANUEL, lawyer; b. N.Y.C., Feb. 28, 1904; s. Morris and Rose (Berkowitz) R.; A.B., N.Y. U., 1932; LL.B., Fordham U., 1926; postgrad. in polit. sci., Columbia U., 1932-36; m. Mildred Russell, Feb. 7, 1935; children—Richard, William. Admitted to N.Y. bar, 1927, U.S. Supreme Ct. bar, 1934; individual practice law, N.Y.C., 1927-31, 38—; partner firm Dwyer & Redfield, 1931-38; co-founder, gen. counsel N.Y. Civil Liberties Union, 1955-1967; counsel Artists Equity Assn. N.Y., 1950-1974, Internat. Assn. Arts, 1955-1965, Percy Grainger Library Soc. 1977—. Past member adv. com. Bd. Edn., City of N.Y.; co-founder, Riverdale Soc. Ethical Culture, 1950; active Boy Scouts Am., Riverdale Art Com. Recipient citation Artists Equity Assn. N.Y., 1974. Mem. N.Y. County Lawyers Assn., Am. Arbitration Assn. Clubs: Riverdale Camera, N.Y.-N.J. Trail Conf. (legal com.), Appalachian Mountain, Woodland Trail Walkers, Westchester Trails Assn.; Campo Beach Assn. (dir.) (Westport, Conn.). Democrat. Author: Artists Estates and Taxes. Contbr. articles and book revs. to law and other jours. Home: 3900 Greystone Ave Riverdale NY 10463 Office: 111 Broadway New York NY 10006

REDFIELD, PETER SCRANTON, financial services co. exec.; b. Cambridge, Mass., Apr. 21, 1931; s. Scranton H. and Marie (Dibell) R.; B.A., Colgate U., 1953; m. Alice Daukas, June 15, 1957; children—Charles Scranton, Ann Marie, Sara Chadwick. Asso. McKinsey & Co., San Francisco, 1962-66; dir. adminstrv. services Transamerica Corp., San Francisco, 1966-67; co-founder, dir., pres., chief exec. officer ITEL Corp., San Francisco, 1967-79; dir. Alexander & Baldwin Inc., Honolulu, Fred S. James & Co. Inc., Chgo., ITEL Corp., Pacific Resources, Honolulu, Riegel Textile Corp., Greenville, S.C. Trustee Colgate U., 1974—. Served as lt. (j.g.) USNR, 1953-56. Clubs: Villa Taverna, Pacific Union, (San Francisco); Menlo Circus (Atherton); Burlingame Country (Hillsborough, Calif.); Links (N.Y.C.). Office: 1 Embarcadero Center San Francisco CA 94111

REDFORD, DONALD BRUCE, historian, archaeologist; b. Toronto, Ont., Can., Sept. 2, 1934; s. Cyril Fitzjames and Kathleen Beryl (Coe) R.; B.A., U. Toronto, 1957, M.A., 1958; Ph.D., Brown U., 1965; m. Margaret Gillings, Sept. 6, 1958; children—Christopher, Philip. Lectr., Brown U., 1960-61; lectr. U. Toronto, 1961-64, asst. prof. history and archaeology, 1965-67, asso. prof., 1967-69, prof., 1969—; site supr. Brit. Sch. Archaeol. Excavations, Jerusalem, 1964-67; dir. Soc. Study Egyptian Antiquities Expdn. to Karnak, Egypt, 1970-72; dir. Akhenaten Temple Project, Luxor, Egypt, 1972—; research asso. Univ. Museum, U. Pa., Royal Ont. Mus. Killam grantee, 1975-79; Smithsonian Fgn. Currency grantee, 1973-76, 1979. Fellow Royal Soc. Can. Author: History and Chronology of the Egyptian 18th Dynasty, 1967; A Study of the Biblical Joseph Story, 1970; Papyrus and Tablet, 1973; The Akhenaten Temple Project, I, 1977; discovered Temple of Akhenaten at Luxor, 1976. Office: U Toronto 280 Huron St Toronto ON M5S 1A1 Canada*

REDFORD, EMMETTE SHELBURN, educator; b. San Antonio, Sept. 23, 1904; s. Samuel Shelburn and Clara Cordelia (Dollahite) R.; student S.W. Tex. State Coll., 1922; B.A., U. Tex., 1927, M.A., 1928; Ph.D., Harvard, 1933; LL.D., Austin Coll., 1966, Tex. Christian U., 1970; m. Claire Bowers, Jan. 2, 1933; children—Emmette Samuel (dec.), Claire (Mrs. Dean Aring). Pub. sch. tchr., 1923-25; tutor, then instr. U. Tex., 1927-29; asst. prof. govt. Tex. Christian U., 1930-31; tutor, then instr. govt. Harvard, 1931-33; faculty U. Tex., 1933—, prof. govt., 1939-63, Ashbel Smith prof. govt., 1963-70, Ashbel Smith prof. govt. and pub. affairs, 1970—; vis. prof. Duke, 1954-55, Columbia, summer 1957, Syracuse U., summers 1965, 67. Research specialist Nat. Resources Com., 1936; asst. regional price exec., asst. dep. adminstr. for rationing OPA, 1942-45; cons. Office Temporary Controls, 1947, Nat. Security Resources Bd., 1950, Econ. Stblzn. Agy., 1951, joint econ. com. U.S. Senate, 1959, Pres. Adv. Com. Govt. Orgn. and Bur. Budget, 1960, U.S. Dept. Agr., 1966, 67, Nat. Adv. Commn. Selective Service, 1966; mem., chmn. com. on personnel Adminstrv. Conf. U.S., 1961-62, mem. 1968-70; mem. Nat. Council on Humanities, 1966-70; mem. recombinant adv. com. NIH, 1976—. Pres. U. Coop. Soc., Austin, 1947-71, U. Toggery, Austin, 1958-66. Recipient Sr. Research award Social Sci. Research Council, 1958-59. Mem. Am. (pres. 1960-61), Southwestern (pres. 1966-67), So. polit. sci. assns., Southwestern Social Sci. Assn., Am. Soc. Pub. Adminstrn., Am. Acad. Pub. Adminstrn., Phi Beta Kappa, Phi Kappa Phi. Mem. Disciples of Christ Ch. Club: Cosmos (Washington). Author: Field Adminstration of Wartime Rationing, 1947; Adminstration of National Economic Control, 1952; Ideal and Practice in Public Administration, 1958; The General Passenger Fare Investigation, 1960; Congress Passes the Federal Aviation Act, 1961; American Government and the Economy, 1965; The Role of Government in the American Economy, 1966; Democracy in the Adminstrative State, 1969; The Regulatory Process, 1969; co-author Politics and Government in the United States, 1965, rev. edit., 1968. Editor: Public Adminstration and Policy Formation, 1956. Contbr. articles to profl. jours. Home: 3001 Clearview Dr Austin TX 78703

REDFORD, ROBERT, actor; b. Santa Monica, Calif., Aug. 18, 1937; student U. Colo., Pratt Inst. Design, Am. Acad. Dramatic Arts. Theatrical appearance in Tall Story, Sunday in New York, Barefoot in the Park; films include Barefoot in the Park, Butch Cassidy and the Sundance Kid, Big Fauss and Little Halsey, Tell Them Willie Boy Is Here, Downhill Racer, Jeremiah Johnson, The Hot Rock, The Candidate, The Way We Were, The Sting, The Great Gatsby, The Great Waldo Pepper, Three Days of the Condor, All the President's Men, A Bridge Too Far, The Electric Horseman, 1979; owner ski resort Sundance, Provo, Utah. Address: care Pickwick 545 Madison Ave New York NY 10022

REDGRAVE, LYNN, actress; b. London, Eng., Mar. 8, 1943; d. Michael Scudemore and Rachel (Kempson) Redgrave; ed. Queensgate Sch., London, also Central Sch. Speech and Drama, London; m. John Clark, Apr. 2, 1967; children—Benjamin, Kelly. Theatrical appearances include Midsummer Night's Dream, The Tulip Tree, Andorra, Hayfever, Much Ado About Nothing, Mother Courage, Love for Love (all with Nat. Theatre Co. of Gt. Britain, 1963-66), Black Comedy, N.Y.C., 1967, Zoo, Zoo, Widdershins Zoo, Edinburgh Festival, 1969, The Two of Us, London, 1970, Slag, London, 1971, A Better Place, Dublin, 1972, Born Yesterday, Greenwich, 1973; N.Y. appearances include Black Comedy, 1967, My Fat Friend, 1974, Mrs. Warren's Profession, 1975, Knock, Knock, 1976, Hellzapoppin, 1976, California Suite, 1977, St. Joan, 1977; appeared in Twelfth Night, Stratford Conn. Shakespeare Festival, 1978; film appearances include Tom Jones, Girl with the Green Eyes, Georgy Girl, The Deadly Affair, Smashing Time, The Virgin Soldiers, Last of the Mobile Hotshots, Don't Turn the Other Cheek, Every Little Crook and Nanny, Everything You Always Wanted to Know About Sex, The National Health, The Happy Hooker, The Big Bus; TV appearances include Centennial, 1978, The Muppets, Gaugain the Savage, Bliss, Housecalls, 1979; co-host Not for Women Only, nat. TV syndication, 1977—; rec. albums include Make Mine Manhattan, 1978, Cole Porter Revisited, 1979. Recipient N.Y. Film Critics award, Golden Globe award, Oscar nomination for best actress, all for Georgy Girl, 1967; named Runner-Up Actress, All Am. Favorites, Box Office Barometer, 1975; Sarah Siddons award as Chgo.'s best stage actress of 1977, 1978. Address: care Diamond Artists Ltd 9200 Sunset Blvd Suite 909 Los Angeles CA 90069

REDGRAVE, VANESSA, actress; b. London, Jan. 30, 1937; d. Michael and Rachel (Kempson) R.; student Central Sch. Speech and Drama, London, 1955-57; m. Tony Richardson, Apr. 28, 1962 (div.); children—Natasha Jane, Joely Kim. Prin. theatrical roles include: Helena in Midsummer Night's Dream, 1959, Stella in The Tiger and the Horse, 1960, Katerina in The Taming of the Shrew, 1961, Rosaline in As You Like It, 1961, Imogene in Cymbeline, 1962, Nina in The Seagull, 1964, Miss Brodie in The Prime of Miss Jean Brodie, 1966; other plays include: Cato Street, 1971, Threepenny Opera, 1972, Twelfth Night, 1972, Anthony and Cleopatra, 1973, Design for Living, 1973, Macbeth, 1975, Lady from the Sea, 1976; film roles include: Leonie in Morgan-A Suitable Case for Treatment (Best Actress award Cannes Film Festival 1966), 1965, Sheila in Sailor from Gibraltar, 1965, Anne-Marie in La Musica, 1965, Jane in Blow Up, 1967, Guinevere in Camelot, 1967, Isadora in Isadora Duncan (Best Actress award Cannes Film Festival), 1968; other films include: The Charge of The Light Brigade, 1968, The Seagull, 1968, A Quiet Place in the Country, 1968, Daniel Deronda, 1969, Dropout, 1969, The Trojan Women, 1970, The Devils, 1970, The Holiday, 1971, Mary Queen of Scots, 1971, Murder on the Orient Express, 1974, Winter Rates, 1974, 7% solution, 1975, Julia, 1977, Agatha, 1978, Yanks, 1978, Bear Island, 1979; bd. govs. Central Sch. Speech and Drama, 1963—. Decorated comdr. Order Brit. Empire; recipient Drama award Evening Standard, 1961, Best Actress award Variety Club Gt. Brit., 1961, 66, Brit. Guild TV Producers and Dirs., 1966; Golden Globe award, 1978, Acad. award for best supporting actress, 1977. Author: Pussies and Tigers, 1964. Address: 1 Ravenscourt Rd London W6 England*

REDHEAD, PAUL AVELING, physicist; b. Brighton, Eng., May 25, 1924; B.A. with honors in Physics, Cambridge (Eng.) U., 1944, M.A., 1948, Ph.D., 1969; m. Doris Packman, 1948; children—Janet, Patricia. Sci. officer dept. naval ordnance Brit. Admiralty, 1944-45, services electronics research lab., 1945-47; research officer NRC Can., Ottawa, Ont., 1947-69, dir. planning group, 1970-72, dir.-gen. (planning), 1972-73, dir. dev. physics, 1973—, group dir. phys./chem. sci. labs., 1974—. Fellow Royal Soc. Can., IEEE, Am. Phys. Soc.; mem. Am. Vacuum Soc. (past pres., Medard W. Welch award 1975), Chem. Soc., Can. Assn. Physicists. Author: Physical Basis of Ultrahigh Vacuum, 1968; contbr. numerous articles to profl. jours.; patentee in field. Home: 1958 Norway Crescent Ottawa ON K1H 5N7 Canada Office: Nat Research Council Can Ottawa ON K1A OR6 Canada

REDHEFFER, RAYMOND MOOS, mathematician, educator; b. Chgo., Apr. 17, 1921; s. Raymond L. and Elizabeth (Moos) R.; S.B., Mass. Inst. Tech., 1943, S.M., 1946, Ph.D., 1948; m. Heddy Gross Stiefel, Aug. 25, 1951; 1 son, Peter Bernard. Research asso. Radiation Lab., Mass. Inst. Tech., 1942-45, Research Lab. of Electronics, 1946-48; instr. Harvard, Radcliffe, 1948-50; mem. faculty U. Calif. at Los Angeles, 1950—, prof. math., 1960—; guest prof. Tech. U. Berlin, 1962, Inst. for Angewandte Math., Hamburg, 1966, Math. Inst. U. Karlsruhe, 1971-72. Peirce fellow Harvard, 1948-50; sr. postdoctoral fellow NSF, Goettingen, Germany, 1956; Fulbright research scholar Vienna, 1957, Hamburg, 1961-62; U.S. sr. scientist Alexander von Humboldt Found., Karlsruhe, 1976; math. cons. IBM-Eames exhibits, Los Angeles, Seattle, Chgo., 1960-61. Recipient award for distinguished teaching U. Calif. at Los Angeles Alumni Assn., 1969. Mem. Am. Math. Soc., Math. Assn. Am., IEEE (sr. mem.), Deutsche Akademie der Naturforscher (Leopoldina), Mass. Inst. Tech., U. Calif. at Los Angeles (life) alumni assns., Sigma Xi. Author: (with Ivan Sokolnikoff) Mathematics of Physics and Modern Engineering, 1958; (with Charles Eames) Men of Modern Mathematics, 1966; (with Norman Levinson) Complex Variables, 1970. Film author, animator (with Charles Eames) Alpha, Two Laws of Algebra, Exponents, Newton's Method of Fluxions, 1972-74. Contbr. articles to profl. jours. Home: 176 N Kenter Ave Los Angeles CA 90049

REDIG, DALE FRANCIS, dentist, assn. exec.; b. Arcadia, Iowa, Mar. 24, 1929; s. Philip F. and Clara (Bohnenkamp) R.; student U. Iowa, 1949-51, D.D.S., 1955, M.S., 1965; m. Diane Marie Murphy, June 13, 1953; children—Mary Catherine, John Francis, Ann Bennett. Pedodontist, Des Moines, 1955-61; mem. faculty U. Iowa Coll. Dentistry, 1961-69, asso. prof. pedodontics, 1968-69, head dept., 1964-69; Fulbright lectr. U. Baghdad, 1963-64; dean U. Pacific Sch Dentistry, 1969-78; exec. dir. Calif. Dental Assn., 1978—. Mem. dental edn. com. USPHS, 1967-71, dental health research and edn. adv. com., 1972-74; dir. dental div. Des Moines United campaign, 1958; bd. dirs. Des Moines Health Center, 1956-61, pres., 1961; pres. Iowa Soc. Dentistry for Children, 1964-65; bd. dirs. Am. Fund for Dental Health, 1976—, v.p., 1976—. Served with USAAF, 1946-49. Mem. Am. Dental Assn. (ednl. cons. Vietnam 1968, mem. council dental edn. 1974—), Am. Soc. Dentistry Children, Am. Acad. Pedodontics (dir. 1972-75), Am., Internat. colls. dentists. Office: 6151 W Century Blvd Suite 900 Los Angeles CA 90045

REDIKER, ROBERT HARMON, physicist; b. Bklyn., June 7, 1924; s. Moe J. and Estelle (Rosenwasser) R.; S.B., Mass. Inst. Tech., 1947, Ph.D., 1950; m. Jane Susan Friend, June 4, 1950 (div. Aug. 1976); children—Richard J., Donald E. Research asso. physics Mass. Inst. Tech., 1950-51, staff Lincoln Lab., Lexington, Mass., 1951-52, 53-57, asst. group leader semi-conductor physics, 1957-59, group leader applied physics, 1959-66, prof. dept. elec. engring., Cambridge, 1966-76, adj. prof., 1976—, asso. head optics div. Lincoln Lab., 1970-72, head optics div., 1972—; research asso. physics Ind. U., 1952-53. Vice pres. Newton Lower Falls Improvement Assn., 1968-71. Mem. spl. group optical masers Def. Dept., 1966-73, working group D (lasers), 1973-76, working group C (imaging and display), 1979—, adv. group on electron devices, high energy laser rev. group, 1973-75; mem. ad hoc com. on materials and processes for electron devices Nat. Acad. Scis., 1970-72, mem. evaluation panel Nat. Bur. Standards, 1975-78. Served with Signal Corps, AUS, 1943-46. Fellow IEEE (chmn. com. solid state devices 1961-63, sec. treas. group electron devices 1965-66, vice chmn. 1967; awards bd. 1976-79, chmn. Liebmann awards com. 1977-78; David Sarnoff award 1969), Am. Phys. Soc.; mem. Sigma Xi, Alpha Epsilon Pi. Jewish. Author, patentee in field. Home: 24 Whites Ave Watertown MA 02172 Office: Mass Inst Tech Lincoln Lab Lexington MA 02173

REDING, PAUL FRANCIS, clergyman; b. Hamilton, Ont., Can., Feb. 14, 1925; s. Thomas Augustine and Florence (Fleming) R.; grad. St. Augustine's Sem., Toronto, Ont., 1943-50. Ordained priest Roman Catholic Ch.; now bishop, Hamilton. Address: 700 King St W Hamilton ON L8P 1C7 Canada

REDINGER, WALTER FRED, sculptor; b. Ont., Can., Jan. 6, 1940; s. Frederich and Frony (Lang) R.; student Ont. Coll. Art, Toronto, Beal Spl. Art Sch., London; m. Marian Jean Manchester, June 24, 1961; children—Jennifer, Jeffrey. Represented Can. at Venice (Italy) Biennale, 1972; artist in residence U. Western Ont., London, Can. Recipient sculpture prize Montreal Mus.; various awards Can. Council. Mem. Can. Artists Representation, Royal Can. Acad. Address: Route 3 West Lorne ON N0L 2P0 Canada

REDL, FRITZ, psychoanalyst; b. Klaus, Austria, Sept. 9, 1902; s. Gustav and Rosa (Schwarz) R.; Ph.D., U. Vienna, 1925; tng. Wiener Psychoanalyses Inst., 1925-36; D.Sc. Edn. (hon.), Wheelock Coll., 1969; Ph.D. (hon.), U. Tuebingen, West Germany, 1971; m. Helen Burnstein, 1959. Came to U.S., 1936, naturalized, 1943. Tchr. Vienna pub. schs., research asso. Gen. Edn. Bd., Rockefeller Found., Progressive Edn. Assn., N.Y.C., 1936-38; lectr. mental hygiene U. Mich., 1938-41; cons. guidance dept. Cranbrook Sch. for Boys, Bloomfield Hills, Mich., 1938-41; research asso. div. for child devel. and tchr. personnel Am. Edn. Assn., U. Chgo., 1939-40; prof. social work Wayne U., 1941-53; chief Child Research br. NIH, Bethesda, Md., 1953-59; prof. behavioral scis. Wayne State U., 1959-75, Distinguished prof. emeritus; Pinkerton guest prof. Sch. Criminal Justice, N.Y. State U., Albany, 1975-76; adj. prof. edn. Mass. State Coll., North Adams, 1976—; vis. prof. dept. child psychiatry U. Utrecht (Holland), 1971; fellow Center for Advanced Study in

Behavioral Scis., Ford Found., Stanford, Calif., 1960-61; cons. div. for mental hygiene, USPHS, 1946-49. Mem. Am. Psychoanalytical Assn., Am. Orthopsychiat. Assn., Am. Psychol. Assn., Am. Assn. Group Therapy, Am. Assn. Applied Anthropology, AAAS, Nat. Probation Assn., Phi Delta Kappa. Author (with others) publs. relating to field; latest: Mental Hygiene in Teaching (with William Wattenberg), 1951; Children Who Hate (with David Wineman), 1951; Controls From Within (with David Wineman), 1952; When We Deal With Children, 1966. Contbr. chpts. to books. Principal investigator on research project USPHS on the use of group medium for clinical work with disturbed children, 1948-51; lecturing in edn., mental hygiene, group work, group therapy and other subjects throughout U.S., 1936—. Home: 100 Porter St North Adams MA 01247

REDLICH, FREDRICK C., psychiatrist, educator; b. Vienna, Austria, June 2, 1910; s. Ludwig Johann and Emma (Eysner) R.; student U. Vienna, 1928-30; internat. exchange student Wittenberg Coll., Springfield, Ohio, 1930-31; M.D., U. Vienna, 1935; m. Herta Glaz; children—Erik, Peter. Came to U.S., 1938, naturalized, 1943. Intern, Allgemeines Krankenhaus, Vienna, 1935-36; resident Neurologisch-Psychiatrische Universitetsklinik, Vienna, 1936-38; asst. physician Iowa State Hosp., 1938-40; resident neurol. unit Boston City Hosp., 1940-42; asso. psychiatrist New Haven Hosp., 1942-48, psychiatrist-in-chief, 1948-77; teaching fellow neurology Harvard U., 1941-42; instr. psychiatry Yale U., 1942-44, asst. prof., 1944-48, asso. prof., 1948-50, prof. psychiatry, 1950—, chmn. dept. psychiatry, sch. medicine, 1950-77, dean Sch. Medicine, 1967-72, asso. provost med. affairs, 1967-72, dir. Behavioral Scis. Study Center, 1973-77; prof. dept. psychiatry and behavioral scis. Sch. Medicine, U. Calif. at Los Angeles, 1977—; chief of staff Brentwood VA Hosp., Los Angeles, 1977—; dir. Conn. Mental Health Center, 1964-67. Served as capt. U.S. Army, 1944. Mem. Am. Psychiat. Assn., Am. Orthopsychiat. Assn., Am. Psychosomatic Soc., Am. Psychoanalytical Soc. Club: Yale. Author: Psychotherapy with Schizophrenics: The Inside Story; Initial Interview in Psychiatric Practice; (with D. X. Freedman) Social Class and Mental Illness: Theory and Practice of Psychiatry; also numerous articles in med. jours. Home: 1529 Bel Air Rd Los Angeles CA 90024

REDLICH, NORMAN, lawyer, educator; b. N.Y.C., Nov. 12, 1925; s. Milton and Pauline (Durst) R.; A.B., Williams Coll., 1947, LL.D. (hon.), 1976; LL.B., Yale, 1950; LL.M., N.Y. U., 1955; m. Evelyn Jane Grobow, June 3, 1951; children—Margaret Bonny-Claire, Carrie Ann, Edward Grobow. Admitted to N.Y. bar, 1951; practiced in N.Y.C., 1951-59; asso. prof. law N.Y. U., 1960-62, prof. law, 1962-74, asso. dean Sch. Law, 1974-75, dean, 1975—, editor-in-chief Tax Law Rev., 1960-66, mem. adv. com. Inst. Fed. Taxation, 1963-68; exec. asst. corp. counsel N.Y.C., 1966-68, 1st asst. corp. counsel, 1970-72, corp. counsel, 1972-74; asst. counsel Pres. Commn. on Assassination Pres. Kennedy, 1963-64; chmn. com. on admissions and grievances U.S. 2d Circuit Ct. Appeals, 1978—. Chmn. commn. on law and social action Am. Jewish Congress, 1978—; mem. Borough Pres.'s Planning Bd. Number 2, 1959-70; counsel N.Y. Com. to Abolish Capital Punishment, 1958-77. Mem. N.Y.C. Bd. Edn., 1969. Mem. bd. overseers Jewish Theol. Sem., 1973—; trustee Law Center Found. of N.Y. U., 1975—, Freedom House, 1976—, Lawyers Com. for Civil Rights under Law, 1976—, Vt. Law Sch., 1977—. Served with AUS, 1943-45. Decorated Combat Infantryman's Badge. Mem. Assn. Bar City N.Y. (exec. com. 1975—). Author: Professional Responsibility: A Problem Approach, 1976; also articles in field. Home: 29 Washington Sq New York City NY 10011 Office: NY U School of Law Washington Sq New York City NY 10003

REDMAN, JOHN C., economist; b. Nancy, Ky., Jan. 31, 1921; s. John Marshall and Gertie (Whitis) R.; B.S., Berea Coll., 1943; M.S., U. Ky., 1946, Ph.D., 1951; postgrad. U. Chgo., 1956-57; m. Nora Litton, Dec. 5, 1942; 1 dau., Barbara Jean. Tchr. rural public schs., Ky., 1941; prof. agr. Western Ky. U., 1946-47; asso. prof. agrl. econs. Miss. State U., 1947-50; prof. agrl. econs. U. Ky., Lexington, 1950—; vis. prof. Gokhale Inst. Econs. and Politics, Poona, India, 1967; gen. mgr. U. Ky. Credit Union. Served with USMC, 1943-45. Social Sci. Research Council fellow, 1956-57; Fulbright scholar, 1965. Mem. Am. Agrl. Econs. Assn. (sec.-treas. 1970—), Am. Econ. Assn., So. Agrl. Econ. Assn., Credit Union Nat. Assn. (dir.), Ky. Credit Union League (dir.), Phi Kappa Phi, Gamma Sigma Delta. Presbyterian. Author: (with B. Redman) Micro-Economics-Resource Allocation and Price Theory, 1979; contbr. articles to profl. jours. Home: 337 Blueberry Ln Lexington KY 40503 Office: Univ of Ky Lexington KY 40506

REDMAN, WILLIAM CHARLES, energy systems scientist; b. Washington, June 19, 1923; s. Lewis Daniel and Mary Eva (Ridgell) R.; B.S., Georgetown U., 1943; M.S., Yale U., 1947, Ph.D. (F.E. Loomis fellow), 1949; m. Eileen Marie Keenan, June 26, 1948; children—Timothy, Brian, Marilyn. Physicist metall. lab. U. Chgo., 1944-46; physicist naval reactor div. Argonne (Ill.) Nat. Lab., 1949-54, energy systems scientist reactor engring., applied physics and engring. divs. and office of dir., 1955—, now dep. dir. energy conversion programs; lectr. Fournier Inst. Tech., 1952-54, pres., 1954-55; guest scientist U.K. Atomic Energy Authority, Winfrith, 1959-60. Served with U.S. Army, 1944-46. Recipient Ordnance Devel. award USN, 1945. Fellow Am. Nuclear Soc. (dir. 1975-78, exec. com. 1975-77), Am. Phys. Soc. Author: (with other) Techniques in Fast Reactor Critical Experiments, 1970. Cons. editor Reactor Physics Constants, 1963; co-editor Fast Critical Experiments and their Analysis. 1966; contbr. numerous articles on basic physics, energy systems to profl. publs.; patentee in field. Home: 608 S Monroe St Hinsdale IL 60521 Office: Bldg 310 9700 S Cass Ave Argonne IL 60439

REDMOND, DOUGLAS ROLLEN, forester; b. Upper Musquodoboit, N.S., Can., Aug. 30, 1918; s. Alfred Jones and Edith Pauline (McIvor) R.; B.Sc., U. N.B., 1949; M.F., Yale, 1950, Ph.D., 1954; m. Hazel Augusta Redmond, July 7, 1943; children—Sharon Redmond Noonan, Roderick Douglas, Peter Herbert, Ian Geoffrey. Provincial forest pathologist, N.S., 1950-51; officer in charge forest pathology research Can. Dept. Agr., Fredericton, N.B., 1951-57; chief forest research div. Can. Forestry Br., Ottawa, 1957-60; dir. forest research Canadian Dept. Forestry, Ottawa, 1960-65; sci. adviser Dept. Forestry and Rural Devel., Ottawa, 1965-69; dir. forestry relations Can. Dept. Environ., Ottawa, 1969-75; dir. Nat. Forestry Insts., 1975-79, sr. adviser Can. Forestry Service, 1979—; hon. lectr. forestry pathology U. N.B., 1951-57. Served with RCAF, 1941-45. Decorated D.F.C. Recipient Edward Bernhard Fernow award Am. Forestry Assn.-Deutscher Forstverein, 1975. Mem. Am. Forestry Assn. (life), Can. Inst. Forestry, Ont., Commonwealth forestry assns., Can. Pulp and Paper Assn., Sigma Xi. Contbr. papers in field. Home: 643 Tillbury Ave Ottawa ON K2A 0Z9 Canada Office: Environment Canada Ottawa ON K1A 0H3 Canada

REDMOND, KENT CLIFFORD, educator; b. N.Y.C., Jan. 6, 1914; s. Harry A. and Matilda M. (Fischer) R.; A.B., U. Calif. at Los Angeles, 1939; Ph.D., U. So. Calif., 1954; m. Doris Margaret Timm, June 15, 1951; children—Shawn Timothy, Eileen Elizabeth. Historian, Holloman Air Devel. Center, 1954-55; asso. command historian Air Research and Devel. Command, 1955-59; asso. prof. history State Coll., Worcester, Mass., 1959-63; prof. history Fairleigh Dickinson U., Florham-Madison (N.J.) Campus, 1963—; cons. MITRE Corp., Bedford, Mass., 1963—. Served with USAAF, 1942-45. Mem. Am. Hist. Assn., Orgn. Am. Historians, Conf. on Brit. Studies, Pi Alpha Theta, Beta Theta Pi. Author: Integration of the Holloman-White Sands Missile Test Ranges, 1947-53, 1959; Air Defense Management, 1950-60: The Air Defense Systems Integration Division, 1961. Home: 74 Noe Ave Madison NJ 07940

REDMOND, RICHARD EUGENE, coop. exec.; b. Bklyn., Mar. 26, 1927; s. John Richard and Mary (Keenan) R.; student St. Francis Coll., 1945, Holy Cross Coll., 1945-46; B.S. in Agr., Cornell U., 1952; m. Margaret Mary Bailey, June 16, 1951; s. Christine, John, Ann, Mary K., Paul, Daniel, Leo, Owen. Dairy farmer, Scipio Center, N.Y., 1952—; dir. Dairylea Milk Mktg. Coop., Pearl River, N.Y., 1966—, mem. exec. com., 1972-78, corp. sec., 1972-75, 78—, pres., 1975-78. Pres., Cayuga County (N.Y.) Farm Bur., 1963-65; chmn. agrl. tech. adv. com. Dairy Internat. Trade, 1974—; dir. Nat. Council Farmer Coops., 1978—; v.p. N.Y. State Council Farmer Coops. Mem. adv. council N.Y. State Coll. Agr., Cornell U., 1976—; chmn. Scipio Republican Com., 1969-72. Mem. Coop. Mktg. Assn. (dir. 1973-76), Am. Inst. Cooperation (dir. 1974-75), Nat. Milk Producers Fedn. (dir. 1971-74), Nat. Forensic Soc., Holy Name Soc. Home: Black St Scipio Center NY 13147 Office: 1 Blue Hill Plaza Pearl River NY 10965

REDMOND, ROBERT FRANCIS, educator; b. Indpls., July 15, 1927; s. John Felix and Marguerite Catherine (Breinig) R.; B.S. in Chem. Engring., Purdue U., 1950; M.S. in Math., U. Tenn., 1955; Ph.D. in Physics, Ohio State U., 1961; m. Mary Catherine Cangany, Oct. 18, 1952; children—Catherine, Robert, Kevin, Thomas, John. Engr., Oak Ridge Nat. Lab., 1950-53; scientist, adviser-cons. Battelle Meml. Inst., Columbus, Ohio, 1953-70; prof. nuclear engring. Ohio State U., Columbus, 1970—, asso. dean Coll. Engring., dir. Engring. Experiment Sta., 1977—; v.p. Argonne Univs. Assn., 1976-77, trustee, 1972—; mem. Ohio Power Siting Commn., 1978—. Served with AUS, 1945-46. Mem. Am. Nuclear Soc. (chmn. Southwestern Ohio sect.), AAAS, Am. Soc. Engring. Edn., Sigma Xi, Tau Beta Pi. Contbr. articles profl. jours. Home: 3112 Brandon Rd Columbus OH 43221

REDMOND, ROLAND LIVINGSTON, lawyer; b. Tivoli, N.Y., Sept. 13, 1892; s. Geraldyn and Estelle (Livingston) R.; A.B., Harvard, 1915; LL.B., Columbia, 1917; m. Sara Delano, June 5, 1915 (div.); children—Sylvie R. Griffiths, Sheila R. Perkins, Joan R. Read, Cynthia R. Mead; m. 2d, Lydia Bodrero, Dec. 2, 1957. Admitted to N.Y. bar, 1919, began practice at N.Y.C. with Carter, Ledyard and Milburn, mem. firm 1925-55, counsel to firm, 1956—. Pres. Met. Museum Art, 1947-64, now trustee emeritus; trustee emeritus Pierpont Morgan Library, N.Y. Pub. Library, Am. Geog. Soc. Served as 1st lt. F.A., U.S. Army, 1917-19, AEF in France. Decorated Order Orange-Nassau (Netherlands); Legion of Honor (France); comdr. Order of Dannebrog (Denmark). Mem. Am., N.Y. State bar assns., Assn. Bar City N.Y. Roman Catholic. Clubs: Recess, Links, Harvard (N.Y.) Office: 2 Wall St New York City NY 10005

REDMOND, WILLIAM ALOYSIUS, state legislator; b. Chgo., Nov. 25, 1908; s. William P. and Gertrude (Crowe) R.; B.S., Marquette U., 1931; J.D., Northwestern U., 1934; m. Rita Riordan, Mar. 6, 1943; children—Bill, Mary, Colleen. Admitted to Ill. bar; atty. Sch. Bd. Dists. 2 and 100, Bensenville Library; mem. Ill. Ho. of Reps., 1959—, speaker 79th-81st sessions. Ill. County chmn. DuPage County Democrats. Served to lt. comdr. USNR, 1941-45. Mem. Am., Ill., DuPage County bar assns. Clubs: K.C., Lions. Home: 250 Tioga St Bensenville IL 60106 Office: 18 N Center St Bensenville IL 60106

REDMONT, BERNARD SIDNEY, fgn. corr., broadcaster; b. N.Y.C., Nov. 8, 1918; s. Morris Abraham and Bessie (Kamerman) R.; B.A., Coll. City N.Y., 1938; M.J., Columbia U., 1939; m. Joan Rothenberg, Mar. 12, 1940; children—Dennis Foster, Jane Carol. Reporter, book reviewer Brooklyn Daily Eagle, 1936-38; free lance correspondent, Europe, 1939, Mexico City, 1939-40; telegraph editor, editorial writer Herkimer (N.Y.) Evening Telegram, 1941-42; newswriter U.S. Office of Inter-Am. Affairs, Washington shortwave radio newscasts to Latin Am., 1942-43, dir. News div., 1944-46; staff correspondent, bur. chief U.S. News & World Report, Buenos Aires and Paris, 1946-51; columnist Continental Daily Mail, Paris, France, 1951-53; chief correspondent English Language World News Service Agence France-Presse, Paris, France, 1953-65; European corr., Paris news bur. chief Westinghouse Broadcasting Co., Paris, 1961-76; corr., bur. chief CBS News, Moscow, 1976-79, corr., Paris, 1979—. Served with USMCR, 1943-44. Decorated Purple Heart, chevalier Legion of Honor (France). Pulitzer Traveling fellow. Mem. Overseas Press Assn. (award best radio reporting from abroad 1968, 73), Nat. Press Assn., Anglo-American Press Assn. of Paris (pres. 1961, treas. 1970-73, sec. 1974-76). Unitarian. Office: CBS News 37 Rue Marbeuf 75008 Paris France

REDMONT, DENNIS FOSTER, newspaperman; b. Washington, Dec. 8, 1942; s. Bernard Sidney and Joan (Rothenberg) R.; B.A., Oberlin (Ohio) Coll., 1962; M.S. in Journalism, Columbia, 1963; m. Maria Manuela Paixao de Magalhaes, Apr. 16, 1968; children—Michael Andrew, Rodrigo Brian. Editor World Services, A.P., N.Y.C., 1963-65, corr., Lisbon, 1965-67, newsman, Rome, 1967-70, chief bur., Rio de Janeiro, 1970-75, chief bur., Rome, 1975—. Trustee Overseas Sch. of Rome. Recipient Carl Dipman award in journalism Oberlin Coll., 1963; Internat. fellow Columbia, 1962-63. Mem. Brazil Fgn. Press Assn. (pres. 1974-75), Fgn. Press Assn. Rome. Club: Overseas Press (N.Y.C.). Home: 59 Via Alessandro Poerio Rome Italy Office: 5 Piazza Grazioli Rome Italy

REDO, S(AVERIO) FRANK, surgeon; b. Bklyn., Dec. 28, 1920; s. Frank and Maria (Guida) R.; B.S., Queens Coll., 1942; M.D., Cornell U., 1950; m. Maria Lappano, June 27, 1948; children—Philip, Martha. Intern in surgery N.Y. Hosp., N.Y.C., 1950-51, asst. resident surgeon, 1951-56, resident surgeon, 1956-57, asst. attending surgeon, 1958-60, asso. attending surgeon, 1960-66, surgeon in charge pediatric surgery, 1960, attending surgeon, 1966—; practice medicine specializing in surgery; clin. asso. prof. surgery Cornell U. Med. Coll., 1963-72, prof., 1972—. Served to capt. USAAF, 1942-46. Diplomate Am. Bd. Thoracic Surgery, Am. Bd. Surgery. Fellow A.C.S., Am. Coll. Chest Physicians; mem. Harvey Soc., Pan Am. Med. Assn., Soc. Univ. Surgeons, Am. Acad. Pediatrics, Am. Fedn. for Clin. Research, Internat. Cardiovascular Soc., Am. Surg. Assn., Am. Assn. Thoracic Surgery, Soc. for Surgery Alimentary Tract, Am. Soc. Artificial Internat. Organs, Am. Acad. Pediatrics, Assn. Advancement Med. Instrumentation, Soc. Thoracic Surgeons, Internat. Soc. Surgery, N.Y. Gastroent. Soc., N.Y. Acad. Sci., N.Y. Cardiovascular Soc., N.Y. Acad. Medicine, N.Y. Soc. Thoracic Surgery, N.Y. Pediatric Soc., Med. Soc. County N.Y., Queens Coll. Alumni Assn. (gov. 1962—), Sigma Xi. Author: Surgery in the Ambulatory Child, 1961; Principles of Surgery in the First Six Months of Life, 1976; Atlas of Surgery in the First Six Months of Life, 1977; contbr. articles to profl. jours; patentee in field. Home: 435 E 70th St New York NY 10021 Office: 525 E 68th St New York NY 10021. *My life is based on the principles of doing as much for others as possible and doing no harm; to offer advice only when asked; to apply myself unstintingly, but not selfishly, to my work; to learn from my mistakes; to strive for perfection; and to always have a project and a dream.*

REDPATH, ROBERT UPJOHN, JR., ins. exec.; b. South Orange, N.J., Aug. 25, 1906; s. Dr. Robert Upjohn and Clara May (Sloneker) R.; grad. Phillips Acad., 1924; student U. Mich., summer 1925; A.B., Yale, 1928, postgrad. Law Sch., 1928-29; postgrad. New Sch. Social Research, N.Y.U., Columbia, Am. Coll. C.L.U.s; m. Nancy Shaw Miller, June 28, 1930; children—Robert Upjohn III, Nancy M., William M., Jean C. (Mrs. Henry P. Becton, Jr.). With Lawyers Mortgage Co., N.Y.C., 1929-33; life underwriter, 1933—; dir. Ohio Casualty Corp., Hamilton, Ohio Life Ins. Co., Hamilton. Lectr. gen. semantics Denver U., 1952; tchr. gen. semantics Adult Schs. of South Orange-Maplewood and Montclair, N.J., 1954-61; trustee South Orange-Maplewood (N.J.) Adult Sch., 1965—. Chmn. planning and devel. bd. Village of South Orange, 1947-49. Trustee, pres. bd. Inst. Gen. Semantics, 1946—; co-founder, trustee Blue Hill Found., 1941-76, New Eyes for the Needy, Short Hills, N.J., 1969-74; bd. mgrs. Vocat. Services br. YMCA, N.Y.C., 1944—; mem. bd. pensions U.P. Ch. of U.S.A., 1947-62. Trustee Phillips Acad., 1950-52, Susquehanna U., 1960—, Ethel Walker Sch., 1952-55, Rosemary Hall Found., 1960-63, Phillips Acad. C.L.U. Mem. Million Dollar Round Table (life), Nat. Assn. Life Underwriters, Yale Alumni Assn. (active alumni affairs, Yale medal 1968), Beta Theta Phi, Elihu. Presbyn. Clubs: Graduates, (New Haven); Essex County Country; Yale (N.Y.C.). Home: 423 N Ridgewood Rd South Orange NJ 07079 also 3502 Estero Blvd Fort Myers Beach FL 33931 Office: 666 Fifth Ave New York City NY 10019

REDSTONE, LOUIS GORDON, architect; b. Poland, Mar. 16, 1903; came to U.S., 1923; s. Abraham Aaron and Anna (Gordon) Routenstein; B.S. in Architecture, U. Mich., 1929; M.Arch., Cranbrook Acad. Arts, 1948; m. Ruth R. Rosenbaum, June 25, 1939; children—Daniel Aaron, Eliel Gordon. Engaged in practice architecture, Israel, 1933-37; started firm Louis G. Redstone Assos. Inc., architects/engrs./planners, Detroit, 1937, pres., 1945—. Del. internat. congresses, Caracas, Tokyo, Moscow and Buenos Aires; exec. com. Pan Am. Fedn. Architects, 1955-70; juror archtl. and artists exhbns., profl. adviser archtl. competitions sponsored by Dow Chem. Co.; mem. Mich. Commn. on Art in State Bldgs., 1975—. Recipient Patron award Mich. Found. for Arts, 1977. Fellow AIA (pres. Detroit 1965; Gold medal outstanding contbn. to profession), Mich. Soc. Architects (bd. mem.; Gold medal 1978), Engring. Soc. Detroit, Bldg. Research Inst. Author: Art in Architecture, 1968; New Dimensions in Shopping Centers and Stores, 1973; The New Downtowns—Rebuilding Business Districts, 1976; Hospitals and Health Care Facilities, 1978; contbr. articles to profl. mags. and newspapers. Home: 19303 Appoline St Detroit MI 48235 Office: 28425 W Eight Mile Rd Livonia MI 48152. *The architect must be a positive force in creating surroundings that enhance and fulfill all human needs, in which the arts become an integral part of man's daily environment. He must implement this approach by studying the specific needs and requirements of those who will use the building. These needs must then be satisfied within an aesthetically designed and functional enclosure that is in harmony with its surroundings. This basic concept must not be limited in application to individual buildings; it must be extended to the wider horizon of the total urban environment.*

REDSTONE, SUMNER MURRAY, theatre exec., lawyer; b. Boston, May 27, 1923; s. Michael and Belle (Ostrovsky) R.; B.A., Harvard, 1944, LL.B., 1947; m. Phyllis Gloria Raphael, July 6, 1947; children—Brent Dale, Shari Ellin. Admitted to Mass. bar, 1947, U.S. Ct. Appeals 1st Circuit bar, 1948, 8th Circuit bar, 1950, 9th Circuit bar, 1948, D.C. bar, 1951, U.S. Supreme Ct. bar, 1952; law sec. U.S. Ct. Appeals for 9th Circuit, San Francisco, 1947-48; instr. law and labor mgmt. U. San Francisco, 1947; spl. asst. to U.S. atty. gen., Washington, 1948-51; partner firm Ford, Bergson, Adams, Borkland & Redstone, Washington, 1951-54; exec. v.p. N.E. Drive-In Theatre Corp., Boston, 1954-67; pres. N.E. Theatre Corp., 1967—; chmn. met. div. N.E. Combined Jewish Philanthropies, Boston, 1963; mem. corp. New Eng. Med. Center, 1967—. Trustee Children's Cancer Research Found., Art Lending Library; sponsor Boston Mus. Sci.; bd. dirs. Will Rogers Meml. Fund, Boston Arts Festival; bd. overseers Sidney Farber Cancer Center. Served to 1st lt. AUS, 1943-45. Decorated Army Commendation medal; recipient William J. German Human Relations award Am. Jewish Com. Entertainment and Communication Div., 1977; named one of ten outstanding young men Greater Boston C. of C., 1958. Mem. Am. Congress Exhibitors (exec. com. 1961—), Theatre Owners Am. (asst. pres. 1960-63, pres. 1964-65), Nat. Assn. Theatre Owners (chmn. bd. dirs. 1965-66); mem. Am., Boston bar assns., Harvard Law Sch. Assn., Am. Judicature Soc. Mason. Clubs: University, Variety New Eng., Harvard (Boston). Home: 98 Baldpate Hill Rd Newton Centre MA 02159 Office: 31 St James Ave Boston MA 02116

REDWINE, JACK THEODORE, food co. exec.; b. Cass City, Mich., July 1, 1919; s. James T. and Anna S. (Cawthon) R.; A.B., U. Mich., 1940, J.D., 1947; postgrad. Harvard, 1970; m. Avis Ann Foege, Jan. 19, 1943; children—James T., Joe D., Julia A. Admitted to Mich. bar, 1947, Ill. bar, 1948; atty. Quaker Oats Co., Chgo., 1947-64, counsel, 1964-72, v.p., gen. counsel, 1972—. Served as 1st lt. AUS, 1942-46. Mem. Am., Ill., Chgo. bar assns., Am. Judicature Soc., Assn. Gen. Counsel, Practicing Law Inst. (corporate law dept. adv. council), Food and Drug Law Inst. (industry trustee). Home: 2444 Central Park Ave Evanston IL 60201 Office: 345 Merchandise Mart Chicago IL 60654

REECE, EVERETTE ARTHUR, aircraft mfg. co. exec.; b. Greenwood, Nebr., July 27, 1914; s. Henry Arthur and Mabel Ann (Wiedman) R.; student U. Nebr., 1932, Iowa State U., 1933; B.B.A., Washington U., St. Louis, 1964; m. Irene May Parrish, Dec. 3, 1929; children—Darlene Louis Reece LeClair, Ronald Arthur, Donald Ray. With McDonnel Douglas Aircraft Corp., and predecessor, 1940—, v.p. mfg., then acting pres., 1969-76, v.p., gen. mgr. McDonnell Douglas Can. Ltd., Toronto, 1976—; mem. Bd. Trade Met. Toronto. Mem. Can. Export Assn. (dir.), McDonnell Douglas Mgmt. Club, Air Industries Assn. Can., Can. C. of C. Club: Canadian (Toronto). Home: 25 Warrender Ave Islington ON M9B 5Z4 Canada Office: McDonnell Douglas Can Ltd PO Box 6013 Toronto AMF ON L5P 1B7 Canada

REECE, JOE WILSON, educator, govt. ofcl.; b. Elkin, N.C., Mar. 1, 1935; s. Thad Marshall and Anita (Hobson) R.; B. Nuclear Engring., N.C. State U., 1957, M.S., 1961; Ph.D., U. Fla., 1963; m. Nancy Lee Fletcher, Aug. 25, 1955; children—James Thad, Joel Wade. Instr. engring. mechanics N.C. State U., Raleigh, 1958-61; asst. prof. mech. engring. Auburn (Ala.) U., 1963-67, asso. prof., 1967-76, prof., 1976—; dep. dir. operating reactors div. U.S. Nuclear Regulatory Commn., 1976-78; cons. U.S. Army Missile Command, Combustion Engring. Co., others. Campus drive chmn. Auburn United Fund, 1969, chmn. bd., 1971. Named Disting. Classroom Tchr., N.C. State U. Sch. Engring., 1961: Outstanding Faculty Mem., Auburn U. Sch. Engring., 1965, 73. Registered profl. engr., Ala. Mem. Am. Soc. Engring. Edn. (pres. S.E. sect. 1977), ASME, Ala. Acad. Sci., Scabbard and Blade, Sigma Xi, Phi Kappa Phi, Tau Beta Pi, Phi Eta Sigma, Sigma Pi Sigma, Theta Tau, Pi Tau Sigma. Methodist (lay leader 1967, chmn. trustees 1972). Clubs: Civitan (pres. 1968), Saugahatchee Country (Auburn); Dixie Sailing (Montgomery, Ala.). Home: 242 Conrey Dr Auburn AL 36830

REED, A(LFRED) BYRON, apparel mfr.; b. Indpls., June 30, 1916; s. Alfred Lumpkin and Myrtle (Wood) R.; B.S., Butler U., 1939; postgrad. U. Chgo., 1946-47; m. Mary Ellen Myers, Sept. 1, 1950; 1 son, Charles W. Asst. brokerage mgr. Conn. Gen. Life Ins. Co., Chgo., 1939-41; sales mgr., marketing mgr., asst. gen. mgr. Vassar Co., Chgo., 1946-57; gen. mgr. women's div., Munsingwear, Inc., Mpls., 1958-66, pres., chief exec. officer, 1966-79, chmn., 1979—, also dir.; dir., trust com., exec. com. 1st Nat. Bank Mpls., Hoerner Waldorf Co. St. Paul, 1973-77, Murphy Motor Freight; mem. mgmt.-labor textile adv. com. U.S. Dept. Commerce. Chmn., Nat. Alliance Businessmen, Mpls., 1972; mem. Adv. Council U.S.-Japan Econ. Relations, Washington; adviser Council Fin. Aid to Edn.; chmn. U.S. Savs. Bond Drive, 1975-76. Bd. dirs. Better Bus. Bur. Mpls., 1973-74, Minn. Pvt. Coll. Fund, Mpls. YMCA; trustee Butler U. Served to lt. USNR, 1942-46. Mem. Am. Apparel Mfrs. Assn. (chmn. bd. dirs., exec. com.), U.S. C. of C. (internat. policy com., internat. trade subcom.), Mpls. C. of C. (dir.), Phi Delta Theta. Republican. Episcopalian. Clubs: Union League (N.Y.C.); Minneapolis, Minikahda (Mpls.). Home: 4523 Wooddale Ave Edina MN 55424 Office: 718 Glenwood Ave Minneapolis MN 55405

REED, ADRIAN FARAGHER, anatomist, physician; b. Terre Haute, Ind., Dec. 22, 1906; s. Charles Fenwick and Helena Maria (Faragher) R.; B.A., DePauw U., 1928; M.A., Cornell U., 1931, Ph.D., 1933; M.D., Tulane U., 1943; m. Mary Cecelia Reese, Dec. 28, 1935. Asst. anatomist Cornell U. Med. Sch., Ithaca, N.Y., 1929-30, instr. 1930-33; mem. faculty dept. anatomy Tulane U. Sch. Medicine, New Orleans, 1933-56, prof., 1945-56; house physician McLeod Infirmary, Florence, S.C., 1956-60; fellow, asso. prof. dept. internal medicine Tulane U. Med. Sch., 1960-62, prof., 1962-72; prof., head dept. anatomy La. State U., Shreveport, 1968-77, prof. emeritus, 1977—; vis. prof. Bowman Gray Sch. Medicine, 1945. NIH grantee. Mem. Am. Assn. Anatomy, So. Soc. Anatomy, Sigma Xi, Alpha Omega Alpha. Democrat. Methodist. Contbr. articles to profl. jours. Office: PO Box 33932 La State Univ Shreveport LA 71130

REED, ALFRED, composer, conductor; b. N.Y.C., Jan. 25, 1921; s. Carl Mark and Elizabeth (Strasser) Friedman; student Juilliard Sch. of Music, 1946-48; B.M., Baylor U., 1955, M.M., 1956; Mus. D., Internat. Conservatory of Music, Lima, Peru, 1968; m. Marjorie Beth Deley, June 20, 1941; children—Michael Carlson, Richard Judson. Composer, arranger, N.Y.C., 1941—; exec. editor Hansen Publs., N.Y.C., 1955-66; prof. music U. Miami (Fla.) Sch. of Music, 1966—; condr. Tri-State Music Festival, Okla., 1956-57, 60-66, 70, 73, Midwest Nat. Band Clinic, 1960-75, Bemidji (Minn.) Summer Music Camp, 1970-71, 75, Mid-East Instrumental Music Conf., Pitts., 1957-60, Canadian Music Educators Assn., Edmonton, Alta., 1975. Served with AUS, 1942-46. Mem. ASCAP, Am. Bandmasters Assn., Am. Fedn. Musicians, Nat. Band Assn., Music Educators Nat. Conv. Composer: Russian Christmas Music, 1944, Symphony for Brass and Percussion, 1952; Rhapsody for Viola and Orch., 1956, Choric Song, 1966, Titania's Nocturne, 1967, A Festival Prelude, 1962, Passacaglia, 1968, Music for Hamlet, 1973, Armenian Dances, 1974-75, Punchinello, Overture to a Romantic Comedy, 1974, Testament of an American, 1974, First Suite for Band, 1975, Othello, A Symphonic Portrait in Five Scenes, 1976, Prelude and Capriccio, 1977, Second Symphony, 1978, Siciliana Notturno, 1978, Second Suite for Band, 1978, The Enchanted Island, 1979, others. Home: 1405 Ancona Ave Coral Gables FL 33146 Office: Sch of Music Univ of Miami Coral Gables FL 33124. *As a composer, my desire has always been to achieve both a depth and intensity of communication between myself, my music and my audiences that would enable me to express something of value as regards myself and my time that, hopefully, would give rise to a deeply felt response on the part of my fellow human beings. I suppose this is true of the arts in general, and all artists, regardless of their medium of expression, but music, for me at least, has been the supreme expression of all time, for all men.*

REED, ALFRED S(HELDON), JR., publisher; b. Westfield, N.J., Aug. 2, 1926; s. Alfred Sheldon and Jenn (Winslow) R.; B.S. in Physics, Lafayette Coll., 1953; student in mktg. and fin. Harvard U. Bus. Sch.; m. Nancy Marion Snell, June 15, 1951; children—Alfred S. III, Kristin W., Tracey S., Jennifer L., Katharine S. Mgmt. trainee Longlines div. AT&T, 1953-54; advt. salesman Whitney Publs., N.Y.C., 1954-56, Aero. Digest Pub. Co., 1956-57, Crain Communications, 1957-59; advt. salesman Chem. Engring. mag. McGraw-Hill Inc., Boston, sales mgr., N.Y.C., 1966-69, pub., 1969—. Chmn. PTA, Hopkinton, Mass., 1962, Republican Town Com., Hopkinton, 1963, Hopkinton Sch. Bldg. Com., 1965; pres. Chowder & Marching Club, Bedford Village, N.Y., 1974-75. Served with USNR, 1943-46; PTO, ETO. Mem. Bus. and Profl. Advertisers Assn. (cert. bus. communicator), Am. Inst. Chem. Engrs. Office: 1221 Ave of Americas New York NY 10020

REED, CARROLL EDWARD, educator; b. Portland, Oreg., Nov. 21, 1914; s. Edward R. and Cora (Schienle) R.; B.A., U. Wash., 1936, M.A., 1937; Ph.D., Brown U., 1941; m. Elizabeth Eshom, Dec. 26, 1938; children—John, Carolyn, Robin Day, Janet, Paul, Carl, Michelle Rimer. Mem. faculty U. Wash., 1946-66, prof., 1959-66; asst. in German, Brown U., 1938-41, instr., 1941-42; cryptanalyst War Dept., 1942-46; asst. prof. U. Ga., 1946; prof., chmn. dept. German and Russian, U. Calif., Riverside, 1966-69; prof. U. Mass., 1969—, head dept. German, 1971-76; lectr. Columbia, 1950. Fulbright research scholar, Germany, 1953-54. Mem. Modern Lang. Assn., Am. Dialect Soc., Linguistic Soc. Am., Pa. German Soc., Am. Assn. Tchrs. German, Can. Linguistic Assn., Phi Beta Kappa. Author: Linguistic Atlas of Pennsylvania German, 1954; Dialects of American English, 2d edit., 1977. Editor: The Learning of Language, 1971. Contbr. articles to profl. jours. Home: 190 Shays St Amherst MA 01002

REED, CHARLES ALLEN, educator, anthropologist, zoologist; b. Portland, Oreg., June 6, 1912; s. C. Allen and Gladys (Donohoe) R.; student Whitman Coll., 1929-30; B.S., U. Oreg., 1937; Ph.D., U. Calif. at Berkeley, 1943; m. Lois Wells, Aug. 18, 1951; children—C. Allen, Robert M., Brian W. Instr. biology U. Oreg., 1936-37; lectr. anatomy U. Calif. Med. Sch. at Berkeley, 1943; instr. biology Reed Coll., 1943-46; asst. prof. zoology U. Ariz., 1946-49; asst. prof., asso. prof. zoology U. Ill. Sch. Pharmacy, 1949-54, 55-61; research asso. anthropology U. Chgo., 1954-55; asso. prof. biology Yale, 1961-66; prof. biology and anthropology U. Ill. Chgo. Circle Campus, 1966-67, prof. anthropology, 1967—, acting head dept., 1967-70. Mem. Catlow Caves archeol. expdn. U. Oreg., 1937; Iraq-Jarmo archeol. expdn. Oriental Inst. U. Chgo., 1954-55; Iranian prehistoric project Oriental Inst., 1960; U. Istanbul-Chgo. Prehistoric project, Turkey, 1970. curator mammals and reptiles Peabody Mus., Yale, 1961-66; dir. Yale prehistoric expdn. to Nubia, 1962-65; research asso. vertebrate anatomy Field Mus. Natural History, Chgo., 1966—; mem. U.S. com. Nat. Acad. Scis. for Internat. Union for Quaternary Research, 1967-74. Fellow Am. Assn. Anthropologists (life), Asso. Current Anthropology, AAAS (life); mem. Am. Soc. Mammalogists (life), Am. Soc. Ichthyologists and Herpetologists (life), Am. Assn. Phys. Anthropology, Am. Soc. Zoologists, Am. Soc. Anatomists, Soc. Study Evolution, Soc. Vert. Paleontology, Am. Soc. Naturalists, Am. Assn. Quaternary Research, Chgo. Acad. Scis. (bd. sci. govs.), Deutsche Gesellschaft für Säugertierkunde, Phi Beta Kappa, Sigma Xi. Editor: Origins of Agriculture, 1977. Contbr. articles to profl. jours. Home: 423 N Cuyler Ave Oak Park IL 60302 Office: U Ill Chgo Circle Box 4348 Chicago IL 60680

REED, CHARLES ELI, elec. co. exec.; b. Findlay, Ohio, Aug. 11, 1913; s. Joseph O. and Katharine (Switzer) R.; B.S., Case Inst. Tech., 1934; Sc.D., Mass. Inst. Tech., 1937. Asst. prof. chem. engring. Mass. Inst. Tech., 1937-42; research asso. Research Lab. Gen. Electric Co., 1942-45, engring. mgr. chem. div., 1945-52, gen. mgr. silicone products dept., 1952-59, gen. mgr. metall. products, 1959-60, gen. mgr. chem. and metall. div., 1960, v.p., 1962—, v.p. and group exec., 1968-71, sr. v.p., 1971—; Marburg lectr. ASTM, 1956. Recipient honor award Comml. Devel. Assn., 1971. Mem. AAAS, Am. Chem. Soc., Am. Inst. Chem. Engrs., Nat. Acad. Engring., Sigma Xi, Tau Beta Pi. Author: (with H.S. Mickley, T.K. Sherwood), Applied Mathematics in Chemical Engineering, 1957. Home: The Inwood 3200 Park Ave Bridgeport CT 06604

REED, CHARLES EMMETT, physician, educator; b. Boulder, Colo., Mar. 13, 1922; s. Charles E. and Helene (Hadady) R.; student Harvard, 1943; M.D., Columbia, 1945; m. Janice Tullock, July 19, 1962; children—Jocelyn, David, Marian, James, Walter, Barbara, Lawrence. Intern, Colo. Gen. Hosp., Denver, 1945-46; resident medicine Roosevelt Hosp., N.Y.C., 1948-51; pvt. practice Corvallis (Oreg.) Clinic, 1951-61; mem. faculty U. Wis. Med. Sch., 1961—, prof. medicine, 1967-78; prof. medicine Mayo Med. Sch., Rochester, Minn., 1978—, cons. Mayo Clinic. Served with AUS, 1946-48. Diplomate Am. Bd. Internal Medicine, Am. Bd. Allergy and Immunology (co-chmn. 1972-75). Mem. Am. Acad. Allergy (pres. 1973-74), A.C.P. Co-editor: Allergy Principles and Practice, 1978; mem. editorial bd. jour. Allergy; editor Jour. Allergy and Clin. Immunology, 1977—. Contbr. articles to profl. jours. Home: 2403 Merrihills Dr SW Rochester MN 55901

REED, CHARLES FOSTER, veterinarian, educator; b. Middleport, Ohio, Mar. 15, 1923; s. Charles Foster and Olivia (Keesey) R.; D.V.M., Ohio State U., 1951, M.S., 1956; m. Sarah Christine Barham, June 27, 1944; children—Nancy Olivia, Scott Hayward. Practice vet. medicine, Cleve., 1953; instr. Coll. Vet. Medicine, Ohio State U., 1953-57, asst. prof., 1957-61, asso. prof., 1961-62; asso. dean, prof. Coll. Vet. Medicine, Mich. State U., East Lansing, 1962-76; asso. dean Coll. Vet. Medicine, U. Tenn., Knoxville, 1976—. Served with AUS, 1943-46, to 1st lt. USAF, 1951-53. Recipient Creativity award Nat. Univ. Extension Assn., 1966; Distinguished Vet. Alumnus award Ohio State U., 1975. Mem. Am., Mich. (pres. 1971) vet. med. assns., Phi Zeta. Home: 8 Boxwood Sq Knoxville TN 37919

REED, CHARLES HANCOCK, textile distbg. co. exec.; b. Richmond, Va., Dec. 25, 1900; s. Charles Clinton and Lyllian (Hancock) R.; student U. Va., 1918; B.S., U.S. Mil. Acad., 1922; grad. Command and Gen. Staff Sch., 1941, Cav. Sch., 1932; m. Janice Cannon, Dec. 27, 1924. Commd. 2d. lt. U.S. Army, 1922, advanced through grades to col., 1943; comdr. 2d Armored Cav. Regt., ETO, 1944-47; sec. Gen. Army Field Forces, 1947-49; ret., 1949; treas. Williams & Reed, Inc., Richmond, 1949-50, pres., 1950—; pres. George W. Delks Co., Smithfield, Va., 1950—, Fosters, Mathews Co., 1950—; dir. Bank of Va., Richmond, Woodstock Corp., Richmond. Pres. Va. Fair, 1965—. Bd. visitors Va. Poly. Inst., 1949-59; vice rector Radford (Va.) Coll., 1950—. Decorated D.S.C., Silver Star with clasp, Bronze Star, Purple Heart, Legion of Merit; Croix de Guerre with palms, chevalier Legion of Honor (France). Mem. Nat. Assn. Textile and Apparel Wholesalers (pres. 1965-66), Nat. Assn. Wholesaler-Distbrs. (pres. 1970). Democrat. Home: Foundry Pl Midlothian VA 23113 Office: 3703 Carolina Ave Richmond VA 23222

REED, CLARENCE C., surgeon, rancher; b. Lewisville, Ohio, June 26, 1902; s. John C. and Rosa (McVay) R.; A.B., Mt. Union Coll., 1920; M.D., U. Chgo., 1925, postgrad. studies, Berlin, Vienna, London; m. Elvira Arman, Dec. 21, 1973; 1 dau. by previous marriage, Linda. Resident in surgery U. Chgo., 1926-29; practice medicine specializing in surgery, Downey, Calif., 1933—; sr. attending surgeon St. Francis Hosp., Lynwood, Calif., 1945—, Dominguez Valley Hosp., Compton, Calif., 1962, Downey Community Hosp., 1970—; cattle rancher, San Luis Obispo County (Calif.), 1942—; asst. prof. surgery U. So. Calif., 1934-44. Founder Reed Meml. Found., 1959, Reed Neurol. Research Center at Med. Sch. U. Calif. at Los Angeles, 1965, Reed Surg. Bldg. at U. Chgo., 1966. Served with AUS, 1919. Recipient Highest award Merit, U. Calif. at Los Angeles Med. Sch., 1972. Diplomate Am. Bd. Plastic Surgery. Fellow A.C.S., Am. Soc. Abdominal Surgeons; mem. AMA, Sigma Nu, Mu Sigma Nu. Mason (Shriner). Home: 1300 Oxford Rd San Marino CA 91108. *The motivating force in my life may be explained in a few words: giving the best possible care to sick people. This has brought honor and success but I regard these as much less important than having contributed to the alleviation of human misery.*

REED, CLARENCE RAYMOND, assn. exec.; b. Shamokin, Pa., Sept. 23, 1932; s. Benton Howard and Gerda Maude (Hoover) R.; B.A., U. Pa., 1954, M.B.A. with distinction, 1958; grad. Stonier Grad. Sch. Banking, 1969; m. Joan Ann Engle, June 25, 1955; children—Ann Elizabeth, Susan Engle. With Prudential Ins. Co. Am., 1954; with Robert Morris Assos., Phila., 1958—, asst. sec., 1959-60, sec.-treas., 1960-74, exec. mgr., 1961-74, exec. v.p., 1974—; mem. faculty loan mgmt. seminar Ind. U., 1971-72. Chmn., Shares in Edn., 1968; pres. Council Springfield (Pa.) Twp. Home and Sch. Assns., 1969-70. Served with AUS, 1954-56. Mem. Credit Mgmt. Assn. Delaware Valley, Am. Soc. Assn. Execs., Am. Mgmt. Assn., Central Home and Sch. Assn. (pres. 1966-67), Wharton M.B.A. Alumni Assn. Presbyn. (fin. sec. 1970, 79, ruling elder 1972-74, chmn. 50th anniversary com. 1974, trustee 1977-79). Clubs: Union League (Phila.); Exchequer (Washington); Rotary. Home: 32 Thornridge Rd Springfield PA 19064 Office: Phila Nat Bank Bldg Philadelphia PA 19107

REED, DARWIN CRAMER, med. center adminstr.; b. Artesia, N.Mex., July 24, 1915; s. Darwin W. and Candace (Cramer) R.; A.B., Wichita U., 1937; M.D., Washington U., St. Louis, 1941; M.S., U. Pa., 1954; m. Martha Gene Thalmann, Aug. 15, 1940; children—Geney Catherine (Mrs. Robert Joe Watson), Darwin Kim. Intern, St. Francis Hosp., Wichita, Kans., 1941-42, resident, 1946-48; resident U. Pa. Hosp., Phila., 1952-54, Med. Coll. Va. Hosp., 1954-55; practice medicine, Wichita, 1948-52; partner Wichita Urology Group, Kans., 1955-70; dean Coll. Health Related Professions, Wichita State U., 1970-73, v.p. for health edn., 1973-77; prof. surgery, vice chancellor U. Kans. Sch. Medicine, Wichita, 1975-78; sr. v.p. med./prof. devel. Wesley Med. Center, Wichita, 1978—. Mem. Kans. Bd. Healing Arts, 1964-67; chmn. dean's com. Wichita VA Hosp., 1975-78. Chmn. bd. trustees Wichita State U., 1966-68. Served to lt. col. M.C., USAAF, 1942-46. Diplomate Am. Bd. Urology. Fellow A.C.S.; mem. Am., Pan Am. med. assns., Am. Urologic Assn., Am. Cancer Soc. (pres. Kans. div. 1960-61, 65-66). Methodist. Home: 720 Stratford St Wichita KS 67206

REED, DAVID ANDREW, hosp. adminstr.; b. Butler, Pa., Feb. 24, 1933; s. Sherman W. and Caroline (Janner) R.; A.B., Allegheny Coll., 1955; M.S., U. Pitts., 1961; m. Virginia Rogers, Dec. 1, 1956; children—Kristine Lynn, Katherine Louise, Elizabeth Anne, Amy Janner. Adminstrv. resident Titusville (Pa.) Hosp., 1959, Cin. Gen. Hosp., 1960-61; asst. adminstr. Warren (Pa.) Gen. Hosp., 1961-62, Western Pa. Gen. Hosp., Pitts., 1962-63; with Cin. Gen. Hosp., 1963-69, adminstr., 1964-69; asso. prof. hosp. adminstrn. U. Cin. Coll. Medicine, 1966-69, preceptor program med. and hosp. adminstrn. U. Pitts. Grad. Sch. Pub. Health, George Washington U., also Zavier U., 1966-69; pres. Lenox Hill Hosp., N.Y.C., 1969-78; v.p., chief exec. officer Good Samaritan Hosp., Phoenix, 1978—; instr. Sch. Pub. Health, Columbia U. Past pres. Greater Cin. Hosp. Council; bd. govs. Greater N.Y. Hosp. Assn.; del. Am. Hosp. Assn. Bd. dirs. Urban League Cin. Served with AUS, 1955-57. Fellow Am. Coll. Hosp. Adminstrs.; mem. Hosp. Adminstrs. Club N.Y.C. (pres.), Hosp. Assn. N.Y., Phi Gamma Delta. Presbyterian. Clubs: Cincinnati; Union League, Scarsdale Golf. Author articles. Home: 8732 N 66th St Paradise Valley AZ 85253 Office: 1033 E McDowell Rd Phoenix AZ 85006

REED, DAVID BENSON, bishop; b. Tulsa, Feb. 16, 1927; s. Paul Spencer and Bonnie Frances (Taylor) R.; A.B., Harvard, 1948; M.Div., Va. Theol. Sem., 1951, D.D., 1964; D.D., U. of South, 1972; m. Susan Henry Riggs, Oct. 30, 1954; children—Mary, Jennifer, David, Sarah, Catherine. Ordained priest Episcopal Ch., 1952; missionary priest in Panama and Colombia, 1951-58; with Nat. Ch. Exec. Office, 1958-61; mission priest, S.D., 1961-63; missionary bishop of Colombia, 1964-72; bishop coadjutor Diocese of Ky., Louisville, 1972-74, bishop of Ky., 1974—; 1st pres. Anglican Council Latin Am., 1969-72. Bd. dirs. Norton Childrens Hosp., Louisville; trustee, regent U. of South. Democrat. Home: 1823 Ballard Mill Ln Louisville KY 40207 Office: 421 S 2d St Louisville KY 40202

REED, DAVID WOODERSON, educator; b. Bolivar, Mo., May 7, 1921; s. Arthur Clyde and Dixie (Wooderson) R.; B.S. in Edn., U. Mo., 1942; A.M., U. Mich., 1943, Ph.D. (fellow 1946-48), 1949; m. Anita Marcine Davison, Aug. 21, 1940; children—Betty Ann, Anita Sue, David Alan. Tchr. English, União Cultural, Brasil-Estados Unidos, São Paulo, 1944; instr. English, U. Mo., 1945-46; mem. faculty U. Calif. at Berkeley, 1948-70, prof. English, 1961-64, prof. linguistics, 1964-70, chmn. dept., 1964-69; prof. linguistics Northwestern U., Evanston, Ill., 1970—, chmn. dept., 1971-73, dir. program Oriental and African langs., 1978—; Gast prof. Albert Ludwigs U., Freiburg, Germany, 1956-57; head Linguistic Atlas of Pacific Coast, 1952—; Fulbright sr. lectr., Germany, 1956-57; Rockefeller fellow, 1942-43; recipient Life Service award S.W. Bapt. Coll., Bolivar, Mo., 1958. Mem. Linguistic Soc. Am. (life), Internat. Linguistic Assn., Am. Dialect Soc., Am. Name Soc., Sigma Xi. Author: The History of Inflectional n in English Verbs before 1500, 1950; also articles. Founding editor Lang. Learning, 1947-48; mng. editor Names, 1958-59. Home: 2666C Prairie Ave Evanston IL 60201 Office: Northwestern U 2016 Sheridan Rd Evanston IL 60201. *The happiest and most fulfilled people are those who are constantly aware of their feelings and whose empathy allows them to be honest in communicating feelings to others. Success is an inner state that arises from knowledge that one's behavior conforms as nearly as possible with his values.*

REED, DOEL, art educator, etcher; b. Logansport, Ind., May 21, 1894; s. William and Anna (Anderson) B.; Art Acad., Cincinnati, 1916-17, 1919-20; student Paris, France, 1926, 1930-31; m. Elizabeth Jane Sparks, Oct. 21, 1920; 1 dau., Martha Jane. Prof. emeritus, former chmn. art dept. Okla. State U.; lectr. Assn. of Am. Colls. Art Project. Works owned by Bibliotheque Nationale, Paris, Victoria and Albert Mus., London, N.Y. Pub. Library Print Room, Library of Congress, Washington, Honolulu Acad. Fine Arts, Phila. Art Mus., Carnegie Inst. Fine Arts, Seattle Art Mus., Philbrook Art Mus., Okla. State Office Bldg. (mural), Met. Mus. Art N.Y.C., Dayton Art Mus., Butler Art Inst., Youngstown, Rockhill Nelson Mus., Kansas City, Joslyn Art Mus., Omaha, Dallas Mus. Fine Arts, Houston Art Mus., El Paso Mus. Art, U. Wyo. Art Mus., U. N.Mex. Art Mus., Beaumont Art Mus., Pa. Acad. Art, Phila. Bd. regents Mus. N.Mex.; spl. aquatint and 35 proofs for Soc. Am. Graphic Artists, 1978; mem. Hardwood adv. bd. U. N.Mex. Recipient awards: Henry B. Shope, Annual, 1949; Appelbaum, 1950; Jourdan Memorial, New Orleans, 1951; First Prize for Graphics, 1951; Audubon Gold Medal of Honor, 1951; Purchase award (casein), Joslyn Mus., 1952; Lovis Schwitzer award, L.S. Ayres Purchase award John Herron Art Museum, 1952; Black and White award Conn. Acad. Fine Arts, 1953; Boston Printmakers award, 1953; John Taylor Arms Meml. medal Audubon Artists, N.Y., 1954; M.C. Hewgley Award, Philbrook Art Center, 1957; NAD prize, 1961; purchase prize DePauw U., Nat. Print Exhbn., 1961; 1st award oils Fine Arts Mus. N.Mex., 1962; Samuel F.B. Morse medal NAD, 1965, Gumbacher award Allied Artists Am., 1972, award for achievement and excellence in visual arts Gov. of N.Mex., others. Mem. Soc. Am. Etchers, Chgo. Soc. Etchers, Ind. Soc. Print Makers, Print Makers Soc. Calif., Allied Artists Am., Nat. Soc. Painters in Casein and Acrylic (Michael M. Engel Meml. award 1978). Served with 47th Inf., 4th Div., World War I. Author: Doel Reed Makes an Aquatint, 1967. Address: PO Box 1244 Taos NM 87571

REED, DONNA, actress; b. Denison, Iowa; d. William R. and Hazel Mullenger; grad. Denison High Sch.; student Los Angeles City Coll., 1938-40; m. William Tuttle, Jan. 30, 1943 (div. 1944); m. 2d, Anthony I. Owen, June 15, 1945; children—Penny Jane, Anthony R., Timothy G., Mary Anne. In motion pictures: The Get-Away, Shadow of the Thin Man, The Bugle Sounds, The Courtship of Andy Hardy, 1941; Mokey, Apache Trail, Calling Dr. Gillespie, Eyes in the Night, Dr. Gillespie's Criminal Case, 1942; The Human Comedy, The Man From Down Under, Thousands Cheer, See Here, Private Hargrove, 1943; Gentle Annie, 1944; Picture of Dorian Gray, They Were Expendable, Faithful in My Fashion, 1945; It's a Wonderful Life, Green Dolphin Street, 1946; Beyond Glory, 1947; Chicago Deadline, 1948; The Hero, 1950; Scandal Sheet, 1951; Hangman's Noose, 1952; Barbarossa, 1952; Trouble Along the Way, The Caddy, Gun Fury, From Here to Eternity, 1953; Last Time I Saw Paris, The Far Horizons, 3 Hours to Kill, They Rode West, 1954; Ransom, Backlash, 1955; Benny Goodman Story, 1956; Beyond Mombasa, 1957; star The Donna Reed Show, ABC-TV, 1957-66. Recipient award best supporting actress Acad. Motion Picture Arts and Scis., 1954; named Princess Young Victory, Flathead Indian Tribes, 1952. Address: care Columbia Studios 300 S Colgems Sq Burbank CA*

REED, EUGENE D., elec. engr., lab. adminstr.; B.S., U. London, 1942; Ph.D. in Elec. Engring., Columbia, 1952. With Bell Labs., 1947—, exec. dir., 1966—; v.p. components Sandia Labs., Albuquerque, 1975—. Served with AUS, World War II. Fellow IEEE; mem. Nat. Acad. Engring. Contbr. papers to tech. jours. Home: 1319 Wagon Train Ct SE Albuquerque NM 87123 Office: PO Box 5800 Albuquerque NM 87115

REED, EVERETT CARLTON, indsl. textiles and plastics mfg. co. exec.; b. Woonsocket, R.I., Aug. 1, 1916; s. Everett T. and Ethel R. (Smith) R.; B.S. in Textile Engring., Lowell Technol. Inst., 1939, D.Sc.(hon.), 1975; m. Dorothy Robinson, Sept. 3, 1968; children—Deborah, David, Everett. With Albany (N.Y.) Internat. Corp., 1939—, chmn. bd., chief exec. officer, 1975—; dir. United Bank Corp. N.Y., State Bank of Albany. Hon. gov. Albany Med. Center Hosp.; dir. Gov. Clinton council Boy Scouts Am., Albany; trustee Siena Coll. Mem. Associated Industries N.Y. State, Am. Mgmt. Assn.

Club: Ft. Orange, Schuyler Meadows, Wolferts Roost Country. Home: 14 Sky Hollow Dr Albany NY 12204 Office: Albany Internat Corp PO Box 1907 Albany NY 12201

REED, FRANK OTHEMAN, clergyman, ednl. adminstr.; b. Auburn, N.Y., June 8, 1906; s. Harry Lathrop and Elsie Maynard (Otheman) R.; B.A., Yale, 1927; B.Th., Auburn Theol. Sem., 1932; M.Litt., Mansfield Coll., Oxford (Eng.) U., 1934; m. Grace Lovering Hosic, Sept. 1, 1932; children—David Hosic, Nancy Truesdale (Mrs. William P. Kellett), Margaret Otheman (Mrs. J. Lawrence Dunlap). Tchr. secondary sch. Hampton (Va.) Inst., 1927-29; ordained to ministry Presbyn. Ch., 1932; pastor in Trumansburg, N.Y., 1935-43, Ossining, N.Y., 1943-58; asso. prof. practical theology Auburn Theol. Sem. in assn. Union Theol. Sem., N.Y.C., 1958-71, adminstrv. dir. Auburn program, 1958-64, sec.-treas. Auburn Sem., 1964-71, dir. summer courses Union Theol. Sem., 1961-64; spl. asst. to pres. Eisenhower Coll., Seneca Falls, N.Y., 1971-72. Trustee, Presbytery Westchester (N.Y.), 1946-55, stated clk., 1957-60, moderator, 1954; stated clk. Presbytery Hudson River, 1961; asst. stated clk. Synod N.Y., 1959-64, stated clk., 1964-74; trustee Synod of N.E., 1974-75; moderator Presbytery Geneva, 1937; pres. Tompkins County Ministerial Assn., 1937. Pres. Ossining Council Social Agys., 1947; chaplain Ossining Police Dept., 1952-58; mem. Intersem. Commn. Tng. Rural Ministry, pres., 1962-64; municipal agt. for aging, Salisbury, Conn., 1973—. Bd. mgrs. Nat. Temperance Soc. and Publ. House, 1967—. Mem. Northeastern Assn. for Ch. and Soc. (pres. 1969-71), Hymn Soc. Am. (exec. com. 1971-76), Phi Beta Kappa. Rotarian. Address: PO Box 297 Salisbury CT 06068

REED, FREDERICK MCMASTER, lawyer, bus. exec.; b. Rutland, Vt., July 28, 1924; s. Reginald H. and Lucy (Pratt) R.; student Burr and Burton Sem., Manchester, Vt., Ill. Inst. Tech., 1943-44, U. Vt., 1946-47; LL.B., Albany Law Sch., 1950; m. Laurel Hansen, May 24, 1946; children—Mary, Martha Jo, Dorothy. Admitted to Vt. bar, 1950; partner Daniels & Reed, Montpelier, 1951-59; spl. counsel atty. gen. Vt., 1954, dep. atty. gen. Vt., 1955, atty. gen., 1956-60; gen. counsel Rock of Ages Corp., 1960—, clk. corp., 1965-67, v.p., 1967—; pvt. practice law, partner Bing & Reed, Williston, Vt., 1971-75; individual practice, 1975—; gen. counsel, sec. G.S. Blodgett Co., Inc., Burlington, Vt., 1974—, also dir.; sec., dir. Wyman's Inc. Montpelier; dir. Blodgett Supply Co., Inc., Burlington. Sec. Vt. Civil & Mil. Affairs, 1969-71; past prin. aide to gov. Vt. Chmn. Eastern Regional Conf. Attys. Gen., 1958. Trustee, Kellogg-Hubbard Library. Served as staff sgt., inf. AUS, 1943-45. Mem. Nat. Assn. Attys. Gen. (exec. com. 1957). Episcopalian. Home: Van Sicklen Rd Williston VT 05495 Office: Taftcor Bldg Williston VT 05495

REED, FREDRIC WILSON, banker; b. San Antonio, Nov. 8, 1913; s. Wilson Ham and Elsbeth (Hensel) R.; student Am. Inst. Banking, 1933-42, Grad. Sch. Banking, Rutgers U., 1957-59, Tex. A. and M. U., 1963, Am. Mgmt. Assn., N.Y.C., 1969; m. Carolyn Mae Cook, Aug. 15, 1937; 1 dau., Vicki Lynn (Mrs. David Rice). With Huth Seed Co., San Antonio, 1931-33; with Fed. Res. Bank Br., San Antonio, 1933-42, 46-54, San Antonio, El Paso, Dallas, 1956-64, v.p. in charge, El Paso Br., 1964—; bd. govs. Fed. Res. System, Wahsington, 1955; instr. Am. Inst. Banking Sch., 1960-61, N.M. Sch. Banking. Served to capt. USAAF, 1942-45. Decorated Bronze Star medal. Methodist. Rotarian. Home: 4433 N Stanton St El Paso TX 79902

REED, GEORGE FARRELL, physician; b. Oswego, N.Y., Oct. 25, 1922; s. George C. and Frances (Farrell) R.; A.B., Colgate U., 1944; M.D., Syracuse U., 1946; m. Jane Margaret Luke, June 28, 1947; children—Sally F., Lucy F., Nancy L., Margaret F. Intern, Syracuse U. Med. Center, 1946-47, USPHS, 1947-49; resident Mass. Eye and Ear Infirmary, Boston, 1949-52; practice medicine specializing in otolaryngology; faculty Harvard Med. Sch., Mass. Eye and Ear Infirmary, 1952-65; prof., chmn. dept. otolaryngology State U. N.Y. Upstate Med. Center, Syracuse, 1965-76, prof., 1976—, now dean Coll. Medicine, exec. v.p. Upstate Med. Center, mem. liaison com. on continuing med. edn. Bd. dirs. Clarke Sch. for Deaf, 1957-71. Diplomate Am. Bd. Ophthalmology and Otolaryngology (dir. 1956—, pres. 1976—). Mem. A.C.S., AMA, Am. Acad. Ophth© and Otolaryngology (rep. council med. splty. socs., sec. for continuing edn. 1968—), Am. Laryngol. Assn., Am. Laryngol., Rhinol. and Otol. Assn., Am. Soc. Head and Neck Surgery (pres. 1976-77), Am. Council Otology (pres. 1976-77), Am. Bronch-Esophageal Assn., Soc. Univ. Otolaryngologists (pres. 1975-76, Am. Acad. Facial Plastic and Reconstructive Surgery, Soc. Acad. Chmn. Otolaryngology (sec. 1974-75), Am. Assn. Med. Colls. (council deans). Home: 6982 Colonial Dr Fayetteville NY 13066 Office: Office of Dean Coll Medicine State U NY Upstate Med Center Syracuse NY 13210

REED, GEORGE FRANCIS, architect; b. Miami, Fla., Sept. 25, 1928; s. George Francis and Lillian Lucille (Hellerman) R.; B.S. in Architecture, Ga. Inst. Tech., 1951, B.Arch., 1953. Draftsman-designer Rufus Nims Architect, Miami, 1954-56; asso. architect Robert B. Browne Architect, Miami, 1957-60; pvt. practice architecture, Miami, 1961—; chmn. Miami Design Rev. Bd., 1967; Dade County (Fla.) Housing and Urban Devel. Adv. Bd., 1968—; pres. South Fla. Inter-Profl. Council, 1970-71; mem. Dade County Art In Public Bldgs. Adv. Bd., 1974-77; mem. Dade County Community Devel. Adv. Bd., 1975—; mem. Dade County Housing Planning Adv. Bd., 1977—. Pres. Coconut Grove Assn., Miami, 1972-73. Served to ensign USCGR, 1952. Recipient various awards for archtl. design and public service Soc. Am. Foresters, 1967, 70, 73, South Fla. Inter-Profl. Council, 1968, 69, 70, Met. Dade County, 1968, 77, 78, Housing Corp. Am., 1971. Fellow AIA (Fla. Assn. awards 1964, 67, 68, 69, 73, Fla. South chpt. awards 1964, 66, 67, 68, 75, 78, pres. Fla. South chpt. 1967). Office: 3050 Bird Ave Coconut Grove Miami FL 33133

REED, GEORGE FRANKLIN, lawyer, ins. exec.; b. Beaver, Pa., Jan. 19, 1935; s. Harold Francis and Mary Lou (Eckles) R.; student Mercersburg Acad., 1950-52; B.A., Princeton, 1956; J.D., U. Pa., 1959; m. Anne Stewart Dixon, May 5, 1962; children—George Franklin, Peter, Carolyn. Admitted to Pa. bar, 1960; asso. firm Morgan, Lewis & Bockius, Phila., 1960-67; gen. counsel Pa. Ins. Dept., Harrisburg, 1967-69; ins. commr. Commonwealth of Pa., Harrisburg, 1969-71; sr. v.p., counsel Am. Gen. Ins. Co., Houston, 1971—; chmn., dir. Am. Gen. Capital Mgmt., Inc., and also officer, director of nineteen registered investment companies managed by AGCM, 1976—. Chmn. state employees div. Tri-County United Fund, Harrisburg, 1969, bd. dirs., 1970-71. Mem. cabinet Gov. Raymond P. Shafer, 1969-71. Bd. regents Mercersburg Acad. Served with AUS, 1959-60, Pa. N.G., 1960-65. Recipient Distinguished Service award Harrisburg Jr. C. of C., 1969. Mem. Am., Tex., Pa. (chmn. young lawyers sect. 1968-69), Phila. (sec. Jr. Bar Conf. 1962-63) bar assns., Houston C. of C. (dir. 1974-75), Investment Company Institute (member of board of governors, 1977—). Republican. Presbyn. (elder). Clubs: Houston, Lakeside Country; Princeton (N.Y.C.). Home: 514 Clear Spring Dr Houston TX 77079 Office: 2727 Allen Pkwy Houston TX 77019

REED, GEORGE JOSEPH, govt. ofcl.; b. Haigler, Nebr., May 31, 1914; s. Edwin W. and Cleo (Randall) R.; A.B., Pasadena Coll., 1938, LL.D., 1953; postgrad. Eastern Nazarene Coll., 1957, U. So. Calif., 1948; m. Lois C. Goetze, Oct. 10, 1938; 1 son, George C. Probation officer Los Angeles County (Calif.), 1938-43; field rep. Calif. Youth Authority, Sacramento, 1946-49; dep. dir. Minn. Youth Correction Dept., 1948-53, chief div. delinquency prevention and parole, 1949-53; mem. U.S. Bd. Parole, 1953-65, chmn. bd., 1957-61; chief Parole and Probation of Nev., Carson City, 1965-67; dir. Lane County Juvenile Dept., Eugene, Oreg., 1968-69; chmn. U.S. Bd. Parole, Dept. Justice, Washington, 1969-73, vice chmn., 1973—. Adminstr. Interstate Compact Nev., 1965-67; mem. Commn. Model Code for Administering State Correctional System, 1966—. Chmn. gen. bd. Ch. of the Nazarene, 1970—. Served with USNR, 1942-45. Grantee for project Improved Parole Decision Making, 1970-72. Fellow Am. Soc. Criminology, Am. Acad. Criminology; mem. Nat. Parole Council (chmn. 1960-64), Nat. Council Crime and Delinquency (trustee, mem. profl. council 1950—), Am. Congress Corrections, Am. Law Inst., Am. Bar Assn. (mem. commn. to improve corrections 1970—, commn. improving adminstrn. correctional facilities). Club: Nat. Exchange (com. chmn. 1959-63). Contbr. chpts. to textbooks, articles to profl. publs. Home: 4201 Cathedral Ave NW Washington DC 20016 Office: 101 Indiana Ave NW Washington DC 20001

REED, GORDON WIES, mfg. exec.; b. Chgo., Nov. 20, 1899; s. Frank and Mary Catherine (Wies) R.; B.S., U. Ill., 1922; m. Naomi Bradley, Sept. 18, 1928; 1 son, Thomas; m. 2d, Genevieve Funston, Oct. 7, 1967. Vice pres. Hanley Co., Bradford, Pa., 1925-41; pres. Tex. Gulf Producing Co., Houston, 1941-45, chmn. bd., 1945-66; dir. AMAX Inc. (formerly Am. Metals Climax, Inc.), Greenwich, Conn., 1966—; dir. Putnam Trust Co., Greenwich, Conn. Asst. dir. aluminum magnesium div. W.P.B., 1941-45, spl. asst. to chmn., 1945, spl. asst. to chmn. surplus property bd., 1945, spl. asst. to chief of staff, USAF, 1950-60; chmn. Reed Com. on MATS, USAF, 1960. With Asso. Hosp. Service of N.Y., 1947-61. Trustee Greenwich Hosp. Assn. Republican (chmn. Conn. finance com.). Methodist (chmn. community ch.). Clubs: University, Links (N.Y.C.); Round Hill (Greenwich, Conn.); Blind Brook (Port Chester, N.Y.). Home: 100 Clapboard Ridge Rd Greenwich CT 06830 Office: AMAX Inc AMAX Center Greenwich CT 06830

REED, H. CARLYLE, newspaper pub.; b. Glendale, Ariz., July 9, 1915; s. Henry Clay and Blanche (List) R.; ed. Ariz. State Coll., Tempe, 1932-33, Woodbury Bus. Coll., 1933; m. Eleanor Pitkin, Mar. 31, 1962; children—Carolyn Scott, Darlene Harden; stepsons—Stan Pitkin, David Pitkin. Asst. editor Glendale News, 1934-36; with Central Ariz. Light & Power Co., 1936-38; pub. El Cajon (Calif.) Valley News, 1938-53; co-pub. La Mesa (Calif.) Scout, also gen. mgr. Intercity Press, pubs. and printers, 1938-52; pub. El Cajon Valley News, 1953-54; propr. Carlyle Reed & Assos., pub. relations cons., 1954-56; legis. rep. San Diego Union and Tribune, 1956; spl. rep. of dir. Calif. Dept. Water Resources, 1956-57; publishers ofcl. rep. Union-Tribune Pub. Co., San Diego, also legis. rep. Copley Newspapers, 1957-64; asst. to publisher Union Tribune, 1964-66; pub. Sacramento Union, 1966-75, pub. emeritus, 1975—, editorial columnist, 1978—; editorial columnist Panax Newspapers, 1978—; pres. Carlyle Reed & Assos., Sacramento, 1976—; v.p. Sierra Pub. Co., Sacramento, 1977—. Disaster acting gov. Calif., 1967—; mem., past chmn. Sacramento Host Com.; adv. bd. Golden Empire council Boy Scouts Am. Mem. adv. com Sacramento State U.; bd. dirs. Sacramento Symphony Assn. Mem. Sacramento City-County C. of C. (past bd. dirs., mem. exec. com.), Calif. Newspaper Pubs. Assn. (pres. 1977), Calif. Press Assn. (dir., pres. 1979), Sigma Delta Chi. Episcopalian. Clubs: Grandfathers of Am., Sutter (Sacramento); Del Paso Country. Home: 5094 Keane Dr Carmichael CA 95608 Office: 301 Capitol Mall Sacramento CA 95812. *We are engaged in this nation in a noble experiment in self-government by means of a republic in which the ultimate decisions rest with all of the people. Its yet-to-be achieved success is dependent on those people acting with full and accurate information and in a responsible manner. A career dedicated to attempting to accomplish some part of this goal becomes one of greatest importance and satisfaction.*

REED, H(ORACE) CURTIS, ins. co. exec.; b. Oneida, N.Y., May 6, 1917; s. Murry Eugene and Gertrude E. (Hicks) R.; student Hamilton Coll., Clinton, N.Y., 1934; B.S. in Bus. Adminstrn., Clarkson Coll. Tech., 1938; m. Loraine McVicar, Dec. 20, 1941; children—Janice Louise (Mrs. C.J. McNeill), Allan Curtis, Donald McVicar. With Travelers Ins. Co., 1946-59, dir. tng., sales research and promotion, 1950-54, sec., dir. group sales Travelers Nat. and Canadian Orgn., 1955-59; exec. v.p. Fed. Life and Casualty Co., Battle Creek, Mich., 1959-68, also dir.; pres., gen. mgr., dir. West Coast Life Ins. Co., San Francisco, 1968-73; pres., dir. First Farwest Corp., Portland, Oreg., 1974-75; chmn. bd., dir. First Farwest Life Ins. Co.; pres. Farwest Ins. Group, 1976-77; pres., dir. La Jolla Assos. Ltd. (Calif.), 1978—; v.p. Life Ins. Co. Calif., La Jolla, 1978—. Trustee, San Francisco Theol. Sem., 1972-75. Served from pvt. to maj. AUS, 1941-45. Named Man of Year Hartford (Conn.) Jr. C. of C., 1952, Outstanding Industrialist of Year Mich., 1967; recipient Golden Knight award Clarkson Coll., 1973. Home: 324 Via Chica Ct Solana Beach CA 92075 Office: 11011 N Torrey Pines Rd La Jolla CA 92038

REED, HUGH, JR., lawyer; b. Centre, Ala., Aug. 1, 1910; s. Hugh and Clyde (Walden) R.; A.B., U. Ala., 1931, LL.B., 1934, J.D., 1969; m. Iris McGritt, Aug. 10, 1950. Admitted to Ala. bar, 1934; currently partner firm Reed & Reed, Centre; dir. Cherokee County Bank, Centre Mfg. Co. Mem. Ala. Bar Assn., Am. Bar Assn., Sigma Phi Epsilon, Phi Alpha Delta. Democrat. Methodist. Clubs: Cherokee County Country, Founders of U. Ala. Home: 202 Iris Dr Centre AL 35960 Office: 120 S River St Centre AL 35960

REED, IRVING STOY, elec. engr., computer scientist, educator; b. Seattle, Nov. 12, 1923; s. Irving McKenny and Eleanor Doris (Stoy) R.; student U. Alaska, 1940-42; B.S. in Math., Calif. Inst., Tech., 1944, Ph.D., 1949; m. Bernice Margaret Schmidt, Dec. 11, 1965; children—Henry, Mark, Thomas, Irving, Ann. Asso. group leader Lincoln Lab., M.I.T. Lexington, 1951-60, cons., 1972—; sr. staff mem. Rand Corp., Santa Monica, Calif., 1960-63, cons., 1963—; asso. prof. elec. engring. and computer sci. U. So. Calif., Los Angeles, 1963-64, prof., 1964—; Charles Lee Powell prof. computer engring., 1978—; research affiliate Jet Propulsion Lab., Calif. Inst. Tech., Pasadena, 1967—; dir. Tech. Service Corps., Santa Monica, Calif., 1967—; cons. to com. on undersea warfare Nat. Acad. Scis., 1971-73. Served with USNR, 1944-46. Fellow IEEE; mem. Nat. Avad. Engring., Am. Math. Soc., Math. Assn. Am., N.Y. Acad. Scis., Soc. Indsl. and Applied Math. Club: Masons. Author: (with Bartee and Lebow) Theory Design of Digital Machines, 1962. Contbr. articles on math., computer logic, coding theory, radar detection theory to profl. jours. Patentee computer circuits and systems; research pioneer in automatic processing of radar data, multiple-error-correcting communication codes, logical design of digital computers. Home: 348 15th St Santa Monica CA 90402 Office: Dept Elec Engring U So Calif Los Angeles CA 90007. *Undoubtedly my broad interests, creativity and tenacity to bring work to a successful concludion are a direct result of the freedom and rigours of a frontier background and the guidance of rather remarkable parents.*

REED, ISHMAEL SCOTT, writer; b. Chattanooga, Feb. 22, 1938; s. Bennie Stephen and Thelma (Coleman) R.; m. Carla Blank; children—Timothy Brett, Tennessee Maria. Dir., Reed & Cannon Co.; co-pub. Y'Bird mag. Author: (novels) The Free-Lance Pallbearers, 1967, Yellow Back Radio Broke Down, 1969, Mumbo Jumbo, 1972, The Last Days of Louisiana Red, 1974, Flight to Canada, 1976; Shrovetide in Old New Orleans, 1978; (poetry) Catechism of the Neo-American HooDoo Church, 1970, Conjure, 1972, Chattanooga, 1973; Secretary to the Spirits, 1978; editor (anthology) 19 Necromancers From Now, 1970. Collaborator (with Carla Blank and Suzushi Hanayagi) in multi media Bicentennial mystery The Lost State of Franklin; sr. lectr. U. Calif. at Berkeley; mem. usage panel Am. Heritage Dictionary. Pres., Before Columbus Found. Recipient award Nat. Inst. Arts and Letters, 1975, ACLU, 1978; winner Poetry in Pub. Places contest, 1975, Michaux award, 1978; Nat. Endowment for Arts writing fellow, 1974; Guggenheim fellow, 1975. Mem. Author's Guild Am., P.E.N. Address: 2140 Shattuck Ave Room 311 Berkeley CA 94704

REED, J. WALTER, advt. agy. exec.; b. Bklyn., Mar. 14, 1933; s. Philip and Kate (Lichtman) R.; M.S. in Math., Bklyn. Coll., 1956; m. Eileen Zucker, Dec. 22, 1957; children—Lauren Beth, Philip. Acctg. clk. Katz Agy., N.Y.C., 1956-57; estimator, time buyer Harry B. Cohen Inc., N.Y.C., 1957-60; time buyer Foote, Cone & Belding Advt. Inc., N.Y.C., 1960-62, media supr., 1963-69, asso. media dir., 1969-74, v.p., media dir., 1974-78, sr. v.p. media and adminstrv. services, 1978—, also mem. exec. com.; broadcast supr. Lawrence C. Gumbinner, N.Y.C., 1963; dir. Walstrom/FCB. Mem. budget adv. com., Roslyn Sch. Dist., 1969-79; v.p. Strathmore Civic Assn., 1972-74; commr. civil preparedness Village of East Hills (N.Y.), 1973-74. Served with U.S. Army, 1953-55. Mem. Am. Assn. Advt. Agys. (chmn. radio/TV com.), Internat. Radio and TV Soc., Radio/TV Arts and Scis. Democrat. Jewish. Home: 25 Primrose Ln East Hills NY 11577 Office: Foote Cone & Belding 200 Park Ave New York NY 10017

REED, JERRY, musician, composer, singer; b. Atlanta, Mar. 20, 1937; m. Priscilla Mitchell; children—Seidina, Lottie. Part time disc jockey Radio sta. WGST, Atlanta, 1953-55; with Capitol Records, Atlanta, 1955-59; Columbia Records, Nashville, 1961-63; RCA Records, Nashville, 1963—; music for films W.W. and the Dixie Dance Kings, Gator, Smokey and the Bandit; personal appearances with Masters Festival of Music. Records include Amos Moses, When You're Hot, You're Hot, East Bound and Down. Composer: Guitar Man, U.S. Male, Tupelo Mississippi Flash, When You're Hot, You're Hot. Address: care Jerry Reed Enterprises 1107 18th Ave S Nashville TN 37212

REED, JOHN ALTON, judge; b. Washington, June 29, 1931; s. John Alton and Emma Powers (Ball) R.; A.B., Duke U., 1954, LL.B., 1956; m. Louisa Wardman, June 6, 1953; children—Donna, Joanne, Deborah. Admitted to Fla. bar, 1956; asso. firm Fowler-White, Tampa, Fla., 1956-57; partner firm Rush, Reed & Marshall, Orlando, Fla., 1957-67; judge Fla. 4th Dist. Ct. Appeal, 1967-73, chief judge, 1971-73; judge U.S. Dist. Ct. for Middle Dist. Fla., Orlando, 1973—. Mem. Am., Orange County, Fla. bar assns., Am. Judicature Soc. Republican. Episcopalian. Home: 1100 S Orlando Ave Maitland FL 32751 Office: 80 N Hughey Ave Orlando FL 32801

REED, JOHN FRANKLIN, instrument mfg. co. exec.; b. Winfield, Mo., Aug. 10, 1917; s. Claude F. and Inez (Crenshaw) R.; B.S. in Mining Engring., Mo. Sch. Mines and Metallurgy, 1940; m. Ann M. Walter Aug. 31, 1940; children—John Franklin, James D., Thomas W., William C., Robert D. Indsl. engr. Tenn. Coal Iron R.R. Co., 1940-42; time study methods engr. McDonnell Aircraft Corp., 1943; prodn. planner, chief estimator Fairchild Aircraft Co., 1944; joined Manning, Maxwell & Moore, Inc., Stratford, Conn., 1944, works mgr., Tulsa, then Shaw Box, Crane and Hoist div., Muskegon, Mich., 1951-57, gen. mgr., 1957-59, v.p., gen. mgr., 1959, exec. v.p., 1959-62, pres., chief exec. officer, dir., 1962-65; pres., dir. Manning, Maxwell and Moore of Can., Ltd., Galt, Ont., 1962-65; exec. v.p. Hupp Corp., 1965-67, pres., dir., 1967-68; pres., chief exec., dir. Hercules Galion Products, Inc. (O.), 1968-69; chmn., chief exec. officer, dir. Canrad-Hanovia Inc., Newark, 1969—. Registered profl. engr., Mo. Mason. Club: Imperial (Naples, Fla.). Home: 745 Willowhead Dr Naples FL 33940 Office: Canrad-Hanovia Inc 100 Chestnut St Newark NJ 07105

REED, JOHN FREDERICK, educator; b. Rockport, Maine, Nov. 18, 1911; s. Marshall Everett and Linthel C. (Ripley) R.; A.B., Dartmouth, 1933; M.A., Duke, 1935, Ph.D., 1936; m. Mildred Gant Stites, Dec. 29, 1934 (dec.); children—John Francis, Robert Marshall, James Roger; m. 2d, Beatrice Costello Crosby, Nov. 10, 1969. Instr. natural scis. Amarillo (Tex.) Coll., 1936-38; from instr. to asso. prof. biology Baldwin-Wallace Coll., 1938-46; from asst. prof. to prof. botany U. Wyo., 1946-56; mem. faculty U. N.H., 1956-62, prof. botany, dean Grad. Sch., 1956-62, dean Coll. Liberal Arts, 1959-61, v.p., 1961, acting pres., 1961-62; pres. Fort Lewis Coll., Durango, Colo., 1962-69, pres. emeritus, 1969—, prof. botany, 1962-69; sect. head ecology and systematic biology NSF, 1969-70; prof. Coll. Environ. Scis. U. Wis., Green Bay, 1970—, chmn. concentration in eco-systems analysis, 1970-72, dean acad. affairs, 1975-77. Technician, Pedo-bot. Mission to Ruanda-Urundi, Africa, 1951-52; cons. environ. biology NSF, 1956-58; mem. Com. on Radioactive Waste Mgmt. NRC; mem. council NIH Nat. Inst. Dental Research, 1959-63, mem. dental tng. com., 1967-68; mem. commn. on plans and objectives for higher edn. Am. Council on Edn.; chmn. U.S. nat. com. for internat. biol. program Nat. Acad. Scis.-NRC, 1972-74; mem. U.S. com. for man and the biosphere UNESCO, 1974-76, U.S. nat. commn. for UNESCO, 1972-78; mem. com. on internat. environ. programs Nat. Acad. Scis.-NRC, 1973-75. Fellow AAAS; mem. Ecol. Soc. Am. (sec. 1953-57, pres. 1963), Brit. Ecol. Soc., Am. Soc. Range Mgmt., Phi Beta Kappa, Sigma Xi, Phi Delta Kappa, Phi Kappa Phi, Phi Sigma. Address: 2745 N Nicolet Dr Green Bay WI 54301 Office: Coll Environmental Scis U Wis-Green Bay 120 S University Circle Dr Green Bay WI 54302

REED, JOHN HATHAWAY, contracting co. exec., former ambassador; b. Fort Fairfield, Maine, Jan. 5, 1921; s. Walter and Eva Ruth (Seeley) R.; B.S., U. Maine, 1942, LL.D. (hon.), 1960; LL.D. (hon.), Ricker Coll.; grad. Harvard Naval Supply Sch., 1944; m. Cora Mitchell Davison, Mar. 24, 1944; children—Cheryl, Ruth. Officer, Reed Farms, Inc., Fort Fairfield, Maine, 1948—; pres. Aroostook Raceway, Inc., 1958-59; adv. com. Fort Fairfield br. No. Nat. Bank of Presque Isle; mem. Nat. Transp. Safety Bd., Washington, 1967—, chmn., 1969-75; ambassador to Sri Lanka, Colombo, 1975-77; dir. govt. relations Asso. Builders & Contractors, Inc., Washington, 1978—; chmn. exec. com. Nat. Govs. Conf. Rep., Fort Fairfield to Maine Legislature, 1954-56; mem. Senate, 1957-59, pres. Senate, 1959-60; gov. Maine, 1960-67. Pres. bd. Community Gen. Hosp., Fort Fairfield, 1952-54, No. Maine Fair, 1953-59; trustee Ricker Coll., 1953-60, Oak Grove Sch., Vassalboro, Maine. Served to lt. (j.g.), USNR, 1942-46. Mem. Am. Legion, VFW, Grange, Maine Assn. Agrl. Fairs (pres. 1956). Republican. Congregationalist. Clubs: Driving (pres. 1950-53) (Fort Fairfield); Capital Hill, Rotary, Masons, K.P. Home: 410 O St SW Washington DC 20024 Office: 444 N Capital St NW Washington DC 20001

REED, JOHN SHEDD, ry. exec.; b. Chgo., June 9, 1917; s. Kersey Coates and Helen May (Shedd) R.; student Chgo. Latin Sch., Hotchkiss Sch.; B.S. in Indsl. Adminstrn., Yale, 1939; grad. Advanced Mgmt. Program, Harvard, 1955; m. Marjorie Lindsay, May 4, 1946;

children—Ginevra, Keith, Helen, Peter, John Shedd. With A.T. & S.F. Ry., 1939—, test dept. asst., successively spl. rep. to gen. supt. transp., Chgo., transp. insp., Amarillo, Tex., trainmaster, Slaton, Tex., Pueblo, Colo., supt. Mo. div., Marceline, Mo., asst. to v.p., Chgo., exec. asst. to pres., 1957-59, v.p. finance, 1959-64, v.p. exec. dept., 1964-67, pres., 1967-78, chief exec. officer, 1968—, chmn. bd., 1973—, dir., 1963—; pres., dir. Santa Fe Industries, Inc., 1968-78, chmn. bd., chief exec. officer, 1973—; dir. No. Trust Co., Kraft, Inc. Served with USNR, 1940-45. Clubs: Chicago, Old Elm, Shoreacres, Onwentsia (Lake Forest). Home: 301 W Laurel Ave Lake Forest IL 60045 Office: 80 E Jackson Blvd Chicago IL 60604

REED, JOHN WESLEY, lawyer, educator; b. Independence, Mo., Dec. 11, 1918; s. Novus H. and Lilian (Houchens) R.; A.B., William Jewell Coll., 1939; LL.B., Cornell U., 1942; LL.M., Columbia, 1949, Jur. Sc.D., 1957; m. Dorothy Elaine Floyd, Mar. 5, 1961; children—Alison A., John M. (dec.), Mary V., Randolph F., Suzanne M. Admitted to Mo. bar, 1942, Mich. bar, 1953; with firm Stinson, Mag, Thomson, McEvers & Fizzell, Kansas City, Mo., 1942-46; asso. prof. law U. Okla., 1946-49; asso. prof., then prof. law U. Mich., 1949-64, prof. law, 1968—; prof. law, dean Law Sch., U. Colo., 1964-68; dir. Inst. Continuing Legal Edn., prof. law Wayne State U., 1968-73; vis. prof. N.Y. U., 1949, U. Chgo., 1960, Yale, 1963-64; mem. Salzburg (Austria) Seminar Am. Studies, 1962, chmn., 1964. Mem. bd. mgrs. of ministers and missionaries benefit bd. Am. Baptist Chs./U.S.A., 1967-74, 76—, pres., 1967-74; mem. com. visitors Judge Adv. Gen.'s Sch., U.S. Army, 1971-77. Trustee Kalamazoo Coll., 1954-64, 68-74. Acad. fellow Internat. Soc. Barristers; mem. Colo. (bd. govs. 1964-68), Am. (council litigation sect.) bar assns., Assn. Am. Law Sch. (mem. exec. com. 1965-67), Am. Acad. Jud. Edn. (v.p.). Author: (with W.W. Blume) Cases and Statutes on Pleading and Joinder, 1952; (with others) Introduction to Law and Equity, 1953; Annual Advocacy Handbooks, 1963-74, 79—; also articles. Editor-in-chief Cornell Law Quar., 1941-42. Home: 3586 E Huron River Dr Ann Arbor MI 48104 Office: Hutchins Hall Ann Arbor MI 48109

REED, JOSEPH WAYNE, JR., educator; b. St. Petersburg, Fla., May 31, 1932; s. Joseph Wayne and Gertrude (Cain) R.; B.A., Yale, 1954, M.A., 1958, Ph.D., 1961; m. Lillian Craig (Kit), Dec. 10, 1955; children—Joseph McKean, John Craig, Katherine Hyde. Research asst. Yale Library, 1956-57; instr. Wesleyan U., Middletown, Conn., 1960-61, asst. prof., 1961-67, asso. prof., 1967-71, prof. English, 1971—, chmn. dept., 1971-73, 75-76; vis. lectr. Yale, 1974; lectr. U.S. Dept. State and USIS, Can., India, Nepal, 1974. Painter, group shows include Ponce Museum, P.R., 1970, Soc. Miniature Painters, Engravers and Sculptors, Washington, 1971, Nat. Miniaturists Show, Nutley, N.J., 1972; one man show Portal Gallery, London, Eng., 1971, USIS Library, New Delhi, 1974. Served to lt. (j.g.) USNR, 1954-56. Mem. Modern Lang. Assn., Elizabethan Club, The Johnsonians. Democrat. Episcopalian. Author: English Biography in the Early Nineteenth Century, 1801-38, 1966; Faulkner's Narrative, 1973. Editor: Barbara Bodichon's American Diary, 1972; (with W.S. Lewis) Horace Walpole's Family Correspondence, 1973; (with F.A. Pottle) Boswell, Laird of Auchinleck, 1977. Home: 45 Lawn Ave Middletown CT 06457

REED, JOYCE ANN BORDEN, engring. cons. co. exec.; b. Montreal, Que., Can., Nov. 8, 1939; d. Alfred Ernest and Alice (Greenfield) Borden; B.C.L., McGill U. (Can.), 1962; m. Gordon Arthur Daniel Reed, Aug. 24, 1964; children—Barbara Alison, John Harold Borden. With No. Electric Co. Ltd., Montreal, 1962—, sec., counsel, 1975, dir., 1974; v.p., gen. counsel, corporate sec. SNC Enterprises Ltd., 1974—, Surveyer, Nenninger & Chenevert Inc. and subsidiaries. Bd. dirs. Mechanics Inst. Library, Montreal. Mem. English Speaking Union (dir., pres. Montreal br., chmn. Que. br. 1979-80), Chartered Inst. Secs., Am. Assn. Corporate Secs., Can., Que. bar assns., Internat. Law Assn., Internat. Licensing Assn. Home: 60 Melbourne Ave Montreal PQ H3P 1G1 Canada Office: 1 Place des Jardins Montreal PQ Canada

REED, KENNETH G., petroleum co. exec.; b. 1917; ed. U. Tex.; married. With Amerada Petroleum Corp., Tulsa, 1948-70, sr. v.p., 1967-70; exec. v.p. internat. operations Amerada Hess Corp., N.Y.C., 1970; pres., chief exec. officer APEXCO, Inc., Tulsa, 1971-77; pres., chief exec. officer Natomas Internat. Corp., 1977—, also dir.; exec. v.p. exploration and prodn. Natomas Co., San Francisco, 1977—, also dir.; dir. Natomas N. Am. Inc., 1st Nat. Bank & Trust Co., Tulsa. Address: Natomas Co 601 California St San Francisco CA 94108

REED, KIT (LILLIAN CRAIG), writer; b. San Diego, June 7, 1932; d. John Rich and Lillian (Hyde) Craig; B.A. in English, Coll. Notre Dame, Balt., 1954; m. Joseph Wayne Reed, Jr., Dec. 10, 1955; children—Joseph, John, Katherine. Reporter St. Petersburg (Fla.) Times, 1954-55, New Haven Register, 1956-59; free-lance, 1959—. Vis. prof. English, Wesleyan U., 1974—; USIS lectr. in India, 1974. Named New Eng. Newspaperwoman of Year, New Eng. Women's Press Assn., 1958, 59; Guggenheim fellow, 1964-65; grantee Abraham Woursell Found., 1966-71; Rockefeller fellow Aspen (Colo.) Inst. for Humanistic Studies, 1976. Mem. P.E.N., Authors Guild, Writers Guild Am. (East). Roman Catholic. Author: Mother Isn't Dead, She's Only Sleeping, 1961; At War as Children, 1964; The Better Part, 1967; Mr. Da V. and Other Stories, 1967; Armed Camps, 1969; Cry of the Daughter, 1971; Tiger Rag, 1973; Captain Grownup, 1976; The Killer Mice, 1976; The Ballad of T. Rantula, 1979; Magic Time, 1980; (radio play) The Bathyscaphe, 1979; also short stories. Address: 45 Lawn Ave Middletown CT 06457

REED, LESTER JAMES, educator, biochemist; b. New Orleans, Jan. 3, 1925; s. John T. and Sophie (Pastor) R.; B.S., Tulane U., 1943, D.Sc. (hon.), 1977; Ph.D., U. Ill., 1946; m. Janet Louise Gruschow, Aug. 7, 1948; children—Pamela, Sharon, Richard, Robert. Research asst. NDRC, Urbana, Ill., 1944-46; research asso. biochemistry Cornell U. Med. Coll., 1946-48; faculty U. Tex., Austin, 1948—, prof. chemistry, 1958—; research scientist Clayton Found. Biochem. Inst., 1949—, asso. dir., 1962-63, dir., 1963—. Mem. Nat. Acad. Scis. U.S., Am. Soc. Biol. Chemists, Am. Chem. Soc. (Eli Lilly & Co. award in biol. chemistry 1958), Phi Beta Kappa, Sigma Xi. Contbr. articles profl. jours. Home: 3502 Balcones Dr Austin TX 78731

REED, PAUL ALLEN, artist; b. Washington, Mar. 28, 1919; s. Charles Miler and Lula Rachael (Annadale) R.; student San Diego State Coll., 1936, Corcoran Sch. Art, 1937; m. Esther Kishter, July 10, 1939; children—Jean Reed Roberts, Thomas, Robert. Asst. art dir. USAF mag., N.Y.C., 1942-44; artist B.D. Adams Advt. Agy., Montclair, N.J., 1944-48; asst. art dir. M.F. Dreher Advt. Agy., N.Y.C., 1948-50; free lance graphics designer, Washington, 1950-62; graphics dir. U.S. Peace Corps, Washington, 1962-71; asst. prof. Corcoran Sch. Art, Washington, 1971—; exhibited in one man shows at Corcoran Gallery Art, 1966, Washington U., 1967, Ariz. State U., 1971, Phoenix Art Mus., 1977; represented in permanent collections at Nat. Coll. Fine Arts, Corcoran Gallery, San Francisco Mus. Art, Detroit Inst. Art; artist in residence Phoenix Art Mus., 1976. Home: 3541 N Utah St Arlington VA 22207

REED, PHILIP DUNHAM, former corp. exec.; b. Milw., Nov. 16, 1899; s. William Dennis and Virginia Brandreth (Dunham) R.; B.S. in Elec. Engring., U. Wis., 1921, LL.D., 1950; LL.B. cum laude, Fordham U., 1924; LL.D., Union Coll., 1941, Bklyn. Poly. Inst., 1942, Swarthmore Coll., 1954; D.C.S., N.Y. U., 1950; E.D., Rensselaer Poly. Inst., 1941; m. Mabel Mayhew Smith, July 16, 1921; children—Philip Dunham, Kathryn Virginia. With Pennie, Davis, Marvin & Edmonds, lawyers, 1921-22; v.p., patent counsel Van Heusen Products, Inc., 1922-26; with law dept. Gen. Electric Co., 1926-37, asst. to pres. and dir., 1938-39, chmn. bd., 1940-42, 45-58, chmn. fin. com., 1946-59, ret., dir. emeritus, 1968—; dir. Fed. Res. Bank of N.Y., 1959-65, chmn. bd., 1960-65; dir. Tiffany and Co., Cowles Communications, Inc.; past dir. Am. Express Co., Bankers Trust Co., Bigelow-Sanford Inc., Eurofund Internat. Inc., Elfun Trusts, Kraft Corp., Met. Life Ins. Co., Otis Elevator Co., Scott Paper Co.; sr. cons. to dir. of priorities Office Prodn. Mgmt., 1941, dept. dir. materials div., July-Dec. 1941; cons. U.S. del. Conf. on World Orgn., San Francisco, 1945. Vice chmn. bus. adv. council Dept. Commerce (now Bus. Council), 1951-52, mem., 1940—; mem. U.S. adv. com. on info., 1948-61; chmn. U.S. del. Anglo-Am. Council on Productivity, 1948-52; trustee Com. for Econ. Devel., mem. research, policy com., 1946-75, chmn., 1948-49; bd. dirs. Internat. Exec. Service Corps., 1964—, chmn. exec. com., 1966-74; trustee Eisenhower Exchange Fellowships, 1953-75, vice chmn., 1955-75, chmn. fin. com. 1956-58; trustee Winston Churchill Found. of U.S., 1970-75. Chief bur. industries WPB, Jan.-July 1942; dep. chief of U.S. Mission for Econ. Affairs, London, Eng., 1942-43, chief of mission with rank of minister, Oct. 1943-Jan. 1945. Recipient President's Certificate of Merit award, 1947; decorated officer Legion of Honor (France), 1947, comdr., 1951. Mem. Internat. C. of C. (exec. com. U.S. council 1945—, chmn. 1945-48, pres. chamber 1949-51, now hon. pres.), Council on Fgn. Relations (dir. 1946-69, dir. emeritus 1969—). Republican. Conglist. Clubs: University, Links (N.Y.C.); Apawamis (Rye, N.Y.); Blind Brook (Port Chester, N.Y.); Bohemian (San Francisco); Clove Valley Rod and Gun (Dutchess County, N.Y.); Mill Reef (Antigua, W.I.). Home: Rye NY 10580 Office: 375 Park Ave New York City NY 10022

REED, REX, author, critic; b. Ft. Worth, Tex., Oct. 2, 1938; s. Jimmy M. and Jewell (Smith) R.; B.A., La. State U., 1960. Film critic Holiday mag., Women's Wear Daily, 1968-71; music critic Stereo Rev., 1968-75; syndicated columnist Chgo. Tribune-N.Y. Times Syndicate, 1971—; film critic N.Y. Daily News, 1971-75; appeared in film Myra Breckenridge, 1970, Superman, 1978. Author: Do You Sleep in the Nude?, 1968; Conversations in the Raw, 1969; Big Screen, Little Screen, 1971; People Are Crazy Here, 1974; Valentines and Vitriol, 1977; Travolta to Keaton, 1979. Address: care NY Daily News 220 E 42d St New York NY 10017*

REED, REX RAYMOND, telephone co. exec.; b. Peterson, Iowa, Mar. 19, 1922; s. Charles Bernard and Dagmar Helen (Heick) R.; student Morningside Coll., 1940-41, U. Notre Dame, 1943-44; B.S. in Gen. Engring., Iowa State U., 1947; m. Rita Compton, Dec. 3, 1944; children—Julie, Nancy, Linda. With Northwestern Bell Telephone Co., various locations, 1947-60, 61-66, employee info. mgr., pub. relations dept., Omaha, 1957-58, gen. comml. mgr., comml. dept., Fargo, N.D., 1958-60, asst. v.p. personnel and employment, 1961-62, asst. v.p. personnel, Nebr. area, 1962-64, asst. v.p. personnel and labor relations, 1964-66; with AT&T Corp., N.Y.C., 1960-61, 66-70, dir. labor relations, personnel dept., 1970-71, asst. v.p. labor relations, 1971—, v.p. labor relations and corporate policy seminar, 1975—; dir. Ind. Bell Telephone Co. Mem. Madison (N.J.) Bd. Edn., 1969-70, pres., 1971-75. Trustee, Menninger Found., Topeka, 1979—, Morristown (N.J.) Meml. Hosp., 1977—. Served with USMC, 1943-46, to capt., 1951-53. Mem. Bus. Roundtable (chmn. labor-mgmt. com. 1977-77), Labor Policy Assn. (chmn. 1979—), Inst. Collective Bargaining (bd. dirs. 1976—). Club: Morris Golf (Morristown, N.J.). Home: 100 Garfield Ave Madison NJ 07940 Office: 295 N Maple Ave Basking Ridge NJ 07920

REED, RICHARD JOHN, educator; b. Braintree, Mass., June 18, 1922; s. William Amber and Gertrude (Volk) R.; B.S., Cal. Inst. Tech., 1945; Sc.D., Mass. Inst. Tech., 1949; m. Joan Murray, June 10, 1950; children—Ralph Murray, Richard Cobden, Elizabeth Ann. Research staff Mass. Inst. Tech., Cambridge, 1949-54; prof. meteorology U. Wash., Seattle, 1954—; cons. U.S. Navy, USAF, U.S. Army, NSF, NASA, Nat. Oceanic and Atmospheric Adminstrn. Served with USNR, 1942-46. Recipient Meisinger award Am. Meterol. Soc., 1964. Mem. Nat. Acad. Scis., Am. Meteorol. Soc. (councilor 1967-74 pres. 1972; 2d Half Century award 1972), Am. Geophys. Union, AAAS. Editor: Jour. Applied Meteorology, 1966-68. Contbr. articles to profl. jours. Home: 13216 42d Ave NE Seattle WA 98125

REED, ROBERT DANIEL, publisher; b. Pottsville, Pa., May 24, 1941; s. Robert Daniel and Thelma June (Weiss) R.; m. Kathy Sonja Cvitanich, Dec. 15, 1963; children—Robert Duane, Alan Andrija, Tanya, Kathy. Purchasing mgr. Ogden Tech. Labs., Sunnyvale, Calif., 1962-69; mktg. mgr. Plaza Press, Sunnyvale, 1969-70; pub. R & E Research Assos., Inc., San Francisco, 1971—, also pres. Served with U.S. Army, 1959-61. Mem. Center for Democratic Instns., Nat. Small Bus. Assn., Calif. Inventors Council, Smithsonian Instn., Soc. for Scholarly Pub. Lutheran. Inventor electro mech.-electronics devices. Author: We Care Cookbook, 1974; (handbooks) How and Where To Research Your Ethnic-American Cultural Heritage: 1, Irish Americans, 2, Black Americans, 3, Mexican Americans, 4, Chinese Americans, 5, Japanese Americans, 6, Native Americans; also published more than 500 books on human rights and Am. history. Home: 18581 McFarland Ave Saratoga CA 95070 Office: 936 Industrial Ave Palo Alto CA 94303. *Spend your life doing what you like to do, by putting all your efforts into it. Don't be afraid to take a chance. Remember, if life gets dull-Risk it a bit.*

REED, ROBERT GEORGE, III, petroleum co. exec.; b. Cambridge, Mass., Aug. 9, 1927; s. Robert George and Marjorie (Furber) R.; B.A., Dartmouth Coll., 1949; grad. Advanced Mgmt. Program, Harvard Bus. Sch., 1970; m. Maggie L. Fisher, Mar. 22, 1974; children—Sandra R. McNickle, Valerie, Jonathan J., John-Paul. Prin., Robert G. Reed Co., Boston, 1949-57; trainee Tidewater Oil Co., Phila., 1957, asst. mgr., N.Y.C., 1958, mktg. mgr. Eastern div., 1958-61, home office mktg. mgr., Los Angeles, 1961-64, asst. gen. mgr. Western div., 1964; retail mktg. mgr. Cities Service Oil Co., Tulsa, 1964-66, v.p. mktg., dir., 1966-72; group v.p. refining, mktg. and transp. Tesoro Petroleum Corp., San Antonio, 1972-76, exec. v.p., 1976-79; chmn. bd., chief exec. officer Clark Oil & Refining Corp., Milw., 1979—. Bd. dirs. Milw. Symphony, DePaul Rehab. Hosp. Served with USNR, 1945-46. Mem. Nat. Petroleum Refiners Assn. (dir. 1973—), Am. Petroleum Inst. (gen. com. mktg. 1963-64, 69-76, budget and planning com. 1969-77). Clubs: Milw. Country, Milw. Athletic, Univ. Home: 2505 N Wahl Ave Milwaukee WI 53211 Office: 8530 W National Ave Milwaukee WI 53227

REED, ROBERT HOLBROOKE, educator; b. Anadarko, Okla., Sept. 29, 1922; s. Otie Watson and Mattie Elizabeth (Ratliffe) R.; B.S., U. Calif. at Berkeley, 1949, M.S., 1953, Ph.D., 1961; m. Luise Antonina Rosalewski, June 11, 1950; children—Elisabeth Luise, Susan Holly. Agrl. economist U. Honolulu, 1952-53; mgmt. trainee Del Monte Foods Co., San Francisco, 1953-54, plant foreman, Emeryville, Calif., 1954-55; agrl. economist, asso. exptl. sta. econ. research service U.S. Dept. Agr. and U. Calif. at Berkeley, 1955-60; research economist United Fruit Co., LaLima, Honduras, 1960-61; agrl. economist Econ. Research Service, Berkeley, 1962-65; prof. agrl. econs. U. Wis., Madison, 1965—; cons. in field, Columbia, 1966, Ecuador, 1976, Azores, 1979; prof. U. Wis./AID, Universidade Fed. do Rio Grande do Sul, Porto Alegre, Brazil, 1968-72; vis. scholar U. Calif. at Berkeley, 1974. Served with AUS, 1940-45; ETO. Grantee U. Calif., Econ. Research Service, 1974—. Mem. Nat. and Internat. Agrl. Econs. Assn., Am. Econ. Assn., Am. Mgmt. Assn. Club: British (Porto Alegre). Author: Economia de Comercializacao, 1971. Home: 904 Arden Ln Madison WI 53711. *Personal achievement, however measured, is a major component of a free society, characterized by the remarkable challenges of rapid scientific and social developments of recent years.*

REED, ROBERT OLIVER, actor; b. London, Eng., Feb. 13, 1938; s. Peter and Marcia (Andrews) R.; student Homewood House, Ewell Castle Sch.; children—Mark Thurloe, Sarah. Prin. films include Women in Love, The Devils, Oliver, Three Musketeers, Tommy, Royal Flash, Prince and the Pauper. Vice pres. Rosslyn Park Rugby Club, 1973—. Served with Brit. Army. Named Master Arts and Sci., Musketeer, (France). Club: White Elephant (London). Office: Omega Prodns Suite 505A Triumph House 189 Regent St London England

REED, ROBERT STUART, newspaper syndicate exec.; b. Kansas City, Mo., Sept. 13, 1928; s. Robert Willard and Myrtle Viola (Stuart) R.; B.S., U. Oreg., 1949; m. Judith Ann Benton, May 10, 1957; children—Ann, Robert. News editor Goodland (Kans.) News, 1949-50; reporter Spokane Spokesman-Rev., 1950-52; sales mgr. classified advt. Seattle Times, 1952-56; editor, co-pub. San Leandro (Calif.) News, 1956-60; Western sales rep. Hall Syndicate, San Francisco, 1962-68, gen. mgr. Eastern ops., N.Y.C., 1968-73; pres. Chgo. Tribune-New York News Syndicate, Inc., N.Y.C., 1974—. Vice chmn. San Leandro Redevel. Agy., 1957-58. Recipient Best Editorial award Calif. Newspaper Pubs. Assn., 1958. Mem. Sigma Delta Chi, Phi Kappa Psi. Republican. Episcopalian. Home: 69 Michael Rd Stamford CT 06903 Office: 220 E 42d St New York NY 10017

REED, RONALD SWAIN, JR., U.S. atty.; b. St. Joseph, Mo., Sept. 11, 1932; s. Ronald Swain and Sally Virginia (Juden) R.; A.B., U. Mo., 1954, LL.B., 1958; m. Nancy Jane Jones, Dec. 7, 1963; children—Houck Scarritt, Katherine Ramsey. Admitted to Mo. bar, 1958; asst. pros. atty. Buchana County, Mo., 1958-60, chief asst. pros. atty., 1959-60; mem. firm Reed & Reed, St. Joseph, 1960-69, Morton, Reed & Counts, St. Joseph, 1969-77; U.S. atty. Western Dist. Mo., 1977—; mem. Ho. of Reps., 1965-70; spl. counsel City of St. Joseph Personnel Bd., 1975; legal adviser to Buchana County Ct., 1972-77. Bd. dirs. Calla E. Varner Ednl. Found., 1969—, pres., 1972—; bd. dirs. Buchana County Social Welfare Bd., 1972—, pres., 1974—; del. Democratic Nat. Conv., 1960, 76; mem. Dem. Mo. Central Com., 1972-77. Served to 1st lt. ARty., U.S. Army, 1954-56; Korea. Recipient Outstanding Good Govt. award St. Joseph Jr. C. of C., 1965, award for outstanding service St. Joseph State Hosp., 1967. Mem. Am., Mo. (Spl. Services award 1968) bar assns. Club: St. Joseph Country. Home: 2602 Francis St Saint Joseph MO 64501 Office: 549 US Courthouse 811 Grand Ave Kansas City MO 64106

REED, ROY MARVIN, clergyman; b. near Coalgate, Okla, June 17, 1926; s. James Herschel and Roxie (Wooley) R.; M. in Bible, Missionary Bapt. Sem., 1954; M.Th., Okla. Missionary Bapt. Sem., 1958, Th.D., 1959; m. Doris Scroggs, July 25, 1945; children—Timothy, Jeanie Reed Cash, Philip, Tammy. Ordained to ministry, Am. Bapt. Assn.; pastor Landmark Bapt. Ch., England, Ark., 1945-47, Dierks (Ark.) Bapt. Ch., 1947-50, Pauline Bapt. Ch., Monticello, Ark., 1950-55, Calvary Bapt. Ch., Duncan, Okla., 1955-62; 1st Missionary Bapt. Ch., Bellflower, Calif., 1962—; pres. Calif. Missionary Bapt. Sem., Bellflower, 1962—. Moderator Bapt. Gen. Assembly of Okla., 1956-62; pres. Am. Bapt. Assn., 1976-77. Named Outstanding Citizen, Tulare (Calif.) C. of C., 1964. Mem. Am. Bapt. Assn. Theol. Schs. (treas.). Clubs: Masons, Lions. Author: The Glorious Church, 1954; Christian Engagements, 1962. Editor Bapt. Sentinel, 1962—. Home: 9322 Rosser St Bellflower CA 90706 Office: PO Box 848 Bellflower CA 90706

REED, RUDDELL, JR., educator; b. Glenville, W.Va., Nov. 2, 1921; s. Ruddell and Emma Beatrice (Brannon) R.; A.B., Glenville State Coll., 1946; B.S. in Mech. Engring., W.Va. U., 1949, M.S., 1950; Ph.D., Ga. Inst. Tech., 1965; m. Geneva C. Proctor, June 3, 1944; children—Jacqueline (Mrs. Jeffry V. Conopask), Ruddell III. Asst. prof. N.C. State Coll., Raleigh, 1950-55; mgr. exptl. planning, mgr. exptl. materials control Wright Aero. div. Curtiss-Wright Corp., Woodridge, N.J., 1955-57; asso. prof. U. Fla., 1957-63; prof. Purdue U., 1963—, Ball Brothers prof. engring., 1972-76; productivity cons., U.S., Europe, S.E. Asia. Troop chmn. Boy Scouts Am., Gainesville, Fla., 1959-61. Bd. dirs. McClure Research Park, West Lafayette Econ. Devel. Commn. Served to 1st lt. USAAF, 1943-45. Decorated D.F.C., Air medal with three oak leaf clusters; named Alumnus of Year, Glenville State Coll., 1973. Registered profl. engr., N.C., Fla. Fellow Am. Inst. Indsl. Engrs. (dir. N.E. Fla. 1960-63, dir. sr. student chpt. relations 1967-69, dir. Central Ind. 1969-71, dir. pre-coll. student relations 1973—), Royal Soc. Health, Nat. Soc. Profl. Engrs., Soc. Mfg. Engrs., Internat. Material Mgmt. Soc. (dir. research 1968-69, chmn. edn. 1971-73), Am. Soc. Engring. Edn., Sigma Xi, Pi Tau Sigma, Alpha Pi Mu. Mason, Kiwanian. Author: Plant Layout: Factors, Principles and Techniques, 1961; Plant Location, Layout and Maintenance, 1967; Material Flow Systems, 1974; Cost Facts Approach to Profit Improvement, 1972. Mem. editorial bd. Am. Inst. Indsl. Engrs. Transactions, 1969-70. Contbr. articles profl. jours. Home: 726 Chelsea Rd West Lafayette IN 47906

REED, SCOTT, state supreme ct. justice; b. Lexington, Ky., July 3, 1921; s. Wilbur Scott and Florence (Young) R.; J.D., U. Ky., 1945; m. Charlotte Sue Charles, Oct. 12, 1946; 1 son, Geoffrey Scott. Admitted to Ky. bar, 1944; practice in Lexington, 1944-64; partner firm Wallace, Turner & Reed, 1954-64; atty., Fayette County, 1952; judge 1st div. Fayette Circuit Ct., 1964-69; justice Ct. Appeals Ky., 1969-75; chief justice Supreme Ct. Ky., 1976-77, justice, 1977—; acting asso. prof. U. Ky. Law Sch., 1948-56. Recipient Algernon Sydney Sullivan medallion U. Ky., 1945. Nat. Coll. Judiciary fellow, 1965. Mem. Am., Ky., Fayette County bar assns., Am. Law Inst., Spindletop Faculty Alumni Assn., Lexington Civil War Roundtable, Order of Coif, Phi Delta Phi. Mem. Disciples of Christ Ch. Kiwanian. Club: Cricket (Lexington). Editor-in-chief Ky. Law Jour., 1944. Author prefaces. Office: State Capitol Bldg Frankfort KY 40601

REED, SIDNEY GEORGE, JR., physicist; b. New Orleans, July 3, 1921; s. Sidney George and Nellie (Donnelly) R.; B.S., Loyola U., New Orleans, 1941; M.S., U. Notre Dame, 1942; Ph.D., Cath. U., 1951; m. Eleanor Mary Merrill, Aug. 28, 1947; children—Mary Elizabeth, Monica, Jacqueline; m. 2d, Betty E. Cowan, Aug. 18, 1978. Physicist, Naval Ordnance Lab., 1950-51, 52-54; asst. prof. physics Loyola U., New Orleans, 1951-52; with Office Naval Research, 1954-67, research dir., 1965-67; head Office Planning and Policy Studies NSF, Washington, 1967-69; sci. dir. Hydronautics, Inc., Laurel, Md., 1969-72; asst. chief scientist Office Naval Research, Arlington, Va., 1972—. Lectr., Georgetown U., 1962-69. Served with

USNR, 1943-46. Mem. Am. Phys. Soc., Am. Geophys. Union, AAAS, Am. Inst. Aeros. and Astronautics, Sigma Xi. Roman Catholic. Home: 11104 Waycroft Way Rockville MD 20852 Office: Office of Naval Research Arlington VA 22217

REED, STANLEY FORMAN, ret. Supreme Ct. justice; b. Mason County, Ky., Dec. 31, 1884; A.B., Ky. Wesleyan Coll., 1902, LL.D., 1941; A.B., Yale U., 1906, LL.D., 1938; studied law U. Va., Columbia U., U. Paris; LL.D., Columbia U., 1940, U. Ky., 1940, U. Louisville, 1947; m. Winifred Elgin; children—John A., Stanley Forman. Practiced law, Maysville and Ashland, Ky., 1910-29; mem. Ky. Gen. Assembly, 1912-16; gen. counsel Fed. Farm Bd., 1929-32, RFC, 1932-35; solicitor gen. U.S., 1935-38; chmn. Pres.'s Com. on Civil Service Improvement, 1939-41; former dir. Commodity Credit Corp., trustee Export-Import Bank, Washington; asso. justice Supreme Ct. U.S., 1938-57.

REED, STANLEY FOSTER, lectr., editor, publisher; b. Bogota, N.J., Sept. 28, 1917; s. Morton H. and Beryl (Turner) R.; student George Washington U., 1939-40, Johns Hopkins, 1940-41; m. Stella Swingle, Sept. 28, 1940; children—Nancie, Beryl Ann, Alexandra. With Bethlehem Steel Corp., Balt., 1940-41; cons. engr., 1942-44; founder, pres. Reed Research, Inc., Washington, 1945-62; pres. Reed Research Inst. Creative Studies, Washington, from 1951, now chmn.; founder, chmn. LogEtronics, Inc., Washington, 1955; founder, pres., chmn. Tech. Audit Corp., Washington, 1962; founder, editor, pub. Mergers & Acquisitions, The Jour. Corp. Venture, 1965—; founder, editor, pub. Directors and Boards, Jour. Corp. Action, 1976—; chmn., pres. Info. for Industry, Inc., McLean, Va.; co-chmn. semi-ann. Merger Week; lectr. numerous U.S. and fgn. groups and instns. including Union Theol. Sem., U. Pa., Pa. State U., U. Colo., Georgetown U., Rensselaer Poly. Inst., Am. U., Claremont Coll., So. Meth. U., Pace U., Wayne State U., U. Oreg., U. Conn., St. John's U., Pepperdine U., Northwestern U., Loyola U., San Francisco State U., U. Pitts., U. R.I., Marquette U., Vanderbilt U., Boston U., U. Cin., Gustavus Adolphus Coll., U. Mo., Mich. State U., Lehigh U., Calif. Inst. Tech., Denver U., George Washington U., Elmhurst Coll.; vis. fellow Wilton Pk. Conf., Eng., 1968. Bd. dirs. Nat. Patent Council, 1970—. Registered profl. engr., D.C. Mem. Soc. Naval Architects and Marine Engrs., Am. Econ. Assn., Soc. for Internat. Devel. Clubs: N.Y. Yacht; International (Washington). Contbr. articles leading jours.; chpts. in books. Inventor. Patentee. Home: 1621 Brookside Rd McLean VA 22101 Office: Box 36 McLean VA 22101

REED, STUART MARSHALL, r.r. corp. exec.; b. Howell, Mich., July 24, 1925; s. Charles P. and Ora N. Reed; B.S., U. Mich., 1949, M.B.A., 1950; m. Joann Irene Utley, July 2, 1949; children—Paul S., Robert U., Thomas C., Barbara J. Various positions Ford Motor Co., Dearborn, Mich., 1953-59; mgr. quality control Cummins Engine Co., Columbus, Ind., 1959-61; v.p. mfg., treas. CP Electronics, Columbus, 1961-63; mgr. product cost analysis Am. Motors Corp., Detroit, 1963-65, plant mgr. Kelvinator div. Grand Rapids, Mich., 1965-66, gen. plant mgr., Milw., 1966-68, v.p. mfg., Detroit, 1968-75, group v.p., 1975-79; pres., chief operating officer Consol. Rail Corp., Phila., 1979—; dir. 1st Nat. Bank, Kenosha, Wis. Served with Signal Corps, AUS, 1944-46. Mem. Nat. Freight Traffic Assn., Soc. Automotive Engrs., Am. Soc. Quality Control. Presbyterian. Office: Consol Rail Corp 6 Penn Center Plaza Philadelphia PA 19104

REED, THEODORE HAROLD, zool. park dir.; b. Washington, July 25, 1922; s. Ollie William and Mildred Marie (Body) R.; D.V.M., Kans. State Coll., 1945; m. Mary Elizabeth Crandall, Apr. 20, 1945 (dec. Nov. 1978); children—Mark Crandall, Mary Alyce. Practice vet. medicine, Ceylon, Minn., also Caldwell, Idaho, Ashland and Portland, Oreg.; vet. Nat. Zool. Park, 1955-57, acting dir., 1956-58, dir., 1958—. Mem. Internat. Wild Waterfowl Assn., Am. Assn. Zool. Parks and Aquariums, Internat. Union Dirs. Zool. Gardens, East African Wildlife Soc., Wild Fowl Trust. Home: 4301 Massachusetts Ave NW Washington DC 20016 Office: National Zoological Park Washington DC 20008

REED, THOMAS CARE, business exec.; b. N.Y.C., Mar. 1, 1934; s. Gordon W. and Naomi (Bradley) R.; B.S. in Mech. Engring., Cornell U., Ithaca, N.Y., 1956; M.S. in Elec. Engring., U. So. Calif., 1959; m. Leslie Jean Papenfus, June 12, 1956; children—Carolyn, Gordon, Andrew. Engaged in weapons physics Law Radiation Lab., U. Calif. at Livermore, 1959-62; cons., 1962-66; founder, mng. partner Supercon, Ltd., Houston, 1962-65; pres. Quaker Hill Devel. Corp., San Rafael, Calif., 1965—; dir. telecommunications and command and control systems Dept. Def., 1974-75; sec. of the air force, 1976-77. Del. Rep. Nat. Conv., 1968, 72; mem. Rep. Nat. Com. for Calif., 1968-72. Served to 1st lt. USAF, 1956-59. Mem. Alpha Delta Phi, Tau Beta Pi. Clubs: St. Francis Yacht, Pacific Union (San Francisco); Ramada (Houston); Metropolitan (Washington). Home: Alexandria VA Office: Quaker Hill Devel Corp 530 D St San Raphael CA 94901

REED, TRAVIS DEAN, public relations cons.; b. Trinity, Tex., Sept. 27, 1930; s. Travis and Alma (Rains) R.; student Tex. A. and M. Coll., 1948-51, U. Houston, 1951-53; m. Caroline Mae McDonald, June 15, 1957; children—Anne McDonald, Lisa Gayle. Reporter, Houston Post, 1951-53; Washington bur. corr. McGraw-Hill Pub. Co., 1955-61, Boston Herald-Traveler, 1961-62; with Newhouse News Service, Washington, 1962-79, chief corr., 1964-67, editor, 1967-79; public relations cons., Washington, 1979—. Served to lst lt. AUS, 1953-55. Clubs: Nat. Press, Washington Press, Federal City, Gridiron (Washington). Home: 1304 Oberon Way McLean VA 22102 Office: 1800 M St NW Suite 790 S Washington DC 20036

REED, VINCENT EMORY, ednl. adminstr.; b. St. Louis, Mar. 1, 1928; s. Artie David and Velma Veander (Body) R.; B.S. in Edn., W.Va. State Coll., 1952, H.L.D. (hon.), 1977; M.A., Howard U., Washington, 1965; D.P.A. (hon.), Southeastern U., Washington, 1976; postgrad. Wharton Sch., U. Pa., 1969; Ph.D. (hon.), Georgetown U., 1977; m. Frances Bullitt, Sept. 20, 1952. Football coach W.Va. State Coll., 1955; mem. staff D.C. Pub. Schs., 1962—, asst. supt. secondary schs., 1971-74, asso. supt. state office, 1974-75, supt. schs., 1975—; dir. Home Fed. Savs. and Loan Assn. Bd. dirs. D.C. Jr. Achievement, D.C. Goodwill Industries, Nat. Cathedral Sch., Washington YMCA, Neediest Kids; vol. worker S.E. Boys' Club, S.E. Youth Football Assn. Served as 1st lt. AUS, 1953-55; Korea. Named All-Am. Football Player, Pitts. Courier, 1951; recipient Superior Service award D.C. Bicentennial Assembly, 1976; Outstanding Achievement award W.Va. State Coll., 1976, Alumnus of Year, 1976; Outstanding Community Service award NAACP, 1977; many others. Mem. Nat. Assn. Secondary Sch. Prins., Am. Assn. Sch. Personnel Adminstrs., Nat. Assn. Sch. Security Officers, Am. Soc. Bus. Ofcls., NAACP, NEA. D.C. PTA, Washington Sch., Club, Phi Delta Kappa, Kappa Alpha Psi. Baptist. Clubs: Pigskin, Kiwanis. Author articles, book revs. Home: 7115 16th St NW Washington DC 20012 Office: 415 12th St NW Washington DC 20004

REED, VIVIAN, singer, actress, dancer; b. Pitts.; d. Clyde and Lucile (Wilkens) Reed; student Juilliard Sch. Music. Appeared on Broadway, TV and in nightclubs; prin. Bubbling Brown Sugar: recorded Don't Bother Me I Can't Cope, Lead, That's Entertainment. Mem. Actors Equity, AFTRA, Screen Actors Guild. AGVA. Baptist. Address: care Mecca Records 1560 Broadway Suite 1410 New York NY 10019*

REED, WALLACE ALLISON, physician; b. Covina, Calif., May 19, 1916; s. Wallace Allison and Mary Julia (Birdsall) R.; A.B., U. Calif., Los Angeles, 1937; postgrad. U. Cologne, 1937-38, U. Freiburg, Breisgau, 1938-39; M.D., U. So. Calif., 1944; m. Maria Eva Wiemers, Jan. 20, 1938; children—Ellen E., Barbara R. (Mrs. David Maurice Knize), Wallace J., Michael E., Kathryn L., Vicki T. Intern, Santa Fe Coast Lines Hosp., Los Angeles, 1943-44; resident Los Angeles County Gen. Hosp., 1946-47; asst. to head dept. anesthesiology Los Angeles County Gen. Hosp., 1946-47; clin. instr. surgery U. So. Calif. Sch. Medicine, 1946-47; practice medicine, specializing in anesthesiology, Phoenix, 1948—; hon. staff mem. Good Samaritan Hosp., Meml. Hosp., Maricopa County Gen. Hosp.; mem. asso. staff Doctors Hosp., Childrens Hosp., St. Lukes Hosp.; co-founder John L. Ford, M.D., Surgicenter, 1970. Vice pres. Maricopa Found. for Med. Care, 1970-74, pres., 1975-76; mem. House Ways and Means Com. adv. council Nat. Health Inst., 1975—; mem. accreditation council for ambulatory health care Joint Commn. on Accreditation of Hosps., 1975-79, vice-chmn. Accreditation Assn. for Ambulatory Health Care, 1979—; mem. panel for study Nat. Health Ins., Congl. Gen. Accounting Office. Bd. dirs. South Phoenix Montessori Sch., pres. bd. dirs., 1971-75; bd. dirs. Central Ariz. Health Systems Agy., 1975-78. Served from lt. to capt. M.C., AUS, 1944-46. Recipient Pinal award Ariz. Psychiat. Soc., 1967-68, Gerard B. Lambert Merit award for innovative ideas that improve patient care John L. Ford M.D., 1972. Diplomate Am. Bd. Anesthesiology. Fellow Am. Coll. Anesthesiologists; mem. Am. Soc. Anesthesiologists (ad hoc com. ambulatory surg. care), Ariz., Maricopa County socs. anesthesiologists, AMA, Internat. Anesthesia Research Soc., Acad. Anesthesiology (pres. 1969, dir. 1966-72), Soc. for Advancement Free-Standing Ambulatory Surg. Care (pres. 1974-75, dir.), Ariz. Med. Assn. (dir. 1972-78), Maricopa County Med. Soc. (pres. 1964, dir., Salsbury medal 1967, 71, Thomas Dooley medal 1970), Am. Assn. Founds. for Med. Care (dir. 1970-74), Guedel Assn. (pres. 1972). Methodist. Home: 4716 N Dromedary Rd Phoenix AZ 85018 Office: 1040 E McDowell Rd Phoenix AZ 85006

REED, WALTER DUDLEY, lawyer, air force officer; b. Dallas Center, Iowa, June 1, 1924; B.C.S., Drake U., 1948, J.D., 1950; LL.M., McGill U., 1964; postgrad. Hague Acad., Netherlands, 1960; m. Dorothy Ann Kelly; children—Elizabeth K., William S., Joseph H., Anne T. Commd. 2d lt. USAAF, 1944, advanced through grades to maj. gen. USAF, 1974; admitted to Iowa bar, 1950, U.S. Supreme Ct. bar, 1964; staff judge adv., asst. staff judge adv. various orgns., 1951-62; mem. internat. law div. Hdqrs. USAF, 1963-67, chief, 1970-73; legal officer Am. embassy, Bangkok, Thailand, 1967-69; dir. civil law Hdqrs. USAF, Washington, 1973, asst. judge adv. gen., 1973-77, judge adv. gen., 1977—; mem. U.S. del. Diplomatic Conf. on Reaffirmation and Devel. Internat. Humanitarian Law Applicable to Armed Conflict, 1974-77. Decorated Legion of Merit with oak leaf cluster, Air Force Commendation medal with two oak leaf clusters, Republic of Korea Presdl. Unit citation. Mem. Am., Fed., Inter-Am. bar assns., Am. Soc. Internat. Law, Internat. Inst. Space Law, Judge Adv. Assn. Contbr. articles to legal jours. Home: 9436 Victoria Dr Upper Marlboro MD 20870 Office: Hdqrs USAF/JA Washington DC 20330

REED, WILLIAM EDWARD, govt. ofcl., educator; b. Columbia, La., July 15, 1914; s. William Reed and Virginia (Barnes) R.; B.S., So. U., 1937; M.S., Iowa State U., 1941; Ph.D., Cornell U., 1946; m. Mattye Marie Scott, Aug. 27, 1942; children—Edwarda Marie (Mrs. Lucien L. Johnson), Carol Ann, Beverlyn Bernetiae, County agrl. agt. Agr. and Home Econs. Extension Service, La. State U., 1937-41; lectr. soil sci. and chemistry So. U., 1942-47; agrl. research specialist U.S. Econ. Mission to Liberia, 1947-49; dean agr. Agrl. and Tech. Coll. N.C., 1949-61; mem. U.S. del. Russia; rep. ICA in Togo, 1961; asst. dir. AID Mission to Nigeria, 1961-68; mem. U.S. del. to UN Conf. on Application Sci. and Tech., 1963; dep. dir. AID Mission to Ethiopia, 1968-72; fgn. service officer in residence N.C. A. & T. State U., Greensboro, 1972-74, spl. asst. to chancellor for internat. programs, 1974-76, asso. dean research and spl. projects, 1976-78, dir. internat. programs, 1978—. State rep. Sisters Cities Internat.; trustee S.E. Consortium for Internat. Devel.; bd. govs. Internat. Sch., U. Ibadan. Mem. AAAS, Am. Chem. Soc., Nat. Planning Assn., Am. Fgn. Service Assn., Am. Freedom Assn. (dir.), Am. Security Council (adv. bd.), Atlantic Council U.S.A. (adv. bd.), Sigma Xi, Phi Kappa Phi, Beta Kappa Chi, Sigma Pi Phi, Gamma Sigma Delta. Episcopalian. Home: 2711 McConnell Rd Greensboro NC 27401

REED, WILLIAM GARRARD, ret. bus. exec.; b. Shelton, Wash., Feb. 3, 1908; s. Mark E. and Irene (Simpson) R.; A.B., U. Wash., 1929; student Harvard U. Bus. Sch., 1929-30; m. Eleanor Henry, July 11, 1935; children—Susan Henry, William Garrard, Mary Simpson. Former chmn. Crown Simpson Pulp Co., Simpson Timber Co., Simpson Lee Paper Co., Simlog Corp.; former pres. Lumbermen's Merc. Co., State Bank Shelton, Malahat Logging Co. (Can.); former exec. v.p. Rayonier, Inc., N.Y.C.; now mng. partner Simpson Reed & Co.; propr. Graysmarsh Farm; dir. Olympia Oyster Co., Boeing Co., Mem. Wash. Rep. Nat. Com., 1940-44; head U.S. del. Econ. Commn. for Europe, 1960; pres. Seattle Found., 1959-61, United Good Neighbor Fund, 1952-53; mem. pres.'s council Calif. Inst. Tech., 1968-70; adv. bd. U. Wash. Grad. Bus. Sch., 1960-70; bd. dirs. Stanford Research Inst., 1957-65, Seattle Art Mus., 1955-73, Harvard Bus. Sch. Assn., 1964-67. Served to lt. comdr. USNR, 1942-45. Decorated Bronze Star. Mem. Psi Upsilon. Episcopalian (sr. warden 1966-68). Clubs: Links, Univ. (N.Y.C.); Pacific Union (San Francisco); Univ., Golf, Rainier (Seattle). Office: 2210 Exchange Bldg Seattle WA 98104

REED, WILLIAM JOHN, steel co. exec.; b. Sault Ste Marie, Can., Dec., 1929; s. William Harburn and Edith Eleanor (Nesom) R.; student Mich. Tech. U., 1949; BA with honours in Bus. Adminstrn., U. Western Ont., 1953; m. Betty Lou Levine, Sept. 6, 1952; children—Wendy, Leslie, Lori, David. With Algoma Steel Corp., Ltd., Sault Ste Marie, 1953—, comptroller, 1972—. Chmn., Community Services Bd., 1965-73. Home: 136 Caddy Ave Sault Sainte Marie ON P6A 6H9 Canada Office: 503 Queen Sault Sainte Marie ON Canada

REED, WILLIAM LAFOREST, educator; b. Defiance, Ohio, Jan. 9, 1912; s. Harold E. and Margaret (Schlotter) R.; B.A., Hiram Coll., Hiram, Ohio, 1934; B.D., Yale, 1937, Ph.D., 1942; fellow Am. Sch. Oriental Research, Jerusalem, 1937-38; m. Annetta Doria Pendergast, Dec. 31, 1935; 1 son, Russell Maurice. Mem. faculty Tex. Christian U., 1946-56, 68—, prof. religion, chmn. dept., 1968-75, Weatherly prof. religion, 1974—; prof. O.T., Lexington Theol. Sem., 1956-68; dir. Am. Sch. Oriental Research, 1951-52; sr. archaeologist AID, Amman, Jordan, 1964; archaeologist and/or dir. excavations in Jordan: Jericho, 1952, Dibon, 1952, Qumran Caves, 1952, Gibeon, 1959, 62, Elealeh, 1962, Saudi Arabia, 1962, 67, Yemen, 1972. Ordained to ministry Christian Ch., 1939. Trustee Am. Sch. Oriental Research, 1953-56, 63-69, exec. asst. to pres., 1956-66, treas., 1966-68; mem. council Soc. Bibl. Lit., 1963-69. Served to maj. Chaplains Corps, AUS, 1942-46. Decorated Bronze Star. Distinguished prof. Tex. Christian U., 1953-56; faculty grantee Am. Assn. Theol. Schs., 1961-62; research grantee Am. Philos. Soc., 1962, 67, 72; Garfield fellow Hiram Coll., 1973. Mem. Am. Acad. Religion, Am. Oriental Soc., Soc. Bibl. Lit., Theta Phi. Author: The Old Testament Asherah, 1949; The Excavations at Dibon in Moab, 1964; co-author: Ancient Records from North Arabia, 1970. Co-editor: Translating and Understanding the Old Testament. Contbr., editor jours. in field. Home: 6212 Whitman Ave Fort Worth TX 76133

REED, WILLIAM VERNON, architect; b. Monticello, Ill., Nov. 4, 1907; s. Carl Seward and Ida (Vaughan) R.; B.Arch. cum laude, U. Ill. at Urbana, 1930; certificate Beaux Arts Inst. Design, 1930; M. Arch. (grad. fellow), Mass. Inst. Tech., 1933; m. Giuliana Nardi, June 21, 1947; children—Carl Christopher, Giuliana Virginia Maria Reed Keller. Mem. faculty U. Ill. at Urbana, 1930-31, U. Man. (Can.), 1931-32, Mass. Inst. Tech., 1933-34; cons. fgn. housing, housing div. PWA, 1935-36; prin. project planner S.E. region U.S. Housing Authority, 1937-40; dir. div. housing standards Office Def. Housing Coordinator, Washington, 1940-42; mem.-in-charge tech. investigations President's Housing Mission to Great Britain, 1943; dep. housing expediter, dir. tech. office Nat. Housing Agy., 1946-47; v.p. So. Calif. Homes, 1947-48, IBEC Housing Corp., N.Y.C. and San Juan, P.R., 1948-57; practice architecture, San Juan, 1957-75; prin. Reed, Torres, Beauchamp, Marvel, 1963-75; vis. lectr. univs. in U.S. and P.R.; prin. works include P.R. comprehensive plan for outdoor recreation, 1970; (with E.L. Barnes) El Monte Urban Renewal Project, Rio Piedras, P.R., 1960-68; Quintana High Rise Housing Project, Rio Piedras, 1966; Commonwealth Housing Center, Rio Piedras, 1965; Dorado (P.R.) Beach Hotel staff housing, 1965; Housing Investment Corp. Bldg., Rio Piedras, 1962; Psychiat. Treatment Center, Ponce, P.R., 1963. Dir. Nat. Housing Conf., 1965—. Mem. council Casa del Libro, 1960-75; mem. citizen's adv. com. to mayor of San Juan, 1965-68; mem. citizen's com. Nuevo Centro de San Juan, 1967-75, treas., 1970-71. Adv. bd. P.R. Salvation Army. Served to maj. USMCR, 1942-45. Allerton Am. travelling scholar, 1929; fellow Lake Forest Found. Architects and Landscape Architects, 1930; Francis Plym fellow, 1935-36. Fellow A.I.A. (pres. P.R. 1968-70); mem. Am. Inst. Planners, Am. Arbitration Assn. (arbitrator 1976—), Inst. de Arquitectos P.R., Colegio de Ingenieros, Arquitectos Y Agrimensores P.R., Tau Beta Pi, Beta Theta Pi. Club: Cosmos (Washington). Author: New Homes for Old, 1940; also articles. Home: 3537 Mineola Dr Sarasota FL 33579

REED, WILLIS, profl. basketball coach; b. Hico, La., June 25, 1942; s. Willis and Inell R.; ed. Grambling Coll.; m. Geraldine Oliver (div.); children—Carl, Veronica. Center, forward N.Y. Knickerbockers Nat. Basketball Assn. team, 1964-74, coach, 1977—; Mem. Nat. Basketball Assn. All-Star team, 1965-71, 73; mem. World Championship team, 1970; recipient Most Valuable Player awards for playoffs and all-star games, 1970; Nat. Basketball Assn. Rookie of Year, 1965, NBA Playoffs Most Valuable Player, 1970, 73. Author: (with Phil Pepe) The View from the Rim, 1971. Home: Bernice LA Office: NY Knickerbockers 4 Pennsylvania Pl New York NY 10010

REEDER, CLIFTON LEE, physician; b. Texas City, Ill., Nov. 13, 1918; s. Owen and Nora (Mills) R.; M.D., U. Ill., 1941; m. Florence Fenske, May 15, 1942; children—Susan Carol, James Owen. Intern, Grant Hosp., Chgo., 1941-42; asst. med dir., later med. dir. Fed. Life Ins. Co., Chgo., 1946; asst. med. dir. Continental Assurance Co., 1947-50, med. dir., 1950-63, dir. underwriting, 1955-68, v.p., 1958; pres., dir. Nat. Ben Franklin Life Ins. Co., 1969; acting chief div. health planning and resource devel. Ill. Pub. Health Dept., 1967-71; cons., 1971—; med. dir., chief adminstrv. officer Bodimetric Profiles div. Am. Service Bur., 1972-75, chief exec. officer Bodimetric Profiles div., 1975—; dir., v.p. Am. Service Bur. dir. Ill. Coop. Health Data System, Inc. Chmn., Gov.'s Council to State Health Agy., 1968-71. Bd. dirs. Chgo. Found. for Med. Care; bd. dirs., sec., mem. exec. com. Ill. Found. for Med. Care, 1975-77. Served from 1st lt. to lt. col. M.C., AUS, 1942-46. Mem. AMA, Chgo. Med. Soc. (chmn. exec. com. 1967, mem. council 1974—, pres.-elect. 1977), Am. Life Conv. (chmn. med. sect. 1963-64, sec. 1965-69), Ill. Med. Soc. (mem. constn. and by laws com.). Club: Tavern (Chgo.). Home: 734 N Merrill Ave Park Ridge IL 60068

REEDER, DON DAVID, physicist; b. Dubuque, Iowa, Aug. 18, 1935; s. Herbert Charlton and Evelyn Gladys (Rassmussen) R.; B.S., U. Ill., 1958; M.S. in Physics, U. Wis., 1961, Ph.D., 1966; m. Carol Ann Bender, Feb. 16, 1958; children—Julia Ann, Linda Sue. Asst. prof. physics U. Wis., Madison, 1966-68, asso. prof., 1968-72, prof., 1972—. Served with USNR, 1958-60. NATO fellow, 1974. Mem. AAUP, AAAS, Am. Inst. Physics. Home: 5 Veblen Pl Madison WI 53705 Office: 1150 University Ave Madison WI 53706

REEDER, JAMES PRYOR, lawyer; b. Knoxville, Tenn., Dec. 30, 1896; s. James Pryor and Katherine (Howard) R.; A.B., U. Tenn., 1919, LL.B., 1922; m. Maxine Gowdy, Dec. 3, 1929; children—Joan Howard (Mrs. Gordon H. Raynor), Nancy Lee (Mrs. F. Edward Kunkel), Maxine (Mrs. W.E. Bixby), Mary Frances (Mrs. John J. Walsh). Teller, mgr. sav. bank dept. Holston Nat. Bank, Knoxville, 1914-24; admitted to Tenn. bar, 1922, Fla. bar, 1933; partner firm Mershon, Sawyer, Johnston, Dunwody & Cole, and predecessors, Miami, Fla., 1946—; hon. Peruvian consul, 1941-46; village judge, Miami Shores, Fla., 1941-51. Exec. v.p., dir. Childrens Home Soc., Southeastern div. Bd. dirs. local A.R.C.; bd. dirs., treas. Greater Miami Boys Club Found. Mem. Am., Fla., Dade County bar assns., Sigma Nu, Phi Delta Phi, Phi Kappa Phi. Presbyterian. Clubs: Kiwanis (charter), Miami Shores Country. Home: 352 NE 98th St Miami FL 33138 Office: SE First Nat Bank Bldg Miami FL 33131

REEDER, LEE, lawyer; b. LaPorte, Ind., Oct. 14, 1909; s. David Huse and Maude Angela (Warner) R.; student Kansas City Jr. Coll., 1926-28; J.D., U. Mo., Kansas City, 1932; m. Madaline Flo Brown, June 8, 1935; children—Douglas Lee, Jennifer Ann, Madeline Brown, Jr. Admitted to Mo. bar, 1932, since practiced in Kansas City; dir. numerous firms; trustee United Med. Properties Trust; spl. counsel, dir. C.L.C. of Am., 1962-78; chmn., counsel W.S.C. Group, Inc. Mem. spl. adv. com. to ICC. Chmn. Citizens Sch. Plant Com., Kansas City, 1950, Citizens Com. on Human Relations, 1950-52, Sch. Bond Com. Kansas City Sch. Dist., 1948; chmn. bd. Youth Symphony of Heart of Am., City Commn. Human Relations, 1952-60; bd. dirs., gen. counsel Heart of Am. council Boy Scouts Am., Eagle Scout, scoutmaster, troop committeeman. Trustee, chmn. Law Found. U. Mo., Kansas City, 1972-75; trustee, chmn. Leelanau Schs., 1972-75; trustee, gen. counsel Am. Humanics. Recipient Silver Beaver award Boy Scouts Am. Mem. Am. (pub. utility sect.), Mo. (dir. dept. adminstrv. law 1960), Kansas City bar assns., Motor Carrier Lawyers Assn. (pres. 1952-53), Lawyers Assn. Kansas City, ICC Practitioners Assn. (chmn. nat. assn. ethics com. 1960-62), Delta Theta Phi, Alpha Phi Omega (hon.), Bench and Robe Soc. Clubs: Kansas City, Carriage (Kansas City), Rotary. Home: 824 W 53d Terr Kansas City MO 64112 Office: 1221 Baltimore Ave Kansas City MO 64105

REEDER, OLIVER HOWARD, paint products mfg. exec.; b. Balt., Sept. 19, 1916; s. Charles Howard and Nannie Dryden (Kensett) R.; A.B., Princeton, 1939; m. Nancy Hardcastle Fisher, Apr. 18, 1942; children—Nancy Fisher, Ellen Dryden. With Balt. Copper Paint Co., Balt., 1939—, tech. dir., treas., 1939-47, pres., 1947—, chmn., 1959—; v.p. Balt. Copper Paint div. Glidden-Durkee Div. SCM Corp., 1969—; pres. Jotun-Balt. Copper Paint Co., Inc., 1974-76, v.p., 1976—; dir. Wm. H. Whiting Co., Savs. Bank Balt. Pres. Hosp. for Consumptives of Md.; trustee Gilman Sch., Balt., 1948-65, Johns Hopkins Hosp.,

1957—, Walters Art Gallery, 1978—; pres. Md. Hosp. Laundry, 1970—, trustee, 1975—. Fellow Am. Inst. Chemists; mem. Am. Chem. Soc., Soc. Naval Architects and Marine Engrs., Phi Beta Kappa, Sigma Xi. Home: 1300 Dulany Valley Rd Towson MD 21204 Office: 501 Key Hwy Baltimore MD 21230

REEDER, PEARL ANN, editor; b. Tipton County, Ind., Aug. 21, 1900; d. Walter Scott and Margaret Louetta (Shaw) Reeder; student U. of Ind., 1918, U. Chgo., 1920. Tchr., Tipton County, Ind., 1918-22; editorial work Union Spl. Machine Co., Chgo., 1922-29, Eagle Mag., South Bend, Ind., 1930; editor Hobbies Mag., Chgo., 1930—. Mem. D.A.R., Bus. and Profl. Women's Club Chgo., Nat. Early Am. Glass Club, Nat. Soc. Watch and Clock Collectors, Nat. Button Soc., Doll Collectors Am. Methodist. Home: 1130 S Michigan Ave Chicago IL 60605 Office: 1006 S Michigan Ave Chicago IL 60605

REEDER, WILLIAM GLASE, museum adminstr., zoologist; b. Los Angeles, Feb. 4, 1929; s. William Hedges and Gladys Ella (Glase) R.; B.A., UCLA, 1950; M.A., U. Mich., 1953, Ph.D., 1957; m. Lynn Roseberry Rohrer, Jan. 27, 1951; children—Elisabeth H., Jeffrey W., Heather L., Kathleen A. Asst. curator ornithology and mammalogy Los Angeles County Mus., 1949-51; vis. asst. prof. zoology UCLA, 1955-56; curatorial asst. Mus. Zoology, U. Mich., 1956-58; asst. prof. zoology U. Wis., Madison, 1958-62, asso. prof., 1962-66, prof., 1966-78, dir. Zool. Mus., 1967-78; prof. zoology, dir. Tex. Meml. Mus., U. Tex., Austin, 1978—. Mem. Am. Soc. Mammology, Am. Soc. Zoologists, Soc. Study Evolution, Soc. Systematic Zoology, Am. Arachnological Soc., Brit. Arachnological Soc., Soc. Vertebrate Paleontology, AAAS. Research, publs. in systematic biology and ecology. Home: 7014 Greenshores Dr Austin TX 78732 Office: 2400 Trinity St Austin TX 78705

REEDY, GEORGE EDWARD, educator, author, lectr.; b. East Chicago, Ind., Aug. 5, 1917; s. George Edward and Mary (Mulvaney) R.; B.A. in Sociology, U. Chgo., 1938; m. Lillian Greenwald, Mar. 22, 1948; children—Michael Andrew, William James. Reporter, Phila. Inquirer, summer 1937; Congl. corr. U.P.I., 1938-41, 46-51; staff cons. armed services preparedness subcom. U.S. Senate, 1951-52, staff dir. minority policy com., 1953-54, staff dir. majority policy com., 1955-60; spl. asst. to Vice Pres. Lyndon B. Johnson, 1961-63; press sec. to Pres. Johnson, 1964-65; pres. Struthers Research and Devel. Corp., Washington, 1966-68; v.p. planning Struthers Wells Corp., N.Y.C., 1966-68, also dir.; spl. cons. to President, 1968-69; writer, lectr., cons. 1969—; dean, Nieman prof. Coll. Journalism, Marquette U., Milw., 1972—. Former fellow Woodrow Wilson Internat. Center for Scholars, Smithsonian Instn., Washington; fellow in communication Duke, 1973-74. Mem. Pres.'s Nat. Adv. Commn. Selective Service, 1966-67, Marine Sci., Engring. Resources, 1967-68. Mem. diocesan council Washington Diocese, Episcopal Ch. Served with USAAF, 1942-45. Author: Who Will Do Our Fighting for Us?, 1969; The Twilight of the Presidency, 1970; The Presidency in Flux, 1973; numerous mag. and syndicated newspaper articles. Home: 2307 E Newberry Blvd Milwaukee WI 53211

REEDY, GEORGE PATRICK, ins. co. exec.; b. Stamford, Conn., Feb. 12, 1935; s. George Joseph and Alice V. (Smith) R.; B.S., Fordham U., 1959; m. Margaret J. Laughlin, June 3, 1961; children—George Thomas, Colleen M. Sr. auditor Ernst & Ernst, C.P.A.'s, N.Y.C., 1959-63; treas. Diesel Engring. Corp., N.Y.C., 1963-66; controller Grand Bahama Devel. Corp., Freeport, Bahamas, 1966-68; treas., v.p. John P. Maguire & Co., 1969-73; treas., controller Comml. Union Assurance Cos., Boston, 1973—, 1st sr. v.p., 1979—, also dir.; pres. CUPAC, Inc.; dir. Comml. Union Leasing Corp. Asst. treas. United Community Planning Corp., Boston. Served with USMC, 1954-56. C.P.A., N.Y. Roman Catholic. Home: 14 Capt Forbush Ln Acton MA 01720 Office: 1 Beacon St Boston MA 02108

REEDY, JAMES HAUGH, ret. retail bus. exec.; b. N.Y.C., Mar. 30, 1907; s. James J. and Delia (Haugh) R.; student N.Y. U.; m. Marie M. McLaughlin, Feb. 6, 1934; children—Virginia Marie (Mrs. E. F. Baxter, Jr.), Barbara Ann (Mrs. J.C. Fraser), Margaret Rose (Mrs. T.J. Hayes), James Haugh. Mdse. mgr. Allied Stores Corp., N.Y.C., 1934-41, mng. dir., 1941-48, group mgr., 1948—, v.p., 1951-63, sr. v.p., 1963-72, dir., 1960-72, dir. emeritus, 1972—; pres. Dey Bros. & Co., Syracuse, 1941-52, chmn. bd., 1952-56. Clubs: Union League; Scarsdale Golf (Hartsdale, N.Y.). Home: 37 Paddington Rd Scarsdale NY 10583

REEDY, JERRY EDWARD, editor, writer; b. Aberdeen, S.D., Feb. 4, 1936; s. Robert Emmett and Helen Mary (Issenhuth) R.; A.B., U. Notre Dame, 1958; M.A., U. S.D., 1961; m. Susan Mary Rogers, June 22, 1968; children—Megan Marie, Erin Elizabeth, Matthew Robert-Emmett. Area editor Red Wing (Minn.) Daily Republican Eagle, 1959-60; with Better Homes & Gardens mag. Meredith Pub. Co., Des Moines, 1961-69, asso. editor, 1966-67, spl. assignments editor, 1967-69; editor-in-chief, contbg. author Odyssey Mag., Chgo., 1969-78; freelance editor, writer and photographer for nat. mags. and maj. met. daily newspapers, 1978—; instr. in English U. S.D., 1960-61, in mag. writing Drake U., 1966-68, Barat Coll., 1976-77. Pres., Com. on Community Life, Chgo., 1976-78. Recipient certificates of excellence Chgo. Communications Collaborative, 1976; Addy Gold 1st place award for mags. Am. Advt. Fedn., 1976; 1st pl. awards of excellence for overall quality and for photojournalism Chgo. Assn. Bus. Communicators, 1977. Mem. Soc. Am. Travel Writers, Midwest Writers. Roman Catholic. Home and office: 3542 Pine Grove Chicago IL 60657

REEDY, JOHN LOUIS, publisher; b. Newport, Ky., Oct. 16, 1925; s. Albert William and Margaret R. (Moser) R.; A.B., Notre Dame U., 1948; postgrad. Holy Cross Coll., Washington, 1948-52; postgrad. journalism, Marquette U., Milw., 1953. Joined Congregation Holy Cross, Roman Catholic Ch., 1943, ordained priest, 1952; exec. editor Ave Maria Press, Notre Dame, Ind., 1953-54, editor-pub., 1954-70, pub., 1970—. Pres. bd. dirs. Urban League South Bend and St. Joseph County, Ind., 1974-76. Recipient award outstanding contbn. Cath. journalism Cath. Press Assn., 1966. Co-author: The Perplexed Catholic: A Guide Through Confusion, 1966. Home: 215 Carroll Hall Notre Dame IN 46556 Office: Ave Maria Press Notre Dame IN 46556

REEDY, ROBERT HAROLD, hosp. exec.; b. Yankton, S.D., Aug. 25, 1930; s. Thomas Harold and Alice (Meslo) R.; B.A., Yankton Coll., 1952; Phys. Therapist, Med. Coll. Va., 1953; grad. hosp. exec. devel. program St. Louis U., 1975; m. June Alice Snow, Sept. 25, 1953; children—Michael Thane, Susan Renee. Dir. phys. therapy Lutheran Hosp., Ft. Wayne, Ind., 1954-63, adminstrv. asst., 1963-72, exec. v.p., 1972-77, pres., 1977—. Recipient cert. recognition Tri-State Hosp. Assembly, 1969; cert. appreciation Lions Club, 1978. Mem. Ind. Hosp. Assn., Am. Hosp. Assn. (cert. Inst. Hosp. Law 1976, 78), Am. Coll. Hosp. Adminstrs. Lutheran. Club: Olympia. Office: 3024 Fairfield Ave Fort Wayne IN 46807

REEMTSMA, KEITH, physician; b. Madera, Calif., Dec. 5, 1925; B.S., Idaho State Coll.; M.D., U. Pa., 1949; Med.Sci.D., Columbia U., 1958; children—Lance Brewster, Dirk Van Horn. Asst. surgery Columbia Coll. Phys. and Surg., 1957; faculty Tulane U. Sch. Medicine, 1957-66, prof. surgery, 1966; prof., head dept. surgery U. Utah Coll. Medicine, Salt Lake City, 1966-71; chmn. dept. surgery, Valentine Mott prof. surgery, Johnson and Johnson distinguished prof. surgery Columbia U., N.Y.C., 1971—. Mem. Soc. Clin. Surgery, Am. Surg. Assn., Soc. U. Surgeons, A.C.S., So. Soc. for Clin. Research, Am. Fedn. for Clin. Research, Am. Assn. for Thoracic Surgery, Soc. for Vascular Surgery, Internat. Cardiovascular Soc., So. Thoracic Surg. Assn., New Orleans Surg. Soc., Surg. Assn. La., AMA, La. State, Orleans Parish med. socs., Alpha Omega Alpha. Contbr. articles to profl. jours. Office: Dept Surgery Columbia U 622 W 168th St New York City NY 10032

REEP, EDWARD ARNOLD, artist; b. Bklyn., May 10, 1918; s. Joseph and Elsie (Abramson) R.; student Art Center Coll. Design, 1936-41; m. Karen Patricia Stevens, Dec. 9, 1942; children—Susan Kay, Cristine Elyse, Janine J., Mitchell Jules. Shows include: Whitney Mus. Am. Art Ann., N.Y.C., 1946-48, Los Angeles County Mus. Ann., 1946-60, Corcoran Gallery Art Biennial, Washington, 1949, Nat. Gallery Art, Washington, 1945; represented in permanent collections: Los Angeles County Mus., U.S. War Dept., Grunwald Graphic Arts Collection, U. Calif., Los Angeles, Lytton Collection, Los Angeles, State of Calif. Collection, Sacramento; instr. painting and drawing Art Center Coll. Design, Los Angeles, 1946-50, Chouinard Art Inst., Los Angeles, 1950-69; prof. painting, chmn. dept., artist in residence E. Carolina U., 1970—; cons. editor Van Nostrand Reinhold Pub. Co. Guggenheim fellow, 1945-46; Nat. Endowment for Arts grantee, 1975. Mem. AAUP, Nat. Watercolor Soc. (past pres.), Los Angeles Art Assn. Democrat. Author: The Content of Watercolor, 1968. Home: 201 Poplar Dr Greenville NC 27834 Office: Sch Art East Carolina U Greenville NC 27834. *I once was consumed by the desire to become an artist. I feel no differently today. There is work ahead. If I had set goals for myself I no longer can recall what they may have been; I go along painting as well or as inventively as I can. Never have I sacrificed living life as I feel I must for my art. My work is a reflection of my life—experiences real and imagined.*

REES, ALBERT (EVERETT), found. exec.; b. N.Y.C., Aug. 21, 1921; s. Hugo R. and Rosalie (Landman) R.; B.A., Oberlin Coll., 1943; M.A., U. Chgo., 1947, Ph.D., 1950; m. Candida Kranold, July 15, 1945; 1 son, David; m. 2d, Marianne Russ, June 22, 1963; children—Daniel, Jonathan. Instr. Roosevelt Coll., Chgo., 1947-48; asst. prof. econs. U. Chgo., 1948-54, asso. prof., 1954-61, prof., chmn. dept., 1961-64; prof. econs. Princeton U., 1966-79, chmn. dept., 1971-74, provost, 1975-77; pres. Alfred P. Sloan Found., N.Y.C., 1979—; dir. Nabisco, Inc.; staff Council Econ. Advisors, 1954-55; dir. Council on Wage and Price Stability, 1974-75; dir. Nabisco, Inc. Mem. Am. Econ. Assn., Indsl. Relations Research Assn. Author: Real Wages in Manufacturing, 1890-1914, 1961; The Economics of Trade Unions, 1962; (with George P. Shultz) Workers and Wages in an Urban Labor Market, 1970; The Economics of Work and Pay, 1973. Editor: Jour. Polit. Economy, 1954-59. Home: 32 Turner Ct Princeton NJ 08540 Office: 630 Fifth Ave New York NY 10020

REES, FRANK WILLIAM, JR., architect, hosp. cons.; b. Rochester, N.Y., June 5, 1943; s. Frank William and Elizabeth (Miller) R.; B.Arch., U. Okla., 1970; m. Joan M. Rees, Apr. 1, 1967; children—Michelle, Christopher. Sales mgr. Radio Sta. KOFM, Oklahoma City, 1967-70; project architect Benham-Blair & Affiliates, Inc., 1970-75; pres., chmn. bd. Weatherscan Radio Network, 1973-78; pres., founder Rees Assos., Inc., Architects, Planners, Cons.'s, Oklahoma City, 1975—; chmn. bd. Weatherscan Internat., 1972-78, Weatherdial, Inc., 1972-78; condr. seminars on hosp. planning or code compliance Am., La., Ark., Miss., Mo., Okla. hosp. assns., Ariz. State U., 1978. Bd. dirs. Bishop Kelley Found. Served with Okla. N.G., 1967-73. Decorated Okla. N.G. Commendation medal, Republic of Vietnam Commendation medal. Mem. AIA, Am., Okla. hosp. assns., Oklahoma City C. of C. Club: Boomer Dinner (v.p.). Home: 9200 Candlewood St Oklahoma City OK 73132 Office: 5500 N Western Ave Suite 103 Oklahoma City OK 73118

REES, MINA SPIEGEL, univ. adminstr.; b. Cleve., Aug. 2, 1902; d. Moses and Alice Louise (Stackhouse) Rees; A.B., Hunter Coll., 1923, Sc.D., 1973; A.M., Columbia, 1925, LL.D., 1971; Ph.D., U. Chgo., 1931; Sc.D. (hon.), Mt. Holyoke Coll., 1962, Wilson Coll., Wheaton (Mass.) Coll., Oberlin Coll., 1964, U. Rochester, 1971, Nazareth Coll. of Rochester, 1971, U. Mich., 1970, Carnegie Mellon U., 1972, Mt. Sinai Sch. Medicine, 1972, U. Ill., 1972; Litt.D. (hon.), Rutgers U., 1965; LL.D. (hon.), Miami U., 1970; L.H.D. (hon.), N.Y. U., 1971, Marymount Coll., 1971, City U. N.Y., 1974; m. Leopold Brahdy, June 24, 1955. Instr. math. Hunter Coll., 1926-32, asst. prof., 1932-40, asso. prof., 1940-50, prof., dean faculty, 1953-61; prof., dean grad. studies City U. N.Y., 1961-68, provost Univ. grad. div., 1968-69, pres. Univ. grad. div., 1969-71, pres. Grad. Sch. and Univ. Center, 1971-72, pres. emeritus, 1972—. Tech. aide, adminstrv. asst. to chief applied math. panel, nat. def. research com. Office Sci. Research and Devel., 1943-46; head, math. br. Office Naval Research, 1946-49, dir. math. scis. div., 1949-52, dep. sci. dir., 1952-53; mem. math. div. NRC, 1953-56, mem. exec. com., 1954-56; councillor Soc. for Indsl. and Applied Math., 1955-58; mem. gen. scis. adv. panel. Dept. Def., 1957-61; mem. adv. bd. Computation and Exterior Ballistics Lab., 1958-61; adv. commn. for math. Nat. Bur. Standards, 1954-58, chmn., 1954-57; mem. adv. panel for math. scis. NSF, 1955-58; adv. bd. Sch. Math. Study Group, 1962-64; mem. N.Y. Adv. Council Grad. Edn., 1962-72; mem. Commn. Humanities, 1963-64; mem. Nat. Sci. Bd., 1964-70; chmn. Council Grad. Schs. in U.S., 1970. Mem. exec. com., trustee Woodrow Wilson Nat. Fellowship Found.; bd. dirs. Asso. Hosp. Service N.Y., 1962-75, Lenox Hill Neighborhood Assn., Health Services Improvement Fund (N.Y. Blue Cross-Blue Shield). Awarded fellowship U. Chgo., 1930-31; recipient King's Medal for Service in Cause of Freedom (Eng.); President's Certificate of Merit (U.S.); Elizabeth Blackwell gold medal Hobart and William Smith Coll.; named Profl. Woman of Year by Bus. and Profl. Women N.Y., 1961; N.Y. Pub. Service award for profl. achievement, 1964; achievement award Am. Assn. U. Women, 1965; Pres.'s medal Hunter Coll., 1971; Alumni medal U. Chgo., 1971; Chancellor's medal City U. N.Y., 1972. Fellow A.A.A.S. (v.p. 1954, bd. dirs. 1957-60, 66-72, chmn. bd. dirs. 1972, pres.-elect 1970, pres. 1971), N.Y. Acad. Scis.; mem. Am. Math. Soc. (trustee 1955-59), Math. Assn. Am. (2d v.p. 1963-65; recipient 1st award for distinguished service to math.), Soc. for Indsl. and Applied Math. (dir. Inst. for Math. and Soc. 1973—), Sigma Xi, Phi Beta Kappa (mem. triennial council united chpts. 1940-46, senator, mem. exec. com. 1970—), Pi Mu Epsilon. Clubs: Cosmopolitan, Princeton (N.Y.C.). Contbr. to math. publs. Home: 301 E 66th St New York City NY 10021

REES, PAUL STROMBERG, clergyman; b. Providence, Sept. 4, 1900; s. Seth Cook and Frida Marie (Stromberg) R.; A.B., U. So. Calif., 1923, D.D. (hon.), 1944; D.D. (hon.), Asbury Coll., 1939, North Park Coll., Chgo., 1965; Litt.D., Houghton Coll., 1953; L.H.D., Seattle Pacific Coll.; m. Edith Alice Brown, June 3, 1926; children—Evelyn Joy Rees Moore, Daniel Seth, Julianna Rees Robertson. Ordained to ministry, 1921; asso. pastor Pilgrim Tabernacle, Pasadena, Calif., 1920-23; ministerial supt. Detroit Holiness Tabernacle, 1928-32; pastor 1st Covenant Ch., Mpls., 1938-58; v.p. at large World Vision Internat., Monrovia, Calif., 1958-75, bd. dirs., 1960—, dir. Pastors' Conf. Ministry, 1964-75, editor World Vision Mag., 1964-72, contbg. editor, 1972-74, editor at large, 1974-78. Moderator, Evang. Covenant Ch. Am., 1948, v.p., 1950-55; v.p. World Evang. Fellowship; minister to ministers Billy Graham Crusades, London, 1954, Glasgow, 1955, N.Y.C., 1957, Sydney, Australia, 1959; columnist Covenant Companion, 1959-72; adviser World Council of Chs. Assembly, New Delhi, India, 1961, Uppsala, Sweden, 1968; speaker World Congress on Evangelism, Berlin, 1966, Nat. Congress on Evangelism, Mpls., 1969. Trustee Asbury Coll., 1935-65, Asbury Theol. Sem., 1967—; bd. dirs. William Penn Coll., 1950-58, Christianity Today, 1958—, Paul Carlson Found., 1965-72, Bread for the World, 1976—. Recipient Freedoms Found. award 1951. Mem. Nat. Assn. Evangs. (bd. adminstrn. 1942—, pres 1952-54), Phi Beta Kappa. Author: If God Be For Us, 1940; Things Unshakable, 1947; The Radiant Cross, 1949; The Face of Our Lord, 1951; Stir Up the Gift, 1952; Prayer and Life's Highest, 1956; Christian: Commit Yourself, 1957; The Adequate Man, 1958; Stand Up in Praise to God, 1960; Triumphant in Trouble, 1962; Proclaiming the New Testament—Philippians, Colossians, Philemon, 1964; Men of Action in the Book of Acts, 1966; Don't Sleep Through the Revolution, 1969. Editor: Nairobi to Berkeley, 1967. asso. editor The Herald, 1955-75, contbg. editor, 1975—; contbg. editor Christianity Today, 1958-75; cons. editor Eternity mag., 1960-77. Home: 2121 N Ocean Blvd Boca Raton FL 33431 also 2527 Mayapple Ct Northbrook IL 60062 Office: World Vision Internat 919 W Huntington Dr Monrovia CA 91016. *I am convinced that the Christian world-view answers more questions, resolves more doubts, subdues more fears, meets more needs, humbles more pride, preserves more dignity, holds more hope than any other.*

REES, REES BYNON, dermatologist; b. Bakersfield, Calif., Feb. 2, 1915; s. Rees Bynon and Edna (Wetterman) R.; A.B., U. Calif. at Berkeley, 1936; M.D., U. Calif. at San Francisco, 1940; m. Natalie Kuznetsova, Aug. 31, 1957; children—Daniel Lodge, David Wetterman. Tng. in dermatology U. Calif. Hosp., 1940-43; hon. staff mem. St. Luke's Hosp., chief dermatology, 1954-70; clin. prof. U. Calif. Sch. Medicine, 1962—, chmn. div. dermatology, 1954-66; cons. Shriners Hosp. Crippled Children, Mt. Zion Hosp., U.S. Army; spl. research antifolic compounds for psoriasis. Dir. div. med. services Nat. Program Dermatology, 1969—. Co-recipient Taub Internat. award, 1968; recipient Clark W. Finnerud award Dermatology Found., 1973. Diplomate Am. Bd. Dermatology (pres. 1972). Mem. Am. Acad. Dermatology (v.p. 1966, Dome lectr. 1974, pres. 1978), Am. (dir. 1970— pres. 1974-75), Pacific (hon. mem.; pres. 1965), San Francisco (pres. 1949-52) dermatol. assns., AMA (chmn. sect. on dermatology 1968-69; mem. com. on cutaneous health and cosmetics 1970-73), Calif. Med. Assn. (chmn. sect. dermatology 1952), San Francisco Med. Soc. (dir. 1960); hon. mem. Danish, Bulgarian, Polish, N.Am. Clin., Southwestern, Pacific dermatol. socs. Asso. editor Jour. Investigative Dermatology, 1965-67. Editor: Dermatoses Due to Environmental and Physical Factors, 1963; mem. editorial bd. Jour. Western Medicine, 1969-79. Home: 3111 Bel Air Dr Las Vegas NV 89109 Office: 1820 E Desert Inn Rd Las Vegas NV 89109

REES, SHERREL JERRY EVANS, assn. exec.; b. Wenatchee, Wash., Oct. 3, 1926; s. Daniel Ivor and Margaret Amenda (Merriman) R.; student San Diego Jr. Coll., 1946-48; m. Joan Louise Dorsey, Mar. 18, 1977; children—Sherrel Rees Brewster, Susan Rees Stover, Daniel Michael. Farmer, Stevens County, Wash., 1950-60; office mgr. Spokane County Agr. Stablzn. and Conservation Service, Dept. Agr., Spokane, Wash., 1960-66; exec. sec. Wash. Assn. Wheat Growers, Ritzville, 1966-68; exec. v.p. Nat. Assn. Wheat Growers, Washington, 1970—; exec. v.p. Nat. Assn. Wheat Growers Found.; bd. dirs. Farm Film Found.; mem. steering com. Nat. Farm Coalition; advisor to U.S. del. Internat. Wheat Council, London; mem. Tech. Adv. Com. on Grain and Feed for Trade Negotiations; mem. com. on changing internat. realities Nat. Planning Assn.; mem. adv. com. Agr. Council Am. Served with USN, 1945-46. Mem. Washington Soc. Assn. Execs. Presbyterian. Club: Nat. Democratic. Editor Report From Washington, 1970—; asso. editor Wheat Grower, 1978—. Home: 13827 Overton Ln Silver Spring MD 20904 Office: 415 2d St NE Suite 300 Washington DC 20002

REES, THOMAS MANKELL, former congressman; b. Los Angeles, Mar. 26, 1925; s. Caradoc and Mildred (Melgaard) R.; B.A., Occidental Coll., 1950; m. Leanne Boccardo, Apr. 16, 1960; children—Evan Boccardo, James Caradoc. Admitted to Calif. bar, D.C. bar; pres. Compania del Pacifico, Inc., Los Angeles, 1951-70; mem. Calif. Assembly, 1955-62; mem. Calif. Senate from Los Angeles County, 1962-65; mem. 89th-94th Congresses from 23d Calif. Dist., mem. banking, currency and housing com., chmn. internat. trade investment and monetary policy subcom., mem. com. on D.C.; U.S. adv. to U.S. del. ann. meetings World Bank and Inter-Am. Bank, 1967-76; adv. to U.S. del. UN Trade and Devel. Meeting, Nairobi, Kenya, 1976; practice law, Washington, 1977—; Mem. Nat. Commn. Supplies and Shortages on Nat. and Internat. Levels; mem. adv. com. on internat. investment, tech. and devel. Dept. State; chmn. small bus. and internat. trade task force Pres. Carter's White House Conf. on Small Bus. Bd. dirs., mem. exec. com. Am. Near East Refugee Aid; bd. dirs. New Directions. Del. Democratic Nat. Convs., 1956, 60, 64, 68. Served with inf. AUS, World War II; ETO. Decorated Bronze star medal. Mem. Former Mems. Congress, Calif. State Soc., Los Angeles County Mus. Art Assos. Home: Washington DC Office: 1101 Connecticut Ave Washington DC 20036

REES, WARREN JAMES, justice Iowa Supreme Ct.; b. Anamosa, Iowa, Aug. 2, 1908; s. Barlow Granger and Anna Marie (Lowe) R.; student Grinnell Coll., 1926-27; m. Alma Davis, Aug. 20, 1938; children—Mary Ann Rees Lyman, William E (dec.). Admitted to Iowa bar, 1934; clk. Dist. Ct. of Jones County (Iowa), 1929-32; practiced in Anamosa, 1934-63; county atty. Jones County, 1939-44; judge 18th and 8th Dist. Cts., 1963-69; chief judge 8th Jud. Dist. Ct., 1967-69; asso. justice Iowa Supreme Ct., Des Moines, 1969—. Republican county chmn., 1938-50; mem. Rep. Central Com. of Iowa, 1948-52; del. Rep. Nat. Conv., 1948; trustee Cornell Coll., Mt. Vernon, Iowa. Mem. Am., Iowa, Jones County bar assns., Am. Judicature Soc. Clubs: Masons, Shriners, Odd Fellows, K.P., Lions. Home: 608 W Crane St Anamosa IA 52205 Office: Supreme Ct Bldg State Capitol Des Moines IA 50319

REES, WILLIAM MASON, ins. co. exec.; b. Bklyn., Mar. 17, 1916; s. Gomer H. and Pauline M. (Mason) R.; B.A., Yale, 1937; m. Marianna Adair, Nov. 2, 1940. With Chubb & Son, Inc., N.Y.C., 1937—, chmn. bd., dir., 1970—; chmn. bd., dir. Fed. Ins. Co., N.Y.C., 1970—; chmn. bd., dir. Vigilant Ins. Co., 1970—; chmn. bd., dir. Chubb Corp., 1970—; chmn., dir. Gt. No. Ins. Co., 1966—; dir. numerous cos. including Pacific Indemnity Co., Colonial Life Ins. Co. Am., Bellemead Devel. Corp., United Mchts. & Mfrs., Inc., Citibank, N.A., Ingredient Tech. Corp. Trustee, John and Mary R. Markle Found.; bd. visitors Tulane U. Served to lt. col. C.E., AUS, 1942-45. Mem. Am. Ins. Assn. (past chmn.), Assocs. Harvard Grad. Sch. Bus. Adminstrn. (dir.). Clubs: Down Town Assn., Links (N.Y.C.); Piedmont Driving (Atlanta). Office: 100 William St New York NY 10038

REESE, ALGERNON BEVERLY, ophthalmologist; b. Charlotte, N.C., July 28, 1896; s. Algernon Beverly and Mary Cannon (Wadsworth) R.; B.S., Davidson Coll., 1917; D.Sc. (hon.), 1946; M.D., Harvard, 1921; student U. Vienna, 1925-26; M.D. (hon.), U.

Melbourne, 1952; LL.D., Duke, 1957; m. Joan Leeds, Sept. 26, 1942; children—Algernon Beverly, III, Rigdon Leeds, Jonathan Wadsworth. Externe, Allgemeines Krankenhaus, Vienna, 1921, 1925-26; resident Mass. Eye and Ear Infirmary, Boston, 1924; Roosevelt Hosp., N.Y.C., 1921-23, N.Y. Eye and Ear Infirmary, 1923-27; chief eye clinic Cornell U. Med. Coll., N.Y.C., 1929-31, N.Y. Eye and Ear Infirmary, 1929-31, pathologist 1925-31; former attending ophthalmologist Vanderbilt Clinic, N.Y.C.; attending surgeon, pathologist Inst. Ophthalmology of Presbyn. Hosp.; cons. ophthalmologist, pathologist Eye Inst., N.Y.C.; cons. ophthalmologist to hosps. in N.Y. met. area. Roosevelt Hosp., Flushing Hosp., St. Clare's Hosp., Stamford (Conn.) Hosp., Southampton (L.I.) Hosp., Greenwich (Conn.) Hosp. Assn., St. Luke's Hosp., Manhattan Eye, Ear and Throat Hosp., N.Y. Eye and Ear Infirmary, Lenox Hill Hosp.; clin. prof. ophthalmology, emeritus Coll. Phys. and Surgs., Columbia; former mem. com. on ophthalmology Div. of Med. Sci., NRC.; DeSchweinitz lectr., 1946; Proctor lectr., 1949; Jackson lectr., 1954; Bedell lectr., 1955; Gifford lectr., 1955, Snell lectr., 1956, Schoenberg lectr., 1959, Montgomery (Royal Coll. Surgeons, Dublin) lectr., 1962. Pres., dir. Ophthalmic Publishing Co.; cons. to Surgeon Gen. U.S. Army; mem. bd. sci. counselors Nat. Inst. Neurol. Diseases and Blindness, HEW. Bd. dirs. Nat. Soc. for Prevention Blindness; adv. panel Research to Prevent Blindness. Received Hon. Key, Am. Acad. Ophthalmology, 1955; Merit citation Davidson Coll., 1948; Lucian Howe medal Am. Ophthalmol. Soc., 1950; Howe prize in ophthalmology U. Buffalo, 1956; Lucien Howe medal, eye sect. AMA, 1961, also Herman Knapp medal, 1972; Bowman medal Ophthal. Soc. U.K., 1971; Vail medal Internat. Soc. Eye Surgeons, 1971; Trustees award Research to Prevent Blindness, 1973. Fellow A.C.S., AMA (chmn. eye sect. 1956-57), Am. Ophthalmol. Soc. (pres. 1960), Am. Acad. Ophthalmology and Otolaryngology (pres. 1954-55), Assn. Research in Ophthalmology (Proctor medal 1958), N.Y. Acad. Med. (chmn. eye sect. 1939), N.Y. State and County Med. Soc. (chmn. eye sect. 1937), N.Y. Ophthalmol. Soc. (pres. 1949), Gonin Soc., Phi Beta Kappa (hon.), Kappa Alpha (So.), Omicron Delta Kappa, Phi Beta Pi; hon. mem. Greek, Cuban, Mexican, Australian, Chilean, Panamanian, French, New Zealand ophthal. socs. Clubs: Bedford Golf and Tennis, Pilgrims. Author: Tumors of the Eye, 1951, 62, 76; Tumors of Eye and Adnexa (Fascicle 38, Armed Forces Inst. Pathology), 1956; contbr. med. jours. and The Eye and Its Diseases, The Treatment of Cancer and Allied Diseases. Mem. editorial bd. Am. Jour. Ophthalmology. Home: 42 Bisbee Ln Bedford Hills NY 10507

REESE, ANNE CATHERINE OHLSON (MRS. EDWIN LEE REESE), librarian; b. Niagara Falls, N.Y., July 15, 1943; d. John Edward and Annetta Katrina (Diekhoff) Ohlson; B.A., U. Mich., 1964, M.A. in L.S., 1965; m. Edwin Lee Reese, Nov. 11, 1967; 1 dau., Catherine Suzanne. Head librarian Toledo Mus. Art, 1965—. Mem. Spl. Libraries Assn., Art Research Libraries of Ohio, Coll. Art Assn., Art Libraries Soc. N.Am. Presbyn. Home: 2401 Berdan St Toledo OH 43613 Office: PO Box 1013 Toledo OH 43613

REESE, BRUCE ALAN, educator; b. Provo, Utah, Aug. 3, 1923; s. David J. and Bessie (Johnson) R.; student Brigham Young U., 1941-43; B.S. in Mech. Engring., U. N.Mex., 1944; Ph.D., Purdue U., 1953; m. Barbara Taylor, June 20, 1945; chilren—Bruce Taylor, Michael David, Pamela Kay. Mem. faculty Purdue U., Lafayette, Ind., 1946—, asso. prof., 1955-57, prof. mech. engring., 1957-73, head Sch. Aeros. and Astronautics, 1973—; dep. dir. Nike Zeus Research and Devel., also tech. dir. Nike X Project Office, U.S. Army, 1961-63; dir. Jet Propulsion Center, Purdue U., 1965-73. Cons. aerospace govt. agys., industry; mem. sci. adv. bd. USAF, 1969-76, mem. adv. group fgn. tech. div., 1970-74, adv. group air systems div., 1973-76; mem. or cons. to sci. adv. panel U.S. Army, 1967—, chmn., 1976-77, chmn. tank and automotive command sci. adv. group, 1970-74, mem. missile command adv. com., 1972-76. Active Boy Scouts Am., 1959-67. Served to ensign USNR, 1943-46. Mem. Am. Inst. Aeros. and Astronautics (chmn. central Ind. sect. 1964-65), ASME (chmn. aircraft gas turbine 1965-68), Sigma Xi, Phi Kappa Phi, Pi Tau Sigma, Tau Beta Phi. Mem. Ch. Jesus Christ of Latter Day Saints. Research on heat transfer, gas dynamics, hybrid fueled rockets, laser diffusers, slurry fuel combustion. Home: 1228 Ravinia Rd West Lafayette IN 47906 Office: School Aeronautics and Astronautics Purdue U Lafayette IN 47907

REESE, CHARLES LEE, JR., publisher, editor; b. Wilmington, Del., Apr. 7, 1903; s. Charles Lee and Harriet Stedman (Bent) R.; grad. Wilmington Friends Sch., 1920; B.A., U. Va., 1924; grad. study, Cambridge U., Eng., 1924-25; m. Harriet Hurd Curtis, Oct. 2, 1926; children—Charles Lee, Sara C. Pryor, Peter A. Karthaus; m. 2d, Annette Mason Bush, Sept. 16, 1972. Mng. editor Popular Radio, N.Y.C., 1925-26; mem. editorial staff Time (mag.), 1927; with News-Journal papers since 1927, editor 1934-47, exec. editor, v.p., 1947-55, pres. News-Jour. Co., 1955-68, chmn. bd., 1966-72, vice chmn. bd., 1972-78. Bd. dirs. Wilmington Med. Center; pres. Lalor Found.; hon. dir., past pres. Wilmington Music Sch.; past pres. Hist. Soc. Del.; hon. trustee Wilmington Soc. of Fine Arts (past pres.). Clubs: Wilmington, Greenville Country. Author: Old Swedes Church; (with Alfred E. Bissell) Further Notes on the Pursuit of Salar; The Horse on Rodney Square; Merger: Events Leading up to the Formation of the Wilmington Medical Center. Editor: Delaware History mag., 1946-70; The Autobiography of Christopher L. Ward. Home: 82 Cokesbury Village Hockessin DE 19707 Address: Orange and Girard Sts Wilmington DE 19801

REESE, DELLA (DELLOREESE PATRICIA EARLY), singer; b. Detroit, July 6, 1931; d. Richard and Nellie Early; student Wayne U. m. Vermont Adolphus Bon Taliaferro (div.); m. 2d, Leroy Basil Gray (div.). Singer in choirs, 1938—; summers with Mahalia Jackson troupe, 1945-49; organized gospel group while student at Wayne U.; club appearances, Detroit, later joined Erskine Hawkins, N.Y.C.; solo artist, 1957—, appearing radio shows with Robert Q. Lewis, on TV with Jackie Gleason, Ed Sullivan, McCloud, Twice in a Lifetime, Police Woman, Petrocelli, Sanford & Son; appeared in TV series Chico & the Man, 1976-78, also others; hostess TV variety show Della, 1969-70; substitute hostess Tonight Show; role in motion picture Let's Rock, 1958; appeared in theatre in The Last Minstrel Show, 1978; recordings for Jubilee, RCA Victor Records, ABC Paramount Records. Voted Most Promising Singer of Yr., 1957. Address: care William Morris Agy 151 El Camino Dr Beverly Hills CA 90212

REESE, EVERETT D., banker; b. Columbus, Ohio, Jan. 15, 1898; s. David T. and Sarah (Davis) R.; B.S., Ohio State U., 1919; LL.D., Rutgers U., 1964, Ohio State U., 1971; D.Pub.Service, Ohio No. U., 1968; m. Martha Grace Miller, Sept. 4, 1924 (dec. May 1970); children—John Gilbert, Phoebe Lang (Mrs. John D. Lewis), Thekla Alice (Mrs. Donald B. Shackelford), David Everett; m. 2d, Pendery Spear Haines, Aug 29, 1971. Instr. sch. commerce Ohio State U., Columbus, 1919-20, Ga. Sch. Tech., Atlanta, 1920-21; part-time instr. Denison U., Granville, Ohio, 1922-23, 39-40; with Park Nat. Bank of Newark (Ohio), 1921—, pres., dir., 1926, chmn. bd., 1956-79, chmn. exec. com., 1979—; chmn. bd. 1st Nat. Bank, Cambridge, Ohio, 1955-73, hon. chmn., 1955-73; chmn. bd. First Fed. Savs. & Loan Assn., Newark, 1934-78, chmn. emeritus, 1978—; chmn. bd. City Nat. Bank & Trust Co., Columbus, 1959-68; chmn. bd. First Banc Group of Ohio Co., 1969-73, dir., 1973-78; dir. Suburban Motor Freight, Inc., Liqui-Box (all Columbus). Lectr., Sch. Banking U. Wis., 1949-56; mem. faculty Grad. Sch. Banking, Rutgers U., 1950-58; served with Internat. Exec. Service Corps. Trustee emeritus Mt. Carmel Hosp., Columbus, Dawes Arboretum, Newark, Ohio, Denison U., Granville, Ohio, Children's Hosp. of Columbus; trustee Evans Found., Newark. trustee, pres. Columbus Gallery Fine Arts, 1973-75; chmn. bd. trustees Piney Woods (Miss.) Country Life Sch.; bd. dirs. Pub. Welfare Found., Inc., Washington; chmn., exec. com. Pres.'s club Ohio State U., 1963-78, chmn. emeritus, 1978—. Recipient Disting. Service award Ohio State U., 1964; Ayres Leadership award Stonier Grad. Sch. Banking, Rutgers U., 1967; Distinguished Citizen award Columbus C. of C.; Preston Davis award, Columbus; Outstanding Citizen of 1979 Columbus Bd. Realtors. Mem. Ohio (pres. 1941-42), Am. (pres. 1953-54) bankers assns., Sigma Chi, Phi Alpha Kappa, Delta Sigma Pi, Beta Gamma Sigma, Alpha Kappa Psi. Presbyterian. Clubs: Univ. (N.Y.C.); Columbus, Rocky Fork Hunt and Country, Columbus Country, Athletic, Faculty, Rotary (Columbus), Masons (33 deg.), K.T., Shriners. Home: 6 Sessions Village Columbus OH 43209 Office: 100 E Broad St Columbus OH 43215

REESE, FRANCIS EDWARD, chem. co. exec.; b. Monaca, Pa., Nov. 3, 1919; s. Francis Edward and Vivian Iris (Hancuff) R.; B.S. in Chem. Engring., Purdue U., 1941; m. Katherine Mary McBrien, June 29, 1946; 1 son, Francis Edward III. With Monsanto Co., St. Louis, 1941—, research engr. plastics div., 1941-48, chief devel. engring. plastics div., 1948-53, asst. gen. mgr. plastics div., 1953-56, dir. engring. plastics div., 1956-59, asst. gen. mgr. plastics div., 1959-61, asst. gen. mgr. hydrocarbons div., 1961-65, asst. gen. mgr., hydrocarbons and polymers div., 1965-66, gen. mgr. internat. div., 1966-68, corp. v.p., 1968-74, gen. mgr., hydrocarbons and polymers div., 1968-71, gen. mgr. polymers and petrochems. div., 1971-73, gen. mgr. internat. div., 1973-74, dir., 1973—, group v.p., 1974-79, sr. v.p., 1979—. Mem. engring. found. adv. council U. Tex. Registered profl. engr., Mo. Fellow AAAS; mem. Am. Inst. Chem. Engrs., Am. Chem. Soc., Nat. Soc. Profl. Engrs., Soc. Chem. Industry, Tau Beta Pi, Phi Lambda Upsilon. Home: 12914 Topping Estates North Dr St Louis MO 63131 Office: 800 N Lindbergh Blvd St Louis MO 63166

REESE, JACK EDWARD, univ. chancellor; b. Hendersonville, N.C., Apr. 12, 1929; s. William James and Alyce Genevieve (Pace) R.; A.B. in English, Berea (Ky.) Coll., 1951; M.A., U. Ky., 1953, Ph.D., 1961; m. Nancy Anne Larsen, Aug. 31, 1957; children—Matthew Bradley, Kristin Alyce. Teaching asst. U. Ky., 1957-58, vis. prof., summer 1968; mem. faculty U. Tenn., Knoxville, 1961—, asso. prof. English, dean grad. studies, asso. vice chancellor acad. affairs, 1972-73, chancellor, 1973—; acad. adminstrv. intern Am. Council Edn., U. Ariz., 1969-70. Chmn. Tenn. Arts Commn., 1967-68; mem. Gov. Tenn. Adv. Com. Minority Econ. Devel., 1974—. Served with USNR, 1953-57. Mem. Southeastern Renaissance Conf., Phi Kappa Phi. Episcopalian. Contbr. articles to profl. jours. Office: 506 Andy Holt Tower U Tenn Knoxville TN 37916*

REESE, JAY RODNEY, electronics mfg. co. exec.; b. Phila., May 7, 1926; s. Joseph Hammond and Ethel (Allen) R.; B.S.E.E., Princeton U., 1950; m. Ninetta Ruth Spearman, June 19, 1965. Chief sales engr. transistor div. Nat. Union Radio Corp., Hatboro, Pa., 1950-55; v.p. Tex. Instruments Inc., Dallas, 1955-73; pres., chief exec. officer Recognition Equipment Inc., Irving, Tex., 1973—, also dir.; dir. Trammell Crow Distbn. Co. Mem. exec. bd. Edna Gladney Home, Ft. Worth; pres. North Tex. Radio for the Blind; treas. Dallas Taping for the Blind; mem. Dallas Citizens Council. Served with U.S. Army, 1944-46. Mem. IEEE, Electronics Industries Assn., Dallas C. of C. (dir.). Club: Northwood Country. Home: 10010 Strait Ln Dallas TX 75229 Office: 2701 E Grauwyler St Irving TX 75061

REESE, JOHN GILBERT, lawyer; b. Newark, Ohio, July 7, 1925; s. Everett David and Martha Grace (Miller) R.; student Phillips Acad. Andover, 1941-43; B.A., Ohio State U., 1949, J.D., 1952; m. Louella Catherine Hodges, Sept. 9, 1951; children—Martha Grace, Sarah Sherwood, Gilbert Hodges, Lucius Everett, Megan. Admitted to Ohio bar, 1952, since practiced in Newark; partner Reese, Paugh, McNenny & Price, 1966—. Dir. Park Nat. Bank of Newark; State Savs. Co., Columbus, Southgate Devel. Corp., B & L Motor Freight, Inc., Capitol Corp.; chmn. bd. First Fed. Savs. & Loan Assn. of Newark. Safety dir. City of Newark, 1955; mem. Newark City Council, 1956-57; city atty., 1958-62. Chmn. nat. council Ohio State U. Coll. Law; pres. Thomas J. Evans Found.; trustee Central Ohio Tech. Coll.; mem. governing com. Licking County Found. for Pub. Giving; trustee Dawes Arboretum, Columbus Mus. Art; trustee, pres. YMCA. Served with M.C., AUS, 1943-46. Named Outstanding Man of Year Jr. C. of C., 1955. Mem. Am., Ohio, Licking County (pres.) bar assns., Newark Area C. of C. (pres.), Newark Fedn. Musicians. Presbyterian. Clubs: Columbus, Presidents of Ohio State U. (Columbus, Ohio); Moundbuilders Country (Newark); Granville (Ohio) Tennis, Elks, Rotary. Home: 693 Tall Oaks Ct Newark OH 43055 Office: 36 N 2d St Newark OH 43055

REESE, KENNETH WENDELL, diversified co. exec.; b. Orange, Tex., Aug. 1, 1930; s. Richard W. and Florence (Mulhollan) R.; B.B.A., U. Houston, 1954; m. Mary A. Broom, Aug. 22, 1955; children—Jimmy, Michael, Gary. Asst. treas. Firestone Tire & Rubber Co., Akron, Ohio, 1968-70, treas., 1970—, v.p., 1973-75, exec. v.p. finance, 1975; sr. v.p. fin. Tenneco Inc., Houston, 1975-78, exec. v.p., 1978—. Served to 1st lt. AUS, 1954-56. Mem. U. Houston Athletic Lettermans Assn. Baptist. Clubs: Champions Golf, Petroleum, Woodlands (Houston). Home: 5623 Boyce Springs Houston TX 77066 Office: Tenneco Bldg Houston TX 77001

REESE, LYMON CLIFTON, educator; b. Murfreesboro, Ark., Apr. 27, 1917; s. Samuel Wesley and Nancy Elizabeth (Daniels) R.; B.S., U. Tex. at Austin, 1949, M.S., 1950; Ph.D. (Gen. Edn. Bd. Calif. fellow, NSF fellow), U. Calif. at Berkeley, 1955; m. Eva Lee Jett, May 28, 1948; children—Sally Reese Melant, John, Nancy. Rodman, Internat. Boundary Commn., San Benito, Tex., 1939-41; layout engr. E.I. DuPont Co. de Nemours & Co., Inc., Pryor, Okla., Childersburg, Ala., 1941-42; surveyor U.S. Naval Constrn. Bns., Aleutian Islands, Okinawa, 1942-45; field engr. Asso. Contractors & Engrs., Houston, 1945; draftsman Phillips Petroleum Co., Austin, 1946-48; research engr. U. Tex., Austin, 1948-50; asst. prof. civil engring. Miss. State Coll., State College, 1950-51, 53-55; asst. prof. U. Tex., Austin, 1955-57, asso. prof., 1957-64, prof., 1964—, chmn. dept., 1965-72, asso. dean engring. for program planning, 1972-79; cons. Shell Oil Co., Shell Devel. Co., 1955-65, Dames & Moore, 1970—, McClelland Engrs., Houston, 1970—, Assn. Drilled Shaft Contractors, 1971—, Fla. Dept. Transp., 1975—, others; Taylor prof. engring. Tex. U., 1972—. Served with USNR, 1942-45. Recipient Thomas Middlebrooks award ASCE, 1958; Joe J. King Profl. Engring. Achievement award, 1977. Registered profl. engr., Tex. Fellow ASCE (Karl Terzaghi lectr. 1976); mem. Nat. Acad. Engring., Am. Soc. Engring. Edn., Nat. Soc. Profl. Engrs., ASTM, Sigma Xi, Tau Beta Pi, Chi Epsilon, Phi Kappa Phi. Baptist (deacon). Contbr. articles to profl. jours. Home: 11512 Tin Cup Dr #109 Austin TX 78750 Office: Dept Civil Engring U Tex Austin TX 78712

REESE, RAYMOND CASTLE, structural engr.; b. Pittsfield, Mass., Dec. 22, 1893; s. John Miles and Minnie Victoria (Castle) Rees; B.S., Mass. Inst. Tech., 1920; postgrad. Harvard U., 1916-20; D.Sc., U. Toledo, 1977; m. Florence Miller, Dec. 30, 1920; children—Carolyn Reese Clark, Allen M., Virginia Reese White. From draftsman to chief draftsman, bldg. dept. Gen. Electric Co., Pittsfield, 1907-20; pvt. practice indsl. engring., Pittsfield, 1920-22; chief engr. Bldg. Products Co., Toledo, 1922-64; pvt. practice structural engring., Toledo, 1922—; partner, cons. Raymond C. Reese Assos., Toledo, 1960-73; lectr. Toledo U., 1924-52; chmn. bd. Nat. Bd. Accreditation in Concrete Constrn., 1973—; mem. commn. I Recommendations pratiques Comite Europeen du Beton, mem. commn. III flexion-compression; exec. com. com. tall bldgs. Internat. Assn. Bridge and Structural Engrs.-ASCE, 1969—, group coordinator, 1969—; past mem. bldg. research div. Nat. Bur. Standards; past chmn. bldg. code requirements for minimum design loads in bldgs. Am. Nat. Standards Inst.; past dir. Toledo Concrete Improvement Bd.; editorial com. codes developing countries UNESCO, 1963-64. Vice pres. Northwestern Ohio chpt. Arthritis Found., 1971-75. Named Man of Year, Engring. News Record, 1966. Registered profl. engr., Ohio, Mich., Ind., Ill., N.Y., Ark., Pa., Wis. Fellow Am. Inst. Cons. Engrs., Brit. Instn. Civil Engrs.; hon. life mem. Am. Conceret Inst. (past pres.; Alfred E. Lindau award 1957, Henry L. Kennedy award 1964, Arthur Y. Moy Meml. award Mich. chpt. 1976, Henry C. Turner Nat. award 1977), ASCE (past chmn. exec. com. structural div., past chmn. com. masonry and reinforced concrete of structural div.); mem. Concrete Reinforcing Steel (past chmn. engring. practice com.; award 1953, salute 1977), ASTM (25 year award 1969), Nat., Ohio, Toledo (past pres.; Engr. of Year award 1962) socs. profl. engrs., Internat. Soc. Bridge and Structural Engrs. (past chmn. U.S. activities com.), Cons. Engrs. Ohio, Mass. Inst. Tech. Alumni Assn., Reinforced Concrete Research Council (past mem. exec. com.), Am. Soc. Engring. Edn. (life), Prestressed Concrete Inst., Internat. Assn. Shell Structures, Réunion Internationale des Laboratoires D'Essais et de Recherches Sur les Materiaux et les Constructions. Clubs: Toledo, Rotary. Author: (with Sutherland) Reinforced Concrete Design, 1943; also handbooks, reports, sects. books, articles. Home: 3821 Sulphur Spring Rd Toledo OH 43606

REESE, WILLIAM LEWIS, educator; b. Jefferson City, Mo., Feb. 15, 1921; s. William Lewis and Lillian Amelia (Fisher) R.; A.B., Drury Coll., 1942; B.D., U. Chgo., 1945, Ph.D., 1947; student Yale, 1955-56; m. Louise Weeks, June 11, 1945; children—Claudia, Patricia, William Lewis III. Asst. prof. philosophy Drake U., 1947-49, asso. prof. philosophy, 1949-57, head dept., 1954-57; asso. prof. philosophy Grinnell Coll., 1957-60; vis. prof. philosophy Iowa State U., 1958; prof. philosophy, chmn. dept. U. Del., Newark, 1960-67, H. Rodney Sharp prof. philosophy, 1965-67; prof. philosophy State U. N.Y. at Albany, 1967—, chmn. dept., 1968-74. Tully Cleon Knoles lectr. U. Pacific, 1962. Del., U.S. Nat. Commn. for UNESCO, 1963; gen. mem. 4th East-West Philosophers Conf., 1964. Recipient Ford Found. Study award, Argentina, 1967; Fulbright lectr., Argentina, summer 1971; Inst. for Humanistic Studies fellow, 1977-78. Mem. AAUP, Am. Philos. Assn., Metaphysical Soc. Am. (sec.-treas. 1962-65). Disciple of Christ. Author, contbr.; Studies in C.S. Peirce, 1952; (with Charles Hartshorne) Philosophers Speak of God, 1953; The Ascent from Below, 1959; (with Eugene Freeman) Process and Divinity, 1964; Dictionary of Philosophy and Religion: Eastern and Western Thought, 1980; gen. editor: Philosophy of Science, The Delaware Seminar, vols. 1, 2, 1963, vol. 3, 1967. Contbg. editor: Philosophical Interrogations, 1964; co-editor: Metaphilosophy; editorial bd. State U. N.Y. Press. Contbr. articles profl. jours. Home: Font Grove Rd Slingerlands NY 12159 Office: Dept Philosophy State Univ NY Albany NY 12203. *To have before one always the realistic sense that if one has been successful in one way he has failed in others, and that one's failures surely outnumber his successes.*

REESE, WILLIS LIVINGSTON MESIER, ednl. adminstr.; b. Bernardsville, N.J., June 16, 1913; s. William Willis and Augusta (Bliss) R.; grad. St. Paul's Sch., N.H., 1931; A.B., Yale, 1935, LL.B., 1938; LL.D., Louvain (Belgium), 1972; m. Frances Gallatin Stevens, June 26, 1937; children—William Willis, Frances Gallatin, John Rathbone, George Bliss, Alexander Stevens. Admitted to N.Y. bar, 1938; law clk. Judge Thomas Swan, 1938-39; asso. Winthrop, Stimson, Putnam & Roberts, N.Y.C., 1939-41; from asst. prof. to Charles Evans Hughes prof. law Columbia, 1946—, dir. Parker Sch. Fgn. and Comparative Law, 1955—. Lectr. Hague Acad. Internat. Law, 1964, 76, mem. curatorium, 1975—; U.S. del. Hague Conf. Pvt. Internat. Law, 1956, 60, 64, 68, 72, 76; reporter restatement (2d) conflict laws Am. Law Inst. Bd. dirs. N.Y. Legal Aid Soc., 1951-71; chmn. Community Action for Legal Services, 1967-70; mem. N.Y. Law Revision Commn., 1973—. Pres. bd. trustees Millbrook Sch., 1968-77; pres. Five Towns United Fund, 1959, chmn. bd., 1958, 60. Served as capt. AUS, 1941-46. Mem. Am. Assn. Comparative Study Law (sec., dir.), Joint Conf. Legal Edn. (1st v.p.), Assn. Bar City of N.Y., Internat. Law Assn. (Am. br.), Am. Bar Assn., Am. Soc. Internat. Law, Am. Fgn. Law Assn. (pres. 1964-67), Am. Assn. UN (pres. Five Towns chpt. 1962-63, 77—), Acad. Polit. Sci. (life), Inst. Internat. Law, Phi Beta Kappa, Order of Coif. Episcopalian (sr. warden, sec. standing com. Diocese N.Y. 1963-65). Clubs: Century, Rockaway Hunting. Union. Author: (with Rosenberg) Cases and Materials on Conflict of Laws, 1971. Editorial bd. law book dept. Little, Brown & Company. Home: 345 Meadowview Ave Hewlett NY 11557 Office: 345 W 116th St New York NY 10027

REESING, JOHN PALMER, JR., educator; b. Gatesville, Tex., Sept. 15, 1920; s. John Palmer and Anne (Baines) R.; B.A., Baylor U., 1941; M.A., Tulane U., 1942; Ph.D., Harvard, 1954. Mem. faculty George Washington U., 1946-49, 54—, prof. English, 1962—, chmn. dept. English, 1963-70, 75—, acting chmn., 1972-73; instr. English, Oberlin Coll., 1953-54. Served to 1st lt. AUS, 1942-46. Mem. Modern Lang. Assn. Am., Modern Humanities Research Assn., Internat. Assn. U. Profs. English, Renaissance Soc. Am. Episcopalian. Author: Milton's Poetic Art, 1968. Address: Dept English George Washington Univ Washington DC 20052

REEVE, EDWARD WILKINS, educator, organic chemist; b. Westmont, N.J., July 31, 1913; s. Edward White and Roxana (Wilkins) R.; B.S. in Chem. Engring., Drexel Inst. Tech. (now Univ.), 1936; Ph.D. in Chemistry, U. Wis., 1940; m. D. Lotus Marsh, Feb. 3, 1940; children—Roslyn Diane, Sheryl Anne, Donald Wilkins. Instr., U. Md., College Park, 1940-41, faculty, 1945—, prof. chemistry, 1951—; tech. aide OSRD, Washington, 1941-45, cons., 1949-52. Recipient Alumni citation for outstanding achievements Drexel U., 1956. Mem. Am. Chem. Soc., AAAS, Washington Acad. Scis., Sigma Xi, Alpha Chi Sigma, Phi Kappa Phi, Tau Beta Pi. Research, publs., patents on chemistry of aryltrichloromethylcarbinols, pinacol rearrangement, catalytic hydrogenation organic compounds. Home: 4708 Harvard Rd College Park MD 20740

REEVE, ERNEST BASIL, physiologist, educator; b. Liverpool, Eng., May 5, 1912; s. William Ernest and Irene (Gill) R.; B.A., Oxford U., 1935, B.M., B.Ch., 1938; F.R.C.P., London, 1969; children—Jonathan, Sarah. Came to U.S., 1953. Mem. sci. staff Med. Research Council London Clin. Research Unit, Guy's Hosp., 1940-52; faculty U. Colo. Med. Sch., Denver, 1953—, prof. medicine, 1962—, head div. lab. medicine, 1961-77; vis. prof. physiology Columbia, 1953. Mem. com. on shock NRC, 1957-68. Mem. Central Soc. for Clin. Research, Am., Brit. physiol. socs., Western Assn. Physicians, Med. Research Soc. (London). Author: (with R.T. Grant)

Observations on the General Effects of Injury on Man with Special Reference to Wound Shock, 1951. Contbr. articles to profl. jours. Home: 1420 S Cherry St Denver CO 80222 Office: Dept Medicine U Colo Health Scis Center 4200 E 9th Ave Denver CO 80262

REEVE, GEORGE WASHINGTON, realtor; b. Globe, Ariz., Feb. 22, 1940; s. Guy Walter and Nevada Jane (Elrod) R.; student Grand Canyon Coll., Phoenix, 1958-59, Phoenix Coll., 1959-60, Ariz. State U., 1960-61; m. Patricia Lanore Miller, Apr. 11, 1968; children—Jack Gregory Clay, Derek Dion, Rhonda Renee. With Del E. Webb Corp., Phoenix, 1962—, gen. mgr. comml. div., then v.p., 1966-71, exec. v.p., 1971—. Campaign chmn. Phoenix United Way, 1974, bd. dirs., 1973-77; bd. dirs. Gompers Meml. Rehab. Center, 1971-73; dean's adv. com. Ariz. State U. Coll. Bus., 1976-77. Named Citizen of Year, Phoenix Real Estate Bd., 1975; One of 10 Outstanding Young Men of Am., U.S. Jaycees, 1976. Mem. Inst. Real Estate Mgmt., Ariz. Assn. Realtors, Phoenix Real Estate Bd., Bldg. Owners and Mgmt. Assn., Phoenix Metro C. of C. (dir. 1976-79, pres. bd. 1978-79). Republican. Clubs: Phoenix Country, Kiva, Plaza (dir.). Author articles in field. Home: 5521 W Cactus Rd Glendale AZ 85304 Office: 3800 N Central Ave Phoenix AZ 85012

REEVE, JOHN PAXTON, paper co. exec.; b. Neenah, Wis., Oct. 22, 1912; s. Howard Dickenson and Lucy (Buckland) R.; B.A., Lawrence U., 1934; m. Jean Shannon, Sept. 3, 1937; children—James, Elizabeth, Barbara. With Appleton (Wis.) Papers div. NCR, 1934—, sales and advt. dept. asst., sales rep., personnel mgr., mill mgr., 1947-55, v.p., 1952-55, exec. v.p., 1955-62, pres., 1962-65, pres., chief exec. officer, 1965-77, also dir., v.p. parent co.; dir. 1st Nat. Bank, Appleton, George Banta Co., Wis. Electric Power Co., Milw. Trustee Lawrence U. Mem. Beta Theta Pi. Congregationalist. Clubs: Rotary, Riverview. Home: 212 N Green Bay Rd Appleton WI 54911

REEVES, ALBERT LEE, lawyer, exec.; b. Steelville, Mo., May 31, 1906; s. Albert L. and Martha (Ferguson) R.; B.A., William Jewell College, 1927; J.D., U. Mo., 1931; m. Eleanor Louise Glasner, Oct. 3, 1935; children—Elaine L., Martha E., Nancy L. Instr., Baylor Coll., Belton, Tex., 1927-28; admitted to Mo. bar, 1931, former partner, now of counsel firm Cummings, Sellers, Reeves & Conner, Washington; admitted to D.C. bar, 1949; sr. v.p., sec., mem. exec. com., dir. Utah Internat., Inc. and subsidiaries and affiliates, 1958-75; sr. v.p. cons. Marcona Corp., Marcona Internat., San Francisco, 1975-76; dir. KQED, 1970-76, French Bank Calif. Mem. 80th U.S. Congress from 5th Dist., Mo. Treas. Jackson County Republican Com., 1934-36; mem. chancellor's assos. Calif. State Univ. and Colls.; bd. dirs. St. Luke's Hosp. Served from capt. to lt. col. C.E., AUS, 1942-46; CBI, Decorated Order of Cristobal Colon, Order of Juan Pablo Duarte (Dominican Republic); Order of Maritime Merit, San Francisco Port Authority, 1967. Mem. Am., Mo., Fed. bar assns., Bar Assn. D.C., Am. Soc. Polit. Law, Acad. Polit. Sci., Mil. Order World Wars, World Affairs Council No. Cal. (pres. 1966-69), S.A.R., Pi Kappa Delta, Kappa Sigma, Phi Delta Phi, Delta Sigma Rho. Episcopalian. Mem. DeMolay Legion of Honor. Clubs: Nat. Lawyers, World Trade (pres., dir. 1965-69, hon. life mem.), Metropolitan (Washington); San Francisco Golf; Burlingame Country, Pauma Valley Country, Bankers. Home and office: PO Box 657 Pauma Valley CA 92061

REEVES, CHARLES HOWELL, educator; b. Schenectady, Nov. 23, 1915; s. Howell H. and Justina (Smith) R.; A.B., Union Coll., Schenectady, 1937; Ph.D. in Classics, U. Cin., 1947; m. Lucille Jane Pritchard, Dec. 22, 1945; children—Jane L. (Mrs. Hugh J. McGee), Frances E. (Mrs. David M. Herring), Helen Ann, Ruth M. (Mrs. Timothy C. Connell), Justina P., Charles Howell. Instr. classics Ind. U., 1946-49; asst. prof. Classics, Johns Hopkins, 1949-52; asso. prof., then prof. classics U. Okla., 1952-66; prof. classics Case Western Res. U., 1966—, chmn. dept., 1966-77. Served to lt. USNR, 1942-45. Mem. Am. Philol. Assn., Am. Inst. Archaeology, Classical Assn. Middle West and South, Soc. Ancient Greek Philosophy, Virgilian Soc., Phi Beta Kappa. Author articles on Greek tragedy. Home: 1791 Cadwell Ave Cleveland Heights OH 44118 Office: Dept Classics Case Western Res Univ Cleveland OH 44106

REEVES, EDWARD DUER, oil co. exec.; b. N.Y.C., July 26, 1909; s. Edward Duer and Beatrice (Oltrogge) R.; B.A., Williams Coll., 1930; postgrad. Princeton; m. Elsie Kean, July 6, 1932; children—Edward Duer, Mabyn Kean, Beatrice Meserole, Elva Gordon. With Standard Oil Co. (N.J.) affiliate Esso Research & Engring. Co. (formerly Standard Oil Devel. Co.), 1930-58, exec. v.p., dir., 1949-58; exec. v.p., dir. Esso Standard Oil Co., 1958-59; v.p., dir. Humble Oil & Refining Co., 1959-62; exec. v.p., dir. Esso Research & Engring. Co., 1962-64; pres., dir. Reeves Assos., Inc., Summit, N.J., 1965-74; chmn. dir. Reeves Enterprises, Inc., Summit, 1974—. Author: Management of Industrial Research, 1967. Office: 226 Oak Ridge Ave Summit NJ 07901

REEVES, FRANK BLAIR, architect; b. Beaumont, Tex., June 5, 1922; s. William Garland and Hazel Ann (Blackburn) R.; B.Arch., U. Tex., 1948; postgrad. Archtl. Assn., London, 1945; M.Arch., U. Fla., 1953; m. Mary Nell Gibson, Aug. 3, 1948; 1 son, William Gibson. Asso. architect Stone and Pitts, Architects, Beaumont, Tex., 1946-49; mem. faculty dept. architecture U. Fla., 1949—, dir. grad. program in archtl. preservation, 1970—; supervising architect Hist. Am. Bldgs. Survey, 1958-71; cons archtl. preservation, 1960—; pres. Preservation Inst., Nantucket; bd. dirs. Research and Edn. Center in Archtl. Preservation; adv. Fla. Div. Archives, History and Records Mgmt., 1966—; mem. Fla. Bicentennial Commn., 1972-76. Served with U.S. Army, 1943-46. Fellow AIA (state preservation coordinator; Fla. Assn. spl. citation for preservation 1976); mem. Nat. Trust Hist. Preservation (trustee), Fla. Trust Hist. Preservation (v.p.), Soc. Archtl. Historians, Fla. Hist. Soc., Assn. Preservation Tech., Delta Tau Delta. Democrat. Methodist. Contbr. articles to Jour. AIA. Office: Dept Architecture U Fla Gainesville FL 32611

REEVES, FRANKLIN DELANO (DELL), singer, songwriter, musician; b. Sparta, N.C., July 14, 1933; student Appalachian State Coll.; m. Ellen Schiell; children—Anne Delano, Kari Elizabeth Bethany. Appeared with WTOP, Galax, Va. and later with Chester Smith TV program, Calif.; host TV program Country Carnival, 1960; regular appearances in Las Vegas; mem. WSN Grand Ole Opry, 1966—; leader musical groups Doodle-Bugs and Good-Time Charlies; songs recorded include: Girl on the Billboard, A Dime at a Time, Looking at the World through a Windshield, The Philadelphia Fillies; movie appearances include: Sam Whiskey, Forty-Acre Feud, Cottonpickin' Chickenpickers. Office: care Buddy Lee Attractions Inc 38 Music Sq E Nashville TN 37203*

REEVES, GEORGE PAUL, bishop; b. Roanoke, Va., Oct. 14, 1918; s. George Floyd and Harriett Faye (Foster) R.; B.A., Randolph-Macon Coll., 1940; B.D., Yale U., 1943; D.D., U. of South, 1970, Nashotah House, 1970; m. Adele Beer, Dec. 18, 1943; children—Cynthia Reeves Pond, George Floyd II. Ordained priest Episcopal Ch., 1948, consecrated bishop, 1969; chaplain U.S. Naval Res., 1943-47, Fla. State U., 1947-50; rector All Saints Ch., Winter Park, Fla., 1950-59, Ch. of Redeemer, Sarasota, Fla., 1959-65, St. Stephens Ch., Miami, Fla., 1965-69; bishop of Ga., Savannah, 1969—. Mem. Phi Beta Kappa. Office: 611 E Bay St Savannah GA 31401

REEVES, HAZARD EARLE, accoustical engring. exec.; b. Balt., July 6, 1906; s. Hazard E. and Susan (Perryclear) R.; B.S., Ga. Inst. Tech., 1928; m. Annette Brown, Nov. 11, 1943; children—Hazard Earle, Alexander G. Research engr. Columbia Phonograph Co., N.Y.C., 1928-29; asst. chief engr. Stanley Rec. Co., N.Y.C., 1929-30; sound dir. Harvard Film Found., 1930-31; ind. sound rec. activities, 1931-33; founder, pres., dir. Reeves Sound Studios, Inc. and asso. firms, N.Y.C., 1933-60; founder, pres. Audio Devices, Inc., N.Y.C., 1936-43; co-founder, pres. Reeves-Ely Labs., Inc., 1942-45, including subsidiaries Am. Transformer Co., Waring Co., Winsted Hardware Co., Reeves-Hoffman Crystal Co., Reeves Instrument Co., Hudson Am. Co.; pioneered devel. stereophonic magnetic sound, 1946; founder, chmn. bd. Reeves Industries, Inc. (formerly Reeves Soundcraft Corp.), N.Y.C., 1947-67; founder, dir., pres. Cinerama, Inc., N.Y.C., 1950-60; organizer, chmn. bd. Reeves Telecom Corp., N.Y.C. 1960—; chmn. bd. Reatron Corp., Detroit, Reeves Teletype, N.Y.C.; dir. Tuxedo Assn., Tuxedo Park, N.Y., Reeves Industries, Inc., Squiers-Sanders, Inc. Mem. elec. engring. adv. com. Ga. Inst. Tech. Trustee Psychiat. Research Found., Ga. Tech. Found., Am. Found. Blind. Recipient of Alumni Distinguished Service award Ga. Inst. Tech., 1957. Fellow Soc. Motion Picture and TV Engrs.; mem. Motion Picture Pioneers, Newcomen Soc. N.Y., N.Y. So. Soc. (exec. com.), Motion Picture Pioneers, N.C. Soc. of New York (trustee), Anak Soc., Tau Beta Pi. Clubs: Economic, Georgia Technology Metropolitan. Union League (N.Y.C.); Tuxedo (Tuxedo Park, N.Y.); North Woods (Minerva, N.Y.); Mipissis Salmon. Home: Tuxedo Park NY 10987 Office: 1211 Ave of Americas New York NY 10036

REEVES, J. E., JR., mfg. co. exec.; b. Woodruff, S.C., Aug. 19, 1939; s. John E. and Jeneil (Beason) R.; grad. N.Y. U., 1962; m. Katherine R. Feighner, Nov. 27, 1965; children—John E. III, Katherine Mercer, Michael Gordon. With Reeves Bros., Inc., 1964—, corp. v.p., 1970-75, pres. Comfy div., 1971-72, head finished goods sales div., 1972-75, corp. pres., N.Y.C., 1975—, also mem. exec., planning adv., pension and profit sharing trust coms. Bd. dirs. Reeves Bros. Found., Greater N.Y. councils Boy Scouts Am.; exec. com. Scouting for Handicapped; mem. budget and fin. coms. United Fund; patron Mental Health Assn. N.J. Served with U.S. Army, 1962-64. Mem. Conf. Bd., NAM, Am. Arbitration Assn., Am. Textile Mfrs. Inst. Republican. Methodist. Clubs: Beacon Hill, Hemisphere, Lint Head Assos. Home: 35 Ox Bow Ln Summit NJ 07901 Office: 1271 Ave Americas New York NY 10020

REEVES, JOHN EDWIN, indsl. textiles co. exec.; b. Mt. Airy, N.C., June 15, 1913; s. Marvin Coke and Myrtle (Spaugh) R.; B.S. Textiles, N.C. State U., Raleigh, 1935; LL.D. (hon.), Clemson U., 1963; m. Jeneil Beason, July 2, 1938; children—John Edwin, Carolyn, Jane. With Reeves Bros. Inc., N.Y.C., 1934—, pres., chmn. bd., chief exec. officer, 1967, chmn. exec. com., 1975—. Mem. Am. Textile Mfg. Inst. (pres. 1972). Clubs: Baltusrol Golf, Biltmore Country, Sparantburg Country, Bay Hill. Address: 115 Summit Ave Summit NJ 07901

REEVES, NORMAN PENNINGTON, retail chain exec.; b. Knightstown, Ind., Nov. 23, 1912; s. Norman Wilmont Chesterfield and Mabell (Pennington) R.; B.S. in Pharmacy, Butler U., Indpls., 1936, LL.D. (hon.), 1979; m. Evelyn Fort, Mar. 16, 1935; children—Delinda Reeves Caldwell, John Douglas. With Hook Drugs, Inc., Indpls., 1945—, v.p. ops., 1959-72, pres., 1972—, chmn. bd., chief exec. officer, 1978—, also dir.; dir. 1st Nat. Bank, Knightstown, Salt Creek Realty Corp.; past mem. Ind. Bd. Pharmacy. Mem. Ind. State Police Bd., 1973—; bd. dirs., past pres. Crossroads Rehab. Center, Indpls.; bd. dirs., exec. com. United Way Greater Indpls.; mem. finance com. Community Hosp., Indpls.; mem. dean's adv. council Krannert Grad. Sch. Indsl. Adminstrn., Purdue U., 1974-75; past mem. Knightstown Pub. Sch. Bd. Mem. Nat. Assn. Chain Drug Stores (dir. 1976—), Ind. Retail Council (dir., exec. com.), Greater Indpls. Progress Com., Amateur Trap Shooting Assn. Clubs: Downtown Kiwanis, Columbia, Shriners, Masons, K.P. Home: 116 S Jefferson St Knightstown IN 46148 Office: Hook Drugs Inc PO Box 26285 Indianapolis IN 46226

REEVES, ROBERT GRIER LEFEVRE, scientist, educator; b. York, Pa., May 30, 1920; s. Edward LeGrande and Helen (Baker) R.; student Yuba Coll., 1938-40; B.S., U. Nev., 1949; M.S., Stanford, 1950, Ph.D., 1965; m. Elizabeth Bodette Simmons, June 11, 1942; children—Dale Ann, Edward Boyd. Geophysicist, geologist U.S. Geol. Survey, 1949-69 with assignments as project chief iron ore deposits of Nev., tech. adviser Fgn. Aid Program, vis. prof. econ. geology U. Rio Grande do Sul, Brazil, staff geologist for research contracts and grants and profl. staffing, Washington; prof. geology Colo. Sch. Mines, Golden, 1969-73; staff scientist Earth Resources Observation Systems Data Center, U.S. Geol. Survey, Sioux Falls, S.D., 1973-78; prof., chmn. earth sci. U. Tex. of Permian Basin, Odessa, 1978—, dean Coll. Sci. and Engring., 1979—; co-leader Am. Geol. Inst. Internat. Field Inst. to Brazil, 1966; vis. geol. scientist Boston Coll., Boston U., 1967; sr. Fulbright lectr. U. Adelaide (Australia), 1969. Served to maj. Signal Corps, AUS, 1941-46; ETO. Recipient Outstanding Service award U.S. Geol. Survey, 1965. Fellow Geol. Soc. Am., AAAS, Geol. Soc. Brazil; mem. Am. Inst. Mining, Metall. and Petroleum Engrs. (sec. Washington 1964), Am. Soc. Photogrammetry (editor-in-chief Manual of Remote Sensing), Am. Assn. Petroleum Geologists, Soc. Econ. Geologists, Soc. Ind. Profl. Earth Scientists. Contbr. articles profl. jours. Home: 2130 Westbrook Odessa TX 79761 Office: U Tex of Permian Basin Odessa TX 79762

REEVES, ROBERT LLOYD, dentist; b. Oxnard, Calif., June 16, 1923; s. Claude Lamar and Aubrey Della R.: student U. So. Calif., 1941-43, D.D.S., 1945: m. Margaret Emma Clare, Oct. 6, 1948; children—David B., Martin A., Robert Lloyd, Thomas B. Instr., U. So. Calif. Sch. Dentistry, 1948-50, asst. prof., 1950-51, asso. prof., 1951-59, prof. periodontics, 1959—, chmn. sect. periodontics, 1950-66, 76—. Served with U.S. Army, 1946-48. Diplomate Am. Bd. Periodontology (exec. sec.-treas.). Fellow Am. Acad. Periodontology (pres.-elect), Am. Coll. Dentists; mem. ADA, Western Soc. Periodontology, Am. Assn. Dental Schs., Omicron Kappa Upsilon. Office: U So Calif Sch Dentistry Los Angeles CA 90007

REEVES, ROSSER SCOTT, III, advt. agy. exec.; b. N.Y.C., Aug. 20, 1936; s. Rosser and Elizabeth (Street) R.; acad. degree with honors, Westminster Sch., 1954; postgrad. Yale, 1954-55; B.S. with honors in Architecture, U. Va., 1961; m. Colin McRae Squibb, Dec. 14, 1963; 1 dau., Elizabeth Robinson. Asso. real estate firm Douglas L. Elliman & Co., N.Y.C., 1961-62; investment banker Lazard Freres & Co., N.Y.C., 1962-67; founder, mng. partner R.S. Reeves & Co., N.Y.C., 1967-68; sr. mng. partner Bacon, Stevenson & Reeves, N.Y.C., 1968-70; chmn. bd. Quantum Corp., N.Y.C., 1970-75; pres. Rosser Reeves Holdings, Ltd., N.Y.C., 1975—; exec. v.p., dir. Rosser Reeves, Inc., advt., N.Y.C., 1976—; mem. N.Y. Stock Exchange, 1967-69; mng. partner Wall St. Leasing Asso., 1968-70; chmn. bd. Internat. Subsea Devel. Corp., N.Y.C., 1969-75, Mil. Armament Corp., 1972-75. Trustee Youth Consultation Service, N.Y.C., 1968-72. Mem. Scarab. Clubs: Racquet and Tennis, N.Y. Stock Exchange Lunch (N.Y.C.). Home: 115 E 87th St New York NY 10028 Office: 605 Third Ave New York NY 10016

REEVES, WILLIAM BOYD, lawyer; b. Easley, S.C., Mar. 24, 1932; s. William C. and Elise B. (Brooks) R.; B.A., Furman U., 1954; LL.B., Tulane U., 1959; m. Rose Mary Weil, Sept. 7, 1957 (dec. Nov. 1977); 1 dau., Gabrielle; m. 2d, Gladys Frances Brown, Nov. 24, 1978. Admitted to La. bar, 1959, Ala. bar, 1960, U.S. Supreme Ct., 1971; law clk. to U.S. Dist. Judge, So. Ala., 1959-61; asso. firm Armbrecht, Jackson & DeMouy, 1961-65; partner Armbrecht, Jackson, DeMouy, Crowe, Holmes & Reeves, Mobile, 1965—. Chancellor St. Lukes Episcopal Ch. and Sch., 1973—. Served to capt. U.S. Army, 1954-56. Mem. Am. Bar Assn., Ala. State Bar, La. State Bar, Mobile Bar Assn. (v.p. 1978-79), Internat. Assn. Ins. Counsel, Maritime Law Assn. U.S., Ala. Defense Lawyers Assn. (past pres.), Southeastern Admiralty Law Inst. (past pres.). Clubs: Athelstan, Mobile Country, Internat. Trade, Bienville, Propeller, Mason. Home: 3755 Rhonda Dr S Mobile AL 36608 Office: 1101 Merchants Nat Bank Bldg Mobile AL 36602

REEVES, WILLIAM CARLISLE, educator; b. Riverside, Calif., Dec. 2, 1916; s. William Claude and Alice (Brant) R.; B.S., U. Calif. at Berkeley, 1938, Ph.D., 1943, M.P.H., 1949; m. Mary Jane Moulton, July 6, 1940; children—William C., Robert F., Terrence M. Entomologist, research asst., research asso. Hooper Found., U. Calif. Med. Sch., San Francisco, 1941-49; faculty Sch. Pub. Health, U. Calif. at Berkeley, 1946—; prof. epidemiology, 1956—, dean Sch. Pub. Health, 1968-71, chmn. dept. epidemiology, 1949-68, 75—; cons. to govt. agys. Mem. AAAS, Am. Pub. Health Assn., Am. Soc. Tropical Medicine and Hygiene, Am. Entomol. Soc., Am. Epidemiol. Soc., Am. Mosquito Assn. Author: (with W. McD. Hammon) Epidemiology of Arthropod-Borne Viral Encephalities in Kern County, California, 1943-52, 1962; also numerous articles. Research on biol. factors controlling spread viral diseas by arthropod vectors. Home: 2846 Kinney Dr Walnut Creek CA 94598 Office: Sch Pub Health U Calif Berkeley CA 94720

REFF, THEODORE, art historian; b. N.Y.C., Aug. 18, 1930; s. Irving and Alice (Pinkowitz) R.; B.A., Columbia U., 1952; M.A., Harvard U., 1953, Ph.D., 1958; m. Arlene Gottesman, June 25, 1961; children—Lisa, Jonathan. Mem. faculty Columbia U., 1957—, prof. art history, 1964—; cons. Time-Life Library of Art. Fellow Guggenheim Found., Am. Council Learned Socs., Am. Philos. Soc., Inst. Advanced Study. Mem. Coll. Art Assn. Am. (dir.). Editor: Cezanne Watercolors, 1963; co-editor: Unpublished Letters of Toulouse-Lautrec, 1969; author: Notebooks of Edgar Degas, 2 vols.; 1976, Manet: Olympia, 1976; Degas: The Artist's Mind, 1977. Home: 435 Riverside Dr New York NY 10025 Office: 814 Schermerhorn Hall Columbia Univ New York NY 10027

REFIOR, EVERETT LEE, labor economist; b. Donnellson, Iowa, Jan. 23, 1919; s. Fred C. and Daisy E. (Gardner) R.; B.A., Iowa Wesleyan Coll., 1942; postgrad. U. Glasgow, 1945; M.A., U. Chgo., 1955; Ph.D., U. Iowa, 1962; m. Marie Emma Culp, Sept. 12, 1943; children—Gene A., Wendell F., Paul D., Donna M. Instr. econs. and bus. Iowa Wesleyan Coll., 1947-50; teaching asst. U. Iowa, 1950-51, research asst. Bur. of Labor and Mgmt., 1951-52, instr. mgmt. and social sci., 1954-55; asso. prof. econs., acting head dept. Simpson Coll., 1952-54; asst. prof. econs. U. Wis. at Whitewater, 1955-62, asso. prof., 1962-64, prof., 1964—, chmn., 1966-75. Founder, pres. Whitewater chpt. World Federalists Assn., 1960-68, 76-78, midwest regional v.p., 1961-63, 67-69, regional pres., 1969-71, 75—, nat. exec. council, 1968-76, 78—, del. World Congress, Ottawa, 1970, Brussels, 1972, Paris, 1977; mem. Gov.'s Commn. on UN, 1971—; mem. Wis. Conf. Bd. Social Concerns, Meth. Ch., 1961-68, 70-76. Democratic precinct committeeman, Whitewater, 1966—; chmn. Walworth County Dem. Com., 1968-72; vice chmn. 1st Congl. Dist. Dem. Com., 1975-78; vice chmn. Wis. Dem. Platform Com., 1978—; bd. dirs. Wis. Protestant Legislative Council, 1965-69. Served with AUS, 1943-46. Mem. Am., Midwest econ. assns., Indsl. Relations Research Assn. (adv. bd. Wis. chpt. 1964—), Assn. U. Wis. Faculties, ACLU, SANE, Fedn. Am. Scientists, Walworth County UN Assn. (vice chmn. 1977—). Methodist (lay speaker). Home: 205 N Fremont St Whitewater WI 53190. *Life is too precious to be spent on ourselves. We show love for our Creator by what we do for others. Happiness is a by-product.*

REGAN, DONALD THOMAS, securities exec.; b. Cambridge, Mass., Dec. 21, 1918; B.A., Harvard, 1940; m. Ann G. Buchanan, July 11, 1942; children—Donna, Donald, Richard, Diane. With Merrill Lynch, Pierce, Fenner & Smith, Inc., and predecessor, 1946—, sec., dir. adminstrv. div., 1960-64, exec. v.p., 1964-68, pres., 1968-70, chmn., chief exec. officer, 1971—; chmn. bd., chief exec. officer Merrill Lynch & Co. Inc., 1973—. Vice chmn., dir. N.Y. Stock Exchange, 1972-75. Trustee Charles E. Merrill Trust; chmn. bd. trustees U. Pa., 1974-78, life trustee, 1978—; mem. policy com. Bus. Roundtable; trustee Com. for Econ. Devel. Served to lt. col. USMCR, World War II. Mem. Investment Bankers Assn. Am. (v.p., gov. 1965-67), Council Fgn. Relations. Clubs: Army-Navy, Metropolitan (Washington); Bond (gov.), Economic (N.Y.C.); Baltusrol Golf; Burning Tree (Bethesda, Md.). Author: A View from the Street, 1972. Office: One Liberty Plaza 165 Broadway New York NY 10006

REGAN, GERALD AUGUSTINE, govt. ofcl. Nova Scotia; b. Windsor, N.S., Can., Feb. 13, 1929; s. Walter Edward and Rose M. (Greene) R.; LL.B., Dalhousie U.; m. A. Carole Harrison, Nov. 17, 1956; children—Gerald, Geoffrey, Miriam, Nancy, David, Laura. Created Queen's counsel; mem. N.S. Legislature, 1967—; premier N.S., 1970-78, pres. exec. council, 1970—; leader N.S. Liberal Party, 1965—; chmn. exec. com. Commonwealth Parliamentary Assn., 1973-77. Roman Catholic. Office: House of Assembly PO Box 1617 Halifax NS Canada*

REGAN, JOHN K., judge; b. 1911; B.S., St. Louis U.; LL.B., Benton Coll. Law. Admitted to bar, 1935; sr. judge U.S. Dist. Ct. for Mo. Eastern Dist., then judge U.S. Temporary Emergency Ct. of Appeals, 1977—. Mem. Am. Bar Assn. Office: US Ct Appeals US Court and Custom House 1114 Market St Saint Louis MO 63101*

REGAN, JOHN MACVEIGH, JR., ins. co. exec.; b. Mpls., June 7, 1921; s. John MacVeigh and Mary Philomena (Morgan) R.; B.A. in Econs., Yale U., 1943; student Advanced Mgmt. Program, Harvard, 1959; m. Prudence B. Sanford, June 17, 1949; child- ren—John M., Deborah S., Peter M., Robert C., Prudence R., William M. With Marsh & McLennan, Inc., N.Y.C., 1946—, v.p., 1955-67, sr. v.p., 1967-68, exec. v.p., 1968-71, pres., chief exec. Officer, 1971, chmn. bd., 1972—, also dir.; pres. Marsh & McLennan Cos., 1972-73, chief exec. officer, 1973—, chmn., 1976—, also dir.; dir. A.C. Nielsen Co. Trustee, Inner City Scholarship Fund, N.Y. Law Sch., Conn. Coll., U. Notre Dame. Served to 1st lt. U.S. Army, 1943-46; ETO. Decorated Purple Heart. Mem. Am. Inst. Property and Liability (vice-chmn.), Underwriters/Ins. Inst. Am., The Conf. Bd., Pilgrims U.S. Clubs: Econ., River (N.Y.C.); Watch Hill Yacht; Misquamicut. Home: 1120 Fifth Ave New York NY 10028 Office: 1221 Ave of Americas New York NY 10020

REGAN, PETER FRANCIS, III, physician, educator; b. Bklyn., Nov. 11, 1924; s. Peter Francis, Jr., and Veronica (Tierney) R.; M.D., Cornell U., Ithaca, N.Y., 1949; m. Laurette Patricia O'Connor, June 18, 1949; children—Peter, Stephen, William, Elizabeth, John, Carol.

Intern in medicine N.Y. Hosp., 1949-50, asst. resident psychiatry Payne Whitney Psychiat. Clinic, 1950, 53-54, resident 1954-56; asst. prof. psychiatry Cornell U. Med. Coll., 1956-58; prof., head dept. psychiatry U. Fla. Coll. Medicine, chief psychiat. service Univ. Teaching Hosp., 1958-64; v.p. for health affairs, prof. psychiatry State U. N.Y. at Buffalo, 1964-67, exec. v.p. univ., prof. psychiatry, 1967-69, exec. v.p., acting pres. univ., prof. psychiatry, 1969-70, prof. psychiatry, 1970—; vice chancellor acad. programs State U. N.Y., 1970-71; project dir. Center for Ednl. Research and Innovation, OECD, 1972-74. Served as capt. M.C., AUS, 1951-52. Diplomate Am. Bd. Psychiatry and Neurology. Fellow Am. Psychiat. Assn.; mem. AMA, Alpha Omega Alpha. Author: (with F. Flach) Chemotherapy in Emotional Disorders, 1960; (with E. Pattishall) Behavioral Science Contributions to Psychiatry. Contbr. articles to profl. jours. Address: 426 Woodbridge Ave Buffalo NY 14214

REGAN, THEODORE MILTON, JR., advt. exec.; b. Phila., May 6, 1931; s. Theodore Milton and Mary Dorothy (Weir) R.; A.B., Haverford Coll., 1956; m. Mary Anne Trainer, Nov. 29, 1958; children—Theodore Milton III, Tracey, Jeffrey, Ann, Alison. With N.W. Ayer ABH Internat., N.Y.C., 1956—, asso. dir. creative services, now exec. v.p., also dir. Served with USMC, 1950-52. Mem. Triangle Soc. Roman Catholic. Clubs: Merion Golf, Martins Dam. Home: 30 Highview Dr Radnor PA 19087 Office: 1345 Ave of Americas New York City NY 10019

REGAZZI, JOHN HENRY, financial co. exec.; b. N.Y.C., Jan. 4, 1921; s. Caesar B. and Jennie (Moruzzi) R.; B.B.A., Pace Coll., 1951; C.P.A., N.Y., 1950; m. Doris Litzau, Feb. 16, 1946; children—Mark, Dale. Audit mgr. Price Waterhouse & Co., C.P.A.'s, N.Y.C., 1954-62; comptroller Am. Broadcasting Cos., Inc., N.Y.C., 1962-70; treas. AVNET, Co., N.Y.C., 1970—. Bd. dirs. River Dell (N.J.) Regional High Sch. Bd. Edn., 1959-65, v.p., 1961-62, pres., 1962-65; treas. Oradell (N.J.) Free Pub. Library; chmn. Oradell chpt. A.R.C. Fund, 1966, 68; councilman Borough of Oradell, 1979—. Served with USAAF, 1942-45. Mem. Am. Inst. C.P.A.'s (editorial adv. com.), Nat. Assn. Accountants, Financial Execs. Inst. Lion. Club: Oradell Swim (treas., trustee). Author numerous articles. Home: 637 Park Ave Oradell NJ 07649 Office: AVNET Inc 767 Fifth Ave New York NY 10022

REGEIMBAL, NEIL ROBERT, SR., journalist; b. Mpls., Mar. 16, 1929; s. Louis Odlin and Marie Elizabeth (O'Neill) R.; B.S. in Journalism, U. Md. 1951; m. Mary Elizabeth Sutton, Aug. 18, 1950; children—Neil Robert, James Michael, Claire Marie, Stephen Louis, Mary Suzanne, Elizabeth Anne. With AP, Washington, 1949-50; asso. editor Takoma (Md.) Jour., 1950-51; reporter Washington Times-Herald, 1951-54; Washington corr. Chilton Publs., 1954-71, Wash. bur. chief, v.p., 1975—; dir. public relations Motor Vehicle Mfrs. Assn., Detroit, 1971-75; editor Oil and Gas Jour., Washington, 1975. Recipient Tom Campbell Editorial Achievement award, 1968, 69, 71, 78. Mem. White House Corrs. Assn., Sigma Delta Chi. Republican. Roman Catholic. Club: Nat. Press. Home: 13811 Marianna Dr Rockville MD 20853 Office: 1093 Nat Press Bldg Washington DC 20045

REGENSTEIN, LOUIS, lawyer; b. Atlanta, Feb. 9, 1912; s. Louis and Venia (Liebman) R.; A.B. cum laude, Harvard, 1933, J.D. cum laude, 1936; m. Helen Lucile Moses, July 30, 1939; children—Lewis Graham, Jonathan Kent. Admitted to Ga. bar, 1935; asso. firm Kilpatrick, Cody, Roger, McClatchey & Regenstein, Atlanta, 1936-41, partner, 1941—; dir. cos. including Nat. Automobile Ins. Co., Peoples Fin. Corp., Selig Enterprises, Inc., Thomas Paint Mfg. Co., Coronet Industries, Inc., Hix Green Co., Fox Mfg. Co. Mem. nat. adv. com. Ga. del. White House Conf. on Aging, 1961; lectr. tax insts., 1946—; pres. bd. Atlanta Legal Aid Soc., 1952-53. Mem. exec. com. Ga. Republican Party, 1950-58. Bd. dirs. Multiple Sclerosis Soc., 1950-60, Community Service for Blind, Atlanta United Appeal; bd. dirs., chmn. Am. Jewish Com.; bd. dirs. Clark Coll., vice chmn.; bd. dirs. NCCJ, Greater Atlanta Community Council, Regenstein Found., Harris Found., Fox Found., Green Found.; mem. pres.'s council Agnes Scott Coll.; mem. exec. com. High Mus. Art; mem. exec. com., treas. Atlanta Coll. Art. Served to lt. col. AUS, 1941-45. Mem. Am., Ga., Atlanta bar assns., Am. Judicature Soc., Nat. Legal Aid and Defenders Assn., World Peace Through Law Center, Atlanta C. of C. (past dir.), Newcomen Soc., Council on Foreign Relations, Atlanta Symphony Guild (dir.). Clubs: Atlanta Lawyers, Standard, Harvard, Atlanta City (dir.), Commmerce (Atlanta). Editor: Harvard Law Rev., 1935-36. Contbr. articles on taxation to profl. jours. Home: 3691 Tuxedo Rd NW Atlanta GA 30305 Office: Equitable Bldg Atlanta GA 30303

REGENSTEINER, ELSE FRIEDSAM (MRS. BERTOLD REGENSTEINER), textile designer, educator; b. Munich, Germany, Apr. 21, 1906; d. Ludwig and Hilda (Nelson-Bachhofer) Friedsam; tchrs. degree Deutsche Frauenschule, Munchen, 1925; student U. Munich, Inst. Design, Chgo.; m. Bertold Regensteiner, Oct. 3, 1926; 1 dau., Helga (Mrs. Herman L. Sinaiko). Came to U.S., 1936, naturalized, 1942. Instr., Hull House, Chgo., 1941-45, Inst. Design, Chgo., 1942-46; asst. prof. Sch. Art Inst. Chgo., 1945-57, prof., 1957-71, prof. emeritus, 1971—; textile designer for industry; partner Reg Wick Studios, 1945—; also lectr.; exhibited one man shows throughout U.S., 1946—; represented in permanent collection Art Inst. Chgo., Cooper Union Mus., N.Y.C. Cons. Am. Farm Sch., Thessaloniki, Greece, 1972—. Recipient 1st prize for drapery and upholstery Internat. Textile Exhbn., 1946; five citations merit Am. Inst. Decorators, 1947, 48, 50, others. Fellow Collegium Craftsmen of Am. Crafts Council; mem. Am. Craftsmen's Council, Handweavers Guild Am. (dir. 1970-78). Author: The Art of Weaving, 1970; Program for a Weaving Study Group, 1974; Weaver's Study Course—Ideas and Techniques, 1975. Contbr. articles to profl. mags. Address: 1416 E 55th St Chicago IL 60615

REGIER, JON LOUIS, clergyman; b. Dinuba, Calif., May 24, 1922; s. John and Adeline (Roth) R.; A.B., Huntington (Ind.) Coll., 1944; B.D., McCormick Theol. Sem., 1947; student U. Mich. Sch. Social Work; D.D., Payne Theol. Sem., Wilberforce, Ohio, 1959; m. Joyce Palmer, June 12, 1948; children—Jon Denniston, Marjorie Grace, Susan Marie, Luke Roth. Ordained to ministry Presbyn. Ch., 1947; asso. dir. Dodge Christian Community House, Detroit House, Detroit, 1947-49; head resident Howell Neighborhood House, pastor Howell Meml. Ch., Chgo., 1949-58; lectr. social group work McCormick Theol. Sem., Chgo., 1952-58; exec. sec. div. home missions Nat. Council Chs., 1958-64, asso. gen. sec., chief exec. officer div. of Christian life and mission, 1965-73; exec. dir. N.Y. State Council Chs., Syracuse, 1973—. Del. to Assembly of Div. World Mission and Evangelism, World Council Chs., mem. exec. com. world mission and evangelism, del. World Conf. Ch. and Soc., Geneva, 1966; founding mem. IDOC, Internat., Rome, pres., 1972; founding mem. IDOC/N. Am., 1967. Exec. council div. edn. and recreation Welfare Council Met. Chgo., 1953; mem. hard-to-reach youth research com., 1953-58; mem. Chgo. Youth Commn., 1954-58; chmn. spl. study on delinquency, 1956-58; exec. com. Citizens' Crusade Against Poverty, 1964—; exec. com. Citizens Adv. Center, 1967—; adv. mem. div. criminal justice State N.Y., 1977; trustee North Conway Inst.; bd. dirs. Literacy Vols. Greater Syracuse, 1976, Urban League Onondaga County, 1976; mem. Human Rights Commn. Syracuse and Onondaga County, N.Y. State Commr. Edn. Interfaith Adv. Council. Mem. Nat. Fedn. of Settlements and Neighborhood Centers (dir. 1954-58), Nat. Assn. Social Workers (exec. council Chgo. chpt. 1955-58), Soc. Propagation of Gospel Among Indians and Others of N.Am., Nat. Assembly for Social Policy and Devel. (founding mem.). Home: 5251 Wethersfield Rd Jamesville NY 13078 Office: 3049 E Genesee St Syracuse NY 13224

REGNERY, HENRY, pub.; b. Hinsdale, Ill., Jan. 5, 1912; s. William Henry and Frances Susan (Thrasher) R.; B.S., Mass. Inst. Tech., 1934; student U. Bonn. Germany, 1934-36; M.A., Harvard, 1938; LL.D., Mt. Mary Coll., Milw.; m. Eleanor Scattergood, Nov. 12, 1938; children—Susan, Alfred S., Henry F., Margaret. Staff Am. Friends Service Com., 1938-41; officer Joanna Western Mills Co., 1941-47, now dir.; founder Henry Regnery Co., 1947, pres. 1947-66, chmn. bd., 1967-1977; founded Gateway Editions, Ltd. (Book publishers) 1977 (now Regnery/Gateway Inc.), pres., 1977—.

REGNIER, J(OSEPH) RONALD, lawyer; b. Manchester, N.H., Apr. 8, 1906; s. Joseph Telesford and Loretta Centenna (Shattuck) R.; B.A., Trinity Coll., Hartford, Conn., 1930; LL.B., Yale, 1933; m. Kathleen R. Gates, Mar. 25, 1939; children—Roger G., Marcia Regnier Marks, Gwen L., Paul S. Admitted to Conn. bar, 1933, since practiced in Hartford; mem. firm Regnier, Taylor, Curran and Langenbach, 1952—. Former trustee Hartford YMCA; corporator Hartford Hosp., St. Francis Hosp., Newington Childrens Hosp. Fellow Am. Bar Found.; mem. Am. Bar Assn. (ho. of dels. 1958-74, Conn. state del. 1963-69, bd. govs. 1969-72), Internat., Hartford County (pres. 1954-55) bar assns., Conn. Bar (pres. 1960-61), Am. Judicature Soc. (past dir.), Internat. Assn. Ins. Counsel. Clubs: Hartford Golf (pres. 1963-65), Hartford University (pres. 1950-52). Home: 25 Norwood Rd West Hartford CT 06117 Office: 41 Lewis St Hartford CT 06103

REGULA, RALPH STRAUS, lawyer, congressman; b. Beach City, Ohio, Dec. 3, 1924; s. O.F. and Orpha (Walter) R.; B.A., Mt. Union Coll., 1948; LL.B., William McKinley Sch. Law, 1952; m. Mary Rogusky, Aug. 5, 1950; children—Martha, David, Richard. Sch. adminstr. Stark County Bd. Edn., 1948-55; admitted to Ohio bar, 1952; practiced law, Navarre; mem. Ohio Ho. of Reps., 1964-65, Ohio Senate, 1965-72; mem. 93d-96th Congresses from 16th Dist. Ohio. Partner Regula Bros. Mem. Pres.'s Commn. on Fin. Structures and Regulation, 1970-71; mem. Ohio Bd. Edn., 1960-65; mem. adv. bd. Walsh Coll., Canton, Ohio Trustee Mt. Union Coll., Alliance, Ohio, Stark County Hist. Soc., Stark County Wilderness Soc. Served with USNR, 1944-46. Recipient Community Service award Navarre Kiwanis Club, 1963; Meritorious Service in Conservation award Canton Audubon Soc., 1965; Ohio Conservation award Gov. James Rhodes, 1969; named Outstanding Young Man of Yr., Canton Jr. C. of C., 1957, Legis. Conservationist of Yr., Ohio League Sportsmen, 1969. Republican. Episcopalian. Office: 401 Cannon House Office Bldg Washington DC 20515

REH, CARL WILLIAM, civil engr.; b. Chgo., Nov. 4, 1917; s. Paul Pius and Anna (Klausegger) R.; B.S. in Civil Engring., Ill. Inst. Tech., 1939; m. Regina Vanden Bosch, Dec. 27, 1941; children—Carl Michael, Katherine Reh DeLisle, Elizabeth Reh Elliott, James C., Thomas A. With Ill. Dept. Pub. Health, 1941; civil engr. Bur. Yards and Docks, U.S. Navy, 1942-45; with Greeley and Hansen, engrs., Chgo., 1945—, partner, 1957—; mem. engring. adv. bd. Met. Sanitary Dist. Greater Chgo., 1960-62; engring. adv. bd. Ill. Inst. Tech., 1972—; mem. water engring. conf. com. U. Ill., 1972—; mem. U. Ill. NSF Project Steering Com., 1976. Mem. Water and sewer com. Village of Lincolnshire, Ill., 1974-77, trustee, 1977—. Registered profl. engr., Ill.; diplomate Am. Acad. Environ. Engrs. Fellow ASCE, Am. Cons. Engrs. Council; mem. Nat. Soc. Profl. Engrs., Am. Water Works Assn., Water Pollution Control Fedn. Roman Catholic. Clubs: Tower, Union League (Chgo.). Home: 47 Coldstream St Lincolnshire IL 60015 Office: 222 S Riverside Plaza Chicago IL 60606

REH, FRANCIS FREDERICK, bishop; b. N.Y.C., Jan. 9, 1911; s. Gustave A. and Elizabeth (Hartnagel) R.; student Cathedral Coll., N.Y.C., 1924-30; B.A., St. Joseph's Sem., Yonkers, N.Y., 1932; S.T.L. cum laude, N.Am. Coll., Rome, 1936; J.C.D. summa cum laude, Pontifical Gregorian U., Rome, 1939; LL.D., Iona Coll., New Rochelle, N.Y., 1962. Ordained priest Roman Catholic Ch., 1935; asst. pastor St. Ann's Ch., Nyack, N.Y., summer 1936; asst. chancellor Archdiocese of N.Y., asst. pastor St. Patrick's Cathedral, N.Y.C., 1939-41; defender Bond of Marriage, promoter justice Tribunal of Archdiocese of N.Y., 1939-46; prof. moral theology and canon law St. Joseph's Sem., 1941-51, rector, 1958-62; vol. chaplain Childrens Village, Dobbs Ferry, N.Y., 1942-51; vice chancellor Archdiocese N.Y., asst. prof. St. Patricks Old Cathedral, N.Y.C., 1951-54; papal chamberlain, 1954; vice rector N.Am. Coll., Rome, 1954-58, rector, 1964-68; domestic prelate, 1956; vicar del. Mil. Ordinariate of U.S. for armed forces in Mediterranean Area, 1957; attended Cardinal Spellman at conclave, Rome, 1958; protonotary apostolic, 1959; moderator Clergy Confs. for Archdiocese N.Y., 1959-62; bishop of Charleston, S.C., 1962-64; bishop of Saginaw, Mich., 1968—. Mem. liaison com. St. Johns Provincial Sem. for Bishops of Mich. Province, 1969; Episcopal adviser Midwestern Div. for Spanish Speaking, 1969; chmn. com. for canonical affairs Nat. Conf. Cath. Bishops, 1969; chmn. Spiritual Founders Day of Mich. Week, 1970. Home: 1555 S Washington Ave Saginaw MI 48601 Office: 2555 Wieneke Rd Saginaw MI 48603*

REHARK, RUSSELL JOHN, container mfg. co. exec.; b. Cleve., Feb. 24, 1911; s. John and Clementine (Burian) R.; student Cleve. Coll. Western Res. U., 1929; m. Elinore Kolos, Aug. 31, 1935; children—Richard, Marianne, Elaine, Jeanne, John. Gen. bookkeeper, asst. mgr. safe deposit dept. Union Trust Co., Cleve., 1927-37; pub. accountant Ernst & Ernst C.P.A.'s, Cleve., 1942-46; successively internal auditor, tax accountant, asst. treas., treas. Greif Bros. Corp., Delaware, Ohio, 1946—, also mem. fin. and pension fund coms. Republican. Roman Catholic. Club: K.C. Home: 430 Sandusky St Delaware OH 43015 Office: 621 Pennsylvania Ave Delaware OH 43015

REHDER, ROBERT RICHARD, coll. dean; b. Chgo., Aug. 18, 1930; s. Frederick W. and Elsie (Beilfus) R.; A.B., DePauw U., 1952; postgrad. U. Ill., 1952-53; M.B.A., Ind. U., 1958; Ph.D., Stanford, 1961; m. Lynne G. Wonderlin, Aug. 21, 1954; children—Mark Richard, David Frederick. Asst. prof., adminstrv. asst. to pres.'s office Stanford, 1963-66; vis. asso. prof. Duke U., 1967; asso. prof. U. N.C. at Chapel Hill, 1966-69; dean, prof. Sch. of Bus. and Adminstrv. Scis., U. N.Mex., 1969—; vis. research prof. U. Western Australia, Perth, 1977; cons. Westinghouse Learning Corp., N.Y.C., Sutter HIlls Corp., Calif., W.R. Grace, Inc., Peru; dir. Public Service Co. N.Mex.; mem. Stanford faculty team to establish first grad. sch. of bus. in Latin Am., Lima, Peru, 1963-65; moderator exec. program Aspen Inst. for Humanistic Studies, 1976. Mem. tech. adv. com. to urban obs., Albuquerque, 1970—; co-dir. systems simulation program Carolina Population Center, Chapel Hill., 1968-69; mem. regional adv. council Small Bus. Adminstrn.; vis. lectr. Institut Superieur De Gestion, Paris, 1973-74. Trustee Nat. Council on Philanthropy, 1976—. Served with M.C., AUS, 1954-56. NSF Found. fellow for computer and soc. sci. research, 1968; Wilton Park fellow, Eng., 1962. Mem. Am. Sociol. Assn., Acad. Mgmt., Inst. Mgmt. Scis., Soc. Gen. Systems Research. Author: Latin American Managemnet: Development and Performance, 1968. Contbr. articles in field to profl. jours. Home: 1424 Stagecoach Rd Albuquerque NM 87123

REHFELD, ROBERT WILLIAM, forest products co. exec.; b. Sheboygan, Wis., Nov. 18, 1917; s. Alvin Arthur and Hazel R. (Bachman) R.; B.A. in Acctg., U. Wis., 1939; m. Jean Ellen Lentz, Aug. 31, 1945; children—Robert William, James Allan, Thomas Arthur. With Arthur Andersen & Co., 1939-51, sr. accountant, Los Angeles, 1945-46, mgr., San Francisco, 1946-51; treas.-controller S.W. Forest Industries, Inc., Phoenix, 1951-61, v.p., treas., 1961—; dir. Ariz. Blue Shield. Bd. dirs. Jr. Achievement; trustee Phoenix Gen. Hosp. Served to lt. (s.g.) USN, 1941-45. C.P.A., Ariz., Calif. Mem. Am. Inst. C.P.A.'s, Ariz. Soc. C.P.A.'s, Fin. Execs. Inst. Republican. Episcopalian. Clubs: Phoenix Country, White Mountain Country, Ariz. Home: 510 W Coronado Rd Phoenix AZ 85003 Office: 3443 N Central Ave Phoenix AZ 85012

REHM, JOHN ALFRED HARRISON, advt. exec.; b. Chgo., Apr. 2, 1902; s. Benjamin and Roselen (Swingley) R.; student Chgo. Acad. Fine Arts, extension classes Northwestern U.; m. Alice Ethelwyn Kirk, Sept. 20, 1924; children—Susan (Mrs. Roderick C. Richards), Nancy (Mrs. Walter L. Greene). Reporter, rewriteman Hearst Newspapers, 1920-22; divisional advt. dir. The Great Atlantic & Pacific Tea Co., 1923-25; with Paris & Peart Advt. Agy., N.Y.C., 1925-58, partner, 1934-58, exec. v.p., treas., 1956-58, pres., treas., 1958; vice chmn. bd., dir. Gardner Advt. Co., 1959-62, also chief exec. officer, dir. N.Y. subsidiary; bus. mgmt. cons., 1962—. Club: Wee Burn Country (Darien, Conn.). Home: 2 Cobblers Green New Canaan CT 06840

REHM, JOHN BARTRAM, lawyer; b. Paris, France, Nov. 23, 1930; s. George Edward and Mary Bartram (Torr) R.; A.B., magna cum laude, Harvard, 1952; LL.B., Columbia, 1955; m. Diana Mary Aed, Dec. 19, 1959; children—David Bartram, Jennifer Aed. Admitted to N.Y. state bar, 1955, D.C. bar, 1969; practiced in Washington, 1956—; atty.-adviser U.S. Dept. State, Washington, 1956-61, asst. legal adviser econ. affairs, 1961-63; gen. counsel Office of Pres.'s Spl. Rep. for Trade Negotiations, Washington, 1963-69; partner firm Busby, Rivkin, Sherman, Levy & Rehm, 1969-77, Busby & Rehm, 1977-78, Busby, Rehm and Leonard, 1979—. Mem. Am. Bar Assn., Phi Beta Kappa. Democrat. Contbr. articles to profl. publs. Home: 5005 Worthington Dr Westmoreland Hills MD 20016 Office: 1629 K St NW Suite 1100 Washington DC 20006

REHM, WARREN STACEY, JR., biophysicist; b. Lancaster, Pa., Oct. 16, 1907; s. Warren Stacey and Grace (Irwin) R.; B.S., U. Tex., Austin, 1930, Ph.D., 1935; M.D., U. Chgo., 1941; M.D. (h.c.), U. Uppsala (Sweden), 1975; m. Barbara Campbell, Apr. 17, 1942; 1 dau., Valerie E. (Mrs. Richard Wheelock Lownes). Research asst. plant physiology U. Chgo., 1935-37; instr. physiology Sch. Medicine, U. Louisville, 1940-42, asst. prof., 1942-45, asso. prof., 1945-48, prof., 1948-58, biophysicist, 1958-61, chmn. dept., 1961-64; prof. physiology and biophysics, chmn. dept. Sch. Medicine, U. Ala., Birmingham, 1964-78, prof. emeritus, 1978—; research prof. medicine U. Louisville Sch. Medicine, 1978—; cons. Warner-Lambert Pharm. Co. Recipient Guggenheim award, 1960. Mem. AAAS, Physiol. Soc., Soc. Exptl. Biology, Biophys. Soc. Contbr. sci. papers to books and jours. Home: 800 S 4th St Louisville KY 40203 Office: Louis Med Center U Louisville Louisville KY 40232

REHME, ROBERT G., film co. exec.; b. Cin., May 5, 1935; s. Gordon W. and Helen H. (Hewkel) R.; ed. U. Cin.; m. Kay Yazell, Jan. 5, 1964; children—Robin, Tracy. Theatre mgr. RKO Theatres, Cin.; advt. mgr. Cin. Theatre Co.; publicist United Artists Pictures; dir. advt. and publicity United Artists Pictures and Paramount Pictures; pres. Avco Embassy Pictures Corp., Los Angeles. Mem. Am. Film Inst., Acad. Motion Picture Arts and Scis. Democrat. Presbyterian. Club: Variety. Office: 956 Seward St Los Angeles CA 90038

REHNER, HERBERT ADRIAN, writer, educator; b. Vincennes, Ind., Dec. 14, 1926; s. Herbert O. and Anna-Blanche (Chapman) R.; A.B., Ind. State U., M.A., 1948; LUD, Royal Acad. Dramatic Art, U. London, 1949, student Acad. Arts and Design in Mex., Litt.D., 1960; Litt.D., Brantridge Forest Sch., Eng., 1967. Tchr., Ind. State U., 1947-48; lectr. Royal Acad. Dramatic Art, 1949-50; head theatre dept. Wilson br. Chgo. City Coll., 1950-68, head speech dept., 1959-68, chmn. and prof. speech and drama, 1968—; producer, dir. Shawnee Summer Theatre, Greene County, 1960; pres. Ind. Acad. Dramatic Art, 1953-56; producer, dir., profl. tour of You Can't Take It With You for Dept. Def., Europe, 1959; programs over radio sta. WBOW and WIHI, 1964-68; summer producer White Barn Profl. Theater, Terre Haute, Ind.; cultural rep. Internat. Theater Inst., Chgo., 1955; dir. All City Chicago Drama Festival, 1957; dir. Shakespeare on TV, 1961, 69; producer Guys and Dolls, Chgo., 1960; Westward the River hist. drama, 1967; mgr. theatre tour to S. Pacific, Dept. Def., 1971; dir TV variety hour, Seoul, Korea, 1971; prod. Profl. Performing Equity Co., Drama Guild, Chgo., 1972-75; mng. producer Sta. WKKC, Chgo., 1978—; producer profl. world premiere of Sinbad, 1979; designer profl. theatre, Bloomfield, Ind., 1979. Contracted to develop 5 curricula, also design performing arts center for new univ., Iran, 1973. Recipient Fulbright grant to study in Eng. and Europe; James Yard award for human relations NCCJ, 1960; named Chgo. Tchr. of Yr., 1965; Kate Moremont travel grantee, 1965. Mem. Speech Assn. Am., Sadlers Wells-Old Vic. Assn., Soc. Midland Authors, ANTA (Chgo. bd. 1960-61), Theta Chi, Theta Alpha Phi (nat. pres. 1974-76, nat. council 1977—), Blue Key. Club: Players (hon.) (N.Y.C.). Author: Sons of the Prairie, 1950; Pastime of Eternity, 1948; The Dramatic Use of Oral Interpretation and Choral Speaking, 1951; The Constant Heritage, 1952; Out of this Land, 1954; Practical Public Speaking, 1957; Communication Through Speaking, 1959, rev., 1961, 62, 65, 68, 77, 78; Speaking in Public, 1961; Activities in Living and Speaking, 1965, rev., 67, 73; nat. editor Cue mag., 1962-64. Home: Valhalla Star Route 1 Owensburg IN 47453 Office: 6904 S Harvard Ave Chicago IL 60621. *I have grown to believe that the only real and lasting happiness comes from personal service. Expecting any form of gratitude defeats the purpose of what you accomplish with your gift of service. The love that flows back and forth is essential for well being. It truly surpasses understanding and creates a goodness that fills up every space available in life. You cannot just take away—you must give something back.*

REHNQUIST, WILLIAM HUBBS, Supreme Ct. justice; b. Milw., Oct. 1, 1924; s. William Benjamin and Margery (Peck) R.; B.A., M.A., Stanford, 1948, LL.B., 1952; M.A., Harvard, 1949; m. Natalie Cornell, Aug. 29, 1953; children—James, Janet, Nancy. Admitted to Ariz. bar; law clk. to former justice Robert H. Jackson, U.S. Supreme Ct., 1952-53; with firm Evans, Kitchel & Jenckes, Phoenix, 1953-55; mem. firm Ragan & Rehnquist, Phoenix, 1956-57; partner firm Cunningham, Carson & Messenger, Phoenix, 1957-60; partner firm Powers & Rehnquist, Phoenix, 1960-69; asst. atty.-gen. office of legal counsel Dept. of Justice, Washington, 1969-71; asso. justice U.S. Supreme Ct., 1971—. Mem. Nat. Conf. Commrs. Uniform State Laws, 1963-69. Served with USAAF, 1943-46; NATOUSA. Mem. Fed., Am. Maricopa (Ariz.) County bar assns., State Bar Ariz., Nat. Conf. Lawyers and Realtors, Phi Beta Kappa, Order of Coif, Phi Delta Phi.

Lutheran. Contbr. articles to law jours., nat. mags. Office: Supreme Ct US Washington DC 20543

REHNSTROM, VERNLEY RAE, electric utility exec.; b. Linn Grove, Iowa, June 28, 1926; s. C. Elim and Myrtle (Halvorsen) R.; student Buena Vista Coll., Storm Lake, Iowa, 1943-44; B.S.C., State U. Iowa, 1949. Staff, then sr. auditor Arthur Andersen & Co., C.P.A.'s, Chgo., 1949-56; with Pub. Service Co. Ind., 1956—, comptroller, 1966—, v.p., 1968-74, v.p. fin., 1974-77, sr. v.p. fin., 1977—. Served with USNR, 1944-46. Mem. Fin. Execs. Inst., Beta Gamma Sigma. Republican. Home: 2517 Parkwood Indianapolis IN 46224 Office: 1000 E Main St Plainfield IN 46168

REHR, BRUCE ROGER, mut. fund exec.; b. Reading, Pa., June 29, 1928; s. Garrett John and Anna (Fry) R.; B.A., Dickinson Coll., 1950; m. Nancy Lou Bain, July 21, 1951; children—Roger Bruce, Linda Jane, Garrett Henry, Scott Lambert. Vice pres. J.L. Hain & Co., Reading, Pa., 1950-68; pres., chief exec. officer Penn Sq. Mgmt. Corp., Reading, 1968—; chmn. Penn Sq. Mut. Fund, 1968—; dir. Wyomissing New Home Fed. Savs. & Loan Assn. Pres., Borough Council, Wyomissing Hills, Pa., 1964-72; bd. dirs. YMCA, Reading, 1970—; bd. mgrs. Reading Hosp., 1968—; exec. bd. Daniel Boone council Boy Scouts Am., 1968—; trustee, v.p. Dickinson Coll., Carlisle, Pa. Served with Adj. Gen. Corps, U.S. Army, 1950-52. Mem. No-Load Mut. Fund Assn. (dir., treas.), Phi Beta Kappa, Omicron Delta Kappa, Sigma Chi. Republican. Lutheran. Clubs: Iris (Wyomissing, Pa.); Wyomissing, Berkshire Country (Reading). Home: 92 Grandview Blvd Wyomissing Hills Reading PA 19609 Office: 451 Penn Sq Reading PA 19601

REICH, ALAN ANDERSON, govt. ofcl.; b. Pearl River, N.Y., Jan. 1, 1930; s. Oswald David and Alma Carolyn (Anderson) R.; B.A., Dartmouth, 1952; diploma Oxford U., 1953; M.A., Russian Inst., Middlebury Coll., 1953; M.B.A., Harvard, 1959; m. Gay Ann Forsythe, Dec. 19, 1954; children—James, Jeffrey, Andrew, Elizabeth. Exec., Polaroid Corp., Cambridge, Mass., 1960-70; dep. asst. sec. ednl. and cultural affairs Dept. State, Washington, 1970-75; spl. asst. to sec. HEW, 1976-77; dep. asst. sec. commerce, dir. Bur. East-West Trade, Dept. Commerce, 1977—. Chmn. Sudbury (Mass.) Community United Fund, 1962, 66; mem. U.S. del. WHO Gen. Assembly, 1970; pres., bd. dirs. Nat. Paraplegia Found.; chmn. bd. dirs. Paraplegia Research; bd. dirs. People-to-People Com. for Handicapped, Synergistic Tech., Inc., Tech. Devel. Corp., Internat. Cardiology Found.; trustee Technology and Research Found. Served to 1st lt. inf. AUS, 1953-57. Recipient United Fund award, Ann. Alumni award New Eng. Prep. Sch. Athletic Council, 1977. Reynolds fellow Oxford U. Mem. Paralyzed Vets. Am., Beta Theta Pi. Home: 6017 Copely Ln McLean VA 22101 Office: Bur East-West Trade Dept Commerce Washington DC 20230

REICH, DAVID LEE, librarian; b. Orlando, Fla., Nov. 25, 1930; s. P.F. and Opal Katherine (Wood) Reichelderfer (now Reich); Ph.B. magna cum laude, U. Detroit, 1961; A.M. in L.S. (Carnegie Library Sci. Endowment scholar), U. Mich., 1963; m. Kathleen Johanna Weichel, Aug. 2, 1954 (div. Sept. 1964); 1 son, Robert Weichel. Tchr. English, Jefferson Davis Jr. Sch., San Antonio, 1961-62; dir. engring. library Radiation Inc., Melbourne, Fla., 1963-64; asst. to dir. libraries Miami-Dade Jr. Coll., Miami, Fla., 1964-65; dir. learning resources Monroe County Community Coll., Monroe, Mich., 1965-68; dep. dir. Dallas Pub. Library, 1968-73; dep. chief librarian The Chgo. Pub. Library, 1973-74, commr., 1975-78; dir. Mass. Bd. Library Commrs., Boston, 1978—; library cons. Macomb County Community Coll., Warren, Mich., 1967; chmn. adv. com. to library tech. asst. program El Centro Coll., Dallas, 1969-71. Mem. Inter-Task Working Group, Goals for Dallas, 1968-70; mem. Dallas Area Library Planning Council, Goals for Dallas, 1970-73. Mem. adv. council dept. library sci. No. Ill. U. Served as sgt. AUS, 1952-55. Recipient Disting. Alumnus award U. Mich., 1978; William B. Calkins Found. scholar, Orlando, 1963. Mem. Am. Assn. community and Jr. Colls., A.L.A. (council mem.-at-large 1968-72, 75-79), So., Southwest, Fla. (sec.-treas. coll. and spl. libraries div. 1965), Ill., Mass. (exec. bd. 1979—) library assns., Chief Officers State Library Agys., Assn. Coll. and Research Libraries, Alumni Assn. U. Mich. (pres. L.S. alumni 1973). Co-author: The Public Library in Non-traditional Education, 1974. Contbr. articles to library jours. Home: 3 Stonehill Dr Apt 2E Stoneham MA 02180

REICH, DONALD RAYMOND, educator; b. Two Rivers, Wis., Apr. 4, 1930; s. Raymond Veit and Leona (Schmoock) R.; A.B., U. Wis., 1952; postgrad. Heidelberg (Germany) U., 1958-59; Ph.D., Harvard, 1961; m. Cary Fellows, June 19, 1957; children—Liese, Elizabeth, John. Teaching fellow Harvard, 1959-61, dean Summer Sch. Arts and Scis., 1961; asst. prof. Oberlin (Ohio) Coll., 1961-67, asso. prof., 1967-68, prof., 1968-74, asso. dean, 1967-68, dean, 1968-74, dir. Peace Corps Tng. Program, 1963; v.p., provost Bklyn. Coll., City U. N.Y., 1974-79, prof., 1974—. Chmn., Oberlin Civil Service Commn., 1967-70. Voting mem. U. Wis. Meml. Union, 1968—. Served from 2d lt. to 1st lt., AUS, 1953-55. Fellow Center for Advanced Study in Behavioral Scis., 1965-66, Am. Council Learned Socs., 1965-66. Mem. AAUP, Am. Polit. Sci. Assn., Law and Soc. Assn. Home: 405 Parkside Ave Brooklyn NY 11226

REICH, EDGAR, educator; b. Vienna, Austria, June 7, 1927; s. Jonas and Luna Sarah (Lunenfeld) R.; came to U.S. in 1938, naturalized, 1944; B.E.E., Poly. Inst. Bklyn., 1947; M.S., Mass. Inst. Tech., 1949; Ph.D., U. Calif. at Los Angeles, 1954; m. Phyllis Masten, June 10, 1949; children—Eugene, Frances. Research asst., Servomechanisms Lab., Mass. Inst. Tech., Cambridge, 1947-49; mathematician Rand Corp., Santa Monica, Calif., 1949-56; mem. Inst. Advanced Study, Princeton, N.J., 1955-56; prof. math. U. Minn., Mpls., 1961—, head Sch. Math., 1969-71. Mem. Forschungsinstitut für Mathematik, Swiss Poly. Inst., Zurich, 1971-72, 78-79. Fulbright research scholar, Denmark, 1960-61; Guggenheim fellow, 1960-61, NSF Postdoctoral fellow, 1954-55; recipient Silver plaque Alpine Motoring Contest, 1968, Bronze medal U. Jyväskylä, 1973. Mem. Am. Math. Soc., Math. Assn. Am. Contbr. profl. jours. Home: 1961 E River Rd Minneapolis MN 55414

REICH, JACK EGAN, ins. exec.; b. Chgo., June 17, 1910; s. Henry Carl and Rose (Egan) R.; student Purdue U., 1928-31; LL.D. (hon.), Butler U., 1973; m. Jean Grady, Apr. 30, 1935; children—Rosemary (Mrs. Jerry Semler), Judith (Mrs. Dan Hoyt). With Inland Steel Co., East Chicago, Ind., 1925-31; field dir. gross income tax and employment security divs. State of Ind., 1933-40; field dir. Ind. C. of C., 1940-52, exec. v.p., 1952-62; chmn., pres. Indpls Water Co., 1962-67, now mem. exec. com., dir.; chmn. bd., chief exec. officer Am. United Life Ins. Co.; dir., past pres. Assn. Ind. Life Ins. Cos.; dir. Ins. Systems Am.; dir., exec. com. Am. Fletcher Corp., Am. Fletcher Nat. Bank & Trust Co. Bd. dirs., past pres. Greater Indpls. Progress Com.; bd. govs., past chmn. Asso. Colls. Ind.; bd. govs., past chmn. bd., pres. United Way Greater Indpls.; past mem. bd. lay trustees St. Mary-of-the-Woods Coll.; bd. dirs. Indpls. Neighborhood Housing, Inc.; mem. adv. bd. Jr. League Indpls., St. Vincent Hosp. Mem. Ind. (dir., past chmn.), Indpls. (dir.) chambers commerce, Hosp. Devel. Assn. (past dir. adv. com.), Nat. Alliance Businessmen (past met. chmn.), Pi Kappa Alpha. Clubs: Columbia, Indpls. Athletic, Indpls. Press, Meridian Hills Country, 100 Club (Indpls.). Home: 7404 N Pennsylvania St Indianapolis IN 46240 Office: One W 26th St Indianapolis IN 46206

REICH, JOHN, theatre dir.; b. Vienna, Austria, Sept. 30, 1906; s. Leopold and Martha (Baxter) R.; Baccalaureate with highest honors, Realgymnasium I. Vienna, 1925; Director's Diploma, U. Vienna, 1931; Ph.D., Cornell U., Ithaca, N.Y., 1944; m. Friederike Karoline Kurzweil, Oct. 31, 1932 (dec. Feb. 1945); m. 2d, Karen Ruth Lasker, July 9, 1957. Came to U.S., 1938, naturalized, 1944. Asst. producer, dir. Burgtheater, Vienna, 1931-32; producer, dir. Reinhardt Theatres, Vienna, 1932-38, also Salzburg Festival, summer 1934-37; asst., then asso. prof. Ithaca (N.Y.) Coll., 1938-44; vis. prof. N.Y. U., 1945-46, Smith Coll., 1946-48; dramatic dir. CBS-TV, 1945-46; lectr. Barnard Coll., 1951-53, Columbia, 1953-56, asst. prof., 1956-57; producing dir. Goodman Theatre and Sch. of Drama, Art Inst. Chgo., 1957-72, Goodman Resident Profl. Co., 1969-72; guest dir. U. Miami, U. Ga., U. Kans., Pa. State U., Cornell U., U. Santa Clara, U. So. Calif., NYS U., Stony Brook, Dallas Theatre Center, Calif. Actors Theatre, Mo. Repertory Theatre, Great Lakes Shakespeare Festival, Julliard; N.Y. stage prodns. include Faust (Goethe), Hypochondriac (Moliere), Dream (Shakespeare-Purcell), Henry IV (Pirandello), Mrs. Warren's Profession (Shaw), The Sacred Flame (Maugham). Mem. Fulbright Selection Commn., 1949; mem. Mayor's Com. Econ. and Cultural Devel., 1964. Recipient Ford Found. award for stage and theatre direction, 1959, treas. theatre communications group, 1961. Decorated chevalier de l'Ordre des Arts et des Lettres (France); Grand Badge of Honor (Austria). Fellow Am. Theatre Assn.; mem. Nat. Theatre Conf., ANTA (Man of Year award Chgo., 1961). Roman Catholic. Club: Cliff Dwellers. Home: 724 Bohemia Pkwy Sayville NY 11782. *I was trained to serve—to stimulate thought, warm the heart, spread knowledge of and compassion for the human condition.*

REICH, KENNETH IRVIN, journalist; b. Los Angeles, Mar. 7, 1938; s. Herman S. and Ruth Alberta (Nussbaum) R.; B.A., Dartmouth Coll., 1960; M.A. (Woodrow Wilson fellow), U. Calif., Berkeley, 1962; m. Nov. 14, 1970; children—Kathleen, David. With UPI, Sacramento, 1962-63, Life mag., 1963-65; with Los Angeles Times, 1965—, polit. writer, 1972—; instr. UCLA Extension, 1979. Co-chmn. Campaign for Dartmouth Coll., San Fernando Valley, 1979; mem. community adv. bd. Chandler Sch. Served with U.S. Army Res., 1956-65. Daniel Webster Nat. Honor fellow Dartmouth Coll., 1956-60. Club: Dartmouth Alumni (Los Angeles chpt.). Contbr. articles to mags. Office: Times-Mirror Sq Los Angeles CA 90053

REICH, MORTON MELVYN, marketing communications co. exec.; b. Phila., Aug. 11, 1939; s. Morris and Lillian (Rabinowitz) R.; student Charles Morris Price Sch. Advt. and Journalism, 1961-62; student Temple U., 1963-68; m. Geraldine Joan Krassan, May 31, 1964; children—Hope, Marla. Asst. dir. pub. relations Goodwill Industries, Phila., 1962-63; dir. promotion and information services Yellow Cab Co., Phila., 1963-66; dir. corporate employee commmunications Philco-Ford Co., Phila., 1966-68; exec. v.p. J.M. Korn & Son Inc., Phila., 1968-75; pres. Richard Yeager Assos., Moorestown, 1975—, Reich, Robinson, Inc., Phila., 1975-76; sr. v.p. Kalish & Rice, Phila., 1976-79; exec. v.p., owner Mktg. Communications Mgmt., Phila., 1979—; tchr. Charles Morris Price Sch.; lectr. in field. Served with USN, 1957-60. Recipient Distinguished Alumni award Charles Morris Price Sch., 1973, Creative Marketing award Readers Digest, 1974, Nat. Jr. C. of C. award, 1972. Mem. Phila. Jr. C. of C. (dir. 1962-65), Advt. Chairmen Phila. Fellowship Commn., others. Contbr. articles to profl. jours. Home: 1813 Rolling Ln Cherry Hill NJ 08003 Office: Mktg Communications Mgmt 1420 Walnut St Philadelphia PA 19102

REICH, NATHANIEL EDWIN, physician, artist, educator; b. N.Y.C., May 19, 1907; s. Alexander and Betty (Feigenbaum) R.; B.S., N.Y. U., 1927; student Marquette U. Coll. Medicine, 1927-29; M.D., U. Chgo., 1932; m. Joan Finkel, May 22, 1943; children—Andrew, Matthew. Intern, resident pathologist City Hosp., N.Y.C., 1931-33; cons. cardiologist Kingsbrook Jewish Med. Center Hosp., mem. exec. bd.; cons. cardiology Unity Hosp.; attending physician Kings County Hosp., Bklyn., State U. Hosp.; faculty State U. N.Y. Downstate Med. Center, 1938—, asso. clin. prof. medicine, 1952-74, clin. prof., 1974—; vis. prof. San Marcos U. Coll. Medicine, Lima, 1968; medico-care program, vis. prof. U. Afghanistan, 1970; vis. prof. U. Indonesia, 1972, U. Sri Lanka, 1975; asst. attending physician N.Y. Postgrad. Hosp., Columbia, 1940; cons. Catholic Diocese Bklyn. and Queens, Long Beach Meml. Hosp., Kings Hwy. Hosp., Flatbush Gen. Hosp., Interboro Gen. Hosp., Linden Gen. Hosp., Bklyn.; cardiac cons. U.S. R.R. Retirement Bd., 1965—, HEW, 1965—; program cons. Acad. Family Physicians, 1973; lectr. univs. Rome, Moscow, Rijeka, Haiti, Jerusalem, Cairo, Athens, Bangkok, Bucharest, Manila, Lisbon, Witwatersrand, Capetown, Natal, Lima, Buenos Aires, Rio de Janeiro, Quito, U. Madras, Madras, India, 1969, Spain, 1971, Auckland, N.Z., Sydney, Australia, also Japan Med. Assn., Philippine Heart Assn., Royal Thai Air Force Med. Service, China Med. Assn., Shanghai, 1978, Nat. Taiwan U., Taipei, 1978; chmn. internat. cardiology sect. Congress Chest Diseases, Cologne, Germany, 1956; impartial specialist N.Y. State Dept. Labor, U.S. Fed. Employees; cons. N.Y. State Bur. Disability Determinations, N.Y.C. Office Vocat. Rehab.; chief med. examiner SSS, 1942-44 (Presdl. commendation). Exhibited one-man show L.I. U., 1961, N.Y.U. Loeb Center, 1962, 72, 74, Greer Gallery, 1962, 64, St. Charles, La., 1964, Prospect Park Cent. Art Show, 1966, Art Inst. Boston, 1970, 76, George Wiener Gallery, 1972; group shows Little Studio, 1952, Mus. Modern Art, Paris, 1970, Bodley Gallery, 1965, 69, others; represented permanent collections Huntington Hartford collection N.Y. Cultural Center 1969, Washington County Mus. of Fine Arts, Hagerstown, Md., Evansville (Ind.) Mus. Arts, Joe and Emily Lowe Mus. U. Miami, Coral Gables, Fla., also several univs., and many pvt. collections. Served from 1st lt. to maj. M.C., AUS, 1944-47. Recipient St. Gaudens award, 1923; 1st prize Art Assn., A.M.A., 1948, Literary Soc., 1949. Diplomate Am. Bd. Internal Medicine. Am. Bd. Legal Medicine, 1958. Fellow A.C.P., Royal Soc. Medicine, Am. Coll. Cardiology, Am. Coll. Angiology (med. honor awards 1956, 59), Am. Coll. Legal Medicine, Am. Coll. Chest Physicians (chmn. exhibits com. 1961, cardiovascular rehab. com. 1965, coronary disease com. 1968, pres. N.Y. state chpt. 1970), Am. Acad. Comp. Medicine; mem. Am. Arbitration Assn., N.Y. State Med. Soc. (vice chmn. space med. sect. 1967, 75, chmn. chest sect. 1972), AMA, Internat. Soc. Internal Medicine, World Med. Assn., Am. Heart Assn. (council on thrombosis), N.Y. Heart Assn., N.Y. Cardiol. Soc. (pres., chmn. exec. bd.), Am. Geriatrics Soc., Am. Soc. Law and Sci., Am. Med. Authors Soc., AMA (physicians Recognition award 1970, 74, 77), Kings County Med. Soc. (chmn. radio com., cultural, program and social coms.), Am. Soc. Internal Medicine, Royal Soc. Health, N.Y.C. Hosp. Alumni Soc., Phi Delta Epsilon, Kappa Alpha (hon.), Sigma Psi (hon.). Clubs: Temple (v.p.); Doctors (vice chmn. bd. govs. Bklyn.); Explorers. Author: Diseases of the Aorta, 1949; The Uncommon Heart Diseases, 1954; (with Dr. R. E. Fremont) Chest Pain: Systematic Differentiation and Treatment, 1959; numerous articles cardiology and internal medicine, contbr. to 3 encys. Home: 1620 Ave I Brooklyn NY 11230 Office: 135 Eastern Pkwy Brooklyn NY 11238

REICH, PETER MARIA, journalist; b. Vienna, Austria, June 9, 1930; s. Hanns Leo and Nelly (Pollitzer) R.; came to U.S., 1937, naturalized, 1943; student U.S. Mil. Acad., 1948; B.J., Northwestern U., 1951, postgrad., 1952; m. Betty Jane Kosberg, Feb. 16, 1952 (div. May, 1969); children—Carol Elizabeth, Holly Lynn, James Peter. With Chgo. Am. newspaper (name later changed to Chgo. Today), 1952-74, aerospace editor, 1959-74; editorial page columnist, nat.-fgn. desk writer Chgo. Tribune newspaper, 1974—; numerous appearances radio and TV. Recipient nat. award for aerospace reporting USAF Assn., 1966, James M. Strebig Meml. award, 1977, AP writing awards, 1963, 66, 69. Mem. Aviation/Space Writers Assn. (award for outstanding aviation/space writing 1970, 71, 76, 77, 78, 79), Press Vets. Assn., South Pole Soc., Cape Kennedy Moonwatchers. Methodist. Home: 5455 N Sheridan Rd Apt 3811 Chicago IL 60640 Office: Nat Fgn Desk Chicago Tribune Chicago IL 60611. *Nothing is impossible; what man can imagine, man can do.*

REICH, ROBERT SIGMUND, landscape architect; b. N.Y.C., Mar. 22, 1913; s. Ulysses S. and Adele G. R.; B.S., Cornell U., 1934, Ph.D., 1941; postgrad. U. So. Calif., 1951; m. Helen Elizabeth Adams, May, 1945; children—Barbara, Betsy, Bobby, Billy. Instr. landscape design Cornell U. Inst. Land Design, 1936-39, 40-41; instr. landscape design U. Conn., 1939-40; instr. La. State U., 1941-46, asst. prof. landscape architecture, 1946-49, asso. prof., 1949-60, prof., 1960—, Alumni prof., 1967—, head dept. landscape architecture, 1964-79, dir. Sch. Landscape Architecture, 1979—; instr. Shrivenham (Eng.) Am. U., 1946, Biarritz (France) Am. U., 1947; vis. lectr. Tulane U., 1958-67; judge, instr. Nat. Council Garden Clubs, 1956—; mem. com. to establish City/Parish Beautification Commn., 1961; mem. area and facilities com. Baton Rouge Recreation and Parks Commn., 1957—; mem. task force on parks, recreation and tourism Goals for La. Program; mem. com. to establish Chicot State Park Arboretum, Ville Plate, La., 1964, mem. steering com., 1964-75; examiner La. Bd. Examination for Landscape Architects, 1957—. Bd. dirs. Hubbard Edn. Trust, Weston, Mass., 1967—. Served with U.S. Army, 1942-45. Recipient Teaching award of merit Gamma Sigma Delta, 1963. Fellow Am. Soc. Landscape Architects (trustee 1968-71, 3d v.p. 1971-73); mem. S.W. Park and Recreation Tng. Inst. (dir. 1975-77, award of merit 1968), Phi Kappa Phi, Pi Alpha Xi, Omicron Delta Kappa, Sigma Lambda Alpha. Methodist. Author: Landscape and You, 1953. Home: 333 E Boyd Dr Baton Rouge LA 70808 Office: Sch Landscape Architecture La State U Baton Rouge LA 70803

REICH, STEVE, composer; b. N.Y.C., 1936; grad. Cornell U.; studied composition with Bergsma and Persichetti at Julliard Sch. Music, Mills Coll. (with Berio and Milhaud); studied Inst. for African Studies, U. Ghana, 1970, Am. Soc. for Eastern Arts Summer Sch., U. Wash., 1973; m. Beryl Korot; children—Ezra, Michael. Composer mus. works including Piano Phase, Violin Phase, It's Gonna Rain, Come Out, Four Organs, Phase Patterns, Drumming, Six Pianos, Clapping Music, Music for Mallet Instruments Voices and Organ, Music for 18 Musicians, Music for a Large Ensemble; performer with own ensemble throughout U.S. and Europe; recs. with Columbia, Odyssey, Angel, Deutsche Grammophon, ECM-Warner Bros.; commns. from Holland Festival, Radio Frankfurt, San Francisco Symphony. Author: Writings about Music, 1974. Guggenheim fellow, 1978; Rockefeller Found. grantee, 1976, 79; Nat. Endowment Arts grantee, 1974, 76.

REICH, THEOBALD, surgeon; b. Svidnik, Czechoslovakia, Jan. 1, 1927; came to U.S., 1939, naturalized, 1953; s. David J. and Susan (Ritter) R.; B.A., N.Y. U., 1948; M.D., St. Louis U., 1951; m. Ida E. Westerman, May 21, 1961; children—David J., A.H. Jonathan. Intern, Bellevue Hosp., N.Y.C., 1951-52; research biochemist, div. labs. and research N.Y. State Dept. Health, N.Y.C., 1952-53; asst. to chief resident Bellevue Hosp., 1955-59; fellow in surgery N.Y. U. Sch. Medicine, N.Y.C., 1959-61; instr. surgery, 1960-67; attending surgeon, research project dir. Misericordia Hosp., N.Y.C., 1961-65; asst. prof. surgery N.Y. U. Sch. Medicine, 1967-73, prof. surg. research, 1973—; dep. chief surgeon N.Y.C. Police Dept., 1970—. Served with M.C., U.S. Army, 1953-55. Dept. Def. grantee, 1967, NSF grantee, 1974; NIH grantee, 1961; Rippel Found. grantee, 1974; Engring. Found. grantee, 1974; Rehab. Services Adminstrn. grantee, 1977; diplomate Nat. Bd. Med. Examiners, Am. Bd. Surgery. Fellow A.C.S.; mem. N.Y. Acad. Medicine, Am. Physiol. Soc., Biomed. Engring. Soc., N.Y. Surg. Soc., N.Y. Soc. Cardiovascular Surgery, Am. Heart Assn., AMA, N.Y. Police Dept. Superior Officers' Council. Contbr. articles to profl. jours.; patentee in field. Home: 100 Bleeker St New York NY 10012 Office: Inst Rehab Medicine NY U Med Center 400 E 34th St New York NY 10016

REICHARDT, CARL E., banker; b. 1931; A.B., U. So. Calif., 1956; postgrad. Stanford U., Northwestern U. Grad. Mgmt. Banking, So. Meth. U. Southwestern Grad. Sch. Banking. Program mgr. ops. and lending Citizens Nat. Bank, 1955-59; sr. statis. analyst N.Am. Aircraft, 1959-60; area exec. v.p. Union Bank, 1960-70; with Wells Fargo Realty Advisors, 1970—; v.p. non bank subsidiaries Wells Fargo & Co., 1973—; exec. v.p. real estate industries group Wells Fargo Bank, San Francisco, 1975-78, corp. pres., 1978—, also dir.; chmn. bd., dir. Wells Fargo Mgmt. Investors; dir. Golden West Mobile Homes, Hosp. Corp. Am. Office: Wells Fargo Bank 464 California St San Francisco CA 94120*

REICHARDT, PAUL EDWARD, gas co. exec.; b. Phila., Apr. 26, 1918; s. Louis Joseph and Pauline (Bier) R.; B.S. in Chem. Engring., Drexel U., 1940; m. Sybil Dorothy Dengler, Nov. 30, 1940; children—David L., Bruce A., Kathryn A. (Mrs. John Clark Wade), Wayne D., Mark E. With Washington Gas Light Co., 1940—, chief chemist, 1942-46, spl. asst. to pres., 1962-64, v.p. corporate planning and services, 1964-69, dir., 1967—, pres., 1969—, chief exec. officer, 1973—, chmn. bd., 1974—, pres., dir. subsidiaries Frederick Gas Co., 1969—, Shenandoah Gas Co., 1969—, Hampshire Gas Co., 1970—, Crab Run Gas Co., 1970—, Brandywood Estates Inc., 1971—, Rock Creek Properties, 1971—, Wash. Gas Approved Services, Inc. 1973—, also chmn. bd., chief exec. officer all subsidiaries, 1974—; dir. Robertshaw Controls Co., Fed. Res. Bank Richmond. Mem. Met. Washington Bd. Trade; trustee, sec.-treas., chmn. budget and fin. com. Bioenergy Council; trustee Fed. City Council; trustee, chmn. Center for Mcpl. and Met. Research; past trustee Inst. Gas Tech., Chgo.; bd. dirs. Gas Research Inst., ARC; trustee Consortium of Univs. Washington Met. Area. Registered profl. engr., D.C. Fellow Am. Inst. Chemists (Honor award 1974); mem. Am. Gas Assn. (treas. 1970-73, chmn. govt. relations com. 1976-79, chmn. bd. 1975-76), AAAS, Am. Chem. Soc., Md.-D.C. Utilities Assn. (pres. 1972-73, dir. 1972-73), U.S. C. of C., D.C. Soc. Profl. Engrs., Gas Men's Roundtable D.C., Newcomen Soc. N.Am., Smithsonian Assos. Presbyn. Rotarian. Club: University (Washington). Home: 9634 Weathered Oak Ct Bethesda MD 20034 Office: 1100 H St NW Washington DC 20005

REICHBERG, DAVID, business exec.; b. Newark, Apr. 19, 1926; s. Jacob and Sadie (Goldin) R.; B.A., Rutgers U., 1950; M.A., Columbia, 1951; m. Mary Fine, Aug. 7, 1979; children—Debra, Gregory, Ethan, Brian. Sales analyst Tidewater Oil Co., N.Y.C., 1951-54; dir. marketing Popular Mdse. Co., Passaic, N.J., 1954-61; pres. Reston & Carroll, Inc., N.Y.C., 1961-63; v.p. Harry Schneiderman, Inc., Chgo., 1963-64; exec. v.p. Altman, Vos & Reichberg, N.Y.C., 1964-74, pres., 1974-76, dir., 1964-79; chmn. Overseas Discount Shopping Service, Inc., 1974-78; pres. Direct Mass Mktg., Inc., 1976—, Syndicated Group Plans, Inc., 1976—, Assn. Informed Travelers, Inc., 1978—; chmn. Group Direct Mktg. Inc., 1976-78, Overseas Discount

Shopping Service, 1974-79; dir. New Corp. Mem. Com. on City Waterfront and Waterways, N.Y.C., 1972—, chmn., 1974—; pres. Am. Family Inst., Inc., 1976—. Served with AUS, 1944-46. Clubs: Rutgers U., Williams U., Columbia U., (N.Y.C.); Princeton U. Home: 228 Overlook Rd New Rochelle NY 10804

REICHEK, JESSE, artist; b. Bklyn., Aug. 16, 1916; s. Morris and Celia (Bernstein) R.; student Inst. Design, Chgo., 1941-42; diploma Academie Julian, Paris, 1951; m. Laure Guyot, May 16, 1950; children—Jonathan, Joshua. Exhibited one man shows at Galerie Cathiers d'Art Paris, 1951, 59, 68, U. Calif. at Berkeley, 1954, Betty Parsons Gallery, N.Y.C., 1958, 59, 63, 65, 67, 69, 70, Molton Gallery, London, 1962, Am. Culture Center, Florence, Italy, 1962, Bennington Coll., 1963, U. N.Mex., 1966, U. So. Calif., 1967, Axiom Gallery, London, 1968, Yoseido Gallery, Tokyo, 1968, Los Angeles County Mus. Art, 1971, exhibited in group shows Bklyn. Mus., 1959, Mus. Modern Art, N.Y.C., 1962, 65, 69, Knox-Albright Art Gallery, 1962, Art Inst. Chgo., 1963, Cin. Art Mus., 1966, Balt. Art Mus., 1966, Yale Art Gallery, 1967, Grand Palais, Paris, 1970, Nat. Mus. Art, Santiago, Chile, 1970, art and tech. exhibit Los Angeles County Mus. Art, 1971, Maeght Found., St. Paul de Vence, France, 1971, Mus. Modern Art, Paris, 1971; represented in permanent collections Mus. Modern Art, Art Inst. Chgo., Bibliotheque Nationale, Paris, Victoria & Albert Mus., London, Los Angeles County Art Mus., Grunwald Graphic Arts Found., U. Calif. at Los Angeles, San Diego Mus. Art, Amon Carter Mus., Fort Worth; instr. dept. architecture U. Mich., 1946-47; prof. Inst. Design Ill. Inst. Tech., 1951-53; prof. dept. architecture U. Calif. at Berkeley, 1953—. Cons., Nat. Design Inst. Ford Found. project, Ahmedabad, India, 1963, San Francisco Redevel. Agy. Embarcadero Center, 1966—; lectr. Nat. Inst. Architects Rome, 1960, U. Florence, 1960, U. Naples, 1960, Israel Inst. Tech., 1960, Greek Architects Soc., Athens, 1960, U. Belgrade, 1960, Mass. Inst. Tech., 1965, U. N.Mex., 1964, Am. Cultural Center, Paris, 1960, 64, Gujarat Inst. Engrs. and Architects, 1963, U. Colo., 1961, Harvard, 1962, U. Minn., 1962, U. Coll. London, 1967, Inst. Contemporary Arts, London, 1967, Ecole Nationale des Beaux-Ats, 1967; artist in residence Tamarind Lithography Workshop, 1966, Am. Acad. in Rome, 1971-72; research prof. Creative Arts Inst. U. Calif., 1966-67; artist in residence IBM Los Angeles Sci. Center, 1970-71. Served to capt. C.E., AUS, 1942-46. Author: Jesse Reichek-Dessins, 1960; La Monte de la Nuit, 1961; Fontis, 1961; Etcetera, 1965; Le Bulletin Des Baux, 1972; e.g., 1976. Home: 5925 Red Hill Rd Petaluma CA 94953

REICHEL, FRANK HARTRANFT, JR., mfg. co. exec.; b. Bklyn., Mar. 2, 1928; s. Frank Hartranft and Marian (Reed) R.; B.A., Yale U., 1948, Ph.D. in Chemistry, 1951; m. Beatrice A. Hinson, Mar. 26, 1955; children—Beatrice Lynn, Frank Hartranft, III. Chemist, Monsanto Co., Miamisburg, Ohio. 1951-52; dir. research Ketchikan Pulp Co. (Alaska) 1952-63; asst. to exec. v.p. F.M.C. Corp., Phila., 1963-65; pres., chmn. bd. A.V.C. Corp., Radnor. Pa., 1965-76, chmn. bd., chief exec. officer, 1976—; dir. Davison Sand & Gravel Co., Raybestos-Manhattan, Inc. Bd. mgrs. Franklin Inst. Mem. Am. Chem. Soc., Chem. Market Research Assn., TAPPI. Republican. Episcopalian. Clubs: Links, Yale (N.Y.C.); Union League, Phila. Country (Phila.); Merion Cricket; Bay Head Yacht. Home: 720 Spring Mill Rd Villanova PA 19085 Office: PO Box 303 Two Radnor Corporate Center Radnor PA 19087

REICHEL, WALTER EMIL, advt. exec.; b. Irvington, N.J., Dec. 12, 1935; s. Walter Edwin and Flora Maria (Pfister) R.; B.A., Columbia, 1959; M.A., N.Y. U., 1971, postgrad., 1971—; m. Priscilla Tedesco, Feb. 1, 1969; 1 son, Bradley Joseph. With Benton & Bowles, N.Y.C., 1959-67, v.p., 1965-67, asso. media dir., 1965-67; with Ted Bates & Co., Inc., N.Y.C., 1967—, sr. v.p., 1973—, exec. dir. media and programs, 1974—, also dir. Mem. Am. Assn. Advt. Agys. (broadcast com.), Advt. Information Services (dir.). Home: 449 1/2 Henry St Brooklyn NY 11231 Office: 1515 Broadway New York City NY 10036

REICHERT, DAVID, lawyer; b. Cin., Nov. 23, 1929; s. Victor E. and Louise F. (Feibel) R.; B.A., Bowling Green State U., 1951; J.D., U. Cin., 1954; m. Marilyn Frankel, May 31, 1959; children—James G., Steven F., William M. Admitted to Ohio bar, 1954, U.S. Supreme Ct. bar, 1963; partner firm Gould, Reichert & Strauss, and predecessors, Cin., 1956-61, partner, 1961—; dir. numerous corps. Pres. brotherhood Rockdale Temple, Cin., 1960-61, temple treas., 1973-75, v.p., 1975-79, pres., 1979—; mem. Ohio Solid Waste Adv. Group, 1974; treas. Contemporary Arts Center, Cin., 1973-75, pres., 1976-77. Served with U.S. Army, 1954-56. Mem. Cin. Print and Drawing Circle (pres. 1974-76), Zeta Beta Tau, Omicron Delta Kappa, Sigma Tau Delta, Phi Delta Phi. Club: Lit. Monthly columnist Scrap Age mag., 1966-74; bd. editors U. Cin. Law Rev., 1953-54. Office: 2613 Carew Tower Cincinnati OH 45202

REICHERT, KURT, social worker; b. Karlsbad, Czechoslovakia, June 5, 1916; s. Leo Rosenthal and Else (Morgenstern) R.; came to U.S., 1938, naturalized, 1943; B.A., Carleton Coll., 1941; M.A., U. Chgo., 1946; Ph.D., U. Minn., 1955; m. Elizabeth Bednasz, Dec. 29, 1941; 1 dau., Julie. Social worker Jewish Family and Community Service, Chgo., 1942-45; social worker, student supr. Scholarship and Guidance Assn., Chgo., 1947-48; asst. prof. chief psychiat. social worker U. Minn. Med. Sch. and Hosps., 1948-52; social work cons. home service Hennepin County (Minn.) chpt. A.R.C., 1949-50; social work cons. cultural affairs div. U.S. High Commn. Germany, 1952; lectr. social work Sch. Social Work, U. Minn., 1952-54, research asso., 1954-55; dir. Office Pub. Health Social Work, N.Y. Dept. Health, 1955-64; asso. prof. social work and research Bryn Mawr Coll., 1964-67; dir. div. standards and accreditation Council Social Work Edn., 1967-70; dean Sch. Social Work San Diego State U., 1970-74, prof., 1974—; cons., spl. lectr. pub. health Syracuse Sch. Social Work, 1959-61. Chmn. com. social work Gov. Minn. Adv. Council Mental Health, 1949-51; chmn. casework div. Minn. Welfare Conf., 1950-51; chmn. health, mental health and rehab. sect. N.Y. State Welfare Conf., 1957-58. Bd. dirs. Albany Child Guidance Clinic, 1958-60, N.Y. State Welfare Conf., 1958-60. Fellow Am. Pub. Health Assn.; mem. Nat. Assn. Social Workers (mem.-at-large bd. dirs. 1959-61, 60-62, pres. 1963-64), Acad. Certified Social Workers, Council Social Work Edn., Nat. Conf. Social Welfare, Internat. Conf. Social Work, Nat. Rehab. Assn. Home: 5317 Wilshire Dr San Diego CA 92116 Office: Sch Social Work San Diego State U San Diego CA 92182

REICHERT, NORMAN VERNON, transp. co. exec.; b. Berwyn, Ill., Apr. 17, 1921; s. John G. and Valeria (Hoffman) R.; B.S. in Bus. Adminstrn., Northwestern U., 1943; postgrad. Harvard, 1943-44; m. Wilma Eleanor Catey, Feb. 5, 1944; children—Susan, Norman Vernon. Accountant, Arthur Young & Co., Chgo., 1946-50; mem. central finance staff, controller styling div. Ford Motor Co., Dearborn, Mich., 1950-61; asst. treas. Philco Ford Corp., Phila., 1961-69; asst. treas. United Air Lines, Inc., Chgo., 1969-72; v.p. fin. Trailer Train Co., Am. Rail Box Car Co., Chgo., 1972—; v.p. fin., dir. Railgon Co., Chgo.; dir. Hamburg Industries, Inc., Augusta, Ga., Calpro, Inc., Riverside, Calif. Served to lt. USNR, 1943-46. C.P.A., Ill. Mem. Am. Inst. C.P.A.'s, Fin. Execs. Inst., Beta Alpha Psi, Sigma Alpha Epsilon. Clubs: Union League, Knollwood, Execs. Home: 921 Grandview Ln Lake Forest IL 60045 Office: 300 S Wacker Dr Chicago IL 60606. *Each day we must start over. One cannot live on yesterday's accomplishments, but instead, must establish new goals. Last year's champion is soon forgotten as we focus on the current achiever. This is the way I try to approach each new day. And, at the end of each day, I assess my efforts in relation to the goals I had established for that day.*

REICHERT, PHILIP, med. cons.; b. N.Y.C., Mar. 29, 1897; s. Nathaniel and Charlotte (Fishel) R.; A.B., Coll. City N.Y., 1918; M.D., Cornell U., 1923; m. Helen F. Keane, Sept. 29, 1939. Fellow, then asst. Rockefeller Inst. Med. Research, 1923-25; acting dir. Witkin Found. Cardiol. Research, 1938-40; became v.p., dir. profl. div. Doherty, Clifford, Steers & Shenfield, N.Y.C., 1947; nat. sec., trustee, gov. Am. Coll. Cardiology, N.Y.C., 1949-59, exec. dir., 1959-69; dir. research Yorktown Products Corp., N.Y.C., 1956—; dir. course med. advt. and promotion N.Y. U., 1956—. Served as sgt. U.S. Army, World War I; maj. detached duty, M.C., Res., World War II. Diplomate Nat. Bd. Med. Examiners. Fellow A.C.P. (life), Am. Coll. of Legal Medicine (trustee), Am. Coll. Cardiology (distinguished fellow); N.Y. Acad. Medicine; mem. Assn. Mil. Surgeons, N.Y. Microscopical Soc., Soc. History of Medicine. Author numerous articles profl. jours. Address: 480 Park Ave New York NY 10022. *What makes it tick? My basic characteristic is curiosity. As a youngster I got into the repairing of watches and clocks. At Rockefeller Institute I did research on the single cell respiration of bacteria; in practice I became a heart specialist.*

REICHERT-FACILIDES, OTTO ERNST, architect; b. Gorlitz, Germany, July 28, 1925; s. Walter A. and Margret (Schulz) R.; diploma engring., Technische Hochschule, Karlsruhe, Germany, 1950; M.Arch., Harvard, 1958; m. Nuria Vandellos, May 27, 1955; children—Mark, Kent, Christopher, Christina. Came to U.S., 1957, naturalized, 1960. Dir. city planning dept. Offenbach on Main, Germany, 1953-57; architect, planner Reichert-Facilides Assos., 1957; instr. city planning and housing Technische Hochschule, Karlsruhe, 1952-53, Sch. Adminstrn., Frankfurt on Main, Germany, 1954-55; chmn. exhibit com. Nat. Conf. Am. Soc. Planning Ofcls., 1966; organizer exhibits World Congress Internat. Fedn. Town Planning and Housing, Phila., 1968. Fulbright scholar Columbia, 1950-51; recipient awards Spain, Germany, U.S. Mem. AIA (dir., v.p. Phila. chpt.), Am. Inst. Planners, Pa. Soc. Architects (dir.). Lutheran. Rotarian. Home: 6 Summit Pl Philadelphia PA 19128 Office: Suite 410 Academy House 1420 Locust St Philadelphia PA 19102

REICHL, ERNST, book designer; b. Leipzig, Germany, May 2, 1900; s. Julius and Rosa (Tuchmann) R.; came to U.S., 1926, naturalized, 1930; Ph.D., U. Leipzig, 1924; m. Miriam Brudno, July 31, 1945; 1 dau., Ruth Reichl Hollis. House designer Alfred A. Knopf, N.Y.C., 1926-27; art dir. Doubleday, Doran, 1928-31; corporate designer H. Wolff Book Mfg. Co., 1931-42; type dir. Foote, Cone & Belding, N.Y.C., 1943-45; pres. Archway Press, Inc., 1945-53; pres. Ernst Reichl Assos., N.Y.C., 1953—; asso. adj. prof. N.Y. U., 1961-70. Mem. Am. Inst. Graphic Arts (dir. 1940-44), Type Dirs. Club N.Y.C., The Typophiles. Author: Legibility - A Typographic Book of Etiquette, 1948. Designer of Ulysses by James Joyce, 1933; designer The Holy Bible, New Internat. Version, 1973. Office: 156 Fifth Ave New York NY 10010

REICHLE, FREDERICK ADOLPH, surgeon; b. Neshaminy, Pa., Apr. 20, 1935; s. Albert and Ernestine R.; B.A. summa cum laude, Temple U., 1957, M.D., 1961, M.S. in Biochemistry, 1961, M.S. in Surgery, 1966. Intern, Abington Meml. Hosp., 1962; resident Temple U. Hosp., Phila., 1966, surgeons, 1966—; practice medicine specializing in surgery, Phila., 1966—; asso. attending surgeons Epis. Hosp., St. Marys Hosp., St. Christophers Hosp. for Children; cons. VA Hosp., Wilkes Barre, Pa.; cons. Germantown Dispensary and Hosp.; prof. surgery, chief peripheral vascular sect., dept. surgery Temple U. Sch. Medicine, 1976—. Recipient Surg. Residents Research Paper award Phila. Acad. Surgery, 1964, 66, Gross Essay prize, 1976; Am. Heart Assn. grantee, 1973; diplomate Am. Bd. Surgery. Fellow A.C.S., Coll. Physicians Phila.; mem. Am. Surg. Assn., Soc. Univ. Surgeons, AMA, Pa. Med. Soc., Assn. Acad. Surgery, N.Y. Acad. Sci., AAAS, Am. Fedn. Clin. Research, Nat. Assn. Professions, Am. Gastroent. Assn., Am. Assn. Cancer Research, Am. Heart Assn., Phila. Acad. Surgery, Heart Assn. Southeastern Pa., Internat. Soc. Thombosis and Haemostasis, Nat. Kidney Found., Soc. for Surgery Alimentary Tract, Soc. Vascular Surgery, Colleguim Internationale Chirurgie Digestivae, Am. Soc. Pharmacology and Exptl. Therapeutics, Am. Inst. Ultrasound in Medicine, Am. Physiol. Soc., Soc. Internationale de Chirurgie, Am. Soc. Abdominal Surgeons, Surg. Hist. Soc., Am. Aging Assn., Am. Geriatrics Soc., Gerontol. Soc., Am. Diabetes Assn., Surg. Biology Club, Alpha Omega Alpha, Sigma Xi, Phi Tho Sigma. Contbr. articles to profl. jours. Home: 771 Easton Rd Warrington PA 18976 Office: 3400 N Broad St Philadelphia PA 19140

REICHLIN, SEYMOUR, physician, educator; b. N.Y.C., May 31, 1924; s. Henry and Celia (Rosen) R.; student Coll. City N.Y., 1940-41; A.B., Antioch Coll., 1945; M.D., Washington U., St. Louis, 1948; Ph.D., U. London, 1954; m. Elinor Thurman Dameshek, June 24, 1951; children—Seth David, Douglas James, Ann Elise. Intern N.Y. Hosp., 1948-49; asst. resident Barnes Hosp., St. Louis, 1949-50; asst. resident N.Y. Hosp., 1950-51; chief resident Barnes Hosp., 1951-52; research fellow physiology dept. Maudsley Hosp., London, Eng., 1952-54; instr. psychiatry Washington U., 1954-55, asst. prof. psychiatry and medicine, 1955-60; asso. prof. medicine U. Rochester, 1960-66, prof., 1966-69; prof., head dept. med. and pediatric spltys. Sch. Medicine U. Conn., 1969-71, prof., head dept. physiology, 1971-72; prof. medicine Tufts U., 1972—; practice medicine specializing in clin. endocrinology, St. Louis, 1955-60, Rochester, 1961-69, Hartford, Conn., 1969-71, Boston, 1972—; sr. physician New Eng. Med. Center, 1972—; cons. Genesee and Rochester Gen. Hosp., 1960-69, Hartford Hosp., 1970—, New Britain (Conn.) Gen. Hosp., 1970-72. Mem. endocrinology study sect. NIH, 1966-70; adv. panel FDA, 1977—. Bd. dirs. Founds. Fund, New Haven, 1968-70. Served with AUS, 1943-44. Commonwealth Fund fellow, 1952-54; Lowell M. Palmer fellow, 1954-56. Mem. Central Soc. Clin. Research, Am. Soc. Clin. Investigation, Assn. Am. Physicians, Am. Physiol. Soc., Endocrine Soc. (Eli Lilly award 1972, pres. 1975-76), Brit. Soc. Endocrinology, Am. Psychosomatic Soc., Am. Thyroid Assn., Internat. Brain Orgn., Assn. for Research in Nervous and Mental Disease (pres. 1976), Alpha Omega Alpha. Club: Interurban. Editorial bd. Endocrinology, 1969-74, New Eng. Jour. Medicine, 1976—. Contbr. profl. jours., texts, monographs. Home: 420 Concord Rd Weston MA 02193 Office: 171 Harrison Ave Boston MA 02111

REICHMAN, OWEN HOWARD, neurol. surgeon; b. Washington, Oct. 1, 1932; s. Owen G. and Stella May (Cheshire) R.; B.A. in Math., U. Utah, 1952, M.D., 1956; m. Nancy Lou Topping, July 20, 1953; children—Howard Reed, Mark Vernon, Kathleen, Owen Stanley, Russell Wayne, Shirley Anne, Douglas James. Rotating intern Latter-day Saint Hosp., Salt Lake City, 1956-57, resident in surgery, 1959-60; resident in pathology Bklyn. Hosp., 1957-58; N.Y. Heart Assn. vis. fellow cardiovascular surgery Columbia-Presbyn. Med. Center, N.Y.C., 1958-59; from resident in surgery to chief resident, asst. in neurol. surgery U. Colo. Med. Center, Denver, 1960-64; practice medicine specializing in neurol. surgery, Salt Lake City, 1964-73; from asst. clin. to asst. clin. prof. neurosurgery U. Utah Med. Sch., 1965-73; asso. prof., prof. neurosurgery Loyola U. Med. Sch., Chgo., 1973—, chief div. neurol. surgery, 1977—; mem. staff Foster G. McGaw Hosp., Maywood, Ill., 1973—; attending neurosurgeon Hines (Ill.) VA Hosp., 1973—. Diplomate Am. Bd. Neurol. Surgery. Fellow A.C.S.; mem. AMA, Ill., Chgo. med. socs., Internat. Soc. Research in Stereoencephalotomy, Am. Assn. Neurol. Surgeons, Congress Neurol. Surgeons, Soc. Neurol. Surgeons, Rocky Mountain, Western, Central neurosurg. socs., Chgo. Neurol. Soc. Contbr. med. jours. Home: 188 Sunnyside St Elmhurst IL 60126 Office: 2160 S 1st Ave Maywood IL 60153

REICHMANN, JAMES BELL, clergyman, educator; b. Everett, Wash., Jan. 14, 1923; s. Linden Nicholas and Eva (Bell) R.; B.A., Gonzaga U., 1946, M.A., 1947; S.T.L., Gregorian U., Rome, 1954, Ph.D., 1960. Joined Soc. of Jesus, 1940, ordained priest Roman Catholic Ch., 1953; asst. prof. philosophy Mt. St. Michael's Coll., Spokane, Wash., 1962-65; mem. faculty Seattle U., 1955-58, 60-62, 65—, prof. philosophy, 1970—, chmn. dept., 1969-79. Mem. Am. Cath., Jesuit philos. assns., Northwest Philosophy Conf. (pres. 1966-67). Address: Seattle U Seattle WA 98122

REICHNER, MORGAN STEPHENS AIKEN, business exec.; b. Phila., Aug. 29, 1905; s. Louis Irving and Cephise H. (Aiken) R.; student Princeton, 1927; m. Christine B. Cadwalader, Jan. 25, 1930; 1 dau., Aiken Cadwalader; m. 2d, Phoebe Logan, Oct. 4, 1940; m. 3d, Eleanor W. Wheeler, Oct. 9, 1948. Exec., Batten, Barton, Durstine & Osborn, N.Y. City, 1927-34; v.p. Kimball, Hubbard & Powel, 1934-37; pres. Morgan Reichner & Co., 1937-41, Morgan Reichner, Inc., bus. cons., 1947-51, Wildlife Research Co. Inc.; trustee Am. Econ. Found., 1951-64; pres., exec. dir. Nat. Schs. Com. for Econ. Edn., 1964—. Trustee Adelphi U., Garden City, L.I., N.Y. Planning officer OSS, ETO, 1942-44; asst. dir. intelligence O.W.I., E.T.O., London, 1944-45. Served as lt. comdr. USNR, World War II. Mem. Soc. Cin., Colonial Wars Soc., S.R., War 1812 Soc., U.S. C. of C., St. Nicholas Soc. N.Y.C. Clubs: Princeton, Leash (N.Y.C.); Westminster Kennel; Fishers Island (N.Y.) Country, Fishers Island Yacht; Round Hill (Greenwich, Conn.); Nassau (Princeton); Imperial Poona Yacht (London). Author: Your Money; Economic Story of Man; co-author The Many Faces of Freedom. Editor: Principles We Live By. Home: 43 Grahampton Ln Greenwich CT 06830 Office: 143 Sound Beach Ave Old Greenwich CT 06870

REID, ARTHUR LEONARD, banker; b. Manchester, Eng., Mar. 13, 1900; s. Arthur John and Mary Jane (Wheatley) R.; grad. Am. Inst. Banking, 1921; m. Marjory L. Warner, Aug. 9, 1922, (dec. 1951); 1 son, John Warner; m. 2d, Isabelle L. Levesque, Oct. 21, 1959. With Mohawk Nat. Bank, Schenectady, 1917—, pres., 1951-59, chmn. bd., 1959—, also dir.; treas. Orchard Park Estates Inc., Schenectady, 1960—, Niskarama Corp., Saratoga County, N.Y., 1960—. Trustee Citizens Public Expenditures, Albany, N.Y.; bd. dirs. Am. Cancer Soc., Heart Soc., Easter Seal Soc. N.Y. Episcopalian (sr. warden 1926—). Clubs: Mohawk, Willows Country (Schenectady); Chatiemac (North Creek, N.Y.). Home: 1216 Waverly Pl Schenectady NY 12308 Office: 216 State St Schenectady NY 12308

REID, AUBREY KARL, JR., ins. co. exec.; b. Center Harbor, N.H., May 16, 1927; s. Aubrey Karl and Alice Mae (Brown) R.; B.S., U. N.H., 1949; children—Aubrey Karl III, Mary Jay (Mrs. Richard Powers), Stephen Martin, Sharon Ann; m. Dorothy Austin; stepchildren—David Austin Jr., Donna Austin, Debra Austin, Dean Austin. With Paul Revere Cos., Worcester, Mass., 1949—, v.p., dir. agys., 1969-71, v.p. sales and mktg., 1971-74, pres., dir., 1974—; pres., dir. Paul Revere Life Ins. Co., Paul Revere Variable Annuity Ins. Co., Paul Revere Protective Life Ins. Co., Paul Revere Equity Sales Co., PR Land Corp., PR Realty Corp., PR Fin. Corp.; dir. Paul Revere Corp. (Holding Co.), Paul Revere Equity Mgmt. Co.; corporator Worcester County Instn. for Savs.; chmn. bd. mgrs. Paul Revere Variable Annuity Contract Accumulation Fund. Bd. dirs. Downtown Worcester Devel. Corp.; corporator Worcester Art Mus.; trustee Central New Eng. Coll., Worcester; gen. chmn. United Way of Central Mass., 1980. Mem. Life Ins. Assn. Mass. (dir.), Worcester Area C. of C. (dir.), Worcester Econ. Club (pres., exec. com.), Nat. Assn. Life Underwriters, Chief Execs. Club, Newcomen Soc. Mason (Shriner). Clubs: Worcester Country, Worcester; Plaza. Home: 6 Crocker Hill Dr Paxton MA 01612 Office: 18 Chestnut St Worcester MA 01608

REID, BENJAMIN LAWRENCE, author, educator; b. Louisville, May 3, 1918; s. Isaac Errett and Margaret (Lawrence) R.; A.B., U. Louisville, 1943, D.H.L., 1970; A.M., Columbia, 1950; Ph.D., U. Va., 1957; m. Jane Coleman Davidson, July 15, 1942; children—Jane Lawrence (Mrs. Michael A. McAnulty), Colin Way. Faculty, Iowa State Coll., Ames, 1946-48, Smith Coll., Northampton, Mass., 1948-51, Sweet Briar (Va.) Coll., 1951-57; prof. English, Mt. Holyoke Coll., 1957—, Andrew Mellon prof. humanities, 1972—. Fulbright Research grantee, 1963-64; Am. Council Learned Socs. fellow, 1966-67; sr. fellow Nat. Endowment for Humanities, 1971-72. Recipient Pulitzer prize for John Quinn and His Friends, 1969. Mem. AAUP, Modern Lang. Assn. Author: Art by Subtraction: A Dissenting Opinion of Gertrude Stein, 1958; William Butler Yeats: The Lyric of Tragedy, 1961; The Man from New York; John Quinn and His Friends, 1968; The Long Boy and Others: Eighteenth Century Studies, 1969; Tragic Occasions: Essays on Several Forms, 1971; The Lives of Roger Casement, 1976; also essays, short stories, verse to lit. revs. Home: 1 Greenwood Ln South Hadley MA 01075

REID, BRYAN SEABORNE, JR., business exec.; b. Chgo., June 26, 1925; s. Bryan Seaborne and Margaret (Brittingham) R.; B.S., Northwestern U., 1945; m. Marian M. Vilas, May 14, 1949 (div. 1978); children—Bryan Seaborne III, Andrew V., Nancy M., Alexander B.; m. 2d, Rosemary Burt, 1979. Salesman, Bacon, Whipple & Co., mem. N.Y. Stock Exchange, 1947-57, partner, 1958-63; chmn. Paxall, Inc., Chgo., 1963—; dir. LaSalle Nat. Bank. Mem. nat. adv. bd., Boy Scouts Am., treas., 1970-78; trustee, sec. Chgo. Hist. Soc.; trustee, vice chmn. Art Inst. Chgo.; vice chmn. bd. dirs., mem. exec. coms. Northwestern Meml. Hosp.; trustee Northwestern U., 4th Presbyn. Ch. Served to ensign USNR, 1943-46. Clubs: Chicago, Mid-Day, Wayfarer's, Commonwealth, Commercial, Casino, Racquet, (Chgo.); East India (London). Office: 100 W Monroe St Chicago IL 60603

REID, DANIEL PETER, aircraft co. exec.; b. St. Paul, Feb. 1, 1925; student U. Minn.; m. Cheryl L. Yonda, Sept. 26, 1975; children—Daniel Peter, Frederick W. With Trans World Airlines, Inc., 1946—, v.p. sales and services, then sr. v.p., gen. mgr., N.Y.C., 1970-76, sr. v.p. ops., 1976-77, also dir.; v.p., program exec.-internat. Lockheed Calif. Co., Burbank, 1978—; dir. Thomson Newspapers, Inc. Served with U.S. Army, 1943-45. Decorated Bronze Star, Purple Heart. Mem. Nat. Rifle Assn. (life). Clubs: Union League (N.Y.C.); Olympic, Mzuri Safari (San Francisco); Mt. Kenya Safari (Nanyuki, Kenya). Office: Box 551 Burbank CA 91520

REID, DONALD SIDNEY, composer; b. Staunton, Va., June 5, 1945; s. Sidney Boxley and Mary Frances (Craun) R.; student Dunsmore Bus. Coll., 1963-64; m. Gloria Elaine Fairchild, Oct. 23, 1964; children—Donald Sidney II, Langdon Fairchild. Song writer Am. Cowboy Pub. Co., Nashville, 1972-78; rec. artist Statler Bros. Prodns., Staunton, Va., 1961—. Bd. dirs. Happy Birthday USA,

1970-78. Recipient Broadcast Music Inc. award, 1973-78, Country Music Assn. awards, 1972-77, Nat. Assn. Rec. Arts and Scis. awards, 1965-74, gold album for Best of Statler Brothers, 1977, platinum album Best of Statler Brothers, 1978. Rec. artist: Class of '57, 1972; Thank You World, 1974; Pictures, 1971; Do You Remember These, 1972; I'll Go To My Grave Loving You, 1975; Whatever Happened to Randolph Scott, 1973; She's Been Like a Mother To Me, 1974; Do You Know You Are My Sunshine, 1978. Mem. Country Music Assn. (asst. treas. 1980). Office: PO Box 2703 Staunton VA 24401

REID, EDWARD SNOVER, lawyer; b. Detroit, Mar. 24, 1930; s. Edward S. and Margaret (Overington) R.; B.A., Yale U., 1951; LL.B., Harvard U., 1956; m. Carroll Grylls, Dec. 30, 1953; children—Carroll Kercheval, Richard Gerveys, Jane Franklin, Margaret Wetherill. Admitted to Mich. bar, 1957, N.Y. bar, 1958; asso. Davis, Polk & Wardwell, N.Y.C., 1957-64, partner, 1964—; dir. Gen. Mills, Inc., 1974—; trustee Bklyn. Savs. Bank, 1974—. Mem. N.Y.C. Bd. Higher Edn., 1971-73; trustee Bklyn. Inst. Arts and Scis., 1966—, chmn., 1974-79; mem. governing com. Bklyn. Mus., 1973—; bd. dirs. Met. Opera Assn., 1973—, Bklyn. Bot. Garden Corp., 1977—. Served as lt. USMC, 1951-53. Mem. Am. Bar Assn., N.Y. State Bar Assn., Assn. Bar City N.Y. Home: 22 Garden Pl Brooklyn NY 11201 also Quogue NY also Stratton Mountain VT Office: Chase Manhattan Plaza New York NY 10005

REID, EDWIN KITCHEN, lawyer; b. Albany, Ga., Nov. 16, 1912; s. William Adolphus and Carrie Ida (Kitchen) R.; A.B., Syracuse U., 1936; J.D., Duke, 1939; m. Betty Ann Thombs, Sept. 3, 1943; children—Kathy, Linda (dec.), Edwin. Admitted to N.Y. bar, 1941, D.C. bar, 1970; asso. Barry, Wainwright, Thatcher & Symmers, N.Y.C., 1939-43; asso. Dow & Symmers, N.Y.C., 1943-44, partner, 1946-52; partner Zock, Petrie, Sheneman & Reid, N.Y.C., 1952-72, Zock, Petrie, Reid, Curtin & Byrnes, 1972-75, Zock, Patrie, Reid & Curtin, 1975—; asst. legal rep. U.S. War Shipping Adminstrn., U.K., N. Ireland, Europe, 1944-46; sometime spl. master U.S. Dist. Ct. for So. Dist. N.Y.; lectr. law and medicine Law Sci. Inst., Crested Butte, Colo., 1960. Chmn. adv. council for law enforcement, Bergen County, 1955-57; mem. Juvenile Conf. Commn. Demarest, Bergen County, N.J., 1966, chmn., 1967—. Councilman, Boro of Demarest, 1954-57; mayor Boro Demarest, 1961-64; chmn. 13th Assembly Dist. N.J., N. Valley, Passiac Valley Republican Fedn., 1967-68. Mem. Bar Assn. City N.Y., Assn. Trial Lawyers Am., N.Y. State Trial Lawyers Assn., Fed. Bar Assn., Am. Maritime Law Assn., Am. Arbitration Assn. (arbitrator), Phi Beta Kappa, Delta Kappa Epsilon. Clubs: Knickerbocker Country (Tenafly, N.J.); Whitehall (N.Y.C.). Home: Apt 11 Brentwood Manor 201 Piermont Rd Cresskill NJ 07626 Office: 19 Rector St New York NY 10006

REID, EVANS BURTON, chemist, educator; b. Brock Twp., Ont., Can., Mar. 29, 1913; s. William Thomas and Ethel Elizabeth (Burton) R.; B.Sc. with first class honors, McGill U., 1937, Ph.D. cum laude, 1940; m. Isabel Sue Lewin, Apr. 2, 1942 (dec. Nov. 3, 1962); 1 son, Nicholas Evans David; m. 2d, Dorothy Pearson, Aug. 12, 1963. Came to U.S., 1941, naturalized, 1944. Grad. asst. chem. engring. McGill U., 1937-38, demonstrator organic chemistry, 1938-40; research chemist Dominion Tar & Chem. Co., Montreal, 1940-41; instr. chemistry Middlebury Coll., 1941-43, asst. prof., 1943-46; asst. prof. chemistry Johns Hopkins, 1946-54; cons. Tainton Products, Balt., 1951-54; Merrill prof. chemistry, chmn. dept. Colby Coll., 1954-78, prof. emeritus, 1978—, acting dean faculty, 1967-68, dir. Coll. NSF Summer Sci. Inst., 1958—; cons. to NSF, 1963-65; corporator Maine Med. Care Devel., Inc., 1968—; Smith-Mundt vis. prof. chemistry U. Baghdad, 1960-61. Mem. screening panel for Nat. award in pure chemistry, 1953. Recipient J. Shelton Horsley award Va. Acad. Scis. (with Albert W. Lutz), 1955. Mem. Am. Chem. Soc. (exec. com. Md. sect. 1951-54, chmn. Me. 1956, 62, 71), Chem. Soc. London, Sigma Xi. Mason. Adv. council World Who's Who in Sci., 1968. Contbr. to profl. jours and encys. Home: 11 Highland Ave Waterville ME 04901

REID, GEORGE WILLARD, educator; b. Indpls., Dec. 18, 1917; s. Lloyd W. and Elsie (Gravedinkel) R.; B.S. in Civil Engring., Purdue, 1942, C.E., 1950; S.M., Harvard, 1943; student Johns Hopkins, 1949-50; m. Barbara Ricks, Feb. 21, 1944; children—Judy, George, Andy Carter. Instr., Purdue U., 1942-43; san. insp. Harvard, 1942-43; asst. prof. civil engring. U. Fla., 1943-44; san. engr. Ind. Health Dept., 1944-45, USPHS, 1945-46; asso. prof. san. engring. Ga. Inst. Tech., 1946-50; faculty U. Okla., 1950—, prof. civil engring., 1956—, Regents prof., 1972—, chmn. dept., 1959—, also coordinator san. sci. and dir. bur. water resources research; cons. USPHS, USAF, State of Okla., Interstate Water Compact Commn.; cons. U.S. Senate Select Com. Water Resources; gov. long range and research council on water resources and Okla. tech. adviser to Peace Corps; mem. cons. bd. Dept. of Interior; active WHO and AID research activities. Mem. ASCE, Am. Water Works Assn., Triangle, Sigma Xi, Chi Epsilon, Tau Beta Pi. Episcopalian. Rotarian. Author numerous articles in field. Home: 3840 Bristol Norman OK 73069

REID, GEORGE WILLIAMS, pub. co. exec.; b. Cleve., Mar. 31, 1925; s. Hugh Thomas and Mildred (Williams) R.; B.A., Dartmouth, 1950; LL.B., Cornell U., 1953; m. Jean Tower, Dec. 27, 1950; children—William T., Karen E. Admitted to N.Y. bar, 1954; pvt. practice law, Buffalo-Niagara Falls, 1953-59; asst. sec., asst. gen. counsel Glidden Co., Cleve., 1959-68; sec., gen. counsel Western Pub. Co., Inc., Racine, Wis., 1968—, v.p., 1974—. Village trustee, Village of Wind Point, 1970—. Bd. dirs. Wis. Nature Conservancy, 1972-76. Served with USNR, 1943-46. Mem. Am., N.Y. bar assns., Am. Soc. Corporate Secs., Delta Tau Delta, Phi Delta Phi. Club: North Shore Tennis (pres., dir.) (Racine). Home: 470 Windridge Dr Racine WI 53402 Office: 1220 Mound Ave Racine WI 53404

REID, HAROLD WILSON, entertainer; b. Augusta County, Va., Aug. 21, 1939; s. Sidney Boxley and Mary Frances (Craun) R.; grad. high sch.; m. Brenda Lee Armstrong, Oct. 15, 1960; children—Kimberley, Karmen, Kodia, Kasey, Harold Wilson II. Mem. group Statler Bros., 1961—; pres. Statler Bros. Prodns., Staunton, Va., 1973—; pres. Am. Cowboy Pub. Co., Staunton, 1973—. Bd. dirs. Happy Birthday U.S.A., 1973—. Recipient several Grammies, Country Music Assn. awards, Broadcast Music Inc. Writer award, 1973-75. Recs. songs including Bed of Roses, Class of '57, What Ever Happened to Randolph Scott. Address: PO Box 2703 Staunton VA 24401

REID, HOCH, lawyer; b. Chanute, Kans., Dec. 27, 1909; s. James W. and Anna (Hoch) R.; A.B., Amherst Coll., 1931; LL.B., Columbia, 1934; m. Mona McMillan, July 3, 1937; children—Wallis H., Luanna Reid. Admitted to N.Y. bar, 1935, since practiced in N.Y.C.; partner firm Valicenti, Leighton, Reid & Pine, 1942-75, Burke & Burke, Daniels, Leighton & Reid, 1976-78, Townley & Updike, 1978—; mem. staff Navy Price Adjustment Bd., 1944-46. Sec. Capital Shares, Inc., Capamerica Fund, Inc. Trustee, Village of Pleasantville, N.Y., 1961-63, chmn. library bd., 1955-61, village atty., 1963-68. Mem. exec. bd. Lawyers Com. on Am. Policy Toward Vietnam, 1967-75; mem. social policy com., planning com. on aging Fedn. Protestant Welfare Agys.; mem. com. agrl. missions Nat. Council Chs., 1962—, chmn., 1962-76; bd. dirs. Bethel Methodist Homes, Ossining, N.Y., 1948—, pres., 1962-75; bd. dirs. Agrl. Missions, Inc., 1950—, pres., 1962-76; bd. dirs., mem. exec. com. Japan Internat. Christian U. Found.; pres., trustee Open Space Inst., 1969-72; trustee Natural Area Council, 1975—. Mem. Am., N.Y. State bar assns., Bar Assn. City N.Y., New Eng. Soc. N.Y., World Peace Through Law Center, Sawmill River Audubon Soc., Nature Conservancy. Congregationalist. Clubs: Canadian, Met. (N.Y.C.). Author: How to Use Investment Company Shares in Estate Planning, 1972; Paying Up for Services, 1976. Home: 18 Church St Pleasantville NY 10570 Office: 405 Lexington Ave New York NY 10017

REID, JACKSON BROCK, psychologist; b. Honea Path, S.C., Sept. 18, 1921; s. Alexander Mack and Ann Orr (Brock) R.; B.S., The Citadel, 1942; postgrad. Ariz. State Coll., Flagstaff, 1948; Ph.D., UCLA, 1951, postgrad., summer 1951; m. Avis Boykin Long, Jan. 12, 1947; step-children—Jules Heywood Long, Barbara Banning Long. Asst. prof. ednl. psychology U. Tex., Austin, 1951-55, asso. prof., 1955-59, prof., 1959—, asso. dean for grad. studies in edn., 1965-73, coordinator ESEA programs U.S. Office Edn., 1969—, chmn. dept. ednl. psychology, 1972—; cons. in field. Served to capt. U.S. Army, 1942-47. Cert., lic. psychologist, Tex.; Office Edn. grantee, 1966-73. Fellow Am. Psychol. Assn.; mem. AAAS, Am. Ednl. Research Assn., Interam. Soc. Psychology, AAUP, Southwestern Psychol. Assn. (sec.-treas. 1965-66, pres. 1967-68), Tex. Psychol. Assn., Ret. Officers Assn., Nat. Psoriasis Found., ACLU, Common Cause, Fund for Peace, Nat. Abortion Rights Action League, Sigma Xi. Clubs: U. Tex. Faculty Center; Lighthouse Resort and Club (Sanibel Island, Fla.). Research, publs. in learning theory, behavioral effects of radiation and drugs, child and adolescent behavior, programmed instn., computer-assisted instrn., 1951—. Office: Dept Ednl Psychology U Tex Austin TX 78712

REID, JAMES SIMS, physician, inventor, mfg. exec.; b. Yazoo City, Miss., Nov. 22, 1894; s. William H. and Sallie (Luse) R.; student (mech. engring.) Miss. Agrl. and Mech. Coll. (Starkville, Miss.), bus. coll. Atlanta, U. Tenn.; M.D., U. Louisville, 1916; m. Felice Crowl, Aug. 16, 1924; children—James Sims, George McKay, Margaret C. With Bd. of Health, Cleve., 2 yrs.; formed Easy-on-Cap (for automobiles) Co., 1921, serving as pres. until 1928; founded Standard Products Co., mfrs. rubber window channel and weatherstrips, plastic interior and exterior trim, other automotive products, with plants in U.S., Can., Europe, S.Am., later chmn. bd. and chief exec. officer, now chmn. bd. Served with U.S. Army, World War I; disch. with rank of capt.; cooperated in development and improvement of M-1 carbine, World War II. Mason. Clubs: Union, Tavern, Detroit Athletic. Inventor products and appliances pioneering in fields served by cos. he established. Home: Hudson OH 44236 Office: Standard Products Co 2130 W 110th St Cleveland OH 44102

REID, JAMES SIMS, JR., mfr. automobile parts; b. Cleve., Jan. 15, 1926; s. James Sims and Felice (Crowl) R.; A.B. cum laude, Harvard, 1948, LL.B., 1951; m. Donna Smith, Sept. 2, 1950; children—Sally, Susan, Anne, Jeanne. Admitted to Mich., Ohio bars, 1951; practice law, Detroit, 1951-52, Cleve., 1953-56; with Standard Products Co., Cleve., 1956—, pres., 1962—, also dir. Home: 2603 Fairmont Blvd Cleveland Heights OH 44106 Office: 2130 W 110th St Cleveland OH 44102

REID, JOHN EDWARD, lawyer, forensic cons.; b. Chgo., Aug. 16, 1910; s. Thomas and Margaret (Hanley) R.; student Loyola U., Chgo., 1930-31; J.D., DePaul U., 1936; m. Margaret McCarthy, July 26, 1941. Began testing subjects with polygraph Chgo. Police Sci. Crime Detection Lab., 1940, inventor polygraph for detection false rises in blood pressure, 1944; revised questioning technique in lie detector tests, 1947; established John E. Reid & Assos. Lab for Lie Detection, Chgo., 1947; founder Reid Coll. for Detection of Deception; devised Reid Report and Reid Survey psychol. questionnaires to determine job applicant and employee honesty. Mem. Chgo. Crime Commn. Fellow Am. Acad. Forensic Scis.; mem. Am. Polygraph Assn. (dir.), Ill. Polygraph Soc., Am. Acad. Polygraph Examiners (past pres.), Internat. Assn. Arson Investigators, Spl. Agts. Assn. (past pres.). Author: (with Fred. E. Inbau) Lie Detection and Criminal Interrogation; Criminal Interrogation and Confessions; Truth and Deception, The Polygraph (Lie Detector) Technique; also articles on lie detection, criminal interrogation. Home: 7306 N Bell Ave Chicago IL 60645 Office: 215 N Dearborn St Chicago IL 60601

REID, JOHN THOMAS, animal scientist; b. Cumberland, Md., Mar. 14, 1919; s. Frank Ernest and Sarah Pierce (Tipton) R.; B.S., U. Md., 1941; M.S., Mich. State U., 1943, Ph.D., 1946; m. Alice Evelyn Smalley, June 8, 1945; children—J. Douglas, Sarah R., Nancy S., Gwen L., Cindy A. Asst. prof. Mich. State U., 1944-45; asso. prof. Rutgers U., 1945-48; asso. prof. Cornell U., 1948-51, prof., 1951-77, Liberty Hyde Bailey prof., 1977—; Sir John Hammond Meml. lectr., 1972. cons. in field. Active Council Agrl. Sci. and Tech., Internat. Union Nutritional Sci., Am. Grassland Council, NSF. Recipient Nutrition Research award Am. Dairy Sci. Assn., 1950; Borden award, 1957; Merit award Am. Grassland Council, 1965; Guggenheim fellow, 1955-56. Mem. Brit. Soc. Nutrition, Am. Inst. Nutrition, Am. Soc. Animal Sci. (Morrison award 1967), Brit. Soc. Animal Prod. Methodist. Contbr. articles to profl. jours. Office: 158 Morrison Hall Cornell U Ithaca NY 14853

REID, JOSEPH EDMONDSON, oil co. exec.; b. Meridian, Miss., Mar. 18, 1929; s. Benjamin Franklin and Lottie (James) R.; B.S. in Petroleum Engring., La. State U., 1951; M.B.A., Harvard, 1956; m. Bobby Jean Ray, Sept. 6, 1955; children—Lisa R., Joseph T., Taylor L., Leslie C., David H. Exploitation engr. Shell Oil Co., 1953-54; mgr. oil and gas div. Cabot Corp., 1956-67; asst. to chmn. Panhandle Eastern Pipe Line Co., 1967-68; exec. v.p. subsidiary Trunkline Gas Co., Houston, 1968-72; pres., dir. Superior Oil Co., Houston, 1978—; pres. Superior Oil Internat., 1972—; chmn. bd., dir. Falconbridge Nickel Mines Ltd.; dir. Greenway Bank & Trust Co., Houston, Western Platinum Ltd., 1st City Nat. Bank of Houston, Southwestern Group Fin. Inc., Can. Superior Oil. Trustee Gray County Sch. Bd., 1966-67. Served as 2d lt. USAF, 1951. Mem. Am. Assn. Petroleum Geologists, Am. Inst. Mining Engrs., Am. Assn. Petroleum Landmen, Ind. Petroleum Assn. Am. (v.p. Houston area 1974-75). Baptist. Mason. Home: 651 Shady Hollow St Houston TX 77056

REID, KATE, actress; b. London, Eng., Nov. 4, 1930; d. Walter C. and Helen Isabel (Moore) R.; ed. Havergal Coll., Toronto Conservatory Music, U. Toronto; awarded Ph.D.; D.Litt. (hon.), York U., 1970; m. Austin Willis, July 13, 1953 (div. 1962); children—Reid, Robin. Stage debut in Years Ago, Gravenhurst, Ont., Can., summer 1948; toured Eng. as Lizzie in The Rainmaker; appeared as Catherine Ashland in The Stepmother, London, 1958; with Stratford (Ont.) Shakespearean Festival of Can.; appeared in As You Like It, Othello, 1959, Romeo and Juliet, A Midsummer Night's Dream, 1960, Henry VIII, Love's Labour's Lost, 1961, The Taming of the Shrew, Macbeth, 1962, Juno and the Paycock, 1973, Leaving Home, 1973, Freedom of the City, 1974, Romeo and Juliet, 1974, Cat on a Hit Tin Roof, 1974, Mrs. Warren's Profession, 1976, The Apple Cart, 1976; N.Y.C. debut as Martha in matinee co. of Who's Afraid of Virginia Woolf?, 1962; appeared in The Comedy of Errors, Troilus and Cresida, Cyrano de Bergerac, 1963, Dylan, 1964; movie appearances include The Andromeda Strain, The Rainbow Boys; various TV appearances. Recipient Order of Can. Address: care Reid Willis 14 Binscarth Rd Toronto ON M4W 1Y1 Canada*

REID, LOREN DUDLEY, educator; b. Gilman City, Mo., Aug. 26, 1905; s. Dudley Alver and Josephine (Tarwater) R.; A.B., Grinnell Coll., 1927; A.M., State U. Iowa, 1930, Ph.D., 1932; m. Mary Augusta Towner, Aug. 28, 1930; children—Jane Ellen, John Christopher, Stephen Dudley Towner, Don Anthony. Tchr. Vermillion (S.D.) High Sch., 1927-29; instr. State U. Iowa, 1931-33; tchr. Westport High Sch., Kansas City, Mo., 1933-35; English instr. U. Mo., 1935-37, asst. prof., 1937-39; asst. prof. and later asso. prof. of speech, Syracuse U., 1939-44; prof. of speech, U. Mo., 1944—, chmn. dept. speech, 1947-52; vis. prof. speech, U. So. Calif., summer, 1947; summer lectr. La. State U., 1949, Mich., 1950, 56, State U. Iowa, 1952, Denver, 1960, Oklahoma, 1962; vis. prof. U. Utah, summer 1952, San Diego State Coll., summer 1954, U. So. Calif., summer 1954; European staff U. Md., 1952-53, summer, 1955, 1961-62, London, U. Mich., summer 1957, State U. Iowa, summer 1958; Carnegie vis. prof. U. Hawaii, 1957. Recipient Alumni Achievement award Grinnell Coll., 1962; Distinguished prof. awards U. Mo., 1970, 71. Fellow Royal Hist. Soc.; mem. Eastern Pub. Speaking Conf., Speech Assn. Am. (exec. sec. 1945-51, pres. 1957), N.Y. State (pres. 1942-44, recipient special award for outstanding service 1967), Central States (exec. sec. 1937-39, Disting. Service award 1979) speech assns., AAUP, Mo. State Tchrs. Assn., Hansard Soc. London, Assn. Phonétique Internationale, Conf. on Brit. Studies, Sigma Delta Chi, Kappa Tau Alpha. Democrat. Episcopalian. Clubs: University of Missouri (pres. 1947). Author: Charles James Fox: An Eighteenth Century Parliamentary Speaker, 1932; Course Book in Public Speaking (With Gilman and Aly); Speech Preparation (with Gilman and Aly), 1946; Fundamentals of Speaking (with Gilman and Aly), 1951; Teaching Speech in High School, 1952; Teaching Speech, rev. edit., 1960, 4th edit., 1971; First Principles of Public Speaking, 1960, rev. edit., published in 1962; Studies in American Public Address, 1961; Speaking Well, 3d edit., 1976; Hurry Home Wednesday (Mo. Writers Guild award 1979, Mo. Library Assn. Lit. award 1979), 1978; Charles James Fox (James A. Winans award 1969, Golden Anniversary award 1970), 1969; also mem. editorial bd. Speech Monographs, 1960-62, Speech Tch., 1964-66, Quar. Jour. Speech, 1966-68. Contbr. profl. jours. Home: 200 E Brandon Rd Columbia MO 65201

REID, MORRIS WILLIAM, mfg. co. exec.; b. Central Butte, Sask., Can., Oct. 24, 1925; s. John William and Birdie Ethel (Walters) R.; m. Evelyn May Pully, June 30, 1945; children—Donna, Brenda, Robert. Came to U.S., 1961. Dir. sales Cockshutt Farm Equipment Co. Ltd., Brantford, Ont., 1958; with J.I. Case Co., Racine, Wis., 1958-79, gen. sales mgr., 1961, v.p., dir. mktg., 1961-67, exec. v.p., 1967-72, chmn. bd., 1972-79; ret., 1979; dir. Wis. Electric Power Co., Marine Bank Milw., Dickie John Co., Auburn, Ill., Harris Metals Co., Racine; exec. dir. Alta. (Can.) Safety Council, 1955; pres. Constrn. Indsl. Mfrs. Chmn. bd. trustees Alverno Coll., Milw., 1979-80. Am. Recipient Fairmarketing award of yr. Nat. Advt. and Mktg. Assn., 1963; Mktg. Man of Yr., Sales and Mktg. Execs.-Internat., 1964; Citizen of Yr. award VFW, 1977. Mem. Am. Ordnance Assn., Sales and Mktg. Execs.-Internat., Sales and Mktg. Execs. Assn., Farm Indsl. Equipment Inst. (pres. 1975), Am. Soc. Agrl. Engrs., Racine C. of C. Presbyterian. Mason. Home: 138 El Dorado Dr Racine WI 53402

REID, PAUL VICTOR, orthodontist; b. Chgo., Nov. 6, 1909; s. Wilfred E. and Eleanor (Weber) R.; D.D.S., U. Mich., 1929, M.S., 1931; m. Eleanor M. Brokaw, July 24, 1932. Instr. orthodontics U. Mich., 1929-31; asso. Dr. A. F. Jackson, Phila., 1931-42; pvt. practice orthodontics, 1946—; clin. prof., chmn. dept. orthodonics U. Pa., 1952-68, Served from lt. (j.g.) to lt. comdr., Dental Corps, USNR, 1942-46. Dir. Am. Bd. Orthodontics, 1958, treas., 1959-62, v.p., 1963-64, pres., 1964-65. Mem. Am. Dental Assn., Am. Assn. Orthodontists (pres. elect 1967, pres. 1968-69), Xi Psi Phi, Omicron Kappa Upsilon, Phi Kappa Phi, Phi Sigma. Club: Merion Golf. Home: 631 Black Rock Rd Bryn Mawr PA 19010 Office: 864 Country Line Rd Bryn Mawr PA 19010

REID, ROBERT NEWTON, lawyer, mortgage cons.; b. Ottawa, Ill., Mar. 28, 1908; s. Robert Joseph and Mae (Newton) R.; Ph.B., U. Chgo., 1929, J.D., 1930. Admitted to Ill. bar, 1930, U.S. Supreme Ct. bar, 1949, Md. bar, 1961, D.C. bar, 1961; practiced in Chgo., 1930-39; with Follansbee, Shorey & Schupp, 1933-39; govt. atty. FCA, Washington, 1939-42; atty., counsel RFC, Fed. Nat. Mortgage Assn., 1942-49; asst. gen. counsel Fed. Nat. Mortgage Assn., 1949-50, gen. counsel, 1950-70, spl. counsel, 1970-73, v.p., 1950-59, 68-73, dir., 1954-59, cons., 1973—. Served from 2d lt. to lt. col. Judge Adv. Gen. Corps, AUS, 1942-46. Decorated Legion of Merit. Mem. Am., Fed., D.C. bar assns., Am. Judicature Soc., Supreme Ct. Hist. Soc., Res. Officers Assn. (life), Am. Legion, S.A.R. (life), Ret. Officers Assn. (life), Mil. Order of World Wars (life), English Speaking Union, Delta Sigma Phi (life), Phi Alpha Delta. Mason. Clubs: Nat. Lawyers (life), Nat. Aviation, University (Washington). Home: University Club 1135 16th St NW Washington DC 20036 Office: 3900 Wisconsin Ave NW Washington DC 20016

REID, ROSS, lawyer, business exec.; b. Spokane, Wash., Mar. 9, 1917; s. William George and Margaret (Gamble) R.; A.B., Whitman Coll., 1938; student U. Wash. Sch. Law, 1938-40; J.D., Northwestern U., 1942; m. Sara Falknor, Dec. 31, 1940 (div.); 1 dau., Heather (Mrs. Edmund A. Schaffzin); m. 2d, Marney Sick Meeker, Jan. 19, 1966. Admitted to Ill. bar, 1941, N.Y. bar, 1943, D.C. bar, 1960; asso. firm Root, Clark, Buckner & Ballantine, N.Y.C., 1942-53; mem. firm Dewey, Ballantine, Bushby, Palmer & Wood, and predecessors, N.Y.C., 1954-62; v.p., dir., gen. counsel Beechnut Life Savers, Inc., 1962-68; sr. v.p., dir., gen. counsel, exec. com. Squibb Corp., 1968—; dir. Allegheny Power System, Inc.; trustee Emigrant Savs. Bank; mem. N.Y State Lawyers Com. to Support Ct. Reorgn., 1958-60. Chmn. bd. Am. Heart Assn., 1972-74, now mem. bd. dirs.; chmn. N.Y. Heart Assn., 1964-72, now mem. bd. dirs., exec. com.; bd. dirs. Internat. Cardiology Found.; bd. mem., 1st v.p. Internat. Soc. and Fedn. Cardiology; trustee Whitman Coll., Robert A. Taft Inst. Govt., Food and Drug Law Inst. Served with USAAF, 1945. Recipient Gold Heart award Am. Heart Assn., 1970. Fellow Am. Bar Found.; mem. Am., N.Y., New York County bar assns., Assn. Bar City N.Y. (chmn. membership com. 1961-64, exec. com. 1962-66), Jud. Conf. Second Circuit (exec. sec. plans com. 1960-64), Am. Judicature Soc., Order of Coif, Beta Theta Pi, Delta Sigma Rho, Delta Theta Phi. Clubs: University, West Side Tennis (N.Y.C.); Coral Beach and Tennis (Bermuda); Seattle Tennis. Home: 142 E 71st St New York NY 10021 Office: 40 W 57th St New York NY 10019

REID, SPENCER BEAL, army med. officer; b. Salt Lake City, Mar. 25, 1921; s. Walter Spencer and Martha (Beal) R.; B.S., U. Calif., Berkeley, 1943; M.D., George Washington U., 1946; m. Jane Hurd Milburn, May 23, 1970; children—Claudia, Spencer, Peter, Thomas, Clarissa. Intern, D.C. Gen. Hosp., 1947; resident Letterman Gen. Hosp., San Francisco, 1954; commd. 1st lt. M.C., U.S. Army, 1947, advanced through grades to maj. gen., 1979; service in Gen., Korea; dep. comdr., dir. profl. services, dir. med. edn. Walter Reed Army Med. Center, Washington, 1972-75; comdg. gen. Madigan Army Med. Center, Tacoma, 1975-77; comdr. U.S. Army 7th Med. Command, Europe and chief surgeon U.S. Forces, Europe, 1977—. Decorated Legion of Merit; recipient Alumni Achievement award George Washington U., 1976. Fellow Am. Coll. Obstetricians and Gynecologists; mem. AMA, Assn. U.S. Army (chpt. exec. council), Assn. Mil. Surgeons U.S., Am. Acad. Med. Dirs., Phi Gamma Delta,

Phi Chi. Mormon. Club: Rotary. Home: Quarters 26 San Jacinto Ave Patrick Henry Village Heidelberg Germany Office: 7th Med Command Europe Heidelberg Germany APO New York NY 09102

REID, TOY FRANKLIN, chem. co. exec.; b. York County, S.C., Jan. 13, 1924; s. Toy Fennell and Nellwyn Marteal (Mulliken) R.; B.S., U. S.C., 1943; B.S. in Chem. Engring., U. Ill., 1947; M.S., Ga. Inst. Tech., 1948; m. Martha Josephine Eggerton, May 31, 1947; children—Martha Josephine, Toy Franklin (dec.), Mark Eggerton. With Eastman Kodak Co., 1948—, supt. cellulose esters div. Tenn. Eastman Co., 1963-65, plant mgr. Carolina Eastman Co., 1965-69: asst. works mgr. Tenn. Eastman Co., also 1st v.p. Bays Mountain Constrn. Co., 1969-70, asst. to pres. Tenn. Eastman Co., 1970-72, v.p., 1972-73, sr. v.p., 1973-74, v.p. Eastman Kodak Co., asst. gen. mgr. Eastman Chems. div., also dir. Eastman Chem. Products, Inc., 1974-79, exec. v.p. Eastman Kodak Co., gen. mgr. Eastman Chems. div., 1979—, also dir., mem. exec. com. parent co.; dir. 1st Nat. Bank of Sullivan County. Bd. dirs. Holston Valley Community Hosp., Community Chest Kingsport, Inc., Jr. Achievement of Kingsport; trustee Holston Conf. Colls. of United Meth. Ch. Served to capt., USAAF, 1943-46. Mem. Am. Inst. Chem. Engrs., Chem. Mfrs. Assn. (dir.), Soc. Chem. Industry, Nat. Soc. Profl. Engrs. Clubs: Ridgefields Country (Kingsport). Home: 2141 Heatherly Rd Kingsport TN 37660 Office: PO Box 511 Kingsport TN 37664

REID, WHITELAW, bus. exec. b. Purchase, N.Y., July 26, 1913; s. Ogden and Helen Miles (Rogers) R.; ed. Lincoln Sch., New York City, 1918-27, St. Paul's Sch., Concord, New Hampshire, 1927-32; B.A., Yale U., 1932-36; m. Joan Brandon, July 1948 (div. Sept. 1959); children—Brandon, Carson; m. 2d, Elizabeth A. Brooks, Nov. 1959; children—John Graham, Gina Rogers. With various depts. of the N.Y. Herald Tribune, 1938- 40, fgn. corr., Eng., 1940, asst. to editor, 1946, editor, v.p., 1947- 52, editor, pres., 1952-55, chmn., 1955-58, dir., 1946-65; pres., dir. Reid Enterprises; chmn., dir. Drinx Plus Co., Inc., 1957-75. Vice chmn. Yale Alumni Bd., 1962-64. Pres. Fresh Air Fund, 1946-62, dir., 1946—; chmn. N.Y. State Com. Pub. Employee Security Procedures, 1956-57; mem. com. Pres.' Citizen Advisers on Mut. Security Program, 1956-57; dist. commr. Purchase Pony Club, 1964-70; dir. Freedom House, until 1978; pres. Yale Westchester Alumni Assn., 1960-62, now dir.; mem. U. council Yale, chmn. publs. com., 1965-70; fellow Pierson Coll., Yale, 1949—. Mem. U.S. Nat. Commn. UNESCO, 1955-60; ambassador to Inauguration of Pres. Ponce, Eduador, 1956. Served to lt. as naval aviator USNR. Mem. Book and Snake (Yale Univ.), Council on Fgn. Relations, Nat. Inst. of Social Sci., Pilgrims U.S., Naval Aviation Commandery, N.Y. State Horse Council. (dir., pres. 1975—) Golden's Bridge Hounds (hon. sec. 1976-79, dir.), Delta Kappa Epsilon. Independent Republican. Clubs: Amateur Ski, Century Assn. (N.Y.C.); Windham Mountain (N.Y.); St. Regis (N.Y.) Yacht; Metropolitan (Washington); Manursing Island; Overseas Press, Silurians, Pilgrims. Home: Ophir Farm Purchase NY 10577 Office: Reid Enterprises Purchase NY 10577

REID, WILLARD MALCOLM, educator, parasitologist; b. Ft. Morgan, Colo., Oct. 9, 1910; s. Willard and Caroline (Riggs) R.; B.S., Monmouth Coll., 1932, D.Sc., 1960; postgrad. Heidelberg (Germany) U., 1933; M.S., Kan. State Coll., 1937, Ph.D., 1941; postgrad. Brown U., 1937-38, U. Mich., 1939; m. Janet Helen Sharp, Sept. 4, 1937; children—Caroline (Mrs. Ted R. Ridelhuber), Donald Malcolm, Willard Sharp, Nancy Jane (Mrs. Jerry Robbins), Judith Ann. Instr., Assiut (Egypt) Coll., 1933-35; prof. biology, dept. head Monmouth Coll., 1937-51; Fulbright research prof. U. Cairo (Egypt), 1951-52; head poultry unit U.S. State Dept. AID, 1952-55; parasitologist poultry sci. dept. U. Ga., Athens, 1955—, Distinguished Alumni Found. prof., 1964-78, Disting. Alumni Found. prof. emeritus, 1978—; poultry cons. Eli Lilly Co., Mathtech; internat. cons. on poultry disease control, coccidiosis. Mem. Am. Soc. Parasitologists, Am. Soc. Zoologists, Poultry Sci. Assn., Am. Assn. Avian Pathologists, Am. Soc. Protozoologists. Author textbook on sci. writing; also numerous articles. Research on morphology, physiology and control poultry cestodes and protozoa; devel. immunity and poultry flock parasite control; growth and devel. of parasites under germfree conditions. Home: 240 Burnett St Athens GA 30601

REID, WILLIAM HILL, educator, mathematician; b. Oakland, Calif., Sept. 10, 1926; s. William Macdonald and Edna (Hill) R.; B.S., U. Calif. at Berkeley, 1949, M.S., 1951; Ph.D., U. Cambridge (Eng.), 1955, Sc.D. (hon.), 1968; A.M., Brown U., 1961; m. Elizabeth Mary Emily Kidner, May 26, 1962; 1 dau., Margaret Frances. Lectr., Johns Hopkins, 1955-56; NSF fellow Yerkes Obs., Williams Bay, Wis., 1957-58; mem. faculty Brown U., 1958-63, asso. prof. applied math., 1961-63; mem. faculty U. Chgo., 1963—, prof. applied math., 1965—; cons. research labs. Gen. Motors Corp., 1960—. Served with AUS, 1954-56. Fulbright Research scholar Australian Nat. U., 1964-65. Fellow Cambridge Philos. Soc.; mem. Am. Math. Soc., Am. Phys. Soc., Sigma Xi. Contbr. profl. jour. Home: 5619 S Dorchester Ave Chicago IL 60637

REID, WILLIAM JAMES, educator; b. Detroit, Nov. 14, 1928; s. James Macknight and Sophie Amelia (Schneider) R.; B.A., U. Mich., 1950, M.S.W., 1952; D.S.W., Columbia U., 1963; m. Audrey D. Smith, Dec. 13, 1972; children by previous marriage—Valerie, Steven. Caseworker-in-charge Family Service of Westchester, Mt. Kisco, N.Y., 1956-59; asst. prof. social work U. Chgo., 1962-65, prof., 1968-75, George Herbert Jones prof., 1975—; dir. Center for Social Casework Research, Community Service Soc., N.Y.C., 1965-68. Served with U.S. Army, 1952-56. Russell Sage fellow, 1959-60; NIMH career tchr., 1960-62. Mem. Nat. Assn. Social Workers, Council Wocial Work Edn., Phi Beta Kappa. Author: Brief and Extended Casework, 1969; Task-Centered Casework, 1972; Task-Centered Practice, 1977; The Task-Centered System, 1978; editor Social Work Research and Abstracts, 1977—. Office: 969 E 60th St Chicago IL 60637

REIDENBAUGH, LOWELL HENRY, sports editor; b. Lititz, Pa., Sept. 7, 1919; s. Harry Martin and Marian Marie (Nies) R.; A.B., Elizabethtown (Pa.) Coll., 1941; m. Ruth Elizabeth Cameron, Nov. 23, 1944; children—Karen Lee, Kathy Jean (Mrs. William J. Schuchman). Gen. reporter Lancaster (Pa.) Intelligencer Jour., 1941-42; sports writer Phila. Inquirer, 1944-47; mem. staff The Sporting News, St. Louis, 1947—, mng. editor, 1962—. Served with AUS, 1942-43. Home: 2106 St Clair St Brentwood MO 63144 Office: 1212 N Lindbergh Blvd Saint Louis MO 63166

REIDY, JOHN JOSEPH, lawyer; b. Youngstown, Ohio, Mar. 8, 1905; s. John W. and Katherine (Mullane) R.; LL.B., U. Notre Dame, 1927; m. Madelon Deacon, Nov. 11, 1931; children—John Joseph, Nancy (Mrs. James J. Richards), David L. Admitted to Ohio bar, 1928; practice in Cleve., 1928-31; head lease and legal dept. Gt. Atlantic and Pacific Tea Co., Cleve., 1931-41; partner firm Falsgraf, Reidy, Shoup, and Ault, Cleve., 1941-71, Baker, Hostetler & Patterson, Cleve., 1971—. Mem. charter commn., Bay Village, Ohio, 1946. Trustee Cath. Charities Corp., 1950—; Cleve. chmn. Notre Dame Found., 1960-65. Bd. dirs. nat. alumni bd. Notre Dame Univ. Named Notre Dame U. Cleve. Alumni Man of Year, 1955. Clubs: Cleve. Athletic; Westwood Country (Rocky River, Ohio). Home: 12900 Lake Ave Lakewood OH 44107 Office: Union Commerce Bldg Cleveland OH 44115

REIDY, WILLIAM EDWARD, food mfg. co. exec.: b. Chgo., July 31, 1931; s. Edward William and Kathryn Therese (O'Donnell) R.; B.S., U. Notre Dame, 1953; m. Barbara Mary Beck, Nov. 30, 1957; children—Kathleen Marie, William Edward, Mary Barbara, Daniel Beck. With IBM, Chgo., 1958-65, industry mktg. mgr., 1963-65; with Kraft, Inc., 1965—, exec. v.p. tech. services, Glenview, Ill., 1976-79, sr. v.p. corp. strategy and devel., Glenview, 1979—; dir. Glenview State Bank; mem. overseers' com. to visit office for info. tech. Harvard Coll. Bd. mgrs. Chgo. Boys Clubs: bd. govs. Winnetka (Ill.) Community House; bd. dirs. Chgo. Platform Tennis Charities. Served with USN, 1953-57: China. Mem. Assn. Corp. Growth, Grocery Mfrs. Am., Planning Exec. Inst., World Future Soc. Republican. Roman Catholic. Clubs: North Shore Country, Tavern. Home: 1066 Mount Pleasant Rd Winnetka IL 60093 Office: Kraft Ct Glenview IL 60025

REIF, FREDERICK, physicist, educator; b. Vienna, Austria, Apr. 24, 1927; s. Gerschon and Clara (Gottfried) R.; came to U.S., 1941, naturalized, 1946; B.A., Columbia, 1948; M.A., Harvard, 1949, Ph.D., 1953. Staff, Lincoln Lab., Mass. Inst. Tech., 1952-53; faculty U. Chgo., 1953-60, asst. prof., 1955- 60; faculty U. Calif. at Berkeley, 1960—, prof. physics, 1964—. Alfred P. Sloan Research fellow, 1955-59; Miller Research prof., 1964-65. Fellow Am. Phys. Soc.; mem. AAAS. Author: Fundamentals of Statistical and Thermal Physics, 1965. Contbr. articles to profl. jours. Address: Physics Dept Univ Cal Berkeley CA 94720

REIFFEL, LEONARD, sci. cons., physicist; b. Chgo., Sept. 30, 1927; s. Carl and Sophie (Miller) R.; B.Sc., Ill. Inst. Tech., 1947, M.Sc., 1948, Ph.D., 1953; m. Judith Eve Blumenthal, 1952 (div. 1962); children—Evan Carl, David Lee; m. 2d, Nancy L. Jeffers, 1971. Physicist, Perkin-Elmer Corp., Conn., 1948; engring. physicist U. Chgo. Inst. Nuclear Studies, 1948-49; with Ill. Inst. Tech. Research Inst., Chgo., 1949-65, dir. physics research, 1956-63, v.p., 1963-65; cons. to Apollo program NASA Hdqrs., 1965-70, cons., 1970—; tech. dir. Manned Space Flight Expts. Bd., 1966-68; chmn. bd. Instructional Dynamics, Inc., 1966—, INTERAND Corp., 1969—, TELESTRATOR Industries, Inc., 1970-73; sci. editor WBBM-CBS radio, Chgo., sci. cons./commentator WBBM-TV, 1971-72, host Backyard Safari, 1971-73; sci. feature broadcaster WEEI-CBS radio, Boston, 1965-75; syndicated newspaper columnist World Book Ency. Sci. Service, Inc. (later Universal Sci. News, Inc.), 1966-72, Los Angeles Times Syndicate, 1972-76; sci. cons. CBS Network, 1967-71. Cons. Korean Govt. on establishment atomic energy research program; mem. adv. com. isotope and radiation devel. AEC, com. research reactors Nat. Acad. Scis., 1958-64; responsible for world's 1st indsl. nuclear reactor, 1956; cons. U.S. Army, 1976—. Bd. dirs. Student Competitions on Relevant Engring. Named Outstanding Young Man of Year Chgo. Jr. C. of C., 1954, 61; recipient Merit award Chgo. Tech. Socs., 1968; Peabody award for radio edn., 1968; IR-100 award for inventing Telestrator, 1970; award for coverage space events Aviation Writers Assn., 1971; IR-100 award for invention underwater diver communications system, 1972, also for invention Audiografix, 1973; Distinguished Alumni Achievement award Ill. Inst. Tech., 1974. Fellow Am. Phys. Soc.; mem. AAAS, Sigma Xi, Tau Beta Pi, Eta Kappa Nu. Author numerous sci. papers; (novel) The Contaminant, 1979. Home: 602 W Deming Pl Chicago IL 60614 Office: 666 N Lake Shore Dr Chicago IL 60611

REIFLER, CLIFFORD BRUCE, physician; b. Chgo., Dec. 28, 1931; s. Eugene Alan and Harriet (Offer) R.; A.B., U. Chgo., 1951; B.S., Northwestern U., 1953; M.D., Yale U., 1957; M.P.H., U. N.C., 1967; m. Barbara Karnuth, Sept. 11, 1954; children—Margery Sue, Cynthia Jean, Angela Harriet. Intern, Univ. Hosps., Ann Arbor, Mich., 1957-58; resident in psychiatry Strong Meml. Hosp., Rochester, N.Y., 1958-61; mem. faculty U. N.C. Med. Sch., 1963-70, asso. prof. psychiatry, 1969-70, asso. prof. mental health Sch. Pub. Health, 1969-70, sr. psychiatrist, chief mental health sect. Student Health Service, 1963-70; prof. health services, prof. psychiatry, prof. preventive medicine and community health U. Rochester (N.Y.) Med. Sch., 1970—, dir. health and safety, 1974—, dir. univ. health service, 1970—; bd. dirs. Genesee Valley Group Health Assn., 1972—; cons. in field. Served with M.C., USAF, 1961-63. Fellow Am. Coll. Health Assn. (pres. 1976-77), Am. Psychiat. Assn., Am. Pub. Health Assn.; mem. Soc. Adolescent Medicine, Am. Occupational Medicine Assn. Co-author: Mental Health on the Campus-A Field Study, 1973; co-author: The Alternative Services: Their Role in Mental Health, 1975; Old Folks at Home-A Field Study of Nursing and Board-and-Care Homes, 1976. Contbr. profl. jours. Home: 143 Palmerston Rd Rochester NY 14618 Office: Univ Health Service 250 Crittenden Blvd Box 617 Rochester NY 14642

REIFSNYDER, CHARLES FRANK, lawyer; b. Ottumwa, Iowa, Sept. 6, 1920; s. Charles L. and Lena (Emery) R.; A.B., George Washington U., 1944, LL.B., 1946; m. Sally Ann Evans, Dec. 27, 1948; children—Daniel Alan, Jeremy Evans; m. 2d, Nancy Lee Laws, Mar. 4, 1960; 1 son, Frank Laws. Admitted to D.C. bar, 1945; sec. to Judge T. Alan Goldsborough, U.S. Dist. Ct., Washington, 1945, law clk. to Chief Judge Bolitha J. Laws, 1946-47; asst. U.S. atty., Washington, 1947-51; spl. asst. to Atty. Gen. U.S., 1950-51; asso. firm Hogan & Hartson, Washington, 1951-58, partner, 1959—. Chmn. personnel security rev. bd. ERDA (formerly AEC); trustee Legal Aid Agy. (now Pub. Defender Service), Washington, 1960-67; bd. dirs. Nat. Coll. State Judiciary, 1968-70. Fellow Inst. Jud. Adminstrn., N.Y.C., 1967-68. Fellow Internat. Soc. Barristers, Am. Bar Found.; mem. Am. (chmn. spl. com. on coordination jud. improvements 1971-74, mem. spl. com. on atomic energy law 1969-73, chmn. sect. jud. adminstrn. 1967-68, del. 1968-69), Fed., Fed. Energy (chmn. com. natural gas 1967-68, 2d v.p. 1978—), D.C. (dir. 1955-56) bar assns., Am. Arbitration Assn. (nat. panel arbitrators), Am. Judicature Soc. (dir. 1972-76), Am. Law Inst., Phi Delta Phi, Sigma Nu. Episcopalian. Clubs: Met., Univ., Nat. Lawyers, Barristers, Lawyers (Washington); Annapolis (Md.) Yacht; Gibson Island (Md.); Farmington Country (Charlottesville, Va.). Home: Gibson Island MD 21056 Office: Hogan & Hartson 815 Connecticut Ave NW Washington DC 20006

REIFSNYDER, WILLIAM EDWARD, meteorologist; b. Ridgway, Pa., Mar. 29, 1924; s. Howard William and Madolin (Boyer) R.; B.S. in Meteorology, N.Y. U., 1944; M.F., U. Calif., Berkeley, 1949; Ph.D., Yale U., 1954; m. Marylou Bishop, Dec. 19, 1954; children—Rita, Cheryl, Gawain. Meteorologist, Pacific S.W. Forest and Range Expt. Sta., 1952-55; mem. faculty Yale U., 1965—, prof. forest meteorology and biometeorology, 1967—; cons. World Meteorol. Orgn. Bd. dirs. Am. Youth Hostels. Service with USAAF, 1943-47. Cert. cons. meteorologist. Fellow AAAS; mem. Am. Meteorol. Soc., Soc. Am. Foresters, Internat. Soc. Biometeorology. Author: Hut Hopping in the Austrian Alps; Footloose in the Swiss Alps; The High Huts of the White Mountains; Weathering the Wilderness; regional editor for Americas, Agrl. Meteorology, 1977—. Address: Stantack Rd Middletown CT 06457

REIGHARD, HOMER LEROY, govt. ofcl., physician; b. Martinsburg, Pa., Dec. 1, 1924; s. David F. and Cora E. (Steele) R.; B.S., Franklin and Marshall Coll., 1945; M.D., Temple U., 1948; M.P.H., Harvard U., 1961; m. Barbara Jane Suttell, Dec. 14, 1951; children—Carol, Janet, Paul. Intern, Temple U. Hosp., Phila., 1948-49, physician-in charge accidents dispensary, 1949-50; med. officer CAA, Washington, 1953-59; practice medicine, Bethesda, Md., 1953-60; chief med. standards div. FAA, 1959-61, spl. asst. to civil air surgeon, 1962-63, dep. fed. air surgeon, 1963-75, fed. air surgeon, 1975—. Served with M.C., USAF, 1950-53. Recipient Meritorious Service award FAA, 1970. Fellow Aerospace Med. Assn.; mem. AMA, Med. Soc. D.C., Phi Beta Kappa. Developer passenger screening system to identify potential hijackers. Home: 10215 Hatherleigh Dr Bethesda MD 20014 Office: 800 Independence Ave SW Washington DC 20591

REILING, HENRY BERNARD, educator; b. Richmond, Ky., Feb. 5, 1938; s. Henry Bernard and Lucille Frances (Fowler) R.; B.A., Northwestern U., 1960; M.B.A., Harvard U., 1962; J.D., Columbia U., 1965; m. Carol-Lina Maria Schuetz, June 4, 1962; children—Christina Lucille, Maria Hays, Carolina Alexis. Admitted to N.Y. bar, 1965; mem. faculty Columbia U. Bus. Sch., 1965-76, prof., 1974-76; vis. asso. prof. Harvard U. Bus. Sch., 1972-73, prof., 1976—, Eli Goldston prof. bus. adminstrn., 1978—; vis. prof. Stanford U. Bus. Sch., 1974-75. Trustee Riverside Ch., N.Y.C., 1976-77. Mem. Am., N.Y. bar assns., Bar Assn. City N.Y., Am. Finance Assn., Financial Mgmt. Assn., Nat. Tax Assn., Tax Inst. Am., Beta Gamma Sigma. Club: Union (N.Y.C.). Contbr. bus. and law jours. Home: 28 Meriam St Lexington MA 02173 Office: Harvard Business Sch Boston MA 02163

REILLY, CHARLES NELSON, actor; b. N.Y.C., Jan. 13, 1931; s. Charles J. and Signe E. Reilly; student U. Conn. Actor appearing on Broadway and TV; mem. road co. Annie Get Your Gun, also 22 off-Broadway prodns.; Broadway prodns. include How to Succeed in Business Without Really Trying (Tony award), Bye Bye Birdie, Hello, Dolly, Skyscraper, God's Favorite; dir. The Belle of Amherst, 1977; starred TV series The Ghost and Mrs. Muir, The Golddiggers, Lidsville; motion picture credits include Two Tickets to Paris, The Tiger Makes Out; tchr. Herbert Bergoff Sch., N.Y.C., The Faculty, Los Angeles; performed in concerts at Carnegie Hall, Philharmonic Hall. Named best actor Variety Critics Poll, 1962; recipient Tony nomination for Skyscraper, Emmy nomination for Ghost and Mrs. Muir. Office: care William Morris Agency Inc 151 E Camino Beverly Hills CA 90212*

REILLY, DANIEL PATRICK, bishop; b. Providence, May 12, 1928; s. Francis E. and Mary (Burns) R.; student Our Lady of Providence Sem., 1943-48, Grand Seminarire, St. Brieuc, France, 1948-53, Sch. Bus. Adminstrn., Harvard U., 1954-55, Sch. Bus. Adminstrn., Boston Coll., 1955-56. Ordained priest Roman Catholic Ch., 1953; asst. pastor Cathedral Saints Peter and Paul, Providence, 1953-54; asst. chancellor Diocese of Providence, 1954-56, sec. to bishop, 1956-64, chancellor, 1964-72, adminstr., 1971-72, vicar gen., 1972-75; became monsignor, 1965, consecrated bishop, 1975; bishop of Norwich, Conn., 1975—; state chaplain K.C., 1976—; Episcopal moderator Nat. Cath. Cemetery Corp., 1977—. trustee St. Joseph's Hosp., 1964-75, Providence Coll., 1969-75, Our Lady of Providence Sem. Coll., Warwick, R.I., 1969-75, Cath. Mut. Relief Soc. Omaha, 1979—; bd. dirs. United Way of Southeastern Conn., 1976—, Conn. Drug and Adv. Council, 1978—, New Eng. Conf. of Cath. Hosp. Assn., 1978—. Recipient Annual award NCCJ, 1972. Club: Rotary. Home: 274 Broadway Norwich CT 06360 Office: 201 Broadway Box 587 Norwich CT 06360

REILLY, DAVID HENRY, univ. dean; b. Paterson, N.J., Nov. 7, 1936; s. David Henry and Ethel Taylor (Alt) R.; B.A., U. Vt., 1959; Ed.M., Rutgers U., 1962, Ed.D., 1965; m. Jean Lockwood, July 2, 1960; children—David Scott, Chris Robert, Sandra Jean. Remedial reading instr. Drake Sch. of N.J. Neuro-Psychiat. Inst., Princeton, 1959-62, jr. fellow psychol. services at inst., summer 1962-63; research asst., N.J. Bur. Research Neurology and Psychiatry, also sch. psychologist Woodbridge (N.J.) sch. system, 1962-63; clin. psychologist, then research asso. N.J. Bur. Research Neurology and Psychiatry, 1963-64, 65; sch. and research psychologist Woodbridge sch. system, 1964-65; post doctoral fellow clin. child psychology Devereux Found., Devon, Pa., 1965-66; mem. faculty U. N.C., Chapel Hill, 1966—, prof. psychology, 1974—, chmn. dept. sch. psychology program, 1969-74, dean Sch. Edn., 1974—. Mem. N.C. Bd. Examiners Practicing Psychologists, 1973—, treas., 1975, chmn., 1976. Research grantee NIMH, 1963. Diplomate Am. Bd. Profl. Psychology. Fellow Am. Psychol. Assn.; mem. Southeastern, N.C. (pres.-elect 1979-80) psychol. assns., N.C. Sch. Psychology Assn. (pres. 1976-77). Contbr. articles to profl. jours. Home: 909 Fairridge Dr Jamestown NC 27282 Office: Sch Edn Univ NC Greensboro NC 27412

REILLY, FRANK KELLY, educator; b. Chgo., Dec. 30, 1935; s. Clarence Raymond and Mary Josephine (Ruckrigel) R.; B.B.A., U. Notre Dame, 1957; M.B.A., Northwestern U., 1961, U. Chgo., 1964; Ph.D., 1968; m. Therese Adele Bourke, Aug. 2, 1958; children—Frank Kelly III, Clarence Raymond II, Therese B., Edgar B. Trader, Goldman Sachs & Co., Chgo., 1958-59; security analyst Tech. Fund, Chgo., 1959-62; asst. prof. U. Kans., Lawrence, 1965-68, asso. prof., 1968-72; prof. bus., asso. dir. div. bus. and econ. research U. Wyo., Laramie, 1972-75; prof. fin. U. Ill., Urbana, 1975—. Bd. dirs. Heart of Am. Growth Fund, Kansas City, Mo., 1971—. Arthur J. Schmidt Found. fellow, 1962-65, U. Chgo. fellow, 1963-65. Chartered fin. analyst. Mem. Midwest Bus. Adminstrn. Assn. (pres. 1974-75), Am., Southwestern, Western (exec. com. 1973-75), Eastern (exec. com. 1979—) fin. assns., Fin. Analysts Fedn., Fin. Mgmt. Assn. (v.p. 1977-78, 79-80), Nat. Bur. Econ. Research, Beta Gamma Sigma. Roman Catholic. Author: Investment Analysis and Portfolio Management, 1979. Editor: Readings and Issues in Investments, 1975. Asso. editor Fin. Mgmt., 1977—, Quar. Rev. Econs. and Bus., 1979—. Fin. Rev., 1979—. Home: 54 Chestnut Ct Champaign IL 61820 Office: Coll Commerce U Ill Urbana IL 61801. *Any success I have enjoyed is due to the talents God has given me and my belief that I have an obligation to maximize the output from those talents by hard work, while never forgetting that my family comes first because they have always provided me with the love and support necessary for success and happiness.*

REILLY, FRANK THOMAS, retail co. exec.; b. Newark, June 8, 1928; s. Francis Patrick and Cora Belle (Perry) R.; B.S., Lowell (Mass.) Textile U., 1951; M.S., N.Y. U., 1952; m. Elizabeth Mulligan, May 9, 1951; children—Frank P., Mary E., Patricia M., Kathleen A., Nancy J., Thomas K., Carol S. Buyer, Brooks Bros., N.Y.C., 1952-62; v.p., mdse. mgr. Saks Fifth Ave., N.Y.C., 1962-70; pres. Wallachs's Inc., N.Y.C., 1970-74, Brooks Bros., 1974—; dir. Garfinckel, Brooks Bros., Miller Rhoads Inc. Bd. dirs. Deafness Research Found.; trustee Overlook Hosp., Summit, N.J. Recipient Good Scout award N.Y. council Boy Scouts Am., 1966; Outstanding Service award Lighthouse for Blind. Clubs: N.Y. Athletic, University (N.Y.C.); Rock Spring Country (dir.). Office: 346 Madison Ave New York NY 10017*

REILLY, GEORGE LOVE ANTHONY, educator; b. Montclair, N.J., Oct. 17, 1918; s. James Joseph and Anna F. (Love) R.; A.B. cum laude, Seton Hall U., 1940; A.M., Harvard, 1942; Ph.D., Columbia, 1951; m. Ethel M. Ehrlich, Aug. 29, 1953; children—Mary Anne, Elizabeth Ruthe, Georgette Louise. Instr. Caldwell (N.J.) Coll., 1946-48, Rutgers U., New Brunswick, N.J., 1948-51; mem. faculty Seton Hall U., South Orange, N.J., 1951—, prof. history, 1960—, chmn. dept., 1961—; faculty Irish Studies seminar Columbia, 1974—. Served to 1st lt. F.A., AUS, 1942-45. Mem. Nat. Geog. Soc., Am., Am. Cath. hist. assns., Conf. on Brit. Studies, Victorian Studies Assn., N.J. Hist. Soc. Democrat. Roman Catholic. Club: Harvard (N.J.). Author: Camden and Amboy Railroad in New Jersey Politics, 1951; Sacred Heart in Bloomfield, 1953; A Century of Catholicism, 1956; Neighbors in New Jersey, 1963; History of Seton Hall University, 1980; co-author: Shepherds of Newark, 1978; also articles. Adv. editor Cath. Hist. Rev., 1957-61; editorial bd. Avocate, Newark, 1968—. Home: 273 Scotland Rd South Orange NJ 07079

REILLY, GERARD DENIS, judge; b. Boston, Sept. 27, 1906; s. Thomas F. and Anne C. (O'Reilly) R.; A.B., Harvard, 1927, LL.B., 1933; m. Eleanor Fahey, July 15, 1939; children—Gerard Denis (dec.), John Fahey, Margaret Anne Reilly Heffern. State House corr. for the Pawtucket Times, Providence Jour., 1927-29; night copy editor Boston Traveler, 1929-30; admitted to Mass. bar, 1933, D.C. bar, 1946; asso. firm Goodwin, Procter & Hoar, Boston, 1933-34; reviewing atty. Home Owner's Loan Corp., 1934; became atty. U.S. Dept. of Labor, 1934, asst. solicitor, 1935, adminstr. Pub. Contracts Div., 1936-37, solicitor, 1937-41; mem. NLRB, 1941-46; mem. firm Reilly, Johns & Zimmerman and predecessor firms, 1946-70; asso. judge D.C. Ct. Appeals, 1970-72, chief judge, 1972-76. Lectr. constl. law Cath. U., 1946-47; counsel Senate com. on labor and pub. welfare, 1947; dir. Reed & Prince Mfg. Co., Worcester, Mass., 1963-70. Fellow Am. Bar Found.; mem. Am., D.C., Boston bar assns. Roman Catholic. Clubs: Nat. Lawyers, Cosmos, Palaver, Harvard (Washington); Bass River Yacht. Office: DC Court House 500 Indiana Ave St NW Washington DC 20001

REILLY, JAMES DUNN, mining exec.; b. Edinburgh, Scotland, Sept. 30, 1908; s. Edward and Jean Inglis (Dunn) R.; brought to U.S., 1910, naturalized, 1918; ed. pub. schs., West Terre Haute, Ind.; m. Alice Hankins, Jan. 25, 1934. Worked in dairy, Terre Haute, 1923; coal mine jobs, advancing from coal loader to fire boss, Terre Haute; became sect. foreman, Walter Bledsoe mine, 1937, asst. supt., 1940; supt. Piney Fork Mine of Hanna Coal Co., 1942, gen. supt., 1945-46, gen. mgr., 1946; v.p. ops. Hanna Coal div. Pitts. Consol. Coal Co., 1947; now pres. Ohio div. Hanna Coal div. Consol. Coal Co.; past pres. Hanna Coal Co.; past chmn. bd. Pike Natural Gas Co., St. Clair Oil Co., Reilly Chevrolet-Cadillac Co. Bd. dirs. Ohio Valley Indsl. and Bus. Devel. Corp., Ohio River Valley Water Sanitation Commn., Ohio Reclamation Assn. Decorated Legion of Honor (France). Mem. Am. Inst. Mining and Metall. Engrs. (pres., dir.), Soc. Mining Engrs. (pres.). Home: Rand Ave St Clairsville OH 43950 Office: 219 E Main Pittsburgh PA 15222

REILLY, JOSEPH WILLIAM, newspaper editor; b. Chgo., May 5, 1939; s. Wilfred John and Helen Regina (McNulty) R.; student U. Ill.; m. Celeste O'Connor, Oct. 10, 1964; children—Brian, Patricia, Kirsten. Reporter, City News Bur. of Chgo., 1961-62; reporter, asst. city editor Chgo. Sun-Times, 1962-74, met. editor, 1974—; v.p., dir. City News Bur. Chgo. Served with USAF, 1957-61. Recipient Marshall Field award, 1972. Mem. Sigma Delta Chi. Roman Catholic. Club: Chgo. Press. Home: 117 N Monroe Hinsdale IL 60521 Office: 401 N Wabash Chicago IL 60611

REILLY, WILLIAM FRANCIS, chem. co. exec.; b. N.Y.C., June 8, 1938; s. William F. and Genevieve R.; A.B. cum laude, U. Notre Dame, 1959; M.B.A., Harvard U., 1964; m. Ellen Chapman, Nov. 19, 1966; children—Anthony Chapman and Jane Wasey (twins). Mgr. fin. analysis W. R. Grace & Co., N.Y.C., 1964-67, asst. to pres., 1969-71, chief exec. officer Bekaert Textile div., 1971-74, group exec., merchandise products group, 1974-75, dep. chief exec. consumer products group, 1974-75; asst. finance adminstr. City of N.Y.C., 1967-69; pres. Herman's World of Sporting Goods, Carteret, N.J., 1976-77; v.p. W. R. Grace & Co., N.Y.C., 1977—, pres. Home Center Div., 1979—. Served to 1st lt. U.S. Army, 1959-61. Home: 1192 Park Ave New York NY 10028 Office: 1114 Ave of the Americas New York NY 10036

REILY, GEORGE WOLF, III, banker; b. Harrisburg, Pa., Dec. 27, 1905; s. George Wolf, Jr. and Louise Haxall (Harrison) R.; student Yale U., 1930; m. Barbara Fleming, June 3, 1939; children—George Wolf, IV, Daniel H., Louise H. (Mrs. William C. Miles), Barbara F., John E. Sec., Harrisburg Nat. Bank & Trust Co., 1936-54, v.p., 1954-64, vice chmn., chief exec. officer, 1964-67, chmn. bd., 1967-69; chmn. bd. Commonwealth Nat. Bank, Harrisburg, 1970-77, chmn. emeritus, 1977—, also dir. Chmn. bd. trustees Eagles Mere Presbyn. Co.; mem. Harrisburg City Planning Commn., 1942-69; treas. Scranton for Pres. Com., 1964; pres., trustee Harrisburg Acad.; trustee Fisher Meml. Fund, Harrisburg Found., Harrisburg Hosp., 1946-71, Harrisburg State Hosp., 1963-69; trustee emeritus Harrisburg Cemetery Assn. Mem. Scotch-Irish Soc. Am. (past pres.), Soc. Colonial Wars (life), SAR. Home: Route 4 Harrisburg PA 17112 Office: 10 S Market Sq Harrisburg PA 17108

REILY, PHILIP KEY, investing co. exec.; b. Washington, Aug. 24, 1924; s. Philip Joseph and Esther (Maddox) R.; B.S. in Chemistry, Lehigh U., 1948; m. Janet Patricia Wiedorn, Feb. 1, 1946; children—Philip Key III, Kathleen (Mrs. Wayne P. Childres), David, Richard, Janet, Jeffery, Meredith (Mrs. Arthur Adams Nelson III), William, Sara, Reid; m. 2d, Maryjane Sherman, Sept. 12, 1968; 1 son, Jonathan. Vice pres. Atlantic Research Corp., Alexandria, Va., 1955-65; dir. tech. services Dept. Commerce, 1967-69; exec. v.p. E.W. Axe & Co., Inc., Tarrytown, N.Y., 1970-75, pres., dir., 1975—; pres., dir. Axe-Houghton Stock Fund, Inc., Tarrytown, 1975—. Chmn. sci. com. Met. Washington Bd. Trade, 1962-64; trustee Marymount Coll., Tarrytown, Bermuda Biol. Sta. for Research, St. Georges; bd. dirs. Phelps Meml. Hosp., Tarrytown. Chmn. tech. adv. bd. Ohio Bd. Regents, 1966-68. Served with AUS, 1942-45. Home: Milton Harbor House Rye NY 10580 Office: Axe Castle Tarrytown NY 10591

REIMER, C. NEIL, labor union ofcl.; b. Ukraine, July 3, 1921; s. Cornelius Johann and Marie (Dyck) R.; student U. Sask.; m. Merry Elaine Spurko, Mar. 9, 1945; children—Janice, Gregory. Engaged in pvt. bus., 1939-40; oil refinery operator Consumers Coop. Refinery, 1943-51; rep. Oil Workers Internat. Union, 1951-54, Canadian dir., later dir. Oil, Chem. and Atomic Workers Internat. Union, 1954-63, now nat. dir. Mem. Canadian Labour Congress (v.p. 1954-74, chmn. energy policy com.). Pres., Alta. New Democratic Party, 1962-63, provincial leader, 1963-68. Home: 8203 101st Ave Edmonton AB Canada Office: Suite 300 10603 100th Ave Edmonton AB Canada

REIMER, MELVIN ADOLPH, ins. co. exec.; b. Tavener, Tex., Oct. 8, 1916; s. Emil Hugo and Hattie Louise (Gerke) R.; B.S., Sam Houston U., 1938; m. Wilhelmina Ruth Brown, July 17, 1939; children—Gary Paul, Elizabeth Ann, Dorothy Lea, David Lloyd, James Henry. Coach, tchr. pub. schs., Boling, Tex., 1939-41, 45-48; salesman to vice chmn. bd. dirs. Amicable Ins. Co., Waco, Tex., 1948—. Life trustee Boling High Sch. Served with USN, 1941-45; PTO. Mem. Nat., Tex., Houston socs. life underwriters. Methodist. Clubs: Masons, Shriners, Lions (chpt. pres. 1951-52). Home: Box 29 East Bernard TX 77435 Office: Box 1849 Waco TX 76703. *We become what we think about all day long. Anything is possible if we truly believe.*

REIMERS, ARTHUR JOHN, feed mfg. co. exec.; b. St. Louis, Dec. 27, 1926; s. Arthur John and Ceridwen and (Morgan) R.: B.S. in Bus. Adminstrn., Washington U., St. Louis, 1949; grad. Dartmouth Coll. Grad. Sch. Credit and Fin. Mgmt., 1963; m. Marjorie Ritter, July 22, 1950: children—Ellen, Arthur, Nancy. With Ralston purina Co., St. Louis, 1949—, regional credit mgr., then asst. treas., 1953-75, treas., 1975—; dir. Commerce Bank St. Louis. Treas., chmn. bd. dirs. Girl Scout council Greater St. Louis; mem. investment com. St. Louis YMCA. Mem. Fin. Execs. Inst. Presbyterian. Clubs: Forest Hills Country (past pres., dir.); Mo. Athletic. Home: 563 Briar Ridge St Louis MO 63131 Office: 835 S 8th St St Louis MO 63102

REIMS, CLIFFORD WALDEMAR, music educator; b. Bklyn., May 1, 1924; s. Sven Waldemar and Jenny Helen (Nelson) R.; A.B. in Music, Bucknell U., 1949; M.Mus. in Voice, Ind. U., 1951; D.M.A. in Opera, U. So. Calif., 1971; m. Georgette Louise Howell, May 30, 1952; children—Kathryn Louise, Karen Helen, Eric Howell. Asst. prof. Auburn U., 1952-57; asst. prof., dir. opera Ohio U., 1957-60, U. So. Miss., 1961-63, Ohio State U., 1963-66; asso. prof., dir. opera theater Calif. State U. at Fullerton, 1966-71; prof., chmn. voice dept., dir. opera theatre Roosevelt U., Chgo., 1972—; gen. dir. Hattiesburg (Miss.) Civic Opera, 1961-62; artistic adviser Springfield (Ohio) Civic Opera, 1963-66; opera, recital and oratorio singer, 1947—; dir., condr. various opera and little theater groups, 1953—. Served with AUS, 1943-46. Decorated Purple Heart; named Outstanding Grad. in Opera, U. So. Calif., 1971; scholar Opera Leadership Sch., Tanglewood, Mass., 1958. Mem. Nat. Opera Assn. (dir. 1965—, pres. 1970-72), Nat. Assn. Tchrs. Singing, Oprill (charter, pres. 1980), Phi Eta Sigma, Omicron Delta Kappa, Phi Mu Alpha, Sigma Alpha Epsilon. Contbr. articles to profl. jours.; translator operas. Home: 1815 S Highland Ave Lombard IL 60148 Office: 430 S Michigan Ave Chicago IL 60605. *It has always been my intent to develop not only those students who will become performers in the musical arts, but to promote an enthusiastic understanding among those who will become the audiences of our artistic future. With the gradual shortening of our work week, the necessity of a strongly developed artistic life becomes more and more visible. If I have been able to develop both professional and competent amateur talent for operatic performances and the audiences necessary to maintain them, I will consider my job well done.*

REIN, CATHERINE AMELIA, corp. officer, lawyer; b. Lebanon, Pa., Feb. 7, 1943; d. John and Esther (Scott) Shultz; B.A. summa cum laude, Pa. State U., 1965; J.D. magna cum laude, N.Y. U., 1968; m. Barry B. Rein, May 1, 1965. Admitted to N.Y. bar, 1968, U.S. Supreme Ct. bar, 1971; asso. firm Dewey, Ballantine, Bushby, Palmer & Wood, N.Y.C., 1968-74; with Continental Group, N.Y.C., 1974—, sec., sr. atty., 1976-77, sec., asst. gen. counsel, 1978—, v.p., gen. counsel Continental diversified ops., Stamford, Conn., 1978—. Mem. Am. Bar Assn., Assn. Bar City N.Y., Am. Soc. Corp. Secs. Episcopalian. Home: 2684 Crest Ln Scotch Plains NJ 07076 Office: 633 3d Ave New York NY 10017

REIN, MARTIN, educator, social worker; b. N.Y.C., Apr. 17, 1928; s. Max and Esther (Strenger) R.; B.A., Bklyn. Coll., 1950; M.S., Columbia, 1954; Ph.D., Brandeis U., 1961; m. Mildred Steinberg, Dec. 5, 1947; children—Glen, Lisa. Program dir. Brownsville Boys Club, 1950-52; supr. Teen Age Gang Project, James Weldon Johnson Community Center, N.Y.C., 1954-56; br. dir. East Tremont YM-YWHA, 1956-59; lectr. sociology Clark U., 1960-62; prof. social work and social research Bryn Mawr Coll., 1962-70; prof. urban studies and planning Mass. Inst. Tech., 1970—; cons. President's Com. on Juvenile Delinquency, 1962-64, President's Manpower Report, 1967, President's Commn. on Income Maintenance, 1968; research asso. Center for Environmental Studies, London, 1969-70, summer 1971. Mem. rev. com. on met. mental health programs NIMH, 1968—; mem. Social Services Task Force, HEW, 1966, 68. NIMH research fellow, 1959-61; sr. research Fulbright fellow London Sch. Econs., 1966-67; Ford Found. research grantee, 1969-70. Mem. Nat. Assn. Social Workers, Nat. Conf. Social Welfare, Am. Sociol. Soc. Author: An Organizational Analysis of Planned Parenthood and its Local Affiliates, 1961; The Network of Agencies Providing Child Protective Services in Massachusetts, 1964; (with R. Morris and R. Binstock) Feasible Planning for Social Change, 1966; (with Peter Marris) Dilemmas of Social Reform, 1967, rev. edit., 1972; Social Policy: Issues of Choice and Change, 1970; (with Sar Levitan) Work and Welfare Go Together, 1972; Social Science and Public Policy, 1976. Home: 40 Crafts Rd Chestnut Hill MA 02167 Office: Dept Urban Studies and Planning Mass Inst Tech Cambridge MA 02139

REINA, RUBEN E., anthropologist, educator; b. Huinca Renanco, Còrdoba Province, Argentina, Dec. 5, 1924; s. Domingo and Margarita (Videla) R.; B.A., Nat. Coll., Argentina, 1945; postgrad. U. Córdoba, 1947; B.A., U. Mich., 1950; M.A., Mich. State U., 1951; Ph.D., U. N.C., 1957; M.A. (hon.), U. Pa., 1971; m. Betty Burton, Sept. 1, 1951; children—Mark Owen, Randall Lester, Roger Andrew. Instr., U. N.C., 1954-56; asst. prof. U. P.R., 1956; asst. prof. anthropology U. Pa., Phila., 1957-62, asso. prof., 1962-67, prof., 1967—, chmn. undergrad. program in anthropology, 1959-64, chmn. grad. program, 1971-73, chmn. dept., 1971-76; field work in Guatemala, P.R., Argentina, Spain; expdn. to Iran; cons. Latin Am. program Ford Found., Argentina, 1965-67. Recipient DiTella Found. award, 1958; NSF grantee, 1960-62; Ford Found. fellow, 1965; Am. Philos. Soc. and U. Mus., U. Pa. grantee, 1968-73. Mem. Am. Anthrop. Assn., Phila. Anthrop. Soc., AAAS, Assn. Applied Anthropology. Author: Relationship of Community Culture and National Change, 1960; (with T. Cochran) Entrepreneurship in Argentine Culture, 1962; Espiritu de Empresa en Argentina, 1965; The Law of the Saints, 1966; Parana: The Social Boundaries of an Argentine City, 1973; (with Robert M. Hill II) Traditional Guatemala Pottery, 1978; also articles. Office: Anthropology Dept Univ Museum U Pa Philadelphia PA 19104

REINDEL, JOHN DONALD, auto parts co. exec.; b. Detroit, Sept. 24, 1910; s. George J. and Emily (Zopf) R.; A.B., U. Mich., 1932; postgrad. Detroit Coll. Law, 1933-34; m. Erma Paglia Pasque, Aug. 1972; 1 dau. by previous marriage, Marcia E. Reindel Fenton. Sales engr. Sheller Mfg. Co., 1935-57, v.p. sales, 1957-62, v.p. sales, dir., 1962-67; sr. v.p. Sheller-Globe Corp., Detroit, 1967-69, exec. v.p., dir., Toledo, 1969-77, vice-chmn., dir., 1977—; dir. Kralinator Filters, Ltd.-Can. Mem. Detroit Bd. Commerce. Chmn. spl. projects com. United Found., 1967; coordinator Armed Forces Activities, 1967. Served to lt. col. USAAF, 1942-46. Decorated Bronze Star medal. Mem. Econ. Club Detroit, Chi Psi. Presbyterian. Clubs: Detroit, Country of Detroit, Detroit Athletic, Detroit Golf, Recess, Tennis House, Renaissance (Detroit). Home: 910 Whittier Rd Grosse Pointe MI 48236 Office: 1641 Porter St Detroit MI 48230

REINDOLLAR, ROBERT MASON, JR., civil engr.; b. Easton, Md., June 6, 1918; s. Robert Mason and Elizabeth (Swank) R.; C.E., Cornell U., 1946; m. Valaska L. Yazel, Nov. 7, 1942; children—Elizabeth Ann, Nancy L., Valerie L. Engr., Whitman Requardt & Assos., Balt., 1938-41; airport planning engr. Trans World Airlines, N.Y.C., 1946-47; field engr. Portland Cement Assn. Pa., Phila., 1947-51, dist. engr., Pa., Md., Del., 1951-56; asso. Rummel, Klepper & Kahl, Balt., 1957-59, partner, 1959-78; cons. engr., Easton, Md., 1978—. Bd. dirs. Automobile Club Md. Served to capt. USAAF, 1941-46; ETO. Decorated Air medal with 3 oak leaf clusters, D.F.C.; registered profl. engr., Pa., Md., D.C. Fellow Am. Cons. Engrs. Council; mem. Cons. Engrs. Council Md. (pres. 1964-65, dir. 1966-69), Md. Assn. Engrs. (pres. 1962—), Soc. Am. Mil. Engrs. (pres. Balt. chpt. 1963—), ASCE, Nat. Soc. Profl. Engrs., Engrs. Club Balt., Pa. Assn. Cons. Engrs. (pres. 1967-68), Phi Kappa Phi, Tau Beta Pi, Chi Epsilon, Delta Tau Delta. Home: Rt 1 Box 208 Miles River Rd Easton MD 21601

REINE, FRANCIS JOSEPH, clergyman; b. Evansville, Ind., Sept. 22, 1914; s. Frank Henry and Emma (von Handorf) R.; B.A., St. Meinrad (Ind.) Sem., 1936; S.T.B., Gregorian U., Rome, Italy, 1938; S.T.L., Cath. U. Am., 1940, S.T.D., 1942. Ordained priest Roman Catholic Ch., 1940, named papal chamberlain, 1958, named domestic prelate, 1964; asst. pastor in Indpls., 1942-45; inst. liturgy Cath. U. Am., summer 1945; instr. theology and psychology Marian Coll., Indpls., 1945-51; instr. religion, counselor Our Lady of Providence High Sch., Clarksville, Ind., 1951-54; pres. Marian Coll., 1954-68; pastor Assumption Ch., Indpls., 1968-73, St. Christopher Ch., Speedway, 1973—. Clergy examiner, censor of book Archdiocese of Indpls., 1947—. Mem. Nat. Cath. Theol. Soc. K.C. Home: 5301 W 16th St Speedway IN 46224

REINECKE, JEAN OTIS, indsl. designer; b. Ft. Scott, Kans., July 9, 1909; s. Henry Hamon and Mary Estella (Knight) R.; student Kans. State Tchrs. Coll.; 1 dau., Barbara J. Art dir. Gen. Displays, Inc., 1927-33, partner, 1933-35; exec. v.p., treas. Barnes & Reinecke, Inc., 1935-47; pres. Reinecke & Assos., 1947—. Guest lectr. Northwestern U., Ill. Inst. Tech., Calif. Inst. Tech., Chgo. Art Inst., U. Calif. at Los Angeles, Mass. Inst. Tech., others. Recipient design awards Am. Designers Inst., Modern Plastics, Art Dirs. Club; Koppers award, 1956, others. Fellow Am. Soc. Indsl. Designers (chmn. bd., pres.). Clubs: Fin 'n' Feather, Riverside. Author articles tech. publs. Office: 3790 Berwick Dr Flintridge CA 91011

REINER, CARL, actor, writer; b. Bronx, N.Y., Mar. 20, 1922; s. Irving and Bessie (Mathias) R.; student Sch. Fgn. Service, Georgetown U., 1943; m. Estelle Lebost, Dec. 24, 1943; children—Robert, Sylvia A., Lucas. Appeared on Broadway and with road co. Call Me Mister, 1947-48, on Broadway in Inside U.S.A., 1948-49, Alive and Kicking, 1950; TV actor, 1950—, appeared Your Show of Shows, 1950-54, Caesar's Hour, 1954-58; master ceremonies Keep Talking, 1958-59; writer-actor Dinah Shore Show, 1960; producer, writer The Dick Van Dyke Show, The New Dick Van Dyke Show; dir. films Oh, God!, 1977, The One and Only, 1978, The Jerk, 1979; appeared in movie The End, 1978. Served with AUS, 1942-46. Recipient Emmy award, 1957, 58, 62, 63. Author short stories, novels Enter Laughing, Something Different, Broadway; screenplay The Thrill of It All; films The Gazebo Recs., Where's Poppa?, The Comic, Enter Laughing; (with Mel Brooks) The 2000 Year Old Man, The 2001 Year Old Man, The 2013 Year Old Man; exec. producer Heaven Help Us, 1976. Office: care Paramount Pictures Corp 5451 Marathon St Hollywood CA 90038*

REINER, IRVING, mathematician, educator; b. Bklyn., Feb. 8, 1924; s. Max and Mollie (Bolotin) R.; B.A., Bklyn. Coll., 1944; M.A., Cornell U., 1945, Ph.D., 1947; m. Irma Ruth Moses, Aug. 22, 1948; children—David, Peter. Mem. Inst. for Advanced Study, Princeton, N.J., 1947-48, 54-56; mem. faculty U. Ill. at Urbana, 1948-54, 56—, prof. math., 1958—; sabbatical leave U. London, fall 1966, spring 1973, U. Paris, U. London, U. Warwick, spring 1977. Guggenheim fellow U. Paris (France), 1962-63. Recipient Distinguished Alumnus award Bklyn. Coll., 1963; NATO sr. fellow in sci., 1977. Mem. Am. Math. Soc. (editor procs. 1966-70), Math. Assn. Am., Sigma Xi, Pi Mu Epsilon (nat. councillor 1967-72). Author: (with C.W. Curtis) Representation Theory of Finite Groups and Associative Algebras, 1962; Introduction to Matrix Theory and Linear Algebra, 1971; Maximal Orders, 1975. Editor procs. Symposium Representation Theory of Finite Groups, 1970; editor: Ill. Jour. Math., 1978—. Contbr. articles to profl. jours. Home: 101 E Michigan Ave Urbana IL 61801

REINER, LEOPOLD, pathologist; b. Leipzig, Germany, Jan. 22, 1911; came to U.S., 1939, naturalized, 1945; s. Joel and Golda Rivka (Michlewitsch) R.; student U. Freiburg, 1930, U. Leipzig, 1930-33; M.D., U. Vienna, 1936; m. Lillian Irene Myers, Sept. 22, 1946. Intern, N.J. Hosp., Camden, 1939-40, resident, 1940-46; resident in pathology Beth Israel Hosp., Boston, 1946-48, asst. pathologist, 1948-52, asso. pathologist, 1952-55, acting pathologist, 1955-56; dir. dept. pathology Bronx-Lebanon Hosp. Center, N.Y.C., 1956—; instr., asso. pathology Harvard Med. Sch., 1950-56; vis. asso. prof. pathology, 1956-72; prof. pathology Albert Einstein Coll. Medicine, 1972-79, prof. emeritus, 1979—; vis. scientist Tel Hashomer Hosp., Israel, 1965. Diplomate Am. Bd. Pathology. Fellow N.Y. Acad. Medicine; mem. Am. Assn. Pathologists, Internat. Acad. Pathology, Histochem. Soc., Harvey Soc., AMA, Soc. Clin. Pathologists, N.Y. Pathology Soc., N.Y. Pathologists Club. Contbr. articles on cardiovascular pathology to profl. jours. Home: 277 Old Colony Rd Hartsdale NY 10530 Office: 1276 Fulton Ave Bronx NY 10456

REINER, ROB, actor, writer; b. N.Y.C., Mar. 6; s. Carl and Estelle (Lebost) R.; student U. Calif. at Los Angeles; m. Penny Marshall, 1971. Scriptwriter, The Summer Brothers Smothers Show, Headmaster, All in the Family, Robert Young and the Family Special, The Super, Three for the Girls; film appearances: Enter Laughing, 1967, Halls of Anger, 1970, Where's Poppa?, 1970, Summertree, 1971, Fire Sale, 1977, How Come Nobody's on Our Side, 1977; with Phil Mishkin created and wrote summer TV series The Super, 1972; regular on TV series All in the Family, 1971-78, Free Country, 1978, other TV appearances include: That Girl, Good Heavens, The Odd Couple, The Rockford Files, The Partridge Family, The Beverly Hillbillies. Winner Emmy award, 1974. Mem. AFTRA. Office: care Creative Artists Agy Inc 1888 Century Park E Suite 1400 Los Angeles CA 90067*

REINERT, CARL M., univ. ofcl.; b. Boulder, Colo., July 4, 1913; s. Francis John and Emma Caroline (Voegtle) R.; A.B., St. Louis U., 1935, A.M., 1938, Ph.L., 1938; S.T.L., St Mary's (Kans.) Coll., 1945; student Marquette U., summer 1948. Entered Soc. of Jesus, 1931; consecrated priest Roman Catholic Ch., 1944; tchr. Creighton Prep. Sch., Omaha, 1938-41; asst. prin. Campion High Sch., Prairie du Chien, Wis., 1946-50, prin., 1950; pres. Creighton U., 1950-62, pres. Devel. Found., 1962—. Home: 2500 California St Omaha NE 68178

REINERT, PAUL CLARE, educator; b. Boulder, Colo., Aug. 12, 1910; s. Francis John and Emma (Voegtle) R.; A.B., St. Louis U., 1933, A.M., 1934; Ph.D., U. Chgo., 1944; LL.D., St. Ambrose Coll., 1951, Xavier U., 1954, Washington U., 1955, Colo. Coll., 1956, Loyola U., 1957, U. Mo., 1957, John Carroll U., 1961, U. Notre Dame, 1964, St. Josephs Coll., 1964; Ped.D., Bradley U., 1956; L.H.D., Manhattan Coll., 1963; Litt.D., McKendree Coll., 1966, St. Norbert Coll., 1975; LL.D., St. Anselm's Coll., 1967, Coll. Mt. St. Joseph of Ohio, 1970, Loyola U., New Orleans, 1973, So. Ill. U., 1973, Creighton U., 1976; L.H.D., Lindenwood Colls., 1972, DePaul U., 1973, Carroll Coll., 1974, St. Francis Coll., 1974, Canisius Coll., 1975, Brandeis U., 1975, Wittenberg U., 1976, Ursuline Coll., 1976, U. Portland, 1977, Tarkio Coll., 1977, P.C.S., Regis Coll., 1977;

Ed.Adm.D., Drury Coll., 1973. Entered Soc. of Jesus, 1927, ordained priest, 1940; instr. classical langs. and English, Creighton U. High Sch., Omaha, Neb., 1934-37; instr. edn. and registrar St. Mary's Coll., St. Marys, Kan., 1938-41; prof. edn. St. Louis U., 1950—, dean Coll. Arts and Scis., 1944-48, dir. summer sessions, 1945-48, v.p., 1948, pres., 1949-74, chancellor, 1974—; chmn. St. Louis Edn. TV Commn., 1955-57. Mem. President's Com. Edn. Beyond High Sch., 1956-57; co-chmn. Mayor's Commn. Equal Employment Opportunities, 1963-65; mem. Pres. Nixon's Task Force on Edn., 1968-69; bd. dirs. St. Louis Civic Alliance for Housing, 1969-71. Bd. dirs. Assn. Am. Colls., 1970—, chmn., 1972; trustee Ednl. Testing Service, 1969—; bd. dirs. Midwest Research Inst., 1962—; pres. Midtown, Inc., 1972—; mem. Mo. Commn. for Humanities, 1975—. Mem. N. Central Assn. Colls. and Secondary Schs. (pres. 1956-57), Nat. Cath. Ednl. Assn. (pres. coll. and univ. dept. 1956-58, v.p. 1964-65, pres. 1968-70, exec. bd. 1956-65), Am. Council Edn. (dir. 1965-68), Assn. Urban Univs. (pres. 1950-51), Nat. Council Ind. Colls. and Univs. (pres. 1973), Cath. Commn. on Intellectual and Cultural Affairs, NEA, Assn. for Higher Edn., Ind. Colls. and Univs. Mo. (pres. 1974), Jesuit Edn. Assn. (pres. 1966-70), Phi Beta Kappa, Phi Delta Kappa. Author: The Urban Catholic University, 1970; To Turn the Tide, 1972. Address: St Louis U 221 N Grand Blvd St Louis MO 63103

REINERT, RAYMOND EDWARD, hosp. adminstr.; b. Columbus, Ohio, Dec. 9, 1920; M.D., Ohio State U., 1945. Intern, St. Francis Hosp., Columbus, 1945-46; resident VA Hosp., Cleve., 1948-50; resident VA Hosp., Topeka, 1950-51, psychiatrist, 1951-61, chief of staff, 1961-69; dir. VA Hosp., St. Cloud, Minn., 1969—. Served to capt. M.C., AUS, 1946-48. Mem. Am. Psychiat. Assn. Office: VA Hosp St Cloud MN 56301

REINERTSEN, NORMAN, transit bus mfg. co. exec.; b. Bklyn., Mar. 27, 1934; s. Berthin and Malene Katherine (Dahl) R.; B.E.E., CCNY, 1960; m. Elizabeth E. O'Shea, Aug. 30, 1958; children—Michael, Christopher, Katherine. Various positions Grumman Aerospace Corp., 1960-75, gen. mgr. Great River ops., 1975-77, v.p. automotive Grumman Allied, Delaware, Ohio, 1977—, sr. v.p. Olson Bodies, Inc., 1977-79, exec. v.p. Grumman Flexible, Delaware, 1979—. Served with AUS, 1955-57. Registered profl. engr., Calif. Mem. Air Force Assn. Club: Northport Yacht. Home: 185 Rustic Pl Columbus OH 43214 Office: Grumman Flexible Corp 970 Pittsburgh Dr Delaware OH 43015

REINES, FREDERICK, physicist, educator; b. Paterson, N.J., Mar. 16, 1918; s. Israel and Gussie (Cohen) R.; M.E., Stevens Inst. Tech., 1939, M.S., 1941; Ph.D., N.Y. U., 1944; D.Sc. (hon.), U. Witwatersrand, 1966; m. Sylvia Samuels, Aug. 30, 1940; children—Robert G., Alisa K. Mem. staff Los Alamos Sci. Lab., 1944-59, group leader Theoretical div., 1945-59; dir. AEC expts. on Eniwetok Atoll, 1951; prof. physics, head dept. Case Inst. Tech., 1959-66; prof. physics U. Calif. at Irvine, 1966—, also dean phys. scis., 1966-74. Mem. Cleve. Symphony Chorus, 1959-62. Guggenheim fellow, 1958-59; Sloan fellow, 1959-63. Fellow Am. Phys. Soc., AAAS; mem. Am. Assn. Physics Tchrs., Argonne U. Assn. (trustee 1965-66), Am. Acad. Arts and Scis., Phi Beta Kappa, Sigma Xi (Stevens honor award 1972), Tau Beta Pi. Contbr. numerous articles to profl. jours. Contbg. author Effects of Atomic Weapons, 1950; Methods of Experimental Physics, 1961. Co-discoverer elementary nuclear particle, free antineutrino, 1956. Home: 2655 Basswood St Newport Beach CA 92660 Office: U Calif at Irvine Irvine CA 92717

REINGOLD, HAIM, educator; b. Lodz, Poland, Mar. 16, 1910; s. Shmaryahu and Esther (Rudnianski) R.; student N.Y. U., 1931; A.B., U. Cin., 1933, M.A., 1934, Ph.D. in Math., 1938; m. Leah Jacobson, Apr. 16, 1942 (dec. Mar. 1964); children—Edward M., Arthur L.; m. 2d, Badonna Levinson, Nov. 16, 1966; 1 son, David A. Came to U.S. 1930, naturalized, 1942. Teaching asst. U. Cin., 1936-38; head dept. math. Our Lady of Cin. Coll., 1938-42; supr. math. Ill. Inst. Tech., 1942-43, asst. prof., 1943-47, asso. prof., 1947-56, prof., 1956—, chmn. dept. math., 1951—; adj. prof. math. Ind. U. Northwest, 1975—. Mem. Am. Math. Soc., Math. Assn. Am., Am. Soc. Engring. Edn. (chmn. math. div. 1955-56, mem. council 1957-59), AAAS, Soc. Engring. Sci., Sigma Xi (chpt. pres. 1966-67). Jewish. Author: (with Andres, Miser) Basic Mathematics for Engineers, 1944; Basic Mathematics for Science and Engineering. 1955. Home: 1329 E 55th St Chicago IL 60615

REINHARD, ERWIN ARTHUR, educator; b. Poth, Tex., Jan. 29, 1931; s. Erwin John and Agnes Pauline (Miculka) R.; student St. Marys U., 1952-53; B.S., U. Tex., Austin, 1956, M.S. (Tex. Found. fellow), 1959, Ph.D. (NSF fellow, W. Alton Jones fellow), 1968; postgrad. U. Pitts., 1959-62; m. Irene Cecilia Salzman, Aug. 11, 1951; children—Nicolette Reinhard Cunningham, Lisa, Francis, Erwin, Tracie, Katherine. Nuclear research scientist Westinghouse Electric Corp., Bettis Atomic Power Lab., West Mifflin, Pa., 1959-63; prof. elec. engring. U. Ala., University, 1963—; cons. Army Missile Command, Huntsville, Ala., NASA, Huntsville. Pres. elementary PTA, 1963-66; active Warrior council Boy Scouts Am., 1968-70. Served with U.S. Army, 1950-52. Named Outstanding Elec. Engring. Instr., 1971, 75; recipient Outstanding Commitment to Teaching award U. Ala. Nat. Alumni Assn., 1978. Mem. Am. Soc. Engring. Edn., Nat. Soc. Profl. Engrs., IEEE, Sigma Xi, Eta Kappa Nu, Tau Beta Pi. Democrat. Roman Catholic. Author: Basic Electric Circuits for Engineers, 1967; Basic Electronics for Engineers and Scientists, 1972; contbr. articles to profl. jours. Home: 276 Woodland Hills Tuscaloosa AL 35405 Office: PO Box 6169 University AL 35486

REINHARD, HAROLD JOSEPH, hosp. adminstr.; b. Macon, Ga., May 1, 1924; s. Milton Edward and Julia Elizabeth (Noonan) R.; student Coll. William and Mary, 1947-49; M.D., Thomas Jefferson Med. Sch., 1953; postgrad. U. Pa., fall 1954, Coll. Phys. and Surg. Columbia, fall 1959; m. Eileen Patricia Murray, June 17, 1950; children—Shiela, Ellen, Kerry, Jerome, Michael, Mark. Intern St. Vincent Hosp., Bridgeport, Conn., 1953-54; resident Warren (Pa.) State Hosp., 1954-57, mem. staff, 1957-60, clin. dir., 1960-69, supt., 1969—. Cons. Warren Gen. Hosp. Family Service, 1965. Pres. Am. Cancer Soc. Warren County, 1965. Served with USMCR, 1943. Diplomate Am. Psychiat. Soc. Fellow Am. Psychiat. Soc.; mem. Pa. Psychiat. Soc. (sec.-treas. 1970—), Warren County Med. Soc. (pres. 1969), Pa. Med. Soc., AMA, Northwestern Pa. Psychiat. Soc., Am. K.C. Clubs: Conewango Valley Country, Conewango. Home and Office: Box 240 Warren PA 16365

REINHARD, JOHN FREDERICK, educator, scientist; b. N.Y.C., Aug. 26, 1908; s. Frederick Augustus and Viva (Duncan) R.; B.S., N.Y.U., 1933, M.S., 1934, Ph.D., 1941; m. Ingeborg Schneid, Aug. 31, 1950; children—John F., Peter Alan, Edwin Russell. Research asst. immunology N.Y.U., N.Y.C., 1933-35, instr. bacteriology, 1935-38, pharmacology, 1938-42; pharmacologist Wellcome Research Labs, Burroughs Wellcome & Co., Tuckahoe, N.Y., 1942-47; dir. pharmacol. research Nepera Chem. Co. (later Warner-Lambert Research Inst.), Yonkers, N.Y., 1947-52, Warner Inst. Therapeutic Research (later Warner-Lambert Research Inst.), Morris Plains, N.J., 1952-54; dir. dept. pharmacology Mead Johnson Research Labs., Evansville, Ind., 1954-55; dir. biol. research Baxter Labs, Inc., Morton Grove, Ill., 1955-56; head dept. pharmacology Wallace & Tiernan, Inc., Belleville, N.J., 1956-62, Strasenburgh Labs. div., Rochester, N.Y., 1962-63; prof., chmn. dept. pharmacology Coll. Pharmacy, Northeastern U., Boston, 1963-75; prof. pharmacology Mass. Coll. Pharmacy, Boston, 1975-79, emeritus prof., 1979—; cons. Kendall Co., Boston, 1967—. Fellow AAAS, N.Y. Acad. Medicine (asso. fellow); mem. Am. Soc. Pharmacology and Exptl. Therapeutics, Soc. Exptl. Biology and Medicine, N.Y. Acad. Scis., Sigma Xi (pres.), Rho Chi, Delta Chi. Republican. Conglist. Contbr. profl. jours. Home: 41 Bay View Rd Wellesley MA 02181 Office: 179 Longwood Ave Boston MA 02115

REINHARD, KEITH LEON, advt. agy. exec.; b. Berne, Ind., Jan. 20, 1935; s. Herman L. and Agnes V. R.; student public schs., Berne; m. Rose-Lee Simons, Nov. 7, 1976; children by previous marriage—Christopher, Timothy, Matthew, Geoffrey, Jacqueline. Comml. artist Kling Studios, Chgo., 1954-56; mgr. tech. communications dept. Magnavox Co., Ft. Wayne, Ind., 1957-60; creative/account exec. Biddle Co., Bloomington, Ill., 1961-63; exec. v.p., dir. creative services Needham, Harper & Steers, Inc., Chgo., 1964—, also dir. Episcopalian. Office: 401 N Michigan Ave Chicago IL 60611

REINHARDT, JOHN EDWARD, govt. ofcl.; b. Glade Spring, Va., Mar. 8, 1920; s. Edward Vinton and Alice (Miller) R.; A.B., Knoxville Coll., 1939; M.S., U. Wis., 1947, Ph.D., 1950; m. Carolyn Lillian Daves, Sept. 2, 1947; children—Sharman W. (Mrs. Neil Lancefield), Alice N. (Mrs. Robert Jeffers), Carolyn C. Prof. English, Va. State Coll., Petersburg, 1950-56; cultural affairs officer USIS, Manila, 1956-58; dir. Am. Cultural Center, Kyoto, Japan, 1958-63; cultural attache USIS, Tehran, Iran, 1963-66; dep. asst. dir. Office East Asia and Pacific, USIA, Washington, 1966-68, 70-71, asst. dir. Office Asst. Dir. for Africa, 1968-70; ambassador to Nigeria, 1971-75, asst. sec. state for pub. affairs, 1975-77; dir. USIA, Washington, 1977-78, U.S. Internat. Communication Agy., Washington, 1978—. Served as officer AUS, 1942-46. Mem. Am. Fgn. Service Assn. (v.p. 1969—), Modern Lang. Assn. Methodist. Clubs: Cosmos, Internat. (Washington). Home: 6801 Laverock Ct Bethesda MD 20034 Office: USICA 1750 Pennsylvania Ave NW Washington DC 20547

REINHARDT, SIEGFRIED GERHARD, artist; b. Germany, July 31, 1925; s. Otto Fredrick and Minni (Kukat) R.; came to U.S., 1928, naturalized, 1936; A.B. in English Lit., Washington U., St. Louis, 1950; L.H.D. (hon.), London Inst., 1970, Occidental U., 1974, Concordia Sem. in Exile, 1977; m. Hariet Fleming Reinhardt, Apr. 25, 1948. Designed, executed stained glass windows with Emil Frei, Inc., Kirkwood, Mo., 1949—; artist in resident So. Ill. U., Carbondale, 1950-54, 68-69; tchr. painting Washington U., 1955-70; artist in residence St. Louis Community Coll. at Meramec, 1971—; exhibited in one man shows at Midtown Galleries, N.Y.C.; represented in permanent collections at Whitney Mus., N.Y.C., St. Louis City Art Mus., Mo. Hist. Soc., Smithsonian Instn., Vatican Mus.; executed murals at Concordia Sr. Coll., Ft. Wayne, Ind., Jefferson Nat. Expansion Meml. Mus., New City Bank, St. Louis, Internat. Lithographers and Photo-engravers Union Bldg., St. Louis, City Hall, Nevada, Mo., U. Mo., Rolla, Fabick Tractor Co., Fenton, Mo., Meramec Community Coll., St. Louis, City of Kirkwood; important works include The Man of Sorrows, 1955, Crucifixion, 1961; commd. to create 11 lithographs for Ency. Brit.'s Propaedia, 1973. Served with AUS, 1944-46. Recipient Washington U. Alumni citation, 1969; named One of Nineteen Outstanding Young Artists, Life mag., 1950. Mem. Assn. Profl. Artists, St. Louis Artists Guild, Mo., St. Louis chambers commerce. Lutheran. Home: 635 Craig Woods Kirkwood MO 63122

REINHARDT, STEPHEN ROY, lawyer; b. N.Y.C., Mar. 27, 1931; s. Gottfried and Silvia (Hanlon) R.; B.A. cum laude, Pomona Coll., 1951; LL.B., Yale, 1954; m. Mary T. Wainwright, Nov. 24, 1956; children—Mark, Justin, Dana. Admitted to Calif. bar, 1958; law clk. to U.S. Dist. Judge Luther W. Youngdahl, Washington, 1956-57; atty. O'Melveny & Myers, Los Angeles, 1957-59; partner Fogel Julber Reinhardt Rothschild & Feldman, L.C., Los Angeles, 1959—. Mem. exec. com. Democratic Nat. Com., 1969-72, nat. Dem. committeeman for Calif., 1976—; pres. Los Angeles Recreation and Parks Commn., 1974-75; mem. Coliseum Commn., 1974-75; pres. Los Angeles Police Commn., 1978—. Served to 1st lt. USAF, 1954-56. Mem. Am. Bar Assn. (labor law council 1975-77). Home: 9544 Lime Orchard Rd Beverly Hills CA 90210 Office: 5900 Wilshire Blvd Los Angeles CA 90036

REINHARDT, WILLIAM OSCAR, med. sch. adminstr.; b. Colo., Apr. 18, 1912; s. Herman O. and Mildred (Davis) R.; A.B., U. Calif. at Berkeley, 1932, M.D., 1938; m. Elizabeth E. Parker, Mar. 16, 1940; children—William P., Susan Shelley. Staff dept. anatomy U. Calif. Sch. Medicine, San Francisco, 1939—, prof. anatomy, 1952—, chmn. dept., 1956-63, dean Sch. Medicine, 1963-66, asso. dean, 1969—, acting dean, 1977-78. Spl. research fellow Nat. Heart Inst., 1954-55; vis. prof. U. Bristol (Eng.), 1954-55, U. Indonesia, Djakarta, 1955-56, Kyoto (Japan) U., 1961, Nat. Def. Med. Center, Taipei, Taiwan, 1966-67. Mem. Am. Assn. Anatomists, Soc. Exptl. Biology and Medicine, AAAS, AAUP, Am. Physiol. Soc., Sigma Xi, Alpha Omega Alpha. Office: University of California School of Medicine San Francisco CA 94143

REINHARDT, WILLIAM PARKER, chem. physicist; b. San Francisco, May 22, 1942; s. William Oscar and Elizabeth Ellen (Parker) R.; B.S. in Basic Chemistry, U. Calif., Berkeley, 1964; A.M. in Chemistry, Harvard U., 1966, Ph.D. in Chem. Physics, 1968; m. Katrina Hawley Currens, Mar. 14, 1979. Instr. chemistry Harvard U., 1967-69, asst. prof. chemistry, 1969-72, asso. prof., 1972-74; prof. U. Colo., Boulder, 1974—, chmn. dept. chemistry, 1977—; vis. fellow Joint Inst. for Lab. Astrophysics of Nat. Bur. of Standards and U. Colo., 1972, 74, fellow, 1974—. Recipient Camille and Henry Dreyfus Tchr. Scholar award, 1972; Fresenius award Phi Lamba Upsilon, 1977; Alfred P. Sloan fellow, 1972; J.S. Guggenheim Meml. fellow, 1978; Council on Research and Creative Work faculty fellow, 1978. Mem. Am. Chem. Soc., Am. Phys. Soc., AAAS, AAUP, Phi Beta Kappa, Sigma Xi (nat. lectr. 1980-81). Research, numerous publs. in theoretical chem. physics, theoretical atomic and molecular physics; asso. editor Phys. Rev. A, 1979—. Home: 1596 Wildwood Ln Boulder CO 80303 Office: JILA-440 U Colo Boulder CO 80309

REINHART, BRUCE LLOYD, educator, mathematician; b. Wernersville, Pa., Oct. 20, 1930; s. Russell Lloyd and Ruth (Snyder) R.; B.A., Lehigh U., 1952; M.A., Princeton, 1954, Ph.D., 1956; m. Virginia May Seems, Jan. 29, 1955; children—Gail, Davis, Hugh. Instr., Princeton, 1955-56, U. Chgo., 1956-58; research asso. U. Mich., Ann Arbor, 1958-59; faculty U. Md., College Park, 1959—, prof. math., 1965—; research scientist Research Inst. for Advanced Studies, Balt., 1959-64. NATO fellow U. Strasbourg (France), 1961-62; Fulbright fellow U. Pisa (Italy), 1965-66. Mem. Am. Math. Soc., Math. Assn. Am., Société Mathématique de France, A.A.A.S. Publs. on geometric study of ordinary differential equations on a surface using asso. family of curves and points, also analogous structures in higher dimensions (foliations). Home: 6604 44th Ave Hyattsville MD 20782 Office: Math Dept U Md College Park MD 20742

REINHEIMER, ROBERT, JR., architect; b. Mercury, Tex., Aug. 8, 1917; s. Robert and Frances Curry (Bell) R.; A.S., Tarleton State Coll., Stephenville, Tex., 1936; m. Dalma Louise Rawls, July 23, 1938 (dec. Nov. 16, 1978); children—Patricia Reinheimer McKinney, Frances Reinheimer Steinhauser. Draftsman, Stanley Brown, architect, Marshall, Tex., 1937-38; draftsman, designer Bayard Witt, Architect, Texarkana, Tex., 1939-40, 42-43; bldg. insp. Public Housing Adminstrn., Texarkana, 1941; prin. Reinheimer & Crompton, Texarkana, 1944—. Chmn. Bd. Appeals Texarkana, 1959-62; mem. Bd. Adjustment Texarkana, 1970—. Fellow AIA (pres. N.E. Tex. chpt. 1961-62; recipient citations); mem. Tex. Soc. Architects (chmn. profl. devel. com. 1969-71, v.p. 1967), Mem. Ch. of Christ. Clubs: Rotary, Texarkana Country. Works include design Little River Meml. Hosp., Texarkana YWCA, Walnut St. Ch. of Christ. Home: 1115 Canadian St Texarkana TX 75501 Office: 601 Pine St Texarkana TX 75501

REINKE, RALPH LOUIS, publishing co. exec.; b. Elmhurst, Ill., June 22, 1927; s. Louis Fred and Malinda Marie (Beckmann) R.; student U. Ill., 1945-46; B.S., Concordia Tchrs. Coll., 1949; M.A., Northwestern U., 1952; postgrad. (AAL Ins. Co. fellow) U. Chgo., 1956-63; Litt.D., Concordia Sem., 1972; m. Lois Hermine Borneman, Aug. 28, 1948; children—Janice (Mrs. William Eisenloeffell III), Stephan, Sharon. Prin. St. John Elem. Sch., Houston, 1949-56; asso. prof. psychology and edn. Concordia Coll., River Forest, Ill., 1956-68; asst. gen. mgr. Concordia Pub. House, St. Louis, 1968-71, pres., 1971—. Pres. Lutheran Edn. Assn., 1968-70, Lutheran Editors and Mgrs. Assn., 1972; chmn. lit. commn. Mo. Synod, Lutheran Ch., 1967-69. Mem. sch. bd. selecting com., Oak Park, Ill., 1965-67. Served with USNR, 1944-46. Mem. Am. Assn. Ednl. Researchers, Am. Mgmt. Assn., Phi Delta Kappa. Author: Christian Spelling Series, 2d edit., 1971. Home: 4332 Berrywick St Saint Louis MO 63128 Office: 3558 S Jefferson St Saint Louis MO 63118

REINKEMEYER, SISTER AGNES M., coll. dean, author; b. Rich Fountain, Mo., Dec. 29, 1923; d. Hubert U. and Clara (Fick) Reinkemeyer; B.S. magna cum laude, St. Louis U., 1952, M.S., 1957; Ph.D., U. Calif. at Berkeley, 1966. Mem. Sisters of St. Mary, now v.p. governing bd.; staff nurse, head nurse, supr. various nursing services, St. Louis, 1952-57; instr. St. Louis U., 1957-63, asst. prof., 1963-66, asso. prof. Grad. Sch., 1966-68, now adj. prof.; prof., dean Coll. Nursing, Seton Hall U., South Orange, N.J., 1968—; cons. nursing service orgns. and colls. of nursing; lectr., research critic, book reviewer. Regional reviewer, legis. adv. com. Council of Baccalaureate and Higher Degree Programs, 1970. Recipient Certificate of Recognition, HEW, 1969; Alumni Merit award St. Louis U., 1975. Fellow Am. Acad. Nursing; mem. Am. Nurses Assn., Am. Assn. Higher Edn., Am. Assn. Deans of Colls. and U. Schs. Nursing, Pi Lambda Theta, Sigma Theta Tau. Mem. rev. panel Image jour.; contbr. articles profl. jours. Office: 1100 Bellevue Ave Saint Louis MO 63117

REINMUTH, JAMES ELROY, univ. adminstr.; b. Yakima, Wash., May 31, 1940; s. Elroy V. and Anita G. R.; B.S., U. Wash., 1963; M.S., Oreg. State U., 1965, Ph.D., 1969; m. Maren I. Clifton, June 19, 1966; children—Hilary Jane, Jennifer Carrie. Mem. faculty Coll. Bus. Adminstrn., U. Oreg., Eugene, 1967—, prof., 1972—, dean Coll. Bus. Adminstrn., 1976—. Mem. Am. Statis. Assn., Am. Inst. Decision Scis., Sigma Xi. Presbyterian. Author: Statistics for Management and Economics, 3d edit, 1978. Contbr. articles to profl. jours. Home: 580 E 40th Ave Eugene OR 97405 Office: Univ of Oreg Eugene OR 97403

REINSCH, EMERSON GERALD, constrn. co. exec.; b. Stuttgart, Ark., Oct. 14, 1903; s. Emil Goethal and Cora (Johnson) R.; B.S. in Econs., Wharton Sch. Commerce and Fin., U. Pa., 1925; m. Dolores G. Gillican, June 10, 1942: 1 dau., Lola Calvin. Mem. Sales dept. Harmon Nat. Real Estate Co., N.Y.C., 1925-31; comml. agt. N.Y. Telephone Co., N.Y.C., 1931-35; pres. Reinsch Constrn. Corp., Arlington, Va., 1935—; dir. United Va., First & Citizens Nat. Bank, Arlington. Mem. spl. commn. to Europe for Housing study for Nat. Apt. Owners Assn., Washington, 1959; chmn. Arlington County Minimum Housing Code, 1961-65; chmn. fin. Arlington Republican Com., 1963; bd. Dirs. Nat. Orthopaedic and Rehab. Hosp., pres. 1966-69. Mem. Nat. (dir. 1951-68), No. Va. (pres. 1956), apt. owners assns., No. Va. Builders (pres. 1958), Nat. Home Builders (dir. 1958-62), No. Va. Builders Assn. (pres. 1956), Home Builders Assn. Met. Washington (pres. 1959), Phi Kappa Alpha, Kiwanian (dir. 1960). Home: 4525 35th St N Arlington VA 22207 Office: 2040 Columbia Pike Arlington VA 22204

REINSCH, JAMES LEONARD, radio and TV exec.; b. Streator, Ill., June 28, 1908; s. Henry Emil and Lillian (Funk) R.; B.S., Northwestern U., 1934; m. Phyllis McGeough, Feb. 1, 1936; children—Penelope Luise (Mrs. Bohn), James Leonard. With radio sta. WLS, Chgo., 1924; chmn. bd. Cox Broadcasting Corp.; dir. 1st Nat. Bank Atlanta. Former chmn. U.S. Adv. Commn. Information; radio adviser to White House, 1945-52; TV and radio cons. Democratic Nat. Com., exec. dir. Democratic Nat. Conv., 1956, 60-64, also arrangements dir., 1968, TV-radio dir. Dem. presdl. campaign, 1960; mem. Carnegie Commn. on Future Public Broadcasting. Bd. dirs., exec. com. Am. Cancer Soc. Recipient D.F. Keller award Northwestern U., Distinguished Bus. Mgmt. award Emory U., 1968, award Am. Women in Radio and TV, 1975. Mem. Atlanta Art Assn., Internat. Radio and TV Soc. (Gold medal 1973), Sigma Delta Chi, Di Gamma Kappa. Clubs: Capital City, Peachtree Golf (Atlanta); Burning Tree (Washington); Broadcast Pioneers (N.Y.C.); Nat. Capital Democratic (Washington); Rotary. Author: Radio Station Management, 1948, rev. edit., 1960. Home: 3671 Northside Dr NW Atlanta GA 30305 Office: 53 Perimeter Center E Atlanta GA 30346

REIS, ARTHUR ROBERT, JR., men's furnishing mfr.; b. N.Y.C., Dec. 8, 1916; s. Arthur M. and Claire (Raphael) R.; B.A. Princeton, 1939; m. Muriel Henle, Sept. 25, 1953; children—Arthur, Diane, Pamela. Joined Pan. Am. Airways, 1940, asst. to v.p., 1943; joined Robert Reis & Co., N.Y.C., 1946, pres., 1947—, dir., 1947—. Mem. N.Y. State Com. on Refugee Relief Act of 1953. Trustee, mem. exec. com. Storm King Sch., Cornwall-on-Hudson, N.Y. Served from pvt. to capt. Air Transport Command, USAAF, 1943-46; asst. chief of staff Central Pacific Wing. Decorated B.S.M. Mem. Young Pres.' Orgn. (co-founder), N.Y.C. of C. (exec. com.). Clubs: Century Country (Purchase, N.Y.); Vineyard Haven Yacht (Martha's Vineyard, Mass.). Home: 1136 Fifth Ave New York City NY 10028 Office: 350 5th Ave New York City NY 10001

REIS, DONALD JEFFERY, neurologist, neurobiologist, educator; b. N.Y.C., Sept. 9, 1931; s. Samuel H. and Alice (Kiesler) R.; A.B., Cornell U., 1953, M.D., 1956. Intern, N.Y. Hosp., N.Y.C., 1956; resident in neurology Boston City Hosp.-Harvard Med. Sch., 1957-59; Fulbright fellow, United Cerebral Palsy Found. fellow, London and Stockholm, 1959-60; research asso. NIMH, Bethesda, Md., 1960-62; spl. fellow NIH, Nobel Neurophysiology Inst., Stockholm, 1962-63; asst. prof. neurology Cornell U. Med. Sch., N.Y.C., 1963-67, asso. prof. neurology and psychiatry, 1967-71, prof., 1971—. Mem. Am. Physiol. Soc., Am. Neurol. Assn., Am. Pharmacol. Soc., Am. Acad. Neurology, Harvey Soc., Telluride Assn., Am. Soc. Clin. Investigation, Phi Beta Kappa, Sigma Xi, Alpha Omega Alpha. Contbr. articles to profl. jours.; mem. editorial bd. various profl. jours.

Home: 190 E 72d St New York NY 10021 Office: 1300 York Ave New York NY 10021

REIS, HERBERT K., govt. ofcl.; b. Ill., Oct. 2, 1932; B.S., Northwestern U., 1954; J.D., Yale, 1957. Admitted to D.C. bar, N.Y. State bar, U.S. Supreme Ct. bar; atty. State Dept., Washington, 1957-71, supervisory atty.-adviser, 1962-63, fgn. affairs officer, 1965-66, asst. legal adviser for UN officer, 1966-68; sr. counsellor for internat. law U.S. Mission to UN, N.Y.C., 1971—. Mem. Am. Soc. Internat. Law, Phi Beta Kappa. Office: US Mission to UN 799 United Nations Plaza New York City NY 10017

REISCHAUER, EDWIN OLDFATHER, educator; b. Tokyo, Japan, Oct. 15, 1910 (parents Am. citizens); s. August Karl and Helen (Oldfather) R.; A.B., Oberlin Coll., 1931; A.M., Harvard U., 1932, Ph.D., 1939; student U. Paris, 1933-35; m. Adrienne Danton, July 5, 1935; children—Ann Heinemann, Robert Danton, Joan; m. 2d, Haru Matsukata, Feb. 4, 1956. Studies abroad on Harvard-Yenching Inst. fellowship in France, Japan, China, 1933-38; instr. Harvard U., 1939-42, asso. prof. Far Eastern langs., 1946-50, prof., 1950-61, U. prof., 1966—, dir. Harvard-Yenching Inst., 1956-61; sr. research analyst, Dept. State, summer 1941, War Dept., 1942-43; chmn. Japan-Korea Secretariat and spl. asst. to dir. Office of Far Eastern Affairs, Dept. of state, 1945-46; mem. Cultural Sci. Mission to Japan, 1948-49; U.S. ambassador to Japan, Tokyo, 1961-66. Chmn. bd. trustees Harvard-Yenching Inst., 1970—. Served as lt. col., Mil. Intelligence Service, War Dept. Gen. Staff, 1943-45. Awarded Legion of Merit. Mem. Assn. for Asian Studies, (pres. 1955-56), Japan Acad. (hon.), Phi Betta Kappa. Author: Japan, Past and Present, 1946, rev. edit., 1963; The United States and Japan, 1950, rev. edit., 1957, 65; Translations from Early Japanese Literature (with Joseph Yamagiwa), 1951; Wanted; An Asian Policy, 1955; Ennin's Diary; The Record of a Pilgrimage to China in Search of the Law, 1955; Ennin's Travels in T'ang China, 1955; (with J.K. Fairbank) East Asia, The Great Tradition, 1960; (with others) East Asia; The Modern Transformation, 1965; Beyond Vietnam; The United States and Asia, 1967; Japan, The Story of a Nation, 1970, rev. edit., 1974; (with Fairbank and Craig) East Asia: Tradition and Transformation, 1973; Toward the 21st Century: Education for a Changing World, 1973; The Japanese, 1977. Home: 863 Concord Ave Belmont MA 02178 Office: 1737 Cambridge St Cambridge MA 02138

REISER, MORTON FRANCIS, educator, psychiatrist; b. Cin., Aug. 22, 1919; s. Sigmund and Mary (Roth) R.; B.S., U. Cin., 1940, M.D., 1943; grad. N.Y. Psychoanalytic Inst., 1960; m. Lynn B. Whisnant, Dec. 19, 1976; children—David E., Barbara, Linda. Intern King's County Hosp., Bklyn., 1944; resident Cin. Gen. Hosp., 1944-49; practice medicine, specializing in psychiatry, Cin., 1947-52, Washington, 1954-55, N.Y.C., 1955-69; mem. faculty Cin. Gen. Hosp., also U. Cin. Coll. Medicine, 1949-52, Washington Sch. Psychiatry, 1953-55; faculty Albert Einstein Coll. Medicine, Yeshiva U., N.Y.C., 1955-69, prof. psychiatry, 1958-69, dir. research dept. psychiatry, 1958-65; chief div. psychiatry Montefiore Hosp. and Med. Center, N.Y.C., 1965-69; chmn. dept. psychiatry Yale Med. Sch., 1969—, prof., 1969-78, Charles B. G. Murphy prof., 1978—; cons. Walter Reed Army Inst. Research, 1957-58, High Point Hosp., Port Chester, N.Y., 1957-69, com. WHO, 1963; mem. profl. adv. com. Jerusalem Mental Health Center, 1972—; mem. clin. program projects rev. com. NIMH, 1970—, chmn., 1973-74; also lectr.; mem. Josiah Macy, Jr. Found. Commn. on Present Condition and Future Acad. Psychiatry, 1977. Recipient Stella Fels Hoffheimer Meml. prize U. Cin. Coll. Medicine, 1943. Diplomate Am. Bd. Psychiatry and Neurology. Fellow Am. Coll. Psychiatrists, Am. Psychiat. Assn.; mem. Am. Soc. Clin. Investigation, Am. Psychosomatic Soc. (pres. 1960-61), Am. Fedn. Clin. Research, Am. Assn. Chairmen Depts. Psychiatry (exec. com. 1971—, pres. 1975-76), Acad. Behavioral Medicine Research (exec. council 1978), Am. Psychoanalytic Assn. (pres.-elect 1980—), Internat. Psycho-Analytical Assn., Assn. for Psychophysiol. Study of Sleep, Internat. Coll. Psychosomatic Medicine (pres. 1975), Psychiat. Research Soc., A. Graeme Mitchell Undergrad. Pediatric Soc., World Psychiat. Assn. (organizing com. sect. psychosomatic medicine 1967), Sigma Xi, Phi Eta Sigma, Pi Kappa Epsilon, Alpha Omega Alpha. Editor: American Handbook of Psychiatry, vol. IV, 1975. Editor-in-chief, Psychosomatic Medicine, 1962-72; editorial bd. AMA Archive of Gen. Psychiatry, 1961-71; Psychiatry Medicine and Primary Care, 1978; contbr. articles to profl. jours. and books. Home: 99 Blake Rd Hamden CT 06517 Office: 25 Park St New Haven CT 06519

REISINI, NICOLAS, export-import co. exec.; b. Athens, Greece, July 7, 1905; s. Gregory and Sofia (Zeldinas) R.; Ingenieur des Travaux Publics, U. Paris (France), 1959, Ingenieur Docteur, 1959, Docteur en Scis. Economiques, 1960; m. Magda Ladanyi, Oct. 29, 1955; children—Krisztina, Nicolas, Andrew. Came to U.S., 1945, naturalized. 1963. Pres. Robin Internat., Inc., N.Y.C., 1950—, pres. Cinerama, Inc., 1959-63, chmn. bd., 1963-64. Decorated grand cross Order St. Denis (Greece); comdr. Belgian Crown. Fellow N.Y. Acad. Scis., Royal Soc. Encouragement Arts (London, Eng.). Home: 1016 Fifth Ave New York NY 10028 also Duck Hollow House Tuxedo Park NY 10987 Office: 1016 Fifth Ave New York NY 10028

REISLER, RAYMOND, lawyer, arbitrator; b. Bklyn., Nov. 28, 1907; s. Frank O. and Fannie R.; B.A., Cornell U., 1927, postgrad. Law Sch., 1926-27; J.D., Columbia U., 1929; postgrad. (fellow) Nat. Coll. Judiciary, 1975; m. Harriet Spitzer, Sept. 10, 1933; children—Nancy, Raymond. Admitted to N.Y. State bar, 1930, U.S. Supreme Ct. bar, 1957; asso. firm Ruston & Snyder, Bklyn., 1930-34, partner, 1934-36; prin. firm Raymond Reisler, successor firm to Ruston & Snyder, 1936-67; judge Criminal Ct. N.Y.C., 1967-77; acting justice N.Y. State Supreme Ct., 1977; counsel firm Buchman, Buchman & O'Brien, N.Y.C., 1978—; referee N.Y. State Commn. on Jud. Conduct, appellate div. N.Y. State Supreme Ct., N.Y. State Bd. Tax Appeals, N.Y. State Dept. Health, N.Y. State Public Health Council; hearing officer state and city govt. agys.; trial officer N.Y.C. Housing Authority; trial examiner N.Y.C. Bd. Edn.; arbitrator Am. Arbitration Assn.; dep. asst. atty. gen. State of N.Y., 1952-65; lectr. St. Johns' U. Law Sch., 1957-62; mem. faculty Bklyn. Law Sch., 1963-68; speaker in field. Life mem. emeritus Cornell U. Council. Fellow N.Y. Bar Found.; mem. Am. Bar Assn. (chmn. nat. joint conf. lawyers, ins. cos. and adjusters 1963-67, chmn. nat. conf. unauthorized practice law 1961), N.Y. State Bar Assn. (exec. com. 1951-63, chmn. com. unlawful practice law 1955-64, plaque for service 1964, resolution of appreciation 1964), Bklyn. Bar Assn. (pres. 1960-61, mem. trustee council 1961—, Scroll of Appreciation 1961, 72, Gold Medal award 1973), Queen's County Bar Assn. (jud. council), Assn. Bar City N.Y., Fed. Bar Council, Cornell Law Alumni Assn., Columbia Law Alumni Assn., Judges Assn. of Criminal Ct. City N.Y., Iota Theta, Sigma Alpha Mu (nat. pres. 1959-61). Clubs: Princeton, K.P. (dep. grand chancellor 1941-42, hon. life. mem. 1979—, Meml. award 1979). Contbr. articles to profl. jours. Office: 10 E 40th St Suite 2000 New York NY 10016

REISMAN, ARNOLD, educator; b. Lodz, Poland, Aug. 2, 1934; s. Isadore and Rose (Joskowitz) R.; came to U.S., 1946, naturalized, 1955; B.S., UCLA, 1955, M.S., 1957, Ph.D., 1963; m. Judith Ann Gelernter, Mar. 12, 1955 (div. 1978); children—Miriam Jennie, Ada Jo, Deborah Fawn, Nina Michelle. Design engr. Los Angeles Dept. Water and Power, 1955-57; asso. prof. Calif. State U., Los Angeles, 1957-66; prof. U. Wis., Milw., 1966-68; prof. ops. research Case-Western Res. U., Cleve., 1968—; vis. prof. Hebrew U., Jerusalem, 1975; affiliate faculty Japan-Am. Inst. Mgmt. Sci., Honolulu, 1975—; U. Hawaii, Honolulu, 1971; asso. research engr. Western Mgmt. Sci. Inst., UCLA, 1964-65; coordinator programs between Inst. Mgmt. Scis. and AAAS, 1971—; examiner N. Central Assn. Colls., Univs. and Secondary Schs., 1971; v.p. Univ. Assos., Inc., Cleve., 1968-75; expert witness solicitor gen., Dept. Labor, 1969-70, U.S. Equal Opportunities Commn., 1976-79; cons. to asst. sec. HEW, 1971-72, Office Program Planning and Evaluation, U.S. Office Edn., 1972-73; cons. in gen. field systems analysis to numerous corps. and instns. U.S. del. to Internat. Fedn. Ops. Research Socs., Conv., Dublin, Ireland, 1972; Review Bd. mem. Lake Erie Regional Transp. Authority, 1974-75; mem. del. assembly Jewish Community Fedn. Cleve., 1974—; mem. Shaker Heights (Ohio) Citizens adv. com., 1972—; bd. dirs., founder Greater Cleve. Coalition on Health Care Cost Effectiveness. Trustee Hillel Found. Named Cleve. Engr. of Yr., 1973; registered profl. engr., Calif., Wis., Ohio; NSF fellow, 1963. Fellow AAAS (council), Soc. Advanced Med. Systems; mem Ops. Research Soc. Am., Inst. Mgmt. Scis., ASME, Am. Soc. Engring. Edn., AAUP, Am. Inst. Indsl. Engrs., N.Y. Acad. Scis., Sigma Xi, Phi Delta Kappa. Author: Managerial and Engineering Economics, 1971; Systems Approach and The City, 1972; Industrial Inventory Control, 1972; Health Care Delivery Planning, 1973; Systems Analysis in Health Care Delivery, 1979; Materials Management for Health Care Delivery, 1980. Series editor Operations Management; asso. editor Socio Economic Planning Sciences. Contbr. numerous articles to profl. jours. Home: 18428 Parkland Dr Shaker Heights OH 44122 Office: Case Western Reserve University Department Operations Research Sears Bldg Cleveland OH 44106

REISMANN, HERBERT, educator, engr.; b. Vienna, Austria, Jan. 26, 1926; s. Henrik and Olga (Pokorny) R.; B.S. in Aero. Engring., Ill. Inst. Tech., 1947, M.S., 1949; Ph.D. in Engring., U. Colo., 1962; m. Edith Falber, Aug. 14, 1952; children—Sandra Jean, Barbara Anne. Project engr. Convair, Ft. Worth, 1951-53; prin. structures engr. Republic Aviation Corp., Hicksville, N.Y., 1954-56; chief engr. systems analysis, chief solid mechanics Martin Marietta Corp., 1957-64; prof. engring. State U. N.Y. at Buffalo, 1964—. Cons. NASA, Bell Aero Systems Corp. Asso. fellow Am. Inst. Aeros. and Astronautics (award best tech. paper 1962); mem. ASME, Internat. Assn. Bridge and Structural Engring., AAUP, Sigma Xi, Tau Beta Pi. Co-author: Elastokinetics, 1974. Contbr. articles to profl. jours. Home: 71 Chaumont Dr Williamsville NY 14221 Office: Parker Engring State U NY Buffalo NY 14214

REISS, ALBERT JOHN, JR., educator; b. Cascade, Wis., Dec. 9, 1922; s. Albert John and Erma Amanda (Schueler) R.; student Mission House Coll., 1939-42; Ph.B., Marquette U., 1944; M.A., U. Chgo., 1948, Ph.D., 1949; m. Emma Lucille Hutto, June 11, 1953; children—Peter C., Paul Wetherington, Amy. Tchr. social scis. Union Free High Sch., 1944-45; social research analyst Ill. Bd. Pub. Welfare Commr., 1946-47; instr. sociology U. Chgo., 1947-49, asst. prof., 1949-52; asso. dir. Chgo. Community Inventory (U. Chgo.), 1948-51, acting dir., 1951-52; asso. prof. sociology Vanderbilt U., 1952-58, prof., 1954-58, chmn. dept., 1952-58; prof. sociology and dir. Iowa Urban Community Research Center, State U. Iowa, 1958-60; prof. sociology, dir. survey research labs. U. Wis., 1960-61; prof. sociology, dir. U. Mich. Center for Research on Social Orgn., Ann Arbor, 1961-70, chmn. dept. 70; prof. sociology Yale U., 1970—, prof. social sci. Inst. Social and Polit. Sci., 1970—, also William Graham Sumner prof. sociology. Chmn. Census Com. on Enumeration Areas. Chgo., 1950-52, Nashville, 1952-58; mem. tech. adv. com. Chgo. Plan Commn., 1951-52; cons. USAF Human Resources Research Inst., 1952-54. Served as pvt., meteorology program, A.C., AUS, 1943-44. Fellow Am. Sociol. Assn. (chmn. methodology sect. 1960, council and exec. com. 1962-65), Ohio Valley Sociol. Soc. (pres. 1966), Am. Statis. Assn., Sociol. Research Assn. (pres. 1969), Nat. Conf. Family Relations (mem. editorial bd. 1950-52, treas. 1952), Soc. for Study Social Problems (pres. 1968), Soc. Social Research (pres. 1949), Ill. Acad. Criminology (treas. 1950). Author: A Survey of Probation Needs and Services in Illinois, 1947; Reader in Urban Sociology (with Paul K. Hatt), 1951; Mobility of Chicago Workers (with Evelyn R. Kitagawa), 1951; Social Characteristics of Rural and Urban Communities, 1950, (with Otis Dudley Duncan), 1956; Cities and Society, 1958; Occupations and Social Status, 1960; The Police and the Public, 1971. Asst. editor Am. Jour. Sociology, 1950-52. Home: 45 Center Rd Woodbridge CT 06525 Office: Yale U Dept Sociology New Haven CT 06520

REISS, ALVIN, writer; b. Ft. Sill, Okla., Oct. 31, 1932; s. Clarence Gustav Alvin and Mabel Alma (Craig) R.; student U. Oreg., 1950-51, So. Oreg. Coll., 1969; m. Audrey Spencer, Sept. 1, 1951 (div. 1974); children—Belinda, Karen. With Union Pacific and Denver & Rio Grande, 1951-61, chief clk., 1955-61; with KBOY-FM, Medford, Oreg., 1961-68, FM program dir., 1966-68; news dir. KYJC, Medford, 1969-73; staff writer Medford Mail Tribune, 1969—; screen writer Larry Lansburgh Films, Inc., 1972. Recipient John Masefield Meml. award Poetry Soc. Am., 1970, regional award for playwriting, Oreg., 1965, Ala., 1963. Mem. Am. Theater Critics Assn., Poetry Soc. Am., Mensa, Soc. Profl Journalists, Sigma Delta Chi (pres. So. Oreg. chpt. 1977-78). Author: (play) The Smallest Giant, 1963, also stories, poetry. Home: 115 F St Jacksonville OR 97530 Office: care Kathryne Walters Lit Agts 782 West End Ave Penthouse 2 New York NY 10025

REISS, ERIC, physician; b. Vienna, Austria, Feb. 29, 1924; s. Leo Josef and Marianne (Schrecker) R.; brought to U.S., 1939, naturalized, 1944; B.S., Randolph Macon Coll., 1943; M.D., Med. Coll. Va., 1948; m. Louise Marie Zibold, Oct. 7, 1950; 1 son, Eric Leo. Intern Phila. Gen. Hosp., 1948-50; asst. resident Barnes Hosp., 1954-55; Am. Cancer Soc. scholar metabolism div. dept. medicine Wash. U. Sch., Medicine, 1955-60, instr. medicine, 1956-58, asst. prof. medicine and preventive medicine, 1958-62, dir. Irene Walter Johnson Inst. Rehab., 1958-64, asso. prof. medicine, preventive medicine, 1962-64; chmn. dept. medicine Michael Reese Hosp. & Med. Center, Chgo., 1964-71; prof. medicine Chgo. Med. Sch., 1964-66, U. Chgo., 1969-72; prof., vice chmn. dept. medicine U. Miami (Fla.) Sch. Medicine, 1972—. Served to maj. AUS, 1943-44, 1950-54. Fellow A.C.P.; mem. Endocrine Soc., Am., So. socs. for clin. investigation, Soc. Exptl. Biology and Medicine, Am. Soc. Nephrology, Am. Fedn. Clin. Research, Central Soc. for Clin. Research, Assn. Am. Physicians, Phi Beta Kappa, Alpha Omega Alpha. Democrat. Author: The Treatment of Burns, 1957; research in parathyroid hormone physiology. Home: 6400 SW 102d St Miami FL 33156 Office: PO Box 875 Biscayne Annex Miami FL 33152

REISS, HAROLD, advt. exec.; b. N.Y.C., Feb. 22, 1912; s. Rudolph and Helen (Fantl) R.; student N.Y. U.; m. Victoria Hughes, Jan. 28, 1955; children—Nancy, Thomas, Richard. With Friend-Reiss Advt., Inc., N.Y.C., 1933—, vice chmn., 1938-64, pres., 1967-71; v.p. Muller, Jordan, Herrick, Inc., N.Y.C., 1971—. Home: 222 E 19th St New York NY 10003 Office: 666 Fifth Ave New York NY 10019

REISS, HOWARD, educator, scientist; b. N.Y.C., Apr. 5, 1922; s. Isidor and Jean (Goldstein) R.; A.B. in Chemistry, N.Y.U., 1943; Ph.D. in Chemistry, Columbia, 1949; m. Phyllis Kohn, July 25, 1945; children—Gloria, Steven. With Manhattan Project, 1944-46; instr., then asst. prof. chemistry Boston U., 1949-51; with Central Research Lab., Celanese Corp. Am., 1951-52, Edgar C. Bain Lab. Fundamental Research, U.S. Steel Corp., 1957, Bell Telephone Labs., 1952-60; asso. dir., then dir. research div. Atomics Internat., div. N.Am. Aviation, Inc., 1960-62; dir. N.Am. Aviation Sci. Center, 1962-67, v.p. co., 1963-67, v.p. research aerospace systems group N.Am. Rockwell Corp., 1967-68; vis. lectr. chemistry U. Calif. at Berkeley, summer 1957; vis. prof. chemistry U. Calif. at Los Angeles, 1961, 62, prof., 1968—; vis. prof. U. So. Calif., 1964, 67. Cons. to chem.-physics program, Air Force Cambridge Research Cambridge Research Labs., 1950-52; chmn., editor proc. Internat. Conf. Nucleation and Interfacial Phenomena, Boston; mem. Air Force Office Sci. Research Physics and chemistry Research Evaluation Groups, 1966—; mem. Oak Ridge Nat. Lab. Reactor Chemistry Adv. Com., 1966-68; adv. com. math. and phys. scis. NSF, 1970-72, ARPA Materials Research Council, 1968—. Guggenheim Meml. fellow, 1978. Fellow Am. Phys. Soc. (exec. com. div. chem. physics 1966-69); mem. Am. Chem. Soc. (chmn. phys. chemistry sect. N.J. sect. 1957, Richard C. Tolman medal 1973, prize in Colloid and surface chemistry 1980), Nat. Acad. Sci., Sci. Research Soc. Am., AAUP, Phi Beta Kappa, Sigma Xi, Phi Lambda Upsilon. Author articles, editor in field. Editor Jour. Statis. Physics, 1968—, Jour. Colloid Interface Sci.; editorial adv. bd. Internat. Jour. Phys. and Solids, Solids,, Jour. Solid State Chemistry, Jour. Phys. Chemistry, Jour. Nonmetals, Chemistry. Author: The Methods of Thermodynamics, 1965. Office: Dept Chemistry U Calif Los Angeles CA 90024

REISS, JOHN C., bishop; b. Red Bank, N.J., May 13, 1922; s. Alfred and Sophia (Telljohann) R.; student Immaculate Conception Sem., 1941-46; S.T.L., Cath. U., 1947, J.C.D., 1953; B.A., Seton Hall U., 1947. Ordained priest Roman Catholic Ch., 1947; asst. chancellor Diocese Trenton, N.J., 1954, sec., master ceremonies, 1953-62, vice chancellor, 1956-62, officialis, 1962—, aux. bishop, 1967—. Mem. Mayor Trenton Adv. Commn. Civil Rights, 1962-68. Office: 701 Lawrenceville Rd Trenton NJ 08638

REISS, KENNETH MOSLEY, publisher; b. Schenectady, July 8, 1936; s. Edgar Allen and Margaret Jane (Mosley) R.; B.A., U. Conn., 1957; m. Sylvia Dale, Aug. 19, 1978; children by previous marriage—Goeffrey, Michael, Elizabeth. Asst. news editor Am. Druggist, Hearst mags., 1957, merchandising editor, 1958; asso. editor Sales and Mktg. Mgmt. mag. Bill Communications, N.Y.C., 1959, sr. editor, 1961, dir. promotion, 1964-69, asst. to pub., 1969-70, asso. pub., pub., 1971—, pres., 1976—. Mem. Internat. Newspaper Advt. Execs., Nat. Premium Sales Execs., Internat. Newspaper Promotion Assn., Sales Execs. Club of N.Y. Office: 633 3d Ave New York NY 10017

REISS, PAUL JACOB, educator; b. Lake Placid, N.Y., Aug. 10, 1930; s. Julian J. and Daisy M. (Smith) R.; B.S., Holy Cross Coll., 1952; M.A., Fordham U., 1954; Ph.D., Harvard, 1959; m. Rosemary A. Donohue, June 25, 1955; children—Catherine, Paul, Gregory, Mark, Julia, David, Steven, Martha. Tutor, Harvard, 1954-57; instr., asst. prof. Marquette U., 1957-63, chmn. dept. sociology, 1961-63; asso. prof. sociology Fordham U., Bronx, N.Y., 1963-75, prof., 1976—, chmn. dept. sociology and anthropology, 1964-68, dean Liberal Arts Coll., 1968-69, v.p. acad. affairs, 1969-75, exec. v.p., 1975—. Exec. dir. Julian Reiss Found., Lake Placid, N.Y. Fellow Am. Sociol. Assn.; mem. Assn. for Sociology of Religion (pres.), Nat. Council on Family Relations. Democrat. Roman Catholic. Editor: Sociological Analysis: A Journal in the Sociology of Religion, 1961-68. Contbr. articles to profl. jours. Home: 1 Hillside Rd Bronxville NY 10708 Office: Fordham U Bronx NY 10458

REISTLE, CARL ERNEST, JR., petroleum engr.; b. Denver, June 26, 1901; s. Carl E. and Leonora I. (McMaster) R.; B.S., U. Okla., 1922; postgrad. Harvard Sch. Bus. Adminstrn., 1948; m. Mattie A Muldrow, June 23, 1922; children—Bette Jean (Mrs. George F. Pierce), Mattie Ann (Mrs. James Tracy Clark), Nancy L. (Mrs. Wilson Hayes Holliday), Carl Ernest III. Petroleum chemist U.S. Bur. Mines, 1922-29, petroleum engr., 1929-33; chmn. East Tex. Engring. Assn., 1933-36; engr. in charge Humble Oil & Refining Co., 1936-40, chief petroleum engr., 1940-45, gen. supt. prodn., 1945-46, mgr. prodn. dept., 1946-51, dir., 1948-51, dir. in charge prodn. dept., 1951-55, v.p., 1955-57, exec. v.p., 1957-61, pres., 1961-63, chmn. bd., chief exec. officer, 1963-66, ret., 1966, cons., 1966-69; dir. Eltra Corp.; dir., chmn. exec. com. Olinkraft, Inc., 1967-78. Bd. dirs. Tex. Tech Coll., Lubbock, 1966-69, U. Okla. Research Inst., Norman. Recipient Anthony F. Lucas Gold medal Am. Inst. Mining, Metall. and Petroleum Engrs., 1958. Mem. Am. Petroleum Inst., Am. Inst. Mining, Metall. and Petroleum Engrs. (pres. 1956), Sigma Xi, Tau Beta Pi, Sigma Tau, Alpha Chi Sigma. Clubs: Ramada, Petroleum, River Oaks Country. Contbr. numerous articles to profl. jours. Home: 3196 Chevy Chase Houston TX 77019 Office: 1100 Milam Bldg Suite 4601 Houston TX 77002

REISTRUP, JEANNE MOSS, interior designer; b. Glasgow, Mo., Aug. 11, 1905; d. Samuel and Jennie (Easley) Moss; student U. Ill., 1923-27; study in Europe, 1931; m. James Reistrup, July 23, 1931 (dec. Apr. 1973); children—Paul H., John V. Head bur. interior decorating Davidson Bros., Sioux City, Iowa, 1928-31; owner firm Jeanne Moss Reistrup, 1933—; tchr. interior decorating YWCA, Catholic U.; lectr. in field. Chmn. bd. Reistrup Arts Assn. Recipient Woman of Achievement award, Sioux City, 1946. Fellow Am. Inst. Designers (nat. by-laws com., nominating com., chmn. nat. conf. 1953, chmn. exhibit Nat. Housing Center, 1959, chmn. bd. govs., corr. sec. D.C. chpt. 1971—), Am. Soc. Interior Designers (life mem.; chmn. by-laws and ethics com. Potomac chpt.) mem. Nat. Symphony Orch. Women's Com., YWCA, P.E.O., Delta Zeta. Clubs: Fortnightly (past pres.), Morningside Coll. Faculty Women's (past pres.). Author articles in field. Home: 3701 Connecticut Ave NW Washington DC 20008

REISTRUP, PAUL HANSEN, railroad exec.; b. Sioux City, Iowa, May 24, 1932; s. James and Laura (Moss) R.; B.S., U.S. Mil. Acad., 1954; m. Mary Winn Caffey, Oct. 11, 1958; children—Paul Hansen, Gordon Petersen, John Moss, Catherine Laura. Various positions engring., operating, and passenger depts. B.&O. R.R., Balt., 1957-67; v.p. Ill. Central Gulf R.R., 1967-73, sr. v.p., 1973-75, also dir.; pres. Nat. R.R. Passenger Corp., Washington, 1975-78, dir., 1976-78; dir. Assn. Am. R.R.'s, 1976-78; dir., mem. fin. com. Trailer Train Co., 1969-74, Am. Railbox Car Co., 1974—; v.p. R.L. Banks and Assos., Inc., Washington, 1978—. Vice pres., mem. exec. bd. Nat. Capitol Area council Boy Scouts Am. Served to 1st lt. U.S. Army, 1954-57. Mem. Transp. Research Forum. Clubs: Army and Navy (Washington); Army and Navy Country (Arlington, Va.). Office: 900 17th St NW Washington DC 20006

REITAN, DANIEL KINSETH, educator; b. Duluth, Minn., Aug. 13, 1921; s. Conrad Ulfred and Joy Elizabeth R.; B.S.E.E., N.D. State U., 1946; M.S.E.E., U. Wis., 1949, Ph.D., 1952; m. Marian Anne Stemme, July 16, 1946; children—Debra Leah, Danielle Karen. Control engr. Gen. Electric Co., Schenectady, N.Y., 1946-48;

transmission line engr. Gen. Telephone Co., Madison, Wis., 1949-50; mem. faculty Coll. Engring. U. Wis., Madison, 1952—, prof. elec. and computer engring., 1962—, dir. power systems simulation lab., 1968—; cons. in field. Served with U.S. Army, World War II. Recipient Outstanding Tchr. award Polygon Engring. Council. Registered profl. engr., Wis. Mem. IEEE, IEEE Power Engring. Soc., Conf. Internat. des Grands Reseaux Electriques a Haute Tension, Am. Soc. Engring. Edn., Wis. Acad. Scis., Am. Wind Energy Assn., Sigma Xi, Tau Beta Pi, Eta Kappa Nu, Kappa Eta Kappa. Lutheran. Contbr. articles to profl. jours. Patentee in field. Office: Elec and Computer Engring Dept 1425 Johnson Dr Madison WI 53706. *I believe that one's career professionalism and perseverance are key factors in success. In one's personal life, the family should be the center, but not the circumference, about which all activities revolve.*

REITAN, PAUL HARTMAN, mineralogist, educator; b. Kanawha, Iowa, Aug. 18, 1928; s. John Olsen and Anna (Meldahl) R.; A.B., U. Chgo., 1953; Ph.D., U. Oslo, 1959; m. Reidun Engebretsen, Sept. 28, 1962; children—Kirsten Berit, Eric Hartmann. Geologist, U.S. Geol. Survey, 1953-56; instr. U. Ill., Chgo., 1954-55; state geologist Geol. Survey of Norway, Oslo, 1956-60; asst. prof. mineralogy Stanford (Calif.) U., 1960-66; asso. prof. SUNY, Buffalo, 1966-69, prof., 1969—, acting provost Faculty Natural Sci. and Math., 1975-76, provost, 1976-78, dean, 1978-79. Served with M.C., AUS, 1946-49. Salisbury fellow, 1953-55; Fulbright fellow, 1955-56, NATO sr. fellow, 1972; G. Unger Vetlesen fellow, Oslo, 1973. Fellow Geol. Soc. Am., Mineral. Soc. Am.; mem. Am. Geophys. Union, Geochem. Soc., Internat. Assn. Geochemistry and Cosmochemistry, Nat. Assn. Geology Tchrs., Norsk Geol. Forening, AAAS, Sigma Xi. Contbr. articles to profl. jours. Home: 120 Walton Dr Buffalo NY 14226 Office: State U NY Buffalo NY 14260

REITEMEIER, RICHARD JOSEPH, physician; b. Pueblo, Colo., Jan. 2, 1923; s. Paul John and Ethel Regina (McCarthy) R.; A.B., U. Denver, 1944; M.D., U. Colo., 1946; M.S. in Internal Medicine, U. Minn., 1954; m. Patricia Claire Mulligan, July 21, 1951; children—Mary Louise, Paul, Joseph, Susan, Robert, Patrick, Daniel. Intern, Corwin Hosp., Pueblo, 1946-47; resident Henry Ford Hosp., Detroit, 1949-50, Mayo Found., Rochester, Minn., 1950-53; cons. internal medicine and gastroenterology Mayo Clinic, Rochester, 1954—, chmn. dept. internal medicine Mayo Clinic and Mayo Med. Sch., 1967-74, prof., 1971—, bd. govs. Mayo Clinic, 1970-74; trustee Mayo Found., 1970-74: St. Mary's Hosp., Rochester, 1976—. Served with U.S. Army, 1947-49. Recipient Alumni award U. Colo. Sch. Medicine. Diplomate Am. Bd. Internal Medicine (chmn. 1978-79, rep. to Federated Council Internal Medicine 1977—, liaison com. grad. edn. 1979—). Fellow A.C.P. (regent 1979—, gov. for Minn. 1975-79), Am. Gastroenterol. Assn., AMA, Am. Clin. and Climatol. Assn., Am. Fedn. Clin. Research, Am. Soc. Clin. Oncology, Am. Assn. Cancer Research, Am. Assn. Study Liver Disease, Alpha Omega Alpha. Republican. Roman Catholic. Author: (with C. G. Moertel) Advanced Gastrointestinal Cancer, Clinical Management and Chemotherapy, 1969; contbr. numerous articles to med. jours. Home: 707 12th Ave SW Rochester MN 55901 Office: 200 1st Ave SW Rochester MN 55901

REITER, STANLEY, educator, economist; b. N.Y.C., Apr. 26, 1925; s. Frank and Fanny (Rosenberg) R.; A.B., Queens Coll., 1947; M.A., U. Chgo., 1950, Ph.D., 1955; m. Nina Sarah Breger, June 13, 1944; children—Carla Frances, Frank Joseph. Research asso. Cowles Commn., U. Chgo., 1949-50; mem. faculty Stanford, 1950-54, Purdue U., 1954-67; prof. econs. and math. Northwestern U., 1967—, now Morrison prof. econs. and math. Coll. Arts and Scis., Morrison prof. managerial econs. and decision scis. Grad. Sch. Mgmt.; cons. in field. Trustee Roycemore Sch., Evanston, Ill., 1969—, treas., 1970—. Served with inf., AUS, 1943-45. Decorated Purple Heart. Fellow Econometric Soc.; mem. Soc. Indsl. and Applied Math., Inst. Mgmt. Scis., Ops. Research Soc. Am. Home: 2138 Orrington Ave Evanston IL 60201

REITH, CARL JOSEPH, apparel industry exec.; b. Peoria, Ill., Jan. 11, 1914; s. Joseph and May (Kolb) R.; ed. high sch.; m. Jennie S. Habbinga, Apr. 3, 1936; 1 dau., Joyce Elaine. Sales, office staff Peoria Creamery Co. (Ill.), 1932; with Kroger Co., 1934-60, successively asst. br. accountant, office mgr., accountant, Terre Haute, Ind., also Atlanta, adminstr., coordinator tng. and mgmt. devel. programing Gen. Offices, Cin., gen. merchandising mgr. St. Louis br., br. mgr., Indpls., br. mgr., Cin., 1934-57, v.p., 1957-60; pres., chief exec. officer Colonial Stores, Inc., 1960-67, also dir.; pres. Oxford Industries, 1967-78, now dir.; vice chmn. bd., dir. mem. exec. com. Lanier Bus. Products, 1978—; dir. Ga. Internat. Ins. Co., Fulton Nat. Bank of Atlanta, Atlanta and West Point R.R. Adv. bd. Salvation Army, Atlanta. Bd. dirs. Atlanta Symphony Guild; trustee Atlanta Art Assn. Mem. Mo., Indiana (pres., v.p., 1951-55), chain store councils, Ind. (bd. 1954-55), Indpls. (bd. 1950), Ga. (indsl. devel. council), Atlanta (v.p., dir. 1964-67) chambers commerce. Clubs: Augusta (Ga.) Nat. Golf, Piedmont Driving; Capital City, Peachtree Golf (Atlanta), Masons, Shriners, Rotary. Home: Atlanta GA Office: Oxford Industries Inc 222 Piedmont Ave NE Atlanta GA 30312

REITHEL, FRANCIS JOSEPH, educator; b. Portland, Oreg., Apr. 6, 1914; s. John A. and Mary R. (Samberg) R.; B.A., Reed Coll., 1936; student Oreg. State Coll., 1936-37; M.A., U. Oreg. Med. Sch., 1938, Ph.D., 1942; m. Mary C. Dickson, Sept. 28 1939, 1 dau., Nancy; m. 2d, Katharine Hunter Miller, June 7, 1974. Instr. biochemistry St. Louis U. Sch. Medicine, 1942-44, Washington U. Sch. Medicine, 1944-45; research asso. bio-organic chemistry Calif. Inst. Tech., 1945-46; mem. faculty dept. chemistry U. Oreg., 1946—, prof., 1955—, head dept., 1956-63; program dir. molecular biology NSF, 1959-60; spl. research fellow Nat. Heart Inst., Bethesda, Md., 1960-61. Fellow Fund Advancement Edn., 1953-54; USPHS spl. research fellow U. Rome, 1967-68; vis. prof. U. Sussex, 1975-76. Fellow AAAS, Am. Soc. Biol. Chemists, Am. Chem. Soc. (chmn. Oreg. 1959), Pacific Slope Biochem. Conf. Author: Concepts in Biochemistry; also articles in field. Home: 2600 Floral Hill Dr Eugene OR 97403. *For more than a hundred years science has provided a medium through which men and women of any background or station in life could participate in a world of the intellect. In the last thirty years, society has strongly endorsed such activities. At the same time, events have suggested that social responsibility for science be assumed by scientists. I am truly grateful for the opportunity to participate in the intellectual effervescence in biochemistry during those years. I have tried to honor the social responsibilities that accompanied the privileges.*

REITHERMAN, WOLFGANG, animated motion picture producer; b. Munich, Bavaria, June 26, 1909; s. Philipp and Rosina Marie (Kuhner) R.; came to U.S., 1911, naturalized, 1919; student Pasadena Jr. Coll., 1927-28, Chouinard Art Sch., 1930-31; m. Janie Marie McMillan, Nov. 26, 1946; children—Richard Wolfgang, Robert King, Bruce Philip. Animator Walt Disney Studios, 1932-37, dir. animator, 1937-41, dir., producer, 1948—. Served as pilot USAAF, 1941-45. Decorated D.F.C., Air medal with oak leaf cluster. Mem. Am. Acad. Motion Picture Arts and Scis. Home: 2 Skyline Dr Burbank CA 91501 Office: Walt Disney Productions 500 S Buena Vista Burbank CA 91521

REITMAN, ROBERT STANLEY, vending, food service and wholesaling exec.; b. Fairmont, W.Va., Nov. 18, 1933; s. Isadore and Freda A. (Layman) R.; B.S., W.Va. U., 1955; J.D., Case Western Res. U., 1958; m. Sylvia K. Golden, Dec. 24, 1955; children—Scott Alan, Alayne Louise. Admitted to Ohio bar, 1958; mem. firm Burke, Haber & Berick, Cleve., 1958-60, partner, 1960-68; exec. v.p. AAV Cos. (formerly Am. Automatic Vending Corp.), Solon, Ohio, 1968-70, pres., vice-chmn., 1970—, also chief exec. officer, 1973—; dir. Mercury Aviation Co., Cleve. Mem. Republican fin. com. Cuyahoga County, 1968-78; gen. co-chmn. Jewish Welfare Fund, Cleve., 1975-79; div. chmn., team capt. United Torch Drive, 1974—; mem. del. assembly, trustee United Torch Services, 1976—; mem. employment com. Jewish Vocat. Service, Cleve., 1974—; trustee B'nai B'rith Hillel Found., Cleve., 1975-80, Cleve. Jewish News, 1976-79, Mt. Sinai Hosp., Cleve., 1976—, Ednl. TV Sta. WVIZ, Cleve., 1976—, Cleve. Zool. Soc., Jewish Community Fedn. Cleve., 1975—. Mem. Am. Bar Assn., Nat. Automatic Merchandising Assn., Cleve. Growth Assn., Am. (regional del. 1959-75), Western Res. (officer, trustee 1958-75) kennel clubs, Zeta Beta Tau, Tau Epsilon Rho. Clubs: Beechmont Country; Pine Lake Trout; Commerce; Muirfield Village Golf; Masons, B'nai B'rith. Contbr. articles to trade jours. Home: 6699 Gates Mills Blvd Gates Mills OH 44040 Office: 31100 Solon Rd Solon OH 44139

REITZ, J(ULIUS) WAYNE, ednl. cons.; b. Olathe, Kans., Dec. 31, 1908; s. Julius Adam and Minnie Mae (Hayes) R.; B.S., Colo. State U., 1930; M.S., U. Ill., 1935, Ph.D., U. Wis., 1941; LL.D., Tusculum Coll., 1955, U. Miami, 1956, Colo. State U., 1961; D.Sc., Jacksonville U., 1959; L.H.D., U. Fla., 1967; m. Frances Huston Millikan, Sept. 1, 1935; children—Margaret Ann, Marjorie Hayes. Acting extension economist Colo. State Coll., 1930-31; asst. extension economist U. Ill., 1931-33; jr. economist FCA, Washington, 1933-34; mem. faculty U. Fla., 1934-44, 1949-55, prof. agrl. econs., 1940-44, provost for agr., 1949-55, pres., 1955-67; dir. div. grad. programs U.S. Office Edn., Washington, 1967-71; Rockefeller Found. cons. to rector Mahidol U., Bangkok, Thailand, 1971-73; dir. Council Internat. Studies and Programs, U. Fla., Gainesville, 1975—; dir. Jacksonville br. Fed. Res. Bank of Atlanta; econ. cons. United Growers and Shippers Assn., Orlando, Fla., 1944-48; chief citrus fruit div. Prodn. and Marketing Adminstrn., USDA, Washington, 1948-49; mem. Nat. Citrus Adv. Com., 1947-48; mem. adminstrv. com. Interam. Inst. Agrl. Scis., Turrialba, Costa Rica, 1952-56; bd. dirs. Escuela Agricola Panamericana, Honduras, 1954—; mem. Pres.'s Pub. Adv. Com. Trade Negotiations; cons. bd. agrl. scis. Rockefeller Found.; mem. study com. on NIH. Recipient Significant Sig award Sigma Chi, 1955; named Man of Year Fla. Agr. Progressive Farmer, 1957; decorated Cross Balboa, Republic Panama, 1961; Order of North Star, Sweden, 1979. Mem. Assn. State Univs. and Land-Grant Colls. (chmn. council presidents 1961), Nat. Commn. on Accrediting, Fla. Blue Key, Phi Alpha Delta, Alpha Phi Omega, Phi Kappa Phi, Alpha Zeta, Gamma Sigma Delta, Sigma Chi. Democrat. Presbyterian. Club: Cosmos. Author bulls. and articles on farm mgmt., farm finance and marketing, and univ adminstrn. to profl. jours. Home: 2105 NW 27 Terr Gainesville FL 32605 Office: JWR Union U Fla Gainesville FL 32611

REIZEN, MAURICE S., state ofcl., Mich.; b. Detroit, Feb. 24, 1919; s. Max and Minna (Chad) R.; B.A., U. Mich., Ann Arbor, 1940, M.S. in Pub. Health, 1946: tchrs. certificate Wayne State U., 1946; M.D., U. Rochester (N.Y.), 1950; m. Leanor Grossman, July 18, 1943; children—Mark E., Nancy E. Reizen Serlin, Bruce J. Intern Grace Hosp., Detroit, 1950-51: pvt. group practice Warren, Mich., 1951-66; dir. Ingham County (Mich.) Health Dept., 1966-70; dir. Mich. Dept. Pub. Health, Lansing, 1970—; asso. prof. medicine Coll. Human Medicine, Mich. State U., East Lansing, 1966—; non-resident lectr. U. Mich., Ann Arbor, 1974—. Served with USAAF, 1941-45. Fellow Am. Acad. Family Physicians; mem. AMA (physicians Recognition award 1969), Mich. Med. Soc. (citation 1978), Assn. State and Territorial Health Officers (pres. 1974). Home: 1915 Tomahawk Rd Okemos MI 48864 Office: 3500 N Logan St Lansing MI 48909

REKATE, ALBERT C., physician; b. Buffalo, June 12, 1916; s. Gustave E. and Fannie (Hummell) R.; M.D., U. Buffalo, 1940; m. Elizabeth Foster, June 12, 1943; 1 dau., Suzanne (Mrs. R. Willis Post). Intern, E.J. Meyer Meml. Hosp., 1940-41, med. resident, 1941-44; asst. prof. medicine State U. N.Y. at Buffalo, 1954-61, asso. prof., 1961-65, prof., 1965—, dir. rehab. medicine, 1965-72, acting dean Sch. Health Related Professions, 1965-66, asso. dean, 1966-74, acting chmn. dept. rehab. medicine, 1972-75; asso. dir. medicine E.J. Meyer Meml. Hosp., 1957-63, head dept. rehab. medicine, 1964-69, dir. primary rehab. center, 1965-69, acting head cardiology, 1966-69, dir., 1970-72. Pres., chmn. Research for Health in Erie County; bd. dirs. Buffalo Hearing and Speech Center. Served with M.C., AUS, World War II. Diplomate Am. Bd. Internal Medicine. Mem. Am., Western N.Y. (pres. 1954-55) heart assns., Assn. Am. Med. Colls., N.Y. State Heart Assembly, N.Y. Acad. Scis., Med. Union (pres. 1974-75), Buffalo Acad. Medicine (pres. 1969-70), Erie County Med. Soc., Med. Alumni Assn. U. Buffalo (pres. 1960-61). Contbr. articles to profl. jours. Home: 122 Hickory Hill Rd Williamsville NY 14221 Office: 462 Grider St Buffalo NY 14215

RELIC, PETER DONALD, govt. ofcl.; b. Cleve., May 22, 1936; s. Peter aNd Mary (Makar) R.; A.B., Bowdoin Coll., 1958; M.A., Case Western Res. U., 1961; Ed.D., Harvard U., 1973; m. Mary Jo Mehl, Oct. 22, 1966; children—Rebecca, Matthew, Peter. Tchr., Hawken Sch., Cleve., 1959-68; prin. Hawken Upper Sch., Cleve., 1963-68, Kyoto Internat. Sch., Japan, 1968-70; dir. edn. Middlesex County House of Correction, Billerica, Mass., 1971-72; asst. supt. schs., Pearl River, N.Y., 1972-75; supt. schs., Hamilton, Ohio, 1975-77; dep. asst. sec. for edn., HEW, Washington, 1977—; U.S. del. to UNESCO, OAS; cons. in field. Bd. dirs. YMCA, Hamilton, Ohio, 1975-77, Hamilton Safety Council, 1975-77, Univ. Regional Broadcasting, Dayton, Ohio, 1975-77, Tchrs. Center, Greenwich, Conn., 1974. Named Educator of Yr., Nat. Assn. Adminstrs. State and Fed. Edn. Programs, 1979. Mem. Am. Assn. Sch. Adminstrs., Assn. Supervision and Curriculum Devel., Nat. Soc. Study Edn., Phi Beta Kappa. Democrat. Roman Catholic. Contbr. articles to profl. jours. Home: 11921 Goya Dr Potomac MD 20854 Office: 310-G Humphrey Bldg Washington DC 20202

RELMAN, ARNOLD SEYMOUR, physician; b. N.Y.C., June 17, 1923; s. Simon and Rose (Mallach) R.; A.B., Cornell U., 1943; M.D., Columbia, 1946; m. Harriet Morse Vitkin, June 26, 1953; children—David Arnold, John Peter, Margaret Rose. House officer New Haven Hosp., Yale, 1946-49; NRC fellow Evans Meml., Mass. Meml. hosps., 1949-50; practice medicine, specializing in internal medicine, Boston, 1950-68, Phila., 1968-77; asst. prof., prof. medicine Boston U. Sch. Medicine, 1950-68, dir. Boston U. Med. Services, Boston City Hosp., 1967-68; prof. medicine, chmn. dept. medicine U. Pa.; chief med. services Hosp. of U. Pa., 1968-77; editor New Eng. Jour. Medicine, Boston, 1977—; physician Peter Bent Brigham Hosp., Boston, 1977—; prof. medicine Harvard Med. Sch., 1977—. Cons., NIH, USPHS. Recipient Columbia Bicentennial Med. Alumni award, 1967. Diplomate Am. Bd. Internal Medicine. Fellow Am. Acad. Arts and Scis., A.C.P.; mem. Assn. Am. Physicians (council), Am. Physiol. Soc., AMA, Mass. Med. Soc., Inst. Medicine of Nat. Acad. Scis. (council 1979—), Am. Soc. Clin. Investigation (past pres.), Am. Fedn. Clin. Research (past pres.), Phi Beta Kappa, Alpha Omega Alpha. Editor: Jour. Clin. Investigation, 1962-67; (with F.J. Ingelfinger and M. Finland) Controversy in Internal Medicine, Vol. 1, 1966, Vol. 2, 1974. Contbr. articles profl. jours. Office: New Eng Jour Medicine 10 Shattuck St Boston MA 02115

RELSON, MORRIS, patent lawyer; b. N.Y.C., Apr. 14, 1915; s. Benjamin and Minnie Relson; B.S., CCNY, 1935; M.A., George Washington U., 1940; J.D., N.Y. U., 1945; m. Rita L. Rubenstein, Apr. 5, 1941; children—Katherine D., David M., Peter J. Elec. engr. Nat. Park Service, 1936-37; patent examiner U.S. Patent Office, 1937-41; admitted to N.Y. State bar, 1945; patent agt. and atty. Sperry Gyroscope Co., Gt. Neck, N.Y., 1941-48; partner firm Darby & Darby, P.C., and predecessor, N.Y.C., 1948—; dir. Letraset USA Inc., Letraset Corp. Mem. Am. Bar Assn., Am. Patent Law Assn., N.Y. Patent Law Assn. (pres. 1976-77). Author, patentee in field. Home: 27 Tain Dr Great Neck NY 11021 Office: 405 Lexington Ave New York NY 10017

REMAK, HENRY HEYMANN HERMAN, educator; b. Berlin, Germany, July 27, 1916; s. Hans Ismar and Hedwig (Salz) R.; student Hochschule für Politik, Berlin, 1933-34; Certificat d'etudes francaises, Universite de Bordeaux, France, 1934; Licencie-es-Lettres, Universite de Montpellier, France, 1936; M.A., Ind. U., 1937; Ph.D., U. Chgo., 1947; Dr. h.c., U. Lille (France), 1973; m. Ingrid Miriam Grunfeld, Aug. 3, 1946; children—Roy Andrew, Steven Bruce, Renee June, Ronald Frank. Came to U.S., 1936, naturalized, 1943. Teaching asst. Ind. U., 1938-39, instr. German and Spanish, Indpls., 1939-43, instr., asst. prof., asso. prof., prof. German, Bloomington, 1946—, prof. comparative lit., 1963—, chmn. West European studies, 1966-71, vice chancellor, dean faculties, 1969-74; dir. Middlebury German Sch., 1967-71; Fulbright vis. prof. Universite de Lille, France, 1962-63, Universität Hamburg, Germany, 1967; vis. prof. U. Wis., summer 1964, Middlebury German Summer Sch., 1958, 60. Served to ensign U.S. Mcht. Marine, 1944-46. Recipient Herman F. Lieber award for distinguished teaching Ind. U., 1962; Guggenheim fellow, 1967-68; Nat. Endowment for Humanities research fellow, 1977-78, 78-79. Mem. AAUP, Modern Lang. Assn. Am. (editorial bd. publs. 1966-71), Internat. Comparative Lit. Assn. (pres., coordinating com.), Ind. Covered Bridge Soc., Sigma Alpha Mu (nat. scholarship chmn. 1960-66). Jewish. Asso. editor German Quar., 1958-62; editor Yearbook of German and Comparative Literature, 1961-78. Contbr. articles to profl. jours. Home: 1212 Maxwell Ln Bloomington IN 47401

REMBAR, CHARLES ISAIAH, lawyer, writer; b. Oceanport, N.J., Mar. 12, 1915; s. Louis S. and Rebecca (Schneider) Zaremba; A.B., Harvard, 1935; LL.B., Columbia, 1938; m. Billie Ann Olsson, Feb. 23, 1944; children—Lance Richard, James Carlson. Admitted to N.Y. bar, 1938; atty. govt. agencies, 1938-42, 45; law sec. N.Y. Supreme Ct., 1946; practice law, N.Y.C., 1947—. Served with USAAF, 1942-44. Recipient George Polk Meml. award for outstanding book of 1968, 1969. Mem. Assn. Bar City N.Y. (chmn. spl. com. on communications), Authors League, P.E.N. Clubs: Century Assn., Harvard (N.Y.C.). Author: The End of Obscenity, 1968, Perspective, 1975. Editor: Columbia Law Rev., 1936-38. Contbr. articles to various periodicals. Home: 190 Inwood Rd Scarsdale NY 10583 Office: 19 W 44th St New York City NY 10036

REMBERT, WILLIAM ADAIR, JR., lawyer; b. Seattle, Dec. 1, 1910; s. William Adair and Sarah Elizabeth (Stevenson) R.; B.S., Davidson Coll., 1931; LL.B., U. Tex., Austin, 1934; m. Jean Merriam, Feb. 14, 1970; children by previous marriage—William, Sally. Admitted to Tex. bar, 1934; practiced law, Dallas, 1935-40, 46—. Served with AUS, 1941-46; war crimes investigator Third Army, discovered Hitler correspondence in salt mine, Alt Aussee, Austria, 1945. Mem. Internat. Assn. Ins. Counsel, State Bar Tex. (vice chmn. grievance com. 1954-59, vice chmn. unauthorized practice of law com. 1958-69), S.A.R. Presbyterian. Club: Dallas Country. Home: 4205 Glenwood Dallas TX 75205 Office: 1313 Praetorian Bldg Dallas TX 75201

REMBOLT, RAYMOND RALPH, pediatrician, ret. hosp. adminstr., educator; b. Grand Island, Nebr., May 8, 1911; s. William Gustav and Lillian Elizabeth (Hershey) R.; A.B., U. Nebr., 1933, M.D., 1937; m. Mae Ione Street, Sept. 9, 1938; children—David, Diana, Richard. Extern, Evang. Covenant Hosp., Omaha, 1936-37; pediatric intern U. Minn. Hosps., Mpls., 1937-38; pvt. practice pediatrics Lincoln (Nebr.) Clinic, 1938-42, Lincoln Children's Clinic, 1947-48; resident dept. pediatrics State U. Iowa, 1946-47, successively asst. prof. pediatrics, asso. prof. pediatrics, 1948-52, prof. pediatrics, 1952-77, dir. U. Hosp. Sch., 1952-77, dir. State Services for Crippled Children, U. Iowa, 1948-52, dir. Birth Defects Center, 1966-70. Pres. Iowa Soc. Crippled Children and Adults, Inc., 1956-57; profl. adv. council Nat. Soc. Crippled Children and Adults, 1962-76; mem. nat. profl. services program com. Nat. United Cerebral Palsy Assns., 1966-72; mem. nat. adv. council div. developmental disabilities HEW, 1972-73, chmn. subcom. on univ. affiliated facilities, 1972-73, cons. to subcom., 1973. Served from lt. to lt. comdr., USNR, 1942-46. Fellow Am. Acad. Pediatrics (Iowa chmn. 1958-60), Am. Acad. Neurology, Am. Acad. Cerebral Palsy (sec.-treas. 1956-58, pres. 1960), Internat. Cerebral Palsy Soc. (spl. mem.). Methodist. Clubs: Optimist Internat. (boy's work dir. 9th dist. 1956-57, gov. 9th dist. 1957-58, dir. Internat. 1958-59, v.p. Internat. 1958-59, pres. Internat. 1961-62, chmn. leadership Tng. com. 1967-70, chmn. achievement com. 1970-72), Masons, Shriners. Home: PO Box 98 North Liberty IA 52317

REMER, VERNON RALPH, travel cons.; b. Urbana, Iowa, July 14, 1918; s. Ralph William and Kittie (Weisbard) R.; B.S., U. Iowa, 1939; m. Jane V. Bush, Sept. 19, 1941; children—Richard Charles, Linda Jane (Mrs. Joseph W. Hidy). With Central Life Assurance Co., Des Moines, Iowa, 1939—, sr. v.p., 1972-77; travel cons., 1977—; pres. Urbana Savs. Bank, 1944-64, dir., 1944-67. Precinct committeeman Republican party, 1952-60; mem. Polk County Rep. Central Com., 1953-56. Fellow Life Office Mgmt. Assn.; mem. Life Ins. Mktg. and Research Assn. (dir. 1971-74, chmn. agy. mgmt. conf. com. 1971—), Am. Soc. Travel Agts. (diploma), Sigma Nu. Congregationalist. Clubs: Masons, Des Moines. Home: 13018 Pomard Way Poway CA 92064

REMICK, LEE (MRS. WILLIAM RORY GOWENS), actress; b. Quincy, Mass., Dec. 14; d. Frank E. and Margaret (Waldo) Remick; student Barnard Coll., 1953; m. William A. Colleran, Aug. 3, 1957 (div. 1969); children—Kate, Matthew; m. 2d, William Rory Gowans, Dec. 18, 1970. Broadway debut in Be Your Age, 1953, other Broadway plays include Anyone Can Whistle, 1964, Wait Until Dark, 1966; films include A Face in the Crowd, 1956, The Long Hot Summer, 1957, Anatomy of a Murder, 1959, Wild River, 1959, Sanctuary, 1960, Experiment in Terror, 1961, Days of Wine and Roses, 1961, The Wheeler Dealers, 1962, Baby The Rain Must Fall, 1963, Hallelujah Trail, 1965, No Way to Treat a Lady, 1967, The Detective, 1968, Hard Contract, 1969, Loot, 1972, A Delicate Balance, 1973, Hennessy, 1974, The Omen, 1976, Telefon, 1977, The Europeans, 1979; appeared in TV prodn. Jennie, Lady Randolph Churchill, 1975; TV series Wheels, 1978; TV mini-series Haywire, 1980. Address: care Internat Creative Mgmt 8899 Beverly Blvd Los Angeles CA 90048

REMICK, OSCAR EUGENE, educator; b. Ellsworth, Maine, Aug. 24, 1932; s. Horace and Blanche (Rich) R.; A.B., Eastern Coll., 1954; B.D. magna cum laude, Eastern Baptist Theol. Sem., 1957; M.A., U.Pa., 1957; Ph.D., Boston U., 1966; student Columbia U., 1959-61, Andover Newton Theol. Sem., 1957-58, Heidelberg (Germany) U., 1958-59; postdoctoral study, India, 1967; D.D., Assumption Coll., 1971, Allegheny Coll., 1974; m. Emma L. Lorance, Dec. 18, 1959; children—Mark Stephen, John Andrew, Paul Thomas. Ordained minister Baptist Ch., 1957, ministerial standby United Presbyn. Ch. U.S.A.; minister United Baptist Ch., Tophsham, Maine, 1961-63; part-time instr. philosophy Bates Coll., 1962-63; minister First Congregational Ch., Paxton, Mass., 1963-66; asst. prof. philosophy and theology Assumption Coll., 1966-67, asso. prof., 1967-69, prof. religious studies, 1969—, v.p., acad. dean, coordinator acad. affairs, 1968-71, co-dir. ecumenical Inst. Religious Studies, 1967-71. Minister theol. studies First Baptist Ch., Worcester, Mass., 1966-71; pres Chautauqua (N.Y.) Instn., 1971-77; lectr. State U. N.Y., 1972—, prof. philosophy, dean for arts and humanities, dir. internat. edn., 1977—; theologian-in-residence First Presbyn. Ch., Jamestown, N.Y. Pres. Worcester Area Council Chs., 1970-71; mem. N.Y. State Council on Arts. Bd. dirs. No. Chautaugua County YMCA, CAPS. Mem. Am., Am. Cath. philos. assns., Am. Philos. Assn., Coll. Theology Soc., Soc. Advancement Continuing Edn. for Ministry, Am. Acad. Clergy, Paul Tillich Soc. N. Am. (dir.), Am. Assn. Higher Edn., Soc. Sci. Study Religion, Am. Conf. Acad. Deans, Am. Acad. Religion, N.Am. Acad. Ecumenists, Soc. for Arts, Religion and Contemporary Culture. Author: Value in the Thought of Paul Tillich; Christianity and Other Major Religions, 1968; India and Hinduism, 1968; Responding to God's Call, 1970; The Hidden Crisis in Education, 1971. Office: Dean Arts Humanities and Internat Edn State U NY Fredonia NY 14063

REMINGTON, FRANK JOHN, lawyer; b. Schenectady, Feb. 10, 1922; s. Michael John and Margaret (Flood) R.; student Union Coll., 1946; B.S., U. Wis., 1947, LL.B., 1949; postgrad. U. Mich., 1949; m. Susan S. Stone, Apr. 29, 1944; children—Michael, James, Thomas, Patrick, Ann, Frank. Admitted to Wis. bar, 1949; mem. law faculty U. Wis., 1949—, asst. prof. law, 1949-52, asso. prof., 1952-55, prof., 1955—; prof. U. Minn., 1970-71; project dir. Am. Bar Found. Survey Adminstrn. Criminal Justice in U.S., 1956-59; bd. dirs. Police Found.; chmn. Wis. Public Defender Bd., 1978—; Wis. athletic rep. to Big 10; mem. rules infractions com. Nat. Collegiate Athletic Assn.; mem. standing com. rules of practice and procedure U.S. Supreme Ct. Wis. athletic rep. Western Coll. Hockey Assn. Served with USAAF, 1943-46. Decorated D.F.C., Air medal. Mem. Am. Bar Assn., Wis. Bar Assn., Am. Law Inst., Internat. Assn. Chiefs of Police, Wis. Nordic Ski Found. (pres.). Roman Catholic. Author: Cases and Materials on Criminal Law and Its Procedures, 1969; (with others) Criminal Justice Administration, 1969; editor: Am. Bar Found. Series on Adminstr. of Criminal Justice in U.S., 1965-70. Home: 1224 Dartmouth Rd Madison WI 53705 Office: U Wis Law Sch Madison WI 53706

REMINGTON, PAUL ELLSWORTH, utility cons.; b. Boulder, Colo., Nov. 29, 1894; s. Walter Wood and Sarah Lucinda (Porter) R.; B.A. magna cum laude, U. Colo., 1917; m. Nondus Idona Maurer, Sept. 1, 1979. With Mountain States Tel. & Tel. Co., 1912-58, auditor disbursements, 1924-28, chief accountant, 1928-36, comptroller, 1936-51, v.p., 1951-58; pub. utility cons., 1958—; lectr. Bus., U. Colo., 1960-65. Sec., dir., trustee, chmn. bldg. com. Denver Met. YMCA, 1950—. Mem. Nat. Accounting Assn. (past nat. dir., pres. Denver), Phi Beta Kappa, Phi Beta Kappa Assos., Beta Gamma Sigma, Beta Alpha Psi, Delta Sigma Pi, Acacia. Methodist. Clubs: Kiwanis, Univ. (Boulder); Lakewood Country (Denver); Masons (32 deg.), Shriners. Home: 350 Ponca Pl Boulder CO 80303

REMINI, ROBERT VINCENT, educator, historian; b. N.Y.C., July 17, 1921; s. William Francis and Lauretta (Tierney) R.; B.S., Fordham U., 1943; M.A., Columbia U., 1947, Ph.D., 1951; m. Ruth Theresa Kuhner, Oct. 9, 1948; children—Elizabeth Mary, Joan Marie, Robert William. Instr., Fordham U., 1947-51, asst. prof., 1951-59, asso. prof., 1959-65; prof. dept. history U. Ill., Chgo. Circle, 1965—, chmn. dept., 1965-66, 67-71; vis. lectr. Columbia, 1959-60. Served with USNR, 1943-46. Recipient Encaenia award Fordham U., 1963; grantee Am. Council Learned Socs., 1964, Am. Philos. Soc., 1966; Guggenheim fellow, 1978-79. Mem. Am. (council 1979—), So. hist. assns., Orgn. Am. Historians. Author: Martin Van Buren and the Making of the Democratic Party, 1959; The Election of Andrew Jackson, 1963; Andrew Jackson, 1966; Andrew Jackson and the Bank War, 1968; The Revolutionary Age of Andrew Jackson, 1976 (award of merit Friends of Am. Writers); Andrew Jackson and the Course of American Empire, 1767-1821, 1977; co-author We the People: A History of the United States, 1975, The Era of Good Feelings and the Age of Jackson, 1816-1841, 1979, also articles, chpts. in books. Editor: the Decline of Aristocracy in the Politics of New York, 1965; The Presidency of Andrew Jackson, 1967; The Age of Jackson, 1972; spl. editor Am. history Crowell-Collier Co., 1960-68, 72-73; editorial bd. Jour. Am. History, 1969-72; editorial cons. Papers of Andrew Jackson, 1972—. Home: 215 9th St Wilmette IL 60091 Office: Dept History U Ill Chicago Circle Chicago IL 60680

REMKE, ROBERT LANG, food co. exec.; b. N.Y.C., Feb. 14, 1925; s. Hugo Edward and Janet (Lang) R.; B.A., Northwestern U., 1945, M.B.A., 1948; m. Joyce Dix, Oct. 2, 1948; children—Katherine Joy Remke Blagden. With Procter & Gamble Co., 1948-75, mgr. instl. cleaning products div., Cin., 1969-75; exec. v.p., then pres. R.J. Reynolds Foods div. RJR, Inc., Winston-Salem, N.C., 1975-77, chmn. bd., chief exec. officer, 1977—; tchr. sales mgmt. Chgo. campus Northwestern U., 1956-57. Mem. Indian Hill (Ohio) Sch. Bd., 1971-75, pres., 1972-73; bd. dirs., v.p., exec. com. N.C. Sch. Arts Found., 1976—; past mem. session, elder Indian Hill Presbyn. Ch. Served to lt. (j.g.) USNR, 1943-46. Mem. Beta Gamma Sigma. Republican. Clubs: University (Mexico City); Old Town, Twin City (Winston-Salem); Masons. Home: 1020 Kent Rd W Winston-Salem NC 27104 Office: PO Box 3037 Winston-Salem NC 27102

REMPEL, ARTHUR GUSTAV, conservationist, educator; b. Ukraine, Russia, Jan. 5, 1910; s. Gustav Aron and Elisabeth (Dirks) R.; brought to U.S., 1923, naturalized, 1931; A.B., Oberlin Coll., 1934; Ph.D., U. Calif. at Berkeley, 1938; m. Lucile Elma Sommerfield, June 19, 1934; children—Robert Arthur (dec.), Herbert Frank, Paul Leonard (dec.), Margaret Louise, Roland Richard. Acting curator Mus. Zoology and Anthropology, Oberlin (Ohio) Coll., 1931-34; teaching asst. zoology U. Calif. at Berkeley, 1934-38; mem. faculty Whitman Coll., 1938—, prof. biology, 1949-75, prof. biology emeritus, 1975—. Vis. asso. prof. biology U. Calif. at Berkeley, summer 1949; vis. prof. biology U. Wash., summers 1957, 58, vis. prof., summers 1966, 67; ranger-historian Whitman Nat. Monument, summers 1953, 54; ranger naturalist Yosemite Nat. Park, summer 1955; research asso. zoology Wash. State U., summer 1956. Mem. AAUP, AAAS, Nat. Geog. Soc., Nat. Parks and Conservation Assn., Friends of the Earth, Nature Conservancy, Save the Redwoods League, Defenders of Wildlife, East African Wild Life Soc., Wilderness Soc., Audubon Soc., Phi Beta Kappa, Sigma Xi. Congregationalist. Home: 635 University St Walla Walla WA 99362

REMPEL, AVERNO MILTON, ednl. adminstr.; b. Saskatoon, Sask., Can., Feb. 15, 1919; s. George S. and Lena (Schultz) R.; B.A., U. Sask., 1940, B.Ed., 1949; M.Ed., U. Omaha, 1951; Ph.D., State U. Iowa, 1954; m. Wendlyn Otti Reimer, July 6, 1944; children—Donna Lynn, Deborah Ann, Gerard Taves. Came to U.S., 1949. Sch. prin., tchr., Lipton, Sask., Can., 1941-43; tchr. Steinbach (Man.) Collegiate Inst., 1943-46; prin. schs., Steinbach, 1946-49; instr. U. Omaha, 1950-51; research asst. State U. Iowa, 1951-54, sec. Interdepartmental Com. on World Affairs, 1952-54; dean State Tchrs. Coll., Minot, N.D., 1954-57; exec. asst. div. edn. Purdue U., 1957-62, head dept. edn., 1962-64; pres. Eastern Oreg. Coll., La Grande, 1964-73; asst vice chancellor Oreg. System of Higher Edn., Eugene, 1974—. Mem. exec. com. Nat. Commn. on Accrediting, v.p., 1972—; bd. dirs. Nat. Council for Accreditation Tchr. Edn. Bd. dirs. United Fund, 1964—. Mem. Internat. Council Edn. For Tchrs., Am. Ednl. Research Assn., AAUP, Assn. For Supervision and Curriculum Devel., Oreg. Edn. Assn. (ednl. policy com.), Am. Assn. State Colls. and Univs. (rep. nat. commn. on accrediting), Am. Assn. Colls. for Tchr. Edn. (rep. to nat. council for accreditation of higher edn.), Union County C. of C. (dir.), Kappa Delta Pi, Phi Sigma Pi, Phi Delta Kappa. Clubs: Rotary, Lions, Kiwanis. Contbr. articles to profl. jours. Home: 2405 Olive St Eugene OR 97405

REMPFER, ROBERT WEIR, educator; b. Parkston, S.D., Apr. 14, 1914; s. William Christian and Helen Irene (Weir) R.; B.S. summa cum laude, U. S.D., 1933; M.S., Northwestern U., 1934; Ph.D. in Math., U. Ill., 1937; m. Gertrude Marjorie Fleming, Sept. 25, 1942; children—Richard Fleming, Jean Trudi, Anne Louise (dec.), William Curry, Rhoda Anne. Mem. faculty Rensselaer Polytech. Inst., 1937-44; with Manhattan Project, Columbia, 1944-45; math. physicist Farrand Optical Co., N.Y., 1945-50; prof. math. Antioch Coll., 1950-53, Fisk U., 1953-57; prof. math. Portland (Oreg.) State U., 1957—, chmn. dept., 1957-61; adj. prof. biostatistics U. Oreg. Dental Sch., 1969—. Translator, Cons.' Bur., Plenum Pub. Corp., 1969—; v.p. Applied Math. Assos., Inc., Portland, 1962-71; dir. NSF Summer Insts., Portland State U., 1958, 63, 64; lectr. Oreg. Acad. Sci., 1963-64. Mem. AAUP (pres. Oreg. State Fedn. 1962-63), NAACP (life), Soc. Indsl. and Applied Math., Math. Assn. Am. (lectr. 1960-63), Am. Math. Soc. Home: Box 268B Route 1 Forest Grove OR 97116 Office: Portland State U Math Dept Portland OR 97207

REMSEN, CHARLES CORNELL, JR., lawyer, indsl. property cons.; b. Newark, Dec. 3, 1908; s. Charles Cornell and Edna (Fisk) R.; E.E., Cornell U., Ithaca, N.Y., 1930; LL.B., George Washington U., 1934; m. Elizabeth Havens Atwood, July 1, 1933; children—Elizabeth Havens Remsen Fetz, Charles Cornell III, Derek Minor. Admitted to D.C. bar, 1934, N.Y. bar, 1941; examiner U.S. Patent Office, 1931-36; partner firm Dicke & Remsen, N.Y.C., 1936-46; with ITT, N.Y.C., 1942-75, asst. v.p., 1960-74, gen. patent counsel, 1961-73; v.p., dir. ITT Farnsworth Research Corp., 1960-75; v.p. Internat. Standard Electric Corp., 1961-74, ITT Industries, Europe Inc., 1964-75; partner firm Bierman & Bierman, N.Y.C., 1976—. Mem. N.Y. Patent Law Assn., Electronics Industry Assn., Am. Belgian Assn. (dir. 1948-49), Nat. Fgn. Trade Council, Assn. Corporate Patent Counsel (sec.-treas. 1967-69), Internat. (U.S. patent com.), U.S. (patent adv. com.) chambers commerce, Pacific Indsl. Property Assn. (gov. 1973—, pres. 1974), Alpha Tau Omega, Eta Kappa Nu. Episcopalian. Clubs: Cornell (N.Y.C.); Cosmos (Washington). Home: Millbrook Rd New Vernon NJ 07976 Office: care Bierman and Bierman 437 Madison Ave New York NY 10022

RENAUD, BERNADETTE MARIE ELISE, author; b. Ascot Corner, Que., Can., Apr. 18, 1945; d. Albert and Aline (Audet) R.; diploma Présentation de Marie, Granby, Que., 1962-64; m. Pierre La Brosse, May, 1973. Librarian asst. Schs. of Waterloo (Que.), 1964-67, tchr. primary schs., 1967-70; adminstrv. sec. Assn. Medi-Tech-Sci., Montreal, Que., 1972-76; author: Emilie La Baignoire A Pattes, 1976 (Can. Council Children's Lit. prize 1976, Assn. Advancement of Scis. and Technics of Documentation award 1976); adaptations of 7 children's classics, 1977; 14 Short Stories for Young Children, 1978; Le Chat de l'Oratoire, 1978; Emilie la baignoire à pattes (album), 1978; La maison tête de pioche, 1979; La révolte de la courte pointe, 1979; mem. adminstrv. bd. Communication-Jeunesse, 1977—. Chief sub-scouts St. Hyacinthe Boy Scouts, Waterloo, 1963-67. Canada

RENCHARD, WILLIAM SHRYOCK, banker; b. Trenton, N.J., Jan. 1, 1908; s. John A. and Lillian C. (Smith) R.; A.B., Princeton, 1928; m. Alice Marie Fleming, Dec. 7, 1935; children—Alice Eugenia (Mrs. Tony G. Ziluca), Christine F. (Mrs. Byron Keith Huffman, Jr.), Cynthia W. (Mrs. Seth Barton French III). Clk., National Bank of Commerce, N.Y.C., 1928-29; successively clk., asst. sec., asst. v.p. Chem. Bank & Trust Co., 1930-46, v.p., 1946-55; exec. v.p. Chem. Corn Exchange Bank, N.Y.C., 1955-60; pres., dir. Chem. Bank N.Y. Trust Co., 1960-66; chmn., chief exec. officer, dir. Chem. Bank N.Y., 1966-73, chmn. exec. com., 1973-78, now chmn. dirs.' adv. com.; dir. N.Y. Life Ins. Co., Borden Inc., N.Y.C., Amenada Hess Corp., N.Y.C., Baldwin Securities Corp., N.Y.C., Cleve.-Cliffs Iron Co.; trustee C.I. Realty Investors, Boston, Consol. Edison Co. N.Y., Inc. Bd. dirs. United Hosp. Fund N.Y.; bd. dirs., pres. Manhattan Eye, Ear and Throat Hosp., N.Y.C.; hon. chmn., trustee emeritus N.Y.C. Citizens Budget Commn., Inc.; mem. council Internat. Exec. Service Corps, N.Y.C. Served as lt. USNR, 1943-45. Mem. Navy Price Adjustment Bd., Apr.-Dec. 1945. Mem. Newcomen Soc. Eng., Pa. Soc. (v.p.), Nat. Inst. Social Scis., UN Assn. U.S.A. (gov.), Pilgrims U.S. Republican. Episcopalian. Clubs: Rolling Rock (Ligonier, Pa.); Meadowbrook (Jericho, L.I.); Univ., Pinnacle, Bond, Links (N.Y.C.); The Creek (gov.) (Locust Valley, L.I.); Alfalfa (Washington); Garden of the Gods (Colorado Springs, Colo.); Lyford Cay (Bahamas). Home: Hegeman's Ln Old Brookville NY 11545 Office: 277 Park Ave New York City NY 10017

RENCHER, DONALD L., U.S. atty.; b. Hawthorne, Calif., July 6, 1941; s. Joseph Lynn and Aften (Flake) R.; B.A., Brigham Young U., Provo, Utah, 1965; J.D., U. Utah, 1968; m. Eileen Bunnell, June 4, 1964; children—Rachel, Jennie and Jefferson (twins), Lynette, Carley. Admitted to Utah bar, 1968; mem. firm Kunz, Kunz & Rencher, Ogden, 1968-77; mem. Utah Ho. of Reps., 1971-77, minority whip, 1973-75, speaker, 1975-77; U.S. atty., Salt Lake City, 1977—. Bd. dirs. Utah Symphony; trustee Utah State Library Commn.; chmn. rules com. Democratic State Conv., 1972. Mem. Am. Bar Assn., Fed. Bar Assn., Utah Bar Assn. Mormon. Office: US Attorney's Office 350 S Main St Salt Lake City UT 84101

RENDA, DOMINIC PHILLIP, airline co. exec.; b. Steubenville, Ohio, Dec. 25, 1913; s. Joseph J. and Catherine (Roberta) R.; B.S. in Bus. Adminstrn., J.D., Ohio State U., 1938; children—Dominique Patricia, Dominic Phillip, Patrick Blake. Admitted to Ohio bar, 1938; practice law, Steubenville, 1938-41; adminstrv. asst. to mem. Congress, 1941-42; with Western Air Lines, Inc., Los Angeles, 1946-68, asst. sec., 1947, v.p. legal, 1954-65, sr. v.p. legal, corp. sec., 1958-68; pres. Air Micronesia, Inc., Los Angeles, 1968-73; sr. v.p. internat. and pub. affairs Continental Air Lines, Inc., 1968-73; exec. v.p., dir., mem. exec. com. Western Air Lines, 1973-76, pres., mem. exec. and nominating coms., 1976—, chief exec. officer, mem. compensation com., 1979—; dir. Bank of Montreal (Calif.). Mem. bus. adminstrn. adv. council Coll. Adminstrv. Sci., Ohio State U., 1974—, mem. alumni adv. bd., 1976—; bd. councilors Sch. Internat. Relations U. So. Calif., 1967—; trustee Peace Found., Ponape, Caroline Islands, 1976—; bd. dirs. So. Calif. region NCCJ; chmn. devel. com. Marymount High Sch., 1977—. Served to lt. comdr. USNR, 1942-46. Mem. Calif., Ohio state bars, Am., Los Angeles County (past trustee) bar assns., Los Angeles Area C. of C. (dir.), Phi Alpha Delta (pres. Los Angeles 1965-66). Clubs: Los Angeles Chancery (pres. 1966-67), Los Angeles Athletic, Bel-Air Country, Riviera Country, Calif., Marina City. Office: 6060 Avion Dr Los Angeles CA 90045

RENDA, RANDOLPH BRUCE, univ. dean; b. Tokat, Turkey, Mar. 31, 1926; s. Abdurrahman and Adviye (Adams) R.; came to U.S., 1945, naturalized, 1956; B.S., Purdue U., 1952, M.S. 1957, Ph.D. (Proctor and Gamble fellow), 1959; m. Martha McDowell Hill, Aug. 30, 1948; children—William, Suzan, Bennett, Lyle, Bruce. Project engr. Nat. Castings Co., Indpls., 1951-53; instr. mfg. processes Purdue U., Lafayette, Ind., 1953-55, instr. mech. engring., 1955-59; asst. prof. U. Ky., 1959-60, Swarthmore (Pa.) Coll., 1960-61; asso. prof. U. Ky., 1961-65; prof., chmn. mech. engring. U. Louisville, 1966-72, asso. dean, dir. Inst. Indsl. Research, 1972-74; dean Sch. Engring. and Tech., Purdue U. at Indpls., 1974—. Cons. Spindletop Research, Inc., Lexington, Ky., Besmar Assos., Knoxville, Pratt & Whitney Co., West Hartford, Conn., Glove Valve Co., Delphi, Ind. Trustee St. Francis Sch., Louisville, 1968-70. Mass. Inst. Tech. summer fellow, 1960; NSF fellow, 1961; NASA/Case Inst. summer fellow, 1964, 65. Mem. Am. Soc. M.E. (pres. 1969), Louisville Engring. Socs. Council, Am. Soc. Engring. Edn., Nat., Ky. socs. profl. engrs., Soc. Engring. Sci., Sigma Xi, Sigma Tau, Pi Tau Sigma. Rotarian. Club: Columbia. Home: 4515 Somerset Way South Carmel IN 46032 Office: Sch Engring and Tech Purdue U at Indpls 799 W Michigan St Indianapolis IN 46202

RENDELL-BAKER, LESLIE, educator, anesthesiologist; b. St. Helens, Eng., Mar. 27, 1917; s. Frank Nelder and Ada (Gill) Rendell-B.; M.B., B.S., Guy's Hosp. Med. Sch., London, Eng., 1941; m. Rosemary Carr Hogg, Aug. 17, 1946; children—Sheila Diane, Helen Rosemary, Frances Nelda. Came to U.S., 1957, naturalized, 1963. Resident anesthesia Brit. Army of Rhine Hosps., 1945-46, Guy's Hosp., London, 1946-48; sr. asst. (asso. prof.) anesthesiology Welsh Nat. Sch. Medicine, Cardiff, 1948-57; Fulbright asst. prof. anesthesiology U. Pitts., 1955-56; from asst. prof. to asso. prof. Western Res. U. Sch. Medicine, Cleve., 1957-62; dir. dept. anesthesiology Mt. Sinai Hosp., N.Y.C., 1962—, prof., chmn. dept. anesthesiology, 1966—. Chmn. sect. com. Z79 standards for anesthesia and respiratory equipment Am. Nat. Standards Instn., 1962-68, vice chmn., 1969—, mem. exec. com. med. devices standards mgmt. bd., 1973—, bd. dirs., 1976—; chmn. classification panel on anesthesiology devices FDA, 1972-76. Served to capt. Royal Army Med. Corps, 1942-46. Diplomate Am. Bd. Anesthesiology. Fellow faculty anesthetists Royal Coll. Surgeons; fellow Royal Soc. Medicine, Assn. Anaesthetists Gt. Britain and Ireland; mem. Am. Soc. Anesthesiologists (chmn. com. equipment and standardization 1962-68), Am. Soc. for Testing and Materials, Nat. Fire Protection Assn., N.Y. Acad. Medicine, N.Y. Acad. Scis., Am., Brit. med. assns., Assn. Advancement Med. Instrumentation (mem. standards bd., co-chmn. subcom. on sterile disposable devices and ethylene oxide sterilization, mem. subcom. on sterilization), A.A.A.S. Author: (with W.W. Mushin) Principles of Thoracic Anesthesia, 1953; (with W.W. Mushin and Thompson) Automatic Ventilation of the Lungs, 3d edit. 1979. Editor chpts. in books; Inventor baby endotracheal connector, pediatric face masks and equipment. Home: 9 Autenreith Rd Scarsdale NY 10583 Office: Dept Anesthesiology Mount Sinai Hosp 100th St and Fifth Ave New York NY 10029

RENDTORFF, ROBERT CARLISLE, physician, educator; b. Carlisle, Pa., Mar. 22, 1915; s. Walter and Meta (Kordenat) R.; A.B., U. Ill., 1937, M.S., 1939; Sc.D., Johns Hopkins, 1944, M.D., 1949; m. Kathryn Seiler, June 15, 1937 (dec. Feb. 1979); 1 dau., Linda; m. 2d, Fanny Coker, June 2, 1979; stepchildren—Elizabeth Coker, Kennith Coker. Entomologist, U. Ill., Champaign, 1938-39; instr. virology lab. U. Mich. Ann Arbor, 1942-44; malariologist-entomologist, div. malariology Ministry Health, Maracay, Venezuela, 1946; asst. prof. community medicine U. Tenn., Memphis, 1955-58; asso. prof., 1958-65, prof., 1965—; dir. div. communicable disease Memphis-Shelby County Health Dept., 1967-75; acting health officer Memphis-Shelby County Health Dept., 1979—. Served as surgeon, USPHS, NIH Lab. Tropical Diseases, 1950-55. Editor: Tenn. Med. Alumnus, 1968—; research in entomology, parasitology, virology, epidemiology of acute communicable diseases. Home: 276 Buena Vista St Memphis TN 38112

RENEHAN, ROBERT FRANCIS XAVIER, educator; b. Boston, Apr. 25, 1935; s. Francis Xavier and Ethel Mary (Sullivan) R.; A.B., Boston Coll., Chestnut Hill, Mass., 1956; A.M., Harvard, 1958, Ph.D., 1963; m. Joan Lee Axtell-Damerow, Sept. 9, 1966; children—Martin, Sharon, Stephen, Judith, John. Instr. Greek and Latin, U. Calif. at Berkeley, 1963-64; instr. Harvard, 1964-65; asst. prof. Boston Coll., 1966-69, asso. prof., 1969-71, prof., 1971-77, chmn. dept. classical studies, 1969-77; prof. Greek and Latin, U. Calif. at Santa Barbara, 1976—. Nat. Endowment for Humanities Sr. fellow, 1972-73. Mem. Am. Philol. Assn. Author: Greek Textual Criticism, 1969; Leo Medicus, 1969; Greek Lexicographical Notes, 1975; Studies in Greek Texts, 1975. Asso. editor Classical Philology, 1976—. Contbr. numerous articles to profl. jours. Office: Dept of Classics Univ of Calif Santa Barbara CA 93106

RENEKER, ROBERT WILLIAM, diversified industry exec.; b. Chgo., Aug. 4, 1912; s. William Turner and Mary Ethel (Gilmour) R.; Ph.B., U. Chgo., 1933; spl. course Harvard, 1954; m. Eva Elizabeth Congdon, Mar. 2, 1935; children—William Carl, David Lee. With purchasing dept. Swift & Co., Chgo., 1934-44, asst. office of v.p. charge purchasing, 1944-46, tech. product sales, 1946-50, asst. in office of pres., 1950-55, 1955-64, pres., 1964-73, chief exec. officer, 1967-73, also dir.; pres., chief exec. officer Esmark, Inc., 1973, chmn., chief exec. officer, 1973-77; dir. Continental Ill. Bank, Gen. Dynamics Co., Chgo. Tribune, Trans Union Co., Jewel Cos., Inc., U.S. Gypsum Co., Lawter Chem., Inc., Morton Norwich. Nat. bd. dirs. Boy Scouts Am.; bd. dirs. Mus. Sci. and Industry; chmn. bd. trustees U. Chgo. Mem. United Ch. Clubs: Chicago, Commercial, Economics, Mid-Am., Chgo. Sunday Evening. Home: 1300 Lake Shore Dr Chicago IL 60610 Office: 2716 1 First Nat Plaza Chicago IL 60603

RENFREW, CHARLES BYRON, dist. judge; b. Detroit, Oct. 31, 1928; s. Charles Warren and Louise (McGuire) R.; A.B., Princeton, 1952; J.D., U. Mich., 1956; m. Susan Wheelock, June 28, 1952; children—Taylor Allison Ingham, Charles Robin, Todd Wheelock, James Bartlett. Admitted to Calif. bar, 1956; asso. firm Pillsbury, Madison & Sutro, San Francisco, 1956-65, partner, 1965-72; U.S. dist. judge No. Dist. Calif., San Francisco, 1972—; mem. exec. com. 9th Circuit Jud. Conf., 1976-78; Congl. liaison com. 9th Circuit Jud. Council, 1976—; mem. spl. com. to propose standards for admission to practice in fed. cts. U.S. Jud. Conf., 1976—; co-chmn. San Francisco Lawyers Com. for Urban Affairs, 1971-72; mem. San Francisco Com. for Performing Arts Center, 1970—; bd. dirs. Internat. Hospitality Center, 1961-74, pres., 1967-70; bd. dirs. San Francisco Symphony Found., 1964—, pres., 1971-72; bd. dirs. Council for Civic Unity, 1968-72, pres., 1971-72; bd. dirs. Opportunity Through Ownership, 1969-72, 150 Parker St. Sch., 1969-71, Marin Country Day Sch., 1972-74, Jr. Achievement San

Alexandria, 1969), Westwood Country (v.p. 1977-78). Contbr. articles to legal jours. Home: 4008 Harris Pl Alexandria VA 22304 Office: 1775 Pennsylvania Ave Washington DC 20006

REPLINGER, JOHN GORDON, architect; b. Chgo., Nov. 9, 1923; s. Roy Lodawick and Dorothy Caroline (Thornstrom) R.; B.S. in Architecture with highest honors, U. Ill., Urbana, 1949, M.S. in Architecture, 1952; m. Dorothy Thiele, June 26, 1945; children—John Gordon, Robert Louis, James Alan. Designer-draftsman, L. Morgan Yost, Architect, Kenilworth, Ill., 1949-50; instr. U. Ill., 1951-53, asst. prof. architecture, 1953-57, asso. prof. architecture, 1957-61, prof. architecture, 1961—, prof. housing research and devel., 1972—, asso. head dept. for acad. affairs, 1970-71; practice architecture, Urbana, 1951—; cons. mem. housing com. AIA Commn. on Envrion. and Design. Served with USAAF, 1943-45. Decorated Air medal with oak leaf cluster; recipient Sch. medal AIA, 1949, List of Tchrs. Ranked as Excellent by Their Students award U. Ill., 1976, 77, 78; Allerton Am. travelling scholar, 1948; registered architect, Ill. Mem. Urban Land Inst., Nat. Trust Hist. preservation. Home: 4 Burnett Circle Urbana IL 61801 Office: Dept Architecture U Ill Urbana IL 61801

REPLOGLE, FREDERICK ALLEN, mgmt. psychologist; b. Rossville, Ind., Dec. 15, 1898; s. William H. and Elizabeth (Metzger) R.; B.A., Manchester Coll., Ind., 1921, LL.D., 1956, M.A., Northwestern U., 1927; Ph.D., U. Chgo., 1936; m. Georgia Miller, Sept. 8, 1926; children—Justin, Carol Ann (Mrs. Christian Nielsen). Pub. sch. adminstrn., Ind., 1921-26; asso. dir. research Meth. Bd. of Edn., Chgo., 1928-31; dean, prof. edn. and psychology McPherson Coll., 1931-35; dean, head sociology dept. Oklahoma City U., 1935-38; personnel dir. Macalester Coll., St. Paul, 1938-43; supr. Chgo. region psychol. services Stevenson, Jordan & Harrison, Chgo., 1943-45; founding partner Rohrer, Hibler & Replogle, Inc., mgmt. psychologists, 1945—, dir. Chgo. region, 1945-68, cons., 1968—. Pres. bd. trustees, former chmn. bd. YMCA Met. Chgo.; former bd. mem. nat. bd., former vice chmn. YMCA, N.Y.C.; mem. adv. council U. Chgo. Sch. Bus.; hon. mem. bd., past chmn. bd. Chgo. Theol. Sem.; vice chmn. bd. trustees George Williams Coll., Chgo.; hon. trustee Manchester Coll.; vice chmn. Ch. Fedn. Greater Chgo.; v.p., bd. dirs. Protestant Found. Greater Chgo.; bd. dirs. World Without War Council Inc. Diplomate Am. Bd. Profl. Psychology. Fellow Am. Psychol. Assn., AAAS; mem. Soc. Advancement Mgmt., Mid-Western, Ill., Chgo. psychol. assns., Am. Guidance and Personnel Assn., Religious Edn. Assn. (dir.). Clubs: Execs., Univ., Plaza (Chgo.); Rotary. Home: 19200 Dixie Hwy Flossmoor IL 60422 Office: 55 E Monroe St Chicago IL 60603

REPLOGLE, THOMAS HARVEY, naval officer; b. Pitts., June 4, 1929; s. Ned Ellsworth and Kathrine Joyce (Baer) R.; B.S., U.S. Navy Postgrad. Sch., Monterey, Calif., 1963; m. Mary Jane Martens, May 29, 1971; children—Susan, Terri, Jannett, Kim, Carol, Margaret, Thomas Harvey. Commd. ensign U.S. Navy, 1951, advanced through grades to rear adm., 1975; fighter pilot in Korea, Vietnam; comdr. U.S.S. America, 1973-74; chief staff 7th Fleet, 1974-75; insp. gen. Atlantic Fleet, 1975-78; comdr. Tactical Wings Atlantic, Naval Air Sta., Oceana, Va., 1978—. Decorated Legion of Merit, D.F.C., Bronze Star, Air medal (23), Navy Commendation medal (5). Mem. U.S. Naval Inst., Assn. Naval Aviation. Address: Comdr Tactical Wings Atlantic Naval Air Sta Oceana VA 23460

REQUARTH, WILLIAM HENRY, surgeon; b. Charlotte, N.C., Jan. 23, 1913; s. Charles William and Amelia (George) R.; A.B., Millikin U., 1934; M.D., U. Ill., 1938, M.S., 1939; m. Nancy Charlton, 1948 (div. 1966); children—Kurt, Betsy, Jeff, Jan. Intern St. Luke's Hosp., Chgo., 1938-39; resident Cook County Hosp., Chgo., 1940-42, 46-48; pvt. practice medicine, specializing in surgery, Decatur, Ill., 1950—; clin. prof. surgery U. Ill. Med. Sch., 1962—. Mem. Chgo. Bd. Trade. Chmn. trustees Millikin U.; chmn. James Millikin Found.; bd. dirs. Decatur Meml. Hosp. Served to comdr. USNR, 1941-46. Diplomate Am. Bd. Surgery. Mem. A.C.S., Central, Western surg. assns., Chgo., Ill. (pres. 1970-71) surg. socs., Am. Soc. Surgery Hand, Am. Soc. Surgery Trauma, Soc. Surgery Alimentary Tract, Warren Cole Soc., Nat. Pilots Assn. (pres. 1960-61), Soaring Soc. Am., Sportsman Pilot Assn., Internat. Aerobatic Club. Author: Diagnosis of Abdominal Pain, 1953; The Acute Abdomen, 1958; also contbg. author chpts. books. Home: 477 S Edward St Decatur IL 62521 Office: 1 Memorial Dr Decatur IL 62526

RERES, MARY EPIPHANY, univ. dean; b. Kansas City, Mo., Jan. 31, 1941; d. Mathew and Mary Ellen (Connelly) R.; B.S. in Nursing, Creighton U., Omaha, 1963; M.Psychiat. Nursing, U. Nebr., 1965; Ed.D., Columbia U., 1970. Staff nurse Nebr. Psychiat. Inst., 1963-65; clin. specialist Norfolk (Nebr.) State Hosp., 1965-66; instr. Creighton U. Sch. Nursing, 1966-68; prof. nursing, medicine and edn. U. Va., 1970-77; prof., dean Sch. Nursing, UCLA, 1977—, prof.-at-large Med. Sch., 1977—; pres. Human Services Tng. and Research Corp., 1974—; co-chmn. Gov. Calif. Mental Health and Mental Retardation Adv. Bd., 1973-76; cons. in field. Recipient Outstanding Alumni award Creighton U. Sch. Nursing, 1972. Mem. Am. Acad. Nursing, Am. Nurses Assn., Am. Assn. Colls. Nursing, Western Interstate Colls. Higher Edn., Delta Sigma Rho, Alpha Sigma Nu, Sigma Theta Tau. Democrat. Roman Catholic. Co-author: Your Future in Nursing Careers, 1972. Home: 6410 Surfside Way Malibu CA 90265 Office: School of Nursing Univ Calif Los Angeles Los Angeles CA 90024

RESCH, GLENN ALLAN, profl. hockey player; b. Moose Jaw, Sask., Can., Oct. 7, 1948; s. Joseph Albert and Ella Bertine (Nesvold) R.; came to U.S., 1967; B.S. (athletic scholarship), U. Minn., Duluth, 1971; m. Diane Kay Anderson, Oct. 5, 1972; 1 dau., Holly Jan. Player minor league hockey teams, 1967-72; goalie New Haven Nighthawks, 1972-73, Ft. Worth Wings, 1973-74, N.Y. Islanders, 1974—; instr. Duluth Hockey Sch., 1973-77, Hicke Bros. Hockey Sch., Regina, Sask., 1974-77. Home: Box 207 Emily MN 56447 Office: 1155 Conklin St Farmingdale NY 11735

RESEN, FREDERICK LAWRENCE, editor, publisher; b. N.Y.C., July 17, 1923; s. Fred and Olga (Dowick) R.; B.S. in Chem. Engring., U. Colo., 1950; m. Margaret Jenkins, Nov. 26, 1952; children—John Frederick, Emily. Chem. engr. Dow Corning Corp., Midland, Mich., 1950-51; refining editor Oil and Gas Jour., Houston, 1951-58, N.Y.C., 1958-59; editor, pub. Chem. Engring. Progress, N.Y.C., 1959—; staff dir. publs. Am. Inst. Chem. Engrs., 1978—; editorial dir. Internat. Chem. Engring., 1964-72; editorial cons.; cons. editor Am. Oxford Ency., 1960. Mem. adv. com. Internat. Exposition of Chem. Industries, 1966-75. Served with USN, 1941-45. Fellow Am. Inst. Chem. Engrs.; mem. Chem. Pub. Relations Soc. (v.p. 1972-74), Am. Chem. Soc., Am. Soc. Bus. Press Editors, Pi Kappa Alpha, Tau Beta Pi. Republican. Conglist. (Sunday Sch. tchr., trustee 1975). Clubs: Silver Spring Country (Ridgefield, Conn.); Chemists (N.Y.C.). Author: Wilton Congregational Church From 1726, 1975. Home: 38 Pheasant Run Wilton CT 06897 Officg: 345 E 47th St New York NY 10017

RESHETAR, JOHN STEPHEN, JR., polit. scientist; b. Mpls., July 14, 1924; s. John Stephen and Mary (Gaedos) R.; B.A., Williams Coll., 1945; M.A., Harvard U., 1946, Ph.D., 1950; m. Helene Taranez, June 12, 1955. Instr. polit. sci. Princeton U., 1947-51, lectr., 1951-55; research fellow Harvard U. Russian Research Center, 1950-52; research asso. Fgn. Policy Research Inst., U. Pa., 1955-57; mem. faculty polit. sci. U. Wash., Seattle, 1957—, asso. prof., 1957-62, prof., 1962—, prof. Russian and East European Studies, 1973—; vis. lectr. in polit. sci. Yale U., 1956-57. Ford Found. faculty fellow, 1953-54. Mem. Am. Acad. Polit., Social Sci., Am., Pacific N.W. polit. sci. assns., Am. Assn. Advancement Slavic Studies, Western Slavic Assn. (pres. 1965-66), Ukrainian Acad. Arts, Scis. in U.S., Phi Beta Kappa. Author: The Ukrainian Revolution, 1917-1920, 1952; Problems of Analyzing and Predicting Soviet Behavior, 1955; A Concise History of the Communist Party of the Soviet Union, 1960; The Soviet Polity, 1971, 2d edit., 1978. Home: 9828 41st Ave NE Seattle WA 98115 Office: Dept of Polit Sci U of Wash Seattle WA 98195

RESHEVSKY, SAMUEL HERMAN, chessplayer; b. Ozarkow, Poland, Nov. 26, 1911; s. Jacob and Shaindel (Eibeschitz) R.; came to U.S., 1920, naturalized, 1925; Ph.B., U. Chgo., 1933; m. Norma Mindick, June 24, 1941; children—Sylvia, Joel, Marcia Gloria. U.S. champion, 1936, 38, 40, 42, 46, 70-71, tie 1972; winner numerous internat. tournaments, including Margate, 1935, Havana, Cuba, 1953, Stardust 1st Nat. Open, 1967, Buenos Aires, Argentina, 1968; winner match with Bobby Fischer, 1961; investment analyst, 1957-74; TV broadcaster, performer, 1972-74; writer on chess for N.Y. Herald Tribune, N.Y. Times, Chess Rev., Chess Life and Rev., Med. Opinion & Rev. Annotator 1st Piatigorsky Cup, 1965. Author: Reshevsky on Chess, 1948; How Chess Games Are Won, 1962; Learn Chess Fast, 1969; Reshevsky on Games, 1972; Reshevsky Teaches Chess, 1973; Great Chess Upsets, 1975; Spassky-Fischer Games—The Art of Positional Play, 1976. Home: 5 Hadassah Ln Spring Valley NY 10977

RESIKA, PAUL, painter; b. N.Y.C., Aug. 15, 1928; s. Abraham and Sonia (Zeltzer) R.; student Sol Wilson, N.Y.C., 1940-44, Hans Hofmann Sch., N.Y.C., 1945-47, Venice, Italy, 1950-53; m. Blair Phillips, Sept. 5, 1967; children—Nathan Anthony, Sonia Phillips. One-man shows include: George Dix Gallery, N.Y.C., 1948, Peridot Gallery, N.Y.C., 1964, 65, 67, 68, 69, 70, Washburn Gallery, N.Y.C., 1971, 73, Hopkins Center, Dartmouth Coll., 1972, Graham Gallery, N.Y.C., 1976; group shows include: Jacques Seligmann Gallery, N.Y.C., 1947, 48, Hirschl & Adler, N.Y.C., 1962, Wadsworth Atheneum, Hartford, Conn., 1964, Museum Modern Art, N.Y.C., 1966, Rijsakademie, Amsterdam, 1968, Smithsonian Inst., Washington, 1968-70, Boston U., 1972, Mus's. Omaha and Lincoln, 1973, Ingber Gallery and travelling, Eastern U.S. and Midwest, 1975-77, Am. Acad. Arts and Letters, N.Y.C., 1976, 77, NAD, N.Y.C., 1977, Graham Gallery, 1977, 79, Long Point Gallery, Provincetown, Mass., 1977, 79; represented in permanent collections, including: U. Nebr. Art Gallery, Indpls. Mus. Art, Goddard Art Center, Ardmore, Okla., Chase Manhattan Bank, N.Y.C., Dartmouth Coll., Colby Coll., NAD; adj. prof. art Cooper Union, 1966-77; instr. Art Students League, 1968-69; artist-in-residence Dartmouth Coll., 1972; faculty Skowhegan Sch. Painting and Sculpture, 1973, 76; chmn. M.F.A. program Parsons Sch. Design, 1978—. Recipient award Am. Acad. Arts and Letters, 1977; Louis Comfort Tiffany grantee, 1959; Ingram Merrill grantee, 1969. Mem. NAD (asso.). Office: care Graham Gallery 1014 Madison Ave New York NY 10021

RESLER, REXFORD ADRIAN, forester, assn. exec.; b. Danville, Ill., Jan. 13, 1923; s. Eugene Everett and Teressa D. (Danner) R.; B.S., Oreg. State U., 1953, M.S., 1954; m. Leona Mae Brewer, Apr. 30, 1948; 1 son, Scott Dana. With Forest Service, Dept. Agr., 1954-78, dep. regional forester Pacific NW, 1970-71, regional forester Pacific NW 1971-72, asso. chief Forest Service, Washington, 1972-78, ret., 1978; exec. v.p. Am. Forestry Assn., Washington, 1978—; bd. dirs. Oreg. Bd. Forestry, 1971-72. Bd. dirs. local council Boy Scouts Am., 1979—. Served with AC, U.S. Army, 1941-45. Fellow Soc. Am. Foresters; mem. Soil Conservation Soc. Am., Am. Hort. Soc., Soc. Range Mgmt., Am. Forestry Assn., Trail Riders Assn. Internat., Yosemite Inst., Fed. Exec. Inst., St. Regis Fellowship, Xi Sigma Pi, Phi Kappa Phi. Methodist. Clubs: Rotary (adv. council), Cosmos (adv. council) (Washington); Lord Calvert Yacht (Solomons Island, Md.). Contbr. articles to profl. jours. Office: 1319 18th St NW Washington DC 20036. *My life and career has been greatly influenced by a deep appreciation and respect for the land. My profl. career has been devoted to the mgmt. of public forest and rangelands and as an assn. exec. concerned with the protection and wise use of the nation's renewable natural resources. That experience has convinced me that man can, and must, live harmoniously with nature. Pursuit of that objective is not only the key to survival; it is also the key to maintaining the productivity of the land on which our soc. depends.*

RESNICK, MILTON, artist; b. Bratslav, Russia, Jan. 8, 1917; s. Michael and Molly (Miller) R.; studied in Paris, N.Y.; m. Patricia Passlof, Apr. 25, 1961. Came to U.S., 1923, naturalized, 1928. Exhibited one man shows at DeYoung Mus., 1955, Poindexter Gallery, 1955, 57, 59, Howard Wise Gallery, 1960, 61, 64, Holland Gallery, Chgo., 1959, Reed Coll., 1969, Ft. Worth Art Center, 1971, Milw. Art Center, 1972, Kent State U., 1973, Max Hutchinson Gallery, 1972; represented in permanent collections at Mus. Modern Art, Whitney Mus., Cleve. Mus., Wadsworth Atheneum, Johnson Wax Collection, Denver Mus., Raleigh (N.C.) Mus., Bundy Mus., Nat. Collection Fine Arts, Washington, Roswell (N.Mex.) Mus. and Art Center; vis. prof. U. Calif., Berkeley, 1955-56, U. Wis., 1966-67. Served with AUS, 1941-45. Address: 80 Forsyth St New York NY 10002*

RESNICK, ROBERT, physicist, educator; b. Balt., Jan. 11, 1923; s. Abraham and Anna (Dubin) R.; A.B., Johns Hopkins, 1943, Ph.D. (Pres.'s Fund scholar 1946-49), 1949; m. Mildred Saltzman, Oct. 14, 1945; children—Trudy, Abby, Regina. Physicist, NACA, Cleve., 1944-46; asst. prof., asso. prof. physics U. Pitts., 1949-56; asso. prof., prof. physics Rensselaer Poly. Inst., Troy, N.Y., 1956—, chmn. interdisciplinary sci. curriculum, 1973—, Edward P. Hamilton Distinguished prof. sci., 1975—; hon. research fellow Harvard, 1964-65; Fulbright prof., Peru, 1971; mem. Commn. on Coll. Physics, 1960-68. Recipient Distinguished Service citation Am. Assn. Physics Tchrs., 1967, Hans Christian Oersted medal, 1974, Esso award for outstanding teaching, 1953; Distinguished Faculty award Rensselaer Poly. Inst., 1971. Fellow Am. Phys. Soc.; mem. Am. Assn. Physics Tchrs., Am. Soc. Engring. Edn., AAAS, AAUP, Phi Beta Kappa, Sigma Xi. Author: A Manual for Laboratory Physics, 1954; Physics for Students of Science and Engineering, 1960; (with D. Halliday) Physics, 1966, 2d edit., 1976; Introduction to Special Relativity, 1968; (with R. Eisberg) Notes on Quantum Theory, 1968, Notes on Modern Physics, 1969, Quantum Physics of Atoms, Molecules, Solids, Nuclei and Particles, 1974; (with D. Halliday) Fundamentals of Physics, 1970, 2d edit., 1974; (with others) Student Study Guide for Physics, 1970, 2d edit., 1977; Basic Concepts in Relativity and Early Quantum Theory, 1972; (with others) Sourcebook for Programmable Calculators, 1978; books translated into numerous fgn. langs. Adv. bd., project staff Physical Science for Non-Scientists, 1964-68, pub., 1968; co-dir. project Physics Demonstration Experiments, 1962-70, pub., 1970; Workshop on Apparatus for College Physics, 1964-65, pub., 1966; Videotapes in Physics Instruction, 1975-78, pub., 1978; dir. Physics Demonstration and Laboratory Apparatus Workshop, 1960-61, pub., 1961; adv. editor John Wiley & Sons, Inc., 1967—. Research publs. in aerodynamics, nuclear physics, atomic physics, upper atmosphere physics. Home: 13 Oxford Rd Troy NY 12180

RESNIK, HARVEY LEWIS PAUL, psychiatrist; b. Buffalo, Apr. 6, 1930; s. Samuel and Celia (Greenberg) R.; B.A. magna cum laude, U. Buffalo, 1951; M.D., Columbia, 1955; grad. Phila. Psychoanalytic Inst., 1967; m. Audrey Ruth Frey, Aug. 30, 1964; children—Rebecca Gabrielle, Henry Seth Maccabee, Jessica Ruth. Intern Phila. Gen. Hosp., 1955-56, resident, 1956-57; resident Jackson Meml. Hosp., Miami, Fla., 1959-61; fellow U. Pa. Hosp., 1961-62, mem. staff, 1962-67; instr. Sch. Medicine, U. Pa., 1962-66, instr. med. hypnosis Grad. Sch. Medicine, 1963-65; clin. dir. psychiatry E. J. Meyer Meml. Hosp., Buffalo, 1967, dir., 1968; asso. prof. psychiatry Sch. Medicine, State U. N.Y. at Buffalo, 1967, prof., 1968-70, dep. chmn. dept. psychiatry, 1968-69; chief Nat. Center for Studies of Suicide Prevention, NIMH, 1969-74, chief mental health emergencies sect., 1974-76; with Reproductive Biology Research Found., St. Louis, 1971; clin. prof. psychiatry Sch. Medicine, George Washington U., 1969—; professorial lectr. Sch. Medicine, Johns Hopkins, 1969—; prof. community health Fed. City Coll., 1971-75; med. dir. Human Behavior Found., 1975—; instr. Del. Valley Group Therapy Inst.; cons. Marriage Council Phila., Phila. Gen. Hosp., Pa. Hosp., Danville State Hosp., WHO, Nat. Naval Med. Center, A.R.C., Nat. Cancer Inst., Mental Health Assn. Southeastern Pa. Served to capt. USAF, 1957-59; ETO; capt. USNR. Diplomate Am. Bd. Psychiatry and Neurology. Fellow Am. Psychiat. Assn., Am. Coll. Psychiatrists; mem. Am. Assn. Marriage Counselors, AMA, Montgomery County, Prince Georges County med. assns., Phila. Psychoanalytic Soc., AAAS, Phi Beta Kappa, Beta Sigma Rho (grand Vice-warden 1963). Jewish. Mason. Club: Cosmos (Washington). Author: Suicidal Behaviors: Diagnosis and Management, 1968; (with M. E. Wolfgang) Treatment of the Sexual Offender, 1971; Sexual Behaviors: Social, Clinical and Legal Aspects, 1972; (with B. Hathorne) Suicide Prevention in the Seventies, 1973; (with H.L. Ruben) Emergency Psychiatric Care, 1974; (with others) The Prediction of Suicide, 1974; Emergency and Disaster Aid, 1976. Editor: Bull. Suicidology, 1969-74. Contbr. articles on hypnosis, sexual offenders, marriage and sexual dysfunction treatment, suicide, death and dying, emergency psychiatric care. Office: Suite U-3 6201 Greenbelt Rd College Park MD 20740 also Suite B6 3233 Superior Ln Bowie MD 20755

RESNIK, MICHAEL DAVID, educator; b. New Haven, Mar. 20, 1938; s. Howard Beck and Muriel (Spitzer) R.; B.A., Yale U., 1960; M.A., Harvard U., 1962, Ph.D., 1964; m. Janet Mildred Depping, June 14, 1960; children—David, Dmitri, Sarah. Asst. prof. U. Hawaii, Honolulu, 1964-67; vis. asst. prof. Washington U., St. Louis, 1966-67; asso. prof. U. N.C., Chapel Hill, 1967-75, prof., 1975—, chmn. dept. philosophy, 1975—; asst. philosopher U. Hawaii, Social Sci. Research Inst., Honolulu, 1966-67; co-prin. investigator NSF grant, 1966-67; participant Sloan Found. grant, 1978-80. Mem. Am. Philos. Assn., Assn. Symbolic Logic, N.C. Philos. Soc. (sec.-treas. 1977-79, pres. 1979-81), Am. Farrier Assn., Phi Beta Kappa. Author: Elementary Logic, 1970; contbr. articles in field to profl. jours. Home: Route 1 Pegasus Farm Chapel Hill NC 27514 Office: Dept Philosophy U NC Chapel Hill NC 27514

RESNIK, REGINA, operatic singer; b. N.Y.C., Aug. 30, 1924; d. Sam and Ruth R.; B.A., Hunter Coll., 1942; m. Harry W. Davis, July 18, 1946; 1 son, Michael Philip; m. 2d, Arbit Blatas, 1975. Debut as Lady Macbeth, 1942; mezzo-soprano debut Met. Opera Co., N.Y.C., 1946; regular guest Vienna State Opera, La Scala, Milan, Italy, Covent Garden, Salzburg, Deutsche Opera, Berlin, Teatro Colon, Buenos Aires, Bayreuth, Germany, Munich Saatsoper, Chgo., Phila., San Francisco, others; co-dir., starred in Carmen at Hamburg Opera, 1971, in Electra, 1971, in Falstaff at Nat. Opera Poland, 1975; condr. seminars on opera New Sch. for Social Research; dir. The Medium (Menotti), The Telephone (Menotti), The Rise and Fall of the City Mahagonny (Weill). Decorated comdr. French Acad. Arts, Scis. and Letters; recipient awards including U.S. Pres.'s medal, Kannersängerin (Austria). Home: 50 W 56th St New York City NY 10019 Office: care London Records Inc 539 W 25th Ave New York NY 10001*

RESNIKOFF, GEORGE JOSEPH, univ. dean; b. N.Y.C., Mar. 25, 1915; s. Isador and Jenny (Rapaport) R.; B.S., U. Chgo., 1950; M.S., Stanford, 1952, Ph.D., 1955; m. Florence Lisa Herman, Apr. 4, 1953; 1 son, Carl. Asso. prof. Ill. Inst. Tech., 1957-61, prof., 1961-64; prof. math. and statistics Calif. State U. at Hayward, 1964—, dean of sci., 1969-72, dean grad. studies, 1972—. Served with AUS, 1942-46. Fellow AAAS, Am. Statis. Assn., Inst. Math. Statistics (exec. sec.). Contbr. articles to profl. jours. Home: 5654 Maxwelton Rd Oakland CA 94618 Office: 25800 Carlos Bee Blvd Hayward CA 94542

RESO, SIDNEY J(OSEPH), oil co. exec.; b. New Orleans, La., Feb. 12, 1935; s. James Anthony and Josephine (Shindler) R.; B.S. in Petroleum Engring., La. State U., 1957; grad. exec. program U. Va., 1971; m. Patricia Marie Armond, Aug. 20, 1955; children—Robin M., Cyd N., Gregory S., Christopher M., Renee E. With Humble Oil and Refining Co. (now Exxon Co., U.S.A.), 1957-65, 69-72, 73-75, div. mgr., Houston, 1973-74, mgr. prodn. dept. ops., 1974-75; chief engr. prodn. dept. Esso Standard Oil (Australia) Ltd., Sydney, New South Wales, 1965-67, mgr. natural gas dept., 1967-69; dir. Esso Australia, Ltd., Sydney, 1972-73; v.p. Esso Europe Inc., London, 1975-78; v.p. Exxon Corp., N.Y.C., 1978—; dir. Exxon Prodn. Research Co., Houston. Mem. Am. Petroleum Inst., Soc. Petroleum Engrs., Tau Beta Psi, Pi Epsilon Tau. Roman Catholic. Club: Country of Darien (Conn.). Office: 1251 Ave of Americas New York NY 10020

RESTALL, ROBIN L., advt. agy. exec.; b. Chigwell, Eng., Mar. 24, 1937; s. Leslie William and Eugenie Lucy Louise (Smith) R.; student Oxford Mgmt. Sch., 1964; m. Mariela Espinosa, Dec. 20, 1978; children—Matthew Bennett, Emma Jane, Millicent Iliana, David Alfonso. With J. Walter Thompson Co., 1960—, dir. client services, Madrid, Spain, 1970-74, v.p., dir. client services, Caracas, Venezuela, 1974-77, sr. v.p. internat., Chgo., 1977—. Served with RAF, 1955-60. Fellow Zool. Soc.; mem. Inst. Practitioners Advt., Am. Mgmt. Assn., Assn. Am. Advt. Agys. Author, illustrator numerous articles on birds; author: Finches, 1975. Home: 2100 Lincoln Park W Chicago IL 60614 Office: 875 N Michigan Ave Chicago IL 60611. *I believe with all my heart in the value of sharing knowledge.*

RESTEMEYER, WILLIAM EDWARD, elec. engr., educator; b. Cin., Apr. 28, 1916; s. William Edward and Lillian A. (Schmidt-Goesling) R.; E.E. with honors, U. Cin., 1938, M.A. with honors, 1939; postgrad. UCLA, 1960, U. Mich., 1961; D.Sc. (hon.), Capitol Inst. Tech., 1976; m. Virginia Lee Harris, Apr. 21, 1943; children—William E., Virginia Lee. Teaching fellow U. Cin., 1939-40, instr., 1940-42, asst. prof., 1942-52, asso. prof., 1952-61, prof., 1961—, asst. dept. head dept. elec. and computer engring., 1976-77; vis. scientist Ohio Acad. Sci.; cons. Avco, General Electric Co., NASA, NATO, NSF. Chmn. bd. mgmt. Campus YMCA. Served to lt. (j.g.) USN, 1945. Mem. Am. Soc. Engring. Edn. (nat. officer), AAAS, IEEE, Math. Assn. Am., Internat. Math. Union, Sigma Xi, Omicron Delta Kappa, Tau Beta Pi, Eta Kappa Nu, Phi Eta Sigma, Alpha Sigma Lambda, Pi Kappa Alpha. Clubs: Masons, Scottish Rite. Contbr. articles to profl. jours. Home: 516 Probasco St Cincinnati OH 45220 Office: Coll Engring Univ of Cin Cincinnati OH 45221

RESTON, JAMES BARRETT, author, newspaperman; b. Clydebank, Scotland, Nov. 3, 1909; s. James and Johanna (Irving) R.; brought to U.S., 1910; student Vale of Leven Acad., Alexandria, Scotland, 1914-20; B.S., U. Ill., 1932, LL.D. (hon.), 1962; Litt.D., Colgate U., 1951, Oberlin Coll., 1955, Rutgers U., 1957; LL.D. (hon.), Dartmouth, 1959, N.Y. U., 1961, Boston Coll., 1963, Brandeis U., 1964; D.H.L., Kenyon Coll., 1962, Columbia, 1963, U. Mich., 1965, Harvard, 1970, Stanford, 1972, U. Utah, 1973, Kent State U., 1974, Colby Coll., 1975, Yale U., 1977; hon. degrees U. Md., Northeastern U., 1976; m. Sarah Jane Fulton, Dec. 24, 1935; children—Richard Fulton, James Barrett, Thomas Busey. With Springfield (Ohio) Daily News, 1932-33; with publicity dept. Ohio State U., 1933; publicity dir. Cin. Baseball Club, 1934; reporter A.P., N.Y.C., 1934-37, London, 1937-39; reporter London (Eng.) bur. N.Y. Times, 1939-41, Washington bur., 1941—, chief Washington corr., 1953-64, asso. editor, 1964-68, exec. editor, 1968-69, v.p., 1969-74, columnist, cons., 1974—, also dir. N.Y. Times Co.; co-pub. The Vineyard Gazette, 1968—. Recipient Pulitzer Prize for nat. corr., 1945, nat. reporting, 1957; Overseas Press Club award for interpretation internat. news, 1949, 51, 55; George Polk Meml. award for nat. reporting, 1953; U. Mo. medal, 1961; J.P. Zenger award, 1964; Elijah Parrish Lovejoy award, 1974; decorated Legion d'Honneur, Order St. Olav (Norway), Order of Merit (Chile). Clubs: Century (N.Y.C.); Metropolitan (Washington); Chevy Chase (Md.). Office: New York Times 1000 Connecticut Ave Washington DC 20036

RESTON, THOMAS BUSEY, govt. ofcl.; b. N.Y.C., July 4, 1946; s. James Barrett and Sarah Jane (Fulton) R.; B.A. cum laude, Harvard U., 1968; J.D., U. Va., 1974. Free-lance fgn. corr. for polit. and econ. affairs, 1968-70; admitted to Va. bar, 1974, D.C. bar, 1974; practice civil rights, public interest law, asso. firm Hogan & Hartson, Washington, 1974-76; mem. Carter-Mondale Transition Team, Washington, 1976-77; dep. asst. sec. for public affairs Bur. Public Affairs, Dept. State, Washington, 1977—. Sec., Democratic Party Va., 1972-77. Mem. Am. Bar Assn., Va. State Bar, D.C. Bar. Episcopalian. Office: Bur Public Affairs Dept State 21st and C St NW Washington DC 20520

RESTREPO, RODRIGO A., mathematician; b. Medellin, Colombia, Nov. 6, 1930; s. Gonzalo and Enriqueta (Londono) R.; B.A., Lehigh U., 1951; Ph.D., Calif. Inst. Tech., 1955. Instr. to prof. dept. math. U. B.C., Vancouver, 1956—; vis. asst. prof. Stanford (Calif.) U., 1958-59, Cienes, Chile, 1963-64; vis. prof. Fed. U. Rio de Janeiro, 1970-71. Mem. Can. Math. Soc., Phi Beta Kappa.*

RESWICK, JAMES BIGELOW, rehab. engr.; educator; b. Ellwood City, Pa., Apr. 16, 1922; s. Maurice and Katherine (Parker) R.; S.B. in Mech. Engring., Mass. Inst. Tech., 1943, S.M., 1948, Sc.D., 1952; D.Eng. (hon.), Rose Poly. Inst., 1968; m. Irmtraud Orthlies Hoelzerkopf, Dec. 27, 1973; children—(by previous marriage) James Bigelow, David Parker (dec.), Pamela Patchin. Asst. prof., then asso. prof., head machine design and graphics div. Mass. Inst. Tech., 1948-59; Leonard Case prof. engring., dir. Engring. Design Center, Case Western Res. U., 1959-70; dir. Rehab. Engring. Center, Rancho Los Amigos Hosp.; prof. biomed. engring. and orthopaedics U. So. Calif., also dir. of research dept. orthopaedics; engring. cons. on automatic control, product devel., automation and bio-med. engring. Mem. com. prosthetics research and devel. Nat. Acad. Scis., 1962—, chmn. design and devel. com.; mem. bd. rev. Army Research and Devel. Office, 1965—; mem. applied physiology and biomed. engring. study sect. NIH, 1972—. Chmn. Mayor's Commn. for Urban Transp., Cleve., 1969. Served to lt. (j.g.) USNR, 1943-46; PTO. NSF sr. postdoctoral fellow Imperial Coll., London, Eng., 1957. Recipient Product Engring. Master Designer award, 1969; Isabelle and Leonard H. Goldenson award United Cerebral Palsy Assn., 1973. Fellow IEEE; mem. ASME (honor award for best paper 1956, sr. mem.), Am. Soc. Engring. Edn., Instrument Soc. Am., Biomed. Engring. Soc. (sr. mem.; pres. 1973, dir.), Am. Acad. Orthopedic Surgeons (asso.), Inst. Medicine of Nat. Acad. Scis., Nat. Acad. Engring., Internat. Soc. Orthotics and Prosthetics, Orthopaedics Research Soc., Rehab. Engring. Soc. N.Am. (founding pres.), Sigma XI. Author: (with C.K. Taft) Introduction to Dynamic Systems, 1967; also articles. Editor: (with F.T. Hambrecht) Functional Electrical Stimulation, 1977; series on engring. design, 1963—. Patentee in field. Office: Rancho Los Amigos Hosp 7601 E Imperial Hwy Downey CA 90242 also Orthopaedic Hosp 2400 S Flower St Los Angeles CA 90007

RETAN, GEORGE WALTER, pub. co. exec.; b. Galeton, Pa., Aug. 24, 1920; s. George Austin and Julia Edith (Walters) R.; student Mansfield State Tchrs. Coll., 1938-40; B.A., U. Pa., 1945; m. Elizabeth Wood, Oct. 27, 1956; children—Katherine Allison, Lucy Elizabeth. Asst. to sales mgr. Bobbs-Merrill Co., 1953-57; with Random House, N.Y.C., 1957-78, div. v.p., 1969-78, editor-in-chief, 1969-78, pres. Beginner Books div., 1978; v.p., pub. Western Pub. Co., Inc., N.Y.C., 1978—. Served with U.S. Army, 1942-45. Mem. Children's Book Council (pres. 1979), Phi Beta Kappa. Presbyterian. Author: Wanted: Two Bikes, 1948; The Steam Shovel that Wouldn't Eat Dirt, 1948; Mystery of the Haunted Cliff, 1949; The Snowplow That Tried to Go South, 1950; Favorite Tales of Monsters and Trolls, 1977. Office: 850 3d Ave New York NY 10022

RETTGERS, FORREST I., mfg. co. exec., assn. exec.; b. Reading, Pa., Nov. 20, 1921; s. I. B. and Laura T. (Hartenstein) R.; student Millersville (Pa.) State Tchrs. Coll., 1947-50, Tex. Western Coll., El Paso, 1951-54; A.B. in History with 1st honors, U. Md., 1958, postgrad. in History, 1959; postgrad. in Personnel Mgmt., George Washington U., 1960, M.A. in Internat. Relations, 1964; postgrad. in Internat. Econs., Am. U., 1966-67; m. Virginia M. Felix, Apr. 3, 1943; children—Robyn Stone, Pamela Vandervort, Bonnie J. Rep. of Sec. Army to U.S. Senate, spl. contact to Senate Appropriations Com., 1956-60, rep. of Sec. Def. to Congress, 1964-66; dep. asst. sec. for internat. security affairs Dept. Def., Washington, 1960-61; adminstrv. asst. to Senator Harry F. Byrd, Jr. of Va., 1966-72, chief-of-staff, 1966-72; pres. Midwestern Industries, Inc., Washington, 1972—; sr. v.p. policy/program div. NAM, Washington, 1974-76, sr. v.p. ops., 1976-77, exec. v.p., 1977—; pres. Adminstrv. Assts. and Exec. Secs. Assn. U.S. Senate, 1970-72. Chmn. bd. trustees Heritage Found., 1973—. Served to col. U.S. Army, 1940-60. Decorated Legion of Merit, Bronze Star with clusters, Purple Heart; recipient Disting. Alumni award U. Md., 1978. Mem. VFW. Clubs: Masons, Exchange of Capitol Hill (bd. govs. 1968-72). Office: NAM 1776 F St NW Washington DC 20006. *In dealing with the Congress, I have always used the following guiding principle: There are no permanent friends; there are no permanent enemies. There are only permanent interests in the U.S. Congress. In dealing with people throughout my life, I have always spoken and acted as if the only thing that I have in life worth protecting is my good name. I therefore have been guided by honesty and integrity and have helped individuals on all occasions, never once giving a thought to whether they, in turn, could ever help me.*

RETZLER, KURT EGON, diversified mgmt. co. exec.; b. Bechkerek, Yugoslavia, Mar. 31, 1927; s. Joseph J. and Melinda (Beno) R.; came to U.S., 1950, naturalized, 1954; B.B.A. with distinction, U. Mich. at Ann Arbor, 1955, M.B.A. with distinction, 1956; m. Rali Tjotis, Aug. 3, 1957; children—Jo Elaine, Kurt Steven. C.P.A., Arthur Andersen & Co., Detroit, 1956-63; asst. controller Carlson Cos., Inc., Mpls., 1963-65, controller, 1965-74, v.p., 1974—, v.p. corp. acquisitions and devel., 1974—, mem. fin. com., 1974—; dir. Premium Corp. Am., Inc., Mpls., 1967—, Gold Bond Stamp Co., 1967—, Luxury Mdse. Corp., Mpls., 1969—, Commonwealth Premium Co., Ltd., Toronto, Ont., Can., 1967—; dir., mem. exec. com. Superior Fiber Products, Inc., T.G.I. Friday's Restaurants, Ardan Wholesale Inc.; dir. Jason/Empire, Inc.; dir., officer Country Kitchen Internat., Inc. Treas., PTA, Golden Valley, Minn., 1967. Served with AUS, 1951-53. C.P.A., Mich., Minn. Mem. Financial Execs. Inst. (dir. Twin Cities chpt. 1969—, treas. 1971-72), Nat. Assn. Accountants, Am. Inst. C.P.A.'s, Minn. Assn. C.P.A.'s, Am. Accounting Assn., Assn. for Corp. Growth, Beta Gamma Sigma, Phi Kappa Phi, Beta Alpha Psi. Home: 1100 Heritage Ln Wayzata MN 55391 Office: Carlson Companies Inc 12755 B State Hwy 55 Minneapolis MN 55444

REUBEN, ALLAN HERBERT, lawyer; b. Pitts., June 24, 1931; s. Monte M. and Miriam (Barthfield) R.; B.A. summa cum laude, U. Pitts., 1953; LL.B. magna cum laude, Harvard U., 1956; m. Gladys Winkler, May 25, 1956; children—John David, Patricia Anne, Catherine Ellen. Law clk. to judge U.S. Ct. Appeals, 3d Circuit, 1956-57; admitted to Pa. bar, 1957; asso. firm Wolf, Block, Schorr & Solis-Cohen, Phila., 1957-65, partner, 1965—; lectr. Banking Law Inst., 1969. Trustee Lawyers Com. Civil Rights Under Law, 1976—; chmn., mem. governing bd. employment discrimination referral project Phila. Bar Assn.-Lawyers Com. Civil Rights Under Law, 1971-75; bd. dirs. Pub. Interest Law Center Phila., 1975—; mem. S.E. regional planning council Pa. Gov.'s Justice Commn., 1973-78, exec. com., 1974-78; mem. exec. com. S.E. regional adv. com. Pa. Com. on Crime and Delinquency, 1979—; trustee Community Legal Services Phila., 1971, 1980—; bd. dirs. Pa. Legal Services Center, 1978—, chmn. evaluation com.; bd. commrs. Cheltenham Twp., Pa., 1972—; bd. dirs. Phila. Am. Jewish Com., 1965—, v.p., 1973-77; mem. Jewish Community Relations Com., Phila., 1965—, bd. dirs., 1973—, chmn. civil rights com., 1975—; bd. govs. Renal Youth Rehab. Program, 1976—. Mem. Am. Judicature Soc., Am., Fed., Pa., Phila. (co-chmn. subcom. riots in N. Phila. 1965, chmn. subcom. invasion of privacy by electronic means 1966-70, 72-78, chmn. speakers Law Day 1966, chmn. speakers bur. 1967, chmn. civil rights com. 1971, 1980—, chancellor's commn. on abortion 1971-72, public relations com. 1965—, speakers panel 1965—, chmn. com. fin. 1966-67, exec. com. 1969-70, 72, sec. 1973, editor Phila. Lawyer 1969-74, co-chmn. editorial bd. 1974—) bar assns., Phi Beta Kappa. Mem. Harvard Law Rev., 1956. Home: 7914 Ivy Ln Elkins Park PA 19117 Office: Packard Bldg Philadelphia PA 19102

REUBEN, DAVID ROBERT, psychiatrist, author; b. Chgo., Nov. 29, 1933; s. Clifford Kalman and Frances (Harris) R.; student U. Chgo., 1949-50; B.S., U. Ill., 1953, M.D., 1957; m. Barbara Hatounian, July 1, 1961; children—David Robert, Catherine, Amy Giselle. Intern, Cook County Hosp., 1957-58, resident psychiatry, Chgo., 1958-59; research asso. psychiatry Harvard Med. Sch., Boston, 1960; practice medicine specializing in psychiatry, San Diego, 1961-72; cons. nat. security. Served to capt. USAF, 1959-61. Mem. AMA, Calif., Fla. med. assns. Mem. Armenian Apostolic Ch. Clubs: Castillo Country (San Jose), Nat. Radio, Cariari Country, Masons. Author: Everything You Always Wanted To Know About Sex, 1969; Any Woman Can!, 1971; How To Get More Out of Sex, 1974; The Save Your Life Diet, 1975; (with Barbara Reuben) The Save Your Life Diet High Fiber Cookbook, 1976; Everything You Always Wanted to Know About Nutrition, 1978. Office: care Harold Matson Co 22 E 40th St New York NY 10016

REUBEN, DON H., lawyer; b. Chgo., Sept. 1, 1928; s. Michael B. and Sally (Chapman) R.; B.S., Northwestern U., 1949, J.D., 1952; m. Evelyn Long, Aug. 27, 1948 (div.); children—Michael Barrett, Timothy Don, Jeffrey Long, Howard Ellis; m. 2d, Jeannette Hurley Haywood, Dec. 13, 1971; stepchildren—Harris, Jeannette, Edward. Admitted to Ill. bar, 1952; practiced with firm Kirkland & Ellis, Chgo., 1952-78, sr. partner, until 1978; sr. partner Reuben & Procter, Chgo., 1978—; gen. counsel for Tribune Co. and subsidiaries, Chgo. Bears Football Club, Inc., Roman Cath. Archdiocese of Chgo.; spl. asst. atty. gen. State of Ill., 1963-64, 69—; counsel spl. session Ill. Ho. of Reps., 1964, for Ill. treas. for congl., state legis. and jud. reapportionment, 1963—; spl. fed. ct. master, 1968-70. Dir. Lake Shore Nat. Bank. Mem. citizens adv. bd. to Sheriff Cook County, 1962-66; mem. jury instrns. com., 1963-68, com. rules Ill. Supreme Ct., 1963-73; mem. pub. relations com. Nat. Conf. State Trial Judges; mem. Chgo. Better Schs. Com., 1968—, Chgo. Crime Commn., 1970—; mem. supervisory panel Fed. Defender Program. Mem. nat. legacy com. Multiple Sclerosis Soc., also vice chmn. Central region; bd. dirs. Lincoln Park Zool. Soc., United Cerebral Palsy Assn. Chgo.; mem. citizens bd. Loyola U., Chgo.; trustee Northwestern U.; exec. com. U. Chgo. Mem. Ill., Chgo. (chmn. subsom. on propriety and regulation of contingent fees com. devel. law 1966-69) Am. (standing com. on fed. judiciary 1973-79), bar assns., Am. Law Inst., Am. Judicature Soc., Fellows Am. Bar Found. (Rule 23 com.), Bar Assn. 7th Fed Circuit, Am. Coll. Trial Lawyers Am., Am. Arbitration Assn., (nat. panel arbitrators), Internat. Acad. Trial Lawyers, Ill. Trial Lawyers Assn., Assn. Trial Lawyers Am., Phi Eta Sigma, Beta Alpha Psi, Beta Gamma Sigma, Order of Coif. Clubs: Univ., Chgo., Tavern, Mid-Am., Chgo. Yacht; Mid-Day; Comml.; Dunham Woods Riding. Lectr. on libel, slander, privacy and freedom of press. Home: 2430 Lake View Ave Chicago IL 60614 Office: 11 S LaSalle St Suite 2001 Chicago IL 60603

REUBER, GRANT LOUIS, banker; b. Mildmay, Ont., Can., Nov. 23, 1927; s. Jacob Daniel and Gertrude Katherine (Wahl) R.; B.A., U. Western Ont., 1950; A.M., Harvard, 1954, Ph.D., 1957; postgrad. Cambridge U., 1954-55; m. Margaret Louise Julia Summerhayes, Oct. 21, 1951; children—Rebecca, Barbara, Mary. Mem. research dept. Bank Can., Ottawa, 1950-52; mem. Can. Dept. Finance, Ottawa, 1955-57; mem. faculty U. Western Ont., London, 1957—, prof. econs., 1962—, head dept., 1963-69, dean faculty Social Sci., 1969-75, academic v.p., provost, 1975-78; sr. v.p., chief economist Bank of Montreal (Que., Can.), 1978-79; dep. minister fin. Can., 1979—; mem. Royal Commn. Banking and Finance, Toronto, 1962-63; chmn. Ont. Econ. Council, 1973-78; cons. Dept. Fin., 1967-69, Nat. Council Applied Econ. Research, New Delhi, India, 1965, Canadian Internat. Devel. Agy., 1968-69; hon. research asso. econs. Harvard, 1968-69; cons. devel. centre OECD, 1969-72. Fellow Royal Soc. Can.; mem. Canadian Econs. Assn. (chmn. founding com., 1966-67, pres., 1967-68). Author: (with R.J. Wonnacott) The Cost of Capital in Canada, 1961; (with R.E. Caves) Canadian Economic Policy and the Impact of International Capital Flows, 1970; Private Foreign Investment in Development, 1973. Contbr. articles to profl. jours. Home: 6 Lakeview Terr Ottawa ON K1S 3H4 Canada Office: Dept Fin Place Bell 160 Elgin St Ottawa ON K1A 0G5 Canada

REULER, MAURICE, lawyer; b. Denver, Mar. 1, 1923; s. Maurice and Hilda R.; B.A., U. Denver, 1945, LL.B. cum laude, 1947; LL.M., U. Mich., 1948; married, Aug. 1, 1961; children—Jody, Stephanie. Admitted to Colo. bar; individual practice law, 1948-54; mem. firm Mason, Reuler and Peek, Denver, 1954—; instr. U. Denver, 1950-60; mem. Colo. Bd. Law Examiners, 1968—, chmn., 1974—. Fellow Am. Bar Found., Am. Acad. Matrimonial Lawyers; mem. Am. (mem. ho. of dels., 1976), Colo., Denver (chmn. unauthorized practice law com. 1957-58, mem. bd. govs. 1964-67, 70-71, pres. 1972-73) bar assns., U. Mich. Alumni Assn. Colo. (pres. 1956-57), U. Denver Law Sch. Alumni Assn. (pres. 1957-58). Jewish. Contbr. articles to profl. jours. Home: 22 Brookside Dr Littleton CO 80121 Office: 2450 Western Fed Savs Bldg Denver CO 80202

REUSCHE, ROBERT FREDERICK, banker; b. New Rochelle, N.Y., Nov. 22, 1927; s. Frank Louis and Marjorie (Ryan) R.; B.S., Ohio State U., 1949; M.B.A., U. Chgo., 1955; m. Mary Lumsden Westbrook, Apr. 28, 1951; children—Emily, Anne, Robert. Securities salesman John B. Joyce & Co., Columbus, Ohio, 1949-50; with No. Trust Co., Chgo., 1951—, 2d v.p., 1961-63, v.p., 1963-68, sr. v.p., 1968-74, exec. v.p., 1974—. Trustee Chgo. Home for Incurables; pres. Ravinia Festival Assn., 1979—. Served with AUS, 1950-51. Clubs: Economic (Chgo.); Exmoor (Highland Park, Ill.). Home: 1279 W Inverlieth Rd Lake Forest IL 60045 Office: 50 S LaSalle St Chicago IL 60690

REUSCHLEIN, HAROLD GILL, univ. dean; b. Burlington, Wis., Dec. 2, 1904; s. Joseph Felix and Frances (Gill) R.; A.B., U. Iowa, 1927; LL.B., Yale, 1933; J.S.D., Cornell, 1934; LL.D., Dominican Coll., 1955, Dickinson Sch. Law, 1970, LaSalle Coll., 1971, Creighton U., 1975; L.H.D., Villanova U., 1972; m. Marcella Christien, Apr. 24, 1930; 1 dau., Mary Frances, Instr. history N.Y. U., 1930-32; asst. gen. counsel Fidelity Mut. Life Ins. Co., 1934; prof. law Georgetown U., 1934-46, U. Notre Dame, 1946-47, Syracuse U., 1947-48, U. Pitts., 1948-53; dean Sch. Law, Villanova U., 1953-72; Ryan Distinguished prof. law St. Mary's U., 1972—; vis. prof. Case Western Res. U., 1967-68; admitted to Wis. bar, 1936, bar Supreme Ct. U.S., 1944, Pa. bar, 1955. Choirmaster, organist First Meth. Episcopal Ch., New Haven, 1927-33, Ch. St. Bernard of Clarivaux, Pitts., 1948-53; dir. Pub. Health Law Project, U. Pittsburgh. Served as col. Judge Adv. Gen. Dept., World War II; chief Office Legislative Service Hdqrs., AAF. Awarded Legion of Merit. Decorated Papal Knight of the Holy Sepulchre, Knight St. Gregory the Great. Mem. Am., Wis., Pa. bar assns., Order of Coif, Pi Kappa Alpha, Pi Gamma Mu. Roman Catholic. Clubs: Cosmos (Washington); Lotos (N.Y.C.). Author: The Schools of Corporate Reform, 1950; Jurisprudence-Its American Prophets, 1951; Cases on Unincorporated Business, 1952; Cases on Agency and Partnership, 1962; Handbook of Law of Agency and Partnership, 1977. Home: 8915 Data Point Dr San Antonio TX 78229

REUSS, HENRY S., congressman; b. Milw., Feb. 22, 1912; s. Gustav A. and Paula (Schoellkopf) R.; A.B., Cornell U., 1933; LL.B., Harvard, 1936; m. Margaret Magrath, Oct. 24, 1942; children—Christopher, Michael, Jacqueline, Anne. Admitted to Wis. bar, 1936, practiced in Milw., 1936-55; lectr. Wis. State Coll., Milw., 1950, 51; asst. corp. counsel Milwaukee County, 1939-40; asst. gen. counsel OPA, Washington, 1941-42; dep. gen. counsel Marshall Plan, Paris, France, 1949; spl. prosecutor Milw. County Grand Jury, 1950; personal counsel to Sec. State in reapportionment case Wis. Supreme Ct. 1953; member 84th to 96th congresses from 5th Wis. Dist., chmn. com. banking, fin. and urban affairs, joint econ. com.; chmn. internat. econs. subcom. Mem. Resources Bd., Washington, 1948-52. Mem. Milw. Sch. Bd., 1953-54; chmn. clubs and orgns. com. Milw. March of Dimes, 1953. Mem. council Cornell U.; dir. Am. Youth Hostels. Served from 2d lt. to capt. 63d, 75th Inf. Divs., AUS, 1943-45; chief price control br. Office Mil. Govt. Germany, 1945. Decorated D.S.M. Mem. Children's Service Soc. (dir.), Jr. Bar Assn. Milw. (vice chmn.), Milw. County (chmn. constn. and citizenship com.), Milw. bar assns., Chi Psi Alumni Assn. (v.p.). Clubs: Milwaukee City. Alumni overseer Harvard Law Rev., 1956-60. Author: The Critical Decade, 1964, Revenue-Sharing, 1970, On the Trail of the Ice Age, 1976; To Save Our Cities, 1977.

REUSS, ROBERT PERSHING, telephone co. exec.; b. Aurora, Ill., Mar. 23, 1918; s. George John and Mary Belle (Gorrie) R.; B.S., U. Ill., 1939; postgrad. Harvard Bus. Sch., 1943; M.B.A., U. Chgo., 1950, D.B.A., Blackburn Coll., 1976; m. Mildred Louise Daly, Dec. 22, 1940; children—Lynn Ann (Mrs. David Bohmer), Robert Cameron. Pres., chief exec. officer, dir. Central Telephone & Utilities Corp., 1972-76, chmn., 1977—; staff Am. Tel. & Tel. Co., 1955-58, asst. comptroller, 1958-59; v.p. Ill. Bell Telephone Co., 1959-72, dir., 1970-72; dir. Am. Nat. Bank and Trust Co., Chgo., Amsted Industries. Sec., Ill. Commn. for Econ. Devel. 1965-73. Bd. dirs. Jr. Achievement Chgo., 1970—, pres., 1971-73; bd. govs. Midwest Stock Exchange; trustee Rush-Presbyn.-St. Luke's Med. Center, Chgo., Blackburn Coll., Carlinville, Ill. Served to lt. (s.g.) USNR, 1943-46; PTO. Mem. Chgo. Assn. Commerce and Industry (dir. 1971—), Newcomen Soc., Phi Kappa Phi. Presbyterian (deacon, trustee). Clubs: Commercial, Mid-Am., Chicago, Economic (Chgo.); Chicago Golf (Wheaton, Ill.); Farmington Country (Charlottesville, Va.); Country of Fla. (Delray Beach). Home: 6 Oak Brook Club Dr Oak Brook IL 60521 Office: 5725 E River Rd Chicago IL 60631

REUSSWIG, FREDERICK WEBSTER, cons. civil engr.; b. Olean, N.Y., Feb. 8, 1924; s. Edgar Charles and Louise Ward (Webster) R.; B.S.C.E., Mass. Inst. Tech., 1949; m. Elizabeth Jane Knothe, June 14, 1945; children—Michael Alan, Patricia Ann, David Frederick, Catherine Ann. Engr., Niagara Mohawk Power Corp., Buffalo, 1949-54, 55-63, sr. engr., 1963; asst. to pres. Moog Valve Co., E. Aurora, N.Y., 1954-55; with Stanley Cons., Inc., Muscatine, Iowa, 1963—, head ops. div., 1970-78, head corp. devel. and services, 1978—, v.p., 1968-75, sr. v.p., 1975—, also past dir. Past mem. adv. bd. Coll. Engring., U. Iowa; past edn. counselor M.I.T.; mem. adv. council Mgmt. Center, U. Iowa. Served with USAAF, 1943-46. Decorated knight comdr. Republic Liberia, 1967; registered profl. engr., 6 states. Fellow ASCE (pres. Buffalo sect. 1954), Am. Cons. Engrs. Council; mem. Nat. Soc. Profl. Engrs., ASME, Muscatine C. of C. Republican. Club: Geneva Country. Home: 1215 Northwood Ln Muscatine IA 52761 Office: Stanley Bldg Muscatine IA 52761

REUTER, FRANK THEODORE, educator; b. Kankakee, Ill., Mar. 18, 1926; s. Frank Theodore and Evelyn Marie (Scott) T.; B.S., U. Ill., 1950, M.A., 1959, Ph.D., 1960; m. Kathleen Ann Pester, June 16, 1951; children—Mark, Stephen, Christopher, Ann, Katherine. Instr., West Liberty (W. Va.) State Coll., 1960-62; asst. prof. Texas Christian U., Fort Worth, 1962-66, asso. prof., 1966-71, prof. history, 1971—, dean Grad. Sch., 1970-75. Served with USNR, 1944-46. Mem. Orgn. Am. Historians, Am. Hist. Assn., Soc. Historians Am. Fgn. Relations, Phi Alpha Theta. Roman Catholic. Author: West Liberty State College: The First 125 Years, 1963; Catholic Influence on American Colonial Policies, 1898-1904, 1967. Home: 3617 Winifred Dr Fort Worth TX 76133

REUTHER, ALFRED RICHARD, JR., energy co. fin. exec.; b. Grosse Pointe Farms, Mich., Sept. 12, 1934; s. Alfred Richard and Alberta (Kansier) R.; B.A., Mich. State U., 1956; M.A., George Washington U., 1958; m. Jane Lewis Weaver, Sept. 12, 1958; children—Sarah Brooke, William Sommers. With Chase Manhattan Bank, N.Y.C., 1958-59; credit analyst Detroit Bank & Trust, 1959-61; supr. econ. analysis Ford Motor Credit Co., Dearborn, Mich., 1961-70; asst. treas. Mich. Consol. Gas Co., Detroit, 1970-73; treas. Mich. Consol. Gas Co., Detroit, 1973-79; asst. treas. Am. Natural Resources, Detroit, 1979—. Mem. Grosse Pointe (Mich.) City Council, 1968-75; pres. Children's Center, Detroit, 1976-79; v.p. Mental Health Assn. Mich., 1979. Mem. Am. Gas Assn., Econ. Club Detroit, Fin. Analyst Soc. Detroit. Republican. Congregationalist.

Club: Country of Detroit. Home: 81 Lewiston Grosse Pointe Farms MI 48236 Office: One Woodward Detroit MI 48226

REUTHER, RONALD THEODORE, mus. adminstr.; b. Miami, Fla., Dec. 25, 1929; s. Frederick G. and Grace E. (Roehll) R.; B.A., U. Calif., Berkeley, 1951, postgrad., 1952-53; postgrad. U. Ariz., 1952; m. Mary B. Howard, Apr. 14, 1956; children—Catherine, Paul, Jon, Victoria. Mgr., Micke Grove Zoo, Lodi, Calif., 1957-58; gen. curator Cleve. Zoo, 1959-62, asst. dir., 1965-66; dir. Indpls. Zoo, 1962-64, San Francisco Zoo, 1966-73, Phila. Zoo, 1973-78; dir. devel. The Exploratorium, San Francisco, 1979—; program chmn. 1st Internat. Congress Zool. Parks, Mexico City, 1967; trustee San Francisco Inst. Animal Behavior; cons. Zoo Plan Assn., Wichita, Kans., 1972—. Served with USAF, 1953-56. Mem. Am. Assn. Zool. Parks and Aquariums (pres. 1968-70), Internat. Union Dirs. Zool. Gardens, Internat. Wild Waterfowl Assn. (dir.), Am. Ornithol. Union, Am. Soc. Mammalogists, Am. Inst. Biol. Scis., Cooper Ornithol. Soc., Fauna Preservation Soc., Calif. Acad. Scis., Aircraft Owners and Pilots Assn., Res. Officers Assn., Phila. Zool. Soc. Club: Rotary. Home: 56 Vendola Dr San Rafael CA 94903 Office: 3601 Lyon St San Francisco CA 94123

REUTTER, EBERHARD EDMUND, JR., educator; b. Balt., May 28, 1924; s. Eberhard Edmund and Irene Louise (Loewer) R.; B.A., Johns Hopkins, 1944; M.A., Columbia, 1948, Ph.D., 1950; m. Bettie Marie Lytle, Aug. 16, 1947; 1 son, Mark Douglas. Dir. Tokyo Army Edn. Program Sch., 1945-47; head math. dept. Barnard Sch., N.Y.C., 1947-49; mem. faculty Tchrs. Coll., Columbia, 1950—, prof., 1957—; vis. prof. U. Alaska, 1960, 66, U. P.R., 1954, U. So. Calif., 1960; speaker, cons. Coordinator spl. edn. projects NAACP Legal Def. Fund, 1965-68; mem. edn. panel Am. Arbitration Assn. Chmn. citizens adv. com. Emerson (N.J.) Bd. Edn., 1954-57. Served from pvt. to 1st lt. inf. AUS, 1943-46. Mem. Nat. Orgn. Legal Problems of Edn. (pres. 1967), AAUP, Am. Assn. Sch. Adminstrs., NEA, Am. Assn. Sch. Personnel Adminstrs., Internat. Personnel Mgmt. Assn., Phi Beta Kappa, Kappa Delta Pi, Phi Delta Kappa. Author: The School Administrator and Subversive Activities, 1951; Schools and the Law, rev. edit., 1970; (with W.S. Elsbree) Staff Personnel in the Public Schools, 1954; (with R.R. Hamilton) Legal Aspects of School Board Operation, 1958; (with W.S. Elsbree) Principles of Staff Personnel Administration in Public Schools, 1959; (with L.O. Garber) The Yearbook of School Law, 1967, 68, 69, 70; Legal Aspects of Control of Student Activities by Public School Authorities, 1970; (with R.R. Hamilton) The Law of Public Education, 1970, 2d edit., 1976, supplement, 1979; The Courts and Student Conduct, 1975; also articles, chpts. in books. Home: 316 Grand Blvd Emerson NJ 07630 Office: Teachers Coll Columbia Univ New York NY 10027

REVEAL, ERNEST IRA, food co. exec.; b. Huntington, W.Va., Oct. 27, 1915; s. Ernest I. and Edna Virginia (Wiltrout) R.; B.A., Northwestern U., 1937; m. Hazel V. Holt, Apr. 30, 1945; children—Ernest I., Charles H. Mng. editor Domestic Engring. Publ., Chgo., 1945-49; sales devel. mgr. Uarco Bus. Forms, Chgo., 1949-54; gen. mgr. Todd Co., Rochester, N.Y., 1954-60; chmn. R.T. French Co., Rochester, 1975—; dir. Lincoln 1st Bank of Rochester, Schlegel Mfg. Co., Rochester, Gleason Works, Rochester, Sykes Datatronics, Rochester, Welch Foods, Inc., Westfield, N.H., Rochester Telephone Co., Reckitt & Colman, Ltd. of London. Chmn. United Community Chest Campaign, 1977; bd. dirs. Rochester Philharmonic Orch.; bd. trustees U. Rochester, Rochester Inst. Tech. Mem. Grocery Mfrs. Am. Republican. Presbyterian. Office: 1 Lincoln First Sq Rochester NY 14604

REVEL, JEAN PAUL, educator, cell biologist; b. Strasbourg, France, Dec. 7, 1930; s. Gaston Benjamin and Suzanne (Neher) R.; Baccalaureat des Scis., U. Strasbourg, 1949; Ph.D., Harvard, 1957; m. Helen Ruth Bowser, July 27, 1957; children—David, Daniel, Steven. Came to U.S., 1953, naturalized, 1962. Teaching fellow Harvard Med. Sch., 1953-56, Whitney fellow biochemistry, 1956-57; Whitney fellow anatomy Cornell U. Med. Sch., 1957-58, research fellow anatomy, 1958-59; mem. faculty Harvard Med. Sch., 1959-71, prof. anatomy, 1969-71; prof. biology Calif. Inst. Tech., Pasadena, 1971—, Albert Billings Ruddock prof. biology, 1978—. Fellow AAAS; mem. Am. Assn. Anatomists, Am. Soc. Cell Biology (pres.), Soc. Gen. Physiology, Histochem. Soc., N.Y. Acad. Scis., Soc. for Neurosci., Sigma Xi (nat. lectr. 1975-77). Mem. editorial bd. Jour. Cell Biology, Jour. Histochemistry and Cytochemistry, Jour. Supramolecular Structure, Jour. Ultrastructure Research; adv. editor Internat. Rev. Cytology. Home: 1201 Linda Ridge Ln Pasadena CA 91103

REVERCOMB, EVERETT EUGENE, assn. exec.; b. Washington, Jan. 28, 1914; s. Luke Woodward and Effie (Davis) R.; A.B., Duke, 1935; m. Dorothy Elouise Faidley, Sept. 29, 1940; children—Everett Eugene, Steven Lee. Auditor, Nat. Assn. Broadcasters, 1935-43, asst. treas., 1946-50; adminstrv. asst. George Washington U., 1950-52; comptroller Nat. Assn. Home Builders, 1952-56; sec.-treas. Nat. Assn. Broadcasters, 1956—. Active Boy Scouts Am.; past pres. McLean (Va.) Civic Assn. Served to lt. (s.g.) USNR, 1943-46. Lion, Mason. Home: 6523 Ridge St McLean VA 22101 Office: 1771 N St NW Washington DC 20006

REVERDIN, BERNARD J., lawyer; b. Baden, Switzerland, June 21, 1919; s. Jean and Germaine R.; LL.B., U. Geneva, 1942; postgrad. Harvard Law Sch., 1949; m. Anne-Cecile Pictet, Mar. 1, 1952; children—Caroline, Brigitte, Nathalie. Came to U.S., 1948, naturalized, 1954. Admitted to bar, Switzerland, 1945, N.Y. bar, 1955; atty., legal asst. Geneva Govt., 1945-48; asso. Sullivan & Cromwell, N.Y.C., 1949-51; asso. Lovejoy, Wasson, Lundgren & Ashton, N.Y.C., 1951-62, partner, 1962—; dir. subsidiaries of European corps. Vice pres., treas., bd. dirs. Friends of Cuttington Coll., Liberia; bd. dirs. Pestalozzi Found. Am., Inc. Mem. Am. Fgn. Law Assn. (dir.), N.Y. Bar Assn., Swiss Soc. N.Y. Contbr. articles to profl. jours. Home: 11 Beech Hill Rd Huntington NY 11743 also New York City NY Office: 250 Park Ave New York NY 10017

REVERE, ANNE, actress; b. N.Y.C., June 1903; d. C. T. and Harriette (Winn) Revere; grad. Wellesley Coll.; m. Samuel Rosen, 1935. Actress motion pictures, including Song of Bernadette, National Velvet, Sunday Dinner for a Soldier, Fallen Angel, Dragonwyck, Gentlemen's Agreement, Place in the Sun, Great Missouri Raid; also roles in theatre prodns. Double Door, Children's Hour, Cue for Passion, Toys in the Attic; TV shows include Search for Tomorrow, Six Million Dollar Man, Baretta, Sesame Street. Recipient Academy Award as best supporting actress, 1945; Tony award for performance Toys in the Attic, 1960. Office: care Jeff Hunter 119 W 57th St New York NY 10019. *An actor's art is wafted on the wind.*

REVI, ALBERT CHRISTIAN, editor; b. N.Y.C., July 31, 1924; s. Leo Charles and Mathilda Marie (Dausch) R.; ed. privately; m. Lois McClarin, Mar. 2, 1974. Owner Art Glass Studios, antiques, Dallas, 1952-66; editor Spinning Wheel mag., Hanover, Pa., 1966—; dir. Am. Antiques and Crafts Soc., 1972—. Elk. Author: 19th Century Glass, 1959; American Press Glass and Figure Bottles, 1961; American Cut and Engraved Glass, 1965; American Art Nouveau Glass, 1967. Editor: Spinning Wheel's Complete Book of Antiques, 1974; Spinning Wheel's Complete Book of Dolls, 1975. Home: 209 DeGuy Av Hanover PA 17331 Office: Spinning Wheel Fame Ave Hanover PA 17331

REVILLE, CHARLES OLIVER, JR., publisher; b. Balt., Aug. 29, 1924; s. Charles Oliver and Mary Madelon (Schmick) R.; A.B. in Chemistry, Princeton, 1948; student U. Md. Law Sch., 1949; m. Janet Marie Sherman, June 17, 1950; children—Charles Oliver III, Nancy Marie, Ann Elizabeth, Cynthia Ruth. Sales rep. Proctor and Gamble, 1948-49; spl. hosp. rep. Sharp and Dohme, Inc., pharms., 1949-51; sales rep. Merck, Sharp and Dohme, 1953; with Williams and Wilkins Co., Balt., pubs. sci. books, 1953—, pres., chief exec. officer, 1969—. Pres., Epilepsy Assn. Central Md., 1973—. Served with USNR, 1944-48, 51-53. Mem. Soc. Indsl. and Applied Math. (trustee). Republican. Presbyn. (trustee). Home: 124 Aylesbury Rd Timonium MD 21093 Office: 428 E Preston St Baltimore MD 21202

REVILLE, EUGENE THOMAS, ednl. adminstr.; b. Buffalo, Jan. 9, 1932; s. James and Agnes (Murphy) R.; B.S. in Elementary Edn., N.Y. State Coll. Tchrs. at Buffalo, 1953; M.Ed. in Adminstrn., U. Buffalo, 1961; m. Joan Schmelzinger, Aug. 18, 1956; 4 children. Prin., Buffalo Bd. Edn., 1962-66, adminstr. chief project, 1966-71, asso. supt. instructional service, 1971-75, supt. schs., 1975—. Contbr. articles to profl. jours. Home: 99 Bedford Pl Buffalo NY 14216 Office: Room 712 City Hall Buffalo Public School Dist Buffalo NY 14202

REVZIN, MARVIN E., oral surgeon; b. Detroit, May 28, 1922; s. Samuel and Sarah (Baxter) R.; B.A., Wayne State U., 1942, M.A., 1952; D.D.S., U. Detroit, 1951, M.S., 1954; m. Elaine Marion Levy, Feb. 14, 1948; children—Michael, Susan. Intern, Detroit Receiving Hosp., 1951-52, resident, 1952-54; asso. oral surgeon, dir. dental edn. Henry Ford Hosp., Detroit, 1954-62; mem. hosp. adv. com. USPHS Hosp., Detroit, 1963-67; mem. deans com. Vets. Hosp., Dearborn, Mich., 1967; dir. dental edn. Am. Dental Assn. Project Vietnam, 1967-73; external assessor U. Malaya, 1973; grad. lectr. speech pathology Wayne State U., 1947-51; lectr. oral surgery U. Detroit Sch. Dentistry, 1954-62, prof., chmn. dept. oral surgery and radiology, 1962-65, asst. dean, prof., chmn. dept., 1965-66, asso. dean, prof., chmn. dept., 1966-67, acting dean, 1967; asso. dean for hosp. affairs, prof., chmn. oral surgery U. So. Calif. Sch. Dentistry, Los Angeles, 1970-75; dean, prof. oral and maxillofacial surgery U. Mo. Sch. Dentistry, Kansas City, 1975—; first oral surgeon Project Hope, Indonesia, 1961; cons. USPHS Hosp., Detroit, 1963-67, U.S. Naval Hosp., San Diego, 1973-75, VA Hosp., Long Beach, Calif., 1974-75, VA Center, Leavenworth, Kans., 1975-76, VA Hosp., Kansas City, 1976, VA Hosp., Topeka, 1976; mem. exec. com. Profl. Staff Assn., Los Angeles County/U. So. Calif. Med. Center, 1970-75; mem. dental hygiene adv. com. Johnson County (Kans.) Community Coll., 1975-76. Mem. profl. adv. com. for health care Mayor's Com., Detroit, 1966-67; bd. dirs. Truman Med. Center; trustee U. Kansas City, Mo. Cancer Found. Served with USAAF, 1941-45. Recipient Outstanding Tchr. awards U. Detroit, 1962-64, Mayor's Commendation award City of Detroit, 1967, Chuong My Bio Tihn, Govt. of S. Vietnam, 1973, Meritorious award medal Vietnam Council on Fgn. Relations, 1973, Cogswell award in oral surgery, 1973, Service award Marsh Robinson Acad. Oral Surgeons, 1975; named Man of Year, U. Detroit. Diplomate Am. Bd. Oral Surgeons (sec.-treas. 1972—, v.p. 1977, pres. 1978). Fellow Am. Coll. Dentists, Internat. Assn. Oral Surgeons; mem. ADA (chmn. council Nat. Bd. Dental Examiners 1977), Mich., Mo. dental assns., Detroit (pres. 1963-64), Greater Kansas City dental socs., Am. (com. chmn.), Gt. Lakes, So. Calif. socs. oral surgeons, Chalmers J. Lyons Acad. Oral Surgeons (pres. 1961), AAAS, Internat. Assn. for Dental Research, Am. Speech and Hearing Assn., AAUP, So. Calif. Acad. Oral Pathology, Soc. for Internat. Devel., Fedn. Dentaire Internat., Arista, Omicron Kappa Upsilon. Editor: Detroit Dental Bull., 1956-64; mem. editorial bd. Jour. of Dental Edn., 1970—, Jour. of Oral Surgery, 1971—. Contbr. articles to dental jours. Home: 10249 Cedarbrooke Ln Kansas City MO 64131 Office: U Mo 650 E 25th St Kansas City MO 64108

REW, THOMAS FREDERICK, ret. air force officer; b. Bklyn., Mar. 18, 1922; s. Thomas John and Lucy Harriett (Davey) R.; B.S. in Edn., Springfield Coll., 1950; grad. Indsl. Coll. of Armed Forces, 1970; m. Marie E. Hartigan, Mar. 21, 1948; children—Thomas Edward, William John, Fredric Thomas, Maureen Ellen. Served as enlisted man U.S. Army Air Force, 1942-43, commd. 2d lt., 1943, advanced through grades to maj. gen., 1976; instr. pilot, chief standardization div. 17th Bomb Wing, 1951-66; squadron comdr. Dow AFB, Bangor, Maine, 1966-68; dir. ops. 2d Bombardment Wing, Barksdale AFB, La., 1968-69; dir. ops. and vice comdr. 380th Bombardment Wing, Plattsburgh, N.Y., 1970-71, comdr. 17th Bombardment Wing, Wright Patterson AFB, Ohio, 1971-72, 97th Strategic Bomb Wing, Blytheville AFB, Ark., 1972-73; comdr. 72d Provisional Wing, Anderson AFB, Guam; commanded 1st wave of B-52 sorties over Hanoi, 1972; chief of staff 2d Air Force, Barksdale AFB, La., 1973-74; comdr. 45th Air Div., Pease AFB, N.H., 1974-75, 3d Air Div., Anderson AFB, Guam, 1975-76, ret., 1976. Decorated D.S.M., Legion of Merit, D.F.C., Meritorious Service Medal with 1 oak leaf cluster, Commendation Medal with 3 oak leaf clusters. Mem. Order of Daedalians, Ret. Officers Assn., Air Force Assn. Baptist. Club: Caterpillar. Home: 64-73 Bridgewood Rd Columbia SC 29206

REWAK, WILLIAM JOHN, univ. ofcl., clergyman; b. Syracuse, N.Y., Dec. 22, 1933; s. William Alexander and Eldora Venetia (Carroll) R.; B.A., Gonzaga U., 1957, M.A. in English, 1958; M.A. in Theology, Regis Coll., Toronto, Ont., Can., 1965; Ph.D. in English, U. Minn., 1970. Joined S.J., Roman Catholic Ch., 1951, ordained priest, 1964; tchr. English, Bellarmine Coll. Prep. Sch., 1958-61; asst. prof. English, U. Santa Clara, 1970-71, rector Jesuit Community, 1971-76, univ. pres., 1976—. Bd. dirs. O'Connor Hosp. Found., San Jose, Calif., 1977—, Ind. Colls. No. Calif., 1977—; bd. govs. NCCJ of Santa Clara County (Calif.), 1978—. Mem. Assn. Ind. Calif. Colls. and Univs. (exec. com. 1978—), MLA, Coll. English Assn., Am. Assn. Univ. Adminstrs. Democrat. Contbr. articles to theol. and critical jours., poetry, short stories to lit. jours. Home and Office: U Santa Clara Santa Clara CA 95053

REWALD, JOHN, art historian; b. Berlin, Germany, May 12, 1912; s. Bruno and Paula (Feinstein) R.; student U. Hamburg, 1931, U. Frankfort on the Main, 1931- 32; Docteur es-Lettres, U. Paris, 1936; m. Estelle Haimovici, 1939 (div.); 1 son, Paul (dec.); m. 2d, Alice Bellony, 1956 (div.). Came to U.S., 1941, naturalized, 1947. Curator pvt. collection John Hay Whitney; asso. Museum Modern Art, N.Y.C., 1943—; prof. dept. art Univ. of Chgo., 1963-71, grad. center City U. N.Y., 1971—; co-dir. exhbn. Cezanne—The Late Work, Mus. Modern Art, N.Y.C., 1977, Grand Palais, Paris, 1978; A.W. Mellon lectr. Nat. Gallery Art, Washington, 1979. Decorated knight Legion of Honor, 1954; comdr. French Order Arts and Letters, 1979. Author: Gauguin, 1938; Maillol, 1939; Georges Seurat, 1943; Camille Pissarro, Letters to His Son Lucien, 1943; Sculptures of E. Degas, 1944; History of Impressionism, 1946; Renoir Drawings, 1946; Pierre Bonnard, 1948; Paul Cezanne, 1948; Post-Impressionism-From Van Gogh to Gauguin, 1956; Gauguin Drawings, 1958, others. Home: 1075 Park Ave New York NY 10028

REXINE, JOHN EFSTRATIOS, educator; b. Boston, June 6, 1929; s. Efstratios John and Athena (Glekas) R.; A.B. magna cum laude, Harvard, 1951, A.M., 1953, Ph.D., 1964; m. Elaine Lavrakas, June 16. 1957; children—John Efstratios Jr., Athena Elisabeth, Michael Constantine. Instr. humanities Brandeis U., 1955-57; instr. classics Colgate U., 1957-60, asst. prof. classics, 1960-64, asso. prof., 1964-68, prof, 1968—, Charles A. Dana prof. classics, 1977—, chmn. dept. classics, 1964-72, dir. div. univ. studies, 1969-72, dir. div. humanities, 1972—, chmn. dept. classics, slavic and Oriental langs., 1972-73, acting chmn., 1976, asso. dean faculty, 1973-74, acting dean faculty, 1977-78; dir. Colgate-IBM Corp. Inst. Liberal Arts Program for Execs., 1969-71, 1978, 79; vis. prof. Greek and classical mythology Coll. Year in Athens, Greece, fall 1972-73; Fulbright-Hays sr. research scholar Am. Sch. Classical Studies, Athens, 1979-80. Mem. program bd. div. Christian edn. Nat. Council Chs. Christ, 1969-72; v.p. Inst. for Byzantine and Modern Greek Studies, 1974—. Trustee Greek Orthodox Theol. Sch., 1955-57. Danforth Found. Tchr. Study grantee Harvard, 1959-60, Helicon Soc. Gold Medal award, 1962; Fulbright scholar to Greece, 1951-52; Am. Numis. Soc. fellow, summer 1955; Colgate U. Asian Studies faculty fellow, 1965-66; Archon Didaskalos tou Genous of Ecumenical Patriarchate of Constantinople, 1967. Mem. Am. Philol. Assn., Mediaeval Acad. Am., Am. Classical League, Classical Assn. Atlantic States, Classical Assn. Empire State, Helicon Soc. (pres. 1956-57), Hellenic Soc. Humanistic Studies (hon.); Phi Beta Kappa, Eta Sigma Phi (trustee 1977—). Author: Solon and His Political Theory, 1958; Religion in Plato and Cicero, 1959, rev. edit., 1968; (with Andreas Kazamias, Paul Nash, Henry Perkinson) The Educated Man, 1965; (with Thomas Spelios, Harry J. Psomiades), A Pictorial History of Greece, 1967. Contbg. editor The Hellenic Chronicle, 1952—; book rev. editor Athene, 1957-67; book rev. editor The Orthodox Observer, 1957-72, book rev. columnist, 1972—, mng. editor, 1959-60; asso. editor Greek Orthodox Theol. Rev., 1960-67, editorial adv. bd., 1967—; asst. editor Helios, 1976-79; asso. editor Diakonia, 1971—; editor Classical Outlook, 1977-79; book rev. editor classics and modern Greek The Modern Lang. Jour., 1977—. Home: RD 2 Spring St Box 78B Hamilton NY 13346

REXROTH, KENNETH, author, critic, painter; b. South Bend, Ind., Dec. 22, 1905; s. Charles Marion and Delia (Reed) R.; student pub. schs.; studied New Sch., Art Students' League, Art Inst. Chgo.; m. Andree Dutcher, 1927 (dec. 1940); m. 2d, Marie Kass, 1940 (div. 1948); m. 3d, Marthe Whitcomb, 1949 (div. 1961); children—Mary, Katharine; m. 4th, Carol Tinker, 1974. Exhibited one-man shows, Los Angeles, Santa Monica, Calif., N.Y.C., Chgo., Paris, San Francisco; San Francisco corr. The Nation, 1953-68; columnist San Francisco Examiner, 1960-68; co-founder San Francisco Poetry Center; creative writer prose and poetry. Spl. lectr. U. Calif. at Santa Barbara. Recipient Commonwealth Club medal; Eunice Tietjens award Poetry mag.; Shelly Meml. award Poetry Soc. Am.; Longview award; Chapelbrook award; Nat. Acad. award; William Carlos Williams award; Copernicus award Am. Acad. Poets, 1975, others; Guggenheim fellow, 1948-49; Amy Lowell fellow, 1958; Fulbright sr. fellow in Japan, 1974-75; Nat. Endowment Arts grantee, 1977. Author: In What Hour, 1940; The Phoenix and the Tortoise, 1944; The Signature of All Things, 1949; The Art of Worldly Wisdom, 1949; The Dragon and the Unicorn, 1952; 100 Poems From the Japanese, 1954; 100 Poems from the Chinese, 1956; 30 Spanish Poems, 1956; Thou Shalt Not Kill; (poems) In Defense of the Earth, 1956; 100 Poems From the Greek and Latin, 1959; The Bird in the Bush (essays), 1959; Assays, 1962; The Homestead Called Damascus, 1962; Natural Numbers, (poems), 1965; An Autobiographical Novel, 1966; Complete Collected Shorter Poems, 1966; Beyond the Mountains, (plays), 1966; Classics Revisited 1968; Collected Longer Poems, 1968; Love and The Turning Year: 100 More Poems from the Chinese, 1969; Poems of Pierre Reverdy, transl. 1969; The Alternative Society essays, 1970; With Eye and Ear (essays), 1970; American Poetry in the 20th Century, 1971; Sky Sea Birds Trees Earth House Beasts Flowers, 1971; (essays) The Elastic Retort, 1973; New Poems, 1974; Communalism From Its Origins to the 20th Century (history), 1975. others. Contbr. poems, articles to various mags. Translator: 100 French poems, 1971; (with Ling Chung) The Orchid Boat: The Women Poets of China, 1973; 100 More Poems from the Japanese, 1976; (with Ikuko Atsumi) The Burning Heart, The Women Poets of Japan; The Silver Swan, 1977; On Flower Wreath Hill, 1977; The Poems of Marichiko, transl. 1977; Selected Poems of Shiraishi Kazuko, transl. 1977; The Morning Star, 1979; (with Ling Chung) The Complete Poems of Li Ch'ing Chao, 1979. Address: 1401 E Pepper Ln Santa Barbara CA 93108

REY, ANTHONY MAURICE, hotel exec.; b. N.Y.C., Mar. 31, 1916; s. Anthony A. and Madeleine (Lauper) R.; student N.Y. U., 1933-34, L'Ecole Hoteliere, Lausanne, Switzerland, 1934-35; m. Dorothea M. Carley, June 2, 1934; children—Anthony Maurice, Donna Christine R. Naame, Jamie Elisabeth R. Di Giovanni, Andrea Michele (dec.), Cynthia Anne Higbee. With Waldorf-Astoria Hotel, N.Y.C., 1934-58; gen. mgr., v.p. Astor Hotel, N.Y.C., 1958-65; pres., dir. Chalfonte Haddon Hall, 1965-76; pres., dir. Resorts Internat. Hotel Casino Co., 1976-80; v.p. Resorts Internat. Inc., 1979—; dir. Guarantee Bank, Atlantic City; sec. E.J.H. Co. Commr., bd. dirs. Atlantic Area council Boy Scouts Am., 1965—; commr., vice chmn. Atlantic County Improvement Authority, 1965-74; bd. dirs. Miss Am. Pageant, 1966—; chmn. exec. com. Atlantic City Conv. Bur., 1967—, chmn. bd., 1975—; trustee So. N.J. Devel. Council, 1971—; chmn. Conv. Liaison Council, 1967-74; bd. dirs. Atlantic County United Fund, 1967-69; trustee Internat. Restaurant and Hotel Union Pension Trust, 1975-76. Served with USNR, 1942-45. Decorated Bronze Star, Presdl. citation; named N.J. Innkeeper of Year, 1971; named to Hospitality Hall of Fame, 1969—; hon. dept. fire chief N.Y.C., 1963—. Mem. Greater Atlantic City (pres. 1969-71, chmn. bd. 1971-73), N.J. (dir. 1973—) chambers commerce, Internat. Hotel Sales Mgmt. Assn., Am. (industry adv. council 1974—, chmn. resort com. 1978, chmn. bd. 1979), N.J. (pres. 1971-72, chmn. bd. 1972-75, trustee, life mem.) hotel-motel assns., Atlantic City Hotel Assn. (trustee 1976—), N.Y. U. Hotel and Restaurant Soc. (hon. life), Hotel and Restaurant Mgmt. Soc. Fairleigh Dickenson U. (life), Waldorf Astoria Disting. Alumni Assn. (chmn. 1973—), Am. Legion. Episcopalian. Clubs: Skal, Lambs (N.Y.C.); Circus Saints and Sinners (life); Seaview Country (Absecon, N.J.). Home: 1 S Somerset Ave Ventnor NJ 08406 Office: Resorts Internat Hotel Casino Boardwalk and North Carolina Ave Atlantic City NJ 08404

REY, WILLIAM KENNETH, engr., educator; b. N.Y.C., Aug. 11, 1925; s. William and Frances Sophia (Sauer) R.; B.S. in Aero. Engring., U. Ala., 1946, M.S. in Civil Engring., 1949; postgrad. U. Ariz., 1961; m. Ruth Jeanette Vickery, Nov. 27, 1946; children—Jeanette Rey Todd, William Kenneth. Instr. math. U. Ala., 1946-47, instr. engring. mechanics, 1947-49, asst. prof. engring. mechanics, 1949-52, asso. prof. aero. engring., 1952-58, prof. aero. engring., 1958-60, prof. aerospace engring., 1960—, acting head dept., 1972, dir. high sch. relations, 1970—, asst. dean engring., 1976—; cons. research NACA, NASA, Army and Air Force depts. Recipient Dist. Scouter award Boy Scouts Am., 1970; registered profl. engr., Ala. Asso. fellow AIAA; mem. Nat. Soc. Profl. Engrs., Am. Soc. Engring. Edn., Air Force Assn., Capstone Engring. Soc. (exec. dir. 1976—), Theta Tau (grand regent, nat. pres. 1963-66, grand marshal 1968-72), Tau Beta Pi, Omicron Delta Kappa, Sigma Gamma Tau, Pi

Mu Epsilon. Baptist (deacon). Clubs: Kiwanis (dir. Tuscaloosa, Ala., 1969-74, 76—, 1st v.p. 1976-77, pres. 1978-79, zone chmn. 1975-78), Univ. (gov. Tuscaloosa 1970-77, pres. 1976). Contbr. NACA and NASA reports, revs., lab. manual. Home: 77 Woodland Hills Tuscaloosa AL 35405 Office: PO Box 1968 University AL 35486

REYBURN, HAROLD ORBRA, accountant; b. Granby, Mo., May 3, 1915; s. Robert D. and Nettie (Burnett) R.; B.C.S., Okla. Sch. Accountancy, 1939; m. C. DeLyte Tallman, Dec. 3, 1938 (div.); children—A. Kim, Donna DeLyte (Mrs. Michael G. Griffith), Thomas M.; m. 2d, Linda K. Terrill, Apr. 16, 1970. Accountant, St. Louis Mining & Smelting Co., 1933-34, Shell Oil Co., 1934-40; with Frazer & Torbet, C.P.A.'s, Tulsa, 1940-44; partner Nicholson, Reyburn & Co., C.P.A.'s, Tulsa, 1944-57, Coopers & Lybrand, Tulsa, 1957-78; instr. Okla. Sch. Accountancy, nights 1940-54; pres. Caywood Oil & Gas Co., 1951-58; adv. dir. Utica Nat. Bank & Trust Co., 1979—; dir. Nash Oil Co., 1949-59, Consol. Oil Co., 1949—, Bovaird Supply Co., 1978—; v.p. Microfilm Service, Inc., 1950-58. Chmn. mayor's adv. com. City of Tulsa, 1966-67; treas., dir. Skelly Stadium Corp., Tulsa, 1965-75; trustee, mem. exec. com. Tulsa Psychiat. Center, 1959—; treas., 1959-73, pres., 1973, chmn. bd., 1974-77; treas., dir. Tulsa Sci. Center, 1969-76. C.P.A., Okla., Tex. Mem. Am. Inst. C.P.A.'s, Okla. Soc. C.P.A.'s (pres. 1953-54), Tulsa C. of C. (dir. 1970-76), Nat. Assn. Accountants (pres. Tulsa 1953-54). Baptist (treas., mem. finance com., brotherhood deacons 1941—). Clubs: Tulsa, Southern Hills Country (Tulsa). Contbr. to profl. jours. Home: 2949 S Delaware Ave Tulsa OK 74114 Office: 4038 First National Tower Suite 4038 Tulsa OK 74103

REYER, RANDALL WILLIAM, anatomist; b. Chgo., Jan. 23, 1917; s. William Cleveland and Elsie Mary (Hardy) R.; A.B., Cornell U., 1939; M.A., 1942; Ph.D., Yale U., 1947; m. Carolyn Elizabeth Murray, June 12, 1943; children—Elizabeth Ann, Mary Louise. Instr. biology Conn. Wesley U., 1946-47; instr. zoology Yale U., New Haven, 1947-50; asst. prof. anatomy U. Pitts., 1950-57; asso. prof. anatomy W.Va. U., Morgantown, 1957-67, prof., 1967—, acting chmn. dept., 1977-78. NIH research grantee, 1951-79. Mem. Am. Assn. Anatomists, Am. Soc. Zoologists, Internat. Soc. Devel. Biologists, Soc. for Devel. Biology, Assn. for Research in Vision and Ophthalmology, So. Soc. Anatomists, Am. Inst. Biol. Scis., Assn. Am. Med. Colls., Sigma Xi, Phi Beta Kappa, Phi Kappa Phi, Pi Kappa Alpha, Phi Rho Sigma. Presbyterian. Research on devel. and regeneration of lens in amphibian eye, 1948-79. Home: 1316 Fairfield St Morgantown WV 26505 Office: Dept Anatomy Med Center WVa U Morgantown WV 26506

REYES-GUERRA, DAVID RICHARD, engrs. orgn. ofcl., civil engr.; b. London, Eng., Oct. 4, 1930; s. Antonio and Linda Elizabeth (Hardesty) Reyes-G.; B.S. in Civil Engring., The Citadel, 1954; M.Engring., Yale, 1955; m. Maria Marta Aris, Jan. 2, 1953; children—David Richard, Elizabeth, Anne, Daniel, John, Paul. Project engr. United Fruit Co., Guatemala, 1955-57; prof. gen. engring. U. Ill., Urbana, 1958-68; exec. dir. Jr. Engring. Tech. Soc., N.Y.C., 1968—, Engrs. Council for Profl. Devel. N.Y.C., 1970—; cons. engr. in adminstrn., pub. relations. mgmt., edn. splty. internat. field. Registered profl. engr. Mem. Am. Soc. C.E., Am. Soc. Engring. Edn., Nat. Soc. Profl. Engrs. Contbr. articles profl publs. Office: Engrs Council for Profl Devel 345 E 47th St New York NY 10017

REYES HEROLES, JESUS, former Sec. Interior Mexico; b. Tuxpan, Veracruz, Mex., Apr. 3, 1921; s. Jesus Reyes Martinez and Juana Heroles Lombera; LL.B. with special honors, Nat. Autonomous U. Mex., 1944; postgrad. U. Buenos Aires and La Plata, Colegio Libre de Estudios Superiores de Buenos Aires, 1945; m. Gloria Gonzalez Garza, May 8, 1951; children—Jesus, Federico. Assessor, Dept. Labor and Social Planning, Mexico City, 1944; substitute pres. special group no. 1 Fedl. Bd. Reconciliation and Arbitration, Mexico City, 1946; sec. gen. Mexican Book Inst., 1949-53; assessor Office of Pres., Mexico City, 1952-58; chief economic studies Mexican Nat. Railroads, Mexico City, 1953-58; tech. subdir. gen. Mexican Inst. Social Security, Mexico City, 1958-64; dir. gen. Petroleos Mexicanos, Mexico City, 1964-70; dir. gen. Diesel Nacional, S.A., Constructora Nacional de Carros de Ferrocarril, S.A., Siderurgica Nacional, S.A., Mexico City, 1970-72; dir. gen. Mexican Inst. Social Security, 1975-76; Sec. Interior (Fedl. Govt.), Mexico City, 1976-79; various professorial positions, colls. in Mex., 1944-67; pres. Interamerican Center for Studies in Social Security; bd. dirs. Fondo para la Historia de las Ideas Revolucionarias de Mex. Various positions in the Partido Revolucionario Institucional (PRI), 1939-60; rep. XLV legis. Congreso de la Union; pres. Nat. Exec. Com. PRI. Hon. mem. Spanish Royal Acad. Hist., mem. Mex. Acad. Hist., Mex. Soc. Geography and Statistics, College Lawyers. Partido Revolucionario Institucional. Author various studies in politics, economics, including El Liberalismo Mexicano (3 volumes) 1957, 58, 61.

REYNAL, JEANNE AMALIE, artist; b. White Plains, N.Y., Apr. 1, 1903; d. Eugene Sugny and Adelaide Fitzgerald R.; m. Thomas Sills, Aug., 1952. Exhibitions include: Loeb Student Center N.Y. U., 1961, PVI Gallery, N.Y.C., 1964, San Francisco Mus. Art Traveling Exhbn., 1964, SS Joachim and Anne Ch., Queens Village, N.Y., Betty Parsons Gallery, N.Y.C., 1971, Newport Art Assn., 1971, Craft Horizons, 1971, 76, Bodley Gallery, N.Y.C., 1976, 79; represented in permanent collections: Ford Found., White Plains, Mus. Modern Art, N.Y.C., Walker Art Center, Mpls., Whitney Mus. Am. Art, N.Y.C., Rockefeller U.; commd. works include: Our Lady of Fla., Palm Beach, 1962, Cliff House, Avon, Conn., 1962, Nebr. State Capitol, Lincoln, 1965, 66. Address: 240 W 11th St New York NY 10014

REYNER, ANTHONY STEPHEN, educator, geographer; b. Tabor, Czechoslovakia, June 15, 1912; s. Sigmund and Leonie (Stearns) R.; Dr.Jur. and Sc.Pol. (cum laude), Charles U., Prague, Czechoslovakia, 1935; Sc.M., U. Chgo., 1941; m. Virginia I. Michalski, Sept. 22, 1948; children—Mary L., John L. Came to U.S., 1939, naturalized, 1948. Officer in charge, ASPT, Iberian studies Grinnell Coll., 1942-43; chief Portuguese unit FEA, 1943-45; prof. geography, head dept. U. P.R., 1945-46, Howard U., 1946—. Chief UN mission to Costa Rica, 1951-52; vis. prof. U. Md., 1946, Catholic U., 1960, 61; cons. radio sta. WETA, 1960—; cons. internat. boundaries Office Geographer, State Dept., 1957—, lectr. Fgn. Service Inst., 1960—; lectr. Indsl. Coll. Armed Forces, 1958—, Am. Council Edn., Washington Internat. Center, 1948—. Served as maj. USAF, 1950-53. Grantee NSF, 1958, 60, African Studies Assn., 1961, 62, Nat. Council Learned Socs., 1963, Social Sci. Research Council, 1964. Fellow Royal Geog. Soc., African Studies Assn.; mem. Assn. Am. Geographers, Nat. Council Geog. Edn., Am. Geog. Assn. Author: (with G. Etzel Pearcy) World Political Geography, 1957; (with G. T. Renner) Global Geography, 1958; (with Charles A Fisher) Essays in Political Geography, 1968; (with C. G. Widstrand) African Boundary Problems, 1969; also numerous articles in profl. jours. U.S. and fgn. countries. Home: 4535 Q Pl NW Washington DC 20007

REYNERTSON, JOHN LEROY, tool mfg. exec.; b. Chgo., Sept. 7, 1926; s. H. Stanley and Irene Margret (Beamer) R.; B.C.S. in Retail Merchandising, Drake U., 1949; postgrad. Northwestern U., Loyola U., Chgo.; m. Patricia Jean Weber, Aug. 28, 1948; children—Raymond, Gloria, Donald, Mariann, John Leroy, Ronald. Trainee, S.S. Kresge Co., 1949-51; asst. furniture buyer Wieboldts' Stores, 1951-56; buyer Montgomery Ward, 1956, nat. retail-mail order sales mgr.—appliance group, nat. mdse. mgr. freezers, air conditioners, ranges and space heaters, until 1969; pres. Hand Tool div. Dresser Industries, Inc., Franklin Park, Ill., 1969-73, 77—, Bay State Abrasives div., 1974-77, Ops. div. Tool Group, 1973-74. Founding chmn. Vill. Community Chest, Itasca, Ill.; Cub Scout leader, Boy Scouts Am., chmn. Served to sgt. inf. U.S. Army, 1944-46; PTO. Mem. Pres's. Assn. (dir.), Hand Tools Inst., Am. Supply and Machinery Mfrs.' Assn., Nat. Hardware Mfg. Assn. Roman Catholic. Clubs: Chgo. Yacht, Lincolnshire (Ill.) Racquet. Home: 9 Essex Ln Lincolnshire IL 60015 Offic 3201 N Wolf Rd Franklin Park IL 60131*

REYNOLDS, A. WILLIAM, diversified mfg. co. exec.; b. Columbus, Ohio, June 21, 1933; s. William M. and Helen (McCray) R.; A.B., Harvard, 1955; M.B.A., Stanford, 1957; m. Joanne McCormick, June 12, 1953; children—Timothy, Virginia, Mary. Controller, Crawford Door Co., Ecorse, Mich., 1959-61, pres., 1961-66; asst. to exec. v.p. TRW, Inc., Cleve., 1966-67, v.p., group exec. aftermarket ops., 1967-70, exec. v.p., 1971—; dir. Society Nat. Bank, Cleve., Soc. Corp., Cleve.; dir. Automotive Info. Council. Mem. vis. com. Case-Western Res. U. Grad. Sch. Bus.; trustee Hathaway Brown Sch., Cleve. Mem. Soc. Automotive Engrs., Motor and Equipment Mfrs. Assn. (past chmn.). Episcopalian. Office: 23555 Euclid Ave Cleveland OH 44117

REYNOLDS, ANDREW JACKSON, hosp. adminstr.; b. Monroe, La., Nov. 8, 1930; s. Frank Albert and Elizabeth (Guinn) R.; B.S. in Engring., U.S. Naval Acad., 1954; LL.B., Ark. Law Sch., 1962; certificate in hosp. adminstr. U. Ala., 1970; m. Dolores March, June 12, 1954; children—Michelle, Michael, Lisa. Civil engr. U.S. C. E., Little Rock., Ark., 1958-62; constrn. mgr.; engr. Langley Research Center, NASA, Hampton, Va., 1962-67; civil engr. Bur. of Research and Engring. U.S. Post Office, Washington, 1967; asso. adminstr. St. Vincent Infirmary, Little Rock, Ark., 1967-73, adminstr., 1973—. Bd. dirs. Aldersgate Methodist Camp., 1973—. Served with USMC, 1954-58. Mem. Ark. Hosp. Assn. (treas. 1971, dir. 1973—, chmn. council of govt. relations 1971—, pres. 1978), Vis. Nurse Assn. (pres. 1974, dir. 1972-74). Roman Catholic. Home: 2913 Imperial Valley Dr Little Rock AR 72212 Office: St Vincent Infirmary Little Rock AR 72201

REYNOLDS, BENEDICT MICHAEL, surgeon; b. N.Y.C., Sept. 12, 1925; s. Benedict and Delia (Coan) R.; student Columbia U., 1942-43, U. Rochester, 1943-44; M.D., N.Y. U., 1948; m. Alice Marie Hodnett, May 3, 1952; children—Benedict, John, Ann Marie, Mary Alice, Daniel. Intern, Bellevue Med. Center, N.Y.C., 1948-49, surg. resident, 1951-55; asst. in surgery N.Y. U., N.Y.C., 1953-55; instr. surgery Albert Einstein Coll. Medicine, Bklyn., 1955-56, asst. prof. surgery, 1956-58, clin. asst. prof., 1958-71, vis. prof. surgery, 1977; prof. surgery N.Y. Med. Coll., N.Y.C., 1971—; practice medicine specializing in surgery, Bronx, 1955—; dir. surgery Misericordia Hosp. Med. Center, Bronx, 1962—, Fordham Hosp., 1964-76; chmn. dept. surgery Lincoln Hosp., Bronx, 1976—; attending surgeon Flower and Fifth Ave Hosp., N.Y.C., 1972—, Met. Hosp., N.Y.C., 1972—; cons. Community Gen. Hosp. of Sullivan County, 1972—. Served with USN, 1943-45, 49-51. Diplomate Am. Bd. Surgery, Pan Am. Med. Assn. Fellow N.Y. Acad. Medicine, A.C.S.; mem. AMA, N.Y. State Med. Soc., N.Y. Acad. Sci., Soc. Surgery Alimentary Tract, N.Y. and Bklyn. Regional Chpt. on Trauma, Internat. Soc. Lymphology, N.Y. Surg. Soc., Am. Gastroent. Assn. Roman Catholic. Contbr. articles in field to med. jours. Home: 150 Overhill Rd Bronxville NY 10708 Office: 600 E 233d St Bronx NY 10466

REYNOLDS, BURT, actor; b. Waycross, Ga., Feb. 11, 1936; s. Burt Reynolds; ed. Fla. State U., Palm Beach Jr. Coll.; m. Judy Carne (div. 1965). Actor numerous stage prodns. including Mister Roberts, Look, We've Come Through, The Rainmaker; movie appearances include Angel Baby, 1961, Armored Command, 1961, Operation CIA, 1965, Navajo Joe, 1967, Impasse, 1969, 100 Rifles, 1969, Sam Whiskey, 1969, Skullduggery, 1970, Deliverance, 1972, Fuzz, 1972, Everything You've Always Wanted to Know about Sex But Were Afraid to Ask, 1972, Shamus, 1973, The Man Who Loved Cat Dancing, 1973, White Lightning, 1973, The Longest Yard, 1974, At Long Last Love, 1975, W.W. and the Dixie Dance Kings, 1975, Hustle, 1975, Lucky Lady, 1975, Silent Movie, 1976, Nickelodeon, 1976, Smokey and the Bandit, 1977, Semi-Tough, 1977, Hooper, 1978, Starting Over, 1979; dir., actor Gator, 1976, The End, 1978; TV appearances include M Squad, Riverboat, Pony Express, Branded; regular appearances Gunsmoke, 1962-65; star series Hawk, 1966, Dan August, 1970-71; owner ranch, Jupiter, Fla. Mem. Dirs. Guild Am. Address: 8730 Sunset Blvd Suite 201 Los Angeles CA 90069

REYNOLDS, CHARLES MCKINLEY, JR., banker; b. Thomasville, Ga., Jan. 11, 1937; s. Charles McKinley and Johnnie (Hadley) R.; student Morehouse Coll., 1954-56; mortuary sci. certificate Wayne State U., 1962; postgrad. Atlanta U., 1965-66; m. Estella Mary Henry, Aug. 19, 1956; children—Eric Charles, Gregory Preston. Tchr., Southside Jr. High Sch., Albany, Ga., 1962-65; nat. bank examiner Treasury Dept., Atlanta, 1965-71; exec. v.p. Citizens Trust Co., 1971, pres., 1971-74; now pres., chief exec. officer, Atlantic Nat. Bank, Norfolk, Va.; treas. Pathways, Inc. Exec. sec. Temporary Devel. Agy., Albany, Ga., 1963-65, Atlanta Leadership Inst., 1966-67; asst. commr. Central dist. Boy Scouts Am., Atlanta, 1969—; mem. Atlanta Coalition on Current Community Affairs; mem. housing task force Gov.'s Goals for Ga. Program; mem. Met. Rapid Transit Authority Commn.; pres. West Manor PTA, Atlanta, 1968-69. Bd. dirs. ARC, Atlanta Model Cities Housing Devel. Corp., Butler St. YMCA, United Appeal, Norfolk State Coll., Nat. Alliance Businessmen; chmn. bd. Boggs Acad., Keysville, Ga. Served with USAF, 1956-60. Mem. Nat. Bankers Assn. (pres. 79—), Ga., Albany (v.p. 1965) tchr. and edn. assns., Social Sci. Work Study Group (pres. 1964-65), Norfolk C. of C. (dir., v.p. govtl. affairs), Tidewater Area Bus. and Contractors Assn. Nat. Bus. League, Alpha Phi Alpha, Epsilon Nu Delta, Gamma Omicron Lambda (chpt. asst. sec. 1964-65). Clubs: Criterion (sec. 1963-65); Morehouse College Alumni. Home: 4504 Kelley Ct Virginia Beach VA 23462

REYNOLDS, COLLINS JAMES, III, aviation co. exec.; b. N.Y.C., Feb. 28, 1937; s. Collins James and Alta Roberta (Carr) R.; student govt. and econs. Harvard, George Washington U.; m. Harriet Virginia Blackburn (div. 1965); children—Collins James IV, Quentin Scott; m. 2d, Carol Ann Miller, June 24, 1967; children—Justin Blake, Carson Jonathan. Data processing supr. missile and space vehicle div. Gen. Electric, Phila., 1961; contract adminstr. Allison div. Gen. Motors, Indpls., 1962-65; dir. Peace Corps, Mauritania, 1966-67, Sierra Leone, 1971-74; dir. div. ops. Gen. Learning Corp., Washington, 1968-71; trustee, sec., treas., exec. dir. Center for Research and Edn., Denver, 1974-79; v.p., gen. mgr. Air Rescue Am., Inc., Denver, 1979—; cons. Econ. Devel. Adminstrn., OECD; project dir. Model Cities Edn. Plan, HUD, Gen. Learning, Balt.; project dir. Dept. Labor/HEW Remedial Edn. and Job Placement Program, Transcentury Corp., Washington; program mgr. Ft. Lincoln New Town Sch. System, Washington; supervising dir. tng. VISTA, Boston, N.Y.C., Atlanta; dir. adminstrn. Job Corps, Kansas City. Co-founder The Bridge Internat. Sch., 1977. Served as aviator USMCR, 1956-60. Club: Explorers (N.Y.C.). Founder, editor, pub. The Bridge. Patentee in field. Home: 1615 Krameria St Denver CO 80220 Office: Air Rescue Am 3333 Quebec St Suite 4000 Denver CO 80207

REYNOLDS, DANA DRUMMOND, devel. exec.; b. Flemington, W.Va., Nov. 22, 1908; s. Wayland Fuller and Inez (Brohard) R.; A.B., W.Va. U. 1930; postgrad. George Washington U., 1943, 46, Am. U., 1948; m. Lorna Woollacott Murphy, Sept. 12, 1933; children—Winifred W. (Mrs. R. Garcia), Deirdre A. (Mrs. Chester Eugene Peters), Lorna Jean, John Dana. Editorial asst. Agr. Extension Service, W.Va. U., 1927, asst. editor, 1928, acting editor, 1929; staff office of info. Dept. Agr., 1930-33, 36-43, 46-48; staff President's Inter-Agy. Com. for Upper Monongahela Valley, acting sec. for preparation of report, 1934-35; liaison agrl. information Dept. Agr.-ECA, 1949-50; food and agrl. specialist ECA-Mut. Security Agy., 1951-52; chief agr. instns. br. FOA-ICA, 1953-58; adv. com. sci. communications service Inter-Am. Inst. Agrl. Scis., Turrialba, 1955-58; dep. food and agr. officer U.S. Ops. Mission to Libya, 1958-60, extension tng. adviser to Afghanistan, 1960-63; cons. AID, other orgns., 1963- 68; pvt. cons. internat. devel. strategy, 1968-70; pres. Internat. Center for Dynamics of Devel., 1971—; organized world conf. Country Strategies to Involve People in Devel., 1975, Center co-sponsor with UN Inst. for Tng. and Research 2 internat. Symposia on Nat. Strategies To Build Support for Devel. in Context of New Internat. Econ. Order, 1979; currently consulting and planning with nat. and internat. ofcls. on proposal for Internat. Decade of Strategy of Change. Weekly agrl. news report ABC Network, 1947-48. Served from seaman to lt., USNR, 1944-45. Mem. Soc. for Internat. Devel., Center for Study Dem. Instns., Am. Acad. Polit. and Social Sci., World Future Soc., Common Cause, New Directions, Kappa Tau Alpha. Editor symposium papers Popular Participation in Nat. Devel.; Unity and Development in the Middle East. Address: 4201 S 31st St Arlington VA 22206. *The world is wrestling with increasingly complex issues in a new era of burgeoning population, pressures for equity within and among nations, disruptions of families, uprooting of millions of people, diminishing resources—and violent reactions by persons frustrated in trying to adjust to these problems. It is proposed that national and international leaders join in an International Decade of Strategy of "change" to re-examine the institutions and processes to cope with the issues of this new era. The aim: peaceful "change" with protection of human rights.*

REYNOLDS, DAVID PARHAM, metals co. exec.; b. Bristol, Tenn., June 16, 1915; s. Richard S. and Julia L. (Parham) R.; student Princeton; m. Margaret Harrison, Mar. 25, 1944; children—Margaret A., Julia P., Dorothy H. With Reynolds Metals Co., Louisville, 1937—, salesman, 1937-41, asst. mgr. aircraft parts div., 1941-44, asst. v.p., 1944-46, v.p., 1946-58, exec. v.p., 1958-69, exec. v.p., gen. mgr., 1969-75, vice chmn., chmn. exec. com., 1975-76, chmn. bd., chief exec. officer, 1976—, also dir.; chmn. bd., dir. Robertshaw Control Co.; dir. Reynolds Metals Devel. Corp., Reynolds Jamaica Mines Ltd., Reynolds Internat., Inc., United Va. Bankshares, Eskimo Pie Corp. Trustee Lawrenceville (N.J.) Sch. Mem. Aluminum Assn. Home: 8905 Tresco Rd Richmond VA 23229 Office: 6601 Broad Street Rd Richmond VA 23261

REYNOLDS, DEBBIE (MARY FRANCES REYNOLDS), actress; b. El Paso, Tex., Apr. 1, 1932; m. Eddie Fisher, Sept. 26, 1955 (div. 1959); children—Carrie, Todd; m. 2d, Harry Karl, Nov., 1960 (div. 1975). Active high sch. plays; screen debut Daughter of Rosie O'Grady; motion pictures include This Happy Feeling, Three Little Words, Tender Trap, Tammy and The Bachelor, Mating Game, Say One For Me, It Started With a Kiss, Singing in the Rain, Catered Affair, The Gazebo, The Rat Race, Susan Slept Here, Pepe, Pleasure of His Company, Mary, Mary, My Six Loves, How the West was Won, Molly Brown, The Singing Nun, Divorce American Style, What's the Matter With Helen?, 1971, That's Entertainment!, 1974, That's Entertainment, Part 2, 1976; star TV program The Debbie Reynolds Show, 1969, Broadway show Irene, 1973-74; nightclub performer, 1961—; appeared in Annie Get Your Gun, Los Angeles, San Francisco, 1977. Named Miss Burbank, 1948, Los Vegas Entertainer of Yr. award. Author: If I Knew Then, 1963.*

REYNOLDS, DONALD WORTHINGTON, publisher; b. Ft. Worth, Sept. 23, 1906; s. Gaines Worlie and Anna Louise (Elfers) R.; B.J., U. Mo., 1927. Pub., Southwest-Times Record, Ft. Smith, Ark., Okmulgee (Okla.) Times, 1940—, Bartlesville (Okla.) Examiner, 1947—, Las Vegas (Nev.) Rev. Jour., 1949—, Ely (Nev.) Times and Carson City (Nev.) Appeal, 1950—, Blackwell (Okla.) Jour. Tribune and Rogers (Ark.) News, 1955—, Chickasha (Okla.) Express, 1956—, Gutherie (Okla.) Leader, 1958—, Hawaii Tribune-Herald of Hilo, 1961—, Pawhuska (Okla.) Daily Jour.-Capital, 1964—, Guymon (Okla.) Daily Herald, 1966—, Aberdeen (Wash.) Daily World, 1968, The Daily Report, Ontario, Calif., Shepherdsville (Ky.) Pioneer News, 1977, Pomona (Calif.) Progress-Bull., Frederick (Okla.) Daily Leader, Borger (Tex.) News Herald, 1977, Pauls Valley (Okla.) Daily Democrat, Wewoka (Okla.) Daily Times, 1967—, Jacksonville (Tex.) Progress, 1978, Cleburne (Tex.) Times Rev., 1976, Red Bluff (Calif.) Daily News, 1968—, Bonneville (Ark.) Democrat, 1968—, Moberly (Mo.) Monitor Index and Democrat, Holdenville (Okla.) News, 1969—, Weatherford (Tex.) Democrat, 1967, Washington (Ind.) Times Herald, 1972—, Sherman (Tex.) Democrat, 1977, Springdale (Ark.) News, Kailua-Kona (Hawaii) West Hawaii Today, 1968—, Henryetta (Okla.) Freelance, Gainesville (Tex.) Daily Register, Sweetwater (Tex.) Reporter, 1973—, Glasgow (Ky.) Daily Times, Vallejo (Calif.) Times-Herald, North Bay TV Cable Co., Inc., Vallejo; pres. Donrey Outdoor, Inc., Las Vegas, Reno, Albuquerque, Spokane, Tulsa, Oklahoma City and Ft. Smith; owner, operator radio stas. KFSA, Ft. Smith, 1946—, KBRS, Springdale, Ark., 1949—, KORK, Las Vegas, and KOLO, Reno, 1955—, KOLO-TV, Reno, 1954—, Wichita (Kans.) Donrey Outdoor Co., 1973—. Hon. disch., maj. M.I., 1945. Awarded Legion of Merit, Bronze Star, Purple Heart, 5 combat stars; Broadcaster of Year award Nev. Broadcasting Assn., 1978. Mem. Nat. Assn. Radio-TV Broadcasters, Am. Soc. Newspaper Editors, Am., So. newspaper pubs. assns., Am. Legion, Sigma Delta Chi, Pi Kappa Alpha. Clubs: Overseas Press (San Francisco); Hillcrest Country (Bartlesville); Tulsa, Dallas Athletic; Hardscrabble Country (Ft. Smith); Prospector's (Reno); Pacific (Honolulu). Home: PO Box 70 1111 N Bonanza Las Vegas NV 89101 Office: Donrey House 920 Rogers Ave PO Box 1359 Fort Smith AR 72902

REYNOLDS, EARL, hotel exec.; b. Warrensburg, Mo., Jan. 22, 1916; s. Henry Elonzo and Flora (Thomas) R.; student U. Mich., 1970; m. Mildred Naomi Deely, June 18, 1939; 1 son, Robert Earl. With Muehlehach Hotel, Kansas City, Mo., 1937-71, v.p., gen. mgr., 1969-71; mgr. The Raphael, San Francisco, 1971—. Vice chmn. adv. council, career devel. div. Am. Hotel-Motel Ednl. Inst.; mem. Mo. Right to Work. Hon. fellow Harry S. Truman Inst. Served with AUS, 1945-46. Life mem. Hotel-Motel Greeters Internat. (pres. 1969-70); mem. Am. Hotel-Motel Assn., Hotel Sales Mgmt. Assn., Kansas City C. of C. Democrat. Bapist. Mason. Club: Cosmopolitan (Kansas City, Mo.). Home: 4310 W 93d Terr Prairie Village KS 66207 Office: The Raphael 386 Geary St San Francisco CA 94102

REYNOLDS, EDWARD STORRS, pathologist; b. Orange, N.J., Dec. 3, 1928; s. Edward Storrs and Jean MacBean (Hadden) R.; B.A., Williams Coll., 1950; M.D., Washington U., St. Louis, 1954; m. Elizabeth Ann Gilliatt, June 22, 1950; children—Jean Elizabeth, Peter Morgan, William Storrs, Margaret Alice. Intern, Peter Bent Brigham Hosp., 1954-55, chief resident in pathology, 1955-56, asst. in pathology, 1961-63, asso., 1963-70, sr. asso., 1970-76; postdoctoral research fellow Peter Bend Brigham Hosp. and Harvard U., 1956-59; instr. Harvard U. Med. Sch., 1962-65, asst. prof. pathology, 1965-71, asso. prof., 1971-76; prof., chmn. dept. pathology U. Tex Med. Br., Galveston, 1976—; mem. bd. sci. counselors Nat. Inst. Environ. Health Sci. Scoutmaster Minuteman council Boy Scouts Am., 1965-74. Served with M.C., U.S. Army, 1959-61. Recipient Research Career Devel. award NIH, 1966-76; NRC-Nat. Acad. Sci. nat. research fellow, 1957-59. Mem. Am. Assn. Pathologists, Am. Soc. Pharmacology and Exptl. Therapeutics, Soc. Toxicology, Biophys. Soc., Am. Soc. Cell Biology, AAAS, Tex. Med. Assn., Tex. Soc. Pathologists. Unitarian. Contbr. numerous articles on chem. mechanisms of cellular injury, renal transplantation and other topics in field to profl. jours. Home: 1823 Bayou Shore Dr Galveston TX 77550 Office: Keiller Bldg U Tex Med Br Galveston TX 77550

REYNOLDS, EDWIN LOUIS, lawyer; b. Chevy Chase, Md., Apr. 13, 1901; s. Edwin Clark and Julia Vincenze (Solyom) R.; C.E., Lehigh U., 1922; LL.B., George Washington U., 1927; m. June Cooper, Oct. 26, 1929; 1 dau., Dorothy Holly. Asst. examiner U.S. Patent Office, 1922-29, prin. examiner, 1939-40, law examiner, 1940-49, solicitor, 1949-55; admitted to D.C. bar, 1928, of U.S. Ct. of Appeals bar, Dist. Ct. of D.C., U.S. Ct. of Custom and Patent Appeals; chief tech. adviser U.S. Ct. Customs and Patent Appeals, 1955-61; first asst. commr. patents, 1961-69; mem. firm Newton Hopkins and Ormsby, Atlanta; asso. prof. patent law Georgetown U., 1950-61. Mem. Order of Coif. Home: 325 White Oak Rd Greenville SC 29609 Office: Equitable Bldg Atlanta GA 30303

REYNOLDS, EMMETT ROBINSON, telecommunications cons., ret. army officer; b. Union Springs, Ala., Nov. 21, 1919; s. Emmett Robinson and Minnie Lou (Sims) R.; B.S., U.S. Mil. Acad., 1943; M.S., U. Ill., 1948; postgrad. Army Command and Gen. Staff Coll., 1955-56, Indsl. Coll. Armed Forces, 1959-60; M.B.A., George Washington U., 1962; m. Betty June Baker, Jan. 23, 1943; 1 dau., June. Commd. 2d lt. U.S. Army, 1943, advanced through grades to brig. gen., 1969; comdr. Signal Co., 81st Inf. Div., 1944-45; exec. officer, dep. dir. Signal Corps Engring. Labs., Ft. Monmouth, N.J., 1948-51; radio frequency mgr. Office Army Chief Signal Officer, Washington, 1951-55; comdg. officer 17th Signal Operations Bn., West Germany, 1956-59; radio frequency mgr. Office Joint Chiefs of Staff, Washington, 1960-63; chmn. Allied Radio Frequency Agy., London, Eng., 1963-65; signal officer 7th U.S. Army, West Germany, 1965-67; comdg. officer 7th Army Communications Command, West Germany, 1966-67; dep. asst. chief of staff for communications-electronics Mil. Assistance Command, Vietnam, 1967-68; asst. mgr. for ops. Nat. Communications System, Washington, 1968; dep. dir. Army Spl. Study of Communications in S.E. Asia, Hawaii, 1968-69; dep. asst. chief of staff for communications-electronics U.S. Army, Washington, 1969-73; ret., 1973; telecommunications cons. Stanford Research Inst., also Battelle Meml. Inst., 1973—, Gen. Research Corp., 1975—, Nat. Sci. Labs., 1976—. Decorated D.S.M., Legion of Merit with oak leaf cluster, Bronze Star, Army Commendation medal, Philippine Liberation medal, Philippine Pres. Unit citation. Mem. Armed Forces Communications-Electronics Assn., Ret. Officers' Assn., Assn. Grads. U.S. Mil. Acad. Methodist. Home: 1525 Dartmouth Ct Green Island Hills Columbus GA 31904

REYNOLDS, ERNEST WEST, physician, educator; b. Bristown, Okla., May 11, 1920; s. Ernest West and Florence (Brown) R.; B.S., U. Okla., 1942, M.D., 1946, M.S., 1952. Intern Boston City Hosp., 1946-47; resident Grady Meml. Hosp., Atlanta, 1949-50; practice medicine, Tulsa, Okla., 1953-54; prof. medicine U Mich., 1965-72; prof. medicine, dir. cardiology U. Wis., 1972—; dir. Kellogg Found. Comprehensive Coronary Care Project, 1967-72; chmn. NIH Cardiovascular Study Sect. A, 1972-73. Served to capt. AUS, 1947-49. Diplomate Am. Bd. Internal Medicine. Mem. Am. Heart Assn. (fellow council clin. cardiology), mem. Central Soc. Clin. Research. Mem. editorial bd. Am. Heart Jour. Contbr. articles to profl. jours. Home: 17 Red Maple Trail Madison WI 53717 Office: U Wis 600 Highland Dr Madison WI 53792

REYNOLDS, FRANK, news correspondent; b. East Chicago, Ind., Nov. 29, 1923; s. Frank James and Helen (Duffy) R.; student Ind. U., Wabash Coll.; m. Henrietta Mary Harpster, Aug. 23, 1947; children—Dean, James, John, Robert, Thomas. With sta. WJOB, Hammond, Ind., 1947-50, WBKB-TV, Chgo., 1950, WBBM-CBS, Chgo., 1951-63; corr. ABC, Chgo., 1963-65, Washington corr., 1965-78; chief anchorman World News Tonight, ABC, 1978—. Lectr. Council Fgn. Relations. Served with AUS, 1943-45; ETO. Recipient George Foster Peabody award, 1969. Mem. Chgo. Council Fgn. Relations. Club: Nat. Press (Washington). TV documentaries; Viet Nam, Africa, Middle East, Latin Am. Office: care ABC News 1330 Ave of Americas New York NY 10019*

REYNOLDS, FRANK MILLER, govt. ofcl.; b. Tulsa, Jan. 8, 1917; s. Frank Miller and Grace (Shields) R.; A.B., LL.B., U. Okla., 1939; LL.M., George Washington U., 1942; B.S., Georgetown Sch. Fgn. Service, 1946; m. Barbara G. MacWilliams, Dec. 7, 1946; children—Susan G., Ellen M., Frank M. Admitted to Okla. bar, 1940; mem. firm Flippo & Reynolds, Tulsa, 1940; elec. engr. Bur. Ships, Dept. of Navy, 1942-43; with office Gen. Counsel Dept. of Navy, 1946; chief negotiator, dep. dir. contract div., Office Naval Research, 1947-54; dep. dir., dir. resources div. Office Asst. Sec. Def., 1954-57; asst. sec. Inst. for Defense Analyses, 1957-61; sec., treas. Logistics Management Inst., Washington, 1961-65, v.p., 1966-76; dir. adminstrv. affairs Uniformed Services U. Health Scis., Bethesda, Md., 1976-78, dir. resource mgmt., 1978—; professorial lectr. mgmt. research George Washington U. Sch. Engring., 1956—. Served with radio div. Naval Research Lab., 1944-46. Mem. Okla. Bar Assn. Delta Upsilon. Home: 9107 River Rd Potomac MD 20854 Office: 4301 Jones Bridge Rd Bethesda MD 20014

REYNOLDS, FRED CURTIS, physician; b. Texarkana, Tex., Feb. 19, 1908; s. Joel Burr and Nellie (Sain) R.; A.B., Washington U., 1931, M.D., 1934; m. Phyllis M. Terry, Feb. 1, 1945; children—Mary Ann, Barbara Jane, Fred Curtis. Intern surgery Barnes Hosp., St. Louis, 1934-35; asst. resident surgery, 1935-36, neurosurgery fellow, 1936-37; preceptorship orthopedic surgery under Dr. E.B. Mumford, Indpls., 1937-43; practice medicine, specializing orthopedic surgery, St. Louis, 1946—; staff Barnes Hosp. Group, 1946—; asst. Washington U. Sch. Medicine, 1946-55, prof. orthopedic surgery, 1956-72, prof. emeritus, 1972—; chmn. residency review com. orthopedic surgery Am. Bd. Orthopedic Surgery, 1958-61, v.p. bd., 1961, pres., 1962-64; mem. com. on skeletal system NRC, 1958-63, 66-70; mem. surgery study section NIH, 1962-65; mem. tng. grant com. NIH, 1968-72; team physician St. Louis Football Cardinals, 1962-72. Trustee Orthopaedic Research and Edn. Found., 1968-74. Served with M.C., U.S. Army, 1943-46. Recipient Alumni citation Washington U., 1978. Mem. A.C.S. (gov. 1956-59, 65-68), Am. Surg. Assn., AMA, Am. Orthopedic Assn., Clin. Orthopedic Soc. (pres. 1960), Am. Acad. Orthopedic Surgeons (chmn. instructional course com., editor instructional course lectures, 1959-61, chmn. com. on grad. edn. 1961-64; pres. 1965, mem. com. on chymopapain 1974), Assn. Orthopedic Chmn. (pres. 1972), St. Louis Med. Soc. (hon.). Editor: Fractures, Dislocations and Sprains (Key, Conwell), rev. edit., 1960; editorial bd. Jour. Bone and Joint Surgery, 1954-61; contbr. articles to profl. publs.; Fred C. Reynolds chair orthopedic surgery at Washington U. named in his honor, 1978. Home: 10094 Briarwood Saint Louis MO 63124 Office: 4960 Audubon Ave Saint Louis MO 63110

REYNOLDS, FREDERICK JAMES, librarian; b. Ft. Wayne, Ind., Jan.7, 1911; s. Fred Hugh and Katherine (Epert) R.; A.B., Ind. U., 1941; B.L.S., Western Res. U., 1946; m. Winifred Irene Hoppe, Oct. 14, 1933. Bookmobile operator Ft. Wayne Pub. Library, 1930-34, head Allen County extension dept., 1935-41, asst. head librarian, 1941-59, head librarian, 1959-79, librarian emeritus, 1979—. Bd. dirs. Historic Fort Wayne, 1967—; mem. exec. com., chmn. publs. com., v.p. Allen County-Ft. Wayne Hist. Soc., 1960-62; hon. mem. Ind. Am. Revolution Bicentennial Commn. Recipient Silver medallion from gov. for work in connection with Ind. Sesquicentennial Observance, 1967. Mem. Ind. Library Assn. (dir.), Soc. Ind. Pioneers, Civil War Round Table, U.S., Ft. Wayne humane socs., Allen County Soc. Prevention Cruelty to Animals (past pres.), Acres, Inc., Audubon Soc., Izaak Walton League, Wilderness Soc., Defenders of Wild Life, Ft. Wayne Cat Fanciers, Ft. Wayne Zool. Soc., Ind., Huntington County, Whitley County, Elkhart County, Washington County, Wells County, DeKalb County, Wabash County, Lake County, No. Ind., Ind. Jewish, Ft. Wayne r.r. hist. socs., Ft. Wayne C. of C., Lindenwood Cemetery Assn. (dir.), Ft. Wayne Library Assn., Newberry Library Assos., Alliance for Animals, Inc. Presbyterian. Clubs: Quest; Downtown Kiwanis; Fortnightly (past pres.); Junto (past pres.). Home: 926 W Rudisill Blvd Fort Wayne IN 46807 Office: 900 Webster St Fort Wayne IN 46802

REYNOLDS, GARDNER MEAD, civil engr.; b. Ithaca, N.Y., Oct. 29, 1918; s. Minos Mead and Ruth Louise (Gardner) R.; B.C.E., Cornell U., 1948; m. Kathleen Kane, July 31, 1945; children—Marcia, Stephen, Timothy, Richard. With Dames & Moore, civil engrs., 1948—, partner, 1954—, mng. partner cons. div., N.Y.C., 1960-74, sr. partner, chmn. exec. com., Los Angeles, 1974—; partner Dames & Moore-U.K., Dames & Moore Australia; dir. Chiyoda/Dames & Moore. Mem. Planning Bd. Wyckoff (N.J.), 1965-68. Served with USAAF, 1942-46. Decorated Purple Heart. Fellow ASCE (nat. dir. 1966-68; chmn. exec. com. engring. mgmt. div. 1977); mem. Asso. Soil and Found. Engrs. (1st v.p., past treas., pres. 1978-79), Deep Founds. Inst. (trustee), Los Angeles-Tehran Sister City Affiliation (vice chmn.), Iran-Am. Chamber Industry and Commerce (dir.), The Beavers, Am. Arbitration Assn., World Dredging Assn. Clubs: Palos Verdes Golf, Breakfast (Palos Verdes, Calif.). Home: 2740 Via Campesina Palos Verdes Estates CA 90274 Office: 445 S Figueroa St Los Angeles CA 90071

REYNOLDS, GENE, TV producer, dir.; b. 1925; m. Bonnie Jones (div.). Actor in motion pictures including: Thank You, Jeeves, 1936, In Old Chicago, 1937, Boys Town, 1938, They Shall Have Music, 1939, Edison the Man, 1940, Eagle Squadron, 1942, The Country Girl, 1954, The Bridges at Toko-Ri, 1955, Diane, 1955; exec. producer TV series Room 222, 1969-74, Anna and the King, 1972, Karen, 1975; producer TV pilot The Ghost and Mrs. Muir, 1968-70, Roll Out!, 1973-74; exec. producer Lou Grant, 1977-78; producer TV series MASH, 1972-76, exec. producer, 1976—; producer, dir. TV movie People Like Us, 1976. Recipient Emmy award Nat. Acad. TV Arts and Scis., 1975, 76; Dirs. Guild award for TV comedy (2); (with others) Peabody award for MASH. Mem. Dirs. Guild Am. *

REYNOLDS, HERBERT HAL, educator; b. Frankston, Tex., Mar. 20, 1930; s. Herbert Joseph and Ava Nell (Taylor) R.; B.S., Trinity U., San Antonio, 1952; M.S., Baylor U., Waco, Tex., 1958, Ph.D., 1961; m. Joy Myrla Copeland, June 17, 1950; children—Kevin Hal, Kent Andrew, Rhonda Sheryl. Entered USAF, 1948, advanced through grades to col., 1966; service in Japan, Europe; dir. research Aeromed. Lab., Alamogordo, N. Mex., 1961-67; dir. Air Force Human Resources Lab., San Antonio, Tex., 1968; ret., 1968; exec. v.p., dean Baylor U., 1969—. Mem. AAAS, Am., Tex. psychol. assns., Sigma Xi. Contbr. articles profl. jours. Address: Baylor Univ Waco TX 76703. *I learned that through diligence I could accomplish many things that less disciplined persons could not and that intelligence and discernment must be coupled with strong determination to achieve one's goals.*

REYNOLDS, JACK, television news corr.; b. Bklyn., Dec. 27, 1933; B.S. in Econs., Fordham U., 1955. With NBC, mgr. ops. Asia, Tokyo, 1967-68, bur. chief, Saigon, 1968-69, mgr. news, Tokyo, 1970, Far East corr., Hong Kong, 1974—. Recipient Christopher award for documentary The Case People of the Philippines, 1973. Office: care NBC News 30 Rockefeller Plaza New York NY 10020*

REYNOLDS, JACK, profl. football player; b. Cin., Nov. 22, 1947; s. Earl N. and Carolyn Elizabeth (Churchill) R.; ed. U. Tenn.; m. Patricia K. Cunningham, Jan. 4, 1972. Mem. Los Angeles Rams, 1970—; player Pro Bowl, New Orleans, 1976. Named All-Pro, 1975. Office: care Los Angeles Rams 10271 W Pico Blvd Los Angeles CA 90064*

REYNOLDS, JAME H., lawyer; b. Dubuque, Iowa, Mar. 24, 1939; s. Harold F. and Ruth M. (Young) R.; B.A., Loras Coll., 1961; J.D., U. Iowa, 1965; m. Joann E. Mormann, Dec. 30, 1967; children—John F., Joshua J., Elizabeth A. Admitted to Iowa bar; asst. Dubuque County Atty., 1965-67; mem. firm Reynolds, Kenline, Brietbach, McCarthy, Clemens & McKay, 1967-77; U.S. Atty. No. Dist. Iowa, Sioux City, 1977—. Chmn. bd. dirs. Aquinas Inst. Theology, Dubuque; candidate for Iowa atty. gen., 1972, 74. Mem. Am. Bar Assn., Assn. Trial Lawyers Iowa (gov.), Iowa, Dubuque County bar assns. Democrat. Roman Catholic. Home: 440 Summer Dubuque IA 52001 Office: Box 4710 Federal Bldg Cedar Rapids IA 52001

REYNOLDS, JOHN TODD, educator, surgeon; b. Dwight, Ill., Sept. 26, 1909; s. Peter J. and Mary (Todd) R.; B.S., U. Ill., 1930, M.S., M.D., 1932, grad. tng. pathology, 1932. Intern Cook County Hosp., Chgo., 1933-34; resident surgery U. Ill. Research and Ednl. Hosp., 1935-38; emeritus prof. surgery U. Ill. Coll. Medicine, 1977—, Rush Med. Coll., 1979—; attending surgeon Presbyn-St. Luke's Hosp., Chgo., 1952, Research and Ednl. Hosp., 1952—. Diplomate Am. Bd. Surgery. Mem. Soc. Univ. Surgeons, Am., Western, Pan-Pacific surg. assns., Central, Chgo., Internat. surg. socs., Kansas City Anatomical Soc. (hon.), Inst. Medicine Chgo., A.C.S., So. Mich. Acad. Medicine (hon.), Am., Chgo. heart assns., Miss. Valley, Chgo., Ill. med. socs., Pan-Am. med. assns., Soc. Surgery Alimentary Tract, Warren H. Cole Soc., Cardiovascular Surgeons Club. Clubs: Tavern, University (Chgo.). Author papers in field. Home: 12 E Scott St Chicago IL 60610 Office: 664 N Michigan Ave Chicago IL 60611

REYNOLDS, JOHN W., dist. judge; b. Green Bay, Wis., Apr. 4, 1921; s. John W. and Madge (Flatley) R.; B.S., U. Wis., 1946, LL.B., 1949; m. Patricia Ann Brody, May 26, 1947 (dec. Dec. 1967); children—Kate M., Molly, James; m. 2d, Jane Conway, July 31, 1971; children—Tom, Jacob, Frances, John III. Admitted to Wis. bar, 1949, since practiced in Green Bay; atty. gen., Wis., 1959-63; gov. State of Wis., 1963-65; U.S. dist. judge Eastern Dist. Wis., 1965-71, chief judge, 1971—. Mem. Am., Wis., Brown County bar assns. Office: Fed Bldg Milwaukee WI 53202

REYNOLDS, JOSEPH ALLEN, JR., banker; b. Montgomery, Ala., May 1, 1925; s. Joseph Allen and Nan Earl (Daniel) R.; student Auburn U., 1942-43, Millsaps Coll., 1943-44; A.B., U. Ala., 1948, LL.B., 1950; postgrad. Northwestern U., 1960, Rutgers U., 1963, Columbia, 1970, Ind. U., 1973; m. Jane St. Clair Ball, Sept. 13, 1952; children—Joseph Allen III, Fred Ball, Jane Ball. Admitted to Ala. bar, 1950, also U.S. Supreme Ct.; with First Ala. Bank, Montgomery, 1956—, v.p., 1961-66, dir., 1963—, exec. v.p., 1966—. Pres. Tukabatchee Area council Boy Scouts Am., 1960-62; pres. United Appeal Montgomery 1964; mem. advisory com. bd. trustees Ala. State U. Mem. adv. bd. Montgomery Extension, U. Ala. Bd. dirs. Landmarks Found. Montgomery. Served to lt. (j.g.) USNR, 1943-46. Recipient Distinguished Service award Montgomery Jr. C. of C., 1961, Silver Beaver award Boy Scouts Am., 1963; named Ala.'s Outstanding Young Banker, 1963; hon. citizen of Escuintla, Guatemala; Hon. alumnus Huntingdon Coll., Montgomery. Mem. Ala., Montgomery County bar assns., Newcomen Soc. N.Am., U. Ala. Nat. Alumni Assn. (past pres.), Soc. Pioneers of Montgomery, Omicron Delta Kappa, Phi Delta Phi, Pi Mu Epsilon, Phi Delta Theta. Episcopalian. Club: Montgomery Country. Home: 2430 Woodley Rd Montgomery AL 36111 Office: 8 Commerce St Montgomery AL 36104

REYNOLDS, JOSHUA PAUL, educator; b. High Falls, N.C., Oct. 17, 1906; s. Herbert William and Fanny (Ozment) R.; B.S., Guilford Coll., 1928; M.S., U. N.C., 1929; Ph.D., Johns Hopkins U., 1934; m. Rebecca Ward, June 8, 1937; children—Joshua Paul, William Lee. Teaching fellow U. N.C., 1928-29, acting asst. prof. zoology, 1932-33, vis. instr. summers 1932-39, 47; instr. biology Guilford Coll., 1929-31; successively asst. prof., asso. prof., prof. biology Birmingham So. Coll., 1934-49; Gen. Edn. Bd. fellow for research zool. lab. U. Pa., 1940-41, 48-49; prof. zoology Fla. State U., 1949-64, asst. dean, 1951-54, asso. dean Coll. Arts and Scis., 1954-58, dean, 1958-64; dean faculty U. N.C. at Wilmington, 1964-71, vice chancellor acad. affairs, 1971, adj. prof. biology, 1971—. Fellow AAAS; mem. N.C. Acad. Sci., Assn. Southeastern Biologists (treas. 1953-56), Am. Genetics Soc., Am. Soc. Human Genetics, Am. Soc. Zoology, Phi Beta Kappa, Sigma Xi. Mem. Society of Friends. Presbyn. Rotarian. Author articles in field. Home: 1813 Azalea Dr Wilmington NC 28403

REYNOLDS, JULIAN LOUIS, business exec.; b. Winston-Salem, N.C., May 3, 1910; s. Richard S. and Julia Louise (Parham) R.; student Wharton Sch. of Finance, U. Pa., 1928-29, Duke, 1929-30; LL.D., U. Ark., 1956; m. Glenn Parkinson, Jan. 25, 1941; children—Glenn Parkinson (Mrs. Martin). With Reynolds Metals Co., Richmond, Va., 1931—, now exec. v.p., dir.; mgr. export div., 1934-39, mgr. seal and label div., 1939-40, v.p. and gen. sales mgr., 1940-48, v.p. in charge operations, 1948-56, exec. v.p., 1956-59, dir., 1936—; chmn., chief exec. officer Reynolds Internat., Inc., 1959—; v.p. Eskimo Pie Corp., 1942-53, pres., 1953—, also dir. Presbyterian. Clubs: Commonwealth, Country of Va. (Richmond); Athletic (N.Y.C.). Office: Reynolds Metals Co 6601 W Broad St Richmond VA 23261*

REYNOLDS, LLOYD GEORGE, economist, educator; b. Wainwright, Alberta, Can., Dec. 22, 1910; s. George F. and Dorothy (Carl) R.; A.B., U. Alberta, 1931, LL.D., 1958; A.M., McGill U., 1933; Ph.D., Harvard, 1936; m. Mary F. Trackett, June 12, 1937; children—Anne Frances, Priscilla Dorothy, Bruce Lloyd. Came to U.S., 1934, naturalized, 1940. Instr. econs. Harvard, 1936-39; asso. polit. economy Johns Hopkins, 1939-41, asso. prof., 1941-45; asso. prof. econs. Yale, 1945-47, prof. econs., 1947-52, Sterling prof. econs., 1952—, chmn. dept. econs., 1951-59; dir Econ. Growth Center, 1961-67; vis. fellow All Souls Coll., Oxford, 1967-68. Mem. adv. bd. Pakistan Inst. Devel. Econs., 1965-73; cons. to Social Sci. Research Center, U. P.R., 1951-65; dir. Nat. Bureau Econ. Research, 1958—. Research dir. labor studies 20th Century Fund, 1940-43; research sec., com. on employment Social Sci. Research Council, 1941-42; co-chmn. appeals com. N.W.L.B., 1943-45; cons. Bur. of Budget, 1945-47; Guggenheim fellow, 1954-55, 1966-67; dir. program in econs. and bus. adminstrn. Ford Found., 1955-57. Fellow Am. Acad. Arts and Scis.; mem. Indsl. Relations Research Assn. (pres. 1955), Am. Econ. Assn. (v.p. 1959, exec. com. 1952-54), Am. Acad. Polit. Sci., Am. Statis. Assn. Clubs: Graduates (pres. 1961-64), (New Haven); Harvard (Boston); Century (N.Y.C.); Cosmos (Washington); Mill Reef (Antigua). Author: The British Immigrant in Canada, 1935; Control of Competition in Canada, 1940; Labor and National Defense, 1941; An Index to Trade Union Publications, 1945; Labor Economics and Labor Relations, 1949; The Structure of Labor Markets, 1951; The Evolution of Wage Structure, 1956; Economics: A General Introduction, 1963; Wages, Productivity and Industrialization in Puerto Rico, 1965; The Three Worlds of Economics, 1971; Agriculture in Development Theory, 1975; Image and Reality in Economic Development, 1977; contbr. articles to profl. jours. Home: 75 Old Hartford Turnpike Hamden CT 06517 Office: Yale University New Haven CT 06520

REYNOLDS, MARYAN EVELYN, librarian; b. Mpls., Feb. 17, 1913; d. William Albert and Mabel Evelyn (Thyng) Reynolds; A.B., U. Minn., 1936; B.S., U. So. Calif., 1940. Circulation asst. Madera (Calif.) County Free Library, 1940-41; supt. brs. Kern County Free Library, Bakersfield, Calif., 1941-43; head Richland (Wash.) Pub. Library, 1950-51; field librarian Wash. State Library, Olympia, 1943-50, state librarian, 1951-75. Sec., Gov.'s Commn. on Status of Women, 1962-70. Named Woman of Achievement, Seattle Matrix, 1975; Distinguished Alumna, U. So. Calif. Sch. Library Sci., 1975. Mem. A.L.A. (council, 1951-55), Pacific Northwest (v.p., pres. 1969-71), Wash. library assns., Am. Assn. U. Women (pres. Olympia 1962-64), State Capitol Hist. Assn., Am. Assn. State Libraries (pres. 1965-66, exec. bd. 1964-67), Am. Assn. Pub. Adminstrn., League Women Voters, Delta Kappa Gamma. Club: Soroptimist (Olympia). Home: 3128 Villa Ct SE Olympia WA 98503

REYNOLDS, NORMAN EBEN, lawyer; b. Muskogee, Okla., Dec. 1, 1919; s. Norman Eben and Elizabeth (Boyd) R.; A.B., U. Okla., 1941, LL.B., 1947; m. Margaret Maxey Cooper, Nov. 21, 1953; children—Norman Eben III, Margaret Boyd, Nancy Elizabeth, Robert Cooper. Admitted to Okla. bar, 1942, also U.S. Supreme Ct.; partner firm Reynolds, Ridings & Hargis, Oklahoma City, 1947—. Dir. Oharco Corp. Mem. Okla. Ho. of Reps., 1949-55; spl. legal cons. Gov. Okla., 1959-63; spl. justice Okla. Supreme Ct., 1961. Pres. trustees Heritage Hall, 1970. Served with AUS, 1942-46. Named Outstanding Young Man in Oklahoma City, 1951. Mem. Comml. Law League Am. (past nat. sec.), Am. (co-chmn. nat. conf. lawyers and collection agys. 1979), Okla., Oklahoma County bar assns., Am. Judicature Soc., Mil. Order World Wars, Phi Beta Kappa (past pres. alumni assn.), Sigma Alpha Epsilon (past pres. alumni assn.). Episcopalian (sr. warden 1971). Clubs: Kiwanis (pres. 1968), Sooner Dinner (pres. 1969) (Oklahoma City). Home: 2212 NW 56th St Oklahoma City OK 73112 Office: 2808 First Nat Bank Bldg Oklahoma City OK 73102

REYNOLDS, ORR ESREY, sci. assn. exec.; b. Balt., Mar. 3, 1920; s. Floyd Wilson and Mildred Alma (Esrey) R.; B.S., U. Md., 1941, M.S., 1942, Ph.D., 1946; m. Marjorie Ellen Johnson, June 12, 1971; children—Caroline Orr Reynolds Gaver, Christi Potts Reynolds Rapps. Asst. physiologist NIH, Bethesda, Md., 1943; dir. biol. scis.

div. Office of Naval Research, Washington, 1946-57; dir. for sci. Office Sec. Def., Washington, 1957-62; dir. bioscience program NASA, Washington, 1962-70; exec. sec.-treas. Am. Physiol. Soc., Bethesda, 1970—. Served with USNR, 1944-46. Recipient medal for exceptional service NASA, 1970; Semmelweis medal Semmelweis Med. U., Budapest, Hungary, 1978. Mem. Am. Physiol. Soc., Am. Soc. Zoologists, Aerospace Med. Assn., Internat. Acad. Astronautics, AAAS, Am. Inst. Biol. Scis., Washington Acad. Scis. Clubs: Cosmos, Rotary. Office: Am Physiol Soc 9650 Rockville Pike Bethesda MD 20014

REYNOLDS, PHILIP REEVES, ins. co. exec.; b. Norwalk, Conn., June 28, 1927; s. Carlton Mortimer and Frances Reeves (Collings) R.; B.A., Yale U., 1948; m. Catherine Greenway Cox, July 20, 1957; children—Mary, Frances, Philip. With Travelers Ins. Co., Hartford, Conn., 1955—, sr. v.p., 1970—; dir. Vestaur Securities, Inc., Phila. Trustee, Child and Family Services, Hartford, Hartford Coll. Women, Elizabeth Colt Bequest; bd. dirs. Conn. Health and Ednl. Facilities Authority. Served with U.S. Army, 1950-52. Home: 43 Montclair Dr West Hartford CT 06107 Office: 1 Tower Sq Hartford CT 06115

REYNOLDS, RICHARD S., JR., business exec.; b. Winston-Salem, N.C., May 27, 1908; s. Richard S. and Louise (Parham) R.; student Davidson Coll.; B.S., U. Pa., 1930; m. Virginia Sargeant; children—Richard S. III, Sargeant (dec.). Became mem. N.Y. Stock Exchange, 1930; with two partners formed banking firm Reynolds & Co., N.Y. City, 1930; asst. to pres. Reynolds Metals Co., Richmond, Va., 1938, treas., 1938-44, v.p., treas., 1944-48, pres., 1948-63, 71-75, chmn. bd., 1963-71, chmn. bd., pres., 1971-75, chmn. bd., chief exec. officer, 1975-76, chmn. exec. com., 1976-77, hon. chmn. bd., 1977—; chmn. bd. Robertshaw Controls Co., 1955-78, chmn. exec. com., 1957-59, chmn., 1959-78; dir. Central Nat. Bank, Richmond, Lawyers Title Ins. Corp. Trustee U. Richmond; trustee emeritus U. Pa. Mem. Aluminum Assn. (past pres.), Bus. Council. Presbyn. Clubs: The Brook, The Jockey (N.Y.C.); Metropolitan (Washington); Country of Va., Commonwealth (Richmond); Buck's (London); Farmington Country; Deep Run Hunt. Office: 6601 W Broad St Richmond VA 23261

REYNOLDS, ROBERT LESTER, ch. ofcl.; b. Webster, Mass., Nov. 27, 1917; s. Joseph and Lillian Mabel (Brown) R.; B.A., Atlantic Union Coll., 1941; M.A., Boston U., 1949, Ph.D., 1970; m. Beatrice Nelson, Aug. 17, 1941; children—Carole (Mrs. Richard Clark), Robert Craig. Dean of boys Shenandoah Valley Acad., New Market, Va., 1941-43; dean men Atlantic Union Coll., 1943-46; dean men, asst. bus. mgr., dir. devel. and pub. relations, dean students Pacific Union Coll., Angwin, Calif., 1946-59; pres. Atlantic Union Coll., 1960-68, Walla Walla Coll., College Place, Wash., 1968-76; gen. field sec. Gen. Conf. Seventh-day Adventists, Washington, 1976—; mem. Gen. Conf. com. Seventh-day Adventists, also mem. bd. higher edn. and bd. regents Gen. Conf. Mem. Am. Hist. Assn., Phi Alpha Theta, Phi Delta Kappa. Rotarian. Home: 2204 Badian Dr Silver Spring MD 20904

REYNOLDS, RUSSELL SEAMAN, JR., recruiting cons.; b. Greenwich, Conn., Dec. 14, 1931; s. Russell Seaman and Virginia Dare (Carter) R.; B.A., Yale, 1954; postgrad. N.Y. U., 1958-61; m. Deborah Ann Toll, July 21, 1956; children—Russell Seaman III, Jeffrey Toll, Deborah Chase. Asst v.p. Nat. div. J.P. Morgan & Co., Inc., Morgan Guaranty Trust Co. of New York, 1957-66; partner William H. Clark Assos., Inc., N.Y.C., 1966-69; pres. Russell Reynolds Assos., Inc., N.Y.C., 1969-71, chmn. bd., 1971—. Former trustee Westminster Sch., Hotchkiss Schs.; trustee Hurricane Island Outward Bound Sch.; mem. Greater N.Y. adv. bd. Salvation Army; bd. dirs. Bruce Museum Assos. Served as 1st lt. SAC, USAF, 1954-57. Mem. Greenwich Hist. Soc. (v.p.), Soc. Colonial Wars. Clubs: Round Hill, N.Y. Yacht, Indian Harbor Yacht, Links, Yale, Recess, California, Mill Reef; Amateur Ski of N.Y. Home: 39 Clapboard Ridge Rd Greenwich CT 06830 Office: 245 Park Ave New York NY 10017

REYNOLDS, SAMUEL WILLIAMS, coal co. ofcl.; b. Omaha, Aug. 11, 1890; s. Joel Barlow and Emily (Van Blarcom) R.; student pub. schs., Omaha; m. Louise Northrup, July 15, 1916; children—Louise (Mrs. Richard L. Haugh), Emily (Mrs. Joe H. Baker) Aurel (Mrs. Ira Couch, Junior). Pres. Reynolds- Updike Coal Co., Omaha, 1924—; dir. Nebr. Savs. & Loan Assn. Served as U.S. senator to fill interim until election following death of Sen. Hugh Butler, 1954. Served with AC, 1917-18; col. Army Specialist Corps, World War II. Recipient Freedom Found. award for 1952 Missouri River flood fight, 1953. Mem. Am. Legion. Mason (Shriner). Home: 6625 State St Omaha NE 68152 Office: Grain Exchange Bldg Omaha NE 68102

REYNOLDS, THOMAS HEDLEY, coll. pres.; b. N.Y.C., Nov. 23, 1920; s. Wallace and Helen (Hedley) R.; grad. Deerfield (Mass.) Acad., 1938; A.B., Williams Coll., 1942, LL.D. (hon.), 1978; M.A. in History, Columbia U., 1947, Ph.D. in History, 1953; LL.D., U. Maine, 1968, Bowdoin Coll., 1969, Colby Coll., 1969; m. Jean Fine Lytle, Apr. 24, 1943; children—Thomas Scott, David Hewson, John Hedley, Tay. Instr. history Hunter Coll., 1947-48; staff historian ARC, Washington, 1948-49; mem. faculty Middlebury Coll., 1949-67, chmn. dept. history, 1957-67, dean of coll., 1964-67; pres. Bates Coll., Lewiston, Maine, 1967—; bd. dirs. Liberty Mut. Ins. Cos., 1977—. commr., Edn. Commn. of States, 1969—; mem. Higher Edn. Council, 1971—; mem. Maine Edn. Council; mem. Commn. Maine's Future, 1975—; dir. New Eng. Bd. Higher Edn., 1976—, mem. exec. com., 1977—. Mem. Vt. Historic Sites Commn., 1964-66; mem. New Eng. Colls. Fund, pres., 1971-72; mem. Maine Council Humanities and Pub. Policy, 1977—. Trustee WCBB Ednl. TV, 1974—; bd. dirs. Nat. Assn. Ind. Colls. and Univs., 1977. Served to capt. AUS, 1942-46; col. Res. Mem. Am. Hist. Assn., Am. Antiquarian Soc., AAUP, Acad. Polit. Sci., Maine, Vt. hist. socs., Maine Parnters Alliance for Progress. Home: 256 College St Lewiston ME 04240 Office: Office of Pres Bates College Lewiston ME 04240

REYNOLDS, THOMAS LEE, educator; b. Guilford County, N.C., Apr. 11, 1918; s. Herbert William and Fanny (Ozment) R.; B.S., Guilford Coll., 1938; M.A. in Math., U. N.C., 1947, Ph.D., 1951; m. Raye Seaford, July 17, 1943; children—Pamela (Mrs. Michael Smith), Richard, Patricia. Pub. sch. tchr., Concord, N.C., 1938-41; prof. math., head dept. Millsaps Coll., Jackson, Miss., 1950-60, Coll. William and Mary, 1960—; math. cons. Ministry Edn. Turkey, summer 1966. Served with USAAF, 1941-45. Mem. Math. Assn. Am., Nat. Council Tchrs. Math. Co-author: SMSG Calculus, summer 1964. Home: 1184 Jamestown Rd Williamsburg VA 23185

REYNOLDS, VIRGIL LLOYD, retail store exec.; b. Fort Bend, County, Tex., June 29, 1916; s. William E. and Ada R.; student public schs., Fort Bend County; m. Ida Wenzel, Nov. 19, 1936; children—Sandra Davenport, Dianne Walger. With J. Weingarten, Inc., Houston, v.p. sales and merchandising, 1968-72, sr. v.p. merchandising after 1972, now exec. v.p. merchandising. Chmn. United Fund Drive, 1966. Mem. Super Market Inst., Coop. Supermarket Research Group. Lutheran. Home: 15055 Memorial St Apt 105 Houston TX 77024 Office: 600 Lockwood St Houston TX 77011

REYNOLDS, WALTER BARTON, ret. judge; b. Elmira, N.Y., July 25, 1901; s. Melvin A. and Alice (Breese) R.; student U. Pa., 1920-21; LL.B., Cornell U., 1925; m. Mary Drinkwater, Sept. 11, 1926; children—Virgina (Mrs. Paul McLane), Suzanne (Mrs. Truman Fudge). Admitted to Ky. bar, 1925, N.Y. bar, 1927; practiced law Elmira, 1927-37; dist. atty. Chemung County, Elmira, N.Y., 1937-50; asso. firm Reynolds, Cramer & Donovan, Elmira, 1950-56; justice N.Y. State Supreme Ct., Elmira, 1955-58, asso. justice appellate div. 3d jud. dept., Albany, 1958-77. Mem. N.Y. State (chmn. jud. sect., 1962, mem. exec. com.), Chemung County (pres. 1954-55) bar assns., N.Y. State Dist. Attys. Assn. (pres. 1943; hon. life), Assn. Supreme Ct. Justices State N.Y. (pres. 1965, mem. exec. com. 1966—). Republican. Episcopalian. Mason, Elk. Clubs: Ft. Orange (Albany), Elmira Country, Princess Anne Country (Virginia Beach, Va.). Home: 83 Decker Pkwy W Elmira NY 14905

REYNOLDS, WARREN LIND, educator; b. Gull Lake, Sask., Can., Nov. 29, 1920; s. Raymond R. and Ellen (Lindgren) R.; B.A., U. B.C., 1949, M.A., 1950; Ph.D., U. Minn., 1955; m. Rose Marie Palone, Sept. 4, 1946; children—Allan Joseph, Lawrence Warren, Michael Lee. Mem. faculty U. Minn., 1954—, prof. chemistry, 1967—; vis prof. U. Oreg., 1959, U. B.C., 1964. Served with RCAF, 1942-45. Bursary, Nat. Research Council Can., 1949; NSF sr. postdoctoral fellow, 1962-63; Fulbright-Hayes research scholar, 1972-73. Mem. Am. Chem. Soc., Am. Phys. Soc., Faraday Soc., AAAS, Minn. Acad. Sci., Phi Lambda Upsilon. Author: Mechanisms of Electron Transfer, 1966. Home: 1898 Eustis St St Paul MN 55113 Office: Dept Chemistry Univ Minn Minneapolis MN 55455

REYNOLDS, WILEY RICHARD, banker; b. N.Y.C., Dec. 4, 1917; s. Wiley Richard and Nettie H. (Hood) R.; grad. Hotchkiss Sch., 1936; A.B., Yale, 1940; m. Janet Raymer, June 20, 1942; children—Wiley Richard, III, Suzanne Raymer, Judith Underhill, Thomas Hood. With First Nat. Bank, Palm Beach, 1940—, dir., 1941—, pres., 1948-65, chmn. 1948-65, chmn. 1948-65, exec. dir., 1965—; Philippine rep. Internat. Exec. Service Corps, 1966, Indonesian dir. for corps, 1968, Turkey, 1977, Taiwan, 1979. Pres. Palm Beach Pvt. Sch., 1961-65. Mem. bd. Civic Assn. Episcopal. Clubs: Seminole Golf (Juno Beach, Fla.); Garden of the Gods. Cheyenne Mountain Country (Colorado Springs, Colorado); River, Downtown Assn. (N.Y.C.); Lyford Cay (Nassau); Union (Sydney, Australia); Bath and Tennis, Everglades (bd. govs.) (Palm Beach); Army and Navy of Manila. Home: 291 El Vedado Way Palm Beach FL 33480 Office: First Nat Bank Palm Beach FL 33480

REYNOLDS, WILEY RICHARD, banker; b. N.Y.C., Dec. 4, 1917; s. Wiley Richard and Nettie H. (Hood) R.; grad. Hotchkiss Sch., 1936; A.B., Yale, 1940; m. Janet Raymer, June 20, 1942; children—Wiley Richard, III, Suzanne Raymer, July Underhill, Thomas Hood. With First Nat. Bank, Palm Beach, 1940—, dir., 1941—, pres., 1948-65, chmn. 1948-65, chmn. 1948-65, exec. dir., 1965—; dir. SE First Nat. Bank Miami. Philippine rep. Internat. Exec. Service Corps, 1966, Indonesian dir. for corps, 1968, Turkish dir., 1977, Philippine dir., 1978. Pres. Palm Beach Pvt. Sch., 1961-65. Mem. bd. Civic Assn. Episcopal. Clubs: Seminole Golf (Juno Beach, Fla.); Garden of the Gods, Cheyenne Mountain Country (Colorado Springs, Colorado); River, Downtown Assn. (N.Y.C.); Lyford Cay (Nassau); Union (Sydney, Australia); Bath and Tennis, Everglades (bd. govs.) (Palm Beach). Home: 291 Elvedado Rd Palm Beach FL 33480 Office: First Nat Bank Palm Beach FL 33480

REYNOLDS, WILLIAM CRAIG, mech. engr.; b. Berkeley, Calif., Mar. 16, 1933; s. Merrill and Patricia Pope (Galt) R.; B.S. in Mech. Engring., Stanford U., 1954, M.S. in Mech. Engring., 1955, Ph.D. in Mech. Engring., 1957; m. Janice Erma, Sept. 18, 1953; children—Russell, Peter, Margery. Asst. prof. mech. engring. Stanford U., 1957-62, asso. prof., 1962-68, prof., 1968—, chmn. dept. mech. engring., 1972—, founder, inst. chmn. for energy studies, 1974—. NSF sr. scientist fellow, Eng., 1964. Fellow ASME; mem. AAUP, Am. Phys. Soc., Nat. Acad. Engring., Sigma Xi, Tau Beta Pi. Author books, including: Energy Thermodynamics, 2d edit., 1976; contbr. numerous articles to profl. jours.; research in fluid mechanics and applied thermodynamics. Office: Stanford U Dept Mech Engring Stanford CA 94305

REYNOLDS, WILLIAM FRANCIS, educator; b. Boston, Jan. 31, 1930; s. William Leo and Grace Regina (Devlin) R.; A.B. summa cum laude, Holy Cross Coll., 1950; A.M., Harvard, 1951, Ph.D., 1954; m. Pauline Jane Fitzgerald, Aug. 5, 1962; children—Nancy, Jane. Instr., Holy Cross Coll., Worcester, Mass., 1954-55; instr. Mass. Inst. Tech., Cambridge, 1955-57; asst. prof. math. Tufts U., Medford, Mass., 1957-60, asso. prof., 1960-67, prof., 1967—, Walker prof. math., 1970—. NSF grantee, 1965-74. Mem. Am. Math. Soc., Math. Assn. Am., AAAS, Sigma Xi. Contbr. articles to math. jours. Home: 3 Preble Gardens Rd Belmont MA 02178 Office: Dept Math Tufts U Medford MA 02155

REYNOLDS, WILLIAM GLASGOW, lawyer; b. Dover, Tenn., July 15, 1911; s. John Lacey and Harriett Edwina (Glasgow) R.; A.B., Vanderbilt U., 1932, J.D. summa cum laude, 1935; m. Nancy Bradford du Pont, May 18, 1940; children—Katherine Glasgow (Mrs. John M. Sturges, Jr.), William Bradford, Mary Parminter (Mrs. John Schofield Savage), Cynthia du Pont (Mrs. Kermit Nelson Farris). Admitted to Tenn. bar, 1935, D.C. bar, 1964, also U.S. Supreme Ct., 1945; gen. practice, Nashville, 1934-35; with E. I. du Pont de Nemours & Co., 1935-71, chief counsel advt., pub. relations and central research depts., 1954-71; with firm Morris, Nichols, Arsht & Tunnell, Wilmington, Del., 1972—; resident counsel Remington Arms Co., Bridgeport, Conn., 1940-41; with Office Gen. Counsel, U.S. Navy, 1942-43, Exec. Office Sec. Navy, 1944, Office Asst. Sec. Navy, 1945. Permanent mem. jud. conf. 3d Jud. Circuit U.S., 1955—; rep. chem. industry Water Resources Policy Com., 1950; mem. adv. com. Patent Office, Dept. Commerce, 1954; mem. Internat. Conf. Indsl. and Municipal Air Pollution, 1949; mem. Nat. Com. Assay U.S. Mints, 1958, chmn., 1958; Am. indsl. rep. Com. Experts on Internat. Trademark Treaties, 1969-71, U.S. Govt. rep., 1972-73; del. numerous internat. confs. Dir. Del. Trust Co., Wilmington, 1974—, mem. exec. com., 1976—, trust com., 1976—. Mem. vis. com. Law Sch., Vanderbilt U., 1968, mem. chancellor's council, 1968—, chmn. Law Sch. devel. council, 1968. Alternate del. Republican Nat. Conv., 1956; mem. Rep. Nat. Com. Assos., 1956-65. Bd. dirs., sec. Rencourt Found. Del., 1955—; bd. dirs. United Community Fund No. Del., 1948-53, exec. com., 1949-51; trustee, chmn. bldg. com. Children's Home, Claymont and Wilmington, 1946-47, pres., 1947-51; bd. dir., mem. bldg. com. Del. Art Center, 1948-64. Recipient Founders medal Vanderbilt U. Law Sch., 1935, U.S. Navy commendations, 1943, 45. Mem. Mfg. Chemists Assn. (chmn. lawyers adv. com. 1954), U.S. Trademark Assn. (chmn. bd., pres. 1964-65), Assn. Internationale pour la Protection de la Propertie Industrielle, Am., Fed., D.C., Del. bar assns., Del., Tenn. trial lawyers assns., Nashville Bar and Library Assn., Navy League U.S., Vanderbilt Alumni Assn. (bd. dirs. 1961-64), Vanderbilt Law Alumni (pres. 1970-71), Am., Pa. Bonsai societies, Order of Coif, Phi Kappa Psi. Episcopalian (past warden, vestryman, chmn. bldg. com.). Clubs: Confrerie des Chevaliers du Tastevin (grand officier Wilmington chpt. 1972, mem. nat. council 1973, grant intendant Eastern U.S. 1975; delége general 1976, grand pelier gen. U.S. 1977, of N. Am. 1978); Chevy Chase (Md.) Country; Union League N.Y.; Aurora Gun, Greenville Country (bd. dirs. 1962-65), Vicmead Hunt (Greenville, Del.); Wilmington. Author: The Law of Water and Water Rights in the Tenn. River Valley, 1934; Local Restrictions on the Pollution of Inland Waters, 1948; Trademark Management—A Guide for Businessmen, 1955; Trademark Selection, 1960; The Chemical Engineer and Public Liability Law, 1962; A Brief for Corporate Counsel, 1964; Legal Servicing of Industrial Publicity, 1967; Planning a Bonsai Collection, 1968; Reynolds History Annotated, 1978; also numerous articles, treatises. Home: Old Kennett Rd Greenville DE 19807 Office: 1702 Am International Bldg Wilmington DE 19801

REYNOLDS, WILLIAM HAROLD, educator, choral condr., music critic; b. Hermosa Beach, Calif., July 19, 1925; s. Frank Harold and Elma Katherine (Williams) R.; B.A. with highest honors, UCLA, 1949; M.F.A., Princeton U., 1952; m. Mary Lee Kingman, June 19, 1949; children—Christopher, Joel, Ellen, Anne Marie, Susan, Martha. Asst. music critic Los Angeles Times, 1948-50; asst. instr. music Princton (N.J.) U., 1951-52; instr. music Vassar Coll., Poughkeepsie, N.Y., 1952-54; asst. prof. U. Calif., Riverside, 1954-60, asso. prof., 1960-66, prof., 1966—, chmn. dept. music, 1961-67, 77—, chmn. acad. senate, 1968-70, mem. statewide acad. council, 1968-70; asso. Danforth Found., 1958—. Recipient E. Harris Harbison prize for disting. teaching Danforth Found., 1969; Disting. Teaching award U. Calif., Riverside, 1971; Riverside Arts Council award for music, 1979; Am. Philos. Soc. grantee, 1960-61, 75-76; Statewide U. Calif. Humanities Inst. grantee, 1967-68; Creative Arts Inst. grantee, 1974; Danmarks Nat. Bank grantee, 1975. Mem. Coll. Music Soc. (v.p. 1972-75, pres. 1975-77), Internat., Am. musicol. socs., Am. Choral Dirs. Assn., Calif. Choral Condrs. Guild (pres. Riverside-San Bernardino chpt. 1956-57), Phi Beta Kappa (hon.). Contbr. articles on Danish composers to Grove's Dictionary of Music. Democrat. Episcopalian. Home: 741 Spruce St Riverside CA 92507. *Music is a field of great diversity, involving historical scholarship as well as the creative areas of performance and composition. It has been my good fortune to be able to combine scholarship and performance so that music is for me not merely an academic field nor a life of concert giving: it is both, and thus truly a liberal art.*

REYNOLDS, WILLIAM WALTER, clergyman; b. Columbia, N.C., Oct. 25, 1926; s. William Thomas and Vedia Mae (Swain) R.; A.B., Free Will Bapt. Bible Coll., 1951; m. Evelyn Lucille Furlough, July 9, 1945; children—Samuel Thomas, Judith Gail (Mrs. Richard Ivey Reeves, Jr.), Charles Stephen. Ordained to ministry Free Will Bapt. Ch., 1949; pastor Sylvan Park Ch., Nashville, Tenn., 1950-51, 1st Ch., Goldsboro, N.C., 1951-53, Hickory Chapel, Ahoskie, N.C., 1953-56, Bethany Ch., Ayden, N.C., 1956-59, Hull Rd. Ch., Snow Hill, N.C., 1959-63, Shady Grove Ch., Dunn, N.C., 1963-66; mgr. Free Will Bapt. Press Found., Inc., Ayden, 1966—. Moderator Central Conf. Original Free Will Bapt. Ch. N.C., 1961-63; pres. state conv. chs. Original Free Will Bapt. N.C., 1963-65; chmn. denominations State Bd. Superannuation, 1959-70, treas., dir., 1970—; v.p. Ch. Finance Assn., Inc., 1964—; mem. exec. com. Christian Action League N.C., 1973—. Served with AUS, 1945-46; PTO. Democrat. Club: Kiwanis. Home: 139 Ange St PO Box 514 Winterville NC 28590 Office: 811 N Lee St Ayden NC 28513

REYNOLDS, WYNETKA ANN, univ. provost; b. Coffeyville, Kans., Nov. 3, 1937; d. John E. and Glennie King; B.S. in Biology and Chemistry, Kans. State Tchrs. Coll., 1958; M.S. in Zoology (NSF predoctoral fellow 1958-62), U. Iowa, 1960; Ph.D., State U. Iowa, 1962; m. Rex Reynolds, Jr., Sept. 13, 1958; children—Rachel Rebacca, Rex King. Asst. prof. Ball State U., Muncie, Ind., 1962-65; mem. faculty U. Ill. Med. Center, Chgo., 1965-79, prof. anatomy, 1973-79, research prof. ob-gyn., 1973-79, asso. vice chancellor research, dean Grad. Coll., 1977-79; provost Ohio State U., Columbus, 1979—; mem. com. nutrition mother and pre-sch. child Food and Nutrition Bd., Nat. Acad. Scis., 1973—, mem. council Inst. Lab Animal Resources, 1979—; mem. grad. record exams. com. Advanced Biology Test, 1974—; mem. animal resources rev. com., primate research centers, research resources NIH, 1977—. Recipient award Central Assn. Obstetricians and Gynecologists, 1968; Disting. Alumna award Kans. State Tchrs. Coll., 1972. Asso. fellow Am. Coll. Obstetricians and Gynecologists; mem. AAAS, Am. Assn. Anatomists, Am. Diabetes Assn., Endocrine Soc., Perinatal Research Soc., Soc. Exptl. Biology and Medicine, Soc. Gynecol. Investigation, Sigma Xi. Presbyterian. Author numerous papers in field. Home: 4324 Langport Rd Columbus OH 43220 Office: 204 Adminstrn Bldg 190 N Oval Mall Columbus OH 43210

REYNOLDSON, WALTER WARD, state supreme ct. chief justice; b. St. Edward, Nebr., May 17, 1920; s. Walter Scorer and Mabel Matilda (Sallach) R.; B.A., State Tchrs. Coll., 1942; J.D., U. Iowa, 1948; m. Janet Aline Mills, Dec. 24, 1942; children—Vicki (Mrs. Gary Kimes), Robert. Admitted to Iowa bar, 1948; practice in Osceola, 1948-71; justice Iowa Supreme Ct., 1971-78, chief justice, 1978—; lectr. seminar Sch. Law, Drake U., 1968; county atty., Clarke County, Iowa, 1953-57. Trustee Clarke County Community Hosp., Osceola; pres. bd. dirs. Osceola Ind. Sch. Dist. Served with USNR, 1942-46. Recipient Osceola Community Service award, 1968. Mem. Iowa (chmn. com. on legal edn. and admission to bar 1964-71), Am. bar assns., Iowa Acad. Trial Lawyers, Am. Coll. Trial Lawyers. Contbg. author: Trial Handbook, 1969. Home: Rural Route 2 Osceola IA 50213 Office: State Capitol Bldg Des Moines IA 50319

REZNICK, MORRIS MARTIN, lawyer; b. Cleve., Apr. 11, 1923; s. Joseph and Miriam (Baum) R.; B.S., Ohio U., 1947; J.D., Cleve. Marshal Law Sch., 1951; m. Shirley Inbender, Apr. 4, 1948; children—Martha, Brad. Admitted to Ohio bar, 1951; asso. firm. Bernard S. Goldfarb, Cleve., 1952-58, 60-66; house counsel Midwest Builders Co., University Heights, Ohio, 1958-60; partner firm Goldfarb and Reznick, Cleve., 1966—. Served with U.S. Army, 1943-46. Decorated Bronze Star, Purple Heart. Mem. Am., Ohio bar assns., Bar Assn. Greater Cleve. Home: 23803 Edgehill Dr Beachwood OH 44122 Office: 55 Public Sq Cleveland OH 44113

REZNIKOFF, WILLIAM STANTON, biochemist; b. N.Y.C., Apr. 29, 1941; s. Paul and Dorothy Eliza (Grout) R.: student U. Ghana, Accra, 1961-62; B.A., Williams Coll., Williamstown, Mass., 1963; Ph.D., Johns Hopkins U., 1967; m. Catherine Anne Armstrong, May 6, 1967; children—Sarah Anne, Joseph William, Charles Paul. NIH postdoctoral fellow dept. bacteriology and immunology Harvard U. Med. Sch., Boston, 1968-70; asst. prof. biochemistry U. Wis., Madison, 1970-75, asso. prof., 1975-78, prof., 1978—; cons. in field; instr. Cold Spring Harbor Lab., summer 1975; mem. Madison Common Council Com. on Recombinant DNA, 1977-78. Recipient Career Devel. award NIH, 1972-77, Harry and Evelyn Steenbock Career Devel. award U. Wis., 1974-78; NIH predoctoral fellow, 1963-67, postdoctoral fellow, 1968-69; Med. Research Found. Boston postdoctoral fellow, 1970; NSF grantee, 1970-72, 79—; NIH grantee, 1972-79. Mem. Am. Soc. Microbiology, Am. Soc. Biol. Chemists, Phi Beta Kappa. Contbr. articles to profl. jours.; editor: (with Jeffrey Miller) The Operon, 1978; editorial bd. Jour. Bacteriology, 1972-79. Home: 3930 Manitou Way Madison WI 53711 Office: Dept Biochemistry U Wis Madison WI 53706

REZNOWSKI, LORNE ANTHONY, polit. party ofcl., educator; b. Winnipeg, Man., Can., Jan. 5, 1929; s. Lorne William and Anna Angela (Brokowski) R.; B.A. cum laude, Loyola Coll., Montreal, Que., 1950; S.T.L., Catholic U. of Am., 1957; M.A., U. Ottawa, 1961; m. Dorothy Joan Heslop, Aug. 22, 1959; children—Lorne Anthony, Tanya Joanne, Theodore David, Daniella Maria, Gabriella Natasha. Prof. English lit. U. Ottawa (Ont.), 1961-65; prof. English lit. St. Pauls Coll., U. Man., Winnipeg, 1966—; nat. leader Social Credit Party of Can., 1978—, nat. sec., 1971-72. Deacon, Ukrainian Cath. Ch., 1970. Mem. Can. Assn. U. Tchrs. Office: St Pauls Coll U Man Dysart Rd Winnipeg MB R3T 2N2 Canada. *I firmly believe that one should never compromise his principles no matter what the immediate gain may be. I don't believe those principles should be swayed by Gallup polls or opinion surveys. My principles are not rooted in the prevailing secular humanism but in the Christian tradition.*

RHAME, WILLIAM THOMAS, land devel. co. exec.; b. Wantagh, N.Y., Aug. 14, 1915; s. Frank Phipps and Eleanora May Sanger (Davis) R.; B.A., U. Cin., 1936; M.B.A., Harvard, 1938, D.C.S., 1942; m. Thelma Scorgie, Aug. 12, 1939 (div. 1964); children—Frank Scorgie, Frederick Taylor. Mem. faculty Harvard Grad. Sch. Bus. Adminstrn., 1938-40; partner Robert Heller & Assos., Cleve., 1940-45; bus. cons., N.Y.C., 1945-48; pres. Texstar Corp., San Antonio, 1948-65, Cosmin Corp., San Antonio, 1965—, Merger Consultants of Am., Inc., 1965—; chmn. finance com., dir. ICN Pharms., Inc., Irvine, Calif., 1960-76; dir. T.O. Corp., Cosmin Corp., Coro, Inc., Roc, Inc., Hallmark Realty Corp., Mountain Top Estates Inc. Pres. Guadalupe Com. Center, 1956-57, The Argyle, 1957-58; bd. dirs. Mind Sci. Found.; Mem. Phi Beta Kappa, Sigma Alpha Epsilon, Sigma Sigma, Tau Kappa Alpha. Republican. Episcopalian. Clubs: San Antonio Country, Argyle, University. Home: 411 Arcadia Pl San Antonio TX 78209 Office: 1635 North East Loop 410 San Antonio TX 78209

RHEIN, JOSEPH P., business exec.; b. Pitts., Oct. 1, 1926; s. Joseph Peter and Mabel Florence (McKinney) R.; B.S., U. Pitts., 1948; m. Janet Houston, June 21, 1952; children—Susan L., Nancy A., Robert H. With Price Waterhouse Co., C.P.A.'s, 1948-59, L.B. Foster Co., 1959-67, Gen. Refractories Co., 1967-69; with SPS Technologies Inc., Jenkintown, Pa., 1969—, v.p. fin., 1969—; dir. Indsl. Valley Bank & Trust Co., Phila. Pres. Penn Valley Civic Assn., 1979-80. Served with U.S. Army, 1946-47. C.P.A., Pa. Mem. Fin. Execs. Inst., Pa. Inst. C.P.A.'s. Club: Seaview Country. Home: 241 McClenaghan Mill Rd Wynnewood PA 19096 Office: SPS Technologies Inc Benson East Jenkintown PA 19046

RHEIN, MURRAY HAROLD, mgmt. cons.; b. N.Y.C., June 7, 1912; s. Aaron and Celia (Hagler) R.; B.A., U. Ark., 1932, postgrad., 1932-33; m. Miriam Eisenstadt, Dec. 22, 1940; children—Alan A., Barbara (Mrs. Allan D. Kramer). Jr. exec. R.H. Macy & Co., N.Y.C., 1934-39; with Platt & Munk Co., N.Y.C., 1940-78, sales mgr., 1958-64, exec. v.p., 1964-67, pres., 1967-77; v.p. Questor Edn. Products Co., 1969-78; with M & M Rhein, mgmt. consultants to pub. industry, 1978—. Served with USCGR, 1943-46. Jewish (trustee, v.p. temple). Home and office: 740 Midfield Rd Woodmere NY 11598

RHEINBOLDT, WERNER CARL, educator; b. Berlin, Sept. 18, 1927; s. Karl Leo and Gertrud Anna (Hartwig) R.; came to U.S., 1956, naturalized, 1963; Dipl.Math., U. Heidelberg (Ger.), 1952; Dr.rer.nat., U. Freiburg (Ger.), 1955; m. Cornelie J. Hogewind, 1959; children—Bernd Michael, Matthew Cornelius. Mathematician, Computer Lab., Nat. Bur. Standards, Washington, 1957-59; dir. Computer Center, asst. prof. math. Syracuse (N.Y.) U., 1959-62; dir. Computer Sci. Center, U. Md., 1962-65, prof. math. and computer sci., 1965-78, dir. interdisciplinary applied math. program, 1974-78; A.W. Mellon prof. math. U. Pitts., 1978—; vis. prof. Gesellschaft für Mathematik und Datenverarbeitung, Bonn, W. Ger., 1969; adv. panel computer sci. NSF, 1972-75; adv. com. Army Research Office, 1974-78; chmn. applied math. com. NRC, 1979—; cons. editor Acad. Press, N.Y.C., 1967—; cons. in field. Served with German Army, 1943-45. Grantee NSF, 1960-62, 65—, NASA, 1963-73, Office Naval Research, 1972—. Mem. Soc. Indsl. and Applied Math. (editor 1964—, v.p. publs. 1976, pres. 1977-78, council 1979-80), Math. Assn. Am., Am. Math. Soc., AAAS, Assn. Computing Machinery. Lutheran. Author: (with J. Ortega), Iterative Solution of Nonlinear Equations in Several Variables, 1970; Methods of Solving Systems of Nonlinear Equations, 1974; also articles. Office: Dept Math and Statistics Univ Pitts Pittsburgh PA 15260

RHEINGOLD, ARNOLD MORTON, ins. co. exec.; b. N.Y.C., June 23, 1931; s. Herman and Shirley R.; student CCNY, 1949-51; ins. course certs.; m. Patricia R. Reilly, Apr. 9, 1961; children—Lawrence, Heather, Stuart. Agt., Equitable Life Assurance Soc., 1954-58; brokerage supr. Berkshire Life, 1958-59, Guardian Life, 1959-63; gen. agt. Empire State Life Mut., Bayside, N.Y., 1963-66, regional v.p., 1966-71, v.p., dir. mktg., 1971-76; v.p. mktg. Internat. Life Ins. Co. of N.Y., Buffalo, 1976-78, exec. v.p., 1978—; tchr. Life Underwriter Trainer Coll., 1956-63. Served with U.S. Army, 1951-53. C.L.U. Mem. Nat. Assn. Life Underwriters, Am. Coll. Life Underwriters, Am. Soc. Life Underwriters. Republican. Jewish. Home: 116 Presidio Pl Williamsville NY 14221 Office: 120 Delaware Ave Buffalo NY 14202

RHIND, JAMES THOMAS, lawyer; b. Chgo., July 21, 1922; s. John Gray and Eleanor (Bradley) R.; student Hamilton Coll., 1940-42; A.B. cum laude, Ohio State U., 1944; LL.B. cum laude, Harvard, 1950; m. Laura Haney Campbell, Apr. 19, 1958; children—Anne Constance, James Campbell, David Scott. Japanese translator U.S. War Dept., Tokyo, Japan, 1946-47; congl. liaison Fgn. Operations Adminstrn., Washington, 1954; admitted to Ill. bar, 1950, since practiced in Chgo.; atty. Bell, Boyd, Lloyd, Haddad & Burns, 1950-53, 55—, partner, 1958—. Dir. Kewaunee Sci. Equipment Corp., Statesville, N.C., VSI Corp., Pasadena, Cal., Fred. S. James & Co., Inc., Chgo., Lindberg Corp., Chgo., Microseal Corp., Zion, Ill. Commr. Gen. Assembly United Presbyn. Ch., 1963; vice chmn., trustee Hamilton Coll., Clinton, N.Y.; trustee U. Chgo.; chmn. Cook County Young Republican Orgn., 1957; Ill. Young Rep. nat. committeeman, 1957-58; v.p., mem. bd. govs. United Rep. Fund Ill., 1965—. Pres., Ill. Childrens Home and Aid Soc., 1971-73, now trustee; vice chmn. Ravinia Festival Assn., 1971-75, now sec., trustee; bd. dirs. E.J. Dalton Youth Center, 1966- 69; governing mem. Orchestral Assn., Chgo.; mem. Ill. Arts Council. 1971-75; mem. exec. com. div. Met. Mission and Ch. Extension Bd., Chgo. Presbytery, 1966-68. Served with M.I., AUS, 1943-46. Mem. Am., Ill., Chgo. (bd. mgrs. 1967-69), Fed. bar assns., Chgo. Council on Fgn. Relations, Japan Am. Soc. Chgo., Legal Club Chgo., Law Club Chgo., Phi Beta Kappa, Sigma Phi. Presbyterian (elder). Clubs: Chicago, Glen View, Commercial, Attic, Economic (Chgo.). Home: 830 Normandy Ln Glenview IL 60025 Office: 135 S LaSalle St Chicago IL 60603

RHIND, JOHN ARTHUR, life ins. co. exec.; b. Toronto, Ont., Can., May 1, 1920; s. John E. and Sybil (Gayford) R.; M.B.A., U. Toronto, 1953; M.B.A., 1953; m. Katharine Elizabeth Greene, Sept. 24, 1948; children—Susan, Ian, Alexander. With Nat. Life Assurance Co. Can., Toronto, 1945-47, 48-76, chmn. bd., chief exec. officer, 1975-76; econ. statistician Mills, Spence & Co., investment dealers, Toronto, 1947-48; pres., chief exec. officer Confedn. Life Ins. Co., Toronto, 1976—; dir. Econ. Investment Trust Ltd., Slough Estate (Can.) Ltd., IAC Ltd., Campbell Soup Co. Ltd. Trustee Toronto Western Hosp. Served as officer Canadian Army, 1942-45. Mem. Health Ins. Assn. Am. (trustee), Canadian Life Ins. Assn. (past pres.). Clubs: Badminton and Racquet, Toronto Golf, Univ. (Toronto); Osler Bluff Ski. Home: 38 Edgar Ave Toronto ON M4W 2A9 Canada Office: 321 Bloor St E Toronto ON M4W 1H1 Canada

RHINEHARDT, FRED HINTON, apparel mfg. co. exec.; b. Piedmont, Ala., Oct. 7, 1929; s. Albert Lester and Ollie (Miller) R.; B.S., Auburn U., 1954; m. Barbara Gilliland, July 20, 1957; children—Jann, Jill, Eric. With Alatex Inc., Andalusia, Ala., 1954—, sales account exec., 1962-74, v.p., 1974-75, pres., 1975—; dir. Comml. Bank of Andalusia. Vice chmn. Covington County (Ala.) Republican Party, 1974-79. Served with USAF, 1947-50. Mem. Am. Apparel Mfrs. Assn., C. of C. of Andalusia (pres. 1978). Presbyterian. Club: Rotary (pres. club 1978) (Andalusia). Office: Alatex Inc River Falls St Andalusia AL 36420

RHINELANDER, FREDERIC WILLIAM TEMPLETON, ednl. adminstr.; b. Oxford, Eng., Nov. 16, 1931 (parents Am. citizens); s. Frederic William and Constance (Templeton) R.; A.B., Harvard, 1953; M.Ed., 1964; m. Nancy Crocker Powell, Oct. 26, 1957; children—Frederic William II, Mary F., Elizabeth T., Alexandra C. Clk., State St. Bank & Trust Co., Boston, 1953-54; export supr. Gen. Radio Co., Concord, Mass., 1956-61; tchr., bus. mgr. Fenn Sch., Concord, 1961-66; headmaster Glenelg (Md.) Country Sch., 1966-77; asso. dir. Council for Am. Pvt. Edn., 1977-78, dir. for state activities, 1978—; headmaster St. John's Parish Sch., Olney, Md., 1978—. Pres. Assn. Ind. Md. Schs., 1971-73, bd. dirs., 1971-76; pres. Md.-CAPE, 1975-78; mem. Md. Title IV Adv. Council, 1975-77; advisory bd. Md. Facilitators Project/Nat. Diffusion Network, 1977-78. Bd. dirs. Howard County Symphony Soc., Council Am. Pvt. Edn. Served with AUS, 1954-56. Mem. Elementary Sch. Headmasters Assn. Clubs: Lunenberg (N.S.) Yacht; Schooner Assn. N.S. (Armdale). Home: Folly Quarter Rd Glenelg MD 21737 Office: St John's Parish Sch Olney MD 20832

RHINESMITH, STEPHEN HEADLEY, assn. exec.; b. Mineola, N.Y., Dec. 13, 1942; s. Homer Kern and Winifred Long (Headley) R.; B.A. (Baker scholar), Wesleyan U., 1965; M. in Pub. and Internat. Affairs, (Heinz fellow) U. Pitts., 1966, Ph.D. (NDEA fellow), 1972; m. Kathleen Alys Law, Aug. 28, 1965; children—Chrisopher Law, Colin Headley. Dir. internat. services McBer and Co., Cambridge, Mass., 1969-71; pres. intercultural programs AFS Internat., N.Y.C., 1972—; cons. Peace Corps, 1968-72, World Bank, 1976—; vis. fellow Fletcher Sch. Law and Diplomacy, Tufts U., 1970-71; mem. U.S. Nat. Commn. for UNESCO, 1974—; adv. com. fgn. aid AID, 1979—. Bd. dirs. Symphony for UN, Friendship Force. Mem. Council Fgn. Relations, Am. Mgmt. Assn., Nat. Acad. Polit. and Social Sci. Clubs: University (N.Y.C.); Met. (Washington). Author: Bring Home the World: A Management Guide for Community Leaders of International Programs, 1975. Home: 443 Highbrook Ave Pelham Manor NY 10803 Office: 313 E 43d St New York NY 10017

RHOADS, GERALDINE EMELINE, editor; b. Phila., Jan. 29, 1914; d. Lawrence Dry and Alice Fegley (Rice) Rhoads: A.B., Bryn Mawr Coll., 1935; unmarried. Publicity asst. Bryn Mawr (Pa.) Coll., 1935-37; asst. Internat. Students House, Phila., 1937-39; mng. editor The Woman mag., N.Y.C., 1939-42; editor Life Story mag., 1942-45; editor Today's Woman mag., N.Y.C., 1945-52, Today's Family Mag., N.Y.C., 1952-53; lectr. Columbia U., 1954-56, asso. editor Readers Digest, 1954-55; producer NBC, 1955-56; asso. editor Ladies Home Jour., 1956-62, mng. editor, 1962-63, exec. editor McCall's mag., 1963-66; editor Woman's Day mag., 1966—, v.p., 1972-77; v.p. CBS Consumer Publs., 1977—; dir. Anchor Hocking Corp. Recipient award for profl. achievement Diet Workshop Internat., 1977; Elizabeth Cutter Morrow award YWCA Salute to Women in Bus., 1977. Mem. Nat. Home Fashions League, Washington Press Club (dir.), Fashion Group (bd. govs. 1977-79, chmn. bd. govs. 1978—), Am. Soc. Mag. Editors (chmn. exec. com. 1971-73), N.Y. Women in Communications (Matrix award 1975), Women's Forum, YWCA. Home: 865 1st Ave New York NY 10017 Office: 1515 Broadway New York NY 10036

RHOADS, JAMES BERTON, archivist, former govt. ofcl.; b. Sioux City, Iowa, Sept. 17, 1928; s. James Harrison and Mary (Keenan) R.; student Southwestern Jr. Coll., 1946-47, Union Coll., Lincoln, Neb., 1947-48; B.A., U. Cal., Berkeley, 1950, M.A., 1952; Ph.D., Am. U., 1965; m. S. Angela Handy, Aug. 12, 1947; children—Cynthia Patrice Neven, James Berton, Marcia Marie. With Gen. Services Adminstrn.-Nat. Archives and Records Service, Washington, 1952-79, asst. archivist for civil archives, 1965, dept. archivist U.S., 1966-68, archivist U.S., 1968-79; chmn. Nat. Archives Trust Fund Bd., 1968-79; chmn. adminstrv. com. Fed. Register, 1968-79; chmn. Nat. Hist. Publs. and Records Commn., 1968-79; mem. Fed. Council on Arts and Humanities, 1970-79. Trustee Woodrow Wilson Internat. Center for Scholars, 1972-79; v.p. Intergovtl. Council UNESCO Info. Program, 1977-79. Recipient Meritorious and Disting. Service awards GSA, 1966, 68, 79 Fellow Soc. Am. Archivists (pres., 1974-75); mem. Am. Hist. Assn., Internat. Council Archives (pres. 1976-79), Am. Antiquarian Soc., Orgn. Am. Historians, Mass. Hist. Soc. (corr.), Phi Alpha Theta, Phi Kappa Phi. Club: Cosmos. Home: 6502 Cipriano Rd Lanham MD 20801

RHOADS, JONATHAN EVANS, surgeon; b. Phila., May 9, 1907; s. Edward G. and Margaret (Ely) Paxson R.; A.B., Haverford Coll., 1928, D.Sc. (hon.), 1962; M.D., Johns Hopkins U., 1932; D. Med. Sci., U. Pa. 1940, LL.D. (hon.), 1960; D.Sc. (hon.), Swarthmore Coll., 1969, Hahnemann Med. Coll., 1978, Duke U., 1979; D.Sci. (Med.) (hon.), Med. Coll. Pa., 1974; Litt.D. (hon.), Thomas Jefferson U., 1979; m. Teresa Folin, July 4, 1936; children—Margaret Rhoads Kendon, Jonathan Evans, George Grant, Edward Otto Folin, Philip Garrett, Charles James. Intern, Hosp. of U. Pa., 1932-34, fellow, instr. surgery, 1934-39, asso. surgery, surg. research U. Pa. Med. Sch., Grad. Sch. Medicine, 1939-47, asst. prof. surg. research, 1944-47, asst. prof. surgery, 1946-47, asso. prof., 1947-49; J. William White prof. surg. research U. Pa., 1949-51, prof. surgery Grad. Sch. Medicine, 1950—, prof. surgery and surg. research U. Pa. Sch. Med., 1951-57, prof. surgery, 1957-59, provost U. Pa., 1956-59, John Rhea Barton prof. surgery, chmn. dept. surgery, 1959-72, prof. surgery, 1972—, asst. dir. Harrison dept. surg. research, 1946-59, dir., 1959-72; dir. surgery Pa. Hosp., 1972-74; surg. cons. Bryn Mawr (Pa.), Children's Hosp. Phila., Monmouth Med. Center, Germantown (Pa.), Phila. VA hosps.; mem. staff Hosp. of U. Pa. Dir. J. E. Rhoads & Sons, Inc. Mem. bd. pub. edn. City of Phila., 1965-71. Mem. bd. mgrs. Haverford Coll., chmn., 1963-72, pres. corp., 1963-78; bd. mgrs. Friends Hosp. of Phila.; v.p. sci. affairs, trustee Inst. Med. Research; trustee emeritus Bryn Mawr Coll. Cons., Bur. State Services, VA, 1963; nat. adv. gen. medical scis. council USPHS, 1963; cons. to div. of medical scis. NIH, 1962-63; adv. council Life Ins. Med. Research Fund., 1961-66. Pres. Phila. div., 1955-56; chmn. adv. commn. on research on pathogenesis of cancer Am. Cancer Soc., 1956-57, del., 1956-61, dir. at large, 1965—, pres., 1969-70, past officer dir., 1970-77, hon. life mem., 1977—; chmn. surgery adv. com. Food and Drug Adminstrn., 1972-74; chmn. Nat. Cancer Adv. Bd., 1972-79. Mem. Am. Bd. Surgery, 1963-69, sr. mem., 1969—. Recipient Roswell Park medal, 1973; Papanicolaou award, 1977; Phila. award, 1976. Fellow Am. Med. Writers Assn., Am. Philos. Soc. (sec. 1963-66, pres. 1976—), A.C.S. (regent, chmn. bd. regents 1967-69, pres. 1971-72), Royal Coll. Surgeons (Eng.) (hon.), Royal Coll. Surgeons Edinburgh (hon.), Deutsches Gesellschaft für Chirurgie (corr.), Assn. Surgeons India (hon.), Royal Coll. Physicians and Surgeons Can. (hon.), Coll. Medicine South Africa (hon.), Polish Assn. Surgeons (hon.); mem. Hollandsche Maatschappij der Wetenschappen (fgn.), Am. Pub. Health Assn., Assn. Am. Med. Colls. (chmn. council acad. socs. 1968-69, distinguished service mem. 1974—), Fedn. Am. Socs. Experimental Biology Am. Assn. Surgery Trauma, AMA (co-recipient Goldberger award 1970), Pa., Phila. County (pres. 1970) med. socs., Coll. Physicians Phila. (v.p. 1954-57, pres. 1958-60), Phila. Acad. Surgery (pres. 1964), Phila. Physiol. Soc. (v.p. 1945-46), Am. (pres. 1972-73, Disting. Service medal), Pan Pacific (v.p. 1975—), So. surg. assns., The Internat. Surg. Group (pres. 1958), Internat. Fedn. Surg. Colls. (v.p. 1972-78, pres. 1978—), Fellows of Am. Studies, Soc. of U. Surgeons, Soc. Clin. Surgery (pres. 1966-68), Am. Assn. for Cancer Research, AAAS, Am. Physiol. Soc., Internat. Soc. Surgery, N.Y. Acad. Scis., Surgeons Travel Club (pres. 1976), Am. Inst. Nutrition, World Med. Assn., Am. Acad. Arts and Scis., Soc. for Surgery Alimentary Tract (pres. 1967-68), Soc. Surg. Chmn. (pres. 1966-68), Phi Beta Kappa Assos., Alpha Omega Alpha, Sigma Xi, Phi Beta Kappa. Author, co-editor: Surgery: Principles and Practice, 1957, 61-65, 70; contbg. author: Trends in Modern American Society; (with J.M. Howard) The Chemistry of Trauma. Mem. editorial bd. Annals of Surgery (chmn. 1971-73), Jour. Surg. Research, 1960-71; editor Jour. Cancer, 1972—. Contbr. articles to med. jours. and chpts. to books. Home: 131 W Walnut Ln Philadelphia PA 19144 Office: 3400 Spruce St Philadelphia PA 19104

RHOADS, WILLIAM G., ofcl. AID; b. Pasadena, Calif., Sept. 8, 1929; s. Samuel and Helen (Vail) R.; B.S., Mass. Inst. Tech., 1951, postgrad., 1956-59. Economist textile fibers dept. Du Pont Co., 1951-54; group leader Latin Am., Am. Friends Service Com., Phila., 1954-56; asst. prof. econs. Williams Coll., 1960-65; joined U.S. Fgn. Service, 1965; asst. dir., rep. AID, Dept. State, Colombia, 1965-69, Uruguay, 1969-73; dep. asst. adminstr. AID, Washington, 1974-78, in Port-au-Prince, Haiti, 1978—. Mem. Am. Econ. Assn., Nat. Tax Assn. Mem. Soc. of Friends. Home: 9508 Wheelpump Ln Philadelphia PA 19118 Office: AID Dept State Washington DC 20523

RHODEN, ELMER CARL, theatre exec.; b. Lemars, Iowa, May 15, 1893; s. Charles A. and Ellen J. (Johnson) R.; student Omaha U., Nebr. U.; m. Hazel M. Schiller, May 5, 1920; children—Elmer Carl, Clark S.; m. 2d, Esther Burger Geyer, Apr. 6, 1971. With Gen. Film Co., Omaha, 1912-20; organized Midwest Film Distributors, 1920, mgr. until 1927; organized Midwest Theatre Co., 1927, pres. until 1929; div. mgr. Fox Midwest Theatres, Inc., 1929-54; pres. Nat. Theatres, Inc., 1954-58, chmn. bd., 1958-59; chmn. bd. Commonwealth Theatres, Inc., also dir.; pres. Rhoden Investment Co.; dir. City Nat. Bank & Trust Co.; owner ranches in Calif., Mo. Bd. dirs. St. Luke's Hosp., Kansas City, Mo., Dinner Playhouse, Inc. Served as flying cadet, U.S. Army, World War I. Recipient Look Film Achievement award, 1956. Mem. Phi Sigma Kappa. Episcopalian. Clubs: River, Saddle and Sirloin, Kansas City Country, (Kansas City, Mo.); Rancheros Visitadores (Santa Barbara, Calif.); Palm Beach, Everglades (Palm Beach, Fla.); Bath and Tennis. Home: 1236 W 57th Kansas City MO 64113 Office: 215 W 18th St Kansas City MO 64108

RHODES, ALFRED WILLIAM, ins. co. exec.; b. Manchester, Eng., Dec. 20, 1922; s. William Henry and Agnes Anna (King) R.; came to U.S., 1930, naturalized, 1943; B.S., Hofstra U., 1947; m. Joan Helen LaVine, Oct. 12, 1947; children—Alfred William, Ellen Jeanne Rhodes McGinnis, Thomas John, Phyllis Irene, Kenneth James. With John Hancock Mut. Life Ins. Co., Boston, 1942—, regional supr., 1953-54, field v.p., 1954-69, 2d v.p., 1969-71, v.p., 1971-74, sr. v.p., 1974—; dir. Hanseco Ins. Co., John Hancock Distbrs. Inc. Pres., Needham (Mass.) Youth Soccer Program, 1974—; host family Mass. chpt. Am. Field Service, 1971-72, pres., 1972-75; mem. Town of Needham Finance Com., 1973-79. Served with AUS, 1943-46. Decorated Bronze Star. Mem. Nat. Assn. Life Underwriters, Gen. Agts. and Mgrs. Conf., Life Underwriter Tng. Council (trustee), Life Ins. Mktg. and Research Assn. (trustee), C.L.U.'s. Episcopalian. Club: Needham Pool and Racquet. Home: 163 Paul Revere Rd Needham MA 02194 Office: John Hancock Mut Life Ins Co John Hancock Pl PO Box 111 Boston MA 02117

RHODES, ALLEN FRANKLIN, drilling co. exec.; b. Estherville, Iowa, Oct. 3, 1924; s. Edwin James and Esther (Butler) R.; B.S. in Mech. Engring., Villanova Coll., 1947; M.A. in Mgmt., U. Houston, 1950; m. Carol Jean Haisler, Mar. 31, 1962; children—James Fleming, Stephen Haisler. With Hughes Tool Co., 1947-52; from dir. engring. to pres. McEvoy Co., Houston, 1952-63; with Rockwell Mfg. Co., Pitts., 1963-71, v.p. research and engring., 1966-71; v.p. corp. planning and devel. ACF Industries, Inc., 1971-74; pres., chief exec. officer McEvoy Oilfield Equipment Co., Houston, 1974-79; exec. v.p., chief operating officer Goldrus Marine Drilling Co., 1979—; partner Rhoman Engring. Co., Houston, 1949-78; cons. Rice U., 1950-53. Pub. mem. pipeline safety com. Dept. Transp., 1969-74. Republican del. Harris County, Tex., 1952-62; Trustee, United Engring. Trustee, Inc., 1978—. Served to lt. (j.g.) USNR, 1943-46. Named Boss of Year, Houston chpt. Nat. Secretaries Assn., 1961; recipient award appreciation Houston Engring. and Sci. Soc., 1962. Registered profl. engr., Tex. Fellow Instn. Mech. Engrs., ASME (pres. 1970, Thurston award 1978); mem. Am. Nat. Standards Inst. (dir. 1970—, v.p. 1973), S.A.R., Tau Beta Pi. Episcopalian. Author, patentee in field. Home: 73 E Broad Oaks Dr Houston TX 77056 Office: 900 First Nat Bank Bldg Houston TX 77002

RHODES, ANDREW JAMES, med. microbiologist; b. Scotland, Sept. 19, 1911; s. William Thomas and Maud (Innes) R.; M.D., U. Edinburgh, 1934. Intern, U. Edinburgh, 1934, lectr. bacteriology, 1935-41; prof. bacteriology U. London, 1945; prof. virology U. Toronto (Ont., Can.), 1947; practice medicine, specializing in med. microbiology and public health, Toronto, 1947—; med. dir. Pub. Health Labs., Ont. Govt., Toronto, 1970-76, cons. virology, 1976—. Decorated Centennial medal Can., 25th Anniversary medal. Life mem. Can. Pub. Health Assn. Defries award 1975); mem. Can. Med. Assn., Can. Soc. Microbiologists, Am. Soc. for Microbiology, Royal Soc. Can. Anglican. Author: (with C.E. Van Rooyen) Virus Diseases of Man, 2 edits., 1940, 48; Text Book of Virology, 5 edits., 1949-68. Contbr. numerous articles to med. jours. Home: 79 Rochester Ave Toronto ON M4N 1N7 Canada

RHODES, CHARLES KIRKHAM, physicist; b. Mineola, N.Y., June 30, 1939; s. Walter Cortlyn and Evelyn (Kirkham) R.; B.E.E., Cornell U., 1963; M.E.E., M.I.T., 1965, Ph.D. in Physics, 1969; m. Mary M. Cannon, Oct. 23, 1976; children—Lisa, Gregory, Edward. Research asst. Chalmers U., Gothenburg, Sweden, 1963; research asso. radiation lab. Columbia U., 1969; staff specialist Control Data Corp., Melville, N.Y., 1969-70; physicist Lawrence Livermore Lab./U.Calif., 1970-75; lectr. dept. applied sci. U. Calif., Davis, 1971-75; program mgr. Molecular Physics Center, Stanford Research Inst. and cons. prof. dept. elec. engring. Stanford U., 1975-78; prof. physics U. Ill., Chgo. Circle, 1978—; cons. atomic and molecular physics, laser research. NSF fellow, 1963-68. Fellow Am. Phys. Soc.;

mem. Joint Council on Quantum Electronics, IEEE (sr.; editor spl. issue 1979), Sigma Xi, Tau Beta Pi, Eta Kappa Nu. Editor: Excimer Lasers, 1979. Home: 237 E Delaware Pl Apt 10A Chicago IL 60611 Office: U Ill Chgo Circle Dept Physics PO Box 4348 Chicago IL 60680

RHODES, DONALD HENRY, lawyer, former state legislator; b. Norfolk, Va., Mar. 17, 1933; s. Early Clemons and Ivy Mae (Harris) R.; B.S. in Edn., U. Va., 1955, J.D., 1961; postgrad. Pa. State U., 1955-56; m. Anna Margaret Young, June 13, 1959; children—Donald Henry, Chester Clemons. Dir. field services and summer rehab. center Va. Soc. Crippled Children and Adults, 1956-58, bd. dirs., 1958—; admitted to Va. bar, 1961; asst. city atty., Norfolk, 1961-62; asso. firm Kellam & Kellam, Virginia Beach, Va., 1962-66, partner, 1967-68; partner Guy, Rhodes, Betz, Smith & Dickerson and predecessor firm, Virginia Beach, 1969-75, Rhodes & Watson, 1975—; mayor of Virginia Beach, 1970-72, mem. city council, 1970-73; mem. Va. Ho. of Dels., 1974-75. Pres. Thalia Civic League, Virginia Beach, 1967; v.p. Tidewater chpt. March of Dimes; exec. bd. Tidewater council Boy Scouts Am., 1973-76. Bd. dirs. Tidewater Mental Health Assn., 1965-70. Mem. Am., Va., Virginia Beach, Norfolk-Portsmouth bar assns., Va. State Bar, Delta Theta Phi, Phi Kappa Psi. Clubs: Princess Anne Ruritan (pres. 1968-69); Sertoma (pres. 1967-68), Cavalier Golf and Yacht (Virginia Beach). Home: 621 Heron Point Circle Virginia Beach VA 23452 Office: 101 Yorktown Commerce Center 228 N Lynnhaven Rd Virginia Beach VA 23452

RHODES, DONALD ROBERT, elec. engr., educator; b. Detroit, Dec. 31, 1923; s. Donald Eber and Edna Mae (Fulmer) R.; B.E.E., Ohio State U., 1945, M.S., 1948, Ph.D., 1953; children—Joyce Rhodes Holbert, Jane, Roger Charles, Diane. Research asso. Ohio State U., Columbus, 1945-54; research engr. Cornell Aero. Lab., Buffalo, 1954-57; head basic research dept. Radiation, Inc., Orlando, Fla., 1957-61; sr. scientist, Melbourne, Fla., 1961-66; Univ. prof. elec. engring. N.C. State U., Raleigh, 1966—. Co-founder Central Fla. Community Orch., Winter Park, 1961, pres., 1961-62. Recipient Benjamin G. Lamme medal Ohio State U., 1975; Eminent Engr. award Tau Beta Pi, 1976. Fellow AAAS, IEEE (John T. Bolljahn award 1963, pres. Antenna and Propagation Soc. 1969); mem. Sigma Xi, Theta Tau, Eta Kappa Nu, Sigma Pi Sigma. Author: Introduction to Monopulse, 1959; Synthesis of Planar Antenna Sources, 1974. Home: 625 Cardinal Gibbons Dr Apt 101 Raleigh NC 27606 Office: PO Box 5275 Raleigh NC 27650

RHODES, FRANK HAROLD TREVOR, geologist, univ. pres.; b. Warwickshire, Eng., Oct. 29, 1926; s. Harold Cecil and Gladys (Ford) R.; naturalized, 1976; B.Sc., U. Birmingham, 1948, Ph.D., 1950, D.Sc., 1963; LL.D., Coll. Wooster, 1976, Nazareth Coll. Rochester, 1979; m. Rosa Carlson, Aug. 16, 1952; children—Jennifer, Catherine, Penelope, Deborah. Came to U.S., 1968. Post-doctoral fellow, Fulbright scholar U. Ill., 1950-51, vis. lectr. geology summers 1951-52; lectr. geology U. Durham, 1951-54, asst. prof., 1954-55, asso. prof., 1955-56; dir. U. Ill. Field Sta., Wyo., 1956, prof. geology, head geology dept., 1956-68, dean faculty of sci. U. Wales, Swansea, 1967-68; prof. geology and mineralogy Coll. Lit., Sci. and Arts, U. Mich., 1968-77, dean, 1971-74, v.p. for acad. affairs, 1974-77; pres. Cornell U., Ithaca, N.Y., 1977—, Gurley lectr., 1960; Bownnocker lectr. Ohio State U., 1966; Case lectr. U. Mich., 1976. Dir. NSF, Am. Geol. Inst., summer field inst., 1963; mem. Australian vice-chancellors' visitor to Australian univs., 1964. Trustee, Carnegie Found. for Advancement Teaching, 1978—; bd. overseers Meml. Sloan-Kettering Cancer Center. NSF sr. vis. research fellow 1965-66. Fellow Geol. Soc. (council 1963-66) (Bigsby medal, 1967); mem. Palaeontol. Assn. (v.p. 1963-68), Brit. Assn. Advancement Sci., Geol. Soc. Am., Am. Assn. Petroleum Geologists, Soc. Econ. Paleontologists and Mineralogists, Phi Beta Kappa (hon.). Author: The Evolution of Life, 1962, 2d edit., 1976; Fossils, 1963; Geology, 1972; The Paleobiology of Conodonts, 1973; Evolution, 1974. Contbr. articles to sci. jours. Office: Office of Pres Cornell U Ithaca NY 14853

RHODES, GEORGE, air force officer; b. Corrine, W.Va., Feb. 15, 1923; s. Toney and Lessie M. (Keatley) R.; student Officer Candidate Sch., 1940-43, Air Tactical Sch., 1949, U. Md., 1954-62, Air Command and Staff Coll., 1956-57, Armed Forces Staff Coll., 1959-60, Indsl. Coll. Armed Forces, 1965-66, George Washington U., 1965-66; m. Vinnice Pruitt, Aug. 30, 1942; children—Michael, Richard, John, Keith. Commd. 2d lt. USAAF, 1943, advanced through grades to lt. gen. USAF, 1975; aircraft maintenance staff adviser, dir. materiel Chinese Tech. Service Command, Taiwan, 1957-59; chief financial mgmt. br. Directorate Maintenance Engring., dir. materiel, requirements and programs br., chief requirement and programs br. Office Dep. Chief of Staff, Systems and Logistics, Hdqrs. USAF, Washington, 1960-65; dep. comdr. materiel, comdr. 7101st Materiel Squadron, Wiesbaden Air Base, Germany, 1966-67; dir. maintenance engring., dep. chief of staff materiel USAF in Europe, Lindsey Air Sta., Germany, 1967-69; dir. materiel mgmt., vice comdr. San Antonio Air Materiel Area, Kelly AFB, Tex., 1969-71; asst., later dep. chief of staff for materiel mgmt. Hdqrs. Air Force Logistics Command, Wright-Patterson AFB, O., 1971-73, chief staff, 1973-75, now vice comdr.; asst. dep. chief staff systems and logistics Hdqrs. U.S. Air Force, Washington, 1975. Decorated Legion of Merit, Meritorious Service medal, D.S.M., Air Force Commendation medal, Army Commendation medal, Distinguished Unit Badge of China. Mem. Soc. Logistics Engrs., Air Force Assn. Baptist. Office: Hdqrs USAFLC/CV Wright-Patterson AFB OH 45433

RHODES, IRWIN SEYMOUR, lawyer; b. Cin., Nov. 21, 1901; s. Solomon and Lina (Silberberg) R.; B.A., U. Cin. 1921; LL.B., Harvard, 1924; M.A., Xavier U., 1962; m. Mary Elizabeth Frechtling, Dec. 12, 1941. Admitted to Ill. bar, 1924, Ohio bar, 1925, D.C. bar, 1978; pvt. practice Chgo., 1924-29, Cin., 1929—. Editor Pub. Utilities and Carrier Service, 1926-29; contbg. editor Ohio Jurisprudence, 1933-35; chmn. com. for Preservation John Marshall Papers, 1953, mem. editorial bd., 1953-59, chmn. spl. com., 1957-59; co-dir. Irwin S. and Elizabeth F. Rhodes Legal History Collection, U. Okla. Cons. jud. recs. Gen. Services Adminstrn., 1969. Bd. fellows U. Okla., 1970—. Mem. Am. (chmn. Communist tactics, strategy and objectives com. 1962), Cin. (chmn. com. for preservation legal hist. documents 1961), Fed. (nat. law observance com.) bar assns., Cin. Law Library Assn., Md., Cin. hist. socs., Phi Beta Kappa (hon.). Clubs: Cosmos (Washington); Harvard, Harvard Business School, Cincinnati. Author articles in field. Author-editor: The Papers of John Marshall, a Descriptive Calendar; Papers of Roger Brooke Taney. Home: 3815 Erie Ave Cincinnati OH 45208 also 2122 Massachusetts Ave NW Washington DC 20008

RHODES, JAMES ALLEN, gov. of Ohio; b. Jackson County, Ohio, Sept. 13, 1909; s. James Allen and Susan (Howe) R.; student Ohio State U.; m. Helen Rawlins, Dec. 18, 1941; children—Suzanne, Saundra, Sharon. Columbus city auditor 1941-44, mayor 1944-53; auditor Ohio, 1953-62; gov. of Ohio, 1963-70, 75—. Republican nominee for gov. Ohio 1954. Past pres. Nat. Amateur Athletic Union; del. Pan-Am. Sports Congress, Internat. Sports Fed.; mem. Columbus Bd. Edn., 1937-40; founder Nat. Caddie Assn., Inc., All-Am. Newspaper Boys Scholarships, Inc., Columbus Boys Club. Mem. Profl. Golfer's Assn. Adv. Com., U.S. Olympic Com. Presbyterian. Mason (32 deg.). Kiwanian. Author: Johnny Shiloh, 1958; The Trial of Mary Todd Lincoln, 1959; The Court Martial of Commodore Perry, 1960. Office: Office of Governor State House Columbus OH 43215*

RHODES, JOHN BOWER, JR., mgmt. cons.; b. Pitts., July 8, 1925; s. John Bower and Mary Lucile (Lewis) R.; B.S. in Mech. Engring., Princeton U., 1946; postgrad. N.Y. U. Law Sch., 1953-55; m. Joan Ann Black, June 11, 1955; children—John Bower, III, Mark Lewis, Lydia Black. With internat. ops. California Texas Oil Co., N.Y.C., 1946-59, mgr. ops. in Arabia, 1947-50, India, 1955-59; mng. officer Europe, Booz, Allen & Hamilton Internat. NV, Zurich, Switzerland, 1959-63, Dusseldorf, W.Ger., 1963-68; v.p. internat. affairs Booz, Allen & Hamilton Inc., N.Y.C., 1968-70, sr. v.p., 1970—, also dir.; chmn. Booz, Allen & Hamilton Internat., N.Y.C., 1971—; dir. Amerace Corp., Amtrol Inc. Mgr. N.Y. Inst. for Edn. of Blind, 1976—. Served with USMC, 1943-45, 51-52. Mem. Internat. C. of C. (U.S. council), Inst. Mgmt. Cons. (founder), Council Fgn. Relations, Orgn. Econ. Coop. and Devel. (U.S. bus. and industry advisory com.). Clubs: Industrie (Dusseldorf); Princeton, Colonial, Racquet (N.Y.C.); Duquesne (Pitts.), Nantucket (Mass.) Yacht. Office: 245 Park Ave New York NY 10017

RHODES, JOHN JACOB, Congressman; b. Council Grove, Kans., Sept. 18, 1916; s. John Jacob and Gladys Anne (Thomas) R.; B.S., Kans. State U., 1938; LL.B., Harvard U., 1942; m. Mary Elizabeth Harvey, May 24, 1942; children—John Jacob, Thomas H., Elizabeth C., James S. Admitted to Kans. bar, 1942, Ariz. bar, 1945; v.p., dir. Farm & Home Life Ins. Co.; mem. 83d-96th congresses from 1st Dist. Ariz., chmn. Republican policy com. 89th-93d congresses, house minority leader, 1973—; chmn. platform com. Nat. Rep. Conv., 1972, permanent chmn., 1976. Mem. Ariz. Bd. Pub. Welfare, 1951-52. Served with AUS, World War II, Col., ret. Mem. Mesa C. of C. (pres. 1950), Kans., Ariz., D.C. bar assns., S.A.R., Am. Legion, Beta Theta Pi. Republican. Methodist. Clubs: Masons (33 deg.), York Rite, Scottish Rite, Elks, Moose, Rotary, Ariz., Mesa Golf and Country, Capitol Hill; Burning Tree (Bethesda, Md.); Congressional Country. Office: H-230 Capitol Bldg Washington DC 20515

RHODES, KENT, publishing co. exec.; b. Bklyn., Feb. 5, 1912; s. Clarence and Louise (Rhodes) Klinck; B.S., Amos Tuck Sch., Dartmouth, 1933; L.H.D. (hon.), Mercy Coll., 1978; m. Christina Riordan, July 19, 1952; children—David Christian, Jean Louise, Brian Mark. Editor, pub. Dartmouth Pictorial, 1931-33; with Time Inc., 1933-44; with Reader's Digest Assn., Inc., Pleasantville, N.Y., 1944-78, dir., 1965-78, exec. v.p., 1970-75, pres., 1975-76, chmn. bd., 1976-78, sr. counsellor, 1978—; pres. Mag. Pubs. Assn., N.Y.C., 1979—; dir. Internat. Exec. Service Corps., 1973-78. Bd. dirs. Reader's Digest Found., 1970—, pres., 1974-77, chmn. bd., 1978—; trustee Outward Bound, 1966—, pres., 1971-72, chmn. bd., 1973; bd. dirs. Hurricane Island (Maine) Outward Bound Sch., 1971-77, Harvey Sch., Katonah, N.Y., 1966-77, Internat. House, 1977—, Inst. Internat. Edn., 1978—; mem. Presdl. Commn. on Postal Service, 1976-77. Recipient William Caxton Human Relations award Am. Jewish Com., 1965. Mem. Mag. Pubs. Assn. (dir. 1956-78, chmn. 1958-60), Assn. Publ. Prodn. Mgrs. (founder, 1st pres. 1939—), Nat. Inst. Social Sci., Westchester County Assn. (dir. 1972—, vice chmn. 1975-77, chmn. 1978—), Direct Mail Mktg. Assn. (dir. 1964-72, vice chmn. 1971), Zeta Psi. Clubs: University (N.Y.C.); Sleepy Hollow (Scarborough, N.Y.); Fishers Island (N.Y.) Country. Home: 860 United Nations Plaza Apt 19A New York NY 10017 Office: Mag Pubs Assn 575 Lexington Ave New York NY 10022

RHODES, RICHARD LEE, author; b. Kansas City, Kans., July 4, 1937; s. Arthur and Georgia Saphronia (Collier) R.; B.A. cum laude, Yale U., 1959; m. Linda Iredell Hampton, Aug. 30, 1960 (div. 1974); children—Timothy James, Katherine Hampton; m. 2d, Mary Magdalene Evans, Nov. 26, 1976. Contbg. editor Harper's mag., N.Y.C., 1970-74; contbg. editor Playboy mag., Chgo., 1974—. Served with USAF, 1959, 60-61. Guggenheim fellow, 1974-75; Nat. Endowment for Arts grantee, 1978-79. Author: The Inland Ground, 1970; The Ungodly, 1973; The Ozarks, 1974; Holy Secrets, 1978; Looking for America, 1979; The Last Safari, 1980; contbr. articles to nat. mags. Address: care TCA Lit Agy 200 W 57th St Suite 1401 New York NY 10019

RHODES, WILLARD, ethnomusicologist; b. Deshler, Ohio, May 12, 1901; s. John Osborne and Lula (Sheely) R.; A.B., B.Mus., Heidelberg Coll., 1922; student Wittenberg Coll., 1922-23; M.A., Columbia, 1925; student Mannes Sch. Music. 1923-25, Ecole Normale de Musique, Paris, 1925-27; m. Lillian Hansen, July 6, 1940; 1 dau., Joy Cooper. Conductor, chorus master Am. Opera Co., 1927-30; asst. conductor Cin. Summer Opera Co., 1928-33; pianist-accompanist on concert tours, pvt. teaching, Chgo. 1930-35; dir. music Pub. Schs., Bronxville, N.Y. 1935-37; asso. music Columbia, 1937-46, asst. prof., 1946-49, asso. prof., 1949-54, prof. music, 1954-69, prof. emeritus music, 1969—. Edn. specialist, music cons. Bur. Indian Affairs, 1938—; collector, editor Music North Am. Indian Library Congress, 1952; vis. prof. U. Hawaii, 1970; vis. research prof. Centre for Nigerian Cultural Studies, Ahmadu Bello U., Zaria, 1974. Fulbright sr. research fellowship, S. Rhodesia, 1958-59; Am. Inst. Indian Studies research grantee for research in carnatic music, India, 1965-66. Fellow African Studies Assn., Am. Inst. Indian Studies; mem. Internat. Inst. for Comparative Music Research and Documentation (mem. scientific bd.), Am. Anthrop. Soc., Am. Musicol. Soc., Am. Folklore Soc., African Music Soc., Am. Ethnol. Soc. (councilor 1959), Music Library Assn., Soc. Ethnomusicology (pres. 1955-57), Soc. Asian Music (pres.), Internat. Folk Music Council (pres. 1967—). Congregationalist. Club: Century (N.Y.C.). Author: (with others) Musikgeschicte in Bildern; (with R. Gordon Wasson) Maria Sabena and Her Mazatec Mushroom Velada, 1974. Editor, annotator: Ethnic Folkways Library. Contbr. articles to profl. jours. Home: 13615 Redwood Dr Sun City AZ 85351

RHODES, WILLIAM LUTHER, JR., state justice; b. Loris, S.C., May 14, 1918; s. William Luther and Gussie Jane (Worley) R.; B.A., Duke U., 1939; LL.B., U. S.C., 1942, J.D., 1970; m. Margaret Elizabeth Rentz, Apr. 23, 1947; children—Nancy Elizabeth, Jane, Jennifer Ethel. Admitted to S.C. bar, 1942; practiced law, Hampton, S.C., 1946-60; resident judge 14th Jud. Circuit Ct. of S.C., 1960-75; asso. justice S.C. Supreme Ct., 1975—. Mem. S.C. Ho. of Reps., 1950-60, chmn. ways and means com. Served with USAAF, 1942-46. Baptist. Home: 301 Palmetto Ave E Varnville SC 29944 Office: PO Box 128 Hampton SC 29924

RHODY, FRANK G., publishing co. exec.; b. Tower City, Pa., Feb. 20, 1911; s. Frederick G. and Gertrude (Workman) R.; grad. Peirce Sch., Phila., 1931; LL.D. (hon.), Susquehanna U., 1977; m. Sara E. Keim, Aug. 17, 1940; children—John F., Thomas W. Mem. bd. publ. Lutheran Ch. in Am., Phila., 1928—, adminstrv. sec., 1947-58, asso. exec. sec., 1958-66, exec. sec., 1966—, gen. mgr., 1972—; gen. mgr. Fortress Press, Phila. Mem. Protestant Church-Owned Pubs. Assn. (dir.). Club: Union League (Phila.). Home: 5249 Apache Ln Drexel Hill PA 19026 Office: 2000 Queen Ln Philadelphia PA 19129

RHULE, JOHN DAVIS, indsl. equipment mfg. co. exec.; b. Pitts., Apr. 22, 1925; s. Warren Alexander and Grace Irene (Davis) R.; B.S. in Engring., U. Mich., 1946; LL.B., U. Pitts., 1952; divorced; children—Kathleen, John, Allen, Lori. Admitted to Pa. bar, 1952; contract negotiator U.S. Army Ordnance Dept., Pitts., 1952-54; tech. buyer Westinghouse Electric Co., 1954-56; atty. Teller Co., Butler, Pa., 1956-58; sec., corp. counsel Mesta Machine Co., Pitts., 1958—; dir. Mesta Communications, Inc., Apollo Fabricators, Inc. Served with USNR, 1946-49. Mem. Am. Bar Assn., Am. Soc. Corp. Secs., Assn. Iron and Steel Engrs., Lic. Execs. Soc., Allegheny County Bar Assn. Republican. Presbyterian. Office: Mesta Machine Co 7th Ave West Homestead PA

RHYNE, CHARLES SYLVANUS, lawyer; b. Charlotte, N.C., June 23, 1912; s. Sydneyham S. and Mary (Wilson) R.; student Duke 1928-29, 32-35, LL.D., 1958, LL.B., George Washington U., 1937, D.C.L., 1958; LL.D., Loyola U. of Cal., 1958, Dickinson Law Sch., 1959, Ohio No. U., 1966, De Paul U., 1968, Centre, 1969, U. Richmond, 1970, Howard U., 1975; m. Sue Cotton, Sept. 16, 1932 (dec. Mar. 1973); children—Mary Margaret, William Sylvanus; m. 2d, Sarah P. Hendon, Oct. 2, 1976; 1 dau., Sarah Wilson. Admitted to D.C. bar, 1937, since practiced in Washington; sr. partner Rhyne & Rhyne; gen. counsel Nat. Inst. Municipal Law Officers; professorial lectr. on aviation law George Washington U., 1948-53; gen. counsel Fed. Commn. Jud. and Congl. Salaries, 1953-54; spl. cons. Pres. Eisenhower, 1959-60. Dir. Nat. Savs. & Trust Co. Mem. Internat Commn. Rules Judicial Procedures, 1959-61, Pres.'s Commn. on UN, 1969-71; spl. ambassador, personal rep. for Pres. U.S. to UN High Commr. for Refugees, 1971. Trustee Geo. Washington U., 1957-67, Duke U., 1961—. Recipient Grotius Peace award, 1958; Freedoms Found. award for creation Law Day-U.S.A., 1959; Alumni Achievement award George Washington U., 1960; Nat. Bar Assn. Stradford award, 1962; gold medal Am. Bar Assn., 1966; Whitney M. Young award, 1972; Harris award Rotary, 1974; U.S. Dept. State appreciation award, 1976; D.C. Distinguished Service award, 1976; Nansen Ring for refugee work, 1976. Mem. World Peace Through Law Center (pres. 1963—), Am. (pres. 1957-58, chmn. ho. dels. 1956-58, chmn. commn. world peace through law 1958-66, chmn. com. aero. law, 1946-48, 51-54, chmn. internat. and comparative law sect., 1948-49, chmn. UN com., chmn. commn. on nat. inst. justice 1972—; nat. chmn. Jr. Bar Conf. 1944-45), D.C. (pres. 1955-56), Inter-Am. (v.p. 1957-59) bar assns., Am. Bar Found. (pres. 1957-58, chmn. fellows 1958-59), Am. Judicature Soc. (dir.), Am. Law Inst., Am. Soc. Internat. Law, Nat. Aero. Assn. (dir. 1945-47), Washington Bd. Trade, Duke U. Alumni Assn. (chmn. nat. council 1955-56, pres. 1959-60), Delta Theta Phi, Order of Coif, Omicron Delta Kappa, Scribes. Clubs: Metropolitan, Nat. Press, Barristers, Congressional, Nat. Lawyers. Author: Civil Aeronautics Act, Annotated, 1939; Airports and the Courts, 1944; Aviation Accident Law, 1947; Airport Lease and Concession Agreements, 1948; Cases on Aviation Law, 1950; The Law of Municipal Contracts, 1952; Municipal Law, 1957; International Law, 1971; Renowned Law Givers and Great Law Documents of Humankind, 1975; International Refugee Law Day, 1976; Law and Judicial Systems of Nations, 1978; editor: Municipalities and Law in Action, NIMLO Municipal Law Rev., Municipal Law Jour., Municipal Law Court Decisions, Municipal Ordnance Rev., Municipal Attorney. Contbr. articles in field. Home: 1404 Langley Pl McLean VA 22101 Office: 1000 Connecticut Ave NW Suite 800 Washington DC 20036

RIASANOVSKY, NICHOLAS VALENTINE, educator, historian; b. Harbin, China, Dec. 21, 1923; came to U.S., 1938, naturalized, 1943; B.A., U. Oreg., 1942; A.M., Harvard U., 1947; D.Phil., Oxford (Eng.) U., 1949; m. Arlene Ruth Schlegel, Feb. 15, 1955; children—John, Nicholas, Maria. Mem. faculty U. Iowa, 1949-57; mem. faculty U. Calif. at Berkeley, 1957—, prof. history, 1961—, Sidney Hellman Ehrman prof. European history, 1969—; vis. research prof. USSR Acad. Scis., Moscow, 1969, Leningrad, 1974. Served to 2d lt. AUS, 1943-46. Decorated Bronze Star; recipient Silver medal Commonwealth Club Calif., 1964; Rhodes scholar, 1947-49; Fulbright grantee, 1954-55; Guggenheim fellow, 1969; sr. fellow Nat. Endowment Humanities, 1975. Mem. Am. Assn. Advancement Slavic Studies (pres. 1973-77), Am. Hist. Assn. Author: Russia and the West in Teaching of the Slavophiles: A Study of Romantic Ideology, 1952; Nicholas I and Official Nationality in Russia, 1825-1855, 1959; A History of Russia, 1963; The Teaching of Charles Fourier, 1969; A Parting of Ways: Government and the Educated Public in Russia, 1801-1855, 1976; also articles. Co-editor: Calif. Slavic Studies, 1960—. Home: 874 Contra Costa Ave Berkeley CA 94707

RIBEIRO, LENOR DE SA, physician, hosp. adminstr.; b. Soa Goncalo, Brazil, Sept. 25, 1919; s. Americo J. Ribeiro and Coneicao S. Corres de Sa; B.A., Peter Second Coll., Rio de Janeiro, Brazil; B.S., Juruena Inst. Rio De Janeiro, 1941; M.D., U. Rio de Janeiro, 1947; m. Maria J. Aguiar, Nov. 4, 1949; children—Silvia, Roberto, Elizabeth, Monica. Naturalized U.S. citizen, 1963. Intern St. John's Hosp., Lowell, Mass., 1951-52; resident physician Tewksbury (Mass.) Hosp., 1953-54; resident pathologist St. Elizabeth Hosp., Youngstown, Ohio, 1954-56; from staff physician to med. dir., clin. dir., asst. supt. and supt. Nashville Met. Bordeaux Hosp., 1956—; asst. prof. medicine U. Rio de Janeiro, 1949-51; faculty dept. medicine Vanderbilt U. Hosp., Nashville, 1965—; prof. dept. med. Meharry Med. Coll., Nashville, 1965. Chmn. Health and Safety Com. Middle Tenn., Nashville Mayor's Task Force on Drug Abuse; active dist. health and safety com. Middle Tenn. council Boy Scouts Am.; mem. bd. Council on Aging. Recipient Outstanding Civil Servant award Nashville Real Estate Bd., 1965; award Boy Scouts Am., 1971, Long Rifle award, 1978; Outstanding Contbns. to Nursing award Tenn. League for Nursing, 1978; Exemplary Service Record award Tenn. Health Care Assn., 1978; Outstanding Community Service award Metro County Council Nashville and Davidson County, 1978. Mem. Am. Acad. Med. Adminstrs., Tenn. Med. Assn., Am. Psychiat. Assn., Nashville Acad. Medicine, Middle Tenn. Hosp. Council, Am. Coll. Hosp. Adminstrs. (past chmn. young adminstrs. club, chmn. task force on minorities), Pan-Am. Assn. Tenn. (pres. 1968-69), Tenn. Hosp. Assn. (lic. practical nurse liaison com., Meritorious Service award 1979). Address: County Hosp Rd Nashville TN 37218

RIBENBOIM, PAULO, mathematician; b. Recife, Brazil, Mar. 13, 1928; s. Moyses and Anna (Drechsler) R.; Came to Can., 1962, naturalized, 1969; B.Sc., U. Federal do Rio de Janeiro (Brazil), 1948; Ph.D., U. Sao Paulo (Brazil), 1957; D.Sc. (hon.), U. Caen (France), 1979; m. Huguette Demangelle, Dec. 19, 1951; children—Serge Charles, Eric Leonard. Researcher, U. Nancy (France), 1950-52, Instituto de Matemática, Rio de Janeiro, 1952-53, 56-59, U. Bonn (Germany), 1954-56; vis. asso. prof. math., Fulbright fellow U. Ill., 1959-62; prof. Queen's U., Kingston, Ont., Can., 1962—; vis. asso. prof. U. Pierre Marie Curie, Paris, 1969-70. Can. Council grantee, 1977. Fellow Royal Soc. Can.; mem. Am. Math. Soc., Can. Math. Soc., Soc. Math. France, Soc. Math. Switzerland, Mexican Math. Soc., Iranian Math. Soc. Author books, including: L'Arithmétique des Corps, 1972; 13 Lectures on Fermat's Last Theorem, 1979; research, numerous publs. in math.; editor Queen's Papers in Pure and Applied Math., 1964—, Can. Jour. Math., 1977—, Math. Reports Acad. Sci. Can., 1978—. Office: Dept Math Queen's U Kingston ON K7L 3N6 Canada

RIBICOFF, ABRAHAM A., U.S. Senator; b. New Britain, Conn., Apr. 9, 1910; s. Samuel and Rose (Sable) R.; student N.Y. U.; LL.B. cum laude, U. Chgo., 1933; m. Ruth Siegel, June 28, 1931 (dec.);

children—Peter, Jane; m. 2d, Lois Mathes, 1972. Admitted to Conn. bar, 1933; mem. Conn. Ho. of Reps., 1938-42; municipal judge, Hartford, Conn., 1942-43, 45-47; chmn. Conn. Assembly of Municipal Court Judges, 1942; mem. 81st—82d congresses from 1st Conn. Dist., mem. com. fgn. affairs; gov. Conn., 1955-61; sec. HEW, 1961-62; mem. U.S. Senate from Conn., 1963—, mem. fin., joint econ. coms., chmn. govt. affairs com. Democrat. Author: Politics: The American Way, 1967; America Can Make It, 1972; The American Medical Machine, 1972. Home: Cornwall Bridge CT 06754 Office: Room 337 Russell Senate Office Bldg Washington DC 20510

RIBICOFF, IRVING S., lawyer; b. New Britain, Conn., Apr. 16, 1915; s. Samuel and Rose (Sable) R.; B.A. summa cum laude, Williams Coll., 1936; LL.B., Yale, 1939; m. Belle Krasne, June 27, 1955; children—Dara K., Sarai K. Admitted to Conn. bar, 1939, since practiced in Hartford; instr. in pub. speaking Williams Coll., 1934-36; atty. reorganization div. SEC, 1939-41; chief price atty. for Conn. OPA, 1942-44; partner Ribicoff & Kotkin, and predecessors, 1941-78, firm Schatz & Schatz, Ribicoff & Kotkin, Hartford, 1978—. Mem. Hartford County Grievance Com., 1957-61, chmn., 1960-61. Bd. dirs. Law Sch. Fund of Yale, Hartford Festival Music, Hartford Jewish Fedn., Symphony Soc. Greater Hartford; exec. com. Yale Law Sch. Assn.; trustee Greater Hartford YMCA; bus. adv. com. N.E. Colls. Fund. Mem. Am., Conn. (mem. fed. bench-bar relations com. 1967—, chmn. 1967-69; mem. specialization com. 1969—, chmn. 1969-74), Hartford County bar assns., N.E. Law Inst. (adv. council), Fed. Bar Assn. (Conn. pres. 1964-75), Order of Coif, Phi Beta Kappa. Home: 56 Scarborough St Hartford CT 06105 Office: One Financial Plaza Hartford CT 06103

RIBLE, ULYSSES FLOYD, ret. architect; b. Chgo., Nov. 22, 1904; s. Ulysses Oscar and Bessie E. (Doty) R.; B.Arch., U. So. Calif.; grad. fellow architecture, U. Pa., 1928; m. Ruth Stone, Morton, May 26, 1935; children—Morton, Justin. Instr. archtl. design U. So. Calif., 1930-33; pvt. practice architecture, Beverly Hills, Calif., 1933-43; asso. prof. U. Kans., 1943-44; partner Allison & Rible, Los Angeles, 1944-66, Allison, Rible, Robinson & Ziegler, architects, 1966—. Mem. bd. examiners AIA, 1954-56; mem. Calif. Bd. Archtl. Examiners, 1952-56, pres., 1955-56; chmn. Calif. State Profl. Licensing Com., 1961-63. Mem. archtl. review bd. U.S. Dept. Def., 1963-72; jurist AIA 2d Biennial Library Awards, 1964, jurist 4th Ann. Archtl. Achievement Awards, 1968. Bd. councilors Sch. Politics Internat. Relations U. So. Calif., 1963—, chmn., 1970-72. Recipient award Pub. Bldgs. Adminstrn. U.S. competition, 1939; Distinguished Service award U.S. Jr. C. of C., 1939; design award AIA, 1951, 54; Legion Honor Order DeMolay. Fellow AIA (pres. So. Calif. chpt. 1954, nat. bd. dirs. 1957-60, chmn. nat. judiciary bd. 1963-66, pres. Calif. council, 1964, sec. coll. fellows, 1968-70; Distinguished Service award Calif. council 1960, Edward C. Kemper award 1970; vice chancellor coll. fellows 1970-72, chancellor 1972-73); mem. Econ. Round Table of Los Angeles (pres. 1947), Beverly Hills Jr. C. of C. (pres. 1938). Mason (32), Rotarian (pres. Wilshire club, Los Angeles, 1967-68). Club: Pauma Valley Country. Home: PO Box 125 Pauma Valley CA 92061

RIBLET, WILLIAM BREEZE, mfg. co. exec.; b. Elkhart, Ind., Sept. 23, 1938; s. William Roy and Mary (Breeze) R.; B.S. Acctg., Miami U., Oxford, Ohio, 1960; m. Janet Margaret Avey, Aug. 25, 1962; children—Leslie Ann, Jonathan William. With Riblet Products Corp., 1962—, successively purchasing agt., exec. v.p. mfg., div. pres., now exec. v.p. and pres RPI div., also corp. dir., Elkhart, Ind. Bd. dirs. Assn. for Disabled of Elkhart County (Ind.), 1976-79. Served with USMC. Republican. Episcopalian. Clubs: Elcona Country (dir. 1978—, pres. 1980) (Elkhart); Elks. Home: 3609 Gordon Rd Elkhart IN 46514 Office: 29618 CR 12 W PO Box 1645 Elkhart IN 46515

RIBMAN, RONALD BURT, playwright; b. N.Y.C., May 28, 1932; s. Samuel M. and Rosa (Lerner) R.; B.B.A., U. Pitts., 1954, M.Litt., 1958, Ph.D., 1962; m. Alice S. Rosen, Aug. 27, 1967; 2 children. Asst. prof. English lit. Otterbein Coll., 1962-63. Served with AUS, 1954-56. Recipient Obie award, 1966; Rockefeller Found grantee, 1966, 68; Guggenheim fellow, 1970; Nat. Endowment Arts fellow, 1974; recipient award Rockefeller Found., 1975; Emmy award nominee, 1967. Author plays including: Harry, Noon and Night, 1965; The Journey of the Fifth Horse (Obie award), 1966; The Ceremony of Innocence, 1967; Passing Through From Exotic Places, 1969; Fingernails Blue as Flowers, 1971; A Break in the Skin, 1972; The Poison Tree (Straw hat award), 1976; Cold Storage (Elizabeth Hull-Kate Warriner award Dramatists Guild 1977), 1977; The Final War of Oily Winter, CBS-TV, 1967; writer screenplay The Angel Levine, 1970. Address: care Dramatists Guild 234 W 44th St New York NY 10036

RIBOUD, JEAN, oil service and electronics co. exec.; b. Lyon, France, Nov. 15, 1919; s. Camille and Helene (Frachon) R.; grad. Faculte de Droit, Ecoles des Scis. Politiques, Paris, 1939; m. Krishna Roy, Oct. 1, 1949; 1 son, Christophe. Exec. v.p. Schlumberger Ltd., 1963-65, pres., chief exec. officer, 1965-75, chmn. bd., 1972-75, chmn. bd., pres., chief exec. officer, 1975—; mem. internat. council Morgan Guaranty Trust Co. Clubs: Links, Sky, Links Golf (N.Y.C.); Desert Forest Golf (Carefree, Ariz.); Augusta (Ga.) Nat. Golf; La Boulie (Paris). Office: 277 Park Ave New York City NY 10017

RICCARDO, JOHN JOSEPH, automotive co. exec.; b. Little Falls, N.Y., July 2, 1924; s. Peter and Mary (Cirillo) R.; student N.Y. Coll. for Tchrs., 1942; B.A., U. Mich., 1949, M.A., 1950; LL.B. (hon.), No. Mich. U., 1971; Sc.D., Lawrence Inst. Tech., 1972; m. Thelma L. Fife, Aug. 5, 1950; children—Mary Catherine, Teresa Anna, Margaret Lynn, Peter Douglas, John Christopher. Mgr., Touche, Ross, Bailey & Smart, Detroit, 1950-59; financial staff exec. internat. ops. Chrysler Corp., Highland Park, Mich., 1959-60, gen. mgr. Export-Import div., 1960-61, v.p., ops. mgr. Chrysler Can., 1961-62, exec. v.p. Chrysler Can., 1962-63, gen. sales mgr. Dodge div., 1963-64, asst. gen. mgr. Dodge div., 1964-65, asst. gen. mgr. Chrysler-Plymouth div., 1965-66, v.p. mktg., 1966, group v.p. domestic automotive, 1967, group v.p. U.S. and Can. automotive, 1967-70, pres., 1970—, dir., 1967—, chmn. bd., to 1979. Mem. Nat. Bus. Council for Consumer Affairs; mem. automotive sub-council Nat. Indsl. Pollution Control Council. Lay chmn. Archdiocesan Devel. Fund, Detroit, 1968; gen. chmn. Meadowbrook Music Festival and Theater, Rochester, Mich., 1971; v.p., mem. exec. com. United Found., Detroit. Bd. dirs., mem. devel. council U. Mich. Served with AUS, 1943-45; CBI. Decorated French Legion of Honor; C.P.A., Mich. Mem. Am. Inst. C.P.A.'s, Mich. Assn. C.P.A.'s, Motor Vehicle Mfrs. Assn (vice chmn.), Sales and Mktg. execs., Hwy. Users Fedn. (dir.), Phi Beta Kappa. Clubs: Bloomfield Hills Country; Detroit Athletic (pres. 1975), Detroit. Office: Chrysler Corp 12000 Oakland Ave Highland Park MI 48203

RICCHIUTO, D. EDWARD, advt. exec.; b. Jersey City, Mar. 30, 1930; s. Angelo and Concetta (D'Amico) R.; B.B.A., Pace Coll., 1951; M.B.A., Coll. City N.Y., 1953; m. Louise Jean Maino, Apr. 25, 1955; children—Edward, Steven. Partner Bklyn. Deer Distbn., 1951-53; exec. v.p. Hicks & Griest, Inc., N.Y.C., 1963—; pres. H. & G. Promotions, Inc., N.Y.C., 1959—; pres., chief exec. officer Hicks & Greist Advt. Inc., 1973—, chief exec. officer, 1974—; v.p., dir. Ricchi Realty Co., Jersey City, 1960—; exec. v.p., dir. Ramm-Retail Action Micro Market, Inc.; partner A & D Mgmt. Real Estate, Greenwood Village Mgmt., Norwood Gardens Mgmt., Franklyn Gardens Realty; dir. I.S. Kogan Pub. Relations. Mem. Internat. Radio and TV Soc., Sale Execs. Club N.Y.C., Internat. Platform Assn. Clubs: N.Y. Athletic; White Beaches Country. Home: 480 Linden Ct Ridgefield NJ 07657 Office: 850 3d Ave New York City NY 10022

RICCI, JERRI, artist; b. Perth Amboy, N.J.; d. Ulysses Anthony and Caroline (Ricci) Ricci; student Mt. St. Mary's Acad., Plainfield, N.J., 1931-34, N.Y. Sch. Applied Design, 1935; Art Students League N.Y., 1935-38; m. Arnold W. Knauth, II, May 29, 1948. Four one man shows Milch Galleries, N.Y.C., one Fairleigh Dickenson Coll.; exhbns. Addison Gallery, Andover, Mass., Artists for Victory, N.Y.C., Toledo Mus. Art, Milch Galleries; represented in permanent collections Parrish Mus., Southampton, L.I., Am. Acad. Arts and Letters, N.Y.C., Clark U., Worcester, Mass., Butler Art. Inst., Youngstown, Ohio, Ranger Fund. Recipient Gold Medal of Honor, Allied Artists, 1942, Arthur E. Friedrichs award, 1948; E.J. Tonsberg prize Rockport (Mass.) Art Assn., 1942, Hayward Neidringhaus award, 1945; Clara Stroud award Am. Water Color Soc., 1947, Herbert Pratt purchase prize, 1950, Charles H. Stuart Meml. purchase prize, 1953; William Publicover award North Shore Art Assn., 1949; purchase Butler Art, Inst., 1950; Bronze Medal of Honor, Corcord (Mass.) Art Assn., 1953; Silver Medal, Catherine Lorrilard Wolfe Club, N.Y.C. 1954; Clara Obrig award N.A.D., 1954. Mem. N.A.D., North Am. Water Color Soc., Audubon Artists, Allied Artists Am., Phila. Water Color Club, Rockport, North Shore, St. Augustine art assns. Home: 1 Atlantic Ave Rockport MA 01966

RICCIARELLI, KATIA, soprano; b. Rovigo, Italy, Jan. 18, 1946; grad. summa cum laude Benedetto Marcello Conservatory, Venice, Italy. Debuts include: Mimi in La Boheme, Mantua, Italy, 1969, I Due Foscari, Lyric Opera, Chgo., 1972, Mimi in La Boheme, Covent Garden, London, 1974, Suor Angelica, La Scala, Milan, 1976, Mimi in La Boheme, Met. Opera Co., N.Y.C., 1975; appeared throughout U.S., Europe including: San Francisco Opera, Paris Opera, Verona Festival; leading roles in Otello, Luisa Miller, Aida, Lucia di Lammermoor, Marriage of Figaro, Don Carlos, Anna Bolena; recordings include: Suor Angelica, Simon Boccanegra, La Boheme, I Due Foscari. Office: care Columbia Artists Mgmt Inc 165 W 57th St New York NY 10019

RICE, (ETHEL) ANN, editor; b. South Bend, Ind., July 3, 1933; d. Walter A. and Ethylan Maude (Worden) Rice; A.B., Nazareth Coll., Kalamazoo, 1955. Editorial asst. Ave Maria mag., Notre Dame, Ind., 1955-63, asst. editor, 1963-64; asst. editor Today mag., Notre Dame, 1963-64; asst. editor Scott, Foresman & Co., Chgo., 1964-67; editor U. Notre Dame Press, 1967—. Democrat. Roman Catholic. Home: 410 W Marion St South Bend IN 46601 Office: U Notre Dame Press Notre Dame IN 46556

RICE, CHARLES DAVIS, chem. co. exec.; b. Bklyn., Sept. 25, 1941; s. Charles Davis and Regina Lester R.; student Colgate U., 1963; postgrad. Harvard Bus. Sch., 1963-65; m. Diane Montgomery, Dec. 31, 1965; children—Luke, Kate. Successively fin. analyst, cost acctg. mgr., asst. to controller Allied Cherm. Corp., Morristown, N.J., 1965-70; cons., asso., mng. asso. Booz, Allen & Hamilton, N.Y.C., 1970-75; controller M&T Chems., Inc., Rahway, N.J., 1975-77, v.p. fin., treas., Woodbridge, N.J., 1977—. Home: 708 Shackamaxon Dr Westfield NJ 07090 Office: 1 Woodbridge Center Woodbridge NJ 07095

RICE, CLARE IRWIN, electronics co. exec.; b. Rice Lake, Wis., Nov. 3, 1918; s. Chris Nilson and Ingeborg (Haug) R.; B.S. in Elec. Engring., U. Wis., 1943; B.S. in Law, St. Paul Coll. Law, 1950; m. Sylvia Elaine Spurrier; children—Karen, Carol Rice-Phillips, David Alan. Supr. aircraft radio engring. N.W. Airlines, Inc., Mpls., 1946-51; staff engr. Aero. Radio, Inc., Washington, 1951-53; aviation sales mgr., gen. mgr. avionics Bendix Radio Div., Balt., 1953-62; pres. Sunbeam Electronics, Inc., Ft. Lauderdale, Fla., 1962-66; v.p. Nova U., Ft. Lauderdale, 1966-68; asst. v.p., v.p., sr. v.p. Collins Radio group, pres. Collins Avionics group Rockwell Internat. Corp., Cedar Rapids, Iowa, 1968—; dir. First Nat. Bank, Bank of Commerce, Mchts. Nat. Bank, Cedar Rapids. Vice pres. bd. dirs. Greater Ft. Lauderdale C. of C., 1964-68; chmn. United Way, Cedar Rapids, 1973-74; trustee Coe Coll., Cedar Rapids; bd. dirs. St. Lukes Hosp., Cedar Rapids. Served from ensign to lt. comdr., USNR, 1943-46. Registered profl. engr., Minn., D.C. Sr. mem. IEEE; mem. Am. Mgmt. Assn., Iowa Mfrs. Assn. (bd. dirs. 1975—), Gen. Aviation Mfrs. Assn. (dir. 1970—, vice chmn. 1978). Republican. Presbyn. (elder). Clubs: Wings (N.Y.C.); Nat. Aviation (Washington); Cedar Rapids Country, Elmcrest Country (Cedar Rapids). Home: 100 Thompson Dr SE Cedar Rapids IA 52403 Office: 400 Collins Rd NE Cedar Rapids IA 52406

RICE, DAVID LEE, univ. pres.; b. New Market, Ind., Apr. 1, 1929; s. Elmer J. and Katie (Tate) R.; B.S., Purdue U., 1951, M.S., 1956, Ph.D., 1958; m. Betty Jane Fordice, Sept. 10, 1950; children—Patricia Denise Rice Dawson, Michael Alan. Dir. research, educator Ball State U., Muncie, Ind., 1961-66; v.p. Coop. Ednl. Research Lab., Inc., Indpls., 1965-67, also research coordinator, bur. research HEW, Washington; dean campus Ind. State U., Evansville, 1967-71, pres. campus, 1971—; adminstrv. asst. Gov.'s Com. on Post High Sch. Orgn. Mem. State Citizens Advisory Bd. Title XX Social Security Act; bd. dirs. Ind. Forum; bd. commrs. Evansville Housing Authority; mem. South Ind. Conf. Div. Church Related Colls.; chmn. Mayors Riverboat Com.; pres. Leadership Evansville, 1978-79; v.p. S.W. Ind. Pub. TV, 1972—; mem. Buffalo Trace council Boy Scouts Am., 1968—. Served with inf. U.S. Army, 1951-53. Decorated Combat Infantryman's Badge; recipient Service to Others award Salvation Army, 1972, Citizen of Year award Westside Civitan Club, 1972, Boss of Year award Am. Bus. Womens Assn., 1976. Mem. Am. Assn. Higher Edn., Am. Ednl. Research Assn., Nat. Soc. Study Edn., Alpha Kappa Psi, Alpha Zeta, Phi Delta Kappa. Methodist. Clubs: Petroleum, Rotary. Contbr. articles to profl. jours. Home: 611 Mels Dr Evansville IN 47712 Office: Ind State U - Evansville Campus Office of Pres 8600 University Blvd Evansville IN 47712*

RICE, DENIS TIMLIN, lawyer; b. Milw., July 11, 1932; s. Cyrus Francis and Kathleen (Timlin) R.; A.B., Princeton U., 1954; J.D., U. Mich., 1959; children—James Connelly, Tracy Ellen. Admitted to Calif. bar, 1960, since practiced in San Francisco; asso. firm Pillsbury, Madison & Sutro, 1959-61, Howard & Prim, 1961-63; prin. firm Howard, Prim, Rice, Nemerovski, Canady & Pollak, 1964—; sec., dir. Marin Sun Printing Co., Inc., San Rafael, Calif., Gensler & Assos., Inc., San Francisco. Sec., San Francisco Democratic Assn., 1960-61; councilman City of Tiburon, Calif., 1968-72, mayor, 1970-72; dir. Marin County Transit Dist., 1970-72, 77—, chmn., 1979—; supr. Marin County, 1977—, chmn., 1979—; commr. Marin Housing Authority, 1977—; mem. San Francisco Bay Conservation and Devel. Commn., 1977—; dir. Bay Area Council, Inc. Served to 1st lt. AUS, 1955-57. Recipient Freedom Found. medal, 1956. Mem. State Bar Calif. (vice chmn. exec. com. bus. law sect.), Am. (fed. regulation of securities com.), San Francisco bar assns., Princeton Alumni Assn. No. Calif. (pres. 1968-69), Am. Judicature Soc., Order of Coif, Phi Beta Kappa, Phi Delta Phi. Clubs: Univ., Bankers, Olympic (San Francisco); Tiburon Peninsula, Corinthian Yacht (Tiburon); Nassau (Princeton, N.J.). Home: 1463 Vistazow Tiburon CA 94920 Office: Hartford Bldg Suite 2900 650 California St San Francisco CA 94108

RICE, DONALD BLESSING, JR., research inst. exec.; b. Frederick, Md., June 4, 1939; s. Donald Blessing and Mary Celia (Santangelo) R.; B.S. in Chem. Engring., U. Notre Dame, 1961, D.Engring. (hon.), 1975; M.S. in Indsl. Adminstrn., Purdue U., 1962, Ph.D. in Econs., 1965; m. Susan Fitzgerald, Aug. 25, 1962; children—Donald Blessing III, Joseph John, Matthew Fitzgerald. Dir. cost analysis Office Sec. Def., Washington, 1967-69, dep. asst. sec. def. resource analysis, 1969-70; asst. dir. Office Mgmt. and Budget, Exec. Office Pres., 1970-72; pres. Rand Corp., Santa Monica, Calif., 1972—; mem. Nat. Sci. Bd., 1974—; chmn. Nat. Commn. Supplies and Shortages, 1975-77; mem. nat. adv. com. oceans and atmosphere Dept. Commerce, 1972-75; mem. adv. panel Office Tech. Assessment, 1976—; adv. council Coll. Engring., U. Notre Dame, 1974—; mem. Def. Sci. Bd., 1977—; dir. Def. Resource Mgmt. Study (for sec. def. and Pres.), 1977-79. Served to capt. AUS, 1965-67. Recipient Sec. Def. Meritorious Civilian Service medal, 1970; Ford Found. fellow, 1962-65. Mem. Am. Econ. Assn., AAAS, Inst. Mgmt. Scis. (past pres.), Tau Beta Pi. Author articles. Home: 518 Georgina Ave Santa Monica CA 90402 Office: 1700 Main St Santa Monica CA 90406

RICE, DOROTHY PECHMAN (MRS. JOHN DONALD), med. economist; b. Bklyn., June 11, 1922; d. Gershon and Lena (Schiff) Pechman; student Bklyn. Coll., 1938-39; B.A., U. Wis., 1941; D.Sc. (hon.), Coll. Medicine and Dentistry N.J., 1979; m. John Donald Rice, Apr. 3, 1943; children—Kenneth D., Donald B., Thomas H. With hosp., and med. facilities USPHS, Washington, 1960-61; med. econs. studies Social Security Adminstrn., 1962-63, health econs. br. Community Health Service, USPHS, 1964-65; chief health ins. research br. Social Security Adminstrn., 1966-72, dep. asst. commr. for research and statistics, 1972-75; dir. Nat. Center for Health Statistics, Rockville, Md., 1976—. Recipient Social Security Adminstrn. citation, 1968, Disting. Service medal HEW, 1974, Jack C. Massey Found. award, 1978. Fellow Am. Public Health Assn. (domestic award for excellence 1978), Am. Statis. Assn.; mem. Inst. Medicine, Am. Econ. Assn., Population Assn. Am., LWV. Developer health ins. research program Social Securities Adminstrn. Contbr. articles to profl. jours. Home: 8410 Barron St Takoma Park MD 20012 Office: Nat Center Health Statistics 3700 East-West Hwy Hyattsville MD 20782

RICE, EDWARD EARL, former govt. ofcl., author; b. Saginaw, Mich., Feb. 6, 1909; s. William Edward and Katherine Marie (Meyer) R.; student U. Wis., 1926-28; B.S., U. Ill., 1930, postgrad., 1934-35; postgrad. U. Mex., 1931; Coll. Chinese Studies and pvt. tutors, Peking, China, 1935-37; m. Mary June Kellogg, Oct. 26, 1942. Passed fgn. service exams., 1932; apptd. fgn. service officer, 1935, lang. attache, Peking, 1935-37; vice consul, Canton, China, 1938-40; consul, Foochow, China, 1940-42; 2d sec. Am. Embassy, Chungking, China, 1942-45; asst. chief div. Chinese affairs Dept. of State, 1946-48; asst. chief div. Philippine affairs, 1948-49; 1st sec., consul Am. Embassy, Manila, 1949-51; student Nat. War Coll., 1951-52; consul gen., Stuttgart, Germany, 1952-56; fgn. service insp., 1956-58; dep. dir. personnel Dept. of State, 1959, mem. policy planning council, 1959-61, dep. asst. sec. of state for Far Eastern affairs, 1962-63; consul gen., minister Hong Kong, 1964-67; diplomat-in-residence with rank of prof. U. Calif. at Berkeley, 1968-69, research asso. Center for Chinese Studies, 1969—; vis. prof. Marquette U., 1973. Adv. U.S. del. 3rd, 4th and 5th sessions Econ. Commn. for Asia Far East, 1948, 1949. Recipient Commonwealth Club gold medal for non-fiction, 1973. Mem. Beta Gamma Sigma. Author: Mao's Way, 1972. Home: 1819 Lagoon View Dr Tiburon CA 94920 Office: Center for Chinese Studies Univ of Calif Berkeley CA 94720

RICE, ELROY LEON, educator, ecologist; b. Edmond, Okla., Jan. 31, 1917; s. Ernest C. and Bertha (Rieckhoff) R.; A.B. in Math., Central State Coll., Edmond, 1934-38; M.S. in Botany, U. Okla., 1942; Ph.D. in Botany, U. Chgo., 1947; m. Esther Mae Wilson, July 28, 1945; children—Linda J., Clifford R. Mem. faculty U. Okla., 1948—, prof. botany, 1962—, David Ross Boyd prof., 1967—. Mem. sci. improvement com. Okla. Curriculum Improvement Commn., 1958—. Bd. dirs. Grassland Research Found., 1958-66. Served with USAAF, 1943-46. Recipient Alumni Teaching award U. Okla., 1955, Regents Teaching award, 1966. Mem. Okla. Acad. Sci. (chmn. biol. sci. sect. 1953, chmn. sci. teaching sect. 1959), Southwestern Assn. Naturalists (pres. 1970), Ecol. Soc. Am., Am. Soc. Plant Physiologists, AAAS, Am. Inst. Biol. Scis., Nature Conservancy, Scandinavian Soc. Plant Physiology, Brit. Ecol. Soc., Sigma Xi. Author articles in field. Home: 1727 Cruce St Norman OK 73069

RICE, EUGENE FRANKLIN, JR., educator; b. Lexington, Ky., Aug. 20, 1924; s. Eugene Franklin and Lula Allen (Piper) R.; grad. Phillips Exeter Acad., 1942; B.A., Harvard, 1947, M.A., 1948, Ph.D., 1953; postgrad. Ecole Normale Supérieure, 1951-52; m. Charlotte Bloch, Aug. 26, 1952; children—Eugene Franklin, John Arthur, Louise. Instr. history Harvard, 1953-55; from asst. prof. to prof. history Cornell U., 1955-64; prof. history Columbia, 1964—, William R. Shepherd prof., 1974—, chmn. dept. history, 1970-73. Cons. editor Alfred A. Knopf, Inc., Random House, Inc.; Am. Council Learned Socs. fellow; mem. Inst. for Advanced Study, Princeton, N.J., 1962-63; Nat. Endowment for Humanities sr. research fellow, resident in post-classical studies Am. Acad. in Rome, 1974-75. Served with AUS, 1942-45. Guggenheim fellow, 1959-60; Fulbright research fellow, 1959-60. Fellow Am. Acad. Arts and Scis.; mem. Renaissance Soc. Am. (exec. dir.), Am. Hist. Assn. (v.p. for research), Am. Soc. Reformation Research. Author: The Renaissance Idea of Wisdom, 1958; The Foundations of Early Modern Europe, 1970; The Prefatory Epistles of Jacques Lefèvere d'Etaples, 1972. Contbr. articles to profl. jours. Home: 560 Riverside Dr New York NY 10027

RICE, FREDERICK ANDERS HUDSON, educator; b. Bismarck, N.D., Feb. 19, 1917; s. Frederick Llewelyn and Karen (Brende) R.; B.A. in Math. and Physics, Dalhousie U., 1937, M.Sc. in Biochemistry, 1945; Ph.D. in Chemistry, Ohio State U., 1948; m. Margaret MacKenzie Carson, Jan. 27, 1949. Sci. master Kings Coll., Windsor, N.S., Can., 1938-41; asst. prof. microbiology Johns Hopkins Sch. Hygiene and Pub. Health, 1948-54; chief high polymer sect. Naval Propellant Plant, Indian Head, Md., 1954-55, asso. chief chem. div., 1955-57, chief fund processing div., 1957-59; chief research br. Office Q.M. Gen., U.S. Army, 1959-62; mem. staff Army Materiel Command, Arlington, Va., 1962-63; prof. chemistry Am. U., Washington, 1963—. Recipient Sr. Fulbright award London Sch. Hygiene and Tropical Medicine, 1952-53; NIH career research award, 1963-68; Hillebrand prize Washington chem. soc., 1972. Mem. Am. Chem. Soc., AAAS, Chem. Soc. London, Biochem. Soc. London, Soc. Exptl. Biology and Medicine, N.Y., Washington acads. sci., U.S. Polo Assn., Sigma Xi, Alpha Chi Sigma. Contbr. articles to profl. jours. Home: 8005 Carita Ct Bethesda MD 20034 Office: Dept Chemistry Am U Washington DC 20016

RICE, GENE EDWARD, savs. and loan assn. exec.; b. Greenleaf, Kans., June 26, 1930; s. Edward E. and Myrtle (Hogan) R.; B.S. in Bus. Adminstrn., Ariz. State U., 1957; grad. Grad. Sch. Savs. and Loan, Ind. U., 1961; m. Lola Margaret Long, Apr. 23, 1951; children—Mary Pat, Nancy Jo, Michael, Paul, Ann, Mathias, Barry,

Regina. With First Fed. Savs. & Loan Assn. Phoenix, 1954—, v.p., 1962-63, exec. v.p., sr. v.p., now pres., also dir.; formerly pub. interest dir. Frontier Fidelity Savs. & Loan Assn., Las Vegas, 1967—; dir. Mountain Bell. Treas., dir. Casa Grande (Ariz.) Jaycees, 1957; pres. Casa Grande C. of C., 1960-61; treas. Phoenix Thunderbirds, 1966-67. Mem. Casa Grande City Council, 1960-62. Bd. dirs. Phoenix Catholic Social Service, 1967-71, Phoenix Jr. Achievement, 1963-64; mem. advisory bd. Bishops Fund, United Fund; chmn. Ariz. dr. Negro Coll. Fund; bd. dirs. Maricopa County Sheriffs Posse, Ariz. Jr. Rodeo Assn.; trustee Pro Rodeo Hall of Fame. Served with USN, 1949-53. Mem. Am. Savs. and Loan Inst. (nat. pres. 1969), Savs. and Loan League Ariz. (pres. 1967-68, dir.), Phoenix Jaycees (life), Profl. Rodeo Cowboys Assn., Delta Sigma Pi. Elk, Kiwanian (pres. Aurora club 1964). Clubs: Phoenix Country, Kiva (Phoenix). Home: PO Box 2263 Phoenix AZ 85002 Office: 3003 N Central Ave Phoenix AZ 85012

RICE, GEORGE WASHINGTON, lawyer; b. Abbeville, La., Oct. 2, 1905; s. George W. and Minnie (Street) R.; B.A., U. Tex., 1927, LL.B., 1928; m. Jimmie Lee Paige, Jan. 9, 1937; children—George Washington, Sue (Mrs. Frank Gatlin). Admitted to Tex. bar, 1928; practiced in Houston, 1941—; mng. partner Butler, Binion, Rice, Cook & Knapp and predecessor firm, 1941—; dir. Midhurst Corp., Rycade Corp., Bankers Credit Life Ins. Co., Bankers Credit Life of Am. Ins. Co., L.L. Ridgway Enterprises, Inc., Rowan Internat., Inc., Rowandrill, Inc., Rowan Leasing, Inc., Ryeade Overseas Oil Co., Lignum Oil Co. Mem. Alpha Tau Omega. Home: 3744 Inwood Dr Houston TX 77019 Office: 1100 Esperson Bldg Houston TX 77002

RICE, GEORGIA RUTH, state edn. ofcl.; b. Ross, N.D., June 4, 1936; d. Joseph and Karoline (Stolefa) Dobrovolny; ed. Eastern Mont. Coll., 1957, U. N.D., 1963, U. Wash., 1967, U. Idaho, 1968, No. Mont. Coll., 1970, Mont. State U., 1975. Tchr. public schs.; asst. traffic edn. and pupil transp. safety supr. Mont. Office Public Instrn., Helena, 1975-76, pupil transp. safety supr., 1976-79, state supt., 1979—; cons. on filmstrips, films and ednl. programs to cos.; mem. Mont. Bd. Public Edn.; bd. regents Mont. Library Commn.; mem. Mont. Tchrs. Retirement Bd.; mem. Mont. Bd. Land Commrs. Recipient Disting. Service award Mont. Pupil Transp. Conf., Outstanding Service award Mont. Sch. Bjs. Contractors Assn. Mem. NEA, LWV, Mont. Edn. Assn., Am. Fedn. Tchrs., Mont. Fedn. Tchrs., Nat. Pupil Transp. Assn., PTA (life). Democrat. Presbyterian. Office: State Capitol Room 106 Helena MT 59601*

RICE, JAMES EDWARD, profl. baseball player; b. Anderson, S.C., Mar. 8, 1953; m. Corine Gilliard, 1972; 1 child, Chauncy. With Boston Red Sox, 1974—; public relations rep. So. Bank & Trust Co., Greenville, S.C. Named Most Valuable Player and Rookie of Yr., Internat. League, 1974; Most Valuable Player, Am. League, 1978; named to Am. League All-Star Team, 1977, 78, 79; co-winner Tucson Pro-Am Golf Tournament, 1977. Office: care Boston Red Sox 24 Yawkey Way Boston MA 02215*

RICE, JOHN RISCHARD, educator, mathematician; b. Tulsa, June 6, 1934; s. John C. Kirk and Margaret (Rischard) R.; B.S., Okla. State U., 1954, M.S., 1956; Ph.D., Calif. Inst. Tech., 1959; m. Nancy Bradfield, Dec. 19, 1954; children—Amy Lynn, Jenna Margaret. NRC-Nat. Bur. Standards fellow Nat. Bur. Standards, Washington, 1959-60; sr. research mathematician Gen. Motors Research Labs., Warren, Mich., 1960-64; prof. math. and computer sci. Purdue U., 1964—; nat. lectr. in numerical math. Assn. Computer Machinery, 1966, George E. Forsythe lectr., 1975; chmn. signum, 1977-79. Mem. Assn. Computing Machinery, Am. Math. Soc., Soc. for Indsl. and Applied Math. Author: The Approximation of Functions, Vol. 1, 1964, Vol. 2, 1968; Introduction to Computer Science, 1969; Computers-Their Impact and Use, 1975; also articles; editor-in-chief ACM Transactions Mathematical Software. Research approximation of functions using nonlinear methods, error analysis and math. software. Home: 112 E Navajo St West Lafayette IN 47906

RICE, JOSEPH ALBERT, banker; b. Cranford, N.J., Oct. 11, 1924; s. Louis A. and Elizabeth J. (Michael) R.; B.Aero. Engring., Rensselear Poly. Inst., 1948; M.Indsl. Engring., N.Y. U., 1952, M.A., 1968; m. Katharine Wolfe, Sept. 11, 1948; children—Walter, Carol, Philip, Alan. With Grumman Aircraft Engring. Corp., 1948-53; with IBM, N.Y.C., 1953-65, mgr. ops., real estate, constrn. divs., 1963-65; dep. group exec. N.Am. comml. telecommunications group, pres. telecommunications div. ITT, N.Y.C., 1965-67; sr. v.p. Irving Trust Co., N.Y.C., 1967-69, exec. v.p., 1969-72, sr. exec. v.p., 1972-73, vice chmn., 1973-74, pres., 1974—, also dir.; exec. v.p. Irving Bank Corp., 1971-74, vice chmn., 1974-75, pres., 1975—, also dir. Bd. dirs., treas. Greater N.Y. Fund; trustee Rensselaer Poly. Inst. Served to 1st lt. C.E., AUS, 1943-46. Mem. Assn. Bank Holding Cos. (dir. 1978). Clubs: University (N.Y.C.); Sleepy Hollow Country (Scarborough, N.Y.). Office: 1 Wall St New York NY 10015

RICE, JOSEPH DAVID, journalist; b. Roanoke, Va., Apr. 26, 1942; s. Joseph Abraham and Constance (Wells) R.; B.A., Ohio State U., 1964; m. Janet M. Cossette, Dec. 30, 1974; children—Peter C., Christopher J. Reporter, Cleve. Press, 1964-68; state house reporter Ohio Scripps-Howard Bur., Columbus, 1968-69; polit. writer Akron (O.) Beacon Jour., 1969-73, Plain Dealer, Cleve., 1973—. Profl. Journalism fellow, 1971-72; corr. C.S. Monitor, 1970—. Mem. Ohio Legis. Corrs. Assn., Sigma Delta Chi. Roman Catholic. Home: 21888 Westchester Rd Shaker Heights OH 44122 Office: 1801 Superior Ave Cleveland OH 44114

RICE, KINGSLEY LORING, JR., advt. agy. exec.; b. Evanston, Ill., Apr. 26, 1931; s. Kingsley Loring and Mary Jane McIntosh (Judson) R.; A.B. in English, Williams Coll., 1952; m. Ann Roesing, June 20, 1953; children—Douglas K., Philip R., Jaine E., Charles J. Media buyer, research analyst, account exec., Leo Burnett Co., Inc., Chgo., 1956-62; advt. plans prodn. mgr., dir. advt. Hills Bros. Coffee Co., San Francisco, 1962-68; v.p., account supr., dir. account mgmt. Hoefer, Dieterich and Brown, San Francisco, 1968-77; pres., chief operating officer D'Arcy-MacManus & Masius, San Francisco, 1977—, also dir. Trustee Reed Union Sch. Dist., 1964-69, also chmn.; bd. dirs. San Francisco Vol. Bur., 1972—; community adv. Jr. League of San Francisco, 1976-78. Served with USN, 1952-56. Recipient Silver Medal award Am. Advt. Fedn. Mem. San Francisco Advt. Club (pres. 1969-70), Bay Area Council, San Francisco C. of C., Illuminators Inc., Nashville Songwriters Assn., Tiburon (Calif.) Peninsula Found. Republican. Congregationalist. Clubs: Bankers, Olympic. Writer song: Time You Found Out, 1978. Home: 187 Stewart Dr Tiburon CA 94920 Office: 433 California St San Francisco CA 94104*

RICE, LAWRENCE HARVEY, univ. dean; b. Clifton, Idaho, Feb. 6, 1931; s. Ira Quince and Myra (Winegar) R.; B.A., Utah State U., 1955, M.A., 1956; Ph.D., Mich. State U., 1963; m. Clarice Hendricks, Dec. 5, 1951; children—Alice Carlyn, Steven Lawrence, Patricia Carol. Mem. faculty Idaho State U., Pocatello, 1962—, prof. English, 1962—, chmn. dept. English, 1964-67, dean Grad. Sch., 1973—. Served with AUS, 1951-53. Mem. Modern Lang. Assn. (asso. bibliographer 1973-75), Council of Grad. Schs., Western Assn. Grad. Schs., Phi Kappa Phi. Contbr. articles to profl. jours. Home: Route 5 Piedmont Rd Pocatello ID 83201 Office: Box 8075 Idaho State U Pocatello ID 83209

RICE, MICHAEL STEPHEN, communications co. exec.; b. Madison, Minn., Nov. 3, 1941; s. Edward William and Gertrude (Schonberg) R.; A.B. magna cum laude, Harvard U., 1963; B.A. (Rhodes scholar), Oxford U., 1965. Radio mgr. Sta. WGBH Ednl. Found. (Sta. WGBH-TV, WGBX-TV, WGBH Radio), Boston, 1965-67, TV program mgr., 1967-73, v.p., gen. mgr., 1973-78; dir. program on communications and society Aspen Inst. for Humanistic Studies, Washington, 1978—. Mem. Mid-Atlantic Dist. Rhodes Scholar Selection Com., 1975—; mem. Harvard vis. com. Office Info. Tech., 1974—. Club: St. Botolph. Editorial bd. Pub. Telecommunications Rev., 1974—. Home: 2823 Q St NW Washington DC 20007 Office: Aspen Inst 2101 Massachusetts Ave NW Washington DC 20036

RICE, PHILIP JOSEPH, JR., physicist; b. Middletown, Conn., Feb. 28, 1917; s. Philip Joseph and Sarah (Moran) R.; A.B., Brown U., 1940; M.S., Case-Western Res. U., 1942; M.S., Yale, 1946, Ph.D., 1948; m. Jean Ann Mattern, Apr. 7, 1956; children—Monica, Adrienne. Mem. tech. staff Radiation Lab., Mass. Inst. Tech., 1942-45, Bell Telephone Labs., 1948-52; mgr. electron devices lab. Stanford Research Inst., Menlo Park, Calif., 1952-62, mgr. phys. electronics lab., 1962-66, program mgr., engring. scis. and indsl. devel., 1966—, gen. mgr. tech. innovation, 1971, lab. dir., 1976—. Trustee Western Electronic Edn. Fund. Mem. IEEE (sr. mem., V. K. Zworykn award 1963), Am. Phys. Soc., Sigma Xi. Author tech. papers, articles. Co-inventor videograph printing process. Home: 118 Heather Dr Atherton CA 94025 Office: Stanford Research Inst Menlo Park CA 94025

RICE, PHILIP MORRISON, univ. dean; b. Los Angeles, Aug. 9, 1916; s. Roger Leavitt and Lela Idele (Morrison) R.; student Harvard, 1933-34; A.B., Pomona Coll., 1938; A.M. (Waddell fellow), U. N.C., 1947, Ph.D., 1949; L.H.D., Claremont Grad. Sch., 1973; m. Harriett Elizabeth Willis, July 25, 1942; children—Ashley Leigh (Mrs. Jon Crawford), Carol (Mrs. James Searing), Harriett. From asst. in history to prof. N.C. State Univ., 1948-59, dir. summer sessions, 1957-59; TV polit. analyst WUNC and WRAL, Carolina Networks, 1957-59; prof. history, chmn. dept. Kans. State U., Manhattan, 1959-64; dean, prof. history Claremont (Calif.) Grad. Sch., 1964-72; dean. prof. history U. South Fla., Tampa, 1972-74; dean grad. sch. U. Conn., Storrs, 1974-78. Cons. Calif. Scholarship Commn., Mt. Angel Coll. Pres. Western Assn. Grad. Schs., 1970-71; exec. com. Council Grad. Schs., 1969-72, African-Am. Inst., N.Y.C., 1970—. Bd. dirs. World Affairs Council, 1964-66, George Washington Nat. U., 1968—. Grantee Ford Found. and Kan. State U. for research in Russian history and history of tech., 1953-59; Phillips-Lippincott fellow, 1959-60. Served to comdr. USNR, 1940-45; comdr. Res. Fellow AAAS; mem. Am., So. hist. assns., conf. Slavic and East European Studies, Am. Canadian Soc. Study Higher Edn., Northeastern Assn. Grad. Schs. (pres. 1977-78), Am. Inst. Indian Studies (trustee), British Soc. History Sci., History Sci. Soc., Soc. History Tech., Newcomen Soc., Orgn. Am. Historians, Am. Acad. Polit. Sci., Acad. Polit. Sci., Am. Assn. Higher Edn., Econ. History Soc. (Eng.), Sigma Phi Alpha, Phi Alpha Theta. Episcopalian. Clubs: West Coast Yacht; Harvard of So. Cal. Author: Internal Improvements in Virginia, 1775-1860, 1949; Understanding History, 3d edit., 1970; Guide To A History of Civilization, 1970; also monographs. Home: 930 Fairway Dr Bakersfield CA 93309

RICE, RAYMOND MAIN, physician; b. Bancroft, Nebr., Dec. 28, 1901; s. Eugene Taylor and Fannie (Dalton) R.; student Coll. of Idaho, 1919-21; B.S., U. Nebr., 1924, M.D., 1929; LL.D. (hon.), Butler U., 1978; m. Charlotte Zurmuehlen, Sept. 1, 1931 (dec. 1973); children—Raymond Dalton and Ronald Bennett (twins); m. 2d, Adele Fehsenfeld, Dec. 15, 1973. Intern, Cleve. Municipal Hosp., 1929-30; practice of medicine, Council Bluffs, Iowa, 1930-36; instr. medicine U. Nebr. Coll. Medicine, 1930-36; with Eli Lilly & Co., Indpls., 1936-66, successively dir. med. div. research labs., asso. exec. dir. research, exec. dir. med. research, 1936-60, v.p. med. affiars, 1960-64, group v.p. sci. and medicine, 1964-66; v.p. Pharm. Mfrs. Assn. Found., 1966-73; asso. medicine Ind. U. Sch. Medicine, 1943-50, asst. prof. medicine, 1950—; cons. physician Marion County Gen. Hosp. Trustee Butler U., Community Hosp. of Indpls.; bd. govs. James Whitcomb Riley Found. Mem. AMA, Am. Rheumatism Assn., Am. Fedn. Clin. Research, AAAS, N.Y. Acad. Scis., Ind. Med. Assn., Marion County Med. Soc., Phi Rho Sigma. Episcopalian. Clubs: Columbia, Crooked Stick Golf, Meridian Hills Country (Indpls.); Imperial Golf, Royal Poinciana Country (Naples, Fla.). Address 8465 Quail Hollow Rd Indianapolis IN 46260 also 3430 Gulf Shore Blvd Naples FL 33940

RICE, RICHARD LEE, architect; b. Raleigh, N.C., May 4, 1919; s. Robert Edward Lee and Grace Lucille (Betts) R.; B.S. in Archtl. Engring., N.C. State U., 1941; grad. U.S. Army Command and Gen. Staff Coll., 1961; m. Cora Belle Stegall, Apr. 12, 1946; children—Richard Lee, Westwood Carter, David Sinclair. Asso., Cooper-Shumaker, Architects, Raleigh, 1946-47; prin. Richard L. Rice, Architect, Raleigh, 1947-48; asso. Cooper, Haskins & Rice, Architects and predecessor, Raleigh, 1948-52, partner, 1953-54; partner Haskins & Rice, Architects, Raleigh, 1954—; v.p. N.C. Design Found., 1973; pres. N.C. Archtl. Found., 1975; mem. Raleigh Arts Commn., 1978—. Pres. Wake County (N.C.) Hist. Soc., 1973-74; mem. N.C. Gov.'s Com. for Facilities for Physically Handicapped, 1970-73. Served with inf. and C.E., U.S. Army, 1941-46; ETO; col. USAR, ret. Decorated Silver Star. Legion of Merit, Bronze Star, Purple Heart. Fellow AIA (pres. N.C. chpt. 1970, Dist. Service award N.C. chpt. 1975); mem. Raleigh Council Architects (pres. 1950), Nat. Trust for Hist. Preservation, N.C. Symphony Soc., N.C. State Art Soc., Raleigh C. of C., Res. Officers Assn. U.S., Ret. Officers Assn. U.S., N.C. State U. Gen. Alumni Assn. (pres., chmn. bd. 1960-61), Phi Eta Sigma, Phi Kappa Phi. Democrat. Baptist. Clubs: Carolina Country, Lions, Torch, Raleigh Sports (Raleigh). Archtl. works include: renovations Raleigh Meml. Auditorium, 1964 (SE Regional AIA award of merit 1964), 1978, Auditorium, Reidsville, N.C., 1975, 3 high schs., Wake County, N.C., 1975-77, Civic Center, Raleigh (asso. architect), 1977, stack addition Wilson Library U. N.C., Chapel Hill, 1977, jr. high sch., Reidsville, 1979. Home: 1525 Canterbury Rd Raleigh NC 27608 Office: 2515 Fairview Rd PO Box 6398 Raleigh NC 27628

RICE, ROBERT MAURICE, mfg. co. exec.; b. Indpls., Dec. 21, 1925; s. Luther G. and Mildred (Williams) R.; B.S. in Bus. Adminstrn. cum laude, Wagner Coll., 1949; m. Geraldine T. Scilipoti, Nov. 26, 1944; children—Gregory S., Randall M., Robin V., Deborah L. Fin. analyst Home Life Co., N.Y.C., 1949-51, Am. Airlines Co., N.Y.C., 1951-52, Sylvania Electric Co., N.Y.C., 1953-54; with internat. div. Ford Motor Co., 1954-67, dir. finance Ford Denmark, Copenhagen, 1958-60, mng. dir. chmn. bd., 1962-67, mng. dir. chmn. bd. Ford Norway, 1960-62; v.p., asst. controller Internat. Telephone and Telegraph, Brussels, Belgium, 1967-70; sr. v.p. finance and devel. CBS, Inc., N.Y.C., 1970-74; v.p. finance Rockwell Internat., Inc., Pitts., 1974-76; owner, gen. mgr. Bridge Center, San Diego, 1977—. Served with USNR, 1943-45. Mem. Financial Execs. Inst., Council Fin. Execs. Club: El Niguel (Calif.) Country. Home: 10478 Russell Rd La Mesa CA 92041

RICE, ROGER DOUGLAS, TV exec.; b. Spokane, Wash., Feb. 20, 1921; s. Leland L. and Bernice B. (Metcalf) R.; B.S., U. Wash., 1944; m. Molly Herron, Feb. 22, 1946; children—Stephannie Lee, Roger Douglas. With KING Radio, Seattle, 1947-51, 53-54; sta. mgr. KTVW-TV, Seattle, Tacoma, 1954-55; gen. sales mgr. WIIC-TV, Pitts., 1955-66, gen. mgr., 1966-68; v.p., gen. mgr. Cox Broadcasting Corp. KTVU, San Francisco, Oakland, Calif., 1973-74; pres., chief exec. officer TV Bur. Advt., N.Y.C., 1974—. Chmn., U.S./Japan Cultural Exchange, 1974; mem. Japan-U.S. Friendship Commn. Mem. Nat. Assn. Broadcasters (bd. dirs. TV code rev. bd. 1971-74, Internat. Radio TV Soc., Broadcast Rating Council (dir.). Clubs: Greenwich (Conn.) Country, St. Francis Yacht (San Francisco); Allegheny Country (Sewickley, Pa.). Home: 45 Sutton Pl South New York City NY 10022 Office: TV Bur Advt 1345 Ave of the Americas New York City NY 10019

RICE, STANLEY TRAVIS, JR., poet; b. Dallas, Nov. 7, 1942; s. Stanley Travis and Margaret Nolia (Cruse) R.; B.A., San Francisco State U., 1964, M.A., 1965; m. Anne O'Brien, Oct. 14, 1961. Prof. English and creative writing San Francisco State U., 1964—, asst. dir. Poetry Center, 1964-72; author: Some Lamb, 1975; Whiteboy, 1976. Recipient Joseph Henry Jackson award San Francisco Found., 1968; Edgar Allen Poe award Acad. Am. Poets, 1977; grantee Nat. Endowment Arts, 1966, writing fellow, 1972. Home: 40 Yorkshire Oakland CA 94168 Office: 1600 Holloway St San Francisco CA 94132

RICE, STEPHEN O(SWALD), communication engr.; b. Shedds, Oreg., Nov. 29, 1907; s. Stephen and Selma (Bergren) R.; E.E., Oreg. State U., 1929, Sc.D. (hon.), 1961; m. Inez Biersdorf, Feb 26, 1931; children—Carole, Joan, Stephen. Mem. tech. staff Bell Telephone Labs., N.Y.C., 1930-58, Murray Hill, N.J., 1958-72, ret., 1972; Gordon McKay vis. lectr. in applied physics Harvard U., 1958. Mem. IEEE (Mervin J. Kelly award 1965), Nat. Acad. Engring. Research, publs. on random processes, elec. circuit theory, signal modulation, electromagnetic waves.

RICE, STUART ALAN, educator, chemist; b. N.Y.C., Jan. 6, 1932; s. Harry L. and Helen (Rayfield) R.; B.S., Bklyn. Coll., 1952; M.A., Harvard, 1954, Ph.D., 1955; m. Marian Ruth Coopersmith, June 1, 1952; children—Barbara, Janet, Jr. fellow Harvard, 1955-57; faculty U. Chgo., 1957—, prof. chemistry, 1960-69, Louis Block prof. phys. scis., 1969—, chmn. dept. chemistry, 1971-76, Frank P. Hixon disting. service prof., 1977—, dir. Inst. Study Metals, 1962-68. Guggenheim fellow, 1960-61; Falk-Plautt lectr. Columbia, 1964; Riley lectr. Notre Dame U., 1964; NSF sr. postdoctoral fellow, 1965-66; USPHS spl. postdoctoral fellow U. Copenhagen, 1970-71; Univ. lectr. chemistry U. Western Ont., 1970; Seaver lectr. U. So. Calif., 1972; Noyes lectr. U. Tex., Austin, 1975; Foster lectr. State U. N.Y., Buffalo, 1976; Frank T. Gucker lectr. Ind. U., 1976. Mem. Am. Chem. Soc. (award Pure Chemistry 1963, Leo Hendrik Backeland award 1971), Nat., Am. acads. scis., Am. Phys. Soc., AAAS, Faraday Soc. (Marlowe medal 1963), N.Y. Acad. Scis. (A. Cressy Morrison prize 1955), Danish Acad. Sci. and Letters (fgn.). Author: Polyelectrolyte Solutions, 1961; Statistical Mechanics of Simple Liquids, 1965. Bd. dirs. Bull. Atomic Scientists; also numerous articles. Home: 5421 Greenwood Ave Chicago IL 60615

RICE, TIMOTHY MILES BINDON, writer, broadcaster; b. Amersham, Eng., Nov. 10, 1944; s. Hugh Gordon and Joan Odette (Bawden) R.; student Lancing Coll., Sussex, 1958-62; m. Jane McIntosh, Aug. 19, 1974; children—Eva Jane Florence, Donald Alexander Hugh. Solicitor's articled clk. Pettit & Westlake, London, 1963-66; mgmt. trainee E.M.I. Records Manchester Sq., London, 1966-68; record producer Norrie Paramor Orgn., London, 1968-69; ind. writer, record producer, London, 1969—; broadcaster Capital Radio London, 1973—, BBC Radio and TV, Ind. TV (U.K.), 1974—; composer libretto Joseph and The Amazing Technicolor Dreamcoat, 1968, expanded for stage, 1973; composer libretto Jesus Christ Superstar, 1970, extra material for film, 1973, libretto Evita, 1976; author: Heartaches Cricketers' Almanac, (with Jo Rice) Guinness Book of British Hit Singles, (with Andrew L. Webber) Evita. Clubs: Marylebone Cricket, Heartaches Cricket. Address: 118 Wardour St London W1V 4BT England*

RICE, VICTOR ALBERT, mfg. co. exec.; b. Hitchin, Hertfordshire, Eng., Mar. 7, 1941; s. Albert Edward and Rosina Emmeline (Pallant) R.; m. Sharla C. Rice, June 25, 1970; children—Gregg, Kristin, Jonathan. With Ford Motor Co., U.K., 1957-64, Cummins Engines, U.K., 1964-67, Chrysler Corp., U.K., 1968-70; comptroller N. European ops. Perkins Engines Group Ltd., Peterborough, U.K., 1970, dep. mng. dir. ops., 1974-75; comptroller world-wide Massey-Ferguson Ltd., Toronto, Ont., Can., 1975-77, v.p. staff ops., 1977-78, pres., 1978—, dir., 1978—. Mem. Farm and Indsl. Equipment Inst. (dir.), Bd. of Trade Met. Toronto, Fin. Execs. Inst., Am. Mgmt. Assn. (mem. Pres.' Assn.), Brit. Inst. Mktg., Inst. Dirs. (U.K.). Anglican. Clubs: Royal Canadian Yacht, Toronto Golf; Carlton (London).

RICE, WILLIAM ALAN, pub. relations exec.; b. New Haven, Aug. 17, 1931; s. William Jennings Bryan and Dorothy (Montagnon) R.; m. Ruthmary Zander, Apr. 27, 1957; children—Pamela Ann, William Zander. With N.Y. News, 1949-73, sci. editor, 1970-73; pub. relations exec. Boeing Aerospace Co., Seattle, 1973—. Served with USAF, 1950-53. Recipient Claude Bernard Sci. Journalism award Nat. Soc. Med. Research, 1972; Cecil award Nat. Arthritis Found., 1971; Med. Writing award, Am. Soc. Anesthesiology, 1972, Journalism award N.Y. Newspaper Guild, 1968. Mem. Nat. Assn. Sci. Writers, Aviation/Space Writers Assn., Overseas Press Club Am. Home: 21511 SE 20th St Issaquah WA 98027 Office: PO Box 3999 Seattle WA 98124

RICH, ADRIENNE, writer; b. Balt., May 16, 1929; d. Arnold Rice and Helen Elizabeth (Jones) R.; A.B., Radcliffe Coll., 1951; Litt.D. (hon.), Wheaton Coll., 1967, Smith Coll., 1979; m. Alfred Conrad (dec. 1970); children—David, Paul, Jacob. Tchr. workshop YM-WHA Poetry Center, N.Y.C., 1966-67; vis. lectr. Swarthmore Coll., 1967-69; adj. prof. writing div. Columbia, 1967-69; lectr. Coll. City N.Y., 1968-70, instr., 1970-71, asst. prof. English, 1971-72, 74-75; Fannie Hurst vis. prof. creative lit. Brandeis U., 1972-73; prof. English Douglass Coll., Rutgers U., 1976—. Adv. bd. The Feminist Press, Old Westbury, N.Y., Woman's Bldg., Los Angeles. Recipient Yale Series of Younger Poets award, 1951; Ridgely Torrence Meml. award Poetry Soc. Am., 1955; Nat. Inst. Arts and Letters award poetry, 1961; Bess Hokin prize Poetry mag., 1963, Eunice Tietjens Meml. prize, 1968; Shelley Meml. award, 1971; Nat. Book award, 1974. Guggenheim fellow, 1952, 61; Amy Lowell traveling fellow, 1962; Bollingen Found. translation grantee, 1962; Nat. Translation Center grantee, 1968; Nat. Endowment for Arts grantee, 1970; Ingram Merrill Found. grantee, 1973-74; Lucy Martin Donnelly fellow Bryn Mawr Coll., 1975. Author: A Change of World, 1951; The Diamond Cutters and Other Poems, 1955; Snapshots of a Daughter-in-Law, 1963; Necessities of Life: Poems 1962-65, 1966; Leaflets; Poems 1965-68, 1969; The Will to Change, 1971; Diving into the Wreck, 1973; Poems Selected and New, 1950-74, 1975; Of Woman Born: Motherhood as Experience and Institution, 1976; The Dream of a Common Language: Poems 1974-1977, 1978; On Lies,

Secrets and Silence: Selected Prose 1966-1978, 1979; contbg. editor: Chrysalis: A Magazine of Women's Culture; contbr. to numerous anthologies. Contbr. numerous articles, revs. to jours. and mags. Address: care WW Norton 500 Fifth Ave New York NY 10036

RICH, ALAN, music critic, author; b. Boston, June 17, 1924; s. Edward and Helen (Hirshberg) R.; A.B., Harvard, 1945; M.A., U. Cal. at Berkeley, 1952; Alfred Hertz Meml. Traveling fellow in music, Vienna, Austria, 1952-53. Asst. music critic Boston Herald, 1944-45, N.Y. Sun, 1947-48; contbr. Am. Record Guide, 1947-61, Saturday Rev., 1952-53, Mus. Am., 1955-61, Mus. Quar., 1957-58; tchr. music U. Cal. at Berkeley, 1950-58; program and music dir. Pacifica Found., FM radio, 1953-61; asst. music critic N.Y. Times, 1961-63; chief music critic, editor N.Y. Herald Tribune, 1963-66; music critic, editor N.Y. World Jour. Tribune, 1966-67; contbg. editor Time mag., 1967-68; music and drama critic, arts editor N.Y. mag., 1968—; tchr. New Sch. for Social Research, 1972-75, 77—; artist-in-residence Davis Center for the Performing Arts City U. N.Y., 1975-76. Recipient Deems Taylor award ASCAP, 1970, 73, 74. Mem. Music Critics Circle N.Y. (sec. 1961-63, chmn. 1963-64), N.Y. Drama Critics Circle, Am. Theatre Critics Assn. Author: Careers and Opportunities in Music, 1964; Music: Mirror of the Arts, 1969; also articles. Home: 113 River Rd Grand View-on-Hudson NY 10960 Office: 755 2d Ave New York City NY 10017

RICH, ALEXANDER, molecular biologist; b. Hartford, Conn., Nov. 15, 1924; s. Max and Bella (Shub) R.; A.B. magna cum laude in Biochem. Scis., Harvard U., 1947, M.D. cum laude, 1949; m. Jane Erving King, July 5, 1952; children—Benjamin, Josiah, Rebecca, Jessica. Research fellow Gates and Crellin Labs., Calif. Inst. Tech., Pasadena, 1949-54; chief sect. phys. chemistry NIMH, Bethesda, Md., 1954-58; vis. scientist Cavendish Lab., Cambridge (Eng.) U., 1955-56; asso. prof. biophysics Mass. Inst. Tech., Cambridge, 1958-61, prof. biophysics, 1961—, William Thompson Sedgwick prof. biophysics, 1974—; Fairchild Disting. scholar Calif. Inst. Tech., Pasadena, 1976; mem. com. career devel. awards NIH, 1964-67, mem. postdoctoral fellowship bd., 1955-58; mem. com. exobiology space sci. bd. NAS, 1964-65, mem. U.S. nat. com. Internat. Orgn. Pure Applied Biophysics, 1965-67; mem. vis. com. dept. biology Weizmann Inst. Sci., 1965-66; mem. life scis. com. NASA, 1970-75, mem. lunar planetary missions bd., 1968-70, mem. biology team Viking Mars Mission, 1969—; mem. corp. Marine Biol. Lab., Woods Hole, Mass., 1965-77; mem. sci. rev. com. Howard Hughes Med. Inst., Miami, Fla., 1978—; mem. vis. com. biology div. Oak Ridge Nat. Lab., 1972-76; mem. sci. adv. bd. Stanford Synchrotron Radiation Project, 1976—; mem. sci. adv. bd. Mass. Gen. Hosp., Boston, 1978—; mem. U.S. Nat. Sci. Bd., 1976—; mem. bd. govs. Weizmann Inst. Sci., 1976—; mem. research com. Med. Found., Boston, 1976—; mem. U.S.-USSR Joint Commn. on Sci. and Tech., Dept. State, Washington, 1977—. Served with USN, 1943-46. Recipient Skylab Achievement award NASA, 1974, Theodore von Karmin award Viking Mars Mission, 1976, Presidential award N.Y. Acad. Scis., 1977; NRC fellow, 1949-51; Guggenheim Found. fellow, 1963; mem. Pontifical Acad. Scis., The Vatican, 1978. Fellow Am. Acad. Arts and Scis., AAAS; mem. Nat. Acad. Scis., Am. Chem. Soc., Biophys. Soc. (council 1960-69), Am. Soc. Biol. Chemists, Am. Crystallographic Soc., Internat. Soc. for Sty of Origin of Life, Phi Beta Kappa. Editor: Structural Chemistry and Molecular Biology (with Norman Davidson), 1968; editorial bd. Biophys. Jour., 1961-63, Currents Modern Biology, 1966-72, Science, 1963-69, Analytical Biochemistry, 1969—, Bio-Systems, 1973—, Molecular Biology Reports, 1974—, Procs. Nat. Acad. Sci., 1973—; editorial advisory bd. Jour. Molecular Biology, 1959-66; contbr. articles to profl. jours. Office: Dept Biology Mass Inst Tech Cambridge MA 02139

RICH, ARTHUR LOWNDES, educator; b. Woodcliff, N.J., May 7, 1905; s. Frank Joseph and Ruth (Lowndes) R.; A.B., Rutgers U., 1926; A.M., Columbia, 1928; Ph.D., N.Y.U., 1940; diploma Julliard Sch. Music, 1928; licentiate Royal Schs. Music (Royal Acad. Music, Royal Coll. of Music), London, 1939; spl. study Harvard, 1943, Christiansen Choral Sch., 1948; 52; m. Helen Wall, July 26, 1934; children—Arthur Lowndes, Ruth Anne. Prof. music Catawba Coll., Salisbury, N.C., 1928-43; dir. music Belhaven Coll., Jackson, Miss., 1943-44; dir. music Mercer U., Macon, Ga., 1944—, Roberts prof. music, 1945-74, prof. emeritus, dir. concert series and cultural affairs, 1974—. Choral condr., adjudicator Ga. and S.E.; music critic Macon News; corr. Mus. Am.; pres. Tudor Apts., Biscayne Apts., Inc. Bd. dirs. Macon Arts Council, Macon Grand Opera Assn., Middle Ga. Symphony Orch. Life hon. mem. Community Concert Assn. (dir.), Macon Piano Tchrs. Guild (pres.); mem. Am. Assn. Coll. and U. Concert Mgrs., Nat. Assn. Schs. Music, Phi Mu Alpha Sinfonia Soc., Macon Morning Music Club (hon.), Macon Federated Music Club (hon.). Baptist. Author: Lowell Mason, the Father of Singing Among the Children, 1945. Contbr. articles to ednl., music jours., reference books. Home: 369 Candler Dr Macon GA 31204

RICH, AVERY EDMUND, plant pathologist, educator; b. Charleston, Maine, Apr. 9, 1915; s. Nathan Harold and Myrtle (Schermerhorn) R.; B.S., U. Maine, 1937, M.S., 1939; Ph.D., Wash. State U., 1950; m. Erma Pauline Littlefield, June 15, 1938; children—Alice Ann Rich Fowler, Donna Rich Moody. Asst. agronomist R.I. State Coll., Kingston, 1943-47; instr. plant pathology Wash. State U., Pullman, 1947-50, asst. prof., 1950-51; asso. prof. plant pathology U. N.H., Durham, 1951-57, prof., 1957—, asso. dean life scis. and agr., 1972—. Mem. Am. Phytopath. Soc., Sigma Xi. Mem. United Ch. of Christ. Home: 13 Burnham Ave Durham NH 03824 Office: 210 Taylor Hall U NH Durham NH 03824

RICH, BERNARD (BUDDY), drummer; b. Bklyn., June 30, 1917; m. Marie Rich, Aug 1952; 1 dau. Appeared with parents in vaudeville act Wilson and Rich, at early age; appeared in Pinwheel on Broadway, at age 4, toured Australia at age of six; with Joe Marsala at Hickory House, 1938, other bands include Bunny Berigan, 1938, Artie Shaw, 1939, Tommy Dorsey, 1939-42, Benny Carter, 1942, 44-46; organized own band, 1946, toured with Jazz at the Philharmonic, 1947; with Ventura and Chubby Jackson in the Big Four, 1951; with Harry James, 1953-54, European tour, 1957; actor TV, 1957-58, also singer and tap dancer. Served with USMCR, 1942-44. Recipient Metronome mag. award, 1948, award Down Beat mag., 1941, 42, 44, 67, 70-72, gold award Esquire mag., 1947, critics poll award Down Beat, 1953-54, 68; named to Down Beat Hall of Fame, 1974. Recs. include Bird and Diz, Jazz Off the Air, Jam Session, Jazz Scene, Stick It, The Roar of '74, A Difficult Drummer, Mercy, Mercy, Take It Away. Address: care Super Zig-Mar/Taurus GC 22170-3 James Allen Circle Chatsford CA 91311*

RICH, BUDDY. see Rich, Bernard

RICH, CHARLES ALLAN, singer; b. Forrest City, Ark., Dec. 14, 1932; s. Wallace Neville and Helen Margaret (West) R.; student U. Ark.; m. Margaret Ann Greene, May 25, 1952; children—Renee Annette Rich Karber, Charles Allan, Laurie Lynn, Jack Michael. Farmer nr. West Memphis, Ark.; appeared in piano bars and clubs, Memphis; session musician Sun Records; rec. artist Epic Records; recorded Behind Closed Doors (Gold record), 1973, The Most Beautiful Girl (Platinum record). Recipient Grammy award as best country male vocalist, 1973; named Male Vocalist of Yr., Country Music Assn., 1973; Entertainer of Yr., 1974; Favorite Country Male Vocalist, 1974; Pop Single Male Vocalist, Billboard mag., 1974. Office: Charlie Rich Enterprises Inc 8229 Rockcreek Pkwy Cordova TN 38018

RICH, DANIEL, polit. scientist, educator; b. N.Y.C., June 1, 1943; s. Max and Lillian (Cianciulli) R.; B.A., Bklyn. Coll., 1964; M.P.I.A., U. Pitts., 1966; Ph.D., Mass. Inst. Tech., 1971; m. Nancy S. Johnson, Aug. 20, 1966; children—Jennifer Leslie, Andrew Owen. Mem. staff div. spl. tng. U. Pitts., 1964-66; instr. dept. polit. sci., div. urban affairs U. Del. at Newark, 1970-71, asst. prof., 1971-75, asso. prof., 1975—, asso. dean Coll. Urban Affairs and Pub. Policy, 1973-78, acting dean, 1978—; cons. research Gen. Electric Corp., 1967; cons. on action for community devel., Boston, 1968; researcher Nat. Opinion Research Council, 1967; research cons. Center Policy Alternatives Mass. Inst. Tech., 1975-77. Fellow AAAS (sec. sect. social econ. scis. 1973-77); mem. Am. Inst. Aeros. and Astronautics (cons. pub. affairs 1969-70), Newcomb-Cleve. Prize Com., Am. Soc. Pub. Adminstrn. (mem. com. sci. tech. govt. 1973—), Sci. Pub. Policy Studies Group (dir. 1971-73), Am. Polit. Sci. Assn. Editor (with S.A. Lakoff) Private Government, 1973. Contbr. articles in field to profl. jours. and anthologies. Home: 805 Chrysler Ave Newark DE 19711 Office: Coll Urban Affairs and Pub Policy Univ Delaware Newark DE 19711

RICH, ERIC, plastics co. exec.; b. Znojmo, Czechoslovakia, Oct. 1, 1921; s. Sandor and Alice (Shifferes) Reich; ed. U. Coll., Wales, Bangor, U.K.; m. Ilse L.B. Renard, Nov. 14, 1959; children—Susan Frances, Sally Dora, Charles Anthony. Came to U.S., 1955, naturalized, 1962. Export sales mgr. Pilot Radio, Ltd., London, Eng., 1945-49; dir. Derwent Exports, Ltd., London, 1949-55; export sales mgr. Am. Molding Powder & Chem. Corp., N.Y.C., 1956-58; with Gering Plastics Co. div. Monsanto Chem. Co., Kenilworth, N.J., 1958-67; v.p., gen. mgr. Goldmark Plastics Internat., Inc., New Hyde Park, N.Y., 1967—. Served with RAF, 1941-45. Decorated Gallantry medal, 1939-43, Star, Atlantic Star. Home: 111 7th St Garden City NY 11530 Office: Nassau Terminal Rd New Hyde Park NY 11040

RICH, FRANCES LUTHER, sculptor; b. Spokane, Jan. 8, 1910; d. Charles H. and Irene (Luther) R.; A.B., Smith Coll., 1931; student Cranbrook (Mich.) Acad. Art, Claremont (Calif.) Coll., Columbia U., Boston Museum Sch.; pupil of Malvina Hoffman, Carl Milles. Monuments and reliefs include: Firestone of St. Francis Assisi, St. Margaret's Episcopal Ch., Palm Desert, Calif., 1970, Mt. Hymettus, St. Francis Pierce Coll., Athens, Greece, 1970, St. Francis of Assisi, Smith Coll., Northampton, Mass., 1978, Madonna and Child, Holy Trinity Ch., Bremerton, Wash., 1969, Milles St. Francis, Millesgarden, Lidingo, Sweden, also mausoleum doors, fountains; portrait busts at Smith Coll., Army-Navy Nurse Monument in Arlington Nat. Cemetery, Washington; bas reliefs Union Bldg. at Purdue U., St. Cecilia's Ch., Stanwood, Wash., St. Peter's Episc. Ch., Redwood City, Calif.; bronze pelican Pelican Bldg., U. Calif., Berkeley, 1958; bronze Healer foyer David L. Reeves Meml. Library Cottage Hosp., Santa Barbara, Calif., 1973; marble bust Alice Stone Blackwell for Boston Pub. Library, 1960; bronze bust Katharine Hepburn as Cleopatra, Am. Shakespeare Theatre, Stratford, Conn., 1962, Theatre of Smith Coll., 1978; ten foot bronze Christ of Sacred Heart, St. Sebastian Ch., W. Los Angeles; ten foot bronze of Our Lady of Combermere at Madonna House, Ont., Can., 1960; 15 bronze Birds in Flight for aviary wall Living Desert Reserve, Palm Desert, Calif., 1978; bas relief portrait plaque of Laura W.L. Scales for Smith Coll., 1978; thirty inch bronze crucifix Grace Cathedral, San Francisco, 1979, numerous others in public and pvt. collections; one-woman exhbns. include: Santa Barbara Mus. Art, 1952, Calif. Palace Legion of Honor, 1955, Palm Springs (Calif.) Desert Mus., 1969, 77; group exhbns. include: DeYoung Mus., 1952, Merrill Collection show, 1954, Botolph Soc. Liturgical show, Boston, 1954, Liturgical Arts show, Denver, 1955, Nat. Decorators show, San Francisco, 1956, Internat. Orchid show, Santa Barbara, 1958, First Nat. Biennale Contemporary Religious Art, Seton Hall Coll., Greensburg, Pa., 1950, Nat. Liturgical Art Week show Seattle World's Fair, 1962, Palm Springs Desert Mus., 1969, 77; others; executed numerous portrait busts, also fountains, small bronzes and silvers for pvt. collections; dir. pub. relations Smith Coll., 1947-50. Served to lt. comdr. USNR, 1942-46. Mem. Archtl. League N.Y., Amvets, Smith Coll. Alumnae Assn. Club: Cosmopolitan (N.Y.C.). Address: Shumway Ranch nr Pinyon Crest PO Box 213 Palm Desert CA 92260

RICH, GARRY LORENCE, artist; b. Neosho, Mo., Nov. 11, 1943; s. Evelyn L. Simpson; B.F.A., Kansas City Art Inst., 1966; M.A., N.Y. U., 1969. Exhibited in numerous one man shows; represented in numerous permanent collections at maj. museums. Max Beckman fellow Nat. Endowment of Arts, 1966, 74, Anderson fellow; N.Y. State Council Arts grantee, 1975. Home: 167 Crosby St New York City NY 10012 Office: c/o Max Hutchinson Gallery New York City NY 10013

RICH, GILES SUTHERLAND, judge; b. Rochester, N.Y., May 30, 1904; s. Giles Willard and Sarah Thompson (Sutherland) R.; S.B., Harvard, 1926; LL.B., Columbia, 1929; m. Gertrude Verity Braun, Jan. 10, 1931 (dec.); 1 dau., Verity Sutherland Grinnell; m. 2d, Helen Gill Field, Oct. 10, 1953. Admitted to N.Y. bar, 1929; registered to practice U.S. Patent Office, 1934; practice of law, N.Y.C., 1929-56, specializing patent and trademark law; partner Williams, Rich & Morse, 1937-52, Churchill, Rich, Weymouth & Engel, 1952-56; asso. judge U.S. Ct. Customs and Patent Appeals, 1956—; lectr. patent law Columbia, 1942-56, N.Y. Law Sch., 1952; adj. prof. Georgetown U. Law Sch., 1963-69. Recipient Jefferson medal N.J. Patent Law Assn., 1955; Kettering award Patent Trademark and Copyright Inst. George Washington U., 1963, Founders Day award for distinguished govt. service, 1970; Freedman Found. award Am. Inst. Chemists, 1967; Eli Whitney award Conn. Patent Law Assn., 1972. Mem. Assn. Bar City, N.Y., Am. Bar Assn., Am., N.Y. (pres. 1950-51), Rochester (hon. life), Los Angeles (hon.) patent law assns., Nat. Lawyers Club (hon.). Clubs: Harvard, Cosmos (Washington). Author articles in field. Home: 4949 Linnean Ave NW Washington DC 20008 Office: US Ct Customs and Patent Appeals 717 Madison Pl NW Washington DC 20439

RICH, JOHN, motion picture and TV producer-dir.; b. Rockaway Beach, N.Y., July 6, 1925; s. Louis and Jennie (Rich) R.; A.B., U. Mich., 1948, M.A., 1949; m. Andrea Louise; children—Catherine Lee, Anthony Joseph, Robert Lawrence. Bd. dirs. Directors Guild Am.; sec. Dirs. Guild Ednl. and Benevolent Found., 1959—; founding trustee Dirs. Guild-Producers Pension Plan, chmn. bd. 1964-65, 68-69; Served to capt. USAAF, 1943-46. Recipient Outstanding Comedy Direction awards Acad. TV Arts and Scis. for The Dick Van Dyke Show, 1963, All in the Family, 1972, 73; Sesquicentennial award U. Mich., 1967; Dirs. Guild Am. award for most outstanding directorial achievement, 1972; Golden Globe awards for All in the Family, 1972, 73, Emmy award, 1972; Christopher award for Henry Fonda as Clarence Darrow, 1974. Mem. Phi Beta Kappa, Phi Kappa Phi.

RICH, JOHN FLETCHER, lawyer; b. Lincoln, R.I., Apr. 3, 1908; s. William G. and Bessie G. (Fletcher) R.; A.B., Dartmouth Coll., 1930; LL.B., Harvard U., 1933; m. Dorothy N. Pettingell, Dec. 23, 1933; children—Nancy W., Cynthia C., Susan D., William P. Admitted to N.Y. State bar, 1934, Mass. bar, 1933 and since practiced in Buffalo, N.Y. and Boston; now counsel Rich, May, Bilodeau, & Flaherty, Boston; chmn. New Eng. Gas & Electric, trustee New Eng. Gas and Electric Assn.; dir. Palm Beach Co., Algonquin Gas Trans. Co., Western Union Corp., Liberty Mut. Ins. Co., Baybanks, Inc. Trustee, Wentworth Inst. Mem. Am., Mass., Boston bar assns., Phi Beta Kappa. Conglist. Clubs: Athletic (N.Y.C.); Union, Harvard (Boston). Home: Jaffrey NH 03452 Office: 675 Massachusetts Ave Cambridge MA 02139

RICH, JOHN HENDERSON, newsprint co. exec.; b. Yonkers, N.Y., Oct. 29, 1910; s. William Slack and Ethel Louise (Barguet) R.; B.S. in Chemistry, Syracuse U., 1933; m. Ruth Elizabeth Kinne, Sept. 7, 1935; children—John Henderson, Cynthia R. Rich Brenner, Linda Rich Bell, Nancy Rich Dietz. Chemist, Brownville Bd. Co. (N.Y.), 1933-34; chemist, mech. supt. Foster Paper Co., Utica, N.Y., 1934-36; chemist Newton Falls Paper Co. (N.Y.), 1936-39, asst. plant mgr., 1939-45; v.p. mfg. Plastic Film Corp., Plainfield, Conn., 1945-50; mgr. converting operation Riegel Paper Co., Milford, N.J., 1950-60; with Garden State Paper Co., 1960—, pres., Garfield, N.J., 1968-75, vice chmn. bd., Saddle Brook, N.Y., 1975—, also dir.; dir. Newspring Trucking Co., Bruno & D'Elia Inc.; bd. dirs. Syracuse Pulp and Paper Found., N.Y. State Coll. Forestry Found. Mem. TAPPI, Paper Industry Mgmt. Assn. (Man of Year 1975), Am. Paper Inst. Republican. Christian Scientist. Home: 6A N Lakeview Dr Whispering Pines NC 28327 Office: 111 N 4th St Richmond VA 23219

RICH, JOHN PARKER, machine mfr.; b. Swanton, Vt., July 10, 1906; s. John Parker and Florence Marion (Rich) R.; student Hotchkiss Prep. Sch., Lakeville, Conn.; B.S. in Mech. Engring., Mass. Inst. Tech., 1929; m. Olive Frances Hussey, Sept. 30, 1933; children—John Parker III, Philip Dewey. Engr. Groveton Paper Co. (N.H.), 1930-31; with Improved Machinery Inc. subs. Ingersoll-Rand Co., Nashua, N.H., 1931-71, dir., 1936-71, exec. v.p., 1946-51, pres., 1951-71; mgmt. cons., 1971—; v.p., dir. Richwood Corp. (Vt.). Trustee Anctil Found. Mem. Squam Lake Assn. (pres. 1957), Twenty Assos. Conglist. Mason (32 deg.). Club: Nashua Country (dir., gov.). Contbr. articles to profl. jours. Patentee in field. Home: 67 Berkeley St Nashua NH 03060

RICH, LINVIL GENE, educator; b. Pana, Ill., Mar. 10, 1921; s. Orville Cadell and Lillian Muriel (Watkins) R.; B.S. in Civil Engring., Va. Poly. Inst., 1947, M.S. in San. Engring, 1948, Ph.D. in Biochemistry, 1951; m. Peggy Jane Burton, June 17, 1944; children—Linvil Burton, Graham Watkins. Asso. prof. civil engring. Va. Poly. Inst., 1951-55; prof. civil engring. Ill. Inst. Tech., 1956-60; head dept. civil engring. Clemson (S.C.) U., 1960-61, dean engring., 1961-72, prof. environ. systems engring., 1972—. Cons. U.S. Army, EPA. Registered profl. engr., Va., W.Va., Ill., S.C. Diplomate Am. Acad. Environ. Engrs. Fellow ASCE; mem. Am. Soc. Engring. Edn. Water Pollution Control Fedn., Sigma Xi, Chi Epsilon, Tau Beta Pi, Phi Kappa Phi, Phi Sigma, Phi Lambda Upsilon. Author: Unit Operations of Sanitary Engineering, 1961; Unit Processes of Sanitary Engineering, 1963; Environmental Systems Engineering, 1973. Home: PO Box 1185 Clemson SC 29631

RICH, MARIA F., arts adminstr.; b. Vienna, Austria, June 18, 1925; d. Richard and Else (Koerner) Fritz; came to U.S., 1942, naturalized, 1945; Baccalaureate Degree, Stockholm, Sweden, 1942; m. Martin Rich, Mar. 28, 1953; 1 dau., Monica Jane. Vol., Met. Opera, 1959-61, asst. adminstr. Central Opera Service of Met. Opera Nat. Council, 1962-65, exec. dir., 1965—, editor bull., 1965—, founder bicentennial opera program, 1973; cons. to opera cos., Nat. Endowment Arts, Nat. Opera Inst., others; lectr. on opera, performing arts, arts adminstrn.; guest lectr. Columbia U., N.Y.C.; rep of Am. opera to Internat. Music Council Congress; opera rep. White House Festival of Arts, 1965; organizer ann. nat. opera confs. Vol., N.Y. Hosp., N.Y.C., 1967-70; mem. com. Parents Assn. Lenox Sch., N.Y.C., 1963-70. Recipient 1st Verdi medal of achievement Met. Opera Nat. Council, 1977. Mem. Pres's. Council Arts Orgns. (founding), Council Nat. Arts Orgns'. Execs. (founding), Nat. Music Council. Contbr. articles to opera jours.; editor: Who's Who in Opera, 1976; originator editor 11 opera directories, also Career Guide for Young American Singers. Home: 57 W 58th St New York NY 10019 Office: Central Opera Service Met Opera Lincoln Center New York NY 10023

RICH, MICHAEL JAMES, advt. exec.; b. Chgo., July 23, 1928; s. Daniel Catton and Bertha (James) R.; student Cornell U., 1946-49; M.B.A., U. Chgo., 1951; student John Marshall Law Sch., 1953-55; m. Mary Alice Bullen, Apr. 4, 1952; children—Stephen, Daniel, Felicia. With Navy Cyclotron Lab., U. Chgo., 1951-53, Rubel, Rich and Humphrey, Chgo., 1953-65, Arthur Andersen and Co., C.P.A.'s, Chgo., 1965-67; sr., v.p. dir. Leo Burnett Co., Chgo., 1967—. Co-chmn. jr. bd. NCCJ, 1963-66. Bd. dirs., treas. Barren Found., 1962—. Mem. Am. Inst. C.P.A.'s. Episcopalian (vestryman, sr. warden, finance dir.). Home: 2451 Partridge St Northbrook IL 60062 Office: Leo Burnett Co Prudential Plaza Chicago IL 60601

RICH, PATRICK JEAN JACQUES, aluminum co. exec.; b. Strasbourg, France, Mar. 28, 1931; s. Henri and Marianne Marguerite (Thull) R.; Diplomé Sciences Politiques, U. Strasbourg, 1952, Diplomé Ectudes Economie, 1953, Licencie en Droit, 1954; spl. student (Fulbright Smith-Mundt scholar), Harvard U., 1954; m. Louise Dionne, July 8, 1961; children—Jean Luc, Eric, Nathalie. With Alcan Aluminium Ltd., 1959—; treas. Bauxites du Midi, 1961-63; with treasury dept. Alcan Industries Ltd., U.K., 1963-65; sec.-treas., v.p. Alcan Argentina S.A., 1965-68; chief fin. officer Alcan Aluminio Iberico S.A., Madrid, 1968-69; mng. dir. Angeletti & Ciucani Fonderia Laminatoio S.P.A., Italy, 1969-71; area gen. mgr. Alcan's Latin Am. ops., 1971-75; regional exec. v.p. for Europe, Near East, Africa, Latin Am., Alcan Aluminium Ltd., 1975-78, regional exec. v.p. Western Hemisphere, 1978—; pres., chief exec. officer Aluminum Co. Can., Ltd., Montreal, Que., 1978—, also dir.; dir. various subs. Alcan group. Served with French Army, 1956-59. Decorated Croix Valeur Militaire. Home: 765 Lexington Ave Westmount PQ H3Y 1K8 Canada Office: PO Box 6090 Montreal PQ H3C 3H2 Canada

RICH, PAUL IAN, machinery mfg. co. exec.; b. N.Y.C., Dec. 9, 1924; s. Irving Marcus and Frances (Shaffer) R.; B.S., N.Y. U., 1950; student Akron U., 1958, N.Y. U., 1961-62; m. Barbara Anne Chuckran, Dec. 26, 1951 (div. Feb. 1979); 1 son, Marcus Paul; m. 2d, Kay D. Kilgast, June 2, 1979. Asst. to controller Am. Standard Corp., N.Y.C., 1951-57; subsidiary auditor Firestone Tire & Rubber Co., Akron, O., 1957-59; budget dir. Allied Chem. Corp., N.Y.C., 1959-62; mgr. budgets Mobil Oil Co., N.Y.C., 1962-64; group controller ITT Corp., N.Y.C., 1964-71; controller Chicago Pneumatic Tool Co., N.Y.C., 1972-74, v.p., operating exec., 1975-77; v.p., dir. Builders Specialties of Fla., Inc., Orlando, 1977—. lectr. Am. Mgmt. Assn., 1959-64. Served with USAAF, 1943-46. Mem. Financial Execs. Inst. (dir. 1967-68), Budget Execs. Inst. Clubs: Aspetuck Valley Country (Weston, Conn.); Wanango Country (Reno, Pa.); Tuscawilla Country (Winter Springs, Fla.); Franklin. Home: 994 Shetland Ave Winter Springs FL 32707 Office: 4257 Daubert St Orlando FL 32803

RICH, WILLIS FRANK, JR., banker; b. Ft. Dodge, Iowa, July 26, 1919; s. Willis Frank and Agnes Reed (Paterson) R.; B.A., Princeton, 1941; m. Jo Ann Rockwell, Apr. 12, 1947; children—Ronald Rockwell, Roxanne, Andrew Paterson. Credit analyst Northwestern Nat. Bank, Mpls., 1947-52, asst. cashier, 1952-55, asst. v.p., 1955, v.p., 1955-57, pres. N.W. Nat. Bank, Bloomington-Richfield, Minn., 1952-58, v.p., cashier, 1957-60, v.p. div. A, 1960-68, sr. v.p. nat. and internat. divs., 1968-73; exec. v.p. Comml. Bank, Mpls., 1973—; dir. Internat. Dairy Queen, 1962-64, Inland Marine Corp., 1962-69, Larson Industries, Inc., 1969—, Schaper Mfg. Co., 1967-71, N.W. Internat. Bank, 1968—, N.W. Growth Fund, 1974-79, Lease N.W., 1974—, Canadian-Am. Bank, 1977—. Pres. Viking council Boy Scouts Am., 1970-71, trustee found., 1971—; mem. exec. bd. Minn. Community Research Council. Served with AUS, 1941-46. Decorated Bronze Star. Mem. Res. City Bankers, Robert Morris Assos. (nat. pres. 1977-78). Episcopalian (trustee St. Stephen's Found., 1965-68). Clubs: Minneapolis; Woodhill; Swan Lake Country. Home: 4770 Manitou Rd Tonka Bay MN 55331 Office: 620 Marquette Ave Minneapolis MN 55480

RICHARD, BETTI, sculptor; b. N.Y.C., Mar. 16, 1916; d. Edwin H. and Therese (Schramm) Richard; student Art Students' League, Paul Manship; m. Franz Matsch, July 2, 1953. Exhibited throughout U.S. and Europe, 1942—; important works Bronze Doors Ch. of Immaculate Conception, Bronx, Bronze Statue Cardinal Gibbons, Balt., marble madonna House of Theology, Centerville, Ohio, 3 ornamental panels Bellingrath Gardens, Mobile, Ala., marble madonna with child Rosary Hill Coll., Buffalo, St. Francis statue Our Lady of Angels Convent, Aston, Pa., St. Francis statue St. Francis Interfaith Center, Denver, medals Met. Opera House; St. Francis statue, also 2 altar figures St. Francis of Assisi Ch., N.Y.C.; other works in Phoenix Art Mus., San Joachin Pioneer Mus. and Haggin Art Galleries, Stockton, Cal., Eureka (Ill.) Coll., Austrian embassy, Tokyo, Hackley Sch., Tarrytown, N.Y., Met. Opera, N.Y.C., Aksarben Race Track, Omaha. Bd. dirs. Fine Arts Fedn. N.Y. Recipient Barnett prize Nat. Acad., 1947, Gold medal for sculpture Allied Artists, 1956, Lindsay Morris prize, 1974, John Gregory award Nat. Sculpture Soc., 1960. Fellow Nat. Sculpture Soc. (sec. 1971-73, rec. sec. 1979—); mem. Allied Artists Am. Studio: 131 E 66th St New York NY 10021. *I believe that there is a supreme, universal law of cause and effect, referred to in the Bible: "As ye sow so shall ye also reap." This alone, and the fact that we are all one with each other, as well as with great nature, should become the basis for right action at all times and under all circumstances.*

RICHARD, CALVIN AIRD, pub. co. exec.; b. Pitts., Aug. 14, 1930; s. Virgil and Elizabeth Drummond (Aird) R.; B.S., Ariz. State U., 1956. Research mgr. Phoenix Republic and Gazette, 1956-61; with Omaha World-Herald, 1962—, adminstrv. asst. to pres., 1968-70, bus. mgr., 1971—, dir., 1973—. Trustee World-Herald Good Fellows Charities, 1962—, Omaha Safety Council, 1970—, United Community Services, 1972—, Children's Meml. Hosp., 1975—, Western Heritage Soc., 1974—. Served with USAF, 1948-52. Mem. Am. Newspaper Publs. Assn., Omaha C. of C., Nat. Rifle Assn. Republican. Methodist. Clubs: Masons, Shriners. Home: 421 S 78th St Omaha NE 68114 Office: Omaha World-Herald 14th and Dodge St Omaha NE 68102

RICHARD, JOHN BENARD, librarian; b. Gulfport, Miss., Nov. 2, 1932; s. John Jesse and Helen Lucille (Schott) R.; student Perkinston Jr. Coll., 1950-52; B.S., Miss. So. Coll. (now U. So. Miss.), 1954; M.S. in Library Sci., La. State U., 1959; m. Sandra Davis Mosley, Dec. 19, 1970; children—John Blake, Elizabeth Carol; 1 stepson, Brian Davis Mosley. Prep. dept. head La. State U., Baton Rouge, 1959-60; library dir. La. State U., Alexandria, 1960-76, mem. faculty, 1960-76; dir. East Baton Rouge Parish Library, Baton Rouge, 1977—; mem. La. Bd. Library Examiners, 1970-76, 78—; chmn. feasibility study com. La.'s Gov.'s Conf., 1971-72; La. del. to White House Conf. on Library and Info. Services, 1979; cons. to libraries. Mem. La. Council for Music and Performing Arts, 1970-76; bd. dirs. Kent House Found., Alexandria, 1971-76, Central La. Art Assn., 1971-76; mem. Rapides Art Council, Alexandria, 1971-76. Served with U.S. Army, 1954-57; ETO. Named Outstanding Citizen of Yr., Alexandria Daily Town Talk, 1975. Mem. La. Library Assn. (1st v.p. 1968-69, pres. 1969-70, chmn. conf. 1975, 79), ALA (La. Library assn. rep. 1970-72), Southwestern Library Assn. (new directions task force, 1971-73). Roman Catholic. Club: Rotary (Baton Rouge). Home: 10719 Landsbury Dr Baton Rouge LA 70809 Office: 7711 Goodwood Blvd Baton Rouge LA 70806

RICHARD, KEITH, musician; b. Dartford, Kent, Eng., Dec. 18, 1943; s. Bert and Doris Richards; student Sidcup Art Sch.; m. Anita Pallenberg; children—Marlon, Dandelion. Lead guitarist, vocalist Rolling Stones, 1962—; films include Sympathy for the Devil, 1970; Gimme Shelter, 1970; Ladies and Gentlemen, the Rolling Stones, 1974. Composer: (with M. Jagger) Satisfaction, Sympathy for the Devil, Street Fighting Man, Brown Sugar, Jumpin' Jack Flash, others. Address: 75 Rockefeller Plaza New York NY 10019

RICHARD, RALPH STEPHENSON, investment banker; b. Opequon, Va., Feb. 4, 1919; s. Charles Atwell and Courtney Elizabeth (Stephenson) R.; B.C.S., Strayer Coll. Accountancy, Washington, 1940, M.C.S., 1941; B.B.A., Southeastern U., Washington, 1953, M.B.A., 1954; m. Dorothy Baker Rutherford, June 8, 1939; children—Ralph Stephenson, David A., Mary Louise. With Hohnston, Lemon & Co., Inc., Washington, 1939—, exec. v.p. 1973—; treas. Washington Mut. Inventors Fund, 1966—; treas., dir. Washington Investors Plans, 1966—; v.p., treas. St. Mary's Devel. Corp., 1978—. Trustee Fairfax (Va.) Hosp. Assn.; chmn. trustees Southeastern U.; pres., bd. dirs. Kiwanis Found. Arlington, Va. Chartered fin. analyst. Clubs: Congl. Country (Bethesda, Md.); Farmington Country Charlottesville, Va.); University (Washington); Washington Golf and Country (Arlington), Kiwanis, Shriners. Home: 3218 N George Mason Dr Arlington VA 22207 Office: 900 Southern Bldg NW Washington DC 20005

RICHARDS, ALLEN B., corp. exec.; b. Detroit, June 22, 1927; s. Thomas O. and Ruth A. R.; B.S., Northwestern U., 1951; M.S., Mont. State U., 1954; Ph.D., Iowa State U., 1958; m. Eleanor C. Bailey, June 30, 1951; children—Thomas A., William C., Claire L. With Gen. Mills, Inc., 1961-69, asst. treas., 1968-69; with Gould, Inc., 1969-74, v.p. adminstrn., 1973-74; v.p. adminstrn. Crown Zellerbach, N.Y.C., 1974-75; sr. v.p. fin. adminstrn. Am. Express Co., N.Y.C., 1975—. Served with AUS, 1945-47. Mem. Fin. Execs. Inst., Nat. Assn. Accts., Inst. Mgmt. Scis. Clubs: N.Y. Athletic; Tavern (Chgo.).

RICHARDS, ARTHUR V., bus. exec.; b. N.Y.C., 1939; s. James V. and Isabel R.; B.B.A., St. John's U., 1963, LL.B., 1966; m. Nancy Richards, Dec. 31, 1960; children—Pamela A., Arthur J. Asst. sec. Melville Corp., Harrison, N.Y., 1970-77, sec., gen. atty., 1977—. Served with USAF, 1958-60. Mem. Am. Soc. Corp. Secs., Assn. Bar of City of N.Y. Home: 63 Kipp St Chappaqua NY 10514 Office: 3000 Westchester Ave Harrison NY 10528

RICHARDS, BENJAMIN BILLINGS, II, librarian; b. Dubuque, Iowa, Mar. 24, 1917; s. Clarence Whitaker and Lora Emma (Lindenberg) R.; student Loras Coll., 1934-36; A.B., U. No. Iowa, Cedar Falls, 1939; B.S. in L.S., Case Western Res. U., 1941; M.A. in Am. Studies, Claremont (Cal.) Grad. Sch., 1951; postgrad. U. Chgo. Grad. Library Sch., 1951-53, U. Pitts., 1967; m. Alice Louise Nagy, June 17, 1942; 1 dau., Janet Alden (Mrs. MacFarland). With purchasing dept. Revere Copper & Brass Co., Inc., Chgo., 1936-38; jr. librarian Iowa Traveling Library, Des Moines, 1939-40; librarian Knox Coll., 1946-58; asst. Pomona Coll. Library, 1949-50; faculty U. Okla. Sch. Library Sci., summer 1958; prof., chmn. div. library edn. and library services Kans. State Tchrs. Coll., Emporia, also librarian William Allen White Meml. Library, 1959-63; librarian Chatham Coll., Pitts., 1963-69, Tex. Woman's U., Denton, 1969-72; dir. Western N.Y. Library Resources Council, 1973—. Co-founder chmn. Midwest Acad. Librarians Conf., 1955-56; adminstrv. chmn. William Allen White Childrens Book Award, 1959-63. Served to lt. USNR, 1941-45; PTO. Mem. Am. (life), Ill. (chmn. coll. sect. 1952-53), Kans. (v.p., pres.-elect 1963-64), Pa. (v.p., pres.-elect coll. and univ. sect. 1968-69), N.Y. library assns., Assn. Coll. and Research Libraries (Tri-State pres. 1966-67), Am. Assn. U. Profs. (v.p., pres.-elect Tex. Woman's U. chpt. 1972-73), Carl Sandburg Assn., Order Bookfellows, Pitts. Bibliophiles, Sigma Tau Delta, Beta Phi Mu. Episcopalian. Editor: The Stepladder, poetry quar., Galesburg, Ill., 1952-58; California Gold Rush Merchant: The Journal of Stephen Davis, 1956. Home: 42 Lancaster Ave Buffalo NY 14222

RICHARDS, DARRIE HEWITT, investment co. exec.; b. Washington, May 31, 1921; s. George Jacob and Esmee (MacMahon) R.; student Brown U., 1937-39; B.S., U.S. Mil. Acad., 1943; M.S., Princeton, 1949; m. Patricia Louise Moses, Jan. 1, 1947; children—Hilary Wade, Craig Hewitt, Lynn Cotter. Commd. 2d lt. U.S. Army, 1943, advanced through grades to maj. gen., 1970, ret., 1974; mem. Army Gen. Staff Logistics, 1962-66; brigade comdr., logistics staff officer, Europe, 1966-68; comdr. Qui Nhon (Vietnam) Support Command, 1968-69; comdr. Western Area Mil. Traffic Mgmt. and Terminal Service, 1969-70; asst. dep. chief staff for logistics Dept. Army, 1970-73; dep. dir. Def. Supply Agy., 1973-74, ret.; v.p. Capital Resources Inc., Washington, 1974-75; asso. Devel. Resources, Inc., Alexandria, Va., 1975-79; pres. the Montgomery Corp., Alexandria, 1976—. Decorated D.S.M. with oak leaf cluster, Legion Merit with 3 oak leaf clusters, Bronze Star, Air medal with 3 oak leaf clusters; Order Chung Mu (Republic Korea); Distinguished Service Order, Honor medal 1st class (Vietnam). Mem. Def. Mgmt. Assn. (v.p. 1973-74), Nat. Def. Transp. Assn. (pres. A Frame chpt. 1960-61), Am. Def. Preparedness Assn. (nat. council 1974—), Assn. U.S. Army (pres. Heidelburg chpt. 1967-68), alumni assns. U.S. Mil Acad., Princeton, Brown U. Episcopalian. Author publs. on devel allied strategy in World War II, also nat. transp. policy. Home: 212 Wilkes St Alexandria VA 22314 Office: 427 N Lee St Alexandria VA 22314

RICHARDS, EARLE BLAKE, former newspaper exec.; b. St. Thomas, Ont., Can., Aug. 17, 1915; s. Emery A. and Frances (Erb) R.; B.A. with honours in Bus. Adminstrn., U. Western Ont., 1939; chartered accountant, 1942; m. Anne Margaret Bowes Taylor, Apr. 3, 1943; children—Barbara (Mrs. B.R.A. Gibbings), Gordon, Robert. With Clarkson Gordon & Co., chartered accountants, Toronto, 1939-49; with Toronto Globe & Mail, 1949-79, exec. v.p., dir. Globe & Mail Ltd. Served to lt. Royal Canadian Navy, 1942-45. Mem. Canadian Daily Newspaper Pubs. Assn. (past pres.), Delta Upsilon. Mem. United Ch. of Can. Kiwanian. Home: 5 Pine Forest Rd Toronto ON M4N 3E6 Canada

RICHARDS, FRED TRACY, corp. exec.; b. Waverly, N.Y., Feb. 8, 1914; s. Parke and Lois (Tracy) R.; B.S. in Engring. with honors, Princeton U., 1935; m. Gladys Bucher Albright, Aug. 1, 1942 (div. 1973); children—Fred Tracy, John Harvey; m. 2d, Jean Hunter, June 16, 1973. Supr. maintenance way, spl. purchasing agt. Pa. R.R. Co., Phila., 1935-47; chmn. bd., chief exec. officer Central Supply Co. Va. Inc., Phila., 1947-55; asst. to chmn. Avco Corp., Greenwich, Conn., 1955-79; pres. Richards Resources, Inc., Stamford, Conn., 1979—. Pres., bd. dirs. U.S.O. N.Y. Served to lt. col. C.E., AUS, 1942-46. Club: Princeton (N.Y.C.). Presbyterian. Home and Office: 125 Saw Mill Rd Stamford CT 06903

RICHARDS, GALE LEE, educator; b. Long Run, W.Va., July 31, 1918; s. Robert Amaziah and Edna Jane (Scott) R.; B.A. (Pixley scholar), U. Akron, O., 1940; M.A. (C.S. Knight Meml. scholar), U. Ia., 1942, Ph.D., 1950; m. Barbara Lee Neely, Apr. 19, 1944; children—Robin Lee, Wendell Scott, Jeffrey Marshall. Instr. speech U. Akron, 1941-42; asst. prof. speech Drake U., 1947-48; asst. prof. English, U. Nev., 1948-52; asst. prof. speech U. Wash., 1952-58; asso. prof. speech U. So. Calif., 1958-65; prof. communication Ariz. State U., Tempe, 1965—. Pub. relations cons. Red Feather campaign United Fund, Los Angeles, 1955-58; mgmt. and tng. cons. various profl. and comml. orgns., 1955—. Bd. dirs. Phoenix Little Theatre. Served to lt. USNR, 1942-45; PTO. Recipient Distinguished Alumni award Radio Sta. WSUI, 1942. Mem. Speech Communication Assn. (adminstrv. council, legislative council), Internat. Communication Assn. (adminstrv. council), Western Speech Communication Assn. (2d v.p. 1956, 71, pres. Execs. club 1975), Ariz. Communication and Drama Assn. (pres. 1967), Blue Key, Phi Kappa Phi, Delta Sigma Rho. Democrat. Methodist. Rotarian. Cons. editor Western Speech, 1957-61, 62-65, 69-72, Jour. of Communication, 1961-67. Contbr. articles profl. jours. Home: 614 E Bishop Dr Tempe AZ 85282

RICHARDS, GILBERT FRANCIS, mfg. exec.; b. Prairieburg, Ia., Nov. 2, 1915; s. Raymond D. and Theresa (O'Connor) R.; student Tilton Acad.; LL.D. (hon.), Ursinus Coll., 1973; m. Mary Elizabeth Hanchett, May 13, 1959; children—Patricia (Mrs. Timothy Roorda), Michael, Sheri Stanton (Mrs. C.R. Taylor), Jan Stanton (Mrs. Ted Johnson), Lauri Stanton (Mrs. James Cleary), James Stanton, Mary Elizabeth. Dist. mgr. Permanente Cement Co., 1944-45; dist. sales mgr. Kaiser Gypsum Co., 1945-48, gen. sales mgr., 1948-52; gen. sales mgr. Kaiser Metal Products, 1952-56; v.p. sales Sharples Corp., 1956-58; sales mgr. Airframe, The Budd Co., 1958-59, v.p. sales, 1959-65, v.p., gen. mgr. automotive div., 1965-68, pres., gen. mgr. automotive div., 1968-71; pres., chief exec. officer Budd Co., 1971-74, chmn. bd., chief exec. officer, 1974—; dir. Transport Indemnity Co., Los Angeles, Fed. Mogul Corp.; supervisory bd. Thyssen Industrie AG. Bd. dirs. United Found., Detroit Renaissance. Mem. Soc. Automotive Engrs. Clubs: Economic (dir.) (Detroit); Bloomfield Hills (Mich.) Country; Eldorado Country (Calif.), Marrakesh Country (Calif.); Economic (N.Y.C.); Nat. Press; Yondotega. Home: 1009 Stratford Ln Bloomfield Hills MI 48013 Office: 3155 W Big Beaver Rd Troy MI 48084

RICHARDS, HERBERT EAST, clergyman, educator; b. Hazleton, Pa., Dec. 30, 1919; s. Herbert E. and Mabel (Vannaucker) R.; A.B., Dickinson Coll., 1941; B.D., Drew U., 1944; M.A., Columbia, 1944; D.D., Coll. of Ida., 1953; postgrad. Union Theol. Sem., 1941-48, Bucknell U., 1943-44; m. Lois Marcey, Jan. 1, 1942; children—Herbert Charles, Marcey Lynn, Robyn Lois, Fredrick East, Mark Allen. Ordained to ministry Methodist Ch., 1944; pastor in Boiling Springs, Pa., 1937-40, Westchester, Pa., 1940-41, Basking Ridge, N.J., 1941-47; mem. faculty Drew U. and Theol. Sem., 1944-51, asso. prof. homiletics and Christian criticism, chmn. dept., asst. dean, 1947-51; spl. lectr. religion Howard U., 1947; minister 1st Meth. Cathedral, Boise, Idaho, 1951-69, 1st United Meth. Ch., Eugene, Oreg., 1969-78, Tabor Heights United Meth. Ch., Portland, Oreg., 1978—; weekly radio broadcaster sta. KBOI, sta. KIDO, 1941—, weekly TV broadcaster CBS, 1945—, ABC, 1969—, NBC, 1973; pres. Inspiration, Inc., TV Found., 1965—, TV Ecology, 1973; producer Life TV series, ABC, 1974-75, also BBC, Eng., Suise Romande Geneva Suise. Chmn. Idaho bd. ministerial tng. Meth. Conf., 1954-60, chmn. TV, Radio and Film Commn., 1954-62, Oreg. Council Pub. Broadcasting, 1973; del. Idaho Conf. Meth. Gen. Conf., 1956, del. Jurisdictional Conf., 1956, del. World Meth. Council, 1957, mem. Gen. Conf., 1956—, mem. Jurisdictional Conf., 1956—; meml. chaplain Ida. Supreme Ct., 1960; chaplain Idaho Senate, 1960-68. Mem. Commn. on Centennial Celebration for Idaho, 1962-63; committeeman Boy Scouts Am. Bd. dirs. Eugene chpt. ARC, 1954-73; adv. bd. Medic-Alert Found. Accredited news reporter Nat. Assn. Broadcasters, 1978. Recipient Alumni citation in religious edn. Dickinson Coll., 1948; Golden Plate award Am. Acad. Achievement; named Clergyman of Year, Religious Heritage Am., 1965. Mem. Am. Acad. Achievement (bd. govs. 1967—), Am. Found. Religion and Psychiatry (charter gov.), Greater Boise Ministerial Assn. (pres.), Eugene Ministerial Assn. (pres. 1978), AAUP, Civil Air Patrol (chaplain Idaho wing, lt. col.). Mason (32 deg., Shriner), Elk, Rotarian (editor Key and Cog). Contbr. articles to religious publs. Composer (oratorios) Prophet Unwilling, 1966; Meet Martin Luther, 1968; Dear Jesus Boy, 1973. Home: 10172 SE 99th Dr Portland OR 97266 Office: Tabor Heights United Methodist Ch 6161 SE Stark St Portland OR 97215. *When a person presses his face against the window pane of life, he becomes as a child waiting for his father's return; simple, trusting and infinitely wiser. In our present time of growth/conflict, such a face-pressing is essential to get us safely from where we are to where we ought to be!*

RICHARDS, JEANNE HERRON, artist; b. Aurora, Ill., Apr. 8, 1923; d. Robert Watt and Ida (Herron) R.; B.F.A., U. Iowa, 1952, M.F.A., 1954. One-woman shows include: U. Nebr. Art Galleries, Lincoln, 1959, U. Ill., Champaign-Urbana, 1969; group shows include: Library of Congress, 1947-61, Corcoran Gallery, Washington, 1974; represented in permanent collections: Lessing J. Rosenwalt Collection, Library of Congress, Nat. Collection Fine Arts, Smithsonian Instn.; instr. art State U. Iowa, 1955-56; instr. U. Nebr., 1957-59, asst. prof., 1959-63; instr. Ascension Acad., Alexandria, Va., 1967-68. Served with USNR, 1943-46. Fulbright grantee, 1954-55. Mem. Soc. Am. Graphic Artists, Soc. Washington Printmakers, Gamma Phi Beta. Address: 9526 Liptonshire Dallas TX 75238

RICHARDS, JOHN HALL, chem. biologist, educator; b. Berkeley, Calif., Mar. 13, 1930; s. Alvin Carl and Verna Lodema (Hall) R.; B.S. with highest honors, U. Calif. at Berkeley, 1951, Ph.D. (NSF fellow), 1955; B.Sc. (Rhodes scholar), Oxford (Eng.) U., 1953; m. Marian Scofield, June 26, 1954; children—Kathleen Richards Eloy, Jennifer Richards Mcray, Julia Richards Hall, Cynthia Claire; m. 2d, Minnie McMillan, June 21, 1975. Instr. Harvard U., 1955-57; asst. prof. organic chemistry Calif. Inst. Tech., 1957-61, asso. prof., 1961-70, prof., 1970—. Cons. E. I. du Pont de Nemours & Co., McGraw-Hill Book Co.; cons. USPHS, 1965-69. Recipient Lalor award, 1956; Alfred P. Sloan Found. grantee, 1960-62, 62-64. Mem. Am. Chem. Soc., Chem. Soc. Eng., N.Y. Acad. Scis., Phi Beta Kappa, Sigma Xi. Club: Leander Rowing (Henley-on-Thames, Eng.). Home: 677 Deodar Ln Bradbury CA 91010 Office: Calif Inst Tech Pasadena CA 91125

RICHARDS, JOHN NOBLE, ret. architect; b. Warren, Ohio, Apr. 23, 1904; s. Charles J. and Carrie May (Noble) R.; B.Arch., U. Pa., 1931; D.Arts, Bowling Green State U., 1977; m. Norma Hayes, Apr. 12, 1938. With Bellman, Gillett & Richards, architects and engrs., Toledo, 1922-62, sr. partner, 1951-62; sr. partner Richards, Bauer & Moorhead, 1962-76; univ. architect U. Toledo, Defiance Coll., Heidelberg Coll.; works include Student Union Bldg. and Mershon Auditorium Ohio State U., MacGruder Meml. Hosp., Port Clinton, Ohio, Ritter Planetarium U. Toledo, Lebanon Correctional Instn., Med. Coll. Ohio, Toledo, Riverside Hosp., Toledo; dir., chmn. bldg. com. Otis Avery Browning Masonic Meml. Complex. Past pres. Art Interests, Inc.; exhibited watercolors, Toledo, Phila., Kent State U., Bowling Green, Tiffin, Van Wert, Ohio; past dir. Peoples Savs. Assn. Mayor of Ottawa Hills, 1965-71. Chmn. bd. Downtown Toledo Assos., Toledo Townscapes, 1975—; chmn. Toledo Arts Commn., 1965-71; mem. Gov.'s Com. for Handicapped; adv. com. Ohio Arts Commn., 5th dist. Gen. Services Adminstrn.; float judge Tournament Roses Parade, 1975; past bd. dirs. Toledo Symphony Orch. Assn., Village Players, Toledo Conv. Bur.; adv. bd. Sch. Fine Arts U. Cin. Life trustee YMCA; trustee Bowling Green State U. Found.; mem. president's council Bowling Green State U., 1978; mem. Pres.'s Council Toledo Mus. Art. Recipient Stewardson traveling scholarship to France, Italy, Germany, Eng.; Cret medal, Archtl. Soc. medal, U. Pa.; Gold medal Architects Soc. Ohio, 1971; Paul Harris fellow Rotary Internat., 1979; registered architect, Ohio, Mich., Ind., W.Va., N.J., Mo., Pa. Fellow AIA (dir. 1949-52, 1st v.p. 1956-58, pres. 1958-60, chancellor Coll. of Fellows 1968-70); hon. fellow Royal Inst. Canadian Architects, Philippine Inst. Architects; mem. Royal Inst. Brit. Architects, NAD (asso.), Mex. Soc. Architects, Nat. Sculpture Soc. (affiliate profl. mem.), Toledo Area C. of C. (pres. 1962, chmn. bd. 1964), Newcomen Soc., Archtl. League N.Y., Northwest Ohio Water Color Soc., Toledo Zool. Soc. (trustee), Ohio Commodores Assn., Tau Sigma Delta, Alpha Rho Chi, Phi Kappa Phi (hon.), Scarab. Episcopalian. Mason (33 deg., Shriner, Jester), Rotarian. Clubs: The Toledo (past pres.), Tile (pres.), Inverness Golf (Toledo); University (Columbus). Home: 3921 Brookside Rd Toledo OH 43606

RICHARDS, JOHN RAYMOND, lawyer; b. Tulsa, Aug. 25, 1918; s. Chester Raymond and Bertha (Gayman) R.; B.A., U. Okla., 1942, LL.B., 1942; m. Cecile Little Davis, Mar. 20, 1948; children—Ann Gayman, Barbara Jane, Philip Raymond, Julia Neal. Admitted to Okla. bar, 1942; gen. law practice, Tulsa, 1946-47; asst. county atty. Tulsa County, 1947-49; mem. firm Houston Klein & Davidson, 1949-71; partner firm Grigg Richards & Paul, 1971—; head dept. law Okla. Sch. Accountancy, 1947-53; judge Ct. on Judiciary, State of Okla., 1966-77. Mem. First CSC Tulsa, 1954-56; mem. Mayor's Study Com. Civil Service Charter Amendment, 1956. Pres. Young Republicans, Tulsa County, 1948. Chmn., trustee Tulsa Police and Fire Acad. Trust. Served from 2d lt. to capt., AUS, 1942-46. Recipient Outstanding Sr. Lawyer award Tulsa County Bar Assn., 1958, certificate of merit Okla. Bar Assn., 1959. Mem. Fed., Am., Okla. (com. chmn.), Tulsa County (com. chmn., past v.p.) bar assns., Am. Judicature Soc., Delta Chi. Presbyterian (elder). Club: Summit (Tulsa). Home: 4153 S New Haven Pl Tulsa OK 74135 Office: Thurston Nat Bldg Tulsa OK 74103

RICHARDS, LISLE FREDERICK, architect; b. Merrick, N.Y., Dec. 28, 1909; B.Arch., U. So. Calif., 1934. Draftsman, H.C. Nickerson, 1935, Lawrence Test, 1936-40, Raimond Johnson, 1937, with Richards & Logue architects; practice as L.F. Richards, Santa Clara, Cal., 1947—; prin. works include Labor Temple, San Jose, Calif., 1948, Swimming Center, Santa Clara, 1949, C.W. Haman Sch., Santa Clara, 1952, Scott Lane Sch., Santa Clara, 1953, W.A. Wilson Sch., Santa Clara, 1954, Westwood Sch., Santa Clara, 1955; Civic Center, Santa Clara, 1962, Santa Clara Internat. Swim Center 1970. Mem. Santa Clara County Appeals Bd., 1952; mem. Santa Clara Code Com., 1954. Fellow AIA (pres. Coast Valleys chpt. 1956, pres. Calif.

Council 1958, Distinguished Service award 1959). Home: 145 Tait Ave Los Gatos CA 95030

RICHARDS, LLOYD GEORGE, theatrical dir., univ. adminstr.; b. Toronto, Ont., Can.; s. Albert George and Rose Isabella (Coote) R.; came to U.S., 1923; student Wayne U., 1943-44; m. Barbara Davenport, Oct. 11, 1957; children—Scott, Thomas. Actor on radio, TV and theater, 1943—, including Broadway plays: The Egghead, 1957, Freight, 1956; disc jockey, Detroit; dir. for radio, TV, film and theater, including Broadway plays: A Raisin in the Sun, 1958, The Long Dream, 1960, The Moon Besieged, 1962, I Had a Ball, 1964, The Yearling, 1966, Paul Robeson, 1977-78 and TV prodns. include: segment of Roots: The Next Generation, 1979, Bill Moyers' Jour., 1979, Robeson, 1979; artistic dir. Nat. Playwrights Conf., Eugene O'Neill Meml. Theater Center, Waterford, Conn., 1969—; prof. theatre and cinema Hunter Coll., 1972—; dean Yale U. Sch. Drama, 1979—, artistic dir. Yale Repertory Theater, 1979—; pres. Theater Devel. Fund; head actor tng. N.Y. U. Sch. Arts, 1966-72; lectr. in field; bd. dirs. Theatre Communications Group, U.S. Bicentennial World Theatre Festival; cons. to various founds.; mem. various profl. adv. groups, task forces; mem. Rockefeller Found. Playwrights Selection Com., Ford Found. New Am. Plays Program Com., com. on profl. theater tng. Nat. Endowment for Arts. Served with USAAF, 1943-44. Mem. Soc. Stage Dirs. and Choreographers (pres.), Actors Equity Assn., AFTRA, Dirs. Guild Am. Office: 222 York St New Haven CT 06520

RICHARDS, LORENZO ADOLPH, physicist; b. Fielding, Utah, Apr. 24, 1904; s. Calvin Willard and Louisa (Madsen) R.; B.S., Utah State U., 1926, M.A., 1927, D.Sc. (hon.), 1974; Ph.D., Cornell U., 1931; D.Tech. Sci. (hon.), Israel Inst. Tech., Haifa, 1952; m. Zilla Linford, Sept. 3, 1930; children—Lorenzo Willard, Paul Linford, Mary (Mrs. Robert L. Armstead). Instr. physics Cornell U., 1927-34; research physicist Battelle Meml. Inst., 1935; asst. prof., then asso. prof. physics Ia. State U., 1935-39; sr. physicist U.S. Salinity Lab., 1939-42; Nat. Def. Research fellow, group supr. Cal. Inst. Tech., 1942-45; chief physicist U.S. Salinity Lab., Dept. Agr., Riverside, Cal., 1945-66; cons., physicist charge research and devel. Lark Instruments, 1966—; prof. in residence dept. soils and plant nutrition U. Calif. at Riverside, 1968-69. Tech. observer rocket ordnance, staff comdr. chief S.W. Pacific Area, 1944. Vice pres., dir. Moistomatic, Inc., 1954-62. Lectr. Internat. Symposium Desert Research, Jerusalem, 1952; cons. Ministry Agr., Egypt, 1952; cons. Ford found., 1962; lectr. U. Alexandria (Egypt), 1962. Recipient Ordnance Devel. award Navy Dept., 1945, Presdl. Certificate of Merit, 1948, Superior Service award Dept. Agr., 1959. Fellow AAAS, Am. Soc. Agronomy (pres. 1965); Stevenson award 1949); mem. Am. Phys. Soc., Soil Sci. Soc. Am. (charter, chmn. div. 1, 1938, pres. 1952), Am. Geophys. Union (chmn. com. physics soil water 1947-50), Internat. Soc. Soil Sci. (del., gen. lectr. 4th Internat. Congress 1950, v.p. commn. I, 1955-56, chmn. com. saline soils 1950-55, gen. lectr. 7th Internat. Congress 1960, hon. mem., permanent mem. council 1968—), Western Soc. Soil Sci. (pres. 1950), Sigma Xi, Phi Kappa Phi. Mem. Ch. of Jesus Christ of Latter-day Saints. Author numerous research papers in field, sect. in books. Editor: Diagnosis and Improvement of Saline and Alkali Soils, 1954. Home: 4455 5th St Riverside CA 92501 Office: PO Box 424 Riverside CA 92502

RICHARDS, PAUL LINFORD, educator, physicist; b. Ithaca, N.Y., June 4, 1934; s. Lorenzo A. and Zilla (Linford) R.; A.B., Harvard, 1956; Ph.D., U. Calif. at Berkeley, 1960; m. Audrey Jarratt, Aug. 24, 1965; children—Elizabeth Anne, Mary Ann. Research fellow Cambridge U., 1959-60; mem. tech. staff Bell Telephone Labs., 1960-66; prof. physics U. Calif. at Berkeley, 1966—; Guggenheim Found. fellow Cambridge (Eng.) U., 1973-74. Cons. U.S. govt. agys., bus. corps. Fellow Am. Phys. Soc.; mem. Phi Beta Kappa, Sigma Xi. Contbr. articles to tech. jours. Home: 900 Euclid Ave Berkeley CA 94708

RICHARDS, RALPH JULIAN, JR., former pharm. mfrs. assn. exec., army officer; b. Sapulpa, Okla., Sept. 1, 1921; s. Ralph Julian and Alva Ruth (Marshall) R.; B.A., George Washington U., 1951, M.S., 1966; M.B.A., Harvard U., 1953, D.Bus. Adminstrn., 1964; postgrad. Army War Coll., 1965-66; m. Jeanne Tailleur Joullian, Dec. 25, 1940; children—Jeanne Anne (Mrs. Jerry Land), Barbara Jayne (Mrs. Robert A. Felker). Commd. 2d lt. U.S. Army, 1942, advanced through grades to maj. gen., 1971; asst. chmn. personnel plans and policy br., personnel div. Surgeon Gen.'s Office Hdqrs., 1947-51; dir. ops. and mgmt., office dependents med. care, 1956-58; chief plans br., operations and maintenance div. Office Dep. Chief of Staff for Logistics, 1960-62; chief operating funds div. Hdqrs. Army Materiel Command, 1962-65; comdr. Tooele Army Depot, 1966-67; comdr. Gen. U.S. Army Fin. Center, 1967-70; asst. comptroller Army, Fin. and Comptroller Info. Systems, Washington, 1970-73; dir. Comptroller Systems, Washington, 1973-74; ret., 1974; asst. v.p. for planning Pharm. Mfrs. Assn., Washington, 1974-79; ret., 1979. Decorated D.S.M., Legion of Merit with 3 oak leaf clusters, Bronze Star medal. Mason (32 deg.). Home: 9312 Falls Bridge Ln Potomac MD 20854

RICHARDS, REUBEN FRANCIS, banker; b. N.Y.C., Aug. 15, 1929; s. Junius A. and Marie Renouard (Thayer) R.; grad. St. Mark's Sch., 1948; A.B., Harvard, 1952; m. Elizabeth Brady, Nov. 28, 1953; children—Reuben Francis, Timothy T., Andrew H. With Citibank, N.A., N.Y.C., 1953—, exec. v.p., 1970—; dir. G.D. Searle & Co., Potlatch Corp., Nat. Distillers & Chem. Corp. Served with USNR, 1948-50. Clubs: Racquet and Tennis, The Links (N.Y.C.); Essex Hunt (Peapack, N.J.); Somerset Hills (N.J.) Country. Home: Black River Rd Far Hills NJ 07931 Office: 399 Park Ave New York NY 10043

RICHARDS, RICHARD, lawyer; b. Cedar Rapids, Iowa, Dec. 9, 1916; s. Dean William and Kathryn (Bozman) R.; A.B., U. So. Calif., 1939, J.D., 1942; student Harvard Law Sch., 1940; m. Bernice Hoaglin, Nov. 7, 1944; children—Kimball Dean, Leslie Melina. Admitted to Calif. bar, 1942, since practiced in Los Angeles; sr. partner firm Richards, Watson, Dreyfuss & Gershon; senator from Los Angeles County to Calif. Legislature, 1954-62. Chmn. Los Angeles County Dem. Central Com., 1950, 52; del. Dem. Nat. Conv., 1948, 52, 56, 60, 64; nominee for U.S. Senate, 1956, 62. Spl. counsel State Alaska, 1968—. Mem. State Bar Calif., Los Angeles Bar Assn. Home: 2681 Glendower Ave Los Angeles CA 90027 Office: Security Pacific Bldg 333 S Hope St Los Angeles CA 90071

RICHARDS, RICHARD DAVISON, ophthalmologist; b. Grand Haven, Mich., Mar. 10, 1927; s. Marshall Foster and Alice Magdalene (Davison) R.; A.B., U. Mich., 1948, M.D., 1951; M.Sc., State U. Iowa, 1958; m. Alice Marian Durham, June 15, 1950; children—William O., Margaret Ann, Robert F. Intern, State U. Iowa Hosps., 1951-52, resident, 1952-53, 55-57; asst. prof. ophthalmology State U. Iowa, 1958-60; prof., chmn. dept. ophthalmology U. Md., 1960—; med. dir. Eye Bank Md. Inc., 1962-72; pres. Md. Soc. for Prevention Blindness, 1975-79. Served with M.C., U.S. Army, 1952-54. Mem. Md. Ophthalmol. Soc., Med. Eye Bank Md., Med-Chirurg Faculty Md., Am. Ophthalmol. Soc., Am. Acad. Ophthalmology, Assn. Research in Ophthalmology, A.C.S., Assn. Univ. Profs. Ophthalmology, So. Med. Assn. (Md. councilor). Research in radiation cataracts and other biochem. changes in cataracts. Office: Dept Ophthalmology U Md Hosp 22 S Greene St Baltimore MD 21201

RICHARDS, RICHARD KOHN, physician, educator; b. Lodz, Poland, June 16, 1904; s. Stanley K. and Johann (Nachmann) R.; student U. Hamburg, 1923-28, 29-30, M.D., 1931; student U. Berlin, 1928-29; m. Erika Nord, Apr. 14, 1946; 1 dau., Evelyn Jean. Came to U.S., 1935, naturalized, 1941. Intern St. George Hosp., Hamburg, Germany, 1930-31; asst. pharmacology U. Hamburg 1930-33, asso. in medicine, 1934-35; research fellow Michael Reese Hosp., Chgo., 1935-36; research pharmacologists Abbott Labs., Chgo., 1936-57, dir. exptl. therapy, 1957-63, research adviser, 1963-66; limited pvt. practice, 1945-66; mem. med. faculty Northwestern U. Med. Sch., Chgo., 1945-72, prof. pharmacology, 1959-72; prof. pharmacology emeritus U. Hamburg, 1963—; med. cons. St. Francis Hosp., Evanston, Ill., 1959-66; cons. prof. anesthesiology, medicine and pharmacology Stanford Med. Sch., 1967—; cons. Palo Alto (Calif.) VA Hosp., 1966—; cons. to research and govt. instns., univs. and hosps. Recipient Research medal Internat. Coll. Anesthetists, 1938. Fellow A.C.P.; mem. Am. Pharmacol. Soc., Am. Physiol. Soc., AMA, Am. Soc. Anesthetists, French Therapeutic Soc. Contbg. author: Therapeutics in Internal Medicine, 1952; Chemical Modulation of Brain Functions, 1973; also numerous articles. Editor, contbr.: Clinical Pharmacology, 1968; editorial bd. Clin. Pharmacology and Therapeutics, also Rational Drug Therapy; bd. Archives Internat. Pharmacodynamie. Research in hypnotics, local anesthetics, exptl. and clin. toxicology and therapy, side effects of drugs, convulsive and anticonvulsive drug action; discovered novel drugs for treatment epilepsy. Home: 1580 Wakefield Terr Los Altos CA 94022 Office: Stanford Med Sch Stanford CA 94305

RICHARDS, RILEY HARRY, ins. co. exec.; b. North Judson, Ind., Oct. 6, 1912; s. Harry J. and Chestie (Johnson) R.; A.B., U. Calif. at Berkeley, 1934; M.B.A., Harvard U., 1937; m. Eloise Quinn Smith, May 4, 1940; children—Roy, Lynne. Fin. analyst Savs. Bank Trust Co. N.Y.C., 1937-40, SEC, Washington, Phila., 1940-45; accountant U.S. Steel Corp., Pitts., 1945-47; with Equitable Life Ins. Co. Iowa, Des Moines, 1947—, v.p. finance, 1961-73, v.p., sec., treas., 1973-76, sr. v.p., sec.-treas., 1976-77, also dir., mem. exec. com.; dir. F.M. Hubbell Sons & Co. Mem. Des Moines Plan and Zoning Commn., 1959-70, chmn., 1968-69; mem. bd. pensions U.P. Ch. in U.S.A., 1960-72, chmn. finance com., 1963-72; trustee United Presbyn. Found., 1979—; bd. regents Life Officers Investment Seminar, 1969-70; trustee Thompson Trust, 1976—, Frederick M. Hubbell Estate, 1977—. Chartered fin. analyst. Mem. Am. Council Life Ins. (chmn. fin. sect. 1970), Greater Des Moines C. of C., Des Moines Soc. Fin. Analysts (pres. 1965-67), Sigma Alpha Epsilon. Republican. Mason (32 deg., Shriner), Rotarian. Clubs: Des Moines Golf and Country, Des Moines. Home: 5500 Harwood Dr Des Moines IA 50312 Office: 604 Locust St PO Box 1635 Des Moines IA 50306

RICHARDS, ROBERT BENJAMIN, chem. engr., mfg. co. exec.; b. Scranton, Pa., Nov. 18, 1916; s. Emrys and Ida Mae (Williams) R.; B.S. in Chem. Engring., Pa. State U., 1939, M.S. in Organic Chemistry, 1941, Ph.D. in Organic Chemistry, 1946; m. Jean Urie, May 22, 1943; children—Catherine Jean, James Emrys. With Gen. Electric Co., 1947—, mgr. engr. atomic power equipment dept., San Jose, Calif., 1957-67, mgr. nuclear fuels engring., 1968-73, mgr. internat. bus. devel., 1973-74, gen. mgr. fast breeder reactor dept., Sunnyvale, Calif., 1974—. Registered profl. engr., Calif. Fellow Am. Inst. Chem. Engrs. (R.E. Wilson award 1970), Am. Nuclear Soc.; mem. Atomic Indsl. Forum, Nat. Acad. Engring. Republican. Episcopalian. Editor: (with Sidney Stoller) Fuel Reprocessing vol. II, AEC Reactor Handbook, 1961. Contbr. articles in field to profl. jours. Home: 15142 Sobey Rd Saratoga CA 95070 Office: 310 DeGuigne Dr Sunnyvale CA 94086

RICHARDS, ROBERT LEROY, assn. exec.; b. Harrisburg, Pa., May 14, 1920; s. Lester Lewis and Marie Emma (Ripper) R.; A.B., Gettysburg Coll., 1943; postgrad. Biarritz (France) Am. U., 1946; m. Suzanne C. Baptisti, Aug. 31, 1943; children—Lynn Susan Richards Browne, Marcia Ann Richards Allen. Asst. dir. Pa. Med. Soc., Harrisonburg, 1947-58; exec. dir. Am. Soc. Internal Medicine, San Francisco, 1958-60; exec. adminstr. Ill. State Med. Soc., Chgo., 1960-67; pres. Nat. Confectioners Assn., Chgo., 1967-69; gen. mgr. Am. Hotel and Motel Assn., N.Y.C., 1969-73, exec. v.p., 1974—; instr., chmn. bd. regents Inst. Orgn. Mgmt., 1969-70. Served with U.S. Army, 1943-46. Decorated Silver Star, Purple Heart. Mem. N.Y. Soc. Assn. Execs. (pres.), Am. Soc. Assn. Execs. (trustee), U.S. C. of C. (chmn. assn. com.), Med. Soc. Execs. Assn. Republican. Lutheran. Clubs: Kiwanis, Nassau County, Athletic Assn. Ill. Home: 10 Summit Dr Manhasset NY 11030 Office: 888 7th Ave New York NY 10019

RICHARDS, ROBERT WADSWORTH, civil engr.; b. Beacon, N.Y., Jan. 26, 1921; s. Parke and Lois Richmond (Tracy) R.; B.S., Princeton U., 1943, Civil Engr., 1944; m. Cynthia Elizabeth Pigot, May 31, 1952; children—Sarah Palmer Richards Padgett, III, Robert Wadsworth, Tracy Leigh. Instr. civil engring. Swarthmore (Pa.) Coll., 1944-45; research engr. Budd Co., Phila., 1945-50; asso. charge Atlanta Office, Howard, Needles, Tammen & Bergendoff, cons. engrs., 1950—. Registered profl. engr., N.Y., N.J., Pa., Ga., Fla., N.C., S.C., Ala., Miss. Fellow ASCE; mem. Am. Soc. Engring. Edn., Soc. Am. Mil. Engrs. (dir. Atlanta post), Am. Rd. and Transp. Builders Assn., Franklin Inst. Clubs: Princeton Campus; Branches. Contbr. articles to tech. and bus. jours. Home: 1051 Winding Branch Ln Dunwoody GA 30338 Office: 3001 N Fulton Dr NE Suite 919 Atlanta GA 30305

RICHARDS, ROGER CLAUDE, savs. and loan exec.; b. Windsor, Ont., Can., Mar. 11, 1920; s. Claude Silvie and Beatrice Stephanie (Beaune) R.; student Wayne State U., 1949-51, Detroit Coll. Law, 1951-53; grad. Grad. Sch. Savs. and Loan Ind. U., 1958-61, Advanced Mgmt. Program U. So. Cal., 1969; m. Jill Pianin, June 24, 1978; 1 son, Lawrence. Joined Met. Fed. Savs. and Loan, Detroit, 1953, mng. officer, 1954-71, exec. v.p., 1954-65, dir., 1964—, pres., 1965-79, chmn. bd., 1977—; dir. Midwest Title Co., Peckham Co., Realtec Industries. Trustee Am. Savs. and Loan Inst., 1967—, also dist. gov. Mem. Mich. Housing Devel. Authority, 1967-70, chmn., 1970—; mem. Gov.'s Spl. Commn. on Land Use; chmn. Neighborhood Housing Rehab. Com.; trustee New Detroit; bd. dirs. Project Hope. Served with USNR, 1940-45. Mem. U.S. Savs. and Loan League (chmn. mgmt. com. 1969-70, dir.), Mich. Savs. and Loan League (pres. 1971-72), Detroit Real Estate Bd. Kiwanian. Club: Detroit. Office: 31550 Northwestern Hwy Farmington Hills MI 48018

RICHARDS, VICTOR, surgeon; b. Ft. Worth, June 4, 1918; s. Julius Kelly and Minnie (Cambert) R.; A.B., Stanford, 1935, M.D., 1939; m. Jennette O'Keefe, June 7, 1941; children—Lane R. Kress, Victoria R. Burris, Victor Frederick, Peter Cromwell. Intern Stanford Hosp., 1938-39, asst. resident, 1939-42, resident surgery, 1942-43; successively instr., asst. prof., asso. prof. surgery Stanford, 1943-55, prof., chmn. dept., 1955- 58; now clin. prof. surgery U. Calif., San Francisco, also at Stanford; chief surgery Children's Hosp. of San Francisco; cons. surgery USPHS, San Francisco, Travis AFB, U.S. Naval Hosp., Oak Knoll, Calif., Letterman Gen. Hosp., San Francisco; pvt. practice medicine, San Francisco. Mem. surgery study sect. B, NIH, 1964-68. Commonwealth research fellow, 1950-51. Diplomate Am. Bd. Surgery (mem. bd. 1964-68), Am. Bd. Thoracic Surgery. Fellow A.C.S.; mem. AMA (chmn. surg. sect. 1968-70, del. surg. sect. 1971), Am. Surg. Assn., Internat., Pacific Coast, San Francisco surg. socs., Soc. U. Surgeons, Soc. Exptl. Medicine and Biology, Am. Thoracic Assn., Pan Pacific Surg. Assn. (v.p. 1972—), Am. Cancer Soc. (pres. San Francisco br. 1972-74), Sigma Xi, Alpha Omega Alpha. Clubs: Commonwealth, St. Francis Yacht, Bohemian (San Francisco). Author: Surgery for General Practice, 1955; Abdominal Pain, 1958; Cancer The Wayward Cell, 1972. Mem. editorial bd. Calif. Medicine, Am. Jour. Surgery, Family Physician, Jour. Family Practice, Continuing Edn. for Physicians; editor Oncology, 1967-76. Home: 2714 Broadway San Francisco CA 94115 Office: 3838 California St San Francisco CA 94118

RICHARDS, VINCENT PHILIP HASLEWOOD, librarian; b. Sutton Bonington, Nottinghamshire, Eng., Aug. 1, 1933; s. Philip Haslewood and Alice Hilda (Moore) R.; came to Can., 1956, naturalized, 1961; A.L.A., Ealing Coll., London, 1954; B.L.S. with distinction, U. Okla., 1966; m. Ann Bearshall, Apr. 3, 1961; children—Mark, Christopher, Erika. Joined Third Order Mt. Carmel, Roman Catholic Ch., 1976; with Brentford and Chiswick Public Libraries, London, 1949-56; asst. librarian B.C. (Can.) Public Library Commn., Dawson Creek, 1956-57; asst. dir. Fraser Valley Regional Library, Abbotsford, B.C., 1957-67; chief librarian Red Deer (Alta., Can.) Coll., 1967-77; dir. libraries Edmonton (Alta.) Public Library, 1977—; pres. Faculty Assn. Red Deer Coll., 1971-72, bd. govs., 1972-73. Vice pres. Jeunesses Musicales, Red Deer, 1969-70; bd. dirs. Red Deer TV Authority, 1975-76. Served with Royal Army Ednl. Corps, 1951-53. Cert. profl. librarian, B.C. Mem. Library Assn. (U.K.) (chartered), Can. Library Assn., Library Assn. Alta., Pacific N.W. Library Assn., Council Adminstrs. Large Urban Public Libraries, Fellowship St. Alban and St. Sergius. Progressive Conservative. Club: Rotary. Contbr. articles to profl. jours., 1954—. Office: 7 Sir Winston Churchill Sq Edmonton AB T5J 2V4 Canada. *Dedication to public service, in spite of its frustrating aspects, diversity of experience, people and places, and the avoidance of overspecialization are great contributors to an enjoyable working life.*

RICHARDS, WALTER DUBOIS, artist-illustrator; b. Penfield, Ohio, Sept. 18, 1907; s. Ralph DuBois and Ruby Mildred (Smith) R.; grad. Cleve. Sch. Art, 1930; m. Glenora Case, June 20, 1931; children—Timothy, Henry Tracy. With Sundblom Studios, Chgo., 1930-31, Tranquillini Studios, Cleve., 1931-36, Charles E. Cooper Studios, N.Y.C., 1936-50; freelance artist, 1950—; executed paintings and illustrations for leading indsl. corps., nat. mags.; designed U.S. postage stamps including Frederick Douglas 25 cent stamp, block of 4 stamps on beautification of Am., Am. bald eagle-Mus. Natural History with commemorative, Cape Hatteras Nat. Parks Centennial block of four, Paul Lawrence Dunbar Am. Poets commemorative, block of 4 15 cent stamps Am. trees, 1978, block of 4 Am. Architecture 15 cents stamps; co-designer anti-pollution block of four stamps; exhibited Cleve. Mus. Art, Art Inst., Chgo., Met. Mus., N.Y.C., Pa. Acad. Fine Arts, Bklyn. Mus., N.A.D., Whitney Mus., 200 Years Watercolor Painting, Met. Mus., 1966, 200 Years Am. Illustration, N.Y. Hist. Soc., 1976; represented in permanent collection Whitney Mus., New Britain Mus. Am. Art, Cleve. Mus. Art. Bd. dirs. Rowayton Art Center. Recipient highest award in lithography Cleve. Mus. Art, ann. 1935-38; Spl. Honor, USAF, 1964. Mem. Am. (2d v.p. 1965-67), Conn. watercolor socs., N.A.D. (asso.), Soc. of Illustrators. Clubs: Fairfield Watercolor Group (pres., founder), Westport Artists. Address: 87 Oak St New Canaan CT 06840

RICHARDSON, ARTHUR LEON BERTRAM, lawyer; b. Schenectady, Jan. 2, 1912; s. Arthur Howard and Avis (Larsen) R.; B.S. in Elec. Engring., Harvard. 1934; J.D., George Washington U., 1939; m. Marjorie Bush, May 16, 1931; children—Arthur B. L., Marion Katherine. Admitted to bar D.C., 1938, N.Y. 1948; patent atty. Gen. Electric Co., 1939-44; asso. law firm Charles W. Hills, Chgo., 1944; mgr. patent dept. Sylvania Electric Products, Inc., N.Y.C., 1945 50, gen. atty., 1950-53, gen. counsel, 1953-54, sec., gen. counsel, 1954-59, v.p., 1959-60, sr. v.p., 1960-61; v.p., gen. counsel C.I.T. Fin. Corp., 1961-76, dir., exec. com., 1962-76, sec., 1965-76; dir. Nat. Bank N.Am. Mem. Am. Bar Assn., Assn. Bar City N.Y., Am. Patent Law Assn., Am. Soc. Corp. Secs., Order of the Coif, Assn. Gen. Counsel, Am. Judicature Soc., N.Y. Patent Law Assn., Phi Delta Phi. Clubs: Nassau Country (Glen Cove, L.I.); Metropolitan (Washington); Harvard (N.Y.C.). Home and Office: 198B Heritage Village Southbury CT 06488

RICHARDSON, ARTHUR M., banker; b. Rochester, N.Y., Dec. 29, 1926; s. Saul Milton and Gertrude (Rubin) R.; B.S. in Fin., Ohio State U., 1949; m. Jane Carol Fruend, June 23, 1963; children—Susan M., Nancy A. With Loeb, Rhodes Co., 1949-51; auditor Security Trust Co., Rochester, 1951-63, v.p., 1963-66, head of mktg., 1966-70, exec. v.p., 1970-74, pres., chief exec. officer, 1974—, also dir.; exec. v.p. Security N.Y. State Corp., 1970-73, pres., chief exec. officer, dir., 1973—; dir. Thomas W. Finucane Corp., Rochester Area Health Maintenance Corp. Bd. dirs. Rochester Mus. and Sci. Center, Temple B'rith Kodesh, Meml. Art Gallery, Citizens Tax League, Downtown Devel. Corp., Highland Hosp.; mem. corp. United Community Chest; mem. exec. com. United Community Chest; mem. Monroe County Human Relations Commn.; active U. Rochester Assos., Nathaniel Rochester Soc.; mem. President's bd. advs. for J.F. Kennedy Center for Performing Arts. Recipient LeRoy Snyder award. Mem. Rochester Soc. N.Y. State Bankers Assn., Am. Inst. Banking, Assn. Bank Holding Cos., Rochester C. of C. (trustee), Automobile Club Rochester (dir.). Republican. Jewish. Clubs: Genesee Valley; Irondequoit Country. Office: Security NY State Corp 1 East Ave Rochester NY 14638

RICHARDSON, BRITTAIN DAVID, petroleum co. exec.; b. Shreveport, La., Feb. 22, 1927; s. Brittain Douthit and Dorothy Caroline (Spaugh) R.; student Centenary Coll. of La., 1946-53; m. Mary Alice Robertson, Feb. 24, 1951; children—Dana, Christian David, Caroline, Rebecca. With fingerprint div. FBI, Washington, 1944-45; accountant United Gas Corp., Shreveport, 1948-53; cashier Murphy Oil Corp., El Dorado, Ark., 1953-64, asst. treas., 1964-72, treas., 1973—; treas. Deltic Farm & Timber Co., Inc.; sec.-treas., dir. Eastridge Devel. Co., Inc. Served with USNR, 1945-46. Mem. Am. Petroleum Inst. Club: El Dorado Country. Home: 1700 W Cedar St El Dorado AR 71730 Office: 200 Jefferson Ave El Dorado AR 71730

RICHARDSON, CHANNING BULFINCH, educator; b. Cambridge, Mass., Oct. 13, 1917; s. Norman Egbert and Agnes (Clough) R.; B.A., Amherst Coll., 1939; student Harvard, 1939-41; Ph.D., Columbia, 1952; m. Comfort Cary Richardson, Oct. 30, 1948; children—Margaret Morris, Ann Poore, David Channing, Eric Cary. Instr., UN liaison officer Columbia, 1948-49; with UNRRA in Germany, 1946, UN Arab Refugee Agy., Gaza, Palestine, 1949; instr. govt. Columbia, 1950-52; mem. faculty Hamilton Coll., 1952—, Bristol prof. internat. affairs, 1962—. chmn. dept. govt., 1968-78. Mem. Kenya Inst. Adminstrn., 1963-64, Salzburg Seminar Am. Studies, 1963, Refugee Services, Nigeria, 1968. Cutting fellow Columbia, 1950; Ford fellow, Rhodesia, 1957-58. Mem. African Studies Assn., Am. Polit. Sci. Assn., Am. Soc. Internat. Law, Internat. Studies Assn., E. Africa Wild Life Soc., Am. Friends Service Com.,

Appalachian Mountain Club. Democrat. Mem. Soc. of Friends (clk.). Home: 303 College Hill Rd Clinton NY 13323

RICHARDSON, DEAN EUGENE, banker; b. West Branch, Mich., Dec. 27, 1927; s. Robert F. and Helen (Husted) R.; A.B., Mich. State U., 1950; LL.B., U. Mich., 1953; postgrad. Stonier Grad. Sch. Banking, 1965; m. Barbara Trytten, June 14, 1952; children—Ann Elizabeth, John Matthew. With Indsl. Nat. Bank, Detroit, 1953-55; with Mfrs. Nat. Bank, Detroit, 1955—, v.p. adminstrn., 1964-66, sr. v.p., 1966-67, exec. v.p., 1967-69, pres., chief exec., 1969—, also chmn., dir.; chmn. bd. dirs. Mrs.-Detroit Internat. Corp., 1973—; gov. Adela Corp. of Luxembourg, Atlantic Internat. Bank of London; dir. Detroit Edison Co., R.P. Scherer Corp., Tecumseh Products Co. Served with USNR, 1945-46. Mem. Mich., Detroit bar assns., Assn. Res. City Bankers, Am. Inst. Banking, Mens Forum, Robert Morris Assos., Econ. Club Detroit (dir.), Newcomen Soc. N.Am. Episcopalian. Mason (K.T.) Clubs: Detroit Athletic, Detroit, Country of Detroit. Office: Mfrs Nat Corp 100 Renaissance Center Detroit MI 48243

RICHARDSON, DOUGLAS WINSLOW, chem. co. exec.; b. Boston, Mar. 14, 1923; s. W.S. and Margaret (Boun) R.; student Lawrenceville Sch., 1941; B.A., U. Va., 1948, J.D., 1951; m. Barbara Jean Coulston, Oct. 6, 1956; children—Douglas Winslow, Claudia Coulston. With N.Y.C. R.R., 1951; mem. legal staff Hughes Aircraft Co., 1952-55; adminstrv. asst. to pres. Lubrizol Corp., 1955-61, sec., 1962-72, v.p. adminstrn., sec., 1972—, vice chmn. bd. dirs., 1977—. Trustee Kelvin and Eleanor Smith Found.; pres., trustee Lubrizol Found., The Andrews Sch.; mem. vis. com. Sch. Mgmt., Case Western Res. U.; regional dir. The Lawrenceville Sch. Served with AUS, 1943-46. Mem. Pi Kappa Alpha. Clubs: Cleve. Country (trustee), Union (Cleve.). Home: 62 Wychwood Dr Moreland Hills OH 44022 Office: 29400 Lakeland Blvd Wickliffe OH 44092

RICHARDSON, EDGAR PRESTON, ret. mus. dir.; art historian; b. Glens Falls, N.Y., Dec. 2, 1902; s. George Lynde and Grace (Belcher) R.; A.B. summa cum laude, Williams Coll., 1925, D.H.L., 1947; student of painting, Pa. Acad. of Fine Arts, 1925-28; Dr. of Arts (hon.), Wayne U., 1951; Litt.D., Union Coll., 1957, U. Laval, 1955; D.H.L., U. Del., 1963; A.F.D., U. of Pa., 1966; m. Constance Coleman, Sept. 15, 1931. Edn. sec. Detroit Inst. of Arts, 1930-33, asst. dir., 1933-45, dir., 1945-62; dir. H. F. du Pont Winterhur Mus., 1962-66. Trustee Archives of Am. Art, 1954-74, H. F. du Pont Winterthur Mus., 1955-76, Library Co. Phila.; pres. Pa. Acad. of Fine Arts, 1968-70, Smithsonian Arts Commn., 1962-71, Nat. Portrait Gallery Commn., 1965—. Decorated chevalier Legion of Honor (France); chevalier Order of Leopold (Belgium); Smithson medal Smithsonian Instn. Benjamin Franklin fellow Royal Soc. Arts. Mem. Am. Philos. Soc., Hist. Soc. Pa. (v.p. 1975), Am. Antiquarian Soc., Colonial Soc. Mass. (corr.), Franklin Inn, Century Assn. Phi Beta Kappa. Author: Way of Western Art, 1939; American Romantic Painting, 1944; Washington Allston, A Study of the Romantic Artist in America, 1948, 67; Painting in America, 1956, rev. edit., 1966; A Short History of Painting in America, 1963; Andrew Wyeth. 1966; American Art, An Exhibition from the Collection of Mr. and Mrs. John D. Rockefeller 3d, 1976. Editor, The Art Quar., 1938-67. Editorial bd., Magazine of Art, 1944-53; Art in America. 1953, Pa. Mag. History and Art, 1973—, Editorial cons. Am. Art Jour., 1969—. Home and Office: 285 Locust St Philadelphia PA 19106

RICHARDSON, ELLIOT LEE, govt. ofcl.; b. Boston, July 20, 1920; s. Edward P. and Clara (Shattuck) R.; A.B. cum laude, Harvard, 1941, LL.B. cum laude, 1947; hon. degrees, U. N.H., Emerson Coll., Springfield Coll., Lowell Tech. Inst., U. Pitts., Yeshiva U., Ohio State U., Lincoln U., Temple U., Mich. State U., Gallaudet Coll.; L.H.D., Mass. Coll. Optometry, Brandeis U., Whittier Coll.; m. Anne Francis Hazard, Aug. 2, 1952; children—Henry Shattuck, Anne Hazard, Michael Elliot. Admitted to Mass. bar, 1949; law clk. Judge Learned Hand, 1947-48, Justice Felix Frankfurter, 1948-49; asso. firm Ropes, Gray, Best, Coolidge & Rugg, Boston, 1949-53, 54-56; lectr. law Harvard, 1952; asst. to Senator Leverett Saltonstall, 1953-54; asst. sec. for legislation HEW, 1957-59; U.S. atty. Mass., 1959-61; spl. asst. to atty. gen. of U.S., 1961; partner firm Ropes & Gray, Boston, 1961-64; lt. gov. State of Mass., 1965-67, atty. gen., 1967-69; under sec. of state Dept. State, Washington, 1969-70; Sec. HEW, 1970-73; sec. def., Jan.-May 1973; atty. gen. U.S., May-Oct. 1973; fellow Woodrow Wilson Internat. Center for Scholars, 1974-75; ambassador to Ct. St. James's, U.K., London, Eng., 1975; sec. Dept. Commerce, 1976-77; ambassador-at-large, spl. rep. of Pres. for Law of the Sea Conf., 1977—. Past v.p., dir. Mass. Bay United Fund; mem. adv. council Trustees of Reservations; bd. govs. A.R.C.; past pres., dir. World Affairs Council Boston; past dir. Salzburg Seminar in Am. Studies, United Community Services of Met. Boston; past chmn. Greater Boston United Fund Campaign; past trustee Mass. Gen. Hosp., Radcliffe Coll., Cambridge Drama Festival, Brookline (Mass.) Pub. Library; past mem. bd. overseers Harvard Coll.; past chmn., mem. overseers com. to visit Harvard John F. Kennedy Sch. Govt., past mem. overseers coms. to visit Harvard U. Press, Dept. Govt., Law Sch., Med. and Dental Schs. Served to 1st lt., 4th Inf. Div., AUS, 1942-45. Decorated Bronze Star medal, Purple Heart with oak leaf cluster. Fellow Am. Acad. Arts and Scis., Am. Bar Found.; mem. Am., Mass., Boston bar assns., Harvard Alumni Assn. (past dir.), Council on Fgn. Relations (gov.), D.A.V., V.F.W., Am. Legion. Office: Dept State 2201 C St NW Washington DC 20520*

RICHARDSON, ESTHER HARBAGE COLE, art mus. trustee; b. Phila., Nov. 11, 1895; d. John Albert and Elizabeth MacIntosh (Young) Harbage; student U. Wyo.; m. Dr. Russell Richardson. Apr. 18, 1940 (dec.); children—Jane (Mrs. Paul A. McShane), Basil Smith Cole, Jr. Dir. bur. mdse. information Gimbels, Phila., 1935-43; dir. Clubwomen's Centre, Phila., 1943-47; cons. customer relations, 1947-50. Clinic relations com., bd. dirs. Cerebral Palsy Assn., Phila. and vicinity. Trustee Phila. Mus. Art, 1952—. Mem. Fashion Group Inc. of N.Y. (Phila. regional dir. 1946-48. permanent chmn. costume wing Phila. Mus. Art), Phila. Art Alliance. Episcopalian. Home: Rittenhouse Claridge Philadelphia PA 19103

RICHARDSON, FRANK CHARLES, educator; b. Detroit, Apr. 22, 1928; s. Herbert A. and Mary M. (Finnell) R.; B.A. in French, U. Mich, 1950, M.A. in Romance Langs., 1953, Ph.D. in Comparative Lit., 1960. Instr. English, Ecole Normale d'Albertville (France), 1950-51; instr. French and German, U. Mich., Ann Arbor, 1952-54, 1955-56; instr. French and German, U. Mich., Flint, 1956-60, asst. prof., 1960-64, asso. prof., 1965-68, prof., 1969—, also prof. comparative lit., 1976—, chmn. dept. fgn. langs., 1965—. Chmn. Vietnam New Mobilization Com., Flint, 1969-70. Fulbright fellow, 1950-51, 54-55. Mem. ACLU (chmn. Flint 1966-69, vice chmn. 1969-71, dir. Mich. 1966-69), AAUP (exec. bd. Flint 1972-76), Modern Lang. Assn., Ams. for Democratic Action, Phi Beta Kappa, Phi Kappa Phi. Author: Kleist in France, 1962. Researcher in contemporary European theatre. Home: G-5138 Lapeer Rd Burton MI 48509

RICHARDSON, FRANK KELLOGG, state justice; b. St. Helena, Calif., Feb. 13, 1914; s. Channing Alonzo and Jessie May (Kellogg) R.; student U. Pa., 1931-32; A.B., with distinction, Stanford U., 1935, LL.B., 1938; LL.D. (hon.), Western State U., San Diego, 1976, Mid-Valley Coll. Law, Los Angeles, 1977; m. Elizabeth Kingdon, Jan. 23. 1943; children—Stuart Channing, Paul Kellogg, Eric Kingdon, David Huntington. Admitted to: Calif bar, 1938; individual practice law, Oroville, Calif., 1939-42, Sacramento, Calif., 1946-71; presiding justice Calif. Ct. of Appeal, 3d Dist., 1971-74; asso. justice Calif. Supreme Ct., Sacramento, 1974—; prof. law U. Pacific. 1946-51; trustee McGeorge Coll. Law, 1959—; bd. visitors, mem. exec. com. law sch. Stanford (Calif.) U., 1966-69. Pres. Methodist Hosp. Sacramento, 1965-71, Sacramento Community Welfare Council, 1956-57, Sacramento YMCA, World Affairs Council Sacramento, 1970-71; bd. regents U. Pacific, 1975—. Served with USAAF, 1942-43, U.S. Army, 1943-45. Fellow Am. Coll. Probate Counsel; Mem. Calif. Judges Assn., State Bar Calif. (mem. exec. com. 1965-69), Presiding Justices Cts. Appeal, Sacramento County Bar Assn. (pres. 1962-63), Phi Beta Kappa. Methodist. Clubs: Commonwealth, Sutter (hon.), Del Paso Country (hon.). Home: 4140 Elderberry Ln Sacramento CA 95825 Office: 350 McAllister St San Francisco CA 94102

RICHARDSON, HAROLD BELAND, baseball club exec.; b. Harris County, Ga., Oct. 27, 1922; s. Walter Fentress and Vera (Moore) R.; student pub. schs., Columbus, Ga.; m. Tommye Ruth Chapman, Dec. 19, 1948; 1 dau., Cynthia Ruth Casey. Concession mgr. S. Atlantic League, Columbus (Ga.) Club, 1946-48, bus. mgr. Jacksonville (Fla.) Club, 1949-52, gen. mgr., 1952-58; gen. mgr. Am. Assn., Houston Club, 1958-61; bus. mgr. Nat. League, Houston Club, 1961-67, gen. mgr., 1967-75, dir., v.p., 1965—; gen. mgr. San Francisco Giants, 1976—. Served with USN, 1942-46. Democrat. Home: 854 Balboa Ln Foster City CA 94404 Office: Candlestick Park San Francisco CA 94124

RICHARDSON, HAROLD WELLINGTON, minister, educator; b. Malden, Mass., June 13, 1907; s. Francis Henry and Mabelle Frances (Palmer) R.; A.B., Bates Coll., 1930, L.H.D., 1956; B.D., Colgate-Rochester Div. Sch., 1933; M.A., U. Mich., 1945, Ph.D., 1952; LL.D., Hanover Coll., 1953; D.D., Franklin Coll., 1975; m. Mildred Lovina Tourtillott, June 25, 1932; children—Elizabeth (Mrs. Ethan Ruben), Constance (Mrs. Joe Ned VanValer), Carol (Mrs. Terence Eads). Ordained to ministry Baptist Ch., 1933; minister First Bapt. Ch., Herkimer, N.Y., 1934-40, Port Huron, Mich., 1940-45, Jackson, Mich., 1945-49; pres. Franklin (Ind.) Coll., 1949-64; exec. sec. Am. Bapt. Bd. Ednl. Ministries, 1964-73; ch. and edn. cons., 1973—. Mem. Am. Psychol. Assn., Phi Beta Kappa, Phi Kappa Phi, Phi Delta Kappa. Home: 477 S Oakwood Dr Greenwood IN 46142

RICHARDSON, HENRY SMITH, JR., chem. co. exec.; b. Greensboro, N.C., May 16, 1920; s. H. Smith and Grace (Jones) R.; B.A., Yale, 1942; m. Adele Greig, Jan. 24, 1945; children—Adele Magruder (Mrs. Ray), Stuart, Ann Page (Mrs. Johnson), Cary (Mrs. Paynter), Peter, Henry Smith III. With Vick Chem. Co., N.Y.C., 1946-61, asst. to pres., 1950-53, v.p., 1953-57, pres., 1957-61; chmn. bd., also exec. personnel com. Richardson-Merrell, Inc., 1961—; chmn., dir. Piedmont Mgmt. Co., Inc.; dir. Reins. Corp. N.Y., Piedmont Adv. Corp., Piedmont Financial Co., Richardson Corp., Pacific Fidelity Life Ins. Co. Trustee Richardson Found. Served as lt. (j.g.), USNR, 1944-46. Mem. Torch Honor Soc., Phi Beta Kappa. Office: Richardson-Merrell Inc 10 Westport Rd Wilton CT 06897*

RICHARDSON, HERBERT HEATH, mech. engr.; b. Lynn, Mass., Sept. 24, 1930; s. Walter Blake and Isabel Emily (Heath) R.; S.B., S.M. with honors, Mass. Inst. Tech., 1955. Sc.D., 1958; m. Barbara Ellsworth, Oct. 6, 1973. Research asst., research engr. Dynamic Analysis and Control Lab., Mass. Inst. Tech., 1953-57, instr., 1957-58, mem. faculty, 1958—, prof. mech. engring., 1968—, head dept., 1974—; with Ballistics Research Lab., Aberdeen Proving Ground, 1958; chief scientist Dept. Transp., 1970-72; sr. cons. Foster-Miller Assos. Served as officer U.S. Army, 1968. Recipient medal Am. Ordnance Assn., 1953, Gold medal Pi Tau Sigma, 1963; Meritorious Service award and medal Dept. Transp., 1972. Registered profl. engr., Mass. Fellow ASME (Moody award fluids engring. div. 1970); mem. N.Y. Acad. Sci., Am. Soc. Engring. Edn., Advanced Transit Assn., Sigma Xi, Tau Beta Pi. Author: Introduction to System Dynamics, 1971; also articles. Home: 4 Latisquama Rd Southboro MA 01772 Office: Room 3-173 Mass Inst Tech Cambridge MA 02139

RICHARDSON, JAMES ABNER, III, mgmt. cons.; b. Johnston, S.C., Jan. 17, 1908; s. James Abner and Eva Douglas (Blair) R.; B.S. in Mech. Engring., U. Cal. at Berkeley, 1933; M.B.A., Harvard, 1949; grad. Indsl. Coll. Armed Forces, 1953; m. Barbara Fuller, Dec. 23, 1933 (div. 1945); children—Judith B. (Mrs. Andrew Whitman), Wendy J. (Mrs. William Thompson); m. 2d, Mary Louise Maloney, Sept. 1, 1947; 1 son, James K. Research engr. Shell Oil Co., 1933-40; commd. 2d lt. U.S. Army, 1941, advanced through grades to maj. gen., 1962; assigned War Dept., then Europe during World War II; served in Far East Command, Korean War; comdg. gen. 7th Logistical Command, Korea, 1959-60; dir. procurement Army Gen. Staff and Sec. Army's Office, 1960- 63; insp. gen. U.S. Army, 1963-66; ret., 1966; v.p. F. R. Schwab Assos., Inc., 1967-69; practice as ind. mgmt. cons., 1969—; chmn. bd., dir. J. Watson Noah & Assos. Inc., 1973—. Decorated Legion of Merit with 2 oak leaf clusters, Bronze Star, D.S.M.; Order Brit. Empire; UN medal. Mem. Assn. U.S. Army, Am. Ordnance Assn., Harvard Bus. Sch. Club Wash. (dir., pres.), Alpha Sigma Phi. Address: 4551 LaSalle Ave Alexandria VA 22304

RICHARDSON, JAMES MILTON, bishop; b. Sylvester, Ga., Jan. 8, 1913; s. James Milton and Pallie (Stewart) R.; A.B., U. Ga., 1934; B.D., Emory U., 1936, M.A., 1942; postgrad. Va. Theol. Sem., 1938, D.D., 1965; LL.D., John Marshall Law Sch., 1948; D.D., Episcopal Theol. Sem. Ky., 1960, U. South, 1961, Episcopal Theol. Sem. Southwest, 1976; m. Eugenia Preston Brooks, June 14, 1940; children—James Milton, Eugenia Brooks (Mrs. James W. Nash), Joan Stewart (Mrs. James R. Doty), Preston Brooks. Ordained to ministry P.E. Ch., 1938; rector St. Timothy's Ch., Atlanta, 1938-40; asst. rector, then rector St. Luke's Ch., Atlanta, 1940-52; dean Christ Ch. Cathedral, Houston, 1952-65; bishop Episcopal Diocese Tex., 1965—. Chmn. bd. trustees St. Stephen's Episcopal Sch., 1965—, Episcopal Theol. Sem. S.W., St. Luke's Episcopal Hosp.; trustee Ch. Pension Fund, Ch. Life Ins. Corp., Ch. Ins. Co., Ch. Hymnal Corp., Episcopal Radio-TV Found., U. of South, Baylor Coll. Medicine. Mem. Blue Key, Phi Beta Kappa, Phi Kappa Phi, Omicron Delta Kappa, Alpha Tau Omega (worthy grand chaplain 1945-52, 56—, nat. pres. 1952-56). Home: 14 Shadowlawn Circle Houston TX 77005 Office: 520 San Jacinto St Houston TX 77002

RICHARDSON, JEAN, junior coll. pres.; b. Electra, Tex., Sept. 21, 1925; s. Robert Bruce and Sue (Dale) R.; B.S., N. Tex. State U., Denton, 1947, M.S., 1947; Ph.D., U. Tex., Austin, 1952; m. Beatrice Elinor Hudson, Dec. 27, 1947; B-Elin Kallas. Instr. econs., then dir. div. bus. and econs. Del Mar Coll., Corpus Christi, 1947-61, v.p., dean coll., 1961-66, pres., 1966—. Chmn. Corpus Christi City Charter Commn., 1953-55. Served with USAAF, 1943-45. Recipient Disting. Service award Corpus Christi Jr. C. of C., 1960. Mem. So. Assn. Colls. and Schs. (chmn. admissions com. 1973), Tex. Public Community/Jr. Coll. Assn., Tex. Jr. Coll. Tchrs. Assn., Corpus Christi C. of C. (dir. 1967-70). Mem. Christian Ch. (Disciples of Christ). Club: Corpus Christi Rotary (pres. 1970). Office: 101 Baldwin Blvd Corpus Christi TX 78404

RICHARDSON, JOHN, JR., assn. exec.; b. Boston, Feb. 4, 1921; s. John and Hope (Hemenway) R.; A.B., Harvard U., 1943;, J.D., 1949; m. Thelma Ingram, Jan. 19, 1945; children—Eva Selek (Mrs. Charles Teleki), Teren (Mrs. E.W. de Cossy), Hope H., Catherine, Hetty L. Admitted to N.Y. bar, 1949; law asso. Sullivan & Cromwell, N.Y.C., 1949-55; with Paine, Webber, Jackson & Curtis, investment bankers, N.Y.C., 1955-69, gen. partner, 1958-61, ltd. partner, 1961-69; pres. Free Europe, Inc. (Radio Free Europe), 1961-68; asst. sec. state for ednl. and cultural affairs Dept. State, 1969-77, also acting asst. sec. state for pub. affairs, 1971-73; exec. dir. for social policy Center for Strategic and Internat. Studies, also research prof. internat. communication Sch. Fgn. Service, Georgetown U., 1977-78; pres., exec. dir. Youth for Understanding, Inc., 1978—; spl. adviser Aspen Inst. Humanistic Studies, 1977—. Mem. Council Fgn. Relations, 1957—; founder Polish Med. Aid Project, 1957-61; pres. Internat. Rescue Com., 1960-61, bd. dirs., 1958-61, 78—; chmn. N.Y.C. Met. Mission, United Ch. of Christ, 1966-69. Bd. dirs. Kennedy Center for Performing Arts, 1970-77, Inter-Am. Found., 1970-77, East-West Center, 1975-77, Fgn. Policy Assn., 1958-68, 77—, Japan-U.S. Friendship Commn., 1976-77, Global Perspectives in Edn., 1977— bd. dirs. Freedom House, 1963-69, dir., pres., 1977—. Served with Paratroops, World War II. Mem. NAACP. Home: 5206 Lawn Way Chevy Chase MD 20015 Office: 3501 Newark St Washington DC 20016

RICHARDSON, JOHN BURDETTE, pathologist; b. Winnipeg, Man., Can., Apr. 6, 1936; B.Sc., McGill U., Montreal, 1958, M.D., C.M., 1962, Ph.D., 1971; children—Eric, Karen, Celia, Eva. Asst. pathologist Montreal Children's Hosp., 1967-68; mem. faculty McGill U. Med. Sch., 1971—, prof. pathology, chmn. dept., 1977—, prof. pharmacology, 1971—; pathologist-in-chief Royal Victoria Hosp., Montreal, 1976—. Fellow Royal Coll. Physicians Can. Office: McGill Univ 3775 University St Montreal PQ H3A 2B4 Canada

RICHARDSON, JOHN HAMILTON, aircraft co. exec.; b. Auburn, N.Y., July 30, 1922; s. John and Marion E. (Kuhn) R.; student Princeton, 1941-43, U. W.Va., 1946, U. Calif. at Los Angeles, 1950, Mass. Inst. Tech., 1959; m. Dorothy Parmer, Dec. 4, 1944 (div. Nov. 1956); m. 2d, Barbara Nott, Dec. 1, 1956 (div. July 1966); m. 3d, Barbara Manning, July 20, 1966. With Hughes Aircraft Co., Culver City, Calif., 1948—, v.p. mktg., 1960-61, v.p., asst. aerospace group exec., 1961-65, v.p. aerospace group, 1965-67, sr. v.p., 1967-69, sr. v.p. ops., 1969-76, sr. v.p., asst. gen. mgr., 1976—, exec. v.p., 1977—. Served to 1st lt. USAAF, World War II. Decorated Air medal. Clubs: Los Angeles Country; de Caza y Pesca Las Cruces (Baja, C.A.); Burning Tree (Bethesda, Md.); Balboa (Mazatlan, Mexico); Eldorado Country (Palm Desert, Calif.). Home: 10372 Sunset Blvd Los Angeles CA 90024 Office: Hughes Aircraft Co Centinela and Teale Sts Culver City CA 90230

RICHARDSON, JOHN MARSHALL, physicist, govt. ofcl.; b. Rock Island, Ill., Sept. 5, 1921; s. George Warren and Eloise (Hanna) R.; B.A., U. Colo., 1942; M.A., Harvard U., 1946, Ph.D., 1951, postgrad. Kennedy Sch. Govt., 1966-67; m. Barbara Bennett, July 22, 1944; children—John Jeffrey, Gregory Bennett, Wendy Laurel, Nancy Brooks. Asst. research physicist Denver Research Inst., U. Denver, 1950-52; successively physicist, sect. chief, div. chief, dep. dir. radio standards Nat. Bur. Standards, Dept. Commerce, Boulder, Colo., 1952-67; dir. Office Standards Rev. Dept. Commerce, Washington, 1967-70; exec. sec. com. telecommunications Nat. Acad. Engring., 1968-69; dep. dir., then acting dir. Office Telecommunications, Dept. Commerce, 1970-76, dir., 1976-78, chief scientist Nat. Telecommunications and Info. Adminstrn., 1978-79; sr. staff officer Nat. Acad. Scis.-NRC, Washington, 1979—; occasional lectr. U. Denver, U. Colo., Nat. Bur. Standards. Served wtih USNR, 1943-46. AEC predoctoral fellow, 1949-50; recipient Boulder Scientist award Sci. Research Soc. Am., 1959; Gold medal exceptional service Dept. Commerce, 1964. Fellow IEEE, AAAS, Am. Phys. Soc.; mem. Internat. Union Radio Sci. Club: Cosmos (Washington). Author tech. papers physics, communications tech. Editorial bd. Telecommunications Policy. Home: 7116 Armat Dr Bethesda MD 20034 Office: Nat Acad Scis NRC 2101 Constitution Ave Washington DC 20418

RICHARDSON, JOHN WILLIAM, JR., univ. dean; b. Springville, Tenn., Feb. 23, 1907; s. John and Emily (Walters) R.; B.S., Murray (Ky.) State Coll., 1931; M. Ed., Duke, 1940; D. Ed., N.Y.U., 1957; m. Myrtle Parke, June 24, 1935. High sch. prin., Tenn., 1937-45; mem. staff Tenn. Dept. Edn., 1945-50, acting dir. div. high schs., 1948-50; asst. exec. sec. Tenn. Edn. Assn., 1950-59; prof. edn. Memphis State U., 1959—, dean Grad. Sch., 1960—, acting pres., 1972-73. Pres., exec. bd. Chickasaw council Boy Scouts Am.; bd. regents Memphis Sch. Banking; trustee WKNO-TV, Lambuth Coll. Mem. Nat. (life), Tenn. edn. assns., Tenn. PTA (life), Tenn. Pub. Sch. Officers Assn., So. Council Tchr. Edn., Tenn. Assn. School Adminstrs. (past pres.), Kappa Delta Pi, Phi Delta Kappa, Omicron Delta Kappa (hon.). Home: 5300 Sycamore Grove Lane Memphis TN 38117

RICHARDSON, L. JANETTE, educator; b. Ontario, Oreg., Aug. 18, 1925; d. Joel Henry and Helen King R.; B.A., U. Oreg., 1946, M.A., 1953; Ph.D., U. Calif., Berkeley, 1962. Tchr. English and drama Gresham (Oreg.) High Sch., 1947-56; asst. prof. rhetoric and comparative lit. U. Calif., Berkeley, 1962-67, asso. prof., 1967-74, prof., 1974—, chmn. dept. comparative lit., 1974-79. Mem. Mediaeval Acad. Am., MLA, Am. Comparative Lit. Assn., Mediaeval Assn. Pacific, Philol. Assn. Pacific Coast. Author: Blameth Nat Me, 1970; contbr. articles to profl. jours. Home: 6044 Monroe Ave Oakland CA 94618 Office: Dept Comparative Lit U Calif Berkeley CA 94720

RICHARDSON, LLOYD MERRITT, assn. exec.; b. Santa Cruz, Calif., Aug. 31, 1933; s. Norval Sweet and Ethel Irene (Lloyd) R.; B.A., Western Wash. State Coll., 1958, B.A. in Edn., 1958; M.S., U. Wyo., 1964; Ed.D., No. Ill. U., 1969; postdoctoral study U. Colo., 1969-70, Mich. State U., 1972; m. Joyce Elaine Bennink, July 14, 1953; children—Cheryl Lynn, Mark Lloyd, Lori Elaine. Tchr., coach, adminstr. pub. schs., Wash., Calif. and Ill., 1958-67; mem. faculty Aurora (Ill.) Coll., 1967—, asso. prof. edn., 1970-75, pres., 1974-78; presdl. interchange exec. Dept. Interior, 1978-79; v.p. programs Council for Advancement of Small Colls., Washington, 1979—; cons. elementary sci. instrn.; dir. environ. edn. and elementary sci. curriculum projects. Recipient numerous fellowships and grants NSF. Mem. Phi Delta Kappa. Mem. Advent Christian Ch. Kiwanian. Office: One Dupont Circle Washington DC 20036

RICHARDSON, LYON NORMAN, ret. educator; b. Andover, Ohio, July 20, 1898; s. Norman Goff and Ella (Lyon) R.; B.A., Western Res. U., 1921, M.A., 1925; Ph.D., Columbia, 1931; m. Helen Hartman, Aug. 11, 1923; 1 dau., Cora Ella (Mrs. John C. Scott, Jr.). Editor Kinsman (Ohio) Jour., 1917-22; prin. Andover (Ohio) High Sch., 1923; adv. editor The New Students' Reference Work, 1924-28; with Western Res. U., 1923, as instr. English, Adelbert Coll., 1923-25, 27-35, Sch. of Edn., 1928-33, Cleve. Coll., 1927-29, asst. dean Adelbert Coll., 1929-35, asst. prof., 1935-43, asso. prof. Adelbert Coll. and Grad. Sch., 1943-46. prof., 1946-69, prof. emeritus English and Am. studies, 1969—, chmn. grad. program Am. studies, 1947-69; dir. U. Libraries, 1946-67; vis. prof. English, Kent State Coll., 1931, Ohio U., 1938, Duquesne U., 1969-71. Served in S.A.T.C., Western Res. U.,

World War. Hon. fellow Cleve. Med. Library Assn.; mem. Modern Lang. Assn. (chmn. Am. lit. sect. 1965), Am. Studies Assn. (mem. nat. exec. council 1959-61), Phi Beta Kappa, Pi Kappa Alpha. Mason. Clubs: Professional, Faculty, Rowfant. Author: History of Early American Magazines (1741-89), 1931, reprinted 1966. Adv. editor: How and Why Library, 1934. Editor: The American Magazine (1741), 1937; The General Magazine (1741), 1938; Henry James, 1941, reprinted 1966; The Heritage of American Literature, 2 vols. (with G.H. Orians and H. R. Brown), 1951. Contbr. numerous reviews and articles. Home: 2050-A Via Mariposa Laguna Hills CA 92653

RICHARDSON, MARK EDWIN, II, lawyer, trade assn. exec.; b. Phila., Mar. 26, 1928; s. Mark Edwin and Adelaide Estelle (Wright) R.; A.B., Western State Coll., Gunnison, Colo., 1951; J.D., George Washington U., 1956; m. Barbara Lillemore Wulff, Aug. 29, 1953; 1 son, Mark Edwin III. Admitted to D.C. bar, 1956, U.S. Supreme Ct. bar, 1960; trial atty., then sr. trial atty. Bur. Litigation, FTC, 1957-62; asst. gen. counsel Electronic Industries Assn., 1962-64, N.A.M., 1964-66; pres. Am. Footwear Industries Assn., Arlington, Va., 1966-78; counsel firm McKean, Whitehead Wilson & Richardson, P.C., Washington, 1978—; teaching asso. Am. U., 1963, Washington and Lee U., 1979. Served with USMCR, 1945-46. Mem. Am., Inter-Am., Fed. bar assns., Washington, N.Y. State, Am. socs. assn. execs., Am. Mktg. and Mgmt. Assn., Am. Acad. Polit. and Social Sci. Clubs: Lawyers, Capitol Hill. Home: 8700 Hidden Hill Ln Potomac MD 20854 Office: 1900 L St NW Washington DC 20036

RICHARDSON, MIDGE TURK, magazine editor; b. Los Angeles, Mar. 26, 1930; d. Charles Aloysius and Marie Theresa (Lindekin) Turk; B.A., Immaculate Heart Coll., Los Angeles, 1951, M.A., 1956; postgrad. U. Calif., Santa Barbara, Duquesne U., U. Pitts.; m. Hamilton Farrar Richardson, Feb. 8, 1974. Mem. Immaculate Heart Community, Roman Cath. Ch., 1948-66; asst. to dean Sch. Arts, N.Y. U., 1966-67; coll. editor Glamour mag., N.Y.C., 1967-74; editor-in-chief Co-Ed mag., also editorial dir. Forecast and Co-Ed mags., N.Y.C., 1974-75; exec. editor Seventeen mag., N.Y.C., 1975-79, editor, 1979—; lectr. Tishman seminars Hunter Coll., N.Y.C., 1975-77; host, guest TV and radio programs. Bd. dirs. YMCA, N.Y.C., 1972-73, Timothy Dwight Sch., N.Y.C., 1979—, Girl Scout council Greater N.Y., N.Y.C., 1979—; mem. women's com., nominating com. Girl Scouts council Greater N.Y., 1976-79, bd. dirs., 1979—; trustee Internat. House, 1979—. Mem. Am. Soc. Mag. Editors, Fashion Group, Cosmetic, Toiletry and Fragrance Assn. Democrat. Clubs: Murray Hill Racquet, River Seventh Regiment Tennis. Author: The Buried Life, 1971; Biography of Gordon Parks, 1971; also articles. Office: 850 3d Ave New York NY 10022

RICHARDSON, PETER DAMIAN, mech. engr.; b. West Wickham, Eng., Aug. 22, 1935; came to U.S., 1958; s. Reginald W. and Marie S. R.; B.Sc. in Engring., Imperial Coll., U. London, 1955, A.C.G.I., 1955, Ph.D. (Unwin scholar), 1958, D.I.C., 1958, D.Sc. in Engring., U. London, 1974. Demonstrator dept. mech. engring. Imperial Coll., U. London, 1955-58; vis. lectr. Brown U., 1958-59, research asso., 1959-60, asst. prof. engring., 1960-65, asso. prof., 1965-68, prof., 1968—, chmn. exec. com. Center Biomed. Engring., 1972—; cons. to industry, U.S. govt. agys; on leave at U. London, 1967, U. Paris, 1968, Orta Dogu Teknik Universitesi, Ankara, Turkey, 1969, Medizinischen Fakultat, RWTH, Aachen, Germany, 1976. Recipient Sr. Scientist award Alexander Von Humboldt Found., 1976. Mem. ASME, Am. Soc. Engring. Edn., Am. Soc. Artificial Internal Organs, European Soc. Artificial Organs. Contbr. numerous articles on engring., physics, geology, biology and medicine to profl. publs.; acting editor asaio Jour., 1979—. Office: Box D Brown U Providence RI 02912

RICHARDSON, RICHARD JUDSON, polit. scientist; b. Poplar Bluff, Mo., Feb. 16, 1935; s. Jewell Judson and Naomi Fern (Watson) R.; B.S., Harding Coll., 1957; cert. U. Dublin, 1958; M.A., Tulane U., 1961, Ph.D., 1967; m. Sammie Sue Cullum, Dec. 29, 1961; children—Jon Mark, Anna Cecile, Ellen Elizabeth, Megan Leigh. Instr., Tulane U., 1962-65; asst. prof. polit. sci. Western Mich. U., Kalamazoo, 1965-67, asso. prof., 1967-69; vis. asso. prof. U. Hawaii, 1967-68; asso. prof. U. N.C. Chapel Hill, 1969-72, prof., 1972-77, Burton Craige prof., 1977—, asso. chmn. dept., 1972-73, chmn. dept., 1975—; adj. prof. Duke U., Durham, 1972-74; cons. in field. Del., County Democratic Conv., 1972; chmn. bldg. fund YMCA, 1976; chmn. Carolina Challenge for endowment U. N.C., Chapel Hill, 1979-80. Recipient Edward S. Corwin award Am. Polit. Sci. Assn., 1967; Tanner Disting. Teaching award U. N.C., 1972; Edgar Stern fellow, 1959-61; Nat. Endowment Humanities grantee, 1970. Mem. N.C. Polit. Sci. Assn. (pres. 1978-79), Am. Polit. Sci. Assn., So. Polit. Sci. Assn. Author: (with Kenneth Vines) The Politics of Federal Courts, 1971; (with Darlene Walker) People and the Police, 1973; (with Marian Irish, James Prothro) The Politics of American Democracy, 1976. Home: 1701 Fountainridge Chapel Hill NC 27514 Office: Dept Political Science Univ of North Carolina Chapel Hill NC 27514

RICHARDSON, ROBERT CHARLWOOD, III, cons., ret. air force officer; b. Rockford, Ill., Jan. 5, 1918; s. Robert Charlwood, Jr. and Lois (Farman) R.; B.S., U.S. Mil. Acad., 1939; grad. Nat. War Coll., 1956; m. Anne Waln Taylor, Sept. 13, 1952; children—Anne Newbold, Robert Charlwood, Lydia Farman. Commd. 2d lt. U.S. Army, 1939, advanced through grades to brig. gen. USAF, 1960; squadron comdg. officer Ascension Island, 1942-43; Army Air Force Bd., Orlando, Fla., 1943- 44; assigned U.K. and France, 1944-45; comdg. officer 365th Fighter Group, 9th Air Force, 1945-46; assigned joint war plans com. Joint Chiefs Staff, 1946-49, NATO, Washington and Paris, 1949-54; U.S. mil. rep. European Def. Community, 1954-55; comdg. officer 83d and 4th Fighter Wing, Tactical Air Command, 1956-58; assigned plans div. Hdqrs. USAF, 1958-61; mil. rep. NATO Council Paris, 1962-64; dep. chief staff for sci. and tech. Air Force Systems Command, 1964-66; dep. comdr., field command Def. Atomic Support Agy., Sandia Base, 1966-67, ret. 1967; sr. asso. Schriever & McKee Assos., Inc., 1967-70; policy cons., pres. Encabulator Corp., 1970; pres. Global Activities Ltd.; v.p. Cons.'s Internat. Inc., 1973-77; pres. Exim Corp., 1977—. Bd. dirs. Am. Cause, Security and Intelligence Fund; exec. dir. Am. Fgn. Policy Inst., 1976—. Decorated Legion of Merit with oak leaf cluster, Air medal, Army Commendation medal; Croix de Guerre with silver star (France). Contbr. numerous articles on atomic warfare, NATO, strategy and concepts. Home: 212 S Saint Asaph St Alexandria VA 22314 also Bath NH 03740

RICHARDSON, ROBERT JOHN, chem. co. exec.; b. North Bay, Ont., Can., Aug. 17, 1928; s. Willard Peard and Annabel (Dickey) R.; B.A.Sc. with honors in Chem. Engring. U. Toronto, 1950; Sc.D. in Chem. Engring., Mass. Inst. Tech., 1954; m. Jane Ripley Elderkin, June 8, 1957; children—Robin, Nancy, William. Dir. sta. Sch. Chem. Engring. Practice, Mass. Inst. Tech., Bangor, Me., 1954; with Du Pont of Can. Ltd., 1954—, mgr. textile div., 1968-69, dir. chems. group, 1969-70, dir. corporate planning, mem. co.'s policy com., 1970-71, exec. v.p., dir., 1971, pres., chief exec. officer, 1972-75, chmn. bd., chief exec. officer, 1975-76; v.p. fin. E.I. duPont de Nemours & Co. Inc., Wilmington, Del., 1976-80, sr. v.p., dir., 1980—; dir. Bell Can., Toronto-Dominion Bank, Del. Trust. Mem. Chem. Inst. Can., Soc. Chem. Industry, Am. Inst. Chem. Engrs., Canadian-Am. Com. Office: EI duPont de Nemours & Co Inc Wilmington DE 19898

RICHARDSON, RUPERT NORVAL, educator; b. nr. Caddo, Tex., Apr. 28, 1891; s. Wills Baker and Nannie (Coon) R.; A.B., Hardin-Simmons U., Abilene, Tex., 1912; Ph.B., U. Chgo., 1914; A.M., U. Tex., 1922, Ph.D., 1928; m. Pauline Mayes, Dec. 28, 1915; 1 son, Rupert Norval. Prin. high sch., Cisco, Tex., 1914-16, Sweetwater, 1916-17; prof. history Hardin-Simmons U., 1917—, dean students, 1926-28, v.p., 1928-38, exec. v.p., 1938-40, acting pres., 1943-45, pres., 1945-53, pres. emeritus, prof., 1953-78, Piper prof., 1963—; asso. prof., prof. hist. U. Tex., 8 summers, also 1940-41. Mem. So. Bapt. Edn. Commn., 1952-55; mem. Tex. Hist. Survey Com., 1953-67, pres., 1961-63. Served 2d lt. U.S. Army, 1918. Recipient Cultural Achievement in Lit. award West Tex. C. of C., 1967; Ruth Lester award Tex. Hist. Survey Com., 1972; award Am. Assn. State and Local History, 1976; citation Tex. Soc. Architects, 1978. Fellow Tex. State Hist. Assn. (pres. 1969-70, Leadership award 1976); mem. Am., Miss. Valley hist. assns., Southwestern Social Sci. Assn. (adv. editor 1929-31, pres. 1936-37), Tex. Philos. Soc. (pres. 1962-63). Baptist. Mason, Lion (past pres., dist. gov.). Author: The Comanche Barrier to the South Plains Settlement, 1933; (with C. C. Rister) The Greater Southwest, 1934; Texas: the Lone Star State, 1943; Adventuring with a Purpose, 1952; The Frontier of Northwest Texas, 1963; Colonel Edward M. House: The Texas Years, 1964; Famous Are The Halls: Hardwin-Simmons University as I Have Seen It, 1964; Caddo, Texas: The Biography of a Community, 1966; Along the Texas Old Forts Trail, 1972. Editor: West Tex. Hist. Assn. Yearbook, 1929—. Contbr. hist., ednl. publs. Home: 2220 Simmons Ave Abilene TX 79601. *Seeking always to keep busy, to avoid dawdling, to be of service, especially to a university with which I was officially linked for 61 years.*

RICHARDSON, SCOVEL, judge; b. Nashville, Feb. 4, 1912; s. M. Scovel and Capitola W. (Taylor) R.; A.B., U. Ill., 1934, A.M., 1936; J.D., Howard U., 1937; LL.D., Lincoln U., 1973; m. Inez Williston, July 3, 1937; children—Frances Elaine, Alice Inez, Mary Louise and Marjorie Linda (twins). Admitted to Ill. bar, 1938, Mo. bar, 1945, to U.S. Supreme Ct. bar, 1943; with Lawrence & Richardson, Chgo., 1938-39; asso. prof. law Lincoln U., St. Louis, 1939-43, dean, prof. law 1944-53; sr. atty. OPA, Washington, 1943-44; mem. U.S. Bd. Parole, Washington, 1953-54, chmn., 1954-57; judge U.S. Customs Ct., N.Y.C., 1957—, presiding judge 3d div., 1966-70. Trustee Colgate U., Howard U.; sec., bd. govs. New Rochelle Hosp. Med. Center. Recipient citation, Urban League St. Louis, 1953, Nat. Bar Assn., 1967, Wisdom award Honor, 1970, Internat. Trade Service award, 1973, Meritorious service cert. Am. Bar Assn. standing com. on customs law, 1974. Mem. Am., Nat., Mo., St. Louis bar assns., Am. Law Inst., Am. Judicature Soc., Nat. Council Crime and Delinquency, Inst. Jud. Adminstrn., Assn. Bar City N.Y., Sigma Pi Phi, Kappa Alpha Psi. Presbyn. (elder). Office: US Customs Court 1 Federal Plaza New York NY 10007

RICHARDSON, STEWART BALMER, pub. co. exec.; b. N.Y.C., Feb. 20, 1926; s. George Allen and Edith (Sturtevant) R.; A.B., Washington and Lee U.; M.A., Columbia U.; m. Jeanne Everitt, Mar. 8, 1951 (div. 1969); m. 2d Sarah Gately, Oct. 16, 1969; children by previous marriage—Scott, Wendy. Editor Houghton Mifflin Co., Boston, 1951-52, Henry Holt Co., N.Y.C., 1952-53; exec. editor Rinehart and Co., N.Y.C., 1955-56; sr. editor Alfred A. Knopf, N.Y.C., 1956-59; v.p. J.B. Lippincott Co., Phila., 1959-66; editor-in-chief Doubleday and Co., N.Y.C., from 1972; now v.p., asso. pub. Anchor Press. Served with AUS, 1943-46; ETO. Decorated Silver Star, Bronze Star with cluster, Purple Heart. Clubs: Century Assn., Coffee House, Union (N.Y.C.). Office: Anchor Press 245 Park Ave New York NY 10017

RICHARDSON, SYLVIA ONESTI, physician; b. San Francisco, Sept. 12, 1920; d. Silvio J. and Johanna (Kristoffy) Onesti; B.A., Stanford, 1940; postgrad. U. Wash., 1940-41; M.A., Columbia U., 1942; M.D., McGill U., 1948; m. William R. Richardson, Sept. 8, 1951; children—William Charles, Christopher Lee. Intern Children's Meml. Hosp., Montreal, 1948-49; resident Children's Med. Center, Boston, 1949-50; instr. spl. edn. Columbia, 1942-43; supr. hearing handicapped New Rochelle (N.Y.) Pub. Schs., 1942-43; clin. fellow in medicine Boston Children's Med. Center, 1949-51, dir. speech clinic, 1950-52, asso. physician, 1951-52, research fellow in surgery, 1954-55; instr. speech dept. Boston U., 1950-52, San Diego State Coll., 1952-54; teaching fellow in medicine Harvard U., 1951-52; cons. dept. child health and maternal welfare State of Mass., 1951-52; asst. clin. prof. pediatrics State U. N.Y., Downstate Med. Center, Bklyn., 1957-58; asso. prof. pediatrics and psychiatry, dir. child study center U. Okla. Sch. Medicine, 1958-65; asst. clin. prof. pediatrics U. Cin. Sch. Medicine, 1965-67, asso. prof., 1967—, dir. learning disabilities program Center for Developmental Disorders, 1966—; cons. dept. child health and maternal welfare State of Okla., 1957-65; spl. cons. Nat. Inst. Nervous Diseases and Blindness, 1960-62; spl. cons. on mental retardation Okla. State Dept. Pub. Welfare, 1963-65; cons. Bur. State Services, USPHS, Bur. Edn. Handicapped, U.S. Office Edn. Mem. Okla. gov.'s com. White House Conf., 1960, White House Conf. on Children, 1970, Okla. citizen's com. Adequate Higher Edn., 1958-62. Recipient award for mental health planning Gov. of Okla., 1966; Distinguished Service award Internat. Assn. Children with Learning Disabilities, 1969; Old Master award Purdue U., 1972; named Okla. Woman of the Year, 1964; Talisman Service award Ohio Assn. Children with Learning Disabilities, 1974; Newell Kephart award for services to exceptional children, 1976. Fellow Am. Speech and Hearing Assn. (mem. exec. council 1957-59; chmn. elect ho. of dels. 1965, pres. 1973), Royal Soc. Health; mem. A.M.A., Mass. (co-founder, pres. 1950-52), Okla. (exec. council), Ohio speech and hearing assns., Oklahoma County Council Mentally Retarded Children (bd. dirs. 1960-65), Oklahoma County Mental Health Assn. (profl. adv. bd. 1961-65), Okla. Hearing Soc. (v.p., bd. dirs. 1959-61), Soc. Research in Child Devel., Assn. Children with Learning Disabilities (profl. adv. bd.), Council Exceptional Children, Cin. Pediatric Soc., Am. Bd. Examiners in Speech Pathology and Audiology, Am. Montessori Soc. (ednl. adv. bd.). Editor, Children's House mag., 1966-67; mem. editorial bd. Acad. Therapy Quar., Jour. Child Psychiatry and Human Devel., Acta Symbolica. Home: 4141 Bayshore Blvd Apt 1701 Tampa FL 33611

RICHARDSON, THOMAS FRANKLIN, banker; b. Hackensack, N.J., Dec. 31, 1922; s. Luther Locke and Ruth (Fisher) R.; A.B., Colgate U., 1945; m. Patricia Gill, Oct. 12, 1963; children—Yvonne Richardson Farley, Jennifer Richardson de Rham. With Union Trust Co., New Haven, 1947—, investment analyst, asst. trust office, asst. v.p., v.p., pres., dir., 1947-67, chief exec. officer, 1967—; pres., chief exec. officer, dir. N.E. Bancorp, 1973-78, chmn. bd., chief exec. officer, 1978—; dir. Caldor, Inc., Stamford Water Co. Pres., Stamford Hosp., 1969-72, Fairfield County Boy Scouts Am., 1973-74. Served with USNR, World War II and Korea. Mem. U.S. C. of C., Am., Conn. bankers assns. Episcopalian. Clubs: Circumnavigators, Landmark of Stamford (dir.); Graduates Club Assn. (New Haven). Office: 300 Main St Stamford CT 06904

RICHARDSON, WILLIAM ALAN, editor, pub., fin. exec.; b. Johannesburg, S. Africa, Oct. 9, 1907 (parents Am. citizens); s. Elliott Verne and Adelaide (Palmer) R.; student Harvard, 1927-30; m. Doris Ira Railing, Dec. 30, 1965; children by previous marriage—Nancy, Craig. Partner Richardson & Putnam, investment counsel, N.Y.C., 1932-33; editor Med. Econs., 1933-57; lectr. med. econs. L.I.U. Coll. Medicine, 1947-48, Yale U. Med. Sch., 1955; v.p. Soc. Bus. Mag. Editors, 1958; speaker, author, 1940—; editor-in-chief Med. Econs., Hosp. Physician, also RN, 1957-69; v.p. Med. Econs. Book Div., Inc., 1960-69; dir. Heritage Fund, Inc., 1968- 69; pres., chmn. bd. Med. Econs., Inc., 1959-68; cons. Med. Econs., Inc., 1969-73; chmn. bd. Richardson & Roebuck, Inc., asset mgmt., Greenwich, Conn., 1970-71; pres. Richardson & Co., Vero Beach, Fla., 1971—. Asso. mem. Conn. Med. Soc., Soc. Profl. Bus. Cons. Clubs: N.Y. Yacht (N.Y.C.); Watch Hill (R.I.) Yacht. Author: A Study of Britain's National Health Service, 1949. Editor: Personal Money Management for Physicians, 1969. Home: 955 Roland Miller Dr Vero Beach FL 32960

RICHARDSON, WILLIAM CHASE, univ. adminstr.; b. Passaic, N.J., May 11, 1940; s. Henry Burtt and Frances (Chase) R.; B.A., Trinity Coll., 1962; M.B.A., U. Chgo., 1964; Ph.D., 1971; m. Nancy Freeland, June 18, 1966; children—Elizabeth, Jennifer. Research asso., instr. U. Chgo., 1967-70; asst. prof. health services U. Wash., 1971-73, asso. prof., 1973-76, prof., 1976—, chmn. dept. health services, 1973-76, asso. dean, 1976, acting dean, 1977-78, asso. dean Sch. Public Health, 1979—; mem. Wash. State Nursing Adminstrn. Bd., Wash. State Employees Ins. Bd.; cons. in field. Kellogg fellow, 1965-67. Fellow Am. Public Health Assn.; mem. Assn. Tchrs. Preventive Medicine, Am. Hosp. Assn. (gen. council 1978-80, chmn. council on research and devel. 1979-80). Author books, including: Ambulatory Use of Physicians Services, 1971; Health Program Evaluation, 1978; contbr. articles to profl. jours. Home: 16525 Shore Dr NE Seattle WA 98155 Office: U Wash (SC-30) Seattle WA 98195

RICHARDSON, WILLIAM ROWLAND, army officer; b. Taichow, Kiangsu, China, Mar. 25, 1929 (parents Am. citizens); s. Robert Price and Agnes Davidson (Rowland) R.; B.S., U.S. Mil. Acad., 1951; M.S. in Bus. Adminstrn., George Washington U., 1968; m. Mary Bailey, June 16, 1951; children—William Rowland, David S., John M. Commd. 2d lt. U.S. Army, 1951, advanced through grades to maj. gen., 1975; chief of staff Americal Div., Vietnam, 1971; dep. comdg. gen. Ft. Leonard Wood, Mo., 1971-72; asst. comdt. Army Inf. Sch., Ft. Benning, Ga., 1972-74; comdr. 193d Inf. Brigade, Ft. Amador, C.Z., 1974-77; dir. requirements Office Dep. Chief Staff for Ops., Dept. Army, Washington, 1977—. Decorated Silver Star, Legion of Merit, Bronze Star, Commendation medal, Air medal, D.F.C., Purple Heart. Mem. Assn. U.S. Army, Assn. Grads. U.S. Mil. Acad., Kappa Sigma. Presbyterian. Club: Kiwanis. Home: 732 Oberlin Rd Augusta GA 30909 Office: Office of Dep Chief Staff for Ops Dept of Army Washington DC 20310

RICHARDSON, WILLIAM SHAW, chief justice Hawaii; b. Honolulu, Dec. 22, 1919; s. Wilfred Kelelani and Amy (Wung) R.; A.B., U. Hawaii, 1941; J.D., U. Cin., 1943, LL.D., 1967; widower; children—Corinne, Barbara, William. Admitted to Hawaii bar, 1946, since practiced in Honolulu; lt. gov. Hawaii, 1962-66; chief justice of Hawaii, 1966—. Chmn. Democratic Party Hawaii, 1956-62. Dir. Episcopal Diocese Honolulu. Chmn. Conf. of Chief Justices, 1972-73. Bd. dirs. Nat. Center for State Cts. Served with AUS, 1943-46 Mem. Bar Assn. Hawaii (pres. 1961), Res. Officers Assn. (pres. Honolulu 1950), Am. Bar Assn. (ho. dels. 1961). Mem. Epiphany Ch. (sr. warden). Mason. Club: Hawaiian Civic (dir.) (Honolulu). Home: 3335 Loulu St Honolulu HI 96822 Office: Hawaii Supreme Ct Alliolani Hale Honolulu HI 96813*

RICHART, FRANK EDWIN, JR., civil engr., educator; b. Urbana, Ill., Dec. 6, 1918; s. Frank Erwin and Fern (Johnson) R.; B.S., U. Ill., 1940, M.S., 1946, Ph.D., 1948; postgrad U. Mich., 1940-41; D.Sc., U. Fla., 1972; m. Elizabeth Goldthorp, Feb. 21, 1945; children—John Douglas, Betsy, Willard Clark. Research asst., then asso. dept. civil engring. U. Ill., 1946-48; asst. prof. mech. engring. Harvard, 1948-52; asso. prof. dept. civil engring. U. Fla., 1952-54, prof., 1954-62; prof. civil engring, U. Mich., 1962-77, W. J. Emmons Distinguished prof., 1977—, chmn. dept., 1962-69; cons. Moran, Proctor, Mueser, Rutledge, N.Y.C., summers 1953-55, 57, also Office Engrs., U.S. Army, NASA. Served to lt. comdr. USNR, 1941-46. Fellow ASCE (T.A. Middlebrooks award 1956, 59, 60, 67, Wellington prize 1963, Terzaghi lectr. 1974); mem. Nat. Acad. Engring., Earthquake Engring. Research Inst. Contbr. tech. papers to profl. jours. Home: 2210 Hill St Ann Arbor MI 48104

RICHENBURG, ROBERT BARTLETT, artist; b. Boston, July 14, 1917; s. Frederick Henry and Spray (Bartlett) R.; student Boston U., George Washington U., Corcoran Sch. Art, Art Students League N.Y., Ozenfant Sch. Fine Arts, Hans Hofmann Sch. Art; m. Libby Chic Peltyn, Nov. 11, 1942 (dec. 1978); 1 son, Ronald P. Tchr. painting Schrivenham Am. U., Eng., 1945; instr. Coll. City N.Y., 1947-52; instr. Cooper Union, 1954-55; instr., dir. Bklyn.-Queens Central YMCA, 1947-51; instr. N.Y. U., 1960-61; instr. Pratt Inst., Bklyn., 1951-64; asso. prof. art Cornell U., Ithaca, N.Y., 1964-67; prof. art Hunter Coll., N.Y.C., 1967-70, Aruba (Netherlands Antiles) Research Center, 1970; chmn. dept., prof. art Ithaca Coll., 1970—, mem. council on arts; exhibited one man shows Hendler Gallery (Phila.), N.Y. Artists Gallery, Tibor DeNagy Gallery, Hansa Gallery (N.Y.), Dwan Gallery, Los Angeles, Santa Barbara (Cal.) Mus., Dayton Art Inst., Dana Arts Center Colgate U., Ithaca Coll. Mus. Art, others; exhibited in group shows Mus. Modern Art, Solomon Guggenheim Mus. (N.Y.C.), Chrysler Art Mus., Yale Art Gallery, Whitney Mus. (N.Y.C.), Univ. Art Mus., Austin, Tex., Balt. Mus., Cocoran Mus. Art, Washington, Bklyn. Mus., Knox Albright Mus., Buffalo, Larry Aldrich Mus., Seattle Art Mus., Boston Mus. Fine Arts, numerous others; represented in permanent collections Chrysler Mus. Art, Norfolk Mus. Art, Coll. of William and Mary, Whitney Mus., Phila. Mus. Art, Pasadena Mus. Fine Art, Mus. Modern Art, Univ. Art Mus., U. Cal. at Berkeley, U. Tex. Art Mus., Austin, Ithaca Coll. Mus., Hirschorn Mus., Smithsonian Instn., Washington, many others; panelist various orgns. Served with AUS, 1942-45. Mem. Am. Assn. U. Profs., Coll. Art Assn., Internat. Platform Assn., Art Students League N.Y. (life). Club: Club (N.Y.C.). Home: 121 E Remington Rd Ithaca NY 14850 Office: Dept Art Ithaca Coll Ithaca NY 14850

RICHERT, EARL HARVEY, newspaper editor; b. Deschutes, Oreg., Sept. 20, 1914; s. Phil A. and May (Lawyer) R.; B.S. in Edn., Okla. A. and M. Coll., 1936; m. Margaret A. Vincent, Sept. 11, 1937; children—Bonnie Ruth (Mrs. Remley), Carol Jean (Mrs. Reininga). Reporter Okla. News, Oklahoma City, 1936-39; polit. writer Indpls. Times, 1939- 44; Washington corr. Scripps-Howard Newspapers, 1944-51; editor Evansville (Ind.) Press, 1951-59, Scripps-Howard Newspaper Alliance, Washington, 1959-69; editor-in-chief Scripps-Howard Newspapers, 1969—. Clubs: Congressional Country, Internat., Gridiron, Nat. Press. Home: 5214 Farrington Rd Washington DC 20016 Office: 777 14th St NW Washington DC 20005

RICHETTE, LISA AVERSA, judge; b. Phila., Sept. 11, 1928; d. Domenico and Maria (Giannini) Aversa; B.A. summa cum laude, U. Pa., 1949; LL.B., Yale U., 1952; m. Lawrence J. Richette, Apr. 15, 1958 (div. Apr. 1971); 1 son, Lawrence Anthony, II; m. 2d, Vero Ajello, Dec. 14, 1972. Admitted to Pa. bar, 1954; research asso. Yale U. Law Sch., 1952, instr., 1952-54; asst. dist. atty., Phila., 1954-64; chief family ct. div. Dist. Atty.'s Office, Phila., 1956-64; judge Ct. Common Pleas Phila., 1972—; lectr. Temple U. Law Sch., 1972—, adj. prof. law, 1972—; clin. prof. law Villanova (Pa.) U. Law Sch., 1970-72. Bd. dirs., co-founder bd. dirs. Tenn-Aid, Inc.; Phila. YWCA, Nat. Commn. Child Abuse; pres. Phila. Health and Welfare Council, 1958-60. Decorated Star of Solidarity (Italy). Mem. Phila. Bar Assn. (vice chmn. chancellor's commn. on drug abuse 1972-75), Justinian Soc., U. Pa. Women's Alumna Soc. (pres. 1966-70), Mortar Bd., Phi Beta Kappa, Phi Alpha Theta. Author: The Throwaway Children, 1969. Address: 1503 One East Penn Sq Philadelphia PA 19107

RICHEY, CHARLES R., fed. judge; b. Middleburg, Ohio, Oct. 16, 1923; s. Paul D. and Miriam (Blaine) R.; A.B., Ohio Wesleyan U., 1945; LL.B., Case Western Res. U., 1948. Admitted to Ohio bar, D.C. bar, Md. bar, U.S. Supreme Ct. bar; practiced law, Washington and Md., 1950-71, founder firm Richey and Clancy, Chevy Chase, Md., 1964; judge U.S. Dist. Ct. for D.C., 1971—; mem. panel U.S. Ct. Appeals for D.C. Circuit, 1972-75, 77-79; gen. counsel Md. Public Service Commn., 1967-71; adj. prof. Georgetown U. Law Center, 1976—; lectr. in field. Affiliate mem. D.C. Urban Renewal Council and Citizens Housing Com., 1961-64; mem. Montgomery County Bd. Appeals, 1965-67, chmn., 1966-67; vice chmn. Montgomery County Charter Revision Commn., 1967-68. Recipient award for outstanding and dedicated public service Montgomery County, 1968, 77; cert. disting. citizenship Gov. Md., 1971; Ann. award of Merit, Adminstrv. Law Judges U.S., 1979. Fellow Am. Bar Found.; mem. Supreme Ct. Hist. Soc. (founding), Am. Bar Assn. (mem. exec. com. Nat. Conf. Fed. Trial Judges 1976—, vice chmn. conf. 1978-79, chmn. adv. com. Project ADVOCATE 1977-78), Assn. Trial Lawyers Am. (award as outstanding fed. trial judge U.S. 1979), Am. Judicature Soc., Montgomery County Bar Assn. (hon.), Soc. Benchers of Case Western Res. U. Sch. Law, Phi Delta Phi, Phi Gamma Delta, Omicron Delta Kappa, Delta Sigma Rho, Pi Delta Epsilon. Methodist. Clubs: Nat. Lawyers; Univ., Masons. Contbr. articles to law revs. Home: 800 25th St NW Washington DC 20037 Office: US Courthouse Room 4317 Constitution Ave and John Marshall Pl NW Washington DC 20001

RICHEY, CHARLES ROBERT, U.S. judge; b. Middleburg, Ohio, Oct. 16, 1923; s. Paul Dorrence and Mariam (Blaine) R.; A.B., Ohio Wesleyan U., 1945; LL.B., Case-Western Res. U., 1948; m. Agnes Mardelle White, Mar. 25, 1950; children—Charles Robert, William Paul. Admitted to Ohio bar, 1949, D.C. bar, 1951, U.S. Supreme Ct. bar, 1952, Md. bar, 1964; legis. counsel former Congresswoman Frances P. Bolton, Ohio, 1948-49; practice in Washington and Chevy Chase, Md., 1950-71; founding partner firm Richey & Clancy, Chevy Chase, 1964-71; gen. counsel Md. Pub. Service Commn., 1967-71; judge U.S. Dist. Ct. D.C., 1971—; sat by designation as mem. U.S. Ct. Appeals for D.C., 1972-75, 77-79; lectr. speech, debate coach Am. U., 1954-55; adj. prof. trial practice Georgetown Law Center, 1976—; mem. faculty Nat. Coll. State Judiciary, 1973-74, Fed. Jud. Center, 1977—, U.S. Atty. Gen.'s Advocacy Inst., Washington, 1977; spl. counsel, councilmanic redistricting Montgomery County Govt., 1965-66, vice chmn. Charter Revision Commn., 1967-68. Gen. counsel Boys' Clubs Greater Washington, 1969-71, bd. dirs., 1957-71; affiliate mem. D.C. Urban Renewal Council and Citizens Housing Commn., 1961-64; chmn. parents assn. Sidwell Friends Sch., Washington, 1968-70; mem. Montgomery County Bd. Appeals, 1965-67, chmn., 1966-67; trustee Immaculata Coll., Washington, 1970-73, Suburban Hosp., Bethesda, Md., 1967-71. Recipient Outstanding and Dedicated Public Service award Montgomery County, Md., 1966, 68; Distinguished Citizenship award Gov. Md., 1971; Merit award Adminstrv. Law Judges of U.S., 1979. Fellow Am. Bar Assn. (chmn. com. on alcohol and drug abuse 1973-76, chmn. com. on sentencing probation and parole 1975-77, mem. council criminal justice sect. 1975—, chmn. nat. adv. com. Project Advocate 1976—); mem. D.C., Md. bar assns., Am. Judicature Soc., Assn. Trial Lawyers Am. (faculty Nat. Coll. Advocacy 1975-77, Outstanding Fed. Trial Judge award 1979), Nat. Conf. Fed. Trial Judges (officer, mem. exec. com. 1975—), Supreme Ct. Hist. Soc. (founding mem.), Soc. of Benchers of Case Western Res. U. Sch. Law, Omicron Delta Kappa, Delta Sigma Rho, Pi Delta Epsilon, Phi Delta Phi, Phi Gamma Delta (gen. counsel 1960-63). Methodist. Clubs: Masons (33 deg.), Nat. Lawyers, Univ. (Washington). Contbr. articles to profl. jours. Home: 800 25th St NW Washington DC 20037 Office: US Dist Court 4317 Constitution Ave and John Marshall Pl NW Washington DC 20001

RICHEY, HERBERT SOUTHALL, coal co. exec.; b. Cleve., June 26, 1922; s. Francis O. and Helen (Betteridge) R.; student Case Inst. Tech., 1940-42; B.S., U. Mich., 1944; m. Martha T. Ewig, June 20, 1944; children—Suzanne, Francis O. II. With Valley Camp Coal Co., Cleve., 1946—, pres., 1960—, chief exec. officer, 1964—, chmn. bd., 1967-79, also dir., mem. exec. com., until 1979; pres. Triple C. Enterprises, Bath, Ohio, 1979—, Richey Coal Co., Bath, 1979—; dir., mem. exec. com., compensation com. Union Savs. Assn.; dir., alt. mem. exec. com., chmn. audit com., compensation com. Oglebay Norton Co.; dir. compensation com. Sifco Industries, Inc., chmn. audit com.; dir., chmn. audit com. Banner Industries. Trustee, mem. exec. com., finance com. Center for Human Services, Cleve.; bd. dirs. Nat. Center for Productivity, Washington, 1976-77. Served to lt. USNR, 1943-46. Mem. C. of C. of U.S. (chmn. 1976-77, chmn. exec. com. 1977-78, mem. sr. council, budget, exec., U.S.-Can., public affairs, pension plan investment coms., investment advisory council), Nat. Coal Assn. (dir., chmn. 1971-72), Ohio (dir.), W.Va. (dir.) coal assns., Bituminous Coal Operators Assn. (exec. com., dir.). Clubs: Union (Cleve.); Duquesne (Pitts.); Sharon Golf (Akron, Ohio). Home: 1500 Cleveland-Mass Rd Bath OH 44210 Office: Box 171 Bath OH 44210

RICHEY, MARY ANNE REIMANN, judge; b. Shelbyville, Ind., Oct. 24, 1917; d. H. Wallace and Emma (Nading) Reimann; student Purdue U., 1937-40; J.D., U. Ariz., 1951; m. William K. Richey, Oct. 8, 1959; 1 dau., Anne Marie Richey. Admitted to Ariz. bar, 1951; dep. county atty. Pima County (Ariz.), 1952-54; asst. U.S. atty. Dist. Ariz., Tucson, 1954-59, U.S. atty., 1960; judge Superior Ct. Pima County, 1964-76, asso. presiding judge, 1972-76; U.S. dist. judge for Dist. Ariz., 1976—. Mem. Jud. Qualification Commn., 1970-76, Criminal Code Revision Commn., 1973-76, Gov's Commn. on Status of Women, 1971-73; co-chmn. Supreme Ct. Com. to Revise Civil Jury Instrns., 1971-73. Mem. adv. bd. Salvation Army, 1968—; pres. bd. dirs. YWCA, Tucson, 1968-69. Served with WASP, 1944-45. Mem. Am., Pima County bar assns., State Bar Ariz. Home: 2800 E River Rd Tucson AZ 85718 Office: US Dist Ct Room 303 US Courthouse Tucson AZ 85701

RICHEY, PHIL HORACE, mfg. co. exec.; b. Detroit, July 30, 1923; s. Lawrence Kennedy and Hazel Annsonia (Stuckey) R.; B.A. with distinction, U. Mich., 1948; m. Patricia Suzzane White, Aug. 25, 1967; children—Karen L. Richey Forrester, Ann C. Richey Zepke; stepchildren—Gregory F. Lloyd, Charles E. Lloyd III. With Detrex Chem. Industries Inc., Detroit, 1948-56, group v.p., 1962-71; with Allied Research Products Co., 1956-59, v.p. fin., 1958-59; with U.S. Chem. Milling Co., Manhattan Beach, Calif., 1959-61, v.p., 1960-61; with Olin Corp., Stamford, Conn., 1971—, corp. v.p., pres. Winchester group, 1977—; dir. Ramset-Australia. Served as 1st. lt. AUS, 1942-46. Mem. Small Arms and Ammunition Inst., Wildlife Mgmt. Inst., Phi Kappa Phi, Beta Gamma Sigma. Republican. Congregationalist. Clubs: Union League (N.Y.C.); Quinnipiqck (New Haven). Home: 46 Mill Stream Stamford CT 06903 Office: 275 Winchester Ave New Haven CT 06511

RICHEY, ROBERT LEE, architect; b. Oklahoma City, July 11, 1923; s. Horace Lee and Beulah (Wear) R.; B.Arch., U. Tex., 1949; M.Arch., Harvard, 1952; m. Elizabeth DeWitt Green, Sept. 9, 1950; children—Anne MacMurray, Elizabeth Graham, Margaret Wilson, Sarah Sansom. Partner, Nayfach-Richey, Architects, San Antonio, 1949-51; asso. Lawrie & Green, Architects, Harrisburg, Pa., 1952-61, partner, 1961-73, now dir.; partner Camco Realty Co., Harrisburg, 1969—; prin. Richey & Assos., 1973—, Rivermist Properties, 1973—; v.p. 200 N 3d, Inc., 1973—; mem. State Bd. Archtl. Examiners, 1976—. Bd. dirs. Harrisburg Community Theatre, 1955-61, v.p., 1958-61; bd. dirs. Harrisburg Art Assn., 1956-61, v.p., 1959-61; bd. dirs. Family and Childrens Service, 1961—, mem. exec. com., 1968-70, 1st v.p., 1970; bd. dirs. Harrisburg Symphony Assn., 1962—, pres., 1970—; v.p., trustee St. Timothy's Sch., Stevenson, Md. Served to lt. (j.g.) USNR, 1942-45. Mem. AIA (pres. Central Pa. chpt. 1962-63), Pa. Soc. Architects, Chi Phi. Republican. Methodist. Important works include Locust Ct. Bldg., Bell Telephone Co., Presbyn. Apts., 100 Pine Street Bldg., Harrisburg; St. Mark's Ch., Hanover, Pa.; Millersville (Pa.) State Coll. Dormitory. Home and Office: 2909 N Front St Harrisburg PA 17110

RICHEY, ROBERT WAYNE, ednl. adminstr.; b. Bradley, Ill., July 6, 1928; s. Robert Walter and Ina Lee (Thompson) R.; B.A. with honors, So. Ill. U., 1954, M.A., 1958; m. Anita Joann Sweeney, Jan. 7, 1950; children—Robert Bruce, Rebecca Lynn, Pamela Ann, Mary Beth (dec.). Budget officer State of Kans., Topeka, 1956-66; exec. sec. Iowa Bd. Regents, Des Moines, 1966—. Mem. Iowa Coordinating Council for Post High Sch. Edn., 1969—; mem. Iowa Planning Council on Developmental Disabilities, 1974—; mem. nat. adv. council Nat. Center for Higher Edn., 1974—; mem. Iowa Higher Edn. Facilities Commn., 1967-71; mem. adv. com. to Nat. Commn. on Correctional Edn., 1974-76. Served with U.S. Army, 1946-47. Mem. State Higher Edn. Exec. Officers, Nat. Assn. Governing Bds. for Colls. and Univs., Am. Soc. Public Adminstrn., Coll. and Univ. Personnel Assn. Home: 1441 7th Des Moines IA 50314 Office: Grimes State Office Bldg Des Moines IA 50319*

RICHEY, THOMAS ADAM, advt. exec.; b. Cleve., Feb. 3, 1934; s. Clyde and Elsie (Long) R.; B.S., Kent (Ohio) State U., 1960; m. LaVerle C. Augdahl, May 1, 1976; children—Kelly Rae, Michael Adam; children by previous marriage—Thomas John, Robert Joseph. Field rep. Gen. Motors Acceptance Corp., 1960-65; salesman Sebrite Corp., 1965-67; with Nationwide Advt. Service, Inc., Cleve., 1967—, regional mgr., 1969-71, v.p., 1971-73, exec. v.p., 1973—. Mem. Employment Mgmt. Assn. Clubs: Lost Nation Country, Elks. Home: 8525 Palamino Trail Chesterland OH 44026 Office: The Penthouse Cleve Plaza Cleveland OH 44115

RICHLER, MORDECAI, author; b. Montreal, Que., Can., Jan. 27, 1931; s. Moses Isaac and Lily (Rosenberg) R.; student Sir George Williams U., 1948-50; m. Florence Wood, July 27, 1959; children—Daniel, Noah, Emma, Martha, Jacob. Author: (novels) The Acrobats, 1954; Son of a Smaller Hero, 1955; A Choice of Enemies, 1957; The Apprenticeship of Duddy Kravitz, 1959; Stick Your Neck Out, 1963; Cocksure, 1967; St. Urbain's Horseman, 1971; (essays) Notes on an Endangered Species, 1974; (stories) The Street, 1975; (childrens book) Jacob Two-Two Meets The Hooded Fang, 1975; (film) The Apprenticeship of Duddy Kravitz (Acad. award nomination 1974, Writers Guild of Am. award 1974), 1974; also articles. Vis. prof. Carleton U., Ottawa, Ont., 1972-74; asso. judge for Can., Book-of-the-Month Club, 1974, also mem. editorial bd., N.Y. Recipient Gov.-Gen.'s award for lit., 1968, 71, Paris Rev. Humour prize, 1968. Guggenheim fellow, 1961, various Can. Council fellows. Club: Montreal Press. Address: 1321 Sherbrooke St W Apt 80C Montreal PQ H3Y 1J4 Canada

RICHMAN, ALAN, mag. editor; b. Bronx, N.Y., Nov. 12, 1939; s. Louis and Sonia (Carity) R.; B.A., Hunter Coll., 1960; m. Kelli Shor, June 21, 1964; children—Lincoln Seth Shor, Matthew Mackenzie Shor. Reporter, Leader-Observer, weekly newspaper, N.Y.C., 1960-61; asst. editor Modern Tire Dealer, publ., N.Y.C., 1962-64; asso. editor ASTA Travel News, N.Y.C., 1964-65; pub. relations rep. M.J. Jacobs, Inc., advt. agy., N.Y.C., 1965-66; mng. editor Modern Floor Coverings, N.Y.C., 1966-68; editor Bank Systems & Equipment, N.Y.C., 1968-79; editor Health Care Products News, N.Y.C., 1976; asso. pub. Bank Systems & Equipment, 1969-71, co-pub., 1971-73, pub. 1973—; editorial dir. Nat. Jeweler, N.Y.C., 1979—. Served with AUS, 1961-62. Recipient Jesse H. Neal certificate merit Am. Bus. Press, 1973. Mem. N.Y. Bus. Press Editors Assn. Author: Czechoslovakia in Pictures, 1969; A Book on the Chair, 1968. Home: 5 Clayton Rd Morganville NJ 07751 Office: 1515 Broadway New York NY 10036

RICHMAN, HAROLD ALAN, educator; b. Chgo., May 15, 1937; s. Leon H. and Rebecca (Klieman) R.; A.B., Harvard, 1959; M.A., U. Chgo., 1961; Ph.D., 1969; m. Marlene M. Forland, Apr. 25, 1965; children—Andrew, Robert. Asst. prof., dir. Center for Study Welfare Policy, Sch. Social Service Adminstrn., U. Chgo., 1967-69, dean, prof. social welfare policy Sch. Social Service Adminstrn., 1969-78, Hermon Dunlop Smith prof., dir. Center for Study Welfare Policy, 1978—, chmn. Univ. Com. Pub. Policy Studies, 1974-77, cons. gov. Ill., Sec. HEW; mem. Pres.'s Commn. Mental Health, 1977-78; mem. com. children and pub. policy Nat. Acad. Scis., 1977—. Bd. dirs. Chgo. Com. Fgn. and Domestic Policy, 1969-78, Southeast Chgo. Commn., 1970—, Jewish Fedn. Met. Chgo., 1970-75, Welfare Council Met. Chgo., 1970-72, Erikson Inst. Early Childhood Edn., 1972-79, Nat. Urban Coalition, 1975—, Inter-Univ. Center for Humanities and Social Scis., Dubrovnik, Yugoslavia, 1972-79. Served to capt. USPHS, 1961-63. White House fellow, Washington, 1965-66; recipient Distinguished Service citation HEW, 1970. Mem. White House Fellows Assn. (v.p. 1976-77), Am. Pub. Welfare Assn., Council Social Work Education, Chmn. editorial bd. Social Service Rev., 1970-79. Contbr. articles to profl. jours. Home: 1220 E 50th St Chicago IL 60615 Office: 969 E 60th St Chicago IL 60637

RICHMAN, JOAN, TV producer; b. St. Louis, Apr. 10, 1939; d. Stanley M. and Barbara (Friedman) R.; B.A., Wellesley (Mass.) Coll., 1961. Asst. producer WNDT, N.Y.C., 1964-65; researcher, CBS News, N.Y.C., 1961-64, researcher spl. events units, 1965-67, mgr. research Republican and Democratic nat. convs., 1968, asso. producer news coverage, including funerals Martin Luther King, Jr. and Robert Kennedy, flights of Apollo 7 and 8, 1968; producer spl. events CBS News, 1969-72; sr. producer The Reasoner Report, ABC News, 1972-75; exec. producer CBS Sports Spectacular, 1975-76, CBS News weekend broadcasts, 1976—; Recipient Nat. TV Acad. Arts and Scis. Emmy award for CBS News space coverage, 1970-71, 71-72; Alumnae Achievement award Wellesley Coll., 1973. Mem. Nat. Acad. TV Arts and Scis., Wellesley Coll. Alumnae Assn. (pres. class of 1961, 1966-70). Home: 228 W 22d St New York NY 10011 Office: CBS News 524 W 57th St New York NY 10019

RICHMAN, JOHN MARSHALL, food co. exec.; b. N.Y.C., Nov. 9, 1927; s. Arthur and Madeleine (Marshall) R.; B.A., Yale, 1949; LL.B., Harvard, 1952; m. Priscilla Frary, Sept. 3, 1951; children—Catherine Richman Roddy, Diana H. Admitted to N.Y. State bar, 1953, Ill. bar, 1973; asso. firm Leve, Hecht, Hadfield & McAlpin, N.Y.C., 1952-54; mem. law dept. Kraft, Inc., 1954-63, gen. counsel Sealtest Foods div., 1963-67, asst. gen. counsel, 1967-70, v.p., gen. counsel, 1970-73, sr. v.p., gen. counsel, 1973-75, sr. v.p. adminstrn., gen. counsel, 1975-79, dep. chmn., 1979, chmn. bd., chief exec. officer, 1979—. Congregationalist. Clubs: Executives, Econ., Mid-Am. (Chgo.); Union League (N.Y.C.); Westmoreland Country (Wilmette, Ill.). Office: Kraft Inc Kraft Ct Glenview IL 60025

RICHMAN, MARTIN FRANKLIN, lawyer; b. Newark, Feb. 23, 1930; s. Samuel L. and Betty E. (Goldstein) R.; stepson Doris (Bloom) R.; B.A. magna cum laude, St. Lawrence U., 1950; LL.B. magna cum laude, Harvard U., 1953; m. Florence E. Reif, May 6, 1962; children—Judith, Andrew. Admitted to N.Y. bar, 1953; law clk. to Judge Calvert Magruder and Chief Justice Earl Warren, 1955-57; asso., mem. firm Barrett Smith Schapiro Simon & Armstrong and predecessors, N.Y.C., 1957-66, 69—; dep. asst. atty. gen. Office Legal Counsel, Dept. Justice, Washington, 1966-69. Public mem. Adminstrv. Conf. U.S., 1970-76; bd. dirs. Community Action for Legal Services, 1977-79; trustee St. Lawrence U., 1979—. Served with U.S. Army, 1953-55. Recipient Alumni citation St. Lawrence U., 1972. Fellow Am. Bar Found.; mem. Am. Bar Assn. (council sect. adminstrv. law 1975-79), Fed. Bar Assn., N.Y. State Bar Assn., N.Y. County Lawyers Assn., Assn. Bar N.Y.C. (sec. and mem. exec. com. 1976-79, chmn. com. fed. legislation 1972-75, com. lawyer's pro bono obligations 1977—), Am. Law Inst. Office: 26 Broadway New York NY 10004

RICHMAN, MILTON SAUL, newspaperman; b. N.Y.C., Jan. 29, 1922; s. Samuel Abraham and Clara (Ganbarg) R.; student pub. schs., N.Y.C. Minor league baseball player, 1939-41; with UPI, 1944—, sports columnist, 1964—, sports editor, 1973—. Served with M.C., AUS, 1942-44. Recipient Headliners award, 1957. Mem. Assn. Profl. Baseball Players Am., Baseball Writers Assn. Am., Profl. Football Writers Assn. Am., Boxing Writers Assn. Club: Headliners. Home: 175 W 13th St New York NY 10011 Office: UPI 220 E 42d St New York NY 10017

RICHMAN, PETER MARK, actor, painter, writer; b. Phila., Apr. 16, 1927; s. Benjamin and Yetta Dora (Peck) R.; B.S. in Pharmacy, Phila. Coll. Pharmacy and Sci., 1951; student Lee Strasberg, N.Y.C., 1952-54; m. Theodora Helen Landess, May 10, 1953; children—Howard Bennett, Kelly Allyn, Lucas Dion, Orien, Roger Lloyd. Appeared in little theater, Phila., 1946-51, on radio and TV, 1948-51, Grove Theater, Nuangola, Pa., 1952, Westchester Playhouse, 1953; appeared in Broadway plays: End As A Man, 1953, Hatful of Rain, 1956-57, Masquerade, 1959; off-Broadway: End As A Man, 1953, The Dybbuk, 1954, The Zoo Story, 1960-61; numerous other theater appearances, including starring roles in stock; motion pictures: Friendly Persuasion, 1955, The Strange One, 1956, Black Orchid, 1958, The Dark Intruder, 1965, Agent for HARM, 1965, For Singles Only, 1967; appeared on TV series as Nick Cain in Cain's Hundred, 1961-62, as David in David Chapter III for CBC, 1966, as Duke Page in series Longstreet, 1971-72; guest star appearances on numerous TV shows, including: Marcus Welby, Bonanza, Twilight Zone, Mannix, The FBI, starred in TV movies: House on Greenapple Road, 1968, McCloud, 1969, Yuma, 1970, Wide World of Entertainment-Nightmare at 43 Hillcrest, 1974, Mallory, 1975, The Islander, 1978, Greatest Heroes of the Bible, 1979, as Robert Mardian in Blind Ambition, 1979; one-man shows of paintings: Am. Masters Gallery, 1967, Orlando Gallery, 1966, McKenzie Gallery, 1969, 73, Rasjad Hopkins Gallery, 1971, Goldfield Gallery, 1979 (all Los Angeles), Crocker Mus. others; group shows include: Adele Bednarz Gallery, Los Angeles, 1968, Dohan Gallery, Los Angeles, 1966, Celebrity Art Exhibits, 55-city tour, 1964-65; represented in permanent collections: Crocker Museum, Sacramento, SUNY, Albany, also numerous pvt. collections in U.S. and abroad; playwright: Heavy Heavy What Hangs Over?, 1971; mem. Actors Studio, 1954—; dir. plays: Apple of His Eye, 1954, Glass Menagerie, 1954. Mem. adv. bd. Valley Youth Orch. Assn. Served with USN, 1945-46. Registered pharmacist, Pa., N.Y. mem. Screen Actors Guild, Actors Equity Assn., AFTRA, Assn. Can. TV and Radio Artists, Acad. Motion Picture Arts and Scis. Office: care David Shapira 9100 Wilshire Blvd Beverly Hills CA 90210. *I have always been grateful be able to work in more than one medium. In a way they are all related, each solidifying and nurturing the other. I have a strong belief in God...and spiritual values. This, along with my marriage, children, and family life, has helped me enormously to express my own individuality as an artist.*

RICHMAN, ROBERT MAXWELL, author, arts center exec.; b. Connersville, Ind., Dec. 22, 1914; s. Leslie Cecil and Mildred Caldwell (Tingley) R.; A.B., Western Mich. U., 1937; A.M. (Gilmore fellow), U. Mich., 1938; m. Maida McFee, Sept. 2, 1939; children—Michael, Robin, Renn Richman Beukema. Instr. English, U. Mich., 1938-45; asso. prof. English, Adelphi U., 1945-47; founder, trustee, pres. Inst. Contemporary Arts, N.Y.C., 1945-47, Washington, 1946—, artistic dir., 1945-70; lit. and arts editor New Republic mag., 1951-54; co-founder, chmn. Univ. Consortium, 1962-66; chmn. Internat. Congress Artists and Writers, 1958-68; presdl. appointee, chmn. Pres.' Eisenhower, Kennedy and Johnson Fine Arts Commn., 1956-65; mem. exec. com. bd. trustees Nat. Cultural Center, 1958-63, J.F. Kennedy Center for Performing Arts, 1963-65; co-founder, trustee Center Arts Indian Am., Santa Fe, 1966-75; founding trustee Opera Soc. Washington, 1958-68, Meridian House Internat., 1959-70; trustee Arena Stage, Washington, 1958-68. Decorated knight Order Brit. Empire; recipient Hopwood Major Poetry award, 1945; named to Honors List of Artists and Writers, Pres. Kennedy, 1961, Pres. Johnson, 1965; recipient certificates by heads of state of France, Italy, Japan, India, USSR, Chile, also various citations by maj. profl. socs. in arts and humanities; fellow U. Chgo. Com. on Social Thought, 1960-63; Ford Found. fellow, 1964. Fellow Internat. Inst. Arts and Letters (life); mem. Tau Kappa Alpha. Club: Cosmos (Washington). Author: Noh Dance and Early Poems, 1947; Fable of Moles and Bees, 1948; Arts at Mid-Century, 1954; Colours of Darkness, 1964; Endangered Phoenix, 1976; Seamusic and Seascapes, 1979; An Eloquent Geology, 1979; Aspects of the Several Arts, 1980; Rites of the Arts, 1981. Home: Tobermory Cranberry Isles ME 04625 Office: 3102 R St NW Washington DC 20007

RICHMAN, SUMNER, educator; b. Boston, Dec. 15, 1929; s. Abraham and Ethel (Kramer) R.; B.A., Hartwick Coll., 1951; M.A., U. Mass., 1953; Ph.D., U. Mich., 1957; m. Joyce L. Clements, Aug. 17, 1952; children—Nancy, Robert, Jeffrey. Instr., Lawrence U., Appleton, Wis., 1957-59, asst. prof., 1959-65, asso. prof., 1965-70, prof. biology, 1970—; instr. Marine Biol. Lab., Woods Hole, Mass., 1969-71. Mem. register of experts in aquatic scis. FAO, 1970—. Chmn. Fox Valley Council on Human Rights, 1968-70. NSF grantee,

1958, 62. Mem. Am. Inst. Biol. Scis., AAAS, Ecol. Soc. Am., Am. Soc. Limnology and Oceanography, Internat. Congress Limnology, Sigma Xi. Contbr. articles profl. jours. Home: 1625 Ravinia Pl Appleton WI 54911

RICHMOND, DAVID WALKER, lawyer; b. Silver Hill, W.Va., Apr. 20, 1914; s. David Walker and Louise (Finlaw) R.; LL.B., George Washington U., 1937; m. Gladys Evelyn Mallard, Dec. 19, 1936; children—David Walker, Nancy L. Admitted to D.C. bar, 1936, Ill. bar, 1946, Md. bar, 1950; partner firm Miller & Chevalier, Washington; lectr. fed. taxation. Served from ensign to lt. comdr. USNR, 1942-46. Decorated Bronze Star; recipient Alumni Achievement award George Washington U., 1976. Fellow Am. Bar Found., Am. Coll. Trial Lawyers; mem. Am. Law Inst., Am. Bar Assn. (chmn. taxation sect. 1955-57, ho. of dels. 1958-60). Republican. Methodist. Mason. Clubs: Union League (Chgo.); Metropolitan, (Washington). Contbr. to profl. jours. Home: 551 Putting Green Ln Longboat Key FL 33548 Office: 1700 Pennsylvania Ave NW Washington DC 20006

RICHMOND, FREDERICK WILLIAM, congressman, industrialist; b. Boston, Nov. 15, 1923; s. George and Frances (Rosen) R.; student Harvard, 1942-43; A.B., Boston U., 1945; LL.D., Pratt Inst.; 1 son, William McNeir. Engaged in import-export bus., 1945-49; chmn. bd. Brubaker Tool Corp., Millersburg, Pa., 1950-57; chmn. exec. com., dir. Nat. Valve & Mfg. Co., Pitts., 1955-75, Landers, Frary & Clark, New Britain, Conn., 1958-60; chmn. bd. Houston Oil Field Material Co., Inc., 1958-62, Pub. Service Radio Network, Inc., N.Y.C., 1961-65; pres. F. W. Richmond & Co., Inc., 1961—; dir. Walco Nat. Corp., N.Y.C., and subsidiaries, Carthage Machine Co., N.Y., Fed. Forge Inc., Lansing, Mich., Gen. Industries, Elyria, Ohio, Capitol Machine Co., Columbus, Ohio, Mitts & Merrill Inc., Saginaw, Mich., Nat. Casket Co., Boston; chmn. bd. Walco-Linck Corp., Clifton, N.J., 1961—. Mem. City Council, City of N.Y., 1973-75; mem. 94th-96th Congresses from 14th N.Y. Dist. Chmn. emeritus Gov.'s Com. on Sch. Achievement; mem. N.Y.C. Commn. on Human Rights, 1962-67; pres. Community Improvement Corp. of Manhattan, Neighborhood Study Clubs, Inc.; chmn. N.Y.C. Com. for Employment Ex-offenders; pres. Frederick W. Richmond Found.; hon. chmn. Young Audiences, Inc. Chmn. emeritus Carnegie Hall Corp., N.Y.C.; trustee Citizens Union, Citizens Budget Commn.; mem. N.Y. Council Arts. Served with USNR, 1943-45. Recipient Outstanding Young Man award Jr. C. of C., N.Y.C., 1955. Mem. Urban League Greater N.Y. (hon. pres.). Democrat. Author: The Need for Businessmen to Become Active in Politics: Corporate Integration. Office: 743 Fifth Ave New York NY 10022 also 147 Remsen St Brooklyn NY 11201

RICHMOND, HENRY RUSSELL, cons.; b. Ft. Riley, Kan., July 13, 1915; s. Henry Russell and Ruby (Fowler) R.; B.Mech. and Elec. Engring., Tulane U., 1937; postgrad. U. So. Cal., 1955; m. Margaret Eloisa Wertz, Nov. 7, 1939; children—Margaret Eloisa (Mrs. James T. Fox), Henry Russell III, Douglas W., Patricia (Mrs. Thomas Mehlberg). Engr., Cal. Electric Power Co., 1938-41; with Bonneville Power Adminstrn., 1941-54, field operations officer, 1963-66, dep. adminstr., 1966-67, acting adminstr., 1967, adminstr., 1967-72; asst. to gen. mgr. Gt. Lakes Carbon Corp., Los Angeles, then sales mgr., 1954-63; dir. Kaiser Aluminum & Chem. Corp., Oakland, Cal.; cons. Boeing Co., Seattle, 1972—. Mem. Pacific N.W. River Basins Commn., 1967—; chmn. U.S. entity Columbia River Treaty, 1967—. Cited by sec. of interior, 1967. Home: 12640 Abra Dr San Diego CA 92128

RICHMOND, JAMES ELLIS, food co. exec.; b. Chgo., Feb. 16, 1938; s. Kenneth E. and Irene M. (Anderson) R.; B.B.A., Case Western Reserve U., 1960; m. Karen Ann Ryder, Oct. 6, 1956; children—Scott, Brian, Ann, Susan. Sr. auditor Ernst & Ernst, Cleve., 1960-64; treas. Cook United, Inc., Cleve., 1964-75; treas. Fairmont Foods Co., Houston, 1975—. C.P.A., Ohio. Mem. Am. Inst. C.P.A.'s., Ohio Soc. C.P.A.'s. Lutheran (treas. 1970-75). Home: 1906 Thousand Pines St Humble TX 77339 Office: 333 W Loop N Houston TX 77024

RICHMOND, JULIUS BENJAMIN, physician, govt. ofcl.; b. Chgo., Sept. 26, 1916; s. Jacob and Anna (Dayno) R.; B.S., U. Ill., 1937, M.S., M.D., 1939; m. Rhee Chidekel, June 3, 1937; children—Barry J., Charles Allen, Dale Keith (dec.). Intern Cook County Hosp., Chgo., 1939-41, resident, 1941-42, 46; resident Municipal Contagious Disease Hosp., Chgo., 1941; mem. faculty U. Ill. Med. Sch., Chgo., 1946-52, prof. pediatrics, 1950-53, dir. Inst. Juvenile Research, 1952-53; prof., chmn. dept. pediatrics Coll. Medicine, State U. N.Y. at Syracuse, 1953-65, dean med. faculty, chmn. dept. pediatrics, 1965-70; prof. child psychiatry and human devel., prof., chmn. dept. preventive and social medicine Harvard Med. Sch., 1971—, also faculty Harvard Sch. Pub. Health; psychiatrist-in-chief Children's Hosp. Med. Center, Boston, 1971—; dir. Judge Baker Guidance Center, Boston, 1971-77; asst. sec. health and surgeon gen. HEW, 1977—; mem. Pres.'s Commn. on Mental Health, 1977—. Nat. dir. Project Head Start, dir. Office Health Affairs OEO, 1965-66. Served to flight surgeon USAAF, 1942-46. Recipient Agnes Bruce Greig Sch. award, 1966; C. Anderson Aldrich award Am. Acad. Pediatrics, 1966; Parents Mag. award, 1966; Distinguished Service award Office Econ. Opportunity, 1967; Martha May Eliot award Am. Pub. Health Assn., 1970. Fellow Am. Orthopsychiat. Assn.; distinguished fellow Am. Psychiat. Assn.; hon. mem. Am. Acad. Child Psychiatry; asso. mem. New Eng. Council Child Psychiatry; mem. Inst. Medicine of Nat. Acad. Scis., AMA, Am. Pediatric Soc., Am. Acad. Pediatrics, Soc. Pediatric Research, Am. Psychosomatic Soc., Am. Pub. Health Assn., Sigma Xi, Alpha Omega Alpha, Phi Eta Sigma. Author: Pediatric Diagnosis, 1962; Currents in American Medicine, 1969. Home: 79 Beverly Rd Chestnut Hill MA 02167 Office: 200 Independence Ave SW Washington DC 20201

RICHMOND, SAMUEL BERNARD, educator; b. Boston, Oct. 14, 1919; s. David E. and Freda (Braman) R.; A.B. cum laude, Harvard, 1940; M.B.A., Columbia, 1948, Ph.D., 1951; m. Evelyn Ruth Kravitz, Nov. 26, 1944; children—Phyllis Gail, Douglas Emerson, Clifford Owen. Mem. faculty Columbia, 1946-76, asso. prof., 1957-60, prof. econ. and statistics, 1960-76, asso. dean Grad. Sch. Bus., 1971-72, acting dean, 1972-73; dean Owen Grad. Sch. Mgmt., Vanderbilt U., 1976—; vis. prof. U. Sherbrooke (Que.), 1967, U. Buenos Aires (Argentina), 1964, 65, Case Inst. Tech., Cleve., 1958-59, Fordham U., N.Y.C., 1952-53; dir. IMS Internat. Inc., N.Y.C., P.S.T. Group Inc., N.Y.C., Corbin Ltd., N.Y.C.; past dir. Brandon Applied Systems Co., N.Y.C., Sci. Resources Inc., N.Y.C.; cons. to maj. comml., ednl., profl. and govtl. orgns. Trustee Ramapo Coll. N.J., 1975-76. Served to 1st lt. USAAF, 1943-45. Recipient Honor award CAB, 1971. Mem. Am. Statis. Assn. (chmn. adv. com. research to CAB 1966-74, dir. 1965-67), Am. Econ. Assn., Inst. Mgmt. Sci., Ops. Research Soc. Am., Beta Gamma Sigma. Author: Operations Research for Management Decisions, 1968; Statistical Analysis, 1957, 2d. edit., 1964; Regulation and Competition in Air Transportation, 1961. Home: 5404 Camelot Rd Brentwood TN 37027 Office: Owen Grad Sch Mgmt Vanderbilt U Nashville TN 37203

RICHTER, BURTON, physicist, educator; b. N.Y.C., Mar. 22, 1931; s. Abraham and Fanny (Pollack) R.; B.S., Mass. Inst. Tech., 1952, Ph.D., 1956; m. Laurose Becker, July 1, 1960; children—Elizabeth, Matthew. Research asso. Stanford, 1956-60, asst. prof. physics, 1960-63, asso. prof., 1963-67, prof., 1967—; cons. NSF, AEC. Recipient E.O. Lawrence medal ERDA, 1975; Nobel prize in physics, 1976. Fellow Am. Phys. Soc., N.Y. Acad. Sci.; mem. Nat. Acad. Sci. Research elementary particle physics. Contbr. articles to profl. publs. Office: Stanford U Stanford CA 94305

RICHTER, CHARLES FRANCIS, seismologist; b. nr. Hamilton, Ohio, Apr. 26, 1900; student U. So. Calif., 1916-17; A.B., Stanford, 1920; Ph.D., Calif. Inst. Tech., 1928; D.Sc. (hon.), Calif. Luth. Coll., 1977; m. Lillian Brand, July 18, 1928 (dec. Nov. 1972). Asst. Seismol. Lab., Carnegie Insts. of Washington, Pasadena, Calif., 1927-36; asst. prof. seismology Calif. Inst. Tech., 1937-47, asso. prof., 1947-52, prof., 1952-70, emeritus, 1970—; mem. Lindvall, Richter & Assos., Los Angeles, cons. Mem. Calif. Bd. Registration Geologists and Geophysicists, 1973-77, Calif. Atty. Gen.'s Environ. Task Force. Fulbright research scholar Tokyo U., Japan, 1959-60. Fellow Geol. Soc. Am., Royal Astron. Soc., Am. Geophys. Union, Royal Soc. New Zealand; mem. Town Hall Los Angeles, Seismol. Soc. Am. (hon., medalist 1977), Assn. Engr. Geologists (hon.), Sigma Xi. Author: (with B. Gutenberg) Seismicity of the Earth, rev. edit., 1954; Elementary Seismology, 1958. Contbr. to Internal Constitution of the Earth, rev. edit., 1951. Pub. earthquake magnitude scale, 1935. Home: 594 Villa Zanita Altadena CA 91001 Office: 825 W Colorado Blvd Suite 200 Los Angeles CA 90041

RICHTER, DONALD PAUL, lawyer; b. New Britain, Conn., Feb. 15, 1924; s. Paul John and Helen (Racoske) R.; A.B., Bates Coll., 1947; LL.B., Yale U., 1950; m. Jane Frances Gumpright, Aug. 10, 1946; children—Christopher Dean, Cynthia Louise. Admitted to N.Y. bar, 1951, Conn. bar, 1953; asso. firm Winthrop, Stimson, Putnam & Roberts, N.Y.C., 1950-52; partner firm Murtha, Cullina, Richter and Pinney, Hartford, Conn., 1954—. Trustee Bates Coll., 1962—, Manchester (Conn.) Meml. Hosp., 1963—, Hartford Sem. Found., 1973—, Suffield Acad., 1974—; bd. dirs. Met. YMCA Greater Hartford, 1970—, pres., 1976—; mem. nat. council YMCA, 1978—; bd. dirs. Church Homes, 1967; trustee, v.p. Silver Bay Assn., 1971—. Served with USNR, 1943-46. Fellow Am. Coll. Probate Counsel; mem. Am., Conn. bar assns., Phi Beta Kappa, Delta Sigma Rho. Congregationalist. Rotarian. Home: 140 Boulder Rd Manchester CT 06040 Office: 101 Pearl St Hartford CT 06103

RICHTER, EARL EDWARD, heat exchanger mfg. co. exec.; b. Twin Lakes, Wis., Oct. 16, 1923; s. John Benjamin and Emma Augusta (Kautz) R.; B.B.A., U. Wis., Madison, 1948; m. Carlista Mae Dean, Sept. 12, 1943; children—Susan Dianne, Robert Dean. With Modine Mfg. Co., Racine, Wis., 1948—, v.p., gen. mgr., 1963-74, pres., 1974—, chief operating officer, 1974, chief exec. officer, 1974—; dir. M&I Am. Bank & Trust Co. Served with USAAF, 1943-45. C.P.A., Wis. Mem. Racine Mfrs. Assn. (dir.), Conf. Board, Am. Mgmt. Assn., Wis. Mfrs. and Commerce Assn. (dir.). Lutheran. Clubs: Racine Country; Milw. Athletic. Home: 3735 Indiana Ln Racine WI 53405 Office: 1500 Dekoven Ave Racine WI 53401

RICHTER, GEORGE HOLMES, educator; b. Gainesville, Tex., May 22, 1904; s. George Alexander and Edna (Scott) R.; A.B., Rice Inst., 1926, A.M., 1927, Ph.D., 1929; m. Dorothy Dean Hannon, June 17, 1929; 1 dau., Katherine Scott. NRC fellow Cornell U., 1929-31; instr. chemistry Rice Inst., 1931-37, asst. prof., 1938-45, asso. prof., 1945-47, prof., 1947—, chmn. dept., 1947-61, dean, 1950-61, dean Grad. Sch., 1961-72. Mem. Deutsche Chemische Gesellschaft, Am. Chem. Soc. (chmn. Southeastern Tex. sect. 1944), Houston Philos. Soc., Phi Beta Kappa, Sigma Xi, Phi Lambda Upsilon. Club: Rice Faculty. Author: Textbook of Organic Chemistry, 1938; Laboratory Manual of Elementary Organic Chemistry, 1940. Contbr. to tech. jours. Home: 1904 Canterbury Houston TX 77030

RICHTER, GEORGE ROBERT, JR., lawyer; b. Blue Island, Ill., July 8, 1910; s. George Robert and Edith (Mason) R.; A.B., U. So. Calif., 1930, LL.B., 1933; m. Betty Jane Dempsey, May 12, 1938; children—Georgann, Craig Wallace. Admitted to Calif. bar, 1933; asso. firm Mathes & Sheppard, Los Angeles, 1933-34, 36-41, partner, 1941-45; with legal dept. Security-1st Nat. Bank, Los Angeles, 1935-36; partner Sheppard, Mullin, Richter & Hampton, Los Angeles, 1945—. Chmn. exec. com. Nat. Conf. Commrs. Uniform State Laws, 1957-59, pres., 1959-61; chmn. Calif. Commn. Uniform State Laws, 1960-73. Mem. Am. (ho. of dels. 1959-61, chmn. com. comml. laws 1955-59, chmn. conf. personal fin. law 1964—, chmn. sect. corp., banking and bus. law 1962-63, chmn. com. class actions 1974-76), Los Angeles County (chmn. com. legal problems in disaster 1956-57, chmn. sect. comml. law and bankruptcy 1968-69) bar assns., State Bar Calif. (chmn. com. uniform comml. code 1949-50), Assn. Bar City N.Y., Am. Law Inst., Scribes. Clubs: Chancery (Los Angeles); Stock Exchange; Big Canyon Country (Newport Beach, Calif.). Mem. permanent editorial bd. Uniform Comml. Code, 1954—. Home: 10 Rue Biarritz Newport Beach CA 92660 Office: 333 S Hope St 48th Floor Los Angeles CA 90071 also 500 Newport Center Dr Newport Beach CA 92660

RICHTER, GOETZ WILFRIED, pathologist, educator; b. Berlin, Germany, Dec. 19, 1922; s. Werner and Ursula (Meyer) R.; came to U.S., 1939, naturalized, 1944; B.A., Williams Coll., 1943; M.D., Johns Hopkins U., 1948; postgrad. (Lewis Cass Ledyard fellow) Cornell U., 1951-53; m. Mary Lucretia Henry, Dec. 28, 1946; children—James W., Elizabeth M., Marianne. Intern N.Y. Hosp., Cornell Med. Center, N.Y.C., 1948-49, asst. resident, 1949-51; practice medicine specializing in pathology, N.Y.C., 1955-67, Rochester, N.Y., 1967—; asst. prof. pathology Cornell U. Med. Coll., N.Y.C., 1955-58, asso. prof., 1958-67; vis. investigator Rockefeller Inst., N.Y.C., 1956-57; asso. attending pathologist N.Y. Hosp., N.Y.C., 1957-67; prof. pathology U. Rochester (N.Y.) Sch. Medicine, 1967—, pathologist Strong Meml. Hosp., 1967—. Sci. cons. to NIH, 1963—. Served with U.S. Army, 1944-46, USNR, 1953-55. Diplomate Am. Bd. Pathology. Rockefeller Found. traveling fellow, 1957-58. Mem. Am. Assn. Pathologists, Fedn. Socs. Exptl. Biology, Internat. Acad. Pathology, Soc. Exptl. Biology and Medicine, Harvey Soc., Am. Soc. Cell Biology, Electron Microscopy Soc. Am., N.Y. Electron Microscope Soc. (pres. 1965-66), AAAS, Sigma Xi, Phi Beta Kappa, Phi Beta Pi. Editor (founder) Internat. Rev. Exptl. Pathology, 1962—. Editorial bd. Am. Jour. Pathology, 1966—, Beiträge zur Pathologie, 1971-78, Pathology Research and Practice, 1978—. Author monographs, articles in profl. jours. Research in exptl. pathology, especially at subcellular level, disorders of iron metabolism. Home: 155 Avon Rd Rochester NY 14625 Office: 601 Elmwood Ave Rochester NY 14642

RICHTER, HARRY LENWOOD, JR., ins. co. exec.; b. Bethlehem, Pa., Oct. 17, 1940; s. Harry Lenwood and Ruth Naomi R.; student Gettysburg Coll., 1962; m. Anita Grace Oliver, Jan. 28, 1961; children—Stuart Matthew, Todd Andrew. Trainee, Am. Casualty Co., Reading, Pa., 1962-64; with Ins. Co. of N.Am., INA Reinsurance, INA Corp., INA Internat. Corp., 1964-77; sr. v.p. Reliance Ins. Co., Phila., 1977—. Republican. Lutheran. Home: 420 James St King of Prussia PA 19406 Office: 4 Penn Center Plaza Philadelphia PA 19101

RICHTER, JOHN BEST, stock broker; b. Phila., Mar. 18, 1924; s. Thomas D. and Anna Regina (Best) R.; B.S., U. Pa., 1948; m. Eleanor Muldoon, Oct. 27, 1948; children—Mary Ann (Mrs. Frank Morell), Susan, Margaret Mary, John Bernard, Ellen, Joseph, Michael. Investment research and investment banking Butcher & Sherrerd, Phila., 1948-61, partner, 1961-73; partner Butcher & Singer, Phila., 1973-76; sr. v.p. Butcher & Singer, Inc., 1976-77; mgr. corp. services dept. McDonald & Co., Bala Cynwyd, Pa., 1977-78; 1st v.p., mgr. invested asset dept. Paine, Webber, Jackson & Curtis, Inc., Bala Cynwyd, 1978-79; v.p. Federated Securities Corp., Bala Cynwyd, 1979—. Served to capt. AUS, 1943-46, 51-52; CBI. Decorated Bronze Star medal. Mem. Securities Industry Assn. (governing council, past chmn. Mid Atlantic Dist.), Investment Bankers Assn. (past gov., past chmn. Eastern Pa. group), Nat. Assn. Securities Dealers (past chmn. Dist. 11), Mcpl. Bond Club of Phila. (past pres.), Bond Club, Investment Traders Assn. Clubs: Wall Street (N.Y.C.); Whitemarsh Valley Country; Seaview (N.J.) Country, Wissahickon Skating. Home: 2016 Hilltop Rd Flourtown PA 19031 Office: 701 GSB Bldg Belmont and City Aves Bala Cynwyd PA 19004

RICK, CHARLES MADEIRA, JR., geneticist, educator; b. Reading, Pa., Apr. 30, 1915; s. Charles Madeira and Miriam Charlotte (Yeager) R.; B.S., Pa. State U., 1937; A.M., Harvard U., 1939, Ph.D., 1940; m. Martha Elizabeth Overholts, Sept. 3, 1938; children—Susan Charlotte Rick Baldi, John Winfield. Asst. plant breeder W. Atlee Burpee Co., Lompoc, Calif., 1936, 37; instr., jr. geneticist U. Calif., Davis, 1940-44, asst. prof., asst. geneticist, 1944-49, asso. prof., asso. geneticist, 1949-55, prof., geneticist, 1955—; chmn. coordinating com. Tomato Genetics Coop., 1950—; mem. genetics study sect. NIH, 1958-62; mem. Galapagos Internat. Sci. Project, 1964; mem. genetic biology panel NSF, 1971-72; mem. nat. plant genetics resources bd. Dept. Agr., 1975—; Carnegie vis. prof. U. Hawaii, 1963; vis. prof. Universidade Sao Paulo, Brazil, 1965; vis. scientist U. P.R., 1968; centennial lectr. Ont. Agr. Coll. U. Guelph (Ont., Can.), 1974. Fellow Calif. Acad. Sci., AAAS (Campbell award 1959); mem. Nat. Acad. Scis., Bot. Soc. Am. (Merit award 1976), Am. Soc. Hort. Sci. (M.A. Blake award 1974, Vaughan Research award 1946). Contbr. articles in field to books and sci. jours. Office: U Calif Davis CA 95616

RICKART, CHARLES EARL, educator, mathematician; b. Osage City, Kans., June 28, 1913; s. Charles Day and Ola May (Brewer) R.; B.A., U. Kans., 1937, M.A., 1938; Ph.D., U. Mich., 1941; m. Annabel Esther Erickson, Mar. 31, 1942; children—Mark Charles, Eric Alan, Thomas Melvin. Peirce instr. math. Harvard, 1941-43; mem. faculty Yale, 1943—, prof. math., 1959—, chmn. dept., 1959-65, Percey F. Smith prof. math., 1963—. Mem. AAAS, AAUP, Conn. Acad. Arts and Scis., Sigma Xi. Author: General Theory of Banach Algebras, 1960; Natural Function Algebras, 1979. Home: 131 Whitney Ridge Terr North Haven CT 06473 Office: Dept Math Yale Univ New Haven CT 06520

RICKELS, KARL, physician, educator; b. Wilhelmshaven, Germany, Aug. 17, 1924; s. Karl E. and Stephanie (Roehrhoff) R.; M.D., U. Muenster, 1951; m. Rosalind Wilson, June 27, 1964; children—Laurence Arthur, Stephen W., Michael R. Came to U.S., 1954, naturalized, 1960. Intern, Dortmund (Germany) Hosp., 1951-52; postgrad. tng. U. Erlangen, U. Frankfurt, City Hosp. Kassel, 1952-54; resident in psychiatry Mental Health Inst., Cherokee, Iowa, 1954-55, Hosp. U. Pa., Phila., 1955-57; instr. U. Pa., Phila., 1957-59, asso., 1959-60, asst. prof., 1960-64, asso. prof., 1964-69, prof. psychiatry, 1969—, prof. pharmacology, 1973—, Stuart and Emily B.H. Mudd prof. human behavior and reprodn., 1977—, dir. psychopharmacology research unit, 1964—, attending physician, dir. psychopharmacology research unit, 1964—; chief psychiatry Phila. Gen. Hosp., 1975-77. Fellow Am. Coll. Neuropsychopharmacology (charter), Acad. Psychosomatic Medicine, Am. Psychiat. Assn., Collegium International Neuro-Psychopharmacologicum, Royal Soc. Medicine; mem. AMA, Am. Soc. Clin. Pharmacology and Therapeutics, Soc. Pharmacology and Exptl. Therapeutics, Am. Psychosomatic Soc. Contbr. numerous articles to profl. publs. Home: 1518 Sweetbriar Rd Gladywne PA 19035 Office: 203 Piersol Bldg Hosp of U Pa 3400 Spruce St Philadelphia PA 19104

RICKER, JOHN BOYKIN, JR., fin. holding co. exec.; b. Augusta, Ga., Nov. 20, 1917; s. John B. and Emily Clark (Denny) R.; B.A., Southwestern Coll., 1938; m. Jane Duncan Darling, Sept. 30, 1950; children—John, Robb Duncan. Mgr. Cotton Fire and Marine Underwriters, Memphis, 1955-63; pres., chief exec. officer Marine Office of Am., N.Y.C., 1964-74; chmn. bd., pres., chief exec. officer Continental Corp., N.Y.C., 1976—; dir. Phoenix Assurance Co. N.Y., Phoenix Assurance Co., Ltd., Almaden Vineyards, Inc., Ins. Corp. of Ireland, Ltd., Mfrs. Hanover Trust Co., Continental Corp., Continental Ins. Cos. Bd. dirs. Jr. Achievement, Memphis, 1961-63; Southwestern Coll., 1967-71; bd. dirs. Youth Services of Memphis, treas., v.p., 1959-63; div. comdr. Shelby United Neighbors Campaign, 1961; bd. dirs. United Way Tri State and Economic Devel. Council N.Y.C.; trustee Coll. Ins. Served with USNR, 1942-46. Decorated Bronze Star. Mem. Property Casualty Ins. Council, Am. Inst. Property and Liability Underwriters (trustee), N.Y. C. of C., Am. Inst. Marine Underwriters (past pres.), Asso. Aviation Underwriters (past dir.), U.S. Salvage Assn. Republican. Episcopalian. Clubs: Baltusrol Country, India House. Home: 25 Devon Rd Essex Fells NJ 07021 Office: 80 Maiden Ln New York NY 10038

RICKERD, DONALD SHERIDAN, found. exec.; b. Smiths Falls, Ont., Can., Nov. 8, 1931; s. Harry M. and Evelyn Mildred (Sheridan) R.; student St. Andrews U. (Scotland), 1951-52; B.A., Queen's U. (Can.), 1953; B.A. (Rotary Found. fellow), Oxford U. (Eng.), 1955, M.A., 1963; postgrad., Osgoode Hall Law Sch. (Can.), 1959; m. Julie Rekai, Dec. 8, 1968; 1 son, Christopher. Called to Ont. bar, 1959, created Queen's counsel, 1978; asso. firm Fasken & Calvin, Toronto, 1957-61; registrar, lectr. history, asst. prof. law Faculty of Adminstrv. Studies, York U., Toronto, 1961-68; pres. Donner Canadian Found., also W.H. Donner Found., Inc. N.Y.C., 1968—. Chmn. council Ont. Coll. Art, Toronto; mem. bd. Central Hosp., Toronto; mem. Royal Commn. Concerning Certain Activities of Royal Can. Mounted Police, 1977—. Mem. Canadian Bar Assn., County of York Law Assn., Toronto Lawyers Club, Bd. Trade Met. Toronto, United Oxford and Cambridge Univ. Club (London, Eng.). Club: Univ. (Toronto). Home: 21 Elm Ave Toronto ON M4W 1M9 Canada Office: 630 Fifth Ave Room 2452 New York NY 10020

RICKETSON, FRANK HENRY, JR., found. trustee; b. Leavenworth, Kans., Oct. 2, 1895; s. Frank H. and Mary M. (Connor) R.; student U. Ky., 1916-17; LL.B., U. Denver, 1919; m. Maizie Donnegan (dec.); 1 son, Frank Henry III. Staff writer Kansas City Star and Denver Post, then engaged in motion picture prodn.; pres. Fox Inter-Mountain Theatres, 1934-56, Roxy Theatre Co., 1956-62; v.p., gen. mgr. Nat. Theatres, 1956-62; pres. Nat. War Fund of Colo., 1941-46; dir. Pub. Service Co. of Colo., 1946-78, United Banks Colo., Inc., 1944-78, Cheyenne Newspapers, Inc. Trustee, John F. Kennedy Center for Performing Arts, 1958-68; chmn. emeritus Central City Opera House Assn.; pres. Roundup Riders of Rockies, 1947-73, chmn. bd., 1973—. Past campaign mgr., pres., chmn. bd. Mile High United Way (hon. mem. award 1964); v.p. United Community Funds and Councils Am. Hon. life trustee U. Denver; trustee Denver Mus., Natural History. Recipient Denver Creativity award, 1957, Civis Princeps, Regis Coll., 1961, Internat. Sertoma, outstanding citizen award, 1964, Nat. Exec. award Delta Sigma Phi; citation NCCJ, 1973. Mem. Phi Delta Theta, Phi Alpha Delta, Tau Kappa Alpha, Delta

Sigma Pi. Clubs: Denver Country, Denver, Denver Athletic. Author: The Management of Motion Picture Theatres, 1938; Opportunity Needs Selling, 1946; Europe After the Marshall Plan, 1952; Gems From a Thousand Sources, 1964. Home: 1373 Fillmore Denver CO 80206

RICKETTS, JOHN ADRIAN, educator, chemist; b. Lakewood, Ohio, Feb. 29, 1924; s. Edwin Virgil and Florence (Magaw) R.; B.S., Ind. U., 1948; M.S., Western Res. U., 1950, Ph.D., 1953; m. Lucille Reininga, Feb. 5, 1948; children—Thomas Grant, Sarah Margaret. Mem. faculty DePauw U., 1952—, prof. chemistry, 1962—, Simeon Smith prof. chemistry, 1976—; summer vis. prof. Western Res. U., 1961, Ind. U., 1964, Purdue U., 1967; vis. prof. chemistry Univ. Coll., Dublin, 1976; vis. scientist Am. Chem. Soc., 1960—; cons. to industry. Served with AUS, 1943-45. Mem. Am. Chem. Soc., Electrochem. Soc., Faraday Soc., Sigma Xi, Alpha Chi Sigma, Phi Lambda Upsilon, Lambda Chi Alpha. Contbr. articles in field. Home: 702 Highridge St Greencastle IN 46135

RICKEY, GEORGE WARREN, artist, sculptor, educator; b. South Bend, Ind., June 6, 1907; s. Walter J. and Grace (Landon) R.; student Trinity Coll., Glenalmond, Scotland, 1921-26; B.A., Balliol Coll., Oxford U., 1929, M.A., 1940; postgrad. Académie Lhote, Paris, 1929-30, Inst. Fine Arts, N.Y. U., 1945-46, State U. Ia., 1947, Inst. Design, Chgo., 1948-49; hon. doctorates Union Coll., Schenectady, 1973, Ind. U., 1974, Kalamazoo Coll., 1977, York U. (Can.), 1978; m. Edith Leighton, May 24, 1947; children—Stuart Ross, Philip J. L. Tchr. Groton Sch., 1930-33, artist-in-residence Olivet Coll., 1937-39, Kalamazoo Coll., 1939-40, Knox Coll., 1940-41; head dept. art, Muhlenberg Coll., 1941-42, 46-48; asso. prof. design Ind. U., 1949-55; prof. Tulane U., 1955-61, head dept., 1955-59; prof. art Sch. Architecture Rensselaer Poly. Inst., Troy, N.Y., 1962-65; sculptor DAAD Art Program, Berlin, Germany, 1968-69, 71-72. Exhibited Denver Mus., 1945, 48, Met. Mus. Art, 1951, Pa. Acad. Ann., 1952-54, Whitney Mus., 1952-53, 64, Mus. Modern Art, 1959, Albright-Knox Gallery, 1965, Mus. Modern Art Internat. Council, 1965, Stedelijk Mus., Amsterdam, Holland, 1965, Mus. Tel Aviv, 1965, St. Louis Bicentennial Sculpture Exhbn., 1965, Annely Juda Fine Art, London, 1973-74, Dag Hammerskjold Plaza, N.Y.C., 1977, other U.S. and fgn. galleries; one man shows John Herron Art Mus., Indpls., 1953, Delgado Mus., New Orleans, 1955, Kraushaar Gallery, 1955, 1959, Amerika Haus, Hamburg, Germany, 1957, Santa Barbara Mus., 1960, Kunstverein, Dûsseldorf, Germany, 1962, Kunsthalle, Hamburg, 1962, Inst. Contemporary Arts, Boston, 1964, Corcoran Gallery, Washington, 1966, Kestner Gesellschaft, Hannover, Nationalgalerie, Berlin, Calif. Inst. Tech., Amerika Haus, Berlin, 1979, Guggenheim Mus., 1979, numerous others; represented in permanent collection Dallas Mus., Kunsthalle, Hamburg, Whitney Mus., Mus. Modern Art, Albright-Knox Gallery, Tate Gallery, London, U. Glasgow, U. Heidelberg, Corcoran Gallery of Arts, Washington, others, also pvt. collections; executed commn. Ft. Worth City Hall, 1974, Fed. Courthouse, Honolulu, 1976, Tech. U., Ulm, Germany, 1977, Ruhr U., Bochum, Ger., 1978, K.B. Plaza, New Orleans, 1978; recipient Fine Arts medal AIA, 1972, Skowhegan medal for sculpture Skowhegan Sch. Painting and Sculpture, 1973; Ind. Arts Commn. award for sculpture, 1975; Creative Arts Award medal Brandeis U., 1979; Guggenheim fellow, 1960-62. Mem. Nat. Inst. Arts and Letters, Coll. Art Assn. Episcopalian. Club: Century Assn. (N.Y.C.). Author: Constructivism: Origins and Evolution, 1967. Contbr. to publs. in field. Home: RD 2 East Chatham NY 12060

RICKEY, GERARD BRANDON, lawyer; b. Dallas, May 28, 1941; s. Harry Wynn and Sara Patterson (Brandon) R.; B.A., So. Methodist U., 1963, J.D., 1966; m. Dorothy Jean Matthew, Aug. 21, 1965. Admitted to Tex. bar, 1966, since practiced in Dallas; asso. firm Woodruff, Hill, Kendall & Smith, 1966-72; partner firm Pace, Chandler & Rickey, 1974—. Served with AUS, 1958-66. Mem. Dallas Bar Assn., Tex. Trial Lawyers Assn., Pi Kappa Alpha, Phi Eta Sigma, Phi Beta Kappa, Delta Theta Phi. Asso. editor Southwestern Law Jour., 1966. Home: 3215 Hanover St Dallas TX 75225 Office: 3400 Republic Nat Bank Bldg Dallas TX 75201

RICKEY, MARTIN EUGENE, nuclear physicist, educator; b. Memphis, Aug. 4, 1927; s. Albert Knox and Nell Matile (Ritnour) R.; student U. Tenn., 1944-45, 46-47; B.S., Southwestern U. at Memphis, 1949; postgrad. Columbia, 1949-50; Ph.D., U. Wash., 1958; m. Barbara Ruth Weibel, July 6, 1961 (div.); children—Ruth Marie, Albert Edwin, Kirsten Emilia. Technician Brookhaven (N.Y.) Nat. Lab., 1951-52, jr. physicist, 1952-54; asst. prof. physics U. Colo., 1958-62, asso. prof., 1962-65; asso. prof. Ind. U., 1965-68, prof., 1968—, dir. cyclotron facility, 1971-72. Mem. vis. staff Los Alamos Sci. Lab., 1970—; cons. Han-Meitner Inst., Berlin, Germany, 1972—. Served with USNR, 1945-46. Recipient Sebastian Karrar prize U. Wash., 1955, U.S. Sr. Scientist award Alexander von Humboldt Found. (West Germany), 1975. Fellow Am. Phys. Soc.; mem. Sigma Xi. Democrat. Unitarian. Designer Ind. U. cyclotron facility. Home: 3171 Piccadilly St Bloomington IN 47401 Office: Swain Hall West Ind U Bloomington IN 47401

RICKLES, DON, comedian, actor; b. L.I., N.Y., May 8, 1926; grad. Am. Acad. Dramatic Arts, N.Y.C.; m. Barbara Rickles; children—Mindy Beth, Lawrence Corey. Star TV show The Don Rickles Show, 1971-72, C.P.O. Sharkey, 1976-77; appeared in movie Kelly's Heroes, Enter Laughing, others; appeared as comedian in Eden Roc Hotel, Miami Beach, Fla., Sahara Hotel, Las Vegas, Nev., Copacabana, N.Y., numerous other nightclubs; appearances on most TV variety shows; rec. albums include Hello Dummy, Don Rickles Speaks. Address: William Morris Agy Inc 151 El Camino Beverly Hills CA 90212*

RICKLIN, ARTHUR H., hosp. adminstr.; b. N.Y.C., Aug. 30, 1934; s. Solomon and Betty (Hirsch) R.; B.S., N.Y. U. Sch. Edn., 1956, postgrad. (Lavanburg Cornerhouse scholar) Sch. Public Adminstrn. 1964-69; m. Janet Jacobson, Nov. 24, 1954; children—Jonathan H., Leslie J. Chief phys. therapist Misericordia Hosp., Bronx, N.Y., 1958-64; adminstrv. asst. Misericordia-Fordham Hosp., Affiliation, Bronx, 1964-65; dir. Albert Einstein Hosp. Evelyn & Joseph I. Lubin Rehab. Center, Bronx, 1965-66; asst. adminstr. Hosp. of Albert Einstein Coll. Medicine, Bronx, 1967-72, sr. asst. adminstr., 1972-73, adminstr., 1973-79; asso. dir. Montefiore Hosp. Med. Center, Bronx, 1979—; prin. asso. dept. rehab. medicine, asso. dept. community health Albert Einstein Coll. Medicine; asst. prof. allied health div. phys. therapy Ithaca Coll., 1973—; clin. asso. Health Professions Inst., Herbert H. Lehman Coll., CUNY; chmn. com. on weekend admission policies for Bronx Profl. Standards Rev. Orgn., 1979; cons., lectr. in field. Lic. physiotherapist, lic. nursing home adminstr., N.Y. State. Mem. Am. Hosp. Assn., Am. Public Health Assn., Hosp. Execs. Club N.Y., Greater N.Y. Hosp. Assn., Am. Phys. Therapy Assn. (vice-chmn. Greater N.Y. Dist. 1965-67, dist. dir. 1968-72, Disting. Service award of N.Y. State chpt. 1972), Royal Soc. Health (London), Public Health Assn. N.Y.C., Am. Soc. Law and Medicine, Am. Coll. Utilization Rev. Physicians. Home: 19 Lookout Pl Ardsley NY 10502 Office: Montefiore Hosp and Med Center 111 E 210th St Bronx NY 10467

RICKOVER, HYMAN GEORGE, govt. ofcl; b. Jan. 27, 1900; s. Abraham and Rachel Rickover; B.S. U.S. Naval Acad., 1922; M.S in Elec. Engring., U.S. Naval Postgrad. Sch., Columbia, 1929; numerous hon. degrees; m. Ruth D. Masters (dec. 1972); 1 son, Robert Masters; m. 2d, Eleonore Ann Bednowicz, 1974. Commd. ensign, U.S. Navy, 1922, advanced through grades to adm., 1973; qualified submariner, 1931; served in U.S.S. La Vallette, U.S.S. Nevada, 1922-27, U.S.S. S-9, U.S.S. S-48, 1929-33; assigned to Office Insp. of Naval Materiel, Phila., 1933-35; engring. officer in U.S.S. New Mexico, 1935-37; comdg. officer U.S.S. Finch, 1937; assigned to Navy Yard, Cavite, Philippines, 1937-39; head elec. sect. Bur. Ships, Navy Dept., Washington, 1939-45; indsl. mgr., Okinawa, also comdg. officer Naval Repair Base, 1945; insp. gen. 19th Fleet, San Francisco, 1945-46; assigned to atomic submarine project with AEC, Oak Ridge, 1946, continued in devel. atomic submarine Bur. of Ships, from 1947; responsible for devel. and constrn. world's 1st atomic submarine U.S.S. Nautilus, 1st nuclear powered electric utility sta. at Shippingport, Pa.; now dir. div. naval reactors U.S. Dept. Energy, also dep. comdr. for nuclear propulsion Naval Sea Systems Command. Decorated D.S.M. with gold star, Legion of Merit with gold star, hon. comdr. mil. div. Most Excellent Order Brit. Empire; recipient numerous awards including Egleston medal Columbia Engring. Alumni Assn., 1955, Cristoforo Columbo gold medal, 1957, Pupin medal, 1958; spl. gold medal U.S. Congress, 1959; Enrico Fermi award for contbn. to atomic sci. AEC, 1965. Author: Education and Freedom, 1959; Swiss Schools and Ours: Why Theirs Are Better, 1962; American Education-A National Failure, 1963; Eminent Americans—Namesakes of the Polaris Submarine Fleet, 1972; How the Battleship Maine Was Destroyed, 1976; also numerous articles. Office: Div Naval Reactors US Dept Energy Washington DC 20845

RICKS, CAPPY ROBERT, advt. exec.; b. Ogden, Utah, Nov. 22, 1925; s. Espen F. and Grace (Salmon) R.; B.A., U. Wash., 1952; m. Mary Ruth Bertagnole, Sept. 3, 1948; children—Robyn Ann, Roger Edward, Randi Lou. Pres. Cappy Ricks & Assos., Inc., Seattle, 1954-63; sr. v.p. Botsford, Constantine & McCarty, Inc., Seattle, 1963-67; exec. v.p. Ricks-Ehrig, Inc., advt., Seattle, 1967—. Office: 4th and Vine Bldg Seattle WA 98121

RICKS, DONALD JAY, agrl. economist; b. Lansing, Mich., Sept. 14, 1936; s. Glenn L. and Evelyn N. R.; B.S. with highest honors, Mich. State U., 1958, M.S., 1960; Ph.D., Oreg. State U., 1965; m. Joanne M. Burr, Aug. 24, 1968; children—Mark, Craig. Instr. in econs. Oreg. State U., 1962-63, asst. in agrl. econs., 1963-64; asst. prof. agrl. econs. Mich. State U., 1964-70, asso. prof., 1970-76, prof., 1976—, extension mktg. economist, 1973—, project leader, extension mktg., 1976—; cons. on projects in Spain, Costa Rica, Panama, Colombia, Switzerland, Poland, Germany, Belgium, and Eng. Recipient State Extension Team award, 1971. Mem. Am. Agrl. Econs. Assn., Extension Specialists Assn., Phi Kappa Phi, Epsilon Sigma Phi, Phi Eta Sigma, Alpha Zeta. Contbr. numerous articles to various publs. Home: 1051 Barry Rd Haslett MI 48840 Office: Room 20 Agr Hall Mich State U East Lansing MI 48823

RIDDEL, JOSEPH NEILL, educator; b. Grantsville, W.Va., Sept. 11, 1931; s. James F. and Selma (Stump) R.; A.B., Glenville State Coll. (W.Va.), 1953; M.S., U. Wis., 1956, Ph.D., 1960; m. Virginia Lee Johnson, Apr. 17, 1957; children—Kevin Joe, Valerie Anne, Vanessa Lee. Instr., later asst. prof. Duke, 1960-64; vis. asst. prof. U. Calif., Riverside, 1964-65; asso. prof., then prof. State U. N.Y. at Buffalo, 1965-72; prof. English, U. Cal. at Los Angeles, 1973—. Served with AUS, 1953-55. Guggenheim fellow, 1976. Mem. Modern Lang. Assn., English Inst. Democrat. Author: The Clairvoyant Eye: The Poetry and Poetics of Wallace Stevens, 1965; C. Day Lewis, 1971; The Inverted Bell: Modernism and the Counterpoetics of William Carlos Williams, 1974. Home: 5044 Vanalden Ave Tarzana CA 91356 Office: Dept English U Calif Los Angeles CA 90024

RIDDELL, JAMES GILMOUR, broadcasting exec.; b. Paisley, Scotland, Apr. 8, 1912; s. John and Elizabeth (Gilmour) R.; m. Fadellis Bradley, May 2, 1936; children—Suzanne (Mrs. Bruce D. Netzer), and Sandra (dec.). Came to U.S. 1921, naturalized, 1940. With Radio Station WXYZ, Detroit, 1931—, successively office boy, traffic mgr., comml. mgr., gen. sales mgr., 1931-46, gen. mgr., 1946-48, pres., gen. mgr. WXYZ, Inc., 1950—; exec. v.p. ABC, 1958-59, v.p. in charge of Western div., 1959-70; dir. Los Angeles Life Ins. Co., Glen-Glenn Sound, Henry Engring. Co., Storer Broadcasting Co. Gen. chmn. Internat. Broadcasting Awards, 1964-65. Adv. council Jr. Achievement, 1956-58; chmn. Gen. Brotherhood Week, Detroit, 1956, Crusade for Freedom, Radio and TV, Detroit, 1956; mem. Detroit Tomorrow com., 1957; adv. com. Better Bus. Bur., 1957-58. Recipient Blessed Martin award Inter-Racial Council of Detroit, 1957. Mem. Radio and TV Execs. Soc., Radio Pioneers Soc., Broadcast Pioneers (dir.), Soc. TV Pioneers, Mich. Assn. Radio and TV Broadcasters, Nat. Assn. Broadcasters, Western Golf Assn. (dir.), Assn. Golf Presidents, Detroit Advt. Golf Assn., Detroit Dist. Golf Assn. (gov.), Hollywood C. of C. (dir.), Radio and TV Execs., Inc., Calif. C. of C., Acad. TV Arts and Scis., So. Cal. Broadcasters Assn. Advt. Assn. W. Clubs: New York Athletic: Detroit Athletic, Detroit Adcraft; Variety, Oakland Hills Country, Red Run Golf (past pres.), Huron River Fishing and Hunting (Detroit); Advertising (Los Angeles); Advertising (Hollywood, Calif.); Bel Air Country; Question; Santa Anita Turf; LaQuinta Country (dir.); Hollywood Park Turf. Home: PO Box 668 La Quinta CA 92253

RIDDELL, JOSEPH MURRAY, JR., dermatologist: b. Iron River, Mich., Jan. 1, 1917; s. Joseph Murray and Elsie (Quirt) R.; B.A., U. Tex., 1941; M.D., Baylor U., 1946; m. Patricia Sue Hengy, May 29, 1943; children—Patricia Sue, Joseph Murray III, Mary Jane Riddell Deal, Robert Clarence, James Alexander. Intern, Baylor U. Hosp., Dallas, 1946-47; resident U. Ill., Chgo. Hosps., 1949-51; practice medicine specializing in dermatology, Fort Worth, 1952—; mem. staff Harris, St. Joseph's, John Peter Smith hosps.; clin. prof. dermatology U. Tex. Southwestern Med. Sch., 1973-77. Diplomate Am. Bd. Dermatology. Episcopalian. Mem. AMA, Tex. Med. Assn., Tarrant County Med. Soc., Tex. Dermatol. Soc. (pres. 1973), Am. Acad. Dermatology. Editor: The Texas Dermatologist, 1972-76. Home: 4015 Hilding Dr E Fort Worth TX 76109 Office: 800 5th Ave Fort Worth TX 76104

RIDDELL, MATTHEW DONALD RUTHERFORD, cons. engr.; b. Toronto, Ont., Can., Mar. 13, 1918; s. Matthew Rutherford and Edith (Downs) R.; S.B., Harvard U., 1940, M.S. in San. Engring., 1946; m. Dorothy Jane Williams, Oct. 2, 1948; children—James, David, Ann. With Greeley & Hansen, Chgo., 1946—, partner, 1957—; mem. water resources tech. adv. com. Northeastern Ill. Planning Commn., 1968—. Pres., bd. dirs. Glenview (Ill.) Pub. Library, 1970-71. Served with USNR, 1941-46. Named Chgo. Civil Engr. of Year, 1975; registered profl. engr., Ill., Mich., Wis., Minn., N.Y., S.D., Md., Fla. Fellow Am. Cons. Engrs. Council; mem. Am. Acad. Environ. Engrs. (trustee 1969-75, pres.-elect 1979-80), Am. Water Works Assn., Central States Water Pollution Control Assn., Inter-Am. Assn. San. Engring., Am. Public Works Assn., Inst. Water Resources (pres. 1979-80), Cons. Engrs. Council Ill., Ill., Nat. socs. profl. engrs., Phi Beta Kappa, Delta Omega, Tau Beta Pi. Clubs: Chgo. Corinthian Yacht, Union League (Chgo.); North Shore Country (Glenview, Ill.). Home: 1215 Elm St Glenview IL 60025 Office: 222 S Riverside Plaza Chicago IL 60606

RIDDELL, RICHARD HARRY, lawyer; b. Seattle, Nov. 29, 1916; s. Charles F. and Kathryn (Wykoff) R.; A.B., Stanford, 1938; LL.B., Harvard, 1941; m. Dolores Gloyd, Feb. 10, 1970; children by previous marriage—Dorothea (Mrs. Carroll D. Parry II), Wendy, Kathryn, Mark W. Admitted to Wash. bar, 1941; partner Riddell, Williams, Ivie, Bullitt and Walkinshaw, and predecessors, Seattle, 1941—. Dir. King Broadcasting Co., Seattle. Served to maj. USAAF, 1941-45. Mem. Am., Seattle-King County (pres. 1963-64), Wash. State (pres. 1976-77) bar assns. Clubs: Rainier (Seattle), Seattle Tennis. Home: 1620 43d E Seattle WA 98112 Office: Seattle First Nat Bank Bldg Seattle WA 98154

RIDDER, BERNARD HERMAN, JR., newspaper pub.; b. N.Y.C., Dec. 8, 1916; s. Bernard Herman and Nell (Hickey) R.; B.A., Princeton U., 1938; m. Jane Delano, Feb. 24, 1939; children—Laura, Paul A., Peter, Robin, Jill. Advt. dir. Duluth News-Tribune, 1941-42, gen. mgr., 1947-52, pub., 1952-72; pub. St. Paul Dispatch-Pioneer Press, 1959-73; pres. Ridder Publs., Inc., 1969—; chmn. bd. Knight-Ridder Newspapers, 1979—; dir. Asso. Press, 1954-64; chmn. bd. Minn. Vikings Football Club; dir. Seattle Times, Great Lakes Paper Co., Ltd. Sr. v.p. U. Minn. Found.; bd. dirs. Profl. Golf Assn. Tour. Served from ensign to lt., USNR, 1942-45. Recipient Journalism award U. Minn., also Regents award. Mem. U.S. Golf Assn. (mem. exec. com. 1958-64). Clubs: Royal and Ancient Golf (St. Andrews, Scotland); Burning Tree Golf (Washington); Somerset Country (St. Paul). Home: 233 Salem Church Rd Saint Paul MN 55118 Office: 55 E 44th St Saint Paul MN 55101

RIDDER, BERNARD J., publisher; b. N.Y.C., June 29, 1913; s. Joseph E. and Hedwig (Schneider) R.; grad. Princeton U., 1936; m. Georgia G. Buck, Oct. 9, 1936; children—Bernard J., Laurance M. Gen. newspaperwork, Aberdeen, S.D., Grand Forks, N.D., St. Paul and Duluth, Minn., and N.Y.C., 1934—; editor and pub. Jour. of Commerce, N.Y.C., 1946-55; pub. Star-News, Pasadena, Calif., 1956-74; chmn. bd. Ridder Publs. Inc., 1974-76; pres. Twin Coast Newspapers Inc., 1956-76; dir. Knight-Ridder Newspapers Inc. Home: 612 S San Rafael Pasadena CA 91105 Office: 301 E Colorado Blvd Pasadena CA 91101

RIDDER, ERIC, newspaper pub.; b. Hewlett, L.I., N.Y., July 1, 1918; s. Joseph E. and Hedwig (Schneider) R.; ed. Portsmouth Priory Sch., Portsmouth, R.I.; student Harvard, 1936-37; m. Ethelette Tucker, 1939 (div.); children—Eric, Susan; m. 2d, Madeleine Graham, 1955. Entire career in newspaper work; v.p., dir. Twin Coast Newspapers, Inc.; dir. Seattle Times Co. Chmn. bd. Grenville Baker Boys Club. Trustee, treas. South St. Seaport Mus.; mem. council Maritime Coll., Ft. Schuyler, Bronx, N.Y. Republican. Roman Catholic. Clubs: Racquet and Tennis, Seawnahaka-Corinthian Yacht, Piping Rock, N.Y. Yacht, India House (N.Y.C.); Royal Swedish Yacht, Rainier. Home: Feeks Ln Locust Valley NY 11560 Office: 110 Wall St New York NY 10005

RIDDER, JOSEPH BERNARD, newspaper pub.; b. N.Y.C., May 3, 1920; s. Bernard Herman and Nell (Hickey) R.; B.A., Coll. William and Mary, 1943; m. Virginia Dunne, Dec. 30, 1950. Gen. mgr. St. Paul Dispatch-Pioneer Press, 1949-52; pub. San Jose (Calif.) Mercury-News, 1952-77, pres., 1977. Exec. v.p. Music and Arts Found. Santa Clara County, 1966—; bd. dirs. O'Connor Hosp. Found., Partnership for Arts in Calif.; sec. Calif. advisory com. U.S. Commn. Civil Rights; trustee Santa Clara U., 1974-80. Served with USNR, World War II. Mem. Inter-Am., Internat. press assns., Calif., Am. newspaper pubs. assns. Clubs: Pacific-Union (San Francisco); Burlingame Country; San Jose Country, Sainte Claire (San Jose). Home: Saratoga Hills Rd Saratoga CA 95070 Office: 750 Ridder Park Dr San Jose CA 95190

RIDDER, PAUL ANTHONY, newspaper publisher; b. Duluth, Minn., Sept. 22, 1940; s. Bernard H. and Jane (Delano) R.; B.A. in Econs., U. Mich., 1962; m. Constance Louise Meach, Nov. 6, 1960; children—Katherine Lee, Linda Jane, Susan Delano, Paul Anthony. With Aberdeen (S.D.) Am. News, 1962-63, Pasadena (Calif.) Star News, 1963-64; with San Jose (Calif.) Mercury News, 1964—, bus. mgr., 1968-75, gen. mgr., 1975-77, pub., 1977—, pres., 1979—; sec.-treas. Western Newspaper Indsl. Relations Bur., 1979. Exec. v.p. Santa Clara County United Way, 1979; bd. regents Santa Clara U.; mem. adv. bd. San Jose State U. Recipient Second Ann. Disting. Citizen award Santa Clara County council Boy Scouts Am., 1976; Community Service award NCCJ, 1979; named San Jose Outstanding Young Man of Year, San Jose Jr. C. of C., 1970. Mem. Santa Clara County Mfrs. Group (bd. dirs. 1979), San Jose C. of C. (chmn. bd. dirs. 1975), Young Presidents Orgn. Clubs: Rotary, San Jose Country; Sainte Claire; La Rinconada Country (Los Gatos, Calif.); Cypress Point (Pebble Beach, Calif.). Home: 14751 Quito Rd Saratoga CA 95070 Office: 750 Ridder Park Dr San Jose CA 95190

RIDDER, WALTER THOMPSON, newspaper corr.; b. N.Y.C., Apr. 1, 1917; s. Victor Frank and Marie (Thompson) R.; student Columbia U., 1934-36; B.S., Harvard, 1939; m. Marie Stix Wasserman, May 22, 1948; children—Ellen, Stephanie, Victor F. II, Pamela. Reporter, Duluth Herald-News-Tribune, 1940-41; Washington corr. St. Paul Pioneer Press-Dispatch, 1941-42, 1944-45, 46—; war corr. St. Paul, Duluth newspapers and N.Am. Newspaper Alliance in ETO, 1945-46, fgn. corr., 1947-48; chief field br., info. div. OSR, ECA, 1950-52; Washington corr. Ridder Publs., Inc., also dir.; pub. Gary (Ind.) Post-Tribune, 1966-72; dir. Knight-Ridder Newspapers. Served as tech. sgt. AUS, 1942-43. Decorated Award of Merit, War Dept.; St. Olav's Medal from King Haakon of Norway; Order Merit (W. Ger.). Mem. Overseas Writers, Delta Psi, Sigma Delta Chi. Unitarian. Clubs: Metropolitan, National Press (Washington); Burning Tree; Overseas Press of Am. (N.Y.C.); Gridiron. Contbr. to nat. mags. Home: 4509 Crest Ln McLean VA 22101 Office: 1195 National Press Bldg Washington DC 20045

RIDDLE, DONALD HUSTED, coll. chancellor; b. Bklyn., Jan. 22, 1921; s. William Ewing and Ruth (Husted) R.; A.B., Princeton U., 1949, M.A. (Woodrow Wilson fellow), 1951, Ph.D. (Ford Found. fellow), 1956; m. Leah Dunlap Gallagher, June 20, 1942; children—Susan Lee and Judith Lee (twins). Asst. prof. dept. govt. Hamilton Coll., 1952-58; dir. research, asso. prof., prof. politics Eagleton Inst. Politics, Rutgers U., 1958-65; dean faculty John Jay Coll. Criminal Justice, City U. N.Y., 1965-68, pres., 1968-76; chancellor U. Ill. at Chgo. Circle, 1976—; staff asst. Conn. Commn. on State Govt. Orgn., 1949; staff mem. Survey Field Services, Dept. Interior, 1950; staff mem. U.S. Senator Paul H. Douglas, 1955-56; cons. N.Y. State Spl. Com. on Constl. Revision and Simplification, 1958. Mem. bd. edn., Princeton, N.J., 1962-64; mem. Mayors Criminal Justice Coordinating Council, N.Y.C., 1968-73. Served to 1st lt. USAAF, 1942-46. Mem. AAUP, Am. Polit. Sci. Assn., Am Studies Assn., Phi Beta Kappa. Author: The Truman Committee: A Study in Congressional Responsibility, 1964. Editor, co-author: The Problems and Promise of American Democracy., 1964; Contemporary Issues of American Democracy, 1969. Editor: American Society in Action, 1965. Home: 400 E Randolph St Chicago IL 60601 Office: Box 4348 Chicago IL 60680

RIDDLE, HUGH, JR., airport mgr.; b. Chgo., June 1, 1932; s. Hugh and Katherine Lucille (Madison) R.; B.A. in Bus. Adminstrn., Lake Forest (Ill.) Coll., 1961; m. Hope Corine Hansen, June 21, 1958; children—Hugh, III, Gordan Scott, Charles Hansen. Asst. mgr. stas. Midway Airlines, Inc., Chgo., 1951-56; air traffic controller FAA, Chgo., 1956-66, ops. and standards specialist, 1966-69, spl. asst. to dir. Bur. Nat. Capital Airports, 1969-71, airport service liaison officer, 1971-73; airport mgr. Washington Nat. Airport, 1974—; aviation adv. com. No. Va. Community Coll., 1969-74; pres. Air Traffic Control Assn., 1968-70. Recipient Service award FAA, 1960, 68, 72, 73. Columnist Jour. Air Traffic Control, 1965-67. Home: 8301 Stonewall Dr Vienna VA 22180 Office: Washington Nat Airport Washington DC 20001

RIDDLE, NELSON SMOCK, composer, conductor, arranger; b. Hackensack, N.J., June 1, 1921; s. Nelson Smock and Marie Albertin (Rieber) R.; ed. pub. schs., N.J.; m. Doreen Moran, Oct. 10, 1945; children—Nelson Smock, Rosemary Ann, Christopher Robert, Bettina Marie, Cecily Jean, Maureen Alicia. Mem. Jerry Wald Band, 1940, Charlie Spivak Band, 1940-43, Tommy Dorsey Band, 1944-45; staff arranger NBC, Hollywood, Calif., 1947-50; music dir. Capitol Records, 1951-62, Reprise Records, 1963—, Route 66, TV series, 1960; guest condr. Hollywood Bowl, 1954-60; Atlanta Symphony Orch. 1963; music dir. Presdl. Inauguration ceremonies, 1961, numerous TV spls. Judge, U. So. Calif. Songfest, 1959, U. Calif. at Los Angeles, Spring Song, 1960, Loyola U. at Los Angeles Spring Song, 1961; patron, hon. chmn. alumni assn. Los Angeles Conservatory Music, 1959. Served with AUS, 1945-47. Recipient Emmy nominations, 1954, 55, 56, 57, Oscar nominations, 1960, Grammy award for composition Cross Country Suite, 1958; commd. to write Three Quarter Suite, Modern Brass Ensemble, 1962; recipient Golden Record for Lisbon Antigua, 1956. Mem. Motion Picture Acad. Arts and Scis., TV Acad. Arts and Scis., TV Acad. Arts and Scis. (bd. govs. 1962-64), Nat. Assn. Recording Artists Soc., Screen Actors Guild, Am. Soc. Music Arranger, Screen Composers Assn., Acad. Motion Picture Arts and Scis., AFTRA, Am. Guild Authors and Composer, Calif. Copyright Conf., Broadcast Music. Composer scores for Merry Andrew, 1957; Johnny Concho, 1956; Oceans 11, 1960; Lolita, 1961; Hole in the Head, 1958; Lisbon, 1957; Girl Most Likely, 1956; Come Blow Your Horn 1962; Paris When it Sizzles, 1963; Four for Texas, 1963; Cross Country Suite, 1958; Three-Quarter Suite, 1962; Theme and Variations, 1971; Goin' Coconuts, 1978; Harper Valley PTA, 1978; TV scores for Untouchables, 1959; Naked City, 1961; Sam Benedict, 1962; Route 66, 1960; How To Break up a Happy Divorce, 1976; 79 Park Avenue, 1977. Address: PO Box 68 Los Angeles CA 90028*

RIDDLE, STURGIS LEE, clergyman; b. Stephenville, Tex., May 26, 1909; s. Lee and Linda (McKinney) R.; B.A. magna cum laude, Stanford U., 1931; student Gen. Theol. Sem., N.Y.C., 1931-32; B.D. cum laude, Episcopal Theol. Sch., Cambridge, Mass., 1934; D.D., Seabury Western Theol. Sem., Evanston, Ill., 1957; m. Elisabeth Pope Sloan, Oct. 14, 1939. Ordained deacon P.E. Ch., 1934, priest, 1935; Episcopal chaplain U. Calif., 1934-37; instr. church Div. Sch. of Pacific, 1934-37; rector Caroline Ch., Setauket, L.I., 1937-40; asst. minister St. Thomas Ch., N.Y.C., 1940-46; rector St. James Ch., Florence, Italy, 1947-49; dean Am. Cathedral of Holy Trinity, Paris, France, 1949-74, dean emeritus, 1974—; hon. minister St. Bartholomew's Ch., N.Y.C., 1974—; exchange preacher Trinity Ch., N.Y.C., 1956-57, 62, St. Bartholomew's Ch., N.Y.C., 1958, 63, 73, St. John's Cathedral, Denver, 1959, Grace Cathedral, San Francisco, 1960, Nat. Cathedral, Washington, 1961, Trinity Ch. Boston, 1964, St. Andrew's Cathedral, Honolulu, 1965, St. John's Ch., Washington, 1966, 67, 68, 70, 73, St. Thomas' Ch., N.Y., 1968, 73, St. Paul's Cathedral, Boston, 1969; clerical dep. Europe to Gen. Conv. P.E. Ch., 1949-60, 64, 70. Hon. gov. Am. Hosp. in Paris; fellow Morgan Library, N.Y.C.; trustee bd. fgn. parishes. Decorated Legion of Honor (France); grand cross and grand prelate Sovereign Order St. John of Jerusalem (Knights of Malta); grand cross Ordre du Milice de Jesus Christ; Patriarchal Order Mt. Athos. Mem. France-Am. Soc., Am. Soc. French Legion of Honor, Phi Beta Kappa. Episcopalian. Clubs: Union, University, Pilgrims, Paris-American (N.Y.C.). Author: One Hundred Years, 1950; contbg. Author We Believe in Prayer, 1958, That Day with God, 1965. Home: 870 Fifth Ave New York NY 10021

RIDDLEBERGER, HUGH COMPTON, educator; b. Woodstock, Va., May 5, 1916; s. Ralph Heiskell and Frances (Waddy) R.; grad. Trinity Sch., 1934; B.S., Hamilton Coll., 1938; L.H.D., Trinity Coll., Hartford, Conn., 1959; m. Jane Joscelyn, Oct. 28, 1942; children—Susan (dec.), Hugh Compton III, Patricia, Elizabeth. Master Trinity Sch., N.Y.C., 1938-41, asst. headmaster, 1945-47, headmaster, 1955-63; asst. headmaster Trinity-Pawling Sch., Pawling, N.Y., 1947-55; headmaster Grosse Pointe U. Sch., 1963-69; exec. dir. Cleve. Council Ind. Schs., 1969-70; headmaster Landon Sch., Bethesda, Md., 1970—. Served as lt. USNR, 1942-45. Mem. Country Day Sch. Headmasters Assn., Headmasters Assn. U.S. Club: Congressional Country. Home: 6210 Alcott Bethesda MD 20034 Office: Landon School Bethesda MD 20034

RIDDLES, JAMES ARNOLD, univ. librarian; b. Cleve., Nov. 2, 1917; s. Parker W. and Nellie (Rice) R.; B.A., Ariz. State Coll., 1940; student Garrett Bibl. Inst., 1941-42, Pendle Hill, Wallingford, Pa., 1942-43; M.S. in L.S., U. So. Calif., 1947; m. Margaret Neil Branum, Apr. 8, 1943; children—David, Cynthia, James Arnold, Asst. Librarian Riverside (Calif.) Coll., 1947-49, acting librarian, 1949-50; children's librarian San Diego Pub. Library, 1950-53, br. librarian, 1953-59; mem. library staff U. Pacific, 1960—, acting dir., 1965, dir. libraries, 1966-79. Pres. Riverside Interracial Club, 1948-50; chmn. Stockton chpt. Am. Civil Liberties Union, 1966-68, 76-78; chmn. coll. com. No. Calif., Am. Friends Service Com., 1961-64. Served with M.C., AUS, 1945-46. Hon. life mem. PTA; life mem. ALA (pres. Golden Empire dist. 1968-69); mem. Calif. Library Assn., Family Service League. Mem. Soc. of Friends (clk. quar. meeting 1967-68). Home: 1821 Princeton St Stockton CA 95204

RIDENHOUR, JOSEPH CONRAD, textile co. exec.; b. Rowan County, N.C., Aug. 12, 1920; s. Martin Luther and Mary Virginia (Schaeffer) R.; student Duke, 1938-40; L.H.D., Lenoir Rhyne Coll., 1974; m. Julia Claire Thorne, Dec. 21, 1943; 1 dau., Janis Claire, Asst. sec. Cannon Mills Co., Kannapolis, N.C., 1953-63, asst. v.p., 1959-60, v.p., 1960-71, sr. v.p., dir. mktg., 1971—, also dir. Mem. Kannapolis Bd. Edn., 1954-65; sec. Home Mission Found., N.C. synod United Lutheran Ch. in Am., 1953-68, dir. 1953—, pres., 1968—; mem. bd. Luth. Theol. So. Sem., 1964—. Served with arty, AUS, World War II; ETO. Home: Oaklynn 420 Idlewood Dr Kannapolis NC 28081 Office: Cannon Mills Co Kannapolis NC 28081

RIDEOUT, PATRICIA IRENE, operatic, oratorio, concert singer; b. St. John, N.B., Can., Mar. 16, 1931; d. Eric Aubrey and Florence May (Chase) R.; ed. U. Toronto Opera Sch., Royal Conservatory Music, 1952-55; m. Rolf Edmund Dissmann, Sept. 3, 1955 (dec. 1975). Singer, Can. Opera Co., Toronto, 1954—; leading roles operas, Stratford, Ont., Vancouver, B.C., Guelph, Ont., 1956—, CBC, 1958—. Mem. Actors Equity Assn., Assn. Radio and TV Artists, Toronto Heliconian Club. Unitarian. Home: 485 Summerhill Ave #2 Toronto ON M4W 2E3 Canada

RIDEOUT, PHILIP MUNROE, pub. co. exec.; b. Boston, June 24, 1936; s. Allen MacDonald and Allene Lucille (Holman) R.; B.A., Williams Coll., 1958; m. Sylviane R.L. Eldin, Aug. 7, 1959; 1 dau., Nicole MacDonald. With Addison-Wesley Pub. Co., 1961-77, gen. mgr. W.A. Benjamin, Inc., Menlo Park, Calif., 1972-77, gen. mgr. health scis. div. Addison-Wesley Co., Menlo Park, 1975-77; pres. Cummings Pub. Co., Inc., Menlo Park, 1968-77; v.p. Coll. Mktg. Group, Inc., 1977-78; editor-in-chief Larousse U.S.A., Inc., N.Y.C., 1979—. Served with U.S. Army, 1958-61. Mem. S.A.R. Unitarian. Home: 104-40 Queens Blvd Apt A17J Forest Hills NY 11375 Office: 572 Fifth Ave New York NY 10036

RIDER, MORRETTE LEROY, musicologist, ednl. adminstr.; b. New Cumberland, Pa., May 3, 1921; s. Ira M. and Rhoda Anna (Morrette) R.; student U. Pa., 1938-39; B.Mus., U. Mich., 1942, M.Mus., 1947; D.Ed., Columbia U., 1955; postgrad. L'Ecole Monteux, Hancock, Maine, 1950-52, Berkshire Music Center, 1949, 65, U. Vienna (Austria), 1958, U. Rochester, 1964; m. Wanda Nigh, Jan. 6, 1946; 1 dau., Rhonda. Asst. prof. music Hope Coll., 1947-50, asso. prof., 1950-55, prof., 1955-67, dean for acad. affairs, 1968-75; adminstrv. asst. to pres. U. Wash., 1967-68; dean Sch. Music U. Oreg., 1975—; pres. Ship's Carpenter Mfg. Co., Holland, Mich., 1957-65; curriculum cons. Music Hochschulen, W. Ger., 1979; cons. to state arts councils; mem. exec. bd. Mich. Council for Arts, 1957-66; mem. exec. bd. Eugene (Oreg.) Jr. Symphony Assn. Served with U.S. Army, 1942-45; CBI. Time-Life grantee, 1964, 66; Den Uyl Found. grantee, 1965; Ford Found.-Am. Council Edn. grantee, 1967-68. Mem. Am. Symphony Orch. League, Nat. Sch. Orch. Assn. (exec. bd.), Nat. Assn. Schs. Music (vice-chmn. N.W. div. 1976-78, chmn. div. 1978—, exec. bd. 1978—), Music Educators Nat. Conf., Am. String Tchrs. Assn. (pres. Mich. chpt. 1963-65), Music Tchrs. Nat. Assn., CBI Vets.' Assn., Coll. Music Assn., Mich. Sch. Band and Orch. Assn. (hon. life mem.), Eugene Symphony Orch. Assn. (exec. bd.), Eugene-Univ. Music Assn. (exec. bd.), U.S. Power Squadrons, Phi Mu Sinfonia, Pi Kappa Lambda (founder 2 chpts.). Republican. Methodist. Contbr. articles to profl. jours., U.S., Europe; writer, producer: History of the Symphony Orchestra, Music of the 20th century, Time-Life TV programs, 1966-67; Jazz in America, Music Since 1900, radio programs, 1975-76; condr. numerous orch. concerts throughout U.S., 1950—. Home: 1847 Fircrest Dr Eugene OR 97403 Office: Sch Music U Oreg Eugene OR 97403

RIDER, ROWLAND VANCE, educator; b. Syracuse, N.Y., Aug. 23, 1915; s. William Morrison and Grace (Vance) R.; B.A., Amherst Coll., 1937; M.A., Syracuse U., 1938; Sc.D., Johns Hopkins U., 1947; m. Agatha Ann Siegenthaler, June 13, 1948. Jr. statistician N.Y. Health Dept., Albany, 1938-39; mem. faculty Johns Hopkins, 1947—, asso. prof., 1957-65, prof. population dynamics, biostatistics, maternal and child health Sch. Hygiene and Pub. Health, 1965—. Chief adviser West Pakistan Research and Evaluation Center, Lahore, 1964-67. Served with AUS, 1942-45; ETO. Decorated Bronze Star (2), Purple Heart. Fellow Am. Pub. Health Assn.; mem. Am. Statis. Assn., Biometric Soc., Internat. Union Sci. Study Population, AAAS, Population Assn. Am., Sigma Xi. Home: 2233 Lake Ave Baltimore MD 21213

RIDGE, MARTIN, historian, educator; b. Chgo., May 7, 1923; s. John and Ann (Lew) R.; A.B., Chgo. Tchrs. Coll., 1943; A.M., Northwestern U., 1949, Ph.D., 1951; m. Marcella Jane VerHoef, Mar. 17, 1948; children—John Andrew, Curtis Cordell, Wallace Karsten. Asst. prof. history Westminster Coll., New Wilmington, Pa., 1951-55; prof. asst. prof. to prof. San Diego State Coll., 1955-66; prof. history Ind. U., Bloomington, 1966—; vis. prof. U. Calif., Los Angeles, summer 1963, Northwestern U., summer 1959; editor Jour. Am. History, 1966-77; sr. research asso. Huntington Library, 1977; bd. dirs. Calif. Hist. Landmarks Commn., 1954-64; cons. in field. Served with U.S. Maritime Service, 1943-45. William Randolph Hearst fellow, 1950; fellow Social Sci. Research Council, 1952, Guggenheim Found., 1965, Am. Council Learned Socs., 1960; Newberry fellow, 1964; Huntington fellow, 1974; recipient Best Book award Phi Alpha Theta, 1963. Mem. Am. Hist. Assn. (Best Book award Pacific Coast br. 1963), Orgn. Am. Historians, Western, So. history assns., Agrl. History Soc., Social Sci. History Soc. Democrat. Author: Ignatius Donnelley: Portrait of a Politician, 1962; co-author: California Work and Workers, 1963; The American Adventure, 1964; America's Frontier Story, 1969; Liberty and Union, 1973. Address: Huntington Library San Marino CA 91108

RIDGELY, JOSEPH VINCENT, English scholar, educator; b. Montgomery, Ala., June 23, 1921; s. Raymond Grover and Eelje Frances (Scriven) R.; B.A., U. Fla., 1942, M.A., 1946; M.A., Johns Hopkins U., 1948, Ph.D., 1956; m. Janetta Somerset, July 27, 1956; 1 dau., Julia Frances Somerset. Asst. prof. English, Columbia U., N.Y.C., 1958-63, asso. prof., 1963-70, prof., 1970—. Served with USAAF, 1942-45. Mem. AAUP, Modern Lang. Assn. Am., Phi Beta Kappa, Phi Kappa Phi. Clubs: Faculty House Columbia U., Johns Hopkins. Author: Wiliam Gilmore Simms, 1962; John Pendleton Kennedy, 1966; editor works of E.A. Poe and W.G. Simms; contbr. articles on Am. lit. to profl. jours. Home: 4819 Keswick Rd Baltimore MD 21210 Office: Dept English and Comparative Lit Columbia U New York City NY 10027

RIDGEWAY, FRANK EDWARD, cartoonist, writer; b. Danbury, Conn., Apr. 7, 1930; s. Frank Edward and Jeanette (Wilson) R.; student Art Student League N.Y., 1949-50, Sch. Visual Arts N.Y., 1951-52; m. Nancy Ann Villane, Apr. 1, 1954. Cartoonist mag. single panel cartoons Sat. Eve. Post, True, Cosmo, Ladies Home Jour., 1950-58; cartoonist Mr. Abernathy comic strip for King Features Syndicate, N.Y.C., 1957—, Simpkins cartoon panel for Eagle Features Syndicate, 1975—; instr. cartoon course Famous Artist Sch., 1956-57. Mem. Nat. Cartoonist Soc., Artists and Writers, Cartoonist Artist Profl. Soc. Office: King Features Syndicate 235 E 45th St New York NY 10017*

RIDGEWAY, JAMES FOWLER, journalist; b. Auburn, N.Y., Nov. 1, 1936; s. George L. and Florence (Fowler) R.; A.B., Princeton U., 1959; m. Patricia Carol Dodge, Nov. 1966; 1 son, David Andrew. Asso. editor New Republic, Washington, 1962-68, contbg. editor, 1968-70; editor Hard Times, 1968-70, Elements, 1974—; asso. editor Ramparts, 1970-75. Asso. fellow Inst. for Policy Studies, 1973-77; mem. Pub. Resource Center, 1977—; staff writer Village Voice, 1973—. Served with Army N.G., 1959. Author: The Closed Corporation, 1969; Politics of Ecology, 1970; The Last Play, 1973; New Energy, 1975; Energy-Efficient Community Planning, 1979; (with Alexander Cockburn) Smoke, 1978, Political Ecology, 1979. Home: 3103 Macomb St NW Washington DC 20008

RIDGLEY, ROBERT LOUIS, lawyer; b. Ft. Wayne, Ind., Mar. 4, 1934; s. Charles Herbert and Margaret (Sparling) R.; A.B., Cornell U., 1956; J.D., Harvard, 1959; m. Marilyn A. Hester, Aug. 24, 1957; children—Gregory C., Derek W. Admitted to Oreg. bar, 1959; practice in Portland, 1960—; asso. firm Stoel, Rives, Boley, Fraser and Wyse, and predecessors, 1960-66, partner, 1966. Mem. Nat. Adv. Council for Edn. Disadvantaged Children, 1969-70; mem. Nat. Commn. on Reform of Secondary Edn. Mem. Multnomah County Republican Exec. Com., 1962-66, alt. del. Nat. Conv., 1964. Chmn. bd. dirs. Portland Sch. Dist.; bd. dirs. Cornell U. Council, Nat. Pub. Affairs Center for TV; trustee Cornell U., 1970-76, Lewis and Clark Coll., 1975—; chmn. bd. visitors Northwestern Sch. Law, 1975-76. Served to 1st lt., arty. AUS, 1959-60. Named Jr. First Citizen Portland, 1968. Mem. Nat. (dir.), Oreg. (pres.) sch. bds. assns., Ripon Soc. (Oreg. pres. 1969). Co-editor: Pleading and Practice Handbook, 1964. Home: 4927 SW Downsview Ct Portland OR 97221 Office: 900 SW 5th Ave Portland OR 97204

RIDGWAY, ROZANNE LEJEANNE, ambassador; b. St. Paul, Aug. 22, 1935; d. H. Clay and Ethel Rozanne (Cote) Ridgway; B.A., Hamline U., 1957, LL.D., 1978. Entered Fgn. Service, 1957; assigned Dept. State, Washington, 1957-59, 64-67, 70-73, Am. embassy, Manila, 1959-61, U.S. Consulate Gen., Palermo, Italy, 1962-64, Am. embassy, Oslo, 1967-70; dep. chief mission Am. embassy, Nassau, 1973-75; dep. asst. sec. state, ambassador for oceans and fisheries affairs, 1975-77; ambassador to Finland, 1977—. Recipient Profl. awards Dept. State, 1967, 70, 75; named Person of Year, Nat. Fisheries Inst., 1977. Home: 4100 Cathedral Ave NW Washington DC 20016 Office: Am Embassy Helsinki APO New York NY 09664

RIDING, LAURA. see Jackson, Laura (Riding)

RIDKER, NORMAN LEE, mag. pub.; b. Chgo., Sept. 18, 1938; s. Jack Wolfe and Estelle R. (Markus) R.; B.A., U. Calif., Los Angeles, 1961. Mem. Peace Corps, 1961-63; editor Harriscope Corp., 1966-68; pres. Fancy Publs., Inc. and Macro/Comm Corp., pubs. Pvt. Pilot, Cat Fancy, Aero and Dog Fancy mags., Beverly Hills, Calif., 1968—. Home: 428 S Spalding Dr Beverly Hills CA 90212 Office: 8322 Beverly Blvd Los Angeles CA 90048

RIDLEN, JULIAN LEON, lawyer, state ofcl.; b. Macon County, Ill., Feb. 4, 1940; s. Charles F. and Doris O. (Franklin) R.; B.A., Anderson Coll., 1963; J.D., George Washington U., 1967; m. Susanne Lee Smith, June 1, 1963. Tchr., Emerson Inst., Washington Hall Jr. Coll., Washington, 1966-68; admitted to Ind. bar, 1967, U.S. Dist. Ct. bar, 1967; legal researcher NEA, Washington, 1967-68; judge Logansport City Ct., Logansport, Ind., 1969-78; partner firm Smith & Ridlen, Logansport, 1968—; state treas. State of Ind., Indpls., 1979—. Chmn. Cass County Bicentennial Com., 1974-76; pres. Cass County Youth Services Bur., 1971; v.p. bd. dirs. United Fund, 1972; pres. Cass County chpt. ARC, 1971-73; v.p. Mental Health Assn., 1971-73; mem. Cass County Bd. Election Commrs., 1970; mem. staff Republican Nat. Com., 1963-64. Mem. Nat. Assn. State Treas., Nat. Assn. State Auditors, Comptrollers and Treasurers, Am. Bar Assn., Ind. Bar Assn., Cass County Bar Assn., Cass County Hist. Soc. (pres. 1974-78), Phi Alpha Delta. Presbyterian. Clubs: Kiwanis, Elks, Eagles, Moose. Home: 613 Wheatland Ave Logansport IN 46947 Office: 242 State Office Bldg Indianapolis IN 46204

RIDOUT, GODFREY, composer, educator; b. Toronto, Ont., Can., May 6, 1918; s. Douglas Kay and Amy Phyllis (Bird) R.; student Upper Can. Coll., Toronto, 1932-36, Toronto Conservatory of Music, 1937-39; grad. composition U. Toronto, 1939-40; LL.D., Queen's U., Kingston, Ont., 1967; m. Freda Mary Antrobus, Aug. 5, 1944; children—Naomi (Mrs. Terrence Thomas), Victoria (Mrs. Terrence Kett), Michael. Composer, condr. scores Nat. Film Bd., Ottawa, 1940-43, CBC, Toronto, 1941—; prin. compositions: Ballade for viola, string orch., 1938; Two Etudes for String Orch., 1946; Esther, dramatic symphony for soli, choir, orch., 1952; Cantiones Mysticae, soprano and orch., 1953; The Dance, choir and orch., 1960; Pange Lingua, choir and orch., 1961; Fall Fair, orch., 1961; Cantiones Mysticae No. 2, soprano and orch., 1962; Cantiones Mysticae No. 3, baritone choir and orch., 1973; Jubilee, orch., 1973; Concerto Grosso, string orch. and piano, 1974; George III, His Lament, orch., 1976; The Lost Child, opera for TV, 1976; mem. teaching staff Toronto Conservatory Music, 1940—; spl. lectr. music U. Toronto, 1948-61, asst. prof., 1961-65, asso. prof., 1965-71, prof., 1971—. Comml. arranger, 1945-50. Recipient Centennial medal Govt. Can., 1967. Fellow Royal Canadian Coll. Organists (hon.); mem. Composers, Authors, Pubs. Assn. Can. (dir. 1966-73). Compositions have been performed frequently in N.Am., Europe, 1939—. Home: 71 Rowanwood Ave Toronto ON M4W 1Y8 Canada Office: Faculty of Music U Toronto Toronto ON M5S 1A1 Canada

RIEDEBURG, THEODORE, mgmt. cons.; b. Milw., June 7, 1912; s. Theodore and Elva Pauline (Wolf) R.; B.S., Marquette U., 1934, M.S., 1936; m. Margaret Anna Louise Oertel, Dec. 24, 1937; children—Theodore, Charles Howard. Dist. sales mgr. Philip Morris & Co., 1937-42; asst. mgr. fumigants dept. Dow Chem. Co., Midland, Mich., 1942-45; sales mgr. agrichems. Westvaco Chem., N.Y.C., 1945-50; mng. dir. Theodore Riedeburg Assos., White Plains, N.Y., 1950—. Pres., Citizens League White Plains (N.Y.), 1962. Fellow Soc. Profl. Mgmt. Cons. (past pres.); mem. Inst. Mgmt. Cons. (founder, dir.), Am. Chem. Soc., Entomol. Soc. Am., Weed Sci. Soc., Am. Arbitration Assn., Chemists Club N.Y.C. Contbr. articles to profl. jours. Home: 63 Walton Ave White Plains NY 10606 Office: 6 Corporate Park Dr White Plains NY 10604

RIEDEL, ALAN ELLIS, mfg. co. exec., lawyer; b. Bellaire, Ohio, June 28, 1930; s. Emil George and Alberta (Schaefer) R.; A.B. magna cum laude, Ohio U., 1952; J.D., Case Western Res. U., 1955; grad. Advanced Mgmt. Program, Harvard, 1971; m. Ruby P. Tignor, June 21, 1953; children—Ralph A., Amy L., John T. Admitted to Ohio bar, 1955, Tex. bar, 1968; asso. firm Squire, Sanders & Dempsey, Cleve., 1955-60; with Cooper Industries Inc. and predecessor, 1960—, gen. counsel, Mt. Vernon, Ohio, 1963-68, sec., 1963-68, v.p. indsl. relations, 1968-73, sr. v.p. adminstrn., Houston, 1973—; dir. Standards Products Co., Cleve. Mem. Mt. Vernon City Council, 1964-67. Bd. dirs., mem. exec. com. Jr. Achievement of S.E. Tex., 1975—. Recipient Distinguished Service award Mt. Vernon Jr. C. of C., 1965. Mem. Ohio Bar Assn. (chmn. sect. corp. counsel 1967), Order of Coif, Phi Beta Kappa, Omicron Delta Kappa, Delta Tau Delta. Home: 13515 Pebblebrook Dr Houston TX 77024 Office: Cooper Industries Inc 2 Houston Center Houston TX 77002

RIEDL, JOHN ORTH, educator; b. Milw., June 10, 1905; s. Lucas Henry and Olive (Orth) R.; A.B., Marquette U., 1927, A.M., 1928, Ph.D., 1930; postgrad. Toronto, 1930, 37, Columbia, 1934, 36, U. Breslau, Germany, 1938-39; m. Clare Carmelita Quirk, Aug. 17, 1932; children—Annelore, John Orth, Joseph, Paul, Rose Virginie, William. Faculty dept. philosophy Marquette U., 1930-46, 54-66, asso. prof., 1944-46, prof., 1954-66, dean Grad. Sch., 1954-60; prof. philosophy, dean faculty Queensborough Community Coll., 1966-75; prof. emeritus, 1975—, dean in charge, 1966-67; cons. Mgmt. Research Service, Gen. Electric Co., Crotonville, N.Y., 1960; chief Catholic affairs Office Mil. Govt. for Germany, 1946-48, chief edn. br., 1948-49, chief edn. br. Office U.S. High Commr. for Germany, 1949-52, pub. affairs officer Pub. Affairs Field Center, Freiburg, Germany, 1952-53; research writer, N.Y.C., 1953-54; staff and faculty USNR Officers Sch. Milw., 1957-58; staff U.S. Naval War Coll., Newport, R.I., 1962. Mem. com. on citizen consultations U.S. Nat. Commn. UNESCO, 1957-61, bd. fgn. scholarships, 1958-63. Served from lt. (j.g.) to lt. comdr. USNR, 1942-45. Mem. Metaphys. Soc. Am., Am. Philos. Assn., Am. Cath. Philos. Assn. (pres. 1935), Midwest Conf. on Grad. Study and Research (chmn. 1958), NCCJ (commn. on ednl. orgns. 1957-61), Das Delphische Institut. Mainz, Germany (hon. com. 1953), Assn. Higher Edn., Cath. Commn.

Intellectual and Cultural Affairs, Societe Thomiste Belgium, Hegel Soc. Am., Charles S. Peirce Soc., Soc. for Phenomenology and Existential Philosophy, Internat. Soc. Neoplatonic Studies, Alpha Sigma Nu. Home: 42-19 219th St Bayside NY 11361

RIEDY, JOHN K., business exec.; b. Chgo., June 29, 1916; s. Elmer B. and Evelyn (Marcoe) R.; m. Mary Eileen Grogan, Feb. 8, 1941; children—Robert D., John M., Michael J. Vice pres. Florsheim Shoe Co., Chgo., 1957-66, pres., 1967-70, now chmn. bd.; pres. Interco, Inc., St. Louis, 1970—; dir. First Nat. Bank St. Louis, Pet Inc., Union Electric Co. Home: 200 S Brentwood Blvd Clayton MO 63105 Office: 10 Broadway Saint Louis MO 63102

RIEFLER, DONALD BROWN, banker; b. Washington, Nov. 10, 1927; s. Winfield W. and Dorothy (Brown) R.; B.A., Amherst Coll., 1949; grad. Stonier Banking Sch., Rutgers U., 1960; m. Patricia Hawley, Oct. 12, 1957; children—Duncan, Linda, Barbara. With Morgan Guaranty Trust Co. of N.Y., N.Y.C., 1952—, v.p., 1962-68, sr. v.p., 1968-77, chmn. sources and uses of funds com., 1977—; dir. Nat. Reinsurance Corp., Niagara Mohawk Power Corp. Served with U.S. Army, 1950-52. Mem. Am. Bankers Assn., Public Securities Assn. Club: Creek (Locust Valley, N.Y.). Home: 837 Orchard Ln Oyster Bay NY 11771 Office: 23 Wall St New York NY 10015

RIEGEL, KENNETH, tenor; b. West Hamburg, Pa., Apr. 29, 1938; s. Robert Lee and Arline (Shollenberger) R.; ed. Manhattan Sch. Music, N.Y.C., 1960; studied with Wellington Wolfe, Reading, Pa. Apprentice, Tanglewood, 1960; operatic debut with Santa Fe Opera, 1965; debut N.Y.C. Opera, 1969, leading roles in La Traviata, Cosi fan Tutte, Der Rosenkavalier, Maria Stuarda, The Young Lord, others; concert appearances Boston, Chgo., Pitts., Am. symphony orchs., Phila. Orch., N.Y. Philharmonic, Columbus (Ohio) Symphony, Houston Symphony, San Francisco Symphony, Cleve. Orch., Netherlands Orch., Los Angeles Philharmonic, Toronto Symphony, Denver Symphony; appearances with Seattle Opera, Portland (Oreg.) Opera, Charlotte (N.C.) Opera, Houston Opera, also Tanglewood, Lincoln Center Mozart, Spoleto, Ravinia, Salzburg (Austria) festivals; debut Met. Opera in Les Troyens, 1973; debut Vienna State Opera in La Traviata, 1977; debut Chgo. Opera in Meistersinger, 1977; debut Paris Opera in Les Contes Hoffmann, 1978; appeared in film version of Don Giovanni, 1978; world premiere of 3-act version of Lulu, Paris Opera, 1979; rec. artist Columbia Records. Served with AUS, 1961-64. Commd. maj. work by Composer Stephen Douglas Burton, Songs of the Tulpehocken, for Am. Bicentennial, 1976. Address: care Thea Dispeker 59 E 54th St New York NY 10022

RIEGEL, KURT WETHERHOLD, fed. pollution control research and devel. adminstr.; b. Lexington, Va., Feb. 28, 1939; s. Oscar Wetherhold and Jane Cordelia (Butterworth) R.; B.A., Johns Hopkins U., 1961; Ph.D., U. Md., 1966; m. Lenore R. Engelmann, Nov. 15, 1974; children—Tatiana Suzanne, Samuel Brent Oscar. Asst. prof. astronomy UCLA, 1966-74; prof. astronomy U. Calif. Extension, Los Angeles, 1968-74; mgr. energy conservation program Fed. Energy Adminstrn., Washington, 1974-75; chief tech. and consumer products energy conservation Dept. Energy, Washington, 1975—, dir. consumer products div., conservation and solar energy, 1979; asso. dep. asst. adminstr. environ. engring. and tech. EPA, 1979—; cons. Aerospace Corp., El Segundo, Calif., 1967-70, Rand Corp., Santa Monica, Calif., 1973-74; vis. fellow U. Leiden (Netherlands), 1972-73. Mem. Casualty Council Underwriters Labs., Nat. Radio Astron. Observatory Users Com., 1968-74. Mem. AAAS, Am. Phys. Soc., Sierra Club, Audubon Soc., Internat. Radio Sci. Union, Am. Astron. Soc., Internat. Astron. Union. Contbr. articles to profl. jours. Address: Box 2807 Washington DC 20013

RIEGEL, WILLIAM MURCHIE, forest products industry exec.; b. N.Y.C., Jan. 25, 1928; s. John L. and Margaret Winslow (Murchie) R.; student Williams Coll., 1946-50; m. Nancy Bailey, Sept. 30, 1970; children—William Murchie, Guy R., Katherine B., Margaret W. Exec. v.p. Riegel Paper Co., N.Y.C., 1950-72; pres. Riegel Products Co., Milford, N.J., 1972-77; exec. v.p., gen. mgr. Paper Products Group, S.W. Forest Industries, Inc., Phoenix, 1972-77; pres. Amax Forest Products, Inc., Greenwich, Conn., 1977—. Served with USNR, 1952-55. Clubs: Paradise Valley Country; Duxbury Yacht. Home: 14 Surplus St Duxbury MA 02332 Office: Amax Inc Amax Center Greenwich CT 06830

RIEGLE, DONALD WAYNE, JR., U.S. senator; b. Flint, Mich., Feb. 4, 1938; s. Donald Wayne and Dorothy (Fitchett) R.; student Flint Jr. Coll., 1956-57, Western Mich. U., 1957-58; B.A., U. Mich., 1960; M.B.A., Mich. State U., 1961; postgrad. Harvard U., 1964-66; LL.D., St. Benedict's Coll., Defiance Coll.; m. Lori L. Hansen, May 20, 1978. Sr. pricing analyst with IBM Corp., 1961-64; faculty Mich. State U., 1962, Boston U., 1965, Harvard, 1965-66; cons. Harvard/Mass. Inst. Tech. Joint Center Urban Studies, 1965-66; mem. 90th-94th congresses, 7th Dist. Mich., mem. internat. relations com.; U.S. senator from Mich., 1977—. Named one of America's 10 Outstanding Young Men, U.S. Jr. C. of C., 1967, one of Two Best Congressmen of Year, The Nation mag., 1967. Author: O Congress, 1972. Democrat. Office: 300 Metropolitan Bldg 432 N Saginaw St Flint MI 48502 also Senate Office Bldg Washington DC 20515

RIEKE, WILLIAM BETTEN, aerospace exec.; b. Onawa, Iowa, Dec. 10, 1913; s. Ray Edgar and Adrienne (Betten) R.; student U. Okla., 1931-32; m. Violet Mae Lindsey, Oct. 2, 1948; children—Marilyn Rieke Johnson, Joann Elizabeth. With Dun & Bradstreet, Inc., 1934-41; with Lockheed Aircraft Corp. and Lockheed-Ga. Co., 1941-62, pres. Lockheed Aircraft Internat., Inc., 1962-64; dep. asso. adminstr. Office Manned Space Flight NASA, 1964-65, asst. adminstr. for industry affairs, 1965-66; exec. v.p. Lockheed Missiles & Space Co., 1967-69, pres., 1974-76, chmn., 1976-78; exec. v.p. Lockheed Aircraft Corp., 1969-74, group v.p. Lockheed Corp., 1976—. Home: 1655 Candace Way Los Altos CA 94022 Office: 1111 Lockheed Way Sunnyvale CA 94086

RIEKE, WILLIAM OLIVER, univ. adminstr.; b. Odessa, Wash., Apr. 26, 1931; s. Henry William and Hutoka S. (Smith) R.; B.A. summa cum laude, Pacific Luth. U., 1953; M.D. with honors, U. Wash., 1958; m. Joanne Elynor Schief, Aug. 22, 1954; children—Susan Ruth, Stephen Harold, Marcus Henry. Instr. anatomy U. Wash. Sch. Medicine, Seattle, 1958, asst. prof., 1961-64, adminstrv. officer, 1963-66, asso. prof., 1964-66; prof., head dept. anatomy Coll. Medicine U. Iowa, Iowa City, 1966-71, dean protem Coll. Medicine, 1969-70, chmn. exec. com., 1969-70; vice chancellor for health affairs, prof. anatomy U. Kans. Med. Center, Kansas City, 1971-73, exec. vice chancellor, prof. anatomy, 1973-75; affiliate prof. biol. structure U. Wash. Sch. Medicine, Seattle, 1975—; pres. Pacific Lutheran U., Parkland, Wash., 1975—. Mem. interdisciplinary gen. basic sci. test com. Nat. Bd. Med. Examiners, 1968-72, chmn. anatomy test com., 1972-75, mem. at large, 1975-79; spl. cons. NIH, 1970-72; mem. adv. com. Inst. Medicine, Nat. Acad. Scis., 1974-76; mem. Commn. on Colls., NW Assn. Schs. and Colls., 1979—. Named Distinguished Alumnus, Pacific Luth. U., 1970, Pi Kappa Delta, 1977. Fellow A.C.P.; mem. Am. Assn. Anatomists, Am. Soc. Cell Biology, AAAS, Sigma Xi, Alpha Kappa Psi, Beta Gamma Sigma. Lutheran (mem. ch. council 1967-70). Editor: Procs. 3d Ann. Leucocyte Culture Conf. 1969; editorial bd. Am. Jour. Anatomy, 1968-71. Home: 13511 Spanaway Loop Rd Tacoma WA 98444 Office: Office of Pres Pacific Lutheran U Tacoma WA 98447

RIELLY, JOHN EDWARD, fgn. policy assn. exec.; b. Rapid City, S.D., Dec. 28, 1932; s. Thomas J. and Mary A. (Dowd) R.; B.A., St. John's U., Collegeville, Minn., 1954; postgrad. (Fulbright scholar) London Sch. Econs. and Polit. Sci., 1955-56; Ph.D., Harvard U., 1961; m. Elizabeth Downs, Dec. 28, 1958 (annulled 1976); children—Mary Ellen, Catherine Ann, Thomas Patrick, John Downs. Faculty dept. govt. Harvard U., 1958-61; with Alliance for Progress programs Dept. State, Washington, 1961-62; fgn. policy asst. to Sen. then Vice Pres. Hubert Humphrey, Washington, 1963-69; cons. office European and internat. affairs Ford Found., N.Y.C., 1969-70; sr. fellow Overseas Devel. Council, Washington, 1970-71; exec. dir. Chgo. Council on Fgn. Relations, 1971-74, pres., 1974—; cons. NSC; mem. adv. bd. Grad. Sch. Arts and Scis., Harvard U.; mem. Am. Council on Germany, Nat. Com. on U.S.-China Relations, China Council of Asia Soc.; Trilateral Commn., commn. on U.S.-Brazilian Relations; past pres. Nat. Council Community World Affairs Orgns. Trustee St. John's U. Mem. Am. Polit. Sci. Assn., Council on Fgn. Relations, N.Y.C. Clubs: Mid-Am.; Michigan Shores (Chgo.); Harvard (N.Y.C.). Contbr. articles to profl. jours.; editor: Development Today: A New Look at U.S. Relations with Poor Countries, 1972; American Public Opinion and U.S. Foreign Policy, 1975, 2d edit., 1979; editorial bd. Fgn. Policy Quar., 1974—. Home: 2021 Kenilworth Ave Wilmette IL 60091 Office: 116 S Michigan Ave Chicago IL 60603

RIELY, JOHN WILLIAM, lawyer; b. Richmond, Va., Mar. 9, 1917; s. Henry Carrington and Marie Antoinette (Evans) R.; B.A., U. Va., 1938; LL.B., Harvard U., 1941; m. Jean Roy Jones, July 2, 1941; children—Caroline A., Henry Carrington. Admitted to Va. bar, 1941; asso. firm Hunton & Williams, and predecessors, Richmond, 1941-42, 45-48, partner, 1949—; dir., gen. counsel Bank of Va. Co. and subsidiaries; dir. Commonwealth Natural Resources, Inc. Past pres. Historic Richmond Found.; trustee RPI Found. Served to lt. comdr. USNR, 1942-45. Mem. Jud. Council Va., Am. Bar Found., Richmond, Va., Am. bar assns., Bar Assn. City N.Y. Democrat. Episcopalian. Clubs: Commonwealth, Country of Va., Downtown. Home: 3 Roslyn Rd Richmond VA 23226 Office: PO Box 1535 Richmond VA 23212

RIENER, MAX. see Caldwell, (Janet) Taylor

RIENZI, THOMAS MATTHEW MICHAEL, army officer; b. Phila., Feb. 5, 1919; s. Luigi and Ethel (Johnson) R.; student mech. engring. Lehigh U., 1937-38; B.S. in Mil. Sci., U.S. Mil. Acad. 1942; M.S. in Elec. Engring., U. Ill., 1948; certificate in mgmt. U. Pitts., 1965; M.A. in Internat. Affairs, George Washington U., 1966; m. Claire M. Moore, Aug. 11, 1945; children—Thomas Matthew, Claire Mary. Commd. 2d lt. U.S. Army, 1942, advanced through grades to lt. gen., 1965; chief supply and maintenance div. signal sect. U.S. Army Pacific, Hawaii, 1961; signal officer XVIII Airgorne Corps, Ft. Bragg, N.C., 1961-63; exec. officer to chief signal officer, chief communications-electronics, Washington, 1963-65; chief Combat Surveillance Office, Material Command, Washington, 1965-66; commdg. gen., comdt. Signal Center and Sch., Ft. Monmouth, N.J., 1966-68; comdg. gen., dep. comdg. gen 1st Signal Brigade, S.E. Asia, Vietnam/Thailand/Laos, 1968-70, also dep. chief staff communications-electronics U.S. Army, Vietnam; comdg. gen Strategic Communications Command, Pacific, also dep. chief of staff communications-electronics U.S. Army Pacific, 1970-72; dir. telecommunications and command and control Dept. of Army, Washington, 1972—; dep. dir. gen. NATO Integrated Communications System Mgmt. Agy., Brussels, 1977—. Permanent deacon Roman Cath. Ch., 1979—. Decorated D.S.M. with oak leaf cluster, Legion of Merit with oak leaf cluster, Bronze Star with oak leaf cluster, Air medal with 5 oak leaf clusters (U.S.); Breast Order of Yun Hui Ribbon (Nationalist China); Chung Mu Order of Merit (Korea); Nat. Order Vietnam Knight (Vietnam): recipient Papal award, 1970. Mem. Assn. U.S. Army (ann. mem.), Armed Forces Communications-Electronics Assn. (nat. officer 1972—); life mem. Assn. Grads. U.S. Mil. Acad.; mem. U. Lehigh Alumni Assn., U. Ill. Alumni Assn., George Washington U. Alumni Assn. Author: History of Communications-Electronics in Vietnam War, 1972; also articles. Home: 676 Elepaio St Honolulu HI 96816

RIEPE, DALE MAURICE, educator; b. Tacoma, June 22, 1918; s. Roland and Martha (Johnson) R.; B.A., U. Wash., 1944; M.A., U. Mich., 1946, Ph.D., 1954; postgrad. (Rockefeller-Watamull-McInerny fellow), U. Hawaii, 1949, Banaras and Madras, India, Tokyo and Waseda, Japan; m. Charleine Williams, 1948; children—Kathrine Leigh, Dorothy Lorraine. Instr. philosophy Carleton Coll., 1948-51; asst. prof. U. S.D., 1952-54; asso. prof. U. N.D., 1954-59, prof., 1959-62, chmn. dept., 1954-62; prof., chmn. C.W. Post Coll., 1962-63; prof. philosophy State U. N.Y., Buffalo, 1963—, chmn. dept. social scis., asso. dean Grad. Sch., 1964—; exchange lectr. U. Man., 1955; vis. lectr. Western Wash. Coll., 1961. Marine instr. electricity Naval Tng. Program, Seattle, 1943-45; Fulbright scholar, India, 1951-52, Fulbright lectr., U. Tokyo, 1957-58; Carnegie Corp. fellow Asian Studies, 1960-61; grantee 4th East-West Philosophers Conf., 1964, Penrose fund Am. Philos. Soc., 1963, State U. N.Y. Research Found., 1965, 66, 67, 69, 72, 73, Bulgarian Acad. Sci., 1975; Am. Inst. Indian Studies research fellow, 1966-67; mem. nat. screening bd. South Asia, Fulbright Selection, 1968-70, Asia, 1970-72, chmn. Fulbright Selection Com. for Asia, 1972; exchange lectr. Moscow State U., 1979; cons., India, 1979. Mem. com. overseers Chung-an U., Korea. London Sch. Oriental and African Studies grantee, 1971. Fellow Royal Asiatic Soc.; mem. Conf. Asian Affairs (sec. 1955), Am. Oriental Soc., Am. Philos. Soc., Indian Inst. Psychology, Philosophy and Psychical Research (hon. adviser), Soc. for Am. Philosophy (chmn. 1960), Am. Inst. Indian Studies (trustee 1965-66), Soc. for Creative Ethics (sec.), Am. Archaeol. Soc., ACLU, Far Eastern Inst., AAAS, Am. Archeol. Soc., Am. Math. Soc., Am. Soc. Comparative and Asian Philosophy, Asiatic Soc. (Calcutta), Soc. for Philos. Study Dialectical Materialism (founding sec.-treas. 1963—), Soc. for Philos. Study Marxism (publs. sec. 1973—), United Univ. Profs of State U. N.Y. at Buffalo (v.p.), Alpha Pi Zeta. Clubs: Racquet, Buffalo (Buffalo). Author: The Naturalistic Tradition in Indian Thought, 1961; The Philosophy of India and its Impact on American Thought, 1970; East-West Dialogue, 1973; Indian Philosophy Since Independence, 1979; The Owl Flies by Day, 1979; also articles in field. Editor: Phenomenology and Natural Existence, 1973; Philosophy and Political Economy. Co-editor: The Structure of Philosophy, 1966; Radical Currents in Contemporary Philosophy, 1970; Reflections on Revolution, 1971; Philosophy at the Barricade, 1971; Contemporary East European Philosophy, 1971; Explorations in Philosophy and Society, 1978; editorial com. Chinese Studies in History, 1970—, Chinese Studies in Philosophy, 1970—; publs. bd. Conf. for Asian Affairs. Editor various series. Editorial bd. Philos. Currents and Revolutionary World, 1972; Soviet Studies in Philosophy. Home: 48 Capen Blvd Buffalo NY 14214 Office: 605 Baldy Hall State U NY Buffalo NY 14261

RIEPE, JAMES SELLERS, investment co. exec.; b. Bryn Mawr, Pa., June 25, 1943; s. Henry Brunt and Marjorie (Sellers) R.; B.S., Wharton Sch., U. Pa., 1965, M.B.A., 1967; m. Gail Nelms Petty, Sept. 14, 1968; children—Christina, James. Mem. audit staff Coopers & Lybrand, C.P.A.'s, Phila., 1967-68; asst. to pres. Wellington Mgmt. Co., Phila., 1969-72, v.p., 1972-75; exec. v.p. Vanguard Group, Inc., Valley Forge, Pa., 1975—, dir., 1979—; exec. v.p. Wellington Fund, Valley Forge, 1975—, dir., 1979—. Mem. U. Pa. Gen. Alumni Soc. (v.p., exec. com., chmn. alumni council on admissions). Clubs: Sunnybrook Golf, Racquet. Home: 1535 Keystone Dr Hatfield PA 19440 Office: PO Box 876 Drummers Ln Valley Forge PA 19482

RIES, AL, advt. exec.; b. Indpls., Nov. 14, 1929; s. Theodore F. and Elsie (Moeller) R.; A.B. in Liberal Arts, De Pauw U., 1950; m. Mary Lou Morrissey, May 6, 1968; 1 dau., Laura Marie. Vice pres., account supr. firm Needham, Louis & Brorby, N.Y.C., 1956-62; account supr. Marsteller, Inc., N.Y.C., 1962-63; chmn. firm Trout & Ries Advt., Inc., N.Y.C., 1963—. Mem. Bus./Profl. Advt. Assn. (past pres.). Clubs: Sales Execs. (dir.), Advt. of N.Y. (dir.) (N.Y.C.). Home: 34 Hemlock Dr Kings Point NY 11024 Office: 1212 Ave of Americas New York NY 10036

RIES, HERMAN ELKAN, JR., phys. chemist; b. Scranton, Pa., May 6, 1911; s. Herman Elkan and Henrietta (Brenner) R.; B.S., U. Chgo., 1933; Ph.D., 1936; m. Elizabeth Hamburger, Aug. 17, 1940 (dec. July 1979); children—Walter Elkan, Richard Alan. Head lab. instr. phys. chemistry U. Chgo., 1934-36; head phys. chemistry sect. Sinclair Refining Co. Research Labs., 1936-51; asst. dir. catalysis research div., 1948-50; research asso. Standard Oil Co. (Ind.), Whiting, 1951-72; vis. prof. Inst. for Chem. Research, Kyoto U. (Japan), 1972-74; research asso. dept. biology U. Chgo., 1974—; cons. in surface chemistry, 1972—; faculty participant in research Argonne Nat. Labs., 1978; cons. petroleum and water pollution UN Indsl. Devel. Orgn., 1973—; lectr. Institut Francais du Petrol, Paris, 1951-57; vis. scientist, lectr. Cavendish Lab., U. Cambridge, Eng., 1964. Asso. sec. 1st Internat. Congress on Catalysis, 1956; coordinator critical data on monolayers Nat. Acad. Sci.-NRC-Nat. Bur. Standards, 1965—; lectr. World Congress on Surface Chemistry, London, 1957, Brussels, Belgium, 1964, Barcelona, Spain, 1968, Zurich, Switzerland, 1972, Moscow, USSR, 1976; plenary lectr. Chem. Soc. Japan, 1973; Welch Found. lectr., 1978-79. Recipient Ipatieff award Am. Chem. Soc., 1950, certificate of merit div. colloid and surface chemistry, 1975. Mem. Am. Chem. Soc. (nat. awards com. 1965-68, 73-75; co-chmn. phys. chemistry group Chgo. sect. 1948-49; coms. continuing edn., environment Chgo. sect. 1970-71; reviewer Jour. Phys. Chemistry 1960—; exec. com. petroleum div. 1951-52; adv. com. colloid div. 1956—; exec. com. div. colloid and surface chemistry 1964), AAAS (adv. bd. Gordon Research Confs. 1947-51; program com. Gordon Research Conf. 1960—; chmn. Gordon Research Conf. on Interfaces 1960), Faraday Soc. (London), Chem. Soc. Japan, Am. Inst. Chemists, Am. Soc. Lubrication Engrs. (fundamentals com. 1960), N.Y. Acad. Scis., Sigma Xi, Phi Beta Kappa. Clubs: Catalysis, Quadrangle (Chgo.). Author: Structure and Sintering Properties of Cracking Catalysts and Related Materials, 1952; Physical Adsorption, 1953; Monomolecular Films, 1973; Direct Measurement of Adsorption of Radiostearic Acid onto Vapor-Deposited Metal Films, 1964; Electron Microscope Studies of Monolayers of Lecithin, 1975. Editorial bd. Jour. Colloid and Interface Sci., 1970-73. Contbr. to profl. jours. Patentee in field. Home: 5660 Blackstone Ave Chicago IL 60637 Office: Erman Biology Center Dept Biology Univ Chgo 1103 E 57th St Chicago IL 60637

RIES, JANE SILVERSTEIN, landscape architect; b. Denver, Mar. 10, 1909; d. Harry Shevelson and Eva Wilson (Sickman) Silverstein; student U. Colo., 1927-28; degree, Lowthorpe Sch. Landscape Architecture Women, Groton, Mass., 1932; m. Henry Francis Ries, Aug. 18, 1953. Pvt. practice landscape archtecture, Colo., Wyo., Nebr., 1935—; landscape architect Skidmore, Owings & Merrill, Architects, N.Y.C., 1945-46; mem. Mayors Citizen Adv. Bd. Denver City Parks, 1952-54; mem. urban environment subcom. Denver Planning Office, 1963-74; chmn. Colo. Bd. Examiners Landscape Architects, 1968; mem. horticulture adv. com. Denver Bot. Garden, 1971—. Served to lt. j.g. USCG, 1943-45. Fellow Am. Soc. Landscape Architects.; charter mem. Women's Forum Colo. Republican. Landscape architect residences, churches, schs., apts., museums, parks, comml. bldgs. Home and office: 737 Franklin St Denver CO 80218. *I have found this a very satisfying and happy profession: to meet the challenge of assisting a client to utilize outdoor space for practical enjoyment. Having a part in improving the environment is indeed stimulating.*

RIESENKONIG, HERMAN FRANK, lithographer; b. N.Y.C., Jan. 29, 1911; s. Hans and Carrie (Seyferth) R.; E.E., Rensselaer Poly. Inst., Troy, N.Y., 1932; m. Lois M. Sterling, Sept. 7, 1935; children—Peter, Pamela, John. With Lithoprint Co. N.Y., Inc., N.Y.C., 1932—, pres., 1935—, also dir. Active Scarsdale (N.Y.) Vol. Fire Dept. Presbyterian. Clubs: Scarsdale Golf, Town (Scarsdale). Inventor specialized equipment for lithoprint process. Home: 27 Fox Meadow Rd Scarsdale NY 10583 Office: 145 Hudson St New York NY 10013

RIESER, LEONARD MOOS, coll. adminstr.; b. Chgo., May 18, 1922; s. Leonard Moos and Margaret (Wallerstein) R.; S.B., U. Chgo., 1943; Ph.D., Stanford, 1952; A.M. (hon.), Dartmouth, 1963; m. Rosemary Littledale, July 16, 1944; children—Leonard, Timothy Savage, Abigail Clara. Research asst., then research asso. Stanford, 1949-52; mem. faculty Dartmouth, 1952—, prof. physics, 1960—, dir. grad. study, 1961-66, dean arts and scis., provost, 1967-71, v.p., dean of faculty, 1971—. Pres. New Eng. Conf. Grad. Edn., 1965; mem. com. grants Research Corps, N.Y., 1961-66. Served with AUS, World War II. Mem. AAAS (chmn. com. sci. edn. 1965, dir. 1967-71, pres. 1973, chmn. bd. 1974, chmn. com. new directions 1975—), Interciencia Assn. (v.p. 1976—), Am. Assn. Physics Tchrs., Am. Phys. Soc., Sigma Xi. Home: Elm St Norwich VT 05055 Office: Wentworth Hall Dartmouth Coll Hanover NH 03755

RIESMAN, DAVID, lawyer, social scientist; b. Phila., Sept. 22, 1909; s. David and Eleanor L. (Fleisher) R.; A.B., Harvard U., 1931, LL.B., 1934, research fellow, 1934-35; LL.D., Marlboro Coll., 1954, Grinnell Coll., 1957, Temple U., 1962, U. Sussex (Eng.), 1965; L.H.D., Williams Coll., 1977, St. Ambrose Coll., 1966, Franklin and Marshall Coll., 1976; D.C.L., Lincoln U., 1962: Ed.D., R.I. Coll., 1959; D.Litt., Wesleyan U., 1960; D.H.L., Oakland U., 1967; LL.D., Muhlenberg Coll., 1967, U. Calif. at Berkeley, 1968, U. Pa., 1972, Fordham U., 1972, Lafayette Coll., 1974; m. Evelyn Hastings Thompson, July 15, 1936; children—Paul, Jennie, Lucy, Michael. Admitted to Mass. and D.C. bars, 1935, N.Y. bar, 1939; law clk. to Mr. Justice Brandeis, U.S. Supreme Ct., 1935-36; practice with Lyne, Woodworth & Evarts, Boston, 1936-37; prof. law U. Buffalo, 1937-41; vis. research fellow Columbia U. Law Sch., 1941-42; dep. asst. dist. atty. N.Y. County, 1942-43; asst. to treas. and war contract termination dir. Sperry Gyroscope Co., Lake Success, L.I., 1943-46; vis. asso. prof. coll. social scis. U. Chgo., 1946-47, prof. social scis., 1949-58; dir. research project on mass communications Com. Nat. Policy, Yale U., 1948-49; Deiches lectr. Johns Hopkins U., 1954; Henry Ford II prof. social scis. Harvard U., 1958—; fellow Center for Advanced Study in Behavioral Scis., 1968-69; mem. Inst. Advanced Study, Princeton, N.J., 1971-72; mem. Carnegie Commn. for Study Higher Edn., 1967—. Adv. council Marlboro (Vt.) Coll., Hampshire Coll., Amherst, Mass. Hon. fellow New Coll., Sarasota, Fla., Cowell Coll., U. Calif., Santa Cruz. Mem. Am. Anthrop. Soc., Am. Sociol. Soc., Soc. Applied Anthropology, Am. Assn. Pub. Opinion Research. Author: The Lonely Crowd: A

Study of the Changing American Character, 1950; Faces in the Crowd, 1952; Thorstein Veblen, 1953; Individualism Reconsidered and Other Essays, 1954; Constraint and Variety in American Education, 1956; Abundance for What? and Other Essays, 1963; (with Evelyn Thompson Riesman) Conversations in Japan: Modernization, Politics and Culture, 1967; (with Christopher Jencks) The Academic Revolution, 1968; (with Joseph Gusfield and Zelda Gamson) Academic Values and Mass Education: the Early Years of Oakland and Monteith, 1970; (with Seymour M. Lipset) Education and Politics at Harvard, 1975; (with Gerald Grant) The Perpetual Dream: Experiment and Reform in the American College, 1978; (with Gerald Grant and others) On Competence: A Critical Analysis of Competence-Based Reforms in Higher Education, 1979; also articles in profl. jours.; editor: (with Verne Stadtman) Academic Transformation, 1973; bd. editors Am. Quar., Sociology of Edn., Ethos, Communication, Univs. Quar., Rev. of Edn. Home: 49 Linnaean St Cambridge MA 02138

RIFENBURGH, RICHARD PHILIP, cons. and investment co. exec.; b. Syracuse, N.Y., Mar. 3, 1932; s. Russell D. and Edna (MacKenzie) R.; student Wayne State U.; m. Doris Anita Hohn, June 24, 1950; children—David, Susan, Robert. With Mohawk Data Scis. Corp., Herkimer, N.Y., 1964-74, pres., 1970-74, chmn., 1974; pres., chief exec. officer Moval Mgmt. Corp., Herkimer, 1968—; pres., treas., dir. Fill-R-Up Systems, Inc., Pompano Beach, Fla., 1968—; treas., dir. Mohawk Valley Community Corp., also Library Bur. div., Herkimer, 1976-78, chmn. exec. com., 1978—; pres., chief exec. officer Mayer China Co., Beaver Falls, Pa., 1979—, also dir. Served with USAF, 1951-55. Address: 133 N Pompano Beach Blvd PH-1 PO Box 1146 Pompano Beach FL 33061

RIFFLE, JACK BURDETTE, ins. co. exec.; b. Rochester, N.Y., Sept. 19, 1928; s. Arvis B. and Eleanor (Taft) R.; B.A., Hamilton Coll., Clinton, N.Y., 1950; m. Suzanne Gregg, Apr. 2, 1955; children—Roberta, Gregg, Martha, Scott. Dist. sales mgr. Kemper Ins. Co., 1950-52, spl. risks rep., 1955-56; mgr. Scautub Ins. Agy., Schenectady, 1956-58; dist. sales mgr. Allstate Ins. Co., Rochester, 1958-65; with Utica Mut. Ins. Co. (N.Y.), 1965—, exec. v.p., 1972—, pres., 1974—, chief exec. officer, 1979—, also dir.; pres., chief exec. officer Graphic Arts Mut. Ins. Co., 1979—, also dir.; pres., chief exec. officer Utica Nat. Life Ins. Co., 1979—; dir. Ins. Claims Services, Inc.; bd. dirs. Ins. Info. Inst., 1979—, Alliance Am. Insurers, 1979—, Property Loss Research Bur., 1979—. Area pres. Boy Scouts Am., 1977—; pres. Utica United Way, 1977-79, now bd. dirs.; bd. dirs. N.Y. State Traffic Safety Council, 1970—, Nat. Crime Prevention Assn., 1976—; trustee Hamilton Coll. Served with USNR, 1952-55. Recipient Silver Beaver award Boy Scouts Am., 1976, Silver Antelope award, 1979. Mem. Utica C. of C. (dir. 1976—). Clubs: Ft. Schuyler, Ft. Schuyler Yacht Squadron; Yahnundasis Golf; City Midday (N.Y.C.). Home: 2 Wedgewood Rd New Hartford NY 13413 Office: PO Box 530 Utica NY 13503

RIFKIN, HAROLD, physician; b. N.Y.C., Sept. 10, 1916; s. Jack and Rose (Zuckoff) R.; B.A., U. Mo., 1935; M.D., Dalhousie U., 1940; m. Beatrice Weiss, Nov. 25, 1945; children—Janet, Matthew, Phyllis. Intern, Jewish Hosp. Bklyn., 1940-41; resident in internal medicine Montefiore Hosp., N.Y.C., 1942-43, 45-47; practice medicine specializing in internal medicine and diabetes, N.Y.C., 1947—; clin. prof. medicine Albert Einstein Coll. Medicine, N.Y.C., 1955—; prof. clin. medicine N.Y. U., 1974—; cons. Loeb Center, Montefiore Hosp., N.Y.C., 1960—, chief div. diabetes, 1955—; attending physician N. Central Bronx Hosp., Bellevue Hosp., Univ. Hosp., Lenox Hill Hosp. Served with U.S. Army, 1943-45. Diplomate Am. Bd. Internal Medicine. Fellow N.Y. Acad. Medicine, N.Y. Acad. Scis., A.C.P.; mem. Am. (bd. dirs. 1973—), N.Y. (past pres., bd. dirs. 1950—) diabetes assns., N.Y. County, N.Y. State med. socs., AMA, Am. Soc. for Clin. Research, Harvey Soc. Jewish. Author: Diabetic Glomerulo Sclerosis, 1949; editor: Diabetes Mellitus, Theory and Practice, 1970. Contbr. articles to profl. jours. Office: 35 E 75th St New York NY 10021

RIFKIND, SIMON HIRSCH, lawyer; b. Meretz, Russia, June 5, 1901; s. Jacob and Celia (Bluestone) R.; brought to U.S., 1910, naturalized, 1924; B.S., Coll. City N.Y.; LL.B., Columbia U.; Litt.D., Jewish Theol. Sem., 1950; LL.D., Hofstra Coll., 1962, Brandeis U., 1977, CCNY, 1978; m. Adele Singer, June 12, 1927; children—Richard Allen, Robert Singer. Admitted to N.Y. bar, 1926, Ill. bar, 1957; legislative sec. to U.S. senator Robert F. Wagner, 1927-33; partner firm Wagner, Quillinan and Rifkind, N.Y.C., 1930-41; fed. judge So. N.Y. Dist., 1941-50; mem. firm Stevenson, Rifkind & Wirtz, Chgo., 1957-61; partner Paul, Weiss, Rifkind, Wharton & Garrison, 1950—. Dir. Revlon, Inc., Sterling Nat. Bank & Trust Co. N.Y.; Herman Phleger vis. prof. law Stanford, 1975. Spl. master Colo. River litigation U.S. Supreme Ct.; chmn. Presdl. R.R. Commn., 1961-62; mem. State Commn. Govtl. Operations City N.Y., 1959-61; co-chmn. President's Commn. on Patent System, 1966-67; mem. mayors mediation panel N.Y. City teachers strike, 1963. Mem. Bd. Higher Edn. City N.Y., 1954-66. Chmn. adminstrv. bd. Am. Jewish Com., 1953-56, chmn. exec. bd., 1956-59; former chmn. bd., now hon. chmn. exec. com. Jewish Theol. Sem.; bd. dirs. Beth Israel Med. Center, N.Y.C., 1972—; chmn. bd. Charles H. Revson Found., Inc., Tudor Found., Inc.; bd. dirs., treas. Norman and Rosita Winston Found., Inc. Adviser to Gen. Eisenhower on Jewish matters in Am. occupation zone, 1945. Recipient Medal of Freedom, 1946. Mem. Assn. Bar City N.Y., Am. Coll. Trial Lawyers (regent 1967-71, pres. 1976-77), Phi Beta Kappa. Democrat. Jewish. Club: Harmonie (N.Y.C.). Home: 936 Fifth Ave New York City NY 10021 Office: 345 Park Ave New York NY 10022

RIGAU, MARCO ANTONIO, judge; b. Ponce, P.R., Mar. 5, 1919; s. Juan M. and Carmen (Gaztambide) R.; B.A., U. P.R., 1940, LL.B. cum laude, 1942; M.A. in Govt., Harvard U., 1947; m. Alice Jimenez, Dec. 16, 1942 (div. Apr. 1968); children—Alma Carmen, Marco Antonio, Maria Alicia; m. 2d, Lucy Torres, Nov. 2, 1968. Admitted to P.R. bar, 1945; asst. atty. gen. P.R., 1947; legis. counsel Legis. Assembly P.R., 1948-49; spl. asst. to gov. P.R., 1949-51, exec. asst., 1951-58; partner firm Rigau, Goldman & Santiago, San Juan, 1959-61; asso. justice Supreme Ct. P.R., 1961—. Served to capt. U.S. Army, 1942-45. Decorated Bronze Star, Combat Inf. Badge. Mem. P.R. Bar Assn., Am. Judicature Soc., Harvard U. Alumni Assn., Internat. Law Assn., Am. Soc. Internat. Law, Inst. Jud. Adminstrn. Office: Supreme Court Bldg San Juan PR 00904

RIGBY, PAUL CRISPIN, artist, cartoonist; b. Melbourne, Australia, Oct. 25, 1924; s. James Samuel and Violet Irene (Wood) R.; came to U.S., 1977; student Sandringham, Australia, Brighton Tech. Sch., Australia, Art Schs., Victoria, Grafton Studios, Australia; m. Marlene Anne Cockburn, Nov. 16, 1956; children—Nicole, Pia, Peter, Paul, Danielle. Free lance artist, 1940-42; illustrator West Australian News, Ltd., 1948-52; editorial cartoonist Daily News Australia, 1952-69; daily cartoonist London Sun and News of the World, London, 1969-74; editorial cartoonist New York Post, 1977—; illustrator numerous books; represented in exhbns. of painting in Australia, Europe and U.S.A. Served with Royal Australian Air Force, 1942-46. Recipient Walkley award (Australia), 1960, 61, 63, 66, 69. Mem. Ch. of Eng. Clubs: Rolls Royce Owners; Royal Freshwater Bay Yacht; Met. Painters and Sculptors, Bentley Drivers. Home: 531 Main St Apt 621 Roosevelt Island New York NY 10044 Office: 210 South St New York NY 10002

RIGDON, VERNON DREW, pipe line co. exec.; b. Ashland, La., Oct. 11, 1924; s. Orie R. and Mollie L. (Joyner) R.; B.S., Centenary Coll. La., 1949; m. Marilyn L. Allen; children—Samuel D., Ethel L., Terri V., Donald C., William A., Lisa L. With internal auditing dept. Tex. Eastern Transmission Corp., Shreveport, La., 1949-56; asst. to treas., controller Pioneer Natural Gas Co., Amarillo, Tex., 1957-59; treas. Pioneer Gathering System, Inc., Amarillo, 1958-59; with Mgmt. Service Corp., Amarillo, 1959-60; staff asst. to asst. treas. Panhandle Eastern Pipe Line Co., Houston, 1960-66, asst. treas., 1966-74, treas., 1974-78, treas. subs. Trunkline Gas Co., 1977-78; v.p., treas. Panhandle Eastern and Trunkline Gas Co., Kansas City, 1979—. Served with USMC, 1942-45. Decorated Bronze Star medal, Purple Heart. C.P.A., Tex. Mem. Am. Inst. C.P.A.'s, Tex. Soc. C.P.A.'s, Fin. Execs. Inst. (v.p. 1977—). Lutheran. Home: 10035 N Charlotte St Kansas City MO 64155 Office: PO Box 1348 Kansas City MO 64141

RIGER, MARTIN, lawyer, educator; b. N.Y.C., June 19, 1910; s. Isidor and Mary (Becker) R.; A.B., Cornell U., 1931; LL.B., Columbia, 1934; m. Anne Cohen, Aug. 17, 1943; children—Andrea, Stephanie. Admitted to N.Y. bar, 1935, Ohio bar, 1955, D.C. bar, 1975, U.S. Supreme Ct. bar, 1940; practice in N.Y.C. and Washington, 1934-38; supervising atty. reorgn. div. SEC, 1938-39, asst. dir., 1939-41, dir., 1941-42, asst. dir. corp. fin. div., 1946-47; with Federated Dept. Stores. Inc., Cin., 1947-71, sec., gen. counsel, 1960-71, v.p., 1964-71; prof. law Georgetown U. Law Center, Washington, 1971-76, prof. law emeritus, 1976—; counsel Arnold & Porter, Washington, 1971-76. Served to lt. comdr. USNR, 1942-46. Mem. Am. Bar Assn., Assn. Bar City N.Y., Am. Law Inst., Phi Beta Kappa. Editor-in-chief Columbia Law Rev., 1933-34. Home: 666A Heritage Village Southbury CT 06488 also 6711 Starkeys Pl Lake Worth FL 33463

RIGG, DIANA, actress; b. Doncaster, Yorkshire, Eng., July 20, 1938; d. Louis and Beryl (Helliwell) Rigg; attended St. Christopher's Sch., Great Missenden, Buckinghamshire, Eng.; grad. Fulneck Girl's Sch., Pudsey, Yorkshire; studied two years at Royal Acad. Dramatic Art; m. Menahem Gueffen, July 6, 1973 (div. Sept. 1976); 1 dau., Rachael Atlanta Sterling. Made stage debut as Natella Abashwilli in The Caucasian Chalk Circle at the Theatre Royal, York, Eng., summer, 1957; after appearing in repertory in Chesterfield and Scarborough, joined Royal Shakespeare Co., Stratford-on-Avon, 1959; made Stratford debut as Andromache in Troilus and Cressida, summer 1960; made London debut at Aldwych Theatre in Ondine, 1961; other appearances in repertory at Aldwych Theatre include: Phillipe Trincante in The Devils, Gwendolen in Becket, Bianca in The Taming of the Shrew, 1961, Madame de Tourvel in The Art of Seduction, 1962, Monica Stettler in The Physicists, 1963; at the Royal Shakespeare, Stratford-on Avon, played Helena in A Midsummer Night's Dream, Bianca in The Taming of the Shrew, Lady Macduff in Macbeth, Adriana in The Comedy of Errors, Cordelia in King Lear, 1962; toured the provinces, spring, 1963, in A Midsummer Night's Dream, subsequently appearing at The Royal Shakespeare and at the Aldwych in The Comedy of Errors, Dec., 1963; again played Cordelia in King Lear at the Aldwych, Feb., 1964, prior to touring with both plays for the Brit. Council in Europe, USSR, and U.S.; during this tour made first appearance in N.Y.C. at the State Theatre, May, 1964, in the same plays; played Viola in Twelfth Night at Stratford, June, 1966, and Heloise in Abelard and Heloise at Wyndham's, May, 1970, and Brooks Atkinson, N.Y.C., Mar., 1971; joined The Nat. Theatre, 1972; appeared in Jumpers, 'Tis Pity She's a Whore and as Lady Macbeth in Macbeth, 1972; Celimene in The Misanthrope, 1973; Eliza Doolittle in Pygmalion, Albery, 1974; rejoined Nat. Theatre for U.S. tour of The Misanthrope at Kennedy Center, Washington, St. James Theatre, N.Y.C., 1975, at Old Vic, 1975, also Governor's Wife in Phaedra Britannica, 1975; film appearances include: A Midsummer Night's Dream, Assassination Bureau, On Her Majesty's Secret Service, Julius Caesar, The Hospital, Theatre of Blood, A Little Night Music, 1977; first appeared on TV, 1964, as Adriana in The Comedy of Errors, also appeared in The Hothouse, 1964, Women Beware Women, 1965; co-starred as Emma Peel in Brit. TV series The Avengers, 1965-67; appeared in TV movie Married Alive, 1970, then in series Diana, 1973-74, TV movie In This House of Brede, 1975, TV series Three Piece Suite, 1977. Nominated for Tony award as best actress in a dramatic play for Broadway appearance in Abelard and Heloise, also for the Misanthrope, Emmy nominations, 1967, 68, 75; recipient Plays and Players award as best performance by actress for Phaedra Britannica. Office: care Phil Gersh Agy Inc 222 N Canon Dr Beverly Hills CA 90210*

RIGG, HORACE ABRAM, JR., educator; b. Phila., Apr. 22, 1909; s. Horace Abram and Maud (Wynkoop) R.; A.M., Harvard, 1932; guest fellow Trinity Coll., Cambridge U., Eng., 1932, 33; student Ludwig-Maximillians Universitaet, Munich, Germany, 1932-33; student in Oriental studies U. Pa., 1934-35; Ph.D., Harvard, 1937, univ. fellow in philosophy, 1931-32, traveling univ. fellow in history, 1932-33; m. Ruth Bowman Lyman, Nov. 24, 1934; children—Alexandra (Mrs. John N. Samaras), Diana, Jonathan Lyman, Margaret R. Stewart, Peter Whitney (dec.). Asso. prof. history of religion Case Western Res. U., 1937-44; prof. history of religion, 1944-47, Severance prof. history of religion, 1947-65; chmn. dept. Bibl. lit. and history religion, 1937-58; research Harvard, 1948-49, prehistoric cave research, France, 1956; prehistoric Bushmen studies So. Rhodesia, 1959, 61, 62; research asso. Carl Mackley Houses, Fed. Housing Project No. 1, Phila., 1933-34; co-ordinating editor history of religion, Ency. Americana, 1946-47. Spl. advisor Selective Service Bd. No. 41, Cleve., 1941-43; fgn. service Middle East sect. OSS, 1943-44. Mem. Archaeol. Inst. Am., Cleve. Soc. (past sec.-treas. and pres.), Am. Oriental Soc., Am. Soc. Ch. Hist., Am. Geog. Soc., Am. Soc. Bibl. Lit. and Exegesis, Cleve. Chamber Music Soc., Internat. Soc. African Culture (trustee). Editor, contbr. Bibl. dictionaries. Contbr. papers, monographs, and revs. to jours., ency. Home: Newfoundway RFD 1 Union ME 04862 Died Dec. 25, 1978.

RIGGS, ARTHUR JORDY, lawyer; b. Nyack, N.Y., Apr. 3, 1916; s. Oscar H. and Adele (Jordy) R.: A.B., Princeton U., 1937; LL.B., Harvard, 1940; m. Virginia Holloway, Oct. 15, 1942; children—Arthur James, Emily Adele Freeman, Keith Holloway, George Bennett. Admitted to Mass. bar, 1940, Tex. bar, 1943; asso. Warner, Stackpole, Stetson & Bradlee, Boston, 1940-41; now mem. firm Johnson, Bromberg, Leeds & Riggs, Dallas; staff Solicitor's Office, U.S. Dept. Labor, 1941-42. Cert. in labor law Tex. Bd. Legal Specialization. Mem. Am., Dallas bar assns., State Bar of Tex., Southwestern Legal Found., Phi Beta Kappa. Home: 4116 Amherst St Dallas TX 75225 Office: 4400 Republic Nat Bank Tower Dallas TX 75201

RIGGS, DONALD EUGENE, univ. librarian; b. Middlebourne, W.Va., May 11, 1942; B.A., Glenville State Coll. 1964; M.A., W.Va. U., 1966; M.L.S., U. Pitts., 1968; Ed.D., Va. Poly. Inst. and State U., 1975; postgrad. U. Colo., 1977-78; m. Jane Francine Vasbinder, Sept. 25, 1964; children—Janna Jennifer, Krista Dyonis. Head librarian, tchr. sci. Warwood (W.Va.) High Sch., 1964-65; head librarian, audiovisual dir. Wheeling (W.Va.) High Sch., 1965-67; sci. and econs. librarian California State Coll. of Pa., 1968-70; dir. library and learning center Bluefield State Coll., 1970-72; dir. libraries and media services Bluefield State Coll., Concord Coll., Greenbrier Community Coll., and So. campus W.Va. Coll. of Grad. Studies, 1972-76; dir. libraries U. Colo., Denver, Met. State Coll., and Community Col. of Denver—Auraria Campus, 1976-79; univ. librarian Ariz. State U., 1979—; adj. prof. Calif. State Coll., 1968-70, W.Va. U., 1970-72, U. Colo., 1977-79; fed. relations coordinator Am. and W.Va. library assns., 1970-75; chmn. bd. dirs. Central Colo. Library System, 1976-79; chmn. Colo. Council Acad. Libraries, 1977-78; exec. bd. Colo. Alliance Research Libraries, 1978-79; cons. to libraries. Named Outstanding Young Educator, Ohio County Schs., 1966. Mem. ALA, Ariz. Library Assn., Colo. Library Assn. (pres. 1978-79), W.Va. Library Assn. (pres. 1975-76), Assn. Coll. and Research Libraries (pres. Tri-State chpt. 1972-74), Beta Phi Mu, Chi Beta Phi, Phi Delta Kappa, Phi Kappa Phi. Contbr. articles to profl. publs.; editor W.Va. Libraries, 1973-75; asso. editor Southeastern Librarian, 1973-75. Home: 2120 E Knoll Circle Mesa AZ 85203 Office: Ariz State U Temple AZ 85281

RIGGS, JAMES LEAR, educator; b. Webster City, Iowa, Sept. 23, 1929; s. Max Elwood and Dixie Ann (Wyckoff) R.; B.S., Oreg. State U., 1951, M.S., 1958, Ph.D., 1962; m. Doris Jean Miller, Dec. 23, 1951; children—James Randall, Robin Lee. With Mater Machine Works, 1958; asst. prof. indsl. engring. Oreg. State U., 1959-62, asso. prof., 1962-67, prof., 1967—, head dept., 1968—; affiliate faculty Japan-Am. Inst. Mgmt. Sci., Hawaii; dir. D & K Frozen Foods, Inc.; cons. editor McGraw-Hill; cons. in field. Served with USMC, 1951-56. Recipient Carter award for Outstanding Teaching, 1967; Fulbright lectr., Yugoslavia, 1975. Registered profl. engr., Calif. Mem. Am. Soc. Engring. Edn., World Confedn. Productivity Sci. (v.p. 1977—), Inst. Mgmt. Sci., Am. Inst. Indsl. Engrs., Sigma Xi, Alpha Pi Mu. Republican. Presbyterian. Author: Economic Decision Models, 1968; Production Systems: Planning, Analysis and Control, 2d edit., 1976; Industrial Organization and Management, 6th edit., 1979; The Art of Management, 1974; Introduction to Operations Research and Management Science, 1975; Engineering Economics, 1977; also articles. Home: 1210 SW Timian St Corvallis OR 97330

RIGGS, LORRIN ANDREWS, psychologist, educator; b. Harput, Turkey, June 11, 1912 (parents Am. citizens); s. Ernest Wilson and Alice (Shepard) R.; A.B., Dartmouth, 1933; M.A., Clark U., 1934, Ph.D., 1936; m. Doris Robinson, Aug. 28, 1937; children—Douglas Rikert, Dwight Alan. NRC fellow biol. scis. U. Pa., 1936-37; instr. U. Vt., 1937-38, 39-41; with Brown U., 1938-39, 41—, successively research asso., asst. prof., asso. prof., 1938-51, prof., 1951-77, L. Herbert Ballou Found. prof. psychology, 1960-68, Edgar J. Marston Univ. prof. psychology, 1968-77, emeritus, 1977—. Recipient Howard Crosby Warren medal Soc. Exptl. Psychologists, 1957; Friedenwald award Assn. Research Ophthalmology, 1966; Prentice medal Am. Acad. Optometry, 1973; Kenneth Craik award St. John's Coll., Cambridge U., 1979. Guggenheim fellow, 1971-72. Mem. Am. (div. pres. 1962-63; Distinguished Sci. Contbn. award 1974), Eastern (pres. 1975-76) psychol. assns., AAAS (v.p., chmn. sect. 1, 1964), Internat. Brain Research Orgn., Optical Soc. Am. (Tillyer medal 1969, dir. 1976—), Nat. Acad. Scis., Am. Physiol. Soc., Internat. Soc. Clin. Electroretinography, Assn. for Research in Vision and Ophthalmology (pres. 1977), Soc. Exptl. Psychologists, Am. Acad. Arts and Scis., Sigma Xi (chpt. pres. 1962-64). Asso. editor Jour. Optical Soc. Am. Club: University (Providence). Author sci. articles on vision and physiol. psychology. Home: 9 Diman Pl Providence RI 02906

RIGGS, ROBERT EDWON, educator; b. Mesa, Ariz, June 24, 1927; s. Lyle Alton and Goldie Esther (Motzkus) R.; B.A., U. Ariz., 1952, M.A., 1953, LL.B., 1963; Ph.D. in Polit. Sci., U. Ill., 1955; m. Hazel Dawn Macdonald, Sept. 1, 1949; children—Robert, Richard, Russel, Rodney, Raymond, Reisa, Preston. Instr., then asst. prof. polit. sci. Brigham Young U., 1955-60; research specialist Bur. Bus. and Pub. Research, U. Ariz., 1960-63; admitted to Ariz. bar, 1963; mem. firm Riggs & Riggs, Tempe, 1963-64; mem. faculty U. Minn., 1964-75, prof. polit. sci., 1968-75, dir. Harold Scott Quigley Center Internat. Studies, 1968-70; prof. law J. Reuben Clark Law Sch., Brigham Young U., 1975—. Democratic precinct chmn., 1970-72, 76—; mayor, Golden Valley, Minn., 1972-75; Dem. candidate for U.S. Congress from 3d dist., 1974. Bd. dirs. Minn. UN Assn., 1967-74, Utah Legal Services Corp., 1978—. Served with AUS, 1945-47. Rotary Found. fellow Oxford (Eng.) U., 1952-53; James W. Garner fellow U. Ill., 1953-55; Rockefeller research fellow Columbia U., 1957-58. Mem. Phi Beta Kappa, Order of Coif, Phi Kappa Phi, Delta Sigma Rho, Phi Alpha Delta. Mem. Ch. of Jesus Christ of Latter-day Saints (missionary in Eng. 1947-49). Author: Politics in the United Nations, 1958; The Movement for Administrative Reorganization in Arizona, rev. edit., 1964; (with Jack C. Plano) Forging World Order, 1967, Dictionary of Political Analysis, 1973; US/UN: Foreign Policy and International Organization, 1971; (with Plano and others) Political Science Dictionary, 1973; (with I. J. Mykletun) Beyond Functionalism: Attitudes toward International Organization in Norway and the U.S., 1979. Home: 1158 S 350 W Orem UT 84057. *Effort, a consistent direction, and dependability will carry anyone a long way. A sense of responsibility to others will make the way worth going.*

RIGGS, ROBERT LARIMORE, tennis player; b. Los Angeles, Feb. 25, 1918; s. Gedion Wright and Agnes (Jones) R.; student Prespreterian Coll., Clinton, S.C., 1938-39, Rollins Coll., Miami, 1939-40; children—Robert Larimore, Lawrence A., John W., James D., Dorothy P., William S. Profl. tennis player, 1941-75; U.S. jr. champion, 1935; mem. U.S. Davis Cup tennis team, 1938-39; tennis champion singles, doubles, also mixed doubles catagories, Wimbledon, Eng., 1939; U.S. tennis champion, 1939-41; U.S. and world profl. champion, 1945, 46, 47, 48; U.S. sr. champion, 1972. Promotor profl. tennis tour of world champions, 1949-51; exec. v.p. Am. Photograph Co., nat. portrait studio chain, 1954-72; promotor Bobby Riggs vs. Margaret Smith Court tennis match, 1973, Bobby Riggs vs. Billie Jean King tennis match, 1973. Served with USNR, World War II; PTO. Winner twenty-nine U.S. nat. tennis championships. Office: 508 E Ave Coronado CA 92118*

RIGGS, ROBERT OWEN, ednl. adminstr.; b. Gallatin, Tenn., Oct. 15, 1942; s. Clyde O. and Sue L. (Culbreath) R.; B.A., Vanderbilt U., 1964; M.Ed., Memphis State U., 1968, Ed.D., 1970; m. Judith Mathis, July 1968; children—Robert Owen, Susan Lea. Asst. to chancellor U. Tenn., Martin, 1970-71; dir. budget and planning Memphis State U., 1971-72; asst. to pres. James Madison U., Harrisonburg, Va., 1972-73, asso. dean, 1973-74, dean, 1974-76; pres. Austin Peay State U., Clarksville, Tenn., 1976—; dir. 1st Trust & Savs. Bank. Served with USMC, 1964-67. Named Outstanding Young Man Clarksville Jaycees, 1976. Mem. Am. Assn. for Higher Edn., Am. Ednl. Research Assn., Assn. for Instl. Research, Am. Assn. of State Colls. and Univs, Alpha Phi Omega, Phi Kappa Pi, Phi Delta Kappa, Phi Kappa Sigma. Methodist. Clubs: Rotary, Clarksville Country. Contbr. articles to profl. jours. Home: 703 College St Clarksville TN 37040 Office: Austin Peay State U College St Clarksville TN 37040

RIGGS, THOMAS JEFFRIES, JR., mfg. exec.; b. Logan, W.Va., June 1, 1916; student Marshall Coll., Huntington, W.Va., 1935, Duke, 1935-36, U.S. Naval Acad., 1936-37; B.S. in Metall. Engring., U. Ill.,

1941; grad. Army Gen. Staff and Command Sch., Ft. Leavenworth, Kans., 1943; m. Maxine L. Nickell, Dec. 8, 1939; children—Thomas Jeffries III, Julia Lee; m. 2d, Virginia Griggs Barrett, Nov. 12, 1948; children—Robin Rhys, Geoffrey Godwyn, Rory Balfour, Merry Murray. Sales engr. Linde Air Products Co., 1941; personnel supr. Ford, Bacon & Davis, Inc., Chgo., 1947-49, bus. rep., N.Y.C., 1949-50; gen. mgr., later v.p. Tele-Trip Policy Co., Inc., N.Y.C., 1950-53; with F. L. Jacobs Co., Detroit, 1953—, successively gen. sales mgr., exec. v.p., pres., 1954-56; exec. v.p., gen. mgr. Gabriel Co., Cleve., 1956-58; pres. Thomas J. Riggs, Jr. and Assos., Inc., mgmt. cons., Cleve., 1958-59; group v.p. Textron, Inc., Providence, 1959-72; exec. v.p., dir. Katy Industries, Inc., Elgin, Ill.; dir. HMW Industries, Inc., Stamford, Conn., 1972-75; pres., chief exec. officer Lawson-Hemphill, Inc., Central Falls, R.I., 1975—; dir. Internat. Paper Box Machine Co., Nashua, N.H. Chmn. Radio Free Europe R.I. Del. White House Conf. on Small Bus., 1980. Served 2d lt. to lt. col. Corps Engrs., AUS, 1941-46; lt. col. to col. M.I., Office Mil. Attache, Mex., 1946-47. Decorated Silver Star, Purple Heart; Croix de Guerre (Belgium, France). Mem. Am. Textile Machinery Assn. (dir. exec. com. 1978—), N.Y. Soc. Mil. and Naval Officers of World Wars, Res. Officers Assn., Young Pres.'s Orgn., Sigma Chi. Episcopalian (vestryman). Clubs: Army-Navy (Washington); Detroit; Hope, Agawam Hunt (Providence). Home: 6 Olive St Providence RI 02906 Office: 96 Hadwin St Central Falls RI 02863. *My personal philosophy is three-dimensional—to achieve and maintain the following priorities: 1) a business climate based on mutual respect and recognition; 2) the financial wherewithal to insure the domestic comforts and educational requirements of my family; 3) the necessary time to enjoy and serve my home, friends, church and chosen community.*

RIGHTER, CARROLL BURCH, astrologer; b. Salem, N.J., Feb. 2, 1900; s. John Charles and Mary Caroline (Burch) R.; student U. Pa., 1918-19; LL.B., Dickinson Sch. Law, 1922, LL.D., 1971. Law clk. firm Norman Grey, Esq., Phila., 1923-25; practicing astrologer, Hollywood, Calif., 1938—; syndicated columnist, 1950—; lectr., 1939—; founder, pres. Carroll Righter Astrological Found., Inc., Los Angeles, 1963—; practicing astrologer Eng., Netherlands, Ger. and France, 1977-79. Chmn. jr. com. Phila. Summer Concert Orch., 1928; chmn. Profl. Players, Phila., 1929; exec. sec. bd. Pa. Grand Opera Co., 1925-30. Mem. Chirothesian Ch. of Faith (chmn. bd., pres. 1968—). Author: Astrology and You, 1957; Astrological Guide to Health and Diet, 1968; Astrological Guide to Marriage and Family Relations, 1970; Dollar Signs, 1972; prepared Monthly astrological forecasts, 1951-75. Home: 1801 N Curson St Hollywood CA 90046 Office: PO Box 1921 Hollywood CA 90028

RIGHTER, JAMES HASLAM, ret. newspaper pub.; b. Phila., Sept. 1, 1916; s. James A. M. and Marie E. (Haslam) R.; student U.S. Naval Acad., 1935-37, Drexel U., 1938-41; div. 1973; children—Edward B., Kate B.; m. 2d, Catherine M. Oehler, May 21, 1975. Sales engr. indsl. sales dept. Phila. Electric Co., 1939-41; with Buffalo Evening News, 1946-71, asst. bus. mgr., 1949-50, asst. treas., dir., 1950-56, pub., v.p., treas., dir., 1956-71; asst. treas. radio sta. WBEN, Inc., 1953-57, asst. sec., treas., dir., 1957-64, treas., sec., dir., 1964-71; mem. exec. com., dir. First Empire State Corp., Buffalo, Mfrs. & Traders Trust Co., Buffalo; trustee Erie County Savs. Bank. Past chmn. adv. council Sch. Journalism, Syracuse U.; past pres. Buffalo Main St. Assn.; mem. bd. advisers Children's Hosp. Buffalo; past chmn. bd. trustees Villa Maria Coll. Buffalo; bd. dirs., chmn. Buffalo Philharmonic Orch. Soc.; trustee Forest Lawn Cemetery. Served from ensign to lt. comdr. USNR, 1942-46. Mem. N.Y. State Pubs. Assn. (past pres.), Navy League U.S. (past pres.), Niagara Frontier Council. Episcopalian. Clubs: Saturn, Buffalo Country (Buffalo); Adirondack League (Old Forge, N.Y.); Coral Beach (Bermuda). Home: 71 Little Robin Rd West Amherst NY 14228

RIGHTER, WALTER CAMERON, bishop; b. Phila., Oct. 23, 1923; s. Richard and Dorothy Mae (Bottomley) R.; B.A., U. Pitts., 1948; M.Div., Berkeley Div. Sch., New Haven, 1951, D.D., 1972; m. Marguerite Jeanne Burroughs, Jan. 26, 1946; children—Richard, Rebecca. Ordained priest Episcopal Ch., 1951, consecrated bishop, 1972; lay missioner St. Michael's Ch., Rector, Pa., 1947-48; priest-in-charge All Saints Ch., Aliquippa, Pa., 1951-54; rector Ch. of Good Shepherd, Nashua, N.H., 1954-71; bishop Diocese of Iowa, Des Moines, 1972—; N.H. del. Nat. Council Chs., 1963. Mem. N.H. com. White House Conf. on Youth, 1962, Regional Crime Commn., Hillsboro County, N.H., 1969-71; trustee Nashua Library, 1968-71. Fellow Coll. Preachers, Washington Cathedral. Home: 2300 Terrace Rd Des Moines IA 50312 Office: 225 37th St Des Moines IA 50312

RIGLER, PATRICIA HANGES, holding co. exec.; b. Oklahoma City, Feb. 26, 1937; d. James and Athena (Petropoulos) Hanges; student Oklahoma City U., 1959-60, Oklahoma City Southwestern Coll., 1975-77; divorced; 1 son, Bradley D. Adminstrv. asst. Liberty Real Estate Investment Trust, Oklahoma City, 1962-64; office mgr. James R. Tolbert & Assos., Oklahoma City, 1964-67; adminstrv. asst. Scrivner-Boogart, Inc., Oklahoma City, 1968-70; with Anta Corp., Oklahoma City, 1970—, corp. sec., 1976—; dir. PPD Corp., Newark. Mem. Am. Soc. Corp. Secs., Downtown Bus. and Profl. Women's Assn., Oklahoma City Met. Bd. Realtors, NOW, Friends of the Poor. Democrat. Mem. Greek Orthodox Ch. Club: Das. of Penelope. Office: 2400 First National Center Oklahoma City OK 73102

RIGLEY, HAROLD TOWNSEND, union ofcl.; b. N.Y.C., July 2, 1913; s. William F. and Anna M. (Townsend) R.; student pub. schs., N.Y.C.; m. Catherine C. Knoud, Aug. 26, 1946; children—Harold T., John, Robert. Bus. rep. Consol. Edison Co., N.Y.C., 1930-55; nat. rep. Utility Workers Union Am., AFL-CIO, 1955-58, sec.-treas. Local Union, N.Y.C., 1958-62, pres., 1962-71, nat. pres., Washington, 1971—; mem. exec. bd. AFL-CIO. Mem. Pres.'s Com. Employment Handicapped, 1957-77; mem. exec. bd. Greater N.Y. council Boy Scouts Am., 1970—. Mem. Am. Arbitration Assn. (dir.). Democrat. Roman Catholic. Club: N.Y. Turner. Office: 815 16th St NW Washington DC 20006

RIGSBEE, WILLIAM ALTON, ins. co. exec.; b. Durham, N.C., July 10, 1926; s. Coley Leonard and Julia (Hackney) R.; B.A., Duke U., 1946-50; m. Shirley M. Morgan, July 12, 1952; children—William Alton, Stephen R., James M. Asst. sec. Home Security Life Ins. Co., Durham, 1950-56; v.p. Franklin Life Ins. Co., Springfield, Ill., 1956-61; pres. Midland Nat. Life Ins. Co., Sioux Falls, S.D., 1961—, chmn. bd., 1966—, also dir.; pres., chmn. bd., dir. Investors Life Ins. Co.; dir. Northwestern Bell Telephone Co., Northwestern Nat. Bank of Sioux Falls. Bd. dirs. Sioux Falls Downtown Devel. Corp. Served to sgt. U.S. Army, 1944-46; ETO. Republican. Congregationalist. Clubs: Country, Racquet. Home: 1200 Tomar Rd Sioux Falls SD 57105 Office: One Midland Plaza Sioux Falls SD 57101

RIKER, WILLIAM HARRISON, educator; b. Des Moines, Sept. 22, 1920; s. Ben H. and Alice (Lenox) R.; B.A., DePauw U., 1942; Ph.D., Harvard, 1948; L.H.D., Lawrence U., 1975; Ph.D. (hon.), U. Uppsala (Sweden), 1977; m. Mary Elizabeth Lewis, Apr. 24, 1942; children—Katharine, William Harrison, Mary. Mem. faculty Lawrence U., Appleton, Wis., 1948-62, prof. polit. sci., 1958-62; Wilson prof. polit. sci. U. Rochester, 1962—, chmn. dept. polit. sci., 1962-78, dean grad. studies, 1979—; Mem. Bd. Zoning Appeals, Rochester, 1965-73. Vice chmn. Outagamie County (Wis.) Democratic Party, 1956-60. Recipient Uihlein award for excellence in teaching Lawrence U., 1962; Ford fellow, 1952-53; Rockefeller fellow, 1955-56; fellow Center Advanced Study Behavioral Sci., 1960-61; Fairchild distinguished scholar Calif. Inst. Tech., 1973-74. Mem. Am. Acad. Arts and Scis., Nat. Acad. Scis. Author: Democracy in the United States, 2d edit., 1964; The Theory of Political Coalitions, 1962; Federalism, 1963; Soldiers of the States, 1957; The Study of Local Government, 1958; Introduction to Positive Political Theory, 1972. Home: 75 Windemere Rd Rochester NY 14610

RIKER, WILLIAM KAY, pharmacologist; b. N.Y.C., Aug. 31, 1925; s. Walter Franklin and Eleanore Louise (Scafard) R.; B.A., Columbia U., 1949; M.D., Cornell U., 1953; m. Carmela Louise DePamphilis, Dec. 21, 1947; children—Eleanor Louise, Gainor, Victoria. Intern, 2d (Cornell) Med. Div., Bellevue Hosp., 1953-54; practice medicine, specializing in pharmacology, Phila., 1954-69, Portland, Oreg., 1969—; instr., asst. prof. dept. pharmacology U. Pa. Sch. Medicine, 1954-61; spl. fellow dept. physiology U. Utah Sch. Medicine, 1961-64; asso. prof., prof., chmn. dept. pharmacology Woman's Med. Coll., Phila., 1964-69; prof., chmn. dept. pharmacology U. Oreg. Sch. Medicine, U. Oreg. Health Scis. Center, 1969—: mem. neurol. disorders program project com. NIH, 1975—. Served with USNR, 1943-46. Recipient Christian R. and Mary F. Lindback Found. award for disting. teaching, 1968. Pa. Plan scholar, 1957-61; Nat. Inst. Neurol. Diseases and Blindness spl. fellow, 1961-64; USPHS (NIH) research grantee, 1958—. Mem. Am. Soc. Pharmacology and Exptl. Therapeutics (sec.-treas. 1978—), Western Pharmacol. Soc. (pres. 1976), Japanese Pharmacol. Soc., Assn. Med. Sch. Pharmacologists (sec. 1976-78), Epilepsy Assn. Am., Pharm. Mfrs. Assn. Found. (chmn. pharmacology-morphology adv. com., sci. adv. com.). Editor Jour. Pharmacology and Exptl. Therapeutics, 1969-72; contbr. articles to biomed. jours. Home: 01661 SW Radcliffe Rd Portland OR 97219 Office: 3181 SW Sam Jackson Park Rd Portland OR 97201

RIKHOFF, JAMES CORNWALL, pub. co. exec.; b. Chgo., May 8, 1931; s. Harold Franklin and Blanch Marie (Bowlus) R.; student Denison U., 1949-51; B.A., Ohio State U., 1956; B.A. in Fgn. Trade, Am. Inst. Fgn. Trade, 1957; m. Janet Mae Finlay, Mar. 17, 1956; children—Erika Viktoria, Christina Anne, James Cornwall. Export specialist Am. Hosp. Supply Corp., Flushing, N.Y., 1957-58; pub. relations adviser Olin Corp., N.Y.C., 1959-64, mgr., 1964-68, dir. 1968-75, pres., chmn. bd. Winchester Press, Inc. div. Olin Corp., N.Y.C., 1969-75; chmn. bd., pres. Winchester Adventures, Inc., 1973-75; pres. Conservation Communications Co., 1975—; pres., chmn. bd. Nat. Sporting Frat. Ltd., 1976—, Amwell Press, Inc., 1976—. Chmn. bd. Nat. Found. Conservation and Environ. Officers, Inc., pres., 1974-77, chmn. bd., 1974—; bd. dirs. Game Conservation Internat.; bd. dirs. Am. Field Sports Soc. Inc., pres., chmn. bd., 1974-76; trustee Hunting Hall of Fame, 1975. Served with AUS, 1952-54; PTO. Mem. African Safari Club N.Y. (Conservation Legion of Merit Silver medal 1974, pres. 1970-71), Boone and Crockett Club, Amwell Valley Hounds (joint-master 1971-77), Shikar-Safari Club Internat., Internat. Profl. Hunters Assn., Phi Delta Theta, Delta Phi Epsilon. Club: Leash (N.Y.C.). Author: Mixed Bag, 1979; (with Thomas E. Hall, George R. Watrous) The History of Winchester Firearms, 1866-75, 1975. Contbr. chpts., editor: Compact Book of Hunting, 1964; editor: (with Eric Peper) Hunting Moments of Truth (anthology), 1973; (with Peper) Fishing Moments of Truth (anthology), 1973, Monthly columnist The Am. Rifleman, 1978—; contbr. numerous articles on conservation, game mgmt., ecology, hunting and fishing, horses and firearms to profl. jours. Home: 49 Dewey Rd High Bridge NJ 08829 Office: 65 Old Route 22 Clinton NJ 08809

RIKHOFF, JOHN LAWRENCE, pub. co. exec.; b. Indpls., Sept. 15, 1934; s. Frank Joseph and Leona Margaret (Colby) R.; B.A., DePauw U., 1956; m. Karen Knutson, Oct. 11, 1956; children—Jeffrey Jon, Gregory Scott, Robert Alan. Coll. salesman Houghton Mifflin Co., 1958-66, sales mgr. dictionary div., 1966-69, dir. mktg. dictionary div., 1969-75, v.p., dir., 1975; pres. William Collins Pubs., Inc., Cleve., 1975—. Served with U.S. Army, 1956-58. Mem. Am. Mgmt. Assn., Am. Mktg. Assn. Home: 4125 Diane Dr Fairview Park OH 44126 Office: 2080 W 117th St Cleveland OH 44111

RIKLIS, MESHULAM, mfg. exec.; b. Turkey, Dec. 2, 1923; s. Pinhas and Betty (Guberer) R.; grad. high sch., Israel; student U. Mexico, 1947: B.A., Ohio State U., 1950, M.B.A., 1966; m. Judith Stern, Dec. 17, 1944; children—Simona (Mrs. Irwin Ackerman), Marcia (Mrs. Benjamin Kletter), Ira Doron. Came to U.S., 1947, naturalized, 1955. Co-dir. youth activities and mil. tng. Hertzlia High Sch., Tel-Aviv, 1942; tchr. Hebrew Talmud Torah Sch., Mpls., 1951; research dept. Piper, Jaffray & Hopwood, 1951-53, sales rep., 1953-56; vice chmn. McCrory Corp., 1960-69, vice chmn. exec. com., dir., 1970—, chmn., 1975—; chmn., pres. Rapid-Am. Corp., 1957—; dir. H.L. Green Co. Served Brit. 8th Army, 1942-46. Mem. Pi Mu Epsilon. Jewish. Home: 781 Fifth Ave New York City NY 10022 Office: 888 7th Ave New York City NY 10019

RILES, WILSON CAMANZA, ednl. adminstr.; b. Alexandria, La., June 27, 1917; B.A., No. Ariz. U., 1940; M.A., 1947, LL.D., 1976; LL.D., Pepperdine Coll., 1965, Claremont Grad. Sch., 1972, U. So. Calif., 1975, U. Akron, 1976; L.H.D., St. Mary's Coll., 1971, U. Pacific, 1971, U. Judaism, 1972; m. Mary Louise Phillips, Nov. 13, 1941; children—Michael, Narvia Riles Bostick, Wilson, Phillip. Tchr. elementary schs., adminstr. pub. schs. Ariz., 1940-54; exec. sec. Pacific Coast region Fellowship of Reconciliation, Los Angeles, 1954-58; with Calif. Dept. Edn., 1958—, dep. supt. pub. instrn., 1965-70, supt. pub. instruction, 1971—; dir. Wells Fargo Bank, Wells Fargo Co., Pacific Gas and Electric Co. Ex-officio mem. bd. regents U. Calif.; ex-officio trustee Calif. State Univs. and Colls.; pub. trustee Nutrition Found.; nat. adv. council Nat. Schs. Vol. Program; mem. council Stanford Research Inst.; adv. bd. Cap Calif. Congress Parents and Tchrs.; trustee Am. Coll. Testing Program; mem. Edn. Commn. of States; past 2d v.p. Nat. PTA. Served with USAF, 1943-46. Recipient awards. Mem. Nat. Council Ednl. Research, Council Chief State Sch. Officers, Cleve. Conf., NAACP (Springarn medal 1973), Nat. Acad. Pub. Adminstrn., Found. Teaching Econs., Phi Beta Kappa. Club: Commonwealth of Calif. Address: State Dept Education 721 Capitol Mall Sacramento CA 95814

RILEY, ANTHONY WILLIAM, educator; b. Radcliffe-on-Trent, Eng., July 23, 1929; s. Cyril Frederick and Winifred Mary (White) R.; B.A. with honors, U. Manchester (Eng.), 1952; Dr.Phil., U. Tübingen (Germany), 1958; m. Maria Theresia Walter, July 16, 1955; children—Christopher, Katherine, Angela. Lectr., U. Tübingen, 1957-59, 60-62; asst. lectr. Queen Mary Coll., U. London (Eng.), 1959-60; asst. prof. German lang. and lit. Queen's U., Kingston, Ont., Can., 1962-65, asso. prof., 1965-68, prof., 1968—, head dept. German lang. and lit., 1967-76, acting head dept., 1979-80. Served with Brit. Army, 1947-49. Summer fellow Weil Inst. for Studies in Religion and the Humanities, Cin., 1965; Can. Council Leave fellow, 1969-70, 76-77. Mem. Canadian Assn. U. Tchrs. German (v.p. 1973-75, pres. 1975-76), Canadian Comparative Lit. Assn., Modern Lang. Assn. Am., Deutsche Schillergesellschaft, Thomas Mann Gesellschaft (Zürich), Humanities Assn. Can. Author: Elisabeth Langgässer Bibliographie mit Nachlassbericht, 1970; also articles on Thomas Mann, Alfred Döblin, Hermann Hesse, Elisabeth Langgässer, F.P. Grove; editorial bd. seminar A Jour. of Germanic Studies, 1971-76; co-editor: The Master Mason's House (F.P. Grove), 1976; editor: Der Oberst und der Dichter/Die Pilgerin Aetheria (Alfred Döblin), 1978. Home: 108 Queen Mary Rd Kingston ON K7M 2A5 Canada Office: Dept German Queen's U Kingston ON K7L 3N6 Canada

RILEY, CONRAD MILTON, physician, educator; b. Worcester, Mass., Aug. 10, 1913; s. Robert Sanford and Katharine (Higgins) R.; B.A., Yale U., 1934; M.D., Harvard U., 1938; m. Janet MacLeod Burbank, July 20, 1935 (dec. Feb. 1976); children—Kitty Chapin (Mrs. Jonathan Clark), Patricia L. (Mrs. Gerard Lenthall), Christopher M., Janet Josephine (Mrs. James Aardal); m. 2d, Ruth G. Moore, July 4, 1976 (dec. Oct. 1977); m. 3d, Nancy D. Mikesell, June 14, 1978. Intern, Presbyn. Hosp., N.Y.C., 1938-40, Boston Children's Hosp., 1941-42; resident Babies Hosp., N.Y.C. 1942-43; from instr. to asso. prof. pediatrics Columbia Coll. Physicians and Surgeons, 1946-59; prof. pediatrics U. Colo. Med. Sch., 1960-77, emeritus, 1977—, prof. preventive medicine, 1961-77, emeritus, 1977—, chmn. dept. preventive medicine, 1961-66, asso. dean admissions, 1973-77; mem. sci. adv. bd. Nat. Kidney Found., 1952-70. Bd. dirs. Riverdale Neighborhood House, N.Y.C., 1956-59, chmn., 1958-59; bd. dirs. Met. Council Community Service, Denver, 1966-72, Rocky Mountain Planned Parenthood, 1976-78; trustee Denver Zool. Soc., 1972—. Served to lt. USNR, 1943-46. Mem. Am. Pediatric Soc. (sec. 1960-63, v.p. 1976-77), Am. Acad. Pediatrics. Described, with others, familial dysautonomia (Riley-Day syndrome), 1949. Home: 590 Circle Dr Denver CO 80206

RILEY, DANIEL EDWARD, air force officer; b. Flint, Mich., Aug. 18, 1915; s. Daniel Edward and Elva (Kirby) R.; B. Aero. Engring., U. Detroit, 1940; M.B.A., U. Mich., 1951; postgrad. Indsl. Coll. of Armed Forces, 1959; m. Margaret E. Marengo, Nov. 28, 1938; children—Dennis M., Patricia A., Daniel R. Commd. 2d lt. USAAF, 1936, advanced through grades to maj. gen. USAF, 1968; chief of plans and operations 7290th Procurement Squadron at Rhein/Main Air Base, Germany, 1951-1952; dep., later chief of procurement and prodn. div. Hdqrs. USAF in Europe, also comdr. 7290th Procurement Squadron, 1952-54; dep. chief of staff materiel Directorate of Procurement and Prodn., Hdqrs. USAF, 1954-58; program dir. MACE missile Air Research and Devel. Command, Wright-Patterson AFB, Ohio, 1959-60; vice comdr. Electronics Systems div. AFSC, Bedford, Mass., 1965; comdr. Air Force Contract Mgmt. Div., Los Angeles, 1965-69; asst. dir. Def. Supply Agy., Washington, 1969—; asst. to pres. Novatronics Inc., Pompano Beach, Fla., 1976-77. Decorated Legion of Merit with 2 oak leaf clusters. Mem. Am. Inst. Aeros. and Astronautics, Armed Forces Mgmt. Assn., Air Force Assn., Am. Ordnance Assn., Indsl. Coll. Armed Forces Assn., Beta Gamma Sigma, Phi Kappa Phi. Home: 1408 Oak Forest Dr Ormond Beach FL 32074

RILEY, DAVID CLYDE, meat packing co. exec.; b. Geneva County, Ala., Oct. 16, 1926; s. Washington Monroe and Ada (May) R.; attended Butler U., 1952-55; m. Patricia J. Thomas, Oct. 30, 1952; children—David Bruce, Margaret Ann. With Hygrade Food Products Corp., 1944—, in processing and sales positions, 1944-68, became gen. mgr. Detroit div., 1968, v.p., gen. sales mgr., 1969, v.p., gen. mgr. div. processed meats, 1970, exec. v.p., 1973, pres. div. meat products, 1974, pres., chief exec. officer, 1974—, also dir.; dir. Liberty State Bank & Trust. Served with USNR. Mem. Am. Meat Inst. (dir., mem. exec. com.), Econ. Club Detroit. Mason (Shriner, K.T.). Club: Detroit Athletic. Office: Hygrade Food Products Corp PO Box 4771 Detroit MI 48219*

RILEY, HAROLD MARVIN, agrl. economist; b. Holton, Kans., Nov. 13, 1922; s. Mart H. and Bertha B. (Brockelman) R.; B.S., Kans. State U., 1947, M.S., 1948; Ph.D., Mich. State U., 1954; m. Dorothy Hibbs, Jan. 29, 1944; children—Betty, James. Mem. faculty Mich. State U., 1954—, prof. agrl. econs., 1960—, chmn. dept., 1973-78, asso. dir. Inst. Internat. Agr., 1967-69. Served with U.S. Army, 1943-46. Mem. Am. Agrl. Econs. Assn., Internat. Assn. Agrl. Economists. Co-author monographs, papers on mktg. and econ. devel. Home: 1351 Albert St East Lansing MI 48823 Office: Room 216 Agriculture Hall Mich State Univ East Lansing MI 48824

RILEY, HENRY CHARLES, banker; b. Newton, Mass., Mar. 23, 1932; s. Charles Matthew and Marion Anna (Armstrong) R.; A.B., Yale, 1954; M.B.A., Boston Coll., 1965; m. Patricia Ann Buchanan, Mar. 3, 1962; children—Lauren Elizabeth, Carolyn Ann, Julie Louise. With Bay Bank Harvard Trust Co., Cambridge, Mass., 1958—, treas., sec., 1967-70, v.p., treas., 1970-72, sr. v.p., sec., 1972—. Treas., trustee Longy Sch. Music; asst. treas. Mt. Auburn Hosp. Served with USNR, 1956-57. Mem. Boston Coll. Grad. Bus. Alumni Assn. (past dir., pres.), Cambridge C. of C. (dir., treas., v.p. 1975—). Episcopalian. Clubs: Rotary (dir. club 1976—, pres. 1978-79); Yale, Harvard (Boston). Home: 33 York Way Westwood MA 02090 Office: PO Box 300 Cambridge MA 02139

RILEY, JACK, actor, writer; b. Cleve., Dec. 30, 1935; s. John A. and Agnes C. (Corrigan) R.; B.S. in English, John Carroll U., 1961; m. Ginger Lawrence, May 18, 1975; 1 dau., Jamie. Mem. Rolling Along of 1960, Dept. Army Travelling Show; co-host Baxter & Riley, Sta.-WERE, Cleve., 1961-65; numerous TV appearances, including: as Mr. Carlin on Bob Newhart Show, CBS-TV, 1972-78, Occasional Wife, series, NBC, 1966, Mary Tyler Moore, 1972, Barney Miller, 1979, Diff'rent Strokes, 1979; appeared in feature films including: Catch-22, 1969, McCabe and Mrs. Miller, 1970, Long Goodbye, 1972, Calif. Split, 1974, World's Greatest Lover, 1978, High Anxiety, 1978, Butch and Sundance—The Early Years, 1979; play: West Coast premier of Small Craft Warnings, 1975; TV writer: The Many Sides of Don Rickles, ABC-TV, 1969, Don Rickles Show, ABC-TV, 1968, Mort Sahl Show, Sta.-KTTV, Los Angeles, 1967; writer comedy material for Tim Conway, Pat McCormick, Mitzi Gaynor, Mike Douglas Show; writer commls. for Blore & Richman Inc., Los Angeles, 1966-79; instr. in comedy acting Sherwood Oaks Coll. Served with U.S. Army, 1958-61. Mem. Screen Actors Guild, Actor's Equity, AFTRA, Writers Guild Am., Acad. Motion Picture Arts and Scis., Acad. TV Arts and Scis. Office: care Artist's Agy 190 N Canon Dr Beverly Hills CA 90210

RILEY, JAMES EDWIN, airline exec.; b. New Haven, June 3, 1926; s. James Edwin and Edith Louise (Howell) R.; A.B., Wesleyan U., Middletown, Conn., 1949; LL.B., Yale U., 1952; m. Carol Edith Chadwick, June 25, 1955; children—Madelein, Pamela, Melissa. Admitted to Conn. bar, 1952, D.C. bar, 1963, Pa. bar, 1971, Tex. bar, 1978; atty. Office Gen. Counsel, Navy Dept., Washington, 1953-58; successively atty., div. counsel, asst. gen. atty. Collins Radio Co., Cedar Rapids, Iowa, 1958-62; counsel Office Manned Space Flight, NASA, Washington, 1962-66; legal counsel Univac div. Sperry Rand Corp., Blue Bell, Pa., 1967-75; v.p., gen. counsel Braniff Internat. Airways, Inc., 1976-77, sr. v.p., gen. counsel, 1977—; chmn. privacy and security com. Computer and Bus. Equipment Assn., 1974-76, chmn. plans and policy com., 1970-71. Served with USAAF, 1944-45. Mem. Am., Fed. bar assns. Address: Braniff Internat PO Box 61747 Dallas-Fort Worth Airport TX 75261

RILEY, JAMES JOSEPH, union exec.; b. Cleve., Nov. 12, 1919; s. Frank James and Mary Jane (Connor) R.; B.S., Western Res. U., 1940; m. Ruth Marie Pearce, Apr. 10, 1939; children—Janet M., Nancy C., Catherine A., James F., Thomas M., Dennis J., Ruth E., Mary H., John R. Mem. Cleve. Motion Picture Operators Union, Local 160, 1941—; partner Electric Speed Indicator Co., weather instrument maker, Cleve., 1965-67; bus. agt. Internat. Alliance of Theatrical Stage Employees and Moving Picture Operators of U.S. and Can., Cleve., 1967-78, internat. gen.-sec. treas., N.Y.C., 1978—, internat. trustee, 1969-78. Served to lt. USNR, 1943-46; PTO. Roman Catholic. Editor Bull., Internat. Alliance Quar., 1978—. Home: 15801 Edgecliff Rd Cleveland OH 44111 Office: Suite 601 1515 Broadway New York NY 10036

RILEY, JANET MARY, lawyer; b. New Orleans, Sept. 20, 1915; d. John Nichols and Odile (Hymel) Riley; B.A. cum laude, Loyola U., New Orleans, 1936; J.D., 1952; B.S. in L.S., La. State U., 1940; LL.M. (fellow 1959-60), U. Va., 1960. Tchr., Orleans Parish pub. schs., 1937-39; asst. circulation dept. New Orleans Pub. Library, 1940-41; admitted to La. bar, 1953, U.S. Supreme Ct. bar, 1960; asst. librarian Loyola U., 1941-43, law librarian Law Sch., 1945-56, mem. teaching faculty, 1956—, prof. law, 1971—, bd. regents, 1970-72, chmn. univ. senate, 1970-72; librarian Camp Plauche, 1943-45, LaGarde Gen. Hosp., 1945; mem. Orleans Parish Juvenile Ct. Adv. Com., 1971—, chmn., 1977-78; steering com., legis. com. Gov. La. Task Force Women and Credit, 1973-76, Gov. La. Conf. Women, 1976, La. Atty. Gen.'s Task Force to Draft Brochure on Community Property for Marriage License Applicants, 1975; mem. com. to draft pattern jury instrn. for civil trials La. Supreme Ct., 1968-72. Bd. dirs. Community Relations Council Greater New Orleans, 1966—, 1st v.p., 1972-73. Mem. La. State Bar Assn. (sec. sect. internat. comparative and mil. law 1955-58, adv. com. bd. admissions 1964-66, 67-68), League Women Voters, St. Thomas More Catholic Lawyers Assn., La. State Law Inst. (council 1971, reporter 1972-78), AAUP, La. Com. Humanities, Cardinal Key, Assn. Henri Capitant, Nat. Assn. Women Lawyers, Assn. Women Attys. Greater New Orleans, Blue Key, Phi Kappa Phi, Phi Alpha Delta, Beta Phi Mu. Democrat. Roman Catholic. Author: Louisiana Community Property, 1972; contbg. author: Essays on the Civil Law of Obligations, 1969; Right in the Marketplace, 1975-76. Contbr. to legal publns. Address: 3413 Vincennes Pl New Orleans LA 70125

RILEY, JEANNIE C. STEPHENSON (MRS. MITCHELL E. RILEY), vocalist, entertainer; b. Stamford, Tex., Oct. 19, 1945; d. Oscar W. and Nora (Moore) Stephenson; grad. high sch., Anson, Tex.; m. Mitchell E. Riley, Dec. 20, 1963; 1 dau., Kim Michelle. Vocalist, rec. artist popular music; TV appearances include Bob Hope, Hollywood Palace, Joey Bishop, Am. Bandstand, Happening '68, Upbeat, Top of Pops (Eng.) shows. Rec. Harper Valley P.T.A. voted no. 2 single, recipient gold record Rec. Industry Assn. Am., 1968, also recipient gold record for Harper Valley P.T.A. Album, 1968; Harper Valley P.T.A. voted no. 1 Country and Western single Country Music Assn., 1968; voted most promising female vocalist pop field Record World Poll, 1968, Cash Box Poll, 1968; recipient Gold Cartridge award. Mem. Country Music Assn., Nat. Acad. Rec. Arts and Scis. Address: care Gene Scott PO Box 454 Brentwood TN 37027*

RILEY, JOSEPH HARRY, banker; b. Pitts., May 13, 1922; s. Joseph John and Frances P. (Wacker) R.; B.C.S., Benjamin Franklin U., 1950; postgrad. Grad. Sch. Banking, Rutgers U., 1954; m. Anna Belle Hepler, May 2, 1957; 1 dau., Michelle Patricia. With Nat. Savs. & Trust Co., Washington, 1947—, exec. v.p., 1970-73, sr. exec. v.p., 1973-76, pres., 1976—; dir. Columbia Real Estate Title Co. Treas., Heroes; bd. dirs. Anthony Francis Lucas Spindletop Found., Anson Mills Found., Benning Park Found., Gainesville Found., Jr. Achievement Washington, Boys Club Greater Washington, St. Ann's Infants Home: bd. dirs., pres. Kiwanis Found.; past pres. Met. Washington Bd. Trade. Served with USMCR, 1942-46, 50-51. Mem. D.C. Bankers Assn. (past pres.), Am. Bankers Assn., Mortgage Bankers Assn., Washington Conv. and Visitors Bur. (past pres.), Soc. Friendly Sons St. Patrick. Clubs: Congressional Country, University, Metropolitan (Washington); Burning Tree. Home: 10116 Iron Gate Rd Potomac MD 20854 Office: 15th and New York Ave Washington DC 20005. *If one guideline stood out in my life it would be my belief in contributing. I feel you should voluntarily offer to give of yourself in any endeavor in which you are a participant whether it be business, community or social. If you fail to make such an effort you have forfeited the right to complain regardless of the final result.*

RILEY, LAWRENCE JOSEPH, clergyman; b. Boston, Sept. 6, 1914; s. James and Ellen (Ryan) R.; A.B., Boston Coll., 1936; S.T.B., Gregorian U., 1939; S.T.D., Catholic U. Am., 1948; LL.D., Stonehill Coll., 1957, Boston Coll., 1965. Ordained Priest, Roman Cath. Ch., 1940; prof., rector St. John's Sem., Boston, 1941-66; prof. Emmanuel Coll., 1965-66; chaplain Harvard Cath. Club, 1950-54; vice officialis Met. Tribunal, Archdiocese of Boston, 1950-76, sec. Archbishop of Boston, 1951-58, aux. bishop of Boston, 1971—; pastor Most Precious Blood Parish, Hyde Park, Mass., 1966—; synodal judge Met. Tribunal Boston. Mem. Cath. Theol. Soc. Am. (past pres.), Mariological Soc. Am., Canon Law Soc. Am., Dante Alighieri Soc. Mass. (past v.p.), Nat. Cath. Edn Assn. Address: 43 Maple St Hyde Park MA 02136

RILEY, MATILDA WHITE (MRS. JOHN W. RILEY, JR.), sociologist; b. Boston, Apr. 19, 1911; d. Percival and Mary (Cliff) White; A.B., Radcliffe Coll., 1931, M.A., 1937; D.Sc., Bowdoin Coll., 1972; m. John Winchell Riley, Jr., June 19, 1931; children—John Winchell III, Lucy Ellen Riley Sallick. Research asst. Harvard U., 1932; v.p. Market Research Co., Am., 1938-49; chief cons. economist WPB, 1941; research specialist Rutgers U., 1950, prof., 1951-73, emeritus prof., 1973—, dir. sociology lab., 1959-73; prof., chmn. dept. sociology and anthropology Bowdoin Coll., Brunwick, Maine, 1973—, Daniel B. Fayerweather prof. polit. econ. and sociology, 1974—; on leave as assoc. dir. Nat. Inst. on Aging, 1979—; mem. faculty Harvard, summer 1955; staff asso., dir. aging and society Russell Sage Found., 1964-73, staff sociologist, 1974-77; chmn. com. on life course Social Sci. Research Council, 1977—; sr. research asso. Center for Social Scis., Columbia U., 1978—; vis. prof. N.Y. U., 1954-61; cons. Nat. Council on Aging, Acad. for Ednl. Devel. Mem. study group NIH, 1971—, Social Sci. Research Council Com. on Middle Years, 1973-77. Trustee The Big Sisters Assn. Recipient Lindback Research award Rutgers U., 1970; Social Sci. award Andrus Gerontology Center, U. So. Calif., 1972—; fellow Advanced Study in Behavioral Scis., 1978-79. Fellow AAAS (chmn. sect. on social and econ. scis. 1977-78); mem. Inst. Medicine of Nat. Acad. Scis. (sr.), Am. Sociol. Assn. (exec. officer 1949-60, v.p. 1973—), Am. Assn. Pub. Opinion Research (sec., treas. 1949-51), Eastern Sociol. Soc. (v.p. 1968-69, pres. 1977-78), Sociol. Research Assn., Phi Beta Kappa, Phi Beta Kappa Assos. Author: (with P. White) New Product Research, Gliding and Soaring; (with Riley and Toby) Sociological Studies in Scale Analysis, 1954; Sociological Research, vols. I, II, 1964; (with others) Aging and Society, vol. I, 1968, vol. II, 1969, vol. III, 1972; (with Nelson) Sociological Observation, 1974; Aging from Birth to Death, 1979; (with Merton) Sociological Traditions from Generation to Generation, 1980; editorial com. Ann. Rev. Sociology, 1978—; contbr. articles to profl. jours. Home: PO Box 248 Brunswick ME 04011 Office: Bowdoin Coll Brunswick ME 04011

RILEY, N. ALLEN, research co. exec.; b. Urbana, Ill., Aug. 15, 1915; s. Lee Williams and Irene Elain (Fleischer) R.; B.S., U. Chgo., 1937, Ph.D., 1947; D.Sc. (hon.), Chapman Coll., 1976; m. Dorothy G. Califf, Feb. 14, 1942; 1 son, Michael Allen. Instr. dept. geology U. Chgo., 1946-47, asst. prof., 1947-48; with Chevron Oil Field Research Co., La Habra, Calif., 1948—, lab. dir., 1963-68, exec. v.p., 1968-71, pres., 1971—. Served from 2d lt. to lt. col. A.C., U.S. Army, 1941-46. Mem. Soc. Exploration Geophysicists, Am. Geophys. Union, Sigma Xi. Home: 1106 Miramar Pl Fullerton CA 92631 Office: PO Box 446 LaHabra CA 90631

RILEY, PATRICK GAVAN DUFFY, journalist, found. exec.; b. Middletown, Ohio, May 2, 1927; s. Frank Jerome and Sylva (Hornback) R.; A.B., St. Paul's Coll., Washington, 1949; M.S., Columbia U., 1951; postgrad. London Sch. Econs., 1954-56; Ph.L., Pontifical U. of St. Thomas, Rome, 1973; m. Annamaria Paltrinieri, Oct. 11, 1958; children—Anthony J. G., Patrick J., Joseph R.S., Miles F.C., Anna Maria, Brendan S.T., Gavin T.T. From copy boy to society reporter N.Y. Times, 1949-54; sub-editor Reuters, London, 1955-56; corr. UPI, 1956-59, assigned Paris, 1956-58, London, 1958-59; with Nat. Cath. News Service, 1959-76, European corr., 1962-74, fgn. editor, 1974-76; editor Nat. Cath. Register, Washington, 1976-79; exec. De Rance Found., 1979—; author weekly column Val Patrick, The Universe, London, 1966-68, monthly column Columbia mag., 1966-68; weekly columnist Nat. Catholic Register, 1975-76; radio news corr. CBS, Rome, 1967-69. Served with AUS, 1952-53. Mem. Associazione della Stampa Estera in Italia. Roman Cath. Club: Nat. Press (Washington). Author: (with others) Council Daybook, vol. I, 1963, vol II, 1964, vol. III, 1965. Home: 7821 Mary Ellen Pl Milwaukee WI 53213 Office: 7700 W Blue Mound Rd Milwaukee WI 53213

RILEY, PAUL HARBERT, gas co. exec.; b. Shinnston, W.Va., Mar. 15, 1918; s. Benjamin Franklin and Agnes Beauty (Harbert) R.; B.A., Fairmont State Coll., 1940; grad. Inst. Gas Tech., 1959, exec. course U. Va., 1961; m. Mary Gene Brown, Apr. 27, 1940; children—James Lynn, Paul Thomas. Serviceman, Lumberport-Shinnston Gas Co., 1940; measurement engr. South Penn Natural Gas Co., Parkersburg, W.Va., 1941-46; supt. transmission Owens, Libbey-Owens Gas Co., Charleston, W.Va., 1946-52; with Commonwealth Natural Gas Co., Richmond, Va., 1952—, v.p., chief engr., 1960-69, pres., 1969-73, chmn., 1973—, also dir.; dir. United Va. Bank. Pres., Robert E. Lee council Boy Scouts Am., 1977-78, Jr. Achievement Richmond, 1969-70; bd. dirs. Better Bus Bur. Richmond, 1971-73, United Givers Fund, Richmond, 1972-74; trustee Richmond Meml. Hosp., 1973—. Served with AUS, 1945-46. Mem. Southeastern Gas Assn. (pres. 1971), Richmond C. of C. (dir. 1976-79), So. Gas Assn. (dir. 1974-77). Methodist. Clubs: Rotary (pres. 1976-77), Commonwealth (Richmond); Stonehenge Golf and Country; Country of Va. Home: 11620 Drysdale Dr Richmond VA 23235 Office: 200 S 3d St Richmond VA 23219

RILEY, PAUL HUNTER, govt. ofcl.; b. Washington, July 3, 1918; s. Eugene and Pearl Riley; B.S., Ind. U., 1942; m. Patricia W. Riley, May 17, 1975; children—Sharon, Lauren, Christine, Paula; 1 stepson, Robert Hill. Chief of classification and wage adminstrn. Dept. Agr., Washington, 1946-50; chief mgmt. analysis div. Bur. of Budget, Washington, 1950-59; dir. supply mgmt. policy Dept. Def., Washington, 1959-61, now dep. asst. Sec. of Def. Served with U.S. Army, 1942-46. Decorated Bronze Star. Mem. Nat. Def. Transp. Assn., Soc. Logistics Engrs. Contbr. articles to profl. jours. Home: 4014 Ellicott St Alexandria VA 22304 Office: The Pentagon Washington DC 20301

RILEY, RAY ALLEN, city adminstr.; b. Little Rock, Nov. 4, 1937; s. Jack and Janet Elizabeth (Vick) R.; student U. Ark., 1954-56; B.A., Ouachita Baptist U., 1961; M.P.A., U. Kans., 1967; m. Mary Jane McClure, Sept. 23, 1967; children—Robert, Maggie. Asst. city mgr. City of Lawrence (Kans.), 1967-68; city mgr. City of Olathe (Kans.), 1968-72; city adminstr. City of Ft. Smith (Ark.), 1972-78; city mgr. City of Beaumont (Tex.), 1978—. Served to 1st lt. arty. U.S. Army, 1961-64. Mem. Internat. City Mgmt. Assn., Tex. City Mgmt. Assn. Methodist. Club: Rotary. Home: 5935 Gladys St Beaumont TX 77704 Office: 801 Main St Beaumont TX 77706*

RILEY, RICHARD WILSON, gov. S.C.; b. Greenville, S.C., Jan. 2, 1933; s. Edward Patterson and Martha Elizabeth (Dixon) R.; B.A., Furman U., 1954; J.D., U. S.C., 1960; m. Ann Osteen Yarborough, Aug. 23, 1957; children—Richard Wilson, Anne Y., Hubert D., Theodore D. Admitted to S.C. bar, 1959; partner firm Riley& Riley, Greenville, 1959-78; gov. S.C., 1978—; spl. asst. to subcom. U.S. Senate Jud. Com., 1960; mem. S.C. Ho. of Reps., 1963-66; mem. S.C. Senate senate from Greenville-Laurens Dist., 1966-76. Vice pres. S.C. Young Democrats, 1968. Served to lt. (j.g.) USNR, 1954-56. Named Outstanding Young Man of Greenville and S.C., Jr. C. of C., 1965. Mem. S.C., Greenville bar assns., Furman U. Alumni Assn. (pres. 1968-69). Rotarian. Home: 200 Sunset Dr Greenville SC 29605 Office: Office of Gov State House Columbia SC 29211

RILEY, ROBERT BARTLETT, architect; b. Chgo., Jan. 28, 1931; s. Robert James and Ruth (Collins) R.; Ph.B., U. Chgo., 1949; B.Arch., Mass. Inst. Tech., 1954; m. Nancy Rebecca Mills, Oct. 5, 1956; children—Rebecca Hill, Kimber Bartlett. Chief designer Kea, Shaw, Grimm & Crichton, Hyattsville, Md., 1959-64; prin. partner Robert B. Riley, A.I.A., Albuquerque, 1964-70; compus planner, asso. prof. architecture, dir. Center Environ. Research and Devel., U. N.Mex., 1966-70; prof. landscape architecture, head dept. landscape architecture U. Ill., Urbana-Champaign, 1970—; mem. rev. panel landscape architects Fed. Civil Service-Nat. Endowment Arts. Served with USAF, 1954-58. Nell Norris fellow U. Melbourne (Australia), 1977. Mem. AIA (Design award Md. 1962, N.Mex. 1968; Environ. Service award N.Mex. 1970), Am. Soc. Landscape Architects, Phi Beta Epsilon. Unitarian. Asso. editor Landscape mag., 1967-70. Home: 407 E Mumford Dr Urbana IL 61801 Office: 205 Mumford Hall Univ Ill Urbana IL 61801

RILEY, RUSSELL LOWELL, univ. ofcl.; b. Mendon, Mo., Feb. 11, 1911; s. Fred and Lucille (Daily) R.; B.S., sch. bus. and pub. adminstrn. U. Mo., 1934; grad. F.A. Sch. Ft. Sill, Okla., 1943; Command and Staff Sch., Ft. Leavenworth, Kans., 1945; m. Betty Thalheimer; children—Robert, Kathleen, Frederick, Marie Lucille, Linda Beth. Salesman, mdse. mgr. Montgomery Ward & Co., 1934; sales rep. for Swift & Co., 1935-37; personnel officer Social Security Bd., 1938-39; econ. clk. and div. chief U.S. R.R. Retirement Bd., 1937, 39-41; asst. chief, clearance div. U.S. Office Export Control, 1941; asst. chief civilian personnel div., hdqrs. USAAF, 1942-43; exec. asst. War Assets Adminstrn., 1946-48; exec. officer Dept. of State, 1948, asst. chief, div. libraries and insts., 1949-50, dep. dir. Office Ednl. Exchange, 1951-52, dir. Internat. Ednl. Exchange Service, 1953-58; dir. personnel Econ. Stablzn. Agy., also OPS, 1951; asst. adminstr. Internat. Info. Adminstrn., 1952-53; U.S. consul gen. to Malta, 1958-60, to Johannesburg, S. Africa, 1960-64, charge d'affaires, 1964-65; counselor Am. embassy, Monrovia, Liberia, 1964-66; consul gen. to Nfld., Labrador and French Islands of St. Pierre and Miquelon, 1966-68; asst. to vice chancellor U. Calif., Irvine, 1968—. Chmn. European Conf. Cultural Officers, 1956. Served as lt. col. F.A., AUS, ETO, 1941-46. Decorated D.S.M.; recipient merit citation Nat. Civil Service League, 1958. Mem. Am. Fgn. Service Assn., Acacia. Methodist, Mason. Home: 11771 Carlisle Rd Santa Ana CA 92705 Office: Univeristy of Cal Irvine CA 92717. *Plan pessimistically-operate optimistically. Remember that rocks are jagged and crevices are deep near the top.*

RILEY, STEPHEN THOMAS, historian, librarian; b. Worcester, Mass., Dec. 28, 1908; s. John and Mary (Ward) R.; A.B., Clark U., 1931, A.M., 1932, Ph.D. in Am. History, 1953; grad. U. Pa. Army Specialized Tng. Program, 1943-44; m. Alice Amelia Riehle, July 2, 1949. Asst. librarian Mass. Hist. Soc., Boston, 1934-47, librarian, 1947-62, dir., 1957-76, dir. emeritus, 1977—; mem. Mass. Revolutionary War Bi-Centennial Commn., 1965—, Mass. Gov.'s Commn. on Need of New Mass. Archives Bldg.; 1974, Mass. Archives Adv. Com., 1978—; mem. advisory com. Adams Family Papers, 1956—, George Washington Papers, 1969—, Daniel Webster Papers, 1966—; mem. vis. com. Boston Coll. Library, 1964, 67-68, Harvard U. History Dept., 1962-68, Harvard U. Press, 1965-71; cons. N.Y. State Hist. Assn., 1978. Bd. Dirs. Freedom Tr., Boston, 1965—. Served with U.S. Army, 1942—44, USAAF, 1944-45. Fellow Am. Acad. Arts and Scis., Soc. Am. Archivists, Royal Soc. Arts and Mfrs. (London); mem. Archives Am. Art (adv. com. New Eng. br. 1972—), Am. Antiquarian Soc., Bibliographical Soc. Am., Bostonian Soc., Colonial Soc. Mass., Mass. Hist. Soc., New Eng. Hist. Geneal. Soc. (corr. sec. 1973—), Weston (Mass.) Hist. Soc. (pres. 1977—), Phi Beta Kappa. Democrat. Roman Catholic. Clubs: Club of Odd Vols., St. Botolph (Boston); Grolier (N.Y.C.). Author: The Massachusetts Historical Society, 1791-1959, 1959; Stephen Thomas Riley: the Years of Stewardship, 1976. contbr. articles, revs. to hist. jours. Home: 334 Wellesley St Weston MA 02193 Office: 1154 Boylston St Boston MA 02215

RILEY, WARREN BARBOUR, mfg. co. exec.; b. Flushing, N.Y., May 7, 1925; s. James Gordon and Elizabeth Hutchinson (Southgate) R.; B.S., Yale, 1947; m. Patricia Ann Bourquardez, Jan. 29, 1947; children—James Gordon, Warren Barbour, Susan Patricia, Robert A.B. Engr., Bethlehem Steel Co., Bethlehem and Steelton, Pa., 1947; partner William E. Hill & Co., mgmt. consultants, N.Y.C., 1948-60; dir. marketing and corporate planning Bendix Corp., Detroit, 1960-65; v.p. corporate planning and marketing Federal-Mogul Corp., Detroit, 1965-68; v.p. Bemis Co., Inc., Mpls., 1968—; dir. Badger Meter Inc., Milw. Served to lt. USNR, 1943-45, 51-53. Mem. IEEE (sr.), Instrument Soc. Am. (sr.), Am. Mgmt. Assn., Am. Mktg. Assn., Yale Engring. Assn., NAM, Inst. Mgmt. Scis., AAAS. Clubs: Yale (N.Y.C.); Minneapolis; Wayzata Country. Contbr. chpt. to Handbook of Industrial Research Management, 1959, also articles to bus. and trade mags. Home: 4030 Heathcote Rd Wayzata MN 55391 Office: 800 Northstar Center Minneapolis MN 55402

RILL, JAMES FRANKLIN, lawyer; b. Evanston, Ill., Mar. 4, 1933; s. John Columbus and Frances Eleanor (Hill) R.; A.B. cum laude, Dartmouth Coll., 1954; LL.B., Harvard, 1959; m. Mary Elizabeth Laws, June 14, 1957; children—James Franklin, Roderick M. Legis. asst. Congressman James P. S. Devereux, Washington, 1952; admitted to D.C. bar, 1959, since practiced in Washington; asso. firm Steadman, Collier & Shannon, 1959-63; partner firm Collier, Shannon & Rill, 1963-69, Collier, Shannon, Rill & Edwards, 1969—; dir. The Winston Group, Inc., Washington, Marshall Durbin Food Corp., Birmingham, Ala. Trustee, Bullis Sch., Potomac, Md. Served to 1st lt. arty. AUS, 1954-56. Mem. Am. (past chmn. legis. com. sect. antitrust law, chmn. Robinson-Patman Act com., vice chmn. com. agy. adjudication sect. adminstrv. law), D.C. bar assns., Phi Delta Theta. Clubs: Federal City, Met., Potomac Valley Country. Contbr. articles to profl. jours. Home: 7305 Masters Dr Potomac MD 20854 Office: Suite 308 1055 Thomas Jefferson St NW Washington DC 20007

RIMERMAN, MORTON WALTER, utility exec.; b. Wilmington, Del., Aug. 7, 1929; B.S., LaSalle Coll., 1958; M.B.A., Drexel U., 1962; m. Helen Holland, Sept. 1960; 1 dau., Jennifer. With Phila. Electric Co., 1948—, asst. treas., 1970-73, treas., 1973—. Served with U.S. Army, 1951-53. Mem. Am. Gas Assn., Fin. Analysts of Phila. Address: Phila Electric Co 2301 Market St Philadelphia PA 19101

RIMOIN, DAVID LAWRENCE, physician; b. Montreal, P.Q., Can., Nov. 9, 1936; s. Michael and Fay (Lecker) R.; B.Sc., McGill U., 1957, M.Sc., 1961, M.D., C.M., 1961; Ph.D., Johns Hopkins U., 1967; m. Mary Ann Singleton, Sept. 1, 1962; 1 dau., Anne Walsh. Rotating intern Royal Victoria Hosp., Montreal, 1961-62, asst. resident medicine, 1962-63, fellow in med. genetics, 1964-67; asst. prof. pediatrics and medicine, chief genetics clinic Sch. Medicine, Washington U., St. Louis, 1967-70; chief med. genetics Harbor Gen. Hosp., Torrance, Calif., 1970—; asso. prof. pediatrics and medicine UCLA, 1970-73, prof. pediatrics and medicine, 1973—; cons. staff Cedars-Sinai Med. Center, Los Angeles, Orthopaedic Hosp., Los Angeles, Shriner's Hosp., Los Angeles, Fairview State Hosp., Costa Mesa. Recipient research career devel. award NIH, 1967-70; Ross Outstanding Investigator award Western Soc. Pediatric Research, 1976; E. Mead Johnson award Am. Acad. Pediatrics, 1976. Diplomate Nat. Bd. Med. Examiners, Am. Bd. Internal Medicine; licentiate Med. Council Can. Fellow A.C.P.; mem. Am. Fedn. Clin. Research (nat. council 1972-73, sec.-treas., 1973-74), Am. Soc. Clin. Investigation, Am. Soc. Human Genetics (dir. 1977-78), Soc. Pediatric Research, Endocrine Soc., Am. Diabetes Assn., Western Assn. Physicians, Wester Soc. Clin. Research (pres. 1978-79), Sigma Xi, Alpha Omega Alpha. Author: (with R.N. Schimke) Genetic Disorders of the Endocrine Glands, 1971. Asso. editor Metabolism 1970, Am. Jour. Human Gentics, 1974—, Med. Genetics Today, 1974, Jour. Clin. Endocrinology and Metabolism, 1975, Genetics Forms of Hypogonadism, 1975, Disorders of Connective Tissue, 1975, New Chromosomal and Malformation Syndromes, 1975. Home: 3141 Deluna Dr Rancho Palos Verdes Peninsula CA 90274 Office: 1000 W Carson St Torrance CA 90509

RIMROTT, FRIEDRICH PAUL J., engr., educator; b. Halle, Germany, Aug. 4, 1927; s. Hans and Margarete (Hofmeister) R.: Dipl. Ing., U. Karlsruhe (Germany), 1951; M.A.Sc., U. Toronto, 1955; Ph.D., Pa. State U., 1958; Dr.Ing., U. Darmstadt (Germany), 1961; m. Doreen McConnell, Apr. 7, 1955; children—Karla, Robert, Kira, Elizabeth-Ann. Came to Can., 1952. Asst. prof. engring. mechanics Pa. State U., 1958-60; mem. faculty dept. mech. engring. U. Toronto, 1960—, asso. prof., 1962-67, prof., 1967—; vis. prof. Tech. U. Vienna (Austria), 1969-70, Tech. U. Hanover (Germany), 1970, U. Bochum (Germany), 1971, U. Wuppertal (Germany), 1978; dir. German Lang. Sch. (Metro Toronto) Inc., 1967—. N.R.C. postdoctorate fellow, 1959, N.R.C. sr. research fellow, 1969-70, Alexander von Humboldt sr. fellow, 1962. Asso. fellow Canadian Aero. and Space Inst.; mem. Canadian Congress Applied Mechanics (mem. central com., chmn. congress com. 1967, 69, 71, 77), N.Y. Acad. Scis., Am. Acad. Mechanics, Canadian Metric Assn. (pres.), Canadian Soc. Mech. Engring. (pres.), Soc. German Engrs. (Germany), Soc. for Applied Math. and Mechanics (Germany) (dir.), Canadian Council on Multiculturalism. Editor: (with J. Schwaighofer) Mechanics of the Solid State, 1968; (with L.E. Jones) Proceedings CANCAM 67, 1968; (with J.T. Pindera, H.H.E. Leipholz, D.E. Grierson) Experimental Mechanics in Research and Development, 1973; (with W. Eichenlaub) Was Du ererbt . . . , 1978. Home: 6 Thurgate Crescent

Thornhill ON L3T 4G3 Canada Office: Dept Mech Engring Univ Toronto Toronto ON M5S 1A4 Canada

RINALDO, MATTHEW J., congressman; b. Elizabeth, N.J., Sept. 1, 1931; s. Matthew John and Ann (Papaccio) R.; B.S., Rutgers U., 1953; M.B.A., Seton Hall U., Newark, 1959; D.P.A., N.Y. U., 1971. Pres., Union Twp. Zoning Bd. Adjustment, 1962-63; mem. Union County Bd. Freeholders, 1963-64; mem. N.J. Senate, 1968-73; mem. 93d-96th Congresses from 12th Dist. N.J. Instr. Rutgers U. Extension Div., 1961-71. Bd. dirs. Union County Heart Assn., UNICO. Recipient Man of Year award Union, Plainfield and Maplewood chpts. UNICO Nat.; Health Freedom award, award Rod and Gun Editors Met. N.Y.; named Outstanding Young Man of Year, Union County Jaycees, C.; Knight of Year, Union council K.C.; Citizen of Year award B'nai B'rith; also honored by N.J. State Fireman's Mut. Benevolent Assn., Cath. War Vets., Hadassah, Union County Heart Assn., Policemen's Benevolent Assn., VFW, State Grand Jurors Assn., others. Republican. Roman Catholic. K.C. (4 deg.), Lion, Elk. Home: 142 Headley Terr Union NJ 07083 Office: 2338 Rayburn House Office Bldg Washington DC 20515

RINDER, GEORGE GREER, retail co. exec.; b. Chgo., Feb. 3, 1921; s. Carl Otto and Jane (Greer) R.; M.B.A., U. Chgo., 1942; m. Shirley Laurine Latham, Dec. 21, 1946; children—Robert Latham, Carl Thomas, Susan Jane. With Gen. Electric Co., 1941-42; with Marshall Field & Co., Chgo., 1946—, asst. to gen. mgr., 1959-62, v.p., comptroller, 1962-67, v.p. finance, 1967-71, exec. v.p. fin., 1971-74, exec. v.p., 1974-78, sr. exec. v.p., 1978—, also dir. Bd. dirs. United Charities Chgo. Served to capt. AUS, 1942-46. C.P.A., Ill. Mem. Fin. Execs. Inst., Phi Beta Kappa, Delta Upsilon, Beta Gamma Sigma. Clubs: Chicago, University, Carlton, Economic (Chgo.); Hinsdale (Ill.) Golf; LaGrange (Ill.) Country. Home: 736 Cleveland Rd Hinsdale IL 60521 Office: 25 E Washington St Chicago IL 60690

RINDER, IRWIN DANIEL, educator, sociologist; b. N.Y.C., Dec. 20, 1923; s. Aaron and Anita (Tieger) R.; B.A., U. Idaho, 1947; M.A., U. Chgo., 1950, Ph.D., 1953; m. Marion Hart, Oct. 3, 1969; children by previous marriage—Lenore, Tamara, Rose, Deborah, Elliott; stepchildren—Ingrid (Mrs. John Brooke), Carl, Charlotte, Marjorie. Instr., Wis. State Coll., Milw., 1952-57; from asst. prof. to prof. U. Wis.-Milw., 1957-68; prof. sociology Macalester Coll., St. Paul, 1968—. Served with USAAF, 1943-45. Fellow Am. Sociol. Assn.; mem. Midwest Sociol. Soc. (dir. 1963-65, 70-72), Soc. Study Social Problems (chmn. com. psychiat. sociology 1965-67). Author: Study Guide to Introductory Sociology, rev. edit., 1970; also articles. Book rev. editor Sociol. Quar., 1960-70; asso. editor Clearinghouse for Sociol. Lit., 1966—; editorial bd. Indian Jour. Sociology, 1968—. Home: 1539 Portland Ave Saint Paul MN 55104

RINEHART, MORRIS LAWLER, air conditioning co. exec.; b. Rushville, Ill., Feb. 25, 1914; s. Herman Chester and Dorothy (Lawler) R.; B.S., Northwestern U., 1935; postgrad. Chgo.-Kent Coll. Law, 1935-37, Loyola U., Chgo., 1937-38, Harvard Bus. Sch., 1954; m. Muriel Ruth Kamis, Dec. 23, 1944; children—Deirdre Sue, Karla Jean, Gayla Dawn, Debra Joan, Todd Cary Palmer, Mimi Kay. Tax accountant U.S. Gypsum Co., Chgo., 1935-41; asst. sec., gen. tax mgr. Butler Bros., Chgo., 1941-49; asst. v.p., asst. treas. Am. Airlines, Inc., N.Y.C., 1949-59; v.p. Carrier Corp., Syracuse, N.Y., 1959—. Past mem. adv. com. to commr. IRS; mem. tax adv. com. N.Y. commr. taxation and finance. Bd. dirs. Syracuse Symphony Orch.; trustee Syracuse Research Corp. Named Ky. col. Mem. Am. Soc. Corporate Secs., Nat. Assn. Bus. Economists, Am. Finance Assn., Newcomen Soc., Tax Execs. Inst. (past pres.), SAR, Phi Kappa Sigma, Beta Gamma Sigma, Beta Alpha Psi. Democrat. Presbyn. Mason (32 deg., K.T., Shriner), Lion. Clubs: University (N.Y.C.); Onondaga Golf and Country (Fayetteville, N.Y.); Century (Syracuse, N.Y.). Home: Henneberry Rd RD 2 Jamesville NY 13078 Office: Carrier Tower Syracuse NY 13221

RINEHART, RAYMOND GEORGE, mfg. co. exec.; b. Waukegan, Ill., Mar. 31, 1922; s. Horace A. and Irene (Love) R.; student Northwestern U., 1941; m. Winifred Collins, May 24, 1947; children—R. Michael, Judith, John, Susan, Patricia, Robert. With Clow Co., Oak Brook, Ill., 1941—, pres. Streator div., 1962-67, pres. Clow, 1967—, chief exec. officer, 1968—, pres., chmn., 1976-77, also dir.; dir. Kewaunee Sci. Equipment Corp., VSI Corp., 1st Fed. Savs. and Loan Assn., Chgo. Chmn., ARC, 1973-75; asso. Rehab. Inst. Chgo., 1970—; sponsor United Settlement Appeal, 1971—; mem. Community Fund Corp., 1972—; chmn. exec. com. Coll. Bus. Adminstrn., U. Notre Dame, 1971—, chmn., 1978; bd. dirs. Crusade of Mercy, Oak Brook and Hinsdale, 1972. Served with USAAF, 1942-46. Mem. Nat. Clay Pipe Inst. (dir. 1960-72), Chgo. Assn. Commerce and Industry (dir. 1971), Ductile Iron Pipe Research Assn. (treas. 1967). Clubs: Chicago, Metropolitan, Commercial (Chgo.); Hinsdale Golf; Butler Nat. Golf (Oak Brook). Home: 605 E 3d St Hinsdale IL 60521 Office: 1211 W 22d St Oak Brook IL 60521

RINES, ROBERT HARVEY, lawyer; b. Boston, Aug. 30, 1922; s. David and Lucy (Sandberg) R.; B.S. in Physics, Mass. Inst. Tech., 1942; J.D., Georgetown U., 1947; Ph.D., Nat. Chiao Tung U., 1972; D.J., NE Coll. Law, 1974; m. Carol Williamson, Dec. 29, 1972; 1 son, Justice Christopher; children by previous marriage—Robert Louis, Suzi Kay Ann. Asst. examiner U.S. Patent Office, 1946; admitted to Mass. bar, 1947, D.C. bar, N.H. bar, U.S. Supreme Ct. bar, FCC, Tax Ct., U.S. and Canadian patent office bars; partner Rines & Rines, Boston, 1947—; dir. Blonder Tongue Labs., Inc., Megapulse, Inc., Astro Dynamics, Inc., Prototech Co., Inc., PTC Research Found., A & M Electronic Reps., Inc., Sportsmans Handbook, Air Science Corp., KR Assos.; Gordon McKay lectr. patent law Harvard, 1956-58; lectr. inventions and innovation Mass. Inst. Tech., 1962—; pres., prof. law Franklin Pierce Law Center, 1973—. Mem. commerce tech. adv. bd. Dept. Commerce, 1963-67, mem. nat. inventors council, 1963-67; mem. N.H. Gov.'s Crime Study Com., 1976—. Campaign chmn. United Fund, Belmont Mass., 1960; com. mem. Nat. Inventors Hall of Fame, 1974—; adv. bd. Harvard-Mass. Inst. Tech. Biomed. Engring. Center, 1976—; bd. dirs. New Eng. Aquarium, Aaron Richmond Concerts, Inc., Allor Found., Inst. Applied Pharmacology. Served from 2d lt. to capt. AUS, 1942-46. Registered profl. engr., Mass. Mem. Acad. Applied Sci. (pres.), I.E.E.E. (sr.), A.A.A.S., Am. Bar Assn., Am. Patent Law Assn., Sci. Research Soc. Am., Aircraft Owners and Pilots Assn., Nat. Acad. Engring. (patent com. 1969—, cons. to exec. officer 1979-80), Sigma Xi. Unitarian (trustee 1954-56). Clubs: Harvard (Boston); Torquay Co. Theatrical Productions, Chemists (N.Y.C.); Mass. Institute Technology Faculty (Cambridge); Nat. Lawyers; Capitol Hill (Washington); Explorers; Highland (Scotland). Author: Create or Perish; Legal Incentives to Economic and Technological Expansion in the Republic of China; A Private Citizen's Commentaria on the American Role in the Far East; A Study of Current World-Wide Sources of Electronic and Other Invention and Innovation. Patentee in electronics. Home: 13 Spaulding St Concord NH 03301 Office: 10 Post Office Sq Boston MA 02109 also 81 N State St Concord NH 03301

RING, GERALD J., real estate developer, ins. exec.; b. Madison, Wis., Oct. 6, 1928; s. John George and Mabel Sarah (Rau) R.; student public schs., Madison; m. Armella Marie Dohm, Aug. 20, 1949; children—Michael J., James J., Joseph W. With Sub-Zero Freezer Co., Madison, 1948-70, mfr.'s rep., 1954-70; founder, sec.-treas. Parkwood Hills Corp., Madison, from 1965, Park Towne Devel. Corp., Madison, from 1969; chmn. bd. CUNA Mut. Ins. Soc., CUNA Mut. Ins. Group, CUNA Mut. Investment Corp., CUDIS Ins. Soc., all Madison; chmn. bd. CUMIS Ins. Soc., mem. exec. com.; treas. CUNADATA Corp.; bd. dirs. Wis. Credit Union League, 1958-79, pres., 1965-67; mem. Wis. Credit Union Rev. Bd., 1967—, chmn., 1973-76; dir. CUNA Credit Union Nat. Assn., Inc., 1964—. Chmn. Greater Madison C. of C., 1980, bd. dirs., 1976—. Served with USMC, 1951-53. Mem. Aircraft Owners and Pilots Assn. Roman Catholic. Club: Rotary. Home: 721 Anthony Ln Madison WI 53711 Office: 6622 Mineral Point Rd Madison WI 53705

RING, JAMES WALTER, physicist; b. Worcester, N.Y., Feb. 24, 1929; s. Carlyle Conwell and Lois (Tooley) R.; A.B., Hamilton Coll., 1951; Ph.D. (Root fellow), U. Rochester, 1958; m. Agnes Elizabeth Muir, July 18, 1959; 1 son, Andrew James. Asst. prof. physics Hamilton Coll., 1957-62, asso. prof., 1962-69, prof., 1969—, Winslow prof., 1975—, chmn. dept. physics, 1968—; attached physicist Atomic Energy Research Establishment, Harwell, U.K., 1965-66, Phys. Chemistry Lab. Oxford (Eng.) U., 1973. NSF grantee, 1959-66; NSF sci. faculty fellow, 1965-66. Mem. Am. Phys. Soc., Am. Assn. Physics Tchrs., Phi Beta Kappa, Sigma Xi. Contbr. articles to profl. jours. Office: Hamilton Coll Dept Physics Clinton NY 13323

RING, LEONARD M., lawyer; b. Tauragena, Lithuania, May 11, 1923; s. Abe and Rose (Kahn) R.; came to U.S., 1930, naturalized, 1930; student N. Mex. Sch. Mines, 1943-44; LL.B., DePaul U., 1949, J.D., 1971; m. Donna R. Cecrle, June 29, 1959; children—Robert Steven, Susan Ruth. Admitted to Ill. bar, 1949, since practiced in Chgo.; spl. asst. atty. gen. State Ill., 1967-72; spl. atty. Ill. Dept. Ins., 1967-73; spl. trial atty. Met. Sanitary Dist. Greater Chgo., 1967-77; lectr. civil trial, appellate practice, tort law Nat. Coll. Advocacy, San Francisco, 1971, 72; guest lectr. civil trial practice U. Chgo. Law Sch., 1973; mem. com. jury instrns. Ill. Supreme Ct., 1967-71, 74—; nat. chmn. Attys. Congl. Campaign Trust, Washington, 1975-79. Trustee Roscoe Pound-Am. Trial Lawyers Found., Cambridge, Mass., 1974—; chmn. bd. trustees Avery Coonley Sch., Downers Grove, Ill. Served with U.S. Army, 1943-46. Decorated Purple Heart. Fellow Am. Coll. Trial Lawyers, Internat. Acad. Trial Lawyers, Internat. Soc. Barristers; mem. Soc. Trial Lawyers, Appellate Lawyers Assn. (pres. 1974-75), Assn. Trial Lawyers Am. (nat. pres. 1973-74), Ill. Trial Lawyers Assn. (pres. 1966-68), Chgo. Bar Assn. (bd. mgrs. 1971-73), Am. Bar Assn., Ill. Bar Assn., Lex Legio (pres. 1976-78). Club: Oak Brook Polo (Ill.); Met. (Chgo.). Author: (with Harold A. Baker) Jury Instructions and Forms of Verdict, 1972; contbr. articles to profl. jours. Home: 6 Royal Vale Dr Oakbrook IL 60521 Office: 111 W Washington St Chicago IL 60602

RINGENBERG, LAWRENCE ALBERT, coll. dean; b. Stryker, Ohio, Aug. 21, 1915; s. Albert and Elizabeth (Rupp) R.; A.B., Bowling Green U., 1937, B.S. in Edn., 1937; A.M., Ohio State U., 1939, Ph.D., 1941; m. Viola Brown, Dec. 23, 1942; children—Richard Ray, Joanne Joy, Lawrence Albert, John Jay. Asst. math., fellow Grad. Sch. Ohio State U., 1937-41; asst. prof. math. Tusculum (Tenn.) Coll., 1941; asst. prof. math. U. Md., 1946-47; prof., head dept. math. Eastern Ill. U., 1947-67, dean Coll. Arts and Sci., 1961—, acting v.p. acad. affairs, 1977-78. Served to capt. AUS, 1941-46; lt. col. Res., ret. Mem. Math. Assn. Am., Nat. Council Tchrs. Math., Am. Assn. for Higher Edn. Author textbooks and articles in field. Home: 203 W Grant Ave Charleston IL 61920. *He knows not what he yet may do/Who works and to high aims is true.*

RINGER, JULES JACOB, lawyer, oil co. exec.; b. Cohoes, N.Y., Nov. 17, 1937; s. Samuel and Edith Lillian (Kelman) R.; B.S. in Econs., Wharton Sch., U. Pa., 1958; J.D., Cornell U., 1961; m. Judith Anne Waldman, Sept. 1, 1968; children—Jason Samuel, Jill Edith. Admitted to N.Y. bar, 1962, Tex. bar, 1974, U.S. Supreme Ct. bar, 1973; with firm Le Boeuf, Lamb & Leiby, N.Y.C., 1962-67; with legal dept., Levin-Townsend Computer Corp., N.Y.C., 1967-73; with firm Beldock, Levine & Hoffman, N.Y.C., 1973-74; v.p., counsel Earth Resources Co., Dallas, 1974—. Bd. dirs. Dallas Civic Opera, 1975—; pres. Dallas Squash Racquets Assn., 1976-77; exec. com. Dallas Symphony Orch. Guild, 1977—. Served with U.S. Army, 1962. Mem. Am., N.Y. State, Dallas bar assns., State Bar Tex., Assn. Bar N.Y.C. Jewish. Clubs: Harmonie (N.Y.C.); Columbian (Dallas); Masons. Home: 7030 Azalea Ln Dallas TX 75230 Office: 1200 One Energy Sq Dallas TX 75206

RINGER, ROBERT KOSEL, physiologist, educator; b. Ringoes, N.J., Feb. 21, 1929; s. Louis and Louise Eleanor (Kosel) R.; B.S., Rutgers U., 1950, M.S., 1952, Ph.D., 1955; m. Joan Lois Harwick, Aug. 18, 1951; 1 son, Kevin James. Asst. prof. Rutgers U., New Brunswick, N.J., 1955-57; asst. prof. physiology Mich. State U., East Lansing, 1957-61, asso. prof., 1961-64, prof., 1964—. Cons. Unilever Research Labs., Sharnbrook, Eng., 1966. Mem. Am. Physiol. Soc., Am. Assn. Avian Pathologists, World's Poultry Sci. Assn., Poultry Sci. Assn., Am. Assn. Accreditation Lab. Animal Care (trustee 1969—), Sigma Xi, Alpha Zeta. Contbr. numerous articles to profl. jours. Home: 2607 Rockwood Dr East Lansing MI 48823

RINGER, WALTER MARDEN, business exec.; b. Mpls., Jan. 1, 1887; s. Charles Wesley and Frances (Marden) R.; student pub. schs., Mpls.; m. Elinor Fisher, Nov. 14, 1914; children—Edwin, Walter Marden, Charles, Isabel, Elinor. Salesman Swift & Co., 1904-09, Meinrath Brokerage Co., 1909-12; organized, mgr. Ringer-Fist Co., Mpls., 1912-16; grocery buyer, 1916-22; organized Red Owl Stores, Mpls., 1922-24; mgr. package cereal dept. Gen. Mills, 1923-26; pres. Foley Mfg. Co., 1926, now dir., chmn. bd. Hon. mem. Bus. Council, Washington. Trustee Hamline U., St. Paul, pres. bd. trustees, 1965—. Dir. for Europe, FOA, 1953-54; vice chmn. small bus. adv. com. Dept. Commerce, 1943-46. Mem. NAM (v.p. 1953-56), Minn. Employers Assn. (dir. 1945-47). Republican. Methodist. Clubs: Minneapolis, Minikahda, Woodhill. Home: 2482 Lafayette Rd Wayzata MN 55391 Office: 3300 5th St NE Minneapolis MN 55418

RINGHAM, RODGER FALK, machinery co. exec.; b. St. Paul, Apr. 25, 1920; s. Clarence H. and Augusta (Falk) R.; B.S. in Aero. Engring., U. Minn., 1942; m. Helen Gavin, Feb. 10, 1943; children—Rodger Falk, Lawrence G., Helen Elizabeth Ringham Gray. Engr., Chance Vought Aircraft Corp., Stratford, Conn., Dallas, 1942-52, v.p., Dallas, 1953-69; sales mgr. Marshall, Neil & Pauley, Inc., Dallas, 1952-53; v.p. Internat. Harvester Co., Chgo., Washington, 1969—; mem. research adv. coms. NASA, 1960-69; mem. adv. com. Fed. Energy Agy., 1975—, other govt. agys.; exchange lectr. Instn. Mech. Engrs., Gt. Britain. Registered profl. engr. Asso. fellow AIAA (dir. 1967-69); mem. Engine Mfrs. Assn. (dir. 1974—), Soc. Automotive Engrs. (dir. 1974—, pres. 1976, rep. Internat. Fedn. Auto Engrs. Socs.), Am. Nat. Standards Inst. (v.p. 1973-77), Soc. Am. Mil. Engrs. (v.p. 1977—), NAM, Am. Soc. Agrl. Engrs., Motor Vehicle Mfrs. Assn. (engring. adv. com.). Contbr. tech. articles to profl. jours. Home: 7002 Woodland Dr Dallas TX 75225

RINGLER, IRA, pharm. co. exec.; b. Bklyn., Feb. 11, 1928; s. Louis and Bessie (Diamond) R.; B.S., Ohio State U., 1951; M.Nutritional Scis., Cornell U., 1953, Ph.D. in Biochemistry, 1955; m. Nancy Moss, June 6, 1954; children—Susan, Julie, Ralph; m. 2d, Edgra Kessel, Nov. 29, 1969. With Lederle Labs., Pearl River, N.Y., 1957-75, dir. research, 1969-75; v.p. research mgmt. and corp. devel. Abbott Labs., N. Chicago, Ill., 1975-76, v.p. pharm. products research and devel., 1976—. Served with U.S. Army, 1946-48. Mem. Am. Soc. Pharmacology and Exptl. Therapeutics, Endocrine Soc., Am. Soc. Biol. Chemists, Am. Chem. Soc., Internat. Soc. Biochem. Pharmacology, Sigma Xi, Phi Kappa Phi. Home: Plum Tree Rd Barrington Hills IL 60010 Office: Abbott Labs 14th and Sheridan Rds North Chicago IL 60064

RINGLER, LENORE, ednl. psychologist; b. N.Y.C., Feb. 8, 1928; d. Albert Haendel and Ida (Brafstein) Haendel; B.A., Bklyn. Coll., 1949; M.A., Queens Coll., 1954; Ph.D., N.Y. U., 1965; m. Jerry Ringler, June 19, 1949; 1 son, Adam. Tchr., then reading specialist N.Y.C. Bd. Edn., 1949-65; prof. N.Y. U., 1965—, chmn. dept. ednl. psychology, 1974-79; ednl. cons. Psychol. Corp. Mem. Citizens Com. for Children. Grantee U.S. Office Edn., 1968-69. Mem. Am. Psychol. Assn., Am. Ednl. Research Assn., Internat. Reading Assn. (past pres. Manhattan council), Orton Soc. (exec. bd. No. N.J. chpt. 1975-76), Pi Lambda Theta (research fellow 1963-64), Kappa Delta Pi. Author: Skills Monitoring System-Reading, 1977; also articles; contbr. to tests. Office: 933 Shimkin Hall New York U New York NY 10003

RINGLER, ROBERT LLOYD, biochemist; b. Chase, Mich., Mar. 27, 1922; s. Lloyd and Minnie (Hoover) R.; B.A. with honors, Central Mich. U., 1951; Ph.D. in Biochemistry, Mich. State U., 1955; m. Virginia Marie Morrow, Jan. 11, 1947; 1 son, Robert Lloyd. Asst. prof. biochemistry N.C. State U., Raleigh, 1955-57; sr. asso. enzyme div. Edsel B. Ford Inst. Med. Research, Henry Ford Hosp., Detroit, 1957-61; mem. staff Nat. Heart, Lung and Blood Inst., and predecessor, NIH, Bethesda, Md., 1961—, chief instl. research programs, 1967-68, spl. asst. to dir., 1968-69, dep. dir. inst., 1969-78, dep. dir. Nat. Inst. on Aging, 1978—; mem. Nat. Commn. Diabetes, 1974-75, Diabetes Mellitus Coordinating Com., 1975; chmn. Nat. Heart, Blood Vessel, Lung and Blood Program Adv. Com., 1972-73; chmn. cardiovascular diseases area U.S.-USSR Joint Com. Health, Moscow, 1974. Served with USCG, 1941-45. Recipient 75th Anniversary award Central Mich. U., 1967; Superior Service Honor award HEW, 1970. Fellow Am. Coll. Cardiology; mem. Am. Soc. Biol. Chemists, Am. Heart Assn. (exec. com. council basic sci.), Sigma Xi. Contbr. articles to med. jours. Home: 12109 Otis Dr Rockville MD 20852 Office: Bldg 31 Room 5C02 NIH 9000 Rockville Pike Bethesda MD 20205

RINGLER, WILLIAM ANDREW, JR., educator; b. Montclair, N.J., May 17, 1912; s. William Andrew and Anna (Holzborn) R.; A.B., Princeton, 1934, A.M., 1935, Ph.D., 1937; m. Evelyn Anne Dressner, June 25, 1946; children—Anne Marie (Mrs. Peter Bower), Robert William, Susan Jane. Instr. English, Princeton, 1937-41, asst. prof., 1941-42, 46-50; prof. English, Washington U., St. Louis, 1950-62; prof. U. Chgo, 1962-79, prof. emeritus, 1980—; Charles K. Colver lectr. Brown U., 1953; H.E. Huntington Library sr. research asso., 1959-60, 79—. Mem. nat. com. Shakespeare Anniversary Com., 1964. Served to maj. USAAF, 1942-46. Guggenheim fellow, 1947-48, 57-58; fellow Folger Shakespeare Library, 1952; Fulbright sr. scholar, Australia, 1972; Huntington Library-NEH fellow, 1976-77. Mem. Renaissance English Text Soc. (chmn. editorial com. 1965-70), Phi Beta Kappa. Democrat. Author: Stephen Gosson, A Biographical and Critical Study, 1942; The Poems of Sir Philip Sidney, 1962; also articles. Editor, Translator: (with Walter Allen, Jr.) John Rainolds Oratio in Laudem Artis Poeticae, 1940. Home: 1644 Oakdale St Pasadena CA 91106 Office: Huntington Library San Marino CA 91108

RINGO, BOYD COLBURN, civil engr.; b. Tulsa, Okla., May 16, 1927; s. Boyd Riley and Helen (Colburn) R.; B.S. in Archtl. Engring., Washington U., 1950, M.S. in Civil Engring., 1954; Ph.D. in Civil Engring., U. Mich., 1964; postgrad Mich. State U., 1956-58; m. Marie Helen Smolicek, Sept. 13, 1948; children—Kim Ellen, Lynn Ann, William Colburn. Archtl. draftsman Gallmaier Engring. Co., Oklahoma City, 1950-51; asst. project engr. Granco Steel Products Co., Granity City, Ill., 1951-52; structural designer Sverdrup & Parcel Consulting Engrs., St. Louis, 1952-54; instr. dept. civil engring. Mich. State U., E. Lansing, 1954-57, asst. prof., 1957-61; asst. prof. dept. civil engring. U. Cin., 1961-64, asso. prof., 1964-67, prof., 1967—; cons. to various indsl. and mfg. firms, 1955—; reviewer for McGraw Hill Book Co., 1966; judge for Lincoln Arc Welding Found. Competition, 1964, 69; lectr. on Concrete structure, slabs-on-grade, tornadoes and structural damage to Civil Defense and the community, 1954—. Committeeman Dan Beard council Cub Scouts Am., 1968-79, asst. scoutmaster, 1972-79; Sunday Sch. tchr. Faith Lutheran, Cin., 1972-74; fin. com. Roselawn Luth. Ch., 1979—. Served with USN, 1945-46. Recipient Entry of Merit award Lincoln Arch Welding Found., 1975; registered profl. engr., Mich., Mo., Ohio. Mem. ASCE (faculty adviser 1962-64, reviewer Jour. for structural div. 1968-72), Am. Inst. Steel Constrn. (Spl. Citation award 1972), Am. Soc. Engring. Edn. (Western Electric Fund award for Teaching Excellence 1976), Tau Beta Pi, Chi Epsilon, Pi Mu Epsilon. Author: (with J.F. McDonough and C.J. Keaney) Use of Computer by the Practicing Civil Engr., 1967; contbr. articles on structural design and engring. edn. to profl. jours.; developed the structural curriculum for undergrad. and grad. courses at U. Cin. Home: 9098 Arrowhead Ct Cincinnati OH 45231 Office: Mail Loc 71 University Cincinnati Cincinnati OH 45221

RINGOEN, RICHARD MILLER, mfg. exec.; b. Ridgeway, Iowa, May 15, 1926; s. Elmer and Evelyn Louise (Miller) R.; student U. Dubuque (Iowa), 1944-45, Marquette U., Milw., 1945-46; B.S. in Elec. Engring., U. Iowa, 1947, M.S., 1948; m. Joan Marie Brandt, June 7, 1953; children—David, John, Daniel. Vice pres. Collins Radio, Cedar Rapids, Iowa, 1948-59; dir. spl. projects Martin-Marietta Co., Denver, 1959-70; v.p., gen. mgr. Ball Brothers Research Corp., Boulder, Colo., 1970-74; corp. v.p. ops. Ball Corp., Muncie, Ind., 1974-78, pres., chief operating officer, 1978—, also dir.; dir. Am. Nat. Bank & Trust Co.; chief exec. officer, dir. Tally Corp., 1973-78. Pres., Arapohoe County (Colo.) Sch. Bd., 1963-70; div. chmn. United Way, 1977-78. Served with USN, 1944-46. Mem. Glass Packaging Inst., Can Mfrs. Inst., Muncie C. of C. Methodist. Club: Rotary Internat. Patentee in communications, navigation and electronics circuitry. Office: Ball Corp 345 S High St Muncie IN 47302

RINGWOOD, GWEN PHARIS, author; b. Anatone, Wash., Aug. 13, 1910; B.A., U. Alta., 1934; M.A., U. N.C., 1939; m. John Brian Ringwood, 1939; children—Stephen Michael, Susan Frances Leslie, Carol Blaine, Patrick Brian. Sec. to Elizabeth Sterling Haynes, dept. extension U. Alta., 1935; author plays Carolina Playmakers, Chapel Hill, N.C., 1937-38. Recipient Canadian drama award; Ottawa Little Theatre Workshop ann. Canadian playwriting competition prize for Lament for Harmonica, 1958. Mem. Canadian Theatre Centre. Author: (novel) Younger Brother, 1950; Pascal, 1972; (plays) Still Stands the House, 1938; Dark Harvest, 1945; The Courting of Marie Jenvrin, 1951; Lament for Harmonica, 1960; Chris Axelson, 1939; The Jack and the Joker, 1945; The Drowning of Wasyl Nemitchuk, 1946; The Rainmaker, 1945; Widger, 1950; Stampede, 1946; The Deep Has Many Voices, 1966; The Stranger, 1970; (librettos) Look Behind You Neighbour, 1961; The Road Runs North, 1968; (plays)

The Lodge, 1975, A Remembrance of Miracles, 1977; Stage Voices, 1978; Transitions I, 1978; numerous radio and TV plays for CBC; contbr.: Best One Act Plays of 1939, 1940; American Folk Plays, 1939; International Folk Plays, 1949; Canadian Short Stories, 1952; Cavalcade of the North, 1958; Canada on Stage, 1960; Stories From Across Canada, 1966; Puerto Ricans Read in English, 1971; Sign Posts, 1974; Canadian Theatre Review, 1975; Ten Short Canadian Plays, 1975; The Magic Carpets of Antonio Angelini, 1979; The Sleeping Beauty and the Golden Goose, 1979; Mirage, 1979; Pasque Flower in Canada's Lost Plays, 1979. Home: PO Box 4329 Williams Lake BC Canada

RINK, SUSAN, coll. pres.; b. Tulsa, Aug. 8, 1927; d. Raymond B. and Helen (McEvoy) Rink; B.A. in Biology, Clarke Coll., Dubuque, Iowa, 1948; M.A. in Biology, Purdue U., 1963; M.A. in Counseling Psychology, Northwestern U., 1971, Ph.D., 1973. Joined Sisters of Blessed Virgin Mary, Roman Catholic Ch., 1948; instr. sci. Holy Angels Acad., Milw., 1951-53; chmn. dept. sci. Xavier High Sch., St. Louis, 1953-66; chmn. biology dept. Clarke Coll., 1966-69, asst. prof., 1969; lectr. edn. Mundelein Coll., Chgo., 1969-71; mem. staff counseling lab. Northwestern U., 1970-71; dir. div. continuing edn. Mundelein Coll., 1971-73, asso. prof. edn., 1973—, acad. dean, 1973-75, pres., 1975—. Mem. higher edn. com. Blessed Virgin Mary Commn.; v.p. Asso. Colls. Ill.; corp. mem. Health Care Service Corp. Northwestern U. scholar, 1971; recipient Distinguished Service award Northwestern U. Sch. Edn., 1975. Mem. Am. Assn. Higher Edn., Pi Lambda Theta, Kappa Gamma Pi. Club: Econ. (Chgo.). Home: 2223 Farwell Chicago IL 60645

RINK, WESLEY WINFRED, banker; b. Hickory, N.C., June 14, 1922; s. Dewey Lee and Mabel E. (Yount) R.; B.S. in Accountancy, U. Ill., 1947, M.S., 1948; m. Doreen M. Warman, Sept. 7, 1946; children—Rebecca S., Christopher L. Accountant, Glidden Co., Chgo., 1948-58; adminstrv. mgr. Central Soya Co., Chgo., 1958-65; v.p., comptroller State Nat. Bank, Evanston, Ill., 1965-71; exec. v.p., dir. Pioneer Trust & Savs. Bank, Chgo., 1971-76; corp. v.p., Exchange Bancorp., Inc., Tampa, 1977—. Served to capt. USAAF, 1942-46. Home: 523 Garrard Dr Temple Terrace FL 33617 Office: 600 Florida Ave Tampa FL 33602

RINKER, MARSHALL EDISON, cement co. exec.; b. Cowan, Ind., Dec. 8, 1904; s. Jacob E. and Alberta May (Neff) R.; student Ball State Tchrs. Coll., Muncie, Ind., 1921-23; m. Vera Lea Keesling, Nov. 26, 1925; children—Marshall Edison, David B., John J. With Rinker Materials Corp., and predecessor, pres., chmn. bd. Rinker Materials Corp., West Palm Beach, Fla., Rinker Portland Cement Corp., Rinker Southeastern Materials Inc. Chmn. W. Palm Beach Community Chest, 1954; bd. dirs. W. Palm Beach chpt. A.R.C., 1930-50; trustee Stetson U., DeLand, Fla.; chmn. bd. deacons Baptist Ch., W. Palm Beach, 1960-62. Mem. Nat. Concrete Masonary Assn. (pres. 1954), Nat. Ready Mixed Concrete Assn. (pres. 1973), Fla. Concrete and Products Assn. (pres. 1967), W. Palm Beach C. of C. (pres. 1954-55). Clubs: Rotary, Everglades, Old Guard Soc. (Palm Beach); Garden of Gods (Colorado Springs, Colo.); Ocean Reef (Key Largo, Fla.); Cirtus (Orlando, Fla.); River (Jacksonville, Fla.). Home: 561 Island Dr Palm Beach FL 33480 Office: 433 7th St West Palm Beach FL 33401

RINSKY, DAVID STUART, ins. exec.; b. Newark, Sept. 15, 1944; s. Irving and Elsie Ann (Millman) R.; B.A., Seton Hall U., 1967; M.A., New Sch. Social Research, 1969; postgrad. Syracuse Inst. Orgn. Mgmt., 1967-71; m. Trudy Dianne Schneider, Aug. 21, 1966; children—Eric Neil, Robert Michael, Gregory Scott. Asst. exec. v.p. Plainfield (N.J.) Area C. of C., 1967-69; v.p. Greater Newark C. of C., 1969-73, pres., 1974-79; v.p. public affairs Prudential Ins. Co. Am., Newark, 1979—. Bd. dirs. Greater Newark Urban Coalition, Symphony Hall, Inc. Named One of 10 Outstanding Young Man Am., U.S. Jaycees, 1978. Mem. Am. C. of C. Execs. (dir., lectr.), N.J. Mortgage and Fin. Assn. (dir.). Office: Prudential Plaza Newark NJ 07101

RINSLEY, DONALD BRENDAN, psychiatrist; b. N.Y.C., Jan. 31, 1928; s. Louis and Annamay (Hindle) R.; A.B. with honors, Harvard U., 1949, postgrad., 1949-50; M.D., Washington U., St. Louis, 1954; diploma in child psychiatry (hon.) Menninger Found., 1975; m. Jacqueline Ann Louk, May 28, 1955. Intern in pediatrics St. Louis Children's Hosp., 1954-55; fellow in psychiatry Menninger Found., Topeka, 1955-56, 58-60; staff psychiatrist Dept. Justice, U.S. Med. Center for Fed. Prisoners, Springfield, Mo., 1956-58; resident psychiatrist Topeka State Hosp., 1955-56, 58-60, asst. chief adolescent unit, childrens sect. 1960-68, chief, 1968-70, dir. sect., 1970-75; asso. chief psychiatry edn. Topeka UA Hosp., 1975—; cons. psychiatrist C.F. Menninger Meml. Hosp., 1976—; asst. in pediatrics Washington U. Sch. Medicine, St. Louis, 1954-55; faculty gen. psychiatry Menninger Sch. Psychiatry, Topeka, 1960—, faculty child psychiatry, 1968—, exec. com. faculty in child psychiatry, 1969-75, 77-79; asso. clin. prof. psychiatry U. Kans. Sch. Medicine, 1970-77, clin. prof., 1977—; sr. asst. surgeon to surgeon USPHS, 1956—. Recipient Edward A. Strecker Meml. award Inst. Pa. Hosp., 1968. Spencer Found. fellow in advanced studies Menninger Found., 1976-79, fellow in interdisciplinary studies, 1979—; diplomate Am. Bd. Psychiatry and Neurology. Fellow Am. Psychiat. Assn. (br. chmn. com. research, 1964-65), Am. Coll. Psychoanalysts, Royal Soc. Health, AAAS, N.Y. Acad. Scis., Am. Orthopsychiat. Assn., Am. Assn. Childrens Residential Centers; mem. Assn. for Research Nervous and Mental Disease, Am. Soc. Adolescent Psychiatry, Am. Acad. Psychoanalysis, Am. Acad. Child Psychiatry, Canadian Psychiat. Assn. (corr.), Am. Assn. Psychiat. Services for Children, Argentine Assn. Child and Adolescent Psychiatry and Psychology (hon.), Sigma Xi (zone cons. to chpt. at large 1969-71, mem. com. on membership at large 1972-75). Editorial bd. Psychiat. Quar., Adolescent Psychiatry, Bull. Menninger Clinic, Argentine Jour. Child and Adolescent Psychiatry and Psychology. Contbr. articles to profl. jours. Home: 4521 W 33d St Terr Topeka KS 66614 Office: 2200 SW Gage Blvd Topeka KS 66622

RINTA, EUGENE FRIDOLPH, assn. exec.; b. Fairport Harbor, Ohio, Oct. 7, 1912; s. Michael and Maria (Saari) R.; B.S., Ohio U., 1938; m. Saga H. Lindberg, Dec. 18, 1946; children—Kerstin G. Speller, Karen M. Spinner, Michael K. Spl. agt. FBI, Atlanta, N.Y.C., Cleve. and Washington, 1938-46; fiscal analyst Council State C. of C., Washington, 1949-52, research dir., 1953-59, exec. dir., 1959-78; dir. Gemcor Inc.; also writer fed.-fiscal affairs. Pres., Ohio U. Fund, 1974—. Mem. Nat. Tax Assn., Govt. Research Assn., Soc. Former Spl. Agts. FBI, Ohio U. Alumni Assn. (dir., nat. pres. 1968-70), Beta Theta Pi. Lutheran. Home: 113 River Forest Ln Washington DC 20022 Office: 499 S Capitol St SW Washington DC 20003

RINTELS, DAVID W., writer; b. Mass., June 25, 1938; s. Jonathan B. and Ruth (Wyzanski) R.; A.B. magna cum laude, Harvard U., 1959. Scriptwriter numerous stage and TV prodns. including Clarence Darrow, Washington: Behind Closed Doors, Fear on Trial, The Senator, The Defenders. Recipient Writers Guild Am. award, 1970, 76; Christopher award; Gavel award Am. Bar Assn., 1970, 74, 75; Emmy award for outstanding TV script, 1975, 76. Mem. Writers Guild Am. West (dir. 1970-75, pres. 1975-77, chmn. com. on censorship and freedom of expression), Clarence Darrow Found. (dir., v.p.), Population Edn., Inc. (dir.). Home: 2002 Old Ranch Rd Los Angeles CA 90049

RINZLER, CAROL GENE EISEN, editor; b. Newark, Sept. 12, 1941; d. Irving Y. and Ruth (Katz) Eisen; A.B., Goucher Coll., 1962; m. Carl Rinzler, July 21, 1962 (div. 1976); children—Michael Franklin, Jane Ruth. Free lance writer, 1965—; editor Charterhouse Books, Inc., N.Y.C., 1971-73, pub., 1973-74; feature editor Glamour Mag., N.Y.C., 1974-77; instr. pub. and current writers courses N.Y. Woman's Sch., 1974-77, asso. dean for curriculum, 1976; book critic Washington Post and syndicated, 1974—; book columnist Ladies' Home Jour., 1977—. Mem. Friends of Scarlett O'Hara, Women's Media Group, Nat. Book Critics Circle. Democrat. Jewish. Club: Cosmopolitan (N.Y.C.). Author: Frankly McCarthy, 1969; Nobody Said You Had to Eat Off the Floor, 1971; The Girl Who Got All the Breaks, 1980. Contbr. to anthologies, articles and revs. to mags. and newspapers. Home: 1215 Fifth Ave New York NY 10029

RIOCH, DAVID MCKENZIE, inst. ofcl.; b. Mussoorie, U.P., India, July 6, 1900; s. David and Minnie (Henly) R.; student Philander-Smith Naini Tal, U.P., India, 1913-15; A.B., Butler U., 1920; M.D., Johns Hopkins Med. Sch., 1924; L.H.D., Exptl. Coll., Inst. Behavioral Research, 1973; m. Margaret Jeffrey, Dec. 23, 1938. House officer Peter Bent Brigham Hosp., Boston, 1924-26; asst. resident in medicine Strong Meml. Hosp., Rochester, N.Y., 1926-28; med. fellow NRC, 1928-30; med. fellow dept. anatomy, Ann Arbor, Mich., also Central Inst. for Brain Research, Amsterdam, Holland, 1928-29, lab. of physiology, Oxford, Eng., 1929-30; instr. lab. physiology Oxford U., 1930; asso. in physiology Johns Hopkins U. Med. Sch., 1930-31; asst. prof. anatomy Harvard U., 1931-38; chmn. dept. neuropsychiatry Washington U. Med. Sch., 1938-42, prof. neurology, 1938-43; dir. research Chestnut Lodge Sanitarium, Rockville, Md., 1943-51; fellow Washington Sch. Psychiatry, 1943-54, dir. div. neuropsychiatry Walter Reed Army Inst. Research, Walter Reed Army Med. Center, Washington, 1951-70; coordinator Adult Learning Center, Inst. for Behavioral Research, Silver Spring, Md., 1970-73, prin. scientist, 1973—; mem. Inst. for Advanced Study, Princeton, N.J., 1958-59; vis. prof. dept. psychiatry U. Chgo., 1968—; vis. lectr. dept. psychiatry Johns Hopkins U. Sch. Medicine, 1970-72, vis. lectr. emeritus, 1972—. Served with RCAF, 1918. Recipient Exceptional Civilian Service award Dept. Army, 1961, Achievement award, 1961; Walter Reed medal Walter Reed Army Med. Center, 1970; Van Giesen award N.Y. State Psychiat. Inst., 1973; Thomas W. Salmon award N.Y. Psychiat. Soc., 1976. Fellow N.Y. Acad. Scis., Am. Psychiat. Assn., Am. Neurol. Assn. (hon.), Am. Acad. Arts and Scis., Washington Acad. Medicine, Washington Acad. Sci.; mem. Am. Psychopath. Assn., AAAS, Am. Assn. Anatomists, Am. Physiol. Soc., Am. Assn. Research in Nervous and Mental Diseases, Am. Acad. Neurology (asso.), Psychonomic Soc., Pavlovian Soc., Phi Beta Kappa, Alpha Omega Alpha. Writer on neuroanatomy and physiology and neuropsychiat. research. Home: 5525 Surrey St Chevy Chase MD 20015 Office: Inst Behavioral Research Silver Spring MD 20910

RIOPELLE, ARTHUR JEAN, psychologist; b. Thorp, Wis., Apr. 22, 1920; s. Wilfred Gaspar and Ann Marie (Schroeder) R.; B.S., U. Wis., 1941, M.S., 1948, Ph.D., 1950; m. Mary Jane Astell, May 2, 1942; children—Mary Ann, James Michael, Jean Elizabeth. Asst. prof., asso. prof. Emory U., 1950-57; dir. psychology div. U.S. Army Med. Research Lab., Ft. Knox, Ky., 1957-59; dir. Yerkes Labs. Primate Biology, Orange Park, Fla., 1959-62; dir. Delta Regional Primate Research Center, Covington, La., 1962-71; prof. psychology La. State U., Baton Rouge, 1972—, Boyd prof., 1977—; mem. Internat. Union for Conservation of Nature, Conf. New World Primates, Wild Animal Propagation Trust, NRC panel on manganese, Com. Biol. Effects of Pollution, La. Bd. Examiners of Psychologists, 1972-75; mem. panel on Air Force tng. Nat. Acad. Sci.-NRC, 1955-56, primate research study sect. Am. Inst. Biol. Scis.-NASA, 1959-63; chmn. sub-com. on man Lunar Receiving Lab. Study, 1970-71; chmn. U.S.-Japan Conf. Primate Research, 1963-64; chmn. sub-com. primate standards Inst. Lab. Animal Resources, NRC, 1964-69. Served with USAAF, 1942-46; ETO. Mem. Am. Psychol. Assn., Am. Physiol. Soc., So. Soc. Philosophy and Psychology, Internat. Primatological Soc., AAAS, Am. Inst. Biol. Scis., Psychonomic Soc., Southeastern Psychol. Assn., Southwestern Psychol. Assn., Sigma Xi, Phi Kappa Phi, Sigma Chi. Editor Jour. Gen. Psychology, 1978; asst. editor Animal Behavior, 1962-65; cons. editor Jour. Genetic Psychology and Genetic Psychology Monograph, 1967—; contbr. chpts.: Marvels of Animal Behavior, 1972, Dewsbury's Comparative Psychology, 1973. Home: 9710 Highland Rd Baton Rouge LA 70810 Office: Dept Psychology La State U Baton Rouge LA 70803

RIORDAN, DALE PATRICK, govt. ofcl.; b. Kingston, Pa., July 4, 1948; s. James Francis and Sophia Anne (Czarnomski) R.; B.A. in Econs., U. Md., 1972, M.A., 1973, postgrad., 1976—; m. Marta J. Taylor, Nov. 11, 1978. Research asst. Urban Inst., Washington, 1972-73; spl. asst. to under sec. HUD, Washington, 1977-78, spl. asst. to sec., 1978-79; asst. to chmn. Fed. Home Loan Bank Bd., 1979—; dir. Office Corp. Planning, Govt. Nat. Mortgage Assn., 1978; grad. teaching asst. U. Md., 1972-73; faculty Hood Coll., Frederick, Md., 1975-76. Served with USMC, 1968-70. Decorated Vietnamese Cross of Gallantry. Mem. Omicron Delta Epsilon, Phi Kappa Phi. Democrat. Roman Catholic. Home: 3100 Connecticut Ave NW Washington DC 20008 Office: 451 7th St SW Washington DC 20410

RIORDAN, HENRY PATRICK, lawyer; b. N.Y.C., Apr. 2, 1924; s. Henry Joseph and Wilhelmina (Brown) R.; LL.B., Fordham U., 1949; m. Aileen Mary Donnelly, Apr. 15, 1950; children—Michael Henry, Thomas John, James Anthony, Timothy, Mary Aileen, Christine Mary. Admitted to N.Y. bar, 1949, since practiced in N.Y.C.; partner firm Cravath, Swaine & Moore, 1961—. Served with AUS, 1943-46. Mem. Am., N.Y. State bar assns., Assn. Bar City N.Y., Fordham Law Alumni Assn. Club: Wall St. (N.Y.C.).

RIORDAN, JAMES QUENTIN, oil co. exec.; b. Bklyn., June 17, 1927; s. James A. and Ruth M. (Boomer) R.; B.A., Bklyn. Coll., 1945; LL.B., Columbia, 1949; m. Gloria H. Carlson, June 23, 1951; children—Nancy, Susan, James, Ruth. Admitted to N.Y. bar, 1951; U.S. Supreme Ct., 1954; atty. Winthrop, Stimson, Putnam & Roberts, N.Y.C., 1949-51; mem. staff Ways and Means sub-com., Washington, 1951-52; atty. tax div. Justice Dept., Washington, 1952-55; atty. Chadbourne, Parke, Whiteside & Wolff, N.Y.C., 1955-57; tax counsel Socony Mobil Oil Co., N.Y.C., 1957-59, planning asso., 1959-60, mgr. planning, 1961-62; v.p. Mobil Latin Am., 1963-64, pres. internat. div., 1965-69, exec. v.p. fin., 1969—, also dir., mem. exec. com.; dir. Dow Jones & Co., Inc., Marcor, Inc., Montgomery Ward; trustee Bklyn. Savs. Bank; adv. bd. Chem. Bank. Bd. dirs. Com. Econ. Devel.; trustee Bklyn. Inst. Arts and Scis. Mem. N.Y. City Bar Assn. Clubs: Pinnacle, Rembrandt (N.Y.C.); Westchester Country. Office: 150 E 42d St New York City NY 10017

RIPLEY, BETTY FARRALLY, dancing tchr.; b. Bradford, Yorkshire, Eng., May 5, 1915; d. Arthur and Ada (Sugden) Hey; student Harrogate Ladies Coll., Eng., 1929-33, Torch Sch. of Dance, Leeds, Eng., 1933-36; m. John Hudson Farrally, Nov. 21, 1942 (dec.); 1 son, Richard Blaise. Founder, dir. Canadian Sch. of Ballet, Winnipeg, B.C., 1939—, founder br., Kelowna, B.C., 1959; dir. Royal Winnipeg Ballet Co.; co-dir. ballet div. Banff (Alta.) Centre, 1950-75. Mem. Royal Acad. Dancing. Home: Rural Route 4 Lakeshore Rd Kelowna BC Canada Office: 1157 Sutherland St Kelowna BC Canada

RIPLEY, HERBERT SPENCER, psychiatrist; b. Galveston, Tex., June 29, 1907; s. Herbert S. and Caroline (Kenison) R.; A.B., U. Mich., 1929; M.D., Harvard U., 1933; certificate in psychoanalysis Columbia U., 1949; m. Elizabeth Stuart Smith, July 20, 1940; children—Caroline Bird, Nancy Stuart. Intern U. Chgo., 1933-34; jr. asst. resident psychiatry N.Y. Hosp., 1934-35, asst. resident psychiatry, 1935-37, resident psychiatry, 1937-38, asst. attending psychiatrist, 1938-42; asst. prof. psychiatry Cornell, 1946-49; prof. psychiatry U. Wash., 1949-77, prof. emeritus, 1977—, chmn. dept., 1949-69; attending physician psychiatry service U. Hosp.; cons. Children's Orthopedic Hosp., Seattle VA Hosp. Trustee, Seattle Psychoanalytic Inst. Served from capt. to lt. col. M.C., AUS, 1942-46. Mem. Am. Coll. Psychiatrists, AMA, Am. Psychiat. Assn., Am. Fedn. Clin. Research, World Fedn. Mental Health, World Med. Assn., Am. Psychoanalytic Assn., North Pacific Soc. Neurology and Psychiatry, Am. Psychosomatic Soc., Am. Coll. Psychoanalysts (pres. 1979-80), AAAS, Assn. Am. Med. Coll., Alpha Omega Alpha, Sigma Xi. Clubs: Harvard (N.Y.C.); Rainier (Seattle). Author articles med. psychiatry. Home: 3707 47th Pl NE Seattle WA 98105 Office: U Wash Sch Medicine Seattle WA 98195

RIPLEY, RANDALL BUTLER, polit. scientist, educator; b. Des Moines, Jan. 24, 1938; s. Henry Dayton and Aletha (Butler) R.; B.A., DePauw U., 1959; M.A., Harvard, 1961, Ph.D., 1963; m. Grace A. Franklin, Oct. 15, 1974; children—Frederick Joseph, Vanessa Gail. Teaching fellow Harvard, 1960-62; mem. staff Brookings Inst., Washington, 1963-67, research asst., 1963-64, research asso., 1964-67; intern Office of Democratic Whip, U.S. Ho. of Reps., Washington, 1963; asso. prof. dept. polit. sci. Ohio State U., Columbus, 1967-69, prof., chmn., 1969—; lectr. Cath. U., Washington, 1963-64; professorial lectr. Am. U., Washington, 1964-67; vis. prof. U. Okla., 1969—. Active various polit. campaigns. Woodrow Wilson fellow, 1959-60, Danforth fellow, 1959-63; recipient Sumner prize Harvard, 1963. Mem. Am. (sec. 1978), Midwest polit. sci. assns., Phi Beta Kappa. Democrat. Author: Public Policies and Their Politics, 1966; Party Leaders in the House of Representatives, 1967; Majority Party Leadership in Congress, 1969; Power in the Senate, 1969; The Politics of Economic and Human Resource Development, 1972; Legislative Politics U.S.A., 1973; American National Government and Public Policy, 1974; Congress: Process and Policy, 1975, 2d edit., 1978; Policy-making in the Federal Executive Branch, 1975; Congress, the Bureaucracy, and Public Policy, 1976, 2d edit., 1980; National Government and Policy in the United States, 1977; A More Perfect Union, 1979; contbr. articles to profl. jours. Home: 2685 Berwyn Rd Columbus OH 43221

RIPLEY, SIDNEY DILLON, 2D, zoologist, museum dir.; b. N.Y.C., Sept. 20, 1913; s. Louis Arthur and Constance Baillie (Rose) R.; B.A., Yale U., 1936, M.A., 1961, LL.D., 1975; Ph.D., Harvard U., 1943; D.H.L., Marlboro Coll., 1965, Williams Coll., 1972; D.Eng., Stevens Inst. Tech., 1977; D.Sc., George Washington U., 1966, Catholic U., 1968, U. Md., 1970, Cambridge (Eng.) U., 1974, Brown U., 1975, Trinity Coll., 1977; LL.D., Dickinson Coll., 1967, Hofstra U., 1968; m. Mary Moncrieffe Livingston, Aug. 18, 1949; children—Julie Dillon (Mrs. Robert S. Ridgely), Rosemary Livingston, Sylvia McNeill. Staff, Acad. Natural Sci., Phila., 1936-39; vol. asst. Am. Mus. Natural History of N.Y., 1939-40; teaching asst. Harvard, 1941-42; asst. curator bds. Smithsonian Instn., Washington, 1942, sec., 1964—; lectr. Yale, 1946-49, asso. curator, 1946-52, asst. prof., 1949-55, curator, 1952-64, asso. prof. zoology, 1955-61, prof. biology, 1961-64; expdns. to South Pacific, S.E. Asia, India, Nepal, Bhutan; dir. Peabody Mus. Natural History, 1959-64. U.S. del. Stockholm Conf. on Human Environment, 1972. Dir. Research Corp. Trustee Henry Francis du Pont Winterthur Mus., White Meml. Found., Forman Sch., George Washington U.; pres. Internat. Council of Bird Preservation; bd. dirs. World Wildlife Fund, chmn. U.S., 1975—. Served as civilian OSS, 1942-45. Decorated Order White Elephant, Freedom medal (Thailand); grand cross Order al Merito Civil (Spain); comdr.'s cross Order of Dannebrog (Denmark); comdr. Order Golden Ark (Netherlands); comdr. Order of Merit (Poland); officier Ordre des Arts et Lettres (France); Knight comdr. Order Brit. Empire; recipient Gold medal N.Y. Zool. Soc., 1966; Gold medal Royal Zool. Soc. Antwerp, 1970; Gold medal Holland Soc. N.Y., 1977; Thomas Jefferson award Am. Soc. Interior Designers; F.K. Hutchinson medal Garden Club Am., 1979; Fulbright fellow, 1950; Guggenheim fellow, 1954; NSF fellow, 1954. Fellow AAAS, Am. Ornithologists Union, Zool. Soc. India; mem. Nat. Acad. Scis., Internat. Council Museums, Council Fgn. Relations, Am. Naturalists Soc., Brit. Ornithol. Union, French (hon.), Argentine (hon.), S. African (corr.), New Zealand, Cooper ornithol. socs., Soc. Systematic Zoology, Bombay Natural History Soc., Soc. Study Evolution, Wilson Soc., Internat. Wild Waterfowl Assn., AIA (hon.), Soc. Cincinnati (hon.), Sigma Xi. Author: Trail of the Money Bird, 1942; Search for the Spiny Babbler, 1953; A Paddling of Ducks, 1959; (with L. Scribner) Ornithological Books in Yale Library, 1961; Synopsis Birds India and Pakistan, 1961; Land and Wildlife of Tropical Asia, 1964; (with Sálim Ali) A Handbook of Birds of India and Pakistan, 10 vols., 1968-74, vol. 1 revised edit., 1978; The Sacred Grove, 1969, 2d edit., 1978; Paradox of the Human Condition, 1975; Rails of the World, 1977. Home: 2324 Massachusetts Ave NW Washington DC 20008 also Litchfield CT 06759 Office: 1000 Jefferson Dr The Mall Washington DC 20560

RIPLEY, THOMAS HUNTINGTON, govt. ofcl.; b. Bennington, Vt., Nov. 18, 1927; s. Robert Milton and Sue Constance (Huntington) R.; grad. N.Y. State Ranger Sch., 1946; B.S., Va. Poly. Inst., 1951, Ph.D., 1958; M.S., U. Mass., 1954; m. Anne Cabell Browning, June 16, 1948; children—Elizabeth (Mrs. William McDonald Stromeyer), James Huntington, Constance Frances. Grad. fellow U. Mass., 1951-53; project leader Mass. Div. Fisheries and Game, 1953-56; instr. biology Va. Poly. Inst., 1956-57; research project leader Va. Commn. Game and Inland Fisheries, Blacksburg, 1957-58; wildlife staff specialist Dept. Agr. Forest Service, Southeastern Forest Expt. Sta., Asheville, N.C., 1958-59, project leader, 1959-65, asst. dir., 1965-67, asst. to dep. chief, Washington, 1967-69, chief wildlife and range ecology research br., 1969; forest resource analyst TVA, Knoxville, 1969-70, dir. div. forestry, fisheries and wildlife devel., Norris, Tenn., 1970-79, mgr. Office Natural Resources, 1979—; adj. prof. dept. forestry and wildlife Va. Poly. Inst., dept. forestry U. Tenn.; mem. curriculum adv. com. Sch. Forestry, U. Fla.; mem. President's Recreation Adv. Study Commn. on Measurement of Outdoor Recreation, Washington. Served with USNR, 1946-47. Recipient Phi Sigma Grad. award for biol. research, 1958. Fellow Soc. Am. Foresters, Am. Inst. Biol. Scis., Wildlife Soc., Am. Forestry Assn. (dir., v.p.), Knoxville Tech. Soc., Internat. Union Forestry Research Orgns., Sigma Xi, Alpha Zeta, Phi Sigma, Phi Kappa Phi, Omicron Delta Kappa. Clubs: Cosmos (Washington); Explorers (fellow) (N.Y.C.). Contbr. articles to profl. jours. Home: 7134 Cheshire Dr Knoxville TN 37919 Office: TVA Ridgeway Rd Norris TN 37828

RIPP, JUDITH ELLEN, mag. editor; b. N.Y.C., Sept. 10, 1940; d. Max and Gertrude (Roth) Seelenfreund; B.A., Cornell U., 1961; m. Seymour Leichman, Oct. 25, 1970 (div. 1978); 1 son, Samuel Andrew. Mem. reference dept. Collier's Ency., N.Y.C., 1961-63; asst. movie editor Parents Mag., N.Y.C., 1964-67, movie editor, 1967-78, media editor, 1978—. Recipient award for excellence Marin County Motion Picture and TV Council, 1974. Office: 52 Vanderbilt Ave New York NY 10019

RIPPEL, HARRY CONRAD, mech. engr.; b. Phila., Feb. 19, 1926; s. Philip and Emma (Metzger) R.; B.M.E., Drexel U., Phila., 1952, M.S., 1957; m. Dorothy Ann Tartala, Nov. 20, 1948; children—Linda Jean, Richard Peter. With Franklin Inst. Research Labs., Phila., 1952—, Inst. fellow, 1978—. Active local Boy Scouts Am.; Sunday sch. tchr., layreader St. James Episcopal Ch., Phila. Served with AUS, World War II; ETO. Decorated Bronze Star. Registered profl. engr., Pa. Fellow ASME, Am. Soc. Lubrication Engrs.; mem. Sigma Xi, Pi Tau Sigma. Author manuals and articles in field. Home: 1434 Sharon Park Dr Sharon Hill PA 19079 Office: Franklin Inst Research Labs 20th and The Parkway Philadelphia PA 19103

RIPPEL, JULIUS ALEXANDER, business and found. exec.; b. Newark, July 22, 1901; s. Albert A. and Caroline (Greig) R.; B.S., Dartmouth, 1923; D.H.L. (hon.), Med. Coll. Pa., 1972; Sc.D. (hon.), Georgetown U. Sch. Medicine; L.H.D. (hon.), Upsala Coll.; m. Carol W. Richards, 1924; children—Susan J., Eric R. With J.S. Rippel & Co., Newark, 1923-38, v.p., 1933-38; pres. Julius A. Rippel, Inc., Newark, 1938-55, Rippel & Co., 1955—; dir. Elizabethtown Gas Co., Nat. Utilities and Industries Corp. Pres., dir., trustee Fannie E. Rippel Found., 1953—. Recipient Outstanding Citizen award Advt. Club Newark, 1943; Hosp. Achievement award N.J. Hosp. Assn., 1969; Heart award N.Y. Cardiology Soc., 1969; award of merit Am. Heart Assn., 1970; Dignity of Man award Kessler Inst. for Rehab., 1971; citation of merit Upper N.J. chpt. Nat. Multiple Sclerosis Assn., 1971; award of merit Mt. Carmel Guild, 1972; certificate of appreciation Assn. for Advancement Med. Instrumentation, 1974; Thanks award St. Michael's Med. Center, 1974; Citizens award Acad. Medicine N.J., 1976; Achievement award Ariz. State U., 1977; named Albert Gallatin fellow N.Y. U., 1977. Mem. Am. Hosp. Assn. (hon.), Phi Beta Kappa Assos., Kappa Sigma. Clubs: Baltusrol Golf (Springfield, N.J.); Morris County Golf (Convent, N.J.); Essex (Newark). Home: Madison NJ 07940 Office: 299 Madison Ave Morristown NJ 07960

RIPPERGER, EUGENE ARMAN, educator; b. Stover, Mo., July 7, 1914; s. William Lawrence and Winnie (Agnew) R.; B.S. in Civil Engring., Kans. State U., 1939; M.S., U. Tex., 1950; Ph.D., Stanford, 1952; m. Elizabeth Nancy Morley, June 23, 1940; children—Ann Ripperger Jolly, Emily Ripperger Eddins, Jane. Research engr. Portland Cement Assn., Chgo., 1939-42; research engr. U.S. Army C.E., Cin., 1942- 43; instr. to prof. U. Tex., Austin, 1946—; dir. Engring. Mechanics Research Lab.; cons., editor, lectr. Served to lt. USNR, 1943-46. Registered profl. engr., Tex. Fellow ASME; mem. IEEE, Soc. for Exptl. Stress Analysis. Contbr. articles profl. jours. Home: 3700 Highland View Dr Austin TX 78731

RIPPETEAU, DARREL DOWNING, architect; b. Clay Center, Nebr., Jan. 14, 1917; s. Claude LaVerne and Eva (Downing) R.; B.A. in Architecture, U. Nebr., 1941; m. Donna Doris Hiatt, Jan. 8, 1939; children—Bruce Estes, Darrel Downing, Jane Upson. Staff architect FHA, Omaha, 1941-42; project mgr., mng. partner firm Sargent-Webster-Crenshaw & Folley, Watertown, Schenectady, Buffalo, Syracuse, N.Y., Burlington, Vt., Bangor, Maine, 1946—; dir. Archtl. Corp. Atlanta, Nat. Bank No. N.Y., Watertown, Assn. Island Recreational Corp. commr. N.Y. State Council Architecture, 1974-76; mem. profl. adv. council Coll. Architecture, U. Nebr., 1975—. Mem. nat. fin. com. Republican Party, 1971-73; bd. dirs. Thousand Islands Mus., Clayton, N.Y., 1973—. Served to maj. U.S. Army, 1942-46. Recipient North Country citation St. Lawrence U., Canton, N.Y., 1971; Sears-Roebuck scholar, 1936-37; U. Nebr. Dept. Architecture grantee, 1940-41; Nebr. master U. Nebr., 1971. Fellow AIA (nat. dir. 1969-73, trustee AIA Found. 1970-73); mem. Empire State (dir.), Greater Watertown (past pres.) chambers commerce, N.Y. State Assn. Indsl. Devel. Agencies (past v.p.), N.Y. State Assn. Architects (pres. 1968-69), Bldg. Research Inst., Res. Officers Assn. (past pres.), Am. Tree Farm Assn., Jefferson County Hist. Soc. (dir. 1974—), Glenn Curtiss Mus., Hammondsport, N.Y., Aviation Pioneers. Republican. Presbyterian. Clubs: OX5, Black River Valley (Watertown); Grenadier Golf (dir.) (Thousand Islands, Rockport, Ont., Can.). Prin. works include Justice Bldg., Albany; N.Y. State Office Bldg., Watertown; Toomey Abbott Towers, Syracuse; State U. N.Y., Cortland; U.S. P.O. Facility, Syracuse. Home: 246 Flower Ave W Watertown NY 13601 Office: 2112 Erie Blvd E Syracuse NY 13224

RIPPY, FRANCES MARGUERITE MAYHEW, educator; b. Ft. Worth, Sept. 16, 1929; d. Henry Grady and Marguerite Christine (O'Neill) Mayhew; B.A., Tex. Christian U., 1949; M.A., Vanderbilt U., 1951, Ph.D., 1957; postgrad. (Fulbright scholar), U. London, 1952-53; m. Noble Merrill Rippy, Aug. 29, 1955; children—Felix O'Neill, Conrad Mayhew, Marguerite Hailey. Instr. Tex. Christian U., 1953-55; instr. to asst. prof. Lamar State U., 1955-59; asst. prof. English, Ball State U., Muncie, Ind., 1959-64, asso. prof., 1964-68, prof., 1968—, coordinator English doctoral studies, 1966—, editor Ball State U. Forum, 1960—; vis. asst. prof. Sam Houston State U., 1957; vis. lectr., prof. U. P.R., summers 1959, 60, 61; cons.-evaluator N. Central Assn. Colls. and Secondary Schs., 1973—. Recipient McClintock award, 1966; Danforth grantee, summer 1964, asso., 1965—; Ball State U. research grantee, 1960, 62, 70, 73, 76. Mem. MLA, Coll. English Assn., Johnson Soc. Midwest (sec., 1961-62), AAUP, Nat. Council Tchrs. English, Am. Soc. 18th Century Studies. Contbr. articles to profl. jours., chpt. to anthology. Home: 4709 W Jackson St Muncie IN 47304. *I have found all of the worlds which the above biographical paragraph touches upon—familial, academic, literary—lively and stimulating and thoroughly satisfying. Each world demands a great deal and offers a great deal in return.*

RIPSTEIN, CHARLES BENJAMIN, surgeon; b. Winnipeg, Man., Can., Dec. 13, 1913; s. Hyman Mendel and Bertha (Benjamin) R.; B.S., U. Ariz., 1936; M.D., C.M., McGill U., 1940; m. Barbara Adelman, Dec. 26, 1950; children—Ellen Joan, Linda Hope. Came to U.S., 1949. Intern medicine Royal Victoria Hosp., Montreal, 1940-41; residency in surgery Royal Victoria and Montreal Gen. hosps., 1945-48; demonstrator surgery McGill U., 1948-49; asso. prof. surgery State U. N.Y., Bklyn., 1949-52, prof. surgery, 1952-54; prof. surgery, also exec. officer dept. surgery Albert Einstein Coll. Medicine, Yeshiva U., 1954-58, prof. clin. surgery, 1958—; clin. prof. surgery U. Miami Sch. Medicine, 1972; chief divs. gen. and thoracic surgery Bronx Municipal Hosp. Center, N.Y.C., 1954-58; dir. surg. service Beth-El Hosp., Bklyn., 1958—; dir. surgery Brookdale Hosp. Center, Bklyn.; cons. in surgery Maimonides Hosp., Bklyn., Bronx VA Hosp.; attending surg. Lebanon Hosp.; clin. prof. surgery U. Miami (Fla.); cons. cardiac surgery Health Ins. Plan N.Y.; vis. prof. surgery U. Tel Aviv (Israel), 1969-70. Served as squadron leader Royal Canadian Air Force, 1941-45. Diplomate Am. Bd. Surgery, Am. Bd. Thoracic Surgery, Am. Bd. Colon and Rectal Surgery. Fellow A.C.S., Royal Coll. Surgeons (Can.), N.Y. Acad. Medicine, Am. Coll. Chest Physicians; mem. AMA, Soc. U. Surgeons, Am. Assn. for Thoracic Surgery, Am. Heart Assn., N.Y. Surg. Soc., Alpha Omega Alpha, Zeta Beta Tau. Author chpt. on cardiac surgery in textbook. Home: 1150 NW 14th St Miami FL 33136

RIS, HANS, zoologist, educator; b. Bern, Switzerland, June 15, 1914; s. August and Martha (Egger) R.; diploma high sch. teaching U. Bern, 1936; Ph.D., Columbia, 1942; came to U.S., 1938, naturalized, 1945; m. Hania Wislicka, Dec. 26, 1947 (div. 1971); children—Christopher Robert, Annette Margo. Lectr. zoology Columbia U., 1942; Seessel fellow in zoology Yale U., 1942; instr. zoology Johns Hopkins U., 1942-44; asst. Rockefeller Inst., N.Y.C., 1944-46, asso., 1946-49; asso. prof. zoology U. Wis., Madison, 1949-53, prof., 1953—. Mem. Am. Acad. Arts Scis., Nat. Acad. Scis., AAAS. Researcher mechanisms of nuclear div., chromosome structure, cell ultrastructure, electron microscopy. Home: 5117 Minocqua Crescent Madison WI 53705 Office: Zoology Research U Wis Madison WI 53706

RIS, WILLIAM KRAKOW, lawyer; b. Dubuque, Iowa, June 11, 1915; s. Rinehart F. and Anna W. (Krakow) R.; A.B., U. Colo., 1937, LL.B., 1939; m. Patty S. Nash, Dec. 28, 1940; children—Frederic N., William Krakow. Admitted to Colo. bar, 1939; practice in Denver, 1939-43, 46—; pres. Wood, Ris & Hames, P.C., 1948—; mem. Commn. on Jud. Qualifications, 1973—, chmn., 1977. Served with AUS, 1943-46. Fellow Am. Bar Found., Am. Coll. Trial Lawyers; mem. Colo. Bar Assn. (pres. 1962-63), Denver Law Club (pres. 1956-57), Order of Coif. Episcopalian. Home: 635 Eudora St Denver CO 80220 Office: 1100 Denver Club Bldg 518 17th St Denver CO 80202

RISHEL, JOSEPH J., museum curator; b. Clifton Springs, N.Y., May 15, 1940; s. Joseph J. and Venus E. (Zarr) R.; B.A., Hobart Coll., 1962; M.A., U. Chgo., 1968; m. Anne d'Harnoncourt, June 19, 1971. Instr. art history Wooster Coll., 1966-67; asst. curator earlier painting and sculpture Art Inst. Chgo., 1968-71; curator European Painting Before 1900, curator John G. Johnson Collection, Phila. Mus. Art, 1971—. Office: Phila Mus Art PO Box 7646 Philadelphia PA 19101

RISHEL, RICHARD CLINTON, banker; b. Oreland, Pa., June 7, 1943; s. Herbert Beale and Evelyn (Lauer) R.; B.A., Pa. State U., 1965; postgrad. Drexel Inst. Tech., 1965-66; m. Carol Staub, Apr. 3, 1965; children—Christian Daniel, Peter James. Credit analyst 1st Pa. Banking & Trust Co., Phila., 1965-69; comml. lending officer Nat. Bank of Chester County, West Chester, Pa., 1969; asst. v.p. Continental Bank of Norristown (Pa.), 1969-70, sec., 1970-71, v.p., 1971-73, sr. v.p., chief fin. officer, 1973-75, exec. v.p., chief fin. officer, 1975—. Bd. dirs. Pa. Economy League. Mem. Bank Adminstrn. Inst., Fin. Execs. Inst. Office: 1500 Market St Philadelphia PA 19102

RISI, LOUIS J., JR., food processing co. exec.; b. Highland Park, Ill., July 2, 1937; s. Louis J. and Ann E. Risi; B.S., Bradley U., 1959; m. Mary Jean Anson, Jan. 15, 1955; children—Steven, Janet, Andrew. With Arthur Young & Co., Chgo., 1959-69, mgr., 1965-69; pres., dir. Norin Corp., Miami, Fla., 1969—; dir. Chgo. Rock Island R.R., Maple Leaf Mills Ltd., Midland Nat. Bank, Norris Grain Co. Mem. Am. Inst. C.P.A.'s, Fin. Execs. Inst. Clubs: Ocean Reef Yacht, Kings Bay Yacht, Bath, Jockey, Bankers. Home: 10915 SW 53d Ave Miami FL 33156 Office: 12100 NE 16th Ave North Miami FL 33161

RISK, J. FRED, banker; b. Ft. Wayne, Ind., Dec. 1, 1928; s. Clifford and Estella (Kline) R.; B.S. cum laude, Ind. U., 1949, LL.B., 1951; postgrad. Nortwestern U.; m. Viola Jean Tompt, July 12, 1953; children—Nancy Jean, John Thomas. With Harris Trust & Savs. Bank, Chgo., 1951-54, W.T. Grimm & Co., 1954-56; with Ind. Nat. Bank of Indpls., 1956—, exec. v.p. dir., 1965-68, pres., 1968—, chmn., 1971-76; chmn. Mutz Corp., 1976—; dir. Steak n Shake, Inc., Standard Locknut, Inc., Northwestern Mut. Life Ins. Co., Lacy Diversified Industries, Inc., Excepticon, Inc., L.R. Nelson Corp., Ransburg Corp., Franklin Corp., Forum Fin., Inc., Cosco, Inc. Bd. dirs. Hanover Coll., 1966—; chmn. Indpls. Center for Advanced Research. Served as capt. inf., AUS, 1950-51. Mem. Am., Ind., Res. City bankers assns., Ind., Indpls. bar assns. Methodist. Clubs: Indpls. Athletic, Meridian Hills Country (Indpls.). Home: 7801 N Pennsylvania St Indianapolis IN 46240 Office: 1853 Ludlow Ave Indianapolis IN 46201

RISMAN, MICHAEL, lawyer, securities com. exec.; b. Everett, Mass., Apr. 2, 1938; s. Morris Charles and Doris (Rosenbaum) R.; B.A., U. Mich., 1960; LL.B., Georgetown U., 1964; m. Rebecca R. Fuchs, Mar. 23, 1974; 1 stepson, Ian Carleton Murray; 1 son, Matthew Craig. Staff mem. Democratic Nat. Com., Washington, 1964; admitted to D.C. bar, 1964; atty. U.S. Fgn. Claims Settlement Commn., Washington, 1964-66, SEC, Washington, 1966-67; counsel Seaboard Planning Corp., 1967-72, pres., 1970-72; v.p. Seaboard Corp., Beverly Hills, Calif., 1970-72; sec. B.C. Morton Realty Trust, 1967-71; with Arlington Corp., Santa Monica, Calif., 1979—; dir. Competitive Capital Fund, Income Fund Boston, Inc., Admirality Fund, Seaboard Leverage Fund, 1970-74. Home: 1133 Centinela Ave Santa Monica CA 90403 Office: 3350 Ocean Park Blvd Suite 106 Santa Monica CA 90405

RISOM, JENS, furniture design exec.; b. Copenhagen, Denmark, May 8, 1916; s. Sven J. and Inger Risom; student Krebs, St. Annae, and Niels Brock Bus. Coll., Kunshaandv Skolen, Denmark; m. Iben Haderup, Dec. 12, 1939 (dec. Jan. 1977); children—Helen Ann, Peggy Ann, Thomas Christian, Sven Christian; m. 2d, Henny Panduro, May 12, 1979. Came to U.S., 1938, naturalized 1944. Freelance furniture designer; pres. Jens Risom Design, Inc. (became subsidiary Dictaphone Corp. 1970), N.Y.C., 1946-73; v.p. Dictaphone Corp., 1970-72; pres. Design Control, Inc., New Canaan, Conn., 1973—; cons. design, mktg., space planning. Trustee R.I. Sch. Design, New Canaan Library, others. Served with AUS, 1943-45. Recipient Archtl. League award, Am. Inst. Internat. Design awards, also numerous Danish and Am. design awards. Mem. Indsl. Designers Soc. Am. Home and office: 103 Chichester Rd New Canaan CT 06840 also Block Island RI 02807

RISON, CLARENCE HERBERT, mfg. exec.; b. Central Falls, R.I., Feb. 25, 1904; s. Herbert Thomas and Sophie (Raithel) R.; LL.B., Northeastern U., Boston, 1938; m. Ebba R. Rydberg, Dec. 5, 1931; children—Carolyn Anne, John Brooks. Instr., Northeastern U., 1941-42, 1942-43; instr. Tech. Inst., Providence YMCA, 1940-41; treas. Grinnell Corp., 1944—, dir., exec. com., 1948—, v.p. fin., 1964-68, pres. corp., 1968-70, vice chmn., 1970—; hon. dir. AMICA Mut. Ins. Co. Mem. NAM (dir. 1958-61), Nat. Assn. Credit Men (dir. 1938-41), R.I. Assn. Credit Men. Baptist (clk. 1945-55). Mason. Clubs: Squantum, Turks Head, Dunes, Hope. Home: 56 President Ave Providence RI 02906 Office: 260 W Exchange St Providence RI 02901

RISS, ROBERT BAILEY, corp. exec.; b. Salida, Colo., May 27, 1927; s. Richard Roland and Louise (Roberts) R.; B.S., U. Kans., 1949; children—Edward Stayton, G. Leslie, Laura Bailey, Juliana Warren. Founder, chmn. bd., pres. Republic Industries, Inc., Kansas City, Mo., 1969—; pres. Riss Internat. Corp., Kansas City, 1950—, chmn. bd., 1964—; pres., chmn. bd. Grandview Bank and Trust Co., 1969—; chmn. bd., treas. Columbia Properties, Inc., 1969—; dir. Johnson Motor Lines, Inc., Charlotte, N.C., Employers Reinsurance Corp., Kansas City, 1974—; dir. ERC Corp., Centennial Life Ins. Co., United Mo. Bank. Mem. Kansas City Crime Commn., 1955-56; mem. advisory com. Am. Field Service, 1968-72; pres. Boys' Club of Kansas City, 1955-56; bd. dirs. Downtown, Inc., Kansas City, 1970—; mem. exec. com., bd. dirs. Kansas City Area Council Boy Scouts Am., 1971—; bd. govs. Agrl. Hall of Fame, 1975—; trustee Kansas U. Endowment Assn., 1970—; mem. exec. com., advisory bd. Sch. of Bus., U. Kans., 187—. Mem. Kans. U. Alumni Assn. (pres. 1969-70, bd. dirs. 1968-74). Clubs: University, Kansas City, Mission Hills Country. Home: 9202 W 71st St Merriam KS 66204 Office: 903 Grand Ave Kansas City MO 64106

RISSE, GUENTER BERNHARD, physician, educator; b. Buenos Aires, Argentina, Apr. 28, 1932; s. Francisco B. and Kaete A. R.; M.D., U. Buenos Aires, 1958; Ph.D., U. Chgo., 1971; m. Alexandra G. Paradzinski, Oct. 14, 1961; children—Heidi, Monica, Alisa. Intern, Mercy Hosp., Buffalo, 1958-59; resident in medicine Henry Ford Hosp., Detroit, 1960-61, Mt. Carmel Hosp., Columbus, Ohio, 1962-63; asst. dept. medicine U. Chgo., 1963-67; asst. prof. dept. history of medicine U. Minn., 1969-71; asso. prof. dept. history of medicine and dept. history of sci. U. Wis., Madison, 1971-76, prof., 1976—, chmn. dept. history of medicine, 1971-77. Served with Argentine Armed Forces, 1955. NIH grantee, 1971-73; WHO grantee, 1979. Mem. Am. Assn. History of Medicine, History Sci. Soc., Soc. Health and Human Values, Internat. Acad. History Medicine, Deutsche Gesellschaft fur Geschichte der Medizin, Société Internat. History Medicine. Author: Paleopathology of Ancient Egypt, 1964. Editor: Modern China and Traditional Chinese Medicine, 1973; Medicine Without Doctors, 1977; editorial bd. Jour. History of Medicine, 1971-74, Clio Medica, 1973—, M.D. Publs., 1979—. Home: 4825 Holiday Dr Madison WI 53711 Office: 1305 Linden Dr Madison WI 53706

RISSER, JAMES VAULX, JR., journalist; b. Lincoln, Nebr., May 8, 1938; s. James Vaulx and Ella Caroline (Schacht) R.; B.A., U. Nebr., 1959, certificate in journalism, 1964; J.D., U. San Francisco, 1962; m. Sandra Elizabeth Laaker, June 10, 1961; children—David James, John Daniel. Admitted to Nebr. bar, 1962; with firm Perry, Perry, Witthoff & Guthery, Lincoln, 1962-64; reporter Des Moines Register and Tribune, 1964—, Washington corr., 1969—, bur. chief, 1976—. Profl. Journalism fellow Stanford U., 1973-74; recipient award for distinguished reporting pub. affairs Am. Polit. Sci. Assn., 1969; Thomas L. Stokes award for environ. reporting Washington Journalism Center, 1971, 79; Pulitzer prize for nat. reporting, 1976, 79; Worth Bingham Found. prize for investigative reporting, 1976; Raymond Clapper Meml. Assn. award for Washington reporting, 1976, 78. Mem. Newspaper Farm Editors Am. (Farm Editor of Yr. award 1979), White House Corr. Assn., Nebr. Bar Assn., Sigma Delta Chi (Distinguished Service award 1976). Democrat. Unitarian. Clubs: Washington Press, Gridiron. Home: 3717 Jocelyn St NW Washington DC 20015 Office: 952 Nat Press Bldg Washington DC 20045

RISSER, PAUL GILLAN, botanist; b. Blackwell, Okla., Sept. 14, 1939; s. Paul Crane and Jean (McCluskey) R.; B.A., Grinnell Coll.; M.S. in Botany, U. Wis., also Ph.D. in Botany and Soils; m. Jeannine Hale, May 10, 1979; children—David, Mark, Stephen. From asst. prof. to prof. botany U. Okla., also asst. dir. biol. sta., chmn. dept. botany and microbiology; dir. Okla. Biol. Survey; program dir., ecosystem studies NSF. Trustee, Pioneer Multi-County Library Bd. Mem. Ecol. Soc. Am. (sec.), Brit. Ecol. Soc., Soc. Range Mgmt., Southwestern Assn. Naturalists (pres.), Torrey Bot. Club, Am. Inst. Biol. Sci. Presbyterian. Author: (with Kathy Cornelison) Man and the Biosphere, 1979; (with others) The True Prairie Ecosystem, 1980; research, numerous publs. in field. Home: Rural Route 1 Box 149 J Norman OK 73069 Office: U Okla 770 S Oval Norman OK 73019

RIST, JOHN MICHAEL, classicist; b. Romford, U.K., June 7, 1936; s. Robert Ward and Phoebe (May) R.; B.A., Cambridge (Eng.) U., 1959. M.A., 1963; m. Anna Therese Vogler, July 30, 1960; children—Peter, Alice, Thomas, Rebecca. Prof. classics and philosophy U. Toronto (Ont., Can.). Fellow Royal Soc. Can. Mem. New Democratic Party. Author books, including: Plotinus; The Road to Reality, 1967; Epicurus, 1972; On The Independence of Matthew and Mark, 1978; contbr. numerous articles to profl. jours. Home: 39 Saint Hilda's Ave Toronto ON M4N 2P5 Canada Office: Dept Classics U Toronto ON M5S 1A1 Canada

RISTICH, MIODRAG, psychiatrist; b. Belgrade, Yugoslavia, July 19, 1938; s. Teodosije and Gordana (Isailovic) R.; came to U.S., 1967, naturalized, 1975; M.D., U. Belgrade, 1962; m. Yvonne Muriel Cunliffe, May 6, 1967; children—Katharine Alexandra, Elizabeth Victoria. Intern U. Hosp., Belgrade, 1962-63; gen. practice medicine, Dalj, Yugoslavia, 1964; psychiat. resident Severalls Hosp., Colchester, Essex, Eng., 1964-67; med. dir. Cambridge (Minn.) State Hosp., 1967-72; dir. Willowbrook Devel. Center, S.I., N.Y., 1972-74; psychiatrist Inst. Basic Research in Mental Retardation, S.I., 1974-76; practice medicine specializing in psychiatry N.Y.C., 1974—. Mem. Am. Psychiat. Assn., AMA, Am. Assn. Mental Deficiency, Royal Coll. Psychiatrists. Eastern Orthodox. Home: 37 Sunrise Ln Upper Saddle River NJ 07458 Office: 133 E 73d St New York NY 10021

RISTINE, RICHARD OSBORNE, found. exec.; b. Indpls., Jan. 19, 1920; s. Harley Thomson and Helen (Osborne) R.; A.B. summa cum laude, Wabash Coll., 1941, LL.D., 1971; LL.B., Columbia, 1944; LL.D., Ind. State U., 1976; m. Mary Lou Durrett, Sept. 21, 1946; children—Richard Osborne, Thomas Harley, James Durrett. Admitted to N.Y. bar, 1944, Ind. bar, 1944; asso. firm Baker & Daniels, Indpls., 1946-48; partner firm Wernle & Ristine, Crawfordsville, Ind., 1948-65; counsel Wernle, Ristine & Ayers, Crawfordsville, 1965—; pres. Elston Bank & Trust Co., Crawfordsville, 1965-67; v.p. L.S. Ayres & Co., Indpls., 1967-72; sec. Lilly Endowment Inc., Indpls., 1972—, v.p., 1972-75, exec. v.p., 1975—; chmn. Fed. Home Loan Bank Indpls., 1969—; dir. Meridian Mut. Ins. Co., Indpls., 1969—, chmn., 1975—; dir. Elston Bank & Trust Co., Indpls. Water Co. Vice pres. Ind. Employment Security Bd., 1969—. Pres., Mental Health Assn. Ind., 1968-69. Mem. Ind. Senate, 1951-60; lt. gov. Ind., 1961-65. Bd. dirs. Ind. State Arts Commn., 1970-72, Hist. Landmarks of Ind., 1978—, Ind. State Symphony Soc., 1969-72, 78—, United Way of Greater Indpls., 1978—; trustee Wabash Coll., 1958—, treas., 1965-75. Served to capt. USAAF, 1943-46. Mem. Ind. Hist. Soc. (trustee 1971—), Ind. Acad., Ouiatenon Club, Phi Beta Kappa, Phi Delta Phi, Beta Theta Pi. Republican. Presbyn. (elder). Home: 2144C Boston Ct Indianapolis IN 46208 Office: 2801 N Meridian St Indianapolis IN 46208

RITCHESON, CHARLES RAY, educator, diplomat; b. Maysville, Okla., Feb. 26, 1925; s. Charles Frederick and Jewell (Vaughn) R.; B.A., Okla. U., 1946; postgrad. Zurich U. (Switzerland), 1946-47, Harvard U., 1947-48; Ph.D. (Fulbright fellow), Oxford U. (Eng.), 1951; D.Litt. (hon.), Leicester U. (Eng.); m. Shirley Marie Spackman, June 13, 1953 (div. July 1964); children—Charles Brendan, Mark Frederick; m. 2d, Alice Luethi, Oct. 11, 1965; children—Philip Luethi, Steven Whitefield, Andrew Shepherd, Peter Lorentz. Asst. prof. history Okla. Coll. for Women, 1951-52, asso. prof., 1952-53; asso. prof. Kenyon Coll., Gambier, Ohio, 1953-60, became prof., 1960, chmn. dept. history, 1964; chmn., dir. grad. studies in history So. Meth. U., 1965-70, dir. Center Ibero-Am. Civilization, 1967-68, dir. with rank of dean Library Advancement, 1970-71; Colin Rhys Lovell prof. Brit. history U. So. Calif., 1971-74, Lovell distinguished prof., 1977—; cultural attaché U.S. Embassy, London, 1974-77; pres. So. Conf. on Brit. Studies, 1967-70; pres. Pacific Coast br. Conf. on

Brit. Studies, 1971-73; exec. sec. Nat. Conf. Brit. Studies, 1973-74; Fulbright prof. Edinburgh U., Cambridge U., 1963-64. Sr. adviser Norton Simon Found., 1972-74; chmn. U.S.-U.K. Ednl. Commn., 1974-77; ofcl. observer Brit. Bicentennial Liaison Com., 1974-76; mem. Harmsworth com. Oxford, 1974-77; mem. Kennedy Scholar Selection Com., 1975-77; mem. internat. adv. council Univ. Coll., Buckingham, Eng.; mem. Gov.'s Commn. Bicentennial of Am. Revolution, 1969-71; mem. U.K.-U.S. Bicentennial Fellows Selection Com., 1975-77. Chmn., Tex. Scholars for Rockefeller, 1968; trustee Am. Sch. in London, 1974-77, Anthony Eden Fund, 1975-77; v.p. Am. Friends of Covent Garden; adv. council Ditchley Found.; chmn. Brit. Inst. U.S., 1979—. Served to lt. (j.g.) USNR, 1942-45. Recipient Social Sci. Research Council grant-in-aid, 1955; Social Sci. Research Council Faculty fellow, 1956-59; Eli Lilly-Clements Library fellow, 1960; Am. Council Learned Socs. fellow, 1963-64. Fellow Royal Hist. Soc.; mem. Am. Hist. Assn., Conf. Brit. Studies (exec. sec. 1968-70), Anglo-Am. Historians (exec. com.), Anglo-Am. Assos. (exec. com.), Am. Soc. for 18th Century Studies (exec. com.), Tex. Inst. Letters, Phi Beta Kappa, Delta Chi, Phi Gamma Mu. Episcopalian. Clubs: Bel-Air Beach (Los Angeles); Brooks' Beefsteak, Athenaeum, Garrick (London); Pilgrims (N.Y.C.). Author: British Politics and the American Revolution, 1954; Era of the American Revolution, 1968; British Policy Toward the U.S., 1783-1795, 1968. Editorial bd. Jour. 18th Century Studies; bd. dirs. History Tchr. Contbr. articles to learned jours. Home: 741 S Bristol Ave Los Angeles CA 90049 Office: History Dept U of So Calif Los Angeles CA 90007

RITCHEY, SAMUEL DONLEY, JR., retail store exec.; b. Derry Twp., Pa., July 16, 1933; s. Samuel Donley and Florence Catherine (Litsch) R.; B.S., San Diego State U., 1955, M.S., 1963; postgrad. (Sloan Found. fellow), Stanford, 1964; m. Sharon Marie Anderson, Apr. 6, 1956; children—Michael Donley, Tamara Louise, Shawn Christopher. Store mgr. supermarkets Lucky Stores Inc., San Diego and Phoenix, 1957-61, store supr. Gemco div., 1965-66, dist. mgr. Gemco, 1966-68, nonfood mdse. mgr. parent co., 1968-69, div. mgr. Gemco, v.p. parent co., 1969-72, sr. v.p. Lucky Stores, Inc., Dublin, Calif., 1972-75, exec. v.p., 1975-78, pres., chief operating officer, 1978—, also dir.; grad. mgr. San Diego State U., 1961-63; lectr. in field. Bd. dirs. Sloan Alumni Adv. Bd., Stanford U., Bay Area Council Boy Scouts Am. Mem. Western Assn. Food Chains (sec., dir.), Food Mktg. Inst. (dir.). Home: 991 Ocho Rios Dr Danville CA 94526 Office: Lucky Stores Inc 6300 Clark Ave Dublin CA 94566

RITCHI, ROLAND A., judge; b. Halifax, N.S., Can., June 19, 1910; s. William Bruce Almon and Lilian Constance (Stewart) T.; ed. U. King's Coll., Halifax, N.S., Pembroke Coll., Oxford (Eng.) U.; m. Mary Lippincot Wylde, May 6, 193; 6; 1 dau., Elizabeth Stewart. Called to bar N.S., 1934, created queen's counsel, 1950; read law with J. M. Stewart, Queen's Counsel; asso. firm Stewart, Smith, Mackeen & Rogers, Halifax, 1934-40; partner firm Daley, Ritchi, Black & Moriera and predecessor; puisne judge Supreme Ct. Can., Ottawa, Ont., 1959—. Chancellor U. King's Coll.; hon. Dalhousie U., U. King's Coll. Served to capt. Royal Can. Airforce, 1940-43. Hon. fellow Pembroke Coll., Oxford U. Mem. N.S. Barristers Soc. (1st v.p.), Can. Bar Assn. Anglican. Clubs: Rideau, Halifax (all Halifax); Royal Ottawa Golf (Aylmer, Que.). Office: Supreme Ct Bldg Wellington St Ottawa ON K1A 0J1 Canada*

RITCHIE, ALBERT EDGAR, Canadian diplomat; b. Andover, N.B., Can., Dec. 20, 1916; s. Stanley W. and Beatrice (Walker) R.; B.A., Mt. Allison U., 1938, LL.D., 1966; B.A. (Rhodes scholar), Oxford (Eng.) U., 1940; LL.D. St. Thomas U., 1967; m. Gwendolin L. Perdue, Dec. 20, 1941; children—Gordon R., Heather G. (Mrs. Leonidas Zourdoumis), Donald I., Holly P. (Mrs. David Dale). Joined Canadian Ministry External Affairs, 1944; dep. undersec. of state for external affairs, 1964-66; Canadian ambassador to U.S., 1966-70; undersec. state for external affairs, 1970-74; spl. adviser to Privy Council, Office of Can., 1974-76; Canadian ambassador to Ireland, 1976—. Recipient Outstanding Achievement award for the pub. service of Can., 1973; decorated companion Order of Can., 1975. Office: 65 St Stephen's Green Dublin Ireland

RITCHIE, ALEXANDER BUCHAN, lawyer; b. Detroit, Apr. 19, 1923; s. Alexander Stevenson and Margaret (May) R.; B.A., Wayne State U., 1947, LL.D., 1949; m. Glady Bilkow, Aug. 12, 1944; children—Alexander K., Barbara Sharon. Admitted to Mich. bar, 1949, since practiced in Detroit; asst. gen. counsel Maccabees Mut. Life Ins. Co., 1952-65; sec. Wayne Nat. Life Ins. Co., 1966-67; partner firm Fenton, Nederlander, Dodge & Ritchie, Profl. Corp., Detroit, 1967-77; spl. asst. atty. gen. State of Mich., 1974-77; v.p., gen. counsel Maccabees Mut. Life Ins. Co. Mem. Detroit Region Bd. Edn., 1971—; mem. Detroit Bd. Police Commrs., 1974-77. Bd. dirs. Drs. Hosp., 1974—. Served with AUS, 1943-46. Lutheran. Home: 12479 Riad St Detroit MI 48224 Office: 25800 Northwestern Hwy Southfield MI 48037

RITCHIE, ALEXANDER CHARLES, educator, physician; b. Auckland, New Zealand, Apr. 2, 1921; s. Percy Charles and Olive Muriel (Hodge) R.; M.B., Ch.B., U. Otago, 1944; D.Phil., U. Oxford, 1951; m. Susan Liszauer, Oct. 10, 1956. Miranda Fraser asso. prof. comparative pathology McGill U., Montreal, Que., 1954-61; prof. U. Toronto (Ont., Can.), 1961—, head dept. pathology, 1961-74; pathologist-in-chief Toronto Gen. Hosp., 1961-75; cons. pathologist several hosps. Toronto. Recipient Centennial Decoration Can., 1967; Can. Jubilee medal, 1977. Fellow Royal Coll. Physicians and Surgeons Can., Royal Coll. Pathologists (Eng., Australia), Coll. Am. Pathologists; mem. Canadian Assn. Pathologists (pres., 1967-69). Club: York. Home: 625 Avenue Rd Toronto ON M4V 2K7 Canada

RITCHIE, CEDRIC ELMER, banker; b. Upper Kent, N.B., Can., Aug. 22, 1927; s. E. Thomas and Marion (Henderson) R.; student pub. schs., Bath, N.B.; m. Barbara Binnington, Apr. 20, 1956. With Bank of N.S., Bath, 1945—, chief gen. mgr., Toronto, 1970—, pres., 1972-79, chief exec. officer, 1972—, chmn. bd., 1974—, also dir.; chmn. bd. Bank N.S. Channel Islands Ltd., Bank N.S. Trust Co. Channel Islands Ltd., Bank of N.S. Trust Co. (U.K.) Ltd., Bank of N.S. Trust Co. W.I. Ltd., Empire Realty Co. Ltd., Bank N.S. Trust Co. (Bahamas) Ltd., Bank N.S. Trust Co. (Caribbean) Ltd., BNS Internat. (U.K.) Ltd., Bank of N.S. Internat. Ltd., Bank N.S. Trust Co. (Cayman) Ltd.; pres. Bluenose Investments Ltd., Nova Scotia Corp.; dir. numerous companies; mem. Can. Econ. Policy Com. Bd. govs. Olympic Trust Can. Recipient Human Relations award Can. Council Christians and Jews, 1976. Clubs: Caledon Ski, Canadian, Donalda, Empire, Mt. Royal, Mid Ocean, National, Toronto, York. Office: Bank of NS 44 King St W Toronto ON M5H 1E2 Canada

RITCHIE, DANIEL LEE, broadcasting exec.; b. Springfield, Ill., Sept. 19, 1931; s. Daniel Felix and Jessie Dee (Binney) R.; B.A., Harvard U., 1954, M.A., 1956. Exec. v.p. MCA, Inc., Los Angeles, 1967-70; pres. Archon Pure Products Co., Los Angeles, 1970-73; exec. v.p. Westinghouse Electric Corp., Pitts., 1975-78; pres. corp. staff and strategic planning Westinghouse Broadcasting Co., 1978-79, pres., chief exec. officer, 1979—. Served with U.S. Army, 1956-58. Address: 90 Park Ave New York NY 10016

RITCHIE, JOHN, educator; b. Norfolk, Va., Mar. 19, 1904; s. John and Edith (Kensett) R., Jr; B.S., U. Va., 1925, LL.B., 1927; J.S.D., Yale U., 1931; LL.D. (hon.), Coll. William and Mary, 1979; m. Sarah Dunlap Wallace, Apr. 20, 1929; children—John, Albert. Admitted to Nebr. bar, 1927, Ill. bar, 1957; with Ritchie, Chase, Canaday & Swenson, 1927-28; asst. prof. law Furman U., 1928-30, U. Wash., 1931-36; prof. law U. Md., 1936-37; prof. law U. Va., 1937-52, asst. dean, 1941-49; admitted to Va. bar, 1942, Mo. bar, 1952, Wis. bar, 1953; dean law sch., Kirby prof. law Washington U., 1952-53; prof., dean Sch. Law, U. Wis., 1953-57; dean Law Sch., Northwestern U., Chgo., 1957-72, John Henry Wigmore prof., 1966—, emeritus dean, 1972—; prof. law U. Va., 1972-74, now scholar-in-residence; vis. distinguished prof. U. Tenn., 1974, U. Okla., 1975, Coll. William and Mary, 1976; mem. Ill. Jud. Adv. Council, 1964-68; dir. Am. Council on Edn., 1965-68. Bd. dirs. United Charities Chgo., 1966-72. Served to col. U.S. Army, 1942-45. Decorated Bronze Star. Fellow Am. Bar Found.; mem. Am., Va., Ill., Chgo. bar assns., Assn. Am. Law Schs. (pres. 1964), Law Club Chgo., Judge Advs. Assn. (pres. 1951-52), Phi Beta Kappa, Order of Coif (nat. pres. 1952-55), Omicron Delta Kappa, Phi Kappa Psi, Phi Delta Phi. Episcopalian. Clubs: Wayfarers, Colonnade, Greencroft. Co-author: Decedent's Estates and Trusts, 1955, 5th edit., 1977; author: The First Hundred Years: A Short History of the School of Law of the University of Virginia for the Period 1826-1926, 1978. Editorial bd. Found. Press. Contbr. various legal publs. Home: 1848 Westview Rd Charlottesville VA 22903 Office: Sch Law U Va Charlottesville VA 22903

RITCHIE, MICHAEL BRUNSWICK, film dir. and producer; b. Waukesha, Wis., Nov. 28, 1938; s. Benbow Ferguson and Patricia (Graney) R.; A.B., Harvard U., 1960; m. Georgina Tebrock, Feb. 2, 1963; children—Lauren, Steven, Jessica. Television dir., 1963-68; dir. films Downhill Racer, 1969, Prime Cut, 1972, The Candidate, 1972, Smile, 1975, Bad News Bears, 1976, Semi Tough, 1977; dir., writer film An Almost Perfect Affair, 1979; dir. TV shows Man from U.N.C.L.E., Dr. Kildare, The Big Valley, Felony Squad, Run for Your Life; producer The Bad News Bears Go to Japan, 1978; pres. Rhee Prodns., Tamalpais Films. Films invited to Venice Film Festival and U.S. Film Festival. Mem. Dirs. Guild Am. Home: 366 Summit Ave Mill Valley CA 94941 Office: care Marvin Freedman Freedman & Freedman 1801 Ave of Stars Los Angeles CA 90067*

RITCHIE, REEVES ESTES, utility exec.; b. Amarillo, Tex., July 8, 1914; s. Robert Estes and Mary (Reeves) R.; student bus. adminstrn. U. Ark., 1933-34, George Washington U., 1934-35; m. Gladys M. Cook, Jan. 31, 1936; children—Robert Estes II, Nancy Marie. With Ark. Power & Light Co., Little Rock, 1936—, v.p., dir. personnel, 1960-62, exec. v.p., 1962, pres., 1962—, chmn. bd., chief exec. officer, 1976—, chmn. bd., 1977—. Mem. Ark. Council on Econ. Edn.; mem. Ozark Folk Cultural Center Commn. Bd. dirs., past pres. Southeastern Electric Exchange. Mem. NAM, Little Rock (past pres.), Ark. (dir., past pres.) chambers commerce. Mem. Christian Ch. Mason (33 deg., Shriner). Clubs: Little Rock, Little Rock Country, (Little Rock). Office: Ark Power & Light Co Capitol and Broadway PO Box 551 Little Rock AR 72203

RITCHIE, RICHARD LEE, railroad exec.; b. Grand Rapids, Mich., July 20, 1946; s. Robert George and Gertrude (Dryer) R.; B.A., Mich. State U., 1968, M.B.A., 1972; m. Marlene Barton, Nov. 16, 1969; children—Gabrielle Gay, Steven Barton. Sr. accountant Peat, Marwick, Mitchell & Co., Detroit, 1968-69, 72-74; mgr. corporate accounting Grand Trunk Western R.R., Detroit, 1974-76, treas., 1976—; prof. Oakland Community Coll., Farmington, Mich. Served with AUS, 1969-71. C.P.A., Mich. Mem. Am. Inst. C.P.A.'s, Mich. Assn. C.P.A.'s, Am. Accounting Assn., Beta Alpha Psi, Beta Gamma Sigma. Jewish. Home: 4238 Fieldbrook West Bloomfield MI 48033 Office: 131 W Lafayette Blvd Detroit MI 48226

RITCHIE, RONALD STUART, mem. Can. parliament, ecomonist; b. Charing Cross, Ont., Can., July 4, 1918; s. Thomas Duncan and Maggie (Sterritt) R.; B.A. (Gold medallis in Econs. and Polit. Sci.), U. Western Ont., 1938; M.A., Queens U., 1960; m. Phyllis Plaskett, Feb. 4, 1950; children—Beverly Janet, Barbara Diane, Patricia Ann, Karen Heather, Margot Lynn. Life underwriter Standard Life Assurance Co., London, Ont., 1938-39; lectr. econs. dept. Ont. Agrl. Coll., Guelph, 1940-41; exec. asst. to dep. chmn. Wartime Prices and Trade Bd., 1941-44, dep. chief prices div., 1945-47; mgr. Ottawa Civil Service Recreational Assn., 1944-45; with Imperial Oil Ltd., N.Y.C., 1947, head econs. and statistics group, Toronto, 1948-50, asst. mgr. coordination and econs. dept., 1950-52, asst. div. mgr. Ont. mktg. div., Toronto, 1953-55, mgr. B.C. mktg. div., Vancouver, 1955-58, asst. gen. mgr. mktg. dept., Toronto, 1958, mgr. employee relations, 1958-60, exec. asst. to bd. spl. projects, 1962-63, dir., 1963-74, sr. v.p., 1970-74; exec. dir. Royal Commn. on Govt. Orgn., 1960-62; prin. asst. Office of Leader of Opposition, Ottawa, 1974-75; cons. economist, 1976-79; mem. Can. Ho. of Commons for York East, 1979—, apptd. parliamentary sec. to minister fin., 1979. Canadian del. Commonwealth Conf., Lahore, Pakistan, 1954; del. ILO, Geneva, 1960. Mem. Internat. Inst. Applied Systems Analysis, Vienna, 1973-76; chmn. Atlantic Council of Can., 1962; mem. Ont. Council on Univ. Affairs, 1974-79. Chmn. bd. dirs. Inst. Research on Pub. Policy, 1972-74; bd. dirs. Orthopedic and Arthritic Hosp., Toronto; bd. govs. Atlantic Inst., Paris; chmn. bd. govs. U. Guelph, 1968-71; mem. nat. exec. com. Canadian Inst. Internat. Affairs, 1959-73; mem. adv. com. Inst. for No. Studies, Saskatoon, 1970-74; mem. adv. council Faculty of Adminstrv. Studies, York U., Toronto, 1972-76; bd. govs. Ditchley Found.; bd. dirs. North-South Inst.; mem. exec. com., bd. dirs. Can. Council Christians and Jews; bd. govs. Found. for Internat. Tng. in Third World Countries. Mem. Canadian Econs. Assn., Can. Inst. Pub. Affairs (dir.), Canadian Polit. Sci. Assn., Canadian Hist. Assn., Club of Rome. Mem. United Ch. of Can. Clubs: U. Toronto; Rideau (Ottawa). Author: NATO: The Economics of an Alliance, 1956; An Institute For Research on Public Policy, 1971; The Ritchie Report on Canada's Postal Service, 1978. Editor, pub. The Canadian Conservative. Contbr. articles to profl. jours. Office: Room 465 West Block House of Commons Ottawa ON K1A 0A7 Canada

RITLAND, OSMOND JAY, aerospace co. exec., ret. air force officer; b. Berthoud, Colo., Oct. 30, 1909; s. Osmund Ovedius and Jennie Olena (Tesdell) R.; student San Diego State Coll., 1928-31; grad. AC Advanced Flying Sch., Kelly Field, Tex., 1933, Second Command Class, Ft. Leavenworth, Kans., 1946; student Indsl. Coll. Armed Forces, Washington, 1953-54; m. Martha Alsup, Mar. 20, 1936; children—Kathleen Virginia, Martha Susan. Engring. officer, fighter pilot 95th Pursuit Squadron AC, U.S. Army, March Field, Calif., 1933-35; pilot United Air Lines, 1935-39; commd. 2d lt. Reg. AAC, 1939, advanced through grades to maj. gen. USAF, 1959; engring. officer, pilot 9th Bombardment Squadron, Hamilton Field, Calif., 1939-40; exptl. flight test pilot, exec. officer flying br. Wright Field, Dayton, Ohio, 1940-44; comdg. officer Assam Air Depot, India, 1944-46; asst. chief aircraft project sect. engring. div. Wright Field, 1946-48, chief of lab. engring. div., Aircraft Lab., Wright Field, 1948-50; comdg. officer 4925th test group (atomic), Kirtland AFB, N.Mex., 1950-53; chief atomic energy div. Hdqrs. USAF, 1954-55; spl. asst. to Dep. Chief Staff Devel., Hdqrs. USAF, 1955-56, vice comdr. air force ballistic missile div., 1956-59, comdr., 1959-61, comdr. space systems div., 1961-62, dep. to comdr. for manned space flight, 1962-64, dep. comdr. for space Air Force Systems Command, 1964-65; v.p. reliability and launch operations, missile and space systems div. Douglas Aircraft Co., Inc., Huntington Beach, Calif., 1965-68, v.p., gen. mgr. launch ops. McDonnell Douglas Astronautics Co., 1968-72; spl. asst. to v.p. and gen. mgr. space systems div. Lockheed Missiles & Space Co., 1972-73. Decorated Legion of Merit (2), D.F.C., Air medal, Bronze Star, D.S.M. (2); recipient Gen. H.H. Arnold award, 1963; Exceptional Service medal NASA. Fellow Am. Inst. Aeros. and Astronautics; mem. Am. Ordnance Assn. (chmn. bd. Los Angeles chpt. 1972-73), Order of Daedalians. Club: Explorers (fellow) (N.Y.C.). Home: PO Box 274 Rancho Santa Fe CA 92067

RITT, MARTIN, dir., actor; b. N.Y.C., Mar. 2, 1920; s. Morris and Rose Ritt; student Elon Coll., also Group Theatre, N.Y.C. Broadway appearances include Golden Boy, 1937, Plant of the Sun, 1938, The Gentle People, 1939, Two on an Island, 1939, They Should Have Stood in Bed, 1942, The Eve of St. Mark, 1942, Winged Victory, 1943 (also on tour), Men of Distinction, 1953, Maya, 1953, The Flowering Peach, 1954, Born Yesterday (Phila.), 1955; motion picture appearances in Winged Victory, 1944, End of the Game, 1976, Hollywood on Trial, 1977; Broadway prodns. directed include Mr. Peebles and Mr. Hooker, 1946, Yellow Jack, 1947, The Big People (Conn. and Mass.), 1947, Set My People Free, 1948, The Man, 1950, Cry of the Peacock, 1950, Golden Boy, Boy Meets Girl, The Front Page (all Phila.), 1954, A View From the Bridge, 1955, A Memory of Two Mondays, 1955; motion pictures directed Include Edge of the City, 1957, The Long Hot Summer, 1958, The Sound and the Fury, 1959, The Black Orchid, 1959, Five Branded Women, 1960, Paris Blues, 1961, Adventures of a Young Man, 1962, The Outrage, 1964, The Spy Who Came in from the Cold, 1966, Hombre, 1967, The Brotherhood, 1968, Sounder, 1972, Pete 'n' Tillie, 1972, Casey's Shadow, 1978, Norma Rae, 1979; co-producer, dir. of Hud, 1963, The Molly Maguires, 1970, The Great White Hope, 1970; dir., producer Conrack, 1974, The Front, 1976; dir. TV series Danger, also plays for U.S. Steel Hour, Playwrites Theatre, Actors Studio Theatre; TV appearances in Danger, Starlight Theatre. Served with USAAF, World War II. Recipient Peabody award; nominated for Oscar award. Mem. Screen Directors Guild, AFTRA, Actors Equity Assn., Screen Actors Guild. Address: care George Chasin Chasin-Park-Citron 9255 Sunset Blvd Los Angeles CA 90069*

RITT, PAUL EDWARD, electronics co. exec.; b. Balt., Mar. 3, 1928; s. Paul Edward and Mary (Knight) R.; B.S. in Chemistry, Loyola U., Balt., 1950, M.S. in Chemistry, 1952; Ph.D. in Chemistry, Georgetown U., 1954; m. Dorothy Ann Wintz, Dec. 30, 1950; children—Paul Edward, Peter M., John W., James T., Mary Carol, Matthew J. Research asso. Harris Research Lab., Washington, 1950-52; aerospace research chemist Melpar, Inc., Falls Church, Va., 1952-60, research dir., 1960-62, v.p. research, 1962-65, v.p. research and engring., 1965-67; v.p., gen. mgr. Tng. Corp. Am., 1965-67; pres. applied sci. div., applied tech. div. Litton Industries, Bethesda, Md., 1967-68; v.p., dir. research Gen. Telephone & Electronics Labs., Waltham, Mass., 1968—; instr. U. Va., 1956-58, Am. U., 1959—. Fellow Am. Inst. Chemists; mem. Am. Phys. Soc., Am. Inst. Physics, Am. Chem. Soc. Contbr. articles to profl. jours.; patentee in field. Home: 36 Sylvan Ln Weston MA 02193 Office: 40 Sylvan Rd Waltham MA 02154

RITTENHOUSE, FRANKLIN PIERCE ROSS, lawyer; b. Wheeling, W.Va., 1926; s. George F. and Pauline (Irwin) R.; B.A., U. Nev.; LL.B., Stanford, 1951; m. Natalie R. Stevenson, Sept. 9, 1953; 1 dau., Allison. Admitted to Nev. bar, 1951; mem. Bonner & Rittenhouse, Las Vegas, 1951-54; asst. to U.S. atty., 1954-55; U.S. dist. atty. Nev. dist., 1955-58; partner McNamee, McNamee & Rittenhouse, Las Vegas, 1958-78; probate commr. Dist. Cts. Nev., Las Vegas, 1978—; municipal ct. judge, 1962-65. Mem. Am., Nev. bar assns., Sigma Alpha Epsilon, Phi Alpha Delta. Republican. Presbyn. Home: 1339 Cashman Dr Las Vegas NV 89102 Office: 200 E Carson Ave Las Vegas NV 89102

RITTENHOUSE, JOSEPH WILSON, elec. products mfg. co. cons.; b. Neosho, Mo., Jan. 22, 1917; s. George Eddy and Nannie Stewart (Morgan) R.; B.S. in Elec. Engring., Purdue U., 1939; M.S. in Elec. Engring., U. Mo., 1949; m. Jane Eileen Peterson, June 3, 1939; children—Joseph Wilson II, John David, Jane Eileen, Judith Anne, James Jay, Jeffrey Lee. Mem. staff radio sta. WBAA, Purdue U., Lafayette, Ind., 1936-39; various engring. positions James R. Kearney Corp., St. Louis, 1939-43; mem. faculty elec. engring. dept. Sch. Mines and Metallurgy, U. Mo. at Rolla, 1947-54, asso. prof. elec. engring., 1952-54; tech. dir. hi-voltage equipment div. Joslyn Mfg. and Supply Co., Cleve., 1954-65, div. gen. mgr., 1965-69, group v.p. elec. products, 1969-73, pres. Joslyn Mfg. & Supply Co., Chgo., 1973-78, chmn., 1973-79, dir., 1970-79, cons., 1979—; dir. Scholl, Inc., Midland Bancorp, Sears Bank & Trust Co. Guest speaker at meetings of profl. and other socs. Mem. indsl. devel. com. City Council, Aurora, Ohio, 1960-62. Served as officer Signal Corps, AUS, 1943-46; maj. Res., ret. Registered profl. engr., Mo. Fellow IEEE (mem., chmn. numerous coms.); mem. Nat., Ill. socs. profl. engrs., Am. Soc. Engring. Edn., Conf. Internationale des Grands Reseaux Electriques, Nat. Elec. Mfrs. Assn. (bd. govs. 1970—, vice chmn. 1974—), Cleve. C. of C., Sigma Xi, Eta Kappa Nu (nat. adv. bd. 1955-57), Tau Beta Pi, Tau Kappa Alpha, Lambda Chi Alpha. Presbyn. Clubs: University, Metropolitan, Tower (Chgo.). Co-author: Electric Power Transmission, 1953. Contbr. articles to profl. publs. Patentee in field. Home: Route 1 Box 26 Barrington IL 60010

RITTER, ALFRED FRANCIS, JR., newspaper and broadcasting exec.; b. Norfolk, Va., Dec. 31, 1946; s. A. Francis and Lucille Gray (Thomas) R.; A.B., Coll. William and Mary, Williamsburg, Va., 1968; m. Caroline Buchanan O'Keefe, Aug. 10, 1968; children—Alfred Francis, III, Caroline O'Donnell. With Goodman & Co., C.P.A.'s, Norfolk, 1971-76; with Landmark Communications, Inc., Norfolk, 1976—, v.p., controller, 1977-78, v.p. fin., chief fin. officer, 1978—; dir. TeleCable Corp. and subs., 1978—. Chmn. Internat. Azalea Festival, 1979; bd. dirs. Health-Welfare-Recreation Planning Council Hampton Roads, Norfolk Goodwill Industries. Served to lt. USNR, 1968-71. C.P.A., Va. Mem. Am. Inst. C.P.A.'s, Broadcast Fin. Mgmt. Assn., Inst. Newspaper Controllers and Fin. Officers, Va. Soc. C.P.A.'s (chpt. dir. 1978-79). Episcopalian. Clubs: Norfolk Yacht and Country, Harbour. Home: 1331 Armistead Bridge Rd Norfolk VA 23507 Office: 150 W Brambleton Ave Norfolk VA 23501

RITTER, ALLAN GERALD, lawyer; b. Williamsport, Pa., June 7, 1888; s. Walter E. and Margaret A. (Wallis) R.; A.B., Dickinson Sem., 1905; Ph.B., Bucknell U., 1909, A.M., 1911; student U. Mich. Law Sch., 1911-12, Stanford Law Sch., 1912; m. Ila E. Coombe, Aug. 13, 1915; 1 dau., Margaret Jane (Mrs. Edwin S. Ross). Admitted to Calif. bar, 1913, since practiced in Los Angeles; trustee emeritus Al Malaikah Auditorium Co. Bd. dirs. emeritus Los Angeles unit Shrine Crippled Children's Hosp. Mem. Am., Calif., Los Angeles Bar assns., Phi Delta Phi, Kappa Sigma (worthy grand master 1935-37; chmn. trustees endowment fund). Mason (K.T.; Red Cross Constantine; 33 deg., Shriner, past potentate). Club: Los Angeles Country. Home: 328 21st St Santa Monica CA 90402 Office: 3946 Wilshire Blvd Los Angeles CA 90010

RITTER, DONALD LAWRENCE, engr., congressman; b. N.Y.C., Oct. 21, 1940; s. Frank and Ruth R.; B.S. in Metall. Engring., Lehigh U., 1961; M.S. in Phys. Metallurgy, M.I.T., 1966, Sc.D., 1966; m. Edith Duerksen; children—Jason, Kristina. Mem. faculty Calif. State Poly. U., also contract cons. Gen. Dynamics Co., 1968-69; mem. faculty dept. metallurgy and materials scis., asst. to v.p. for research Lehigh U., 1969-76; mgr. research program devel., 1976-78; mem. 96th Congress from 15th Dist. Pa. Sci. exchange fellow U.S. Nat. Acad. Scis.-Soviet Acad. Sci., Balkov Inst., Moscow, 1967-68. Bd. dirs. Baum Art Sch. of Allentown Art Mus. Mem. Am. Soc. Metals, Am. Soc. Engring. Edn., Sigma Xi, Alpha Sigma Mu, Pi Mu Epsilon. Republican. Unitarian. Club: Elks. Contbr. articles to metallurgy jours. Home: RD 1 Coopersburg PA 18036 Office: 124 Cannon House Office Bldg Washington DC 20515

RITTER, GEORGE WILLIAM, lawyer; b. Vermillion, Ohio, June 30, 1886; s. John and Louise (Hauth) R.; student Cleve. Law Sch., 1903-06; LL.B., Baldwin U., Berea, Ohio, 1906; LL.D., Baldwin-Wallace Coll., 1946, U. Toledo; m. Mary Fowler, June 30, 1911. Admitted to Ohio bar, 1907, since practiced in Ohio; dir. law City of Toledo, 1928-29; v.p., gen. counsel Overland Corp., Toledo, 1936—; partner law firm Ritter, Boesel, Robinson & Marsh. Trustee Toledo Hosp., Toledo Mus. Art, Baldwin-Wallace Coll. Mem. Toledo, Ohio, Lucas County, Am., Cleve., Toledo bar assns., Assn. Bar City of N.Y. Republican. Conglist. Clubs: Toledo, Inverness, Country (Toledo); Big Creek Hunting and Fishing (Can.); Bath, Surf, Indian Creek Country, Com. 100 (Fla.); Castalia Trout; La Gorce Country. Home: 4555 Forestview Dr Ottawa Hills OH 43615 (winter) The Kenilworth Apt 501 10205 Collins Ave Bal Harbour FL 33154 Office: 240 Huron St Toledo OH 43604

RITTER, JOHNATHAN SOUTHWORTH, actor; b. Burbank, Calif., Sept. 17, 1948; s. Tex and Dorothy Fay (Southworth) R.; B.A., U. So. Calif., 1971; m. Nancy Karen Morgan, Oct. 16, 1977. Appeared in films The Barefoot Executive, 1970, The Other, 1972, Nickelodeon, 1976, Hero at Large, 1980; appeared in plays Desire Under the Elms, The Glass Menagerie, Butterflies Are Free, Nevada, As You Like it, The Tempest, Feiffer's People; appeared on TV shows Mary Tyler Moore Show, Rhoda, Phyllis, The Bob Newhart Show, The Rookies, Who's Happy Now (Theatre in America), The Lie (Playhouse 90), also on Hawaii Five-O, The Waltons, Kojak, Streets of San Francisco; star TV series Three's Company (nominated Emmy award), others. Bd. dirs. United Cerebral Palsy Assn. Mem. Screen Actors Guild, AFTRA, Actor's Equity. Office: care Robert Myman 9454 Wilshire Blvd #800 Beverly Hills CA 90212

RITTEREISER, ROBERT PETER, brokerage co. exec.; b. N.Y.C., July 15, 1938; s. Frederic Edward and Elizabeth Loretta (Collins) R.; B.B.A., Baruch Sch. CCNY, 1965; grad. advanced mgmt. program Harvard U., 1977; m. Mary P. McKenna, Oct. 3, 1959; children—Cathleen, Daniel, Patricia, Suzanne, R. J. With Merrill Lynch, Pierce, Fenner & Smith Inc., N.Y.C., 1958—, pres. Goodbody Inc., subs., N.Y.C., 1971-74, dir. ops. parent co., 1974-76, regional v.p., 1976-79, exec. v.p. ops., 1979—, also dir.; dir. Nat. Securities Clearing Corp., Chgo. Bd. Options Exchange; mem. bd. advs. N.Y. Inst. Fin. Clubs: Indian Tr. (Franklin Lakes, N.J.); Harvard Bus. Sch., Bd. Room (N.Y.C.). Author: Margin Regulations and Practice, 1971. Office: 165 Broadway New York NY 10080

RITTERHOFF, C(HARLES) WILLIAM, steel co. exec.; b. Balt., Nov. 1, 1921; s. Ernest F. and Anna M. (Luerssen) R.; B.S. in Mech. Engring., Mass. Inst. Tech., 1947; grad. Advanced Mgmt. Program, Harvard, 1973; m. Margery A. McKenney, June 24, 1944; children—Leslie, William, James. Asst. engr. mech. dept., then various supervisory positions Bethlehem Steel Co., Sparrows Point, Md., 1948-57, asst. supt. Sparrows Point plate mills, 1957-60, asst. chief engr. plant engring. dept., 1960-63, asst. chief engr. Burns Harbor project, 1963, asst. gen. mgr., 1963-67, gen. mgr. Burns Harbor plant, 1967-70, v.p. manufactured products and West Coast steel plants, 1970-71, v.p. steel operations-prodn., 1971-74, dir., 1974—, exec. v.p., 1974-77, vice chmn., 1977—. Mem. Am. Iron and Steel Inst., Assn. Iron and Steel Engrs., NAM (dir.), Hwy. Users Fedn. (dir.). Home: RD 4 Bethlehem PA 18015 Office: Bethlehem Steel Corp Bethlehem PA 18016

RITTERMAN, STUART I., speech pathologist, educator; b. Bklyn., May 21, 1937; s. Nathan and Ettie (Fried) R.; B.A., N.Y. U., 1959; postgrad. CUNY, 1962-64; Ph.D., Case Western Res. U., 1968; 1 dau., Moriah. Speech clinician Bklyn. Coll. Clinic, CUNY, Bklyn., g963, Bergen Pines County Hosp., Paramus, N.J., 1963-64; Vocat. Rehab. adminstrn. trainee Cleve. Hearing and Speech Center, 1964-66; speech clinician Benjamin Rose Hosp., Cleve., 1965-66; NIH career investigator trainee Case Western Res. U., Cleve., 1966-68, research asso. in dental edn., 1967-68; asst. prof. dept. communication disorders U. Okla. Med. Center, Oklahoma City, 1968-69, dir. diagnostic services in speech pathology, 1968-69; asst. prof. speech pathology and audiology inst. U. South Fla., Tampa, 1969-71, asso. prof., 1972-76, prof., 1976—, dir. diagnostic services, 1969-71, dir. research in communicology, 1976—, acting dir. program in speech pathology and audiology Coll. Social and Behavioral Sci., 1971, dir., 1971—; cons. speech pathology Fla. Bur. for Crippled Children, Tampa. HEW grantee, 1971; Office of Edn. grantee, 1971; Fla. Dept. Edn. grantee, 1971. Fellow Royal Soc. Health, Acad. for Forensic Application of Communication Process; mem. Am. Speech and Hearing Assn., Fla. Speech and Hearing Assn., Internat. Soc. Phonetic Sci., Internat. Assn. Logopedics and Phoniatrics, Fla. Acad. Sci., Inst. for Advanced Study of Communication Process. Contbr. articles to profl. jours. Home: 181 Ellerbee Rd Zephyrhills FL 33599 Office: U South Fla CBA 241 Tampa FL 33620

RITTHALER, GERALD IRVIN, diversified co. exec.: b. Fremont, Nebr., May 27, 1930; s. Irvin Peter and Jessie (Vaughan) R.; B.A., Wayne State Coll., 1953; postgrad. Drake U., 1958; m. Barbara Jane Brown, Aug. 17, 1952; children—Daniel Vaughan, Elizabeth Ann, John Charles. Staff acct. Dennis West, C.P.A., Shenandoah, Iowa, 1953-55; office mgr. Imperial Chem. Co., Shenandoah, 1955-57; asst. comptroller Boss Hotels Co., Des Moines, 1957-62; tax supr. Ernst & Ernst, Houston, 1963-65; tax mgr. Gulf & Western Industries, Inc., N.Y.C., 1965-67, v.p., 1967-79, sr. v.p., 1979—. Mem. Am. Inst. C.P.A.'s, C. of C. U.S. (tax com.). Presbyterian. Office: 1 Gulf & Western Plaza New York NY 10023

RITTS, ROY ELLOT, JR., physician; b. St. Petersburg, Fla., Jan. 16, 1929; s. Roy Ellot and Dorothy (Bliss) R.; A.B., George Washington U., 1948, M.D., 1951; m. Hilda Joan Stump, June 19, 1953 (div. 1978); children—Leslie Sue, Graham Douglas, Ian Christopher; m. 2d, Kristin Gunderson, 1979. Intern, D.C. Gen. Hosp., 1951; fellow infectious diseases George Washington U., 1952, resident medicine George Washington U. Hosp., 1953; asso. prof. microbiology Georgetown U. Sch. Medicine, 1958-61, chmn. dept., 1959-64, professorial lectr. medicine, 1960, prof. microbiology and tropical medicine, 1961-64; dir. Inst. Biomed. Research, A.M.A., 1964-68, asst. dir. div. sci. activities, 1964-66, dir. med. research, 1966-68; professorial lectr. microbiology U. Chgo., 1964-68; chmn. dept. microbiology Mayo Clinic, 1968-79, head microbiology research, 1979—; prof. microbiology and oncology Mayo Grad. Sch. Medicine, Mayo Med. Sch., U. Minn.; asst. medicine Peter Bent Brigham Hosp., 1954; research fellow medicine Harvard, 1954; vis. investigator, research asso. Rockefeller Inst., 1955-58; cons. clin. pathology NIH; cons. immunology Nat. Naval Med. Center, Bethesda, Md., lectr. microbiology Naval Dental Sch., 1958-64; mem. Am. Bd. Med. Microbiology, 1965-67; chmn. sci. adv. com. FDA, HEW, 1970-71, chmn. nat. adv. com. on diagnostic products, 1972-74, mem. commr.'s steering com., 1974-75, nat. food and drug adv. com., 1976-78; mem. nat. working party on therapy of lung cancer Nat. Cancer Inst., 1972-75, mem. carcinogenesis rev. com. A, 1974-79, mem. gastrointestinal tumor study group 1975-80, immunology com. radiation therapy oncology group, 1974-79; chmn. immunology standards com. WHO/Internat. Union Immunology Socs., 1973—; cons. cancer immunology VA Central Office, 1974—; mem. Am. Bd. Med. Lab. Immunology, 1976—. Served from ensign to lt. (j.g.), M.C., USNR, 1948-56. Life Ins. Fund for Med. Research fellow, 1954-57. Diplomate Am. Bd. Microbiology. Fellow Royal Soc. Tropical Medicine, Am. Acad. Microbiology, Royal Soc. Health, A.C.P., Am. Coll. Chest Physicians, Assn. Clin. Scientists, Infectious Disease Soc. Am.; mem. Reticuloendothelial Soc., SAR, Am. Assn. Pathologists, Am. Fedn. Clin. Research, Am. Soc. Clin. Oncology, Am. Soc. Exptl. Pathology, Am. Soc. Microbiology, Am. Rheumatism Assn., Soc. Gen. Microbiology (Eng.), Soc. Exptl. Biology and Medicine, Am. Assn. Immunologists, Am. Soc. Cancer Research, Internat. Assn. Study of Lung Cancer (dir. 1974-76, sec. 1976-79), Am. Soc. Surg. Oncology, Brit. Soc. Immunologists, Sigma Xi, Sigma Chi, Phi Chi, Alpha Chi Sigma, Alpha Omega Alpha. Contbr. articles on tumor and cellular immunology, immunotherapy to med. and sci. publs. Office: Dept Microbiology Mayo Clinic Rochester MN 55901

RIVARD, JEAN, lawyer; b. Quebec, Que., Can., Dec. 22, 1926; s. Antoine and Lucille (Garneau) R.; B.A., Jesuits Coll., Quebec, 1947; LL.L., Laval U., 1950; m. Janine Raymond, Nov. 17, 1953; children—Louise, Michele, Line, Pierre, Guy. Called to bar Que., 1950, created Queen's counsel, 1964; practice in Quebec City and Montreal; sr. partner Flynn, Rivard, Cimon, Lessard & LeMay, 1966—; dir. Pagé Ltee; lectr. law Laval U., 1962-66. Mem. Canadian, Que. bar assns., Que. Dist. Bar (sec. 1958-59), Motor Carriers Lawyers Assn. Home: 1438 Des Gouverneurs Sillery PQ Canada Office: 2 Chauveau Quebec PQ Canada also 2020 University St #1738 Montreal PQ Canada

RIVER, LOUIS PHILIP, surgeon; b. San Francisco, Mar. 12, 1901; s. Louis Philip and Amy (Hopkins) R.; S.B., U. Chgo., 1922, M.D., 1925; m. Elizabeth Lambert, Sept. 18, 1928; children—Louis, George, Amy (Mrs. T. Valenzuela), Valerie (Mrs. A.W. Vaughan III). Intern Presbyn. Hosp., Chgo., 1924-25; pvt. practice, Oak Park, Ill., 1925-72; attending surgeon Oak Park Hosp., 1928—, Cook County Hosp., Chgo., 1937-74; clin. prof. surgery Stritch Med. Sch., Loyola U., Chgo., 1952—; prof. surgery Cook County Postgrad. Med. Sch., 1937-72. Served to lt. col. M.C., AUS, 1942-46; ETO. Diplomate Am. Bd. Surgery. Fellow A.C.S., Internat. Coll. Surgeons (pres. U.S. sect. 1974, internat. corp. sec. 1973-77). Contbr. articles to surg. jours. Home: 165 N Kenilworth Ave Oak Park IL 60301 Office: 715 Lake St Oak Park IL 60301

RIVERA, GERALDO, broadcast journalist; b. N.Y.C., July 4, 1943; s. Cruz Allen and Lillian (Friedman) R.; B.S., U. Ariz., 1965; J.D., Bklyn. Law Sch., 1969; postgrad. (Smith fellow) U. Pa., 1969, Sch. Journalism, Columbia, 1970; m. Sherryl Raymond, Dec. 31, 1976; 1 son, Gabriel Miguel. Admitted to N.Y. State bar, 1970; mem. anti-poverty neighborhood law firms Harlem Assertion of Rights and Community Action for Legal Services, N.Y.C., 1968-70; with Eye Witness, WABC-TV, N.Y.C., 1970-75; host Goodnight America program, Good Morning America program ABC-TV, 1974-78; spl. corr. ABC News, 1978—. Chmn. One-to-One Assn. Retarded Children. Recipient numerous awards including 7 Emmy awards; Kennedy Journalism award, 1973, 75; named Broadcaster of Year, N.Y. State A.P., 1971, 72, 74. Mem. N.Y. State bar assn. Jewish. Author: Willowbrook, 1972; Island of Contrasts, 1974; Miguel, 1972; A Special Kind of Courage, 1976. Home: 1330 Ave of Americas New York NY 10019 Office: 77 W 66th St New York NY 10023

RIVERA, JOSE DE, sculptor; b. West Baton Rouge, La., Sept. 18, 1904; pupil drawing John W. Norton; Litt.D. (hon.), Washington U., St. Louis, 1974. Exhibited in numerous one man and group shows, including: Whitney Mus., Seattle World's Fair, Battersea Park, London, Eng., Arts Club, Chgo., The White House, Washington, U. N.Mex., Los Angeles County Mus., Phila. Mus. Art; maj. retrospective shows La Jolla (Calif.) Mus. Contemporary Art, 1972; Whitney Mus., 1972; numerous commns. including U. Rochester, City of Lansing (Mich.); represented in permanent collections in maj. museums throughout U.S. including, Mus. Modern Art, N.Y.C., Met. Mus. Art, N.Y.C., Art Inst. Chgo., Smithsonian Instn., Tate Gallery, Eng., Art Gallery Toronto (Ont., Can.), Hirshhorn Mus., Washington, others. Mem. dept. art Nat. Inst. Arts and Letters, grantee, 1959. Recipient Watson F. Blair prize Chgo. Art Inst., 1957, Creative Arts medal Brandeis U., 1969, sculpture commn. Am. Iron and Steel Inst., 1965. Address: care Grace Borgenicht Gallery 1018 Madison Ave New York City NY 10003

RIVERA, TOMÁS, univ. ofcl.; b. Crystal City, Tex., Dec. 22, 1935; s. Florencio and Josefa (Henandez) R.; A.A. in English, SW Tex. Jr. Coll., 1956, B.S. in Edn., 1958, M.Ed., 1964; student NDEA Spanish Inst., 1962, 63; M.A. in Spanish Lit., U. Okla., 1969, Ph.D. in Romance Langs. and Lit., 1969; m. Concepción Garza, Nov. 27, 1978; children—Ileana Imelda, Irasema, Florencio Javier. Migrant worker until 1957; tchr. public secondary schs., Tex., 1957-65; instr. and chmn. dept. fgn. langs. SW Tex. Jr. Coll., 1965-66; teaching asst. dept. modern langs. U. Okla., 1966-68, instr., dir. lang. labs., 1968-69, asst. dir. Spanish studies program in Madrid, summer 1969; asso. prof. Spanish, San Houston State U., Tex., 1969-71; prof. Spanish lit., dir. div. fgn. langs., lit. and linguistics U. Tex., San Antonio, 1971-73, prof. Spanish, asso. dean Coll. Multidisciplinary Studies, 1973-76, v.p. for adminstrn., 1976-78; exec. v.p., acting v.p. acad. affairs U. Tex., El Paso, 1978-79; chancellor U. Calif., Riverside, 1979—; lit. judge; speaker; cons. in field; mem. exec. com. Nat. Council Chicanos in Higher Edn., 1976—, v.p., 1978; mem. task force on Hispanic arts Nat. Endowment Arts, 1977-79; trustee Carnegie Found. Advancement of Teaching, 1976-80; mem. bd. fgn. scholarships Dept. State, 1978—; mem. adv. com. Allied Health Professions, coordinating bd. state univ. and coll. system, Tex., 1979—; bd. dirs. Hubert H. Humphrey Inst. Public Affairs, U. Minn., 1979—, Tex. Commn. on Humanities, 1979—, Nat. Center Higher Edn. Mgmt. Systems, 1979—. Bd. dirs. Inman Christian Center, San Antonio, 1972-77, Commn. for Mexican-Am. Affairs, Archdiocese of San Antonio, 1972-77, Am. Issues Forum, San Antonio, 1975-76, Assn. Advancement Mexican Ams., Houston, 1977-79. Recipient Premio Quinto Sol., 1970-71; Project Milestone Recognition award Assn. Supervision and Curriculum Devel., 1977; Danforth Found. asso., 1971. Mem. Sigma Delta Pi (pres. U. Okla. chpt. 1968) Democrat. Roman Catholic. Clubs: Kiwanis (hon.), Sembradores de Amistad (hon.; Sembrador of Yr. 1974), Con Safo Artists San Antonio (hon.). Author books, the most recent being: Always and Other Poems, 1973; (with others) A Public Trust, 1979; contbr. articles, fiction to profl. publs.; subject of profl. publs. Office: Office of Chancellor U Calif Riverside CA 92507

RIVERA, VICTOR MANUEL, clergyman; b. Penuelas, P.R., Oct. 16, 1929; s. Victor and Filomena (Toro) R.; student Modern Bus. Coll. P.R., 1937, DuBose Meml. Ch. Tng. Sch., 1938; B.D., Ch. Div. Sch. Pacific, 1944, D.D., 1965; postgrad. St. Augustine Coll., Eng., 1957; m. Barbara Ross Starbuck, Dec. 1944; 3 children. Ordained deacon Episcopal Ch., 1943, priest, 1944; curate St. John's Cathedral, Santurce, P.R., 1944-45; rector St. Paul's Ch., Visalia, Calif., 1945-68; consecrated bishop San Joaquin, Fresno, Calif., 1968. Address: Episcopal Ch Diocese San Joaquin 4159 E Dakota Ave Fresno CA 93726

RIVERA-DUENO, JAIME, pediatrician; b. Ponce, P.R., Nov. 20, 1935; s. Dionisio and Josefina R.-D.; B.A., Inter Am. U., 1956; M.D., U. P.R., 1960; m. Carmen Lydia Rodriguez, July 24, 1975; children—Denise, Glenda, Jaime, Camilie. Intern, Univ. Hosp., Rio Piedras, P.R., 1960-61, resident, 1964-66; practice medicine specializing in pediatrics, Rio Piedras, 1966—; asst. sec. for maternal-infant care P.R. Dept. Health, 1969-72; regional health adminstr. HEW, Region II, N.Y.C., 1972-74; sec. health Commonwealth of P.R., 1977—; asst. prof. pediatrics U. P.R. Sch. Medicine, 1966-70; mem. adv. com. on child devel. Nat. Acad. Sci., Washington, 1971-75. Mem. Gov.'s Com. on Population, 1969, P.R. Childrens Commn., 1970. Served with USAF, 1961-64. Recipient Jaycee's Ten Outstanding Young Men award, 1975. Mem. P.R. Med. Assn. Mem. New Progressive Party. Roman Catholic. Home: K-622 Cond Montebello Trujillo Alto PR 00760 Office: Dept Health Bldg A Psychiatry Hosp Area Rio Piedras PR 00935

RIVERS, ELIAS LYNCH, educator, Hispanist; b. Charleston, S.C., Sept. 19, 1924; s. Elias Lynch and Dorothy (Reid) R.; B.A., Yale, 1948, M.A., 1950, Ph.D., 1952; M.A. (hon.), Dartmouth, 1962; m. Phyllis Arlene Pirl, Mar. 17, 1945; children—Elias Lynch, Franklin Seabrook, Cornelia Foote; m. 2d, Georgina Sabat, Sept. 19, 1969. Instr. Spanish, Yale, 1951-52; mem. faculty Dartmouth, 1952-62, prof. Spanish, chmn. dept. Romance langs. and lit., 1961-62; prof. Spanish, Ohio State U., 1962-64; prof. Spanish, Johns Hopkins U., 1964-78, chmn. Romance langs., 1968-74; prof. Spanish, chmn. dept. SUNY, Stony Brook, 1978—. First sec. gen. Asociacion Internacional de Hispanistas, 1962—. Served with AUS, 1943-46. Howard fellow, 1956-57; Guggenheim fellow, 1959-60; Fulbright fellow, Spain, 1964-65; NEH fellow, 1967-68, 70-71. Mem. Modern Lang. Assn., Acad. Lit. Studies. Socialist. Episcopalian. Author articles, books on Spanish poetry of 16th and 17th centuries. Office: Dept Hispanic Langs SUNY Stony Brook NY 11794

RIVERS, EURITH DICKINSON, JR., broadcasting exec.; b. Mineral Springs, Ark., May 12, 1915; s. Eurith Dickinson and Margaret Lucile (Lashley) R.; ed. Ga. State U., Woodrow Wilson Law Sch.; m. Marie Georgine Bie, May 3, 1952; children—Eurith Dickinson, III, Rex B., Maria Kells, Lucile, Georgia. Admitted to Ga. bar, 1932; asst. atty. gen. State of Ga.; legal dir. Ga. Welfare Dept., Atlanta; chief judge Ga. Indsl. Commn., Atlanta, then chmn. bd.; chmn. bd. Stars, Nat., N.Y.C., Stars, Inc., Miami Beach, Fla., WGOV, Inc., Valdosta, Ga., WEDR, Inc., Miami, Fla., Seminole Broadcasting Co. (Fla.), KWAM Inc., Memphis, WGUN, Inc., Atlanta, WEAS, Inc., Savannah, Ga., Sounds of Service, Inc., Suncoast Broadcasting Corp., Deesown Corp., Fla.; dir. Farmer's and Merchant's Bank, Lakeland, Ga. Served with USNR, World War II. Mem. Ga., Fla., Tenn., Ark. assns. broadcasters, Ga., Am. bar assns., Am. Judicature Soc. Clubs: La Gorce Country, Rod and Reel, Bankers, Racquet, Coral Reef Yacht, Com. of loo (Miami Beach); Silver Springs Shores Country, Valdosta (Ga.) Country, Masons, Shriners. Home: Route 7 Box 427 Ocala FL 32671 Office: 6825 SW 70th Ave Ocala FL 32670

RIVERS, JOAN, entertainer; b. 1937; d. Meyer C. Molinsky; B.A., Barnard Coll., 1958; m. Edgar Rosenberg, July 15, 1965; 1 dau., Melissa. Formerly fashion coordinator Bond Clothing Stores; debut entertaining, 1960; mem. From Second City, 1961-62; TV debut Tonight Show, 1965, Las Vegas debut, 1969; originator, author screen play TV movie The Girl Most Likely To . . ., ABC, 1973; co-author, dir. film Rabbit Test, 1978; author: Having a Baby Can Be a Scream, 1974. Address: PO Box 774 Los Angeles CA 90049 also care Katz-Gallin Assos 9255 Sunset Blvd Los Angeles CA 90069

RIVERS, LARRY, artist; b. N.Y.C., 1923; grad. N.Y. U.; student painting with Hans Hofmann; m. Augusta Berger, 1945 (div.); 1 son; m. 2d, Clarice Price, 1961; 2 children. Exhibited one man shows, N.Y.C. galleries, 1949—; group shows Vanguard Gallery, Paris, France, 1953, Am. Fedn. Arts traveling exhbn., 1954-55, Mus. Modern Art, N.Y.C., 1956, Museum de Arte Moderne, Sao Paulo, Brazil, 1957, Art Inst. Chgo., Mpls. Inst. Arts, spl. exhbn. sponsored Mus. Modern Art, Japan; permanent works in collections William Rockhill Nelson Gallery Art, Kansas City, Mpls. Inst. Arts, State U. Coll. Edn., New Paltz, N.Y., Bklyn. Mus. Art, Met. Mus. Art, Mus. Modern Art, Whitney Mus. Am. Art, N.Y.C., R.I. Sch. Design, Providence, N.C. Mus. Art, Raleigh, Corcoran Gallery Art, Washington, also pvt. collections; stage designer play The Toilet; appearance film Pull My Daisy; executed mural History of the Russian Revolution. Recipient spl. awards Corcoran Gallery Art, 1954, Arts Festival, Spoleto, Italy, also Newport, R.I., 1958. Author: Drawings and Digressions, 1979. Address: 92 Little Plains Rd Southampton NY 11968 also care Marlborough Gallery 40 W 57th St New York NY 10022*

RIVERS, MARIE BIE, broadcasting exec.; b. Tampa, Fla., July 12, 1928; d. Norman Albion and Rita Marie (Monrose) Bie; student George Washington U., 1946; m. Eurith Dickinson Rivers, May 3, 1952; children—Eurith Dickinson, III, Rex B., M. Kells, Lucy L., Georgia. Engaged in real estate bus., 1944-51, radio broadcasting, 1951—; pres. Sta. WGUN, Atlanta, 1969—, Sta. KWAM-AM-FM, Memphis, 1969—, Sta. WEAS-AM-FM, Savannah, Ga., 1969—, Sta. WGOV-AM-FM, Valdosta, Ga., 1969—, Sta. WSWN-AM-FM, Belle Glade, Fla., 1969—, Sta. WXOS, Islamorada, Fla., 1969—, also real estate cos. Stars, Inc., Deesown, Inc., Suncoast Inc.; sec. Sta. WEDR, Miami, Fla. Youth dir. Fla. Appaloosa Horse Club, 1972—. Clubs: La Gorce Country (Miami Beach, Fla.); Coral Reef Yacht (Coconut Grove, Fla.); Silver Springs (Fla.) Country. Home: Route 7 Box 427 Ocala FL 32670 Office: 7055 SW 70th Ave Ocala FL 32671

RIVERS, SAMUEL CARTHORNE, musician, composer; b. El Reno, Okla., Sept. 25, 1930; studied composition at Boston Conservatory Music; m. Bea Rivers. Plays tenor and soprano saxophone, piano, bass clarinet, flute and viola; played with Jaki Byard, Joe Gordon, 1950's, with Miles Davis, 1964, with Cecil Taylor, 1967-71, and later with McCoy Tyner; founder Studio Rivbea, N.Y.C., 1971; performer with trio, 1973—; began teaching, 1967; composer-in-residence Harlem Opera Soc., 1968—; lectr. Conn. Coll., 1972; artist-in-residence Wesleyan U., 1970-73; performed at Newport Jazz Festival, 1973, Montreaux, 1973, Antibes, 1974; guest soloist San Francisco Symphony, 1975; albums include: Sizzle, Hues, Streams, Crystals, Involution, Contours. Winner Downbeat Critics poll for flute, 1978, 79. Office: Studio Rivbea 24 Bond St New York NY 10012*

RIVERS, WILLIAM LAWRENCE, educator; b. Gainesville, Fla., Mar. 17, 1925; s. Lucius and Minnie (Gable) R.; B.A., La. State U., 1951, M.A., 1952; Ph.D., Am. U., 1960; m. Sarah Alford, Feb. 4,

1949; children—Gail, Marianne. Reporter, editorial writer State-Times, Baton Rouge, 1950-52; reporter, editorial columnist News-Herald, Panama City, Fla., 1952-53; instr. La. State U., Baton Rouge, 1953-54; reporter, editorial writer, Sunday editor Morning Advocate, Baton Route, 1954; faculty U. Miami, Coral Gables, 1955-58, U. Tex., Austin, 1959-60, 61-62; Washington corr. The Reporter, 1960-61; prof. dept. communications Stanford, 1962—; columnist The Progressive Mag., Stanford, 1971-73. Bd. dirs. Media and Consumer Found., 1973-75. Served with USMC, 1943-46. Am. Polit. Sci. Assn. fellow, 1954-55; recipient Distinguished Teaching award U. Tex., 1962; Walter J. Gores Faculty Achievement award Stanford, 1975. Mem. Am. Polit. Sci. Assn., Assn. for Edn. in Journalism. Club: Nat. Press (Washington). Author: The Opinionmakers, 1965, (with Theodore Peterson and Jay Jensen) The Mass Media and Modern Society, rev. edit., 1971; (with Wilbur Schramm) Responsibility in Mass Communication, 1969; The Adversaries: Politics and the Press, 1970; (with others) Backtalk: Press Councils in America, 1972; Other Voices: The New Journalism in America, 1974; Finding Facts: Interviewing, Observing, Using Reference Sources, 1975; Writing, Craft and Art, 1975. Contbr. articles to profl jours. Home: 665 Alvarado Row Stanford CA 94305 Office: Dept Communication Stanford U Stanford CA 94305

RIVES, ALBERT GORDON, lawyer; b. Brimingham, Ala., Apr. 12, 1901; s. John R. T. and Mamie Lillian (Gordon) R.; LL.B., U. Ala., 1924; m. Hester Maude Burchfield, May 22, 1926 (dec. Aug. 4, 1963); m. 2d, Margaret Gordon Crawford Jackson, Mar. 9, 1968. Asst. dir. athletics U. Ala., 1924; admitted to Ala. bar, 1925, since practiced in Birmingham; sr. partner firm Rives, Peterson, Pettus, Conway, Elliott and Small, 1958—. Messenger to Baptist World Congress, Rio de Janeiro, 1960. Served to lt. comdr. USNR, World War II. Mem. Am., Ala., Birmingham bar assns., Internat. Assn. Ins. Counsel, Am. Judicature Soc., World Peace Through Law Center, SAR, SCV, Ala. Hist. Soc., Phi Alpha Delta, Sigma Chi. Baptist (chmn. bd. trustees). Mason (Shriner). Clubs: Bath and Tennis (Palm Beach, Fla.); Mountain Brook; Vestavia Country, Relay House, The Club (Birmingham). Home: 3415 Pine Ridge Rd Mountain Brook Birmingham AL 35213 Office: 8th Floor 1st Nat-So Natural Bldg Birmingham AL 35203. *Quiet thinking of the past, present and future, while alone.*

RIVES, RICHARD TAYLOR, judge; b. Montgomery, Ala., Jan. 15, 1895; s. William Henry and Alice Bloodworth (Taylor) R.; student Tulane U., 1911-12; studied law in office of Hill, Hill, Whiting and Stern, Montgomery; LL.D., U. Notre Dame, 1966, Samford U., 1975; m. Jessie Hall Dougherty, July 23, 1918 (dec. Nov. 23, 1973); children—Richard Taylor, Callie Dougherty Smith; m. 2d, Martha Blake Frazer, June 18, 1976. Admitted to Ala. bar, 1914; gen. practice, Montgomery; judge Fifth Circuit, U.S. Ct. Appeals, 1951-59, chief judge, 1959-60, judge, 1960-66, sr. U.S. circuit judge, 1966—. Served in N.G., Mexican Border, 1916-17, as 1st lt. Signal Corps., AEF, 1917-19. Del. Democratic Conv., Chgo., 1940. Mem. Montgomery (former pres.), Ala. (pres. 1939), Am. bar assns., Am.. Legion, Order of Coif (hon.). Presbyterian. Mason. Office: PO Box 1070 Montgomery AL 36102*

RIVET, CHARLES LANDRY, lawyer; b. New Orleans, July 7, 1920; s. Charles J. and Elma (Landry) R.; LL.B., Loyola U. of South, 1948; m. Rosemary Grenier, Dec. 1, 1945 (div. Mar. 1969); children—Charles G., Pierre G., Randy G., Arianne M. Admitted to La. bar, 1948; law clk. La. Supreme Ct., 1948-49; practiced in New Orleans, 1949—; mem. firm Rivet & Rivet, and predecessors, 1955—; judge ad hoc Civil Dist. Ct. Parish Orleans, 1970—. Mem. bd. commrs. New Orleans City Park, 1954—, sec., 1975—; sec. Orleans Parish Law Library Commn., 1965—. Mem. citizens adv. council Nat. Police Hall of Fame. Mem. Am., N.Y.C., La., New Orleans (sec. 1952-70) bar assns., Am. Judicature Soc., Am. Mus. Natural History, Delta Theta Phi. K.C. Home: 2003 Napoleon Ave New Orleans LA 70115 Office: 404 Cotton Exchange Bldg New Orleans LA 70130

RIVETTE, GERARD BERTRAM, mfg. co. exec.; b. Syracuse, N.Y., May 18, 1932; s. George Francis and Helen (McCarthy) R.; A.B., B.S., Syracuse U., 1954; grad. student U. Buffalo, 1957-59, Rutgers U., 1962-65; m. Patricia Anne Yates, June 20, 1953; children—Kevin Gerard, Brian Yates. Owner-mgr. Rivette Sales and Service, Syracuse, 1950-54; sales rep. Sperry-Rand, Inc., Elmira, N.Y., 1954-55; with Hewitt-Robins Inc., Buffalo, 1955-62, mgr. conveyor equipment sales, Passaic, N.J., 1962-65, pres. Hewitt-Robins (Can.) Ltd., Montreal, 1965-69, also dir.; Canadian regional mgr. Hewitt-Robins Inc., 1965-69; pres., chmn. bd. Conergics Corp., Kansas City, Kans., 1970—; pres. Mid-West Conveyer Co., 1970—, Alpine Metals Co., Salt Lake City, Con Cal Corp., Orange, Calif.; chmn. bd. Versa Corp., Mt. Sterling, Ohio, 1972—, Baker Erection Co., Kansas City, Mo., 1971—; chmn. bd., pres. Ferguson Conveyor Corp., Livonia, Mich., 1972—, Stearns Mfg. Corp., Flat Rock, Mich.; pres. Conveyor Corp. Am., Ft. Worth, 1978—; dir. Comml. Nat. Bank, Kansas City, Kans. Councilman local Boy Scouts Am., 1965. Bd. dirs. Kansas City chpt. Jr. Achievement. Mem. Am. Inst. Mining, Metall. and Petroleum Engrs., Conveyer Equipment Mfrs. Assn. (dir.), Kansas City Civic Council, Kans. C. of C. Home: 2100 W 61st Terr Mission Hills KS 66208 Office: 450 E Donovan Rd Kansas City KS 66115

RIVIERE, PAUL FRANKLIN, sec. of state Ark.; b. Drew County, Ark., July 17, 1947; s. Frank and Maybell (Barnett) R.; B.A., George Washington U., 1971; J.D., U. Ark., Little Rock, 1975; m. Carolyn Lee Moore, 1973; children—Mary Catherine, Rebecca Lee. Staff asst. to U.S. Senator John L. McClellan, 1968-71; adminstrv. asst. Ark. Jud. Dept., 1971-74; mem. Ark. Gov.'s Commn. on Crime and Law Enforcement, Little Rock, 1974-76; legal asst. to Ark. Sec. of State, Little Rock, 1977-78; sec. of state State of Ark., Little Rock, 1979—. Bd. dirs. Big Bros. of Pulaski County (Ark.), Am. Legion Boys State of Ark., 1975-77. Democrat. Mem. Bible Ch. Office: 256 State Capitol Little Rock AR 72201

RIVINUS, EDWARD FLORENS, publisher; b. Phila., Nov. 27, 1915; s. Edward Florens and Marion Willis (Martin) R.; A.B., Princeton U., 1937, postgrad., 1949-50; M.A., George Washington U., 1967; m. Esther Lloyd Hayward, Sept. 29, 1939; children—Edward M., Mariannia M., Frank F., David L., Emily H., Andrew P. With Hutchinson Rivinus & Co., ins. brokers, Phila., 1938-40; with fgn. service officer 1946-70; dir. Smithsonian Instn. Press, Washington, 1974—. Served with F.A., AUS, 1941-46. Decorated Croix de Guerre (France); recipient Superior Honor award Dept. State, 1970. Mem. Washington Pubs. Soc., Audubon Naturalist Soc. Central Atlantic States (pres. 1971-74, chmn. bd. 1974-77). Republican. Contbr. articles to environ. and sports jours. Home: 606 Boyle Ln McLean VA 22101 Office: Smithsonian Instn Press A and I Bldg Smithsonian Instn Washington DC 20560

RIVKIN, ALLEN, writer; b. Hayward, Wis., Nov. 20, 1903; s. Samuel Richard and Rose (Rosenberg) R.; B.A., U.. Minn., 1920-25; m. Laura Hornickel (profl. name Laura Kerr), Nov. 10, 1952. Freelance mag. writing, 1925-31; writer numerous screen and television plays, 1932—. Founder and pres., Motion Picture Industry Council; founder, pres., dir. Screen Writers Guild, Inc.; founder, v.p., dir. Writers Guild Am. West, Inc., dir. pub. affairs, 1965—; treas. Writers Guild Found.; sec. Writers-Producers Pension Fund, 1965-66; chmn. ofcl. U.S. del. Cannes Film Festival; liaison rep. to legal adv. com. for motion pictures, television Am. Bar Assn. Vice pres. Hollywood Guilds Festival Com., 1962-63. Nat. dir. com. arts Democratic Nat. Com., 1955-63; dir. entertainment, pub. relations Dem. Nat. Conv., Los Angeles, 1960; dir. Hollywood for Roosevelt, 1936-44, Hollywood for Truman, 1948, Hollywood for Stevenson, 1952-56, Hollywood for Kennedy, 1960. Recipient Valentine Davies award, 1963, Morgan Cox award, 1972. Mem. Dramatists Guild, Acad. Motion Picture Arts and Scis., Sigma Alpha Mu. Author: (with Leonard Spigelgass) I Wasn't Born Yesterday, 1935; (with Laura Kerr) Hello, Hollywood, 1962. Mng. editor: Who Wrote the Movie . . . and What Else Did He Write?, 1970. Editor Writers Guild Newsletter, 1965—. Office: Box 1644 Beverly Hills CA 90213

RIVKIN, DONALD H., lawyer; b. Davenport, Iowa, May 24, 1924; s. Samuel W. and Florence N. (Fryer) R.; B.A., Yale, 1948, J.D., 1952; M.A. (Rhodes scholar), Oxford (Eng.) U., 1950; m. Lois Borwick Herman, Dec. 29, 1953; children—David W., Judith F., Daniel H. Admitted to N.Y. bar, 1953, D.C. bar, 1960, U.S. Supreme Ct., 1966; asso. Cravath, Swaine & Moore, N.Y.C., 1952-56, Solinger & Gordon, N.Y.C., 1956-59; mem. Rivkin Sherman and Levy, and predecessor firms, N.Y.C., 1959—. Cons. Fund for Republic, Study of Polit. Process, 1957-61; mem. interreligious cooperation coms. Anti-Defamation League, 1960—; counsel Operation Crossroads Africa, 1960—, also bd. dirs.; U.S. State Dept. rep. Conf. on Internat. Conv. on Travel Agy. Contract, Internat. Inst. for Unification Pvt. Law, Rome, Italy, 1967; cons. adv. com. pvt. internat. law U.S. State Dept., 1968—. Served with AUS, 1943-46. Mem. Assn. Bar City N.Y. (chmn. com. internat. law 1978—), Am. Soc. Internat. Law, Council Fgn. Relations, Order of Coif, Internat. Law Assn., Assn. Am. Rhodes Scholars (dir., treas.), Am. Trust for Oxford U. (treas.), Phi Beta Kappa, Phi Delta Phi. Clubs: Yale (N.Y.C.); Federal City (Washington). Author articles in field. Home: 16 W 77th St New York City NY 10024 also One Bluewater Hill Westport CT 06880 Office: 750 3d Ave New York NY 10017

RIVKIN, ELLIS, educator; b. Balt., Sept. 7, 1918; s. Moses Isaacher and Beatrice (Leibowitz) R.; B.A. with honors, Johns Hopkins U., 1941; Ph.D., 1946; B.H.L., Balt. Hebrew Coll., 1945, D.H.L. (hon.), 1975; m. Zelda Zafren, June 29, 1941; children—Roslyn Rivkin Weinberger, Sharon Rivkin Kilburn. Instr. Jewish history Gratz Coll., 1946-49; asst. prof. Hebrew Union Coll.-Jewish Inst. Religion, 1949-51, asso. prof., 1951-53, prof., 1953—, Adolph S. Ochs prof. Jewish history, 1965—; vis. prof. Antioch Coll., 1963; vis. prof. Jewish history Dropsie U., 1969; Joseph Rosenblatt lectr. U. Utah, 1967, vis. prof. Jewish history, summer 1973; vis. prof. Judaic studies So. Methodist U., 1977. Pres., Globalist Research Found., 1979—. Cyrus Adler post-doctoral research fellow Dropsie Coll. Hebrew and Cognate Learning, 1946-48; Guggenheim fellow, 1962-63; grantee Am. Philos. Soc., 1965; Am. Council Learned Socs., 1965. Mem. Am. Hist. Soc., Econ. History Assn., Medieval Acad. Am., Central Conf. Am. Rabbis, Jewish Publ. Soc. (mem. publ. com.), Phi Beta Kappa. Editorial bd. Studies Bibliography and Booklore, Jewish Quar. Rev. Author: Leon da Modena and the Kol Sakhal, 1952; The Dynamics of Jewish History, 1970; The Shaping of Jewish History: A Radical New Interpretation, 1971; A Hidden Revolution: The Pharisees' in Search of the Kingdom Within, 1978. Home: 7610 Reading Rd Cincinnati OH 45237

RIVLIN, ALICE MITCHELL, economist; b. Phila., Mar. 4, 1931; d. Allan C. G. and Georgianna (Fales) Mitchell; B.A., Bryn Mawr Coll., 1952; M.A., Radcliffe Coll., 1955, Ph.D., 1958; m. Lewis Allen Rivlin, 1955 (div. 1977); children—Catherine Amy, Allan Mitchell, Douglas Gray. Research fellow Brookings Instn., Washington, 1957-58, staff econ. studies div., 1958-66, sr. fellow, 1969-75; dir. Congl. Budget Office, 1975—; dep. asst. sec. program coordination HEW, Washington, 1966-68, asst. sec. planning and evaluation, 1968-69. Staff, Adv. Commn. on Inter-govtl. Relations, 1961-62. Mem. Am. Econ. Assn. Author: The Role of the Federal Government in Financing Higher Education, 1961; (with others) Microanalysis of Socioeconomic Systems, 1961; The U.S. Balance of Payments in 1968, 1963; Systematic Thinking and Social Action, 1971; (with others) Setting National Priorities: The 1974 Budget, 1973. Home: 2842 Chesterfield Pl NW Washington DC 20008 Office: Congl Budget Office US Congress Washington DC 20515

RIVLIN, BENJAMIN, educator; b. Bklyn., July 10, 1921; s. Moses and Esther (Ribnick) R.; B.A., Bklyn. Coll., 1942; M.A., Harvard, 1947, Ph.D., 1949; m. Leanne Green, July 9, 1957; 1 son, Marc Alexander. With OSS, 1943-45; teaching fellow Harvard, 1948; mem. trusteeship dept. UN Secretariat, 1948, 50, 52; research asso. Hoover Commn., 1948; mem. faculty Bklyn. Coll. of City U. N.Y., 1949-75, prof. polit. sci., 1962—, chmn. dept., 1966-70; exec. officer Ph.D. program City U. N.Y., 1970-75, dean research and univ. programs Grad. Sch. and Univ. Center, 1975-78; dir. Inter-Univ. Doctoral Consortia Project, N.Y. U., N.Y.C., 1978—; vis. lectr. Johns Hopkins Sch. Advanced Internat. Studies, 1956; vis. prof. African and Middle East Insts., Columbia U., 1963-68. Trustee Inst. for Mediterranean Affairs. Served with AUS, 1942-45. Grantee Social Sci. Research Council, 1951, 54, 64; Fulbright scholar, France and N. Africa, 1956-57. Fellow African Studies Assn., Middle East Studies Assn.; mem. Internat. Studies Assn. (pres. Middle Atlantic region 1978—), Am. Polit. Sci. Assn. Club: N.Y. City. Author: The United Nations and The Italian Colonies, 1950; Self-Determination and Dependent Areas, 1955; (with J.S. Szyliowicz) The Contemporary Middle East: Tradition and Innovation, 1965; also articles. Office: NY U 6 Washington Sq N New York City NY 10003

RIVLIN, RONALD SAMUEL, educator; b. London, Eng., May 6, 1915; s. Raoul and Bertha (Aronsohn) R.; B.A., St. John's Coll., Cambridge U., 1937, M.A., 1939, Sc.D., 1952; m. Violet Larusso, June 16, 1948; 1 son, John Michael. Came to U.S., 1952, naturalized, 1955. Research physicist Gen. Electric Co., Eng., 1937-42; sci. officer Telecommunications Research Establishment, Ministry Aircraft Prodn., Eng., 1942-44; research physicist, head phys. research, supt. research British Rubber Producers Research Assn., 1944-52; head research group Davy-Faraday Lab., Royal Instn., London, 1948-52; cons. Naval Research Lab., Washington, 1952-53; prof. applied math. Brown U., 1953-63, L. Herbert Ballou U. prof., 1963-67, prof. applied math. and engring sci., 1963-67, chmn. div. applied math., 1958-63; prof. associé U. Paris, 1966-67; Centennial Univ. prof., dir. Center for Application of Math., Lehigh U., Bethlehem, Pa., 1967—; Russell Severance Springer vis. prof. U. Calif., Berkeley, 1977; co-chmn. Internat. Congress Rheology, 1963. Recipient Panetti prize, 1975. Guggenheim fellow, 1961-62. Fellow Am. Acad. Mechanics, Am. Phys. Soc.; mem. Soc. Natural Philosophy (chmn. 1963-64), Am. Acad. Arts and Scis., Washington Acad. Scis., Inst. Physics (gov. 1974-76), Am. Math. Soc., Soc. Rheology (exec. com. 1957-59, 71-77, Bingham medal 1958, v.p. 1971-73, pres. 1973-75; nat. com. theoretical and applied mechanics 1973—, chmn. 1976—), ASME (mem. exec. com. applied mechanics div. 1975—, vice-chmn. and sec. 1978-79), Internat. Union Theoretical and Applied Mechanics (gen. assembly 1975—, chmn. U.S. del. 1978), Council Sci. Soc. Pres. (sec.-treas. 1975, exec. bd. 1975-77). Contbr. articles profl. jours. Editorial com. Jour. Rational Mechanics and Analysis, 1952-57, Archive for Rational Mechanics and Analysis, 1957-72, Jour. Math. Physics, 1960, Jour. Applied Physics, 1960-63, Acta Rheologioa, 1963—, Internat. Jour. Biorheology, 1972—, Mechanics Research Communications, 1974—, Jour. Non-Newtonian Fluid Mechanics, 1975—, Meccanica, 1975—. Home: Merryweather Dr RD4 Bethlehem PA 18015 Office: Center for Application Math Lehigh U 203 E Packer Ave Bethlehem PA 18015

RIXEY, CHARLES WOODFORD, cons. co. exec.; b. Ferrelview, Mo., Apr. 15, 1926; s. Joseph Woodford and Genevieve (Hoskins) R.; A.B. in Econs., William Jewell Coll., 1948; M.B.A. in Mktg., Wharton Sch. U. Pa., 1950; M.S. in Ops. Research, U.S. Navy Postgrad. Sch.. 1961; m. Mary Joe, June 6, 1948; children—Susan, Sallie, Joseph. Served as enlisted man U.S. Navy, 1944-46, commd. 951, advanced through grades to rear adm., 1975; Served in war theaters, World War II, Korea and Vietnam; exec. officer Navy Fleet Material Support Office, 1972-73; project mgr. Navy Surface Ship Maintenance Project, Washington, 1973-75; asst. chief of stdff U.S. Atlantic Fleet, Norfolk, Va., 1975-77; vice comdr. Navy Supply System, Washington, 1977-78; ret., 1978; prin., program mgr. Am. Mgmt. Systems, Inc., Arlington, Va., 1978—. Serve Decorated Legion of Merit with 2 oak leaf clusters, Bronze Star with combat V, numerous other mil. decorations; recipient citation for ach. William Jewell Coll., 1979. Mem. Sigma Xi, Sigma Pi Sigma, Mu Sigma Alpha, Phi Gamma Delta. Presbyterian. Home: 1003 Potomac Ln Alexandria VA 22308 Office: 1515 Wilson Blvd Arlington VA 22209

RIZZO, FRANCIS LAZZARO, former mayor Phila.; b. Phila., Oct. 23, 1920; s. Raffaele and Theresa (Erminio) R.; m. Carmella Silvestri, 1942; children—Francis Silvestri, Joanna Ellen. Patrolman, City of Phila., 1943-51, sgt., 1951-54, capt., 1954-59, insp., 1959-64, dep. police commr., 1964-67, police commr., 1967-71; mayor City of Phila., 1972-80; chmn. Delaware Valley Regional Planning Commn., 1972—. Recipient Phila. Crime Commn. award for lowest crime rate among ten largest cities, 1969; J. Edgar Hoover award VFW, 1969; Honor award U.S. Secret Service, 1969; numerous civic and regional awards. Mem. S.E. Pa. Police Chiefs Assn., Fraternal Order Police, Sons of Italy. Democrat. Roman Catholic. Club: Lions. Office: Room 215 City Hall Philadelphia PA 19107*

RIZZOLI, HUGO V(ICTOR), neurosurgeon; b. Newark, Aug. 20, 1916; s. Angelo R. and Clelia (Carlucci) R.; A.B., Johns Hopkins U., 1936, M.D., 1940; m. Dec. 21, 1949; children—Hugo V., Pamela, Paul, Robert. Intern, Balt. City Hosp., 1940-41; resident in gen. surgery and neurosurgery Johns Hopkins U. Hosps., 1941-44; practice medicine specializing in neurosurgery, Washington, 1947-71; prof., chmn. neurosurgery George Washington U. Med. Center, Washington, 1969—; mem. staff George Washington U. Hosps. Served with M.C., U.S. Army, 1944-46. Recipient Comdrs. award for Civilian Service, U.S. Army, 1979; diplomate Am. Bd. Neurol. Surgery (bd. mem. 1970-76). Mem. AMA, Am. Assn. Neurol. Surgery, Am. Acad. Neurol. Surgery, Soc. Neurol. Surgeons, Neurol. Surgery Soc. N.Am., Congress of Neurol. Surgeons. Roman Catholic. Club: Congl. Country. Author: (with D. N. Horwitz) Post Operative Complications in Neurosurgical Practice 1967; contbr. articles on neurol. surgery to med. jours. Office: George Washingtin U Sch Medicine Dept Neurol Surgery Washington DC 20037

RIZZUTO, PHILIP FRANCIS, sportscaster; b. Bklyn., Sept. 25, 1918; s. Philip F. and Mary Rizzuto. Baseball player with N.Y. Yankees, 1941-42, 46-56, now radio-TV announcer N.Y. Yankees baseball games; mem. Am. League All-Star Team, 1942, 50-53. Named Most Valuable Player, Am. League, 1950. Office: care NY Yankees Bronx NY 10451*

ROACH, JAMES ROBERT, coll. adminstr.; b. Rock Rapids, Iowa, Aug., 25, 1922; s. Paul Ramsey and Doris (Kline) R.; B.A., U. Iowa, 1943; A.M., Harvard, 1948, Ph.D., 1950. Mem. faculty, adminstrn. U. Tex. at Austin, 1949—, prof. govt., 1965—, dir. spl. programs, 1965-69, vice provost, dean interdisciplinary programs, 1971-72, dean div. gen. and comparative studies, 1972-74; counselor for cultural affairs Am. embassy, New Delhi, 1974-78; Fulbright vis. lectr. polit. sci. Rajasthan U. (India), 1961-62. Mem. Bd. Fgn. Scholarships, 1965-74, chmn., 1969-71; mem. U.S. Commn. for UNESCO, 1966-69. Served with USNR, 1943-46. Fulbright research grantee, 1951-52, Ford Found. fgn. fellow, 1956-57. Mem. Am. Polit. Sci. Assn., Assn. Asian Studies, Phi Beta Kappa, Kappa Tau Alpha, Sigma Delta Chi, Phi Kappa Psi. Democrat. Conglist. Home: 8604 Dorotha Ct Austin TX 78759 Office: Dept of Govt U Tex Austin TX 78712

ROACH, JOHN ROBERT, archbishop; b. Prior Lake, Minn., July 31, 1921; s. Simon J. and Mary (Regan) R.; B.A., St. Paul Sem., 1946; M.A., U. Minn., 1957. Ordained priest Roman Catholic Ch., 1946; instr. St. Thomas Acad., 1946-50, headmaster, 1951-68; named domestic prelate, 1966; rector St. John Vianney Sem., 1968-71; aux. bishop St. Paul and Mpls., 1971; consecrated bishop, 1971; pastor St. Charles Borromeo Ch., Mpls., 1971-73, St. Cecilia Ch., St. Paul, 1973-75; archbishop of St. Paul, 1975—; appointed vicar for parishes, 1971; vicar for clergy, 1972—; Episc. moderator Nat. Apostolate for Mentally Retarded, 1974. Mem. Priests Senate, 1968-72; pres. Priests Senate and Presbytery, 1970; chmn. Com. on Accreditation Pvt. Schs. in Minn., 1952-57; mem. advisory com. Coll. Entrance Exam. Bd., 1964; Episc. mem. Bishops and Pres.'s Com.; chmn. Bishops Com. to Oversee Implementation of the Call to Action Program; trustee St. Paul Sem., 1971—, now chmn.; trustee Cath. U. Am., Coll. St. Catherine; chmn. bd. trustees St. Thomas Acad., Coll. St. Thomas; v.p. Nat. Conf. Cath. Bishops, 1977, chmn. ad hoc com. on call to action, 1977. Mem. Minn. Cath. Edn. Assn. (past pres.), Assn. Mil. Colls. and Schs. U.S. (past pres.), N.Central Assn. Colls. and Secondary Schs. (past mem. advisory com.), Am. Council Edn. (del. 1963-65), Nat. Conf. Cath. Bishops (adminstrv. com., priestly formation com., chmn. vocations com.), U.S. Cath. Conf. Office: 226 Summit Ave Saint Paul MN 55102

ROACH, MAXWELL LEMUEL, musician; b. Elizabeth City, N.C., Jan. 10, 1924; s. Alphonzo and Cressie (Saunders) R.; student Manhattan Sch. Music, N.Y.C.; m. Mildred Wilkinson, Jan. 14, 1949 (div.); children—Daryl, Maxine; m. 2d, Abbey Lincoln, Mar. 3, 1962 (div.). Adapted use of tympani in jazz; musician, specializing percussion instruments; with Charlie Parker, 1946-48, later appeared with Thelonious Monk, Bud Powell, Dizzy Gillespie; co-leader Max Roach-Clifford Brown Quintet, with Sonny Rollins, Harold Land, 1954-56, later with Booker Little, Ray Bryant, Eric Dolphy; appearances at Paris Jazz Festival, 1949, Newport Jazz Festival, 1972; prof. music U. Mass., 1973—; producer, dir. and choreographer. Recipient Best Record of the Year award Down Beat mag., 1956; winner Down Beat poll, 1955, 57, 58, 59, 60, metronome poll., 1951-54. Mem. Jazz Artists Guild Inc. (organizer). Composer Freedom Now suite (integration of jazz and dance). Address: Dept Music and Fine Arts Fine Arts Center U Mass Amherst MA 01003*

ROACH, THOMAS ADAIR, lawyer; b. Akron, Ohio, May 1, 1929; s. Edward Thomas and Mayme Bernice (Turner) R.; B.A., U. Mich., 1951, J.D., 1953; m. Sally Jane Bennett, July 11, 1953; children—Thomas, David, James, Dorothy, Steven, Patrick. Admitted to Mich. bar, 1953, since practiced in Detroit; asso. firm McClintock, Donovan, Carson & Roach, and predecessor, Detroit, 1956-62, partner, 1962—. Dir., mem. exec. com. Muskegon Bank & Trust Co.; dir. Ferndale Labs., Inc., Acme Abrasive Co. Vice chmn.

14th Congl. Dist. Democratic Orgn., 1971-75; chmn. platform and resolution com. Mich. Dem. Party, 1971-74, treas., 1975—, permanent chmn. Dem. State Conv., 1976; mem. platform com. and drafting subcom. Dem. Nat. Conv., 1972. Bd. regents U. Mich., 1975—. Served to capt. USCGR, 1953-56; res. group comdr., Detroit, 1974-77; pres. 9th Dist. Res. Policy Bd., 1976-77. Mem. Am. Judicature Soc., Soc. Hosp. Attys., Am., Fed., Mich., Detroit bar assns., Engring. Soc. Detroit, Res. Officers Assn., Navy League, Order of Coif. Episcopalian. Clubs: Thomas M. Cooley, Torch, U. Mich. (gov. 1970-74), Economic (Detroit); University (Ann Arbor, Mich.). Home: 151 Textile Rd Ann Arbor MI 48104 Office: 2150 Guardian Bldg Detroit MI 48226

ROACH, WESLEY LINVILLE, ins. co. exec.; b. Norlina, N.C., Oct. 8, 1931; s. Joseph Franklin and Florence G. (Sink) R.; B.S., Wake Forest U., 1953, J.D., 1955; m. Mary Jon Gerald, Aug. 13, 1955; children—Gerald, Mary Virginia. Admitted to N.C. bar, 1955; with Pilot Life Ins. Co., Greensboro, N.C., 1958—, gen. counsel, 1971—, v.p., 1973—, sec., 1974—; dir., sec. Gt. Eastern Life Ins. Co.; chmn., dir. N.C. Life & Accident & Health Ins. Guaranty Assn., Va. Life, Accident & Health Guaranty Assn., S.C. Life, Accident & Health Guaranty Assn.; sec. JP Investment Mgmt. Co., Jefferson-Pilot Equity Sales, Inc., Spl. Services Agy., Inc. Mem. finance com. Greensboro United Fund, 1964-65; nat. chmn. coll. fund, alumni council Wake Forest U., 1971-76, pres. nat. alumni council, 1975-76, trustee univ., 1978—. Trustee So. Bapt. Theol. Sem., Louisville. Served with USNR, 1955-58. Mem. Am., N.C., Greensboro bar assns., Assn. Life Ins. Counsel, Greensboro C. of C. (chmn. nat. legis. com. 1973—). Democrat. Baptist (finance com. 1963-66, chmn. bd. deacons 1974-76). Home: 3006 Alamance Rd Greensboro NC 27407 Office: PO Box 20727 Greensboro NC 27420

ROACH, WILLIAM RUSSELL, bus. exec.; b. Bedford, Ind., Jan. 1940; s. George H. and Beatrice M. (Schoenlaub) R.; B.S., U. Calif. at Los Angeles, 1961; m. Margaret R. Balogh, 1961; children—Kathleen L., Keith W. Internal auditor Hughes Aircraft Co., Los Angeles, 1961-62, Lockheed Aircraft Corp., Los Angeles, 1962; sr. accountant Haskins & Sells, Los Angeles, 1962-66; asst. to group v.p. Lear Siegler, Inc., 1966-71; v.p. fin., sec. Paul Hardeman Engrs. & Constructors, Inc., Los Angeles, 1971-72; exec. v.p., corporate sec., dir. Optimum Systems Inc., Santa Clara, Calif., 1972-79; pres., dir. Banking Systems Inc., Dallas, 1976-79; pres., dir. BancSystems, Inc., Santa Clara, 1976-79, DMA/Optimum, Honolulu, 1978-79; pres. W.R. Assos., Menlo Park, Calif., 1979—. Mem. Am. Inst. C.P.A.'s, Calif. Soc. C.P.A.'s, Los Angeles Jr. C. of C., Town Hall, Theta Delta Chi. Club: Commonwealth (San Francisco). Home: 48 Lowery Dr Atherton CA 94025 Office: 1259 El Camino Real Suite 1001 Menlo Park CA 94025

ROACHE, EDWARD FRANCIS, mfg. co. exec.; b. Morristown, N.J., May 2, 1923; s. Vincent D. and Cecelia R. (Kennedy) R.; B.S. in Economics, Fordham U., 1947; postgrad. Sienna Coll., 1953; m. Beth Davidson, Aug. 8, 1948; children—Marc E., Steven P., Kevin J. With Gen. Electric Co., 1947—, mem. fin. mgmt. program, corporate audit staff, mgr. fin. various depts., gen. mgmt. assignments in electronics, computers, aircraft engine and internat. ops., Syracuse, N.Y., Phoenix, Lynn, Mass., Fairfield, Conn., 1978—, v.p., gen. mgr. internat. constrn. bus. div., 1978—; dir. Gen. Electric Co., Spain, Italy, Australia, Philippines, S. Korea, U.K. Served with USMC, 1943-46. Mem. Fin. Execs. Inst. Club: Pinnacle. Home: 1161 Mill Hill Rd Southport CT 06490 Office: 10 Wright St Westport CT 06880

ROACHE, MILTON ORIS, JR., mech. engr.; b. Norfolk, Va., Sept. 25, 1922; s. Milton Oris and Alberta (Wetter) R.; student Rutgers U., 1943-44, Drexel Inst. Tech., 1944; B.M.E., Va. Poly. Inst., 1947; m. Mildred Traynham, Sept. 4, 1948; children—Edward Randolph, David Lawson, Margaret Sydnor. Engr., C. & O. Ry. Co., Richmond, Va., 1948-50; design engr. Hankins & Anderson, 1950-55; partner Roache & Mercer, Roache, Mercer & Faison, Richmond, 1955-71, pres., 1972—. Chmn. bd. trustees Henrico County Library, 1970-71, 75—. Served with inf., AUS, 1943-46. Decorated Bronze Star, Purple Heart. Fellow Am. Cons. Engrs. Council; mem. Am. Soc. Heating, Refrigeration and Air Conditioning Engrs. Presbyterian. Club: North Richmond Kiwanis (past pres.). Home: 3008 Birchbrook Rd Richmond VA 23228 Office: 2507 Willard Rd Richmond VA 23229

ROADEN, ARLISS LLOYD, univ. pres.; b. Bark Camp, Ky., Sept. 27, 1930; s. Johnie Samuel and Ethel Nora (Killian) R.; A.B., Carson Newman Coll., 1951; M.S., U. Tenn., 1958, Ed.D., 1961; m. Mary Etta Mitchell, Sept. 1, 1951; children—Janice Arletta Roaden Skelton, Sharon Kay. With Oak Ridge Inst. Nuclear Studies, 1957-59, Auburn U., 1961-62; mem. faculty Ohio State U., 1962—, prof. edn., 1967—, acting dean Coll. Edn., 1968-70, vice provost for research, dean Grad. Sch., 1970-74; pres. Tenn. Technol. U., 1974—; summer vis. prof. Marshall U., 1961, U. So. Calif., 1964, Ind. U., 1967; cons. ednl. instns., 1961—. Chmn. bd. govs. Phi Delta Kappa Found., 1969—; pres. Tenn. Coll. Assn., 1978; chmn. sci. and tech. com. Am. Assn. State Colls. and Univs. Served with AUS, 1951-53. Research grantee Phi Delta Kappa Internat., 1968; named Distinguished Alumnus Cumberland Coll., 1970; recipient Distinguished Alumni and Faculty Centennial medallion Coll. Edn., 1970, Distinguished Service award Council Grad. Students, 1974 (both Ohio State U.), others. Mem. Am. Assn. Higher Edn., AAAS, Acad. Polit. and Social Scis., Am. Ednl. Research Assn. (chmn. publs. com.), Nat. Soc. Study Edn., Nat. Assn. State Colls. and Land Grant Univs., Phi Kappa Phi, Phi Delta Kappa (Distinguished Service award Ohio State U. chpt. 1974), Kappa Phi Kappa, Kappa Delta Pi. Democrat. Baptist. Lion, Rotarian. Co-author: The Research Assistantship: Recommendations for Colleges and Universities, 1975. Contbr. articles to profl. jours. Editor: Problems of School Men in Depressed Urban Areas, 1967. Home: 1155 N Dixie Ave Tenn Technological U Cookeville TN 38501

ROADMAN, GEORGE H., coll. pres.; b. Merrittstown, Pa., Oct. 8, 1920; s. George C. and Hazel (Lint) R.; student Calif. State Tchrs. Coll.; M.A., Ph.D., U. Pitts.; hon. degree Palmer Coll.; m. Betty Roberts, Aug. 7, 1943; children—George William, Emmilou, John. Tchr., Redstone Township schs., 1941-42; prof. history California (Pa.) State Coll., 1946-47, dean instrn., now pres., prof. Mem. Pa. Bd. Pvt. Correspondence Schs.; pres. California Community Sch. Bd.; mem. Washington County Planning Commn.; mem. Monongahela Valley Progress Council; dist. chmn. Boy Scouts Am.; bd. dirs. Monongahela Valley United Fund; bd. mgrs. Brownsville (Pa.) Gen. Hosp. Served to capt., F.A., AUS, 1942-46; ETO. Decorated Bronze Star medal. Mem. Am. Hist. Assn. Presbyn. Contbr. articles hist. jours. Office: Office of Pres California State Coll 3d Ave California PA 15419*

ROARK, ELIJAH BUCK, JR., tobacco co. exec.; b. Halifax, Va., Mar. 14, 1925; s. Elijah Buck and Maggie Y. (Hodnett) R.; diploma Phillips Bus. Coll., 1949; evening student U. Richmond, Richmond Poly. Inst.; corr. student LaSalle Extension U., Chgo.; m. Ruth N. Hughes, June 21, 1947; children—Charlie Larry, Betty Ruth. Field accountant Keystone Constrn. Co., Huntington, W.Va., 1949-50; mil. pay supr., chief clk. Army Finance, Camp Pickett, Va., 1951-52; accountant Universal Leaf Tobacco Co., Inc., Richmond, Va., 1953-60, auditor, 1961-67, controller 1968—. Past mem. adv. com. John Tyler Community Coll., Richmond. Served with AUS, 1943-46. Certified internal auditor. Mem. Inst. Internal Auditors (pres. 1970-71, gov. Richmond chpt. 1971—), Smithsonian Assos. Methodist (past lay leader, past ch. sch. supt.). Home: 8930 Rockdale Rd Richmond VA 23235 Office: Universal Leaf Tobacco Co Inc Hamilton St at Broad Richmond VA 23230

ROB, CHARLES GRANVILLE, surgeon, educator; b. Weybridge, Eng., May 4, 1913; s. Joseph William and Alice Maud (Smith) R.; M.A., Cambridge (Eng.) U., 1934, M.D., 1937, M. Chir., 1941; M. Chir. (hon.), Trinity Coll., Dublin, Ireland, 1961; m. Mary Beazley, June 23, 1941; children—Joseph Michael, Peter James, Caroline Mary, Sarah Rebecca. Came to U.S., 1960. Student, surg. resident appointments St. Thomas's Hosp. Med. Sch., 1934-41; surgeon St. Thomas's Hosp., 1946-50; prof. surgery U. London, also surgeon St. Mary's Hosp., 1950-60; prof. surgery, chmn. dept. U. Rochester Sch. Medicine, also surgeon-in-chief Strong Meml. Hosp., 1960-78; prof. surgery E. Carolina U. Sch. Medicine, Greenville, N.C., 1978—. Served to lt. col. Brit. Army, 1941-46. Decorated Mil. Cross. Mem. A.C.S., Royal Coll. Surgeons (Eng.), Am. Surg. Assn., Soc. Univ. Surgeons. Home: 230 Country Club Dr Greenville NC 27834

ROBARDS, JASON NELSON, JR., actor; b. Chgo., July 22, 1922; s. Jason Nelson and Hope (Glanville) R.; studied Am. Acad. Dramtic Arts, 1946; m. Eleanore Pitman, May 7, 1948; children—Jason III, Sarah Louise, David; m. 3d, Lauren Bacall, July 4, 1961 (div.); 1 son, Sam; m. 4th, Lois O'Connor; children—Shannon, Jake. Broadway plays include: Stalag 17, 1951-53, The Chase, 1952, The Iceman Cometh, 1956, Long Day's Journey Into Night, 1956-58, The Disenchanted, 1958, Henry IV, Part I, Stratford (Ont., Can.), 1958, Macbeth, Stratford, Conn., The Disenchanted, 1958-59, Toys in the Attic, 1960, Big Fish, Little Fish, 1961, A Thousand Clowns, 1962, After the Fall, 1964, But for Whom, Charlie, 1964, Hughie, 1964, The Devils, 1965, We Bombed in New Haven, 1968, The Country Girl, 1972, A Moon for the Misbegotten, 1973, Long Day's Journey Into Night, 1976, A Touch of the Poet, 1977-78; motion picture appearances include: The Journey, 1959, By Love Possessed, 1961, A Thousand Clowns, Big Hand for the Little Lady, 1966, Any Wednesday, 1966, St. Valentine's Day Massacre, 1967, Night They Raided Minsky's, 1968, Hour of the Gun, 1967, Loves of Isadora, 1969, Once Upon a Time in the West, 1969, Ballad of Cable Hogue, 1970, Johnny Got His Gun, 1971, Murders in the Rue Morgue, 1971, The War Between Men and Women, 1972, Pat Garrett and Billy the Kid, 1973, All the President's Men, 1976, Julia, 1977, Comes a Horseman, 1978, Hurricane, 1979, Melvin and Howard, 1979; TV appearance in For Whom the Bell Tolls, CBS, 1959; starred TV prodn. The Iceman Cometh, 1961, One Day in the Life of Ivan Denisovitch, 1963, Washington Behind Closed Doors, 1977. Bd. dirs. Am. Acad. Dramatic Arts, 1957—. Served with USN, 1939-46. Recipient Presidential citation; ANTA award for outstanding contbn. to living theater, 1959, Antoinette Perry award as best actor, 1959, Obie award, 1956, Acad. awards for best supporting actor, 1976, 77, N.Y. Film Critics Circle award for best supporting actor, 1976. Club: Players (N.Y.C.). Address: care STE Representation Ltd 888 7th Ave New York NY 10019

ROBB, CHARLES SPITTAL, lt. gov. Va.; b. Phoenix, June 26, 1939; s. James Spittal and Francis Howard (Woolley) R.; student Cornell U., 1957-58; B.B.A., U. Wis., 1961; J.D., U. Va., 1973; m. Lynda Bird Johnson, Dec. 9, 1967; children—Lucinda Desha, Catherine Lewis, Jennifer Wickliffe. Admitted to Va. bar, 1973, U.S. Supreme Ct. bar, 1976; law clk. to John D. Butzner, Jr., U.S. Ct. Appeals, 1973-74; atty. Williams Connolly & Califano, 1974-77; lt. gov. Va., 1978—; v.p., dir. LBJ Co., 1971—, No. Va. Radio Co., 1978—; chmn. Va. Forum on Edn., 1978—, Concerned Citizens of the Commonwealth, 1978—; vice-chmn. Local Govt. Adv. Commn., 1978—; mem. exec. com., chmn. So. Region, chmn. intergovtl. affairs com., vice chmn. econ. devel. com. Nat. Conf. Lt. Govs., 1979-80; chmn. Am. Council Young Polit. Leaders del. to Peoples Republic of China, 1979. Mem. various bds. U. Va., 1974—, U. Richmond, 1974—, Hampton Inst. Tech., 1977—; mem. nat. Capital Area exec. bd. Boy Scouts Am., 1976—, chmn. No. Va. Scout Expo, 1976, 77; mem. Fairfax County bd. Am. Cancer Soc., 1976—; profl. gifts chmn. United Way of Fairfax County, 1976; dep. gen. counsel, asst. parliamentarian Democratic Nat. Com. Platform Com., 1976; mem. Fairfax County Dem. Com., 1975—, Dem. State Central Com., 1976—. Served with USMC, 1961-70; co. comdr., aide to comdg. gen., 2d Marine Div.; social aide to White House, Washington; inf. co. comdr., Vietnam. Decorated Bronze Star, Vietnam Service medal with 4 Stars; Vietnamese Cross of Gallantry with Silver Star; recipient Raven award, 1973, Seven Socs. Orgn. award U. Va. Mem. Am., Va. bar assns., Va. Trial Lawyers Assn., Res. Officers Assn., USMC Res. Officers Assn., Am. Legion, Raven Soc., Omicron Delta Kappa. Episcopalian. Office: Office of Lt Gov State Capitol Richmond VA 23219

ROBB, DAVID BUZBY, JR., lawyer, bank exec.; b. Phila., Nov. 30, 1935; s. David B. and Sarah C. (Carson) R.; B.A., Princeton U., 1958; LL.B., U. Va., 1963; grad. Advanced Mgmt. Program, Harvard U., 1978; m. Patricia Ann Robb, Sept. 14, 1979; children—David S., Stephen C. Admitted to Pa. bar, 1963; asso. firm Ballard, Spahr, Andrews & Ingersoll, Phila., 1963-69; v.p., gen. counsel Provident Nat. Corp., Phila., 1969-75; v.p., gen. counsel Provident Nat. Bank, 1969-75, sr. v.p., gen. counsel, 1975-76, sr. v.p., chief operating officer trust div., 1976—; dir., chmn. Provident Capital Mgmt., Inc.; dir., vice-chmn. Provident Instl. Mgmt. Corp. Sr. v.p., sec. Independence Sq. Income Securities Inc., Phila., 1972—. Mem. bd. mgrs. Phila. City Inst., 1973—. Served with USNR, 1958-60. Episcopalian. Clubs: Union League (Phila.); Martins Dam. Home: 738 Wolcott Dr Apt B-2 Philadelphia PA 19118 Office: Provident Nat Bank 17th and Chestnut Sts Philadelphia PA 19103

ROBB, FELIX COMPTON, assn. exec.; b. Birmingham, Ala., Dec. 26, 1914; s. Felix Compton and Ruth (Nicholson) R.; A.B. summa cum laude, Birmingham-So. Coll., 1936, L.H.D., 1979; M.A., Vanderbilt U., 1939; student George Peabody Coll., 1939-40; Ed.D., Harvard U., 1952; D.Ped., W.Va. Wesleyan Coll., 1968; LL.D., Mercer U., 1968, U. S.C., 1978; D.H.L., U. Ala. System, 1975; m. Virginia Lytle Threlkeld. Tchr. jr. high sch., Irondale, Ala., 1936-37; tchr. Ensley High Sch., Birmingham, Ala., 1937-38; instr. English, Birmingham-So. Coll., 1940-42, successively alumni sec., registrar, 1946; asst. to pres. Peabody Coll., 1947-51, acting dir. Library Sch., 1947-48, acting dean of coll., 1948-49, asso. prof. higher edn., 1950-53, prof., 1953-66, acting dir. surveys and field services, summer 1951, dean instrn., 1951-61, coll. pres., 1961-66; dir. So. Assn. Colls. and Schs., Atlanta, 1966-79, exec. dir., 1979—; coordinator edn. project in Korea, 1956-58. Dir. Carnegie fellowships in teaching, 1950-60; dir. Peabody Bldg. Fund Campaign, 1958; chief of staff The Study of Coll. and Univ. Presidency, 1958-60; mem. Tenn. Adv. Council on Tchr. Edn. and Certification, 1954-58; case writer Inst. for Coll. and Univ. Adminstrs., Harvard, 1955; nat. selection com. Fulbright awards, 1955-57; dir workshops in TV, ednl. TV program series, Nashville; chmn. gov.'s conf. edn. beyond high sch., 1958; mem. com. specialized personnel Dept. Labor, Tenn. Commn. Human Relations, 1964-66; exec. com. Met. Action Commn., 1965-66; chmn. S.E. Manpower Adv. Com., 1965-68; mem. bd. So. Edn. Reporting Service, 1961-69; trustee, chmn. scholarship com. Presser Found.; mem. Cleveland Conf., Colloquium on Higher Edn. Served to lt. USNR, 1943-46. Mem. So. Council Tchr. Edn. (pres. 1956-57), Phi Beta Kappa, Omicron Delta Kappa, Phi Delta Kappa, Kappa Phi Kappa, Pi Gamma Mu, Kappa Alpha, Kappa Delta Pi. Methodist (chmn. adminstrv. bd. 1974). Rotarian. Home: 377 Camden Rd NE Atlanta GA 30309 Office: 795 Peachtree St NE Atlanta GA 30308

ROBB, JAMES ALEXANDER, lawyer; b. Huntingdon, Que., Can., May 3, 1930; s. Alexander George and Irma Mary (Martin) R.; B.A., McGill U., 1951, B.C.L., 1954; postgrad. U. Montreal, 1961-63; m. Katherine Ann Teare, June 26, 1960; children—Laura, John, Andrew. Called to Que. bar, 1955, created queen's counsel; lectr. comml. law and taxation Sir George Williams U., 1958-60; partner Stikeman, Elliott, Tamaki, Mercier & Robb, Montreal, 1967—. Dir. Potchett Investment, Ltd., Robapharm (Can.), Ltd., C. Itoh & Co. (Can.) Ltd., Lincoln, Manson, Ltd., YKK Can. Ltd., Hitachi Sales Corp. Can. Ltd. Mem. Westmount Sch. Bd., Sch. Council of Island of Montreal; mem. Protestant Sch. Bd. Greater Montreal, mem. central parents com.; chmn. bd. trustees Martlet Found., 1967-69; v.p. Que. Liberal Party, 1976—; mem. adv. com. McGill U. Centre for Study of Regulated Industries. Mem. Bar Que., McGill Grad. Soc. (past hon. sec. Montreal br.), Consumers Assn. Can. (chmn. regulated industries program). Clubs: University (Montreal); Kanawaki Golf (Caughnawaga, Que.). Home: 9 Renfrew Ave Westmount PQ H3Y 2X3 Canada Office: 1155 Dorchester Blvd W Montreal PQ H3B 3V2 Canada

ROBB, JOHN DONALD, JR., lawyer; b. N.Y.C., Jan. 11, 1924; s. John Donald and Harriet (Block) R.; student Yale, 1941-42, U. N.Mex., 1942-44; B.S.L., U. Minn., 1948, LL.B., 1949; m. Peggy Hight, Feb. 8, 1946; children—John Donald III, Linda Celeste, Ellen Bea, Bradford Hight, George Geoffrey, David McGregor. Admitted to N.Mex. bar, 1950, since practiced in Albuquerque; sr. partner firm Rodey, Dickason, Sloan, Akin & Robb and predecessors, 1958—. Mem. nat. adv. com. OEO; legal services program, exec. com., v.p. Nat. Legal Aid and Defender Assn., 1966-72; exec. com. Albuquerque Legal Aid Soc., 1963-71. Bd. dirs. Navajo Legal Services Bd., 1967-68, Council on Legal Edn. for Profl. Responsibility. Served to lt. (j.g.) USNR, 1942-46; PTO. Recipient Distinguished Service award Albuquerque United Community Fund, 1960, Outstanding Man of Year award Albuquerque Jr. C. of C., 1956. Mem. Am. (chmn. standing com. legal aid and indigent defendents 1966-72, chmn. spl. com. atomic energy law 1974-76), Albuquerque, N.Mex. bar assns., Albuquerque Lawyers Club. Home: 7200 Rio Grande Blvd NW Albuquerque NM 87107 Office: PO Box 1888 Albuquerque NM 87103

ROBB, JOHN WESLEY, educator; b. Los Angeles, Dec. 1, 1919; s. Edgar Milton and Alta (Boger) R.; A.B., Greenville Coll., 1941; Th.M., U. So. Calif., 1945, Ph.D., 1952; L.H.D., Hebrew Union Coll.-Jewish Inst. Religion, 1977; m. Ethel Edna Tosh, June 13, 1942; children—Lydia Joan (Mrs. Elliot), Judith Nadine. Asst. prof. philosophy and religion Dickinson (Pa.) Coll., 1948-51; fellow Fund for Advancement Edn., 1951-52; asso. prof. U. So. Calif., at Los Angeles, 1954-62, chmn. dept. religion, 1954-67, prof., 1962—, asso. dean humanities Coll. Letters, Arts and Scis., 1963-68, Leonard K. Firestone prof., 1974, 75. Served as lt. (j.g.) USNR, 1945-47, to lt., 1952-54. Recipient award for excellence in teaching U. So. Calif., 1960, 74; Dart award for acad. innovation, 1974. Mem. Religious Edn. Assn., Am. Acad. Religion (v.p. 1966, pres. 1967), Am. Philos. Assn., AAUP (v.p. Calif. Conf. 1977, pres. 1978-79), Phi Kappa Phi, Phi Chi Phi, Theta Phi, Pi Epsilon Theta. Methodist. Author: Inquiry Into Faith, 1960. Co-editor: Readings in Religious Philosophy; The Reverent Skeptic, 1979. Home: 1807 W 27th St San Pedro CA 90732

ROBB, LYNDA JOHNSON, writer; b. Washington, Mar. 19, 1944; d. Lyndon Baines and Claudia Alta (Taylor) Johnson; B.A. with honors, U. Tex., 1966; m. Charles Spittal Robb, Dec. 9, 1967; children—Lucinda Desha, Catherine Lewis, Jennifer Wickliffe. Writer, McCall's mag., 1966-68; contbg. editor Ladies Home Jour., Downe Communications, Inc., N.Y.C., 1969—. Lectr. in field. Bd. dirs. Reading Is Fundamental, 1968—, L.Q.C. Lamar Soc., 1974—, Washington Performing Arts Soc., 1974, Lyndon B. Johnson Family Found., 1969—; chmn. Pres.'s Adv. Com. for Women, 1979—. Mem. Zeta Tau Alpha. Democrat. Episcopalian. Office: 641 Lexington Ave New York NY 10022

ROBB, ROGER, judge; b. Bellows Falls, Vt., July 7, 1907; s. Charles Henry and Nettie May (George) R.; A.B., Yale, 1928, LL.B., 1931; m. Mary Ernst Cooper, 1932; 1 son, Charles Cooper; m. 2d, Lillian Nordstrom, 1943. Admitted to D.C. bar, 1931; asst. U.S. atty., D.C., 1931-38; pvt. practice, Washington, 1938-69; partner Robb, Porter, Kistler & Parkinson, and predecessor firms, 1951-69; U.S. circuit judge U.S. Ct. Appeals D.C. Circuit, 1969—. Asso. counsel spl. Ho. com. investigate NLRB, 1939-40; counsel AEC Personnel Security Bd., 1954; mem. com. on admissions and grievances U.S. Dist. Ct. for D.C., 1953-69; spl. hearing officer U.S. Dept. Justice, 1956-68. Mem. Commn. on Revision Fed. Ct. Appellate System, 1973-75. Trustee Legal Aid Agy. of D.C., 1960-68, chmn. bd., 1965-67. Fellow Am. Bar Found., Am. Coll. Trial Lawyers; mem. Am., D.C. (v.p. 1953-54) bar assns., Phi Beta Kappa. Clubs: Yale (N.Y.C.); George Town, Chevy Chase (Washington). Home: 1700 Hoban Rd Washington DC 20007 Office: US Courthouse Washington DC 20001

ROBBIE, JOSEPH, lawyer, profl. football team exec.; b. Sisseton, S.D., July 7, 1916; s. Joseph and Jennie (Ready) R.; A.B., U. S.D., 1943, J.D., 1946; LL.D., Biscayne Coll., 1970, U. S.D., 1979; D.Arts and Scis. (hon.), Mt. Marty Coll., 1979; m. Elizabeth Ann Lyle, Dec. 28, 1942; children—Diane, David (dec.), Janet (Mrs. John R. Glode), Joseph Michael, Kathleen (dec.), Lynn, Deborah, Timothy, Brian, Daniel, Kevin. Admitted to S.D. bar, 1946, Minn. bar, 1951; practice in Mitchell, S.D., 1948-53, Mpls., 1953—; founder, 1965, pres., gen. mgr. Miami Dolphins, Ltd., 1965—. Mem. Fla. Bd. Bus. Regulation, 1977; mem. exec. com. Hubert H. Humphrey Inst. Pub. Affairs, 1977—. Regional counsel, acting regional enforcement dir. OPS, Mpls., 1951-52, regional dir., 1952-53; author Minn. Municipal Commn. Act., 1959-60, 1st chmn. commn., 1959-65; regional v.p. Nat. Municipal League, 1977; charter mem., sec.-treas. Twin Cities Met. Planning Commn., 1957-65; spl. counsel com. for hearings to create Dept. Urban Affairs, U.S. Senate, 1961; exec. dir., legal counsel Commn. Municipal Annexation and Consol. Minn. Legislature, 1961-63; asst. prof. econs. Dakota Wesleyan U., 1946-48; spl. instr., debate coach Coll. St. Catherine, St. Paul, 1953-54. Chmn. Harry S. Truman Library Fund Drive, 1956; v.p., presiding officer Am. Lebanese Syrian Asso. Charities, 1966-68, bd. dirs., 1959—; chmn. Community Relations Bd. Dade County, 1973; mem. tourist devel. adv. council Bd. Broward County Commrs., 1977; chmn. nat. alumni fund drive Dakota Dome, U. S.D., 1972; co-chmn. fund drive Curley High Sch., Miami, 1973, Gesu Ch., 1973; hon. chmn. Century of Service Fund campaign, Yankton, S.D., 1978; com. to raise funds Carleton Coll., Northfield, Minn., 1973; mem. S.D. Legislature, 1949-51, joint caucus leader; chmn. S.D. Democratic Party, 1948-50; candidate gov. S.D., 1950, U.S. Congress from Minn., 1956, 58; v.p. Catholic Charities, Archdiocese of Miami; bd. dirs. St. Jude Children's Research Hosp., Memphis, 1959—; bd. dirs. Boys Town Miami, 1969—, Operation Self-Help, 1969-71, United Fund, 1972—, Am. Health Found., 1975—, Dakota Dome Devel. Corp.; mem. adv. bd. Fla. Meml. Coll., Miami, 1967—; trustee Biscayne Coll., 1970-71,

76—, chmn. devel. bd., 1976, mem. adv. com. sports adminstn.; trustee Dade Found., 1972-75, Jackson Meml. Hosp., 1973—; chmn. bd. dirs. Cath. Service Bur., 1977—; mem. citizens' bd. U. Miami; mem. adv. council Coll. Arts and Letters, U. Notre Dame, 1973; mem. council advisors Fla. State U. System, 1975—; bd. dirs. USO, 1976—, Jesuit Program for Living and Learning, 1978—. Served with USNR, 1941-45. Decorated Bronze Star; recipient Nathan Burkan Meml. award for essay copywright law, 1946; J. Ernest O'Brien Commendation award Nat. Assn. Tobacco Distbrs., 1966; Good Samaritan award Variety Club Miami, 1971; Alumni award excellence No. State Coll., 1971; Outstanding Alumnus award Sisseton (S.D.) High Sch., 1971; Silver Medallion award Fla. Region NCCJ, 1973; Citation for meritorious pub. service Dept. of Navy, 1974; Horatio Alger award, 1979, others; named Pro Football Exec. of Year, L.I. Athletic Club, 1973; Miami Dolphins recipient Nat. Football League World Championship, 1972-73; Pop Warner Football Father of Year award, 1976. Hon. fellow Hebrew U., 1973. Mem. No. State Coll. Alumni Assn. (nat. fund raising chmn.), Miami C. of C. (gov.). Kiwanian. Clubs: Jockey, LaGorce Country, Miami, Ocean Reef, Palm Bay, Standard of Greater Miami, Tiger Bay; Minneapolis Golf, Pool and Yacht. Office: 330 Biscayne Blvd Miami FL 33132

ROBBINS, ANTHONY, state health officer; b. N.Y.C., Jan. 9, 1941; s. I.D. and Carolyn (Marx) R.; B.A., Harvard U., 1952; M.D., Yale U., 1966; M.P.A., John F. Kennedy Sch. Govt., Harvard U., 1969; m. Jennifer Lauterbach, June 8, 1963; children—John, Richard. Intern dept. medicine Beth Israel Hosp., Boston, 1966-67, asst. resident, 1967-68; asst. physician Harvard U. Health Services, 1968-70; clin. instr. Harvard Med. Sch., 1969-70; fellow Center for Community Health and Med. Care, Sch. Pub. Health, 1968-70; clin. and research fellow Mass. Gen. Hosp., 1968-70; asst. physician Royal Victoria Hosp., Montreal, Can., 1970-72; asst. prof. dept. epidemiology and health McGill U., 1970-72; dir. Community Health Centre Project, McGill Centre for Health Care Research, 1970-72; jr. scientist Nat. Health Research, Can., 1971-72; dir. profl. relations and community health devel. New Eng. Regional Med. program, Burlington, Vt., 1972-73; commr. Vt. Health Dept., 1973-76; exec. dir. Colo. Dept. Health, Denver, 1976-78; dir. Nat. Inst. Occupational Health and Safety, Rockville, Md., 1978—; clin. asso. prof. coll. medicine U. Vt., 1973-76; asso. clin. prof. dept. preventive medicine U. Colo. Med. Center, 1976-78; cons. in field. Mem. Am. Pub. Health Assn., Vt., Mass med. socs., AAAS, Med. Com. for Human Rights. Contbr. articles to med. jours. Office: Nat Inst Occupational Safety and Health Parklawn Bldg 5600 Fishers Ln Rockville MD 20257

ROBBINS, BILLY ALVIN, lawyer; b. Hot Springs, Ark., Oct. 18, 1926; s. William Thomas and Tressie Alva (Nelson) R.; B.S. in Elec. Engring., U. Ark., 1951; J.D., U. So. Calif., 1957; m. Juanita Ruth Pennell, June 19, 1953; children—Brick Arin, Lance Aris. Admitted to Cal. bar, 1958; practiced law, Los Angeles, 1958—; with patent dept. Hughes Aircraft Co., Culver City, Calif., 1953-58; asso. firm Nilsson, Robbins, Dalgarn, Carson Berliner & Wurst (and predecessor firms), Los Angeles, 1960—; adj. prof. law Southwestern U., Los Angeles, 1972—; lectr. in field. Pres. Woodland Hills Coordinating Council, 1959-60. Served with USNR, 1944-46, USAF, 1951-53. Mem. Woodland Hills Jr. C. of C. (v.p. 1961), IEEE (legal counsel Los Angeles Council 1958—). Methodist (trustee, ofcl. bd.). Mason. Clubs: Woodland Hills Country, Los Angeles Athletic, Calabasas Park Tennis. Home: 4517 Park Allegra Calagasas CA 91302 Office: 707 Wilshire Blvd Los Angeles CA 90017

ROBBINS, CAROLINE, educator; b. Sipson, Eng., Aug. 18, 1903; d. Rowland Richard and Rosa Marion (Harris) R.; B.A., London U., 1924, Ph.D., 1926; fellow U. Mich., 1927; LL.D., Smith Coll., 1971; Litt. D., Wilson Coll., 1971; m. Stephen Herben, Sept. 21, 1932 (dec.). Came to U.S., 1926, naturalized, 1933. Instr., Western Res. U., 1927-28, 1st Flora Mather Stone prof., 1976; mem. faculty Bryn Mawr Coll., 1929—, successively instr., asst. prof., 1929-48, asso. prof., 1948-60, chmn. dept. history, 1957-68, Marjorie Walter Goodhart prof. history, 1960-70; Alice Freeman Palmer prof. U. Mich., 1958. Recipient Lindback award for distinction in teaching, 1971. Guggenheim fellow, 1953-54. Fellow Royal Hist. Soc.; mem. Am. (council 1964), Mass. (hon.), Pa. (council 1970—, v.p. 1977—), hist. assns., Renaissance Soc. Am., AAUP, AAUW, League Women Voters, Radner Hist. Soc. (v.p. 1948-57, pres. 1957-64), Inst. Early Am. History and Culture (council), Conf. Brit. Studies (pres. 1971-73). Author: The Eighteenth Century Commonwealthman (Herbert Baxter Adams prize Am. Hist. Assn.), 1959; editor: Diary of John Milward, M.P. 1666-1668, 1938; Two Republican Tracts, 1969. Chmn., The Papers of William Penn, 1967—. Contbr. articles to profl. jours. Home: 815 The Chetwynd Rosemont PA 19010 Office: Penn Papers 1300 Locust St Philadelphia PA 19107

ROBBINS, CHARLES EDWARD, bus. assn. exec.; b. Perry, Okla., July 19,1906; s. William Marion and Mary (Swan) R.; student U. Okla., 1924; B.A., DePauw U., 1928; postgrad. U. Cin., 1930-31, U. Chgo., 1938-39; m. Pauline Frederick, Mar. 29, 1969; 1 son by previous marriage, Charles Edward. Reporter, Indpls. Star, 1928-29; reporter Wall St. Jour., Cin., 1929-34, mng. editor, N.Y.C., 1934-35, Midwest mgr., Chgo., 1935-41; with bus. dept. N.Y. Times, 1941-49; v.p. Bozell & Jacobs, N.Y.C., 1949-53; exec. mgr. Atomic Indsl. Forum, N.Y.C., 1953-72, pres., 1972-74, dir., 1973—; cons. and lectr. internat. bus. and energy, 1974—; sr. counsellor UN Internat. Bus. Council, N.Y.C., 1978—; lectr. internat. bus. and energy. Served to lt. USNR, 1943-46. Mem. Atomic Indsl. Forum, Am. Nuclear Soc., UN Assn., Fgn. Policy Assn., N.Y. Soc. Profl. Journalists, Phi Gamma Delta, Sigma Delta Chi. Episcopalian. Clubs: Univ. (N.Y.C., Washington). Home: PO Box 323 Saugatuck Sta Westport CT 06880

ROBBINS, CORNELIUS (VAN VORSE), ednl. adminstr.; b. Wilmington, Del., Nov. 2, 1931; s. Cornelius V. and Irene (Tatman) R.; B.A. in Polit. Sci., U. Del., 1953, M.Ed. in Social Scis., 1961; Ed.D. in Ednl. Adminstrn., U. Pa., 1964; m. Janet Porter, Aug. 8, 1953; children—Eva Robbins Burke, Susan, Laurel, Melissa. Mem. faculty U. Del., 1957-58; tchr. Marshallton (Del.) Sch. Dist., 1958-60, Mt. Pleasant (Del.) Sch. Dist., 1960-62; asst. to dir. sch. study councils U. Pa., 1962-64; dean instrn. Ocean County Coll., 1965-67; dean of coll. Community Coll. of Delaware County (Pa.), 1967-69; sr. asso., coll. div. dir. McManis Assos., Washington, 1969-70; pres. Genesee Community Coll., 1970-75; asso. chancellor for community colls. SUNY, 1975—; cons. Middle States Assn. Colls.; area liaison officer U.S. Mil. Acad., 1972; chmn. SUNY West Pres.'s Council and mem. Chancellor's Council, 1973. Served with U.S. Army, 1954-56. Recipient Outstanding Educator's award N.Y. State Assn. Jr. Colls., 1975. Mem. Am. Assn. Higher Edn., Am. Assn. Polit. and Social Scis., Futuristic Soc., Genesee County C. of C. (v.p. 1974), Phi Delta Kappa. Contbr. articles to profl. publs. Office: Room T-705 SUNY Plaza Albany NY 12246

ROBBINS, DANIEL, author, educator, art museum dir.; b. N.Y.C., Jan. 15, 1933; s. David and Ora (Laddon) R.; A.B., U. Chgo., 1951; M.A., Yale, 1956; student Inst. Fine Arts, N.Y. U., 1956-58, Ph.D., 1974; Fulbright fellow Inst. Art and Archaeology, U. Paris, 1958-59; m. Eugenia Scandrett, Dec. 6, 1959; children—Juliette, Miranda. Curator Nat. Gallery Art, Washington, 1960-61, Guggenheim Mus., N.Y.C., 1961-65; dir. Mus. Art, R.I. Sch. Design, Providence, 1965-71, Fogg Art Mus., Harvard, 1971-75; vis. prof. art history Brown U., 1966-71; vis. research prof. art Dartmouth, 1975—; sr. fellow Nat. Endowment for Humanities, 1976; vis. prof. Yale, 1977; Williams Coll., 1977; lectr. fine arts Harvard, 1971—; cons. Vt. Ho. of Reps., 1979; mem. adv. panel mus. program NEA. Trustee Am. Fedn. Arts. Guggenheim fellow, 1978. Author: Albert Gleizes, 1964; Jacques Villon, 1976; Cubist Drawings, 1978. Home: RD 2 Peth Rd Randolph VT 05060 Office: Carpenter Hall Dartmouth Coll Hanover NH 03755

ROBBINS, DAVID WALTER, JR., chem. co. exec.; b. W. Baden, Ind., Nov. 1, 1919; s. David Walter and Martha (Hagen) R.; B.S. in Bus. Adminstrn., Ind. U., 1942, M.S., 1943; m. Edith Petit, Dec. 24, 1949; children—Marie-France, Jack, Regis, Corinne, Nathalie. Dep. dir. Joint Export-Import Agy. U.S./ U.K., Frankfurt, Ger., 1947-48; v.p. Continental Ore Corp., N.Y.C., 1948-52, Internat. Ore & Fertilizer Corp., N.Y.C., 1948-52; exec. v.p., dir. W.R. Grace & Co., N.Y.C., 1952—; adv. bd. Chem. Bank, N.Y.C. Served with AUS, 1943-46. Mem. Ind. U. Sch. Bus. Acad. Alumni Fellows, Beta Gamma Sigma. Clubs: University (N.Y.C.); Westchester Country (Rye, N.Y.). Address: 1114 Ave Americas New York City NY 10036

ROBBINS, DONALD GOODRICH, JR., sewing machine mfr.; b. Newton, Mass., May 5, 1915; s. Donald Goodrich and Ann (Wheelock) R.; A.B., Darmouth, 1936; M.S., Mass. Inst. Tech., 1938; m. Anne Patrick, Oct. 14, 1936; children—Ann Wheelock, Henry Beveridge, Bruce Loomis, Laurence Goodrich, Patricia. With Singer Mfg. Co., N.Y.C., 1938—, asst. v.p., 1951-54, dir., 1954-55, v.p., dir., 1955-60, v.p., 1960-64, treas., 1960-70, v.p. indsl. products div., 1964-67, chief financial officer, 1967-75, sr. v.p., dir., 1970-77; sr. v.p. Singer Sewing Machine Co., 1970—. Office: 30 Rockefeller Plaza New York City NY 10020

ROBBINS, DONALD MICHAEL, lawyer; b. Woonsocket, R.I., Oct. 2, 1935; s. Robert Sidney and Nancy Ruth (Medoff) R.; student Brandeis U., 1953-55; A.B., U. Mich., 1957; LL.B., Boston U., 1960; m. Esther Sharp, Aug. 30, 1959; children—Jeffrey, Benjamin. Admitted to Mass. bar, 1961, R.I. bar, 1962; individual practice law, 1961-68; v.p., sec., gen. counsel Hasbro Industries, Inc., Pawtucket, R.I., 1968—. Bd. dirs., former chmn. Big Bros. R.I.; bd. dirs. Jewish Family and Children's Service, Bur. Jewish Edn., Temple Emanu-El. Mem. Am. Soc. Corporate Secs., Mass., R.I. bar assns. Home: 670 Elmgrove Ave Providence RI 02906 Office: 1027 Newport Ave Pawtucket RI 02861

ROBBINS, FREDERIC JOHN, steel co. exec.; b. Kankakee, Ill., June 17, 1910; s. John F. and Rose M. (Preisel) R.; B.S., Colo. State Coll. Edn., 1933; Sc.D., Pomona Coll.; m. Doris A. Whitmer, Aug. 26, 1938; children—Franklyn W., Melodie M. (Mrs. James Rice), Phillip L. Metallurgist, Lindberg Steel Treating Co., Chgo., 1934-36; metall. engr. Bliss & Laughlin, Harvey, Ill., 1936-43; v.p., tech. dir. Pendleton Tool Industries (formerly Proto Tool Co., now Ingersoll Rand), Los Angeles, 1943-57; pres. Sierra Drawn Steel Corp., Los Angeles, 1946-60, Metall. Consultants, Inc., Montebello, Calif., 1954-60, dir., 1954—; pres. Phillips-Robbins, Inc., Los Angeles, 1958-62; pres., chief exec. officer, dir. Bliss & Laughlin Industries, Inc., Oak Brook, Ill., 1960-73; dir. Emhart Corp., Electronic Mem. and Mag. Corp., Fredor Industries. Trustee Pomona Coll., Claremont, Calif., 1976—; past nat. trustee, del. First World Met. Congress. Registered profl. engr., Calif. Mem. Am. Soc. Metals, Newcomen Soc. N. Am., Am. Soc. Metals, ASTM, Soc. Automotive Engrs. Club: Rotary. Home: Box 1957 Rancho Santa Fe CA 92067 Office: Suite 202 Picklair Bldg Rancho Santa Fe CA 92067

ROBBINS, FREDERICK CHAPMAN, physician; b. Auburn, Ala., Aug. 25, 1916; s. William J. and Christine (Chapman) R.; A.B., U. Mo., 1936, B.S., 1938; M.D., Harvard, 1940; D.Sc. (hon.), John Carroll U., 1955, U. Mo., 1958; LL.D., U. N.Mex., 1968; m. Alice Havemeyer Northrop, June 19, 1948; children—Alice, Louise. Sr. fellow virus disease NRC, 1948-50; staff research div. infectious diseases Children's Hosp., Boston, 1948-50, asso. physician, asso. dir. isolation service, asso. research div. infectious diseases, 1950-52; instr., asso. in pediatrics Harvard Med. Sch., 1950-52; dir. dept. pediatrics and contagious diseases Cleve. Met. Gen. Hosp., 1952-66; asso. pediatrician U. Hosps., Cleve., 1952—; prof. pediatrics Case-Western Res. U., 1952—, dean Sch. Medicine, 1966—; vis. scientist Donner Lab., U. Calif., 1963-64. Served as maj. AUS, 1942-46; chief virus and rickettsial disease sect. 15th Med. Gen. Lab.; investigations infectious hepatitis, typhus fever and Q fever. Decorated Bronze Star, 1945; received 1st Mead Johnson prize application tissue culture methods to study of viral infections, 1953; co-recipient Nobel prize in physiology and medicine, 1954; Med. Mut. Honor Award for 1969. Diplomate Am. Bd. Pediatrics. Mem. Am. Epidemiol. Soc., Am. Acad. Arts and Scis., Am. Soc. Clin. Investigation (emeritus mem.), Am. Acad. Pediatrics, Soc. Pediatric Research (pres. 1961-62, emeritus mem.), Am. Assn. Immunologists, Soc. Exptl. Biol. and Medicine, Am. Pediatric Soc., Nat. Acad. Scis., Nat. Inst. Medicine, Am. Philos. Soc., Phi Beta Kappa, Sigma Xi, Phi Gamma Delta. Home: 2467 Guilford Rd Cleveland Heights OH 44118 Office: 2119 Abington St Cleveland OH 44106

ROBBINS, HAROLD, author; b. N.Y.C., May 21, 1916; student pub. schs., N.Y.C.; m. Lillian Machnivitz (div.); m. 2d, Grace Palermo; children—Caryn, Adreana. In food factoring bus. until 1940; shipping clk. Universal Pictures, N.Y.C., 1940-46; author: Never Love a Stranger, 1948; The Dream Merchants, 1949; A Stone for Danny Fisher, 1952; Never Leave Me, 1953; 79 Park Avenue, 1955; Stiletto, 1960; The Carpetbaggers, 1961; Where Love Has Gone, 1962; The Adventurers, 1966; The Inheritors, 1969; The Betsy, 1971; The Adventures, 1972; The Pirate, 1974; Lonely Lady, 1976; Dreams Die First, 1977; Memories of Another Day, 1979. Home: South of France Office: care Simon & Schuster 1230 6th Ave New York NY 10009

ROBBINS, HENRY ZANE, pub. relations exec.; b. Winston-Salem, N.C., Jan. 17, 1930; s. Romulus Mayfield and Vera Ethel (Daniel) R.; A.B., U. N.C., 1952; student Emory U., 1952; m. Barbara Anne Brown, Jan. 19, 1955; children—Zane Scott, Jill Stewart, Gail Ruth. Reporter, Atlanta Constn., 1952; exhibit specialist Gen. Electric Co., Schenectady, 1952, employee relations specialist, Cin., 1955, editor, Schenectady, 1955, account supr., Winston-Salem, 1956-58, group supr., Schenectady, 1958-60; v.p., gen. mgr. Burson-Marsteller, Pitts. and Chgo., 1960-70; pres., chief exec. officer SLEH-Robbins Inc., Chgo., 1970-72, also dir.; pres., chief exec. officer Beveridge Kraus Robbins & Manning, Chgo., 1973-75, also dir.; pres., dir., chief exec. officer Beveridge and Robbins Inc., Chgo., 1975-78; pres., chief exec. officer Financial Advt. of Ill., Inc., Chgo.; mng. dir. Sports Mgmt. Group, Chgo., 1975-78; dir. communications Arthur Andersen & Co., Chgo. and Geneva, Switzerland, 1978—, sr. adminstrn. exec., 1979—. Mem. journalism adv. com. William Rainey Harper Coll.; pub. relations com. Chgo. Met. Crusade Mercy; mem. Nat. Task Force on Environment; cons. sec. Dept. Health, Edn. and Welfare, 1970; chmn. pub. relations com. Honor Am. Day Com., 1970; counselor Council of Mojave, 1972-74; gen. chmn. Chgo. Children's Classic Golf Tournament, 1974—; chmn. Chgo. fin. com. Am.'s Freedom Train, 1976; chmn. fund devel. com. Presbytery of Chgo., 1977—, maj. mission fund, 1977-79; dist. commr. Boy Scouts Am., 1976-79, chmn. Wildcat dist., 1980—, mem. exec. bd. N.E. Ill. council, 1980—. Mem. Republican Citizens Com. Ill., 1960-61, Allegheny County (Pa.) Rep. Com., 1962-65. Trustee, Roycemore Sch., Evanston, 1971-74; trustee, v.p. devel. Child and Family Services Chgo.; bd. dirs. Fellowship of Christian Athletes, U. N.C. Alumni Ill., Little Sisters of Poor, Stockbrokers Assn. Chgo. Served to 1st lt. AUS, 1952-54. Mem. Pub. Relations Soc. Am. (counselors sect.), Nat. Investor Relations Inst., Midwest Travel Writers Assn., Chgo. Ednl. TV Assn., Pub. Relations Counselors Roundtable, Am. Mgmt. Assn., Envrion. Writers Assn. Am., Chgo. Assn. Commerce and Industry, Art Inst. Chgo., Chi Psi. Republican. Presbyn. (elder). Clubs: Press, University, Whitehall, Publicity (Chgo.); Pickwick (Niles, Mich.); Sunset Ridge Country (Winnetka, Ill.); Curtis Curling (Wilmette, Ill.). Contbr. articles to profl. jours. Home: 2759 Broadway Ave Evanston IL 60201 Office: 69 W Washington St Chicago IL 60602

ROBBINS, HERBERT ELLIS, educator; b. New Castle, Pa., Jan. 12, 1915; s. Mark Louis and Celia (Klebansky) R.; A.B., Harvard, 1935, Ph.D., 1938; Sc.D., Purdue U., 1974; m. Mary Dimock, 1943 (div. 1955); children—Mary Susannah, Marcia (Mrs. Weston T. Borden); m. 2d, Carol Hallett, 1966; children—Mark Hallett, David Herbert, Emily Carol. Instr. math. N.Y. U., 1939-42; asso. prof. math. statistics U. N.C., 1946-50, prof., 1950-52; prof. math. statistics Columbia, 1953-66, 68—; prof. math. U. Mich., Ann Arbor, 1966-68; mem. Inst. Advanced Study, 1938-39, 52-53; Guggenheim fellow, 1952, 75. Served with USNR, 1942-46. Mem. Inst. Math. Statistics (pres. 1966), Internat. Statis. Inst., Nat. Acad. Scis., Am. Acad. Arts and Scis. Author: (with R. Courant) What is Mathematics?, 1941; (with Y.S. Chow and D. Siegmund) Great Expectations: The Theory of Optimal Stopping, 1971; (with J. Van Ryzin) Introduction to Statistics, 1975. Contbr. profl. jours. Office: Dept of Math Statistics Columbia U New York City NY 10027

ROBBINS, HULDA DORNBLATT, printmaker; b. Atlanta, Oct. 19, 1910; d. Adolph Benno and Lina (Rosenthal) Dornblatt; student Phila. Mus's. Sch. Indsl. Art, 1928-29, Prussian Acad., Berlin, 1929-31, Barnes Found., Merion, Pa., 1939. Poster designer and maker ITE Circuit Breaker Co. Inc., Phila., 1944; instr. serigraphy Nat. Serigraph Soc. Sch., N.Y.C., 1953-60; instr. creative painting Atlantic County Jewish Community Centers, Margate and Atlantic City, N.J., 1960-67; one-man shows Lehigh U. Art Galleries, 1933, ACA Galleries, Phila., 1939, 8th St. Gallery, N.Y.C., 1941, Serigraph Gallery, N.Y.C., 1947, Atlantic City Art Center, 1961, 71; numerous group shows 2d Nat. Print ann. Bklyn. Mus., Carnegie Inst., Library of Congress, LaNapoule Art Found., Am. Graphic Contemporary Art; represented in permanent collections, including Met. Mus. Art, N.Y.C., Mus. Modern Art, N.Y.C., Bibliotheque Nationale, Smithsonian Instn., Art Mus. Ont. (Can.), Victoria and Albert Mus., London, U.S. embassies abroad, Lehigh U., Princeton (N.J.) Print Club. Recipient Purchase prize Prints for Children, Mus. Modern Art, N.Y.C., 1941; prize 2d Portrait of Am. Competition, 1945, 2d prize Paintings by Printmakers, 1948. Mem. Am. Color Print Soc., Print Club, Graphics Soc., Serigraph Soc. (mem. founding group, charter sec., Ninth Ann. prize 1948, 49). Home and Office: 16 S Buffalo Ave Ventnor NJ 08406. *To cherish and express living through devotion to art.*

ROBBINS, JEROME, choreographer, director; b. N.Y.C., Oct. 11, 1918; s. Harry and Lena (Rips) R; student N.Y. U., 1935-36; D.F.A. (hon.), Ohio U., 1974; studied ballet, modern, Spanish and Oriental dance. Debut as dancer Sandor-Sorel Dance Center, 1937; dancer Broadway musicals Great Lady, Stars in Your Eyes, Keep Off the Grass, Straw Hat Review, 1938-40; dancer Ballet Theatre, N.Y.C., 1940-44, soloist 1941-44; choreographer ballets for Ballet Theatre, 1944-48; choreographer New York City Ballet, 1949—, asso. artistic dir., 1949-59, ballet master, 1969—; ballets: U.S.A., 1958-61 (also founder and artistic dir.), Am. Ballet Theatre, Joffrey Ballet, Royal Swedish Ballet, Batsheva Ballet, Royal Danish Ballet, Boston Ballet, Nat. Ballet Can., Harkness Ballet, Royal Ballet (London), Australian Ballet, San Francisco Ballet, Pa. Ballet, Dance Theatre of Harlem, Paris Opera Ballet, Bayerischen Staatsoper Munich; ballets include: Fancy Free, 1944, Interplay, 1945, The Cage, 1951, Fanfare, 1953, Afternoon of a Faun, 1953, N.Y. Export: Opus Jazz, 1958, Moves, 1959, Les Noces, 1965, Dances at a Gathering, 1969, In the Night, 1970, The Goldberg Variations, 1971, Watermill, 1972, Dybbuk Variations, 1974, Concerto in G (later in G Major), 1975, Ma Mere l'oye, 1975, Chansons Madecasses, 1975, Other Dances, 1976, Tricolore, 1978, A Sketch Book, 1978, The Four Seasons, 1979, Le Bourgeois Gentilhomme, 1979; choreographer Broadway musicals On the Town (based on ballet Fancy Free), 1945, Billion Dollar Baby, 1946, High Button Shoes, 1947, Miss Liberty, 1949, Call Me Madam, 1950, The King and I, 1951, Two's Company, 1952; dir. and choreographer stage musicals Peter Pan, 1954, Bells Are Ringing, 1956, West Side Story (Donaldson and Antoinette Perry awards), 1957, Gypsy, 1959, Fiddler on the Roof (Antoinette Perry awards for choreography and direction), 1964, TV versions Peter Pan, 1955-60 (Emmy award); co-dir. (with George Abbott) Pajama Game (stage version), 1952; prodn. supr. Funny Girl (stage version), 1964; choreographer motion pictures The King and I, 1956, West Side Story (Academy Awards for choreography and direction, Screen Dirs. Guild award, Laurel award), 1960; dir. plays Oh Dad Poor Dad Mama's Hung You in the Closet and I'm Feeling So Sad, 1962, Mother Courage and Her Children, 1963. Mem. panel N.Y. Council on Arts, 1973-77, Nat. Council on Arts, Nat. Endowment for Arts, 1974—. Recipient numerous awards for productions including: 5 Donaldson awards, 4 Antoinette Perry awards, 2 Academy Awards, and Sylvania, Emmy, Dance Magazine, Box Office Blue Ribbon, Evening Standard Drama (London), Screen Dirs. Guild, Laurel, Drama Critics, and City of Paris awards, Capezio Dance award, 1976, Handel Medallion, N.Y.C., 1976; named best choreographer, Theatre des Nations, 1959; decorated chevalier Order Arts and Letters, 1964. Office: 117 E 81st St New York NY 10028 also NYC Ballet NY State Theater Lincoln Center New York NY 10023

ROBBINS, JEROME WALTER, mfg. co. exec.; b. N.Y.C., July 26, 1925; s. Mayer and Rose (Reiter) R.; student Cornell U., 1943-44; B.S., U.S. Naval Acad., 1947; student Grad. Sch. Bus., Columbia, 1950-51; m. Patricia Davis, Oct. 9, 1949; children—Cynthia, Richard. Enlisted in USNR, 1943, commd. ensign, 1947, advanced through grades to lt., 1953, ret., 1960; advt. mgr. Norman M. Morris Corp., N.Y.C., 1950-58, nat. sales mgr., marketing dir., 1958-62; asst. to pres., dir. planning Bulova Watch Co., N.Y.C., 1962-65; pres., chief exec. officer Elgin Nat. Watch Co. (Ill.), 1965-68, also dir.; v.p. Brunswick Corp., Chgo., 1968-70, pres. Mac Gregor div., 1970-71; pres., chief exec. officer HMW Industries, Inc. (formerly Hamilton Watch Co.), 1971—, chmn. bd., dir., 1973—. Mem. N.Y.C. Sales Execs. Club, Chgo. Econ. Club. Club: Rotary. Home: 700 N Wilton Rd New Canaan CT 06840

ROBBINS, JERRY HAL, univ. adminstr.; b. DeQueen, Ark., Feb. 18, 1939; s. James Hal and Barbara I. (Rogers) R.; B.A. in Math., Hendrix Coll., 1960; M.Ed., U. Ark., 1963, Ed.D., 1966. Tchr. math. and music Clinton (Ark.) pub. schs., 1960-61; prin. Adrian (Mo.) High Sch., 1961-63; exec. sec. Ark. Sch. Study Council, Fayetteville, 1963-65; mem. faculty U. Miss., University, 1965-74, prof. ednl. adminstrn., 1970-74, chmn. dept. ednl. adminstrn., 1970-74; dean Coll. Edn., U. Ark., Little Rock, 1974-79; asso. v.p. for acad. affairs Ga. State U., Atlanta, 1979—. Mem. NEA, Am. Assn. Sch. Adminstrs., Am. Assn. Colls. Tchr. Edn. (dir. 1979—), Nat. Assn.

Secondary Sch. Prins., So. Regional Council Ednl. Adminstrn. (pres. 1970-71), Phi Delta Kappa, Kappa Delta Pi (v.p. chpt. devel. 1978—). Methodist. Author: (with S.B. williams, Jr.) Student Activities in the Innovative School, 1969, School Custodian's Handbook, 1970, Adminstrator's Manual of School Plant Administration, 1970. Home: 90 Forest Pl Atlanta GA 30328 Office: 132 Sparks Hall Georgia State Univ Atlanta GA 30303

ROBBINS, JOHN CLAPP, mgmt. cons.; b. Cleve., Jan. 22, 1921; s. John Clapp and Esther Turner (Holland) R.; A.B., Harvard U., 1942; m. Louise Severance Nash, Jan. 10, 1951 (div. Oct. 1974); children—Anne Millikin, Julia Severance, John Nash; m. Beatrice Blair, Aug. 2, 1975. Copy boy, reporter, writer, promotion editor Cleve. Press, 1946-57; exec. internat. div. Mobil Oil Corp., N.Y.C., Istanbul, 1957-70; chief exec. officer Planned Parenthood/World Population, N.Y.C., 1970-75; prin. mgmt. cons. Stanford Research Inst., 1976—. Bd. dirs. Am. Hosp. of Istanbul. Served to capt. AUS, 1942-45. Decorated Bronze Star, Purple Heart; Reid fellow, 1953. Mem. Internat. Planned Parenthood Fedn. London. Republican. Unitarian. Club: Harvard (N.Y.C.). Author: Too Many Asians, 1959. Home: 1056 Fifth Ave New York NY 10028 Office: Menlo Park CA 94025

ROBBINS, LAURENCE LAMSON, physician; b. Burlington, Vt., Mar. 26, 1911; s. George E. and Grace L. (Lamson) R.; student Ohio Wesleyan Coll., 1929-32; B.S., U. Vt., 1935, M.D., 1937, Sc.D. (hon.), 1973; m. Ruth Dick, Feb. 18, 1932; children—Dick L., Carol, Janice. Rotating intern Mary Fletcher Hosp., Burlington, 1937-38, resident, instr. pathology and roentgenology, 1938-39; resident radiology Mass. Gen. Hosp., 1939-41, radiologist, 1941-46, radiologist-in-chief, 1946-71, radiologist, 1971—, Aubrey O. Hampton lectr., 1972; asso. clin. prof. radiology Harvard Med. Sch., 1954-60, clin. prof., 1960-69, prof. radiology, 1969—. Holmes lectr. N.E. Roentgen Ray Soc., 1956; vis. prof. Brazilian Coll. Radiology, 1972. Nat. Adv. Com. Radiation, 1964-67; adv. council radiation protection Dept. Pub. Health, 1965—; sci. adv. bd. cons. Armed Forces Inst. Pathology, 1968—; mem. med. radiation adv. com. Bur. Radiol. Health, USPHS, 1968—, chmn., 1962—; cons. to surgeon gen. Navy, 1972—. Bd. dirs. James Picker Found., 1963—, pres. bd. 1964-69. Mem. Radiol. Soc. N.A. (pres. 1959; Gold medal 1968), N.E. Roentgen Ray Soc. (pres. 1953-54), AMA (chmn. radiology 1955), Am. Bd. Radiology (pres. 1960-63, trustee 1954-72), Am. Roentgen Ray Soc., Am. Coll. of Radiology (Gold medal 1970), Alpha Omega Alpha. Author: Roentgen Interpretation, 1955. Editor: Golden's Diagnostic Radiology, 1959. Home: 98 Cambridge St Winchester MA 01890 Office: 265 Charles St Boston MA 02114

ROBBINS, MARTY (MARTIN DAVID ROBINSON), musician; b. Glendale, Ariz., Sept. 26, 1925; s. Jack Joe and Emma (Heckle) R.; grad. high sch.; m. Marizona Baldwin, June 16, 1945; children—Ronny, Janet. Mem. Grand Ole Opry, Nashville, 1954—; artist CBS Records, 1952-72, MCA Records, 1972-74, Columbia Records, 1975—; pres. Marioposa Music, 1960—, Maricopa Music, 1960—, Maricana Music, 1960—, Charger Records, 1970—, all Nashville; composer over 500 songs; starred in 8 movies; operator cattle farm, Franklin, Tenn., 1965—; star syndicated TV show Marty Robbins' Spotlight, 1977—; also auto racer. Recipient gold records, platinum records, Gold Guitars, ASCAP awards, BMI awards, Grammy awards; Gold Trustees' medal for outstanding contbn. to Western heritage through music Nat. Cowboy Hall of Fame, 1979. Mem. Nat. Assn. Stock Car Racing, Am. Fedn. Musicians, Country Music Assn., Acad. Country and Western Music Assn., AFTRA, Screen Actors Guild. Composer: A White Sport Coat, 1955; El Paso, 1956; Devil Woman, 1962; You Gave Me a Mountain, 1966; Don't Worry, 1960; My Woman, My Woman, My Wife, 1970. Author: (novel) Small Man, 1966. Home: Brentwood TN 37027 Office: 713 18th Ave South Nashville TN 37203

ROBBINS, PAUL HEBERT, engr.; b. Syracuse, N.Y., Feb. 15, 1914; s. James H. and Jessie E. (Lair) R.; B.S. Syracuse (N.Y.) Univ., 1935; S.M., Mass. Inst. Tech., 1936; postgrad. Columbia, 1938-41; D.Eng., Rose Poly. Inst., 1964, Norwich U., 1979; m. Hester Becker, Apr. 24, 1937; children—Susan Jane, David Paul. Draftsman and estimator Pitts. Bridge & Iron Works, 1936-37; mem. civil engring. faculty Cooper Union, 1937-41, U. Me., summers 1938, 39, 40, N.Y. U., summer 1939; lectr. civil engring. Cooper Union, 1941-46; cons. engring. tng. City of N.Y., 1941-43, expert examiner (engring.), 1938-42; dir. civilian tng. N.Y. Port of Embarkation, 1943-45, dir. tng. and employee relations, 1945-46; exec. dir. Nat. Soc. Profl. Engrs., Washington, 1946-72; sec. Nat. Soc. Profl. Engrs. Ednl. Found. Mem. several adv. coms. to Fed. Govt. Bd. visitors Norwich U. Served as cons. on tng. U.S. Army Transp. Corp, 1944-46. Received War Dept. Commendation for Meritorious Service, 1946. Registered profl. engr. Fellow AAAS; mem. Soc. Am. Mil. Engrs., Nat. Soc. Profl. Engrs., Jr. Engring. Tech. Soc. (dir.), Am. Soc. Engring. Edn., Tau Beta Pi (dir. fellowships), Phi Kappa Phi, Delta Sigma Rho, Sigma Tau. Republican. Conglist. Clubs: University, Columbia, Rotary. Author: (with B.B. Talley) Photographic Surveying, 1944. Home: 1601 Myrtle Rd Silver Spring MD 20902 Office: 2029 K St NW Washington DC 20006

ROBBINS, RAY CHARLES, corp. exec.; b. Syracuse, N.Y., Sept. 15, 1920; s. Frederick and Mary Elizabeth R.; children—Sandra Robbins Jannetta, Ray Charles. With Lennox Industries, Inc., 1940—, pres. Lennox-Can. div., 1967-76, corp. exec. v.p., Marshalltown, Iowa, 1969-71, pres., chief exec. officer Lennox world wide, 1971-77, chmn. bd. Lennox-Can., 1976—, chmn. bd., chief exec. officer Lennox Industries, Inc., 1977-80, chmn. bd., 1980—; dir. Central Nat. Bancshares, Inc., Des Moines, 1978—, Fin. Security Ins. Co., Des Moines, 1976—, Marshalltown Savs. and Loan Assn., 1971-77, Central Nat. Bank & Trust Co., Des Moines, 1971-78, Northeastern Ins. Co. of Hartford, Hawkeye Security Ins. Co., 1976-78. Bd. dirs. Metro Toronto Big Bros., 1964-69, Queensway Gen. Hosp., 1957-69; bd. govs., mem. exec. com. Iowa Coll. Found., 1975-78; v.p., mem. exec. bd. Mid Iowa County Boy Scouts Am., 1974-78; dir. Texx Found., 1979—; mem. Pres.' Phys. Fitness Council, 1979—; exec. bd. Circle 10 Council Boy Scouts Am., 1979—. Mem. ASHRAE (dir. 1973-74, v.p. 1975-76, chmn. bd. 1977, dir. 1974-75, dir. at large 1976, dir. State of Iowa 1977-78, dir. State of Tex. 1979-80), Nat. Assn. Mfrs. (dir.), Nat. Mgmt. Assn. (mem. exec. adv. com.), Gas Appliance Mfrs. Assn. (past dir.). Club: Brookhaven Country. Home: 16510 Fallkirk Dallas TX 75248 Office: Lennox Industries Inc Promenade Tower Box 400450 Dallas TX 75240

ROBBINS, ROBERT R., educator; b. Dayton, Ohio, Feb. 17, 1909; s. Bert O. and Lulu (Beamer) R.; A.B., Ohio State U., 1932, M.A., 1934, Ph.D., 1941; grad. study, Alliance Francaise, Paris, France, 1933, Harvard, 1937-38, Acad. Internat. Law, The Hague, 1936, U. Mich.; A.M.L.D., Fletcher Sch. Law and Diplomacy, 1940; A.M., Columbia, 1943; m. Rebecca Nichols, Sept. 3, 1941 (dec. Apr. 1970); children—Sarah Brooks (Mrs. Lorenzo M. Horne), David Sears. Instr., asst. prof. govt. Tufts Coll., 1935-42; asst. prof. polit. sci. Ohio State U., 1946; specialist on dependent area affairs U.S. Dept. State, 1946-47, exec. chief, 1948-49; exec. asst. to dir. gen. Internat. Refugee Orgn., 1947-48; officer-in-charge non-self-governing Territories Affairs, 1949-53, dep.-dir. Office Dependent Area Affairs, 1953-56; Carnegie fellow Council on Fgn. Relations, Inc., N.Y.C., 1956-57; research asso. Columbia U., 1956-57; prof. polit. sci., 1957—, chmn. dept. polit. sci. Tufts U., 1957-69, prof. Fletcher Sch. Law and Diplomacy, 1957-74, Jackson prof. polit. sci., 1958-74, prof. emeritus, 1974—. U.S. mem. working com. Caribbean Commn., 1949-54, acting U.S. sr. commr., 1953; alternate U.S. commr. S. Pacific Commn., 1951—, acting sr. commr., 1951, U.S. acting sr. commr., 1953, to S. Pacific Conf., 1950, 53; mem. U.S. delegations U.N. meetings, including 4th, 8th, 9th, 10th Gen. Assemblies; U.S. mem. UN Vis. Mission to Togolands, 1955; 1st legistive counsel Congress Micronesia, 1965; spl. polit. adviser Trust Ty. Pacific Islands, 1965-66. Mem. corp. Lawrence Meml. Hosp.; bd. dirs. Royall House Assn.; mem. alumni council Tufts U.; chmn. bd. trustees Unitarian-Universalist Ch. of Medford, vice chmn. bd. dirs. CLF Unitarian Universalist, 1978—. Served from lt. (j.g.) to comdr. USNR, 1942-46, comdg. officer, 1954, Internat. Affairs Co. Mem. Am. Soc. Internat. Law, Am. Polit. Sci. Assn., New Eng. Polit. Assn. (pres. 1970), ACLU, Phi Mu Alpha Sinfonia. Editor: State Government and Public Responsibility, Vol. 1, 1959, Vol. 2, 1960, Vol. 3, 1961, Vol. 4, 1962, Vol. 5, 1964, Vol. 6, 1965. Contbr. articles to profl. jours., Ency. Americana. Home: 51 Mystic St West Medford MA 02155. *Continual change being the immutable natural law, one should avoid use of the words "ever", "never," and "always" in human affairs. Human beings must plan for the future and fortunately without prescience. Strength and steadfastness derive from the thought that life's vicissitudes, however painful, can be interesting and will pass.*

ROBBINS, ROGER RANSOM, bus. exec.; b. Ventura, Calif., Apr. 17, 1923; s. Lowell W. and Jennie Rhea (Ransom) R.; B.S., U. So. Calif., 1948; m. Geraldine Solaman, May 17, 1947; children—Lowell, Todd. Chief accountant Los Angeles Shopping News, 1948-49; with Purex Corp., Ltd., Lakewood, Calif., 1950—, now exec. v.p. grocery, drug and toiletries. Served with AUS, 1942-45. Home: 3558 Bravata Dr Huntington Beach CA 92649 Office: 5101 Clark Ave Lakewood CA 90712

ROBBINS, ROSSELL HOPE, medievalist; b. Wallasey, Eng., July 22, 1912; s. Rossell Casson and Alice (Hope) R.; B.A. with honours, Liverpool (Eng.) U., 1933, dip. edn., 1934; Ph.D., Emmanuel Coll., Cambridge (Eng.) U., 1937; licentiate Guildhall Sch. Music, London, 1932, Matthay Sch. Music, Liverpool, 1935; m. Helen Ann Mins, June 9, 1939; came to U.S., 1937, naturalized, 1944. Dir. studies Cambridge U., 1935-37; instr. Bklyn. Coll., 1942; staff cons. Nat. Inst. Social Relations, Washington, 1946; asst. prof., then asso. prof. Bklyn. Poly. Inst., 1946-54; vis. prof. U. N.C., 1958; Can. Council prof. Mt. Allison U., 1965; vis. prof. Duke, 1965, Sir George Williams U., 1968; internat. prof. State U. N.Y. at Albany, 1969—; Beckman prof. U. Calif. at Berkeley, 1966; Regents' prof. U. Calif. at Riverside, 1968-69; vis. scholar Univ. Center in Va., Richmond, 1966, California (Pa.) State Coll., 1969; First Thomas Kirby lectr. La. State U., 1976; vis. lectr. throughout U.S., Can., Europe, Japan, 1957—, Brit. U. Tchrs. English, 1962; overseas speaker Brit. Assn. Advancement Sci., 1963, Humanities Assn. Can., 1966, 69, Internat. Musicol. Soc., Ljubljana, 1967, Federation internationale des langues et littératures modernes, Islamabad, 1969, Sydney (Australia), 1975, Internat. Assn. U. Profs. English, Istanbul, 1971; faculty asso. Columbia, 1956-66. Served with U.S. Army, 1943-46. Commonwealth Fund fellow N.Y. U., 1937-39; Noble fellow Liverpool U., 1939-40; Guggenheim fellow, 1955-56; Ford vis. fellow Harvard, 1958, 59; State U. N.Y. research fellow, 1971, 72, sr. fellow Inst. Humanistic Studies, 1977. Fellow Medieval Club N.Y. (pres. 1977-79), Royal Soc. Lit.; mem. AAUP, Mediaeval Acad., Modern Lang. Assn. (chmn. Middle English bibliography com. 1959—, chmn. div. 22, 1975-78), Renaissance Soc., Internat. Assn. U. Profs. English, Modern Humanities Research Assn., Anglo-Norman Text Soc., Early English Text Soc., N.Y. Folklore Soc., Internat. Court Lit. Assn., New Chaucer Soc., Middle English Text Soc. (U.S. dir.). Author: (with C. Brown) The Index of Middle English Verse, 1943; Christopher Marlowe: Dr. Faustus, 2d edit., 1967; The T.S. Eliot Myth, 2d edit., 1964; Secular Lyrics of the XIV and XV Centuries, 2d edit., 1955; Historical Poems of XIV and XV Centuries, 1959; Encyclopedia of Witchcraft and Demonology, 15th edit., 1978; The Hundred Tales, 2d edit., 1962; Early English Christmas Carols, 1961; (with J. Cutler) Supplement to the Index of Middle English Verse, 1966; The Chaucerian Apocrypha, 1973; Poems Dealing with Contemporary Conditions, 1975; Chaucer at Albany, 1975; Witchcraft: Introduction to the Literature, 1978; also numerous articles; gen. editor: Old English and Middle English, Lexikon des Mittelalters, 1975; Middle English Texts & Contexts, 1975; hon. gen. editor: The Index of Middle English Prose, 1978; mem. editorial bd. Medievalia of Humanistica; Vita etc in Chaucer and Middle English Studies in Honour of Rossell Hope Robbins, 1974. Address: Katsbaan Onderheugel 6163 Shear Rd Saugerties NY 12477 also 8 W 13th St New York City NY 10011

ROBBINS, WARREN MURRAY, mus. dir.; b. Worcester, Mass., Sept. 4, 1923; s. Harry Leo and Pauline (Sharfman) R.; B.A., U. N.H., 1945, D.H.L., 1979; M.A., U. Mich., 1949; L.L.D., Lebanon Valley Coll., 1975; D.H.L., Internat. Coll., 1979. Aviation editor, feature writer Worcester Gazette, 1945; tchr. pvt. schs., N.H., Am. Sch. System, West Germany, 1948-50; lectr. U.S. Cultural program, Germany, 1950; editor, edn. advisor U.S. High Commn. to Austria, 1951-55; consul for cultural and pub. affairs, Stuttgart, Germany, 1955-57; attache, chief Am. cultural program, Bonn, Germany, 1958-60; asst. staff dir. U.S. Adv. Commn. on Edn. and Cultural Relations, Dept. State, Washington, 1960-61, asst. to dep. asst. sec. of state for edn. and cultural relations, 1961-62; course chmn. Fgn. Service Inst., Dept. State, 1962-63; founder, dir. Center for Cross Cultural Communication, Washington, 1962—, Mus. African Art, Washington, 1963—; lectr. in field; tutor Internat. Coll. Bd. dirs. Duke Ellington Sch. Arts, Big Brothers, Iscari Found., D.C. Citizens for Better Public Edn., African Student Aid Fund, Inst. Study Nat. Behavior; mem. adv. council Dept. of State Bur. of African Affairs, 1971-72; mem. D.C. Commn. Arts and Humanities, 1975-79, arts adv. com. Library Congress. Served to lt. CAP, USAF Aux., 1943-45. Recipient award Delta Sigma Theta, 1972; decorated Order of Merit (Republic of Cameroon); named Washingtonian of Year, 1975. Mem. Am. Assn. Mus., Am. Assn. Art Mus. Dirs., Capitol Hill Restoration Soc. Clubs: Cosmos, Explorers, Capitol Press. Author: African Art in American Collections, 1966. Editor Kontinente, 1952-55; contbg. editor Transformation, 1949-50; editorial adv. bd. African Arts Jour.; editor, pub. exhbn. catalogues: The Sculptor's Eye, Traditional Art of Nigerian Peoples, The Language of African Art, Tribute to Africa, Creative Heritage of Africa. Contbr. articles to mags. and newspapers. Office: 316-332 A St NE Washington DC 20002

ROBBINS, WILLIAM ANDERSEN, magazine editor; b. N.Y.C., May 15, 1925; s. Harry William and Adele Hunter (Andersen) R.; B.A., Hamilton Coll., Clinton, N.Y., 1949; postgrad. Columbia U., 1949-50; m. Ruth Hubbell Eddy, May 5, 1951; children—Carol Elizabeth, Scott Andersen. Founder, co-editor Gambit mag., 1951-52; asso. editor Prentice-Hall Co., 1952-55; asso. editor, mng. editor various publs. Mag. Mgmt. Co., 1955-58; editor-in-chief Banner mags., 1958-59; articles editor, then mng. editor Pageant mag., 1959-63, exec. editor, 1963-65; sr. editor, then mng. editor Redbook mag., N.Y.C., 1965-78, exec. editor, 1978—; mem. faculty N.Y. U., summer 1967. Sec. Shorewood Civic Assn., Shelter Island, N.Y., 1967—. Served with AUS, 1943-46. Decorated Combat Inf. badge, Purple Heart. Mem. Am. Soc. Mag. Editors, Phi Beta Kappa. Clubs: Hot, Quintet of Hot Club (co-founder) (Scarsdale, N.Y.). Home: 28 Jones St New York City NY 10014 Office: Redbook Mag 230 Park Ave New York City NY 10017

ROBBINS-LEET, MILDRED, civic worker; b. N.Y.C., Aug. 9, 1922; d. Samuel Milton and Isabella (Zeitz) Elowsky; B.A., N.Y.U., 1942; m. Louis J. Robbins, Feb. 23, 1941 (dec. 1970); children—Jane, Aileen; m. 2d, Glen Leet, Aug. 9, 1974. Pres. women's div. United Cerebral Palsy, N.Y.C., 1951-52, bd. dirs., 1953—, chmn. bd., 1953-55; rep. Nat. Council Women U.S. at UN, 1957-64, 1st v.p., 1959-64, pres., 1964-68, hon. pres., 1968-70; sec., v.p. conf. group U.S. Nat. Orgns. at UN, 1961-64, 76—, vice chmn. sec., 1962-64, mem. exec. com., 1961-65, 75—, chmn. hospitality info. service, 1960-66; vice chairperson exec. com. NGO's with UN Office Pub. Info., 1976-78, chmn. ann. conf., 1977; chairperson com. on water, desertification, habitat and environment Conf. NGO's with consultative status with UN/ECOSOC 1976—; mem. exec. com. Internat. Council Women, 1960-73, v.p., 1970-73; chmn. program planning com., women's com. OEO, 1967-72; chmn. com. on natural disasters N.Am. Com. on Environment, 1973-77; N.Y. State chairperson UN Day, 1975; with Leet & Leet, cons. women in devel., 1979. Co-chmn. Vols. for Stevenson, N.Y.C., 1956; vice chmn. task force Nat. Democratic Com., 1969-72; commr. N.Y. State Commn. on Powers Local Govt., 1970-73. Vice chmn. Coll. for Human Services; bd. dirs. Am. Arbitration Assn., Save the Children Fedn.; sec. Inst. for Mediation and Conflict Resolution, Spirit of Stockholm, Hotline Internat.; rep. Internat. Peace Acad. at UN, 1974-77, Internat. Soc. Community Devel., 1977—; del. at large 1st Nat. Women's Conf., Houston, 1977; chmn. task force on internat. interdependence N.Y. State Women's Meeting, 1977; bd. dirs. New Directions; mem. Task Force on Poverty, 1977—; chmn. Task Force on Women, Sci. and Tech. for Devel., 1978; U.S. del. UN Status of Women Commn.; U.S. del. UN Conf. Sci. and Tech. for Devel., 1979. Author articles. Editor: Measure of Mankind, 1963. Home: 54 Riverside Dr New York NY 10024 also 2 Briar Oak Dr Weston CT 06883 Office: 790 Madison Ave New York NY 10021

ROBENALT, JOHN ALTON, lawyer; b. Ottawa, Ohio, May 2, 1922; s. Alton Ray and Kathryn (Straman) R.; B.A., Miami U., 1943; LL.B., Ohio State U., 1948, J.D., 1948; m. Margaret Morgan Durbin, Aug. 25, 1951; children—John F., William A., James D., Robert M., Mary K., Margaret E., Thomas D. Admitted to Ohio bar, 1948; asst. atty. gen. Ohio, 1949-51; practice in Lima, Ohio, 1951-59; acting municipal judge Lima Municipal Ct., 1955-59; partner firm Robenalt, Daley, Balyeat & Balyeat, 1959—. Chmn. Lima March of Dimes, 1957-58. Bd. dirs. Lima Civic Center, pres., 1971-72; bd. dirs. Lima Rotating Fund; trustee Allen County Regional Transit Authority, Lima, pres., 1975—. Served with AUS, 1943-45. Mem. Am., Ohio, Allen County (pres. 1969-70) bar assns., Am. Legion, Delta Tau Delta, Phi Delta Phi. Clubs: Lima Automobile (dir., pres. 1975—), Lima, Shawnee Country (pres. 1968-70), Elks, Rotary (Lima). Home: 324 S Cole St Lima OH 45805 Office: 110-112 N Elizabeth St Lima OH 45801

ROBERSON, JOE E., aluminum mfg. co. exec.; b. Birmingham, Ala., Dec. 13, 1927; s. Earle C. and Lurline (Cox) R.; B.S. in Indsl. Engring., Ga. Inst. Tech., 1949; children—David, Paul, Catherine. Plant mgr. Reynolds Metals Co., Richmond, Va., and St. Louis, 1949-63; pres. Johnston Foil Co., St. Louis, 1963-69; with Alumax Corp., 1969—, pres. Alumax Extrusion, St. Charles, Ill., 1969-70, Alumax Mill Products, Inc., San Mateo, Calif., 1970—, also dir.; dir. Decatur Aluminum Co. Mem. Aluminum Assn., Nat. Assn. Aluminum Distbrs. Republican. Presbyterian. Club: Bayshore Tennis. Home: 10 Rinconada Circle Belmont CA 94002 Office: Alumax Mill Products Inc 400 S El Camino Real San Mateo CA 94402

ROBERSON, NATHAN RUSSELL, physicist; b. Robersonville, N.C., Dec. 13, 1930; s. Nathan Russell and Myrtle (Taylor) R.; B.S., U. N.C., 1954, M.S., 1955; Ph.D., Johns Hopkins U., 1960; m. Ruth Haislip, June 19, 1954; children—David Wintner, Michael Taylor, Mary Russell. Jr. instr. Johns Hopkins U., 1955-60; research asso. Princeton U., 1960-63; asst. prof. physics Duke U., Durhan, N.C., 1963-68, asso. prof., 1968-74, prof., 1974—; bd. dirs. Triangle Univs. Computation Center, 1975—. Treas. N.C. Council Chs., 1974-79. Mem. Am. Phys. Soc., Am. Assn. Physics Tchrs., Phi Beta Kappa. Presbyterian. Contbr. articles on physics to profl. jours. Home: 3406 Ogburn Ct Durham NC 27705 Office: Dept Physics Duke U Durham NC 27706

ROBERSON, ROBERT EARL, ins. co. exec.; b. La Fayette, Ga., Sept. 8, 1917; s. Zebulon Spencer and Ollie (Browne) R.; A.B., Berry Coll., 1938; M.A., Emory U., 1940; LL.B., La Salle U., 1943; m. Ruth Grace, Dec. 3, 1943; children—John Lawrence, Nancy Ann. Admitted to Miss. bar, 1943; with Am. Mut. Liability Ins. Co., Wakefield, Mass., 1942—, adjustor, 1942-55, v.p., 1956-61, sr. v.p., 1962-63, pres., 1964—, chmn., 1975—; dir. State St. Bank & Trust Co., Boston, Allandale Mut. Ins. Co., Providence, Am. Mut. Re-ins. Co., Chgo., Fed. Paper Board Co., N.Y.C. Mem. corp. Northeastern U., Morgan Meml. Goodwill Enterprises. Clubs: Union League (N.Y.C.); Union, Comml., Algonquin (Boston). Author: Mark Twain the Critic, 1940. Home: 16 Chatham Way Lynnfield MA 01940 Office: Am Mutual Liability Ins Co Wakefield MA 01880

ROBERT, GILBERT O'DAY, banker; b. Cohoes, N.Y., Sept. 28, 1925; s. Gilbert H. and Marie (O'Day) R.; student Dartmouth, 1943-44; A.B., Siena Coll., 1949; m. Rosemarie Alice Mitchell, Oct. 1, 1949; children—Alice Marie, Gilbert Mitchell. Real estate broker appraiser, 1949-60; appraiser N.Y. State Bd. Equalization and Assessment, 1960-63; asst. treas. Albany Savs. Bank, 1963-68, v.p., 1968-69, sr. v.p., 1969-72, exec. v.p., 1972-74, pres., 1975—, trustee 1975—; pres. SBNY Mut. Service Corp. Mem. Albany County Bd. Realtors. Mem. exec. com. Gov. Clinton council Boy Scouts Am.; bd. dirs. Albany Area chpt. ARC; trustee Albany Meml. Hosp., 1976—, Coll. St. Rose, 1976—. Served to ensign USNR, 1943-46, to lt., 1950-52. Mem. Mortgage Bankers Assn., Albany Area C. of C. (dir. 1975—). Clubs: Schuyler Meadows Country, Hudson River, Univ., Ft. Orange (Albany). Home: 19 Loudon Heights N Loudonville NY 12211 Office: 20 N Pearl St Albany NY 12201

ROBERT, HENRY FLOOD, JR., museum ofcl.; b. El Dorado, Ark., Feb. 26, 1943; s. Henry Flood and Margery (Hay) R.; B.F.A., Ariz. State U., 1970, M.F.A., 1973; diploma Inst. Arts Adminstrn., Harvard U., 1977; m. Mary Beth Parkey, Apr. 20, 1968; children—Spencer Flood, Erika Ashley. Dir., Meml. Union Gallery, Ariz. State U., 1969-70, asst. dir. Univ. Art Mus., 1970-72; asst. dir. Loch Haven Art Center, Orlando, Fla., 1973-74; dir. Montgomery (Ala.) Mus. Fine Arts, 1974-79, Joslyn Art Mus., Omaha, 1979—; guest curator Soleri Exhbn., Whitney Mus. Am. Art, Corcoran Gallery Art, Mus. Contemporary Art; exhbn. dir. Art Inc.: American Paintings from Corp. Collections. Mem. Internat. Council Museums, Am. Assn. Museums (visitation com. for accreditation), Assn. Art Mus. Dirs. Episcopalian. Author: Paolo Soleri: Arcology and the Future of Man, 1975; Venetian Drawings from the Collection of Janos Scholz, 1976; Corporate Collections in Montgomery, 1976; American Paintings: 1900-1939, 1976; The George Verdak Collection: Eras of the Dance, 1976; Anne Goldthwaite 1869-1944, 1977; Walter Gaudnek

Retrospective, 1978. Home: 514 S 91st St Omaha NE 68114 Office: 2200 Dodge St Omaha NE 68102

ROBERT, STEPHEN, investment firm exec.; b. Haverhill, Mass., June 13, 1940; s. Samuel Robert; A.B. with honors, Brown U., 1962; postgrad. London Sch. Econs., 1962-63, Columbia Bus. Sch., 1963-65; children—Tracey Alexandra, Elisabeth Amory. Security analyst, Faulkner Dawkins and Sullivan, 1965-67; v.p. Oppenheimer Funds, N.Y.C., 1968-76, chief portfolio mgr., 1969-72; partner Oppenheimer & Co., 1970—, pres., 1979—, exec. v.p. Oppenheimer Mgmt. Corp.; pres.; dir. Oppenheimer Properties Securities Corp., 1974—; dir. Oppenheimer Asset Mgmt., 1975—; dir. Admiralty Funds, 1975-76. Dir., chmn. fin. com. Wiltwyck Sch., 1968-78; trustee Bradford Coll., 1977-78; mem. large gifts com. Brown U. Club: Harmonie (N.Y.C.). Office: 1 New York Plaza New York NY 10005

ROBERTI, MARIO ANDREW, energy co. exec.; b. Denver, May 12, 1935; s. Emil and Elvira (Ligrano) R.; B.S., Loyola U., Los Angeles, 1957, J.D., 1960; m. Patricia Ann Ludwig, Apr. 27, 1963; children—Andrea Louise, Paul Richard, Robert Raymond. Admitted to Calif. bar, 1961; dep. atty. gen. State of Calif., 1961-69; atty. Pacific Lighting Corp., Los Angeles, 1969-71; asst. gen. counsel, asst. sec. McCulloch Oil Corp., Los Angeles, 1971-76; v.p., gen. counsel Pacific Resources, Inc., Honolulu, 1976—. Trustee Hawaii Sch. Girls. Mem. Fed. Energy Bar Assn., Ind. Refiners Assn. Am., Hawaii Bar Assn. (chmn. corp. counsel sect. 1979), Calif. Bar Assn. Democrat. Roman Catholic. Clubs: Pacific, Outrigger Canoe (Honolulu). Office: 733 Bishop St Honolulu HI 96813

ROBERTS, ARTHUR, physicist; b. N.Y.C., July 6, 1912; s. Abraham and Rose (Bloch) R.; B.S., Coll. City N.Y., 1931; M.A., Columbia U., 1933; grad. Manhattan Sch. Music, 1933; Ph.D., N.Y. U., 1936; m. Janice Banner, May 21, 1935; children—Judith Roberts Neale, Richard M. Research asso. Harvard-Mass. Inst. Tech., 1937-42; tchr. New Eng. Conservatory Music, 1938-40; group leader Radiation Lab., Mass. Inst. Tech., 1942-46; asso. prof. physics State U. Iowa, 1946-50; asso. prof., then prof. U. Rochester (N.Y.), 1950-60; physicist Argonne (Ill.) Nat. Lab., 1960-67, Fermi Nat. Accelerator Lab., Batavia, Ill., 1967-79, U. Hawaii, Honolulu, 1980; mem. faculty U. Chgo., 1964-67; sci. liaison Office Naval Research, London, 1954-55; physicist Rutherford Lab., Chilton, Eng., 1974-75; bd. dirs. Contemporary Concerts, Inc., 1965—; music dir. Light Opera Co., Chgo., 1967-79. Recipient Presdl. Certificate of Merit, 1947; certificate of award nuclear medicine New Eng. Soc. Nuclear Medicine, 1976. Fellow Am. Phys. Soc.; mem. Phi Beta Kappa, Sigma Xi. Pioneer radioactive iodine in thyroid; author papers nuclear physics, beta-ray spectroscopy, nuclear spins and moments, high-energy particle physics. Home: 6633 Kauna St Honolulu HI 96825 Office: Physics Dept U Hawaii 2505 Correa Rd Honolulu HI 96822

ROBERTS, AUBREY ADDISON, fin. and mgmt. cons.; b. Bridgetown, Va., Apr. 1, 1915; s. Charles Edward and Nancy Elizabeth (Wilkins) R.; B.S., Coll. William and Mary, 1935, LL.D., 1974; LL.B., Temple U., 1940; m. Doris Lorraine Lawrence, Nov. 20, 1944; children—Karen Elizabeth (Mrs. Thomas DeVol), Randolph Lawrence, Leslie Virginia. Admitted to Va. bar, 1937; claim adjuster Liberty Mut. Ins. Co., 1937-38; asso. counsel Reliance Ins. Co. (formerly Fire Assn. Phila.), 1938-47, sec., 1947-52, v.p., treas., 1952, exec. v.p., 1962-64, pres., chief exec. officer, 1964-74, chmn. bd., chief exec. officer, 1974-76; pres., chmn. bd. Reliance Standard Life Ins. Co., 1963-76; pres. Pilot Ins. Co., Toronto, 1962-76; owner, operator A. Addison Roberts Assos., 1977—; chmn. bd. United Pacific Ins. Co., 1972-76, United Pacific Life Ins. Co., 1972-76; dir. Gino's, Inc., First Pa. Corp., Phila., First Pa. Bank & Trust Co., WHYY Inc., Drexel Utility Fund., Germantown Savs. Bank, Phila. Reins. Co., Commonwealth Land Title Ins. Co. Past chmn. bd. dirs. Am. Com. for Econ. Edn.; bd. govs. Pa. Economy League; past chmn. bd. trustees Temple U.; bd. dirs., exec. com., gen. chmn. 1973 United Fund Torch dr. United Way Phila.; past bd. dirs. Greater Phila. Partnership; past chmn. bd. Am. Cancer Soc. Phila.; bd. dirs. Crime Commn. Phila., Phila. Mus. Art; bd. visitors, bd. dirs. Coll. William and Mary; bd. mgrs. Pa. Hosp., Univ. Mus., U. Pa. Mem. Ins. Info. Inst. (dir., past chmn. bd.), Am. Ins. Assn. (dir., past chmn. bd.), Ins. Inst. Am. (dir.), Nat. Assn. Casualty and Surety Execs. (pres. 1968, dir.), Ins. Fedn. Pa. (past pres., dir.), S.R. Clubs: Racquet, Rittenhouse (Phila.); Gulph Mills Golf; Waynesborough Country. Home: 254 Curwen Rd Rosemont PA 19010 Office: 4 Penn Center Plaza Suite 627 Philadelphia PA 19103

ROBERTS, BONNY K., lawyer, former judge; b. Sopchoppy, Fla., Feb. 5, 1907; s. Thomas and Florida (Morrison) R.; J.D., U. Fla., 1928; LL.D., U. Miami, 1954; m. Mary Newman, Aug. 20, 1937; children—Mary Jane, Thomas Frederick. Admitted to Fla. bar, 1928; practiced in Tallahassee, 1928-49; justice Supreme Ct. of Fla., 1949-77, chief justice, 1953-54, 61-63, 71-72, ret., 1977; sr. partner firm Roberts, Miller, Baggett and LaFace, 1977—; v.p., dir. Tallahassee Bank & Trust Co., 1948-49. Mem. awards jury Freedoms Found. at Valley Forge, 1962; mem. Fla. Constl. Revision Commn., 1966, 77, chmn. subcom. on human rights; chmn. Jud. Council Fla., 1962—; mem. exec. com. Nat. Conf. Chief Justices, 1966, dep. chmn., 1972-73. Chmn. trustees Fla. State U. Found.; bd. counselors Fla. Presbyn. Coll. Served as lt. comdr. USCG, 1942-45, shipping commr. Port Jacksonville, Fla., 1943-45. Recipient Distinguished Citizen award Stetson U. Coll. Law. Mem. Internat. (patron), Inter-Am., Am. (UN com., world order under law com.; ofcl. ct. rep. London meeting 1957), Fla. (past v.p.), Tallahassee (past pres.) bar assns., Am. Judicature Soc., Am. Law Inst., Newcomen Soc. Eng., Am. Legion (mem. nat. distinguished guests com.), Alpha Kappa Psi, Fla. Blue Key, Gold Key, Soc. of Wig and Robe, Phi Alpha Delta, Delta Chi. Mason (Shriner), Elk, Odd Fellow, Kiwanian. Democrat. Presbyn. Home: MSS Box 3005 Tallahassee FL 32303 Office: Chmn Jud Council of Fla Supreme Court Bldg Tallahassee FL 32304 also 101 E College Ave Tallahassee FL

ROBERTS, BRADLEY HOUSE, advt. exec.; b. New Rochelle, N.Y., Jan. 23, 1927; s. Ernest House and Grace (Notton) R.; A.B., Hamilton Coll., 1950; m. Jean Edgerton Hypes, Oct. 21, 1950 (dec. 1971); children—Bradley House, Barbara Kimball (Mrs. David Gainza), Sarah Hypes. Advt. brand mgr. Swift & Co., 1950-52; sales and advt. mgr. Earle-Chesterfield Mill Co., Asheville, N.C., 1953; comml. mgr. Skyway Broadcasting Co., Asheville, 1953-56; account exec. Compton Advt. Inc., Chgo., 1956-57; with Needham, Harper & Steers, Inc., 1957—, exec. v.p., 1966—, vice chmn., mng. dir. Needham, Harper & Steers, Los Angeles, also dir.; dir. U.S.P.-Needham Pty. Ltd., Melbourne, Australia, U.S.P. Needham, S.E. Asia Pte., Ltd., Singapore. Mem. Bd. Parks and Recreations, Lake Forest, Ill., 1964-65; vice chmn. fund raising drive Los Angeles Jr. Achievement, 1966; bd. dirs. Big Rock Property Owners Assn., Malibu, Calif., 1966-67. Bd. dirs. Civitan Internat. Assn., 1953-56, Scholarship Fund Found. Ill., 1962-65, Jr. Achievement; adv. bd. Art Center Coll. of Design, 1974—; founding bd. dirs. Hollywood Presbyn. Med. Center Served with USNR, 1945-46. Mem. Los Angeles C. of C., Westwood C. of C., Am. Assn. Advt. Agys. (chmn. and gov. Western region, dir.-at-large, leader of yr. award Western region 1979), Alpha Delta Phi. Clubs: Winter (dir. 1963-66) (Lake Forest); Riviera Country, Calif. (Los Angeles). Home: 20283 Inland Ln Malibu CA 90265 Office: 10889 Wilshire Blvd Los Angeles CA 90024

ROBERTS, BRUCE EVERETT, cons. engr.; b. Chanute, Kans., May 22, 1917; s. Everett Earl and Belle M. (Jones) R.; B.S. in Civil Engring., Kans. State U., Manhattan, 1939; m. Marcelle Braden, Aug. 9, 1941; children—Stephen Kent, Craig Arnold. Civil engr. Cheyenne County, Kans., 1939-40; constrn. engr. Frazier-Bruce on Weldon Springs (Kans.) Ordnance Plant, 1940; field engr. with Consoer-Townsend Co. for Parsons (Kans.) Ordnance Plant, 1940-41; with Wilson & Co., engrs. and architects, Salina, Kans., 1946—, dir., 1950—, project mgr., 1959—, exec. partner, 1959—; pres., dir. Wilson-Murrow Co., 1963—; dir. Planters State Bank, Salina; co-owner B&R Ranch; past chmn. Kans. Bd. Engring. Examiners. Served to lt. USNR, 1942-45. Recipient Disting. Service award Kans. State U. Coll. Engring., 1979; registered profl. engr. and land surveyor, Kans. Mem. Am. Soc. Profl. Engrs., ASCE, Am. Cons. Engrs. Council, Am. Rd. and Transp. Builders Assn., Internat. Rd. Fedn., Nat. Soc. Profl. Engrs., Profl. Engrs. in Pvt. Practice, Am. Water Works Assn., Am. Soc. Photogrammetrists. Clubs: Salina Country, Masons, Elks. Home: 201 Greenway Rd Salina KS 67401 Office: PO Box 1648 631 E Crawford St Salina KS 67401

ROBERTS, BRUCE OWEN, heavy industry mfg. co. exec.; b. Aurora, Ill., June 18, 1926; s. Albert James and Berneice (Stark) R.; B.S. in Mech. Engring., U. Wis., 1950; m. Dolores A. Westphal, Aug. 9, 1947; children—Dianne Roberts Caporale, Gary Bruce. With Gen. Electric Co., 1950—, gen. mgr. aviation service dept., 1964-68, gen. mgr. appliance motor dept., 1968-70, v.p. Corp. Facility Services, 1970-72, v.p., gen. mgr. AC motor and generator div., Schenectady, 1972-74, v.p., gen. mgr. large transformer bus. div., Pittsfield, Mass., 1974—; dir. First Agrl. Bank, Pittsfield, Locke Insulators, Inc., Balt., Electric Mut. Liability Ins. Co., Electric Ins. Co., Lynn, Mass. Bd. dirs. Berkshire Med. Center, Pittsfield, 1975—. Served with USAAF, 1944-45. Mem. Central Berkshire C. of C. (dir. 1975—). Clubs: Country of Pittsfield; Mohawk Golf (Schenectady). Home: 91 Stonehenge Rd Pittsfield MA 01201 Office: 100 Woodlawn Ave Pittsfield MA 01201

ROBERTS, BURNELL RICHARD, paper co. exec.; b. Wis., May 6, 1927; s. Roy C. and Ann (Jones) R.; B.B.A., U. Wis., 1950; M.B.A., Harvard, 1957; m. Karen H. Ragatz, Aug. 8, 1953; children—Evan, Kari, Paul, Nancy. With Bendix Aviation Corp., 1953-58; with Gen. Tire & Rubber Co., 1957-62, treas., controller subsidiary A.M. Byers Co., Pitts., 1962-66; asst. to exec. v.p. Mead Corp., 1966-68, controller, v.p. finance, 1968-71, group v.p., pres. Mchts. group, 1971-74, group v.p., pres. Mead Paper, 1974—, sr. v.p. Mead Corp., 1979—; dir. Chemineer Corp., Dayton, B.C. Forest Products, Vancouver, Northwood Pulp & Paper, Prince George, B.C.; dir., chmn. Brunswick Pulp & Paper (Ga.). Bd. dirs. Goodwill Industries, Dayton; trustee Central State U., Wilberforce, Ohio, Dayton Art Inst.; adv. bd. Sinclair Coll., Dayton; adv. council Miami U., Oxford, Ohio. Served with USNR, 1944-46. Mem. Fin. Execs. Inst., Nat. Assn. Accountants, Am. Paper Inst. (exec. com. printing and writing div.). Club: Harvard Business School (Dayton). Office: Mead World Hdqrs Courthouse Plaza NE Dayton OH 45463

ROBERTS, BURTON BENNETT, state justice; b. N.Y.C., July 25, 1922; s. Alfred S. and Cecila (Schanfein) R.; B.A., N.Y. U., 1943, LL.M., 1953; LL.B., Cornell U., 1949. Admitted to N.Y. State bar, 1949; asst. dist. atty. N.Y. County, 1949-66; chief asst. dist. atty. Bronx County, Bronx, N.Y., 1966-68, acting dist. atty., 1968-69, dist. atty., 1969-72; justice Supreme Ct. State N.Y., 1973—. Pres. Bronx div. Hebrew Home for Aged, 1967-72. Served with U.S. Army, 1943-45. Decorated Purple Heart, Bronze Star with Oak leaf cluster. Mem. Assn. Bar City N.Y., Am. Bar Assn., N.Y. Bar Assn., Bronx City Bar Assn., N.Y. State Dist. Attys. Assn. (pres. 1971-72). Jewish (exec. bd. temple). Home: 136 E 55th St New York NY 10022 Office: 100 Center St New York NY 10013

ROBERTS, CHALMERS MCGEAGH, reporter; b. Pitts., Nov. 18, 1910; s. Franklin B. and Lillian B. (McGeagh) R.; A.B., Amherst Coll., 1933, L.H.D., 1963; m. Lois Hall, Sept. 11, 1941; children—David H., Patricia E., Christopher C. Reporter, Washington Post, 1933-34, Asso. Press., Pitts. bur., 1934-35, Toledo News-Bee, 1936-38, Japan Times, Tokyo, 1938-39; asst. mng. editor Washington Daily News, 1939-41; Sunday editor Washington Times-Herald, 1941; staff OWI, London, Washington, 1941-43; staff Life mag., 1946-47, Washington Star, 1947-49; staff writer Washington Post, 1949-71, reporter local and nat. news, 1949-53, chief diplomatic corr., 1953-71, contbg. columnist, 1971—. Served from pvt. to capt. USAAF, 1943-46. Decorated Order of Merit (Germany); recipient Sigma Delta Chi award, 1953; Washington Newspaper Guild nat. news award, 1954, 60; citation Overseas Press Club, 1955; Washington Newspaper Guild Front Page grand prize, 1957, 60; Raymond Clapper Meml. award, 1957; Edward Weintal prize for diplomatic reporting, 1975; Frank Luther Mott Research award Kappa Tau Alpha, 1978. Mem. Am. Newspaper Guild, State Dept. Corrs. Assn. (pres. 1958-59), Council on Fgn. Relations. Author: Washington Past and Present, 1950; Can We Meet the Russians Half Way?, 1958; The Nuclear Years: The Arms Race and Arms Control 1945-70, 1970; First Rough Draft: A Journalist's Journal of Our Times, 1973; The Washington Post: The First 100 Years, 1977. Contbr. articles popular mags. Home: 6699 MacArthur Blvd Washington DC 20016

ROBERTS, CHARLES RILES, petroleum co. exec.; b. Sadler, Tex., Jan. 19, 1934; s. McKinley Charles and Nettie Bell (Perryman) R.; B.B.A., U. Tex., 1956; LL.B., J.D., U. Denver, 1961; m. Kathryn Mowrey, Apr. 11, 1968; children—Leslie Ann, Lindsey Charles. Admitted to Colo. bar, 1961, Tex. bar, 1974; mem. legal dept. Continental Oil Co., Denver, 1961-68, exec. asst. to pres., N.Y.C., 1967-68; v.p., sec., gen. counsel Western Crude Oil Inc., Denver, 1968-71, Tesoro Petroleum Corp., San Antonio, 1971-78; sr. v.p., sec., gen. counsel Valero Energy Corp., San Antonio, 1978—; Mem. adv. bd. Internat. and Comparative Law Center, also Internat. Oil and Gas Ednl. Center at Southwestern Legal Found. Served with AUS, 1953-55. Mem. Am., Tex., Colo., Bexar County, Denver bar assns., Order St. Ives, Phi Theta Kappa, Phi Sigma Upsilon, Phi Delta Phi. Republican. Clubs: Denver Law, University, Shriners (Denver); Town, Plaza, Oak Hills Country (San Antonio). Home: 3502 Marymont St San Antonio TX 78217 Office: 730 McCullough St San Antonio TX 78292

ROBERTS, CLYDE FRANCIS, assn. exec.; b. Lawrence, Mass., Sept. 10, 1924; s. Clyde F. and Blanche (Fellows) R.; B.S.B.A., Boston U., 1947; postgrad. Am. U., Beirut, 1954; m. May 18, 1947; 1 dau., Michele. Commd. Fgn. affairs officer Dept. State, 1948-57; v.p. Nat. Assn. Mfrs., Washington, 1957-75; pres. Indsl. Fasteners Inst., Cleve., 1975—; past dir. Am. Nat. Metric Council. Served with U.S. Army, 1943-45; Africa, Sicily, Italy, Greece. Mem. Nat. Indsl. Council. Roman Catholic. 18827 Cliff Circle Fairview Park OH 44126 Office: 1505 E Ohio Bldg Cleveland OH 44114

ROBERTS, DENNIS JOSEPH, II, state ofcl., lawyer; b. Providence, May 30, 1941; s. Thomas Hagan and Florence Elizabeth (McCabe) R.; A.B., Fordham U., 1963; LL.B., Boston Coll., 1966; m. Brenda Judith Bride, Sept. 9, 1967; children—Thomas, Jane. Admitted to R.I. bar, 1966, U.S. Supreme Ct. bar, 1978; 1st legal counsel R.I. Consumers Council, Providence, 1966-78; founder, chmn. bd. R.I. Legal Services, Inc., Providence, 1967-68; gen. counsel, dir. R.I. Group Health Assn., Providence, 1966-78; spl. asst. atty. gen. Gen., Providence, 1977-78, R.I. atty. gen., 1978—. Mem. Nat. Assn. Attys. Gen. (charitable trusts, anti-trust and criminal law enforcement com. 1979—, vice chmn. com. on hist. preservation 1979—), Nat. Dist. Attys., R.I. Bar Assn. Democrat. Roman Catholic. Club: Providence Rotary. Article, book rev. editor Boston Coll. Indsl. and Comml. Law Rev., 1965-66. Office: R I Dept Atty Gen 250 Benefit St Providence RI 02903

ROBERTS, DONNA MAE TWICHELL, editor; b. Oak Ridge, Nov. 15, 1945; d. Lewis Paxson and Mae (Cleek) Twichell; B.A., Colo. Women's Coll., 1967; divorced; 1 dau., Adria Lynn. Copy editor Am. U. Fgn. Area Studies, Washington, 1968-69; editorial asst. Rocky Mountain Med. Jour., Denver, 1971-73; asst. editor Plastics Machinery and Equipment mag., Denver, 1973; asst. editor Sch. Foodservice Jour., Denver, 1973-75, editor, 1975—, dir. publs. Am. Sch. Foodservice Assn., 1977—, dir. communications, 1978—. Mem. Internat. Foodservice Editorial Council (dir. 1977-78), Women in Communications, Am. Soc. Bus. Press Editors, Am. Soc. Assn. Execs. Home: 10243 E Yale St Aurora CO 80014 Office: 4101 E Iliff Ave Denver CO 80222

ROBERTS, DORIS, actress; b. St. Louis, Nov. 4, 1930; student N.Y. U., 1950-51; studied with Sanford Meisner, Neighborhood Playhouse, N.Y.C., 1952-53, Lee Strasberg, Actors' Studio, N.Y.C., 1956; m. William Goyen, Nov. 10, 1963; 1 son by previous marriage, Michael. Profl. stage debut, Ann Arbor, Mich., 1953; appeared in summer stock, Chatham, Mass., 1955; Broadway debut in The Time of Your Life, 1955; other Broadway and off-Broadway appearances include: The Desk Set, 1955, The American Dream, 1961, The Death of Bessie Smith, 1961, The Office, 1965, The Color of Darkness, 1963, Marathon 33, 1963, Secret Affair of Mildred Wilde, 1972, Last of the Red Hot Lovers, 1969-71, Bad Habits (Outer Circle Critics award 1974), 1973; film appearances include: Something Wild (movie debut), 1961, Barefoot in the Park, 1968, No Way to Treat a Lady, 1973, A Lovely Way to Die, 1969, Honeymoon Killers, 1969, A New Leaf, 1970, Such Good Friends, 1971, Little Murders, 1971, Heartbreak Kid, 1972, Hester Street, 1975, The Taking of Pelham, One, Two, Three, 1974, The Rose, 1979, Good Luck, Miss Wyckoff, 1979; TV debut on Studio One, 1958; appeared on TV series: Mary Hartman, Mary Hartman, 1975, Mary Tyler Moore Hour, 1976, Soap, 1978-79, Angie, 1979—; other TV appearances include: The Defenders, CBS Playhouse, Neil Simon Comedy Hour, Lily Tomlin Comedy Hour; appeared in TV films: The Story Teller, 1979, Ruby and Oswald, 1978, It Happened One Christmas, 1978, Jennifer: A Woman's Story, 1979. Mem. Screen Actors Guild, AFTRA, Actors Equity, Dirs. Guild. Office:

ROBERTS, DORIS EMMA, epidemiologist, cons.; b. Toledo, Dec. 28, 1915; d. Frederic Constable and Emma Selina (Reader) R.; nursing diploma Peter Bent Brigham Sch. Nursing, Boston, 1938; B.S., Geneva Coll., Beaver Falls, Pa., 1944; M.P.H., U. Minn., 1958; Ph.D., U. N.C., 1967. Staff nurse Vis. Nurse Assn., New Haven, 1938-40; sr. nurse Neighborhood House, Millburn, N.J., 1942-45; supr. Tb Baltimore County Dept. Health, Towson, Md., 1945-46; Tb cons. Md. State Dept. Health, 1946-50; cons., chief nurse Tb program USPHS, Washington, 1950-57; cons. div. nursing USPHS, 1958-63; chief nursing practice br. Health Resources Adminstrn., HEW, Bethesda, Md., 1966-75; adj. prof. Sch. Pub. Health, U. N.C., 1975—. Cons., WHO. Mem. Pub. Citizen, Inc. Mem. Democratic Nat. Com. from Md., 1970-71. Served with USPHS, 1945-75. Recipient Distinguished Alumna award Geneva Coll., 1971; Distinguished Service award USPHS, 1971. Fellow Am. Pub. Health Assn. (v.p. 1978-79, Distinguished Service award 1975, Sedgwick Meml. medal 1979); mem. Inst. Medicine of Nat. Acad. Scis., Common Cause, Delta Omega. Home: 6111 Kennedy Dr Chevy Chase MD 20015

ROBERTS, EDWARD BAER, educator; b. Chelsea, Mass., Nov. 18, 1935; s. Nathan and Edna (Podradchik) R.; B.S., Mass. Inst. Tech., 1958, M.S., 1958, M.S. in Mgmt., 1960, Ph.D., 1962; m. Nancy Helen Rosenthal, June 14, 1959; children—Valerie Jo, Mitchell Jonathan, Andrea Lynne. Founding mem. systems dynamics program Mass. Inst. Tech., 1958—, instr., 1959-61, asst. prof., 1961-65, asso. prof., 1965-70, prof., 1970—, David Sarnoff prof. mgmt. of tech., 1974—, asso. dir. research program on mgmt. sci. and tech., 1963-73, chmn. tech. and health mgmt. program, 1973—; co-founder, pres. Pugh-Roberts Assos., Inc., Cambridge, Mass., 1963—, also dir.; dir. Mass. Inst. Tech.-Boston VA Joint Center on Health Care Mgmt., 1976—; dir. Med. Info. Tech. Inc., Cambridge; cons. Assn. Am. Med. Colls., also numerous corps.; mem. Task Force on Nuclear Medicine, ERDA, 1975-76. Mem. Am. Econs. Assn., IEEE, Inst. Mgmt. Sci. (pres. Boston chpt. 1962-63), Sigma Xi, Tau Beta Pi, Eta Kappa Nu, Tau Kappa Alpha. Author: The Dynamics of Research and Development, 1964; (with others) Systems Simulation for Regional Analysis, 1969, The Persistent Poppy, 1975, The Dynamics of Human Service Delivery, 1976; prin. author, editor Managerial Applications of System Dynamics 1978; editorial bd. IEEE Trans. on Engring. Mgmt., 1968—, Indsl. Mktg. Mgmt., 1975—, Health Care Mgmt. Rev., 1976-78; contbr. over 60 articles to profl. jours. Home: 17 Fellsmere Rd Newton MA 02159 Office: 50 Memorial Dr Cambridge MA 02139

ROBERTS, EDWIN ALBERT, JR., journalist; b. Weehawken, N.J., Nov. 14, 1932; s. Edwin Albert and Agnes Rita (Seuferling) R.; student Coll. William and Mary, 1952-53, N.Y. U., evenings 1955-58; m. Barbara Anne Collins, June 14, 1958; children—Elizabeth Adams, Leslie Carol, Amy Barbara, Jacqueline Harding. Reporter, N.J. Courier, Toms River, 1953-54, Asbury Park (N.J.) Press, 1954-57; reporter Wall Street Jour., N.Y.C., 1957, editorial writer, 1957-63; news editor Nat. Observer, Silver Spring, Md., 1963-68, columnist, 1968-77; editorial writer, columnist Detroit News, 1977-78, editorial page editor, 1978—. Recipient Distinguished Reporting Bus. award U. Mo., 1969; Pulitzer prize for distinguished commentary, 1974. Mem. Am. Soc. Newspaper Editors, Nat. Conf. Editorial Writers, Detroit Press Club. Clubs: Econ. Detroit, Detroit Athletic; Explorers. Author: Elections, 1964, 1964; Latin America, 1965; The Smut Rakers, 1966; Russia Today, 1967. Editor anthology America Outdoors, 1965. Office: 615 Lafayette Blvd Detroit MI 48231

ROBERTS, ELLEN ELIZABETH MAYHEW, publisher; b. Knoxville, Tenn., Oct. 5, 1946; s. Elliott P. and Sue (Abraham) R.; B.A., Reed Coll., 1969. Asst. editor St. Martin's Press, 1969-70, Lothrop, Lee & Shepard Co., 1970-71; asso. editor Prentice-Hall, Inc., Englewood Cliffs, N.J., 1971-73, dir. Children's Books, 1973—; lectr. children's lit. and pub. Central Mo. State U., William Paterson Coll., U. Houston, Fairleigh Dickinson U. Mem. ALA, Children's Book Council, Am. Inst. Graphic Arts, Am. Printing History Assn., Woman's Nat. Book Assn., Printing Women N.Y., Assn. Childhood Edn., Am. Assn. Sch. Librarians. Home: 414 W 121st St New York City NY 10027 Office: Prentice-Hall Inc Englewood Cliffs NJ 07632

ROBERTS, ELLIOTT CLIFTON, hosp. adminstr.; b. Balt., Jan. 20, 1927; s. Charles Patrick and Margianna Lillian (Ledeatte) R.; B.S., Morgan State Coll., 1951; M.A. in Hosp. Adminstrn., George

Washington U., 1963; m. Shirley D. Roberts; children—Elliott Clifton, Jay Timothy, Charles Patrick, Sondra Lynn, Erroll Anthony. Bus. mgr. Provident Hosp., Balt., 1953-55, asst. adminstr., 1955-60; chief accountant Crownsville (Md.) State Hosp., 1960-63, asst. supt., 1963-65; exec. dir. Mercy Douglass Hosp., Phila., 1965-69, Harlem Hosp. Center, N.Y.C., 1969-72; commr. hosp. Detroit Gen. Hosp., 1972-77; asst. sec. La. Dept. Health and Human Resources, dir. Office of Charity Hosp. at New Orleans, 1977—; asst. adj. prof. Columbia Sch. Pub. Health and Adminstrv. Medicine, 1970-72, Grad. Sch. Pub. Adminstrn. N.Y. U., 1971-72; adj. prof. Wayne State U. Sch. Medicine, 1973-77; asst. prof. dept. public health and preventive medicine La. State U., 1977—. Served with AUS, 1945-47, to 1st lt., 1951-53. Mem. Am. Coll. Hosp. Adminstrs., Am. Hosp. Assn., Kappa Alpha Psi. Episcopalian. Home: 266 Walnut St New Orleans LA 70118 Office: Charity Hosp at New Orleans 1532 Tulane Ave New Orleans LA 70140

ROBERTS, ELMER A., banker; b. Crawford, Tex., Oct. 12, 1921; s. Clyde Howell and Ninnie Lou (Hay) R.; student Baylor U., 1939-41; m. Annette Stewart, Dec. 9, 1945; 1 dau., Nancy. Dep. clk. McLennan County, 1945-50; mgr. County Title Co., 1951-54; controller City of Waco (Tex.), 1954-58, dir., 1958-64, city mgr., 1965-71; v.p. 1st Nat. Bank of Waco, 1971-72, pres., from 1972, now chmn.; v.p. S.W. Sprayer & Chem. Co., 1964; dir. S. Amsler Co. of Crawford, Inc. Bd. dirs. YMCA, United Fund, ARC, Baylor Stadium. Served with USAF, 1942-45. Named outstanding pub. ofcl., Waco Jr. C. of C., 1960. Mem. Internat. City Mgrs. Assn., Waco C. of C. (dir.), Municipal Finance Officers Assn. U.S. and Can. Mason. Office: 1st Nat Bank of Waco 811 Washington Ave Waco TX 76703*

ROBERTS, ELVY BENTON, former army officer, ins. co. exec.; b. Manchester, Ky., Aug. 21, 1917; s. Farris Frank and Iola (Hatton) R.; B.S., Eastern Ky. U., 1939; B.S., U.S. Mil. Acad., 1943; postgrad. U.S. Army War Coll., 1959; m. Drucilla Wilson, Dec. 19, 1943; children—Catharine W. (Mrs. John E. Repine), Sandra (Mrs. Colin Hallford), William A. Commd. 2d lt. U.S. Army, 1943, advanced through grades to lt. gen., 1973; chief of staff 11th Air Assault Div., 1963-65; comdg. gen. 1st Air Cav. Div., 1969-70; asst. dep. chief of staff for mil. operations Dept. Army, Washington, 1971-72; joint chiefs staff rep. U.S. del. on force reduction negotiation, Vienna, 1973; comdr. 6th U.S. Army, Presidio of San Francisco, 1973-75; ret., 1975; v.p. Johnson & Anton Inc., 1976-79; dir. Altair Assos, San Francisco, 1976—. Decorated D.S.M. with oak leaf cluster, Silver Star medal with oak leaf cluster, Legion of Merit with oak leaf cluster, D.F.C., Bronze Star medal with V and 2 oak leaf clusters. Mem. World Affairs Council, Assn. U.S. Army, Army Aviation Assn. Am., 1st Cav. Div. Assn. Rotarian. Clubs: St. Francis Yacht, Bohemian, Commonwealth of Calif. (San Francisco). Home: 129 Eliseo Dr Greenbrae CA 94904

ROBERTS, ERNEST ROTH, mgmt. cons. co. exec.; b. Mezokovesd, Hungary, Mar. 14, 1917; s. Ignatius and Rosalie (Schwar) Roth; came to U.S., 1946, naturalized, 1948; Diploma Engring., Swiss Fed. Inst. Tech., 1942, Dr. of Tech. Sci., 1945; m. Verna Jo Sellers, June 9, 1951; children—Karen Verna, Peter Zsolt, Larry Michael. Vice pres. Solid Rocket Co., Sacramento, 1960-64; v.p. devel. Aerojet-Gen. Corp., El Monte, Calif., 1964-70, group v.p., 1974—; pres. Envirogenics Co. div. Aerojet Gen. Corp., El Monte, 1970-73; chmn., chief exec. officer Chemico Corp. subsidiary Aerojet Gen. Corp., N.Y.C., 1973-74. Bd. dirs. Parent Assn. of Calif. Inst. Tech., 1972. Served with AUS, 1941-47. Recipient Meritorious Pub. Service citation USN, 1960, certificate of Commendation USN, 1960, C. N. Hickman award Am. Rocket Soc., 1959. Registered profl. engr., Calif., N.Y. Fellow Am. Inst. Aeros. and Astronautics (asso.); mem. ASME, Am. Mgmt. Assn. Clubs: Burning Tree Country, Metropolitan (Washington). Home: 26991 El Ciervo Mission Viejo CA 92675 Office: 9100 E Flair Dr El Monte CA 91734

ROBERTS, EUGENE LESLIE, JR., editor; b. Goldsboro, N.C., June 15, 1932; s. Eugene Leslie and Margeret (Ham) R.; A.A., Mars Hill (N.C.) Jr. Coll., 1952; B.A., U. N.C., 1954; Niemen fellow in Journalism, Harvard U., 1961-62; m. Susan Jane McLamb, Feb. 23, 1957; children—Leslie Jane, Margaret Page, Elizabeth Susan, Polly Ann. Local govt. reporter Goldsboro News-Argus, 1956-58; maritime reporter Norfolk Virginian-Pilot, 1958-59; state capitol corr. The News & Observer, Raleigh, N.C., 1959-61, Sunday editor, 1962-63; labor writer Detroit Free Press, 1963-64, city editor, 1964-65; chief So. corr. N.Y. Times, 1965-67, war corr., South Vietnam, 1968-69, nat. editor, 1969-72; exec. editor Phila. Inquirer, 1972—; v.p., dir. Phila. Newspapers, Inc. Mem. Am. Soc. Newspaper Editors, Soc. Profl. Journalists, Sigma Delta Chi. Author: (with Jack Nelson) The Censors and The Schools, 1963; (with David R. Jones) Assignment America, 1973. Home: 1022 Clinton St Philadelphia PA 19107 Office: 400 N Broad St Philadelphia PA 19101

ROBERTS, FRANCES CABANISS, historian; b. Gainesville, Ala., Dec. 19, 1916; d. Richard H. and Mary (Watson) R.; B.S., Livingston State U., 1937; M.A., U. Ala., 1940, Ph.D., 1956; postgrad. Vanderbilt U., 1949-50. Tchr. pub. schs., Huntsville, Ala., 1937-52; teaching fellow U. Ala., Huntsville, 1952-53, faculty, 1953—, prof. history, 1961—, chmn. dept., 1966-70, dir. Acad. Advisement Center, 1972—. Bd. mem. Huntsville Civic Symphony, Twickenham Hist. Preservation Assn.; Ala. state dir. on exec. bd. So. Heritage Found., 1964-65; bd. dirs. Burritt Mus., Huntsville; mem. Huntsville Historic Preservation Commn., 1972—, Commn. Restoration Capitol Bldg., 1973, Ala. Com. on Humanities and Pub. Policy, 1972—. Recipient Livingston State U. Alumni award, 1964; Ala. Historic Commn. award, 1969; N.Ala. Bar Assn. Liberty Bell award, 1970; Life Sharer's award Kiwanis, 1973; Service award U. Ala., Huntsville, 1975; award of merit Am. Assn. State and; Alumni Faculty Appreciation award, 1976. Mem. Ala. Ednl. Assn., Huntsville Hist. Soc. (exec. bd. 1950—), Ala. Council Social Studies (pres. 1947-48), Am., Ala. (pres. 1968-69, exec. bd. 1951—), So., N. (exec. bd. 1956-64) hist. assns., Golden Key, Kappa Delta Pi, Phi Alpha Theta (scholarship award 1973), Phi Kappa Phi. Author: Shadows on the Wall, The Life and Works of Howard Weeden, 1962; Civics for Alabama Schools, 1968, rev., 1970. Home: 603 Randolph Ave Huntsville AL 35801

ROBERTS, FRANCIS JOSEPH, ret. army officer, ednl. adminstr.; b. Holyoke, Mass., July 26, 1918; s. Francis Raymond and Mary (Curry) R.; B.S., U.S. Mil. Acad., 1942; postgrad. Harvard U., 1964; m. Mary Murray Prickett, May 30, 1942; children—Murray Francine Roberts Graff, Laurel Virginia Roberts Manning, Randall Curry, Phillip Raymond. Commd. 2d lt. U.S. Army, 1942, advanced through grades to brig. gen., 1966; comdg. officer B Battery, 358th F.A., 1942-43, ops. and tng. staff officer, 1943-45; ops. and tng. staff officer Hdqrs. III Corps, 1946; instr. tactics U.S. Mil. Acad., 1946, instr. academics, 1950-53, grad. mgr. athletics, dir. athletics, 1956-59; intelligence staff officer Amphibious Force U.S. Atlantic Fleet, 1946-48; personnel staff officer Hdqrs. 101st Airborne Div., 1948, asst. chief of staff, 1948-49; plans and ops. staff officer Hdqrs. I Corps, 1953-54; comdg. officer 159th F.A., 1954; plans and policy staff officer J-3, Hdqrs. Far East Command, 1954-55; chief personnel services div. Office Asst. Chief of Staff for Personnel, Washington, 1960-61; mil. asst. to dep. sec. def., Washington, 1961-64; comdg. officer 4th Inf. Div. Arty., 1964-66; chief war plans SHAPE, 1966, chief strategic plans br., 1966-68; chief of staff Alaskan Command, 1968-69; comdg. gen. II Field Force Vietnam, 1969-70; chief staff Hdqrs. II Field Force, Vietnam, 1970-71; chief Europe-Middle East-Africa Div. Orgn. Joint Chiefs Staff, 1971-72, ret., 1972; dean of cadets N.Y. Mil. Acad., 1971-72, supt., 1972—. Vice pres. AMP 45, Harvard; trustee Am. Child Guidance Found.; bd. dirs., mem. exec. com. U.S. Olympic Com.; mem. exec. com. Eastern Collegiate Athletic Conf.; mem. Western Alaska council Boy Scouts Am. Decorated D.S.M., D.F.C., Silver Star, Legion of Merit with 3 oak leaf clusters, Bronze Star with oak leaf cluster and Valor device, 10 Air medals, Croix de Guerre avec Etoile de'Argent, Legion of Honor; Army Distinguished Order 1st Class medal, Gallantry Cross with Palm, Nat. Honor Medal (Vietnam); Royal Army Aiguillette (Thailand), others. Mem. Assn. Grad. West Point (trustee), Harvard Alumni Assn. Grads. Nat. War Coll., U.S. Srs. Golf Assn., Internat. Srs. Amateur Golf Soc., Assn. U.S. Army (chpt. pres., chmn. nat. resolutions com., bd. advs.). Clubs: Army-Navy Country (Washington); Pinehurst (N.C.) Country; Union League (N.Y.C.); Harvard-Radcliffe of Hudson Valley (pres. 1976—); Touchdown of Am. (dir.). Address: NY Mil Acad Cornwall on Hudson NY 12520

ROBERTS, FRANCIS WARREN, former educator; b. Menard, Tex., Dec. 3, 1916; s. William Clyde and Exia Ethel (Frazier) R.; A.B., Southwestern U., 1938; D.Litt. (hon.), 1972; Ph.D., U. Tex., 1956; m. Patricia Lomasney, Jan. 1, 1943; children—Jeffrey W., Victoria Roberts. Instr. in English, U. Tex., Austin, 1954-56, asst. prof., 1958-59, asso. prof., 1959-66, prof., 1967—, dir. Humanities Research Center, 1962-78, ret., 1978. Served with USNR, 1940-41, 42-45, 50-54; comdr. ret. Fulbright grantee, 1956-58 77. Mem. Modern Humanities Research Assn., Tex. State Hist. Assn., Collectors Inst., Tex. Inst. Letters (sec.-treas. 1976-78), Tex. Folklore Soc., S. Central Modern Lang. Assn. (pres. 1974-75). Clubs: Grolier (N.Y.C.); American (London); Army and Navy (Washington). Author: Bibliography of D.H. Lawrence; editor: (with V.De Sola Pinto) The Complete Poems of D.H. Lawrence, 1964; (with Harry T. Moore) D.H. Lawrence and His World, 1966; Phoenix II: Uncollected Unpublished and Other Prose Work by D.H. Lawrence, 1968; gen. editor (with J.T. Boulton) Cambridge U. Press critical edit. of D.H. Lawrence works; others. Home: 2305 Windsor Rd Austin TX 78703

ROBERTS, GEORGE ADAM, metallurgist; b. Uniontown, Pa., Feb. 18, 1919; s. Jacob Earle and Mary M. (Bower) R.; student U.S. Naval Acad., 1935-37; B.Sc., Carnegie Tech., 1939, M.Sc., 1941, D.Sc., 1942; m. Betty E. Matthewson, May 31, 1941; children—George Thomas, William John, Mary Ellen; m. 2d, Jeanne Marie Polk. Technician Bell Telephone Labs., N.Y.C., 1938; research dir. Vasco Metals Corp. (formerly Vanadium Alloys Steel Co.), Latrobe, Pa., 1940-45, chief metallurgist, 1945-53, v.p., 1953-61, pres., 1961-66; pres., dir. Teledyne, Inc. (merger with Vasco Metals Corp.), Los Angeles, 1966—; hon. lectr. Societe Francaise de Metallurgie, 1960. Pres., Am. Soc. Metals Found. Edn. and Research, 1955-56, trustee, 1954-59, 63-64; mem. Greater Latrobe Sch. Bd., 1959-64. Recipient silver medal from Paris, 1955. Fellow Metall. Soc. Am. Inst. Mining, Metall. and Petroleum Engrs., Am. Soc. for Metals (chmn. Pitts. chpt. 1949-50, internat. pres. 1954-55, Gold medal 1977); mem. Nat. Acad. Engring., Metal Powder Industries Fedn. (dir. 1952-55, pres. 1957-61), Am. Iron and Steel Inst., Soc. Mfg. Engrs., Tau Beta Pi, hon. life mem. several fgn. socs. Methodist. Author: Tool Steels, 1944, 62. Contbr. articles trade jours. Office: 1901 Ave of the Stars Suite 1808 Los Angeles CA 90067

ROBERTS, GEORGE BERNARD, JR., realtor, state legislator; b. Andover, Mass., June 13, 1939; s. George Bernard and Helene F. (Eversen) R.; B.S., U. N.H., 1964, M.P.A., 1967; m. Margaret Fay Edmunds, Aug. 26, 1967; children—Abigail Emerson, Jessica Swift. Partner, Roberts Assos., Gilmanton, N.H., 1966—; mem. N.H. Ho. of Reps., 1967—, majority leader, 1971-73, speaker, 1975-76, 77-78, 79-80. Republican. Home: Smith Meeting House Rd Gilmanton NH 03237 Office: State House Concord NH 03301

ROBERTS, HARRY VIVIAN, educator; b. Peoria, Ill., May 1, 1923; s. Harry V. and Mary (Pickels) R.; B.A., U. Chgo., 1943, M.B.A., 1947, Ph.D., 1955; m. June H. Hoover, Nov. 19, 1943; children—Andrew H., Mary D. Market researcher McCann-Erickson, Inc., Chgo., 1946-49; mem. faculty Grad. Sch. Bus., U. Chgo., 1949—, prof. statistics, 1959—; cons. in field, 1950—. Mem. rezoning commn., Village of Homewood, Ill., 1956-60, 71-73, mem. zone bd. appeals, 1962-75, chmn., 1973-75, mem. plan commn., 1970-73. Served with AUS, 1943-45. Fellow Am. Statis. Assn. (census adv. com. 1973-78, asso. editor Jour. 1977—); mem. Royal Statis. Soc., Inst. Math. Statistics, Am. Econ. Assn., AAAS. Author: (with James H. Lorie) Basic Methods of Marketing, 1951; (with Allen Wallis) Statistics: A New Approach, 1956; Conversational Statistics, 1974; also articles. Home: 1353 Burr Oak Rd Homewood IL 60430 Office: Grad Sch Bus Univ Chgo Chicago IL 60637

ROBERTS, HENRY REGINALD, life ins. co. exec.; b. Toronto, Ont., Can., June 2, 1916; s. Alfred Reginald and Margaret (Creighton) R.; B.A. in Math. and Physics, U. Toronto, 1937; L.H.D. (hon.), Clarkson Coll. Tech., 1965; LL.D., Trinity Coll., 1970, U. Hartford, 1971; m. Margaret Elizabeth Fisher, May 23, 1940; children—Michael Alfred, Barbara Elizabeth, William Henry, Margaret Jane. Came to U.S., 1945, naturalized, 1954. With Mfrs. Life Ins. Co., Toronto, 1937-42; with Conn. Gen. Life Ins. Co., Hartford, 1945—, 2d v.p., 1958-60, exec. v.p., 1960-61, pres., 1961-76, also dir.; chmn. bd. Aetna Ins. Co., 1966-76; pres., dir. Conn. Gen. Ins. Corp. parent co., 1967-76, chmn. bd., 1976—; dir. Gen. Foods Corp., So. New Eng. Telephone Co. Adv. com. bus. programs Brookings Instn. Chmn. bd. trustee Kingswood-Oxford Sch.; trustee Hartford Grad. Center, Conn. Ednl. Telecommunications Corp., Met. Hartford YMCA; corporator St. Francis Hosp., Mt. Sinai Hosp., Hartford Hosp., Conn. Inst. Blind; past chmn. Ins. Assn. Conn.; mem. council Internat. Execs. Service Corps. Fellow Soc. Actuaries; mem. Am. Council Life Ins., Greater Hartford C. of C. (past chmn.). Office: Conn Gen Life Ins Co Hartford CT 06152

ROBERTS, IRVING, cons. engr.; b. Bklyn., Jan. 9, 1915; s. Isidor and Tillie (Dolin) R.; B.S., City Coll. N.Y., 1934; M.A., Columbia, 1935, Ph.D., 1937; m. Doris Hoxter, July 8, 1966; children by previous marriage—Ellen and Susan (twins). Teaching asst., later research asst. Columbia, 1935-39; phys. chemist, chem. engr. Weiss & Downs, Inc., N.Y.C., 1939-43; group leader Manhattan Project, N.Y.C., 1943-45; process div. engr. Elliott Co., Jeannette, Pa., 1945-50; cons. engr. on steel, aluminum, low temperatures, 1950-56; dir. planning corp. planning dept. Reynolds Metals Co., Richmond, Va., 1956-61, v.p., 1961-78; cons. engr., Richmond, 1978—; pres. Fan Garden Shop, Inc., Richmond, 1972—. Mem. Am. Inst. Chem. Engrs., Am. Chem. Soc., ASME, Am. Rhododendron Soc. Author: Home Landscaping You Can Design Yourself, 1972. Author papers. Patentee in field. Home: 3 Westwick Rd Richmond VA 23233 Office: 14100 Patterson Ave Richmond VA 23233

ROBERTS, JACK, U.S. judge; b. Sweetwater, Tex., Feb. 18, 1910; s. Benjamin F. and Sally (Hopkins) R.; LL.B., U. Tex., Austin, 1933; m. Bonnie Abernathy, June 23, 1943; 1 son, Jack. Admitted to Tex. bar, 1933; practice in Austin, 1933-42; dist. atty. Travis County, Tex., 1946-48; judge 126th Jud. Dist., Austin, 1948-66; U.S. dist. judge Western Dist. Tex., 1966—. Bd. dirs. Holy Cross Hosp., Austin. Served with AUS, 1942-45. Hon. mem. Order of Coif. Mason (33 deg., K.T., Shriner). Home: 1201 Claire Ave Austin TX 78703 Office: 200 W 8th St Austin TX 78701

ROBERTS, JACK EARLE, lawyer, ski resort operator, wood products co. exec., real estate developer; b. Los Angeles, Nov. 5, 1928; s. James Earle and Illa Ann (Morgan) R.; B.S. in Accounting and Bus. Adminstrn., Brigham Young U., 1952; J.D., George Washington U., 1955, LL.M. in Taxation (Teaching fellow), 1956; m. Marilyn Humphreys, Sept. 13, 1954; children—Ronda, Cyndi, Scott, Robynne, Craig. Admitted to Calif. bar, 1957, since practiced in Los Angeles; atty. Office Chief Counsel, IRS, Los Angeles, 1956-60; mem. firm Roberts, Carmack, Johnson, Paulson & Harmer, Los Angeles, 1961-78; pres. Park West Ski Resort, Snyderville, Utah, 1975—; pres., dir. Accudyne Corp., Los Angeles, 1972—, Richmark Corp., Los Angeles, 1972-77; chmn., dir. Comml. Wood Products Co., Los Angeles, 1968—; pres., dir. Snyderville Devel. Co., Inc. (Utah), 1978—. Pres. Westwood Republican Club, 1968; mem. Calif. State, Los Angeles County Rep. central coms., 1974-77. Bd. dirs. Ettie Lee Homes for Boys, sec. 1971-78. C.P.A., Ariz. Mem. Am., Los Angeles County bar assns., State Bar Calif., D.C. Bar, Calif. Soc. C.P.A.'s. Contbr. articles on legal subjects to tech. jours. Home: Box 1598 Park West UT 84060 Office: 10880 Wilshire Blvd Suite 1800 Los Angeles CA 90024

ROBERTS, JAMES MCGREGOR, profl. acad. exec.; b. Moncton, N.B., Can., Nov. 24, 1923; s. Roland M. and Edith M. (Shields) R.; came to U.S., 1949, naturalized, 1956; B.Commerce, U. Toronto (Ont., Can.), 1949; m. Thelma E. Williams, May 6, 1944; 1 dau., Jana M. Auditor, Citizens Bank, Los Angeles, 1949-54; auditor Acad. Motion Picture Arts and Scis., Hollywood, Calif., 1954—, controller, 1956-71, exec. dir., 1971—, exec. sec. acad. found., 1971—. Served as pilot Royal Can. Air Force, World War II. Mem. Beverly Hills (Calif.) C. of C. Home: 450 S Maple Dr Beverly Hills CA 90212 Office: 8949 Wilshire Blvd Beverly Hills CA 90211

ROBERTS, JAMES MILNOR, JR., assn. exec.; b. Pitts., Sept. 16, 1918; s. James Milnor and Elizabeth (Bennett) R.; student Lehigh U., 1936-40, U.S. Army Command and Gen. Staff Coll., 1962, Nat. Def. U., 1963, Army War Coll., 1970; m. Virginia Lee Sykes, Mar. 15, 1947; children—James Milnor III, Mary Lee, Deborah Lee, Todd Osborn. Commd. 2d lt. inf. U.S. Army, 1940, advanced through grades to maj., 1944, discharged, 1945, mem. Res., 1946-70; with 1st battle group U.S. Army Res. 314th Inf. Regt., Pitts., 1947-62; comdr. combat command sect. 79th Command Hdqrs., Pitts., 1962-64; with Office Chief Info., Dept. Army, Washington, 1964-67; comdr. 99th Army Res. Command, Pitts., 1967-70, promoted to maj. gen., 1971; dep. chief U.S. Army Res., Washington, 1970-71, chief, 1971-75; exec. dir. Res. Officers Assn. U.S., Washington, 1975—, pub. The Officer mag., 1975—; v.p. Nat. Intelligence Study Center. Chmn., Young Republicans, Allegheny County, Pa., 1952-54; exec. v.p. Wind Symphony Orch., Pitts., 1961-62; bd. dirs. Pitts. Civic Light Opera, 1958-70; nat. co-chmn. Coalition for Peace Through Strength. Decorated D.S.M., Legion of Merit, Bronze Star; Croix de Guerre with silver star (France); Mil. Cross (Czechoslovakia); named Significant Sig, Sigma Chi, 1973. Mem. Res. Officers Assn. (past chpt. officer), Am. Security Council (dir.), Soc. Am. Mil. Engrs. (v.p. at large), Assn. U.S. Army, Mil. Order World Wars, Ret. Officers Assn., SAR, VFW, Am. Legion, Washington Soc. Assn. Execs. Episcopalian. Clubs: Army-Navy (Washington); Pitts., Masons (Pitts.); Ft. Myer (Va.) Officers. Home: 3133 S 14th St Arlington VA 22204 Office: 1 Constitution Ave NE Washington DC 20002

ROBERTS, JANET LOUISE (ALSO LOUISA BRONTE, REBECCA DANTON, JANETTE RADCLIFFE), author, librarian; b. New Britain, Conn., Jan. 20, 1925; d. Walter Nelson and Marjorie Mae (Miller) R.; B.A., Otterbein Coll., 1946; M.S.L.S., Columbia U., 1966. Reference librarian Dayton and Montgomery County (Ohio) Public Library, 1966—; author numerous books, including: Jewels of Terror, 1970; The Weeping Lady, 1971; Ravenswood, 1971; Love Song, 1971; Dark Rose, 1971; The Devil's Own, 1972; The Curse of Kenton, 1972; Marriage of Inconvenience, 1973; Rivertown, 1972; Marriage of Inconvenience, 1972; Rivertown, 1972; My Lady Mischief, 1973; The Dancing Doll, 1973; The Dornstein Icon, 1973; The Golden Thistle, 1973; Isle of the Dolphins, 1973; La Casa Dorada, 1973; The Cardross Luck, 1974; The First Waltz, 1974; Castlereagh, 1975; Jade Vendetta, 1976; Wilderness Inn, 1976; Island of Desire, 1977; Isle of the Dolphins, 1978; Ravens-Wood, 1978; Black Pearls, 1979; as Rebecca Danton: Sign of the Golden Goose, 1972, Black Horse Tavern, 1972, Fire Opals, 1977, Amethyst Love, 1977, Ship of Hate, 1977, Star Sapphire, 1979; as Louisa Bronte: Lord Satan, 1972, Her Demon Lover, 1973, Greystone Tavern, 1975, Gathering at Greystone, 1976, The Valette Heritage, 1979, The Van Rhyne Heritage, 1979; as Janette Radcliffe: The Blue-Eyed Gypsy, 1974, The Moonlight Gondola, 1975, Gentleman Pirate, 1975, The Heart Awakens, 1977, Lions and Lovers, 1979. Mem. ALA, Ohio Library Assn., Mystery Writers Am. Office: Dayton and Montgomery County Public Library 215 E 3d St Dayton OH 45402*

ROBERTS, JAY, pharmacologist; b. N.Y.C., July 15, 1927; s. Harry and Evelyn R.; B.S., L.I. U., 1949; Ph.D., Cornell U., 1953; m. Marion Camenson, June 18, 1950; children—Hunt, Kathy. Asst. prof., then asso. prof. pharmacology Cornell U. Med. Coll., 1956-66; prof. pharmacology U. Pitts. Med. Sch., 1966-70; prof. pharmacology, chmn. dept. Med. Coll. Pa., 1970—; cons. to industry. Mem. NIH Study Sect. Served with USNR, 1945-46. Postdoctoral fellow N.Y. Heart Assn., 1953-57, USPHS, 1953-55; recipient Lindback distinguished teaching award, 1973. Fellow Am. Coll. Cardiology, Coll. Physicians Phila.; mem. Internat. Study Group Research Cardiac Metabolism, AAAS, Am. Soc. Pharmacology and Exptl. Therapeutics, Soc. Exptl. Biology and Medicine, Cardiac Muscle Soc., Am., N.Y., Southeastern Pa. heart assns., Harvey Soc., Greater Phila. Com. Med.-Pharm. Scis., Worcester Found. Exptl. Biology, Myo-Bio Club Phila., Assn. Med. Sch. Pharmacology, Phila. Physiol. Soc., Am. Coll. Clin. Pharmacology (charter), Am. Fedn. Clin. Research, Am. Soc. Gerontology, AAUP, Sigma Xi. Contbr. numerous articles profl. jours.; reviewer for numerous sci. jours. Home: Benson House 730 Montgomery Ave Rosemont PA 19010 Office: Med Coll Pa 3300 Henry Ave Philadelphia PA 19129

ROBERTS, JEANNE ADDISON, educator; b. Washington; d. John West and Sue Fisher (Nichols) Addison; A.B., Agnes Scott Coll., 1946; M.A., U. Pa., 1947; Ph.D., U. Va., 1964; m. Markley Roberts, Feb. 19, 1966; children—Addison Cary Steed Masengill, Ellen Carraway Masengill Coster. Instr., Mary Washington Coll., 1947-48; instr., chmn. English, Fairfax Hall Jr. Coll., 1950-51; tchr. Am. U. Assn. Lang. Center, Bangkok, Thailand, 1952-56; instr. Beirut (Lebanon) Coll. for Women, 1956-57, asst. prof., 1957-60, chmn. English dept., 1957-60; instr. lit. Am. U., Washington, 1960-62, asst. prof., 1962-65, asso. prof., 1965-68, prof., 1968—, dean faculties, 1974; lectr. Howard U., 1971-72; seminar prof. Folger Shakespeare Library Inst. for Renaissance and 18th Century Studies, 1974—. Danforth Tchr. grantee, 1962-63; Folger Sr. fellow, 1969-70. Mem. Modern Lang. Assn., Renaissance Soc. Am., Milton Soc., Shakespeare Assn. Am. (trustee 1978—), AAUP (pres. Am. U. chpt. 1966-67), Phi Beta Kappa, Mortar Board, Phi Kappa Phi. Episcopalian. Editor: (with James G. McManaway) A Selective Bibliography of Shakespeare: Editions, Textual Studies, Commentary,

1975; author: Shakespeare's English Comedy: The Merry Wives of Windsor in Context, 1979; contbr. articles to scholarly jours. Home: 4931 Albemarle St NW Washington DC 20016 Office: Dept Lit Am U Washington DC 20016

ROBERTS, JOHN D., chemist, univ. adminstr.; b. Los Angeles, June 8, 1918; s. Allen Andrew and Flora (Dombrowski) R.; A.B., U. Calif. at Los Angeles, 1941, Ph.D., 1944; Dr. rer. nat. h.c., U. Munich, 1962; D.Sc., Temple U., 1964; m. Edith Mary Johnson, July 11, 1942; children—Anne Christine, Donald William, John Paul, Allen Walter. Instr. chemistry U. Calif. at Los Angeles, 1944-45; NRC fellow chemistry Harvard, 1945-46, instr. chemistry, 1946; instr. chemistry Mass. Inst. Tech., 1946, asst. prof., 1947-50, asso. prof., 1950-52; vis. prof. Ohio State U., 1952, Stanford U., 1973-74; prof. organic chemistry Calif. Inst. Tech., 1953-72, Inst. prof. chemistry, 1972—, dean of faculty, v.p., provost, 1980—, chmn. div. chemistry and chem. engring., 1963-68, acting chmn., 1972-73; Foster lectr. U. Buffalo, 1956; Mack Meml. lectr. Ohio State U., 1957; Falk-Plaut lectr. Columbia, 1957; Reynaud Found. lectr. Mich. State U., 1958; Bachmann Meml. lectr. U. Mich., 1958; vis. prof. Harvard, 1958-59, M. Tishler lectr., 1965; Reilly lectr. Notre Dame U., 1960; Am.-Swiss Found. lectr., 1960; O.M. Smith lectr. Okla. State U., 1962; M.S. Kharasch Meml. lectr. U. Chgo., 1962; K. Folkers lectr. U. Ill., 1962; Phillips lectr. Haverford Coll., 1963; vis. prof. U. Munich, 1962; Sloan lectr. U. Alaska, 1967; Distinguished vis. prof. U. Iowa, 1967; Sprague lectr. U. Wis., 1967; Kilpatrick lectr. Ill. Inst. Tech., 1969; Pacific Northwest lectr., 1969; E.F. Smith lectr. U. Pa., 1970; vis. prof. chemistry Stanford, 1973-74; S.C. Lind lectr. U. Tenn.; Arapahoe lectr. U. Colo., 1976; Mary E. Kapp lectr. Va. Commonwealth U., 1976; R.T. Major lectr. U. Conn., 1977; Nebr. lectr. Am. Chem. Soc., 1977; dir., cons. editor W.A. Benjamin, Inc., 1961-67; cons. E.I. du Pont Co.; mem. adv. panel chemistry NSF, 1958-60, chmn., 1959-60, chmn. divisional com. math., phys. engring. scis., 1962-64, mem. math. and phys. sci. div. com., 1964-66; chemistry adv. panel Air Force Office Sci. Research, 1959-61; chmn. chemistry sect. Nat. Acad. Scis., 1968-71, chmn. Class I, 1976-78. Recipient Alumni Profl. Achievement award U. Calif. at Los Angeles, 1967; Guggenheim fellow, 1952-53, 55-56; recipient Am. Chem. Soc. award pure chemistry, 1954; Harrison Howe award, 1957; Roger Adams award in organic chemistry, 1967; Alumni Achievement award U. Calif. at Los Angeles, 1967; Nichols medal, 1972; Tolman medal, 1975; Michelson-Morley award, 1976; Norris award, 1978. Mem. Am. Chem. Soc. (chmn. organic chemistry div. 1956-57; exec. com. organic div. 1953-57; Nebr. lectr. Nebr. sect.), Nat. Acad. Scis., Am. Philos. Soc., Am. Acad. Arts and Scis., Sigma Xi, Phi Lambda Upsilon, Alpha Chi Sigma. Author: Basic Organic Chemistry, Part I, 1955; Nuclear Magnetic Resonance, 1958; Spin-Spin Splitting in High-Resolution Nuclear Magnetic Resonance Spectra, 1961: Molecular Orbital Calculations, 1961; (with M.C. Caserio) Basic Principles of Organic Chemistry, 1964, 2d edit., 1977; Modern Organic Chemistry, 1967; (with R. Stewart and M.C. Caserio) Organic Chemistry-Methane To Macromolecules, 1971. Cons. editor McGraw-Hill Series in Advanced Chemistry, 1957-60; editor-in-chief Organic Syntheses, vol. 41; editorial bd. Tetrahedron, Nouveau Chimie. Office: Calif Inst Tech Pasadena CA 91125

ROBERTS, JOHN MILTON, educator; b. Omaha, Dec. 8, 1916; s. John Milton and Ruth (Kohler) R.; A.B., U. Nebr., 1937; student U. Chgo., 1937-39; Ph.D., Yale, 1947; m. Marie Louise Kotouc, May 22, 1941; children—Tania, Andrea; m. 2d, Joan Marilyn Skutt, Oct. 22, 1961; children—James, John. Asst. prof. anthropology U. Minn., 1947-48, Harvard, 1948-53; asso. prof., then prof. U. Nebr., 1953-58; prof. Cornell U., 1958-71; Andrew W. Mellon prof. anthropology U. Pitts., 1971—; prof. comparative cultures Naval War Coll., 1969-70. Served as officer AUS, 1942-45. Decorated Silver Star, Bronze Star. Fellow Center Advanced Study Behavioral Scis., 1956-57. Mem. Am. Anthrop. Assn., Am. Ethnological Soc. (past pres.), Am. Sociol. Assn., Am. Psychol. Assn., Linguistic Soc. Am., Royal Anthrop. Inst., Soc. Am. Archaeology, Northeastern Anthrop. Assn. (past pres.), Soc. Cross-Cultural Research (past pres.), Anthrop. Assn. Study of Play (pres.), Phi Beta Kappa, Sigma Xi. Author: Three Navaho Households, 1951; co-author: Studies of an Elementary Game of Strategy, 1967; Zuni Law, 1954. Contbr. articles to profl. jours. Home: 122 Kent Dr Pittsburgh PA 15241

ROBERTS, JUSTIN, journalist; b. N.Y.C., June 10, 1919; s. Louis and Claire (Meyers) R.; B.A., Wayne U., 1941; m. Lois Elinore Schneider, Sept. 5, 1943; children—Donn Roberts, Alta (Mrs. Paul Nelson), Sarah Roberts. With N.Y. Daily Mirror, 1935-36, INP, 1936-41, Acme Newspictures, N.Y.C., 1941-50; editor Calif. newspapers, 1953-61; editor, writer Contra Costa Times Lesher Newspapers, Walnut Creek, Calif., 1961—; condr. investigation Bay Area Rapid Transit Dist., 1972-73. Recipient nat. journalism award Nat. Soc. Profl. Engrs., 1972, A.P. Writing award, 1974, Journalism award State Soc. Profl. Engrs., 1976. Club: Contra Costa Press. Home: 3009 S Apple Ct Antioch CA 94509 Office: 2640 Shadelands Dr Walnut Creek CA 94596

ROBERTS, KENNETH LEWIS, banker; b. Dungannon, Va., Dec. 12, 1932; s. Clarence Eugene and Katherine (Osborne) R.; B.A., Vanderbilt U., 1954, LL.B., 1959; m. Anne Foster Cook, Sept. 10, 1955; children—Stephen Cook, Kenneth L., Patrick Foster. Admitted to Tenn. bar; asso. prof. law Vanderbilt U., 1959-60; asso. Waller, Lansden & Dortch, Nashville, 1960-66; exec. v.p. Commerce Union Bank, Nashville, 1966-71; pres., chief exec. officer, dir. Central Nat. Bank, Richmond, Va., 1971-76, First Am. Nat. Bank, Nashville, 1976—; dir. First Amtenn Corp., 1976—, vice chmn., 1976-77, pres., chief exec. officer, 1977—; past pres., dir. Central Nat. Corp.; dir. A.H. Robins Co., Inc., Thalhimer Bros., Inc. Mem. regional adv. com. on banking policies and practices Comptroller of Currency, 1974—. Trustee Vanderbilt U.; bd. dirs. St. Thomas Devel. Found., Nashville Symphony, Tenn. Performing Arts Mgmt. Corp., Blair Sch. Music, Leadership Nashville; mem. exec. bd. Middle Tenn. council Boy Scouts Am. Served to lt., Chem. Corps, AUS, 1955-57. Mem. Am., Tenn., Nashville bar assns., Am., Va. (bank mgmt. com. 1975—) bankers assn., Assn. Res. City Bankers Young Pres.'s Orgn., Retail Mchts. Assn. Greater Richmond (dir. 1975—). Nashville C. of C. (treas.). Clubs: Cumberland, Rotary, Belle Meade Country. Home: 3800 Woodlawn Dr Nashville TN 37215 Office: First American Center Nashville TN 37237

ROBERTS, LORIN WATSON, educator, botanist; b. Clarksdale, Mo., June 28, 1923; s. Lorin Cornelius and Irene (Watson) R.; B.A., U. Mo. at Columbia, 1948, M.A., 1950, Ph.D. in Botany, 1952; m. Florence Ruth Greathouse, July 10, 1967; children—Michael Hamlin, Daniel Hamlin, Margaret Susan. Asst. prof., then asso. prof. botany Agnes Scott Coll., Decaur, Ga., 1952-57; vis. asst. prof. Emory U., 1952-55; mem. faculty U. Idaho, 1957—, prof. botany, 1967—; Fulbright research prof. Kyoto (Japan) U., 1967-68; research fellow U. Bari (Italy), 1968; Cabot fellow Harvard, 1974; Fulbright teaching fellow North-Eastern Hill U., Shillong, Meghalaya, India, 1977; pres. botany sect. 1st Internat. Congress Histochemistry and Cytochemistry, Paris, 1960. Served with USAAF, 1943-46. Decorated chevalier de l'Ordre du Merite Agricole (France), 1961. Fellow AAAS; mem. N.W. Sci. Assn. (pres. 1970-71), Bot. Soc. Am., Histochem. Soc., Tissue Culture Assn., Internat. Assn. Plant Tissue Culture, Internat. Soc. Plant Morphologists, Am. Inst. Biol. Scis., Idaho Acad. Scis., Sigma Xi, Phi Kappa Phi, Phi Sigma. Author: Cytodifferentiation in Plants, 1976; contbr. articles to profl. jours. Home: 920 Mabelle Ave Moscow ID 83843

ROBERTS, MARC JEFFREY, educator; b. Bayonne, N.J., Feb. 11, 1943; s. Wilfred Rogow and Dorothy (Shanbam) R.; B.A., Harvard, 1964, Ph.D. in Econs., 1969; Fulbright fellow, U. Newcastle-Upon-Tyne, 1964-65; m. Ann Tager Stein, Dec. 22, 1963; children—Jennifer Sophie, Justine Elizabeth, Clement Seth, Zachery Ethan. Asst. prof. dept. econs. Harvard, Cambridge, Mass., 1969-72, asso. prof., 1972-75, prof. polit. economy and health policy Sch. Pub. Health, 1975—. Cons., Nat. Water Commn., EPA, HEW, Mass. Dept. Pub. Health. Mem. Nat. Air Pollution Commn., Am. Lung Assn.; mem. com. energy and environment Nat. Acad. Scis. Danforth fellow. Mem. Am. Econ. Assn., Fedn. Am. Scientists (council), Am. Acad. Arts and Scis. (chmn. com. on environ. alteration), Phi Beta Kappa. Democrat. Editor: (with R. Caves) Regulating the Product, 1975. Contbr. articles profl. jours. Home: 164 Highland Ave Newton MA 02160 Office: Sch Pub Health 677 Huntington Ave Kresge Bldg 408 Harvard U Cambridge MA 02115

ROBERTS, MARGUERITE, educator, author; b. Rockport, Ind., Mar. 15, 1904; d. Judge Ralph Elmer and Alice Enfield (Saunders) Roberts; A.B., U. Evansville, 1924; A.M., Harvard, 1928, Ph.D., 1943; postgrad. Ind. U., Cambridge U., U. Chgo., Weymouth Coll., Eng. Dean women, asst. prof. English, McMaster U., Can., 1937-46; lectr. English, U. Toronto, 1946-47; dean, Westhampton Coll., U. Richmond, 1947-65, prof. English, 1947-74, chmn. dept. English, 1965-74; research fellow Radliffe Coll., Cambridge, Mass., spring 1961; rep. of Fulbright program and leaders program sponsored by Dept. State; mem. Def. Adv. Com. on Women in the Services, 1965-68. Mem. Canadian Authors, 1938-49; mem. panel Gov. Gen. Awards for Lit. in Can., 1946-49; del. Can. U. Women to Internat. Conf., Internat. Fedn. U. Women, Stockholm, Sweden, 1939. Mem. adv. com. Can. Red Cross, Hamilton, Ont., World War II. Recipient Alumni Certificate of Excellence, U. Evansville, 1977. Mem. AAUW, Am. Deans Assn., English-Speaking Union, Phi Beta Kappa. Clubs: Woman's (pres. 1970-71, dir.), Virginia Writers (v.p. 1970, pres. 1975-77) (Richmond); Radcliffe, Harvard of Va. Author: Tess in the Theater, 1950, Japanese edit., 1970; Hardy's Poetic Drama and the Theatre, 1965, also articles in learned jours. Asso. editor Dean's Jour., 1942-49. Address: 15 Towana Rd Richmond VA 23226

ROBERTS, MELVILLE PARKER, JR., surgeon, educator; b. Phila., Oct. 15, 1931; s. Melville Parker and Marguerite Louise (Reimann) R.; B.S., Washington and Lee U., 1953; M.D. (James Hudson Brown research fellow), Yale U., 1957; m. Sigrid Marianne Magnusson, Mar. 27, 1954; children—Parker, Julia Pell, Erik Emerson. Intern, Yale Med. Center, 1957, neurosurg. resident, 1958-60, 62-64, Am. Cancer Soc. fellow in neurosurgery, 1962-64, instr., 1964; asst. prof. surgery U. Va. Sch. Medicine, Charlottesville, 1965-69; practice medicine specializing in neurol. surgery, Hartford, Conn., 1970—; mem. staff Hartford Hosp., John Dempsey Hosp., Newington Children's Hosp.; asst. prof. surgery U. Conn. Sch. Medicine, Farmington, 1970-71, asso. prof., 1972-75, asso. prof. neurology, chmn. div. neurosurgery, 1973—, prof. surgery, 1975—, acting chmn. dept. neurology, 1973-77, acting chmn. dept. surgery, 1974-77, William Beecher Scoville prof. neurosurgery, 1976—; cons. neurosrugeon VA Hosp., Newington, Conn., Milford Hosp. Served as capt. M.C., U.S. Army, 1960-61. Diplomate Am. Bd. Neurol. Surgery. Fellow A.C.S.; mem. Am. Assn. Neurol. Surgeons, Soc. Neurol. Surgeons, Congress. Neurol. Surgeons, Assn. for Research in Nervous and Mental Diseases, Am. Assn. Anatomists, Am. Acad. Neurology, New Eng. Neurosurg. Soc., Assn. Am. Med. Colls., AMA, Sigma Xi. Episcopalian. Author: Atlas of the Human Brain in Section, 1970; mem. editorial bd. Conn. Medicine, 1973—; contbr. articles to profl. jours. Home: 10 Mountain Spring Rd Farmington CT 06032 Office: 85 Jefferson St Hartford CT 06106

ROBERTS, MELVIN JOHN, banker; b. Denver, May 6, 1908; s. G.H. and Myra (Sowles) R.; student U. Colo., 1925-26; Ph.B., Yale, 1930; postgrad. U. Denver, 1930-33; grad. Rutgers U. Sch. Banking, 1938; m. Elizabeth Daly, July 5, 1939 (dec. May 1944); children—Melvin S., Elizabeth D. (Mrs. Roland D. Ball); m. 2d, Edith Malo, Mar. 5, 1957; 1 son, Peter G.M.; stepchildren—Frank Freeman Foster, William R. Easton III. Asst. trust officer Colo. Nat. Bank, 1930-42, exec. v.p., dir., 1958-62, pres., 1962-70, chmn. bd., 1970-75, chief exec. officer, 1962-72; v.p., treas. Capitol Life Ins. Co., 1945-58, dir., 1958—; pres. Colo. Nat. Bankshares, Inc., 1968-75, chmn. bd., 1975-76. Former chmn. Denver Planning Bd.; former pres. Colo. Pub. Expenditure Council; bd. dirs., treas. Denver Regional Transit Dist., 1973—; trustee U. Denver, Social Sci. Found., Com. Econ. Devel. Republican. Presbyn. Clubs: Denver Country, Mile High, University (Denver). Home: 222 Gaylord St Denver CO 80206 Office: Colo National Bank Denver 17th and Champa Sts Denver CO 80217

ROBERTS, MERRILL JOSEPH, economist, educator; b. Glendive, Mont., Aug. 10, 1915; s. Merrill Joseph and Inez (Ludgate) R.; B.A., U. Minn., 1938; M.B.A., U. Chgo., 1939, Ph.D., 1952; m. Janet Hunter Dion, Aug. 31, 1941; children—David, Michael, James, Patricia. Teaching asst. U. Minn., 1939-40; transp. economist OPA, 1941, Dept. Agr., 1942-46, TVA, 1946-48; asst. prof. transp. and econs., then asso. prof. U. Fla., 1948-54, prof., 1955-58; asso. prof. transp. U. Calif. at Los Angeles, 1954-55; vis. prof. econs. Mich. State U., 1956-57; prof. transp. and pub. utilities, head dept. U. Pitts., 1958-61, prof. transp. Grad. Sch. Bus., 1958-72, prof. econs., 1960-72, chmn. faculty, 1960-63; dir. Bur. Bus. Research, 1963-66; v.p., dir. econs. div. Wilbur Smith and Assos., 1972-75; prof., chmn. transp., bus. and pub. policy U. Md., 1975—; research cons. Nat. Transp. Policy Study Commn., 1977-79; mem. com. applications of econs. Transp. Research Bd., Nat. Acad. Scis., 1973—; econ. adv. Estudio Integral de Transport de Bolivia, 1979; mem. adv. panel, r.r. merger project Rail Services Planning Office, ICC; dir. study Penn Central R.R. bankruptcy U.S. Senate, 1971-72. Econ. cons. numerous fgn. govts. including New Zealand, Thailand, Singapore, Hong Kong, Korea, Spain, Nicaragua, Algeria; cons. transp. to bus. and govt. agys.; research staff Commn. Money and Credit, 1959-60; mem. Venezuelan Commn. Economica Ferroviaria Nacional, 1959-60; participant transp. study conf. Nat. Acad. Sci.-NRC, 1960; research staff Nat. Planning Assn. study, 1962-63; participant Am. Assembly Conf. on the Future of Am. Transp., 1971; mem. research com. Transp. Assn. Am., 1965-72; mem. commn. econs. Transp. Research Bd., 1972—; v.p. Am. Transp. Research Forum, 1960-63; mem. legis. com. Allegheny Regional Adv. Bd., 1959-72; bd. dirs. Port Authority Allegheny County, 1962-69. Bd. visitors Amy Transp. Sch., 1959-60. Served to lt. (s.g.) USNR, 1942-46. Mem. Am. Econs. Assn. (sec.-treas. transp. and pub. utilities group 1957-61, chmn. 1963), Am. Soc. Traffic and Transp. (founder mem.), Nat. Def. Transp. Assn. (life), Delta Nu Alpha, Phi Delta Theta, Beta Gamma Sigma. Presbyterian. Club: Cosmos (Washington). Author: (with T.C. Bigham) Citrus Fruit Rates, 1950; (with T.C. Bigham) Transportation, 1952; Taxation of Railroads and Other State-Assessed Companies in Florida, 1957; Evaluation of Rate Regulation, 1959; Transportation in Region in Transition, 1962; Freight Transport Coordination, 1966; The Penn Central and Other Railroads, 1973. Contbr. numerous articles to profl. jours. Home: 230 New Mark Esplanade Rockville MD 20850

ROBERTS, MILLARD GEORGE, educator; b. Schenevus, N.Y., Dec. 10, 1917; s. Elmer Jay and Madge Ethel (Roberts) R.; student Wyoming Sem., Kingston, Pa., 1934-35; B.A., Syracuse U., 1939; student Yale Div. Sch., 1939-41; B.D., U. Chgo., 1942, Ph.D., 1947; D.D., Hartwick Coll., 1959; m. Louise Evelyn Acker, Jan. 6, 1942; children—Mary Barbara, Ann Helen, Robert North, Richard Bradford. Ordained to ministry Presbyn. Ch., 1943; asso. pastor Bryn Mawr Community Ch., Chgo., 1946-49; pastor First Presbyn. Ch., Olean, N.Y., 1949-52; asst. to the pastor Brick Presbyn. Ch., N.Y.C., 1952-55; pres. Parsons Coll., Fairfield, Iowa, 1955-67. Chmn. Crusade for Freedom, Western N.Y. state, 1950; dir. Olean YMCA, 1950-52, Salvation Army, 1949-52; mem. exec. com. United Fund of Iowa, 1956-67. Served as maj., chaplain, USAAF, 1943-46; maj. N.Y. State N.G., 1949-52; sr. staff chaplain Iowa N.G., 1956—, col. ret., 1965. Mem. Iowa State Fulbright Com., 1963—. Awarded Army Commendation Medal, Presdl. Citation. Recipient Citizenship award, U. Chgo., 1960; Arents Pioneer medal Syracuse U., 1966. Mem. Mil. Chaplains Assn. U.S. (nat. chmn. 1948, editor The Military Chaplain, 1954-56), Young Presidents Orgn., Mil. Order Fgn. Wars, Am. Legion (chaplain 1954), Phi Beta Kappa, Phi Kappa Phi, Delta Sigma Rho, Pi Gamma Mu, Alpha Chi Rho. Presbyn. (finance com. Presbytery of N.Y.; adviser N.Y. Presbytery Council). Mason, Rotarian. Clubs: University (N.Y.C. and Chgo.); Des Moines; Lake Placid. Home: Snowdon Southside Oneonta NY 13820

ROBERTS, NEIL FLETCHER, mgmt. cons. co. exec.; b. Salem, Oreg., Feb. 4, 1914; s. Harold D. and Rhoda (Haynes) R.; A.B., Dartmouth, 1935; M.B.A., Harvard, 1937; m. Lee (Roberts) R., June 23, 1937; children—Stephen L., Susan A. (Mrs. J.B. Persson). With United Bank Denver N.A. (formerly U.S. Nat. Bank, merger with Denver Nat. Bank 1959, became Denver U.S. Nat. Bank), 1937—, v.p., 1948-54, exec. v.p., 1954-62, pres., 1962-69, vice chmn., 1971—, chief exec. officer, 1969-71; v.p. United Banks Colo., Inc. (formerly Denver U.S. Bancorp., Inc.), 1964-70, exec. v.p., 1971-72, pres., 1972-77, chief exec. officer, 1974-79, chmn. bd., 1977-79; v.p. Sheehan Internat., Denver, 1979—; chmn. United Mortgage Co., 1971-74, dir., 1968-71, 74-77; chmn. United Banks Service Co., 1971-75, dir., 1975-77. Trustee, Mile High United Way, 1971-79, chmn., pres., 1969-71. Served as lt. (j.g.) USNR, 1944-46. Mem. Phi Kappa Sigma. Episcopalian. Club: Colo. Harvard Bus. Sch. Home: 3165 S Hills Ct Denver CO 80210 Office: 2310 United Bank Center 1700 Broadway Denver CO 80217

ROBERTS, NORBERT JOSEPH, physician; b. Alabama, N.Y., June 6, 1916; s. Cory Rudell and Bertha (McTigue) R.; student Canisius Coll., Buffalo, 1934-36; M.D., U. Buffalo, 1940; M.S., U. Minn., 1949; m. Winifred Irene Dolan, Oct. 23, 1943; children—Norbert Joseph, Jerome M., Kevin J., Beth Ann, Mary Ann. Intern Buffalo Gen. Hosp., 1940-41, resident pathology, 1941-42; fellow internal medicine Mayo Found. for Med. Edn. and Research, 1946-49; sr. physician Exxon Corp., N.Y.C., 1949-52, asso. med. dir., 1955-74, med. dir., 1974—; med. dir. Pa. R.R., 1952-55; asst. prof. dept. community medicine Sch. Medicine, U. Pa., 1953-73; asso. clin. prof. dept. community medicine Mt. Sinai Med. Sch., N.Y.C., 1974—; lectr. N.Y.U. Inst. Environ. Medicine, 1955—. Chmn. exec. com. Nat. Assn. Drug Abuse Problems, 1972—; bd. dirs. N.Y. League for Hard of Hearing, 1974—, Nat. Assn. Mental Health, 1976—, Nat. Fund for Med. Edn.; trustee Exxon Edn. Found., 1976—. Served from 1st lt. to maj., USAAF, 1942-46; ETO. Diplomate, vice chmn. Am. Bd. Preventive Medicine; diplomate Am. Bd. Internal Medicine. Fellow A.C.P., Am. Coll. Preventive Medicine, N.Y. Acad. Scis. (bd. govs., chmn. environ. health sect.), Am. Acad. Occupational Medicine; mem. West Side Clin. Soc. N.Y.C. (past pres.), N.Y. Acad. Medicine (past sect. chmn.), Soc. for Occupational and Environ. Health (v.p., dir.), Med. Execs. (past pres.), Am. Occupational Med. Assn. (past pres.), Soverign Mil. Order Malta (master knight). Roman Catholic. Clubs: Hemisphere, University (N.Y.C.). Contbr. articles to profl. jours. Home: Rivermere Bronxville NY 10708 Office: 1251 Ave of Americas New York NY 10020

ROBERTS, (GRANVILLE) ORAL, clergyman; b. nr. Ada, Okla., Jan. 24, 1918; s. Ellis Melvin and Claudius Priscilla (Irwin) R.; student Okla. Bapt. U., 1942-44, Phillips U., 1947; m. Evelyn Lutman, Dec. 25, 1938; children—Rebecca Ann (dec.), Ronald David, Richard Lee, Roberta Jean. Ordained to ministry Pentecostal Holiness Ch., 1936, trans. ordination to United Meth. Ch., 1968; evangelist, 1936-41; pastor, Fuquay Springs, N.C., 1941, Shawnee, Okla., 1942-45, Toccoa, Ga., 1946, Enid, Okla., 1947; began worldwide evangelistic ministry thru crusades, radio, TV, printed page, 1947; founder Oral Roberts Evangelistic Assn., Inc.; founder Univ. Village Retirement Center, City of Faith Med. and Research Center; founder, pub. Abundant Life monthly mag., Daily Blessing, quar. mag.; founder pres. Oral Roberts U., Tulsa, 1963—; appears on weekly half-hour TV program, quar. one-hour TV spl.; dir. Bank Okla. Club: Rotary. Author over 50 books including If You Need Healing, Do These Things, 1947; God is a Good God, 1960; If I Were You, 1967; Miracle of Seed-Faith, 1970; (autobiography) The Call, 1971; The Miracle Book, 1972; A Daily Guide to Miracles, 1975; Better Health and Miracle Living, 1976; How to Get Through Your Struggles, 1977; Receiving Your Miracle, 1978; also numerous tracts and brochures. Office: Oral Roberts University 7777 S Lewis Ave Tulsa OK 74171

ROBERTS, PERNELL, actor; b. Waycross, Ga., May 18; student U. Md.; m. Cara Knack; 1 son. Appeared in summer stock theater, making profl. debut in The Man Who Came to Dinner, Olney (Md.) Theater; actor Arena Stage, Washington, 1950; appeared in off-Broadway prodns. including Am. Lyric Theatre, Shakepearewrights Co.; Broadway debut: Tonight in Samarkand, 1953; Broadway appearances include: The Lovers, A Clearing in the Woods; appeared in summer tours of Camelot, The King and I; appeared in musical version of Gone with the Wind, Los Angeles Civic Light Opera; toured in Captain Brassbound's Conversion, The Music Man; appeared on TV series Bonanza, 1959-65, Trapper John, M.D., 1979—; appeared in mini-series Captains and the Kings, 1976; film appearances include: Desire Under the Elms, The Sheepman, Ride Lonesome, The Magic of Lassie; TV films include: Dead Man on the Run, The Lives of Jenny Dolan, The Deadly Tower, Charlie Cobb: Nice Night for a Hanging. Served with USMR. Recipient Drama Desk award for role in Macbeth, 1955. Office: care Public Relations 20th Century Fox TV PO Box 900 Beverly Hills CA 90213*

ROBERTS, RACHEL, actress; b. Llanelly, Wales, Sept. 20, 1927; d. Richard Rhys and Rachel Ann Roberts; B.A. in English, U. Wales; student Royal Acad. Dramatic Art; m. Alan Dobie, 1955 (div. 1960); m. 2d, Rex Harrison, 1962 (div. 1971). Joined Shakespeare Meml. Theatre, Stratford-on-Avon, 1951; appeared Watergate Theatre, London, 1953; theater appearances include Alpha Beta, London, Eng., The Visit and Chemin de Fer, 1973, New Phoenix Repertory Co., N.Y.C., The Effect of Gamma Rays on Man-in-the Moon Marigolds, Los Angeles, 1971, Once a Catholic, 1979; films include The Good Companions, 1957, The Weak and the Wicked, Valley of Song, Our Man in Havana, 1959, Saturday Night and Sunday Morning, 1961, Girl on Approval, This Sporting Life, 1963, Doctors' Wives, 1971, O Lucky Man, 1973, Alpha Beta, 1976, Foul Play, 1978, others; also revues also numerous TV appearances including Jonathan North, Circus, Time, Sunday Out of Season, Shadow Squad, regular on The Tony Randall Show, ABC-TV, 1976-78. Recipient Clarence Derwent award; Brit. Acad. award for Saturday Night and Sunday Morning, This Sporting Life; London Evening Standard best actress award Alpha Beta. Address: care Internat Creative Mgmt 8899 Beverly Blvd Los Angeles CA 90048*

ROBERTS, RAY, congressman; b. nr. McKinney, Tex., Mar. 28, 1913; s. Roy C. and Margaret (Burton) R.; student Tex. A. and M. Coll., 1930-31, North Tex. State Coll., 1931-32, U. Tex., 1933-35; m. Elizabeth Bush, Nov. 12, 1946; 1 dau., Kay (Mrs. Tom Murray II). Mem. staff Speaker Sam Rayburn, U.S. Ho. of Reps., 1940-42; mem. Tex. Senate from 9th Dist., 1955-62; elected 87th Congress to fill unexpired term of Speaker Rayburn, 1962; mem. 88th-96th congresses from 4th Tex. Dist. Served to capt. USNR, World War II; PTO, ETO. Democrat. Home: 509 Tucker St McKinney TX 75069 Office: 2184 Rayburn House Office Bldg Washington DC 20515*

ROBERTS, RAY CROUSE, JR., economist, educator; b. Burlington, N.C., Jan. 8, 1929; s. Ray Crouse and Bessie (Cloniger) R.; A.B., Duke, 1950; M.S., U. N.C., 1957, Ph.D., 1961; m. Alice Suzanne Molnar, June 24, 1952; children—David, Rebecca, Eric, Mark. Indsl. engr. Glen Raven Cotton Mills (N.C.), 1952-54; asst. prof., asso. prof., prof. econs. Old Dominion Coll., Norfolk, Va., 1956-67, chmn. dept. econs., 1962-67; vis. asso. prof. econs. Duke, 1964-65; dean Sch. Bus. Adminstrn., Winthrop Coll., Rock Hill, S.C., 1967-69; Frederick W. Symmes prof. econs. Furman U., Greenville, S.C., 1969—, chmn. dept. econs., 1969-73; cons. Office of Adminstrn., U.S. Patent and Trademark Office. Served to 1st lt. USMCR, 1950-52; col. Res. ret. Mem. So. Econ. Assn., Indsl. Relations Research Assn., Am. Arbitration Assn. (nat. labor panel), S.C. Acad. Sci. Democrat. Methodist. Home: Route 7 11 Dundee Ln Greenville SC 29609

ROBERTS, RICHARD WATERS, assn. exec.; b. Kansas City, Mo., June 6, 1928; s. Ernest Woodson and Josephine (Waters) R.; B.A., Yale U., 1950; LL.B., U. Va., 1956; m. Elizabeth Shelby Elliott, Apr. 16, 1966; children—Richard Waters, Elizabeth Arnold. Admitted to N.Y. bar, 1957; asso. firm White & Case, N.Y.C., 1956-67; atty. CBS, N.Y.C., 1967-69; sr. atty. Texaco, Inc., White Plains, N.Y., 1969-78; v.p. Nat. Fgn. Trade Council, N.Y.C., 1978-79, pres., 1979—. Served to 2d lt. U.S. Army, 1951-54. Decorated Bronze Star. Mem. Assn. Bar City N.Y. Home: 1125 Park Ave New York NY 10028 Office: 10 Rockefeller Plaza New York NY 10020

ROBERTS, ROBERT, JR., lawyer; b. Minden, La., Sept. 20, 1903; s. Robert and Olive (Goodwill) R.; B.A., La. State U., 1923, LL.B., 1925; m. Mary Hodges Marshall, Apr. 25, 1929 (dec.); children—Robert III, Mary Susan (Mrs. Robert O'Neal Chadwick), Olive G. (Mrs. William H. Forman, Jr.). Admitted to La. bar, 1925, since practiced in Shreveport; mem. legal dept. Ark. Natural Gas Corp., 1934-53, chief atty., 1939-53; mem. law firm Blanchard, Walker, O'Quin & Roberts, and predecessor, 1953—. Dir., Ark. La. Gas Co., Md. Co., Inc., Shadyside Co., Ltd., Franklin, La. Chmn. Shreveport Council Social Agys., 1945-46. Pres. bd. trustees Southfield Sch., 1953-54; bd. govs. La. Civil Service League. Mem. Am., La. (mem. ho. dels. 1957-58), Shreveport (pres. 1962) bar assns., La. State U. Found., Order of Coif. Episcopalian (past jr. warden). Clubs: Shreveport Country, Shreveport (pres. 1973); Boston Club (New Orleans). Home: 724 Elmwood St Shreveport LA 71104 Office: First National Bank Bldg Shreveport LA 71163

ROBERTS, ROSALEE ANN, pub. relations exec.; b. Omaha, Dec. 17, 1943; d. Leo Joseph and Madeline Mary (Elder) Ohlinger; B.A. cum laude, Duchesne Coll. Sacred Heart, 1965; m. Robert Wesley Roberts, Oct. 21, 1967; 1 dau., Catherine Anne. Advt. copywriter Bozell & Jacobs, Inc., Omaha, 1967-68; account exec. J. Lipsey and Assos., Inc., 1969; promotion mgr. Sta. KETV, 1969-73; dir. pub. relations Bozell & Jacobs, Inc., 1973—. Trustee Omaha Community Playhouse; bd. dirs. Nebr. chpt. Arthritis Found.; mem. adv. panel Met. Arts Council, Douglas County chpt. ARC; pres. Met. Actors' Guild, Inc., 1976-77; mem. adv. bd. Western Heritage Mus. Recipient award Omaha Fedn. Advt., 1975, and others. Mem. Omaha Fedn. Advt. (bd. dirs. 1972-73), Am. Women in Radio and Television, Pub. Relations Soc. Am. (accredited), Omaha C. of C., Pub. Relations Soc. Am., Omaha Press Club. Republican. Roman Catholic. Office: 10250 Regency Circle Omaha NE 68114. *To accept life as it comes, with problems, joys and sorrows and look forward to tomorrow.*

ROBERTS, ROYSTON MURPHY, chemist; b. Sherman, Tex., June 11, 1918; s. Charles Stanly and Leska (Murphy) R.; B.A., Austin Coll., 1940, D.Sc., 1965; M.A., U. Ill., 1941, Ph.D., 1944; m. Phyllis Arlene Benson, Sept. 18, 1943; children—Richard, David, Stanly, Jean Ellen. Chemist, Merck & Co., Inc., 1945-46; research asso. UCLA, 1946-47; asst. prof. chemistry U. Tex., 1947-50, asso. prof., 1951-60, prof., 1961—; vis. prof. U. Marburg (Ger.), summer 1967; Fulbright research fellow Poly. Inst., Bucharest, Romania, 1976; cons. in chemistry. Am. Chem. Soc.-Petroleum Research Fund. research fellow U. Zurich (Switzerland), 1959-60. Mem. Am. Chem. Soc., Chem. Soc. (London), Sigma Xi, Alpha Chi Sigma, Phi Kappa Phi, Phi Lambda Upsilon. Presbyterian (elder). Author: Introduction to Modern Experimental Organic Chemistry, 1969, 3d ed., 1979. Contbr. articles to profl. jours. Home: 841 E 38th St Austin TX 78705 Office: Dept Chemistry U Texas Austin TX 78712. *A large part of the credit for any success I may have achieved must be attributed to the good fortune of being born in the USA, growing up in a strong Christian family, and being married to a wonderful woman who has been loving, unselfish and supportive of all of my efforts. Having lived in both Western and Eastern Europe, I feel strongly that the freedom of democracy is essential to individual fulfillment, but I am increasingly concerned that Americans are forgetting the moral and ethical principles on which our country was founded.*

ROBERTS, S.M., advt. exec.; b. Detroit, Aug. 11, 1934; s. Jacob and Florence (Moskovitz) Robinowitz; B.A. in Journalism, Wayne State U., 1956; m. Carol Knight Stross, Dec. 16, 1956; children—Bradley Alan, Tracey Knight, Kristin Sophia. Writer, producer radio and TV, W.B. Doner & Co., Southfield, Mich., 1956-60, account exec., 1960-64, v.p., account supr., 1967—, exec. v.p., mgmt. supr., partner, 1973—. Served with AUS, 1957-59. Mem. Zeta Beta Tau. Club: Franklin Hill Country. Home: 3412 Bloomfield Shore Dr Orchard Lake MI 48033 Office: 26711 Northwestern St Southfield MI 48075

ROBERTS, SAMUEL JACOB, state justice; b. Bklyn., Feb. 18, 1907; s. Jacob and Anna (Wexler) R.; B.S. in Econs., U. Pa., 1928, LL.B., 1931; LL.D., Gannon Coll., 1963, Dickinson Sch. Law, 1966, Villa Maria Coll., 1968, Phila. Coll. Osteo. Medicine, 1971; m. Helen G. Blumberg, Dec. 14, 1934 (dec. 1963); 1 dau., Barbara (Mrs. Louis I. Pollock); m. 2d, Marian S. Zurn, Dec. 12, 1970. Admitted to Pa. bar, 1931; practice in Erie, 1931-52; asst. dist. atty. Erie County, 1935-38; referee in unemployment compensations, also spl. dep. atty. gen. Commonwealth Pa., 1939-52; judge Orphans Ct. Erie County, 1952-63, presiding judge, 1953-63; justice Supreme Ct. Pa., 1963—. Trustee, Gannon Coll.; bd. incorporators Hamot Hosp., St. Vincent Hosp. Served to lt. comdr. USNR, 1944-46. Recipient 16th Ann. Max C. Currick Brotherhood award; award of Merit, Erie County Social Agys.; named Man of Year 11th Ann. award Erie Tchrs. Assn. Mem. Am. Bar Assn. (various coms). Clubs: Kahkwa Country, Erie, University, Aviation; Concordia (Pitts.); Franklin Inn (Phila.); Erie County Motor (dir.). Contbr. to various legal publs. Home: 1630 S Shore Dr Erie PA 16505 Office: Court House Erie PA 16501

ROBERTS, SHEPHERD MCGREGOR, SR., steel mcht.; b. Chgo., Apr. 19, 1893; s. Charles Aaron and Cora (Hicks) R.; student pub. schs.; m. Marguerite Dixon, May 26, 1917; children—Charles S., Shepherd M., John H. With Crerar, Adams & Co., ry. supplies, Chgo., 1911-16; v.p. C. A. Roberts Co., Chgo., 1917, 1926, pres., 1926-62, chmn. bd. dirs., 1962—. Served as lt., Ordnance Dept., U.S. Army, 1917-19. Mem. Steel Service Center Inst., Farm Equipment Inst. Aux. Clubs: Glen View, Question, Chgo. (Chgo.); Paradise Valley Country (Phoenix). Home: 126 Woodley Rd Winnetka IL 60093 Office: 2401 25th Ave Franklin Park IL 60131. *Honest co-operation with your fellow man.*

ROBERTS, SIDNEY, biol. chemist; b. Boston, Mar. 11, 1918; s. Samuel Richard and Elizabeth (Gilbert) R.; B.S., Mass. Inst. Tech., 1939; M.S., U. Minn., 1942, Ph.D., 1943; m. Clara Marian Szego, Sept. 14, 1943. Instr. physiology U. Minn. Med. Sch., 1943-44, George Washington U. Med. Sch., 1944-45; research asso. Worcester Found. Exptl. Biology, Shrewsbury, Mass., 1945-47; asst. prof. physiol. chemistry Yale U. Med. Sch., 1947-48; mem. faculty U. Calif. Med. Sch., Los Angeles, 1948—, prof. biol. chemistry, 1957—; mem. adv. panel regulatory biology NSF, 1955-57, adv. panel metabolic biology, 1957-59; mem. metabolism study sect. NIH, 1960-63; basic sci. study sect. Los Angeles County Heart Assn., 1958-63; cons. VA Hosp., Long Beach, Calif., 1951-55, Los Angeles, 1958-62; air conservation tech. adv. com. Los Angeles County Lung Assn., 1972-76. Served to 2d lt. AUS, 1944-48. Guggenheim fellow, 1957-58. Fellow AAAS; mem. Am. Physiol. Soc., Endocrine Soc. (v.p. 1968-69; Ciba award 1953), Brit. Biochem. Soc., Soc. Neurosci., Am. Chem. Soc. (exec. com. div. biol. chemistry 1956-59), Am. Soc. Biol. Chemists, Am. Soc. Neurochemistry, Internat. Soc. Neurochemistry, Sigma Xi. Author articles, revs., editor med. jours. Home: 1371 Marinette Rd Pacific Palisades CA 90272 Office: Dept Biol Chemistry Univ Calif Med Sch Los Angeles CA 90024

ROBERTS, SIDNEY I., lawyer; b. Bklyn., Nov. 29, 1913; s. David I. and Ray (Bleicher) Robinovitz; B.B.A., Coll. City N.Y., 1935; LL.B. magna cum laude, Harvard, 1938; m. Arlene Lee Aron, June 4, 1961; 1 son, Russell Lewis. With Michael Schimmel & Co., C.P.A.'s, N.Y.C., 1938-39, S.D. Leidesdorf & Co., C.P.A.'s, N.Y.C., 1939-49; admitted to N.Y. bar, 1938; with firm Roosevelt, Freidin & Littauer, N.Y.C., 1950-56, Anderson & Roberts, N.Y.C., 1956-57, Roberts & Holland, N.Y.C., 1957—; adj. prof. law Columbia U., 1971-78; mem. adv. bd. Internat. Bur. Fiscal Documentation. C.P.A., N.Y. Mem. Internat., Am. (sect. on taxation, council dir. 1970-73, chmn. com. on cooperation with state and local bar assns. 1968-70, chmn. com. on taxation of fgn. income 1963-64), N.Y. State (tax sect. exec. com. 1967—, chmn. com. on tax sect. planning 1968-70, chmn. com. on tax policy 1970-72) bar assns., Assn. Bar City of N.Y., N.Y. State Soc. C.P.A.'s, Internat. Fiscal Assn. (mem. exec. com. 1972-77, pres. U.S.A. br. 1972-73). Jewish. Author: (with William C. Warren) United States Tax Income Taxation of Foreign Corporations and Nonresident Aliens, 1966; (with others) Annotated Tax Forms: Practice and Procedure, 1970; contbr. articles to profl. jours. Home: 145 Central Park W New York City NY 10023 Office: 1301 Ave of the Americas New York City NY 10019

ROBERTS, STEPHEN JAMES, veterinarian; b. Indpls., Aug. 5, 1915; s. James Flanders and Elizabeth (Johnston) R.; D.V.M., Cornell U., 1938; M.S., Kans. State U., 1942; m. Betty Jane Harris, Dec. 28, 1938; children—Stephen James, Gail H. Instr., Kans. State U., 1938-42; asst. prof. vet. medicine Cornell U., 1942-44, asso. prof. 1944-46, prof., 1946-65, chmn. dept. vet. medicine, 1965-72, prof. emeritus, 1972—; practice vet. medicine, Woodstock, Vt., 1972—; mem. Vt. Bd. Veterinary Examiners, 1979-81; coach Cornell Polo Team, 1947-72. Co-chmn. Woodstock Planning Commn., 1974-79; pres. bd. trustees Universalist Ch., Woodstock, 1976-77, Ottauquechee Health Center, Woodstock, 1977-80. Recipient award Borden Milk Co. 1965. Mem. AVMA (jud. council 1962-73), Am. Coll. Theriogenologists, Am. Soc. Theriogenologists, Vt. Vet. Med. Assn., Am. Assn. Equine Practitioners, Am. Assn. Bovine Practitioners, Phi Zeta, Phi Kappa Phi. Clubs: Rotary, Quechee Polo. Author: Veterinary Obstetrics and Genital Diseases, 1956, 2d rev. edit., 1971. Home and Office: Prosper Rd Woodstock VT 05091

ROBERTS, STEVEN VICTOR, newspaper reporter; b. Bayonne, N.J., Feb. 11, 1943; s. Will Rogow and Dorothy (Schanbam) R.; B.A., Harvard, 1964; m. Corinne Claiborne Boggs, Sept. 10, 1966; children—Lee Harriss, Rebecca Boggs. Research asst. Washington bur. N.Y. Times, N.Y.C., 1964-65, reporter met. staff, 1965-69, chief Los Angeles bur., 1969-74, chief Athens (Greece) bur., 1974-77, reporter Washington bur., 1977—; TV appearances, N.Y.C., Los Angeles; radio commentaries Nat. Public Radio. Mem. Harvard Alumni Assn. (dir. 1973-75), Am. Newspaper Guild. Jewish. Author: Eureka, 1974. Contbr. articles to mags. Home: 5315 Bradley Blvd Bethesda MD 20014 Office: 1000 Connecticut Ave NW Washington DC 20036

ROBERTS, THEODORE HARRIS, banker; b. Gillette, Ark., May 14, 1929; s. D. Edward and Gertrude (Harris) R.; B.A. in Govt., Northwestern State U., Natchitoches, La., 1949; M.A. in Polit Sci., Okla. State U., 1950; student U. Chgo. Grad. Sch. Bus., 1954-55; m. Elisabeth Law, July 17, 1953; children—Susan, William, Julia, John. With Harris Trust and Savs. Bank, Chgo., 1953—, sr. v.p., comptroller, 1968-71, exec. v.p., sec., 1971-75, exec. v.p., 1975—; exec. v.p., sec., treas. Harris Bankcorp, Inc., 1971—; chmn. adv. com. Fed. Deposit Ins. Corp., 1968-69; mem. Bd. Banks and Trust Cos. of State of Ill., 1974-76. Served to 1st lt. AUS, 1950-53. Mem. Fin. Execs. Inst. (bd. dirs. Chgo. chpt. 1970-73), Am. Bankers Assn. (com. to rev. presdl. commn. on financial structure and regulation 1970-71), Chgo. Clearing House Assn. (steering com.), Assn. Modern Banking in Ill. (chmn., dir., exec. com.), Assn. Res. City Bankers. Clubs: Bankers, Chicago, Exmoor Country, Economic, Monroe, University (Chgo.). Home: 475 Greenwood Ave Lake Forest IL 60045 Office: 111 W Monroe St Chicago IL 60690

ROBERTS, THOMAS HUMPHREY, JR., seed co. exec.; b. DeKalb, Ill., May 23, 1924; s. Thomas H. and Eleanor (Townsend) R.; student U. Ill., 1941-43, U. Chgo., 1943-45; B.S., Iowa State U., 1949; M.B.A., Harvard U.; m. Nancy Jean Barker, Mar. 12, 1974; children—Tom, Cathy, Shawn, Mike. With DeKalb Agresearch Inc. (Ill.), 1949—, exec. v.p., 1960-61, pres., 1961-76, chmn., chief exec. officer, 1961—; dir. Internat. Minerals Corp. Trustee Rush Presbyterian-St. Luke's Med. Center, Chgo. Served with armed forces, 1943-47. Episcopalian. Home: 9 Arrowhead Ln DeKalb IL 60115 Office: DeKalb Agresearch Sycamore Rd DeKalb IL 60115

ROBERTS, TONY (DAVID ANTHONY ROBERTS), actor; b. N.Y.C., Oct. 22, 1939; s. Kenneth and Norma R.; B.S., Northwestern U., 1961; 1 dau, Nicole. Movie debut in The Million Dollar Duck, 1971; other film appearances include: Star Spangled Girl, 1971, Play It Again, Sam, 1972, Serpico, 1974, The Taking of Pelham One Two Three, 1974, Annie Hall, 1977, Lovers Like Us, 1977, Just Tell Me What You Want; TV movie The Lindbergh Kidnapping Case, 1976; regular on TV series The Edge of Night, 1963-65, Rosetti and Ryan, 1977; other TV appearances include: Night Gallery, Phyllis, Love American Style, The Defenders, Storefront Lawyers, Snafu, The Girls in the Office, Love Boat, If Things Were Different; Broadway debut in Something about a Soldier, 1962; toured with nat. co. of Come Blow Your Horn, 1962; other stage appearances: Take Her, She's Mine, 1964, Never Too Late, The Cradle Will Rock, 1963, Barefoot in the Park, The Last Analysis, 1964, Don't Drink the Water, 1966, How Now, Dow Jones (nominated for Tony award), 1967, Play It Again, Sam (nominated for Tony award), 1969, Sugar, 1972, Murder at the Howard Johnson's, 1979, They're Playing Our Song, 1980, Losing Time; London debut in Promises, Promises (London Critics Poll award as Best Actor in Musical), 1969; toured with nat. co. Promises, Promises, 1970; appeared in The Tempest and Darkroom with Yale Repertory Theatre, New Haven, 1973-74; in Absurd Person Singular at Kennedy Center, Washington and on Broadway, 1974; in Hamlet at Otterbein Coll. (Ohio) Winter Drama Festival, 1975; Taming of the Shrew, Atlanta, 1978; Let 'Em Eat Cake, Berkshire Theatre Festival; Serenading Lovie, Acad. Festival Theatre. Served in U.S. Army. Mem. Actors Equity Assn. (governing council 1968-74). Office: care William Morris Agy 1350 Ave of Americas New York NY 10019

ROBERTS, WALTER HERBERT BEATTY, anatomist; b. Field, B.C., Can., Jan. 24, 1915; s. Walter McWilliam and Sarah Caroline (Orr) R.; came to U.S., 1956, naturalized, 1965; M.D., Coll. Med. Evangelists (later Loma Linda U.), 1939; m. Olive Louise O'Neal, Sept. 1, 1937; children—Gayle, Sharon. Intern, St. Paul's Hosp., Vancouver, B.C., 1938-40; med. dir. Rest Haven Hosp. Sanitarium and Hosp., Sidney, Vancouver Island, B.C., 1940-53; post doctoral trg. White Meml. Hosp., Los Angeles, 1946-47, hosp., Edinburgh, Scotland, 1953-55; instr. in anatomy Loma Linda U., 1955-58, asst. prof. anatomy, 1959-62, asso. prof., 1962-70, prof., 1971—, chmn. dept. anatomy, 1974—. Mem. Am. Assn. Anatomists, Sigma Xi, Alpha Omega Alpha. Adventist. Home: 11366 Campus St Loma Linda CA 92354 Office: Dept Anatomy Loma Linda U Stewart St Loma Linda CA 92350

ROBERTS, WALTER ORR, solar astronomer; b. West Bridgewater, Mass., Aug. 20, 1915; s. Ernest Marion and Alice Elliott (Orr) R.; A.B., Amherst Coll., 1938, D.Sc. (hon.), 1959; M.A., Harvard, 1940, Ph.D., 1943; D.Sc. (hon.), Ripon Coll., 1958, Colo. Coll., 1962, C.W. Post Coll. L.I. U., 1964, Carleton Coll., 1966, Southwestern at Memphis, 1968, U. Colo., 1968, U. Denver, 1969, U. Alaska, 1975; m. Janet Naomi Smock, June 8, 1940; children—David Stuart, Alan Arthur, Jennifer Roberts McCarthy, Jonathan Orr. Operator High Altitude Obs., Climax, Colo., 1940-47, dir. charge solar research program, 1947-50, dir. High Altitude Obs., Boulder, also Climax, Colo., 1940-60; instr. Harvard, 1947-48, Radcliffe Coll., 1947-48; research asso. Harvard Coll. Obs., 1948-73; dir. Nat. Center for Atmospheric Research, 1960-70, research asso., 1975—; prof. astro-geophysics U. Colo., Boulder, 1957—; dir. program in food, climate and world's future Aspen Inst. for Humanistic Studies, 1974—. Trustee Univ. Corp. Atmospheric Research, 1959, pres., 1960-73; trustee Mitre Corp., 1960—, Upper Atmosphere Research Corp., 1971-74. Chmn. com. on arctic sci. and tech. Nat. Acad. Scis., 1972-73, mem. com. on internat. environ. programs, 1971-77; mem. com. cons. Report on the State of the Human Environment UN Stockholm Conf., 1972; mem. U.S. Nat. Commn. for UNESCO, 1964-67; mem. def. sci. bd. Dept. Def., 1972-75; mem. adv. panel for NSF Journalistic History, 1972; mem. adv. com. World Meteorol. Orgn., 1963-68; mem. bur. com. effects solar terrestrial disturbances in lower atmosphere Spl. Com. Solar-Terrestrial Physics, 1972—; mem. subcom. U.S.-USSR coop. program man's impact on environment Dept. State, 1973—; mem. visiting com. Smithsonian Astrophys. Observatory, 1975-78; mem. founding bd., chmn. task force sci. and tech. Civilian/Mil. Inst., Air Force Acad., 1975—; mem. Council on Sci. and Tech. for Devel., 1977—. Trustee Max C. Fleischmann Found., 1967—, Charles F. Kettering Found., 1964-70, Amherst Coll., 1964-70; trustee Aspen Inst. for Humanistic Studies, 1970—, sec. Marconi Internat. Fellowship Council, 1974—; trustee Internat. Fedn. Insts. Advanced Study, 1971—, chmn. program com.; bd. dirs. Internat. Inst. Environment and Devel., 1971-76, Worldwatch Inst., 1975—. Recipient Hodgkins medal Smithsonian Instn., 1973. Fellow AAAS (dir. 1963-70, pres. 1967, mem. com. on arid lands 1973—), Am. Acad. Arts and Scis., Royal Astron. Soc.; mem. Aspen Soc. Fellows, Am. Rocket Soc., Am. Astron. Soc. (mem. council), Am. Meteorol. Soc., Internat. Astron. Union, Colo.-Wyo. Acad. Sci., Am. Geophys. Union, Am. Philos. Soc., Fedn. Am. Scientists, AIAA, Internat. Acad. Astronautics, Internat. Soc. Ecol. Modelling, Bio-Energy Council, World Future Soc., Council Fgn. Relations, Royal Soc. Arts, Sigma Xi, Phi Beta Kappa, Sigma Pi Sigma. Club: Century Assn. (N.Y.C.); Rocky Mountain Harvard; Explorers. Asso. editor Jour. Geophys. Research, 1960-64; editorial bd. Science, 1970-72, Jour. Planetary and Space Sci. Home: 1829 Bluebell Ave Boulder CO 80302

ROBERTS, WARREN AUSTIN, oil co. exec.; b. Pitts., Nov. 28, 1915; s. Warren Austin and Laura H. (Dennis) R.; B.S. in Chem. Engring., Carnegie Inst. Tech., 1937; m. Margaret E. Fry, Mar. 19, 1942; children—Warren Austin III, Margaret Ann. With Phillips Petroleum Co., 1937—; dist. supt., Hobbs, N.Mex., Los Angeles, 1953-60, div. mgr., Oklahoma City, 1960-63, vice chmn. operating com., Bartlesville, Okla., 1963-66, chmn. operating com., 1966-68, v.p. exploration and prodn. dept., 1968-69, sr. v.p., 1969-71, exec. v.p., 1971—, also dir.; dir. 1st Nat. Bank Bartlesville. Past pres. Cherokee Area council Boy Scouts Am.; past mem. nat. bd. dirs. Camp Fire Girls; chmn. tech. adv. council, deep sea drilling project Scripps Inst. Oceanography; chmn. indsl. adv. council, geothermal resource project U. Calif. at Riverside, 1969-70; mem. Nat. Acad. Sci. panel on drilling technique Project Mohole, 1958-64; mem. Okla. Air Pollution Council, 1967-72; dir. U.S. nat. com. World Energy Conf. Served from 2d lt. to maj., C.E., USAAF, 1942-46. Registered profl. engr., Okla. Mem. Am. Petroleum Inst. (chmn. com. on pub. affairs 1972-74, dir.), Mid-Continent Oil and Gas Assn. (dir.), Okla. Petroleum Council (pres. 1965-66, Distinguished Achievement award 1962, 71), Nat. Soc. Profl. Engrs., Oklahoma City C. of C. (chmn. oil and gas div. 1962, 63), Bartlesville C. of C. (dir.). Home: 1208 Swan Dr Bartlesville OK 74003 Office: Phillips Bldg Bartlesville OK 74004

ROBERTS, WILLARD EUGENE, mgmt. cons., ret. steel co. exec.; b. West Pittston, Pa., Oct. 30, 1908; s. Walter E. and Bertha (Ruggles) R.; A.B., Rider Coll., 1929; m. Ruth M. Vanderbilt, Feb. 19, 1938; 1 son, Paul Vanderbilt. Pub. accountant Lybrand, Ross Bros. & Montgomery, Phila., 1929-44; controller Carpenter Tech. Corp., Reading, Pa., 1944-56, sec.-treas., 1956-66, v.p. finance, sec., 1966-73, also dir.; mem. Pa. policy bd. Am. Mut. Ins. Co., 1959—; pres. Wyomissing Property Corp. Trustee Community Gen. Hosp., Rider Coll. Mem. Newcomen Soc., Reading C. of C. (past pres., nat. councilor), Am. Inst. C.P.A.'s. Clubs: Wyomissing; Iris; Berkshire Country. Home and office: 1021 Parkside Dr N Wyomissing PA 19610

ROBERTS, WILLIAM B., mfg. co. exec.; b. Detroit, Aug. 23, 1939; s. Edwin Stuart and Marjorie Jean (Wardle) R.; B.A., Mich. State U., 1961; J.D. with distinction, U. Mich., 1963; m. Cathleen Anne Thompson, Sept. 1, 1962; children—Bradford William, Brent William, Katrina Marjorie. Admitted to Mo. bar, 1964; mem. firm Thompson & Mitchell, St. Louis, 1963-67; atty. Monsanto Co., 1967-70; exec.

v.p., sec., gen. counsel Chromalloy Am. Corp., Clayton, Mo., 1970-78, exec. v.p.-adminstrn., gen. counsel, sec., 1978—; co-owner Ed Roberts Cadillac, Inc., Mansfield, Ohio, SpiralCool Co., Bellevue, Ohio; mem. exam. com. of policyowners Northwestern Mut. Life Ins. Co., Milw., 1978. Bd. dirs., asso. mem. Internat. Comparative Law Center, Southwestern Legal Found.; trustee S.E.A.S., Inc. Mem. Am., Mo., St. Louis (chmn. antitrust sect. 1973) bar assns., Delta Theta Phi. Methodist. Clubs: Clayton, Mo. Athletic, Forest Hills Country (St. Louis). Home: 1516 Chesterfield Lakes Rd Chesterfield MO 63017 Office: 120 S Central St Clayton MO 63105

ROBERTS, WILLIAM C., savs. and loan assn. exec.; b. N.Y.C., Jan. 19, 1925; s. Arthur Ernest and Mary Alda (Ferris) R.; B.B.A., U. Mich., 1949, M.B.A., 1950; m. Rhoda Roberts, Aug. 19, 1949; children—Robyn Anne, William Curtis, Kenneth Charles. Jr. accountant Chirnside, Roberts, Langston, C.P.A.'s, 1950-53; mortgage broker in Broward and Dade counties, Fla., 1953-64; pres. United Fed. Savs. & Loan Assn., Ft. Lauderdale, Fla., 1965—, also dir.; dir. Investors Mortgage Co., Fla. Devel. Corp. Chmn. Ft. Lauderdale Zoning Bd.; v.p. Ft. Lauderdale Apt. House Assn.; bd. dirs. Henderson Clinic, Ft. Lauderdale. Served with AUS, 1943-46. Mem. U.S., Fla. (past chmn.) savs. and loan leagues. Episcopalian. Club: Ft. Lauderdale Rotary (past pres.). Address: 3600 N Federal Hwy Fort Lauderdale FL 33308

ROBERTSON, A. BRUCE, ret. judge; b. Victoria, B.C., Can., Sept. 23, 1904; s. Harold Bruce and Helen McGregor (Rogers) R.; B.A., U. Toronto, 1925; m. Jean Keefer Campbell, Feb. 15, 1924; children—Joan Marjorie (Mrs. H. T. DeLong), Harold Barnard. Called to B.C. bar, 1928; with firm Robertson, Douglas & Symes, 1928-46; gen. solicitor, then gen. counsel B.C. Electric Co. Ltd., 1946-60, v.p., 1948-60, sr. v.p., 1960-61; v.p. parent co. B.C. Power Corp., Ltd., 1948-60, pres., chmn. bd., 1961-63, also dir.; dir. Wilshire Oil Co. Tex., 1957-67, pres., 1965; asso. counsel firm Russell & DuMoulin, Vancouver, 1964-67, with firm, 1979—; justice Ct. Appeal for B.C., Vancouver, 1967-79. Bd. dirs. Save the Children Fund, B.C. Clubs: Vancouver, Vancouver Lawn Tennis and Badminton; Union (Victoria). Home: 1329 Balfour Ave Vancouver BC V6H 1X8 Canada Office: 17th Floor 1075 W Georgia St Vancouver BC V6E 3G2 Canada

ROBERTSON, ABEL ALFRED LAZZARINI, JR., pathologist; b. St. Andrews, Argentina, July 21, 1926; s. Abel Alfred Lazzarini and Margaret Theresa (Anderson) R.; came to U.S., 1952, naturalized, 1957; B.S., Coll. D.F. Sarmiento, Buenos Aires, Argentina, 1946; M.D. cum laude, U. Buenos Aires, 1951; Ph.D., Cornell U., 1959; m. Irene Kirmayr Mauch, Dec. 26, 1958; children—Margaret Ann, Abel Martin, Andrew Duncan, Malcolm Alexander. Fellow tissue culture div. Inst. Histology and Embryology, U. Buenos Aires Sch. Medicine, 1947-49; surg. intern Hosp. Ramos Mejia, Buenos Aires, 1948-50; fellow in tissue culture research Ministry of Health, Buenos Aires, 1950-51; resident Hosp. Nacional de Clinicas, Buenos Aires, 1950-51; head blood vessel bank and organ transplants Research Center, Ministry of Health, Buenos Aires, 1951-53; fellow dept. surgery and pathology Cornell U. Sch. Medicine, N.Y.C., 1953-55; asst. vis. surgery U. Hosp. N.Y., N.Y.C., 1955-60; asst. prof. research surgery N.Y. U. Postgrad. Med. Sch., N.Y.C., 1955-56; asst. vis. surgeon Bellevue Hosp., N.Y.C., 1955-60; asso. prof. research surgery N.Y. U. 1956-60, asso. prof. pathology Sch. Medicine and Postgrad. Med. Sch., 1960-63; staff mem. div. research Cleve. Clinic Found., 1963-73, prof. research, 1972-73; asso. clin. prof. pathology Case Western Res. U. Sch. Medicine, Cleve., 1968-72, prof. pathology, 1973—, dir. interdisciplinary cardiovascular research, 1975—; research fellow N.Y. Soc. Cardiovascular Surgery, 1957-58; mem. research study subcom. of heart com. N.E. Ohio Regional Med. Program, 1969—. Recipient Research Devel. award NIH, 1961-63. Fellow Am. Coll. Cardiology, Am. Coll. Clin. Pharmacology, Am. Heart Assn. (nominating com. council on arteriosclerosis 1972), Royal Microscopical Soc., Royal Soc. Promotion Health (Gt. Britain), Am. Geriatrics Soc., N.Y. Acad. Scis., Cleve. Med. Library Assn.; mem. AAAS, Am. Assn. Pathologists, AAUP, Am. Inst. Biol. Scis., Am. Judicature Soc., Am. Soc. Cell Biology, Am. Soc. Exptl. Pathology, Am. Soc. Nephrology, Assn. Am. Physicians and Surgeons, Assn. Computing Machinery, Electron Microscopy Soc. Am., Internat. Acad. Pathology, Internat. Cardiovascular Soc., Internat. Soc. Cardiology (sci. council on arteriosclerosis and ischemic heart disease 1960-64), Internat. Soc. Nephrology, Internat. Soc. Stereology, Pan Am. Med. Assn. (life, councillor in angiology 1966-72), Reticuloendothelial Soc., Soc. Cryobiology, Tissue Culture Assn., Ohio Soc. Pathologists, Electron Microscopy Soc. Northeastern Ohio (pres., trustee 1966-68), Heart Assn. Northeastern Ohio, N.Y. Soc. Cardiovascular Surgery, N.Y. Soc. Electron Microscopists, Cuyahoga County Med. Soc., Cleve. Soc. Pathologists, Sigma Xi. Mem. internat. editorial bd. Atherosclerosis, Jour. Exptl. and Molecular Pathology, 1964—. Contbr. articles to profl. jours. Home: 3596 Beverly Hills Dr Rocky River OH 44116 Office: 2085 Adelbert Rd Cleveland OH 44106

ROBERTSON, CHANNING REX, chem. engr., educator; b. Los Angeles, Nov. 26, 1943; s. Jack Richard and Marjorie Lucille (Johannes) R.; B.S. with honors, U. Calif., 1965; M.S., Stanford U., 1968, Ph.D., 1970; m. Donna Deene Reinecke, Aug. 21, 1965; children—Jodie Lynn, Jesse Ian. Research scientist Marathon Oil Co., Littleton, Colo., 1969-70; asst. prof. chem. engring. Stanford U., 1970-74, asso. prof., 1974-78, prof., chmn. dept. chem. engring., 1978—; cons. in field; guest prof. Institüt für Biomedizinische Technik der Universität und der Eidgenössichen Technischen Hochschule Zürich, 1977. Mem. Am. Inst. Chem. Engrs., Phi Beta Kappa, Tau Beta Pi. Research, numerous publs. on application of chem. engring. principles to biol. and med. problems. Office: Dept Chem Engring Stanford U Stanford CA 94305

ROBERTSON, CLIFF, actor, writer, dir.; b. La Jolla, Calif. Stage appearances include Mr. Roberts, Late Love, The Lady and the Tiger, The Wisteria Tree, Orpheus Descending.; films include Picnic, Autumn Leaves, Battle of the Coral Sea, As the Sea Rages, Underworld, U.S.A., The Big Show, All in a Night's Work, The Interns, PT 109, The Best Man, 633 Squadron, Masquerade, The Honey Pot, The Devil's Brigade, Charly (Oscar award 1969), The Great Northfield Minnesota Raid, The Game (Emmy award 1968), Ace Eli and Rodger of the Skies, Too Late the Hero, Man on a Swing, 3 Days of the Condor, Out of Season, Obsession, Shoot, TV movies include Man Without a Country, Days of Wine and Roses, The Two Worlds of Charlie, Washington: Behind Closed Doors; writer, dir., actor film J.W. Coop. Address: care Internat Creative Mgmt 40 W 57th St New York NY 10019*

ROBERTSON, DAVID WYATT, lawyer, educator, univ. admnstr.; b. Little Rock, Sept. 8, 1937; s. Lee W. and Thelma (Iueen) R.; B.A., La. State U., 1960, LL.B., 1961; LL.M., Yale U., 1965, S.J.D., 1968. Admitted to La. bar, 1961, D.C. bar, 1961, Tex. bar, 1976, U.S. Supreme Ct. bar, 1978; legis. asst. to Sen. Russell B. Long, Washington, 1961-62; asst. prof. law La. State U., Baton Rouge, 1962-64; lctr. law Leeds (Eng.) U., 1965-66; asso. prof. U. Tex., Austin, 1966-68, prof., 1968—; of counsel firm Mandell & Wright, Houston, 1979—. Mem. Assn. Am. Law Schs., Am. Law Inst., Maritime Law Assn. U.S., Order of Coif, Omicron Delta Kappa. Author: Admirality and Federalism, 1970; contbr. articles to profl. jours. Office: U Tex Sch Law 2500 Red River Rd Austin TX 78705

ROBERTSON, DEWAYNE CONNELL, hosp. adminstr.; b. Paw Paw, W.Va., Mar. 8, 1932; s. Lawrence Paul and Virginia Pearl (Smith) R.; B.S. in Biology, Shepherd Coll., 1953; m. Verna Lee Rudolph, Dec. 17, 1955; children—Steven Wayne, Kevin Earl. Adminstrv. asst. med. research VA, Dallas, 1965-68, adminstrv. asst. to chief of staff, 1968-70; asst. med. center dir. trainee VA, Albuquerque, 1970-71, asst. dir. med. center; Vancouver, Wash., 1971-73, Syracuse, N.Y., 1973-75, Little Rock, 1975-76; dir. VA Med. Center, Canandaiqua, N.Y., 1976—; clin. asso. Sch. Allied Health Profls., Ithaca (N.Y.) Coll.; mem. mental health-mental retardation regional council, bd. dirs. Finger Lakes Health System Agy.; bd. dirs. Genesee Region Health Edn. Council. First v.p. Ontario County (N.Y.) United Way, 1976—; bd. dirs. Greater Rochester (N.Y.) United Way, 1978—. Served with U.S. Army, 1953-55. Recipient cert. merit State of Ark., 1976. Mem. Inter Agy. Inst. for Fedn. Health Care Execs., Greater Canandaiqua C. of C. Methodist. Club: Am. Legion (Ark. cert. merit 1976). Home: East St Canandaiqua NY 14424 Office: VA Med Center Fort Hill Ave Canandaiqua NY 14424

ROBERTSON, DURANT WALTE, JR., educator; b. Washington, Oct. 11, 1914; s. Durant Waite and Emma (Jones) R.; B.A., U. N.C., 1935, M.A., 1937, Ph.D. 1945, D.Litt., 1973; m. Betty McLean Hansen, July 17, 1937; children—Susanna, Durant Waite III, Douglas. Instr. U. Md., 1938-42, U. N.C., 1942-44, Yale, 1945-46; from instr. to prof. English, Princeton, 1946—, now Murray prof. English lit., 1970—. Fellow Am. Council Learned Socs., 1945-46; Guggenheim fellow, 1957. Fellow Mediaeval Acad. Am.; mem. AAAS, Renaissance Soc. Am. Author: (with B.F. Huppe) Piers Plowman and Scriptural Tradition, 1951; A Preface to Chaucer, 1962; (with B.F. Huppé) Fruyt and Chaf, 1963; Chaucer's London, 1968; The Literature of Medieval England, 1970; Abelard and Heloise, 1972. Translator St. Augustine, On Christian Doctrine, 1958. Contbr. articles to learned jours. Home: 93 Maclean Circle Princeton NJ 08540

ROBERTSON, FRANK LEWIS, clergyman; b. Covington, Ga., Apr. 22, 1917; s. Herman W. and Nell (Hutchins) R.; A.B., Emory U., 1940; M.Div., Yale, 1942; postgrad. Columbia; D.D., LaGrange Coll., 1961; L.H.D., Ky. Wesleyan U., 1973; LL.D., Union Coll., 1974; Litt.D., Lambuth Coll., 1976; m. LuReese Ann Watson, June 18, 1941; children—Jane Robertson Westerfield, Frank Lewis. Ordained to ministry United Methodist Ch., 1942; pastor Baker Village Ch., Columbus, Ga., 1942-47, 1st Meth. Ch., Hawkinsville, Ga., 1947-51, Douglas, Ga., 1951-55, St. Luke Ch., Columbus, 1955-60; dist. supt. United Meth. Ch., Savannah, Ga., 1960-64; pastor Mulberry St. Meth. Ch., Macon, Ga., 1964-69, 1st Meth. Ch., Valdosta, Ga., 1969-72; bishop Louisville area United Meth. Ch., 1972—. Trustee Lake Junaluska Assembly, N.C., Ky. Wesleyan Coll., Lindsey Wilson Coll., Ky., Union Coll., Barbourville, Ky. Rotarian, Kiwanian. Home: 800 S 4th St Louisville KY 40203 Office: 1115 S 4th St Louisville KY 40203

ROBERTSON, GEORGE LEVEN, assn. exec.; b. Alexandria, La., Feb. 7, 1921; s. Ernest E. and Cornelia (La Croix) R.; B.S., La. State U., 1941; M.S., A. and M. Coll. Tex., 1947; Ph.D. (Gen. Edn. Bd. fellow 1949-50), U. Wis., 1951; m. Florence Horne, Feb. 7, 1943; children—Linda, Malcolm Ernest, Judy Elaine. Grad. asst. animal husbandry A. and M. Coll. Tex., 1941-42, instr., then asst. prof., 1946-49, asso. prof., 1951-55; grad. asst. U. Wis., 1949-51; prof. animal sci., head dept. La. State U., 1955-77, chmn. grad. council, 1961; exec. dir. Honor Soc. of Phi Kappa Phi, 1977—. Trustee Baton Rouge Gen. Hosp. Served to capt. AUS, 1942-46; col. Res. Named Outstanding Tchr., A. and M. Coll. Tex. Sch. Agr., 1948-49. Fellow AAAS; mem. Am. Soc. Animal Sci. (pres. So. sect. 1967-68), AAUP, Sigma Xi, Alpha Zeta, Phi Kappa Phi (nat. pres.-elect 1974-77), Gamma Sigma Delta, Omicron Delta Kappa. Club: Masons. Home: 7017 Perkins Rd Baton Rouge LA 70808

ROBERTSON, GERALD LESLIE, foundry co. exec.; b. St. Joseph, Mo., Aug. 8, 1934; s. James Leo and Laura Elizabeth R.; student Gen. Motors Inst., 1952-56; grad. mgmt. program Harvard U., 1974; m. Joan Alice Brock, Aug. 16, 1956; children—Stephen, Christopher, Julianne, Scott. Supr. central foundry div. Gen. Motors Co., Defiance, Ohio, 1952-58; methods engr. Diamond Nat. Corp., Middleton, Ohio, 1958-60; indsl. engr. Mead Containers, Cin., 1960-62, mgr. dist. mfg. Durham, N.C., 1962-66, Chgo., 1966-68; gen. mgr. Xenia Services, Zurich, Switzerland, 1968-72; v.p., gen. mgr. soil pipe ops. Mead Corp., Birmingham, Ala., 1973-74; exec. v.p. Mead Indsl. Products Co., Birmingham, 1974-75; pres. Lynchburg Foundry Co. (Va.), 1975—; dir. United Va. Bank/1st Nat., 1975—. Bd. dirs. United Way of Central Va., 1975-79, campaign vice chmn., 1975, campaign chmn., 1976, pres., 1977; bd. dirs. Jr. Achievement, Lynchburg, 1977—, pres., 1979. Mem. Foundry Ednl. Found., Am. Foundryman's Soc., Iron Castings Soc., Va. Mfr.'s Assn. (dir. 1978-79), Va. Bus. Council, Am. Mgmt. Assn., Lynchburg C. of C. (dir. 1978-79). Roman Catholic. Office: Lynchburg Foundry Drawer 411 Lynchburg VA 24505

ROBERTSON, GREGG W., diversified co. exec.; b. Sydney, Australia, Jan. 16, 1934; s. Alexander and Lillian R.; B.A. in Econs., Fairleigh Dickinson U., 1964; m. Elizabeth Stimper, Apr. 30, 1957; children—Gregg W., Lisa. Asst. treas. Oritani Savs. and Loan Assn., Hackensack, N.J., 1959-64; asst. v.p. Bankers Trust Co., N.Y.C., 1964-69; asst. treas. Dillingham Corp., Honolulu, 1970-73, treas., 1974-77, treas., v.p. fin., 1977—, chief fin. officer, 1979—. Mem. Fin. Execs. Inst. Clubs: Olympic (San Francisco); Outrigger Canoe (Honolulu). Home: 1603 Kalaniuka Circle Honolulu HI 96821 Office: PO Box 3468 Honolulu HI 96801

ROBERTSON, HORACE BASCOMB, JR., educator; b. Charlotte, N.C., Nov. 13, 1923; s. Horace Bascomb and Ruth (Montgomery) R.; B.S., U.S. Naval Acad., 1945; J.D., Georgetown U., 1953; M.S., George Washington U., 1968; m. Patricia Lavell, Aug. 11, 1947; children—Mark L., James D. Commd. ensign U.S. Navy, 1945, advanced through grades to rear adm., 1972; line officer, 1945-55; law specialist, 1955-68; spl. counsel to sec. Navy, Washington, 1964-67, judge adv., 1968-76; spl. counsel to chief naval ops., Washington, 1970-72; dep. judge adv. gen. Navy Dept., Washington, 1972-75, judge adv. gen., 1975-76; prof. law Duke, 1976—. Decorated D.S.M. Mem. Am., Fed. (nat. council) bar assns., Am. Soc. Internat. Law. Methodist. Home: 5 Stoneridge Circle Durham NC 27705 Office: Duke U Sch Law Durham NC 27706

ROBERTSON, ISIAH, profl. football player; b. New Orleans, Aug. 17, 1949; B.A., So. U. With Los Angeles Rams (Nat. Football League), 1971—; played in Pro Bowl (Nat. Football League All-Star Game) following 1971 season, 1973-77 seasons. Office: care Los Angeles Rams 10271 W Pico Blvd Los Angeles CA 90064*

ROBERTSON, JAMES DAVID, anatomist; b. Tuscaloosa, Ala., Oct. 13, 1922; s. Floyd Earl and Gladys (Williams) R.; B.S., U. Ala., 1942; M.D., Harvard U., 1945; Ph.D., Mass. Inst. Tech., 1952; m. Doris Elizabeth Kohler, Oct. 21, 1946; children—Karen Lee, Elizabeth Ann, James David. Lab. teaching asst. biology U. Ala., 1940-42; intern 4th Med. Service, Boston City Hosp., 1945-46; resident pathology U. Kans. Sch. Medicine Hosp., 1952-55; part-time practice medicine, specializing internal medicine, Lowndsboro and Hayneville, Ala., 1947-48; asst. physician U.S. VA Hosp., Montgomery, Ala., 1948; asst. physician med. dept. Mass. Inst. Tech., 1948-49, research fellow Am. Cancer Soc., 1949-52; asst. prof. pathology and oncology dept. pathology and oncology Med. Sch. U. Kans., Kansas City, 1952-55; hon. research asso. dept. anatomy U. Coll. London (Eng.) 1955- 60; asso. biophysicist, biophysicist research lab. McLean Hosp., Belmont, Mass., 1960-66; asst. prof. neuropathology Med. Sch. Harvard, 1960-64, asso. prof. (with tenure), 1964-66; prof., chmn. dept. anatomy Duke, Durham, N.C., 1966—, James B. Duke prof. anatomy, 1975—; vis. prof. Inst. Physiol. Chemistry, U. Wurzburg, W. Ger., 1978-79, also other univs.; chmn. exec. com. Internat. Cell Membrane Confs., Frascati, Italy, 1965-70, mem. exec. com., 1970—; past mem. cell biology study sec. NIH, now cons.; cons. NSF; past mem. panel IV, Internat. Cell Research Orgn. Served to lt. (j.g.), M.C., USNR, 1942-45, 48-49. Recipient W.B. Saunders award in pathology and bacteriology, 1943; Alexander von Humboldt Soc. sr. scientist award, W. Ger., 1978; Kellogg Found. scholar U. Ala., 1942-43, First Pomerat Meml. lectr. U. Tex., 1966. Mem. Electron Microscope Soc. Am., Am. Assn. Anatomists, Anat. Soc. Gt. Britain and Ireland, Physiol. Soc., Research Def. Soc., Internat. Assn. Cell Biology, Biophys. Soc., Neurochem. Soc., Biophys. Soc., Soc. Neurosci., Pan Am. Assn. Anatomists, Southeastern Electron Microscopy Soc., So. Soc. Anatomists, British Biophysical Soc., Am. Soc. Cell Biology, Soc. For Devel. Biology, Internat. Neurochem. Soc., AAAS, Am. Cryst. Assn., Sigma Xi, Phi Beta Kappa, Alpha Omega Alpha, Phi Eta Sigma. Past mem. editorial bd. Anat. Rec.; mem. editorial bd. Jour. Neurobiology, Lipid Research; mem. editorial bd. Jour. Cell Biology, 1965-68, editorial cons., 1968—; cons. editor Scott Forsman Co., Wiley-Intersci. Home: 32 Oak Dr Durham NC 27707

ROBERTSON, JAMES IRVIN, JR., educator, historian; b. Danville, Va., July 18, 1930; s. James Irvin and Mae (Kympton) R.; B.A., Randolph-Macon Coll., 1955; M.A., Emory U., 1956, Ph.D., 1959; m. Elizabeth Green, June 1, 1952; children—Mae Elizabeth, James Irvin III, Howard Wells. Editor, Civil War History, U. Iowa, 1959-61; exec. dir. U.S. Civil War Centennial Commn., 1961-65; asso. prof. history U. Mont., 1965-67; C.P. Miles prof. history Va. Poly. Inst. and State U., Blacksburg, 1977—, chmn. dept. history, 1969-77; vis. prof. history U. Nebr., summer 1971; hist. cons. New Market Battlefield Meml. Park. Registrar for Episcopal Diocese Southwestern Va., 1971—. Mem. awards com. Mus. of Confederacy, 1970—. Certified football ofcl. Atlantic Coast Conf. Mem. Am., So. hist. assns., Orgn. Am. Historians, Va. Hist. Soc. (exec. com.). Author: The Stonewall Brigade, 1963; Civil War Books: A Critical Bibliography, 2 vols., 1967-68. Contbr. articles profl. jours. Home: 405 Stonegate Dr NW Blacksburg VA 24060

ROBERTSON, JAMES MACPHIE, ins. co. exec.; b. North Sydney, N.S., Can., Apr. 27, 1926; s. George Browe and Margaret Jessie (MacPhie) R.; grad. Sydney Acad., North Sydney; m. Margaret Adeline Mackley, Aug., 1952; children—Catherine L., George M., Andrew J. With ManuLife, 1950—, v.p. Can. ops., 1972-73, v.p. mktg. ops., 1973-74, sr. v.p., 1974-76, exec. v.p., Toronto, Ont., 1976—, also dir.; dir. A/P Cons. Services, ManEquity, Inc. ManEquity Mgmt. Corp., ManuLife Computer Corp. Ltd., ManuLife Investment Mgmt. Corp., ManuLife Service Corp. Pres. Can. Opera Co.; bd. dirs. Ont. Heart Found. Served with Can. Parachute Corps, 1945-46. C.L.U. Liberal. Mem. United Ch. Canada. Clubs: Royal Can. Yacht, Toronto Cricket Skating and Curling. Office: 200 Bloor St E Toronto ON M4W 1E5 Canada

ROBERTSON, JAMES MUELLER, educator; b. Champaign, Ill., Apr. 18, 1916; s. William Spence and Gertrude (Mueller) R.; B.S. in C.E., U. Ill., 1938; M.S., U. Iowa, 1940, Ph.D., 1941; m. Margaret Dillinger, Oct. 23, 1943; children—Bruce Dillinger, Alan Spence. Asst. physicist U.S. Navy Dept., Taylor Model Basin, 1941-42; asst. prof. engring. mechanics Pa. State U., 1942-46, asso. prof., 1946-47, asso. prof. civil engring., 1947-49, prof. engring. research, also dir. Water Tunnel, 1949-54; research engr. Douglas Aircraft, Santa Monica, Calif., 1944-45; prof. theoretical and applied mechanics U. Ill. at Urbana-Champaign, 1954—. Mem. adv. com. Bur. Ordnance, U.S. Navy, 1950-54, chmn., 1950-53, mem. adv. com. Basic Research Underwater Ballistics, 1951-55; prin. scientist Ill. State Water Survey, Urbana summers, 1955-57; sr. research scientist Intersci. Research Inst., Champaign, 1966-72; cons. U.S. Army Waterways Expt. Sta., 1957, Consol. Papers, 1960-61, Goodyear Aircraft, 1962, research dept. Caterpillar Tractor Co., 1963-71, Westvaco Research Lab., 1966-68, Kennecott Exploration, 1971-72, Nat. Distillers & Chem. Corp., 1972, Continental Can Co., 1973; vis. lectr. hydraulic engring. Kans. State U., 1967; course instr. TAPPI, 1969; lectr. U. Tenn. Space Inst., 1973; vis. prof. civil engring. Colo. State U., 1974. Fellow ASCE (chmn. hydraulics research com. 1954-55, 58, Hilgard prize in hydraulics 1955), ASME (chmn. cavitation com. 1967-69, mem. polyphase flow com.; certificate for 25 years as reviewer for Applied Mechanics Revs. 1972); mem. AIAA, Internat. Assn. Hydraulic Research, Sigma Xi, Phi Eta Sigma, Chi Epsilon, Tau Beta Pi, Phi Kappa Phi. Clubs: Univ., Urbana Town, Champaign Ski. Author: Hydrodynamics in Theory and Application, 1965. Editor: (with G.F. Wislicenus) Cavitation State of Knowledge, 1969. Contbr. articles to tech. Jours., chpts. in books. Hydrodynamic designer research water tunnel Pa. State U., 1946-49. Home: 1706 Pleasant St Urbana IL 61801 Office: 216 Talbot Laboratory University of Illinois Urbana IL 61801

ROBERTSON, JOHN MARSHALL, JR., gas pipeline co. exec.; b. Houston, Sept. 10, 1924; s. John Marshall and Annie Goforth (Toland) R.; B.S., Tex. A & M U., 1948; postgrad. Harvard U. Bus. Sch., 1972; m. Margaret Jean Anderson, June 11, 1948; children—Barbara Jean, John Marshall, III, Thomas Allan. Design engr. Parkersburg Rig & Reel Co., Houston, 1948-50; engr. Tenn. Gas Transmission Co., Houston, 1950-61, sales rep., 1961-65, sr. v.p., 1980—; v.p. East Tenn. Natural Gas Co., Knoxville, 1965-67; v.p. Midwestern Gas Transmission Co., Houston, 1967-72, pres., 1972-80, also dir. Served with AUS, 1942-46. Mem. Midwest, So. gas assns. Club: Houston. Office: PO Box 2511 Houston TX 77001

ROBERTSON, JOSEPH H., pulp and paper products co. exec.; b. Neepawa, Man., Can.; ed. Brandon Coll., U. Man., U. Toronto (Ont., Can.). With Domtar Inc., Montreal, Que., Can., 1941—. Asst. gen. mgr. Howard Smith Div. (name changed to Domtar Fine Papers Ltd. 1968) Domtar Pulp & Paper Ltd., 1961-62, gen. mgr., 1962-66, v.p., gen. mgr., 1966—, pres. Domtar Pulp & Paper Products Ltd., 1974—, exec. v.p. Domtar Inc., 1979—. Vice pres., treas. Reddy Meml. Hosp., Montreal. Mem. Canadian Pulp and Paper Assn. (past chmn. tech. sect., mem. exec. com.), TAPPI, Montreal Amateur Athletic Assn. Clubs: Cornwall Golf and Country, St. James (Montreal). Office: care Domtar Inc Corporate Communications Dept 395 deMaisonneuve Blvd W Montreal PQ H3A 1L6 Canada

ROBERTSON, JOSEPH MOORMAN, assn. exec.; b. Glen Dean, Ky., Jan. 11, 1916; s. William James and Emma (Moorman) R.; A.B., Western Ky. U., 1946; M.A., U. Ala., 1947; student U. Minn., 1947-49; m. Virginia Mansfield, Dec. 21, 1940; children—William J.,

Sally, Susan. Asst. prof. U. Ala., 1949-50; research asst. Ky. Dept. Revenue, 1950-52; commr. taxation, dir. tax research Minn. Dept. Taxation, 1952-61; part-time instr. polit. sci. U. Minn. extension div., 1952-61; chief govts. div. Bur. of Census, Dept. Commerce, 1961; asst. sec. Dept. Agr., 1961-71; dir. Bur. Intergovtl. Personnel Programs, U.S. CSC, 1971-76; exec. dir. Nat. Assn. Schs. Pub. Affairs and Adminstrn., Washington, 1976—; chmn. gen. adminstrn. bd. Dept. Agr. Grad. Sch., 1961—. Bd. dirs. Nat. Tng. and Devel. Service, 1977—. Served to capt. AUS, 1941-45. Fellow pub. adminstrn. So. Regional Tng. Program, 1946-49. Mem. Am. Soc. Pub. Adminstrn. (pres. Nat. Capital area; nat. council 1965-67; editorial bd. 1966-69), Nat. Assn. Tax Adminstrs. (chmn. research sect. 1952, exec. com. 1959), Fedn. Tax Adminstrs. (trustee 1958), Nat. Tax. Assn., Am. Soc. Pub. Adminstrn. (exec. bd. Minn. 1957-59), Am. Polit. Sci. Assn., Conf. on Pub. Service. Home: 9409 Kingsley Ave Bethesda MD 20014 Office: Suite 306 1225 Connecticut Ave NW Washington DC 20036

ROBERTSON, LAWRENCE VERNON, JR., assn. exec.; b. Tucson, June 28, 1938; s. Lawremce Vernon and Lemma (Starling) R.; B.A., Stanford U., 1960, J.D., 1964; m. Judith Ann Williams, Oct. 12, 1963; children—Lawrence Vernon, III, Brenton John. Admitted to Ariz. bar, Nev. bar, D.C. bar; asso. firm Robertson, Childers, Burke & Drachman, Tucson, 1964-66, Stompoly & Even, P.C., Tucson, 1977-78; asst. dir. negotiated trusts Pacific Maritime Assn., San Francisco, 1966-67; sec., gen. atty. S.W. Gas Corp., Las Vegas, Nev., 1967-72; v.p. legal and regulation Tucson Gas & Electric Co., 1972-77; v.p., gen. counsel, sec. Interstate Natural Gas Assn. Am., Washington, 1978—. Bd. dirs. Ariz. Civic Theatre, 1973-76, pres., 1975-76; mem. Tucson Crime Commn., 1972-74, Pima Health Planning Council, 1972-74; bd. dirs. Palo Verde Mental Health Found., 1975-78. Mem. Am., D.C., Fed. Energy bar assns., state bars Ariz., Nev., Phi Beta Kappa. Contbr. articles to legal jours. Home: 6305 Evermay Dr McLean VA 22101 Office: 1660 L St NW Washington DC 20036

ROBERTSON, LEON FOREST, engr., ret. glass co. exec.; b. Bethany, Mo., Feb. 12, 1906; s. Oscar C. and Bertha (Riley) R.; B.M.E., U. Nebr., 1931; m. Jane E. Small, June 3, 1936; children—Anna May, James Leon. Engr., Dravo Corp., 1931-35, Frazier-Simplex, 1935-40; chief engr., v.p. in charge engring. research Brockway Glass Co., Inc. (Pa.), 1940-68, sr. v.p., 1968-71, also dir. Fellow Am. Ceramic Soc.; mem. Pa. Soc. Profl. Engrs., Am. Inst. Mining, Metall. and Petroleum Engrs., Pa. Municipal Authority Assn. Home: 1051 12th Ave Brockway PA 15824

ROBERTSON, LESLIE EARL, structural engr.; b. Los Angeles, Feb. 12, 1928; s. Garnet Roy and Tina (Grantham) R.; B.S., U. Calif., Berkeley, 1952; m. Sharon Michiko Hibino, Feb. 12, 1969; children—Jeanne, Christopher Alan, Sharon Miyuki. Structural engr. Kaiser Engrs., Oakland, Calif., 1952-54, John A. Blume, San Francisco, 1954-57, Raymond Internat. Co., N.Y.C., 1957-58; managing partner firm Skilling, Helle, Christiansen, Robertson, N.Y.C., Seattle, Anchorage, 1958—; chmn. com. risks and liabilities Kinetic Energies Resource Council, 1975—. Served with USNR, 1944-46. Fellow ASCE (Raymond C. Reese Research prize 1974); mem. Nat. Acad. Engring. Author papers in field. Home: PO Box 8284 New Fairfield CT 06810 Office: 230 Park Ave Room 1216 New York NY 10017

ROBERTSON, MARION GORDON, religious broadcaster; b. Lexington, Va., Mar. 22, 1930; s. A. Willis and Gladys Churchill (Willis) R.; J.D., Yale U., 1955; M.Div., N.Y. Theol. Sem., 1959; B.A., Washington and Lee U., 1950; m. Adelia Elmer, 1954; children—Timothy, Elizabeth, Gordon, Ann. Pres., host, TV program The 700 Club, 1968—. Regent, MeLody Land Sch. of Theology, 1975—. Served to 1st lt., USMC, 1950-52. Recipient Merit Citation, Nat. Conf. Christian and Jews, 1975; named Broadcaster of the Year, Religious Heritage of Am., 1976. Mem. Nat. Religious Broadcasters (dir. 1973—), Nat. Assn. Broadcasters, Phi Beta Kappa, Sigma Alpha Epsilon, Phi Alpha Delta. Baptist. Author: Shout It From The Housetops, 1972; My Prayer for You, 1977. Office: Pembroke Four Virginia Beach VA 23463*

ROBERTSON, MICHAEL SWING, mfg. co. exec.; b. Boston, July 20, 1935; s. Charles Stuart and Elizabeth (Swing) R.; A.B., Harvard U., 1957, grad. Advanced Mgmt. Program, 1979; m. Margaret Filoon, Sept. 17, 1960; children—Michael Swing, Ashlee Whipple, Christopher Filoon, Andrew Stuart. With Robertson Factories, Inc., 1962—, exec. v.p., 1968-73, pres., 1973-79, chmn. bd., 1979—. Vice-pres. adv. council Coll. of Bus. and Industry, Southeastern Mass. U., Taunton, Mass., 1979—; selectman Town of Berkley (Mass.), 1974—, chmn., 1979; bd. dirs. Mass. Easter Seal Soc., 1977—, v.p., 1979; bd. dirs. Taunton YMCA; bd. deacons Pilgrim Congl. Ch., Taunton; Republican nominee U.S. Senate from Mass., 1976. Mem. Nat. Assn. Mfrs., Chgo. Drapery Market Assn. (past pres.). Clubs: Taunton Rotary, Falmouth Yacht, N.Y. Yacht, Racquet (Chgo.), Harvard Varsity. Home: 25 Swing Dr Berkley MA 02780 Office: 33 Chandler Ave Taunton MA 02780. *Accept responsibility with enthusiasm and gratitude. Our freedom of choice is unmatched in history, compelling us to remain true to our beliefs.*

ROBERTSON, NAT CLIFTON, chemist; b. Atlanta, July 23, 1919; s. Henry Booker and Eura Allen (Williams) R.; A.B., Emory U., 1939, Sc.D., 1970; Ph.D., Princeton, 1942; m. Elizabeth Bates Peck, Nov. 29, 1946; children—Henry Bartlett, Mary Amanda, Paul Edward. Research asso. OSRD, 1942-43; chemist Standard Oil Co. (N.J.), 1943-47; group leader Celanese Corp. Am., 1947-51; dir. petrochems. dept. Nat. Research Corp., 1951-55; v.p., dir. research Escambia Chem. Corp., 1955-58; v.p. Spencer Chem. div. Gulf Oil Corp. (formerly Spencer Chem. Co.), Kansas City, Mo., 1958-66; v.p. Air Products & Chems., Inc., Allentown, Pa., 1966-69, sr. v.p., 1969-77, also dir.; dir. Marion Labs., C.H. Kline & Co. Trustee Midwest Research Inst.; bd. dirs. Kans. Research Found., 1963-66, pres., 1963-64. Mem. Am. Chem. Soc., Dirs. Indsl. Research, Indsl. Research Inst., Phi Beta Kappa, Sigma Xi. Democrat. Presbyn. Clubs: Nassau; Princeton (N.Y.C.). Home: 156 Philip Dr Princeton NJ 08540

ROBERTSON, RICHARD BENTLEY, cons. engr.; b. Prairieton, Ind., May 8, 1920; s. Augustus Lane and Mary Agnes (Bentley) R.; B.S. in Mech. Engring., Purdue U., 1942; m. Verna Jean; children—Patricia Ann, Linda Marie, Kathryn Jean, Richard Bentley, Sheila Renee. Jr. engr. Curtis-Wright Corp., Columbus, Ohio, 1942-43; engr. United Air Lines, 1943-48; partner Bovay Engrs., Houston, 1948-62, exec. v.p., dir., 1962—. Served as 1st lt. AUS, 1944-46. Named Distinguished Engring. Alumnus, Purdue U., 1975; registered profl. engr., Ark., Calif., La., Tex., Wash. Mem. ASME (pres. 1974-75), Nat. Soc. Profl. Engrs., Houston Engring. and Sci. Soc. (pres. 1969-70), Engrs. Council Houston (pres. 1973-74), Pi Tau Sigma (hon.), Tau Beta Pi (hon.). Methodist. Home: 15354 Terrell Rd Baton Rouge LA 70816 Office: 10305 Airline Hwy Baton Rouge LA 70895

ROBERTSON, ROBERT, malacologist; b. Great Waldingfield, Suffolk, Eng., Nov. 14, 1934; s. David William and Katharine Anne (West) R.; came to U.S., 1952; A.B., Stanford U., 1956; Ph.D., Harvard U., 1960; m. Marian Esther Ropes, Oct. 3, 1959 (dec. Feb. 25, 1975); 1 dau., Pamela Lucinda. Mem. staff Acad. Natural Scis. Phila., 1960—, chmn. dept. malacology, 1969-72, curator malacology, 1976—. Pres., Inst. Malacology, 1973-75. Grantee NSF, 1968-71, 76—. Fellow AAAS; mem. Marine Biol. Assn. U.K., malacological socs. London, Japan, Australia, Am. Malacological Union. Co-editor-in-chief Malacologia, 1973—; contbr. articles to profl. jours. Home: 125 W Spruce St Moorestown NJ 08057 Office: Acad Natural Scis 19th and Parkway Philadelphia PA 19103

ROBERTSON, ROBERT GORDON, Can. govt. ofcl.; b. Davidson, Sask., Can., May 19, 1917; s. John Gordon and Lydia Adelia (Paulson) R.; B.A., U. Sask., 1938; B.A. Juris, Oxford U., 1940; M.A., U. Toronto, 1941; L.L.D., U. Sask., 1959, McGill U., 1963, U. Toronto, 1973, U. Dalhousie, 1977; Di de l'univ., U. Laval, 1975; m. Beatrice Muriel Lawson, Aug. 14, 1943; children—John Lawson, Karen Martha. Mem. staff Dept. External Affairs, Govt. of Can., 1941-45; sec. to Office of Prime Minister, 1945-49; mem. staff Privy Council Office, 1949-53; dep. minister of No. Affairs and Nat. Resources, commr. Northwester Territories, 1953-63; clk. Privy Council, sec. to cabinet, 1963-75, sec. to cabinet for fed.-provincial relations, 1975—. Decorated Companion of Order of Can. Fellow Royal Soc. Can. Mem. United Ch. of Can. Home: 20 Westward Way Ottawa ON K1L 5A7 Canada Office: 59 Sparks St Ottawa ON K1A 0A3 Canada

ROBERTSON, ROBERT ROY, JR., banker; b. Stamford, Tex., Sept. 2, 1932; s. Robert Roy and Fay Lucille (Williams) R.; B.A., Rice U., 1955; M.B.A., U. Tex., Austin, 1960; m. Helen E. Harris, Aug. 9, 1955 (div. Oct. 1968); children—Susan, Shelley; m. 2d, Virginia A. Kennedy, Aug. 23, 1969; children—Jennifer, Jeanine. With First City Nat. Bank Houston, 1960-78, sr. v.p., mgr. nat. dept., 1971-78; sr. v.p., sr. credit adminstr. First City Bancorp. Tex., Houston, 1978—; dir. First Clear Lake Bank, Houston. Mem. United Fund, 1964-66, 73, div. vice chmn., 1966; treas. Traffic Safety Council Greater Houston, 1969-70. Bd. dirs., pres. Houston Shakespeare Soc., 1965-66; trustee Tax Research Assn. Houston and Harris County, 1966-69; bd. dirs. Vols. in Tech. Assistance. Served with USNR, 1955-57. Mem. Houston C. of C., Rice Alumni Assn. (exec. bd. 1972—, also chmn. com. for self-study and goal setting), Beta Gamma Sigma. Episcopalian. Clubs: Houston (pres. 1974), Houston Racquet. Home: 3011 Ella Lee Ln Houston TX 77019 Office: 1111 Fannin St Houston TX 77002

ROBERTSON, STOKES VERNON, state justice; b. Hattiesburg, Miss., Nov. 9, 1912; s. Stokes V. and Sudie (Burt) R.; student Millsaps Coll., 1929-32; B.A., U. Miss., 1933, LL.B., 1935; m. Una Lurline Caldwell, July 14, 1945; children—Stokes Vernon III, David George, Helen Caldwell. Admitted to Miss. bar, 1935; partner firm Robertson and Robertson, Jackson, 1935-55; chancery judge, Hinds County, Miss., 1955-65; asso. justice Supreme Ct. of Miss., Jackson, 1966-77, presiding justice, 1978—. Trustee Belhaven Coll., Jackson. Served with AUS, 1940-45, 51-52. Mem. Kappa Alpha, Omicron Delta Kappa, Sigma Upsilon, Pi Kappa Delta, Phi Delta Phi. Presbyn. (deacon 1938-50, elder 1951—). Kiwanian. Home: 2246 N Cheryl Dr Jackson MS 39211 Office: Justice Bldg Jackson MS 39205

ROBERTSON, STUART A., cons. actuary; b. Montesano, Wash., Feb. 28, 1918; s. George Duncan and Anna (McLeod) R.; student U. Idaho, 1934-35, U. Wash., 1935-37; m. Marjory Belle Moch, Nov. 24, 1939; children—Richard S., Ann (Mrs. David Luther Corn) (dec.). Vice pres. Great Northwest Life Ins. Co., Spokane, 1937-47; actuarial asst. No. Life Ins. Co., Seattle, 1947-49; actuary Northwestern Life Ins. Co., Seattle, 1949-50; cons. actuary, chmn. and chief exec. officer Milliman & Robertson, Inc., Seattle, 1950—; chmn. bd. M&R Services, Inc., computer services, Seattle, 1970—. Fellow Soc. Actuaries (bd. govs. 1972-75), Conf. Actuaries Pub. Practice; mem. Am. Acad. Actuaries, Actuarial Club Pacific States (pres. 1963), Seattle Actuarial Club (pres. 1958), Sr. Actuaries Club. Episcopalian. Clubs: Wing Point Golf and Country (Bainbridge Island); Wash. Athletic, Harbor, Univ. Kiwanis (Seattle). Home: 14320 Sunrise Dr NE Bainbridge Island WA 98110 Office: 1301 5th Ave Seattle WA 98101

ROBERTSON, SYDENHAM BROOKS, utility co. exec.; b. Richmond, Va., Sept. 1, 1917; s. Joseph William and Nancy Lucrecia (Brooks) R.; B.S. in Bus. Adminstrn., U. Richmond, 1938; Basic Advanced Mgmt. Program, U. Va., summer 1965; m. Patsy Leona Phillips, Apr. 28, 1945; children—Joseph Brooks, Michael Sparks. With Va. Elec. and Power Co., Richmond, 1938—, asst. chief accountant, 1952-53, chief accountant, 1953, supr. gen. accounting and payroll, 1954-57, system supr. plant accounting and property records, 1957-65, asst. sec., 1965-72, sec., 1972—. Served to capt. AUS, 1942-46. Mem. Am. Soc. Corporate Secs., Ret. Officers Assn. (pres. Richmond chpt. 1970), Am. Radio Relay League, Phi Delta Theta. Baptist. Club: Salisbury Country (Richmond). Home: 1800 Oakengate Ln Salisbury Midlothian VA 23113 Office: One James River Plaza Richmond VA 23261

ROBERTSON, WARREN J., food co. exec.; b. Whitinsville, Mass., Mar. 31, 1926; s. James A. and Alma (Matz) R.; B.S. in Econs., U. Pa., 1949; grad. Advanced Mgmt. Program, Harvard; m. Helen I. Horne, May 6, 1950; children—James W., David B., Ellen Sue, Theodore J. Mgr. data processing Nabisco, Inc. (formerly Nat. Biscuit Co.), N.J., 1957-62, asst. controller, 1962, controller, 1962-68, dir. finance, 1968-69, v.p. finance, 1969-74, sr. v.p. finance, 1974-75, sr. v.p., 1975-78, exec. v.p.-adminstrn., 1978—. Served with USAAF, 1944-46. Mem. Fin. Execs. Inst. Home: 79 Penwood Rd Basking Ridge NJ 07920 Office: Nabisco Inc East Hanover NJ 07936

ROBERTSON, WILLIAM DIXON, JR., naval officer; b. Lexington, N.C., Aug. 27, 1926; s. William Dixon and Mary Norman (Hargrave) R.; B.S., U.S. Naval Acad., 1947; postgrad. Indsl. Coll. Armed Forces, 1970-71; M.S., George Washington U., 1971; m. Frances Warthen Tuttle, Sept. 27, 1952; children—Dixon, Frances. Served as enlisted man and midshipman U.S. Navy, 1943-47, commd. ensign, 1947, advanced through grades to rear adm., 1974; served in various sea assignments, 1947-74, comdr. guided missile cruiser, 1972-74; dir. div. strategic forces Navy Systems Analysis Office, Washington, 1969-70; dir. profl. edn. U.S. Naval Acad., 1971-72, mem. admissions bd., 1971-72, chmn. bd., 1972; vice-dir. Def. Intelligence Agy., Washington, 1974—. In various ednl. and adminstrv. positions Trinity Meth. Ch., Alexandria, Va., 1962—. Decorated Bronze Star, Def. Superior Service medal, Nat. Intelligence medal, Meritorious Service medal, Joint Commendation medal with oak leaf cluster. Mem. Smithsonian Instn., Nat. Geog. Soc., U.S. Naval Inst. Clubs: Army-Navy Country, Forest Lake (Columbia, S.C.). Home: 3904 Terry Pl Alexandria VA 22304 Office: Pentagon Washington DC 20301

ROBERTSON, WILLIAM F(ARQUHAR), mktg. communications agy. exec.; b. Phila., Aug. 6, 1941; s. James Campbell and Frances Margaret (Farquhar) R.; B.S. in Econs., U. Pa., 1964; m. Elaine Ruth Cook, May 22, 1965; children—Sydney, Lauren, Amy, Hilary. Grad. trainee Ford Motor Co., 1964-66; new products devel. mgr. E. I. DuPont Co., Wilmington, Del., 1966-71; v.p., dir. mkgt. Vantage House div. Bristol Myers Co., Cherry Hill, N.J., 1971-73; pres., chief exec. officer Mel Richman Inc., Bala Cynwyd, Pa., 1973—; dir. MRI, Mktg.; cons. in field. Bd. visitors Valley Forge Mil. Acad. Republican. Presbyterian. Club: Union League (Phila.). Home: 409 Redleaf Rd Wynnewood PA 19096 Office: 15 N Presidential Blvd Bala Cynwyd PA 19004

ROBERTSON, WILLIAM FRANKLIN, publishing co. exec.; b. Richmond, Va., Sept. 1, 1917; s. Joseph William and Nancy Lucretia (Brooks) R.; B.S., U. Richmond, 1938; m. Avis Dorothy Stillman, Aug. 7, 1943; children—Lynne Brooks, William Elden. Circulation route supr. Richmond News Leader, 1935-40; office mgr. Richmond Newspapers, Inc., 1941-46, credit mgr., controller, 1946-66, asst. treas., 1966-68, treas., asst. sec., 1968—; v.p., treas., asst. sec. Media Gen., Inc.; asst. treas. S.E. Media, Inc.; treas. Cablevision of Fredericksburg, Inc.; asst. treas., asst. sec. Media Gen. Financial Services, Inc.; asst. sec. Tribune Co., Inc., WFLA, Inc., Beacon Press, Inc., Marketgraphics, Inc., S.E. Bldg. & Realty Co. Inc., Garden State Paper Co. Inc., Piedmont Pub. Co. Inc., Golden Triangle Printing Co., Metro-Guide, Inc., Mega Advt. Inc. Pres., trustee Lakewood Manor, Inc.; trustee Va. Bapt. Homes, Bapt. Ministers Relief Fund of Va. Served to lt. USNR, 1943-45. Decorated Letter of Commendation with ribbon (2). Mem. Inst. Newspaper Controllers and Finance Officers (dir.), Adminstrv. Mgmt. Soc. (pres. Richmond chpt. 1964-65), Financial Execs. Inst., Phi Delta Theta. Baptist. Home: 1500 W 45th St Richmond VA 23225 Office: 333 E Grace St Richmond VA 23219

ROBERTSON, WILLIAM OSBORNE, physician; b. N.Y.C., Nov. 24, 1925; s. William Osborne and Barbara Konvalinka (Bennett) R.; B.A., U. Rochester, 1946, M.D., 1949; m. Barbara Foster Simpson, Feb. 23, 1952; children—Kathy, Lynn, Kerry, Douglas, Andrew. Intern, Strong Meml. Hosp., Rochester, N.Y., 1949-51, resident, 1951-52; resident Grace New Haven Hosp., 1954-56; acting med. dir. Ross Labs., Columbus, Ohio, 1956-59; mem. faculty Ohio State Coll. Medicine, 1956-63, asso. prof. pediatrics, 1961-63; mem. faculty dept. pediatrics U. Wash., Seattle, 1963—, prof., 1972—, asso. dean, 1967-72, med. dir., 1963-67, acting chmn. dept. pediatrics, 1972-73, head div. ambulatory pediatrics, 1975-77, 78-79; dir. med. edn. div. Children's Orthopedic Hosp., 1971—, dir. poison control center, 1971—; mem. staffs Children's, Harborview, Univ. hosps.; mem. advisory com., chmn. Wash. Alaska Regional Med. Program; bd. dirs. Wash. Med. Edn. and Research Found., 1968-73. Served with USNR, 1952-54. Mem. Am. Acad. Pediatrics (chmn. edn. com. 1971-73), Am. Acad. Clin. Toxicology, King County Med. Soc. (pres. 1971-72), Wash. State Med. Assn. (pres. 1975-76), Phi Beta Kappa, Alpha Omega Alpha. Contbr. articles to profl. publs. Home: 18724 40th Pl NE Seattle WA 98155 Office: U Wash Sch Medicine PO Box 5371 Seattle WA 98195

ROBESON, MARK D., motor carrier co. exec.; b. Columbus, Kans., Sept. 6, 1911; s. Daniel Webster and Minnie (Colvin) R.; B.A., U. Kans., 1935; m. Katherine M. Willard, Jan. 23, 1937; children—Mark D., Daniel F. Trust cons. City Nat. Bank & Trust Co., Kansas City, Mo., 1936-47; 1st v.p. Riss & Co., Kansas City, Mo., 1947-53; chmn. fin. com. Yellow Freight System, Inc., Shawnee Mission, Kans., 1953—, also dir. Chmn. Western Hwy. Inst., San Francisco, 1969; bd. dirs., v.p. Nat. Safety Council, Chmn., 1979-80; trustee Am. Trucking Assn. Found.; pres. Am. Trucking Assns., Inc., 1969; regional dir. Office Emergency Transp., 1967—; mem. Urban Transp. Adv. Council, 1968-74; mem. Pres.'s Transp. Task Force, 1969—; mem. exec. com. transp. research Nat. Acad. Scis., 1979. Chmn. Kans. Econ. Devel. Commn., 1963-65. Bd. dirs. ENO Found., Westport, Conn., 1974—; bd. dirs. Kan. Council Econ. Edn., 1970-72, pres., 1972-74; hon. chmn. YWCA, Kansas City, 1973—. Served to lt. USNR, 1942-45. Mem. Transp. Assn. Am. (dir. 1968—, Seley award 1979), Nat. Def. Transp. Assn. (v.p., dir. 1974-79). Home: 6420 Sagamore Rd Mission Hills KS 66208 Office: Yellow Freight System Inc 10990 Roe Blvd Shawnee Mission KS 66207

ROBICHAUD, GERARD ALARIC, newspaperman; b. Chicopee Falls, Mass., Mar. 19, 1912; s. Joseph A. and Flordia M. (Demers) R.; B.S., N.M. Sch. Mines, 1933; postgrad. Boston U., 1934-35; m. Pauline C. Wilkinson, Oct. 15, 1938; 1 dau., Judith (deGuevara). Mining, civil engr., 1933-34; reporter Holyoke (Mass.) Transcript-Telegram, 1935-36; N.E. night mgr. United Press, Boston, 1936-37; became Washington corr. for U.P., 1937, Chgo. Sun, 1943; chief Washington bur., Chgo. Sun-Times (formerly Sun), 1946-50, editorial writer 1951-59; Latin Am. corr. for Chgo. Daily News, 1959, editorial writer, 1966-73; dir. Chgo. Daily News/Sun-Times News Service, 1973-75; free-lance fgn. corr., 1975—. Mem. Am. Acad. Polit. and Social Sci., Mil. Order Carabao (Washington), Fgn. Corrs. Assn. Mexico, Sigma Delta Chi (profl. chpt.). Clubs: Chicago Press; American (Rio de Janeiro); Nat. Press Club (chmn. bd. govs. 1950). Contbr. reviews, articles and poetry to nat. mags. Home: Apdo 162 Oaxaca Mexico Office: 401 N Wabash Ave Chicago IL 60611

ROBICHAUD, HEDARD J., lt. gov. N.B. (Can.); b. Shippegan, N.B., Feb. 11, 1911; s. John G. and Amanda (Boudreau) R.; B.A., St. Joseph U., Memramcook, N.B., 1931; LL.D. (hon.), U. St. Thomas, 1972, U. N.B., 1972, Mt. Allison U., 1974; D.C.S. (hon.), U. Moncton, 1964; m. Gertrude Leger, Oct. 27, 1937; children—Doris, Mona, Linda, John, Robert, Eric, Anne, Louise, Richard. Engaged in fishing business, 1931-38; insp. Can. Dept. Fisheries, 1938-46; dir. fisheries div. N.B. Dept. Industry and Devel., 1946-53; founder Fishermen's Loan Bd., 1948; mem. Can. Ho. of Commons from Gloucester Country, 1953-68, Can. Senate, 1968-71; minister fisheries, 1963-68; dir. Nat. Sea Products Ltd., 1968—; spl. ambassador to inauguration of Pres. Allende of Chile, 1970; lt. gov. N.B., 1971—. Decorated hon. knight of grace Order St. John Jerusalem, 1973. Roman Catholic. Club: Fredericton Garrison. Home: 238 Waterloo Row Fredericton NB E3B 1Z3 Canada Office: Legislative Bldg Fredericton NB E3B 5H1 Canada

ROBICHAUD, LOUIS JOSEPH, Canadian senator; b. St. Anthony, N.B., Oct. 21, 1925; s. Amedee and Annie (Richard) R.; B.A., Sacred Heart U., 1947, Dr. Polit. Sci., 1960; postgrad. Laval U., 1947-49; LL.D., U. N.B., 1960, St. Joseph's U., 1961, U. Montreal, 1961, U. Ottawa, 1962, St. Dunstan's U., 1964, U. St. Thomas, 1965, McGill U., 1967, Dalhousie U., 1969; D.C.L., Mt. Allison U., 1961, Moncton U., 1973; m. Lorraine Savoie, Aug. 9, 1951; children—Jean Claude, Paul, Louis-Rene, Monique. Admitted to N.B. bar, Queen's counsel, 1960; practiced in Richibucto, N.B., 1952-60; mem. N.B. Legislature, 1952-71, financial critic, 1957-58, leader of opposition, 1958-60, 70-71, premier, 1960-70, atty. gen. N.B., 1960-65; minister of youth, 1968-70; mem. Privy Council, 1967—; chmn. Canadian sect. Internat. Joint Commn., 1971-73; summoned to Senate of Can., 1973—; leader Liberal Party of N.B., 1958-71; dir. Assumption Mut. Life Ins. Co. Past pres. Ottawa Valley chpt. Kidney Found. Can., bd. dirs. found. Decorated companion Order of Canada; recipient gold medal Laval U. Alumni Assn., 1963. Mem. N.B. Barristers Soc., Canadian Forestry Assn. (dir.). Roman Catholic. Mem. Liberal Party. Home: 2365 Georgina Dr Ottawa ON Canada Office: Senate of Can Ottawa ON K1A 0A4 Canada

ROBICHAUD, MICHEL, fashion designer; b. Montreal, Que., Can., June 9, 1939; s. Emile and Charlotte (Laberge) R.; student Comml. Trade Sch., Montreal, 1958-59; m. Lucienne Lafreniere, Mar. 7, 1963.

Province of Que. scholar Chambre Syndicale de la couture parisienne, 1960-61; probationer Nina Ricci's Workshop, 1962; designer at Guy Laroche House of Fashion, 1962; presented first Couture Collection, Montreal, 1963; ofcl. presentation new uniforms for Air Can. hostesses, 1964, uniforms for Expo 67 hostesses, 1965; presented travel wardrobe in Paris, Brussels, Milan and London, 1966; first line of women pret-a-porter, 1968; founder Boutique pret-a-porter, 1968; presented spring capsule collection at Quebec Delegation in Paris, 1969; participant Montreal-Mode, 1973; launched first Canadian perfume Brumante, 1973; chmn. com. for creation all 1976 Olympic uniforms, 1975; launched first collection pret-a-porter for men, 1976, swimwear for Canadian Beach Wear, 1976, first leather collection, 1977, first collection men's accessories, 1977. Office: 2195 Crescent St Montreal PQ H36 2C1 Canada

ROBIDOUX, OMER ALFRED, missionary, bishop; b. St. Pierre Jolys, Man., Can., Nov. 19, 1913; s. Joseph and Jeanne (Tanguay) R.; B.A., U. Ottawa, 1940; D.D., U. Man., 1970. Oblate of Mary Immaculate, 1934; ordained priest Roman Catholic Ch., 1939, consecrated bishop, 1970; worked with natives in Lestock (Sask.) Missions and Schs., 1941-51, Lebret (Sask.) Missions and High and Elementary Sch., 1951-58, Winnipeg Assiniboia High Sch. and Missions, 1958-65; prin. Assiniboia Sch., Winnipeg, 1958-65; tchr. adult edn. programs, 1965-70; bishop of Churchill, 1970—. Bd. dirs. Churchill Health Centre, 1972—, mem. exec. com., 1974—; chmn. Churchill Community Devel. Corp., 1974—, Churchill No. Studies Centre, 1976—. Cadet instr. Army, 1943-65. Home: Box 10 Churchill MB R0B 0E0 Canada

ROBILLIARD, WALTER HENRY, heat transfer products co. exec.; b. Faribault, Minn., Aug. 3, 1921; s. Charles Morton and Virginia Harriet (Schutt) R.; student Grinnell (Iowa) Coll., 1939-41, U. Minn., 1942-43; m. Caroline Ann Gilbert, May 30, 1941; children—Walter Henry, Bonnilee Robilliard. Sr. accountant Holloway, Knutson & Bowers, C.P.A.'s, Mpls., 1942-45; agt. IRS, 1945-54; with Minn. and Ont. Paper Co., Mpls., 1954-66, sec.-treas., 1961-66; v.p., treas. McQuay-Perfex Inc., St. Louis Park, Minn., 1966—; dir. Foto-Mark, Inc., Mpls. Past pres. Minn. Arabian Horse Assn. C.P.A., Minn. Mem. Am. Inst. C.P.A.'s, Fin. Execs. Inst., Min. Soc. C.P.A.'s. Republican. Congregationalist. Club: Masons. Home: Route 3 Box 218A Buffalo MN 55313 Office: 5401 Gamble Dr St Louis Park MN 55416

ROBIN, EUGENE DEBS, biologist, physician; b. Detroit, Aug. 23, 1919; s. Benedict and Anna (Cooper) R.; A.A., U. Chgo., 1939; S.B., George Washington U., 1946, S.M., 1947, M.D., 1951; m. Evelyn Cowen, Aug. 23, 1942; children—Anna Rosa, Donald Allan. Intern Peter Bent Brigham Hosp., Boston, 1951-52; chief med. resident Peter Bent Brigham Hosp., Boston, 1954-55, asso. dir. cardiovascular tng., 1958-59; instr. medicine Harvard, 1955-58; asso. prof. medicine U. Pitts., 1959-63, prof. medicine, 1963-70; prof. medicine and physiology Stanford U. Sch. Medicine, 1970—; cons. to Gov. Pa. Tb care, 1968-70, Pneumoconiosis, 1964-66; vis. prof. medicine Washington U., St. Louis, 1964; vis. research prof. Cardiovascular Research Inst., San Francisco, 1964; vis. prof. Tufts U., 1968, Stanford, 1969; Towsley prof. medicine U. Mich., 1974; Farquarson prof. medicine U. Toronto, 1976; Eppinger prof. medicine Harvard U., 1977; vis. prof. medicine French Govt., 1978. Chmn., pulmonary adv. com. Nat. Heart and Lung Inst., NIH, 1971—, mem. cardiovascular and pulmonary study sect., 1976—. Bd. dirs. Nat. Tb and Respiratory Disease Assn.; trustee Mt. Desert Island Biol. Lab. Mem. Am. Assn. Physicians, Am. Soc. Clin. Investigation, Am. Physiol. Soc., Am. Thoracic Soc. (pres. 1970—), Assn. Am. Physicians, Sigma Xi, Alpha Omega Alpha. Contbr. chpts. to books, articles to med. jours. Home: 878 Miranda Green Palo Alto CA 94306 Office: Stanford U Med Center Stanford CA 94305

ROBIN, RICHARD SHALE, educator; b. Stamford, Conn., Apr. 18, 1926; s. Edwin Joseph and Eva (Effron) R.; B.A., Harvard, 1948, Ph.D., 1958; m. Joann Wilma Cohan, Jan. 29, 1961; children—David Seth, Deborah Elizabeth. Instr. philosophy U. Conn., Storrs, 1958-62; asst. prof. Mt. Holyoke Coll., South Hadley, Mass., 1962-66, asso. prof., 1966-71, prof., 1971—, chmn. dept., 1967—; mem. grad. faculty, U. Mass. at Amherst, 1963—. Grantee Harvard, 1960-61, Henry P. Kendall Found., 1962, Mt. Holyoke Coll., 1969-70, 75-76; Danforth asso., 1967—. Mem. Charles S. Peirce Soc. (pres. 1965-67), Charles S. Peirce Found., Am. Philos. Assn., AAUP, Soc. Advancement Am. Philosophy (exec. circle). Co-editor, co-author Studies in the Philosophy of Charles Sanders Peirce, 1963; editor Annotated Catalogue of the Papers of Charles S. Peirce, 1967; editor trans. Charles S. Peirce Soc.; bd. advs. Peirce edition project; bd. cons. Arisbe Papers. Home: 78 Woodbridge St South Hadley MA 01075

ROBINETT, BETTY JANE, linguist; b. Detroit, June 23, 1919; d. Henry Guy and Beulah (Reid) Wallace; B.A., Wayne State U., 1940; M.A., U. Mich., 1941, Ph.D., 1951; m. Ralph F. Robinett, Apr. 10, 1952 (div. 1960); 1 son, Richard Wallace. Instr., adminstrv. asst. English Lang. Inst., U. Mich., Ann Arbor, 1945-50; cons. Dept. Edn., San Juan, P.R., 1950-51, 52-57; lectr. English, U. Mich., 1951-52; asso. prof. English InterAm. U., San German, P.R., 1957-59; asst. prof. English and linguistics Ball State U., Muncie, Ind., 1959-63, asso. prof., 1963-67, prof., 1967-68; prof. dept. linguistics U. Minn., Mpls., 1968—, dir. program in English as a second lang., 1968—, acting asst. v.p. acad. affairs, 1979—, chmn. Univ. Senate Consultation Com., 1977-78. Internat. Programs travel grantee, 1972, 77; recipient Morse-Amoco award for Excellence in Teaching, 1977. Mem. Tchrs. of English to Speakers of Other Langs. (pres., 1974), Assn. Tchrs. English as Second Lang., Am. Assn. Applied Linguistics, Linguistic Soc. Am., AAUP. Author: (with C.H.Prator) Manual of Am. English Pronunciation, 1972; Teaching English to Speakers of Other Languages, Substance and Technique, 1978. Home: 1909 E River Terr Minneapolis MN 55414 Office: Dept Linguistics U Minn 320 16th Ave SE Minneapolis MN 55455. *The ability to listen for and to respond quickly to special moments of inspiration has been of inestimable help to me. In this I am following the example set by my parents, to whom I owe much. The old saying, "whatever is worth doing is worth doing well," was ingrained in me from a child, and it has been the basis of my conduct since. It has also been a hope of mine that I could help other women who are beginning their professional lives.*

ROBINS, E. CLAIBORNE, pharm. mfr.; b. Richmond, Va., July 8, 1910; s. Claiborne and Martha (Taylor) R.; A.B., U. Richmond, 1931; B.S., Med. Coll. Va. Sch. Pharmacy, 1933, D.Pharm. Sci., 1958, LL.D., 1960; m. Lora McGlasson, June 24, 1938; children—Lora Elizabeth Robins Porter, E. Claiborne, Ann Carol (Mrs. John Cheves Haskell, Jr.). Chmn. bd. A.H. Robins Co., Inc., Richmond; pres. Monroe-Prestwould Corp.; dir. Thalhimers Bros., Inc. Trustee emeritus Richmond Meml. Hosp., United Givers Fund, Crippled Children's Hosp.; mem. exec. com., trustee U. Richmond, past pres. alumni council. Recipient Disting. Service award U. Richmond, 1960; Dean M. McCann award Pharm. Wholesalers Assn., 1968; Hugo H. Schaefer medal Am. Pharm. Assn., 1969; Liberty Bell award Richmond Bar Assn., 1970; Sertoma Club award, 1970; Thomas Jefferson award Pub. Relations Soc. Am., 1970; named Pharmacist of Year, Va. Pharm. Assn., 1967; Bus. Leader of Year, Sales and Mktg. Execs. Richmond, 1969; Disting. Service award Va. State Chamber, 1972; Jackson Davis award for disting. service to higher edn. in Va., 1976; Edward A. Wayne medal for Disting. Service, Va. Commonwealth U., 1978. Mem. Pharm. Mfrs. Assn. (past chmn.), NAM, Va. Mfrs. Assn., Va. Pharm. Assn., Newcomen Soc. N.A., Richmond C. of C. (past pres.), Med. Coll. Va. Alumni Assn. (past pres., dir.), Phi Beta Kappa, Alpha Kappa Psi, Omicron Delta Kappa, Phi Delta Chi, Kappa Psi, Lambda Chi Alpha, Beta Gamma Sigma (hon.). Baptist (mem. bd. adminstrn.). Clubs: Rotary (past dir.), Commonwealth Forum, Country of Va. Home: Clear View River Rd Richmond VA 23226 Office: 1407 Cummings Dr Richmond VA 23220

ROBINS, ELI, psychiatrist, biochemist, educator; b. Houston, Feb. 22, 1921; B.A., Rice U., 1940; M.D., Harvard, 1943; m. Lee Nelken, Feb. 22, 1946; children—Paul, James, Thomas, Nicholas. Intern Mt. Sinai Hosp., N.Y.C., 1944; resident Mass. Gen. Hosp., Boston, 1944-45, McLean Hosp., Waverley, Mass. 1945-46, Pratt Diagnostic Hosp., Boston, 1948-49; instr. neuropsychiatry Washington U. Sch. Medicine, St. Louis, 1951-53, asst. prof. psychiatry, 1953-56, asso. prof., 1956-58, prof., 1958-66, Wallace Renard prof., 1966—, head dept. psychiatry, 1963-75. Fellow Am. Psychiat. Assn. (life), Am. Coll. Neuropsychopharmacology (hon.); mem. Am. Soc. Clin. Investigation, Am. Soc. Biol. Chemists, Psychiat. Research Soc., Am. Psychopath. Assn. Author: (with M.T. Saghir) Male and Female Homosexuality: A Comprehensive Study, 1973; editor: (with others) Ultrastructure and Metabolism of the Nervous System, 1962; (with K. Leonhard) Classification of Endogenous Psychoses; contbr. to profl. jours. Home: 1 Forest Ridge Saint Louis MO 63105 Office: 4940 Audubon Ave Saint Louis MO 63110

ROBINS, GERALD BURNS, educator; b. Salem, Ark., Jan. 24, 1924; s. Gerald Alfred and Lucille (Burns) R.; B.S. in Edn. cum laude, U. Ark., 1948, M.S., 1950; Ed.D., U. Ga., 1954; m. Fay Ann Kennan, Sept. 1, 1946; children—Gerald Kennan, James Dow. Asst. prof., chmn. dept. distbv. edn., chmn. dept. bus. edn. U. Ga., 1950-57, prof. higher edn., 1970-73; pres. Augusta (Ga.) Coll., 1957-70, Tex. A&I U., Kingsville, 1973-77, sr. prof., 1977—; cons. Air Force ROTC, 1954; chmn. edn. com. Ga.-S.C. Nuclear Council, 1969; acad. dean Civil Air Patrol Cadet Officers Sch., 1970-71. Trustee Lawton B. Evans Ednl. Fund, Barrett Sch. Nursing, Augusta Prep. Sch. Served with USAAF, 1943-46; lt. col. USAF Res. (ret.). Decorated Air medal. Recipient Distinguished Alumnus award U. Ark., 1974. Donaghey fellow, 1943; Kellogg fellow, 1953-54. Mem. Am. Assn. State Colls. and Univs. (com. on studies), Assn. Tex. Colls. and Univs. (commn. on acad. affairs), Internat. Assn. U. Pres.'s, Internat. Council Edn. for Teaching, Nat. Assn. Intercollegiate Athletics (rep. Lone Star Conf.), Kleberg (Tex.) Hist. Commn., Ret. Officers Assn. (life), Navy League, Kappa Sigma (alumni advisor), Kappa Delta Pi, Phi Kappa Phi, Omicron Delta Kappa, Psi Chi, Phi Delta Kappa (emeritus mem., charter chpt. pres.). Mason (32 deg.). Clubs: Rotary (club pres., scholarship trustee), Pinnacle, Kingsville Country. Author: Understanding the College Budget, 1973; Campus 1980, 1975. Home: 515 University Blvd Kingsville TX 78363

ROBINS, JOHN SAMUEL, coll. dean; b. Cimarron, Kans., Oct. 25, 1925; s. Samuel Benton and Ida Mae (Woodward) R.; B.S., Kans. State U., 1949; Ph.D., U. Calif. at Davis, 1951; m. I. Kathryn Rose, Aug. 15, 1946; children—Stephen, Susan, Linda, Barbara, Kayren, Sharon. Agrl. scientist Dept. Agr., 1951-65; agrl. adminstr. Wash. State U., Pullman, 1965-70, dean Coll. Agr., 1973—, agrl. adminstr. Coop. State Research Service, Dept. Agr., 1970-73. Served with USAAF, 1944-45. Home: SE 1100 Spring St Pullman WA 99163

ROBINSON, AGNES SOUTAR, educator, ednl. psychologist; b. Chgo., Mar. 20, 1918; d. Forrest Glen and Roselle (Burns) Soutar; A.B. with honors, Calif. State U., San Francisco, 1949; M.A. in Sch. Adminstrn., Calif. State U., Sacramento, 1952; Ed.D. in Ednl. Psychology, U. of the Pacific, 1957; children—Harold H., Forrest G., Ross A. Tchr. primary pub. schs. Sacramento City Sch. Dist., 1949-51, speech therapist, 1951-54, sch. psychologist, dir. spl. edn., 1955-62; asst. to dep. supt. spl. programs, 1962-66, asst. supt. curriculum devel., 1966-68; asso. prof. edn. adminstrn. Calif. State U., Sacramento, 1968-71, prof. ednl. adminstrn., 1971-79, prof. emeritus, 1979—, chmn. dept. ednl. adminstrn., 1973-76. Cons., Peat, Marwick, Mitchell & Co., also sch. dists., ednl. agys. Vice chmn. Calif. Adv. Com. on Program and Cost Effectiveness, 1969-71; chmn. edn. com. Sacramento Community Commn. for Women, 1971-72; mem. Calif. adv. com. U.S. Commn. Civil Rights, 1974-77. Named Edn. Alumnus of Year, U. Pacific, 1974. Mem. Assn. Calif. Sch. Adminstrs., AAUP, Am. Psychol. Assn., Assn. for Supervision and Curriculum Devel., AAUW. Home: 4336 Palacio Way Fair Oaks CA 95628

ROBINSON, ALEXANDER COCHRANE, III, architect; b. Edgeworth, Pa., Nov. 2 1891; s. Alexander Cochrane and Emma Payne (Jones) R.; A.B., Princeton, 1914; B. Arch., Columbia, 1917; m. Marjory Woods, Jan. 14, 1918; children—Emma Jones (Mrs. Robert Crawford Morris), Gertrude Marjory (Mrs. Lee Clark), Alexander Cochrane, Sylvia Crane (Mrs. Richard L. Cruess). Asso. George H. Schwan, Pitts., 1919-20, Abram Garfield, Clev., 1920-26; mem. firm Garfield, Harris, Robinson & Shafer, architects, Cleve., 1926-57. Asso. of com. on classification personnel Adj. Gen.'s Office, 1917-19. Mem. Cuyahoga County Planning Commn., 1934-46, Nat. Capital Planning Commn, 1957-63, Joint Landmarks Commn., Washington, 1963-73. Trustee Cleve. Sch. Art, Cleve. Philharmonic Orch., Weatern Res. U., Music Sch. Settlement (pres. 1958-62), Childrens' Services (pres. 1942-46), Youth Bur. Cleve. (pres. 1949-52), Musical Arts Assn. Fellow A.I.A. (chancellor coll. fellows 1954, mem., 1926—; sec. 1943-47; pres. Cleve. chpt. 1935-37). Clubs: Rowfant, Mid-Day, Union (Cleve.); Cosmos (Washington). Home: Wade Park Manor 1890 E 107th St Cleveland OH 44106 Office: Keith Bldg Cleveland OH 44115

ROBINSON, ALICE GRAM, editor, pub.; b. Omaha, Nebr.; d. Andrew Peter and Carrie (Jensen) Gram; student U. Ore., U. Cal.; m. Norborne Thomas Nelson Robinson, Jr.; 1 son, Norborne Thomas Nelson, III. Press dept. Nat. Woman's Party; mem. Brewer, Taylor, Gram Co., pub. relations; spl. Washington writer Good Housekeeping, Fashion Art, Farmer's Wife mags., others; editorial dept. Community Center, Washington; dir., women's div. Rep. Nat. Com.; founder, pub. Congressional Digest, Washington; pres. C.D. Corp. Mem. Acad. Polit. Sci., Am. Contract Bridge League (life master), Kappa Alpha Theta. Christian Scientist. Clubs: Women's Nat. Press (a founder), City Tavern. Author: Congressional Committee Method of Classroom Study, 1948. Home: 3210 Q St NW Washington DC 20007 Office: 3231 P St NW Washington DC 20007

ROBINSON, ALLYN PRESTON, JR., emeritus coll. pres., lectr.; b. Center Moriches, N.Y., Mar. 24, 1909; s. Allyn Preston and Madeline Joy (Penny) R.; B.A., Columbia U., 1931; B.D., Union Theol. Sem., 1933; H.H.D., Wiberforce U., 1956; D.H.L., Dowling Coll., 1977; D.Litt., Adelphi U., 1977; m. Elizabeth Schenck, Sept. 15, 1934; children—Sarah Elizabeth Robinson Munson, Allyn Preston. Ordained to ministry, Congregational Ch., 1933; minister Puritan Congl. Ch., Wilkes-Barre, Pa., 1933-38, United Ch., Raleigh, N.C., 1938-46; instr. English, N.C. State Coll., 1944-46; dir. N.C. region NCCJ, 1946-49, Greater N.Y. area, 1956-65, dir. com. on religious orgn., 1949-56; dean Adelphi Suffolk Coll., Oakdale, N.Y., 1965-68; pres. Dowling Coll., Oakdale, N.Y., 1968-77, pres. emeritus, 1977—; guest prof. Inter-Am. U. of San German (P.R.). Cons. police tng. programs, labor mgmt. Chmn., Islip Housing Authority, 1971-77; exec. council Boy Scouts Am., 1965-77; sec. L.I. Regional Adv. Council on Higher Edn.; trustee nat. bd. NCCJ; Lisle Found. Recipient Edn. award NCCJ, Gov. of L.I. award L.I. Pub. Relations Assn., L.I. Distinguished Leadership award, certificate of spl. achievement HUD, citation Town of Islip, citation Suffolk County, award Suffolk Human Rights Commn. Clubs: Lions (hon. pres.), Watauga (Raleigh); Princeton (N.Y.C.). Author: Our Moral and Religious Resources, 1954; And Crown Thy Good, 1955; American Catholics: A Protestant Jewish View, 1959; Roots of Anti-Semitism in American Life, 1960; When Christmas Brings Conflict, 1962. Home: 465 Pebble Creek Dr Cary NC 27511 Office: Dowling Coll Office of the Pres Emeritus Oakdale Long Island NY 11769. *To give oneself to life-long learning, to have compassion, to care about people and to develop the human skills that allow one to work effectively with people. These, to me, are the marks of a true educator or a successful administrator.*

ROBINSON, ARTHUR BROUHARD, chemist, educator; b. Chgo., Mar, 24, 1942; s. Edward Hill and Zelma Adrian (Brouhard) R.; B.S., Calif. Inst. Tech., 1963; Ph.D., U. Calif., San Diego, 1967; m. Laurelee Ruth Wahl, Mar. 21, 1972. Asst. prof. biology U. Calif., San Diego, Sch. Medicine, 1968-72; sr. research asso. Stanford U., Palo Alto, Calif., 1972-74, vis. scholar, 1968-72; asst. dir., v.p. Linus Pauling Inst. Sci. and Medicine, Menlo Park, Calif., 1973-75, dir., pres., 1975—. Republican. Contbr. articles in field to profl. publs. Home: 3 Siskiyou Pl Menlo Park CA 04915 Office: 2700 Sand Hill Rd Menlo Park CA 94025

ROBINSON, ARTHUR HOWARD, educator; b. Montreal, Que., Can., Jan. 5, 1915 (parents Am. citizens); s. James Howard and Elizabeth (Peavey) R.; B.A., Miami U., Oxford, Ohio, 1936, Litt.D., 1966; M.A., U. Wis., 1938; Ph.D. in Geography, Ohio State U., 1947; m. Mary Elizabeth Coffin, Dec. 23, 1938; children—Stephen Michael, Patricia Anne. Sec. to mem. Ohio Bd. Liquor Control, 1936; asst. geography U. Wis., 1936-38, Ohio State U., 1938-41; chief map div. OSS, 1941-46; mem. faculty U. Wis., 1945—, prof. geography, 1951-80, prof. emeritus, 1980—, chmn. dept., 1954-58, 66-68, Lawrence Martin prof. cartography, 1967—, dir. Univ. Cartographic Lab., 1966-73; hon. cons. cartography Library of Congress, 1974—. Chief map officer Quebec and Cairo confs., World War II; cartographic cons. Field Enterprises Edn. Corp.; pres. Internat. Cartographic Assn., 1972-76. Guggenheim research fellow, Eng., 1964, 78. Served to maj. AUS, 1944-45. Decorated Legion of Merit. Mem. Assn. Am. Geographers (council 1960-65, pres. 1963), Am. Congress Surveying and Mapping (hon.; chmn. cartography div. 1971), Am. Geog. Soc. Author: Look of Maps, 1952; Elements of Cartography, 4th edit., 1978; Elements of Geography, 1957, 5th edit., 1967; Fundamentals of Physical Geography, 3d edit., 1977; The Nature of Maps, 1976; also articles. Editor: Am. Cartographer, 1974-76. Home: 101 Burr Oak Ln Mount Horeb WI 53572

ROBINSON, AUBREY EUGENE, JR., U.S. dist. judge; b. Madison, N.J., Mar. 30, 1922; s. Aubrey Eugene and Mabel (Jackson) R.; B.A., Cornell U., 1943, LL.B., 1947; m. Sara E. Payne, Dec. 31, 1946 (dec.); children—Paula, Sheryl; m. 2d, Doris A. Washington, Mar. 17, 1973. Admitted to N.Y. and D.C. bars, 1948; practice with law firms in Washington, 1948-65; asso. judge Juvenile Ct. D.C., 1965-66, U.S. Dist. Ct. for D.C., 1966—. Gen. counsel Am. Council Human Rights, 1953-55, dir., 1955; mem. D.C. Commrs.'s Com. Child Placement Regulations, 1954-62. Mem. D.C. Pub. Welfare Adv. Council, 1963-65; mem. Washington Urban League Adoption Project, 1959; mem. membership steering com. Health and Welfare Council D.C., 1961-66; mem. budget steering com. Health and Welfare Council Nat. Capital Area, 1963-66; mem. exec. com. Interreligious Com. Race Relations, 1966-67; exec. com., bd. dirs. D.C. Citizens for Better Pub. Edn., 1964-66. Trustee United Planning Orgn. D.C., 1963-66, Washington Center Met. Studies, 1967-74; bd. dirs. Family and Child Services Washington, 1954-63, v.p., 1958-61; bd. dirs. Family Service Assn. Am., 1958-68, Washington Action for Youth 1962-64, Barney Neighborhood Settlement House, 1962-64, Eugene and Agnes E. Meyer Found, 1969—, Consortium Univs. Washington Met. Area, 1969-74. Served with AUS, 1943-46. Mem. Am. Bar Assn. (mem. com. cts. and community 1972—, mem. adv. com. judges function 1970-72), Nat. Conf. Fed. Trial Judges (chmn. 1973). Office: US Court House 3d and Constitution Ave NW Washington DC 20001

ROBINSON, BOB LEO, real estate exec.; b. Franklin, Tenn., Sept. 9, 1933; s. W.A. and Cornelia Irene (Lampley) R.; B.S. in Indsl. Mgmt., Tenn. Tech. U., 1955; M.B.A., Calif. Western U., 1976; m. Carolyn Overton, Dec. 18, 1955; children—Richard Glenn, Leigh Ann, Elizabeth Lynne. Quality control engr. Gates Rubber Co., Nashville, 1960; tech. rep. Home Ins. Co., 1961-65; civilian staff adminstrv. asst. Dept. Army, Nashville, 1965; exec. asst. to pres. Sullivan's Dept. Stores, Nashville, 1966-69; dir. engrng. and devel. Venture Out in Am., Knoxville, Tenn., 1969; v.p., then exec. v.p. Hosp. Corp. Am., Nashville, 1970-79; pres., chief exec. officer CORIM Real Estate Group Inc., Nashville, 1979--, Fidelity Trust Co., Nashville, 1974—; pres. Internat. Bus. and Investment Services, Nashville, 1978; gen. partner Union Sq. Ltd., Jacksonville, Fla., 1973; dir. Am. Travel Service, World Health Cons.; speaker in field. Mem. Mayor Nashville Blue Ribbon Com., 1975-77; commr. City of Brentwood (Tenn.), 1969-71, vice mayor, 1969-71, interim mayor, 1971, mem. planning commn., 1970-71; chmn. bldg. fund St. Cecilia Acad., Nashville, 1978; vice chmn. Audubon council Boy Scouts Am., 1968. Served as officer U.S. Army, 1955-60. Decorated Army Commendation medal; recipient numerous public service awards; cert. property mgr. Mem. Internat. Inst. Hosp. Cons., Nat. Assn. Realtors, Inst. Real Estate Mgmt., Tenn. Assn. Realtors, Army Aviation Assn. Am., Res. Officers Assn. Republican. Baptist. Clubs: Md. Farms Racquet and Country, Shriners. Office: 170 2d Ave Nashville TN 37201

ROBINSON, BROOKS CALBERT, JR., former profl. baseball player, TV commentator; b. Little Rock, May 18, 1937; s. Brooks Calbert and Ethel (Denker) R.; student Little Rock U., 1956-57; m. Constance Louise Butcher, Oct. 8, 1960; children—Brooks David, Christopher Leslie, Michael Patrick, Diana Agnes. Profl. baseball player with Balt. Orioles, 1955-77; sports commentator (Orioles games) Sta. WMAR-TV, Balt., 1978-79; spl. asst. mktg. dept. Crown Central Petroleum Corp., 1979—; v.p. Personal Mgmt. Assos., 1979—. Selected Most Valuable Oriole, 1960, 62, 64, 71; named Am. League's Most Valuable Player, 1964, Most Valuable Player in Major League All-Star game at St. Louis, 1966; Most Valuable Player 1970 World Series; recipient Hickock Athlete of Yr. award, 1970; Balt. Decade award, 1970. Address: Lutherville MD 21093

ROBINSON, CALVIN, educator, author; b. Lowell, Mass., Sept. 18, 1905; s. Julius Louis and Rose (Miller) R.; J.D., Northeastern U., 1926; LL.M., Boston U., 1927; m. Sylvia Berman, Aug. 2, 1936; children—Marjorie Deborah (Mrs. Samuel A. Oolie), Richard Berman. Admitted to Mass. bar, 1927, Supreme Court U.S. bar, 1963; pvt. law practice, Lowell, 1927-45; founder Robinson Bar Review (sch.), Boston, 1929, dir., 1929—; lectr., practical psychology, 1930—; lectr. bus. law Am. Inst. of Banking, 1944-46. Trustee, Lowell Hist. Soc., Lowell City Library; corp. mem. Lowell YWCA; bd. dirs.

Emergency Adjustment Services to Ex-Offenders. Mem. Am., Mass. State, Lowell bar assns., Am. Judicature Soc., Bigelow Assn. Masters of Law, Boston U. Law Sch. Assn., Acad. Polit. Sci., Mass. Library Trustees Assn., Internat. Inst. Arts and Letters. Author: Give Yourself One Day, 1952 (Brit. edit.), 1956. Author publs. on legal subjects. Contbr. to various mags. Home: 193 Lincoln Pkwy Lowell MA 01851 Office: 174 Central St Lowell MA 01852. *In learning how to live, I found that you do not have full control over your life. Life is too big for that. The best you can do is to make the most of any given situation. And that depends on your attitude. If you have the right attitude, you will fight all the harder when life gets tough for you. The more you fight, the stronger you become. And the stronger you become, the more sure you feel of yourself. You build an inner strength with which to fight again. Constructive fighting is a part of life's program for achievement. To do the best you can with yourself, to refuse to give in no matter how hard the fight may be, to act as if you were the master of your fate-that is to make the most of life.*

ROBINSON, CHESTER HERSEY, educator; b. Yonkers, N.Y., Nov. 8, 1918; s. Sherman Alexander and Alice (Hersey) R.; A.B., Union Coll., Schenectady, 1940; Ph.D., Stanford, 1950; m. Marguerite Davis, Dec. 14, 1945 (div. Oct. 1976); children—Barry, Roslyn; m. 2d, Heidemarie Höfler, Dec. 30, 1976. Asst. registrar Stanford, 1949-50; dir. div. extension and summer session Miami U., Oxford, Ohio, 1950-54; asso. dir. Sch. Gen. Studies, Hunter Coll, 1954-60, dir. Sch. Gen. Studies, Bronx campus, 1960-66, dean, 1966-68; dean Sch. Gen. Studies, Herbert H. Lehman Coll., City U. N.Y., 1968—. Served to lt. USNR, 1942-46. Mem. NEA, Beta Theta Pi, Phi Delta Kappa. Presbyn. Elk. Home: 500 E 63d St New York NY 10021 Office: Herbert H Lehman Coll City U NY Bedford Park Blvd W Bronx NY 10468

ROBINSON, CLARK LEE, advt. exec.; b. Chillicothe, Ohio, Dec. 31, 1922; s. Ellwyn W. and Marea (Caldwell) R.; B.F.A., Miami U., Oxford, Ohio, 1947; m. Beatrice Barna, June 14, 1947; children—Laura, Drew, Diane, Kevin, Kerry. Asst. art dir. McCann-Erickson, 1947-49; art dir., then exec. art dir. Fuller & Smith & Ross, 1949-55; exec. art dir. McCann-Erickson, 1955-58; group art dir. Cunningham & Walsh, 1959; v.p., creative dir. Ketchum, MacLeod & Grove, 1959-63; pres. Robinson, Donion & West, Inc., N.Y.C., 1963-70; sr. v.p. Friedlich, Fearon & Strohmeier, Inc., N.Y.C., 1970-72; pres. Clark L. Robinson, Inc., 1972—. Pres. Art Dirs. Club Cleve., 1951-52. Served as bomber pilot USAAF, World War II. Decorated D.F.C., Air medal; recipient 60 art dirs. awards; created best read advt. Mem. Nat. Soc. Art Dirs. (1st v.p. 1953-60), Art Dirs. Club N.Y.C., Phi Delta Theta, Omicron Delta Kappa, Delta Phi Delta. Home and office: 157 Huckleberry Hill Wilton CT 06897

ROBINSON, CLARK SHOVE, physicist; b. Reading, Mass., May 13, 1917; s. Clark Shove and Florence (Ciani) R.; S.B., Mass. Inst. Tech., 1938, Ph.D., 1942; m. Rachel Goldsmith, Mar. 29, 1942; children—Clark Shove III, Christine (Mrs. Edward Franquemont). Research asso. Mass. Inst. Tech. Radiation Lab., 1941-43; vacuum tube developer Evans Signal Lab., Belmar, N.J., 1943-46; research prof. physics and nuclear physics U. Ill. at Champaign-Urbana, 1946-76; adj. prof. physics Mont. State U., Bozeman, 1976—; chmn. translations editorial com. Am. Inst. Physics, 1977—. Served to capt. Signal Corps, AUS, 1942-46. Fellow Am. Phys. Soc. Club: Appalachian Mountain (life) (Boston). Translator sci. Russian, 1963—; editor Soviet Jour. Particles and Nuclei, 1972-78, Soviet Jour. Nuclear Physics, 1976—. A designer, constructor 300-million volt betatron, 1946-50. Home: Box 1765 Bozeman MT 59715 Office: Physics Dept Mont State U Bozeman MT 59715

ROBINSON, DANIEL THOMAS, health co. exec.; b. Los Angeles, June 17, 1925; s. George Thomas and Helen Theresa (Walsh) R.; B.S., U. So. Calif., 1948; M.B.A., U. Calif. at Los Angeles, 1950; m. Diane W. Robinson; children—Marc David, Mattheu Curtis. Vice pres. Dart Industries, Inc., Los Angeles, 1962-63; sr. v.p. Bergen Brunswig Corp., Los Angeles, 1972—; dir. K.D.L. Corp. Past pres., bd. dirs. Trojan Club, U. So. Calif.; past pres. Cardinal and Gold, U. So. Calif.; bd. councillors U. So. Calif. Mem. Am. Coll. Pharmacists (dir., past pres.), Am., Man. surg. trade assns., Health Industries Assn. Author: Medical Marketing of Seventies, 1968; Marketing Challenges of Biomedical Industry, 1969; Biomedical Marketing, 1975; Biomedical Representation, 1976. Home: 6336 Vista del Mar Playa Del Rey CA 90291 Office: 1900 Ave of Stars Los Angeles CA 90067

ROBINSON, DAVID ADAIR, neurophysiologist; b. Boston, Dec. 9, 1925; s. Edwin Whitmore and Gladys (Mansley) Colby; B.A., Brown U., 1947; M.S., Johns Hopkins U., 1956, Dr.Engring., 1958; m. Alice Maude Webster Lang, Aug. 8, 1956. Project engr., dir. engring., v.p. charge research Airpax Electronics Inc., Ft. Lauderdale, Fla., 1951-61; mem. faculty Johns Hopkins U. Med. Sch., 1961—, prof. ophthalmology depts. ophthalmology and biomed. engring., 1975—; mem. vis. sci. study sect. div. research grants NIH, 1966-70, engring. in biology and med. tng. com., 1971-73; mem. communicative sci. cluster President's Biomed. Research Panel, 1975; mem. planning com. sensori-motor disorders vision Nat. Eye Inst., NIH, 1976; cons. in field. Served to ensign USN, 1947-49. Research grantee Nat. Eye Inst., 1969—, Research to Prevent Blindness, 1975-77. Mem. Assn. Research Vision and Ophthalmology, Soc. Neurosci., Bárány Soc. Democrat. Editorial bd. Jour. Neurophysiology, Vision Research, Investigative Ophthalmology. Research and publs. on neurophysiology oculomotor system. Office: Wilmer Inst 601 N Broadway Baltimore MD 21205

ROBINSON, DAVID ZAV, found. exec.; b. Montreal, Que., Can., Sept. 29, 1927; s. Benjamin and Antonia (Seiden) R.; A.B., Harvard, 1946, A.M., 1947, Ph.D., 1950; m. Nan Senior, Sept. 6, 1954; children—Marc, Eric. Asst. dir. research Baird-Atomic Inc., Cambridge, Mass., 1949-59, 60-61; sci. liaison officer Office Naval Research, London, Eng., 1959-60; sci. advisor Office of the Pres., Washington, 1961-67; v.p. acad. affairs N.Y. U., 1967-70; v.p. Carnegie Corp. N.Y., N.Y.C., 1970—; dir. Urban Research Corp., Chgo., 1968-75; cons. Congressional Office of Tech. Assessment, 1975-78; mem. com. women in sci. NRC, 1975—; mem. vis. com. dept. chemistry Harvard U., 1977—, physics dept. Princeton U., 1970-76. Mem. N.Y. Energy Research and Devel. Authority, 1971-77; mem. N.Y.C. Bd. Higher Edn., 1976—. Mem. Optical Soc. Am., Am. Contract Bridge League. Club: Harvard (N.Y.C.). Home: 10 Washington Mews New York City NY 10003 Office: 437 Madison Ave New York City NY 10022

ROBINSON, DEAN WENTWORTH, chemist, educator; b. Boston, July 22, 1929; s. Lawrence Dean and Doris Elizabeth (Prowse) R.; B.S., U. N.H., 1951, M.S., 1952; Ph.D., Mass. Inst. Tech., 1955; children—Dean Wentworth, Amy E., Jonas W. Mem. faculty Johns Hopkins, 1955—, prof. chemistry, chmn. dept., 1976—. Guggenheim fellow, 1966; Fulbright fellow, 1966. Mem. Am. Chem. Soc., AAAS. Author research papers. Home: 2209 Deerfern Crescent Baltimore MD 21209 Office: Chemistry Dept Johns Hopkins U Baltimore MD 21218

ROBINSON, DONALD JOHN, lawyer; b. Chgo., Aug. 24, 1934; s. Stafford John and Anne (Hinrichs) R.; B.S., U. Notre Dame, 1955; LL.B., Columbia, 1958; m. Rebecca Jean Young, June 30, 1973; 1 son, Nicholas John III; children by previous marriage—Ann Lee, Donald John, Christopher William, Susan Lenore. Admitted to N.Y. bar, 1960; mem. staff SEC, N.Y.C., 1960-65; asso. firm Caldwell, Trimble & Mitchell, N.Y.C., 1966-67, Nixon Mudge Rose Guthrie Alexander & Mitchell, N.Y.C., 1968-69; partner firm Hawkins, Delafield & Wood, N.Y.C., 1969—. Chmn., lectr. Practicing Law Inst., 1969—; mem. Task Force on Municipal Bond Market, Twentieth Century Fund; trustee Mus. of City of N.Y. Mem. Am., N.Y. State bar assns., Municipal Finance Officers Assn. (chmn. com. for revision disclosure guidelines for offerings of securities by state and local govts.), Assn. Bar City of N.Y. (com. on mcpl. affairs 1978—, chmn. 1979—). Clubs: Wall Street, River (N.Y.C.). Contbr. articles to profl. publs. Home: 160 E 65th St New York NY 10021 Office: 67 Wall St New York NY 10005

ROBINSON, DONALD KEITH, physicist, educator; b. Truro, N.S., Can., Aug. 29, 1932; s. Travis Sylvanus and Georgietta (Carter) R.; B.Sc., Dalhousie, Halifax, N.S., 1954, M.Sc., 1956; postgrad. Cambridge (Eng.) U., 1956-57; D.Phil., Oxford (Eng.) U., 1960; m. Margaret Tompkins Bainbridge, June 12, 1965; children—Gregory Kenneth, Claire Carter. Research asso. Brookhaven (N.Y.) Nat. Lab., 1960-62, asst. physicist, 1962-63, asso. physicist, 1963-66; asso. prof. physics Case Western Res. U., 1966-71, prof., 1971—. Mem. Am. Phys. Soc., AAUP. Research in exptl. particle physics with bubble chambers and electronic counters, boson resonances, neutral K-meson decays, polarized proton interactions, proton-antiproton interactions. Home: 2602 E Overlook Rd Cleveland OH 44106 Office: Dept Physics Case Western Res U Cleveland OH 44106

ROBINSON, DONALD WALTER, coll. dean; b. Rockford, Ill.; s. Walter John and Viola (Anderson) R.; A.B., Carthage Coll., 1950; M.A., Bradley U., 1951, Ph.D., 1957; m. Betty Jane Zink, May 30, 1948; children—Deborah Beth, Galen Don, Darci Lynn, Gregory John. Various positions coll. and pub. sch. adminstrn., 1952-58; specialist in coll. adminstrn. U.S. Office of Edn., Washington, 1959-62; dir. mental retardation research centers program Nat. Inst. Child Health and Human Devel., Bethesda, Md., 1962-65; asst. dean, prof. higher edn. So. Ill. U., Carbondale, 1965-70; dean Coll. Edn., Youngstown (Ohio) State U., 1970-72; dean Coll. Edn., prof. psychology and higher edn. Okla. State U., Stillwater, 1972—; cons. examiner N. Central Assn. Schs. and Colls.; cons. Higher Edn. Execs. Assos., USPHS, U.S. Office Edn. Bd. dirs. Marymount Coll., Arlington, Va., 1962-66. Served with USAAF, 1944-46. Mem. North Central Assn. Colls. and Schs. (dir. 1975-79, chmn. council research and service 1977-79), Am. Psychol. Assn., Am. Ednl. Research Assn., Am. Assn. Higher Edn. Presbyterian (elder). Home: 6310 Canterbury Dr Stillwater OK 74074

ROBINSON, EARL HAWLEY, composer, writer, singer, condr., lectr.; b. Seattle, July 2, 1910; s. Morris John and Hazel (Hawley) R.; B.Mus., U. Wash., 1933; m. Helen Worris, Feb. 17, 1937 (dec. June 1963); children—Perry Morris, James; m. 2d, Ruth Martin, May 5, 1965 (div. 1975). Wrote music for Fed. Theater shows, N.Y.C., 1936-39 (including Processional, Life and Death of an American, Sing for Your Supper); condr. American Peoples' chorus, 1937-42; Guggenheim fellowship and renewal to make musical setting of The People, Yes, by Carl Sandburg, 1940-41; music dir. Elisabeth Irwin High Sch., N.Y.C., 1957-66; condr. Extension Chorus, U. Calif. at Los Angeles, 1967-68; tchr. sound and music for film and theatre U. Calif. at Los Angeles extension, 1969-71; music for radio theater, films, TV, also singing on radio and TV; lectrs. and concerts in U.S., Can., Europe; songs for 20th Century-Fox film, Walk in the Sun; songs for Paramount film California, MGM film Romance of Rosie Ridge; song and background score for documentary film The Roosevelt Story, Eagle Lion film Texas Story, Gen. Motors indsl. film Giants in the Land; composed, sang, narrated Fox short film Muscle Beach; produced and appeared with children's chorus in film When We Grow Up; music coordinator Paramount film Up Tight, 1968; score and songs for Universal NBC film The Great Man's Whiskers; ABC Movie of the Week, Maybe I'll Come Home In The Spring, 1971, Adventures of Huckleberry Finn, ABC-TV, 1975, The Pumpkin Who Couldn't Smile, CBS, 1979. Mem. Authors League Am., Am. Fedn. Musicians, ASCAP, Am. Guild Authors and Composers (alt. council), Composers and Lyricists Guild, Universal Life Alliance. Composer: (cantatas) Ballad for Americans; The Lonesome Train; Tower of Babel; In the Folded and Quiet Yesterdays; Giants in the Land; The Town Crier; Preamble to Peace; Illinois People (commd. by State of Ill. for Sesquicentennial Year 1968); Strange Unusual Evening; Grand Coulee Dam; Ride the Wind; Song dance Cantatas for children, Good Morning, Come Along; When We Grow Up; songs for children's musical Gingerbread John; composer of score for Los Angeles Coronet Theatre Prodn. of Dark of the Moon; (score for ballet) Bouquet for Molly; (operas) Sandhog, David of Sassoun; (symphonic poem with tenor voice) A Country They Call Puget Sound; To the Northwest Indians, a Symphonic Narrative; Concerto for Five String Banjo; (piano concerto) A New Human; (musicals) Washington Love Story, One Foot in America; Earl Robinson's America; (for symphonic band) Soul Rhythms, Salt Water Song, A Country They Call Puget Sound; (songs) The House I Live In, Joe Hill, Abe Lincoln, Song of the Free Men, A Man's a Man for A'That, Free and Equal Blues, Toward the Sun, Spring Song, Hold Fast to Your Dreams, Same Boat Brother, Black and White, Hurry Sundown, Janie, All the Words Are New, Johnny's Gone, Johnny Got His Gun, Body Count, My Fisherman—My Laddy-o, The Animal Kingdom, The People Painter, Suppose, Four Hugs a Day, I Appreciate Me, Where It Is, Song of Sassoun, Let David Go . . . Author: Folk Guitar in 10 Sessions, 1965. Musical editor: Young Folk Song Book, 1963; Songs of the Great West, 1967; Songs of Brecht and Eisler, 1966. Office: 3937 Bledsoe Ave Los Angeles CA 90066. *It has taken me all of my 69 years to realise truly, that I am totally responsible for what happens to me, my successes, my "failures" . . . I created them and will continue creating until—and after I move off this particular plane of existence. I enjoy most deeply being good for people, and am increasingly allowing them to be good for me. In this good, responsible and creative space I am realising that I am a winner, in a scene where there need be no losers. My life is working well.*

ROBINSON, FARREL RICHARD, pathologist, toxicologist; b. Wellington, Kans., Mar. 23, 1927; s. Farrel Otis and Norine (Sloan) R.; B.S., Kans. State U., 1950, D.V.M., M.S., 1958; Ph.D., Tex. A. and M. U., 1965; m. Mimi Agatha Hathaway, June 5, 1949; children—Farrel Richard, Kelly S., E. Scott, Brian A. Served with USN, 1945-46; commd. 2d lt. USAF, 1951, advanced through grades to lt. col., 1971; vet. pathologist Aerospace Med. Research Labs., Wright-Patterson AFB, Ohio, 1958-68; chief Vet. Pathology div. Armed Forces Inst. Pathology, Washington, 1968-74; ret., 1974; scientist asso. Univs. Asso. for Research and Edn. in Pathology, Inc., 1972-74; asst. clin. prof. pathology George Washington U. Sch. Medicine, 1972-74, instr. NIH Grad. Program, 1973-74; prof. toxicology-pathology Sch. Vet. Medicine, Purdue U., 1974—, dir. Animal Disease Diagnostic Lab., 1978—, head dept. vet. sci., 1978—; cons. vet. pathology USAF surg. gen. and asst. surg. gen. for vet. services, 1970-74; life mem. adv. bd. C.L. Davis Found. for Advancement Vet. Pathology. Decorated USAF Commendation medal, Meritorious Service medal; recipient Aerospace Med. Research Labs. Scientist of Year award, 1967. Diplomate Am. Coll. Vet. Pathologists, Am. Bd. Vet. Toxicology (v.p. 1971-74, pres. 1976-79). Mem. AVMA, Am. Coll. Vet. Toxicologists, Wildlife Disease Assn., Conf. Research Workers in Animal Disease, Soc. Pharmacol. and Environ. Pathologists, Soc. Toxicology, Am. Animal Health Assn., Sigma Xi, Phi Kappa Phi, Alpha Zeta, Pi Zeta. Democrat. Methodist. Mem. editorial bd. Human and Vet. Toxicology, 1976—. Contbr. sci. articles to profl. jours. Home: 201 W 600 N West Lafayette IN 47906 Office: Animal Disease Diagnostic Lab Purdue U West Lafayette IN 47907

ROBINSON, FAYE, lyric soprano; b. Houston, Feb. 11, 1943; d. Robert Ernest and Deltessa (Steen) Lee; B.A., Bennett Coll., Greensboro, N.C., 1964; postgrad. Tex. So. U., N. Tex. State U. Debut, Aix-en-Provence, France, 1974; appearances with N.Y.C. Opera, Dusseldorf Opera, Teatro Colon, Buenos Aires, Hamburg (W. Ger.) Staatsoper, Can. Opera Co., also with Chgo., San Francisco, Cleve., N.Y., Nat., Detroit, Amsterdam (Netherlands), Phila., Los Angeles, Cin., Boston and Toronto orchs.; festival appearances at Blossom, Caramoor, Israel, Aspen and Ambler festivals; prin. roles include Violetta in La Traviata, Gilda in Rigoletto, Liu in Turandot, Pamina in The Magic Flute, Queen Shemakha in Le Coq d'Or, Micaela in Carmen, Constanze in The Abduction from the Seraglio and Tomyris in Die Grossmutige Tomyris. Recipient 1st prize San Francisco Opera Auditions, 1969. Mem. Am. Guild Mus. Arts. Baptist. Address: care Thea Dispeker 59 E 54th St New York NY 10022

ROBINSON, FLORENCE CLAIRE CRIM, composer, conductor, educator; b. Carbondale, Ill., Oct. 26, 1932; d. Alonzo V. and Doddridge M. (Taylor) Crim; B.A., So. Ill. U., Carbondale, 1950, Ph.D., 1963; M.A., Denver U., 1956; posgrad. Northwestern U., 1950-51, U. Colo., 1960-62; m. Carl Robinson, Aug. 9, 1951 (div. 1970); children—Carl Emil, Joan Gayle, Tchr. music, then coordinator music Denver pub. schs., 1953-65; asso. prof. music So. Ill. U., 1965-67; prof. music edn., chmn. music dept. Bishop Coll., Dallas, 1967-71; prof. music Clark Coll., Atlanta, also chmn. dept., 1971—, chmn. div. arts and humanities, 1976—; vis. prof. Emory U., 1974, Fisk U., 1969, 70, 71, U. Colo., 1963-65, Atlanta U., 1974-79; hostess Florence Robinson Radio Show, Atlanta, 1971-73, The Many Sides of Black Music, syndicated, 1974—; profl. piano accompanist; TV music tchr. KRMA, Denver, 1961-63; condr., cons., composer, lectr. Mem. Human Relations Commn., Denver, 1965. Mem. NEA, Music Educators Nat. Conf., AFTRA, Kappa Delta Pi, Pi Lambda Theta, Mu Phi Epsilon, Alpha Kappa Alpha, Phi Kappa Phi. Cons. ednl. albums black music, 1977. Home: 2885 Pine Needle Dr Atlanta GA 30344 Office: Div Arts and Humanities Clark Coll Atlanta GA 30314. *It has always been my belief that being merely good in all endeavors is not enough; I have always worked to be the best I could be. It is also very important that I do whatever I feel is right for me. I discovered long ago that when one likes and respects oneself, there is rarely difficulty in obtaining respect and loyalty from others.*

ROBINSON, FRANCIS ARTHUR, opera co. exec.; b. Henderson, Ky., Apr. 28, 1910; s. Robert Lee and Beulah Katherine (Cox) R.; B.A. cum laude, Vanderbilt U., 1932, M.A., 1933; Litt.D. (hon.), Westminster Choir Coll., 1969. With Nashville Banner, 1933-38, Sunday editor, 1935-38; writer, actor, producer Sta. WSM, Nashville, 1933-38; co. mgr., press rep. Cornelia Otis Skinner, 1938-39, Playwrights' Co., N.Y.C., 1938-40; press rep. Katharine Cornell, 1940-42, 46-48, Boston Symphony Orch., Berkshire Festival at Tanglewood, 1947-48; tour dir. Met. Opera Co., N.Y.C., 1948-80, head box office and subscription, 1950-62, asst. mgr., 1952-76, press dir., 1954-77; trustee Manhattan Sch. Music, 1969—, Vanderbilt U., 1970—. Chmn. music com., vestryman, warden St. Thomas Episcopal Ch., N.Y.C., 1974—. Served to lt. USNR, 1942-45. Recipient Handel medallion City of N.Y., 1972. Mem. Assn. Theatrical Press Agts. and Mgrs. (v.p. 1954-57). Author: Caruso: His Life in Pictures, 1957; Celebration: The Metropolitan Opera, 1979; author, narrator Biographies in Music, 1960-75, Heifetz for Bell Telephone program NBC, 1971; intermissions Met. Opera Telecasts, 1977—, host, 1978—; writer Bing Salute for Texaco-CBS TV, 1972. Home: 220 Central Park S New York NY 10019 Office: Met Opera House Lincoln Center New York NY 10023

ROBINSON, FRANK, profl. baseball coach; b. Beaumont, Tex., Aug. 31, 1935; s. Frank and Ruth (Shaw) R.; student Xavier U., Cin.; m. Barbara Ann Cole, Oct. 28, 1961; children—Frank Kevin, Nichelle. Baseball player Cin. Reds, 1956-65, Balt. Orioles, 1966-71, Los Angeles Dodgers, 1972, Calif. Angels, 1973-74; player Cleve. Indians, 1974-76, mgr., 1975-77; coach Calif. Angels, 1977, Balt. Orioles, 1978—. Named Rookie of Year, Nat. League, 1956, Most Valuable Player, Nat. League, 1961, Am. League, 1966; mem. Nat. League All-Star Team, 1956, 57, 59, 61, 62, Am. League All-Star Team, 1966, 67, 69-71, 74. Author: (with Al Silverman) My Life is Baseball, 1968. Address: Balt Orioles Meml Stadium Baltimore MD 21218*

ROBINSON, FRANK D., corp. exec.; b. Eng., 1917; ed. Columbia U., 1940. Pres., dir. Diebold, Inc.; treas., dir. Ohio Med. Indemnity Mut. Inc. Treas., trustee Aultman Hosp. Office: 818 Mulberry Rd SE Canton OH 44711

ROBINSON, GAIL, coloratura soprano; b. Meridian, Miss., Aug. 7, 1946; attended Memphis State U.; m. Henno Lohmeyer. Opera debut with Memphis Opera Theatre, 1967; Met. Opera debut as Genie in Die Zauberflote, 1970; appearances with maj. cos. in Europe and N. Am. including: Lyric Opera Chgo., New Orleans Opera, Phila. Grand Opera; now resident mem. Met. Opera. Winner Nat. Council Audition, Met. Opera, 1968; Rockefeller Found. grantee. Office: care Columbia Artists Mgmt Inc 165 W 57th St New York NY 10019*

ROBINSON, GEORGE WAYNE, steel co. exec.; b. Pitcairn, Pa., Nov. 12, 1913; s. George Wayne and Ann (Snyder) R.; grad. Robert Morris Sch., 1937; m. Alda Margaret Waina, July 8, 1939; children—George, Diana, Deborah. Asst. to purchasing agt. Robert Shaw Thermostat Co., Youngwood, Pa., 1937-39; mgr. Price Waterhouse & Co., Pitts., 1939-56; v.p. treas., dir. Lochinvar Industries, 1955-56; comptroller, asst. treas. Sharon Steel Corp. (Pa.), 1956-60, v.p., comptroller, 1962-64, adminstrv. v.p., 1964-66, exec. v.p., dir., 1966-69; pres. Teledyne Ohio Steel, 1969-78, chmn., 1978-79; ret., 1979; partner McCartan Kelly & Co., C.P.A.'s, Pitts., 1960-62. Prof., Robert Morris Sch., Pitts., 1942-45. C.P.A., Pa., Ohio, W.Va. Mem. Am. Inst. Accountants, Am. Iron and Steel Inst., Am. Ordnance Assn., Pa. Soc., Ohio Mfrs. Assn. (trustee), Am. Iron and Steel Engrs., Newcomen Soc. Clubs: Duquesne (Pitts.); Shawnee Country; Lakeview Country. Home: 3657 Miramonte Dr Lima OH 45806

ROBINSON, GILBERT ASA, public relations exec.; b. N.Y.C., May 25, 1928; s. M.A. and E.L. (Lebovit) R.; B.S. in Econs., Roanoke Coll., Salem, Va., 1950; m. Patricia Lee Armstrong, June 13, 1964; 1 dau., Nancy Lee. Asst. to chmn. Nat. Citizens Com. Ednl. TV, 1952-55; spl. asst. to sec. commerce, 1955-60; pres. Gilbert A. Robinson Inc., pub. relations counseling, N.Y.C., 1960-70, 71—; v.p. communications Gulf & Western Industries, Inc., 1970; chmn. Pub. Relations Bd., N.Y.C., 1972-76; polit. cons. to Gov. Rockefeller, 1964-66, 70, Senator Percy, 1967-68, Mayor Lindsay, 1965. Chmn. N.Y. Bd. Trade, 1976, pres., 1977—; bd. dirs. N.Y. State Vehicle Pollution

Control Corp., Laymen's Nat. Bible Com.; mem. Mayor N.Y.C. Com. Urban Fellowships. Republican candidate for Congress, 1962. Served with AUS, 1946-47. Mem. Pub. Relations Soc. Am., Am. Assn. Polit. Consultants (dir.), Blue Key. Republican. Christian Scientist. Clubs: Gipsy Trail (Carmel); Atrium (N.Y.C.). Coordinator Am. Nat. Exhbn., Moscow, USSR, 1959. Home: Gipsy Trail Carmel NY 10512 Office: Galleria Bldg 115 E 57th St New York NY 10022

ROBINSON, GON ZALA, tobacco co. exec.; b. Andrews, N.C., July 7, 1921; s. Oscar Patton and Martha Jane (Martin) R.; student Western Carolina U.; m. Charlotte Louise Wingfield, Oct. 4, 1942; 1 son, Richard Haynes. Asst. to controller Beaunit Corp., Elizabethton, Tenn., 1948-66; controller, v.p., corp. sec. Austin Co., Inc., Greeneville, Tenn., 1966—, also dir. Past city councilman, Greenville; mem. Greeneville City Planning Commn., since 1974; ruling elder Presbyn. Ch., Greeneville, 1967—. Served to 1st lt. U.S. Army, 1942-46, 51-53; Korea. Mem. Greene County C. of C. (dir.). Clubs: Link Hills Country (dir.), Greeneville Rotary (past pres., dir.). Home: 1610 Brentwood Dr Greeneville TN 37743 Office: Austin Co Hall & Cutler Sts Greeneville TN 37743

ROBINSON, GWYNN HERNDON, fin. exec.; b. N.Y.C., Sept. 16, 1920; s. E. Gwynn and Corinne (Herndon) R.; grad. Choate Sch., Wallington, Conn., 1938; student Mass. Inst. Tech., 1940; m. Natalie Thompson, Dec. 31, 1959; children—Catherine, Gwynn; 1 stepdau., Kendall Thompson Fewell. Mgr. exports Rochester Ropes Inc., N.Y.C., 1946-48, Mathieson Chem. Corp., 1948-51; mng. partner Feldt & Robinson, ind. oil producers, Colorado Springs, Colo., 1953-57; with Northrop Corp., 1958-67, v.p., mgr. European ops., 1965-67; pres. Diners Club Internat., sr. v.p. Diners Club, Los Angeles, 1967-70; pres. Internat. Market Mgmt., Inc., Los Angeles, 1970-73; v.p. Boyden Assos., Inc., Los Angeles, 1973-77; sr. v.p. Eastman & Beaudine, Inc., Los Angeles, 1977-79, THinc Cons. Group Internat., Los Angeles, 1979—. Bd. dirs. Air Acad. Found. Served to col. USAAF, 1941-45, USAF, 1951-53; N. Africa, ETO; maj. gen. Res. Decorated D.S.M., Legion of Merit, Purple Heart, D.F.C., Air medal with clusters. Mem. Air Force Assn. (past regional v.p., dir.), Am. Fighter Pilots Assn. (life), Res. Officers Assn., Am. Inst. Aeros. and Astronautics (asso), Delta Psi. Clubs: Army-Navy (Washington); Mass. Inst. Tech. Southern Calif.; St. Anthony, River (N.Y.C.). Home: 9912 Durant Dr Beverly Hills CA 90212 Office: 1900 Ave of the Stars Los Angeles CA 90067

ROBINSON, H. ELMO, savs. and loan assn. exec.; b. Denver, May 24, 1916; s. Henry E. and Gwendolyn Mory (Pettibone) R.; B.S.B.A., U. Fla., 1939, LL.B., 1942, J.D., 1970; m. Claire Reynolds, May 7, 1977; children—Sandra Robinson Doeherty, Robby, Denise Robinson Joyner. Sr. partner firm Caldwell, Pacetti & Robinson, West Palm Beach, Fla., 1967-69, Wood, Cobb, Robinson & Letts, West Palm Beach, 1969-75; individual practice law, West Palm Beach, 1960-67; spl. re-evaluation of Fla. under Fla. Cabinet and Gov., 1967-69; pres. First Fed. Savs. & Loan Assn. of Palm Beaches, West Palm Beach, 1975—; dir. First Fed. Savs. of Palm Beaches, 1958—. Bd. dirs., chmn. Palm Beach Community Trust Fund, 1977—; bd. dirs., pres. Mental Health Assn.; bd. dirs., v.p. Fla. Mental Health Assn.; mayor City of West Palm Beach, 1952-53. Served with AC, U.S. Army, 1942-45; ETO. Named 1 of 5 Outstanding Young Men in Fla., Fla. Jaycees, 1952. Mem. Am. Bar Assn., Fla. Bar Assn., Greater West Palm Beach C. of C. (dir. 1976—), West Palm Beach Jaycees (past pres.), SAR, Fla. Blue Key, Phi Beta Pi. Democrat. Clubs: Kiwanis, JDM Country, NPB Country, Tuscawilla. Home: 801 Lake Shore Dr Apt 711 Lake Park FL 33403 Office: 215 S Olive Ave West Palm Beach FL 33402*

ROBINSON, HAMILTON BURROWS GREAVES, educator; b. Phila., Feb. 16, 1910; s. William J. and Kathryn (Burrows) R.; D.D.S., U. Pa., 1934; M.S. (Rockefeller fellow), U. Rochester, 1936; D.Sc. (hon.), Georgetown U., 1975; m. Katherine Long, Oct. 1, 1929; children—William Edward, Marian Kay (Mrs. P.W. Burnside), Peter Jay. Asst. prof. pathology Washington U., St. Louis, 1937-41, asso. prof., 1941-44; prof. dentistry Ohio State U., 1944-58, dir. postgrad. dental div., 1947-52, dir. clin. teaching, 1950-52, asso. dean, 1952-58, chief dental staff Univ. Hosp., 1952-58; dean, prof. oral pathology and diagnosis U. Mo.-Kansas City, 1958—, acting chancellor, 1967-68, dean Sch. Dentistry, 1968-75, dean emeritus, 1975—; vis. prof. UCLA, 1975—; Webb Johnson lectr. Royal Coll. Surgeons (London), 1961; cons. to asst. chief med. officer (dentistry) VA Central Office, 1970-75, Kansas City VA Hosp., Leavenworth (Kans.) VA Hosp., 1958-75, Long Beach (Calif.) VA Hosp., 1975—; staff Kansas City Gen. Hosp., 1958-75, Mercy Hosp., 1958-75; former cons. Surgeon Gen. USAF, U.S. Naval Med. Center, Bethesda, Md., Surgeon Gen. U.S. Army and Navy; lectr. Naval Regional Med. Center, San Diego; pres. Am. Bd. Oral Pathology, 1952-53; mem. nat. adv. council community health USPHS, 1962-66, nat. adv. council dental research, 1972-76; bd. sci. councillors Nat. Inst. Dental Research, 1962-66. Pres. Columbus Bd. Health, 1946-54. Chmn. Council Fedn. Assn. Schs. Health Professions, 1969-70. Bd. dirs. Kansas City Gen. Hosp. and Med. Center, 1967-75; trustee U. Kansas City, 1968-75. Recipient Tufts Univ. award for leadership oral pathology, 1959; Callahan medal, 1964; Jarvie-Burkhart medal, 1967; Internat. Research award Mass. Dental Soc., 1975. Hon. fellow Internat. Coll. Dentists, Am. Acad. Gen. Dentistry; mem. Am. Cancer Soc. (dir. Mo.), Pierre Fauchard Acad. (pres. 1958-59, Fauchard medal 1950), Am. Acad. Dental Medicine (hon.), Fedn. Dentaire Nationale Francais (hon.), Am. (1st v.p. 1971-72), Mo., Kansas City (hon.) dental socs., Internat. Assn. Dental Research (pres. 1959-60), Am. Soc. Oral Surgeons (hon.), Am. Acad. Oral Pathology (pres. 1952-53), Am. Assn. Dental Schs. (pres. 1967-68), Am. Soc. Dental Anesthesiology (hon.), Mo. (hon.), Kansas City (hon.) dental hygiene socs., Sigma Xi, Omicron Kappa Upsilon, Omicron Delta Kappa, Phi Kappa Phi, Sigma Phi Alpha. Author: Oral Diagnosis and Treatment Planning (with K.H. Thoma), 1960; Tumors of the Oral Regions, 1958; Color Atlas of Oral Pathology (with R.A. Colby and D.A. Kerr), 1971. Editor: Jour. Dental Research, 1935-58, Jour. Ohio Dental Soc., 1951-58; asso. editor Oral Surg., Oral Medicine, Oral Pathology, 1948-56; chmn. bd. editors Dental Survey, 1969—, editor, 1975—. Contbr. tech. articles to trade publs., profl. jours. Home: 3243 San Amadeo St Laguna Hills CA 92653

ROBINSON, HAMPTON CARROLL, JR., surgeon; b. Missouri City, Tex., Oct. 20, 1914; s. Hampton Carroll and Dannie Joe (DeWalt) R.; student U. Houston, 1931-36, U. Tex. at Austin, 1934-36; M.D., Baylor U., 1940; m. Patricia Welder, July 12, 1947 (dec. June 1965); children—Hampton Carroll, Patricia W. Robinson, Patrick Welder, Justin Hughes; m. 2d, Mary Louise Fenton, May 29, 1967. Intern, Research Hosp., Kansas City, Mo., 1940-41; resident St. Joseph's Infirmary, Houston, 1941; practice medicine, specializing in surgery, Houston, 1946—; chmn. Houston Acad. Medicine, 1956-62, Tex. Bd. Health, 1963-75; mem. cons. staff Tex. Children's, Meth., Hermann hosps.; clin. asst. prof. surgery Baylor Coll. Medicine, 1949—; adj. prof. community health U. Tex. Health Sci. Center, Houston, 1971—. Bd. dirs. Houston Soc. for Performing Arts; trustee Houston Symphony Soc., Houston Found., U. St. Thomas, Tex. Childrens Hosp. and Catholic Community Services. Served with AUS, USAAF, 1941-45. Decorated Knight of Malta; recipient Commendation award Sec. War, 1945, Brotherhood award NCCJ, 1964. Mem. AMA, Tex. Med. Assn., Harris County Med. Soc., Houston C. of C. (dir.). Clubs: River Oaks Country, Houston Country, Ramada; El Dorado (Indian Wells, Calif.). Home: Inwood Manor 9-B 3711 San Felipe Houston TX 77027 Office: Park Plaza Profl Bldg Tex Med Center Houston TX 77025

ROBINSON, HARLO LYLE, lawyer; b. Shelley, Idaho, Mar. 10, 1925; s. Clarence and Vilate (Hanny) R.; student Idaho State Coll., Pocatello, 1943, Weber Coll., Ogden, Utah, 1946-47; B.S., U. Utah, 1949; LL.B., U. Calif. at Berkeley, 1952; m. Janet Alderson, Dec. 28, 1969; children—Tracy E., James H., Thomas A., Harlo Todd. Admitted to Calif. bar, 1953, Hawaii bar, 1970; atty. Thelen, Marrin, Johnson & Bridges, San Francisco, 1952-54; lectr. bus. law U. Calif. at Berkeley, Japan, Korea, 1954-56; atty. U.S. Steel Corp., San Francisco, 1956-63; partner Robinson & Mills, San Francisco, 1964-68; atty. Dillingham Corp., Honolulu, 1968—, sec., gen. counsel, 1971-75; individual practice law, 1975-77; fiscal control mgr. Robert Pomeroy Co., Tehran, Iran, 1977-79; prime contract adminstr. and legal officer Ralph M. Parsons Co., Jeddah, Saudi Arabia, 1979—. Mem. adv. bd. Internat. and Comparative Law Center of Southwestern Legal Found., Dallas. Served with USNR, 1943-46. Mem. Am., Calif., Hawaii bar assns. Home: 696 Kalanipuu St Honolulu HI 96825

ROBINSON, HAROLD BARRETT, bishop; b. Nelson, Eng., June 14, 1922; s. Harold and Mary (Barrett) R.; came to U.S., 1922, naturalized, 1945; B.A., U. Calif. at Los Angeles, 1943; S.T.B., Gen. Theol. Sem., 1946, S.T.D., 1967, L.H.D. (hon.), 1979; m. Marie A. Little, May 17, 1952; children—Mary Elizabeth, Martha Marie Anne Victoria, Jane Barrett. Ordained priest Episcopal Ch., 1946; curate, rector in San Diego, 1946-62; dean St. Paul's Cathedral, Buffalo, 1962-68; bishop coadjutor Diocese Western N.Y., 1968-70, bishop, 1970—; chmn. bd. Epis. Radio/TV Found. chaplain Buffalo Fire Dept. Mem. Mayor Buffalo Adv. Com. Chmn. Bd. De Veaux Sch., Ch. Home, Ch. Mission of Help. Club: Saturn (Buffalo). Home: 1112 Delaware Ave Buffalo NY 14209 Office: 1114 Delaware Ave Buffalo NY 14222

ROBINSON, HAROLD FRANK, ednl. adminstr.; b. Bandana, N.C., Oct. 28, 1918; s. Fred Herbert and Geneva (Jarrett) R.; B.S. with high honors, N.C. State Coll., 1939; M.S., 1940; Ph.D., U. Nebr., 1948; D.Sc., 1966; m. Katherine Palmer, Feb. 9, 1944; children—Karen Elizabeth Dail, Mary JoAnne. Seed specialist N.C. Crop Improvement Assn., 1940-41; mem. faculty N.C. State Coll., 1945-68; prof., head dept. genetics, 1958-62; dir. Inst. Biol. Scis., also asst. dir. Agrl. Expt. Sta., 1962-65; adminstrv. dean for research N.C. State U., 1965-68; vice chancellor Univ. System Ga., 1968-71; provost Purdue U., 1971-74; chancellor Western Carolina U., Cullowhee, N.C., 1974—; cons. internat. maize program Rockefeller Found., 1955-65. Exec. dir. President's Sci. Adv. Com. Panel on World Food Supply, 1966-67; mem. consultants bur. Nat. Commn. Undergrad. Edn. Biol. Scis., 1963-65; mem. N.C. Bd. Sci. and Tech., 1965-68; mem. President's Sci. Adv. Com. Internat. Tech. Coop. and Assistance, 1967-68; chmn. panel food crisis in Indonesia, Nat. Acad. Scis., 1968, mem. bd. sci. and tech. in internat. devel., 1968-72, mem. panel Korea tech. assistance study, 1969, mem. world food and nutrition study, 1976—; Purdue U. rep. Univ. Corp. for Atmospheric Research, 1971-74; mem. planning com. on world food, health and population Nat. Acad. Scis.-NSF, 1974-75; mem. world food and nutrition study Nat. Acad. Scis., 1976—; mem. com. agrl. devel. Bd. Internat. Food and Agrl. Devel., 1977—; mem. joint council food and agrl. scis. U.S. Dept. Agr., 1978—; mem. study group of exec. com. Joint Council Food and Agrl. Scis., 1978—. Trustee Coll. Entrance Exam. Bd., 1971-75, mem. finance com., 1975; bd. dirs. Mountain Area Health Edn. Found., Asheville, N.C., 1975—, chmn., 1979—; mem. Nat. Plant Genetics Resources Bd., 1975—; chmn. joint adv. com. U. N.C.-Community Coll. System-pvt. instns., 1976—; chmn. instl. heads of So. Conf., 1979-80. Served with USNR, 1942-45. Recipient award Nat. Council Comml. Plant Breeders, 1964. Fellow Am. Soc. Agronomy, AAAS; mem. Am. Inst. Biol. Scis., Assn. Allied Health Professions, Am. Assn. State Colls. and Univs. (com. on allied health professions 1975—, chmn. com. on agr. 1976-79, chmn. agr., renewable resources and rural devel. com. 1978-79, mem. team to study higher edn. in Cuba 1978), Biometric Soc., Genetics Soc. Am., N.C. Assn. Colls. and Univs. (exec. com. 1978—) N.C. Acad. Scis., Sigma Xi, Gamma Sigma Delta, Phi Kappa Phi, Phi Sigma, Omicron Delta Kappa. Asso. editor Crop Sci., 1962- 65. Research, publs. quantitative genetics, heterosis in maize genetics, population and food supply. Office: Office of Chancellor West Carolina U Cullowhee NC 28723

ROBINSON, HAROLD NYLE, controls co. exec.; b. McCorkle, W.Va., Mar. 8, 1925; s. Richard Moses and Emmer (McClure) R.; B.S. in Bus. Adminstrn., W.Va. U., 1950; m. Mary Lou Williams, Aug. 26, 1949; children—David Lynn, Diane Susan, R. Gregory. With Ernst & Ernst, C.P.A's, Pitts., 1949-59; with Robertshaw Controls Co., Richmond, Va., 1959—, controller, 1963—, v.p., 1978—. Dist. treas. Robert E. Lee council Boy Scouts Am., 1963-66, asst. scoutmaster, 1964—, mem. exec. bd., 1969—; pres. Huguenot High Sch. P.T.A., 1968-70; mem. budget and allocations com. United Way Greater Richmond. Served with USNR, 1943-46. C.P.A., Pa. Mem. Inst. Internal Auditors (pres. Richmond chpt. 1963-64), Planning Execs. Inst. (pres. Richmond chpt. 1965-66), Financial Execs. Inst. (pres. Va. chpt. 1969-70), Am., Pa. insts. C.P.A.'s, Va. Soc. C.P.A.'s, Tau Kappa Epsilon, Alpha Kappa Psi. Republican. Methodist. Clubs: Executives (treas., bd. dirs. 1966-68, pres., bd. dirs. 1968-69), Willow Oaks Country, Southampton Recreation Assn. (Richmond). Home: 7741 Marilea Rd Richmond VA 23225 Office: 1701 Byrd Ave Richmond VA 23261

ROBINSON, HARRY MAXIMILIAN, JR., physician; b. nr. Balt., Dec. 13, 1909; s. Harry and Verna (Wilson) R.; B.S., U. Md., 1931, M.D., 1935; m. Maurice Hardin, July 3, 1937 (dec. Dec. 1964); children—E. Ann, Harry Maximillian III; m. 2d, Elizabeth Shema Rehm, June 6, 1965. Intern U. Md. Hosp., 1935-36, asst. resident physician, 1936-37, pres. staff, 1959-60; fellow in medicine Johns Hopkins Hosp., 1937-40; prof. head dermatology div. U. Md., 1953—; pvt. practice, Balt.; chief dermatologist St. Agnes Hosp., 1947—, South Balt., 1948—; dermatologist Md. penal insts. Med. examiner Balt. Boy Scouts Am., 1955-60; cons. Balt. VA hosps., chmn. physicians com. Balt. United Appeal; chmn. adv. com. FDA, 1963-71; mem., spl. cons. com., 1968—; mem. Gov. (Md.) Com. Community Health, 1963-70. Served to lt. col. AUS, 1942-45. Recipient Clarke Finnerad award Am. Dermatol. Found., 1977. Mem. Am. Acad. Dermatology (dir. 1957-60; Gold medal for research 1970, Clark Finnerud award 1976), So. (councilor 1956-61, chmn. dermatology sect. 1977-78), Am. (mem. com. evaluation of phys. impairment 1965—) med. assns., Balt. City Med. Soc. (v.p. 1960-61, pres. 1962-63), Am. Dermatologic Assn. (v.p. 1975-76), Med. and Chirurg. Faculty Md. (council 1963—), U. Md. Alumni Assn. (pres. 1958-60). Presbyterian (elder). Author textbook in field, profl. publs. Mem. editorial bd. Cutis, 1975—, Current Prescribing, 1975—. Home: 107 W Lake Ave Baltimore MD 21210 Office: 3506 N Calvert St Baltimore MD 21218

ROBINSON, HENRY SCHRODER, archaeologist; b. Bklyn., June 6, 1914; s. Francis George and Lily Augusta (Schroder) R.; A.B., Duke U., 1936; Ph.D., Princeton U., 1941; m. Rebecca Cooper Wood, Dec. 21, 1953; children—Helen Cooper, Geoffrey Martin, Anne Wood. Instr. classics U. Okla., 1941-42, asst. prof., 1946-48, 1948-51, prof., 1953-58, asso. dean Grad. Coll., 1954-58; asst. dir. Am. Sch. Classical Studies at Athens (Greece), 1958-59, dir., 1959-69, field dir. Corinth excavations, 1959-66; prof. Case Western Res. U., 1970-78, Harold North Fowler prof. classical studies, 1971-78; mem. Inst. Advanced Study, Princeton, N.J., 1952-53, 69-70. Served with Transp. Corps, U.S. Army, 1942-45. John Simon Guggenheim Found. fellow, 1969-70. Mem. Archaeol. Inst. Am., Am. Philol. Assn., Soc. Promotion Hellenic Studies (London), Deutsches Archaolgisches Institut (Berlin), Associazione Internazionale di Archeologia Classica (Rome), Phi Beta Kappa. Quaker. Author: The Athenian Agora, V, Pottery of the Roman Period—Chronology, 1959. Office: Dept Classics Case Western Cleveland OH 44106

ROBINSON, HERBERT WILLIAM, corp. exec., economist; b. Hull, Yorkshire, Eng., Jan. 2, 1914; s. Herbert and Mary Elizabeth (Ellis) R.; B.Sc., (London), U. Coll. of Hull (Eng.), 1935; Ph.D., London Sch. Econs., 1937; D.Phil., Balliol Coll., Oxford U., 1939 m. Elsie Caroline Roenfeldt, May 8, 1948; children—Denise Patricia, Keith Brian. Came to U.S., 1943, naturalized, 1948. Sr. lectr. math. statistics, econ. theory, trade cycle theory, indsl. orgn. U. Coll., Hull, 1939; asst. to Lord Cherwell, Prime Minister's Pvt. Office, 1939-42; asst. to Lord Layton, Ministry Prodn., 1942-43; Brit. staff mem. Combined Prodn. and Resources Bd., U.S., U.K., Can., 1943-44; dep. dir. statistics, econ. and statistics div. Ministry Agr. and Fisheries, 1945; chief econ. trends VA, 1948; chief operational analysis div. UNRRA Mission to Poland, 1946-67; loan and econs. depts. Internat. Bank Reconstrn. and Devel., 1947-51; dep. div. dir. Office Program and Requirements, Def. Prodn. Adminstrn., 1951-53; pres. Council Econ. and Industry Research, Inc., Washington, 1954-57, pres. renamed corp. C-E-I-R, Inc., 1958-67, chmn. bd., 1954-67; v.p. Control Data Corp., 1968-70; pres. Internat. Mgmt. Systems Corp., 1970—. Trustee Washington Tech. Inst., 1967-72. Fellow Assn. Inc. Statisticians, Royal Statis. Soc. (mem. council 1943, 44); mem. Am. Soc. for Cybernetics (dir. 1967-75), Am. Econ. Assn., Inst. Mgmt. Scis., Am. Statis. Assn., Ops. Research Soc., Econometric Soc., Lambda Alpha, Alpha Kappa Psi. Clubs: Cosmos (Washington); Fountain Hills (Ariz.). Author articles, reports on econ. subjects. Home and Office: Box 17107 Fountain Hills AZ 85268. *Hard work, intense concentration, planning based on discerning future trends, plus a deep interest in and love for people means success even if combined only with common sense.*

ROBINSON, HOWARD OLIS, banker; b. Edinburg, Tex., Dec. 9, 1926; s. Howard Olin and Emma D. (Patridge) R.; B.B.A., U. Tex., 1950; grad. Sch. Bus. Adminstrn., So. Meth. U., 1963, diploma Grad. Sch. Banking, 1970; m. Dorothy Nell Jordan, June 11, 1949; 1 son, Randall Howard. Agt. IRS, U.S. Treasury, Corpus Christi, Tex., 1949-53; partner R.R. Co. of Tex., Corpus Christi, 1953-57; dir. data processing Hess Oil & Chem., Woodbridge, N.J., 1957-67; sr. v.p. First Nat. Bank, Dallas, 1967—. Served with USNR, 1943-45. Methodist. Home: 7634 Rolling Acres Dallas TX 75248 Office: PO Box 83124 Dallas TX 75283

ROBINSON, HUBERT NELSON, bishop, African Methodist Episcopal Ch.; b. Urbana, Ohio, Apr. 29, 1909; s. John Henry and Rovilla Ontario (Hill) R.; A.B., Ohio State U., 1935; B.D., Hamma Sch. Theology, 1934; D.D., Wilferforce U., 1942, Allen U., 1946; m. Mary Magdalene Isley, Oct. 15, 1929; 1 dau., Cassandra (Mrs. Walter Hampton). Ordained deacon African Methodist Episcopal Ch., 1932, elder, 1934, bishop, 1964; pastor chs. Ohio, 1934-44, St. James Ch., Pitts., 1944-48, St. James Ch., Cleve., 1948-55, Ebenezer A.M.E. Ch., Detroit, 1955-64; bishop of Africa, 1964-68, of Ala., 1968-72, of Fla., 1972-76; bishop, Detroit-Chgo.-Indpls. area, 1976—; chmn. gen. bd. A.M.E. Ch. Chmn. Gen. Conf. Commn.; editor hymn book in Shangani dialect in Mozambique; pres. Detroit Ministerial Assn., 1960. Dir. Columbus Urban League. Mem. NAACP (nat. life mem.), Lambda Mu, Kappa Alpha Psi. Democrat. Mason, Elk. Home: 5281 W Outer Dr Detroit MI 48235 Office: 7220 N Illinois St Indianapolis IN 46260

ROBINSON, HUGH GRANVILLE, army officer; b. Washington, Aug. 4, 1932; s. James Hill and Wilhelmina (Thomas) R.; student Williams Coll., 1949-50; B.S., U.S. Mil. Acad., 1954; M.S., Mass. Inst. Tech., 1959; m. Karen Arlette Wiggs, Dec. 21, 1954; children—Hugh Granville, Susan K. Commd. 2d lt. U.S. Army, 1954, advanced through grades to brig. gen., 1978; platoon leader, co. comdr. Co. B, 185th Engrs. Bn., Korea, 1955; platoon leader, ops. officer 74th Engr. Co., Korea, 1955-56, br. chief Engr. Supply Control Office, St. Louis, 1956-58; chief Catalog and Authorization div. Engr. Supply Control Agy., Orleans, France, 1960-62, co. comdr. 553d Engr. Bn., Orleans, 1962-63; chief combat br. War Plans div. Engr. Strategic Studies Group, Washington, 1963-65; Army asst. to armed forces aide to Pres., Washington, 1965-69; comdr. 39th Engr. Bn., Vietnam, 1969-70; br. chief war plans div. Office Dep. Chief Staff for Ops., Washington, 1970-71; assigned Nat. War Coll., 1972; comdr. 3d regt. U.S. Corps Cadets, West Point, N.Y., 1973-74; comdr. U.S. Army Engr. Sch. Brigade, Fort Belvoir, Va., 1974-76, dist. engr., Los Angeles, 1976-78; dep. dir. civil works office Chief of Engrs., Washington, 1978—. Chmn. ways and means com. Takoma PTA, 1964-65. Mem. Am. Soc. Mil. Engrs. (past sec. Orleans chpt.). Episcopalian. Address: 5906 Dalecarlia Pl NW Washington DC 20016

ROBINSON, HUGH R., mktg. co. exec.; b. Syracuse, N.Y., Sept. 18, 1922; s. Frank J. and Gladys (Hunt) R.; B.S., Syracuse U., 1949; m. Evelyn De Mattia, Nov. 24, 1949; children—Susan, Hugh R., Patrice. Dist. mgr. Syracuse China, 1949-59; with Royal Worcester Porcelain Co., N.Y.C., 1959—, v.p. sales, 1971-75, pres., 1975-76; pres. Royal Worcester Spode, Inc., 1977—, Lance Internat., N.Y.C., 1977—; dir. Lance Corp. Served with USAAF, 1942-46. Mem. Brit. Am. C. of C., Brit. China Importers Assn. (v.p.), Sales Execs. Club N.Y., Alumni Assn. Syracuse U. Home: 12 Drislane Rd Briarcliff Manor NY 10510 Office: 225 Fifth Ave New York NY 10010

ROBINSON, IRA CHARLES, pharm. co. exec.; b. Webster, Fla., Aug. 27, 1940; s. William Levy and Mary (Howard) R.; B.S. in Pharmacy, Fla. A. and M. U., 1961; Ph.D., U. Fla., 1966; m. Clarice Elizabeth James, Aug. 11, 1962; children—Ira Charles II, Patricia Clarice, Krishwin Amicus, Charmalyn Elan. Staff mfg. pharmacist Student Health Service, U. Fla., 1963-66; tech. asst. to v.p. research, project leader pharm. research, medicinal products research div. Chas. Pfizer & Co., Inc., Groton, Conn., 1967-69, sr. research scientist, Bklyn., 1966-67; dean Sch. of Pharmacy, prof. pharmaceutics Fla. A. and M. U., 1969-72; dean Coll. Pharmacy and Pharmacal Scis., Howard U., Washington, 1972-77, prof., 1972-76; pres., chmn. bd. Universal Pharm. Systems, Inc., Washington, 1977—; exec. dir. Nat. Pharm. Found., 1973-79, pres., 1979—; state splty. dir. Am. Bd. Diplomates in Pharmacy, 1976—; mem. adv. com. to program in med. scis. Fla. A. and M. U., Fla. State U., U. Fla. Coll. Medicine, 1970-72. Mem. com. drug abuse Fla. Med. Assn., 1970-72; mem. Fla. Tripartite Com. Continuing Edn. Pharmacists, 1970-72, Fla. Tripartite Com. on Internship in Pharmacy, 1971-72. Fellow Am. Found. Pharm. Edn., Am. Coll. Apothecaries; mem. AAAS, Am., Nat., Fla. (mem. legislative com. 1970-72), D.C. pharm. assns., Am. Assn. Colls. Pharmacy (mem. nominations com. 1971-72, govt. service com.

1970-72, sec.-treas. council deans 1973-77, chmn. dist. 1973-74), Am. Soc. Cons. Pharmacists, Fla. Soc. Hosp. Pharmacists (hon.), Collegio Pharmaceutico National de Cuba (hon.), Alpha Phi Omega, Sigma Xi, Phi Beta Sigma, Rho Chi. Roman Catholic. Editorial bd. Evaluation and the Health Professions, 1977—. Inventor sustained release pharm. tablets. Home: 1436 Primrose Rd NW Washington DC 20012

ROBINSON, IRWIN ZELIG, music pub. co. exec., lawyer; b. Bklyn., Apr. 20, 1932; s. Charles and Edith (Weiss) R.; B.B.A., Bernard Baruch Sch. Bus., Coll. City N.Y., 1957; LL.B., Bklyn. Law Sch., 1961; m. Joan Arrow, July 3, 1957; children—Paul Martin, Carole Heidi. Mgr. bus. affairs Zodiac Music Corp., music pub., N.Y.C., 1957-62; admitted to N.Y. bar; partner firm Parks, Robinson & Talbert, N.Y.C., 1962-64; house-counsel Screen Gems Columbia Music Inc., subsidiary Columbia Pictures Industries Inc., music pub., N.Y.C., 1964-67, mgr. bus. affairs, 1967-69, v.p. bus. affairs, 1969-70, v.p., gen. mgr., from 1970; v.p., gen. mgr. Screen Gems-EMI Music, Inc., also dir.; pres. Chappell Music Co., Inc., 1977—; lectr. on counseling clients in the performing arts Practising Law Inst., 1975; lectr. bus. of music Berklee Sch. Music, Boston, 1978; mem. com. for devel. music bus. curriculum N.Y. U., 1978. Mem. Baldwin (N.Y.) Citizens' Com., rep. at monthly sch. bd. meetings, 1959-61; chmn. music industry fund dr. Am. Cancer Soc., 1972-75; career guidance counselor Williams Coll., Mass., 1978. Served with AUS, 1952-54; ETO. Mem. N.Y. State Bar Assn., ASCAP (dir.), Nat. Music Pubs. Assn. (dir.). Jewish. Mem. B'nai B'rith. Club: Friars. Home: 1441 Dartmouth St Baldwin NY 11510 Office: 711 Fifth Ave New York City NY 10022

ROBINSON, JAMES ANTHONY, lawyer; b. Bristow, Okla., Jan. 19, 1929; s. Maurice A. and Florence (Makoske) R.; B.S., Okla. State U., 1949; LL.B., U. Okla., 1953; m. Betty L. Robinson. Admitted to Okla. bar, 1953; practice in Tulsa, 1954—; gen. counsel Bank of Okla. N.A., 1964-66, sr. v.p., 1966-68; pres. City Nat. Bank, 1968; atty. firm Rogers, Bell & Robinson, 1968-74, Robinson, Boese & Davidson, 1974—. Dir. Sand Springs State Bank; adv. dir. City Bank & Trust; dir. Merc. Bank and Trust, Boulder Bank & Trust, Am. Bank of Okla., Pryor, 1st Nat. Bank, Claremore, Okla., S.W. Tulsa Bank. Legal counsel C. of C.; commr. Tulsa City-County Library. Served with USAF, 1950-51. Clubs: Tulsa, Southern Hills Country (Tulsa). Office: PO Box 1046 Tulsa OK 74101

ROBINSON, JAMES ARTHUR, coll. pres.; b. Blackwell, Okla., June 9, 1932; s. William L. and Ethel Bell (Hicks) R.; A.B., George Washington U., 1954, D.P.S. (hon.), 1977; M.A., U. Okla., 1955; Ph.D., Northwestern U., 1957; LL.D. (hon.), Kyungpook (Korea) Nat. U., 1979; m. Lucia Adelaide Walton, Dec. 11, 1965; children—Adelaide Ethel, William Luke Walton. Instr. polit. sci. Northwestern U., 1958-59, asst. prof., 1959-62, asso. prof., 1962-64; prof. polit. sci. Ohio State U., Columbus, 1964-71, dir. Mershon Center, 1967-70, v.p. acad. affairs, provost, 1969-71; pres., prof. polit. sci. Macalester Coll., St. Paul, 1971-74; pres., prof. polit. sci. U. West Fla., Pensacola, 1974—. Trustee, chmn. Episcopal Day Sch.; bd. dirs. Nat. Center Higher Edn. Mgmt. Systems. Congl. fellow Am. Polit. Sci. Assn., 1957-58. Mem. Nat. Commn. Coop. Edn., Fla. Assn. Colls. and Univs. (past chmn.). Democrat. Episcopalian. Club: Cosmos (Washington); University (N.Y.C.). Author: National and International Decision Making, 1961; Congress and Foreign Policy Making, rev. edit., 1967; House Rules Committee, 1964. Home: 180 Dean Rd Pensacola FL 32503

ROBINSON, JAMES DIXON, III, business exec.; b. Atlanta, Nov. 19, 1935; s. James Dixon and Josephine (Crawford) R.; B.S., Ga. Inst. Tech., 1957; M.B.A., Harvard U., 1961; m. Bettye Ann Bradley, May 30, 1957; children—Emily English, James Dixon. With Morgan Guaranty Trust Co., N.Y.C., 1961-68, asst. to chmn. and pres., 1967-68; gen. partner White, Wld & Co., 1968-70; exec. v.p. Am. Express Co., N.Y.C., 1971-73, pres., dir., 1975-76, chmn. bd., 1977—, also chief exec. officer; dir. Bristol-Myers Co., Coca Cola Co., Am. Express Internat. Banking Corp., N.Y.C., Union Pacific Corp., Trust Co. Ga. Bd. mgrs., pres. Meml. Hosp. for Cancer and Allied Diseases; trustee Meml. Sloan Ketterin Cancer Center; mem. council Rockefeller U.; bd. dirs., treas. Bus. Council for Internat. Understanding. Served to lt. (j.g.) USNR, 1957-59. Mem. Overseas Devel. Council (dir.), Council Fgn. Relations. Clubs: Links (gov.), River, Recess, Racquet and Tennis, Economic (N.Y.C.); Linds Golf, Augusta (Ga.) Nat. Golf; Piedmont Driving, Capital City (Atlanta). Office: Am Express Plaza New York NY 10004*

ROBINSON, JAMES KENNETH, congressman; b. nr. Winchester, Va., May 14, 1916; s. Ray and Ida Helen (Robinson) R.; B.S., Va. Poly. Inst., 1937; m. Kathryn Rankin, Mar. 28, 1946; children—James Kenneth (dec.), Patrick M., Keveney M., Helen Ray, James, J. Kelly, Sallie. Mem. 92d-95th congresses from 7th Dist. Va. Adviser Va. Poly. Inst. Agr. Coll., 1961—. Mem. Va. Senate, 1965-70. Bd. dirs. Apple Blossom Festival, Winchester Meml. Hosp. Served to maj. Inf. AUS, World War II. Named Farmer of Year, Progressive Farmer mag., 1964. Mem. Va. Poly. Inst. Alumni Assn. (dir.), Winchester, Va. chambers commerce, Am. Legion, Winchester Hist. Soc., Va. Farm Bur., Izaak Walton League. Republican. Quaker. Rotarian, Moose, Elk. Home: Merrimans Ln Route 4 Winchester VA 22601 Office: House Office Bldg Washington DC 20515

ROBINSON, JAMES KENNETH, lawyer, govt. ofcl.; b. Grand Rapids, Mich., Nov. 27, 1943; s. Kenneth W. and Margurite I. (Anderson) R.; B.A., Mich. State U., 1965; J.D., Wayne State U., 1968; children—Steven James, Renee Elizabeth. Admitted to Mich. bar, 1968, U.S. Supreme Ct. bar, 1977; law clk. Judge George C. Edwards, U.S. Ct. of Appeals, 6th Circuit, 1968-69; asso. firm Miller, Canfield, Paddock & Stone, Detroit, 1969-71; partner firm Honigman Miller, Schwartz & Cohn, Detroit, 1972-77; U.S. atty. Eastern Dist. of Mich., Detroit, 1977—; adj. prof. law Wayne State U. Law Sch., 1973—; chmn. Mich. Supreme Ct. Com. on Rules of Evidence, 1975—. Mem. Am., Mich., Detroit (dir.), Fed. (dir.) bar assns. Office: 817 Federal Bldg Detroit MI 48226

ROBINSON, JAMES WILLIAM, mgmt. cons.; b. Bklyn., Feb. 22, 1919; s. Charles Edward and Adelaide (Reimer) R.; A.B., Cornell U., 1940, LL.B., 1942; m. Dorothy L. Luckow, July 5, 1946; 1 dau., Joan Barbara. Admitted to N.Y. bar, 1942; practice in N.Y.C., 1946—; asso. atty. Whitman, Ransom & Coulson, 1946-57; with W.Va. Pulp & Paper Co., N.Y.C., 1957-69, sec., 1966-69; prin. Georgeson & Co., N.Y.C., 1969—. Served to capt. AUS, 1942-46. Decorated Bronze Star medal. Mem. Am., NY. State bar assns., Assn. Bar City N.Y., Am. Soc. Corporate Secs., Phi Delta Phi, Lambda Chi Alpha. Club: North Hempstead Country. Editor: Tender Offers Handbook. Home: 66 Woodedge Rd Plandome NY 11030 Office: 100 Wall St New York City NY 10005

ROBINSON, JAMES WILLIAM, educator; b. Kidderminister, Eng., July 12, 1923; s. James William and Eva (Lane) R.; came to U.S., 1955, naturalized, 1963; B.Sc. with honors, U. Birmingham (Eng.), 1949, Ph.D., 1952, D.Sc., 1977; m. Winifred Nixon, Jan. 8, 1946; children—James William, Linda Juanita, Sandra Jacqueline Robinson Hendrix. Sr. sci. officer Brit. Civil Service, Birmingham, 1952-55; sr. chemist Esso Research Co., Baton Rouge, 1955-63; tech. adv. Ethyl Corp., Baton Rouge, 1963-64; prof. chemistry La. State U., Baton Rouge, 1964—, mgr. Environ. Sci. Inst., 1971—. Chmn., Coll. Town Civic Assn., 1968-75. Served with RAF, 1942-45. Guggenheim fellow, 1974-75. Mem. Soc. Applied Spectroscopy (pres. S.E. sect. 1970), Am. Inst. Chemistry (chmn. La. sect. 1978), Sigma Xi, Alpha Xi Sigma, Omicron Delta Kappa. Author: Atomic Absorption Spectroscopy, 1966, rev. edit., 1975; Undergraduate Instrumental Analysis, 1970, rev. edit., 1972; editor: Spectroscopy Letters, 1965—; Environ. Sci. and Engring., 1971—, Chem. Rubber Co. Handbook Spectroscopy, Vol. I and II, 1974; asst. editor Analytica Chemica Acta, Applied Spectroscopy, 1969. Home: 375 Amherst Dr Baton Rouge LA 70808. *1) Successful people exalt their colleagues and are modest about themselves. Little people diminish their collegues and exalt themselves. 2.) Each person's world is inhibited by some fact, but more fantasy. Destroy other people's fantasies at your own risk. 3.) If you want to know how you look to the rest of the world, look to see how the rest of the world looks to you. 4.) Influence is something you have till you try to use it.*

ROBINSON, JAY T(HURSTON), painter; b. Detroit, Aug. 1, 1915; s. Carter Boston and Marie Rose (Steger) R.; B.A., Yale U., 1937; M.F.A., Cranbrook Acad. Art, 1943; m. Dorothy June Whipple, Sept. 15, 1937 (dec. 1968); children—Theodore Carter, Thomas Whipple, James Jay; m. 2d, Anne Frances Helen Posch, Nov. 5, 1970. One-man shows include: Guggenheim Mus. Non-Objective Painting, N.Y.C., 1947, Milch Galleries, N.Y.C., 1948, 51, 53, 54, 55, 56, J.B. Speed Art Mus., Louisville, 1953, Dayton Art Inst., 1953, Phila. Art Alliance, 1957, Monede Gallery, N.Y.C., 1961, 62, Raymond Burr Galleries, Beverly Hills, Calif., 1963, xxth Century West Gallery, N.Y.C., 1968, E. Kuhlik Gallery, N.Y.C., 1971; group shows include: Guggenheim Mus., 1947, 49; Carnegie Inst., Pitts., 1949, Des Moines Art Center, 1950, Butler Inst., Youngstown, Ohio, 1953, also Audubon Artists, N.Y.C., Corcoran Gallery, Washington, Mich. Artists, Detroit, Nat. Acad. Design, N.Y.C., Pa. Acad., Phila., Provincetown (Mass.) Annual, Va. Biennial, Richmond; represented in permanent collections, including: Detroit Inst. Art, Houston Mus. Fine Art, Witte Meml. Mus., San Antonio, Berea Coll., Goucher Coll., Fish U., others, also collections of corps., including IBM, Repbulic Steel Co., Prentice-Hall Pub.; portrait painter, designer china and textiles, indsl. designer. Served with OSS, 1943, USN, 1943-46. Recipient Louis Comfort Tiffany Found. award, 1950, also various purchase awards Am. Acad. Arts and Letters, 1951-64. Mem. Artist Equity Assn. N.Y. Illustrator books: Seventeenth Summer, (Maureen Daly), 1948; The New York Guide Book, 1964; contbr. illustrations to other books. Home and Studio: 60 Church St Pleasantville NY 10570. *I have always been drawn to the theme of Man in His Environment. By extension to our own, I love jazz music, many of whose players I have painted; classic cars; Japanese gardens; good company and active social life. Travel enables me to see what others have done and are doing, all of us alike in trying to cope as best we can. In painting, I can not only portray but participate in what goes on on our planet.*

ROBINSON, JOHN ALAN, educator; b. Halifax, Eng., Mar. 9, 1930; s. Harry and Clara (Pilkington) R.; B.A. in Classics with honours, Corpus Christi Coll., Cambridge (Eng.) U., 1952; M.A., 1955; M.A. in Philosophy, U. Ore., 1953; M.A., Princeton, 1955, Ph.D., 1956; m. Gwen Groves, Dec. 18, 1954; children—Alan Groves, Hugh Parke Custis, Gwen Owen. Came to U.S., 1952. Operations research analyst E.I. du Pont de Nemours & Co., Inc., 1956-60; post-doctoral research fellow U. Pitts., 1960-61; mem. faculty Rice U., 1961-67, prof. philosophy, 1964-65, prof. computer sci. and philosophy, 1965-66, prof. computer sci., 1966-67; distinguished prof. logic and computer sci. Syracuse U., 1967—; cons. to applied math. div. Argonne Nat. Lab., 1961-67, Stanford Linear Accelerator Center, 1966-68. Served with RAF, 1948-49. Guggenheim Found. fellow, 1967-68; hon. research fellow U. Edinburgh, 1967—. Mem. Assn. Symbolic Logic, Assn. Computing Machinery, Am. Philos. Assn. Contbr. articles profl. jours. Office: 313 Link Hall Syracuse U Syracuse NY 13210

ROBINSON, JOHN ALEXANDER, football coach; b. Chgo., July 25, 1935; s. Matthew and Ethlyn (Alexander) R.; B.S., U. Oreg., 1958; m. Barbara Lee Amirkhan, July 31, 1960; children—Teresa, Lynn, David, Christopher. Asst. football coach U. Oreg., Eugene, 1960-71, U. So. Calif., Los Angeles, 1971-74, Oakland (Calif.) Raiders, 1975; head foobal coach U. So. Calif., 1976—. Served with U.S. Army, 1958-59. Named Dist. 9 Coach of Year, Am. Coaches Assn., 1976. Roman Catholic. Home: 1900 E Brookdale St La Habra CA 90631 Office: Heritage Hall U So Calif Los Angeles CA 90007

ROBINSON, JOHN BECKWITH, econ. devel. cons., former govt. ofcl.; b. Portland, Oreg., May 23, 1922; s. Jewell King and Arvilla Agnes (Beckwith) R.; B.A., U. Oreg., 1944; postgrad. U. Shrivenham (Eng.), 1945, Oxford (Eng.) U., 1946, Am. U., 1947; m. Dilys Walters, Sept. 8, 1945; children—John Gwilym, David Gwyn. Staff, Bur. Budget, 1948, 51-52; sr. program and budget officer UNESCO, 1948-51; chief personnel policy Mut. Security Agy., Washington, 1952-54, program officer, Guatemala, 1954-59, planning officer, later acting asst. dep. dir. for program and planning, Washington, 1959-61; dep. U.S. rep. devel. assistance com. OECD, 1961-64; asst. dir. devel. policy, Pakistan, 1964-68; dep. dir. North Coast Affairs, AID, State Dept., Washington, 1969-71; dep. mission dir. U.S. Econ. Aid Program, Colombia, 1971-73, mission dir., Dominican Republic, 1973-76, Honduras, 1976-79; prin. J.B. Robinson & Assos., devel. cons., Washington and London, 1979—; mem. faculty, fellow Harvard U., 1968-69; cons. NATO, 1951, UN, 1959. Served to 1st lt., inf., AUS, 1943-46; ETO. Episcopalian. Clubs: Sind (Karachi, Pakistan); Country (Santo Domingo). Home: 1300 NE 16th St Portland OR 97232 Office: 700 7th St SW Room 612 Washington DC 20024 also 145 A Abbey Rd London NW6 4SP England

ROBINSON, JOHN EDMUND, dentist; b. Kearny, N.J., Nov. 27, 1924; s. John Edmund and Norma (McDonald) R.; D.D.S., State U. N.Y., Buffalo, 1952; m. Mary Bolinski, Nov. 23, 1946. Practice dentistry, specializing in maxillofacial prosthetics, North Syracuse, N.Y., 1952-56; instr. dental surgery Zoller Dental Clinic, U. Chgo. Hosps. and Clincs, 1957-58, asst. prof. dental surgery, 1958-64, asso. prof., 1964-70, prof., 1970—, head unit maxillofacial prosthetic rehab., 1964—; cons. U. Ill. Center for Craniofacial Anomalies, 1968—. Served with USNR, 1943-46; PTO. Fellow Am. Coll. Dentists, Inst. Medicine Chgo., N.Y. Acad. Scis., Midwest Acad. Prosthodontists, Am. Acad. Maxillofacial Prosthetics (pres. 1970-71), Fedn. Prosthodontic Orgns. (pres. 1973-74). Home: 5530 S Shore Dr Apt 5C Chicago IL 60637 Office: 950 E 59th St Chicago IL 60637. *My philosophy in life has been to try to be fair and honest in all things. It is a difficult course to take.*

ROBINSON, JOHN HAMILTON, civil engr.; b. Kansas City, Mo., Feb. 14, 1927; s. David Beach and Aileen March (Weaver) R.; B.S., U. Kans., 1949; m. Patricia Ann Odell, June 17, 1949; children—John Hamilton, Patricia Ann, Donna Marie, Clinton Odell. With Black & Veatch, cons. engrs., Kansas City, Mo., 1949—, partner, 1956—, exec. partner, 1971—. Trustee Johnson County Community Coll.; deacon elder 2nd Presbyn. Ch., Kansas City, Mo. Served with USNR, 1945-46. Registered profl. engr., Kans., Mo., Minn., Colo., N.Y., N.J., Ohio, La., Ind., Mass., Mich., N.H., Tenn., Iowa, Va. Mem. Cons. Engrs. Council Mo. (dir. 1972—, pres. 1976-77), ASCE (com. fellows), Mo. Soc. Profl. Engrs., Kans. Engring. Soc. (dir., chmn. standards council), Am. Water Works Assn., Water Pollution Control Fedn., Tau Beta Pi, Sigma Tau, Omicron Delta Kappa, Beta Theta Pi. Clubs: Mission Hills Country, Vanguard, Mercury, Optimists. Home: 3223 W 67th St Mission Hills KS 66208 Office: 1500 Meadow Ln Pkwy Kansas City MO 64114

ROBINSON, JOHN LEWIS, educator; b. Leamington, Ont., Can., July 9, 1918; s. William John and Emily Laverne (Dunphy) R.: B.A., Western Ont. U., 1940; M.A., Syracuse U., 1942; Ph.D., Clark U., 1946; m. M. Josephine Rowan, Oct. 14, 1944; children—David, Jo-Anne, Patricia. Geographer, Northwest Ters. Adminstrn., Ottawa, Ont., 1943-46; prof., head dept. geography U. B.C., Vancouver, 1946-68, prof. geography, 1968—. Recipient citation of merit Assn. Am. Geographers, 1966; Massey medal Canadian Geog. Soc., 1971. Mem. Canadian Assn. Geographers (pres. 1956, citation for service to profession 1976). Author: Resources of the Canadian Shield, 1969; British Columbia: A 100 Years of Geographical Change, 1973. Contbr. articles to profl. jours. Home: 1911 Acadia Rd Vancouver BC Canada Office: U BC Dept Geography Vancouver BC V6T 1W5 Canada

ROBINSON, JOHN MINOR, lawyer, business exec.; b. Uniontown, Pa., Mar. 18, 1910; s. John M. and Martha (Downs) R.; A.B., Harvard, 1932, LL.B, 1935. Admitted to Calif. bar, 1936; asso. firm Macdonald & Pettit, 1935-41; partner firm Musick, Peeler & Garrett, 1947-77; v.p., sec. Consol. Western Steel div. U.S. Steel Corp., and predecessors, 1941-57; dir. MAPCO, Inc., St. John d'el Rey Mining Co., Ltd., Trust Co. of West. Clubs: Calif. (past pres.), Los Angeles Country (Los Angeles); Pacific Union (San Francisco); Cypress Point (Pebble Beach, Calif.); The Old Capital (Monterey, Calif.); Royal and Ancient Golf of St. Andrews (Fife, Scotland). Home: Oleada Rd Pebble Beach CA 93953 Office: One Wilshire Blvd Los Angeles CA 90017

ROBINSON, JOSEPH ALBERT, corp. exec.; b. Kenton, Ohio, May 10, 1938; s. George Lowell and Georgia Eileen Robinson; B.B.A., U. Cin., 1961; m. Sharon R. Jolliff, May 17, 1964; children—Jeffrey Allen, Mark Joseph. Audit mgr. Arthur Andersen & Co., C.P.A.'s, Cleve., 1961-72; controller Standard Products Co., Cleve., 1972-76, v.p. fin., 1976—. Served with U.S. Army, 1961-62. C.P.A., Ohio. Mem. Am. Inst. C.P.A.'s, Fin. Execs. Inst., Ohio Soc. C.P.A.'s. Methodist. Club: Cleve. Athletic. Home: 575 Marygate St Bay Village OH 44140 Office: 2130 W 110th St Cleveland OH 44102

ROBINSON, JOSEPH LEE, oboist; b. Lenoir, N.C., June 20, 1940; s. Roy Lee and Nina Elizabeth R.; A.B. cum laude, Davidson Coll., 1962; M.P.A., Woodrow Wilson Sch. Public and Internat. Affairs, Princeton U., 1966; m. Mary Kathryn McQuilkin, June 20, 1970; children—Kathryn Grace, Jody Diana. First oboist Mobile (Ala.) Symphony, 1966-67; prin. oboist Atlanta Symphony, 1967-73; asst. prof. music U. Md., 1973-74; instr. oboe and chamber music N.C. Sch. Arts, 1974-78; solo oboist N.Y. Philharm., N.Y.C., 1978—; bd. dirs. Winston-Salem (N.C.) Symphony, 1974-78; founder, dir. John Mack Oboe Camp, 1976-78; mem. Moravian Music Festival Music Com., Winston-Salem, 1977. elder Central Presbyterian Ch., Atlanta, 1973. Recipient Disting. Alumni award Brevard Music Center, 1972; Fulbright grantee, 1962-63. Home: 2 Heritage Ct Demarest NJ 07627 Office: Avery Fisher Hall Broadway at 65th St New York NY 10023

ROBINSON, JOSEPH WILLIAM, polit. scientist, educator; b. St. Paul, June 16, 1908; s. Joseph William and Emma (Weston) R.: A.B., Stanford U., 1930, M.A., 1931, Ph.D., 1936; postgrad. Harvard U., U. Chgo., U. Calif. at Los Angeles; m. Jeanne Elizabeth Keever, Mar. 21, 1936 (dec. Feb. 1963); children—William Weston, Alren Leonard. Acting instr. Stanford, 1930-36; instr. U. Idaho, 1935-36; asso. U. Calif. at Los Angeles, 1935-36; instr. Purdue U., 1937-39, asst. prof., 1939-41, asso. prof., 1941-44, prof., 1944-47; prof., chmn. dept. polit. sci. and internat. relations Whittier (Calif.) Coll., 1947—, dir. Whittier European program, Copenhagen, 1970-71, Rio Hondo Coll., 1975—; dir. exec. com. Inst. World Affairs, U. So. Calif., 1950—; vis. prof. U. So. Calif., summer 1964, 68, March AFB Grad. Program, 1968, extension div. U. Calif., 1963-69; lectr., speaker; with Ind. Commn. Interstate Coop., 1939-40, OPA, 1944-45. Trustee, Coro Found. Mem. Am., So. Calif. (pres. 1960, exec. com. 1958—), Midwest, Western polit. sci. assns., Los Angeles World Affairs Council, Los Angeles Com. Fgn. Relations, Town Hall Los Angeles, Am. Soc. Internat. Law, AAUP, Commn. Study Orgn. Peace, Am. Assn. UN, Pi Sigma Alpha, Sigma Delta Chi, Omicron Delta Kappa, Alpha Tau Omega. Club: Los Angeles Athletic. Author: What Does Ideology Signify, 1942; General International Organization, 1957; Royal Commissions of Inquiry, 1947; The Institute of World Affairs, Past and Present, 1959; The Background and Purposes of International Organization, 1967; The Roots of International Organization, 1968; also articles. Contbr. encys., proc. profl. jours. Home: 4734 41st Ave SW Seattle WA 98116

ROBINSON, JULIA BOWMAN, mathematician; b. St. Louis, Dec. 8, 1919; d. Ralph Bowers and Helen (Hall) Bowman; A.B., U. Calif., Berkeley, 1940, M.A., 1941, Ph.D., 1948; m. Raphael Mitchel Robinson, Dec. 22, 1941. Jr. mathematician RAND Corp., Santa Monica, Calif., 1949-50; lectr. math. U. Calif., Berkeley, 1960, 63-64, 66, 69-70, 75, prof., 1976—. Mem. Am. Math. Soc., Assn. Symbolic Logic, AAAS, Nat. Acad. Scis. Democrat. Home: 243 Lake Dr Berkeley CA 94708 Office: Dept Math Univ Calif Berkeley CA 94720

ROBINSON, KATHERINE PRENTIS WOODROOFE (MRS. M. RICHARD ROBINSON, JR.), editor; b. Detroit, Oct. 20, 1939; d. Robert William and Lindsay Prentis Woodroofe; B.A. magna cum laude, Smith Coll., Northampton, Mass., 1961; m. M. Richard Robinson, Jr., May 17, 1968. With Scholastic Mags., Inc., N.Y.C., 1961—, asst. editor Lit. Cavalcade Mag., 1963-64, asso. editor, mng. editor Scholastic Scope Mag., 1965-67, editor, 1967—; also editor Scope Play Series, 1971, 75, Scope Activity Kits, 1975, 76, 77, 78, 79. Home: 156 W 88th St New York City NY 10024 Office: Scholastic Scope 50 W 44th St New York City NY 10036

ROBINSON, KENNETH LEON, agrl. economist; b. Olympia, Wash., July 2, 1921; s. Charles Leon and Elsie Beulah (Caspar) R.; B.S., Oreg. State Coll., 1942; M.S., Cornell U., 1947; postgrad. (Elmhirst fellow) Oxford (Eng.) U., 1948-49; Ph.D., Harvard U., 1952; m. Jean Ruth Anderson, July 10, 1954; children—James Carl, Alan Eric. Asst. prof. agrl. econs. Cornell U., 1951-54, asso. prof., 1954-59, prof., 1959—; Fulbright lectr. U. Sydney (Australia), 1964; vis. prof. U. Calif., Berkeley, 1968; vis. scientist Internat. Inst. Tropical Agr., Ibadan, Nigeria, 1973-74. Served with U.S. Army, 1942-45. Mem. Am. Agrl. Econs. Assn., Internat. Assn. Agrl. Economists. Author: (with W.G. Tomek) Agricultural Product Prices, 1971. Home: 128 N Sunset Dr Ithaca NY 14850 Office: 40 Warren Hall Cornell U Ithaca NY 14853

ROBINSON, LEN (TRUCK), profl. basketball player; b. Jacksonville, Fla., Oct. 4, 1951; student Tenn. State U. With Washington Bullets (Nat. Basketball League), 1974-76, Atlanta Hawks (Nat. Basketball Assn.), 1977, New Orleans Jazz (Nat. Basketball Assn.), 1978, Phoenix Suns (Nat. Basketball Assn.), 1979—. Office: care New Orleans Jazz Louisiana Superdome PO Box 53213 New Orleans LA 70153*

ROBINSON, LLOYD B., soft drink mfg. co. exec.; b. Portland, Oreg., Sept. 16, 1941; s. George E. and Lillian M. (Beam) R.; B.A. in Indsl. Mgmt., U. Oreg.; J.D., Lewis and Clark Coll.; m. Barbara Monroe, Nov. 29, 1968; children—Tracy, Kristin, James, John Emily. Admitted to Oreg. bar; retail rep. Shell Oil Co., Portland, 1962-65; mktg. dir. U-Haul Rental System, Portland, 1965-69; dir. internat. mktg., gen. counsel Port of Portland, 1969-76; pres., chief exec. officer Alpac Corp., Seattle, 1976—; dir. No. Comml. Co. Bd. dirs. Safety Tng. and Research Assn. Wash. Mem. Young Presidents Orgn., Oreg. State Bar Assn., Am. Bar Assn., Wash. Soft Drink Assn., Pepsi-Cola Bottlers Assn., Nat. Soft Drink Assn. (exec. bd.), Republican. Presbyterian. Clubs: Seattle Golf, Wash. Athletic, Rainier, Multnomah Athletic. Office: 2300 26th Ave S Seattle WA 98144

ROBINSON, LUCIUS FRANKLIN, JR., lawyer, b. Hartford, Conn., Oct. 3, 1895; s. Lucius F. and Elinor (Cooke) R.; A.B., Yale, 1918, M.A. (hon.), 1953; LL.B., Harvard, 1921; m. Augusta James McLane, Apr. 29, 1922; children—Elinor (Mrs. George S. Greene), Augusta (Mrs. John deK. Alsop), Amy James (Mrs. G. David Campbell-Harris), Anne Trumbull (Mrs. Alden Y. Warner, Jr.). Lt. 301st F.A., U.S. Army, 1917-19; admitted to Conn. bar, 1922; partner Robinson, Robinson & Cole, Hartford, Conn., 1925—. Former dir. various financial and indsl., ednl. and charitable corps. Former pres. various state and municipal commns. and agys.; pres. Miss Porter's Sch., 1943-64; pres. Yale U. Council, 1948-51. Recipient Mory's Cup, 1951, Yale medal, 1953, Nathan Hale, 1957; fellow Corp. of Yale U., 1953-59; fellow Saybrook Coll. Fellow Am. Bar Found.; mem. Am., Conn. (pres. 1956-57), Hartford County (pres. 1943-45) bar assns. Clubs: Century, Yale (N.Y.C.); Graduates, Mory's (New Haven); Maidstone, Devon Yacht (gov.) (L.I.); Gilpins, Monday Evening (Hartford). Home: Farmington CT 06032 Office: 799 Main St Hartford CT 06103

ROBINSON, MAGNUS EUGENE, ins. co. exec.; b. Norfolk, Nebr., May 28, 1927; s. Franklin Guy and Lillian Jane (Johnson) R.; B.S., U. Nebr., 1951; LL.B., J.D., U. Mo., Kansas City, 1954; LL.M., N.Y. U., 1959; m. Lois Katherine Elwell, Aug. 26, 1951; children—Linda Jane, Graham Scott, Laura Ann. Admitted to Mo. bar, 1954, Kans. bar, 1954, N.Y. bar, 1963; with Shell Oil Co., Houston, 1959-68, asst. treas., 1963, treas., 1963-68; gen. mgr. Polymers div. Shell Chem. Co., Houston, 1968-72; v.p., treas. INA Corp., Phila., 1972-75; v.p., treas. IU Internat. Corp., Wilmington, Del., 1975—. Mem. Am. Inst. C.P.A.'s, Am. Bar Assn. Home: 926 Black Rock Rd Gladwyne PA 19036 Office: IU International Corp 1105 N Market St Wilmington DE 19801

ROBINSON, MARSH EDWARD, educator, oral surgeon; b. Sioux City, Iowa, Oct. 30, 1916; s. James Edward and Edna Barbara (Jepson) R.; A.B., U. Calif. at Los Angeles, 1938; D.D.S., U. So. Calif., 1942, M.D., 1946. Research asso. dept. anatomy U. So. Calif. Sch. Medicine, 1943-49, asso. prof. dept. pathology Sch. Dentistry, 1949-54, prof. oral surgery, 1954—, head dept., 1954-70, head emeritus, 1970—, prof., head dept. oral surgery Sch. Medicine, 1958—; cons. VA Los Angeles, U.S. Naval Hosp., San Diego, 1954-68; chief oral surgery service Los Angeles County Gen. Hosp., Orthopedic Children's Hosp.; sr. staff Santa Monica Hosp. Bd. dirs. Los Angeles County Heart Assn. Served as capt. M.C., AUS, 1946-48. Diplomate Am. Bd. Oral Surgery. Fellow Am. Coll. Dentists, A.C.S; mem. AMA, Am. Soc. Oral Surgeons, Am. Dental Assn., Am. Soc. Maxillofacial Surgeons, So. Calif. Acad. Oral Pathology (founding mem., pres. 1958). Home: 3003 Santa Monica Blvd Santa Monica CA 90404 Office: Univ of Southern California Los Angeles CA 90007

ROBINSON, MARSHALL ALAN, found. exec.; b. Berkeley, Calif., Feb. 16, 1922; s. Webster Richard and Evelyn (Casey) R.; A.B., U. Calif. at Berkeley, 1943; M.A., Ohio State U., 1948, Ph.D., 1950; m. Ynid Douglas Rankin, June 5, 1944 (div. 1973); children—Joan Douglas (Mrs. James Saalfield), Margaret Elaine, Richard Webster; m. 2d, Flavia Derossi, Oct. 1974. Instr. econs. Ohio State U., 1948-50; asst. prof. econs. Tulane U., 1951-53; research asso. Nat. Bur. Econ. Research, 1951-52; asst. prof. econs. Dartmouth, 1953-55; sr. staff mem., asst. to pres. Brookings Instn., 1955-60; prof. econs., dean Grad. Sch. Bus., U. Pitts., 1960-63; dir. econ. devel. and adminstrn. program Ford Found., 1964-67, program officer in charge higher edn. and research, 1967-71, dep. v.p. edn. and research, 1971-73, v.p. resources and environ., 1973-79; pres. Russell Sage Found., N.Y.C., 1979—. Served to 1st lt. USMCR, 1943-45; PTO. Mem. Am. Econs. Assn., Am. Fin. Assn., Council on Fgn. Relations, Alpha Delta Phi. Author: An Introduction to Economic Reasoning, 1956, 2d edit., 1967; The National Debt Ceiling, 1959. Home: 870 United Nations Plaza Apt 35C New York NY 10017 Office: Russell Sage Foundation 633 3d Ave New York NY 10017

ROBINSON, MARTHA STEWART, lawyer, educator; b. Topeka, Mar. 2, 1914; d. Robert Bigger and Lenora (Stubbs) Stewart; A.B. cum laude, Washburn U., 1934, LL.B., 1940; LL.M., Stanford U., 1953; m. Albrecht Marburg Yerkes, July 3, 1940 (dec. 1963); children—Robert Stewart, William Marburg; m. 2d, Stephan B. Robinson, Jr., July 17, 1971. Admitted to Kans. bar, 1940, Calif. bar, 1945; individual practice law, Los Angeles, 1946-55; instr. law Southwestern U. Sch. Law, Los Angeles, 1946-55; cons. Los Angeles Superior Ct. Com. on Standard Jury Instrns., 1957-64; prof. law Loyola U. Sch. Law, Los Angeles, 1965—; judge pro tempore Los Angeles County Superior Ct., 1963; chmn. remedies sect. Am. Law Schs., 1973, 74. Mem. Am. Law Inst., Am., Calif., Los Angeles County (chmn. legal ethics com. 1975-76, trustee 1976-78), bar assns., Women Lawyers Assn. Los Angeles (past pres.). Home: 625 Old Mill Rd Pasadena CA 91108 Office: Loyola U Law Sch 1440 W 9th St Los Angeles CA 90019

ROBINSON, MARY FRANCES MCFEETERS, educator; b. Ithaca, N.Y., Dec. 16, 1918; d. Milo Crow and Elma (Taylor) McFeeters; A.B., Wilson Coll., 1940; M.A., Syracuse U., 1947, Ph.D. in Romance Langs., 1954; French Govt. scholar, 1950-51; m. Paul Signor Robinson, Dec. 26, 1955; children—Pauline Minta, Ellen Frances. High sch. lang. tchr. upstate N.Y., 1941-45; instr. French, Syracuse U., 1946-50; mem. faculty Wake Forest Coll., 1952—, prof. French, 1968—, chmn. dept. Romance langs., 1967-74, 78—. Syracuse U. fellow, 1951-52. Mem. Am. Assn. Tchrs. French, Modern Lang. Assn., S. Atlantic Modern Lang. Assn. Baptist. Home: 1939 Faculty Dr Winston-Salem NC 27106

ROBINSON, MAURICE RICHARD, publisher; b. Wilkinsburg, Pa., Dec. 24, 1895; s. Richard Bradley and Rachel S.C. (Calderwood) R.; A.B., Dartmouth, 1920; m. Florence Liddell, June 2, 1934; children—Richard, Susan, Barbara, Florence, William. Founded Western Pa. Scholastic, 1920, title changed to Scholastic, 1922, Scholastic Mags., Inc., pubs. 27 elementary and secondary sch. classroom periodicals, pubs., distbrs. books, recs., filmstrips to schools, pres., pub., 1922-63, chmn. bd., chief exec. officer, 1963-75, chmn. bd., 1975—. Served from pvt. to 2d lt. U.S. Army, 1917-19. Recipient Pa. award for excellence in edn., 1969; Henry Johnson Fisher award, 1970. Mem. Assn. Am. Pubs. (pres. 1962-63), Delta Tau Delta. United Presbyn. Clubs: Cosmos (Washington); Apawamis (Rye, N.Y.); University (N.Y.C.). Home: 55 Witherbee Pelham NY 10803 Office: 50 W 44th St New York NY 10036

ROBINSON, MAURICE RICHARD, JR., pub. co. exec.; b. Pitts., May 15, 1937; s. Maurice Richard and Florence (Liddell) R.; B.A. magna cum laude, Harvard, 1959; postgrad. St. Catharines Coll., Cambridge U., 1959-60; m. Katherine Woodroofe, May 17, 1968. Tchr. English, Evanston Twp. (Ill.) High Sch., 1960-62; asst. editor Lit. Cavalcade, Scholastic Mags., Inc., N.Y.C., 1962-63, editor Scholastic lit. units, 1963-64, editor Scope mag., 1964-67, editorial dir. English, 1967-71, pub. sch. div., 1971-74, pres., chief exec. officer, 1974—, also dir.; chmn. bd. Advanced Typographic Systems. Mem. Nat. Council Tchrs. English, N.Y. Acad. Public Edn., Assn. Am. Pubs. (dir. 1978—). Clubs: University, Pubs. Lunch, Harvard (N.Y.C.); Quogue Field. Home: 156 W 88th St New York NY 10024 Office: 50 W 44th St New York NY 10036

ROBINSON, MAX, television news broadcaster; b. Richmond, Va., May 1, 1939; s. Maxie Cleveland and Doris (Jones) R.; student Oberlin Coll., 1957-58, Ind. U., 1959-60; LL.D. (hon.), N.C. A&T State U., 1979; m. Beverly Hamilton, Apr. 1, 1973; children—Mark, Maureen, Michael, Malik. Corr., cameraman Sta. WTOP-TV, Washington, 1965, anchorman, 1969-78; corr. Sta. WRC-TV, Washington, 1965-69; anchorman ABC Network News, N.Y.C., 1978—; asso. prof. communicative arts Fed. City Coll., 1968-72. Served with USAF, 1959-60. Recipient Journalist of Year award Capital Press Club, 1967; NEA award, 1966; Nat. Emmy award, 1967, Regional Emmy award (2), 1967; award Ohio State U., 1967; Outstanding News Reporting award D.C. C. of C., 1978; Communication and Leadership award Toastmasters Internat., 1978, Chgo. State U., 1979, Congress Nat. Black Chs., 1979; named Hon. Citizen Indpls., 1978, Houston, 1978, Cin., 1979, Atlanta, 1979; Max Robinson Day decreed in D.C., 1978, Richmond, 1978; Nat. Media award Capital Press Club, 1979; decorated knight comdr. Order African Redemption (Liberia), 1972. Mem. Sigma Delta Chi. Office: 190 N State Chicago IL 60601

ROBINSON, MILTON BERNIDINE, clergyman, editor; b. Forest City, N.C., June 29, 1913; s. Plato and Connie (McEntire) R.; A.B., Johnson C. Coll., Charlotte, N.C., 1963; M.S., A. and T. State U., Greensboro, N.C., 1967; D.D. (hon.), Livingstone Coll., Salisbury, N.C., 1973; m. Lois Mosley, Oct. 28, 1933; children—Evelyn (Mrs. Lois Mercer), Essie (Mrs. McDaniel), Connie (Mrs. Mae Foust), Milton Bernidine, Arthur, Charles, Annie (Mrs. Walker Evans), Bettie (Mrs. Francis McKesson), Priscilla (Mrs. Doretha Hodge), Phylias, Kenneth. Formerly farmer, sch. bus driver, Pullman porter, editor, brick mason, builder; ordained to ministry A.M.E. Zion Ch., 1949; pastor St. John A.M.E. Zion Ch., Rutherford, N.C., 1965—; tchr. Rutherford County Carver High Sch., 1965-69; editor Star of Zion, 1969—. Del. gen. conf. A.M.E. Zion Ch., 1960, 64, 68, 72, connectional mem. bd. Christian edn., home-ch. div., 1968—; del. World Meth. Conf., 1971; mem. governing bd. Nat. Council Chs. Christ in U.S.A., 1972—. Chmn. Rutherford County Human Relations Council, 1968-69. Second vice chmn. Rutherford County Democratic Exec. Com., 1970-74. Chmn. trustees Doggett Grove A.M.E. Zion Ch., Forest City, N.C.; trustee Winston-Salem State U., Clinton Jr. Coll., Rock Hill, S.C. Mem. NAACP. Mason. Home: Route 3 Box 472 Forest City NC 28043 Office: 401 E 2d St Charlotte NC 28230

ROBINSON, PAUL HERON, JR., group ins. exec., mut. fund broker; b. Chgo., June 22, 1930; s. Paul Heron and Virginia Jane (Croft) R.; B.S. in Pub. Affairs, U. Ill., 1953; m. Martha Courtney Bidwell, June 29, 1953; 1 dau., Virginia Louise. Founder, pres. Robinson Inc., specialist brokerage firm for banks and profl. assns., Chgo., 1960—, Robinson Adminstrv. Services, Inc., 1971—, Robinson-Coulter Ltd., London, 1972—. Exec. v.p. United Republican Fund Ill. Exec. bd. Chgo. Area council Boy Scouts Am. Served as lt. (j.g.) USNR, 1953-55; Korea. Mem. U.S. C. of C., Navy League U.S., Inst. Dirs. (London), Delta Kappa Epsilon. Clubs: Capitol Hill, Army and Navy (Washington); Chicago, Union League (Chgo.); Shoreacres (Lake Bluff, Ill.). Author financial articles. Home: Shoreacres Lake Bluff IL 60044 Office: 209 S LaSalle St Chicago IL 60604

ROBINSON, PAUL IRWIN, physician, state ofcl., ret. army officer; b. Waltonville, Ill., Sept. 15, 1904; s. James W. and Anna B. (Elliston) R.; B.S., Washington U., 1926, M.D., 1928; student Armed Forces Indsl. Coll., 1939-40; m. Marjorie F. Halliburton, Dec. 31, 1928; children—L. Jane (widow of Maj. H.B. Dierdorff, Jr.), Judy A. (Mrs. Robert B. Hydeman). Commd. 1st lt. M.C., U.S. Army, 1928, advanced through grades to maj. gen., 1955; intern Fitzsimons Army Hosp., Denver, 1928-29; various assignments, U.S., Hawaii, 1929-38; med. supply, fiscal positions Office Surgeon Gen., 1930-44; dep. surgeon Far East Theatre, 1945; chief personnel div. Office Surgeon Gen., 1947-51; comdr. St. Louis Med. Depot, 1946-47, Fitzsimons Army Hosp., 1951-54, Madigan Army Hosp., Tacoma, 1955, Letterman Army Hosp., San Francisco, 1955-56; surgeon 8th Army, Korea, 1954-55; exec. dir. dependents med. care program for Army, Navy, Marine Corps, USAF, USPHS, Coast Guard, Coast and Geodetic Survey, 1956-58; physician and coordinator med. relations Met. Life Ins. Co., 1958-59, asso. med. dir., 1959-60, med. dir., 1960-61, chief med. dir., 1961-65, v.p., chief med. dir., 1965-69; chief profl. div. Med. Services Adminstrn., Ala. Dept. Pub. Health, 1970-71, dir. med. services adminstrn., 1971-74. Decorated D.S.M., Legion of Merit with oak leaf cluster; Mil. medal of Merit (Philippines); Taiguk medal (Korea). Diplomate Am. Bd. Preventive Medicine. Fellow Am. Coll. Preventive Medicine, A.C.P., Am. Coll. Hosp. Adminstrs. (hon.), N.Y. Acad. Medicine; mem. Assn. Life Ins. Med. Dirs. Am. (pres. 1963), Am. Geriatrics Soc., (pres. 1967; Thewlis award), Ind. Med. Assn., Am. Pub. Health Assn., Internat. Soc. Internal Medicine, AMA, Assn. Mil. Surgeons, Ala. Ret. Officers Assn. (pres. Montgomery chpt. 1973), Sigma Xi, Phi Beta Pi. Contbr. Phi Beta Pi. Contbr. to med. publs. Home: 3303 Royal Carriage Dr Montgomery AL 36116

ROBINSON, PAUL MINNICH, clergyman; b. Denver, Jan. 26, 1914; s. John Amos and Nora Edna (Minnich) R.; A.B., Juniata Coll., 1935, D.D., 1948; Th.B., Princeton Theol. Sem., 1938; S.T.M., Luth. Sem., Phila., 1941; LL.D., Bridgewater Coll., 1953; m. Mary Elizabeth Howe, June 29, 1938; children—Margaret (Glick), Thomas Barton. Ordained to ministry Ch. of Brethren; pastor First Ch. of the Brethren, Ambler, Pa., 1936-40, Hagerstown, Md., 1940-53; pres. Bethany Theol. Sem., Chgo., 1953-75, pres. emeritus, 1975—; pastor Crestmanor Ch. of Brethren, South Bend, Ind., 1975—; moderator Ch. of Brethren, 1955-56, chmn. commn. on higher edn. Ch. of Brethren, 1963-64; mem. exec. com. Moslem-Christian Cooperation; pres. Ch. Fedn. Greater Chgo., 1957-60; mem. Brethren delegation Nat. Council Chs. Pres., Ecumenical Inst., Chgo., 1960-64; trustee Juniata Coll. Mem. Am. Assn. Theol. Sems. (exec. com., treas. 1964-68), Assn. Chgo. Theol. Sems. (pres.), Chgo. Theol. Faculties Union (pres.), Assn. Theol. Profs., Practical Fields, Tau Kappa Alpha. Rotarian. Club: Torch. Author: Call the Witnesses, 1974. Editorial asso. The Pulpit. Contbr. articles religious jours. Home: 1328 Berkshire Dr South Bend IN 46614 Office: 1342 Berkshire Dr South Bend IN 46614. *Life is a trust, in which each person is given the investment of abilities to be developed into skills, energies to be converted into activity, and time to allow all life's resources to find meaningful fulfillment. The use of the gifts which are our natural endowment not selfishly, but for the common good, becomes both priority and commitment for anyone who would leave the world a better place.*

ROBINSON, PETER CLARK, mktg. exec.; b. Brighton, Mass., Nov. 16, 1938; s. Richard and Mary Elizabeth (Cooper) R.; B.S. in Fgn. Service, Georgetown U., 1961; M.B.A., Babson Inst., 1963; m. Sylvia Phyllis Petchek, Aug. 26, 1961 (div. 1974); children—Marc Louis, Nicholas Daniel, Andrea Suzanne. Asst. supt. prodn. Mass. Broken Stone Co., Weston, 1961-62, night shift supt., 1962-65, v.p. ops., 1968, v.p., 1969-75, also dir.; gen. supt. Berlin Stone Co., 1965-67, v.p. ops., 1968; v.p. Holden Trap Rock Co., to 1975, also dir.; pres. J.P. Burroughs & Sons, Inc. aggregate div. subs. Blount, Inc., Saginaw, Mich. and Montgomery, Ala., 1975-78; v.p. corp. mktg. Blount, Inc., Montgomery, 1978-79, v.p. corp. planning and mktg., 1979—. Mem. Nat. Crushed Stone Assn., Am. Mktg. Assn., Am. Mgmt. Assn., Am. Soc. Agrl. Engrs., Newcomen Soc., Engring. Soc. Detroit. Clubs: Econ. (Detroit); Saginaw; Capital City (Montgomery). Office: 9520 Executive Park Dr Montgomery AL 36111

ROBINSON, PREZELL RUSSELL, coll. pres.; b. Batesburg, S.C., Aug. 25, 1922; s. Clarence and Annie (Folks) R.; A.B. in Sociology, St. Augustine's Coll., 1946; M.A. in Social Sci. and Psychology, Cornell U., 1951, Ed.D. in Sociology-Ednl. Adminstrn., 1956; D.C.L. (hon.), U. South, 1970; L.H.D., Cuttington U. Coll., Monrovia, Liberia; LL.D. (hon.), Bishop Coll.; m. Lulu Harris, Apr. 9, 1950; 1 dau. Tchr. social sci., French, Bettis Jr. Coll., Trenton, S.C., 1946-48; sucessively registrar, tchr., acting prin. high sch., acting dean jr. coll., instr., dir. adult edn. Voorhees Jr. Coll., Denmark, S.C., 1948-56; prof. sociology, dean coll. St. Augustine's Coll., Raleigh, N.C., 1956-64, exec. dean, 1964-66, acting pres., 1966-67, pres., 1967—; pres. United Negro Coll. Fund, Inc.; bd. dirs. Learning Inst. N.C.; scholar-in-residence Nairobi (Kenya) U., 1973; vis. lectr., Dept. State del. to African nations, 1971, 73, 78; Dir. Wachovia Bank & Trust Co. Mem. exec. com. N.C. Edn. Com. on Tchr. Edn.; mem. N.C. Bd. Edn.; chmn. bd. Assn. Episcopal Colls. Mem. Mayor's Community Relations Com.; vice chmn. Wake County div. Occoneechee council Boy Scouts Am., 1959-67, chmn. Wake Occoneechee council, 1963-66, mem. exec. com., 1965—; vice chmn. Wake County chpt. ARC; chmn. edn. div. United Fund of Raleigh, mem. budget com., 1965—; mem. exec. com. Wake County Libraries. Trustee Voorhees Coll. Fulbright fellow to India, summer 1965. Served with AUS, 1942. Recipient Distinguished Alumni award Voorhees Coll., 1967; decorated Star of Africia (Liberia); recipient numerous service awards and citations. Mem. AAAS, Nat. Assn. Collegiate Deans and Registrars, Am. Acad. Polit. and Social Sci., Am., N.C. (exec. com.) sociol. socs., Central Intercollegiate Athletic Assn. (exec. com.), N.C. Assn. Ind. Colls. and Univs. (dir.), Raleigh C. of C., So. Sociol. Assn., Am. Acad. Polit. Sci., Nat. Geog. Soc., N.C. Lit. and Hist. Soc., N.C. Hist. Soc., Phi Delta Kappa, Phi Kappa Phi, Alpha Kappa Mu, Phi Beta Lambda, Delta Mu Delta. Protestant Episcopalian (lay reader). Contbr. articles to profl. publs. Office: St Augustine's Coll Raleigh NC 27611

ROBINSON, RAYMOND HENRY, educator, historian; b. Clearfield, Pa., July 23, 1927; s. Isaac Hartley and Helen (Bailey) R.; B.A., Pa. State U., 1949, M.A., 1950; Ph.D., Harvard, 1958. Instr. history Pottsville Center, Pa. State U., 1950-51; mem. faculty Northeastern U., 1952-57, 61—, prof. history, 1962—, chmn. dept., 1961—; asst. prof. bus. history Northwestern U., 1957-61. Organist St. Andrew's Episcopal Ch., Framingham, Mass., 1961—. Mem. Am. Hist. Assn., Orgn. Am. Historians, Wellesley (bd. dirs.), Clearfield County hist. socs., Bostonian Soc., Am. Guild Organists, Phi Beta Kappa, Phi Kappa Phi, Phi Alpha Theta, Pi Gamma Mu, Phi Mu Alpha, Phi Eta Sigma. Author: The Growing of America, 1789-1848, 1973; (with Donald M. Jacobs) America's Testing Time, 1848-1877, 1973. Contbr. to Ency. Americana, Notable American Women. Home: 61 Sheridan Rd Wellesley MA 02181 Office: Meserve Hall Northeastern Univ Boston MA 02115

ROBINSON, RAYMOND KENNETH, mag. editor; b. N.Y.C., Dec. 4, 1920; s. Louis Harry and Lillian (Hoffman) R.; B.A., Columbia, 1941; postgrad. Columbia Law Sch., 1941-42; m. Phyllis Cumins, Sept. 18, 1949; children—Nancy, Stephen, Tad. Mng. editor Mag. Mgmt., 1950-56; editor Real mag., 1956-57; mng. editor Pageant mag., 1957-59; sr. editor Coronet mag., 1959-61; articles editor Good Housekeeping mag., 1961-69; mng. editor Seventeen mag., 1969-79, exec. editor, 1979—. Served with AUS, 1942-46. Mem. Authors Guild, Soc. Mag. Editors (exec. com.). Author: Mario Lanza Story, 1960; Ted Williams, 1962; Stan Musial: Baseball's Durable Man, 1963; Speed Kings of the Basepaths, 1964; Greatest World Series Thrillers, 1965; Greatest Yankees Of Them All, 1968; Baseball's Most Colorful Managers, 1969; Baseball, paperback series, 1958-75. Home: 530 E 90 St New York NY 10028 Office: 850 3d Ave New York NY 10022

ROBINSON, RICHARD EARL, U.S. dist. judge; b. Omaha, Feb. 3, 1903; s. Richard and Jane (Hanna) R.; LL.B., Creighton U., 1927; m. Florence Rich, May 22, 1929; children—Thomas E., John L. Admitted to Nebr. bar, 1927, practiced in Omaha until 1956; U.S. dist. judge for Dist. Nebr., 1956—, chief judge, 1957-72, now sr. judge. Mem. Omaha Airport Commn., 1950-51; finance commr., Omaha, 1951. Recipient Brandeis award Brandeis U. Club of Omaha, 1957; Alumni Merit award Creighton U., 1967. Home: 6247 Underwood Ave Omaha NE 68132 Office: PO Box 1457 Omaha NE 68101

ROBINSON, RICHARD NORMAN, aircraft co. exec.; b. Estherville, Iowa, Dec. 26, 1922; s. Merle Haynes and Dorothy (Tredway) R.; student Estherville Jr. Coll., 1940-41, Bakersfield Jr. Coll., 1946-48, U. Minn., 1948-50; D.Aero. Sci., Embry-Riddle Aero. U., 1972; m. Hilda Virginia Laney, Feb. 19, 1948; children—Sandra Mae, Norye Layne; m. 2d, Mary Kathryn Lowe, Nov. 24, 1973. Sales mgr. Courtesy Enterprises, 1951-54; field engr. Gardner-Denver, 1954- 57; with Cessna Aircraft Co., Wichita, Kans., 1958-67; domestic sales mgr., 1961-65; gen. sales mgr., 1965-67; v.p. marketing aircraft div. Rockwell-Standard Corp., 1967-68; pres. Aero Comdr. div. N.Am. Rockwell Corp., 1968-69, pres. Gen. Aviation div., Bethany, Okla., 1969-73; group gen. mgr. Fairchild Burns Co. (Fairchild Burns Aero Seat div., Fairchild Indsl. Products div., Fairchild Stratos div.) all divs. Fairchild Industries, Germantown, Md., 1973—; v.p. Swearingen Aviation Corp., San Antonio, 1973-76; Western div. sales mgr. Cessna/Citation, Wichita, 1976—. Served with USAAF, 1942-45, AUS, 1945-46. Mem. Gen. Aviation-Mfrs. Assn., Nat. Aviation Trades Assn., Sales and Mktg. Execs., Aerospace Industry Assn. Home: 501 Circle Lake Dr Wichita KS 67209 Office: Cessna Aircraft Co PO Box 1107 Wichita KS 67201

ROBINSON, ROBERT ALEXANDER, orthopaedic surgeon; b. Rochester, N.Y., Jan. 9 1914; s. Robert Clarence and Anna (Bill) R.; student Harvard U., 1932-35; M.D., Columbia Coll. Physicians and Surgeons, 1939; m. Beatrice Clark, June 21, 1941; children—Ann, Barbara, Robert Alexander, Elizabeth. Rotating intern Bklyn. Hosp., 1939-41, resident gen. surgery, 1941-42; asst. resident orthopaedics Strong Meml. Hosp., Rochester, 1946, resident orthopaedics, 1947-48; resident orthopaedics Rochester Gen. Hosp., 1946-47; house surgeon Robert Jones and Agnes Hunt Orthopaedic Hosp., Oswestry, Eng., 1948-49; instr. orthopaedic surgery Sch. Medicine and Dentistry, U. Rochester, 1949-51, asst. prof., 1951-53; prof. orthopaedic surgery Johns Hopkins U., also orthopaedic surgeon in charge Johns Hopkins Hosp., 1953-79, Disting. Service prof., 1977—; trustee Orthopaedic Research and Edn. Found., 1970-74, pres., 1975-77. Trustee Easter Seal Research Found., 1975-77. Served in M.C., AUS, 1942-46, sta. and field hosps., comdg. officer, chief surgery 90th Field Hosp., Tacloban, Leyte, Philippines, 1946. Diplomate Am. Bd. Orthopaedic Surgery. Fellow Am. Acad. Orthopaedic Surgeons, A.C.S.; mem. Soc. Univ. Surgeons, Am., Brit. (corr.) orthopaedic assns., Am. Surg. Assn., Société Internationale de Chirugie Orthopedique et de Traumatologie. Home: 314 Broxton Rd Baltimore MD 21212 Office: 600 N Wolfe St Baltimore MD 21205

ROBINSON, ROBERT ARMSTRONG, pension fund exec.; b. Waterbury, Conn., Sept. 11, 1925; s. Robert and Ethel (Armstrong) R.; A.B. magna cum laude, Brown U., 1950, M.A., 1952; postgrad. U. Ill., 1954-55; Litt. D., Episcopal Theol. Sem. Ky., 1971; D.C.L., U. South, 1972; m. D. Ann Harding, June 7, 1947; 1 dau., Gayllis Robinson Ward. Instr. English, Brown U., 1950-53; instr. English, asst. prof. rhetoric U. Ill., 1953-56; trust officer Colonial Bank & Trust Co., Waterbury, 1956-63, v.p., trust officer, 1963-65, sr. trust officer, 1965-66; v.p., sec. Ch. Pension Fund and Affiliates, Ch. Life Ins. Corp., Ch. Ins. Co., Ch. Agy. Corp., Ch. Hymnal Corp., 1966-67, exec. v.p., 1967-68, pres., dir., 1968—; dir. Seabury Press, Inc. Trustee, Hillspeak, Eureka Springs, Ark., Episcopal Ch. Bldg. Fund, Washington Nat. Cathedral, Episcopal Theol. Sem., Ky.; mem. exec. com. N.Y. councils Boy Scouts Am., Ch. Pensions Conf.; mem. econ. adv. bd. Columbia U. Grad. Sch. Bus. Adminstrn. Served with inf. AUS, 1943-46. Decorated Purple Heart with oak leaf cluster. Mem. Conn. Bankers Assn. (v.p., head trust div.), Am. Numis. Assn., Newcomen Soc., Phi Beta Kappa. Republican. Episcopalian (vestryman). Clubs: St. Andrew's Soc., Brown, Union League, Church (N.Y.C.); Country of Darien; Athenaeum (London); Pilgrims. Home: 251 Laurel Rd New Canaan CT 06840 Office: 800 2d Ave New York NY 10017

ROBINSON, ROBERT BLACQUE, assn. exec.; b. Long Beach, Calif., Apr. 24, 1927; s. Joseph LeRoi and Frances Hansel R.; student Oreg. State Coll., 1946; B.A., UCLA, 1950; m. Susan Amelia Thomas, Jan. 21, 1960; children—Victoria, Shelly, Blake, Sarah. Partner, Pritchard Assos., Mgmt. Cons., Honolulu, 1957-58; asst. dir. Econ. Planning and Coordination Authority, Hawaii, 1959; dep. dir. Dept. of Econ. Devel., State of Hawaii, 1960-62; with Pacific Concrete and Rock Co., Ltd., Honolulu, 1963-77, exec. v.p., 1966-68, pres., 1968-75, chmn., 1976-77; pres. C. of C. of Hawaii, Honolulu, 1977—; dir. Pacific Concrete and Rock Co., Ltd., 1964-79, Bank of Honolulu, 1973—, Fed. Home Loan Bank of Seattle, 1973-76. Bd. govs. Hawaii Employers Council, 1969-74, mem. exec. com., 1969-74, vice chmn., 1973-74; dir. Aloha United Fund, 1970-76, sec., 1972, v.p., 1973-76; bd. dirs. Oahu Devel. Conf., 1970-75; dir. Jr. Achievement Hawaii, 1967-73, pres., 1969; dir. Hawaii Ednl. Council, 1974-75; mem. Interagency Energy Conservation Council, State of Hawaii, 1978—. Served with USNR, 1945-46; lt. comdr. USNR, ret. Mem. Japan-Am. Conf. of Mayors and C. of C. Pres. (mem. Am. exec. com. 1974—), C. of C. Hawaii (dir. 1972-75, chmn. 1975), Navy League, Engring. Assn. Hawaii, Sigma Chi. Clubs: Pacific, Kaneohe Yacht, Rotary. Home: 1437 Kalaepohaku St Honolulu HI 66816 Office: 735 Bishop St Honolulu HI 96813

ROBINSON, ROSCOE ROSS, physician, educator; b. Oklahoma City, Aug. 21, 1929; s. Roscoe and Tennie (Ross) R.; B.S., Central State U., Edmond, Okla., 1949; M.D., U. Okla., 1954; m. Ann Allen, Aug. 24, 1952; children—Susan, Brooke. Intern in medicine Duke U. Med. Center, Durham, N.C., 1954-55, jr. asst. resident in medicine, 1955-56, chief resident, instr. medicine, 1957-58, asso. in medicine, 1960-62, asst. prof. medicine, dir. div. nephrology, 1962-65, asso. prof. medicine, dir. div. nephrology, 1965-69, prof. medicine, dir. div. nephrology, 1969-78, Florence McAlister prof. medicine, dir. div. nephrology, 1978—, asso. v.p., 1976—; chief exec. officer Duke U. Hosp., 1976—; Am. Heart Assn. research fellow, vis. fellow dept. medicine Columbia-Presbyn. Med. Center, N.Y.C., 1956-57; chief resident, instr. medicine VA Hosp., Durham, 1957-58, clin. investigator, 1960-62, attending physician, 1962—; cons. nephrology VA Hosp., Fayetteville and Asheville, N.C., Research Triangle Inst., Research Triangle Park, N.C., 1964—; nat. cons. to surgeon gen. USAF, 1970—; chmn. N.C. Kidney Council, Region 21, Dept. HEW, 1977—. Served to capt. M.C., USAF, 1958-60. Diplomate Nat. Rd. Med. Examiners, Am. Bd. Internal Medicine (asso. mem. 1975-78, mem. 1979—, chmn. test com. on nephrology 1979—). Fellow A.C.P.; mem. Am. Clin. and Climatol. Assn., Am. Fedn. Clin. Research (councillor So. sect. 1968-71), Assn. Am. Physicians, European Dialysis and Transplant Assn., Am. Heart Assn., N.C. Heart Assn. (sr. investigator 1962-74, exec. com., bd. dirs. 1971-72), Am. Soc. Clin. Investigation, So. Soc. Clin. Investigation (councillor 1977—), Am. Physiol. Soc., Am. Soc. Artificial Internal Organs (councillor 1968-71), Internat. Soc. Nephrology (editor Kidney Internat. jour 1971—, exec. com. 1972-78, council 1978—), Am. Soc. Nephrology (councillor 1977—), Nat. Kidney Found. (mem. sci. adv. bd. 1970-75), Kidney Found. N.C., Soc. Med. Adminstrs., Alpha Omega Alpha. Mem. editorial bd. Archives Internal Medicine, 1970—, Perspectives in Nephrology and Hypertension, 1972—, Mineral and Electrolyte Metabolism, 1977—; mem. editorial com. Fogerty internat. com. Monograph on Prevention of Kidney and Urinary Tract Disease; cons. editor renal diseases Cecil Textbook of Medicine, 15th edit.; contbr. articles to profl. jours. Home: 3929 Nottaway Rd Durham NC 27707 Office: Duke U Med Center Box 3708 Durham NC 27710

ROBINSON, RUTH OLEVIA, lawyer; b. New Orleans, Feb. 22, 1944; d. Julian H. and Melba Evelyn (Brazier) R.; B.A., Albright Coll., 1965; J.D., Vanderbilt U., 1968. Admitted to D.C. bar; exec. dir. Dixwell Legal Rights Assn., New Haven, 1968-72; mem. faculty Sch. of Law Antioch Coll., Washington, 1972-73; asst. counsel House Com. on the Judiciary, Subcom. on Constl. Rights and Civil Rights, Washington, 1973-74; asst. counsel div. legislation and legal counsel Dept. Labor, Washington, 1974-76, counsel for spl. legal services, 1976-77; exec. dir. Occupational Safety and Health Rev. Commn., Washington, 1977-79; chief exec. officer, sec. to council Council of D.C., Washington, 1979—; lectr. George Washington U. Sch. Law, 1976-77. Recipient Harriet Tubman award for community service; Disting. Alumnus award Albright Coll. Mem. Bar of D.C., Washington Women's Network. Methodist. Home: 3100 Connecticut Ave NW Washington DC 20008 Office: District Bldg 14th and E Sts NW Washington DC 20004

ROBINSON, S. BENTON, ins. co. exec.; b. Parsons, Kans., June 5, 1928; s. Arthur Winston and Mary Idella (Butler) R.; B.S. cum laude, W.Va. State Coll., 1950; M.B.A., U. Chgo., 1970; m. Dymple Orita McIntyre, Nov. 23, 1952; children—Benton Lewis, Karen Denise, Arthur Winston. With Supreme Life Ins. Co. Am., Chgo., 1950—, internal auditor, 1955-62, controller, 1962, v.p., controller, 1963-68, 1st v.p., 1968-73, sr. v.p., asso. actuary, 1973—, also dir. Mem. citizens com. U. Ill., 1974—; corp. co-chmn. United Negro Coll. Fund, Chgo., 1970-71; bd. dirs., v.p. United Charities Chgo., 1962—; sec. exec. program U. Chgo., 1974—. Served with USNR, 1946-48. Mem. Alpha Phi Alpha. Home: 1641 E 92d St Chicago IL 60617 Office: 3501 S King Dr Chicago IL 60653

ROBINSON, S. MONTE, corp. exec.; b. Murray, Utah, Aug. 9, 1924; s. William A. and Cora (Mumford) R.; student U. Utah, 1943, U. Calif. at Berkeley, 1943-44; B.S., U. Calif. at Los Angeles, 1948; m. Gertrude Turner, Feb. 1, 1946; children—Christine Ann, Kevin Thomas. Staff accountant Price Waterhouse & Co., Los Angeles, 1948-52; asst. controller Earle M. Jorgensen Co., Los Angeles, 1952-53, controller, 1953-58, treas., controller, 1958-64, v.p., treas., 1964-66, dir., mem. exec. com., 1966—, sr. v.p. finance, 1975—. Served with AUS, 1943-45. Decorated Bronze Star. Mem. Am. Inst. C.P.A.'s, Calif. Soc. C.P.A.'s, Financial Execs. Inst. Home: 9263 Otto St Downey CA 90240

ROBINSON, S. WARNE, variety store exec.; b. Monogahela, Pa., Apr. 2, 1916; s. Samuel B. and Edith (Warne) R.; B.S., Coll. William and Mary, 1937; postgrad. U. Pitts., 1939; m. Mary Helen Stoudt, Feb. 29, 1976. With G.C. Murphy Co., McKeesport Pa., 1937—, mdse. investment controller, 1958-68, treas., mdse. investment controller, 1968, asst. v.p., treas., mdse. investment controller, 1968-70, v.p., 1970-73, dir., 1970—, vice chmn., 1973-74, chmn. bd., 1974—, chief exec. officer, 1975—; dir. McKeesport Nat. Bank. Bd. dirs. Goodwill Industries, Pitts., 1974-77. Served to capt. USAAF, 1942-46. Mem. Pa. C. of C. (dir.), Flat Hat Soc., Theta Delta Chi, Omicron Delta Kappa, Alpha Kappa Psi. Home: 640 Robinwood Dr Pittsburgh PA 15216 Office: 531 5th Ave McKeesport PA 15132

ROBINSON, SMOKEY, singer, composer; b. Detroit, Feb. 19, 1940; m. Claudette Rogers; children—Berry William, Tamla Claudette. Formed group Smokey Robinson and the Miracles; with Miracles, 1957-72; performed Detroit nightclubs; co-founder Tamla record label, 1959; numerous singles and album recs. including Sweet Harmony, 1973, Virgin Man, 1974, Agony and the Ecstasy, 1975, Quiet Storm, 1976, Open, 1976, There will Come a Day (I'm Gonna Happen to You), 1977; appearances at clubs, colls., also network TV shows including Hullabaloo, Ed Sullivan Show, American Bandstand, Shindig; star own TV spl., 1971; solo albums include Smokey, 1973; A Quiet Storm; Smokey's Family Robinson; Deep in My Soul; v.p. Motown Record Corp. Office: care Randy Dunlap 6255 Sunset Blvd Los Angeles CA 90028*

ROBINSON, SPOTTSWOOD WILLIAM, III, judge, lawyer; b. Richmond, Va., July 26, 1916; s. Spottswood William, Jr. and Inez (Clements) R.; student Va. Union U., Richmond, 1932-34, 35-36, LL.D., 1955; LL.B. magna cum laude, Howard U., 1939; m. Marian Bernice Wilkerson, Mar. 5, 1936; children—Spottswood William IV, Nina Cecelia (Mrs. Oswald G. Govan). Admitted to Va. bar, 1943, U.S. Supreme Ct., 1948; faculty Howard U., 1939-48, asso. prof. law, 1945-48, on leave, 1947-48, prof., dean Law Sch., 1960-63; mem. firm Hill & Robinson, Richmond, 1943-44, Hill, Martin & Robinson, 1944-55; sole practitioner, Richmond, 1955-60; legal rep. for Va., NAACP Legal Def. and Ednl. Fund, 1948-50, Southeast regional counsel, 1951-60; judge U.S. Dist. Ct. D.C., 1964-66, U.S. Ct. Appeals D.C., 1966—. Vice pres., gen. counsel Consol. Bank & Trust Co., Richmond, 1963-64. Mem. U.S. Commn. on Civil Rights, 1961-63. Named to Richmond Afro-Am. Honor Roll, 1946; recipient testimonial of merit in jurisprudence Phi Phi chpt. Omega Psi Phi, 1946, annual alumni award (in law), Howard U., 1951, annual non-mem. citizenship award Beta Gamma Lambda chpt. Alpha- Phi Alpha, 1951, social action achievement award Phi Beta Sigma, 1953, citation Beta Theta Sigma chpt. Delta Sigma Theta, 1954, citation Richmond chpt. Frontiers of Am., 1954, award Md. Conf. NAACP, 1959. Mem. Am., Nat. (testimonial of merit 1948), Va., Old Dominion bar assns., Bar Assn. D.C. (hon.), Nat. Lawyers Club (hon.). Episcopalian. Office: US Courthouse 3d and Constitution Ave NW Washington DC 20001*

ROBINSON, SUGAR RAY (WALKER SMITH ROBINSON), profl. fighter; b. Detroit, May 3, 1921; s. Walker and Leila (Hurst) Smith; student Detroit pub. schs.; m. Edna M. Holly, July 3, 1943 (div. 1960); children—Ray II, Ronnie; m. 2d, Millie Wiggins Bruce, May 25, 1965. Welter-weight champion, 1946; middleweight champion, 1951; now entertainer, actor TV commercials. Chmn. bd. dirs. Sugar Ray Robinson's Youth Found., 1969—. Served with AUS, 1952-45. Methodist. Author: Sugar Ray, 1970. Office: care Sugar Ray Robinson Youth Found 1905 10th Ave Los Angeles CA 90018*

ROBINSON, THOMAS BULLENE, civil engr.; b. Kansas City, Mo., Feb. 28, 1917; s. David Beach and Aileen March (Weaver) R.; B.S., Kans. U., 1939; M.S., Columbia, 1940; m. Suzanne Callaway, May 24, 1941; children—Suzanne (Mrs. Robert B. Burdick), Thomas Bullene, Alice (Mrs. Peter A. Levy). Asst. engr. Black & Veatch, cons. engr., Kansas City, 1940-43, prin. asst. engr., prin. engr., 1946-56, partner, 1956-65, asst. mng. partner, 1965-72, mng. partner, 1973—; chmn. bd. Black & Veatch Internat.; dir. Commerce Bank of Kansas City, Bus. Men's Assurance Co. Past pres. Heart of Am. United Campaign; trustee Kansas City U., Midwest Research Inst. Served to lt. Civil Engr. Corps, USNR, 1943-46. Recipient Honor award for distinguished service in engring. U. Mo., 1971; Distinguished Service citation U. Kans., 1975. Diplomate Am. Acad. Environ. Engrs. Fellow ASCE, Am. Cons. Engrs. Council (pres. 1970-71); mem. Nat. Acad. Engring., Kansas City C. of C. (dir. 1968-71), ASME, Nat. Soc. Profl. Engrs., Am. Water Works Assn. (hon.), Am. Pub. Works Assn., Am. Pub. Health Assn., Water Pollution Control Fedn., Sigma Xi, Tau Beta Pi, Sigma Tau, Beta Theta Pi. Clubs: Kansas City, University, Mission Hills Country (Kansas City). Home: 6401 Norwood Rd Shawnee Mission KS 66208 Office PO Box 8405 1500 Meadow Lake Pkwy Kansas City MO 64114

ROBINSON, WALTER GEORGE, mus. exec.; b. London, June 18, 1911 (derivative citizen); s. Walter and Annie (Ledger) R.; student N.Y. U., 1943; D.F.A. (hon.), Mpls. Coll. Art and Design; m. Ruth V. Holden, Sept. 14, 1941. Engaged in investment bus., N.Y.C., 1928-33; with Bass River Savs. Bank, South Yarmouth, Mass., 1934-60, pres., 1952-60; dir. Cape & Vineyard Electric Co., 1958-60, Hyannis Trust Co., until 1960; pres. Mpls. Soc. Fine Arts, governing and supporting orgn. for Mpls. Inst. Arts, Mpls. Coll. Art and Design, Children's Theatre Co., 1960-72, vice chmn., treas., sec., 1972-75; acting pres. Mpls. Coll. Art and Design, 1974-75; dir. resource devel. Mus. Fine Arts, Boston, 1975-77; arts mgmt. and funding cons., 1977—; trustee Farmers & Mechanics Savs. Bank. Vice pres. Cape Cod Hosp., 1955-60; chmn. Mpls. Com. for Urban Environment, 1968-70, 72—; mem. Minn. State Arts Council, 1967-73, Minn. Heritage Preservation Commn., 1972-75; chmn. Mpls. Bicentennial Commn., 1974-75; mem. Minn. Com. on Esthetic Environment, 1973-75. Founding dir. E.B. Kelley Found., Pocasset, Mass., 1954—; bd. dirs. Mpls. Sch. Art, 1962-63, Tyrone Guthrie Theatre Found., Mpls., 1960-70; trustee Northwestern Hosp., Mpls., 1967-74, Am. Assn. Museums, 1973-75. Clubs: Skylight, Mpls., Minn. (Mpls.); St. Botolph (Boston). Home and Office: 10 Wampatuck Rd Dedham MA 02026

ROBINSON, WALTER MCLAREN, JR., lawyer, ins. co. exec.; b. Louisville, Mar. 13, 1923; s. Walter McLaren and Emma (Hagerty) R.; B.A., Vanderbilt U., 1942; LL.B., Harvard, 1948; m. Margaret Ann Craig, Oct. 4, 1949; children—Ann Craig, Emmie Bridges, Elizabeth Wade, Walter McLaren III. Admitted to N.Y. State bar, 1948, Tenn. bar, 1950; asso. firm Cravath, Swaine & Moore, N.Y.C., 1948-50; with Nat. Life & Accident Ins. Co., Nashville, 1950—, asst. gen. counsel, 1953-61, asso. gen. counsel, 1961-65, v.p., gen. counsel, 1965-71, sr. v.p., gen. counsel, 1971-74, exec. v.p., 1974-77, also dir.; sec.-treas. NLT Corp., Nashville, 1968-74, v.p., gen. counsel, 1974-77, pres., 1977—, also dir.; dir. WSM, Inc., Nashville, Great So. Life Ins. Co., Houston, Guardsman Life Ins. Co., Des Moines. Mem. exec. com. Mid Cumberland Comprehensive Health Planning Council, 1968-74. Bd. dirs. Nashville Council Community Services, 1965-68, Vanderbilt U. Med. Center, 1970—; mem. exec. com. Middle Tenn. council Boy Scouts Am., 1972—; chmn. health and ednl. facilities bd. Met. Govt. of Nashville and Davidson County, 1974—; trustee Watkins Inst., 1974—. Served from pvt. 1st lt. F.A., AUS, 1942-46; ETO. Mem. Assn. Life Ins. Counsel, Nashville Area C. of C. (bd. govs. 1967-69, 79—), Phi Beta Kappa, Omicron Delta Kappa, Episcopalian. Clubs: Belle Meade Country, Cumberland, Coffee House, Round Table, Exchange (pres. 1964-65) (Nashville). Home: 15 White Bridge Rd Nashville TN 37205 Office: National Life Center Nashville TN 37250

ROBINSON, WAYNE, editor, author; b. Syracuse, N.Y., Sept. 19, 1916. Reporter, feature writer Phila. Bull., 1936-70, editor and writer, 1961—. Author: Barbara, A Story of an American Tank Through World War II in Europe, 1962 (translated and pub. in France, Holland, Italy and Portugal). Home: Narberth PA 19072 Office: The Bulletin 30th and Market Sts Philadelphia PA 19101

ROBINSON, WILKES COLEMAN, found. ofcl., lawyer; b. Anniston, Ala., Sept. 30, 1925; s. Walter Wade and Catherine Elizabeth (Coleman) R.; A.B., U. Ala., 1948; LL.B., U. Va., 1951, J.D., 1970; m. Julia Von Poelnitz Rowan, June 17, 1956; children—Randolph C., Peyton H., Wilkes Coleman. Admitted to Ala. bar, 1950, Va. bar, 1962, Mo. bar, 1966; asso. firm Bibb & Hemphill, Anniston, Ala., 1951-53; city recorder City of Anniston, 1953-55; judge Juvenile and Domestic Relations Ct. of Calhoun County (Ala.), 1954-56; atty. legal dept. GM&O R.R., Mobile, Ala., 1956-58; commerce counsel, asst. gen. atty. Seaboard Air Line R.R., Richmond, Va., 1958-66; commerce counsel Monsanto Co., St. Louis, 1966-70; gen. counsel, v.p. Marion Labs., Inc., Kansas City, Mo., 1970-79; pres. Gt. Plains Legal Found., Kansas City, Mo., 1980—. U.S. appeal agt. Draft Bd.; bd. govs. Kansas City Philharmonic Orch., 1975-77. Served with USNR, 1943-44. Mem. Am. Bar Assn., Ala. Bar Assn. Va. Bar Assn., Mo. Bar Assn., Lawyers Assn. Kansas City, Variety Club Internat. of Kansas City, Phi Beta Kappa (treas. Kansas City, Mo.). Episcopalian. Clubs: Stadium (Kansas City, Mo.); Masons; Brookridge Country (Overland Park, Kans.). Home: 10139 Craig Dr Overland Park KS 66212 Office: Suite 1022 127 W 10th St Kansas City MO 64105

ROBINSON, WILLIAM DODD, physician, educator; b. Hoosac, N.Y., Aug. 8, 1911; s. William Goodwin and Catherine Bradford (Dodd) R.; A.B., Albion Coll., 1931; M.D., U. Mich., 1934, research fellow internal medicine, 1938-40; m. Anna Louise Ebert, Sept. 8, 1932; children—William Harvey, David Wells, Peter Dodd. Intern, resident, instr. dept. internal medicine U. Mich., 1934-38, asst. prof. internal medicine, in charge Rackham Arthritis Research unit, 1944-53, asso. prof. medicine, 1946-52, prof. internal medicine, 1952-79, prof. emeritus, 1979—, chmn. dept. internal medicine, 1958-75; mem. sci. adv. com. Nat. Vitamin Found., 1957-60; cons. Surg. Gen., USPHS, 1954-61; field studies internat. health div. Rockefeller Found., Tenn., Spain, Mexico, 1940-43; instr. medicine Vanderbilt U., 1943-44. Bd. dirs. Mich. chpt. Arthritis and Rheumatism Found. Cons. to surgeon gen. U.S. Army, 1945-46; nat. adv. arthritis and metabolic diseases council USPHS, 1963-67. Diplomate Am. Bd. Internal Medicine (mem. bd. 1961-66). Master A.C.P.; mem. AMA (mem. council food and nutrition 1966-67), Am. Rheumatism Assn., Assn. Am. Physicians, Central Soc. Clin. Research, Am. Fedn. Clin. Research, Mich. Rheumatism Soc., Phi Beta Kappa, Sigma Xi, Sigma Chi, Phi Rho Sigma, Alpha Omega Alpha, Phi Kappa Phi. Editor U. Mich. Med. Bull. 1950-54, Rheumatism Reviews, 1952-56, Jour. Lab. and Clin. Medicine, 1955-60. Home: 2735 Overridge Dr Ann Arbor MI 48104 Office: 1405 Ann St Ann Arbor MI 48109

ROBINSON, WILLIAM EDWARD, JR., baseball club exec.; b. Paris, Tex., Dec. 15, 1925; s. William Edward and Hazel Robinson; ed. pub. schs.; m. Bette Jane Farlow, Oct. 6, 1955; children—William Edward III, Marc F., Paul R., John Andrew. Profl. baseball player Am. League, 1947-57; field dir. Balt. Orioles, 1957-61; farm dir., asst. gen. mgr. Houston Astros, 1961-65; dir. player devel. Kansas City Athletics, 1966-67; dir. player devel. Atlanta Braves, 1967-72, gen. mgr., exec. v.p., 1972-76; exec. v.p. Tex. Rangers, Arlington, 1976—; dir. Tex. Mgmt., Inc. Served with USN, 1943-46. Clubs: Masons, Shriners. Office: PO Box 1111 Arlington TX 76010

ROBINSON, WILLIAM FRANKLIN, fin. co. exec.; b. Hammond, Ind., Feb. 10, 1916; s. William P. and Pauline M. (Hopkins) R.; B.A. with high honors, Ind. U., 1942, J.D., 1944; m. Betty Jo Powell, Sept. 15, 1946; children—William Franklin, Stephen Powell, Michael Paul. Admitted to Ind. bar, 1944, Mich. bar, 1946, Calif. bar, 1957; spl. atty. Office Chief Counsel, IRS, Washington and Detroit, 1944-46; pvt. practice, Detroit, 1946-51; asst. gen. counsel, asst. sec. Montgomery Ward & Co., Inc., Chgo., 1951-56; v.p., gen. counsel, sec. Transam. Fin. Corp., Los Angeles, 1956—, also dir.; spl. instr. Wayne State U. Law Sch., also U. Detroit, 1947-51. Mem. sch. bd. Calumet City, Ill., 1954-55. Mem. Calif. Loan and Fin. Assn. (chmn. laws and regulations com.), Nat. Consumer Fin. Assn., Conf. Personal Fin. Law, Am., Los Angeles County bar assns., State Bar Calif., Acacia, Phi Beta Kappa, Phi Delta Phi. Club: Friendly Hills Country (Whittier). Contbr. articles to profl. jours., chpts. to textbooks. Home: 8217 Lindante Dr Whittier CA 90603 Office: 1150 S Olive St Suite 2033 Los Angeles CA 90015

ROBINSON, WILLIAM INGRAHAM, lawyer; b. Kansas City, Mo., Sept. 2O, 1909; s. Ernest Franklin and Mary (Kip) R.; A.B., U. Mo., 1931; J.D., U. Mich., 1934; m. Virginia Burch, Sept. 5, 1942; children—Mary Kip (Mrs. Forney Fleming), William Ingraham. Admitted to Calif. bar, 1935, Okla. bar, 1940, Kans. bar, 1946; gen. practice, San Francisco, 1935-40; asst. gen. counsel Ind. Oil Co., Tulsa, 1940-41; partner firm Adams, Jones, Robinson & Malone, Wichita, 1946—; dir. 1st Nat. Bank in Wichita. Democratic candidate 4th Congl. Dist. Kans., 1960; chmn. Sedgwick County (Kans.) Dem. Com., 1962-66; Dem. candidate for U.S. Senator, 1968. Trustee

Wichita State U., 1967-76, chmn., 1970—; trustee Wichita Art Mus., 1966-70; trustee Wichita Art Assn., 1960—, pres., 1978-79. Served with Armed Forces, 1941-45. Mem. Am., Wichita (past bd. dirs., v.p.) Kans., Okla., Calif. bar assns., Am. Judicature Soc., Soc. Internat. Law, Phi Delta Phi. Home: 3343 Country Club Pl Wichita KS 67208 Office: PO Box 1034 Wichita KS 67201

ROBINSON, WILLIAM PETERS, polit. scientist, educator, state legislator; b. Norfolk, Va., Mar. 15, 1911; s. William Carl and Avis (Peters) R.; A.B., Howard U., 1932, M.A., 1935; Ph.D., N.Y. U., 1950; 1 son, William Peters. Instr. dept. polit. sci. Howard U., Washington, 1935-39; analyst program surveys div. Dept. Agr., Washington, 1939-44; prof. dept. social scis. So. U., Baton Rouge, 1944-46; dir. Sch. Arts and Scis., dir. vets. affairs Alcorn (Miss.) Coll., 1946-48; asst. to pres., prof. polit. sci. Morris Brown Coll., Atlanta, 1948-50; chmn. dept. polit. sci. Central State Coll., Wilberforce, Ohio, 1950-58, editor Research Bull., 1954-58; chmn. dept. polit. sci. Tex. So. U., Houston, 1958-62; prof. polit. sci., head dept. Norfolk (Va.) State Coll., 1962—, chmn. div. social scis., 1965—, pres. faculty senate, 1970-71; mem. Va. Ho. of Dels., 1970—. Cons. Washington Office, OEO for Va., 1963—; cons. Desegregation Inst., Elizabeth City State U., 1972—; lectr. U. N.H., 1972. Mem. Overall Adv. Council on Needs Handicapped Children and Adults; chmn. steering com. Concerned Citizens of Norfolk; mem. Va. Adv. Legis. Council Study Commn. on Pub. Welfare; mem. exec. com. Advance Norfolk; co-chmn. Com. of 60 for Better Norfolk; mem. exec. council Tidewater council Boy Scouts Am. Coordinator, Voter Registration Project, Norfolk; chmn., dir. Conf. Newly Elected Black Local Ofcls. of Va. Bd. dirs. Med. Center Hosps. Recipient Brookings Instn. Center for Advanced Study award, 1966, award YMCA, Norfolk, 1969, Phi Delta Kappa, 1970, Lamplighter award Ednl. Assn. Norfolk, 1972, Outstanding Contbn. to Humanity award Delver Women's Club, Richmond, Va., 1972, award for distinguished achievement Howard U. Alumni Assn., 1970, certificate of appreciation Norfolk Jaycees, 1974, certificate of merit Va. State Coll., 1974, also others. Mem. Am. (exec. council), So., Southwestern polit. sci. assns., Am. Acad. Polit. Sci., Am. Acad. Polit. and Social Scis., Assn. for Study Afro-Am. Life and History (exec. council, program dir.), Am. Sociol. Assn., Assn. Social and Behavioral Scientists (Presdl. Service award 1974), Assn. Social Sci. Tchrs. (pres. 1954-55), Nat. Conf. Black Polit. Scientists (past pres.), Norfolk Mission Coll. Alumni Assn. (pres.), Nat. Municipal League (governing council), Pi Alpha Theta, Phi Sigma Alpha. Co-editor: Negro History Bull. Contbr. articles to profl. jours. Home: 958 Anna St Norfolk VA 23502

ROBINSON, WILLIAM WHEELER, editor; b. Elizabeth, N.J., Oct. 4, 1918; s. Henry Pearson and Clare Stearns (Wheeler) R.; B.A., Princeton, 1939; m. Jane Dimock, Feb. 27, 1942; children—William Wheeler, Martha (Mrs. Henry R. Hinckley III), Alice. Traffic rep., traffic dept. Eastern Airlines, N.Y.C., 1939-41; mgr. pub. relations Elco Yacht Div., Bayonne, N.J., 1945-47; sportswriter Newark Evening News, 1947-55; sportswriter, syndicated columnist Newark Star-Ledger, 1955-57; asso. editor Yachting Mag., N.Y.C., 1957-67, editor, exec. v.p., 1967-78, editor-at-large, 1979—; mem. exec. bd. Sea Ventures, Ft. Hancock, N.J., 1974-77; writer radio, TV shows on boating; freelance writer. Vice pres. Rumson (N.J.) Community Appeal, 1952; mem. Rumson-Fair Haven (N.J.) Regional Bd. Edn., 1955-60; mem. Rumson Environ. Commn., 1973-77. Served with USNR, 1941-45. Decorated Bronze Star with gold star. Mem. Met. Squash Racquets Assn. (v.p. 1973-75), Cruising Club Am. (historian 1972-77), Corinthians (master afterguard 1951-52). Clubs: Princeton of N.Y. (v.p., gov.), N.Y. Yacht, Century Assn., Royal Bermuda Yacht, Rumson Country, Seabright Beach. Author: The Science of Sailing, 1960; New Boat, 1961; A Berth to Bermuda, 1961; Where the Trade Winds Blow, 1963; Expert Sailing, 1965; Over the Horizon, 1966; The World of Yachting, 1966; Better Sailing for Boys and Girls, 1968; (with H.L. Stone) The America's Cup Races, 1970; Legendary Yachts, 1971, rev., 1978; The Sailing Life, 1974, Right Boat for You, 1974; Great American Yacht Designers, 1974; America's Sailing Book, 1976; A Sailor's Tales, 1978. Contbr. numerous articles to profl. jours. Home: 14 Oyster Bay Dr Rumson NJ 07760 Office: care Yachting 1 Park Ave New York NY 10016

ROBISON, ANDREW CLIFFE, JR., museum curator; b. Memphis, May 23, 1940; s. Andrew Cliffe and Elfrieda (Barnes) R.; A.B., Princeton U., 1962, Ph.D., 1974; B.A. (Marshall Scholar), Oxford U., 1965, M.A., 1968; m. Lynn Louise Pedigo, June 8, 1974. Instr. philosophy U. Ill., 1970-73, asst. prof. philosophy, 1973-75; curator, head dept. prints and drawing Nat. Gallery Art, Washington, 1974—; Fulbright research scholar, India, 1965-66. Danforth fellow, 1966-70. Mem. Print Council Am. (pres. 1975—), Coll. Art Assn., Am. Philos. Assn., Phi Beta Kappa. Club: Grolier. Author: Giovanni Battista Piranesi: Prolegomena to the Princeton Collections, 1970; Paper in Prints, 1977; Master Drawings, 1978; Giovanni Battista Piranesi: The Early Architectural Fantasies, 1978. Contbr. articles and revs. to Nouvelles dl'estampe, The Print Collectors Newsletter, The Art Bull., Master Drawings, others. Office: Nat Gallery of Art Washington DC 20565

ROBISON, G(EORGE) ALAN, pharmacologist, educator; b. Lethbridge, Alta., Can., Nov. 4, 1934; came to U.S., 1957, naturalized, 1971; s. Douglas Charles and Margaret Elizabeth (Barr) R.; B.Sc., U. Alta., 1957: M.S., Tulane U., 1960, Ph.D., 1962; postgrad. Western Res. U., 1962-63; m. Jill Jeanine Seaman, Mar. 12, 1956; children—James Darcy, Amelia N'Orlean. Research asso. Vanderbilt U., Nashville, 1963-64, instr., 1964-66, asst. prof., 1966-69, asso. prof., 1969-72; prof. pharmacology U. Tex. Med. Sch., Houston, 1972—, chmn. dept. pharmacology, 1972—; Pfizer fellow Clin. Research Inst., Montreal, Que., Can., 1970; investigator Howard Hughes Med. Inst., 1970-72; mem. bd. sci. advs. Nelson Research & Devel. Co., Irvine, Calif., 1972—; mem. pharmacology study sect. NIH, 1973-77; prin. organizer, 1st Gordon Research Conf. on Cyclic AMP, Phymouth, N.H., 1970; sci. sec. 1st Internat. Conf. on Cyclic AMP, Milan, Italy, 1971, 4th Internat. Conf., Brussels, Belgium, 1980. Recipient E.L. Woods Meml. prize Can. Found. for Advancement Pharmacy, 1957: Disting. Alumnus award Tulane U., 1977; J. Murray Luck award Nat. Acad. Sci., 1979. Mem. Am. Humanist Assn., Am. Chem. Soc., Am. Soc. for Pharmacology and Exptl. Therapeutics, Endocrine Soc., N.Y. Acad. Scis., Sigma Xi. Author: (with R.W. Butcher, E.W. Sutherland) Cyclic AMP, 1971; editor: (with P. Greengard) Advances in Cyclic Nucleotide Research, 1972—; mem. editorial bd. Archives of Biochemistry and Biophysics, 1972-78, Biochem. Pharmacology, 1973—, Jour. Cyclic Nucleotide Research, 1975—, Current Contents, 1977—, Jour. Pharmacol. Exptl. Therapeutics, 1978—, Jour. Cardiovascular Pharmacology, 1978—. Home: 250 Stoney Creek Dr Houston TX 77024

ROBISON, JAMES EVERETT, bus. cons.; b. Aldred, N.D., Nov. 22, 1915; s. John J. and Myrtle (Klundt) R.; A.B., U. Minn., 1938; M.B.A. Harvard U., 1940; Sc. D. (hon.), Suffolk U., 1968; m. Jeanette Hoffman, June 6, 1942; 1 dau., Martha Ann Davies. Sales dept. Nashua Mfg. Co., N.Y.C., 1940-46, Textron, Inc., N.Y.C., 1947-53; chief textile br. OPS, Washington, 1951; pres., dir. Indian Head, Inc., N.Y.C., 1953-67, chmn. bd., chief exec. officer, 1967-72, chmn. fin. com., 1971-76; pres. Lonsdale Enterprises, Inc., 1976—; dir. Continental Oil Co., Thyssen-Bornemisza N.V., Dominion Bridge, Ltd., Houbigant, Inc., Narragansett Capital Corp. Mem. com. univ. resources Harvard U., 1966-69, vis. com. Grad. Sch. Bus. Adminstrn., 1966-72, 73—, chmn. bd. Assos. Harvard Bus. Sch., 1968-70; trustee Air Force Aid Soc., 1968—, fin. com., 1969—; bd. dirs. Bus. Com. for Arts, 1973—; trustee Com. Econ. Devel., 1965-74, Calif. Inst. Tech., 1970—. Served to maj. USAAF, 1942-46. Decorated D.F.C., Air Medal with three oak leaf clusters; recipient Distinguished Service award Harvard Bus. Sch. Assn., 1969; Outstanding Alumni award U. Minn., 1974. Mem. Conf. Bd., Harvard Bus. Sch. Assn. (exec. council 1968-71), Am. Textile Mfrs. Inst. (dir. 1961-64), Soaring Soc. Am., U.S. C.of C., Air Force Res. Assn., Phi Delta Theta. Clubs: Harvard, Racquet and Tennis, Economic, Harvard Bus. Sch. Greater N.Y. (past dir., pres. 1967-68) (N.Y.C.); Stanwich (Greenwich, Conn.); Stowe (Vt.) Country; Bedford (N.Y.) Golf and Tennis: Lyford Cay (Bahamas). Home: Windmill Farm 12 Spruce Hill Rd Armonk NY 10504 Office: 20 Haarlem Ave White Plains NY 10603

ROBISON, OLIN CLYDE, coll. pres.; b. Anacoco, La., May 12, 1936; s. Audrey Clyde and Ruby (Cantrell) R.; B.A., Baylor U., 1958, LL.D., 1979; D.Phil., Oxford (Eng.) U., 1963; m. Sylvia Margaret Potter, Apr. 10, 1959; children—Gordon Reece, Blake Elliott, Mark Edward. Dean students San Marcos (Tex.) Acad., 1963-64; regional officer Peace Corps, Washington, 1964-65, dir. univ. affairs, Washington, 1965-66; spl. asst. dep. under-sec. for polit. affairs Dept. State, Washington, 1966-68; asso. provost for social scis. Wesleyan U., Middletown, Conn., 1968-70; provost, dean faculty, sr. lectr. govt. and legal studies Bowdoin Coll., Brunswick, Maine, 1970-75; pres., prof. polit. sci. Middlebury (Vt.) Coll., 1975—; cons. State Dept., 1968-72, 77—; adv. bd. Investment Co. Am.; cons. Am. Council Life Ins., Washington Forum, Met. Life Ins. Co. Bd. dirs. Atlantic Info. Center for Tchrs., London, 1970-77; exec. com. New Eng. Colls. Fund; mem. Am. Com. on East-West Accord, Washington; chmn. Vt. com. Rhodes Scholarship Trust, 1976-77; bd. dirs. Am. Council Young Polit. Leaders, 1968-78, Atlantic Council U.S., 1973-78; chmn. U.S. Adv. Commn. on Public Diplomacy, 1978—; adviser U.S. del. Conf. on Security and Coop. in Europe, Belgrade, 1977-78. Named Ehrenburger, Johannes Gutenberg Universität, Mainz, Germany, 1977. Rockefeller Found./Aspen Inst. fellow, 1978-79; Presdl. fellow Aspen Inst. Humanistic Studies, 1979-80. Mem. Internat. Inst. Strategic Studies (London), Soc. Values in Higher Edn., Council Fgn. Relations, Royal Inst. Internat. Affairs London (fgn. asso.), UN Assn. U.S. (panel on approaches to collective security), Atlantic Treaty Assn. (Atlantic edn. com. 1972—). Baptist. Clubs: Federal City (Washington); Univ. (N.Y.C.); St. Botolph (Boston). Home: 3 South St Middlebury VT 05753 Office: Middlebury Coll Middlebury VT 05753

ROBISON, PAUL FREDERICK, lawyer; b. Miltonvale, Kans., June 28, 1919; s. Rheuben G. and Hazel I. (Austin) R.; student Kans. State U., 1937-38, Miltonvale Wesleyan U., 1938-39; B.A., Washburn U., Topeka, 1946, LL.B., 1947; postgrad. George Washington U. Sch. Law, 1954-55; m. Roberta L. Shannon, Dec. 24, 1941; children—Pamela Ann (Mrs. John Vantress), Paula Lee (Mrs. Larry Honchen). Admitted to Kans. bar, 1947, Alaska bar, 1948, also U.S. Supreme Ct.; practice Anchorage, 1948—; sr. atty. Robison, McCaskey & Frankel, 1955—; city atty., 1950-51; mem. Alaska senate, 1953-54, exec. asst. to Gov. Frank B. Heintzelman, 1955-56. Mem. Nat. Commn. Uniform Laws. Pres. Alaska Real Estate Investment Corp.; sec., dir. Alaska Gas & Service Corp., Alaska Pipeline Co. Pres., Alaska council Boy Scouts Am., 1955, mem. exec. com. Western Region, 1956—, mem. nat. exec. com., 1956, nat. bd., 1956—; author bill for Alaska Legislative Council, 1st chmn., 1953-55; del. Rep. Nat. Conv., 1956; author Statehood Plank Alaska resulting in statehood, 1958. Served to lt. col. AUS, 1941-45. Decorated Legion of Merit. Mem. Anchorage C. of C. (past v.p., dir.), Alaska State Chamber, Alaska Press Club, Cook Inlet Hist. Soc. Office: 921 W 6th St Anchorage AK 99501

ROBISON, PAULA JUDITH, flutist; b. Nashville, June 8, 1941; d. David Victor and Naomi Florence R.; student U. So. Calif., 1958-60; B.S., Juilliard Sch. Music, 1963: m. Scott Nickrenz, Dec. 29, 1971; 1 dau., Elizabeth Hadley Nickrenz. Soloist with various maj. orchs., including N.Y. Philharmonic; mem. Orpheus Trio, 1970—; prin. ann. recital series: Paula and..., 1976—; co-dir. chamber music Spoleto Festivals, Charleston, S.C. and Spoleto, Italy; mem. faculty Juilliard Sch. Music. Recipient First prize Geneva Internat. Competition, 1966; named Musician of Month, Musical Am., 1979; Martha Baird Rockefeller grantee, 1966. Mem. Cousteau Soc., Chamber Music Soc. Lincoln Center (founding). . *I believe that artists must be warriors for beauty - pure and simple - and I hope I'll always be able to devote my life to this noble cause.*

ROBITSCHER, JONAS, psychiatrist, educator; b. N.Y.C., Oct. 28, 1920; s. Jonas and Elsa (Eisinger) R.; A.B., Brown U., 1942; J.D., George Washington U., 1948, M.D., 1955; m. Jean Begeman, June 1, 1950; children—Jan, Christine, John. Intern, George Washington U., 1955-56; psychiat. resident Inst. Pa. Hosp., Phila., 1956-59; psychoanalytic tng. Inst. Phila. Assn. Psychoanalysis, 1970; practice medicine, specializing in psychiatry, psychoanalysis and forensic psychiatry, Phila., 1959-63, Bryn Mawr, Pa., 1963-72; lectr. law and psychiatry Villanova U. Law Sch., 1965-72; asst. prof. clin. psychiatry U. Pa. Sch. Medicine, 1968-72; Henry Luce prof. law and behavioral scis. Emory U., Atlanta, 1972—. Program dir. social-legal uses of forensic psychiatry NIMH, 1970-72, prin. investigator dangerousness in psychiat. commitment study, 1974—. Fellow Am. Coll. Legal Medicine, Inst. Soc., Ethics and Life Scis., Am. Psychiat. Assn. (commn. on jud. action 1974—, Isaac Ray award); mem. Am. Bar Assn. (commn. on mentally disabled 1973—), Am. Acad. Psychiatry and the Law (councillor), Phi Beta Kappa, Alpha Omega Alpha. Author: Pursuit of Agreement: Psychiatry and the Law, 1966. Editor: Eugenic Sterlization, 1973. Home: 779 Clifton Rd NE Atlanta GA 30307 Office: Law Sch Emory U Atlanta GA 30322

ROBLIN, DANIEL ARTHUR, JR., corp. exec.; b. Buffalo, Oct. 3, 1918; s. Daniel Arthur and Emma (Goldstein) R.; B.S. in Metallurgy, Lehigh U., 1939; m. Gloria Landsman, May 22, 1949; children—Diane Seigler, Daniel Arthur III. With Am. Smelting & Refining Co., 1939-41; v.p. Buffalo Housewrecking Co., also chmn. Seaway Steel Corp., 1946-57; pres. Roblin Inc., 1957-61; pres., chmn. Roblin Industries Inc., 1961—; dir. Niagara Frontier Transit Co., Marine Midland Trust Co., Western N.Y., Bisonite Corp., Rand Capitol Corp.; trustee Erie County Savs. Bank. Pres. Erie County chpt. Nat. Found. Infantile Paralysis, 1953-55; mem.-at-large Boy Scouts Am., 1954—, v.p. Erie County council, 1954-57; chmn. Buffalo and Erie County Econ. Devel. Corp., 1962-69; exec. com., bd. dirs. Greater Buffalo Devel. Found., 1964—; treas., mem. exec. com. Erie County Republican Com., 1951-66. Trustee Edward J. Meyer Meml. Hosp., 1956-64, Buffalo Gen. Hosp., 1966—; mem. exec. com., bd. dirs. Buffalo Philharmonic Orch., 1965-68; exec. com., trustee State U. N.Y. at Buffalo Found., 1966—, chmn., 1973—; co-chmn. Buffalo and Erie County Labor/Mgmt. Council; bd. advisers Villa Maria Coll., 1967-72; mem. adminstrn. bd. advisers Canisius Coll. Sch. Bus., Buffalo, 1969; chmn. exec. com. Erie County Indsl. Devel. Agy. Served with USNR, 1941-46. Mem. Am. Iron and Steel Inst., Greater Buffalo Area (dir. 1967-69, v.p. 1968-69), Empire State chambers commerce, NAM (dir. 1977—). Clubs: Buffalo, Westwood Country (Buffalo); Marco Polo, Harmonie, Metropolitan (N.Y.C.); Capitol Hill (Washington). Home: 50 Danbern Ln Williamsville NY 14221 Office: 241 Main St Buffalo NY 14203

ROBLIN, GLORIA LANDSMAN (MRS. DANIEL A. ROBLIN, JR.), psychologist, educator; b. N.Y.C., Apr. 29, 1925; d. Benjamin F. Landsman and Helen (Siegler) Lehman; B.A., Barnard Coll., 1945; M.A., Columbia U., 1947; Ph.D., SUNY, Buffalo, 1963; m. Daniel A. Roblin, Jr., May 22, 1949; children—Diane Roblin Finlayson, Daniel Arthur III. Instr. psychology dept. U. Richmond (Va.), 1946-48, Columbia U., N.Y.C., 1948-49, Med. Coll. SUNY, Buffalo, 1963-65; research psychologist Research Found., SUNY, Buffalo, 1973—, professorial lectr. Coll. Arts and Scis., 1965—, clin. asso. prof. psychiatry Med. Coll., 1972, clin. prof., 1975—, coordinator, instr. programs on human sexuality, clin. hypnosis and psychopathology. Bd. dirs. Psychiat. Clinic, Buffalo, 1956-62, pres., 1961-63, spl. cons., 1962—; bd. dirs. Nat. Council Jewish Women, 1954-60, chmn. social legislation, v.p., 1956-57; mem. speakers bur. Erie County Republican Com., 1950—; bd. dirs. United Way, 1972—, Mental Hygiene Community Services of Erie County, 1979—; mem. council Religious Studies Center of Canisius Coll., 1970—. Fellow Soc. for Sci. Study of sex (dir.); mem. Am. Psychol. Assn., N.Y. State Psychol. Assn., AAUP, Psychol. Assn. Western N.Y., Am. Soc. Clin. Hypnosis, Soc. Clin. and Exptl. Hypnosis, Am. Assn. Sex Educators, Counselors and Therapists, Sex Info. and Ednl. Council U.S., Sigma Xi. Clubs: Buffalo, Westwood Country (Buffalo); Barnard of Western N.Y. (past pres.); Met., Harmonie (N.Y.C.). Home: 50 Danbern Ln Williamsville NY 14221 Office: Dept Psychiatry Med Coll State U NY Buffalo NY 14214

ROBOCK, STEFAN HYMAN, economist; b. Redgranite, Wis., July 31, 1915; s. Samuel and Elizabeth (Kushner) R.; B.A., U. Wis., 1938; M.A., Harvard U., 1941, Ph.D. (Adminstrn. fellow), 1948; Prof. Honoris Causa, U. Recife, Brazil, 1956; M. Honoris Causa, E.S.T.E., San Sebastian, Spain, 1974; m. Shirley Bernstein, June 17, 1946; children—Alan David, Jerry, Lisa. Economist, Nat. Resources Planning Bd., Washington, 1940-41, antitrust div. U.S. Dept. Justice, Washington, 1941-42, Boston, 1948-49; chief economist TVA, Knoxville, 1949-54; devel. adviser UN, Brazil, 1954-56; prof. bus. Ind. U., Bloomington, 1960-67; R.D. Calkins prof. internat. bus. Columbia U., N.Y.C., 1967—; internat. economist Dept. Commerce, 1975-76; dir. Serial Fed. Savs. and Loan Assn.; cons. fgn. countries, 1959—. Adv. bd. World Trade Inst., 1979—. Served with USNR, 1942-46. Mem. bd. sci. and tech. Nat. Acad. Sci., 1969-72. Mem. Soc. Internat. Devel. (mem. council 1966-69), Am. Econ. Assn., Acad. Internat. Bus., Latin Am. Studies Assn., Phi Kappa Phi, Beta Gamma Sigma, Phi Eta Sigma. Club: Columbia Tennis. Author: Brazil's Developing Northeast, 1963; Brazil: A Study in Development Progress, 1975; International Business and Multinational Enterprises, 1977. Editorial bd. Columbia Jour. World Bus., 1975—, Jour. Internat. Bus. Studies, 1977—. Home: 560 Riverside Dr Apt 21J New York NY 10027

ROBSION, JOHN MARSHALL, JR., former congressman, lawyer; b. Barbourville, Ky. Aug. 28, 1904; s. John Marshall and Lida (Stansberry) R.; grad. Union College Acad., Barbourville, 1919; J.D., George Washington U., 1926; LL.D., Union Coll., 1969; m. Laura Selinda Edwards, July 15, 1949. Admitted to Ky. bar, 1926, practiced in Barbourville, 1926-29, Louisville, 1935-42, 46-52, 58—; chief law div. U.S. Bur. Pensions, 1929-32, Bd. Vets. Appeals, 1932- 35; spl. circuit judge, 1946-52; mem. 83d-85th Congresses from 3d Ky. Dist., mem. judiciary com. 1953-59, mem. com. on coms., 1955-58; del. Interparliamentary Union Conf., Helsinki, 1955, Bangkok, 1956, London, 1957; del. Republican Nat. Conv., 1956, 60; Rep. nominee Gov. Ky., 1959. Pres. Louisville Community Concert Series, 1960-63; chmn. Great Decisions Louisville area, 1960-61; former pres. bd. Salvation Army, Louisville area; trustee Union Coll.; dist. commr. Boy Scouts Am. Served with AUS, 1942-46; mem. staff Gen. Mark Clark, Italy, Austria. Mem. Amvets, Am. Legion, VFW (dist. comdr.), DAV, Mil. Order World Wars (past comdr. Louisville chpt.), Louisville Ampitheatre Prodn. (pres. 1961), Louisville Bar Assn. (past 1st v.p.), Sigma Nu. Republican (gen. counsel for Ky.; mem. exec. com. Louisville). Mem. Christian Ch. (deacon, sec. ofcl. bd.) Clubs: Masons, Pendennis (Louisville); Lincoln of Ky. (past pres.), Highland Men's (past pres.), Young Rep. of Ky. (past pres.). Home: 2500 E Las Olas Blvd Fort Lauderdale FL 33301 Office: Citizens Plaza Louisville KY 40202

ROBSON, EDWIN ALBERT, U.S. sr. judge; b. Chgo., Apr. 16, 1905; s. Clarence T. and Alice B. (Andres) R.; LL.B., DePaul U., 1928; m. Leah M. Kinne, Sept. 15, 1928; children—Edwin Albert, Clark K., David K. Admitted to Ill. bar, 1928; practiced with Kinne, Scovel & Robson, Chgo., 1928-45; judge Superior Ct. Cook County, 1945-51, dir., organizer central assignment system and pretrial conf. of civil cases, 1948-50, chief justice, 1950-51; judge Ill. Appellate Ct. 1951-58; judge U.S. Dist. Ct. for No. Dist. of Ill. Ct., 1958—, chief judge, 1970—. Mem. Nat. Panel on Multidist. Litigation, 1968—. Mem. Am. Judicature Soc., Am., Ill., Chgo. bar assns., Phi Alpha Delta. Methodist. Clubs: Law, Legal, Union League, Standard (Chgo.). Home: 2418 Iroquois Rd Wilmette IL 60091 Office: 219 S Dearborn St Chicago IL 60604

ROBSON, JOHN EDWIN, lawyer, pharm. co. exec.; b. N.Y.C., June 21, 1930; s. Edwin O. and Elizabeth (Stone) R.; B.A., Yale U., 1952; LL.B., Harvard U., 1955; m. Margaret Elizabeth Zuehlke, Dec. 3, 1960; children—Matthew Stone, Douglas O'Neil. Admitted to Ill. bar, 1955, also D.C. bar; mem. firm Leibman, Williams, Bennett, Baird & Minow, Chgo., 1957-66 (merged with Sidley & Austin), 1969-75; cons. on econ. matters Bur. Budget, Washington, 1966-67; gen. counsel Dept. Transp., Washington, 1967-68, under sec., 1968-69; chmn. CAB, Washington, 1975-77; exec. v.p. G.D. Searle & Co., Skokie, Ill., 1977—. Bd. govs., bd. visitors St. John's Coll. Served with AUS, 1955-57. Mem. Ill. State, Chgo., D.C., Fed. bar assns., Harvard Legal Aid Soc., Delta Kappa Epsilon. Clubs: Elihu, Chancery. Home: Chicago IL Office: GD Searle & Co PO Box 1045 Skokie IL 60076

ROBSON, JOHN MERCEL, educator; b. Toronto, May 26, 1927; s. William Renton Mercel and Christina Henderson (Sinclair) R.; B.A., U. Toronto, 1951, M.A., 1953, Ph.D., 1956; m. Ann Provost Wilkinson, Aug. 8, 1953; children—William, John, Ann Christine. Instr. English, U. B.C., 1956-57; asst. prof. English, U. Alta., 1957-58; mem. faculty dept. English, Victoria Coll., U. Toronto, 1958—, prof., 1967—, prin. Victoria Coll., 1971-76. Guggenheim Found. fellow, 1969-70. Fellow Royal Soc. Can.; mem. Brit. Studies Conf., Rhetoric Soc. Am., Dickens Soc., Victorian Studies Assn., Assn. Can. Univ. Tchrs. English, Can. Assn. Univ. Tchrs. Author: The Improvement of Mankind: The Social and Political Thought of J.S. Mill, 1968; editor: The Collected Works of J.S. Mill, 1963—. Home: 66 Woodlawn Ave W Toronto ON M4V 1G7 Canada Office: 27 Birge Carnegie Victoria Univ Toronto ON M5S 1K7 Canada

ROBUSTO, C. CARL, univ. adminstr.; b. Bridgeport, Conn., Nov. 29, 1916; s. Rocco and Lena (Carruozzo) R.; B.S., St. John's U., 1939; M.A., Columbia U., 1946; M.S., N.Y.U., 1950; Ph.D., Fordham U., 1954; m. Dorothea Van Nostrand, June 25, 1944; children—Mrs. Edward De Lorenzo, Edward J. Prof. math. and physics St. John's U., 1946—, chmn. physics dept., 1954-56, dean The Jr. Coll., 1962-67, dean Sch. Gen. Studies, 1968-71, acad. v.p. S.I. campus, dean Notre Dame Coll., 1971-77, acad. v.p. Queens campus, 1977-80, exec. v.p.,

1980—. Served with USNR, 1941-46. Mem. Am. Assn. Jr. Colls., Nat. Council Math. Teachers, Math. Assn. Am. Author: Business Mathematics, 1952; College Algebra and Trigonometry, 1954; Introduction to College Mathematics, 1956; College Mathematics: Unified Approach, 1958. Home: 171-97 St Brooklyn NY 11209

ROBY, FRANK HELMUTH, elec. equipment mfg. co. exec.; b. Indpls., May 5, 1911; s. William Ellsworth and Gertrude Louise (Helmuth) R.; B.E.E., Purdue U., 1933, D.Eng. (hon.), 1967; m. Mary Jane Rogo, May 18, 1950; children—Joan E. and John A. (twins). Vice pres. mktg., dir. Square D Co., Detroit, 1933-58; from exec. v.p. to pres. Fed. Pacific Electric, Newark, 1958-65; chmn. bd., pres. Sola Basic Industries unit Gen. Signal, elec. and electronic equipment, Milw., 1965—; sr. v.p., group exec. parent co., Stamford, Conn., 1977—; dir. Shaler Co., Waupun, Wis., Nat. Rivet & Mfg. Co., Waupun, 1st Fed. Savs. & Loan of Wis., Milw., Realist, Inc., Menomonee Falls, Wis.; lectr. in field. Bd. dirs. Milw. Blood Center. Served to maj. Signal Corps, AUS, 1942-44. Recipient James H. McGraw medal for elec. men. Mem. IEEE, Nat. Elec. Mfrs. Assn. (past gov.), Am. Nat. Standards Inst. (Howard Coonley Gold medal, past pres.), Electronic Industries Assn. (past dir.). Clubs: Milw. Country, Milw. Athletic. Contbr. tech. papers to profl. publs. Home: 2204 W Kenboern Dr Milwaukee WI 53209 Office: PO Box 753 Milwaukee WI 53201

ROCA, PAUL MCLENNAN, lawyer; b. Nebraska City, Nebr., Dec. 16, 1911; s. Lautaro and Stella (McLennan) R.; A.B., U. Ariz., 1933; student No. Ariz. U., 1931, U. Nebr., 1932, U. Calif., 1933-34; J.D., George Washington U., 1941; D.C.L. (hon.), Ch. Div. Sch. of Pacific, 1974; m. Elizabeth A. Yeager, Nov. 22, 1938 (div. 1974); children—Mariana M. (Shulstad), Ellen E. (Tomkins), Michael P.; m. 2d, Lucile Johannessen West, Mar. 1, 1975. Admitted to Va. bar, 1937, D.C. bar, 1940, Ariz. bar, 1941; sec. U.S. Senator Carl Hayden, 1934-41; practice law, Phoenix, 1941—, partner firm Lewis and Roca, 1948—; chief counsel Blood Systems, Inc. Pres., Legal Aid Soc., 1964; trustee Phoenix Little Theatre; pres., trustee DeMund Found. Mem. standing com. Episcopal Diocese Ariz., 1961-75, chancellor diocese, 1970-77, dep. to gen. conv., 1961-76, chmn. standing commn. on structure of Episc. Ch., 1973-76. Mem. Phoenix Community Council, pres., 1950, 68; active United Red Feather Fund, Legal Aid, Boy Scouts Am. Trustee Ch. Div. Sch. of Pacific, Berkeley, Calif., 1972-77. Mem. Am., Maricopa County (pres. 1948), Fed. bar assns., State Bar of Va., D.C. Bar, State Bar Ariz., Assn. Life Ins. Counsel, Internat. Assn. Ins. Counsel, Fedn. Ins. Counsel, Am. Law Inst., United Brotherhood of Carpenters and Joiners, Order of Coif, Phi Beta Kappa. Episcopalian. Author: Life Insurance Law of Arizona, 1958; Paths of the Padres through Sonora, 1967; Spanish Jesuit Churches in Mexico's Tarahumara, 1979. Home: 158 N Country Club Dr Phoenix AZ 85014 Office: 100 W Washington Phoenix AZ 85003

ROCCO, ALEX, actor; b. Cambridge, Mass., Feb. 29, 1936; s. Alesandra Sam and Mary (Di Biase) Petricone; student pvt., public schs., Bordentown (N.J.) Mil. Acad.; m. Sandra Elaine Garrett, Mar. 24, 1966; children—Maryann Petricone, Marc Rocco, Jennifer Rocco, Lucien Rocco. Appeared as Moe Greene in The Godfather, 1976; TV appearances include: That Girl, Cannon, Kojak, Lotsa Luck, The Rookies, Twigs, Hustling (TV film), The Blue Knight, Three for the Road (TV movie and series), Alan King's Final Warning. Served with U.S. N.G., 1952-55. Mem. Screen Actors Guild, AFTRA, Actors Equity. Mem. Bahai Faith. Office: care Jay Julien 9 E 41st St New York NY 10017. *For world unity and peace, and "the oneness of mankind", let us dwell on this thought..."One planet, one people...please!"*

ROCEK, JAN, educator, chemist; b. Prague, Czechoslovakia, Mar. 24, 1924; s. Hugo and Frida (Loebl) Robitschek; M.S., Tech. U., Prague, 1949, Ph.D., 1953; m. Eva Trojan, June 26, 1947; children—Martin, Thomas. Came to U.S., 1960, naturalized, 1966. Scientist, Czechoslovak Acad. Sci., Prague, 1953-57, sr. scientist, 1957-60; vis. scientist U. Coll., London, Eng., 1958; research fellow Harvard, 1960-62; asso. prof., then prof. Cath. U. Am., 1962-66; prof. chemistry U. Ill., Chgo. Circle, 1966—, acting dean Grad. Coll., 1969-70, dean Grad. Coll., 1970-79, asso. mem. Inst. Advanced Studies, 1968-69; vis. scholar Stanford U., 1979-80. Mem. Am. Chem. Soc., AAAS, Chem. Soc. (London), Czechoslovak Soc. Arts and Scis. in Am., AAUP, Sigma Xi (pres. chpt. 1976-77), Phi Kappa Phi. Contbr. articles to profl. jours. Home: 2636 Laurel Ln Wilmette IL 60091 Office: Box 4348 Chicago IL 60680

ROCH, ROBERT HOOVER, lawyer; b. Jacksonville, Tex., Dec. 10, 1937; s. Lewis Marshall and Gladys Irene (Hoover) R.; B.S. in Commerce cum laude, Tex. Christian U., 1958; J.D. cum laude, Baylor U., 1961; m. Margaret Lynn LeGrand, Apr. 18, 1964; children—Sharon Elaine, Carolyn Diane. Admitted to Tex. bar, 1961, since practiced in Houston; asso. firm Hill, Brown, Kronzer & Abraham, 1961-66; partner firm Fisher, Roch & Gallagher, 1966—; adv. Am. Bd. Trial Advs.; lectr. law S. Tex. Coll. Law, 1966-72. Fellow Tex. Bar Found.; mem. State Bar Tex. (grievance com. 1968-71, chmn. 1970-71, dir. 1976-79), Am., Houston bar assns., Assn. Trial Lawyers Am., Am. Judicature Soc., Houston Trial Lawyers Assn., Alpha Chi, Delta Tau Delta, Phi Alpha Delta. Methodist (adminstrv. bd. 1969-76). Home: 48 Sugarberry Circle Houston TX 77024 Office: 2600 Two Houston Center Houston TX 77002

ROCHBERG, GEORGE, composer, educator; b. Paterson, N.J., July 5, 1918; s. Morris and Anna (Hoffman) R.; B.A., Montclair State Tchrs. Coll., 1939, L.H.D., 1962; B.Mus., Curtis Inst. Music, 1948; M.A., U. Pa., 1949; Mus.D. (hon.), Phila Mus. Acad., 1964; m. Gene Rosenfeld, Aug. 18, 1941; children—Paul Bernard (dec.), Frances Ruth. Mem. faculty Curtis Inst. Music, 1948-54; Fulbright fellow Am. Acad., Rome, 1950-51; editor, dir. publs. Theo. Presser Co., Bryn Mawr, Pa., 1951-60; prof. music U. Pa., 1960-68, Annenberg prof.; commd. to compose ballet music for Anna Sokolov, Lincoln Center Fund, 1965. Recordings include: Tableaux, Trio for Violin, Piano, Cello, Night Music, Symphony No. 1, Robert Whitney conducting, also Symphony No. 2, with Werner Torkanowsky conducting, String Quartet No. 2 with Phila. String Quartet; Contra Mortem et Tempus: Serenata d Estate, Blake Songs; String Quartet No. 1, 2 and 3 recorded by Concord Quartet; numerous others. Served to 2d lt., inf. AUS, 1942-45; ETO. Decorated Purple Heart with cluster; recipient Gershwin Meml. award, 1952, Soc. for Publ. Am. Music award, 1956, Koussevitzky commn., 1957, Naumberg Rec. award, 1961, Nat. Inst. Arts and Letters grant, 1962, Fromm Found. commn., 1965; Guggenheim fellow, 1957, 1966-67; Nat. Endowment for Arts grantee, 1972-73. Mem. Am. Musicological Soc., ASCAP, Internat. Webern Soc. (v.p.). Composer: Symphony No. 1, 1948-49; Night Music, 1949; String Quartet No. 1, 1952; Serenata d Estate, 1955; Symphony No. 2, 1956; La Bocca della Verita, 1958; String Quartet No. 2, 1959-61; Blake Songs, 1961; Time-Span (II), 1962; Trio for Violin, Cello and Piano, 1963; Zodiac, 1964; Black Sounds, 1965; Contra Mortem et Tempus, 1965; Music for the Magic Theater, 1965; Symphony No. 3, 1969; Tableaux for chamber ensemble, 1968; String Quartet No. 3, 1972; Violin Concerto premiered by Isaac Stern, 1975; Piano Quintet (Nat. Endowment for Arts commn.), 1975; Symphony No. 4, 1976; (monodrama) Phaedra, 1976; String Quartet No. 4 (1st place Kennedy Center Friedheim award 1979); others. Office: U Pa Music Bldg Philadelphia PA 19104. *I have always clung fast to these fundamentals: that music was given man so he could express the best he was capable of; that the best he was capable of had to do with his deepest feelings; that his deepest feelings are rooted in what I believe to be a moral order in the universe which underlies all real existence.*

ROCHBERG, SAMUEL, physician; b. Paterson, N.J., Apr. 19, 1915; s. Morris and Anna (Hoffman) R.; A.B., U. Md., 1935, M.D., 1939; m. Toba Kleiman, Sept. 1, 1940; children—Richard, Dianne (Mrs. James Sagner), Robert (dec.). Intern Passaic (N.J.) Gen. Hosp., 1939-40; resident Columbia-Presbyn. Hosp., N.Y.C., 1940-42; anesthesiologist-in-chief Sinai Hosp., Balt., 1946—, James L. Kernan Hosp., Balt.; instr. Johns Hopkins Med. Sch., 1962—, U. Md., 1965—; med. dir. Chesapeake Life Ins. Co., 1956—. Mem. Am. Soc. Anesthesiology, Balt. Med. Soc. Jewish religion (pres. congregation). Home: 1815 Greenberry Rd Baltimore MD 21209 Office: James L Kernan Hospital Baltimore MD 21215

ROCHE, BURKE BERNARD, mfg. co. exec.; b. Billings, Mont., Oct. 26, 1913; s. John Francis and Bertha B. (Buchanan) R.; B.Philosophy, Loyola U., Chgo., 1936; postgrad. Northwestern U. Sch. Law, 1937; LL.B., De Paul U., 1939, J.D., 1973; m. Mary Constance Kayser, Aug. 5, 1950. Admitted to Ill. bar, 1940; with Binks Mfg. Co., Franklin Park, Ill., 1946—, v.p., 1948-49, pres., 1949—, chief exec. officer, 1973—; dir. Binks-Bullows, Ltd., Walsall Staffs, Eng., Binks-Bullows (Australia) Pty., Sydney, Binks de Mexico S.A., Mexico City; pres., treas. Binks Japan, Ltd., Tokyo; pres. Binks Research and Devel. Corp., Boulder, Colo.; pres., chmn. Binks Internat. S.A., Brussels, Binks Italia S.r.l., Zingonia, Italy; chmn. Binks Internat. (Deutschland) GmbH, Krefeld, Germany; pres. Binks Mfg. Co. of Can. Ltd., Toronto, Ont. Bd. dirs. Catholic Charities, Chgo.; Eastern lt. of U.S. Assn. Knights and Ladies of Equestrian Order of Holy Sepulchre of Jerusalem. Served to lt. USNR, 1943-46. Mem. Am. Mgmt. Assn., Am. Inst. Mgmt., Soc. Plastics Industry, Am. Hereford Assn., Chgo. Bar Assn. Republican. Roman Catholic. Clubs: Chgo. Athletic Assn., Union League of Chgo., Carlton, Loyola U. Pres's., Econ. of Chgo. (Chgo.). Home: 2400 Windsor Mall Apt 3-K Park Ridge IL 60068 Office: 9201 W Belmont Ave Franklin Park IL 60131

ROCHE, EAMONN KEVIN, architect; b. Dublin, Ireland, June 14, 1922; s. Eamon and Alice (Harding) R.; B.Arch., Nat. U. Ireland, 1945, hon. D.Sc., 1977; postgrad. Ill. Inst. Tech., 1948; m. Jane Tuohy, June 10, 1963; children—Eamon, Paud, Mary, Ann, Alice. Came to U.S., 1948, naturalized, 1964. With Eero Saarinen and Assos., Hamden, Conn., 1950-66; partner Kevin Roche, John Dinkeloo and Assos., Hamden, 1966—; prin. works include Ford Found. Hdqrs., 1967, Oakland (Calif.) Mus., 1968, Nat. Fisheries Center and Aquarium, Washington, maj. expansion program Met. Mus. Art, K.C. Hdqrs. and Coliseum, New Haven, 1969, Creative Arts Center, Wesleyan U., Middletown, Conn., 1971, Aetna Life Ins. Com. computer bldg., Hartford, Conn., 1971, Fine Arts Center, U. Mass., 1971, Fiat Hdqrs., Turin, Italy, Denver Center for Performing Arts, 1973, John Deere & Co. West Office Bldg., Moline, Ill., 1975, Union Carbide Corp. World Hdqrs., Conn., Gen. Foods Corp. Hdqrs., N.Y.C., 1977. Mem. Fine Arts Commn., Washington; trustee Am. Acad. in Rome, 1968-71, Woodrow Wilson Center for Scholars in Smithsonian Instn. Recipient Brunner award Am. Inst. Arts and Letters, 1965; Creative Arts award Brandeis U., 1967; medal of honor N.Y. chpt. AIA, 1968; A.S. Bard award City Club N.Y., 1968; award Gov. Calif., 1968; N.Y. State award Citizens Union N.Y., 1968; total design award Am. Soc. Interior Design. Mem. Nat. Inst. Arts and Letters, Académie d'Architecture (grand gold medal 1977); asso. NAD. Office: 20 Davis St Hamden CT 06517

ROCHE, GEORGE CHARLES, III, coll. pres.; b. Denver, May 16, 1935; s. George Charles, Jr. and Margaret (Stewart) R.; B.S., Regis Coll., Denver, 1956; M.A., U. Colo., 1961, Ph.D., 1965; m. June Bernard, Feb. 11, 1955; children—George Charles, IV, Muriel Eileen, Margaret Clare. Tchr. jr. and sr. high schs., Salida, Colo., 1958-60; mem. faculty U. Colo., 1963-64, Colo. Sch. Mines, 1964-66; dir. seminars Found. Econ. Edn., N.Y.C., 1966-71, trustee, 1971—; pres. Hillsdale (Mich.) Coll., 1971—; chmn. acad. adv. council Charles Edison Meml. Youth Bd. Served to 1st lt. USMCR, 1956-58. Recipient Freedom Leadership award Freedoms Found., 1972. Mem. Am. Hist. Assn., Am. Acad. Polit. and Social Sci., Young Pres.'s Orgn., Am. Assn. Pres.'s Ind. Colls. and Univs., Mt. Pelerin Soc., Phila. Soc. Author: Power, 1967; American Federalism, 1967; Education in America, 1969; Legacy of Freedom, 1969; Frederic Bastiat: A Man Alone, 1971; The Bewildered Society, 1972; The Balancing Act: Quota Hiring in Higher Education, 1974; also articles, newspaper column. Address: Hillsdale Coll Hillsdale MI 49242

ROCHE, GERARD RAYMOND, mgmt. cons.; b. Scranton, Pa., July 27, 1931; s. Joseph Arthur and Amelia Jane (Garcia) R.; B.S. in Accounting, U. Scranton, 1953; M.B.A., N.Y. U., 1957; m. Marie Terotta, Apr. 27, 1957; children—Mary Margaret, Anne Elizabeth, Paul Joseph. Mgmt. trainee AT&T, Phila., 1953; account exec. ABC-TV, N.Y.C., 1955-59; mktg. dir. plastics div. Mobil Chem. Co., Macedon, N.Y., 1959-64; pres. Heidrick & Struggles, Inc., N.Y.C., 1964—; dir. Ideal Ins. Co. Trustee Marywood Coll., Scranton. Served to lt. USN, 1953-55. Mem. Assn. Exec. Recruiting Cons. (past pres.), Alpha Sigma Nu (past treas.). Roman Catholic. Clubs: University, Sky, Yale, Sleepy Hollow Country (gov.). Home: 111 Paulding Dr Chappaqua NY 10514 Office: 245 Park Ave New York NY 10017

ROCHE, JOHN OWENS, advt. writer; b. Houghton, Mich., July 19, 1916; s. Clarence Louis and Louise Marie (Rothering) R.; student Mich. Tech. U., 1934-35, 36-40, Columbia U., 1946-48; m. Maud Rives Wellman, Apr. 18, 1948; children—Louise Rothering, Matthew James, Roderic Wellman, John Owens, William Allen. Reporter, Albert Lea (Minn.) Tribune, 1945-46; copywriter Montgomery Ward, N.Y.C., 1946-47; copy dir. John Wiley & Sons, N.Y.C., 1947-50; advt. dir. Simmons-Boardman Pub. Co., N.Y.C., 1950-53; v.p., creative dir. Gardner Advt., Inc., St. Louis, N.Y.C., 1954-60; copy supr. Donahue & Coe, N.Y.C., 1960-63; copy supr., v.p. Doherty, Clifford, Steers & Shenfield, N.Y.C., 1963-66; copywriter J. Walter Thompson, Inc., N.Y.C., 1966-69, v.p., creative dir. Deltakos, N.Y.C., San Francisco, 1969-75; v.p., creative dir., dir. Barnum Communications, Inc., San Francisco, 1975-77; v.p., copy supr., dir. Vicom Assos., San Francisco, 1977-78. Served to lt. comdr. USNR, 1940-45; PTO. Club: Indian Valley Golf (Novato, Calif.). Home: 164 Camino de Herrera San Anselmo CA 94960

ROCHE, JOHN P., educator; b. Bklyn., May 7, 1923; s. Walter John and Ruth (Pearson) R.; A.B., Hofstra Coll., 1943; A.M., Cornell U., 1947, Ph.D., 1949; D.Litt., Ripon Coll., 1974; m. Constance Ratcliff Ludwig, June 21, 1947; 1 dau., Joanna Ratcliff (Mrs. J.F. Solomon). Instr., asst. prof., asso. prof. polit. sci. Haverford Coll., 1949-56; prof. politics Brandeis U., Waltham, Mass., 1956-70, Herter prof. politics and history, 1970-73, chmn. dept. politics, 1956-59, 61-65, dean faculty arts and scis., 1959-61, chmn. grad. com. Am. Civilization, 1963-65; Henry R. Luce prof. civilization and fgn. affairs, academic dean Fletcher Sch. Law and Diplomacy, Medford, Mass., 1973—, acting dean, 1978-79; Fulbright lectr., France, 1959; vis. prof. Columbia, Cornell U., Mass. Inst. Tech., U. Chgo., Swarthmore Coll.; cons. Vice Pres. Hubert H. Humphrey, Dept. State; spl. cons. to Pres. U.S., 1966-68. Nat. chmn. Americans for Democratic Action, 1962-65; mem. exec. com. Civil Liberties Union Mass., 1961-66; mem. Nat. Council on The Humanities, 1968-70; mem. Presdl. Commn. on Internat. Broadcasting, 1972-73; mem. U.S. Bd. for Internat. Broadcasting, 1974-77. Trustee Woodrow Wilson Center for Scholars, Smithsonian Instn., 1968-75, Dubinsky Found., 1972—. Served with USAAF, 1943-46. Recipient Moses Coit Tyler prize Cornell U., 1949. Fellow Rockefeller Found., 1961-62, 65-66, Found. For Advancement Edn., 1954-55, Hudson Inst., 1970—. Mem. Am. Polit. Sci. Assn. (past mem. exec. council), Council on Fgn. Relations, Phi Beta Kappa, Sigma Delta Chi, Phi Alpha Theta. Mem. Soc. Friends. Author: (with M.S. Stedman, Jr.) The Dynamics of Democratic Government, 1954; Courts & Rights, 1961, rev. edit., 1965; The Quest for the Dream: Civil Liberties in Modern America, 1963; Shadow and Substance: Studies in the Theory and Structure of Politics, 1964; Origins of American Political Thought, 1966; American Political Thought: Jefferson and the Progressives, 1967; John Marshall, 1967; Sentenced to Life: Reflections on Politics, Education and Law, 1974; (with M.S. Stedman and E. Meehan) The Dynamics of Modern Government, 1966; American Nationality, 1607-1978: An Overview, 1978; contbg. author: The American Revolution: A Heritage of Change, 1975; The Legacy of Vietnam, 1976. Nationally syndicated columnist, 1968—. Home: 15 Bay State Rd Weston MA 02193 Office: Fletcher Sch Medford MA 02155

ROCHE, JOHN THOMAS, business exec.; b. N.Y.C., June 6, 1932; s. Thomas P. and Helen C. (Paulakovic) R.; B.B.A., St. John's U., 1953; m. Claire Ten Eyck, Sept. 12, 1955; children—Bradley, Kevin, Bryan. With Kidder, Peabody & Co., Inc., N.Y.C., 1955—, asst. treas., 1965-67, v.p., 1967-75, exec. v.p., 1975—; dir. Depository Trust Co. Served with U.S. Army, 1953-55. Clubs: Huntington Country, Westhampton (N.Y.) Country. Office: 10 Hanover Sq New York NY 10005

ROCHE, MAURICE WILLIAM, pharm. co. exec.; b. New London, Conn., Apr. 1, 1928; s. Maurice Michael and Anne Mary (McGarry) R.; B.Ch.E., Rensselaer Poly. Inst., 1951; m. Dolores Robert, Nov. 28, 1953; children—Marie, Dolores, Ellen, William, Robert, Mark. In various mfg. and adminstrn. positions Pfizer Inc., Groton, Conn., 1953-57, Bklyn., 1957-62; pres. Pfizer Co. Ltd., Montreal, Que., Can., 1962-69; chmn., mng. dir. Pfizer Ltd., Sandwich, Eng., 1969-72; pres. Pfizer Europe, Brussels, 1972—. Pres. Am. Overseas Meml. Day Assn. of Belgium, 1976-77. Served with USN, 1945-46, U.S. Army, 1952-53. Decorated Bronze Star. Mem. Pharm. Mfrs. Assn. Can., Am. C. of C., Association Belgo Americaine, Tau Beta Pi, Phi Lambda Upsilon. Roman Catholic. Clubs: Cercle des Nations, Golf du Bercuit. Home: 40 Ave du Manoir Waterloo Belgium 1410 Office: 55 rue du Moulin a Papier Brussels Belgium 1160

ROCHE, THOMAS FRANCIS, lawyer; b. Chgo., May 2, 1927; s. Martin J. and Gladys (Murphy) R.; J.D., Loyola U., 1955; m. Beatrice Point, May 30, 1948; children—Thomas, Kathleen, James. With trust dept. LaSalle Nat. Bank, Chgo., 1950-55; admitted to Ill. bar, 1955, since practiced in Chgo.; partner firm Halfpenny, Hahn & Roche, 1970—; lectr. in field. Trustee Catholic Charities Chgo.; pres. Citizens for Kids. Served with U.S. Army, 1945-47. Named Automotive Man of Yr., 1979. Mem. Am., Ill., Chgo. bar assns., Chgo. Assn. Commerce and Industry. Democrat. Roman Catholic. Author: Wholesaler-Distributor Stock Valuation Study, 1968; also articles. Home: 218 Timber Ln LaGrange Park IL 60525 Office: 111 W Washington St Chicago IL 60602

ROCHELEAU, GILLES ROGER, city ofcl. Can.; b. Hull, Que., Can., Aug. 28, 1935; s. J.-Avila and Blanche (Naubert) R.; student in Adminstrn., Ottawa (Ont., Can.) U., 1955-57, in Adminstrn., Inst. Specialized Careers, Montreal, Que., 1957-58, LaSalle Acad., Ottawa., 1952, Bourget Coll., Rigaud, Que., 1947-51; m. June 25, 1956; 1 son, Gilles-Celine. Chmn. bd. Gil-Ber Inc., Hull, Que., 1963, Ba-Ro-Ma Inc., Hull, 1970—, Ma-Roc Inc., Hull, 1965—; alderman City of Hull, 1967-74, dep. mayor, 1968, mayor, 1974—. Chmn., Hull Mcpl. Housing Corp., 1969-74, 78-79; bd. dirs. Nat. Arts Center, 1974-79; mem. Outaouais Regional Community, 1974-79; chmn. bd. trustees Olympiques Hockey Club, 1976-79; gov. Que. Jr. Maj. Hockey League, 1978; mem. Provincial-Mcpl. Fiscal Reform, 1979; chmn. Mchts. Assn., Hull, 1962-67, Centennial Festivities, Hull, 1967; treas. Outaouais Regional Econ. Council, Hull, 1966-69. Roman Catholic. Home: 295 St-Joseph Blvd Hull PQ J8Y 3Y5 Canada Office: PO Box 1970 Sta B Hull PQ J8X 3Y9 Canada

ROCHELEAU, RONALD DELPHIS, forest products co. exec.; b. Atlanta, Nov. 13, 1941; s. Delphis Joseph and Edith Lisbeth (Tompkins) R.; B.A., Harvard U., 1963; M.B.A., Columbia U., 1971; m. Sheila Darlene Grummick, Nov. 5, 1972. Mem. audit staff Arthur Young & Co., 1971-73; with Diamond Internat. Corp., N.Y.C., 1973—, asst. treas., 1975-77, treas., 1977—. Served to lt. USN, 1963-69. Office: Diamond Internat Corp 733 3d Ave New York NY 10017

ROCHELL, CARLTON CHARLES, librarian; b. Lawrenceburg, Tenn., Nov. 2, 1933; s. William Frank and Mae (Crews) R.; B.S. in Math., George Peabody Coll., 1959; M.L.S., Fla. State U., 1961, A.M.D. in L.S., 1974, Ph.D. in L.S. and Govt., 1976; m. Rebecca Anne Ridley, Sept. 9, 1961; children—Carlton Charles, Anne Leslie. Reference librarian, spl. asst. to dir. Nashville Pub. Library, 1957-60; dir. Hattiesburg (Miss.)-Forest County Pub. Library, 1961-63, Pub. Library Anniston and Calhoun County (Ala.), 1963-65, Pub. Library Knoxville and Knox County (Tenn.), 1965- 68, Atlanta Pub. Library, 1968-76; dean libraries N.Y. U., 1976—; library service and bldg. cons., 1965—; chmn. N.Y. Regents Library Adv. Bd., 1977—; pres. N.Y. Met. Reference and Research Library Agy., 1978—; humanities in libraries cons., 1975—; N.Y. del. White House Conf. on Libraries and Info. Services, mem. steering com., 1979; cons. Nat. Endowment for Humanities. Served with USNR, 1953-57. Recipient spl. citation City Anniston, 1965; Effie award N.Y. Chpt. Am. Mktg. Assn., 1976; Andy award Advt. Club N.Y., 1976; Council on Library Resources fellow, 1973. Mem. ALA (awards com. Lippincott Jury; standards com. 1970, treas. 1966, John Cotton Dana Publicity award 1976), Southeastern (chmn. pub. library div. 1971-72), Ala. (past v.p., pres. elect. pub. library div. 1965) library assns. Democrat. Episcopalian. Contbr. articles to profl. jours. Office: Bobst Library 70 Washington Sq S New York NY 10012

ROCHER, LUDO, educator; b. Hemiksem, Belgium, Apr. 25, 1926; s. Jules and Anna Van Den (Bogaert) R.; B.A., U. Ghent, Belgium, 1946, M.A., 1948, LL.D., 1950, Ph.D., 1952; m. Rosane Debels, Apr. 1, 1961. Agrege, U. Ghent, 1958-59; prof. sanskrit and comparative philology U. Brussels, 1959-67; prof. sanskrit U. Pa., Phila., 1966—, chmn. dept. Oriental studies, 1967-75, chmn. dept. South Asia regional studies, 1975-78; dir. Center for Study of South and S.E. Asia, U. Brussels, 1961-67. Served with Belgian Army, 1950-52. Research fellow Nat. Found. for Sci. Research, Belgium, 1952-58. Fellow Royal Acad. for Overseas Scis. Belgium; mem. Am. Oriental Soc., Assn. for Asian Studies, Royal Asiatic Soc. (Eng.). Author: A Hindu Legal Digest, 1956; Manual of Modern Hindi, 1958; Bibliography of Hindu Law, 1963; Smrticintamani, 1976; Paulinus a S. Bartholomaeo on the Sanskrit Language, 1977; contbr. articles to profl. jours. Home: 226 W Rittenhouse Sq Philadelphia PA 19103

ROCHESTER, DUDLEY FORTESCUE, physician; b. Bennington, Vt., May 21, 1928; s. Edward Fortescue and Gwendolen Florence (Wolfe) R.; B.A., Columbia U., 1950, M.D., 1955; m. Lois Boochever, 1950; children—Gwendolen, Carolyn. Intern, Presbyn. Hosp., N.Y.C., 1955-56, resident, 1956-58; research fellow Belleview Hosp., N.Y.C., 1958-60; asst. prof. medicine Columbia U., 1965-72, asso. prof., 1972-76; dir. pulmonary disease tng. program USPHS, N.Y.C., 1972-76; prof., head pulmonary-allergy div. U. Va., 1976—; dir. Tb service Blue Ridge Hosp. Served to capt. M.C., USAR, 1956-63. NIH grantee, 1974—, 1977—. Fellow A.C.P.; mem. Am. Physiol. Soc., Am. Fedn. Clin. Research, Harvey Soc., Am. Thoracic Soc. (pres. Eastern sect. 1973-74), N.Y. Trudeau Soc. (v.p. and pres.-elect 1975-76), N.Y. Lung Assn. (dir.), AMA, Va. Med. Assn., Albemarle County (Va.) Med. Assn., Alpha Omega Alpha. Episcopalian. Cons. editor Am. Jour. Medicine. Home: 103 Shawnee Ct Charlottesville VA 22901 Office: Box 225 U Va Med Center Charlottesville VA 22908

ROCHETTE, LOUIS, ship bldg. co. exec.; b. Quebec City, Que., Can., Feb. 19, 1923; s. Évariste and Blanche (Gaudry) R.; M. Commerce, Laval U. (Que.), 1948; m. Nicole Barbeau, Oct. 12, 1968; children—Louise, Ann, Guy. Chief auditor retail sales tax Govt. Que., Quebec City, 1953-55; treas. Davie Shipbldg., Ltd., Lauzon, Que., 1955-65; exec. v.p. Marine Industries, Ltd., Montreal, Que., 1965-76; chmn., chief exec. officer Davie Shipbldg. Ltd., Lauzon, Que., 1976—, Soconav Ltd., Montreal, 1976—. Gov. Council for Canadian Unity; past chmn. Lloyd's Com. for Can. Served as pilot RCAF, 1943-45; ETO. Chartered Accountant, Que. Mem. Inst. Chartered Accountants Can., Canadian Shipbldg. and Ship Repairing Assn. (past chmn.). Author: Le Reve Separatiste, 1969. Home: 5 Jardins Merici Apt 701 Quebec City PQ G1S 4N7 Canada Office: Davie Shipbldg Ltd PO Box 130 Levis PQ G6V 6N7 Canada

ROCHLIN, PAUL R., lawyer; b. Balt., Dec. 14, 1934; s. Jack and Sara (Levin) R.; A.A., U. Balt., 1955, J.D., 1958; m. Joyce Tretick Sopher, Aug. 9, 1973; children—Gregory Joseph, Jennifer David. Admitted to Md. bar, 1959, since practiced in Balt.; pres. firm Rochlin & Settleman, P.A., 1962—. Mem. budgetary com. Asso. Jewish Charities, 1969—. Bd. dirs. Balt. Jewish Council, 1969-75. Served with AUS, 1958, 61-62. Mem. Md., Balt. bar assns., Md. Trial Lawyers Assn., Nu Beta Epsilon. Republican. Jewish religion. Mason. Home: 3410 Philips Dr Baltimore MD 21208 Office: 110 E Lexington St Baltimore MD 21202

ROCHLIS, JAMES JOSEPH, mfg. co. exec.; b. Phila., Apr. 12, 1916; s. Aaron and Gussie (Pearlene) R.; ed. pub. schs.; m. Riva Singer, Mar. 21, 1943; children—Jeffrey A., Susan J. Salesman Mid-City Tire Co., Phila., 1945-46, gen. mgr., 1946-49; pres. Ram Rubber Co., Phila., 1948-49; rep. Blair & Co., Phila., 1949-61, bus. analyst, 1955-61; dir., chmn. exec. com. Mono-Sol Corp., Gary, Ind., 1959—; pres., chief exec. officer, dir. Baldwin-Montrose Chem. Co., Inc., N.Y.C., 1961-68; v.p. Chris-Craft Industries, Inc., N.Y.C., 1968-69, exec. v.p., 1969—, dir., 1958—, pres. Baldwin-NAFI Industries div., 1968—; pres. Chris-Craft Internat., 1977—, Chris-Craft Corp., Pompano Beach, Fla., 1969-71; dir. Montrose Chem. Co. Calif., Torrance and Mexico, 1961—; dir. Piper Aircraft Corp., Lock Haven, Pa., Chris-Craft Pacific, Inc., Calif. Mem. AIAA, Fin. Analysts Soc. Phila., Soc. Naval Architects and Marine Engrs. Club: Atrium (N.Y.C.). Home: 150 E 69th St New York City NY 10021 Office: Chris Craft Industries Inc 600 Madison Ave New York City NY 10022

ROCHON, EDWIN WATERBURY, mag. editor, author; b. Butte, Mont., Jan. 29, 1918; s. Clarence G. and Edna (Waterbury) R.; B.A., Princeton, 1940; M.A., Columbia, 1962; m. Thelma Parrish, Mar. 7, 1943. Copy reader N.Y. Herald Tribune newspaper, 1948-52, N.Y. Daily News, 1961-63; columnist N.Y. World-Telegram and Sun, 1953-61; fin. editor House and Home mag., N.Y.C., 1963—, mng. editor, 1977—; staff editor Bus. Week mag., 1980—. Served with arty. AUS, 1941-45; lt. col. Res. ret. Republican. Episcopalian. Club: Princeton (N.Y.C.). Author short stories This Week mag., 1951-65, including Scandal Aboard Flight 13, 1965. Home: 310 1st Ave New York NY 10009 Office: 1221 6th Ave New York NY 10020. *I have spent my life with words. The noblest are duty, honor, country. . .and the sweetest are music, wine, and beauty.*

ROCHWARGER, LEONARD, fin. services co. exec.: b. Buffalo, Aug. 3, 1925; s. Max and Sarah (Wallace) R.; B.S., U. Buffalo, 1949; m. Arlene Rassuk, June 19, 1949; children—Jeffrey Alan, Michelle, Chief auditor Western N.Y. State, Buffalo, 1949-61; sr. partner S. L. Horowitz & Co., Buffalo, 1961-65; pres., dir., chief exec. officer Firstmark Corp., Buffalo, after 1965, now chmn.; chmn. bd., pres. Indpls. Morris Plan Corp., Firstmark Fin. Corp.; chmn. bd. Israel Am. Leasing Ltd.; dir. Marine Midland Bank-Western, Nat. Fuel Gas Co., Niagara Frontier Services, Inc., Gen. chmn. United Way Buffalo and Erie Co.; trustee, past chmn. bd. regents Canisius Coll.; chmn. United Jewish Appeal, Buffalo, 1969; past. pres., life dir. Buffalo Jewish Center; nat. bd. dirs. NCCJ; bd. dirs., v.p. Nat. Jewish Welfare Bd.; bd. dirs., mem. exec. com.; United Way Buffalo and Erie County; pres. Jewish Fedn. Greater Buffalo; bd. dirs. Council Jewish Fedns. Served with AUS, 1943-46. Decorated Bronze Star, Conspicious Service Cross. Mem. Am. Assn. Equipment Lessors (past pres., dir.), Beta Gamma Sigma. Jewish. Mem. B'nai B'rith (dir. 1960-63). Home: 81 Nottingham Terr Buffalo NY 14216 Office: 135 Delaware Ave Buffalo NY 14202

ROCK, ARTHUR, venture capitalist; b. Rochester, N.Y., Aug. 19, 1926; s. Hyman A. and Reva (Cohen) R.; B.S., Syracuse U., 1948; M.B.A., Harvard U., 1951; m. Toni Rembe, July 19, 1975. Gen. partner Davis & Rock, San Francisco, 1961-68, Arthur Rock & Assos., San Francisco, 1969—; chmn. bd. Sci. Data Systems, Inc., 1962-69 (merged with Xerox Corp. 1969), dir. Xerox Corp., 1969-72; chmn. exec. com., dir. Intel Corp., Santa Clara, Calif.; chmn. bd. Xynetics, Inc., Santa Clara, Qantel Corp., Hayward, Calif.; chmn., dir. Diasonics, Inc., Sunnyvale, Calif.; mem. exec. com., dir. Teledyne, Inc., Los Angeles; dir. Republic Geothermal, Inc., Santa Fe Springs Calif. Bd. dirs. San Francisco Opera Assn., Am. Soc. for Technion. Served with AUS, 1944-45. Office: 1635 Russ Bldg San Francisco CA 94104

ROCK, JOSEPH ALOYSIUS, univ. adminstr.; b. Phila., July 28, 1915; s. Michael J., Jr. and Helen Marie (Doyle) R.; A.B., Georgetown U., 1938, M.A., 1941, Ph.D., 1957; Ph.L., Woodstock (Md.) Coll., 1939; S.T.L., Boston Coll., 1946. Joined Soc. of Jesus, 1932, ordained priest Roman Catholic Ch., 1945; mem. faculty Georgetown U., 1940-42, 50-57, dir. student personnel, 1951-57; mem. faculty U. Scranton, 1946-47, 57—, dean Evening Coll., 1957-61, dean Grad. Sch., 1957-66, acad. v.p., 1966-75, v.p. emeritus, prof. history, 1975—. Formerly mem. pres.'s bd. Caldwell (N.J.) Coll. for Women. Trustee Coll. Misericordia; bd. dirs. Allied Services Handicapped. Mem. Nat. (exec. com. 1954-55, 56-57), Jesuit (pres. 1952-54) assns. student personnel adminstrs., Eastern Assn. Deans and Advisers Men, Jesuit Ednl. Assn. (commn. grad. schs.), Nat. Cath. Ednl. Assn., C. of C. (dir.), Am. Hist. Assn., Alpha Sigma Nu, Pi Gamma Mu, Phi Alpha Theta, Phi Delta Kappa. Address: U Scranton Scranton PA 18510

ROCK, VIRGINIA JEANNE, educator; b. Detroit, Sept. 23, 1923; d. Frank William and Lydia (Fanslow) Rock; came to Canada, 1965; A.B., U. Mich., 1944, M.A., 1947; Ph.D. (Carnegie fellow, AAUW fellow), U. Minn., 1961. Instr. English, U. Louisville, 1947-49; Duke U. scholar, 1949-50; asst. prof. Lake Erie Coll., Painesville, Ohio, 1950-53; instr. communications U. Minn., Mpls., 1954-57; asst. prof. English, Montclair (N.J.) State Coll., 1958-60; asst. prof. Am. thought and lang. Mich. State U., East Lansing, 1960-62, 64-65; Fulbright-Hays vis. prof. Jagiellonian U., Kraków, Poland, 1962-64; mem. faculty York U., Downsview, Ont., Can., 1965—, asso. prof., 1967-73, prof. English, 1973—, also master Stong Coll., 1969-78. Mem. Canadian Assn. Am. Studies (pres. 1970-72), Modern Lang. Assn., Assn. Canadian Univ. Tchrs. English, Am. Studies Assn., Soc. Study So. Lit. Contbr. articles to profl. jours., also biog. essays to I'll Take My Stand, 1977, 79. Home: 87A Walmer Rd Toronto ON M5R 2X6 Canada Office: Stong Coll York U Downsview ON M3J 1P3 Canada

ROCK, WILLIAM RAY, educator; b. Mercersburg, Pa., Apr. 8, 1930; s. David Ray and Mildred Cecilia (Glee) R.; B.A., Gettysburg Coll., 1951; M.A., Duke, 1953, Ph.D., 1956; m. Suzanne Joyce Beck, June 18, 1955; children—Stephen, Anne, Brian. Instr. history Duke, 1957-58; from instr. to prof. history Bowling Green (Ohio) State U., 1958—. Served with AUS, 1955-57. Recipient Distinguished Faculty award Bowling Green State U., 1967. Mem. Am. Hist. Assn. Lutheran. Author: Appeasement on Trial, 1966; Neville Chamberlain, 1969; British Appeasement in the 1930s, 1977. Home: 14543 Sand Ridge Rd Bowling Green OH 43402

ROCKBURNE, DOROTHEA G., artist; b. Verdun, Que., Can.; d. Alfred and Dorothea (Powelle) Rockburne; student Black Mountain Coll. One-women shows include; New Gallery, Cleve., 1972, Bykert Gallery, N.Y.C., 1971, 72, 73, Galleria Toselli, Milan, Italy, 1972, 73, 74, U. Rochester (N.Y.) Art Gallery, 1972, Galleria D'Arte, Bari, Italy, 1972, Lisson Gallery, London, 1973, Daniel Weinberg Gallery, San Francisco, 1973, Galerie Charles Kriwin, Brussels, 1975, Galleria Scheme, Florence, Italy, 1975, John Weber Gallery, N.Y.C., 1976, 78, Tex. Gallery, Houston, 1979; group shows include: Sch. of Mus. Fine Arts, Boston, 1971, U. Rochester, 1972, San Francisco Mus. Art, 1973, Fogg Mus., Cambridge, Mass., 1973, N.Y. Cultural Center, 1973, Centro Communitario di Brera, Milan, 1973, Whitney Mus. Am. Art, N.Y.C., 1972, 73, 77, Mus. Modern Art, N.Y.C., 1974, 75, 77, Corcoran Gallery of Art, Washington, 1975, Städtisches Mus., Leverkusen, W. Ger., 1975, Art Gallery of Ont., Toronto, Can., 1975, Phila. Coll. Art, 1976, Balt. Mus. Art, 1976, Renaissance Soc. of U. Chgo., 1976, Lowe Art Mus., U. Miami (Fla.), 1976, Seibu Mus. Art, Tokyo, 1976, Art Inst. Chgo., 1976, N.Y. Mus., N.Y.C., 1977, Drawing Center, 1977, Whitney Mus. Art, 1977, 79, Kassel, W. Ger., 1977; represented in permanent collections: Milw. Art Center, Mus. Modern Art, Whitney Mus. Am. Art, Fogg Mus., Oberlin (Ohio) Coll., Phila. Mus. Art, High Mus. Art, Atlanta, Houston Mus. Fine Arts. Guggenheim fellow, 1972; Nat. Endowment for Arts grantee, 1973; recipient Witowsky prize 72d Am. Exhbn., Art Inst. Chgo., 1976.

ROCKEFELLER, BLANCHETTE HOOKER (MRS. JOHN D. ROCKEFELLER, 3D), orgn. exec.; b. N.Y.C., Oct. 2, 1909; d. Elon Huntington and Blanche (Ferry) Hooker; A.B., Vassar Coll., 1931; m. John D. Rockefeller 3d, Nov. 11, 1932 (dec. July 1978); children—Sandra Ferry, John Davison IV, Hope Aldrich (Mrs. Hope Spencer), Alida Davison. Mem. Nat. Council on the Humanities, 1974—. Trustee Mus. Modern Art, 1953—, pres., 1959-62, 72—. Mem. Am. adv. com. to Japan Found., 1972—. Trustee Community Service Soc., 1933-57, vice chmn., 1952-57; trustee Brearly Sch., 1947-56, Vassar Coll., 1949-56, Juilliard Sch., 1973—. Mem. Japan Soc., Asia Soc., Met. Opera Guild, Philharmonic Symphony Soc., Friends of Japan House Gallery, Friends of Asia House Gallery. Club: Cosmopolitan. Home: 1 Beekman Pl New York City NY 10022

ROCKEFELLER, DAVID, banker; b. N.Y.C., June 12, 1915; s. John Davison, Jr. and Abby Greene (Aldrich) R.; B.S., Harvard, 1936, LL.D., 1969; Ph.D., U. Chgo., 1940; LL.D., Columbia, 1954, Bowdoin Coll., 1958, Jewish Theol. Sem., 1958, Williams Coll., 1966, Wagner Coll., 1967, Harvard, 1969, Pace Coll., 1970, St. John's U., 1971, U. Liberia, 1979; m. Margaret McGrath, Sept. 7, 1940; children—David, Abby A., Neva (Mrs. Walter J. Kaiser), Margaret D., Richard G., Eileen M. Sec. Mayor Fiorello H. La Guardia, 1940-41; asst. regional dir. Office Def., Health and Welfare Services, 1941-42; 2d v.p. Chase Nat. Bank, 1948-49, v.p., 1949-51, sr. v.p., 1951-55, merged with Bank of Manhattan, exec. v.p. Chase Manhattan Bank, 1955-57, vice chmn. bd. dirs., 1957-61, pres., chmn. exec. com., 1961-69, chief exec. officer, 1969-80, chmn. bd., 1969—, also dir.; dir. Rockefeller Center, Inc. Chmn. Downtown Lower Manhattan Assn., 1958—. Served to capt. AUS, 1942-46. Trustee, chmn. bd. Rockefeller U., 1950-75, chmn. exec. com., 1975—; vice chmn., trustee Rockefeller Bros. Fund; hon. trustee Rockefeller Family Fund; life trustee U. Chgo.; trustee, vice chmn. exec. com. Mus. Modern Art; mem. bd. overseers Harvard Coll., 1954-60, 62-68, 73-74. Awarded Legion of Honor (France); Order of Merit (Italy); recipient award of merit N.Y. chpt. A.I.A., 1965; Medal of Honor for City Planning, N.Y.C., 1968; Charles Evans Hughes award Nat. Conf. Christians and Jews, 1974. Mem. Internat. Exec. Service Corps (dir., chmn. 1964-68), Center Inter-Am. Relations (dir., hon. chmn.), Council Fgn. Relations (dir. 1949—, v.p. 1951-70, chmn.), Am. Philos. Soc., Congress on Liberty. Clubs: Harvard, University, Century, Links, Knickerbocker. Author: Unused Resources and Economic Waste, 1940; Creative Management in Banking, 1964. Address: 1 Chase Manhattan Plaza New York NY 10015

ROCKEFELLER, EDWIN SHAFFER, lawyer; b. Harrisburg, Pa., Sept. 10, 1927; s. Edwin S. and Nancy (McCullough) R.; grad. George Sch., 1944; B.A. magna cum laude, Yale, 1948, LL.B., 1951; m. Marilie Gould Wallace, Dec. 22, 1952; children—Ben Wallace, Edwin Palmer. Admitted to Conn. bar, 1951, D.C. bar, 1956, also U.S. Supreme Ct.; staff FTC, 1956-61; practice in Washington, 1961—; chmn. adv. bd. antitrust and trade regulation report Bur. Nat. Affairs. Served as 1st lt. Judge Advocate Gen.'s Corps, AUS, 1953-56. Mem. Am. (chmn. antitrust sect. 1976-77), D.C. bar assns., Phi Beta Kappa, Phi Delta Phi. Clubs: Capitol Hill, Chevy Chase, Metropolitan (Washington); Yale (N.Y.C.). Author: Desk Book of FTC Practice and Procedure, 1972, 3d edit., 1979; Antitrust Questions and Answers, 1974. Office: 1625 K St NW Washington DC 20006

ROCKEFELLER, GODFREY STILLMAN, textile printing co. exec.; b. N.Y.C., May 1, 1899; B.A., Yale U., 1921; m. Halen Gratz; children—Godfrey A., Marion Rockefeller Stone, Audrey Rockefeller Blair, Lucy Rockefeller Stewart, Peter R. Faculty, Yale-in-China, 1921-22; with indsl. dept. Nat. Comml. Bank & Trust Co., Albany, N.Y., 1925-28; ltd. partner Clark Dodge & Co., 1929-40; dir., v.p., pres., chmn. bd. Cranston Print Works Co., N.Y.C., 1930—; with indsl. div. Marshall Plan Hdqrs., Paris, 1946; dir. Freeport Minerals Co., Istel Fund, Inc. Served as 2d lt. U.S. Army, 1918; to lt. col. USAAF, 1943-45. Home: Mead Ln Greenwich CT 06830 Office: 1412 Broadway New York City NY 10018

ROCKEFELLER, JOHN DAVISON, IV, gov. W.Va.; b. N.Y.C., June 18, 1937; s. John Davison III and Blanchette Ferry (Hooker) R.; B.A., Harvard U., 1961; student Japanese lang. Internat. Christian U., Tokyo, 1957; postgrad. in Chinese, Yale U. Inst. Far Eastern Langs.; m. Sharon Percy, April 1, 1967; children—Jamie, Valerie, Charles. Apptd. mem. nat. adv. council Peace Corps, 1961, spl. asst. to dir. corps, 1962, ops. officer in charge work in Philippines, until 1963; desk officer for Indonesian affairs Bur. Far Eastern Affairs, U.S. State Dept., 1963, later asst. to asst. sec. state for Far Eastern affairs; cons. Pres.'s Commn. on Juvenile Delinquency and Youth Crime, 1964; field worker Action for Appalachian Youth program, from 1964; mem. W.Va. Ho. of Dels., 1966-68; sec. of state W.Va., 1968-72; pres. W.Va. Wesleyan Coll., Buckhannon, 1973-75; gov. State of W.Va., 1977—; mem. exec. com. Nat. Govs. Assn. Trustee U. Chgo., 1967—; chmn. White House Conf. Balanced Nat. Growth and Econ. Devel., 1978—, Pres.'s Commn. on Coal Industry, 1978—. Contbr. articles to mags. including Life, N.Y. Times Sunday mag. Home: Gov's Mansion 1716 Kanawha Blvd E Charleston WV 25305 Office: State Capitol Charleston WV 25305

ROCKEFELLER, LAURANCE S., business exec., conservationist; b. N.Y.C., May 26, 1910; s. John Davison, Jr. and Abby Greene (Aldrich) R.; B.A., Princeton U., 1932; LL.D., State U. Sch. Forestry at Syracuse U., 1961; D.Pub. Service, George Washington U., 1964, U. Vt., 1968; L.H.D. (hon.), Tex. Tech. Coll., 1966; m. Mary French, Aug. 15, 1934; children—Laura Rockefeller Chasin, Marion French Rockefeller Weber, Lucy Rockefeller Waletzky, Laurance. Chmn. Rockefeller Center, Inc., 1953-56, 58-66, now dir.; chmn. Rockefeller Bros. Fund, Caneel Bay Plantation, Inc., Rockresorts, Inc., Woodstock Resort Corp., Grand Teton Lodge Co., Olohana Corp.; dir. Reader's Digest Assn., 1973—. Chmn., Citizens Adv. Com. on Environ. Quality, 1969-73; pres. Am. Conservation Assn., Jackson Hole Preserve, Palisades Interstate Park Commn., 1970-77; hon. chmn. N.Y. Zool. Soc., chmn. Outdoor Recreation Resources Rev. Commn., 1958-65, White House Conf. on Natural Beauty, 1965; life mem. corp. Mass. Inst. Tech.; charter trustee Princeton U.; trustee Alfred P. Sloan Found., Greenacre Found., Nat. Geog. Soc.; chmn. Meml. Sloan-Kettering Cancer Center; bd. dirs. Community Blood Council Greater N.Y., Nat. Park Found. Served from lt. (j.g.) to lt. comdr. USNR, 1942-45. Decorated commandeur de Ordre Royal du Lion, Belgium, 1950; comdr. most excellent Order Brit. Empire; recipient Conservation Service award U.S. Dept. Interior, 1956, 62, Horace Marden Albright Scenic Preservation medal, 1957; Distinguished Service medal Theodore Roosevelt Assn., 1963; Audubon medal, 1964; Nat. Inst. Social Scis. award, 1959, 67; Alfred P. Sloan, Jr. Meml. award Am. Cancer Soc., 1969; Medal of Freedom, 1969. Clubs: River, Princeton, Univ., Brook, Links, Boone and Crockett, Knickerbocker (N.Y.C.); Cosmos, Met. (Washington). Office: 30 Rockefeller Plaza New York NY 10020*

ROCKEFELLER, MARGARETTA FITLER MURPHY (HAPPY), widow of former v.p. U.S.; m. Nelson Aldrich Rockefeller, May 1963; children—Nelson A., Mark F.

ROCKEFELLER, MARY FRENCH (MRS. LAURANCE S. ROCKEFELLER), assn. ofcl.; b. N.Y.C., May 1, 1910; d. John and Mary Montague (Billings) French; student Vassar Coll., 1927-29, Art Students League N.Y.C., 1929-34; m. Laurance Spelman Rockefeller, Aug. 15, 1934; children—Laura Rockefeller Chasin, Marion Rockefeller Weber, Lucy Rockefeller Waletzky, Laurance. Mem. nat. bd. YWCA, 1951—, vice chmn. fgn. div., 1955-64, chmn. Am. Centennial Observance and Celebration, 1956, co-chmn. nat. convocation on racial justice, 1972; chmn. World Service Council, 1958-64, chmn. world relations com., 1964-73; mem. council Found. Child Devel.; trustee Spelman Coll., Atlanta, 1946-70, hon. trustee, 1970—; trustee Whitney Mus. of Am. Art, Woodstock Hist. Soc., Calvin Coolidge Found., Gordon-Conwell Theol. Sem., Fgn. Policy Assn.; trustee, v.p. YWCA of City N.Y., 1971—; mem. distbn. com. N.Y. Community Trust, 1969—; bd. dirs. N.Y. Community Fund, Inc., 1969—. Recipient Gold medal Nat. Inst. Social Scis., 1972. Mem. N.Y. Zool. Soc., Hort. Soc. N.Y., Am. Craftsmen Council, Met. Mus. Art, Mus. Modern Art, Philharmonic Symphony, Park Assn. N.Y.C., Women's Nat. Republican Club. Clubs: Women's City, Cosmopolitan, Colony (N.Y.C.) Home: 834 Fifth Ave New York City NY 10021

ROCKEFELLER, W.C., cons. engr.; b. Ogden, Utah, Apr. 2, 1910; s. William V. and Julia (Tullis) R.; B.S., Cal. Inst. Tech., 1932, M.S., 1934; m. Verna Margaret Rood, July 17, 1937; children—Alan Frank, Gail Frances. Instr., Cal. Inst. Tech., 1932-37; cons. aero. engr., 1934-38; chief of aerodynamics Vultee Aircraft, Inc., 1938-42; asst. chief engr. Avion, Inc., 1942-44; gen. mgr. Alvin R. Adams & Assos., 1944-48; dir., exec. asst. to chmn. bd. Consol. Vultee Aircraft Corp., 1947-53; v.p., dir. Airfleets Inc., 1949-56; v.p., dir. San Diego Corp., 1952-56; v.p., dir. Nut-Shel Co., 1952-56, Hidden Splendor Mining Co., 1954-58; v.p. Atlas Corp., 1954-58; v.p., dir. MVT Industries, Inc., 1960-64; v.p. Sonico, Inc., 1964-69; pres. Via Computer, Inc., 1969—; asso. Calif. Inst. Tech., 1975—. Recipient Lawrence B. Sperry award Inst. Aero. Scis., 1936. Fellow Inst. Aero. Scis. Contbr. articles to various engring. publs. Home: 12983 Caminito del Pasaje Del Mar CA 92014

ROCKEFELLER, WILLIAM, lawyer; b. N.Y.C., Dec. 4, 1918; s. William Avery and Florence (Lincoln) R.; grad. St. Paul's Sch., 1936; A.B., Yale, 1940; student U. Wis., 1940-41; LL.B., Columbia, 1947; m. Mary D. Gillett, July 3, 1947; children—Mary Gillett Fogarty, Edith McKee Laird, Sarah Stillman Bogdanovitch. Admitted to N.Y. bar, 1948; asso. firm Dorr, Hammond, Hand & Dawson, 1947-55; asso. firm Shearman & Sterling, N.Y.C., 1955-57, partner, 1957—. Dir. Cranston Print Works Co. (R.I.), Indian Spring Land Co. (Conn.), Oneida Ltd. Trustee, sec. Meml. Sloan-Kettering Cancer Center; bd. dirs. Am. Soc. Prevention Cruelty to Animals, pres., 1956-64; chmn. Met. Opera Assn., Geraldine R. Dodge Found.; trustee Paul Smith's Coll. Served to lt. comdr. USNR, 1941-46. Decorated Bronze Star; recipient gold medal Nat. Inst. Social Sci., 1977. Mem. Am., N.Y. bar assns., Assn. Bar City N.Y., Zeta Psi, Phi Delta Phi. Episcopalian. Clubs: Met. (Washington); DownTown Assn., N.Y. Yacht, Links, Brook, Anglers', Metropolitan Opera, Westminster Kennel (N.Y.C.); American Yacht (Rye). Home: 84 Grandview Ave Rye NY 10580 Office: 153 E 53 St New York NY 10022

ROCKLER, WALTER JAMES, lawyer; b. Mpls., Nov. 25, 1920; s. Nathan and Evelyn R.; A.B., U. Chgo., 1940; J.D., Harvard U., 1942; m. Aino Allenkand, Aug. 21, 1949; children—Elliot, James, Nicolas, Julia. Admitted to Ill. bar, 1947, N.Y. bar, 1950, D.C. bar, 1952, U.S. Supreme Ct., 1953; prosecutor Nuremberg War Crime Trials, 1947-49; asso. firm Chapman, Bryson, Walsh & O'Connor, N.Y.C., 1949-51, 53, Paul, Weiss, Rifkind, Wharton and Garrison, N.Y.C., 1951-53; partner firm Lederer, Livingston, Kahn & Adsit, Chgo., 1954-60; counsel Altheimer & Gray, Chgo., 1961; partner Pennish, Steele & Rockler, Chgo., 1962-64, Cotton, Watt, Rockler & Jones, Chgo., 1964-66, Arnold & Porter, Washington, 1966—; dir. Office of Spl. Investigation, Dept. Justice, 1979—. Served with USMC, 1943-46. Decorated Bronze Star. Mem. Chgo. Bar Assn., Am. Bar Assn., D.C. Bar Assn. Democrat. Jewish. Home: 11129 Stephalee Ln Rockville MD 20852 Office: 1229 19th St Washington DC 20036

ROCKOFF, NEIL FREDERICK, broadcasting exec.; b. Bayonne, N.J., Mar. 19, 1938; s. Herman C. and Florance (Laden) R.; B.A., U. Vt., 1962; m. Deborah Hoch, July 2, 1967; children—Cherie, Cindy. Research analyst HR TV Reps., N.Y.C., 1965-66; asst. dir. research Blair Radio Reps., N.Y.C., 1966-67; dir. mktg. and research Christal Co., N.Y.C., 1967-68; salesman CBS Radio, N.Y.C., 1968-69; gen. sales mgr. Sta. WEEI, Boston, 1969-70; Eastern sales mgr. CBS-FM, N.Y.C., 1970-71; sta. mgr. KNX-FM, Los Angeles, 1971-72; v.p., gen. mgr. Sta. WLAK-FM, Chgo., 1972-75; v.p., gen. mgr. Sta. WHN, N.Y.C., 1975-79; v.p. radio div. Storer Broadcasting Co., Inc., N.Y.C., 1978—; pres. Force Communications Investment Corp., 1979—. Chmn. bd. N.Y. Market Radio Broadcasters; v.p. bd. Country Music Assn. Home: PO Box 1967 Rancho Santa Fe CA 92067 Office: 7867 Convoy Ct Suite 303 San Diego CA 92111

ROCKRISE, GEORGE THOMAS, architect; b. N.Y.C., Nov. 25, 1916; s. Thomas S. and Agnes M. (Asbury) R.; B. Arch., Syracuse U., 1938; M.S. in Architecture, Columbia, 1941; m. Margaret Lund Paulson, June 12, 1948 (dec. Aug. 1957); children—Christina, Peter; m. 2d, Sally S. Griffin, Dec. 1959 (div.); 1 dau., Celia. Univ. fellow architecture Columbia, 1940-41; architect Army and Navy, Panama, 1941-45; designer Edward D. Stone, N.Y.C., 1945-46, UN Hdqrs. Planning Commn., 1946-47; archtl. asso. Thomas D. Church, San Francisco, 1948-49; pvt. practice, 1949—; chmn. bd. Rockrise, Odermatt, Mountjoy Assos., architects and planners; lectr. Sch. Architecture, U. Calif., 1949-53; adviser to faculty com. Sch. Architecture, U. Venezuela, Caracas, 1954. Mem. San Francisco Art Commn., 1952-55; cons. architect U.S. Dept. State, Japan, 1957-58, W. Ger., Brazil, 1978-79; vis. lectr. Cornell U., Clemson Coll., 1961, Syracuse U., U. Utah, Stanford U., 1962-65; lectr. urban design Spanish Ministry Housing and Devel., Madrid, 1978; mem. San Francisco Planning Commn., 1961-62; adviser to sec. for design HUD, 1966-67; participant State Dept. AID Urban Seminars Latin Am., 1971. Mem. pres.'s adv. com. U. Mass., 1971; mem. adv. council San Francisco Planning Urban Renewal Assn. Recipient AIA nat. award for residential work, 1953, 59, prog. architecture award citation, 1956, award of honor and award of merit AIA Homes for Better Living Program, 1956, regional awards for residential architecture AIA, 1957, others; Fulbright-Hays scholar, Rome, 1978; Fulbright fellow in urban design U. Rome, 1978-79. Fellow AIA (pres. No. Calif. chpt. 1961, nat. v.p. from 1969, mem. nat honor awards jury, mem. nat. commn. urban design and planning 1978); mem. Am. Soc. Planning and Housing Ofcls., Am. Inst. Cert. Planners, Am. Soc. Landscape Architects, Nat. Assn. Housing and Redevel. Ofcls., Delta Kappa Epsilon, Tau Sigma Delta, Lambda Alpha. Home: 468 Vallejo St San Francisco CA 94133 Office: 405 Sansome St San Francisco CA 94111. *My adult life as architect and planner has been devoted to the construction and improvement of the man-made environment. I have come to believe through this endeavor, that it is concern and responsibility of all thinking persons, whether professional or laity, to understand the forces for change in the environment and to work for the protection and enhancement of our cities and the natural environment.*

ROCKWELL, ALVIN JOHN, lawyer; b. Kalamazoo, Dec. 29, 1908; s. John S. and L. B. (DeVall) R.; A.B., DePauw U., 1929; postgrad. London Sch. Econs., 1929-30; J.D., Harvard, 1933; m. Anne Hayward, Aug. 24, 1933; 1 son, John Sargent. Admitted to Mass. bar, 1933, Calif. bar, 1948; spl. asst. to U.S. atty. gen., 1940-43; gen. counsel NLRB, 1944-45; legal adviser to U.S. Mil. Govt., Germany, 1946-48; partner firm Brobeck, Phleger & Harrison, San Francisco, 1948-79, of counsel, 1979—. Trustee De Pauw U., 1958—, San Francisco Law Library, 1975—; pres. San Francisco Bar Assn. Found., 1979—; mem. Commn. on Uniform State Laws, 1962-69. Fellow Am. Bar Found., Am. Law Inst., Harvard Law Sch. Assn. No. Calif. (past pres.), World Affairs Council No. Calif. (past pres.), Phi Beta Kappa. Clubs: Commonwealth, Pacific-Union, Bohemian (San Francisco); Cosmos (Washington). Home: 45 Scenic Way San Francisco CA 94121 Office: Spear St Tower 29th Floor One Market Plaza San Francisco CA 94105

ROCKWELL, BRUCE MCKEE, banker; b. Denver, Dec. 18, 1922; s. Robert B. and Florence (McKee) R.; B.A., Yale, 1945; m. Virginia Packard, Apr. 22, 1950; children—David, Jane, Sarah. Exec. sec. to mayor of Denver, 1947-52; public relations and advt. account exec. William Kostka & Assos., 1952-53; with Colo. Nat. Bank, Denver, 1953—, pres., 1970-75 chmn., chief exec. officer 1975—, also dir.; exec. v.p. Colo. Small Bus. Investment Co.; vice chmn. Colo. Nat. Bankshares, Inc., 1975-76, chmn., 1976—, also dir.; dir. Colo. & So. R.R., Burlington No., Inc.; mem. Colo. adv. bd. Mountain Bell Telephone Co.; pres., dir. Lenders Mortgage Corp.; dir. VISA U.S.A. Inc. Pres. Downtown Denver Inc., 1977—; chmn. Denver Urban Renewal Authority, 1958-68; mem. nat. council Salk Inst., 1978—; trustee Nat. Jewish Hosp., 1977—, Com. for Econ. Devel., 1979—, Denver Symphony Orch.; Orch., 1974-77, Denver Art Mus., 1965-72. Served to ensign USMC, 1945-46. Named Colo. Bus. Man of Yr., Colo. Bus. Mag., 1976. Mem. Am., Res. City (dir. 1975—), Colo. bankers assns., Colo. Assn. Commerce and Industry (dir. 1977—, v.p. 1979), Denver C. of C. 1973-74). Clubs: University, Press, Petroleum, Tennis (Denver). Home: 815 Vine St Denver CO 80206 Office: Colo Nat Bank 17th and Champa Sts Denver CO 80202

ROCKWELL, GEORGE BARCUS, financial cons.; b. Chgo., Jan. 5, 1926; s. Thomas S. and Irene G. (Barcus) R.; A.B. in Econs., Harvard U., 1949, grad. Advanced Mgmt. Program, 1967; m. Lois Ladd, Sept. 10, 1950; children—Susan, Cindy. Salesman, IBM, 1949, products mgr., 1956, asst. mgr., Boston, 1958, mgr., Albany, N.Y., 1960; v.p., div. head computer services State St. Bank & Trust Co., Boston, 1963, v.p., head mut. funds div., 1966, sr. v.p., 1968, bank sales coordinator, 1968, exec. v.p., 1968, pres., 1970-75, vice chmn. bd. State St. Boston Fin. Corp., 1975-76, also dir.; v.p., dir. fin. industries Arthur D. Little, Inc., Cambridge, Mass., 1976—; v.p., dir. Webster-Atlas Bldg. Corp., Keane Assos., Inc.; pres., dir. State St. Bank Boston Internat., State St. Boston Securities Service Corp., State St. Boston Credit Co., Inc., SSB Investments, Inc.; dir., exec. com. Nat. BankAmericard Inc., 1970-75. Bd. overseers Boys' Clubs Boston, 1969-75; trustee council Boston U. Med. Center, 1969-74; trustee Lahey Clinic, 1973—. Served to 1st lt., inf., AUS, 1944-46. Mem. Greater Boston C. of C. (bd. dirs. 1969—), Harvard Bus. Sch. Assn. Boston (bd. govs. 1969-72). Clubs: Wellesley Country; Commercial, Economic (Boston). Home: 376 Glen Rd Weston MA 02193 Office: Acorn Park Cambridge MA 02140

ROCKWELL, JAMES MITCHELL, army officer; b. Wellsville, N.Y., June 26, 1928; s. John Hobart and Mary Margaret (Higgins) R.; B.S., U.S. Mil. Acad., 1951; M.S., George Washington U., 1966; postgrad. U. Pitts., 1970-72; m. Ann Alberta Scott, June 6, 1951; children—Mary M., James Mitchell, Rebecca A., Scott T., Jessamyn L. Commd. 2d lt. U.S. Army, 1951, advanced through grades to maj. gen., 1975; comdr. inf. co., Korea, 1952; comdr. signal bn. 1st inf. div., Vietnam, 1966; comdr. 1st Signal Brigade, Korea, 1973; dir. communications-electronics systems office of asst. chief of staff for communications-electronics Dept. Army, 1973-74; dep. dir. Telecommunications Command and Control Dept. Army, Washington, 1974-75; vice dir. Def. Communications Agy., Washington, 1975-78; dir. Joint Tactical Communications Office, Ft. Monmouth, N.J., 1978—. Decorated Silver Star, D.F.C., Legion of Merit (2), Bronze Star (3), Air medal (14). Mem. Armed Forces Communications-Electronics Assn., Am. Soc. Pub. Adminstrn. Roman Catholic. Lone Home: 17 Allen Ave Fort Monmouth NJ 07703 Office: Joint Tactical Communications Office Fort Monmouth NJ 07703

ROCKWELL, JOHN SARGENT, music critic; b. Washington, Sept. 16, 1940; s. Alvin John and Anne Sargent (Hayward) R.; B.A., Harvard U., 1962; postgrad. U. Munich, 1962-63; M.A., U. Calif., Berkeley, 1964, Ph.D., 1972. Music and dance critic Oakland (Calif.) Tribune, 1969; asst. music and dance critic Los Angeles Times, 1970-72; freelance music critic N.Y. Times, 1972-74, staff music critic, 1974—; lectr. in field. Harvard-German Govt. fellow, 1962-63; Woodrow Wilson fellow, 1963-64. Mem. Music Critics Assn. (treas.), Phi Beta Kappa. Home: 376 Broome St New York City NY 10013 Office: NY Times 229 W 43d St New York City NY 10036. *Criticism is not something you do after you've failed at something else, it is a creative act in itself. It's not something necessarily negative or carping, but a positive act of discrimination, analysis and celebration. To be a music critic means to encounter music openly, and to relate the genesis and perception of sound to the life of the individual and society.*

ROCKWELL, LANDON GALE, educator; b. N.Y.C., Jan. 3, 1914; s. Alphonso David and Carolyn Reynolds (Gale) R.; A.B., Dartmouth, 1935; student Harvard, 1936-37; A.M., Princeton, 1938, Ph.D., 1942; m. Ruth Adams, Aug. 5, 1939; children—Sandra Adams, Winthron Adams; m. 2d, Heidi Hockstrasser, Feb. 11, 1967. Instr. Princeton, 1938-40, U. Cin., 1940-42; asst. prof. Williams Coll., 1946-50; asso. prof., head dept. govt. Hamilton Coll., 1950—, James S. Sherman prof. polit. sci., 1955—; vis. prof. U. Tex., 1959. Moderator Aspen (Colo.) Inst. Humanistic Studies Seminar, 1960-62. Bd. dirs. Keene Valley (N.Y.) Hosp.; trustee, pres. Keene Valley Library Assn. Served to lt. comdr. USNR, 1942-46. Mem. Am., N.Y. State (pres. 1953-54) polit. sci. assns., Am. Civil Liberties Union, Soc. Mayflower Descs. Democrat. Conglist. Club: Am. Alpine (N.Y.C.). Contbr. articles profl. jours. Home: College Hill Rd Clinton NY 13323

ROCKWELL, PERRY JACK, JR., educator, psychologist; b. Williamsport, Pa., Nov. 24, 1924; s. Perry J. and Erma (Decker) R.; B.S., U. Wis., 1949, M.S., 1950, Ph.D., 1958; m. Kathleen Jean Tremmel, Apr. 16, 1949 (div. July 1971); children—Perry Jack III, Barbara Jean; m. 2d, Lauralee Kemper Eherenman, Aug. 9, 1975. Tchr., Cook County (Ill.) Sch. Dist. 141, 1950-51, Savanna (Ill.) city schs., 1952-56; asst. prof. Coll. Pacific, Stockton, Calif., 1958-60, Ind. U., 1960-65; prof. Atlanta U., 1965-66; prof. U. Wis.-Platteville, 1966—, head dept. ednl. psychology, 1967-74; vis. lectr. U. Iowa, 1976-77. Served with USNR, 1942-45, 51-52. Mem. Am. Personnel and Guidance Assn. (pres. Wis. 1970-71), N.E.A., Phi Delta Kappa. Home: 1290 W Hill Ave Platteville WI 53818

ROCKWELL, R(ONALD) JAMES, JR., laser and electro-optics cons.; b. Cin., May 7, 1937; s. Ronald James and Mary Cornelius (Thornton) R.; B.S., U. Cin., 1960, M.S., 1964; m. Diane Lundin, Feb. 3, 1968; children—James Gregory, Christopher Derrick. Directing physicist, asso. prof. laser scis., laser research labs. Med. Center, U. Cin., 1963-76; dir. continuing edn. services Electro-Optical Systems Design Jour., Cin., 1976-77; v.p. laser/electro-optics Control Dynamics, Inc., Cin., 1977-79; pres. Rockwell Assos., Inc., cons. lasers, optics and electro-optics, Cin., 1979—; exec. sec. Laser Inst. Am., 1976-77, dir., 1972—, pres., 1974; exec. com. safe uses lasers com. Am. Nat. Standards Inst., 1971—; dir. Laserworks, Inc.; cons. WHO. Mem. IEEE, N.Y. Acad. Scis., Newcomen Soc., Sigma Xi (nat. lectr. 1971-75), Delta Tau Delta (dir. acad. affairs, nat. bd. dirs. 1975—). Methodist. Co-author: Lasers in Medicine, 1971; contbr. articles profl. jours., editor jours. in field. Designer, builder portable laser entertainment system in laser light artistic shows; patentee in field. Home: 6282 Coachlite Way Cincinnati OH 45243 Office: PO Box 43018 Cincinnati OH 45243

ROCKWELL, STEVEN KENT, mfg. co. exec.; b. Washington, Sept. 11, 1944; s. Willard F. and Constance Babcock (Templeton) R.; B.A. in Econs., Lafayette Coll., 1966; ed. Wharton Sch. Fin. and Commerce, U. Pa., 1969; m. Dorothy Carol Dingfelder, Sept. 13, 1969; children—Steven Kristofer, Jonathan Corey. Pres., Keystone Aircraft Sales Co., Pitts., 1969-74; dir. bus. planning, utility and indsl. ops. Rockwell Internat., Pitts., 1975, v.p., gen. mgr. mcpl. and utility div., 1976-77, pres. Utility Products Group, 1977—, also dir.; dir. Global Real Estate Investment Trust. Bd. dirs. Forbes Health System, Pitts.; trustee Lafayette Coll. Served with U.S. Army, 1967. Mem. Am. Mgmt. Assn., Am. Mgmt. Research Inst., Am. Gas Assn., Am. Public Works Assn., Gas Appliance Mfg. Assn., Am. Water Works Assn. (dir.), Pa. Mcpl. Authority Assn. Clubs: Duquesne, Pitts. Athletic, Fox Chapel Golf. Home: Pasadena Dr Extension Pittsburgh PA 15215 Office: 400 N Lexington Ave Pittsburgh PA 15208

ROCKWELL, THEODORE, III, nuclear engr.; b. Chgo., June 26, 1922; s. Theodore G. and Paisley (Shane) R.; B.S., Princeton, 1943, Chem.E., 1944; grad. courses, Oak Ridge, 1944-49; D.Sc. (hon.), Tri-State U., 1960; m. Mary Juanita Compton, Jan. 25, 1947; children—Robert C., William T., Lawrence E., Juanita C. Process improvement engr. Manhattan Project, Oak Ridge, 1944-45; head shield engring. group Oak Ridge Nat. Lab., 1945-49; nuclear engr., naval reactors br. AEC, also nuclear propulsion divs. Navy Bur. Ships, 1949-55, tech. dir., 1955-64; prin. officer, dir. MPR Assos., Inc., Washington, 1964—; research asso. Johns Hopkins U. Center Fgn. Policy Research, 1965-66. Chmn. Atomic Indsl. Forum Reactor Safety Task Force, 1966-72; mem. adv. group artificial heart program NIH, 1966; cons. to Joint Congl. Com. on Atomic Energy, 1967. Mem. adv. council dept. chem. engring. Princeton U., 1966-72. Recipient Distinguished Civilian Service medal U.S. Navy, 1960; Distinguished Service medal AEC, 1960. Registered profl. engr., D.C. Fellow Am. Soc. Psychical Research; mem. Parapsychol. Assn., AAAS. Presbyterian (elder). Club: Cosmos (Washington). Co-founder Princeton Engr. Editor: Reactor Shield Design Manual, 1956. Co-author: Arms Control Agreements/Designs Verification, 1968. Editor: Shippingport Pressurized Water Reactor, 1958. Contbr. sci. articles to profl. publs., non-tech. articles nat. mags. Holder patents, patent applications for neutron-absorbing cermets, process for leaching uranium from slags, process for prodn. boron-containing plastic sheet, others. Home: 3403 Woolsey Dr Chevy Chase MD 20015 Office: MPR Assos Inc 1140 Connecticut Ave NW Washington DC 20036

ROCKWELL, WILLARD FREDERICK, JR., mfg. exec.; b. Boston, Mar. 3, 1914; s. Willard Frederick and Clara (Thayer) R.; B.S., Pa. State U., 1935, I.E., 1955; LL.D. (hon.), Grove City Coll., Lambuth Coll.; D. Eng. (hon.), Tufts U., Carnegie-Mellon U., Washington and Jefferson Coll.; m. Constance Templeton, July 16, 1942; children—Patricia Lynne R. Boorn, Willard Frederick lll, Steven Kent, George Peter, Russell Alden. Cost accountant Pitts. Equitable Meter Co., 1935-36, mgr. engring., 1937-39, v.p., controller, 1939-43, v.p., gen. mgr., 1945-47; asst. to controller Timken-Detroit Axle Co., Detroit, 1936-37; pres. Rockwell Mfg. Co., Pitts., 1947-64, vice chmn. bd., chief exec. officer, 1964-71, chmn. bd., 1971-73, also dir.; pres. Rockwell-Standard Corp., 1963-67, dir., 1942-67; chmn. bd., chief exec. officer N. Am. Rockwell Corp., 1967-73; chmn. bd. Rockwell Internat. 1973-79, chmn. exec. com., dir., 1979—; dir. The El Paso Co., Mellon Bank N.A., Mellon Nat. Corp., Lone Star Industries, Inc., Planning Research Corp., Magic Chef, Inc., Pitts. Athletic Co., Inc. (Pitts. Pirates), El Paso Products Co. Trustee U.S. council Internat. C. of C.; mem. Greater Pitts. Airport Adv. Bd.; trustee Am. Enterprise Inst. for Pub. Policy Research, Aerospace Edn. Found.; chmn. exec. com. Tax Found., Inc.; trustee U. So. Calif., Grove City (Pa.) Coll., Point Park Coll., Carnegie Mus. Natural History; bd. dirs. World Affairs Council Pitts.; chmn. bd. govs. Ford's Theatre, Washington. Served to capt., ordnance, AUS, World War II. Registered profl. engr., Pa., Calif. Fellow Royal Soc. Arts; mem. Natural Gas and Petroleum Assn. Can., Am. Petroleum Inst., Engrs. Soc. Western Pa., Gas Appliance Mfrs. Assn. (pres. 1956, dir.), Smithsonian Assos., Am. Soc. M.E., Am. Inst. Indsl. Engrs., Mil. Order World Wars, Pitts. Athletic Assn., Pa. C. of C. (past pres., dir.), Pitts. C. of C. (past v.p. dir.), Am. Ordnance Assn., Am. Water Works Assn., Pa. Soc., Soc. Automotive Engrs., S.A.R., Conf. Bd., Omicron Delta Kappa, Kappa Sigma, Delta Sigma Pi. Clubs: Duquesne, University, Longue Vue (Pitts.); University (N.Y.C.); Rolling Rock (Ligonier, Pa.); Bath, Indian Creek (Miami Beach); Chicago; Detroit Athletic; California (Los Angeles); Cat Cay (Bahamas); Laurel Valley Golf (Ligonier, Pa.). Office: 600 Grant St Pittsburgh PA 15219

ROCKWOOD, RUTH H., emeritus educator; b. Chgo., Oct. 15, 1906; d. Charles Edward and Myrtle Isabelle (Wheeler) Humiston; A.B., Wesllesley Coll., 1927; M.S., U. Ill., 1949; Ed.D., Ind. U., 1960; m. George Herbert Rockwood, Apr. 14, 1928 (dec.); children—Charles Edward, Nancy Hoyt Rockwood Haigh, Alice Frances Rockwood Bethke. Adminstrv. asst., instr. U. Ill. Library Sch., 1949-52; Fulbright lectr. Chulalongkorn U., Bangkok, Thailand, 1952-53; vis. asst. prof. Ind. U. Library Sch., 1958-59; prof. library sci. Fla. State U., 1953-79, prof. emeritus, 1979—. Mem. Southeastern Library Assn., ALA, Fla. Library Assn., Assn. Am. Library Schs., Adult Edn. Assn., AAUP, Fla. Assn. Media in Edn., Beta Phi Mu. Club: Pilot (Tallahassee). Home: 1616 Woodgate Way Tallahassee FL 32312 Office: Sch Library Sci Fla State U Tallahassee FL 32306

ROD, DONALD OLAF, librarian; b. Roland, Iowa, July 14, 1915; s. Mikkel O. and Ada (Birkeland) R.: A.B., Luther Coll., 1938; B.L.S., U. Mich., 1940; m. Elsie Victoria Siemers, June 3, 1944; children—Michael Olaf, Catherine Marie, John Thomas. Asst. cataloger gen. library U. Mich., 1938-40; asst., asso. librarian Luther Coll., 1940-43; librarian Augustana Coll., Rock Island, Ill., 1943-53; dir. library services U. No. Iowa, 1953—. Mem. adv. com. on library services Iowa Dept. Pub. Instrn., 1954-59; cons. coll. library bldgs. and adminstrn. Cons.-examiner North Central Assn. Colls. and Secondary Schs., 1973—. Bd. dirs. Norwegian-Am. Mus. Traveling fellowship to Europe, A.L.A., 1947. Recipient Distinguished Service award Luther Coll., 1969. Mem. A.L.A. (mem. council 1961-65, standards com., chmn. coll. and univ. library bldgs. com. 1970-71), Am. Assn. U. Profs. (chmn. Iowa conf. 1958), Iowa Library Assn. (pres. 1957-58). Lutheran. Home: 2603 Iowa St Cedar Falls IA 50613

RODALE, ROBERT DAVID, editor, publisher; b. N.Y.C., Mar. 27, 1930; s. Jerome Irving and Anna Apollonia (Andrews) R.; student Lehigh U., 1947-52; m. Ardath Harter, June 23, 1951; children—Heather, Heidi, David, Maria, Anthony. Chief exec. officer Rodale Press, Inc., Emmaus, Pa., editor Organic Gardening and Farming, 1952—, Prevention, 1964—, The New Farm, 1978—, Rodale's New Shelter, 1980—. Pres., Lehigh Valley Conservancy, 1974—; chmn. Lehigh County Velodrome Commn., 1974—; asst. treas., asst. sec. East Pa. Sch. Authority, 1967—; mem. shooting sports com. U.S. Olympic Com., 1969-75. Pres., Soil and Health Found., Emmaus. Recipient Distinguished Internat. Shooter badge Dept. Def., 1963. Author: Sane Living in a Mad World, 1972; The Best Health Ideas I Know, 1974. Editor: The Challenge of Earthworm Research, 1961; The Basic Book of Organic Gardening, 1971. Home: RD 2 Box 313 Allentown PA 18103 Office: 33 E Minor St Emmaus PA 18049

RODD, THOMAS, banker; b. 1913; A.B., Yale, 1935; married. With Morgan Guaranty Trust Co., 1935-76, exec. v.p., 1965-71, vice chmn., 1971-76, mem. dirs. adv. council, 1977—; dir. Panhandle Eastern Pipe Line Co. Served to capt. USMCR, 1943-45. Address: 23 Wall St New York NY 10015

RODDA, PETER ULISSE, geologist, curator, educator; b. Albuquerque, Nov. 18, 1929; s. Peter and Mary Edwina (Rodin) R.; B.A., U. Calif., Los Angeles, 1952, Ph.D., 1960; m. Ramona Jewell Strang, June 25, 1963; 1 son, Peter Grant. Teaching asst. U. Calif., Los Angeles, 1954-57; research scientist Bur. Econ. Geology, U. Tex., Austin, 1958-71, asso. prof. dept. geology, 1963-71; curator, chmn. dept. geology Calif. Acad. Scis., San Francisco, 1971—; adj. prof. geology dept. Calif. State U., San Francisco, 1972—. Recipient NSF grant, 1958. Fellow Calif. Acad. Scis., Geol. Soc. Am.; mem. Am. Assn. Petroleum Geologists, Calif. Malacozoological Soc., Paleontol. Soc. Contbr. articles profl. jours. Office: Golden Gate Park San Francisco CA 94118

RODDENBERRY, EUGENE WESLEY (GENE), writer, producer; b. El Paso, Tex., Aug. 19, 1921; s. Eugene Edward and Caroline Glen (Golemon) R.; A.A., Los Angeles City Coll.; student U. Miami, Columbia, U. So. Cal.; D.H.L., Emerson Coll., Boston, 1973; m. Majel Leigh Hudec, Aug. 6, 1969; children—Darlene Roddenberry Cervantes, Dawn Alison Roddenberry Compton, Eugene Wesley. Pilot, Pan Am. World Airways, 1945-49; sgt. Los Angeles Police Dept., 1949-53; freelance TV and motion picture writer, 1953-62; producer TV and motion pictures, 1962—; writer, producer movie Pretty Maids All in a Row, 1970; Star Trek - The Motion Picture, 1979; creator, producer Star Trek, The Lieutenant, Questor, Genesis II; pres. Norway Prodns., Inc. Served with USAAF, 1941-45. Decorated D.F.C., Air Medal. Recipient writing and prodn. awards Writers Guild Am., Nat. Acad. TV Arts and Scis., other TV orgns. Mem. Writers Guild Am. (past mem. exec. council), TV Acad. Arts and Scis. (past gov.), Assn. for Profl. Law Enforcement, ACLU. Co-author: The Making of Star Trek, 1968; Star Trek - The Motion Picture: A Novel, 1979. Clubs: Explorers (N.Y.C.); Bel-Air Country, La Costa Country. Home: 9147 Leander Pl Beverly Hills CA 90210 Office: Paramount Pictures 5451 Marathon St Hollywood CA 90038. *To be different is not necessarily to be ugly; to have a different idea is not necessarily to be wrong. The worst possible thing that can happen to humanity is for all of us to begin to look and talk and act and think alike. The best measure of maturity and wisdom in a human is the recognition of value received on hearing another say: "I disagree with you, for the following reasons . . . ."*

RODDEY, OTHA CHARLES, engring. co. exec.; b. Crossett, Ark., Jan. 7, 1924; s. Otha Columbus and Ann Laura (Holland) R.; B.S., La. State U., 1947; M.S., M.I.T., 1951; m. Hilda Blaine, Oct. 7, 1951; children—Leah Ann, Mary Robin. Devel. engr. Esso Standard Oil Co., Baton Rouge, 1949-51; process engr. Southwestern Engring. Co., Los Angeles, 1951-53, sales engr., 1953-54, mgr. sales, 1955-58; mgr. sales Nichols Constrn. Co., Baton Rouge, 1958-61; with Ralph M. Parsons Co., 1961—, exec. v.p., Pasadena, Calif., 1978, pres., 1979—. Served to capt. U.S. Army, 1943-46. Mem. Am. Inst. Chem. Engrs., Beavers, Sigma Xi, Phi Eta Sigma, Tau Beta Pi, Phi Lambda Upsilon, Phi Kappa Phi, Omicron Delta Kappa. Republican. Presbyterian.

Clubs: Annandale Golf, Seven Lakes Country. Home: 7746 Bowen Dr Whittier CA 90602 Office: 100 W Walnut St Pasadena CA 91124

RODDIS, LOUIS HARRY, JR., ret. naval officer, cons. engr., business exec.; b. Charleston, S.C., Sept. 9, 1918; s. Louis Harry and Winifred Emily (Stiles) R.; B.S., U.S. Naval Acad., 1939; M.S., Mass. Inst. Tech., 1944. Commd. ensign U.S. Navy, 1939, advanced through grades to capt., 1957; various assignments, sea duty, 1939-41, Pearl Harbor, 1941; assigned Phila. Naval Shipyard, 1944; staff of comdr. Joint Task Force I, atomic weapons tests, Bikini, 1946; assigned Clinton Labs., Manhattan Engring. Dist. (now Oak Ridge Nat. Lab.), 1946; staff bur. ships Dept. Navy, Washington, nuclear ship propulsion program AEC, assisted nuclear reactor design U.S.S. Nautilus, 1947-55; dep. dir., div. reactor devel. AEC, 1955-58. Pres., dir. Pa. Electric Co., Johnstown, Pa., 1958-67, chmn. 1967-69; dir. nuclear power activities Gen. Pub. Utilities Corp., N.Y.C., 1967-69; vice chmn. Consol. Edison Co. N.Y., 1969, 73-74, pres., 1969-73, also trustee; pres., chief exec. officer John J. McMullen Assos., Inc., N.Y.C., 1975-76, asso. co. Panero-Tizian Assos., Inc., 1975-76; cons. engr., 1976—. Mem. Pres.'s Adv. Council on Energy Research and Devel., 1973-75; cons. U.S. Dept. of State, Disarmament Commn., 1960-61, U.S. Maritime Adminstrn., 1959-62; chmn. maritime research adv. com. Nat. Acad. Scis.-NRC, 1958-60; mem. Gov.'s Com. of 100 for Better Edn., 1962-64, Gov.'s Council Sci. and Tech., 1963-65; mem. Pa. Indsl. Devel. Authority, 1961-68; pres. Atomic Indsl. Forum, 1962-64; mem. adv. com. Rockefeller U., 1972—; mem. energy research adv. bd. Dept. Energy. Bd. dirs. Edison Elec. Inst., 1959-62, 69-72, Mercy Hosp., Johnstown, 1959-67, Metal Properties Council. Recipient outstanding service award AEC, 1957; Arthur S. Flemming career award Washington C. of C., 1958; Outstanding Citizen award Johnstown Inter-Service Club Council, 1963. Registered profl. engr., Pa., D.C., N.Y., N.J., S.C.; chartered engr. U.K. Fellow Royal Instn. Naval Architects; mem. Am. Soc. M.E. (Fellowship award), I.E.E.E., Am. Nuclear Soc. (pres. 1969-70, Fellowship award 1970), Soc. Naval Engrs., Am. Soc. Naval Archts. and Marine Engrs., Nat. Acad. Engring., Nat. Soc. Profl. Engrs., Am. Soc. Heating, Refrigeration and Air-Conditioning Engrs., N.Y. C. of C., Newcomen Soc. N.Am., Edison Electric Assn. (dir. 1969-73), Am. Gas Assn. (dir. 1973-74), Commerce and Industry Assn. N.Y. (bd. dirs. 1969-74), Sigma Xi. Clubs: University (Pitts.); Army Navy (Washington); Army-Navy Country (Arlington, Va.); Rotary (Charleston); Chemists (N.Y.); Mantoloking (N.J.) Yacht. Author tech. articles on nuclear power and energy subjects. Home and office: 110 Broad St Charleston SC 29401

RODDIS, RICHARD STILES LAW, lawyer, educator; b. Washington, Mar. 18, 1930; s. Louis Harry and Winifred Emily (Stiles) R.; A.B., San Diego (Calif.) State Coll., 1951; J.D., U. Calif. at Berkeley, 1954; m. Joanne Margreta Hagen, Aug. 16, 1953; children—Kathryn Hazel, Linda Marie, Victoria Anna, Margaret Mae, Richard Louis Martin. Admitted to Calif. bar, 1955, U.S. Supreme Ct. bar, 1959; dep. atty. gen. Calif., San Francisco, 1954-58, dep. atty. gen., chief sect. bus. law and investment frauds unit, Los Angeles, 1961-63; practiced law, San Diego, 1958-61; chief dep. ins. commr. Calif., Los Angeles, 1963-65, ins. commr. State of Cal., 1966-68; prof. law U. Wash., Seattle, 1968—, dean Sch. Law, 1970-78; dir. Unigard Mut. Ins. Co., Seattle; adviser U.S. Dept. Transp., 1968-70, Nat. Conf. Commrs. on Uniform State Laws, 1971-72; chmn. Gov. Wash. Task Force on Catastrophic Health Care Costs, 1973-74; mem. steering com. medical injury compensation study Inst. Medicine, Nat. Acad. Scis., 1976. Bd. dirs. Saul Haas Found.; trustee Lutheran Bible Inst. Mem. State Bar Calif., Nat. Assn. Ins. Commrs. (chmn. blanks com., chmn. laws and legis. com., vice chmn. exec. com. 1966-68). Republican. Lutheran. Home: 12735 42d Ave NE Seattle WA 98125

RODEHORST, WAYNE, coll. pres.; b. Pleasanton, Nebr., Dec. 18, 1929; s. Arthur William and Harriet Elsie (Valentine) R.; B.F.A., Kearney (Nebr.) State Coll., 1951, M.F.A., 1958; Ph.D., Mich. State U., 1964; LL.D., Lake Erie Coll., Painesville, Ohio, 1972; m. Mary Lou Bartruff, June 2, 1951; children—Rhett Arthur, Morgan Wayne, Damon Le. Tchr., then supt. schs., Wilcox, Nebr., 1951-59; prin. Plattsmouth (Nebr.) High Sch., 1959-62; successively dir. liberal arts, dean instrn., v.p. Macomb County Community Coll., Macomb, Mich., 1964-67; pres. Lakeland Community Coll., Mentor, Ohio, 1967—. Exec. bd. N.E. Ohio council Boy Scouts Am., 1968-69; bd. dirs. Lake County Mental Health Clinic, 1969-76, Blue Cross N.E. Ohio, 1970-75, East Surburban Concerts, 1978-79; trustee Grand River Acad., 1969-76, Lake County Free Clinic, 1971-75; mem. corp. bd. Holden Arbortum, 1970-79. Recipient various Boy Scout awards, service awards; Kellogg fellow, 1962. Mem. Am. Assn. Community and Jr. Colls., Assn. Community Coll. Trustees, Kappa Pi. Methodist. Clubs: Grand River Yacht, Rotary, Gyro Internat., Masons. Author curriculum materials. Home: 7365 Holly Park Mentor OH 44060 Office: Lakeland Community Coll Mentor OH 44060

RODEMACHER, W.D., utilities exec.; b. Lake Charles, La., 1907. Chmn., chief exec. officer, dir. Central La. Electric Co., Pineville, La.; chmn., dir. La. Intrastate Gas Corp., South La. Prodn. Co.; pres., chief exec. officer, chmn. bd. mem. exec. com., dir. Central La. Energy Corp. Office: PO Box 111 Alexandria LA 71301

RODENBERG, SIDNEY DAN, educator; b. St. Louis, Apr. 5, 1926; s. Martin and Etta (Goldfried) R.; A.B. in Zoology, Washington U., St. Louis, 1948, A.M. in Microbiology, 1950, Ph.D. in Botany (NSF fellow), 1953; M.A. (hon.), U. Pa., 1971; m. Dolores Knight, Dec. 21, 1950; children—Nancy, Wendy, Amy, Philip. Mem. faculty U. Pa., 1953-75, asso. prof. microbiology, 1961-69, prof., 1969-75, dean Sch. Allied Med. Professions, 1969-75; prof. health sci., dean Coll. Health Related Professions, Wichita State U., 1976—. Chmn. Upper Merion Student Loan Fund, 1962-64, chmn. Upper Merion Parent-Tchr. Council, 1962-63; mem. Upper Merion San. Bd., 1965-66; mem. health manpower review and study commn. Pa. Regional Comprehensive Health Planning Council, 1971-74; mem. task force on allied health edn. Pa. Dept. Edn., 1972; mem. Pa. Gov.'s Com. on Health Edn., 1974-75; mem. accreditation rev. bd. Nat. Accrediting Agy. for Clin. Lab. Services, 1974—. Bd. dirs. Upper Merion Area Sch. System, 1969-75, pres., 1974-75. Served with AUS, 1944-46. NSF Postdoctoral fellow, 1966-67; recipient Lindback award Lindback Found., 1964. Mem. AAAS, Am. Inst. Biol. Scis., Am. Soc. Microbiology, Am. Soc. Allied Health Professionals (dir. 1973—, mem. adv. com. regional tng. insts. 1972-74, treas. 1974-76, pres. 1977-79), Sigma Xi. Home: 6710 E 10th St Wichita KS 67206 Office: Coll Health Related Professions Wichita State Univ Wichita KS 67208

RODERICK, DAVID MILTON, steel co. exec.; b. Pitts., May 3, 1924; s. Milton S. and Anna (Baskin) R.; B.S. in Econs. and Finance, U. Pitts.; m. Elizabeth J. Costello, Jan. 31, 1948; children—David Milton, Patricia Ann, Thomas Kevin. Asst. to dir. statistics U.S. Steel Corp., Pitts., 1959-62, accounting cons.-internat. projects, 1962-64, v.p. accounting, 1964-67, v.p. internat., 1967-73, chmn. finance com., 1973-75, pres., 1975-79, chmn., chief exec. officer, 1979—, dir., 1975—; dir. Procter & Gamble Co., Aetna Life & Casualty Co. Mem. exec. bd. Allegheny Trails council Boy Scouts Am.; pres., trustee Tax Found., Inc.; bd. dirs. United Way of Allegheny County, Pitts. Symphony Soc.; trustee Mercy Hosp., Carnegie-Mellon U., Carnegie Inst., Shady Side Acad., Nat. Safety Council, Hwy. Users Fedn.; mem. adv. council Japan-U.S. Econ. Relations; bd. govs. United Way Am. Mem. Am. Iron and Steel Inst., Pa. Bus. Roundtable, Econ. Club N.Y., Nature Conservancy (corp. relations com.), Newcomen Soc. N.Am. Clubs: Rolling Rock, Laurel Valley Golf (Ligonier, Pa.); Fox Chapel Golf, Pitts. Field, Duquesne (Pitts.); Pine Valley Golf (N.J.). Co-author: Industrial Internal Auditing. Office: 600 Grant St Pittsburgh PA 15230

RODERICK, DORRANCE DOUGLAS, ret. newspaper publisher; b. Brooklyn, Iowa, Dec. 24, 1900; s. Taliesin Evan and Mary (Dorrance) R.; A.B., U. Okla., 1922; m. Olga Burnett, Aug. 14, 1922; children—Frances Rozelle, Dorrance Douglas. Reporter, Tulsa World, 1918; asst. editor AP, Oklahoma City, 1922; with advt. dept. Wichita (Kans.) Eagle, 1923; advt. and bus. mgr. Lubbock (Tex.) Jour., 1924-25, pub., 1926-29; pub. Lubbock Avalanche, 1926-29, El Paso Herald and Times, 1929-31, El Paso Times, 1931-75; ret., 1975; pres. El Paso Times, Inc. Newspaper Printing Corp., Newspaper Realty Corp., Sta. KROD-TV-AM, 1940-60; chmn. bd. Times Enterprises, Inc.; dir., mem. exec. com. El Paso Nat. Bank; dir. Trans Tex. Bancorp. Mem. Tex. Good Neighbor Commn., 1943-57, chmn., 1943; pres. Roderick Found., Inc.; bd. dirs. El Paso Mus. Art, United Fund, Radford Sch. for Girls, Armed Services YMCA; trustee Phi Gamma Ednl. Found; bd. dirs. U. Tex. El Paso Pres.'s Assos., Providence Meml. Hosp., Tex. Daily Press League. Served to maj. AUS, 1943-45. Recipient Human Relations award NCCJ, 1967; Citizen of Year award Bd. Realtors, 1971. Mem. El Paso Indsl. Bd. (dir.), El Paso Symphony Assn. (pres. 1923-63, chmn. bd. 1963—), El Paso Hist. Soc. (trustee), VFW, Phi Gamma Delta, Sigma Delta Chi, Phi Mu Alpha, Phi Alpha Tau. Episcopalian (vestryman). Clubs: Masons (33 deg.), Shriners (potentate 1938), Jesters, Cabiri, Internat., Ormsbee (pres. 1934-36), Kiwanis (gov. S.W. dist. 1935), Knife and Fork (pres. 1938-39), Coronado Country, El Paso, Pioneer. Home: 857 River Oaks Dr El Paso TX 79912 Office: Suite 9A El Paso Nat Bank Bldg El Paso TX 79901

RODES, ELMER OWEN, JR., cons. engr.; b. Harrisonburg, Va., June 17, 1923; s. Elmer O. and Alma Rose (Kaylor) R.; B.S. in Mining Engring., Va. Poly. Inst., 1947; m. Betty B. Dumas, Sept. 6, 1947; children—Katherine P. Rodes Wilkerson, Mary Elizabeth. Partner, Robert L. Brown & Assos., engrs., Roanoke, Va., 1950-53, Sowers, Knowles & Rodes, cons. engrs., Roanoke, 1953-59, Sowers, Rodes & Whitescarver, cons. engrs., Roanoke, 1959—. Trustee Greenvale Nursery Sch., Roanoke, 1970—, pres., 1973-77. Served to 1st lt. U.S. Army, 1943-46. Fellow Am. Cons. Engrs. Council (treas., trustee 1973-75); mem. Cons. Engrs. Council Va. (pres. 1967-68), Nat. Soc. Profl. Engrs., Am. Soc. Plumbing Engrs., Va. Assn. Professions, Omicron Delta Kappa, Pi Kappa Alpha, Tau Beta Pi. Presbyterian. Clubs: Rotary, Hunting Hills Country. Home: 3030 Hemlock Ln SW Roanoke VA 24014 Office: PO Box 4038 Roanoke VA 24015

RODEWALD, PAUL GERHARD, lawyer; b. Newton, Wis., May 16, 1899; s. Ferdinand Adolph and Elise (Tasche) R.; A.B., Ripon Coll. 1921, LL.D., 1978; LL.B., Harvard, 1924; m. Lillian Young, Aug. 17, 1927; children—William Young, Mary Louise (Mrs. Fred L. Forni), Paul Gerhard. Admitted to Pa. bar, 1924, also U.S. Supreme Ct.; partner firm Buchanan, Ingersoll, Rodewald, Kyle & Buerger, and predecessors, 1930—. Trustee Ripon Coll., 1957-76, chmn. bd., 1965-69. Mem. Am., Pa., Allegheny County bar assns., Am. Law Inst., Phi Beta Kappa, Pi Kappa Delta, Delta Sigma Rho. Republican. Presbyn. Clubs: Harvard-Yale-Princeton, Duquesne, University (Pitts.). Home: 508 Edgerton Pl Pittsburgh PA 15208 Office: 57th Floor 600 Grant St Pittsburgh PA 15219

RODGERS, B. THOMAS, acct.; b. Hillsboro, N.D., Dec. 18, 1928; s. Benjamin Thomas and Marguerite Helen (Brueckner) R.; B.S.C., U. N.D., 1950, LL.B., 1952; m. Sandra Grigsby, Mar. 12, 1976; children—Kathryn, Douglas, Philip, James, Jane. Admitted to N.D. bar; v.p. fin. McGraw-Edison Co., Chgo., from 1973; now v.p. fin. Nashua Corp. (N.H.). Served with U.S. Army, 1946-47. Home: Nathan Lord Rd Amherst NH 03031 Office: 44 Franklin St Nashua NH 03061

RODGERS, CHARLES HOOD, mfg. co. exec.; b. Glasgow, Scotland, Jan. 19, 1914; s. Thomas and Agnes (Hood) R.; came to U.S., 1920; B.B.A, St. John's U., 1939; m. Helen V. Cook; 1 son, Thomas C. Vice-pres., treas. Servomechanisms, Inc., Los Angeles, 1950-57; v.p. fin. Condec Corp., Old Greenwich, Conn., 1957—; dir. Lunkenheimer Corp., Cin., Hammond (Ind.) Valve, N.R.M. Corp., Akron, Ohio, Consol. Controls Corp., Bethel, Conn., Unimation Inc., Danbury, Conn. Mem. Fin. Execs. Inst., Am. Mgmt. Assn. Home: 83 Hawthorne Rd New Canaan CT 06840 Office: Old Greenwich CT 06870

RODGERS, CLIFTON EUGENE, landscape architect; b. Beaver, Pa., Mar. 19, 1915; s. George Barr and Iris (Musgrave) R.; B.S. in Landscape Architecture, Pa. State U., 1938; m. Jean Fiorita, Nov. 22, 1951; children—Courtonne, Lee Ann, Clifton E., Chase. Mng. partner Clifton E. Rodgers Assos., Planning Cons., Landscape Architects, Beaver Falls and Harrisburg, Pa., 1946—; partner Rodgers and Frederick, Engrs., Architects, 1960—; dir., sec. Rivercrest Inc., 1974—; pres. Mahoning Devel., Inc.; vis. lectr. depts. landscape architecture and city regional planning Pa. State U.; planning cons., govt. devel. agencies and pvt. devel. cos., Pa.; tech. advisor Philippine Govt. and Congl. Hearings on War Damages, Washington; del. Internat. Congress Landscape Architects, Paris, 1973, Vienna, 1974. Pres. Internat. Assn. Torch Clubs, 1979-80. Served with USNR, 1944-46. Recipient Scarab award for design excellence Pa. Dept. Architecture, 1936. Fellow Am. Soc. Landscape Architects. Republican. Presbyterian. Contbr. articles and reports in field. Office: PO Box 2057 4101 N 6th St Harrisburg PA 17105

RODGERS, DAN, advt. co. exec.; b. N.Y.C., Jan. 10, 1920; s. Louis and Augusta (Goldstein) R.; ed. pub. schs., N.Y.C.; m. Ruth Steigerwald, Apr. 13, 1943 (dec. May 1964); children—Sanda Lynn, Cathy Allyn, Michael (dec.), Elly; m. 2d, Doris Kanner Lazare, Dec. 16, 1965; children—Laura, Todd. With Raymond Spector Co., advt., N.Y.C., 1937-42, E.T. Howard Inc., advt., N.Y.C., 1945-48; v.p., account supr. Milton Biow Co., advt. N.Y.C., 1949-56; sr. v.p. account group head, mem. bd. dirs. and exec. com. Ted Bates & Co., Inc., advt., N.Y.C., 1956-63; v.p. mem. finance and operations coms. Am. Home Products Corp., N.Y.C., 1963-66, chmn., dir. John F. Murray div. Am. Home Products Corp., 1971—. pres., dir. Revlon, Inc., N.Y.C., 1966-69; chmn. bd., chief exec. officer G.J. Holding Corp., 1970-71. Served with USAAF, 1942-45. Office: 685 3d Ave New York City NY 10017

RODGERS, EUGENE, writer; b. Bklyn., July 22, 1939; s. Thomas Aquinas and Catherine (Slattery) R.; B.S., Villanova U., 1961; postgrad. U. Wis., 1961-63; m. Carol Diane Huber, 1977; 1 son, Eric Eugene. Research asst. sci. writing U. Wis., Madison, 1961-63; pub. info. officer U.S. Antarctic Research Program, 1963-65; freelance writer, Washington, 1965-67; mgr. sci. pub. relations Westinghouse Electric Corp., Pitts., 1967-75; editor Atomic Indsl. Forum Inc., Washington, 1975-76; speechwriter ERDA, Washington, 1976, IBM Corp., Armonk, N.Y., 1977, United Techs. Corp., Hartford, Conn., 1979—. Home: 39 Drumlin Rd West Simsbury CT 06092 Office: United Techs Bldg Hartford CT 06101

RODGERS, FRANK, librarian; b. Darlington, Eng., July 28, 1927; came to U.S., 1956; s. Charles Bede and Frances (Page) R.; B.A. with honours, King's Coll., U. Durham, 1947; diploma librarianship, Univ. Coll., London U., 1952; m. Sarah Louise Edelson, Dec. 18, 1971; children—Hilda Marie, Norah Frances. Librarian, Poplar Tech. Coll., London, 1951-53, St. Martin's Sch. Art, London, 1953-56; sr. librarian adult services div. Akron (Ohio) Public Library, 1956-59; asst. reference librarian U. Ill., 1959-64; chief reference librarian, then asst. dir. public services Pa. State U. Libraries, 1965-69; dir. Portland (Oreg.) State U. Library, 1969-79; dir. libraries U. Miami (Fla.), 1979—; mem. Oreg. Adv. Council Libraries, 1973-74; bd. dirs. Pacific N.W. Bibliog. Center, 1973-77; tech. adv. com. libraries Columbia Regional Assn. Govts., 1976-79; vis. fellow U. Southampton (Eng.), 1975-76, pres. Oreg. Library Assn., 1974-75. Served with Brit. Army, 1947-49. Grantee Council Library Resources, 1975-76. Fellow Library Assn. U.K.; mem. ALA. Author, editor various library publns., guides. Home: 5630 Twin Lakes Circle South Miami FL 33143 Office: Univ Miami Library Coral Gables FL 33124

RODGERS, FRANKLYN, publishing exec.; b. Johnstown, Pa., Feb. 1, 1936; s. Leon T. and Martha (Findley) R.; B.S. in Econs., U. Pa., 1958; m. Cintra Scott, Feb. 28, 1959; children—Andrew, Jeffrey. With Charles Scribner's Sons, N.Y.C., 1962—, exec. v.p., treas., 1970—, also dir.; pres. Scribner Book Cos., 1977—; sec., treas. Scribner Bookstores, Inc.; sec. Book Warehouse, Inc., Publishers Realty Co. Bd. dirs. Nat. Energy Found. Served to lt. (j.g.) USNR, 1958-62. Mem. Phi Gamma Delta (pres. 1957), Sphinx Sr. Soc. Author articles. Home: Van Beuren Rd Morristown NJ 07960 Office: 597 Fifth Ave New York NY 10017

RODGERS, JOANN ELLISON, journalist; b. Balt., Jan. 10, 1941; d. Max Milton and Dorothy (Hirschhorn) Ellison; B.S. magna cum laude, Boston U., 1962; M.S. cum laude, Columbia, 1964; m. George Greeley Rodgers, Sept. 15, 1963 (div. 1978); children—Adam, Jared. Reporter, then city editor Boston U. News, 1959-62; reporter, reviewer Patriot Ledger, Quincy, Mass., 1961-63; stringer N.Y. Herald Tribune, 1963; with News Am., Balt., 1964—, med. and life sci. writer, 1966—, columnist Extra mag., 1971—; nat. sci. writer Hearst Headline Service, 1966—; med. columnist, feature writer Balt. mag., 1970-71; writer column Sci. Beat, Hearst Newspapers, 1974; freelance writer; mem. Council for Advancement Sci. Writing, 1977—. Pres. Hebbville P.T.A., 1973-75. Recipient Lasker Med. Journalism award, 1965, A.M.A. Med. Journalism award, 1965, Md.-Del. Council for Alcohol Studies award, citation Md. div. Am. Cancer Soc., Med. Journalism award for excellence Md. Optometric Assn., 1974, citation Arthritis Found; Blakeslee award Am. Heart Assn., 1975, 77; Sci. Writing award Cystic Fibrosis Found., 1976. Mem. at large Nat. Assn. Sci. Writers (sec.-treas.). Jewish. Home: 12104 Ridge Valley Dr Owings Mills MD 21117 Office: News American South and Lombard Sts Baltimore MD 21203

RODGERS, JOHN, educator, geologist; b. Albany, N.Y., July 11 1914; s. Henry D. and Louise W. (Allen) R.; B.A., Cornell U., 1936, M.S., 1937; Ph.D., Yale, 1944; unmarried. Geologist, U.S. Geol. Survey, 1938-46, intermittently, 1946—; sci. cons. U.S. Army Engrs., 1944-46; instr. geology Yale, 1946-47, asst. prof., 1947-52, asso. prof., 1952-59, prof., 1959-62, Silliman prof., 1962—; vis. lectr. Coll. de France, Paris, 1960. Sec.-gen. commn. on stratigraphy Internat. Geol. Congress, 1952-60; commr. Conn. Geol. and Natural History Survey, 1961-71. NSF Sr. postdoctoral fellow, France, 1959-60; exchange visitor Geol. Inst., Acad. Scis. USSR, 1967; Guggenheim fellow, Australia, 1973-74; recipient medal of freedom U.S. Army, 1947. Fellow Geol. Soc. Am. (councillor 1962-65, pres. 1970), A.A.A.S.; mem. Am. Acad. Arts and Scis., Am. Assn. Petroleum Geologists, Conn. Acad. Sci. and Engring. (charter), Conn. Acad. Arts and Scis. (pres. 1969), Am. Geophys. Union, Nat. Acad. Scis., Geol. Soc. London (hon.), Société géologique de France (asso. mem., v.p. 1960), Acad. Scis. USSR (hon. fgn. mem.), Academia Real de Ciencias y Artes Barcelona (fgn. corr. mem.), Sigma Xi. Club: Elizabethan (New Haven). Author: (with C.O. Dunbar) Principles of Stratigraphy, 1957; The Tectonics of the Appalachians, 1970; also articles in field. Editor: Symposium on the Cambrian System, 3 vols., 1956, 61. Asst. editor Am. Jour. Sci., 1948-54, editor, 1954—. Address: Dept Geology Yale U New Haven CT 06520

RODGERS, JOHN BARNEY, architect; b. Norfolk, Va., Sept. 8, 1905; s. John Gilmour and Agnes Platt (Barney) R.; B.A., Princeton, 1926, M.F.A. in Arch., 1928; student of L. Mies Van Der Rohe, 1933-34; m. Ruth Easton, Mar. 18 1933; children—Anne E. (Mrs. Jackson T. Witherspoon III), Elizabeth B. With Skidmore, Owings & Merrill, architects, San Francisco, 1946-70, partner, 1948-70; prin. works include Mt. Zion Hosp., San Francisco, Cedars of Lebanon Hosp., Los Angeles, U.S. mil. installations in Japan, Okinawa, Guam, Philippines, Shell Oil Bldg., Melbourne, St. James project for Australian Mut. Provident Soc., Melbourne, Qantas Wentworth Hotel, Sydney, Australia, Kimberly Clark paper mill, Fullerton, Cal., Crown Zellerbach office bldg., San Francisco, Union Sq. Hyatt Hotel, Qantas Bldg., urban renewal planning for San Francisco and Sacramento, modernization San Francisco Civic Center Auditorium-Opera House and Veterans Bldg., San Francisco, also work on retirement communities; pvt. practice architecture, N.Y.C. and Chgo., 1935-42; asso. architect C.E., AUS, 1942-44, Navy Dept., 1944-45; asso. prof. arch. Ill. Inst. Tech., 1938-42; Mem. San Francisco Art Commn., 1951-53. Exec. bd. Bay Area council Boy Scouts Am., chmn. camping com., 1966-68, properties and devel. coms., 1968-75; chmn. architects com. Bay Area United Crusade, 1960-63, 70. Mem. A.I.A. (emeritus). Clubs: Pacific Union (San Francisco); Burlingame (Calif.) Country; Inverness (Calif.) Yacht. Home: 3200 Ralston Ave Burlingame CA 94010

RODGERS, JOHN EX, ins. co. exec.; b. Norton, Kans., Feb. 21, 1935; s. Alcide Edward and Freda (Van Diest) R.; B.S., U. Kans., 1958; M.B.A., Harvard, 1961; m. Patricia Andrus Hanson, Mar. 31, 1962; children—Scott, Todd. Mgr. advt. brands Procter & Gamble, Toronto, 1961-64; with New Eng. Mut. Life Ins. Co., Boston, 1964—, treas., 1970-75, v.p., 1972-79, sr. v.p., 1979—; corporator Provident Instn. Savs., Boston, 1972-78. Mem. finance com. Boston Archtl. Center, 1971—, chmn. finance com., 1975—, bd. dirs., 1975-79; asst. treas. Boston Symphony Orch., 1977—. Mem. Town Meeting, Wellesley, Mass., 1972-74. Trustee Forsyth Dental Center, Boston, 1970—, v.p., 1974—; bd. dirs. Shady Hill Sch. Served to 2d lt., inf. AUS, 1959. Internat. Farm Youth Exchange del., France, 1955. Mem. Harvard Bus. Sch. Assn. Boston (bd. govs. 1968, pres. 1975), Cambridge Hist. Soc. (dir.), Boston Com. Fgn. Relations (exec. com.). Club: Boston Econ. Home: 68 Lake View Ave Cambridge MA 02138 Office: 501 Boylston St Boston MA 02117

RODGERS, MARY (MRS. HENRY GUETTEL), composer; b. N.Y.C., Jan. 11, 1931; d. Richard and Dorothy (Feiner) R.; student Wellesley Coll., 1948-51; m. Julian B. Beaty, Jr., 1951 (div. 1957); children—Richard Rodgers, Linda Mackay, Constance Peck; m. 2d, Henry Guettel, Oct. 14, 1961; children—Adam, Alexander. Composer music, lyrics Some of My Best Friends Are Children, 1952; book and lyrics Three to Make Music, 1957; Mary Martin children's spl. Easter NBC-TV, 1957; music, lyrics Davy Jones Locker, 1957; composer Once Upon a Mattress, Broadway, 1959, Hot Spot, Broadway, 1963, Mad Show, New Theatre, 1966-67; Pinocchio for Bil Baird Marionettes, 1974; asst. to producer Philharmonic Young People's Concerts, CBS-TV, 1957-70; contbg. composer, editor Free To Be You and Me; author screenplay Freaky Friday. Trustee, Phillips Exeter Acad.; mem. adv. council Nat. Inst. Environ. Health Scis. Mem. ASCAP, Dramatists Guild (council), Authors League (council), Authors Guild, Writers Guild. Author: The Rotten Book, 1969; Freaky Friday, 1972; (with Dorothy Rodgers) A Word to the Wives, 1970; A Billion for Boris, 1974; monthly column Of Two Minds, McCall's mag., 1971-78. Club: Cosmopolitan. Home: 115 Central Park West New York City NY 10023

RODGERS, WILLIAM WOODSON, lawyer; b. Moberly, Mo., July 2, 1907; s. William and Elizabeth (Harris) R.; A.B., U. Mo., 1929; B.S., U. Okla., 1930, LL.B., 1933; m. Marguerite Louise Gurley, Mar. 9, 1935; children—William Woodson, James R. Admitted to Okla. bar, 1933; practice in Oklahoma City, 1933-37, Blackwell, 1937—; partner firm Rodgers, Rodgers & Boyd, 1938—. Chmn. bd. Security Bank & Trust Co., Blackwell, 1970—. Pres., Blackwell Council Youth; bd. regents No. Okla. Coll., Tonkawa, 1951—; past regent Okla. Baptist U.; past mayor Blackwell. Mem. Am., Okla., Kay County bar assns., Am. Judicature Soc., Blackwell C. of C., Phi Beta Kappa, Phi Delta Phi. Baptist. Rotarian (past pres. Blackwell). Home: 323 S 2d St Blackwell OK 74631 Office: Security Bank Bldg Blackwell OK 74631

RODIMER, FRANK JOSEPH, clergyman; b. Rockaway, N.J., Oct. 25, 1927; s. Frank Grant and Susan Elizabeth (Hiler) R.; student St. Charles Coll., Catonsville, Md., 1944-45; B.A., St. Mary's Coll.-Sem., Balt., 1947; postgrad. Immaculate Conception Sem., Darlington, N.J., 1947-50; S.T.L., Cath. U. Am., 1951, J.C.D., 1954. Ordained priest Roman Catholic Ch., 1951; asst. chancellor, 1954-64; chancellor, 1964-77; apptd. papal chaplain, 1963; apptd. 6th Bishop of Paterson (N.J.), 1977, ordained, 1978. Home: 178 Derrom Ave Paterson NJ 07054 Office: 777 Valley Rd Clifton NJ 07013*

RODINO, PETER WALLACE, JR., congressman; b. Newark, June 7, 1909; s. Peter and Margaret (Gerard) R.; LL.B., U. Newark (now Rutgers U.), 1937; LL.D., Lehigh U., 1975, Rutgers U., 1975, N.Y. Law Sch., 1975, Princeton U., 1975, Seton Hall U., 1976, Bklyn. Law Sch., 1976, Yeshiva U., 1979, Potomac Sch. Law, 1979; L.H.D., LeMoyne Coll., 1974, Gov.'s State U., 1977, Jersey City State Coll., 1977, Georgetown U., 1977; D.C.L., St. John's U., 1974; m. Marianna Stango, Dec. 27, 1941; children—Margaret (Mrs. Charles Stanziale, Jr.), Peter III. Admitted to N.J. bar, 1938; practiced gen. law Newark; mem. 81st-96th Congresses from 10th N.J. Dist., dean N.J. congl. delegation, chmn. House Com. on Judiciary, sr. mem. Select House Com. on Narcotics Abuse and Control. Del., Intergovtl. Com. for European Migration, 1962—, chmn., 1971-72; mem. Pres.'s Select Commn. Immigration Refugee Policy, Nat. Commn. for Rev. Antitrust Laws and Procedures; del. North Atlantic Assembly, 1962—, chmn. sci. and tech. com., to 1972, chmn. working group control narcotics; congl. observer Disarmament Conf., Geneva, 1958. Served with 1st U.S. Armored Div., in North Africa, Italy, with Mil. missions, Italian Army, discharged as capt., 1941-46. Decorated Bronze star (U.S.); Knight grand cross Order of Merit (Republic of Italy); Gold medal Knights of Lithuania; Knight Sovereign Order Malta; Knight comdr. Equestrian Order of St. Agata (Republic of San Marino); others; recipient citation for outstanding service Free Polish Govt. Guglielmo Marconi award Order Sons of Italy in America, 1967; A. Philip Randolph Inst. award, 1975; Humanitarian award Internat. B'nai B'rith, 1975; Hubert H. Humphrey Civil Rights award Leadership Conf. on Civil Rights, 1978, numerous others. Office: 970 Broad St Newark NJ 07102 also Room 2462 House Office Bldg Washington DC 20515. *The real security of this nation lies in the integrity of its institutions and the informed confidence of its people.*

RODMAN, CHARLES GILBERT, business exec.; b. Owego, N.Y., May 1, 1921; s. Lawrence L. and Lorena (Root) R.; B.S. in Econs., Wharton Sch. of U. Pa., 1943; LL.B., Harvard, 1949; m. Jane E. McCarthy, June 12, 1946; children—Lawrence L., Sarah J., Andrew C., John W. Admitted N.Y. bar, 1949; with firm Sullivan & Cromwell, N.Y.C., 1949-52; with Grand Union Co., 1952-76, exec. asst. to pres., 1957-60, v.p. operations, 1960-65, exec. v.p., 1965-66, pres., 1966-74, chmn. bd., 1974-76, also chief exec. officer, dir.; trustee Estate of W.T. Grant Co., Bankrupt, 1976—; dir. United Jersey Banks, Hackensack, N.J., United Jersey Banks, N.J. Bell Telephone Co.; dir. Nat. Assn. Food Chains, 1970-76. Mem. planning bd. Village of Ridgewood, N.J., 1965-67. Trustee Valley Hosp., Ridgewood, N.J.; bd. fellows Fairleigh Dickinson U., 1966-69. Home: 110 Sheridan Terr Ridgewood NJ 07450

RODMAN, GEORGE BUSH, educator; b. Frankfort, Ky., Sept. 11, 1911; s. Edmund Berry and Mary Talbot (Dudley) R.; B.A., Centre Coll. Ky., 1932; M.A., U. Va., 1934; Ph.D., U. Wis., 1940; m. Elizabeth Carleton Sperry, Aug. 19, 1939; children—George Bush, James Sperry. Instr., U. Ark., 1940-43; asst. prof. English, U. Wis., 1946-47, asso. prof., 1947-54, prof., 1954—, chmn. dept. extension div., 1946-64, Center System, 1964-79. Served to lt. USNR, 1943-46. Mem. Omicron Delta Kappa, Delta Kappa Epsilon. Editor: (with Robert Doremus and Edgar Lacy) Patterns in Writing, 3d edit., 1963. Home: 5134 Whitcomb Dr Madison WI 53711

RODMAN, HARRY EUGENE, educator, architect, acoustical cons.; b. Plainfield, Iowa, Sept. 29, 1913; s. Harry Irwin and Iva (Reade) R.; B. Archtl. Engring., Iowa State U., 1936; M.Arch., Harvard, 1937; m. Marion G. Rooney, Feb. 14, 1942; children—Harry Eugene, Bruce Ervin, Gerald Reade, Blair Douglas. Instr. Wash. State U., 1937-41; designer Austin Co., Cleve., 1941-45; asso. architect U. Ill. at Urbana, 1945-46; mem. faculty Rensselaer Poly. Inst., 1946-78, prof. architecture, 1955-78; vis. prof. Sch. Architecture and Environ. Design, Calif. Poly. State U., 1979—; profl. practice, Troy, N.Y., 1946—; cons. in field, 1946—. Chmn. N.Y. State Bd. Examiners Architects, 1962-64; bd. dirs. Nat. Council Archtl. Registration Bds., 1964-71, sec., 1967-71, chmn. com. exams., 1965-70; sec. Nat. Archtl. Accrediting Bd., 1969-70; mem. tech. adv. com. Illuminating Engring. Research Inst., 1972—; mem. U.S. nat. com. Internat. Commn. on Illumination. Mem. exec. bd. Uncle Sam council Boy Scouts Am., 1956-70. Fellow A.I.A. (pres. Eastern N.Y. chpt. 1952, bd. dirs. 1953); mem. N.Y. State Assn. Architects (bd. dirs. 1954); asso. Acoustical Soc. Am.; mem. Allied Arts Com., Illuminating Engring. Soc. (vice chmn. Mohawk-Hudson sect. 1956, bd. mgrs. 1971—), Am. Arbitration Assn. (panel constrn. arbitrators), Sigma Xi, Tau Beta Pi, Tau Sigma Delta, Scarab. Contbr. to profl. jours. Home: RD 2 Petersburg NY 12138

RODMAN, HUGH BURGESS, educator; b. Louisville, Nov. 10, 1908; s. Paul E. and Edna (Burgess) R.; student St. Mary's (Kans.) Coll., 1925-27; B.A., Xavier U., 1933, M.A., 1934. Joined Soc. of Jesus, 1929, ordained priest Roman Cath. Ch., 1942. Instr. Loyola U., Chgo., 1937-38; asst. dean John Carrol U., 1944-56, Xavier U., 1956-58; asso. dean Loyola U., Chgo., 1958-70. Democrat. Home: 6525 Sheridan Rd Chicago IL 60626

RODMAN, JAMES PURCELL, astrophysicist, educator; b. Alliance, Ohio, Nov. 11, 1926; s. Clarence James and Hazel (Purcell) R.; B.S., in Physics, Chemistry and Math., Mt. Union Coll., 1949; M.A. in Nuclear Physics, Washington U., St. Louis, 1951; Ph.D. in Astrophysics, Yale U., 1963; m. Margaret Jane Kinsey, Aug. 14, 1950; children—William James, Jeffrey Kinsey, David Lawrence, Gretchen. Sec., Alliance Ware, Inc., 1954-55, Alliance Machine Co., 1959-69; v.p., treas. Alliance Tool Co., 1951-54, pres., 1954-59; instr. dept. physics and math. Mr. Union Coll., Alliance, 1951-59, asso. prof. physics, 1962-66, prof., 1966—, head dept. physics, 1963-65, head dept. physics and astronomy, 1965-74, 77—, dir. Clarke Obs., 1953—, dir. Computer Center, 1967-74, 77, recipient Gt. Tchr. award, 1976; research asso. dept. astronomy Yale U., 1963-68; cons. astrophys. engr. astron. instrumentation, 1962—; dir. United Nat. Bank & Trust Co. Mem. Alliance Bd. Edn., 1957-59, pres. 1959; exec. com. Buckeye council Boy Scouts Am., 1963-77, mem. nat. scouting com., 1973-77; dep. sheriff Stark County, 1972—; spl. police officer Alliance Police Dept., 1974—, tech. ins., 1976—; exec. com. Stark County Disaster Services, 1976-78, chmn., 1979; trustee Western Res. Acad., 1969—. Served with USNR, 1944-45. Recipient Alliance Mayor's Award as outstanding citizen, 1978. Fellow AAAS, Royal Astron. Soc.; mem. Am. Phys. Soc., Am. Astron. Soc., Astron. Soc. Pacific, Am. Assn. Physics tchrs., Optical Soc. Am., Am. Geoghys. Union, Nantucket Maria Mitchell Assn. (pres. 1974), Sigma Xi. Republican. Clubs: Masons (32 deg. Shriner, K.T.), Corinthian Yacht, Cape May (N.J.) Beach, Alliance Country. Contbr. articles to profl. jours. Home: 1125 Fernwood Blvd Alliance OH 44601 also 1613 Beach Ave Cape May NJ 08204

RODMAN, LEROY ELI, lawyer; b. N.Y.C., Feb. 22, 1914; s. Morris and Sadie (Specter) R.; A.B., Coll. City N.Y., 1933; J.D. (James Kent scholar), Columbia, 1936; m. Toby Chertcoff, Mar. 14, 1943; children—John Stephen, Lawrence Bernard. Admitted to N.Y. bar, 1937; practiced in N.Y.C., 1937-42, 46—; law sec. to U.S. dist. judge, Bklyn., 1936; law asst. Am. Law Inst., N.Y.C., 1937; chief, food enforcement unit N.Y. Regional Office, OPA, 1942-43; mem. firms Lawrence R. Condon, 1937-42, Joseph & Rodman, 1946-53; mem., sr. partner firms Rodman, Maurer, & Dansker, 1964-73, Carro, Spanbock, Londin, Rodman, & Fass, 1973-78, Rodman & Rodman, 1978—. Tchr. fed. taxation Pace Coll., N.Y.C., 1953-55; dir., v.p., sec. Francosteel Corp., N.Y.C.; exec. bd. sec. Daval Steel Products. Bd. dirs. Manhattan council Boy Scouts Am., 1960—, v.p., 1961-68, pres., 1972-75, exec. bd. Greater N.Y. councils, 1972—, recipient certificates of service including Silver Beaver award, 1962. Served to capt. JAG Dept., AUS, 1943-46. Fellow Am. Coll. Probate Counsel; mem. Am. Bar Assn, N.Y. County Lawyers Assn., Assn. Bar City N.Y., Judge Adv. Assn., Phi Beta Kappa. Jewish (trustee, v.p. synagogue, pres. brotherhood 1958-60). Clubs: Univ. (N.Y.C.); Metropolis Country (sec. 1976-77, v.p. 1977-78, exec. bd. 1978—) (White Plains, N.Y.). Editorial bd. Columbia Law Rev., 1934-36. Contbr. articles to legal jours. Home: 535 E 86th St New York NY 10028 Office: 260 Madison Ave New York NY 10016. *Sincere and conscientious attention to all responsibilities, both professional and volunteer.*

RODMAN, MORTON JOSEPH, educator; b. Boston, Jan. 28, 1918; s. John J. and Sarah (Feldman) R.; B.S., Mass. Coll. Pharmacy, 1939; postgrad. Am. U., 1946, Boston U., 1949; Ph.D., Georgetown U., 1950; m. Beatrice Sher, Aug. 22, 1943 (dec.); children—John, Peter, Michael, William, Marcia, Elizabeth; m. 2d, Tessa Abramsky, July 30, 1974. Instr. New Eng. Coll. Pharmacy, 1939-41; chief purchasing officer drugs and chems. VA, Washington, 1946-47; asst. prof. pharmacology Rutgers U., 1950-53, asso. prof., 1953-57, prof. pharmacology, chmn. dept. pharmacology Coll. Pharmacy, 1957—; prepared, delivered TV series Science Scrapbook, 1957, Drugs and Your Mind, 1958, radio lecture series Drugs and Your Nervous System, 1959, The Dependent Society: The Use and Abuse of Drugs and Alcohol, 1970. Cons. poison accident activities hosps., health depts.; toxicology cons. USPHS Accident Prevention Program; cons. neuropharmacology and psychopharmacology VA; scientist USPHS Commd. Res., 1960—; vis. scientist NSF, Am. Assn. Colls. Pharmacy, 1963-65; mem. narcotic drug study commn. N.J. Legislature; narcotics study group Hosp. and Health Council Greater Newark; lectr. centennial meeting Pharm. Soc. Gt. Britain, 1963; mem. pharmacy adv. com. N.J. Blue Cross, 1970. Served to capt. 125th Inf. Regt., AUS, 1942-46. Recipient Man of Year award Rho Pi Phi, 1960; Lindback Found. award for distinguished teaching, 1962. Mem. A.M.A. (sci. affiliate; cons. council drugs), Am. Pub. Health Assn. (cons. 1960), Am. Pharm. Assn., A.A.A.S., Am. Assn. U. Profs., N.Y. Acad. Sci., Walter Reed Soc., Sigma Xi, Rho Chi, Rho Pi Phi, Delta Sigma Theta. Author: (with D.W. Smith) Pharmacology and Drug Therapy in Nursing, 1968, rev., 1979; (with J.R. DiPalma) Basic Readings in Drug Therapy, 1972, More Readings in Drug Therapy, 1973; (with D.W. Smith) Clinical Pharmacology in Nursing, 1974; (with A.M. Overbach) Drugs Used With Neonates During Pregnancy, 1975; Basic Drug Therapy, 1979; compiler Poisons and Antidotes sect. Physicians Desk Reference, rev. edit., 1960. Contbr. articles popular publs., sci. and profl. papers to jours. Home: 41 Wayland Dr Verona NJ 07044 Office: Rutgers Univ PO Box 789 Piscataway NJ 08854

RODMAN, NATHANIEL FULFORD, JR., pathologist; b. Norfolk, Va., July 24, 1926; s. Nathaniel F. and Elizabeth Lee (Jones) R.; student M.I.T., 1944-45; B.A., Princeton U., 1947; M.D., U. Pa., 1951; m. Martha Elizabeth Shmidheiser, June 13, 1951; children—Mary Hall, Nathaniel Fulford III, William S.; m. 2d, Jeanne Marjorie Andrew, Oct. 28, 1970; 1 dau., Anne Blount. Instr. pathology U. N.C., Chapel Hill, 1958-59, asst. prof., 1959-64, asso. prof., 1964-70; prof. U. Iowa, Iowa City, 1970-74; prof., chmn. dept. pathology W.Va. U., Morgantown, 1974—. Served with USN, 1944-45, to lt. M.C., 1953-55. Nat. Heart and Lung Inst. Research Career Devel. awardee, 1967-70. Mem. AMA, Internat. Acad. Pathology, Am. Assn. Pathologists, Am. Soc. Clin. Pathologists, Coll. Am. Pathologists, Electron Microscope Assn. Am., Assn. Pathology Chairmen, Internat. Soc. Haemostasis and Thrombosis, Am. Soc. Cytology, W.Va., Med. Assn., Monongalia County Med. Soc. Democrat. Episcopalian. Asso. editor Microvascular Research, 1974-77. Home: 804 Augusta Ave Morgantown WV 26505 Office: Dept Pathology WVa U Med Center Morgantown WV 26506

RODMAN, SUMNER, ins. exec.; b. Malden, Mass., Aug. 5, 1915; s. Nathan Markel and Sara Ruth (Slater) R.; A.B. cum laude, Harvard, 1935; m. Helen Rhoda Morris, July 2, 1942; children—Peter Warren, John Slater. Agt., Aetna Life and Casualty Co., Boston, 1935—; chmn. bd. Rodman Ins. Agy., Inc., Chestnut Hill, Mass.; life ins. adviser, 1953—. Pres., Boston Life Ins. and Trust Council, 1958-59. Bd. dirs. Jewish Family and Children's Service, Boston, 1953—, Boston Estate and Bus. Planning Council, 1960—, Youth Tennis Found. New Eng., 1963—, Simons-Gutman Found., 1965—; trustee Combined Jewish Philanthropies of Greater Boston, 1967—. Served to capt. AUS, 1941-46; ETO. C.L.U. Inst. fellow, 1952, 61. C.L.U. Mem. Am. Coll. Life Underwriters (trustee 1971-74), Boston Life Underwriters Assn. (pres. 1965-66), Am. Soc. C.L.U.'s (pres. 1972-73), Million Dollar Round Table (life), New Eng. Lawn Tennis Assn. (dir. 1966-68), World Affairs Council, Golden Key Soc. Jewish (v.p. temple). Clubs: Masons; Harvard, Harvard Varsity (Boston); Newton (Mass.) Squash and Tennis; Wightman Tennis Center (Weston, Mass.); Beefeater. Home: 94 Vine St Chestnut Hill MA 02167 Office: 1330 Boylston St Chestnut Hill MA 02167

RODNAN, GERALD PAUL, physician; b. N.Y.C., Oct. 3, 1927; s. Sam and Charlotte (Donner) R.; student N.Y. U., 1943-45; M.D., L.I. Coll. Medicine, 1949; m. Joan Bernstien, May 28, 1950; children—Leslie Ann, Andrew, Meredith Carol. Intern, Maimonides Hosp., Bklyn., 1949-51; asst. resident, resident medicine Duke U., 1951-53; clin. investigator Nat. Inst. Arthritis and Metabolic Diseases, 1953-55; mem. faculty U. Pitts. Med. Sch., 1955—, prof. medicine, 1967—. Served with USPHS, 1952-55. Diplomate Am. Bd. Internal Medicine (gov.). Fellow A.C.P.; mem. Am. Rheumatism Assn. (pres. 1975-76), Am. Fedn. Clin. Research, Central Soc. Clin. Research, Am. Assn. History Medicine, Scleroderma Club (founder), Alpha Omega Alpha. Jewish. Editor: Primer on the Rheumatic Diseases, 7th edit., 1973; editorial bd. Arthritis and Rheumatism, Clinics on Rheumatic Diseases; editor Bull. Rheumatic Diseases. Home: 1306 Murray Ave Pittsburgh PA 15217 Office: 985 Scaife Hall Dept Medicine Univ Pitts Med Sch Pittsburgh PA 15261

RODNICK, DAVID, anthropologist, educator; b. New Haven, May 10, 1908; s. Louis David and Bryna (Kaplan) R.; B.S., N.Y. U., 1931; M.A., Yale U., 1933; Ph.D., U. Pa., 1936; m. Elizabeth Wright Amis, Mar. 24, 1945; 1 dau., Amie Bowman. Asst. dir. Inst. Internat. Social Research, Princeton, N.J., 1955-59; chmn., prof. div. social scis. Inter Am. U., P.R., 1959-61; prof. sociology and anthropology Iowa Wesleyan Coll., 1961-63; sr. sociologist Ops. Research, Inc., Washington, 1963-65; prof. sociology and anthropology Tex. Technol. U., Lubbock, 1965-75; vis. prof. U. Hamburg (W. Ger.), 1975-77, cons., 1977—; cons. Columbia U. Project in Contemporary Cultures, 1947-51. Social Sci. Research Council grantee; Fulbright Sr. Research prof. in Norway and Germany. Fellow Am. Sociol. Assn., Am. Anthrop. Assn., Soc. Applied Anthropology, AAAS; mem. Soc. Internat. Devel., Soc. History of Tech., Am. Acad. Polit. and Social Sci., Internat. Studies Assn. Author: The Fort Belknap Assiniboine, 1938, reprinted, 1978; Postwar Germans, 1948; The Norwegians, 1955; An Introduction to Man and His Development, 1966; The Strangled Democracy, 1970; Essays on an America in Transition, 1972; Man's Quest For Autonomy, 1974; A Portrait of Two German Cities: Lübeck and Hamburg, 1979; contbr. articles to profl. jours. Home: 4806 17th St Lubbock TX 79416

RODNICK, ELIOT HERMAN, psychologist, educator; b. New Haven, Nov. 27, 1911; s. Louis D. and Bertha (Caplan) R.; A.B., Yale, 1933, Ph.D., 1936; m. Helen Percival Hollander, Nov. 20, 1940; children—Jonathan Eliot, Marion Percival. Asst. research Yale, 1934-36; research psychologist, research service Worcester (Mass.) State Hosp., 1936-46, dir. psychol. research, chief psychologist, 1946-49; acting dir. Worcester Child Guidance Clinic, 1946-47, instr. Mt. Holyoke Coll., 1939; asst. prof. psychology Clark U., 1942-46, asso. prof. 1946-49 vis. lectr. summer session, U. Wis., 1949, Harvard, 1952, U. Colo., 1958; prof. psychology, dir. clin. tng. psychology Duke U., 1949-57, chmn. dept. psychology, 1951-61; prof. psychology, dir. clin. tng. psychology U. Calif. at Los Angeles, 1961-79, prof. emeritus, 1979—; cons. psychologist VA 1949—, mem. central office adv. com. to chief, dept. psychiatry and neurology, 1957-61; mem. mental health study sect. NIH, 1954-57, behavorial sci. study sect., 1957, mental health projects rev. commn., 1957-60, chmn. spl. mental health grants rev. com., 1960-62; dir. Los Angeles Psychiat. Service, 1961-66; dir. Didi Hirsch Mental Health Center, 1973—; cons. Calif. Dept. Mental Hygiene; mem. com. on research tng. in biol. scis. Nat. Inst. Mental Health, 1962-66, chmn., 1965-66; mem. mental health council Western Commn. Higher Edn., 1961-66; adv. com. abuse of stimulant and depressant drugs FDA, 1966-68; sci. add. com. on drug abuse U.S. Dept. Justice, 1968-75. Cons. Narcotics Control Commn. N.Y., 1969—. Commd. officer USPHS. Recipient Stanley Dean prize for outstanding research in schizophrenia, 1967; Wilbur Lucius Cross medal for outstanding profl. performance Yale Grad. Sch. Assn., 1975. Mem. N.Y. Acad. Scis., Am. (dir. 1962-65, Distinguished Contbn. to Clin. Psychology award 1976), Calif. (Distinguished Sci. Contbns. in Psychology award 1975), Western (pres. 1966-67), Los Angeles County, N.C. (past pres.) psychol. assns., Am. Orthopsychiat. Assn. (dir. 1966-69, pres. 1967-68), AAAS, AAUP, Phi Beta Kappa, Sigma Xi. Club: Cosmos (Washington). Editorial bd.: Am. Jour. Orthopsychiatry, 1954-57, Jour. Personality, 1955-60, Jour. Abnormal and Social Psychology, 1957-62, Am. Jour. Community Psychology, 1972-77, Family Process, 1977—. Home: 21446 Rambla Vista Malibu CA 90265 Office: Dept Psychology U Cal 405 Hilgard Ave Los Angeles CA 90024

RODOCANACHI-ROIDI, STAMATY, steel co. exec.; b. Genoa, Italy, May 6, 1911; s. Dimitri Rodocanachi and Maria Corradi; indsl. engr. degree Universita di Ingegneria di Genova, Genoa, Italy, 1934. Mgr. Italsider, Italy, 1935-45; with Compagnia Tecnica Internazionale S.p.A., 1946—, exec. v.p., 1947—; vice chmn. Tubos de Acero de Mexico S.A., Mexico City, 1969—. Served with Italian Army, 1936-37. Clubs: Jockey (Buenos Aires, Argentina); Yacht (Genoa). Home: 1220 Monte Libano Mexico DF 10 Mexico Office: 15 Calle Paris Mexico DF 4 Mexico

RODRIGUES, PERCY, actor. Appeared on TV program Peyton Place, also appearances Most Wanted, Star Trek, Sanford & Son; theatrical appearance in Blues for Mr. Charlie, 1968; appeared in films The Sweet Ride, 1968, The Plainsman, 1967, The Heart Is a Lonely Hunter, 1970, Come Back, Charleston Blue, 1972; appeared in TV movies The Lives of Jenny Dolan, 1975, The Last Survivors, 1975, Genesis II, 1973, Most Wanted, 1976, Enigma, 1977; appeared in TV series The Silent Force, 1971, ltd. series Executive Suite, 1976-77, The Moneychangers, 1976. Address: care Robert Raison Assos 9575 Lime Orchard Rd Beverly Hills CA 90210*

RODRIGUEZ, FERDINAND, chem. engr.; b. Cleve., July 8, 1928; s. Jose and Concha (Luis) R.; B.S., Case Western Res. U., 1950, M.S., 1954; Ph.D., Cornell U., 1958; m. Ethel V. Koster, July 28, 1951; children—Holly Edith, Lida Concha. Devel. engr. Ferro Corp., Bedford, Ohio, 1950-54; asst. prof. chem. engring. Cornell U., 1958-61, asso. prof., 1961-71, prof., 1971—; on sabbatic leave at Union Carbide Corp., 1964-65, Imperial Chem. Industries, Ltd., 1971, Eastman Kodak Co., 1978-79; cons. to industry. Served with U.S. Army, 1954-56. Recipient Excellence in Teaching award Cornell Soc. Engrs., 1966. Mem. Am. Chem. Soc., Am. Inst. Chem. Engrs., Soc. Rheology. Lutheran. Author: Principles of Polymer Systems, 1970; contbr. numerous articles to profl. jours.; songwriter. Home: 107 Randolph Rd Ithaca NY 14850 Office: 144 Olin Hall Cornell U Ithaca NY 14853

RODRIGUEZ, JOHN RAUL DAVIS, singer, songwriter; b. Sabinal, Tex., Dec. 10; s. Andre and Isabel Rodriguez; ed. public schs. Performed at Alamo Village Resort, Brackettville, Tex., 1970-71; guitarist with Tom. T. Hall and the Storytellers, 1972; solo artist, 1972—; compositions include: Pass Me By, You Always Come Back to Hurting Me, Ridin' My Thumb to Mexico; albums include: Introducing Johnny Rodriguez, All I Ever Meant to do Was Sing, Just Get Up And Close the Door, Love Put a Song in My Heart, Reflecting, Sketches. Recipient 4 Gold Album awards. Office: care Jim Halsey Co Inc Corp Pl Penthouse 5800 E Skelly Dr Tulsa OK 74135*

RODRIGUEZ, JUAN GUADALUPE, entomologist; b. Espanola, N.Mex., Dec. 23, 1920; s. Manuel D. and Lugardita (Salazar) R.; B.S., N.Mex. State U., 1943; M.S., Ohio State U., 1946, Ph.D., 1949; m. Lorraine Ditzler, Apr. 17, 1948; children—Carmen, Teresa, Carla, Rosa. Asst. entomologist U. Ky., Lexington, 1949-55, asso. entomologist, 1955-61, prof. entomology, 1961—; adv. entomology Universidade de San Carlos, Guatemala, 1961; vis. scientist Warsaw U., 1961; sec. V Internat. Congress Acarology, 1978; del. internat. confs. Vienna, Moscow, San Jose, Costa Rica, Nottingham, Eng., Prague, Saalfelden, Austria. Bd. dirs. Lexington chpt. NCCJ. Served with inf., AUS, World War 11. Recipient Disting. Research award U. Ky. Alumni Assn., 1963; Thomas Poe Cooper award U. Ky. Coll. Agr., 1972. Mem. Am. Inst. Biol. Scis., Acarological Soc. Am. (gov.), Ky. Acad. Sci., AAAS, Can. Entomol. Soc., Ont. Entomol. Soc., Am. Entomol. Soc. (br. sec.-treas. 1963-65, br. com. man at large 1968-71), Order Ky. Cols., Sigma Xi (pres. U. Ky. chpt. 1977, Gamma Alpha, Gamma Sigma Delta. Roman Catholic. Editor: Insect and Mite Nutrition, 1972; Recent Advances in Acarology, vols. I and II, 1979; editorial bd. Internat. Jour. Acarology; contbr. articles to profl. jours. Home: 1550 Beacon Hill Rd Lexington KY 40504

RODRIGUEZ, MARIO EDGARDO, health ins. co. exec.; b. Ponce, P.R., Nov. 24, 1923; s. Buenaventura and Manuela (Olmo) R.; B.B.A., U. P.R., 1949; postgrad. U. Pa., 1958-60, Northwestern U., 1961; m. Maria Cristina Jusino, Dec. 6, 1953; children—Cristina Maritza, Myra Cristina, Mario Edgardo, Edgardo Aramis. With Govt. Devel. Bank for P.R., San Juan, 1949-75, v.p. operations, 1962-72, comptroller, 1965-72, sr. v.p., comptroller, 1972-75; sr. v.p. Housing Investment Corp., Hato Rey, 1975-78; fin. dir. Seguros de Servicios de Salud, Inc., 1978—. Served to 1st lt., S.C., AUS, 1943-46, 50-52; Korea. C.P.A., P.R. Mem. P.R. Coll. C.P.A.'s, Investment Bankers Assn., Bank Adminstrn. Inst. Home: 389 Emory St Reparto U Rio Piedras PR 00926 Office: 203 Ponce de Leon Ave Hato Rey PR

RODRIGUEZ-BOU, ISMAEL, former univ. chancellor, cons.; b. Orocovis, P.R., Sept. 28, 1911; s. Francisco Rodriguez and Cristina Bou; B.A. in Edn., U. P.R.; M.A., Columbia U. Tchrs. Coll.; Ph.D., U. Tex.; postgrad. Central U. Madrid; hon. degree Catholic U. Dominican Republic, 1975; m. Gloria Ponsa Feliu, Oct. 28, 1948; children—Dora Sylvia, Ismael, Gloria M. Elementary and high sch. prin.; asst. supr. schs. P.R.; mem. faculty U. P.R., prof. psychology, chancellor, 1974-78; cons. to pres. Inter-Am. U. P.R., 1978—; sec., dir. ednl. research Superior Ednl. Council; cons. in field. Recipient Encomienda de Isabel La Catolica (Spain). Hon. mem. Tchrs. Assn. P.R., Am. Ednl. Research Assn., Acad. Puertorriquena de la Lengua, Phi Delta Kappa. Author papers in field. Home: 800 Vesta Dos Pinos Rio Piedra PR 00923

RODWIN, LLOYD, educator; b. N.Y.C., Sept. 14, 1919; s. Abraham and Nettie (Small) R.; B.S.S., Coll. City N.Y., 1935-39; certificate in housing New Sch. Social Research, 1939-40; fellow N.Y. Law Sch., 1940-41; M.A., U. Wis., 1945; M.P.A. (Littauer fellow 1945-46), Harvard, 1947, Ph.D., 1949; m. Nadine Suzanne Posniak, Dec. 26, 1943; children—Victor George, Marc André, Julie Ann. Intern U.S. Housing Authority, 1941; adminstrv. asst. Div. Def. Housing Coordination, 1941-43; research asst. U. Wis., 1944-45; research asso. city and regional planning Mass. Inst. Tech., 1946-47, asst. prof., 1947-51, asso. prof., 1951-59, prof. land econs., dept. city and regional planning, 1959-73, Ford Internat. prof., 1973—; dir. spl. program for urban and regional studies of developing areas Sch. of Architecture and Planning, 1967—, head dept. urban studies and planning, 1970-74; chmn. faculty com. Joint Center Urban Studies, Mass. Inst. Tech. and Harvard, 1959-69; Fulbright sr. lectr. U. Liverpool, 1951-52; vis. lectr. New Sch. Social Research, 1951, U. Calif., summer 1952, U. P.R., 1954; Guggenheim fellow, 1964-65; vis. prof. U. Calif. at Berkeley, 1969; vis. fellow Churchill Coll., vis. asso. Martin Center Archtl. and Urban Studies, Cambridge (Eng.) U., 1974. Bd. dirs. Cambridge Center Adult Edn., 1954-59, Regional Sci. Research Inst. Served as pvt. AUS, 1944. Mem. Am. Econ. Assn., Regional Sci. Assn., Am. Inst. Planners, Internat. Fedn. Housing and Town Planning, Inter-Am. Soc. Planners, Nat. Housing Conf. Author: The British New Towns Policy, 1956; Housing and Economic Progress, 1961; Nations and Cities, 1970. Editor: The Future Metropolis, 1961; Planning Urban Growth and Regional Development, 1968. Asso. editor Daedalus, Jour. Am. Acad. Arts and Scis., 1961-66. Bd. editors The New Atlantis, 1968-69. Home: 15 Arlington St Cambridge MA 02140

ROE, BENSON BERTHEAU, surgeon, educator; b. Los Angeles, July 7, 1918; s. Hall and Helene Louise (Bertheau) R.; A.B., U. Calif., Berkeley, 1939; M.D. cum laude, Harvard U., 1943; m. Jane Faulkner St. John, Jan. 20, 1945; children—David B., Virginia St. John. Intern Mass. Gen. Hosp., Boston, 1943-44, resident, 1946-50; Nat. Research fellow, dept. physiology Harvard Med. Sch., 1947; Moseley traveling fellow U. Edinburg (Scotland), 1951; instr. surgery Harvard Med. Sch., 1950; asst. clin. prof. surgery U. Calif., San Francisco, 1951-58, chief cardiothoracic surgery, 1958—, prof. surgery, 1966—; pvt. practice medicine specializing in cardiothoracic surgery, San Francisco, 1952—; cons. thoracic surgery VA Hosp., San Francisco Gen. Hosp.; cons. Baxter Labs., Ethicon, Inc. Bd. dirs. United Bay Area Crusade, 1958-70, mem. exec. com., 1964-65; bd. dirs. chmn. exec. com. San Francisco chpt. Am. Cancer Soc., 1955-57; bd. dirs. San Francisco Heart Assn., 1964-72, pres., 1964-65, chmn. research com., 1966-71; mem. various coms. Am. Heart Assn., 1967—. Served with USNR, 1944-46. Diplomate Am. Bd. Surgery, Am. Bd. Thoracic Surgery (dir. 1971—, chmn. program com. 1977, chmn. exam. com. 1978, chmn. long-range planning com., vice chmn. bd. 1979—). Fellow Am. Coll. Cardiology, A.C.S. (chmn. adv. council thoracic surgery, program chmn. thoracic surgery); mem. Am. Assn. Thoracic Surgery, AMA (residency rev. com. for thoracic surgery), Am., Pacific Coast surg. assns., Calif. Acad. Medicine (pres. 1974), Calif. Med. Assn., Howard C. Naffziger Surg. Soc., Internat. Cardiovascular Soc., Mid Century Surgeons Club, Samson Thoracic Surg. Soc., San Francisco County Med. Soc., Thoracic Surgery Dirs. Assn. (pres. 1979-80), San Francisco Surg. Soc., Soc. Thoracic Surgeons (council 1971—, pres. 1972), Soc. Univ. Surgeons, Soc. Vascular Surgery (past v.p.), Western Soc. Clin. Research, Chilean Soc. Cardiology, Am. Soc. Artificial Internal Organs, Harvard Med. Alumni Assn. (pres. No. Calif. chpt. 1974). Mem. editorial bd. Annals of Thoracic Surgery, 1969—. Contbr. numerous articles to profl. jours. Office: Dept Surgery U Calif San Francisco CA 94143. *Spawned in the Puritan Ethic and raised in the cross-fire between integrity and ruthless competition, I rapidly became addicted to ridiculous work habits and the pursuit of remote goals, sometimes substituting diligence and persistence for natural talent. Secret expectations of recognition and reward from this behavior overlooked political reality and led to some disappointments. Nevertheless, the satisfactions derived from measures to improve professional quality and accountability are well worth the frustrations and trauma suffered along the pathway.*

ROE, CHARLES RICHARD, baritone; b. Cleve., May 24, 1940; s. Andrews Rogers and Margaret (Dalton) R.; B.Mus., Baldwin-Wallace Coll., 1963; M.Mus., U. Ill., 1964; children by previous marriage—Charles Andrews, Richard Nevins, Robert Arthur. Instr. in music Tex. Tech. U., 1964-68; asst. prof. music Eastern Mich. U., 1968-74; vis. asso. prof. U. So. Calif., 1976-77, asso. prof., 1979—; vis. prof. and artist in residence Western Mich. U., 1978-79; leading singer N.Y.C. Opera, 1974—; appeared in leading roles with: Mich. Opera Theater, Ft. Worth Opera, Ky. Opera, Miss. Opera, Lake George Opera; appeared with symphonies: Phila., Cleve., Detroit, Toledo, Wichita, Duluth. Mem. Am. Guild Musical Artists, Actors Equity, Nat. Assn. Tchrs. Singing (S.W. region Singer of Year 1966), AAUP. Office: care Sch Music U So Calif Los Angeles CA 90007

ROE, INA LEA, editor; b. Wheat, Tenn., Nov. 25, 1930; d. William Ernest and Lucile Marie (Zimmerman) Gallaher; B.A., B.S., U. Tenn., 1952; M.S., Temple U., 1961; m. Donald Roe, Aug. 15, 1961. Technologist for doctors, Knoxville, Tenn., 1952-58; technologist Meml. Hosp., Chattanooga, 1958-59; mem. faculty dept. med. tech. Temple U., 1961-75, prof., 1973-75, clin. prof., 1975—; editor-in-chief Am. Jour. Med. Tech., Houston, 1970—; cons. med. lab. sci. edn. programs, 1970—. Mem. bd. Nat. Accrediting Agy. Clin. Lab. Scis., 1969-76, chmn. rev. bd., 1975-76. Recipient Mendelson award Am. Soc. Med. Tech. Edn. and Research Fund, 1975. Mem. Am. (named Outstanding Med. Technologist of Year 1973), Pa. (pres. 1972-73), Tenn. socs. med. tech., Acad. Clin. Lab. Scientists and Physicians, Alpha Mu Tau, Sigma Kappa. Author articles in field. Home: Route 1 Box 236-A Spring City TN 37381

ROE, JERROLD MELVIN, investments exec.; b. Industry, Ill., May 29, 1933; s. William Sampson and Lena (Flinn) R.; B.A. in Commerce, U. Notre Dame, 1955; postgrad. Loyola U. Law Sch., Chgo., 1958-58, Georgetown Grad. Law Sch., 1959; m. Marilyn Matacia, Jan. 17, 1959; children—Michael, Emily, Timothy, Kathleen, Daniel, Jennifer. Mgr. accounting operations Md. div. Litton Industries, 1958-60; asso. Robert Heller Assos., Cleve., 1960-64; v.p. planning Greatamerica Corp., also exec. v.p. First Western Bank, Los Angeles, 1964-68; chmn. bd. Minn. Nat. Life Ins. Co., 1968; pres. G.S.I. Inc., Chgo., 1973—. Served to lt. (j.g.) USNR, 1955-57. Clubs: California (Los Angeles); Union League (Chgo.); Butler National Golf (Oak Brook, La Jolla Country: Springs Country (Rancho Mirage, Calif.). Home: 1580 El Camino Del Teatro La Jolla CA 92037 Office: 222 N Dearborn St Chicago IL 60601

ROE, KENNETH ANDREW, engring. co. exec.; b. Perry, N.Y., Jan. 31, 1916; s. Ralph Coats and Esther Mae (Bishop) R.; B.A., Columbia U., 1938; B.S. in Chem. Engring., Mass. Inst. Tech., 1941; M.S. in Mech. Engring., U. Pa., 1946; D.Eng. (hon.), Stevens Inst. Tech., 1978; m. Hazel Winifred Thropp, Feb. 22, 1942; children—Ralph Coats, Randall Brewster, Kenneth Keith, Hollace Lindsey, Willis Barton. With Burns and Roe, Inc., N.Y.C., 1938—, exec. v.p., 1953-64, pres., 1963—, chmn. bd., 1971—; trustee, past chmn. exec. com. council engring. affairs, mem. com. acad. affairs of bd. trustees Manhattan Coll.; mem. bd. overseers U. Pa. Coll. Engring. and Applied Scis.; trustee, mem. exec. com. Stevens Inst. Tech.; mem. engring. council Columbia U., founding mem. Columbia Engring. Affiliate; bd. dirs., investment adv. com. U.S. nat. com. World Energy Conf. Trustee Round Hill Community Ch., Greenwich, Conn., 1972—; adv. council Bergen council Boy Scouts Am., 1974; past chmn. N.J. Conf. Promotion Better Govt.; past trustee Brit.-Am. Found. Served to lt. comdr. USNR, 1941-45. Recipient Karl Kayan award Columbia U., 1977. Registered profl. engr., 27 states; certificate Nat. Council Engring. Examiners. Fellow AAAS, Inst. Mech. Engrs. (Eng.), Inst. Engrs. (Australia); hon. mem. ASME (past v.p., pres.; Engring. award 1965); mem. Nat. Acad. Engring., Engrs. Joint Council (1st v.p. 1976-77, pres. 1978—), Am. Nuclear Soc., Am. Inst. Aeros. and Astronautics, IEEE, Nat., N.J. socs. profl. engrs., TAPPI (asso.), Electro-Chem. Soc., Am. Chem. Soc. (sr.), Am. Mgmt. Assn. (pres. assn.), Am. Soc. Quality Control, Am. Inst. Chem. Engrs., Pub. Utilities Assn. Virginias, ASCE, Am. Soc. Engring. Edn., Columbia U. Engring. Alumni Assn. (life; chmn. fund 1978-79), Brit. Nuclear Energy Soc. Author numerous papers, articles in field. Home: Baldwin Farms North Greenwich CT 06830 Office: 550 Kinderkamack Rd Oradell NJ 07649

ROE, RICHARD C., home furnishings mfg. co. exec.; b. Des Moines, Iowa, Jan. 4, 1930; s. Lloyd E. and Mary E. (Nuzum) R.; B.S. in Indsl. Engring., Iowa State U., 1952; m. Sally McGlothlen, Dec. 27, 1952; children—Stephen James, Julie Ann. Indsl. engr. Maytag Co., Newton, Iowa, 1952-56; gen. mgr. mfg. Schnadig Corp., Chgo., 1956-66; group v.p. Sealy, Inc., Chgo., 1966—; pres. Sealy Spring Corp., 1972—, Sealy Furniture Corp., 1978—. Mem. vestry St. Philips Episcopal Ch., Palatine, Ill.; active local NCCJ. Registered profl. engr., Iowa, Ind., Ill. Mem. Am. Mgmt. Assn., Nat. Soc. Profl. Engrs., Am. Inst. Indsl. Engrs. Republican. Clubs: Merchants and Mfrs. (Chgo.) (bd. govs.); Elks. Patentee in field. Home: 1620 Pheasant Trail Inverness IL 60067 Office: 470 Merchandise Mart Chicago IL 60654

ROE, ROBERT A., congressman; b. Wayne, N.J., Feb. 28, 1924; s. Robert A. and Lillian (Thornton) R.; student Oreg. State U., Wash. State U. Former corp. exec.; mayor Wayne Township, 1956-61; mem. gov.'s cabinet, commr. conservation and econ. devel. State of N.J., Trenton, 1963-69; mem. 91st-96th congresses from 8th N.J. Dist.; mem. Pub. Works and Transp. Com., chmn. subcom. on econ. devel., mem. oversight and rev. subcom., surface transp. subcom., mem. Sci. and Tech. Com., subcoms. energy research and prodn., energy devel. and applications. Committeeman, Wayne Twp. Gov. Body, 1955-56; mem. Passaic County Bd. Chosen Freeholders, 1959-63, dir., 1962-63. Mem. exec. bd. Altaha council Boy Scouts Am., mem. nat. council; trustee Chilton Meml. Hosp.; mem. pres.'s adv. bd. Tombrock Coll., West Paterson, N.J.; mem. community adv. council William Paterson Coll. N.J. Served with AUS, World War II; ETO. Named Man of Year, N.J. Jr. C. of C., 1959, Water Conservationist of Yr., N.J. State Fedn. Sportsmen's Clubs, 1966, Ann. Golden Medal award Garden Clubs N.J., 1969, State of Israel Bonds Scroll of honor, 1971, D.A.V. citation, 1971, citations Nat. Small Bus. Assn., 1972, Pres.'s Com. Employment Handicapped, 1972, Nat. Humanitarian award Joint Handicapped Council Nat. Soc. Handicapped, 1972, Disting. Service award Nat. Council Urban Econ. Devel., 1975, numerous leadership and service awards. Hon. fellow Am. Acad. Med. Adminstrs.; mem. Wayne C. of C. (past pres.), V.F.W., Am. Legion. Optimist, Elk. Office: House Office Bldg Washington DC 20515

ROE, THOMAS ANDERSON, bldg. supply co. exec.; b. Greenville, S.C., May 29, 1927; s. Thomas Anderson and Leila (Cunningham) R.; B.S., Furman U., 1948; diploma in bus. mgmt. LaSalle Extension U., 1956; m. Bette Verner Bain, Oct. 14, 1950; children—Elizabeth Overton Roe Mason, Thomas Anderson, III, Philip Stradley, John Verner. Cancer research asst. Furman U., 1947-48; with Builder Marts of Am., Inc., Greenville, 1948—, pres., 1961-69, chmn. bd., 1969—, chief exec. officer, 1969-78; chmn. bd. First Piedmont Corp., First Piedmont Bank & Trust Co., 1967-74; pres. Greenville Housing Found., 1971-72; mem. Greenville County Redevel. Authority, 1971-75. Vice chmn. S.C. Republican Party, 1963-64; mem. Nat. Rep. Finance Com., 1963-64; hon. asst. sgt. at arms Rep. Nat. Conv., Chgo., 1960; bd. dirs. Greenville chpt. ARC, Nat. Found. Ileitis and Colitis; trustee Christ Ch. Episcopal Sch., 1970-72; past bd. dirs. Greenville United Cerebral Palsy, Greenville chpt. ARC; mem. Com. on Monetary Research and Edn. (Greenwich); active Little Theater Prodns. Named Builder of Yr., Greenville Home Builders Assn., 1962. Mem. Nat. Assn. Home Builders (mem. internat. housing com.), Greenville Home Builders Assn. (v.p. 1962-63), Nat. Lumber Bldg. Material Dealers Assn., Carolina (pres. 1965-66), Greenville (pres.) bldg. material dealers assns., Greenville C. of C. (dir. 1967-70, pres. 1970). Clubs: Players (pres. 1951), Sertoma (pres. local club 1960-61, Distinguished Service award 1959, Superior Leadership award 1961), Green Valley Country, Altamount (dir.), Poinsett, Piedmont Economics (pres.). Home: Altamount Rd Paris Mountain Box 4255 Greenville SC 29609

ROE, THOMAS COOMBE, utility co. dir.; b. Dover, Del., Sept. 22, 1914; s. John Moore and Elizabeth Lindale (Cooper) R.; B.S. in Elec. Engring., U. Del., 1935; m. Emma Lillian Scotton, Oct. 16, 1937; children—Thomas C., Margaret Ruth. With Eastern Shore Public Service, 1936-43; with Delmara Power & Light Co., 1943—, pres. subs., 1971-76, chmn. bd., 1976-79, dir., 1971—. Served with AUS, 1941-45. Mem. Salisbury Area C. of C. (past pres.). Republican. Methodist. Club: Rotary (past pres.). Office: 800 King St Wilmington DE 19899

ROE, WILLIAM PRICE, metals co. exec.; b. Dover, Del., Aug. 25, 1923; s. William Price and Grace Lee (Elliott) R.; student U. Pa., 1941-43; B.A., Vanderbilt U., 1947, M.S., 1948, Ph.D., 1951; m. Esther Jean Salmons, Feb. 23, 1943; children—Kathy Gibson, Janis Elliott. Chemist, Union Carbide Corp., South Charleston, W.Va., 1948-49; research metallurgist Titanium div. Nat. Lead Co., Sayreville, N.J., 1951-56; head phys. metallurgy sect. So. Research Inst., Birmingham, Ala., 1956-57; metallurgist Central Research dept. ASARCO, Inc., South Plainfield, N.J., 1957-60, research supt., 1960-63, mgr., 1963-69, dir. research, 1969-74, v.p., dir., 1974—; dir. Internat. Lead Zinc Research Orgn., Inc. Mem. com. visitors Sch. Engring., Vanderbilt U., 1975—. Served with AUS, 1943-46. Mem. Zinc Inst. (dir.), Selenium-Tellurium Devel. Assn. (dir.), Am. Inst. Mining, Metall. and Petroleum Engrs., Indsl. Research Inst., AAAS, Am. Soc. Metals. Club: Baltusrol (Springfield, N.J.). Home: 1041 Minisink Way Westfield NJ 07090 Office: ASARCO Inc 901 Oak Tree Rd South Plainfield NJ 07080

ROEBLING, MARY G., banker; b. West Collingswood, N.J.; d. I.D., Jr. and Mary W. (Simon) Gindhart; student bus. adminstrn., econs. and fin. U. Pa., econs. and fin. N.Y. U.; LL.D. (hon.), Ithaca Coll., 1954; D.S. in Bus. Adminstrn. (hon.), Bryant Coll.; D.Sc. (hon.), Muhlenberg Coll.; H.H.D. (hon.), Wilberforce U.; D.F.A. (hon.), Rider Coll.; D.C.S. (hon.), St. John's U.; m. Siegfried Roebling (dec.); children—Elizabeth (Mrs. D.J. Hobin), Paul. Chmn. bd. Nat. State Bank N.J., N.Y. World's Fair Corp., 1964-65; dir. Companion Life Ins. Co., N.Y., Tattersall Co., Trenton. Mem. adv. com. U.S. commr. gen. for Expo '67; pub. gov. Am. Stock Exchange, 1958-62; mem. Regional Adv. Com. on Banking Policies and Practices; econ. ambassador State N.J. Chmn., N.J. Citizens for Clean Water, 1969-70; mem. Ann. Assay Commn., 1971, Nat. Bus. Council on Consumer Affairs; mem. adv. com. N.J. Museum. Life trustee George C. Marshall Research Found., N.J. Dental Service Plan; mem. nat. adv. council Nat. Multiple Sclerosis Soc.; trustee Invest-in-America; adv. bd. Assn. U.S. Army; bd. govs. Del. Valley Council; vice chmn. N.J. Savs. Bond Com.; mem. 4th dist. Adv. Council Naval Affairs; bd. govs. Swedish Hist. Found.; nat. bd. Jr. Achievement Inc.; emeritus mem. adv. com. on women in services Dept. Def.; civilian aide to Sec. Army N.J.; citizens adv. council Com. on Status of Women; bd. dirs. Am. Mus. Immigration; chmn. N.J. Hospitalized Vets.'s Service; comptroller Trenton Parking Authority; founder Donnelly Meml. Hosp. Women's Com. Decorated Royal Order Vasa (Sweden); commendatore Order Star Solidarity (Italy); recipient Brotherhood award NCCJ; Nat. Assn. Ins. Women award; Distinguished Service award Marine Corps League; Golden Key award N.J. Fedn. Jewish Philanthropies; Spirit of Achievement award women's div. Albert Einstein Coll. Medicine; Holland award N.J. Fedn. Women's Clubs; Outstanding Civilian Service medal Dept. Army, 1969; Humanitarian award N.J. chpt. Nat. Arthritis Found., 1970; Four Chaplains award, 1969; Trenton chpt. Nat. Secs. Boss of Year award, 1969, Internat. Boss of Year award, 1972; Golden Plate award Am. Acad. Achievement; Jerusalem Holy City of Peace award State of Israel; others. Mem. Nat. Def. Transp. Assn. (v.p., life mem.), U.S. Council of I.C.C. (trustee), N.J. Conf. Christians and Jews, Swedish Colonial Soc., League Women Voters, Am. Inst. Banking, N.J. Investment Council, Am. Bankers Assn., Soc. Mayflower Descs., Colonial Daus. 17th Century, Trenton C. of C., N.J. Firemen's Mut. Benevolent Assn. (hon. life), D.A.R., Geneal. Soc. Pa., Bus. and Profl. Women's Club, Daus. Colonial Wars, Pilgrim John Howland Soc. Clubs: Zonta, Trenton Country, Lake Placid, Sea View Country, Contemporary (Trenton); Overseas Press (asso.); Am. Newspaper Women's (asso.), 1925 F Street (Washington). Home: 777 W State St Trenton NJ 08618 Office: 28 W State St Trenton NJ 08605. *Each day I Seek . . . to preserve my physical health; to grow in mental strength; to allocate my time wisely to most important things; to serve God and my church; to love all human beings, whatever their needs wherever they may be; to take pride in my homeland and my community, and work for their best interests; to be a dutiful daughter, a wise parent, a kind sister, a good neighbor, an efficient banker, a more tolerant, more generous, more ideal American woman.*

ROEBUCK, CARL ANGUS, educator; b. Toronto, Ont., Can., Feb. 23, 1914; s. Walter Martin and Maude Valerie (Brand) R.; B.A., U. Toronto, 1935, M.A., 1936; Ph.D, U. Chgo., 1941; student Am. Sch. Classical Studies, Athens, Greece, 1937-40; L.H.D., U. Vt., 1966; m. Mary Thorne Campbell, Apr. 9, 1947. Came to U.S., 1948, naturalized, 1952. Tchr. classics and ancient history Dalhousie U., 1943-48; faculty U. Chgo., 1948-52; chmn. classics dept. Northwestern U., 1954—, prof., 1957-62, John Evans prof. classics, 1962—; archaeol. work, Greece, Turkey, 1946-47, 54; mem. Inst. Advanced Study, Princeton, 1953-54. Guggenheim fellow, 1952-53; sr. fellow Nat. Endowment Humanities, 1968-69. Mem. Archaeol. Inst. Am. Author: The Asklepeion and Lerna, 1951; Ionian Trade and Colonization, 1959; The World of Ancient Times, 1966; editor: The Muses at Work, 1969.

ROEDDE, WILLIAM ADOLPH, librarian; b. Vancouver, B.C., Can., May 10, 1925; s. William August and Viola Maude (White) R.; B.A., U. B.C., 1950; B.L.S., McGill U., 1951; m. Helen Mary Gowans, May 1, 1950; children—Gretchen, Stephen. Librarian, Ft. William (Ont.) Pub. Library, 1951-53; dir. Northwestern Regional Library, Thunder Bay, Ont., 1953-58; asst. dir. provincial library service Ont. Dept. Edn., Toronto, 1958-60, dir., 1960—. Served with Royal Canadian Navy, 1944-46. Can. Council fellow, 1959. Mem. Canadian, Ont. library assns., Inst. Profl. Librarians. Home: 16 Oneida Ave Toronto ON M5J 2E3 Canada Office: 7th Floor 77 Bloor St W Toronto ON Canada

ROEDEL, PAUL ROBERT, steel co. exec.; b. Millville, N.J., June 15, 1927; s. Charles Howard and Irene (Voorhees) R.; B.S. in Accounting, Rider Coll., 1949; m. June Gilbert Adams, June 25, 1951; children—Beth Anne, Meg Adams. With Carpenter Tech. Corp., Reading, Pa., 1949—, asst. controller, 1957-65, controller, 1965-72, treas., 1972-73, v.p. fin., 1973-75, exec. v.p., 1975-79, pres., 1979—, dir., 1973—; dir. Am. Bank & Trust Co. Pa., Gen. Public Utilities Corp., 1979—. Bd. dirs. Hawk Mountain council Boy Scouts Am., Children's Home of Reading; trustee, treas. Reading Musical Found., 1969; bd. dirs., treas. Reading Center City Devel. Fund, 1976. Served with USNR, 1945-46. Mem. Fin. Execs. Inst., Am. Iron and Steel Inst., Reading-Berks C. of C. Home: 416 Wheatland Ave

Shillington PA 19607 Office: Carpenter Tech Corp 101 Bern St Reading PA 19603

ROEDEL, PHILIP MORGAN, govt. ofcl.; b. San Jose, Calif., Aug. 24, 1913; s. Wilhelm vonBrinken and Alice (Morgan) R.; A.B., Stanford, 1935, A.M., 1952; m. Geraldine Harney, June 30, 1939; children—David H., Deborah Ann (Mrs. Knutson). With Calif. Dept. Fish and Game, 1936-69, dir. marine fisheries research program Calif. Fisheries Lab., 1957-69; dir. Bur. Comml. Fisheries, Dept. Interior, 1970; dir. Nat. Marine Fisheries Service, Nat. Oceanic and Atmospheric Adminstrn., Dept. Commerce, 1970-73, coordinator marine recreation, 1973-75; fisheries advisor AID, 1975—; commr. Internat. No. Pacific Fisheries Commn., 1971-74. Sec., Calif. Marine Research Com., 1963-69; mem. or chief del. various U.S. fisheries dels., 1965—. Bd. dirs. Gulf and Caribbean Fisheries Inst. Served with AUS, 1943-46. Fellow Am. Inst. Fishery Research Biologists. Club: Cosmos (Washington). Contbr. articles to profl. jours. Home: 4932 Sentinel Dr Washington DC 20016 Office: AID Washington DC 20523

ROEDER, GEORGE ALBERT, JR., banker; b. Hackensack, N.J., Sept. 28, 1920; s. George Albert and Gertrude (Miller) R.; B.S. in Econs., U. Pa., 1942; M.B.A., Harvard, 1947; m. Anne T. Connor, June 7, 1947; children—Jane Anne, Russell K. With Chase Manhattan Bank, N.Y.C., 1947—, successively trainee, asst. cashier, asst. v.p., v.p., sr. v.p., 1947-61, exec. v.p., 1961-69, vice chmn., dir., 1969—; dir. Allied Stores Corp., Nat. Reins. Corp., Alliance Holdings, Ltd. Bd. dirs. United Fund Greater N.Y. Served from pfc. to maj. USMCR, 1942-45. Decorated Bronze Star. Mem. Phi Delta Theta. Home: 6 Dogwood Dr Madison NJ 07940 Office: 1 Chase Manhattan Plaza New York NY 10015

ROEDER, JOHN ANTHONY, educator; b. Buffalo, Sept. 17, 1917; s. Louis Frank and Dorothea (Stengel) R.; B.E., U. Buffalo, 1959, M.Ed., 1961; Ed.D., SUNY, Buffalo, 1972; m. Betty Schutrum; children—Wendy Roeder Sciolino, John D., Beth L. Roeder Sigrist. Tool and die maker, designer, engr., 1937-54; tchr. Trott Vocat. High Sch., Niagara Falls, N.Y., 1954-57; asst. prof. mech. tech., Erie Community Coll., Buffalo, 1957-61; prof., tchr. trainer N.Y. State Edn. Dept., Buffalo, 1961-62; prof. vocat. tech. edn. SUNY, Buffalo, 1962—; regional planner N.Y. State Edn. Dept., 1971; coordinator Leadership Inst., 1971-72; cons. Erie County Vocat. Study, 1964. Mem. North Forest Civic Assn.; trustee St. Johns Luth. Home for Children; bd. dirs. Protestant Home for Children, 1976—, Lutheran Social Services, Jamestown, N.Y., 1979—. Mem. Soc. Mfg. Engrs., Am. Vocat. Assn. (Life), N.Y. State Assn. Vocat. Indsl. Ednl. Orgns. (adviser), Assn. Vocat. Ednl. Adminstrs., N.Y. State Vocat. Tchrs. Assn. (leadership award 1972), Creative Problem Solving Found. Clubs: Masons, Shriners. Home: 92 Clearfield Dr Williamsville NY 14221 Office: 1300 Elmwood Ave Buffalo NY 14222. *If I can, as a professor, leader and family man, touch others, listen and educate; and if they can in turn communicate their ideas to me, we have both benefitted, and I have succeeded.*

ROEDER, ROBERT GAYLE, biochemist; b. Boonville, Ind., June 3, 1942; s. Frederick John and Helene (Bredenkamp) R.; B.A. summa cum laude (Gilbert scholar), Wabash Coll., 1964; M.S., U. Ill., 1965; Ph.D. (USPHS fellow), U. Wash., 1969; m. Suzanne Himsel, July 11, 1964; children—Kimberly, Michael. Am. Cancer Soc. fellow dept. embryology Carnegie Instn. Washington, Balt., 1969-71; asst. prof. biol. chemistry Washington U., St. Louis, 1971-75, asso. prof., 1975-76, prof., 1976—, prof. genetics, 1978—, James S. McDonnell prof. biochem. genetics, 1979—; cons. USPHS, 1975-79. NIH grantee, 1972—; NSF grantee, 1975-79; recipient Dreyfus Tchr.-Scholar award Dreyfus Found., 1976. Mem. AAAS, Am. Chem. Soc. (Eli Lilly award 1977), Phi Beta Kappa. Home: 919 S Bemiston Saint Louis MO 63105 Office: 660 S Euclid Saint Louis MO 63110

ROEHL, JOSEPH E., lawyer; b. Albuquerque, Feb. 17, 1913; s. H.C. and Elizabeth J. (Walsh) R.; B.A., U. N.Mex., 1936, postgrad., 1936-37; LL.B., U. Tex., 1946; m. Jeanne F. Scott, Nov. 1, 1938; children—James F., Jerrald J., Virginia J. News columnist, bus. mgr. N.Mex. Lobo, Albuquerque, 1934-36; spl. events, sports announcer sta. KOB, Albuquerque, 1935-37; advt. mgr. N.Mex. Sentinel, Santa Fe, 1938-40; owner operator Gas Palace, Albuquerque, 1940-42; asst. adminstr. OPA, 1942-44; promotion, merchandising mgr. sta. KNOW, Austin, Tex., 1945-46; librarian Supreme Ct. Tex., Austin, 1945-46; admitted to Tex. bar, 1946, N.Mex. bar, 1946; practice in Albuquerque, 1946—; law clk. U.S. Circuit Judge Sam G. Bratton, Albuquerque, 1946-47; asso. Simms & Modrall, 1947-53; mng. partner Modrall, Seymour, Sperling, Roehl & Harris, 1953-74; sr. partner Modrall, Sperling, Roehl, Harris & Sisk, 1953—; chmn. com. uniform jury instrns. Supreme Ct. N.M., 1962—; dir. Mountain States Mut. Casualty Ins. Co., 1977—. Pres., gen. mgr. Rio Grande Lumber Co., 1959-68; pres. Rico, Inc. Recipient First Nat. award for state bar activities, 1962. Mem. Fellows Am. Bar Assn., Am., Tex., N.Mex. bar assns., Sigma Chi. Roman Catholic. Elk. Co-author: New Mexico Civil Jury Instruction, 1966. Contbr. articles on law office econs. and mgmt. profl. jours.; speaker before profl. groups. Home: 4010 Avenida La Resolana NE Albuquerque NM 87110 Office: Public Service Building Albuquerque NM 87103

ROEHM, MACDONELL, JR., petroleum services co. exec.; b. Semerang, Indonesia, July 6, 1939; s. MacDonell and Mary Bennett (Cobb) R.; B.A., Colgate U., 1961; M.B.A., Harvard U., 1966; m. Nedra Ann Zeth, May 11, 1974. Fin. analyst Exxon Corp., 1966-68; asso. Lazard Freres, N.Y.C., 1968-71; gen. partner J. Bush & Co., N.Y.C., 1971-73; v.p. planning and devel. Cerro Corp., N.Y.C., 1973-75; v.p., treas. N L Industries, Inc., N.Y.C., 1976-79; sr. v.p. ops., devel. and planning N L Petroleum Services/N L Industries, Inc., Houston, 1979—. Served with U.S. Navy, 1961-64. Decorated Silver Star, Bronze star, Purple Heart. Office: 1717 S James Pl Houston TX 77056

ROEHR, JUERGEN HERMANN, chem. corp. exec.; b. Hirschberg, Germany, Sept. 29, 1931; came to U.S., 1971; s. Joachim Eggert and Elfriede Elise (Luecke) R.; B.S., U. Marburg, 1955, M.S., 1958, Ph.D., 1961; m. Sibylle Charlotte Mewes, Apr. 8, 1960; children—Joachim E., Stefan J. With Hoechst AG, Germany, 1962-71, prodn. mgr., 1969-71, Am. Hoechst Corp., 1971—, group v.p. prodn., tech. planning, Somerville, N.J., 1974-77, group v.p., Bayport works mgr., Houston, 1978—, also dir.; dir. Burdett Oxygen Co., Norristown, Pa., 1975—, C-R-O, Inc., Menomonee Falls, Wis., 1973—, Baybrook Nat. Bank, Friendswood, Tex., 1978—, Mem. Am. Chem. Soc., Soc. Chem. Industry, Nat. Petroleum Refiners Assn. (dir.). Clubs: Golfcrest Country (Pearland, Tex.), Roxiticus Country (Mendham, N.J.). Office: Am Hoechst Corp PO Box 58160 Houston TX 77058

ROELS, OSWALD ALBERT, oceanographer, educator; b. Temse, Belgium, Sept. 16, 1921; s. Ghisleen and Elvire (Heirwegh) R.; came to U.S., 1958, naturalized, 1965; B.S., U. Louvain (Belgium), 1940, M.S., 1942. Ph.D., 1944; m. Dorothy Mary Broadhurst, Sept. 16, 1950; 1 dau., Margaret Ann Roels Talarico. Sr. research asso. Lamont-Doherty Geol. Obs., Columbia, Palisades, N.Y., 1960-76; prof. Inst. Marine and Atmospheric Scis., City U. N.Y., 1969-76, adj. prof., 1976—; adj. prof. Rockefeller U., N.Y.C., 1969—; vis. research prof. Laval U., Quebec, Can., 1972—; dir. mariculture research Mariculture Research, Port Aransas (Tex.) Marine Lab., U. Tex. Marine Sci. Inst., 1976—. Served with Belgian Army, 1940. Recipient Postdoctoral award U. Brussels, 1945, U. Liverpool (Eng.), 1946, Sorbonne, 1957; Research Career Devel. award NIH, 1962-65; fellow WHO, 1957; Hoffman-LaRoche vis. lectr., 1974. Mem. AAAS, Am. Chem. Soc., Am. Inst. Nutrition, Am. Soc. Biol. Chemists, Am. Soc. Limnology and Oceanography, Chemici Lovanienses, Inst. Environ. Scis., Inst. Food Tech., Internat. Conf. Biochem. Lipids, Marine Tech. Soc., N.Y. Acad. Scis., N.Y. Lipid Club, Photoelectric Spectrometry Group Gt. Britain. Author numerous articles in field. Asso. editor Nutrition Revs., 1961-68. Home: 28 Hewit Dr Corpus Christi TX 78404 Office: Port Aransas Marine Lab UTMSI Port Aransas TX 78373

ROEMER, ELIZABETH, educator, astronomer; b. Oakland, Calif., Sept. 4, 1929; d. Richard Quirin and Elsie (Barlow) Roemer; B.A. with Honors (Bertha Dolbeer scholar), U. Calif. at Berkeley, 1950, Ph.D. (Lick Obs. fellow), 1955. Tchr. adult class Oakland pub. schs., 1950-52; lab technician U. Calif. at Mt. Hamilton, 1954-55; grad. research astronomer U. Calif. at Berkeley, 1955-56; research asso. Yerkes Obs., U. Chgo., 1956; astronomer U.S. Naval Obs., Flagstaff, Ariz., 1957-66; asso. prof. dept. astronomy, also in lunar and planetary lab. U. Ariz., Tucson, 1966-69, prof., 1969—. Chmn. working group on orbits and ephemerides of comets commn. 20 Internat. Astron. Union, 1964-79, v.p. comm. 20, 1979—, v.p. commn. 6, 1973-76, pres., 1976-79. Mem. adv. panels Office Naval Research, Nat. Acad. Scis.-NRC, NASA. Recipient Dorothea Klumpke Roberts prize U. Calif. at Berkeley, 1950, Mademoiselle Merit award, 1959; asteroid (1657) named Roemera, 1965; Benjamin Apthorp Gould prize Nat. Acad. Scis., 1971. Fellow AAAS (council 1966-69, 72-73), Royal Astron. Soc. (London); mem. Am. Astron. Soc. (program vis. profs. astronomy 1960-75, council 1967-70, chmn. div. dynamical astronomy 1974), Astron. Soc. Pacific (publs. com. 1962-73, Comet medal com. 1968-74; Donohoe lectr. 1962), Internat. Astron. Union, Am. Geophys. Union, Brit. Astron. Assn., Phi Beta Kappa, Sigma Xi. Research and numerous publs. on astrometry and astrophysics of comets and minor planets including 79 recoveries of returning periodic comets; visual and spectroscopic binary stars, computation of orbits of comets and minor planets, photog. astrometry. Office: Lunar and Planetary Lab U Ariz Tucson AZ 85721

ROEMER, MILTON IRWIN, physician, educator; b. Paterson, N.J., Mar. 24, 1916; s. Jacob and Mary (Rabinowitz) R.; B.A., Cornell U., 1936, M.A., 1939; M.D., N.Y. U., 1940; M.P.H., U. Mich., 1943; m. Ruth Rosenbaum. Sept. 1. 1939; children—John, Beth. Intern, Barnert Meml. Hosp., Paterson, 1940-41; with N.J. Health Dept., Trenton, 1941-42, USPHS, Washington, 1943-48; mem. faculty Yale U. Med. Sch., 1949-51; with WHO. Geneva, 1951-53, Sask. (Can.) Health Dept., 1953-56; mem. faculty Cornell U., 1957-61; prof. health adminstrn. U. Calif. Sch. Pub. Health, Los Angeles, 1962—; cons. in field. Diplomate Am. Bd. Preventive Medicine. Mem. Inst. Medicine, Am. Pub. Health Assn. (award for excellence in internat. health 1977), Am. Coll. Preventive Medicine, Internat. Epidemiol. Assn., Physicians Forum, Group Health Assn. Am., Phi Beta Kappa, Sigma Xi, Alpha Omega Alpha, Phi Kappa Phi, Delta Omega. Author numerous books, including: Rural Health Care, 1976; Health Care Systems in World Perspective, 1976; Comparative National Policies on Health Care, 1977. Home: 365 S Westgate Ave Los Angeles CA 90049 Office: Univ Calif Sch Pub Health Los Angeles CA 90024

ROEN, SHELDON R., publisher; b. N.Y.C.; s. Morris Rosenthal and Gussie (Weininger) R.; B.S., City U. N.Y., 1950, M.A., 1951; Ph.D., Columbia U., 1955; postgrad. New Sch. Social Research, 1951-53, Harvard Sch. Pub. Health, 1961-62; m. Selma Lois Pollets, Feb. 21, 1954; children—Randa M., Marjorie A., Harris L. Tchr. pub. schs., N.Y.C., 1950-53; chief Clin. Psychology Service, Ft. Sill, Okla., 1955-58; instr. Cameron Coll., Okla. A. and M. U., 1956-58; asst. prof. U. N.H., 1958-60; asst. chief psychol. services Mass. Mental Health Center, Boston, 1960-63; instr. Harvard, 1961-63, research asso. Med. Sch., 1960-63, dir. research S. Shore Mental Health Center, Quincy, Mass., 1962-66; asso. prof. dept. psychology Tchrs. Coll., Columbia, N.Y.C., 1966-72, dir. Psychol. Consultation Center, 1966-72; chmn. bd., pres. Human Scis. Press, N.Y.C., 1972—. Lectr., L.I. U., summer 1958, Tufts U., 1961-62; mem. N.H. Gov.'s Com. on Spl. Edn., also Study Com. on Mental Health Reorgn., 1961-62; cons. VISTA program OEO, 1966-67; mem. juvenile problems research rev. com. NIMH, 1968-69; mem. research rev. com. Title III, Elementary and Secondary Edn. Act project application Ohio Dept. Edn., 1969-72; mem. mental health coordinating com. local sch. dist. 5, N.Y.C., 1969-72; mem., research dir. work incentive program for welfare recipients Wharton Sch. Pa., U.S. Dept. Labor, 1969-72; mem. mental health and community control com. N.Y. Psychologists for Social Action, 1969-72. Chmn. bd. trustees Bristol Acres Sch., Taunton, Mass., 1965-67. Diplomate Am. Bd. Examiners in Profl. Psychology. Fellow Am. Psychol. Assn. (mem. com. pre-coll. behavioral scis. 1968-71, founder div. 27 community psychology div. 1969, chmn. subcom. pre-high sch. behavioral sci. 1969-72), Am. Pub. Health Assn., Am. Orthopsychiat. Assn. (com. on research edn. 1965-67), Am. Sociol. Assn.; mem. New Eng. (steering com. 1965-68), N.H. (legis. chmn. 1961-62) psychol. assns. Authors, editor books. Editor: Mass. Psychol. Assn. Newsletter, 1963-65; Community Mental Health Jour.; contbr. articles to profl. jours. and chpts. to books. Office: Human Scis Press 72 Fifth Ave New York NY 10011

ROEPER, ALBERT PETER, chem. co. exec.; b. N.Y.C., Sept. 2, 1916; s. Peter and Frida (Bossert) R.; certificate Pace Inst., 1939; student N.Y. U., 1940-42, 47-48; B.B.A., Pace Coll., 1952; m. Ruth Lillian Haas, July 17, 1943; children—Barbara, Robert. With Bank of N.Y., N.Y.C., 1933-40; controller J.H. Bunnell & Co., N.Y.C., 1940-42, 46-51, Self Winding Clock Co., N.Y.C., 1951-54; v.p., treas. Flight Refueling, Inc., Balt., 1954-62; treas. Thiokol Corp., Bristol, Pa., 1962—, also v.p. fin., dir. Served to capt. USAAF, 1942-46. Mem. Nat. Assn. Accountants (past nat. dir., past pres. Balt.), Fin. Execs. Inst. Club: Met. (N.Y.C.). Home: 568 Countess Dr Yardley PA 19067 Office: Thiokol Corp Newtown PA 18940

ROERICK, WILLIAM (GEORGE), actor, author; b. New Jersey, Dec. 17, 1912; s. William George and Josephine (Clark) R.; B.S., Hamilton Coll., Clinton, N.Y., 1934, D.F.A. (hon.), 1971; student Berkshire Playhouse Drama Sch., 1935. Broadway appearances include Romeo and Juliet, 1935, St. Joan, 1936, Hamlet, 1936, Our Town, 1938, The Land is Bright, 1941, This is the Army, 1942-45, Magnificent Yankee, 1946, Tonight at 8:30, 1948; Right Honourable Gentleman, 1961, Marat/Sade, 1967, The Homecoming, 1967, Waltz of the Toreadors, 1973, Night of the Iguana, 1976-77; film appearances include This is the Army, The Harder They Fall, Love Machine, Sporting Club, Separate Peace, 92 in the Shade, The Other Side of the Mountain; numerous TV appearances; co-author: The Happiest Years (play), 1949, A Passage to E.M. Forster (dramatic reading), 1970; author TV scripts for Mama, Claudia, Crime Photographer, Climax; bd. dirs. E.W. Root Art Center, Clinton, Plays for Living. Head zoning com. W. Hollywood Homeowners Assn.; vestryman St. Matthias Ch., Los Angeles. Served with AUS, 1942-45. Mem. Actors Equity Assn. (council 10 years), Screen Actors Guild. AFTRA, Dramatists Guild, Actors Fund Am. Home: 145 W 79th St New York City NY 10024 also Lost Farm Tyringham MA 01264

ROESCH, CLARENCE HENRY, banker; b. Egg Harbor City, N.J., Aug. 22, 1925; s. Joseph Aloysius and Bertha (Heumann) R.; B.B.A., N.J. Coll. Commerce, 1949; certificate Am. Inst. Banking, 1961; postgrad. Rutgers U., 1961; grad. Trust Sch., Bucknell U., 1971; m. Helen Regina Owens, Sept. 25, 1954; children—Kathleen Marie, Helena Patricia, Maryanne Cornelia. Bookkeeper, teller, head teller, asst. sec., trust officer, auditor Egg Harbor Bank & Trust Co., 1949-61; bank examiner Phila. Fed. Res. Bank, 1962-65; chief auditor Am. Bank & Trust Co. of Pa., Reading, 1966—, v.p. audit dept., auditor, 1968—; mem. faculty Berks County chpt. Am. Inst. Banking, 1966-68; instr. bank auditing Bank Adminstrn. Inst., U. Richmond, 1968. Mem. budget com. Berks County chpt. United Way, 1967-73. Bd. dirs., Berks Reading council Camp Fire Girls, 1966-78, chmn. finance com., 1973, 75, treas., 1975. Recipient John Johnston award as outstanding banker N.J., 1955, award U.S. Savs. Bond Com., 1961; Luther Halsey Gulick award for vol. services Camp Fire Girls, 1975. Certified internal auditor, data processing auditor. Mem. Inst. Internal Auditors (dir. central Pa. chpt.), Berks County Bankers Assn., Travelers Protective Assn., Berks Reading C. of C., Bank Adminstrn. Inst. (past pres., dir. Penn-Jersey chpt.), Am. Inst. Banking (past chpt. pres.). Home: 24 Medinah Dr Flying Hills Reading PA 19607 Office: 35 N 6th St Reading PA 19603

ROESCH, RAYMOND AUGUST, univ. pres., clergyman; b. Jenkintown, Pa., Sept. 16, 1914; s. Aloysius Adam and Anna Estelle (Fleck) R.; B.A., U. Dayton, 1936; M.A., Cath. U. Am., 1945; postgrad. Columbia, 1949; Ph.D., Fordham U., 1954; D. Pedagogy (hon.), Coll. of Steubenville, 1976; H.H.D. (hon.), Wright State U., 1979. High sch. tchr. Cathedral Latin Sch., Cleve., 1936-41; ordained priest Roman Catholic Ch., 1944; guidance dir. Chaminade High Sch., Mineola, N.Y., 1945-49; parish priest St. Mary's Ch., Mt.Vernon, N.Y., 1949-51; prof. psychology, chmn. dept. U. Dayton, 1951-59, pres., 1959—. Dir. Winters Nat. Bank & Trust Co. Pres., Dayton-Miami Valley Consortium, 1968—. Sec. bd. trustees Ohio Higher Edn. Assistance Commn.; mem. Ednl. Commn. of States, 1969—; mem. provincial council Cin. province, Soc. of Mary; mem. adv. council ROTC Affairs, 1963-66; mem. Ohio Higher Edn. Facilities Commn., 1968-78, 79—. Bd. dirs. Serenity Found., Dayton, Dayton Met. YMCA, 1975, Dayton ARC, 1979; chmn. bd. Ohio Found. Independent Colls., 1976—; bd. dirs. Montgomery Mental Health Assn., v.p., 1975-76, pres., 1976-77; trustee Good Samaritan Hosp., Dayton, Mary Manse Coll., Toledo; trustee; govs. bd. Ohio Scholarship Fund; mem. Dayton Area Progress Council, 1979. Recipient Distinguished Civilian Service award, 1969; Outstanding Service to Civic Affairs award Am. Soc. for Pub. Adminstrn., 1972; Distinguished Alumnus award, 1973; named to U. Dayton Hall of Fame, 1979. Mem. AAAS, Am., Am. Cath. psychol. assns., N.E.A., Ohio Coll. Assn. (pres. 1967-68), Assn. Am. Colls. (mem. commn. faculty and students 1965), Ind. Colls. and Univs. Ohio (v.p. 1968), Assn. Urban Univs. (v.p. 1976—), Phi Delta Kappa, Tau Alpha Pi. Rotarian. Home: 300 College Park Ave Dayton OH 45409

ROESGEN, JOHN FRANCIS, corp. exec.; b. Williamsport, Pa., June 3, 1928; s. Jacob Hubert and Margaret (Sparks) R.; B.S. in Econs., Villanova U., 1951; m. Marie G. Patrick, Sept. 20, 1952; children—John, Barbara, Susan, Richard, Nancy. Successively audit asst., senior, mgr. pub. accounting Arthur Andersen & Co., Phila., 1951-65; asst. controller Weyerhaeuser Co., Tacoma, Wash., 1965-70, comptroller Am. Home Products Corp., N.Y.C., 1970-75; sr. v.p., controller McKesson-Robbins Drug Co., San Francisco, 1975—. C.P.A., Pa. Mem. Am. Inst. C.P.A.'s, Financial Execs. Inst. Home: 357 Hartford Rd Danville CA 94526 Office: One Post St San Francisco CA 94104

ROESGEN, WILLIAM NEWELL, editor; b. Williamsport, Pa., May 15, 1931; s. Jacob H. and Margaret (Sparks) R.; B.S. in Social Sci., Fordham U., 1953; m. Joan Danneker, July 23, 1954; children—Susan, Richard, Andrew, Theodore. Mng. editor S. Haven (Mich.) Daily Tribune, 1954-58, Burlington (Vt.) Daily News, 1958-60, Sandusky (Ohio) Register, 1960-64; group editor Sandusky-Kingsport Group, 1962-74; editor Kingsport (Tenn.) Times-News, 1964-74, Billings (Mont.) Gazette, 1974—; asso. prof. journalism E. Tenn. State U., part-time 1966-74. Juror Pulitzer Prize, 1977-78; discussion leader Am. Press Inst. Mem. Am. Soc. Newspaper Editors. Home: 3653 Quimet Circle Billings MT 59102 Office: Billings Gazette Billings MT 59103

ROESLER, ROBERT HARRY, newspaper editor; b. Hammond, La., Oct. 5, 1927; s. Albert N. and Hilda (Schwartz) R.; student Tulane U.; m. Cloe Alferez, May 7, 1955; children—Kim, Bob, Toby. Mem. sports staff Times Picayune, New Orleans, 1949—, sports editor, 1964—. Served with USNR, World War II, Korean conflict. Mem. Profl. Football Writers Assn. Am. (pres. 1976, 77), Basketball Writers Assn., Am. Legion. Club: Press (pres. New Orleans 1959-60, sports writing awards). Home: 6958 Colbert St New Orleans LA 70124 Office: Times Picayune 3800 Howard Ave New Orleans LA 70125

ROESNER, LARRY AUGUST, civil engr.; b. Denver, Mar. 14, 1941; s. Walter George and Sarah Jane (Merrick) R.; B.A., Valparaiso (Ind.) U., 1963; M.S., Colo. State U., 1965; Ph.D., U. Wash., Seattle, 1969; m. Kathleen Ann Fahrenbruch, Dec. 13, 1964; children—David John, Kevin Walter, Nathan August, Melissa Jane. Part-time grad. research asst. Colo. State U., 1963-65, U. Wash., 1965-68; asso. engr., then sr. engr. Water Resources Engrs., Inc.. Walnut Creek, Calif., 1968-73, prin. engr., Walnut Creek, then Springfield, Va., 1973—; mem. exec. com. Urban Water Resources Research Council; guest lectr., cons. in field. Registered profl. engr., Calif., Va., Mich. Mem. ASCE (Outstanding Service award Student chpt. 1963, Nat. Walter L. Huber Civil Engring. Research prize 1975), Am. Geophys. Union. Republican. Lutheran. Author research reports, tech. revs. Home: 3721 Merlin Way Annandale VA 22003 Office: 8001 Forbes Pl Springfield VA 22151

ROESSLER, ROBERT LOUIS, physician, educator; b. Neillsville, Wis., Sept. 2, 1921; s. Julius Otto and Elizabeth Wilhelmina Anna (Pirwitz) R.; Ph.B., U. Wis., 1942; M.D., Columbia U., 1945; m. Eleanor Ramsdell, Nov. 6, 1946 (div.); children—Ronald, Christina, Erich; m. 2d, Martha Dukes Yow, July 27, 1974. Intern, Englewood (N.J.) Hosp., 1945-46; resident psychiatry VA Hosp., Madison, Wis., 1946-48, Strong Meml. Hosp., Rochester, N.Y., 1948-49; instr. psychiatry U. Rochester Med. Sch., 1949-50; asst. prof. psychiatry U. Wis. Med. Sch. 1950-52, asso. prof., 1952-60, prof., 1960-64, chmn. dept., 1957-61; prof. psychiatry Baylor Coll. Medicine, 1964—. Fellow Am. Coll. Psychiatrists, Am. Psychiat. Assn.; mem. AAAS, AAUP, Am. Psychosomatic Soc., Houston Psychiat. Soc., N.Y. Acad. Scis., Soc. Psychophysiol. Research (dir. 1966-73, pres. 1971-72), Wis. Psychiat. Assn. (pres. 1957-58), Sigma Xi. Editor: (with N.S. Greenfield) Physiological Correlates of Psychological Disorder, 1962; contbr. sci. papers to profl. jours. Office: 1200 Moursund Ave Houston TX 77030

ROESSLER, RONALD JAMES, lawyer; b. Kansas City, Mo., Aug. 10, 1939; s. Robert Louis and Eleanor Florence (Ramsdell) R.; B.A. in Govt., Miami U., 1961; postgrad. Law Sch., Duke U., 1961-62; J.D. Wis. Law Sch., 1964; LL.M., George Washington U., 1968; m. Sally Jo Canfield, Aug. 18, 1962; children—Martha Lee, Elizabeth Ramsdell. Admitted to Wis. bar, 1964, D.C. bar, 1970, W.Va. bar,

1971, Md. bar, 1972; atty. Dept. Agr., Washington, 1964-66, Office Gen. Counsel, CIA, Washington, 1966, 68-69, C & P Tel. Co., Washington, 1969-73; v.p., gen. counsel Alexander & Alexander Inc., Balt., 1972—. Bd. dirs. No. Va. chpt. Big Brothers Va., 1969-72. Served with USAF, 1966-68. Mem. Am., Fed., Wis., D.C., W. Va., Md. (chmn. com. on corp. law depts.) bar assns., Am. Judicature Soc. Home: 4303 Crab Orchard Rd Glen Arm MD 21057 Office: 300 E Joppa Rd Baltimore MD 21204

ROESSNER, GILBERT GEORGE, savs. and loan assn. exec.; b. Irvington, N.J., Apr. 27, 1918; s. John K. and Emma Dora (Kurz) R.; B.S., Rutgers U., 1940; 5 year diploma Am. Savings and Loan Inst.; grad. Internat. Sch. Bldg. Socs. Inst., Eng., 1964; m. Dorothy Anne Hector, Oct. 24, 1942; children—Dorothy Anne (Mrs. John W. Atherton, Jr.), Martha, Gilbert George, Jane (Mrs. John M. Ritchie), Barbara (Mrs. Steven W. Anderson), Katherine Kurz. With City Fed. Savs. & Loan Assn., Elizabeth, N.J., 1941—, dir., 1955, exec. v.p., 1958-69, pres., 1969—, chief exec. officer, 1970—, chmn., 1978—; mem. Fed. Savs. and Loan Adv. Council, 1974-75; mem. council Fed. Home Loan Mortgage Corp., 1977-79. Pres. Overlook Hosp. Assn., Summit, N.J., 1963; chmn. N.J. Bd. Higher Edn., 1973-75. Served with USNR, 1942-45. Mem. Nat. Savs. and Loan League (pres. 1973-74), N.J. Council Fed. Savs. Assns. (pres. 1964-65). Clubs: Baltusrol Golf (Springfield, N.J.); Beacon Hill (Summit); Lost Tree (North Palm Beach, Fla.); N.Y. Yacht. Home: 15 Norwood Ave Summit NJ 07901 Office: 1141 E Jersey St Elizabeth NJ 07201

ROESSNER, ROLAND GOMMEL, architect, educator; b. Terre Haute, Ind., Nov. 19, 1911; s. Elmer George and Florence Carol R.; B. Arch., Miami U., Oxford, Ohio, 1935; M. Arch., U. Cin., 1942; m. Virginia Gail Humberger, Nov. 17, 1943 (dec. Oct. 1955); 1 son, Roland Gommel. Asso., Grunkeymeyer & Sullivan & Assos., architects, engrs., Cin., 1935-42; designing architect; pvt. practice architecture schs., pvt. residences R. Gommel Roesener A.I.A., St. Petersburg, Fla., 1945-47, Austin, Tex., 1947—; asso. Creer & Roessner, cons. architects, Austin, 1958-63; owner R. Gommel Roessner, design cons., 1977—; prof. architecture U. Tex. Sch. Architecture, Austin, 1947—, chmn. design dept., 1954-67; mem. grad. faculty, 1958—, also acting dir., 1966, chmn. architecture scholarship com., 1960-67, founder, dir. profl. residency program, 1971—, mem. credit union bd., 1977—; profl. adviser community standards com. Dept. Commerce; mem. naval scholarship com. U. Tex., 1965-67, also mem. Naval Res. research unit; adviser design State (Tex.) Bd. Archtl. Registration, 1960-68. Served to lt. comdr. CEC, USNR, 1942-45. Recipient numerous awards, citations in Am., fgn. publs. for architecture. Registered architect, Ohio, Fla., Tex. Fellow AIA (mem. design com.); mem. Am. Concrete Inst., Am. Mil. Inst., Tex., Ohio, Fla. assns. architects, Nat. Council Archtl. Registration Bds., Univ. Coop. Soc. (chmn. bd. dirs.), Am. Legion, VFW A'telier, Delta Phi Delta, Alpha Rho Chi, Delta Upsilon. Methodist (trustee). Clubs: Optimist; Westwood Country; U. Tex. Faculty; Headliners, Tarryhouse. Contbr. articles to profl. publs. Home: 3416 Pecos Apt A Austin TX 78703

ROETHEL, DAVID ALBERT HILL, assn. exec.; b. Milw., Feb. 17, 1926; s. Albert John and Elsie Margaret (Hill) R.; B.S., Marquette U., 1950, M.S., 1952; certificate Oak Ridge Sch. Reactor Tech., 1953; m. Suzanne Harding Berger, Aug. 22, 1953; children—Elizabeth Jane, Susan Margaret. Chem. engr. naval reactors br. AEC, Washington, 1952-57; mgr. profl. relations, asst. to exec. sec. Am. Chem. Soc., Washington, 1957-72; exec. dir. Nat. Registry in Clin. Chemistry, Washington, 1967-72; exec. dir. Am. Assn. Clin. Chemists, Washington, 1968-70, Am. Orthotic and Prosthetic Assn., 1973-76, Am. Acad. Orthotists and Prosthetists, 1973-76, Am. Bd. Certification in Orthotics and Prosthetics, 1973-76; exec. dir., fellow Am. Inst. Chemists, Washington, 1977—, exec. dir. Nat. Certification Commn. in Chemistry and Chem. Engring., 1977—; sec., vice chmn., then chmn. Intersoc. Com. on Health Lab. Services, 1966-72; v.p. Pensions for Profls., Inc., Washington, 1970-72. Chmn. Engrs. and Scientists Joint Commn. on Pensions, 1979; mem. Sci. Manpower Commn., 1978-79, sec.-treas., 1979. Mem. Md. Gov.'s Com. on Sci. Devel., 1969, Served with U.S. Army, 1944-46; CBI. Mem. Am. Chem. Soc., Am. Inst. Chemists, AAAS, Chemists Club, Alpha Chi Sigma, Sigma Gamma Chi, Pi Mu Epsilon. Club: Sports Car Am. (dir. 1964-67, 75-77, vice chmn., sec. 1967, 1975-76, local officer, 1960-74). Office: 7315 Wisconsin Ave Am Inst Chemists Washington DC 20014

ROETTGER, NORMAN CHARLES, JR., U.S. judge; b. Lucasville, Ohio. Nov. 3, 1930; s. Norman Charles and Emma Eleanora (Addis) R.; B.A., Ohio State U., 1952; LL.B. magna cum laude, Washington and Lee U., 1958; children—Virginia, Peggy. Admitted to Ohio, Fla. bars, 1958; asso. firm Frost & Jacobs, Cin., 1958-59; asso. firm Fleming, O'Bryan & Fleming, Ft. Lauderdale, Fla., 1959-63, partner, 1963-69, 71-72; dep. gen. counsel HUD, Washington, 1969-71; judge U.S. Dist. Ct., So. Dist. Fla., Ft. Lauderdale, 1972—. Served to lt. (j.g.) USN, 1952-55, to capt. Res., 1972. Mem. Am., Fed., Fla., Broward County bar assns., Order of Coif, Omicron Delta Kappa, Kappa Delta Rho. Presbyterian. Clubs: Masons; Coral Ridge Yacht (Ft. Lauderdale). Home: 2231 NE 15th Ct Fort Lauderdale FL 33304 Office: US Courthouse 299 E Broward Blvd Fort Lauderdale FL 33301

ROEVER, LUIS CONRAD, bus. exec.; b. N.Y.C., Jan. 29, 1919; s. Luis K. and Anita H. (Sumner) R.; B.S., Harvard Coll., 1941; M.B.A.. Harvard U., 1946; m. Mary Emily Cifri, Nov. 9, 1946; children—Diane Louise. Geoffrey Paul. Analyst, Smith, Barney & Co., N.Y.C., 1947-48; treas. Textron P.R., Ponce, 1948-54; controller Electronics Corp. Am., Cambridge, Mass., 1954-58; treas., v.p. Purity Supreme, Inc., Billerica, Mass., 1958-78; pres., chief exec. officer Milton Savs. Bank (Mass.), 1978—. Commr. rail services Mass., 1974-76; corporator Milton Hosp., 1978—. Served with M.I., U.S. Army, 1942-45. Mem. Fin. Execs. Inst., Planning Execs. Inst. Club: Harvard (Hingham). Home: 29 Howland Ln Hingham MA 02043 Office: 40 Adams St Milton MA 02186

ROGAT, MORRIS EDWARD, lumber co. exec.; b. Cleve., Aug. 26, 1908; s. Carl and Mollie (Youdovin) R.; E.E., Cleve. Coll., 1932; postgrad. Fenn Coll., 1941-43, John Huntington Inst. (Cleve.), 1944; m. Dorothy Katz, Nov. 28, 1933 (dec. Oct. 1971); children—Richard, Hannah (Mrs. M. Kuhn), Beverly (Mrs. G.A. Praver), Carl, Joseph; m. 2d, Dorothy Shiff, June 4, 1972. Ednl. dir. Am. Tng. Inst., Cleve., 1937-67; dir. tng. Grossman div. Evans Products Co., Braintree, Mass., 1967-72, dir. consumer edn., 1972—; lectr. mgmt. seminars, various colls., 1953—. Bd. dirs. Grossmans Fed. Credit Union, 1968-69; trustee Port St. Lucie (Fla.) Community Center. Named Ky. col., 1965. Mem. Sales and Marketing Execs. Internat., Am. Soc. Tng. Dirs., Automotive Boosters Club. Jewish. Clubs: Odd Fellows, Lions, Masons, Toastmasters, B'nai B'rith (pres. local lodge). Author: The Key to Power Selling, 1964; The Magic Interface of Salesmanship, 1971. Contbr. profl. jours. Home: 469 SE Seabreeze Ln Port Saint Lucie FL 33452. *Success comes to those who set a goal in their life to accomplish their desires. This can be done only by focusing their eyes on the target. This means to keep thinking constantly of your goal night and day and not be fearful of hard work or failures along the way. I have found this true in my lifetime and I know it works. Of course, you have to be technically prepared to know your product, profession or service.*

ROGERS, A. ROBERT, librarian; b. Moncton, N.B., Can., Sept. 9, 1927; s. Amos R. and Ethel L. (Lutes) R.; B.A., U. N.B., 1948; M.A., U. Toronto, 1950; Diploma in Librarianship, U. London, 1953; Ph.D., U. Mich., 1964; m. Rhoda M. Page, Dec. 18, 1960; 1 son, Mark Alan. Came to U.S., 1956, naturalized, 1965; Asst. librarian U. N.B., 1951-55, librarian, 1955-56; adult asst. home reading services Detroit Pub. Library, 1957-58, adult asst. reference services, 1958-59; asst. to dir. Bowling Green (Ohio) U. Library, 1959-61, acting dir., 1961-64, dir., 1964-69; prof. library sci. Kent State U., 1969—, acting dean Sch. Library Sci., 1977-78, dean, 1978—; vis. prof. library sci. Pahlavi U., Shiraz, Iran, 1976-77. Mem. Adv. Council on Fed. Library Programs, 1971-76, 78—. Trustee Ohio Coll. Library Center, 1967-69. Recipient Gov. Gen.'s Gold medal. Mem. Am. (council 1972-76), Canadian, Ohio (dir. 1968-76, pres. 1979-80, Librarian of Yr. award 1976) library assns., Library Assn. Gt. Britain, Bibliog. Soc. Can., Ohio Coll. Assn. (pres. librarians sect. 1964-65, chmn. library cooperation com. 1966-67). Methodist (ch. sch. supt. 1965-68, chmn. Commn. on Edn. 1973-76, 78—). Author: (poetry) The White Monument, 1955; The Humanities; A Selective Guide to Information Sources, 1974, 2d edit., 1980. Home: 1965 Pine View Dr Kent OH 44240

ROGERS, ADRIAN P(IERCE), clergyman; b. West Palm Beach, Fla., Sept. 12,1931; s. Arden Duncan and Rose Lee (Purcell) R.; B.A., Stetson U., 1954; T.H.M., New Orleans Bapt. Theol. Sem., 1958; D.D. (hon.), Trinity Coll., Clearwater, Fla., 1972; Litt.D. (hon.), Calif. Grad. Sch. Theology, 1979; m. Joyce Louise Gentry, Sept. 2, 1951; children—Stephen, Gayle, David, Janice. Ordained to ministry So. Bapt. Ch., 1951; pastor First Bapt. Ch., Fellsmere, Fla., 1950-54, Waveland (Miss.) Bapt. Ch., 1954-58, Parkview Bapt. Ch., Ft. Pierce, Fla., 1958-64, First Bapt. Ch., Merritt Island, Fla., 1964-72, Bellevue Bapt. Ch., Memphis, 1972—; pres. Fla. Bapt. Pastors Conf., 1970, So. Bapt. Pastors Conf., 1976, So. Bapt. Conv., 1979. Trustee Luther Rice Theol. Sem., 1970—, Union U., Jackson, Tenn, 1974—; hon. mem. staff 8th Congl. Dist. Tenn., 1976. Recipient award of merit City of Memphis, 1976, Key to City, 1976, cert. appreciation, 1979. Democrat. Home: 339 Grove Park S Memphis TN 38117 Office: 70 N Bellevue Memphis TN 38104

ROGERS, ARCHIBALD COLEMAN, architect; b. Annapolis, Md., Sept. 29, 1917; s. William Coleman and Margaret Bemiss (Bryan) R.; grad. Lawrenceville Sch., 1935; B.A., Princeton, 1939, M.F.A. in Architecture, 1942; certificate in Naval Architecture, U.S. Naval Postgrad. Sch., 1943; m. Lucia Bernardine Evans, July 12, 1947; children—Lucia Coleman (Mrs. Murdock), Coleman. Draftsman, Cross & Cross, architects, N.Y.C., 1939-40; founder Rogers, Taliaferro & Lamb, architects, Annapolis, 1946, sr. partner, 1946-69; chmn. RTKL Assos., Inc., architects, planners, Balt., 1969-76; zoning commr. Anne Arundel County, Md., 1946-52; lectr. Va. Theol. Sem., 1967-72; chmn. Symposia on Urban Design, Soviet-Am., 1968, Israeli-Am., 1969, Indian-Am., 1970. Mem. Md. Archtl. Registration Bd., 1958-67; mem. Archtl. Rev. Bd., Washington, 1963-66, Cin., 1965-70. Exec. dir. Greater Balt. Com., 1955; chmn. Anne Arundel County San. Commn., 1965; mem. Md. Arts Council, 1967-68. Trustee Princeton, 1972-76. Served to lt. USNR, 1942-46. Decorated Navy Commendation medal; recipient Young Man of Year award Annapolis Jr. C. of C., 1951, citation for design concept team Nat. Transp. Seminar, Denver, 1969. Fellow A.I.A. (past chpt. pres., com. chmn., nat. pres. 1973-74); mem. Am. Inst. Planners, Soc. Archtl. Historians. Democrat. Episcopalian. Author: Design Concept Teams for Urban Freeways, 1966; The Monticello Fault, 1979. Designer Cin. Downtown Plan, 1964. Home: Belvoir Crownsville MD 21032 Office: Village Sq Village of Cross Keys Baltimore MD 21210

ROGERS, BERNARD WILLIAM, army officer; b. Fairview, Kans., July 16, 1921; s. William Henry and Lora (Haynes) R.; student Kans. State Coll., 1939-40; B.S., U.S. Mil. Acad., 1943; B.A. (Rhodes scholar), Oxford (Eng.) U., 1950; M.A., 1954; grad. Command and Gen. Staff Coll., 1954-55; Army War Coll., 1959-60; m. Ann Ellen Jones, Dec. 28, 1944; children—Michael W., Diane E., Susan A. Commd. lt. U.S. Army, 1943; advanced through grades to gen., 1974; aide to supt. U.S. Mil. Acad., 1945-46; commdt. cadets, 1967-69; aide to high commr. Austria, Gen. Mark W. Clark, 1946-47; bn. comdr., Korea, 1952; exec. to comdr.-in-chief Far East Command, 1953-54; mil. asst. to Chief Staff, U.S. Army, 1956-59; exec. to chmn. Joint Chiefs of Staff, 1962-66; asst. div. comdr. 1st Inf. Div., Vietnam, 1966-67; comdg. gen. 5th Inf. Div., Ft. Carson, Colo., 1969-70; chief legislative liaison Dept. Army, 1970-72, dep. chief for personnel, 1972-74; comdg. gen. U.S. Army Forces Command, 1974-76; chief of staff U.S. Army, 1976-79; supreme allied comdr. Europe, comdr. in chief U.S. European Command, 1979—. Decorated D.S.C., Silver Star, Legion of Merit with 4 oak leaf clusters, D.F.C. with 2 oak leaf clusters, Bronze Star medal with V device, Air medal with 35 oak leaf clusters; hon. fellow Univ. Coll., Oxford U. Mem. Assn. U.S. Army, Legion of Valor, Assn. Am. Rhodes Scholars, Soc. 1st Inf. Div., Phi Delta Theta. Club: Army-Navy Country. Office: Supreme Allied Commander Europe SHAPE BE APO NY 09055

ROGERS, BRYAN ALLEN, hosp. adminstr.; b. Akron, Ohio, Aug. 2, 1925; s. Jesse L. and Helen O. (Baker) R.; B.A., U. Akron, 1949; M.H.A., Washington U., St. Louis, 1954; m. Jean E. Hoffman, Dec. 29, 1950; children—Mark, Amy. Mem. adminstrv. staff Methodist Hosp., Indpls., 1954-72, exec. v.p., adminstr., 1971-72; adminstr. Toledo Hosp., 1972-77, pres., 1977—; adj. instr. health care adminstrn. U. Toledo, Washington U.; charter mem. bus. adv. council Coll. Bus. Adminstrn., U. Toledo; mem. public health council Ohio Dept. Health, 1978—; chmn. task force on cost-effectiveness Blue Cross, 1978-79. Served with AUS, 1943-46. Fellow Am. Coll. Hosp. Adminstrs.; mem. Toledo Area C. of C. (trustee 1979-82). Presbyterian. Club: Toledo Rotary. Home: 4626 Corey Rd Toledo OH 43623 Office: 2142 N Cove Blvd Toledo OH 43606

ROGERS, C. B., lawyer; b. Birmingham, Ala., July 10, 1930; s. Claude B. Rogers and Doris (Hinkley) Rogers Lockerman; A.B., Emory U., 1951, LL.B., 1953; m. Patricia Maxwell DeVoe, Dec. 26, 1962; children—Bruce Lockerman, Evelyn Best, Brian DeVoe. Advitted to Ga. bar, 1953; adj. prof. litigation Emory U., 1968-70; asso., then partner firm Powell, Goldstein, Frazer & Murphy, 1954-76; partner firm Rogers & Hardin, Atlanta, 1976—. Fellow Am. Coll. Trial Lawyers; mem. Lawyers Club Atlanta, Am. Law Inst. Democrat. Episcopalian. Clubs: Ansley, Capital City, Commerce (Atlanta); Downtown Athletic (N.Y.C.). Home: 1829 W Wesley Rd NW Atlanta GA 30327 also Brandon Mill Rd Lakemont GA 30552 Office: 101 Marietta Tower 32d Floor Atlanta GA 30303

ROGERS, CARL RANSOM, psychologist; b. Oak Park, Ill., Jan. 8, 1902; s. Walter A. and Julia (Cushing) R.; B.A., U. Wis., 1924; M.A., Columbia, 1928, Ph.D., 1931; L.H.D., Lawrence Coll., 1956, U. Santa Clara (Cal.), 1971; Litt.D., Gonzaga U., 1968; D.Sc., U. Cin., 1974; Ph.D., U. Hamburg (Germany), 1975; Dr. Social Scis., Leiden U. (Netherlands), 1975; Sc.D., Northwestern U., 1978; m. Helen Elliott, Aug. 28, 1924 (dec. 1979); children—David, Natalie. Psychologist in child study dept. Soc. for Prevention Cruelty to Children, Rochester, N.Y., 1928-30, dir., 1930-39; dir. Rochester Guidance Center, 1939; prof. clin. psychology Ohio State U., 1940-45; dir. counseling services U.S.O., 1944-45; prof. psychology, exec. sec. Counseling Center, U. Chgo., 1945-57; Knapp prof. U. Wis., 1957, prof. psychology and psychiatry, 1957-63; resident fellow Western Behavioral Scis. Inst., La Jolla, Calif., 1964-68, Center Studies of the Person, La Jolla, 1968—; vis. prof. at various times U. Rochester, Columbia Tchrs. Coll., U. Cal. at Los Angeles, Harvard, Occidental Coll., U. Calif. at Berkeley, Brandeis U. Recipient Distinguished Sci. Contbn. award Am. Psychol. Assn., 1956, 1st Distinguished Profl. Contbn. award, 1972; Nicholas Murray Butler medal Columbia, 1955; Distinguished Contbn. award Am. Pastoral Counselors Assn., 1967; Profl. award Am. Bd. Profl. Psychology, 1968; fellow Center Advanced Study in Behavioral Scis., 1962-63; named Humanist of Year, Am. Humanist Assn., 1964. Fellow Am. Acad. Arts and Scis.; mem. Am. Acad. Psychotherapists (pres. 1956-58), Am. Orthopsychiat. Assn. (v.p. 1944-45), Am. Assn. Applied Psychology (pres. 1944-45), Am. Psychol. Assn. (pres. 1946-47), Phi Beta Kappa. Author: Measuring Personality Adjustment in Children, 1931; Clinical Treatment of the Problem Child, 1939; Counseling and Psychotherapy, 1942; Counseling with Returned Servicemen (with J. Wallen), 1946; Client-Centered Therapy, 1951; Psychotherapy and Personality Change (with others), 1954; On Becoming a Person, 1961; The Therapeutic Relationship and its Impact: A Study of Psychotherapy with Schizophrenics (with E.T. Gendlin, D.J. Kiesler, C.B. Truax), 1967; Freedom to Learn, 1969; Carl Rogers on Encounter Groups, 1970; Becoming Partners: Marriage and Its Alternatives, 1972; Carl Rogers on Personal Power, 1977; also numerous articles. Home: 2311 Via Siena La Jolla CA 92037

ROGERS, CHARLES B., artist, gallery exec.; b. Gt. Bend, Kans., Jan. 27, 1911; s. Walter and Sarah (Schoonoever) R.; student (Volker grantee) Nat. Acad. Art; B.F.A., Bethany Coll., 1942; M.F.A., Calif. Coll. Arts and Crafts, 1947; m. Ruth Estella Walker; 1 son, Robert C. Head Sch. Art Bethany Coll., 1947-53; mgr. Huntington Hartford Found., Pacific Palisades, Calif., 1954-66, asst. dir., 1954-66; head Sch. Art Kans. Wesleyan U., 1966-67; dir. Rogers House Museum Gallery, Ellsworth, Kans., 1968—; more than 100 one-man shows including Mus. N.Mex., Santa Fe, Inst. Tech., Rochester, N.Y., Smithsonian Instn., Disney Studios; more than 250 group shows including Denver Art Mus., Derby Gallery, London, Eng., Chgo. Art Inst., Fuji Daimaru Gallery, Kyoto, Japan; represented in permanent collections: Library of Congress & Met. Mus. Art, N.Y.C., Phila. Mus. Art, U. Kans., Kans. State U. works include murals at: U.S. Post Office, Council Grove, Kans., Britton Meml., Ellsworth. Served with USN, 1942-46. Recipient numerous awards including Mikami award Japanese Brush Painting, award Kans. Art Inst., Painters and Sculptors, Los Angeles, Topeka (Kans.) Ann., Nat. Vets. Art, Santa Monica, Calif.; Tiffany Found. grantee, Huntington Hartford Found. grantee. Fellow Am. Inst. Fine Arts; mem. Soc. Am. Graphic Artists, Kans. Fedn. Art (pres.), St. Mary's Coll. (hon.). Author, illustrator: Quill of the Kansan, 1970; The Great West, 1973; Images of the American West, 1975; Country Neighbor, 1977. Home: 102 E Main S Ellsworth KS 67439 Office: Rogers House Museum Gallery Snake Row Ellsworth KS 67439. *A man need not extoll his virtues nor comment on his failings; his friends know the former, and his enemies will search out the latter. The genuine artist labors as diligently on a small piece as he does on a large one. The seed of his growth is in each effort expended. Therefore, it is a redundancy to speak of good or bad art—either it is or is not art.*

ROGERS, CHARLES EDWIN, phys. chemist; b. Rochester, N.Y., Dec. 29, 1929; s. Charles Harold and Maybelle (Johnson) R.; B.S. in Chemistry, Syracuse U., 1954; Ph.D. in Phys. Chemistry, SUNY at Syracuse U., 1957; m. Barbara June Depuy, June 12, 1954; children—Gregory Newton, Linda Frances, Diana Suzanne. Research asso. dept. chemistry Princeton U., 1957-59, Goodyear fellow, 1957-59; mem. tech. staff Bell Telephone Labs., Murray Hill, N.J., 1959-65; asso. prof. macromolecular sci. Case Western Res. U., 1965-74, prof., 1974—; TAPPI fellow SUNY, 1954-57; sr. vis. fellow Imperial Coll., U. London, 1971; cons. to polymer and chem. industries. Served with U.S. Army, 1946-49. Mem. Am. Chem. Soc., Am. Phys. Soc., Fedn. Coatings Socs., Soc. Plastics Engrs., AAAS, Sigma Xi. Contbr. numerous articles to profl. jours.; editor: Permselective Membranes, 1971; Structure and Properties of Block Copolymers, 1977; bd. editors Jour. Membrane Sci., Jour. Polymer Engring. and Sci.; patentee in field; devel. overseas ednl. instns. Home: 8400 Rockspring Dr Chagrin Falls OH 44022 Office: Dept Macromolecular Sci Case Western Res U Cleveland OH 44106

ROGERS, CHARLES MCPHERSON ADUSTON, III, banker; b. Mobile, Ala., Nov. 10, 1932; s. Charles McPherson Aduston and Elisabeth (Benson) R.; B.A., Williams Coll., 1954; LL.B., U. Ala., 1959; m. Gail Whitehurst, June 19, 1954; children—Anne Aduston, Charles McPherson Aduston IV, Bradshaw Aduston. Admitted to Ala. bar, 1959; asso. firm McCorvey, Turner, Johnstone, Adams & May, Mobile, 1959-63, partner, 1963-67; with Am. Nat. Bank, Mobile, 1967—, chmn. bd., chief exec. officer, dir., 1977—. Mem. Ala. Ho. of Reps., 1961-66; trustee Mobile Symphony Orch., 1960-70, pres., 1966-68; trustee Allied Arts Council Met. Mobile, 1966-74, St. Paul's Episcopal Sch., 1967—, United Fund of Mobile County, 1974—, Birmingham Symphony Orch., 1978—; trustee Mobile Big Game Fishing Club, 1968-74, pres., 1969; mem. adv. bd. trustees Mobile Assn. for Retarded Citizens, 1969—; Belgian consul Ala., N.W. Fla., 1970—; mem. Consular Corps of Mobile, 1970—, chmn., 1974-76; mem. City of Mobile Indsl. Devel. Bd., 1974—; pres. Mobile Area council Boy Scouts Am., 1974-77, Area IV, S.W. region, 1979—, recipient Disting. Eagle Scout award, 1977; bd. dirs. Mobile United, 1974—, Mobile Opera Guild, 1979—, Community Chest and Council, 1975—, Univ. Health Services Found., 1976—; mem. adv. bd. U. South Ala. Sch. Bus., 1975—, mem. Policemen and Firefighters Pension and Relief Fund Bd., 1974—; bd. regents Spring Hill Coll., 1978—. Served to 1st lt. USAF, 1955-57. Mem. Am. Bar Assn., Ala. Bar Assn., Mobile Bar Assn., Am. Bankers Assn., Ala. Bankers Assn., Mobile C. of C. (v.p. 1975-78), Phi Delta Phi, Phi Delta Theta. Episcopalian. Clubs: Athelstan, Country of Mobile, Mobile Yacht. Editor-in-chief Ala. Law Rev., 1958-59. Home: 256 College Ln Mobile AL 36608 Office: Am Nat Bank 130 St Joseph St Mobile AL 36629

ROGERS, DALE EVANS (FRANCES OCTAVIA SMITH), singer, actress, author; b. Uvalde, Tex., Oct. 31, 1912; d. Walter Hillman and Bettie Sue (Wood) S.; m. 1st, Thomas Frederick Fox, Mar., 1928 (div. 1930); 1 son, Thomas Frederick; m. 2d, Roy Rogers, Dec. 31, 1947; stepchildren—Cheryl Darlene, Linda Lou, Roy; children—Robin Elizabeth (dec.), John David (dec.), Mary Little Doe, Marion Fleming, Deborah (dec.). Worked as stenographer with ins. co., then as singer on radio programs in Chgo., Louisville, Dallas; became featured singer with Anson Weeks Orch., Chgo.; sang at Chez Paree night club, Chgo.; singer star of CBS weekly radio program News and Rhythm; with Twentieth Century-Fox, fall 1941; entertained at Army and Navy camps; featured vocalist on Edgar Bergen-Charlie McCarthy radio show for thirty-nine weeks; later sang on many popular radio programs, including Jack Carson, Garry Moore, Jimmy Durante; made film debut in Swing Your Partner, 1943; appeared in films West Side Kid, Here Comes Elmer, Hoosier Holiday, In Old Oklahoma; first appearance with Roy Rogers in The Cowboy and the Senorita, 1944; movies include: Lights of Old Santa Fe, 1944, Song of Nevada, 1944, Yellow Rose of Texas, 1944, Sunset in El Dorado,

1945, Utah, 1945, My Pal Trigger, 1946, Under Nevada Skies, 1946, Song of Arizona, 1946, Bells of San Angelo, 1947, The Golden Stallion, 1949, Bells of Coronado, 1950, Pals of the Golden West, 1951, Don't Fence Me In, 1945; appeared on TV on Roy Rogers Show, 1951-56; now appears with Roy Rogers at rodeos and state fairs. Co-chmn. (with Roy Rogers) motion picture, TV and radio com. Nat. Safety Council, 1956. Named the Money-Making Western Star, Motion Picture Herald-Fame Poll, 1947, 50-52; recipient (with Roy Rogers) George Spelvin award in recognition of humanitarian services Masquers' Club, 1956, Pub. Interest award Nat. Safety Council, citations Nat. Assn. Retarded Children, ARC, Muscular Dystrophy Assn., Nat. Nephrosis Found., Am. Legion; award for distinguished service to humanity and to their country Round Table Internat.; award for tour Vietnam Gen. William Westmoreland in Saigon, 1967; named Women of Year, Internat. Orphans Inc., Ch. Woman of Year, Religious Heritage Am. Mem. Am. Bible Soc. (hon. life), Hollywood Christian Group, Lambda Theta. Methodist Episcopalian. Author: Angel Unaware; Christmas Is Always; Dearest Debbie; Finding the Way; Let Freedom Ring!; My Spiritual Diary; No Two Ways About It!; Salute To Sandy; Time Out Ladies; To My Son; Faith at Our House; Where He Leads; Woman at the Well; Cool It or Lose It, 1972; Trials, Tears and Triumph, 1977; Hear the Children Crying, 1978; others. Writer 25 songs including: Will You Marry Me, Mr. Laramie?; Happy Trails to You; Aha, San Antone; The Bible Tells Me So. Recorded more than 30 records for Little Golden and Bell Records. Office: care Art Rush Inc 10221 Riverside Dr Suite 219 North Hollywood CA 91602*

ROGERS, DAVID ELLIOTT, physician, educator, charitable assn. exec.; b. N.Y.C., Mar. 17, 1926; s. Carl Ransom and Helen Martha (Elliott) R.; student Ohio State U., 1942-44, Miami U., Oxford, Ohio, 1944; M.D., Cornell U. Med. Coll., N.Y.C., 1948; Sc.D., Thomas Jefferson U., 1973; m. Cora Jane Baxter, Aug. 13, 1946 (dec. Feb. 1971); children—Anne Baxter, Gregory Baxter, Julia Cushing; m. 2d, Barbara Louise Lehan, Aug. 26, 1972. Intern Johns Hopkins Hosp., 1948-49, asst. resident, 1949-50; USPHS postdoctoral fellow div. infectious disease N.Y. Hosp., N.Y.C., 1950-51, chief resident in medicine, 1951-52, attending physician, 1974—; vis. investigator Rockefeller Inst. Med. Research, N.Y.C., 1954-55; Lowell M. Palmer Sr. fellow in medicine Rockefeller Inst. Med. Research and Cornell U. Med. Coll., 1955-57, asst. prof., 1954-56, chief div. infectious diseases, 1955-59; asso. prof. Cornell U. Med. Coll., 1956-59; prof., chmn. dept. medicine Vanderbilt U., 1959-68; physician-in-chief Vanderbilt U. Hosp., 1959-68; prof., dean med. faculty Sch. Medicine, Johns Hopkins, v.p. univ., med. dir. Johns Hopkins Hosp., 1968-71; pres. Robert Wood Johnson Found., Princeton, N.J., 1972—. Cons. Surgeon Gen., 1958-68, HEW, 1969-72; chmn. sect. Streptococcal-Staphylococcal Disease Commn. Armed Forces Epidemiol. Bd., 1958-69; mem. sci. adv. bd. Mead Johnson Research Center, Evansville, Ind., 1961-68; mem. med. adv. bd. Nat. Bd. Med. Examiners, 1961-64; mem. Tenn. adv. com. U.S. Commn. Civil Rights, 1962-64; mem. adv. com. survey of research and edn. VA-NRC, 1966-68; chmn. nat. sci. adv. council Nat. Jewish Hosp. and Research Center, Denver, 1971-73; mem. sci. adv. bd. Scripps Clinic and Research Found., La Jolla, Cal., 1972-74; vis. prof. numerous univs. Bd. visitors Charles R. Drew Postgrad. Med. Sch., 1971—. Served to lt. (s.g.) M.C., USNR, 1952-54. Recipient John Metcalf Polk prize, Alfred Moritz Michaelis prize Cornell U. Med. Sch., 1948; Distinguished Service award Nashville Jr. C. of C., 1960; One of Ten Outstanding Young Men of Year award U.S. Jr. C. of C., 1961; Centennial Achievement award Ohio State U., 1970; award of distinction Cornell Alumni Assn., 1976; decorated Royal Order of Cedar, Govt. Lebanon, 1972. Fellow A.C.S., A.A.A.S.; mem. Am. Fedn. Clin. Research, Am. Soc. Clin. Investigation, ACP (master), Assn. Am. Physicians (pres. 1974-75), Assn. Profs. Medicine (sec.-treas. 1965-67), Am. Heart Assn., A.A.U.P., So. Soc. Clin. Research, Infectious Disease Soc. Am. (charter), Am. Clin. and Climatological Assn., Interurban Clin. Club, Council Fgn. Relations, Assn. Am. Med. Colls. (Distinguished Service award), Soc. Health and Human Values, Inst. Medicine, Sigma Xi, Alpha Omega Alpha. Clubs: Cosmos, Century Assn. Editorial bd. Clin. Research, 1958-61, Medicine, 1962—; editor Year Book of Medicine, 1966—. Home: RFD 1 Coppermine Rd Princeton NJ 08540 Office: Robert Wood Johnson Found PO Box 2316 Princeton NJ 08540

ROGERS, DONALD LEE, indsl. equipment mfg. co. exec.; b. Dallas, Jan. 28, 1930; s. John Ernest and Maude Kathleen (McCool) R.; B.S. in Elec. Engring., Tex. Agrl. and Mech. U., 1951; M.B.A., Harvard U., 1957; children—Lance H., Celia I., Donna L. With Comet Rice Mills, Dallas, 1953-71, v.p., 1957-66, pres., 1966-68, chmn. bd., 1968-71; chmn. Country Cupboard, Inc., Dallas, 1970-71; pres., chmn. bd. Burgess Industries Inc., Dallas, 1971—. Served to 1st lt. Signal Corps U.S. Army, 1951-53. Mem. Young Presidents' Orgn. Republican. Methodist. Clubs: Dallas Country, Dallas Petroleum. Office: 8101 Carpenter Freeway Dallas TX 75247

ROGERS, ELMER GILLIS, retail stores chain exec.; b. Grassy Meadows, W.Va., Oct. 5, 1922; s. Gillis Robert and Cleva Mae (Stevens) R.; student Tyler Comml. Coll., 1942; children—Cheryl Susan, Dean Gordon. With Neisner Bros., Inc. (acquired by Ames Dept. Stores, Inc., Rocky Hill, Conn. 1978), Rochester, N.Y., 1941—stores mgmt. dir., 1971-74, fin. v.p., treas., 1974-78, dir. adminstrn., 1976-78, dir., 1974-78, dir. manpower planning and career devel. parent co., Rocky Hill, 1979—. Served with U.S. Army, 1943-46. Mem. Rochester C. of C. Republican. Baptist. Club: 4-H. Home: Rocky Hill CT 06067 Office: 2418 Main St Rocky Hill CT 06067

ROGERS, ERNEST PAUL, lawyer; b. nr. Duluth, Ga., Sept. 10, 1903; s. Raymond Clifford and Ora (Bloodworth) R.; student Darlington Sch., Rome, Ga., 1917-21; LL.B., U. Ga., 1926; m. Mary Weems, June 18, 1932; children—Mary Ann (Mrs. John Hammaker), Ronald Weems, Michael Clayton, Ernest Paul. Admitted to Ga. bar, 1927; atty. legal staff Coca-Cola Co., Atlanta, 1927-35; asso. Harold Hirsch & Marion Smith, Atlanta, 1935-39; mem. firm Kilpatrick, Cody, Rogers, McClatchey & Regenstein, 1939—. Pres. Scripto Pencil Co., 1945-46, dir., mem. exec. com., 1936-73; pres. Laow Investment Co., Inc.; dir. Colonial Stores, Inc., 1966-74. Life trustee Darlington Sch., Rome, Ga.; permanent trustee Atlanta Lawyers Found., Inc. Mem. Am. Judicature Soc., Am., Ga., Atlanta bar assns., Kappa Sigma, Phi Delta Phi. Methodist. Kiwanian. Clubs: Atlanta Lawyers (past pres.), Piedmont Driving, Capital City, Commerce (Atlanta). Home: 2933 Andrews Dr NW Atlanta GA 30305 Office: Equitable Bldg Atlanta GA 30303

ROGERS, EUGENE CHARLES, stock broker; b. Bklyn., Sept. 29, 1932; s. Eugene Aloysius and Agnes Hilda (Scharbach) R.; B.B.A., St. John's U., Bklyn., 1954; M.B.A., N.Y. U., 1960; m. Anita Therese Tobin, May 13, 1961; 1 son, Eugene Charles. Staff accountant Haskins & Sells, C.P.A.'s, N.Y.C., 1954-60, Bache & Co., N.Y.C., 1960-62; controller, then chief fin. officer Reynolds Securities Inc., N.Y.C., 1962-72, v.p., treas., 1972—; v.p., treas. Dean Witter Reynolds Inc., 1978—; guest lectr., panelist in field. Served with U.S. Army, 1954-56. C.P.A., N.Y. Mem. N.Y. State Soc. C.P.A.'s, Fin. Execs. Inst., Fin. Club of N.Y. U. Grad. Sch. Bus., Securities Industry Assn. (past pres. fin. mgmt. div.). Roman Cath. Clubs: Rockville Links, Sun and Surf Beach. Home: 15 Whitby Ct Rockville Centre NY 11570 Office: 120 Broadway New York NY 10005

ROGERS, FRANCIS DAY, architect; b. Chgo., Mar. 25, 1912; s. James Gamble and Anne (Day) R.; A.B., Yale U., 1935; student Cambridge U., 1936; B.Arch., N.Y. U., 1941; m. Pauline Washburn, Sept. 19, 1942; children—Deborah Day Rogers Butler, Polly Washburn Rogers Greenberg, Philip Gamble, Nicholas Livingston. Draftsman, James Gamble Rogers, Inc., 1936-37, project mgr., 1939-42, architect, project mgr., 1943-45; spl. cons. Dept. City Planning, N.Y.C., 1942-43; architect, project mgr. Voorhees, Walker, Foley & Smith, architects, 1944-47; partner Rogers, Burgun, Shahine & Deschler, architects, N.Y.C. Chmn. bd. Spelman Coll., Atlanta; exec. com. Met. Mus. of Art; bd. dirs. Commonwealth Fund. Mem. AIA, Marine Hist. Assn. (exec. com.) (Mystic, Conn.). Presbyterian (elder). Clubs: Yale, Union, Century Assn. (N.Y.C.); Grads. (New Haven). Home: 182 E 75th St New York NY 10021 Office: 521 Fifth Ave New York NY 10017

ROGERS, FRANCIS MILLET, educator; b. New Bedford, Mass., Nov. 26, 1914; s. Frank Leo and Laura (Sylvia) R.; A.B., Cornell, 1936; student U. Paris, 1934-35; A.M., Harvard, 1937, Ph.D., 1940; Sheldon traveling fellow, Portugal, Madeira, and Azores, 1938-39; fellow Am. Council Learned Socs., Brazil, 1941; Litt.D., Loyola U., Chgo., 1952, New Bedford Inst. Tech., 1963; L.H.D., Duquesne U., 1953, Assumption Coll., Worcester, 1960, Georgetown U., 1966; LL.D., Miami U., 1953, Stonehill Coll., 1957, Providence Coll., 1960; Dr. (hon.), U. Bahia (Brazil), 1959; m. Nathalie Esselborn, July 25, 1942 (dec. 1968); 1 dau., Sheila Mary; m. 2d, Elsie Bann La Carrubba, Oct. 24, 1970. Jr. fellow Soc. of Fellow, Harvard U., 1940-41, faculty instr. in Romance langs. and lits., 1945-46, asso. prof., 1946-52, prof., 1952-77, Nancy Clark Smith prof. lang. and lit. of Portugal, 1977—; sr. tutor in John Winthrop House, 1946-50, chmn. dept. Romance langs. and lits., 1947-49, 61-66, dean Grad. Sch. Arts and Scis., 1949-55. U.S. mem. adminstrv. bd. Internat. Assn. Univs., 1950-55; pres. 1st Internat. Colloquium on Luso-Brazilian studies, Washington, 1950, sec.-gen. 6th Cambridge, N.Y.C., 1966; chmn. council on jr. year abroad Inst. Internat. Edn., 1951-53; consultative com. Internat. Bull. Luso-Brazilian Bibliography, 1959-73; hon. prof. U. San Marcos, Lima, Peru, 1961. Trustee, Old Dartmouth Hist. Soc. and Whaling Mus., 1970-73, St. John's Sem., Boston, 1968-76. Served to lt. col. USMCR, 1941-45; service in French Morocco, Algeria, Sicily, Italy; col. Res. ret. Decorated Silver Star; chevalier French Legion of Honor, 1950. Mem. Hakluyt Soc., Internat. Acad. Portuguese Culture (corr. academician 1966), Inst. Nav. Washington, Inst. Nav. London, Am. Assn. Tchrs. Spanish and Portuguese, MLA, Hispanic Soc. Am., Portuguese Ednl. Soc. (New Bedford, Mass.), Acad. Scis. Lisbon (corr. academician, hon. mem.), Soc. for History of Discoveries (pres. 1968-69), Phi Beta Kappa, Phi Kappa Phi, Pi Delta Phi, Delta Phi Alpha, Delta Epsilon Sigma (hon.), Phi Lambda Beta (pres. 1968-77). Contbr. articles on Portuguese linguistics, lit. and maritime history in various learned jours. Author: Higher Education in the United States: A Summary View, 1952, 3d edit., 1960; The Obedience of a King of Portugal, 1958; The Travels of the Infante Dom Pedro of Portugal, 1961; The Quest for Eastern Christians, 1962; Europe Informed: An Exhibition of Early Books Which Acquainted Europe with The East, 1966; Precision Astrolabe: Portuguese Navigators and Transoceanic Aviation, 1971; Americans of Portuguese Descent: A Lesson in Differentiation, 1974; The Portuguese Heritage of John Dos Passos, 1976; Atlantic Islanders of the Azores and Madeiras, 1979. Home: 202 Grove St Belmont MA 02178 Office: Widener Library Cambridge MA 02138

ROGERS, FRANK WATERS, lawyer; b. Dendron, Va., Nov. 2, 1892; s. Edward and Otis Alice (Harrison) R.; grad. Episcopal High Sch. in Va., 1909; B.A., U. Va., 1912; LL.B., 1914; m. Anne Newton Jett, June 6, 1922; children—Anne F. (Mrs. Edwin B. Vaden), Virginia H. (Mrs. A. L. Holton, Jr.), Robert J. (dec.), Frank Waters. Admitted to Va. bar, 1913, since practiced in Roanoke; partner firm Woods, Rogers, Muse, Walker & Thornton, 1919—. Dir. emeritus 1st Nat. Exchange Bank Va.; asst. sec. Natural Bridge Va., Inc. Rep. Va. Bar Assn. at trial of Francis Gary Powers, Moscow, Russia, 1960. Pres. Roanoke Symphony Soc., 1955-60. Bd. visitors U. Va., 1962-70, rector, 1966-70; trustee Va. Found. Ind. Colls., 1954-60, Hollins Coll., 1947-70; bd. dirs. Roanoke Pub. Library, 1951-61. Served as 2d lt. (pilot) Air Corps, U.S. Army, 1918-19; AEF. Mem. Am., Va. (pres. 1938), Roanoke (pres. 1927) bar assns. Home: 2222 Stanley Ave SE Roanoke VA 24014 Office: 105 Franklin Rd SW Roanoke VA 24011

ROGERS, FRANKLYN CHRISTOPHER, civil engr.; b. N.Y.C., Apr. 24, 1910; s. David Carroll and Frederika Mary (Frank) R.; student N.Y. U., 1927-28; B.S.C.E., Purdue U., 1931; M.S.C.E., Columbia U., 1946; m. Harriet Louise Van Dusen, Oct. 2, 1937; children—David Van Dusen, Franklyn Christopher, Beatrice Mary, Peter Martin. Design engr. Ambursen engring. Corp., N.Y.C., 1935-43; asso. prof. civil engring. Rutgers U., 1943-46, prof., 1946-50; v.p., dir. Harza Engring. Co., Chgo., 1950-72, prin. asso., 1972—. Registered profl. engr., N.Y., N.J., Calif., Ill., Ind., Md., Va.; Fellow ASCE (Rickey Gold medal 1976); mem. Nat. Soc. Profl. Engrs., Am. Cons. Engrs. Council, Sigma Xi, Tau Beta Pi. Republican. Episcopalian. Co-editor: Current Practice in Design and Construction of Large Gravity Dams 1967; contbr. numerous articles to profl. publs. Home: 5940 Emerald Harbor Dr Longboat Key FL 33548 Office: 150 S Wacker Dr Chicago IL 60606

ROGERS, FRED BAKER, med. educator; b. Trenton, N.J., Aug. 25, 1926; s. Lawrence H. and Eliza C. (Thropp) R.; A.A., Princeton, 1947; M.D., Temple U., 1948; M.S. in Medicine, U. Pa., 1954; M.P.H., Columbia, 1957; spl. student Johns Hopkins, 1962. Intern Temple U. Hosp., Phila., 1948-49, chief resident physician, 1953-54; USPHS fellow Temple U. Sch. Medicine, 1954-55, asst. prof. preventive medicine, 1956-58, asso. prof., 1958-60, prof., 1960—; lectr. epidemiology Columbia Sch. Pub. Health, 1957-68, Sch. Nursing, U. Pa., 1964-67; cons. USN Hosp., Phila., 1964-73. Served with M.C., USNR, 1950-53; ETO, Korea. Diplomate Am. Bd. Preventive Medicine. Fellow A.C.P.; mem. Am. Pub. Health Assn., AMA (chmn. sect. preventive medicine 1963-64), Phila. Art Alliance, Sigma Xi, Alpha Omega Alpha, Phi Rho Sigma. Clubs: Campus (Princeton); Franklin Inn (Phila.); Charaka (N.Y.C.); Osler (London). Author: A Syllabus of Medical History, 1958; Help-Bringers: Versatile Physicians of N.J., 1960; Epidemiology and Communicable Disease Control, 1963; Studies in Epidemiology, 1965; (with A.R. Sayre) The Healing Art, 1966; (with M.E. Cashel) Your Body is Wonderfully Made, 1974. Editorial bd. Am. Jour. Pub. Health, 1967-73. Contbr. articles to profl. jours. Home: 301 W State St Trenton NJ 08618 Office: Temple U Sch Medicine Philadelphia PA 19140

ROGERS, FRED MCFEELY, television producer and host; b. Latrobe, Pa., Mar. 20, 1928; s. James Hillis and Nancy (McFeely) Flagg; Mus.B., Rollins Coll., 1951; M.Div., Pitts. Theol. Sem., 1962; D.H.L., Thiel Coll., 1969; D.Hum., Eastern Mich. U., 1973; Litt.D., St. Vincent Coll., 1973; D.D., Christian Theol. Sem., 1973; L.H.D., Yale, 1974; D.F.A., Carnegie-Mellon U., 1976; L.H.D., Lafayette Coll., 1977; Mus.D., Waynesburg Coll., 1978; m. Sara Joanne Byrd, July 9, 1952; children—James Byrd, John Frederick. Asst. producer NBC, N.Y.C., 1951-53; exec. producer WQED, Pitts., 1953-62; producer, host CBC, Toronto, Ont., 1962-64; exec. producer, host Mister Rogers Neighborhood, Pub. Broadcasting System, Pitts., 1965—; adj. prof. U. Pitts., 1976. Pres. Family Communications, Inc., Pitts.; dir. Latrobe Die Casting Co., Vulcan Inc. Chmn. child devel. and mass media forum White House Conf. on Children. Mem. Esther Island Preserve Assn. Bd. dirs. McFeely Rogers Found., Children's Hosp., Pitts. Recipient Peabody award for finest children's TV program, Nat. Ednl. TV award for excellence in children's programming, and others. Mem. Luxor Ministerial Assn. Presbyn. Author: Mister Rogers Talks About . . .; Tell Me, Mister Rogers; Many Ways to Say I Love You. Five long playing records of original songs; composer Mr. Rogers' Songbook. Office: 4802 5th Ave Pittsburgh PA 15213. *Every person in this life is so much more than meets the eye or ear. I'm continually surprised at the complexity of all those whom I'm fortunate enough to really get to know.*

ROGERS, GAINES MADISON, coll. dean; b. Belton S.C., June 11, 1918; s. James Duckworth and Alice (Gaines) R.; B.S., Clemson Coll., 1942; M.A., U. Va., 1945, Ph.D., 1946; m. Betty Pollay, Mar. 20, 1943; children—Zarita Jeanne, Liza Sabina. Asst. prof. econs. Baylor U., Waco, Tex., 1946-48, chmn. dept. econs., 1948; dean sch. bus. adminstrn. Wake Forest (N.C.) Coll. 1949-68; dean Coll. Bus. and Industry, prof. finance Miss. State U., State Coll., 1968—; former mem. faculty Sch. Consumer Banking, U. Va.; faculty Sch. Banking of South; dir. Depositors Savs. Assn.; local div. Nat. Bank Commerce of Miss. Mem. South Central Export Council; past mem. exec. com. Pushmatahu Area council Boy Scouts Am. Past trustee N.C. Found. Econ. Edn.; bd. dirs. Miss. Econ. Council. Nat. council Small Bus. Mgmt. Devel. Served as 1st lt., signal intelligence officer, AUS, 1942-43. Mem. So. Econ. Assn., So. Bus. Adminstrn. Assn. (past pres.), Am. Assn. Collegiate Schs. Bus. (past chmn. accreditation com.), Miss. Econ. Council, Beta Gamma Sigma, Delta Sigma Pi, Omicron Delta Kappa, Omicron Delta Epsilon, Pi Sigma Epsilon, Phi Kappa Phi, Alpha Sigma Phi. Presbyn. Rotarian. Home: Starkville MS 39759 Office: Drawer 5288 State College MS 39762

ROGERS, GINGER (VIRGINIA KATHERINE MCMATH), dancer, actress; b. Independence, Mo., July 16, 1911; d. William Eddins and Lela Emogene (Owens) McMath; ed. pub. schs. Began as a child dancer, 1926; appeared in motion pictures, 1930—; starred in Broadway prodns. Top Speed and Girl Crazy, 1929-30; danced with Fred Astaire in Flying Down to Rio, 1933; has co-starred with Astaire in numerous motion picture prodns., including Top Hat, Gay Divorcee, Follow the Fleet, Swing Time, Roberta Shall We Dance; has also appeared in Twenty Million Sweethearts, Change of Heart, Chance at Heaven, The Sap from Syracuse, Sitting Pretty, Young Man of Manhattan, Star of Midnight, Top Hat, In Person, Golddiggers of 1933, Stage Door, Vivacious Lady, Having a Wonderful Time, Carefree, The Story of Vernon and Irene Castle, Bachelor Mother, Fifth Avenue Girl, Primrose Path, Lucky Partners, Kitty Foyle, Tom Dick and Harry, Roxy Hart, Major and Minor, Tales of Manhattan, Once Upon a Honeymoon, Lady in the Dark, Tender Comrade, I'll Be Seeing You, Week-end at the Waldorf, Heartbeat, Magnificent Doll, It Had to Be You, Barkleys of Broadway, Perfect Strangers, Storm Warning, Groom Wore Spurs, We Are Not Married, Monkey Business, Forever Female, Dreamboat, Twist of Fate, Black Widow, Teenage Rebel, Tight Spot, O Men O Women, Harlow, The Confession; TV appearances include Bob Hope Show, Perry Como Show; star plays Hello Dolly, 1965, Mame, 1969. Recipient Academy award for Kitty Foyle, 1940. Home: Rogers Rogue River Ranch 18745 Crater Lake Hwy 62 Eagle Point OR 97524

ROGERS, HAMILTON, lawyer; b. Dilley, Tex., Apr. 7, 1914; s. C.W. and Pearl (Pollard) R.; LL.B., U. Tex., 1938; grad. Advanced Mgmt. Program, Harvard, 1952; m. Helen Margaret Dickson, Mar. 21, 1936; children—Hamilton, J. Dick, Nancy Lee, T. Pollard. Admitted to Tex. bar, 1938, practice of law, Ft. Worth, 1938-41; counsel Rowan Oil Co., 1941- 55; v.p., dir. Rowan Oil Co., 1941-55, pres., dir., 1955-58; v.p., dir. Rowan Drilling Co., Inc., 1955-58; v.p., dir. Tex. Pacific Coal & Oil Co., 1958-59, exec. v.p., dir., 1959-61; exec. v.p. Champlin Petroleum Co. (formerly Champlin Oil & Refining Co.), 1961-65, pres., 1965, chmn. bd., 1965-69, also mem. exec. com., dir., Mem. Am. Assn. Petroleum Landmen (past pres.), Tex. Ind. Producers and Royalty Owners Assn., Am., Tex., Ft. Worth bar assns., Tex. Mid-Continent Oil and Gas Assn., Kappa Sigma. Clubs: Rivercrest, Ft. Worth, Petroleum, Shady Oaks Country (Ft. Worth). Home: 5036 Bryce Ave Fort Worth TX 76107 Office: Oil & Gas Bldg Fort Worth TX 76102

ROGERS, HARTLEY, JR., mathematician, educator; b. Buffalo, July 6, 1926; s. Hartley and Margaret (Kinsey) R.; B.A., Yale U., 1946, M.S., 1950; M.A., Princeton U., 1951, Ph.D., 1952; M.A., Cambridge (Eng.) U., 1968; m. Adrianne Thorine Ellefson, Aug. 6, 1954; children—Hartley Raymond, Campbell David Kinsey, Caroline Rebecca. Asst. instr. Princeton U., 1950-52; Benjamin Peirce instr., tutor Eliot House, Harvard U., 1952-55; mem. faculty Mass. Inst. Tech., 1955—, prof. math., 1964—, chmn. faculty, 1971-73, asso. provost, 1974—; vis. fellow Clare Hall, Cambridge U., 1967-68; participant summer workshops African Math. Program, Kenya, 1965-68. Trustee Buckingham, Browne & Nichols Sch., 1975—, Kingsley Trust Asso., 1976-78, mem. jud. nominating commn. Commonwealth of Mass., 1976-79. Henry fellow Trinity Coll., Cambridge U., 1946-47; Guggenheim fellow, 1960-61; NSF sr. postdoctoral fellow, 1967-68. Mem. Assn. Symbolic Logic (v.p. 1964-67), Am. Math. Soc., Math. Assn. Am. (Lester R. Ford award 1965). Episcopalian. Clubs: Scroll and Key, Elizabethan (Yale U.); Signet (Harvard U.); St. Botolph (Boston). Author: Theory of Recursive Functions and Effective Computability, 1967. Editor: Jour. Symbolic Logic, 1960-67, Annals Math. Logic, 1968—, Jour. Computer and System Sci., 1970—; chmn. editorial bd. Mass. Inst. Tech. Press, 1974—. Contbr. articles to profl. jours. Home: 19 Lakeview Rd Winchester MA 01890 Office: Mass Inst Tech Cambridge MA 02139

ROGERS, HENRY C., public relations exec.; b. Irvington, N.J., Apr. 19, 1914; s. Maurice and Mollie (Harrison) Rogosin; student U. Pa., 1932-34, N.Y. U., 1934; m. Rosalind Jaffe, June 16, 1937; children—Macia Medavoy, Ronald Rogers. Founder, chmn. bd. Rogers & Cowan, Inc., Public Relations, N.Y.C., Beverly Hills, Calif. Trustee Los Angeles County Mus. Art, Am. Film Inst.; bd. govs. Los Angeles Music Center. Mem. Public Relations Soc. Am., Filmex Soc. (trustee), ACLU Found. (trustee). Democrat. Jewish. Home: 130 S Cliffwood Ave Los Angeles CA 90049 Office: 9665 Wilshire Blvd Beverly Hills CA 90211

ROGERS, IRVING EMERSON, newspaper publisher; b. Lawrence, Mass., Aug. 20, 1902; s. Alexander H. and Ethel Lynn (Emerson) R.; student Phillips Andover Acad., 1921, Dartmouth, 1925; m. Martha Buttrick, June 16, 1928; children—Irving Emerson, Alexander H. II. Reporter with Lawrence Eagle- Tribune, 1923, pub., pres. treas., 1942—; treas. Consol. Lawrence Eagle-Tribune Trust, both Lawrence; pub., treas. Andover Townsman, North Andover Townsman; gen. mgr. Radio Sta. WLAW, Lawrence, 1937-53; pres., treas. Hildreth & Rogers Co., 1942-53. Chmn. bd. Bon Secours-Lawrence Gen. Joint Hosp. Corp.; chmn. bd. Lawrence Boys Club; trustee Bon Secours Hosp., Rogers Family Found. Mem. N.E. Daily Newspaper Assn. Office: Eagle-Tribune Pub Co PO Box 100 Lawrence MA 01842*

ROGERS, JAMES FREDERICK, banker; b. Centerville, Iowa, June 27, 1935; s. John W. and Mildred Holly (Morris) R.; A.B., U. Mo., 1957; postgrad. Rutgers U. Grad. Sch. Banking, 1972; m. Janet L.

Marsden, July 27, 1957; children—Jennifer Frederica, John William. With Am. Security and Trust Co., Washington, 1959—, sec., 1970-72, v.p. marketing, sec., 1972-76, sr. v.p., cashier, 1976—; mem. Met. Washington Bd. Trade. Mem. Arlington County Planning Commn.; asst. treas. Kennedy Center Performing Arts; trustee Leonard Wood Found., Inst. for Tropical Diseases, New York Ave. Presbyn. Ch. Served as officer AUS, 1958-59. Mem. Am. Soc. Corporate Secs., Kappa Alpha, Phi Delta Phi. Presbyn. Clubs: University, Nat. Press (Washington). Home: 4244 Vacation Ln Arlington VA 22207 Office: 730 15th St NW Washington DC 20013

ROGERS, JOHN EDWARD, med. engring. cons.; b. Los Angeles, Dec. 9, 1926; s. John E. and Bessie M. Rogers; B.S., Inst. Elec. Engrs., Eng., 1952; M.S., West Coast U., 1959; children—Janice, Mark. Electrician Electric Constrn. Co., N.Z., 1943-49; engr. State Hydro Electric Co., N.Z., 1949-51, Tasman Empire Airways, N.Z., 1952-53; research engr. N.Am. Aviation, Los Angeles, 1953-57, research specialist, 1957-62, chief engring., 1962-66; pres. Scimedics, Inc., Los Angeles, 1966-69, Sci. Devels., Inc., Los Angeles, 1966-67; research cons. Rancho Los Amigos Hosp., Downey, Calif., 1969-76, asso. dir. tissue trauma research, 1974-76, project dir. Fracture/Amputee Center, 1969-74; pres. Talley Med. & Indsl. Equipment, Inc., 1975-76; cons. to hosps. and industry Rogers & Assocs., Anaheim, Calif., 1970-79; med. engring. cons. to physicians, patients and hosp. staff, 1965—. Recipient Performance award N.Am. Aviation, 1955, 57; Eminent Engr. award Tau Beta Pi, 1976. Mem. Assn. for Advancement of Med. Instrumentation, AAAS, Am. Congress Rehab. Medicine. Republican. Anglican. Contbr. articles on biomed. engring. to profl. jours.; patentee in field. Introduced original concepts for handicapped care; developed new med. care techniques. Office: 700 N Valley St Suite B Anaheim CA

ROGERS, JOHN JAMES WILLIAM, educator, geologist; b. Chgo., June 27, 1930; s. E. James and Josephine (Dickey) R.; B.S., Calif. Inst. Tech., 1952, Ph.D., 1955; M.S., U. Minn., 1952; m. Barbara Bongard, Nov. 30, 1956; children—Peter, Timothy. Mem. faculty Rice U., 1954-74, prof. geology, 1963-74, chmn. dept., 1971-74, master Brown Coll., 1966-71, Minnie Stevens Piper prof., 1967; W.R. Kenan, Jr. prof. geology U. N.C., Chapel Hill, 1975—. Trustee Gulf Univs. Research Consortium, 1970-73, sec., 1971-73. Fellow Geol. Soc. Am., Mineral. Soc. Am., Geol. Soc. India, AAAS; mem. Am. Assn. Petroleum Geologists, Soc. Econ. Paleontologists and Mineralogists, Geochem. Soc., Nat. Assn. Geology Tchrs., Am. Geophys. Union. Author: (with John A.S. Adams) Fundamentals of Geology, 1966; (with Robert Lankford) Holocene Geology of the Galveston Bay Area; also articles. Office: Dept Geology Mitchell Hall 029A U NC Chapel Hill NC 27514

ROGERS, JOHN S(TANLEY), union ofcl.; b. Scranton, Pa., Nov. 19, 1930; student U. Wis., 1959-61, U. Mich., 1963; student spl. studies Am. U., 1965-66. Harvard U. Bus. Sch., 1967. Rec. sec. Local 1937, United Brotherhood of Carpenters and Joiners of Am., 1954-60, internat. rep., 1958-65, asst. to pres., 1966-74, mem. gen. exec. bd., 1974-78, dir. edn., 1971-74, gen. sec., Washington, 1979—; sec.-treas. Suffolk County (N.Y.) Dist. Council Carpenters, 1957-58; v.p. N.Y. State Bldg. and Constrn. Trades Council, 1979—, N.Y. State Fedn. Labor, 1979—; pres. N.Y. State Council Carpenters, 1979—; vice chmn. N.Y. State Commn. Jobs and Energy; mem. Suffolk County Public Employment Relations Bd.; vis. lectr. George Meany Center Labor Studies. Fund chmn. L.I. action com. Assn. for Help Retarded Children, 1956-60; labor co-chmn, United Cerebral Palsy, N.Y.C., 1977-78. Mem. Harvard Trade Union Alumnae Assn. Author Numerous trade union leadership mans. and instructional materials, 1966-79. Home: 75 Atlantic Pl Hauppauge NY 11787 Office: 101 Constitution Ave NW Washington DC 20001

ROGERS, JON GUY, psychologist, univ. dean; b. Kansas City, Kans., Jan. 17, 1938; s. George Leonard and Bernice Lavere (Farmer) R.; B.A., Kans. State Coll. at Emporia, 1960; M.A., U. Ark., 1963; Ph.D. (NSF fellow, NDEA fellow), U. N.Mex., 1967; m. Kathryn Frances Counts, June 29, 1962; children—Laura Lea, Todd Matthew. Asst. prof. Hendrix Coll., Conway, Ark., 1962-65; staff psychologist Sandia Lab., Albuquerque, 1966-67; staff psychologist Marshall Space Flight Center, NASA, Huntsville, Ala., 1967; prof. psychology, dean Sch. Humanities and Behavioral Sci., U. Ala. at Huntsville, 1968—. Cons. Sandia Corp.; mgmt. cons. IBM Corp., Huntsville Hosp.; mem. Ala. Bd. Psychol. Cons. to Rehab.; speaker Madison County Mental Health Assn. IBEN scholar, 1957. Mem. N.Y. Acad. Sci., Human Factors Soc., Nat. Rehab. Assn., Sigma Xi. Contbr. articles to profl. jours. Home: 2702 Churchill Dr SE Huntsville AL 35801 Office: PO Box 1247 U Ala Huntsville AL 35807

ROGERS, JON GUY, univ. adminstr., clin. psychologist; b. Kansas City, Kans., Jan. 17, 1938; A.B., Kans. State U., 1960; M.A. in Psychology, U. Ark., 1963; Ph.D., U. N.Mex., 1967; m. Kathryn Frances Counts, June 29, 1962; children—Laura Lea, Todd Matthew. Instr., U.S. AFB, 1962-63; asst. prof. psychology Hendrix Coll., 1962-65; NDEA fellow U. N.Mex., 1965-67; research psychologist NASA, Huntsville, Ala., 1967-68; asst. prof. psychology U. Ala., Huntsville, 1968-70, asso. prof., 1971-74, prof., 1975—, dean Sch. Humanities and Behavioral Scis., 1972—; vis. faculty mem. Ark. State Tchrs. Coll., summer 1965; NSF fellow NSF Summer Research, 1963; mem. human factors staff Sandia Corp., summer 1966; cons. Vocat. Rehab. Service; mem. Ala. Gov.'s Coms. on Employment Handicapped. Recipient Profl. award Huntsville Area Com., 1976. Mem. Am. Psychol. Assn., N.Y. Acad. Sci., Human Factors Soc., Nat. Rehab. Assn., Sigma Xi. Methodist. Club: Rotary. Contbr. articles to profl. jours. Home: 2702 Churchill Dr Huntsville AL 35801 Office: PO Box 1247 Huntsville AL 35807

ROGERS, JORDAN THOMAS, trade cons.; b. Hartsville, S.C., May 25, 1921; s. Paul Hamilton and Arabella Toole (Thomas) R.; A.B., U. N.C., 1942; M.S., Mass. Inst. Tech., 1943; M.A., Cath. U. Am., 1972; m. Sarah Louisa Flinn, Oct. 17, 1945 (dec. Nov. 18, 1976); children—Elinor Walker, Arabella Thomas (Mrs. Robert Meadows-Rogers), Sarah Louisa (Mrs. Barry Evans), Jane Elizabeth; m. 2d, Dulcie Mary Nicholson, Sept. 3, 1977 (dec. Oct. 1979). With U.S. Fgn. Service, 1946-73; served in Germany, Hungary, Argentina, Ecuador, 1946-61; minister-counselor, dep. chief of mission Am. embassy, Rawalpindi, Pakistan, 1968-69; dir. Office Regional Econ. Policy, Bur. Inter-Am. Affairs, Dept. State, Washington, 1970-73; dir. Bur. Internat. Commerce, Pa. Dept. Commerce, Harrisburg, 1974-78; owner Venture Internat., internat. trade cons. firm, 1978—. Served to capt. USAAF, 1942-46. Home: 148 Old Ford Dr Camp Hill PA 17011

ROGERS, JOSEPH PATRICK, lawyer; b. Syracuse, N.Y., Sept. 3, 1906; s. Joseph P. and Mary (Ryan) R.; LL.B., Cornell U., 1928; m. Helen Montgomery, Aug. 17, 1935; children—Joseph Patrick, John Otto, Jane (Mrs. Robert J. Corcoran). Admitted to N.Y. bar, 1929, since practiced in Syracuse; partner firm Hiscock, Lee, Rogers, Henley & Barclay, 1948—. Dir., sec. Columbian Rope Co.; dir. Excelsior Ins. Co. N.Y., Vega Industries, Inc.; dir., sec. Newton Line Co., Syracuse Cold Storage Co. Mem. Am., N.Y. State, Onondaga County bar assns., Am. Judicature Soc., Syracuse C. of C. Clubs: Cornell (dir.), University, Century (Syracuse); Skaneateles Country. Home: 301 Highland Ave Syracuse NY 13203 Office: First Trust Bldg Syracuse NY 13201

ROGERS, KENNETH CANNICOTT, physicist, ednl. adminstr.; b. Teaneck, N.J., Mar. 21, 1929; s. Ralph Waldo and Ruth (Geltner) R.; B.S., St. Lawrence U., 1950, M.A., 1952; Ph.D., Columbia U., 1956; M.Engring.(hon.), Stevens Inst. Tech., 1964; m. Katharine Munzer, Aug. 4, 1956; children—Margaret, Christopher, Thomas. Research asso. Lab. Nuclear Studies Cornell U., Ithaca, N.Y., 1955-57; asst. prof. physics Stevens Inst. Tech., Hoboken, N.J., 1957-60, asso. prof., 1960-64, prof., 1964—, head physics dept., 1968-72, acting provost, dean of faculty, 1972, pres., 1972—; dir. First Jersey Nat. Corp., Pub. Service Electric & Gas Co. Fellow Royal Soc. Arts; mem. AAAS, Am. Phys. Soc., IEEE, N.Y. Acad. Scis., Newcomen Soc., N.J. C. of C. (state dir. 1974—), Sigma Xi. Club: Cosmos. Patentee in field. Home: Castle Point Station Hoboken NJ 07030 Office: Stevens Institute Technology Hoboken NJ 07030

ROGERS, KENNETH DYER, educator, physician; b. Cin., May 23, 1921; s. H. Kenneth and Marion (Dubois) R.; A.B., DePauw U., 1942; M.D., U. Cin., 1945; M.P.H., U. Pitts., 1953. Intern U. Iowa Hosps., 1945-46; resident Grady Hosp., Atlanta, 1949-50, Children's Hosp., Cin., 1950-52; practice medicine specializing in pediatrics and pub. health, Pitts., 1952—; instr. pediatrics and preventive medicine U. Cin. Med. Sch., 1951-52; asst. prof. to asso. prof. maternal and child health U. Pitts. Sch. Pub. Health, 1953-60, prof., chmn. dept. community medicine Med. Sch., 1960—. Cons. WHO, NIH, USPHS; mem. preventive medicine and pub. health test com., 1961-68, research advisory com. Nat. Bd. Med. Examiners, 1961-76. Served with USNR, 1942-48. Mem. Am. Acad. Pediatrics, Am. Pediatric Soc., Internat. Epidemiological Assn., Am. Coll. Preventive Medicine (v.p. for gen. preventive medicine 1973-74), Assn. Tchrs. Preventive Medicine (pres. 1969, exec. com. 1964-70). Home: 245 Melwood St Pittsburgh PA 15213

ROGERS, KENNETH RAY, entertainer; b. Houston; s. Edward Floyd and Lucille (Hester) R.; student U. Houston; m. Marrianne Gordon, Oct. 2, 1977. Appeared on American Bandstand; mem. Bobby Doyle Trio, then Christy Minstrels, 1966-67, The First Edition, 1967-76; performed numerous concerts in U.S., Can., Eng., Scotland and New Zealand; starred in own syndicated TV series Rollin; appearances on Tonight Show; recording artist with United Artists Records, 1976—; recs. include Just Dropped In To See What Condition My Condition Was In, But You Know I Love You, Ruby (Don't Take Your Love to Town), Tell It All Brother, Heed the Call, Reuben James, Somethin's Burnin', Love Lifted Me, Homemade Love, Laura, While The Feeling's Good, Lucille, Daytime Friends, Ten Years of Gold, Every Time Two Fools Collide, Love or Something Like It, The Gambler, You Decorated My Life, Coward of the County. Named Cross-over Artist of Year, Billboard mag., 1977, Top Male Vocalist; recipient Country Music Assn. awards, 1978, 79, Grammy award, 1977, Brit. Country Music Assn. award, Acad. Country Music award. Address: care Ken Kragen or Guy Thomas Kragen & Co 1112 N Sherbourne Dr Los Angeles CA 90069

ROGERS, LAWRENCE H., II, gen. mgmt. cons.; b. Trenton, N.J., Sept. 6, 1921; s. Norman Tallman and Nancy (Titus) R.; grad. Lawrenceville Sch., 1939; B.A., Princeton, 1943; student Harvard, 1963; m. Suzanne Long; children—Hallie, Suzanne, Lawrence H. III, Campbell, Natalie, Christian. A pioneer broadcast editorials; built sta. WSAZ-TV Inc.; with Taft Broadcasting Co., Cin., 1960-76, pres., 1963-76; pres., chief exec. officer Omega Communications, Inc., Orlando, Fla., 1977—, chmn. bd., pres. Devel. Communications, Inc., 1976—; dir. Allied Technology Inc., InterOcean Ins. Co., Cin., Oak Industries, Inc. chmn. bd. dirs. Cin. br. Fed. Res. Bank of Cleve.; dir. Cin. Financial Corp., Cardinal Fund, Inc., Columbus, Ohio. Past mem. TV Code Rev. Bd.; treas. TV Bur. Advt., then chmn. bd. dirs.; vice chmn. bd. NBC-TV Affiliates; v.p., dir. Assn. Maximum Service Telecaster, Washington; mem. information com. Nat. Assn. Broadcasters, then editorial com.; mem. TV Code Rev. Bd. Vice chmn. trustees distbn. com. Greater Cin. Found. Former Gov. W.Va. Econ. Devel. Agy. Bd. dirs. Cin. Council World Affairs, Theatre Devel. Fund; gen. chmn. Greater Cin. Fine Arts Fund. Served to capt. F.A., AUS, World War II; ETO. Recipient Distinguished Service award U.S. Jr. C. of C., 1956. Mem. Washington Broadcasting Club, Internat. Radio TV Exec. Soc., Newcomen Soc. Clubs: Queen City (Cin.); Camargo; Brook (N.Y.C.); Rolling Rock (Ligonier, Pa.). Home and office: 4600 Drake Rd Cincinnati OH 45243

ROGERS, LAWRENCE S., psychologist; b. N.Y.C., July 6, 1913; s. Morris O. and Esther (Simon) R.; B.S., Bklyn. Coll., 1933; M.A., Columbia, 1934, Ph.D., 1940; m. Tessie Deich, Aug. 28, 1938; children—Susan M., Michael D. Psychologist, USPHS, 1945; counselor Yale Vocat. Counseling Service, 1946; chief clin. psychologist VA Mental Hygiene Clinic, Denver, 1947-72, chief clinic, 1972-76; clin. prof. psychology U. Colo. Sch. Medicine, 1963—; faculty affiliate Colo. State U., 1969—; clin. affiliate Sch. Profl. Psychology, U. Denver, 1976-77. Chmn. Colo. Bd. Psychologist Examiners, 1961-65; chmn. Intermountain Regional Bd. Am. Bd. Profl. Psychology, 1972-73. Diplomate clinic psychology Am. Bd. Examiners Profl. Psychology. Fellow Am. Psychol. Assn. (council, pres. div. psychologists in pub. service and Rocky Mountain br. 1954-55); mem. Colo. Psychol. Assn. (pres. 1949-50, chmn. bd. dirs. 1956-57, chmn. bd. examiners 1956-57), Colo. Assn. Mental Health (dir. 1953-55, chmn. prof. adv. com. 1955-57), Am. Assn. State Psychology Bds. (pres. 1965-66), Internat. Council Psychologists (sec. 1965-66). Home: 2098 Q Ronda Granada Laguna Hills CA 92653

ROGERS, LEE FRANK, radiologist; b. Colchester, Vt., Sept. 24, 1934; s. Watson Frank and Marguerite Mortimer (Cole) R.; B.S., Northwestern U., 1956, M.D., 1959; m. Donna Mae Brinker, June 20, 1956; children—Michelle, Cynthia, Christopher, Matthew. Commd. 2d lt. U.S. Army, 1959, advanced through grades to maj., 1967; rotating intern Walter Reed Gen. Hosp., 1959-60; resident radiology Fitzsimons Gen. Hosp., 1960-63; ret., 1967; radiologist Baptist Meml. Hosp., San Antonio, 1967-68, U. Tex. Med. Sch., San Antonio, 1968-71; dir. residency tng., radiologist U. Tex. Med. Sch., Houston, 1972-74; prof., chmn. dept. radiology Northwestern U. Med. Sch., Chgo., 1974—. Fellow Am. Coll. Radiology; mem. Am. Roentgen Ray Soc., Assn. U. Radiologists, Radiology Soc. N.Am., Alpha Omega Alpha. Episcopalian. Home: 815 Mt Pleasant St Winnetka IL 60093 Office: 303 E Chicago Ave Chicago IL 60611

ROGERS, LEWIS HENRY, environ. cons.; b. DeFuniak Springs, Fla., Oct. 1, 1910; s. Henry Jewett and Ruby Edwards (Rose) R.; B.Ch.E., U. Fla., 1932, M.S., 1934; Ph.D., Cornell U., 1941; m. Lucile Ellenberg, June 2, 1934; children—Mary Frances Rogers Rasmus, James Lewis. Instr. soil chemistry U. Fla., 1934-36, asst. prof., 1936-39, asso. prof., 1939-46, prof., 1946-48; research supr. Union Carbide Nuclear, Oak Ridge, 1948-52; leader Analyt. div. Kraftco Research Lab., Oakdale, L.I., 1952-54; sr. chemist Air Pollution Found., Los Angeles, 1954-58; asso. dir. Research Lab., Automation Industries, West Orange, N.J. and Los Angeles, 1958-65, dir., 1965-69, dir. corporate research and devel., 1969-71; exec. v.p. Air Pollution Control Assn., Pitts., 1971-78, emeritus, 1978—; environ. cons., 1978—; mem. adv. com. Air Pollution Control Dist., Los Angeles, 1955-58; mem. adv. com. Air Pollution Control Bur., Pitts., 1972-78. Mem. Chatham Twp. (N.J.) Bd. Edn., 1961-63, pres., 1963. Served to maj. USAAF, 1942-46. Mem. Am. Chem. Soc., Air Pollution Control Assn. (hon.), AAAS, Am. Soc. Assn. Execs., Sigma Xi, Sigma Tau, Gamma Sigma Epsilon. Democrat. Methodist. Club: Rotary (Gainesville, Fla.). Contbr. numerous articles to sci. jours. Home: 2607 NW 22d Ave Gainesville FL 32605 Office: Environ Sci and Engring Box 13454 Univ Sta Gainesville FL 32601

ROGERS, LOCKHART BURGESS, educator, chemist; b. Manchester, Conn., July 16, 1917; s. William Lockhart and Mabel (Burgess) R.; A.B., Wesleyan U., Middletown, Conn., 1939; A.M., Princeton, 1940, Ph.D., 1942; m. Eleanor Greene Smith, Sept. 6, 1952; children—Eleanor Smith (Mrs. Peter R. Johnson), Winslow Smith. Instr., then asst. prof. Stanford, 1942-46; group leader Oak Ridge Nat. Lab., 1946-48; from asst. prof. to prof. Mass. Inst. Tech., 1948-61; prof. chemistry Purdue U., 1961-74; Graham Perdue prof. chemistry U. Ga., Athens, 1974—. Mem. adv. com. NSF, NIH, EPA, Army Research Office, Durham, USAF Office Sci. Research; mem. adv. com., analytical div. Oak Ridge Nat. Lab., Lawrence Livermore Lab., Nat. Bur. Standards; mem. commn. equilibrium data Internat. Union Pure and Applied Chemistry 1967-73, 77—, mem. U.S. nat. com., 1968-71; chmn. Gordon Conf. Analytical Chemistry, 1954; mem. com. on analytical chemistry NRC. Mem. Am. Chem. Soc. (awards Chromatography, analytical chemistry; chmn. Northeastern sect. 1959; nat. councilor Northeastern sect. 1957-59, Purdue sect. 1967-74; sec.-treas. analytical div. 1959-61, chmn. 1961), Electrochem. Soc. (chmn. Boston sect. 1959, nat. councilor 1960), Am. Acad. Arts and Scis., Phi Beta Kappa, Sigma Xi, Phi Lambda Upsilon (hon.), Alpha Chi Sigma, Delta Tau Delta. Editorial adv. com. Analytical Chemistry, Talanta, Separation Sci., Jour. Electrochem. Soc. Research trace analysis, electrochemistry and luminescence, analytical separations. Home: 219 Rolling Wood Dr Athens GA 30605

ROGERS, LORENE LANE (MRS. BURL GORDON ROGERS), univ. pres.; b. Prosper, Tex., Apr. 3, 1914; d. Mort M. and Jessie L. (Luster) Lane; B.A., N. Tex. State Coll., 1934; M.A. (Parke, Davis fellow), U. Tex., 1946, Ph.D., 1948; D.Sc., Oakland U., 1972; LL.D. (hon.), Austin Coll., 1977; m. Burl Gordon Rogers, Aug. 23, 1935 (dec. June, 1941). Prof. chemistry Sam Houston State Coll., Huntsville, Tex., 1947-49; research scientist Clayton Found. Biochem. Inst., U. Tex., Austin, 1950-64, asst. dir., 1957-64, prof. nutrition, 1962—, asso. dean Grad. Sch., 1964-71, v.p. univ., 1971-74, pres., 1974—, mem. exec. com. African grad. fellowship program, 1966-71. Vis. scientist, lectr., cons. NSF, 1959-62; cons. S.W. Research Inst., San Antonio, 1959-62; mem. Grad. Record Exams Bd., 1972—, chmn., 1974-75; adv. com. Internat. Tel. & Tel. Corp. Internat. Fellowship, 1973—. Eli Lilly fellow, 1949-50. Recipient U. Tex. Students Assn. Teaching Excellence award, 1963; Distinguished Alumnus award N. Tex. State U., 1972; Outstanding Woman of Austin award, 1971; Distinguished Alumnus award U. Tex., 1976. Fellow Am. Inst. Chemists; mem. A.A.A.S., Am. Chem. Soc. (sec. 1954-56), Am. Inst. Nutrition, Am. Soc. Human Genetics, Assn. Grad. Schs. (internat. edn. com. 1967-71), Sigma Xi, Phi Kappa Phi, Iota Sigma Pi. Research in hydantoin synthesis, intermediary metabolism, biochem. nutritional aspects of alcoholism, mental retardation, congenital malformations. Home: 4 Nob Hill Circle Austin TX 78746 Office: Univ Tex Main Bldg 400 Austin TX 78712

ROGERS, M(AYNARD) L(IVINGSTON), JR. (TEX), editor; b. Houston, Dec. 7, 1942; s. M. L. and Pearl (Bolin) R.; grad. journalism Tex. A. and M. U., 1965; m. Sally F. Shepard, Nov. 24, 1964; children—David, Travis. Asso. pub. Stamford (Tex.) Am., 1965-66; editor-pub. Omaha (Tex.) Times, 1967-68; farm editor Big Spring (Tex.) Herald, 1968-69; farm reporter Houston Post, 1969-70; editor Tex. & Southwestern Horseman, Houston, 1970-72; editor Horseman Mag., Horseman Books, Houston, 1973-77; editor-gen. mgr. Spring Creek Sun-Dispatch, Pinehurst, Tex., 1977—. Mem. com. youth horse show Houston Livestock Show, Rodeo, 1974. Named Writer Best Sports Story Tex. AP, 1968. Mem. Tex. Horse Council (acting pres. 1974), Am. Quarter Horse Assn., Nat. Cutting Horse Assn., Appaloosa Horse Club Inc. Author: Mare Owner's Handbook, 1971; editor award winning newspapers; writings have appeared in Congl. Record. Home: 215 Kelly Dr Magnolia TX 77355 Office: 34703 FM 149 Pinehurst TX 77362

ROGERS, MAC EDWIN, govt. ofcl.; b. Cookeville, Tenn., Apr. 26, 1921; s. Frank L. and Lula (Burroughs) R.; certificate Western Res. U., 1952; student Harvard, 1962; m. Mary Ann Burton, Oct. 1, 1941; children—Pamela, Marc. Brakeman, Pa. R.R., 1941, condr., 1946-48; with Office Brotherhood R.R. Trainmen, Cleve., 1948-54, research and edn. dir., 1954-64; state legislative rep. Ohio, 1964-68; 1st dir. Bur. R.R. Safety, 1968-75; asso. adminstr. Fed. R.R. Adminstrn., Dept. Transp., Washington, 1968-75, fed. programs assistance liaison specialist Southeast area, College Park, Ga., 1975—. Served as officer, inf. AUS, 1942-46. Decorated Combat Inf. badge. Mason (Shriner). Home: 995 Lost Forest Dr Sandy Springs GA 30328 Office: 1720 Peachtree Rd NE Suite 440-A Atlanta GA 30309

ROGERS, MARGUERITE MOILLIET, physicist; b. Minatitlan, Vera Cruz, Nov. 6, 1915; d. Alexander Keir and Odo (Surratt) Moilliet; A.B., Rice U., 1937, M.A., 1937, Ph.D., 1940; m. Fred Terry Rogers, Jr., June 10, 1936 (dec. Feb. 1956); children—Alexander Keir, Fred Terry, Charles Galton, Robert Barclay, Alison Margaret. Instr., U. Houston, 1940-43; head optics sect. Naval Ordnance Plant, Indpls., 1943-45; research asso. U. N.C., 1947-48; sr. physicist Oak Ridge Nat. Lab., 1948-49; research physicist U.S. Naval Ordnance Test Sta., China Lake, Calif., 1949-53; prof., head sci. div. Columbis (S.C.) Coll., 1954-56; lectr. Toyal Tech. Coll., Salford, Eng., 1956-57; head analysis br., aviation ordnance dept. U.S. Naval Weapons Center, China Lake, 1957-62, head air to surface weapons div. weapons devel. dept., 1962-67, head weapons systems analysis div., 1967-74, head systems devel. dept., also asst. tech. dir. systems, 1974—. Fellow Tex. Acad. Sci.; mem. Sci. Research Soc. Am. (treas. China Lake chpt., 1959-60), sec. 1960-61, Am. Physics Soc., AAAS, Phi Beta Kappa, Sigma Xi. Home: PO Box 804 Ridgecrest CA 93555 Office: US Naval Weapons Center Code 31 China Lake CA 93555

ROGERS, MAX TOFIELD, educator; b. Edmonton, Alta., Can., Jan. 12, 1917; s. Harry Earlby and Edith (Tofield) R.; B.Sc., U. Alta., 1937, M.Sc., 1938; Ph.D., Calif. Inst. Tech., 1941; m. Ethel Pearl McMaster, 1943; children—Richard Eugene, Kathleen Elaine. Came to U.S., 1938, naturalized, 1944. Postdoctoral fellow Calif. Inst. Tech., Pasadena, 1941-42; instr. chemistry U. Calif. at Los Angeles, 1942-46; faculty Mich. State U., East Lansing, 1946—, asso. prof., 1948-55, prof., 1955—. Robert Tegler fellow, 1937-38; Guggenheim Found. fellow, 1954-55; NSF sr. postdoctoral fellow, 1962-63. Mem. Am. Chem. Soc. (chmn. phys. chemistry div. 1969-70), Am. Phys. Soc., Chem. Soc. London, A.A.A.S., Am. Assn. U. Profs., Sigma Xi. Home: 915 Lantern Hill Dr East Lansing MI 48823

ROGERS, MILLARD FOSTER, JR., art mus. dir.; b. Texarkana, Tex., Aug. 27, 1932; s. Millard Foster and Jessie Bell (Hubbell) R.; B.A. with honors, Mich. State U., 1954; M.A., U. Mich., 1958; m. Nina Olds, Aug. 3, 1963; 1 son, Seth Olds. Gosline fellow Victoria and Albert Mus., London, Eng., 1959; curator Am. art Toledo Mus. Art, 1959-67; dir. Elvehjem Art Center, prof. art history U. Wis.-Madison, 1967-74; dir. Cin. Art Mus., 1974—. Served with AUS, 1954-56. Mem. Assn. Art Mus. Dirs., Am. Assn. Mus. Author: Randolph Rogers, American Sculptor in Rome, 1971; Spanish Paintings in the

Cincinnati Art Museum, 1978. Address: care Cincinnati Art Museum Cincinnati OH 45202

ROGERS, NATHANIEL SIMS, banker; b. New Albany, Miss., Nov. 17, 1919; s. Arthur L. and Elizabeth (Bouton) R.; A.B., Millsaps Coll., 1941; M.B.A., Harvard, 1947; m. Helen Elizabeth Ricks, July 3, 1942; children—Alice, John, Lewis. With Deposit Guaranty Bank and Trust Co., Jackson, Miss., 1947-69, 1st v.p. 1957-58, pres., dir., 1958-69, chmn. dir. 1st City Nat. Bank Houston, 1969—; dir. Standard Life Ins. Co., Lomas & Nettleton Fin. Corp., Gulf States Utilities Co., Beaumont, Tex., Gt. So. Life Ins. Co. Chmn. Jackson United Givers Fund, 1957, pres., 1959, bd. dirs., 1958-61; pres. Andrew Jackson area council Boy Scouts Am., 1962; trustee Miss. Found. Ind. Colls., 1959-69; past pres., trustee Millsaps Coll.; trustee Methodist Hosp., Houston. Served to lt. (s.g.) USNR, 1942-46. Named Outstanding Young Man of Year, Jackson Jr. C. of C., 1955. Mem. Am. (pres. 1969-70), Miss. (pres. jr. banker sect. 1952-53; pres. 1964-65) bankers assns., Robert Morris Assos. (pres. S.E. chpt. 1954-55 nat. dir. 1959-62), Assn. Res. City Bankers, Jackson C. of C. (pres. 1962), Young Pres.'s Orgn., Millsaps Coll. Alumni Assn. (pres. 1955-56), Newcomen Soc., Omicron Delta Kappa, Kappa Alpha. Methodist (chmn. ofcl. bd.). Home: 3631 Meadow Lake Ln Houston TX 77027 Office: 1001 Main St Houston TX 77002

ROGERS, PAUL GRANT, lawyer, former Congressman; b. Ocilla, Ga., June 4, 1921; s. Dwight L. and Florence (Roberts) R.; B.A., U. Fla., 1942, LL.B., 1948; LL.D. (hon.), Fla. Atlantic U., U. Md., George Washington U.; D.Sc. (hon.), U. Miami, Albany Med. Coll. of Union U.; H.H.D. (hon.), Nova U.; L.H.D. (hon.), N.Y. Med. Coll.; m. Rebecca Bell, Dec. 15, 1962; 1 dau., Rebecca Laing. Admitted to Fla. bar, 1948; partner firm Burns, Middleton, Rogers, Farrell & Faust, 1952-69; mem. 84th-95th Congresses from 11th Dist. Fla., chmn. health and environ. subcom.; partner firm Hogan & Hartson, Washington, 1979—. Served to maj. F.A., AUS, 1942-46. Markle scholar, 1973. Mem. Am., Fla. (gov. jr. sect. 1952-53), Palm Beach County bar assns., Jud. Conf. U.S. (adv. com. on civil rules), Inst. Medicine of Nat. Acad. Scis., Phi Delta Phi, Phi Delta Theta. Methodist (steward). Office: Hogan & Hartson 815 Connecticut Ave NW Washington DC 20006

ROGERS, PETER, advt. agency exec.; b. Hattiesburg, Miss., Jan. 24, 1934; s. Henry Halcomb and Nettie Merle (Hudson) R.; B.S., U. S.Miss., 1957. With production dept. Warwick and Legler, 1960-62, traffic dept. Doyle, Dane and Bernbach, 1962-63; exec. v.p. Trahey Advt., 1963-74; pres. Peter Rogers Assos., N.Y.C., 1974—. Served with U.S. Army, 1957-59. Recipient 4 creativity certificates of distinctions, 1974, 75, 77; Andy award of excellence, 1975, 76, 78; Print awards, 1978, 79; Andy award of merit, 1975, 78, 79; 6 creativity certs. of distinction, 1976, one cert., 1978. Mem. Advt. Club Am. Author: The Blackgama Story, 1979. Home: 215 E 79th St New York NY 10021 Office: 730 Fifth Ave New York NY 10019

ROGERS, PETER PHILIP, environ. engr.; b. Liverpool. Eng., Apr. 30, 1937; s. Edward Joseph and Ellen (Duggan) R.; came to U.S., 1960, naturalized, 1977; B.Engring., Liverpool U., 1958; M.S., Northwestern U., 1961; Ph.D., Harvard U., 1966; m. Rosemarie Rogers, July 11, 1964; children—Christopher, Justin. Asst. engr. Sir Alfred McAlpine & Sons Ltd., Cheshire, Eng., 1958-60; mem. faculty Harvard U., 1966—, Gordon McKay prof. environ. engring., 1974—, prof. city planning, 1974—; prin. Meta Systems Inc., Cambridge, Mass.; mem. Center Population Studies, Harvard U. Sch. Pub. Health, 1974—. Gordon McKay teaching fellow, 1961; Radley research student, 1962-64; doctoral dissertation fellow Resources for Future, 1964-65; recipient Clemens Herschel prize Harvard U., 1964; Guggenheim fellow, 1973. Mem. Am. Geophys. Union, Internat. Assn. Hydrology Socs., Ops. Research Soc., Inst. Mgmt. Sci., Sigma Xi. Club: Delhi Polo (New Delhi). Co-author: Urbanization and Change, 1970; Land Use and The Pipe: Planning for Sewerage, 1976. Home: 20 Berkeley St Cambridge MA 02138 Office: Pierce Hall 121 Harvard U Cambridge MA 02138

ROGERS, RALPH B., business exec.; b. Boston, 1909; ed. Northeastern U.; married. With Cummins Diesel Engine Corp., Edwards Co., Hill Diesel Engine Co., Ideal Power Lawnmower Co., Indian Motocycle Co., Rogers Diesel & Aircraft Corp., Rogers Internat. Corp., Armstrong Rubber Export Corp.; with Tex. Industries Inc., Dallas, 1950—, chmn. bd., pres., chief exec. officer, 1951-75; chmn. bd., 1975—; dir. numerous subsidiaries; dir. Chapparal Steel Co. Chmn. bd. dirs. Tex. Industries Found., Pub. Communication Found. North Tex.; formerly chmn. bd. govs. Pub. Broadcasting Service; trustee Northeastern U., St. Mark's Sch. Tex.; chmn. bd. mgrs. Dallas County Hosp. Dist. Mason. Home: 10621 Strait Ln Dallas TX 75229 Office: 8100 Carpenter Freeway Dallas TX 75247

ROGERS, RICHARD DEAN, judge; b. Oberlin, Kans., Dec. 29, 1921; s. William Clark and Evelyn May (Christian) R.; B.S., Kans. State U., 1943; J.D., Kans. U., 1947; m. Helen Elizabeth Stewart, June 6, 1947; children—Letitia Ann, Cappi Christian, Richard Kurt. Admitted to Kans. bar, 1947; partner firm Springer and Rogers, Attys., Manhattan, Kans., 1947-58; instr. bus. law Kans. State U., 1948-52; partner firm Rogers, Stites & Hill, Manhattan, 1959-75; gen. counsel Kans. Farm Bur. & Service Cos., Manhattan, 1960-75; judge U.S. Dist. Ct., Topeka, Kans., 1975—. City commnr., Manhattan, 1950-52, 60-64; mayor Manhattan, 1952, 64; county atty., Riley County, Kans., 1954-58; state rep., 1964-68; state senator, 1968-75, pres. Kans. Senate, 1975. Served with USAAF, 1943-45. Decorated Air medal, Dfc. Mem. Kans., Am. bar assns., Beta Theta Pi. Republican. Presbyterian. Club: Masons. Home: 3250 Briarwood Dr Topeka KS 66611 Office: 410 Federal Bldg 444 S E Quincy St Topeka KS 66683

ROGERS, RICHARD HUNTER, lawyer; b. Flushing, N.Y., Sept. 11, 1939; s. Royden Harrison and Frances Wilma (Hunter) R.; B.S. in Bus. Adminstrn., Miami U., 1961; J.D., Duke, 1964; m. Kara Jane Parker, Sept. 2, 1961; children—Gregory P., Lynne A., Reade H. Admitted to Ill. bar, 1964, Ohio bar, 1973; atty. Continental Ill. Nat. Bank, Chgo., 1964-65; sr. atty. Brunswick Corp., Chgo., 1965-70; corporate counsel The A. Epstein Cos., Inc., real estate developers, Chgo., 1970-73; v.p., gen. counsel, sec. Price Bros. Co., Dayton, Ohio, 1973—. Pres., Miami U. Alumni Assn., Dayton; trustee Woodhaven, Inc. Mem. Am., Ill., Ohio, Dayton (chmn. corp. law dept. com.), Chgo. bar assns. Club: Miami U. President's. Home: 1169 Cedar Creek Circle Dayton OH 45459 Office: 367 W 2d St Dayton OH 45402

ROGERS, RICHARD RAYMOND, cosmetics mfg. co. exec.; b. Houston, Apr. 15, 1943; s. Julius Ben and Mary Kay R.; student North Tex. State U., 1960-63; m. Janice Lee Zielen, May 25, 1974; children—Terri, Rick, Ryan. Gen. mgr. Mary Kay Cosmetics Inc., Dallas, 1963-65, v.p., 1965-68, pres., chief exec. officer, 1968—. Baptist. Home: 5606 Bent Trail Dallas TX 75248 Office: 8787 Stemmons Freeway Dallas TX 75247

ROGERS, RICHARD WALLACE, feed and food co. exec.; b. St. Louis, Dec. 30, 1922; s. Frank D. and Frieda H. (Poertner) R.; B.S. in Bus. Adminstrn., Washington U., St. Louis, 1948; m. Virginia M. Gessett, Oct. 10, 1944; children—Steven F., Barbara J., David R., James M. Accountant, Ernst & Ernst, C.P.A.'s, St. Louis, 1948-51; asst. controller Rawlings Mfg. Co., St. Louis, 1952-60; controller Nat. Rejectors, Inc., St. Louis, 1960-62; asst. controller, dir. systems and data processing Ralston Purina Co., St. Louis, 1962-69, controller, 1969-72, corporate v.p., controller, 1972—. Mem. lay adv. bd. St. Mary's Hosp. Served to lt. USNR, World War II. Mem. Fin. Exec. Inst. (nat. dir. Midwestern area). Clubs: Norwood Hills Country, Missouri Athletic, Stadium (St. Louis). Home: 6610 Lakeside Hills Dr Florissant MO 63033 Office: 835 S 8th St St Louis MO 63102

ROGERS, ROBERT FRANCIS, television producer; b. Washington, Apr. 4, 1931; s. Robert Francis and Margaret Katherine (McLaughlin) R.; student The Citadel, 1949-50; B.A., Georgetown U., 1953; m. Elizabeth Hunter Buck, Jan. 24, 1953; children—Eileen Margaret, Christopher Thomas, Timothy Francis. Commd. 2d lt. U.S. Army, 1953, advanced through grades to capt., 1959; resigned, 1961; free lance writer, 1961-62; asso. producer, writer NBC News, 1962-67; producer, writer, dir. documentaries NBC, Washington, 1967—. Mem. Nat. Acad. TV Arts and Scis., Writers Guild Am., Dirs. Guild Am., Sigma Delta Chi. Roman Catholic. Club: Kenwood Golf and Country. Contbr. articles and stories to mags. Office: NBC 4001 Nebraska Ave NW Washington DC 20016

ROGERS, ROBERT WENTWORTH, educator; b. Boston, Dec. 1, 1914; s. Lester Frances and Elizabeth (Gill) R.; A.B., U. Mich., 1936; M.A., Harvard, 1937, Ph.D., 1942; m. Jeanne Francis Way, May 18, 1946 (dec. 1955); foster children—Susan Way, Sarah Wentworth; m. 2d, Elizabeth Belcher Yudkin, Nov. 23, 1956; one son, John Parker; foster children—Michael Yudkin, David Yudkin. Instr. English, sr. tutor Dunster House, Harvard, 1946-48; asst. prof. English, U. Ill., Champaign-Urbana, 1948-51, asso. prof., 1951-55, prof., 1955—, exec. sec. dept. English, 1953-57, acting head 1956-57, head dept., 1957-64, dean Coll. Liberal Arts and Scis., 1964-79, dean emeritus, 1979—. Mem. Commn. on Arts and Scis., Nat. Assn. State Univs. and Land Grant Colls., 1972-74. Bd. dirs. Center Research Libraries, 1964-67. Served from ensign to lt. (s.g.), USNR, 1942-46. Guggenheim fellow 1957-58. Mem. Modern Lang. Assn., Nat. Council Tchrs. English (adv. council 1960-62), Midwest Modern Lang. Assn. (pres. 1960- AAUP, Nat. Assn. Chmn. Depts. English (sec.-treas. 1963-64), Council Colls. Arts and Scis. State Univs. and Land Grant Colls. (pres. 1972), Assn. Am. Colls. (dir. 1977-80), Pilgrim Soc. (dir.), Phi Beta Kappa, Phi Kappa Phi, Psi Upsilon. Author: The Major Satires of Alexander Pope, 1955; also articles, revs. Editorial bd. jour. English and Germanic Philology, 1954-66. Home: 601 W Michigan Ave Urbana IL 61801 also Brook Rd Manomet MA 02345

ROGERS, ROBERT WILLIAM, editor, publisher; b. Los Angeles, Oct. 27, 1932; s. Ross Alexander and Anna Kathleen (Lowrey) R.; student Los Angeles City Coll., 1955, Los Angeles Conservatory Music and Arts, 1955-57; m. Mary Ann Galloway, May 16, 1959; children—Michael Richard Smith, Timothy John, Robert William. Sports reporter Los Angeles Examiner, 1951; musician, 1955-62; news stringer, then feature editor Western Outdoor News, Newport Beach, Calif., 1963-68, asso. editor, 1968-72; mktg. dir., then exec. editor Western Outdoors mag., Newport Beach, 1971-77; pub., editor Wyo. Outdoor Reporter, Sheridan, 1977—; pres. Big Horn Publs., Inc.; founder-pres. Wildlife Conservancy, 1973. Served with USNR, 1951-55. Mem. Calif. Trout Inc. (Conservation Communicator award 1975), Outdoor Writers Assn. Am., Ducks Unlimited., Wyo. Wildlife Fedn. (pres. 1979-80), Wildlife Soc. Republican. Roman Catholic. Author: The Basics of Freshwater Fishing, 1973; contbg. author: Petersen's Complete Book of Sportfishing, 1971; contbr. to numerous state, regional and nat. publs. Home: Buffalo WY Office: Big Horn Publs PO Box 1040 Buffalo WY 82834

ROGERS, ROBISON MAX, educator; b. Morgan, Utah, May 1, 1918; s. Curtis W. and Rachel (Robison) R.; B.A., Brigham Young U., 1940, A.M., 1942; Ph.D., Stanford, 1951; m. Florence Francis, Sept. 18, 1941; children—Kay, Francis, Paul, Russell, Joel, Karalee. Instr., Stanford, 1943-44; prof. German, Brigham Young U., 1945—, dir. travel-study program, 1953-58, chmn. dept. langs., 1963-67, chmn. dept. Germanic and Slavic langs., 1967-68, asst. dean humanities, 1969-75, asso. dean humanities, 1975—. Mem. Modern Lang. Assn., Am. Assn. Tchrs. German, Am. Council Teaching Fgn. Langs. Co-author: Interessantes Deutsch, 1958; German Through Conversational Patterns, 2d edit., 1973; Reviewing German, 1969; Scenes from German Drama, 1978. Home: 1167 Ash Ave Provo UT 84601

ROGERS, RODNEY ALBERT, biologist, educator; b. Lucas, Iowa, Aug. 24, 1926; s. Harold A. and Ardis (Allen) R.; B.A., Drake U., 1949, M.A., 1951; Ph.D., U. Iowa, 1955; m. Frances A. Ritchey, July 1, 1956; children—Robert, William. Asst. prof. biology Drake U., Des Moines, 1955-60, asso. prof., 1961-64, prof., 1965—, chmn. biology dept., 1966—; asso. program dir. NSF, 1967-68. Served with AUS, 1944-46; PTO. Mem. A.A.A.S., Am. Inst. Biol. Sci., Am. Soc. Parasitologists, Soc. Am. Microbiologists, Am. Soc. Zoologists, Am. Assn. U. Profs., Am. Soc. Tropical Medicine and Hygiene, Sigma Xi, Omicron Delta Kappa. Home: 4203 40th St Des Moines IA 50310

ROGERS, ROSEMARY, author; b. Panadura, Ceylon, Dec. 7, 1932; d. Cyril and Barbara (Jansze) Allan; B.A., U. Ceylon; div.; children—Rosanne, Sharon, Michael, Adam. Writer features and pub. affairs info. Associated Newspapers Ceylon, Colombo, 1959-62; sec. billeting office Travis AFB, Calif., 1964-69; sec. Solano County (Calif.) Parks Dept., Fairfield, 1969—; part-time reporter Fairfield Daily Republic; author novels: Sweet Savage Love, 1974; Dark Fires, 1975; The Wildest Heart, 1974; Wicked Loving Lies, 1976; The Crowd Pleasers, 1978. Mem. Authors Guild of Authors League Am. Democrat. Episcopalian. Office: care Avon Books 959 Eighth Ave New York NY 10019*

ROGERS, ROY, motion picture actor; b. Cin., Nov. 5, 1912; s. Andrew E. and Mattie Martha (Womach) Slye; m. Arlene Wilkins, 1936 (dec. Nov., 1946); children—Cheryl Darlene, Linda Lou, Roy Jr., Marion, Scottish Ward; m. 2d, Dale Evans; children—Robin (dec.), John, Mary Little Doe, Deborah (dec.). Organized western group Sons of the Pioneers, 1932-38; starred in first movie Under Western Stars, 1938; has since starred in 89 western pictures; former radio singer; appearances TV program series, also spls.; appeared film Mackintosh & T.J., 1977; actor, producer TV films; host TV show The Great Movie Cowboys, 1975; numerous personal appearances rodeos and fairs; rec. artist Capitol Records, 20th Century Records. Pres. Roy Rogers Enterprises; past owner Roy Rogers Apple Valley Inn, resort hotel; Roy Rogers Family restaurants franchised by Marriott Corp.; owner Roy Rogers Western World and Mus., Victorville, Cal. Mem. Musicians Union, AFTRA, Screen Actors' Guild, Am. Guild Variety Artists. Mason. Office: care Art Rush Inc 10221 Riverside Dr North Hollywood CA 91602*

ROGERS, RUTHERFORD DAVID, librarian; b. Jesup, Iowa, June 22, 1915; s. David Earl and Carrie Zoe (Beckel) R.; B.A., U. No. Iowa, 1936, Litt.D., 1977; M.A., Columbia, 1937, B.S. (Lydia Roberts fellow), 1938; D.Library Adminstrn. (hon.), U. Dayton, 1971; m. E. Margaret Stoddard, June 4, 1937; 1 dau., Jane Shelley. Asst. N.Y. Pub. Library, 1937-38; reference librarian Columbia Coll. Library, Columbia U., 1938- 41, acting librarian, 1941-42, librarian, 1942-45; research analyst Smith, Barney & Co., N.Y.C., 1946-48; dir. Grosvenor Library, Buffalo, 1948-52; dir. Rochester Pub. Library 1952-54; chief personnel office N.Y. Library, 1954-55; chief reference dept., 1955-57; chief asst. librarian of Congress, Washington, 1957-62, dep. librarian of Congress, 1962-64; dir. univ. libraries, Stanford U., 1964-69; univ. librarian Yale U., 1969—. Dir. H.W. Wilson Co., 1969—; chmn. bd. dirs. Research Libraries Group, Inc. Mem. Exam. Com. for Pub. Librarians' Certificates, N.Y. State 1951-54; mem. U.S. Adv. Council Coll. Library Resources. Bd. govs. Yale U. Press. Served from pvt. to 1st sgt. Air Transp. Command, USAAF, 1942-43, from 2d lt. to capt., planning officer, chief, spl. Planning Div., Office Asst. Chief Staff, Plans, Air Transport Command, 1943-46. Decorated officier de L'Ordre de la Couronne Belge; recipient U. No. Iowa Alumni Achievement award. Fellow Am. Acad. Arts and Scis.; mem. A.L.A. (chmn. com. Intellectual Freedom 1950-51, mem. 1950-60; 2d v.p. 1965-66, mem. exec. bd. 1961-66, trustee endowment fund), Assn. Research Libraries (dir., pres. 1967-68), N.Y. Library Assn., AAUP, Bibliog. Soc. Am., Assn. Coll. and Reference Libraries, Blue Key, Kappa Delta Pi, Sigma Tau Delta, Theta Alpha Phi. Clubs: Grolier; N.Y. Library, Columbia U., Yale (N.Y.C.); Cosmos, Kenwood Country (Washington); Roxburghe (San Francisco); Book of Cal. Author: Columbia Coll. Library Handbook, 1941; (with David C. Weber) University Library Administration, 1971; also articles in profl. jours. Home: 33 Edgehill Terr New Haven CT 06511 Office: Yale U Libraries Box 1603 A Yale Station New Haven CT 06520

ROGERS, SCOTT A(RTHUR), JR., cement co. exec.; b. Cleve., Mar. 15, 1918; B.A., Dartmouth Coll., 1940; m. Louise Schickler, Sept. 15, 1943; children—Scott A., Virginia Rogers Richmond. Pres., Am. Chain & Cable, Inc., 1972-76, Medusa Corp., 1976-79, Gen. Portland, Inc., Dallas, 1979—, also dir.; dir. Stauffer Chem. Co., Parker-Hannifin Corp. Served with U.S. Army, 1942-45. Office: PO Box 324 Dallas TX 75221

ROGERS, STANLEY, lawyer; b. Los Angeles, Feb. 28, 1934; s. Murray Harold and Rose (Mednick) R.; A.B., Princeton U., 1956; J.D., U. Calif. at Los Angeles, 1959; m. Jane Hope Fegen, Feb. 1, 1959; children—Susan Louise, John Stuart, Kenneth Andrew, Steven Michael. Admitted to Calif. bar, 1960; law clk. to judge Fed. Dist. Ct., Los Angeles, 1959-60; asso. firm Little, Curry & Hagen, Los Angeles, 1960-62; partner firm Rogers and Harris, Los Angeles, 1962—. Trustee Los Angeles County Law Library, 1977-78; mem. Consumer Affairs Commn., County of Los Angeles, 1979; mem. adv. councils local elementary, jr. and high schs.; cubmaster Boy Scouts Am.; pres. Westside Democratic Club, 1962-63; mem. Los Angeles County Central Com., Dem. party, 1967-73, 77—; chmn. del. county com., 1968-72; del. Dem. Nat. Conv., 1968; mem. state com., 1969, 70, 71, 72, 75, 76, 77. Mem. State Bar Calif., Los Angeles County, Beverly Hills bar assns., Am. Arbitration Assn. (arbitrator). Home: 661 Warner Ave Los Angeles CA 90024 Office: 9200 Sunset Blvd Los Angeles CA 90069

ROGERS, STEPHEN, newspaper publisher; b. Lansing, Mich., Feb. 24, 1912; s. Anthony and Anna (Kruszewska) R.; A.B., Mich. State Coll., 1933; m. Athenia A. Andros, Oct. 19, 1935; children—Stephen A., Christopher A., Elizabeth A. Writer, Detroit Times, 1934-35; copy editor N.Y. Herald-Tribune, European edit., Paris, France, 1936-37; spl. writer Newark Ledger, 1937-38; editorial writer, city editor Long Island Daily Press, 1938-41; editor Long Island Star-Jour., 1941-55; pub. Post Standard, Syracuse, N.Y., 1955-58, Herald-Journal, Herald-Am., Syracuse and pres. The Herald Co., 1958—. Dir. N.Y. Dental Service Corp. (N.Y.C.), Mchts. Nat. Bank. Bd. dirs. Crouse-Irving Hosp., Syracuse. Mem. N.Y. State Pubs. Assn. (pres. 1963), Am. Newspaper Pubs. Assn. Roman Catholic. Home: Duguid Rd Fayetteville NY 13066 Office: Syracuse Newspapers Ltd Clinton Sq Box 4915 Syracuse NY 13221*

ROGERS, STEPHEN DOUGLAS, profl. baseball player; b. Jefferson City, Mo., Oct. 26, 1949; s. William Leo Douglas and Constance Annabelle (Rudder) R.; B.A. in Petroleum Engring., U. Tulsa, 1971; m. Barbara Anne Bodnarchuk, Sept. 16, 1972; children—Stephen Jason, Geoffrey Douglas. Pitcher, Montreal Expos (Que., Can.), 1973—. Named mem. Rookie All Star Team and Rookie Pitcher of the Yr., 1973, to All Star Team, 1974, 78, 79. Mem. Soc. Petroleum Engrs., Kappa Sigma. Roman Catholic. Office: care Montreal Expos PO Box 500 Sta M Montreal PQ H1V 3P2 Canada

ROGERS, THEODORE COURTNEY, steel co. exec.; b. Lorain, Ohio, Aug. 25, 1934; s. William Theodore and Leona Ruth (Gerhart) R.; Sc.B., Miami U., 1956; M.B.A. summa cum laude, Marquette U., 1968; postgrad. Johns Hopkins U., 1957; m. Adele Lee Woods, June 15, 1957; children—Pamela Anne, Theodore Courtney. With Armco Inc., 1958—; pres. Olympic Fastening Systems, 1970-71, pres., 1971-74; Bathey Mfg. Co. subs., 1970, group v.p. indsl. products, 1971-74, exec. v.p. Nat. Supply Co. subs., Houston, 1974-76, pres., 1976—, v.p. parent co., 1976-79, group v.p. parent co., 1979—; dir. Ralph M. Parsons Co., chmn. compensation com., 1976, mem. exec. com., 1977—. Mem. internat. bus. com. Houston C. of C., 1976; exec. com., bd. dirs., chmn. personnel com., chmn. sustaining mem. com. Houston Met. YMCA, 1977—; div. chmn. United Fund, 1966-68, key man Pacesetter Houston campaign, 1977, chmn. Vanguard Group, 1978, Pacesetter Group, 1979; chmn. Cancer Fund, 1967; bd. dirs. Houstonian Found., U. Tex. Health Sci. Center Devel., Fisher Inst.; bd. dirs., chmn. spl. projects com. Houston Ballet; bd. dirs., co-chmn. employee edn. task force Houston chpt. Am. Heart Assn., chmn. heart fund drive; mem. Houston Council Human Relations; nat. bd. dirs. Palmer Drug Abuse, 1977—. Served with USN, 1956-58. Mem. Miami U. Alumni Club (bd. dirs. 1976—), Petroleum Equipment Suppliers Assn. (bd. dirs. 1976—), Am. Petroleum Inst., Nat. Ocean Industries Assn. (dir. 1978—), Am. Ordnance Soc., Young Pres.' Orgn. (exec. com.), Miami U. Alumni (dir., program chmn.), Beta Gamma Sigma, Kappa Phi Kappa, Sigma Chi. Presbyterian. Clubs: Ramada, Lakeside Country, Forum (founding) Univ. (chmn. bd. govs. 1977-79, chmn. atheletic com. 1977) (Houston). Home: 206 Millbrook Ln Houston TX 77024 Office: 1455 W Loop S Houston TX 77027

ROGERS, VANCE DONALD, former univ. pres.; b. Frontenac, Minn., May 16, 1917; s. Azzy Floyd and Mary C. (Martinson) R.; student Gustavus Adolphus Coll., St. Peter, Minn., 1934-36; A.B., Hamline U., 1938, LL.D., 1976; postgrad. Northwestern U., 1940-41; M.Div., Garrett Bibl. Inst., 1941; D.D., Neb. Wesleyan U., 1955; LL.D., Mt. Union Coll., 1958; L.H.D., Morningside Coll., 1960; Litt.D., Lane Coll., 1966; L.H.D., U. Nebr., 1968; m. Barbara Marie Yarwood, June 22, 1940; children—Nancy Ann (Mrs. James Steele), Mary Lou (Mrs. Roger Downs). Ordained to ministry Methodist Ch., 1941, minister Meth. Ch., Dundee, Ill., 1941-43, Brookfield, Ill., 1946-53, Trinity Meth. Ch., Lincoln, Nebr., 1953-57; pres. Nebr. Wesleyan U., Lincoln, 1957-77; chmn. bd. Pure Water, Inc., 1978—. Served as lt. comdr. Chaplains Corps, USNR, 1943-46. Mem. Neb. Acad. Scis., Newcomen Soc. N.Am., Am. Legion, Blue Key, C. of C., Phi Kappa Phi, Phi Eta Sigma, Pi Kappa Delta. Republican. Mason (Shriner, K.T.). Clubs: Univ., Lincoln Country, Rotary (Lincoln). Home: 6000 Old Cheney Rd Lincoln NE 68516. *A successful life is one that is: disciplined (body, mind, and spirit); adventuresome (seeking new ideas, innovative approaches to problem solving, and* *new areas of exploration); dedicated (to personal standards that call for mature responses-to ideal patterns of behavior-to moral and spiritual ideals rooted in the Judeo-Christian tradition).*

ROGERS, WARREN JOSEPH, JR., journalist; b. New Orleans, May 6, 1922; s. Warren Joseph and Rose Agatha (Tennyson) R.; student Tulane U., 1940-41, La. State U., 1951; m. Hilda Kenny, Dec. 23, 1943 (dec.); children—Patricia Ann, Sean, Michael (dec.); m. 2d, Alla Bilajiw, Dec. 26, 1973. Copy boy, cub reporter New Orleans Tribune, 1939-41; copyreader, columnist New Orleans Item, 1945-47; reporter A.P., Baton Rouge, 1947-51, Washington, 1951-53, diplomatic corr., Washington, 1953-59; mil., fgn. affairs corr. assignments abroad Wash. Bur. N.Y. Herald Tribune, 1959-63; chief Washington corr. Hearst Newspapers, assignments abroad, 1963-66; Washington editor Look mag., 1966-69, chief Look Washington bur., 1969-70; mil., fgn. affairs corr. Washington bur. Los Angeles Times, 1970-71; Washington columnist Chgo. Tribune-N.Y. News syndicate, 1971-73; v.p. pub. affairs Nat. Forest Products Assn., Washington, 1973-76; editorial dir. Plus Publs., Washington, 1977-78, v.p., editor-in-chief, 1978—; Washington bur. chief Trib. of N.Y., 1977-78; dir. Nat. Press Bldg. Corp.; lectr. mil., fgn. affairs. Served with USMCR, 1941-45. Recipient Overseas Press Club N.Y. Citation, 1963. Mem. Clubs: Nat. Press (pres. 1972), Federal City Club, Gridiron Club. Author: The Floating Revolution, 1962; Outpost of Freedom, 1965; (with others) An Honorable Profession: A Tribute to Robert F. Kennedy, 1968. Home: 1622 30th St NW Washington DC 20007 Office: 2626 Pennsylvania Ave NW Washington DC 20037

ROGERS, WILLARD LEWIS, educator; b. Ottumwa, Iowa, Apr. 14, 1917; s. Perry Pearl and Emma Pauline (Schworm) R.; B.S. in Mech. Engring., Iowa State U., 1942; M.S., Northwestern U., 1949; Ph.D., Stanford U., 1960; m. Janet Louise Hill, May 4, 1944; children—Peggy Jean, Susan Louise. Instr. mech. engring. Iowa State U., 1942-46; lectr. Northwestern U., 1946-51, asst. prof., 1951-55, asso. prof., 1958-59; lectr. Stanford U., 1956-57; prof. aerospace and mech. engring. U. Ariz., 1959—; cons. noise, vibration and energy problems, 1951—. Mem. com. proposal evaluations NSF, 1969, 74; mem. com. noise Tucson Master Tech. Council, 1971. Danforth fellow, 1955-56. Mem. Am. Soc. Engring. Edn. (vice chmn. programs ednl. research and methods div. 1971-72, exec. com. council teaching and learning 1971-72, dir. Ariz.-Nev. regional effective teaching insts. 1967-72, dir. ednl. research and methods div. 1977-78), ASME, Wilderness Soc., Tau Beta Pi, Pi Tau Sigma, Phi Kappa Phi. Co-author: Gas Turbine Analysis and Practice, rev. edit., 1969; Mechanics of Machinery, 4th edit., 1958. Contbr. to profl. jours. Editorial bd. Engring. Edn., 1970-71. Home: 5744 E Holmes St Tucson AZ 85711

ROGERS, WILLIAM CECIL, educator; b. Manhattan, Kans., 1919; s. Charles Elkins and Sadie (Burns) R.; B.A., U. Chgo., 1940, M.A., 1941, Ph.D., 1943; m. Mary Jane Anderson, Aug. 31, 1941; children—Shelley, Faith, Mary Sarah. Asst. to dir. Pub. Adminstrn. Clearing House, Chgo., 1943-47; lectr. internat. relations U. Chgo., 1945-47; asst. prof. U. Va., 1947-48; asso. prof. polit. sci. Western Res. U., 1948-49; dir. World Affairs Center, U. Minn., Mpls., 1949—; dir. Program Information on World Affairs, Mpls. Star and Tribune, 1951-73. Pres. Minn. Jass Sponsors, 1966-67; chmn. Mpls. Com. on Urban Environment, 1976—. Recipient Dwight D. Eisenhower People to People award, 1973, Distinguished service award UN Assn., study grantee Swedish Inst., 1973. Mem. Nat. U. Extension Assn. (past sec.-treas.), Soc. for Citizen Edn. in World Affairs (pres. 1971-72). Author: Community Education in World Affairs, 1956; A Guide to Understanding World Affairs, 1966; Global Dimensions in U.S. Education: The Community, 1972. Home: 143 Orlin Ave SE Minneapolis MN 55414 Office: 306 Wesbrook Hall 77 Pleasant St SE U Minn Minneapolis MN 55455

ROGERS, WILLIAM PIERCE, lawyer; b. Norfolk, N.Y., June 23, 1913; s. Harrison Alexander and Myra (Beswick) R.; A.B., Colgate U., 1934; LL.B., Cornell, 1937; m. Adele Langston, June 27, 1936; children—Dale, Anthony Wood, Jeffrey Langston, Douglas Langston. Mem. editorial bd. Cornell Law Quar., 1935-37; admitted to N.Y. bar, 1937, D.C. bar, 1950; asst. dist. atty., N.Y. County, 1938-42, 46-47; counsel U.S. Senate War Investigating Com., 1947, chief counsel, 1947-48; chief counsel U.S. Senate Investigations Sub-Com. Exec. Expenditures Com., 1948-50; mem. firm Dwight, Royall, Harris, Koegel & Caskey, N.Y.C. and Washington, 1950-53; dep. atty. gen. U.S., 1953-58, atty. gen., 1958-61; partner firm Royall, Koegel, Rogers & Wells, N.Y.C. and Washington, 1961-69; U.S. sec. state, 1969-73; now sr. partner firm Rogers & Wells, N.Y.C. and Washington. U.S. rep. 20th Gen. Assembly, UN, 1967, UN Ad Hoc Com. on South Africa, 1967; mem. Pres.'s Commn. Law Enforcement and Adminstrn., 1965-67. Served to lt. comdr. USN, 1942-46. Fellow Am. Bar Found.; mem. Bar Assn. City N.Y., Am., N.Y. State, Washington bar assns., Am. Law Inst., Order of Coif, Sigma Chi. Clubs: Burning Tree, Country (Bethesda, Md.); Sky, Racquet and Tennis (N.Y.C.); Chevy Chase (Md.); Metropolitan, Alibi (Washington). Home: 7007 Glenbrook Rd Bethesda MD 20014 also 870 UN Plaza New York NY 10017 Office: 200 Park Ave New York NY 10017 also 1666 K St Washington DC 20006

ROGERS, WILLIAM RAYMOND, JR., educator; b. Oswego, N.Y. June 20, 1932; s. William Raymond and A. Elizabeth (Hollis) R.; B.A. magna cum laude, Kalamazoo Coll., 1954; B.D. magna cum laude (Danforth Found. fellow, Blatchford Traveling fellow), U. Chgo. and Chgo. Theol. Sem., 1958; Ph.D., U. Chgo., 1965; M.A. (hon.), Harvard, 1970; m. Beverley Claire Partington, Aug. 14, 1954; children—John Partington, Susan Elizabeth, Nancy Claire. Cons., staff counselor U. Chgo. Counseling and Psychotherapy Research Center, 1960-62; teaching fellow, counselor to students Chgo. Theol. Sem., 1961-62; asst. prof. psychology and religion, dir. student counseling Earlham Coll., Richmond, Ind., 1962-68, asso. prof. psychology and religion, asso. dean of Coll., 1968-70; vis. lectr. in pastoral counseling Harvard Div. Sch., Cambridge, Mass., 1969-70; prof. religion and psychology Div. and Edn. Schs., Harvard, 1970—, faculty chair clin. psychology and pub. practice, 1970-72. Pres. Eastern Ind. Mental Health Services, Inc., Richmond, Richmond Mental Health Assn., Ind. Mental Health Assn. Mem. Am. Acad. Religion, Am. Psychol. Assn., Soc. Religion Higher Edn., Soc. Sci. Study Religion. Mem. Soc. of Friends. Author: The Alienated Student, 1969; Project Listening, 1974; Nourishing the Humanistic in Medicine, 1979. Contbr. articles to profl. jours. Home: 166 Goodman Hill Rd Sudbury MA 01776 Office: Andover Hall HDS Harvard U Cambridge MA 02138

ROGERSON, JAMES RUSSELL, lawyer, corp. exec.; b. Kiantone, N.Y., Oct. 1, 1892; s. David M. and Alberta M. (Campbell) R.; LL.B., Syracuse U., 1914; m. Eleanor E. Olson, Dec. 22, 1917; children—Adele (Mrs. Lyman C. Wynne), Rita (Mrs. Burton N. Lowe). Admitted to N.Y. bar, 1917, since practiced in Jamestown; corp. counsel, Jamestown, 1929-30; chmn. bd. Art Metal, Inc., 1963-68; pres. Phelps Can Co., 1966—; dir., exec. com. Mid Continent Telephone Corp., 1968-76, Jamestown Telephone Corp., 1946-76. Del. Republican Nat. Conv., 1948. Served with U.S. Army, 1917-19; AEF in France. Fellow Am. Coll. Trial Lawyers; mem. Am., N.Y. State, Jamestown bar assns. Presbyn. Home: 924 Lakeview Ave Jamestown NY 14701 Office: 511 W 5th St Jamestown NY 14701

ROGERSON, JOHN BERNARD, JR., astronomer, educator; b. Cleve., Sept. 3, 1922; s. John Bernard and Ruth (Davis) R.; B.S. in Math., Case Inst. Tech., 1951; Ph.D. in Astronomy, Princeton U., 1954; m. Elizabeth M. Van Doren, Jan. 30, 1943; children—John Norman, Jerry Bruce, Alan Martin. Carnegie fellow Mt. Wilson Obs., 1954-56; mem. research staff, faculty Princeton U., 1956—, asso. prof. astrophysics, 1963-67, prof., 1967—. Served with USNR, 1943-46. Recipient Newcomb Cleveland prize AAAS, 1957. Mem. Am. Astron. Soc., Internat. Astron. Union, Sigma Xi. Contbr. articles to profl. jours. Home: 277 Moore St Princeton NJ 08540

ROGET, EINAR LEONARD, govt. ofcl.; b. Superior, Wis., Mar. 12, 1926; s. John E. and Elsie (Carlson) R.; student Superior State Coll., 1946-47; B.S. in Forest Mgmt., Utah State U., 1950; M.Pub. Adminstrn., Harvard, 1960; m. Marjorie Jane Greenberg, Sept. 3, 1947; 1 dau., Janet Louise. Soil conservationist, dist. conservationist Soil Conservation Service, Dept. Agr., Imperial, Calif., 1952-56, Watershed planning specialist, Riverside, Calif., 1956-59, area conservationist N.Mex., 1960-62, asst. state conservationist, Albuquerque, 1962-65, state conservationist, 1965-68, state conservationist, Little Rock, 1968-73, asso. dep. chief Forest Service, Washington, 1973-79, dep. chief Forest Service, 1979—. Served with USMCR, 1944-46. Recipient Dept. Agr. Superior Service award, 1969. Mem. Soil Conservation Soc. Am. (pres.), Soc. Am. Foresters, Soc. Range Mgmt. Presbyn. Home: 8906 Footstep Ct Annandale VA 22003 Office: South Agrl Bldg Washington DC 20250

ROGG, NATHANIEL H., economist, lawyer, assn. exec.; b. N.Y.C., July 27, 1913; s. H.N. and Nettie (Fihrer) R.; B.A. magna cum laude, N.Y. U., 1934, M.A. with honors in Econs., 1935; postgrad. Brookings Inst., 1937-38; J.D. with honors, George Washington U., 1951; m. Genevieve DeVere, Nov. 14, 1964; children—David N., Katherine, Elizabeth, Daniel, Margaret. Econ. adminstr. Fed. Works Agy., Washington, 1935-42; econ. adviser Nat. Housing Agy., Washington, 1946-47, HHFA, Washington, 1947-54; chief economist Nat. Assn. Homebuilders, Washington, 1954—, exec. v.p., 1965-77; dir. Universal Rundle Corp., Sea Pines Inc.; vis. prof. econs. Harvard, 1962-63; adj. prof. Am. U., 1965-66; cons. U.S. League Savs. Assns., 1977—, also cons. in field. Mem. Nat. Commn. Mortgage Interest Rates, 1968-69. Served to lt. comdr. USNR, 1942-46. Mem. Order of Coif, Phi Beta Kappa. Clubs: Cosmos (Washington); Army-Navy Country (Arlington, Va.); Plantation (Hilton Head, S.C.). Author: Urban Housing Rehabilitation in the United States. Home: 1718 Q St NW Washington DC 20009 Office: 1718 Q St NW Washington DC 20009

ROGGE, O(ETJE) JOHN, lawyer; b. Cass County, Ill., Oct. 12, 1903; s. Hermann and Lydia Anna (Satorius) R.; A.B., U. Ill., 1922; LL.B., Harvard, 1925, S.J.D., 1931; m. Nellie Alma Luther, Jan. 1, 1926; children—Genevieve Oetjeanne, Hermann; m. 2d, Wanda Lucille Johnston, Dec. 15, 1940. Admitted to Ill. bar, 1925; practice in Chgo., 1925-30, 31-37; counsel RFC, 1934-37; spl. counsel SEC, 1937-38, asst. gen. counsel, 1938-39; asst. atty. gen. of U.S. in charge criminal div. Dept. Justice, 1939-40; spl. asst. to atty. gen. U.S., 1943-46; former partner firm Weisman, Celler, Spett, Modlin & Wertheimer, N.Y.C.; now in pvt. practice, N.Y.C. Mem. Egypt Exploration Soc., Am. Bar Assn. (mem. com. internat. criminal jurisdiction), N.Y. County Lawyers Assn., Assn. Bar City N.Y., Phi Beta Kappa. Democrat. Author: Our Vanishing Civil Liberties, 1949; Why Men Confess, 1959; The First And The Fifth, 1960; The Official German Report, 1961; Obscenity Litigation in 10 American Jurisprudence Trials, 1965; contbg. author The Rights of the Accused, 1972, Equal Rights for Women, 1978. Contbr. numerous articles to legal jours. Editor Harvard Law Rev. Home: 44 Laurel Ledge Ct Stamford CT 06903 Office: 777 3d Ave New York NY 10017

ROGIN, GILBERT LESLIE, mag. editor, author; b. N.Y.C., Nov. 14, 1929; s. Robert I. and Lillian Carol (Ruderman) R.; student State U. Ia., 1947-49; A.B., Columbia, 1951; m. Ruth Emily Copes, Oct. 20, 1963. Mng. editor Sports Illus., N.Y.C., 1955—. Served with AUS, 1952-54. Recipient award for creative work in lit. Am. Acad. Inst. Arts and Letters, 1972. Author: The Fencing Master, 1965; What Happens Next?, 1971; Preparations for the Ascent, 1980; contbr. short fiction The New Yorker, 1963—. Home: 43 W 10th St New York NY 10011 Office: Sports Illustrated Time and Life Bldg New York NY 10020

ROGLIANO, ALDO THOMAS, pub. co. exec.; b. Tuckahoe, N.Y., Mar. 7, 1925; s. Alfred and Nancy (Morrone) R.; student Syracuse U., 1946-49; m. Bettie Eleanor Fehrs, June 13, 1948; children—Susan (Mrs. James U. Shortley), Betsy (Mrs. George Dyer), Guy, Barbara, Robert. Newstand promotion mgr. Fawcett Publs. Inc., Greenwich, Conn., 1949-54, promotion mgr., 1957-68; promotion mgr. MacFadden Pub. Co., N.Y.C., 1954-57; account exec., promotion mgr. Dell Pub. Co., 1968-71; v.p., dir. pub. relations MacFadden-Bartell Corp., N.Y.C., 1971-74; promotion dir. Internat. Circulation Distbrs., N.Y.C., 1974-77, Kable News Co., 1977-78; v.p., dir. promotion and publicity Publishers Distbg. Corp., a Filmways co., N.Y.C., 1978—. Served with USMCR, 1943-45. Decorated Purple Heart; recipient Pub. Relations Gold Key award, 1971. Mem. Ind. Newsstand Circulation Execs. Assn. Clubs: Stamford Roxbury (Stamford, Conn.); 25-Year. Home: 104 Hubbard Ave Stamford CT 06905 Office: 2 Park Ave New York NY 10016

ROGOFF, KENNETH SAUL, chess player; b. Rochester, N.Y., Mar. 22, 1953; s. Stanley Myron and June Beatrice (Goldman) R.; B.A., M.A. in Econs. (N.Y. State Regents scholar), Yale, 1975; Ph.D. (NSF Grad. fellow in econs.), Mass. Inst. Tech., 1979—; m. Evelyn Jane Brody. Became master U.S. Chess Fedn., 1968, sr. master, 1970, internat. master, 1973, internat. grandmaster, 1978; U.S. jr. champion, 1969-71, N.Y. State champion, 1972; 3d place in world jr. championships, Athens, Greece, 1971; 1st bd. World Champion U.S. Under-27 Team, Haifa, Israel, 1970; 1st place Norristown (Pa.) Internat. Tournament, 1973; 5th place U.S. championship, Chgo., 1974; 2d place U.S. Championship, 1975; 13th place World Chess Championship Interzonal Tournament, Biel, Switzerland, 1976; tchr., condr. chess exhbns.; lectr. chess Yale, 1974-75; economist to bd. govs. Fed. Res. Bd., 1979—. Mem. Phi Beta Kappa. Contbr. articles in field. Home: 435 Hillside Ave Rochester NY 14610

ROGOSHESKE, WALTER FREDERICK, state justice; b. Sauk Rapids, Minn., July 12, 1914; s. August Otto and Ottilia (Fiergolla) R.; B.A., U. Minn., 1937, LL.B., 1939; m. Dorothy Heywood, Sept. 29, 1940; children—James, Thomas, Mark, Paul, Mary Alice. Admitted to Minn. bar, 1940; gen. practice, Sauk Rapids, 1940-50; dist. judge 7th Jud. Dist., 1950-62; asso. justice Supreme Ct. Minn., 1962—; lectr. law U. Minn. Law Sch., 1951-74. Chmn. Mpls.-St. Paul Met. Airports Commn., 1949-50. Mem. Minn. Ho. of Reps., 1943-49. Bd. dirs. Amicus, Inc.; past pres. Big Bros., St. Paul. Served with AUS, 1944-45. Fellow Am. Bar Found.; mem. Am. (chmn. adv. com. prosecution and def. function, criminal law project 1968-71, mem. council sect. criminal justice 1970-74), Minn., 7th Dist. bar assns., Am. Judicature Soc., Inst. Jud. Adminstrn., U. Minn. Law Alumni Assn. (dir.). Lutheran. Home: 138 Canabury Ct Saint Paul MN 55117 Office: Minn Supreme Ct State Capitol Saint Paul MN 55101

ROGOVIN, MITCHELL, lawyer; b. N.Y.C., Dec. 3, 1930; s. Max Shea and Sayde (Epstein) R.; A.B., Syracuse U., 1952; LL.B., U. Va., 1954; LL.M., Georgetown U., 1960; m. Sheila Anne Ender, Jan. 31, 1954; children—Lisa Shea, Wendy Meryl, John Andrew. Admitted to Va. bar, 1953; trial atty. Office Chief Counsel, IRS, 1958-61, asst. to commr., 1961-64, chief counsel, 1964-66; asst. atty. gen. Dept. Justice, 1966-69; partner firm Arnold & Porter, 1969-76, Rogovin, Stern & Huge, 1976—; spl. counsel, dir. CIA, 1975-76; spl. counsel, chmn. CSC, gen. counsel, 1977-78; dir. Nuclear Regulatory Commn.'s Spl. Inquiry into Three Mile Island Accident, 1979—; gen. counsel Common Cause, 1970-75; prof. law Georgetown U. Law Center, 1964-65. Chmn. Center for Law and Social Policy; bd. dirs. Nat. Legal Aid Defenders; co-chmn. Council for Pub. Interest Law; trustee Lawyers Com. for Civil Rights Under Law. Served with USMC, 1954-58. Mem. Am., Fed. (chmn. tax com.), Va., D.C. bar assns., Nat. Acad. Pub. Adminstrn., Council Fgn. Relations, Phi Delta Phi. Democrat. Jewish. Contbr. articles to profl. jours. Home: 4500 Klingle St NW Washington DC 20016 Office: 1730 Rhode Island Ave NW Washington DC 20036

ROHATYN, FELIX GEORGE, investment co. exec.; b. Vienna, Austria, May 29, 1928; s. Alexander and Edith (Knoll) R.; came to U.S., 1942, naturalized, 1950; B.S., Middlebury (Vt.) Coll., 1948; LL.D. (hon.), Adelphi U., Bard Coll.; LL.B. (hon.), N.Y. U., 1979; m. Jeannette Streit, June 9, 1956; children—Pierre, Nicolas, Michael; m. 2d, Elizabeth Fly, May 31, 1979. With Lazard Freres & Co., investment bankers, N.Y.C., 1948—, gen. partner, 1960—; dir. ITT, N.Y.C., Pfizer Co., Owens Ill. Inc., Engelhard Minerals & Chems. Corp.; mem. finance com. Rockefeller Brothers Fund, N.Y.C., 1969—; chmn. Municipal Assistance Corp., N.Y.C. Trustee Middlebury Coll., 1969—; bd. dirs. N.Y.C. Heart Assn., 1968—. Served with AUS, 1951-53; Korea. Home: 770 Park Ave New York NY 10021 Office: 1 Rockefeller Plaza New York NY 10020

ROHER, WILLIAM CARL, chem. co. exec.; b. Bayonne, N.J., July 21, 1927; s. William C. and Jennie (Johnson) R.; B.S. in Physics, Allegheny Coll., 1950; m. Margaret Youtes McCreary; children—Kristina Roher Aikman, Kathleen M., Karen E., William C. Sales serviceman Plastoid Corp., Hamburg, N.J., 1950-52; sales engr. Reaction Motors Co., Danville, N.J., 1952-55. With Gulf Oil Corp. (formerly Spencer Chem. Co.), 1955—, regional v.p., Houston, 1970-73, pres. Gulf Oil Chems. Co. div., 1973—. Bd. dirs. United Way Tex. Gulf Coast. Served to 1st lt. U.S. Army, 1944-46. Mem. Mfg. Chemists Assn. (dir.). Clubs: Petroleum, Lakeside Country (Houston); Duquesne (Pitts.). Office: PO Box 3766 Houston TX 77001

ROHLICH, GERARD ADDISON, civil and environ. engr., educator; b. Bklyn., July 8, 1910; s. Henry Otto and Margaret Loretta (Burns) R.; B.C.E., Cooper Union, 1934, hon. citation, 1971; B.C.E., U. Wis., 1936, M.C.E., 1937, Ph.D. in Civil Engring., 1940; m. Mary Elizabeth Murphy, Sept. 8, 1941; children—Mary Ellen, Gerard A., Thomas Henry, Karl Otto, Catherine Ann, Henry James, Virginia Jean, John Harold, Richard Joseph, James William. Instr. civil engring. Carnegie Inst. Tech., Pitts., 1937-39; asst. prof. civil engring. Pa. State Coll., State College, 1941-43, asso prof., 1945-46; sr. san. engr., office chief of engrs. Dept. War, Washington, 1943-44; chief project engr. Esna Corp., Union, N.J., 1944-45; prof. civil engring. U. Wis., Madison, 1946-72, asso. dean grad. sch., 1963-65, dir. Water Resources Center, 1963-71, Inst. Environ. Studies, 1967-70; C.W. Cook prof. environ. engring., prof. pub. affairs U. Tex., Austin, 1972—; vis. prof. U. Calif., Berkeley, 1963, U. Helsinki (Finland), 1970; Walker-Ames Prof. U. Wash., Seattle, 1972; mem. exec. com. sci. adv. bd. EPA; chmn. Potomac Estuary treatment plant project Nat. Acad. Engring.; chmn. tech. assessment and pollution control com. EPA; cons. WHO; commr. Madison Water Utility, 1961-70; mem. bd. Wis. Dept. Natural Resources, 1966-72. Recipient Benjamin Smith Reynolds award Excellence Teaching Engring., U. Wis., 1962; named Wis. Water Man of Year, Am. Water Works Assn., 1969. Fellow ASCE (Karl Emil Hilgard Hydraulics award 1972); diplomate Am. Acad. Environ Engrs.; mem. Nat. Acad. Engring. Democrat. Roman Catholic. Contbr. articles in field to profl. jours. and books. Home: 2101 Pecos St Austin TX 78703 Office: 86 E Cockrell Hall U Tex Austin TX 78712

ROHM, ROBERT HERMANN, sculptor; b. Cin., Feb. 6, 1934; s. Hermann George and Anna Katherine (Sager) R.; B.Indsl. Design, Pratt Inst., 1956; M.F.A., Cranbrook Acad. Art, 1960; m. Patricia Jean Cutlip, Dec. 6, 1958 (div. 1979); children—Hans Tobin, Kyle Curtis. Instr., Columbus (Ohio) Coll. Art and Design, 1956-59, Pratt Inst., Bklyn., 1960-65; prof. art U. R.I., Kingston, 1965—; one-man shows: O.K. Harris Gallery, N.Y.C., 1970, 72, 73, 75, 77, 80, Parker St. 470 Gallery, Boston, 1970, 72, U. Rochester (N.Y.), 1971, N.S. Coll. Art, Halifax, Can., 1969, Mass. Coll. Art, Boston, 1970; group shows include: Boston Mus., 1974, Whitney Mus., N.Y.C., 1962, 64, 69, 70, 73, Va. Mus., Richmond, 1970, Fogg Mus., Cambridge, Mass., 1971, Seattle Art Mus., 1969, Vancouver Art Mus., B.C., Can., 1970, N.J. State Mus., Trenton, 1969, Inst. Contemporary Art, Boston, 1975, Vassar Coll., 1971; represented in permanent collections: Columbos Gallery Fine Art, Finch Coll., N.Y.C., Pa. State U., Kunsthalle, Zurich, Va. Mus. Fine Arts, Mus. Modern Art, N.Y.C., U. N.Mex., Albuquerque, Albright-Knox Gallery, Buffalo, Whitney Mus. Am. Art, N.Y.C. Grantee Guggenheim Found., 1964, Cassandra Found., 1967, R.I. State Council on Arts, 1973, Nat. Endowment for Arts, 1974. Recipient award Boston 200 Bicentennial Commn., 1975. Mem. AAUP. Office: Fine Arts Center U RI Kingston RI 02881

ROHMAN, DAVID GORDON, educator; b. Whitesboro, N.Y., Apr. 27, 1928; s. Hobart Henry and Margaret (Davies) R.; A.B., Syracuse U., 1948, M.A., 1955, Ph.D., 1960; m. Palma A. Miccoli, Feb. 2, 1951; children—Amy Hope, David Gordon, Emily Katherine, Laura Beth, Margaret Ann, Marc Hobart, Christian Andrew. With Utica (N.Y.) Observer-Dispatch, 1949-51, Utica Daily Press, 1953, Syracuse Post-Standard, 1953-58; lectr. Syracuse U., 1955-58; instr. Mich. State U., East Lansing, 1958-61, asst. prof., 1961- 65, asso. prof., 1965-68, prof., 1968—, asst. dean continuing edn. Colls. Arts and Social Scis., 1963-65, dean Justin Morrill Coll. 1965-75, spl. cons. to pres. for lifelong edn., 1975-79, spl. cons. to dean for lifelong edn., 1979—. Served with AUS, 1951-53. Mem. Phi Beta Kappa, Phi Kappa Phi. Author: Pre-Writing, 1965. Home: 504 Division St East Lansing MI 48823

ROHMANN, CHARLES PETER, mfg. co. exec.; b. Bklyn., Oct. 2, 1924; s. Charles E. and Clara (Petersen) R.; B.M.E., Cooper Union, 1949; M.S., Drexel Inst., 1955; m. Marjorie K. Boschen, Oct. 3, 1949; children—Carl Frederick, Karen Louise, Laura Emily. Engr., Worthington Corp., 1949-52; engring. supr. Mpls.-Honeywell, 1952-63; pres., vice chmn., corporate sec., dir. Fischer & Porter Co., Warminster, Pa., 1963—; dir. Warminster Fiberglass Co., Fischer & Porter (Can.) Ltd., FISPO Mex S.A., Fischer & Porter Pty. Ltd. (Australia), Fischer & Porter Belgium NV, Fischer & Porter BV (Netherlands). Served with AUS, 1943-46. Registered profl. engr., Pa. Mem. ASME, Instrument Soc. Am. Patentee in field. Home: 221 Beatrice St Hatboro PA 19040 Office: County Line Rd Warminster PA 18974

ROHMANN, PAUL HENRY, publishing exec.; b. Bklyn., Feb. 15, 1918; s. Henry August and Elizabeth (Zaiser) R.; B.A., Antioch Coll., 1940; m. Christabel Grover, May 31, 1941; children—Christopher, Eric, Margaret (Mrs. David Moore), Kimberly (Mrs. Mark Cowan). Editor Air Tech. Service Command, U.S. Army Air Force, Wright Field, 1942-45; asst. mgr. Antioch Press, Yellow Springs, Ohio, 1945-57, dir., 1957-69, editor Antioch Rev., 1957-67; asso. dir. Kent (Ohio) State U. Press., 1969-73, dir., 1973—. Contbr. to publs., including New Yorker, Atlantic, Antioch Rev., Scholarly Pub. Home: 11554 Parkman-Windham Rd Garrettsville OH 44231 Office: Kent State U Press Kent OH 44242

ROHMER, ERIC (SCHERER, JEAN-MARIE MAURICE), film dir.; b. Tulle, France, Mar. 21, 1920. Journalist, until 1951; film critic for Revue du cinema, Arts, Temps modernes, La Parisienne; formerly co-editor and founder La Gazette du cinema; formerly co-editor Cahiers du cinema; co-dir. Soc. des Films du Losange; dir. film Le Signe du Lion, 1959; film cycle Six Moral Tales (La Boulangère de Monceau 1962, La Carrière de Suzanne 1963, La Collectionneuse 1967, My Night at Maud's 1969, Claire's Knee 1970, Cloe in the Afternoon 1972); Die Marquise von O, 1975; Perceval le Gallois, 1978; made ednl. films for French TV, 1964-70. Recipient Prix Max-Ophuls for My Night at Maud's, 1970; Prix Louis-Delluc, Prix du Meilleur Film dur Festival de Saint-Sebastien and Prix Melies (all for Claire's Knee), 1971. Author: (with Claude Chabrol) Alfred Hitchcock; L'Organisation de l'espace le Faust de Murnau, 1977; Six Moral Tales, 1980.

ROHN, ROBERT J., physician, educator; b. Lima, Ohio, 1918. M.D., Ohio State U., 1943; m. Ann Rohn; children—Megan Ann, David, Daniel, Matthew. Intern, Ohio State U. Hosp., 1944, asst. resident, 1944-45, resident in internal medicine, 1945-46, asst. resident in hematology, 1948-49, resident in hematology, 1949-50; practice medicine specializing in internal medicine, 1950—; prof. internal medicine, dir. hematology research, cancer coordinator Ind. U., Indpls., now Bruce Kenneth Wiseman chair of medicine. Served to capt. M.C., AUS, 1946-48. Diplomate Am. Bd. Internal Medicine. Mem. A.M.A., Am. Fedn. Clin. Research, Central Soc. for Clin. Research. Office: Sch Medicine Ind U Indianapolis IN 46223

ROHNER, FRANKLIN BOYDEN, lawyer; b. San Francisco, Sept. 18, 1927; s. Franklin Ellery and Fay (Boyden) R.; B.A., Stanford, 1950, LL.B., 1954; m. C. Vanya Foster, Apr. 11, 1970; children—Franklin II, Cynthia, Meredeth, Clayton, Boyden. Admitted to Calif. bar, 1954; research asst. Cal. Supreme Ct., San Francisco, 1956-57; asst. atty. CBS TV Network, Los Angeles, 1958-61, dir. bus. affairs, 1962, mgr. program dept., 1963, v.p. bus. affairs, 1964-65; v.p. CMA Inc., theatrical agy., Los Angeles, 1966-67; partner law firm Shearer, Fields, Rohner & Shearer, Los Angeles, 1968—; dir. Fox Cat Prodns., Chuck Connors Prodns., Bunky Prodns., Inc., R L Sq. Inc. Served with USNR, 1945-46, to 1st. lt., J.A.G. Corp USAF, 1954-56; PTO. Food and Drug Law Inst. fellow 1956. Mem. Stanford Alumni Assn., Los Angeles County Bar Assn., Cal. Thoroughbred Breeders Assn., Town Hall Calif., Chi Psi (pres. 1949-50), Phi Delta Phi. Republican. Presbyn. Clubs: Calif. Yacht, LaQuinta Golf and Country, Ingomar, Olympic. Home: 1023 N Roxbury Dr Beverly Hills CA 90210 Office: Shearer Fields Rohner & Shearer 9255 Sunset Blvd Los Angeles CA 90069

ROHNER, PAUL ERNEST, pharm. co. exec.; b. Jackson County, Ky., Feb. 27, 1937; s. Charles and Eula (Isaacs) R.; B.S. in Commerce and Acctg., U. Cin., 1962, M.B.A. in Fin., 1967; m. Sept. 1, 1956; children—Pamela Lea, Stephen Paul. Adminstrv. asst. to tech. dir. Nat. Lead Co. Ohio, Cin., 1955-62; cost acctg. and budgeting supr. Black Clausen Co., Hamilton, Ohio, 1962-65; controller Ward Mfg. Co., Hamilton, 1966-67; with Eli Lilly & Co., Indpls., 1967-76, adminstr. internat. acctg. ops., 1970-72, internat. controller, 1972-74, treas. Lilly Internat., 1974-76; v.p. fin., worldwide pharm./consumer products group G. D. Searle & Co., Skokie, Ill., 1976-78, corp. treas., 1978—. Home: 1051 Cherokee Rd Wilmette IL 60091 Office: 4711 Golf Rd Skokie IL 60076

ROHNER, RALPH JOHN, educator; b. East Orange, N.J., Aug. 10, 1938; A.B., Cath. U. Am., 1960, J.D., 1963. Admitted to Md. bar, 1964; teaching fellow Stanford (Calif.) U., 1963-64; atty. pub. health div. HEW, 1964-65; prof. Cath. U. Am. Sch. Law, Washington, 1965—, acting dean, 1968-69, asso. dean, 1969-71; staff counsel consumer affairs subcom. U.S. Senate Banking Com., 1975-76; cons. Fed. Res. Bd., 1976—; cons. fed. Deposit Ins. Co., 1978—. Bd. dirs. Migrant Legal Action Program, Inc., Washington, Automobile Owners Action Council, Washington. Mem. Am. Bar Assn., Am. Judicature Soc., Am. Law Inst. Co-author: Consumer Law: Cases and Materials, 1979. Home: 7706 Powhatan St New Carrollton MD 20784 Office: Cath U Sch Law Washington DC 20064

ROHR, DONALD GERARD, educator; b. Toledo, Oct. 10, 1920; s. Lewis Walter and Marie (Pilliod) R.; B.A., U. Toronto (Ont., Can.), 1943, M.A., 1949; Ph.D., Harvard, 1958; m. Joan Willis Michener, Sept. 14, 1948; children—Karen, Kristin. Instr., then asst. prof. Williams Coll., 1953-59; mem. faculty Brown U., 1959—, prof. history, 1963—, chmn. dept., 1960-65, 66-69, 72-74, sec. faculty, 1969-72, asso. dean faculty and acad. affairs, 1976—. Served with AUS, 1943-46; ETO. Mem. Am. Hist. Assn., Conf. Group Central European History, Providence Com. Fgn. Relations (sec. 1974—). Democrat. Roman Catholic. Club: University (Providence). Author: The Origins of Social Liberalism in Germany, 1963; (with Robert Ergang) Europe Since Waterloo, 1967. Home: 71 Grotto Ave Providence RI 02906

ROHRBAUGH, ALBERT HOWARD, mfg. co. exec.: b. York, Pa., May 29, 1920; s. Lake and Alice B. (Krone) R.; B.A., U. Denver, 1948; m. Virginia Brandt, June 18, 1942; children—Richard, Robert, Eric. Vice-pres. fin. Spaulding-Fibre Co., Tonawanda, N.Y., 1960-68; v.p. adminstrn. Struthers-Wells, Warren, Pa., 1968-70; v.p., controller Marsh Instruments, Skokie, Ill., 1970-71; v.p. fin., treas. Magic Chef, Inc., Cleveland, Tenn., 1971—. Served with USAF, 1942-46. Office: Magic Chef Inc 740 King Edward Ave Cleveland TN 37311

ROHRBAUGH, LEWIS HENRY, educator, univ. adminstr.; b. Yatesville, Pa., July 2, 1908; s. Lewis Guy and Mae (Heffelbower) R.; Ph.B., Dickinson Coll., 1930, D.Sc., 1954; postgrad. Cornell U., 1931-32, U. Pa., 1932-34; Ph.D., U. Pa., 1939; D.Sc., Mass. Coll. Pharmacy, 1972; m. Mary Grove, Sept. 1933; 1 dau., Mary Lou; m. 2d, Ruth Elizabeth Bunker, Sept. 22, 1936; children—Stephen Bunker, Lewis Bunker, Joanna Bunker. Dir. boys' work Webster House, Phila., 1932-33; social service sec. U. Pa., asst. head Univ. House, 1933-34; dir. edn. and recreation dept. and state cons. Fed. Transient Bur., 1934-35; dir. edn. and recreation div. Phila. Bd. Pub. Edn. and Fed. Works Agy., 1935-40; spl. asst. to dir., div. vocational edn. Phila. Bd. Pub. Edn., 1941; field supt., mgmt. div. Farm Sec. Adminstrn., Dept. Agr., 1941-42, head profl. sci. and tech. tng. Office of Sec., 1942-43, dir. Grad. Sch., 1943-44, 45-52; asst. to dir. personnel and loaned half-time to UNRRA as cons. in personnel adminstrn. Dept. Agr., Washington, 1944; on leave to UNRRA as dir. personnel Balkans Mission, Cairo, Egypt, then dep. chief of mission for finance and adminstrn., Greece Mission, Athens, 1944-45; dir. U.S. Tech. Cooperation Mission to Iraq, Dept. State, 1952-54; spl. asso. to pres. Am. Council Edn., 1954; v.p., provost U. Ark., 1954-59; cons. adminstrn. and orgn. Internat. Bank Reconstrn. and Devel. mission to Peru, 1958; v.p. acad. affairs Boston U., 1959-62, dir. Med. Center, 1962-73, v.p. for med. affairs, 1962-71, v.p. health and welfare, 1971-73, exec. v.p. Univ. Hosp., 1962-73, prof. Sch. Medicine, Coll. Bus. Adminstrn., now emeritus, cons. Arthur D. Little, Inc., 1973—, Assn. Schs. and Colls. Optometry, 1973—. Mem. Maine Councils on Health, Mental Health and Mental Retardation, 1968—; bd. dirs. Univ. Hosp., 1962-73, New Eng. Primate Center, 1963-73, Mass. Coll. Optometry, 1969-73; bd. visitors Coll. Bus. Adminstrn., 1972—; mem. council on optometric edn. Am. Optometry Assn., 1974-76; Maine rep. bd. trustees New Eng. Coll. Optometry, 1979—. Mem. Assn. Acad. Health Centers (pres. 1970, cons. orgn. and devel. 1973—), Grange, Alpha Chi Rho, Omicron Delta Kappa. Mem. Soc. of Friends. Clubs: Union (Boston); Cosmos (Washington); Megunticook Golf (Camden); Rockport Boat. Home: 2 Sea St Rockport ME 04856 also 4 Pinckney St Boston MA 02114

ROHRLICH, GEORGE FRIEDRICH, social economist; b. Vienna, Austria, Jan. 6, 1914; s. Egon Ephraim and Rosa (Tenzer) R.; Dr.Jur., U. Vienna, 1937; Diplomate, Consular Acad. Vienna, 1938; Ph.D. (Univ. refugee scholar), Harvard U., 1943; m. Laura Ticho, Feb. 3, 1946; children—Susannah Ticho, David Ephraim, Daniel Mosheh. Social economist sect. public health and welfare Supreme Comdr. Allied Powers, Tokyo, 1947-50; socioecon. program analyst and developer U.S. Govt. agys., 1950-59; sr. staff mem. social security div. Internat. Labor Office, Geneva, 1959-64; vis. prof. social econs. and policy Sch. Social Service Adminstrn., U. Chgo., 1964-67; prof. econs. and social policy Sch. Bus. Adminstrn., Temple U., 1967—, founder, dir. Inst. for Social Econs. and Policy Research; sr. lectr. Sch. Social Work, Columbia U., 1968-69; dir. research P.R. Commn. on an Integral Social Security System, San Juan, 1975-76; cons. in field. Former mem. bd. dirs. Health and Welfare Council Greater Phila. Brookings research tng. fellow, 1941-42; Ford Found. travel grantee, 1966; Fulbright scholar, N.Z., 1980. Mem. AAAS, Assn. Social Econs. (pres. 1978-79), Assn. Evolutionary Econs., Am. Econ. Assn., Eastern Econ. Assn., Indsl. Relations Research Assn. (charter), Internat. Soc. Labor Law and Social Security, Am. Risk and Ins. Assn., AAUP. Democrat. Jewish. Club: Harvard of Phila. Author: Social Economics—Concepts and Perspectives, 1974, others; editor books, the most recent being: Environmental Management: Economic and Social Dimensions, 1976; contbr. articles to profl. publs.; co-editor FORUM for Social Economics; editorial adv. bd. Internat. Jour. Social Econs. (U.K.). Home: 7913 Jenkintown Rd Cheltenham PA 19012 Office: Sch Bus Adminstrn Temple U Philadelphia PA 19122

ROHSENOW, WARREN MAX, mech. engr., educator; b. Chgo., Feb. 12, 1921; s. Fred and Selma (Gorss) R.; B.S., Northwestern U., 1941; M.Eng., Yale, 1943, D.Eng., 1944; m. Katharine Towneley Smith, Sept. 20, 1946; children—John, Brian, Damaris, Sandra, Anne. Teaching asst., instr. mech. engring. Yale, 1941-44; mem. faculty Mass. Inst. Tech., 1946—, prof. mech. engring., 1955—, dir. heat transfer lab., 1954—. Chmn. bd. dirs. Dynatech Corp. Served as lt. (j.g.) USNR, 1944-46; mech. engr. gas turbine div. Engring. Expt. Sta., Annapolis, Md. Recipient Pi Tau Sigma gold medal Am. Soc. M.E., 1951; award for advancement sci. Yale Engring. Assn., 1952; merit award Northwestern Alumni, 1955. Fellow Am. Acad. Arts and Scis., Nat. Acad. Engring., Am. Soc. M.E. (Heat Transfer Meml. award 1967, Max Jakob Meml. award 1970); mem. Sigma Xi, Tau Beta Pi, Pi Tau Sigma. Author: (with Choi) Heat Mass and Momentum Transfer, 1961. Editor: Developments in Heat Transfer, 1964; (with Hartnett) Handbook of Heat Transfer, 1973. Home: 47 Windsor Rd Waban MA 02168 Office: Massachusetts Institute of Technology Cambridge MA 02138

ROHWER, OTTO, lawyer; b. Dixon, Calif., May 30, 1905; A.B., U. Calif., 1927; LL.B., Calif. Sch. Jurisprudence, 1930. Mem. firm Downey, Brand, Seymour & Rohwer, Sacramento; ret., 1976. Mem. Am., Sacramento (pres. 1950-51) bar assns., State Bar Calif. Office: 555 Capitol Mall Suite 1050 Sacramento CA 95814

ROIG, LESTER CLARENCE, railroad ofcl.; b. Lakewood, Ohio, Sept. 13, 1923; s. Lester Clarence and Selma (Wilms) R.; A.B., Baldwin-Wallace Coll., 1947; student Va. Poly. Inst., 1943-44; M.A., Bowling Green State U., 1949; m. Mildred Elaine Lent, Oct. 31, 1947; children—Randy Allen, Wendy Ellen, Reed Alan. With Cleve. Electric Illuminating Co., 1949-53, asst. staff economist, 1951-53; with C. & O. Ry., 1953-63, asst. treas., 1962-63; sr. asst. treas. B. & O. Ry., 1963-65; treas. C. & O. Ry. and B. & O. R.R., 1965-73; asst. v.p., treas. Chessie System, Inc., 1974—. Chmn. Eastern group, treasury div. Assn. Am. Railroads, 1966-67, mem. adv. com. treasury div., 1966-78, vice chmn. treasury div., 1970-71, chmn. treasury div., 1971-72; dir. Trail Train Co., Am. Rail Box Car Co.; dir. Toledo Terminal R.R. Co. Served with inf. AUS, 1943-46. Mem. Alpha Sigma Phi. Republican. Methodist. Home: 1931 King James Pkwy Apt 425A Westlake OH 44145 Office: PO Box 6419 Cleveland OH 44101

ROIPHE, ANNE, author, journalist; b. N.Y.C., Dec. 25, 1935; d. Eugene and Blanche (Phillips) Roth; B.A., Sarah Lawrence Coll., 1957; m. Herman Roiphe, Jan. 20, 1967; children—Emily, Katie, Becky; stepchildren—Margaret, Jean. Author: Diggin Out, 1967; Up the Sandbox, 1970; Long Division, 1972; Torch Song, 1977. Contbr. articles to mags. Home: 130 E 95th St New York City NY 10028

ROIZMAN, BERNARD, educator, microbiologist; b. Chisinau, Rumania, Apr. 17, 1929; s. Abram and Liudmilla (Seinberg) R.; came to U.S., 1947, naturalized, 1954; B.A., Temple U., 1952, M.S., 1954; Sc.D. in Microbiology, Johns Hopkins, 1956; m. Betty Cohen, Aug. 26, 1950; children—Arthur, Niels. From instr. microbiology to asst. prof. Johns Hopkins Med. Sch., 1956-65; mem. faculty div. biol. scis. U. Chgo., 1965—, prof. microbiology, 1969—, prof. biophysics, 1970—, chmn. com. virology, 1969—; convener herpesvirus workshop, Cold Spring Harbor, N.Y., 1972—; lectr. Am. Found. for Microbiology, 1974-75. Mem. spl. virus cancer program, devel. research working group Nat. Cancer Inst., 1967-71, cons. inst., 1967-73; mem. steering com. human cell biology program NSF, 1971-74, cons. found., 1972-74; mem. adv. com. cell biology and virology Am. Cancer Soc., 1970-74; chmn. herpesvirus study group for Internat. Commn. Taxonomy of Viruses, 1971—; sci. adv. council N.Y. Cancer Inst., 1971—; med. adv. bd. Leukemia Research Found., 1972-77; mem. herpesvirus working team WHO/FOA, 1972—; mem. bd. sci. consultants Sloan Kettering Inst., N.Y.C., 1975—; mem. study sect. on exptl. virology NIH, 1976-80; mem. task force on virology Nat. Inst. Allergy and Infectious Disease, 1976-77; mem. external adv. com. Emory U. Cancer Center, 1973—, Northwestern U. Cancer Center, 1979—; cons. Institut Merieux, Lyon, France. Trustee Leo Goodwin Inst. for Cancer Research, 1977—. Recipient Lederle Med. Faculty award, 1960-61, Career Devel. award USPHS, 1963-65, Pasteur award Ill. Soc. Microbiology, 1972, Esther Langer award for achievement in cancer research, 1974. Am. Cancer Soc. scholar cancer research at Pasteur Inst., Paris, 1961-62, faculty research asso., 1966-71; traveling fellow Internat. Agy. Research Against Cancer, Karolinska Inst., Stockholm, Sweden, 1970; grantee USPHS/NIH, 1958—, Am. Cancer Soc., 1962—, NSF, 1962-79, Whitehall Found., 1966-74. Hon. fellow Pan Am. Cancer Soc.; mem. Nat. Acad. Scis., Am. Assn. Immunologists, Soc. Exptl. Biology and Medicine, Am. Soc. Microbiology, A.A.A.S., Am. Soc. Biol. Chemists, Internat. Assn. Microbiol. Socs. (internat. microbial genetics commn. 1974—), Brit. Soc. Gen. Microbiology, Internat. Assn. for Comparative Research on Leukemia and Related Diseases. Club: Quadrangle (Chgo.). Author sci. papers, chpts. in books. Mem. editorial bd. Jour. Hygiene, 1958-61, Infectious Diseases, 1965-69, Jour. Virology, 1970—, Jour. Intervirology, 1972—, Archives of Virology, 1975—, Virology, 1976-78, Microbiologica, 1978—; adv. editor Progress in Surface Membrance Sci., 1972—. Home: 5555 S Everett Ave Chicago IL 60637

ROJAS, RICHARD RAIMOND, elec. engr.; b. N.Y.C., Sept. 25, 1931; s. Henry and Emily (Medrek) R.; B.E.E., CCNY, 1952; M.E.E., Drexel Inst. Tech., 1961; postgrad. U. Pa., 1965-70; m. Natalie Avena, July 5, 1954; children—Richard Raimond, Robert. Project engr. Philco Corp., Phila., 1952-60; mgr. dept. hydroacoustics Gen. Atronics Corp., Phila., 1960-69; asso. dir. research for oceanology Naval Research Lab., Washington, 1969—; instr. Pa. State U., 1963-69. Recipient Achievement award Philco Co., 1954, Spl. Achievement award Naval Research Lab., 1975. Mem. Acoustical Soc. Am., Marine Tech. Soc., IEEE, Sigma Xi. Roman Catholic. Home: 9212 Wooden Bridge Rd Potomac MD 20854 Office: Naval Research Lab Washington DC 20375

ROKAW, DANIEL ROY, retail food co. exec.; b. N.Y.C., Oct. 8, 1917; s. Joseph E. and Dora (Rosenberg) R.; B.S. in Accounting and Finance, N.Y. U., 1941, M.B.A. in Indsl. Mgmt., 1950; certificate Signal Corps Contract Termination Sch., 1944; certificate Army Service Forces Accounting and Auditing, 1945; m. Lucille Levy, Feb. 12, 1944 (dec. 1974); children—Nanette, Elyse; m. 2d, Audrey Orenstein, 1976. Auditor Metro Goldwyn Mayer, Inc., N.Y.C., 1935-41; treas. Gen. Builders Supply Corp., N.Y.C., 1946-59; treas. Asso. Food Stores, Inc., N.Y.C., 1959-75, pres., 1975—, now also chmn., chief exec. officer. Investment cons. Chmn. bd. trustees Town and Village Temple, 1960-62, treas., 1955-60. Served to master sgt. Signal Corps, AUS, 1942-46. Mem. Golden Rule Ionic (master 1963). Office: 179-45 Brinkerhoff Ave Jamaica NY 11433

ROKER, ROXIE, actress; b. Miami, Fla., Aug. 28; d. Albert and Bessie R.; B.A. in Drama, Howard U.; postgrad. (Hattie M. Strong Found. fellow) Shakespeare Inst., Stratford-on-Avon, Eng.; m. Sy Kravitz; 1 son, Leonard. Asso. producer Family Living, NBC, 1962-69; co-hostess Inside Bedford-Stuyvesant, Sta. WNEW-TV, N.Y.C., 1967-68; stage debut in chorus of Faith of Our Fathers, Rock Creek Amphitheatre, Washington; appeared off-off Broadway in The Dreamy Kid, 1957; appeared off-Broadway in The Blacks, Negro Ensemble Co., 1961; other Negro Ensemble Co. appearances: Rosalee Pritchett, 1970, Ododo, 1970, The River Niger, 1972 (Obie award 1973); other off-Broadway appearances: Behold! Cometh the Vanderkellans, 1971, Jamimma, 1972; regular on TV series The Jeffersons, 1975—; appeared in TV mini-series Roots, 1977; other TV appearances include: Change at 125th Street, Billy: Portrait of a Street Kid. Recipient Alumni award for disting. postgrad. achievement in field of performing arts. Office: care TAT Communications Inc 1901 Ave of Stars Los Angeles CA 90067*

ROLAND, CHARLES GORDON, physician, med. historian, educator; b. Winnipeg, Man., Can., Jan. 25, 1933; s. John Sandford and Leona (McLaughlin) R.; student U. Toronto (Ont., Can.), 1952-54; M.D., U. Man., 1958, B.Sc., 1958; m. Marjorie Ethel Kyles, 1953 (div. 1973); children—John Kenneth, Christopher Franklin, David Charles, Kathleen Siobhan; m. Connie Rankin, 1979. Intern St. Boniface (Man.) Hosp., 1958-59; practice medicine specializing in anesthesia, Tillsonburg, Ont., 1959-60, Grimsby, Ont., 1960-64; sr. editor Jour. Am. Med. Assn., Chgo., 1964-69; head sect. publns. Mayo Clinic, 1969-70, chmn. dept. biomed. communications, 1970-77; prof. history medicine, prof. biomed. communications, coordinator family practice track, chmn. adminstrv. com. dept. family medicine Mayo Med. Sch., 1971-77, also mem. admissions, edn. and curriculum coordinators coms.; hon. mem. med. staff West Lincoln Meml. Hosp., Grimsby; mem. grants com. Hannah Inst. History of Medicine and Related Scis., Toronto, 1974-77; Jason A. Hannah prof. history of medicine McMaster U., Hamilton, Ont., Can., 1977—. Fellow A.A.A.S. (council 1969—), Am. Med. Writers Assn. (pres. 1969-70); mem. Can. Med. Assn., Can. Coll. Family Practice, Am. Assn. History Medicine (sec.-treas. 1976—), Soc. Internat. d'Histoire de la Medicine, Can. Soc. for History of Medicine, Soc. Med. History Chgo. (sec.-treas. 1966-69), Council Biology Editors, Med. Hist. Club Toronto (pres. 1977-78), Council Communications Socs., Canadian Hist. Assn., Am. Acad. Family Practice, Bibliog. Soc. Can., Am. Osler Soc. (sec.-treas. 1975—), Royal Soc. Medicine (London), Sigma Xi. Clubs: University (Rochester); Osler (London); Alpine of Canada; Literary (Chgo.). Author: Scientific Writing, 1968; William Osler, The Continuing Education, 1969; Good Scientific Writing, 1971; William Osler's The Master Word in Medicine: A Study in Rhetoric, 1972; You and Leukemia: A Day at a Time, 1976; An Annotated Bibliography of Canadian Medical Periodicals, 1826-1975, 1979. Editor: (E.P. Scarlett) In Sickness and In Health, 1972; co-editor: An Annotated Checklist of Osleriana, 1976; mem. editorial adv. bd. Canadian Family Physician, 1964—, Chest, 1966—, Med. Communications, 1971-75, Postgrad. Med. Jour., London, 1967-72, Mayo Clinic Procs., 1969-77, Bioscis. Communications, 1975—. Office: 3H56-HSC McMaster U Med Center 1200 Main St W Hamilton ON L8S 4J9 Canada

ROLAND, CHARLES PIERCE, historian, educator; b. Maury City, Tenn., Apr. 8, 1918; s. Clifford Paul and Grace (Paysinger) R.; student Freed-Hardeman Jr. Coll., 1934-36; B.A., Vanderbilt U., 1938; postgrad. George Washington U., 1947; Ph.D., La. State U., 1951; m. Allie Lee Aycock, Jan. 23, 1948; children—John Clifford, Karen Jean, Charles Franklin. Tchr., Alamo (Tenn.) High Sch., 1938-40; hist. technician Nat. Park Service, Washington, 1940-42, 46-47; asst. to chief historian of the Army, Dept. Army, Washington, 1951-52; instr. history La. State U., Baton Rouge, 1950-51; with dept. history Tulane U., New Orleans, 1952-70, instr., 1952-53, asst. prof., 1953-57, asso. prof., 1957-60, prof., 1960-70, head dept. history, arts and sci., 1963-67, chmn. univ. dept. history, 1967-70; alumni prof. history U. Ky., 1970—; mem. adv. council U.S. Civil War Centennial Commn., 1959-65; mem. adv. com. Office Mil. History, Dept. Army, 1965-69. Served to capt. AUS, 1942-46. Decorated Bronze Star, Purple Heart; recipient La. Lit. award La. Library Assn., 1957; Guggenheim fellow, 1960-61. Mem. So., La., Ky. hist. assns., Orgn. Am. Historians. Author: Louisiana Sugar Plantations During the American Civil War, 1957; The Confederacy, 1960; Albert Sidney Johnston: Soldier of Three Republics, 1964; (with Francis Butler Simkins) A History of the South, 1972; The Improbable Era: The South Since World War II, 1975. Home: 814 Sherwood Dr Lexington KY 40502

ROLAND, GILBERT, actor; b. Chihuahua, Mexico, Dec. 11; s. Francisco and Consuelo (Botana) Alonso; came to U.S., 1913, naturalized, 1942; m. Constance Bennett (div.); children—Gyl, Lorinda; m. 2d, Guillermina Cantu, Dec. 12, 1954. Made motion picture debut in Camille, 1927; starred in films Twelve-Mile Reef, We Were Strangers, Bullfighter and the Lady, Miracle of Fatima, The Furies, The Bad and the Beautiful, My Six Convicts, Cheyenne Autumn, Islands in the Stream, Cabo Blanco, others. Recipient Entertainment Favorite award League of United Latin Am. Citizens, 1969; commended by mayor of Los Angeles, 1969, Cal. State

Legislature, 1968. Served with USAAC, World War II. Office: care Jewel Smith Pub Relations 435 N Roxbury Dr Beverly Hills CA 90210

ROLAND, JOHNNY EARL, profl. athlete, football coach, broadcasting exec., real estate broker; b. Corpus Christi, Tex., May 21, 1943; s. Vernon Lee and Willie Mae (Wells) R.; B.S. in Bus. Adminstrn., U. Mo., 1966; m. Barbara Ann Warren, Aug. 29, 1964 (div.); children—Johnny Earl, James Erwin; m. 2d, Florence Alice McKinley, Mar. 29, 1975 (div.); 1 dau., Cynnamon Aisha. Running back St. Louis Football Cardinals, 1966-72, N.Y. Giants, 1973; asst. coach Green Bay Packers, 1974; coach Notre Dame U., South Bend, Ind., 1975; coach Phila. Eagles Football Club, 1976-79; pres. Bronco Broadcasting Co., Inc., 1974—, Sta. KIRL, St. Charles, Mo.; pres. Pro Sports Coordinators, Inc. Named Rookie-of-the-Year, 1966; pro bowl nominee, 1966-67, Collegiate All Am., 1965, All Big Eight Conf., 1962-65, Prep. All Am., 1960, All State (Tex.), 1960. Mem. NFL Players Assn., Am. Football Coaches Assn., U. Mo. Black Student Alumni Assn. (exec. bd.), Kappa Alpha Psi. Office: Bronco Broadcasting Co Inc PO Box 1374 Saint Charles MO 63301

ROLANDER, CARL ARTHUR, JR., energy cons.; b. McPherson, Kans., May 7, 1920; s. Carl Arthur and Vera Julia (Peterson) R.; J.D., Catholic U., 1949; m. Mildred Elizabeth Donaldson, June 26, 1943; children—Carl Arthur III, Nancy (Mrs. William B. Leroy), Stephen. With FBI, 1940-44; mem. staff U.S. AEC, Washington, 1947-56; v.p. Gen. Atomic div. Gen. Dynamics Corp., San Diego, 1957-67; v.p. Gulf Gen. Atomic Co., San Diego, 1967-70; pres. Gulf Energy & Environmental Systems, San Diego, 1970-72; pres. Gen Atomic Co. and Gen. Atomic Internat., San Diego, 1973-74; sr. v.p. Gulf Oil Corp., Pitts., 1974-76; sr. adv. fellow Mellon Inst. Served with U.S. Army, 1944-46. Recipient Outstanding Service award AEC, 1957. Republican. Episcopalian. Clubs: Allegheny Country; Metropolitan (Washington); Duquesne (Pitts.). Home: Farmhill Rd Sewickley PA 15143

ROLANDI, GIANNA, opera singer; b. N.Y.C., Aug. 16, 1952; d. Enrico G. and Jane E. (Frazier) R.; Mus.B., artist diploma, opera cert., Curtis Inst. Music, 1975. Operatic debut at N.Y.C. Opera, 1975; Met. Opera debut, 1979, mem. Met. Opera, 1979—; mem. N.Y.C. Opera; appeared with major opera cos., symphonies throughout U.S., P.R., Buenos Aires, Argentina. Met. Opera Auditions winner; Rockefeller grantee; Nat. Opera Inst. grantee. Mem. Am. Guild Musical Artists, Jr. League of N.Y.

ROLF, HOWARD LEROY, educator, mathematician; b. Laverne, Okla., Nov. 25, 1928; s. James Walter and Edith (Yoho) R.; B.S., Okla. Baptist U., 1951; M.A., Vanderbilt U., 1953, Ph.D., 1956; m. Anita Jane Ward, June 24, 1961; children—James Scott, Jennifer Jane, Stephanie Kaye, Rhonda Mary. Instr. math. Vanderbilt U., 1954-56, asst. prof., dir. computer center, 1959-64; asst. prof. Baylor U., 1956-57, prof., 1964—, dir. acad. computing, 1968-70, chmn. dept. math., 1971—; asso. prof. Georgetown (Ky.) Coll., 1957-59; cons. in field, Mem. Math. Assn. Am. (chmn. Tex. sect. 1977), Assn. Computing Machinery, Am. Math. Soc., Sigma Xi. Baptist. Home: Box 1456M Route 1 Waco TX 76710

ROLFE, STANLEY THEODORE, educator, civil engr.; b. Chgo., July 7, 1934; s. Stanley T. and Eunice (Fike) R.; B.S., U. Ill., 1956, M.S., 1958, Ph.D., 1962; m. Phyllis Williams, Aug. 11, 1956; children—David Stanley, Pamela Kay, Kathleen Ann. Supr. structural-evaluation sect. ordnance products div. U.S. Steel Corp., 1962-69, div. chief mech. behavior of metals div., 1969; Ross H. Forney prof. civil engring. U. Kans., 1969—, chmn. civil engring. dept., 1975—. Chmn. metall. studies panel ship research com. Nat. Acad. Scis., 1967-70; chmn. Am. Soc. C.E. task force fracture. Recipient Sam Tour award, Am. Soc. Testing Materials, 1971, H.E. Gould Distinguished Teaching award U. Kans., 1972, 75, AWS Adams Meml. Educator award, 1974. Registered profl. engr., Pa. Mem. Am. Soc. C.E., Am. Soc. Testing Materials, Am. Soc. M.E., Soc. Exptl. Stress Analysis, Am. Soc. Engring. Edn., Chi Psi. Conglist. Elk. Author: Fracture and Fatigue Control in Structures—Applications of Fracture Mechanics. Contbr. articles to profl. jours. Home: 2001 Camelback Dr Lawrence KS 66044

ROLFS, BEMISS ALVIN, auto rental co. exec.; b. New Orleans, July 2, 1935; s. Henry A. and Lillian C. (Pitard) R.; student Tulane U., 1956; m. Betty J. Garland, Dec. 28, 1956; children—Richmond Bemiss, Bradley Garland. With Hertz Corp., 1955-66, field mgr., New Orleans, 1962-66; with Nat. Car Rental System Inc., 1966—, div. v.p., Mpls., 1972-74, corp. v.p. car rental ops., 1974-78, exec. v.p. ops., 1978—. Mem. Am. Car Rental Assn. (dir.). Home: 430 Narcissus Ln Plymouth MN 55447 Office: 5501 Green Valley Dr Minneapolis MN 55437

ROLL, EDGAR A., advt. research exec.; b. Elizabeth, N.J., Feb. 5, 1929; s. John and Juanita (Hubert) R.; A.B., Syracuse U., 1952; m. Lucille Krayenhof, June 20, 1953; children—Dorian Lee, John H., Marcia L., Christina C. Salesman, Armstrong Cork Co., Lancaster, Pa., 1952-59; field and phone sales mgr. circulation sales dept. Dow Jones & Co. Inc., N.Y.C., 1959-63, circulation sales mgr. Wall St. Jour., Dow Jones & Co. Inc., 1963-64, circulations sales dir., 1964-69, circulation sales dir., mem. mgmt. com., 1969-74; pres. Advt. Research Found., 1974—. Trustee YMCA, Westfield, N.J. Mem. Direct Mail Advtg. Assn. Inc. (chmn. bd. dirs. 1970-72), Sigma Phi Epsilon. Methodist (mem. ofcl. bd. 1971—, finance com. 1971-72). Clubs: Toastmaster's Internat. (Charlotte, N.C.); Echo Lake Country (Westfield, N.J.). Home: 82 Barchester Way Westfield NJ 07090 Office: 3 E 54th St New York NY 10022

ROLL, IRWIN CLIFFORD, marketing, advt. and public relations co. exec.; b. N.Y.C., Aug. 21, 1925; s. Arnold and Bertha (Vogel) R.; B.B.A. magna cum laude, Coll. City N.Y., 1948; postgrad. Columbia, 1952; m. Marilyn Witlin, Apr. 10, 1949; children—Richard J., Douglas W. Asst. advt. mgr. Standard Motor Products, Inc., Long Island City, N.Y., 1948-50; advt. and sales promotion exec. RCA, Harrison, N.J., 1950-54; account exec. Fuller & Smith & Ross, Inc., N.Y.C., 1954-59, v.p., mgr. account group, 1959-66; pres., dir. Henderson, Roll, Friedlich, Inc., advt. and pub. relations agy., 1966-79; chmn. bd., treas., chief exec. officer, dir. Listfax Corp., nat. computerized info. services co., 1966—; chmn. bd., chief exec. officer, dir. Roll & Kolody, Inc., advt. and public relations, N.Y.C., 1979—. 1943-46; ETO. Mem. Am. Assn. Advt. Agys., Pub. Relations Soc. Am., Beta Gamma Sigma, Alpha Delta Sigma. Club: N.Y. Sales Executives. Home: 11 Cedarwood Rd White Plains NY 10605 Office: 600 3d Ave New York NY 10016

ROLL, LYLE CHARLES, grocery mfg. exec.; b. Easton, Ill., Sept. 13, 1907; s. Sidney R. and Margaret (Hurley) R.; student Ill. Wesleyan U.; Ph.D. in Law (hon.), Mich. State U.; m. Martha Angela Barrett (dec.); m. 2d, Marguerite Swallen. With Kellogg Co., 1927—, sales mgr. Kellogg Co. of Can., 1947-49, asst. to pres. Kellogg Co., 1949-52, v.p., 1952, exec. v.p., 1953-57, pres., gen. mgr., 1957-68, chmn., chief exec., 1963-73, vice-chmn. bd., chmn. exec. com., 1973-79, chmn. emeritus, dir., mem. exec. com., 1979—; dir. Consumers Power Co., J.M. Smuckers Co., Bankers Life Co. Trustee W.K. Kellogg Found., Ill. Wesleyan U. Home: 225 W Columbia Ave Battle Creek MI 49015 Office: Kellogg Co Battle Creek MI 49016

ROLL, MARLIN HENRY, health services facility exec.; b. Pacific Junction, Iowa, July 6, 1927; s. Dorsey Lee and Edythe Marie (Hanfeld) R.; B.A., State U. Iowa, 1949, M.A., 1951, Ph.D., 1959; m. Janice C. Wheeler, Feb. 5, 1949; children—Elizabeth Marie, Clark Stanton, Paul Wheeler, Tiffany Lynne. Asst. prof. ednl. psychology State U. Iowa, 1956-62; exec. dir. South Suburban Pub. Sch. Coop. Assn. of Cook County (Ill.), 1962-64; asso. prof. U. Houston, 1964-66; dir. interagy. commn. on mental retardation Office of Gov., State of Del., Dover, 1966-69; regional adminstr. for mental retardation, supt. dept. mental health State of Mass., 1969-73; dir. Caro (Mich.) Regional Center, 1973—. Fellow Am. Assn. Mental Deficiency; mem. N.E.A. (life), Am. Psychol. Assn., Council on Exceptional Children, Phi Delta Kappa. Address: Caro Regional Center Box A Caro MI 48723

ROLLAND, IAN MCKENZIE, ins. co. exec.; b. Fort Wayne, Ind., June 3, 1933; s. David and Florence (Hunte) R.; B.A., DePauw U., 1955; M.A. in Actuarial Sci., U. Mich., 1956; m. Miriam V. Flickinger, July 3, 1955; children—Cheri L., Lawrence D., Robert A., Carol Ann, Sara K. With Lincoln Nat. Life Ins. Co., Fort Wayne, Ind., 1956—, sr. v.p., 1973-75, pres. Lincoln Nat. Corp., 1975—, pres., chief exec. officer Lincoln Nat. Corp., Lincoln Nat. Life Ins. Co., 1977—; dir. No. Ind. Public Service Co., Lincoln Nat. Bank and Trust Co., Gen. Telephone Co. Ind., Inc., Central Soya Co. Chmn. citizens bd. St. Francis Coll., 1978—; bd. dirs. United Way of Allen County, 1975—; mem. adv. bd. Ind. U.-Purdue U., 1977; mem. Ind. Com. for the Humanities, 1978—. Mem. Soc. Actuaries, Acad. Actuaries, Health Ins. Assn. Am. Home: 3825 Dalewood Dr Fort Wayne IN 46815 Office: 1300 S Clinton Fort Wayne IN 46802

ROLLAND, LUCIEN G., paper co. exec.; b. St. Jerome, Que., Can., Dec. 21, 1916; s. Olivier and Aline (Dorion) R.; student Coll. Jean de Brebeuf, Montreal; Profl. Engr., Ecole Polytech., U. Montreal, B.A., B.A.Sc., C.E., also D.C.Sc. (hon.), 1960; m. Marie de Lorimier, May 30, 1942; children—Nicolas, Natalie, Stanislas, Dominique, Christine, Etienne, David. With Rolland Paper Co. Ltd., 1942—, v.p., gen. mgr., 1952, pres., gen. mgr., 1952—, chief exec. officer, 1978—; chmn., dir. ASEA Ltd., ASEA Industries Ltd., Fine Papers Ltd., Wilson Munroe Co. Ltd.; pres. Dessalu Limitée, Tarascon Holdings Ltd.; v.p., dir. Bank of Montreal; chmn. bd. Atlas-Copco Can. Ltd., Philips Can. Ltd., Can. Pacific Ltd., Bell-Can., U.A.P., Inc., Donohue Inc., Steel Co. of Can. Ltd., INCO Ltd., Canadian Investment Fund Ltd., Munich Reins. Co. Can., Canadian Fund Inc., Gt. Lakes Reins. Co.; mem. Montreal Bd. Trade. Bd. govs. Notre-Dame Hosp., Montreal Children's Hosp., Montreal Gen. Hosp. Decorated knight comdr. Order St. Gregory. Registered profl. engr. Mem. Canadian Mfrs. Assn., Pulp and Paper Research Inst. Can. (dir.), Can. Pulp and Paper Assn. (exec. bd.), Corp. Profl. Engrs., Province of Que., Montreal chambers commerce, Engring. Inst. Can. Home: 90 Summit Circle Westmount PQ H3Y 1N8 Canada Office: PO Box 306 Stock Exchange Tower Suite 3620 800 Place Victoria Montreal PQ H4Z 1H3 Canada

ROLLE, ANDREW F., educator, author; b. Providence, Apr. 12, 1922; s. John B. and Theresa (Maurizio) R.; B.A., Occidental Coll., 1943; M.A., U. Calif. at Los Angeles, 1949, Ph.D., 1953; m. Frances Johanna Squires, Dec. 22, 1945 (div.); children—John Warren, Alexander Frederick, Julia Elisabeth. Am. vice consul, Genoa, Italy, 1945-48; vis. prof. U. Calif. at Los Angeles, 1975, 76; editorial asso. Pacific Hist. Rev. 1952-53; asst. prof. Occidental Coll., 1953-56, asso. prof., 1957-62, prof., chmn. dept. history, 1962, 65-66, 73-74, Cleland prof. history, 1965—; grad. So. Calif. Psychoanalytic Inst., 1976—. Served to 1st lt. M.I., AUS, 1943-45, 51-52. Decorated cavaliere Ordine Merito (Italy); recipient award of merit Am. Assn. State and Local History, 1957; silver medal Italian Ministry Fgn. Affairs, 1963; Commonwealth award for non-fiction, 1969. Huntington Library-Rockefeller Found. fellow, 1954; resident scholar Rockefeller Found. Center, Bellagio, Italy, 1970, 71. Mem. Am. Studies Assn. (past regional sec.-treas., 2d pres.), Phi Beta Kappa. Author: Riviera Path, 1946; An American in California, 1956; The Road to Virginia City, 1960; (with Allan Nevins, Irving Stone) Lincoln: A Contemporary Portrait, 1961; California: A History, 1963, rev. edit., 1969, 78; Occidental College: The First Seventy-Five Years, 1963; The Lost Cause: Confederate Exiles in Mexico, 1965; The Golden State, 1967, rev. edit., 1978; California, A Student Guide, 1965; Los Angeles, A Student Guide, 1965. Editor: A Century of Dishonor (Helen Hunt Jackson), 1964; The Immigrant Upraised, 1968. Editor: Life in California (Alfred Robinson), 1971; The American Italians: Their History and Culture, 1972; Gli Emigrati Vittoriosi, 1973; (with George Knoles others) Essays and Assays, 1973; (with Francesco Cordasco and others) Studies in Italian American Social History, 1975; (with John Caughey and others) Los Angeles: The Biography of a City, 1976; (with Allan Weinstein and others) Crisis in America, 1977. Contbr. to Ency. Brit., Ency. Americana, also jours. Home: 1244 Glen Oaks Pasadena CA 91105

ROLLE, ESTHER, actress; b. Pompano Beach, Fla., Nov. 8; student Spellman Coll., Hunter Coll., New Sch. for Social Research. Dancer, Shogola Obola Dance Co., then mem. Negro Ensemble Co.; off-Broadway debut, The Blacks, 1962; London stage debut, God is a (Guess What?), 1969; numerous stage appearances include: Amen Corner, Blues for Mister Charlie, Don't Play Us Cheap, Macbeth; toured Scandinavia with The Skin of Our Teeth; toured Australia, New Zealand with Black Nativity; toured U.S. with Purlie; film appearances include: To Kill a Mockingbird, 1963, Nothing But a Man, 1964, The Learning Tree, 1969, Cleopatra Jones, 1973; regular on TV series: One Life to Live, Maude, 1972-74, Good Times, 1974-77, 78-79; TV appearances include: N.Y.P.D., Like It Is, East Side, West Side, Dinah's Place; appeared in TV movie Summer of My German Soldier (Emmy award 1979), 1979. Hon. chmn. Pres.'s Com. on Employment of Handicapped. Grand Marshall Cherry Blossom Festival, Washington, 1975. Named Woman of Yr. 3d World Sisterhood, 1976; recipient Emmy award, 1979, Image award NAACP. Address: care Carter Mgmt 9000 Sunset Blvd Los Angeles CA 90069*

ROLLER, DUANE HENRY DUBOSE, educator; b. Eagle Pass, Tex., Mar. 14, 1920; s. Duane Emerson and Doris Della (DuBose) R.; A.B. in History of Sci., Columbia, 1941; M.S. in Physics, Purdue U., 1949; Ph.D. in History of Sci. and Learning, Harvard, 1954; m. Marjorie Fair Williamson, Mar. 15, 1942; 1 son, Duane Williamson. Research and teaching asst. physics Purdue U., 1946-49; vis. fellow gen. edn. Harvard, 1949-50, teaching fellow gen. edn., 1951-54; asst. prof. history of sci., curator DeGolyer Collection, U. Okla., 1954-58, curator history sci. collections, 1958—, asso. prof., 1958-62, McCasland prof. history sci., 1962—, asst. dir. spl. collections univ. library, 1971-78; bd. dirs. U. Okla. Research Inst., 1957-61, v.p., 1967; research asso. Am. Sch. Classical Studies, Athens, 1970-71, 77-78; Sigma Xi nat. lectr., 1977-79; AAAS/NSF Chautauqe lectr., 1978-80. Chmn. U.S. Nat. Com. History and Philosophy Sci., 1964-65. Sr. postdoctoral fellow NSF, 1961-62. Served to lt. comdr. USNR, World War II. Fellow A.A.A.S., Okla. Acad. Sci.; mem. Internat. Acad. History of Sci. (corr.), History of Sci. Soc., Midwest Junto (pres. 1960-61), AAUP, Phi Beta Kappa, Sigma Xi. Author: The De Magnete of William Gilbert, 1959. Co-author: Foundations of Modern Physical Science, 1959; The Development of the Concept of Electric Charge, 1954; A Checklist of the E. DeGolyer Collection in the History of Science and Technology, 1954; The Catalogue of the History of Science Collections of the University of Oklahoma Libraries, 2 vols., 1976. Editor: Landmarks of Science, 1967—; Perspectives in the History of Science and Technology, 1971.

ROLLESTON, WILLIAM FRANCIS, motion picture exec.; b. St. Augustine, Fla., Mar. 23, 1912; s. Frank A. and Caroline (Watts) R.; student pub. schs., St. Augustine, Fla; m. Mary Mayo, Nov. 26, 1936 (div. 1970); children—William F., Penelope. Various positions banks, rys., auto distbrs., also with W.P.A., 1923-38; accountant Marine Studios, Inc., Marineland, Fla., 1938-40, comptroller, 1940-42, v.p., treas., gen. mgr., 1942-61, pres., 1961-66; operational mgr. Marineland Biol. Research Lab., 1953-66; now tourist cons. Dir. St. Augustine Nat. Bank. Mayor, Marineland, Fla., 1942-68; pres. St. Augustine Restoration, Inc., 1968—. Served to capt. AUS, 1942-45. Mem. Fla. Publicity and Pub. Relations Assn. (past pres.), Fla. Attractions Assn. (past pres.), Fla. (past pres.), St. Augustine (p.p.), U.S. (nat. dir. 1947-48) jaycees, Fla. C. of C. (chmn. advt. and tourist div., 1949-54, dir., 1950-57), Discover Am. Travel Orgn. (dir. 1962-64), St. Augustine Hist. Soc., Inst. Sci., Fla. Amateur Golf Assn. (past pres., dir.). Exec. producer: (film) Secrets of the Reef; (TV series) Wonders of the Sea; (film) Order Me an Octopus. Elk. Address: care St Augustine Restoration Inc 5 Cordova St Saint Augustine FL 32084

ROLLIN, BETTY, television journalist, author; b. N.Y.C., Jan. 3, 1936; d. Leon and Ida R.; B.A., Sarah Lawrence Coll., 1957; m. Harold M. Edwards, Jan. 21, 1979. Profl. actress on stage and television, 1958-64; asso. features editor Vogue mag., 1964; sr. editor Look mag., 1965-71; network corr. NBC News, N.Y.C., 1971—. Mem. Womens Media Group. Author: I Thee Wed, 1958; Mothers Are Funnier Than Children, 1964; The Non-Drinkers' Drink Book, 1966; First, You Cry, 1976. Contbr. articles to popular mags. Office: NBC News 30 Rockefeller Plaza New York NY 10020

ROLLINS, ALFRED BROOKS, JR., univ. pres.; b. Presque Isle, Maine, May 28, 1921; s. Alfred Brooks and Clarissa (Jack) R.; B.A., Wesleyan U., Middletown, Conn., 1942, M.A., 1946; Ph.D., Harvard, 1953; m. Ernestine Emma McMullin, Nov. 6, 1942 (dec. Aug. 28, 1972); children—John Douglas, Nancy Jane, James Scott; m. 2d, Faith Kenyon, June 16, 1973 (dec. Mar. 1979). From instr. to prof. history State U., N.Y. at New Paltz, 1948-63; prof., chmn. dept. history State U. N.Y. at Binghamton, 1964-67; dean U. Vt. Coll. Arts and Scis., Burlington, 1967-70, v.p. acad. affairs, 1970-76; pres. Old Dominion U., Norfolk, Va., 1976—. Cons. oral history project John F. Kennedy Library, 1965. Served to 1st lt. USAAF, 1943-46. Decorated D.F.C., Air medal with four clusters. Mem. Am. Hist. Assn., Assn. Am. Historians, Phi Beta Kappa, Chi Psi. Author: Roosevelt and Howe, 1962. Editor with narrative: Franklin D. Roosevelt and the Age of Action, 1960; Woodrow Wilson and the New America, 1965. Contbr. articles to profl. jours. Clubs: Commonwealth (Richmond, Va.); Harbor (Norfolk). Home: 5000 Edgewater Dr Norfolk VA 23508 Office: Old Dominion U Norfolk VA 23508

ROLLINS, CALVIN DWIGHT, educator; b. Clay Center, Nebr., Sept. 14, 1918; s. Calvin and Mary Merle (Eller) R.; A.B., U. Nebr., 1941; D.Phil., U. Oxford (Eng.), 1954; m. Helen D. Abernathy, Oct. 28, 1961; 1 son, Mark Edward. Chmn. dept. philosophy Oberlin (Ohio) Coll., 1957-65; sr. fellow The Inst., Australian Nat. U., Canberra, 1965-67; prof. U. Western Ont. (Can.), London, 1967-68; prof. U. Conn., Storrs, 1968—. Served with USAAF, 1942-46. Rockefeller Postwar fellow Cambridge (Eng.) U., 1947-48; Rhodes scholar Oxford U., 1948-51; Mellon Postdoctoral fellow U. Pitts., 1962-63; Fulbright grantee, vis. prof. Australian Nat. U., 1965. Mem. Am. Philos. Assn., Mind Assn., Aristotelian Soc., Am. Assn. Rhodes Scholars. Editor: Knowledge and Experience, 1963; (with Robert Brown) Contemporary Philosophy in Australia, 1969. Home: 202 Separatist Rd Storrs CT 06268

ROLLINS, J. DONALD, former steel co. exec.; b. Pitts., Dec. 25, 1913; s. M. Clark and Jean W. (Hodgkiss) R.; student Carnegie Inst. Tech., Armour Inst. Tech.; m. 2d, Nancy Boecking; children—Donald Peter, Susan J., Ruth M. Clk.-estimator Am. Sheet & Tin Plate Co., 1934-36; with Carnegie-Ill. Steel Corp., 1936-50, planning engr., 1948-50, asst. chief engr., 1950; with U.S. Steel Corp., 1951—, v.p. facility planning and appropriations, 1960, pres. Am. Bridge div., 1961-69, pres. subsidiary U.S.S. Engrs. & Cons., Inc., 1969-73; exec. v.p. internat. U.S. Steel Corp., 1973-76, group v.p. resource devel., 1976-78, sr. v.p., asst. to chmn. bd., 1978-79, ret., 1979; dir. Equimark. Bd. dirs. Allegheny Trails council Boy Scouts Am. Mem. Am. Iron and Steel Inst., ASME, Assn. Iron and Steel Engrs., Am. Inst. Mining and Metall. Engrs. Clubs: Duquesne, South Hills Country (Pitts.); Rolling Rock (Ligonier, Pa.); Belleview-Biltmore Country (Belleair, Fla.). Home: 1500 Cochran Rd #801 Pittsburgh PA 15243 also 220 Belleview Blvd Apt 805 Belleair FL 33516

ROLLINS, REED CLARK, botanist, educator; b. Lyman, Wyo., Dec. 7, 1911; s. William (Clarence) and Clara Rachel (Slade) R.; A.B., U. Wyo., 1933; S.M., Wash. State Coll., 1936; Ph.D., Harvard (fellow Soc. of Fellows), 1941; m. Alberta Fitz-Gerald, Sept. 23, 1939 (div. 1976); children—Linda Lee White, Richard Clark; m. 2d, Kathryn W. Roby, Apr. 2, 1978. Teaching fellow Wash. State Coll., 1934-36, teaching asst., summer sch., U. Wyo., 1935; teaching asst. biology Harvard, 1936-37; instr. biology, asst. curator Dudley Herbarium, Stanford, 1940-41, asst. prof., curator, 1941-47, asso. prof., curator, 1947-48; asso. geneticist Guayule Research project, Dept. Agr., 1943-45; prin. geneticist Stanford Research Inst., 1946-47; geneticist, div. rubber plant investigations Dept. Agr., 1947-48; asso. prof. botany Harvard U., 1948-54, Asa Gray prof. systematic botany, 1954—, dir. Gray Herbarium, 1948-78; chmn. Inst. Research Gen. Plant Morphology, 1955-65, Inst. of Plant Scis., 1965-69; supr. Bussey Instn., Harvard, 1968-78; chmn. adminstrv. com. Farlow Library and Herbarium, 1974-78; v.p. nat. com. XI Internat. Bot. Congress, Seattle, 1969, v.p. XII, Leningrad, USSR, 1975. Recipient Centenary medal French Bot. Soc., 1954; certificate of merit Bot. Soc. Am.; Congress medal XI Internat. Bot. Congress, 1969, XII, 1975. Fellow A.A.A.S., Linnean Soc. (London); mem. Orgn. Tropical Studies (pres., chmn. bd. 1964-65), Am. Soc. Naturalists (pres. 1966), Am. Acad. Arts and Scis., Am. Inst. Biol. Scis. (mem. governing bd. 1961-63), Am. Soc. Plant Toxonomists (pres. 1951), Bot. Soc. Am. (v.p. 1961), Calif. Bot. Soc. (treas. 1945-48), Genetics Soc. Am., Internat. Assn. Plant Taxonomy (past pres., 25th Anniversary medal 1975), Nat. Acad. Scis., N.E. Bot. Club (past pres.), Soc. Study Evolution. Phi Beta Kappa, Sigma Xi, Sigma Chi, Phi Kappa Phi. Author: rev. edit. of Fernald and Kinsey Edible Wild Plants of Eastern North America; (with E. Shaw) The Genus Lesquerella (Cruciferae) in North America. Past editor-in-chief of Rhodora; editor Contributions from the Gray Herbarium, 1948-78; editor occasional papers Farlow Herbarium, 1974-78. Contbr. articles and tech. papers to profl. jours. Home: 19 Chauncy St Cambridge MA 02138 Office: Gray Herbarium 22 Divinity Ave Cambridge MA 02138

ROLLINS, THEODORE SONNY, musician, composer; b. N.Y.C., Sept. 7, 1930; s. Walter and Valborg (Solomon) R.; ed. high sch., N.Y.C.; m. Dawn Finney, 1956 (div.); m. 2d, Lucille Pearson, Sept. 7, 1959. Condr. Sonny Rollins & Co. Orch.; concert tours Europe, Far East, 1973-79; composed, scored and played music for motion picture Alfie; recs. for Milestone, Fantasy-Prestige; organized Henry Street Settlement Music Sch., 1963. Recipient Critics and Readers award for best tenor saxophone, 1973-76, Downbeat mag. Guggenheim fellow, 1972. Compositions include: Freedom Suite, Doxy, Oleo, Sonnymoon, Suite Imperator, Valse Hot, Kid's Know, Decision, Plain Jane, Wail March, Way Out West, others. Recipient jazz Man of the Year award Downbeat mag., 1962, All Star Jazz poll winner Playboy mag., 1962, others. Home: Route 9G Germantown NY 12526

ROLOFF, MICHAEL, publisher; b. Berlin, Dec. 19, 1937; s. William and Alexandra (Von Alvensleben) R.; came to U.S., 1950, naturalized, 1952; B.A., Haverford Coll., 1958; M.A., Stanford U., 1960. Editor, Farrar, Straus & Giroux, N.Y.C., 1966-70; lit. agt. Lantz-Donadio Agy., N.Y.C., 1970-72; sr. editor Continuum Books, Seabury Press, N.Y.C., 1972-75; pub., mgr. Urizen Books, Inc., N.Y.C., 1975—. Mem. PEN (exec. com. 1977—). Translator numerous books from German, including works by Peter Handke, Hermann Hesse, Nelly Sachs, Franz Xaver Kroetx and H. M. Enzensberger; contbr. to Partisan Rev., N.Y. Times Book Rev., others. Home: 65W Broadway New York NY 10007 Office: 66 W Broadway New York NY 10007

ROLONTZ, ROBERT, communications and entertainment co. exec.; b. Phila., Dec. 14, 1920; s. David E. and Rose (Malis) R.; B.S., Columbia, 1952, postgrad., 1952-54; m. Susan P. Morgan, Aug. 29, 1959; children—Lee Alison, Robert Morgan. Record producer RCA Victor Records, 1955-58; music editor Billboard mag., 1962-63; exec. editor Music Bus. mag., 1964-65; dir. advt. and publicity Atlantic Records, N.Y.C., 1965—, v.p. advt. and publicity, 1969-74; dir. corporate information Warner Communications Inc., N.Y.C., 1974—; v.p. communications Cosmos Soccer Club, N.Y.C., 1977—. Served with USAAF, 1942-45; ETO. Decorated Air medal with clusters. Mem. Music Reporters Assn. (founder, v.p. 1953-55), Record Industry Assn. Am., Nat. Acad. Rec. Arts and Scis. Author: How to Get Your Song Recorded, 1963. Contbr. articles to mags. Office: 75 Rockefeller Plaza New York NY 10019

ROM, IRVING, mfg. co. exec.; b. Bklyn., Sept. 25, 1923; s. Samuel and Bertha (Ruvinsky) R.; B.B.A., Coll. City N.Y., 1949; J.D., N.Y. U., 1954; m. Dorothy Ozeroff, Oct. 16, 1948; 1 dau., Beth Rom Rymer. Admitted to N.Y. State bar, 1954; partner firm Clarence Rainess & Co., N.Y.C., 1961-76; exec. v.p. fin., chmn. exec. com., dir. Bally Mfg. Corp., Chgo., 1976—; adj. asso. prof. Pace U., N.Y.C., 1955-65. Served with USAF, 1943-46. C.P.A., N.Y. Mem. Am. Inst. C.P.A.'s, N.Y. State Soc. C.P.A.'s. Home: 1300 N Lake Shore Dr Chicago IL 60610 Office: 2640 W Belmont Ave Chicago IL 60618

ROM, M. MARTIN, fin. and real estate co. exec.; b. Detroit, Mar. 2, 1946; s. Jack and Thelma (Meyer) R.; B.A. magna cum laude, U. Mich., 1967; m. Barbara Miller, July 12, 1970. Founder, MultiVest, Inc., Southfield, Mich., 1969, pres., 1969-73, chmn. bd., chief exec. officer, 1973-75. Pres. Real Estate Securities and Syndication Inst., Nat. Assn. Realtors, Washington, 1975—, dir., bd. govs., 1972—; pres. Martin Rom Co., Inc., 1976—; dir. Mocatta Corp.; vice chmn. Sports Illustrated Ct. Clubs, Inc., 1977-79; mem. joint com. Nat. Assn. Securities Dealers-Nat. Assn. Realtors, 1975-76; mem. adv. com. on market instruments Commodity Futures Trading Commn. Mem. adv. bd. N.Y. U. Cancer Inst. Mem. Nat. Assn. Securities Dealers (com. on gold regulations 1975-76), Phi Beta Kappa. Author: Nothing Can Replace the U.S. Dollar . . . and It Almost Has, 1975. Adv. bd. Housing and Devel. Reporter, Washington. Home: 5136 Corners Dr West Bloomfield MI 48033 Office: 30400 Telegraph Rd Birmingham MI 48010

ROMAINE, HENRY SIMMONS, life ins. co. exec.; b. N.Y.C., May 30, 1933; s. Theodore Cole and Cornelia (Simmons) R.; B.A., Harvard U., 1954; children—Henry, Hilary. Asst. security analyst Mutual Life Ins. Co., N.Y.C., 1958-60, investment analyst, 1960-61, investment specialist, 1961-64, asst. dir. investments, 1964, dir. investments, 1964-66, asst. v.p. for securities investment, 1966-68, 2d v.p. for securities investment, 1969-71, v.p. for securities investment, 1971-72, sr. v.p., 1972-78, sr. v.p., chief investment officer, 1976-78, exec. v.p., 1978—; dir. Norcen Energy Resources Ltd., N. Am. Life and Casualty Co., MONY Life Ins. Co. of Can.; chmn. bd. MONY Mortgage Investors, 1978—; mem. Lower Manhattan advisory bd. Chem. Bank, 1974—. Served with USN, 1954-57. Mem. Harvard Advanced Mgmt. Assn. Clubs: The Links, Harvard, Bedford Golf and Tennis. Home: 162 Croton Lake Rd Mount Kisco NY 10549 Office: 1740 Broadway New York NY 10019

ROMAN, HERSCHEL LEWIS, geneticist; b. Szumsk, Poland, Sept. 29, 1914; s. Isadore and Anna R.; came to U.S., 1921, naturalized, 1927; A.B., U. Mo., 1936, Ph.D., 1942; m. Caryl Kahn, Aug. 11, 1938; children—Linda, Ann. Instr., U. Wash., 1942-46, asst. prof., 1946-47, asso. prof., 1947-52, prof., 1952—, chmn. dept. genetics, 1959—; vis. investigator Carlsberg Lab., Copenhagen, 1960; vis. prof. Australian Nat. U., Canberra, 1966; cons. in field. Served with AC, U.S. Army, 1943-46. Guggenheim fellow, 1952; Fulbright fellow, 1956. Mem. Am. Acad. Arts and Scis., Nat. Acad. Scis., Genetics Soc. Am. (pres. 1968). Research, publs. on maize genetics, yeast genetics; editor Ann. Rev. Genetics, 1965—. Home: 5619 NE 77th St Seattle WA 98115 Office: Dept Genetics U Wash Seattle WA 98195

ROMAN, LAWRENCE, playwright, screen writer; b. Jersey City, May 30, 1921; s. Isadore and Bessie Dora (Roud) R.; B.A., U. Calif. at Los Angeles, 1943; m. Evelyn Mildred Zirkin, Apr. 29, 1946; children—Steven Mark, Catherine Ann. Began as radio script writer, 1943; wrote first screen play, 1952, first play, 1960; plays written: Under the Yum Yum Tree, 1960, P.S. I Love You, 1965, Buying Out, 1970, Crystal, Crystal Chandelier, 1972; If! If! If!, 1979; screenplays include: Paper Lion, 1968; original screenplays include: A Warm December, 1972, McQ, 1974. Mem. Writers Guild Am., Dramatists Guild, Producers Guild. Jewish. Office: 9157 Sunset Blvd Los Angeles CA 90069

ROMAN, NANCY GRACE, astronomer, govt. ofcl.; b. Nashville, May 16, 1925; d. Irwin and Georgia Frances (Smith) Roman; B.A. (Joshua Lippincott Meml. fellow), Swarthmore Coll., 1946; Ph.D., U. Chgo., 1949; D.Sc., Russell Sage Coll., 1966, Hood Coll., 1969, Bates Coll., 1971, Swarthmore Coll., 1976. Asst., Sproul Obs., Swarthmore Coll., 1943-46; asst. Yerkes Obs., U. Chgo., at Williams Bay, Wis., 1946-48, research asso., 1949-52, instr. stellar astronomy, 1952-55, asst. prof., 1955; research asso. Warner and Swasey Obs., Case Inst. Tech., Cleve., summer 1949; physicist radio astronomy br. U.S. Naval Research Lab., Washington, 1955-56, astronomer, head microwave spectroscopy sect., 1956-58, astronomer cons., 1958-59; head observational astronomy program Office Space Flight Devel., NASA, Washington, 1959-60, chief astronomy and solar physics, geophysics and astronomy programs, 1960-64, chief astronomy programs, physics and astronomy programs, 1964-79, program scientist for space telescope, 1979—; ret., 1979. Trustee Russell Sage Coll., 1973-78; bd. mgrs. Swarthmore Coll., 1979—. Recipient Fed. Woman's award. 1962; citation for pub. service Colo. Woman's Coll., 1966; 90th Anniversary award Women's Ednl. and Indsl. Union, 1967; NASA Exceptional Sci. Achievement award, 1969, NASA Outstanding Leadership medal, 1978. Fellow Am. Astronautical Soc.; mem. Royal Astron. Soc., Am. Astron. Soc., Internat. Astron. Union (editor symposia 1956-58), Astron. Soc. Pacific, Internat. Sci. Radio Union, AAUW. Contbr. articles to sci. periodicals. Research on stellar clusters, high velocity stars, radio astronomy. Office: NASA Hdqrs Code SC-7 Washington DC 20546

ROMAN, STEPHEN B., mining co. exec.; b. Slovakia, Apr. 17, 1921; s. George and Helen Roman; student Agrl. Coll.; m. Betty Gardon, Oct. 20, 1945; 4 sons, 3 daus. Chmn. bd., chief exec. officer, dir. Denison Mines Ltd., Toronto, Ont., Can., chmn. bd., dir. Roman Corp., Ltd., Lake Ontario Cement Ltd.; dir. Crown Life Ins. Co., Guaranty Trust Co. Can., Romandale Farms Ltd., Seagull Internat. Inc. Pacific Tin Consol. Corp. Hon. bd. dirs. Royal Agrl. Winter Fair Assn. Can.; trustee Toronto Sch. Theology. Served with Canadian Army, World War II. Decorated knight comdr. Order St. Gregory. Catholic. Clubs: Empire, Engineers. Office: PO Box 40 Royal Bank Plaza Toronto ON M5J 2K2 Canada

ROMANACH, MARIO JOSE, architect; b. Havana, Cuba, Dec. 2, 1917; came to U.S., 1965; s. Mario Jose and Estela (Paniagua) R.; Architect's Degree, U. Havana, 1945; M.A. (hon.), U. Pa., 1971; m. Josefa E. Romanach, Dec. 14, 1944; children—Maria Cristina, Josefina. With Bosch/Romanach Architects, 1945-54; prin. Mario Romanach Architect, 1954-76; exec. dir. Havana Met. Planning Office, 1954-59; dir. design, asso. Kelly & Gruzen, N.Y.C., 1962-64; partner Romanach Partnership, Phila., 1976—; asso. prof. architecture Cornell U., 1960-62; prof. U. Pa., 1962—; vis. critic, master class Grad. Sch. Design, Harvard U., 1959-60. Recipient Gold medal Colegio National de Arquitectos, Havana, 1947, 55; Progressive Architecture award, 1966, 67; Bard award, 1968. Fellow AIA; mem. Nat. Acad. Design, Pa. Soc. Architects, Phila. Art Alliance, Archtl. League (founding). Archtl. works include: Chatham Towers, N.Y.C., 1966, Residence Luis Vega, Caracas, Venezuela, U. Pa. Student Housing, 1970, Power Plant and Adminstrn. Bldg. CADAFE, Punta Moron, Venezuela, 1977, Residence D. Alger, Pottersville, N.J., 1978. Contbr. articles to Arts and Architecture, Architectural Forum, Progressive Architecture, Arquitectura, Album de Cuba. Home and Office: 2143 Locust St Philadelphia PA 19103

ROMANELL, PATRICK, educator, philosopher; b. Bari, Italy, Oct. 2, 1912; s. Joseph and Mary (Brandonisio) R.; came to U.S., 1920, naturalized, 1928; B.A. magna cum laude, Bklyn. Coll., 1934; M.A., Columbia, 1936, Ph.D., 1937; m. Edna Pellegrino, June 25, 1939. Instr. philosophy Bklyn. Coll., 1936-41, Barnard Coll., 1941; prof. philosophy U. Panama, 1941-44; prof., chmn. philosophy dept. Wells Coll., 1946-52; prof. med. philosophy U. Tex. Med. Br., Galveston, 1952-62; joint prof. philosophy and med. philosophy U. Okla., 1962-65; H.Y. Benedict prof. philosophy U. Tex. at El Paso, 1965—; Fulbright prof. U. Turin, 1952-53; Smith-Mundt prof. U. Ecuador, 1956; Dept. State specialist Central and S.Am., 1961, Chile, Paraguay, Peru, 1975. Cutting Travelling and Carnegie fellow, 1945-46; grantee Am. Philos. Soc., 1957, USPHS, 1960-63. Mem. Am. Philos. Assn., Latin Am. Studies Assn., Am. Assn. History Medicine, Am. Assn. U. Profs., Brazilian Inst. Philosophy, Southwestern (pres. 1961), Chilean, Peruvian philos. socs., Phi Beta Kappa. Author: Philosophy of Giovanni Gentile, 1938; La Polémica entre Croce y Gentile, 1946; Croce Versus Gentile, 1946; (with others) Homenaje a Antonio Caso, 1947; Can We Agree? (with C.D. Leake), 1950; Locke's Letter Concerning Toleration, 1950; Making of the Mexican Mind, 1952; Verso un Naturalismo Critico, 1953; La Formación de la Mentalidad Mexicana, 1954; El Neo-Naturalismo Norteamericano, 1956; Toward a Critical Naturalism, 1958; B. Croce's Guide to Aesthetics, 1965; (with others) Religion in Philosophical and Cultural Perspective, 1967; Para um Naturalismo Dialéctico, 1967; Il Naturalismo Critico, 1969; (with others) Mexican Education in Cultural Perspective, 1971, Humanistic Perspectives in Medical Ethics, 1972. Book editor Jour. Philosophy, 1939-51; mem. editorial bd. Ency. Philosophy, 1962-66. Home: 6767 Fiesta Dr El Paso TX 79912

ROMANI, JOHN HENRY, educator; b. Milan, Italy, Mar. 6, 1925 (parents Am. citizens); s. Henry Arthur and Hazel (Pettengill) R.; B.A., U. N.H., 1949, M.A., 1949; Ph.D., U. Mich., 1955; m. Nina Jean Nichols, Aug. 28, 1954; children—David John, Paul Nichols. Instr. U. N.H., 1950-51; instr. U. Mich. at Ann Arbor, 1954-55, asso. to prof., asst. to asso. dean Sch. Pub. Health, 1961-69, asso. v.p., 1971-75, chmn. health planning and adminstrn., 1975-80, prof., 1971—; asst. prof. Western Mich. U., 1956-57; asso. dir. Cleve. Met. Services Commn., 1957-59; asso. prof. U. Pitts., 1959-61; vice chancellor, prof. U. Wis.-Milw., 1969-71; research fellow Brookings Instn., 1955-56. Task force mem. Nat. Commn. on Orgn. Community Health Services, 1963-66; staff dir. Sec.'s Com. on Orgn. Health Activities, Dept. Health, Edn. and Welfare, 1965-66; dir. Govtl. Affairs Inst., 1969-75, chmn., 1970-72; trustee Pub. Adminstrn. Service, 1969-75, chmn., 1973-75; bd. dirs. Delta Dental Plan Mich., 1972-78, chmn. consumer's adv. council 1975-77; bd. dirs. Centre for Population Activities, 1975—, chmn., 1975—. Mem. Citizens League, Cleve., 1957-59; mem. Ann Arbor Citizens Council, 1965-69; bd. dirs. Southeastern Mich. Family Planning Project, 1975-77. Served with AUS, 1943-46; ETO. Fellow Am. Pub. Health Assn. (chmn. program devel. bd. 1975-77, mem. exec. bd. 1975—, mem. governing council 1975—, pres. 1979), Royal Soc. Health, Am. Polit. Sci. Assn. (life); mem. Am. Acad. Health Adminstrn. (past v.p., dir. 1964-67, 74-76), Am. Soc. Pub. Adminstrn. (past mem. council), Phi Kappa Phi, Pi Sigma Alpha, Pi Gamma Mu, Delta Omega. Author: The Philippine Presidency, 1956. Editor: Changeing Dimensions in Public Administration, 1962. Contbr. articles to profl. jours. Home: 1716 Morton Ave Ann Arbor MI 48104

ROMANO, JOHN, psychiatrist; b. Milw., Nov. 20, 1908; s. Nicholas Vincent and Frances Louise (Notari) R.; B.S., Marquette U., 1932, M.D., 1934; Sc.D. (hon.), Med. Coll. Wis., 1971, Hahnemann Med. Coll., 1974, U. Cin., 1979; m. Miriam Modesitt, May 13, 1933; 1 son, David Gilman. Asst. biochemistry Marquette U. Sch. Medicine, 1929-30; extern psychiatry Milw. County Asylum for Mental Diseases, 1932-33; intern medicine Milw. County Hosp., 1933-34; asst. psychiatry Yale Sch. Medicine, 1934-35; intern, asst. resident psychiatry New Haven Hosp., 1934-35; Commonwealth Fund fellow psychiatry U. Colo., 1935-38; asst. psychiatrist Colo. Psychopathic Hosp., Denver, 1935-38; fellow neurology Boston City Hosp., 1938-39; Rockefeller fellow neurology Harvard Med. Sch., 1938-39, asst. medicine, 1939-40, instr. medicine, 1940-42; asso. medicine Peter Bent Brigham Hosp., 1939-42; Sigmund Freud fellow psychoanalysis Boston Psychoanalytic Soc., 1939-42; dir. dept. psychiatry Cin. Gen. Hosp., 1942-46; prof. psychiatry U. Cin. Coll. Medicine, 1942-46; psychiatrist in chief Strong Meml. Hosp., Rochester, 1946-71; prof. psychiatry, chmn. dept. U. Rochester Sch. Medicine, 1946-71, distinguished univ. prof. psychiatry, 1968-79, disting. univ. prof. emeritus, 1979—; lectr. in field; vis. prof. U. Toronto (Ont., Can.), 1972; physician-in-residence U.S. VA, 1975—; qualified psychiatrist, N.Y. State Dept. Mental Hygiene, 1954—; Salmon lectr. N.Y. Acad. Medicine, 1976; nat. adv. mental health council USPHS, chmn. mental health career investigator selection com., 1956-61; chmn. adv. com. human growth and emotion devel. Social Sci. Research Found., 1953; cons. health div. Ford Found., adv. com. behavioral scis. div., rep., Europe, 1956; cons. surgeon gen., U.S. Army Europe, 1955; exam. com. Examination Medicine, Part II, Nat. Bd. Med. Examiners, 1953-56; bd. psychiat. exams. N.Y. Dept. Mental Hygiene, 1963-65; mem. Commonwealth Fund Advanced Fellowship European Study, 1959-60; mem. med. adv. com. Phillips Exeter Acad., 1964—; mem. Salmon Com. Psychiatry and Mental Health, N.Y. Acad. Medicine, 1970—. Served as vis. neuropsychiat. cons. 8th Service Command AUS, 1943-44; cons. psychiatry AUS, ETO, 1945. Commonwealth Fund advanced fellow European study, 1959-60. Recipient William J. Kerr Lecture award U. Calif. at San Francisco, 1972; William C. Menninger Meml. award A.C.P., 1973; Distinguished Profl. Achievement award Genesee Valley Psychol. Assn., 1975. Diplomate Am. Bd. Psychiatry and Neurology. Fellow Acad. Arts and Scis., Royal Coll. Psychiatrists (hon.); mem. Assn. Research in Nervous and Mental Disease (1st v.p. 1955), Am. Psychiat. Assn. (Psychiatrist of Year Area II 1976, Disting. Service award 1979), Am. League Against Epilepsy, Am. Soc. Research Psychosomatic Problems, Nat. Com. Mental Hygiene, Am. Neurol. Assn., AAAS, Am. Soc. Clin. Investigation, Monroe County Soc. Mental Hygiene (dir.), Group for Advancement Psychiatry, Phi Beta Kappa (hon. Iota chpt. 1979), Sigma Xi, Alpha Omega Alpha. Unitarian. Clubs: Cosmos (Washington); Fortnightly. Editorial bd. Jour. Psychiatric Research, 1961—; Schizophrenia Bull., 1971—. Mem. panel of editors Year Book of Psychiatry and Applied Mental Health, 1972—. Contbr. articles to profl. jours. Home: 240 Chelmsford Rd Rochester NY 14618

ROMANO, UMBERTO, artist, educator; b. Italy, Feb. 26, 1906; s. Andrea and Raffaela (Cerrate) R.; came to U.S., 1914, naturalized, 1926; student N.A.D., 1922-26; Tiffany Found. fellow, 1926; research study of old masters technique Am. Acad. in Rome, 1926-27; m. Clorinda Corcia, June 12, 1941; 1 son, Umberto Roberto, Jr. Founder Romano Sch. Art (Gallery on the Moors), East Gloucester, Mass., 1933; founder Romano Winter Sch. Art, N.Y.C., 1941; head Worcester Art Mus. Sch., 1934-40; illustrations for Dante's Divine Comedy, 1946 (originals exhibited in museum U.S. 1947-49, Europe 1956-67); numerous one-man exhbns., 1928—; dir. Castle Hill Found. Artists Equity Academician, Abbey Found.; bd. dirs. chmn. sch. com. N.A.D., 1st v.p., 1967; works include portrait of Mrs. Sara Delano Roosevelt in Roosevelt Library, Hyde Park, N.Y., Three Centuries of New England History, mural in Springfield (Mass.) P.O., portrait of Gov. Foster Furcolo in Mass. State House, Boston; represented permanent collections Fogg Art Mus., Worcester Art Mus., Springfield Mus. Fine Arts, Addison Gallery (Andover), R.I. Sch. Design, Smith Coll. Mus., Tel Aviv Mus., Pa. Acad. Fine Arts, San Diego Mus., Nat. Acad., Whitney Mus., N.Y., Corcoran Art Gallery, Washington, Cin. Mus., Smithsonian Instn., Brandeis U., U. Maine, Fairleigh Dickinson U., White Mus. at Cornell U., So. Ill. U., Ohio U., Syracuse (N.Y.) U., Nat. Collection Fine Arts, Washington U. Miami, Phoenix Mus., Birmingham (Ala.) Mus., Evansville (Ill.) Mus., Norfolk (Va.) Mus., Chrysler Mus., others; also numerous collections in the U.S., Eng., France and Italy; executed mosaic mural New City and Municipal Cts. Bldg., N.Y.C., 1959-60. Recipient awards including Peabody prize, Chgo. Art Inst.; Pulitzer prize; Crowninshield award, Stockbridge, Mass.; Tiffany Foundation medal; Atheneum prize, Conn. Academy; 1st prize and portrait prize, Springfield Art League; Lewis prize N. Shore Arts Assn.; Suydam Silver Medal; Carnegie award Nat. Acad., 1951; Saltus Gold medal of Honor, Nat. Acad. N.Y., 1959, gold medal, 1961; Allied Artist medal of honor, 1961; Lillian Cotton prize, 1963; 1st prize Rockport Art Assn., 1964; Grumbacher purchase award Audubon Artists, 1967; Century Club medals, 1967, 68. Mem. Internat. Assn. of Fine Arts (v.p. 1965), Nat. Soc. Mural Painters (v.p.), Allied Artists Am. (Emily Lowe prize 1962, 73), Audubon Artists (pres. 1971), Provincetown Art Assn. (v.p. 1963, dir.). Club: Century (N.Y.C.). Illustrator: Great Men, 1979. Home: 162 E 83d St New York NY 10028 also Old Wharf Rd North Chatham MA 02650

ROMANOWITZ, BYRON FOSTER, architect, engr.; b. Covington, Ky., Nov. 14, 1929; s. Harry Alex and Mildred (Foster) R.; B.S. in Civil Engring., U. Ky., 1951; M.F.A. in Architecture, Princeton, 1953; m. Mildred Elaine Gize, June 15, 1957; children—Laura Ann, Mark Walter, Cynthia Ellen. Instr., Sch. Architecture, Princeton, 1954; architect Brock & Johnson, Lexington, 1958-59, Johnson/Romanowitz, architects, Lexington, 1960—; prin. works include U. Ky. campus bldgs., 1959-78, Eastern Ky. U. campus bldgs., 1959-77, Centre Coll., Danville, Ky., campus bldgs., 1967, Georgetown Coll., (Ky.) campus bldgs., 1964-78, Asbury Coll., Wilmore, Ky., 1972-78, Berea Coll. bldgs., 1978, Ashland Community Coll., 1974. Pres., Ky. Bd. Examiners and Registration of Architects, 1975—. Mem. Lexington Urban Renewal Commn., 1963—. Chmn. adv. bd. Salvation Army, 1971-72. Served with USNR, 1955-58; lt. comdr. Res. Recipient award of merit nat. archtl. competition A.I.A./Ednl. Facilities Lab., 1966. Mem. A.I.A. (1st honor awards Ky. archtl. competition 1959, 61, 68, 70, 73, 78; pres. East Ky. chpt. 1965), Ky. Soc. Architects (pres. 1966), Tau Beta Pi, Phi Mu Alpha, Phi Sigma Kappa. Mason, Kiwanian (pres. Lexington 1969). Clubs: Lexington Country, Cotillion (Lexington). Home: 2057 Lakeside Dr Lexington KY 40502 Office: 153 Walnut St Lexington KY 40507

ROMANOWSKI, THOMAS ANDREW, educator; b. Warsaw, Poland, Apr. 17, 1925; s. Bohdan and Alina (Sumowski) R.; came to U.S., 1946, naturalized, 1949; B.S., Mass. Inst. Tech., 1952; M.S., Case Inst. Tech., 1956, Ph.D., 1957; m. Carmen des Rochers, Nov. 15, 1952; children—Alina, Dominique. Research asso. physics Carnegie Inst. Tech., 1956-60; asst. physicist high energy physics Argonne Nat. Lab., Ill. 1960-64, now physicist; prof. physics Ohio State U., Columbus, 1965—. Served with C.E., AUS, 1946-47. Fellow Am. Phys. Soc.; mem. Lambda Chi Alpha. Contbr. articles to profl. jours. Research in nuclear and high energy physics. Patentee in field of electronics. Home: 217 South St Elmhurst IL 60126 Office: 174 W 18th St Columbus OH 43210

ROMANS, DONALD BISHOP, diversified co. exec.; b. Louisville, Apr. 22, 1931; s. Albert D. and Moneta (Bishop) R.; B.A., U. Louisville, 1954; M.B.A., Harvard, 1958; m. M. Yvonne Neff, June 13, 1953; children—Rebecca Ann, Jennifer. Mgr. internal auditing, mgr. data processing, mem. controllers staff Container Corp. Am., Chgo., 1958-62; successively asst. to pres., asst. treas., treas., v.p. fin., sr. v.p. fin. Trans Union Corp., Chgo., 1962—, now exec. v.p.; dir. Drexel Burnham Fund, N.Y. Mem. governing bd. St. Mary Nazareth Hosp., Chgo. Served to capt., inf., USMCR, 1953-56. Clubs: Mid-America, Knollwood, Economic (Chgo.). Home: 336 Crescent Dr Lake Bluff IL 60044 Office: 90 Half Day Rd Lincolnshire IL 60015

ROMANSKY, MONROE JAMES, physician, educator; b. Hartford, Conn., Mar. 16, 1911; s. Benjamin and Henrietta (Levine) R.; A.B., U. Maine, 1933; M.D., U. Rochester, 1937; m. Evelyn Muriel Lackman, Jan. 10, 1943; children—Stephen, Gerald, Michael, Richard. Intern Strong Meml. Hosp.-U. Rochester (N.Y.), 1937-38, asst. resident, 1938-39, James Gleason Research fellow studies on relationship of kidneys to hypertension, 1939-40, chief resident, 1940-41, instr. in medicine, 1941-42; investigator Office Sci. Research and Devel., Surgeon Gen. U.S., 1941-42; chief biochemistry and antibiotic research Walter Reed Army Hosp., 1942-46; asso. prof. Sch. Medicine George Washington U., Washington, 1946—, prof. medicine, 1957—, dir. George Washington U. med. div. D.C. Gen.

Hosp., 1950-69, dir. infectious diseases research lab. and infectious diseases div., 1950-69. Cons. internal medicine antibiotics Walter Reed Army Hosp., Washington, 1946—, VA Hosp., Washington, 1952—, NIH, Bethesda, Md., 1953—, Surgeon Gen. USAF, 1966—; mem. Asian influenza adv. com. D.C., 1956-61; mem. ad hoc adv. com. Bur. Medicine FDA, 1966-67; examiner Am. Bd. Internal Medicine, 1965, 67, 69. Trustees council U. Rochester, 1965—. Served with M.C., AUS, 1942-46. Decorated Legion Merit; recipient Founders award Tau Epsilon Phi, Distinguished Career award U. Maine. Diplomate Am. Bd. Internal Medicine. Fellow A.C.P. (adv. bd. to gov. D.C. 1969—); mem. Am. Soc. Internal Medicine, Am. Fedn. Clin. Research, Soc. Exptl. Biology and Medicine, Am. Soc. Microbiology, Infectious Diseases Soc. (founding council 1963-66), Soc. Med. Cons. to Armed Forces, Washington Acad. Medicine, Sigma Xi, Alpha Omega Alpha. Club: Woodmont Country. Jewish religion. Editorial bd. Antimicrobial Agts. and Chemotherapy, 1961-72. Pioneer work in prolonging action of penicillin, requiring only single daily injection, Romansky Formula, 1944; nutritional studies in obesity as related to weight reduction. Contbr. to profl. jours. Home: 6609 32d Pl NW Washington DC 20015 Office: 5480 Wisconsin Ave Washington DC 20015

ROMARY, JOHN KIRK, educator; b. Topeka, Kans., July 26, 1934; s. John Jacob and Della M. (Leffler) R.; B.S. summa cum laude, Washburn U., 1956; Ph.D. (NSF, NIH fellow), Kans. State U., 1961; m. Alice JoRene Kerns, Jan. 26, 1956; children—David Kirk, Douglas LaVern, Dana Matthew. Asst. prof. chemistry U. Nev., Reno, 1961-63; asso. prof. chemistry Washburn U., Topeka, 1963-67; asst. program dir. NSF, Washington, 1967-68; prof. chemistry, chmn. dept. U. Wis., Whitewater, 1968—. Research cons. Tex. Instruments, Inc., E.I. duPont; cons. NSF, Petroleum Research Fund. Mem. Gov.'s. Commn. on Edn. for Wis. NIH research asso., 1964. Named An Outstanding Young Man Am., 1970. Mem. Am. Chem. Soc., Chem. Soc. London, Am. Inst. Chemists, N.Y. Acad. Sci., Sigma Xi, Phi Kappa Phi, Sigma Pi Sigma, Kappa Mu Epsilon, Phi Lambda Upsilon, Tau Delta Pi. Contbr. articles to sci. jours. Home: Twin Oaks Box 81 Whitewater WI 53190 Office: Dept Chemistry U Wis Whitewater WI 53190

ROMBERG, PAUL F(REDERICK), univ. pres.; b. Nebr., Dec. 31, 1921; s. Alexander and Catherine (Hiebenthal) R.; Ph.D. in Botany, U. Nebr., 1954; m. Rose Mayer, Apr. 23, 1944; children—Catherine, Rose Marie. Asso. prof. botany Wabash Coll., 1952-56, Iowa State U., 1956-62; prof. biology, v.p. acad. affairs Chico State Coll., 1962-67; founding pres. Calif. State Coll. at Bakersfield, 1967-73; pres. San Francisco State U., 1973—. Mem. nat. adv. council on health professions edn. Dept. Health, Edn. and Welfare; mem. Nat. Commn. Future State Colls. and Univs.; cons. NSF. Past pres. YMCA; chmn. San Francisco Consortium, 1973; mem. Fromm Inst. for Life-Long Learning. Recipient Weber-Ernst Bot. award. Mem. A.A.A.S., Am. Assn. State Colls. and Univs. (task force on allied health professions), Am. Coll. Health Assn., Am. Inst. Biol. Scis., San Francisco, Bakersfield (dir.) chambers commerce, Nat. Assn. Biology Tchrs., Sigma Xi, Blue Key, Phi Kappa Phi. Clubs: Commonwealth, University (San Francisco). Address: Office of Pres San Francisco State U 1600 Holloway Ave San Francisco CA 94132

ROME, DONALD LEE, lawyer; b. West Hartford, Conn., May 17, 1929; s. Herman Isaac and Juliette (Stern) R.; S.B., Trinity Coll., 1951; LL.B., Harvard U., 1954; m. Sheila Ward, Apr. 20, 1958; children—Adam Ward, Lisa, Ethan Stern. Admitted to Conn. bar, 1954, U.S. Supreme Ct. bar, 1965; mem. firm Ribicoff and Kotkin, Hartford, Conn., 1954-58, partner, 1958-67; partner firm Rosenberg, Rome, Barnett, Sattin & Santos, and predecessor, Hartford, 1967—; mem. Conn. Gov.'s Study Commn. on Uniform Consumer Credit Code, 1969-70; chmn. Conn. bar advisory com. of attys. to make recommendations to U.S. dist. ct. for proposed changes of bankruptcy rules in dist. Conn., 1975-77; lectr. in law U. Conn., 1965-74; lectr. continuing legal edn. on secured creditors' rights, bankruptcy and uniform comml. code, 1958—. Past bd. dirs. New Eng. region Am. Jewish Com., also Hartford chpt.; past bd. dirs. Hebrew Home for Aged, Hartford; past bd. trustees Temple Beth Israel, West Hartford. Mem. Am. (bus. bankruptcy com. of sect. on corp., banking and bus. law), Conn. (chmn. sect. comml. law and bankruptcy 1977—), Hartford County (continuing legal edn. com.) bar assns., Assn. Comml. Fin. Attys. (pres. 1978—), Am. Arbitration Assn. (mem. panel comml. arbitrators), Fed. Bar Assn. (bankruptcy law com.), Assn. Trial Lawyers Am., Conn. Trial Lawyers Assn., Comml. Law League Am., Harvard Law Sch. Assn. Conn. (pres. 1970-71). Clubs: Univ., Harvard of N.Y.C., Trinity, Masons (32 deg., Scottish Rite, mem. trial commn. Conn. grand lodge 1970—). Author: The Business Workout-A Primer for Participating Creditors, 1979; The New Bankruptcy Act and The Commercial Lender, 1979; co-author: A Comparative Analysis and Study of the Uniform Consumer Credit Code in Relation to the Existing Consumer Credit Law in Connecticut, 1970; contbg. author Connecticut Practice Book, 1978. Home: 46 Belknap Rd West Hartford CT 06117 Office: Rosenberg Rome Barnett Sattin & Santos 37 Lewis St Hartford CT 06103. *We are told by Kipling that success and failure are "imposters". I have found this fundamental teaching to be most helpful in the practice of law and in life generally. Concentration on long term relationships and basic values is so much more important than ephemeral successes and failures.*

ROME, HAROLD JACOB, composer; b. Hartford, Conn., May 27, 1908; s. Louis and Ida (Aronson) R.; B.A., Yale U., 1929, student Law Sch., 1928-30; B.F.A., Sch. Architecture, 1934; m. Florence Miles, Feb. 3, 1939; children—Joshua, Rachel. Composer, lyricist Pins and Needles, produced by Labor Stage, 1937, 39; revue, Sing Out the News, produced by Max Gordon, 1938; musical comedy, The Little Dog Laughed, produced by Eddie Dowling, 1940; score of Lunch Time Follies; spl. material for Star and Garter (produced by Michael Todd); spl. material for Ziegfeld Follies, 1943; music and lyrics for Stars and Gripes Army Show produced by Spl. Service Office, Ft. Hamilton and U.S. Army; music and lyrics for Call Me Mister, produced by Melvyn Douglas and Herman Levin, 1946; also popular songs, Franklin D. Roosevelt Jones, Sunday in the Park, and piano suite, Opus New York, spl. material for Peep Show, produced by Michael Todd, 1950; music and lyrics for Bless You All, 1950; Wish You Were Here (Logan and Hayward producers), 1952; Fanny (Logan and Merrick producers), 1954; Sing Song Man (children's album); A Touch of Rome; Harold Rome Sings Fanny, Rome Antics, And Then I Wrote (albums); Destry Rides Again, 1959; also I Can Get It for You Wholesale, 1962; music and lyrics for The Zulu and The Zayda, 1965, Scarlett, mus. adaptation of Gone With the Wind, Imperial Theatre, Tokyo, 1970, Drury Lane Theatre, London, 1972, Los Angeles Civic Light Opera, 1973. One man show paintings and songs Marble Arch Gallery, N.Y.C., 1964, paintings Bodley Gallery, N.Y.C., 1970. Served with AUS, 1943-45. Mem. Dramatists Guild, AFTRA, ASCAP, Am. Guild Authors and Composers, Composers and Lyricists Guild Am. Clubs: Yale, Players. Democrat. Address: care Chappell & Co 810 7th Ave New York NY 10019

ROME, MORTON PHILLIPS, elec. co. exec., lawyer; b. Phila., Apr. 2, 1913; s. John J. and Etta (Phillips) R.; B.A., U. Pa., 1933, LL.B., 1936; m. Marjorie Taussig, June 20, 1942; children—Mary T., Sally P., Thomas M. Admitted to Pa. bar, 1936; with firm Sundheim, Folz & Sundheim, Phila., 1936-42; partner firm Sundheim, Folz, Kamsler & Goodis, Phila., 1946-51; v.p. contracts Emerson Radio & Phonograph Corp., N.Y.C., 1951-60, dir., 1966, v.p., sec., 1962-66; pres., dir. Emertron, Inc.. Jersey City and Washington, 1960-62; sec., counsel Nat. Union Electric Corp., Greenwich, Conn., 1966—; sec. Onward Mfg. Co., Ltd., Kitchener, Ont., Can., 1973—. Served to capt. U.S. Army, 1942-46. Decorated Commendation ribbon. Mem. Am., Pa., Phila. bar assns., Order of Coif. Clubs: Philmont Country; Princeton (N.Y.C.). Address: 204 Kent Rd Wyncote PA 19095

ROMEO, LUIGI, educator; b. Tropea, Italy, Sept. 20, 1926; s. Pasquale and Beatrice (LoTorto) R.; came to U.S., 1953, naturalized, 1960; B.A. in Fgn. Langs., Wash. State U., 1957; M.A., U. Wash., 1959, Ph.D., 1960. Instr., U. Wash., Seattle, 1959-60, acting asst. prof., 1960-61; asst. prof. U. Toronto (Ont., Can.), 1961-65; asso. prof. U. Colo., Boulder, 1965-68, chmn. adv. com. linguistics, 1967-68, prof., chmn. dept. linguistics, 1969-75; hon. prof. Istituto Superiore Europeo di Scienze Umane, 1968—. U. Colo. faculty fellow, 1970-71, 76-77. Mem. Linguistic Assn. Can. and U.S. (charter), Linguistic Circle Colo., Semiotic Circle Colo. (founder, pres.), Semiotic Soc. Am. Contbg. author: Language Sciences, 1971; Current Trends in Linguistics, 1975; History of Linguistic Thought and Contemporary Linguistics, 1975; author: Ecce Home! A Lexicon of Man, 1979. Mem. adv. bd. Historiographia Linguistica, 1972—; editor-in-chief Ars Semeiotica; editor, pub. Ars Semeiotica Press, Boulder. Contbr. articles profl. jours. Home: PO Box 600 Boulder CO 80306. *The goal of my educational life is to learn something new and useful from anyone who was once my student.*

ROMER, ROBERT HORTON, educator, physicist; b. Chgo., Apr. 15, 1931; s. Alfred Sherwood and Ruth (Hibbard) R.; B.A., Amherst Coll., 1952; Ph.D. in Physics, Princeton, 1955; m. Diana Haynes, June 12, 1953; children—Evan James, David Hibbard, Theodore Haynes. Faculty, Amherst (Mass.), Coll., 1955—, prof. physics, 1966—, chmn. dept., 1966—. Research asso. Duke, 1958-59; guest physicist Brookhaven Nat. Lab., 1963—; vis. prof. physics Voorhees Coll., 1969-70. NSF fellow U. Grenoble (France), 1964-65. Mem. Am. Phys. Soc., Am. Assn. Physics Tchrs. (asso. editor jour. 1968), Phi Beta Kappa, Sigma Xi. Author: Energy—An Introduction to Physics, 1976. Research low temperature physics, solar energy. Home: 104 Spring St Amherst MA 01002

ROMER, ROY R., state ofcl.; b. Garden City, Kans., Oct. 31, 1928; s. Irving Rudolph and Margaret Elizabeth (Snyder) R.; B.S. in Agrl. Econs., Colo. State U., 1950; LL.B., U. Colo., 1952; postgrad. Yale U.; m. Beatrice Miller, June 10, 1952; children—Paul, Mark, Mary, Christopher, Timothy, Thomas, Elizabeth. Engaged in farming in Colo., 1942-52; admitted to Colo. bar, 1952; ind. practice, Denver, 1955-66; mem. Colo. Ho. of Reps., Dist., 1958-62, Colo. Senate, 1962-66; owner, operator Arapahoe Aviation Co., Colo. Flying Acad., Geneva Basin Ski Area; engaged in home site devel.; owner chain farm implement and indsl. equipment stores in Colo.; commr. agr. State of Colo., 1975, state treas., 1977—; chief staff, exec. asst. to gov. Colo., 1975-77; chmn. Gov. Colo. Blue Ribbon Panel, Gov. Colo. Small Bus. Council; mem. agrl. adv. com. Colo. Bd. Agr. Past trustee Iliff Sch. Theology, Denver. Served with USAF, 1952-54. Mem. Colo. Bar Assn. (gov.), Order of Coif. Democrat. Presbyterian. Bd. editors Colo. U. Law Rev., 1960-62. Home: 4600 Montview Blvd Denver CO 80220 Office: 140 State Capitol Bldg Denver CO 80203

ROMERO-BARCELÓ, CARLOS ANTONIO, gov. P.R.; b. San Juan, P.R., Sept. 4, 1932; s. Antonio and Josefina (Barcelo-Bird) Romero-Moreno; B.A., Yale U., 1953; LL.B., U. P.R., 1956; LL.D. (hon.), U. Bridgeport, 1977; m. Kathleen Donnelly, Jan. 2, 1966; children—Juan Carlos, Melinda Kathleen; children by previous marriage—Carlos, Andrés. Admitted to P.R. bar, 1956; mem. firm Herrero-Frank & Romero-Barceló, 1956-58; partner firm Rivera-Zayas, Rivera-Cestero & Rúa, Segurola, Romero & Toledo, San Juan, 1958-63, Segurola, Romero & Toledo, 1963-68; pres. Citizens for State 51, 1965-67; mayor, San Juan, 1969-77; gov. P.R., 1977—. Pres. New Progressive Party, 1974—; Pres., Nat. League Cities, 1975; past dir. U.S. Conf. Mayors. Mem. Nat. Govs.' Assn., So. Govs.' Assn. (vice chmn.). Roman Catholic. Author: Statehood Is For the Poor, 1973. Home and Office: La Fortaleza San Juan PR 00901. *The Puerto Rico of today is not especially wealthy; we are not mighty; our people do not live in total internal harmony. Nevertheless, we do enjoy, individually and collectively, the basic human rights which define a free society. And believe me, the people of Puerto Rico appreciate with every fiber of their being how rare and how precious a blessing freedom is. Moreover, we know why we are free. We know that we are free precisely because we are natural-born citizens of the freest and most open and most culturally diverse nation in the history of mankind: the United States of America.*

ROMEY, WILLIAM DOWDEN, geologist, educator; b. Richmond, Ind., Oct. 26, 1930; s. William Minter and Grace Warring (Dowden) R.; A.B. with highest honors, Ind. U., 1952; student U. Paris, 1950-51, 52-53; Ph.D., U. Calif. at Berkeley, 1962; m. Lucretia Alice Leonard, July 16, 1955; children—Catherine Louise, Gretchen Elizabeth, William Leonard. Asst. prof. geology and sci. edn. Syracuse U., 1962-66, asso. prof., 1966-69; exec. dir. earth sci. ednl. program Am. Geol. Inst., 1969-72; prof., chmn. dept. geology St. Lawrence U., Canton, N.Y., 1971-76, prof., 1976—; ednl. cons., 1962—; Nat. Acad. Sci. visitor USSR Acad. Sci., 1967; vis. geoscientist Am. Geol. Inst., 1964-66, 71; earth sci. cons. Compton's Ency., 1970-71. Bd. dirs. Onondaga Nature Centers, Inc., 1966-69. Served to lt. USNR, 1953-57; lt. comdr. Res. Woodrow Wilson Found. fellow, 1959-60, 61-62; NSF sci. faculty fellow U. Oslo, 1967-68. Fellow Geol. Soc. Am., AAAS; mem. Nat. Assn. Geology Tchrs. (v.p. 1971-72, pres. 1972-73), Assn. Am. Geographers, Am. Geophys. Union, Nat. Sci. Tchrs. Assn., Geol. Soc. Norway, Assn. Educating Tchrs. of Sci., Assn. Humanistic Psychology, Phi Beta Kappa, Sigma Xi, Phi Delta Kappa. Author: (with others) Investigating the Earth, 1967; (with J. Kramer, E. Muller, J. Lewis) Investigations in Geology, 1967; Inquiry Techniques for Teaching Science, 1968; Risk-Trust-Love, 1972; Consciousness and Creativity, 1975; Confluent Education in Science, 1976; co-editor Geochemical Prospecting for Petroleum, 1959; asso. editor Jour. Coll. Sci. Teaching, 1972-74; editor-in-chief Ash Lad Press, 1975—; asso. editor Geol. Soc. Am. Bull., 1979—. Contbr. articles on geology and edn. to profl. publs. Home: 14 W Main St Canton NY 13617 Office: Dept Geology and Geography St Lawrence U Canton NY 13617

ROMINE, JOANNE BARBARA, handwriting analyst, columnist; b. Portland, Oreg. July 28, 1932; d. Ellis Wesley and Josephine Elliot (Porter) Penny; student Portland State Coll., 1960-61, Fullerton Jr. Coll., 1969-70; m. Lester Ronald Romine, July 3, 1948 (div. 1978); children—Deborah Ann (Mrs. Richard Carroll Sinclair), David Lester (dec.), Diane Elizabeth (Mrs. Kenneth Bruce Miller), Douglas Ellis, Daniel Scott, Denise JoLynn. Free-lance writer short humor, poetry, handwriting analysis, Portland, 1959-64; writer syndicated column Clarke Pub. Co., Portland, 1964—; editor Modesto (Calif.) News Bull., newspaper, 1972-73; nationally syndicated columnist Copley News Service, 1974-76; lectr., tchr. handwriting analysis, Calif., 1969—; own TV segment Penny's Write, Sta. WCRA-TV, 1974-75; founder, dir. Internat. Inst. Handwriting Analysis, 1976—. Counselor Outreach Drug Abuse Prevention Center, Santa Ana, 1969-71; vol. counselor Orange County Mental Health Drug Hot Line, 1970, Beyer High Sch., Modesto, 1972; cons. to psychiatrists, psychologists, bus. firms; lectr.-counselor to schs., clubs, chs. bus. assns. Mem. Am. Handwriting Analysts Found., Internat. Platform Assn., Soroptimists, Am. Bus. Women's Assn. Republican. Mem. Ch. of Jesus Christ of Latter-day Saints. Office: PO Box 6482 Modesto CA 95355. *Over the years I have learned that through "understanding" we can have empathy for all people—and that understanding comes when we learn to look and listen with our hearts.*

ROMINE, THOMAS BEESON, JR., cons. engring. firm exec.; b. Billings, Mont., Nov. 16, 1925; s. Thomas Beeson and Elizabeth Marjorie (Tschudy) R.; student Rice Inst., 1943-44; B.S. in Mech. Engring., U. Tex., Austin, 1948; m. Rosemary Pearl Melancon, Aug. 14, 1948; children—Thomas Beeson III, Richard Alexander, Robert Harold. Jr. engr. Gen. Engring. Co., Ft. Worth, 1948-50; design engr. Wyatt C. Hedrick, architect/engr., Ft. Worth, 1950-54, chief mech. engr., 1954-56; pres., chief mech. engr. Thomas B. Romine, Jr. cons. engr. (now Romine Romine & Burgess, Inc. cons. engrs.), Ft. Worth, 1956—. Mem. Plan Commn., City of Ft. Worth, 1958-62; mem. Supervisory Bd. Plumbers, City Ft. Worth, 1963-71, chmn., 1970-71, chmn. Plumbing Code Rev. Com., 1968-69; mem. Mech. Bd., City Ft. Worth, 1974—, chmn., 1976—; chmn. plumbing code bd. North Central Tex. Council Govts., Ft. Worth, 1971-75. Bd. mgrs. Tex. Christian U.-South Side YMCA, Ft. Worth, 1969-74; trustee Ft. Worth Symphony Orch., 1968—, Orch. Hall, 1975—. Served with USNR, 1943-45. Registered profl. engr., Tex., Okla., La., Ga. Fellow ASHRAE (pres. Ft. Worth chpt. 1958, nat. committeeman 1974—), Automated Procedures Engring. Cons., Am. Cons. Engrs. Council (trustee 1970-71, 75, 1st v.p. 1972-73, internat. pres. 1974); mem. Nat. Soc. Profl. Engrs., Tex. Soc. Profl. Engrs. (dir. 1956, treas. 1967), Cons. Engrs. Council Tex. (pres. North Tex. chpt., also v.p. state orgn. 1965, dir. state orgn. 1967), Starfish Class Assn. (nat. pres. 1970-73, nat. champion 1976), Delta Tau Delta, Pi Tau Sigma. Episcopalian (vestryman). Clubs: Colonial Country, Rotary. Author numerous computer programs in energy analysis and heating and air conditioning field; contbr. articles to profl. jours. Home: 3232 Preston Hollow St Fort Worth TX 76109 Office: 300 Greenleaf St Fort Worth TX 76107. *It has long been my belief that, in this technological age, the general public can do little more than accept on faith the propriety of mechanical and electrical systems provided for use in their homes and businesses, and that without an understanding and knowledgeable agent to guide them this faith is often misplaced. It is thus incumbent upon the Professional Engineer to use his expertise in this field to insure competency and safety in those projects under his control, and to assist wherever possible in guiding and influencing appropriate legislation in this regard along sound engineering pathways.*

ROMMEL, WILFRED H., ret. govt. ofcl., lawyer; b. Fargo, N.D., Mar. 6, 1916; s. William and Winifred (Herzer) R.; B.S., N.D. State U., 1937; postgrad. Am. U. Grad. Sch. Pub. Adminstrn., 1938-40; LL.B., George Washington U., 1950; m. Leona P. Stevens, Aug. 17, 1957. Adminstrv. asst. to budget officer Dept. Agr., 1940-42; with U.S. Office Mgmt. and Budget, 1946-75, asst. dir. legis. reference, 1966-75; admitted to D.C. bar, 1950. Served to lt. USNR, 1942-46. Recipient Career Service award Nat. Civil Service League, 1971. Mem. Fed. Bar Assn., Nat. Lawyers Club. Home: 4301 Massachusetts Ave NW Washington DC 20016

ROMNEY, CARL F., seismologist; b. Salt Lake City, June 5, 1924; B.S. in Meteorology, Calif. Inst. Tech.; Ph.D., U. Calif.; m. Barbara Doughty; children—Carolyn Ann, Kim. Seismologist, U.S. Dept. Air Force, 1955-73, asst. tech. dir. Air Force Tech. Applications Center, to 1973; dep. dir. Nuclear Monitoring Research Office, Def. Advanced Research Projects Agy., Arlington, Va., 1973-75, dir., 1975—; tech. adviser U.S. reps. in negotiations Test Ban Treaty; mem. U.S. del. Geneva Conf. Experts, 1958, Conf. on Discontinuance Nuclear Weapons Tests, 1959, 60, negotiations on threshold Test Ban Treaty, Moscow, 1974; mem. U.S. del. Peaceful Nuclear Explosions Treaty, Moscow, 1974-75. Recipient Exceptional Civilian Service awards Air Force, 1959, Dept. Def., 1964; Pres.'s award for Distinguished Fed. Civilian Service, for outstanding contbns. to devel. of control system for underground nuclear tests, 1967. Contbr. articles to tech. jours. Research on earthquake mechanism, seismic noise; generation, propagation, detection seismic waves from underground explosions. Home: 4105 Sulgrave Dr Alexandria VA 22309 Office: 1400 Wilson Blvd Arlington VA 22209

ROMNEY, GEORGE, former govt. ofcl., orgn. exec.; b. Chihuahua, Mex., July 8, 1907; s. Gaskell and Anna (Pratt) R.; student Latter Day Saints High Sch. and Jr. Coll., U. Utah, 1929, George Washington U., 1929-30; m. Lenore LaFount, July 2, 1931; children—Lynn (Mrs. Loren G. Keenan), Jane (Mrs. Bruce H. Robinson), Scott, Willard Mitt. Missionary, Scotland and England, 1927- 28; tariff specialist for U.S. Senator David I. Walsh, 1929-30; apprentice Aluminum Co. Am., 1930, salesman, Los Angeles, 1931; Washington rep. Aluminum Co. Am., also Aluminum Wares Assn., 1932-38; Detroit mgr. Automobile Mfrs. Assn., 1939-41, gen. mgr. assn., 1942-48; v.p. Nash-Kelvinator Corp., 1950-53, exec. v.p., 1953-54, dir., 1953-54; pres., chmn. bd., gen. mgr. Am. Motors Corp., 1954-62, vice chmn., dir. (on leave), until 1962; gov. Mich., 1963-69; sec. HUD, 1969-72; chmn., chief exec. officer Nat. Center Vol. Action, 1973-79; chmn. Volunteer: Nat. Center Citizen Involvement, 1979—; U.S. employer delegate to Metal Trades Industry Confs., 1946-49; mng. dir. Automotive Council War Prodn., 1942-45; chmn. Citizens for Mich., 1959-62; mgmt. mem. War Manpower Commn., Labor-Mgmt. Commn., Detroit area, also pres. Washington Trade Assn. Execs., 1937-38; pres. Detroit Trade Assn., 1941; dir. Am. Trade Assn. Execs., 1944-47; mng. dir. Nat. Auto. Golden Jubilee Com., 1946. Past mem. bd. dirs. NCCJ, United Found., Cranbrook Sch. Named A.P. Industry Man of Year, 1958-61. Past pres. Detroit Stake Ch. Jesus Christ of Latter-Day Saints, now regional rep. Clubs: Athletic, Detroit (Detroit); Burning Tree (Washington); Bloomfield Hills Country. Home: East Valley Rd Bloomfield Hills MI 48013

ROMNEY, HENRY JOHN, found. exec.; b. Frankfurt, Germany, Jan. 23, 1924; s. Alfred Albert and Emmily (Gartner) R.; student Harrow (Eng.) Sch.; B.A., Harvard U., 1946; m. Janet Shearson Adams, Mar. 30, 1948 (div. 1958); children—Diana Adams, Charles Christopher, Cynthia Shearson; m. Elizabeth Mehlfeld, Nov. 1978. Writer, March of Time, N.Y.C., 1952-54; asso. editor Sports Illustrated mag., N.Y.C., 1954-61; spl. asst. to Sec. Interior, Washington, 1961, asst. to sec. interior, 1961-62; head info. service Rockefeller Found., N.Y.C., 1962-76, dir. ednl. pub. program, 1976—. Served with AUS, 1942-45. Decorated Purple Heart with oak leaf cluster. Home: 24 E 81st St New York NY 10028 Office: 1133 Ave of Americas New York NY 10036

ROMNEY, JUNIUS STOWELL, lawyer; b. Colonia Juarez, Mexico, June 10, 1903; s. Junius and Gertrude (Stowell) R.; brought to U.S., 1912; student U. Utah, 1921-23; J.D. with honors, George Washington U., 1930; m. Ruth Stewart, Sept. 4, 1928; children—Junius Stewart, Joseph Barnard, Bruce Stewart, David Stewart. Asso. editor Millennial Star, Liverpool, Eng., 1925-26; asst. chief clk. Bur. of Investigation, Dept. Justice, 1927-28; admitted to D.C. bar, 1930, Utah bar, 1931 and since practiced in Salt Lake City; mem. Romney and Boyer, predecessor firm, 1953-70. Mem. Utah State Soc.

(pres. 1927), Am., Utah, Salt Lake County bar assns., Utah Bar Found. (pres. 1964-65), Tau Kappa Alpha, Phi Alpha Delta. Mem. Ch. Jesus Christ Latter-day Saints. Home: 1010 Douglas St Salt Lake City UT 84105

ROMNEY, MARION GEORGE, religious ofcl., lawyer; b. Colonia Juarez, Chihuahua, Mexico (parents Am. citizens), Sept. 19, 1897; s. George Samuel and Artemesia (Redd) R.; grad. Ricks Acad., 1918, Ricks Normal Jr. Coll., 1920; student Brigham Young U., 1924; B.S., U. Utah, 1926, J.D., 1932; m. Ida Olivia Jensen, Sept. 12, 1924; children—Richard J., Janet Ida (dec.), George J. Admitted to Utah bar, 1929; asst. atty. Salt Lake County, 1935; asst. dist. atty. 4th Jud. dist. State Utah, 1937-38; asst. atty. Salt Lake City, 1940; treas. Zions Securities Corp., 1947-59, chmn. exec. com. bd. dirs., 1961—, dir., 1958—, chmn. bd., 1975—; chmn. bd. Beneficial Life Ins. Co., Hotel Utah Corp., Beneficial Devel. Corp.; dir. Bonneville Internat. Corp., Deseret Mgmt., Peoples 1st Thrift. Missionary Ch. of Jesus Christ of Latter-day Saints, Australia, 1920-23, sec. Australian Mission, pres. New South Wales Conf., 1921-23, bishop 33d Ward, 1935-38, pres. Bonneville Stake, 1938-41, asst. to Council of Twelve Apostles, 1941-51, mem. Council, 1951-72, 2d counselor in 1st presidency, 1972—; mng. dir. Gen. Ch. Welfare Com., 1959, chmn., 1959-63, mem. com. on expenditures, 1963—, supr. Latin Am. mission, 1961-68, supr. Scandinavian, West European, South African missions, 1968-71, dir. Asian missions, 1971-72. Rep., Utah State Legislature, 1935-36; adv. welfare div. Utah State Civil Def. Council, 1950. Trustee Brigham Young U., Provo, Utah. Served as pvt. U.S. Army, 1918. Mem. Am. Bar Assn., Order of Coif, Phi Alpha Delta, Phi Kappa Phi. Home: 1909 Yalecrest Ave Salt Lake City UT 84108 Office: 47 E South Temple St Salt Lake City UT 84111

ROMNEY, SEYMOUR LEONARD, physician, educator; b. N.Y.C., June 8, 1917; s. Benjamin and Anne (Senter) R.; A.B., Johns Hopkins, 1938; postgrad. Mass. Inst. Tech., 1948-49; M.D., N.Y. U., 1942; m. Shirley Gordon, Nov. 4, 1945; children—Benjamin, Mary Clark, Dana, Anne. Intern Beth Israel Hosp., Boston, 1942-43; resident Boston Lying-in Hosp., Free Hosp. for Women, Boston, 1946-51; fellow, instr. Harvard Med. Sch., 1947-51, asst. prof. obstetrics and gynecology, 1951-57; prof., chmn. dept. gynecology and obstetrics Albert Einstein Coll. Medicine, N.Y.C., 1957-72, prof., 1972—, dir. research gynecol. oncology, 1972—; dir. obstetrics and gynecology Bronx Municipal Hosp. Center, N.Y.C., 1957-72. Cons. WHO. Mem. N.Y. State Family Planning Coalition. Bd. dirs. N.Y. Zool. Soc. Served to lt. comdr. M.C., USNR, 1943-45. Diplomate Am. Bd. Obstetrics and Gynecology (examiner), Nat. Bd. Med. Examiners. Mem. Assn. Profs. Obstetrics and Gynecology, Am. Gynecol. Soc., N.Y. Obstet. Soc., Am. Coll. Obstetricians and Gynecologists, Soc. Gynecologic Investigation, Planned Parenthood-World Populations (adv. com.), Am. Assn. Parenthood Physicians, Maternity Center Assn., N.Y. Acad. Medicine, N.Y. Acad. Sci., A.A.A.S., Population Assn. Am. Home: 1081 Orienta Ave Mamaroneck NY 10543 Office: Bronx Municipal Hosp Center-Einstein Coll Medicine Pelham Pkwy and Eastchester Rd Bronx NY 10461

ROMOSER, GEORGE KENNETH, educator; b. Kingston, N.Y., Sept. 14, 1929; s. Carl August and Alva (Becker) R.; A.B., Rutgers U., 1951; A.M., U. Chgo., 1954, Ph.D., 1958; m. Mechthild von Tresckow, Apr. 30, 1967; children—Alexandra Ada, Valerie Anna. Research asst. Nat. Opinion Research Center, 1953; asst. Polit. Sci. Inst., Freiburg U., Germany, 1955-56; instr. Ohio State U., 1957-61; asso. prof. Conn. Coll., 1963-67; asst. prof., asso. prof., prof. polit. sci. U. N.H., Durham, 1961-62, 67—, chmn. dept., 1968-71. Fulbright prof. Faculty of Law, Mainz U., Germany, 1962-63; vis. prof. Free U., Berlin, 1964, Mannheim U., 1968, Johns Hopkins, Bologna, Italy, 1969, Munich U., 1973-74; Fulbright sr. research fellow Munich U., 1974; Rockefeller fellow Aspen Inst. for Humanistic Studies, 1978-79; cons. Com. on Internat. Exchange of Persons, 1965-66; co-founder, chmn. Conf. Group on German Politics, 1968—. Chmn. com. on govtl. reorgn. Democratic party N.H., 1962. Decorated Civilian Knight's Cross (Fed. Republic of Germany). Mem. Internat. Polit. Sci. Assn. (chmn. study group on comparative polit. ideas 1977—), Phi Delta Theta, Pi Sigma Alpha, Delta Phi Alpha, Phi Alpha Theta. Contbr. articles to profl. jours., books. Home: Worster Rd Eliot ME 03903 Office: U NH Durham NH 03824

ROMUALDI, JAMES PHILIP, engring. educator; b. N.Y.C., June 30, 1929; s. Serafino and Jean (Pesci) R.; B.S. in Civil Engring., Carnegie Inst. Tech., 1951, M.S., 1953, Ph.D., 1954; m. Daina M. Mucinieks, June 5, 1958; children—Jean Renee and Jessica Anne (twins), John Philip. Engr., Richardson Gordon and Assos., summer 1955; research engr. U.S. Navy Research Lab., summer 1956; mem. faculty Carnegie Inst. Tech., 1955—, prof. civil engring., 1964—, dir. Transp. Research Inst., 1966—; partner Gen. Analytics, Inc., cons. engrs., Pitts., 1966—. Fulbright fellow Technische Hochschule Karlsruhe, 1954-55. Mem. Am. Soc. C.E. (Young Civil Engr. of Year award Pitts. sect. 1966), Am. Soc. Testing and Materials, Am. Concrete Inst., Am. Soc. Engring. Edn. Inventor crack resistant steel fiber reinforced concrete. Author articles. Home: 5737 Wilkins Ave Pittsburgh PA 15217

ROMZICK, MARGUERITE (MRS. VERNON C. ROMZICK), automobile co. exec.; b. Detroit, Mar. 20, 1938; d. Domenic and Carina (Faricelli) N.; student pub. schs., Detroit; m. Vernon C. Romzick, July 9, 1979. With Gen. Motors Corp., 1956—, exec. sec., 1962-72, asst. corp. sec., 1972—, also sec., dir. 20 U.S. subs. coms.; sec. bd. trustees Gen. Motors Inst., Flint, Mich. Mem. Am. Soc. Corporate Secs. Club: Nomads (dir.) (Detroit). Home: 23355 Beechcrest Dearborn Heights MI 48127 Office: Gen Motors Corp 8-217 GM Bldg Detroit MI 48202

RONA, GEORGE, physician; b. Budapest, Hungary, Mar. 8, 1924; s. Adolf A. and Ilona (Steiner) R.; M.D., U. Budapest, 1949; Ph.D., Hungarian Sci. Acad., 1954; m. Agnes Szilas, Jan. 13, 1950; children—Zoltan, Gabriel. Asso. dir. Pathol. Inst., Med. U., Budapest, 1954-56; prof. pathology McGill U., Montreal, 1971—; dir. labs. Lakeshore Gen. Hosp., 1965-79. Recipient Arthur Weber Meml. prize for work catecholamines and effect of isoproterenol on myocardium, 1976. Mem. Internat. Soc. for Heart Research (pres. Am. sect. 1976—), Canadian Assn. Pathologists, Que. Assn. Lab. Physicians, Am. Assn. Pathology and Exptl. Pathology, Am. Coll. Pathology, Coll. of Pathology (Eng.), Royal Coll. Physicians and Surgeons (Can.), Internat. Acad. Pathology, Am. Soc. Exptl. Pathology. Asso. editor: Jour. of Molecular and Cellular Cardiology, 1969; editorial bd. Basic Research in Cardiology, 1974; series editor Recent Advances in Studies on Cardiac Structure and Metabolism, 12 vols., 1972—. Contbr. articles to profl. jours. Home: 80 Henley Ave Town of Mt Royal Montreal PQ Canada Office: Dept Pathology McGill U 3775 University St Montreal PQ Canada. *Talent must be channeled and directed towards a goal by self-discipline. Much youthful talent is wasted because of lack of control; rarely, if ever, can we compensate for wasted days. Although much time can be saved by profiting from the experience of others, one must venture forth courageously into uncharted waters to discover anything really new and great.*

RONALD, PETER, utility exec.; b. Duluth, Minn., Aug. 26, 1926; s. George W. and Florence (Jones) R.; B.A., U. Va., 1950; m. Mary Locke Boyd, Nov. 25, 1950; children—Peter Webb, Pauline Morton, Samuel Herschel. With Louisville Gas & Electric Co., 1950—, treas., 1962—, v.p., 1969—. Bd. dirs., mem. exec. com. Bus. Devel. Corp. Ky., 1967-75, pres., 1971-72; bd. dirs. Louisville Community Chest, 1967-72, 73—, v.p., 1969-72; bd. dirs., v.p. Louisville Rehab. Center, 1964—, pres., 1970-71; bd. overseers Louisville Country Day Sch., 1967-70; trustee Children's Hosp. Found., 1978—, sec.-treas., 1978—. Served with USNR, 1945-46. Mem. Zeta Psi. Clubs: Louisville Country; Juniper (v.p. 1975, pres. 1976). Home: Mockingbird Valley Rd Louisville KY 40207 Office: 311 W Chestnut St PO Box 32010 Louisville KY 40232

RONALD, WILLIAM, artist; b. Stratford, Ont., Can., Aug. 13, 1926; s. William Stanley and Lillian M. (Plant) R.; hon. grad. Ont. Coll. Art, 1952; pupil Jock Macdonald; m. Helen Marie Higgins, Sept. 6, 1952; children—Suzanne Marie, Dianna Louise. Came to U.S., 1954, naturalized, 1963. One man shows include Hart House, U. Toronto, 1954, Greenwich Gallery, Toronto, 1957, Laing Galleries, Toronto, 1960, Douglass Coll., New Brunswick, N.J., 1960, Kootz Gallery, N.Y.C., 1957-60, 62, 63, Issacs Gallery, Toronto, 1963, David Mirvish Gallery, Toronto, 1965, Princeton Mus., 1963, Dunkelman Gallery, Toronto, 1970, Tom Thompson Meml. Gallery, Owen Sound, Ont., 1971, Brandon (Man.) U., 1972, Morris Gallery, Toronto, 1975, Gustafssen Gallery, Brampton, Ont., Can., 1975, Brampton Pub. Library and Art Gallery, Bramalea, Ont., Can., 1976; retrospective, Ronald-25 Years, exhibited Robert McLaughlin Gallery, Oshawa, Ont., Can., 1975, Musee d'Art Contemporain, Montreal, 1975, Rodman Hall Arts Centre, St. Catharines, Ont., 1975, Beaverbrook Art Gallery, Fredericton, N.B., 1975, Confedn. Centre Art Gallery and Mus., Charlottetown, P.E.I., 1975, Edmonton (Alta.) Art Gallery, 1975, Burnaby (B.C.) Art Gallery, 1976, Art Gallery of Windsor, Ont., 1976, Morris Gallery, Toronto, 1977, 78; group exhbns. include Trinity Coll., Toronto, 1951, Eglinton Gallery, Toronto, 1953, Biennial exhbns. Nat. Gallery Can., 1955, 57-58, Smithsonian Travelling Exhbn., 1956, Riverside Mus., N.Y.C., 1956, Contemporary Canadian Painters, 1957, Carnegie Internat., 1958, Brussels World Fair and Traveling Show, 1958, Sao Paulo Biennale, 1959, Whitney Ann., 1959, Corcoran Biennial, 1962, 63, Toysby Contemporary Artists, 1966, Artists on Campus, York U., Toronto, 1970, Toronto Painting, 1972, Robert McLaughlin Gallery, Oshawa, 1978; represented permanent collections Art Gallery Ont., Toronto, Bklyn. Mus., Carnegie Inst., Guggenheim Mus., Mus. Modern Art, Nat. Gallery Can., Ottawa, R.I. Sch. Design, Albright-Knox Gallery, Buffalo, Aldrich Mus., Ridgefield, Conn., U. B.C., Art Inst. Chgo., Internat. Minerals & Chems. Corp., Skokie, Ill., James A. Michener Found., Allentown, Pa., Montreal (Que.) Mus. Fine Arts, York U., Toronto, David Rockefeller Collection, Nelson A. Rockefeller Collection, U. N.C., Phoenix Art Mus., Balt. Mus., Walker Art Center, Mpls., Williams Coll., Princeton Mus., Queens U., Kingston, Ont., Brandeis U., Wadsworth Atheneum, Hartford, Conn., Whitney Mus. Am. Art, Washington Gallery Modern Art, Newark Mus., N.J. State Mus., Trenton, U. Tex., Can. Council Collection, Can. Art Bank, Windsor Art Mus., Hudson River Mus., Pasadena (Calif.) Mus. Modern Art, Masters Sch., Dobbs Ferry, N.Y., Mercy Coll., Dobbs Ferry, Toronto Dominion Bank, Notre Dame U., U. Okla. Art Mus., Norman, numerous others. Founding mem. Painters Eleven Group, Toronto, 1952; radio and TV broadcaster, 1966—; newspaper columnist, book reviewer. Recipient Ind. Order Daus. Empire scholarship, Can., 1951; Hallmark Art award for watercolor, 1952; Canadian Amateur Hockey Assn. scholarship Can. Found., 1956; Guggenheim Mus. award Canadian painting, 1956; Sr. Arts award Can. Council, 1977. Mem. Royal Canadian Acad. Address: 392 Brunswick Ave Toronto ON M5R 2Z4 Canada summer PO Box 902 Wellfleet MA 02667

RONAN, WILLIAM JOHN, coll. adminstr., pub. ofcl.; b. Buffalo, Nov. 8, 1912; s. William and Charlotte (Ramp) R.; A.B., Syracuse U., 1934; Ph. D., N.Y. U., 1940, LL.D., 1969; certificate Geneva Sch. Internat. Studies, 1933; m. Elena Vinadé, May 29, 1939; children—Monica (Mrs. Bruce Nourie), Diana (Mrs. Alan Quasha). Mus. asst. Buffalo Mus. Sci., 1928-30; with Niagara-Hudson Power Co., 1931; transfer dept. N.Y.C.R.R., 1932; Penfield fellow internat. law, diplomacy and belles lettres, 1935, Univ. fellow, 1936; editor Fed. Bank Service, Prentice-Hall, Inc., 1937; instr. govt. N.Y. U., 1938, exec. sec. grad. div. for tng. in pub. services, 1938, asst. dir., 1940, asst. prof. govt., dir. grad. div. for tng. pub. service, 1940, asso. prof. govt., 1946-47, prof., 1947, dean, grad. sch. pub. adminstrn. and social service, 1953-58. Cons. N.Y.C. Civil Service Commn., 1938; prin. rev. officer, negotiations officer U.S. Civil Service Commn., 1942; prin. div. asst. U.S. Dept. State, 1943; cons. Dept. State, 1948, Dept. Def., 1954; dir. studies N.Y. State Coordination Commn., 1951-58; project mgr. N.Y. U.-U. Ankara project, 1954-59; cons. ICA, 1955, N.Y. State Welfare Conf.; adminstrv. co-dir. Albany Grad. Program in Pub. Adminstrn.; 1st dep. city adminstr. N.Y.C., 1956-57; exec. dir. N.Y. State Temporary Commn. Constl. Conv., 1956-58; sec. to Gov. N.Y., 1959-66, chmn. interdept. com. traffic safety; commr. Port Authority N.Y. and N.J., 1967—, vice chmn., 1972-74, chmn., 1974-77; trustee Met. Savs. Bank; chmn. bd. L.I. R.R., 1966-74. Chmn., Tri-State Transp. Com. (N.Y., N.J., Conn.), 1961-67; chmn. interstate com. New Haven R.R., 1960-63; chmn. N.Y. com. on L.I. R.R., 1964-65; mem. N.Y. State Commn. Interstate Coop., 1961, N.Y. State Com. Fgn. Ofcl. Visitors, 1961, N.Y. State Coordination Commn., 1960, N.Y. Civil Service Commn., Temporary State Commn. on Constl. Conv., 1966-67; chmn. N.Y. State Met. Commuter Transp. Authority, 1965-68, Met. Transp. Authority, 1968-74, Tri-Borough Bridge and Tunnel Authority, 1968-74, N.Y.C. Transit Authority, 1968-74, Manhattan and Bronx Surface Transit Operating Authority, 1968-74; chmn. bd., pres. 3d Century Corp., 1974—; mem. Commn. Critical Choices for Am., 1973—, acting chmn., 1975—; mem. urban transp. adv. com. U.S. Dept. Transp.; sr. adviser Rockefeller family, 1974—; pres. Nelson Rockefeller Collection, Inc.; trustee Power Authority of State of N.Y., 1974-77; cons. to trustees Penn Central Transp. Co.; dir. Security Nat. Bank L.I.; vice chmn. bd., dir. Continental Copper & Steel Industries, Inc.; sec.-treas. Sarabam Corp. N.V.; chmn. N.Y. and N.J. Inland Rail Rate Com. Mem. U.S. FOA, Am. Public Health Assn.; staff relations officer N.Y.C. Bd. Edn. Mem. Nat. Conf. Social Work, Nat. Conf. on Met. Areas, Citizens Com. on Corrections, Council on Social Work Edn., bd. dirs. World Trade Club; adv. bd. World Trade Inst.; mem. 42d St. Redevel. Corp., Assn. for a Better N.Y.; bd. advisers Inst. for Socioecon. Studies, 1977—; dep. dir. policy Nelson Rockefeller campaign for Republican presdl. nomination, 1964. Served as lt. USNR, 1943-46. Dir. Nat. Mgmt. Council, 1951. Mem. Am. Polit. Sci. Assn., Am. Acad. Public Adminstrn., Am. Soc. Public Adminstrn., Civil Service Assembly of U.S. and Canada, Internat. Assn. Met. Research and Devel., Nat. Municipal League, Municipal Personnel Soc., Citizens Union of N.Y., Nat. Civil Service League, Am. Acad. of Polit. and Social Sci., N.Y.C. Assn. Commerce and Industry (dir.), Internat. Inst. Adminstrv. Scis., N.E.A., Am. Fgn. Law Assn., Internat. Union Pub. Transport (mgmt. com.; v.p.) Am. Pub. Transit Assn. (chmn. 1974-76), Nat. Def. Transportation Assn. (v.p. for Mass. transit). Clubs: Metropolitan Opera; Maidstone; Devon Yacht; Knickerbocker, Hemisphere, Harvard; Winged Foot Country; Wings, Traffic, University, Railroad (N.Y.C.). Author: Money Power of States in International Law, 1940; The Board of Regents and the Commissioner, 1948; Our War Economy, 1943 (with others); articles in profl. jours.; adviser Jour. Inst. Socio-Econ. Studies. Home: 655 Park Ave New York NY 10021 also Creek House West Island Glen Cove NY 11542 Office: 30 Rockefeller Plaza Room 5600 New York NY 10020 also Port Authority of NY and NJ 1 World Trade Center New York NY 10048

RONCA, LUCIANO BRUNO, geologist, educator; b. Trieste, Italy, Apr. 26, 1935; s. Hugo Luciano and Olympia (Leeb) R.; came to U.S., 1957, naturalized, 1966; grad. Lyceum-Gymnasium, Trieste, 1953, U. Padua, Italy, 1957; M.S. (Fulbright scholar), U. Kans., 1959, Ph.D., 1963; m. Jane Areta Thorne, June 3, 1958; children—Melinda, Erika, Roxane. Research asso. geophysics U. Kans., 1962-64; gen. phys. scientist A.F. Cambridge Research Labs., Bedford, Mass., 1964-67; sr. scientist Boeing Sci. Research Labs., Seattle, 1967-70; prof. geology Wayne State U., Detroit, 1971—; mem. U. Kans. Antarctic Expedition, 1960-61; researcher U. Bern, Switzerland, 1961-62; vis. scientist Brookhaven Nat. Labs, Upton, N.Y., 1966, Lunar Sci. Inst., Houston, 1970-71; Nat. Acad. Scis. vis. scientist Vernadsky Inst., Moscow, 1976, 79-80. Fellow Geol. Soc. Am., Internat. Assn. Planetologists (treas. 1975-78), Am. Geophysics Union, Antarctican Soc., Am. Polar Soc., Mich. Basin Geol. Soc. Editor-in-charge Modern Geology, 1970—; asso. editor The Moon, 1971—. Contbr. articles to profl. jours. Mount Ronca in Antarctica is named after him. Office: Dept Geology Wayne State U Detroit MI 48202

RONCALLO, ANGELO DOMINIC, judge, former congressman; b. Port Chester, N.Y., May 28, 1927; s. Anthony and Connie (Prochilo) R.; B.A., Manhattan Coll., 1950; J.D., Georgetown U., 1953; m. Priscille Pouliot, May 31, 1952; children—Marc, Paul, John, Jean, James. Admitted to N.Y. bar, 1955; dep. county atty., 1958-60; councilman, Oyster Bay, N.Y., 1965-67; comptroller Nassau County (N.Y.), 1968-72; mem. 93d Congress from 3d N.Y. Dist., 1972-74; justice N.Y. State Supreme Ct., 1978—. Chmn. Oyster Bay Republican Com., 1968-72; bd. dirs. Am. Com. Italian Migration; trustee United Fund L.I.; mem. Bishop Lay Com.; adv. com. Nassau County Heart Fund. Served with AUS, 1944-45. Recipient Ann. Alumni Achievement award Georgetown Alumni Club Met. Washington, 1973. Mem. Delta Theta Phi. Roman Catholic. Clubs: Sons of Italy, Elks. Home: 226 Toronto Ave Massapequa NY 11758

RONDILEAU, ADRIAN, coll. pres., author; b. N.Y.C., May 8, 1912; s. Leon J. and Bessie (Caspere) R.; A.B., Coll. City N.Y., 1932; M.A., Columbia, 1934, Ph.D., 1942; m. Martha L. Denison, Aug. 15, 1936. Instr. social scis. and psychology Central Mich. Coll. 1935-37; adminstr. speech research, adult edn. and curriculum Mich. Dept. Pub. Instrn., 1937-41; dir. vocat. guidance and in-service tng. War Manpower Commn., 1941-43; spl. cons., lectr. Brazilian Ministry Edn. and coordinator Inter-Am. Affairs, Rio de Janeiro and Sao Paulo, Brazil, 1943-46; dean. bus. adminstrn., chmn. econs. dept. Asso. Colls. Upper N.Y., 1946-49; dean liberal arts Pace Coll., 1950-54; pres. Yankton (S.D.) Coll., 1954-62, Mass. State Coll., Bridgewater, 1962—; pres. Mass. State Coll. Council of Presidents, 1976—. Chmn. coll. and univ. com. YMCA 6-State N. Central Area; dir. N. Central Area YMCA; adv. bd. Upper Midwest Research and Devel. Council; pres. S.D. Found Pvt. Colls.; v.p. S.D. Assn. of Colls. and Univs.; mem. Lady Doak Coll. Funds Corp. Trustee Mass. State Colls. Adv. Commn. Rackham Found. fellow, 1935-36; Stevens scholar, 1934-35; Hoe scholar, 1933-34. Mem. N. Central Assn. Colls. and Secondary Schls., S.D. Ednl. Assn., Am. Econ. Assn., Am. Coll. Pub. Relations Assn., Brazil-Am. Cultural Soc. Mass. State Colls. Council Presidents (chmn.), N.E.A., C. of C., Phi Delta Kappa, Pi Kappa Delta. Conglist. Mason (Shriner), Elk, Rotarian (dir.). Author: Research Studies in the Teaching of College Public Speaking (with Donald Hayworth), 1939; Education for Installment Buying, 1943; People and Scenes of Brazil, 1945; Public Higher Education in the City of New York: The Master Plan Study Report (with Donald P. Cottrell), 1950; The Capital Plant Needs of American Higher Education, 1951; also articles. Office: Office of Pres Mass State Coll Bridgewater MA 02324*

RONE, WILLIAM EUGENE, JR., editor; b. Atlanta, Nov. 7, 1926; s. William Eugene and Marguerite (Kellett) R.; A.B., Wofford Coll., 1949; LL.B., U. S.C., 1951; grad. U.S. Army Command and Gen. Staff Coll., 1974; m. Margaret Louise Banks, July 17, 1953; 1 son, James Kellett. With The State, newspaper, Columbia S.C., 1950—, city editor, 1962-65, asso. editor, 1966-69, editorial page editor, 1969—; S.C. corr. So. Edn. Reporting Service, Nashville, 1962-68; columnist Raleigh (N.C.) News & Observer, 1968—, Atlanta Jour.-Constn., 1973—. Chmn. S.C. Athletic Hall of Fame, 1957-61. Served with USNR, 1945-46. Recipient S.C. AP award for reporting in depth, 1962. Mem. Am. Soc. Newspaper Editors, Nat. Conf. Editorial Writers, S.C. Bar, Kappa Sigma, Phi Delta Phi. Episcopalian. Author: Biography of Max Hirsch, 1956. Home: 726 Fairway Ln Columbia SC 29210 Office: care Columbia Newspapers Inc Stadium Rd PO Box 1333 Columbia SC 29202

RONEY, JAY LOUIS, social worker; b. Chester, S.D., Feb. 12, 1913; s. Ray W. and Caroline (Krumm) R.; A.B., Augustana Coll., Sioux Falls, S.D., 1936; M.A., Western Res. U., 1938; m. Jean M. Tollefson, July 15, 1937; children—Susan, Linda, Jennifer. Social caseworker Inst. Family Service (now Family Service Assn.), Cleve., 1938-40; chief of pub. assistance S.D. Dept. Social Security (now Dept. Pub. Welfare), Pierre, 1940-42, dir. dept., 1947-50; exec. sec. Luth. Welfare Soc. Minn., Mpls., 1942-47; regional child welfare rep., children's bur. Social Security Adminstrn., Dept. Health, Edn. and Welfare, Kansas City, Mo., 1950-54, dir. Bur. Pub. Assistance, Washington, 1954-59; dir. Pub. Welfare Project Aging, Am. Pub. Welfare Assn., Chgo., 1959-68; dir. community relations staff Office External Affairs, Social Security Adminstrn., Balt., 1968-78; ret., 1978. Recipient Centennial award Augustana Coll., 1960; certificate honor Western Res. U. Alumni, 1966. Mem. Council Social Work Edn., Am. Pub. Welfare Assn., Nat. Assn. Social Workers. Lutheran. Home: 5146 Driftwood Ct Columbia MD 21044

RONEY, PAUL H., fed. judge; b. Olney, Ill., Sept. 5, 1921; student Petersburg Jr. Coll., 1938-40; B.S. in Econs., U. Pa., 1942; LL.B., Harvard U., 1948; LL.D., Stetson U., 1977; married; 3 children. Admitted to N.Y. bar, 1949, Fla. bar, 1950; asso. firm Root, Ballantine, Harlan, Bushby & Palmer, N.Y.C., 1948-50; with firm Mann, Harrison, Roney, Mann & Masterson, and predecessors, St. Petersburg, Fla., 1950-57; individual practice law, 1957-63; partner firm Roney & Beach, St. Petersburg, 1963-69, firm Roney, Ulmer, Woodworth & Jacobs, St. Petersburg, 1969-70; judge U.S. Circuit Ct. 5th Circuit, St. Petersburg, 1970—; chmn. legal adv. com. Fair Trial-Free Press, 1973-76; mem. Task Force on Cts. and Public, 1973-76; adv. com. on adminstrv. law judges U.S. Civil Service Commn., 1976-77. Served in U.S. Army, 1943-46. Fellow Am. Bar Found.; mem. Am. Bar Assn. (jud. adminstrn. div., chmn. appellate judges' conf. 1978-79, Am. Judicature Soc. (dir. 1972-76), Am. Law Inst., Fla. Bar, St. Petersburg Bar Assn. (pres. 1964-65), Nat. Jud. Coll. (faculty 1974, 75), Jud. Conf. U.S. (subcom. on jud. improvements 1978—). Office: 601 Federal Office Bldg Saint Petersburg FL 33701

RONEY, WILLIAM CHAPOTON, JR., stock broker; b. Detroit, Dec. 19, 1924; s. William Chapoton and Helen (Hurdley) R.; B.S., U. Notre Dame, 1949; m. Catherine Alice Cavanaugh, Feb. 12, 1949; children—William Chapoton, Michael C., Kathleen F., Brian J.

Partner, William C. Roney & Co., mems. N.Y. Stock Exchange, Detroit, 1949—; mem. Am. Stock Exchange; past gov. Detroit Stock Exchange; gov. Midwest Stock Exchange. Past pres. Holy Name Sch. Dads Club, U. Notre Dame Detroit Alumni Club; trustee Hutzel Hosp., Detroit; bd. dirs. Brother Rice High Sch. Dads Club. Mem. Securities Industry Assn. (nat. gov., dir., past vice chmn. Gt. Lakes dist.), Detroit Assn. Stock Exchange Firms (chmn.), Bond Club Detroit. Clubs: Otsego Ski (Gaylord, Mich.); Birmingham Athletic; Orchard Lake (Mich.) Country; Savoyard, Detroit (Detroit). Home: 1075 Timberlake Dr Bloomfield Hills MI 48013 Office: Buhl Bldg Detroit MI 48226

RONGIONE, LOUIS ANTHONY, educator, librarian; b. Aquafondata, Italy, Aug. 23, 1912; s. Joseph J. and Maria Christina (Celino) R.; came to U.S., 1914, naturalized, 1925; A.B., Villanova U., 1936, B.S. in L.S., 1940; postgrad. theology Augustinian Coll., Washington, 1936-39; M.A., Cath. U. Am., 1940; Ped.D. (hon.), Steubenville (Ohio) Coll., 1957. Joined Order of St. Augustine, 1931, ordained priest Roman Cath. Ch., 1939; prof. langs. in high schs., Ill., also N.Y. State, 1940-50; librarian Augustinian Internat. Coll., Rome, 1952-53; mem. faculty Villanova U., 1950, 52—, prof. philosophy, 1953—, dean Grad. Sch., 1956-62, librarian, 1962—, chmn. library sci. dept., 1968-71; aux. chaplain Ft. Wadsworth, S.I., N.Y., 1942-46, also Halloran VA Hosp., S.I.; rector Augustinian Collegiate Sem., Villanova, 1969-71; prior St. Thomas Monastry, Villanova, 1971—. Trustee Am. Inst. Italian Culture; bd. govs. Gallery Living Cath. Authors, 1943-48; mem. council Nursing Sch., St. Joseph Hosp., Reading, Pa., 1959—; bd. advisers Cabrini Coll., Radnor, Pa. Recipient Archbishop's medal, 1937, Paladin jewel, 1938, Grand Cross, 1939. Mem. Nat. Cath. Ednl. Assn., N.E.A., Am., Pa., Cath. (pres. N.Y. State-N.J. unit 1942-45, chmn. library edn. sect. 1965—) library assns., Cath. Audio Visual Educators (pres.), Assn. for Higher Edn., Eastern Assn. Coll. Deans and Advisers Students, Phi Kappa Phi. K.C. (4). Author: The Jubilee Year, 1949; Conferences on the Beatitudes, 1959; Reform and Rejoice, 1974; Let Your Light Shine, 1975; The Liberty Bell's Sister, 1976. Book critic; contbr. to Cath. periodicals, bulls. Address: Villanova U Villanova PA 19085. *Absolute certitude about the existence of a personal God who is both creator and sustainer of the whole human race. The objectivity of truth and standard of morals, both of which must conform to the mind and will of God. The double mandates to love God and our neighbor are inseparable and neither can be substituted for the other.*

RONGREN, ERIC HJALMAR, engring. exec.; b. Chgo., Apr. 4, 1925; s. Hjalmar Nels and Ann Marie (Falser) R.; M.S., Ill. Inst. Tech., 1948; B.B.A., Northwestern U., 1950; m. Cecelia Krueger, Nov. 10, 1951; children—Nancy Elizabeth, Lynn Erica, Margaret Cecile, Karen Anne. Research engr. Celotex Corp., 1948-50; asst. to mgr. engring. research dept. Standard Oil Co. (Ind.), 1950-53; bus. mgr. research dept. Kendall Co., 1953-56; asso. McKinsey & Co., 1956-57; v.p. engring. and research R.R. Donnelley & Sons, Chgo., 1957-67; owner Rongren & Assos., 1967—. Fellow Am. Inst. Chemists; mem. Am. Inst. Chem. Engrs., Am. Chem. Soc. Clubs: Econ., Swedish (Chgo.). Home: 750 Elmwood Dr Glen Ellyn IL 60137 Office: 907 N Elm St Hinsdale IL 60521

RONIS, LEONARD, city transp. ofcl.; b. Cleve., Sept. 5, 1921; s. Max and Lillian (Rubin) R.; A.B., Western Res. U., 1943, A.M., 1950; m. Joan Terr, Dec. 19, 1948; children—Laurel Beth Ronis Krieger, Robert Jeremy. With Greater Cleve. Regional Transit Authority, 1946—, personnel dir., 1959-67, mgr. ops., 1967-70, asst. gen. mgr., 1970-75, gen. mgr., 1975—; mem. com. on supr. devel. Am. Public Transit Assn., 1950-55, chmn. personnel confs., 1958-66, com. on operator tng., 1960-65, com. on personnel, 1965-66, mem. ops. div. adminstrv. com., 1966-69, chmn. ops. div., 1968-69, chmn. steering com. rail transit div., 1970-72, div. ops. adv. com., 1973-74, vice chmn. legis. com., 1973, mem. labor com., 1974—, bd. dirs., 1975—, mem. govt. affairs steering com., 1975—, mem. planning and research com.-subcom. on nat. transp. policy, 1976—, v.p. adminstrn. and fin., 1976-78, v.p. devel. and tech., 1978—. Vice pres. transp. Greater Cleve. Safety Council, 1975—. Served with AUS, 1943-46. Mem. Inst. for Rapid Transit (govt. affairs com. 1971-75), Ohio Public Transit Assn (pres. 1971-73), Transit Devel. Corp. (dir. 1974-76), Transit Data Summaries Group (chmn. 1972—), Transit Devel. Corp. (treas. 1977). Office: Greater Cleve Regional Transit Authority 1404 E 9th St Cleveland OH 44114*

RONK, GLENN EMERY, elec. co. exec.; b. Arcadia, Calif., Sept. 7, 1925; s. Emery Cline and Sarah (Curtis) R.; student U. Calif. at Santa Barbara, 1946-48; B.E. in Mech. Engring. magma cum laude, U. So. Calif., 1950; m. Barbara Lee Hughes, Sept. 12, 1946; children—Connie Lee (Mrs. Michael Frank Panebianco), Edward Curtis, Martin Daniel, William Thomas. Application engr. Westinghouse Electric Corp., Pitts. and Los Angeles, 1950-52; div. sales mgr. Am. Electronics Inc., Los Angeles, 1952-55, div. mgr.-v.p. marketing, 1955-57, v.p., gen. mgr., 1957-59; v.p. marketing Cornell Dubilier Electronics subsidiary Fed. Pacific Electric Co., Newark, 1959-65, pres., 1965-70; pres. Sola Electric, group exec. electronics and communications group unit Gen. Signal Corp., Elk Grove Village, Ill., 1970-80, v.p. parent co., also group exec., Stanford, Conn., 1980—. Served with USAAF, 1943-45. Mem. Electronics Industry Assn. (gov. 1966—, v.p. parts div. 1975), U. So. Cal. Midwest Alumni Club (pres. 1973), Phi Kappa Phi, Tau Beta Pi, Pi Tau Sigma. Republican. Presbyn. Home: 35 Beach Dr Darien CT 06820 Office: Gen Signal Corp High Ridge Park Stanford CT 06904

RONSTADT, LINDA MARIA, singer; b. Tucson, July 15, 1946; d. Gilbert and Ruthmary (Copman) Ronstadt. Recorded numerous albums, including Evergreen, 1967, Evergreen Vol. 2, 1967, Linda Ronstadt, The Stone Poneys and Friends, Vol. 3, 1968, Hand Sown, Home Grown, 1969, Silk Purse, 1970, Linda Ronstadt, 1972, Don't Cry Now (Gold album), 1973, Heart Like a Wheel (Gold album, Platinum album), 1974, Prisoner In Disguise (Gold album, Platinum album), 1975, Hasten Down the Wind (Gold album, Platinum album), 1976, Greatest Hits (Gold album, Platinum album), 1976, Simple Dreams (Gold album, Platinum album), Blue Bayou (Gold single), 1977, Living in the U.S.A. (Gold album, Platinum album), 1978. Recipient Grammy awards for best country vocal female, 1975, best pop vocal female, 1976, Am. Music award, 1978. Address: care Peter Asher Mgmt Inc 644 N Doheny Dr Los Angeles CA 90069

ROOD, JAMES LESLIE, JR., lawyer; b. Richmond Heights, Mo., July 24, 1931; s. James Leslie and Lucille (Pierce) R.; student U. Wis., 1949-52; J.D., U. Chgo., 1955, M.B.A., 1963; m. June Howe, Feb. 2, 1968; children (by previous marriage)—J. David, Karen L.; stepchildren—Sylvia L., J. Harold Runnfeldt. Admitted to Ill. bar, 1955, Mo. bar, 1975; mem. law firm Madigan & Thorsen, Chgo., 1955, 57-59; gen. atty. Fairbanks-Morse & Co., Chgo., 1959-61; v.p., sec. Walter E. Heller & Co., Chgo., 1961-74, also gen. counsel (all Chgo.); v.p., sec., gen. counsel Consol. Aluminum Corp., St. Louis, 1974-76; individual practice law, Chesterfield, Mo., 1976—. Served with AUS, 1955-57. Mem. Fed., Am., Ill., Mo., St. Louis, Chgo. bar assns., Mo. Bar, Am. Soc. Corporate Secs., Am. Arbitration Assn. (nat. panel), Am. Judicature Soc. Club: Execs. (Chgo.). Home and Office: 15021 Conway Rd Chesterfield MO 63017

ROOKE, DAVID LEE, chem. co. exec.; b. San Antonio, Tex., May 2, 1923; s. Henry Levi, Jr. and Annie (Davidson) R.; B.S. in Chem. Engring., Rice Inst., Houston, 1944; postgrad. U. Houston; m. Esthermae Litherland, June 2, 1945; children—Eugene, Mark, Paul, Bruce. With Dow Chem., 1946—, v.p. ops., Midland, Mich., 1977-78, pres., 1978—; v.p. Dow Chem. Corp., 1978—, also dir.; dir. Dow Corning Corp., First Midland Bank & Trust Co. Bd. dirs. Midland County United Community Fund, 1977—; mem. Mich. Com. Jobs and Energy, 1979—; trustee, mem. fin. com. Citizens Research Council Mich., 1979—; nat. exec. bd. Boy Scouts Am., 1979—. Served with USNR, 1944-46. Mem. Am. Inst. Chem. Engrs. Methodist. Office: 2020 Dow Center Midland MI 48640

ROOKS, RAYMOND NEWTON, lawyer; b. Nevada, Mo., Dec. 23, 1910; s. Ola Raymond and Amy Pearl (Ratliff) R.; student Trenton (Mo.) Jr. Coll., 1928-30; B.S. cum laude, U. Ill., 1932, LL.B. cum laude, 1934; m. Ruth Dunlop Darling, June 1, 1940; children—Melissa Darling (Mrs. W.T. Russell), Mary Ratliff, John Newton. Admitted to Ill. bar, 1934; with law and claim dept. North Am. Accident Ins. Co., Chgo., 1934-37; practice law, Chgo., 1937—; mem. firm Rooks, Pitts, Fullagar & Poust, and predecessors, 1943—; resident counsel Elgin, Joliet & Eastern Ry. Co. First dist. commr. character and fitness, 1963-73, chmn., 1971-72. Fellow Am., Chgo. bar founds.; mem. Am. (ho. dels. 1955-56, 60-61), Ill., Chgo. (bd. mgrs. 1949-51, 59-63, treas. 1954-57, pres. 1961-62), 7th Fed. Circuit bar assns., Nat. Conf. Bar Presidents, Am. Law Inst., Am. Judicature Soc., Delta Kappa Epsilon. Republican. Presbyn. Clubs: Legal (pres. 1958-59), Law (pres. 1967-68) (Chgo.); Michigan Shores. Home: 909 Locust Rd Wilmette IL 60091 Office: 208 S LaSalle St Chicago IL 60604

ROONEY, ANDREW AITKEN, writer; b. Albany, N.Y., Jan. 14, 1919; s. Walter S. and Ellinor (Reynolds) R.; student Colgate U., 1942; m. Marguerite Howard, Apr. 21, 1942; children—Ellen, Martha, Emily, Brian. Writer-producer CBS-TV News, 1959—; TV programs include Essay on Doors, Bridges, Women, Hotels, War, Of Black America, The Great American Dream Machine, In Praise of New York City, The Colleges, Mr. Rooney Goes to Washington, Mr. Rooney Goes To Dinner; regular commentator-essayist 60 Minutes, 1978-79; newspaper columnist Chgo. Tribune-N.Y. News Syndicate, 1979—. Served with AUS, 1941-45. Decorated Air medal, Bronze Star. Recipient awards for best written TV documentary, 1966, 68, 71, 75; Retrospective Mus. Modern Art, 1974. Author: (with O.C. Hutton) Air Gunner, 1944; The Story of Stars and Stripes, 1946; Conquerors' Peace, 1947; The Fortunes of War, 1962. Home: 254 Rowayton Ave Rowayton CT 06853

ROONEY, ARTHUR JOSEPH, profl. football club exec.; b. Coulter, Pa., Jan. 27, 1901; s. Daniel and Margaret (Murray) R.; B.C.S., Georgetown U., 1920; student, Duquesne U., 1923; m. Kathleen McNulty, June 10, 1931; children—Daniel, Arthur, Timothy, Patrick, John. Chmn. bd. Pitts. Steelers Profl. Football Club, 1933—; dir. William Penn Raceway, 1962, Pompano Raceway, 1965—; promoter prize fights, 1928—; horse race breeder, 1930—. Mem. Holy Name Soc., St. Vincent De Paul Soc. K.C. Home: 940 N Lincoln Ave Pittsburgh PA 15233 Office: 300 Stadium Circle Pittsburgh PA 15212*

ROONEY, FRED B., former congressman; b. Bethlehem, Pa., Nov. 6, 1925; B.A. in Bus. Adminstrn., U. Ga., 1950; LL.D., Moravian Coll., 1972, Allentown Coll. St. Francis de Sales, 1973, Lehigh U., 1977; m. Evelyn Davis Lisle, Dec. 14, 1963; children—Timothy, Martha, Gregory. Mem. Pa. Senate, Harrisburg, 1958-63; mem. 88th to 95th congresses from 15th Pa. Dist. Bd. dirs. St. Luke's Hosp., Bethlehem. Democrat. Home: 3150 Highland Pl Washington DC 20008

ROONEY, KEVIN DAVITT, govt. ofcl.; b. Springfield, Mass., June 23, 1944; s. Davitt Michael and Elizabeth Isabel (Wlodyka) R.; B.A., St. Marys Coll., 1966; J.D., George Washington U., 1975; m. Annette Eloise Benevento, Nov. 11, 1972; 1 dau., Kathryn Denise. Computer systems analyst VA, Washington, 1967-68, 70-73; admitted to Va. bar, 1975, D.C. bar, 1977; chief legal programs and budget Dept. Justice, Washington, 1973-77, exec. asst. to asso. atty. gen., 1977, asst. atty. gen. for adminstrn., 1977—. Served with U.S. Army, 1968-70. Mem. Am., Fed., Va., D.C. bar assns., Am. Soc. Pub. Adminstrn. Home: 2003 Miracle Ln Falls Church VA 22043 Office: 10th St and Constitution Ave Washington DC 20530

ROONEY, MICKEY (JOE YULE, JR.), actor; b. Bklyn., Sept. 23, 1920; s. Joe and Nell (Brown) Yule; ed. in Dayton Heights and Vine Street grammar sch., also Pacific Mil. Acad. and under tutors; m. Ava Gardner, Jan. 10, 1942 (div. May 1943); m. 2d, Betty Jane Rase, Sept. 30, 1944 (div. 1949); children—Joe Yule, Timothy; m. 3d, Martha Vickers, June 3, 1949 (div.); m. 4th, Elaine Mahnken (div. 1958); m. 5th, Barbara Thomason, Dec. 1958; children—Kerry, Kyle, Kelly Ann, Kimmy Sue; m. 6th, Margie Lang, Sept. 1966 (div. 1967); m. 7th, Carolyn Hockett, 1969; m. 8th, Jan Chamberlin. First appeared in vaudeville with parents; then appeared with Sid Gold; numerous TV programs; motion pictures include Judge Hardy's Children, Hold That Kiss, Lord Jeff, Love Finds Andy Hardy, Boys' Town, Stablemates, Out West with the Hardys, Huckleberry Finn, Andy Hardy Gets Spring Fever, Babes in Arms, Young Tom Edison, Judge Hardy and Son, Andy Hardy Meets Debutante, Strike Up the Band, Andy Hardy's Private Secretary, Men of Boystown, Life Begins for Andy Hardy, Babes on Broadway, A Yank at Eton, The Human Comedy, Andy Hardy's Blonde Trouble, Girl Crazy, Thousands Cheer, National Velvet, Ziegfeld Follies, The Strip, Sound Off, Off Limits, All Ashore, Light Case of Larceny, Drive a Crooked Road, Bridges at Toko-Ri, The Bold and Brave, Eddie, Private Lives of Adam and Eve, Comedian, The Grabbers, St. Joseph Plays the Horses, Breakfast at Tiffany, Somebody's Waiting, Requiem for a Heavyweight, Richard, Pulp, It's a Mad, Mad, Mad, Mad World, Everything's Ducky, The Secret Invasion, The Extraordinary Seaman, The Comic, The Cockeyed Cowboys of Calico County, Skidoo, B.J. Presents, That's Entertainment, The Domino Principle, Pete's Dragon, The Magic of Lassie, others; starred in TV spectacular Pinocchio, 1957; appeared on stage in Sugar Babies, 1979; appeared in TV series The Mickey Rooney Show, Mickey, A Year at the Top. Served with AUS, World War II. Author: I.E. An Autobiography, 1965. Office: care Ruth Webb 9229 Sunset Blvd Suite 509 Los Angeles CA 90069*

ROONEY, MIRIAM THERESA, univ. dean, lawyer; b. Bunker Hill, Charlestown, Mass., July 4; student Harvard U., 1926-28; A.B., Cath. U. Am., 1930, A.M., 1932, Ph.D., 1937; J.D., George Washington U., 1942; L.H.D., Caldwell Coll., 1977; LL.D., St. John's U., 1978. Admitted to D.C. bar, 1942, U.S. Supreme Ct., 1945, N.J. bar, 1962, U.S. Customs Ct., 1971; asst. catalogue div. Boston Pub. Library, 1924-28; successively legal ref. librarian, divisional asst. trade agreements and comml. policy-laws and regulation sect., asst. to legal adviser U.S. Dept. State, 1928-50; lectr. jurisprudence Columbus U. Sch. Law, 1942- 48; asso. prof., law librarian Cath. U. Am., 1948-51; prof., 1st dean Seton Hall U. Sch. Law, 1950-61, research prof. law, 1961- 67; vis. prof. jurisprudence St. John's U. Sch. Law, 1952-58; adviser delegation of Holy See UN Conf. Trade Land-locked Countries, 1965, UN Conf. Law of The Sea, 1973—; Fulbright-Hays prof. Am. law and govt., Vietnam, 1965-66, 67-68; Nat. Assn. Women Lawyers observer UN, 1956-67; World Peace Through Law rep. UN as cons. ECOSOC, 1967-73; adviser internat. law Holy See del. UN, 1973—; mem. U.S. Cath. conf. Com. Internat. Affairs, 1969-73; hearing examiner N.J. Commn. Civil Rights, 1961-62; participant Internat. Congress Comparative Law, Hamburg, 1962, Uppsala, Sweden, 1966, Pescara, Italy, 1970; participant World Peace Through Law Conf., Athens, 1963, Washington, 1965, Belgrad, 1971, World Congress on Philosophy of Law, Brussels, Belgium, 1971, Basel, Switzerland, 1979, Internat. Thomistic Congress, Rome, 1974. Mem. rector's adv. com. Cath. U. Am. Sch. Law, 1958-68. Recipient Outstanding Woman award Nat. Assn. Women Lawyers, 1962; Alumni Achievement for Law award Catholic U. Am., 1962; 1st Pax Urbis ex Jure gold medal World Peace Through Law Center, 1971; Gold medal Internat. Community services, London, 1972, Distinguished Service award Cath. U. Am. Alumni, 1973; Alumni award for law George Washington U., 1974; Pope Paul VI award Pro Ecclesia et Pontifice, 1976; Centennial award Girls' Latin Sch., Boston, 1978. Mem. AAUW (life), Am. (chmn. com. comparative jurisprudence and legal philosophy sect. internat. law 1962-72), InterAm., Internat., Fed. bar assns., Internat. Fedn. Women Lawyers, Nat. Assn. Women Lawyers, Women's Bar Assn. D.C., Internat. Law Assn., Am. Soc. Internat. Law (exec. com. 1960-63), Cath. U. Alumni (v.p. 1963-65, gov.), Am. Fgn. Law Assn., Selden Soc. (London), Assn. World Justice (Louvain), Am. Soc. Legal History (treas. 1964-68), World Peace Through Law Center (charter), Medieval Acad. Am., Kappa Beta Pi (hon. life mem.), Phi Alpha Delta (Seton Hall grad. award 1979). Author: Lawlessness, Law and Sanction, 1937; Introduction to the French Institutionalists, 1970; asso. editor New Scholasticism, 1945-48; adv. editor Natural Law Forum, 1965—; co-area editor Philosophy of Law (Am.), New Cath. Ency., 1960-67; contbr. articles to philos. and legal periodicals. Address: 66 Myrtle Ave Millburn NJ 07041

ROONEY, PAUL GEORGE, mathematician; b. N.Y.C., July 14, 1925; s. Geoffrey Daniel and Doris Elizabeth (Babcock) R.; B.Sc., U. Alta., 1949; Ph.D., Calif. Inst. Tech., 1952; m. Mary Elizabeth Carlisle, June 20, 1950; children—Francis Timothy, Elizabeth Anne, Kathleen Doris, John Edward, James Carlisle. Asst. prof. math. U. Alta., 1952-55; asst. prof. U. Toronto, 1955-60, asso. prof., 1960-62, prof., 1962—; dir. Commonwealth Petroleum Co., Calgary, 1946-59. Bd. dirs. Francis F. Reeve Found., 1954—. Served with Can. Army, 1943-45. Fellow Royal Soc. Can. Mem. Can. Math. Soc. (councillor 1960-64, 66-70, 76—, v.p. 1978—), Am. Math. Soc., Math. Assn. Am. Contbr. articles to profl. jours.; editor-in-chief Can. Jour. Math., 1971-75. Office: Dept Math Univ of Toronto Toronto ON M5S 1A1 Canada

ROONEY, PAUL MONROE, library adminstr.; b. Buffalo, Apr. 16, 1918; s. John Francis and Marguerite (Cass) R.; B.S., State Tchrs. Coll., Buffalo, 1938; B.S. in L.S., U. Buffalo, 1940; m. Elizabeth Dorsey, Jan. 22, 1955; children—James, Thomas. Br. librarian Buffalo Pub. Library, 1940-42; head reference dept. Grosvenor Library, 1945-59; head tech. dept. Buffalo and Erie County Pub. Library, 1959-61, asst. dep. dir., 1961-63, dep. dir., 1963-75, dir., 1975—; chmn. N.Y. State Pub. Librarians Certification Com., 1959-60; trustee Western N.Y. Library Resources Council, 1966—, pres., 1969-70. Served with USAF, 1942-45. Mem. N.Y., Am. library assns., Buffalo and Erie County Hist. Soc. (bd. mgrs.), Grosvenor Soc. (dir.). Roman Catholic. Home: 522 Ashland Ave Buffalo NY 14222 Office: Buffalo and Erie County Pub Library Buffalo NY 14203

ROONEY, ROBERT OWEN, lawyer; b. Chgo., Sept. 27, 1921; s. Owen T. and Margaret (Sullivan) R.; student Loyola U., Chgo., 1939-41, Vanderbilt U., 1944; J.D., DePaul U., 1946; m. June M. Meyers, Nov. 28, 1946; children—Garry O., Kevin M., Maureen, Denise, Owen, Brian. Admitted to Ill. bar, 1947, U.S. Supreme Ct. bar, other cts.; pvt. practice gen. isn. law, Chgo.; mem Fedn. Ins. Counsel, 1952—, v.p., 1958, bd. govs., 1959, sec.-treas., 1960-61, exec. v.p., 1961-62, pres., 1963-64, chmn. bd. govs., 1964-65. Mem. industry coop. com., v.p. Def. Research Inst. Served with Air Transp. Command, 1943-46. Fellow Am. Coll. Trial Lawyers; mem. Am. Ill., Chgo. bar assns., Internat. Assn. Ins. Counsel (chmn. auto ins. com. 1966-68), Am. Judicature Soc., Soc. Trial Lawyers, Am. Legion. K.C. Contbr. articles profl. jours. Home: 1269 Oakmont Ave Flossmoor IL 60422 Office: 2 N LaSalle St Chicago IL 60602

ROONEY, WILLIAM RICHARD, magazine editor; b. New Brunswick, N.J., Mar. 12, 1938; s. William Richard and Bernadette (Huether) R.; B.S. in English, St. Peter's Coll., Jersey City, 1959; m. Rita Ann Scherer, July 20, 1963; children—Karen, Kevin, Brian. Asst., then asso. editor Marine Engring./Log mag., N.Y.C., 1960-64; asso. editor Outdoor Life mag., N.Y.C., 1964-72, mng. editor, 1972-76, sr. editor, 1976-77; editor Am. Forests mag., Washington, 1977—. Served with AUS, 1959-60. Mem. Outdoor Writers Assn. Am. Roman Catholic. Contbr. Complete Outdoors Ency., 1972; others. Home: 7916 Carrie Ln Manassas VA 22110 Office: 1319 18th St NW Washington DC 20036

ROOP, JOHN WESLEY, hosp. adminstr.; b. Blawnox, Pa., Aug. 16, 1920; s. Wilbur George and Mary Walker (Sheeler) R.; A.B., U. Pitts., 1942, M.D., 1945; m. Emily Jeanette Lawrence, Sept. 22, 1944; children—Joel, Kristine (Mrs. Otavio Lima), Janna (Mrs. Allen D. Timm), Rebecca (Mrs. Mark R. Kharasch). Intern, U. Pitts. Med. Center, 1945-46; resident psychiatry Menninger Sch. Psychiatry, Topeka, 1951; practice medicine, specializing in psychiatry, Jamestown, N.Y., 1951-57; clin. dir. Warren (Pa.) State Hosp., 1957-69; Catchment area dir. Mental Health/Mental Retardation, Northampton County, 1969-73; supt. Allentown (Pa.) State Hosp., 1973—. Served to 1st lt. USAF, 1946-48. Diplomate Am. Bd. Psychiatry and Neurology. Fellow Am. Psychiat. Assn., Pa. Psychiat. Soc.; mem. Lehigh Valley Neuropsychiat. Soc. (past pres.). Home: 709 Barrymore Ln Bethlehem PA 18017 Office: Allentown State Hosp Allentown PA 18103. *Whenever I contemplate events of a degree of success in my life, I find it impossible to sort out those successes brought about by effort and determination from those successes resulting from coincidence or good fortune. And just when I come to believe that an accomplishment is the result of dedication and ability, I am made aware of the good luck involved, nearly always as results of kindnesses extended to me by other people. Even my excellent physical health, I realize, is more of an accident than a result of good management on my part.*

ROORDA, JOHN FRANCIS, JR., oil co. exec.; b. Evanston, Ill., Jan. 16, 1923; s. John Francis and Sadie M. (Daley) R.; B.S. in Chem. Engring., Purdue U., 1943, Ph.D., 1949; m. Elizabeth Mulcahy, July 2, 1949; children—Elizabeth Roorda Barker, John F., Ann C. With Shell Oil Co., 1949—; gen. mgr. combined oil products/chem. econs. dept., 1973-74, v.p. planning and econs., 1974-77; v.p. Shell Devel. Co., Houston, 1977-78, v.p. corp. planning, 1978—. Served to lt. (j.g.) USNR, 1943-46. Recipient Disting. Engring. Alumnus award Purdue U., 1976. Mem. Am. Inst. Chem. Engrs., Soc. Chem. Industry, Sigma Xi. Roman Catholic. Office: PO Box 2463 Houston TX 77001

ROOS, DANIEL, educator; b. Bklyn., Apr. 12, 1939; s. Sigmund and Anita (Sperling) R.; B.S. in Civil Engring., M.I.T., 1961, M.S., 1963, Ph.D., 1966; m. Eva Bonis, June 1, 1969; children—Richard Joseph, Linda Suzanne. Mem. faculty M.I.T., Cambridge, 1963—, asso. prof.

civil engring., 1970-76, prof., 1976—, head transp. systems div., 1977-78, dir. Center for Transp. Studies, 1978—; founder, dir. Multisystems Inc., Cambridge, 1965—. Mem. U.S. Task Force on Transp., 1969. Mem. ASCE, Assn. Computing Machinery, Ops. Research Soc. (treas. 1970-71), Transp. Research Bd. (chmn. para-transit com., transp. sci. sect. 1973-74). Author: ICES System Design, 1964; contbr. articles to profl. jours. Developer Dial-A-Ride transp. concept, 1965. Home: 28 Baskin Rd Lexington MA 02173 Office: Center Transp Studies Mass Inst Tech Cambridge MA 02139

ROOS, FREDERICK RIED, film producer; b. Santa Monica, Calif., May 22, 1934; s. Victor Otto and Florence Mary (Stout) R.; B.A., U. Calif. at Los Angeles, 1956; Casting dir., story editor various cos., 1960-70; film producer, 1964—; producer Flight to Fury, Back Door to Hell, 1964-65, The Conversation (Acad. award nomination), Godfather Part II (Acad. award Best Picture), 1973-79, Apocalypse Now, The Black Stallion, 1975-79, Hammett, 1979-80; asso. producer Drive He Said, 1970. Served with AUS, 1957-59. Office: Omni-Zoetrope 1040 N Las Palmas Ave Hollywood CA 90038

ROOS, LAWRENCE K., banker; b. St. Louis, Feb. 1, 1918; s. Sol and Selma (Kalter) R.; B.A., Yale U., 1940; LL.D., U. Mo., 1974; m. Mary Watson, Apr. 30, 1955; children—Pamela, Mary Ellen, Jennifer, Lawrence K. Pres., Mound City Trust Co., 1950-62; chmn. bd. 1st Security Bank, Kirkwood, Mo., 1950-62; supr. St. Louis County, 1962-74; exec. v.p., dir. 1st Nat. Bank, St. Louis, 1975-76; pres. Fed. Res. Bank St. Louis, 1976—. Active Mo. Citizens for Eisenhower, 1952; mem. Mo. Ho. of Reps., 1946-50; Republican candidate for gov. Mo., 1968; chmn. Mo. Com. for Re-election of Pres., 1972; del. Rep. Nat. Conv., 1972; Mo. del. Rep. Nat. Com., 1973-74; active Radio Free Europe, 1954, U.S. Assay Commn., 1955; mem. U.S. Adv. Commn. on Intergovtl. Relations, 1969-74; mem. adv. com. Woodrow Wilson Internat. Center for Scholars, 1974; chmn. bd. East-West Gateway Coordinating Com., 1965-67, 73-75; chmn. Mo., Crusade for Freedom, 1954; mem. Pres.'s Commn. on Jobs for Vietnam Vets., 1971; pres. Wesley House Found., St. Louis, 1955-60; bd. dirs. St. Louis Jewish Hosp., 1975—, Central Inst. for Deaf, 1975—, Maryville Coll., St. Louis, 1975-78, United Way Greater St. Louis, 1955—, St. Louis Regional Commerce and Growth Assn., 1976—, Govtl. Research Inst., St. Louis, 1975—, Nat. Assn. Counties, 1963-72; chmn. St. Louis County Charter Revision Commn., 1979. Served to maj. U.S. Army, ETO. Decorated Bronze Star. Named Mo. Rep. of Year, 1972, Man of Year, St. Louis Globe-Democrat, 1974; recipient Torch of Liberty award Anti-Defamation League, 1974. Home: 943 Tirrill Farms Rd Saint Louis MO 63124 Office: PO Box 442 Saint Louis MO 63166

ROOS, PHILIP, adminstrv. psychologist; b. Brussels, Belgium, Jan. 24, 1930; s. Maurice and Berthe (Matthyssens) R.; came to U.S., 1939, naturalized, 1945; B.S. in Biology and Psychology with highest distinction, Stanford, 1949, postgrad., 1950-51; Ph.D. in Clin. Psychology, U. Tex., 1955; m. Susan Morgan, June 4, 1958; 1 dau., Valerie Gail. Psychology trainee VA Hosp., Waco, Tex., 1953-55; staff psychologist USPHS Hosp., Ft. Worth, 1955-57; asso. prof. psychology Tex. Christian U., 1957-59; chief psychologist Timberlawn Sanitarium, Dallas, 1959-60; dir. psychol. services Tex. Dept. Mental Health and Mental Retardation, 1960-63; supt. Austin (Tex.) State Sch., 1963-67; asso. commr. div. mental retardation N.Y. State Dept. Mental Hygiene, 1967-68; exec. dir. Nat. Assn. Retarded Citizens, N.Y.C., 1969—; asst. clin. prof. Baylor Med. Sch., 1963-67; lectr. U. Tex., 1966-67; cons. in field, 1957—. Mem. Gov. Tex. Com. Mental Retardation, 1964-65, Pres.'s Com. on Employment Handicapped, 1969—; trustee Mental Health Law Project, 1978—; bd. dirs. Nat. Industries for Severely Handicapped, 1977—. Squadron comdr. Civil Air Patrol, 1959, group comdr., 1960. Fellow Am. Assn. Mental Deficiency, Am. Orthopsychiat. Assn.; mem. Am. Psychol. Assn., Council Exceptional Children, Am. Pub. Health Assn., Phi Beta Kappa, Sigma Xi, Psi Chi. Contbr. numerous articles to profl. jours. and books. Home: 6100 Tiffany Park Ct Arlington TX 76016 Office: 2709 Ave E East Arlington TX 76011

ROOSA, ROBERT VINCENT, banker; b. Marquette, Mich., June 21, 1918; s. Harvey Mapes and Ruth Elizabeth (Lagerquist) Rosa; A.B., U. Mich., 1939, M.A., 1940, Ph.D., 1942, D.Sc. in Bus. Adminstration, 1962; LL.D., Wesleyan U., 1963, Williams Coll., 1974; m. Ruth Grace Amende, Mar. 16, 1946; children—Meredith Ann Roosa Inderfurth, Alison Ruth Roosa Cluff. Tchr. econs. U. Mich., Harvard, Mass. Inst. Tech., 1939-43; with Fed. Res. Bank N.Y., 1946-60, v.p. research dept., 1953-54, asst. v.p. securities dept., 1954-56, v.p. research dept., 1956-60; under sec. for monetary affairs U.S. Treasury, 1961-64; partner Brown Bros., Harriman & Co., 1965—; advisory com. Internat. Finance Corp.; dir. Am. Express Co., Am. Express Internat. Banking Corp., Owens-Corning Fiberglas Corp., Texaco, Inc.; chmn. N.Y. Stock Exchange Advisory Com. Internat. Capital Market. Bd. dirs. Nat. Bur. Econ. Research; vice-chmn., trustee Rockefeller Found.; chmn. Brookings Instn.; trustee Sloan Kettering Inst. Cancer Research. Rhodes scholar Magdalen Coll., 1939. Served with AUS, 1943-46. Mem. Council Fgn. Relations (dir.), Conf. Bus. Economists, Am. Econ. Assn., Am. Finance Assn. (pres. 1967), UN Assn. (bd. govs. policy studies), Royal Econ. Soc., Am. Acad. Arts and Scis., Am. Philos. Soc., Phi Beta Kappa. Clubs: Harvard, Economic (pres. 1970-71), Links, Pilgrims of U.S. (N.Y.C.); Century Association, Cosmos (Washington); Manursing Island, Apawamis (Westchester County). Author: Federal Reserve Operations in the Money and Government Securities Market, 1956; Monetary Reform for the World Economy, 1965; The Dollar and World Liquidity, 1967; (with Milton Friedman) The Balance of Payments; Free Versus Fixed Exchange Rates, 1967. Editor: Money, Trade and Economic Growth, 1951. Home: 30 Woodlands Rd Harrison NY 10528 Office: 59 Wall St New York City NY 10005

ROOSA, STUART, former astronaut, investment co. exec.; b. Durango, Colo., Aug. 16, 1933; s. Dewey R.; ed. Okla. State U., U. Ariz.; B.S. in Aero. Engring., U. Colo.; Litt.D., U. St. Thomas, 1971; m. Joan C. Barrett; children—Christopher A., John D., Stuart Allen, Rosemary D. Served as commd. officer USAF, from 1953, advanced through grades to col.; formerly exptl. test pilot, Edwards AFB, Calif.; named astronaut NASA, 1966; mem. support crew Apollo IX; command module pilot Apollo XIV, 1971, backup command module pilot Apollo XVI and XVII; assigned crew tng. space shuttle, until 1976; v.p. Charles K. Campbell Inc., Austin, Tex. Decorated Disting. Service medal NASA, Air Force Command Pilot Astronaut Wings, USAF D.S.M.; recipient Arnold Air Soc.'s John F. Kennedy award, 1971, City N.Y. Gold Medal, 1971. Address: care Charles K Campbell Inc 106 Timberline Office Park 2525 Wallingwood Austin TX 78746

ROOSE, HENRY RASMUSSEN, banker; b. Omaha, Jan. 17, 1917; s. Christian Rasmussen and Camilla (Bech) R.; student Grad. Sch. Banking, U. Wis., 1962-64; m. Esther Marguerite Oglesby, Aug. 27, 1938; children—James C., Bettie Lee (Mrs. Oscar B. Curtis), Patricia L. (Mrs. Paul J. Barber), Robert H. With Standard Oil Co., 1934-38; office mgr. Gt. Western Finance Co., 1938-42; v.p., cashier Douglas County Bank, Omaha, 1942-52; v.p. U.S. Nat. Bank of Omaha, 1952—. Pres., Am. Bapt. Fgn. Mission Soc., 1979—; mem. exec. com., gen. bd. Am. Baptist Chs. in U.S.A.; bd. govs. Nat. Council Chs., 1979—; pres., trustee, mem. exec. com. Nebr. Childrens Home Soc.; bd. dirs. Douglas/Sarpy County chpt., nat. bd. govs. A.R.C., 1970-76, 1st Harriman award for distinguished vol. service, 1974, 1st Henry R. Roose award for vol. services, 1976; trustee Sioux Falls (S.D.) Coll.; bd. dirs. Ad-Sell League of Omaha, 1979-80; chmn. Hosp. Authority, Immanuel Med. Center. Recipient Man of Year award Benson Am. Legion Post, 1962. Mem. Robert Morris Assos., Nat. Assn. Credit Mgmt., Nebr. Assn. Commerce and Industry, Omaha C. of C. (hon. Life), Omaha Sister City Assn. (past pres.). Mason (Shriner), Lion (past pres., past dist. gov.). Home: 5419 Ida St Omaha NE 68152 Office: PO Box 3408 Omaha NE 68103

ROOSEVELT, ARCHIBALD BULLOCH, JR., banker; b. Boston, Feb. 18, 1918; s. Archibald Bulloch and Grace Stackpole (Lockwood) R.; grad. Groton Sch., 1936; B.A., Harvard, 1939; m. Selwa Showker, Sept. 1, 1950; 1 son, Tweed. Newspaperman, 1939-42; joined U.S. Fgn. Service, 1947; attache Am. embassy, Beirut, Lebanon, 1947-49; chief Near East sect. Voice of Am., 1949-50; consul, Istanbul, Turkey, 1951-53; assigned Dept. State, 1953-58; 1st sec., spl. asst. to ambassador to Spain, Madrid, 1958; attaché, spl. asst. Am. embassy, London, Eng., 1962-66; assigned Dept. State, 1966-74; v.p. internat. relations Middle East and Africa, Chase Manhattan Bank, 1975—. Served from 2d lt. to capt. AUS, 1942-47; Clubs: City Tavern (Washington); Garrick (London). Home: 3400 R St NW Washington DC 20007

ROOSEVELT, JAMES, bus. cons.; b. N.Y.C., Dec. 23, 1907; s. Franklin Delano (31st pres. U.S.) and Anna Eleanor (Roosevelt) R.; grad. Harvard U., 1930; LL.D. (hon.), Woodbury U., 1977; Ph.D. (hon.), Calif. Western U.; m. Betsey Cushing (div. 1940); children—Sara Wilford, Kate Roosevelt Whitney; m. 2d, Romelle Schneider (div. 1955); children—Michael, James, Anne Johnston; m. 3d, Gladys Irene Owens, July 9, 1956 (div. Sept. 1969); 1 son, Hall Delano; m. 4th, Mary Lena Winskill, Oct. 3, 1969; 1 dau., Rebecca Mary. Ins. broker, 1930; organizer Roosevelt & Sargent, Inc., Boston, pres. until 1937, resigned 1938; in motion picture industry, 1938-40; reentered Roosevelt & Sargent, Inc. as exec. v.p. establishing west coast office, 1946; pres. James Roosevelt & Co.; mem. 84th-89th congresses from 26th Calif. Dist.; U.S. rep. to ECOSOC, 1965-66; with I.O.S. Mgmt. Co., 1966-70, pres., 1970-71, bus. cons., 1970—; pres. IOS Devel. Co. Ltd.; lectr. Soc. Ecology, U. Calif. at Irvine, Chancellors Club; lectr. polit. sci. Woodbury U., Chapman Coll., others. Democratic nat. committeeman, 1948-52; Dem. candidate for gov. Calif., 1950; v.p. Eleanor Roosevelt Cancer Found.; bd. dirs. Nat. Found.-March of Dimes; trustee Chapman Coll., Orange, Calif. Served from capt. to col., USMCR, 1940-45; brig. gen. Res. ret. Decorated Navy Cross, Silver Star. Clubs: Met., Harvard (N.Y.C.). Author: Affectionately, F.D.R., 1959; My Parents, 1976. Home: 1901 Yacht Resolute Newport Beach CA 92660 Office: 110 Newport Center Dr Suite 200 Newport Beach CA 92660

ROOSEVELT, JOHN A., investment exec.; b. Washington, Mar. 13, 1916; s. Franklin D. and Eleanor (Roosevelt) R.; B.A., Harvard, 1938; m. Irene Boyd McAlpin, 1965; children by previous marriage—Haven C., Anne S. Roosevelt Gibson, Joan L. Roosevelt Schoonmaker. With William Filene's Sons Co., Boston, 1938-41, Grayson-Robinson Stores, Inc., Los Angeles, 1946-48; with Roosevelt, Lee, Magee, Inc., Beverly Hills, Calif., 1953-61; sr. v.p., dir. Bache Halsey Stuart Shields Inc. Trustee Eisenhower Exchange Fellowship Found., State U. N.Y., Marist Coll., Roosevelt U., Chgo.; bd. dirs. Boy Scouts Am. Served with USNR, 1941-46. Decorated Bronze Star. Mem. Am. Legion, Holland Soc. N.Y., Pilgrims of U.S., Huguenot Soc. Am. Republican. Episcopalian. Clubs: Leash, Racquet and Tennis (N.Y.C.); Tuxedo (N.Y.); Mid-Ocean (Bermuda). Home: 333 E 57th St New York City NY 10022 Office: 100 Gold St New York City NY 10005

ROOSEVELT, JULIAN KEAN, investment banker; b. N.Y.C., Nov. 14, 1924; s. George Emlen and Julia (Addison) R.; grad. Phillips Exeter Acad., 1943; A.B., Harvard, 1950; m. F. Madeleine Graham, July 26, 1946; children—Nicholaes Paul, George Emlen III, Robin Addison, Fay Satterfield; m. 2d, Margaret Fay Schantz, Dec. 30, 1957. Vice pres. Sterling Grace & Co. Inc., investment bankers, N.Y.C.; trustee United Mut. Savs. Bank. Mem. exec. bd. U.S. Olympic Com.; mem. Internat. Olympic Com. for U.S.; mem. council N.Y. State Maritime Coll. Trustee Mus. City N.Y. Served with USCGR, 1943-46, USNR, 1947; to 1st lt. F.A., AUS, 1948-55. Mem. Investment Assn. N.Y. (v.p. 1952), Am. Seamen's Friend Soc. (trustee), Am. Hist. Assn. (pres.), U.S. Internat. Sailing Assn. (v.p.), Desc. Signers Declaration Independence (life), Holland Soc. (life), Soc. Colonial Wars, Soc. War 1812, S.A.R. Republican. Episcopalian. Clubs: N.Y. Yacht (life); Bond of N.Y. (N.Y.C.); Seawanhaka Corinthian Yacht (Oyster Bay); Cruising of Am. (life); Storm Trysail; Hanko Yacht; Royal Norwegian Yacht (Oslo); Royal Swedish Yacht; Royal Bermuda Yacht; Transpacific Yacht (Calif.); Imperial Poona Yacht; Royal Danish Yacht; Royal Cork Yacht (Ireland); Fishers Island Yacht; Kanto Yacht (Japan); North American Yacht Racing Union; Sagamore Yacht; Far East Yacht Racing Fedn. Mem. U.S. Olympic Teams 1948, 52, 56, ofcl., 1960, 64, 68, 72, 76; recipient Gold medal, 1952. Home: Bonnie Brae Centre Island Oyster Bay NY 11771 Office: 39 Broadway New York City NY 10006

ROOSEVELT, NICHOLAS, author, consevationist; b. N.Y.C., June 12, 1893; s. J. West and Laura (d'Oremieulx) R.; A.B., Harvard U., 1914; m. Tirzah Maris Gates, June 5, 1936 (dec. May 1961). Attaché, Am. Embassy, Paris, 1914-16; sec. mission to Spain, Am. Internat. Corp., 1916-17; editorial writer N.Y. Tribune, 1921-23; editorial writer, spl. corr. N.Y. Times, 1923-30; vice-gov. Philippines, 1930; U.S. minister to Hungary, 1930-33; mem. editorial staff N.Y. Herald-Tribune 1933-42; dep. dir. OWI, 1942-43; asst. to pub. N.Y. Times, 1944-46. Mem. Calif. Recreation Commn., 1962—. Served as capt. 322d Inf., U.S. Army, 1917-19; attached to Am. Com. to Negotiate Peace, 1919. Republican. Clubs: Century (N.Y.C.); Met. (Washington). Author: The Philippines, a Treasure and a Problem, 1926; The Restless Pacific, 1928; America and England?, 1930; The Townsend Plan, 1936; A New Birth of Freedom, 1938; A Front Row Seat, 1953; Creative Cooking, 1956; Good Cooking, 1959; Theodore Roosevelt: The Man as I Knew Him, 1967; Conservation, Now or Never, 1970. Home: Big Sur CA 93920

ROOSEVELT, THEODORE, III, investmant exec.; b. N.Y.C., June 14, 1914; s. Theodore and Eleanor B. (Alexander) R.; B.A., Harvard U., 1936; m. Anne Babcock, 1940; 1 son, Theodore IV. With E.I. duPont de Nemours & Co., Inc., 1936-41; with Janney Montgomery, Scott, Inc., Phila., 1945—, partner, 1952—; dir. Western Sav. Fund Soc., Delaware Fund, Delta Trend Fund, Delchester Fund, Decatur Income Fund, Provident Ltd., Boque Banks N.C.; sec. commerce Commonwealth of Pa., 1949-51. Pres. Ams. for Competitive Enterprise System, 1951-71; bd. dirs. Episcopal Hosp., 1947—, sec., 1948—; bd. dirs. Acad. Natural Scis., 1957—, v.p., 1959-70; bd. dirs. Wildfowl Found. Served to lt. comdr. USNR, 1941-45. Decorated Air medal; named One of Ten Outstanding Young Men, U.S. Jr. C. of C., 1949. Mem. World Affairs Council, Phila. Conservationists (dir.), Navy League (dir.). Clubs: Phila., Harvard, Cts., Wilderness (v.p. 1958) (Phila.). Home: Silver Spring Farm Paoli PA 19301 Office: 6-20th Floor 5 Penn Center Plaza Philadelphia PA 19103

ROOSEVELT, W. EMLEN, banker; b. N.Y.C., Aug. 29, 1917; s. John Kean and Elise (Weinacht) R.; student Princeton U.; m. Arlene M. King, May 31, 1941 (dec. 1975); children—(Lucy Margaret, Nancy Arlene. Pres., dir. Nat. State Bank, Elizabeth, N.J.; dir. Elizabethtown Gas Co., Elizabethtown Water Co., Hackensack Water Co., Weehawken, N.J., N.J. Life Ins. Co., Saddle Brook, N.J., Nat. Utilities & Industries Corp. Home: Point Pleasant Beach NJ 08742 Office: Nat State Bank Elizabeth NJ 07207

ROOSEVELT, WILLIAM DONNER, investment co. exec.; b. N.Y.C., Nov. 17, 1932; s. Elliott and Elizabeth Browning (Donner) R.; B.A., Harvard U., 1955; m. Ruth Barrons, May 9, 1969; children—Dana, Christopher, Nicholas, Graham. Chmn. bd., chief exec. Standard Precision, Inc., Wichita, Kans., 1962-63, Air Assos. Inc., Wichita, 1958-62; security analyst, dir. spl. situation research Laird & Co., N.Y.C., 1963-66; v.p., dir. Auerbach Pollack & Richardson, Inc., N.Y.C., 1966-71; dir., v.p., dir. research Coenen & Co. Inc., N.Y.C., 1971-72; v.p., dir. Hoenig & Strock Inc., N.Y.C., 1972—. Bd. dirs., past chmn. William H. Donner Found.; bd. dirs. Donner Canadian Found., 1963—, Acad. Religion and Mental Health, 1970-73; trustee Midwest Research Inst., 1973-76; treas. William H. Donner Found., 1978-79. Presdl. fellow Aspen Inst., 1978. Mem. N.Y. Soc. Security Analysts, Fin. Analysts Fedn. Episcopalian. Clubs: Wee Burn Country, Leash, Doubles. Home: Nathan Hale Rd Wilson Point South Norwalk CT 06854 Office: 580 Fifth Ave New York City NY 10036

ROOT, ALAN CHARLES, diversified mfg. co. exec.; b. Essex, Eng., Apr. 11, 1925; came to U.S., 1951, naturalized, 1959; s. Charles Stanley and Lillian (Collins) R.; B.A., Oxford U., 1943; M.A., Cambridge U., 1951; M.B.A., Stanford U., 1953. Research analyst Dow Chem. Co., Midland, Mich., 1954-55; mgr. mktg. research Gen. Electric Co., 1955-61; v.p. bus. planning Mosler Safe Co., Hamilton, Ohio, 1961-70; sr. v.p. ops. services Am. Standard Co., N.Y.C., 1970—; dir. Mosler Safe Co., Mosler de P.R., Cole-Resdevel. Inc. Served to capt. AUS, 1944-48; mem. Am. Inst. Chem. Engrs. (asso. producer TV series Midland sect. 1955), Pilgrims U.S., Newcomen Soc. N. Am. Clubs: West Side Tennis, N.Y. Athletic, University (N.Y.C.). Home: 35 Park Ave New York NY 10016 Office: 40 W 40th St New York NY 10018

ROOT, JOHN O., assn. exec.; b. Flint, Mich., Mar. 10, 1919, s. John C. and Hazel (McEwen) R.; B.S., George Williams Coll., 1946, grad. study group work adminstrn., 1946-48; m. Betty Van Haften, Aug. 3, 1946; children—Jacalyn (Mrs. Daniel Mueller), Rebecca Root Rich, Victoria, John Alan. Phys. dir. Sears YMCA, Chgo., 1946-48; program dir. Harvey Meml. YMCA, 1948-50, exec. sec. YMCA Met. Chgo., 1950-54; asst. gen. sec. (title changed to gen. exec.) program services 1954-62, asso. gen. exec., 1962, pres., 1963—; numerous positions Nat. Bd. YMCA's including exec. com., exec. com. of internat. com.; nat. YMCA rep. exchange program with USSR, 1962, 76. Mem. exec. com. Chgo. Com. Urban Opportunities, Office Econ. Opportunity; mem. adv. bd. Cook (Ill.) County Pub. Aid; mem. adminstrv. com. Chgo. Alliance for Collaborative Effort; mem. Ill. Juvenile Justice and Delinquency Prevention Adv. Council; mem. adv. com. Chgo. Health Systems Agy.; bd. dirs. United Way Met. Chgo., 1978; trustee George Williams Coll., also mem. exec. com. and chmn. nominating com.; chmn. Chgo. Manpower Planning Council. Served to maj. USAAF, 1941-46. Recipient Thomas and Eleanor Wright award Chgo. Commn. on Human Relations, 1976, Outstanding Agy. Profl. award United Way Am., 1978. Mem. Nat. Com. Prevention of Child Abuse (dir., mem. exec. com.). Clubs: Metropolitan, Economic (Chgo.). Home: 155 N Harbor Dr Apt 4410 Chicago IL 60601 Office: YMCA Met Chgo 19 S LaSalle St Chicago IL 60603

ROOT, NINA J., librarian; b. N.Y.C., Dec. 22, 1934; d. Jacob J. and Fannie (Slivinsky) Root; B.A., Hunter Coll., 1955; M.S. in Library Sci., Pratt Inst., 1958; postgrad. U.S. Dept. Agr. Grad. Sch., 1964-65, City U. N.Y., 1970-75. Reference and serials librarian Albert Einstein Coll. Medicine Library, Bronx, N.Y., 1958-59; asst. chief librarian Am. Cancer Soc., N.Y.C., 1959-62; chief librarian Am. Inst. Aeros. and Astronautics, N.Y.C., 1962-64; head reference and library services sci. and tech. div. Library of Congress, Washington, 1964-66; mgmt. cons. Nelson Assos., Inc., N.Y.C., 1966-70; chief librarian Am. Mus. Natural History, N.Y.C.. 1970—; free lance mgmt. cons. and library planning, 1970—. Mem. Vols. of the Shelter, N.Y.C., 1967-75. Recipient Meritorious Service award Library of Congress, 1965. Mem. ALA (preservation com. 1977—, chmn. library/binders com. 1978—), Spl. Libraries Assn. (sec. documentation group N.Y. chpt. 1972-73, 2d v.p. N.Y. 1975—, treas. sci. and tech. group N.Y. 1975-76, mus. arts and humanities div. program planning chairperson-conf. 1977), AAAS, Am. Sci. Info. Sci., Archons of Colophon (convener 1978-79), Soc. Bibliography of Natural History (editor Am. newsletter 1977-79), N.Y. Acad. Scis. (mem. publs. com. 1975—, archives com. 1976—, search com. 1976). Club: Grolier (mem. exhbn. com. 1977—, admissions com. 1979—). Home: 325 E 57th St New York NY 10022 Office: Library of American Museum of Natural History Central Park W at 79th St New York NY 10024

ROOT, OREN, lawyer; b. N.Y.C., June 13, 1911; s. Oren and Aida (de Acosta) R.; A.B., Princeton, 1933; LL.B., U. Va., 1936; LL.D. (hon.), St. Michael's Coll., 1963; m. Daphne Skouras, Feb. 15, 1947; 4 children. Admitted to N.Y. Bar, 1938; mem. firm Root, Barrett, Cohen, Knapp & Smith and predecessors firms, until 1965; counsel Barrett Smith Schapiro & Simon, 1972—; counsel Irving Trust Co., N.Y.C., 1965-72; pres., dir. Charter N.Y. Corp., 1965-70, chmn. bd. dirs., 1970-72. Supt. of banks N.Y., 1961-64. Pres. Nat. Assn. Mental Health, Inc., 1950-52; chmn. Joint Legislature Com. Narcotics Study, N.Y., 1956-58; mem. N.Y. Job Devel. Authority, 1962-64; spl. asst. to gov. N.Y., 1959-60. Chmn. Asso. Willkie Clubs of Am., 1940. Bd. dirs. Internat. Rescue Com.; trustee Vera Inst. Justice. Served to lt. comdr. USNR, 1941-45; staff comdr. Fourth Fleet, 1942-43; participated in Normandy landings on staff comdr. Task Force 122, 1944. Mem. N.Y.C. Bar Assn., Am. Arbitration Assn. (dir.), Delta Psi, Phi Delta Phi. Republican. Roman Catholic. Author: Persons and Persuasions, 1974. Contbr. to Atlantic Monthly, N.Y. Times Mag., Sat. Rev., other periodicals. Office: 26 Broadway New York NY 10004

ROOT, WILLIAM ALDEN, govt. ofcl.; b. Boston, Sept. 20, 1923; s. John Alden and Louise Joy (Eppich) R.; B.A., Colo. Coll., 1943; M. Internat. Affairs, Columbia, 1948, certificate Russian Inst., 1948; m. Constance Hilda Young, Dec. 14, 1945; children—Carl David, Margaret Anne, John Alden, Christine Eppich. Budget examiner Bur. Budget, Washington, 1948-50; mgmt. and budget officer Dept. State, Washington, 1950-52; mgmt. and budget officer, Bonn, Germany, 1952-55; budget officer for Europe, Dept. State, 1955-59; economist Am. embassy, Copenhagen, Denmark, 1959-63; dep. dir. Office East-West Trade, Dept. State, 1964-69; econ. officer Am. embassy, Vietnam, 1969-71, U.S. Mission Berlin, 1971-74; dir. Office Soviet and Eastern European Sci. and Tech. Affairs, State Dept., 1974-76, dir. Office East West Trade, 1976—. Served to lt. (j.g.) USNR, 1943-46. Mem. Phi Beta Kappa. Address: 4024 Franklin St Kensington MD 20795

ROOT, WILLIAM PITT, poet, educator; b. Austin, Minn., Dec. 28, 1941; s. William Pitt and Bonita Joy (Hilbert) R.; B.A., U. Wash., 1964; M.F.A., U. N.C. at Greensboro, 1967; postgrad. (Wallace Stegner Writing fellow) Stanford, 1968-69; m. Judith Carol Bechtold, 1965 (div. 1970); 1 dau., Jennifer Lorca. Asst. prof. Mich. State U., 1967-68; tchr. writing Mid-peninsula Free U., 1969; writer-in-residence Amherst Coll., U. Southwestern La., 1976, U. Mont., 1978; with poet-in-schs. program state art councils, Oreg., Miss., Idaho, Ariz., Vt., Mont., Wyo., Wash., Tex., 1971—; Distinguished writer-in-residence Wichita State U., 1976; vis. writer in residence U. Mont., 1978. Rockefeller Found. grantee, 1969-70; Guggenheim Found. grantee, 1970-71; Nat. Endowment for Arts grantee, 1973-74; U.S./U.K. Bicentennial Exchange Artist, 1978-79. Author: The Storm and Other Poems, 1969; Striking the Dark Air for Music, 1973; Coot and Other Characters, 1977; A Journey South, 1977; Fireclock, 1979; Faultdancing, 1980. Collaborated with filmmaker Ray Rice on poetry films: Song of the Woman and the Butterflyman (Orpheus award 1st Internat. Poetry Film Festival 1975), 7 For a Magician, 1976; Mendocino Songs, 1977; Faces, 1979. Address: care Bruce MacGrew Box E Oracle AZ 85623. *With Rilke I believe the measure of one's life consists in one's growing capability to change life even as one is changed by it, to engage ever more fully in that dance between what we call will and what we call fate until the result is a contagion of vitality powerful enough to dissipate the spell of habits and to recreate in oneself that first spirit which is intuitive, sympathetic, and clear. Poems simply record the complex effort.*

ROOTES, CHARLES WESLEY, mfg. co. exec.; b. Tebbetts, Mo., June 14, 1927; s. David J. and Iva R. (Adkinson) R.; student Westminster Coll., 1947-48, Mo. U., 1949-50; m. Joanne Thesen, Feb. 1, 1951; children—David, Sue Ellen, Timothy. Supervising accountant Ernst & Ernst, St. Louis, 1951-56; controller A.B. Chance Co., Centralia, Mo., 1956-62; asst. controller Spencer Chem. Co., Kansas City, Mo., 1962-63; v.p., treas. Rival Mfg. Co., Kansas City, 1963-77, exec. v.p., dir., 1977—. Served with USAAF, 1945-47. C.P.A., Mo. Mem. Mo. Soc. C.P.A.'s, Fin. Execs. Inst. Presbyterian (trustee, treas. 1967-70). Clubs: Rotary (dir., treas. 1960-61), Centralia Country (pres. 1960-61), Leawood (Kans.) Country. Home: 3509 W 92d St Leawood KS 66206 Office: 36th and Bennington Sts Kansas City MO 64129

ROOTHAAN, CLEMENS CAREL JOHANNES, physicist, educator; b. Nymegen, Netherlands, Aug. 29, 1918; s. Charles M.V. and Wilhelmina F. E. (Straeter) R.; came to U.S., 1946, naturalized, 1955; engring. diploma in physics Inst. Tech., Delft, Netherlands, 1945; Ph.D. in Physics, U. Chgo., 1950; m. Judith Grace Cosin, Jan. 6, 1950; children—Karen S., John P. E., Peter F., Charles M. V., Elizabeth S. Instr., Cath. U. Am., 1947-49; mem. faculty U. Chgo., 1949—, prof. physics, 1959-68, prof. info. scis., 1965-68, dir. Computation Center, 1962-68, Louis Block prof. physics and chemistry, 1968—; cons. to govt. and industry, 1958. Served with Netherlands Army, 1939-40. Netherlands-Am. Found. fellow, 1946-47; Guggenheim fellow Cambridge (Eng.) U., 1957. Fellow Am. Phys. Soc., Internat. Acad. Quantum Chemistry. Club: Quadrangle (U. Chgo.). Spl. research theory atomic and molecular structure. Home: 5235 S University Ave Chicago IL 60615

ROPER, CLYDE FORREST EUGENE, biol. oceanographer, curator; b. Ipswich, Mass., Oct. 1, 1937; s. Howard Gleason and Louise Calvey (Norcross) R.; B.A., Transylvania U., 1959; M.S., U. Miami (Fla.), 1962, Ph.D., 1967; m. Ingrid Hilde Braunohler Sept. 13, 1958; children—Erik C., Christopher T. Research asst. Inst. Marine Scis., 1964-66; asso. curator div. mollusks Nat. Mus. Natural History, Smithsonian Instn., Washington, 1966-72, curator div. mollusks, 1972—. Adj. asso. prof. U. Miami, 1968—; adj. lectr. George Washington U., Washington, 1968—; external examiner Meml. U. Nfld., Can., 1970-73; affiliate grad. faculty U. Hawaii, 1975-76. Rep., Vienna Hills Civic Assn. to Town of Vienna, Va., 1971-73. Recipient Distinguished Alumni award Transylvania U., Lexington, Ky., 1970; named an Outstanding Young Man of Am., 1971. Internat. Oceanographic Fedn. fellow, 1960-61, U.S. Bur. Comml. Fisheries fellow, 1961-64. Mem. Systematics Assn., Soc. Systematic Zoology, Biol. Soc. Washington, Am. Soc. Limnology and Oceanography, Am. Malacological Union, Council Systematic Malacologists, Marine Biol. Assn. (U.K.), Western Soc. Malacologists, Australian Malacol. Soc., Inst. Malacology (sponsor mem.), Am. Polar Soc., Senate of Scientists. Editorial bd. Malacologia, 1970—, Malacological Rev., 1970—, The Mautilus, 1975—, Veliger, 1975; contbr. articles to tech. lit. Office: Nat Mus Natural History Div Mollusks Smithsonian Inst Washington DC 20560

ROPER, JOHN LONSDALE, II, ship bldg., conversion and repair co. exec.; b. Norfolk, Va., Sept. 18, 1902; s. George Wisham and Isabelle Place (Hayward) R.; student Princeton U., 1920-21; m. Sarah Engle Dryfoos, Apr. 7, 1926; children—John Lonsdale III, George Wisham II, Isabel Roper Yates. With Norfolk Shipbldg. & Drydock Corp., 1925—, pres., gen. mgr., 1956-68, pres., chief exec. officer, 1968-73, chmn. bd., 1973—; officer, dir. John L. Roper Estate, Inc., Lonsdale Bldg. Corp., Botetourt Bldg. Corp. Trustee, mem. distbn. com. Norfolk Found.; pres. Norfolk United Fund, then gen. chmn., dir. emeritus; bd. dirs. Urban Coalition of Norfolk. Recipient Disting. Service medal Cosmopolitan Club of Norfolk, 1969. Mem. Hampton Rds. Maritime Assn., Inc. (pres., life dir., Disting. Service award 1973), Am. Bur. Shipping, Am. Inst. Mgmt. (pres.'s council, 1st Marquis award), Soc. Naval Architects and Marine Engrs., Propeller Club U.S. Episcopalian. Clubs: Capitol Hill (Washington); Commonwealth (Richmond, Va.); Whitehall, Princeton (N.Y.C.); Va. (pres.), Norfolk Yacht and Country (dir.) (Norfolk); Princess Anne Country (Virginia Beach, Va.). Office: PO Box 2100 Norfolk VA 24501

ROPER, JOHN LONSDALE, III, shipyard exec.; b. Norfolk, Va., Jan. 19, 1927; s. John Lonsdale II and Sarah (Dryfoos) R.; B.S. in Mech. Engring., U. Va., Charlottesville, 1949; B.S. in Naval Achitecture and Marine Engring., M.I.T., 1951; m. Jane Preston Harman, Sept. 29, 1951; children—Susan Roper Fuller, John Lonsdale, IV, Sarah Preston, Jane Harman, Katherine Hayward. With Norfolk Shipbldg. & Drydock Corp., 1946—, now pres., chief exec. officer, dir.; dir. John L. Roper Corp., Botetourt Bldg. Corp., Cruise Internat., Inc., Dominion Nat. Bank of Tidewater, Maritime Terminals, Inc., Desert Am. Ins. Co., Inc.; pres., dir. Lonsdale Bldg. Corp., Marepcon Corp.-Internat.; bd. dirs., bd. govs. Nat. Maritime Council; bd. dirs. Am. Bur. Shipping; v.p., sec., dir. Schooner Point, Inc. Served with USCG, 1945-46. Mem. Nat. Propeller Club U.S. (dir.), Shipbuilders Council Am. (dir.), Nat. Assn. Mfrs. (dir. So. div.). Episcopalian. Office: PO Box 2100 Norfolk VA 23501

ROPER, PAUL HOLMES, hosp. adminstr.; b. Shamrock, Tex., Aug. 9, 1932; s. Guilt and Mable (Holmes) R.; B.B.A., Tex. A. and M. U., 1954; M.A., State U. Iowa, 1958; m. Dana Furr, Feb. 26, 1955; children—M. Brian, M. Boyce. Orderly, Baylor U. Hosp., Dallas, 1954; asst. adminstr. Bapt. Meml. Hosp., San Antonio, 1958-71, adminstr., 1971—. Served with U.S. Army, 1954-56; Korea. Fellow Am. Coll. Hosp. Adminstrs.; mem. Am. Hosp. Assn., U.S. Power Squadron. Baptist. Home: 1127 Haltown St San Antonio TX 78213 Office: 111 Dallas St San Antonio TX 78286

ROPER, RAYMOND WARREN, JR., assn. exec.; b. Springfield, Mo., Apr. 26, 1940; s. Raymond Warren and Mary (Hacker) R.; B.A. cum laude, Benedictine Coll., 1961; m. Judith Ann Haynes, Jan. 5, 1963; children—Mark Christopher, Sean Gregory, Douglas Warren. Personnel officer Frisco Ry., Springfield, Mo., 1965-69; dept. dir. U.S. Jaycees, Tulsa, Okla., 1969-72, exec. v.p., 1972-74; exec. v.p. Mo. Assn. Realtors, Columbia, 1974-78; sr. v.p. Nat. Assn. Realtors, Chgo., 1978—. Commr. Springfield (Mo.) Human Rights Commn., 1969; cubmaster Boy Scouts Am., 1973-74, mem. dist. finance com., 1974—; mem. Gov.'s Task Force on Med. Malpractice, 1975. Trustee, sec.-treas. U.S. Jaycees War Meml. Fund, 1972-74; trustee U.S. Jaycees Found., 1972-74. Served with AUS, 1963. Mem. Am. Soc. Assn. Execs. (dir. 1979—), Lambda Alpha (Ely chpt.). Roman Catholic. Club: Chgo. Athletic Assn. Home: 22 W 5th St Hinsdale IL 60521 Office: 430 N Michigan IL 60611

ROPP, THEODORE, educator; b. Hollywood, Ill., May 22, 1911; s. Iwrin and Margaret (Esh) R.; A.B. summa cum laude, Oberlin Coll., 1934; A.M., Harvard, 1935, Ph.D., 1937; m. Elizabeth S. Chapman, Sept. 8, 1937; children—Stephen C., Frederick, Paul T. Instr. history Harvard, 1937-38, vis. lectr., 1947-48; faculty Duke, 1938—, prof. history, 1959—. Ernest J. King prof. U.S. Naval War Coll., 1962-63; spl. research compulsory mil. service and mil. conscription in Brit. Commonwealth; mem. Hist. Adv. Com. to sec. army, 1962-65, 69-72; dir., policy adv. com. Hist. Evaluation and Research Orgn., 1963—, chmn. bd. 1965—; prof. U.S. mil. history research collection U.S. Army War Coll., 1972-73; vis. prof. mil. history U.S. Mil. Acad., 1976-77. Trustee Am. Mil. Inst., 1961-78, pres., 1968-71. Social Sci. Research Council fellow, 1958-59. Mem. Am., So. hist. assns., Am. Assn. U. Profs. (pres. N.C. conf. 1959-61, mem. council 1964-67). Author: (with Harold T. Parker) Historical Background of the World Today, 1947; War in the Modern World, 1959. Contbr. to Makers of Modern Strategy, 1943. Home: 302 Woodridge Dr Durham NC 27707

ROREM, NED, composer, author; b. Richmond, Ind., Oct. 23, 1923; s. Clarence Rufus and Gladys (Miller) R.; student Northwestern U., 1940-42, Curtis Inst., Phila., 1942-43; B.A., Juilliard Sch. Music, 1947, M.A., 1949; D.F.A. (hon.), Northwestern U., 1977. Slee prof., composer-in-residence Buffalo U., 1959-61; prof. composition U. Utah, 1965-67. Recipient Music Libraries Assn. award for song Lordly Hudson, 1948; Gershwin Meml. award, 1949; Lili Boulanger award, 1950; Nat. Inst. Arts and Letters award 1968; Pulitzer prize in music, 1977. Fulbright fellow, Paris, 1951-52; Guggenheim fellow, 1957-58, 77-78. Mem. PEN, ASCAP, Am. Acad. and Inst. Arts and Letters. Mem. Soc. of Friends. Composer: symphonies No. 1 (premiere Vienna, Austria), 1951, No. 2 (premiere N.Y.C.) 1959, No. 3 (premiere with Leonard Bernstein and N.Y. Philharmonic) 1959; Lento for Strings, 1950; Design for Orch., 1954, Pilgrims for Strings, 1958; Eagles for Orch., 1958; Lions, 1964; Ideas for Easy Orch., 1961; Piano Concerto No. 2, 1951; 3d Piano Concerto, 1970; Eleven Studies 1959; Water Music, 1966; Sun (for voice and orch., commd. by N.Y. Philharmonic), 1966; Air Music for Orch., 1974 (Pulitzer prize 1976); Assembly and Fall, 1975; Sunday Morning for Orch., 1977; Letters from Paris (for chorus and orch.; commd. by Koussevitzky Found. in Library of Congress); numerous chorus works, latest being Little Prayers; (operas) A Childhood Miracle, 1952, Three Sisters Who Are Not Sisters, 1969, Fables, 1970, Bertha, 1968, Miss Julie (Ford Found. grantee), 1964, Hearing, 1976, Cycles: War Scenes, 1969, Six Songs for High Voice and Orchestra, 1954, Six Irish Poems, 1951; Ariel for Voice, clarinet and piano, 1971, Last Poems of Wallace Stevens for voice, cello and piano, 1971, Serenade for voice, violin, viola and piano, Women's Voices, 1975, The Nantucket Songs, 1979; Day Music and Night Music for Violin, 1972-73; Etudes for Piano, 1975; Book of Hours for flute and harp, A Quaker Reader for Organ, 1976; commns. for U.S. Bicentennial include compositions for Cin. Symphony, N.C. Symphony, Nat. Endowment of the Arts, Am. Harp Soc. Author: The Paris Diary of Ned Rorem, 1966; Music from Inside Out, 1967; The New York Diary, 1967; Music and People, 1968; Critical Affairs, 1970; Pure Contraption, 1973; The Final Diary, 1974; An Absolute Gift, 1978; also articles newspapers, mags. Recs. for Columbia, Decca, Odyssey, Desto, C.R.I., Westminster, Orion. Address: care Boosey & Hawkes 30 W 57th St New York NY 10019

RORER, WILLIAM HERBERT, III, pharm. co. exec.; b. Abington, Pa., June 21, 1936; s. Herbert C. and Adelaide (Brown) R.; B.S., U.S. Naval Acad., 1958; m. Susan W. Straus, June 14, 1958; children—William, Suzanna, Samantha. Commd. ensign U.S. Navy, 1958, advanced through grades to lt., submarine engring. officer, resigned, 1963; with William H. Rorer, Inc., Fort Washington, pa., 1963—, v.p. engring., 1967-74, group v.p., 1976, pres., 1977—, mng. dir., 1959—; mng. dir. Rorer Group Inc., 1968-76; pres., mng. dir. Barcroft Co., 1974-76; pres., mng. dir. Dermik Labs. Inc., 1974-76. Pres., bd. dirs. Fort Washington Indsl./ Park Mgmt. Assn., 1970-72; mem. 13th Congl. Dist. Pa. Service Acad. Selection Bd., 1973-74; trustee Episcopal Acad., Phila., 1970-72, Chestnut Hill Hosp., Phila., 1973-74, Citizens' Crime Commn. Phila., 1978—, Phila. Coll. Pharmacy and Sci., 1978—; bd. dirs. Phila. Drug Exchange, 1972—, pres., 1977-78. Mem. Navy League U.S. (bd. dirs., v.p. Pa. chpt.), Pa. Soc. S.R., Club: Sunnybrook Golf (Plymouth Meeting, Pa.). Office: 500 Virginia Dr Fort Washington PA 19034

RORICK, ALAN GREEN, lawyer; b. Seneca, Mich., Oct. 22, 1918; s. John Porter and Bertha (Green) R.; B.S., U.S. Military Acad., 1940; LL.D., Case Western Res. U., 1947; m. Evelyn Edwards, May 10, 1941; children—Emily, Stephen, Josephine, Mark. Admitted to Ohio bar, 1948; asso. firm Baker & Hostetler, Cleve., 1947-57, partner firm, 1957—, mng. partner, 1974—. Mem. Bd. Edn., Brecksville, Ohio, 1962-67, pres., 1966; councilman Village of Waite Hill, Ohio, 1978—. Served to maj. U.S. Army, 1940-45. Mem. Am. Bar Assn., Ohio Bar Assn., Cleve. Bar Assn., Am. Law Inst. Republican. Mem. United Ch. of Christ. Club: Union. Home: 7610 Eagle Rd Kirtland OH 44094 Office: 1956 Union Commerce Bldg Cleveland OH 44115

RORIE, CONRAD JONATHAN, naval officer; b. Henning, Tenn., Oct. 28, 1930; s. Elvy and Lena (Jenkins) R.; B.S., Union U., Jackson, Tenn., 1952; M.S. in Elec. Engring., U.S. Naval Postgrad. Sch., 1961; Ph.D. in Elec. Engring., Vanderbilt U., 1970; m. Patricia Paris Cunliffe, Feb. 24, 1952; children—Michael Stephen, Catherine Jean, Patrick Jonathan. Enlisted in U.S. Navy, 1952, advanced through grades to rear adm., 1977; comdg. officer U.S.S. Robin, Panama City, Fla., 1957-58, U.S.S. Waxsaw, Key West, Fla., 1958-59, U.S.S. Bridget, San Diego, 1965-67, U.S.S. Dewey, Newport, R.I., 1970-72; comdr. U.S. Naval Surface Weapons Center, Dahlgren, Va., 1974-77; dep. comdr. for surface combatants and dep. comdr. for weapons, systems and engring. Naval Sea Systems Command, Washington, 1977—; mem. numerous naval bds. for officer career devel., including chmn. Weapons Systems Mgr./Ordnance Adv. Bd. to Naval Postgrad. Sch. Decorated Legion of Merit, Meritorious Service medal with gold star, Navy Achievement medal; recipient Am. Spirit of Honor medal, 1952; 150th Ann. Disting. Alumnus award Union U., 1975. Mem. Sigma Xi, Eta Kappa Nu, Alpha Tau Omega. Baptist. Club: Masons. Home: 1430 Mayflower Dr McLean VA 22101 Office: Naval Sea Systems Command Dept of Navy Washington DC 20362

RORKE, LUCY BALIAN, neuropathologist; b. St. Paul, June 22, 1929; d. Aram Haji and Karzouhy (Ousdigian) Balian; A.B., U. Minn., 1951, M.A., 1952, B.S., 1955, M.D., 1957; m. Robert Radcliffe Rorke, June 4, 1960. Intern, Phila. Gen. Hosp., 1957-58, resident anatomical pathology and neuropathology, 1958-62, asst. neuropathologist, 1963-67, chief pediatric pathologist, 1967-68, chief neuropathologist, 1968-69, chmn. dept. anatomical pathology and chief neuropathologist, 1969-73, chmn. dept. pathology, 1973-77; practice medicine specializing in neuropathology, Phila., 1962—; neuropathologist Children's Hosp., Phila., 1965—; cons. neuropathologist Wyeth Research Labs., Radnor, Pa., 1961—, Wistar Inst. Anatomy and Biology, Phila., 1967—; asso. prof. pathology U. Pa. Sch. Medicine, Phila., 1970-73, prof., 1973—, clin. prof. neurology, 1979—; NIH fellow in neuropathology, 1961-62, NIH grantee for study of neonatal brain, 1963-68. Diplomate Am. Bd. Pathology. Fellow Coll. Am. Pathologists; mem. Phila. Gen. Hosp. Med. Staff (pres. 1973-75), Phila. Neurol. Soc. (v.p. 1971-72, editor Transactions 1973, pres. 1975-76), Am. Assn. Neuropathologists (exec. council 1976—, v.p. 1979-80), Am. Neurol. Assn., Am. Acad. Neurology, AMA, Burlington County Med. Soc., Phila. Coll. Physicians. Author: Myelinization of the Brain in the Newborn, 1969. Contbr. articles to profl. jours. Home: 120 Chestnut St Moorestown NJ 08057 Office: Children's Hosp of Philadelphia Philadelphia PA 19104

RORSCHACH, HAROLD EMIL, JR., educator, physicist; b. Tulsa, Nov. 5, 1926; s. Harold Emil and Margaret (Hermes) R.; S.B., Mass. Inst. Tech., 1949, S.M. 1950, Ph.D., 1952; m. Helen Virginia Purdy, July 14, 1951; children—Kimerly, Kelly. Faculty, Rice U., Houston, 1952—, prof. physics, 1961—, chmn. dept., 1966-73. Vis. prof. Baylor U. Med. Sch., 1965-66, 68—; cons. bus., govt., 1975—. Served with USNR, 1945-46. Guggenheim fellow, 1961. Fellow Am. Phys. Soc.; mem. Am. Assn. Physics Tchrs., Sigma Xi. Presbyn. Contbr. articles to profl. jours. Home: 7918 Chevy Chase St Houston TX 77063

RORSCHACH, RICHARD GORDON, lawyer; b. Tulsa, Aug. 9, 1928; s. Harold Emil and Margaret (Hermes) R.; B.S., Mass. Inst. Tech., 1950; M.S., U. Okla., 1952; J.D., U. Houston, 1961; children—Richard Helm, Reagan Cartwright, Andrew Maxwell. Cons. civil engr. firm Freese & Nichols, Fort Worth, 1955, firm Freese, Nichols & Turner, Houston, 1955-56; petroleum engr. Marathon Oil Co., Bay City, Tex., 1956-57, Houston, 1957-61, atty., 1961-64; admitted to Tex. bar, 1961; since practiced in Houston; partner firm Ragan, Russell & Rorschach, Houston, 1968—; mem. exec. com. Colonial Royalties Co., Tulsa, 1970-77, dir., 1977—. Served to 1st lt. C.E., AUS, 1952-54; Korea. Mem. Am. Inst. Mining and Metall. Engrs., ASCE, Houston, Tex., Am. bar assns., Tex. Trial Lawyers Assn., Sigma Xi, Sigma Alpha Epsilon. Republican. Episcopalian (vestry man). Home: 4406 Hazard St Houston TX 77098 Office: 1100 River Oaks Bank & Trust Tower 2001 Kirby Dr Houston TX 77019

RORTY, RICHARD MCKAY, educator; b. N.Y.C., Oct. 4, 1931; s. James Hancock, and Winifred (Raushenbush) R.; B.A., U. Chgo., 1949, M.A., 1952; Ph.D., Yale, 1956; m. Amelie Sarah Oksenberg, June 15, 1954 (div. 1972); 1 son, Jay; m. 2d, Mary R. Varney, Nov. 4, 1972; children—Patricia, Kevin. Instr. philosophy Yale, 1955-57; instr. Wellesley Coll., 1958-60, asst. prof., 1960-61; mem. faculty Princeton, 1961—, prof., philosophy, 1970—; vis. prof. Cath. U. Am., U. Calif. at Santa Barbara, U. Pitts., J.W. Goethe Universität, Frankfurt am Main, Germany. Served with AUS, 1957-58. Guggenheim fellow, 1973-74. Mem. Am. Philos. Assn. (pres. Eastern div. 1979). Author: Philosophy and the Mirror of Nature, 1979. Home: 308 The Western Way Princeton NJ 08540 Office: Dept Philosophy Princeton U Princeton NJ 08540

ROSA, CLARENCE HENRY, architect; b. Lansing, Mich., July 13, 1912; s. George Henry and Eva (Blum) R.; B.S. in Arch., U. Mich., 1936; m. Marcella Vonda Orr, Dec. 31, 1937 (dec. May 1967); children—Tadd Henry, Zosia Eve (Mrs. Gerald Boicourt), Krisia Marie; m. 2d, Clarice Carr Dawson, Oct. 18, 1975. Dep. dir. Mich. Bldg. Div., 1941-69; architect Clarence H. Rosa, Lansing, 1969—. Mem. Lansing Urban Redevel. Bd., 1962-78, chmn., 1967-69; mem. Lansing Model Cities Policy Bd., 1968-72; mem. Lansing Symphony Bd., 1974—, v.p., 1977—; mem. Lansing Bd. Edn., 1955-72, pres., 1959-61, 70-72; mem. Mich. Commn. Architecture, 1971-72; mem. Lansing Center for Arts, 1975—, pres., 1976-78. Fellow AIA (pres. Mid-Mich. chpt. 1946). Mason (Shriner). Club: Civitan (past pres. Lansing). Asso. dir. architecture and engring. Northville (Mich.) State Hosp., 1948-56, Steven T. Mason bldg., Lansing, 1952, State Capitol Complex, Lansing, 1962-69; dir. architecture and engring. Central Mich. U., Mt. Pleasant, 1950-66, Medium Security Correctional Inst., Ionia, Mich., 1958-62, Mich. Secondary Facilities Center, Lansing, 1966-69. Mem. A.I.A. (regional dir. 1972-75), Mich. Soc. Architects (exec. v.p. 1972-76, Gold medal 1972), Mich. Assn. Professions (treas. 1973-78). Home: 1430 Lindbergh Dr Lansing MI 48910 Office: 120 W Ottawa Lansing MI 48933

ROSA, RAYMOND ULRIC, banker; b. New Britain, Conn., Jan. 30, 1927; s. Kenneth E. and Regina (Chenette) R.; A.S., Hillyer Coll., 1949; m. Irene M. Asselin, Feb. 5, 1949; children—R. James, David M., Catherine P., Michael F., Nancy A., Kenneth E. Pvt. practice pub. accounting, Manchester, Conn., 1949-52; auditor, Auditors of Pub. Accounts, State of Conn., Hartford, 1952-65; dir. Fed.-State Relations Dept. Finance and Control, Conn., 1965-69; dep. commr. Finance and Control, Conn., 1969-71; v.p., auditor Soc. Savings, Hartford, 1971—. Mem. Windsor Locks (Conn.) Bd. Finance, 1973—. Treas. Mental Health Assn. Conn., 1974-77, v.p., 1977; bd. dirs. Nat. Assn. Mental Health, 1977—. Served with USNR, 1944-46. Mem. Conn. Soc. C.P.A.'s, Am. Inst. C.P.A.'s, Conn. Soc. Govtl. Accountants, K.C. Roman Cath. Clubs: Officers Club of Conn.; Suffield Country. Home: 44 Center St Windsor Locks CT 06096 Office: 31 Pratt St Hartford CT 06103

ROSALDO, RENATO IGNACIO, educator; b. Minatitlan, Veracruz, Mexico, Apr. 16, 1912; s. Ignacio de Loyola and Emilia (Hernandez) R.; came to U.S., 1930, naturalized, 1940; B.A., U. Ill., 1936; M.A., 1937, Ph.D., 1942; m. Mary Elizabeth Potter, Sept. 10, 1938; children—Renato Ignacio, Richard, Robert. Teaching asst., instr. U. Ill., 1936-45; asst. prof., asso. prof. U. Wis., 1947-55; vis. prof. U. Ariz., 1955-56, mem. faculty, 1956—, prof., 1958—, head dept. Romance langs., 1958-73, dir. Latin Am. Center, 1965-70; vis. prof. Guadalajara (Mexico) Summer Sch., 1955-58, co-dir., 1959-71, acad. coordinator, 1972—; vis. prof. U. Minn., 1945, U. N.Mex., 1949, U. Calif. at Los Angeles, 1957. Coordinator, Ariz.-Mexico West Coast Trade Commn., 1959-63; adv. com. grad. edn. U.S. Office Edn., 1967-68, adv. council grad. edn., 1968—; exec. com. Assembly Border States, 1965-66. Recipient diploma Gov. Ariz., 1959, Gov. Jalisco, Mexico, 1964. Mem. Am. Assn. Tchrs. Spanish and Portuguese (exec. council 1961-63, 68-70, past sec. Ill., past pres. Wis., nat. pres. 1967), Ariz. Fgn. Lang. Assn. (past pres.), Rocky Mountain (past exec. com.), Pacific Coast (past bd. govs., pres. 1970-71) councils Latin Am. Studies, Modern Lang. Assn. Am., Philol. Assn. Pacific Coast, Inst. Internacional de Literatura Iberoamericana (pres. 1969-71, v.p. 1971-73), Rocky Mountain Modern Lang. Assn., Beta Kappa, Sigma Delta Pi, Pi Delta Phi; hon. mem. Assn. de Escritores y Artistas Americanos, Havana, Cuba, Soc. Benjamin Franklin, Academia

Norteamericana de la Lengua Española. Democrat. Catholic. Club: Cosmopolitan (past pres. U. Ill). Author: Flores de Baria Poesia, 1952; co-author: Six Faces of Mexico, 1966; Chicano: Evolution of a Culture, 1973. Contbr. articles on Latin Am., Mexican lit. to jours. Home: 5424 E 10th St Tucson AZ 85711

ROSAN, RICHARD ADAMS, former utilities exec.; b. Bridgeport, Conn., Sept. 24, 1912; s. Robert Rudolph and Nanchen (Adams) R.; A.B., Cornell U., 1933; LL.B., Yale U., 1936; m. Helen Marshall, July 21, 1939; children—Richard M., Nancy Rosan Roblin III, Wendy Rosan Costa. Admitted to Conn. bar, 1936, N.Y. bar, 1937; asso. firm Cravath, Swaine & Moore, N.Y.C., 1936-51; with Columbia Gas System, Wilmington, Del., 1951—, gen. counsel, sec., 1973, dir., 1973—, exec. v.p., gen. counsel, sec., 1974-77; cons. on energy and regulation; mem. adv. com. revision roles of practice and procedure Fed. Energy Regulatory Commn., 1978—; pres. Cecil-Kent Health Services, Inc. Mem. rep. Town Meeting, Greenwich, Conn., 1960-65; mem. Greenwich Planning and Zoning Commn., 1966-69. Served to capt., F.A., AUS, 1942-45; ETO. Decorated Bronze Star, Purple Heart. Mem. Fed. Power (past pres.), Am. bar assns., Am. Gas Assn. (past chmn. legal com.), Order of Coif, Phi Beta Kappa. Congregationalist. (chmn. bd. trustees 1965). Clubs: Congressional Country (Washington); Chester River Yacht and Country (Chestertown). Home: Duckhollow Georgetown MD 21930

ROSATI, JAMES, sculptor; b. Washington, Pa., June 9, 1912; s. Joseph and Lucia (Spagnola) R.; grad. high sch.; m. Carmel Greco, Sept. 1, 1931; children—Margaret Elizabeth (Mrs. Jan Norton), Anthony John, Mary Joset, Phillippe Cecilia (Mrs. Lawrence Tuscano). Exhibited one man shows at Peridot Gallery, N.Y.C., 1954, Otto Gerson Gallery, N.Y.C., 1959-62, Hopkins Art Center Dartmouth Coll., 1963; exhibited in group shows at 9th St. Show, 1951, Whitney Mus., 1952-54, 60, 62, 64, 67, Carnegie Internat., 1958, 61, 64, London County Council, Battersea Park, 1963, Mus. Modern Art Circulating Show, 1964-65, Internat. Council Mus. Modern Art, Paris, Berlin, 1965-66, Colby Coll., 1967, Mus. Contemporary Arts traveling exhbn., 1967-68; represented in permanent collections at Whitney Mus., Yale U., U. Mus., Geighy Chem. Corp., Ardsley, N.Y., N.Y. U. Mus., Hopkins Art Center of Dartmouth Coll., also pvt. collections; prof. sculpture Yale U., 1964—; violinist Pitts. Symphony, 1928-30. Bd. govs. Skowhegan Sch. Painting and Sculpture. Recipient Brandeis Creative Arts award, 1960; Frank Logan Gold medal and prize for sculpture Chgo. Inst., 1962; Arts Club prize Providence, 1962; Guggenheim fellow, 1964; Nat. Arts Council grantee, 1968. Home: 56 7th Ave New York City NY 10011

ROSATO, FRANCIS ERNEST, surgeon; b. Phila., June 2, 1934; s. Ernest Lancelot and Mary Rita (Huggard) R.; student St. Joseph's Coll., Phila., 1952-55; M.D., Hahnemann Med. Coll., Phila., 1959; m. Gertrude Blount Doman, Oct. 27, 1962; children—Ernest, Ann, Gertrude, Frank, Aimee. Resident in surgery U. Pa.; mem. faculty to prof. surgery, 1965-74; prof. surgery, chmn. dept. Eastern Va. Med. Sch., Norfolk, 1974-78; prof., chmn. dept. surgery Jefferson Med. Coll. of Thomas Jefferson U., Phila., 1978—. Advanced clin. fellow Am. Cancer Soc.; diplomate Nat. Bd. Med. Examiners. Fellow A.C.S.; mem. Soc. Univ. Surgeons, Am., So. surg. assns., So. Soc. Clin. Surgeons, Norfolk C. of C. Roman Catholic. Clubs: Phila. Country; Friendly Sons St. Patrick. Contbg. author to Christopher's Textbook of Surgery, Rhodes Textbook of Surgery. Contbr. articles med. jours. Home: 1600 Hagys Ford Rd Narbeth PA 19072 Office: Jefferson Med Coll 1925 Walnut St Philadelphia PA 19107

ROSAVAGE, A. RICHARD, corp. financial exec.; b. Jenkins Twp., Pa., July 10, 1934; s. Alfred and Anna Elizabeth (Benish) R.; B.S. in Accounting, King's Coll., 1956; m. Jeryl Lois Anderson, Feb. 2, 1963; children—Lori Ann, Jill Erica. Mgmt. trainee Westvaco, N.Y.C., 1956-57, accounting supr., 1959-63; sec., asst. treas. Dolly Madison Industries, Inc., Phila., 1963-70; v.p., treas., chief financial officer P.A. & S. Small Co., York, Pa., 1970-72; treas. The Budd Co., Troy, Mich., 1972-74, v.p. fin., 1974-78; v.p. fin., chief financial officer Wheeling-Pitts. Steel Corp., Pitts., 1978—. Served with Security Agy., AUS, 1957-59. Home: 3399 Brookdale Dr Pittsburgh PA 15241 Office: 4 Gateway Center Pittsburgh PA 15222

ROSAZZA, PETER ANTHONY, bishop; b. New Haven, Feb. 13, 1935; s. Aldo Massimiliano and Agatha Dolores (Dinneen) R.; student Dartmouth Coll.; A.A., St. Thomas Sem., Bloomfield, Conn., 1955; B.A., St. Bernard Sem., Rochester, N.Y., 1957; postgrad. Seminaire Saint Sulpice, Paris; M.A., Middlebury Coll., 1967. Ordained priest, Roman Catholic Ch.; now bishop; asst. pastor St. Timothy Ch., West Hartford, Conn., 1961-63; instr. modern langs. St. Thomas Sem., 1963-72; co-pastor Sacred Heart Ch., Hartford, Conn., 1972—; dir. Apostolate to Hispanics for Archdiocese of Hartford, 1972-78; now aux. bishop Archdiocese of Hartford; bd. dirs. Archdiocesan Office Urban Affairs. Mem. Nat. Conf. Cath. Bishops, U.S. Cath. Conf. Home and Office: 49 Winthrop St Hartford CT 06103

ROSBERG, CARL GUSTAF, educator; b. Oakland, Calif., Feb. 28, 1923; s. Carl Gustaf and Ethel (Moore) R.; B.S., Georgetown U., 1948, M.S., 1950; D.Phil., Oxford (Eng.) U., 1954; m. Elizabeth Joanna Wilson, Oct. 23, 1954; children—James Howard, David Nils. Asst. prof., research asso. African studies program Boston U., 1955-58; vis. asst. prof. U. Calif., Berkeley, 1958-59, asst. prof. dept. polit. sci., 1959-63, asso. prof., 1963-67, prof., 1967—, chmn. dept. polit. sci., 1969-74, dir. Inst. Internat. Studies, 1973—. Served with USAAF, 1943-45. Decorated Purple Heart, Air medal. Ford Found. fellow, 1954-55. Mem. Am. Polit. Sci. Assn., Royal African Soc., African Studies Assn. (past pres.), Author: (with John Nottingham) The Myth of Mau Mau: Nationalist in Keny, 1966; (with George Bennett) The Kenyatta Election: Kenya, 1960-61, 1961; eidtor: (with James S. Coleman) Political Parties and National Integration in Tropical Africa, 1964; (with William H. Friedland) African Socialism, 1964; (with Thomas Callaghy) Socialism in Sub-Saharan Africa. Home: 1015 Cragmont Ave Berkeley CA 94708 Office: Dept Polit Sci U Calif Berkeley CA 94720

ROSBERG, DAVID WILLIAM, educator; b. Superior, Wis., Jan. 3, 1919; s. Albert and Hulda (Sundin) R.; B.A., St. Olaf Coll., 1940; postgrad. Tex. A. and M. Coll., 1940-41; M.S., Ohio State U., 1947, Ph.D., 1949; m. Helen Dana McDonald, Nov. 8, 1941; children—David William, Dana Karin. Grad. asst. biology dept. Tex. A. and M. Coll., College Station, 1940-42, lab. asst. Tex. Agr. Expt. Sta., 1942, asst. prof. plant physiology and pathology dept., 1949-54, asso. prof., 1954-58, prof., 1958-60, prof., head dept. plant scis., 1960—; insp. R.R. Perishable Inspection Agy., N.Y.C., 1941; grad. asst. dept. botany Ohio State U., 1946-48, research asst. Research Found., 1948-49; lab. asst. Battelle Meml. Inst., Columbus, O., 1948. Named Distinguished Alumnus, Ohio State U., 1972. Mem. A.A.A.S., Am. Phytopath. Soc., Tex. Acad. Sci., Sigma Xi, Phi Kappa Phi, Gamma Sigma Delta, Home: Route 3 Box 252 Bryan TX 77801 Office: Dept Plant Scis Tex A and M U College Station TX 77843

ROSBERG, JOFFRE WESLEY, advt. exec.; b. Chgo., Apr. 24, 1917; s. Holger John and Astrid (Wingard) R.; student Northwestern U., 1936-38; m. Lorraine Sward, Sept. 21, 1940; children—Jeffrey Wesley, Timothy John. With Henri, Hurst & McDonald, Advt., Chgo., 1937-43; sr. v.p., treas., dir. Buchen Advt. Inc., Chgo., 1946-67, pres., dir., 1968-71; sr. v.p., dir. Meldrum & Fewsmith, Inc., Cleve., 1971—. Speaker on research and marketing, 1956—. Bd. dirs. Bus. Publs. Audit of Circulations; former trustee Center for Marketing Communications. Served with AUS, 1943-46; PTO. Mem. Bus./Profl. Advertisers Assn. (past pres. Chgo., past nat. v.p.), Indsl. Marketers Cleve., Cleve. Advt. Club, Am. Assn. Advt. Agys. Contbr. articles to profl. jours. Home: 2208 Harcourt Dr Cleveland Heights OH 44106 Office: 1220 Huron Rd Cleveland OH 44115

ROSCH, PAUL JOHN, physician; b. Yonkers, N.Y., June 30, 1927; s. Samuel Joseph and Mary (Gang) R.; A.B., Brown U., N.Y. U., 1948; M.A., N.Y. U., 1950; M.D., Albany Med. Coll., 1954; m. Lorraine Marie Hunt, June 27, 1951; children—David Carl, Jonathan Hunt, Jane Ellen, Michael Edward, Richard Joseph, Donna Marie; m. 2d, Marguerite Delamater, Sept. 12, 1972. Fellow, Inst. Exptl. Medicine and Surgery, U. Montreal (Que., Can.), 1951; intern, asst. resident in medicine Johns Hopkins Hosp., 1954-56, resident in medicine, chief dept. metabolism Walter Reed Med. Center, 1956-58; physician-in-charge nuclear medicine St. John's Riverside Hosp., Yonkers, 1959; chief endocrine clinic and attending physician St. Joseph's Hosp., 1959; pres., chmn. Am. Inst. Stress, Yonkers, 1978—; med. dir. Hudson View Nursing Home, Yonkers; cons. in endocrinology, chief endocrine sect. N.Y.C. Hosp. at Elmhurst; asso. attending physician, Mt. Sinai Hosp., N.Y.C.; clin. instr. medicine and asst. physician N.Y. Med. Coll. Flower and Fifth Ave. Hosp., N.Y.C.; vice chief staff St. John's Riverside Hosp. Bd. govs. Jewish Community Center; bd. dirs. Family Service Soc. Served as capt. AUS, 1956-58. Diplomate Am. Bd. Internal Medicine. Fellow Am. Coll. Cardiology, A.C.P., Internat. Acad. Medicine, Am. Coll. Angiology; N.Y. Diabetes Assn.; mem. Westchester Diabetes Assn. (past pres.), Yonkers Acad. Medicine (bd. govs.; past pres), N.Y. Cardiology Soc., N.Y. Acad. Scis., Endocrine Soc., Am. Diabetes Assn., Westchester Soc. Internal Medicine (past pres.), N.Y. State Soc. Internal Medicine (v.p. 1979—), Soc. Nuclear Medicine (dir.), Am. Fedn. Clin. Research, Am. Soc. Internal Medicine, Am. Geriatrics Soc. Republican. Clubs: Elmwood Country (Ardsley, N.Y.); Brant Beach (N.J.) Yacht; Atlantis (Fla.) Country; Breakers Golf (Palm Beach, Fla.). Asst. editor: Health Communications and Informatics; editorial bd. AMA Archives of Internal Medicine, Folia Clinica Internacional. Contbr. articles to profl. jours. Address: 124 Park Ave Yonkers NY 10703 also 221 N County Club Ave Atlantis FL 33462

ROSCH, STANLEY, port ofcl.; b. N.Y.C., June 8, 1918; s. Meyer and Mollie (Silver) R.; B.B.A., Coll. City N.Y., 1938; postgrad. Columbia, 1938-40, George Washington U., 1946-48; m. Lila Kendall Joralemon, 1979; children—Edward Arthur, Brenda Huelani. Accountant, John Berg, C.P.A., Washington, 1945-48; with Young, Lamberton & Pearson, C.P.A.'s, Honolulu, 1948-56, partner, 1953-56; partner Haskins & Sells, C.P.A.'s, Honolulu, 1956-63, Los Angeles, 1963-65; controller Castle & Cooke, Inc., Honolulu, 1965-72, v.p., 1966-69, sr. v.p., 1970-72; sr. v.p. finance, controller World Airways, Inc., Oakland, Calif., 1972-74; dir. fiscal affairs Port of Oakland, 1974—; past pres. Hawaii Soc. C.P.A.'s. Served with USNR, 1942-45. C.P.A., D.C., Hawaii, N.Y., Calif., La. Mem. Am. Inst. C.P.A.'s, Nat. Assn. Accountants, Financial Execs. Inst., Mcpl. Fin. Officers Assn., Assn. Water Transp. Acctg. Officers. Club: Kiwanis. Home: 176 Caldecott Ln Apt 214 Oakland CA 94618 Office: 66 Jack London Sq Oakland CA 94607

ROSCIA, JOHN J., multi-industry co. exec.; b. Utica, N.Y., June 25, 1920; s. Angelo and Ida (Salerno) R.; A.B., Cornell U., 1942, LL.B., 1947; m. Elizabeth Taylor, Jan. 9, 1943; children—Elizabeth, Margaret. Admitted to N.Y. bar, 1947, Calif. bar, 1951; with firm Chadbourne, Parke, Whiteside & Wolff, and predecessors, N.Y.C., 1947-55; asst. gen. counsel Rockwell Internat. Corp., Los Angeles, 1956-60, v.p., gen. counsel, 1961—. Served to capt., F.A., AUS, 1942-46. Mem. Am. Bar Assn., Phi Beta Kappa, Phi Kappa Phi, Delta Sigma Phi. Home: 1660 N Amalfi Dr Pacific Palisades CA 90272 Office: 2230 E Imperial Hwy El Segundo CA 90245

ROSCOE, STANLEY NELSON, psychologist, aero. engr.; b. Eureka, Calif., Nov. 4, 1920; s. Stanley Boughton and Martha Emma (Beer) R.; A.B. in Speech and English, Humboldt State U., 1943; postgrad. U. Calif., Berkeley, fall 1942, spring 1946; M.A. in Psychology, U. Ill., 1947, Ph.D. in Psychology, 1950; m. Margaret Hazel Brookins, Dec. 21, 1948 (dec.); m. 2d, Elizabeth Frances Lage, Mar. 12, 1977; children—Lee Marin Roscoe Bragg, Jack, Catherine Marie. Research asst. U. Ill., 1946-50, research asso., 1950-51, asst. prof., 1951-52, asso. dir. Inst. Aviation, head aviation research lab., 1969-75, prof. psychology and aero. and astronautical engring., 1977-79; prof. N.Mex. State U., 1979—; with Hughes Aircraft Co., Culver City, Calif., 1952-69, 75-77, dept. mgr., 1962-69, sr. scientist, 1975-77; tech. adviser, cons. in field; pres. Illiana Aviation Scis. Ltd., Champaign, Ill. Served with A.C., U.S. Army, 1943-46. Cert. psychologist, Calif. Fellow Human Factors Soc. (pres. 1960-61, Jerome H. Ely award 1968, 73, Alexander C. Williams award 1973, Paul M. Fitts award 1974), Soc. Engring. Psychologists, Am. Psychol. Assn. (Franklin V. Taylor award 1976), Fellow Royal Aero. Soc. (Gt. Brit.); mem. IEEE, AIAA, Inst. Navigation, Assn. Aviation Psychologists (Am. Career award 1978), Sixma Xi, Phi Kappa Phi, Phi Sigma, Chi Sigma Epsilon. Author: Aviation Psychology, 1979; contbr. numerous articles to profl. jours.; editor: Aviation Research Monographs, 1971-72; patentee, inventor in field. Office: Dept Psychology New Mexico State U Las Cruces NM 88003

ROSCOPF, CHARLES BUFORD, lawyer; b. Marvell, Ark., Apr. 21, 1928; s. Emmett Lee and Sally Virginia (King) R.; student Hendrix Coll., 1948-50; J.D., U. Ark., 1954; m. Mary Anne Maddox, Aug. 22, 1954; children—Charles David; Anne Karen. Admitted to Ark. bar, 1954, U.S. Dist. Cts., 1955, 64, U.S. Supreme Ct. bar, 1965; practiced in Helena, Ark., 1954—; asso. firm Burke, Moore & Burke, 1954-58; partner firm Burke & Roscopf, 1958-64; sr. partner firm Roscopf, Raff & Asher and predecessor, 1964-70, Roscopf & Epes, P.A., 1974—; individual practice law, 1970-74; mem. Ark. Ho. of Reps., 1953-58; del. Ark. Constl. Conv., 1968; mem. Ark. Probate Drafting Com. Served with USN, 1946-48, USAF, 1962-68. Mem. Am. Bar Assn., Ark. Bar Assn., Am. Law Inst., Kappa Sigma. Methodist. Clubs: Rotary, Masons, Shriners. Home: 117 Avalon Pl Helena AR 72342 Office: 408 Helena Nat Bank Bldg Helena AR 72342

ROSE, ALBERT, physicist; b. N.Y.C., Mar. 30, 1910; s. Simon and Sarah (Cohen) Rosenblum; A.B., Cornell U., 1931, Ph.D., 1935; m. Lillian Loebel, Aug. 25, 1940; children—Mark Loebel, Jane Susan. Research, RCA Labs., Princeton, N.J., 1935—; dir. research Labs. RCA Ltd., Zurich, Switzerland, 1955-58; mem. planning com. Internat. Confs. on Semiconductors, Internat. Conf. on Photoconductivity, Internat. Conf. on Electrophotography; vis. prof. Stanford U., 1976, Hebrew U., Jerusalem, 1976-77, Boston U., 1977, 78, Polytechnic Inst., Mexico City, 1978, U. Del., 1979. Recipient certificate of merit USN, 1946, TV Broadcasters award, 1945, David Sarnoff Gold medal Soc. Motion Picture and TV Engrs., 1958; Mary Shephard Upson distinguished prof. Cornell U., 1967; Fairchild distinguished scholar Calif. Inst. Tech., 1975. Fellow Am. Phys. Soc., IEEE (Morris Liebman award 1945, Edison medal 1979); mem. Nat. Acad. Engring., Société Suisse de Physique. Author: Concepts in Photoconductivity, 1963; Vision: Human and Electronic, 1974; editorial bd. Phys. Rev., 1956-58, Advances in Electronics, 1948-75, Jour. Physics and Chemistry of Solids, 1958-75; contbr. articles to profl. jours. Patentee in field. Home: 292 Stockton Rd Princeton NJ 08540 Office: RCA Labs Princeton NJ 08540

ROSE, AUGUSTUS STEELE, neurologist; b. Fayetteville, N.C., July 14, 1907; s. Augustus S. and Jean (Evans) R.; student Davidson Coll., 1924-25; B.S. in Medicine, U. N.C., 1930; M.D., Harvard, 1932; m. Grace Duncan, June 24, 1932; children—Ann Duncan (Mrs. Bruce F. Davie), Augustus Steele III, Charles Duncan, Jane Evans. Teaching fellow anatomy U. N.C. Sch. Medicine, 1928-30, Harvard Med. Sch., 1931-32; med. intern Mass. Gen. Hosp., Boston, 1932-34, asst. neurology, 1937-39; jr. physician McLean Hosp., Waverly, Mass., 1934; asso. prof. anatomy U. N.C., 1934-37; asst. to chief dept. therapeutic research Boston Psychopathic Hosp., 1939-51; instr. neurology and psychiatry Harvard Med. Sch., 1939-51; prof. neurology U. Calif. at Los Angeles, 1951-74, prof. emeritus, 1974—, chmn. dept. neurology, dir. Reed Neurol. Research Center, 1970-74; distinguished physician VA, 1974—; mem. staff U. Calif., Harbor Gen., VA, St. John's hosps. Dir. Am. Bd. Psychiatry and Neurology, 1960-68, v.p., 1968; adv. bd. Med. Spltys. Mem. Nat. Adv. Neurol. Disease and Stroke Council, 1968-72; v.p. 9th Internat. Neurol. Congress, 1969; mem. med. adv. bd. psychiatry and neurology services VA Central Office; dir. Epilepsy Found. Am.; mem. med. adv. bd. Nat. Multiple Sclerosis Soc., 1952—, chmn. 1955-60; med. adv. bd. Myasthenia Gravis Found.; med. adv bd. Cal. Epilepsy Soc.; adv. bd. Parkinson's Diseases Found. Mem. nat. council Pomona Coll. Recipient Distinguished Service award U. N.C. Sch. Medicine, 1962. Fellow A.M.A. (chmn. residency rev. com. 1968), Am. Psychiat. Assn.; mem. Am. Neurol. Assn. (pres. 1968-69), Am. Acad. Neurology (pres. 1959-61), Brit. Assn. Neurologists (hon. fgn.), Western Assn. Physicians, Am. Epilepsy Soc. (council 1962-64), World Fedn. Neurology, Alpha Omega Alpha. Presbyn. (ruling elder). Editor: (with C.M. Pearson) Mechanism of Demyelination, 1963. Home: 625 N Crescent Dr Beverly Hills CA 90210 Office: VA Wadsworth Hosp Center Los Angeles CA 90073. *Whatever achievements of success that may have been attained along the road of seeking to become a worthy physician and teacher can be best attributed to an effort to utilize energy and enthusiasm for the tasks of each day. The dominating standard of conduct-whether in a professional or personal setting-has been to strive toward the recognition and understanding of the needs of others.*

ROSE, BEATRICE SCHROEDER (MRS. WILLIAM H. ROSE), harpist; b. Ridgewood, N.J., Nov. 15, 1922: d. Henry William and Ida (LeHovey) Schroder; student Inst. Mus. Art, 1940-41; pupil Lucile Lawrence and Carlos Salzedo; student (scholar) Mannes Coll. Music, 1942-44; m. William Harrison Rose, Apr. 10, 1954; 1 son, Daniel. Concert and radio debut N.Y. World's Fair, 1939; soloist Damrosch Music Appreciation Hour broadcast, 1940, Duke of Windsor's Save the Children Fund, Govt. House, Nassau, Bahamas, 1941; asso. harpist Radio City Music Hall Orch., N.Y.C., 1944-50; various radio and solo performances N.Y. area, 1944-51; concert artist, Italy, U.S., and Can., 1952, 53; prin. harpist Houston Symphony, 1953—; harp instr. U. Houston, 1953—; mem. Contemporary Music Soc., soloist, 1959, 60; soloist Houston Chamber Orch., 1969; dir. Houston Harp Ensemble in Christmas Festival of Harps, PBS, 1978; instr. Shepherd Sch. Music, Rice U., 1977—. Recipient 1st prize Federated Music Clubs Context, 1936; winner N.Y. Hour of Music award, 1945. Mem. Am. Harp Soc., Phi Beta. Author: (with Grace Follet) Outline of Six-Year Harp Course for Elementary, Junior and Senior High School, 1966; Troubadour Harp: A Guide for Teachers and Students, 1976; composer: Enchanted Harp, rev. edit., 1975; also recs. for Houston Symphony, Stokowski, Everest and Capitol records. Home: 1315 Friarcreek Ln Houston TX 77055 Office: care Houston Symphony Jones Hall Houston TX 77002

ROSE, BERNICE BEREND, museum curator; b. Miami Beach, Fla.; d. Berthold and Rose (Kinwiser) Berend; B.A., Hunter Coll., N.Y.C.; M.A., N.Y. U.; married. Asso. curator painting and sculpture Mus. Modern Art, N.Y.C., then curator drawings. Author: Jackson Pollock: Works on Paper, 1967, A Salute to Alexander Calder, 1969, Drawing Now, 1976. Address: 11 W 53d St New York NY 10016

ROSE, CHARLES GRANDISON, III, congressman; b. Fayetteville, N.C., Aug. 10, 1939; s. Charles Grandison, Jr. and Anna Frances (Duckworth) R.; A.B., Davidson Coll., 1961; LL.B., U. N.C., 1964; m. Sara Louise Richardson, June 30, 1962; children—Charles Grandison IV, Sara Louise. Admitted to N.C. bar, 1964; chief prosecutor Dist. Ct., 12th Judicial Dist., 1967-70; mem. 93d-96th congresses from 7th Dist. N.C., mem. agrl. and adminstrn. coms. Pres. N.C. Young Democrats, 1968. Presbyterian. Office: 2435 Rayburn House Office Bldg Washington DC 20515*

ROSE, CHRISTOPHER WALCOTT, mfg. co. exec.; b. Muncie, Ind., Sept. 18, 1942; s. Andrew Walcott and Janet (Kitselman) R.; B.A., Claremont (Calif.) Men's Coll., 1964. Sales mgr. ITT Jabsco Products, Costa Mesa, Calif., 1968-71; gen. mgr. ITT Brydon Brass, Rexdale, Ont., Can., 1971-76, also v.p. marine and reaction components div. ITT Corp.; partner Rollins & Co., Mgmt. Cons., Del Mar, Calif., 1976—; mgr. mfg. and engring. B.M.W.-Monarch div. Trico Industries, Tulsa, 1978—. Home: 3324 E 83d Pl Tulsa OK 74136

ROSE, DANIEL, real estate co. exec., cons.; b. N.Y.C., Oct. 31, 1929; s. Samuel B. and Belle (Bernstein) R.; student Yale U., 1947-50; B.A., Syracuse U., 1952; postgrad. U. Paris; m. Joanna Semel, Sept. 16, 1956; children—David Semel, Joseph Benedict, Emily, Gideon Gregory. With Dwelling Mgrs., Inc., N.Y.C., 1954—, exec. v.p. charge mgmt., 1957-60, pres., 1960—; partner Rose Assos., N.Y.C., 1958—; dir. Dreyfus Tax Deferred Income, Inc., Boston Brit. Properties, Town and City Properties Ltd.; trustee Corporate Property Investors; advisor to sec. HUD, 1972; cons. U.S. commr. edn., 1974; mem. N.Y. Gov.'s Task Force on Housing, 1975; mem. task force on taxation Municipal Assistance Corp., 1976—. Chmn. bd. trustees Horace Mann Sch., 1971-74; trustee, asst. treas., mem. exec. com. Police Athletic League N.Y., also past chmn. Manhattan adv. bd.; former trustee Fedn. Jewish Philanthropies N.Y.; asso. fellow Pierson Coll. of Yale; mem. council fellows New Sch. Social Research, also bd. overseers Center N.Y.C. Affairs; pres. Nat. Jewish Welfare Bd., 1974-78; past pres., chmn. exec. com. YM and YWHA, Bronx; trustee Citizens Union, N.Y.C. Rand Inst.; trustee, treas., mem. exec. com. Citizens Housing and Planning Council N.Y.; mem. adv. bd. NYC Municipal Broadcasting System, 1977-78; vice chmn. Trilling Seminars Columbia U., 1977—; bd. dirs. N.Y. Inst. Humanistic Studies N.Y. U., 1977—. Served with USAF, 1951-54. Mem. Am. Arbitration Assn. (nat. panel), N.Y. Bldg. Supts. Assn. (hon., real estate man of year 1961), Fgn. Policy Assn. (dir., mem. exec. com., chmn. assos), Am. Technion Soc. (dir.), Council Fgn. Relations, Real Estate Bd. N.Y. (gov., chmn. housing programs com.), Assn. Yale Alumni (assembly del.-at-large 1978—). Clubs: Century Assn., Coffee House, Yale (N.Y.C.); Racquet and Tennis (Boston). Home: 895 Park Ave New York NY 10021 Office: 522 Fifth Ave New York NY 10036

ROSE, DAVID, composer, conductor; b. London, June 24, 1910; s. Meyer and Eva R.; student Chgo. Coll. Music; m. Betty Jane Bartholomew, Dec. 28, 1928; children—Melanie, Angela. Pianist, Ted Fio Rio Orch., 1933-35; staff arranger, pianist NBC, Chgo., 1935-38; musical dir. Calif. Melodies series NBC, 1938-42; mus. dir. and condr., composer, 1946—; mus. dir. TV programs Red Skelton Program, 1947, Bob Hope Show, 1959-62, also Bonanza, 14 yrs., The Lonliest Runner, NBC movie, Little House on the Prairie, NBC-TV. Served with USAAF, 1942-45. Recipient Emmy award for Fred Astaire Program, 1959, for Bonanza, 1965, Craftsman episode Little House on the Prairie, 1979; Acad. Motion Pictures Arts and Scis. nomination for Wonder Man; 22 Grammy awards. Mem. ASCAP. Composer: Holiday for Strings, Our Waltz, Dance of the Spanish Onion, The Stripper; (Moss Hart Prodn.) Winged Victory; composer scores for motion pictures including Texas Carnival, Rich, Young and Pretty, The Clown, Bright Road, Jupiter's Darling, Port Afrique, Never Too Late, Hombre, Please Don't Eat the Daisies; scored movie Suddenly Love. Address: 4020 Longridge Ave Sherman Oaks CA 91403

ROSE, DAVID JOHN, educator; b. Victoria, B.C., Can., May 8, 1922; s. David Angus and Nora (Birkett) R.; student Victoria Coll., 1939-40; B.A.Sc., U. B.C., 1947; Ph.D., Mass. Inst. Tech., 1950; m. Constance Vivienne Fox; children—Elizabeth Constance, Victoria Ann (dec.), Hugh Alexander, Andrew David; m. 2d, Renate Papke. Came to U.S., 1947, naturalized, 1958. With B.C. Research Council, Vancouver, 1950-51; tech. staff Bell Telephone Labs., Inc., Murray Hill, N.J., 1951-58; asso. prof. dept. nuclear engring. Mass. Inst. Tech., 1958-60, prof., 1960— (on leave 1969-71); dir. long range planning Oak Ridge Nat. Lab., 1969-71; with Oak Ridge Nat. Lab., 1967-68; vis. staff U.K. Atomic Energy Authority, 1968; faculty Salzburg Seminar in Am. Studies, Austria, 1973; mem. Am. Bar Assn.-AAAS Joint Conf. Lawyers and Scientists, 1975—; mem. com. on nuclear and alternative energy systems Nat. Acad. Scis., 1975—; cons. to Govt. of Brazil, 1975, Govt. of W.Ger., 1976, World Council of Chs., 1976—; cons. on controlled fusion, plasma physics, energy tech., energy policy to U.S. govt., indsl. firms. Served to capt. Canadian Army, 1942-45. Fellow Am. Phys. Soc. (chmn. div. plasma physics 1965-66), Am. Acad. Arts and Scis., AAAS; mem. Am. Nuclear Soc. (Arthur Holley Compton 1975), Sigma Xi, Author: (with M. Clark, Jr.) Plasmas and Controlled Fusion, 1961; also articles. Office: Mass Inst Tech Cambridge MA 02139

ROSE, DAVID SHEPHERD, former bishop; b. Nashville, Mar. 10, 1913; s. Charles Solon and Amy (Payne) R.; B.A., U. of the South, 1936, M.Div., 1938, D.Div., 1959; D.D., Va. Theol. Sem., 1959; m. Frances Lewis Luce, Jan. 6, 1947; 1 son, Hill Luce. Ordained to ministry, Episcopal Ch., 1938; asst. rector St. Mary's Cathedral, Memphis, 1938; asso. rector Christ Ch., Pensacola, Fla., priest in charge St. John's, Werrington, St. Mary's, Milton and St. Andrew's, Destin, Fla., 1939-43; asst. to bishop of Fla., 1946-48; rector Ch. of Good Shepherd, Corpus Christi, 1948-58; suffragan bishop of So. Va., 1958-64; bishop coadjutor of So. Va., 1964-71, bishop of So. Va., Norfolk, 1971-78, ret., 1978; chmn. bd. trustees Va. Theol. Sem., St. Pauls Coll., Lawrenceville, Va., Trustee U. of the South; mem. governing council St. George's Coll., Jerusalem. Served to maj., U.S. Army, 1943-46. Fellow Coll. Preachers. Address: Star Route Box 35 Carrabelle FL 32322

ROSE, EVANS, JR., lawyer; b. Sewickley, Pa., Mar. 10, 1932; s. Evans and Jane Eline (Murphy) R.; A.B., Yale U., 1954; J.D., U. Pitts., 1959; m. Diana Lee Risien, Nov. 28, 1970; children—Virginia, Susan, Jessica, Hilary, Robert. Admitted to Pa. bar, 1960; asso. firm Rose Schmidt Dixon Hasley Whyte & Hardesty and predecessors, Pitts. and Washington, 1960-64, partner, 1964—, sr. partner, 1970—; dir. Sea Breeze Labs., Inc., Tele-Media Co. of Lake Erie, Tele-Media Co. of Key West, L.G. Harkins Co., Inc., H. E. Haller, Inc.; solicitor Borough of Sewickley Heights; sec. Fed. Ct. Nominating Commn. of Pa., 1977—; chmn. Appellate Ct. Nominating Commn. of Pa., 1979—. Trustee West Penn Hosp., Pitts., Carnegie Hero Fund Commn.; chmn. Pa. Republican Fin. Com., 1979—; del. Rep. Nat. Conv., 1976. Served with U.S. Army, 1954-56. Mem. Am. Law Inst., Law Club, Allegheny County (Pa.) Bar Assn., Pa. Bar Assn., Am. Bar Assn. Republican. Episcopalian. Clubs: Duquesne, Rolling Rock, H-V-P, Pitts. Golf (gov.). Article editor U. Pitts. Law Rev., 1958-59. Home: 1035 Devon Rd Pittsburgh PA 15213 Office: 900 Oliver Bldg Pittsburgh PA 15222

ROSE, FRANK ANTHONY, univ. adminstr.; b. Meridian, Miss., Oct. 16, 1920; s. Frank Anthony and Susan Clare (Cooper) R.; A.B., Transylvania U., 1942, LL.D., 1958; B.D., Lexington Sem., 1946; LL.D., Lynchburg Coll., 1951, U. Cin., 1958, U. Ala., 1958, Samford U., 1960; D.H.L., St. Bernard Coll., 1964; D.Sc., W.Va. U., 1965; D.Hum., Am. U., Mexico, 1965, Bapt. Coll. Charleston, 1970; D.Litt., Central Meth. Coll., 1977; m. Tommye Stewart, Oct. 16, 1942; children—Susan Rose Dabney, Frank Anthony, Julian, Elizabeth. Dir. admission, prof. philosophy Transylvania U., Lexington, Ky., 1943-48, advisor to pres., 1948-51, pres., 1951-58; pres. U. Ala., 1958-69; chmn. bd. Univ. Assos., Inc., Washington, 1969—; nat. chmn. for planning and devel. Salk Inst., 1970-74; mem. bd. control, exec. com. So. Regional Edn. Bd., 1958-68; mem. Commn. on Higher Edn. Opportunity in the South, 1964-68. Chmn. bd. trustees Am. Univs. Field Staff, 1968-74; bd. curators Transylvania U.; chmn. Ala. March of Dimes, 1958-65, regional chmn., 1965-69; trustee Salk Inst. Biol. Studies, Nat. Found.; mem. Nat. Citizen Com. on Public TV; mem. adv. panel ROTC affairs, U.S. Army, 1964-68; chmn. bd. visitors U.S. Mil. Acad., West Point, 1968-69; bd. govs. Air Univ., 1960, chmn., 1962; del. U.S. Com. to Atlantic Congress, NATO, 1959; exec. com. Reading is Fundamental, 1969—; nat. adv. com. Council on Med. Health Professions Edn., 1977—; chmn. bd. Christian Ch. Found., 1977-79; mem. policy bd. TACTICS. Mem. Nat. Assn. State Univs. and Land Grant Colls. (exec. com.), Omicron Delta Kappa (nat. pres. 1968), Phi Beta Kappa, Alpha Omega Alpha. Democrat. Club: Cosmos. Home: 1115 Ashgrove Pike Nicholasville KY 40356 Office: 475 L'Enfant Plaza Suite 2100 Washington DC 20024

ROSE, FREDERICK PHINEAS, builder and real estate exec.; b. N.Y.C., Nov. 16, 1923; s. Samuel and Belle (Bernstein) R.; B.C.E., Yale U., 1944; m. Sandra Priest, June 28, 1948; children—Deborah, Jonathan Frederick Phineas, Samuel Priest, Adam Raphael. Vice pres. Rose Assos., Inc., N.Y.C., 1946-60, pres., 1960—; partner Keystone, Centrose Assos., Boston; vice chmn. N.Y. Facilities Devel. Corp., 1970-75; dir. Home Life Ins. Co., 1972—; chmn. publs. com. Commentary Mag.; trustee N.Y.C. Pub. Devel. Co., 1968-75, United Mut. Savs. Bank, 1977—, Consol. Edison Co. N.Y., 1978—; gov. N.Y. Real Estate Bd., 1972-75; mem. Council on Fgn. Relations; mem. Urban Design Council N.Y.C.; mem. U.S. nat. com. Internat. Council for Bldg. Research, U.S. del. to UN Conf. on Housing, Planning and Bldg. Research, 1962-63, 67. Pres. Fedn. Jewish Philanthropies of N.Y., 1974-77; vice chmn. Greater N.Y. Fund, 1974-76; bd. dirs. Henry Kaufmann Campgrounds, 1950-66, pres., 1962-66; trustee N.Y. State Mental Hygiene Fund, 1964-70; trustee Scarsdale (N.Y.) Bd. Edn., pres., 1966-71; trustee Lexington Sch. for Deaf, 1954-70, Asia Soc., 1976—, Mills Coll. Edn., 1960-68, Found. for Coop. Housing, 1967-70, Energy Fund, 1970-75, Citizens Budget Commn., N.Y.C., 1969—, Inst. Pub. Adminstrn., 1970—, Mt. Sinai Sch. Medicine, Hosp. and Med. Center, 1966-73, Childrens Aid Soc., 1964-75; chmn. bd. govs. Assn. Yale Alumni, 1972-75; mem. vis. com. Grad. Sch. Design, Harvard U.; mem. pres.'s council Manhattanville Coll., 1972-74. Served to lt. (j.g.) USNR, World War II. Fellow Jonathan Edwards Coll., Yale U., 1969—, Brandeis U., 1971—; recipient Yale medal, 1976, Urban Leadership award N.Y. U., 1978. Mem. Am. Arbitration Assn. (nat. panel), ASCE. Clubs: Century Assn.; Beach Point Yacht; Old Oaks Country; Yale (N.Y.C.). Home: 72 Brewster Rd Scarsdale NY 10583 Office: Rose Assos Inc 522 Fifth Ave New York NY 10036

ROSE, HARRY MELVIN, physician, educator; b. Niles, Ohio, May 30, 1906; s. Charles Homer and Anna Beatrice (Stevens) R.; A.B., Yale U., 1928; M.D., Cornell U., 1932; m. Elizabeth Dryden Ramage, June 26, 1930 (dec. Apr. 1978); children—Ann Elizabeth (Mrs. Rene Alexandre Isaac), Frank Stevens, Stuart Ramage; m. 2d, Helen R. Buxton, July 30, 1979. Intern, Springfield (Mass.) Hosp., 1932; asst. physician N.Y. State Tb Hosp., Raybrook, 1933-35, sr. physician, 1935-38; intern Presbyn. Hosp., N.Y.C., 1938, resident bacteriology, 1938-42, mem. hosp. staff, 1943—, attending microbiologist 1950-72; faculty Columbia U., 1940-73, prof. microbiology, 1950-73, John E. Borne prof. med. and surg. research, chmn. dept. microbiology, 1952-73; active staff Lakes Region Gen. Hosp., Laconia, N.H., 1973—, Huggins Hosp., Wolfeboro, N.H., 1973—; mem. Nat. Bd. Med. Examiners, 1958-62. Mem. Commn. on Influenza, Armed Forces Epidemiological Bd., 1949-71; cons. Sec. of War on epidemic diseases, 1941-46; cons. to surg. gen., 1956-72; cons. med. com. U.S. Army Chem. Corps Adv. Council, 1962-66. Recipient award Gairdner Charitable Found., Can., 1959. Diplomate in pub. health and med. lab. microbiology Am. Bd. Microbiology, Am. Bd. Internal Medicine. Fellow A.C.P., Am. Pub. Health Assn., Am. Acad. Microbiology; mem. A.M.A., Assn. Am. Physicians, A.A.A.S., Am. Assn. Immunologists, Am. Soc. Clin. Investigation, Harvey Soc., Soc. Exptl. Biology and Medicine, Am. Soc. Microbiologists, Am. Rheumatism Assn. (hon.), N.Y. Soc. Electron Microscopists, N.Y. Acad. Medicine, N.Y. Acad. Scis., N.H. Med. Soc., Alpha Omega Alpha, Sigma Xi, Nu Sigma Nu. Club: Saint Andrew's Golf (Hastings-on- Hudson). Editor-in-chief Jour. Immunology, 1968-72. Home: Rural Route 1 Box 224 Center Harbor NH 03226 Office: Sandwich Health Center Sandwich NH 03227

ROSE, HERMAN, artist; b. Bklyn., Nov. 6, 1909; s. Charles and Bella (Washelevsky) Rappaport; student N.A.D., 1927-29; m. Tilly Lomsky, Mar. 15, 1934 (div.); children—George, Andrew; m. 2d, Elia Braca, Oct. 18, 1955. Mem. staff art project Works Progress Adminstrn., 1934-39; tchr. Hofstra Coll., 1959-60, Bklyn. Coll., 1949-51, 58-61, New Sch., 1954-55; instr. New Sch. Social Research, 1963—; artist-in-residence U. Va., 1966, U. N.Mex., 1970-71, Queens Coll., 1974; one man shows include Egan Gallery, 1946-47, A.C.A. Gallery, 1952-55, Forum Gallery, 1962, Zabriskie Gallery, 1967-69, 71-74; group shows include Fifteen Americans, Mus. Modern Art, 1952, Mus. Modern Art, Barcelona, 1955, Mus. Modern Art, Paris, 1955, Tate Mus., 1956, Pa. Acad., 1953, Whitney Mus., 1948, 49, 53, 55, 56, Nat. Ins. Arts and Letters; works in permanent collection Mus. Modern Art, Whitney Mus., U. Tex., U. Calif., Smithsonian Instn. Print Collection, U. Nebr., Hirshchorn Mus. and Sculpture Garden. Recipient Yaddo scholarship, 1955, Longview award, 1959, 60, 61; awards Inst. Arts and Letters, 1972; Nat. Endowment for the Arts, 1976, Childe Hassam, 1970. Mem. N.A.D. (Benjamin Altman 1st prize landscape 1976, Henry Ward Ranger Fund purchase 1977). Office: Zabriskie Gallery 29 W 57th St New York NY 10021

ROSE, HORACE CHAPMAN, lawyer; b. Columbus, Ohio, Feb. 11, 1907; s. Henry Nelson and Grace (Chapman) R.; A.B., Princeton, 1928; LL.B., Harvard, 1931; m. Katherine Cast, Oct. 1, 1938; 1 son, Jonathan Chapman. Sec. to Oliver Wendell Holmes, asso. justice Supreme Ct. U.S., 1931-32; admitted to Ohio bar, 1933, D.C. bar, 1946; asso. with Jones, Day, Cockley & Reavis (formerly Tolles, Hogsett & Ginn), Cleve., 1933-38; partner Jones, Day Reavis & Pogue, Cleve., Washington, 1939-42, 46-52, 56-76, of counsel, 1977—; dir. Office of Contract Settlement, Washington, 1946; asst. sec. treasury, 1953-55, under sec. treasury, 1955-56. Dir. Gould Inc., Chgo. Trustee Cleve. Orch., Cleve. Council World Affairs, Western Res. Acad., Episcopal Ch. Found.; trustee emeritus Princeton U., Brookings Instn. Served to col. AUS, 1942-45. Decorated Legion of Merit. Mem. Am., Ohio, Cleve. bar assns., Am. Law Inst. (council), Phi Beta Kappa. Republican. Episcopalian. Clubs: Union, Tavern, Kirtland Country (Cleve.); Princeton (N.Y.C.); Metropolitan, Burning Tree, Chevy Chase (Washington). Home: 12407 Fairhill Rd Cleveland OH 44120 also 2701 31st St NW Washington DC 20008 Office: Union Commerce Bldg Cleveland OH 44114 also 1735 Eye St NW Washington DC 20006

ROSE, HUGH, mfg. co. exec.; b. Evanston, Ill., Sept. 10, 1926; s. Howard Gray and Catherine (Wilcox) R.; B.S. in Physics, U. Mich., 1951, M.S., 1952; m. Mary Moore Austin, Oct. 25, 1952; children—Susan, Nancy, Gregory, Matthew, Mary. With Caterpillar Tractor Co., Peoria, Ill., 1952-66; v.p., mktg. mgr. Cummins Engine Co., Columbus, Ind., 1966-69; pres. Cummins Northeastern, Inc., Dedham, Mass., 1969—; pres., dir. Diesel Leasing, Inc.; dir. Northeastern Supply, Inc. Bd. dirs. Jordan Hosp., Plymouth, Mass. Served with USAAF, World War II. Mem. Soc. Vertebrate Paleontology, Puppeteers of Am., Beacon Soc. Clubs: Mo. Athletic, Madison Square Garden, Duxbury Yacht, Algonquin. Home: Governor Wentworth Rd Amherst NH 03031 Office: 100 Allied Dr Dedham MA 02026

ROSE, ISRAEL HAROLD, educator, mathematician; b. New Britain, Conn., May 17, 1917; s. Abraham and Dora (Dubrow) R.; student Coll. City N.Y., 1934-36; A.B., Bklyn. Coll., 1938, A.M., 1941; Ph.D., Harvard, 1951; m. Pearl Nitzberg, Jan. 24, 1942 (div. Feb. 1956); 1 son, Steven Philip; m. 2d, Susan Ann Lazarus, Mar. 26, 1961; children—Dora, Eric. Tutor, instr. Bklyn. Coll., 1938-41; instr. Pa. State Coll., 1942-46; asst. prof. U. Mass., 1948-54, asso. prof., 1954-60; faculty Hunter Coll., 1960-68, prof. math., 1965-68, chmn. dept., 1966-68; prof. math. Lehman Coll., City U. N.Y., 1968—, chmn. dept., 1968-72. Vis. asst. prof. Mt. Holyoke Coll., 1951-52, vis. asso. prof., 1954-55, 58-59; sci. cons. AID, India, summer 1965. NRC predoctoral fellow Harvard, 1946-48; fellow Fund Advancement Edn., 1952-53. Mem. Am. Math. Soc., Math. Assn. Am. (chmn. Met. N.Y. sect. 1973-75), Nat. Council Tchrs. Math., Assn. Tchrs. Math. New Eng. (pres. Conn. Valley sect. 1956-57), Sigma Xi (pres. Hunter Coll. chpt. 1966-67). Author: A Modern Introduction to College Mathematics, 1959; Algebra: An Introduction to Finite Mathematics, 1963; Vectors and Analytic Geometry, 1968; Elementary Functions: A Precalculus Primer, 1973; (with Esther R. Phillips) Elementary Functions, 1978. Home: 18 Floral Dr Hastings-on-Hudson NY 10706 Office: Lehman Coll Bedford Park Blvd W Bronx NY 10468

ROSE, JAMES MCKINLEY, JR., lawyer, govt. ofcl.; b. N.Y.C., Aug. 8, 1927; s. James McKinley and Helen (Goodwin) R.; grad. Phillips Exeter Acad., 1946; B.A., Princeton, 1951; J.D., Harvard, 1954; m. Anne Louise Bourne, Aug. 19, 1960; children—Anne Clark, Louise Barnes. Admitted to N.Y. bar, 1955, also D.C. bar; with firm Dewey, Ballantine, Bushby, Palmer & Wood, N.Y.C., 1954-57; asst. U.S. atty. So. Dist. N.Y., 1957-61; legal asst. to pres. Atlantic Mut. Ins. Co., 1961-65, sec., counsel, 1965-71; asst. fed. ins. adminstr. U.S. Dept. Housing and Urban Devel., Washington, 1971—. Mem. men's com. Am. Mus. Natural History, 1968-71. Served with AUS, 1946-47. Mem. Bar Assn. City N.Y., N.Y. Dist. Attys. Assn., St. Nicholas Soc. Republican. Episcopalian (vestryman). Clubs: Union (N.Y.C.); Prouts Neck (Maine) Country; Kenwood (washington). Home: 4913 Rodman St NW Washington DC 20016

ROSE, JERZY EDWIN, neurophysiologist; b. Buczacz, Poland, Mar. 5, 1909; s. Henryk and Regina (Deiches) R.; came to U.S., 1940, naturalized, 1943; M.D., Jagiellon U., Cracow, Poland, 1934; m. Hanna Maria Sobkowicz, Mar. 14, 1972. Fellow, Emperor William Inst. Brain Research, Berlin and German Inst. Brain Research, Neustadt, 1936-38; sr. asst. in neurology and psychiatry Stefan Batory U., Wilno, Poland, 1938-39; research asso. Henry Phipps Psychiat. Clinic, Johns Hopkins U., 1940-43; asst. prof., asso. prof. psychiatry and physiology Johns Hopkins U., Balt., 1946-60; prof. neurophysiology U. Wis., Madison, 1960—. Served with M.C., AUS, 1943-46. Mem. Am. Assn. Anatomists, Am. Physiol. Soc., Internat. Brain Research Orgn., Nat. Acad. Scis. Jewish. Home: 4169 Cherokee Dr Madison WI 53711 Office: 283 Med Sci Bldg U Wis Madison WI 53706

ROSE, JOHN CHARLES, physician; b. N.Y.C., Dec. 13, 1924; s. Hugh Stanley and Marie-Louise (Delury) R.; B.S., Fordham U., 1946; M.D. magna cum laude, Georgetown U., 1950, D.Sc. (hon.), 1973; LL.D. (hon.), Mt. St. Mary's Coll., 1973; m. Dorothy Anne Donnelly, June 26, 1948; children—Nancy, Ellen, John Charles, Richard, Christopher. Intern Walter Reed Army Hosp., 1950-51; resident, research fellow Georgetown U., VA hosps., Washington, 1950-54; established investigator Am. Heart Assn., 1954-57; instr., asst. prof. medicine Georgetown U., 1954-57, coordinator med. edn., 1957-58, asso. prof. physiology and biophysics, 1958-60, prof., chmn. dept., 1960-63, dean Sch. Medicine, 1963-73, 78-79, prof. medicine, 1973—. Asso. editor Am. Family Physician, 1955-62, chief med. editor, 1962—; Served to 2d lt. USAAF, 1943-45. Decorated Air medal. Diplomate Am. Bd. Internal Medicine, Am. Bd. Family Practice. Fellow A.C.P.; mem. Am. Physiol. Soc., Biophys. Soc., Soc. Exptl. Biology and Medicine (nat. councillor 1962-63), Am. Heart Assn. (fellow sect. circulation), Am. Assn. Med. Colls., Royal Soc. Medicine. Club: Cosmos (Washington). Contbr. articles to sci. publs. Home: 5710 Surrey St Chevy Chase MD 20015 Office: Georgetown U School of Medicine Washington DC 20007

ROSE, LEONARD, cellist; b. Washington, July 27, 1918; s. Harry and Jennie (Frenkel) R.; grad. Curtis Inst. Music, Phila., 1938; m. Minnie Knopow, Dec. 1, 1938 (dec. June 1964); children—Barbara Jean, Arthur Ira; m. 2d, Xenia Petschek, Jan. 29, 1965. Asst. 1st cellist NBC Symphony; 1st cellist Cleve. Orch., 1939-43; debut N.Y. Philharmonic, 1943, first cellist, 1944-51; soloist recitals Town Hall, N.Y.C., also orchs. including Boston Symphony, Phila. Orch., Chgo. Symphony, St. Louis Symphony, San Francisco Orch., London Symphony, also in Paris, The Hague; ann. tours U.S., Can., Europe; rec. for Columbia Masterworks; mem. faculty Juilliard Sch. Music, N.Y.C., 1947—, Curtis Inst. Music, 1951—. Editor numerous compositions Internat. Music, N.Y.C. Office: care ICM Artists Ltd 40 W 57th St New York City NY 10019

ROSE, MARK ALLEN, educator; b. N.Y.C., Aug. 4, 1939; s. Sydney Aaron and Rose (Shapiro) R.; A.B. summa cum laude, Princeton, 1961; B.Litt., Merton Coll., Oxford (Eng.) U., 1963; Ph.D., Harvard, 1967; divorced; 1 son, Edward Gordon; m. 2d, Rachel Warner Liebes, 1979; 1 stepson, Jonah Liebes. From instr. to asso. prof. English, Yale, 1967-74; prof. English, U. Ill., Urbana, 1974-77, U. Calif., Santa Barbara, 1977—. Woodrow Wilson fellow, 1961; Henry fellow, 1961-62; Dexter fellow, 1966; Morse fellow, 1970-71; Nat. Endowment for Humanities fellow, 1979-80. Mem. Modern Lang. Assn., Renaissance Soc. Am., Shakespeare Soc. Am., Phi Beta Kappa. Author: Heroic Love, 1968; (fiction) Golding's Tale, 1972; Shakespearean Design, 1972; Spenser's Art, 1975. Editor: Twentieth Century Views of Science Fiction, 1976; Twentieth Century Interpretations of Antony and Cleopatra, 1977. Home: 859 Jimeno Rd Santa Barbara CA 93103

ROSE, MARY CARMAN (MRS. ALEXANDER GRANT ROSE), educator; b. Mpls., Feb. 23, 1916; d. Charles M. and Lulu (Gassmann) Carman; B.A., U. Minn., 1937, M.A., 1939; Ph.D., Johns Hopkins, 1949; m. Alexander Grant Rose, Dec. 12, 1942; 1 son, John M. Asst. prof. philosophy George Washington U., 1949-53; asso. prof. philosophy, chmn. dept. philosophy Goucher Coll., Towson, Md., 1953—, Dean John B. Van Meter prof. philosophy, 1961—. Lectr. philosophy, religion. Mem. Am., Am. Cath. Philos. Assns., Am. Aesthetics Soc., So. Soc. for Philosophy and Psychology, AAUP, So. Soc. for Philosophy of Religion, Am. Acad. Religion, Coll. Theology Soc., Sperchial Frontiers Fellowship, Phi Beta Kappa. Roman Catholic. Essays in Christian Philosophy, 1963. Contbr. articles to profl. jours. Home: 402 E Gittings Ave Baltimore MD 21212 Office: Goucher Coll Towson MD 21204

ROSE, MASON H., IV, psychoanalyst; b. Charlevoix, Mich., July 4, 1915; s. Mason Harry III and Catharine (Deibel) R.; grad. Philips Exeter Acad., 1932; student U. Fla., 1932-33, Duke, 1933-34, U. So. Calif., 1934-35; B.A., Inst. Religious Sci., 1943; M.S., Ph.D., Sequoia U., 1953; LL.D. (hon.), Asso. Univs., Hong Kong, 1959; 1 son, Mason Harry V. Tennis profl. The Inn, Charlevoix, 1932-35; lectr. Inst. Religous Sci., 1937-43; pvt. practice psychoanalysis, Los Angeles, 1941—; exec. dir. Nat. Found. Psychol. Research, 1940-60; psychol. cons. Med. Found. Am., 1948-62; leader Humanist Ch. of Religious Sci., 1957—; v.p., dean undergrad. sch. Calif. Inst. Advanced Study, 1959-65; chancellor Pacific Inst. Advanced Studies, 1965—. Chmn. Great Books of Modern World, 1959—; exec. dir. Olympic League Am., 1967—; dir. Center Organic Ecology, 1968—, Everywoman's Village, Disease Prevention and Life Extension Center; cons. World Ecology Corp., 1969—, World Environmental Systems, 1970—. Mem. A.A.A.S., Fedn. Am. Scientists, Soc. Social Responsibility in Sci., Am. Civil Liberties Union, N.A.A.C.P., Internat. Footprinters Assn., Aircraft Owners and Pilots Assn., Helms Athletic Found. (life), So. Calif. Olympic Games Com., Philips Exeter Acad. Alumni Assn., Trojan Football Alumni Assn. Clubs: Athletic, Press (adv. bd. 1952) (Los Angeles). Author: You and Your Personality, 1944; Community Plan for the Returning Serviceman, 1945; Sex Education from Birth to Maturity, 1948; Creative Education, 1953; Humanism as Religion, 1959; The Nutra-Bio-Zyme Soil Management System, 1969; The Nutra-Bio-Zyme Manutrol System, 1970; Bio-N-Gest Sewage Treatment and Water Reclamation System, 1970; Bio-N-Gest Wast Recycling System, 1970; Bio-Dynamics, 1970; The Island Tribe, 1971; New Hopes for the Emotionally Disturbed Child, 1974, 2d edit., 1977; Humanics Health System, 1975; Medical Survey of Nutrition for Pregnancy and Lactation, 1976; How to Provide Optimum Nutrition for You and Your Child, 1978; Suntanning, The World's Most Dangerous Sport, 1979; How to Scare Your Teenager Straight, 1979; (syndicated newspaper column) You and Your Child, 1950-54. TV programs, 1951-52. Home: 1312 N Stanley Ave Los Angeles CA 90046 Office: 1312 N Stanley Ave Los Angeles CA 90046

ROSE, MERLE RICHARD, univ. pres.; b. Fredonia, Pa., Mar. 6, 1933; s. Willis J. and Bertha Mae (Wasser) R.; B.S., Slippery Rock State Coll., Pa., 1955; M.S., Westminster Coll., Pa., 1962; Ph.D., U. Pitts., 1968; m. Clarice Ratzlaff, June 4, 1955; children—Scott

Richard, Eric Timothy, Craig Quentin. Tchr., Lakeview Schs., Sandy Lake, Pa., 1958-60, guidance counselor, 1960-62; asst. to vice chancellor for regional campuses U. Pitts., 1962-64, coordinator regional programs, 1964-69, asst. provost, 1969-72; dep. asst. sec. Def., 1972-74; pres. Alfred (N.Y.) U., 1974-78, Rochester Inst. Tech., 1979—; dir. Monroe Savs. Bank, Rochester, Raymond Corp., Greene, N.Y., Spin-Optics Inc., Rochester. Mem. Nat. USMC Pistol Team, 1962-72; mem. adv. com. Servicemen's Opportunity Coll., Washington; mem. climate research advisory group Nat. Def. U., 1976—; trustee Commn. on Ind. Colls. and Univs. N.Y.; bd. overseers Strong Meml. Hosp., Rochester, N.Y.; bd. dirs. Center for Govt. Research, Rochester, YMCA, Rochester, Otetiana Council Boy Scouts Am.; trustee Anderson Coll., 1978—; mem. ACE Commn. on Mil.-Higher Edn. Relations, 1978—. Served with USMC, 1955-58. Recipient Distinguished Civilian awards U.S. Army, 1971, USAF, 1971. Mem. Am. Ceramics Soc., AAUP, Inter-Univ. Seminar of Armed Forces, Rochester Area C. of C. (dir.), Phi Kappa Phi. Republican. Clubs: Rotary, Rochester Country, Genesee Valley (Rochester). Author: Instructional Technology in the Department of Defense: Now and in the Future, 1976; (with Andrew Dougherty) Educating the American Military Officer. 1975; The Armed Forces: A Learning Society. Office: One Lomb Memorial Dr Rochester NY 14623

ROSE, MICHAEL DAVID, hotel corp. exec.; b. Akron, Ohio, Mar. 2, 1942; s. William H. and Annabel L. (Kennedy) R.; B.B.A., U. Cin., 1963; LL.B., Harvard U., 1966; m. Regina Marie Franco, Dec. 15, 1973; children—Matthew Derek Franco, Gabrielle Elaine Franco. Admitted to Ohio bar, 1966; lectr. U. Cin., 1966-67; atty. firm Strauss, Troy & Ruehlmann, Cin., 1966-72; exec. v.p. Winegardner Internat., Cin., 1972-74; v.p. hotel group Holiday Inns, Inc., Memphis, 1974-76, pres. hotel group, 1976-78, corp. exec. v.p., 1978-79, pres., 1979—; dir. Commerce Union Bank of Memphis. Bd. dirs. Memphis Arts Council, 1979—, Lausanne Sch., 1978—; mem. Future Memphis, 1979—; mem. nat. adv. com. U. Cin., 1979—. Mem. Ohio Bar Assn., Young Pres.'s Orgn., Memphis C. of C. (fin. com. 1979). Clubs: Econ. Memphis, Racquet of Memphis. Office: Holiday Inns Inc 3742 Lamar Ave Memphis TN 38195

ROSE, MILTON CURTISS, lawyer; b. Cleve., June 5, 1904; s. Benjamin Holly and Evelyn (Curtiss) R.; grad. Phillips Exeter Acad., 1923; A.B., Williams Coll., 1927; LL.B., Harvard, 1930; m. Emily White Mason, Sept. 6, 1930; children—Stephen Curtiss, Mason Curtiss, Jonathan Holly. Admitted to N.Y. bar, 1932; asso. Baldwin, Hutchins & Todd, N.Y.C., 1930-38; partner firm Mudge, Rose, Guthrie & Alexander, and predecessor firms, N.Y.C., 1938—. Pres., dir. Straight Enterprises, Inc., Straight Improvement Co., Inc. Vice pres., bd. dirs. William C. Whitney Found.; bd. dirs. Mary Reynolds Babcock Found., Royal Soc. Medicine Found., Gustavus and Louise Pfeiffer Research Found.; life trustee Pfeiffer Coll.; trustee Shaker Community; trustee emeritus Simon's Rock, Inc. bd. dirs., v.p., sec. Mario Negri Inst. Found. Mem. Am., N.Y. State bar assns., N.Y. County Lawyers Assn., Assn. Bar City N.Y. Presbyn. Clubs: Century Assn., Downtown Assn., Grolier, University (N.Y.C.). Home: PO Box 427 Great Barrington MA 01230 Office: 20 Broad St New York City NY 10005

ROSE, NICHOLAS JOHN, mathematician, educator; b. Ossining, N.Y., Apr. 21, 1924; s. Luigi Chiarito and Pellegrina (Giorgio) R.; M.E., Stevens Inst. Tech., 1944; M.S., N.Y.U., 1949, Ph.D., 1956; m. Muriel Freudenberg, Oct. 25, 1946; children—Toni Catherine, Louis Chiarito, Margaret Louise, John Edward. Instr., Stevens Inst. Tech., Hoboken, N.J., 1946-51, asst. prof., 1951-55, asso. prof., 1955-60, prof., head math. dept., 1960-68; prof. N.C. State U., Raleigh, 1968—, head dept. math., 1968-77. Cons. Bell Telephone Lab., 1955-60. Served with USNR, 1943-46. Recipient Outstanding Tchr. award Stevens Inst. Tech., 1959. Mem. Am. Math. Soc., Math. Assn. Am., Am. Soc. Engring. Edn., Soc. Indsl. and Applied Math. Home: 6713 Candlewood Dr Raleigh NC 27612

ROSE, NOEL RICHARD, immunologist, microbiologist; b. Stamford, Conn., Dec. 3, 1927; s. Samuel Allison and Helen (Richard) R.; B.S., Yale U., 1948; M.A., U. Pa., 1949, Ph.D., 1951; M.D., SUNY, Buffalo, 1964; m. Deborah S. Harber, June 14, 1951; children—Alison, David, Bethany, Jonathan. From instr. to prof. microbiology SUNY Sch. Medicine, Buffalo, 1951-73, dir. Center for Immunology, 1970-73, dir. Erie County labs., 1964-70; dir. WHO Collaborating Center for Autoimmune Disorders, Detroit, 1968—; prof. immunology and microbiology, chmn. dept. immunology and microbiology Wayne State U. Sch. Medicine, 1973—; cons. in field. Recipient award Sigma Xi, 1952, Alpha Omega Alpha, 1976, Lamp award, 1975, Faculty Recognition award Wayne State U. Bd. Govs., 1979, Pres.'s award for excellence in teaching, 1979; Josiah Macy fellow, 1979. Fellow Am. Public Health Assn., Am. Acad. Allergy; Am. Acad. Microbiology; mem. Acad. Clin. Lab. Physicians and Scientists, AAAS, Am. Assn. Immunologists, Am. Assn. Pathologists, Am. Soc. Clin. Pathologists, Am. Soc. Microbiology, Brit. Soc. Immunology, Coll. Am. Pathologists, Société Française d'Immunologie, Can. Soc. Immunology, Soc. Exptl. Biology and Medicine, Sigma Xi, Alpha Omega Alpha. Editor: (with others) International Convocation on Immunology, 1969, Methods in Immunodiagnosis, 1973, Principles of Immunology, 1973, 2d rev. edit., 1979, Specific Receptors of Antibodies, Antigens and Cells, 1973, Manual of Clinical Immunology, 1976, Genetic Control of Autoimmune Disease, 1978; contbr. over 250 articles to profl. publs. Home: 1952 Oak Blvd Birmingham MI 48009 Office: Dept Immunology and Microbiology Wayne State U Sch Medicine 540 E Canfield St Detroit MI 48201

ROSE, PETER EDWARD, baseball player; b. Cin., Apr. 14, 1942; s. Harry Rose; m. Karolyn Ann Englehardt (div.); children—Fawn, Peter. With Cin. Reds, 1963-78, Phila. Phillies, 1979—; mem. Nat. League All-Star Team, 1965, 67-71, 73-79. Named Nat. League Rookie of Year, 1963; Most Valuable Player, 1973; Most Valuable Player, World Series, 1975; Nat. League Player of Year, The Sporting News, 1968, Ball Player of Decade, 1979. Author: (with Bob Hertzel) Charlie Hustle, 1975, Winning Baseball, 1976. Office: PO Box 7575 Philadelphia PA 19101*

ROSE, PETER ISAAC, sociologist, educator; b. Rochester, N.Y., Sept. 5, 1933; s. Aaron E. and Lillian (Feld) R.; A.B., Syracuse U., 1954; M.A., Cornell U., 1957, Ph.D., 1959; m. Hedwig Hella Cohen, Mar. 25, 1956; children—Elisabeth Anne, Daniel Eric. Instr., Goucher Coll., 1958-60; faculty Smith Coll., Northampton, Mass., 1960—, prof. sociology, 1967—, chmn. dept. sociology and anthropology, 1967-74, Sophia Smith prof., 1973; mem. grad. faculty U. Mass., 1961—; Fulbright lectr. U. Leicester (Eng.), 1964-65, Kyoto U., Japan, Flinders U., Australia, 1970; vis. prof. Wesleyan U., Middletown, Conn. 1966-67, U. Colo., summer 1968, Yale, spring 1970, Clark U., 1970-71; cons. editor Random House-Alfred A. Knopf, Time-Life Books. Mem. Am. Sociol. Assn. (council 1974-77), Mass. Sociol. Assn., (pres. 1967-68), Soc. Study Social Problems (v.p. 1968-69), Eastern Sociol. Soc. (v.p. 1970-71), Am. Studies Assn. Author: They and We, 1964, rev., 1974; The Subject is Race, 1968; Strangers in their Midst, 1977; co-author Sociology, 1977; Understanding Society, 1978. Editor: The Study of Society, 1967, 4th edit., 1977; The Ghetto and Beyond, 1969; Americans From Africa, 1970; Nation of Nations, 1972; Seeing Ourselves, 1972, 75; Socialization and the Life Cycle, 1979; co-editor Through Different Eyes, 1973. Home: 66 Paradise Rd Northampton MA 01060

ROSE, PHILIP, stage producer, dir.; b. N.Y.C., July 4, 1921; s. Max and Esther Rosenberg; m. Doris Belack, 1946. Began career as singer, performed with St. Louis Municipal Opera, 1945; co-producer A Raisin in the Sun (N.Y. Drama Critics' Circle award), 1959, Nobody Loves an Albatross, 1963, Nathan Weinstein, Mystic, Connecticut, 1966, Does a Tiger Wear a Necktie?, 1969; producer Semi-Detached, 1960, Purlie Victorious, 1961, Brave Giovanni, 1962, Cafe Crown, 1964, The Owl and the Pussycat, 1964, Kings, 1976, The Trip Back Down, 1977, Shenandoah, 1975-77, Angel, 1978; producer, dir. The Ninety-Day Mistress, 1967; producer, dir., co-writer Purlie, 1970-71; co-producer, co-writer, dir. Shenandoah (Tony award for best musical book), 1975. Mem. Actors Equity, AGVA, AFTRA. *

ROSE, REGINALD, TV writer-producer; b. N.Y.C., Dec. 10, 1920; s. William and Alice (Obendorfer) R.; student Coll. City N.Y., 1937-38; m. Barbara Langbart, Sept. 5, 1943; children—Jonathan, Richard, Andrew and Steven (twins); m. 2d, Ellen McLaughlin, July 6, 1963; children—Thomas, Christopher. Author TV plays, 1951—, including Twelve Angry Men, 1954, The Sacco Vanzetti Story, 1959, The Defenders, 1961-65; film scripts include Crime in the Streets, 1956, Twelve Angry Men, 1957, Baxter!, 1973, Somebody Killed Her Husband, 1978, The Wild Geese, 1978; plays include Black Monday, 1962, Twelve Angry Men, 1958, The Porcelain Year, 1965; books include Six TV Plays, 1956, The Thomas Book. 1972; pres. Defender Prodn., Inc., 1961—, also Ellrose Equities. Pres. Reginald Rose Found., 1963—. Served to 1st lt. AUS, 1942-46. Recipient Emmy awards, 1954, 62, 63; numerous others. Address: 20 Wedgewood Rd Westport CT 06880

ROSE, RICHARD CARLISLE, steel co. exec.; b. Ashtabula, Ohio, Sept., 24, 1920; s. Edward P. and Dorothy (Smith) R.; B.B.A., Case Western Res. U., 1942, J.D., 1947; m. Jean Coon, Dec. 29, 1940; children—Richard Carlisle, Theodore Frederick, Wendell Allen, Ralph Edward. Admitted to Ohio bar, 1947; practice in Ashtabula, 1947-57; sec., house counsel True Temper Corp., Cleve., 1957-67; asst. sec., dir. patents Allegheny Ludlum Steel Corp. (named changed Allegheny Ludlum Industries, Inc.), 1967-68, corp. sec., 1968—, v.p., 1975—. Pres., Trade Relations Council U.S., now chmn. bd. Pres., Kingsville (Ohio) Bd. Edn., 1948-62. Served to lt. USNR, 1942-46. Mem. Am. Bar Assn., Am. Iron and Steel Inst. (chmn.-elect 1978), Am. Soc. Corp. Secs. Episcopalian (sr. warden 1957, vestryman 1954-57). Mason (Shriner). Clubs: Duquesne, Long Vue (Pitts.). Home: 939 Lake St Kingsville OH 44048 also Chatham Center Apts Pittsburgh PA 15219 Office: Two Oliver Plaza Pittsburgh PA 15222

ROSE, RICHARD LOOMIS, lawyer; b. Long Branch, N.J., Oct. 21, 1936; s. Charles Frederick Perrott and Jane Mary (Crotta) R.; B.A., Cornell U., 1958; J.D., Washington and Lee U., 1963; m. Marian Frances Irons, Apr. 1, 1960; children—Linda, Cynthia, Bonnie. Mem. firm Townsend & Lewis, N.Y.C., 1963-65, Cummings & Lockwood, Stamford, Conn., 1965—; dir. Vitam Center, Inc. Served as 1st lt. AUS, 1958-60. Mem. Am., Conn. bar assns., Assn. Bar City N.Y., Phi Delta Phi, Omicron Delta Kappa, Phi Delta Theta. Republican. Episcopalian. Clubs: New Canaan Country, Landmark. Editor Washington and Lee Law Rev. Office: 1 Atlantic St Stamford CT 06904

ROSE, ROBERT CARLISLE, banker; b. Gutheria, Okla., Aug. 14, 1917; s. Warren Glenn and Elizabeth Aileen (Landenberger) R.; student public schs.; diploma Sch. Banking, U. Wis., 1962; m. Maejeanne Harker, June 17, 1939; children—Sharon Sue, Barbara Ann. With Am. Nat. Bank, Vincennes, Ind., 1935—, pres., chief exec. officer, 1975—, also dir. Bd. dirs. Vincennes Community Sch. Corp.; sec. Harmony Soc., Vincennes. Served with USNR, World War II. Mem. Ind. Bankers Assn., Independent Bankers Assn. (dir.), Am. Legion, Vincennes C. of C. (dir.). Democrat. Baptist. Club: Elks. Address: Am Nat Bank 302 Main St Vincennes IN 47591

ROSE, ROBERT LEONARD, newspaperman; b. Detroit, Apr. 21, 1924; s. Leonard Cecil and Mildred Ernestine (Brothers) R.; student U. Colo., 1941-42, Drexel Inst. Tech., 1942-43, U. Del., 1943, U. Denver, 1947; m. Beverly Bain McKee, Aug. 1, 1947 (dec. Sept. 1978); 1 son, Michael. Reporter, Daily Plainsman, Huron, S.D., 1947-49; bur. mgr. U.P., St. Paul-Mpls., 1949-53, Des Moines, 1953-56; reporter-rewriteman, asst. city editor Chgo. Daily News, 1956-60, 1st asst. editor, 1961-63, city editor, 1964-66, West Coast bur. chief, 1966-78; polit. editor Spokane Spokesman-Rev., 1979—; bd. dirs. City News Bur., Chgo., Ill. Served with AUS, 1942-46. Mem. Sigma Chi. Episcopalian. Mason (Shriner), Elk. Clubs: Press, LaSalle St. Rod and Gun (Chgo.). Office: Spokesman-Review Spokane WA 99210

ROSE, ROBERT MARC, psychiatrist; b. Chgo., Apr. 28, 1936; s. Henry and Eve (Feldsott) R.; A.B., Bard Coll., 1957; M.D., Harvard U., 1961; m. Sara Perrott, Mar. 1, 1970; children—Ariana, Alyssa. Research trainee in biology Brookhaven Nat. Lab., L.I., N.Y., 1954-55; research asst. in cellular physiology U. Mich., 1955-56; research asst. dept. neuroendocrinology Walter Reed Army Inst. Research, Washington, summers 1958-60, asst. chief dept. neuroendocrinology, 1965-68, chief dept. psychiatry div. neuropsychiatry, 1968-71; intern Boston City Hosp., 1961-62, assisting physician psychiatry service, 1973-77; resident in psychiatry Mass. Mental Health Center, Boston, 1962-64, research asso. psychopharmacology research lab., 1963-64; resident in psychiatry Mass. Meml. Hosp., also sr. teaching fellow in psychiatry Boston U., 1964-65; research asso. dept. psychiatry Univ. Hosp., Boston, 1964-65; asso. prof. psychiatry Boston U., 1971-75, prof., 1976-77, chief dept. psychosomatic medicine, 1971-77; prof., chmn. dept. psychiatry and behavioral scis. U. Tex. Med. Br., Galveston, 1977—; cons. Yerkes Regional Primate Research Center, 1970—. Recipient John Lockwood award Bard Coll., 1957, John Murray award Boston U. Sch. Medicine, 1965; FAA grantee, 1973-78; NIMH grantee, 1975-77, 76-78. Diplomate Am. Bd. Psychiatry and Neurology. Fellow Am. Psychiat. Assn.; mem. AAAS, Am. Psychosomatic Soc. (council 1974-77), Am. Psychopathol. Assn.; Endocrine Soc., Psychiat. Research Soc., Public Responsibility in Medicine and Research (treas. 1974-77), Soc. Neurosci. (council Galveston chpt. 1977-80), Am. Coll. Neuropsychopharmacology, Boylston Soc., Harvard Med. Soc. Jewish. Contbr. numerous articles to profl. publs.; editorial bd. Archives Sexual Behavior, 1975—, Jour. Behavioral Medicine, 1977—, Jour. Human Stress, 1974—, Psychosomatic Medicine, 1971—, Ann. Rev. Medicine, 1978—; asso. editor Hormones and Behavior. Home: 1517 Bayou Shore Dr Galveston TX 77550 Office: U Tex Med Br Galveston TX 77550

ROSE, ROWLAND G., pharm. co. exec.; b. 1916; B.S., N.Y. U., 1937; grad. Advanced Mgmt. Program, Harvard, 1960; m. Elizabeth K. Stewart, Nov. 26, 1942; children—Mary, Rowland G., A. Stewart, W. Duncan, John, James. With W.R. Grace & Co., 1937-40; Am. Overseas Airline, 1945-47, W.R. Grace & Co., 1947-58; with Miles Labs., Inc., 1958—, treas., 1964-67, v.p., chief fin. officer, 1967-75, exec. v.p., 1975-76, dir., mem. exec. and fin. coms., 1969-76, pres., chief operating officer, chmn. fin. com., 1976—, chmn. exec. com., 1978—; dir. First Nat. Bank of Elkhart, Coachmen Industries, Protection Mut. Ins. Co. Served with USNR, 1940-45. C.P.A., N.Y. Address: 1127 Myrtle St Elkhart IN 46514

ROSE, SIDNEY RUDOLPH, lawyer; b. Los Angeles, Aug. 25, 1927; s. Joseph and Goldie (Turetz) R.; student Los Angeles City Coll., 1945, U. N.Mex., 1945-46, U. Calif. at Los Angeles, 1946-48; J.D., U. So. Calif., 1951; m. Leontine R. Flam, Jan. 29, 1950; children—Michael S., James J., Thomas A. Admitted to Calif. bar, 1952; partner firm Flam, Valensi & Rose, Los Angeles, 1952-59; partner Valensi & Rose, Beverly Hills, 1960-70, Century City, 1970—. Vice chmn. Beverly Hills Land Use Citizens Council. Bd. govs. Beverly Hills Municipal League, 1970-74; bd. dirs. Beverly Hills Residents Assn. Served with USNR, 1945-46. Mem. Am., Los Angeles County (trustee 1979-80), Wilshire (charter; dir.), Beverly Hills (bd. govs. 1970—, pres.-elect 1979-80) bar assns., State Bar Calif., Beverly Hills Bar Assn. Law Found. (pres. 1973-74, dir. 1974-76), Am. Judicature Soc., Constl. Rights Found. (lawyers adv. council 1979—), Los Angeles County Mus. Art, UCLA Chancellors Assn., UCLA Alumni Assn., U. So. Calif. Law Alumni Assn., Legion Lex. Office: 1880 Century Park E Suite 1518 Century City Los Angeles CA 90067

ROSE, WILLIAM, screenwriter; b. Jefferson City. Films include Gift Horse (Glory at Sea); Genevieve; The Maggie (High and Dry); Touch and Go; The Ladykillers; Man in the Sky; Davy; The Smallest Show on Earth; It's A Mad, Mad, Mad, Mad World; The Russians Are Coming, The Russians Are Coming; The Flim Flam Man; Guess Who's Coming to Dinner (Oscar award 1967); The Secret of Santa Vittorio. Address: Care William Morris Agy 151 El Camino Beverly Hills CA 90212*

ROSE, WILLIAM ALFRED, lawyer; b. Pulaski, Tenn., Oct. 7, 1900; s. William Alfred and Sarah Lilian (Tardy) R.; A.B., U. Ala., 1921, LL.B., 1923; J.D., Yale U., 1924; m. Anne Elizabeth Travis, May 2, 1942; children—William Alfred, Elizabeth Travis Rose Sledge. Admitted to Ala. bar, 1923, since practiced in Birmingham; ct. apptd. atty. for receiver in extensive litigation in Fed. Dist. and Appellate cts., 1933-37; mem. firm Bradley, Arant, Rose & White, and predecessors, 1935—, specializing financing by govt. bodies. Mem. Am. Bar Assn. (council secs. local govt. law and legal edn.), Ala., Birmingham bar assns., Am. Judicature Soc., Nat. Conf. Commrs. Uniform State Laws (life), Assn. Bar City N.Y., Sons Colonial Wars, S.O.R., St. Andrew's Soc. Middle South, Birmingham Little Theater (pres. 1942-43), Phi Beta Kappa, Phi Delta Phi (pres. 1939-41), Phi Gamma Delta. Episcopalian (treas., mem. exec. council Diocese of Ala. 1946-71, chmn. diocesan endowment fund 1965-71, warden emeritus ch. 1961—). Clubs: Mountain Brook Country, Relay House, Execs. (pres. 1947-48). Contbr. articles to legal jours. Home: 28 Country Club Blvd Birmingham AL 35213 Office: Brown-Marx Bldg Birmingham AL 35203

ROSEBERG, CARL ANDERSSON, educator, sculptor; b. Vinton, Iowa, Sept. 26, 1916; s. Swan Bernard and Selma (Olson) R.; B.F.A., U. Iowa, 1939, postgrad., 1939-41, M.F.A., 1947; postgrad. Cranbrook Acad. Art, summers 1947-48, U. Hawaii, 1950-51, U. Va., summer 1964, Mysore (India) U., summer 1965, Tyler Sch. Art, Temple U., summer 1967; m. Virginia M. Gorman, Aug. 23, 1942. Faculty, Coll. of William and Mary, Williamsburg, Va., 1947—, prof. fine arts, 1966—, William and Mary Heritage fellow, 1968—, mem. faculty com. on Asian House, coll. rep. on Oriental Studies with Richmond Area Univ. Center. Exhibited one man shows at Radford Coll., 1962, Roanoke Fine Art Gallery, 1962-63, Norfolk Mus., 1963, Asheville (N.C.) Gallery Art, 1963, Longwood Coll., 1966, Phi Beta Kappa Hall, William and Mary Coll., 1970; exhibited in numerous group shows; represented in permanent collections at U. Iowa, Springfield (Mo.) Mus., Va. Mus. Fine Arts, Colonial Williamsburg, Chrysler Mus. Norfolk, Rockingham County Citizens Com., Longwood Coll., Farmville, Va., Thalhimer Bros., Inc., others; designer, creator bronze meml. plaque honoring Donald W. Davis for Millington Hall, Coll. William and Mary, 1970, bronze plaque honoring William G. Guy, Rogers Hall, 1975; designer James City County Bicentennial Medallion, 1976. Founding bd. mem. 20th Century Gallery, Williamsburg. Served to comdr. USNR, 1941-45, 50-52; ret. Res. Recipient Thomas Jefferson award, 1971, numerous art awards. Fellow Internat. Inst. Arts and Letters; mem. Audubon Artists Am., Coll. Art Assn., Tidewater Artists Assn., Asian Soc., Res. Officers Assn. Am., Navy League U.S., Lambda Chi Alpha. Presbyn. Mason. Club: Williamsburg German. Home: 110 Hickory Signpost Rd Williamsburg VA 23185

ROSEBERY, DEAN ARLO, educator; b. Stahl, Mo., Sept. 23, 1919; s. Dalton C. and Chloe E. (Sanders) R.; B.S., N.E. Mo. State U., 1941; postgrad. Midshipman Sch. Columbia, 1942; Ph.D. in Aquatic Zoology, Va. Poly. Inst., 1946; m. Amy Ayers, Mar. 19, 1943; children—Frank, Margaret. Asst. chief Div. Fish Va. Commn. Inland Fisheries, 1951; prof. biology N.E. Mo. State U., Kirksville, 1952—, head div. sci., 1962—. Dir. NSF ednl. sponsored projects on campus, 1968—; dir. summer sequential program in ecology; dir. Environmental Edn. Act Fund for Sch. Adminstrs. Mem. State Adv. Com. on Environmental Studies. Chmn. Salvation Army Bd., 1972. Served to lt. USNR, 1942-46. Recipient Mo. Sci. Educator award, 1969. Fellow A.A.A.S. (life); mem. Am. Fisheries Soc., Nat. Geographic, Nat. Sci. Tchrs. Assn., Mo. Sci. Tchrs. Assn., Mo. Tchrs. Assn., Nat. Assn. Biology Tchrs. Methodist (mem. area com. on higher edn.). Rotarian (pres. Internat. Club Kirksville 1968). Home: 1208 E Illinois St Kirksville MO 63501

ROSECRANCE, RICHARD NEWTON, polit. scientist, educator; b. Milw., Oct. 24, 1930; s. Francis Chase and Marjorie N. R.; B.A. in Polit. Sci. with high honors, Swarthmore Coll., 1952; M.A. in Internat. Affairs, Harvard U., 1954, Ph.D. in Govt., 1957; m. Barbara Joan Benjamin, Aug. 26, 1967; children by previous marriage—Gail W., Richard C., Anne W.; stepchildren—Jane Dreeben, Jill Dreeben, Thomas Dreeben. Ford intern in polit. sci. Brown U., 1956-57; instr. polit. sci. UCLA, 1957-58, asst. prof., 1958-62, asso. prof., 1962-67, dir. security studies program, 1962-67; mem. Policy Planning Council, Dept. State, 1967-68; prof., dir. internat. security program, U. Calif., Berkeley, 1967-70; Walter S. Carpenter Jr. prof. internat. and comparative politics Cornell U., Ithaca, N.Y., 1970—; cons. Rand Corp.; Fulbright scholar in internat. relations Australian Nat. U., Canberra, 1954-56, vis. fellow, 1964; Rockefeller fellow Kings Coll. U. London, 1964-65; Guggenheim fellow, 1973-74. Mem. Internat. Inst. Strategic Studies of London, Council Fgn. Relations, Internat. Studies Assn. (pres. 1976), Am. Polit. Sci. Assn. Author: Australian Diplomacy and Japan: 1945-51, 1962; Action and Reaction in World Politics, 1963; Defense of the Realm: British Strategy in the Nuclear Epoch, 1968; International Relations: Peace or War?, 1973; contbr. articles to profl. jours.; editor The Dispersion of Nuclear Weapons, 1964; The Future of the International Strategic System, 1972; America as an Ordinary Country: U.S. Foreign Policy and the Future, 1976. Home: 115 Cayuga Heights Rd Ithaca NY 14850 Office: Center for Internat Studies Uris Hall 160 Cornell U Ithaca NY 14853

ROSELIEP, RAYMOND, clergyman, author; b. Farley, Iowa, Aug. 11, 1917; s. John Albert and Anna Elizabeth (Anderson) R.; B.A., Loras Coll., 1939; postgrad. Cath. U. Am., 1939-43, M.A., 1948;

Ph.D., U. Notre Dame, 1954. Ordained secular priest Roman Catholic Ch., 1943; asst. pastor Immaculate Conception Ch., Gilbertville, Iowa, 1943-45; mng. editor Witness, 1945-46; faculty dept. English, Loras Coll., Dubuque, Iowa, 1946-66; resident chaplain Holy Family Hall, Mt. St. Francis, Dubuque, 1966—. Poet-in-residence Georgetown U., summer 1964. Recipient Montgomery Poetry award Soc. Midland Authors, 1968, Henderson award Haiku Soc. Am., 1977. Mem. Acad. Am. Poets, Hist. Soc. Ia., Delta Epsilon Sigma. Author: Some Letters of Lionel Johnson, 1954; (poetry) The Linen Bands, 1961; The Small Rain, 1963; Love Makes the Air Light, 1965; (poetry and prose) Voyages to the Inland Sea, IV, 1974; (poetry) Flute Over Walden, 1976; (poetry) Light Footsteps, 1976; Walk In Love, 1976; A Beautiful Woman Moves with Grace, 1976; Sun in His Belly, 1977; Step on the Rain, 1977; Wake to the Bell, 1977; (poetry) A Day in the Life of Sobi-Shi, 1978; Sailing Bones, 1978; (prose) Devilish Wine, 1979. Contbr. poetry and revs. to numerous mags. Address: Holy Family Hall 3340 Windsor Extension Dubuque IA 52001. *Whatever success I enjoy as a poet must reflect the philosophy behind my work. Through poems I try to materialize spirit and spiritualize matter. I attempt to project the dissidence at the heart of all life: the clash between darkness and light, good and evil, purposelessness and purpose, avowal and denial, the sacred and the profane, flesh and spirit, death and the thirst for immortality, Yahweh and oblivion. Believing as George Eliot did that "love is the word of all work," I publish my poems so that I might impose fresh order on the disorder of the world. A poem is a plumb line by which all of us can better understand ourselves and the universe. A poem completes and caps our being.*

ROSELLE, WILLIAM CHARLES, librarian; b. Vandergrift, Pa., June 30, 1936; s. William John and Suzanne Esther (Clever) R.; B.A., Thiel Coll., 1958; M.L.S., U. Pitts., 1963; m. Marsha Louise Lucas, Aug. 2, 1959; 1 son, Paul Lucas. Mem. faculty Milton Hershey Sch., Hershey, Pa., 1960-62; trainee Pa. State Library, 1962-63; asst. catalog librarian Pa. State U., 1963-65; engring., math. librarian U. Iowa, 1965-66, library adminstrv. asst., 1966-69, asst. dir. libraries, 1969-71; prof., dir. library U. Wis.-Milw., 1971—; chmn. planning task force on computing U. Wis. System, 1973-74, library planning study com., 1978-79; chmn. computing mgmt. rev. team U. Wis.-Stout, 1976; library cons. Grambling (La.) State U., Viterbo Coll., LaCrosse, Wis., N.C. A. and T. U., Greensboro, Mt. Mary Coll., Milw., U. Ill.-Chgo. Circle; participant library adminstrs. devel. program U. Md., 1973, Mgmt. Skills Inst., Assn. Research Libraries, Kansas City, Mo., 1977; mem. sect. geography and map libraries Internat. Fedn. Library Assns. and Instns., 1978—. Served with AUS, 1958-60. Lic. profl. guide State of Mont. Hon. fellow Am. Geog. Soc.; mem. ALA (life), Iowa (chmn. audit com. 1968-70, chmn. intellectual freedom com. 1969-70), Wis. library assns., Midwest Acad. Librarians Conf. (chmn. 1969-71), A.A.U.P. (treas. U. Ia. chpt. 1969-70), Council Wis. Librarians (chmn. 1973-74), Soc. Tympanuchus Cupido Pinnatus, Milw. Civil War Round Table, Beta Beta Beta, Beta Phi Mu, Phi Alpha Theta, Phi Kappa Phi, Phi Delta Kappa. Luth. Contbr. articles to profl. jours. Home: 324 Sunny Ln Thiensville WI 53092 Office: U Wis Milw Golda Meir Library Milwaukee WI 53201

ROSEMAN, NORMAN BERT, advt. and pub. co. exec.; b. N.Y.C., Apr. 13, 1928; s. Sol and Lillian Russell (Rudinger) R.; m. Marilyn Mandel, June 5, 1955; children—Scott, Jayne. Account exec. Huber Hoge & Sons, Inc., 1952-56; partner Advercom, Inc., N.Y.C., 1956-69; v.p. LIN Broadcasting, 1969-71; v.p. Greybank Advt., N.Y.C., 1971—; pub. Soap Opera Digest, N.Y.C., 1975—. Bd. dirs. N.Y. Fedn. Reform Synagogues; pres. Central Synagogue of Nassau County, 1976-78. Served with USNR, 1945-46. Mem. Nat. Acad. TV Arts and Scis. Club: B'nai B'rith. Home: 22 Pickwick Terr Rockville Centre NY 11570 Office: 420 Lexington Ave New York NY 10017

ROSEMAN, SAUL, biochemist; b. Bklyn., Mar. 9, 1921; s. Emil and Rose (Markowitz) R.; B.S., City Coll. N.Y., 1941; M.S., U. Wis., 1944, Ph.D., 1947; m. Martha Ozrowitz, Sept. 9, 1941; children—Mark Alan, Dorinda Ann, Cynthia Bernice. From instr. to asst. prof. U. Chgo., 1948-53; from asst. prof. to prof. biol. chemistry, also Rackham Arthritis Research Unit, U. Mich., 1953-65; Ralph S. O'Connor prof. biology Johns Hopkins, 1965—, chmn. dept., 1969-73, dir. McCollum-Pratt Inst., 1969-73; cons. NIH, NSF, Am. Cancer Soc., Hosp. for Sick Children, Toronto; sci. counselor Nat. Cancer Inst. Served with AUS, 1944-46. Recipient Sesquicentennial award U. Mich., 1967, T. Duckett Jones Meml. award Helen Hay Whitney Found., 1973, Rosenstiehl award Brandeis U., 1974. Mem. Am. Soc. Biol. Chemists, Am. Acad. Arts and Scis., Nat. Acad. Scis., Am. Chem. Soc., Am. Soc. Microbiologists. Author articles on metabolism of complex molecules containing carbohydrates. Mem. editorial bd. Jour. Biol. Chemistry, Jour. Lipid Research, Jour. Membrane Biology, Developmental Biology, Biochimica et Biophysica Acta, Biochemistry. Home: 8206 Cranwood Ct Baltimore MD 21208

ROSE MARIE, actress; b. N.Y.C., Aug. 15; d. Frank and Stella (Gluscak) Mazzetta; ed. profl. children's schs., also parochial schs.; m. William R. Guy, June 19, 1946 (dec. 1964); 1 dau., Georgiana Marie. Former co-star Dick Van Dyke TV series, Bob Cummings Show, Doris Day TV show; regular panelist Hollywood Sqs.; co-star Broadway mus. comedy Top Banana; appeared various motion pictures, commls., also night clubs. Chmn., Easter Seal Soc. Mem. Screen Actors' Guild, AFTRA, Actors' Equity, Am. Guild Variety Artists. Club: Variety. Home: Van Nuys CA Office: care J Robert Prete Mgmt Co 4805 Sepulveda Blvd Sherman Oaks CA 91403. *My motto for life has always been-I am third. First comes God; second comes everyone else; and I am third!*

ROSEMBERG, EUGENIA, physician, scientist, educator, med. research administr.; b. Buenos Aires, Argentina, Apr. 25, 1918; d. Pedro and Fanny (Hestrin) Rosemberg; came to U.S., 1948, naturalized, 1956; B.S., Liceo Nacional de Senoritas, Buenos Aires, 1936; M.D., U. Buenos Aires, 1944. Intern Hosp. Pirovano, Buenos Aires, 1940-41; resident Hosp. Nacional de Clinicas, U. Hosp., U. Buenos Aires, 1941-44, asso. in pediatrics, 1943-48, instr. in anatomy Med. Sch., 1940-46, instr. pediatrics, 1946-48; practice medicine specializing in pediatrics, 1946-48; research in endocrinology, Balt., 1948-51, Worcester, Mass., 1955—; Mead Johnson fellow dept. endocrinology Johns Hopkins Med. Sch., Balt., 1948-49; vis. scientist Med. Sch., U. Montevideo (Uruguay), 1950; research fellow NIH, Bethesda, Md., 1951-53, Nat. Inst. Arthritis and Metabolic Diseases, 1951-53; research fellow Med. Research Inst. and Hosp., Oklahoma City, 1953; mem. staff Worcester Found. Exptl. Biology, Shrewsbury, Mass., 1953-62; research dir. Med. Research Inst. of Worcester, Inc., 1962—; cons. Center for Population Research, Nat. Inst. Child Health and Human Devel., NIH, 1969-70, chief contraceptive devel. br., 1970-71; prof. pediatrics U. Md. Hosp., Balt., 1970-73; prof. research U. Mass. Med. Sch., Worcester, 1972—; mem. staff Worcester City Hosp., 1955—, dir. clin. research, 1972—. Sec. subcom. on gonadotropins Nat. Pituitary Agy., Nat. Inst. Arthritis and Metabolic Diseases, 1965-69, chmn., 1969—, mem. med. adv. bd., 1969-72, 73—, sec. subcom. on standards endocrinology study sect., 1968. Fellow A.A.A.S.; mem. Am. Med. Women's Assn., Endocrine Soc. U.S. (mem. com. pub. affairs 1971, v.p. 1975-76), Soc. for Research in Biology of Reproduction, Soc. for Study of Reproduction, Am. Fertility Soc., Peru Fertility Soc. (fgn. corr.), N.Y. Acad. Scis., New Eng. Cardiovascular Soc., Am., Mass. heart assns., Argentine Endocrine Soc., Argentine Pediatric Soc., Sociedad Argentine Para El Estudio de la Esterilidad., Pan Am. Med. Women's Alliance, Am. Soc. Andrology (program chmn. 1975-76; exec. council 1976—, chmn. publ. com. 1975—), Internat. Com. for Study Andrology (exec. council 1976-79). Author: Gonadotropins, 1968; (with C.A. Paulsen) The Human Testis, 1970; Gonadotropin Therapy in Female Infertility, 1973; (with C. Gual) Hypothalamic Hypophysiotropic Hormones—Physiological and Clinical Studies, 1973. Mem. editorial bd. Giner, 1970—; Procs. 1st Ann. Meeting Am. Soc. Andrology, supplement, Vol. 8, 1976; Andrologia, 1978—; Jour. Andrology, 1979-82; Internat. Jour. Andrology, 1978—; asso. editor Reproduccion, 1970—, Andrologia jour., 1974-77. Contbr. articles and book chpts. on research in endocrinology to med. texts and jours. Translator: (from Spanish) Diagnosis and Treatment of Endocrine Disorders in Childhood and Adolescence (L. Wilkins). Home: 14 Ashland St Worcester MA 01609 Office: Medical Research Institute 26 Queen St Worcester MA 01610

ROSEMOND, GEORGE P., surgeon, educator; b. Hillsborough, N.C., Aug. 23, 1910; s. Charles Edwin and Bessie (Parrott) R.; B.S., U. N.C., 1932; M.D., Temple U., 1934, M.S. in Surgery, 1939; m. Lois Jean Mason, Aug. 21, 1937 (dec. Mar. 2, 1976); 1 dau., Linda (Mrs. Howard W. Buzzard, Jr.). Intern, Temple U. Hosp., 1934-36, resident, 1936-39; mem. faculty Temple U. Health Scis. Center, 1939—, prof. surgery, 1960—, chmn. div., 1960-73, chmn. dept. surgery, 1963-73; asso. attending surgeon St. Christopher's Hosp. Children, Phila., 1950-74; surgeon Temple U. Hosp., 1939—; mem. med. adv. com. Wilkes-Barre VA Hosp., 1973; mem. ad hoc cancer control adv. com. Nat. Cancer Inst., 1972-73; dir. Blue Cross of Greater Phila., 1977-79. Recipient Humanitarian award Am. Cancer Soc., Owl award Temple U., 1976; St. Francis Surg. award, 1973, others. Diplomate Am. Bd. Surgery, Am. Bd. Thoracic Surgery. Fellow emeritus Am. Coll. Chest Physicians, A.C.S. (sr. mem. Commn. Cancer 1956-71, chmn. nominating com. fellows 1956-71, others; mem. AMA, Am. Assn. Thoracic Surgery (sr.), Am. Surg. Assn., Am. Trudeau Soc., Soc. Surg. Chairmen, Internat. Soc. Surgeons, Phila. Coll. Physicians (pres. 1978-80), Phila. Acad. Surgery (pres. 1968-69), Phila. County Med. Soc. (pres. 1965-66, Strittmatter award 1978), Pa. Med. Soc. (chmn. Phila. delegation 1967-70, pres. 1971-72), Surgeons Travel Club (sec. 1976-79), Laennec Soc. Phila. (pres. 1964), Wainwright Tumor Clinic Assn., Am. Cancer Soc. (nat. del., nat. dir. 1968, pres. Phila. div. 1967-68, nat. v.p., pres. 1974-75, dir. Phila. div. 1977, other com. assignments, hon. Life mem.), Pa. Soc. for Advancement Med. Research (pres. 1967); hon. mem. Venezuela Cancer Soc., Alaska State Med. Soc., others. Cons. editor Breast, 1975—. Home: Box 37 RD 1 Malvern PA 19355 Office: 3401 N Broad St Philadelphia PA 19140

ROSEN, ALEX, coll. dean; b. N.Y.C., July 27, 1915; s. Morris and Celia (Perelstien) R.; B.A., N.Y. U., 1942, Ph.D., 1961; M.Sc., Columbia, 1947; m. Rose S. Shenderoff, Aug. 14, 1939; children—Fred, Robert. Dir. pub. relations 110th St. Community Center, N.Y.C., 1946-48; exec. dir. Elmira Jewish Community Center and Welfare Fund, 1948-53; asso. dir. intergroup relations study Cornell U., 1951-52; asst. dir. bur. personnel and tng. Nat. Jewish Welfare Bd., 1953-58; cons. Council on Social Work Edn., 1958-60; dean Grad. Sch. Social Work N.Y.U., 1960-70; prof. social and community medicine, dir. urban health affairs N.Y.U. Med. Center, 1970—. Served with AUS, 1943-46. Recipient Annisfield-Wolfe award Saturday Rev. mag., 1955. Fellow N.Y. Acad. Medicine; mem. Nat. Assn. Social Workers, Nat. Conf. Social Work, Alpha Kappa Delta. Author: (with John P. Dean) A Manual of Intergroup Relations, 1955. Home: 58 Washington Mews New York City NY 10003 Office: NY U Med Center New York City NY 10003

ROSEN, BERNARD, educator; b. N.Y.C., July 21, 1920; s. Jacob and Rose (Rosansky) R.; B.A., U. Ala., 1940; M.A., 1941; postgrad. U. Ill., 1941-42; m. Adele Berman, July 11, 1942; children—Bernard Arnold, Stephen Louis. Chief profl. and adminstrv. exams. U.S. Civil Service Commn., Chgo., 1946-48, field operations supr., Washington, 1948-53, dep. regional dir., Cin., 1953-54, dir. fed. incentives award program, Washington, 1954-58, regional dir., San Francisco, 1958-62, dep. exec. dir., Washington, 1965-71, exec. dir., 1971-75; dep. dir. personnel State Dept., 1962-63, dir., 1963-64; counselor embassy for adminstrn., Athens, Greece, 1964-65; prof. pub. adminstrn. Am. U., 1975—. Mem. President's Adv. Council Intergovtl. Personnel, 1971—; mem. pub. sector com. Nat. Center for Productivity and Quality of Working Life. Trustee Washington div. Am. Cancer Soc. Served with AUS, 1943-45. Recipient Arthur S. Fleming award, 1955; Civil Service Commr.'s award for distinguished service, 1970. Mem. Am. Soc. Pub. Adminstrn. (nat. council 1958-61, Nat. Capitol chpt. award for exceptional integrity in pub. service 1975), Internat. Personnel Mgmt. Assn., San Francisco Fed. Bus. Assn. (pres. 1961), Phi Beta Kappa. Club: Commonwealth (San Francisco). Home: 4000 Massachusetts Ave NW Washington DC 20016

ROSEN, BERNARD H., chem. engr.; b. N.Y.C., Sept. 29, 1922; s. Max and Dorothy (Hildebrand) R.; B.S. in Chem. Engring., Coll. City N.Y., 1943; M.S., N.Y. U., 1947; postgrad. Harvard, 1943-44, Okla. A. and M., 1949, Ill. Inst. Tech., 1949-50, Columbia, 1955-56; m. Anita Ruth Greenberg, Aug. 26, 1947; children—Jeffrey Paul, Seth Gordon, Lise Ann. Grad. asst. N.Y. U., 1946-47; with Cities Service Research and Devel. Co., 1947—, successively research chem. engr., Tallant, Okla., asso. chemist East Chicago, Ind., chem. engr., Camden, N.J., asst. v.p., N.Y.C., 1947-57, mgr. products devel., Cranbury, N.J., 1957-58, mgr. Cranbury Lab., 1958-65, dir. product and process research Cities Service Oil Co., 1965-71, mgr. research and planning, chems. and metals group Cities Service Co., N.Y.C., 1971-72, dir. research, 1972-76; pres. Cities Service Research & Devel. Co., Cranbury, 1972-76, gen. mgr. tech. systems div., Tulsa, 1976-78, gen. mgr. metal fabrication, Chester, N.Y., 1978—. Served as 1st lt. AUS, 1943-46; capt. Res. Mem. Am. Chem. Soc., Am. Inst. Chem. Engrs., AAAS, Harvard Engring. Soc., N.Y., N.J. acads. sci. Contbr. articles to profl. jours. Patentee in field. Home: 13 Buena Vista Rumson NJ 07760 Office: Cities Service Chester Cable Ops Oakland Ave Chester NY 10918

ROSEN, CHARLES WELLES, pianist; b. N.Y.C., May 5, 1927; s. Irwin and Anita (Gerber) R.; B.A. summa cum laude, Princeton, 1947, M.A., 1949, Ph.D., 1951; Dr. Music honoris causa, Trinity Coll., Dublin, 1976, U. Leeds, 1976. New York debut at Town Hall, 1951; first recording Debussy Etudes, 1951; asst. prof. modern langs. Mass. Inst. Tech., 1953-55; prof. music U. N.Y. State at Stony Brook, 1971—; Messenger lectr. Cornell U., 1975; Ernest Bloch prof. U. Calif. at Berkeley, 1977. Recordings include Bach's Art of Fugue, Beethoven's Last Six Sonatas, Elliott Carter's Double Concerto; concertized throughout Europe and Am. Recipient Nat. Book award, 1972; Edison prize, 1974; Deems Taylor award ASCAP, 1972, 76; nominated for Grammy award for Beethoven's Late Sonatas, 1973, for Beethoven's Diabelli Variations, 1979; Fulbright fellow, 1951-53, Guggenheim fellow, 1973-74. Mem. Nat. Acad. Arts and Scis. Author: The Classical Style: Haydn, Mozart, Beethoven, 1971; Schoenberg, 1975.

ROSEN, FRED, biologist, educator; b. Newark, Dec. 18, 1921; s. Samuel and Leah (Peterman) R.; B.S. in Agrl. Biochemistry, U. Wis., 1944; Ph.D. (Nutrition Found. fellow), Duke U., 1949; m. Rochelle Gruber, Dec. 25, 1949; children—Karen, Amy. Research asso. Ortho Research Found., Raritan, N.J., 1950-56; asso. chief cancer scientist and asso. dir. Grace Cancer Drug Center, Roswell Park Meml. Inst., Buffalo, 1956—, asso. dir. sci. affairs, 1979—; research prof. biochemistry State U. N.Y. at Buffalo, 1959—. Research prof. biology Canisius Coll., Buffalo, 1967—; research prof. chemistry Niagara U., Niagara Falls, N.Y., 1967—. Served with AUS, 1943. USPHS fellow, NIH fellow, 1949-50; NIH research grantee, 1958—. Mem. Am. Chem. Soc., Am. Assn. Cancer Research, Am. Inst. Nutrition. Am. Soc. Biol. Chemists, Endocrine Soc., N.Y. Acad. Scis., Sigma Xi, Phi Lambda Upsilon. Contbr. articles to books, sci. jours. Home: 37 South Ln Orchard Park NY 14127 Office: 666 Elm St Buffalo NY 14203

ROSEN, FRED SAUL, immunologist, educator; b. Newark, May 26, 1930; s. Philip and Amelia (Feld) R.; A.B., Lafayette Coll., 1951, D.Sc. (hon.), 1978; M.D., Western Res. U., 1955; M.A. (hon.), Harvard U., 1972. Intern, Children's Hosp., Boston, 1955-56, resident, 1956-57, 59-60; faculty Harvard U. Med. Sch., 1955—, James L. Gamble prof. pediatrics, 1972—; staff Children's Hosp. Med. Center, Boston, 1955—; dir. Center for Blood Research, Boston, since 1972—; vis. prof. Royal Postgrad. Med. Sch., London, 1974. Served to sr. asst. surgeon USPHS, 1957-59. Mem. Am. Soc. Clin. Investigation, Soc. Pediatric Research, Infectious Disease Soc. Am. (councillor 1972-75), Am. Assn. Immunologists, Brit. Soc. Immunology, Am. Pediatric Soc. Clubs: Harvard of N.Y.C.; United University (London, Eng.). Contbr. numerous articles to sci. publs. Home: 100 Memorial Dr Cambridge MA 02142 Office: 300 Longwood Ave Boston MA 02115

ROSEN, GEORGE, economist, educator; b. Leningrad, USSR, Feb. 7, 1920; s. Leon and Rebecca (Rosenoer) R.: B.A., Bklyn. Coll., 1940; M.A., Princeton U., 1942, Ph.D., 1950; 1 son, Mark. Prof. econs. Bard Coll., Annadale-on-Hudson, N.Y., 1946-50; economist Dept. State, Washington, 1951-54, Council Econ. Indsl. Research, Washington, 1954-55, M.I.T., Cambridge, 1955-59, UN, N.Y.C., 1959-60, Ford Found., N.Y.C., India, 1960-62, Rand Corp., Santa Monica, Calif., 1962-67; chief economist Asian Devel. Bank, Manila, Philippines, 1967-71; prof. econs. U. Ill., Chgo., 1972—, head dept., 1972-77. Ford Found. fellow N.Y. U., 1971-72; U. Ill. grantee, 1977-78. Author: Industrial Change in India, 1958; Some Aspects of Industrial Finance in India, 1962; Democracy and Economic Change in India, 1966, 67; Peasant Society in a Changing Economy, 1975. Home: 821 Mulford St Evanston IL 60202 Office: University of Illinois PO Box 4348 Chicago IL 60680

ROSEN, GERALD HARRIS, physicist, educator; b. Mount Vernon, N.Y., Aug. 10, 1933; s. David A. and Shirley (Schapiro) R.; B.S.E. (Guggenheim Jet Propulsion scholar, Whiton Engring.-Physics scholar), Princeton U., 1955, M.A. (NSF predoctoral fellow), 1956, Ph.D., 1958; m. Sarah Louise Sweet, June 8, 1963; children—Lawrence Alexander, Karlyn Penelope. NSF predoctoral fellow Inst. Theoretical Physics, Utrecht, Netherlands, 1957-58; research asso. dept. aero. engring. Princeton, 1958-59; NSF postdoctoral fellow Inst. Theoretical Physics, Stockholm, Sweden, 1959-60; tech. cons. weapon systems evaluation div. The Pentagon, 1960; prin. scientist Martin-Marietta Aerospace div., Balt., 1960-63; cons. to a tech. v.p. Southwest Research Inst., 1963-66; prof. physics Drexel U., Phila., 1966-73, M.R. Wehr prof. physics, 1973—. Cons. indsl. and govt. agys.; reviewer Math. Revs., 1964—, jours. of Am. Phys. Soc., 1960—. Sponsor San Antonio Chamber Music Soc., 1963-66; mem. Franklin Inst., 1967—, Phila. Art Mus., 1969—. Fellow Am. Phys. Soc., AAAS; mem. Am. Math. Soc. Author: Formulations of Classical and Quantum Dynamical Theory, 1969. Contbr. articles to profl. jours. Patentee in field. Home: 415 Charles Ln Wynnewood PA 19096 Office: Dept Physics Drexel U Philadelphia PA 19104. *The meaning of life has transcended human understanding up to the present time, but there are reasons to believe that future discoveries in science will illuminate the significance of life in nature. We must break completely free of non-rational dogma and illusion, and attempt to solve this mystery with factual clues revealed by scientific progress.*

ROSEN, GERALD ROBERT, editor; b. N.Y.C., Nov. 17, 1930; s. Sol and Essie (Shapiro) R.; B.S., Ind. U., 1951, M.A., 1953; m. Lois Lehrman, May 9, 1958; 1 son, Evan Mark. Intelligence analyst Dept. Def., N.Y.C., 1955-58; asso. editor Challenge: The Mag. of Econ. Affairs, N.Y.C., 1959-61, mng. editor, 1961-64, 65-66; sr. editor Dun's Rev., N.Y.C., 1964-65, nat. affairs editor, 1967-77, exec. editor, 1977—. Served with CIC, U.S. Army, 1953-55. Mem. Soc. Am. Bus. and Econ. Writers, N.Y. Fin. Writers Assn., White House Corrs. Assn. Club: Nat. Press. Home: 1185 Park Ave New York NY 10028 Office: Dun's Rev 666 Fifth Ave New York NY 10019

ROSEN, JAMES MAHLON, painter, art historian, educator; b. Detroit, Dec. 3, 1933; s. Joseph and Lillian R.; B.S., Cooper Union, 1957; M.F.A., Cranbrook Acad. Art, 1958; m. Mignon Evans, Feb. 26, 1978; children—Shira Del, Phyllis Dresser, Jeremy-Joseph. Exhibitions include: Betty Parsons Gallery, N.Y.C., Donald Morris Gallery, Detroit, Dana Reich Gallery, San Francisco, Mus. Modern Art Penthouse Show; represented in permanent collections: Mus. Modern Art, N.Y.C., Whitney Mus. Am. Art, Syracuse U.; mem. faculty dept. art Wayne State U., 1961-63, U. Hawaii, 1965-67; mem. faculty Santa Rosa (Calif.) Jr. Coll., 1967—, now chmn. art history area; artist in residence, guest lectr. Deep Springs Coll., R.I. Sch. Design, Montclair State Coll., San Bernardino State Coll. Served with M.C., U.S. Army, 1953-55. Huntington Hartford Found. grantee; Yaddo Found. grantee; Nat. Endowment Humanities grantee. Author: Notes From a Painter's Journal, 1960; Qualities of Camouflaging, 1970; On the Sheer Nonsense of Liking Anything, 1979. Home: 513 Benton St Santa Rosa CA 95404 Office: 1501 Mendocino Ave Santa Rosa CA 95401

ROSEN, JUDAH BEN, computer scientist; b. Phila., May 5, 1922; s. Benjamin and Susan (Hurwich) R.; B.S. in Elec. Engring., Johns Hopkins U., 1943; Ph.D. in Applied Math., Columbia U., 1952; children—Susan Beth, Lynn Ruth. Research asso. Princeton (N.J.) U., 1952-54; head applied math. dept. Shell Devel. Co., 1954-62; vis. prof. computer sci. dept. Stanford (Calif.) U., 1962-64; prof. computer sci. dept. and math. research center U. Wis., Madison, 1964-71; prof., head computer sci. dept. Inst. Tech., U. Minn., Mpls., 1971—; Fulbright prof. Technion, Israel, 1968-69; lectr.; cons. Argonne (Ill.) Nat. Lab.; mem. Nat. Computer Sci. Bd. NSF grantee, 1969—. Mem. Assn. Computing Machinery, Soc. Indsl. and Applied Math., Math. Programming Soc. Editor: Nonlinear Programming, 1970; asso. editor Soc. Indsl. and Applied Math. Jour. on Control and Orgn., 1965-77; Jour. Computer System Scis., 1966—; contbr. articles to profl. jours. Home: 1904 W 49th St Minneapolis MN 55409 Office: Lind Hall U Minn Minneapolis MN 55455

ROSEN, LEO, lawyer; b. Kaunas, Lithuania, Nov. 25, 1906; s. Paul and Lina (Tubin) R.; came to U.S., 1909; naturalized, 1915; A.B. cum laude, Washington U., St. Louis, 1926; LL.B. cum laude, Yale, 1929; m. Lucille Grullow, June 24, 1931; children—Elizabeth, Michael, Charles. Admitted to N.Y. bar, 1931, since practiced in N.Y.C.; with firm Greenbaum, Wolff & Ernst, 1936—, partner, 1945—. Chmn. law com. Am. Ethical Union, 1956-76; mem. N.Y.C. advisory council State Commn. on Human Rights, 1951-71. Trustee, v.p. Hudson

Guild; bd. dirs., v.p. Brotherhood in Action. Mem. Am., N.Y. State bar assns., N.Y. County Lawyers Assn., Assn. Bar City N.Y. (admissions, arbitration, corp. law coms.), Phi Beta Kappa, Order of Coif. Home: 5245 Fieldston Rd Riverdale NY 10471 Office: 437 Madison Ave New York City NY 10022

ROSEN, LOUIS, physicist; b. N.Y.C., June 10, 1918; s. Jacob and Rose (Lipionski) R.; B.A., U. Ala., 1939, M.S., 1941; Ph.D., Pa. State U., 1944; D.Sc. (hon.), U. N.Mex., 1979; m. Mary Terry, Sept. 4, 1941; 1 son, Terry Leon. Instr. physics U. Ala., 1940-41, Pa. State U., 1943-44; mem. staff Los Alamos Sci. Lab., 1944—, group leader nuclear plate lab., 1949-65, alternate div. leader exptl. physics div., 1962-65, dir. meson physics facility, also div. leader medium energy physics div., 1965—. Mem. Los Alamos Town Planning Bd., 1962-64; mem. Gov.'s Com. on Tech. Excellence in N.Mex., Nat. Acad. Panel on Nuclear Sci., chmn. sub-panel on accelerators; mem. N.Mex. Cancer Control Bd., 1976—, v.p., 1979—; mem. panel on future of nuclear sci. Nat. Acad. Scis., 1976, mem. panel on instl. arrangements for orbiting space telescope, 1976; mem. com. on future nuclear sci. NRC, 1976; mem. U.S.A.-USSR Joint Coordinating Com. on Fundamental Properties of Matter, 1976—. Co-chmn. Los Alamos Vols. for Stevenson, 1956; Democratic candidate for county commr., 1962. Bd. dirs. Los Alamos Med. Center. Recipient E.O. Lawrence award AEC, 1963; Golden Plate award Am. Acad. Achievement, 1964; N.Mex. Disting. Public Service award, 1978; named Citizen of Year, N.Mex. Realtors Assn., 1973; Guggenheim fellow, 1959-60; alumni fellow Pa. State U., 1978. Fellow Am. Phys. Soc. (mem. council 1975-78, chmn. panel on public affairs 1980), AAAS. Author papers in nuclear sci. and applications of particle accelerators. Bd. editors Particle Accelerators; Applications of Nuclear Physics. Home: 1170 41st St Los Alamos NM 87544 Office: PO Box 1663 Los Alamos NM 87544

ROSEN, MARTIN M., investment banker; b. Cin., Aug. 7, 1919; s. Samuel and Sarah (Fradkin) R.; A.B. with high honors, U. Cin., 1940; M.A., U. Minn., 1947; m. Judith Frank Jacobs, Mar. 27, 1949; children—Andrea, Henry Samuel, Yereth, Irene Rochelle, Marshall Aaron, Jania Joy. Economist, U.S. Treasury Dept., 1941-42; dep. chief finance div. U.S. Element, Allied Commn. Austria, 1945-46; with Internat. Bank for Reconstrn. and Devel., 1946-61, dir. dept. operations Far East, 1957-61, dir. operations Far East, Internat. Devel. Assn., 1960-61; exec. v.p. Internat. Finance Corp., 1961-69; pres. First Washington Securities Corp., 1969-72, chmn., 1972—; pres. Model, Roland & Co. Inc., 1972-73, co-chmn., 1973-74; vice chmn. Shields Model Roland, 1974-77; dir. Atlantic Bank of N.Y., LogEtronics, Inc., Bates Mfg. Co., Internat. Developers Inc.; mem. internat. adv. bd. Am. Security & Trust. Lectr. internat. econs. Am. U., 1947; dep. chief finance br. Office Spl. Rep. in Europe, ECA, 1948. Served with AUS, 1942-46. Decorated govts. Colombia, Japan, Mauritania, Senegal. Mem. Am. Econ. Assn., Fgn. Policy Assn. (dir.), Royal Econ. Soc. Clubs: International (Washington); Wall Street, Lotos (N.Y.C.). Contbr. articles to profl. jours. Home: 2115 Paul Spring Rd Alexandria VA 22307 Office: 1735 Eye St NW Washington DC 20006

ROSEN, MELVILLE G., physician; b. Bklyn., Sept. 20, 1923; s. Joseph and Betsy R.; B.S., Tulane U., 1942; M.D., Middlesex U., 1945; m. Norma Smith, Mar. 10, 1946; children—Jane, Joseph. Intern, Unity Hosp., Bklyn., 1976-78: practice medicine specializing in family practice, Deer Park, N.Y., 1949-71; asso. prof. family medicine SUNY Sch. Medicine, Stony Brook, 1971-72, prof., 1972—, vice chmn. dept., 1973-74, acting chmn., 1975, chmn., 1975—; cons. Nassau County Med. Center, Catholic Med. Center, N.Y.C.; v.p. N.Y. State Family Practice Found. of Research and Edn., 1978-79. Served to capt. M.C., U.S. Army, 1953-55. Diplomate Am. Bd. Family Practice. Fellow Am. Acad. Family Practice, Suffolk Acad. Medicine; mem. AMA, Suffolk County Med. Soc. (past pres.), N.Y. State Med. Soc., N.Y. Acad. Sci., Soc. Tchrs. Family Medicine, Assn. Am. Med. Colls., Assn. Chmn. Univ. Family Medicine. Jewish. Asso. editor: The Patient and the Family, 1978. Office: Dept Family Medicine Health Scis Center SUNY Stony Brook NY 11794

ROSEN, MILTON WILLIAM, engr., physicist; b. Phila., July 25, 1915; s. Abraham and Regina (Weiss) R.; B.S. in Elec. Engring., U. Pa., 1937; postgrad. U. Pitts., 1937-38, Calif. Inst. Tech., 1946-47; m. Josephine H. Haar, Feb. 28, 1948; children—Nancy Elizabeth, Deborah Anne, Janet Suzanne. Engr., Westinghouse Electric & Mfg. Co., 1937-38; engr., physicist Naval Research Lab., Washington, 1940-58, sci. officer Viking rocket, 1947-55, head rocket devel. br., 1953-55, tech. dir. Project Vanguard (earth satellite), 1955-58; engr. NASA, 1958-74, chief rocket vehicle devel. programs, 1958-59, asst. dir. for vehicles, 1959-60, dir. launch vehicle and propulsion, 1961-63, sr. scientist office def. affairs, 1963-72, dep. asso. adminstr. for space Sci. (engring.), 1972-74; exec. sec. Space Sci. Bd., Nat. Acad. Scis., Washington, 1974-78, Com. on Impacts Stratospheric Change, 1978—. Chmn., Greater Washington Assn. Unitarian-Universalist Chs., 1966-68. Fellow Am. Rocket Soc. (dir. 1954, James H. Wyld meml award for application of rocket power 1954). Unitarian (chmn. trustees 1962-63). Author: The Viking Rocket Story, 1955. Patentee in field. Home: 5610 Alta Vista Rd Bethesda MD 20034 Office: Nat Acad Scis Washington DC 20418

ROSEN, MYOR, harpist, educator; b. N.Y.C., May 28, 1917; s. Caesar and Rose (Seidenberg) R.; diploma, Juilliard Sch. Music, 1940; m. May 25, 1941; children—Linda, David. Prin. harpist Mexico Symphony Orch., 1941-42, Indpls. Symphony Orch., 1941-42, Mpls. Symphony Orch., 1943-44; staff harpist CBS, Columbia Records and free lanced, 1945-60; prin. harpist N.Y. Philharm., 1960—; faculty Juilliard Sch. Music, 1947-69. Served with U.S. Army, 1945. Mem. Am. Fedn. Musicians, Bohemians. Composer incidental music for NBC series Arts and the Gods, 1946, CBS Camera Three, 1947, Solomon, The King, 1948. Office: New York Philharmonic 65th St and Broadway New York NY 10023

ROSEN, NATHANIEL KENT, cellist; b. Altadena, Calif., June 9, 1948; s. David Leon and Frances Jean (Kaufman) R.; student Pasadena (Calif.) City Coll., 1965-67; Mus.B., U. So. Calif., 1971; m. Jennifer Langham, Aug. 27, 1976. Teaching asst. U. So. Calif., 1968-75; prin. cellist Los Angeles Chamber Orch., 1970-76, Pitts. Symphony, 1977-79; asst. prof. Calif. State U. at Northridge, 1970-76. Recipient 1st prize Naumburg Competition, 1977, 1st prize Moscow Tchaikovsky Competition, 1978; Ford Found. grantee, 1970-71, Rockefeller Found. grantee, 1973-74. Mem. Violoncello Soc. New York, Musicians Union Local 47 (Los Angeles). Office: 165 W 57th St New York NY 10019

ROSEN, NORMAN EDWARD, lawyer; b. Providence, July 2, 1938; s. Albert and Lillian (Korb) R.; A.B., Harvard Coll., 1959; LL.B., Columbia U., 1962; M.A., George Washington U., 1965; m. Estelle Cutler, Sept. 5, 1966; children—James, Vanessa. Trial atty. FTC, 1962-67; asso. firm Paskus, Gordon & Hyman, 1967-69; partner firm Levin, Kreis, Ruskin & Gyory, 1969-72; staff v.p., sr. counsel licensing RCA, N.Y.C., 1972—. Mem. Am. Bar Assn., Assn. Bar City N.Y. Jewish. Clubs: Harvard of N.Y.C., Miramar Yacht. Home: 333 E 23d St Apt 8D New York NY 10010 Office: 30 Rockefeller Plaza New York NY 10020*

ROSEN, PHILIP, educator, physicist; b. N.Y.C., Oct. 31, 1922; s. Louis and Gussie (Brazaza) R.; B. Chem. Engring., City Coll. N.Y., 1944; M.S., Yale, 1946, Ph.D., 1949; m. Jeanne Penn, June 30, 1946; m. 2d, Rose Taubenblatt, Aug. 21, 1966; children—Gary M., Robert M., Ellen S. Asst. prof. Renssalaer Poly. Inst., 1948-51; sr. physicist Johns Hopkins Applied Physics Lab., 1951-54; faculty U. Conn., 1954-57; prof. physics U. Mass., Amherst, 1957—; vis. prof. U. Wis., summer 1965; vis. fellow Yale, 1965-66; also cons. bus. orgns. Spl. fellow Nat. Cancer Inst., Oak Ridge Nat. Lab., 1972-73. Fellow Am. Phys. Soc.; mem. Biophys. Soc., Am. Soc. for Photobiology, Sigma Xi. Research and publs. on propagation of electromagnetic waves in ionized gas; discovered that chem. potential energy is not additive; used variational principles in irreversible phenomena of thermodynamics; calculated entropy flux of electromagnetic radiation and probability of ionization for neutral colliding atoms; explained twin paradox of relativity, band structure DNA, theory of carcinogenesis. Home: 11 Western Ln Amherst MA 01002

ROSEN, RICHARD, publisher; b. N.Y.C., Nov. 10, 1917; s. Abraham and Rae (Armour) R.; B.A., N.Y. U., 1939; m. Ruth Chier, Sept. 13, 1947; children—Richard A., Roger C. Founder Richards Rosen Group, N.Y.C., 1950, co. comprises Richards Rosen Assos., paperbook publs., Richards Rosen Press, hardcover trade pubs., Richard Rosen Realty, realtors. Served to col. AUS, 1942-46. Mem. Am. Personnel and Guidance Assn., ALA, Res. Officers Assn., 21st St. Civic Assn., Gramercy Park Neighborhood Assn. Editor Mil. Research Series, 8 vols., 1970. Home: 137 E 19th St New York City NY 10003 Office: 29 E 21st St New York City NY 10003

ROSEN, ROBERT, math. biologist; b. Bklyn., June 27, 1934; s. Benjamin and Sarah Rebecca (Cooper) R.; B.S., Bklyn. Coll., 1955; Ph.D., U. Chgo., 1959; m. Patsy Lou Guinand, May 21, 1959; children—David Guy, Judith Louise, Jacob Alan. Research asso. U. Chgo., 1960-63, asst. prof. math. biology, 1963-66; asso. prof. math. and biophysics State U. N.Y., Buffalo, 1966-71, prof., 1971-75; Killam prof. physiology and biophysics Dalhousie U., Halifax, N.S., Can., 1975—; vis. fellow Center Study of Dem. Instns., 1971-72; asso. dir. Center Theoretical Biology, 1969-75. Recipient career devel. award USPHS, 1962-68; prin. or co-investigator Air Force Office of Sci. Research, NIH, NASA. Mem. Soc. Math. Biology, Biophys. Soc., Am. Soc. Cell Biology. Author: Optimality Principles in Biology, 1967; Dynamical System Theory in Biology, 1971; editor: Foundations of Mathematical Biology (3 vols.), 1975; Fundamentals of Measurement and Representation of Natural Systems, 1978. Home: 2494 Robie St Halifax NS B3K 4N1 Canada Office: Tupper Bldg Dalhousie U Halifax NS Canada

ROSEN, ROBERT ARNOLD, real estate, investment and communciation co. exec.; b. N.Y.C., June 19, 1936; s. Louis and Helen (Weiss) R.; B.B.A., U. City N.Y., 1957, M.B.A., 1960; postgrad. (Ford Found. scholar), N.Y. U., 1961; m. Florence Cohen, Oct. 23, 1960; children—David S., Kenneth A., Mark A., Emily B. Sales promotion mgr. Leipzig & Lippe, Inc., 1956-58; advt. and sales promotion mgr. Zenith Radio, 1958-63; chmn., pres., founder Am. Bus. Resources Corp., 1963-64; v.p., dir. Royal Bus. Funds Corp., 1964-68; mng. dir. Rosen Assos., 1968—; pres. Robert A. Rosen Co., Inc., N.Y.C., 1968—; v.p. corporate finance div., dir. Brand Grumet & Siegel, Inc., 1969-70; pres. Brand Grumet & Siegel Equities, Inc., 1970; former pres., chief operating officer Bell TV, Inc., N.Y.C.; pres., former chmn. bd. Holmes Protection, Inc.; former chmn. bd., pres. Union Small Bus. Investment Co., 1968-77, Skyway-Laguardia Corp.; dir. past chmn. bd. Okuraya Davos Internat., Inc.; chmn. bd., pres., chief exec. officer, treas. Suburban Broadcasting Corp., 1979—; past chmn. bd. High Energy Processing Corp.; cons. Asian Devel. Bank, Vols. in Tech. Assistance; past cons. Nat. Housing Bank Brazil, Constrn. Bank Iran; lectr. Baruch Coll. Grad. Sch. Bus., U. City N.Y., 1960-63; adj. prof. Fairleigh Dickinson U. Grad. Sch. Bus., 1968-75; pres., dean Internat. Inst. Real Estate Studies Ltd.; dir. Center for Real Estate Studies, Adelphi U.; adj. prof. mgmt. N.Y. U.; mem. faculty New Sch. for Social Research; prin. owner, developer shopping centers, comml. real estate throughout U.S.; chmn. UN Trade and Tech. Adv. Mission to Israel, 1972; mem. Nat. Builder Mktg. Bd. Chmn., Borough Presidents of Manhattan Com. on Narcotics Addiction Control, 1970—; N.Y. mem. adv. council U.S. Air Force Acad., bd. govs. Grad. Sch., Yeshiva U.; mem. Nat. Democratic Club N.Y.C., 1963; bd. dirs. The Film Forum, 1979—. Maj. USAF Res. Mem. AAUP, Am. Arbitration Assn., Nat. Assn. Corp. Real Estate Execs., Nat. Rifle Assn. U.S., Am. Mgmt. Assn., Nat. Def. Exec. Res., Young Presidents' Orgn., Real Estate Bd. N.Y., Internat. Council Shopping Centers, Alpha Delta Sigma, Phi Sigma Delta, Sigma Alpha. Club: Harvard Bus. Sch. (vol. urban cons. program) (N.Y.C.). Mem. hon. editorial bd. Nat. Mall Monitor. Home: 85-29 Wicklow Pl Jamaica Estates NY 11432 Office: 3200 Expressway Dr S Central Islip NY 11722

ROSEN, RONALD STANLEY, lawyer; b. Los Angeles, July 22, 1932; s. Daniel and Florence Edyth (Hirsch) R.; A.B. cum laude, Stanford, 1954, LL.B., 1957; postgrad. (scholar) London Sch. Econs., 1953; m. Judith Berenice Friedman, June 26, 1955; children—Philip James, Matthew Howard. Admitted to Calif. bar, 1958; asst. U.S. atty., So. Dist. Calif., Los Angeles, 1958-59; asso. firm Pacht, Ross, Warne & Bernhard, Los Angeles, 1959-62; partner Silverberg, Rosen & Leon, 1962—; officer, dir. numerous corps. Chmn., Fed. Indigent Def. Com., Los Angeles, 1966-68, Lawyer's Reference Com., Los Angeles, 1969-70. Bd. dirs. Elsie DeWolfe Found.; trustee Young Musicians Found., 1973—. Mem. Am., Los Angeles County, Beverly Hills bar assns., State Bar Calif. (adminstrv. com. 1969—, chmn. 1972—, mem. state bar disciplinary com. 1975—, exec. com. 1975-76, disciplinary referee 1975—), Phi Beta Kappa, Phi Delta Phi. Clubs: Los Angeles, Los Angeles Tennis. Home: Encino CA Office: 2029 Century Park E Century City Los Angeles CA 90067

ROSEN, RUBEN PAUL, fin. exec.; b. Phila., Sept. 30, 1915; s. Frank and Rose (Greck) R.; m. Tallu Leis, June 13, 1937; children—Donald, Lisa Rosen Kaplan. With Progress Lighting, Phila., 1933—, pres., 1938-54, chmn. bd., 1954-60, 63-71, vice chmn. bd., 1960-63, 71-75; chmn. bd. Sarama Industries, Inc., Bala Cynwyd, Pa., 1975—, Poloron Products, Inc., Harrison, N.Y., 1975—. Bd. dirs. Pop Warner Conf., Beth Jacob Schs.; trustee emeritus Nat. Jewish Hosp., Denver; mem. cabinet Greater Phila. com. State of Israel Bonds. Mem. Am. Technion Soc. (dir. Phila. div.). Jewish (dir. temple). Club: Locust (dir.). Home: 50 Belmont Ave Bala Cynwyd PA 19004 Office: 190 Presidential Blvd Bala Cynwyd PA 19004

ROSEN, SAUL, computer scientist; b. Port Chester, N.Y., Feb. 8, 1922; s. George and Bertha (Semmel) R.; B.S., Coll. City N.Y., 1941; M.S., U. Cin., 1942; Ph.D., U. Pa., 1950; m. Winifred Claire Catsiff, Aug. 13, 1950; children—Barbara, Diana, Frances, Janet. Instr., U. Del., 1946-47; lectr. U. Calif., Los Angeles, 1948-49; asst. prof. math. Drexel Inst., Phila., 1949-51; logical design engr. Burroughs Corp., Phila., 1951-52, mgr. applied math. sect., 1956-58; asst. prof. elec. engring. U. Pa., 1952-54; asso. prof. math. Wayne State U., 1954-56; mgr. programming research and devel. Philco Corp., Phila., 1958-60; cons. in computers and programming, Phila., 1960-62; prof. math. and computer sci. Purdue U., West Lafayette, Ind., 1962—, dir. Computing Center, 1968—; dir. Meditech, Inc., Indpls. Served with AUS, 1943-45. Decorated Bronze Star; NSF grantee, 1970. Mem. Assn. Computing Machinery, IEEE Computer Soc., U.S. Chess Fedn., ACLU. Author: Programming Systems and Languages, 1967; editorial bd. Ency. of Computer Sci., 1976; contbr. articles on computers to profl. publs. Home: 341 Smiley St West Lafayette IN 47906

ROSEN, SAUL DAVID, ret. editor; b. Bronx, N.Y., July 4, 1906; s. Joseph and Mary (Kalotkin) R.; student pub. sch., N.Y.; m. Ethel Greenhut, Nov. 28, 1935; children—Kenneth, Joseph. Handicapper, Morning Telegraph. 1929-35, nat. mng. editor, 1948-65, editor, 1965-72; editor Daily Racing Guide, 1935-44; asst. editor-in-chief Triangle Publs. (includes Morning Telegraph, N.Y.C., Daily Racing Form, N.J., Chgo., Los Angeles, Toronto, Vancouver, Miami), 1944-47, nat. mng. editor, 1948-65, editor, 1965-72; cons. N.Y.C. Off-Track Betting Corp. Trustee Nat. Mus. of Racing. Named Big Sport of Turfdom, 1970. Mem. Nat. (Walter Haight award 1976), N.Y. turf writers assns., U.S., N.Y. harness writers assns., Thoroughbred Club Am. Clubs: B'nai B'rith, Silurians. Co-author: (play) Bangtails, 1940. Home: V-Eleven Avon Dr East Windsor NJ 08520

ROSEN, SHERWIN, economist; b. Chgo., Sept. 29, 1938; s. Joe W. and Nell (Rudy) R.; M.A., U. Chgo., 1962, Ph.D., 1966; m. Sharon Ginsberg, June 11, 1961; children—Jennifer, Adria. Mem. faculty dept. econs. U. Rochester (N.Y.), 1964-75, Kenan prof. econs., 1975-77; prof. econs. U. Chgo., 1977—; sr. research fellow Nat. Bur. Econ. Research; vis. prof. U. Buffalo, 1970, Harvard U., 1971-72, Columbia U., 1973, Stanford U., 1976. Fellow Econometric Soc.; mem. Am. Econ. Assn. Contbr. articles to profl. jours. Home: 5714 Kimbark Chicago IL 60637 Office: Dept Econs U Chicago IL 60637

ROSEN, STANLEY HOWARD, educator; b. Warren, Ohio, July 29, 1929; s. Nathan A. and Celia (Narotsky) R.; B.A., U. Chgo., 1949, Ph.D., 1955; student Am. Sch. Classical Studies, Athens, Greece, 1955-56; m. Francoise Harlepp, Sept. 5, 1955; children—Nicholas David, Paul Mark, Valerie. Mem. faculty Pa. State U., 1956—, prof. philosophy, 1966—; Fulbright research prof. U. Paris (France), 1960-61; research fellow Humanities Research Inst., U. Wis., 1963-64; Inst. for Arts and Humanities research sr. fellow Pa. State U., 1972—. Research grantee Am. Philos. Soc., 1961, Earhart Found., 1971, 73. Author: Plato's Symposium, 1968; Nihilism, 1969; G.W.F. Hegel, 1974. Home: 1256 S Garner St State College PA 16801 Office: Sparks Bldg Pa State Univ University Park PA 16802

ROSEN, STUART MARTIN, television producer; b. Joliet, Ill., June 26, 1939; s. David and Ethel Susan (Pitts) R.; B.A., Calif. State U., Long Beach, 1963. Producer, creator, writer, host Dusty's Attic, Sta. KEET-TV, Los Angeles, 1966-67; producer, dir., copywriter, free lance, 1968-70; exec. producer A Christmas Dream Sta. KNXT-CBS, 1971; producer, dir., writers Help Your Sell-F, 1972-74; producer, creator, writer Funky, Sta. KNXT-CBS, 1975, What If?, 1976, exec. producer, writer Guzzle, Gurgle & Gone, 1977, Just for the Health of It, 1979, Zap!, 1979; producer, creator, writer, host Dusty's Treehouse, 1970-78; pres. Peanut Butter and Jelly Productions, Inc., 1978—; pres., Sagen Arts, Inc., 1969-78; guest faculty mem. Calif. State U., Long Beach, 1975-77, Columbia Coll. Broadcasting, 1974-75. Recipient Emmy award Dusty's Treehouse, 1970-75; George Foster Peabody award for Dusty's Treehouse, 1973; Emmy award Funky, 1975; Emmy award It, 1978. Mem. Dirs. Guild Am., AFTRA, Nat. Acad. Rec. Arts and Scis., ASCAP, Acad. Television Arts and Scis. (bd. govs.), Calif. State U. at Long Beach Alumni Assn. (bd. dirs.). Home: 7631 Lexington Los Angeles CA 90046

ROSENBAUM, EDWARD E., physician; b. Omaha, May 14, 1915; s. Sam and Bessie (Mittleman) R.; student Crieghton U., 1932-34; B.S., M.D., U. Nebr., 1938; M.S. in Medicine, U. Minn., 1947; m. Davida Naftalin, Feb. 17, 1942; children—Richard, James, Howard, Kenneth. Intern, Jewish Hosp., St. Louis, 1938-39; resident Michael Reese Hosp., Chgo., 1939-40; fellow internal medicine Mayo Found., 1940-41; 46-48; pvt. practice internal medicine, Portland, Oreg., 1948—; mem. staff St. Vincent's Hosp., 1948—, chief medicine 1958-59; mem. staff Holladay Park Hosp., 1948—, pres. staff 1950-52, chief medicine, 1952-58; faculty U. Oreg. Med. Sch., 1948—, asso. clin. prof. medicine, 1962-69, chief prof. medicine, 1969—, chief Rheumatism Clinic, 1950-62, chief Rheumatology Clinic, 1968-76. Mem. Ore. Council on Aging, 1959-65; del. White House Conf. on Aging, 1961. Mem. Sylvan Sch. Dist. Bd., 1962-63. Served to maj. M.C., AUS, 1941-46; ETO. Decorated Bronze Star. Diplomate Am. Bd. Internal Medicine. Mem. A.M.A. (nat. speakers bur. 1960-65), Oreg., Multnomah County (trustee) med. socs., N.Y. Acad. Scis., Am., N.W. Rheumatism assns., Sigma Xi, Alpha Omega Alpha. Author: (with S.W. Jacob) First Clinical Report on Dimethyl Sulfoxide, 1964; Rheumatology New Directions in Therapy, 1979. Contbr. articles to profl. jours. Home: 4444 SW Fairhaven Dr Portland OR 97221 Office: 333 NW 23d Ave Portland OR 97210

ROSENBAUM, HAROLD DENNIS, physician; b. Fairplay, Ky., Aug. 17, 1921; s. George Leslie and Maud May (Loy) R.; A.B., Berea Coll., 1941; M.D., Harvard U., 1944; children—Robin, Nancy, Paula, Harold Dennis Jr.; m. 2d, Doris M. Fooks, June 12, 1970; children—Stanley Drew, Anthony Dennison-Dorris. Intern, Peter Bent Brigham Hosp., Boston, 1944; attending staff med. outpatient dept. Colo. Gen. Hosp., Denver, 1948-49; resident radiology Denver Gen. Hosp., 1949; resident pathology New Eng. Deaconess Hosp., Boston, 1950, resident radiology, 1950-51; research fellow pediatrics Children's Hosp., Boston, 1952; pvt. practice radiology, Lexington, Ky.; cons. cardiac roentgenology St. Joseph's Hosp., Lexington; radiologist various suburban hosps., 1953-60; prof., chmn. dept. radiology U. Ky. Coll. Medicine, 1960—; assisted orgn. Central Ky. Surg. Heart Clinic for Indigents, 1954, conducted specialized diagnostic services, 1954-61. Chmn. bd. Fayette County unit Am. Cancer Soc. Served to capt. M.C., AUS, 1945-47. Diplomate Am. Bd. Radiology. Fellow Am. Coll. Radiology (chmn. com. on matching plans 1968); mem. Radiol. Soc. N.Am., Am. Roentgen Ray Soc., Soc. Univ. Radiologists, Am. Heart Assn., AMA, Ky., Fayette County med. socs., Ky. (pres. 1965-66), Grass Blue (pres.) radiol. socs. Presbyterian. Editor: Pearls in Diagnostic Radiology. Home: 3605 Gloucester Dr Route 2 Lexington KY 40511

ROSENBAUM, IRVING JOSEPH, rabbi, ednl. adminstr.; b. Omaha, Dec. 20, 1921; s. David and Rose (Lederman) R.; B.A., U. Chgo., 1943; B.H.L., Rabbi, Hebrew Theol. Coll., 1945, D.H.L., 1977; m. Ruth Groner, Feb. 27, 1944; children—Roy, Don, Susan, Alan. Rabbi, 1945; nat. dir. religious dept. Anti-Defamation League of B'nai B'rith, 1944-55; curator Lasker Fellowship Program in Civil Liberties and Civil Rights Brandeis U., 1959-60; exec. v.p. Chgo. Bd. Rabbis, 1960-63, also bd. dirs.; rabbi Chgo. Loop Synagogue, 1963-77; pres. Jewish U. Am., Skokie, Ill., 1977—, Hebrew Theol. Coll., Skokie, 1977—; author weekly column Rabbi at Random in Chgo. Sentinel and other Anglo-Jewish newspapers 1963—; producer, dir. motion picture Your Neighbor Celebrates, 1949. Mem. Mayor's Adv. Com. Urban Affairs, 1963—, Met. Mental Health Planning Council, 1964—; bd. dirs. Hebrew Theol. Coll., Chgo. Conf. on Religion and Race, Jewish Fedn. Met. Chgo., Jewish Council Urban Affairs, Ida Crown Acad. Mem. Religious Edn. Assn. (dir.), Rabbinical Council Am., Chgo. Rabbinical Council. Author: (with O. Tarcov) Your Neighbor Celebrates, 1955; The Holocaust and Halakha, 1974. Contbr. articles to profl. publs. Home: 5743 N Bernard St Chicago IL 60645 Office: 7135 N Carpenter St Skokie IL 60077

ROSENBAUM, IRVING M., dept. store exec.; b. Dresden, Germany, Apr. 20, 1921; s. Max and Clara (Koerner) R.; came to U.S., 1938, naturalized, 1943; B.A. in Econs., New Sch. Social Research, 1953; M.A. in Econs., N.Y. U., 1956; m. Hanni Schein, Oct. 15, 1953; children—Eli M., Daniel S., Michael J. Stockman, S.E. Nichols Inc., N.Y.C., 1938-40, asst. store mgr., 1940-43, store mgr., 1946-48, buyer, 1949-56, mdse. mgr., 1957-60, pres., 1960-72, chmn. bd., 1972—; chmn. bd. F.R. Schreiber Co., Lititz, Pa. Exec. v.p. Solomon Schechter Day Sch., Nassau and Suffolk Counties, 1974—; bd. dirs. United Jewish Appeal, Fedn. Jewish Philanthropies, Israel Bond Orgn. Greater N.Y. Served with U.S. Army, 1943-45. Recipient Prime Minister's medal Israel, 1976. Mem. Nat. Mass Retailing Inst., U.S. C. of C. Club: Lake Mohawk Country (Sparta, N.J.). Home: 22 Glenwood Rd Great Neck NY 11021 Office: 500 8th Ave New York NY 10018. *Only a person who appreciates his own background, traditions and values is able to appreciate those of others.*

ROSENBAUM, ROBERT ABRAHAM, educator; b. New Haven, Nov. 14, 1915; s. Joseph and Goldey (Rostow) R.; A.B., Yale, 1936, Ph.D., 1947; M.A., Wesleyan U., Middletown, Conn., 1954; L.H.D., St. Joseph Coll., 1970; m. L. Louise Johnson, Aug. 1, 1942; children—Robert J., Joseph, David. Henry Fund fellow St. John's Coll., Cambridge (Eng.) U., 1936-37; Gen. Edn. Bd. fellow Reed Coll., 1939-40, from instr. to prof. math., 1940-53; prof. math. Wesleyan U., 1953—, chmn. dept. math., 1953-63, dean sci., 1963-65, provost, 1965-69, v.p. for acad. affairs, 1967-69, chancellor, 1970-73, univ. prof., 1977—; vis. prof. Swarthmore Coll., 1950-51, U. Mass., 1973. NSF fellow Math. Inst., Oxford, Eng., 1958-59. Served with USNR, 1942-45. Hon. alumnus Reed Coll. Fellow AAAS; mem. Math. Assn. Am. (2d v.p. 1961-62, editor 1966-68), Am. Math. Soc., Am. Assn. U. Profs. (chpt. pres. 1959-61), Conn. Acad. Sci. and Engring. (charter mem., treas.), Phi Beta Kappa, Sigma Xi. Home: 29 Long Ln Middletown CT 06457

ROSENBERG, ALEX, educator, mathematician; b. Berlin, Germany, Dec. 5, 1926; s. Theodore and Rela (Banet) R.; came to U.S., 1949, naturalized, 1959; B.A., U. Toronto, 1948, M.A., 1949; Ph.D., U. Chgo., 1951; m. Beatrice Gershenson, Aug. 24, 1952; children—Theodore Joseph, David Michael. From instr. to asso. prof. math. Northwestern U., 1952-61; prof. math. Cornell U., Ithaca, N.Y., 1961—, chmn. dept., 1966-69, mem. com. undergrad. program math., 1966-76, chmn., 1971-73. Mem. Inst. Advanced Study, 1955-57. Recipient Humboldt Stiftung Sr. U.S. Scientist award U. Munich, 1975-76. Mem. Am. Math. Soc. (algebra editor procs. 1960-65, exec. com. 1965-66, trustee 1974—), Math. Assn. Am. Editor: Am. Math. Monthly, 1974-77. Contbr. articles to profl. jours. Home: 608 Highland Rd Ithaca NY 14850

ROSENBERG, ALEXANDRE PAUL, art dealer; b. Paris, France, Mar. 8, 1921; s. Paul and Marguerite Ida (Loevi) R.; Ph.D in Philosophy, Sorbonne, Paris, 1940; m. Elaine Lois Sobel, Feb. 29, 1948; children—Elizabeth Marthe, Marianne Barbara. Came to U.S., 1946. With Paul Rosenberg & Co., N.Y.C., 1946—, pres., 1959—; spl. research European art from Renaissance to 20th century; organizer public exhbns. Served with Free French Forces, 1940-45. Mem. Art Dealers Assn. Am. (pres. 1962-64, 76-78, dir.). Club: Grolier (resident mem. N.Y.). Home and office: 20 E 79th St New York NY 10021

ROSENBERG, ALLEN LEON, banker; b. Los Angeles, Jan. 28, 1909; s. Morris and Rose R.; student Pomona Coll., 1926-28; m. Rose Rosen, Feb. 16, 1930; 1 son, Robert G. Partner, Belvedere Gardens Drug Co., Los Angeles, 1930-33; pres. Thrifty-Payless Drugs, Inc., Phoenix, 1933-42; chmn. Central Ariz. War Price and Rationing Bd. OPA, 1942-44; sec., treas. Allied Grain Co., Phoenix, 1944-56; pres. Allied Sales Co., Phoenix, 1956-63; Ariz. State mgr. Continental Grain Co., Phoenix, 1959-61; sr. v.p., dir. Guaranty Bank, Phoenix, 1962-64; pres. Bank of Scottsdale (Ariz.), 1964-66; pres. Pioneer Bank of Ariz., Phoenix, 1966-69, also chief exec. officer; pres. Gt. Western Bank & Trust, Phoenix, 1970-74, vice chmn. bd., 1974—; exec. dir. Ariz. Community Found., 1978—; dir., sec., mem. exec. com. Sta. KAET-TV, 1975-79. Mem. Phoenix City Council, 1952-53, Ariz. Human Relations Commn., 1964-65; chmn. Phoenix Area Air Service Com., 1962-75; pres. Jr. Achievement of Met. Phoenix, Inc., 1965-67; mem. Ariz. Regional Export Expansion Council, 1967-71; chmn. Phoenix Municipal Aeros. Bd., 1976—; mem. nat. bd. dirs. NCCJ, 1961-64; bd. dirs. Phoenix Symphony Assn., 1968-77, Ariz. Bus. Resource Center, 1976-78; chmn. bd. dirs. Ariz. State U. Found., 1976-78; bd. dirs. Central Ariz. Project Assn.; chmn. Gov.'s Econ. Security Adv. Council, 1978—. Recipient Nat. Jr. Achievement award, 1967; Sertoma Internat. Service to Mankind award, 1967; Alumni Appreciation award Ariz. State U., 1969, Nat. Jewish Hosp./Nat. Asthma Center humanitarian award, 1979. Mem. Am. Soc. Corporate Secs., Phoenix C. of C. (pres. 1964-65), Ariz. Bankers Assn. (pres. 1971-72), Nu Alpha Phi, Beta Gamma Sigma, Sigma Tau. Clubs: Arizona, Phoenix Country, Masons, Shriners. Home: 3600 N 5th Ave Phoenix AZ 85013 Office: PO Box 2012 Phoenix AZ 85001

ROSENBERG, ARTHUR JAMES, business exec.; b. Boston, Dec. 8, 1926; s. Benjamin R. and Lillian (Wolfson) R.; B.S. magna cum laude, Tufts U., 1948; M.A., Harvard, 1951, Ph.D., 1952; m. Naomi C. Solomon, Oct. 16, 1949; children—Deborah L., Janis E., Mia B. Research scientist Merck & Co., Inc., 1951-54; mem. tech. staff Lincoln Lab., Mass. Inst. Tech., Cambridge, 1954-60; pres. Tyco Labs., Inc., Waltham, Mass., 1960-70, Epidyne, Inc., Palos Verdes Estates, Calif., 1972-78; cons., 1970-72. Chmn. Gordon Research Conf. on Chem. and Metallurgy of Semicondrs., 1960-61. Served with USNR, 1944-45. Mem. Am. Chem. Soc. Am. Phys. Soc., Faraday Soc., Electrochem. Soc., I.E.E.E., Am. Inst. Metals. Contbr. numerous articles to profl. jours. Address: 1728 Via Boronada Palos Verdes Estates CA 90274

ROSENBERG, CHARLES ERNEST, historian, educator; b. N.Y.C., Nov. 11, 1936; s. Bernard and Marion (Roberts) R.; B.A., U. Wis., 1956; M.A., Columbia, 1957, Ph.D., 1961; m. Carroll Ann Smith, June 22, 1961 (div. 1977); 1 dau., Leah. Fellow Johns Hopkins, Balt., 1960-61; asst. prof. U. Wis., 1961-63; asso. prof. U. Pa., Phila., 1965-68, prof. history, 1968—, chmn. dept., 1974-75. Bd. dirs. Mental Health Assn. Southeastern Pa., 1973—. Nat. Inst. Health Research grantee, 1964-70; Guggenheim Found. fellow, 1965-66; Nat. Endowment Humanities fellow, 1972-73; Rockefeller Found. humanities fellow, 1975-76. Mem. Inst. Advanced Study, Am. Assn. History of Medicine (William H. Welch medal 1969, council 1974—), History of Sci. Soc. (council 1972-75). Author: The Cholera Years: The United States in 1832, 1849 and 1866, 1962; The Trial of the Assassin Guiteau: Psychiatry and Law in the Gilded Age, 1968; No Others Gods: On Science and Social Thought in America, 1976. Home: 2200 St James St Philadelphia PA 19103 Office: Dept History U Pa Philadelphia PA 19104

ROSENBERG, CLAUDE NEWMAN, JR., investment adviser; b. San Francisco, Apr. 10, 1928; s. Claude Newman and Elza (Wolff) R.; B.A., Stanford, 1950, M.B.A., 1952; m. Louise Jankelson, Dec. 19, 1968; children—Linda Kay, Douglas Claude. Research analyst J. Barth & Co., San Francisco, 1955-62, partner charge research, 1962-70; investment adviser, pres. Rosenberg Capital Mgmt., San Francisco, 1970—; lectr. Grad. Sch. Bus., Stanford; dir. Calif. Casualty Ins. Co., San Francisco. Bd. dirs. Jewish Welfare Fedn., Presbyn. Children's Cancer Research Center, Jewish Community Center; trustee San Francisco Ballet Assn., Univ. High Sch., San Francisco. Served with USNR, 1951-53. Mem. Financial Analysts San Francisco, Alumni Assn. Stanford U. Grad. Sch. Bus. (pres.). Republican. Jewish religion. Clubs: Family, Concordia-Argonaut, Calif. Tennis, Family (San Francisco). Author: Stock Market Primer, 1962, rev., 1970; The Common Sense Way to Stock Market Profit, 1968, rev., 1978; Psycho-Cybernetics and the Stock Market, 1970. Home: 2465 Pacific Ave San Francisco CA 94115 Office: One Market Plaza Spear St Tower Suite 3910 San Francisco CA 94105

ROSENBERG, DAVID HOWARD, mktg. exec., lawyer; b. Terre Haute, Ind., July 2, 1941; s. Al and Pearl (Eshowsky) R.; student N. Tex. State U., Denton, 1963-65; J.D., U. Tex., 1968; m. Helen Claire Stahl, Jan. 29, 1967; children—Lisa Sharon. Michelle Lynn, Alan Jay. Admitted to Tex. bar, 1968; law clk. to U.S. dist. judge, 1968-69; practice in Dallas, 1969-78; pres. Precision Mktg., Inc., Dallas, 1978—; gen. counsel Film Fin. Group, Ltd., 1977. Bd. dirs. Jewish Fedn. Greater Dallas, 1972-74, 76—; trustee N. Am. Jewish Students' Appeal, 1973—. Served with AUS, 1960-63. Recipient I. Zesmer Leadership award Jewish Fedn. Dallas, 1972. Mem. Am., Fed., Tex., Dallas bar assns., Am. Judicature Soc. Home: 5531 Palomar Ln Dallas TX 75229 Office: Suite 510 Campbell Centre 1 8350 N Central Expressway Dallas TX 75206

ROSENBERG, DENNIS MELVILLE LEO, surgeon; b. Johannesburg, South Africa, Jan. 27, 1921; s. Nathan and Dorothy (Lee) R.; came to U.S., 1946, naturalized, 1953; B.Sc. with honors, U. Witwatersrand (South Africa), 1941, M.B., B.Ch., 1945; m. Jeanna Van der Kar, Jan., 1947. Intern, Johannesburg Gen. Hosp., 1946; resident in surgery Tulane U. Ochsner Found. Hosp., 1947-51, Children's Hosp., Johannesburg, 1952; asst. thoracic surgeon Biggs Hosp., Ithaca, N.Y., 1953-54; practice medicine specializing in cardiovascular and thoracic surgery, New Orleans, 1955—; sr. surgeon Touro Infirmary, New Orleans, 1955—, chief dept. cardiovascular and thoracic surgery, 1972—; mem. staffs East Jefferson Gen. Hosp., Metairie, La., St. Charles Gen. Hosp., New Orleans; sr. vis. surgeon Charity Hosp., New Orleans, 1962—; sr. investigator Touro Research Inst., 1964—; asso. prof. surgery Tulane U. Served with M.C., South African Army, 1940-45. Fellow A.C.S.; mem. Am. Coll. Chest Physicians, Am. Coll. Cardiology, AMA, Am. Heart Assn., Am. Assn. Thoracic Surgery, So. Thoracic Surg. Assn., Internat. Cardiovascular Soc., Am. Thoracic Soc., Soc. Thoracic Surgeons, Soc. Vascular Surgery, Soc. Internationale de Cirugie, Royal Soc. Medicine, So. Assn. Vascular Surgery. Home: 3115 Prytania St New Orleans LA 70115 Office: 3600 Prytania St New Orleans LA 70115

ROSENBERG, EDGAR, educator; b. Fuerth, Germany, Sept. 21, 1925; s. Otto and Lilly (Arnstein) R.; B.A., Cornell U., 1949, M.A., 1950; Ph.D., Stanford U., 1958; m. Birthe Terp-Johansen, Sept. 12, 1965. Instr. English, Harvard U., 1957-60, Briggs-Copeland asst. prof., 1960-65; asso. prof. English, Cornell U., Ithaca, N.Y., 1965-69, prof., 1969-70, prof. English and comparative lit., 1970—; vis. prof. English, Stanford U., 1970. Served with U.S. Army, 1944-45. Stanford Creative Writing fellow, 1951-52; Bread Loaf Writing fellow, 1952; Cornell research grantee, 1968, 69, 79; Guggenheim fellow, 1973-74. Mem. Am. Dickens Soc., Dickens Fellowship, Jewish Hist. Soc., MLA. Democrat. Jewish. Author: From Shylock to Svengali, 1960; The Jew in Western Drama, 1968; Tabloid Jews and Fungoid Scribblers, 1973. Contbr. articles to profl. and gen. publs. Home: 201 Forest Dr Ithaca NY 14850 Office: Dept English Cornell Univ Ithaca NY 14853

ROSENBERG, FRANK P., film producer; b. N.Y.C., Nov. 22, 1913; ed. Columbia, N.Y.U. Joined Columbia Pictures, 1929, motion picture and radio writer, exploitation mgr., 1941, dir. advt. publicity, exploitation, 1944, dir. publicity Columbia Pictures Studios, Hollywood, 1946-47, entered prodn. field, 1947; co-producer Man Eater of Kumaon, 1968; asso. producer Where the Sidewalk Ends, 1950; producer Secret of Convict Lake, 1951, Return of the Texan, 1952, The Farmer Takes a Wife, 1953, King of the Khyber Rifles, 1954, Illegal, 1955, Miracle in the Rain, 1956, Girl He Left Behind, 1956, One-Eyed Jacks, 1961, Critic's Choice, 1963, Madigan, 1968, Reincarnation of Peter Proud, 1975; TV exec. producer, producer Schlitz Playhouse programs, 1957-58; exec. producer Arrest and Trial, 1963-64, Kraft Suspense Theatre, 1964-65; v.p. MCA Artists Ltd., 1964; writer Gray Lady Down, 1978. Address: care Producers Guild Am 8201 Beverly Blvd Hollywood CA 90048*

ROSENBERG, HENRY A., JR., petroleum co. exec.; b. Pitts., Nov. 7, 1929; s. Henry A. and Ruth (Blaustein) R.; B.A. in Econs., Hobart Coll., 1952; m. Eleanor Kantor, June 22, 1952; children—Henry A. III, Edward Lee, Frank Blaustein. With Crown Central Petroleum Corp., Balt., 1952—, pres., 1966-75, chmn. exec. com., 1966—, chmn. bd., 1975—, also chief exec. officer; dir. Am. Trading & Prodn. Corp., Union Trust Co. Md., U.S. Fidelity & Guaranty Co. Bd. dirs. Sinai Hosp., Am. Petroleum Inst.; exec. bd. local Boy Scouts Am. Served with AUS, 1952-54. Mem. Nat. Petroleum Refiners Assn. (chmn., dir., exec. com). Office: Blaustein Bldg 1 N Charles St Baltimore MD 21202

ROSENBERG, HERMANN PAUL, lithographing co. exec.; b. Las Vegas, N.Mex., Aug. 25, 1924; s. Hermann Paul and Ruby Shell (Holland) R.; B.B.A., U. Tex., 1945; m. Barbara Rosenberg; children—Nita Rosenberg Levy, Paul, James. Pres. Midland Lithographing Co., Kansas City, Mo., 1961—; pres. Kings Profl. Basketball Club, Inc., Kansas City, 1973—; dir. Traders Bank. Pres. Beth Shalom Congregation, 1973-75; pres. Jewish Fedn. Greater Kansas City, 1974-77; dir. Am. Joint Distribution Com; mem. exec. com. United Jewish Appeal; trustee United Israel Appeal, Community Alcohol Program. Recipient Herbert Lehman award Israel Bond Orgn. Mem. Soc. of Fellows Graphic Arts Tech. Found. (pres. 1971-72), Printing Industry Assn. Kansas City (pres. 1965-66), Graphic Arts Union Employers of Am. (pres. 1971-72), Graphic Arts Internat. Union (co-chmn. early retirement trust); mem. Nat. Basketball Assn. (gov.). Democrat. Jewish. Club: Oakwood Country. Home: 121 W 48th St Apt 2101 Kansas City MO 64112 Office: 1841 Vernon St North Kansas City MO 64116

ROSENBERG, IRWIN HAROLD, physician; b. Madison, Wis., Jan. 6, 1935; s. Abraham Joseph and Celia (Mazursky) R.; B.S., U. Wis., 1956; M.D. cum laude, Harvard U., 1959; m. Civia Muffs, May 24, 1964; children—Daniel, Ilana. Intern, Mass. Gen. Hosp., Boston, 1959-60, resident, 1960-61; research asso. NIH, 1961-64; fellow Thorndike Meml. Lab., Boston, 1964-65; instr. Harvard U. Med. Sch., 1965-67, asst. prof. medicine, 1967-70; asso. prof. U. Chgo., 1970-74, prof., 1974—, head sect. gastroenterology, 1971—; mem. gen. med. study sect. NIH; mem. food and nutrition bd. NRC/Nat. Acad. Scis. Served with USPHS, 1961-64. Mem. Am. Gastroenterol. Assn., Am. Soc. Clin. Nutrition, Am. Soc. Clin. Investigation, AAAS. Office: 950 E 59th St Chicago IL 60637

ROSENBERG, JAMES LEROY, theater educator; b. Sheridan, Wyo., May 19, 1921; s. J.L. Roy and Emily (MacPherson) R.; A.B., U. Calif. at Berkeley, 1951; M.A., U. Denver, 1952, Ph.D., 1954; m. Dorothy Ellen Ayre, June 12, 1949; children—Shelley, Robert, Susan. Mem. English dept. Kans. State U., 1953-61, theatre dept. Tulane U., 1961-62; prof. drama Carnegie-Mellon U., 1962—; mem. drama dept. U. Birmingham (Eng.), 1968-69. Served with AUS, 1942-46. Fulbright fellow, 1968-69. Home: 3230 Beechwood Blvd Pittsburgh PA 15217

ROSENBERG, JAY FRANK, philosopher; b. Chgo., Apr. 18, 1942; s. Sandor and Laura (Fried) R.; B.A., Reed Coll., 1963; M.A., U. Pitts., 1964, Ph.D., 1966; children—Joshua Conrad, Leslie Johanna. Faculty, U. N.C., Chapel Hill, 1966—, prof. philosophy, 1974—, asst. chmn. dept., 1975-76, 77-78. Mem. AAUP, Am. Philos. Assn., So. Soc. for Philosophy and Psychology. John Simon Guggenheim Meml. fellow, 1976-77. Author: The Impoverished Students' Book of Cookery, Drinkery and Housekeepery, 1964, Linguistic Representation, 1974, The Practice of Philosophy, 1978; contbr. essays, papers in philosophy to profl. jours.; editor: (with Charles Travis) Readings in the Philosophy of Language, 1971. Home: 715 Williams Circle Chapel Hill NC 27514 Office: Dept Philosophy Univ North Carolina Chapel Hill NC 27514. *We are amazed when all the jigsaw pieces fit together to form a picture, until we remember that we made the puzzle by sawing up the picture. After all, if there were no solution, would we have gone to all the trouble of inventing the problem? Every age needs a myth. Ours is that we live in an age which no longer needs a myth.*

ROSENBERG, JEROME LAIB, chemist, educator; b. Harrisburg, Pa., June 20, 1921; s. Robert and Mary (Katzman) R.; A.B., Dickinson Coll., 1941; M.A., Columbia, 1944, Ph.D., 1948; m. Shoshana Gabriel, Sept. 15, 1946; children—Jonathan, Judith. Instr. chemistry Columbia, 1946-48; research asso., asst. prof. Inst. Radiobiology and Biophysics, U. Chgo., 1950-53; mem. faculty U. Pitts., 1953—, chmn. dept. biophysics and microbiology, 1969-71, prof. biol. scis., 1976—, dean faculty arts and scis., 1970—, vice provost, 1978—; research chemist S.A.M. Labs., N.Y.C., 1944-46. NSF Sr. fellow Technion, Israel Inst. Tech., 1962-63; AEC fellow phys. sci. U. Chgo., 1948-50. Mem. Am. Assn. U. Profs. (nat. council 1968-69, pres. Pa. div. 1968-69). Author: Photosynthesis, 1965. Editor, reviser: Outline Theory and Problems of College Chemistry (Schaum), 1949, 58, 66, 80; contbr. articles profl. jours. Home: 1029 S Negley Ave Pittsburgh PA 15217

ROSENBERG, JERRY MARTIN, educator; b. N.Y.C., Feb. 5, 1935; s. Frank and Esther (Gardner) R.; B.S., Coll. City N.Y., 1956; M.A., Ohio State U., 1957; certificate, Sorbonne, 1958; Ph.D., N.Y.U., 1963; m. Ellen Young, Sept. 11, 1960; children—Lauren, Elizabeth. Asst. prof. Cornell U. Sch. Indsl. and Labor Relations, 1961-64; asst. prof. Columbia, 1964-68; pvt. practice cons., N.Y.C., 1968-71; asso. prof. City U. N.Y., 1971-74; prof. mgmt., chmn. dept. Poly. Inst. N.Y., N.Y.C., 1974-77; prof. mgmt. Lehman Coll., City U. N.Y., 1977—; testified before U.S. senate on privacy, 1971. Recipient Fulbright and French Govt. awards, 1957. Mem. Am. Psychol. Assn., Jewish (exec. bd. temple). Author: Automation Manpower and Education, 1966; The Computer Prophets, 1969; The Death of Privacy, 1969; Dictionary of Business and Management, 1978. Home: 515 Tulfan Terr Riverdale NY 10463 Office: Bedford Park Blvd W Bronx NY 10468

ROSENBERG, JOHN DAVID, literary critic, educator; b. N.Y.C., Apr. 17, 1929; s. David and Dorothy Lilian (Shatz) R.; B.A., Columbia Coll., 1950; B.A., Clare Coll., Cambridge U., 1953, M.A., 1958; M.A., Columbia U., 1951, Ph.D., 1960; m. Maurine Ann Hellner, June 11, 1972; 1 son, Matthew John. Lectr. in English, Columbia U., N.Y.C., 1953-54, asst. prof., 1962-65, asso. prof., 1966-67, prof. English, 1967—, chmn. Columbia Coll. humanities program, 1970-73, dir. masters program in English, 1976-78, editor-in-chief Columbia Rev., 1949-50; instr. Coll. City N.Y., 1954-62; vis. prof. English, Harvard U., summer 1968, U. B.C., summer 1970, Princeton U., 1978; guest lectr. U.S. Mil. Acad., Cambridge U., Queens U., Northwestern U.; cons. Harvard, Yale, Princeton univs. presses; cons. nat. screening com. Fulbright Program, 1968-69. Recipient Clarke F. Ansley award for Voice in the Wilderness: A Study of John Ruskin, 1960, Council for Research in Humanities grant-in-aid, 1965; Euretta J. Kellett fellow Cambridge U., 1951-53, Edward Coe fellow, 1956-57, Samuel S. Fels fellow, 1959-60; Am. Council Learned Socs. fellow, 1965-66, 79; Lawrence H. Chamberlain fellow, 1965-66; John Simon Guggenheim fellow, 1968-69; vis. fellow Clare Hall, Cambridge U., 1969. Mem. Modern Lang. Assn. Am. (chmn. exec. com. Victorian div. 1970, exec. com. 1979—), AAUP, Tennyson Soc., Ruskin Assn., Camp Rising Sun Alumni Assn., Phi Beta Kappa. Author: The Darkening Glass: A Portrait of Ruskin's Genius, 1961; The Fall of Camelot: A Study of Tennyson's Idylls of the King, 1973; critical edits. of Ruskin, 1963, Mayhew, 1968, Swinburne, 1968, Tennyson, 1975. Contbr. essays and reviews on English lit. to N.Y. Times Book Rev., Harper's Mag., Hudson Rev., and profl. jours. Home: 435 Riverside Dr New York NY 10025 Office: Dept English Columbia U New York NY 10027

ROSENBERG, LEONARD B., lawyer; b. S.I., N.Y., May 11, 1928; s. Max B. and Esther (Katz) R.; B.A., U. Tex., 1947; LL.B., U. Houston, 1953; m. JoAnn Schultz, Sept. 7, 1951; children—Andrea Rosenberg Satter, Wade, Robert, Eric, Lynne. Admitted to Tex. bar, 1952; individual practice law, Houston, 1953-67; partner firm Rosenberg, Zuber & Pulaski, Houston, 1968-72, Foreman, Dyess, Prewett, Rosenberg & Henderson, Houston, 1972—. Trustee Houston Inst. Cancer Research and Treatment, 1974-76, U. Houston Law Sch. Found., 1978—, U. Houston Law Sch. Found., 1978—. C.P.A., Tex. Mem. Am., Houston, Tex. bar assns., Alpha Epsilon Pi, Phi Delta Phi. Jewish. Clubs: Houston, Westwood Country (Houston). Home: 5639 Doliver St Houston TX 77035 Office: 2900 Entex Bldg Houston TX 77002

ROSENBERG, LOUIS, U.S. dist. judge; b. Beaver Falls, Pa., July 5, 1898; s. Morris and Frances (Goldberg) R.; LL.B., Duquesne U., Pitts.; 1 son, Marcis S. Admitted to Pa. bar; spl. atty. Allegheny County Emergency Relief, 1935; spl. dep. atty. gen. Commonwealth Pa., 1936-41; spl. asst. city solicitor City of Pitts., 1941-56, dir. public safety, 1956-61; U.S. dist. judge Western Dist. Judge Pa., Pitts., 1961—, sr. judge. Address: 918 US Post Office and Courthouse Pittsburgh PA 15219

ROSENBERG, MANUEL BERNARD, retail co. exec.; b. Boston, Apr. 26, 1930; s. Israel and Lillian (Wirin) R.; A.B., Harvard U., 1951, M.B.A., 1953; m. Audray Merle Gold, Aug. 28, 1955; children—Peter Neal, Beth Susan. Vice pres. Filene's, Boston, 1967-73; pres., chief exec. officer, Gimbel's, Phila., 1973-75, chmn. bd., chief exec. officer, 1975-77; exec. v.p. Garfinckel, Brooks Bros., Miller & Rhoads, Inc., Washington, 1977-79, pres., 1979—, also dir. Served to lt. USN, 1953-56. Jewish. Club: Univ. (Washington). Home: 417 Spruce St Philadelphia PA 19106 Office: 1629 K St NW Washington DC 20006

ROSENBERG, MAURICE, lawyer, asst. atty. gen. U.S.; b. Oswego, N.Y., Sept. 3, 1919; s. Samuel and Diana (Lishansky) R.; A.B., Syracuse U., 1940; LL.B. (editor-in-chief Law Rev.), Columbia, 1947;

m. Ruth Myers, Dec. 7, 1941 (dec. Nov. 1945); 1 son, David Lee; m. 2d, Gloria Jacobson, Dec. 19, 1948; children—Joan Myra, Richard Sam. Admitted to N.Y. bar, 1947; law sec. to judge N.Y. Ct. Appeals, 1947-49; asso. firm Cravath, Swaine & Moore, N.Y.C., 1949-53, Austrian, Lance & Stewart, N.Y.C., 1953-56; prof. Columbia Law Sch., 1956— (on leave 1979—); dir. Project Effective Justice, 1956-64, dir. Walter E. Meyer Research Inst. Law, 1965-71, Nash prof., 1970-73, Harold R. Medina prof. procedural jurisprudence, 1973—; spl. asst. to Atty. Gen. U.S., 1976; vis. prof. Harvard U., 1969-70; cons. U.S. Dept. Justice, 1977-79, asst. atty. gen. U.S., 1979—; lectr. U.S., Asia and Europe; mem. faculty Nat. Coll. State Trial Judges. Mem. Mayor N.Y.C. Com. on Judiciary, 1962-77; chmn. Adv. Council Appellate Justice, 1970-75, Council on Role of Cts., 1978—; chmn. adv. council Nat. Center for State Cts., 1975-77. Trustee Practising Law Inst. Served with AUS, 1941-45; ETO. Fellow Am. Acad. Arts and Scis., Inst. Jud. Adminstrn.; mem. Am., N.Y. State bar assns., Assn. Bar City N.Y., Assn. Am. Law Schs. (pres. 1972-73), Am. Judicature Soc. Author: (with Harold Korn, Hans Smit and Jack Weinstein) Elements of Civil Procedure, 1962, 3d edit., 1976; (with Willis Reese) Conflict of Laws, 7th edit., 1977; The Pretrial Conference and Effective Justice, 1964; (with Paul Carrington and Daniel Meador) Justice on Appeal, 1976. Editor: Dollars, Delay and the Automobile Victim, 1968, (with Lloyd Ohlin) Law and Social Research, 1977. Clubs: Century (N.Y.C.); Cosmos (Washington). Home: 4970 Sentinel Dr Bethesda MD 20016 Office: Dept Justice 01AJ Washington DC 20530

ROSENBERG, MILTON J., social psychologist; b. N.Y.C., Apr. 15, 1925; s. Jacob and Rae (Dumbrowitz) R.; B.A., Bklyn. Coll., 1946; M.A., U. Wis., 1948; Ph.D., U. Mich., 1954; m. Marjorie Anne King, Sept. 5, 1954; 1 son, Matthew. Instr., U. Wis. at Milw., 1948-49; research asst. and asso. U. Mich., 1949-52, instr. psychology, 1952-54; asst. prof. psychology Yale, 1954-61; asso. prof. Ohio State U., 1961-63; prof. psychology Dartmouth, 1963-65; prof. social psychology U. Chgo., 1965—; chmn. doctoral program in social and organizational psychology, 1976—. Past cons. VA, Nat. Conf. Christians and Jews. Faculty Research fellow Social sci. Research Council 1960-61, Mem. Am. Psychol. Assn., Soc. Psychol. Study Social Issues, Com. Psychology Internat. Relations. Author: (with others) Attitude Organization and Change, 1960, Theories of Cognitive Consistency, 1968, Vietnam and the Silent Majority, 1970, Beyond Conflict and Containment, 1972, also articles chpts in books. Office: Dept Psychology U Chicago Chicago IL 60637

ROSENBERG, NANCY SHERMAN (MRS. LAWRENCE C. ROSENBERG), author; b. N.Y.C., June 21, 1931; d. Monroe and Gertrude (Horn) Sherman; grad. Fieldston Sch., N.Y.C., 1948; B.A., Bryn Mawr Coll., 1952; m. Lawrence C. Rosenberg, July 15, 1951; children—Eric, Mark, Constance, Elizabeth. Author: The Boy Who Ate Flowers, 1960; Gwendolyn the Miracle Hen (Herald Tribune Children Spring Book Festival award 1961), 1961; Gwendolyn and the Weathercock, 1963; (with Dr. Lawrence Rosenberg) The Story of Modern Medicine, 1966; Miss Agatha's Lark, 1968; (with Reuven K. Snyderman) New Parts for People 1968; How To Enjoy Mathematics with Your Child, 1970; (with Dr. Louis Z. Cooper) Vaccines and Viruses, 1971. Home: 28 Fanshaw Ave Yonkers NY 10705

ROSENBERG, NORMAN, surgeon; b. N.Y.C., Apr. 25, 1916; s. Leo and Rose (Kamerman) R.; B.A., U. Pa., 1934; M.D., N.Y. U., 1938; m. Ruth Harriet Feller, Nov. 30, 1940; children—Lois (Mrs. Robert F. Ebin), Ralph. Intern, Mt. Sinai Hosp., N.Y.C., 1939-41, resident, 1942-43; practice medicine, specializing in surgery, New Brunswick, N.J., 1946—; sr. attending surgeon St. Peters Med. Center, New Brunswick, 1946—; chief staff Middlesex Gen. Hosp., New Brunswick, 1959-66, chief vascular surgery, 1960—, dir. dept. surgery, 1975—; cons. surgeon Roosevelt Hosp., Metuchen, N.J., 1956—, Raritan Valley Hosp., Greenbrook, N.J., 1970—, Somerset Hosp., Somerville, N.J., 1952—, J.F. Kennedy Hosp., Edison, N.J., 1969—; clin. prof. surgery Rutgers Med. Sch., Coll. Medicine and Dentistry N.J., New Brunswick, 1972—; cons. Johnson & Johnson Research Center, New Brunswick, 1954—. Trustee Robert Wood Johnson Found. Served to capt. M.C., AUS, 1943-46. Diplomate Am. Bd. Surgery. Fellow A.C.S., Southeastern Surg. Congress; mem. Soc. Vascular Surgery, Internat. Cardiovascular Soc., Soc. Surgeons N.J. Contbr. articles to books and profl. jours. Co-inventor modified bovine arterial graft. Home: 48 North Dr East Brunswick NJ 08816 Office: 10 Lincoln Ave Highland Park NJ 08904

ROSENBERG, NORMAN JACK, agrl. meteorologist; b. Bklyn., Feb. 22, 1930; s. Jacob and Rae (Dombrowitz) R.; B.S., Mich. State U., 1951; M.S., Okla. State U., 1958; Ph.D., Rutgers U., 1961; m. Sarah Zacher, Dec. 30, 1950; children—Daniel Jonathon, Alyssa Yael. Soil scientist Israel Soil Conservation Service, Haifa, 1953-55, Israel Water Authority, Haifa, 1955-57; research asst. Okla. State U., 1957-58; research fellow Rutgers U., 1958-61; asst. prof. agrl. meteorology U. Nebr., Lincoln, 1961-64, asso. prof., 1964-67, prof., 1968—, prof. agrl. engring., 1975—, prof. agronomy, 1976—, leader sect. agrl. meteorology, 1974, dir. Center for Agrl. Meteorology and Climatology, 1979; cons. Dept. State AID, NOAA, Am. Public Health Assn.; mem. numerous ad hoc coms., and mem. standing com. on atmospheric sci. Nat. Acad. Scis./NRC, 1975-78; vis. prof. agrl. meteorology Israel Inst. Tech., Haifa, 1968; Lady Davis fellow Hebrew U., Jerusalem, 1977. NATO sr. fellow in sci., 1968; recipient Centennial medal Nat. Weather Service, 1970. Fellow AAAS; mem. Am. Soc. Agronomy, Am. Meteorol. Soc. (outstanding achievement in bioclimatology award 1978), Arid Zone Soc. India, Sigma Xi, Alpha Zeta, Gamma Sigma Rho. Jewish. Club: Malib Poker Soc. of Lincoln. Author: Microclimate: The Biological Environment, 1974, also numerous articles in profl. jours.; editor: North American Droughts, 1978; tech. editor Agronomy Jour., 1974—. Home: 3145 S 31st St Lincoln NE 68502 Office: 211 Agrl Engring Bldg U of Nebr Lincoln NE 68583

ROSENBERG, PAUL, physicist; b. N.Y.C., Mar. 31, 1910; s. Samuel and Evelyn (Abbey) R.; A.B., Columbia, 1930, M.A., 1933, postgrad., 1933-40; m. Marjorie S. Hillson, June 12, 1943; 1 dau., Gale B.E. Chemist, Hawthorne Paint & Varnish Corp., N.J., 1930-33; grad. asst. physics Columbia, 1934-39, lectr., 1939-41; instr. Hunter Coll., N.Y.C., 1939-41; research asso. elec. engring. Mass. Inst. Tech., Cambridge, 1941; staff mem. Radiation Lab., Nat. Def. Research Com. 1941-45; pres. Paul Rosenberg Assos., cons. physicists, Pelham, N.Y., 1945—; pres. Inst. Nav., 1950-51. Mem. war com. radio Am. Standards Assn., 1942-44; gen. chmn. joint meeting Radio Tech. Commn. for Aeros., Radio Tech. Commn. for Marine Services and Inst. of Nav., 1950; co-chmn. Nat. Tech. Devel. Com. for upper atmostphere and interplanetary nav., 1947-50. Mem. maritime research Adv. com. Nat. Acad. Scis.-NRC, 1959-60; chmn. cartography panel space programs Earth resources survey NRC, 1973-76; chmn. panel on nav. and traffic control space applications study Nat. Acad. Scis., 1968. Bd. dirs. Center for Environment and Man, 1976-79. Fellow AAAS (council 1961-73, v.p. 1966-69), IEEE, Am. Inst. Chemists, Am. Inst. Aeros. and Astronautics (asso.); mem. Am. Phys. Soc., Am. Chem. Soc., Nat. Acad. Engring., Acoustical Soc. Am., Armed Forces Communication Assn., Optical Soc. Am., N.Y. Acad. Scis., Am. Soc. Photogrammetry (Talbert Abrams award 1955), Am. Assn. Physics Tchrs., Sigma Xi, Zeta Beta Tau. Clubs: Beach Point Yacht (Mamaroneck, N.Y.); Columbia U. Contbr. sci., tech. articles to prof. jours. Editorial com. Jour. Aerospace Scis., 1952-60. Patentee in field. Home: 53 Fernwood Rd Larchmont NY 10538 Office: 330 5th Ave Pelham NY 10803

ROSENBERG, PAUL BAYARD, fin. exec.; b. Boston, June 2, 1932; s. Benjamin Robert and Lillian (Wolfson) R.; A.B., Tufts U., 1953; M.B.A., Harvard, 1958; m. Marcia Barbara Fershtman, June 20, 1954; children—Benjamin, James, Gail. Vice pres., treas. Tyco Labs., Inc., Waltham, Mass., 1960-71; v.p., treas. Brookfield Sporting Goods Co., Inc., East Brookfield, Mass., 1971-73; v.p., treas. Healthco. Inc., Boston, 1973-77; v.p. Tech. Ops., Inc., Boston, 1977—. Served with USN, 1953-56. Mem. Phi Beta Kappa. Home: 95 Warren Rd Framingham MA 01701 Office: 1 Beacon St Boston MA 02108

ROSENBERG, RICHARD MORRIS, banker; b. Fall River, Mass., Apr. 21, 1930; s. Charles and Betty (Peck) R.; B.S., Suffolk U., 1952; M.B.A., Golden Gate Coll., 1962, LL.B., 1966; m. Barbara K. Cohen, Oct. 21, 1956; children—Michael, Peter. Publicity asst. Crocker-Anglo Bank, San Francisco, 1959-62; banking services officer Wells Fargo Bank, N.A., San Francisco, 1962-65, asst. v.p., 1965-68, v.p. marketing dept., 1968, v.p., dir. marketing, 1969, sr. v.p. marketing and advt. div., 1970-75, exec. v.p., 1975—; dir. Wells Fargo Mortgage Co., Grayco Land Escrow Ltd. Bd. dirs. Marin Ecumenical Housing Assn.; bd. regents Sch. Bank Marketing, U. Colo. Served from ensign to lt. USNR, 1953-59. Mem. Western States Bankcard Assn., Am. Bankers Assn. (exec. com. marketing/savs. div.), Bank Mktg. Assn. (dir.), State Bar Calif. Jewish. Clubs: San Francisco Press, World Trade. Home: 66 Oakdale Way San Rafael CA 94901 Office: 420 Montgomery St San Francisco CA 94104

ROSENBERG, ROBERT MELVIN, educator, chemist; b. Hartford, Conn., Mar. 9, 1926; s. Abraham and Minnie (Baggish) R.; B.S., Trinity Coll., Hartford, Conn., 1947; Ph.D., Northwestern U., 1951; m. Eleanor Virginia Hobbs, June 7, 1951; children—Charles Albert, Lenore Beth, Margaret Susan, James Steven. Research asso. Cath. U., 1950-51; asst. dermatology Harvard Med. Sch., 1951-53; asst. prof. chemistry Wesleyan U., Middletown, Conn., 1953-56; mem. faculty Lawrence U., Appleton, Wis., 1956—, prof. chemistry, 1967—, chmn. dept., 1961-62, 66-67, 79-80; asso. dean Lawrence and Downer Colls., 1968-72; resident dir. Asso. Colls. Midwest Argonne Semester program Argonne Nat. Labs., 1967-68; vis. asso. prof. Wesleyan U., Summer 1960, Northwestern U., summer 1961; research asso. U. Wis. at Madison, 1974-75. Served with USNR, 1944-46. NSF faculty fellow Oxford (Eng.) U., 1962-63. Mem. Am. Chem. Soc. (chmn. vis. scientists com., div. chem. edn. 1968-69), Chem. Soc. (London), Am. Assn. U. Profs., A.A.A.S., Sigma Xi. Author: Principles of Physical Chemistry, 1977; co-author 2 books; also contbr. articles to sci. publs. 1901 N Nicholas St Appleton WI 54911

ROSENBERG, ROBERT MICHAEL, restaurant exec.; b. Boston, Mar. 4, 1938; s. William and Bertha (Greenberg) R.; B.S., Cornell U., 1959; M.B.A., Harvard, 1963; m. Lorna Meltzer, Mar. 26, 1961; children—James Lee, John Matthew. Pres., dir. Dunkin' Donuts, Inc., Randolph, Mass., 1963—. Bd. dirs. Greater Boston Assn. for Retarded Citizens; bd. overseers Center for Study Foodservice Mgmt., N.Y. U. Served with Mass. N.G., 1963-67. Recipient award for bus. Bryant and Stratton Coll., 1968; named One of Ten Outstanding Young Men of Greater Boston, Greater Boston Jr. C. of C., 1968, Outstanding Man of Year, Greater Boston Assn. for Retarded Citizens, 1968. Mem. Harvard Bus. Sch. Assn., Internat. Franchise Assn. (pres. 1970-71), Cornell Soc. Hotelmen. Mason. Author: (with Madelan Bedell) Profits from Franchising, 1969. Home: 4 Chadwick Rd Weston MA Office: Dunkin' Donuts Inc PO Box 317 Randolph MA 02368

ROSENBERG, RUTH YALOWICH (MRS. ARTHUR EARL ROSENBERG), opera producer; b. Rochester, N.Y., May 28, 1912; d. William and Fanny (Courtheoux) Yalowich; B.A. magna cum laude, U. Rochester, 1935; m. Arthur Earl Rosenberg, Aug. 22, 1939; 1 son, John Saul. Asst. in history U. Rochester, 1935-36; tchr. children's religious choir, 1938-42; pvt. tchr. piano and theory, 1939—; stage dir. religious and lay orgns.; founder, gen. mgr., producer Opera Theatre of Rochester, Inc., 1962—. Mem. housing com. NAACP, 1960, bd. dirs., 1949-56, also dir. publicity and edn. Mem. Music Tchrs. Guild, World Federalists, Phi Beta Kappa. Home: 757 Winton Rd S Rochester NY 14618 Office: PO Box 172 North NY 14514

ROSENBERG, STEVEN AARON, surgeon; b. N.Y.C., Aug. 2, 1940; s. Abraham and Harriet (Wendroff) R.; B.A., Johns Hopkins U., 1960, M.D., 1963; Ph.D., Harvard U., 1968; m. Alice Ruth O'Connell, Sept. 15, 1968; children—Beth Liorah, Rachel Ann. Resident in surgery Peter Bent Brigham Hosp., Boston, 1963-64, 68-69, 72-74; resident fellow in immunology Harvard Med. Sch., 1969-70; clin. asso. immunology br. Nat. Cancer Inst., Bethesda, Md., 1970-72; chief surgery Nat. Cancer Inst., NIH, 1974—, asso. editor Jour., 1974—; mem. U.S.-USSR Coop. Immunotherapy Program, 1974—, U.S.-Japan Coop. Immunotherapy Program, 1975—; clin. asso. prof. surgery George Washington U. Med. Center, 1976—. Served with USPHS, 1970-72. Mem. Soc. Univ. Surgeons, Soc. Surg. Oncology, Surg. Biology Club II, Halsted Soc., Transplantation Soc., Am. Assn. Immunologists, Am. Assn. Cancer Research, Phi Beta Kappa, Alpha Omega Alpha. Contbr. articles to profl. jours. Home: 9015 Honeybee Ln Bethesda MD 20014 Office: Nat Cancer Inst NIH 9000 Rockville Pike Bethesda MD 20014

ROSENBERG, WILLIAM, food chain exec.; b. Boston, 1916. Chmn., Dunkin' Donuts Inc., Randolph, Mass.; founder N.H. Sire Stakes Program; past chmn., trustee Standardbred Breeders and Owners Devel. Agy.; founder, owner Wilrose Farms, Standardbred breeding facility, East Kingston, Kingston, N.H. Mem. Internat. Franchise Assn. (founder, past pres.), Am. Standardbred Breeders Assn. (dir.), New Eng. Standardbred Breeders and Owners Assn. (founder, past pres.), Standardbred Breeders and Owners Assn. N.H. (dir.). Office: PO Box 317 Randolph MA 02368

ROSENBERGER, CAROL, concert pianist; b. Detroit, Nov. 1, 1935; d. Maurice Seiberling and Whilamet (Gibson) Rosenberger; B.F.A., Carnegie-Mellon U., 1955; postgrad. Acad. Performing Arts, Vienna, 1956-59. Internat. concert career, 1964—; New York debut, 1970; appeared several times at Carnegie Hall; soloist Am. Symphony, Nat. Symphony, Royal Philharmonic, San Diego Symphony, Detroit Symphony, Houston Symphony, St. Louis Symphony, Indpls. Symphony, Los Angeles Chamber Orch.; performed world premiere of Buenaventura piano concert with Philippine Philharmonic, 1977, with Am. Symphony, 1977; recital series in Am., European, Asian music capitals; recorded Chopin Preludes, Schubert Sonata Op. 42, Four Impromptus Op. 90, Szymanowski Mazurkas, Hindemith's Four Temperaments with London Royal Philharmonic; mem. artist faculty U. So. Calif.; vis. artist numerous colls. and univs.; chosen to represent Am. women musicians by Nat. Commn. on Observance Internat. Womens Year, 1976. Recipient Steinway Centennial medal, 1954. Mem. Nat. Acad. Rec. Arts and Scis. Contbr. articles to music publs. Home: 721 Adelaide Pl Santa Monica CA 90402 Office: care Walter Gould Century Artists Bureau Inc 866 3d Ave New York NY 10022

ROSENBERGER, DONALD MARKLEY, hosp. cons.; b. Norristown, Pa., Jan. 30, 1913; s. Daniel H. and Jennie K. (Markley) R.; A.B., Oberlin Coll., 1934; postgrad. Coll. William and Mary, 1936-37; m. Helen Louise Leonardson, June 17, 1941; 1 dau., Jane L. Adminstrv. intern Pa. Hosp., Phila., 1937-38; adminstrv. asst. Asso. Hosp. Service, Blue Cross, Phila., 1939; adminstr. Clearfield (Pa.) Hosp., 1939-41; dir. Hamot Hosp., Erie, Pa., 1941-49, Me. Gen. Hosp. and Me. Med. Center, Portland, 1949-58; dir. United Hosps. of Newark, including Presbyn., Babies, Hosp. Crippled Children, Newark Eye and Ear hosps., 1958-70; pres. Donald M. Rosenberger & Assos., Inc., hosp. cons., 1962—; dir. Interax, Inc., Phila. v.p. Hosp. Research and Devel. Inst.; cons. USPHS; mem. jury 1954 A.I.A.'s to judge hosp. architecture; hosp. cons. Am. Pub. Health Assn. Pres. trustees Beard Sch., Orange, N.J., Morristown-Beard Sch., Morristown, N.J.; chmn. sch. devel. com. Town of Raymond (Maine); v.p. Raymond Waterways Assn. Fellow Am. Coll. Hosp. Adminstrs., Am. Pub. Health Assn., Soc. Advancement Mgmt. Internat.; mem. Am. (council design and constrn. 1966), N.J. (trustee, chmn. council adminstrv. practice, pres. 1967-68), Me., Pa. hosp. assns., hosp. adminstrs. clubs N.Y.C. (pres. 1970-71), N.J., Am. Assn. for Hosp. Planning (dir. 1972-77), Soc. Profl. Mgmt. Consultants (v.p.), N.Y. Acad. Scis. (life), Newcomen Soc., Pa. Soc., Pa. German Soc. Episcopalian. Rotarian. Club: Downtown (Newark). Editorial bd. Modern Hosp. mag., Quar. Jour. Hosp. Adminstrn. Address: PO Box 255 Raymond ME 04071

ROSENBERGER, HOMER TOPE, historian, personnel tng. cons.; b. Lansdale, Pa., Mar. 23, 1908; s. Daniel Hendricks and Jennie Kulp Markley R.; grad. Albright Coll., 1929, LL.D., 1955; M.A., Cornell U., Ithaca, N.Y., 1930, Ph.D., 1932; m. Gertrude Pauline Richards, July 14, 1934 (dec. June 1975); children—Arley Jane (Mrs. Harry C. Furminger), Lucretia Hazel (Mrs. Patrick R. Myers); m. 2d, Jean Hershey Richards, Apr. 12, 1977. High sch. hist. tchr., Tidioute, Pa., 1930-31; prof. history and govt. Susquehanna U., summer 1933; adult night sch. instr., Lock Haven, Pa., 1933-35; ednl. research and adminstrn. U.S. Office Edn., 1935-42; supr. tng. Bur. Prisons, U.S. Dept. Justice, 1942-57; chief of tng. Bur. Pub. Rds., U.S. Dept. Commerce, 1957-65; cons. U.S. Post Office Dept., 1969, Pa. Dept. Hwys., 1965-78; mem. safety council U.S. Civilian Conservation Corps, 1938-42; chmn. U.S. Tng. Officers Conf., 1949-50, 55-57, mem. steering com., 1947-67, citation, 1957; mem. Pa. Com. Correctional Staff Tng., 1955-57, cons. on personnel mgmt. to United Hosps., Newark, N.J., 1960-69; mem. adv. com. on counseling, testing and programmed learning Grad. Sch., U.S. Dept. Agr., 1965-66; adviser on devel. adminstrv. competence govt. employees Nigeria, Africa, 1963-64. Bd. dirs. Bur. Rehab., Nat. Capital Area, 1951-79, pres., 1958-61, mem. exec. com., 1967-71, citation, 1968, 79, mem. personnel com., 1975—; mem. Pa. Bd. Pvt. Corr. Schs., 1957-73, chmn., 1972-73. Organizer, moderator Rose Hill Seminars, 1963—; proposed, promoted William Penn Meml., Harrisburg, Pa., 1943-46; v.p. Franklin County (Pa.) Heritage, Inc., 1968-74, dir., 1968—; mem. Pa. adv. bd. rev. Nat. Register Historic Places, 1969—; mem. Pa. Hist. and Mus. Commn., 1972—. Mem. Pa. Fedn. Hist. Socs. (exec. com. 1969-75, chmn. awards com. 1970-74), Pa. Prison Soc. (exec. com., 1949-66, chmn. awards com. 1952-64), Kittochtinny Hist. Soc. (v.p., dir. 1969—), Howard League Penal Reform, London, Pa. Hist. Assn. (mem. council 1945—, chmn. of publs. com. 1946-48, 51-67, pres. 1967-69), Columbia Hist. Soc. (Washington, pres. 1968-76, bd. mgrs. 1953— chmn. exec. com. 1963-68), Pa. Hist. Junto (Washington, founder, past pres., past program chmn., mem. exec. com., citations 1957, 67), Am. Peace Soc. (dir. 1960—, mem. exec. com., 1961-64, chmn. com. on pub. of monographs 1962-64), Pa. German Soc. (pres. 1957-69, dir. 1949—, chmn. nominating com. 1976—), Am. Correctional Assn., Phi Delta Kappa, Phi Alpha Theta, Pi Gamma Mu, Alpha Pi Omega. Club: Cosmos (history com. 1960-65, 70—, awards com. 1977—) (Washington). Mem. United Methodist Ch. Author: Testing Occupational Training and Experience, 1948; What Should We Expect of Education?, 1956; Manuals for Executives, 1956, 58; Recommendations Concerning the Use of Case Material in the Institute of Administration, Ibadan, Nigeria, 1964; Techniques for Getting Things Done, 7th edit., 1964; Letters from Africa, 1965; The Pennsylvania Germans, 1891-1965, 1966; Harriet Lane, 1967; Adventures and Philosophy of a Pennsylvania Dutchman, 1971; (trilogy Horizons of the Humanities) Man and Modern Society: Philosophical Essays, 1972, Grassroots Philosophy for the Modern Mind, 1976, Vignettes of Philosophy: Thirty-Five Vital Subjects, 1977; Mountain Folks: Fragments of Central Pennsylvania Lore, 1974; The Philadelphia and Erie Railroad: It's Place in American Economic History, 1975; The Enigma: How Shall History Be Written?, 1979; also hist. articles, visual edn. and vocational guidance materials, employee tng. courses and occupational tests; many govtl. monographs and reports. Contbg. editor Pa. History, 1943-75, mem. editorial bd., 1975—; mem. editorial bd. Social Studies for Tchrs. and Adminstrs., 1949-59, Pa. Heritage, 1974—. Collector of material on history of Pa. and Pa. Germans. Home: 2121 Massachusetts Ave NW Washington DC 20008 also Rose Hill 12368 Old Pen Mar Rd Waynesboro PA 17268 Office: 1307 New Hampshire Ave NW Washington DC 20036. *To search for truth, to move from success or failure to new projects, to learn from people in many walks of life, to appreciate various kinds of beauty that surround everyone, to change my mind when gaining new understanding, and to have faith in the awe-inspiring mystery beyond mankind have helped me survive.*

ROSENBERGER, WALTER EMERSON, percussionist; b. Rochester, Pa., Nov. 2, 1918; s. Walter Emerson and Frances Mary (Means) R.; diploma timpani and percussion, Juilliard Sch. Music, 1941; m. Bernice Ida Mittlacher, Aug. 15, 1950; children—Joanne, Nancy. Percussionist, Pitts. Symphony Orch., 1941-43, also radio and rec. orchs., N.Y.C.; percussionist N.Y. Philharmonic, 1946—, prin. percussionist, 1972—; original mem. Sauter-Finegan Orch.. 1952; mem. percussion faculty Manhattan Sch. Music, 1974—. Pres. Tenafly Pony League, 1970-72. Served with AUS, 1944-46. Mem. Philharmonic Symphony Soc. N.Y. Presbyterian. Club: Englewood. Address: 11 Woodmere Ln Tenafly NJ 07670

ROSENBLATT, ARTHUR ISAAC, museum dir.; b. N.Y.C., Aug. 31, 1931; s. Harry and Helen (Satz) R.; diploma Cooper Union, 1952; B.Arch., Carnegie-Mellon U., 1956; m. Ruth Anne Turteltaub, Aug. 5, 1956; children—Paul Mark, Judith Alice. Architect, designer Katzman Assos., 1956-57; designer Isadore & Zachary Rosenfield, 1957-60; designer N.Y.C. Civic Center Project, 1960-61; chief designer Irwin Chanin, Architect, N.Y.C., 1963-65; 1st dep. adminstr. N.Y.C. Parks Dept., 1966-68; faculty archtl. and urban problems Sarah Lawrence Coll., Bronxville, N.Y., 1967-69; vice dir. Met. Mus. Art, N.Y.C., 1968-77, v.p., 1977—; mem. Mayor's Urban Design Council, 1975—; lectr. various univs. Mem. citizens housing planning council, N.Y.C., 1966—; vice chmn. community planning bd. no. 8, N.Y.C., 1964-66; trustee Trinity Sch., N.Y.C., 1979—. Served with AUS, 1953-55. Recipient Profl. citation Cooper Union, 1967; Urban Am., Inc. grantee, 1966. Mem. Archtl. League N.Y. (pres. 1970-72), AIA (dir. N.Y. chpt. 1966-68, spl. citation N.Y. chpt. 1979), Cooper Union Alumni Assn. (v.p. 1975-77, pres. 1977—), N.Y. Soc. Architects, Municipal Art Soc. Contbr. articles to archtl. jours., also N.Y. Times, Met. Mus. Bull. Home: 1158 Fifth Ave New York NY 10029 Office: Met Mus Art Fifth Ave & 82nd St New York NY 10028

ROSENBLATT, JOSEPH, poet; b. Toronto, Ont., Can., Dec. 26, 1933; s. Samuel and Bessie R., grad. pub. schs.; m. Faye Carole Smith, Oct. 13, 1969; 1 son, Eliot Howard. Books of poetry include: Voyage of the Mood, 1962, L.S.D. Leacock, 1966, Winter of the Luna Moth, 1968, The Bumblebee Dithyramb, 1972, The Blind Photographer, 1973, Dream Craters, 1974, Vampires & Virgins, 1975, selected Poems, 1976; anthologies include: Enchanted Forest, 1967, Oxford Book of Canadian Verse, 1968, Fourteen Winds, 1970, Nobody But Yourself, 1972, Poets of the Sixties, 1973, Children's Verse, 1974; exhibited ink drawings one-man show, Gadatsy Gallery; contbr. poetry to anthologies, periodicals. Recipient Gov. Gen.'s award for Poetry, 1976. Mem. League of Canadian Poets. Home: 15 Greensides Ave Toronto ON M6G 3P5 Canada

ROSENBLATT, JUDAH ISSER, statistician; b. Balt., Feb. 12, 1931; s. Samuel and Claire (Woloch) R.; B.A., Johns Hopkins U., 1951; Ph.D., Columbia U., 1959; m. Lisa Herzfeld, June 12, 1956; 1 son, Daniel. Asst. prof. Purdue U., 1956-60; asso. prof. U. N.Mex., 1960-68; prof. math. and stats. Case Western Res. U., 1968-72, prof. computer sci., 1972-76, prof. ops. research, prof. biometry, 1974—; cons. in field. Fellow Inst. Math. Stats., Am. Statis. Assn.; mem. Am. Math. Soc., Math. Assn. Am. Author: Modern University Calculus, 1966; Probability and Statistics, 1972; Simplified Computer Programming, 1974. Home: 3129 Monticello Blvd Cleveland Heights OH 44118 Office: Wearn Bldg Case Western Res U Cleveland OH 44106

ROSENBLATT, LESTER, naval architect; b. Apr., 1920; B.S., CCNY; M.S. in Naval Architecture and Marine Engring., U. Mich., 1942. Naval architect John H. Wells, Inc., 1942, 47; co-founder M. Rosenblatt & Son, N.Y.C., Architects and Marine Engrs., N.Y.C., 1947—, pres., 1959—. Recipient Sesquicentennial award, U. Mich., 1967. Mem. Soc. Naval Architects and Marine Engrs. (chmn. N.Y. met. sect. 1961-62, nat. chmn. membership com. 1964-78, mem. council, pres. 1978-80). Home: 8 E 83d St New York NY 10028 Office: 350 Broadway New York NY 10013

ROSENBLATT, LOUIS, musician; b. Phila., Mar. 9, 1928; s. Paul and Celia (Seidman) R.; diploma Curtis Inst. Music, 1951; m. Renate Gisela Reiss, Aug. 2, 1953; children—William Reiss, Richard Henry. Player oboe and solo English horn Houston Symphony, 1954-55, New Orleans Philharmonic-Symphony, 1955-59, Phila. Orch., 1959—; mem. faculty Temple U. Coll. Music. Served with AUS, 1951-54. Recipient C. Hartman Kuhn award, 1978. Mem. Am. Fedn. Musicians, Nat. Acad. Rec. Arts and Scis. Home: 1100 Chelten Ave Philadelphia PA 19126 Office: Phila Orch 230 S 15th St Philadelphia PA 19102

ROSENBLATT, PAUL, coll. dean; b. Bklyn., Feb. 16, 1928; s. Abraham and Mildred (Brower) R.; B.A., Bklyn. Coll., 1949, M.A., 1951; Ph.D., Columbia U., 1960; m. Joan Barbara Shufro, June 17, 1956; children—Abram, David. Instr., Bklyn. Coll., 1955-58; mem. faculty U. Ariz., Tucson, 1958—, prof. English, 1970—, acting head dept. Romance langs., 1973-75, dean Coll. Liberal Arts, 1975—; Regent Hays-Fulbright prof. Am. lit. Fed. U., Rio de Janeiro, Brazil, 1968-69, 72-73; Fulbright prof. U. Cuyo, Mendoza, Argentina, 1969; mem. bd. acad. visitors Am. Grad. Sch. Internat. Mgmt., 1975—; mem. panel pub. programs div. Nat. Endowment Humanities, 1976—; mem. Ariz. Council Humanities and Pub. Policy, 1975—; mem. commn. on arts and scis. Nat. Assn. State Univs. and Land Grant Colls., 1979—. Served with U.S. Army, 1953-55. Danforth fellow, 1974. Mem. Modern Lang. Assn.; hon. life mem. Am. Lit. Assn, Brazil; hon. mem. Nat. Slavic Honor Soc. Co-author: A Certain Bridge: Issac Bashevis Singer on Literature and Life, 1971, rev. edit., 1979; John Woolman, 1969. Editor: (Henry Blake Fuller) The Cliff Dwellers, 1973. Address: 345E Modern Lang Bldg Univ Ariz Tucson AZ 85721

ROSENBLATT, PETER RONALD, lawyer, ambassador; b. N.Y.C., Sept. 4, 1933; s. William and Therese Amalia (Steinhardt) R.; B.A., Yale U., 1954, J.D., 1957; postgrad. fellow Tel-Aviv U., 1971; m. Naomi Henriette Harris, July 1, 1952; children—Therese Sarah, Daniel Harris, David Steinhardt. Admitted to N.Y. bar, 1959, D.C. bar, 1969; teaching asst. history Yale U., New Haven, Conn., 1954-55; asst. dist. atty. N.Y. County, 1959-62; asso. firm Stroock & Stroock & Lavan, N.Y.C., 1962-66; dep. asst. gen. counsel AID, Washington, 1966; mem. White House staff, Washington, 1966-68; jud. officer, chmn. bd. contract appeals U.S. Post Office Dept., Washington, 1968-69; v.p., dir. EDP Technology, Inc., Washington, 1969-71; chmn. bd. Internat. Devel. Services, Washington, 1969-71; spl. cons. to Senator Edmund S. Muskie, 1970-72; practice law, Washington, N.Y.C., 1972-77; personal rep. of Pres. (with rank ambassador) to conduct negotiations on future polit. status of Trust Ter. of Pacific Islands, 1977—; mem. Middle East study group Dem. Adv. Council of Elected Officials, 1974-76. Sec., chmn. exec. com. Coalition for a Democratic Majority, 1973-77; bd. dirs. Com. on Present Danger, 1976-77. Served to 2d lt. Q.M.C., AUS, 1957-58. Mem. Am. Bar Assn., Assn. Bar City N.Y., N.Y. County Lawyers Assn. Jewish.

ROSENBLATT, ROGER, writer; b. N.Y.C., Sept. 13, 1940; s. Milton B. and Mollie Ruth (Spruch) R.; A.B., Univ. Coll. N.Y. U., 1962, postgrad., 1963-68; A.M., Harvard, 1963, Ph.D., 1968; postgrad. Dublin (Ireland) and Trinity Coll., 1965-66; m. Virginia Lee Jones, June 15, 1963; children—Carl, Amy, John. Allston Burr Sr. tutor Harvard, 1967-69, Briggs Copeland instr., 1968-69, asst. prof. English, 1969-73, dir. freshman English, Master Dunster House, 1970-73; dir. edn. Nat. Endowment for Humanities, Washington, 1973-75; lit. editor New Republic mag., Washington, 1975-78; columnist, mem. editorial bd. Washington Post; lectr. Georgetown U., 1975—. Fulbright scholar, 1965-66; Nat. Endowment for Humanities fellow, 1971-72. Clubs: Century (N.Y.C.), Harvard of N.Y., Century of N.Y.; Cosmos (Washington). Author: Black Fiction, 1974. Contbr. articles to newspapers, profl. jours. Home: 3252 N St NW Washington DC 20007 Office: Washington Post 1150 15th St NW Washington DC 20071

ROSENBLITH, WALTER ALTER, scientist, educator; b. Vienna, Austria, Sept. 21, 1913; s. David A. and Gabriele (Roth) R.; came to U.S., 1939, naturalized, 1946; Ingenieur Radiotelegraphiste, U. Bordeaux, 1936, Ing. Radioelectricien, Ecole Supérieure d'Electricité, Paris, 1937; m. Judy Olcott Francis, Sept. 27, 1941; children—Sandra Yvonne, Ronald Francis. Research engr., France, 1937-39; research asst. N.Y. U., 1939-40; grad. fellow, teaching fellow physics U. Calif. at Los Angeles, 1940-43; asst. prof., asso. prof., acting head dept. physics S.D. Sch. Mines and Tech., 1943-47; research fellow Psycho-Acoustic Lab., Harvard U., 1947-51, research asso. otology, 1957—, lectr. otolaryngology Med. Sch. Harvard, also Mass. Eye and Ear Infirmary, 1969—; asso. prof. communications biophysics Mass. Inst. Tech., 1951-57, prof., 1957—, Inst. prof., 1975—, staff Research Lab. Electronics, 1951-69, chmn. faculty, 1967-69, asso. provost, 1969-71, provost, 1971—; dir. Kaiser Industries; cons. com. conservation of hearing and noise in industry Am. Acad. Ophthalmology and Otolaryngology, 1953-64; chmn. com. electronic computers in life scis. Nat. Acad. Scis.-NRC, 1960-64, mem. brain scis. com., 1965-68, chmn., 1966-67; mem. central council Internat. Brain Research Orgn., 1960-68, mem. exec. com., hon. treas., 1962-67; mem. life scis. panel Pres.'s Sci. Adv. Com., 1961-66; mem. council Internat. Union Pure and Applied Biophysics, 1961-69; inaugural lectr. Tata Inst. Fundamental Research, Bombay, 1962; Weizmann lectr. Weizmann Inst. Sci., Rehovoth, Israel, 1962; pres. Commn. on Biophysics of Communication and Control Processes, 1964-69; mem. Pres.'s Com. Urban Housing, 1967-68; cons. communications scis. WHO, 1964, 65; mem. bd. medicine Nat. Acad. Sci., 1967-70, charter mem. Inst. Medicine, 1970—, mem. council, 1970-76, mem. exec. com., 1973—; mem. adv. com. to dir. NIH, 1970-74; mem. governing bd. NRC, 1974-76; mem. adv. com. med. sci. AMA, 1972-74; mem. U.S. Nat. Commn. on Pure and Applied Biophysics, 1965-69; sci. adviser Callier Center for Communication Disorders, 1968—, chmn. sci. adv. council, mem. Found., 1975—. Bd. govs. Weizmann Inst. Sci., 1968—; chmn. com. on research and devel. needs of physically handicapped NRC, 1975-76. Fellow Acoustical Soc. Am., World Acad. Art and Sci., Am. Acad. Arts and Scis. (exec. bd. 1970—), AAAS, IEEE; mem. Biophys. Soc. (council 1969-72, exec. bd. 1957-61), Nat. Acad. Engring., Nat. Acad. Scis., Soc. Exptl. Psychologists, Psychonomic Soc. Contbr. articles and chpts. to profl. publs. Office: Office of Provost Mass Inst Tech Cambridge MA 02139*

ROSENBLOOM, ALFRED A., JR., optometrist, coll. pres.: b. Pitts., Apr. 5, 1921; s. Alfred A. and Corinne (Lorch) R.; B.A. magna cum laude, Pa. State U., 1942; D. Optometry (cum laude), No. Ill. Coll. of Optometry 1948, D. Ocular Sci. (hon.), 1954; M.A., U. Chgo., 1953; m. Sarah Anne Rosenbaum, June, 1948; children—Alfred III, Susan. Instr. lab. courses No. Ill. Coll. of Optometry, Chgo., then prof. of optometry, dir. contact lens and low vision depts., dean, 1956-72, pres., 1972—; instr. dept. edn. reading clinic U. Chgo., summer, 1953, 54; cons. to HEW, Chgo. Lighthouse for the Blind, 1955—; lectr. Brit. Optical Assn., London, 1970, 9th Gerontol. Congress, Kiev, USSR, 1972, Australian Internat. Optometrical Congress, Melbourne, 1974, Coll. of Optometry, U. South Wales; mem. Commn. for Report of Nat. Study of Optometric Edn., 1973; mem. liaison com. on geriatric blindness Am. Found. of the Blind; mem., past chmn. adv. research com. Am. Optometric Found. Served as sgt. M.C., U.S. Army, 1942-46. Fellow Am. Acad. Optometry (editorial council); mem. Am. Optometric Assn. (com. on new acad. facilities), Ill. Optometric Assn. (Optometrist of Year 1967), Southside Optometric Soc., NEA, Assn. Schs. and Colls. Optometry (v.p.), Nat. Soc. Study Edn., AAAS, Contact Lens Soc. Eng., Internat. Reading Assn., Beta Sigma Kappa, Phi Sigma Kappa, Phi Eta Sigma, Phi Sigma Sigma, Phi Theta Upsilon. Clubs: Masons, Shriners. Contbg. author Vision of the Aging Patient; Vision of Children; contbr. numerous articles on optometry and optometric edn. to profl. jours. Office: Office of Pres Ill Coll Optometry 3241 S Michigan Ave Chicago IL 60616

ROSENBLOOM, ARLAN LEE, physician, educator; b. Milw., Apr. 15, 1934; s. Harris Phillip and Esther (Schneider) R.; B.A., U. Wis., 1955, M.D., 1958; m. Edith Kathleen Peterson, Sept. 14, 1958; children—Eric David, Maliah Jo, Disa Lynn, Harris Phillip. Intern, Los Angeles County Gen. Hosp., 1958-59; resident in gen. practice Ventury County Hosp., Ventura, Calif., 1959-60; physician-in-charge Medico Hosp., Kratie, Cambodia, 1960-61; med. officer, Pahang, Malaysia, 1961-62; resident in pediatrics U. Wis. Hosp., Madison, 1962-63, 64-65, fellow in pediatric endocrinology, 1963-64, 65-66; asst. prof. pediatrics U. Fla., Gainesville, 1968-71, asso. prof., 1971-74, prof., 1974—, chief div. endocrinology, 1977—, asso. dir. Clin. Research Center, 1969-74, dir., 1974-80, dir. Nat. Found. March of Dimes Birth Defects Center, 1969-73; vis. prof. McMaster U. Med. Centre, 1974-75. Pres., dir. Fla. Camp for Children and Youth with Diabetes, 1970—; dir. N. Fla. Regional Diabetes Program Children and Youth, 1974—, State cons., 1977—; Dir. U. Fla. Diabetes Edn., Research and Teaching Center, 1977—; clin. and sci. advisory bd. Children's Diabetes Found., Denver, 1978—; med. dir. Gainesville Youth Clinic, 1972-74; mem. advisory com. Nat. Disease and Therapy Index; mem. Fla. Com. Children and Youth, 1972—; data work group chmn. Nat. Diabetes Commn., 1975; mem. epidemiology and disease control study sect. NIH, 1978—. Served with USPHS, 1966-68. Mem. Am. Acad. Pediatrics, Am. Fedn. Clin. Research, Am. Diabetes Assn., Fla. Diabetes Assn. (dir.), Alachua County Med. Soc., Soc. Adolescent Medicine, Internat. Study Group Diabetes in Children/Adolescents, Endocrine Soc., Lawson Wilkins Pediatric Endocrine Soc., Am. Pediatric Soc., Soc. Pediatric Research. Contbr. numerous articles to profl. jours. Home: 2902 SW 1st Ave Gainesville FL 32607

ROSENBLOOM, DANIEL, investment banker, lawyer; b. N.Y.C., Feb. 11, 1930; s. Sol and Florence (Vogel) R.; B.A., U. Va., 1951, J.D., 1954; LL.M., N.Y. U., 1960; m. Linda D. Menken, Aug. 15, 1965 (div. 1979). Admitted to Va. bar, 1954, to N.Y. bar, 1956; atty. Paskus, Gordon & Hyman, N.Y.C., 1957-62; v.p., sec., gen. counsel Phila. & Reading Corp., 1962-68; partner First Manhattan Co., 1968—; dir. Brennand-Paige Industries, Inc. Served as 1st lt. AUS, 1954-56. Mem. Phi Alpha Delta, Phi Epsilon Pi. Jewish. Clubs: Harmonie, City Athletic (N.Y.C.). Home: 775 Park Ave New York NY 10021 Office: 380 Madison Ave New York NY 10017

ROSENBLOOM, MORRIS VICTOR, publisher, pub. relations exec.; b. Pitts., Oct. 25, 1915; s. Alfred A. and Corinne (Lorch) R.; B.A., U. Pitts., 1936; m. Ronda Rose Robins, May 16, 1953 (div. 1974). Dir. research statistics United Brewers Indsl. Found., N.Y., 1937; asst. to pres. Ruffsdale Distilling Co., Braddock, Pa., 1937-39; founder, dir. Am. Industries Surveys, N.Y.C., 1939-41, reactivated as Am. Surveys, 1947, dir., 1947-54, pres., 1955—; pres. of Am. Surveys Internat., 1965—; pres. Assn. for Mgmt. Environ. Resources and Info. Center for Am. Needs, 1975—; sr. economist OPM, 1941-42; prin. indsl. specialist, chief consumers' durable goods and service equipment W.P.B., later asst. to vice chmn. civilian requirements, 1942-43; v.p. charge sales Diamond Prodns. Inc., 1946-47; marketing, sales cons. to pres. Publicker Industries, Inc., Phila., sales mgr. subsidiary, 1947-50; program coordinator, asst. to chmn. NSRB, 1950; spl. asst. dept. adminstr. DPA, 1951-52; founder, exec. dir. Inst. on Econs. Def. Moblzn., sponsored by Am. U., ODM, 1951-52; exec. dir. def. materials operating and policy coms. ODM, 1953; asso. Coates & McCormick, Inc., Washington and N.Y.C., 1954; dir. PR Rev. Pub. Co. Dir. operations Nat. Citizens Com. for Hoover Report; sponsor Atlantic Council; mem. pub. relations adv. com. Fair Campaign Practices Com. Mem. nat council, nat. communications com. Boy Scouts Am., also mem. adv. bd. and chmn. pub. relations com. Nat. Capital Area council; chmn. alumni regional council U. Pitts., 1960-61. Served with USNR, 1943-46; comdg. officer submarine chaser. Recipient Silver Beaver award Boy Scouts Am., 1963. Mem. Am. Acad. Polit. and Social Sci., Am. Legion, Naval Hist. Found., Def. Orientation Conf. Assn. (v.p. 1956-57), Pub. Relations Soc. Am. (dir. Washington chpt., chmn. govt. affairs adv. com., mem. exec. com. counselors sect.), Internat. Pub. Relations Assn., Met. Washington Bd. Trade, Am. Polit. Sci. Assn., Jewish War Vets. U.S.A., Res. Officers Assn. U.S., Ret. Officers Assn., U.S. Naval Inst. and Found., Am. Inst. Mgmt., V.F.W. (nat. publicity, pub. relations com. 1953-55), Internat. Platform Assn., Am. Arbitration Assn., Pi Lambda Phi. Clubs: Army and Navy, Pitt. (Washington). Author: The Liquor Industry, rev. edit., 1937; Bottling for Profit (with A.B. Greenleaf), 1940; Peace Through Strength: Bernard Baruch and a Blueprint for Security, 1953. Contbr. articles to profl. jours.; lectr. Home: Embassy Sq Washington DC 20036 Office: 2000 N St NW Washington DC 20036

ROSENBLUETH, EMILIO, earthquake engr.; b. Mexico City, Mex., Apr. 8, 1926; s. Emilio and Charlotte (Deutsch) R.; C.E., Nat. Autonomous U. Mex., 1947; M.S. in Civil Engring., U. Ill., 1949, Ph.D., 1951; m. Alicia Laguette, Feb. 20, 1954; children—David Arturo, Javier Fernando, Pablo Esteban, Monica Teresa. Surveyor and structural engr., 1945-47; soil mechanics asst. Ministry Hydraulic Resources, also U. Ill., 1947-50; structural engr. Fed. Electricity Commn., also Ministry Navy, 1951-55; prof. earthquake engring. Nat. Autonomous U. Mex., 1956—, regent, 1972—; pres. DIRAC Group Cons., 1970-77; vice-minister Ministry Edn., 1977—; pres. Reúnion Internationale des Laboratoires d'Essais des Materiaux (RILEM), 1965-66; trustee Autonomous Metropolitana U., 1974-77; mem. working group engring. seismology UNESCO, 1965. Fellow ASCE; mem. Mexican Acad. Sci. Research (pres. 1964-65), Mexican Soc. Earthquake Engring., Mex. Soc. Soil Mechanics (trustee), Internat. Assn. Earthquake Engring. (pres. 1973-77), Mexican Assn. Civil Engrs., Mexican Math. Soc., Mexican Geophys. Union, Coll. Engring. Iberoamerican U., Seismol. Soc. Am., Soc. Exptl. Stress Analysis, Latin Am. Assn. Seismology and Earthquake Engring., Assn. Computing Machinery, N.Z. Soc. Earthquake Engring., Sigma Xi; hon. mem. Am. Concrete Inst., Internat. Assn. Earthquake Engring.; fgn. asso. Nat. Acad. Arts and Scis., Nat. Acad. Scis., Nat. Acad. Engring. Co-author: Fundamentals of Earthquake Engineering, 1971. Co-editor: Seismic Risk and Engineering Decisions, 1976. Contbr. to profl. publs. Home: Arquitectura 14 Copilco Mexico 20 DF Mexico Office: Argentina 28 20 Piso of 318 Mexico 1 DF Mexico. *The price of greatness is calumny.*

ROSENBLUM, DONALD EDWARD, army officer; b. N.Y.C., June 3, 1929; s. A. J. and Rose L. R.; B.S., The Citadel, 1951; m. Laura G. Maree, June 19, 1955; children—Alice, Jay, Nancy, Carol, Sarah, David, Anne Patrick. Joined, U.S. Army, advanced through grades to maj. gen., 1974; staff officer Joint Chiefs of Staff, 1967-68; div. support command comdr., Vietnam, 1970-71; dep. dir. ops. Dept. Army, 1974-75; comdg. gen. 24th Infantry div., 1975-77; dep. chief of staff for tng., Tng. and Doctrine Command, Fort Monroe, Va., 1979—. Decorated Legion of Merit, Bronze Star, Air medal, others. Mem. Assn. U.S. Army, Alumni Assn. of the Citadel. Home: 37 Fenwick Fort Monroe VA 23651 Office: Dept Chief of Staff for Tng HqTRADOC Fort Monroe VA 23651

ROSENBLUM, HAROLD ARTHUR, grocery distbn. exec.; b. Sharon, Pa., Jan. 5, 1923; s. H. David and Carol (Thaler) R.; student Western Res. U., 1939-40; A.B. cum laude, Harvard, 1943, J.D., 1949; m. Irene F. Rosen, June 25, 1950; children—Julia M., Mark A., Lee S., Joel N., Ruth C. Admitted to Pa. bar, 1949; with Golden Dawn Foods, Inc., Sharon, 1950—, pres., 1961—; treas., 1961-73. Mem. Mercer County Mental Health/Mental Retardation Bd., 1967—, chmn., 1967-70; chmn. Community Council Com. Mental Health/Mental Retardation, 1965-67, Shenango Valley Jewish Fedn., 1964—; pres. Friends of Buhl Henderson Library, 1973-75; treas. Mercer County Mental Health Assn., 1964-66; bd. dirs. Mercer County Family Guidance Clinic, 1959—, sec., 1961-63, pres., 1963-65; v.p. Mercer County Drug and Alcohol Council, Inc., 1973-74; mem. exec. bd. Shenango Valley Human Relations Council, 1960-68; mem. econ. devel. com. Multi-County Manpower Devel. Corp., 1972-73; mem. Sharon Human Relations Commn., 1969—; sec. Mercer County Comprehensive Health Planning Bd., 1972-74, mem. adv. com., 1971-74; charter mem. Pa. Freedom of Choice in Family Planning; mem. Mercer County Commn. on Drug and Alcohol Abuse, 1973—; mem. adv. bd. Shenango Valley Campus, Pa. State U., 1976; exec. com. Mercer County br. N.A.A.C.P., 1964-71; pres. bd. dirs. Playhouse 600, 1973-76; bd. dirs. Sharon Gen. Hosp., 1964—, sec., 1966-77, chmn., 1977—; mem. Mayor's Com. for Arts, 1973-75. Trustee-at-large Pa. council Union Am. Hebrew Congregations, 1966—; bd. dirs. Shenango Valley Urban League, 1971-73, Pa. Mental Health Assn., 1968-72. Served with AUS, 1943-46. Mem. Nat. Am. Wholesale Grocers Assn. (bd. govs. 1964-66), Shenango Valley C. of C. (bd. dirs. 1969—, treas. 1970). Clubs: Rotary (pres. 1978-79), Sharon Country, University (fin. sec., pres. 1978-79) (Sharon); F.H. Buhl (dir. 1977—). Home: 1700 Hannah Ct Sharon PA 16146 Office: 385 Shenango Ave Sharon PA 16146

ROSENBLUM, MARVIN, educator; b. Bklyn., June 30, 1926; s. Isidore and Celia (Mendelsohn) R.; B.S., U. Calif. at Berkeley, 1949, M.A., 1951, Ph.D., 1955; m. Frances E. Parker, May 30, 1959; children—Isidore, Mendel, Jessie, Rebecca, Sarah. Instr., U. Calif. at Berkeley, 1954-55; asst. prof. U. Va., Charlottesville, 1955-59, asso. prof., 1960-65, prof. math., 1965—; mem. Inst. Advanced Study, 1959-60. Served with USNR, 1944-46. Mem. Am. Math. Soc., Am. Math. Assn., Soc. for Indsl. and Applied Math., Sigma Xi. Jewish religion. Home: Box 241 Route 1 Earlysville VA 22936 Office: Math Astro Bldg U Va Charlottesville VA 22903

ROSENBLUM, MYRON, educator, chemist; b. N.Y.C., Oct. 21, 1925; s. Julius and Miriam (Sandler) R.; A.B., Columbia, 1949; A.M., Harvard, 1950, Ph.D., 1954; m. Rachel S. Jacobson, June 22, 1958; children—Miriam Judith, Jonathan, Leah. Postdoctoral fellow Columbia, 1953-55; asst. prof. Ill. Inst. Tech., 1955-58; faculty Brandeis U., Waltham, Mass., 1958—, prof. chemistry, 1966—. Office: Brandeis U Waltham MA 02154

ROSENBLUM, ROBERT, art historian; b. N.Y.C., July 24, 1927; s. Abraham H. and Lily M. (Lipkin) R.; B.A., Queens Coll., 1948; M.A., Yale U., 1950; Ph.D., N.Y. U., 1956; M.A. (hon.), Oxford U., 1972; m. Jane Kaplowitz, June 23, 1977. Mem. faculty U. Mich., Ann Arbor, 1955-56, Princeton (N.J.) U., 1956-66, Yale U., New Haven, 1966-67; mem. faculty N.Y. U., N.Y.C., 1967—, prof. fine arts, 1967—. Served with U.S. Army, 1945-46. Mem. Coll. Art Assn. Am. Author: Cubism and Twentieth-Century Art, 1960; Transformations in Late Eighteenth Century Art, 1967; Ingres, 1967; Frank Stella, 1971; Modern Painting and the Northern Romantic Tradition, 1975. Office: Inst Fine Arts NY U 1 E 78th St New York NY 10021

ROSENBLUM, VICTOR GREGORY, educator; b. N.Y.C., June 2, 1925; s. George and Vera (Minster) R.; A.B., Columbia, 1945, LL.B., 1948; Ph.D., U. Calif. at Berkeley, 1953; D.H.L., Hebrew Union Coll., 1970; m. Louise Rann, Feb. 21, 1946; children—Susan, Ellen, Laura, Keith, Jonathan, Peter, Warren, Joshua. Admitted to Ill. and N.Y. bars, also U.S. Supreme Ct.; lectr. polit. sci. U. Calif. at Berkeley, 1949-52, asst. prof. polit. sci., 1953-57; asso. prof. polit. sci. Northwestern U., 1958-63, prof. polit. sci. and law, 1963-68, 70—; pres. Reed Coll., Portland, Oreg., 1968-70. Vis. Fulbright lectr. Sch. Law U. Louvain (Belgium), 1966-67, vis. prof., 1978-79; sr. legal cons. project on bankruptcy govtl. studies div. Brookings Instn., 1964-69. Editor-in-chief Adminstrv. Law Rev., 1958-62; staff asso. Govtl. Affairs Inst., Washington, 1952-53; cons., asso. counsel Subcom. on Exec. and Legislative Reorgn., Com. on Govt. Operations, U.S. Ho. of Reps., 1956-57. Bd. dirs. Center for Adminstrv. Justice, 1972-78. Mem. Am. (council sect. adminstrv. law 1962-65, 72-75, chmn. 1977-78), Fed. bar assns., Am. Polit. Sci. Assn., Law and Soc. Assn. (pres. 1970-72), Phi Beta Kappa, Pi Sigma Alpha. Democrat. Jewish. Author: Law As A Political Instrument, 1955; Cases on Constitutional Law: Political Roles of the Supreme Court, 1973. Contbr. to law revs., also law and polit. sci. books. Home: 2030 Orrington Ave Evanston IL 60201 Office: 357 E Chicago Ave Chicago IL 60611

ROSENBLUTH, GIDEON, educator; b. Berlin, Germany, Jan. 23, 1921; s. Martin R. and Marie (Zellermayer) R.; came to Can., 1941, naturalized, 1944; student London Sch. Econs., 1938-40; B.A., U. Toronto, 1943; Ph.D., Columbia U., 1953; m. Annemarie Fischl, June 6, 1944; children—Vera, David. Lectr., Princeton (N.J.) U., 1949-50; asst. prof. econs. Stanford (Calif.) U., 1952-54; asso. prof. econs. Queens U., Kingston, Ont., 1954-62; prof. econs. U. B.C., Vancouver, 1962—. Fellow Royal Soc. Can.; mem. Am., Canadian (pres. 1978-79) econ. assns., Royal Econ. Soc., Can. Assn. U. Tchrs. (pres. 1966-67). Author: Concentration in Canadian Manufacturing Industries, 1957; (with H.G. Thorburn) Anti Combines Adminstration in Canada, 1963: The Canadian Economy and Disarmament, 1967. Office: Dept Econs U BC Vancouver BC V6T 1W5 Canada

ROSENBLUTH, MARSHALL NICHOLAS, physicist, educator; b. Albany, N.Y., Feb. 5, 1927; s. Robert and Margaret (Sondhein) R.; B.A., Harvard, 1945; M.S., U. Chgo., 1947, Ph.D., 1949; m. Arianna Wright, Jan. 26, 1951; children—Alan Edward, Robin Ann, Mary Louise, Jean Pamela. Inst., Stanford, 1949-50; staff mem. Los Alamos Sci. Lab., 1950-56; sr. research adviser Gen. Atomic Corp., San Diego, 1956-67; prof. U. Calif., San Diego, 1960-67; prof. Inst. for Advanced Study, Princeton, N.J., 1967—; lectr. with rank prof. in astrophys. scis. Princeton U., also vis. sr. research physicist Plasma Physics Lab., 1967—; Andrew D. White vis. prof. Cornell U., 1976, cons. AEC, NASA, Inst. Def. Analysis. Served with USNR, 1944-46. Recipient E.O. Lawrence award, 1964, Albert Einstein award, 1967, Maxwell prize, 1976. Mem. Am. Phys. Soc., Nat. Acad. Sci., Am. Acad. Arts and Scis. Home: 284 Mercer St Princeton NJ 08540 Office: Inst for Advanced Study Princeton NJ 08540*

ROSENBORG, RALPH MOZART, artist; b. N.Y.C., June 9, 1913; s. Mozart Wolfgang and Helena Hedvig (Ohlson) R.; pvt. art student, N.Y.C., 1930-33; m. Margaret Ann Taylor, Apr. 26, 1951. Numerous one man shows include: Artists Gallery, 1936-38, Willard Gallery, 1939-42, Phillips Meml. Gallery, 1941, Nierendorf Gallery, 1943, Rose Fried Gallery, 1945, Jacques Seligmann Gallery, 1948, 49, 74, U. Notre Dame Art Mus., 1967, Charles Egan Gallery, 1965, Georgette Passedoit Gallery, 1958-62; exhibited numerous group shows including: New Britain (Conn.) Mus. Am. Art, 1979, Butler Inst. Am. Art, Youngstown, Ohio, 1979, Deutsche Gallery, N.Y.C., 1978; represented in permanent collections including: Whitney Mus. Am. Art, Guggenheim Mus. Art, Hirschorn Art Mus., Newark Art Mus., Mus. Modern Art, Collection of Societe Anonyme-Yale U. Art Mus., Israel Mus., Met. Mus. Art, Wadsworth Atheneum, Rose Art Mus., Phillips Meml. Gallery, various museums and univs, pvt. individuals. Recipient Nat. Council of Arts and Humanities award, 1966, Childe Hassem award Am. Acad. Arts and Letters, 1960. Home: 165 Lexington Ave New York NY 10016. *I would describe my painting as a highly personal and creative effort to interpret nature and the American landscape and its people. I try to create good painting for all people to see and enjoy.*

ROSENCRANS, EVAN WILLIAM, air force officer; b. Sayre, Pa., May 31, 1926; s. Lloyd Calvin and Martha (Meredith) R.; B.S., U.S. Mil. Acad., 1948; M.B.A., George Washington U., 1968; m. Wilma Ruth Buchholz; children—Karen L., Linda M., Cynthia L., Douglas E. Commd. 2d lt. USAF, 1948; advanced through grades to lt. gen. USAF, 1979; pilot 80th Fighter-Bomber Squadron, Korea, 1950-51; flight comdr. RAF Chivenor, U.K., 1953-55; operations officer, comdr. 3597th Combat Crew Tng. Squadron, Nellis AFB, Nev. 1955-56; co-comdr. dept. tactics U.S. Mil. Acad., 1957-59; operations officer, comdr. 531st Tactical Fighter Squadron, Misawa AFB, Japan, 1959-62; operations officer Hdqrs. Pacific Air Forces, Hickam AFB, Hawaii, 1963-65; operations officer, dep. chief staff plans and operations Hdqrs. USAF, 1965; mem. gen. purposes forces br., chmn. spl. study group Joint Chiefs Staff, 1966-67; asst. dep. comdr. operations 37th Tactical Fighter Wing, Phu Cat AFB, Vietnam, 1968-69; vice comdr. 4531st Tactical Fighter Wing, Homestead AFB, Fla., 1969-70; comdr. 354th Tactical Fighter Wing, Myrtle Beach AFB, S.C., 1970-71; dir. inspection Air Force Inspection and Safety Center, 1971-73; comdr. 3d Air Force, RAF Mildenhall, U.K., 1973-77; vice comdr. Air Tng. Command, Randolph AFB, Tex., 197-79; dep. comdr. in chief UN Command Korea, dep. comdr. in chief U.S. Forces Korea, comdr. Air Forces Korea, 1979—. Decorated D.S.M., Legion of Merit with 2 oak leaf clusters, D.F.C. with 3 oak leaf clusters, Air medal with 16 oak leaf clusters. Mem. Air Force Assn. Presbyn. Home and Office: Dep Cinc US Forces Korea APO San Francisco CA 96301

ROSENE, LEE, cosmetic co. exec.; b. Chgo., Nov. 5, 1912; s. David and Belle (Baim) R.; m. Dorothe Ann Rosen, Dec. 20, 1934; children—Sara Lynn Rosene Radell. Alexander. With Max Factor & Co., Hollywood, Calif., 1936—, dir. U.S. sales, 1957—, sr. v.p., 1968—, pres. devel. div., 1970-74, cons., 1974-77; ret., 1977; dir. Argo Petroleum Corp., Los Angeles; pres. Century Towers Assn. Chmn. Hollywood div. United Jewish Welfare Fund, 1971. Bd. dirs. City of Hope. Mem. Am. Mgmt. Assn., Los Angeles World Affairs Council, Century City C. of C. (dir.), Los Angeles C. of C. Clubs: Beverly Hills (Calif.) (pres. 1960—); Brentwood Country, Town Hall, Merchants (v.p.), Variety (Los Angeles). Home: 2222 Ave of Stars Century City CA 90067

ROSENFELD, ARNOLD SOLOMON, editor; b. N.Y.C., Apr. 18, 1933; s. William and Sarah (Cohen) R.; student U. Houston, 1951; Profl. Journalism fellow Stanford, 1967; m. Ruth Doris Lilly, Sept. 30, 1956; children—William Bennett, Jonathan Andrew, Lauren Melissa. Mem. staff Houston Post, 1953-67; asso. editor Detroit mag., Detroit Free Press, 1967; editor Detroit mag., 1968; mng. editor Dayton Daily News, 1968-76, editor, 1976—. Served with AUS, 1951-53. Recipient Editorial Writing award A.P. Mng. Editors Assn. Tex., 1966; Tex. Theta Sigma Phi award, 1969, 72; Media award Nat. Assn. Mental Health, 1976. Mem. Am. Soc. Newspaper Editors. Editor: A Thomason Sketchbook, 1969. Home: 563 E Dale Dr Dayton OH 45415 Office: Dayton Daily News Dayton OH 45401

ROSENFELD, EUGENE SEYMOUR, bldg. co. exec.; b. Chgo., Jan. 26, 1934; s. Irving and Mary (Charatz) R.; B.S., U. Calif. at Los Angeles, 1956; m. Maxine Miller, May 10, 1957; children—Dennis, Michael. Pub. accountant Haskins & Sells, Los Angeles, 1958-63; controller Kaufman & Broad, Inc., Los Angeles, 1963-64, Los Angeles, div. mgr., 1964-68, exec. v.p., 1968-69, pres., dir., 1969-76; owner Anden Corp., Encino, Calif., 1976—. Served with AUS, 1956-58. Home: 19456 Shenango Dr Tarzana CA 91356 Office: 16133 Ventura Blvd Encino CA 91436

ROSENFELD, RONALD MARVIN, advt. exec.; b. Balt., July 13, 1932; s. Bernard and Bessie (Feinglass) R.; student Balt. City Coll., 1949; children—Bonnie, Ned. Copywriter, Applestein, Levinstein & Golnick, Balt., 1955-57; v.p., co-copy chief Doyle Dane Bernbach, N.Y.C., 1957-69; sr. v.p., creative mgmt. supr. J. Walter Thompson, N.Y.C., 1969-70; prin., exec. v.p., co-creative dir. Rosenfeld, Sirowitz & Lawson, N.Y.C., 1970—. Bd. dirs. Daytop Village, drug abuse rehab., 1974-76, Hope for Diabetics Found., 1978. Named to Copywriters Hall of Fame, 1971; recipient numerous awards from Copy Club, Art Dirs. Club, also Clio awards. Co-chmn. One Show. Home: 300 Central Park W New York City NY 10024 Office: 1370 Ave of Americas New York City NY 10019

ROSENFELT, FRANK EDWARD, motion picture co. exec.; b. Peabody, Mass., Nov. 15, 1921; s. Samuel and Ethel (Litvack) R.; B.S., Cornell U., 1948, LL.B., 1950; m. Judith Roman, Nov. 1, 1943; children—Fred, Peter, Karen. Admitted to N.Y. and Mass. bars, 1950, Calif. bar, 1971; atty. RKO Radio Pictures, 1950-55; with Metro-Goldwyn-Mayer, Inc., 1955—, pres., chief exec. officer, dir., 1973—. Served with inf. AUS, World War II. Decorated Purple Heart. Mem. Acad. Motion Picture Arts and Scis. (bd. govs. 1977—), Order of Coif. Bd. editors Cornell Law Quar., 1948-50. Office: 10202 W Washington Blvd Culver City CA 90230

ROSENFIELD, ISADORE, architect; b. Mayaky, Russia, Sept. 7, 1893; s. Haem and Rosse (Keegler) R.; B.S., Harvard, 1918, M.Arch., 1921; m. Leora Kagan, Nov. 28, 1918; children—Zachary, Lenora (Mrs. Roderick Kyle de Camp). Came to U.S., 1910, naturalized, 1916. Asst. prof. architecture N.Y.U., 1932-40; chief architect Dept. Pub. Works, N.Y.C., 1940-45; prof. med. architecture Columbia, practice arch., N.Y.C., 1945—; sr. partner firm Isadore and Zachary Rosenfield (firm now Zachary Rosenfield & Partners), now ret.; design, color cons. U. Minn., Inst. of Design, Chgo.; lectr. med. archtl. planning profl. orgns. and univs. in U.S.; designer P.R. Med. Center, San Juan, Khyber Med. Center, Peshawar, Pakistan. Served with 472d Engrs., U.S. Army, World War I. Fellow A.I.A. (lectr. med. archtl. planning N.Y. chpt. 1944, 1st chmn. com. hosp. research; various profl. honors); mem. Am. Assn. for Hosp. Planning (dir., honor award for distinguished contbn. to hosp. planning and health of Am. people 1975), Am Hosp. Assn. Author: Hospitals-Integrated Design, 2d edit., 1951; Hospital Architecture and Beyond, 1969; Hospital Architecture-Integrated Components, 1971; Lest We Forget, Memoirs, 1977; also articles. Home: 5998 Palisade Ave New York NY 10471. *We are all entitled to make an honest living . . . But we are also obligated to do something to contribute to the quality of our society. That quality we call humanism.*

ROSENFIELD, JAMES HAROLD, TV exec.; b. Boston, July 18, 1929; s. Harold and Beatrice (Garber) R.; B.A., Dartmouth, 1952; m. Nancy Lee Stenbuck, Oct. 19, 1952; children—Laurie Ann, James Harold. TV network sales exec. NBC, N.Y.C., 1954-57; advt. mgr. Polaroid Corp., Boston, 1956-59; v.p. mktg. Airequipt, Inc., New Rochelle, N.Y., 1959-65; TV account exec. CBS, Inc., N.Y.C., 1965-67, dir. daytime sales, 1967-70, v.p. Eastern sales, 1970-75, v.p. network sales adminstrn., 1975-77, v.p., nat. sales mgr., 1977, pres. TV Network Div., 1977—. Bd. dirs. N.Y. Heart Assn. Served with Signal Corps, AUS, 1950-53. Mem. Nat. Acad. TV Arts and Scis., Internat. Radio and TV Soc. (mem. bd.), Advt. Council (mem. bd.). Office: 51 W 52d St New York NY 10019

ROSENFIELD, JOHN MAX, educator; b. Dallas, Oct. 9, 1924; s. John M. and Claire (Burger) R.; student U. Tex., 1941-43; B.A., U. Calif. at Berkeley, 1945; B.F.A., So. Meth. U., 1947; M.F.A., U. Iowa, 1949; Ph.D., Harvard, 1959; m. Ella Hopper, Jan. 2, 1948; children—Sarah, Paul Thomas. Instr. art U. Iowa, 1949, 52-54; asst. prof. U. Calif. at Los Angeles, 1957-60; research fellow Harvard, 1960-65, faculty, 1965—, prof. art, 1968—, Abby Aldrich Rockefeller prof. Oriental art, 1974—, chmn. dept. fine arts, 1971-76. Trustee Mus. Fine Arts, Boston, 1975-77. Served with AUS, 1943-46, 50-51. Mem. Assn. Asian Studies, Coll. Art Assn., Am. Acad. Benares, Am. Acad. Arts and Scis. Author: Dynastic Arts of the Kushans, 1967; Japanese Art of the Heian Period, 1967; Traditions of Japanese Art, 1970; Courtly Tradition of Japanese Art and Literature, 1972. Research history Buddhist art and Japanese art. Home: 75 Coolidge Rd Arlington MA 02174 Office: Fogg Art Mus Harvard Cambridge MA 02138

ROSENGARTEN, THEODORE HARVEY, author; b. Bklyn., Dec. 17, 1944; s. Charles and Hannah (Sokal) R.; A.B., Amherst Coll., 1966; Ph.D., Harvard U., 1975. Grantee ethnic studies Ford Found., 1972-73. Author: All God's Dangers: The Life of Nate Shaw (Nat. Book award contemporary affairs), 1974. Address: Route 1 Box 83A McClellanville SC 29458

ROSENHAUPT, HANS, educator; b. Frankfurt-on-Main, Germany, Feb. 24, 1911; s. Heinrich and Marie (Freudenthal) R.; came to U.S., 1935, naturalized, 1940; student univs. Frankfurt, Berlin, Munich, 1928-33; Ph.D., U. Berne, 1935; LL.D., Colo. Coll., 1963, Valparaiso U., 1963, U. Chattanooga, 1965, Franklin Coll., 1969; Litt.D., Centenary Coll., 1975; Dr.Phil., Johann Wolfgang Goethe U., 1979; m. Maureen Church, Dec. 15, 1945; 1 dau., Elise. Tchr. German and French, Oak Park Jr. Coll., 1935-37, Knox Coll., 1937-38, Colo. Coll., 1938-42, 46-47; lectr. Rotary Internat., 1947-48; asso. dir. admissions Columbia U., 1948-58; nat. dir. Woodrow Wilson Nat. Fellowship Found., 1958-69, pres., 1969—; research asso. com. on future of univ. Columbia U., 1956-57; mem. adv. council German dept. Princeton U. Bd. dirs. Nat. Med. Fellowships, Inc. Served from pvt. to capt., M.I., AUS, 1942-46. Mem. Modern Lang. Assn., AAUP. Clubs: Century, Nassau (Princeton). Author: Isolation in Modern German Literature, 1939; How to Wage Peace, 1949; The True Deceivers, 1954; Graduate Students Experience at Columbia, 1940-56, 1958; contbr. to American Education Today, 1963, Macmillan Ency. Edn., 1973. Home: Mount Lucas Rd Princeton NJ 08540 Office: Box 642 Princeton NJ 08540

ROSENHAUS, MATTHEW BERNARD, toiletries and pharm. co. exec.; b. Bayonne, N.J., Mar. 19, 1912; s. Morris and Sophie (Post) R.; B.A., Rutgers U., 1933; m. Sarah Esther Pollack, Nov. 8, 1934 (dec. Feb. 1968); children—Harriet Rosenhaus Bobrow, Lawrence, Annetta Rosenhaus Chester, Albert; m. 2d, Gila Golan, Sept. 16, 1969; children—Sarita Agnes, Hedy Marisa, Loretta Sonia. Pres., chmn. bd. J.B. Williams Co., Inc., N.Y.C., 1935—; vice chmn. bd. Nabisco, Inc., Columbia Pictures Industries, Inc. Chmn. bd. dirs. Eleanor Roosevelt Cancer Found.; bd. dirs. United Cerebral Palsy Research and Edn. Found.; trustee Fund for Peace, Huxley Inst., N.Y. Acad. Scis., Rutgers U. Found., Synagogue Council Am.; mem. exec. com. Daus. of Jacob Geriatric Center, Bronx; hon. vice-chmn. Anti-Defamation League; hon. life mem. Am. Cancer Soc. Office: 767 Fifth Ave New York NY 10022

ROSENHEIM, EDWARD WEIL, educator; b. Chgo., May 15, 1918; s. Edward Weil and Fannie (Kohn) R.; B.A., U. Chgo., 1939, M.A., 1946, Ph.D., 1953; m. Margaret Morton Keeney, June 20, 1947; children—Daniel Edward, James Morton, Andrew Keeney. Publicity writer Pub. Relations Service, Chgo., 1939-40; instr. Gary (Ind.) Coll., 1946; faculty U. Chgo., 1947—, prof. English, 1962—, asso. chmn. dept. English, 1967-75, dir. broadcasting for univ., 1954-57, dir. Nat. Humanities Inst., 1977—; Distinguished vis. prof. Pa. State U., 1961; Distinguished lectr. Nat. Council Tchrs. English, 1967. Served to capt., inf. AUS, 1941-46. Recipient Quantrell Teaching award U. Chgo., 1953. Willet Faculty fellow, 1962; John Simon Guggenheim Meml. fellow, 1967. Mem. Modern Lang. Assn., AAUP, Johnson Soc. (pres. Central region 1971). Author: What Happens in Literature, 1960; Swift and the Satirist's Art, 1963. Editor: Selected Prose and Poetry of Jonathan Swift, 1938; Jour. Gen. Edn., 1954-56; co-editor Modern Philology, 1968—. Home: 5805 Dorchester Ave Chicago IL 60637

ROSENHEIM, HOWARD HARRIS, pub. co. exec.; b. Williamson, W.Va., Oct. 1, 1915; s. William Spiller and Frances Minerva (Harris) R.; B.S., Northwestern U., 1936, M.B.A., 1954; grad. Advanced Mgmt. Program, Harvard U. Grad. Sch. Bus., 1956; m. Marjorie Jane Griffin, June 30, 1945; children—Cathy (Mrs. Frank Hammer), William Spiller. Civilian dir. indsl. planning div. USAF, Dayton, Ohio, 1947; pres. Internat. Register Co., elec. mfg. co., Chgo., 1948-70; pres. Internat. Accountants Soc., home study sch., Chgo., 1971; pres. Denoyer-Geppert Co., ednl. pub. co., subsidiary Times Mirror Co., Chgo., 1972-79; dir. Extel Corp., Chgo. Vis. prof. bus. Northwestern U., Evanston, Ill., 1956-71, trustee, 1968—; cons. Presdl. Commn. Nat. Air Policy, 1947. Served to maj. USAF, 1942-46. Decorated Legion of Merit; recipient Distinguished Educator award Northwestern U., 1972. Mem. Am. Mktg. Assn., Northwestern U. Alumni Assn. (pres. 1966-68). Methodist (mem. ofcl. bd. 1965—). Clubs: Union League (Chgo.); Park Ridge (Ill.) Country. Contbr. articles to profl. jours. Inventor various time switches. Home: 2411 Farrell Ave Park Ridge IL 60068 Office: 5235 Ravenswood Ave Chicago IL 60640

ROSENHEIM, MARGARET KEENEY, educator; b. Grand Rapids, Mich., Sept. 5, 1926; d. Morton and Nancy (Billings) Keeney; student Wellesley Coll., 1943-45; J.D., U. Chgo., 1949; m. Edward W. Rosenheim, June 20, 1947; children—Daniel, James, Andrew. Admitted to Ill. bar, 1949; mem. faculty Sch. Social Service Adminstrn., U. Chgo., 1950—, asso. prof., 1961-66, prof., 1966—, Helen Ross prof. social welfare policy, 1975—, dean, 1978—; vis. prof. U. Wash., 1965; acad. visitor London Sch. Econs., 1973; cons. Pres.'s Commn. Law Enforcement and Adminstrn. Justice, 1966-67, Nat. Adv. Commn. Criminal Justice Standards and Goals, i972; mem. Juvenile Justice Standards Commn., 1973-76; adv. com. Wis. Inst. Research on Poverty, 1975—. Ford Found. grantee, 1967-68. Mem. Chgo. Bar Assn. Editor, contbr.: Justice for the Child, 1962, reprinted. 1977; Pursuing Justice for the Child, 1976. Contbr. articles and book revs. to profl. jours. Address: 5805 Dorchester Ave Chicago IL 60637

ROSENHOUSE, IRWIN, artist, designer; b. Chgo., Mar. 1, 1924; s. Samuel and Mae (Baer) R.; B.F.A., Cooper Union, N.Y.C., 1950. Designer, Mus. Modern Art, 1954-57, Harcourt, Brace & Co., 1957, Dell Books, 1963; tchr. art Mus. Modern Art, 1967-69, Pratt Graphic Center, N.Y.C., 1972, Bklyn. Coll., 1972-73, Bklyn. Mus. Art Sch., 1974, Nassau Community Coll., 1973-79; lectr. art, book illustration, design; one-man exhbns. in N.Y.C. and Bklyn., also various colls. and museums in U.S.; illustrator: (juveniles) What Kind of Feet Does a Bear Have?, Bad Trouble in Miss Alcorn's Class, Science Book of Magnets, The Rabbi's Bible, Have You Seen Trees?; group exhbns. at numerous museums throughout U.S., also at painting soc. exhbns. Served with U.S. Mcht. Marine, 1944-51. Recipient award Louis Comfort Tiffany Found., Huntington Hartford Found. (2), Billboard Ann., Illustrators Club; 1st prize Rome Collaborative. Address: 256 Mott St New York NY 10012

ROSENKRANTZ, BARBARA GUTMANN, sci. historian; b. N.Y.C., Jan. 11, 1923; s. James and Jeanette (Mack) G.; A.B., Radcliffe Coll., 1944; Ph.D., Clark U., 1970; m. Paul Solomon Rosenkrantz, Apr. 19, 1950; children—Louise, Judith, Deborah. Microbiologist, Springfield (Mass.) Hosp., 1955-57, Wesson Meml. Hosp., Springfield, 1958-63; lectr. Harvard U., 1972-73, asso. prof. history of sci., 1973-75, prof., 1975—; master Currier House, Harvard U.; trustee Clark U. Radcliffe Inst. fellow, 1967-69; NIH/Nat. Library Medicine grantee, 1971-72. Mem. History of Sci. Soc., Am. Hist. Assn., Soc. Am. Historians, Am. Public Health Assn., Sigma Xi. Jewish. Author: Public Health and the State: Changing Views in Massachusetts 1842-1936, 1972; editor: (with William A. Koelsch) American Habitat: A Historical Perspective, 1973. Home: 983 Memorial Dr Cambridge MA 02138 Office: Sci Center 235 Harvard U Cambridge MA 02138

ROSENKRANZ, STANLEY WILLIAM, lawyer; b. N.Y.C., Aug. 20, 1933; s. Jacob and Adele R.; B.S. in Acctg., U. Fla., 1955, J.D. with honors, 1960; LL.M. (Kenneson fellow), N.Y. U., 1961; m. Judith Ossinsky, Aug. 14, 1960; children—Jack Michael, Andrew Lawrence. Admitted to Fla. bar, 1960, Ga. bar, 1970; mem. firm Macfarlane, Ferguson, Allison & Kelly, Tampa, Fla., 1961-68, 71-79, firm Holland & Knight, Tampa, 1979—, firm King & Spalding, Atlanta, 1969-71; adj. prof. Grad. Sch. Law, U. Fla.; dir. Life Savs. and Loan Assn. Served with U.S. Army, 1955-57. Named Young Man of Year, Tampa Jaycees, Fla., 1967. Mem. Am. Bar Assn., Am. Law Inst., Fla. Bar Assn., Ga. Bar Assn. Home: 10 Formosa Ave Tampa FL 33606 Office: 610 Florida Ave Tampa FL 33602

ROSENLICHT, MAXWELL ALEXANDER, mathematician; b. Bklyn., Apr. 15, 1924; s. Martin and Julia (Dalinski) R.; A.B., Columbia, 1947; Ph.D., Harvard, 1950; m. Carla Zingarelli, 1953; children—Nicholas, Alan, Joanna. Nat. Research fellow U. Chgo., U. Mexico, Princeton, 1950-52; asst. prof. math. Northwestern U., 1952-55, asso. prof., 1955-59; prof. math. U. Calif. at Berkeley 1959—, chmn. dept. math., 1973-75. Vis. prof. Rome, 1954-55, Bures, France, 1962-63, Mexico, 1965, Harvard, 1966, Northwestern U., 1968-69. Served with AUS, 1943-46. Mem. Am. Math. Soc. (Cole prize 1960), Sigma Xi. Author: Introduction to Analysis, 1968. Contbr. numerous research articles to profl. jours. Home: 263 Forest Ln Berkeley CA 94708

ROSENN, MAX, fed. judge; b. Plains, Pa., Feb. 4, 1910; s. Joseph and Jennie (Wohl) R.; B.A., Cornell U., 1929; LL.B., U. Pa., 1932; m. Tillie R. Hershkowitz, Mar. 18, 1934; children—Keith S., Daniel Wohl. Admitted to Pa. bar, 1932, also Pa. Appellate Cts., U.S. Supreme Ct., Cts. of Philippines; spl. counsel Pa. Dept. Justice, 1939; asst. dist. atty. Luzerne County, 1942-44, also solicitor various municipal boroughs; partner firm Rosenn & Rosenn, 1947-54, Rosenn, Jenkins & Grenwald, Wilkes-Barre, 1954-70; judge U.S. Ct. Appeals, 3d Circuit, 1970—; sec. Pa. Dept. of Pub. Welfare, 1966-67. Dir., solicitor Franklin Fed. Savings & Loan Assn., Wilkes-Barre; dir. Wyoming Nat. Bank of Wilkes-Barre. Mem. Pa. Bd. Pub. Welfare, 1963—; chmn. Gov's Hosp. Study Commn., Gov.'s Council for Human Services, 1966-67; exec. bd. Commonwealth of Pa., 1966-67; chmn. Commn. Met. Govt., 1957-58; pres. Property Owners Assn. Luzerne County, 1955-57; mem. criminal procedure rules com. Supreme Ct. Pa., 1958—; chmn. Pa. Human Relations Commn., 1969-70, Pa. Com. Children and Youth, 1968-70, Legis. Task Force Structure Pa. Dept. Human Services, 1970; mem. Pa. Commn. to Revise Pub. Employee Laws, 1968-69. Alternate del. Republican Nat. Conv., 1964. Pres. Wyoming Valley Jewish Com., 1941-42; trustee Wilkes-Barre Jewish Community Center, Wilkes Coll., Wilkes-Barre. Served to 1st lt. AUS, World War II. Fellow Am. Coll. Trial Lawyers, Internat. Acad. Trial Lawyers; mem. Am., Pa. (chmn. indsl. relations sect.), Luzerne County bar assns., Anti-Defamation League (pres. Pa.-W.Va.-Del. bd. 1955-58, nat. commr. 1964—), Alpha Epsilon Pi. Jewish religion. Mason (33, Shriner); mem. B'nai B'rith (pres. dist. Grand Lodge 1947-48, life gov.). Author article. Office: US Ct Appeals 197 S Main St Wilkes-Barre PA 18701*

ROSENOW, EDWARD CARL, JR., physician; b. Chgo., Apr. 7, 1909; s. Edward Carl and Lydia Barbara (Senty) R.; B.A., Carleton Coll., 1931, D.Sc., 1967; M.D., Harvard, 1935; M.Sc. in Medicine, Mayo Found. of U. Minn., 1939; D.Sc., MacMurray Coll., 1973; m.

Esther Jane Church, Dec. 25, 1931; children—Susan Jane (Mrs. Vernon Vig), Robert Frank. Intern Faulkner Hosp., Boston, 1935-36; pvt. practice internal medicine, Pasadena, Cal., 1940-57; clin. prof. medicine U. So. Calif. Sch. Medicine, 1941-59, dir. med. extension, 1948; exec. dir. Los Angeles County Med. Assn., 1957-59; exec. v.p. A.C.P., Phila., 1960-77, exec. v.p. emeritus, 1977—; clin. prof. medicine U. Pa. Sch. Medicine, 1960—. Chmn. com. postgrad. activities Calif. Med. Assn., 1949-59; editor-in-chief Audio-Digest, 1954-59; pres., dir. Charles Cook Hastings Home (Tb research), 1954-59. Trustee Carleton Coll., 1966—. Diplomate Am. Bd. Internal Medicine. Master A.C.P. (Alfred Stengel Meml. award 1976); fellow Royal Coll. Physicians Ireland, Royal Soc. Medicine, Royal Coll. Physicians London (Eng.), Royal Australasian Coll. Physicians; mem. Los Angeles Soc. Internal Medicine, Los Angeles Heart Assn., Calif. (council 1954-57), Los Angeles County (pres. 1956) med. assns., AMA (alt. del. 1957-58), Am. Med. Writers Assn. (pres. 1964), Pa., Phila. County med. socs., Internat. Soc. Internal Medicine (pres. elect 1978), Alumni Assn. Mayo Grad. Sch. Medicine (pres. 1965), Carleton Coll. Alumni Assn. (pres. 1966). Episcopalian. Home and office: 1901 Walnut St Philadelphia PA 19103

ROSENOW, JOHN HENRY, physician; b. Chgo., Sept. 16, 1913; s. Edward Carl and Lydia Barbara (Senty) R.; B.A., Carleton Coll., Northfield, Minn., 1934; M.D., Harvard U., 1938; M.S. in Surgery, Mayo Found., U. Minn., 1944; m. Jane Dexter, June 8, 1938; children—Joan (Mrs. Charles Jackson), Peter Dexter, Philip John, Charles Edward, Margaret (Mrs. Theodore Hope), Barbara. Intern, Presbyn. Hosp., Chgo., 1939-40; fellow in surgery Mayo Clinic, 1941-43, 46-47; pvt. practice medicine specializing in gen. surgery, Mpls., 1948-63; part-time editor Modern Medicine Publs., Inc., Mpls., 1955-63, sr. med. editor, 1963-75; clin. instr. surgery U. Minn. Med. Sch., 1955—; civilian med. officer Armed Forces Exam. and Entrance Sta., Mpls., 1975—; mem. staff Northwestern Hosp., Abbott Hosp., Met. Med. Center and Fairview-Southdale hosps., Hennepin County Med. Center. Mem. diocesan standing com. Episcopal Ch., 1961-64, 70-73. Served with M.C., USNR, 1943-46; PTO. Decorated Bronze Star. Diplomate Am. Bd. Surgery. Fellow A.C.S.; mem. Am., Minn. med. assns., Hennepin County Med. Soc., Minn. Surg. Soc., Mpls. Acad. Medicine. Contbr. articles to med. jours. Home: 4609 Casco Ave Minneapolis MN 55424 Office: 210 Federal Bldg Minneapolis MN 55401

ROSENQUIST, JAMES ALBERT, painter; b. Grand Forks, N.D., Nov. 29, 1933; s. Louis A. and Ruth C. (Hendrickson) R.; m. Mary Lou Adams, June 5, 1960; 1 son, John Adams. Engaged as comml. artist painting gas tanks, billboards, 1952-60; exhibited one man shows Green Gallery, N.Y.C., 1962, 64, Mus. Modern Art, 1963, Sonnabend Gallery, Paris, France, 1964, 67, Dwan Gallery, Los Angeles, 1964, Castelli Gallery, N.Y.C., 1965, 66, 68, 69, 70, 73, 74, 78, Nat. Gallery Can., Ottawa, Ont., 1968, Met. Mus. Art, N.Y.C., 1968, Max Protech, Washington, 1974, Nat. Gallery, Victoria, Australia, 1978, Sable-Castelli Gallery, Toronto, 1978, others; exhibited numerous group shows, U.S. and Europe, including 16 Ams. at Mus. Modern Art, 1963, Artist and Object at Guggenheim Mus., 1963, Sao Paulo, Brazil, 1967, Mus. Modern Art, Tokyo, Japan, 1967, Musée des Arts Decoratives, Palais Louvre, 1967, Haywood Gallery, London, 1969, Met. Mus. Art, N.Y.C., 1969-70, Mayer Gallery, London, 1978, U. Mich. Mus., 1978, Fitzwilliam Mus., Cambridge, Eng., 1978; represented in permanent collections Pasadena Mus., Modern Museet, Stockholm, Sweden, Stadtlicht, Amsterdam, Holland, Whitney Mus., Albright-Knox Gallery, Mus. Modern Art, N.Y.C., Met. Mus. Art, N.Y.C., Nat. Gallery Can., Wallraf-Richartz Mus., Cologne, Germany, others; lectr. Yale Sch. Art, 1964; artist in residence Aspen (Colo.) Inst. Humanist Studies, 1965; painting of bomber, F-111. Bd. dirs. Nat. Endowment for Arts. Recipient Norman Waite Harris award Chgo. Art Inst., 1963; Prix di Tella, Argentina, 1965; Graphics prize 6th Internat. Biennial Exhbn. Prints, Nat. Mus. Modern Art, Tokyo, 1968, 7th Internat Expn. Graphics, Moderna Gallery, Ljubliana, Yugoslavia, 1967. Mem. Municipal Art Soc., N.Y. Home: Box 4 Aripeka FL 33502

ROSENQUIT, BERNARD, artist; b. Hotin, Romania, Dec. 26, 1923 (parents Am. citizens); s. Eli and Ida (Schotkin) R.; student (Monitor scholar) Art Students League, N.Y.C., 1947-50, (Mrs. John D. Rockefeller III scholar), Atelier 17, N.Y.C., 1955-56, (Fulbright grantee) Fotainbleau Sch. Fine Arts, France, 1947, (Monitor scholar), Bklyn. Mus. Sch. Fine Arts, 1955-56, Inst. Art and Archaeology, Paris, 1958-59. Instr. painting and drawing Riverdale Neighborhood and Lit. Assn., also Fieldston Sch. Arts Center, Riverdale, N.Y., 1962-64, Five Towns Music and Art Found., Cedarhurst, N.Y., also Bronx House Community Center, N.Y.C., 1961-62; one-man exhbns. include Roko Gallery, N.Y.C., 1951-71; group exhbns. include Honolulu Acad. Fine Arts, Boston Mus. Fine Arts, Bklyn. Mus. Fine Arts, Newark Mus. Art, Toronto Mus. Fine Arts, Oakland (Calif.) Art Mus., U.S. Nat. Mus., Washington, Seattle Mus. Fine Arts, Mus. Modern Art, N.Y.C., New Sch. Social Research, U. So. Ill., others; represented in permanent collections Met. Mus. Art, Bklyn. Mus. Fine Arts, Victoria and Albert Mus., London, Smithsonian Instn., Bryn Mawr Coll., U. Kans. Mus., Dallas Art Assn., Long Beach (N.Y.) Pub. Library, Peabody Coll. Mus., N.Y. Pub. Library; works reproduced book rev. sect. N.Y. Times. Grantee Louis Comfort Tiffany Found., 1959. Mem. Artists Equity Assn., Art Students League., Phila. Print Club. Address: 87 Barrow St New York NY 10014

ROSENSAFT, MELVIN, business exec., mgmt. cons., educator; b. N.Y.C., Jan. 28, 1919; s. Nathan and Yetta (Applebaum) R.; cert. State Tchrs. Coll., Paterson, N.J., 1940; B.S. cum laude, Rider Coll., 1942; M.B.A., Suffolk U., 1978; cert. mgmt. cons. Inst. Mgmt. Cons., 1979; m. Beatrice Golombek, June 27, 1954; children—David Norman, Lester Jay, Emily Susan. Field dep. IRS, Newark, 1942-43; with Gt. Am. Plastics Co., Leominster, Mass., 1944-48, 50-52, 56-71, asst. to pres., 1950-52, v.p. in charge mfg., 1956-62, exec. v.p., gen. mgr., 1962-71; pres., chief operating officer Artefactos Plasticos, Mexico City, 1948-49; pres., mng. dir. Irwin Products, Toronto, Ont., Can., 1949-50; mgr. plastics div. Ideal Plastics Co., Hollis, N.Y., 1953-55; exec. v.p., gen. mgr. Gt. Am. Chem. Corp., Fitchburg, Mass., 1962-71, pres., chief exec. officer, 1971-76, also dir.; pres., chief exec. officer Melvin Rosensaft and Assos., mgmt. cons., Leominster, 1976—; chmn. bd., pres., chief exec. officer Cons. to Mgmt., Inc., 1980—; asso. prof. mgmt. Keene State Coll., 1979—; master lectr. in mgmt. and mktg. Suffolk U. Grad. Sch. Mgmt., 1977—; mem. adj. faculty Fitchburg State Coll., Mt. Wachusett Community Coll.; v.p., gen. mgr. Irwin Corp., N.Y.C., Leominster Plastics Co., Nashua Plastics Co. (N.H.), Fitchburg Realty Corp., Factory St. Realty Corp., Nashua; v.p., dir. F.I.A. Credit Union; dir. Lastomerex Inc., Jefferson, Mass. Mem. adv. on econ. and indsl. devel. City of Leominster; mem. adv. com. Leominster Urban Renewal, Mass. Regional Vocat. Tech. Sch. Pres., trustee, bd. dirs. Fitchburg—Leominster Community Center; bd. dirs. Fitchburg Gen. Hosp.; active ARC, Boy Scouts Am. Served with AUS, 1943-44. Scheie Eye Inst. fellow Presbyn. Hosp., U. Pa. Med. Center, Phila.; lic. real estate broker, Mass. Mem. Commerce Club (past pres.), Fin. Mgmt. Honor Soc., Inst. Mgmt. Sci., Inst. Mgmt. Consultants, Am. Mgmt. Assn., Soc. Profl. Mgmt. Consultants, AAUP, Soc. Plastics Engrs. (profl.), Chem. Soc. Gt. Brit., Soc. Plastics Industry, Leominster C. of C., Delta Mu Delta. Contbr. articles to profl. jours.. *In order to deal effectively with new problems and opportunities, we must be prepared to make a twofold commitment: first, to high moral standards; second, to provide a mechanism to transform our talented young men and women into broadley educated professionals. Our dedication to these goals will determine our destiny.*

ROSENSHINE, ALLEN GILBERT, advt. co. exec.; b. N.Y.C., Mar. 14, 1939; s. Aaron and Anna (Zuckerman) R.; A.B., Columbia Coll., 1960; m. Suzan Weston-Webb, Aug. 31, 1979; children—Andrew, Jonathan. Copywriter, J.B. Rundle, advt., N.Y.C., 1962-65; copywriter Batten, Barton, Durstine & Osborn, N.Y.C., 1965, copy supr., 1967, v.p., 1968, asso. creative dir., 1970, sr. v.p., creative dir., 1975-77, exec. v.p., 1977—, also dir., mem. exec. com.; dir. BBDO Internat.; lectr. gen. studies Bklyn. Coll., 1961-65. Home: 421 E 84th St Port New York NY 10028 Office: 383 Madison Ave New York NY 10017

ROSENSON, JAY HAROLD, tire co. exec.; b. Wilmington, Del., July 21, 1930; s. Joel and Ruth June (Weinberger) R.; B.S. in Chem. Engring., U. Del., 1952; m. Elaine Helen Werstler, Oct. 11, 1962. With plastics div. Firestone Tire & Rubber Co., Akron, Ohio, 1952-73, pres. div., 1970-73, group v.p. chems. and raw materials, 1973—. Home: 1160 S Medina Line Rd Wadsworth OH 44281 Office: 1200 Firestone Pkwy Akron OH 44317

ROSENSON, LEONARD HENRY, lawyer; b. New Orleans, Dec. 2, 1917; s. Louis and Celia (Clein) R.; A.B. magna cum laude, Loyola U., New Orleans, 1937; M.A., La. State U., 1938; LL.B. cum laude, Tulane U., 1941; m. Marilyn Jo Kaffie, Aug. 31, 1952; children—Charles J., Malcolm D., Celia C. Admitted to La. bar, 1941; law clk. U.S. 5th Circuit Ct., 1941-42; sr. atty. OPA, Washington, 1942-45; asst. dist. atty., Orleans Parish, La., 1946-47; practice law, New Orleans, 1946—; partner firm Sessions, Fishman, Rosenson, Snellings & Boisfontaine and predecessors, 1950—. Prof. law Tulane U. Sch. Law, 1970—. Pres., Jewish Fedn. New Orleans, 1951-52. Mem. Order of Coif, Alpha Sigma Nu, Phi Kappa Phi. Home: 5401 St Charles Ave New Orleans LA 70115 Office: 2100 BNO Bldg New Orleans LA 70112

ROSENSTEIN, CLAUDE HOUSTON, lawyer; b. Gonzales, Tex., Aug. 31, 1893; s. Robert Edward and Mary Effie (Gould) R.; LL.B., U. Okla., 1913; m. Helen S. Fist, Jan. 31, 1916; children—Robert H., Mary Helen (Mrs. Samuel Zeligson), Daniel L. Admitted to Okla. bar, 1913; practiced in Tulsa, 1915—; mem. firm Rosenstein, Fist & Ringold. Dir., mem. exec. com. Tulsa Psychiatric Center. Fellow Okla. Bar Found., Am. Bar Found., Am. Coll. Trial Lawyers; mem. Am., Okla., Tulsa County (past pres.) bar assns., Order of Coif, Phi Delta Phi. Mason (33). Clubs: Kiwanis (past pres.), Meadowbrook Country, Tulsa, Petroleum, Summit (Tulsa). Home: 4850 S Knoxville Pl Tulsa OK 74135 Office: Suite 300 525 S Main St Tulsa OK 74103

ROSENSTEIN, SAMUEL MURRAY, U.S. sr. judge; b. Frankfort, Ky., June 7, 1909; s. Robert and Yetta (Urdang) R.; student U. Ky., 1927-28; J.D., U. Cin., 1931; m. Helen Tarbis Levitan, Aug. 22, 1960; children—Elaine Levitan (Mrs. Elaine Sherman), Lawrence Mayer Levitan. Admitted to Ky. bar, 1931; spl. counsel Ky. Dept. Revenue and Welfare, 1935-43; gen. counsel Ky. Fair Bd., 1956-63; asso. late Senator M.M. Logan in law, Frankfort, 1933-35; partner firm Smith, Reed & Leary, Frankfort, 1935-46; partner firm Milliken, Handmaker & Rosenstein, Louisville, 1946-68, sr. mem., 1964-68; judge U.S. Customs Ct., N.Y.C., 1968—, now sr. judge; city prosecutor Frankfort, 1933-41; acting county atty. Franklin County (Ky.), 1941-42; faculty Jefferson Law Sch., Louisville, 1948-50. Mem. Ky. Constn. Revision Assembly, 1964-66. Mem. pres.'s adv. com. Bellarmire Coll., Louisville; mem. bd. Ky. div. Am. Cancer Soc.; pres.'s adv. council Brandeis U. Bd. dirs. Louisville chpt. Nat. Conf. Christians and Jews. Served with AUS, World War II. Recipient Gov. Ky. award, 1967; named Man of Year in Ky., Am. Cancer Soc., 1963. Mem. Am. (past ho. dels.), Ky. (hon. life; sec. 1934-50), Louisville (exec. com. 1967-68) bar assns., Am. Judicature Soc. Home: 2200 S Ocean Ln Fort Lauderdale FL 33316 Office: Federal Bldg 299 E Broward Blvd Fort Lauderdale FL 33301

ROSENSWEIG, ROBERT LAWRENCE, lawyer; b. New Britain, Conn., Aug. 19, 1928; s. Clarence G. and Helen I. (Fagan) R.; B.A., Yale, 1949; LL.B., Fordham U., 1952; m. Gertrude H. Schaefer, Aug. 14, 1954; children—Robert Lawrence, Eric, William. Admitted to Conn. bar, 1952; asso. Shipman & Goodwin, Hartford, 1954-57, partner, 1957—. Chmn., trustee State Bank for Savs. Corporator, Hartford Hosp. Mem. Am., Conn., Hartford County bar assns. Clubs: Hartford, Hartford Golf, 20th Century. Home: 29 Westmont West Hartford CT 06117 Office: 799 Main St Hartford CT 06103

ROSENSWEIG, STANLEY HAROLD, diversified bus. exec.; b. Phila., May 5, 1918; s. Emanuel Martin and Jennie (Hoffman) R.; A.B. in Bus. Adminstrn., George Washington U., 1939; m. 1st, Aug. 20, 1944 (div. Oct. 1967); children—Susan, Ellen, Tod, Lisa; m. 2d, Elaine Gordon Decker, Dec. 4, 1967. Chmn. bd. Electronics Wholesalers Co., Washington, 1959-68, CWF Corp., Washington, 1963-73; pres. Sun Appliance Wholesalers, Washington, 1950-69; pres. Gem Internat., Inc., St. Louis, 1961-65, chmn. exec. com., 1963-66; mng. partner Nat. Theater-Munsey Trust Bldg., Annapolis Roads Country Club Properties (Md.); chmn. bd. Lewis & Thos. Saltz Clothiers, Inc., Washington, 1977—; dir. St. Louis Arena, Inc., Action Leasing, Inc. Trustee Boys' Club, Greater Washington Jewish Community Found.; exec. bd. United Jewish Appeal, Washington; bd. dirs. Jewish Social Services Agy., Washington, Nat. Symphony Orch., Child Guidance Clinic, Washington; co-donor grad. bldg. bio-chemistry Brandeis U., 1964. Served with USCGR, 1941-45. Mem. Young Pres.'s Orgn. Clubs: Standard (Chgo.); Woodmont Country, Circus Saints and Sinners (Washington). Home: 2700 Chesapeake St NW Washington DC 20008 Office: 1409 G St NW Washington DC 20005

ROSENTHAL, AARON, govt. ofcl.; b. N.Y.C., July 12, 1914; s. Zelig and Sarah (Shapinsky) R.; B.A., Coll. City N.Y., 1934, M.S. in Edn., 1935; postgrad. Georgetown U. Law Sch., 1937-39, Am. U., 1950-53; m. Edna Blanche Finkel, Sept. 3, 1940; children—Stephen Mark, Marjorie Ann. Dir. Internal Audit Service, VA, Washington, 1953-58; controller VA, 1958-60; dir. financial mgmt. NASA, 1960-61; comptroller NSF, 1961-69, Nat. Acad. Scis., 1969—. U.S. rep. supr. Radiation Effects Research Found., Hiroshima, Japan; mem. nat. adv. council Nat. Center for Higher Edn. Mgmt. Systems. Trustee, Sci. Service Inc. Served with AUS, 1943-45. Recipient Exceptional Service award VA, 1960; Merit citation Nat. Civil Service League, 1957, Distinguished Service award NSF, 1969. Fellow A.A.A.S.; mem. Am. Soc. Pub. Adminstrn., Fed. Govt. Accountants Assn. Home: 3001 Veazey Terr NW Washington DC 20008 Office: 2101 Constitution Ave Washington DC 20418

ROSENTHAL, ABRAHAM MICHAEL, editor; b. Sault St. Marie, Ont., Can., May 2, 1922; s. Harry and Sarah (Dickstein) R.; came to U.S. 1926, naturalized, 1951; B.S. in Social Sci., Coll. City N.Y., 1944, LL.D., 1974; m. Ann Marie Burke, Mar. 12, 1949; children—Jonathan Harry, Daniel Michael, Andrew Mark. Staff, N.Y. Times, 1944—, UN corr., 1946-54, assigned India, 1954-58, Warsaw, Poland, 1958-59, Geneva, Switzerland, 1960-61, Tokyo, 1961-63, met. editor, 1963-66, asst. mng. editor, 1967-68, asso. mng. editor, 1968-69, mng. editor, 1969-77, exec. editor, 1977—, Recipient citation for work in India, Overseas Press Club, 1956, for work in India and Poland, 1959, for two fgn. affairs mag. articles, 1965; Pulitzer prize for internat. reporting, 1960, Number One award Overseas Press Club, 1960, George Polk Meml. award, 1960, 65, Page One award Newspaper Guild N.Y., 1960; Hon. award Assn. Indians in Am., 1974. Pres., Fgn. Corr. Assn. India, 1957. Author: 38 Witnesses; co-author One More Victim; also articles N.Y. Times magazine, Sat. Eve. Post, Colliers, Fgn. Affairs. Office: care NY Times 229 W 43d St New York City NY 10036

ROSENTHAL, ALBERT HAROLD, educator, former govt. ofcl.; b. Denver, Nov. 26, 1914; s. Max L. and Anna (Schatz) R.; B.A., U. Denver, 1936, LL.D., 1973; A.M. (Rockefeller Found. fellow), U. Minn., 1937; Ph.D. (Littauer fellow), Harvard, 1941. Cons., FSA, 1939-42, personnel officer, 1941-42; ofcl. office exec. dir. U.S. Social Security Bd., 1937-41; cons. Dept. State and Bur. Budget, 1939-42; asst. dir. UNESCO relations staff Dept. State, 1946-49; dir. sch. pub. adminstrn., prof. pub. adminstrn. U. Denver, 1949-51; pub. mem. Gov.'s Adv. Council on Employment Security, Colo., 1949-51; regional dir. Dept. Health, Edn. and Welfare, 1951-64; state chmn. Colo. Fulbright Com., 1950-64; chmn. Denver Fed. Exec. Bd., 1963-64; UN adviser in pub. adminstrn. to Ireland, 1964-65; prof. pub. adminstrn. U. Minn., 1965-67; prof. polit. sci., dir. Program for Advanced Study in Pub. Sci. Policy and Adminstrn., U. N.Mex., Albuquerque, 1967—; head Office Pub. Understanding of Sci., NSF, 1970-71; vis. prof. Trinity Coll., Dublin, 1964-65, U. Okla., 1963—. Mem. Gov.'s Commn. Mental Health, N.Mex., 1969-70; chmn. N.Mex.-Nat. Civil Service League State Council, 1973. Bd. dirs. Met. Council for Community Services, Denver, Am. Med. Center. Served from ensign to lt. comdr., USNR, 1942-46. Recipient Rockefeller Pub. Service award, 1957, Denver Civic Activities Distinguished Pub. Service award, 1956, N.Mex.-Nat. Civil Service League Distinguished Pub. Service award, 1969. Wilton Park fellow, Eng., 1969. Mem. Am. Polit. Sci. Assn., Am. Soc. Pub. Adminstrn. (nat. council 1961-64), Civil Service Assembly, Am. Acad. Polit. and Social Sci., Am. Municipal Assn., Albuquerque C. of C. (Pub. Service award 1969), Phi Beta Kappa (Alumni award 1962), Omicron Delta Kappa, Pi Gamma Mu. Author: Administrative Problems in the Establishment of UNESCO, 1948; The Social Programs of Sweden, 1968; Public Science Policy and Administration, 1973. Bd. editors Pub. Adminstrn. Rev., 1960-63. Contbr. articles to profl. jours. Home: 2204 Lester Dr NE Apt 499 Albuquerque NM 87112

ROSENTHAL, ARNOLD H., advt. agy. exec.; b. Chgo., Jan. 31, 1933; s. Gus and Sara (Ariel) R.; B.A., U. Ill., 1954; children—Michel, Jason. Graphic designer Whitaker-Guernsey Studios, Chgo., 1954-55; art dir. Edward H. Weiss Advt., Chgo., 1956-60; owner Arnold H. Rosenthal & Assos., Chgo., 1960-70; partner, creative dir., pres. Meyer & Rosenthal Inc., mktg. communications, Chgo., 1970-75; sr. v.p., creative dir. Garfield-Linn & Co., Advt., Chgo., 1975—; TV jury chmn. Chgo. Internat. Film Festival, 1977, 78. Bd. dirs. Chgo. Sch. and Workshop for Retarded, Jewish United Fund. Served with AUS, 1955-56. Recipient creative awards Hollywood Radio and TV Soc., Communication Clubs Chgo., N.Y.C., 1960—. Mem. Soc. Typographic Arts (design awards 1958—; pres. 1971-72), Am. Inst. Graphic Arts (spl. award 1974), Jazz Inst. Chgo. (charter), Tau Epsilon Phi, Alpha Delta Sigma. Contbr. articles to profl. publs. Home: 175 E Delaware Pl Chicago IL 60611 Office: 875 N Michigan Ave Chicago IL 60611

ROSENTHAL, ARTHUR JESSE, publisher; b. N.Y.C., Sept. 26, 1919; s. Arthur J. and Grace (Ellinger) R.; B.A., Yale U., 1941; postgrad. Harvard U. Bus. Sch., 1942; m. Margaret Ann Roth, Dec. 12, 1975; children—James, Kathryn, Paul. Spl. asst. to U.S. ambassador to Israel, Jerusalem, 1948; pres., editor-in-chief Basic Books, Inc., N.Y.C., 1949-72; dir. Harvard U. Press, Cambridge, 1972—; founding trustee Bank St. Coll. Edn., 1952-68. Trustee Austen Riggs Center, Stockbridge, Mass., Nat. Commn. on Resources for Youth. Served to capt., M.I., U.S. Army, 1942-46. Clubs: Century Assn. (N.Y.C.); St. Botolph (Boston). Editorial bd. Pub. Interest, 1961-72, Harvard Bus. Rev., Family Process. Home: 8 Follen St Cambridge MA 02138 Office: Harvard U Press 79 Garden St Cambridge MA 02138

ROSENTHAL, BENJAMIN STANLEY, congressman; b. N.Y.C., June 8, 1923; s. Joseph and Ceil (Fischer) R.; student L.I.U., Coll. City N.Y.; LL.B., Bklyn. Law Sch., 1949; LL.M., N.Y.U., 1952; m. Lila Moskowitz, Dec. 23, 1950; children—Debra, Edward. Admitted to N.Y. bar, 1949, practiced in N.Y.C.; elected to 87th Congress in spl. election, 1962; mem. 88th-96th Congresses from 8th Dist. N.Y., mem. fgn. affairs com., mem. govt. ops. com., chmn. commerce, consumer and monetary affairs subcom.; mem. consumer task force Democratic Study Group; dep. house whip; mem. Mems. Congress for Peace Through Law. Participant Anglo-Am. Parliamentary Conf.; congl. del. 34th UN Gen. Assembly, 1979. Served with AUS, 1943-46. Mem. Am., N.Y. State, Queens County bar assns. Democrat-Liberal. Home: 88-12 Elmhurst Ave Elmhurst NY 11373 Office: House Office Bldg Washington DC 20515 also 41-65 Main St Flushing NY 11351

ROSENTHAL, BERNARD GORDON, psychologist, educator; b. Chgo., Feb. 3, 1922; s. B.J. and Sonia (Gordon) R.; B.S., Northwestern U., 1942; M.A., Princeton, 1943, Ph.D., 1944; m. Judith Ann Straka, Sept. 22, 1957; children—Amy, Mark. Instr. Princeton, 1947-48; asst. prof. U. Chgo., 1948-55; asso. prof. Howard U., research asso., lectr. Harvard, 1957-60; vis. prof. Ill. Inst. Tech., 1964-65, prof. social psychology, 1965—. Co-chmn. Greater Boston Com. Sane Nuclear Policy, 1959-60; chmn. Greater Ill. Faculty Com. Vietnam, 1965-66. Served with Morale Services Div., War Dept., 1944-45. Mem. Am. Psychol. Assn. (chmn. program com. div. 9, 1952-53, chmn. Midwest com. race relations 1951-53), Am. Assn. Humanistic Psychology (chmn. Midwest region 1966-68), AAUP, Phi Beta Kappa, Sigma Xi. Club: Princeton (Chgo.). Author: The Images of Man, 1971; Development of Self-Identification in Relation to Attitudes towards the Self in the Chippewa Indians, 1974; Von der Armut der Psychologie-und wie ihr Abzuhelfen ware, 1974; (with others) Confrontation: Encounters in Self and Interpersonal Awareness, 1971; In the Search for Community, 1977; also articles in sci. and scholarly jours. Co-editor: The Human Context, 1969-76, exec. editor Am. Editorial bd., 1971-76; editorial bd. Existential Psychiatry, 1971-73. Home: 801 Hinman Ave Evanston IL 60202

ROSENTHAL, DOUGLAS EURICO, lawyer, govt. ofcl.; b. N.Y.C., Feb. 12, 1940; s. Jacob and Edna Louise (Muir) R.; B.A. summa cum laude, Yale U., 1961, LL.B., 1966, Ph.D. in Polit. Sci., 1970; postgrad. (Henry fellow) Balliol Coll. Oxford (Eng.) U., 1962; M.A., Columbia U., 1963; m. Erica Switzen Kremen, Nov. 12, 1967; children—Benjamin Muir, Rachel Elizabeth. Admitted to N.Y. bar, 1968, U.S. Supreme Ct. bar, 1976; project dir. Russell Sage Found., N.Y.C., 1968-70; asso. firm Fried, Frank, Harris, Shriver & Jacobson, N.Y.C., 1970-74; asst. chief fgn. commerce sect., antitrust div. Dept. Justice, Washington, 1974-77, chief, 1977—; reporter Am. Law Inst.-Am. Bar Assn. Joint Project to Develop Model Lawyer Peer Rev. System. Sgt.-at-arms Democratic Party Presdl. Conv., 1960; committeeman Nassau County (N.Y.) Dem. Party, 1963-65. Recipient Edward S. Corwin award Am. Polit. Sci. Assn., 1971;

Woodrow Wilson fellow, 1963. Mem. Am. Law Inst., Bar Assn. City N.Y., Am. Bar Assn., Am. Soc. Internat. Law, N.Y. State Bar Assn., Confrerie des Chevaliers du Tastevin, Phi Beta Kappa. Jewish. Author: (with Baker and others) Antitrust Guide for International Operations, 1977; Lawyer and Client: Who's in Charge? 1974, 2d rev. edit., 1977; contbr. articles to profl. publs. Home: 3502 Legation St NW Washington DC 20015 Office: Dept Justice Antitrust Div 10th and Constitution Ave NW Washington DC 20530

ROSENTHAL, EARL EDGAR, educator; b. Milw., Aug. 26, 1921; s. Edgar Ernst and Reneé (Wyler) R.; B.S., U. Wis. at Milw., 1943; Ph.D., Inst. Fine Arts, N.Y. U., 1953. Asst. dir. Milw. Art Inst., also Layton Art Gallery, Milw., 1952-53; vis. lectr., dept. art history, U. Chgo., from 1953, prof., 1968—. Served to lt. (j.g.) USNR, 1943-46; PTO. Spanish govt. grantee, 1948-49; Fulbright grantee, Italy, 1949-50; Fulbright grantee, Spain, 1963-64; Guggenheim grantee, Italy, 1963-64. Mem. Hispanic Soc. Am. (corr.), Coll. Art Assn., Soc. Archtl. Historians (dir. 1957-58, 66-69), Academia de San Fernando (Madrid) (corr.). Author: The Cathedral of Granada, 1961. Contbr. articles to profl. publs. Office: Cochrane-Woods Art Center 5540 Greenwood Ave Chicago IL 60637

ROSENTHAL, FRANZ, educator; b. Berlin, Germany, Aug 31, 1914; s. Kurt W. and Elsa (Kirschstein) R.; Ph.D., U. Berlin, 1935. Came to U.S., 1940, naturalized, 1943. Asst. prof. Semitic langs. Hebrew Union Coll., Cin., 1940-48; prof. Arabic, U. Pa., 1948-56; Louis M. Rabinowitz prof. Yale, 1956-67, Sterling prof. Near Eastern langs., 1967—. Served with AUS, OSS, 1943-45. Fellow Am. Acad. Arts and Scis.; mem. Am. Philos. Soc., Am. Oriental Soc. (pres. 1964-65). Author: Aramaistische Forschung, 1939; Technique and Approach of Muslim Scholarship, 1947; Hist. of Muslim Historiography, 1952; Humor in Early Islam, 1956; Ibn Khaldûn, The Muqaddimah, 1958; The Muslim Concept of Freedom, 1960; Fortleben der Antike im Islam, 1965; Knowledge Triumphant, 1970; The Herb: Hashish versus Medieval Muslim Society, 1971; Gambling in Islam, 1975. Home: 80 Heloise St Hamden CT 06517

ROSENTHAL, GARY, hat mfg. co. exec.; b. St. Joseph, Mo., Sept. 13, 1932; s. Ben L. and Eleanor (Feltenstein) R.; B.A., Dartmouth Coll., 1954; m. Marian Levy Kaufman, Jan. 1, 1976; children—John Rosenthal, Debra Rosenthal, Jane Kaufman, Richard Kaufman, Cheryl Kaufman. With Stevens Hat Co., St. Joseph, 1956—, pres., 1972—; pres. subs. Stetson Hat Co. Inc., St. Joseph, 1971—; dir. Commerce Bank, St. Joseph. Served to lt. (j.g.) USNR, 1954-56; Korea. Mem. Headwear Inst. Am. (pres. 1977-79). Clubs: Lions, Elks, Shriners, St. Joseph Country. Home: 43 Stonecrest St Saint Joseph MO 64506 Office: 4500 Stetson Trail Saint Joseph MO 64502

ROSENTHAL, GERALD DAVID, fed. govt. research adminstr.; b. Reading, Pa., Jan. 2, 1934; s. Bernard and Mildred (Cohen) R.; A.B. in Econs., Cornell U., 1958, S.M. in Labor Econs. and Statistics, 1959; Ph.D. in Econs., Harvard U., 1963; m. Susan, Dec. 31, 1972; children—Eric, Signe, David. Mem. faculty dept. econs. Boston U., 1960-61; instr., then asst. prof. econs. Harvard U., Cambridge, Mass., 1962-67, research asst. interfaculty program in econs. and adminstrn. of med. care, 1961-62; sr. asso. Orgn. for Social and Tech. Innovation, Cambridge, Mass., 1968-72; asso. prof. dept. econs., Florence Heller Grad. Sch. Social Welfare Brandeis U., Waltham, Mass., 1967-74, on leave as exec. dir. Health Wage Stabilization Program, Cost Living Council, Washington, 1973-74; dir. Nat. Center for Health Services Research, HEW, Hyattsville, Md., 1974—; mem. Task Force on Health, Nat. Urban Coalition, 1969, planning com. Nat. Health Forum, 1970; chmn. Health Industry Wage and Salary Com., Cost Living Council, 1973-74. Served with U.S. Army, 1955-57. Mem. Am., Mass. (pres. 1972-73) pub. health assns. Home: 5003 Decatur St Hyattsville MD 20781 Office: 3700 East West Hwy Hyattsville MD 20782

ROSENTHAL, JACOB (JACK), editor; b. Tel-Aviv, Palestine, June 30, 1935; s. Manfred and Rachel (Kaplan) R.; came to U.S., 1938, naturalized 1943; A.B., Harvard, 1956; m. Marilyn Wayne Silver, Apr. 6, 1963; children—John, Ann. Reporter, editor Portland Oregonian, Reporter, 1950-61; asst. dir., dir. public info. U.S. Dept. Justice, Washington, 1961-66; exec. asst. to undersec. state, 1966-67; Kennedy fellow Harvard Inst. Politics, 1967-68; prin. author Kerner Commn. Report on Urban Riots, 1968; nat. urban corr. Life mag., 1968-69; urban corr. N.Y. Times, Washington, 1969-73, asst. Sunday editor, mag. editor, 1973-77, dep. editorial page editor, 1977—. Mem. overseers vis. com. for govt. Harvard U., 1975—; for history, 1976—; chmn. Robert F. Kennedy Journalism Awards Com., 1979-80. Recipient Best Editorial award Internat. Labor Assn., 1961; Loeb award for demographic reporting, 1973, others. Office: 229 W 43d St New York NY 10036

ROSENTHAL, JOSEPH AARON, librarian; b. Pitts., Aug. 11, 1929; s. Joseph Aaron and Elizabeth Kathryn (Feight) R.; B.A., Dickinson Coll., 1949; M.A., Pa. State U., 1951; M.S.L.S., Columbia U., 1957. With N.Y. Public Library, 1955-57, 58-70, documents librarian, 1960-64, chief preparation services, 1964-70; spl. recruit Library of Congress, 1957-58; asso. univ. librarian for tech. services U. Calif., Berkeley, 1971-79, univ. librarian, 1979—; speaker in field; cons. Internat. MARC Network Steering Com., 1978-79. Mem. ALA, Assn. Research Libraries, Public Affairs Info. Service, Archons of Colophon, Phi Beta Kappa, Beta Phi Mu. Editor: (with James W. Henderson) Library Catalogs: Their Preservation and Maintenance by Photographic and Automated Techniques, 1960; compiler: (with Edward di Roma) A Numerical Finding List of British Command Papers Published 1833-1961/62, 1967. Office: 245 General Library U Calif Berkeley CA 94720

ROSENTHAL, JULIAN BERNARD, lawyer, assn. ofcl.; b. N.Y.C., July 4, 1908; s. Alex Sidney and Katherine (Goodman) R.; student Columbia, 1925-26; LL.B., Fordham U., 1929; m. Frances Stone, Nov. 14, 1941; children—Brian, John L. Admitted to N.Y. bar, 1931, practiced in N.Y.C., 1931-72, Ga., 1972-78; mem. firm Javits & Javits, 1968-72, of counsel, 1972-74; mem. Air Force Assn., 1945—, life mem., 1946—, sec., 1946-59, chmn. bd. dirs., 1959-60, chmn. constn. com., 1946-71, chmn. resolutions com., 1946-61, permanent bd. dirs., 1960—; chmn. bd. dirs. Aerospace Edn. Council, N.Y.C., 1965-73; mem. Atlanta consumer adv. panel Gulf Oil Corp. Govt. appeal agent SSS, 1943-44. Chmn. steering com. com., Ga. joint legis. com. Am. Assn. Ret. Persons-Nat. Ret. Tchrs. Assn., 1975-78, mem. Ariz. joint state legis. com., 1978—; mem. motion picture div. Democratic Nat. Com., 1940; past treas., dir. Lydia M. Morrison Found.; former sec. bd. dirs. Herbert I. and Shirley C. Rosenthal Found.; former v.p., treas., dir. Vanguard Found.; past trustee, sec. Aerospace Edn. Found.; former bd. dirs. Natser Found.; bd. dirs. Ariz. Recovery Centers Assn. Served with USAAF, 1944-45. Recipient Man of Year award Air Force Assn., 1953. Mem. Am. Bar Assn., State Bar Ga. Address: 17631 Foothills Dr Sun City AZ 85373

ROSENTHAL, LAWRENCE MICHAEL, investment exec.; b. Bklyn., Jan. 2, 1935; s. Albert and Florence Hannah (Zweibel) R.; B.S. in Econs., U. Pa., 1956; postgrad. Harvard, 1956-57; m. Marjorie Bellows Pechenik, Sept. 27, 1959; children—Pamela Beth, Lisa Jan, Eric Michael. With Lehman Brothers, N.Y.C., 1957-61; pres. L.M. Rosenthal & Co., Inc., N.Y.C., 1961-75; pres., dir. Inconcoal Corp., 1976—; dir. Am. Bankers Mortgage Corp., Eldon Industries, Masters, Inc., Terro Constructors, Inc., Potomac Mining, Inc., Owens & Rosenthal Properties, Inc., Number One Music, Inc., Volta Sugar Estates, Ltd., Accra, Ghana; gen. partner Greenleaf Meadows Assos., Park Plaza II Ltd., Palm Lakes, Ltd., Rope Assos. Bd. dirs. Police Athletic League, N.Y.C., Am. Council for Nationalities Service, Brotherhood in Action; trustee L.M. Rosenthal Found. Home: 998 Fifth Ave New York NY 10028 Office: 9 W 57th St New York NY 10019

ROSENTHAL, LEIGHTON A., indsl. laundry and apparel co. exec.; b. Buffalo, Jan. 27, 1915; s. Samuel and Sadie (Dosberg) R.; student Phila. Textile Sch.; grad. U. Pa.; hon. doctorate, Cleve. Coll. Jewish Studies, 1973; m. Honey Rousuck, June 30, 1940; children—Cynthia, Jane. Pres. Cleve. Overall Co., 1956-61, Work Wear Corp., 1961—, Mfg. & Service Co.; dir., mem. exec. com. Union Commerce Bank, Cleve.; dir. Union Commerce Corp. Bd. dirs. Cleve. Automobile Assn. Trustee Cleve. Health Mus., Jewish Community Fedn. Cleve.; bd. dirs. Greater Cleve. Growth Assn. Fellow Am. Assn. Jewish Edn. Clubs: Clevelander, Commerce, Oakwood (Cleve.); Fifth Avenue (N.Y.C.); Poinciana (Palm Beach, Fla.); Marks, Annabels, Burkes (London). Office: 1768 E 25th St Cleveland OH 44114

ROSENTHAL, LUCY GABRIELLE, editor, writer; b. N.Y.C., Jan. 3, 1933; d. Henry Moses and Rachel (Tchernowitz) R.; A.B. (Hopwood award), U. Mich., 1954; M.S., Columbia U. Sch. Journalism, 1955; M.F.A., Yale Sch. Drama, 1961. Asst. editor Radiology mag., Detroit, 1955-57; freelance editorial cons. various pub. houses, lit. agts., N.Y.C., 1957-73; mem. admissions staff U. Iowa Writers Workshop, Iowa City, 1965-68; editor Book-of-the-Month Club, N.Y.C., 1973-74, mem. editorial bd. judges, 1974-79, sr. editorial adv., 1979—; Pulitzer fellow critical writing, 1968. Mem. Authors Guild, Nat. Book Critics Circle, Women's Media Group (dir. 1979—), Eugene O'Neill Meml. Theater Center, Phi Beta Kappa, Phi Kappa Phi. Contbr. articles, reviews to various mags. and periodicals including Book World, Sat. Review, Ms. Mag., Mich. Quar. Review. Office: Book-of-the-Month Club 485 Lexington Ave New York NY 10017

ROSENTHAL, MACHA LOUIS, educator, writer; b. Washington, Mar. 14, 1917; s. Jacob and Ethel (Brown) R.; B.A., U. Chgo., 1937, M.A., 1938; Ph.D., N.Y. U., 1949; m. Victoria Himmelstein, Jan. 7, 1939; children—David, Alan, Laura. Faculty, Mich. State U., 1939-45; faculty N.Y. U., N.Y.C., 1945—, prof., 1961—, dir. Poetics Inst., 1977-79; poetry editor The Nation, 1956-61, Humanist, 1970-78, Present Tense, 1973—; vis. specialist U.S. Cultural Exchange Programs, Germany, 1961, Pakistan, 1965, Poland, Rumania, Bulgaria, 1966; vis. prof. U. Pa., 1974; vis. poet, Israel, 1974. Mem. adv. com. Nat. Book Com., 1964-67, mem. Bollingen award com., 1968-70; chmn. Delmore Schwartz Meml. Award, 1970—; mem. creative arts awards lit. jury Brandeis U., 1976—. Am. Council Learned Socs. fellow, 1942, 50-51; Guggenheim fellow, 1960-61, 64-65. Mem. AAUP, P.E.N., Modern Lang. Assn., Nat. Book Critics Circle. Author: (with A.J.M. Smith) Exploring Poetry, 1955, 73; The Modern Poets: A Critical Introduction, 1960; A Primer of Ezra Pound, 1960; Blue Boy on Skates: Poems, 1964; The New Poets: American and British Poetry since World War II, 1967; Beyond Power: New Poems, 1969; The View from the Peacock's Tail: Poems, 1972; Randall Jarrell, 1972; Poetry and the Common Life, 1974; She: A Sequence of Poems, 1977; Sailing into the Unknown; Yeats, Pound, and Eliot, 1978. Editor: Selected Poems and Two Plays of W.B. Yeats, 1962, 73; The William Carlos Williams Reader, 1966; The New Modern Poetry: An Anthology of American and British Poetry since World War II, 1967, 69; 100 Postwar Poems, British and American, 1968; co-editor Chief Modern Poets of Britain and America, 1970. Contbr. articles and poems to profl. publs. Home: 17 Bayard Ln Suffern NY 10901 Office: Dept English NYU 19 University Pl New York NY 10003

ROSENTHAL, MICHAEL JAY, investment banker; b. N.Y.C., Feb. 16, 1944; s. Joseph and Sylvia (Weisman) R.; B.A., McGill U., Montreal, Que., Can., 1964; M.B.A., Columbia, 1966; J.D., N.Y. U., 1970; m. Barbara Carol Etra, May 29, 1966. Supr. tax dept. Coopers & Lybrand, accountants, N.Y.C., 1966-69; v.p. investment banking dept. Shearson Hayden Stone, Inc., investment bankers, N.Y.C., 1969-72; admitted to N.Y. State bar, 1971; fin. v.p. CertainTeed Corp., Valley Forge, Pa., 1972-73, sr. v.p., 1973-75; sr. v.p., dir., mng. dir. devel. banking dept. Donaldson, Lufkin, Jenrette & Co., Inc., N.Y.C., 1976—. C.P.A., N.Y. Mem. Am. Inst. C.P.A.'s N.Y. State Soc. C.P.A.'s. Home: 25 Fifth Ave New York City NY 10003 Office: 140 Broadway New York City NY 10005

ROSENTHAL, MILTON FREDERICK, corp. exec.; b. N.Y.C., Nov. 24, 1913; s. Jacob C. and Louise (Berger) R.; B.A., City Coll. N.Y., 1932; LL.B., Columbia U., 1935; m. Frieda Bojar, Feb. 28, 1943; 1 dau., Anne Rosenthal Mitro. Admitted to N.Y. bar, 1935; research asst. N.Y. State Law Revision Commn., 1935-37; law sec. Fed. Judge William Bondy, 1937-40; asso. atty. Leve, Hecht & Hadfield, 1940-42; sec., treas. Hugo Stinnes Corp., 1946-48, exec. v.p., treas., 1948-49, pres., dir., 1949-64; pres., dir. Minerals and Chems. Philipp Corp., N.Y.C., 1964-67; pres. Engelhard Minerals & Chems. Corp., N.Y.C., 1967-77, 79—, chmn., 1977—, also dir.; dir. European-Am. Banking Corp., European-Am. Bank & Trust Co., Ferro Corp., Midlantic Banks Inc., Schering-Plough Corp. Bd. dirs. Romanian-U.S. Econ. Council, also chmn. U.S. sect.; bd. dirs. U.S.-USSR Trade and Econ. Council, Inc., Mt. Sinai Med. Center, United Cerebral Palsy Research and Ednl. Found., Inc., Nat. Council for U.S.-China Trade; trustee Mt. Sinai Hosp. Served as 1st lt. JAG dept. U.S. Army, 1942-45. Mem. Assn. Bar City N.Y., Chgo. Bar Assn., Columbia Law Sch. Alumni Assn., Judge Adv. Assn., Fgn. Policy Assn. (dir., gov.), Phi Beta Kappa. Home: Woodlands Rd Harrison NY 10528 Office: 1221 Ave of Americas New York NY 10020

ROSENTHAL, NORMAN, retail store exec.; b. 1919; student Omaha U. With Edison Bros. Stores, Inc., 1937—, v.p., 1961-74, exec. v.p., 1974—, bd. mem., 1968, dir. Chandler, Burts and Wild Pair div. Address: 400 Washington Ave Saint Louis MO 63102

ROSENTHAL, RICHARD ANTHONY, banker; b. St. Louis, Jan. 20, 1933; s. John J. and Bertha Marie (Evers) R.; B.S., Notre Dame U., 1954; grad. Grad. Sch. Banking, U. Wis., 1959-61; m. Marylyn Blair, Apr. 7, 1956; children—Kathleen, John, Mary Lorene, Joseph, Carol Ann, Ellen Elizabeth, Susan Maureen, Mary Pat, Richard Peter. Asst. v.p. Ind. Bank & Trust Co., Ft. Wayne, 1958-59, v.p., 1959-61, 1st v.p., dir., 1961; pres., dir., chief exec. officer St. Joseph Bank & Trust Co., South Bend, Ind., 1961-71, chmn. bd., pres., chief exec. officer, 1971-72, chmn. bd., chief exec. officer, 1972—; dir. Zimmer Paper Products, Inc., Indpls., Beck Corp., Elkhart, Ind., Athey Corp., Raleigh, N.C., Dalton Foundries, Warsaw, Ind., Gen. chmn. United Fund Campaign, 1964; pres. United Community Services, 1968, now mem. exec. com.; mem. Downtown Council of South Bend; chmn. South Bend Civic Center Authority; mem. internat. com. U.S. C. of C.; chmn. South Bend Community Prayer Breakfast, 1973; chmn. adv. bd. Sch. Bus., U. Notre Dame; bd. dirs. Cath. Charities, Diocese Ft. Wayne-South Bend; mem. pres.'s com. U. Notre Dame; trustee St. Joseph's Hosp., South Bend, Ind. Tchrs. Retirement. Served with AUS, 1954-58. Recipient Outstanding Young Man of Year award for South Bend, 1963; named One of Ind.'s 5 Outstanding Young Men, 1963, Notre Dame Man of Year, 1964, Am. Bus. Women's Boss of Year in South Bend, 1964, knight Order Holy Sepulchre by Pope Paul VI. Mem. Chgo. Export Expansion Council, Bank Mktg. Assn., Am., Ind. bankers assns., South Bend-Mishawaka C. of C. (dir., past pres.), chambers commerce, Notre Dame Alumni Assn. (past pres.). Roman Catholic (dir. diocese). Club: St. Joseph Valley Notre Dame. Home: 15675 Hearthstone Dr Mishawaka IN 46544 Office: 202 S Michigan St South Bend IN 46601

ROSENTHAL, RICHARD HENRY, publisher; b. Cin., Feb. 12, 1933; s. Wilbert and Helen (Bauman) R.; B.S., Ohio State U., 1957; m. Lois Reis, Dec. 20, 1959; children—Jennie, David. Sales mgr. Writers Market, 1957-58; editor Writer's Digest, Cin., 1959-63, sch. dir., 1963-67, pub., 1963—, pres., 1974; partner, S. Rosenthal & Rosenthal-Kaufman printing firms. Charter mem. U. Cin. Publ. Com. Mem. Mayor's Cable Television Task Force, 1973; team capt. Determined Young Men, 1970-72; mem. parents bd. Walnut Hills High Sch.; trustee Seven Hills Sch., Jewish Community Center. Served with AUS, 1953-55. Mem. Ohio Valley Direct Mktg. Club (founder, pres. 1975), Alpha Delta Sigma. Jewish. Club: The Board. Home: 8435 Susann Ln Cincinnati OH 45215 Office: 9933 Alliance Rd Cincinnati OH 45242

ROSENTHAL, ROBERT, educator, psychologist; b. Giessen, Germany, Mar. 2, 1933; s. Julius and Hermine (Kahn) R.; came to U.S., 1940, naturalized, 1946; A.B., UCLA, 1953, Ph.D., 1956; m. Mary Lu Clayton, Apr. 20, 1951; children—Roberta, David C., Virginia. Clin. psychology trainee Los Angeles Area VA, 1954-57; lectr. U. So. Calif., 1956-57; acting instr. UCLA, 1957; from asst. to asso. prof., coordinator clin. tng. U. N.D., 1957-62; vis. asso. prof. Ohio State U., 1960-61; lectr. Boston U., 1965-66; lectr. clin. psychology Harvard, 1962-67, prof. social psychology, 1967—. Diplomate clin. psychology Am. Bd. Examiners Profl. Psychology. Fellow AAAS (co-recipient Sociopsychol. prize 1960, Am. Psychol. Assn. (co-recipient Cattell Fund award 1967); mem. Eastern, Mid-western, Mass. (Disting. Career Contbn. award 1979) psychol. assns., Soc. Projective Techniques (past treas.), Phi Beta Kappa, Sigma Xi. Author: Experimenter Effects in Behavioral Research, 1966, enlarged edit., 1976; (with Lenore Jacobson) Pygmalion in the Classroom, 1968; (with others) New Directions in Psychology 4, 1970; Sensitivity to Nonverbal Communication: The PONS Test, 1979; (with Ralph L. Rosnow) The Volunteer Subject, 1975, Primer of Methods for the Behavioral Sciences, 1975. Editor: (with Ralph L. Rosnow) Artifact in Behavioral Research, 1969; Skill in Nonverbal Communication, 1979. Home: 12 Phinney Rd Lexington MA 02173 Office: 33 Kirkland St Cambridge MA 02138

ROSENTHAL, SAMUEL ROBERT, lawyer; b. Manistique, Mich., June 6, 1899; s. Lazarus and Rachel (Blumrosen) R.; A.B. summa cum laude, U. Mich., 1921; J.D., Harvard U., 1924; LL.D. (hon.), Grinnell Coll., 1978; m. Marie-Louise Dreyfus, July 30, 1932; children—Martin Raymond (dec.), Louise (Mrs. James J. Glasser). Admitted to Ill. bar, 1925, since practiced in Chgo.; asso. firm Foreman, Bluford, Steele & Schultz, 1924-26; asso. firm Sonnenschein Carlin Nath & Rosenthal, 1926-36, partner, 1937—; pres. D and R Fund, Chgo. Pres. bd. edn. Highland Park High Sch., 1955-59; pres. Highland Park Community Chest, 1947-48. Bd. mgrs. Highland Park Hosp. Found., 1942-53, life trustee; life trustee Ravinia Festival Assn.; trustee Grinnell Coll., 1962-77, Newberry Library, Chgo., Highland Park Pub. Library, 1962-72; life trustee Michael Reese Hosp. and Med. Center. Fellow Brandeis U. Served lt. U.S. Army World War I. Mem. Am., Ill., Chgo. bar assns., Am. Antiquarian Soc., Am. Bar Found., Am. Coll. Probate Counsel, Phi Beta Kappa. Clubs: Mid-America, Mid-Day, Metropolitan, Caxton (pres. 1974-76), Standard, (Chgo.); Lake Shore Country (Glencoe, Ill.); Pierpont Morgan Library, Grolier (N.Y.). Home: 910 Baldwin Rd Highland Park IL 60035 Office: 8000 Sears Tower Chicago IL 60606

ROSENTHAL, STANLEY LAWRENCE, meteorologist; b. Bklyn., Dec. 6, 1929; s. Louis and Fay (Pokorne) R.; B.S., CCNY, 1951; M.S., Fla. State U., 1953, Ph.D., 1958; m. Mildred Farlow, Aug. 8, 1953; children—Russell K., Sarah Lynn, David Scott. With NOAA, Dept. Commerce, 1960—, chief theoretical studies group Nat. Hurricane and Exptl. Meterol. Lab., Miami, Fla., 1960-75, chief modeling group, 1975-77, chief analytical and theoretical studies group, 1977—, dir. Nat. Hurricane and Exptl. Meterology Lab., 1977—; adj. prof. meteorology U. Miami, Coral Gables, Fla., 1964—. Served with U.S. Army, 1953-55. Recipient Gold medal U.S. Dept. Commerce, 1970. Fellow Am. Meteorol. Soc. (past chmn. Greater Miami br.); mem. Fla. Acad. Scis. (past pres. oceans and atmospheres sect.), AAAS (officer sect. W). Contbr. articles to profl. jours. Home: 13301 SW 99th Pl Miami FL 33176 Office: Gables 1 Tower 1320 S Dixie Hwy Coral Gables FL 33146

ROSENTHAL, TONY (BERNARD), sculptor; b. Highland Park, Ill., Aug. 9, 1914; s. Nathan H. and Bessie (Baumgarden) R.; A.B., U. Mich., 1936; student Art Inst. Chgo., Cranbrook Acad. Arts; m. Halina Kotlowicz, Apr. 2, 1946. Exhibitions Art Inst. Chgo., Met. Mus. Art, Mus. Modern Art, N.Y., Whitney Mus. Am. Art, N.Y., Pa. Acad. Fine Arts, Archtl. League, N.Y., Yale, U. Ill., U. Neb., Biennale Exhbn., Sao Paulo, Brazil, Brussel's Fair, 1958, others; one man exhbns. San Francisco Mus., Western Mus. Assn. Travel Exhbn., Santa Barbara Mus., Long Beach Mus., Catherine Viviano Gallery of N.Y. Kootz Gallery, N.Y.C., M. Knoedler & Co., others; archtl. commns. include: Temple Emanuel, Beverly Hills, 1955, IBM Bldg., 1958, Southland Center, Dallas, IBM Western Hdqrs., Los Angeles, Police Plaza, N.Y.C., Fullerton (Calif.) State Coll., Financial Center Pacific, Honolulu, Holocaust Meml., Buffalo, others; work in permanent collections Milw. Art Center, Ill. State, Los Angeles County, Long Beach, Lincoln (Mass.) Mus., Ariz. State Coll., Mus. Modern Art, N.Y.C., Whitney Mus. Art, Albright Knox Art Gallery, Buffalo, U. Ill., N.Y. U., Yale U., Middelheim Mus., Antwerp, Belgium, others, also pvt. collections. Served with AUS, 1942-46. Awards, prizes San Francisco Mus., 1950, Los Angeles City Exhbn., 1951, 52, Audubon Artists, N.Y., 1953, Pa. Acad. Fine Arts, 1953, Los Angeles County Mus., 1950, 57, Santa Barbara (Cal.) Museum of Art, 1959, Art in Steel award Iron and Steel Inst., 1974-75. Address: 173 E 73d St New York City NY 10021

ROSENTHAL, WILLIAM J., lawyer; b. Balt., Nov. 4, 1920; s. Justin J. and Ray Marian (Stern) R.; A.B., Johns Hopkins U., 1941; LL.B., U. Balt., 1950; m. Margaret Irwin Parker, July 4, 1956; children—Adriane Leigh, Jacqueline Rae, John Justin. Adminstrv. asst. Office Price Adminstrn., Washington, 1941-42; admitted to Md. bar, 1950; asso. firm Earl K. Shawe (name changed to Shawe & Rosenthal 1967), Balt., 1951-67, partner, 1967—; lectr. U. Balt., 1952-56; mem. regional adv. council NLRB. Vets. rep. Md. Constrn. Adv. Council, 1946-49; bd. dirs., treas. Edgar J. Kassan Meml. Fund. Served to lt. USNR, 1942-46; ETO. Decorated Bronze Star. Mem. Am., Balt. bar assns., Spiked Shoe Soc., Omicron Delta Kappa, Pi Delta Epsilon. Club: Suburban of Baltimore County. Contbg. author: The Developing Labor Law; contbr. articles to profl. jours. Expert witness on labor law, legis. and congl. coms. Home: 8207 Cranwood Ct Pikesville MD 21208 Office: Sun Life Bldg Charles Center Baltimore MD 21201

ROSENTHAL, WILLIAM SANFORD, physician, educator; b. N.Y.C., June 21, 1925; s. Louis and Minna (Pollack) R.; B.A., U. Minn., 1946; M.D., State U. N.Y. Downstate Med. Center, Bklyn., 1950; m. Barbara Swift Bakwin, Nov. 24, 1954; children—Keith William, Andrew Robert. Intern Michael Reese Hosp., Chgo., 1950-51; med. resident VA Hosp., Bklyn., 1951-52, 53-55; research asst. Postgrad. Med. Sch., London, Eng., 1955-56, Mt. Sinai Hosp., N.Y.C., 1957-61; mem. faculty N.Y. Med. Coll., 1961—, prof. medicine, 1968—, chief sect. gastroenterology, 1969—, Sarah C. Upham prof. gastroenterology, 1969—; chief sect. gastroenterology Westchester County Med. Center, N.Y. Trustee, Nat. Found. for Ileitis and Colitis. Served with USNR, 1943-45, USAF 1952-53. Mem. Am. Assn. Study Liver Diseases, Am. Fedn. Clin. Research, Am. Soc. Human Genetics, Am. Gastroent. Assn., Am. Inst. Nutrition, A.C.P., Am. Coll. Gastroenterology (pres., editorial staff jour.), Am. Physiol. Soc., Soc. Exptl. Biology and Medicine, N.Y. Gastroent. Assn. (pres.). Contbr. articles to med. jours. Home: 130 E 67th St New York NY 10021

ROSENWALD, WILLIAM; B. CHGO., AUG. 19, 1903; s. Julius and Augusta (Nusbaum) R.: B.S., Mass. Inst. Tech., 1924; student Harvard Coll., 1924-25, London (Eng.) Sch. Econs. and Polit. Sci., 1925-27; hon. Dr. Hebrew Letters, Hebrew Union Coll., 1944; LL.D., Tuskegee Inst., 1964. Dir. Sears, Roebuck & Co., 1934-38; established W.R. Enterprises, 1936; chmn. bd. Am. Securities Corp. Hon. v.p., bd. dirs. Am. Jewish Joint Distbn. Com., Inc.; mem. advisory bd. Israel Edn. Fund; hon. nat. chmn. United Jewish Appeal, Inc.; hon. pres. United Jewish Appeal-Fedn. Jewish Philanthropies Joint Campaign; hon. chmn. bd. United Jewish Appeal Greater N.Y.; mem. adv. com. Jewish Communal Fund N.Y.; life trustee Fedn. Jewish Philanthropies N.Y.; life mem. bd. dirs. Council Jewish Fedns. and Welfare Funds; hon. nat. chmn. Am. Jewish Com. Campaign; hon. v.p. Am. Jewish Com.; v.p. HIAS; hon. trustee Tuskegee Inst.; hon. life trustee Mus. Sci. and Industry, Chgo. Mem. Am. Arbitration Assn., Council Fgn. Relations. Clubs: Harmonie, Sky, Wall Street (N.Y.C.); Tavern (Chgo.); Century Country (White Plains, N.Y.). Office: 122 E 42d St New York NY 10017

ROSENZWEIG, DAVID LEE, bank holding co. exec.; b. Pottsville, Pa., June 17, 1939; s. Saul and Ethel (Joseph) R.; B.S., Youngstown State U., 1962; J.D., Case-Western Res. U., 1968; m. Nancy Beth Rosenzweig, July 25, 1964; children—Susan, Daniel, Jeremy. Admitted to Ohio bar, 1968; asso. firm Squire, Sanders & Dempsey, Cleve., 1968-74; exec. v.p. adminstrn., gen. counsel Union Commerce Corp., Cleve., 1974—; dir., 1976—; dir. Clarion Capital Corp., So. Ohio Bank, Union Capital Mgmt. Corp., Union Commerce Leasing Corp. Mem. Ohio State Bar Assn., Bar Assn. Greater Cleve., Order of Coif. Editor-in-chief Case-Western Res. Law Rev., 1967-68. Home: 21349 Fairmount Blvd Shaker Heights OH 44118 Office: 300 Union Commerce Bldg Cleveland OH 44115

ROSENZWEIG, MARK RICHARD, psychologist; b. Rochester, N.Y., Sept. 12, 1922; s. Jacob Z. and Pearl (Grossman) R.; B.A., U. Rochester, 1943, M.A., 1944; Ph.D., Harvard U., 1949; m. Janine S.A. Chappat, Aug. 1, 1947; children—Anne Janine, Suzanne Jacqueline, Philip Mark. Postdoctoral research fellow Harvard U., 1949-51; asst. prof. U. Calif., Berkeley, 1951-56, asso. prof., 1956-60, prof. psychology, 1960—, asso. research prof., 1958-59, research prof., 1965-66; vis. prof. biology Sorbonne, Paris, 1973-74; mem. exec. com. Internat. Union Psychol. Sci., Internat. Com. for Social Sci. Info. and Documentation. Served with USN, 1944-46. Fulbright research fellow, faculty research fellow Social Sci. Research Council, 1960-61; research grantee NSF, USPHS, Easter Seal Found. Fellow Am. Psychol. Assn., AAAS; mem. Am. Physiol. Soc., Internat. Brain Research Orgn., Soc. Exptl. Psychologists, Soc. for Neuroscience, Société Francaise de Psychologie, Nat. Acad. Sci., NAACP (life), Common Cause, Phi Beta Kappa, Sigma Xi. Author: Biologie de la Mémoire, 1976. Editor: (with P. Mussen) Psychology: An Introduction, 1973, 2d edit., 1977; (with E.L. Bennett) Neural Mechanisms of Learning and Memory, 1976; Ann. Rev. of Psychology, 1968—. Contbr. articles to profl. jours. Office: Dept Psychology U Calif Berkeley CA 94720

ROSENZWEIG, RICHARD STUART, publishing co. exec.; b. Appleton, Wis., Aug. 8, 1935; s. Walter J. and Rose (Bahcall) R.; B.S., Northwestern U., 1957; student Advanced Mgmt. Program, Harvard, 1975. Credit rep. Dun & Bradstreet, Inc., 1958; with Playboy Enterprises, Inc., 1958—, exec. asst. to pres., 1963-73, sr. v.p., dir., 1973—, dir. mktg., 1974—, exec. v.p. publs. group, 1975-77, exec. v.p., head West Coast ops., 1977—; dir. I. Bahcall Industries, Appleton. Bd. dirs. Better Govt. Assn., Chgo. Council Fgn. Relations, Chgo. Film Bd.; mem. Chgo. Forum, Assn. Governing Bds. Univs. and Colls.; trustee Columbia Coll., Chgo., Los Angeles Film Expn.; mem. 2d decade council Am. Film Inst.; bd. dirs. Mus. Contemporary Art, Chgo., Periodical and Book Assn. Am. Served with AUS, 1957. Mem. Am. Mktg. Assn., Hollywood C. of C. Home: 524 N Canon Dr Beverly Hills CA 90210 Office: 8560 Sunset Blvd Los Angeles CA 90069

ROSENZWEIG, ROBERT MYRON, univ. ofcl.; b. Detroit, Aug. 27, 1931; s. Louis and Gertrude (Lifsitz) R.; B.A., U. Mich., 1952, M.A., 1953; Ph.D., Yale U., 1956; m. Adelle Ruth Rotman, Aug. 30, 1953; children—Kathryn Ann, David Michael. Instr. polit. sci. Amherst Coll., 1955-57; with U.S. Office Edn., 1958-62, spl. asst. to commnr., 1961-62; asso. dean Grad. Div., Stanford U., 1962-67, asso. provost of univ., 1967-71, vice provost, adviser to pres., 1971-74, v.p. pub. affairs, 1974—, lectr. polit. sci., 1963—, dir. Center Research Internat. Studies, 1967-68. Mem. Assn. Ind. Calif. Colls. and Univs. (v.p. 1978—). Author: (with H.D. Babbidge, Jr.) Federal Interest in Higher Education, 1962; also articles. Home: 1462 Dana Palo Alto CA 94306 Office: Stanford U Stanford CA 94301

ROSETT, ARTHUR IRWIN, lawyer; b. N.Y.C., July 5, 1934; s. Milton B. and Bertha (Werner) R.; A.B., Columbia U., 1955, LL.B., 1959; m. Susan Hadas Gurfein, June 5, 1956; children—David Benjamin, Martha Jean, Daniel Joseph. Admitted to Calif. bar, 1968, N.Y. State bar, 1960, U.S. Supreme Ct. bar, 1963; law clk. U.S. Supreme Ct., 1959-60; asst. U.S. atty. So. Dist. N.Y., 1960-63; practice law, N.Y.C., 1963-65; asso. dir. Pres.'s Commn. on Law Enforcement and Adminstrn. Justice, 1965-67; acting prof. law UCLA, 1967-70, prof., 1970—. Served with USN, 1956-58. Mem. Los Angeles and Beverly Hills Bar Assn., Am. Law Inst., AAUP. Author: Contract Law and Its Application (with A. Mueller), 1971, 2d, rev. edit., 1976; (with D. Cressey) Justice by Consent, 1976. Home: 641 S Saltair Ave Los Angeles CA 90049 Office: UCLA Law Sch Los Angeles CA 90024

ROSETT, RICHARD NATHANIEL, educator, economist; b. Balt., Feb. 29, 1928; s. Walter and Essie (Stofberg) R.; B.A., Columbia, 1953; M.A., Yale, 1954, Ph.D., 1957; m. Madelon Louise George, June 24, 1951; children—Claudia Anne, Martha Victoria, Joshua George, Sarah Elizabeth, Charles Richard. Instr. Yale, 1956-58; mem. faculty U. Rochester, 1958—, chmn. dept. econs., 1966-74, prof. econs., 1967-74, prof. preventive medicine and community health, 1969-74; prof. bus. econs., dean Grad. Sch. Bus., U. Chgo., 1974—; dir. GATX Corp., Hutchinson Indsl. Corp., Marshall Field Co., McGraw-Edison Co., Nat. Can Corp., Kemper Ins. Co. Trustee, Tax Found., 1975—, Chgo. Coll. Osteo. Medicine, 1976—, Nat. Bur. Econ. Research, 1977—. Served with USNR, 1944-45. Mem. Am. Econ. Assn., Econometric Soc., Am. Statis. Assn., Mont Pelerin Soc., Phi Beta Kappa. Clubs: Cosmos; Economic, Plaza (Chgo.). Editor: The Role of Health Insurance in the Health Services Sector, 1976. Contbr. articles to profl. jours. Home: 5706 Woodlawn Ave Chicago IL 60637

ROSHKIND, MICHAEL, entertainment conglomerate exec.; b. N.Y.C., Oct. 4, 1921; s. Joseph and Sarah (Okun) R.; B.S., Northwestern U., 1941; m. Dorothy Zimberoff, Mar. 24, 1973; 1 dau., Leigh; children by previous marriage—Gary, Teri. News editor NBC, N.Y.C., 1941-42; dir. news, spl. events and sports ABC, N.Y.C., 1942-48; v.p. Weintraub Advt. Agy., 1948-50; exec. v.p. A.A. Schechter Pub. Relations, 1950-60; partner Straus Pub. Relations, 1960-66; v.p. Motown Record Corp., Los Angeles, 1966—; vice chmn., chief operating officer Motown Industries. Broadcasting cons. to Adlai Stevenson, 1942, John F. Kennedy, 1960, Lyndon B. Johnson, 1964; trustee Los Angeles Film Expn. Served with USN, World War II. Decorated Navy Cross. Mem. Record Industry Assn. Am. (dir.), NAACP (life), Motion Picture Acad., Nat. Acad. Rec. Arts and Scis., Overseas Press Club. Home: 2220 Ave of the Stars Los Angeles CA 90067 Office: 6255 Sunset Blvd Los Angeles CA 90028

ROSHKO, ANATOL, educator, aero. scientist; b. Bellevue, Alta., Can., July 15, 1923; s. Peter and Helen (Macen) R.; came to U.S., 1950, naturalized, 1957; B.Sc., U. Alta. (Can.), 1945; M.S., Calif. Inst. Tech., 1947, Ph.D., 1952; m. Aydeth de Santa Ritta Seitz, Dec. 8, 1956; children—Peter, Tamara. Instr. math. U. Alta., 1945-46, lectr. engring., 1949-50; research fellow Calif. Inst. Tech., Pasadena, 1952-55, asst. prof. aeronautics, 1955-58, asso. prof., 1958-62, prof., 1962—; sci. liaison officer Office Naval Research, London, Eng., 1961-62; U.S.-India exchange scientist, Bangalore, 1969; cons. McDonnell-Douglas Corp., 1956—; mem. exec. bd. Wind Engring. Research Council. Served with Canadian Army, 1945. Fellow Am. Inst. Aeros. and Astronautics, Canadian Aeros. and Space Inst., Am. Acad. Arts and Scis.; mem. Am. Phys. Soc., Arctic Inst. N.Am., Nat. Acad. Engring. Author: (with H.W. Liepmann) Elements of Gasdynamics, 1957. Research in gasdynamics, separated flow and turbulence. Home: 3130 Maiden Ln Altadena CA 91001 Office: 1201 E California St Pasadena CA 91125

ROSIER, CLAUDE HARRY, mfg. co. exec.; b. Brooklyn, N.S., Can., Dec. 23, 1915; s. Richard C. and Lillian (Aston) R.; ed. Dalhousie U., 1937; M.E. (hon.), N.S. Tech. Coll., 1939; postgrad. in student mgmt. Northwestern U., 1958; m. Edna Louise Belden, Sept. 27, 1946; children—Wendy Alice, Linda Louise, Ross Cassius, David, Deborah Elizabeth, Christine Margaret. With U.S. Gypsum Co., 1951-59, ops. mgr., 1957-59; with Abitibi-Price Inc., 1959—, v.p., gen. mgr. Abitibi Corp., 1959-61, v.p. bd. products, 1961-63, devel., research and bd. products, 1963-65, sr. v.p. bd. products group, 1965-66, sr. v.p. planning and devel., 1966-68, exec. v.p. corporate affairs, 1968-69, exec. v.p., 1969-73, pres., chief operating officer, 1973-78, vice chmn., 1978—, also dir., 1968—, mem. mgmt. com.; dir. Continental Bank of Can., Crum & Forster of Can. Ltd., Herald Ins. Co., Price Co. Ltd., LAC Ltd., Internat. Minerals & Chem. Corp. (Can.) Ltd. Bd. dirs. Oakville-Trafalgar Meml. Hosp. Served with Royal Canadian Navy, 1941-45. Registered profl. engr., Ont. Mem. Assn. Profl. Engrs. Ont. Mem. Anglican Ch. Mason. Clubs: Toronto; St. James's (Montreal); Mississauga Golf and Country (Port Credit, Ont.); Pinnacle; Oakville Golf. Home: 2260 Chancery Ln Oakville ON L6J 6A3 Canada Office: Box 21 Toronto-Dominion Centre Toronto M5K 1B3 ON Canada

ROSIER, JAMES LOUIS, educator; b. Chgo., Mar. 14, 1932; s. Escol MacFarland and Maudellen (Hamblin) R.; student De Pauw U., 1949-51; B.A., Stanford, 1953, Ph.D., 1957; postgrad. Freie U. Berlin (West Germany), 1954-55; m. Katherine Lee Allen, Sept. 10, 1955; children—Meredith Lee, Paul Carrick, Jessica Holly. Instr. Cornell U., Ithaca, N.Y., 1957-60, asst. prof., 1960-61; asst. prof. U. Mich., Ann Arbor, 1961-63; asso. prof. English U. Pa., Phila., 1963-68, prof. English philology, 1968—, chmn. grad. studies, 1977—. Vis. asso. prof. U. Chgo., 1965; honors examiner Manhattenville (N.Y.) Coll., 1970-71, Swarthmore (Pa.) Coll., 1972-73; cons. Binghamton Med. Studies; external Ph.D. examiner U. Ottawa, 1979. Bd. dirs. Swarthmore Pub. Library, 1965-69. Baker fellow, 1956-57; Am. Council Learned Socs. grantee, 1960, 72; Am. Philos. Soc. grantee, 1964, 71; Guggenheim fellow, 1964-65; mem. sr. common room Univ. Coll., Oxford (Eng.) U., 1961—. Fellow Soc. for Values in Higher Edn.; mem. Modern Lang. Assn. Am. (chmn. Old English 1961-63), Medieval Acad. Am., Soc. Study Medieval Lang. and Lit., Dictionary Soc. (co-founder, exec. bd. 1977—). Author: The Vitellius Psalter, 1962; Poems in Old English, 1962; Philological Essays, 1970; Old English Language and Literature, 1972. Asst. editor Middle English Dictionary, 1961-63. Home: 508 Cedar Ln Swarthmore PA 19081 Office: Dept of English U of Pa Philadelphia PA 19104. *Any profession has its own conventions of participation and boundaries of contributions to knowledge, and these constraints serve well a profession and its members at large. But to make his or her special mark in knowledge itself, an individual may have to break out of the constraints and, risking privations, nurture his or her talent independently.*

ROSKIN, LEWIS ROSS, broadcasting co. exec.; b. Moose Jaw, Sask., Can., July 16, 1920; s. Samuel and Molly (Ross) R.; m. Elizabeth Craig, Feb. 14, 1942; children—Fredrick, Robin, Craig, Deborah, Lance. Announcer, Sta. CJOC, Lethbridge, Alta., Can., 1937-42; program mgr. Sta. CJOB, Winnipeg, Man., Can., 1946-47; program mgr. Sta. CFRN, Edmonton, Alta., 1947-49; gen. mgr. Sta. CJDC, Dawson Creek, B.C., 1949-54; gen. mgr. Sta. CFCN, Calgary, 1954-55; asst. mgr. Sta. CHED, Edmonton, 1955-61; gen. mgr. Sta. CKLG, Vancouver, 1961-65; pres., gen. mgr. Sta. CHQT, Edmonton, 1965—; dir. CHQT Broadcasting Ltd. Served with Can. Army, 1942-45. Mem. Can. Assn. Broadcasters (dir.), Western Assn. Broadcasters (past pres.), Broadcasters Assn. Alta. (past pres., dir.). Jewish. Club: Edmonton Exec. Office: CHQT-AM 10154 103d St Edmonton AB T5J 0X8 Canada

ROSKY, BURTON SEYMOUR, lawyer; b. Chgo., May 28, 1927; s. David T. and Mary W. (Zelkin) R.; student Ill. Inst. Tech., 1944-45; B.S., U. Calif. at Los Angeles, 1948; J.D., Loyola U., Los Angeles, 1953; m. Leatrice J. Darrow, June 16, 1951; children—David Scott, Bruce Alan. Auditor, City Los Angeles, 1948- 51; with Beidner, Temkin & Ziskin, C.P.A.'s, Los Angeles, 1951-52; supervising auditor Army Audit Agy., 1952-53; admitted to Calif. bar, 1954, U.S. Supreme Ct., U.S. Tax Ct.; practiced in Los Angeles, Beverly Hills, 1954—; partner Duskin, Rosky & Fidler; lectr. on tax and bus. problems. Judge pro tem Beverly Hills Mcpl. Ct.; mem. Los Angeles Mayor's Community Adv. Council. Asso. Los Angeles County Mus. Arts, Smithsonian Instn., Am. Mus. Natural History; mem. exec. bd. So. Calif. council Nat. Fedn. Temple Brotherhoods, mem. nat. exec. bd. Served with USNR, 1945-46. C.P.A., Calif. Mem. Am. Arbitration Assn. (nat. panel arbitrators), Am. (charter mem. pres. 1968), Calif. (charter mem., pres. 1963) assns. attys.-C.P.A.'s, Calif. Soc. C.P.A.'s, Calif., Beverly Hills, Century City, Los Angeles County bar assns., Am. Judicature Soc., So. Cal. Fedn. Temple Brotherhoods, Jewish Chautauqua Soc. (life), Tau Delta Phi, Phi Alpha Delta. Jewish (mem. exec. bd. temple, pres. brotherhood). Mason; mem. B'nai B'rith. Contbr. profl. publs. Office: 8383 Wilshire Blvd Beverly Hills CA 90211

ROSKY, THEODORE SAMUEL, ins. co. exec.; b. Chgo., Apr. 14, 1937; s. Theodore and Lora Marie (O'Connell) R.; B.A., State U. Iowa, 1959; m. Jacqueline Reed, Apr. 19, 1958; 1 dau., Laura Marie. Various actuarial positions Conn. Gen. Life Ins. Co., Hartford, 1959-66, asso. actuary, 1967-70, controller, 1970-73, 2d v.p., actuary, 1973, v.p., 1973-78; sec. Puritan Life Ins. Co., 1966-67; exec. v.p. Capital Holding Corp., 1978—; dir. CG Trust Co., 1972-73, Congen Properties, 1971-73, Peoples Life Ins. Co.; instr. State U. Iowa, 1958-59, U. Hartford, 1964-66, U. Conn., 1967-68. Bd. dirs. Hartford Coll. for Women, 1974-78, Louisville and Jefferson County Heart Assn.; bd. pensions Luth. Ch. Am. Recipient award Soc. Actuaries, 1958. Fellow Soc. Actuaries; mem. Am. Acad. Actuaries, Southeastern Actuaries Club. Republican. Lutheran. Club: Pendennis. Home: 2304 Speed Ave Louisville KY 40205 Office: Capital Holding Corp Commonwealth Bldg Louisville KY 40232

ROSLER, LEE, pub. co. exec.; b. N.Y.C., Nov. 2, 1923; s. Julius and Ethel (Agid) R.; B.S.S., Coll. City N.Y., 1948; m. Elaine Rhodes, Sept. 20, 1945; children—David, Michael, Donald. Sales promotion specialist Prudential Ins. Co., Inc., 1952-55; cons. advt. and promotion, 1955-58; successively dir. publs., v.p., pres. Farnsworth Pub. Co. Inc., Rockville Centre, N.Y., 1958—; direct mail cons. to advt. agys. Served with USAAF, 1942-45. Mem. L.I. Direct Marketers Assn. Author: Opportunities in Life Insurance Selling; contbr. numerous articles on direct mail and promotion to profl. jours. Home: 49 Narwood Rd Massapequa NY 11758 Office: 78 Randall Ave Rockville Centre NY 11570

ROSNER, FRED, physician; b. Berlin, Germany, Oct. 3, 1935; s. Sidney and Sara (Feingold) R.; B.A. cum laude, Yeshiva Coll., 1955; M.D., Albert Einstein Coll., 1959; m. Saranne Eskolsky, Feb. 24, 1959; children—Mitchel, Miriam, Aviva, Shalom. Came to U.S., 1949, naturalized, 1955. Intern Maimonides Med. Center, Bklyn., 1959-60, resident in medicine, 1960-62, fellow in hematology, 1962-63, asst. dir. hematology, 1967-70; instr. State U. N.Y. Downstate Med. Center, Bklyn., 1968-70, asst. prof. medicine, 1970; asso. prof. State U. N.Y. at Stony Brook, 1970-78, prof. medicine, 1978—; dir. hematology Queens Hosp. Center, Jamaica, N.Y., 1970-78, dir. medicine, 1978—. Served with USPHS, 1963-65. Recipient Maimonides award Michael Reese Hosp., Chgo., 1969, Bernard Revel Meml. award Yeshiva U., 1971; Maimonides award of Wis., 1977. Diplomate Am. Bd. Internal Medicine. Fellow A.C.P., N.Y. Acad. Medicine; mem. AMA, Am. Assn. History Medicine, N.Y. Soc. Study of Blood, Am., Internat. socs. hematology, Am. Fedn. Clin. Research. Author: Modern Medicine and Jewish Law, 1972; Medicine in the Bible and Talmund, 1977; Biblical and Talmudic Medicine, 1978. Translator, editor several Moses Maimonides med. works including: Moses Maimonides' Treatise on Hemorrhoids and Responsa, 1969; Medical Aphorisms of Moses Maimonides, 1970; Sex Ethics in the Writings of Moses Maimonides, 1974; Moses Maimonides Introduction to the Mishnah, 1975. Contbg. editor Ency. Judaica, 1969—; editorial bd. Medica Judaica, 1970—; contbr. Ency. Bioethics. Contbr. numerous articles tech. lit. Home: 750 Elvira Ave Far Rockaway NY 11691 Office: Queens Hosp Center 82-68 164th St Jamaica NY 11432

ROSNER, JORGE, therapist, inst. exec.; b. N.Y.C., Mar. 10, 1921; s. Samuel and Anna (Blumental) R.; Master Mechanic, Acad. Aeros., 1941; student Cleve. Gestalt Inst., 1967-70; m. Charlotte Francis Heller, Apr. 22, 1949; children—Cindy Ann, Ellen Sue. Supt. tng. internat. div. TWA Airlines, Wilmington, Del., 1946-48; mgr. store ops. Darling Shops, Inc., N.Y.C., 1952-53; pres., founder Display by Jorge, displays and designs, Chgo., 1953-67; founding fellow, treas., mem. faculty Gestalt Inst. Chgo., 1968—, also dir.; pres., founder The Center, Gestalt counseling, Chgo., 1970—; chmn., exec. dir. Gestalt Inst., Toronto, Ont., Can., 1972—; chmn., dir. tng. Gestalt Inst., Amsterdam, Netherlands, 1973—; dir., chmn. tng. Gestalt Inst. Scandinavia, Norway-Denmark-Sweden; mem. faculty Northwestern U. Sch. Medicine, 1973—; guest faculty Gestalt Inst., Denver, 1970, 71, 72, Trollegen Rehab. Center U. Stockholm, 1973; lectr. in field U.S. and Europe, Am. Assn. Psychology, Am. Psychiat. Assn., Ontoanalystical conv., 1969, others. Actor, theatre dir., Chgo., 1965-68; pres. Theatre of Being, Chgo., 1965-68; dir. Willa Jones City Chgo. Passion Play, 1969, 71; mem. Adult Edn. Council, Chgo., 1970-72; founding fellow, bd. dirs. Oasis Midwest Center Human Potential, 1966—; founding mem. Inst. Psychiatry Northwestern U., Chgo., 1976. Served with USAFR. Mem. Contemporary Forum. Home: Route 3 Box 380 Whitewater WI 53190

ROSOFF, ARNOLD Z., advt. exec.; b. Boston, Oct. 4, 1916; s. Frank and Mary (Rabinowitz) R.; B.S., Harvard, 1939; m. Billie Tanner, Aug. 29, 1944; children—Leslie Karen Tanner, Lory Anne, Lynn Ellen. Account exec. David Malkiel Advt., Boston, 1939-41, 45-46; treas. Arnold & Co., Inc., Boston, 1946-52, pres., 1952—, chmn., 1977—. Vice pres., bd. dirs. Businessmen's Club Boston, 1958-62; adviser League Women Voters. Bd. dirs. Norumbega council Boy Scouts Am., 1950-58, Jewish Meml. Hosp., 1964-66, Boston Aid to Blind, 1973—, Mass. Commn. Blind, 1976—; trustee Carroll Sch. for Dyslexic Children, 1974-75, Beth Israel Hosp., 1975—; mem. pres.'s council Brandeis U.; mem. permanent class com. Harvard Class of 1939. Served to maj. USAAF, 1941-45. Decorated D.F.C., Air medal with 2 oak leaf clusters. Mem. Nat. Fedn. Advt. Agencies (past pres.), Advt. Club Greater Boston (bd. dirs.), Nat. Acad. TV Arts and Scis. (dir. New Eng. chpt.). Clubs: Harvard Executive (Boston). Author articles. Home: 20 Shady Hill Rd Newton MA 02161 Office: Park Sq Bldg Boston MA 02116

ROSOFF, LEONARD, surgeon; b. Grand Fork, N.D., May 5, 1912; s. Albert and Sophie (Koblin) R.; B.A., U. So. Calif., 1931; M.D., U. Tex., 1935; m. Marie Louise Aronsfeld, June 1, 1935; 1 son, Leonard. Intern, then resident gen. surgery Los Angeles County Hosp., 1935-40; from instr. to prof. surgery U. So. Calif. Sch. Medicine, 1946—, chmn. dept., 1970-79; chief surg. services, dir. surgery Los Angeles County-U. So. Calif. Med. Center, 1955-77; staff Hosp. Good Samaritan; cons. staff Cedars of Lebanon, Los Angeles Childrens, Huntington Meml. hosps.; lectr. in field. Served with M.C. AUS, 1942-45. Recipient Outstanding Alumnus award U. Tex. Med. Br., 1971. Diplomate Am. Bd. Surgery (dir. 1970-76). Fellow A.C.S. (bd. govs. 1975—, pres. So. Calif. chpt. 1969); mem. Am., Western, Pacific Coast, Los Angeles (pres. 1970) surg. assns., Am. Assn. Surgery Trauma, Soc. Surgery Alimentary Tract (pres. 1979-80), Internat. Soc. Surgery, Collegium Internationale Chirurgiae Digestive, Los Angeles Acad. Medicine. Club: University (Los Angeles). Contbr. articles to med. jours. Research surgery parathyroids, thyroid gland and other endocrine systems, surgery peptic ulcer and other gastrointestinal diseases. Home: 2024 Cummings Ln Los Angeles CA 90027 Office: Dept Surgery Univ So Calif Sch Medicine 1200 N State St Los Angeles CA 90033

ROSOFSKY, SEYMOUR, artist; M.F.A., Art Inst. Chgo. Numerous one-man shows include Galerie du Dragon, Paris, France, Art. Inst. Chgo., U. Wis., U. Chgo., B.C. Holland Gallery, Chgo., Richard Feigen Gallery, Chgo., Gallery Odyssia, Rome and N.Y.C., Transart Gallery, Milan, Italy, I Portici Gallery, Turin, Italy, Hank Baum

Gallery, San Francisco, Richard Gray Gallery, Chgo.; appeared in group shows in N.Y.C., Chgo., Paris, Rome, Turin, Houston, Detroit, Milw., Brussels, Montreal, Washington; represented in permanent collection Mus. Modern Art, N.Y.C., Art Inst. Chgo.; also pvt. collection; rep. by Richard Gray Gallery, Chgo., Galerie du Dragon, Paris, Odyssia Galleries, N.Y.C. and Rome, Hank Baum Gallery, Galeria Minotauro, Caracas, Venezuela. prof. art Loop City Coll., Chgo. Fulbright fellow, 1958-59, Guggenheim fellow, 1962-63, 63-64, Tamarind fellow, 1967, Cassandra Found. fellow, 1972. Address: 1510 W Cullom St Chicago IL 60613

ROSOMOFF, HUBERT LAWRENCE, physician, educator; b. Phila., Apr. 11, 1927; s. Morris and Caroline (Green) R.; A.B., U. Pa., 1948; M.D., Hahnemann Med. Coll., 1952; D.M.S., Columbia U., 1960; children—Richard N., Peter A. Intern, Hahnemann Hosp., Phila., 1952-53; asst. resident surgeon Presbyn. Hosp., N.Y.C., 1953-54; asst. resident neurosurgeon Neurol. Inst. and Presbyn. Hosp., N.Y.C., 1954-55, 57-58, resident neurosurgeon, 1958-59; practice medicine, specializing in neurol. surgery, Pitts., 1959-66, N.Y.C., 1966—; neurologist U.S. Naval Hosp., Bethesda, Md., 1955-57; research physiologist, neurol. surgeon Naval Med. Research Inst., Bethesda, 1955-57, cons., 1957-59; clin. trainee Nat. Inst. Neurol. Diseases and Blindness, USPHS, 1958-59; clin. asst. prof. neurol. surgery U. Pitts. Sch. Medicine, 1959-65, clin. asso. prof., 1965-66; chief Neurol. Surgery Service VA Hosp., Oakland, Pitts., 1959-66; attending neurosurgeon VA Hosp., Leech Farm, Pitts., 1959-64, cons. neurosurgeon, 1964-66; neurosurgeon Presbyn.-U. Hosp., Pitts., 1959-66; cons. Harmarville (Pa.) Rehab. Center, 1961-66, Magee-Womens Hosp., Pitts., 1963-66, Pa. Bur. Vocat. Rehab., 1959-66; prof., chmn. dept. neurol. surgery Albert Einstein Coll. Medicine, Yeshiva U., Bronx, N.Y., from 1966, chmn. dept. neurol. surgery, from 1966; chief dept. neurol. surgery Bronx Municipal Hosp. Center, from 1966; chmn. dept. neurol. surgery Hosp. Albert Einstein Coll. Medicine, from 1966; cons. U. State N.Y. div. vocat. rehab., from 1966; cons. Morrisania City Hosp., Bronx, from 1968; chief dept. neurol. surgery Bronx-Lebanon Hosps., from 1969; now chief neurol. surgery Miami (Fla.), Jackson Meml. hosps.; prof., chmn. dept. neurol. surgery U. Miami (Fla.). Recipient Am. Acad. Neurol. Surgery award, 1956. Diplomate Nat. Bd. Med. Examiners, Am. Bd. Neurol. Surgery. Fellow A.C.S.; mem. Am. Assn. Neuropathologists, AAAS, Am. Assn. Neurol. Surgeons, AMA, Am. Physiol. Soc., Am. Soc. Critical Care Medicine, Assn. Research in Nervous and Mental Diseases, Bronx County Med. Soc., Congress Neurol. Surgeons, Med. Soc. State N.Y., N.Y. Acad. Scis., N.Y. Neurol. Soc., N.Y. Soc. Neurosurgery, Pan Am. Med. Assn., Research Soc. Neurol. Surgeons, Royal Soc. Health, Soc. for Cryobiology, Soc. for Neurol. Surgeons, Soc. for Neurosci., Phi Beta Kappa, Alpha Omega Alpha. Contbr. articles to profl. jours. Address: PO Box 016960 Miami FL 33101

ROSOVSKY, HENRY, economist, educator; b. Danzig, Sept. 1, 1927; s. Selig S. and Sophie (Rosovsky) R.; came to U.S., 1940, naturalized, 1949; A.B., Coll. William and Mary, 1949, LL.D., 1976; A.M. (John E. Thayer scholar), Harvard U., 1953 Ph.D., 1959; L.H.D. (hon.), Yeshiva U., 1977, Hebrew Union Coll., 1978, Colgate U., 1979; m. Nitza Brown, June 17, 1956; children—Leah, Judith, Michael. From asst. prof. to prof. econs. and history U. Calif. at Berkeley, 1958-65, chmn. Center Japanese and Korean Studies, 1962-65; prof. econs. Harvard U., 1965—, Walter S. Barker prof. econs., 1975—, chmn. dept., 1969-72, dean faculty arts and scis., 1973—, asso. dir. East Asia Research Center, 1967-69; vis. prof. Tokyo (Japan) U., 1962, Hitotsubashi U., Tokyo, 1957, Hebrew U., Jerusalem, 1965. Sr. v.p. Am. Jewish Congress, 1975—. Served to 1st lt. AUS, 1946-47, 50-52. Recipient Schumpeter prize Harvard, 1963, jr. fellow Soc. Fellows, 1954-57. Fellow Am. Acad. Arts and Scis.; mem. Am. Econ. Assn., Econ. History Assn., Assn. Asian Studies. Author: Capital Formation in Japan, 1868-1940, 1961; Quantitative Japanese Economic History, 1961; (with K. Ohkawa) Japanese Economic Growth, 1973. Editor: Industrialization in Two Systems, 1966; Discord in the Pacific, 1972; (with H. Patrick) Asia's New Giant, 1976; Explorations in Entrepreneurial History, 1954-56. Home: 37 Beechcroft Rd Newton MA 02158 Office: Univ Hall Harvard Univ Cambridge MA 02138

ROSOW, JEROME MORRIS, inst. exec.; b. Chgo., Dec. 2, 1919; s. Morris and Mary (Cornick) R.; B.A. cum laude, U. Chgo., 1942; m. Rosalyn Levin, Sept. 28, 1941; children—Michael, Joel. Position classification analyst Dept. Army, Washington, 1942-43, orgn. and methods examiner, asst. mgr. wage and salary div., 1948-51; dir. compensation War Assets Adminstrn., Washington, 1946-48; dir. policy, salary stblzn. bd. Econ. Stblzn. Agy., 1952-53; with Creole Petroleum Corp., subsidiary Standard Oil N.J., Caracas, Venezuela, 1953-55; various exec. positions including coordination of compensation, indsl. relations research Standard Oil N.J., N.Y.C., 1955-66; mgr. employee relations dept. ESSO Europe, Inc., London Eng., 1966-69; asst. sec. labor for policy, evaluation and research Dept. Labor, 1969-71; planning mgr. pub. affairs. dept. Exxon Corp., 1971-77; pres. Work in Am. Inst., 1976—. Cons. fed. pay plans U.S. Bur. Budget and U.S. CSC, 1964; mem. bus. adv. research com. Bur. Labor Statistics, 1958-65; chmn. council of compensation Nat. Indsl. Conf. Bd., 1959-66; asso. seminar on labor Columbia, 1961—; dir. N.Y.C. Vocational Adv. Service, 1961—, chmn. finance com., 1962-65; mem. White House Working Group on Welfare Reform, 1969-71; chmn. cabinet com. White House Conf. Children and Youth, 1970-71, chmn. subcabinet com. nat. growth policy; U.S. del OECD Ministers' Conf., Paris, 1970, 74; vice-chmn. Nat. Productivity Commn., 1971; chmn. tech. experts multinat. indsl. relations OECD, Paris, 1972, chmn. subcom. manpower and social affairs; chmn. Pres.'s Advisory Com. Fed. Pay, 1971—; adviser Presidents U.S.; chmn. Am. assembly The Changing World at Work; mem. nat. exec. council Am. Jewish Com. Bd. dirs. Young Audiences; trustee Nat. Com Employment of Youth; adviser Com. Econ. Devel., 1972—; adviser Nat. Planning Assn., 1973—; mem. Nat. Commn. Productivity and Quality of Work, 1975; v.p. Population Edn. Inc., 1975—; mem. Study Group Work and Edn. in China, 1978. cons. comptroller gen. U.S., 1972—, also Ford Found. Served with AUS, 1943-46. Mem. Indsl. Relations Research Assn. (life, exec. bd., pres. 1979). Jewish. Contbg. author: Bargaining Without Boundaries, 1974. Editor: American Men in Government, 1949; The Worker and the Job: Coping with Change, 1974; (with Clark Kerr) Work in America: The Decade Ahead, 1979. Contbr. articles on manpower, compensation, welfare reform, indsl. relations to profl. jours. Home: 117 Fox Meadow Rd Scarsdale NY 10583 Office: 700 White Plains Rd Scarsdale NY 10583

ROSS, ALAN, educator; b. Hamilton, Ohio, Aug. 25, 1926; s. Earl Clarendon and Madeleine (Millikin) R.; A.B. cum laude, Brown U., 1950; M.S., Iowa State Coll., 1952, Ph.D., 1960; m. Barbara Eleanor Mink, Sept 2, 1950; children—Thomas Alan, Catharine May, James Morrissey. Research asso. U. Pitts., 1954-56; asst. prof. State U. N.Y. Syracuse, 1956; asst. prof. U. Ky., 1956-60, asso. prof., 1960-64; asso. prof. Johns Hopkins U., Balt., 1964-67, prof., chmn. biostatistics dept., 1967—; chief biostatis. cons. FAA, 1965—; vis. prof. Yale U., summers 1965-66, U. Pitts., summer 1968, U. Wash., summer 1970, U. Calif. at Berkeley, summer 1972. Served with AUS, 1944-46. Fellow Am. Statis. Assn.; mem. Biometrics Soc., Inst. Math. Statistics, Phi Beta Kappa. Contbr. articles to profl. jours. Home: 308 Thornhill Rd Baltimore MD 21212 Office: 615 N Wolfe St Baltimore MD 21205

ROSS, ALAN O(TTO), psychologist; b. Frankfurt am Main, Germany, Dec. 7, 1921; came to U.S., 1940, naturalized, 1943; s. Walter M. and Elizabeth L. (Keller) R.; B.Social Sci., CCNY, 1949; M.S., Yale U., 1950, Ph.D., 1953; m. Ilse Wallis, Sept. 2, 1950; children—Judith, Pamela. Chief psychologist C. Beers Guidance Clinic, New Haven, 1956-59, Pitts. Child Guidance Center, 1959-67; prof. psychology SUNY, Stony Brook, 1967—; cons. VA, 1967—. Mem. Planning Bd., Village of Poquott, 1970—. Served with U.S. Army, 1943-46, 51-56. Cert. psychologist, N.Y.; diplomate Am. Bd. Profl. Psychology. Fellow Am. Psychol. Assn. (pres. div. clin. psychology 1969-70); mem. Assn. for Advancement of Behavior Therapy, Soc. for Research in Child Devel. Author: The Practice of Clinical Child Psychology, 1959; The Exceptional Child in the Family, 1964; Psychological Disorders of Children, 1974, 2d edit., 1980; Psychological Aspects of Learning Disabilities, 1976; Learning Disability, 1977. Office: Dept Psychology State U NY Stony Brook NY 11794

ROSS, ALEXANDER, artist; b. Dunfermline, Scotland, Oct. 28 1909; s. James and Elizabeth (Anderson) R.; came to U.S., 1912, naturalized, 1921; student Carnegie Tech., 1930-32; M.A. (hon.), Boston Coll., 1953; m. Helen R. Connelly, June 30, 1932; children—Robert Alexander, Arlene, Wendy, Alan. Profl. artist, Pitts., 1934-40; advt. artist, N.Y.C., 1940-42; editorial artist, 1942-65, portrait commissions, 1958—; painter Good Housekeeping mag. covers monthly, 1941-54; dir. creative painting seminar Cath. U. Workshop, 1954; illustrator mags.; illustrator book, Rifle and Plow (50 books of year award), Saints: Adventures in Courage, 1963, Fr. Gilbert's Book of Prayer, others; one-man shows; Eric Gallery N.Y.C., 1973, Carlson Gallery of U. Bridgeport, 1974, Demers Gallery, Hilton Head, S.C., 1972-73, 74, 76, 77, Tenn. Fine Arts Gallery, Nashville, 1974, Thompson Gallery, Phoenix, 1975, Palm Beach (Fla.) Galleries, 1976, Naples (Fla.) Art Gallery, 1978-79, others; represented USAF Acad., USAF Hist. Soc., and pvt. collections. Recipient 1st prize water color New Canaan Outdoor Show, 1964; award Excellence, Soc. Illustrators Show, 1964; Dixie prize Conn. Watercolor Soc., 1964, 71; Ranger Fund Purchase award, 1964; Alexander Crane award, 1965; Sage Allen award, 1967; Adolf and Clara Obrig award NAD, 1972, Merit award NAD, 1973; Walter Biggs Meml. award Nat. Acad., 1975. Mem. NAD (asso.), Silvermine Art Guild, Am. Water Color Soc. (Ford Times award 1973, 76, Marthe T. McKinnon award 1974). Roman Catholic. Contbr. articles to various publs., nat. mags.; narrator film New Directions in Watercolor. Home: Hawthorn Trail Ridgefield CT 06877

ROSS, ALLAN ANDERSON, condr., univ. music dean; b. Amesbury, Mass., Jan. 16, 1939; s. Frank Albert and Ruth Ethel (Anderson) R.; A.B., U. Rochester, 1961; M.M., Ind. U., 1962; Mus.D., 1968; m. Barbara Kay Bedford, Apr. 15, 1962; children—Karen, Judith, Donna, Linda, Jason. Asst. dir. music U. Rochester, 1962-65; instr. music Ind. U., 1967-69, asst. prof. music, dir. undergrad. studies, 1969-73, asso. prof., 1973-76, prof., 1977-79, asst. to dean, 1973-79; dean Shepherd Sch. Music, Rice U., 1979—; dir. music Trinity Methodist Ch., Rochester, N.Y., 1963-65, First United Meth. Ch., Bloomington, Ind., 1969-79; guest condr. and adjudicator at music festivals throughout U.S.; bd. dirs. Riemenschneider Bach Inst., Houston Symphony Orch. NDEA Title IV fellow, 1967-68. Mem. Music Educators Nat. Conf., Am. Choral Dirs. Assn., Coll. Music Soc., Shepherd Soc. (exec. dir.), Pi Kappa Lambda. Author: Techniques for Beginning Conductors, 1976. Home: 2002 Masters Ln Missouri City TX 77459 Office: Shepherd Sch Music Rice U Houston TX 77001

ROSS, ARTHUR, investment banker; b. N.Y.C., Nov. 25, 1910; s. Adolph and Estelle Ross; student Wharton Sch., U. Pa., 1927-30; B.S., Columbia U., 1931; children—Alfred F., Beverly, Clifford Arthur. With Sutro Bros. & Co., mems. N.Y. Stock Exchange, 1932-37; with Central Nat. Corp., 1938—, v.p., 1945-56, exec. v.p., mng. dir., 1956-74, vice chmn., mng. dir., 1974—; vice chmn. Gottesman & Co., N.Y.C., 1974—; mem. exec. com., dir. Dominion Tar & Chem. Co. Ltd., Montreal; mem. N.Y. adv. com. Chase Manhattan Bank; dir. Jefferson Ins. Co., N.Y.C., Grand Union Co.; mem. U.S. del. 38th, 39th, 52d assemblies ECOSOC; fgn. affairs adviser to U.S. Mission to UN; sr. adviser U.S. del. UNESCO 18th Biennial Conf., Paris, 1974; adviser U.S. del. UN Water Conf., Mar del Plata Argentina, 1977; past mem. Nat. Export Expansion Council; expert witness Congressional Sub-com. on Econ. Growth, 1974. Bd. dirs. Barnard Coll., N.Y.C., Parks Council, N.Y.C., Am. Cancer Soc. N.Y., Central Park Community Fund, N.Y.C.; trustee Mt. Sinai Med. Center, Mt. Sinai Sch. Medicine, N.Y.C., Jewish Home and Hosp. for Aged, N.Y.C., Riverdale Country Sch., Guild Hall, East Hampton, L.I., N.Y.; mem. council Cooper-Hewitt Mus.; mem. adv. council Sch. Gen. Studies, Columbia U. Served as lt. USNR, 1942-45; lt. comdr. Res. Mem. UN Assn. U.S.A. (dir.), Center for Strategic and Internat. Studies, Internat. C. of C. (trustee U.S. council), Fgn. Policy Assn. N.Y. (dir.), Internat. Inst. Strategic Studies (London), Nat. Com. on U.S.-China Relations, Asia Soc. (dir.), Beta Gamma Sigma. Club: Century Country (White Plains, N.Y.). Home: 19 E 72d St New York NY 10021 also Apaquogue Rd East Hampton NY 11937 Office: 100 Park Ave New York NY 10017

ROSS, BEATRICE BROOK, artist; b. N.Y.C., Mar. 31, 1927; d. Alexander and Ray (Tenenbaum) Brook; student Hunter Coll., 1943, Coll. City N.Y., 1944, Bklyn. Mus. Art Sch., 1959-60, 64-65; pupil of Ruben Tam, Wang Chi Yuan, Leo Manso; m. Alexander Ross, Dec. 23, 1945; children—Robert Alan, Kenneth Jay, Stefani Lynn. Exhbns. include Women in Art, Huntington, N.Y., 1972, C.W. Post Coll., 1972, 73, Guild Hall Mus., East Hampton, 1971, Lever House, Inc., 1970, J. Walter Thompson Loan Show, 1970, Whitehouse Gallery, 1970, Park Ave. Synagogue, 1970, Locust Valley Ann., 1970, Nat. Arts Club, 1970, Light Show, Loeb Student Center, N.Y. U., 1969, Suffolk Mus., Stoneybrook, N.Y., 1969, 71, N.A.D., 1968, Audubon Artists, 1968, 70, Silvermine Guild, 1968, 71, Port Washington (N.Y.) Library, 1968, 70, 75, Light Environment Happening at Profl. Artists Guild L.I., 1968, (3 man show) Jericho (N.Y.) Gillary Gallery, 1968, Bklyn. Coll., 1968, Huntington Twp. Art League, Cold Spring Harbor, N.Y., 1967, (one man show) Gillary Gallery, Jericho, 1966, 70, 71, 72, 73, Ho. of Reps., 1965, Library of Congress, 1965, Award Winners Show, Merrick (N.Y.) Gallery, 1963, N. Shore Community Art Center ann., Roslyn, N.Y., 1959, 62, 63, Heckscher Mus., 1962, 70, Birchwood Art League, Jericho, N.Y., 1958, 61-62, Hofstra U., 1960, City Center, N.Y.C., 1960, Nassau Democratic County Com. ann., 1958, (1 person show) R.A.A. Gallery, N.Y.C., 1969-70, 77, (two man show) Roosevelt Field Art Gallery, Garden City, N.Y., 1958, Family Show, Bryant Library, Roslyn, N.Y., 1973, Women's Interart Center, N.Y.C., 1974, Family Show, Wantagh (N.Y.) Library, 1975, (4 person show) Port Washington Library, 1976, (2 person show) L.I. U., 1976, C.W. Post Coll. Schwartz Library, 1976, St. Johns U., 1976, Union Carbide, N.Y.C., 1977, Harley U. Center Gallery, Adelphi U., 1976; one person show Lincoln Center, N.Y.C., 1978; represented in pvt. collections; traveling shows in France, Italy and Japan; owner, operator Jean Rosenthal Bea Ross Gallery, Jericho, 1961-64; founder Birchwood Art League, 1958-63; lectr. bd. edn., Ont., Can., 1972. Recipient 1st prize oil Birchwood Art League, 1958; certificate award outstanding contbn. Mid Island Plaza Art League, Hicksville, N.Y. 1961, 2d prize oil, 1962; hon. mention oil Operation Democracy, Inc. ann., Locust Valley, 1967, 1st prize oil, 1970; Benjamin Altman landscape prize N.A.D., 1968; 2d prize Heckscher Mus., Huntington, N.Y., 1970; hon. mention Port Washington Ann., 1971; others. MacDowell fellow, 1975. Mem. Profl. Artists Guild L.I. (v.p. admissions 1971-74, exec. v.p. 1975), Easthampton Guild-Women in Arts, Artists Equity. Home: 19 Briar Ln Jericho NY 11753

ROSS, BILLY IRVAN, educator; b. Murray, Ky., Jan. 21, 1925; s. Enoch Herman and Mary (Ward) R.; student Murray State Coll., 1942-43; B.J., U. Mo., 1948; M.A., Eastern N.Mex., U., 1952; Ph.D., So. Ill. U., 1964; m. Avis Riedlinger, Nov. 26, 1949; 1 son, Randall Irvan. Advt. mgr. High Plains Jour., Dodge City, Kans., 1948-51; dir. publicity Ky. Wesleyan Coll., Owensboro, 1952-55; head advt. sequence journalism U. Houston, 1955-63; pub. partner Galena Park (Tex.) Reporter, 1955-60; prof. advt. and marketing Tex. Tech U., Lubbock, 1964-70, prof., chmn. dept. mass communications, 1970—. Pres., Tex. Journalisn Edn. Council, 1972-73. Mem. fund raising com. Houston Mus. Natural Sci. and Planetarium, 1962; coordinator Don Belding Internat. Grant-in-Aid Fund, 1967—. Served with AUS, 1943-46; now col. Res. (Ret.). Mem. Am. Acad. Advt. (nat. pres. 1960-61), Am. Mktg. Assn., Assn. Edn. in Journalism (exec. com. 1976-77), Am. Soc. Journalism Schs. Adminstrs. (pres. 1976), Am. Council on Edn. for Journalism, Am. Advt. Fedn., Assn. U.S. Army, Res. Officers Assn., Alpha Delta Sigma (nat. pres. 1963-67, 6th degree key 1967), Sigma Delta Chi, Kappa Tau Alpha. Methodist. Rotarian. Author: Advertising Education, 1965; co-author: Toward Professionalism in Advertising, 1969; School Publications, 1974. Contbr. articles to profl. jours. Home: 3429 55th St Lubbock TX 79413

ROSS, BRADFORD, lawyer; b. Cheyenne, Wyo., Sept. 26 1912; s. William Bradford and Nellie (Tayloe) R.; student U. Va., 1930-32; LL.B., George Washington U., 1932-36; m. Dorothy Hardy, Jan 12, 1940; children—William Bradford, David (dec.), John Hardy, Robert Tayloe. Admitted to D.C. bar, 1936; practiced with McNeill & McNeill (D.C.) 1936-38; admitted to Wyoming bar, 1939, practiced with Lacey & Loomis (Cheyenne), 1939-41; gen. counsel Fed. Power Commn., 1946-53; now mem. firm Ross Marsh & Foster, Washington, D.C. Nat. committeeman for Wyo. of Young Democrats of Am., 1933-37; chmn. Laramie County (Wyo.) Democrat Central Com. 1940-41; mem. Wyo. State Legislature, 1941-42. Served from 2d lt. to lt. col. Cav., Wyo. Nat. Guard, 1941-46. Mem. Am., Fed., D.C., Wyo., FCC, Fed. Power Commn. bar assns., Phi Delta Phi, Kappa Sigma. Episcopalian. Home: 3517 Tilden St NW Washington DC 20008 Office: 730 15th St NW Washington DC 20005

ROSS, BRIAN ELLIOTT, news corr.; b. Chgo., Oct. 23, 1948; s. Kenneth Earl and Shirley Louise (Johnston) R.; B.A., U. Iowa, 1971. Corr., KWWL-TV, Waterloo, Iowa, 1971, WCKT-TV, Miami, Fla., 1972-74; news corr. NBC News, Cleve. and N.Y.C., 1974—. Recipient Peabody award, 1974, Columbia-DuPont award, 1975, Sigma Delta Chi award, 1976, Robert F. Kennedy award, 1979. Office: NBC News 30 Rockefeller Plaza New York NY 10020

ROSS, CHARLES, artist; b. Phila., Dec. 17, 1937; s. Fred H. and Gertrude (Hill) R.; A.B. in Math., U. Calif., Berkeley, 1960, M.A. in Sculpture, 1962; m. Elizabeth Ginsberg, 1977. Exhibited in one man shows at Dilexi Gallery, San Francisco, 1961, 65, 66, 68; Dwan Gallery, N.Y.C., 1968, 69, 71, Daytons Gallery 12, Mpls., 1968, John Weber Gallery, N.Y.C., 1972, 77, 79, The Clocktower, N.Y.C., 1974, Utah Mus. Fine Arts, Salt Lake City, 1975, Mus. Contemporary Art, La Jolla, Calif., 1976, Mus. Contemporary Art, Chgo., 1976, Inst. Contemporary Art, Phila., 1977, Susan Caldwell Gallery, N.Y.C., 1977, M.I.T., 1977; exhibited in group shows at Archtl. League of New York, 1967, Albright Knox Art Gallery, Buffalo, 1967, Finch Coll., N.Y.C., 1967, Aldrich Mus., Ridgefield, Conn., 1967, Nelson Atkins Mus., Kansas City, 1968, Milw. Art Center, 1968, Whitney Mus., N.Y.C., 1969, Art Inst. Chgo., 1969, Dwan Gallery, 1969, Art Gallery of Ont., Toronto, 1969, Galeries-pilotes, Lausanne, Switzerland, 1970, Mus. Fine Arts, Boston, 1971, Indpls. Mus. Art, 1974, Neuberger Mus., SUNY, Purchase, 1975, Stadtisches Mus., Leverkusen, Germany, 1975, Phila. Coll. Art, 1977, Hirshhorn Mus., Washington, 1977, John Weber Gallery, 1977, Old Customs House, N.Y.C., 1977, Mus. Natural History, N.Y.C., 1977, Leo Castelli Gallery, N.Y.C., 1978, Yale U. Art Gallery, 1978, Dartmouth Coll. Gallery, 1978; commns. include solar spectrum for Temple of Porat Yeshivat Joseph, Old City, Jerusalem, Israel (in progress), prism and spectrum installation Fed. Bldg., Lincoln, Nebr., 1976, prisms installations U. Pa., 1977, Prestonwood Town Center, Dallas, 1979, Dietrich Found., Phila., 1979; artist in residence U. Utah, 1973-74. New York Center for Game Studies grantee Solar Center, Las Vegas, N.Mex., 1975-78, Individual Artist grantee Nat. Endowment for Arts, 1976-77. Author: Sunlight Convergence Solar Burn (Am. Inst. Graphic Arts award), 1976; films: Sunlight Dispersion, 1972; Solar Eclipse, 1972. Office: c/o John Weber Gallery 420 W Broadway New York NY 10012

ROSS, CHARLES ROBERT, lawyer, cons.; b. Middlebury, Vt., Feb. 24, 1920; s. Jacob Johnson and Hannah Elizabeth (Holmes) R.; A.B., U. Mich., 1941, M.B.A., 1948, LL.B., 1948; m. Charlotte Sells Hoyt, Aug 28, 1948; children—Jacqueline Hoyt, Peter Holmes, Charles Robert. Admitted to Ky. bar, 1949, Vt. bar, 1954, U.S. Supreme Ct. bar, 1968; instr. Oreg. State Coll., 1948-49; practice law, Louisville and Burlington, Vt., 1949-59; chmn. Vt. Pub. Service Commn., 1959-61; commr. FPC, 1961-68; mem. U.S. sect. Internat. Joint Commn., 1962—; mem. Nat. Consumers Energy Com., 1973-74; pub. mem. Adminstrv. Conf. U.S., 1971-74; adj. prof. econs. U. Vt., 1969-74. Served to capt. USAAF, 1942-46. Home: Hinesburg VT 05461 Office: PO Box F Hinesburg VT 05461

ROSS, CLARENCE HOPKINS, lawyer, utility exec.; b. David City, Nebr., Mar. 20, 1900; s. John Gans and Lucy (Clark) R.; A.B., U. Nebr., 1922; LL.B., Harvard, 1925; m. Elizabeth Hall, Feb. 21, 1942; children—Gwen, Elizabeth; m. Mrs. James Flower, May 4, 1973. Admitted to Ill. bar, 1926, since practiced in Chgo.; Washington counsel R.F.C., 1932-33; Washington counsel for Navy Renegotiation Bd., 1943; counsel Ross, Hardies, O'Keefe, Babcock & Parsons. Past chmn. Central Telephone & Utilities Corp. Mem. Am. (past chmn. pub. utility law sect.), Ill., Chgo. bar assns. Clubs: Gulf Stream Golf (Delray Beach); Everglades (Palm Beach, Fla.). Home: 547 Golfview Dr Delray Beach FL 33444 Office: 5725 E River Rd Chicago IL 60031

ROSS, DAVID, III, bus. exec.; b. N.Y.C., Nov. 16, 1940; s. David W. and Florence J. (Shutts) R.; B.A., Yale U., 1962; M.B.A., Harvard U., 1970; m. Ellen M. Glaab. Feb. 8, 1968; 1 son, David, IV. With pension actuarial dept. Penn Mut. Life Ins. Co., Phila., 1962-63, 66-68; internal cons. Alaska Interstate Co., Houston, 1970-72, asst. v.p. econs., 1972-74, asst. treas., 1974-76, treas., 1976—. Mem. Am. Soc. Corp. Planning, Nat. Assn. Bus. Economists. Nat. Soc. Accountants. Club: Harvard Bus. Sch. Office: 2200 Post Oak Tower Houston TX 77056

ROSS, DAVID JAMES, mus. adminstr.; b. Sutton, Surrey, Eng., Sept. 8, 1926; s. James MacBean and Gwendoline Agnes (Cooper) R.; student Simon Fraser U., Vancouver, B.C. Staff Provincial Mus. Alta. (Can.), Edmonton, 1967-68, Glenbow-Alta. Inst., Calgary, 1968-69, Man. (Can.) Mus. Man and Nature, Winnipeg, 1970-75; dir. N.B. (Can.) Mus., Saint John, 1976—. Served with Brit. Royal Marines,

1944-47. Author books, most recent being: Cataloguing Military Uniforms, 1977. Office: NB Mus 277 Douglas Ave Saint John NB E2K 1E5 Canada

ROSS, DAVID PRESTON, JR., publishing co. exec.; b. St. Louis, Feb. 21, 1908; s. David Preston and Irene (Robinson) R.; student Art Inst. Chgo., 1930-31, 37, U. Kans., 1933-34; m. VerLita Laurett Dodsen, Jan. 3, 1935; children—Jacquelyn Jane, Danelle Lita. Free lance comml. artist, Chgo., 1938-40; exhibit dir. Art Project, WPA, Chgo., 1940-42; draftsman Map Office, U.S. Army, Chgo., 1943-45; dir. Community Art Center, Chgo., 1946-50; advt. layout artist N.Y. Age newspaper, N.Y.C., 1950-52; asst. dir. promotion Chgo. Daily Defender Newspaper, 1953-58; exec. asst. dir. Emancipation Centennial Authority, Chgo., 1959-63; pres. and founder Afro-Am. Pub. Co., Inc., Chgo., 1963—; cons. Singer-Soc. Visual Edn., 1965—. Pres. South Side Community Art Center, Chgo., 1953-55. Recipient Best Pub. Service Radio Program award Freedom Found., 1963. Mem. Assn. Study Afro-Am. Life and History, African Assn. Black Studies, Hyde Park-Kenwood Conf., Art Inst. Chgo., Kappa Alpha Psi. Editor: Great Negroes, Past and Present, 1963. Office: 910 S Michigan Ave Chicago IL 60605

ROSS, DIANA, singer, actress, entertainer; b. Detroit, Mar. 26; d. Fred and Ernestine Ross; grad. high sch.; m. Robert Ellis Silberstein, Jan. 1971 (div. 1976); 3 daus. Former lead Singer Diana Ross and the Supremes; films include Lady Sings the Blues, 1972, Mahogany, 1975, The Wiz, 1978; NBC-TV spl. An Evening With Diana Ross, 1977. Recipient citation Vice Pres. Humphrey for efforts on behalf Pres. Johnson's Youth Opportunity Program; citation Mrs. Martin Luther King and Rev. Abernathy for contbn. to SCLC cause; awards Billboard, Cash Box and Record World as worlds outstanding singer; Grammy award, 1970; Female Entertainer of Year NAACP, 1970; Cue award as Entertainer of Year, 1972; Golden Apple award, 1972; Gold medal award Photoplay, 1972; Antoinette Perry award, 1977; nominee as best actress of year for Lady Sings the Blues, Motion Picture Acad. Arts and Scis., 1972; recipient Golden Globe award, 1972. Office: care Shelly Berger 6255 Sunset Blvd Los Angeles CA 90028*

ROSS, DONALD HAMILTON, equipment distbg. co. exec.; b. Beloit, Wis., Apr. 10, 1901; s. Harry Beach and Sofia (Riensland) R.; student U. Mich., 1919-20; B.S., U. Ill., 1924; m. Grace Pajeau, Dec. 12, 1930. With Ross Carrier Co., Inc., Hoboken, N.J., 1925—, treas., 1926—; pres. W.E. Johnson Equipment Co., Donald H. Ross, Inc. Home: Great Hopes Farm Benton Harbor MI 49022 Office: Donald H Ross Inc Benton Harbor MI 49022

ROSS, DONALD KENNETH, cons. engr.; b. St. Louis, Apr. 15, 1925; s. Maurice James and Babe Cyril (Grodsky) R.; B.S. in Elec. Engring., U. Minn., 1946; M.S., M.I.T., 1948; Sc.D., Washington U., St. Louis, 1960; m. Peggy Grosberg, July 1, 1951; 1 dau., Pamela Toder. Research and teaching asst. M.I.T., 1946-48; electronics engr. Mo. Research, Inc., 1949-51; prin. Donald Ross & Assos., St. Louis, 1953-61; pres. Ross & Baruzzini, Inc., St. Louis, 1961—; pres. Hanlon & Assos., Inc., cons. engrs., St. Louis, 1976—; profl. asso. Bldg. Research and Adv. Bd., Nat. Acad. Scis.; lectr. Washington U. Served with USNR, 1943-46, 51-53. Fellow Am. Cons. Engrs. Council; mem. IEEE, Illuminating Engring. Soc., Assn. Profl. Material Handling Cons. (pres. 1976-77), Mo. Assn. Cons. Engrs. (past pres.), Sigma Xi, Tau Beta Pi, Eta Kappa Nu. Patentee solar collector, foucault pendulum, stabilizer amplifier. Office: 7912 Bonhomme Ave Saint Louis MO 63105

ROSS, DONALD MURRAY, zoologist, educator; b. Sydney, N.S., Can., May 21, 1914; s. Murdoch Willard and Jennie (Fail) R.; B.A., Dalhousie U., 1934, M.A., 1936; Ph.D., Cambridge (Eng.) U., 1941, Sc.D., 1966; m. Ruth Emily Green, May 31, 1941; children—Mary Isabel, Andrew John. Sci. officer Sch. Agr., Cambridge U., 1941-46; lectr. zoology Univ. Coll., London, 1946-60; prof. zoology U. Alta. (Can.), 1961—, head dept., 1961-64, dean faculty sci., 1964-76. Recipient Gov. Gen.'s medal Dalhousie U., 1934; scholar of 1851 Exhbn., 1937-41. Fellow Royal Soc. Can., AAAS; mem. Physiol. Soc. (U.K.), Canadian, Am. socs. zoologists, Zool. Soc. (London). Contbr. zool. papers, chpts. in books; producer films on marine biology. Home: 11603 77th Ave Edmonton AB Canada

ROSS, DONALD ROE, U.S. judge; b. Orleans, Nebr., June 8, 1922; s. Roe M. and Leila H. (Reed) R.; LL.B., U. Nebr., 1948; m. Janice S. Cook, Aug. 29, 1943; children—Susan Jane, Sharon Kay, Rebecca Lynn, Joan Christine, Donald Dean. Admitted to Nebr. bar, 1948; practice law, Lexington, Nebr., 1948-53; mem. firm Swarr, May, Royce, Smith, Andersen & Ross, 1956-70; U.S. atty. Dist. Nebr., 1953-56; gen. counsel Republican party Nebr., 1956-58; mem. Rep. Exec. Com. for Nebr., 1952-53, nat. com. mem. Nebr., 1958-70; vice chmn. Republican Nat. Com., 1965-70; U.S. circuit judge 8th Circuit, U.S. Ct. Appeals, 1971—. Mayor City of Lexington, 1953. Home: 9936 Essex Dr Omaha NE 68114 Office: Federal Bldg Omaha NE 68101

ROSS, EDWIN FRANCIS, hosp. adminstr.; b. Struthers, Ohio, June 19, 1917; s. Edwin Francis and Ethel Marie (Wymer) R.; B.S., Mt. Union Coll., 1939; M.H.A., Washington U., St. Louis, 1949; m. Virginia Kerr, Apr. 26, 1941; children—Richard, David. Tchr. public schs., Struthers, Ohio, 1940-42; adminstrv. resident Huron Rd. Hosp., East Cleveland, 1948-49; adminstr. Doctor's Hosp., Cleveland Heights, 1949-53; asst. dir. Univ. Hosp., Cleve., 1953-62; adminstr. Univ. Hosp., Omaha, 1961-66; pres. Fairview Gen. Hosp., Cleve., 1966—; faculty Coll. Medicine, U. Nebr., 1962-66. Pres., Cleve. Area League Nursing. Mem. Greater Cleve. Hosp. Assn. (pres. 1972-74, chmn. exec. council 1974-75), Ohio Hosp. Assn., Am. Hosp. Assn., Am. Coll. Hosp. Adminstrs. Republican. Presbyterian. Clubs: Masons, Kiwanis. Office: 18101 Lorain Ave Cleveland OH 44111

ROSS, ELINOR, soprano; b. Tampa, Fla., Aug. 1, 1932; d. Joe D. and Lillian Rosenthal; student Syracuse U.; m. Aaron M. Diamond; 1 son, Ross. Debuts include Turandot, Met. Opera, N.Y.C., Il Trovatore, Cin. Opera, Cavalleria Rusticana, La Scala, Milan, Tosca, Bolshoi, Moscow; leading soprano roles with Met. Opera, LaScala, Bolshoi, Chgo. Lyric Opera, San Francisco Opera, Tulsa Opera, Cin. Opera, Staatsoper, Vienna, LaFenice, Venice; appeared with symphony orchs. throughout world. Recipient medal of honor, Novosibiresk, Siberia. Jewish. Office: care Herbert Barrett Mgmt Inc 1860 Broadway New York NY 10023

ROSS, FLOYD HIATT, educator, clergyman; b. Indpls., Jan. 19, 1910; s. Roy Menzies and Anna (Hiatt) R.; A.B., Butler U., 1930; B.D., Garrett Bibl. Inst., 1933; M.A., Northwestern U., 1933; Ph.D., Yale, 1935; m. Mary L. Shields, 1934 (dec. 1947); children—David Roy, Bruce Shields; m. 2d, Frances Dewey Jenney (div.); m. 3d, Kashihi Tanaka, 1968; 1 son, Floyd Haruhi. Ordained to ministry Unitarian Ch., 1956; instr. religion So. Meth. U., 1935-36; prof. philosophy, religion Iowa Wesleyan Coll. 1936-40; prof. world religions U. So. Calif., 1940-56, So. Calif. Sch. Theology, 1956-67; now prof. philosophy Calif. State Poly. U. Former exec. dir. Blaisdell Inst. Fulbright research fellow, 1953-54; Rockefeller research fellow, 1958. Mem. Asia Soc., Assn. Asian Studies, Phi Kappa Phi, Theta Phi. Author: Personalism and the Problem of Evil, 1940; Addressed to Christians: Isolationism versus World Community, 1950; (with Frederick, Mayer) Ethics and the Modern World, 1952; Meaning of Life in Hinduism and Buddhism, 1952; England, 1953; U.S.A.; Questions That Matter Most, Asked by the World's Religions, 1954; Man, Myth and Maturity, 1959; Shinto—The Way of Japan, 1965. Home: 5204 Parkfield Ln LaVerne CA 91750 Office: Cal State Poly U Pomona CA 91768

ROSS, FRANK GAYLORD, food co. exec.; b. Sterling, Kans., June 28, 1929; s. Floyd Willis and Olive Myrtle (Hutcheson) R.; student U. Kans., 1947-51; B.B.A., Wichita U., 1957; m. Helen Marie Graves, May 17, 1952; 1 son, Richard Patrick. Chemist, Ross Industries, Inc., Wichita, Kans., 1947-55, accountant, 1955-57, salesman, 1957-69, v.p., treas., 1969-74, exec. v.p., 1974—; v.p., treas. Enchanted Land Broadcasting Co. (KAFE AM-FM radio sta.), Santa Fe, 1970—, Sun Country Radio, Inc., Las Cruces, N.Mex.; dir. First Nat. Bank, Wellington, Kan. Dir. Kans. Wheat Improvement Assn. Mem. Kans. Ho. of Reps., 1961-62. Trustee St. Luke's Hosp., Wellington. Served to lt. col. USAF, 1951-55. Decorated D.F.C., Air medal with 5 oak leaf clusters; named to N.G. All-Am. Team, 1967. Mem. Am. Bonanza Soc. (dir., past pres.), Kans., Wichita (pres. 1977) chambers commerce, Sigma Alpha Epsilon. Republican. Methodist. Elk, Rotarian. Home: 15 Pinecrest Box 369 Wellington KS 67152 Office: 715 E 13th St Box 2696 Wichita KS 67201

ROSS, FREDERICK ARTHUR, life ins. co. exec.; b. Bklyn., June 23, 1923; s. Frederick Eugene and Grace Ruth (Osborne) R.; B.A., Colgate U., 1946; LL.B., Yale U., 1949; m. Phoebe E. Goldsmith, 1944 (dec. 1970); children—Pamela, David, Nancy; m. Bette Holman, 1972; stepchildren—Catherine, Donald, Thomas, Robert Holman. Admitted to N.Y. State bar, 1949; with N.Y. Life Ins. Co., N.Y.C., 1949—, atty., 1949-57, asst. counsel, 1957-60, counsel, 1960-65, asst. gen. counsel, 1965-69, v.p., asso. gen. counsel, 1969—. Bd. dirs. Colgate Alumni Corp. Served with USAAF, 1944-45. Decorated Air medal with 2 oak leaf clusters. Mem. Am., N.Y. State bar assns., Bar Assn. City N.Y., Assn. Life Ins. Counsel, Phi Beta Kappa. Democrat. Mem. United Ch. Christ. Home: 77 Hampton Rd Garden City NY 11530 Office: 51 Madison Ave Room 1005 New York City NY 11010

ROSS, GILBERT IRVING, cons. engr.; b. N.Y.C., Mar. 24, 1902; s. Gustave Charles and Caroline Gertrude (Fleischman) R.; B.S. in Mech. Engring., Yale, 1923; m. Leslie L.M. Harrington, Aug. 31, 1929; children—Gilbert Harrington, Carol Ann (Mrs. Joseph W. Moran), Robert Frederick; m. 2d, Loretta A. Murtagh, Sept. 13, 1975. With Bridgeport Brass Co. (Conn.), 1923-25, English & Mersick Co., New Haven, 1925-28, MacDonald Bros. Inc., Boston, 1928-32; v.p., chief engr., dir. R.A. Lasley Inc., N.Y.C., 1932-38; partner Ross, Wells & Co., engrs. N.Y.C., 1938-40; exec. v.p., gen. mgr. Unexcelled Mfg. Co., N.Y.C., 1944-46; partner Ross & Co., engrs. and consultants, N.Y.C., 1946—; past pres. Am. Inst. Constrn. Engrs. Served to col. AUS, 1940-44; col. Res. ret. Decorated Legion of Merit. Registered profl. engr. 21 states. Fellow ASME; mem. Am. Def. Preparedness Assn., Ret. Officers Assn. Republican. Presbyterian. Club: Yale (N.Y.C.). Author articles, contbr. handbooks. Home: 270 Grace Church St Rye NY 10580 Office: PO Box 526 Rye NY 10580

ROSS, GLENN ROBERT, educator; b. Kerens, Tex., Aug. 6, 1928; s. Henry and Cassie (Busher) R.; B.S., Tex. A. and M. U., 1949, M.S., 1950; Ph.D., U. Denver, 1955; m. Billye Stricklin, Aug. 28, 1950 (dec. Mar. 1966); children—Mark, Robin; m. 2d, Betty Dick Chapin, Aug. 21, 1968. Salesman, Conway & Co., Bryan, Tex., 1949-50; dormitory counsellor Tex. A. and M. U., 1950-51; grad. asst. Counselling Center U. Denver, 1953-55; counseling psychologist U. Tex., 1955-56; asst. dean students, asst. prof. psychology, dir. counseling U. Denver, 1956-59; dean student affairs Ball State U., 1959-62; dean student affairs, prof. ednl. psychology, vice chancellor student affairs U. Nebr., Lincoln, 1962-70, vice chancellor, corp. sec., prof., 1970-73; chancellor U. Ark. at Little Rock, 1973—. Vice chmn. Assn. for Internat. Practical Tng., Inc.; former cons. Social Security Administrn., VA; dir. No. Systems Co., Academic Press. Nebr. gov.'s rep. to Nat. Group Student Loan Programs, 1966; apptd. by sec. state to U.S. Nat. Commn. on UNESCO, 1970, vice chmn., 1975; chmn. U.S. delegation Western Hemisphere meeting UNESCO, Ottawa, 1971; mem. U.S. delegation meeting UNESCO, Bucharest, Rumania, 1973; co-chmn. Ark. Brotherhood Program, 1974-75; mem. Ark. Humanities Council (chmn. 1977-78), Regional Med. Advisory Group, 1976; regional bd. dirs. NCCJ, 1977; mem. Ark. Com. for Future Directions of Higher Edn. Served with USAF, 1951-53; lt. col. res. Mem. Am. Psychol. Assn., Nat. Assn. Deans and Adminstrs. Student Affairs (past mem. exec. council), Am. Assn. State Colls. and Univs. (chmn. urban affairs com.), Am. Personnel and Guidance Assn., Internat. Assn. Univ. Presidents (steering com. N.Am. Council), Am. Coll. Personnel Assn. (pres. 1972-73), Phi Kappa Phi, Beta Gamma Sigma, Phi Kappa Delta, Omicron Delta Kappa. Presbyn. (elder). Contbr. articles to profl. jours. Office: U Ark 33d and University Ave Little Rock AR 72204

ROSS, GLYNN, opera adminstr.; b. Omaha, Dec. 15, 1914; s. Herman and Ida (Carlson) R.; student Leland Powers Sch. Theater, Boston, 1937-39; m. Angelamaria Solimene, Nov. 15, 1946; children—Stephanie, Claudia, Melanie, Anthony. Opera stage dir., U.S., Can., 1939-63; debut San Francisco Opera, 1948; gen. dir. Seattle Opera Assn., Inc., 1964—; bd. dirs. O.P.E.R.A. Am., Nat. Opera Inst.; gen. dir. Pacific N.W. Dance, 1974—; founder, dir. Pacific N.W. Festival, 1975—. Served to 1st lt. AUS, 1942-47. Office: Seattle Opera Assn Inc PO Box 9248 Seattle WA 98109*

ROSS, GRIFF TERRY, ofcl. HEW; b. Mt. Enterprise, Tex., 1920; M.D., U. Tex., 1945; Ph.D. in Medicine, U. Minn., 1961. Intern, John Sealy Hosp., Galveston, Tex., 1945-46; fellow in medicine U. Minn.-Mayo Found., 1955-60; research asso. in path. anatomy Mayo Clinic, Rochester, Minn., 1960; gen. practice medicine, Mt. Enterprise, 1946-53; chief reprodn. research br., clin. dir. Nat. Inst. Child Health and Human Devel., NIH, Bethesda, Md., 1975-76, dep. dir. Clin. Center, NIH, 1976—. Served with M.C., USAF, 1953-55. Diplomate Am. Bd. Internal Medicine. Office: Bldg 10 room 1N216 Nat Insts Health Clin Center 9000 Rockville Pike Bethesda MD 20205

ROSS, HENRY RAYMOND, advt. exec.; b. Toronto, Ont., Can., Nov. 9, 1919; s. Joseph and Mary R.; grad. Ont. Coll. Art, 1936; m. Ann Clarfield, Nov. 5, 1944; children—Ellen Louise, Janice Carol. Pres. Ferris Theaters, Toronto, 1937-39, Ross Enterprises, 1939-44; with F.H. Hayhurst Co., Ltd., Toronto, 1944—, sr. v.p., dir. creative services, 1957-73, sr. v.p., dir. industry, govt. and corporate affairs, 1973—. Pres. Contemporary Paintings, Toronto, 1969—; sr. partner H.M.S. Investments, 1975—; pres. Henry R. Ross Consultants Inc., Toronto, 1979—. Chmn. broadcast com. Inst. Canadian Advt./Assn. Canadian Advertisers, Toronto, 1970—, chmn. talent negotiation com. Bd. dirs. Canadian Advt. Research Found.; trustee Am. Fedn. Musicians. Served with Canadian Army, 1943-44. Mem. Art Dirs. Club Toronto. Club: Donalda Country (Toronto). Home: 127 Munro Blvd Willowdale ON Canada Office: 55 Eglinton Ave E Toronto 12 ON Canada

ROSS, HERBERT DAVID, motion picture dir.; b. Bklyn., May 13, 1925; m. Nora Kaye, Aug. 21, 1959. Dir. motion pictures Warner Bros., Burbank, Calif.; dir. Goodbye Mr. Chips, 1969, The Owl and The Pussycat, 1970, T. R. Baskin, 1971, Play It Again Sam, 1972, The Last of Sheila, 1973, Funny Lady, 1975, The Sunshine Boys, 1975, The Seven Percent Solution, 1976, The Goodbye Girl, 1977, California Suite, 1978; dir., producer The Turning Point, 1977; choreographer Caprichos Am. Ballet Theatre, The Maids, Paean, Ballet of Two Worlds, Spoleto (Italy) Festival, Berlin (Germany) Festival; active in numerous Broadway prodns., including Tree Grows in Brooklyn, House of Flowers, On A Clear Day, The Gay Life, Torarich, Anyone Can Whistle. Recipient Golden Globe award, 1978. Address: care ICM 8899 Beverly Blvd Los Angeles CA 90048*

ROSS, HUGH ALAN, educator; b. Madison, Wis., July 18, 1924; s. Frank A. and Jessee (Spence) R.; B.S., U. Wis., 1947, LL.B., 1950; LL.M., U. Mich., 1954, S.J.D., 1959; m. Jeanne Adair Hardy, Dec. 18, 1948; children—Hugh, Stuart, Catherine. Admitted to Wis. bar, 1950; asso. Spohn, Ross, Stevens & Lamb, Madison, 1950-53; research fellow U. Mich. Law Sch., Ann Arbor, 1953-54; prof. law Case-Western Res. U., Cleve., 1959—, legal counsel, 1959-67, asso. dean, 1978—. Project dir. Am. Bar Found. Research Project on Hospitalization of Mentally Ill. Chmn. com. on protective services Nat. Council on Aging. Served with AUS, 1943-46. Mem. Ohio Bar Assn. Home: 36450 Jackson Rd Chagrin Falls OH 44022 Office: Case Western Res U Cleveland OH 44106

ROSS, IAN MUNRO, elec. engr.; b. Southport, Eng., Aug. 15, 1927; came to U.S., 1952, naturalized, 1960; B.A., Gonville and Caius Coll., Cambridge (Eng.) U., 1948; M.A. in Elec. Engring., Cambridge U., 1952, Ph.D., 1952; m. Christina Leinberg Ross, Aug. 24, 1955; children—Timothy Ian, Nancy Lynn, Stina Marguerite. With Bell Telephone Labs., Inc., and affiliates, 1952—, exec. dir. network planning div., 1971-73, v.p. network planning and customer services, 1973-76, exec. v.p. systems engring. and devel., Murray Hill, N.J., 1976-79, pres., 1979—; dir. Gulton Industries, Inc. Recipient Liebmann Meml. prize IEEE, 1963; Pub. Service award NASA, 1969. Fellow IEEE; mem. Nat. Acad. Engring. Author, patentee in field. Home: 5 Blackpoint Horseshoe Rumson NJ 07760 Office: 600 Mountain Ave Murray Hill NJ 07974

ROSS, JACOB JOHN, JR., lawyer, banker; b. New Kensington, Pa., Apr. 10, 1939; s. Jacob John and Ann Elizabeth (Chovanes) R.; B.A., St. Vincent Coll., Latrobe, Pa., 1961; LL.B., W.Va. U., 1964; postgrad. George Washington U. Coll. Law, 1966; m. Patricia Marie Martonik, July 18, 1964; children—Jacob John, Craig Martin. With firm Hazlett, Gannon and Jacobs, Pitts., summers 1962-63; admitted to W.Va. bar, 1964, Pa. bar, 1970; with Fgn. Claims Settlement Commn., Washington, 1964-66, Office of Comptroller of Currency, Treasury Dept., 1966-69; with Wells Fargo Bank, N.A., San Francisco, 1969-70; with Equibank N.A. (formerly Western Pa. Nat. Bank), Pitts., 1970—, v.p., counsel, 1970-76; mem. firm Parmelee Miller Welsh & Kratz, Pitts., 1976—. Mem. W.Va., Allegheny County bar assns., Bankers Club Pitts., Phi Alpha Delta. Home: 129 Berwyn Rd Pittsburgh PA 15237 Office: Suite 721 301 Fifth Ave Bldg Pittsburgh PA 15222

ROSS, JAMES ALAN, ret. coll. dean; b. Bellingham, Wash., Jan. 30, 1911; s. Albert John and Angela Marie O'Neill; B.A., Western Wash. State Coll., Bellingham, 1936; postgrad. U. Chgo., 1938-39; M.A., Yale, 1942, Ph.D., 1943; m. Dorothy Cecilia Cleary, Feb. 10, 1934; children—Allene (dec.), James Alan, Robert William. Tchr., adminstr. pub. schs., Wash. State, 1931-38; prof. edn. and psychology Western Wash. State Coll., 1946—, dean Grad. Sch., 1960-76, dean emeritus, 1976—; vis. prof. univs. Kyushu and Kyoto (Japan), 1951-52. Served to comdr. USNR, 1943-46. Mem. Am. Psychol. Assn. Club: Bellingham Yacht (commodore 1966). Home: 132 Forest Ln Bellingham WA 98225

ROSS, JAMES ANTHONY, educator; b. Louisville, Ohio, Aug. 16, 1918; s. Nicholas C. and Mary K. (Clapper) R.; student Ashland Coll., 1937-39, B.A., 1946; postgrad. U. Chgo., 1946-47; M.A., Kent State U., 1951; Ph.D., Western Res. U., 1954; m. Mary Elizabeth Wells, Nov. 23, 1950. Instr. Bowling Green State U., 1953-54; asst. prof. Oberlin Coll., 1954-55; prof. Baldwin-Wallace Coll., Berea, Ohio, 1955—, chmn. dept. speech, chmn. faculty, 1970—; communications cons. for bus. and industry, 1959—. Chmn. Div. Speakers and Films Greater Cleve., 1963-64. Served with AUS, 1941-45. Mem. Ohio, Central State speech assns., Speech Communication Assn., Pi Kappa Delta. Contbr. articles profl. jours. Home: 10617 King Coe Ln Strongsville OH 44136 Office: Baldwin-Wallace Coll Berea OH 44017

ROSS, JAMES BARRETT, ins. co. exec.; b. Cleve., Apr. 25, 1930; s. James Barrett and Marjorie (Stutsman) R.; B.A. cum laude, Harvard U., 1951; m. Ann Penney, July 1, 1950; children—James, Scott, Alison, Andrea, Alan, Dana, Ann Elizabeth, Brandon, Mary Ellen, Marjorie, Wendy. With Conn. Gen. Life Ins. Co., 1951-62; pres., dir. Puritan Life Ins. Co., Providence, 1962-68; exec. v.p. mktg. Keystone Custodian Funds Inc., Boston, 1968-73; sr. v.p. Met. Life Ins. Co., N.Y.C., 1973—. Vice pres. West Shore dist. R.I., Boy Scouts Am., 1966-68; mem. Warwick area schs. and scholarship com. Harvard Club R.I., 1964-68; dir. United Fund. R.I., 1967-68, chmn. spl. gifts, 1967, mem. capital funds com., 1967-68; v.p., dir. R.I. Philharmonic Orch., 1964-68; trustee Warwick Pub. Library, 1967-68; bd. dirs. John Hope Settlement House, 1966-68; corporator Sophia Little Home, 1966-68; chmn. Met. Life United Way, 1978, 79. Fellow Life Mgmt. Inst., Soc. Actuaries; mem. Am. Acad. Actuaries, Am. Coll. Life Underwriters, Actuaries Club N.Y. Congregationalist. Clubs: Harvard (N.Y.C.); Milbrook (Greenwich, Conn.). Home: 29 Hillside Rd Greenwich CT 06830 Office: Metropolitan Life Ins Co 1 Madison Ave New York NY 10010

ROSS, JAMES BRENT, publishing co. exec.; b. Williamstown, W.Va., June 12, 1925; s. Claget Howard and Hazel (Bailey) R.; A.B., W.Va. U., 1949; M.S., U. Pitts., 1950; m. Alma Eugenia Lowe, Dec. 26, 1947; children—Anna Elizabeth, William Brent. Editor, W.B. Saunders Co., Phila., 1951-57; mgr. coll. textbook dept. Reinhold Pub. Corp., N.Y.C., 1957-62, gen. mgr. book div., 1962-67, v.p., 1965-68; pub., dir. Chapman-Reinhold Book Corp., 1968; exec. v.p., pub. Pergamon Press, Inc., pres. Pergamon Pub. Co., N.Y.C., 1968-69; pres. Dowden, Hutchinson & Ross, Inc., pubs., Stroudsburg, Pa., 1970—; owner James B. Ross & Assos., pub. cons., 1969—. Trustee, Open Space Inst., Inc., N.Y.C., 1966-72, pres., 1968-70, chmn., 1970-72; bd. govs. Nature Conservancy, Inc., 1952-65, pres., 1958-60, gov. emeritus, 1978—. Served with USNR, 1943-46. Recipient Green Leaf Conservation award Nature Conservancy, 1960. Fellow AAAS; mem. Am. Inst. Biol. Sci. (bd. govs. 1966-71, bd. mem.-at-large 1973-77), Ecol. Soc. Am., Am. Chem. Soc. (life), Am. Ornithologists Union, Sigma Xi. Mason (32 deg., Shriner), Elk, Torch. Home: Box 4102 Mel-Mar Dr RD 4 Stroudsburg PA 18360 Office: 523 Sarah St Stroudsburg PA 18360

ROSS, JAMES FRANCIS, educator; b. Providence, Oct. 8, 1931; s. James Joseph and Teresa Marie (Sullivan) R.; A.B., Cath. U. Am., 1953, M.A. (Basselin Found. fellow), 1954; Ph.D., Brown U., 1958; J.D., U. Pa., 1974; m. Kathleen Marie Fallon, Dec. 1, 1956; children—Seamus, Ellen, Richard Fallon, Therese. Instr., then asst.

prof. philosophy U. Mich., 1959-61; asst. prof. U. Pa., 1962-65, asso. prof., 1965-68, prof., 1968—, chmn. philosophy dept. and grad. group in philosophy, 1966-70. Rackham research fellow U. Mich., 1960-61; NIH spl. research fellow 1970; Nat. Endowment for Humanities fellow, mem. Inst. for Advanced Study, Princeton, 1975-76; vis. prof. Brown U., summer 1977; admitted to Pa. bar, 1975. Recipient Christian B. and Mary L. Linbach Found. award for Distinguished Teaching, 1966; Distinguished Scholarship award Cath. U. Am., 1971. Fellow Soc. Religion in Higher Edn.; mem. Am. Philos. Assn., Am. Cath. Philos. Assn., Am. Theol. Soc., Soc. Theol. Discussion. Roman Catholic. Author: Philosophical Theology, 1969; Introduction to Philosophy of Religion, 1970; translator, editor: Suarez on Formal and Universal Unity, 1964; editor: Studies in Medieval Philosophy, 1971. Home: Grange Ave Little Compton RI 02837 Office: Logan Hall U Pa Philadelphia PA 19104

ROSS, JERROLD, educator; b. N.Y.C., Feb. 8, 1935; s. James M. and Alice (Gubernick) R.; B.S., N.Y. U., 1955, Ph.D., 1963; M.S., Queens Coll., 1959. Music tchr., Syosset, N.Y., 1956-58, Great Neck, N.Y., 1958-61; instr. music edn. N.Y. U., 1961-63; chmn. tchr. edn. dept. N.Y. Coll. Music, 1963-65, pres., 1965-67; head div. music edn. N.Y. U., 1967-74, head div. arts and arts edn., 1974—, mem. senate, 1977-80, dir. Town Hall of N.Y. U., 1971-74, bd. dirs. Town Hall Found., 1973-75. Asst. bd. examiners N.Y.C. Pub. Schs.; cons. to and mem. music com. N.Y. State Edn. Dept. Coll. Proficiency Exam. Program; participant various confs. U.S. Office Edn.; dir. various projects N.Y. State Edn. Dept., Nat. Found on Arts and Humanities, N.Y. State Council on Arts, Andrew W. Mellon Found., Rockefeller Found., Rubin Scholars Program in Israel; v.p. Concert Artists Guild N.Y., 1964-69; bd. dirs. Usdan Center for the Arts, chmn. bd., 1972-77; bd. dirs. Broadway Assn., Am. Assn. for Music Therapists; mem. citizens adv. bd. Radio Sta. WNCN. Mem. Music Educators Nat. Conf. (grad. commn.), Coll. Music Soc. (mem. council 1975-78), Nat. Assn. Schs. Music (govtl. relations com.), N.Y. Musicians Club, Phi Delta Kappa, Phi Mu Alpha Sinfonia (province gov. 1964-70). Club: New York University. Author: Interpreting Music Through Movement, 1963. Home: 2 Washington Sq Village New York NY 10012

ROSS, JOHN, chemist, educator; b. Vienna, Austria, Oct. 2, 1926; s. Mark and Anna (Krecmar) R.; came to U.S., 1940, naturalized, 1945; B.S., Queens Coll., 1948; Ph.D., M.I.T., 1951; m. Virginia Franklin, Aug. 26, 1950; children—Elizabeth, Robert. Research asso. Mass. Inst. Tech., Cambridge, 1950-52, prof., 1966—, F.G. Keyes prof. chemistry, 1971—, chmn. dept. chemistry, 1966-71; NSF fellow Yale U., 1952-53; prof. chemistry Brown U., 1953-66; Guggenheim fellow, 1959-60; Sloan fellow, 1960-64; vis. van der Waals prof. U. Amsterdam, 1966. Bd. govs. Weizmann Inst., Rehovoth, Israel, 1971—. Served to 2d lt., inf. AUS, 1944-46. Fellow Am. Acad. Arts and Scis., Am. Phys. Soc. (chmn. chmn. div. chem. physics 1975-76); mem. Nat. Acad. Scis., Am. Chem. Soc. (chmn. div. phys. chemistry 1971-72), AAAS. Editor: Molecular Beams, 1966. Contbr. articles profl. jours. Home: 21 Longfellow Rd Lexington MA 02173 Office: Dept Chemistry MIT Cambridge MA 02139

ROSS, JOHN, JR., educator, physician; b. N.Y.C., Dec. 1, 1928; s. John and Janet (Moulder) R.; A.B., Dartmouth, 1951, M.D., Cornell U., 1955; children—Sydnie, John, Duncan; m. Lola Romanucci, Aug. 26, 1972; 1 son, Adan. Intern Johns Hopkins Hosp., 1955-56; resident Columbia-Presbyn. Med. Center, N.Y.C., 1960-61, N.Y. Hosp.-Cornell U. Med. center, 1961-62; chief sect. cardiovascular diagnosis cardiology br. Nat. Heart Inst., Bethesda, Md., 1962-68, prof. medicine U. Calif. at San Diego, 1968—, also dir. cardiovascular div., 1968—; cons. Nat. Heart, Lung and Blood Inst., also mem. cardiology adv. com., 1975—. Served as surgeon, USPHS, 1956-63. Fellow Am. Coll. Cardiology (v.p. trustee), A.C.P.; mem. Am. Soc. Clin. Investigation (councillor), Am. Physiol. Soc., Assn. Am. Physicians, Cardiac Muscle Soc., Am. Soc. Pharmacology and Exptl. Therapeutics, Assn. Univ. Cardiologists, Assn. West Physicians (councillor), Interam. Soc. Cardiology (research com.), Council Clin. Cardiology, Am. Heart Assn. Author: Mechanisms of Contraction of the Normal and Failing Heart, 1968, 76; Understanding the Heart and Its Diseases, 1976. Mem. editorial bd. Circulation, 1967-75, Circulation Research, 1971-75, Am. Jour. Physiology, 1968-73, Annals of Internal Medicine, 1974-78, Am. Jour. Cardiology, 1974—, Cardiovascular Medicine, 1976—. Contbr. chpts. to books, sci. articles to profl. jours. Home: 8599 Prestwick Dr La Jolla CA 92037 Office: 2024 Basic Sciences Bldg M-013 Univ California San Diego CA 92037

ROSS, JOHN ALANSON THORLAY, physician; b. Hamburg, Germany, Apr. 20, 1927; M.D., U. Calif., 1955. Intern, San Francisco Gen. Hosp., 1955-56, resident in otorhinolaryngology, 1956-59; chief otolaryngology and resident tng. program, Ft. Miley VA Hosp., San Francisco, 1962-79; chief otolaryngology St. Luke's Hosp., San Francisco; mem. staff St. Francis Hosp., San Francisco; clin. prof. U. Calif. Sch. Medicine, San Francisco. Served with AUS, 1945-47. Fellow A.C.S., Am. Acad. Otolaryngology and Ophthalmology; mem. AMA, Triological Soc., Soc. Univ. Otolaryngologists. Office: Dept Otolaryngology Univ of Calif Sch Medicine San Francisco CA 94143

ROSS, JOHN HAROLD, lawyer, chem. co. exec.; b. Watertown, N.Y., Dec. 8, 1930; s. Rowland Hollingsworth and Augusta (Hynes) R.; B.Sc., U. Notre Dame, 1952; J.D., Georgetown U., 1957; m. Nancy A. Gibbon, Oct. 9, 1954; children—Mary Lynn, John Kevin, Katherine Anne, Peter Hynes, Jennifer Marie, Patricia Ellen, Gerald Anthony, Thomas Patrick, Michael Rowland. Admitted to N.Y. bar, 1958; sec. N.Y. Stock Exchange, N.Y.C., 1957-64; corporate sec. Vanadium Corp. Am., N.Y.C., 1965-67; corporate sec. Foote Mineral Co., Exton, Pa., 1967-75 v.p. legal affairs, 1973-75; sec. Newmont Mining Co., N.Y.C., 1975—. Served to lt. j.g. USNR, 1952-55. Mem. Am. Bar Assn., Am. Soc. Corporate Secs. Home: Heritage Dr Washington Crossing PA 18977 Office: Newmont Mining Co 300 Park Ave New York City NY

ROSS, JOHN MICHAEL, editor; b. Bklyn., Oct. 17, 1919; s. Albert Henry and Dorothy Veronica (Murray) R.; student pub. schs., N.Y.C.; m. Kathleen M. Courtney; children—Donna Patricia, Maureen Courtney Ross Quick. Sports writer Bklyn. Eagle, 1937-41, The Newspaper PM, 1946-47; editor Am. Law Tennis mag., 1947-50, Macfadden Publs., 1950-51, 60-61; contbg. editor Am. Weekly, 1952-60; editor-in-chief Golf mag., 1961-67, Golf Bus. mag., 1963-65, Golfdom mag., 1965-67; v.p. Universal Pub. and Distbn. Corp., 1965-67; pres. Golf Promotions, Inc., 1967-70; pub. Golf Bus. Almanac, also Golf TV Guide, 1969; pub. relations dir. Profl. Golfers Assn. Golf Tour, 1970-71; editor-in-chief Golf mag., 1972-79, asso. pub., 1979—; bd. dirs. World Golf Hall of Fame, 1974—; chmn. Women's Golf Scholarship Fund, 1976—; exec. dir. Internat. Golf Assn., 1977—; co-author: Nothing But The Truth, 1960; editor: Encyclopedia of Golf, 1977. Justice of peace, Newtown, Conn., 1960-64. Served with AUS, 1942-46. Recipient Christopher award for best mag. story, 1957. Mem. Lawn Tennis Writers Assn. (sec. 1949-50), Golf Writers Assn. Am. (gov. 1966-67), Met. Golf Writers Assn. (pres. 1975-76), Am. Soc. Mag. Editors. Roman Catholic. Clubs: Overseas Press (N.Y.C.); Patterson (Fairfield, Conn.). Home: 19 Riverfield Dr Weston CT 06880 Office: 380 Madison Ave New York NY 10017

ROSS, JOHN STONER, educator; b. Ames, Iowa, Sept. 28, 1925; s. Herold Truslow and Rosella (Stoner) R.; B.A., DePauw U., 1947; M.A., U. Wis., 1949, Ph.D., 1952; m. Ann Roberta Cox, June 16, 1948; children—Catherine, David, Martin, Barbara, Gregory, Stephen, Kevin, Eric. Research physicist Ansco, Binghamton, N.Y., 1951-53; asst. prof. Rollins Coll., Winter Park, Fla., 1953-59; asso. prof., 1959-64, prof. physics, head dept., 1965—, dir. grad. program physics, 1963-75. Optical analysis engr. RCA, Patrick AFB, Fla., 1955-58, staff physicist Radiation, Inc., Orlando, Fla., 1958-62. Mem. A.A.A.S., Am. Assn. Physics Tchrs., Optical Soc. Am., Phi Beta Kappa. Home: 508 Langholm Dr Winter Park FL 32789

ROSS, JOHN THEODORE, artist, educator; b. N.Y.C., Sept. 25, 1921; s. Ferdinand J. and Mary Agnes (Higgins) R.; B.F.A., Cooper Union Sch. Art, 1948; postgrad. Columbia, 1953, New Sch. for Social Research, 1950-53; m. Clare Romano, Nov. 30, 1943; children—Christopher, Timothy. Prof. art Manhattanville Coll., Purchase, N.Y., 1964—. Numerous one-man shows including U. Wash., Seattle, 1975, N.J. State Mus., 1975, Arwin Galleries, Detroit, Pa. State U.; exhibited in group shows Pratt Graphic Center, 1975-76, Invitational Print Bienneal, Long Beach, Calif.; rep. in permanent collections Nat. Coll. Fine Arts, Washington, Met. Mus. Art, N.Y.C., Library of Congress, Dallas Mus., others. Served with AUS, 1943-46. Recipient Tiffany grant in printmaking, 1954, Profl. Achievement citation Cooper Union Art Sch., 1954; MacDowell Colony fellow, 1974; Artist in Residence grant N.E.A., 1974-75. Mem. Soc. Am. Graphic Artists, A.A.U.P. Author: The Complete Printmaker, 1972. Home: 110 Davidson Place Englewood NJ 07631 Office: Manhattanville Coll Purchase NY 10577

ROSS, JOSEPH COMER, educator, physician; b. Tompkinsville, Ky., June 16, 1927; s. Joseph M. and Annie (Pinckley) R.; B.S., U. Ky., 1950; M.D., Vanderbilt U., 1954; m. Isabelle Nevins, June 15, 1952; children—Laura Ann, Sharon Lynn, Jennifer Jo, Mary Martha, Jefferson Arthur. Intern Vanderbilt U. Hosp., 1954-55; resident Duke Hosp., 1955-57; research fellow Duke, 1957-58; instr. medicine Ind. U., 1958-60, asst. prof., 1960-62, asso. prof., 1962-66, prof., 1966-70; prof., chmn. dept. medicine Med. U. S.C., 1970—; vis. prof. Vanderbilt U. Sch. Medicine, 1979-80. Mem. cardiovascular study sect. NIH, 1966-70, program project com., 1971-75; mem. ad hoc coms. Nat. Acad. Sci., 1966, 67; mem. Pres.'s Nat Adv. Panel on Heart Disease, 1972; mem. merit rev. bd. in respiration VA Research Service, 1972-76, chmn., 1974-76. Served with AUS, 1945-47. Diplomate Am. Bd. Internal Medicine (bd. govs. 1975—; subsplty pulmonary disease; mem. pulmonary subsplty. bd. 1972-78). Fellow A.C.P., Am. Coll. Chest Physicians (gov. S.C. 1970-76, vice chmn. bd. govs. 1974-75, chmn. bd. govs. 1975-76, exec. council 1974—, pres. elect 1976-77, pres. 1978—, chmn. sci. program com. 1973), Am. Coll. Cardiology; mem. Am. Fedn. Clin. Research (chmn. Midwest sect.), Am. Physiol. Soc., Am. Soc. Clin. Investigation, Assn. Am. Physicians, Assn. Profs. Medicine, Central Soc. Clin. Research, AMA (sect. on med. schs.), S.C. Med. Soc., Am. Thoracic Soc. (nat. councillor 1972-76), So. Soc. Clin. Research, S.C. Lung Assn. (v.p. 1974-75), Am. Soc. Internal Medicine, Phi Beta Kappa, Alpha Omega Alpha. Mem. Ch. of Christ (elder). Club: Country of Charleston. Editorial bd. Jour. Lab. and Clin. Medicine, 1964-70, Chest, 1968-73, Jour. Applied Physiology, 1968-73, Archives of Internal Medicine, 1976—, Heart and Lung, 1977—. Contbr. articles to profl. jours. Office: Med U SC 171 Ashley Ave Charleston SC 29403

ROSS, JOSEPH FOSTER, physician, educator; b. Azusa, Calif., Oct. 11, 1910; s. Verne Ralph and Isabel Mills (Bumgarner) R.; A.B., Leland Stanford Jr. U., 1933; M.D., Harvard, 1936; m. Eileen Sullivan, Dec. 19, 1942; children—Louisa, Elisabeth, Joseph, Jeanne, Marianne. Asst. topographical anatomy Harvard, 1934-37, research fellow biochemistry, 1943-46; med. house officer Huntington Meml. Hosp., 1934-35; Palmer Meml., New Eng. Deaconess hosps., 1935-36; resident pathology Mallory Inst. Pathology, 1936-37; intern Harvard med. service Boston City Hosp., 1937-39; asst. pathology U. Rochester Sch. Medicine, 1939-40; resident pathology Strong Meml. Hosp., Rochester, N.Y., 1939-40; physician, dir. hematology and radioisotope divs. Mass. Meml. Hosp., 1940-54; instr., asst. prof., asso. prof. medicine Boston U., 1940-54; dir. radioisotope unit Cushing VA, Boston VA hosps., 1948-54; prof. medicine U. Calif. at Los Angeles, 1954—, prof. radiobiology, 1954-59, asso. dean, 1954-58, chmn. dept. nuclear med. and radiation biology, 1958-60, dir. Lab. Nuclear Med. and Radiation Biology, 1958-65; prof., chmn. dept. biophysics and nuclear medicine, 1960-65, chief div. hematology, 1969-76; chief staff U. Calif. Hosp., Los Angeles, 1954-58, attending physician, 1954—. U.S. del. Internat. Conf. Peaceful Uses Atomic Energy, Geneva 1955; mem. U.S. Atoms for Peace mission to Latin Am., 1956, U.S. AEC Life Scis. Mission to Greece, Turkey, 1961, radiation biology Mission to USSR, 1965; mem. Calif. Adv. Council on Cancer, 1959—, chmn., 1963-66, 74-77; mem. CENTO Sci. Mission Iran, Turkey, Pakistan, 1963; mem. nat. adv. cancer council Nat. Cancer Inst., 1956-60. Research preservation whole blood OSRD, World War II. Recipient certificate of merit Pres. U.S., 1948; Van Meter award Am. Goiter Soc., 1953; Wilson medalist, lectr. Am. Clin. and Climatol. Assn., 1964. Diplomate Am. Bd. Internal Medicine (mem. bd. 1975-78, sec. conjoint Am. Bd. Nuclear Medicine 1971-72, pres. 1973-77), Am. Bd. Nuclear Medicine. Mem. Am. Soc. Exptl. Pathology, Am. Soc. Clin. Investigation, Assn. Am. Physicians, Am. Acad. Arts and Scis., A.C.P., Biophys. Soc., Radiation Research Soc. (council 1964-65), A.M.A., Internat. Soc. Hematology, Am. Soc. Hematology (pres. 1961-62), Western Assn. Physicians (pres. 1962-63), Soc. Nuclear Med. (trustee 1962-72, pres. So. Calif. chpt. 1964-65; Nuclear Pioneer lectr. 1971, 77, Distinguished Scientist award Western. sect. 1977, dist. v.p. 1976-77, 78-79, del. Calif. Med. Assn. 1978-79), Phi Beta Kappa, Sigma Xi, Alpha Omega Alpha, Theta Xi, Nu Sigma Nu. Clubs: Harvard (Boston); Cosmos (Washington). Presbyn. (exec. com. Westminster Found. So. Calif. 1962-72, pres. 1968). Editorial bd. Blood, Jour. Hematology, 1946-76, Annals Internal Medicine, 1960-70, Jour. Nuclear Medicine, 1968, med. book div. Little Brown Co., 1958-68. med. book series U. Calif. Press, 1962-70. Contbr. articles to profl. jours. Home: 11246 Cashmere St Los Angeles CA 90049 Office: U Calif Sch of Medicine Los Angeles CA 90024

ROSS, KATHARINE, actress; b. Los Angeles, Jan. 29; student Santa Rosa Coll., San Francisco Actors Workshop; appeared in films The Graduate, 1967, Hellfighters, 1969, Butch Cassidy and the Sundance Kid, 1969, Fools, 1970, Tell Them Willie Boy is Here, 1970, Shenandoah, 1965, Mister Buddwing, 1966, The Singing Nun, 1966, Games, 1970, They Only Kill Their Masters, The Stepford Wives, 1975, Voyage of the Damned, 1976, The Betsy, 1978, The Swarm, 1978, The Legacy, 1979; TV appearances include Sam Benedict, Ben Casey, Bob Hope-Chrysler Theatre, The Virginian, Kraft Mystery Theatre, others; appeared in TV movie Wanted: The Sundance Woman, 1976. Recipient Golden Globe award, 1968. Address: The Hiller Agy 9220 Sunset Blvd Hollywood CA 90069*

ROSS, LEON, physician; b. N.Y.C., Jan 3, 1903; s. Simon Meyer and Jennie (Bullock) R.; B.S., Coll. City N.Y., 1924; M.D., N.Y. U., 1930; m. Muriel Lief, Aug. 29, 1934. Tchr. pub. schs., N.Y.C., 1924-26; physician, N.Y.C., 1930-42; with dept. medicine and surgery VA, 1942-72, dir. VA Hosp., Wilkes-Barre, Pa., 1965-72; practice medicine, Princeton, N.J., 1972—; med. div. Trenton Neighborhood Health Center; part-time cons., Trenton. Served to maj. M.C., AUS, 1944-46. Recipient Distinguished Service award VA, 1972; certificate of Appreciation, Am. Legion, 1973. Fellow Am. Coll. Hosp. Adminstrs., Am. Coll. Chest Physicians; mem. A.M.A., Pa., Wyoming Valley (dir.) Tb and health socs., Fed. Hosp. Inst. Alumni Assn., Fed. Ofcls. Assn. (organizer, past pres. Ann Arbor, Mich. and Wilkes-Barre, Outstanding Service award Ann Arbor 1959). Kiwanian. Home and office: Kingston Terr Princeton NJ 08540

ROSS, LEONARD ELLIS, educator; b. Burlington, Iowa, Dec. 15, 1930; s. Lloyd Sylvester and Olive Martha (Bachman) R.; B.A., U. Iowa, 1955, M.A., 1958, Ph.D., 1959; m. Susan Michelle Wilcox, Oct. 23, 1970; children—Jeffrey Bruce, Terry Diane, David Craig. Research asso. U. Iowa, 1959; from instr. to prof. psychology U. Wis., 1956—; vis. prof. Joseph P. Kennedy Found. to Peabody Coll., 1963-64. Coordinator behavioral and social scis. unit U. Wis. Center Mental Retardation and Related Aspects Human Devel. Served with AUS, 1951-53. Recipient Emil H. Steiger teaching award U. Wis., 1962; spl. postdoctoral fellow NIH, 1970. Fellow Am. Psychol. Assn., A.A.A.S.; mem. Psychonomic Soc., Phi Beta Kappa, Sigma Xi. Asso. editor Jour. Exptl. Psychology, 1968-73; cons. editor Jour. Exptl. Child Psychology, 1965-68. Contbr. articles to sci. jours., chpts. in books. Home: 7 Gray Birch Trail Madison WI 53717

ROSS, LEONARD LESTER, anatomist; b. N.Y.C., Sept. 11, 1927; s. Aaron Theodore and Shirley (Smolen) R.; A.B., N.Y. U., 1946, Ph.D., 1954; m. Marcella Gamel, June 23, 1951; children—Jane, Jill. Asst. prof. U. Ala. Med. Coll., 1954-57; asso. prof. Cornell U. Med. Coll., 1957-67, prof., 1969-73; vis. prof. Cambridge U., 1967-68; prof., chmn. dept. anatomy Med. Coll. Pa., Phila., 1973—. Served with M.C., U.S. Army, 1946-47. Recipient Lindback award for teaching, 1976: NIH sr. research fellow, 1967-68. Mem. Am. Assn. Anatomists, Soc. Neurosci., Am. Soc. Cell Biology, N.Y. Soc. Electron Microscopists (pres. 1975-76), AAUP (nat. council 1974-77), Sigma Xi. Asso. editor Anatomical Record, 1976. Office: 3300 Henry Ave Philadelphia PA 19129

ROSS, LOUIS ROBERT, automotive co. exec.; b. Detroit, Mar. 23, 1932; s. Louis Robert and Sadie Madge (Stobbe) R.; B.M.E., Wayne State U., Detroit. 1954; M.B.A., Mich. State U., E. Lansing, 1972; m. Carolyn Ann Lory. June 20, 1953; children—Stephen Charles, Philip Elliott. With Ford Motor Co., 1955—. v.p. Ford Brazil, Sao Paulo. 1973-75, v.p., gen. mgr. tractor div., Troy, Mich., 1975-77, exec. v.p. diversified products ops., 1977-79, exec. v.p. car product devel. N.Am. automotive ops., 1979—; dir. Ford Brazil, 1973-75, Ford Aerospace & Communications Corp., 1977—. Escorts Tractors Ltd. India, 1975-77, Hokkai Ford Tractor Japan, 1975-77. Exec. bd. Detroit council Boy Scouts Am.. 1975-77. Mem. Soc. Automotive Engrs.. Phi Kappa Phi, Beta Gamma Sigma. Presbyterian. Club: Fairlane (Dearborn). Home: Bloomfield Hills MI 48013 Office: Ford Motor Co NAm Automotive Ops Box 1522-A Dearborn MI 48121

ROSS, MALCOLM MACKENZIE, educator; b. Fredericton, N.B., Can., Jan. 2, 1911; s. Charles Duff and Cora Elizabeth (Hewitson) R.; B.A., U. N.B., 1933, Litt.D., 1962; M.A., U. Toronto, 1934; Ph.D., Cornell U., 1941; LL.D., U. St. Thomas, 1978; m. Lois Natalie Hall, June 4, 1938; 1 dau., Julie Martha. Instr., Ind. U. Bloomington, 1941-42; asst. prof., then prof. U. Man. (Can.), 1945-50; prof. Queen's U., Kingston, Ont., 1950-62, head dept., 1957-62; prof. English, Trinity Coll., U. Toronto (Ont.), 1962-64, dean Faculty of Arts, 1964—, acting provost, 1967-68; Thomas McCulloch prof. English, Dalhousie U., Halifax, N.S., 1968—; mem. acad. panel Can. Council, 1966-69; mem. nat. Killam Awards Com., 1972-75, Gov. Gen.'s Awards Jury, 1973-76; adv. bd. Can. Writers Union, 1977-78; mem. publ. com. Humanities Research Council, 1976-79; mem. jury Evelyn Richardson Award, 1978. Bd. dirs. Neptune Theatre, 1972-75, Nat. Library Can., 1977—; mem. Halifax com. Atlantic Symphony Orch., 1969-72; bd. dirs. Inst. Hist. Micro-reprodns., 1978. Guggenheim fellow 1949-50; officer Order of Can., 1976. Fellow Royal Soc. Can. (v.p. sect. II, 1969-70, pres. sect. 1970-71); mem. Can. Assn. Univ. Tchrs., Assn. Can. Univ. Tchrs. of English, Humanities Assn. Can. (pres. 1959), Assn. Univs. and Colls. Can. (chmn. research com. 1957-60), Writers Fedn. N.S. (council 1976), Toronto Arts and Letters Club. Anglican. Author: Milton's Royalism, 1943; Poetry and Dogma, 1954, 69; editor: Our Sense of Identity: A Book of Canadian Essays, 1954; The Arts in Canada, 1958; (with J. Stevens) Man and His World, 1961, In Search of Ourselves, 1967, Images of Man, 1967; editor-in-chief Queen's Quar., 1953-56; editor The New Canadian Library, 1955—; editorial bd. Dictionary of the Bible and the Tradition in English Literature, 1978, English Studies in Can., 1977, Four Decades, 1975, Jour. Can. Ch. Hist. Soc., 1974; adv. editor Lit. History Can., Vol. IV, 1978; contbr. articles and revs. to scholarly jours. Home: 1750 Connaught Ave Halifax NS B3H 4C8 Canada Office: Dalhousie U Halifax NS B3H 3J5 Canada

ROSS, MARION, actress; b. Albert Lea, Minn., Oct. 25; student San Diego State Coll; children—Jim, Ellen. Performed with Globe Theatre, San Diego, LaJolla Summer Theater; Broadway debut in Edwin Booth; starred in touring prodns. of Cactus Flower, My Daughter, Your Son, Shelves; film debut in Forever Female, 1953; films include: The Glenn Miller Story, Legend of the Incas, Sabrina, The Proud and the Profane, Operation Petticoat, Teacher's Pet, Lust for Life, Colossus, The Forbin Project, Airport, Honkey, Grand Theft Auto; TV film: Survival of Dana; appeared in TV series: Life with Father, 1953-55, Paradise Bay, 1965-66, Happy Days, 1974—; appeared in TV mini-series Pearl, 1978; other TV appearances include: The Untouchables, Perry Mason, Mannix, Marcus Welby, M.D., Ironside, Hawaii Five-O, Love, American Style, Petrocelli, Love Boat. Office: care ABC Press Relations 1330 Ave of the Americas New York NY 10019*

ROSS, MARION COLLIER, army officer; b. Moberly, Mo., Jan. 24, 1927; s. Marion Hunter and Irene (Collier) R.; B.S., U.S. Mil. Acad., 1949; grad. Command and Gen. Staff Coll., 1958, Armed Forces Staff Coll., 1963, Army War Coll., 1967; M.S., George Washington U., 1970; m. Ann E. Sylvester, Mar. 31, 1950; children—Benjamin Moore, James Howard, Colleen. Commd. 2d lt. U.S. Army, 1949, advanced through grades to lt. gen., 1978; bn. comdr., Vietnam, 1967, asst. chief staff 1st Cav. Div., 1967-68; regtl. comdg. officer Corps Cadets, West Point, 1968-70; brigade comdr., Ft. Carson, Colo., 1970-71; comdg. gen. 173d Airborne Brigade, Ft. Campbell, Ky., 1971-72; asst. div. comdr. 101st Airborne Div., 1972-73; dep. dir. ops. directorate Office Dep. Chief Staff for Ops. and Plans, Army Dept., Washington, 1973; dir. human resources devel. Office Dep. Chief Staff for Personnel, Army Dept., Washington, 1973-75; comdg. gen. 7th Inf. Div. and Ft. Ord (Calif.), 1975-76; asst. dep. chief staff for ops. and plans, Washington, 1976-78; comdg. gen. I Corps (ROK/US) Group, 1978—. Decorated Silver Star, Legion of Merit with 2 clusters, D.F.C., Bronze Star with V and 2 clusters, Purple Heart. Home: Quarters 15B Fort Myer VA 22211 Office: Hdqrs I Corps (ROK/US) Group APO San Francisco CA 96358

ROSS, MATTHEW HAROLD, lawyer; b. N.Y.C., Aug. 17, 1913; s. Julius and Lena (Levinson) R.; B.S., St. Johns U., 1934; LL.B., U. Va., 1937; m. Mildred Berger, Sept. 11, 1938; children—Allen N., Jane (Mrs. Rand Ross). Admitted to N.Y. State bar, 1938; asso. Leon Lauderstein, N.Y.C., 1937-40; practiced in N.Y.C., 1940-56; partner Blumberg, Singer, Ross, Gottesman & Gordon and predecessor firms,

N.Y.C., 1956—. Trustee, Central Synagogue, 1950-58, pres., 1958-63, hon. pres., 1964—; chmn. bd. trustees Union of Am. Hebrew Congregations, 1973—; bd. govs. Hebrew Union Coll.-Jewish Inst. Religion, 1973; bd. dirs., mem. exec. council Nat. Jewish Community Relations Adv. Council; mem. N.Am. exec. bd. World Union for Progressive Judaism. Mem. Am. Bar Assn., Assn. Bar City N.Y., World Peace Through Law Center. Clubs: Harmonie; Birchwood Country. Mem. editorial staff U. Va. Law Rev., 1937. Home: 16 Sutton Pl New York City NY 10022 Office: 245 Park Ave New York City NY 10017

ROSS, MICHAEL, producer, writer, dir.; b. N.Y.C., Aug. 4, 1923; s. Harry and Bessie (Semel) Rovinsky; B.S., Coll. City N.Y., 1939-42; m. Irene Saslaw, Jan. 12, 1950. Producer-dir. Green Mansions Theatre, Warrensburg, N.Y., 1950-59; cons. Caesar's Hour, TV show, 1954; comedy dir. Perry Como TV Show, 1956; comedy supr. Garry Moore TV show, 1962, 64; story editor, producer All in the Family, 1971-75; co-creator, producer The Jeffersons, 1974—; co-creator, writer, producer Three's Company, 1977—. Served to lt. USAAF, 1943-45; ETO. Decorated Air medal with 4 oak leaf clusters; recipient Emmy award for outstanding achievement in comedy writing for episode of All in the Family, 1973. Mem. Writers Guild Am., Dirs. Guild Am., Actors Equity Assn. Author numerous TV scripts. Office: Three's Company CBS TV City Fairfax and Beverly Blvd Los Angeles CA 90036*

ROSS, MURRAY GEORGE, educator; b. Sydney, N.S., Can., Apr. 12, 1910; s. George Robert and Catherine (MacKay) R.; B.A., Acadia U., 1936, D.C.L., 1960; M.A., U. Toronto, 1938, LL.D., 1970; Ed.D., Columbia, 1948; D.Litt., York U., 1940; D.Un., U. York (Eng.), 1973; LL.D., Laurentian U., 1977; m. Janet Kennedy Lang, May 10, 1940; children—Susan Janet, Robert Bruce, Prof., U. Toronto, 1950-55, v.p., 1955-60; pres. York U., Downsview, Ont., 1960-70, prof. social sci., 1970—, pres. emeritus, 1972—. Dir. Continental Can Co. Can., McGraw Hill Ryerson, Ltd., The Assos. Acceptance Co. Ltd., Time Can., Capital Growth Fund Ltd., Toronto; mem. N.Am. adv. bd. Volvo Co. Chmn. bd. trustees Hist. Series; trustee Sunnybrooke Hosp. Decorated officer Order of Can.; recipient Book award Am. Council on Edn., 1976; Centennial medal, 1976; Queen's Jubilee medal, 1977. Fellow Am. Sociol. Soc. Author: Religious Beliefs of Youth, 1950; The Y.M.C.A. in Canada, 1951; (with C.E. Hendry) New Understanding of Leadership; A Survey and Application of Research, 1957; Case Histories in Community Organization, 1958; The New University, 1961; New Universities in the Modern World, 1965; Community Organization: Theory and Principles and fgn. edits., 1955, 2d edit., 1965; The University: The Anatomy of Academe, 1976. Editor: Towards Professional Maturity, 1948. Contbr. articles to profl. jours. Home: 75 Highland Crescent Willowdale ON Canada Office: Glendon Coll 2775 Bayview Ave Toronto ON Canada

ROSS, NANCY WILSON (MRS. STANLEY P. YOUNG), author; b. Olympia, Wash.; d. Robert James and Lydia (Giles) Wilson; B.A., U. Ore.; student Bauhaus in Dessau, Germany, 1931-32, in Berlin, 1933; spl. student U. Chgo., 1937-38; m. Charles Walton Ross, Jr. (div.); m. 2d, Stanley P. Young, 1942 (dec.). Writer articles and novels, 1932—; war corr., 1945; lectr. on Zen, C.G. Jung Inst., Zûrich, 1964; lectr. Dartington Hall, Devon, Eng., 1977. Mem. Asia Soc. (bd. trustees), Kappa Kappa Gamma, Theta Sigma Phi. Author: Friday to Monday, 1932; Take the Ligtning, 1940; Farthest Reach; Oregon and Washington, 1941; The Waves, 1943; Westward the Women, 1944; The Left Hand Is the Dreamer, 1947; I, My Ancestor, 1950; Times Corner, 1952; Joan of Arc, 1953; The Return of Lady Brace, 1957; The World of Zen: An East-West Anthology, 1960; Heroines of the Early West, 1960; Three Ways of Asian Wisdom; Hinduism, Buddhism, Zen and Their Significance for the West, 1966; Buddhism: A Way of Life and Thought, 1980; introdn. to The Notebooks of Martha Graham, 1973. Home: Applegreen Old Westbury NY 11568

ROSS, NORMAN ALEXANDER, banker; b. Miami, Fla., Jan. 30, 1922; s. Norman DeMille and Beatrice (Dowsett) R.; A.B., Stanford U., 1946; postgrad. Trinity Coll., Oxford (Eng.) U., 1953; D.H.L., Lincoln (Ill.) Coll., 1959, Fisk U., 1978, Roosevelt U., 1979; Litt.D., Lake Forest Coll., 1967; children—Isabel, Susan Diana. Airport mgr. Pan Am. Airways, 1943; asst. to producer Metro-Goldwyn-Mayer, 1943-44; partner Norman Ross & Co., 1947-50; owner Norman Ross Record Club, 1951-52; radio-TV commentator NBC, ABC, Chgo., 1953-64, ABC, WGN and WBKB, Chgo., 1964-68; v.p. pub. affairs First Nat. Bank Chgo., 1968—, sr. v.p. communications dept., 1979—; pres. Ross-McElroy Prodns., Inc., 1962-68; former columnist Chgo. Daily News. Served with inf. AUS, World War II. Decorated cavaliere Dell Ordine Repubblica Italiana; U.S. Army Outstanding Civilian Service medal; officier and cross of chevalier Legion of Honor (France); recipient Peabody award for TV program Off the Cuff, 1964. Mem. Phi Gamma Delta. Clubs: Chgo., Racquet, Oxford, Mid Day, Econ. (Chgo.); Wayfarers. Home: 1550 N State Pkwy Chicago IL 60610 Office: 1 First Nat Plaza Chicago IL 60670

ROSS, OSCAR BURR, agrl. co. exec.; b. Rosalie, Nebr., June 5, 1914; s. Ura S. and Eva May (Copple) R.; B.S.A., U. Nebr., 1936; M.Sc., U. Wis., 1939, Ph.D., 1942; m. Bertha K. Philips, Aug. 24, 1946; children—James Burr, Donald Charles. Instr., U. Tenn., 1936-38; asst. U. Wis., 1938-41, asst. prof., 1941-1943; prof. Okla. State U., 1946-51; gen. mgr. Gooch Feed Mill, Salina, Kans., 1951-58; head dept. animal sci. U. Ill., Urbana, 1958-64; v.p. research, dir. agrl. expt. sta. Okla. State U., Stillwater, 1964-68; now v.p. ConAgra, Inc., Omaha; treas., dir. Western Star Mill Co., Salina, Kans.; dir. Kans. Soya Products Co., Inc. Emporia, Kans. Served to capt. San. Corps, AUS, 1943-46. Mem. Sigma Xi, Alpha Zeta, Gamma Alpha, Gamma Signa Delta. Home: Beaver Lake Plattsmouth NE 68048

ROSS, PATRICK CONROY, rubber co. exec.; b. Iron River, Mich., Aug. 27, 1929; s. William D. and Elsie A. (Thompson) R.; A.B., U. Mich., 1951, M.A., 1976; grad. advanced mgmt. program Harvard U., 1969; m. Ann M. Groves, Feb. 2, 1952; children—Stewart C., Charles E., Nancy J. Merchandising mgr. WWJ-Detroit News, 1956-57; sales mgr. Argus Cameras Co., Ann Arbor, Mich., 1957-62; area dir. Europe, B.F. Goodrich Co., 1962-68, pres. internat. div., Akron, Ohio, 1969-70, pres. B. F. Goodrich Tire Group, Akron, Ohio, 1972—, exec. v.p. B.F. Goodrich Co., 1979—. Mem. Ohio Council Econ. Edn.; bd. dirs. Akron Internat. Inst.; trustee Akron Children's Hosp., Center for Econ. Edn., U. Akron. Served with USAF, 1951-55. Mem. Rubber Mfr.'s Assn. Club: Portage Country (Akron). Office: 500 S Main St Akron OH 44318

ROSS, RICHARD JOHN, educator; b. Ludhiana, Punjab, India, Nov. 6, 1918 (parents Am. citizens); s. John Elliott and Della Bonnie (Pease) R.; B.A., Sterling Coll., 1941; M.A., U. Mich., 1947, Ph.D., 1958; m. Barbara Naftel Grut, Dec. 29, 1945 (dec. May 1969); children—John Harvey, Kathleen Margaret Paul, Charles Theodore. Tchr. English, dramatics Sch. Organic Edn., Fairhope, Ala., 1941-42; instr. English, U. Mich., Ann Arbor, 1946-58, asst. prof., 1958-65, asso. prof., 1965—; reporter Ypsilanti (Mich.) Daily Press, 1951; personnel asst. Kaiser-Frazer Corp., 1951. Served with AUS, 1942-45; ETO. Mem. Phi Kappa Phi. Tech. writer, editor Inst. Sci. and Technology, 1962-63. Contbr. articles to profl. jours. Research in criticism of poetry and fiction. Home: 3449 Craig Rd Ann Arbor MI 48103

ROSS, RICHARD MORROW, JR., banker; b. New Rochelle, N.Y., May 18, 1929; s. Richard Morrow and Eleonore Kimbel (Taylor) R.; A.B., Cornell U., 1952; M.B.A., N.Y. U., 1958; m. Jane Ethel McKim, June 28, 1952; children—Barbara R. Carito, Richard Morrow III. Portfolio mgr. trust dept. Hanover Bank, N.Y.C., 1954-61; security analyst Burton Dana & Co., N.Y.C., 1961-63; asst. mgr. Van Strum & Towne, Phila., 1963-65; sr. v.p., investment officer 1st Eastern Bank, Wilkes-Barre, 1965-73, pres., 1973—, chief exec. officer, 1975—; tchr. bank mgmt. and investments Am. Inst. Banking. Campaign chmn. Wyoming Valley United Fund, 1973; pres. Family Service Assn. Wyoming Valley, 1971-74. Bd. dirs. Wyoming Valley Hosp.; trustee Wilkes Coll.; mem. council Cornell U. Served with AUS, 1952-54. Certified fin. analyst. Mem. Phila. Soc. Fin. Analysts, Pa. Bankers Assn. (governing bd., chmn. agy. relations com., treas. 1978—), Pa. (dir.), Greater Wilkes-Barre (pres. 1974) chambers commerce. Rotarian. Club: Westmoreland (Wilkes-Barre). Home: Shrine View RD 5 Dallas PA 18612 Office: 11 W Market St Wilkes-Barre PA 18701

ROSS, RICHARD STARR, med. sch. dean, physician, cardiologist; b. Richmond, Ind., Jan. 18, 1924; s. Louis Francisco and Margaret (Starr) R.; student Harvard, 1942-43, M.D. cum laude, 1947; m. Elizabeth McCracken, July 1, 1950; children—Deborah Starr, Margaret Casad, Richard McCracken. Intern, asst. resident Osler Med. Service, Johns Hopkins Hosp., 1947-49, asst. resident, 1951-52; research fellow physiology Harvard Med. Sch., 1952-53; resident physician Osler Med. Service, 1953-54; instr. medicine Johns Hopkins Med. Sch., 1954-56, asst. prof. medicine, 1956-59, asso. prof., 1959, asso. prof. radiology, 1960-65, prof. medicine, 1965—, Clayton prof. cardiovascular disease, 1969-75; dir. Wellcome Research Lab., Johns Hopkins; physician Johns Hopkins Hosp.; dir. cardiovascular div. dept. medicine, adult cardiac clinic Johns Hopkins Sch. Medicine and Hosp., dir. myocardial infarction research unit, 1967-75; dean med. faculty, v.p. medicine Johns Hopkins U., 1975—; prin. prof. staff Johns Hopkins Applied Physics Lab., 1970—; Sir Thomas Lewis lectr. Brit. Cardiac Soc., 1969; John Kent Lewis lectr. Stanford U., 1972; dir. Blue Shield Md., 1972-76, Balt. Life Ins. Co.; mem. cardiovascular study sect. Nat. Heart and Lung Inst., 1965-69, chmn., 1966-69, mem. tng. grant com., 1971-73, chmn. heart panel, 1972-73, adv. council, 1974—; mem. Inst. of Medicine, 1976—; bd. dirs. Union Meml. Hosp., 1977—. Served to capt. M.C., AUS, 1949-51. Diplomate Nat. Bd. Med. Examiners, Am. Bd. Internal Medicine. (subsplty. bd. cardiovascular disease). Master A.C.P.; fellow Am. Coll. Cardiology; mem. Boylston Med. Soc., Am. Fedn. Clin. Research, Am. Physiol. Soc., Assn. Am. Physicians, Am. Soc. Clin. Investigation (councillor 1967-69), Am. Clin. and Climatol. Assn. (pres. 1978-79), Assn. U. Cardiologists (councillor 1972-75), Am. Heart Assn. (chmn. sci. sessions program com. 1963-67, chmn. publs. com. 1970-73, pres. 1973, dir. 1973—), Heart Assn. Md. (pres. 1967), Sigma Xi, Alpha Omega Alpha; corr. mem. Brit. Cardiac Soc., Sociedad Peruana de Cardiologie, Cardiac Soc. Australia and New Zealand. Clubs: Peripatetic, Interurban (pres. 1978), Elkridge, 14 West Hamilton, Johns Hopkins. editor: Modern Concepts Cardiovascular Disease, 1961-65; editor: The Principles and Practice of Medicine, 17th-20th edits., 1968-77; editorial bd. Circulation, 1968-74; editorial com. Jour. Clin. Investigation, 1969-73. Home: 214 Wendover Rd Baltimore MD 21218 Office: 720 Rutland Ave Baltimore MD 21205

ROSS, ROBERT JAMES, aircraft co. exec.; b. Farnham, Eng., Jan. 1, 1926; s. James and Anne (Creswell) R.; came to Can., 1952; M.S. (Ministry of Supply scholar), Cranfield Inst. Tech., Eng., 1948; m. Joan Hall, June 4, 1949; children—James Stuart, Elizabeth Susan. Sci. officer Royal Aircraft Establishment, Farnborough. Eng., 1948-52; successively chief aerodynamics, chief flight test engr., chief advanced design engr., dir. research and devel., dir. surveillance systems Canadair Ltd., Montreal, Que., Can., 1952—; past dir. Que. Indsl. Research Centre. Past chmn. Olympic and internat. com. Canadian Canoe Assn., competition sec. Montreal Olympic canoeing events, 1976. Mem. Order Engrs. Que., Instn. Mech. Engrs. (U.K.). Anglican. Author reports in field. Home: 12220 Rue La Corne Montreal PQ H4K 1Y4 Canada Office: PO Box 6087 Station A Montreal PQ H3C 3G9 Canada

ROSS, RODERIC HENRY, life ins. co. exec.; b. Jamestown, N.Y., July 14, 1930; s. Edwin A. and Mary Elizabeth (Dornberger) R.; A.B., Hobart Coll., Geneva, N.Y., 1952, LL.D. (hon.), 1979; C.L.U., 1960; m. Patricia Johnson, Aug. 6, 1955; children—Timothy, Amy, Jane, Christopher. With Phila. Life Ins. Co., 1954—, sr. v.p. mktg., 1972-73, pres., 1973—, also dir.; dir. Hunt Mfg. Co., Phila., Provident Nat. Bank, Phila., Provident Nat. Corp., Phila., Phila. Life Asset Mgmt. Co.; chmn. Ins. Fedn. Pa., 1979. Former vestryman, St. David's Episcopal Ch., Radnor, Pa.; bd. dirs. Old Phila. Devel. Corp., Better Break '77, '78, Phila., Million Dollar Round Table Found., Des Plaines, Ill.; vice chmn. bd. trustees Hobart and William Smith Colls. Served with AUS, 1952-54. Decorated Commendation ribbon with medal pendant; recipient Nat. Quality award Nat. Assn. Life Underwriters, 1961-74. Life mem. Million Dollar Round Table; mem. Am. Soc. C.L.U.'s, Phila. Assn. Life Underwriters. Clubs: Union League, Racquet, Orpheus (Phila.); St. David's (Pa.) Golf; Pine Valley Golf (Clementon, N.J.). Home: 770 Pugh Rd Wayne PA 19087 Office: 111 N Broad St Philadelphia PA 19107

ROSS, RONALD EUGENE, mag. editor; b. Estelline, S.D., June 2, 1937; s. Harvey Monroe and Beulah Leona Ross; B.S., S.D. State U., 1959; m. Mary Richardson, Dec. 5, 1955; children—Rhonda, Steven, Diana, Juliet, Daniel. Agrl. field editor Mont. State U., 1959-61; publs. editor S.D. State U., 1961-63; info. specialist S.D. Dept. Game, Fish and Parks, 1963-65; editor Creative Communications div. Webb Co., St. Paul, also asso. editor Farmer mag., 1967-74; editor Irrigation Age mag., St. Paul, 1974—. Mem. Am. Agrl. Editors Assn., Nat. Agrl. Mktg. Assn. Home: Route 2 Box 6A Welch MN 55089 Office: 1999 Shepard Rd St Paul MN 55116

ROSS, RONALD RICKARD, educator, physicist; b. Mpls., July 11, 1931; s. Manford William and Ida Gunhild (Nelson) R.; A.B., U. Calif., Berkeley, 1956, Ph.D., 1961; m. Adeleen A. Tarr, Apr. 12, 1952; children—Kristine Linn, Susan Kay, Linda Diane. Research asst. Lawrence Radiation Lab., Berkeley, Calif., 1956-61; physicist Lawrence Berkeley Lab., 1961-63; lectr. physics U. Calif., Berkeley, 1961-63, asst. prof., 1963-67, asso. prof., 1967-72, prof., 1971—; staff physicist Lawrence Berkeley Lab., Berkeley, 1963—; vis. prof. U. Heidelberg Inst. for High Energy Physics, 1966-67. Served with USAF, 1950-54. IBM fellow, 1957. Mem. AAAS, AAUP, Am. Phys. Soc., Am. Assn. Physics Tchrs., Fed. Am. Scientists, Sigma Xi, Phi Beta Kappa. Contbr. articles to profl. jours. Office: Physics Dept U Calif Berkeley CA 94720

ROSS, RUSSELL, pathologist; St. Augustine, Fla., May 25, 1929; s. Samuel and Minnie (DuBoff) R.; A.B., Cornell U., 1951; D.D.S., Columbia U., 1955; Ph.D., U. Wash., 1962; m. Jean Long Teller, Feb. 22, 1956; children—Valerie Regina, Douglas Teller. Intern, Columbia-Presbyn. Med. Center, 1955-56, USPHS Hosp., Seattle, 1956-58; spl. research fellow pathology U. Wash. Sch. Medicine, 1958-62, asst. prof. pathology and oral biology U. Wash. Sch. Medicine and Dentistry, 1962-65, asso. prof. pathology, 1965-69, prof., 1969—, adj. prof. biochemistry, 1978—, asso. dean for sci. affairs Sch. of Medicine, 1971-78; vis. scientist Strangeways Research Lab., Cambridge, Eng.; mem. research com. Am. Heart Assn.; mem. adv. bd. Found. Cardiologique Princess Liliane, Brussels, Belgium; vis. fellow Clare Hall, Cambridge U. John Simon Guggenheim fellow, 1966-67; mem. nat. heart, lung and blood adv. council Nat. Heart, Lung and Blood Inst., NIH, 1978-81. Mem. Am. Soc. Cell Biology, Tissue Culture Assn., Gerontol. Soc., Am. Assn. Pathologists and Bacteriologists, Internat. Soc. Cell Biology, Electron Microscope Soc. Am., Am. Soc. Exptl. Pathology, Royal Microscopical Soc., AAAS, Belgian Acad. Medicine (fgn. corr. mem.). Mem. editorial bds. Proceedings Exptl. Biology and Medicine, 1971—, Jour. Cell Biology, 1972-74; asso. editor Jour. Cell Physiology; field editor Blood Vessels, 1973, and other jours. Contbr. articles in field of arteriosclerosis research and wound healing to profl. jours. Home: 4811 NE 42d St Seattle WA 98105 Office: U of Wash Sch Medicine SM-30 Seattle WA 98195. *I have always believed in open, direct communication in society as well as in science, softened with as much tact and sensitivity as possible, but uncompromising in so far as honesty is concerned. A modicum of intelligence combined with a great deal of hard work will go as far as a great deal of brilliance.*

ROSS, RUSSELL MARION, educator; b. Washington, Iowa, June 2, 1921; s. Harold Ellis and Lucille Carrie (Dorris) R.; B.A., U. Iowa, 1942; certificate Harvard, 1945; M.A., U. Iowa, 1946, Ph.D., 1948; m. Shirley Arlene Jackson, June 1, 1944; children—Sheryl Ross, Jule. Instr. dept. polit. sci. U. Iowa, Iowa City, 1946-48, asst. prof., 1948-52, asso. prof., 1952-60, research prof., 1963-64, prof., 1965—, chmn. dept., 1970—; adminstrv. asst. to atty. gen. Iowa, 1960; exec. asst. to Gov. Iowa, 1961-62. Chmn., Regional Planning Commn., 1966-68; pres. Iowa City Community Sch. Bd., 1969-70; chmn. Iowa Campaign Finance Disclosure Commn., 1973-77. Mayor, University Heights, 1954-60. Bd. dirs. Goodwill Industries S.E. Iowa. Served to lt. USNR, 1942-45. Mem. Internat. City Mgrs. Assn. (hon.), Am. Pub. Adminstrn. Soc., AAUP, Am., Mid-West polit. sci. assns., Phi Beta Kappa, Phi Delta Kappa, Pi Sigma Alpha. Kiwanian. Author: Iowa Government and Administration, 1958; State and Local Government and Administration, 1966. Home: 315 Highland Dr Iowa City IA 52240

ROSS, SHELDON JULES, dentist; b. N.Y.C., June 17, 1924; s. Sam and Regina (Rosner) R.; stepson Nathan Sudnow; D.D.S., N.Y. U., 1949; m. Carolyn L. M. Loesch, Apr. 26, 1946; children—Jane, Eric, Ellen, Lisa. Pvt. practice periodontology, N.Y.C., 1949—; prof. periodontics and oral medicine N.Y. U. Sch. Dentistry, 1949—; resident oral medicine Montefiore Hosp., N.Y.C., 1956-57, charge periodontics and oral medicine, 1951-70; attending charge oral medicine and periodontics Beth Abraham Hosp., Bronx, N.Y., 1961—; asso. attending periodontics and oral medicine Cabrini Hosp. and Med. Center, N.Y.C.; lectr. in field; honored lectr. Internat. Odontological Congress, Maringa, Brazil, 1972, 78. Served with AUS, 1942-43. Diplomate Am. Bd. Periodontology, Am. Bd. Oral Medicine. Fellow Am. Coll. Dentists, N.Y. Acad. Dentistry, Am. Acad. Oral Medicine (pres. 1980); mem. ADA, Am. Assn. Dental Editors, Am. Acad. Oral Medicine, Am. Acad. Oral Pathology, Am. Acad. Periodontology, N.E. Soc. Periodontists, Orgn. Tchrs. Oral Diagnosis, Am. Soc. Forensic Dentists, Am. Soc. Esthetics in Dentistry (v.p. 1979), Am. Assn. Hosp. Dentists, Am. Heart Assn., Sci. Research Assn. Am., AAAS, Omega Kappa Upsilon. Editor Jour. Oral Medicine, 1971—, Annals of Dentistry, 1971—; contbr. articles to dental jours., chpts. to textbooks. Home and Office: 40 Twisting Ln Wantagh NY 11793. *When I was 20 I thought knew all the answers. At 30, new questions arose so rapidly, I realized I knew much less. At 50, I now know only one answer, and that is I know almost nothing.*

ROSS, SHERMAN, psychologist; b. N.Y.C., Jan. 1, 1919; s. Max R. and Rachel (Khoutman) R.; B.S., Coll. City N.Y., 1939; A.M., Columbia, 1941, Ph.D., 1943; m. Jean Goodwin, Aug. 18, 1945; children—Norman Kimball, Claudia Lisbeth (Mrs. Overway), Michael Lachlan. Asst. psychology, research psychologist Columbia, 1941-44; asst., then asso. prof. psychology Bucknell U., 1946-50; research fellow N.Y. Zool. Soc., 1948; guest investigator, sci. asso. Jackson Lab., 1947-69; asso. prof., then prof. psychology U. Md., 1950-60; spl. cons. psychopharmacology service center Nat. Inst. Mental Health, 1956-63, asst. chief, 1957; exec. sec. edn. and tng. bd., sci. affairs officer Am. Psychol. Assn., 1960-68; prof. psychology Howard U., 1968—; exec. sec., staff asso., assembly of behavioral and social scis. Nat. Acad. Scis.-NRC, 1968-76; cons. VA, Human Ecology Fund, Stanford Research Inst., Office Naval Research, U.S. Sci. Exhibit, Am. U., HRB-Singer, Inc. Bd. dirs. Interdisciplinary Communications Assos., Washington; adv. council Woodrow Wilson Rehab. Center Found.; mem. Md. Bd. Examiners Psychology, 1957-58. chmn. bd. dirs. Inst. for Research, State Coll., Pa.; trustee Carver Research Found., Tuskegee Inst. Served to lt. (j.g.) USNR, 1944-46; capt. Res. (ret.). Fellow Am. Psychol. Assn., Am. Coll. Neuropsychopharmacology, Royal Soc. Health, Washington Acad. Scis.; mem. Aerospace Med. Assn., A.A.A.S., Am. Soc. Zoologists, Ecol. Soc., Ergonomics Research Soc., Md. Psychol. Assn. (pres. 1973-74), Sigma Xi (pres. U. Md. 1957-58), Phi Kappa Phi, Psi Chi (nat. pres. 1964-68). Club: Cosmos (Washington). Home: 19715 Greenside Terr Montgomery Village Gaithersburg MD 20760 also Glen Mary Rd Bar Harbor ME 04609 Office: Dept Psychology Howard Univ Washington DC 20059

ROSS, STANFORD G., lawyer, govt. ofcl.; b. St. Louis, Oct. 9, 1931; A.B. with honors, Washington U., 1953; J.D. magna cum laude, Harvard U., 1956; m. Dorothy Rabin, June 9, 1958; children—John, Ellen. Admitted to D.C. bar, 1969, Calif. bar, 1956, N.Y. bar, 1959; asso. firm Irell & Manella, Los Angeles, 1956-57; teaching fellow, research asst. Harvard Law Sch., 1957-58; asso. firm Dewey, Ballantine, Bushby, Palmer & Wood, N.Y.C., 1958-61; asst. tax legis. counsel U.S. Dept. Treasury, 1961-63; prof. law N.Y. U., 1963-67; White House staff asst. to Pres. Johnson, 1967-68; gen. counsel U.S. Dept. Transp., 1968-69; partner firm Caplin & Drysdale, Washington, 1969-78; commr. Social Security Adminstrn., Washington, 1978-79; partner firm Califano, Ross & Heineman, Washington, 1980—. Mem. Am. Bar Assn., Fed. Bar Assn., Internat. Fiscal Assn. (council). Democrat. Jewish. Editor Harvard Law Rev., 1954-56. Office: Rm 613-D Independence Ave NW Washington DC 20201

ROSS, STANLEY, editor, publisher; b. N.Y.C., Jan. 18, 1914; s. Harry Paul and Bella R.; student Coll. City N.Y., 1932-36, U. Caracas (Venezuela), 1941-43; m. Eleanore Lyle, July 1, 1948 (dec. Feb. 1960); 1 son, Michael Stanley; m. 2d, Countess Margarita Theresa Parravicini. Editor The Argus, 1932-34; owner of 9 weeklies under corporate name Stanley Ross Assos., 1936; N.Y. Times corr., Venezuela and other S.Am. countries, 1940-43; pub. relations adviser to Pres. of Venezuela, 1941-43; traveled widely through Latin and S.Am. for U.S. mags., 1940-47; AP and NBC corr., Argentina, 1943-45; organized Latin Am. Press Syndicate (serving 700 Latin Am. papers), 1946; founder, pub., editor El Caribe and El Urgente (daily papers), Dominican Republic, 1947-49; pub., editor The Star, Wilmington, Del., 1948-50; editor N.Y. Amsterdam News, 1951; editor in chief, asso. pub. El Diario de Nueva York (daily newspaper), 1955-62; editor-in-chief Bklyn. Eagle, 1962-63, La Prensa, daily, 1961-62; editor, pub. El Tiempo, N.Y.C., 1963-69, 73-75, El Mundo, N.Y.C., 1969-71; also editor in chief L.I. (N.Y.) Post; internat. editor ABC of the Americas and Madrid; cons. on Latin Am. Affairs, Dept.

Justice; lectr. Latin Am. affairs throughout U.S., 1948; author semi-weekly articles appearing in 245 Latin Am. papers. Decorated comdr. Order Ruben Dario (Nicaragua). Mem. Assn. de Escritores Americanos (1st U.S. citizen elected pres. 1946, 47), Nat. Soc. Prevention Juvenile Delinquency (hon. pres.), N.Y. Advt. Club. Republican. Clubs: Masons, Overseas Press. Author: Communism in Latin America, 1947; The War for Trade in Latin America, 1947; Axel Wenner-Gren, The Sphinx of Sweden, 1948. Research in Latin Am. history and polit. economy. Home: 230 E 48th St New York NY 10017 also Juan Ramon Jimenez 8 Madrid 16 Spain Office: Business Week 1221 Ave of Americas New York NY 10020

ROSS, STANLEY RALPH, film writer; b. N.Y.C., July 22, 1935; s. Morris H. and Blanche (Turer) R.; student Pratt Inst., 1950-51; D.D., Universal Life Ch., 1974; m. Neila Hyman, Dec. 14, 1957; children—Andrew Steven, Lisa Michelle Turer, Nancy Ellen. Self-employed photographer, N.Y.C., 1952-56; copywriter Fuller, Smith & Ross, Los Angeles, 1956-60, Universal Pictures, Los Angeles, 1960-61; program exec. ABC-TV, Los Angeles, 1961-63; creative dir. Cole, Fischer & Rogow, Beverly Hills, Calif., 1963-65; self-employed film and TV writer, Beverly Hills, 1965—; pres. Neila Corp. Guest lectr. U. Calif. at Los Angeles, U. So. Calif., Calif. Luth. Coll., Los Angeles Coll., others; cons. Blanc Advt., Mego Toys, N.Y.C. Recipient UNICEF award, 1974, West Los Angeles Coll. Presdl. citation, 1974, Carson (Calif.) citation, 1973, also 3 Emmy nominations, 2 Writers Guild award nominations. Mem. Writers Guild, Screen Actors Guild, AFTRA, ASCAP, Saints and Sinners of Los Angeles (award). Republican. Mem. Universal Life Ch. Author: Games For Planes, 1974; Speak When You Hear The Beep, 1975. Writer for television programs Banacek, Batman, UNCLE, Colombo, All In The Family. Home: 451 Beverwil Dr Beverly Hills CA 90212 Office: 407 N Maple St Beverly Hills CA 90210. *My goal in life has been to have a good time and do only what I care to. I feel that I cannot do something that is alien to my nature and have so refused over the years until I discovered that writing was my true vocation. In the past decade, I have enjoyed myself and had more success than in all my former work years due to this independence. The only other principle I espouse is the law of Karma. For every effect, there is a cause; and every good thing one does is noted in a grand book and the rewards for doing good are reaped here on earth.*

ROSS, STANLEY ROBERT, historian; b. N.Y.C., Aug. 8, 1921; s. Max George and Ethel (Aks) R.; A.B. (scholar), Queens Coll., 1942; M.A., Columbia U., 1943, Ph.D. (Schiff fellow), 1951; m. Leonore Jacobson, Oct. 7, 1945 (div. 1975); children—Steven David, Alicia Ellen, Janet Irene; m. 2d, Geraldine D. Gagliano, Dec. 18, 1977. Instr. history Queens Coll., 1946-48, Bklyn. Coll., spring 1948; from instr. to prof. history U. Nebr., 1948-62; prof. history, chmn. dept. State U. N.Y. at Stony Brook, 1962-66, acting dean Coll. Arts and Scis., 1963-66, dean, 1966-68; prof. history, dir. Inst. Latin Am. Studies, U. Tex., Austin, 1968-71, provost arts and scis., 1971-72, provost, 1972-73, v.p., provost, 1973-76, prof. history, coordinator research program, 1976—; summer tchr. City Coll. N.Y., 1946, Columbia U., 1960, U. Colo., 1962; chmn. Conf. on Latin Am. History, 1968; U.S. nat. mem. commn. on history Pan Am. Inst. Geography and History, 1969-73; mem. joint com. Latin-Am. studies Am. Council Learned Socs.-Social Sci. Research Council, 1968-71. Vice chmn. Suffolk County (N.Y.) Com. to Study Sch. Redistricting, 1965; chmn. Three Village Council Edn., 1966-67. Served to 1st lt. USAAF, 1943-46. Travel grantee State Dept., summer 1947-48; Doherty Found. fellow, 1952-53; Faculty summer grantee U. Nebr., 1955, fellow, 1961; Rockefeller Found. research grantee, 1958-59, 61, 68-69. Mem. Conf. Latin Am. History (chmn. Bolton Prize com. 1965), Am. Hist. Assn., Acad. Am. Franciscan History (corr.), Instituto Mexicano de Cultura (corr.), Latin Am. Studies Assn. (chmn. com. govt. relations), AAUP. Author: Francisco I. Madero, Apostle of Mexican Democracy, 1955, 2d edit., 1977; co-author, co-editor: Historia Documental de México, 2 vols., 1964. Editor: Is the Mexican Revolution Dead?, 1965, rev. edit., 1975; Fuentes de la Historia Contemporánea de México: Periódicos Y Revistas, 2 vols., 1966-67; Latin America in Transition, 1970; (Paul Kennedy) The Middle Beat, 1971; Views Across the Border: The United States and Mexico, 1978; co-editor Críticas constructivas del sistema político Mexicano, 1973; adv. editor The Americas, 1956-70; contbg. editor The Handbook of Latin American Studies, 1960-70; mng. editor Hispanic American Hist. Rev., 1970-75; editorial bd. Hispanic Am. Hist. Rev., 1960-66. Home: 102 Canyon Rim Dr Austin TX 78746

ROSS, STEVEN J., corp. exec.; b. N.Y.C., 1927; ed. Paul Smith's Coll., 1948. Pres., dir. Kinney Services Inc., 1966-72; chmn. bd., pres., chief exec. officer Warner Communications Inc., N.Y.C., 1972—. Bd. dirs. N.Y. Conv. and Visitors Bur., N.Y. State Alliance to Save Energy; mem. bd. sports medicine Lenox Hill Hosp. Office: 75 Rockefeller Plaza New York NY 10019

ROSS, STEVEN SANDER, editor; b. Boston, May 29, 1946; s. Eli Woodrow and Lillian Faye (Arrick) R.; B.S. in Physics (Rabb scholar 1964, Interfraternity scholar 1966), Rensselaer Poly. Inst., 1969; M.S. in Journalism (Marti-Ibanez scholar), Columbia, 1970; m. Nancy Lawrence Bush, June 23, 1970; children—Marion Joyce, Heather Rebecca, Leah Elizabeth. Editor, Air and Water News, McGraw-Hill Pub. Co., N.Y.C., 1970-72, asso. editor Chem. Engring. mag., 1972; editor New Engr. mag. MBA Communications, N.Y.C., 1972-79, corp. v.p., editorial dir., 1978-79; mng. editor Boardroom Reports, 1979—. Dir. spl. projects Environ. Info. Center, N.Y.C., 1972—; adj. prof. journalism Columbia, 1974—. Bd. dirs. N.J. League for Conservation Legislation; v.p. bd. dirs. Armstrong Found.; mem. Environ. Commn. and Planning Bd., Leonia, N.J. Recipient Chmn's. award Profl. Engrs. in Pvt. Practice div. Nat. Soc. Profl. Engrs., 1975; named Citizen of Year N.Y. State Soc. Profl. Engrs., 1978. Fellow Am. Inst. Chemists; mem. ASTM, Am. Astron. Soc., Sigma Delta Chi, Pi Delta Epsilon (pres. chpt. 1968), Phi Sigma Kappa. Democrat. Jewish (v.p., trustee to temple). Co-author: Product Safety and Liability: A Desk Reference, 1979. Editor: Environment Regulation Handbook, 1973—; Land Use Abstracts, 1974, 75; Toxic Substances Sourcebook, 1978. Co-editor: McGraw-Hill's 1972 Report on Business and the Environment, 1972. Home: 120 Irving St Leonia NJ 07605 Office: 500 Fifth Ave New York NY 10036. *I hope you all enjoy your work as much as I enjoy mine.*

ROSS, STUART TENNENT, surgeon; b. East Hampton, N.Y., Jan. 16, 1907; s. Howard V. and Grace (Conover) R.; A.B., Columbia, 1927, M.D., 1930; m. Jean M. Goodman, June 29, 1933; 1 dau., Jane S. Intern, Meth. Hosp., 1930-32; resident United Hosp., 1932-33; practice medicine, Hempstead, N.Y., 1933-46, Garden City, 1946—; attending proctologist Nassau Hosp., Mineola, N.Y., Mercy Hosp., Rockville, N.Y.; asso. prof. clin. surgery Sch. Medicine, SUNY, Stony Brook, 1979—; mem. adv. bd. Med. Specialists. Served to lt. col. M.C., AUS, 1942-46. Decorated Legion of Merit. Diplomate Am. Bd. of Colon and Rectal Surgery (sec. 1955-68, pres. 1968-69). Fellow A.C.S., Internat. Coll. Surgeons, Am. (pres. 1955), Mexican (hon.), N.Y., Pa., N.J. proctologic socs., Pa. Soc. Colon and Rectal Surgery (hon.); mem. World, Am. (ho. dels.) Pan Am. med. assns., Mensa, Nassau Surg. Soc. (pres. 1960), Royal Soc. Medicine (Eng.), Am. Cancer Soc. (dir. Nassau div.), Internat. Soc. U. Colon and Rectal Surgeons (treas. 1965), Pan-Pacific Surg. Assn. Author: (with Harry E. Bacon) Atlas of Operative Technic, Anus, Rectum and Colon, 1954; (with H.E. Bacon, P. Recio) Proctology, 1956; Synopsis of Anorectal Diseases, 1959. Asso. editor: Diseases of Colon and Rectum; editorial cons. Postgrad. Medicine. Contbr. numerous articles to med. jours. Home: 392 Roslyn Rd East Williston NY 11596 Office: 520 Franklin Ave Garden City NY 11530

ROSS, SYDNEY, chemist; b. Scotland, July 6, 1915; s. Jack Clunies and Liza B. (Campbell) R.; came to U.S., 1936; B.Sc., McGill U., 1933-36; Ph.D., U. Ill., 1940. Research asso. Stanford, 1941-45; sr. chemist Oak Ridge Nat. Lab., 1945-48; prof. colloid sci. Rensselaer Poly. Inst., 1948—; cons. surface chemistry. Chmn. Gordon Conf. Chemistry of Interfaces, 1954. Mem. Am. Chem. Soc. (chmn. colloid div. 1951-52), Chem. Soc. London. Author: Inhibition of Foaming, 1950; (with J.P. Olivier) On Physical Adsorption, 1964; also articles. Editor: Physics and Chemistry of Interfaces, vol. 1, 1965, vol. 2, 1971. Home: 2194 Tibbits Ave Troy NY 12180

ROSS, TED L., mfg. co. exec.; b. Albany, Ind., Sept. 16, 1931; s. Dennis M. and Mary (Foustnight) R.; student Springfield (Ill.) Jr. Coll., 1949-51; B.A. in Accounting, U. Ill., 1953, B.S. in Elec. Engring., 1958; m. Patricia Ann McHugh, Aug. 17, 1957; children—Karen M., Mary P., Nancy D. With Sundstrand Corp., Rockford, Ill., 1958—, sec., 1968—, controller, 1970—, v.p. fin., sec., 1978—. Served with U.S. Army, 1953-55. Episcopalian. Office: 4751 Harrison Ave Rockford IL 61101

ROSS, THOMAS BERNARD, govt. ofcl.; b. N.Y.C., Sept. 2, 1929; s. Henry M. and Evelyn (Timothy) R.; B.A., Yale, 1951; Nieman fellow, Harvard, 1963-64; m. Gunilla Ekstrand, Nov. 2, 1963; children—Maria, Anne, Kristina. Reporter, I.N.S., 1955-58, U.P.I., 1958; mem. staff Chgo. Sun-Times, 1958-77, Washington bur., 1958-68, fgn. corr., Beirut, Paris, 1968-70, Washington bur. chief, 1970-77; asst. sec. def. for pub. affairs, 1977—. Served to lt. (j.g.) USNR, 1951-54. Recipient Marshall Field award, 1961, 71. Roman Catholic. Clubs: Elizabethan (New Haven); Gridiron (Washington). Author: (with David Wise) The U-2 Affair, 1962; The Invisible Government, 1964; The Espionage Establishment, 1967. Home: 2911 P St NW Washington DC 20007 Office: The Pentagon Washington DC

ROSS, THURSTON HOWARD, economist; b. Richmond, Ind., Oct. 25, 1894; s. Thomas Edwin and Louise Emma (Busch) R.; B.S., Otterbein Coll., 1917; M.B.A., U. So. Calif., 1922, Ph.D., 1924; m. Bertha Corl, Sept. 25, 1920; 1 son, Thurston Howard. Instr. indsl. mgmt. U. Calif. at Los Angeles, 1921-22; instr. U. So. Calif., 1922-24, asst. prof., 1924-26, asso. prof., 1926-28, prof., chmn. dept. mgmt., 1928-50, dir. Bur. Bus. Research, 1930-50, then dir. Sch. Mdsg.; now engaged in econ. and biometric research. Served as lt. U.S. Army, 1917-19; capt. USNR, World War II; mem. joint mil. transp. com. Joint Chiefs Staff; combined mil. transp. com.; rep. U.S. Navy for logistics at both Que. Confs. and Cairo and Yalta confs.; staff Pacific Fleet, logistics; set up liquidation plan for War Shipping Adminstrn. and reorgn. for U.S. Maritime Commn. Registered profl. engr. Mem. ASME, Am. Legion, Mil. Order World Wars, Am. Soc. Real Estate Counselors, Phi Beta Kappa, Alpha Kappa Psi, Beta Gamma Sigma, Phi Kappa Phi, Blue Key, Skull and Dagger, Artus, Sigma Sigma, Alpha Delta Sigma. Episcopalian. Clubs: Masons; Engrs. (Los Angeles); Univ. (Washington). Author: Real Estate Appraisal, 1927; Some Economic Aspects of Urban Land Valuation; Mathematical Approach to Industrial Valuation; Management and the Business Cycle. Past editor So. Calif. Bus. Rev. Author articles econs. and indsl. mgmt.; lectr. Army-Navy Staff Coll. Home: 14918 La Cumbre Dr Pacific Palisades Los Angeles CA 90272

ROSS, WARREN REINHARD, health communications co. exec.; b. Frankfurt, Germany, July 24, 1926; s. Walter M. and Elizabeth Johanna (Keller) R.; B.S., Coll. City N.Y., 1946; M.S. in Journalism, Northwestern U., 1947; m. Lucile Perry, Dec. 15, 1951; children—Catherine Elizabeth, Ellen Christina, Johanna Margaret. Instr. dept. English, Coll. City N.Y., 1947-49; pub. relations dir. Memphis Community Chest, 1949-50; dir. pub. and profl. information United Cerebral Palsy Assn., 1952-56; account supr., group creative dir. William D. McAdams, advt. agy., N.Y.C., 1956-61; a founder, partner Kallir, Philips, Ross, Inc., N.Y.C., 1962—; now pres. KPR Infor/Media Corp. Active edn. affairs, Rye, N.Y. Trustee Unitarian Universalist Assn., 1971-75. Served with AUS, 1950-52. Mem. Alliance for Continuing Med. Edn., Phi Beta Kappa, Phi Alpha Theta, Pharm. Advt. Council, Urban League of Westchester. Contbr. fiction, articles to mags. Office: 919 3d Ave New York NY 10022

ROSS, WILLIAM DEE, JR., economist; b. Jackson, Miss., May 16, 1921; s. William Dee and Betty (Biggs) R.; B.A., Millsaps Coll., 1942; M.A., Duke U., 1947, Ph.D., 1951; m. Nell Triplett, July 25, 1944; 1 son, William Dee III. Economist, U.S. Mil. Govt. for Germany, Berlin, 1945-46; instr. econs. Duke, 1946-49; asso. prof. econs. La. State U., 1949-54, prof. econs., 1954-56, dean Coll. Bus. Adminstrn., 1956-76; pres. Fin. Con. Services, Inc., Baton Rouge, 1976—; mem. bd., exec. com. Am. Bank, Baton Rouge, 1966—; dir. other corps.; dir. La. Hwy. Fin. Study, La. Legis. Council, 1953-54; cons. Joint House-Senate Hwy. Com., La. Legislature, La. Dept. Hwys., 1955-56; lectr. exec. devel. programs Mich. State U., Ga. Inst. Tech., La. State U.; mem. dept. econs., fin. and adminstrn. Hwy. Research Bd., Nat. Acad. Scis., Washington, 1957-64; mem. adv. council Tax Inst. Am., 1961-63. Bd. dirs., area council Boy Scouts Am. Served to 1st lt. USAAF, 1943-45. Mem. Am. Assn. Collegiate Schs. Bus., Am., So. (exec. com. 1960-62) econ. assns., Nat. Tax Assn. (exec. com. 1960-63, editorial com. Nat. Tax Jour. 1959-62), Am., So. (pres. 1962-63) fin. assns., Southwestern Social Sci. Assn., Omicron Delta Kappa, Beta Gamma Sigma. Methodist. Club: Rotary. Author: (with B.U. Ratchford) Berlin Reparations Assignment, 1947; Financing Highway Improvements in Louisiana, 1955; Business in a Free Society, 1966; contbr. articles to profl. jours. Home: 2738 McConnell Dr Baton Rouge LA 70809

ROSS, WILLIAM EDWIN, advt. agy. exec.; b. N.Y.C., Mar. 26, 1930; s. John R. and Barbara (Bertrand) R.; m. Helene, May 28, 1966; children—Robert, Barbara. TV writer Schwimmer & Scott Co., Chgo., 1952-56; writer-producer North Advt., Chgo., 1956-57; with J. Walter Thompson Co., Chgo., 1957—, exec. v.p., Chgo., 1974-75, gen. mgr. Chgo. office, 1975-77, pres. U.S. Western div., 1977—, also dir. Bd. dirs. Boy Scouts Am., Salvation Army. Served in U.S. Army, 1948-52. Christian Scientist. Contbr. numerous articles to advt. jours. Home: 1242 Lake Shore Dr Chicago IL 60610 Office: 875 N Michigan Ave Chicago IL 60611

ROSS, WILLIAM JARBOE, lawyer; b. Oklahoma City, May 9, 1930; s. Walter John and Bertha (Jarboe) R.; B.B.A., U. Okla., 1952, LL.B., 1954; m. Mary Lillian Ryan, May 19, 1962; children—Rebecca Anne, Robert Joseph, Molly Kathleen. Admitted to Okla. bar, 1954, since practiced in Oklahoma City, asst. municipal counselor Oklahoma City, 1955-60; mem. firm Rainey, Ross, Rice & Binns, 1960—, partner, 1965—. Dir. United Energy Resources Corp., United Gas Pipe Line Co., Hudson Petroleum Corp., Lilbert, Inc. Mem. Mayor's Hist. Preservation Com., 1968—; state chmn. preservation easements com. Okla. Hist. Soc.; bd. dirs. Okla. Symphony Orch. Mem. Am., Okla. bar assns., Okla. Heritage Assn. (chmn. edn. com.), Phi Alpha Delta, Beta Theta Pi. K.C. (4), Rotarian. Clubs: Oklahoma City Golf and Country, Beacon. Home: 6923 Avondale Ct Oklahoma City OK 73116 Office: First Nat Center West Oklahoma City OK 73102

ROSSANO, AUGUST THOMAS, educator; b. N.Y.C., Feb. 1, 1916; s. August Thomas and Rosa (Cosenza) R.; B.S., M.I.T., 1938; M.S., Harvard U., 1941, S.D., 1954; m. Margie Chrisney, Dec. 6, 1944; children—August Thomas III, Marilyn, Pamela, Jeannine, Renee, Christopher, Stephen, Teresa. Commd. lt. (j.g.) USPHS, 1941, advanced through grades to capt., 1955; assigned Hdqrs. USPHS, 1941, 48, Taft Engring. Center, Cin., 1954-59; ret., 1963; prof. air resource engring. U. Wash., Seattle, 1963—; vis. prof. Calif. Inst. Tech., 1960-63. Mem. expert adv. panel on air pollution WHO, Geneva, 1960—, Pan Am. Health Orgn., 1975—; cons. European office WHO, 1960—, U.S. Dept. HEW, 1962—, State of Wash., 1963—, Puget Sound Air Pollution Control Agy., 1967—; cons. govts. U.S., Can., Greece, Czechoslovakia, Mexico, Syria, Iran, Egypt, Brazil, Peru, Chile, Barbados and World Bank; mem. subcom. on hydrogen sulfide NRC. Bd. dirs. Environmental Resources Assos., Bellevue Montessori Sch., Environmental Sci. Service div. E.R.A., N.W. Environmental Scis. Ltd., Inst. Exec. Research, Nat. Air Conservation Commn. Served with C.E., AUS. Recipient Spl. Service award USPHS, 1958; HEW tng. grantee, 1964-70; EPA grantee, 1971—. Diplomate Am. Acad. Environmental Engrs., Am. Bd. Indsl. Hygiene. Mem. Sigma Xi, Delta Omega, Tau Beta Pi. Club: Bellevue Triangle Pool; Alderbrook (Wash.) Golf and Yacht. Author: (with Hal Cooper) Source Testing for Air Pollution Control, 1971. Editor: Air Pollution Control, 1969. Contbr. articles to tech. jours. Patentee pollution control device. Home: 9427 NE 20th St Bellevue WA 98004 Office: More Hall U Wash Seattle WA 98195

ROSSANT, JAMES STEPHAN, architect, planner; b. N.Y.C., Aug. 17, 1928; s. Marcus and Ann (Orbach) R.; student Columbia U., 1948-49; B.Arch., U. Fla., 1951; M. City and Regional Planning, Harvard U., 1953; m. Colette Palacci, Sept. 8, 1955; children—Marianne, Juliette, Cecile, Thomas. Archtl. designer Mayer Whittlesey & Glass, N.Y.C., 1956-61, Whittlesey & Conklin, N.Y.C., 1961-65; partner Whittlesey, Conklin & Rossant, N.Y.C., 1966-67, Conklin & Rossant, N.Y.C., 1967—; lectr. urban planning Columbia, 1968, architecture Pratt Inst., 1963-66; lectr. city planning N.Y. U., 1965, prof. urban design, 1978-79. one-man show Gallery of Architecture, 1975; works include Lake Anne Village and Master Plan for Reston, Va., Metro-North Apts., N.Y.C., Usdan Center for the Arts, Huntington, N.Y., maintenance facilities Am. Airlines, Los Angeles and San Francisco. Served with USNR, 1949-53, AUS, 1953-54. Fellow AIA; mem. Am. Inst. Planners. Home: 114 Sullivan St New York City NY 10012 Office: 251 Park Ave S New York City NY 10010

ROSSBACH, JAY HARRY, JR., cosmetics co. exec.; b. Phila., Dec. 11, 1921; s. J. H. and Sophia (Haas) R.; grad. Berkshire Prep. Sch., 1939; A.B., Brown U., 1943; m. Linda Johnson, Nov. 22, 1971; children by previous marriage—Jay Adam, Elizabeth Cady. With Saks Fifth Ave., N.Y.C., 1946-74, buyer for University Shop, 1946-49, mdse. man children's shops, 1950-74, v.p. Saks Fifth Av., 1956-74, mdsg. mgr. Young Elite Ready to Wear, 1954-72; pres. Rosspeltz Corp., White Plains, N.Y., 1974-76; exec. v.p., gen. mgr. Dahlia Enterprises Ltd., N.Y.C., 1976-78; exec. v.p. Scandia Cosmetics Internat. Inc., 1978-79, J.W. Toiletries, N.Y.C., 1979—. Bd. dirs. N.Y. council Boy Scouts Am. Served to lt. USNR, 1943-46. Clubs: Southampton Golf; Aspatuck Tennis (Westhampton, L.I., N.Y.); Brown Univ. (N.Y.C.). Home: 10 E 70th St New York NY 10021 Office: 600 Madison Ave New York NY 10022

ROSSBERG, ROBERT HOWARD, univ. adminstr., educator; b. Bklyn., Mar. 9, 1926; s. Benjamin William and Mollie (Linn) R.; student U. Mich., 1943-44; B.S., CCNY, 1949; M.A., Columbia U., 1951; Ph.D., N.Y. U., 1956; m. Mary Jo Kogan, June 22, 1947; 1 dau., Susan Lea. Counselor, Fedn. of 1950-51; staff psychologist N.Y. U. Med. Center, 1951-53; asst. chief psychologist, 1953-56; asst. prof. edn. and psychology SUNY, Buffalo, 1956-59, asso. prof., 1959-64, prof., 1964—, dir. grad. programs in counseling and ednl. psychology, 1959-65, asso. dean, 1965-67, dean Faculty Ednl. Studies, 1978—; cons. in field. Served with USAAF, 1944-46. Rehab. Counseling grantee, 1956-60; NDEA grantee, 1959-60; Office Edn. leadership tng. grantee, 1969-70. Mem. Am. Psychol. Assn., AAUP. Author: Youth: Myths and Realities, 1972; contbr. articles to profl. publs.; editorial asso. Urban Edn., 1961-70. Home: 105 Summerview Rd Williamsville NY 14221 Office: 367 Christopher Baldy Hall SUNY at Buffalo Amherst NY 14260

ROSSE, WENDELL FRANKLYN, physician; b. Sidney, Nebr., June 5, 1933; student U. Chgo., 1949-52, M.D. with honors, 1958; B.A., U. Omaha, 1953; student U. Nebr. Sch. Medicine, 1953-55, M.S. in Physiology, Grad. Sch., 1956; m. Simonne Vernier, July, 1959; children—Christopher, Stephanie, Phillipe. Sr. investigator Nat. Cancer Inst. NIH, Bethesda, Md., 1964-66; asst. prof. medicine Duke U. Med. Center, 1966-68, asso. prof. medicine, 1968-72, asso. prof. immunology, 1970-76, prof. medicine, 1972—, prof. immunology, 1976—, chief sect. immunohematology, 1971—, co-dir. blood bank, 1971—, chief hematology-oncology, 1976—; chief med. service Durham (N.C.) VA Hosp., 1973-76; vis. research prof. Institut de Pathologie Cellulaire, Paris, 1974; investigator Howard Hughes Med. Inst., 1976—; mem. regional adv. com. ARC: mem. N.C. Gov's Council on Sickle Cell Syndrome. Recipient Career Devel. award, 1968, Golden Apple Student Teaching award Duke U. Med. Center, 1968. Josiah Macy, Jr., scholar, 1974. Mem. Am. Soc. Hematology (Stratton lectr. 1976), Assn. Am. Physicians, Am. Soc. Clin. Investigation, Am. Fedn. Clin. Research, Nat. Blood Club (pres. 1975), Red Cell Club, N.C. Assn. Blood Banks, N.C. Heart Assn., Sigma Xi, Alpha Omega Alpha. Contbr. numerous articles to med. publs. Home: Box 223 Route 7 4 Timberly Dr Durham NC 27707 Office: PO Box 3934 Duke U Med Center Durham NC 27710

ROSSELL DE LA LAMA, GUILLERMO, govt. ofcl. Mexico; b. Pachuca, Mex., July 22, 1925; degree in architecture, Nat. U. Mexico; m. Emilia Abitia de Rossell; children—Guillermo, Fernando, Mauricio. Chief exec. officer Ministry Nat. Properties Mex., 1958-59; undersec. nat. properties Mex., 1959-64; pvt. archtl. practice; sec. of tourism Mex., 1976—; prof. arcitecture Nat U. Mexico; dir. San Carlos Archtl. mag., Space, Planning and Plastic mag. Decorated Cruz de Marti (Cuba); Orden Cruzairo do Sul (Brazil); Orden de Constantino (Greece); Orden Soberana Imperial Bizanrina de Constantino El Grande; officer Legion of Honor (France); hon. mem. AIA; named hon. citizen Tex. and La. Home: Tinaco No 40 Mexico 20 DF Mexico Office: Ave Juarez No 92 Mexico 1 DF Mexico*

ROSSER, CHARLES D., lawyer; b. Birmingham, Ala., Apr. 28, 1935; s. Alex Hiram and Oneita (Horn) R.; B.S., Birmingham So. Coll., 1961; LL.B., U. Ala., 1963; children—Joan Elizabeth, Charles D. Admitted to Ala. bar, 1963; law clk. to judge U.S. Ct. Appeals, 1963-64; asso. Howell T. Heflin, atty., Tuscumbia, Ala., 1964-66; partner firm Heflin & Rosser, Tuscumbia, 1967-71, Rosser & Munsey, 1971-77, Heflin, Rosser and Munsey, 1977—; spl. asst. atty. gen. Ala., 1968-69. Pres., Sheffield (Ala.) Jr. C. of C., 1964; chmn. Colbert County Cancer Crusade. Served with AUS, 1955-57. Mem. Am., Ala. trial lawyers assns., Am., Ala., Colbert County bar assns., Lamdba Chi

Alpha, Sigma Delta Kappa. Mason, Kiwanian. Club: Turtle Point Yacht and Country (Florence, Ala.). Home: 3310 Harding Ave Muscle Shoals AL 35660 Office: 105 E 2d St PO Box 496 Tuscumbia AL 35674

ROSSER, JAMES MILTON, univ. pres.; b. East St. Louis, Ill., Apr. 16, 1939; s. William M. and Mary E. (Bass) R.; B.A., So. Ill. U., 1962, M.A., 1963, Ph.D., 1969; m. Carmen Rosita Colby, Dec. 27, 1962; 1 son, Terrence. Diagnostic bacteriologist Holden Hosp., Carbondale, Ill., 1961-63; research bacteriologist Eli Lilly & Co., Indpls., 1963-66; coordinator Black Am. studies, instr. health edn., So. Ill. U., Carbondale, 1968-69, asst. prof., dir. Black Am. studies, 1969-70, asst. to chancellor, 1970; asso. vice chancellor for acad. affairs U. Kans., Lawrence, 1970-74, asso. prof. edn. and pharmacology, 1971-74; vice chancellor dept. higher edn. State of N.J., Trenton, 1974-79, acting chancellor, 1977; pres. Calif. State U., Los Angeles, 1979—; cons. Kans. Regional Med. Program, 1972, Ottawa (Kans.) U., 1972, State of Ill. Bd. Higher Edn., 1972, HUD, 1972, St. Johns U., 1972; cons. Commn. on Edn., Nat. Acad. Engring., 1973; mem. tech. resource panel Center for Research and Devel. in Higher Edn., U. Calif., Berkeley, 1975-76; mem. health maintenance orgn. com. Health Planning Council, State of N.J., 1975-79; mem. standing com. on research and devel. bd. trustees Ednl. Testing Service, 1976-77; mem. steering com. and task force on retention of minorities in engring. Assembly of Engring., NRC, 1975—; mem. Bd. Med. Examiners, State of N.J., 1978-79; vis. faculty mem. Inst. Mgmt. of Lifelong Edn., Grad. Sch. Edn., Harvard U., 1979; mem. Commn. on Acad. Affairs Am. Council Edn., 1979—; trustee Life Inst. Medicine and Law, 1979—. Mem. Carbondale Human Relations Commn., 1969-70; bd. dirs. Architects Community Center, Kansas City, Mo., 1972-74; mem. exec. bd. Los Angeles Area council Boy Scouts Am., 1979—; bd. dirs. Hispanic Urban Center, Los Angeles, 1979—. NSF fellow, 1961, NDEA fellow, 1967-68. Mem. Am. Assn. State Colls. and Univs. (mem. com. on urban affairs), Am. Ednl. Research Assn., Am. Public Health Assn., Kappa Delta Pi, Phi Delta Kappa, Phi Kappa Phi, Kappa Alpha Psi. Roman Catholic. Author: An Analysis of Health Care Delivery, 1977. Home: 225 El Cielo Ln Bradbury CA 91010 Office: Calif State U 5151 State University Dr Los Angeles CA 90032

ROSSER, JOHN BARKLEY, mathematician, rocket ballistician; b. Jacksonville, Fla., Dec. 6, 1907; s. Harwood and Ethel (Merryday) R.; B.S., U. Fla., 1929, M.S., 1931, D.Sc. (hon.), 1970; Ph.D., Princeton U., 1934; D.Sc. (hon.) Otterbein Coll., 1971; m. Annetta L. Hamilton, Sept. 7, 1935; children—Edwenna Merryday, John Barkley. Procter research fellow Princeton U., 1933-35, lectr., 1939-40; NRC fellow Harvard U., 1935-36; instr. math. Cornell U., 1936-39, asst. prof., 1939-40, asso. prof., 1940-43, prof., 1943-63, chmn. dept., 1961-62; prof. math. U. Wis., Madison, 1963—, dir. Math. Research Center, 1963-73; ballistician Allegany Ballistics Lab., 1944-46; dir. research Inst. Numerical Analysis, Nat. Bur. Standards, 1949-50, mem. com. for evaluation, 1953; dir. ART project Army Ordnance, 1951-52; mem. Stewart Com. monitoring U.S. space satellite, 1955-58; dir. FOCUS project Inst. Def. Analyses, 1959-61, dir. SCAMP project, summers 1962-63; cons. rocket ballistics govt. agys. and industries; pres. CO- OP, 1959-60, chmn. math. div. NRC, 1960-62; chmn. Conf. Bd. Math. Scis., 1963-65. Guggenheim and Fulbright research fellow U. Paris, 1953-54; recipient Presdl. Certificate of Merit, 1948; Dept. Navy commendation, 1960; Distinguished Civilian award Dept. Army, 1974. Mem. Am. Acad. Arts and Scis., Soc. Indsl. and Applied Math (pres. 1964-66), Am. Math. Soc. (council 1948-51), Math. Assn. Am., Assn. Symbolic Logic (exec. com. 1935-37, 41-44, pres. 1950-53), Assn. Computing Machinery (council 1954-56), Sigma Xi, Phi Kappa Phi. Presbyterian. Clubs: Madison; Cosmos (Washington). Author: (with R. R. Newton and G. L. Gross) Mathematical Theory of Rocket Flight, 1947; Theory and Application of Various Integrals, 1948; (with A. R. Turquette) Many-Valued Logics, 1952; Logic for Mathematicians, 1953; Deux Esquisses de Logique, 1955; Simplified Independence Proofs, 1969; (with Carl de Boor) Pocket Calculator Supplement for Calculus, 1979; author research papers math., computers, mil. rocket development. Home: 4209 Manitou Way Madison WI 53711

ROSSER, RICHARD FRANKLIN, univ. pres.; b. Arcanum, Ohio, July 16, 1929; s. Harold Armand and Margaret (Whitacre) R.; B.A., Ohio Wesleyan U., 1951; M.P.A., Syracuse U., 1952, Ph.D., 1961; m. Donna Eyssen. Mar. 21, 1951; children—Eric, Carl, Edward. Joined U.S. Air Force, 1952, advanced through grades to col., 1968; prof. polit. sci. U.S. Air Force Acad., Colorado Springs, Colo., 1959-73, head dept., 1967-73, ret., 1973; prof. polit. sci., dean Albion (Mich.) Coll., 1973-77; pres. DePauw U., Greencastle, Ind., 1977—. Decorated Legion of Merit with oak leaf cluster. Mem. Am. Polit. Sci. Assn., Internat. Studies Assn., Internat. Inst. Strategic Studies, AAUP, Am. Assn. Advancement Slavic Studies, Phi Beta Kappa, Omicron Delta Kappa. Methodist. Author: An Introduction to Soviet Foreign Policy, 1969. Contbr. articles to profl. jours. Home: 125 Wood St Greencastle IN 46135 Office: DePauw University Greencastle IN 46135

ROSSET, BARNET LEE, JR., publisher; b. Chgo., May 28, 1922; s. Barnet Lee and Mary (Tansey) R.; Ph.B., U. Chgo., 1947; B.A., New Sch. Social Research, N.Y.C., 1952; m. Joan Mitchell, 1947 (div. 1952); m. 2d, Hannelore Eckert, Aug. 1953 (div. 1957); 1 son, Peter; m. 3d, Cristina Agnini, Mar. 11, 1965; children—Tansey, Beckett. Publisher and editor Grove Press, Inc., 1951—. Served to 1st lt. Signal Corps, AUS, 1942-46. Mem. PEN Club. Club: Overseas Press. Office: 196 W Houston St New York NY 10014

ROSSEY, PAUL WILLIAM, supt. schs.; b. Richmond, Ind., July 7, 1926; s. Chris C. and Lela (Longman) R.; B.S., Jersey City State Coll., 1952, D. Letters, 1971; M.A., N.Y. U., 1953, Ed.D. (Kellogg Found. fellow 1955), 1958; children—Joanne (Mrs. George A. Thompson). Head jr. sch. Peddie Sch., Hightstown, N.J., 1952-53; cons., elementary sch. instr., West Hempstead, N.Y., 1953-55; prin. elementary sch., Dobbs Ferry, N.Y., 1955-58; supt. schs., Litchfield, Conn., 1958-60; supt. schs. Scotch Plains-Fanwood, N.J., 1960-67; dist. supt. schs., Nassau County, N.Y., 1967-69; pres. West Chester (Pa.) State Coll., 1969-74; supt. schs., Millburn-Short Hills, N.J., 1974—; lectr. N.Y. U., 1954-67. County dir. Boy Scouts Am.; v.p. YMCA. Bd. dirs. Garbe Found., Community Fund; trustee Pub. Library, N.Y. U., 1970-74, The Peddle Sch., 1974—; mem. exec. com. N.J. Council Edn., 1977—. Served with USNR, 1944-46, USMCR, 1971—. Named Outstanding Alumnus award Jersey City State Coll., 1962; recipient N.Y. U. medallion, 1966, Ernest O. Melby award human relations, 1970. Mem. Am. Assn. Sch. Adminstrs. (chmn. N.J. 1965-67), Am. Council Edn., Aircraft Owners and Pilots Assn., N.J. Assn. Sch. Adminstrs. (exec. com. 1964-67), Horace Mann League U.S. (nat. pres. 1977-78), Kappa Delta Pi, Phi Delta Kappa. Republican. Presbyn. Clubs: Exchange (dir.), N.J. Schoolmasters. Contbr. articles to profl. jours. Home: 1 Shore Edge Ln Short Hills NJ 07078 Office: 434 Millburn Ave Millburn NJ 07041

ROSSI, ALICE SCHAERR (MRS. PETER H. ROSSI), sociologist, educator; b. N.Y.C., Sept. 24, 1922; d. William A. and Emma C. (Winkler) Schaerr; B.A., Bklyn. Coll., 1947; Ph.D. (Gilder fellow), Columbia, 1957; L.H.D., Towson State Coll., 1973; D.Sc., Rutgers U., 1975; LL.D., Simmons Coll., 1977; m. Peter H. Rossi, Sept. 29, 1951; children—Peter Eric, Kristin Alice, Nina Alexis. Research asso. Cornell U., Harvard, U. Chgo., Johns Hopkins, 1951-69; prof. sociology Goucher Coll., Towson, Md., 1969-74, U. Mass., Amherst, 1974—. Mem. acad. adv. bd. Kirkland Coll. Recipient Nat. Inst. Mental Health Career award, 1964-69, 125th Anniversary award State U. N.Y., 1972; Ford Found. Faculty Research fellow, 1976. Mem. Sociologists for Women in Soc. (pres.), A.A.U.P. (chmn. nat. commn. on status of women 1970-73, 2d v.p. 1973-75), Am. Sociol. Assn. (v.p. 1977-78), Social Sci. Research Council (dir. 1970-76, chmn. bd. 1976-77). Author: Essays on Sex Equality, 1970; Academic Women on the Move, 1973; The Feminist Papers, 1973. Contbr. articles to profl. jours. Mem. editorial bd. Am. Sociol. Rev., 1969-72. Home: 34 Stagecoach Rd Amherst MA 01002

ROSSI, ANTHONY GERALD, lawyer; b. Warren, Ohio, July 20, 1935; s. Anthony Gerald and Lena (Guarnieri) R.; B.S., John Carroll U., 1957; J.D., Cath. U. Am., 1961; m. Marilyn J. Fuller, June 22, 1957; children—Diana L., Maribeth, Anthony Gerald III. Admitted to Ohio bar, 1961, since practiced in Warren; partner Guarnieri & Secrest, 1961—; acting judge Warren Municipal Ct. Mem. Mahoning-Shenango Estate Planning Council, 1968—, past sec.; past pres. Warren Olympic Club. Past bd. govs. Cath. U. Am. Law Sch. Council. Served to capt. Transp. Corps, AUS, 1957-65. Mem. Am., Ohio, Trumbull County (pres. 1976-77) bar assns., Am. Arbitration Assn., Ohio Motorist Assn. (corporate mem.). Clubs: K.C., Elks. Home: 1768 Coventry St NE Warren OH 44483 Office: 151 E Market St Warren OH 44481

ROSSI, BRUNO, physicist; b. Venice, Italy, Apr. 13, 1905; s. Rino and Lina (Minerbi) R.; student U. Padua, 1923-25, U. Bologna, 1925-27; hon. doctorate U. Palermo, 1964, U. Durham (Eng.), 1974, U. Chgo., 1977; m. Nora Lombroso, Apr. 10, 1938; children—Florence S., Frank R., Linda L. Asst. physics dept. U. Florence, 1928-32; prof. physics U. Padua, 1932-38; research asso. U. Manchester (Eng.), 1939; research asso. in cosmic rays U. Chgo., 1939-40; asso. prof. physics Cornell U. 1940-43; prof. physics Mass. Inst. Tech., 1946—, Inst. prof., 1966-70, Inst. prof. emeritus, 1970—. Mem. staff Los Alamos Lab., 1943-46, hon. fellow Tata Inst. Fundamental Research, Bombay, India 1971; mem. physics com. NASA; hon. prof. U. Mayor San Andres, La Paz, Bolivia. Recipient Cresson medal Franklin Inst., 1974; decorated Order of Merit (Republic of Italy). Mem. Am. Acad. Arts and Scis. (Rumford prize 1976), Nat. Acad. Sci. (space sci. bd., astronomy survey com.), Deutsche Akademieder Naturforscher Leopoldina, Am. Phys. Soc., Am. Inst. Physics, Accademia dei Lincel (Internat. Feltrinelli award 1971), Internat. Astron. Union, Am., Royal astron. socs., Accademia Patavina di Scienze, Letteree Arti, Accademia Ligure di Scienze e Lettere, Bolivian Acad. Scis. (corr.), A.A.A.S., Am. Philos. Soc., Italian Phys. Soc. (Gold medal 1970), Sigma Xi. Author: Rayons Cosmiques, 1935; (with L. Pincherle) Lezioni di Fisca Sperimentale Elettrologia, 1936; Lezioni di Fisica Sperimentale Ottica, 1937; High Energy Particles, 1952; Optics, 1957; Cosmic Rays, 1964; (with S. Olbert) Introduction to the Physics of Space, 1970. Address: 221 Mt Auburn St Cambridge MA 02138

ROSSI, HARRY, ins. co. exec.; b. Fivizzano, Italy, Nov. 21, 1919; s. Emilio and Clementing (Battini) R. (parents Am. citizens); A.B., Middlebury Coll., 1942; M.B.A., Harvard U., 1946; m. Jane Gorham Caswell, Oct. 29, 1949; children—John, Susan, Lisa. Investment officer Nat. Life Ins. Co., Montpelier, Vt., 1946-53; investment mgr. Occidental Life Ins. Co., Los Angeles, 1954-63; v.p. investment, sr. v.p., exec. v.p. Union Central Life Ins. Co., Cin., 1963-75, pres., 1976—; dir. Central Trust Co., Central Bancorporation, Inc.; lectr. U. So. Calif. Grad. Sch. Bus., 1957-61. Mem. adv. council Catherine Booth Home-Salvation Army, 1967—; mem. finance com. Bethesda Hosp. and Deaconess Assn., 1976—. Served with AUS, 1943-45. Episcopalian. Clubs: Queen City; Bankers. Home: 641 Flagstaff Dr Cincinnati OH 45215 Office: PO Box 179 Cincinnati OH 45201

ROSSI, MARIO ALEXANDER, architect; b. Chgo., Apr. 9, 1931; s. Gastone J. and Irma (Giorgi) R.; B.Arch., Ill. Inst. Tech., 1955; m. Jo Ann Therese Kneip, Apr. 12, 1958; children—John Vincent, Lyn Ann, Paul Alexander, Mara Ann. Architect, Omnimetrics, Los Angeles, 1967-78; prin. works include fin. models for Calif. Fed. Savs. and Loan Assn., Los Angeles, First Nat. City Bank, N.Y.C., Glendale Fed. Savs. and Loan Assn. (Calif.), Wailea, Alexander and Baldwin, Honolulu; research computerized techniques in architecture and econ. feasibility land devel. Served to lt. (j.g.) USNR, 1955-58. Home and Office: 1721 Catalina Ave Seal Beach CA 90740

ROSSI, PETER HENRY, educator; b. N.Y.C., Dec. 27, 1921; s. Peter Maxim and Elizabeth (Porcelli) R.; B.S., Coll. City N.Y., 1943; Ph.D., Columbia, 1951; m. Alice Schaerr, Sept. 29, 1951; children—Peter Eric, Kristin Alice, Nina Alexis. Research asso. Bur. Applied Social Research, Columbia, 1947- 51; asst. prof. Harvard, 1951-55; prof. dept. sociology U. Chgo., 1955-67, dir. Nat. Opinion Research Center, 1960-67; prof. dept. social relations Johns Hopkins, 1967-74, chmn. dept., 1967-70, dir. research, center for met. planning and research, 1972-74; prof. sociology, dir. Social and Demographic Research Inst., U. Mass., Amherst, 1974—. Served with AUS, 1942-45. Faculty Research grantee Social Sci. Research Council, 1959; Carnegie Sr. fellow, 1965. Fellow Am. Sociol. Assn. (sec. 1968-72, pres.-elect 1978-79, pres. 1979-80); mem. Am. Assn. Pub. Opinion Research, Am. Statis. Assn. Author: Why Families Move, 1956; The Politics of Urban Renewal, 1962; The Education of Catholic Americans, 1966; New Media and Education, 1967; Ghetto Revolts, 1970; Cities Under Siege, 1971; Evaluating Social Programs, 1972; Roots of Urban Discontent, 1974; Reforming Public Welfare, 1976; Prison Reform and State Elites, 1977; Evaluation: A Systematic Approach, 1979. Editor: Am. Jour. Sociology, 1957-58; asso. editor Am. Sociol. Rev., 1957-60, Am. Sociologist, 1964-66; editor Social Sci. Research, 1972—. Contbr. articles to profl. and popular jours. Office: Dept Sociology U Mass Amherst MA 01002

ROSSINI, FREDERICK DOMINIC, educator, chemist; b. Monongahela, Pa., July 18, 1899; s. Martino and Costanza (Carrara) R.; B.S., Carnegie Inst. Tech., 1925, M.S., 1926, D.Sc. (hon.), 1948; Ph.D., U. Calif., 1928; D.Engring Sci., Duquesne U., 1955; D.Sc., U. Notre Dame, 1959, Loyola U., Chgo., 1960, U. Portland, 1965; Litt.D., St. Francis Coll., 1962; Ph.D. honoris causa, U. Lund (Sweden), 1974; m. Anne Kathryn Landgraff, June 29, 1932; 1 son, Frederick Anthony. Phys. chemist Nat. Bur. Standards, Washington, 1928-36, chief sect. thermochemistry and hydrocarbons, 1936-50, lectr. Grad. Sch., 1934-50; Silliman prof., head dept. chemistry and dir. chem. and petroleum research lab. Carnegie Inst. Tech., Pitts., 1950-60; prof. chemistry U. Notre Dame, 1960-71; dean coll. sci., asso. dean Grad. sch., 1960-67, v.p. for research, 1967-71, emeritus, 1971—; prof. chemistry Rice U., 1971-75, emeritus, 1975—; Strosacker vis. prof. sci. Baldwin-Wallace Coll., 1973; guest lectr. numerous schs. and colls. U.S. and abroad. Mem. commn. chem. thermodynamics Internat. Union Pure and Applied Chemistry, 1934-73, chmn., 1947-61, Rossini lectr., 1975; mem. com. on phys. chemistry NRC, 1948-62, chmn. div. chemistry and chem. tech., 1955-58, exec. com. office critical tables, 1957-70, chmn., 1963-70, mem. climatic impact com., chmn. panel engines and fuels, 1974-75; cons., cooperating expert for tech. adv. com. Petroleum Industry War Council, Office Rubber Res., OSRD, Atomic Energy program during World War II; cons. NSF, 1952-62, U.S. Army Ordnance Corps, 1954-61; dir. Am. Petroleum Inst. research projects, 1935-60, Mfg. Chemists Assn. research projects, 1955-60; mem. policy advisory bd. Argonne Nat. Lab., 1958-66; mem. U.S. Dept. State cultural mission to Yugoslavia, 1966; pres. World Petroleum Congresses, 1967-75; mem. bur. Internat. Council Sci. Unions Com. Data for Sci. and Tech., 1966-72, pres., 1966-70; chmn. environ. measurements advisory com., mem. exec. com. sci. adv. bd. EPA, 1976-78; cons., 1978—. Pres. Asso. Midwest Univs., 1967-68; trustee Argonne Univ. Assos., 1966-71, v.p., 1968-71. Recipient Hillebrand prize award Chem. Soc. Washington, 1934; Gold medal, Exceptional Service award Dept. Commerce, 1950; Pitts. Jr. C. of C. award in chemistry, 1957; Pitts. award Am. Chem. Soc., 1959; Laetare medal U. Notre Dame, 1965, presdl. citation, 1971; John Price Wetherill medal Franklin Inst., 1965; William H. Nichols medal N.Y. sect. Am. Chem. Soc., 1966; Priestley medal Am. Chem. Soc., 1971; Redwood medal Inst. Petroleum, U.K., 1972; Carl Engler medal Deutsche Gesellschaft für Mineralölwissenschaft und Kohlechemie (W.Ger.), 1976; Nat. Medal Sci. (U.S.A.), 1977. Fellow Am. Inst. Chemists, AAAS (past councilor), Am. Phys. Soc.; mem. Am. Chem. Soc. (past councilor, chmn. petroleum chemistry div. 1954), Chem. Soc. Washington (pres. 1950), Am. Inst. Chem. Engrs., Am. Petroleum Inst. (U.S. nat. com. World Petroleum Congresses 1965-67, 75-79), ASTM (Marburg lectr. 1953), Faraday Soc., Washington Acad. Scis. (editor 1937-70, sec. 1940-43, pres. 1948), Philos. Soc. Washington, U.S. Calorimetry Conf. (Huffman lectr. 1956), Cath. Commn. Intellectual and Cultural Affairs (sec. 1946-47, chmn. 1958-59), Am. Soc. Engring. Edn., Am. Acad. Arts and Scis., Albertus Magnus Guild (pres. 1961-65), Nat. Acad. Scis. (chmn. sci. mission to Romania 1966, adv. com. USSR and Eastern Europe 1966-71, chmn. 1970-71, other coms.), Sigma Xi (exec. com., 1953-58, 67-71, pres. 1963-64, treas. 1971-78, v.p. 1978—), Tau Beta Pi, Phi Kappa Theta, Phi Lambda Upsilon (hon.). Roman Catholic. Club: Cosmos (Washington). Author of 11 books and 252 papers mainly in thermodynamics and thermochemistry, numerical data for sci. and tech., phys. chemistry of petroleum and hydrocarbons. Home and office: 2131 NE 58th Ct Fort Lauderdale FL 33308. *I urge my fellowmen to show trust and faith to all in our daily life and work; to promote freedom of inquiry, of travel, and of individual and business enterprise; to appreciate the fact that knowledge recognizes no geographical boundaries and that no one country has a monopoly on intelligence; to see that proper cooperation among the people of different countries, with due regard for existing equities, is essential for the advancement of man's well-being in the world; and to place quality of performance above all other characteristics—quality of product and service, in science and engineering, in business and commerce, in all levels and phases of government, and in our ordinary dealings and transactions with people.*

ROSSITER, FRANK RAYMOND, historian: b. Abington, Pa., Dec. 21, 1937; s. Frank Augustus and Dorothy Anna (Weiss) R.; A.B., Harvard U., 1959; M.S. in Edn., U. Pa., 1964; Ph.D., Princeton U., 1970. Tchr. social studies Springfield Twp. Sr. High Sch., Montgomery County, Pa., 1963-66; asst. prof. history U. Mich. at Ann Arbor, 1970-75; asso. prof. history and Am. studies U. Tex. at Dallas, 1975—. Served with USN, 1959-62. Woodrow Wilson fellow, 1966-67; Nat. Endowment for the Humanities fellow, 1973-74, 79; ASCAP-Deems Taylor award, 1976. Mem. Am. Hist. Assn., Orgn. Am. Historians, Am. Studies Assn. Democrat. Author: Charles Ives and His America, 1975. Home: 3883 Turtle Creek Blvd Apt 1704 Dallas TX 75219 Office: History Dept U Tex at Dallas Box 688 Richardson TX 75080

ROSSMANN, MICHAEL GEORGE, biochemist, educator; b. Frankfurt, Germany, July 30, 1930; s. Alexander and Nelly (Schwabacher) R.; B.Sc. with honors, Polytechnic, London, 1951, M.Sc. in Physics, 1953; Ph.D. in Chemistry, U. Glasgow, 1956; m. Audrey Pearson, July 24, 1954; children—Martin, Alice, Heather. Fulbright scholar U. Minn., 1956-58; research scientist MRC Lab. Molecular Biology, Cambridge, Eng., 1958-64; asso. prof. biol. scis. Purdue U., West Lafayette, Ind., 1964-67, prof., 1967-78, Hanley Disting. prof. biol. scis., 1978—, prof. biochemistry, 1975—. NIH grantee; NSF grantee; recipient Herbert Newby McCoy award for sci. achievement Purdue U., 1974. Mem. Am. Soc. Biol. Chemists, Am. Chem. Soc., Biophys. Soc., Am. Crystallographic Assn., Brit. Biophys. Soc., Inst. Physics, Chem. Soc. (U.K.), Am. Acad. Arts and Sci. Democrat. Club: Lafayette Sailing. Editor: The Molecular Replacement Method, 1972; editorial bd. Jour. Biol. Chemistry, 1975—; contbr. articles to profl. jours. Home: 1208 Wiley Dr West Lafayette IN 47906 Office: Dept Biol Scis Purdue Univ West Lafayette IN 47907

ROSSMILLER, GEORGE EDDIE, agrl. economist; b. Gt. Falls, Mont., June 8, 1935; s. Albert E. and Romaine (Hennford) R.; B.S., Mont. State U., 1956, M.S., 1962; Ph.D., Mich. State U., 1965; m. Betty Ann Rinio, Dec. 20, 1955; children—David W., Diane J. Research asso. Mich. State U., East Lansing, 1965-66, asst. prof., 1967-71, asso. prof., 1972-76, prof. agrl. econs., 1977—; agrl. attache to OECD, Fgn. Agrl. Service, U.S. Dept. Agr., Paris, 1978-79, Washington, 1979—. Served with U.S. Army, 1956-59. Recipient service citation Korean Ministry of Agrl. and Fisheries, 1973, Office of Prime Minister of Korea, 1977. Mem. Am. Agrl. Econs. Assn., Internat. Assn. Agrl. Economists, Korean Agrl. Econs. Assn. Presbyterian. Author: The Grain-Livestock Economy of West Germany with Projections to 1970 and 1975, 1968; (with others) Korean Agricultural Sector Analysis and Recommended Development Strategies, 1971-1985, 1972; editor: Agricultural Sector Planning: A General System Simulation Approach, 1978. Office: Fgn Agrl Service US Dept Agr Washington DC 20250

ROSSNER, JUDITH, novelist; b. N.Y.C., Mar. 31, 1935; d. Joseph George and Dorothy (Shapiro) Perelman; student City Coll. N.Y., 1952-55; m. Robert Rossner (div.); children—Jean, Daniel; m. 2d, Mordecai Persky. Author: (novels) To the Precipice, 1966; Nine Months in the Life of an Old Maid, 1969; Any Minute I Can Split, 1972; Looking for Mr. Goodbar, 1975; Attachments, 1977; Emmeline, 1980; also short stories. Address: care Julian Bach Agy 747 3d Ave New York NY 10017

ROSSON, GLENN RICHARD, ops. bldg. products and furniture co. exec.; b. Galveston, Tex., Aug. 17, 1937; s. John Raymond and Elsie Lee (Reece) R.; B.B.A., Tex. Tech U., 1959; m. Edwina Lucille Hart, June 2, 1956; children—Darrell Richard, Alex Mark. Supr., accountant Axelson div. U.S. Industries Inc., Longview, Tex., 1960-67, controller, 1968; group financial v.p. U.S. Industries Inc., Dallas, 1969, group chmn., 1969-72, v.p., 1973-74, sr. v.p., 1974, exec. v.p., 1974—, also dir. C.P.A., Tex. Mem. Am. Inst. C.P.A.'s, Tex. Soc. C.P.A.'s, Nat. Assn. Accts. (past nat. dir., past pres. E. Tex. chpt.). Club: Dallas Athletic. Home: 11367 Drummond Dr Dallas TX 75228 Office: 1000 Expressway Tower Dallas TX 75206

ROSS-ROSS, PATRICK ELCHO, steam generator mfg. exec.; b. Cornwall, Ont., Can., Jan. 31, 1930; s. Donald Ronald Decourcy and Kathleen Mary (Carson) R.-R.; B.Eng., McGill U., 1953; m. Diana Beatrice Reid, May 8, 1954: children—Patrick Ian, Beverly Kathleen, Carol Ann, Michael Andrew. Constrn. and service engr. Combustion Engring. Superheater, Ltd., Montreal, Que., 1953-55, design and test engr., 1956-61, mgr. project engring., 1963-67, chief project engr.,

1967-73, dir. operation services, 1974-76, v.p. ops., Ottawa, Ont., 1976—; sr. design engr. on loan to United Engrs. & Constructors, Phila., Shawinigan Engring. Co., 1961-62; dir. Optimum Controls-Can., Ltd. Mem. Assn. Profl. Engrs. Ont. Anglican. Clubs: Baie D'Urfe Curling; Beaconsfield Golf; Royal Ottawa Golf. Home: 151 Bay St Apt 201 Ottawa ON K1R 7T2 Canada Office: 99 Bank St Ottawa ON K1P 6C5 Canada

ROST, DUANE DELBERT, diversified mfg. and service co. exec.; b. Hartley, Iowa, Mar. 13, 1921; s. Alfred C. and Emma C. (Centner) R.; B.S. in Econs., U. Pa., 1947; postgrad. Harvard U. Bus. Sch., i945, Yale U., 1943; m. Patricia Brooks, Dec. 6, 1945; children—Wendy Rost Tibbets, Mark D., Randall J. With Chicopee Mfg. Co. div. Johnson & Johnson, Brunswick, N.J., 1947-67, v.p. fin., dir., 1964-67; exec. v.p., dir. Dresser Industries, Inc., Dallas, 1967—. Served with USCGR, 1942-44, USNR, 1944-46. Mem. Machinery and Allied Products Inst. Home: 609 Guadalajara Circle Irving TX 75062 Office: PO Box 718 Dallas TX 75221

ROSTEN, IRWIN, writer, producer, dir.; b. N.Y.C., Sept. 10, 1924. Mgr. news and pub. affairs Du Mont TV Network, N.Y.C., 1950-54; writer-producer news, pub. affairs Sta. KNXT-CBS, Los Angeles, 1954-60; dir. news, pub. affairs Sta. KTLA, Los Angeles, 1960-63; writer-producer, dir. Wolper Prodns., Inc., Los Angeles, 1963-67; chief documentary dept. MGM Studios, Culver City, Calif., 1967-72; pres., Ronox Prodns., Inc., Los Angeles, 1970—; writer-producer-dir. Nat. Geog. Soc. TV spls.: Grizzly!, The Incredible Machine, The Volga, Legacy of L.S.B. Leakey, Gold!, Mysteries of the Mind; numerous other shows including Trial by Wilderness, Hollywood: The Dream Factory, Kifaru: The Black Rhinoceros, The Wolf Men. Recipient EMMY award Acad. TV Arts, Scis., Writers Guild Am. award, also Peabody award, Christophers award, Ohio State U. award, Saturday Rev. award, CINE Golden Eagle award, also film festival citations. Mem. Writers Guild Am., Acad. TV Arts and Scis., Am. Sci. Film Assn. Office: 2217 Chelan Dr Los Angeles CA 90068

ROSTEN, LEO CALVIN (PSEUDONYM LEONARD Q. ROSS), author, polit. scientist; b. Lodz, Poland, Apr. 11, 1908; s. Samuel C. and Ida (Freundlich) R.; came to U.S., 1910; Ph.B., U. Chgo., 1930, Ph.D., 1937; postgrad. London (Eng.) Sch. Econs. and Polit. Sci., 1934; travel, study, Europe, 1928, 34, 45, 51, 53; D.H.L., U. Rochester, 1973; m. Priscilla Mead, Mar. 30, 1935 (dec.); children—Philip, Madeline, Margaret; m. 2d, Gertrude Zimmerman, Jan. 5, 1960. Instr. English, U. Chgo., 1932-34; pub. lectr., 1932-35; research asst. polit. sci. dept. U. Chgo., 1934-35; fellow Social Sci. Research Council, 1935-36; research staff Pres.'s Com. on Adminstrv. Mgmt., 1936; writer for motion pictures, 1937; dir. Motion Picture Research Project (under grant from Carnegie Corp.), 1939; Rockefeller Found. grantee for study; Hollywood, The Movie Colony, The Movie-makers, 1940; cons. expert to Nat. Def. Adv. Commn. and Office for Emergency Mgmt. (Exec. Office Pres.), 1941; chief motion pictures div. Office Facts and Figures, 1942; dep. dir. OWI, 1942-43; expert cons. Sec. of War's Office, War Dept., 1945, sent to France, Germany, Eng. on spl. mission; sr. staff Rand Corp., 1947-49; lectr. N.Y.U., Stanford, New Sch. Social Research, U. Calif. at Los Angeles, Yale, others; faculty asso. Columbia; Ford vis. prof. polit. sci. U. Calif., 1960-61; cons. Pres.'s Commn. on Nat. Goals, 1960. Recipient George Polk Meml. award, 1955; Freedom Found. award, 1955; Profl. Achievement Alumni award U. Chgo., 1969; hon. fellow London Sch. Econs. and Polit. Sci. Mem. Am. Acad. Polit. and Social Sci., Am. Polit. Sci. Assn., A.A.A.S., Authors League Am. (bd.), Authors' Guild Am., Phi Beta Kappa. Clubs: Chaos (N.Y.C.); Savile, Reform, Garrick (London). Author: The Washington Correspondents; The Education of Hyman Kaplan; The Strangest Places; Hollywood: The Movie Colony, The Movie Makers; The Dark Corner, 1945; The Return of Hyman Kaplan, 1959; Captain Newman, M.D., 1961; The Story Behind the Painting, 1961; The Many Worlds of Leo Rosten, 1964; A Most Private Intrigue, 1967; The Joys of Yiddish, 1968; A Trumpet for Reason, 1970; Rome Wasn't Burned In a Day, 1970; People I Have Loved, Known or Admired, 1970; Leo Rosten's Treasury of Jewish Quotations, 1972; Dear "Herm", 1974; The 3:10 to Anywhere, 1976; O Kaplan! My Kaplan, 1976; The Power of Positive Nonsense, 1977; Passions and Prejudice, 1978. Editor: Religions of Am., 1955, 67, 75; The Look Book, 1975; Infinite Riches: Gems from a Lifetime of Reading, 1979. Writer screenplays Walk East on Beacon, Sleep My Love, The Velvet Touch, The Dark Corner. Contbr. to nat. mags. Office: 36 Sutton Pl S New York NY 10022. *From Captain Newman, M.D.: "Most men debase the 'pursuit of happiness' by transforming it into a narcotic pursuit of 'fun'. But there are those sublimely cursed by discontent, and to them happiness comes only when they push their brains and hearts to the farthest reaches of which they are capable. Nothing is more rewarding then the effort a man makes to matter-to count, to stand for something, to have it make some difference that he lived at all."*

ROSTENKOWSKI, DAN, congressman; b. Chgo., Jan. 2, 1928; s. Joseph P. and Priscilla (Dombrowski) R.; student St. John's Mil. Acad., 1942-46, Loyola U., 1948- 51; m. LaVerne Pirkins, May 12, 1951; children—Dawn Priscilla, Kristie, Gayle, Stacy Lynn. Mem. Ho. of Reps., Ill. Gen. Assembly, 1952, Senate, 1954, 56; mem. 87th-96th congresses from 8th Dist. Ill., chmn. Democratic caucus 90th-91st Congresses, chief dep. majority whip 95th-96th Congresses. Del., Dem. Nat. Convs., 1960, 64, 68, 72, 76. Served with 7th Inf. Div., AUS, 1946-48. Mem. YMCA, VFW. Democrat. K.C. Club: Ill. Athletic. Home: 1372 W Evergreen St Chicago IL 60622 Office: House Office Bldg Washington DC 20515

ROSTKER, BERNARD DANIEL, dir. Selective Service System; b. N.Y.C., Feb. 1, 1944; B.S. in Edn. and Econs., N.Y. U., 1964; M.S. in Econs., Syracuse U., 1966, Ph.D. in Econs., 1970. Economist, Office Sec., Dept. Def., 1968-70; economist Rand Corp., 1970-73, dir. manpower, personnel and tng. programs, 1972-77, sr. economist, 1973-77; dep. asst. sec. for manpower and res. affairs Dept. Navy, 1977-79; dir. SSS, Washington, 1979—. Served with U.S. Army, 1968-70. Office: Selective Service System 600 E St Washington DC 20435*

ROSTKY, GEORGE HAROLD, editor; b. N.Y.C., Feb. 28, 1926; s. Morris and Mary (Wyloge) R.; B.E.E., City Coll. N.Y., 1957; m. Rhoda Thelma Bornstein, June 29, 1950; children—Mark, Lisa. Asso. editor Electronic Design, N.Y.C., 1957-61, editor-in-chief, Rochelle Park, N.J., 1971-78; editorial dir./asso. pub. Electronic Engring. Times, Manhasset, N.Y., 1978—; securities analyst McDonnell & Co., N.Y.C., 1961-62; editorial dir. Mactier Pub. Co., N.Y.C., 1962-71. Served with AUS, 1942-45. Recipient Indsl. Mktg. award for editorial excellence, 1964, Neal awards, 1967, 74, 75, 77. Home: 39 Cumberland Ave Great Neck NY 11020 Office: 333 East Shore Rd Manhasset NY 11030

ROSTOKER, WILLIAM, educator; b. Hamilton, Ont., Can., June 21, 1924; s. Louis and Fanny (Silbert) R.; B.A.Sc., U. Toronto (Ont.), 1945, M.A.Sc., 1946; Ph.D., Lehigh U., 1948; m. Fay M. Tippett, Apr. 2, 1949; children—Gareth, Alan, Glyn, Wendy. Lectr., U. Birmingham (Eng.), 1948-50; asst. prof. metallurgy Ill. Inst. Tech., 1950-51, supervising research metallurgist, 1951-59, sr. sci. adviser Research Inst., 1960-65; prof. metallurgy and bioengring. U. Ill., Chgo. Circle, 1965—, acting dean Grad. Coll., 1968-70. Dir. Automatic Screw Machine Products, Chgo., 1966-71; cons. in field. Recipient Kappa Delta Orthopedic Research award, 1970. Fellow Am. Soc. Metals. Author: The Metallurgy of Vanadium, Embrittlement by Liquid Metals, Interpretation of Metallographic Structures. Contbr. articles to profl. jours. Patentee in field. Home: 2052 W 108th Pl Chicago IL 60643

ROSTOW, ELSPETH DAVIES, coll. dean; b. N.Y.C.; d. Milton Judson and Harriet Elspeth (Vaughan) Davies; A.B., Barnard Coll., 1938; A.M., Radcliffe Coll., 1939; M.A., Cambridge (Eng.) U., 1949; L.H.D. (hon.), Lebanon Valley Coll.; m. Walt Whitman Rostow, June 26, 1947; children—Peter Vaughan, Ann Larner. Lectr. Am. studies Barnard Coll., 1939-41, instr. govt., dir. Am. studies, 1941-43, instr. govt., 1945-47; mem. social sci. faculty Sarah Lawrence Coll., 1945-47; tchr. Salzburg (Austria) Seminar, 1947; supr. in history, Univ. lectr. Cambridge U., 1949-50, 58-59; research asso. dept. econs. and social sci. M.I.T., 1950-52, asst. prof. history, 1952-65, on leave, 1961-65; asso. prof. history Am. U., 1961-69; lectr. grad. history faculty Georgetown U., 1961-62, faculty asso. Fgn. Service Inst., 1967-69; asso. prof. govt. U. Tex., Austin, 1969-76, prof., 1976—, acting dir. Am. studies, 1970-71, chmn. comparative studies, 1972-74, acting dean div. gen. and comparative studies, 1974-75, dean div., 1975-77, dean Lyndon B. Johnson Sch. Public Affairs, 1977—; mem. Pres.'s Adv. Com. for Trade Negotiations, 1978—; mem. Pres.'s Commn. for a Nat. Agenda for the Eighties, 1979—; research asso. OSS, Washington, 1943-45; Geneva corr. London Economist, 1947-49; lectr. Air War Coll., 1963-79, Army War Coll., 1965, 68, 69, 78, 79, Nat. War Coll., 1962, 68, 74, 75, Indsl. Coll. Armed Forces, 1961-65, Naval War Coll., 1971, Fgn. Service Inst., 1974-77, Dept. State, Europe, 1973. Trustee, chmn. nominating com. Sarah Lawrence Coll., 1952-59; bd. dirs., trustee Overseas Edn. Fund, 1961-74; bd. dirs. Barnard Coll., 1962-66, Tex. Arts Alliance, 1976—, London Baines Johnson Found., 1977—; trustee nat. com. The Coll. Bd., 1978—. Recipient award Air U.; Woman of Accomplishment award Harper's Bazaar, 1967; Outstanding Woman award Women in Communications, Austin, 1973. Mem. Nat. Acad. Public Adminstrn., Tex. Philos. Soc., Nat. Assn. Schs. Public Affairs and Adminstrn. (dir. exec. council 1978—), Phi Beta Kappa, Phi Nu Epsilon, Mortar Bd. (hon.), Omicron Delta Kappa. Club: Headliners (Austin). Author: Europe's Economy After the War, 1948; (with others) America Now, 1968; The Coattailless Landslide, 1974; contbr. articles, revs., poems to scholarly jours., newspapers, mags. Home: One Wild Wind Point Austin TX 78746 Office: Drawer Y University Station Austin TX 78712

ROSTOW, EUGENE VICTOR, educator, lawyer, economist; b. Bklyn., Aug. 25, 1913; s. Victor A. and Lillian (Helman) R.; A.B., Yale, 1933, LL.B., 1937, A.M., 1944; postgrad. King's Coll., Cambridge (Eng.) U., 1933-34; M.A., Cambridge U., 1959, LL.D., 1962; LL.D., Boston U., 1976; m. Edna Berman Greenberg; children—Victor A. D., Jessica (Mrs. Dana N. Stevens), Charles Nicholas. Admitted to N.Y. bar, 1938; practice in N.Y.C., 1937-38; mem. faculty Law Sch., Yale, 1938—, prof. law, 1944—, dean, 1955-65, Sterling prof. law and pub. affairs, 1964—, master Trumbull Coll., 1966; under-sec. state for polit. affairs, 1966-69; pres. Atlantic Treaty Assn., 1973-76; vis. prof. U. Chgo., 1941; Pitt prof. Am. history and instns., professorial fellow King's Coll., Cambridge U., 1959-60; William W. Cook lectr. Mich. U., 1958; John R. Coen lectr. U. Colo., 1961; Leary lectr. U. Utah, 1965; Brandeis lectr. Brandeis U., 1965; Rosenthal lectr. Northwestern U., 1965; George Eastman vis. prof., fellow Balliol Coll., Oxford (Eng.) U., 1970-71. Adviser, Dept. State, 1942-44; asst. exec. sec. Econ. Commn. for Europe, UN, 1949-50; mem. Jud. Council of Conn., 1955-66; mem. Atty. Gen.'s Nat. Com. Study Antitrust Laws, 1954-55; mem. adv. council Peace Corps, 1961; cons. undersec. state, 1961-66; chmn. exec. com. Com. on the Present Danger, 1976—. Guggenheim fellow, 1959-60. Decorated chevalier Legion d'Honneur (France) 1960; grand cross Order of Crown (Belgium), 1969. Fellow Am. Acad. Arts and Scis.; mem. Am. Law Inst., Am. Arbitration Assn. (bd.), Am. Planning Assn. (dir.), Phi Beta Kappa, Alpha Delta Phi. Democrat. Jewish religion. Clubs: Elizabethan (Yale); Lawn, Century Assn. (N.Y.C.). Author: Planning for Freedom, 1959; The Sovereign Prerogative, 1962; Law, Power and the Pursuit of Peace, 1968; Peace in the Balance, 1972; The Ideal in Law, 1978. Editor: Is Law Dead?, 1971. Home: 208 S Ronan St New Haven CT 06511 also Peru VT 05152

ROSTOW, WALT WHITMAN, economist, educator; b. N.Y.C., Oct. 7, 1916; s. Victor Aaron and Lillian (Helman) R.; B.A., Yale U., 1936, Ph.D., 1940; Rhodes scholar, Balliol Coll., 1936-38; m. Elspeth Vaughan Davies, June 26, 1947; children—Peter Vaughan, Ann Larner. Instr. econs. Columbia U., 1940-41; asst. chief German-Austrian econ. div. Dept. State, 1945-46; Harmsworth prof. Am. history Oxford (Eng.) U., 1946-47; asst. to exec. sec. Econ. Commn. for Europe, 1947-49; Pitt. prof. Am. history Cambridge (Eng.) U., 1949-50; prof. econ. history Mass. Inst. Tech., 1950-60, staff mem. Center Internat. Studies, 1951-60; dep. spl. asst. to Pres. for nat. security affairs, 1961; counselor, chmn. policy planning council Dept. State, 1961-66; spl. asst. to Pres., 1966-69; U.S. rep., ambassador Inter-Am. com. Alliance for Progress, 1964-66; now prof. econs. and history U. Tex, Austin. Mem. Bd. Fgn. Scholarships, 1969-72. Served as maj. OSS, AUS, 1942-45. Decorated Legion of Merit, Hon. Order Brit. Empire (mil.); recipient Presdl. Medal of Freedom with distinction. Clubs: Cosmos (Washington); Elizabethan (New Haven). Author: The American Diplomatic Revolution, 1947; Essays on the British Economy of the Nineteenth Century, 1948; The Process of Economic Growth, 1953, 2d edit., 1960; (with A. D. Gayer, A.J. Schwartz) The Growth and Fluctuation of the British Economy, 1790-1850, 1953, 2d edit., 1975; (with A. Levin, others) The Dynamics of Soviet Society, 1953; (with others) The Prospects for Communist China, 1954; (with R.W. Hatch) An American Policy in Asia, 1955; (with M.F. Millikan) A Proposal: Key to an Effective Foreign Policy, 1957; The United States in the World Arena, 1960; The Stages of Economic Growth, 2d edit., 1971; View from the Seventh Floor, 1964; A Design for Asian Development, 1965; (with William E. Griffith) East-West Relations: Is Detente Possible?, 1969; Politics and the Stages of Growth, 1971; The Diffusion of Power, 1972; How It All Began, 1975; The World Economy: History and Prospect, 1978; Getting From Here to There, 1978. Editor: The Economics of Take-Off Into Sustained Growth, 1963. Home: 1 Wildwind Point Austin TX 78746

ROSTRON, ROBERT ZELDON, corp. exec.; b. Salt Lake City, July 9, 1929; s. Zeldon John and Catherine (Silotti) R.; B.S., U. Utah, 1950; m. Judith Talbot, Aug. 8, 1967; children—Robert Dell, Douglas John, Jerry Scott, Nancy Lynn, Julie Ann, David Wayne, Glenn Hayden, Sean Talbot. Staff acct. Goddard Sunnival & Griffin, Salt Lake City, 1950-51; with Haskins & Sells, 1953-69, prin., Honolulu, 1965-69; with Amfac, Inc., Honolulu, 1969—, sr. v.p. devel. and planning, 1978, exec. v.p., 1978—. Served with U.S. Army, 1951-53. Mem. Hawaii Soc. C.P.A.'s (dir.), Nat. Assn. Accts., Tax Found. Hawaii (dir.). Clubs: Outrigger Canoe, Pacific. Office: 700 Bishop St Honolulu HI 96813*

ROSTROPOVICH, MSTISLAV, musician; b. Baku, USSR, Mar. 27, 1927; ed. Moscow Conservatory; numerous hon. doctorate degrees; s. Leopold and Sofia (Fedotova) R.; m. Galina Vishnevskaya; children—Olga, Yelena. Debut as violoncellist, 1935; performer world concert tours Moscow Philharmonic Orch.; became faculty mem. Moscow Conservatory, 1953, became prof., 1960, also head cello and double-bass dept.; formerly prof. Leningrad Conservatory; now music dir. Nat. Symphony Orch., Washington. Recipient honors, prizes and awards from numerous countries including Stalin prize, 1951, 53, Lenin prize, 1964. Hon. mem. Brit. Royal Acad. Music. Address: care Nat Symphony Orch John F Kennedy Center Performing Arts Washington DC 20566

ROSTVOLD, GERHARD NORMAN, economist; b. Nashwauk, Minn., Oct. 15, 1919; s. Arndt and Olive Mathilda (Ness) R.; A.B. in Econs.-Accountancy with great distinction, Stanford, 1948, M.A. in Econs., 1949, Ph.D. in Econs., 1955; m. Virginia Fay Faubion, Feb. 3, 1945; children—Roger Mark, Laura Ann, Christine Marie, Ellen Alicia. Instr., Stanford U., 1949-51; price economist OPS, 1951-52; mem. faculty Pomona Coll., 1952-66, Stedman-Sumner prof., 1961-66; with Urbanomics Research Assos., Claremont, 1966—; econs. commentator Sta. KHJ-TV, Los Angeles; econ. cons. to govt., industry. Trustee Sutro Mortgage Investment Trust. Chmn. nat. advisory bd. Council Pub. Lands, also mem. Calif. advisory bd.; mem. Calif. Council Econ. Edn. Served with USAAF, 1942-45. Recipient Wig Distinguished Prof. award Pomona Coll., 1962; Conservation award Dept. Interior, 1975. Mem. Am., Western (pres. 1966-67) econ. assns., Nat. Tax Assn. (pres.), Lambda Alpha. Author: The Southern California Metropolis—1980, 1960; Financing California Government, 1967; The Economics of Energy, 1975; Economics and the Environment, 1975; The Economics of the Public Utility Enterprise, 1976; Understanding How the Economic System Works, 1976; Teacher's Instructional Program for Understanding How the Economic System Works, 1976; Charting Your Path to Economic and Financial Survival in the 1980's, 1979; co-author California Local Finance, 1960; Garcia-Rostvold Work Experience Education Series, 1974; social sci. editor Stone/Leswing Social Sci. Series. Contbr. articles to profl jours. Home: 19712 Oceanaire Huntington Beach CA 92649 Office: PO Box 188 Corona Del Mar CA 92625. *If you have a difficult question or problem, bring it to me. As a professional economist, I will bring objective facts and analysis to bear upon your question or problem, and recommend alternative courses of action. . . . But, never bring me a predetermined answer to be supported by facts and analysis. Scientific objectivity demands that the analyst, from whatever field of knowledge, choose the facts and the analytical framework which translate into a truth, not a preconceived bias.*

ROSZAK, THEODORE, author, editor, educator; b. 1933. Prof. history Calif. State U. at Hayward. Author: Making of a Counter-Culture, 1969; Where the Wasteland Ends: Politics and Transcendence in Post-Industrial Society, 1972; Pontifex: A Revolutionary Entertainment for the Mind's Eye Theater, 1974; Unfinished Animal, 1975; Person/Planet, 1978. Editor: The Dissenting Academy, 1968; (with Betty Roszak) Masculine/Feminine: Readings in Sexual Mythology and the Liberation of Women, 1970; Sources: An Anthology of Contemporary Materials Useful for Preserving Personal Sanity While Braving the Great Technological Wilderness, 1972. Guggenheim fellow, 1971-72. Address: California State Univ Hayward CA 94542

ROSZAK, THEODORE, sculptor; b. Posen, Poland, May 1, 1907; s. Kasper and Praxeda (Swierczynska) R.; came to U.S., 1909, naturalized, 1921; student Art Inst. Chgo., 1922-25, 26-29, N.A.D., N.Y.C., 1925-26, Columbia, 1925-26; m. Florence Sapir, Oct. 24, 1931; 1 dau., Sara Jane. Faculty, Art Inst. Chgo., 1927-29, Sarah Lawrence Coll., Bronxville, N.Y., 1941-56, Columbia, 1970-73; one man exhbn. Venice Bienalle, Italy, 1960, Pierre Matisse Gallery, 1961, Whitney Mus., 1932-66, Century Assn., N.Y.C., 1971, Harold Ernest Galleries, Boston, 1972, Pierre Matisse Gallery, N.Y.C., 1974, Arts Club Chgo., 1975, Fairweather Hardin, Chgo., 1975—; exhibited maj. museums in U.S., Darmstadt and Kassel (Germany), Vienna, Madrid, Paris, London, Antwerp, Brussels, Stockholm, Milan, Zurich, Whitney Mus. Am. Art, 1929-56, World's Fair in Brussels, 1958, retrospective exhbn., N.Y.C., Walker Art Center, Mpls.; permanent collections Whitney Mus. Art, Mus. Modern Art, Norton Mus. Art, Fla., Mus. Modern Art, Saõ Paulo, Brazil, U. Ill., Urbana, U. Ariz., Iowa State U., Tate Gallery, Yale U. Art Gallery, John Barnes Found., N.Y.C., Cleve. Mus. Fine Arts, Solomon Guggenheim Mus., N.Y.C., Art Inst. Chgo., others. Mem. adv. bd. cultural presentations program State Dept., 1960-66; commr. fine arts N.Y.C., 1964-70; mem. Pres.' Fine Arts Commn., 1963-67. Recipient silver medal Posen Expn., 1930; Eisendrath award, 1934, Frank G. Logan medal and award Art Inst. Chgo., 1947-51; purchase award Mus. Modern Art, Saõ Paulo, Brazil, 1951, U. Ill., 1953; George E. Widener Gold medal Pa. Acad. Fine Arts, 1956; Ford Found. study grantee, 1959. Fellow Nat. Inst. Arts and Letters. Office: 1 St Lukes Pl New York NY 10014*

ROSZKOWSKI, STANLEY JULIAN, judge; b. Booneville, N.Y., Jan. 27, 1923; s. Joseph and Anna (Christkowski) R.; B.S., U. Ill., 1949, LL.D., 1954; m. Catherine Mary Claeys, June 19, 1948; children—Mark, Gregory, Dan, John. Sales mgr. Warren Petroleum Co., Rockford, Ill., 1954; admitted to Ill. bar, 1954; mem. firm Roszkowski, Paddock, McGreevy & Johnson, Rockford, from 1955; now dist. judge U.S. Dist. Ct., Chgo.; pres. First State Bank, Rockford, 1963-75, chmn. bd., 1975—. Chmn., Fire and Police Commn., Rockford, 1967-74, commr., 1974—; chmn. Paul Simon Com., 1972, Adlai Stevenson III campaign, 1968-71, Winnebago County Citizens for John F. Kennedy, 1962, Winnebago County Democratic Central Com., 1962-64; bd. dirs. Sch. of Hope, 1960—; mem. Ill. Capital Devel. Bd., 1974—. Served with USAAF, 1943-45. Decorated Air medal with 2 oak leaf clusters. Mem. Am., Ill., Fla., Winnebago County bar assns., Am. Coll. Trial Lawyers, Am. Judicature Soc., Am., Ill. trial lawyers assns., Am. Arbitration Assn. (arbitrator). Club: Forest Hills Country (Rockford). Home: 2435 Cerro Vista Dr Rockford IL 61111 Office: US Courthouse 219 S Dearborn St Chicago IL 60604

ROTA, GIAN CARLO, educator, mathematician; b. Vigevano, Italy, Apr. 27, 1932; s. Giovanni and Gina (Facoetti) R.; came to U.S., 1950; naturalized, 1961; B.A. summa cum laude, Princeton, 1953; M.A., Yale, 1954, Ph.D., 1956; m. Teresa Rondón-Tarchetti, June 23, 1956. Vis. fellow Courant Inst. Math. Scis., N.Y.U., 1956-57; B. Pierce instr. Harvard, 1957-59; asst. prof., then asso. prof. math. M.I.T., 1959-65, prof. math., 1967-74, prof. applied math. and philosophy, 1975—; prof. math. Rockefeller U., 1965-67; vis. prof. U. Calif. at Berkeley, 1961, Courant Inst. Math. Scis., 1964, U. Ill., 1965, Ind. U., 1964, U. Paris, 1972, U. Mex., 1973, Scuola Normale Superiore, 1975, U. Buenos Aires, 1975, U. Strasbourg, 1976, 78; Taft lectr. U. Cin., 1971; spl. vis. prof. U. Colo., 1969—; Andre' Aisenstadt vis. prof. U. Montreal, 1971; Hardy lectr. London Math. Soc., 1973; professore linceo, Rome, 1979; cons. Rand Corp., 1965-71; Sigma Xi nat. lectr., 1980-81; fellow Los Alamos Sci. Lab., 1966—; cons. Brookhaven Nat. Lab., 1969-71. Sloan fellow, 1962-64. Fellow Am. Acad. Arts and Scis., Academia Argentina de Ciencias, Inst. Math. Statistics, AAAS; mem. Am. Math. Assn. (Hedrick lectr. 1967); mem. Am. (council 1967-72), London math. socs., Heidegger Circle, Soc. Indsl. and Applied Math. (v.p. 1975), Am. Philos. Assn., Soc. Phenomenology and Existential Philosophy, AAUP, Unione Mathematica Italiana, Phi Beta Kappa (pres. chpt. 1978—). Roman Catholic. Author: (with G. Birkhoff) Ordinary Differential Equation, 1962; (with H. Crapo) Combinational Geometries, 1970; Finite Operator Calculus, 1975;

MAA Survey in Combinatorics, 1971; also articles combinatorial theory, differential equations, probability, philosophy. Editor Jour. Combinatorial Theory, 1966—, Jour. Math. and Mechanics, 1965-71, Jour. Math. Analysis, 1966—, Utilitas Mathematica, 1973—, Math. Assn. Am. Studies in Combinations, 1978; asso. editor Am. Math. Monthly, 1966-73, Procs. Royal Soc. Edinburgh, 1976—; editor in chief Advances in Mathematics, 1967—, Advances in Applied Math., 1980—; editor Bull. Am. Math. Soc., 1967-73, Ency. of Math., 1974—. Address: 2-351 Mass Inst Tech Cambridge MA 02139

ROTBERG, ROBERT IRWIN, historian, polit. scientist, editor; b. Newark, Apr. 11, 1935; s. Louis and Mildred S. R.; A.B., Oberlin Coll., 1955; M.P.A., Princeton U. 1957; D.Phil. (Rhodes scholar), U. Oxford, 1960; m. Joanna H. Henshaw, June 17, 1961; children—Rebecca T.H., Nicola S.D., Fiona J.Y. Asst. prof. history, research asso. Center for Internat. Affairs, Harvard U., 1961-68; research dir. Twentieth Century Fund, 1968-71; prof. polit. sci. and history M.I.T., 1968—; research asso. Boston U. African Studies Program, 1976—; cons. Dept. State, 1968—, Commrs. of Middlesex County, Mass., 1976-77. Vice pres. Cambridge Civic Assn., 1969-72; chmn. Middlesex County Govtl. Rev. Task Force, 1972; pres. Citizens Com. for Lexington (Mass.) Pub. Schs., 1979; mem. Lexington Sch. Com., 1974-77, Lexington Town Meeting, 1973—. Guggenheim fellow, 1970-71, Hazen Found. fellow, 1976-77. Fellow Royal Geog. Soc.; mem. Am. Hist. Assn. (chmn. nominating com. 1978), African Studies Assn., Social Sci. History Assn. (chmn. local com. 1979), Council on Fgn. Relations. Author: A Political History of Tropical Africa, 1965; The Rise of Nationalism in Central Africa, 1965; Protest and Power in Black Africa, 1970; Joseph Thomson and the Exploration of Africa, 1971; Haiti: The Politics of Squalor, 1971; Africa and Its Explorers, 1971; The Black Homelands of South Africa, 1977; Black Heart: Gore-Browne and the Politics of Multiracial Zambia, 1978; Suffer the Future: Policy Choices in Southern Africa, 1980. Editor: Jour. of Interdisciplinary History, 1970—. Office: Dept Polit Sci 14N-323 Mass Inst Tech Cambridge MA 02139

ROTENBERG, SHELDON, violinist; b. Attleboro, Mass., Apr. 11, 1917; s. Joseph and Jennie (Almer) R.; A.B., Tufts U., 1939, grad. student, 1939-40; violin pupil of Felix Winternitz, Georges Enesco, Maurice Hewitt; m. Hilde Sussmann, Jan. 29, 1950; children—David, Steffi. Violinist, Boston String Quartet, 1948-52; mem. 1st violin sect. Boston Symphony Orch., 1948—; solo performances with Boston Pops Orch., 1939-41; tchr. violin, 1947—; Boston Symphony rep. as soloist, tchr., mem. orch. in State Dept. cultural exchange program with Japan Philharmonic, Tokyo, 1968-69; music adviser, cons. pub. schs., Brookline, Mass. Served to capt. AUS, 1942-46. Mem. Tufts U. Alumni Assn. Home: 60 Browne St Brookline MA 02146 Office: care Boston Symphony Orch Symphony Hall Boston MA 02115

ROTH, ARIEL ADRIAN, educator; b. Geneva, Switzerland, July 16, 1927; s. André Gustave and Hazel Julia (Worden) R.; came to U.S., 1942, naturalized, 1956; B.A., Pacific Union Coll., 1948; M.S., U. Mich., 1949, Ph.D., 1955; postgrad., U. Calif., Berkeley, part time 1956, U. Calif., Riverside, part time 1963-64, 1966-69; m. Lenore Alfreda Hardt, Sept. 1, 1952: children—Lawrence Lionel, John Carleton. Instr. to asso. prof. biology Pacific Union Coll., 1950-57; research asso. Loma Linda U. (Calif.), 1957-58, prof., chmn. dept. biology, 1963-71, acting chmn. Geosci. Research Inst., 1971-73; prof., chmn. dept. biology Andrews U., Berrien Springs, Mich., 1958-63. Vis. prof. Andrews U. Extension, Collonges-sous-Saleve, France. USPHS grantee, 1956-58; AEC, NSF grants as mem. Symbios Research Team to Eniwetok; Nat. Oceanic and Atmospheric Adminstrn. grantee as dir. Loma Linda U. team to Hydro Lab., Bahamas. Mem. A.A.A.S., Western Soc. Naturalists, Geol. Soc. Am., Soc. Econ. Paleontologists and Mineralogists, Am. Assn. Petroleum Geologists, Sigma Xi. Seventh-day Adventist (elder 1961-63, 71-74). Editor, Origins jour., 1973—. Home: 8976 Pigeon Pass Rd Sunnymead CA 92388

ROTH, DANIEL BENJAMIN, lawyer; b. Youngstown, Ohio, Sept. 17, 1929; s. Benjamin F. and Marion (Benjamin) R.; B.S. in Finance, Miami U., Oxford, Ohio, 1951; J.D., Case-Western Res. U., 1956; m. Joann M. Roth; children—William M., Jennifer A. Admitted to Ohio bar, 1956, since practiced in Youngstown; mem. firm Roth, Stephens & Blair, 1969—. Sec., gen. counsel, dir. Nat. Data Processing Corp., Cin., 1961-69; vice chmn., gen. counsel, dir. Toro Enterprises, Inc., Youngstown, 1971—; dir. Mahoning Nat. Bank Youngstown. Profl. singer, appearances including Steve Allen Show, 1952. Liaison officer U.S. Air Force Acad. Bd. dirs. Youngstown Playhouse, Youngstown Speech and Hearing Center, McGuffey Center, Youngstown. Served to 1st lt. USAF, 1951-53; lt. col. Res. Named most outstanding undergrad. mem. Zeta Beta Tau in U.S., 1951. Mem. Am., Ohio, Mahoning County, Lawyer-Pilots bar assns., Youngstown Jr. C. of C. (bd. dirs., 1st v.p. 1958-63), Zeta Beta Tau (nat. v.p. 1964-66), Omicron Delta Kappa, Phi Eta Sigma, Tau Epsilon Rho. Jewish (bd. dirs. temple). Clubs: Youngstown; Squaw Creek Country. Home: 1108 Ravine Dr Youngstown OH 44505 Office: Union Nat Bank Bldg Youngstown OH 44503

ROTH, DAVID JAMES, bus. exec.; b. N.Y.C., Dec. 2, 1941; s. Chester H. and Janet H. (Falk) R.; student Brandeis U., Elon Coll.; m. Mari E. Fletcher, Aug. 16, 1972; children—Naniscah Fletcher, Jennifer. With Kayser-Roth Corp., N.Y.C., 1963—, v.p., dir., 1968—, chmn. finance com., 1972—, vice-chmn. bd., 1973—; dir. Found. Fin. Corp., Found. Life Ins. Co. Am.; pres., dir. Harrison Factors Corp.; chmn. bd. Hammacher Schlemmer; pres., dir. Slipasox, Inc., Lewis & Conger; pres., sec. R.O.S. Corp; founder Wave Energy Systems, Inc. Bd. dirs., pres. Gustave and Sarah Roth Found., United Cerebral Palsy Research and Edn. Found.; trustee, pres. Chester H. and Janet Roth Found. Served with AUS, 1964. Clubs: City Athletic; Old Oaks Country (Purchase, N.Y.). Home: 860 United Nations Plaza New York NY 10017 Office: 640 Fifth Ave New York NY 10019

ROTH, EDWARD STANFORD, mfg. engr.; b. Llanerch, Pa., July 31, 1922; s. Clinton Mende and Edith Louise (Stanford) R.; B.A., Pa. State U., 1947; postgrad. U. Colo., 1949, U. N.Mex., 1956; m. Patricia Ann Heflin, Nov. 18, 1950; children—Vicki Lynn, Douglas Henry. Electromech. design standards Sandia Labs., Albuquerque, 1951-58, indsl. engr., 1958-65, mfg. cons., 1961-65, project leader process devel., 1965-70, project leader exploratory systems, 1970-79; pres. Productivity Services, 1979—; tchr., lectr. U. N.Mex., 1963-66; indsl. cons. Served with AUS, 1943-46. Recipient gold medal Am. Soc. Tool and Mfg. Engrs., 1966, Archimedes Engring. award Calif. Soc. Profl. Engrs., 1977. Registered profl. engr., Calif. Mem. Soc. Mfg. Engrs. (dir. 1969—, nat. sec. 1971-72, treas. 1972-73, v.p. 1973-75, now pres.), Nat. Soc. Profl. Engrs. (chmn. continuing profl. devel. com.), Am. Inst. Indsl. Engrs. Author: Functional Gaging, 1970; Functional Inspection Techniques, 1967. Major contbr. Fundamentals of Tool Design, 1962, Tool and Manufacturers Handbook, 1977. Book and standards reviewer Jour. Quality Technology, 1969. Contbr. articles to profl. publs. Home: 7950 Coors Blvd SW Albuquerque NM 87105 Office: 7950 Coors Blvd SW Albuquerque NM 87105

ROTH, EDWIN MORTON PARKIN, service co. exec.; b. Cleve., Oct. 15, 1927; s. Bernath and Lottie (Klafter) R.; student Ohio State U., 1946-47; B.B.A., Case Western Res. U., 1949; m. DeMaris Reider, May 29, 1949; children—Lacey Jan Roth Cohen, Alden Hope Guren, Corey Bruce, Cullen Andrew. With Weather-Proof Co., Cleve., 1949-50; pres. E.M. Roth & Assos., Cleve., 1950-52; sales mgr. Garland Co., Cleve., 1952-54, PlastiKote, Inc., Cleve., 1954-56; v.p. ITT Consumer Services, Cleve., 1967-75; pres., dir. ITT Service Industries, Cleve., 1970-75, Yellow Cab Co., Kansas City, Mo., 1968-75; v.p., dir. Abbey Casualty Ins. Co., Washington, 1968-75; pres., dir., chief exec. officer APCOA, Inc., 1975—; dir. Tri-american Corp. Mem. del. assembly Jewish Fedn. Cleve.; mem. governing council Am. Jewish Congress; mem. nat. council Joint Distbn. Com.; trustee Cleve. Am. Jewish Com.; chmn. bd. dirs. Mt. Sinai Hosp., Cleve., 1979—; bd. dirs. Menorah Park Home for Aged, Cleve. Hebrew Schs., Inst. Jewish Policy Planning and Research, No. Ohio council Camp Fire Girls; trustee No. Ohio Respiratory Disease Assn.; trustee, exec. com. Jewish Community Fedn.; bd. dirs. Bellefaire Children's Home, pres., 1975-78. Served with USNR, 1945-46. Mem. Am. Assn. Jewish Edn. (dir.), Nat. Parking Assn. (pres. 1976-78, chmn. 1978—), Musical Arts Assn. Cleve., No. Ohio Tennis Assn. Jewish (trustee, v.p. synagogue). Clubs: Commerce, Clevelander, Oakwood Country. Home: 18200 S Park Blvd Shaker Heights OH 44120 Office: 1919 E 13th St Cleveland OH 44114

ROTH, FREDERIC HULL, accountant; b. Cleve., Feb. 20, 1914; s. Stanley Edward and Myrtle (Hull) R.; A.B., Wooster (Ohio) Coll., 1935; M.B.A., Harvard, 1937; m. Emmy Alice Braun, Aug. 17, 1936; children—Frederic Hull, Robert Allan (dec.). With Scovell Wellington & Co., Cleve., 1938-62, sr. supr., 1952-62; partner Coopers & Lybrand Internat. (formerly Lybrand, Ross Bros. & Montgomery), Cleve., 1962—; dir. Magnetics Internat., Inc. Bd. dirs., treas. Cleve. Playhouse, 1964-66, dir., 1967-76; mem. nat. adv. bd. Am. Security Council; trustee Rocky River Library Found. C.P.A., Ohio, La., Va., N.C. Mem. Ohio Soc. C.P.A.'s (pres. Cleve. chpt. 1960-61, state pres. elect 1966-67, pres. 1967-68), Am. Inst. C.P.A.'s (council 1966-70, gov. Cleve. chpt.), Nat. Assn. Accountants, Inst. Internal Auditors, AIM, Tax Club Cleve., Internat. Platform Assn., Cleve. C. of C., Newcomen Soc. N.Am., Western Res. Hist. Soc., Ohio Hist. Soc., Great Lakes Hist. Soc., Early Settlers Assn., Nat. Trust Hist. Preservation, Internat. Soc. Brit. Genealogy and Family History, Order of Founders and Patriots Am., SAR, Mil. Order of Stars and Bars, Sons of Confederate Vets., Sons of Union Vets. of Civil War. Mason (Shriner), Rotarian (bd. dirs. treas. Cleve. club 1966-67), Order of Blue Gavel (dist. treas. 1973-74, chpt. pres. 1973, dist. pres. 1975, eastern v.p. 1976). Republican. Methodist. Clubs: City, Harvard, Univ., Midday, Yacht (treas. 1952-65, fleet capt. 1966, rear commodore 1967, vice commodore 1968, commodore 1969) (Cleve.); Westwood Country (Rocky River); Catawba Island, Union of Clevland, Beaver Creek Hunt. Home: 20661 Avalon Dr Rocky River OH 44116 Office: Union Commerce Bldg Cleveland OH 44115

ROTH, GEORGE LEITH, JR., educator; b. Somerset, Pa., Jan. 5, 1925; s. George Leith and Stella (Ruth) R.; A.B., Franklin and Marshall Coll., 1944; M.A., Princeton, 1946, Ph.D., 1949; m. Ruth Audrey Brooks, Aug. 16, 1952; children—Katherine, Jane. Instr. English, U. Va., 1947-51; faculty English, Va. Mil. Inst., Lexington, 1951—, prof., 1962—, head dept., 1968—. Organist, choirmaster R.E. Lee Meml. Ch., Lexington, 1961—. Mem. Modern Lang. Assn. Am., Nat. Council Tchrs. English, Phi Beta Kappa. Episcopalian. Contbr. American Theory of Satire, 1790-1820, American Literature, vol. XXIX, no. 4, 1958. Home: 108 McDowell St Lexington VA 24450

ROTH, HAROLD LEONARD, publishing co. exec.; b. N.Y.C., Nov. 1, 1919; s. Samuel and Sadie (Wolfe) R.; B.Social Sci., Coll. City N.Y., 1939; M.S.W. (Keith Fund fellow), U. Pa., 1941; m. Marjorie Doris Englander, June 22, 1941; children—Joan (Mrs. Robert Saffa), Richard Lawrence, Peter Alan. Vice pres., dir. Simon and Schuster, Inc., also Pocket Books, N.Y.C., 1950-66; pres., chief exec. officer, dir. Grosset and Dunlap, Inc., N.Y.C., 1966—; chmn. bd. Ace Books, 1977—; dir. Filmways, Inc., 1975-78. Served to capt. AUS, 1942-46. Mem. Assn. Am. Pubs. (dir. 1977—), Am. Booksellers Assn. (liaison com. 1972). Clubs: Dutch Treat, Marco Polo, Players, Publishers Lunch (N.Y.C.). Home: 45 Carleon Ave Larchmont NY 10538 Office: 51 Madison Ave New York NY 10010

ROTH, HARVEY PAUL, publisher; b. N.Y.C., Feb. 20, 1933; s. Lewis Theodore and Harriet (Wallow) R.; A.B., Bklyn. Coll., 1954; LL.B., N.Y. U., 1957; m. Tanya Cohen; children by previous marriage—Andrea, Matthew Jay. Editor, West Pub. Co., N.Y.C., 1959-61; pres. BFL Communications, Inc., Plainview, N.Y., 1961-76; pres. Core Collection Books, Inc., Great Neck, N.Y., 1976—; dir. Nat. Paragon Corp. Admitted to N.Y. bar, 1959. Served with AUS, 1957-58. Home: 9 Ridge Dr E Great Neck NY 11021

ROTH, HENRY, writer; b. Austria-Hungary, Feb. 8, 1906; s. Herman and Leah (Farb) R. (father Am. citizen); B.S., Coll. City N.Y., 1928; m. Muriel Parker, Oct. 7, 1939; children—Jeremy, Hugh. With WPA, then permanent substitute tchr. Theodore Roosevelt night High Sch., N.Y.C., 1939-41; precision metal grinding machine shops, N.Y.C., Providence, Boston, 1941-46; tchr. one-room sch., Montville, Me., 1947-48; attendant Me. State Hosp., 1949-53; waterfowl farmer, 1953-63; pvt. tutor, 1956- 65. Grantee Nat. Inst. Arts and letters, 1965; recipient Townsend Harris medal Coll. City N.Y., 1965. Author: (novel) Call it Sleep, 1934. Address: Box 17 6817 Guadalupe Trail Albuquerque NM 87107

ROTH, HENRY LOGAN, life ins. co. exec.; b. Kansas City, Mo., Apr. 30, 1917; s. Henry and Margaret (Kelly) R.; student U. Nebr., 1934-36, Tex. A. and M. U., 1942-43, U. Pa., 1945; m. Margaret Elaine Quisenberry, Sept. 20, 1943; children—Donald, Susan. Mgr. ins. dept. Globe Investment Co., Los Angeles, 1936-40; pres. Acme Agencies, Inc., Los Angeles, 1940-41; v.p. Beneficial Fire & Casualty Co., Los Angeles, 1952-60; v.p. Fidelity Interstate Life Ins. Co., Phila., 1960-65, dir. 1966—; v.p. Brit. Pacific Life Ins. Co., Vancouver, B.C., Can., 1965-66; v.p. accident and health sales Beneficial Standard Life Ins. Co., Los Angeles, 1940-54, v.p. life sales, 1954-66, sr. v.p., 1966-68, dir. agencies, 1968-69, pres., 1969—, chief exec. officer, 1978—, also dir.; dir. Beneficial Computer Services, Inc., 1970—; chmn. bd. Beneficial Pension Services Corp., 1973-75, dir., 1973—; dir. Beneficial Standard Corp., Calif. Can. Bank, Transit Casualty Co., St. Louis, Direct Mktg. Internat., Ltd.; chmn. bd., dir. Direct Mktg. Corp. Am. Served to lt. (j.g.), USNR, World War II; PTO. Mem. Life Office Mgmt. Assn., Lambda Chi Alpha. Democrat. Roman Catholic. Clubs: Balboa Bay (bd. govs. 1968—) (Newport Beach, Calif.); Mission Hills Country (bd. govs. 1979). Home: 5503 Bellaire Ave North Hollywood CA 91607 Office: 3700 Wilshire Blvd Los Angeles CA 90010

ROTH, HERBERT, JR., corp. exec.; b. S. Bend, Ind., Oct. 7, 1928; s. Herbert and Vita (Augustienovicz) R.; B.S., U.S. Mil. Acad., 1951; M.S., Newark Coll. Engring., 1959; m. Dolores Maloney, June 5, 1951; children—Christine, Diane, Carla. Sr. product planner EDP div. RCA, 1956-61; v.p. Nuclear Corp. Am., Phoenix, 1961-62; v.p. GCA Corp., Bedford, Mass., 1962-66; pres., chief exec. officer Anelex Corp., Boston, 1966-67; dir., chmn. exec. com. Mohawk Data Scis., Corp., Boston, 1967-68; pres., chief exec. officer, dir. LFE Corp. Waltham, Mass., 1968—; dir. Boston Edison Co., Computervision Corp., Tech. Ops., Inc., Phoenix Mut. Life Ins. Co., Adams Russell Co. Inc. Served with U.S. Army, 1951-55. Home: 134 Lake St Sherborn MA 01770 Office: 1601 Trapelo Rd Waltham MA 02154

ROTH, IRVING, airline exec.; b. N.Y.C., Dec. 13, 1913; s. Max and Anna (Greenberg) R.; A.B., Bklyn. Coll. 1934; postgrad. N.Y. U. Columbia, 1935-36; m. Sarah J. Nathan, Aug. 15, 1948; children—Barry N., Catherine A. With FCC, 1935-38; financial analyst pub. utilities div. SEC, 1938-41; rate analyst to chief rates div. CAB, Washington, 1941-61, dir. bur. econ. regulation, 1961-65, dir. bur. econs., 1965-70; v.p. investor relations United Air Lines, Inc., also UAL, Inc., Chgo., 1970—. Served to capt. USAAF 1943-46. Clubs: Aero (pres.), Internat. Aviation (Washington); Wings (N.Y.C.). Home: 1934 Mission Hills Ln Northbrook IL 60062 Office: PO Box 66100 Chicago IL 60666

ROTH, JACK JOSEPH, educator, historian; b. Dec. 17, 1920; s. Max and Dinah (Kraus) R.; B.A., U. Chgo., 1942, Ph.D., 1955; postgrad. Inst. d'études politiques, Paris, France, 1949-50; m. Sheilagh Goldstone; children—Bradford, Heather. Mem. faculty Roosevelt U., 1951-68, prof. history, chmn. dept., 1960-68; prof. history Case Western Res. U., Cleve., 1968—, chmn. dept., 1968-73; vis. asso. prof. history U. Chgo., 1962, professorial lectr. history, 1968; vis. prof. history U. Wis., 1964-65; project dir. The Persistence of Surrealism, Nat. Endowment for Humanities. Served with AUS, 1942-46. Recipient Penrose Fund award Am. Philos. Soc., 1964. Author: The Revolution of the Mind: The Politics of Surrealism Reconsidered, 1977. Translator: (Georges Sorel) Reflections on Violence, 1951; Sorel und die Totalitaren System, 1958; Revolution and Morale in Modern French Thought: Sorel and the Sorelians, 1963; The First World War: A Turning Point in Modern History, 1967; The Roots of Italian Fascism, 1967; Georges Sorel: on Lenin and Mussolini, 1977; The Cult of Violence: Sorel and the Sorelians, 1979. Contbr. articles to profl. jours., chpts. to books. Home: 24301 Bryden Rd Beachwood OH 44122 Office: Dept History Case Western Res U Cleveland OH 44106

ROTH, JAMES FRANK, mfg. co. exec., chemist; b. Rahway, N.J., Dec. 7, 1925; s. Louis and Eleanor R.; B.A. in Chemistry, U. W.Va., 1947; Ph.D. in Phys. Chemistry, U. Md., 1951; children by previous marriage—Lawrence, Edward, Sandra; m. Sharon E. Mattes, June 20, 1969. Research chemist Franklin Inst., Phila., 1951-53, mgr. chemistry lab., 1958-60; chief chemist Lehigh Paints & Chems. Co., Allentown, Pa., 1953-55; research chemist GAF Corp., Easton, Pa., 1955-58; with Monsanto Co., St. Louis, 1960—, dir. catalysis research, 1973-77, dir. process sci. research, 1977—. Served with USN, 1943-46. Recipient Richard J. Kokes award Johns Hopkins U., 1977. Mem. Am. Chem. Soc. (St. Louis sect. St. Louis award 1975, E.V. Murphree nat. award 1976), Catalysis Soc. N. Am., Chgo. Catalysis Club. Contbr. articles to profl. jours.; editorial bd. Jour. Catalysis, 1976—, Catalysis Revs., 1973-79; inventor process biodegradable detergents, for acetic acid; U.S., fgn. patents in field. Office: 800 N Lindbergh Blvd Saint Louis MO 63166

ROTH, JAMES LUTHER AUMONT, physician, educator; b. Milw., Mar. 8, 1917; s. Paul Wagner and Rose Marie (Schulzke) R.; B.A., Carthage Coll., 1938, D.Sc. (hon.), 1957; M.A., U. Ill., 1939; M.D., Northwestern U., 1944, Ph.D., 1945; m. Marion S. Main, June 7, 1938; children—Stephen Andrew, Kristina Marie, Lisa Kathryn. Intern, Mass. Gen. Hosp., Boston, 1944-45; resident Grad. Hosp., 1945-46, 49-50, Hosp. U. Pa., Phila., 1948-49; practice medicine specializing in gastroenterology, Phila., 1950—; instr. physiology Northwestern U., 1942-44; instr. div. gastroenterology Grad. Sch. Medicine, U. Pa., 1950-52, asso., 1952-54, asst. prof., 1954-56, asso. prof., 1956-59, clin. prof. gastroenterology, 1959-68, dir. div., 1961-69, prof. clin. medicine, 1968—, chief gastroenterology clinic Grad. Hosp., 1953-67, chief gastroenterology service, 1961-69, dir. Inst. Gastroenterology, Presbyn. U. Pa. Med. Center, 1965—; cons. USN, Bethesda, Md., 1967—, USAF, 1946-48. Recipient Bronze medal AMA, 1944; certificates of merit Am. Roentgen Ray Soc., AMA, 1958; Disting. Alumni award Carthage Coll., 1979. Fellow A.C.P.; mem. AMA, Pan Am. Med. Assn., N.Y. Acad. Sci., Am. Physiol. Soc., Am. Fedn. Clin. Research, Am. Gastroent. Assn. (chmn. admissions com.), Am. Coll. Gastroenterology (trustee 1977—), Bockus Internat. Soc. Gastroenterology (pres. 1973-75), Digestive Disease Fedn. (dir.), Union League Phila., Sigma Xi, Alpha Omega Alpha; hon. mem. Colombian, Venezuelian, Dominican Republic socs. gastroenterology. Republican. Lutheran. Editorial bd. Gastroenterology 1960-67, Am. Jour. Gastroenterology, 1976-79, Current Therapy, 1972—, Current Concepts in Gastroenterology, 1976—; asso. editor Bockus' 3d edit. Gastroenterology. Contbr. articles to med. jours. Home: 639 Montgomery School Ln Wynnewood PA 19096 Office: 51 N 39th St Philadelphia PA 19104

ROTH, JESSE, endocrinologist; b. N.Y.C., Aug. 5, 1934; B.A., Columbia U., 1955; M.D., Albert Einstein Coll. Medicine, Yeshiva U., 1959. Intern, Barnes Hosp., Washington U., St. Louis, 1959-60, resident, 1960-61; Am. Diabetes Assn. research fellow radioisotope service Bronx (N.Y.) VA Hosp., 1961-63, clin. asso., 1963-65, sr. investigator, 1965-66, chief diabetes sect., clin. endocrinology br., 1966-74; chief diabetes br. Nat. Inst. Arthritis, Metabolism and Digestive Diseases, Bethesda, Md., 1974—; regents' lectr. U. Calif., 1977; G. Burroughs Midler lectr. NIH, 1978. Recipient Eli Lilly award Am. Diabetes Assn., 1974, Ernst Oppenheimer Meml. award Endocrine Soc., 1974, Spl. Achievement award HEW, 1974, David Rumbough Meml. award Juvenile Diabetes Found., 1977, Lita Annenberg Hazen award Mt. Sinai Sch. Medicine, Diaz Cristobal Found. prize, 1979. Office: Diabetes Br Nat Inst Arthritis Metabolism and Digestive Diseases 9000 Rockville Pike Bethesda MD 20205

ROTH, JUNE DORIS SPIEWAK, author; b. Haverstraw, N.Y., Feb. 16, 1926; d. Harry I. and Ida (Glazer) Spiewak; student Pa. State U., 1942-44; grad. Tobe-Coburn Sch. for Fashion Careers, 1945; m. Frederick Roth, July 7, 1945; children—Nancy, Robert. Author: The Freeze and Please Homefreezer Cookbook, 1963; The Rich and Delicious Low-Calorie Figure Slimming Cookbook, 1964; Thousand Calorie Cookbook, 1967; How to Use Sugar to Lose Weight, 1969; Fast and Fancy Cookbook, 1969; How to Cook like a Jewish Mother, 1969; The Take Good Care of My Son Cookbook for Brides, 1969; The Indoor/Outdoor Barbecue Book, 1970; The Pick of the Pantry Cookbook, 1970; Let's Have a Brunch Cookbook, 1971; Edith Bunkers' All in the Family Cookbook, 1972; The On-Your-Own Cookbook, 1972; Healthier Jewish Cookery: The Unsaturated Fat Way, 1972; Elegant Desserts, 1973; Old-Fashioned Candymaking, 1974; Salt-Free Cooking with Herbs and Spices (R. T. French Tastemaker award), 1975; The Troubled Tummy Cookbook, 1976; Cooking for Your Hyperactive Child, 1977; The Food/Depression Connection, 1978; author Spl. Diets, nationally syndicated newspaper column, 1979—. Vice pres. evening group Teaneck (N.J.) br. Nat. Council Jewish Women, 1954, pres., 1955, v.p. day group, 1956. Mem. Authors League Am., Tobe-Coburn Alumni Assn., Internat. Platform Assn., Town and Gown Soc. Fairleigh-Dickinson U., Am. Soc. Journalists and Authors (exec. bd.), Nat. Fedn. Press Women, Nat. Press Club. Address: 1057 Oakland Ct Teaneck NJ 07666

ROTH, L(INWOOD) EVANS, univ. adminstr., biologist; b. Ft. Wayne, Ind., Mar. 8, 1929; s. Reuben E. and Florence E. R.; A.B., Ind. U., 1950; M.S., Northwestern U., 1955; Ph.D., U. Chgo., 1957; m. Nancy Elizabeth Lewis, July 30, 1949; children—Philip Lewis, Stephen Evans. Asst. scientist Argonne Nat. Lab., Lemont, Ill., 1952-60; mem. faculty Iowa State U., 1960-67, asst. dean grad.

studies; mem. faculty Kans. State U., 1967-76, dir. div. biology; vice chancellor for grad. studies and research, prof. U. Tenn., Knoxville, 1976—; bd. dirs. U. Tenn. Research Corp. Mem. Am. Soc. Cell Biology, AAAS, Am. Sci. Affiliation, Sigma Xi, Phi Kappa Phi. Presbyterian. Contbr. numerous articles on cell biology, electron microscopy to profl. jours. Home: 507 Cherokee Blvd Knoxville TN 37919 Office: U Tenn 404 Andy Holt Tower Knoxville TN 37916*

ROTH, MARK STEPHAN, profl. bowler; b. Bklyn., Apr. 10, 1951; s. Sidney and Hilda (Rocker) R.; m. Jackie Dente, May 20, 1979. Profl. bowler; leading money winner, 1977-78; holder 20 Profl. Bowling Assn. titles. Recipient George Young High Average award, 1976, 77, 78; named Bowler of Yr., 1977, 78; Player of Yr., Sporting News, 1977, 78. Mem. Profl. Bowling Assn. Office: care Internat Artists and Athletes Mgmt Ltd 515 Madison Ave New York NY 10022

ROTH, MYRON ALFRED, aviation writer; b. Bklyn., Sept. 12, 1917; s. Jack and Beatrice (Bass) R.; B.S., N.Y. U., 1939, M.A., 1940; M.S. in Internat. Relations, George Washington U., 1969; m. Bernice Beverley Gilinsky, Mar. 4, 1947; children—Michael Baron, Shelley Ann Ferguson, Teri Ellen Chuntz. Commd. 2d lt. USAAF, 1941, advanced through grades to col. USAF, 1961; stationed C.Z., 1941, Ecuador, 1942-43, Colorado Springs, 1943-46, Biloxi, Miss., 1947-50, San Antonio, 1950-52, C.Z., 1952-55, Orlando, Fla., 1955-57, Monterey, Cal., 1957-58, Ankara, Turkey, 1958-61, Washington, 1961-65, Philippines, 1965-67, Montgomery, Ala., 1967-69; ret., 1969; asst. exec. dir. Nat. Aero. Assn., Washington, 1969-77. Dir., World Golf Directory. Decorated Legion of Merit, Air medal, Air Force Meritorious medal. Charles W. Hayden scholar, 1939-40. Mem. Am. Inst. Aeros. and Astronautics, Aviation Space Writers Assn., Nat. Aviation Club, Manila Overseas Press Club, Aero. Club Washington, First Flight Soc., Tuesday Musical, Air Force Assn., Ret. Officers Assn. Exec. editor Nat. Aeros. mag., 1971-74, Jour. Aerospace Edn., 1974—. Home: PO Box 396 Melbourne Beach FL 32951

ROTH, PHILIP, author; b. Newark, Mar. 19, 1933; s. Herman and Bess (Finkel) R.; student Newark Coll. of Rutgers U., 1950-51; A.B., Bucknell U., 1954; M.A., U. Chgo., 1955; m. Margaret Martinson, Feb. 22, 1959 (dec. 1968). Tchr. English, U. Chgo., 1956-58; mem. faculty Iowa Writer's Workshop, 1960-62; writer in residence Princeton U., 1962-63; vis. writer State U. N.Y. at Stony Brook, 1966, 67, U. Pa., 1967-77; short story writer, novelist, works pub. in Harper's, New Yorker, Epoch, Commentary, others, also reprints in Best Am. Short Stories of 1956, 59, 60, O'Henry Prize Stories of 1960. Served with AUS, 1955-56. Recipient Aga Khan prize for fiction, 1958; Guggenheim fellow, 1959-60; award Nat. Inst. Arts and Letters, 1960; Daroff award Jewish Book Council, 1960; Ford Found. grantee, 1965; Rockefeller fellow, 1966. Author: Goodbye, Columbus (Nat. Book award), 1959; Letting Go, 1962; When She Was Good, 1967; Portnoy's Complaint, 1969; Our Gang, 1971; The Breast, 1972; The Great American Novel, 1973; My Life as a Man, 1974; Reading Myself and Others, 1975; The Professor of Desire, 1977; The Ghost Writer, 1979. Address: care Farrar Straus & Giroux 15 Union Sq W New York NY 10022

ROTH, RALPH SHARP, newspaper exec.; b. Montvale, N.J., Jan. 12, 1927; s. David F. and Reva E. (Sharp) R.; B.S., Dartmouth Coll., 1946, M.S. in Bus. Adminstrn. and Engring., 1949; m. Barbara N. Smith, Dec. 23, 1950; children—Harold A., Mark A., Scott D., Kip P. Asst. to v.p. sales Mergenthaler Linotype Co., Bklyn., 1949-57; asst. prodn. mgr. St. Paul Dispatch, 1957-59; pres., pub., dir. Grand Forks (N.D.) Herald, 1959-72; prodn. dir. Ridder Publs., Denver, 1972-75; v.p. prodn. Knight-Ridder Newspapers, Inc., Miami, Fla., 1975-77; pres. Detroit Free Press, 1977—; former dir. Aberdeen Am.-News, Boulder Camera, First Nat. Bank of Grand Forks. Bd. dirs., mem. exec. com. Met. Detroit Conv. and Visitors Bur. Served with USNR, World War II, Korean War; PTO. Mem. Am. Newspaper Pubs. Assn. (prodn. mgmt. com., vice-chmn.), Inland Daily Press Assn. (past pres.), Detroit C. of C. (dir., exec. com.), Econ. Club Detroit (dir.). Presbyterian. Clubs: Masons; Shriners; Renaissance; Detroit, Detroit Athletic; Oakland Hills Country. Home: 30777 Cheviot Hills Dr Franklin MI 48025 Office: 321 W Lafayette St Detroit MI 48231

ROTH, RAYMOND EDWARD, educator, statistician; b. Rochester, N.Y., Oct. 29, 1918; s. George Norbert and Florence Margaret (Kirchgessner) R.; B.S. magna cum laude, St. Bonaventure U., 1940, M.S., 1942; Ph.D., U. Rochester, 1963; m. Mary Elizabeth O'Brien, Nov. 7, 1942; children—Mary Elaine (Mrs. Archie C. Bush, Jr.), Patricia (Mrs. Addison E. Fischer, Jr.), Katherine, Jean A., Joan B. (Mrs. Jay Harrington). With Gen. Electric Co., 1943-46; sci. cons. U. Dayton (Ohio), 1948-50; optics specialist Bausch & Lomb, 1950-52; researcher U. Rochester, 1953-57; mem. faculty St. Bonaventure U., 1958-66, prof. statistics, dir. Computer Center, State U. N.Y. at Geneseo, 1966-68; prof. math Rollins Coll., Winter Park, Fla., 1968—, acting dean faculty, 1969, now Archibald Granville Bush prof. math.; research cons. FAA, 1962-63; vis. scientist Oak Ridge, 1964. Bd. dirs. Fla. Sci. and Engring. Fair, 1972. Fellow U. Okla., Royal Statis. Soc., Biometric Soc., Am. Chem. Soc., Math. Assn. Am., Soc. Indsl. and Applied Math.; mem. Am. Statis. Assn. (Fla. pres. 1972-73), Sigma Xi (pres. Rollins chpt. 1970-73), Mu Alpha Theta, Pi Mu Epsilon. Club: University. Home: 1761 Tippicanoe Trail Maitland FL 32751 Office: Math Dept Rollins Coll Winter Park FL 32789. *It is not important to lead a long life, just a happy, useful, meaningful one.*

ROTH, RAYMOND J(EAN), zoo, aquarium and planetarium dir.; b. Bienne, Switzerland, Mar. 25, 1929; s. Arnold Raymond and Jeannette (Jost) R.; came to Can., 1951, naturalized, 1957; B.Commerce, U. Bienne, 1948; m. Denise Coupal, Aug. 23, 1952; children—Ginette, Michel. With Montreal Park Dept., 1951-64; circulation mgr. Montreal mag., 1964-69; dir. Montreal Zoo, 1969-72, Montreal Aquarium, Planetarium and Zoo, 1972—; mem. mgmt. com. Montreal Soc. Prevention Cruelty to Animals; sec.-treas. Assn. des Parcs Zoologiques du Que. Served with Swiss Army, 1948-51. Fellow Am. Assn. Zool. Parks and Aquariums, Can. Assn. Zool. Parks and Aquarians. Home: 1449 Leclaire St Montreal PQ H1V 2Z4 Canada Office: St Helen's Island Montreal PQ H3C 1A0 Canada. *Zoos have traditionally served as educational and recreational natural history centers. An important additional responsibility has quite recently been assumed by zoos, as a result of the systematic destruction of urban environment by overpopulation and increasing industrialization. Conservation as a way of safeguarding our animal resources (in some cases man's own food supply) is now a vital zoo concern which involves challenging work in the dissemination of knowledge about endangered animal species, and also in programs for breeding some of these animals in captivity.*

ROTH, ROBERT, journalist; b. N.Y.C., Nov. 11, 1901; s. Abraham Lincoln and Sophie (Hafer) R.; student Amherst Coll., 1919-21; m. Katherine Lennehan, July 22, 1928 (dec. July 1958); m. 2d, Edith R. Brill, Oct. 16, 1959. Reporter various newspapers, 1925-33; editor Mt. Vernon (N.Y.) Daily Argus, 1934-42; reporter Phila. Record, 1943-44, Washington corr., 1945-47; reporter, spl. writer Phila. Bull., 1947-49, chief Washington corr., 1954—. Mem. Sigma Delta Chi. Clubs: Nat. Press, Cosmos, Internat., Gridiron (Washington). Home: 2440 Virginia Ave NW Washington DC 20037 Office: Nat Press Bldg Washington DC 20045

ROTH, ROBERT EARL, radiologist, educator; b. Springfield, Ill., Mar. 3, 1925; s. Earl Andrew and Aldine (Schockley) R.; student Columbia, 1943-45; U. Ill., Chgo., 1947. M.D., 1949; m. Joanne Seneff, June 26, 1948; children—Michael Gordon, Nicholas Brian, Andrew John, Emily Dean, Laura Seneff. Intern St. Louis County Hosp., Clayton, Mo., 1949-50; resident U.S. Naval Hosp., San Diego, VA Hosp., and Vanderbilt, Nashville, 1950-54; practice medicine, specializing in radiology, Birmingham, Ala., 1955—; asst. chief radiology VA Hosp., Nashville, 1954-55; asst. prof. radiology, chief radiation therapy U. Ala. Med. Coll., 1957-58, asso. prof., chief radiation therapy, 1958-59, prof., chmn. dept. radiology, 1959-69; acting chief radiology VA Hosp., Birmingham, 1959-69, chmn. dept. radiation oncology, 1959—, also cons. radiology; radiologist-in-chief U. Ala. Hosps. and Clinics, 1959-69, radiation oncologist-in-chief, 1969—. Served to lt., M.C., USNR, 1949-52. Diplomate Am. Bd. Radiology. Fellow Am. Coll. Radiology; mem. AAAS, Am. Soc. Therapeutic Radiologists, Am. Coll. Radiology, Radiol. Soc. N.Am., Am., So. med. assns., N.Y. Acad. Scis., So. Radiol. Conf., Soc. Nuclear Medicine, Ala., Jefferson County med. socs., Pan Am. Cancer Cytology Soc., Ala. Roentgen Ray Soc. (past pres.), Ala. Soc. Radiation Oncologists (sec.-treas.), Birmingham Surg. Soc. Home: 4332 Old Brook Trail Birmingham AL 35243 Office: 619 S 19th St Birmingham AL 35233

ROTH, RUSSELL BURTON, physician; b. Erie, Pa., Nov. 6, 1913; s. Augustus Henry and Florence (Burton) R.; grad. Phillips Acad., Andover, Mass., 1931; A.B., Yale U., 1935; M.D., Johns Hopkins, 1939; LL.D., Gannon Coll., 1973; D.Sc., Edinboro State Coll., 1974; m. Jeanne Guy, Oct. 17, 1964; stepchildren—G. Thomas Gay, Peter Gay. Intern, Johns Hopkins Hosp., 1939-40; asst. pathology Johns Hopkins Hosp., 1940-41, St. Mary's Hosp., Pierre, S.D., 1941-42, Henry Ford Hosp., Detroit, 1942-43, Brady Urol. Inst., Balt., 1943-44; practice medicine specializing in urology, Erie, 1946—; cons. urologist VA Hosp., Erie; cons. various govt. agys. Mem. Pa. Gov's Adv. Health Bd., 1956-72; chmn. Erie County Bd. Health, 1958-76; mem. adv. com. Office Dependent Med. Care, Dept. Def., 1961-69; pub. speaker on sci. and socio-econ. med. subjects, 1946—; mem. Nat. Advisory Council Regional Med. Programs, 1970-73; mem. spl. adv. group VA, 1971-79; mem. steering com. exptl. med. care rev. orgn. HEW, 1971-74, mem. health ins. benefits advisory council, 1975-78. Pres. Hess-Roth Urol. Found., Inc., 1960-71; bd. dirs. Pa. Health Research Inst., Lakes Area Health Edn. Center, 1965—; adv. dir. Internat. Found. Employee Benefit Plans, 1971-74, mem. com., 1971-76; mem. Joint Commn. on Accreditation Hosps., 1975—; trustee Villa Maria Coll., Erie, 1976—. Served to capt. M.C., AUS, 1944-46. Recipient medal of honor Pa. State Coll., 1974, D.A.R., 1974. Fellow A.C.S.; mem. AMA (chmn. fed. med. services com. 1960-64, council on med. service 1965-66, speaker ho. dels. 1969-72, pres. 1973-74), Pa. (council, bd. chmn., speaker ho. dels. 1963-67), Erie County (past sec., pres.) med. socs., Am. Urol. Assn., Am. Assn. Clin. Urologists (pres. 1976), Pa. Soc. Advancement Med. Research (pres. 1956-65). Clubs: Masons (32 deg.), Shriners, Jesters, Rotary, Erie (gov.), Erie Yacht. Contbr. numerous articles on urology and med. socio-econs to profl. jours. Home: 3275 Georgian Ct Erie PA 16506 Office: 225 W 25th St Erie PA 16502

ROTH, SANFORD IRWIN, pathologist; b. McAlester, Okla., Oct. 14, 1932; s. Herman Moe and Blanche (Brown) R.; student Vanderbilt U., 1949-52; M.D., Harvard U., 1956; m. Kathryn Ann Corliss, Sept. 3, 1967; children—Jeffrey Franklin, Elisabeth F., Gregory James, Suzannah Joan. Intern, Mass. Gen. Hosp., Boston, 1956-57, resident in pathology, 1957-60, pathologist, 1962-75; pathologist Armed Forces Inst. Pathology, 1960-62; asst. prof. Harvard Med. Sch., 1962-69, asso. prof., 1969-75; pathologist, prof., chmn. dept. U. Ark. Coll. Medicine, Little Rock, 1975—. Served with M.C., U.S. Army, 1960-62. Mem. AAAS, Internat. Acad. Pathologists, Am. Assn. Pathologists, Am. Soc. Cell Biology, AMA, Coll. Am. Pathology. Home: 39 St Andrews Dr Little Rock AR 72212 Office: 4301 W Markham St Little Rock AR 72205

ROTH, STANLEY, chain store exec.; b. Chgo., Sept. 19, 1898; s. Henry and Lucy (Duschner) R.; Ph.B., U. Chgo., 1918; m. Elsie Erman, Aug. 19, 1920; children—Stanley, Robert Merle. Engaged in personnel, mdsg. and operations research Retail Research Assn., 1919-21; personnel and mdse. mgr. L. S. Ayres & Co., Indpls., 1921-28; v.p., gen. mgr. Gimbel Bros., Milw., 1928- 33; v.p., mng. dir. The Golden Rule, St. Paul, 1934-37; v.p., gen. mdse. mgr. D.A. Schulte, Inc., N.Y.C., 1937-47; exec. v.p. Darling Stores Corp., N.Y.C., 1947-59, pres., dir., 1960-64; pres. dir. Grayson-Robinson Store, Inc., N.Y.C., 1960-64; vice chmn., dir. A.S. Beck Shoe Corp., 1961-64; pres. Apparel Buying Assos., N.Y.C., 1964—, chmn., 1966—. Trustee Jewish Home and Hosp. for Aged, N.Y.C.; established Roth Program Retailing Research, Harvard Grad. Sch. Bus., Roth Program Cardiovascular Research, N.Y. U. Grad. Sch. Medicine. Served as 1st lt. U.S. Army, 1918. Mem. Phi Beta Kappa. Home: 40 Central Park S New York NY 10019 Office: 125 Castle Rd Secaucus NJ 07094

ROTH, STEPHEN ALAN, advt. exec.; s. Herman and Rose (Fingerman) R.; B.B.A., Coll. City N.Y., 1958; postgrad. Fairleigh Dickenson U., 1964-66; m. Paula Susan Goldstein, Oct. 5, 1961; children—Stephanie, Gary, Jill, Gregory. Project supr. NCO div. Dun & Bradstreet, N.Y.C., 1963-65; product planner Sperry Rand, Norwalk, Conn., 1965-66; sr. research analyst SCM Corp., N.Y.C., 1966-68; v.p., dir. market services Doremus & Co., advt. agy., N.Y.C., 1968—. Mem. Inst. for Mgmt. Sci., Am. Marketing Assn., Am. Statis. Assn., Am. Sociology Soc. Home: 19 Divan Way Wayne NJ 07470 Office: 120 Broadway New York City NY 10005

ROTH, TOBY, congressman; b. Oct. 10, 1938; s. Kasper and Julia (Roehrich) R.; B.A., Marquette U., 1961; m. Barbara Fischer, Nov. 28, 1964; children—Toby, Vicky, Barbie. Owner, Toby Roth Realty, Appleton, 1969—; mem. Wis. Ho. of Reps. from 42d Dist., 1972-78; mem. 96th Congress from 8th Wis. Dist., mem. Sci. and Tech. Com., Small Bus. Com., Congressional Rural Caucus, Tourism Caucus, Environ. Study Conf. Served to 1st lt. USAR, 1962-69. Named Wis. Legislator of Yr., Wis. Towns Assn., 1978; Outstanding Rep. Freshman Congressman, 1979. Mem. Wis. Northside Businessmen's Assn. (pres. 1970), Am. Legion. Republican. Club: Optimists (hon.). Office: 1008 Longworth House Office Bldg Washington DC 20515

ROTH, WILLIAM FREDERICK, JR., physician; b. Kansas City, Mo., Feb. 25, 1904; s. William F. and Marie Alma (Beitner) R.; Ph.B., Yale, 1925, M.D., 1929; m. Marian Axtell Cowperthwaite, June 12, 1931 (div. Mar. 1964); children—William Frederick 3d (dec. Sept. 1940), John Cowperthwaite; m. 2d, Dorothy Wilhelmina Hoy Hubbard, July 14, 1972. Commonwealth Fund fellow in psychiatry Boston Psychopathic Hosp. and Harvard Med. Sch., 1932-35; dir. Williamson County Child Guidance Study, Franklin, Tenn., 1935-42; prof. psychiatry U. Kans. Sch. Medicine, 1946-63, chmn. dept. psychiatry, 1946-58; prof. neurology and psychiatry U. Nebr. Coll. Medicine, Omaha, 1964-67, prof. psychiatry, 1967-72, sr. cons in psychiatry, 1972—. Cons. VA, 1946-64, 68-70, Nebr. Pschiat. Inst., 1957-63. Served with USNR, 1942-46; capt. Res. (ret.). Mem. AMA, Central Neuropsychiat. Assn., Am., Mid-Continent psychiat. assns., Am. Coll. Psychiatrists, Am. Orthopsychiat. Assn., Phi Beta Kappa, Nu Sigma Nu. Presbyterian. Office: Nebr Psychiat Inst 602 S 44th Ave Omaha NE 68105

ROTH, WILLIAM MATSON, business exec.; b. San Francisco, Sept. 3, 1916; s. William Philip and Lurline Berenice (Matson) R.; A.B., Yale U., 1939; m. Joan Osborn, Apr. 13, 1946; children—Jessica, Margaret, Anna. Wtih Barber Oil Corp., 1947; with Honolulu Oil Corp., 1948-50, past dir.; chmn. bd. Pacific Nat. Life Assurance Co., 1960-63; v.p. fin., dir. Matson Nav. Co. and subs.'s San Francisco, 1952-61; dep. spl. rep. for trade negotiations, 1963-66; White House spl. rep. for trade negotiations with rank of ambassador, 1967-69; fellow Kennedy Center for Sch. Govt., Harvard U., 1969—. Trustee Carnegie Instn. Washington, Com. for Econ. Devel., German Marshall Fund U.S.; exec. com. Trilateral Commn.; mem. council Yale U. Clubs: Pacific Union, Bohemian, Cypress Point. Address: 215 Market St San Francisco CA 94105

ROTH, WILLIAM V., JR., senator; b. Great Falls, Mont., July 22, 1921; B.A., U. Oreg.; M.B.A., LL.B., Harvard; m. Jane K. Richards; children—William V. III, Katharine Kellond. Admitted to Del. bar; U.S. Supreme Ct., mem. 90th-91st congresses at large from Del.; senator from Del., 1971—; mem. finance, govt. ops. coms., joint econ. com. Chmn. Del. Republican State Com., 1961-64; mem. Rep. Nat. Com., 1961-64. Served to capt. AUS, 1943-46. Decorated Bronze Star medal. Mem. Am., Del. bar assns. Episcopalian. Address: New Senate Office Bldg Washington DC 20510

ROTHAUGE, CHARLES HARRY, educator; b. Balt., Sept. 8, 1919; s. George Harry and Margaret Eva (Heimert) R.; B.Eng., Johns Hopkins, 1940, D. Eng., 1949; m. Lorraine A. Yuckert, Feb. 12, 1971. Electronic engr. design measurement equipment Johns Hopkins Hosp. and Univ., 1940-41; instr. math. and engring. at univ., 1946-49; mem. faculty U.S. Navy Postgrad. Sch., 1949—, prof. elec. engring., 1956—, exec. asst. to chmn., 1960-62, chmn. dept. elec. engring., 1962-70, 75—. Served to major, ordnance dept., AUS, 1941-46. Mem. Am. Inst. E.E., I.R.E., Am. Assn. Engring. Edn., AAUP, Sigma Xi, Tau Beta Pi. Home: 170 Del Monte Blvd Pacific Grove CA 93950 Office: US Naval Postgrad Sch Monterey CA 93940

ROTHBALLER, ALAN BURNS, physician; b. N.Y.C., May 15, 1926; s. Albert Floyd and Helen (Burns) R.; student Princeton U., 1943-44; M.D., U. Pa., 1948; M.Sc. in Neurophysiology, McGill U., 1955. Intern, U. Pa., George Washington U. hosps., 1949-51; spl. tng. neurology and neurosurgery Montreal Neurol. Inst., 1951-56; from asst. prof. to asso. prof. anatomy, from asst. prof. to asso. prof. neurosurgery Albert Einstein Coll. Medicine, 1956-65, vis. prof. anatomy, 1965-68; prof., chmn. dept. neurosurgery, research prof. physiology N.Y. Med. Coll., 1965—; chmn. neurosurgery sect. Westchester County Med. Center, 1971; attending staff Met., Bird S. Coler hosps., 1965—. Served to capt. M.C., AUS, 1949-51. Mem. Am. Physiol. Soc., Harvey Cushing Soc., Research Soc. Neurol. Surgeons, AAAS, Internat. Brain Research Orgn., Sigma Xi, Nu Sigma Nu, Alpha Omega Alpha. Republican. Presbyterian. Spl. research brain control neurohypophysiol. hormones, thirst, fluid and electrolyte metabolism. Co-translator Zûlch's Neuropathology brain tumors, 2d edit., 1965. Home: 318 W 102d St New York NY 10025 Office: NY Med Coll Munger Pavilion Room 553 Valhalla NY 10595

ROTHBART, HERBERT I., lawyer; b. Chgo., Jan. 5, 1929; s. William and Frances (Slifkin) R.; B.A., Drake U., 1950; J.D., Northwestern U., 1953; m. Claire Meyer, June 16, 1957; children—Courtney, Jeffrey, Douglas. Admitted to Ill. bar, 1953; sr. trial atty. FTC, Washington, 1956-61; mem. firm Kahn, Adsit & Arnstein, Chgo., 1962-64; partner firm Getzoff & Rothbart, Chgo., 1965—; dir. Pate Co., E.W. Filkins, Inc. Served with U.S. Army, 1954-56. Mem. Fed., Ill. bar assns., Phi Delta Phi, Omicron Delta Kappa. Home: 105 Carlisle Ave Deerfield IL 60015 Office: 115 S LaSalle St Chicago IL 60600

ROTHBAUM, IRA, advt. exec.; b. Phila., Nov. 23, 1923; s. Samuel and Charlotte (Gross) R.; A.B. in Journalism, U. N.C., 1947; student Columbia U., 1944; m. 2d, Eileen Glickfeld, Dec. 26, 1972; children—Stephen Ira, Peggy Ann, John E. Copywriter, RCA, 1947-49, advt. and sales promotion mgr., 1949-50, divisional sales mgr., 1953; instr. Tulane U., 1952; copywriter N.W. Ayer, Phila., 1953-56, account exec., account supr., Detroit, 1956-63, v.p., sr. v.p., mgmt. supr., N.Y.C., 1963-71; sr. v.p., mgmt. supr. SSC & B, 1971-76; exec. v.p. Keyes, Martin & Co., Inc., Springfield, N.J., 1976-77; asst. to pres. W.B. Doner & Co., Southfield, Mich., 1977—. Served with USNR, 1943-46, 50-52. Home: 26815 Captain's Ln Franklin MI 48025 Office: 26711 Northwestern Hwy Southfield MI 48034

ROTHBERG, ABRAHAM, editor, author, educator; b. N.Y.C., Jan. 14, 1922; s. Louis and Lottie (Drimmer) R.; A.B., Bklyn. Coll., 1942; M.A., U. Iowa, 1947; Ph.D., Columbia, 1952; m. Esther Conwell, Sept. 30, 1945; 1 son, Lewis Josiah. Chmn. editorial bd. Stateside mag., N.Y.C., 1947-49; instr. English, creative writing Columbia, N.Y.C., 1948; instr. English, humanities Hofstra Coll., Hempstead, N. Y., 1947-51; prof. English, St. John Fisher Coll., 1973—; Ford Found. fellow, N.Y.C., 1951-52; editor-in-chief Free Europe Press, N.Y.C., 1952-59; mng. editor George Braziller, Inc., N.Y.C., 1959, New Leader mag., N.Y.C., 1960-61; sr. editor Bantam Books, Inc., N.Y.C., 1966-67; writer, editorial cons.; European corr. Nat. Observer, Washington, Manchester (Eng.) Guardian, 1962-63. Served with AUS, 1943-45. Recipient John H. McGinnis Meml. award for short story, 1970; John H. McGinnis Meml. award for essay, 1973-74. Author: Abraham, Eyewitness History of World War II, 1962; The Thousand Doors, 1965; The Heirs of Cain, 1966; The Song of David Freed, 1968; The Other Man's Shoes, 1969; The Boy and the Dolphin, 1969; The Sword of the Golem, 1971; Aleksandr Solzhenitsyn: The Major Novels, 1971; The Heirs of Stalin: Dissidence and the Soviet Regime, 1953-1970, 1972; The Stalking Horse, 1972; The Great Waltz, 1978. Editor: U.S. Stories, 1949; Flashes in the Night, 1958; Anatomy of a Moral, 1959; A Bar-Mitzvah Companion, 1959; Great Adventure Stories of Jack London, 1967. Contbr. articles, essays, stories, poems to various publs., anthologies, collections. Home: 340 Pelham Rd Rochester NY 14610

ROTHBERG, GERALD, editor, pub.; b. Bklyn., Oct. 29, 1937; s. Abraham and Pauline R.; B.A., Bklyn. Coll., 1960; postgrad. Dickinson Law Sch., 1962; m. Glenda Fay Morris, June 18, 1970; children—Laura, Abigail. Spl. projects editor Esquire mag., 1963-66; owner, editor, pub., founder Circus mag., N.Y.C., 1966—. Home: 11 E 94th St New York NY 10028 Office: 115 E 57th St New York NY 10022

ROTHBERG, SOL, lawyer, industrialist; b. N.Y.C., July 29, 1910; s. Samuel and Ada (Shayne) R.; LL.B., Ind. U., 1933; m. Dorothy Platka, Jan. 9, 1938; children—David, Richard, Samuel. Admitted to Ind. bar, 1933, since practiced in Ft. Wayne; sr. partner firm Rothberg, Gallmeyer, Fruechtenicht & Logan, 1951—; chmn. bd. Bowser, Inc., 1960—, Wabash Smelting, Inc., 1958—, Gen. Smelting Co.; chmn. bd., dir. Summit Labs., Inc.; dir., counsel Ind. Bank & Trust Co., Ft. Wayne, Pierce Industries, Inc., Anderson, Ind., 1972, Milton R. Barrie

Co., Inc., 1976, Energystics Corp. Founder, Ft. Wayne Child Guidance Clinic, 1950, pres., 1953; mem. budget and priority coms. Community Chest and United Fund, Ft. Wayne, 1949; pres. Ft. Wayne Jewish Fedn., 1949; mem. Econ. Devel. Authority Ind., 1972; dir. Allen County Dept. Pub. Welfare, 1936; chmn. United Jewish Appeal, Ft. Wayne, 1953; bd. dirs. Parkview Meml. Hosp. Found.; adv. exec. com. Ind. U. Sch. Bus. Mem. Am. (mem. com. on banking instns. and regulated investment cos., taxation sect.), Ind. (dir. trial sect. 1958), Allen County (treas. 1943) bar assns., Am. Judicature Soc., Bar Assn. 7th Circuit and 6th Circuit. Jewish (pres. congregation 1951). Mem. B'nai B'rith (pres. Ft. Wayne 1943). Clubs: Indiana Univ. Alumni (pres. 1934), Ft. Wayne Country, Quest (Fort Wayne). Home: 4721 Covington Rd Fort Wayne IN 46804 Office: Indiana Bank Bldg Fort Wayne IN 46802

ROTHCHILD, IRVING, educator, physician; b. N.Y.C., Dec. 2, 1913; s. Phillip and Yetta (Fisch) R.; B.A., U. Wis., 1935, M.A., 1936, Ph.D., 1939; M.D., Ohio State U., 1954; m. Rose Kanet, Sept. 27, 1935 (div. 1956); 1 dau., Susan Elizabeth; m. 2d, Ellen Newman, Sept. 6, 1958. Biologist, Hosp. Liquids, Inc., Chgo., 1940-41; chemist Michael Reese Hosp., Chgo., 1941-43; asst. physiologist U.S. Dept. Agr., Beltsville, Md., 1943-48; asst. prof. physiology U. Md., Balt., 1948-49; asst. prof. obstetrics and gynecology Ohio State U., Columbus, 1949-53; asso. prof. obstetrics and gynecology Case Western Res. U., Cleve., 1955-66, prof. reproductive biology, 1966—; asso. obstetrician, gynecologist U. Hosps., Cleve., 1955—; vis. asst. Cleve. Met. Gen. Hosp., 1962—. Mem. AAAS, Am. Soc. Zoologists, Endocrine Soc., Am. Physiol. Soc., Soc. Study Reprodn., Soc. Gynecologic Investigation. Research on physiology of reprodn. Home: 2441 Kenilworth Rd Cleveland Heights OH 44106 Office: Case Western Res U Dept Reproductive Biology Cleveland OH 44106

ROTHE, G. H. RIEDEL, artist; b. Beuthen, Germany, Mar. 15, 1935; d. Harry Alfred and Elisabeth Emma Marie (Kuhfuss) Riedel; came to U.S., 1970; diploma Ernst Barlach Sch., Rheda, 1953; grad. Acad. Design Master Sch., Pforzheim, 1958; m. Curt R. Rothe, Jan. 30, 1958; 1 son, Peter Christian. One-man shows include: German galleries, 1968—, Villa Romana Florenz (Italy), Upstairs Galleries, Los Angeles, Hammer Galleries. N.Y.C.; group shows include: Landesmuseum Münster, Ulm, Haus der Kunst München, Gallerie der Stadt Stuttgart (all Germany); represented in permanent collections staatsgalleries Stuttgart, Karlsruhe, House of Parliament, Bonn, Kunsthalle Düsseldorf (Germany), also numerous corp. collections in U.S.; specialist in mezzotint. Recipient Villa Romana prize, 1968. Mem. Victorian Soc. Am. Club: Nat. Art (N.Y.C.). Author: Dr. Phil Max Bense/Rothe Epischestudie, 1967; Bense with Rothe, Existensmitteilung, 1970.

ROTHE, KENNETH WARREN, univ. pres.; b. St. Louis, Oct. 15, 1940; s. Harold Charles and Juanita (Reynolds) R.; A.B. cum laude with honors in Physics, Middlebury Coll., 1961; M.A., U. Rochester, 1965, Ph.D., 1966; children—Christelie Ann, Dawn Leigh. Research asso. U. Pa., 1966-68, asst. prof. physics, asst. dean coll., 1968-71, asso. prof. physics, 1972-73, asso. dean coll., 1971-73; provost Bowling Green (Ohio) State U., 1973-78; pres., provost Union Experimenting Colls. and Univs., 1978—. Bd. dirs. J. Preston Levis Regional Computer Center, 1973—, chmn., 1974-76; bd. dirs. Toledo Opera, v.p., 1976-78. Woodrow Wilson Found. fellow; NSF Grad. fellow. Mem. AAAS, Am. Phys. Soc., Am. Assn. Higher Edn., Sigma Xi. Episcopalian (chmn. ministries in higher edn. 1970-72). Contbr. articles to sci. jours. Home: 1331 Delta Ave Cincinnati OH 45208

ROTHELL, GEORGE EDWIN, banker; b. Norfolk, Nebr., Dec. 17, 1930; s. Frank Stephen and Margaret Anna (Howorth) R.; B.S. in Bus. Adminstrn., U. Nebr., 1952; m. Elaine Marie Jones; 1 dau., Leslie Elaine. Vice pres. Bank of Am., Los Angeles, 1960-72; mng. dir. Western Am. Bank (Europe) Ltd., London, 1972-77; exec. v.p. United Calif. Bank, Los Angeles, 1977-78, pres., 1978—. Served with USMCR, 1952-56. Address: United Calif Bank 707 Wilshire Blvd Los Angeles CA 90017

ROTHEN, ALEXANDRE, chemist, ret. educator; b. Geneva, Jan. 25, 1900; s. Georges and Mathilde (Favre) R.; came to U.S., 1927, naturalized, 1938; Chem. Engr., U. Geneva, 1924, Ph.D., 1926. Mem. faculty Rockefeller U., 1927-70, prof. phys. chemistry, 1955-70, prof. emeritus, 1970—. Home: 1801 Mont-Pelerin (Vaud) Switzerland. *The following principle which guided me successfully during my academic life was enunciated by the Franciscan monk Roger Bacon: "Do not believe the authorities, throw overboard their doctrines; but have faith in the experimental data which alone stand." I had an unwavering determination in investigating a special field of fundamental research, for over 35 years in spite of violent criticisms by the experts.*

ROTHENBERG, ALBERT, psychiatrist; b. N.Y.C., June 2, 1930; s. Gabriel and Rose (Goldberg) R.; A.B., Harvard U., 1952; M.D., Tufts U., 1956; m. Julia C. Johnson, June 28, 1970; children—Michael, Mora, Rina. Intern Pa. Hosp., Phila., 1956-57; resident in psychiatry Yale U., West Haven (Conn.) VA Hosp., 1957-58, Grace-New Haven Hosp., 1958-59, Yale Psychiat. Inst., New Haven, 1959-60; practice medicine specializing in psychiatry, New Haven, 1960-61, 1963-65, San Juan, P.R., 1961-63, Farmington, Conn., 1975-79; dir. research Austen Riggs Center, Stockbridge, Mass., 1979—; asst. dir. Yale Psychiat. Inst., 1963-64, sr. staff mem., 1964-75, 78—; mem. staff Yale-New Haven Med. Center, VA Hosp., West Haven, U. Conn. Health Center, Farmington; cons. to various jours. in psychiatry; asst. prof. dept. psychiatry Yale U. Sch. Medicine, 1964-68, asso. prof., 1968-74, clin. prof., 1974—; prof. psychiatry U. Conn. Sch. Medicine, Farmington, 1975-79, dir. residency tng., 1976-78, dir. clin. services, 1975-78; prin. investigator Studies in the Creative Process, 1963—; vis. prof. Pa. State U., 1971, adj. prof., 1971-78; vis. prof. dept. Am. studies Yale U., 1974-76. Served with M.C., U.S. Army, 1961-63. Recipient Tufts Med. Alumni award, 1956; Research Scientist Career Devel. award NIMH, 1964, 69; Guggenheim Meml. fellow, 1974-75; diplomate Am. Bd. Psychiatry and Neurology. Fellow Am. Psychiat. Assn., Royal Soc. Health; mem. Conn. Psychiat. Soc., Mass. Psychiat. Soc., Am. Soc. Aesthetics, Soc. Phenomenology and Existentialism, Pan Am. Med. Assn., Sigma Xi. Democrat. Jewish. Author: (with B. Greenberg) Index of Scientific Writings on Creativity: Creative Men and Women, 1974, Index of Scientific Writings on Creativity: General 1566-1974, 1976; (with C.R. Hausman) The Creativity Question, 1976; The Emerging Goddess: The Creative Process in Art, Science and Other Fields, 1979; contbr. numerous articles on the creative process, schizophrenia and psychotherapy to profl. and popular jours.; research on creativity in the arts and sciences. Home: Stockbridge MA 01262 Office: Austen Riggs Center Stockbridge MA 01262

ROTHENBERG, ALLEN W., health service specialist; b. N.Y.C., June 13, 1929; s. George and Hattie (Kessler) R.; B.S., Bklyn. Coll., 1951; M.A., Columbia, 1955, Ed.D., 1968; m. Marcia Lacy; children—David, Debra, Daniel. Recreation leader, tchr. N.Y.C. Bd. Edn., 1949-52, tchr. pub. schs., 1954-55; jr., sr. high sch. counselor, West Hempstead, N.Y., 1956-60, prin. jr. high sch., 1960-66; counselor Queens Coll., 1957-65; dir. spl. services Peace Corps, 1966-69, dep. dir. Philippines, 1969-71, evaluator programs, 1971; cons. tng., eval., and edn., 1971-73; sr. project dir., edn. specialist Psychiat. Insts. Am., 1973; dir. devel. Psychiat. Inst. Washington, also v.p. Psychiat. Inst. Found., 1973—. Chmn. Merrick-Bellmore Human Rights Com., 1960—; ednl. cons. N.Y. chpt. Nat. Conf. Christians and Jews, 1963-65; mem. forming com. Interracial Council Bus. Opportunity, 1964; pres. Logan Circle Community Improvement Assn. Bd. dirs. Compeers, Washington, 1968, Logan Circle Historic Preservation Corp. Served with USCGR, 1952-54. Internat. Paper Co. Found. fellow, Columbia, 1963-64; NDEA grantee, 1957. Mem. N.E.A., Council for Exceptional Children. Club: Army and Navy (Manila). Address: 5437 Potomac Ave NW Washington DC 20016

ROTHENBERG, JEROME (DENNIS), author; b. N.Y.C., Dec. 11, 1931; s. Morris and Estelle (Lichtenstein) R.; B.A., Coll. City N.Y., 1952; M.A., U. Mich., 1953; m. Diane Brodatz, Dec. 25, 1952; 1 son, Matthew. Poet, freelance writer, 1956—; with Mannes Coll. Music, N.Y.C., 1961-70; vis. prof. U. Calif. at San Diego, 1971, 77—, U. Wis.-Milw., 1974-75, San Diego State U., 1976-77, U. Calif., San Diego, 1977-79, U. Calif., Riverside, 1980. Served with AUS, 1953-55. Recipient award in poetry Longview Found., 1960; Wenner-Gren Found. grantee-in-aid for research in Am. Indian poetry, 1968; Guggenheim fellow in creative writing, 1974; NEA poetry grantee, 1976. Mem. P.E.N. Am. Center, New Wilderness Found. Author numerous books of poetry and prose, including: Between, 1967; Technicians of the Sacred, 1968; Poems for the Game of Silence, 1971; Shaking the Pumpkin, 1972; America a Prophecy, 1973; Revolution of the Word, 1974; Poland/1931, 1974; A Big Jewish Book, 1978; A Seneca Journal, 1978; Vienna Blood, 1980. Editor, pub. Hawk's Well Press, N.Y.C., 1958-65, Some/Thing mag., 1966-69, Alcheringa: Ethnopoetics mag., 1970-76, New Wilderness Letter, 1976—. Home: 1026 San Abella Dr Encinitas CA 92024 Office: care New Directions 80 8th Ave New York NY 10011

ROTHENBERG, MELVIN GORDON, mathematician; b. Boston, Apr. 6, 1934; s. Harry and Leah (Gordon) R.; B.A., U. Mich., 1955; M.A., U. Calif., 1957, Ph.D., 1962; m. Marcia Cherko, Sept. 7, 1953; children—Julia, Aaron, Louise. Instr. in math. U. Chgo., 1961-63, asst. prof. math., 1963-66, asso. prof., 1966-69, prof., 1969—. Mem. Am. Math. Soc. Contbr. numerous articles on differential, geometric topology to profl. jours. Office: U of Chgo 5800 Ellis St Chicago IL 60637

ROTHENBERG, ROBERT EDWARD, physician, author; b. Bklyn., Sept. 27, 1908; s. Simon and Caroline A. (Baer) R.; A.B., Cornell U., 1929, M.D., 1932; m. Lillian Babette Lustig, June 8, 1933 (dec. Jan. 1977); m. 2d, Eileen Fein, Nov. 3, 1977; children—Robert Philip, Lynn Barbara (Mrs. Richard L. Kay). Intern Jewish Hosp., Bklyn., 1932-34, attending surgeon, 1955-75; postgrad. study Royal Infirmary, Edinburgh, 1934-35; civilian cons. U.S. Army Hosp., Ft. Jay, N.Y., 1960-66; attending surgeon French Polyclinic Med. Sch. and Health Center, N.Y.C., 1966-76; pres., 1973—, trustee, 1972-76; attending surgeon Cabrini Health Care Center, 1976—; clin. asst. prof. environ. medicine and community health State U. Coll. Medicine, N.Y.C., 1950-60; pvt. practice, 1935—. Pres. Medbook Publs., Inc. Chmn. Med. Group Council, 1947-64; cons. Office and Profl. Employees Internat. Union (local 153) Health Plan, 1960—, United Automobile Workers (local 259) Health Plan, 1960—, Sanitationmens Security Benefit Fund, 1964—; dir. Surgery Internat. Ladies Garment Workers Union; med. adv. bd. Hotel Assn. and Hotel Workers Health Plan, 1950-60, Hosp. Workers Health Plan, 1970-76. Served to lt. col. M.C., AUS, 1942- 45. Diplomate Am. Bd. Surgery. Mem. A.C.S., AMA, Bklyn. Surg. Assn., N.Y. County Med. Soc., Alpha Omega Alpha. Author and/or editor: Group Medicine and Health Insurance in Action, 1949; Understanding Surgery, 1955; New Illustrated Med. Ency., 4 vols., 1959; New Am. Med. Dictionary and Health Manual, 1962; Reoperative Surgery, 1964; Health in Later Years, 1964; Child Care Ency., 12 vols., 1966; Doctor's Premarital Medical Adviser, 1969; The Fast Diet Book, 1970; The Unabridged Medical Encyclopedia, 20 vols., 1973; Our Family Medical Record Book, 1973; The Complete Surgical Guide, 1973; What Every Patient Wants to Know, 1975; The Complete Book of Breast Care, 1975; Disney's Growing Up Healthy, 4 vols., 1975; First Aid—What to Do in an Emergency, 1976; The Plain Language Law Dictionary, 1980. Contbr. articles to med. jours. Home: 35 Sutton Pl New York NY 10022. *Truly great ideas are had by a large number of people. Success, however, is limited to the very few who have the ability to carry them out.*

ROTHER, GEORGE ULRICH, fin. exec.; b. Magdeburg, Germany, Dec. 31, 1933; s. Georg Paul and Johanna Wilhelmina (Horning) R.; came to U.S., 1958, naturalized, 1964; A.A., Real Gymnasium Bad Reichenhall (Germany), 1952; student Santa Ana Coll., 1962, Syracuse U., 1968; children—Michael G., Daniel G., Darin R. J. Teller, Toronto (Ont., Can.) Dominion Bank, 1956-58; head teller Cleve. Trust Co., 1958-60; cost accountant Bendix Corp., Santa Ana, Calif., 1960-63, supr. accounting, 1963-65, plant controller, 1965-67, asst. div. controller, Sidney, N.Y., 1967-68, div. controller, Ft. Lauderdale, Fla., 1968-71, fin. staff exec., Southfield, Mich., 1971-73, corporate controller, 1973-76; treas., controller Bendix Forest Products Corp., San Francisco, 1976-77, v.p., 1977-78, sr. v.p., 1978—, group exec., 1979—; dir. Modern Material Corp., Southfield, Am. Forest Properties, Inc., Arnold, Calif. Mem. Fin. Execs. Inst. Republican. Roman Catholic. Club: Phoenix. Home: 2101 Shoreline Dr Alameda CA 94501 Office: 2740 Hyde St San Francisco CA 94109

ROTHERMEL, DANIEL KROTT, metals co. exec.; b. West Reading, Pa., Mar. 21, 1938; s. Daniel Grim and Ruth Elizabeth (Krott) R.; B.S., Pa. State U., 1960; J.D., Am. U., 1966; m. Sarah Finch, July 9, 1960; children—Anne, Daniel F., K. Melissa. Accountant, Lukens Steel Co., Coatesville, Pa., 1960-61; admitted to D.C. bar, 1967; practiced in Reading, 1966-68; atty. Carpenter Tech. Corp., Reading, 1968-70, resident counsel, 1970-78, asst. sec., 1972-73, sec., 1973—, v.p., gen. counsel, 1978—; dir. Wyomissing New Home Fed. Savs. & Loan Assn. Mem. Inst. Community Affairs, Pa. State U., 1974-78. Served to lt. USNR, 1961-66. Mem. Am., D.C. bar assns., Am. Iron and Steel Inst., Am. Soc. Corp. Secs., U.S., Pa., Reading chambers commerce. Republican. Episcopalian (former mem. bishop's standing com.). Rotarian. Home: RD 1 Box 359-C Reading PA 19607 Office: 101 W Bern St Reading PA 19603

ROTHFIELD, LAWRENCE I., scientist; b. N.Y.C., Dec. 30, 1927; s. Joseph and Henrietta (Brown) R.; A.B., Cornell U., 1947; M.D., N.Y. U., 1951; m. Naomi Fox, Sept. 18, 1953; children—Susan Anne, Lawrence, Jane, John. Intern, resident Bellevue, Presbyn. hosps., N.Y.C., 1951-53, 55-57; successively instr., clin. asst. prof., asst. prof. N.Y. U. Sch. Medicine, 1957-64; asst. to asso. prof. Albert Einstein Coll. Medicine, 1964-68; prof., chmn. dept. microbiology U. Conn. Sch. Medicine, Farmington, 1968—; mem. molecular biology rev. panel NIH, 1970-75; mem. microbiology and immunology adv. com. Pres.'s Biomed. Research Panel, 1975. Served with M.C., AUS, 1953-55. Mem. Am. Soc. Biol. Chemists, Am. Soc. Microbiology (chmn. microbial physiology div. 1975). Author: Structure and Function of Biological Membranes; editorial bd. Jour. Membrane Biology, 1969—, Jour. Biol. Chemistry, 1974—. Home: 540 Deercliff Rd Avon CT 06001 Office: U Conn Health Center Farmington CT 06032

ROTHGERBER, IRA C., JR., lawyer; b. Denver, Apr. 5, 1913; s. Ira C. and Reina (Grunsfeld) R.; B.A., U. Colo., 1934, LL.B., 1935, LL.D., 1975. Admitted to Colo. bar, 1935, since practiced in Denver as partner firm Rothgerber, Appel & Powers; chmn. com. civil jury instrns. Colo. Supreme Ct., 1964-79; dir. First Bank Holding Co., also subs. banks, 1962—. Served with AUS, 1942-46. Decorated Legion of Merit, Bronze Star. Fellow Am. Bar Found.; mem. Am. Judicature Soc., Am., Colo., Denver bar assns., Order of Coif, Phi Alpha Delta. Democrat. Jewish. Clubs: Boulder Country; Denver. Home: 1245 Old Tale Rd Boulder CO 80303 Office: 2450 Colo State Bank Bldg 1600 Broadway Denver CO 80202

ROTHHOLZ, PETER LUTZ, pub. relations exec.; b. Berlin, June 23, 1929; s. Alfred and Bertha (Isner) R.; came to U.S., 1945, naturalized, 1947; B.A., Queens Coll., 1950; postgrad. N.Y. U., 1956-60; certificates U. London, 1949, McGill U., 1950; m. Paula Trachtman, Sept. 16, 1951; 1 dau., Amy Elisabeth; m. 2d, Barbara Peters Margules, July 4, 1971; stepchildren—David, Thomas. With Lissone-Lindeman U.S., Inc., N.Y.C., 1953-56, KLM Royal Dutch Airlines, N.Y.C., 1956-61; exec. v.p. Simmons Tours, Inc., N.Y.C., 1961-62; pres., prin. Peter Rothholz Assos., Inc., N.Y.C., 1962—; mem. faculty div. bus. mgmt. Sch. Continuing Edn. N.Y. U., 1969-70. Mem. exec. com. Pacific Area Travel Assn., Caribbean Tourism Assn. Served with U.S. Army, 1951-52. Fellow Inst. Certified Travel Agts; mem. Pub. Relations Soc. Am., Soc. Am. Travel Writers, Queens Mus. (pres. 1977—), Queens Coll. Alumni Assn. (pres. 1973-75), Phi Alpha Theta. Clubs: N.Y. Publicity (past v.p., dir.), N.Y. U. (bd. govs.). Contbr. articles to various publs. Home: 100-17 67th Dr Forest Hills NY 11375 Office: 380 Lexington Ave New York NY 10017

ROTHING, FRANK JOHN, investment banker; b. Chgo., July 4, 1924; s. Frank Joseph and Eva A. (Buhl) R.; B.S., U. Notre Dame, 1948; C.P.A., U. Ill., 1954; m. Carita Reiss Corbett, June 16, 1951; children—Frank John, Reginald, Peter, James, Richard, Joseph, Thomas, Carita Ann. Pub. accountant Arthur Young & Co., Chgo., 1948-55; v.p. Midwest Stock Exchange, 1955-60, v.p., treas., 1960-66, sr. v.p., 1966-71; exec. v.p., sec., dir. Ill. Co., 1971-74; v.p. 1st Nat. Bank Chgo., 1974-75; exec. v.p. Front St. Securities, Inc., 1975-78; mem. Chgo. Office, SEC, 1978; chmn. bd. Chgo. Bd. Options Exchange Clearing Corp. Mem. Chgo. Bd. Trade. Adviser, Jr. Achievement Chgo.; bd. dirs. St. Elizabeth's Hosp., Chgo.; mem. citizens bd. U. Chgo. Bd. dirs., mem. exec. bd. North Shore Area Boy Scouts Am.; chmn. bd. trustees St. Mary of Woods Coll., Terre Haute, Ind. Served to 1st lt. USAAF, 1943-45. Decorated D.F.C., Air medal. Mem. Am. Inst. Accountants, Ill. Soc. C.P.A.'s, Am. Accounting Assn., Newcomen Soc., Navy League U.S. Clubs: Michigan Shores; Bond of Chicago (dir.), Economic, Illinois Athletic, Notre Dame (dir.), Attic (Chgo.), Home: 630 Linden Ave Wilmette IL 60091 Office: 141 W Jackson Blvd Chicago IL 60604

ROTHKOPF, RICHARD ELLIOT, co. exec.; b. Cleve., Jan. 26, 1945; s. William R. and Ruth (Birnbaum) R.; B.S., Cornell U., 1967; postgrad. M.I.T. Sloan Sch. Mgmt.; m. Ann Fletcher; 1 son, Gray Sebastian. With Mobile Oil Corp., Europe and U.S., 1968-73; fin. controller, then mktg. planning mgr. Nitdorf Computer A.G., Germany, 1973-76; pres. Douglas Dunhill Inc., Chgo., 1976-79, Nat. Express Co., Chgo., 1979—.

ROTHMAN, DAVID J., educator; b. N.Y.C., Apr. 30, 1937; s. Murray and Anne (Beier) R.; B.A., Columbia, 1958; M.A., Harvard, 1959, Ph.D., 1964; m. Sheila Miller, June 26, 1960; children—Matthew, Micol. Asst. prof. history Columbia, N.Y.C., 1964-67, asso. prof., 1967-71, prof., 1971—. Fulbright-Hayes prof. Hebrew U., Jerusalem, 1968-69; vis. Pinkerton Prof. Sch. Criminal Justice, State U. N.Y., at Albany, 1973-74; Samuel Paley lectr. Hebrew U., Jerusalem, 1977. Mem. Com. for Study of Incarceration, 1971-74; co-dir. Project on Community Alternatives, 1978—. Bd. dirs. Mental Health Law Project, 1973—. Recipient Albert J. Beveridge prize Am. Hist. Assn., 1971. Social Sci. Research Council fellow, 1966; HEW fellow, 1968-69; Nat. Endowment for Humanities fellow, 1971-72; NIMH fellow, 1974-75, 78—; Law Enforcement Assistance Adminstrn. fellow, 1975-76. Mem. Am. Hist. Assn., Orgn. Am. Historians, N.Y. Civil Liberties Union (dir. 1973—), Phi Beta Kappa. Author: Politics and Power, 1966; The Discovery of the Asylum, 1971; co-author Doing Good, 1978; Conscience and Convenience: The Asylum and its Alternatives in Progressive America, 1980. Editor: The World of the Adams Chronicles, 1976; (with Sheila M. Rothman) On Their Own: The Poor in Modern America, 1972, The Sources of American Social Tradition, 1975. Office: 522 Fayerweather Hall Columbia U New York City NY 10027

ROTHMAN, DONALD NAHUM, lawyer; b. Balt., May 4, 1923; s. Frank and Minna Beth (Mahr) R.; student U. Va., 1939-41; B.A., Johns Hopkins, 1943; J.D., Harvard, 1948; m. Elizabeth Davidson, Oct. 7, 1944; children—John, Ellen, Thomas, Julie. Admitted to Md. bar, 1948, since practiced in Balt.; asso. firm Simon E. Sobeloff, 1948-52; mem. firm Gordon Feinblatt & Rothman, 1952-72, Gordon, Feinblatt, Rothman, Hoffberger and Hollander, 1972—. Bd. dirs. Mt. Washington Improvement Assn., 1948-75, Balt. Neighborhoods, Inc., 1965-74, Park Sch., 1971-76, Am. Jewish Com., 1968—; bd. dirs., founder Center Stage Assos., 1963—, pres., 1974—. Served to lt. (j.g.) USNR, 1943-46. Fellow Am. Coll. Trial Lawyers; mem. Am., Md. (bd. govs.), Balt. City bar assns., Am. Arbitration Assn. (panelist). Democrat. Clubs: Merchants, Johns Hopkins, Suburban Country. Home: 2207 Cross Country Rd Baltimore MD 21209 Office: Garrett Bldg Redwood and South Sts Baltimore MD 21202

ROTHMAN, KENNETH JOEL, lawyer, state legislator; b. St. Louis, Oct. 11, 1935; s. Herman and Anna (Ollanik) R.; A.B., then LL.B., Washington U., St. Louis; m. Geri Jaffe, Apr. 19, 1965; children—David Aaron, Sarah Ann, Rachel Eve, Daniel Joseph. Admitted to Mo. bar; individual practice law, Clayton, Mo., 1959—; asst. pros. atty., St. Louis, 1959-61; mem. Mo. Ho. of Reps., 1964—, majority floor leader, 1973-76, speaker, 1976—. Served with Air N.G., 1953-62. Recipient Legis. award Mo. Assn. for Mental Health; Mo. Bar award; Mo. Assn. Counties award; Mo. Probation and Parole Officers Assn. award; Conv. and Visitors Bur. of Greater St. Louis award; St. Louis County Bar Assn. award; Mo. Assn. Realtors award, others. Mem. Phi Delta Phi, Eta Sigma Phi, Sigma Alpha Mu. Democrat. Jewish. Club: Masons. Home: 90 Aberdeen Pl Clayton MO 63105 Office: Room 308A State Capitol Bldg Jefferson City MO 65101

ROTHMAN, MELVIN L., judge; b. Montreal, Que., Can., Apr. 6, 1930; s. Charles and Nellie (Rosen) R.; B.A., McGill U., 1951, B.C.L., 1954; m. Joan Elizabeth Presant, Aug. 4, 1954; children—Ann Elizabeth, Claire Presant, Margot Sneyd. Admitted to bar Que., 1954; practiced law, Montreal, 1954—; partner firm Phillips, Vineberg, Goodman, Phillips & Rothman, 1965—; judge Superior Ct., Dist. of Montreal, 1971—. Mem. Jr. Bar of Montreal (pres. 1963-64), Bar of Montreal (council 1964-65), Westmont Liberal Assn. (pres. 1968-70), Institut Philippe Pinel (sec., dir. 1965-70), Liberal Fedn. Can. (v.p. 1963-66). Home: 487 Argyle Ave Westmount PQ Canada Office: Superior Court Court House 10 Craig St E Montreal PQ Canada

ROTHMAN, PHILIP, educator; b. Phila., Oct. 31, 1921; s. Samuel and Reba (Levinthal) R.; B.S., Temple U., 1942, M.Ed., 1948; Ph.D., N.Y.U., 1954; m. Esther Steinberg, Nov. 26, 1947; children—Carol, Barbara, Alex, Jay, Tchr., Phila. pub. schs., 1946-48; mem. faculty Temple U., 1948-50, N.Y.U., 1951-54; mem. faculty Antioch Coll.,

Yellow Springs, Ohio, 1954—, prof. edn., chmn. dept., 1962—; cons. Nat. Council Christians and Jews, U.S. Office Edn.; vis. lectr. Bklyn. Coll., U. Kansas City (Mo.), U. Buffalo. Chmn. Yellow Springs Commn. Human Relations, 1968—. Bd. dirs. Yellow Springs Civil Liberties Union, 1960—, chmn., 1961-63. Served with AUS, 1942-46. Decorated Purple Heart. Mem. Assn. Supervision and Curriculum Devel., AAUP. Contbr. articles profl. jours. Home: 765 Wright St Yellow Springs OH 45387

ROTHMAN, STANLEY, educator; b. Bklyn., Aug. 4, 1927; s. Jack and Rose (Feinberg) R.; B.S., CCNY, 1949; M.A., Brown U., 1951; Ph.D., Harvard U., 1958; m. Eleanor Ruth Berman, Aug. 12, 1956; children—David, Michael. Mem. faculty dept. govt. Smith Coll., Northampton, Mass., 1956—, Marry Huggins Gamble prof. govt., 1978—. Served with USN, 1945-46. Ford Found. grantee, 1962, 74; Social Sci. Research Council grantee, 1966; NIMH grantee, 1970-72; NSF grantee, 1972-74. Mem. Am. Polit. Sci. Assn., Internat. Soc. Polit. Psychology. Jewish. Author: European Society and Politics, 1970; (with G. Breslauer) Soviet Politics and Society, 1977. Home: 67 Country Way Northampton MA 01061 Office: Dept Govt Smith Coll Northampton MA 01063

ROTHMAN, STEPHANIE, motion picture writer-dir.; b. Paterson, N.J., Nov. 9, 1936; d. Theodore Rothman; B.A. in Sociology, U. Calif., 1958, postgrad., 1959; postgrad. cinema U. So. Calif., 1961-64; m. Charles S. Swartz, June 16, 1963. Dir., co-author: (films) It's A Bikini World, 1966, The Student Nurses, 1970, The Velvet Vampire, 1971, Group Marriage, 1972, Terminal Island, 1973, dir., author The Working Girls, 1974; co-author Beyond Atlantis, 1973; v.p. creative affairs Dimension Pictures, Inc., Los Angeles, 1971-74. Fellow Dirs. Guild Am., 1963; grad. fellow U. So. Calif., 1963. Mem. Writers Guild Am.

ROTHMEIER, STEVEN GEORGE, airline exec.; b. Mankato, Minn., Oct. 4, 1946; s. Edwin George and Alice Joan (Johnson) R.; B.B.A., U. Notre Dame, 1968; M.B.A., U. Chgo., 1972. Corp. fin. analyst Northwest Airlines, Inc., St. Paul, 1973, mgr. econ. analysis, 1973-78, dir. econ. planning, 1978, v.p. fin., treas., 1978—; dir. 1st Nat. Bank of St. Paul, Mont. Enterprises, Inc., Tomisato Shoji Tokyo. Served to lt. U.S. Army, 1968-71. Decorated Bronze star. Mem. Air Transport Assn. Am. Republican. Roman Catholic. Club: Decathlon. Office: Minneapolis-St Paul Internat Airport Saint Paul MN 55111. *Success is not an accident; it is a habit. Success is the result of desire, dedication, sacrifice, mental toughness, hard work—and prayer. And you are not successful until you can share your success with others.*

ROTHMULLER, MARKO, baritone; b. Trnjani, Yugoslavia, Dec. 31, 1908; s. Josip and Anka (Hahn) R.; student composition Music Acad., Zagreb, Yugoslavia; with Alban Berg, Vienna, Austria; student voice with Franz Steiner, Vienna; m. Ela Reiss, July 14, 1935 (div. 1970); children—Ilan, Daniel; m. 2d, Catherine Blanchard, Jan. 15, 1971 (div. 1975). Came to U.S., 1948, naturalized, 1958. Operatic appearances at Hamburg-Altona, Germany, 1932, Zurich, Switzerland, 1935-48, State Opera, Vienna, 1946-57, Covent Garden, London, Eng., 1948-54, Teatro Colon, Buenos Aires, Argentina, 1952, 53, N.Y.C. Center Opera, 1948-50, 52, Paris Opera, 1952-, Staedtische Oper, Berlin, Germany, 1954—, Met. Opera, N.Y.C., 1958-61, 64-65; prof. voice Ind. U. Sch. Music; ret., 1979; rec. artist for His Master's Voice, London LP, Decca, Bartok Records. Author: The Music of the Jews, rev. edit., 1967; Pronunciation of German and German Diction for Singers, 1978. Home: 1005 E Wylie St Bloomington IN 47401

ROTHOLZ, MAX B., farm and ranch mgmt. specialist; b. Houston, Dec. 26, 1921; s. Max B. and Lavania Evelina (Abercrombie) R.; B.S., Tex. A. and M. U., 1946; m. Mary Louise Wade, Jan. 10, 1946; children—Rebecca, Michael, James, Don, Lee. Farmer and rancher, Crystal City, Tex., 1946-50; mgr. Doane Agrl. Service, Inc. (Tex.), 1953-55; gen. mgr. Pierce (Tex.) Ranch, 1955—; partner Cometa Cattle Co., Crystal City, 1956—; dir., pres. Rice Belt Warehouse, Inc., El Campo, Tex., 1963—; pres. Am. Rice, Inc., Houston, 1969-76; v.p. W. Tex. Rice, Inc., Alvin, 1973—; dir. Volar Inc., City State Bank, Palacios, Tex., Bay City Bank and Trust Co. Pres., mem. bd. Wharton Ind. Sch. Dist., 1963-76; mem. Tex. com. Agrl. Stblzn. and Conservation Service, U.S. Dept. Agr. Served with U.S. Army, 1943-46. Decorated Bronze Star. Mem. Houston, San Antonio livestock expns., Tex. Mid-Coast Water Devel. Assn. (pres. 1970), Tex. Southwestern Cattle Raisers Assn., Soc. Farm Mgrs. and Rural Appraisers, Nat. Assn. Rural Appraisers, Tex. Soc. Farm Mgrs., Am. Assn. Certified Appraisers, Am. Cattle Raisers Assn., Aircraft Owners and Pilots Assn., Sheriff's Assn. Tex., Tex. Police Assn., Wharton County Boy Builders Assn. Democrat. Presbyterian. Clubs: Lions, Wharton, El Campo, Bay City Country, Elks. Home and Office: Pierce Ranch Pierce TX 77467

ROTHSCHILD, ALAN FRIEND, lawyer; b. Columbus, Ga., Aug. 15, 1925; s. Irwin Bernard and Aleen (Samuels) R.; B.S. in Commerce, U. Va., 1945, LL.B., 1947; m. Eva Garrett Pound, Sept. 21, 1957; children—Alan Friend, William Garrett, Elizabeth Pound. Admitted to Ga. bar, 1948; partner Rosenstrauch & Rothschild, Columbus, 1948-51; asso. Hatcher, Stubbs, Land, Hollis & Rothschild and predecessor, Columbus, 1951-57, partner, 1957—. Mem. adv. bd. First Nat. Bank Columbus; sec. Rothschild Co., 1967—; dir. Rothschild Realty Co. Mem. Gov.'s Commn. on Revision Appellate Cts. Ga., 1976—; mem. Ga. Bd. Bar Examiners, 1979—; chmn. bd. commrs. Med. Center, 1973-74; pres. Community Counseling Center, 1960-62; local co-chmn. NCCJ, 1958; active Boys Club, Jr. Achievement, Three Arts League; trustee St. Francis Hosp., Springer Theatre, Brookstone Sch.; life trustee, 1st v.p. Columbus Mus. Arts and Crafts; bd. dirs. Walter Alan Richards Found., Anne Elizabeth Shepherd Home; pres. Columbus Legal Aid Soc., 1971-73. Fellow Am. Coll. Probate Counsel; mem. Columbus Lawyers Club (pres. 1967), Ga. Bar Assn., Am. Bar Assn. Jewish. Home: 2328 Fairway Ave Columbus GA 31906 Office: 500 Corporate Center Columbus GA 31902

ROTHSCHILD, AMALIE ROSENFELD, artist; b. Balt., Jan. 1, 1916; d. Eugene Isaac and Addye (Goldsmith) Rosenfeld; diploma Md. Inst. Coll. Art, 1934; student N.Y. Sch. Fine and Applied Art, 1934; m. Randolph S. Rothschild, Aug. 3, 1936; children—Amalie R., Adrien R. One-woman shows include: Goucher Coll., Balt., 1968, Balt. Mus. Art, 1971, Nat. Acad. Scis., Washington, 1975, Kornblatt Gallery, Balt., 1978; group shows include: Jewish Mus., N.Y.C., 1952, Corcoran Gallery Art, Washington, 1958, 59; represented in permanent collections: Corcoran Gallery Art, Phillips Collection, Washington, Peale Mus. Balt., Balt. Mus. Art, Honolulu Acad. Arts, Fed. Res. Bank, Richmond, Va.; instr. painting Met. Sch. Art, Balt., 1956-59; lectr. fine arts Goucher Coll., 1960-68; commns. include: archtl. panels Martin Luther King, Jr. Elem. Sch., Balt., 1969; wall hanging Walters Art Gallery, Balt., 1974. Chmn. artists com. Balt. Mus. Art, 1956-58, trustee, 1977—. Mem. Artists Equity Assn. (dir. Md. chpt. 1977—). Democrat. Jewish. Address: 2909 Woodvalley Dr Baltimore MD 21208. *The definition of talent as power of mind and body committed to one for use and improvement describes my purpose in life. Late intellectual motivation followed early practical preparation for commercial art. Continuing self-education through multi-disciplinary reading, directing of energy into daily art-related endeavor, expecting integrity of performance in myself and others—these are my criteria for pursuit of excellence and fulfillment.*

ROTHSCHILD, AUGUST BARNET, lawyer; b. San Francisco, Feb. 10, 1906; s. Robert Barnet and Lillie (Helbing) R.; A.B., U. Calif., 1925, J.D., 1928; m. Kathryn Wolf, Jan. 20, 1942; children—August Barnet, John David, Donald Edward. Admitted to Calif. bar, 1928; asso. atty. in law office, 1928-39; individual practice law, 1939-42; partner firm Shapro & Rothschild, San Francisco, 1945-58; partner firm Rothschild, Phelan & Montali, San Francisco, 1958—; instr. in bankruptcy U. San Francisco, 1937-39, 46. Vice pres. Am. Council Judaism. Served to lt. comdr. USNR, 1942-45. Mem. Am. Bar Assn., Bar Assn. San Francisco (dir. 1961-62), Nat. Bankruptcy Conf. Republican. Jewish. Club: Villa Taverna. Home: 550 Battery St 1413 San Francisco CA 94111 Office: 235 Montgomery St 1520 San Francisco CA 94104

ROTHSCHILD, ERNEST LEO, publishing co. exec.; b. Darmstadt, Germany, Sept. 23, 1922; s. David and Auguste (Levi) R.; came to U.S., 1939, naturalized, 1943; B.A. magna cum laude, N.Y. U., 1948, M.A., 1949; m. Edith Margot Chan, Mar. 9, 1952; children—Anthony Joseph, Deborah Wilma, Vivian Miriam, Philip Elias. Modern lang. editor Am. Book Co., N.Y.C., 1951-69; mng. editor Van Nostrand Reinhold Co., N.Y.C., 1969-70, exec. editor, 1970-72; mng. editor D. Van Nostrand Co., 1972-78, v.p., editorial dir., 1978—; instr. French, N.Y. U., N.Y.C., 1951. Pres. Shelter Rock Jewish Center, Roslyn, N.Y., 1966-68; bd. dirs. N.Y. Met. region United Synagogue Am., 1978—. Served with AUS, 1943-45; ETO, MTO. Mem. Modern Lang. Assn. Am., Am. Council on Teaching of Fgn. Langs., Am. Assn. Tchrs. of German, Phi Beta Kappa. Home: 5 Peppermill Rd Roslyn NY 11576 Office: D Van Nostrand Co 135 W 50th St New York NY 10020

ROTHSCHILD, GEORGE WILLIAM, lawyer, transp. co. exec.; b. Chgo., Mar. 21, 1917; s. Edwin and Hannah (Loeb) R.; A.B. cum laude, Harvard, 1939; J.D. cum laude, U. Chgo., 1942; m. Valerie Jane Myers, Mar. 16, 1946; children—Jane Rothschild Ferguson, John Steven. Admitted to Ill. bar, 1942, N.Y. bar, 1946; asso. Root, Ballantine, Harlan, Bushby & Palmer, N.Y.C., summer 1942, 46-49; atty., asst. and asso. gen. counsel ECA and successor agys., Washington, 1949-55; atty. GATX (formerly Gen. Am. Transp. Corp.), Chgo., 1955-61, gen. counsel, 1961-69, v.p., gen. counsel, 1969-78, sec., dir., 1972-78; spl. counsel Steel Project Program, Econ. Devel. Adminstrn., Dept. Commerce, 1979; counsel firm Coin, Crowley & Nord, Chgo., 1979—; panelist Am. Arbitration Assn. Served from ensign to lt. USNR, 1942-46. Mem. Am., Ill., Chgo. (com. chmn. 1968, 72) bar assns., Order of Coif. Clubs: Cliff Dwellers, Columbia Yacht (Chgo.); Harvard (Chgo., N.Y.C.). Home: 321 Hamilton St Evanston IL 60202 Office: 33 N Dearborn St Chicago IL 60602

ROTHSCHILD, JOSEPH, educator; b. Fulda, Germany, Apr. 5, 1931; s. Meinhold and Henriette (Loewenstein) R.; came to U.S., 1940, naturalized, 1945; A.B. summa cum laude, Columbia Coll., 1951; A.M., Columbia U., 1952; D.Phil. (Euretta J. Kellett fellow), Oxford U., 1955; m. Ruth Deborah Nachmansohn, July 19, 1959; children—Nina, Gerson. Instr. dept. polit. sci. Columbia, N.Y.C., 1955-58, asst. prof., 1958-62, asso. prof., 1962-68, prof., 1968—, Class of 1919 endowed prof., 1978—, chmn. dept., 1971-75. Vice chmn. mem. exec. com. Am. Profs. for Peace in Middle East. Social Sci. Research Council fellow, 1963-64, J.S. Guggenheim fellow, 1967-68, Am. Council Learned Socs. fellow, 1971-72; Chamberlain sr. fellow, 1974; Ford research fellow, summer 1976; Nat. Endowment for Humanities fellow, 1978-79; Lehrman Inst. fellow, 1979-80. Mem. Polit. Sci. Acad., Am. Assn. for Advancement Slavic Studies, Polish Inst. Arts and Scis. in Am., Jewish Publ. Soc. Am., Phi Beta Kappa. Author: The Communist Party of Bulgaria, 1959; Introduction to the Contemporary Civilization in the West, 3d edit., 1960; Chapters in Western Civilization, 3d edit., 1962; Communist Eastern Europe, 1964; Pilsudski's Coup d'Etat, 1966; East Central Europe Between the Two World Wars, 1974. Contbr. articles to profl. jours. Home: 445 Riverside Dr New York NY 10027

ROTHSCHILD, LOUIS SAMUEL, business exec.; b. Leavenworth, Kans., Mar. 29, 1900; s. Louis Philip and Nora (Westheimer) R.; Ph.B., Yale, 1920; m. Emily Bettman, Oct. 7, 1929. With Rothschild & Sons, Inc., Kansas City, Mo. and Oklahoma City, 1920-56, sec., 1931-34, v.p., 1934-42, pres., 1942-55; chmn. bd. Inland Waterways Corp., 1953-59; chmn. Fed. Maritime Bd., maritime adminstr., U.S. Dept. Commerce, 1953-55, under sec. of commerce for transp., 1955-58; pres., dir. Transp. Equities Corp., 1958-61, 65—; pres., dir. Intermediate Credit Corp., 1962-65, Standard R.E. Improvement Co., 1965-75. U.S. del. NATO Planning Bd. for Ocean Shipping, 1953; chmn. Air Coordinating Com., 1955-58; mem. commn. govt. security, 1955-56; U.S. del. ILO conf., 1958. Mem. city planning commn., Kansas City, Mo., 1937-53, chmn., 1946-53. Chmn. Menorah Found. Med. Research; dir. Community Studies, Inc., Midwest Research Inst., Kansas City, Mo.; trustee William Allen White Found. Served with USN, 1918-19. Recipient Presdl. citation, 1958. Home: 4000 Massachusetts Ave NW Washington DC 20016 Office: 1629 K St NW Washington DC 20006

ROTHSCHILD, MICHAEL, economist; b. Chgo., Aug. 2, 1942; s. Edwin Alfred and Ann (Meyer) R.; B.A., Reed Coll., 1963; M.A., Yale U., 1965; Ph.D., M.I.T., 1969; m. Linda Preiss, Sept. 7, 1969; children—David, Daniel. Asst. prof. econs. Harvard U., 1969-73; lectr. Princeton U., 1972-74, asso. prof., 1974-75, prof., 1975-76; prof. U. Wis., Madison, 1976—. Guggenheim fellow, 1975-76. Fellow Econometric Soc.; mem. Am. Econ. Assn. Editor: (with Peter Diamond) Uncertainty in Economics, 1978. Home: 4414 Woods End Madison WI 53711 Office: Econs Dept U Wis Madison WI 53711

ROTHSCHILD, V. HENRY, II, lawyer; b. N.Y.C., Apr. 4, 1908; s. Victor Sidney and Lily (Sulzberger) R.; student Phillips Exeter Acad., 1923-25; A.B. with honors, Cornell U., 1929; LL.B. with honors, Yale U., 1932; m. Ann Eleanor Hatfield, May 29, 1939 (div.); children—Thomas Adams, V. Henry III, Cameron Adams Hatfield (stepson); m. 2d, Jacqueline Dury Roy; stepchildren—Michel, Serge, Christian Roy. Admitted to N.Y. bar, 1932, since practiced in N.Y.C.; asso. Root, Clark, Buckner & Ballantine (now Dewey, Ballantine, Bushby, Palmer & Wood), N.Y.C., 1932-40; engaged in practice of law, specializing in corporate and tax work 1940—. Mem. Salary Stblzn. Bd., 1951-52, chief counsel, 1951, vice chmn., 1952. Hon. trustee Asso. YM-YMCA Greater N.Y. Mem. Am. (mem. sect. corp., banking and bus., com. on employee benefits, tax), N.Y. State (chmn. com. on employee benefits 1968-70, chmn. com. retirement plan 1971-76), N.Y.C. bar assns., Am. Arbitration Assn. (nat. panel), Am. Pension Conf. (steering com. 1966-70, legislation com. 1968—), Phi Beta Kappa, Phi Kappa Phi, Pi Lambda Phi. Clubs: Sky, Yale (N.Y.C.). Author: Pay Contracts with Key Men (with William J. Casey), 1952; Deferred Compensation for Executives (with J. K. Lasser), 1955; Compensating the Corporate Executive (with George Thomas Washington), 3d edit., 1962; Executive Compensation and Federal Securities Legislation (with Myer Feldman), 1957; Financing Stock Purchases, 1957; Expense Accounts for Executives, 1958; Business Gifts as Income, 1961; The New Stock Option, 1965; Top Management Compensation Outlook, 1966; The Restricted Stock Arrangement, 1968; Employee Stock Options and the New Maximum Tax Rate on Earned Income (with Peter Miller), 1971; Stock Option Plans in France, 1972; (with Jack B. Salwen) Stock Option Plans in Transition, 1973; Regulation of Deferred Compensation for Executives by the Pension Reform Act, 1975; Funding Deferred Compensation Arrangements, 1976. Contbr. legal and non-legal publs. Editor Yale Law Sch. Jour., 1930-32. Lectr. Practicing Law Inst., N.Y.U. Inst. Fed. Taxation. Home: 155 E 38 St New York NY 10016 also Truro MA 02666 also Norwich VT 05055 Office: 30 Rockefeller Plaza New York NY 10020

ROTHSTEIN, ASER, educator; b. Vancouver, B.C., Can., Apr. 29, 1918; s. Samuel and Etta (Wiseman) R.; B.A. in Zoology, U.B.C., 1938; student U. Calif. at Berkeley, 1938-40; Ph.D., U. Rochester, 1943; m. Evelyn Paperny, Aug. 18, 1940; children—Sharon Leslie, David Michael, Steven Jay. Came to U.S., 1940, naturalized, 1955. With atomic energy project U. Rochester, 1948—, co-dir., 1965—, mem. faculty Med. Sch., 1946—, prof. radiation biology, 1959—, co-chmn. dept., 1965—; dir. research inst. Hosp. for Sick Children, Toronto, Ont., 1971; prof. med. biophysics U. Toronto Med. Sch., 1972—; vis. prof. Eidgenossische Technische Hochschule, Zurich, 1977. U.S. del. UNESCO Conf., Paris, France, 1957. NSF sr. postdoctoral fellow U. Bern (Switzerland), 1959-60. Fellow AAAS. Home: 33 Harbour Sq Toronto ON M5J 2G2 Canada

ROTHSTEIN, FRED H., bus. exec.; b. Berlin, Nov. 13, 1928; s. Max M. and Margot R.; B.A., UCLA; m. Anita Gallo, Jan. 7, 1976; children—Paul M., Randi E. Mdse. mgr. Kaynee Co., 1953-57, McGregor Sportswear, 1958-61; with Manhattan Industries Inc., 1962—, mdse. mgr. sportswear, then v.p. internat. div., now pres. inernat. div., N.Y.C. Served with U.S. Army, 1950-52. Mem. Young Menswear Assn. of Men's Apparel Industry. Republican. Jewish. Office: 1271 6th Ave New York NY 10020

ROTHSTEIN, JESSE, lawyer; b. N.Y.C., May 30, 1934; s. David and Miriam (Kreiswirth) R.; S.B., Mass. Inst. Tech., 1956; LL.B., Harvard U., 1959; m. Polly Wittenberg, Aug. 30, 1959; children—Amy, Chester. Admitted to N.Y. bar, 1959, since practiced in N.Y.C.; partner firm Amster Rothstein, & Engelberg, 1964—; dir. Certech, Inc. Home: Lincoln Ave Purchase NY 10577 Office: 90 Park Ave New York NY 10016

ROTHSTEIN, SAMUEL, librarian, educator; b. Moscow, Russia, Jan. 12, 1921; s. Louis Israel and Rose (Checov) R.; brought to Can., 1922, naturalized, 1929; B.A., U. B.C., 1939, M.A., 1940; student U. Calif. at Berkeley, 1941-42, B.S. in L.S., 1947; student U. Wash., 1942-43; Ph.D. (Carnegie Corp. fellow 1951-54), U. Ill., 1954, D.Litt., York U., 1971; m. Miriam Ruth Teitelbaum, Aug. 26, 1951; children—Linda Rose, Sharon Lee. Teaching fellow U. Wash., 1942-43; prin. library asst. U. Calif. at Berkeley Library, 1947; mem. staff U. B.C. Library, 1946-51, 54-62, acting univ. librarian, dir. Sch. Librarianship, 1961-62, prof., 1962—, dir. Sch. Librarianship, 1962-70; vis. prof. U. Hawaii, 1969, U. Toronto, 1970, Hebrew U., Jerusalem, 1973. Mem. Commn. Nat. Plan Library Edn., 1963—; mem. asso. com. sci. information Nat. Research Council Can., 1962—; councillor B.C. Med. Library Service, 1961, Pacific div. Canadian Jewish Congress, 1962—, Internat. House Assn. B.C., 1959-60; mem. Canadian Adv. Bd. Sci. and Tech. Information. Bd. dirs. Jewish Community Centre of Vancouver, pres., 1972-74. Served with Canadian Army, 1943-46. Recipient Helen Gordon Stewart award, 1970. Mem. Assn. Am. Library Schs. (pres. 1968-69), Am. (council 1963—), B.C. (pres. 1959- 60), Pacific Northwest (pres. 1963-64), Canadian (council 1958-60) library assns., Bibliog. Soc. Can. (council 1959—), Inst. Profl. Librarians Ont., Canadian Assn. U. Tchrs. Author: The Development of Reference Services, 1955; (with others) Training Professional Librarians for Western Canada, 1957; The University-The Library, 1972; also articles. Co-editor: As We Remember It, 1970. Home: 1416 W 40th Ave Vancouver 13 BC Canada

ROTHWELL, ANGUS B., state ednl. ofcl.; b. Superior, Wis., July 25, 1905; s. John Z. and Eva C. (Barton) R.; student U. Wis., 1925-26, U. Ia., summers 1928-29; B. Edn., Wis. State Coll., Superior, 1930; M.A., Columbia Tchrs. Coll., 1932; M.A. (hon.), Lawrence Coll., 1945; summer student U. Minn., 1935; LL.D. (hon.), Carroll Coll., 1963; m. Florence M. Rothwell, Aug. 8, 1927; children—William S., Jean Ann (Mrs. William Olson), Marilyn Gail (Mrs. E. Lee Geraldson). Elementary sch. prin., Wausau, Wis., 1926-34; curriculum dir., Superior, 1934-35, high sch. prin., 1935-41, supt. schs., 1941-49; supt. schs., Manitowoc, Wis., 1949-61; supt. pub. instrn. Wis., 1961-66; exec. dir. Coordinating Council Higher Edn., 1966-69. Wis. commr. Edn. Commn. of States; chmn. Wis. Coordinating Com. Higher Edn., Wis. Bd. Vocat. and Adult Edn., Wis. Free Library Commn., Wis. Radio Council. Bd. regents U. Wis., Wis. State Coll., Madison. Served to lt. comdr. USNR, 1943-46. Mem. Council Chief State Sch. Officers (dir.). Am. Assn. Sch. Adminstrs., Wis. Supts. Assn., Nat. (chmn. nat. safety commn.), Wis. edn. assns., Phi Delta Kappa. Contbr. articles ednl. jours. Home: 5514 Stadium Dr Madison WI 53705

ROTHWELL, JACK C., JR., banker; b. Borger, Tex., Sept. 29, 1932; s. Jesse Cecil and Ruth Katherine (Bell) R.; B.B.A., U. Tex., 1956, M.B.A., 1956, Ph.D., 1958; postgrad. U. Perugia (Italy), 1957; m. Jo Ann, Aug. 25, 1957; children—Lesli Ann, John Kevin. Lectr. in fin. U. Tex., 1957-58, U. Pa., 1960-62; economist Fed. Res. Bank of Phila., 1958-66; v.p., economist New Eng. Mchts. Bank of Boston, 1966-74; exec. v.p., chief economist Central Nat. Bank of Cleve., 1974—. Mem. Am. Bankers Assn. (exec. com. planning div.), Am. Acad. Polit. and Social Sci., World Affairs Council, Am. Econ. Assn., Nat. Assn. Bus. Economists, Beta Theta Pi. Republican. Episcopalian. Clubs: Algonquin of Boston, Union of Cleve., Kirtland Country, Cohasset Yacht. Office: 800 Superior Ave Cleveland OH 44114

ROTHWELL, WARREN RANDALL, bus. equipment mfg. co. exec.; b. Regina, Sask., Can., Jan. 23, 1917; s. Warren and Ethel (Baker) R.; student U. Man., 1935-37, U. Toronto, 1942; m. June Patricia Knight, Jan. 19, 1942; 1 dau., Patricia June. With Coca-Cola Ltd., Toronto, 1937-47; with Can. Binding Ltd., Toronto, 1947-62, pres., 1950-62; pres. Gen. Binding Corp. (Can.) Ltd., 1952-63; chmn., dir. Gen. Binding Corp., Northbrook, Ill., 1963—; dir. Lakeview Bank, Pioneer Bank, N.W. Nat. Bank, Northbrook Trust and Savs. Bank. Served with RCAF, 1942-45. Mem. Computer and Bus. Equipment Mfrs. Assn., Bus. Records Mfrs. Assn. Republican. Clubs: Shoreacres Golf (Lake Bluff, Ill.); Imperial Golf (Naples, Fla.). Home: 220 E Witchwood Ln Lake Bluff IL 60044 Office: 1 Gen Binding Corp Plaza Northbrook IL 60062

ROTMAN, JOSEPH JONAH, mathematician, educator; b. Chgo., May 26, 1934; s. Ely and Rose (Wolf) R.; B.A., U. Chgo., 1954, M.A., 1956, Ph.D., 1959; m. Marganit Weinberger, Aug. 25, 1978. Research asso. U. Ill. at Urbana, 1959-61, asst. prof., 1961-63, asso. prof., 1963-68, prof., 1968—; vis. prof. Queen Mary Coll., U. London, Eng., 1965-66, Hebrew U., Jerusalem, Israel, 1970; vis. prof., Lady Davis fellow Technion (Israel Inst. Tech.), Haifa, also Hebrew U., Jerusalem, 1977-78. Chmn., Champaign-Urbana Civil Liberties Union, 1975. Mem. Am. Math. Soc., Math. Assn. Am. Club: Urbana Poker and Salami. Author: Theory of Groups, 1965, rev. edit., 1973; Notes on Homological Algebra, 1970; An Introduction to Homological

Algebra, 1979. Editor Proc. Am. Math. Soc., 1970-72, mng. editor, 1972-73. Office: U Ill Urbana IL 61801

ROTMAN, MORRIS BERNARD, pub. relations cons.; b. Chgo., June 6, 1918; s. Louis and Etta (Harris) R.; student Wright Jr. Coll., 1936-37, Northwestern U., 1937-39; m. Sylvia Sugar, Mar. 1, 1944; children—Betty Ruth, Jesse, Richard. Editor Times Neighborhood publs., Chgo., 1938-40; asst. editor City News Bur., 1940-42; mng. editor Scott Field Broadcaster, USAAF, 1942-43; publicity dir. Community and War Fund of Met. Chgo., 1943-45; v.p. William R. Harshe Assos., Chgo., 1945-49, pres., 1949-66, chmn. bd., chief exec. officer, 1966—, name changed to Harshe-Rotman & Druck, Inc., 1962. Chmn. solicitations pub. relations div. Community Fund Chgo., 1948-49, spl. events chmn., 1953; chmn. communications div. Jewish Fedn. Chgo., 1965, Combined Jewish Appeal, 1966; bd. dirs. Rehab. Inst., Center for Sports Medicine, Nat. Commn. Prevention Child Abuse; trustee Roosevelt U. Recipient Prime Minister Israel medal, 1969. Mem. Pub. Relations Soc. Am. (past dir.), Chgo. President's Orgn. (pres. 1970-71), Chief Exec. Forum, World Bus. Council, Chgo. Press Vets. Assn., Sigma Delta Chi. Clubs: Cliff Dwellers, Mid-Am., Standard, Publicity, Press (Chgo.); Bryn Mawr Country; Tamarisk Country (Palm Springs); Headline. Home: 400 E Randolph St Chicago IL 60601 Office: 444 N Michigan Ave Chicago IL 60611 also 300 E 44th St New York NY 10017 also 3345 Wilshire Blvd Los Angeles CA 90010 also 27 Albemarle St London England also 1010 Wisconsin Ave NW Washington DC 20007 also 1900 W Loop S Houston TX 77027

ROTTER, PAUL TALBOTT, life ins. exec.; b. Parsons, Kans., Feb. 21, 1918; s. J. and LaNora (Talbott) R.; B.S. summa cum laude, Harvard U., 1937; m. Virginia Sutherlin Barksdale, July 17, 1943; children—Carolyn Sutherlin, Diane Talbott. Asst. mathematician Prudential Ins. Co. of Am., Newark,, 1938-46; with Mut. Benefit Life Ins. Co., Newark, 1946—, successively asst. mathematician, asso. mathematician, mathematician, 1946-59, v.p., 1959-69, exec. v.p., 1969—. Mem. Madison Bd. Edn., 1958-64, pres., 1959-64. Trustee, mem. budget com. United Campaign of Madison, 1951-55; mem. bd., chmn. advancement com. Robert Treat council Boy Scouts Am., 1959-64. Fellow Soc. Actuaries (bd. govs. 1965-68, gen. chmn. edn. and exam. com. 1963-66; chmn. adv. com. edn. and exam. 1969-72); mem. Brit. Inst. Actuaries (asso.). Am. Acad. Actuaries (v.p. 1968-70 bd. dirs., chmn. edn. and exam. com. 1965-66, chmn. rev. and evaluation com. 1968-74), Asso. Harvard Alumni (regional dir. 1965-69), Actuaries Club N.Y. (pres. 1967-68), Harvard Alumni Assn. (v.p. 1964-66), Phi Beta Kappa Assos., Phi Beta Kappa. Clubs: Harvard N.J. (pres. 1956-57); Harvard (N.Y.C.); Morris County Golf (Convent, N.J.). Home: 15 Noe Ave Madison NJ 07940 Office: 520 Broad St Newark NJ 07101

ROTTIERS, HARRY BERNARD, computer co. exec.; b. Birch Run, Mich., Mar. 8, 1914; s. Bernard and Emelie (Wuelfing) R.; Ph.B., U. Detroit, 1935, J.D., 1937; m. Ruth M. Jeynes, Aug. 17, 1940; chidlren—Robert B., Russell J. Admitted to Mich. bar, 1937; since practiced in Detroit; regional counsel War Assets Adminstrn., Detroit, 1945-51; various positions Burroughs Corp., Detroit, 1951—, sr. v.p. 1974—; sec., dir. Detroit Internat. Bridge Co., 1949-53. Mem. Franklin (Mich.) City Council, 1953-55. Trustee Rehab. Inst. Detroit. Mem. Nat. Security Indsl. Assn., Am., Mich. bar assns., Computer and Bus. Equipment Mfg. Assn. (dir.), Delta Pi Kappa, Delta Theta Phi. Club: Birmingham (Mich.) Country. Home: 2945 Woodward Ave Apt 21 Bloomfield Hills MI 48013 Office: Burroughs Corp Burroughs Pl Detroit MI 48232

ROTTMAN, ELLIS, govt. ofcl.; b. Balt., Apr. 5, 1930; s. Abraham Isaac and Sadie (Harris) R.; B.S., U. Md., 1952; m. Carol Parker Donovan, May 30, 1965; children—Marcus, Lisa, Jason, Adam. Asso. editor Army Times Pub. Co., Washington, 1956-59; editor, dir. pub. relations Am. Fedn. Govt. Employees, AFL-CIO, 1959-65; pub. info. officer U.S. Post Office Dept., 1966-69; editor Manpower mag. Dept. Labor, 1969-75; editor, publs. dir. FDA, Rockville, Md., 1975-78; public info. dir. Labor-Mgmt. Services Adminstrn. Dept. Labor, 1978—. Active Boy Scouts Am. Served with AUS, 1952-54. Recipient Journalism award Internat. Labor Press Assn., AFL-CIO, 1959, 60, 61, 62, 64; award merit Fed. Editors Assn., 1974, 75, 77, 78. Jewish. Home: 901 N Belgrade Rd Silver Spring MD 20902 Office: 2d St and Constitution Ave NW Washington DC 20210

ROUB, BRYAN ROGER, diversified industry financial exec.; b. Berea, Ohio, May 1, 1941; s. Bernard Augustus and Pearl Irene (Koeblitz) R.; student Ohio Wesleyan U., 1962; B.S., Ohio State U., 1966; M.B.A., U. Pa., 1978; m. Judith Elaine Penman, June 19, 1965; children—Paul, Bradley, Michael. Mem. audit staff Ernst & Ernst, Cleve., 1966-70; asst. controller Midland-Ross, Cleve., 1970-73, controller, 1973—, v.p., 1977—. Mem. Fin. Execs. Inst., Am. Inst. C.P.A.'s, Ohio Soc. C.P.A.'s. Club: Westwood Country (Rocky River). Home: 1936 Newbury Dr Westlake OH 44145 Office: Midland-Ross Corp 20600 Chagrin Blvd Cleveland OH 44122

ROUBOS, GARY LYNN, diversified mfg. co. exec.; b. Denver, Nov. 7, 1936; s. Dorr and Lillian Margaret (Coover) R.; B.S. in Chem. Engring. with high honors, U. Colo., 1959; M.B.A. with distinction, Harvard U., 1963; m. Terie Joan Anderson. Feb. 20, 1960; children—Lyndel, Leslie. With Boise Cascade Corp., 1963-71; with Dieterich Standard Corp., Boulder, Colo., 1971-76, exec. v.p., then pres., 1975-76; co. acquired by Dover Corp., N.Y.C., 1975; exec. v.p. Dover Corp., 1975-76, pres.. 1977—. Bd. dirs. Colo. U. Devel. Found., 1976—, Boulder YMCA, 1976. Served to 1st lt. C.E., U.S. Army, 1959-61. Clubs: Boulder Country; Tokeneke (Darien); Board Room (N.Y.C.). Home: Darien CT Office: 277 Park Ave New York NY 10017

ROUDEBUSH, GEORGE M., lawyer; b. Newtonsville, Ohio, Jan. 25, 1894; s. George Milton and Rosalind (Patchell) R.; A.B., Denison U., 1915; LL.B., U. Cin., 1917; m. Harriett McCann, June 28, 1924; children—George Milton, Jane Roudebush Daganhardt, Thomas M. Admitted to Ohio bar, 1917; practice in Cleve., 1919—; partner firm Roudebush, Brown, Corlett & Ulrich, and predecessors, 1919—; dir. corps. Trustee Denison U., 1940—, chmn. fin. com., 1940-73. Served to capt., inf., U.S. Army, 1917-19; AEF in France. Named to Athletic Hall of Fame Denison U., 1975, recipient alumni citation. Mem. Am., Ohio, Cleve. bar assns., Cleve. C. of C. (chmn. fin. com., mem. 100 year club), SAR, Beta Theta Pi. Baptist. Clubs: Cleve. Athletic, Mayfield Country, Midday. Officer coll., profl. football and basketball games 25 years. Home: 20101 Shelborne Rd Shaker Heights OH 44118 Office: Williamson Bldg Cleveland OH 44114

ROUDEBUSH, GEORGE SHOTWELL, lawyer; b. St. Louis, Feb. 18, 1909; s. Alfred Holt and Susan (D'Arcy) R.; A.B., Princeton, 1931; LL.B., Harvard, 1934; m. Dorothy Coleman, Nov.7, 1936; children—Susan, George Shotwell, Mary C. Admitted to Mo. bar, 1934, since practiced in St. Louis; partner firm Jones, Hocker, Gladney & Grand, 1949-60, Bryan, Cave, McPheeters & McRoberts, 1960- 63; v.p., gen. counsel, dir. McDonnell Douglas Corp., 1963-74; counsel Bryan, Cave, McPheeters & McRoberts, 1974—; spl. atty. war div. Dept. Justice, 1943-44. Mem. University City Sch. Bd., 1950-53. Served as 1st lt. USMCR, 1944-45. Mem. Am. Bar Assn., Mo. Bar, Bar Assn. St. Louis (pres. 1962-63). Home: 2127 N Ballas Rd St Louis MO 63131 Office: 500 N Broadway St Louis MO 63102

ROUDIEZ, LEON SAMUEL, JR., educator; b. Bronxville, N.Y., Nov. 18, 1917; s. Leon Samuel and Louise (Horan) R.; Baccalaureat es Scis., U. Paris, 1936, Baccalaureat en Droit, 1938; M.A., Columbia, 1940, Ph.D., 1950; m. Jacqueline Strich, May 7, 1945; children—Genevieve Strich, Francis Horan. Instr. French, Columbia, 1946-50; from instr. to asso. prof. Romance langs. Pa. State U., 1950-59; mem. faculty Columbia, 1959—, prof. French grad. faculties, 1962—, acting chmn. dept., 1968-69, chmn., 1971-74. Served to capt. AUS, 1940-45; Alaska, ETO. Mem. Modern Lang. Assn., Am. Assn. Tchrs. French (exec. council 1953-65). Author: Maurras Jusqu'a L'Action Francaise, 1957; Michel Butor, 1965; French Fiction Today, 1972. Mng. editor, editor French Rev., 1953-65. Home: 38 Taylor Dr Closter NJ 07624 Office: Philosophy Hall Columbia Univ New York City NY 10027

ROUDYBUSH, FRANKLIN, business exec.; b. Washington, Sept. 17, 1906; s. Col. R. Franklin and Frances (Mahon) R.; ed. Consular Acad. and U. Vienna, 1925-26, Ecole Nationale des Langues Orientales Vivantes, Paris, 1926, U. Paris, 1926-28, U. Madrid, 1928; B.F.S., Georgetown U., 1929-30; postgrad. Harvard Bus. Sch., 1930-31; M.A., George Washington U., 1944; Ph.D., U. Strasbourg, 1953; m. Alexandra Brown. Dean, Roudybush Fgn. Service Sch., 1931-42; prof. internat. econ. relations Southeastern U., 1938-45; dir. Pan-Am. Inst., Roudybush Fgn. Service Sch., U.S., France. Attended sessions Council of Europe, and assembly of Schuman Plan Pool for Iron and Steel. Mem. Am. Soc. Internat. Law, Automobile Club Portugal, Delta Phi Epsilon. Clubs: Harvard, Nat. Press, Nat. Yacht, Green, Portmarock Golf; Royal Aberdeen Golf (Scotland); Miramar Golf (Oporto, Portugal); Yacht (Angers); Harvard Bus. Sch., France-Amerique (Paris). Author: The Present State of Western Capitalism, 1959; Diplomacy and Art, 1971; The Twentieth Century; Diplomatic Language; Why the Tragic Collapse of the British Empire; (in French) Training for the Foreign Service. Editor Affairs Mag., 1938-42. Author monographs: An Analysis of the Educational Background and Experience of 828 United States Foreign Service Officers; Evaluative Criteria for Foreign Service Schools and Foreign Service Training; XX Century Diplomacy, The French Educational System, others. Address: 15 Ave du Président Wilson Paris 16 France also Sauveterre de Rouergue 12 Avéyron France

ROUECHÉ, BERTON, writer; b. Kansas City, Mo., Apr. 16, 1911; s. Clarence Berton and Nana (Mossman) R.; B.J., U. Mo., 1933; m. Katherine Eisenhower, Oct. 28, 1936; 1 son, Bradford. Reporter, Kansas City Star, St. Louis Globe-Democrat, St. Louis Post-Dispatch, 1934-44; staff writer New Yorker mag., 1944—. Exec. com. Health Research Com. N.Y.C. Vice chmn. E. Hampton (L.I.) Twp. Planning Bd., 1965-70. Trustee Guild Hall, E. Hampton, Nat. Found. for Infectious Diseases. Recipient Lasker Journalism award med. reporting, 1950, 60; annual award Nat. Council Infant and Child Care, 1956; annual award Am. Med. Writers Assn., 1963; Journalism award AMA, 1970; W.E. Leidt award Episcopal Ch., 1973; J.C. Penney-U. Mo. ann. award, 1978. Fellow Kansas City (Mo.) Acad. Medicine; mem. Am. Epidemiol. Soc. (hon.). Clubs: Devon Yacht (Amagansett N.Y.); Coffee House (N.Y.C.). Author: Black Weather, 1945; Eleven Blue Men, 1954; The Incurable Wound, 1958; The Last Enemy, 1957; The Delectable Mountains, 1959; The Neutral Spirit, 1960; A Man Named Hoffman, 1965; A Field Guide to Disease, 1967; Annals of Epidemiology, 1967; What's Left: Reports on a Diminishing America, 1969; The Orange Man, 1971; Feral, 1974; Fago, 1977; The River World, 1978. Editor: Curiosities of Medicine, 1963. Home: Stony Hill Rd Amagansett NY 11930 Office: 25 W 43d St New York NY 10036

ROUFFA, ALBERT STANLEY, botanist, educator; b. Boston, Mar. 30, 1919; s. Saul and Dorothy (Winesky) R.; B.S., Mass. State Coll., 1941; M.S., Rutgers U., 1947, Ph.D., 1949; m. Bertha Bluestein, June 15, 1943; children—Dorothy Rouffa Keagy, Michael, Paul. Prof. biol. scis. U. Ill., Chgo. Circle Campus, also dir. James Woodworth Prairie Preserve. Served with USAAF, 1941-45. Mem. Bot. Soc. Am., Ecol. Soc. Am., Am. Fern Soc. Home: 4426 Florence Ave Downers Grove IL 60515 Office: Dept Biol Sci U Ill at Chgo Circle Box 4348 Chicago IL 60680

ROUGH, GAYLORD EARL, biologist, educator; b. Cochranton, Pa., Nov. 17, 1924; s. Homer Glenn and Maude (Watson) R.; student DePauw U., 1946-49; B.S. in Biology, U. Pitts., 1950, M.S. in Zoology, 1952, Ph.D., 1961; m. Elzada May Deeter, Aug. 30, 1949; children—Allan Conrad, Linda Sue, Shirley Ann. From instr. biology to asso. prof. Alfred (N.Y.) U., 1952-66, prof. biology, 1966—, chmn. dept. biology, 1969-75, dir. environ. studies program, 1978—; grad. teaching asst. U. Pitts., 1956-57, lectr. biology, 1957-58, vis. investigator, mem. research and teaching staff Pymatuning Lab. of Ecology, summers 1963-70. Served with Med. Dept., AUS, 1943-46. Recipient Phi Sigma Soc. award for meritorious grad. achievement in biol. scis., 1957. Mem. Ecol. Soc., Am. Inst. Biol. Scis., Soc. Ichthyologists and Herpetologists, Pa. Acad. Sci., AAAS, Sigma Xi. Home: 88 S Main St Alfred NY 14802

ROUILLARD, CLARENCE DANA, educator; b. Bath, Maine, July 7, 1904; s. George Frederic and Ellen Maria (Gooch) R.; A.B., Bowdoin Coll., 1924, Litt.D. (hon.), 1964; A.M., Harvard U., 1925; Ph.D., 1936; m. Harriet Page Lane, June 23, 1928. Instr. French, Harvard U., 1925-27, Amherst Coll., 1927-37; asst. prof. French, Univ. Coll., U. Toronto, 1937-45, asso. prof., 1945-49, prof., 1949-72, head dept., 1959-69, head grad. dept. Romance langs., 1956-63, prof. emeritus, 1972—; research officer NRC Can., Ottawa, 1942-45; pres. Alliance Française de Toronto, 1945-49; dir. Fédération de l'Alliance Française des Etats-Unis et du Can., 1945-52; councillor Union des Alliances Françaises au Can., 1951-63. C.R.B. Ednl. Found. fellow, 1930-31; recipient Alliance Française medal, 1947; Officier d'Académie, 1949; Chevalier Légion d'honneur, 1968. Fellow Royal Soc. Can.; mem. Modern Humanities Research Assn., MLA, Internat. Comparative Lit. Assn., Assn. Internat. des Etudes Françaises. Author: The Turk in French History, Thought and Literature, 1520-1660, 1940; editor: Le Notaire du Havre (Georges Duhamel), 1954, Souvenirs de Jeunesse: An Anthology, 1957; contbr. articles to profl. jours. Home: 209 Rosedale Heights Dr Toronto ON M4T 1C7 Canada Office: 185 University College U Toronto - Toronto ON M5S 1A1 Canada

ROULAND, JAY THOMAS, bar assn. exec.; b. Detroit, Aug. 17, 1935; s. John Edward and Esther (Failor) R.; B.A. magna cum laude with high honors in Econs., Kenyon Coll., 1957; J.D., Duke, 1960; m. Suzanne Freeman Rowell, Apr. 18, 1970; children—Christopher Jay, Carolyn Elizabeth, Michael Russell. Admitted to Mich. bar, 1961, also U.S. Supreme Ct., atty. FTC, 1960-62, div. gen. trade restraints, Washington, 1963-67; exec. dir. Fed. Bar Assn., Washington, 1967—, del. to Am. Bar Assn. Ho. of Dels., Honolulu, 1967, dist. v.p. for D.C. dist., 1966-67, nat. chmn. Younger Lawyers, 1965-66. Class agt. Kenyon Coll., 1957—. Cert. assn. exec. Recipient meritorious service award FTC, 1962; spl. commendation for distinguished service Fed. Bar Assn., 1970. Mem. Am. (govt. relations com. 1973-77, chmn. profl. assns. council 1977-79, long-range planning com. 1978-79, survey and research com. 1978-79, cert. assn. exec. study com. 1979-80), Washington (chmn. survey and research com. 1978-79) socs. assn. execs., Nat. Assn. Bar Execs., Am. Bar Assn., Assn. Continuing Legal Edn. Adminstrs. Episcopalian (vestryman 1966-70, del. Va. Diocesan Council 1967-71). Editor Fed. Bar News, 1966-67, mng. editor, 1965-66. Home: 12126 Basset Ln Reston VA 22091 Office: 1815 H St NW Suite 420 Washington DC 20006

ROULSTON, THOMAS HENRY, stockbroker; b. N.Y.C., Apr. 6, 1933; s. Henry Davies and Marjorie (Heather) R.; grad. Choate Sch., 1951; B.A., Dartmouth, 1955; m. Lois Mueller, July 31, 1954; children—Scott Davies, Thomas Henry III, Heather Fuller. Vice pres. Gunn, Carey & Roulston, stockbrokers, Cleve., 1960-63; pres. Roulston & Co., Inc., Cleve., 1963—; vice chmn. Bank Roulston Ltd., Zurich, Switzerland, 1972-76; pres., chmn. Investment Guidance Fund, 1967—. Mem. Ohio Criminal Justice Supervisory Commn., 1970-73; chmn. Adminstrn. of Justice Com., 1968-70. Past trustee Soc. for Crippled Children, Hill House, Health Hill Hosp., Cleve. Council World Affairs; trustee Lakeview Cemetery Assn., Bluecoats Inc. Served as capt. USAF, 1955-58. Mem. Young Presidents Orgn. Clubs: Union, Clevelander, Country, Midday (Cleve.); Metropolitan, Lawyers (N.Y.C.). Home: 2627 Fairmount Blvd Cleveland Heights OH 44106 Office: 4000 Chester Ave Cleveland OH 44114

ROUNDTREE, RICHARD, actor; b. New Rochelle, N.Y., July 9, 1942; s. John and Katheryn R.; student So. Ill. U. Held a succession of odd jobs, then became a salesman at Barney's, men's store, N.Y.C.; in 1967, began modeling for Ebony Fashion Fair; later joined the Negro Ensemble Co. and appeared in the co's. prodns. of Kongi's Harvest, Man, Better Man, and Mau Mau Room; last stage appearance was in The Great White Hope, Phila.; appeared in movies: What Do You Say to a Naked Lady?, 1970, Parachute to Paradies; starred in movies: Shaft, 1971, Shaft's Big Score, 1972, Shaft in Africa, 1973, Embassy, 1972, Charley One-Eye, Earthquake, 1974, Man Friday, 1975, Diamonds, 1975; TV appearances include: Search For Tomorrow, The New Yorkers, Inside Bedford-Stuyvesant, The Dean Martin Show, The Merv Griffin Show; starred in TV series Shaft, 1973-74; appeared in TV movie Firehouse, in TV mini-series Roots; recorded album The Man From Shaft, and single release, Street Brother. Office: Agency Performing Arts Inc 9000 Sunset Blvd Suite 315 Los Angeles CA 90069*

ROUNER, LEROY STEPHENS, clergyman, educator; b. Wolfeboro, N.H., Aug. 5, 1930; s. Arthur Acy and Elizabeth Ward (Stephens) R.; grad. cum laude, Choate Sch., Wallingford, Conn., 1948; student Uppingham Sch. Eng., 1949, Harvard, 1953; B.D. summa cum laude, Union Theol. Sem., 1958; Ph.D., Columbia, 1961; m. Rita Rainsford, May 21, 1955; children—Stephen Rainsford, Timothy Nichols (dec.), Jonathan Kerr, Christina Elizabeth. Lightweight crew coach Harvard, 1953-54, asst. dean freshmen, 1954-56; ordained to ministry United Ch. Christ, 1960; asst. to pres. Union Theol. Sem., 1957-58, tutor, 1958-59; asst. prof. philosophy and theology United Theol. Coll., Bangalore, India, 1962-67; missionary-at-large United Ch. Bd. World Ministries, 1967-69; prof. philos. theology Boston U., 1970—, also dir. Inst. Philosophy and Religion and Chmn. Carroll County (N.H.) Democratic Party, 1969-72. Mem. Phi Beta Kappa. Author: Within Human Experience: The Philosophy of William Ernest Hocking, 1969; The Discovery of Humankind, 1977. Editor, co-author: Philosophy, Religion and the Coming World Civilization, 1966. Contbr. articles profl. jours. Home: High Meadow Farm Center Sandwich NH 03227 also 8 Concord Rd Wayland MA 01778 Office: 745 Commonwealth Ave Boston MA 02215

ROUNES, ARISTIDES K., fgn. service officer; b. Kansas City, Mo., Apr. 25, 1925; s. Charles A. and Sophia G. (Pappas) R.; student Kansas City Jr. Coll., 1946, St. Louis U., 1947; B.A., U. Mo. at Kansas City, 1950; postgrad. U. Chgo., 1950-51; m. Athena A. Tselios, Apr. 23, 1971. Info. specialist, fgn. service officer USIA/USICA, 1951—; exec. officer, attaché Am. embassy, Vientiane, Laos, 1961-63; asst. pub. affairs officer, attaché Am. embassy, Ft. Lamy, Chad, 1963-65; pub. affairs officer, consul Am. consulate, Constantine, Algeria, 1965-66; pub. affairs officer, attaché Am. embassy, Kigali, Rwanda, 1966-67; exec. officer, attaché Am. embassy, Kinshasa, 1967-69; spl. asst. to dir. adminstrn. USIA, Washington, 1969-70, officer charge So. African affairs, 1970; pub. affairs officer, attache Am. embassy, Libreville, Gabon, 1970-72; dep. French br. chief IBS/USIA, 1972-76, E. Africa br. chief, 1976-78; exec. officer Voice of Am. Kavala Relay Sta., 1978—. Recipient Meritorious Service award USIA, 1970. Address: Am Embassy (KRS) APO New York NY 09253

ROUNTREE, JOHN ASA, lawyer; b. Birmingham, Ala., Aug. 9, 1927; s. John Asa and Cherokee Jemison (Van de Graaff) R.; A.B., U. Ala., 1949; LL.B. magna cum laude, Harvard U., 1954; m. Elizabeth Rhodes Blue, Aug. 11, 1951; children—Robert Blue, John Asa. Admitted to Ala. bar, 1954, N.Y. State bar, 1962; asso., then partner firm Cabaniss & Johnston, Birmingham, 1954-62; asso. firm Debevoise, Plimpton, Lyons & Gates, N.Y.C., 1962-63, partner, 1963—. Served to 1st lt., inf., AUS, 1946-47, 51052. Mem. Am., N.Y. State, Ala. bar assns., Assn. Bar City N.Y., Am. Law Inst., Am. Coll. Trial Lawyers, Phi Beta Kappa, Phi Delta Theta. Clubs: Harvard (N.Y.C.); River, Mountain Brook (Birmingham). Home: 439 E 51st St New York NY 10022 Office: 299 Park Ave New York City NY 10017

ROURKE, CHARLES MICHAEL, lawyer, leasing co. exec.; b. Princeton, Ind., Nov. 8, 1937; s. John William and Virginia Lee (Ammerman) R.; B.S., U. San Francisco, 1959, J.D., 1964; m. Patricia Cicone, June 20, 1959; children—Stephanie, Andrea, Monica. Admitted to Calif. bar, 1964; asst. counsel Greyhound Leasing & Financial Corp., 1964-67; sr. v.p., gen. counsel GATX Leasing Corp., San Francisco, 1968—. Served to lt. AUS, 1959-61. Mem. San Francisco, Am. bar assns., State Bar Calif., San Francisco Zool. Soc. Home: 2564 Sherborne Dr Belmont CA 94002 Office: 1 Embarcadero Center San Francisco CA 94111

ROURKE, FRANCIS EDWARD, educator; b. New Haven, Sept. 11, 1922; s. Joseph Francis and Bridget Anna (Malone) R.; B.A., Yale, 1947, M.A., 1948; Ph.D., U. Minn., 1952; m. Lillian Irene Randall, Dec. 27, 1948; children—Katherine, Stephen, Anne. Instr. Yale, 1952-54; mem. faculty Johns Hopkins, 1954—, prof. polit. scis., 1961—, chmn. dept. polit. sci., 1964-70; vis. prof. U. Calif. at Berkeley, 1970-71; dir. Commn. Expansion Higher Edn. in Md., 1961-62. Mem. Balt. Charter Revision Com., 1963-64; vice chmn. Commn. for Modernization Exec. Br. of Md. Govt. Mem. Am. Soc. Pub. Adminstrn. (pres. Md. 1960-61), Am. Polit. Sci. Assn. (treas. 1968-70), Phi Beta Kappa. Club: Johns Hopkins. Author: Intergovernmental Relations in Employment Security, 1952; (with Malcolm Moos) The Campus and the State, 1959; Secrecy and Publicity; Dilemmas of Democracy, 1961; Bureaucratic Power in National Politics, 1965, 3d edit., 1978; (with Glenn Brooks) The Managerial Revolution in Higher Education, 1966; Bureaucracy, Politics, and Public Policy, 1969, 2d edit., 1976; (with others) America and the World, 1970; Bureaucracy and Foreign Policy, 1972; (with others) Retreat from Empire, 1973. Home: 7100 Copeleigh Rd Baltimore MD 21212

ROUS, STEPHEN NORMAN, physician, educator; b. N.Y.C., Nov. 1, 1931; s. David H. and Luba (Margulies) R.; A.B., Amherst Coll., 1952; M.D., N.Y. Med. Coll., 1956; M.S., U. Minn., 1963; m. Margot Woolfolk, Nov. 12, 1966; children—Benjamin, David. Intern, Phila. Gen. Hosp., 1956-57, resident, 1959-60; resident Flower-Fifth Ave. and Met. Hosp., N.Y.C., 1957-59, Mayo Clinic, Rochester, Minn., 1960-63; practice medicine specializing in urology, San Francisco, 1963-68; asso. prof. urology N.Y. Med. Coll., N.Y.C., 1968-72, asso. dean, 1970-72; prof. surgery, chief div. urology Mich. State U., East Lansing, 1972-75; prof., chmn. dept. urology Med. U. S.C., Charleston, 1975—; urologist-in-chief Med. U. S.C. and County hosps., Charleston, 1975—; cons. urologist Saginaw VA Hosp., 1972-75, Charleston VA Hosp., 1975—; chmn. alumni devel. com. Mayo Clinic, 1979—. Mem. East Lansing Planning Commn., 1974-75; vestryman, jr. warden All Saints Episcopal Ch., 1974-75, lay reader, mem. diocesan com. on continuing edn., 1975—, vestryman St. Michael's Episcopal Ch., 1979—, chmn. every mem. canvas, 1979. Diplomate Am. Bd. Urology. Fellow A.C.S., Am. Acad. Pediatrics; mem. Soc. Univ. Urologists, Internat. Soc. Urology, Am. Urol. Assn., AMA, Nat. Urologic Forum, Soc. Pediatric Urology. Republican. Clubs: Seabrook Island. Author: Understanding Urology, 1973; Urology in Primary Care, 1976, Spanish edit., 1978, Russian edit., 1979; contbr. articles to profl. jours. Home: 43 Legare St Charleston SC 29401 Office: Dept Urology Med U SC 171 Ashley Ave Charleston SC 29403

ROUSAKIS, JOHN PAUL, mayor; b. Savannah, Ga., Jan. 14, 1929; s. Paul V. and Antigone (Alexopoulos) R.; B.B.A., U. Ga., 1952; m. Irene Fotopoulos, Sept. 5, 1953; children—Rhonda, Paul, Thea, Tina. Ins. broker, Savannah, 1956—; commr. Chatham County (Ga.), 1965-69, vice chmn., 1969-70; mayor of Savannah, 1970—. Pres. Nat. League Cities; mem. advisory bd. U.S. Conf. Mayors; mem. Advisory Commn. Intergovtl. Relations. Bd. dirs. Nat. Tng. and Del. Ser.; hon. com. Nat. Tribute to Greek Orthodoxy. Served with AUS, 1953-56. Named Outstanding Young Man of Savannah and Outstanding Young Man of Ga., 1962. Mem. Ga. Municipal Assn. (past pres.), Am. Legion, Sertoma Internat., Ahepa. Mason, (Shriner), Elk. Home: 1905 Colonial Dr Savannah GA 31406 Office: City Hall Savannah GA 31401

ROUSE, GEORGE E., geochemist; b. Chugwater, Wyo., May 4, 1934; s. Elverton Frank and Lucy (Wall) R.; geol. engr., Colo. Sch. Mines, 1961, D.Sc., 1968; m. Sue Ellen Werber, June 4, 1961; children—Dorthea Lyn, Valerie Sue, Wendelynn Ann. Mining geologist Anglo Am. Corp. S. Africa, Ltd., 1961-64; geol. engr., sr. project mgr., v.p. Earth Scis., Inc., Golden, Colo., 1968—. Mem. Am. Inst. Mining Engrs., Sigma Xi. With R.E. Bisque, developed theory that stresses at interface of earth's interior (globally) control distbn. of surface features, such as mountains, deep oceanic trenches, mineral belts, island arcs, etc.; theory asserts that quakes, volcanoes, rifts fall into ordered pattern and are not chance happenings; provides possibility for prediction of earthquakes; asserted that intergalactic and interplanetary magnetic fields may react sufficiently with earth's magnetic field to cause core to rotate a little differently than earth does on regular turning around axis. Office: Earth Scis Inc Golden CO 80401

ROUSE, IRVING, educator, anthropologist; b. Rochester, N.Y., Aug. 29, 1913; s. Benjamin Irving and Louise Gillespie (Bohachek) R.; B.S., Yale, 1934, Ph.D., 1938; m. Mary Uta Mikami, June 24, 1939; children—Peter, David. Asst. anthropology Yale Peabody Museum, 1934-38, asst. curator, 1938-47, asso. curator, 1947-54, research asso., 1954-62, curator, 1977—; instr. anthropology Yale, 1939-43, asst. prof., 1943-48, asso. prof., 1948-54, prof., 1954-69, Charles J. MacCurdy prof. anthropology, 1969—. Recipient Medalla Commemorativa del Vuelo Panamericano pro Faro de Colon, Govt. Cuba 1945, A. Cressy Morrison prize in natural sci. N.Y. Acad. Sci., 1951, Viking fund medal Wenner-Gren Found., 1960; Guggenheim fellow, 1963-64. Mem. Am. Anthrop. Assn. (pres. 1967-68), Eastern States Archeol. Fedn. (pres. 1946-50), Assn. Field Archaeology (pres. 1977-78), Soc. Am. Archaeology (editor 1946-50, pres. 1952-53), Nat. Acad. Scis., Am. Acad. Arts and Scis. Author monographs on archaeology of Fla., Cuba, Haiti, P.R., Venezuela. Home: 12 Ridgewood Terr North Haven CT 06473 Office: Box 2114 Yale Sta New Haven CT 06520

ROUSE, MERL L., ins. exec.; b. Urbana, Iowa, Apr. 17, 1909; student Cedar Rapids (Ia.) Bus. Coll.; m. Imogene Rector; children—James, Margaret. With Inter-Ocean Reins. Co., Cedar Rapids, 1928-34, N.Y.C., 1934-36, asst. sec., 1936-39, sec., 1939, v.p., 1940-46, chmn. bd., 1962—; now div. Am. Reins. Co.; v.p., dir. Am. Res. Ins. Co., 1946-51, exec. v.p., 1951-53, pres., 1953-55, merged with Am. Reins. Co., 1955, exec. v.p., dir. Am. Reins. Co., 1955-61, pres., chief exec. officer, 1961-68, chmn. bd., 1968—, chief exec. officer, 1968-75. Mem. N.Y. Bd. Trade, 1961—. Mem. Ins. Info. Inst. Clubs: Wall Street, India House, Knickerbocker, N.Y. Athletic (N.Y.C.). Home: 1040 Fifth Ave New York NY Office: 91 Liberty St New York NY 10006

ROUSE, RICHARD HUNTER, historian; b. Boston, Aug. 14, 1933; s. Hunter and Dorothee (Hüsmert) R.; B.A., State U. Iowa, 1955; M.A., U. Chgo., 1957; Ph.D., Cornell U., 1963; Mary L. Ames, Sept. 7, 1959; children—Thomas, Andrew, Jonathan. Mem. faculty UCLA, 1963—, prof. history, 1975—; advisory bd. Hill Monastic Microfilm Library, St. John's U., Collegeville, Minn. Dir. Summer Inst. in Basic Disciplines for Medieval Studies, 1978. Fellow Am. Council Learned Soc.s, 1972-73, All Souls Coll., Oxford, 1978-79, Guggenheim Found., 1975-76; Rosenbach fellow in bibliography, 1976. Fellow Royal Hist. Soc.; mem. Medieval Assn. Pacific (pres. 1968-70), Mediaeval Acad. Am., (councillor 1977—) Comité international de paléographie, Société international de l'étude de philosophie médiévale. Co-editor: Viator: Medieval and Renaissance Studies. Author: Serial Bibliographies for Medieval Studies, 1969; (with M.A. Rouse) Preachers, Florilegia and Sermons: Studies on the Manipulus Florum of Thomas of Ireland, 1979. Editorial bd. Miedeval Texts. Home: 11444 Berwick St Los Angeles CA 90049 Office: Dept History Univ Calif Los Angeles CA 90024

ROUSE, RICHARD OLIVER, JR., educator, psychologist; b. Boston, July 9, 1920; s. Richard Oliver and Lillian (Seaboyer) R.; A.B., Harvard, 1941; M.A., Yale, 1943, Ph.D., 1949; m. Peggie Gates, Aug. 22, 1953 (dec. June 1968); children—Robert D., Linda G., James M.; m. 2d, Regina M. Solzbacher, Aug. 23, 1971; 1 son, Richard Oliver III. Instr. U. Conn., 1946-48; mem. faculty Williams Coll., 1948—, prof. psychology, 1962-70, Mary A. and William Wirt Warren prof. psychology, 1970—, chmn. dept., 1960-73; research asso. Austen Riggs Center, 1957-64; mem. staff Free Psychiat. Service So. Berkshire County, 1973-75. Served to 1st lt. USAAF, 1942-46. Fellow Am. Psychol. Assn.; mem. Psychonomic Soc., Sigma Xi. Home: Harmon Pond Rd Williamstown MA 01267

ROUSE, ROBERT SUMNER, coll. ofcl.; b. Northampton, Mass., Sept. 2, 1930; s. Charles Edward and Laura Elisabeth (Rowbotham) R.; B.S., Yale, 1951, M.S., 1953, Ph.D. in Chemistry, 1957; m. Nancy Isabella Cox, June 23, 1951; children—R. Daniel, Roland, James, Katherine. Lab. asst., then asst. in instrn. Yale, 1951-56; asst. prof. chemistry Lehigh U., 1956-62; group leader, plastics div. Allied Chems. Corp., 1962-66, tech. supr., 1966-67; prof. chemistry Monmouth Coll., West Long Branch, N.J., 1967—, chmn. chemistry dept., 1967-73, asso. dean faculty, 1968-73, dean faculty, v.p. acad. affairs, 1973—; mem. licensure adv. and approval bd. N.J. Dept. Higher Edn., 1973—; bd. dirs. Assn. Ind. Colls. and Univs. N.J., 1978—. Fellow N.Y. Acad. Scis.; mem. Am. Chem. Soc., Sigma Xi. Methodist. Author: (with Robert O. Smith) Energy: Resource, Slave, Pollutant-A Physical Science Text, 1975. Home: 482 Cedar Ave West Long Branch NJ 07764

ROUSE, ROSCOE, JR., librarian; b. Valdosta, Ga., Nov. 26, 1919; s. Roscoe and Minnie Estelle (Corbett) R.; B.A., U. Okla., 1948, M.A., 1952; M.A. in L.S., U. Mich., 1958, Ph.D., 1962; student (Grolier Soc. scholar) Rutgers U., 1956; m. Charlie Lou Miller, June 23, 1945; children—Charles Richard, Robin Lou. Bookkeeper C & S Nat. Bank, Valdosta, Ga., 1937-41; draftsman R.K. Rouse Co., heating engrs., Greenville, S.C., 1941-42; student asst. U. Okla. and Rice U., 1947-48; asst. librarian Northeastern State Coll., Tahlequah, Okla., 1948-49, acting librarian, instr. library sci., 1949-51; circulation librarian Baylor U., 1952-53, acting univ. librarian, 1953-54, univ. librarian, prof., 1954-63, chmn. dept. library sci., 1956-63; dir. libraries State U. N.Y. at Stony Brook (L.I.), 1963-67; dir. library, prof. Okla. State U., Stillwater, 1967—, chmn. dept. library edn., 1967-74. Vis. prof. U. Okla. Sch. Library Sci., summer 1962, N. Tex. State U., summer 1965; acad. library cons.; mem. AIA-Am. Library Assn. Library Bldg. Awards Jury, 1976. Served from sgt. to 2d lt. USAAF, 1942-45. Decorated Air medal with clusters. Mem. ALA (mem. council 1971-72, 76-80, council com. on coms. 1979-80, chmn. library orgn. and mgmt. sect. 1973-75, bldgs. and equipment sect. exec. bd. 1979-80), Okla. (pres. 1971-72, ALA council rep. 1976-80, Disting. Service award 1979), S.W. (chmn. coll. and univ. div. 1958-60, chmn. scholarship com. 1968-70), Fla. (standing com. on library bldgs. and equipment) library assns., Assn. Coll. and Research Libraries (chmn. univ. libraries sect. 1969-70), Assn. Research Libraries, Center for Research Libraries (council), Internat. Fedn. Library Assns., U. Mich. Sch. Library Sci Alumni Soc. (pres. 1979-80), Beta Phi Mu. Baptist (chmn. bd. deacons 1973). Clubs: Archons of Colophon, Melvil Dui C and M Assn., Stillwater Rotary (dir. 1978-80, pres. 1980-81). Author: A History of the Baylor University Library, 1845-1919. Editor: Okla. Librarian, 1951-52; co-editor Organization Charts of Selected Libraries, 1973. Contbr. articles, book reviews, chpts. to publs. in field. . *It is sometimes a hidden influence in our lives which drives us toward a set goal. We ourselves may not recognize the real source of that urge to fulfill a dream. Only after many years was I able to look back and point to the factors in my youth that pushed me toward my goal of attaining a good education. It was nothing more than fear, an uncertainty dealt out of the Great Depression, the death of my father when I was thirteen, and World War II. Unconsciously I must have concluded that a good, solid education would help to insulate me from the fears and uncertainties of a cold, harsh world. And I was right.*

ROUSE, ROY DENNIS, ednl. adminstr.; b. Andersonville, Ga., Sept. 20, 1920; s. Joseph B. and Janie (Wicker) R.; student Ga. Southwestern Coll., 1937-39; B.S. in Agr., U. Ga., 1942, M.S., 1947; Ph.D., Purdue U., 1949; m. Madge Mathis, Mar. 6, 1946; children—David Benjamin, Sharon. Asst. prof. agronomy and soils Auburn (Ala.) U., 1949-50, asso. prof., 1950-56, prof., 1956-66, asso. dir., asst. dean Sch. Agr. and Agrl. Expt. Sta., 1966-72, dean, dir. Sch. Agr. and Agrl. Expt. Sta., 1972—; mem. Com. of Nine, Dept. Agr., 1970-74. Served to capt. USNR, 1942-67; PTO. Recipient Leadership award Farm-City Com. Ala., 1975; Disting. Service award Catfish Farmers Am., 1976, Ala. Vocat.-Agrl. Tchrs. Assn., 1976, Man of Yr. in Agr. award, 1977; named Hon. State Farmer, Future Farmers Am., 1976. Fellow Am. Soc. Agronomy, Soil Sci. Soc. Am.; mem. So. Assn. Agrl. Scientists (pres. 1976), Assn. So. Agrl. Expt. Sta. Dirs. (chmn. 1974) Assn. Univs. and Land-Grant Colls. (chmn. expt. sta. com. on orgn. and policy 1977), Sigma Xi, Alpha Zeta, Phi Kappa Phi, Xi Phi Xi, Gamma Sigma Delta. Presbyterian. Clubs: Lions, Men's Camellia, Outing (Auburn). Contbr. articles to profl. jours. Home: 827 Salmon Dr Auburn AL 36830

ROUSE, STANLEY HARRY, investment co. exec.; b. Cin., Sept. 4, 1927; s. Clifford S. and Ada Z. (Rolf) R.; student U. Cin., 1945-48; m. Virginia P. Richardson, Apr. 29, 1950; children—Deborah Melissa, Gregory Stanley. Mgr. Westheimer & Co., Cin., 1948-61; v.p., sec. Robinson-Humphrey Co., Inc., Atlanta, 1961-68, 75—; v.p. Courts & Co., Atlanta, 1968-69; sr. v.p., treas. Roberts, Scott & Co., Inc., San Diego, 1969-71; sr. v.p. First Albany Corp., Albany, N.Y., 1971-74; supr. Paul Revere Life Ins. Co., Albany, 1974-75; allied mem. N.Y. Stock Exchange. Mem. exec. com., dad's com. Stephens Coll., Columbia, Mo., 1971-72. Served with USNR, 1945. Mem. Nat. Machine Accountants Assn. (pres. 1957), Nat. Assn. Securities Dealers (regulation T com. N.Y. 1973-74). Club: Commerce (Atlanta). Office: Two Peachtree St NW Atlanta GA 30303

ROUSS, RUTH, lawyer; b. Des Moines, May 21, 1914; d. Simon Jacob and Dora (Goldin) R.; B.A., Drake U., 1934, J.D., 1937; m. Dennis O'Rourke, Jan. 21, 1940; children—Susan Jerene, Kathleen Frances, Brian Jay, Dennis Robert, Ruth Elizabeth, Dolores Ann. Admitted to Iowa bar, 1937, U.S. Supreme Ct. bar, 1945, Colo. bar, 1946, D.C. bar, 1971; legal counsel to Jay N. Darling, Des Moines, 1937-38; atty. Office of Solicitor, Dept. Agr., 1938-45, asst. to solicitor, 1940-45; practice law, Colorado Springs, Colo., 1946—, mem. firm Williams & Rouss, 1946-50, individual practice law, 1950-69, of counsel firm Sutton, Shull & O'Rourke, Colorado Springs and Washington, 1969-72, mem. firm Rouss & O'Rourke, Colorado Springs and Washington, 1972—; dir., sec.-treas. ManExec., Inc. Bd. dirs. Human Relations Commn. City Colorado Springs, 1968-73, chmn., 1971-72; bd. dirs., sec. Colorado Springs Community Planning and Research Council, 1972-78; bd. dirs. Logos, Inc., Colorado Springs, 1972-78, sec., 1976-77, v.p., 1977-78; bd. dirs. Colorado Springs Opera Festival. Mem. El Paso County (Colo.) Bar Assn., Colo. Bar Assn., D.C. Bar Assn., Am. Law Inst. (life), Internat. Fedn. Women Lawyers, Women's Forum Colo., Phi Beta Kappa. Mem. cast, chorus Colo. Opera Festival, 1976, 78; mem. Colorado Springs Chorale, 1976—. Home: 8 Heather Dr Colorado Springs CO 80906 Office: 231 E Vermijo Ave Box 572 Colorado Springs CO 80901 also 1614 20th St Washington DC 20009

ROUSSAKIS, NICOLAS, composer, educator; b. Athens, Greece, June 14, 1934; s. George and Irene (Sommer) R.; came to U.S., 1950, naturalized, 1956; B.A., Columbia U., 1956, M.A., 1960, D. Musical Arts, 1975; m. Vuka Boyovich, June 5, 1971. Works include: Sonata for Harpsichord, 1966, Night Speech (chorus and percussion instruments), 1968, Six Short Pieces for Two Flutes, 1969, Concertino for Percussion and Woodwinds, 1973, Ode and Cataclysm (symphony orch.), 1975, Syrtos (concert band), 1975; Ephemeris (string quartet), 1979; Voyage (chorus), 1979; fellow Yaddo, 1966, 68, 68, 70, MacDowell Colony, 1964, 65, 67, 68, 69, Ossabaw Island Project, Savannah, Ga., 1966; preceptor, music dept. Columbia U., N.Y.C., 1968-70; instr. Barnard and Columbia Colls., 1970-75; asst. prof. Columbia U., 1975-77; lectr. music dept. Rutgers U., New Brunswick, N.J., 1977—; exec. dir. The Group for Contemporary Music; v.p. Am. Composers Concerts; co-founder Am. Composers Orch., 1977—; dir. Composers Recordings, Inc. Recipient award Nat. Inst. Arts and Letters, 1969. Fulbright grantee, 1961-63. Mem. Am. Composers Alliance (pres. 1975—), Coll. Music Soc., Am. Soc. Univ. Composers, Hellenic Council Am. Mem. Greek Orthodox Ch. Home: 209 W 86th St Penthouse 2F New York NY 10024 Office: Music Dept Rutgers U 25 Bishop Pl New Brunswick NJ 08903

ROUSSEAS, STEPHEN WILLIAM, educator; b. Scranton, Pa., Jan. 11, 1921; s. William and Lilliam (Laleas) R.; B.S., Columbia U., 1948, A.M., 1949, Ph.D., 1954; m. Claude Chauvierre, Sept. 22, 1967. Instr. econs. Columbia, 1951-56; asst. prof. U. Mich., 1956-58; vis. lectr. monetary theory Yale, 1959-60; asso. prof. Cornell U., 1961-63; prof. N.Y. U., 1963-69, Vassar Coll., 1969—. Fulbright fellow U. Salonika (Greece), 1954-55. Mem. Am. Econ. Assn. Author: Death of a Democracy: Greece and the American Conscience, 1967; Monetary Theory, 1972; Capitalism and Catastrophe: A Critical Appraisal of the Limits to Capitalism, 1979. Home: 10 Thelberg Rd Poughkeepsie NY 12601

ROUSSEAU, VIATEUR, educator, chemist; b. Baie des Sables, Que., Can., July 5, 1914; s. Anicet and Angeline (Ratte) R.; came to U.S., 1921, naturalized, 1940; B.S., Am. Internat. Coll., 1939; Ph.D., N.Y. U., 1948; m. Noreen Frances Longo, June 21, 1958; children—Michele Monique, Peter Laurence, Jeannine Frances. Analytical chemist Chapman Valve Mfg. Co., 1940-42; asst. in chemistry N.Y.U., 1942-47; instr. Coll. Mt. St. Vincent, N.Y.C., 1947-50, asst. prof., 1950-56; lectr. Iona Coll., New Rochelle, N.Y., 1952-56, asso. prof., 1956-58, prof., 1958—, chmn. sci. div., 1966-68; adj. asst. prof. Fordham U., 1957-59, adj. prof., 1959-73; adj. prof. N.Y.U., 1968. Mem. Am. Chem. Soc., AAUP, Sigma Xi. Author: (with Daniel B. Murphy) Foundations of College Chemistry. Home: 107 Pryer Terr New Rochelle NY 10804

ROUSSELOT, HAROLD ANTHONY, securities and commodities broker; b. N.Y.C., June 13, 1907; s. Louis J. and Louise (Jaeck) R.; A.B., Columbia U., 1929; m. Elsie Muller, Sept. 2, 1931; 1 son, Anthony Denis. Joined Orvis Bros. & Co., 1929, became partner 1938, mng. partner, 1950-55; gov. Am. Stock Exchange, 1954-60; gov. Commodity Exchange, Inc., 1954-64, pres., 1958-60; became partner Francis I. Du Pont & Co., 1955, sr. partner, 1966, mng. partner, 1971; chmn. bd. duPont Glore Forgan Inc., 1971-73; exec. v.p. duPont Walston Inc., 1973-74; sr. adviser, v.p. Drexel. Burnham Lambert, Inc., 1974—; mem. N.Y. Produce Exchange, gov. 1953-58; former mem. Chgo. Bd. Trade, N.Y. Cotton Exchange, Boston Stock Exchange; bd. govs. Assn. Stock Exchange Firms, 1963-71, chmn., 1969-70; bd. govs. Assn. Commodity Exchange Firms, 1972-74. Chmn. com. on athletics Columbia, 1951-60; chmn. Columbia Coll. Council, 1958-59; pres. Columbia Alumni Fedn., 1960-62; trustee Columbia U., 1962—. Served as 1st lt. USAAC, 1942, lt. col. USAAF, 1945. Decorated knight of Malta. Republican. Roman Catholic. Clubs: Univ., N.Y. Stock Exchange, Luncheon (N.Y.C.). Home: 104 E 68th St New York NY 10021 Office: 60 Broad St New York NY 10004

ROUSSELOT, JOHN HARBIN, congressman; b. Los Angeles, Nov. 1, 1927; s. Harbin M. and Mary (Gibson) R.; B.A. in Polit. Sci. and Bus. Adminstrn., Principia Coll., Elsah, Ill., 1949; m. Vyonne Le Masters; children by previous marriage—Craig, Robin, Wendy. Adminstrv. asst. to dir. pub. relations Pacific Finance Corp., 1954-55; pres. John H. Rousselot & Assos., pub. relations cons., 1955-58; dep. to chmn. Cal. Bd. Equalization, 1957; dir. pub. information FHA, 1958-60; dir. pub. relations John Birch Soc., 1963-67; mgmt. cons., 1967-70; mem. 87th Congress 25th Dist. Calif. 91st-93d Congresses from 24th Dist. Cal.; mem. 94th-96th Congresses from 26th Dist. Calif. Mem. exec. com. Calif. Republican Central Com., 1956-57; pres. Young Reps. Calif., 1956-57; vice chmn. Los Angeles County Rep. Central Com., 1956-58; dir. pub. relations Nat. Fedn. Young Reps., 1957—; pub. relations cons.; TV commentator; formerly pub. Am. Opinion Mag. Mem. Pub. Relations Soc. Am., Yale Polit. Union (hon.). Christian Scientist (bd. dirs. br. ch. 1969-70). Club: Capitol Hill (Washington). Home: 1178 Sherwood Rd San Marino CA 91108 Office: 2133 Rayburn House Office Bldg Washington DC 20515*

ROUSSO, ELI LOUIS, clothing co. exec.; b. N.Y.C., Nov. 3, 1920; s. Louis E. and Dora (Cohen) R.; student Fashion Inst. Tech., N.Y.C., 1946, Chic's Sch. Pattern Making, N.Y.C., 1947; m. Julia Saporta, Nov. 15, 1941; children—Doris (Mrs. Albert Taxin), Louis, Susan. Founder, 1946, since pres. Russ Togs, Inc., N.Y.C. Adv. bd. Mfrs. Hanover Trust. Active Mt. Sinai Hosp., Anti-Defamation League, Hebrew U., Jerusalem, Five Towns Community Chest; chmn. bd. overseers Albert Einstein Coll. Medicine; chmn. bd. Sephardic Home for Aged; founder Sephardic Temple, Cedarhurst; pres. Prime Ministers' Club State of Israel Bonds. Served with USNR, 1942-45. Named Ky. col., 1964. Mem. Young Pres. Orgn. Clubs: Friars (N.Y.C.); President Country (West Palm Beach, Fla.); Seawane Country (Hewlett Harbor, N.Y.); Masons. Home: 1534 Broadway Hewlett NY 11557 Office: 1411 Broadway New York NY 10018

ROUTH, PORTER WROE, church exec.; b. Lockhart, Tex., July 14, 1911; s. Eugene Coke and Mary M. (Wroe) R.; A.B., Okla. Baptist U., 1934, LL.D., 1951; student So. Bapt. Theol. Sem., 1937, U. Mo., 1938, George Peabody Coll., 1946-47; D.D., Wake Forest U., 1978; m. Ruth Elizabeth Purtle, June 7, 1936; children—Eugene Charles, Elizabeth Ann, Dorothy Kate, Mary Susan, Leila Ruth. Dir. publicity and instr. polit. sci. Okla. Bapt. U., 1935, dir. univ. press, 1936-37; instr. journalism, editorial staff Shawnee News, 1938- 40; asso. sec. Okla. Bapt. Sunday Sch. and Tng. Union Dept., Oklahoma City, 1940-41, sec. Okla. Bapt. Brotherhood and Promotion Dept., 1942-43; sec. dept. survey, statis. and info. Bapt. Sunday Sch. Bd., Nashville, 1945-51; sr. sec. So. Bapt. Conv., 1946-52, exec. sec. of exec. com., 1951-79; vis. prof. So. Bapt. Theol. Sem., Louisville, 1979; exec. com. Bapt. World Alliance, 1955—, adminstrv. com., 1956—. Mem. Nat. council Boy Scouts Am. Mem. So. Bapt. Hist. Soc., Am. Bible Soc. (dir.); chmn. Gov.'s Advisory Com. on Developmental Disabilities, Tenn. Author: My World Too, 1948; Meet the Presidents, 1952; 77,000 Churches, 1964; Chosen for Leadership, 1976; Waiting in the Wings, 1978; Mission to the World, 1979; editor Okla. Bapt. Messenger, 1943-45, The Quar. Rev., 1945-52. Home: 3426 Hampton Ave Nashville TN 37215 Office: Nashville TN 37219

ROUTHIER, HENRI, clergyman; b. Pincher Creek, Alta., Can., Feb. 28, 1900; s. Jean-Charles and Eulodie (Pelletier) R.; student St. John's Coll., Edmonton, Alta., 1913-18; Ph.D., Gregorian U., Rome, 1922, B.J.C., 1925; D.D., Angelico U., 1926; LL.D. (hon.), Laval U., 1952. Entered Oblate Order, 1918; ordained in Roviano, Rome, 1924; prof. St. John's Coll., Edmonton, 1926-30, rector, 1930-36; provincial supr. Oblate Fathers Alta. and Sask., 1938-44; co-adjutor bishop of Grouard, 1945-53, vicar apostolic Grouard, 1953-67; archbishop Grouard-McLennan, 1967-73. Address: Foyer Grandin 3 St Vital Ave St Albert AB T8N 1K1 Canada

ROUTIEN, JOHN BRODERICK, mycologist; b. Mt. Vernon, Ind., Jan. 23, 1913; s. William Evert and Frances Lolita (Broderick) R.; B.A., DePauw U., 1934; M.A., Northwestern U., 1936; Ph.D., Mich. State Coll., 1939; m. Helen Harrison Boyd, Mar. 11, 1944 (dec. 1965); m. 2d, Constance C. Connolly, Feb. 22, 1967. Instr. botany U. Mo., 1939-42; mycologist Pfizer, Inc., N.Y.C., 1946-77, research adviser, 1974-77; research on molds producing new antibiotics, strain improvement of cultures, identification of fungi. Recipient Comml.

Solvents award in antibiotics, 1950. Mem. Mycol. Soc. Am., Bot. Soc. Am., Soc. Am. Bacteriologists, Soc. Indsl. Microbiology. Editorial bd. Applied Microbiology, 1964-71, Antimicrobial Agts. and Chemotherapy, 1974-77. Patentee in field. Home: Grassy Hill Rd Lyme CT 06371 Office: Pfizer Inc Groton CT 06340

ROUTTENBERG, MAX JONAH, rabbi; b. Montreal, Que., Can., Mar. 22, 1909; s. Harry David and Dora (Garmaise) R.; came to U.S., 1927, naturalized, 1940; student McGill U., 1925-27; B.S.S., N.Y. U., 1931; rabbi, M.H.L., Jewish Theol. Sem., N.Y.C., 1932, D.H.L., 1949, D.D. (hon.), 1966; m. Lilly Soloway, Sept. 24, 1931; children—Ruth, Naomi, Aryeh. Rabbi, Kesher Zion Synagogue, Reading, Pa., 1932-48; exec. v.p. Rabbinical Assembly Am., 1948-51, pres., 1964-66, chmn. Jewish law and standards com., 1960-63, chmn. publs. com., 1976—; exec. v.p. Jewish Theol. Sem., 1951-54, co. chmn. rabbinic cabinet, 1957—, bd. dirs., 1962—, vis. prof. homiletics, 1972—; dir. Sem. Coll. Jewish Music and Cantors Inst., N.Y.C., 1951-54; rabbi Temple B'nai Sholom, Rockville Centre, N.Y., 1954-72, rabbi emeritus, 1972—; program editor TV program The Eternal Light, 1970—; chmn. Nat. Acad. Jewish Studies, 1956-59; mem. fgn. affairs com. N.Y. Bd. Rabbis, 1958—; exec. com. Jewish chaplaincy commn. Jewish Welfare Bd., 1962—; exec. com. Synagogue Council Am., 1962—; mem. Zionist Dist., Rockville Centre, 1954—; chmn. Met. Rabbinical Assembly, 1958-60. Mem. Rockville Centre Commn. Human Rights, 1960—, Nat. Citizens Com. Community Relations Service, 1964—; bd. dirs. United Synagogue Am. Served as chaplain AUS, 1942-45; ETO. Recipient Sabato fellowship Jewish Theol. Sem. Mem. Zionist Orgn. Am. (exec. com.), Am. Jewish Hist. Soc., Histadrut Ivrit Am. Author: Seedtime and Harvest, 1969; Decades of Decision, 1973; One in a Minyan, 1977; also chapter in book. Chmn. editorial bd. Conservative Judaism, 1964—; editor Rabbinical Assembly Proc., 1940; editorial bd. Jewish Digest, 1963—. Home: 79 E Independence Ct Yorktown Heights NY 10598

ROUX, AMBROISE MARIE CASIMIR, utility exec.; b. Piscop, France, June 26, 1921; s. Andre and Cecile (Marchilhacy) R.; student Coll. Stanislas, Paris, 1932-40, Ecole Polytechnique, 1940-41, Ecole des Ponts & Chausées, 1942-44, Ecole Supérieure d'Electricité, 1945-46; m. Françoise Marion, June 17, 1946; children—Christian, Véronique. Engr., Dept. Civil Engring., France, 1944-51; exec. dir. Office Sec. States for Industry and Commerce, 1952-55; sr. v.p. Compagnie Générale d'Electricité, Paris, 1955-63, pres., 1963—, chmn. bd., 1970—, also dir., hon. chmn. Pétrofigaz; chmn. bd. Afnor, 1972—, AGREF, 1976—, Compagnie Industrielle des Télécommunications (CIT-Alcatel), 1966—, Compagnie Electro-Financière, Paris, 1969—; v.p. Crédit Comml. de France, 1974—; dir. Compagnie Financière de Paris & des Pays-Bas, Péchiney Ugine Kuhlmann, Crédit Nat., Société La Radiotechnique, Alsthom-Atlantique, Société Nationale d'Investissement. Decorated comdr. Légion d'Honneur, comdr. Mérite Comml., officer Instrn. Publique. Mem. Fedn. French Industries (vice chmn. 1966-75, 1st vice chmn. 1975—). Home: 17 place des Etats-Unis Paris 75116 France Office: 54 rue la Boétie F75382 Paris Cedex 08 France

ROUZE, ROBERT LLOYD, mfr.; b. Goodridge, Minn., Sept. 10, 1921; s. Samuel D. and Myrtle M. (Ferdinandsen) R.; B.B.A., U. Minn., 1948; m. Ellen E. Korpi, Apr. 16, 1949; children—Christine, Jeffrey, Randolph, Colleen, Steven. With Lybrand, Ross Bros. & Montgomery, Rockford, Ill., 1948-54; treas. Twin Disc, Inc., Racine, Wis., 1966-76, sec.-treas., 1976—. Served with USAAF, 1942-46. C.P.A., Ill., Wis. Mem. Wis. Soc. C.P.A.'s. Home: 1505 Spring Valley Dr Racine WI 53405 Office: 1328 Racine St Racine WI 53403

ROVENSKY, WILLIAM RICHARD, investment banker; b. Pitts.; s. John and Agnes (Benes) R.; U. Pitts.; m. Josephine P. Gale. With Nat. Bank Commerce, N.Y. City, 1919-20; trainee to sr. partner Hornblower & Weeks (firm now Loeb Rhoades) Hornblower mems. N.Y. Stock Exchange), 1920-59, ltd. partner, cons., 1960—. Served in A.S., U.S. Army, 1918-19. Conglist. Clubs: Western University, Metropolitan (N.Y.C.); Greenwich (Conn.) Country; Bath and Tennis, Everglades (Palm Beach). Home: 3 E 77th St New York NY 10021

ROVIN, SHELDON, dentist, univ. dean; b. Detroit, Dec. 6, 1932; s. Samuel H. and Fannie J. (Gooze) R.; D.D.S., U. Mich., 1957, M.S. (USPHS trainee), 1960; m. Nancy May Gold, June 23, 1957; children—Lisa, Suzan, David. Chmn. dept. oral pathology U. Ky., Lexington, 1962-70, dir. office devel. planning evaluation Sch. Dentistry, 1970-73, pres. Senate, 1971; dean Sch. Dentistry, U. Wash., Seattle, 1973-77; curriculum cons. council on dental edn. ADA; cons USPHS Hosp., Lexington, 1963-73, VA hosps., Lexington and Cin., 1964-73, VA Hosp., Seattle, 1973—; VA adminstrv. scholar, Washington, 1977-79; chmn. dept. dental care systems U. Pa., Phila., 1979—. Bd. dirs. Jewish Fedn. Greater Seattle. Served to capt. Dental Corps, AUS, 1960-62. Recipient Great Tchr. award U. Ky., 1969, 4 others; Preventive Dentistry award ADA, 1974; Service award Alpha Omega, 1974. Diplomate Am. Bd. Oral Pathology. Fellow Am. Acad. Oral Pathology; mem. Gnotobiotic Assn., Am. Assn. Dental Schs., Internat. Assn. Dental Research, Omicron Kappa Upsilon. Author: Oral Cancer, 1969; Oral Pathology, 1972; contbr. articles on sci., edn. to profl. jours. Home: 1316 Medford Rd Wynnewood PA 19096. *Be Willing to stand for what you believe when called on even if it may be unpopular, but at the same time keep your mind open to other views.*

ROVINSKY, JOSEPH JUDAH, obstetrician, gynecologist; b. Phila., Sept. 4, 1927; s. Israel and Sarah (Blackman) R.; B.A., U. Pa., 1948, M.D., 1952; m. Judith S. Levin, June 24, 1964; children—Audrey, John, Jill, Michael, Paul, David. Intern, U. Pa. Hosp., Phila., 1952-53; resident in Ob-Gyn, Mt. Sinai Hosp., N.Y.C., 1953-58; practice medicine specializing in Ob-Gyn, 1958—; chmn. dept. Ob-Gyn City Hosp. Center, Elmhurst, N.Y., 1964-74; prof. Ob-Gyn, Mt. Sinai Sch. Medicine, N.Y.C., 1969-74; prof., chmn. dept. Ob-Gyn, Sch. Medicine Health Scis. Center, SUNY, Stony Brook, 1975-79, prof., 1975—; chmn. dept. Ob-Gyn, L.I. Jewish-Hillside Med. Center, 1973—; mem. obstetric adv. com. N.Y.C. Dept. Health, 1964—; chmn. med. care evaluation com. Profl. Standards Rev. Orgn. Queens County (N.Y.), 1977—. Served to capt., M.C., USAF, 1964-66. Diplomate Am. Bd. Ob-Gyn. Mem. Am. Coll. Obstetricians and Gynecologists, A.C.S., Am. Fertility Soc., N.Y. Acad. Medicine, N.Y. Obstetrical Soc., N.Y. Gynecol. Assn., Med. Soc. State N.Y. Jewish. Author: Medical, Surgical and Gynecological Complications of Pregnancy, 1961, 2d edit., 1965; editor: Davis' Gynecology and Obstetrics, 1968-73. Office: 410 Lakeville Rd New Hyde Park NY 11042

ROVIRA, LUIS DARIO, state justice; b. San Juan, P.R., Sept. 8, 1923; s. Peter S. and Mae (Morris) R.; B.A., U. Colo., 1948, LL.B., 1950; m. Lois Ann Thau, June 25, 1966; children—Douglas, Merilyn. Admitted to Colo. bar, 1950; now justice Colo. Supreme Ct., Denver. Mem. Pres.'s Com. on Mental Retardation, 1970-71; chmn. State Health Facilities Council, 1967-76; bd. dirs. YMCA, 1969-78; pres. Lowe Found. Served with AUS, 1943- 46. Mem. Colo. Assn. Retarded Children (pres. 1968-70), Am., Colo., Denver (pres. 1970-71) bar assns., Alpha Tau Omega, Phi Alpha Delta. Republican. Clubs: Athletic, Country (Denver). Home: 4810 E 6th Ave Denver CO 80220 Office: Colo Judicial Bldg Denver CO 80203

ROW, WILLIAM STANLEY, mining co. exec.; b. Curries, Ont., Can., Feb. 1, 1904; s. Frederick and Clara Ann (Putnam) R.; B.Sc. in Mining, McGill U., 1927; m. Helen Shirley Rogers, Feb. 16, 1933; children—James (dec.), Caroline Margaret. With Cerro de Pascoe Copper Corp., 1927-30, Lake Shore Gold Mines Ltd., 1930-37; mgr. Kerr-Addison Mines Ltd., Toronto, Ont., 1937-55, exec. v.p., 1955-58, pres., 1958-66, chmn., 1967—. Registered profl. engr., Ont. Mem. Ont. Mining Assn. (past pres.), Can. Inst. Mining and Metallurgy (chmn. Toronto 1960-61), Am. Inst. Mining, Metall. and Petroleum Engrs., Profl. Engrs. Assn. Ont. Clubs: National; York Downs Golf and Country; Goodwood. Office: PO Box 45 Commerce Ct W Toronto ON M5L 1B6 Canada

ROWAN, CARL THOMAS, columnist; b. Ravenscroft, Tenn., Aug. 11, 1925; s. Thomas David and Johnnie (Bradford) R.; student Tenn. State U., 1942-43, Washburn U., 1943-44; A.B. in Math., Oberlin Coll., 1947, D.Litt., 1962; M.A. in Journalism, U. Minn., 1948; D.Litt., Simpson Coll., 1957, Hamline U., 1958, Coll. Wooster, 1968, Drexel Inst. Tech., 1969; L.H.D., Washburn U., 1964, Talladega Coll., 1965, St. Olaf Coll., 1966, Knoxville Coll., 1966, R.I. Coll., 1970, U. Maine, 1971; LL.D., Howard U. 1964, Alfred U., 1964, Temple U., 1964, Atlanta U., 1965, Allegheny Coll., 1966, Colby Coll., 1968, Clark U., 1971; D. Pub. Adminstrn., Morgan State Coll., 1964; m. Vivien Louise Murphy, Aug. 2, 1950; children—Barbara, Carl Thomas, Geoffrey. Copywriter, Mpls. Tribune, 1948-50, staff writer, 1950-61; dep. asst. sec. State for pub. affairs Dept. of State, 1961-63; U.S. ambassador to Finland, Helsinki, 1963-64; dir. USIA, Washington, 1964-65; syndicated columnist Chgo. Daily News, Pubs.-Hall Syndicate, 1965—. Recipient Sidney Hillman award for best newspaper reporting, 1952; selected one of 10 outstanding young mem of Am., U.S. Jr. C. of C., 1954; award for best gen. reporting on segregation cases pending before U.S. Supreme Ct., Sigma Delta Chi, 1954; fgn. corr. medallion for articles on India, 1955, fgn. corr. medallion for articles on S.E. Asia, coverage of Bandung Conf., 1956; Distinguished Achievement award Regents, U. Minn., 1961; Communications award in Human Relations, Anti- Defamation League B'nai B'rith, 1964; Contbns. to Am. Democracy award Roosevelt U., 1964; Nat. Brotherhood award Nat. Conf. Christians and Jews, 1964; Liberty Bell award Howard U., 1965; George Foster Peabody award for TV spl. Race War in Rhodesia, 1978. Author: South of Freedom (named to A.L.A. ann. list best books), 1953; The Pitiful and the Proud (A.L.A. ann. list best books), 1956; Go South to Sorrow, 1957; Wait Till Next Year, 1960; Just Between Us Blacks, 1974. Office: 1220 19th St NW Washington DC 20036

ROWAN, DAN HALE, actor; b. Beggs, Okla., July 2, 1922; s. Sean (John) and Clella (Hale) R.; extension student U. So. Calif., U. Calif. at Los Angeles.; m. Phyllis Mathis, 1946; children—Thomas Patrick, Mary Ann, Christie; m. 2d, Adriana Van Ballegooygn, June, 1963. Formed team Rowan and Martin, 1952; performed U.S., Eng., Australia; TV appearances; summer TV replacement Dean Martin show, 1966; co-star Rowan and Martin's Laugh-In TV show, 1968-72, also co-producer series; charity performances for Eisenhower Heart Fund, ARC, others. Served as fighter pilot USAAF, 1941-54. Decorated Air medal, Purple Heart, D.F.C. with oak leaf cluster. Club: Bohemian. Office: care Agy for Performing Arts 9000 Sunset Blvd Suite 315 Los Angeles CA 90069*

ROWAN, FORD, television news corr.; b. Houston, May 31, 1943; B.A., Tulane U., 1968; M.A. in Govt., Am. U., 1972; J.D., Georgetown U., 1976. Reporter, anchorman Sta. WDSU-TV, New Orleans, 1964-69; White House corr. Sta. WTOP-TV, Washington, 1969-72; reporter urban affairs Sta. WRC-TV, 1972-75; Washington corr. NBC News, 1974—. Office: care NBC News 30 Rockefeller Plaza New York NY 10020*

ROWAN, GERALD BURDETTE, ins. co. exec., lawyer; b. Powersville, Mo., Feb. 9, 1916; s. M. C. and Blanch (Spidle) R.; A.B., N.W. Mo. State Coll., 1937; LL.B., Mo. U., 1940; m. Mary Elizabeth Turner, Dec. 24, 1939; children—Sandra Josephine (Mrs. Ronald Schweder), Roger Turner. Admitted to Mo. bar, 1940; practice in Marble Hill, 1940-49, Cape Girardeau, 1949-59, Kansas City, 1959—; mem. firm Frye & Rowan, 1940-42, 46-49; mem. firm Oliver & Oliver, 1949-59; with legal dept. Kansas City Life Ins. Co., 1959-76, sr. v.p. tech. services, 1976—, also dir.; pros. atty. Bollinger County, 1946-49; city atty. Cape Girardeau, 1954-59. Pres., Jackson County unit Am. Cancer Soc., 1963-65, 70-73; chmn. Mo. div. Am. Cancer Soc., 1974-76; mem. Mo. Park Bd., 1965-77. Served with F.A., AUS, 1943-45; MTO. Mem. Am., Mo. (com. chmn.), Kansas City bar assns., World Assn. Lawyers, Assn. Life Ins. Counsel, State City Attys. Assn. (past pres.), Mo. Law Sch. Alumni Assn. (past pres.), Order of Coif, Sigma Tau Gamma. Republican. Disciples of Christ. Club: Masons. Home: 4545 Wornall Rd # 303 Kansas City MO 64111 Office: 3520 Broadway Kansas City MO 64111

ROWAN, JAN CHRISTOPHER, editor, architect; b. Warsaw, Poland, Oct. 24, 1924; s. George B. and Zofia (Fajans) R.; came to U.S., 1949, naturalized, 1955; B.Commerce, London Sch. Econs., 1944; student Archtl. Assn. Sch. Architecture, London, 1947-49; B.Arch., McGill U., 1951; m. Ursula Miskolczy, June 12, 1955; children—Christopher George, Timothy Roderick, Peter Oliver. Propr., Jan. C. Rowan, architect, 1955—; features editor Progressive Architecture, 1959-61, mng. editor, 1961-63, editor, 1963-69; exec. v.p. R & S Internat., Inc., 1970-71; pres. Rowan Constrn. Co., 1972—; lectr., instr. Pratt Inst., Cooper Union, R.I. Sch. Design, 1952-56. Served with Brit. Liberation Forces, 1942-47. Recipient Jesse H. Neal Editorial Achievement award Am. Bus. Press, 1967. Address: 71 Gurley Rd Stamford CT 06902

ROWAN, JOHN ROBERT, med. center dir.; b. Joliet, Ill., Aug. 19, 1919; s. Hugh Hamilton and Elizabeth Margaret (Maloney) R.; student Butler U., 1952-53, Ind. U., 1953-54; m. Ruth Elaine Boyle, June 17, 1944; 1 son, Robert J. Personnel specialist VA Br. Office 7, Chgo., 1946; personnel officer VA Hosp., Ft. Benjamin Harrison, Ind., 1946-51; personnel officer VA Hosp., Indpls., 1951-56, asst. dir., 1960-67; asst. mgr. VA Hosp., Iron Mountain, Mich., 1956-60; hosp. adminstrn. specialist VA Central Office, Washington, 1967-69; dir. VA Hosp., Manchester, N.H., 1969-71, VA Hosp., Buffalo, 1971-72, VA Med. Center, Lexington, Ky., 1972—; dir. VA Med. Dist. 11, 1975—. Bd. dirs. Marion County (Ind.) unit Am. Cancer Soc., 1960-67, pres., 1964-66, bd. dirs. Ind. div., 1966-67; bd. dirs. Western N.Y. Regional Med. Program, 1971-72, Eastern Ky. Health Systems Agy., 1976—, United Way of Bluegrass, 1976—; mem. regional advisory council Ohio Valley Regional Med. Program, 1972-76; mem. Ky. Comprehensive Health Planning Council, 1972—. Served in USAAF, 1942-46. Decorated Bronze Star; recipient Meritorious Service citations Ind. dept. DAV, 1964, Ky. dept. Am. Legion, 1975, Ky. dept. VFW, 1976, Eastern Ky. U., 1974, Ky. dept. DAV, 1978, others. Fellow Am. Coll. Hosp. Adminstrs.; mem. Am., Ky. (trustee) hosp. assns., Lexington Hosp. Council, Assn. Mil. Surgeons U.S., Fed. Hosp. Inst. Alumni Assn., Lexington Fed. Exec. Assn. (pres. 1975-76). Roman Catholic. Home: Quarters 8 VA Med Center Leestown Rd Lexington KY 40507 Office: VA Med Center Leestown Rd Lexington KY 40507

ROWAN, RICHARD LAMAR, educator; b. Guntersville, Ala., July 10, 1931; s. Leon Virgle and Mae (Williamson) R.; A.B., Birmingham-So. Coll., 1953; postgrad. Auburn U., 1956-57; Ph.D., U. N.C., 1961; m. Marilyn Walker, Aug. 3, 1963; children—John Richard, Jennifer Walker. Instr., Auburn (Ala.) U., 1956-57, U. N.C., Chapel Hill, 1958-59, 60-61; lectr. U. Pa., Phila., 1961-62, asst. prof., 1962-66, asso. prof. industry, 1966-73, prof. industry, 1973—, co-dir. indsl. research unit; visitor to Faculty Econs. and Politics, Cambridge (Eng.) U., 1972. Mem. personnel com. Del. Valley Settlement Alliance, 1966-68. Served with Transp. Corps U.S. Army, 1953-56. Mem. Indsl. Relations Research Assn. (sec. Phila., 1964-65), Am. Econs. Assn., So. Econs. Assn. Democrat. Episcopalian. Author: (with H.R. Northrup) The Negro and Employment Opportunity, 1965; Readings in Labor Economics and Labor Relations, 1976, 2d edit., 1980; The Negro in the Steel Industry, 1969; The Negro in the Textile Industry, 1970; (with others) Negro Employment in Basic Industry, Vol. 1, Negro Employment in Southern Industry, Vol. IV, Studies of Negro Employment, 1970; Educating the Employed Disadvantaged for Upgrading, 1972; Collective Bargaining: Survival in the 1970's, 1972; Opening the Skilled Construction Trades to Blacks, 1972; Multinational Bargaining in Food and Allied Industries, 1974; Multinational Collective Bargaining Activity: The Factual Record in Chemicals, Glass and Rubber Tires, 1974; Multinational Bargaining in Metals and Electrical Industries, 1975; (with others) The Impact of Government Manpower Programs, 1975; Multinational Bargaining Approaches in the Western European Flat Glass Industry, 1976; Multinational Union Activity in the 1976 U.S. Rubber Tire Strike, 1977; Multinational Union-Management Consultation: The European Experience, 1977; International Enforcement of Union Standards in Ocean Transport, 1977; The Socio-Economic Environment and International Union Aspirations, 1978; (with H.R. Northrup) Multinational Bargaining Attempts: The Record, the Cases, and the Prospects, 1980. Home: 113 Blackthorn Rd Wallingford PA 19086 Office: Wharton Sch U Pa Philadelphia PA 19174

ROWAN, ROBERT BELLARMINE, pub. co. exec.; b. Phila., May 25, 1923; s. Joseph Ignatius and Mary Elizabeth (Hill) R.; A.B., St. Joseph Coll., 1943; postgrad. Coll. City N.Y., 1943-44, N.Y. U., 1944, Am. U., Biarritz, France, 1945; m. Mary Ann Jennings, Nov. 8, 1947; children—Mary Ann, Robert Bellarmine, Marcia, Shawn, Patrick, Michele, Christopher. With W. B. Saunders Co., Phila., 1946—, v.p. sales, 1971-73, exec. v.p., 1973—. Bd. dirs. Union Fire Assn., 1963-69, 78—, Mus. and Planetarium of Franklin Inst.; trustee Bala Cynwyd (Pa.) Library, 1964-70, Lower Merion (Pa.) Acad., 1978—; mem. exec. com. Washington Square Assn., Phila. Served with inf. U.S. Army, 1943-46. Mem. Assn. Am. Pubs. (exec. council tech. sci. med. div.). Democrat. Roman Catholic. Club: Downtown of Phila. (dir.). Office: WB Saunders Co W Washington Sq Philadelphia PA 19105

ROWDEN, MARCUS AUBREY, lawyer, former govt. ofcl.; b. Detroit, Mar. 13, 1928; s. Louis and Gertrude (Lifsitz) Rosenzweig; B.A. in Econs., U. Mich., Ann Arbor, 1950, J.D. with distinction, 1953; m. Justine Leslie Bessman, July 21, 1950; children—Gwen, Stephanie. Admitted to Mich. bar, 1953; trial atty. Dept. Justice, 1953-58; legal advisor U.S. Mission to European Communities, 1959-62; solicitor, asso. gen. counsel, gen. counsel AEC, 1965-74; commr., chmn. U.S. Nuclear Regulatory Commn., Washington, 1975-77; partner firm Fried, Frank, Harris, Shriver and Kampelman, Washington, 1977—. Served with AUS, 1946-47. Recipient Distinguished Service award AEC, 1972. Mem. Am., Fed., Mich., D.C. bar assns., Internat. Nuclear Law Assn., Order of Coif. Home: 7937 Deepwell Dr Bethesda MD 20034 Office: 600 New Hampshire St NW Suite 1000 Washington DC 20037

ROWDEN, WILLIAM HENRY, naval officer; b. Woodsville, N.H., May 12, 1930; s. Henry Thomas and Kathleen Maude (Gochey) R.; B.S., U.S. Naval Acad., 1952, U.S. Naval Postgrad. Sch., 1963; m. Sarah Ives Sumner, Apr. 10, 1956; children—Sarah Jane, Thomas Sumner, John William. Commd. ensign U.S. Navy, 1952, advanced through grades to rear adm., 1976; service in Japan; project mgr. ordnance project Naval Ordnance Systems Command, 1969-73; comdg. officer U.S.S. Columbus, 1973-74; staff weapons systems matters Office Chief Naval Ops., Washington, 1974-77; comdr. Cruiser Destroyer Group 3, 1977—. Decorated Bronze Star, Meritorious Service medal, Joint Service Commendation medal. Mem. U.S. Naval Inst. Methodist. Club: Masons. Home: Quarters V US Naval Air Sta Coronado CA 92125 Office: Comdr Cruiser Destroyer Group Three FPO San Francisco CA

ROWE, CHARLES SPURGEON, editor; b. Fredericksburg, Va., May 28, 1925; s. Josiah Pollard and Genevieve Sinclair (Bailey) R.; A.B., Washington and Lee U., 1947, postgrad. Law Sch., 1947-49; m. Mary Ann Else Huntsman, May 1, 1970; children by previous marriage—Ashley K. Rowe Gould, Charles Spurgeon, Timothy D.; stepchildren—Laura Huntsman, Kathleen Huntsman. Editor, co-pub. Free Lance-Star, Fredericksburg, 1949—, mng. editor, 1949-76; pres. Free Lance-Star Pub. Co., 1949—, Star Broadcasting Corp., radio stas. WFLS AM-FM, Fredericksburg, 1957—; dir. A.P., Fredericksburg Savs. & Loan Assn.; mem. Mary Washington Coll. Bd. Publs.; chmn. regents A.P. Mng. Editors, 1973-75. Chmn. bd. trustees Central Rappahannock Regional Library, 1969-75. Served to lt. (j.g.), USNR, 1943-46; now capt. Res. ret. Recipient George Mason award, 1974; named Outstanding Young Man of 1958, Fredericksburg Jaycees. Mem. A.P. Mng. Editors Assn. (pres. 1969), Am. Soc. Newspaper Editors (dir. 1971-77, 79—), Am., So. newspaper pubs. assns., Va. Press Assn. (dir.), Va. Freedom Info. Council (chmn. 1977-79), Phi Beta Kappa, Omicron Delta Kappa, Phi Delta Phi, Delta Tau Delta, Sigma Delta Chi. Episcopalian. Clubs: Nat. Press, Fredericksburg Country, Dominion. Home: 501 Hanover St Fredericksburg VA 22401 Office: 616 Amelia St PO Box 7267 Fredericksburg VA 22401

ROWE, CLAIR DEVERE, coll. dean; b. Troy Mills, Iowa, Oct. 31, 1924; s. Charles W. and Ida (Schneider) R.; B.A., U. No. Iowa, 1951, M.A., 1954; Ph.D., U. Iowa, 1967; m. Florine Erger, June 30, 1956; children—Paul, Patricia, Janet. Tchr. high sch., Dunkerton, Iowa, 1951-54; dir. distbv. edn., Algona, Iowa, 1954-57; mem. faculty Ball State U., Muncie, Ind., 1957-71, prof. mktg., 1970-71, chmn. dept., 1965-71; dean Coll. Bus. and Pub. Adminstrn., prof. mktg. U. N.D., Grand Forks, 1971—. Served with USAAF, 1943-45. Decorated Air medal with 5 oak leaf clusters, Purple Heart; Marathon Oil industry fellow, 1967; Danforth grantee, summer 1962. Mem. N.D. Council Econ. Edn. (trustee 1971—), Ind. Mktg. Assn. (dir. 1969-71), Nat. Assn. Purchasing Mgmt. (chmn. profl. devel. 1969-71), Grand Forks C. of C., Am. Mktg. Assn., Midwest Bus. Adminstrn. Assn., Beta Gamma Sigma, Delta Pi Epsilon. Clubs: Rotary, Elks, Civitan, Toastmasters. Contbr. articles to bus. jours. Home: 3010 Chestnut St Grand Forks ND 58201

ROWE, CLARENCE JOHN, psychiatrist; b. St. Paul, May 24, 1916; s. Clarence John and Sayde E. (Mabin) R.; B.A., Coll. St. Thomas, 1938; M.B., U. Minn., 1942, M.D., 1943, fellow in psychiatry, 1946-49; m. Patricia A. McNulty, Jan. 15, 1945; children—Padraic, Rory, Kelly Michael. Intern, St. Joseph's Hosp., St. Paul, 1942-43; resident VA Hosp., Mpls., U. Minn. Hosps., Mpls., 1946-49; instr., asst. prof. U. Minn., 1949-54; dir. Hamm Meml. Psychiat. Clinic, St. Paul, 1954-57; pvt. practice psychiatry, St. Paul, 1957—; cons. 3M

Co., 1957-72, Ramsey County Municipal Ct., 1958—, Constance Bultman Wilson Center, Faribault, Minn., 1973—; clin. prof. psychiatry U. Minn. Med. Sch., 1964—; adj. faculty mem. Antioch Coll., 1974—; cons. St. Thomas Acad., 1970—; chmn. Minn. Mental Health Planning Council, 1963-69; mem. Mayor's Com. on Drug Use and Abuse, 1969-71, Gov.'s Council on Employment of Handicapped, 1954-65; mem. adv. bur. hearing and appeals Social Security Adminstrn., 1965—. Trustee St. St. Thomas Acad., 1970-76; bd. dirs. St. Johns U. Inst. Mental Health, Collegeville, Minn., 1954-78. Served with M.C., U.S. Army, 1943-46. Fellow Am. Psychiat. Assn. (chmn. mental health in industry com. 1965-71); mem. AMA, Group for Advancement Psychiatry, Minn. Psychiat. Soc. (pres. 1973-75), Minn. Soc. Adolescent Psychiatry (pres.-elect 1977-78), St. Paul Soc. Psychiatry and Neurology (pres. 1978—). Roman Catholic. Clubs: St. Paul Athletic, Town and Country, Informal. Author: An Outline of Psychiatry, 7th edit., 1980; The Mentally Ill Employee, 1965; (with Allan McLean) The Clergy and Pastoral Counselling, 1969. Home: 1770 Colvin Ave Saint Paul MN 55116 Office: 551 S Snelling St Saint Paul MN 55116

ROWE, DAVID NELSON, educator; b. Nanking, China, Oct. 21, 1905; s. Harry Fleming and Margaret (Nelson) R.; A.B., Princeton U., 1927; A.M., U. So. Calif., 1930; Ph.D., U. Chgo., 1935; student Chinese and Japanese langs., Harvard, 1935-37, Coll. Chinese Studies, Peking, China, 1937-38; M.A. (hon.), Yale, 1950; m. Kathryn Ingram, Apr. 2, 1938; children—Andrew Stewart, Robert Ingram. Asst. instr. dept. history U. So. Calif., 1929-31; research asst. social sci. U. Chgo., 1931-33, fellow history, 1933-35, instr. history, summer 1935; lectr. Far Eastern affairs, Princeton, 1938-43; research analyst Library of Congress, spl. def. unit Dept of Justice, Washington, 1941; spl. asst. to dir. br. research and analysis OSS, 1941-42; spl. research technician, spl. asst. to ambassador, Chungking, China, 41-42; cons. exptl. div. study wartime communications Library of Congress, 1943; asso. with Yale U., New Haven, 1943—, research asso. Inst. Internat. Studies, 1943-51, research asso. dept. fgn. area studies, asso. prof. internat. relations, 1945-50, dir. Staff Officers Sch. for Asiatic Studies, 1945-46, dir. Chinese, Japanese and Russian studies, 1946-48, prof. polit. sci., 1950-74, emeritus prof., 1974—; research prof. polit. sci., 1958-59, dir. grad. studies, Internat. Relations, 1958-60, 65-67, dir. study human resources, 1951-54; asso. govt. Bernard Coll., 1945-46; asso. dir. Princeton Bicentennial Conf. on Chinese Soc. and Culture, 1947; vis. prof. polit. sci. U. Mich., 1937, Nat. Taiwan U., 1954-56; vis. prof. history Trinity Coll., 1962-63; cons. USIS, Dept. of State, Shanghai, China, 1948; rep. The Asia Found., Taipei, Taiwan, 1954-56; distinguished vis. prof. internat. studies Troy State U., 1976. Fellow Trumbull Coll. of Yale U. Mem. internat. secretariat UN Conf., San Francisco, 1945. Nat. co-chmn. Scholars for Nixon-Agnew, 1968; chmn. Nat. Council Scholars, 1969-75; vis. research scholar Inst. Internat. Relations, Republic of China, 1974-75. Ret. col. U.S. Army Res. Awarded Order Brilliant Star, Republic China, 1956, 73, Postwar fellow humanities Rockefeller Found., 1948. Mem. Am. Assn. Tchrs. Chinese Lang. and Culture (exec. com., past pres.), Univ. Profs. for Acad. Order (pres. 1977-78); adj. prof. polit. sci. Ariz. State U., 1980. Author: American Constitutional History, 1933; China among the Powers, 1945; Modern China, a Brief History, 1959; Editor: Journey to the Missouri, 1950; China, an Area Manual, 1954; Czechoslovakia, an Area Manual, 1954; Index to I Wu Shih, Mo. 1960; U.S. China Policy Today, 1979; also articles on Far Eastern affairs. Co-editor index to Soviet Plot in China, 1965. Editor: New Nations, 1968. Office: 19 Spring Rock Rd Branford CT 06405 also 10831 Alabama Ave Sun City AZ 85351

ROWE, DAVID THOMAS, cons. engring. firm exec.; b. Flint, Mich., Aug. 4, 1929; s. Thomas Jenkins and Eva Juanita (Stokoe) R.; B.S. with honors, Mich. Tech. U., 1951; m. July 28, 1951; children—Carrie, Thomas, Rebecca. Vice pres. engring. Gould Engring., Inc., Flint, 1953-62; pres., founder Rowe Engring., Inc., Flushing, Mich., 1962—. Trustee, Flushing Community Schs., 1971-76. Served with U.S. Army, 1951-53. Recipient Disting. Citizen award Davison Jaycees, 1958; registered profl. engr., land surveyor, Mich., Wis.; registered profl. community planner, Mich. Fellow Am. Cons. Engrs. Council (chmn. scholarship com. 1973-74); mem. Mich. Soc. Registered Land Surveyors (sec. 1966-67), Nat. Soc. Profl. Engrs., Mich. Cons. Engrs. Council (pres. 1968), Mich. Soc. Planning Ofcls., Am. Congress Surveying and Mapping, Fed. Water Pollution Control Fedn., Am. Public Works Assn. Methodist. Clubs: Masons, Shriners. Office: Rowe Engring Inc PO Box 202 Flushing MI 48433

ROWE, EDWARD JOHN, educator; b. Racine, Wis., Dec. 28, 1910; s. Felix J. and Mary (Mansite) R.; B.S., U. Wis., 1937, Ph.D., 1941; m. Margaret Forcht, June 25, 1943. Asst. prof. pharmacy, then asso. prof. Indpls. Coll. Pharmacy, 1941-46; prof. pharmacy, head dept. Butler U., 1946—. Recipient Holcomb award Butler U., 1956, Baxter award, 1955, 56, U. Wis. citation, 1974. Mem. Am. Pharm. Assn. (chmn. hist. sect. 1954-55, sec. sect. 1952-53, chmn. tech. sect. Acad. Pharm. Scis. 1965), Am. Inst. History Pharmacy (exec. council 1968-70, pres. 1973-74), Ind. Soc. Hosp. Pharmacy, Ind. Pharm. Assn., Assn. Coll. Honor Socs. (exec. council 1962-64, 65-66, v.p. 1969-70, pres. 1971-72), Sigma Xi, Rho Chi (nat. pres. 1964-66), Phi Lambda Upsilon, Phi Kappa Phi. Bd. authors: Martin, Dispensing of Medication, 1959, 66, 71, 76. Contbr. articles to profl. jours. Home: 5332 Brendonridge Rd Indianapolis IN 46226

ROWE, GEORGE GILES, cardiologist, educator; b. Vulcan, Alta., Can., May 17, 1921; s. James Giles and Cora (Blotz) R.; came to U.S., 1923, naturalized, 1929; B.A., U. Wis., Madison, 1943, M.D., 1945; m. Patsy Barnett, Sept. 12, 1947; children—George Lee, James Andrew, Jane Ellen. Intern, Phila. Gen. Hosp., 1945-46; resident U. Wis., 1950-52; instr. in anatomy Washington U., St. Louis, 1948-50; Am. Heart Assn. research fellow cardiovascular research lab. U. Wis., 1952-54, research asso. in medicine, 1954-55, asst. prof. medicine, 1957-59, asso. prof., 1959-64, prof., 1964—, lab. dir., 1969-76, Markle scholar in med. sci. dept. medicine, 1955-60; vol. research asso. Hamersmith Hosp., London, 1956-57. Served with M.C., U.S. Army, 1946-48. Diplomate Am. Bd. Internal Medicine. Mem. AMA, Wis. State Med. Assn., Dane County (Wis.) Med. Assn., Wis. Heart Assn. (pres. 1969-70), Am. Heart Assn., Assn. Univ. Cardiologists (pres. 1974-75), Central Clin. Research Club (pres. 1968-69). Contbr. numerous articles on congenital and acquired heart disease to profl. publs.; co-editor Cardiovascular Nursing, 1968-71. Home: 5 Walworth Ct Madison WI 53705 Office: 600 N Highland Ave Madison WI 53792

ROWE, HARRISON EDWARD, elec. engr.; b. Chgo., Jan. 29, 1927; s. Edward and Joan (Golden) R.; B.S. in Elec. Engring., Mass. Inst. Tech., 1948, M.S., 1950, Sc.D., 1952; m. Alicia Jane Steeves, Feb. 10, 1951; children—Amy Rogers, Elizabeth Joanne, Edward Steeves, Alison Pickard. Mem. tech. staff Radio Research Lab., Bell Labs., Holmdel, N.J., 1952—; vis. lectr. U. Calif., Berkeley, 1963, Imperial Coll., U. London, 1968; mem. Def. Sci. Bd. Task Force, 1972-74. Bd. dirs. Monmouth (N.J.) Arts Found. Served with USN, 1945-46. Co-recipient Microwave prize, 1972, David Sarnoff award, 1977. Fellow IEEE; mem. Internat. Union Radio Sci., Monmouth Symphony Soc., Monmouth Conservatory Opera Soc., Sigma Xi, Tau Beta Pi, Eta Kappa Nu. Unitarian. Clubs: Shrewsbury Sailing and Yacht, Appalachian Mountain. Author: Signals and Noise in Communication Systems, 1965; asso. editor IEEE Trans. on Communication, 1974-76; patentee in field; contbr. articles to profl. jours. Home: 9 Buttonwood Ln Rumson NJ 07760 Office: Bell Labs Box 400 Holmdel NJ 07733

ROWE, HERBERT JOSEPH, trade assn. exec.; b. Granite City, Ill., Mar. 25, 1924; s. Herbert Bernard and Maude (Klein) R.; student U. Tex., 1942-43, Purdue U., 1943-44; B.S. in Mgmt., B.S. in Marketing, U. Ill., 1948; m. Ann Muter, Dec. 2, 1950; children—Douglas H., Stephen F., James D., Edith L. With Edward Valves, Inc., subsidiary Rockwell Mfg. Co., 1948-50; with Muter Co., Chgo., 1952-71, v.p., 1957-64, pres., 1964-71, treas., 1964-67, chmn. bd., 1965-71, also dir., 1957-71; pres., treas., dir. Wescoil Co., 1964-66, Tri-Axial Corp., 1966-67; v.p., treas. Gen. Magnetic Corp., 1965-67, chmn. bd., 1967-70, dir., 1964-70; chmn. bd., dir. Pemcor, Inc., Westchester, Ill., 1971-75; asso. adminstr. external affairs NASA, 1975-78; v.p. Electronic Industries Assn., 1978—; sec.-treas. Englewood Elec. Supply Wis., Inc., 1972-75, Rahr's Inc., 1972-75. Pres. Pokagon Trails council Boy Scouts Am., 1964-66, pres. Calumet council, 1966-68, region 7 exec. com., 1966-72, vice chmn., 1971-72, bd. dirs. East Central region, 1972-75, mem. nat. program com., 1970-78, nat. cub scouts com., 1970—, SE regional exec. com., 1975-78, membership chmn. Nat. Eagle Scouts Assn., 1976—; recipient Silver Beaver award, 1966, Silver Antelope award, 1969, Distinguished Eagle Scout award, 1971; corp. campaign chmn. Chgo. Met. Crusade Mercy, 1964-68; chmn. Bd. Edn. Caucus, Flossmoor, Ill., 1962; Mem. bd. Flossmoor United Party, 1963-68; Mem. U. Ill. Found., 1967—; mem. advisory com. U. Ill. Coll. Commerce and Bus. Adminstrn., 1968—; bd. dirs. Electronic Industries Found., 1974—; mem. advisory bd. Air and Space Mus., Smithsonian Instn., 1975—. Served with USMCR, 1942-46, 50-52. Recipient NASA team award Bicentennial Expo. on Sci. and Tech., Exceptional Ser. medal, 1978. Mem. Electronic Industries Assn. (hon.; dir. 1967-69, bd. govs. 1969-75, exec. com. parts div. 1966-75, vice chmn. parts div., 1970-74, bd. dirs. consumer electronics div. 1972-75, chmn. world trade com. 1968-70, vice chmn. 1970-73, chmn. membership and scope com. 1972-74), Am. Loudspeaker Mfrs. Assn. (v.p., dir. 1967-68, pres., dir. 1968-70), Assn. Electronic Mfrs. (dir. 1970-73), Field Mus. Natural History, Chgo. Art Inst., Beta Gamma Sigma, Alpha Phi Omega, Sigma Chi (dir. Kappa Kappa corp. 1954-75, sec. 1971-73, pres. 1973-75, Charles J. Kiler award 1975, Grand Consul's citation 1976). Mem. Community Ch. (deacon). Mason (Shriner). Clubs: Flossmoor Country; Washington Golf and Country (Arlington, Va.); Masons, Shriners. Home: 1451 Highwood Dr McLean VA 22101 Office: 2001 I St NW Washington DC 20006

ROWE, JACK DOUGLAS, lawyer; b. Coldwater, Mich., Nov. 14, 1930; s. Herschel Harold and Ellen Moore (Preston) R.; B.A., DePauw U., 1952; LL.B., U. Mich., 1955; m. Amy Lou Lytle, Aug. 11, 1956; children—Andrew, Todd, Scott, Michael. Admitted to Mich. bar, 1955; practiced law Detroit, 1956; asso. firm Erickson, Dyll, Marentay & Slocum, Detroit, 1956, 60-62; mem. firm Joselyn, Rowe, Jamieson, Grinnan, and predecessor firm, Detroit, 1962—; lectr. in field. Pres. Grosse Pointe (Mich.) Little League, 1974; active YMCA Indian Guides. Served with AUS, 1956-60, Judge Adv. Gen. Corps; mem. Am., Mich., Detroit bar assns., Assn. Def. Trial Attys. (pres. 1975-76), Beta Theta Pi, Phi Alpha Delta. Presbyterian (deacon, trustee, elder bds.). Elk. Home: 360 Lincoln Rd Grosse Pointe MI 48230 Office: 1805 Ford Bldg Detroit MI 48226

ROWE, JACK FIELD, electric utility exec.; b. Minn., May 10, 1927; s. William F. and Anna (Stenborg) R.; B.E.E., U. Minn., 1950; m. Mary E. Moen, Mar. 26, 1955; 1 dau., Lizette Ann. With Minn. Power and Light Co., Duluth, 1950—, asst. to pres., 1966-67, v.p., 1967-68, exec. v.p., 1969-74, pres., 1974—, chief exec. officer, 1978—, chmn., 1979—, also mem. exec. com., dir.; mem. exec. com. dir. No. City Nat. Bank, Duluth. Mem. exec. bd. Nat. Electric Reliability Council, 1970-73; vice chmn. Mid Continent Area Reliability Council, 1970-71, chmn., 1972-73. Past bd. dirs., v.p. Duluth Jr. C. of C.; mem. exec. bd. Lake Superior council Boy Scouts Am., 1967-75, exploring chmn., 1968-72; comml. chmn. Duluth United Fund, 1960-61; vice chmn. Duluth United Way, 1975, chmn., 1976; U.S. Savs. Bond chmn. St. Louis County, Minn., 1974-77; chmn. St. Louis County Heritage and Arts Center, 1979—; v.p., bd. dirs. Lyric Block Corp., 1979—; mem. Minn. Bus. Partnership, 1979—; bd. dirs. Minn. Safety Council, 1979—. Served with USNR, 1945-46. Recipient Distinguished Service award Duluth Jr. C. of C., 1960. Registered profl. engr., Minn., Wis. Mem. NAM (dir. 1975-78), IEEE, Duluth C. of C. (pres. 1972-73, exec. com., bd. dirs.), Kappa Eta Kappa. Lutheran. Clubs: Duluth Athletic, Engineers, Rotary (pres. 1974-75), Kitchi Gammi (dir. 1979—) (Duluth), Masons, Shriners. Home: 630 Valley Dr Duluth MN 55804 Office: 30 W Superior St Duluth MN 55802

ROWE, JAMES HENRY, JR., lawyer; b. Butte, Mont., June 1, 1909; s. James Henry and Josephine (Sullivan) R.; A.B., Harvard, 1931, LL.B., 1934; m. Elizabeth Holmes Ulman, Sept. 6, 1937; children—Elizabeth (Mrs. Douglas Costle), Clarissa (Mrs. Stephen Batzell), James III. Engaged as attorney with the Nat. Emergency Council, 1934; sec. to Oliver Wendell Holmes, asso. justice Supreme Ct. of U.S., 1934-35; atty. RFC, 1935, Dept. Labor, 1935-36, power div. Pub. Works Adminstrn., 1936, SEC, 1937; staff Dem. Nat. Com., 1936 campaign; asst. to James Roosevelt, sec. to Pres., 1938; adminstrv. asst. to Pres. of U.S., 1939-41; asst. atty. gen. dept. of Justice, 1941-43; tech. adviser Internat. Mil. Tribunal, Nuernburg, 1945-46; pvt. law practice, 1946—. Dir. Comml. Credit Co. Cons. Bur. of Budget, 1947; mem. First Hoover Commn., 1948-49; pub. mem. Fgn. Service Selection Bd., State Dept. 1948; chmn. commn. to reorganize govt. P.R., 1949; chmn. adv. com. on personnel Sec. State, 1950; counsel Senate Majority Policy com. U.S. Senate, 1956; commr. Franklin Roosevelt Meml. Commn., 1956—, Roosevelt-Campobello Internat. Park Commn., 1967—; mem. Conf. on Pub. Service, 1960-63; chmn. U.S.-P.R. Commn. on Status, 1964-67. Trustee, former chmn. 20th Century Fund; bd. overseers Harvard, 1965-71; bd. visitors Air U., 1964-67; adv. council Sch. Advanced Internat. Studies, Johns Hopkins. Served as lt. USNR, 1943-45. PTO. Decorated two Presdl. citations, Navy Commendation ribbon, battle stars (8). Democrat. Roman Catholic. Home: 3207 Highland Pl Washington DC 20008 Office: 1511 K St Washington DC

ROWE, JAMES PETER, wallboard mfg. co. exec.; b. Stockton, Calif., May 24, 1932; s. James Melvin and Irene Louise (Pezzi) R.; B.S., U. Santa Clara (Calif.), 1954; P.M.D., Harvard U.; m. Emilee Jane Skidmore, Jan. 17, 1957; children—Susan J., James Peter, Thomas B. Zone credit mgr. Kaiser Gypsum Co., Los Angeles, 1965-69; with Kaiser Cement & Gypsum Co., Oakland, Calif., 1969-78, v.p. mktg., 1974-78; pres., chief exec. officer Domtar Gypsum America Inc., Oakland, 1978—. Served to 1st lt. AUS, 1954-56. Clubs: Orinda (Calif.) Country; Oakland Athletic, Athenian-Nile (Oakland). Home: 48 Sandringham Rd Piedmont CA 94611 Office: 1221 Broadway 7th Floor Oakland CA 94612

ROWE, JAMES W., food chain store exec.; b. Chattanooga, Dec. 28, 1923; s. John Howard and Anne Lou (Borders) R.; student advanced mgmt. Northeastern U., 1976; m. Doris Eileen Carlton, Feb. 19, 1946; children—Carlton, Leigh Anne. Vice-pres., sec. Colonial Stores, Atlanta, 1970-77, sr. v.p. adminstrn., 1978, pres., 1979—; sr. v.p., asst. to chief exec. officer Grand Union Co., Elmwood Park, N.J., 1979; dir. Colonial Stores, Grand Union Co. Served with AUS, 1942-45. Republican. Home: 6255 River Overlook Dr NW Atlanta GA 30328 Office: 2251 N Sylvan Rd East Point GA 30344

ROWE, JOHN HOWLAND, educator, anthropologist; b. Sorrento, Maine, June 10, 1918; s. Louis Earle and Margaret Talbot (Jackson) R.; A.B., Brown U., 1939, L.H.D. (hon.), 1969; M.A. in Anthropology, Harvard U., 1941, Ph.D. in Latin Am. History and Anthropology, 1947; Litt.D. (hon.), U. Nacional del Cuzco (Peru), 1954; student U. Paris (France), 1945-46; m. Barbara Bent Burnett, June 6, 1942; children—Ann Pollard, Lucy Burnett; m. 2d, Patricia Jean Lyon, Apr. 24, 1970. Field supr. So. Peru, Inst. Andean Research, 1941-42; prof. de arqueologia, dir. de la Seccion Arqueologica, U. Nacional del Cuzco, 1942-43; rep. in Colombia, Inst. Social Anthropology, Smithsonian Instn., also tchr. U. del Cauca, Popayan, 1946-48; mem. faculty U. Calif. at Berkeley, 1948—, prof. anthropology, 1956—, chmn. dept., 1963-67, curator S. Am. Archaeology Mus. Anthropology, 1949—; cons. UNESCO, Cuzco, Peru, 1975; field research in Maine, 1938, 40, Mass., 1939-41, Fla., 1940, Guambia and Popayan, Colombia, 1946-48, Peru, 1939, 41-43, 46, 54, 58, 59, 61-78; hon. prof. U. del. Cauca 1947; research prof. Mil. Inst. Basic Research Sci., U. Calif. at Berkeley, 1964-65. Served with AUS, 1944-46; ETO. Recipient Diploma de Honor, Soc. Cientifica del Cuzco, 1954, Prémio de Honor, Concejo Provincial de Ica, Peru, 1958; ofcl. Orden El Sol del Peru, 1968; Diploma de Honor, Concejo Provincial del Cuzco, Peru, 1974. Guggenheim fellow, 1958. Mem. Archaeol. Inst. Am., Soc. Am. Archaeology, Soc. des Americanistes de Paris, Soc. Antiquaries London, Am. Anthrop. Assn., Soc. Peruana de Historia, Soc. History Tech., Inst. Andean Studies (pres. 1960—). Author: An Introduction to the Archaeology of Cuzco, 1944; Max Uhle, 1954; Chavin Art, 1962; (with Menzel and Dawson) The Paracas Pottery of Ica, 1964. Editor: Nawpa Pacha, 1963—. Home: 1029 Cragmont Ave Berkeley CA 94708

ROWE, JOSEPH EVERETT, elec. engr.; b. Highland Park, Mich., June 4, 1927; s. Joseph and Lillian May (Osbourne) R.; B.S. in Engring., U. Mich., 1951, B.S. Engring. in Math., 1951, M.S. in Engring., 1952, Ph.D., 1955; m. Margaret Anne Prine, Sept. 1, 1950; children—Jonathan Dale, Carol Kay. Mem. faculty U. Mich., Ann Arbor, 1953-74, prof. elec. engring., 1960-74, dir. electron physics lab., 1958-68, chmn. dept. elec. and computer engring., 1968-74; vice provost, dean engring. Case Western Res. U., Cleve., 1974-76, provost Case Inst. Tech., 1976-78; v.p. tech. Harris Corp., Melbourne, Fla., 1978—; cons. to industry. Mem. adv. group electron devices Dept. Def., 1966—. Recipient Distinguished Faculty Achievement award U. Mich., 1970. Fellow IEEE (chmn. adminstrv. com. group electron devices 1968-69; editor proc. 1971-73), AAAS; mem. Am. Phys. Soc., Am. Soc. Engring. Edn. (Curtis McGraw research award 1964), Sigma Xi, Phi Kappa Phi, Tau Beta Pi, Eta Kappa Nu. Author: Nonlinear Electron-Wave Interaction Phenomena, 1965; also articles. Address: Harris Corp Melbourne FL 32919

ROWE, MAX L., lawyer, mgmt. cons.; b. Dallas City, Ill., Aug. 14, 1921; s. Samuel Guy and Nellie (Moyes) R.; student Knox Coll., Galesburg, Ill., 1939-40; A.B., U. Ill., 1943, J.D., 1946; M.B.A., U. Chgo., 1952; m. Maxine Marilyn Gladson, May 23, 1944; children—Melody Ann (Mrs. Gunn), Susan Elaine, Joyce Lynn, Andrew Blair. Admitted to Ill. bar, 1947, Ind. bar, 1954, also U.S. Supreme Ct.; pvt. practice in Aurora and Urbana, 1947; asst. to sec., asst. treas. Elgin Nat. Watch Co., 1948-50; gen. atty., asst. to pres.-treas. Rival Packing Co., 1950- 51; gen. counsel, asst. sec.-treas. Victor Mfg. & Gasket Co., Chgo., 1951-54; sec. Mead Johnson & Co., Evansville, Ind., 1954-55; asst. to sec. Caterpillar Tractor Co., 1955-62; asso. gen. counsel, sec., asst. treas. Thomas J. Lipton, Inc., and subsidiaries, 1962-68; v.p., treas. Seeburg Corp., Chgo., 1968-69; v.p. finance, law and adminstrn. Nightingale Conant Corp., Chgo., 1970-71; pvt. legal practice, also mgmt. cons., 1968—; v.p. law, sec. Ward Foods, Inc., Wilmette, Ill., 1972-76; dir. Ward-Johnston, Inc., Ward Internat., Inc., Superior Potato Chips, Inc., Quinlan Pretzal Co., Honiron-Philippines, Inc. Instr. extension div. U. Ill., 1960-61, eve. div. Fairleigh Dickinson U., 1966-68; leader Am. Mgmt. Assn., other corp. seminars, 1966—. Treas. Peoria County (Ill.) Republican Central Com., 1958-62; Rep. precinct committeeman Peoria County, 1958-62, Bergen County, N.J., 1966-68; elder Presbyterian Ch., 1975—; mem. nat. adv. council SBA, 1976—; chmn., mem. adv. bd. Ill. Dept. Personnel, 1979—. Served to 2d lt. AUS, 1943-45. Mem. Am. Mgmt. Assn., Conf. Bd., Am., Ill, Chgo. bar assns., Phi Gamma Delta. Republican. Clubs: Union League, Execs. (Chgo.). Office: Suite 5600 200 E Randolph Dr Chicago IL 60601 also 805 Red Bud Ln Wilmette IL 60091

ROWE, NATHANIEL HAWTHORNE, dentist; b. Hibbing, Minn., May 26, 1931; s. Nathaniel Hawthorne and Edna (Bockler) R.; D.D.S., B.S., U. Minn., 1955, M.S.D., 1958; m. Norma Estelle Quinlan, June 24, 1954 (div. July 1978); children—Bradford Scott, Nathaniel Edwin, Lorna Michelle, Jonathan Alan. Teaching asst. dept. oral pathology Sch. Dentistry U. Minn., 1955-56, research fellow, 1956-58, clin. instr., 1958-59; asst. prof. pathology Washington U. Sch. Dentistry, St. Louis, 1959-65, asso. prof., 1965-69, prof. Grad. Sch. Arts and Scis., 1966-69, vis. prof. pathology Sch. Dentistry, 1969-71, chmn. dept. gen. and oral pathology, 1959-68, coordinator oral cancer teaching, 1959-68; asso. research scientist Cancer Research Center, Columbia, Mo., 1967-71; asso. prof. pathology Sch. Medicine U. Mich., Ann Arbor, 1969-76, prof. pathology, 1976—, prof. dentistry Sch. Dentistry, 1968—, asso. dir. Dental Research Inst., 1970—, sr. research scientist Virus Research Group, 1977; cons. staff Jewish Hosp., St. Louis, 1960-68; cons. Ellis Fischel State Cancer Hosp., Columbia, 1967—, sci. adv. bd. Cancer Research Center, 1975—; cons. oral pathology U.S. VA Hosps., St. Louis, 1965-68, Ann Arbor, 1973—, Mo. Dental Assn., St. Louis, 1967-69; civilian profl. cons. Office of Surgeon 5th U.S. Army, 1967—; cons. Bur. Medicine Adv. Panel System, HEW, dental agts. adv. com. FDA, 1968-70; mem. profl. adv. council on cancer Mich. Assn. Regional Med. Programs, 1969-73; mem. policy council Met. Detroit Cancer Control Program, 1976—. Recipient D.E. Listiac award, faculty U. Minn. Sch. Dentistry, 1955; Army Outstanding Civilian Ser. award, 1979; Tiffany Nat. award Am. Cancer Soc., 1979; named Hon. Alumnus Washington U. Sch. Dentistry, 1966. Diplomate Am. Bd. Oral Pathology. Fellow Am. Acad. Oral Pathology (councillor 1971-74, pres. 1977-78), Am. Coll. Dentists; mem. AAAS, N.Y. Acad. Scis., Am. Assn. Cancer Research, ADA (cons. Council on Dental Edn. 1971-72, 75—, mem. commn. on accreditation 1976—), Mich. (cons. com. on cancer control 1971—), Dist. Dental assns., Mich. Soc. Pathologists, Am. Acad. Peridontology, Internat. Assn. Dental Research, Royal Soc. Health (Eng.), Fedn. Dentaire Internationale, Internat. Acad. Pathology, Am. Cancer Soc. (dir. St. Louis City and County unit 1964-68, chmn. profl. edn. com. 1967-68, v.p. 1967-68, dir. 1042 Greenhills Dr Ann Arbor MI 48105 edn com 1973-76 vp unit 1975-76 pres 1976-77) Sigma Xi Xi Psi Phi Omicron Kappa Upsilon Editor: Proc of Symposium: Salivary Glands and Their Secretion 1973; Proc of Symposium: Dental Plaque: Interfaces 1974; Proc of Symposium: Oral and Peioral Ulcerations: Cause and Control Emphasis on Herpes Simples Virus 1975; Proceedings of Symposium: Research in Form and Function 1976 Mem editorial bd Journ Mo Dental Soc 1963-69 Bull Greater St Louis Dental Soc 1964-68 Cancer 1967— Oral Research Abstracts 1967— Jour Dental Research 1971-73; contbr articles to profl jours; also chpts to books Home: 2107 Devonshire Rd Ann Arbor MI 48104

ROWE, PAUL NICHOLAS, lawyer; b. Indpls., Aug. 27, 1904; s. Pierce Edward and Cecelia Elizabeth (O'Toole) R.; student U. Notre Dame, 1923-25; S.B., Harvard, 1927, J.D., 1930; m. Dorothy Margaret Meier, Apr. 18, 1931; children—Edward Francis, Norman Pierce. Admitted to Ind. bar, 1930, since practiced in Indpls.; with firm Baker & Daniels, 1930—, partner, 1939-76, counsel, 1977—; dir., sec. Clowes Fund. Sec., dir. Gov. Ind. Economy Program, 1968-73. Bd. dirs., v.p. Ind. Bar Found., 1965-66; bd. dirs. Ind. Continuing Legal Edn. Forum, 1964-67, pres., 1966. Fellow Am. Bar Found.; mem. Am., Ind. (bd. mgrs. 1955-57, 63-67, pres. 1965-66), Indpls. (treas. 1947, pres. 1953), 7th Circuit bar assns., Assn. ICC Practitioners, Am. Law Inst., Ind., Indpls. chambers commerce. Clubs: Lawyers, Columbia, Athenaeum (Indpls); Nat. Lawyers (Washington). Editor, author: Indiana Taxes, 1953; author: History of Baker & Daniels, 1979. Home: 4930 Laurel Circle Indianapolis IN 46226 Office: Fletcher Trust Bldg Indianapolis IN

ROWE, THOMAS JOSEPH, corp. exec.; b. Newark, June 18, 1915; s. Edward F. and Rose C. (Farley) R.; B.B.A., Rutgers U., 1939; M.B.A., N.Y.U., 1941; grad. student bus. adminstrn., Columbia, 1941-43, 46-47; m. Marie Agnes McKenna, Aug. 18, 1951; children—Elizabeth, Patricia, Mary Ellen, Madeleine, Laurette, Anita, Thomas Joseph. Asst. prof. accounting Rutgers U., 1939-47; asst. to controller Prudential Ins. Co., 1948-50; controller owned and operated stas. div. NBC, 1950-52; dir. budgets ACF Industries, Inc., 1953-54, v.p. charge operations shippers car line div., 1954-60; v.p. finance Knox Glass, Inc., 1960-61; v.p., treas. Glen Alden Corp., N.Y.C., 1961-62; controller Trans World Airlines, Inc., N.Y.C., 1963-66; v.p. fin. Avnet, Inc., N.Y.C., 1967-71; pres., dir. Intermodel Transp. Systems Inc., Hoboken, N.J., 1971-74; exec. v.p., dir. Logetronics Inc., Springfield, Va., 1975-78; pres. Rowe Mgmt. Assos., West Caldwell, N.J., 1978—; dir. Artek Systems Corp., Tesdata Systems Corp. Served to lt. (s.g.) USNR, 1943-45. Mem. Financial Execs. Inst., Beta Gamma Sigma. Republican. Roman Catholic. Clubs: Essex Fells (N.J.) Country; N.Y. University, N.Y. Traffic, Union League (N.Y.C.). Home and Office: 50 Redman Terr West Caldwell NJ 07006

ROWE, VERALD KEITH, toxicologist; b. Warren, Ill., Oct. 5, 1914; s. Earl James and Edna Lilas (Leverington) R.; B.A., Cornell Coll., Mt. Vernon, Iowa, 1936, Sc.D. (hon.). 1971; M.S., State U. Iowa, 1937; m. Mary W. Gardner, Sept. 6, 1937; children—James Keith, Karen Kay. With Dow Chem. U.S.A., Midland. Mich., 1937—, dir. toxicology and indsl. hygiene, 1970-73, research scientist, 1973-78, research fellow, 1978—, dir. toxicological affairs, health and environ. research, 1973—; mem. clearinghouse environ. carcinogens Nat. Cancer Inst.; mem. U.S. Permanent Commn., Internat. Assn. Occupational Health. Diplomate Am. Bd. Indsl. Hygiene. Mem. Soc. Toxicology (pres. 1966-67; Merit award 1976), Am. Acad. Indsl. Hygiene (pres. 1974), Am. Indsl. Hygiene Assn. (Cummings award 1979), N.Y. Acad. Sci., Soc. Occupational and Environ. Health, Internat. Soc. for Ecotoxicology and Environ. Safety, Am. Chem. Soc., Am. Soc. Pharmacology and Exptl. Therapeutics. Club: Elks. Author articles, chpts. in books. Home: 709 Columbia Rd Midland MI 48640 Office: 1803 Bldg Dow Chem Co Midland MI 48640

ROWE, WALLACE PRESCOTT, physician, virologist; b. Balt., Feb. 20, 1926; s. George Davis and Mary Wallace (Buck) R.; student Coll. William and Mary, 1943-44; M.D., Johns Hopkins, 1948; m. Marjorie Louise Power, May 29, 1948; children—Wallace Prescott, Wendy M.D. Intern, N.C. Bapt. Hosp., Winston-Salem, 1948-49; virologist Naval Med. Research Inst., Bethesda, Md., 1949-52; commd. sr. asst. surg. USPHS, 1952, advanced through grades to med. dir., 1961; virologist NIH, Bethesda, Md., 1952—. Instr. Howard U., Washington, 1960-74. Vice chmn. Frederick County (Md.) Human Relations Council, 1968-70. Served with USNR, 1945, 49-52. Recipient Eli Lilly award, 1960, Langer-Teplitz award, 1965, Rockefeller Pub. Service award, 1972, G.H.A. Clowes award, 1973, Ricketts award, 1974, Selman Waksman award in microbiology Nat. Acad. Scis., 1976, Virus Cancer Program award, 1976; Paul Ehrlich-Ludwig Darmstaedter Preis (W. Ger.), 1979; Harvey lectr., 1976. Mem. Nat. Acad. Scis. Office: NIH Bldg 7 Bethesda MD 20014

ROWE, WILLIAM L., educator; B.A., Wayne State U., 1954; B.D., Chgo. Theol. Sem., 1957; M.A., U. Mich., 1958, Ph.D., 1962. Prof. philosophy Purdue U., Lafayette, Ind. Office: Dept Philosophy Purdue U Lafayette IN 47907

ROWE, WILLIAM STANHOPE, banker; b. Cin., Oct. 10, 1916; s. John Jay and Grace (Probasco) R.; grad. Middlesex Sch., Concord, Mass., 1935; A.B., Harvard U., 1939; LL.D. (hon.), Xavier U., 1978; m. Martha Phyllis Whitney, July 8, 1939; children—George Whitney, Nancy Sherlock (Mrs. Edward J. Conner), Jennifer Stanhope (Mrs. Charles L. Rose), Martha Whitney (Mrs. Phillip C. Long). With Fifth Third Bancorp, also Fifth Third Bank (formerly Fifth Third Union Trust Co.), Cin., 1939—, exec. v.p., 1962-63, pres., 1963—, dir.; dir. Cin. Equitable Ins. Co., LeBlond, Inc., Cin. Gas & Electric Co., Taft Broadcasting Co., Diamond Internat. Corp. Mem. advisory bd. Greater Cin. Airport. Trustee Cin. Inst. Fine Arts, Cin. Children's Home, Cin. Mus. Natural History, Greater Cin. TV Ednl. Fund, Children's Hosp. Med Center, Cin. Hist. Soc., Convalescent Hosp. Children and Orphan Asylum; bd. dirs. Cin. Council on World Affairs. Mem. Assn. Res. City Bankers. Club: Cin. Harvard. Home: 4765 Burley Hills Dr Cincinnati OH 45243 Office: Fifth Third Bank Fifth Third Center Cincinnati OH 45202

ROWELL, JOHN AUSTIN, librarian, author, educator, editor; b. Grand Rapids, Mich., Sept. 29, 1929; s. Frances Howard and Esther (Austin) R.; student Aquinas Coll., 1947; A.B., Harvard, 1951; M.Ed., U. Mich.; M.S. in L.S., U. Denver, 1954, LL.D., 1962. State sch. library supr. Mich. State Library, Lansing, 1958-60; state dir. sch. libraries Pa. Dept. Pub. Instrn., Harrisburg, 1960-65; dir. sch. library programs and prof. library sci. Case Western Res. U., Cleve., 1965—; dir. Ohio Valley Folklore Center; editor, editorial cons. various trade and textbook pubs.; cons. R.R. Bowker Co., Am. Seating Co., Bro-Dart Co., Xerox Corp., UN, UNESCO, U. W.I., Jamaica; cons. Nat. Book Com., U.S. Office Edn., State Dept., also project dir. Ednl. Media Selection Centers Project, Bur. Research, U.S. Office Edn., 1968—; cons., chmn. library com. Field Enterprises Ednl. Corp.; mem. adv. bd. World Book Ency.; cons., ednl. film critic. Served with M.C., U.S. Army, 1951-53. Recipient award of merit Pa. Library Assn., 1966; named Man of Year, Pa. chpt. Am. Soc. Pub. Adminstrn., 1965; award Bur. Ind. Pubs. and Distbrs., 1963, Nat. Sch. Bds. Assn., 1961, Daus. Am. Colonists, 1965. Mem. NEA, ALA, Women's Nat. Book Assn., Am. Assn. Sch. Librarians (pres. 1969-71), Pa. Sch. Library Assn. (hon. life mem.), State Sch. Library Suprs. Assn. (pres. 1965-66). Club: Harvard (Cleve.). Author: Glad Eden; The Organization and Operation of Educational Media Selection Centers, 1971; also fiction. Editor Sch. Libraries mag. Home: 19121 S Woodland Rd Shaker Heights OH 44122 Office: Sch Library Sci Baker Bldg Case Western Res U Cleveland OH 44106

ROWEN, HOBART, journalist; b. Burlington, Vt., July 31, 1918; s. Moses G. and Sarah (Rosenberg) R.; B.S. in Social Sci., Coll. City N.Y., 1938; m. Alice B. Stadler, Aug. 5, 1941; children—Judith Diane, James Everett, Daniel Jared. Reporter, N.Y. Jour. Commerce, N.Y.C. 1938-41, Washington corr., 1941-42; with information div. War Prodn. Bd., Washington, 1942-44; corr. Washington bur. Newsweek mag. 1944-65, Bus. Trends editor, 1957-65; financial editor, asst. mng. editor Washington Post, 1966-75, columnist, econs. editor, 1975—. Councilman, Town of Somerset, Md., 1957-65. Recipient spl. achievement award Loeb mag. 1961; distinguished service award for mag. writing Sigma Delta Chi, 1961; John Hancock award for excellence, 1968; A.T. Kearney award, 1968; Gerald Loeb award for best economics column, 1978. Mem. Soc. Am. Business Writers (pres.), Sigma Delta Chi, Tau Delta Phi. Democrat. Jewish. Clubs: Nat. Press, Nat. Economists (Washington). Contbr. articles and columns various mags. and newspapers, including Harpers, New Republic. Author: The Free Enterprisers-Kennedy, Johnson and the Business Establishment, 1964. Office: 1150 15th St NW Washington DC 20071

ROWLAND, ARTHUR RAY, librarian; b. Hampton, Ga., Jan. 6, 1930; s. Arthur and Jennie (Goodman) R.; A.B., Mercer U., Macon, Ga., 1951; M. Librarianship, Emory U., 1952; m. Jane Thomas, July 1, 1955; children—Dell Ruth, Anna Jane. Circulation asst. Ga. State Coll. Library, 1952, circulation librarian, 1952-53; librarian Armstrong Coll., Savannah, Ga., 1954-56; head circulation dept. Auburn U. Library, 1956-58; librarian, asso. prof. library sci. Jacksonville U., 1958-61, Augusta Coll., 1961-76, prof., librarian, 1976—; lectr. library edn. U. Ga., 1962-66. Served with U.S. Navy, 1948-49. Mem. Am., Southeastern (exec. bd. 1971-72), Ga. (2d v.p. 1965-67, 71-73, 1st v.p., pres. elect 1973-75, pres. 1975-77), Central Savannah River Area (past pres., editor union list of serials 1967), Duval County (past v.p.) library assns., Nat., Ga. geneal. socs., Am. Assn. State and Local History, Richmond County (curator 1964—, pres. 1967-69, founder, editor Richmond County History), Ga., Ga. Baptist hist. socs., Nat., Ga. trusts for historic preservation, Historic Augusta (trustee), Kappa Phi Kappa. Baptist. Author: Bibliography of the Writings of Georgia History., 1966; A Guide to the Study of Augusta and Richmond County, Georgia, 1967; (with Helen Callahan) Yesterday's Augusta, 1976; (with James E. Dorsey) A Bibliography of the Writings on Georgia History 1900-1970, rev. edit., 1978. Editor: Reference Services, 1964; Historical Markers of Richmond County, Georgia, rev. edit., 1971; The Catalog and Cataloging, 1969; The Librarian and Reference Service, 1977. Contbr. to profl. jours. Home: 1339 Winter St Augusta GA 30904 Office: Reese Library Augusta Coll 2500 Walton Way Augusta GA 30904

ROWLAND, BENJAMIN ALLEN, corp. exec.; b. Phila., Mar. 17, 1910; s. Benjamin Holl and Mary Allen (Smith) R.; grad. Phillips Andover Acad., 1928; B.A., Yale U., 1932; M.B.A., Harvard U., 1934; m. Sara Briggs, June 18, 1932; children—Edward S., Benjamin Allen, George B., Daniel B., Mary A. (Mrs. Swedlund); m. 2d, Barbara Bearse, July 22, 1963; 1 son, Rodney Douglas. With First Nat. Bank Boston, 1934-36; statistician, investment officer Old Colony Trust Co., Boston, 1936-42; treas., dir. F. S. Gilley & Co., Inc., 1946-50, Chute Worsted, Inc., 1950-52; spl. asst. to sec. commerce 1953-57; pres., treas. Rowlands Industries, Inc., 1958—; past treas. Greater Lawrence Bus. Devel. Corp. (Mass.); dir. Essex Co. Mem., former chmn. Methuen (Mass.) Sch. Com.; past chmn. trustees, chmn. exec. com. Lawrence Gen. Hosp.; past mem. Yale alumni bd.; past pres., chmn. Greater Lawrence United Fund; past trustee Phillips Andover Acad.; bd. dirs. Lawrence YMCA, Lawrence Boys Club; past pres., treas. Merrimack Valley United Fund, also past dir.; mem. exec. com., past pres. Strawbery Banke, Portsmouth, N.H. Served to maj. USAAF, 1942-45; PTO, 1945. Episcopalian (vestryman). Mason (32 deg.). Clubs: Yale (past treas.) (Boston); Wianno (Mass.) (past pres., chmn. bd.), Wianno Yacht; Stratton (Vt.) Mountain Country; Portsmouth Yacht; Hole-in-the-Wall, Port Royal Beach (Naples, Fla.). Home: Wild Rose Ln New Castle NH 03854 Office: 300 Canal St Lawrence MA 01840

ROWLAND, CHARLES SHERMAN, cosmetics co. exec.; b. Ebensburg, Pa., Sept. 4, 1918; s. Charles P. and Mabel (Griffith) R.; B.S., Juniata Coll., 1940; M.S., Pa. State U., 1941, Ph.D., 1944; m. Elizabeth G. Smith, Aug. 15, 1942; children—Susan Rowland Ried, Dean S. With Inmont Corp., Clifton, N.J., 1943-68, dir. corporate research, 1960-65, dir. corporate devel., 1965-68; asst. to v.p. research and devel. Avon Products, Inc., Suffern, N.Y., 1968-69, v.p. research and devel., 1969—, dir. sci. regulatory affairs, 1978—. Mem. Tenafly (N.J.) Bd. Edn., 1961-64. Fellow Am. Petroleum Inst.; mem. Am. Chem. Soc., Soc. Cosmetic Chemists, Assn. Research Dirs., Chemists Club N.Y.C., Phi Lambda Upsilon. Club: Knickerbocker Country (Tenafly). Home: 63 Stonehurst Dr Tenafly NJ 07670 Office: Division St Suffern NY 10901

ROWLAND, FRANK SHERWOOD, educator, chemist; b. Delaware, Ohio, June 28, 1927; s. Sidney and Margaret Lois (Drake) R.; A.B., Ohio Wesleyan U., Delaware, 1948; M.S., U. Chgo., 1951, Ph.D. in Chemistry, 1952; m. Joan Evelyn Lundberg, June 7, 1952; children—Ingrid Drake, Jeffrey Sherwood. Instr. Princeton U., 1952-56; mem. faculty U. Kans., Lawrence, 1956-64, prof. chemistry, 1963-64; prof. chemistry U. Calif. at Irvine, 1964—, chmn. dept., 1964-70; Philips lectr. Haverford Coll., 1975; J.T. Donald lectr. McGill U., 1976; cons. radiation chemistry IAEA, 1969, 74. Mem. vis. com. in chemistry Brookhaven Nat. Lab., 1972-75; mem. vis. com. in chemistry Argonne Nat. Lab., 1974-79, chmn., 1975. Served with USNR, 1945-46. Recipient John Wiley Jones award Rochester Inst. Tech., 1975; Distinguished Faculty Research award U. Calif., Irvine, 1976; Profl. Achievement award U. Chgo., 1977; Gordon Billard award N.Y. Acad. Scis., 1977. Guggenheim fellow, 1962, 74; Erskine fellow U. Canterbury (N.Z.), 1978. Fellow Am. Acad. Arts and Scis.; mem. Nat. Acad. Scis., Am. Chem. Soc. (chmn. div. nuclear chemistry and tech. 1973, chmn. phys. div. 1974 Orange County award 1975, Tolman medal 1976), Am. Phys. Soc. (Leo Szilard award 1979), Am. Geophys. Union, AAAS, Phi Beta Kappa, Sigma Xi (nat. lectr.). Club: Explorers. Co-discoverer theory that fluorocarbons deplete ozone layer of stratosphere; contbr. articles to profl. jours.; editorial bd. Jour. Geophys. Research, 1963-65, Jour. Phys. Chemistry, 1968-77. Home: 4807 Dorchester Rd Corona del Mar CA 92625 Office: Dept Chemistry U Calif Irvine CA 92717

ROWLAND, HERBERT LESLIE, pub. relations exec.; b. N.Y.C., Dec. 4, 1925; s. I. Martin and Matilda (Appelbaum) R.; grad. CCNY, 1948; M.A., Columbia U., 1951; m. Joan Feldman, Apr. 9, 1949; children—Russell Lloyd, Daryl Verne, Julie Anne. Corr., N.Y. Times, 1949-50; editor Where mag., also TV Week mag., 1951-53; gen. mgr. Roger Brown, Inc., N.Y.C., 1954-56; partner Brown & Rowland, N.Y.C., 1957-60; pres. Rowland Co., N.Y.C., 1961—. Served with USAAF, 1944-46. Mem. Pub. Relations Soc. Am. Home: 300 E 74 St New York NY 10021 Office: 415 Madison Ave New York NY 10017

ROWLAND, IVAN WENDELL, coll. dean; b. Pocatello, Idaho, Apr. 1, 1910; s. William N. and Stella M. (Mills) R.; B.S., Idaho State Coll., 1932; M.S., U. Colo., 1947; Ph.D., U. Wash., 1954; m. Helen Thomas, June 1, 1958; 1 dau., Betty Jo Giles. Instr. pub. schs., Ririe, Idaho, also Pocatello, 1933-38; instr. physics Idaho State Coll., 1938-46, prof. pharm. chemistry, 1946-54, dean Sch. Pharmacy, 1954-56; dean Sch. Pharmacy, U. Pacific, 1956—. Mem. Am., Calif. pharm. assns., Rho Chi, Phi Delta Chi (past grand pres.). Club: Commonwealth of Calif. Home: 3355 Fairway Dr Stockton CA 95204

ROWLAND, JOHN CARTER, educator; b. Lancaster, Ohio, Mar. 13, 1926; s. Carter Harrison and Mary Agnes (Mooney) R.; A.B. cum laude, Gannon Coll., 1949; M.A., Pa. State U., 1951; Ph.D., Western Res. U., 1960; m. Wilda Haag, Dec. 26, 1946; children—Mark, Cynthia, Kirk, Lisa. Instr. to prof., chmn. dept. English, Gannon Coll., 1950-67; prof., chmn. dept. English, State U. N.Y. at Fredonia, 1967-72, v.p. acad. affairs, 1972—. Fulbright prof., dir. Am. studies U. Jordan, 1966-67. Served with AUS, 1943-45; ETO. Decorated Croix de Guerre (France); Penrose fellow Am. Philos. Soc., 1966. Mem. AAUP, Johnson Soc., Modern Lang. Assn., Delta Sigma Phi. Rotarian. Editor: Bibliography of the College Teaching of English, 1963, 67. Contbr. articles profl. jours. Home: 4587 W Main Rd Fredonia NY 14063

ROWLAND, LEWIS PHILLIP, educator, neurologist; b. Bklyn., Aug. 3, 1925; s. Henry Alexander and Cecile (Coles) R.; B.S., Yale U., 1945, M.D., 1948; m. Esther Edelman, Aug. 31, 1952; children—Andrew Simon, Steven Samuel, Judith Mora. Intern New Haven Hosp., 1949-50; asst. resident N.Y. Neurol. Inst., 1950-52, fellow, 1953; clin. asso. NIH, Bethesda, Md., 1953-54; practice research medicine, specializing in neurology, N.Y.C., 1954-67, Phila., 1967-73, N.Y.C., 1973—; asst. neurologist Montefiore Hosp., N.Y.C., 1954-57; vis. fellow Nat. Inst. Med. Research, London, Eng., 1956; from asst. prof. to prof. neurology Columbia Coll. Phys. and Surg., 1957-67; prof., chmn. dept. neurology U. Pa., Med. Sch., 1967-73, Columbia Coll. Phys. and Surg., 1973—; from asst. neurologist to attending neurologist Presbyn. Hosp., 1957-67, co-dir. Neurol. Clin. Research Center, 1961-67, dir. neurology service, 1973—. Mem. med. adv. bd. Myasthenia Gravis Found., pres., 1971-73; med. adv. bd. Muscular Dystrophy Assos. Am., Nat. Multiple Sclerosis Soc., Myasthenia Gravis Found., Com. to Combat Huntington's Disease; mem. tng. grants com. Nat. Inst. Neurol. Communicable Diseases and Stroke, NIH, 1971-73, bd. sci. counselors, 1978—. Served with USNR, 1942-44; with USPHS, 1953-54. Diplomate Am. Bd. Psychiatry and Neurology. Mem. Am. Neurol. Assn., Am. Acad. Neurology, Phila. Neurol. Soc. (pres. 1972), Assn. Research Nervous Mental Disease (pres. 1969, trustee 1976—), Assn. U. Profs. Neurology (sec. 1971-74, pres. 1978), multiple sclerosis socs. Eastern Pa. (chmn. med. adv. bd. 1969-73), N.Y.C. (chmn. med. adv. bd. 1977—). Editorial bd. Archives of Neurology, 1968-76; editor-in-chief Neurology, 1977—. Home: 404 Riverside Dr New York NY 10025 Office: Neurological Inst 710 W 168th St New York NY 10032

ROWLAND, RAYMOND EDGAR, bus. exec.; b. Kansas, Ill., Dec. 8, 1902; s. William and Lula Pearl (Estes) R.; student U. Ill., 1921-23; B.S., U. Wis.; m. Connie Lou Melton, July 30, 1928; children—Raymond Edgar, Eleanor Frances and Doris Elaine (twins). Sales div. Ralston Purina Co., 1926-34, plant mgr., Circleville, Ohio, 1934-40, asst. v.p., St. Louis, 1940-43, v.p., 1943-51, pres., 1951-79, chmn. bd., chief exec. officer, 1964-68, dir., 1951-74; dir. Merc. Trust Co.; chmn. bd. Barnes Hosp., St. Louis, 1968—. Bd. dirs. St. Louis Area council Boy Scouts Am., 1962—; trustee Wis. Alumni Research Assn., 1963—. Mem. Alpha Zeta (hon.), Phi Sigma (hon.). Presbyterian. Clubs: Noonday, Bellerive Country, Bogey, St. Louis, Eldorado Country, Crystal Downs Country, Bohemian. Home: 710 S Hanley Rd Clayton MO 63103 Office: 100 N Broadway Saint Louis MO 63102*

ROWLAND, RICHARD CRESWELL, educator; b. Phila., June 29, 1917; s. Sydney Vanferson and Elizabeth (Hollis) R.; B.A., Columbia, 1938; B.A., Oxford (Eng.) U., 1940, D.Phil., 1957; m. Clarissa Mary Lewis, Sept. 8, 1945; children—Elizabeth (Mrs. Douglas Overmyer), Charity, Hugh Richard, David Lewis. Instr. English, Columbia, 1940-41, 46- 53, Sarah Lawrence Coll., 1947; asst. prof. English, Rollins Coll., 1955- 57; mem. faculty Sweet Briar Coll., 1957—, prof. English, 1962—, Charles A. Dana prof. English, 1975—; mem. Summer Inst. Chinese Civilization, Taiwan, 1962. Served to lt., Transp. Corps, AUS, 1941-46; PTO. Fellow in E. Asian Studies, Harvard, 1959-60. Mem. AAUP, Assn. Asian Studies (chmn. S.E. regional conf. 1967), Phi Beta Kappa. Democrat. Home: 546 Elmwood Ave Lynchburg VA 24503

ROWLAND, THEODORE JUSTIN, physicist, educator; b. Cleve., May 15, 1927; s. Thurston Justin and Lillian (Nesser) R.; B.S., Western Res. U., 1948; M.A., Harvard, 1949, Ph.D., 1954; m. Janet Claire Millar, June 28, 1952 (div. 1967); children—Theodore Justin, Dawson Ann, Claire Millar; m. 2d, Patsy Marie Beard, Aug. 21, 1968. Research physicist Union Carbide Metals Co., Niagara Falls, N.Y., 1954-61; prof. phys. metallurgy U. Ill., 1961—; pres., dir. Materials Consultants, Inc.; guest participating faculty Argonne Nat. Lab.; cons. physicist, 1961—, cons. metallurgist, 1976—. Mem. Am. Phys. Soc., Am. Inst. Mining, Metall. and Petroleum Engrs., Am. Chem. Soc. (polymer div.), Am. Soc. for Metals, AAUP, AAAS, Sigma Xi. Contbr. articles to profl. jours. Home: 405 S James St Champaign IL 61820 Office: Metallurgy Dept U Ill Urbana IL 61801

ROWLAND, THOMAS MIFFLIN, coll. adminstr.; b. Phila., Oct. 13, 1924; s. Thomas Mifflin and Gladys Berrell (Cummings) R.; B.S., Temple U., 1948; LL.D. (hon.), Phila. Coll. Osteo. Medicine, 1973. Asst. registrar Phila. Coll. Osteo. Medicine, 1950-52, registrar, dir. admissions, 1952-59, adminstrv. asst. to pres., 1959-65, v.p. for adminstrv. affairs, 1965-73, exec. v.p., 1973-74, pres., 1974—, asst. prof. profl. econs., 1960-75, prof., chmn. dept. community health, 1972—. Chmn. profl. adv. com. Phila. chpt. ARC; 1st vice chmn. Republican City Com., Phila., 1972; del. Rep. Nat. Convs., 1968, 72, 76; mem. Phila. Dist. Atty's. Com. on Alcoholism and Drug Addiction; mem. adv. council Salvation Army Men's Social Service. Served with USAAF, 1943-46; ETO. Recipient Lindback Found. award for Distinguished Teaching, 1973, certificate of merit North City Congress Police Community Relations Program, 1965, Achievement award Lambda Omicron Gamma, 1973, Distinguished Achievement award Golden Slipper Club, 1975, State of Israel award, 1976, Distinguished Guest award Pa. Osteo. Med. Assn., 1977, 1st Distinguished Service award Philadelphia County Osteo. Soc., 1977, Alumni award N.E. High Sch., 1977. Mem. Am. Osteo. Assn. (Andrew Taylor Still Meml. lectr. 1976), Am. Osteo. Hosp. Assn., Temple U., N.E. High Sch. alumni assns., Assn. Schs. Allied Health Professions, Am. Pub. Health Assn., Am. Assn. Colls. Osteo. Medicine, Assn. Am. Med. Colls., Am. Legion, Welsh Soc. (pres. 1966-68), Phila. Hot Stove Leaguers, Sigma Sigma Phi, Phi Sigma Gamma (hon. mem. Zeta chpt.). Republican. Baptist. Clubs: Union League of Phila., Bala Golf, Pa. Soc., Masons. Office: 4150 City Ave Philadelphia PA 19131

ROWLAND, WILLIAM CHARLES, utility co. exec.; b. New Castle, Pa., Dec. 26, 1921; s. David John and Beryl Abigail (Reynolds) R.; B.S., Westminster Coll., 1949; postgrad. U. Mich., 1956; M.B.A., U. Chgo., 1970; m. Leah M. Davis, Aug. 26, 1947; children—Lawrence, Robert. Sta. installer Bell Telephone Co. Pa., New Castle, 1941-48; outside plant engr. Gen. Telephone Co. Pa., Erie, 1949-53, dist. plant engr., Oil City, Pa., 1953-55, gen. plant engr., Erie, 1955-56, gen. plant mgr., 1956-58; operating v.p. Gen. Telephone Co. Wis., Madison, 1958-61, Gen. Telephone Co. Ind., Fort Wayne, 1961-67; pres. Gen. Telephone Co. Ill., Bloomington, 1967-72, Hawaiian Telephone Co., Honolulu, 1972-78; group v.p. GTESC, Los Gatos, Calif., 1978-79, exec. v.p. telephone operating group, Stamford, Conn., 1979—; dir. 1st Hawaiian Bank, Dillingham Corp. Pres., mem. exec. com. Ft. Wayne Conv. and Visitors Bur., Inc., 1966-67; mem. adv. council Ill. State U., Normal, 1968-71; mem. adv. com. Coll. Commerce and Bus. Adminstrn., U. Ill. at Urbana, 1968-72; chmn. regional adv. com. Gov.'s Commn. on Urban Area Govt., 1969-72; gov. mem. Ill. Council on Econ. Edn., 1971-72; mem. Hawaii Joint Council Econ. Edn., 1973—; bd. dirs. Morgan-Washington Home, Bloomington, 1969-72, Ill. Wesleyan U. Assos., Bloomington, 1970-72, United Community Services McLean County (Ill.), 1968-72, Oahu Devel. Conf., 1972-78, Honolulu Symphony, 1975-78; bd. dirs. Aloha United Way, 1972-78, gen. campaign chmn., 1976, pres., 1976-77, chmn. bd., 1977—; trustee Ill. Wesleyan U., 1970-72, Hawaii Loa Coll., 1976; advisory council Coll. Bus. Adminstrn., U. Hawaii at Honolulu, 1972—, mem. advisory com. Advanced Mgmt. Program, 1973—; bd. govs. Goodwill Tng. Center Honolulu, 1973-78; bd. dirs. Bicentennial Hawaii Corp., 1974—, Hawaii Visitors Bur., 1973-75, Downtown Improvement Assn., 1975-78, Hawaii chpt. ARC, 1976-78; bd. govs. Hawaii Employers Council, 1973-78; mem. advisory bd. Nat. Alliance Businessmen, 1974—; bd. dirs. Aloha council Boy Scouts Am., 1975-78. Served with USAAF, 1941-45, AUS, 1950-52. Decorated D.F.C., Air medal with 3 oak leaf clusters. Mem. Ind. Telephone Pioneer Assn., McLean County Assn. Commerce and Industry (dir. 1968-72), C. of C. Hawaii (dir. 1974—), Assn. U.S. Army (pres. 1974-75). Republican. Presbyterian. Clubs: Masons (32 degree), Rotary; Oahu Country, Waialae, Pacific; U. Chgo. Exec. Program. Home: 11 Sunset Hill Rd New Canaan CT 06840 Office: GTE Corp One Stamford Forum Stamford CT 04904

ROWLANDS, DAVID D., city ofcl.; b. Pitts., Mar. 22, 1915; s. Charles Wilson and Laura Isabelle (Dickson) R.; A.B., Westminster Coll. (Pa.), 1937; M.A., U. Chgo., 1940; m. Sarah B. Hamilton, May 25, 1943; children—David D., Jean Louise, Margaret Jane, John Hamilton. Planning dir., asst. to city mgr., Wichita, Kans., 1945-48; city mgr., Mt. Lebanon, Pa., 1949-52, Eau Claire, Wis., 1952-56, Tacoma, 1956-70; exec. v.p. Univ. Dist. Devel. Council, Seattle, 1970-72; city adminstr. City of Huntington Beach (Calif.), 1972-76; vis. prof. Calif. State U. Long Beach, 1976—; instr. tech. municipal adminstrn. Inst. Tng. Municipal Adminstrs. Mem. Gov. Wis. Retirement Study Commn., 1955, Gov. Wash. Adv. Expenditure Council, 1958; chmn. Wash. Adv. Council Higher Edn., 1966; chmn. nat. com. fire def. Nat. League Cities, 1959-62; chmn. Municipal Fire Def. Inst., 1961-62; mem. exec. com. Puget Sound Govtl. Conf.; mem. Task Force on Model Cities, 1969—. Served to capt. AUS, World War II. Mem. Internat. (pres. 1966-67), Pa., Wash. (past pres.) city mgrs. assns., Am. Soc. Planning Ofcls., Mcpl. Fin. Officers Assn. Club: Rotary. Author: Effective Strike Management for Local Government, 1978; Contract Management Techniques and Practices in Local Government, 1979; contbr. articles to profl. publs. Home: 5133 E Emerald Circle Mesa AZ 85206 Office: Center for Public Policy and Adminstrn Calif State U Long Beach CA 90840

ROWLANDS, DAVID THOMAS, physician; b. Wilkes-Barre, Pa., Mar. 22, 1930; s. David Thomas and Anna Jule (Morgan) R.; M.D., U. Pa., 1955; m. Gwendolyn Marie York, Mar. 1, 1958; children—Julie Marie, Carolyn Jane. Intern Pa. Hosp., Phila., 1955-56; resident Cin. Gen. Hosp., 1956-60; asst. prof. U. Colo., 1962-64, Rockefeller U., 1964-66; asso. prof. Duke U., Durham, N.C., 1966-70; prof. pathology U. Pa., Phila., 1970—, chmn. dept. pathology, 1973-78. Served with USNR, 1960-62. Recipient Lederle Med. Faculty award U. Colo., 1964, Jacob Ehrenzeller award Pa. Hosp., 1976. Diplomate Am. Bd. Pathology, Am. Bd. Allergy and Immunology. Mem. Am. Assn. Pathologists, Internat. Acad. Pathology, Am. Soc. Clin. Pathology, Am. Assn. Immunologists. Presbyterian. Mem. editorial bd. Am. Jour. Pathology, 1971—, Developmental and Comparative Immunology, 1977-79. Home: 528 Arbordale Rd Wayne PA 19087 Office: Dept Pathology School of Medicine University of Pennsylvania Philadelphia PA 19174

ROWLANDS, GENA, actress; b. Cambria, Wis., June 19; d. Edwin Merwin and Mary Allen (Neal) Rowlands; student U. Wis., also Am. Acad. Dramatic Art, N.Y.C.; m. John Cassavetes; children—Nicholas, Alexandra, Zoe. Theatrical appearance include The Middle of the Night, 1956; films include The High Cost of Loving, 1958, Lonely Are The Brave, 1962, A Child is Waiting, 1962, Spiral Road, 1962, Faces, 1968, At Any Price, 1970, Minnie and Moscowitz, 1971, Woman Under the Influence, 1973, Two Minute Warning, 1976, Opening Night, 1977, The Brinks Job, 1978, One Summer Night, 1979; TV movies A Question of Love, 1978, Strangers, 1979; numerous other TV appearances. Mem. Actors Equity Assn., Screen Actors Guild, AFTRA, Am. Guild Variety Artists.

ROWLANDS, MARVIN LLOYD, JR., pub. exec.; b. Wellington, Kans., Apr. 30, 1926; s. Marvin Lloyd and Opal Mary (Pilant) R.; B.S. in Journalism, U. Kans., 1950. Wire editor Manhattan (Kans.) Mercury, 1950-51; reporter Leavenworth (Kans.) Times, 1951-56, Topeka (Kans.) Daily Capital, 1956-57, Cin. Times-Star, 1957-58; asso. editor The AMA News, 1958-61, mng. editor, 1961-65, editor Am. Med. News, Chgo., 1965-75; editor-in-chief Modern Healthcare, Chgo., 1975-76; editor Contemporary Surgery and Contemporary Ob/Gyn, N.Y.C., 1976-77; dir. devel. McGraw-Hill Publs. Co., N.Y.C., 1978—. Served with USNR, 1944-46. Mem. Sigma Delta Chi, Omicron Delta Kappa. Baptist. Home: 429 E 52d St New York NY 10022 Office: 1221 Ave of Americas New York NY 10020

ROWLANDS, STANLEY, educator; b. Liverpool, Eng., July 30, 1918; s. Walter Frederick and Florence Ada (Moreton) R.; B.Sc., Liverpool U., 1939, Ph.D., 1942; postgrad. London U., 1952-56; m. Margaret Mary Barton, Aug. 15, 1942; children—Christopher John, Caroline Grace. Sr. lectr. London U., 1945-48, reader, 1952-67; sr. lectr. Edinburgh U., 1948-52; prof. Faculty Medicine, U. Calgary, 1967—, asso. dean, 1969-71; cons. physician nuclear medicine St. Marys Hosp., London, 1962-67; chmn. biomed. engring. com. Med. Research Council Can. Bd. dirs. Theatre Calgary; bd. govs. Paddington Tech. Coll., U. Calgary; v.p. So. Alta. Opera Assn. Licentiate Royal Coll. Physicians. Fellow Inst. Physics; mem. Royal Coll. Surgeons. Contbr. articles profl. jours. Home: 111 Scarboro Ave SW Calgary AB T3C 2H2 Canada

ROWLES, CHARLES ARTHUR, chemist, educator; b. Crandal, Man., Can., May 8, 1915; s. Thomas and Gertrude Mary (Williamson) R.; B.S.A. with distinction, U. Sask., 1935, M.Sc., 1937; Ph.D., U. Minn., 1939; m. Janet M. Gould, Feb. 13, 1976; children—Charles Garfield, Thomas Gordon. Instr., U. Sask., 1939-40; chief chemist, insp. officer Insp. Bd. U.K. and Can., Ottawa, 1940-46; asso. prof. U. Guelph (Ont.), 1946-47; prof., chmn. dept. soil sci. U. B.C., Vancouver, 1955—; tech. adviser Govt. Venezuela under FAO UN, 1963-64. Mem. Chem. Inst. Can., Canadian Soc. Soil Sci. (pres. 1952), Soil Sci. Soc. Am. Contbr. articles to sci. jours. Home: 4660 W 10th Ave Apt 1404 Vancouver BC Canada Office: U BC Vancouver BC Canada

ROWLEY, DONALD A., pathologist-immunologist, educator; b. Owatonna, Minn., Feb. 4, 1923; B.S., U. Chgo., 1945, M.S., 1950, M.D., 1950; m. 1948; 4 children. Sr. asst. surgeon Nat. Inst. Allergy and Infectious Diseases, 1951-54; instr. pathology U. Chgo., 1954-57, asst. prof., 1957-61, asso. prof., 1961-68, prof. dept. pathology, 1969—, dept. pediatrics, 1973—, dir. research La Rabida-U. Chgo. Inst., 1973-78, dir. inst., 1978—, dir. La Rabida Children's Hosp. and Research Center, 1978—; sr. research fellow USPHS, 1959-69; vis. scientist Sir William Dunn Sch. Pathology, Oxford, Eng., 1961-62, 70-71. Mem. Soc. for Exptl. Pathology, Assn. Pathology and Bacteriology, Assn. Immunology. Office: LaRabida U of Chgo Inst 65th and Lake Michigan Chicago IL 60649

ROWLEY, JAMES WALTON, coll. pres.; b. Ravenswood, W.Va., Sept. 30, 1925; s. Paul Foster and Ruth Celestine (McBride) R.; A.B., W.Va. Wesleyan Coll., 1945; M.A., Ohio State U., 1946; M.A. in Edn., U. Ky., 1949, Ed.D., 1950; B.S.C., Ohio U., 1953; m. Nyana Raynes, Dec. 30, 1946; 1 dau., Jana Lou. Instr. in English, Marshall U., Huntington, W.Va., 1946-48; asst. prof. edn. Ohio Wesleyan U., Delaware, 1950-52; prof. edn. Morris Harvey Coll., Charleston, W.Va., 1954-66, v.p., acad. dean, 1966-75; acting pres. Bluefield State, Concord and Greenbrier colls., W.Va., 1975-76; pres. W.Va. Coll. Grad. Studies, Institute, W.Va., 1976—. Postdoctoral fellow Ohio State U., 1954, U. Minn., 1956. Mem. W.Va. Assn. Higher Edn. (past pres.), W.Va. Assn. Acad. Deans (past pres.). Methodist. Home: 3610 Staunton Ave SE Charleston WV 25304 Office: WVa Coll Grad Studies Institute WV 25112

ROWLEY, PETER TEMPLETON, physician; b. Greenville, Pa., Apr. 29, 1929; s. George Hardy and Susan Mossman (Templeton) R.; A.B. magna cum laude, Harvard U., 1951; M.D., Columbia U., 1955; m. Carol Stone, Mar. 19, 1967; children—Derek Stone, Jason Templeton. Intern med. service N.Y. Hosp.-Cornell Med. Center, 1955-56; clin. asso. Nat. Inst. Neurol. Disease and Blindness, NIH, 1956-58; asst. resident, then resident Harvard Med. Service, Boston City Hosp., asst. in medicine Harvard U. Med. Sch. and researcher Thorndike Meml. Lab., 1958-60; hon. research asst. dept. eugenics, biometry and genetics Univ. Coll., U. London, 1960-61; postdoctoral fellow dept. microbiology N.Y. U. Sch. Medicine, 1961-63; asst. prof. medicine Stanford U., 1963-70; asso. prof. medicine pediatrics and genetics U. Rochester, 1970-75, prof. medicine, pediatrics, genetics and microbiology, 1975—, acting chmn. div. genetics, 1975—, dir. genetics and regulation postdoctoral tng. program, 1977—; mem. staff Highland Hosp.; physician, pediatrician Strong Meml. Hosp.; cons. NIH study, 1977-79; med. med. adv. bd. Ahepa Cooley's Anemia Found., 1978—; mem. N.Y. State Exec. and Adv. Coms. on Genetics Diseases, 1979—; WHO vis. scholar Inst. Biol. Chemistry, U. Ferrara (Italy), 1970. Served with USPHS, 1956-58. Recipient Excellence in Teaching award U. Rochester Class of 1976, 1973; NRC fellow, 1960-63; Buswell research fellow, 1970-71, 71-72. Diplomate Am. Bd. Internal Medicine. Fellow A.C.P.; mem. Am. Fedn. Clin. Research, Am. Soc. Hematology, Am. Soc. Human Genetics. Editor: (with M. Lipkin Jr.) Genetic Responsibility: On Choosing Our Children's Genes, 1974. Office: Div Genetics PO Box 641 U Rochester Med Sch 601 Elmwood Ave Rochester NY 14642

ROWLEY, WORTH, lawyer; b. Boston, Aug. 14, 1916; s. Clarence Worth and Catherine Agnes (Foley) R.; J.D., Northeastern U., 1938; m. Jacqueline Magrath, May 4, 1940 (div.); children—Jonathan M., Susannah W., Belinha P., Joshua F.; m. 2d, Jane Pedersen, Apr. 1, 1972; children—Clarence Worth III, Eliza Ann. Admitted to Mass. bar, 1938, D.C. bar, 1958; practice law with father, Boston, 1938-41; with antitrust div. U.S. Dept. Justice, Washington, 1945-58; individual practice law, Washington, 1958-69, partner firm Rowley & Green, Washington, 1969—. Served to lt. (j.g.) USN, 1942-45. Mem. Am. Law Inst., Am. Bar Assn., D.C. Bar Assn. Democrat. Unitarian. Clubs: Nat. Press, Internat., University (Washington); West River Sailing. Home: 2446 Kalorama Rd NW Washington DC 20008 Office: Rowley & Green 1990 M St NW Washington DC 20036

ROWLINGSON, DONALD TAGGART, educator; b. Syracuse, N.Y., Mar. 9, 1907; s. Clyde Adelbert and Mary Sylvia (Taggart) S.; A.B., Allegheny Coll., 1929, D.D., 1962; S.T.B., Boston U., 1932, Ph.D., 1938; student U. Berlin (Germany), 1932-33; m. Louise Kendrick, Aug. 30, 1935; children—Ann (Mrs. Leo Austin, Jr.), Elisabeth (Mrs. Ralph Dorman), John; m. 2d, Lilian Mary Edwards, Jan. 19, 1960. Summer camp leader, 1920-28, camp dir., 1928; ordained to ministry Meth. Ch., 1934; asso. pastor Community Ch., Islington, Mass., 1930-37; mem. Central N.Y. Conf. Meth. Ch., 1934-42, Va. Conf., 1942-49, Central N.Y. Conf., 1949-73; teaching fellow N.T., Boston U., 1935-37; instr. religion, alumni sec. Allegheny Coll., 1937-39; asst. prof. N.T., Candler Sch. Theology, Emory U., 1939-41, asso. prof., 1941-44, prof., 1944-49; prof. N.T., Boston U. Sch. Theol., 1949-72, emeritus prof. N.T., 1972—; adminstrv. asst. 1st Congregational Ch., Winchester, Mass., 1975-76, minister adminstrn., 1977—. Dir. Druid Hills Civic Assn., Atlanta, 1947-49; bd. dirs. Mystic Valley Mental Health Assn., 1975—, v.p., 1977-79; mem. Winchester Interagy. Council, 1976—. Jacob Sleeper fellow Boston U., 1932; fellow German-Am. Student Exchange, 1932-33; Am. Assn. Theol. Schs. fellow, Cambridge, Eng., 1958-59. Mem. Soc. Bibl. Lit. (v.p. So. sect. 1949-50), Nat. Assn. Bibl. Instrs. (council 1948-49), Phi Delta Theta, Omicron Delta Kappa, Kappa Phi Kappa. Author: Introduction to New Testament Studies, 1956; Jesus the Religious Ultimate, 1961; The Gospel-Perspective on Jesus Christ, 1968; also articles. Home: 15 Ridge St Winchester MA 01890 Office: First Congregational Church Winchester MA 01890

ROWNTREE, GRADIE RAYMOND, physician, educator; b. Hart County, Ky., Sept. 25, 1903; s. John and Carrie (Bale) R.; M.D., U. Ark., 1932; M.P.H., Johns Hopkins, 1936; M.S., U. Louisville, 1941; m. Marjorie Wulff, May 23, 1936. Intern, USPHS Hosp., S.I., N.Y., 1946-47; med. field dir. Ky. Dept. Health, Louisville, 1932-37; dep. dir. Louisville Dept. Health, 1938-43, dir., 1944-46; med. dir. Fawcett Printing Corp., Louisville, 1948-68; prof. occupational medicine U. Louisville, 1939—. Chmn. Louisville and Jefferson County Bd. Health, 1956-65. Bd. dirs. Louisville YMCA, 1940-50. Recipient Physicians award for contbn. to nation's physically handicapped Pres. U.S., 1956, Meritorious Service award Indsl. Med. Assn., 1964. Diplomate Am. Bd. Preventive Medicine. Fellow Am. Occupational Med. Assn. (pres. 1961-62), Am. Pub. Health Assn., Am. Acad. Family Physicians (charter, pres. chpt. 1954-55); mem. World, Am., So., Ky. med. assns., Internat. Assn. Occupational Health (permanent commn. 1963—), Royal Soc. Health, Jefferson County Med. Soc. (pres. 1955-56, gov.), Ky. Hist. Soc., Louisville C. of C., S.A.R. (nat. surgeon gen. 1975, pres. Ky. soc. 1975), Ky. Homes Found. (life). Mason (33 deg.). Clubs: Filson (life), Automobile (pres. 1955-56, dir.), Jefferson. Home: 70 Valley Rd Louisville KY 40204

ROWNY, EDWARD LEON, army officer; b. Balt., Apr. 3, 1917; s. Gracyan J. and Mary Ann (Rodgers) R.; B.C.E., Johns Hopkins U., 1937; B.S., U.S. Mil. Acad., 1941; M.A., Yale U., 1949, M.S., 1949; Ph.D. in Internat. Studies, Am. U., 1977; m. Mary Rita Leyko, Dec. 26, 1941; children—Marcia, Peter, Paul, Michael, Grayson. Commd. 2d lt. U.S. Army, 1941, advanced through grades to lt. gen., 1970; participated in African campaign, 1942, European and Middle East campaign, 1944-45, Korean campaign, 1950-52, Vietnam campaign, 1962-63; spl. asst. tactical mobility Dept. Army, 1963-65; comdg. gen. 24th Inf. Div., Europe, 1965-66; dep. chief staff logistics U.S. Army Europe, 1968-69; dep. chief research and devel. U.S. Army, 1969-70; comdg. gen. I Corps, Korea, 1970-71; dep. chmn. NATO Mil. Com., 1971-73; JCS rep. to SALT del., Geneva, 1973—. Decorated D.S.M., Silver Star with 2 oak leaf clusters, Legion of Merit with 4 oak leaf clusters, Combat Inf. badge with star. Registered profl. engr., D.C. Mem. Internat. Inst. for Strategic Studies (London), Knights of Malta. Home: Quarters 6 Fort McNair Washington DC 20319 Office: JCS Rep SALT OJCS The Pentagon Washington DC 20301

ROWSON, RICHARD CAVANAGH, publisher; b. Hollywood, Calif., Apr. 7, 1926; s. Louis Cavanagh and Mable Louise (Montney) R.; A.B., U. Calif., Berkeley, 1946; certificate, Sorbonne, 1949; M.I.A., Columbia U., 1950; m. Elena Louisa Costabile, Nov. 22, 1952; children—Peter Cavanagh, John Cummings. Trainee, Fgn. Policy Assn., 1950; dir. World Affairs Council R.I., 1951-52; with Fgn. Policy Assn., 1951-62, dir. finance and devel., 1960-62; with Radio Free Europe, 1962-69, dir. policy and planning, 1964-69; dir. spl. studies Praeger Pubs., Inc., N.Y.C., 1969-77, pres., 1975-77; pres. Pergamon Press, 1977—; lectr., condr. workshops, roundtables. Served to lt. (j.g.) USNR, 1944-47. Mem. Am. Polit. Sci. Assn., Am. Econ. Assn., Am. Assn. Pub. Opinion Research, N.Y. Acad. Scis., Am. Assn. Advancement Slavic Studies, U. Calif., Columbia U. alumni assns., Soc. Internat. Devel. Democrat. Club: Overseas Press (N.Y.C.). Contbr. articles to profl. jours. Address: 2 Beekman Pl New York NY 10022

ROY, CARMEN, anthropologist; b. Bonaventure, Que., Can., Dec. 25, 1919; B.A., Coll. Marguerite Bourgeoys, Montreal, 1942; M.A., U. Paris, 1951, Ph.D. cum laude (Govt. of Que. and Govt. of France fellows), 1953. Tchr. French, U. Laval, Que., summer 1947; folklore fieldwork Nat. Mus. Can., Quebec, 1948-56, chief folklore sect., 1957-66, chief folklore div., 1966-70, chief Can. Centre Folk Culture Studies, 1970-77, sr. scientist Nat. Mus. of Man, Ottawa, Ont., 1977—. Recipient Centennial medal, 1967; Queen's Jubilee medal, 1977. Fellow Am. Anthrop. Assn.; mem. Internat. Folk Music Council, Am. Folklore Soc., Can. Folk Music Soc. (dir., past pres.), Can. Sociology and Anthropology Assn., Can. Museums Assn., Assn. Recorded Sound Collections, Am. Assn. State and Local History, Internat. Commn. Ethnographic Film, Folklore Studies Assn. Can. (hon. life pres.), Royal Anthrop. Inst. Gt. Britain and Ireland, Ont. Mus. Assn., Société internationale d'Ethnologie européenne, Société des Écrivains canadiens-Ottawa (past pres.), Société des Ecrivains canadiens-Montreal (past dir.), Assn. des Docteurs de l'Université de Paris, Fedn. internationale des Phonotheques, Paris, Société d'Etudes folkloriques du Centre-Ouest (La Rochelle, France), ICOM (France and Can.), Association des Écrivains de Langue française (Mer et de Outre-Mer), La Société historique de la Gaspésie, Société d'Ethnologie française, Société historique acadienne, Alliance francaise, Union des Bretons du Can., Société québécoise d'Ethnologie et de folklore (hon.), Commn. on Urgent Anthrop. Research, Société internationale d'Ethnologie et de Folklore. Author: Contes populaires gaspésiens, 1952; Littérature orale en Gaspésie, 1955; Le Géant Brigandin, 1956; Saint-Pierre et Miquelon, 1962; Présentation du Centre canadien d'études sur la culture traditionnelle, 1973; contbr. articles to profl. jours. Address: Nat Museum of Man 110 Argyle Ave Ottawa ON K1A 0M8 Canada

ROY, CHARLES ROBERT, machinery mfg. co. exec.; b. Duluth, Minn., Oct. 15, 1930; s. John Benjamin and Ruth Laverna (Olsen) R.; B.A., Mich. State U., 1953; m. Patricia Raye Haggins, May 21, 1955; children—Richard, Margaret, John, Joan. Auditor, Price Waterhouse & Co., Milw., 1954; auditor, tax accountant, tax mgr. Arthur Andersen & Co., Milw., 1954-62; tax mgr. Rex Chainbelt, Inc. (name now Rexnord Inc.), West Milwaukee, Wis., 1962-65, asst. sec., 1965-66, asst. sec., chief accounting officer, 1966-68, asst. sec., asst. treas., 1968-69, controller, 1969—. Sec.-treas., bd. dirs. Wis. Heart Assn.; bus. alumni dir., devel. fund dir. Mich. State U. Served with USAF, 1948-49. C.P.A., Wis., 1957. Mem. West Milwaukee C. of C. (dir. 1964), Am. Inst. C.P.A.'s, Wis. Soc. C.P.A.'s (dir. Milw. chpt. 1967), Tax Execs. Inst. (pres. Wis. chpt. 1965), NAM, Fin. Execs. Inst., Mich. State U. Alumni Assn. of Milw., Delta Sigma Phi. Episcopalian. Home: 14245 Heatherwood Ct Elm Grove WI 53122 Office: 4701 W Greenfield Ave West Milwaukee WI 53201

ROY, ELSIJANE TRIMBLE, U.S. dist. judge; b. Lonoke, Ark., Apr. 2, 1916; d. Thomas Clark and Elsie Jane (Walls) Trimble; J.D., U. Ark. at Little Rock, 1939, LL.D. (hon.), 1978; m. James M. Roy, Nov. 23, 1943; 1 son, James Morrison. Admitted to Ark. bar, 1939; atty. Ark. Revenue Dept., Little Rock, 1939-64; mem. firm Reid, Evrard & Roy, Blytheville, Ark., 1947-54, Roy & Roy, Blytheville, 1954-63; law clk. Ark. Supreme Ct., Little Rock, 1963-65, asso. justice, 1975-77; U.S. dist. judge for Eastern and Western Dists. Ark., Little Rock, 1977—; judge Pulaski County (Ark.) Circuit Ct., Little Rock, 1966; asst. atty. gen. Ark., Little Rock, 1967; sr. law clk. U.S. Dist. Ct., Little Rock and Ft. Smith, 1968-73. Mem. med. adv. com. U. Ark. Med. Center, 1952-54. Committeewoman Democratic Party 16th Jud. Dist., 1940-42; vice chmn. Ark. Dem. State Com., 1946-48; mem. chmn. com. Ark. Constnl. Commn., 1967-68. Recipient Disting. Alumna citation U. Ark., 1978; named Ark. Woman of Yr., 1976. Mem. Nat. Assn. Women Lawyers, Am. Bar Assn., Ark. Bar Assn., AAUW, Little Rock (pres. 1939, 42), Ark. (pres. 1940-41) women lawyers, Mortar Bd., P.E.O., Delta Theta Phi. Chi Omega. Club: Altrusa. Home: Riviera Apts Apt 1101 Little Rock AR 72202 Office: US Post Office and Courthouse Little Rock AR 72203

ROY, FABIEN JOSEPH, Canadian politician; b. St. Prosper of Beauce, Que., Apr. 17, 1928; s. Fridolin and Anne-Marie (Goulet) R.; attended St. Georges Sem., Laval U., to 1968; m. Pauline Lessard, Aug. 27, 1960; children—Brigitte, Jean-François, Madeleine, Veronique. Gen. mgr. Caisse d'Etablissement de la Chaudière, 1962-70; mem. council Adminstrn. of Fedn. of Caisses d' Etablissement Que., 1968-70, mem. exec. council, 1968-70, dir. recruitement and sales for Que., 1970; elected dep. from Beauce, 1970, relected dep. nouveau comte de Beauce-Sud, 1973, elected dep. for Beauce, House of Commons, 1979. Sec., Fedn. Chantiers Cooperatifs Quebec-Sud, 1949-52, Sherbrooke, 1952-53; pres. C. of C. St-Prosper, 1963; pres. Credit Assn. Dorchester, 1962-68; regional organizer ralliement creditiste, elections of 1962, 63, 65, 68; provincial v.p. Ralliement, 1964-65; mem. polit. com. Ralliement creditiste, 1964-65; named fin. spokesman Parti Creditiste, 1970; parliamentary leader Ralliement creditiste in the Nat. Assembly of Que., 1972-75; pres. Parti Creditiste, 1973-74; co-founder with Jerome Choquette of P.N.P., 1975; named chief Social Credit Party of Can., 1979—. Mem. Association Internationale des Parlementaires de langue française (Que. del. to internat. congress in Brussels 1974, Gabon 1978), Association des Parlementaires du Commonwealth, Association des Parents catholiques. Office: 11260 1e Ave Saint Georges Est Beauce PQ 65Y 2C3 Canada

ROY, GABRIELLE (MRS. MARCEL CARBOTTE), writer; b. St. Boniface, Man. Can.; d. Leon and Melina (Landry) Roy; student Institut Collegial St. Joseph, St. Boniface, Normal Sch., Winnipeg, Man.; m. Marcel Carbotte, Aug. 30, 1947. Tchr. pub. schs., St. Boniface; free-lance writer for Canadian papers and mags., Montreal, 1939—. Recipient Prixfemina, 1947; Gov. Gen. award; Prix Duvernay; Medaille de L'Academie Francaise; prix David, 1971; Molson award, 1977; Can. award for best short story of 1979; 3 Gov.-Gen. awards; companion Order of Can. Mem. Royal Soc. Can. Author: (novels) The Tin Flute, 1947; Where Nests the Water Hen, 1951; The Cashier; Street of Riches; The Hidden Mountain; The Road Past Altamont, 1966; Windflower, 1970; Enchanted Summer, 1976;

Garden in the Wind, 1977; Children of My Heart, 1978. Address: 135 W Grande Allee Quebec PQ G1R 2H2 Canada

ROY, MAURICE CARDINAL, clergyman; b. Quebec, Can., Jan. 25, 1905; s. Ferdinand and Mariette (Legendre); B.A., Petit Seminaire, Quebec, 1923; D.Th. (D.D.), Laval U., 1927; D.Ph., Institutum Angelicum, 1929; student Institut Catholique and Sorbonne, Paris, 1929-30. Ordained priest Roman Catholic Ch., 1927; prof. theology Laval U., 1930- 46; rector Grand Sem. (Sch. Theology), Laval U., 1946; bishop, Trois- Rivieres, Quebec, 1946-47; bishop ordinary to Canadian Armed Forces, 1946—; archbishop of Quebec, 1947—, cardinal, 1965—; named chmn. Council of Lay Apostolate and Pontifical Commn. Justice and Peace, 1967; sec., faculty of philosophy (Laval), 1930-34; organizer Laval Summer Course of Pedagogy, 1935-37. Served as army chaplain (hon. col.) Canadian Army Overseas, 1939-45. Decorated Order Brit. Empire; chevalier Legion d'Honneur; comdr. de l'Ordre d'Orange-Nassau de Holande; companion Order Can. Primate of Can., 1956. Club: Quebec Garrison. Address: Archbishop's Residence CP 459 Quebec PQ G1R 4R6 Canada

ROY, PHILIP H., pharm. co. exec.; b. Newark, May 25, 1920; s. Joseph P. and Doris (Schellhardt) R.; B.S., Bucknell U., 1942; postgrad. Columbia U., 1946; m. Treva Poling, Dec. 26, 1942; children—Philip, Sandra, Ann, Steven, Peter, Treva, Judy. Auditor, S.D. Leidesdorf & Co., C.P.A.'s, N.Y.C., 1946-51; with Merck & Co., Inc., 1951—, controller, 1968-72, v.p. fin., 1972-76, sr. v.p., 1976—; dir. Arkwright Boston Ins. Co. Trustee Bucknell U., Chilton Meml. Hosp. Served with USNR, 1942-45. C.P.A., N.Y. Mem. Fin. Execs. Inst., Am. Inst. C.P.A.'s. Home: 275 Indian Trail Dr Franklin Lakes NJ 07417 Office: Merck & Co Lincoln Ave Rahway NJ 07065

ROY, RADHA RAMAN, physicist; b. Calcutta, India, Feb. 8, 1921; came to U.S., 1958, naturalized, 1965; s. Debendra Nath and Krishna Kumari R.; B.Sc., U. Calcutta, 1940; M.Sc., U. Calif., 1942; Ph.D., U. London, 1946; m. Marie Louise Angela Goes, June 30, 1956; children—Manik Ratan, Robin Kumar. Prof. physics, dir. nuclear physics lab. U. Brussels, 1949-57; prof., dir. nuclear physics lab. Pa. State U., University Park, 1958-63; prof. Ariz. State U., Tempe, 1963—; cons. in field. Fellow Am. Phys. Soc. Author: Nuclear Physics, 1967, Photons and Leptons Interactions, 1968; Statistical Physics, 1971; contbr. articles to profl. jours. Home: 5926 E Oak St Scottsdale AZ 85257 Office: Ariz State Univ Tempe AZ 85281. *Recognition for good work, if it comes, is as transient as fame, but the way we work can bring self-realization and inner contentment which last.*

ROY, RAYMOND, bishop; b. Fisher Branch, Man., Can., May 3, 1919; s. Charles-Borromée and Zephirina (Milette) R.; B.A. in Philosophy and Theology, U. Man., 1942; student Philos. Sem., Montreal, 1942-43, Major Sem., Montreal, 1943-46, Major Sem. St. Boniface, 1946-47. Ordained priest Roman Catholic Ch., 1947; asst. pastor, then pastor chs. in Man., 1947-50, 53-66; chaplain St. Boniface (Man.) Hosp., 1950-53; superior Minor Sem., St. Boniface, 1966-69; pastor Cathedral Parish, St. Boniface, 1969-72; ordained bishop, 1972; bishop of St. Paul, Alta., Can., 1972—. Club: K.C. Address: 4637 45th Ave PO Box 339 St Paul AB T0A 3A0 Canada*

ROY, ROBERT HALL, educator; b. Balt., Nov. 21, 1906; s. Harry Hall and Mollie (Frederick) R.; B.E., Johns Hopkins, 1928; m. Florence Sentman, Nov. 25, 1930; children—Mollie Frederick, Florence Conard. Apprentice engr., Waverly Press, Inc., Balt., 1928, then successively salesman, engr., chief engr., to 1947, v.p. for engring., 1947-49, dir., 1941-51; instr. in mech. engring., Johns Hopkins, 1939-47, asso. prof. indsl. engring., 1947-49, prof. and chmn. indsl. engring., also asst. dean, Sch. Engring., 1949-53, dean sch. engring., 1953-72; cons. engr., labor arbitrator, 1949—. Mem. Am. Olympic team, 1928. Bd. govs., bd. visitors Wash. Coll., chmn., 1976—. Fellow ASME, Am. Inst. Indsl. Engrs. (recipient Frank and Lillian Gilbreth award 1967); mem. Am. Soc. Engring. Edn. (hon.; pres. 1966-67), AAUP, Phi Beta Kappa, Alpha Tau Omega, Omicron Delta Kappa, Tau Beta Pi. Clubs: Engineers (pres. 1949-50), Johns Hopkins. Author: Management of Printing Production, 1953; The Adminstrative Process, 1958. Co-editor: Operations Research and Systems Engineering, 1960; (with others) Horizons for a Profession, 1964; The Cultures of Management (Book of Yr. award 1978), 1977. Home: 7826 Chelsea St Ruxton MD 21204 Office: The Johns Hopkins University Baltimore MD 21218

ROY, ROSS, advt. agy. exec.; b. Kingston, Ont., Can., July 22, 1898; s. Dr. Emile and Josephine (Pronovost) R.; brought to U.S., 1900, naturalized, 1928; student pub. schs. Wis.; m. Mary Agnes Hillemeyer, June 28, 1927; children—Robert Regis, Arlene Marie, Jon; m. 2d, Celia Christiansen Wormer, June 30, 1960; children—Rex Regis, Ross Regis Roy, Jr.; stepchildren—Chris, Sally, Sigrid. Automobile salesman O'Connell Motor Co., Janesville, Wis., 1919-26; founder Ross Roy, Inc., Detroit, N.Y.C., Windsor, Ont., Can., pres., 1926-60; chmn. bd., exec. officer Ross-B.S.F. & D., Inc. (name changed to Ross-Roy, Inc. 1962), 1960—. Mem. exec. bd. Detroit area council Boy Scouts Am., 1946; nat. bd. dirs. Jr. Achievement, Inc., chmn. bd., dir. S.E. Mich. area; past pres. Mich Soc. Mental Health; v.p. and dir. United Found. Met. Detroit; bd. directors Boys' Clubs Met. Detroit; past pres. Greater Detroit Bd. of Commerce; dir. Detroit Inst. Econ. Edn.; lay trustee U. Detroit; dir. Mich. Colls. Found. Recipient honor medal, Freedoms Found., 1951, Silver Beaver award Boy Scouts Am., 1956, George Washington Honor medal, 1962. Republican. Clubs: Economic, Adcraft, Detroit Athletic, Detroit Boat, Grosse Pointe Yacht, Detroit Country, Grosse Pointe Hunt, Otsego Ski. Home: 511 Sheldon Rd Grosse Pointe Shores MI 48236 Office: 2751 E Jefferson Ave Detroit MI 48207

ROY, RUSTUM, educator; b. Ranchi, India, July 3. 1924; s. Narendra Kumar and Rajkumari (Mukherjee) R.; came to U.S., 1945, naturalized, 1961; B.Sc., Patna (India) U., 1942; M.Sc., Pa. State U., 1944, Ph.D., 1948; m. Della M. Martin, June 8, 1948; children—Neill, Ronnen, Jeremy. Research asst. Pa. State U., 1948-49, mem. faculty, 1950—, prof. geochemistry, 1957—, prof. solid state, 1968—, chmn. solid state tech. program, 1960-67, chmn. sci. tech. and soc. program, 1977—, dir. materials research lab., 1962—; sr. sci. officer Nat. Ceramic Lab., India, 1950; mem. com. mineral sci. tech. Nat. Acad. Scis., 1967-69. com. survey materials sci. tech., 1970-74; exec. com. chem. div. NRC, 1967-70, nat. materials adv. bd., 1970-77, mem. com. radioactive waste mgmt., 1974—, chmn. panel waste solidification, 1976—, chmn. com. USSR and Eastern Europe, 1976—; mem. Pa. Gov.'s Sci. Adv. Com.. chmn. materials adv. panel, 1965—; mem. adv. com. engring. NSF, 1968-72, adv. com. to ethical and human value inplications sci. and tech., 1974-76, adv. com. div. materials research, 1974—; dir. Kirkridge, Inc.. Bangor, Pa.; cons. to industry. Chmn. bd. Dag Hammarskjold Coll., 1973-75; mem. ad hoc com. sci., tech. and ch. Nat. Council Chs., 1966-68. Mem. Nat. Acad. Engring., Mineral. Soc. Am. (award 1957), Am. Chem. Soc. (Petroleum Research Fund award 1960), Royal Swedish Acad. Engring. Scis. (fgn. mem.). Author: Honest Sex, 1968; Crystal Chemistry of Non-metallic Materials, 1974; also articles. Editor-in-chief Materials Research Bull., 1966—; Bull. Sci. Tech. and Soc. Home: 528 S Pugh St State College PA 16801 Office: 202 Materials Research Lab University Park PA 16802. *A continuing search for an accurate perception of the totality of "Reality," and a commitment both to sharing those (slightly changing) perceptions and to living by the highest values embedded in them, is central to my being. Integration of the insights of science and the vehicle of art into the highest religious value systems is the urgent need of our time. As a Christian I seek to increase society's commitment to proclaiming the centrality of other-centered love, and educating and training all citizens in it, even as a partial substitute for its commitment to science.*

ROY, SAKTIDAS, librarian, univ. adminstr.; b. Murshidabad, India, Oct. 11, 1935; s. Prabodh Kumar and Bibha (Nag) R.; came to U.S., 1960; B.A., Calcutta (India) U., 1958; M.S.L.S., Simmons Coll., 1964; m. Papiya Datta, May 6, 1971. Asst. librarian U.S. Info. Library, Calcutta, 1954-60; serials cataloger Harvard U. Bus. Sch., 1960-65, head serial records div. Harvard Coll. Library, 1969-72; librarian Am. Studies Research Center, Hyderabad, India, 1965-67; chief librarian U.S. Library of Congress, New Delhi, India, 1967-68; asst. acquisitions librarian U. Calif. Library, Santa Cruz, 1968-69; head preparations div. Va. Poly. and State U., 1972-73; asst. dir. tech. services, univ. libraries SUNY, Buffalo, 1973-77, dir. univ. libraries, 1977—; vice chmn. bd. trustees Western N.Y. Library Resources Council; bd. dirs. Five Asso. Univ. Libraries. Mem. ALA., Assn. Coll. and Research Libraries, Western N.Y. Library Resources Council. Hindu. Home: Apt 206 4547 Chestnut Ridge Rd Amherst NY 14221 Office: 432 Capen Hall Amherst NY 14260. *I have always tried not to be envious but to be a kind and understanding friend to all who come in contact with me; to be free from false ego and pride; to do my duty with determination, an open mind and a clear conscience; and to be always satisfied with what I achieve.*

ROY, WILL, basso; b. Schenectady; s. William Arnott and Jean C. R.; student Hope Coll.; cert. Curtis Inst. Music, Manhatten Sch. Music; m. Nancy Honegger, June 5, 1959; 1 dau., Carol Genia. Appeared in leading roles: N.Y.C. Opera, Washington Opera, Soc., Ft. Worth Opera, Grand Theatre de Geneve, French Nat. Radio; appeared with symphonies: Florence, Italy, Phila., Pitts; musical comedy appearances: as Emile De Beque in South Pacific, Jud in Oklahoma; created role of Henri in King of Hearts on Broadway; one-man shows of paintings and sculpture: Stecura Gallerie, 1973, Tim Blackburn Gallerie, N.Y.C., 1978; group shows include: Blackburn Gallerie, 1978. Winner Met. Opera Nat. Audition, Concorso di Guiseppe Verdi; Rockefeller Found. grantee, Sullivan Found. grantee. Mem. Curtis Inst. Music Alumni Assn., Am. Guild Mus. Artists (dir.). Unitarian. Home: 95 Brinkerhoff St Ridgefield Park NJ 07660 Office: care Ann Summers Internat Box 95 Sta A Willowdale Toronto ON M2N 5S7 Canada

ROY, WILLIAM ROBERT, physician, lawyer, former congressman; b. Bloomington, Ill., Feb. 23, 1926; s. Elmer Javan and Edna Blanche (Foley) R.; B.S., Ill. Wesleyan U., 1946; M.D., Northwestern U., 1949; J.D. with honors, Washburn U., 1970; m. Jane Twining Osterhoudt, July 1947; children—Robin Jo, Randall Jay, Richelle Jane, William Robert, Renee Jan, Rise Javan. Intern Evanston (Ill.) Hosp., 1949-50; resident Detroit Receiving Hosp., 1950-53; practice medicine, specializing in obstetrics and gynecology, Topeka, 1955-70; pres. med. staff Stormont Vail Hosp., 1965-66; mem. clin. faculty Kans. U. Med. Sch.; mem. 92d-93d congresses from 2d Dist. Kans.; dir. med. edn. and profl. services St. Francis Hosp., Topeka, 1974—. Del. White House Conf. on Children and Youth, 1960; conferee Inst. Urban Affairs, Washburn U. and Brookings Instn., 1968; mem. Goals for Topeka Com., 1968. Democratic candidate for U.S. Senate, 1974, 78. Bd. dirs. Nat. Health Council. Served to capt. USAF, 1953-55. Diplomate Am. Bd. Obstetrics and Gynecology. Fellow Am. Coll. Obstetrics and Gynecology; mem. Kans. (del.), Shawnee County (pres. 1967) med. socs., Inst. Medicine, Nat. Acad. Scis., Sigma Chi. Democrat. Methodist. Clubs: Topeka Country, Rotary. Home: 1561 Lakeside Dr Topeka KS 66604 Office: St Francis Hospital 1700 W 7th St Topeka KS 66606

ROYAL, DARRELL K., athletic dir.; b. Hollis, Okla., July 6, 1924; s. Burley Ray and Katy Elizabeth (Harmon) R.; B.S. in Bus., U. Okla., 1950; m. Edith Marie Thomason, July 26, 1944; children—Marian (Mrs. Abraham Kazen III) (dec.), Mack, David. Former head football coach, now dir. athletics U. Tex. Named Football Writers' Coach of Yr., 1961, 63, Am. Football Coaches Assn. Coach of Yr., 1963, 70, Tex. Sports Writers' Coach of Yr., 1961, 63, 69, 70, Southwesterner of Yr., 1961, 62, 63; named to U. Tex. Longhorn Hall Fame, 1976, Tex. Sports Hall Fame, 1976, Jim Thorpe Okla. Hall of Fame, 1977. Mem. Delta Upsilon. Presbyterian. Author: Darrell Royal Talks Football, 1963. Home: 10507 La Costa Dr Austin TX 78747

ROYALL, ROBERT VENNING, JR., banker; b. Mount Pleasant, S.C., Dec. 11, 1934; s. Robert Venning and Eleanor (Williams) R.; A.B., U. S.C., 1956; postgrad. Stonier Grad. Sch. Banking Rutgers U., 1969; grad. Advanced Mgmt. Program, Harvard U., 1975; m. Edith Gregory Frampton, July 30, 1955; children—Eleanor, Margaret, Edith. With Citizens & So. Nat. Bank, Columbia, 1961—, exec. v.p., Florence, 1968-70, exec. v.p. retail div., Columbia, 1970-74, pres., 1974—, also dir.; dir. Citizens and So. Corp. Pres., Richland County Heart Fund, 1977; trustee Sch. Bus., U. S.C., Winthrop Coll.; past chmn. bd. Heathwood Hall Episcopal Sch.; treas. S.C. Council Econ. Edn.; campaign chmn. United Way of Midlands, 1978, also bd. dirs.; mem. commandant's civilian adv. council 6th Marine Corps. Served to capt. USMCR, 1956-59. Named Young Man of Year, Jr. C. of C., 1961, 65, Outstanding Man of Year, 1968, 1 Of 3 Outstanding Young Men in S.C., 1968, Outstanding Young Banker S.C., 1971. Episcopalian (past trustee diocese S.C., vestryman). Home: 4700 Carter Hill Dr Columbia SC 29206 Office: 1801 Main St Columbia SC 29222

ROYBAL, EDWARD R., congressman; b. Albuquerque, Feb. 10, 1916; student U. Calif. at Los Angeles, Southwestern U., Kaiser Coll., Los Angeles; LL.D. (hon.), Pacific States U., Claremont Grad. Sch.; m. Lucille Beserra, Sept. 27, 1940; children—Lucille (Olivarez), Lillian (Rose), Edward R. With Civilian Conservation Corps, 1934-35; social worker, pub. health educator Calif. Tb Assn., then dir. health edn. Los Angeles County Tb and Health Assn., 1942-49; mem. 88th-96th Congresses from 25th Dist. Calif.; mem. appropriations com., select com. on aging, chmn. subcom. housing and consumer interests; mem. com. on orgn., study and review Democratic Caucus; chmn. Congl. Hispanic Caucus. Mem. L.A. City Council, 1949-62, pres. pro tem, 1961-62. Served with AUS, 1944-45. Recipient Excellence in Pub. Service award Am. Acad. Pediatrics, 1976; Chubb fellow Yale. Mem. Nat. Assn. Latino Elected Ofcls. (chmn.), Am. Mem. Am. Legion. Democrat. Roman Catholic. K.C. Home: Los Angeles CA 90023 Office: Rayburn House Office Bldg Washington DC 20515

ROYDEN, HALSEY LAWRENCE, educator, mathematician; b. Phoenix, Sept. 26, 1928; s. Halsey Lawrence and June (Slavens) R.; B.S., Stanford, 1948, M.S., 1949; Ph.D., Harvard, 1951; m. Virginia Voegeli, June 15, 1948; children—Leigh Handy, Halsey Lawrence, Constance Slavens. Mem. faculty Stanford, 1951—, prof. math., 1958—, acting exec. head dept., 1957-58, asso. dean Sch. Humanities and Scis., 1962-65, acting dean Sch. Humanities and Sci., 1968-69, dean, 1973—; vis. prof. Orta Dogu Teknik Universitesi, Ankara, 1966. Mem. math. scis. div. NRC, 1971-75; mem. adv. com. for research NSF, 1975-77, mem. adv. council, 1978—. Sr. postdoctoral fellow NSF, Swiss Fed. Inst. Tech., Zürich, 1958-59; mem. Inst. for Advanced Study, Princeton, 1969. Recipient Silver medal U. Helsinki, 1970; Guggenheim fellow, 1974. Fellow AAAS; mem. Am. Math. Soc., Math. Assn. Am., Finnish Math. Soc., Am. Inst. Archeology, Phi Beta Kappa, Sigma Xi. Author: Real Analysis, 1963. Editor Pacific Jour. Mathematics, 1955-58, 67-69. Home: 13466 Three Forks Ln Los Altos Hills CA 94022 Office: Mathematics Dept Stanford U Stanford CA 94305

ROYER, BILL, congressman; b. Jerome, Idaho, Apr. 11, 1920; s. Howard Roy and Cecilia Barbara (Schneeberger) R.; student Santa Clara U., 1938-41, Okla. A&M U., 1941; m. Shirley Wilson Bright, June 30, 1941; children—Dennis, William P. Sales mgr. Leonard Realty Co., Redwood City, Calif., 1946-54; owner, broker Royer Realty Co., Redwood City, 1950-66; mem. Redwood City City Council, 1950-66; mayor of Redwood City, 1956-60; mem. bd. suprs. County of San Mateo (Calif.), 1973-79, chmn., 1976; mem. 96th Congress from 11th dist. Calif. Trustee, Peninsula Meml. Blood Bank, Burlingame, Calif. Served to cpl. USAAC, 1943-45. Mem. Santa Clara U. Alumni Assn., Am. Legion. Republican. Roman Catholic. Clubs: Rotary, Elks, Sons of Italy, Order of Eagles. Office: 1022 Longworth Bldg Washington DC 20515

ROYER, CHARLES THEODORE, mayor; b. Medford, Oreg., Aug. 22, 1939; s. Russell Theodore and Mildred Mae (Hampson) R.; B.S., U. Oreg., 1967; postgrad. Harvard U. and Mass. Inst. Tech., 1969-70; m. Rosanne Gostovich, Oct. 19, 1968; children—Jordan, Suzanne. Polit. reporter KOIN-TV, Portland, Oreg., 1966-68; news analyst KING-TV, Seattle, 1970-77; mayor City of Seattle, 1978—. Served with U.S. Army, 1961-63. Recipient Am. Polit. Sci. Assn. fellowship, 1969-70; Washington Journalism Center fellow, 1968; Sigma Delta Chi award, 1976; Edward R. Murrow award, 1976. Democrat. Office: 1200 Municipal Bldg Seattle WA 98104

ROYER, JOHN EVERETT, educator; b. North Manchester, Ind., Dec. 21, 1915; s. Frank and Bertha (Brandenburg) R.; B.S., Manchester Coll., 1938; M.A., Ball State Tchrs. Coll.; Ed.D., Ind. U., 1955; m. Idabelle Bischoff, Aug. 19, 1939; children—John E., Margaret Jane. Instr. Ind. U. Naval Tng. Sch., 1942-44; asst., asso. dean U. Miami Sch. Bus. Adminstrn., 1946-61; chmn. accounting dept. U. Miami, 1961-69, now prof.; tchr. bus. adminstrn., Nassau, Bahamas, 1976-79; supr. C.P.A. rev. course Miami office Haskins & Sells; cons. pension and profit-sharing plans Nat. Life Ins. Co. of Vt.; dir. Southeast Fla. Fin. Corp.; guest lectr. in Colombia, 1969, Mex., 1972. Active United Fund drive. Served to lt. (j.g.) USNR, 1944-45. Mem. Am. Accounting Assn. (chmn. com. to study accounting curricula jr. colls.), Nat. Assn. Accountants, Beta Alpha Psi, Alpha Kappa Psi, Delta Pi Epsilon, Omicron Delta Kappa, Beta Gamma Sigma. Home: 4840 SW 64th Ct South Miami FL 33143 Office: Box 8031 U Miami Coral Gables FL 33124

ROYER, ROBERT LEWIS, utility co. exec.; b. Louisville, Jan. 2, 1928; s. Carl Brown and Martha Helen (Garrett) R.; B.S. in Elec. Engring., Rose Poly. Inst., 1949; m. Carol Jean Pierce, June 24, 1950; children—Jenifer Lea, Todd Pierce, Robert Douglas. With Louisville Gas and Electric Co., 1949—, asst. v.p. ops., 1962-63, asst. v.p., asst. gen. supt., 1963-64, v.p., gen. supt., 1964-69, v.p. ops., 1969-78, exec. v.p., 1978, pres., chief exec. officer, 1978—, also dir.; mem. exec. bd. East Central Area Reliability Council, 1978—; mem. Ky. Energy Resources Commn., 1975—; mem. energy task force Gov.'s Econ. Devel. Commn., 1976—; mem. Ky. Energy Research Bd., 1978—; v.p. Ind.-Ky. Electric Corp., 1979—; dir. Ohio Valley Transmission Corp., Citizens Fidelity Corp., Citizens Fidelity Bank and Trust Corp., Mem. exec. bd. Old Ky. Home Council Boy Scouts Am., v.p. dist. ops., 1970-75, 79—, commr., 1975-79, rep. to nat. council, 1975-79; bd. dirs. East End Boys Club, 1975-78; trustee Spirit of Louisville Found., 1978—; mem. Louisville Devel. Com., 1979—. Served with U.S. Army, 1953-55. Recipient Silver Beaver award Boy Scouts Am., 1975. Registered profl. engr., Ky. Mem. IEEE, Execs. Club Louisville, Louisville C. of C. (dir. 1978—). Methodist. Clubs: Hurstbourne Country, Jefferson, Pendennis. Home: 4014 Norbourne Blvd Louisville KY 40207 Office: PO Box 32010 311 W Chestnut St Louisville KY 40232

ROYKO, MIKE, newspaper columnist; b. Chgo., Sept. 19, 1932; s. Michael and Helen (Zak) R.; student Wright Jr. Coll., 1951-52; m. Carol Joyce Duckman, Nov. 7, 1954 (dec. Sept. 1979); children—M. David, Robert F. Reporter, Chgo. North Side Newspapers, 1956; reporter, asst. city editor Chgo. City News Bur., 1956-59; reporter, columnist Chgo. Daily News, 1959-78, asso. editor, 1977-78; reporter, columnist Chgo. Sun-Times, 1978—. Served with USAF, 1952-56. Recipient Heywood Brown award, 1968, Pulitzer prize for commentary, 1972, Man of Yr. award City of Hope Med. Center, 1979, medal for service to journalism U. Mo. Sch. Journalism, 1979. Mem. Chgo. Newspaper Reporters Assn. Club: LaSalle St. Rod and Gun. Author: Up Against It, 1967; I May Be Wrong but I Doubt It, 1968; Boss—Richard J. Daley of Chicago, 1971; Slats Grobnik and Some Other Friends, 1973. Office: Chgo Sun-Times 401 N Wabash Ave Chicago IL 60611*

ROYLANCE, D.C., lawyer; b. Bismarck, N.D., June 18, 1920; s. William G. and Freda (Zender) R.; LL.B., George Washington U., 1952; m. Joan Stieber, 1954 (dec. 1973); children—Stephen Michael, Kathleen Moore; m. Mary Lou Wagner, 1978. Admitted to D.C. bar, 1952, U.S. Supreme Ct. bar, 1960; now mem. firm Roylance, Abrams, Berdo & Farley, Washington. Mem. Am. Bar Assn., Bar Assn. D.C., Am. Patent Law Assn., Soc. Plastics Engrs., Order of Coif, Phi Alpha Delta. Home: 12210 Glen Mill Rd Potomac MD 20854 Office: 1225 Connecticut Ave Washington DC 20036

ROYSTER, VERMONT (CONNECTICUT), journalist; b. Raleigh, N.C., Apr. 30, 1914; s. Wilbur High and Olivette (Broadway) R.; grad. Webb Sch., Bellbuckle, Tenn., 1931; A.B., U. N.C., 1935, LL.D. 1959; Litt.D., Temple U., 1964, Williams Coll., 1979; L.H.D., Elon Coll., 1968; LL.D., Colby Coll., 1976; m. Frances Claypoole, June 5, 1937; children—Frances Claypoole, Sara Eleanor. Reporter, N.Y.C. News Bur., 1936; reporter Wall St. Jour., 1936, Washington corr., 1936-41, 45-46, chief Washington corr., 1946-48; editorial writer and columnist, 1946-48; asso. editor Wall St. Jour., 1948-51, sr. asso. editor, 1951-58, editor, 1958-71, contbg. editor, columnist, 1971—; sr. v.p. Dow Jones & Co., Inc., 1960-71, dir., 1970—; dir. Wachovia Bank & Trust Co., N.A.; William Rand Kenan prof. journalism and pub. affairs U. N.C., Chapel Hill, 1971—; regular commentator pub. affairs CBS Radio and TV, 1972-77; sr. fellow Inst. Policy Scis., Duke, 1973—. Mem. adv. com. Pulitzer prizes, Columbia, 1967-76; mem. Nat. Commn. Hist. Publs., 1974-76. Bd. dirs. Newspaper Fund, Inc.; trustee St. Augustine Coll., Raleigh, N.C. Commd. ensign USNR, 1940, active duty, 1941-45, Atlantic, Caribbean, Pacific; exec. officer USS LaPrade; comdg. officer USS Jack Miller, USS PC-1262; lt. comdr. Res. Recipient Pulitzer prize for editorial writing, 1953; medal for distinguished service in journalism Sigma Delta Chi, 1958; William Allan White award for distinguished service to journalism, 1971; Loeb Meml. award for contbn. to econ. journalism U. Calif. at Los Angeles, 1975; Elijah Lovejoy award Colby Coll., 1976; Fourth Estate award Nat. Press Club, Washington, 1978. Mem. Am. Soc. Newspaper Editors (pres. 1965-66), Nat. Conf. Editorial Writers (chmn. 1957),

Phi Beta Kappa Assos., Phi Beta Kappa. Episcopalian. Clubs: University (N.Y.C.); Nat. Press (Washington). Author: (with others) Main Street and Beyond, 1959; Journey Through the Soviet Union, 1962; A Pride of Prejudices, pub. 1967; contbr. numerous articles on financial and econ. subjects to periodicals. Appears on pub. affairs programs on TV and radio. Home: 903 Arrowhead Rd Chapel Hill NC 27514

ROYSTER, WIMBERLY CALVIN, univ. dean, mathematician; b. Robards, Ky., Jan. 12, 1925; s. Fred and Ruth (Denton) R.; B.A., Murray State Coll., 1946; M.A., U. Ky., 1948, Ph.D. 1952; m. Betty Jo Barnett, July 1, 1950; children—David Calvin, Paul Barnett. Asst. prof. math. Auburn U., 1952-56; mem. faculty U. Ky., 1956—, prof. math., 1962—, chmn. dept., 1963—, dir. Sch. Math. Scis., 1967-69, dean Coll. Arts and Scis., 1969-72, dean Grad. Sch., coordinator research, 1972—; mem. Inst. Advanced Study, Princeton, 1962. Bd. dirs. Center Research Libraries, Chgo., NRC, 1972—; councillor Oak Ridge Asso. Univs., 1974-78, bd. dirs., 1978—; bd. dirs. Ephraim McDowell Cancer Research Network, Inc. Mem. Am. Math. Soc., Math. Assn. Am., AAAS, Sigma Xi. Contbr. articles profl. jours. Home: 133 Vanderbilt Dr Lexington KY 40503

ROZEL, SAMUEL JOSEPH, mfg. co. exec.; b. Louisville, Apr. 22, 1935; s. Sam and Anna (Sessmer) R.; B.S.L., U. Louisville, 1955, LL.B., 1957; grad. Advanced Mgmt. Program, Harvard U., 1979; m. Jeanne Frances Foulkes, July 3, 1965; children—Brooke Jane, John Samuel. Admitted to Ky. bar, 1958, D.C. bar, 1962, Minn. bar, 1968, Ind. bar, 1970; atty. FTC, Washington, 1962-67; antitrust counsel Honeywell, Inc., Mpls., 1967-69; atty. Magnavox, Fort Wayne, Ind., 1969-71, gen. counsel, 1971, v.p., 1972-75 sec., 1973-75; v.p. U.S. Philips Corp., 1975-77, sr. v.p., 1977—; asso. gen. counsel N.Am. Philips Corp.; sec. governing com. U.S. Philips Trust. Served to capt. Judge Adv. Corps, AUS, 1957-62. Mem. Am., Fed., Ky., Ind. bar assns. Clubs: Union League, Harvard (N.Y.C.); Nat. Lawyers (Washington). Home: 215 S Bald Hill Rd New Canaan CT 06840 Office: 100 E 42d St New York NY 10017

ROZELLE, ALVIN RAY (PETE), commr. Nat. Football League; b. S. Gate, Calif., Mar. 1, 1926; s. Raymond Foster and Hazel Viola (Healey) R.; B.A., U. San Francisco, 1950; 1 dau., Ann Marie. Athletic news dir. U. San Francisco, 1948-50, asst. athletic dir., 1950-52; pub. relations dir. Los Angeles Rams Football Club, 1952-55; partner Internat. Bus. Relations, pub. relations, San Francisco, 1955-57; gen. mgr. Los Angeles Rams Football Club, 1957-60; commr. Nat. Football League, 1960—. Served with USNR, 1944-46. Office: 410 Park Ave New York NY 10022

ROZEN, JEROME GEORGE, JR., entomologist, mus. curator and adminstr.; b. Evanston, Ill., Mar. 19, 1928; s. Jerome George and Della (Kretchmar) R.; student U. Pa., 1946-48; B.A., U. Kans., 1950; Ph.D., U. Calif. at Berkeley, 1955; m. Barbara L. Lindner, Dec. 18, 1948; children—Steven George, Kenneth Charles, James Robert. Entomologist (taxonomy) U.S. Dept. Agr., 1956-58; asst. prof. entomology Ohio State U., 1958-60; asso. curator Hymenoptera, dept. entomology Am. Mus. Natural History, N.Y.C., 1960-65, curator of Hymenoptera, 1965—, chmn. dept., 1960-71, dep. dir. for research, 1972—. Fellow AAAS; mem. Entomol. Soc. Am. (editor misc. publs. 1959-60), Soc. Study Evolution, Soc. Systematic Zoology, N.Y. (pres. 1964-65), Washington entomol. socs. Clubs: Explorers, Cosmos. Home: 55 Haring St Closter NJ 07624 Office: Am Museum Natural History Central Park W at 79th St New York City NY 10024

ROZETT, WALTER PHILIP, corp. exec.; b. N.Y.C., Apr. 15, 1923; s. Arthur J. and Frances (Duderstadt) R.; B.B.A., Iona Coll., 1948; M.B.A., N.Y.U., 1950; M.S. (Sloan fellow), Mass. Inst. Tech., 1960; m. Kathryn T. Davin, Dec. 28, 1946; children—Stephen, Thomas, Robert, John. With CBS, Inc., 1952-67; v.p. fin. Capitol Industries, Inc., Hollywood, Calif., 1967-71; exec. v.p. fin. Bergen Brunswig Corp., 1971-72; sr. v.p. dir. Fluor Corp., Los Angeles, 1972-74; exec. v.p. Envirotech Corp., Menlo Park, Calif., 1974—; dir. Systems Assos., Inc. Served to capt. USAAF, 1943-46. Roman Catholic. Home: 99 Edwards Ln Atherton CA 94025 Office: 3000 Sand Hill Rd Menlo Park CA 94025

ROZIN, PAUL, psychologist; b. Bklyn., Aug. 3, 1936; s. Albert and Rosanne R.; B.A., U. Chgo., 1956; A.M., Harvard U., 1959, Ph.D., 1961; m. Elisabeth Briefer, June 9, 1957; children—Lillian, Seth, Alexander. Asst. prof. psychology U. Pa., Phila., 1963-67, asso. prof., 1967-70, prof., 1970—, also chmn. dept. Home: 672 S Highland Ave Merion PA 19066 Office: Dept Psychology U Pa 3813 Walnut Philadelphia PA 19104

ROZSNYAI, ZOLTAN FRANK, composer, conductor; b. Budapest, Hungary, Jan. 29, 1927; s. Laszlo Lesly and Francisca (Molnar) R.; ed. Franz Liszt Acad. Music; Ph.D. in Music, Pazmany Peter U., 1949; postgrad. U. Vienna, 1959-61; 1 dau. from previous marriage, Christine Monica; m. 2d, Susan C. Daily, Nov. 29, 1971; children—Susanna Francesca, Dorothy-Katherine. Came to U.S., 1961, naturalized, 1967. Concert pianist, 1942-52, organist, 1940-50; music dir. Miskolc Philharmonic Orch., 1949-50, Debrecen Opera, 1950-52; regular condr. Hungarian Nat. Philharmony, 1952-56; founder, 1st music dir. Philharmonia Hungarica, Vienna, 1956-60; music dir. Continental Cinecraft Motion Picture Co., 1961-63; asst. condr. N.Y. Philharmonic Orch., 1962-63; music dir. Cleve. Philharmonic and Utica Symphony Orch., 1963-67, San Diego Symphony Orch., 1967-71, Knoxville Symphony, 1978—; artistic dir. So. Calif. Philharmonic Soc., San Diego, 1971—; artistic head music div. U.S.I.U. Sch. Performing Arts, 1968-71. Full mem. Hungarian Arpad Akademy Arts and Scis., head music div. Recipient diploma and prize Internat. Condrs. Competition in Rome, Italy, 1956, Cultural Merit star Hungary, Golden Key of Detroit, Spl. Peace Bell with citation from Willy Brandt, Berlin, citation of recognition City of N.Y. from Robert Wagner. Recs. with Columbia, Vox, Qualiton, Direct-to-Disk. Composer numerous pieces, orchestrations, transcriptions, film scores. Home: 2461 Palace Dr San Diego CA 92123 Office: care Knoxville Symphony Orch Gay St Knoxville TN

RUB, LOUIS JOHN, banker; b. Bklyn., Oct. 2, 1915; s. Louis C. and Paula K. (Knoll) R.; B.S. in Accouting, then M.B.A., N.Y. U.; m. Marguerite Gustafson, Sept. 5, 1942; children—Christopher L., Peter M., Timothy F., Marguerite L. Asst. sec. East River Savs. Bank, N.Y.C., 1946-49, asst. v.p., 1949-57; exec. v.p. First Fed. Savs. & Loan Assn., Shreveport, La., 1957-58; v.p. Fed. Home Loan Bank N.Y., N.Y.C., 1958-68, exec. v.p., 1968-72; pres. Fed. Home Loan Bank of Pitts., 1973—; mem. faculty N.Y. U., 1946-57, 59-63. Club: Duquesne (Pitts.). Home: 343 Oak Forest Dr Pittsburgh PA 15216 Office: 11 Stanwix St Pittsburgh PA 15222

RUBEL, ARTHUR JOSEPH, anthropologist; b. Shanghai, China, Aug. 29, 1924; came to U.S., 1924; s. Arthur John and Marcella (Crohn) R.; B.A., Mexico City Coll., 1949; M.A., U. Chgo., 1958; Ph.D., U. N.C., Chapel Hill, 1962; m. Phyllis Lavern Howard, Apr. 22, 1954 (dec.); 1 dau., Laura. Behavioral scientist behavioral sci. br. USPHS, 1962-63; asst. prof. U. N.C., Greensboro, 1963-64, U. Tex., Austin, 1964-66; asso. prof. U. Notre Dame (Ind.), 1966-68, prof., 1968-74; population program asst. Ford Found., Mexico City, Mex., 1969; prof. anthropology Mich. State U., East Lansing, 1973—, behavioral sci. coordinator Coll. Human Medicine, 1975—; cons. Ford Found.; mem. social sci. rev. panel NIMH; Disting. vis. prof. Instituto de Investigación Antropológica, Nat. U. Mex., 1980-81. Served with USNR, 1942-46. NIMH fellow, 1960-63, grantee, 1969-71. Fellow Am. Anthrop. Assn., Soc. Applied Anthropology; Soc. Med. Anthropology (pres. 1976), Soc. Cross-cultural Research, So. Anthrop. Assn., Assn. Behavioral Scis. and Med. Edn., Latin Am. Studies Assn. Author: Across the Tracks: Mexican-Americans in a Texas City, 1966. Office: Dept Anthropology Mich State U East Lansing MI 48824

RUBEL, DAVID MICHAEL, naval officer; b. Fargo, N.D., Dec. 2, 1917; s. Harris and Lucille Margret (Rubel) R.; B.S., U.S. Naval Acad., 1941; grad. U.S. Nat. War Coll., 1966; m. Shirley Joann Cane, Oct. 4, 1942; children—Carol-Lynn, William Richard. Commd. ensign USN, 1941, advanced through grades to rear adm., 1969; dean English history and govt. dept. U.S. Naval Acad., Annapolis, 1959-62; comdr. USS Norfolk, 1963, Destroyer Squadron 20, 1964; head strategic objectives plans and policy div. Office Chief Naval Operations, Joint Chiefs Staff, Washington, 1967-69; comdr. amphibious tng. command Pacific Fleet, 1969-70, Command Amphibious Group 3, Western Pacific, 1970-71; mem. staff Chief Naval Operations, Washington, 1971—. Decorated Navy Cross, Legion Merit with 2 gold stars, Bronze Star, Commendation medal; Peruvian Navy Cross; National Order Vietnam 5th Class, Vietnamese Gallantry Cross with palm, Republic Vietnam Campaign medal (Vietnam). Kiwanian. Home: 2071 Via Ladeta La Jolla CA 92037

RUBEL, DONALD CLARKE, securities co. exec.; A.B., Brown U., 1923; LL.D. (hon.) Med. Coll. Pa.; m. Julia Davis Lee, 1925; children—Julia Lee Rubel O'Brien, Walter Lee. Chmn. bd. Parrish Securities div. Bruns, Nordeman, Rea and Co., v.p. parent co. Past pres., trustee Germantown Unitarian Ch.; past chmn. Com. of Seventy, Phila. Com. on Pub. Affairs, South Broad St. USO; past vice chmn. Citizens Charter Com.; past Republican councilman-at-large, Phila.; del. Rep. Nat. Conv., 1960, 64; chmn. Phila. Rep. Policy Com.; treas. Frederick Douglas Meml. Hosp.; pres., bd. dirs. City Trusts; bd. dirs. Lincoln U.; mem. exec. bd. Big Brothers Assn., Pub. Charities Assn.; chmn. bd. corporators Med. Coll. Pa.; pres., trustee Eastern Pa. Psychiat. Inst.; mem. advisory com. West Mt. Airy Neighbors. Served with USMC, World War I. Recipient hon. citation Brown U. Mem. Security Analysts Assn. (Phila. chpt.), Bond Club Phila. Clubs: Union League, Phila. Cricket, Penn, Wagners Run Assn. Home: 606 Westview St Philadelphia PA 19119 Office: 2310 Two Girard Plaza Philadelphia PA 19102

RUBEN, ALAN MILES, lawyer, educator; b. Phila., May 13, 1931; s. Maurice Robert and Ruth (Blatt) R.; A.B., U. Pa., 1953, M.A., 1956, J.D., 1956; m. Betty Jane Willis, May 23, 1965. Admitted to Pa. bar, 1957, Ohio bar, 1972; law clk. Supreme Ct. Pa., 1956-58; pvt. practice law, Phila., 1958-65; asso. counsel Aetna Life & Casualty Co., Hartford, Conn., 1965-69; corporate counsel Lubrizol Corp., Cleve., 1969-70; prof. Cleve.-Marshall Coll. Law, Cleve. State U., 1970—; lectr. law U. Conn. Law Sch., 1968; dep. to city solicitor Phila., 1958-61; dep. atty. gen. State of Pa., 1961-65; spl. counsel to U.S. Senate Subcom. on Nat. Stockpile, 1962; commentator Higher Edn. Issues, WCLV-FM, Cleve., 1975—; mem. nat. panel labor arbitrators Fed. Mediation and Concilliation Service and Am. Arbitration Assn. Bd. dirs. U.S. Olympic Com., 1968-73; chmn. U.S. Olympic Fencing Sport Com., 1969-73; pres. Amateur Fencers League Am., 1968-73; capt. U.S. Pan-Am. Fencing Team, 1971, U.S. Olympic Fencing Team, 1972; bd. dirs. Legal Aid Soc. Cleve. Winner Internat. Inst. Edn. Internat. Debate Championship, 1953, Harrison Tweed Bowl and Am. Law Inst. prizes Nat. Moot Ct. Competition, 1955; Guggenheim scholar, 1949-53. Mem. Assn. Am. Law Schs. (chmn. sect. law and edn.), Am., Ohio, Pa., Cleve., Fed., Phila. bar assns., AAAS, Internat. Indsl. Relations Research Assn., Am. Trial Lawyers Assn., Internat. Soc. Labor Law, AAUP (pres. Ohio conf. 1974-75), Phi Beta Kappa, Pi Gamma Mu. Author: The Constitutionality of Basic Protection for the Automobile Accident Victim, 1968; Unathorized Insurance: The Regulation of the Unregulated, 1968; Arbitration in Public Employee Labor Disputes: Myth, Shibboleth and Reality, 1971; Illicit Sex on Campus: Federal Remedies for Employment Discrimination, 1971; Model Public Employees Labor Relations Act, 1972; Sentencing the Corporate Criminal, 1972; Modern Corporation Law, 1973, rev. edit., 1978; contbr. With an Eye to Tomorrow: The Future Outlook of the Life Insurance Industry, 1968; The Urban Transportation Crisis: The Philadelphia Plan, 1961; Philadelphia's Union Shop Contract, 1961; The Administrative Agency Law: Reform of Adjudicative Procedure and The Revised Model Act, 1963; The Computer in Court: Computer Simulation and the Robinson Patman Act, 1964. Home: 9925 Lakeshore Blvd Bratenahl OH 44108 Office: 18th St and Euclid Ave Cleveland OH 44115

RUBEN, GARY A., advt. agy. exec.; b. Cochem, Germany, Jan. 1, 1924; s. Jules and Erna (Hirsch) R.; came to U.S., 1939, naturalized, 1943; student Indpls. Acad. Comml. Art, 1940-41; m. Irene Jehle, Aug. 12, 1962; 1 dau., Monique L. With advt. dept. Indpls. News, 1940-41; advt. mgr. Greater Indpls. Amusement Corp., 1941-42; pres. Ruben Advt. Agy., Indpls., 1948-68; chmn. bd. Ruben, Montgomery & Assos., 1968-76; pres. Prestige Program Sales Inc., 1973-76; pres. Gary A. Ruben Inc., advt. and mktg. cons., Indpls., 1976—; lectr. advt. Northwood Inst. Trustee Indpls. Children's Mus.; bd. dirs. St. Mary's Home for Children; bd. fellows Northwood Inst. Served with Combat Engrs., AUS, 1943-46. Mem. Nat. Fedn. Advt. Agys. (pres. 1971). Club: Broadmoor Country (Indpls.). Home: 11812 Forest Dr Carmel IN 46032 Office: 1812 N Meridian St Indianapolis IN 46202. *It was years ago, in the late 30's in Vienna, that the cry "Lebensraum", echoed across yet another land. And, a family, judged comfortable by most standards, scattered to the four winds, leaving behind all things material, but salvaging the will to survive and to commence once again in a new land. To a boy in his teens and still dressed in European-style short pants upon arrival in this country, the emotion, the sights, the sounds, and the smells were overwhelming and exciting to say the least. . .so began another chapter in my life. In the ensuing years, I learned the true meaning of individual freedom. And while the echoes of Vienna have become dim, that dim sound will continue to remind me that all worthwhile things in life are earned-not given, and even in adversity, there is opportunity.*

RUBEN, JAMES HARRIS, food co. exec.; b. Pitts., Mar. 5, 1930; s. Jack Eli and Rosalie (Harris) R.; B.S., U. Ill., 1952; m. Ruth Pasik, Feb. 10, 1953; children—Jacqueline, Robin, James, Valerie, Abra, Adam. Store mgr. Walgreen Drug Co., Chgo., 1945-58; div. mgr., exec. v.p. Stineway Ford-Hopkins Drug Co., Chgo., 1958-62; pres., chmn. bd. ShopKo Stores, Inc., Green Bay, Wis., 1962-72; group v.p. Super Valu Stores, Inc., Mpls., 1972-75; group v.p. apparel group Gen. Mills, Inc., Mpls., 1975—; dir. Dependable Feeds, 1974-76; dir. Super Valu, 1972—; dir. AAR Corp., 1978—. Trustee St. Norbert's Coll., 1974—; bd. dirs. Ronald McDonald House. Served with U.S. Army, 1952-54. Clubs: Mpls., Edina Country, Interlachen Country. Office: 9200 Wayzata Blvd Minneapolis MN 55440

RUBEN, LAWRENCE, real estate developer, bldg. co. exec., lawyer; b. Bklyn., Sept. 28, 1926; s. Irving and Minnie (Sruelif) R.; B.A., N.Y. U., 1949; LL.B., Bklyn. Law Sch., 1951; m. Selma Belfer, Dec. 20, 1952; children—Richard Gordon, Lenore Denise, Rochelle Gail. Admitted to N.Y. bar, 1952; gen. practice law, N.Y.C., 1952-53; pres. Ru-Min Constrn. Co., N.Y.C., 1953-54; exec. v.p. Belco Petroleum Corp., N.Y.C., 1954-64, now dir.; sec. Fundamental Bldg. Corp., 1952—, also v.p.; pres. Randall Devel. Co., Aragon Devel. Corp.; partner Lexington Madison Co., Tower Plaza Assos., Devonshire Assos., Sunrise-Sunset Assos., Lawrence Assos.; dir. Progressive Accessories Corp. Chmn., N.Y. Builders and Realtors Fellowship Fund; trustee Nat. Jewish Hosp. of Denver; patron Albert Einstein Coll. Medicine; sponsor Grad. Sch. Sci. and mem. bd. Cardoza Sch. Law at Yeshiva U.; Scarsdale (N.Y.) chmn. United Jewish Appeal, 1974-75. Served with AUS, 1945-46. Mem. Am. Bar Assn. Club: Fenway Golf. Office: 630 3d Ave New York NY 10017

RUBEN, ROBERT JOEL, physician, educator; b. N.Y.C., Aug. 2, 1933; s. Julian Carl and Sadie (Weiss) R.; A.B., Princeton U., 1955; M.D., Johns Hopkins U., 1959; children—Ann, Emily, Karin, Arthur. Intern, Johns Hopkins Hosp., Balt., 1959-60, resident, 1960-64, dir. neurophysiology lab., div. otolaryngology, 1958-64; practice medicine specializing in otorhinolaryngology, N.Y.C., 1964—; mem. staffs hosps. Montefiore Hosp., Hosp. of Albert Einstein Coll. Medicine, Bronx Municipal Hosp., North Central Bronx Hosp., St. Barnabas Hosp., Misericordia Hosp.; asst. prof. otorhinolaryngology N.Y. U. Sch. Medicine, 1966-68; asso. prof., chmn. dept. otolaryngology Albert Einstein Coll. Medicine, N.Y.C., 1968-70, prof., 1970, chmn. dept. otorhinolaryngology, 1970—. Bd. dirs. N.Y. League Hard of Hearing. Served to surgeon USPHS, 1964-66. Recipient Research award Am. Acad. Ophthalmology and Otolaryngology, 1962. Fellow A.C.S., N.Y. Acad. Medicine; mem. Am. Assn. Anatomists, Audiology Study Group N.Y. (pres. 1968-69), Acoustical Soc. Am., AMA, Am. Acad. Ophthalmology and Otolaryngology, Soc. Univ. Otolaryngologists, Am. Otol. Soc. (sec.-treas. research fund 1979—), Assn. Acad. Surgery Triological Soc. (Edmund Prince Fowler award 1973), Soc. for Ear, Nose and Throat Advances in Children (pres. 1973). Editor-in-chief Internat. Jour. Pediatric Otorhinolaryngology, 1979—. Office: 1300 Morris Park Ave Bronx NY 10461

RUBEN, ROBERT JOSEPH, lawyer; b. N.Y.C., Apr. 9, 1923; s. Ira Herbert and Kathleen Marie (Murphy) R.; B.S., Columbia, 1943; M.A., Harvard, 1948; LL.B., Fordham U., 1953; m. Audrey H. Zweig, Nov. 20, 1949; children—Pamela Joan, James Bradford. Exec. trainee Chase Nat. Bank, N.Y.C., 1948-49; economist, 1949-53; admitted to N.Y. bar, 1954; asso. Milbank, Tweed, Hope & Hadley, N.Y.C., 1953-55; asso., partner Shea & Gould, N.Y.C., 1955—; sec. Gen. Battery Corp., Reading, Pa., 1963-73, Fiat Metal Mfg. Co., Inc., Plainview, N.Y., 1961-64. Filtors, Inc., East Northport, N.Y., 1961-64, Trans-Industries, Inc., 1969—; asst. sec. Elgin Nat. Industries, 1975—; dir. Automatic Toll Systems, Inc., 1969—, VTR, Inc., 1966-67. Asst. judge City Ct., Rye, N.Y., 1977—. Trustee Rye Hist. Soc.; bd. dirs. Carver Center, Port Chester, N.Y. Served with AUS, 1943-46. Decorated Combat Inf. medal. Mem. Am., N.Y. State, Westchester County bar assns., Assn. Bar City N.Y., Am. Econ. Assn., Am. Acad. Polit. Sci., Zeta Beta Tau, Beta Gamma Sigma. Mason. Club: Harvard (N.Y.C.). Home: 4 Heritage Ln Rye NY 10580 Office: 330 Madison Ave New York NY 10017

RUBENSTEIN, ALBERT, retail chain exec.; b. Balt., July 23, 1913; s. Frank and Henrietta (Shor) R.; student Tulane U., 1932-34, Columbia U., 1934-35; m. Marion Freedman, Oct. 15, 1944; children—Franklin David, Robin Ann, Marke Ellen. Successively trainee, mgr., supr., merchandiser, gen. mgr. Rubenstein's New Orleans Stores, 1936-38; trainee various depts. Franklin Stores Corp., 1938-40, v.p., 1940-44, exec. v.p., 1944-54, pres., 1954-78, chmn., 1968-78; sr. exec. v.p. Cornwall Equities Ltd., 1974-78; pres. City Enterprises Inc., P.R., Center Enterprises Inc., P.R.; dir. Republic Nat. Bank N.Y.C., Republic N.Y. Corp. Mem. Nat. Council of Nat. Planning Assn.; founder Albert Einstein Coll. Medicine, N.Y.C.; chmn. Stamford Bi-Cultural Sch. Jewish (dir. temple). Clubs: Rockrimmon Country (Stamford); Harmonie (N.Y.C.); Ocean Reef (Key Largo, Fla.). Home: 60 Ocean Dr N Stamford CT 06902 Office: 375 Park Ave Suite 1202 New York NY 10022

RUBENSTEIN, ALBERT HAROLD, educator; b. Phila., Nov. 11, 1923; s. Leo and Jean (Kaplan) R.; B.S. magna cum laude in Indsl. Engrng. (Sr. prize econs.), Lehigh U., 1949; M.S. in Indsl. Engrng., Columbia, 1950, Ph.D. in Indsl. Engrng. and Mgmt., 1954; m. Hildette Grossman, Sept. 11, 1949; children—Michael Stephen, Lisa Joan. Asst. to pres. Perry Equipment Corp., 1940-43; research asso. Columbia, 1950-53; asst. prof. indsl. mgmt. Mass. Inst. Tech., 1954-59; prof. indsl. engrng. and mgmt. scis. Northwestern U., 1959—; pres. Internat. Applied Sci. and Tech. Assos., 1977—; vis. prof. U. Calif., Berkeley; cons. to govt. and industry. Dir. Narragansett Capital Corp. Served with inf. AUS, World War II. Decorated Purple Heart, Combat Inf. badge. Recipient Lincoln Arc Welding Found. prize paper, 1948; Omicron Delta Kappa annual fellow, 1949-50; Fulbright research fellow, 1955. Fellow Soc. Applied Anthropology; sr. mem. IEEE (editor trans. 1959—), Inst. Mgmt. Scis. (dir. studies for coll. on research and devel. 1960—), Inst. Mgmt. Scis. (v.p. research and edn. 1966-68). Author books and articles in field. Home: 2348 Ridge Ave Evanston IL 60201

RUBENSTEIN, ARTHUR HAROLD, physician, educator; b. Johannesburg, South Africa, Dec. 28, 1937; s. Montague and Isabel (Nathanson) R.; came to U.S., 1967; M.B., B.Ch., U. Witwatersrand, 1960; m. Denise Hack, Aug. 19, 1962; children—Jeffrey Lawrence, Errol Charles. Fellow in endocrinology Postgrad. Med. Sch., London, 1965-66; fellow in medicine U. Chgo., 1967-68; asst. prof., 1968-70, asso. prof., 1970-74, prof., 1974—, asso. chmn. dept. medicine, 1975—; attending physician Billings Hosp., U. Chgo., 1968—; mem. study sect. NIH, 1973-77; mem. adv. council Nat. Inst. Arthritis, Metabolism and Digestive Diseases, 1978—. Recipient David Rumbough Meml. award Juvenile Diabetes Found., 1978. Fellow A.C.P., Coll. Physicians (S. Africa), Royal Coll. Physicians (London); mem. Am. Soc. for Clin. Investigation, Am. Diabetes Assn. (Eli Lilly award 1973), Endocrine Soc., Am. Fedn. for Clin. Research, Central Soc. for Clin. Research, Assn. Am. Physicians. Editorial bd. Diabetes, 1973-77; Endocrinology, 1973-77, Jour. Clin. Investigation, 1976—, Am. Jour. Medicine, 1978—; contbr. articles to profl. jours. Home: 5517 S Kimbark Ave Chicago IL 60637 Office: 950 E 59th St Chicago IL 60637

RUBENSTEIN, HERBERT, educator; b. Phila., Dec. 24, 1920; s. Samuel and Olga (Frumkin) R.; B.A., U. Pa., 1942, M.A., 1943; Ph.D., Columbia, 1949; m. Mollie Annette Gross, June 11, 1943; children—Seth Raphael, Abi Beryl. Linguist, Army Specialized Tng. Program, U. Pa. and Ind. U., 1942-45; instr., asst. prof. fgn. langs. Mich. State U., 1949-56; supervisory research psychologist Decision Scis. Lab., USAF, Bedford, Mass., 1960-65; research fellow Harvard, 1964-67; prof. linguistics and psychology Lehigh U., Bethlehem, Pa., 1967—; cons. NIH and NSF; vis. lectr. in psycholinguistics U. Pa., 1968, N.Y. U., 1970; mem. adv. panel social psychology and sociology NSF and adv. panel for biomed. communications NIH. Fellow Am. Council Learned Socs.; mem. Linguistic Soc. Am., Linguistic Circle N.Y., Am. Psychol. Assn., Research Engrng. Soc. Am. Cons. editor Jour. of Verbal Learning and Verbal Behavior, 1966-76, Jour. Exptl. Psychology, 1973-75. Contbr. articles to profl. jours. Home: RD 3 Fire Ln Bethlehem PA 18015

RUBENSTEIN, HOWARD JOSEPH, pub. relations exec.; b. N.Y.C., Feb. 3, 1932; s. Samuel and Ada (Sall) R.; A.B., U. Pa., 1953; student law Harvard, 1953; LL.B. (Dean's scholar), St. Johns Sch. Law, 1959; m. Amy Forman, Dec. 17, 1959; children—Roni, Richard, Stephen. Pres. Howard J. Rubenstein Assos., Inc., pub. relations cons., N.Y.C., 1954—; admitted to N.Y. State bar, 1960. Asst. counsel judiciary com. U.S. Ho. of Reps., 1960; cons. U.S. Fgn. Claims Commn., 1961-62; cons. joint legis. com. child care needs, N.Y., 1965-66; adviser U.S. Small Bus. Adminstrn., 1965-66. Mem. mayor's council econ. bus. advisors, N.Y.C., 1974-77, mayor's com. pub. interest, 1975-77; past dir. Brownsville Boys Club; dir. Provide Addict Care Today, Police Athletic League, Inst. Contemporary Hispanic Art, N.Y.C.; mem. U.S. Internat. Council, 1977—. Mem. Assn. Better N.Y. (mem. exec. com. 1972—), Phi Beta Kappa, Beta Sigma Rho. Jewish (dir. congregation). Home: 141 E 72d St New York NY 10021 Office: 1345 Ave of Americas New York NY 10019

RUBENSTEIN, JERRY G., diversified co. exec.; b. N.Y.C., Apr. 15, 1930; s. Morris and Frieda (Shustek) R.; B.B.A. cum laude in accounting Coll. City N.Y., 1953; m. Bernice Glasner, Sept. 22, 1957; children—Laura, Daniel, Karen. Sr. accountant Stern, Porter, Kingston & Coleman, N.Y.C., 1956-57; comptroller Branch Motor Express Co., Inc., N.Y.C., 1957-64; controller Motor Freight Express Co., York, Pa., 1964-66; v.p. finance Ryder Truck Lines, Jacksonville, Fla., 1966-67, exec. v.p., 1967-69; v.p. land transp., treas. Internat. Utilities Corp., Phila., 1969-70, sr. v.p., 1970-72, exec. v.p., 1972-73, pres., 1973-74, also dir.; owner, pres. Vanguard Enterprises, Inc., Ardmore, Pa., 1975-79, Redstone Corp., Houston, 1975—; control shareholder, pres. Omni Mgmt., Inc., Ardmore. Served with USNR, 1953-56. C.P.A., N.Y. Home: 223 Glenmoor Rd Gladwyne PA 19035 Office: Omni Mgmt Inc 123 Coulter Ave Ardmore PA 19003 also 1845 Walnut St Philadelphia PA 19103

RUBENSTEIN, LEWIS W., artist; b. Buffalo, Dec. 15, 1908; s. Emil and Hannah (Hirschman) R.; A.B., Harvard, 1930, grad. fellow study painting in Europe, 1931-33; m. Erica Beckh, June 28, 1942; children—Daniel B., Emily G. Mem. faculty Vassar Coll., 1939-74, prof. art, 1957-74; exhbns. include Nat. Acad. Design, Whitney Mus. Am. Art, Met. Mus., Am. Watercolor Soc., Library of Congress, Soc. Am. Graphic Artists, USIA, Harvard, Am. U., Vassar Art Gallery, Buffalo Jewish Center, Ford Found., Busch-Reisinger Mus., Fogg Art Mus., Albright-Knox Gallery, Schenectady Mus. Served to lt. USNR, 1942-45. Fulbright grantee, Japan, 1957-58; State Dept. grantee, S. Am., 1961; recipient award Soc. Graphic Artists, 1952, 54, Silvermine Artists, 1959, Empire State Architects, 1950. Mem. Soc. Am. Graphic Artists. Originated Time Painting; films, Time Painting by Lewis Rubenstein, 1956; Psalm 104, 1969; Ceremony for a New Planet, 1972. Home: 153 College Ave Poughkeepsie NY 12603

RUBENSTEIN, MARTIN, broadcasting exec.; b. Bklyn., Oct. 16, 1935; s. Charles and Evelyn R.; B.A. in Polit. Sci., Bklyn. Coll., 1957; LL.B., Columbia U., 1961; m. Cora Gurien, June 12, 1958; children—Deborah, William. Admitted to N.Y. bar, 1962, D.C. bar, 1980. With ABC, 1961-78, dir. legal and bus. affairs ABC News, N.Y.C., 1966-69, v.p., gen. mgr. ABC News, 1969-78; exec. v.p. Mut. Broadcasting System, Inc., Arlington, Va., 1978-79, pres., 1979—. Active, United Cerebral Palsey Assns., Inc., 1964—, nat. v.p., 1975—, chmn. fin. com., 1972—. Served with Air N.G., 1957-63. Mem. Radio TV News Dirs. Assn., Internat. Radio and TV Soc., N.Y. State Bar Assn., Radio Advt. Bur. (dir.), Nat. Assn. Broadcasters (radio bd.), Advt. Council (dir.). Jewish. Office: 1755 S Jefferson Davis Hwy Arlington VA 22202

RUBENSTEIN, RICHARD LOWELL, theologian, educator; b. N.Y.C., Jan. 8, 1924; s. Jesse George and Sara (Fine) R.; student Hebrew Union Coll., Cin., 1942-45; A.B., U. Cin., 1946; M.H.L., rabbi, Jewish Theol. Sem., N.Y.C., 1952; S.T.M., Harvard U., 1955, Ph.D., 1960; m. Betty Rogers Alschuler, Aug. 21, 1966; children by previous marriage—Aaron, Nathaniel (dec.), Hannah Rachel, Jeremy. Rabbi in Brockton, Mass., 1952-54, Natick, Mass., 1954-56; chaplain to Jewish students Harvard U., 1956-68; univ. chaplain to Jewish students U. Pitts. and Carnegie Inst. Tech., 1958-70; adj. prof. humanities U. Pitts., 1969-70; prof. religion Fla. State U., Tallahassee, 1970-77, Disting. prof. religion, 1977—, dir. So. Center for Study of Religion and Culture, 1973—; vis. fellow Ezra Stiles Coll., Nat. Humanities Inst., Yale U., 1976-77; Leonard K. Firestone vis. prof. Sch. Religion, U. So. Calif., 1978; Disting. prof. of yr., Fla. State U., 1977-78; Disting. vis. prof. Calif. State U., Chico, 1979; vis. prof. Hochschule für Jüdische Studien, Heidelberg, W. Ger., 1980—. Mem. nat. adv. bd. Center for Study of So. Culture, U. Miss. Recipient Portico d' Ottavia lit. prize, Rome, 1977. John Phillips fellow Phillips Exeter Acad., 1970; postdoctoral fellow Soc. Religion in Higher Edn.; Nat. Humanities Inst. fellow, Yale U., 1976-77; Rockefeller Found. fellow Aspen Inst. for Humanistic Studies, 1979. Fellow Soc. for Arts, Religon and Contemporary Culture; mem. Rabbinical Assembly Am., Am. Acad. Religion, Soc. Sci. Study Religion, Soc. for Bibl. Lit., Internat. Psychohist. Assn., Western Assn. for Gen. Studies. Clubs: Winewood Country, Springtime (Tallahassee). Author: After Auschwitz-Radical Theology and Contemporary Judaism, 1966; The Religious Imagination, 1967; Morality and Eros, 1970; My Brother Paul, 1971; Power Struggle, 1974; The Cunning of History, 1975; also articles. Editorial bd. The Reconstructionist. Office: Fla State U Tallahassee FL 32306

RUBENSTONE, ALBERT IRVING, physician, educator; b. Elkton, Md., Apr. 21, 1919; s. Jacob and Annie (Diamond) R.; B.A., U. Pa., 1941; M.D., U. Md., 1944; m. Eva Mae Dinenberg, Mar. 25, 1951; 1 dau., Georgette. Intern Mt. Sinai Hosp., Phila., 1944-45, resident pathology, 1945-49, resident internal medicine, 1950-52; asst. pathologist So. div. Albert Einstein Med. Center, Phila., 1949-54, acting dir. labs., also pathologist, 1954-55, asst. dir. labs., also pathologist, 1955-56; asst. pathologist Skin and Cancer Hosp., Phila., 1953-54, cons. pathologist, 1954-56; chief pathology No. div. Phila. Gen. Hosp., 1955-56; asso. pathologist, asst. dir. pathology Michael Reese Hosp. and Med. Center, Chgo., 1956-62; chief lab. service VA Hosp., Phila., 1962-64; asso. dir. labs., pathologist Mt. Sinai Hosp. Med. Center, Chgo., 1964-65, dir. dept. pathology, 1965—; asst. prof. pathology Hahnemann Med. Coll., Phila., 1954-56; asso. pathology Women's Med. Coll., Phila., 1954-56, asst. prof., 1962-64; clin. asst. prof. pathology U. Ill. Med. Sch., 1956-62; prof. pathology Chgo. Med. Sch., 1964-74, chmn. dept., 1968-74; prof. pathology Rush Med. Coll., Chgo., 1975—, chief clin. pathology sect. dept. pathology, 1977—; cons. pathology West Side VA Hosp., Chgo., 1965-69; cons. breast pathology Ill. Registry Anatomic Pathology, 1965—, chmn. exec. com., 1967-68. Diplomate in pathol. anatomy and clin. pathology Am. Bd. Pathology. Mem. Am. Assn. Chmn. Med. Sch. Depts. Pathology, AAUP, AMA, Am. Soc. Cytology, Am. Assn. Pathologists and Bacteriologists, A.C.P., Internat. Acad. Pathology, Pan. Am. Med. Assn., Am. Soc. Clin. Pathologists, Assn. Clin. Scientists, Chgo. Med. Soc., Chgo. Pathol. Soc. (pres. 1968-69), Coll. Am. Pathologists, Ill. Soc. Pathology, Inst. Medicine, Soc. Med. History Chgo., Sigma Xi. Jewish. Author articles, chpts. in textbooks. Home: 633 Echo Ln Glenview IL 60026 Office: Mt Sinai Hosp Med Center California Ave at 15th St Chicago IL 60608

RUBES, JAN LADISLAV, opera singer, actor; b. Volyne, Czechoslovakia, June 6, 1920; s. Jan and Ruzena (Kellnerova) R.; student Prague Conservatory Music, Charles U.; grad. Prague Acad. Music (citation Ministry Culture), 1947; m. Susan Douglas, Sept. 22, 1950; children—Christopher Jan, Jonathan Mark, Anthony Dean. Singer opera houses, Prague, Pilsen, Frankfurt, City Center, Chgo., Toronto; appeared in motion pictures for United Artists, Disney, Canadian Prodns.; tchr., lectr. Music Faculty, Toronto U., York U., U. Sask.; dir. Stratford Shakespearean Festival; star new Canadian feature film shown at Cannes Festival, 1975, Moscow Family Film Festival, Guelph and Stratford Film Festival; author, star Guest What, ednl. TV children's program; film roles include Forbidden Journey, The Incredible Journey, Lions for Breakfast, House on Front Street; musical comedy roles include South Pacific, The Sound of Music, Man of La Mancha; has sung over 80 leading bass roles in 6 langs.; concert tour, U.S. and Can.; dir. touring and program devel. in Ont. for Can. Opera Co., 1974-76. Bd. dirs. Can. Council, Canadian Conf. for Arts, Prologue to Performing Arts. Recipient Canadian Centennial medal, Queen Elizabeth Jubilee medal; named Hon. Citizen of Winnipeg, Man., Saskatoon, Sask., Sydney, N.S., Toronto. Mem. Actors Equity. Office: care David Haber Artists Mgmt 1235 Bay St Suite 500 Toronto ON M5R 3K4 Canada

RUBIN, ABE, coll. pres., podiatrist; b. Winnipeg, Man., Can., Aug. 14, 1911; s. Burrows and Lily R. (Adilman) R.; student U. Man., 1928-32; D.P.M., Ill. Coll. Podiatric Medicine, 1937, Ed.D., 1967; postgrad. U. Chgo., 1952-55; Litt.D., Ohio Coll. Podiatry, 1968; m. Doris Silvia Miller, July 8, 1949; children—Mark B., Hollis Beth. Asso. prof. anatomy Ill. Coll. Podiatric Medicine, 1937-42, dir. clinics, head orthopedic dept., 1947-55; sec. Am. Podiatry Assn., Washington, 1955-62, editor Jour., 1955-70; exec. dir. Council Podiatric Edn., 1962-70; pvt. practice, 1938-42; v.p., dean Ohio Coll. Podiatric Medicine, Cleve., 1970-71, pres., 1971—. Cons. N1H, Nat. Acad. Scis., Inst. of Medicine, others. Served to capt. USAAF, 1942-46. Recipient Gold award Wm. J. Stickel Ann. awards research podiatry, 1954. Fellow Am. Coll. Foot Orthopedists (past pres.), Am. Med. Writers Assn. (chpt. pres.), AAAS; mem. Am. Podiatry Assn., Am. Assn. Colls. Podiatric Medicine (pres. 1970), Am. Pub. Health Assn., Gerontol. Soc., Am. Inst. Parliamentarians. Contbr. articles med. jours. encys. Co-editor: The Podiatry Curriculum. Editorial adv. bd. Jour. Am. Podiatry Assn. Home: 29501 Cedar Rd Mayfield Heights OH 44124 Office: 10515 Carnegie Ave Cleveland OH 44106

RUBIN, ALBERT LOUIS, educator, physician; b. Memphis, May 9, 1927; s. Malcolm M. and Sarah (Bryan) R.; student Williams Coll., 1944-45, Mass. Inst. Tech., 1945-46; M.D., Cornell U., 1950; m. Carolyn Helen Diehl, Sept. 28, 1953; 1 son, Marc. Intern, resident Cornell med. unit Bellevue Hosp., N.Y.C.; mem. faculty Cornell U. Med. Coll., 1951—, prof. biochemistry and surgery, 1969—, dir. Rogosin Labs., 1963—, dir. Rogosin Kidney Center, 1971—, prof. medicine, 1976—; fellow Sch. Advanced Study, Mass. Inst. Tech., 1961-63; med. editorial cons. Time, Inc.; investigator Am. Heart Assn., 1957-62. Served with USNR, 1944-45. Diplomate Am. Bd. Intenal Medicine. Mem. A.C.P., Am. Soc. Biol. Chemists. Alumni Assn. Cornell U. Med. Coll. (pres. 1969-71), Sigma Xi. Author: Physical Diagnosis, 1964. Home: 220 Allison Ct Englewood NJ 07631 Office: 1300 York Ave New York City NY 10021

RUBIN, ALVIN BENJAMIN, judge; b. Alexandria, La., Mar. 13, 1920; s. Simon and Frances (Prussack) R.; B.S. in Bus. Adminstrn., La. State U., 1941, LL.B. 1942; m. Janice Ginsberg, Feb. 19, 1946; children—Michael H., David S. Admitted to La. bar, 1942; practice in Baton Rouge, 1946-66; partner firm Sanders, Miller, Downing, Rubin & Kean, 1946-66; U.S. dist. judge Eastern Dist. La., 1966-77; U.S. circuit judge 5th Circuit Ct. Appeals, 1977—; adj. prof. law La. State U. Law Sch., 1946—; lectr. taxation Am. Law Inst., Tulane U. Tax Inst., Ga. Tax Inst., La. State U. Mineral Law Inst.; arbitrator Fed. Mediation and Conciliation Service, 1964-66. Chmn. Baton Rouge Zoning Study Com.; mem. La. Legislative Adminstrv. Procedure Com. Sec. Baton Rouge United Givers Fund, 1954-66; bd. dirs. C.L.E.P.R., 1970—, New Orleans Jewish Welfare Fedn., 1972-76; mem. vis. com. Law Sch., U. Chgo., 1972-75, U. Miami, 1974—, Harvard, 1975—; past bd. dirs. Baton Rouge chpt. Girl Scouts Am., Mental Health Guidance Center, Community Chest, Community Services Council, Nat. Assn. Crippled Children and Adults; past adv. bd. local Salvation Army, YWCA, Blundon Orphanage; trustee Temple B'nai Israel, 1966-74, Temple Sinai, 1973-76. Served to capt. AUS, 1942-46; ETO. Recipient Golden Deeds award for civic service, 1964; Brotherhood award Nat. Conf. Christians and Jews, 1968. Mem. Am. (bd. editors jour. 1976—, mem. task force competency in legal edn. 1978—, chmn. estate and gift tax com. 1964, chmn. sect. bar activities 1963, chmn. lawyer referral com. 1969-72), La. (chmn. sect. trust estates, probate and immovable property law 1961, chmn. labor law sect. 1957, jr. bar sect. 1955, com. on ct. adminstrn. Jud. Conf.) bar assns., Nat. Acad. Arbitrators, Am. Arbitration Assn., La. Law Inst., Order of Coif, Phi Beta Kappa, Phi Delta Phi, Omicron Delta Kappa, Blue Key (hon.). Mason (32 deg.). Author: (with McMahon) Louisiana Pleadings and Judicial Forms Annotated; (with Janice G. Rubin) Louisiana Trust Handbook. Home: 225 Walnut St New Orleans LA 70118 Office: 500 Camp St New Orleans LA 70130

RUBIN, BENJAMIN NORMAN, textile co. exec.; b. Bklyn., Oct. 12, 1917; s. Joseph and Esther (Kantrowitz) R.; B.S., Columbia, 1938; m. Susanne Fried, June 20, 1943; children—Robert, Irwin. Staff accountant Milton Rindler & Co., 1938-42; pub. accountant Chirlian Parker & Co., N.Y.C., 1942-51; treas. Coleport Fabrics, Inc., N.Y.C., 1951-65; controller Greenwood Mills, Inc., N.Y.C., 1965—; instr. accounting Bklyn. Coll., 1945-47. C.P.A., N.Y. Mem. Am. Inst. C.P.A.'s, N.Y. State Soc. C.P.A.'s, Nat. Assn. Accountants, Alpha Kappa Psi. K.P. Home: 370 Ocean Pkwy Brooklyn NY 11218 Office: 111 W 40th St New York City NY 10018

RUBIN, BERNARD, pharmacologist; b. N.Y.C., Feb. 15, 1919; s. Charles and Anna (Slutskin) R.; B.A., Bklyn. Coll., 1939; Ph.D., Yale U., 1950; m. Betty Schindler, June 17, 1945; children—Stefi G., Robert H. Research asst. microbiology N.Y. City Health Dept., 1940-42, food and drug insp., 1944-45; research asst. pharmacology and chemotherapy Nepera Chem. Co., 1945-48; with Squibb Inst. Med. Research, Princeton, N.J., 1950—, now sr. research group leader pharmacology. Served with U.S. Army, 1942-43. AEC fellow, 1948-50. Mem. Am. Soc. Pharm. and Exptl. Therapeutics, Soc. Expl. Biology and Medicine, Internat. Soc. Hypertension, N.Y. Acad. Scis., AAAS, Am. Heart Assn., Sigma Xi. Home: 2 Pin Oak Dr Lawrenceville NJ 08648 Office: PO Box 4000 Princeton NJ 08540

RUBIN, CARL BERNARD, U.S. dist. judge; b. Cin., Mar. 27, 1920; s. John I. and Ethel (Friedman) R.; B.A., U. Cin., 1942, J.D., 1944; m. Gloria Weiland, Sept. 23, 1945; children—Marc W., C. Barry, Pam G., Robert S. Admitted to Ohio bar, 1944; practiced in Cin., 1944-71; asst. pros. atty. Hamilton County (Ohio), Cin., 1950-60; judge U.S. Dist. Ct. So. Dist. Ohio, 1971—, chief judge, 1979—. Instr. criminal law Chase Coll. Law, Cin., 1965-67; mem. com. on ct. adminstrn. fed. cts. U.S. Jud. Conf., 1975; adj. prof. law U. Dayton Coll. Law, 1976—. Mem. Cin. Civil Service Commn., 1960-66, chmn., 1965-66; pres. S.W. Ohio Regional Transit Authority, 1971. Mem. Am. Contract Bridge League (dir. 1966-73, pres. 1970-71). Office: US Courthouse 5th and Walnut Sts Cincinnati OH 45202

RUBIN, DAVID ROBERT, fin. services co exec.; b. Bklyn., Aug. 3, 1933; s. Benjamin and Ruth M. (Shapiro) R.; B.A. cum laude, Harvard Coll., 1955; M.B.A. with distinction, U. Mich., 1959; m. Roberta Jean Hattis, July 4, 1959; children—Julia Anne, Martha Beth, Laura Rachel, John Andrew. Mgmt. cons. Arthur Young & Co., Chgo., 1959-68; sr. v.p. Midwest Stock Exchange, Chgo., 1968-70, exec. v.p., 1972—; pres. Midwest Stock Exchange Service Corp., Chgo., 1970-72; dir. Midwest Securities Trust Co., Mortgage Backed Securities Clearing Corp., Buckingham Fin. Services. Trustee, Glencoe (Ill.) Village and Sch. Bd. Caucuses, 1970-72, Village of Glencoe, 1976—; chief crusader Crusade of Mercy, Chgo., 1972-77. Served with U.S. Army, 1955-57. C.P.A., Ill. Mem. Am. Inst. C.P.A.'s, Ill. Soc. C.P.A.'s. Clubs: Standard, Old Willow Swim and Tennis. Home: 126 Hazel Glencoe IL 60022 Office: 120 S LaSalle St Chicago IL 60603

RUBIN, EDWARD PERRY, ret. investment counsel; b. Payne, Ohio, Mar. 27, 1903; s. Henry E. and Blanche (Reader) R.; A.B., Heidelberg Coll., 1925, LL.D. (hon.), 1968; grad. work, Harvard, 1926; m. Mary Allene Myers, Nov. 27, 1930; 1 son, Edward P. Pres., dir. Selected Am. Shares, Inc., 1942-70; pres. Selected Investments Co., 1943-55, chmn. bd., 1955-68; chmn. bd. Selected Spl. Shares, Inc., 1968-70; adviser, dir. Security Supvrs., investment counsel, 1969-70, partner, pres. predecessor orgns.; a prin. organizer Selected Am. Shares, Selected Cumulative Shares, Selected Income Shares, Selected Am. Shares, Inc., Selected Spl. Shares, Inc. Adv. gov. Midwest Stock Exchange, 1956-59. Trustee Heidelberg Coll., 1954—, mem. fin. and investment com. 1958—, chmn., 1958, 64-66, 70-73, 76—, chmn. planning com., 1967; trustee Library Internat. Relations, 1960-77. Mem. Investment Co. Inst. (bd. govs. 1949-52, 58-61, 63-67, 68-70, chmn. tax com. 1958-60, 67-70, chmn. instl. studies com. 1963-66), Fin. Writers Assn. Chgo. (pres. 1965-66), Investment Analysts Soc. Chgo., Am. Rose Soc. Episcopalian. Clubs: Bond, Attic, Economic, Heidelberg, Harvard, Execs. (Chgo.); Internat.; 71; Rotary. Writer, lectr. fin. subjects. Home: 459 Sunset Rd Winnetka IL 60093

RUBIN, EDWIN MANNING, advt. exec.; b. Charleston, S.C., May 18, 1927; s. Louis Decimus and Janet (Weinstein) R.; B.A. in History and English, U. Richmond, 1950; M.A. in Writing, Speech and Drama, Johns Hopkins, 1951; m. Jane Leslie Goldman, Apr. 20, 1969; children—Edward M., James E., Joshua D. Trainee, Lennen & Mitchell Advt., N.Y.C., 1952-53; dir. radio-TV Cargill, Wilson & Acree, Inc., Richmond, Va., 1953-60; TV producer Benton & Bowles, Inc., N.Y.C., 1960-62; with Grey Advt., Inc., N.Y.C., 1962—, sr. v.p., creative dir., 1969—. Chmn. TV comml. prodn. com. Am. Assn. Advt. Agys., 1967—; co-chmn. audio-visual and program coms., mem. nat. commn. and exec. com. Anti-Defamation League. Served with AUS, 1944-47. Recipient Sam Dalsimer Human Relations award Anti-Defamation League B'nai B'rith, 1976; also numerous awards for creative work. Mem. Internat. Radio-TV Soc., Nat. Acad. TV Arts and Scis., Council Motion Pictures-E. Coast, Phi Beta Kappa. Home: 970 Park Ave New York NY 10028 Office: 777 3d Ave New York NY 10017

RUBIN, EMANUEL, pathologist; b. N.Y.C., Dec. 5, 1928; s. Jacob and Sophie Rubin R.; B.S., Villanova U., 1950; M.D., Harvard U., 1954; m. Barbara Kurn, Mar. 27, 1955; children—Raphael, Jonathan, Daniel, Rebecca. Intern, Boston City Hosp., 1954-55; resident Children's Hosp. of Phila., 1957-58; research fellow in pathology Mt. Sinai Hosp., N.Y.C., 1958-62, asso. attending pathologist, 1964-68, attending pathologist, dir. hosp. pathology services, 1968-72, pathologist-in-chief, 1972-76; dir. labs. Hahnemann Hosp., Phila., 1977—; prof. pathology Mt. Sinai Sch. Medicine, City U. N.Y., 1966-72, Irene Heinz and John LaPorte Given prof. pathology, chmn. dept., 1972-76; prof., chmn. dept. pathology and lab. medicine Hahnemann Med. Coll., Phila., 1977—, prof., chmn. Coll. Allied Health Professions, 1977—; adj. prof. biochemistry and biophysics U. Pa. Sch. Medicine, Phila., 1977—. Served with USN, 1955-57. Mem. Am. Assn. Pathologists, Internat. Acad. Pathology, Am. Assn. for Study of Liver Diseases, Internat. Assn. for Study of the Liver, A.C.P., Am. Gastroent. Assn., Am. Soc. Biol. Chemistry. Contbr. articles to profl. jours. Home: 1505 Monk Rd Gladwyne PA 19035 Office: 230 N Broad St Philadelphia PA 19102

RUBIN, HARRY, biologist; b. N.Y.C., June 23, 1926; s. Nathan and Nettie (Rubin) R.; D.V.M., Cornell U., 1947; m. Dorothy M. Schuster, Jan. 14, 1952; children—Andrew L., Janet E., Clinton T., Nell A. Veterinarian control foot and mouth disease Dept. Agr., Mexico, 1947-48; officer USPHS, Montgomery, Ala., 1948-52; sr. research fellow Calif. Inst. Tech., Pasadena, 1953-58; prof. virology and molecular biology U. Calif. at Berkeley, 1958—. Recipient Eli Lilly prize, 1961; Lasker award, 1964; Merck Research award, 1964, Rosenthal Cancer award AAAS, 1959; Dyer Lectureship award NIH, 1964. Mem. Nat. Acad. Arts and Scis., Nat. Acad. Scis. Research in regulation of cell metabolism and growth. Home: 1170 Sterling Ave Berkeley CA 94708

RUBIN, IRVING, editor; b. N.Y.C., Apr. 7, 1916; s. Julius and Sadie (Seidman) R.; Ph.G., Bklyn. Coll. Pharmacy, 1936; B.A., Bklyn. Eve. Coll., 1948; Pharm.D. (hon.), Mass. Coll. Pharmacy, 1973; m. Florence Podolsky, Mar. 12, 1949; children—Joanne, Saul Robert. With retail pharmacies, N.Y.C., 1933-38; asso. editor, then mng. editor Pharmacy, Am. Druggist mag., also editorial dir. Blue Price Book, 1938-60; editor, v.p., publ. dir. Pharmacy Times, and predecessor, Port Washington, N.Y., 1960—; pharmacy cons. Med. Times mag., 1978, Resident and Staff Physician, 1978. Mem. exec. council for Remington Honor Medal, 1960—. Trustee Arnold and Marie Schwartz Coll. Pharmacy, Bklyn. Served with AUS, 1941-46; ETO. Decorated Bronze Star; recipient Alumni Achievement award Alumni Assn. Bklyn. Coll. Pharmacy, 1963; Editorial Achievement award Alpha Zeta Omega, 1968, Am. Cancer Soc., 1964; Gold medal Nicholas S. Gesoalde Pharm. Econ. Research Found., 1972; J. Leon Lascoff award Am. Coll. Apothecaries, 1977; named Man of Year, Pharmacy lodge B'nai B'rith, Phila., 1973. Charter diplomate Am. Bd. Diplomates in Pharmacy. Hon. life mem. Am. Coll. Pharmacists; mem. Am. Inst. History Pharmacy (council), Nat. Assn. Retail Druggists, Am. Pharm. Assn. (pres. N.Y. chpt. 1955-56, ho. dels.), Am. Soc. Hosp. Pharmacists, Alumni Assn. Bklyn. Coll. Pharmacy (pres. 1946-48), Alpha Zeta Omega (hon.) Rho Pi Phi, Delta Sigma Theta, Rho Chi, Kappa Psi. Jewish. Author: The Pharmacy Graduate's Career Guide, 1970. Leader nat. drive for U.S. postage stamp in honor of pharmacy, 1972. Home: 39 Ruxton Rd Great Neck NY 11023 Office: 80 Shore Rd Port Washington NY 11050

RUBIN, JOAN ALLEMAN, editorial exec.; b. Hanover, Pa., Oct. 1, 1931; d. Richard B. and Katherine (Eckert) Alleman; B.A., Coll. William and Mary, 1953; m. Robert Rubin, July 30, 1955; children—Thomas, Andrew. Asst. to feature editor, career editor Mademoiselle Mag., N.Y.C., 1954-61; free-lance mag. writer, N.Y.C., 1961-64; editor-in-chief Playbill, N.Y.C., 1964—. Vice pres. Film Modules; affiliated Drama Forum mem. nominating com. Tony award, 1975, 76, 76-77, mem. eligibility com., 1977-78. Mem. Phi Beta Kappa. Club: Corinthian Yacht. Home: 172 Sullivan St New York NY 10012 Office: care Playbill 151 E 50th St New York NY 10022. *I believe that in a lifetime only two or three things are truly important.*

This conviction has enabled me to live and work with realistic priorities and a minimum of anxiety.

RUBIN, LOUIS DECIMUS, JR., educator, writer; b. Charleston, S.C., Nov. 19, 1923; s. Louis Decimus and Janet (Weinstein) R.; student Coll. of Charleston, 1940-42; A.B., U. Richmond, 1946, Litt.D., 1972; M.A., Johns Hopkins U., 1949, Ph.D., 1954; m. Eva M. Redfield, June 2, 1951; children—Robert Alden, William Louis. Instr. Johns Hopkins U., editor Hopkins Rev., 1950-54; fellow criticism Sewanee Rev., 1953-54; exec. sec. Am. Studies Assn., asst. prof. Am. civilization U. Pa., 1954-56; asso. editor Richmond (Va.) News Leader, 1956-57; asso. prof. English, Hollins Coll., 1957-60, prof., chmn. dept., 1960-67; prof. English, U. N.C., 1967—, Univ. Disting. prof., 1973—; editor Hollins Critic, 1963-68; vis. prof. history La. State U., 1957; Fulbright lectr. U. Aix-Marseille, 1960; lectr. Bread Loaf Writer's Conf., 1961; vis. prof. U. N.C., 1965, Harvard U., 1969. Served with AUS, 1943-46. Guggenheim fellow, 1958-59; fellow Am. Council Learned Socs., 1964. Mem. Modern Lang. Assn., So. Hist. Assn., Soc. Study So. Lit. (pres. 1975-76), Phi Beta Kappa. Author: Thomas Wolfe: The Weather of His Youth, 1955; No Place on Earth, 1959; The Golden Weather, 1961; The Faraway Country, 1963; The Teller in the Tale, 1967; The Curious Death of the Novel, 1967; George W. Cable, 1969: The Writer in the South, 1972; William Elliott Shoots A Bear, 1975; Virginia: A History, 1977; The Wary Fugitives, 1978. Editor: Southern Renascence, 1953; The Lasting South, 1957; Teach the Freeman: R.B. Hayes and the Slater Fund for Negro Education, 1959; The Idea of an American Novel, 1961; South: Modern Southern Literature in Its Cultural Setting, 1961; Bibliographical Guide to the Study of Southern Literature, 1969; The Comic Imagination in American Literature, 1973; The Literary South, 1978; co-editor: So. Lit. Jour., 1968—; contbr. articles to periodicals. Address: 702 Gimghoul Rd Chapel Hill NC 27514

RUBIN, MEL, advt. exec.; b. Bklyn., Sept. 6, 1922; s. Henry M. and Ida (Posner) R.; B.S., Coll. City N.Y., 1943; m. Isabelle Irma Cohen, Jan. 6, 1948; children—Nina, Jason, Emily Laura. With D.H. Ahrend Co., 1946-50; owner Shaller-Rubin Co., Inc., N.Y.C., 1950—. Democratic Party committeeman, bd. govs. Gt. Neck Dem. Club, 1964-66. Served to lt. USNR, World War II. Mem. Drug, Chem. and Allied Trades Assn. (dir.), Pharm. Advt. Club, Marketing Exec. Club. Home: 7 Old Colony Ln Great Neck NY 11023 Office: 909 3d Ave New York City NY 10022

RUBIN, MORRIS HAROLD, author; b. N.Y.C., Aug. 7, 1911; s. Jacob and Leah (Abrahamson) R.; B.A., U. Wis., 1934; m. Mary Barbara Sheridan, Sept. 12, 1936. With Portland (Me.) Evening Express, 1929-34, Boston Globe, 1929-34, N.Y. Times, 1935-38, N.Y. Herald Tribune, 1939, Time Mag., 1935-38, Milw. Jour., 1933-35, Wis. State Jour., Madison, 1934-38; editor The Progressive Mag., Madison, 1940-73, pres., pub., 1973-76; editorial cons., free-lance writer, 1976—; trustee, dir. Madison Capital Times; dir. Madison Newspapers, Inc.; aide to Gov. Philip F. LaFollette and Sen. Robert M. LaFollette, Jr., Madison, 1938-40. Founder, Wis. Civil Liberties Union, 1941, pres., 1941-47; v.p. ACLU, 1947. Recipient Sidney Hillman Found. award for outstanding journalism in domestic field for spl. issue on Senator Joseph R. McCarthy, 1954; George Polk Meml. award for distinguished fgn. reporting for spl. issue on Latin Am., 1962. Mem. Madison Newspaper Guild (founder). Editor: McCarthy—The Documented Record, 1954; The Crisis of Survival, 1970. Home: 1208 Bowdoin Rd Madison WI 53705 Office: 408 W Gorham St Madison WI 53703

RUBIN, SAMUEL HAROLD, physician, univ. adminstr.; b. N.Y.C., July 24, 1916; s. Joseph and Esther (Goldfarb) R.; A.B., Brown U., 1938; M.D., St. Louis U., 1943; M.S., U. Chgo., 1957; m. Audrey Arndt, Nov. 20, 1943; children—James E., David A. Intern, Jewish Hosp., St. Louis, 1943-44; resident St. Louis U. Group Hosp., 1944-45, St. Mary's Hosp., Kansas City, Mo., 1945-46; practice medicine, Asbury Park, N.J., 1948-61; vol. faculty mem. N.Y. Med. Coll., 1948-61, asso. prof. dept. medicine, 1962-65, prof., 1965—; chief med. service N.Y. Med. Coll.-Met. Hosp. Center, 1966-71, asso. dean, 1971-72, exec. dean, 1972-74, dean, v.p. acad. affairs, 1975, provost, dean, 1977—; mem. exec. com. Asso. Med. Schs. N.Y. and N.J., 1974—; cons. medicine Jersey Shore Med. Center, 1962—; trustee Med. Library Center N.Y., 1974—. Served with M.C., AUS, 1946-48. NIH program dir. grantee, 1966-71. Diplomate Am. Bd. Internal Medicine. Fellow A.C.P.; mem. N.Y. Acad. Sci. Contbr. articles to med. jours. Home: Scarborough Manor Scarborough NY 10510 Office: NY Medical Coll Elmwood Hall Valhalla NY 10595

RUBIN, SEYMOUR JEFFREY, lawyer; b. Chgo., Apr. 6, 1914; s. Sol and Sadie (Bloom) R.; B.A., U. Mich., 1935; LL.B. magna cum laude, Harvard, 1938, LL.M., 1939; m. Janet Beck, Mar. 26, 1943. Admitted to Ill. bar, 1939, D.C. bar, 1941; legal adviser U.S. dels. to organizing confs. GATT, 1947-48; mem. U.S. Reparations Del., 1945, Inter-Am. Conf. on Problems of War and Peace, 1945; chief U.S. Delegation on Post-War Problems, Portugal, Spain, Sweden, 1946; asst. legal adviser econ. affairs Dept. State, 1946-48; practiced law, Washington, 1948-61; counsel Surrey, Karasik & Morse, 1964-75; cons. U.S. Dept. State, Brookings Instn., 1948-49; chief U.S. del. negotiating Marshall Plan Agreements, 1951-52; dep. adminstr. Mut. Def. Assistance Control Act, 1952-53; mem. Spl. Presdl. Mission to Bolivia, 1961; gen. counsel ICA and AID, 1961-62; U.S. rep. Devel. Assistance Com., 1962-64; cons. Dept. State, U.S. rep. to spl. com. UN Security Council, 1964-65; U.S. rep. UN Commn. on Internat. Trade Law, 1967-69; pub. mem. Commn. on Internat. Rules Jud. Procedure, 1961-62; personal rep. Pres. to Bolivia wih rank of spl. ambassador, 1962; adj. prof. Georgetown U. Law Center, 1964-72; lectr. Sloan Sch. Bus. Adminstrn., Mass. Inst. Tech., 1969; prof. Am. U. Law Sch., 1973—; mem. Inter Am. Juridical Commn., 1974—; U.S. rep. UN Commn. on Transnat. Corps., 1975—; mem. U.S. del. UNETAD Tech. Transfer Conf., 1978; exec. v.p. Am. Soc. Internat. Law, 1975—. Chmn. adv. bd. Council Law and Social Policy; mem. bd. Inst. Internat. and Fgn. Trade, Found. for Coop. Housing, Consumers for World Trade. Recipient Sesquicentennial award U. Mich., 1967; Grand Silver medal Austria, 1967. Mem. Am. Soc. Internat. Law, Council on Fgn. Affairs, Am. Law Inst., Am. Bar Assn., Soc. for Internat. Devel. Democrat. Author: Private Foreign Investment, 1956; The Conscience of the Rich Nations - The Common Aid Effort and the Development Assistance Committee, 1966; (with others) The International Corporation, 1970; Global Companies, 1975. Editor, contbr. Foreign Development Lending—Legal Aspects, 1971. Contbr. articles in field to profl. jours. Home: 1675 35th St NW Washington DC 20007 Office: 2223 Massachusetts Ave NW Washington DC 20008

RUBIN, STANLEY CREAMER, film TV producer-writer; b. N.Y.C., Oct. 8, 1917; s. Michael Isaac and Anne (Creamer) R.; student U. Calif., Los Angeles, 1933-37; m. Elizabeth Margaret von Gerken (actress Kathleen Hughes), July 25, 1954; children—John, Chris, Angela, Michael. Story analyst various film studios, 1939-40; writer Universal Studios, 1940-42; writer-producer on TV, 1948-49; theatrical feature producer RKO Studios, 1949-50, 56-57, 20th Century-Fox Studios, 1950-53, Universal Studios, 1953-55; TV producer CBS, 1957-59, Universal Studios, 1960-63, 71-72, 20th Century Fox Studios, 1967-70, MGM-TV, 1972-77; pres. TBA Prodns., Hollywood, 1978—; theatrical films produced include: The Narrow Margin, 1950, My Pal Gus, 1950, Destination Gobi, 1951, River of No Return, 1952, Promise Her Anything, 1966, The President's Analyst, 1967; TV prodns. include G.E. Theatre, 1959-63, Ghost and Mrs. Muir, 1968-69, Bracken's World, 1969-71; co-producer Babe (Hollywood Fgn. Press Golden Globe award, Christopher medal), 1975, And Your Name is Jonah, 1978. Served with USAAF, 1942-46. Recipient Emmy award for Diamond Necklace, 1949. Mem. Writers Guild Am. (dir. 1941-42), Producers Guild Am. (pres. 1974-79, dir. 1962—), Acad. Motion Picture Arts and Scis., Acad. TV Arts and Scis. Home: 8818 Rising Glen Pl Los Angeles CA 90069 Office: Sunset Gower Studios Hollywood CA 90028

RUBIN, THEODORE ISAAC, psychiatrist; b. Bklyn., Apr. 11, 1923; s. Nathan and Esther (Marcus) R.; B.A., Bklyn. Coll., 1946; M.D., U. Lausanne (Switzerland), 1951; grad. Am. Inst. Psychoanalysis, 1964; m. Eleanor Katz, June 16, 1946; children—Jeffrey, Trudy, Eugene. Resident psychiatrist Los Angeles VA Hosp., 1953, Rockland (N.Y.) State Hosp., 1954, Bklyn. State Hosp., 1955, Kings County (N.Y.) Hosp., 1956; chief psychiatrist Women's House of Detention, N.Y.C., 1957; mem. faculty Downstate Med. Sch., N.Y. State U., 1957-59; pvt. practice, N.Y.C., 1956—; mem. med. bd. Karen Horney Psychoanalytic Clinic, 1964—, also tng. and supervising psychoanalyst, physician-in-charge of Obesity Clinic; mem. faculty Am. Inst. Psychoanalytic Psychoanalysis, 1962—, also tng. and supervising psychoanalyst, New Sch. Social Research, 1967—. Pres. trustees Am. Inst. Psychoanalysis; bd. dirs. League Sch. Seriously Disturbed Children. Served as officer USNR, World War II. Recipient Adolf Meyer award Assn. Improvement Mental Hosps., 1963. Fellow Am. Acad. Psychoanalysis; mem. N.Y. County Med. Soc., Am. Psychiat. Assn., Assn. Advancement Psychoanalysis, Authors Guild. Author: Jordi, 1960; Lisa and David, 1961; In The Life, 1961; Sweet Daddy, 1963; Platzo and the Mexican Pony Rider, 1965; The Thin Book by a Formerly Fat Psychiatrist, 1966; The 29th Summer, 1966; Cat, 1966; Coming Out, 1967; The Winner's Note Book, 1967; The Angry Book, 1969; Forever Thin, 1970; Emergency Room Diary, 1972; Doctor Rubin Please Make Me Happy, 1974; Shrink, 1974; Compassion and Self-Hate, An Alternative to Despair, 1975; Love Me, Love My Fool, 1976; Reflections in a Goldfish Tank, 1977; Alive and Fat and Thinning in America, 1978; also articles, columns. Mem. editorial bd. Am. Jour. Psychoanalysis. Office: 243 E 61st St New York NY 10021

RUBIN, WILLIAM, art curator; b. N.Y.C., Aug. 11, 1927; A.B., M.A., Ph.D., Columbia U.; student U. Paris. Prof. art history Sarah Lawrence Coll., 1952-67; prof. art history Grad. Div., City U. N.Y., 1960-68; chief curator painting and sculpture Mus. Modern Art, 1968-73, dir. painting and sculpture, 1973—; adj. prof. art history Inst. Fine Arts, N.Y. U., 1968—. Decorated chevalier French Legion Honor. Author: Modern Sacred Art and the Church of Assy, 1961; Matta, 1957; Dada, Surrealism and Their Heritage, 1966; Dada and Surrealist Art, 1969; Frank Stella, 1970; Picasso in the Collection of the Museum of Modern Art, 1972; Miró in the Collection of the Museum of Modern Art, 1973; The Paintings of Gerald Murphy, 1974; Anthony Caro, 1975; (with Carolyn Lanchner) André Masson, 1976; Paris-New York: Situation de l'Art, 1978; editor: Cezanne: The Late Work, 1977; Am. editor Art Internat. Mag., 1959-64. Address: Museum Modern Art New York NY 10019

RUBINOFF, IRA, biologist, conservationist; b. N.Y.C., Dec. 21, 1938; s. Jacob and Bessie (Rose) R.; B.S., Queens Coll., 1959; A.M., Harvard U., 1960, Ph.D., 1963; m. Roberta Wolff, Mar. 19, 1961; 1 son, Jason; m. 2d, Anabella Guardia, Feb. 10, 1978. Biologist, asst. dir. marine biology Smithsonian Tropical Research Inst., Balboa, Republic of Panama, 1964-70, asst. dir. sci., 1970-73, dir., 1973—; asso. in ichthyology Harvard U., 1965—; courtesy prof. Fla. State U., Tallahassee, 1976—; mem. sci. adv. bd. Gorgas Meml. Inst., 1964—; trustee Rare Animal Relief Effort, 1976—; bd. dirs. Charles Darwin Found. for Galapagos Islands, 1977—; chmn. bd. fellowships and grants Smithsonian Instn., 1978-79. Fellow Linnean Soc. (London); mem. Am. Soc. Naturalists, Soc. Study of Evolution, N.Y. Acad. Scis., Orgn. Tropical Studies. Club: Cosmos (Washington). Contbr. articles to profl. jours. Home: Box 2281 Balboa Republic of Panama Office: Smithsonian Tropical Research Inst APO Miami FL 34002

RUBINSTEIN, ALVIN ZACHARY, educator; b. Bklyn., Apr. 23, 1927; s. Max and Sylvia (Stone) R.; B.B.A., City Coll. N.Y., 1949; M.A., U. Pa., 1950, Ph.D., 1954; m. Frankie Kimmelman, Nov. 12, 1960. Mem. faculty U. Pa., 1957—, prof. polit. sci., 1966—; vis. lectr. Queen Coll., 1959; vis. prof. U. Calif. at Santa Barbara, summer, 1968, Am. U., Cairo, 1971, Lehigh U., spring, 1973, U. Va., spring 1977; chmn. grad. program internat. relations U. Pa., 1966-70, dir. Anspach Inst. Diplomacy and Fgn. Affairs, 1968-70; cons. Inst. Def. Analysis, 1966-70, Inst. for Fgn. Policy Analysis, 1976; vis. asso. Russian Research Center, Harvard, 1956-57. Ford Found. fellow, 1956-57; Rockefeller Found. grantee, 1961-62; Guggenheim fellow, 1965-66; grantee Am. Philos. Soc., 1958, 59, 68, 73; NSF travel grant, 1970-71; Barra Found. research grant, 1970-71; president scholar Bellagio Study and Conf. Center, Rockefeller Found., Italy, 1974; Earhart Found. research grantee, 1974; Joint Com. on Soviet Studies of Am. Council Learned Socs. and Social Sci. Research Council grantee, 1975; vis. fellow Clare Hall, Cambridge (Eng.) U., 1974-75; NATO research fellow, 1977; Earhart Found. research grantee, 1979. Served to lt. USNR, 1954-56. Author: Communist Political Systems, 1966; (with P. Berton) Soviet Writings on S.E. Asia, 1968; The Soviets in International Organizations, 1964; The Foreign Policy of the Soviet Union, 3d edit., 1972; Yugoslavia and the Nonaligned World, 1970. Co-editor: Soviet and American Policies in the United Nations: A Twenty Five Year Perspective, 1971; editor Soviet and Chinese Influence in the Third World, 1975; Red Star on the Nile: The Soviet-Egyptian Influence Relationship Since the June War, 1977; co-editor: Soviet Foreign Policy Toward Western Europe, 1978; book rev. editor Current History, 1959-69, bd. editors, 1968—; mem. editorial bd. Studies in Comparative Communism, 1973—, ORBIS, 1974, Soviet Union, 1974—. Home: The Mermont Apt 503 Bryn Mawr PA 19010

RUBINSTEIN, ARTUR, pianist; b. Lodz, Poland, Jan. 28, 1887; s. Ignace and Felicia (Heyman) R.; student at Warsaw and Berlin Acad. of Music; studied under Joachim, the violinist, Berlin; studied piano with Rozycki and Barth; Hon. degree in music, Northwestern U., 1949; m. Aniela Miynarska, July 27, 1932; children—Eva, Paul, Alina-Anna, John-Arthur. First concert at 6 in Warsaw; debut with Berlin Symphony Orch. at 13; made first U.S. tour, 1906 (debut with Phila. Orch.); tours throughout Europe, S. Am. Australia, South and North Africa, China, Japan, Java, Philippine Islands, and many other parts of the world; among many other records has recorded entire work of Chopin. Decorated comdr. Legion of Honor (France); officer Order of Santiago (Portugal); Cross of Alfonso XII (Spain); comdr. of the Crown and officer Order of Leopold I (Belgium); Polonia Restituta (Poland); comdr. Chilean Republic; U.S. medal of Freedom; comdr. Order Orange Nassau (Holland); recipient gold medal Royal Philharmonic Soc. London; Grammy awards for best classical album, 1976, for best classical performance, 1959, 63, 65, 72, 76, 77, for best chamber music, 1974-76. Mem. French Académie des Beaux-Arts de l'Instut de France, Acad. Music of Brazil (hon.), Accademia Santa Cecilia (Rome) (hon.). Author: (autobiography) Vol. I, My Young Years, 1973, Vol. II, My Happy Years, 1979. Office: ICM Artists Ltd 40 W 57th St New York NY 10019*

RUBINSTEIN, DAVID, medical educator; b. Montreal, Que., Can., Mar. 4, 1929; s. Louis and Anna (Kooperstock) R.; B.S., McGill U., 1949, M.S., 1951, Ph.D., 1953, M.D., 1957; m. Blanche Goldstein, June 28, 1952; children—Larry, Bruce, Rhonda. Intern Jewish Gen. Hosp., Montreal, 1957-58; research fellow Michael Reese Hosp., Chgo., 1958-59; asst. prof. biochemistry McGill U. Med. Sch., Montreal, 1959-63, asst. prof. exptl. medicine, 1959-70, asso. prof. biochemistry, 1966-67, asso. prof. exptl. medicine, 1970-76, prof. biochemistry, 1971-79, prof. medicine, 1976-79; prof. chmn. dept. biochemistry Dalhousie U., Halifax, N.S., Can., 1979—; vis. prof. Hebrew U., Jerusalem, Israel, 1966-67; asso. scientist Royal Victoria Hosp., Montreal, 1968-79. Fellow Council on Arteriosclerosis; Am. Heart Found.; mem. Am. Soc. Biol. Chemists, Can. Biochem. Soc., Can. Soc. Clin. Investigation, Am. Fedn. Clin. Research, McGill Assn. Univ. Tchrs. (past pres.). Research in lipid and blood metabolism. Home: 31 Northcliffe Ln Halifax NS Canada Office: Sir Charles Tupper Bldg Halifax NS Canada

RUBINSTEIN, HYMAN SOLOMON, neurologist, psychiatrist, psychoanalyst; b. Leeds, Eng., Mar. 16, 1904; s. Myer David and Rose (Schneederman) R.; Ph.G., U. Md., 1924, M.D., 1928, B.S., 1932, Ph.D., 1934; student Henry Phipps Psychiat. Clinic, Johns Hopkins, 1932-35, George Washington U., 1935-36, Washington-Balt. Psychoanalytic Inst., 1946-51; diploma Washington Sch. Psychiatry, 1952; certificate in psychoanalysis, William Alanson White Inst., 1958; m. Ellen Steinhorn, July 21, 1929; children—Madelyn Shapiro, Roberta Herts. Intern, Sinai Hosp., Balt., 1927-29, asst. medicine, 1929-30; instr. neuroanatomy and neurology U. Md., 1930-33; asso. neuroanatomy, chief neurol. clinic, 1933-35; dir. lab. neuroendocrine research Sinai Hosp., 1935-45, chief div. psychiatry, 1945-47, psychiat. research, 1945-51; cons. psychiatry USPHS, 1937-42; cons. psychiatrist U.S. Fed. Ct., 1942-50, Jewish Big Brother League; attending physician neurology and psychiatry U.S. Army Hosp., Aberdeen Proving Ground, 1951-54; faculty Washington Sch. Psychiatry, 1952-56; pvt. practice psychiatry and psychoanalysis; mem. staff Sinai Hosp.; supervising psychiatrist Seton Psychiat. Inst., Balt., 1965-73, chmn. vis. staff, 1972-73. Chmn. commn. on law and social action, 1958-61; chmn. commn. on internat. affairs Md. chpt. Am. Jewish Congress, 1961, pres. Md., 1964-69, mem. nat. governing council of congress, 1958-62, 64—; pres. Med. Students Aid Soc., 1959-63; bd. dirs. Hebrew Immigrant Aid Soc., pres., 1969-71; bd. dirs. Asso. Jewish Charities and Welfare Fund, 1969-71; bd. dirs. Histadrut Council of Greater Balt., pres., 1975—. Named Big Brother of Year for Md. by Jewish Big. Bro. League Balt. and Big Bros. Affiliates of Big Bros. Am., U.S. and Can., 1964; recipient Sidney Hollander award Md. chpt. Am. Jewish Congress, 1973, cert. distinction Alumni Assn. Sch. Pharmacy U. Md., 1974, cert. service to mankind Alumni Assn. Sch. Medicine U. Md., 1978; diplomate Am. Bd. Psychiatry and Neurology. Fellow Am. Acad. Psychoanalysis, Am. Psychiat. Assn., AAAS; mem. AMA, William A. White Psychoanalytic Soc., Soc. Med. Psychoanalysts, Am. Physicians Fellowship for Israel Med. Assn. (pres. Md. chpt. 1957-67, mem. nat. exec. com., nat. v.p.), Israel Med. Assn. (hon. corr. mem.), Alumni Assn. Peabody Conservatory Johns Hopkins U., Sigma Xi, Phi Sigma Delta, Phi Lambda Kappa (nat. bd. govs., nat. pres. 1966-67). Jewish (bd. electors Balt. Hebrew congregation 1966-69). Clubs: Music, Torch (exec. com.) (Balt.). Author: (with C. L. Davis) Laboratory Manual of Neuroanatomy, 1937; Stereoscopic Atlas of Neuroanatomy, 1947; The Study of the Brain, 1953; Inter personal Conflict, 1960. Contbr. The Pituitary Gland, 1938; World Book Ency. Editor-in-chief Quar. Phi Lambda Kappa and Med. Students Aid Soc., 1964-66. Cons. psychiatry Current Med. Digest, 1960-75. Address: 3900 N Charles St Baltimore MD 21218

RUBINSTEIN, JOHN ARTHUR, actor, composer; b. Los Angeles, Dec. 8, 1946; s. Arthur and Aniela (Mlynarski) R.; student U. Calif. at Los Angeles, 1964-67, Julliard Sch. Music, 1973-74; m. Judi West, Dec. 15, 1971; children—Jessica, Michael. Appeared in numerous TV shows, including The Virginian, 1965, CBS Repertory Workshop, 1965, Dragnet, 1965, Ironside, 1965, The Bold Ones, 1969, Storefront Lawyers, 1971, The Young Lawyers, 1971, Nichols, 1971, Mod Squad, 1971, The Psychiatrist, 1969, Mary Tyler Moore Show, 1971, Matt Lincoln, 1971, Cannon, 1972, Hawaii Five-O, 1972, 77, Broadway, My Street, 1974, Barnaby Jones, 1975, 76, Harry O, 1975, The Quest, 1976, Stop the Presses, 1976, Lou Grant Show, 1977, Class of '65, 1977, Wonder Women, 1977; regular Family, 1975-78; appeared in TV movies A Howling in the Woods, 1971, Something Evil, 1972, The Streets of San Francisco (pilot), 1972, God Bless the Children, 1969, All Together Now, 1975, Happily Ever After, 1978, Roots: The Next Generations, 1979, The Gift of the Magi, 1978, A Celebration of the Performing Arts, 1978; star Corey for the People (pilot), 1977; appeared in motion pictures Journey to Shiloh, 1965, The Trouble With Girls, 1969, Getting Straight, 1969, Zachariah, 1971, The Car, 1977, The Boys from Brazil, 1978; stage show appearances include Camelot, 1965-67, South Pacific, 1966, On A Clear Day You Can See Forever, 1968, Mark Taper Forum New Theater for Now, 196B, Metamorphoses, Los Angeles, 1971, on Broadway, Pippin (Theater World award 1972-73); with Los Angeles Philharmonic, L'Histoire du Soldat, 1977; Candida, Boston, 1977, Streamers, Los Angeles-San Francisco, 1978, The Tempest, Los Angeles, 1978. Recipient BMI Varsity Show award (with David Colloff), 1967. Mem. AFTRA, Actors Equity, ASCAP, Screen Actors' Guild, Composers and Lyricists Guild Am. Composer film scores Paddy, 1969; (with Tim McIntire) Jeremiah Johnson, 1972, Kid Blue, 1973; The Candidate, 1972, The Killer Inside Me, 1976; TV show The New Land, 1974, TV movie All Together Now, 1975, TV movie Stalk the Wild Child, 1976, series theme Family, 1976, an episode Harry O, 1976, Emily, Emily (Hallmark Hall of Fame), 1977, The Fitzpatricks series, 1977, The New Maverick, 1978, Wonderland Cove series, 1979, Champions: A Love Story, 1979, Get Patty Hearst, 1979; keyboard player and composer for group Funzone (made record album for First Artists/Mercury Records 1977). Home: 10420 Scenario Ln Los Angeles CA 90024

RUBINSTEIN, LUCIEN JULES, pathologist, educator; b. Antwerp, Belgium, Oct. 15, 1924; s. Emile and Diane (Silberfeld) R.; L.R.C.P., M.R.C.S., M.B., B.S., U. London (Eng.), 1948, M.D., 1952; m. Dorothea Elizabeth Lunzer, 1950; children—Marion Harriet, Edmund John, Francis Marcel; m. 2d, Mary Margaret Herman, 1969. House surgeon, house physician, casualty officer London Hosp., 1948-49, pathology asst., demonstrator chem. pathology, 1949-52, lectr., sr. lectr. morbid anatomy Med. Coll., 1954-61; vis. asst. prof. neuropathology U. Minn., 1959-60; vis. scientist NIH, 1960; attending neuropathologist Montefiore Hosp., N.Y.C., 1961-64; asso. prof. neuropathology Columbia, 1961-64; prof. pathology and neuropathology Stanford Sch. Medicine, 1964—; cons. lab. service VA Hosp., Palo Alto; adviser WHO, Geneva; adv. cons. Nat. Inst. Neurol. Diseases and Stroke, NIH, Bethesda, Md. Served with M.C., Brit. Army, 1952-54. Recipient T.A.M. Ross prize in clin. medicine and pathology London Hosp., 1948. Mem. Am. Assn. Neuropathologists (pres. 1970-71, council mem. 1966-74), Internat. Acad. Pathology, Coll. Pathologists, Mexican Assn. Pathologists (hon.), Soc. Neuroscis., World Fedn. Neurology. Author: (with D.S. Russell) Pathology of Tumors of the Nervous System, 1959; Tumors of the Central Nervous System, 1972. Mem. editorial adv. bd. Acta Neuropathologica, Cancer, Jour. Neuropathology and Exptl. Neurology, Child's Brain, Virchow's Archiv Path. Histology. Contbr. articles to profl. jours. Home: 807 Allardice Way Stanford CA 94305 Office: Stanford Sch Medicine Stanford CA 94305

RUBINSTEIN, MOSHE FAJWEL, educator; b. Miechow, Poland, Aug. 13, 1930; s. Shlomo and Sarah (Rosen) Rubinstein; came to U.S. 1950, naturalized, 1965; B.S., U. Calif. at Los Angeles, 1954, M.S., 1957, Ph.D., 1961; m. Zafrira Gorstein, Feb. 3, 1953; children—Iris, Dorit. Designer, Murray Erick Assos., engrs. and architects, Los Angeles, 1954-56; structural designer Victor Gruen Assos., Los Angeles, 1956-61; asst. prof. U. Calif. at Los Angeles, 1961-64, asso. prof. dept. engring., 1964-69, prof., 1969—, chmn. engring. systems dept., 1970-75, program dir. modern engring. for execs. program, 1965-70; cons. Pacific Power & Light Co., Portland, Oreg., Northrop Corp., U.S. Army, NASA Research Center, Langley, Tex. Instruments Co., Hughes Space System Div., U.S. Army Sci. Adv. Com., Kaiser Aluminum and Chem. Corp., IBM. Recipient Distinguished Teaching award Acad. Senate, U. Calif. at Los Angeles, 1964; Western Electric Fund award Am. Soc. Engring. Edn., 1965; Distinguished Tchr. trophy Engring. Student Soc. U. Calif. at Los Angeles, 1966; Sussmann Chair for Distinguished Visitor, Technion Israel Inst. Tech., 1967-68; Fulbright-Hays fellow, Yugoslovia and Eng., 1975-76. Named Outstanding Faculty Mem., UCLA Engring. Alumni award, 1979. Mem. ASCE, Am. Soc. Engring. Edn., Seismol. Soc. Am., Sigma Xi, Tau Beta Phi. Author: (with W.C. Hurty) Dynamics of Structures, 1964 (Yugoslavian trans. 1973); Matrix Computer Analysis of Structures, 1966 (Japanese transl. 1974); Structural Systems, Statics Dynamics and Stability, 1970; Patterns of Problem Solving, 1975; (with K. Pfeiffer) Concepts in Problem Solving, 1979; research in use of computers in structural systems, analysis and synthesis; problem solving and decision theory. Home: 10488 Charing Cross Rd West Los Angeles CA 90024 Office: Engring Systems Dept Sch Engring and Applied Sci U Calif Los Angeles CA 90024

RUBLOFF, ARTHUR, real estate developer; b. Duluth, Minn.; s. Solomon W. and Mary Rubloff; m. Josephine Sheehan (dec.). Engaged in real estate devel.; chmn. bd. Rubloff Devel. Corp., Chgo., North Kansas City Devel. Co. (Mo.); pioneer, creator North Mich. Ave-Magnificent Mile, Ft. Dearborn, Old North Town; developer Evergreen Park Shopping Plaza, Chgo., Carl Sandberg Village, Chgo.; Bay Shore Properties, San Francisco; creator, developer Southland, Sun Valley, East Ridge, San Francisco; former cons. World Trade Center. Mem. sr. council All Chgo. Citizens' Com.; nat. chmn., dir. Horatio Alger Awards Com., N.Y.C.; mem. citizens bd. U. Chgo.; trustee Goodwill Industries, Roosevelt U., Chgo., Hull House, Chgo.; bd. govs., chmn. H.A.P. Found., Chgo. Heart Assn.; bd. dirs., v.p. Chgo. Boys Clubs; bd. dirs. Lyric Opera, Chgo.; mem. Pres.'s council Lincoln Park Zool. Soc., Chgo.; trustee, mem. found., dir. Jr. Achievement Chgo., trust asso. Chgo. Community Trust; bd. dirs., v.p. Hundred Club of Cook County; dir. citizens bd. Loyola U., Chgo.; mem. bus. adv. council Chgo. Urban League; vice chmn. library council Northwestern U.; life mem. Art Inst. Chgo.; cons. Chgo. council Girl Scouts U.S.A.; past bd. dirs. Jewish Fedn. Met. Chgo.; dir., nat. co-chmn. United Cerebral Palsy Assn., N.Y.C.; chmn., dir. United Cerebral Palsy Greater Chgo.; dir. Chgo. Mayor's Commn. for Sr. Citizens; mem. Inst. Religion and Health, N.Y.C., Lawson YMCA, Chgo., Bergstrom Mus., Neenah, Wis.; mem. Chgo. exec. com. Anti-Defamation League of B'nai B'rith; mem. Chgo. Mayor's Com. Econ. and Cultural Devel.; mem. adv. council Ill. 2000; dir. exec. com. Sr. Centers Met. Chgo.; chmn. sr. citizens services Dept. Human Resources; bd. dirs. Civic Fedns., Rehab. Inst. Chgo., Beverly Art Center, State St. Council; mem. Chgo. Com. Urban Opportunity, Internat. Human Assistance Programs, Inc.; co-chmn. nat. bd. dirs. NCCJ, also co-chmn., Chgo. Decorated Stella Della Solidarieta Italiana award, recipient 1956, 58; award Am. Planning and Civic Assn., 1954, ann. Horatio Alger award Am. Schs. and Colls. Assn., 1955, award North Side Civic Com. Chgo., 1955, award of merit VFW, 1961, Good Am. award Chgo. Com. 100, 1962, Man of Yr. award Cath. War Vets., 1963, Outstanding Civic Leader Chgo., Little Flower Sem. Soc., 1969, Chicagoan of Year award Chgo. Boys Clubs, 1971, Internat. Humanitarian award B'nai B'rith, 1975; named to Hall of Fame, B'nai B'rith Women's Council, 1966. Mem. Internat. Real Estate Fedn. Chgo. Bd. Chgo. Assn. Commerce and Industry (sr. council, policy com.), Nat. Assn. Housing and Redevel. Ofcls., Chgo. Real Estate Bd., NAREB, Nat. Realty Com. (membership com.), Greater North Michigan Ave. Assn. (founder, past pres., dir.), Am. Soc. Real Estate Counselors, U.S. C. of C., French C. of C. of U.S. (asso.), Lambda Alpha. Clubs: Harmonie, Hemisphere, El Morocco, Doubles, Raffles (N.Y.C.); Standard, Executives, Oil Men's (hon.), Monroe, The Arts, Mid-Day, Economics, Mid-America, Plaza, Metropolitan, International, Poinciana (Palm Beach, Fla.); Racquet (Chgo.); (Palm Springs, Calif.); Variety (gov. tent 26, King of Hearts award 1973). Office: 69 W Washington St Chicago IL 60602 also 781 Fifth Ave New York NY 10022

RUBOTTOM, ROY RICHARD, JR., educator; b. Brownwood, Tex., Feb. 13, 1912; s. Roy Richard and Jennie Eleanor (Watkins) R.; B.S., So. Meth. U., 1932, M.A., 1933; postgrad. U. Tex.; LL.D., Southwestern Coll., Winfield, Kans., 1968; m. Billy Ruth Young, Dec. 23, 1938; children—Eleanor Ann (Mrs. Allen Odden), Frank, John. Traveling sec. Lambda Chi Alpha frat., 1933-35; bus. experience, 1935-37; asst. dean of student life U. Tex., 1937-41; v.p. State Nat. Bank, Corsicana, Tex., 1946-47; apptd. fgn. service officer, 1947; sec. of embassy and consul, Bogota, Colombia, 1947-49; officer-in-charge Mexican affairs State Dept., 1950; dep. dir. Middle Am. Affairs, 1951, dir., 1952-53; 1st sec. embassy, Madrid, 1953, counselor of embassy, 1954; dir. U.S. Ops. Mission, Madrid, 1954-56; asst. sec. of state for inter-Am. affairs, 1957-60; U.S. ambassador to Argentina, 1960-62; State Dept. adviser Naval War Coll., Newport, R.I., 1962-64; v.p. So. Meth. U., Dallas, 1964-71, also prof. govt., scholar-in-residence, 1975—, dir. Center of Ibero-Am. Civilization, 1975-77; pres. U. Americas, Puebla, Mex., 1971-73. Active Scouting U.S.A. Served with USNR, 1941-46. Recipient Silver Beaver award Boy Scouts Am., 1976. Mem. Sigma Delta Chi, Lambda Chi Alpha, Pi Sigma Alpha. Methodist. Rotarian. Home: 3429 University Blvd Dallas TX 75205

RUBRIGHT, ROYAL CUSHING, lawyer; b. Denver, Nov. 27, 1909; s. John Compton and Marie (Popovich) R.; B.A., LL.B., U. Colo., 1932, LL.M., 1933; m. Gwennell Morgan, Sept. 8, 1934; 1 child, Lynnell. Admitted to Colo. bar, 1933; since practiced Denver; asso., partner Fairfield & Woods, Denver, 1940—; part-time instr. law U. Denver; spl. lectr. law U. Colo. Fellow Am. Coll. Probate Counsel; mem. Am., Colo., Denver (pres., award of merit) bar assns., Pi Kappa Alpha. Mason. Clubs: Denver Law, 26, City, Rotary, Executives (Denver). Home: 765 Monaco Pkwy Denver CO 80220 Office: 1600 Colo Nat Bldg Denver CO 80202

RUBY, RUSSELL (GLENN), lawyer; b. Albany, Mo., Nov. 19, 1911; s. Gordon Romeo and Minnie (Hazelrigg) R.; student Palmer Coll., 1929-31; B.J., U. Mo., 1933; LL.B., Tulsa U., 1939; m. Elizabeth Bradford Popkin, Feb. 11, 1939 (dec. Aug. 1967); children—Michael Gordon, Adrienne Elizabeth, Glenn Russell; m. 2d, Dorothea King, 1972. Admitted to Okla. bar, 1939; practice in Muskogee, 1940—; spl. agt. FBI, 1942-47. Mem. Okla. Ho. of Reps., 1955-66; mem. Muskogee City Council, 1968-72, 76—, vice mayor, 1968-72, dep. mayor, 1976—; chmn. Muskogee City-County Port Authority, 1974-76; mem. Muskogee Met. Planning Commn., 1968-72, 76—, chmn., 1978-79; bd. dirs. Muskogee Community Concert Assn., Kate Frank Manor, Family Guidance Center. Mem. Am., Okla., Muskogee bar assns., Assn. Fed. Attys. (past pres.), Soc. Former Agts. FBI, S.A.R. Democrat. Episcopalian. Mason (Shriner, Jester). Home: 4500 Girard St Muskogee OK 74401 Office: Commercial Bank Bldg Muskogee OK 74401

RUCCI, EUSTINE PAUL, naval officer, physician; b. Waukesha, Wis., Feb. 4, 1929; s. Samuel J. and Rose M. R.; M.D., Marquette U., 1954; student Naval Sch. Aviation Medicine, 1955; m. Elena Sawyer, June 12, 1954; children—Peter, Robert, Thomas, John. Commd. lt. (jg.), M.C., U.S. Navy, 1954, advanced through grades to rear adm., 1977; intern Naval Hosp., Gt. Lakes, Ill., 1954-55, resident, 1957-60; served in Malta, 1956-57, Morocco, 1963-66; staff obstetrician-gynecologist Naval Hosp., Camp Pendleton, Calif., 1960-63; head assignments and distbn. Bur. Medicine and Surgery, Navy Dept., 1966-68; served on U.S.S. Hancock, 1968-69; asst. chief Ob-Gyn dept. Nat. Naval Med. Center, Bethesda, Md., 1969-70; chief Ob-Gyn service, exec. officer Naval Regional Med. Center, Camp Pendleton, 1970-74; comdg. officer Naval Regional Med. Center, Long Beach, 1974-77; med. tng. and readiness officer, fleet surgeon to staff Comdr.-in-Chief U.S. Atlantic Fleet, Norfolk, Va., 1977-79; asst. chief bur. medicine and surgery Dept. Navy, Washington, 1979—; mem. clin. and adminstrv. medicine staff for grad. med. edn. U.S. Navy. Bd. dirs. Long Beach chpt. ARC, 1974-77; youth counselor YMCA, Oceanside, Calif., 1960-63; coach Little League Baseball, Camp Pendleton, 1970-73; instl. rep. Long Beach council Boy Scouts Am., 1974-79. Decorated Legion of Merit; recipient cert. appreciation Internat. Coll. Surgeons, 1977, commendation Los Angeles County, 1975, award of appreciation City of Long Beach, 1977. Diplomate Am. Bd. Ob-Gyn. Fellow Am. Coll. Obstetricians and Gynecologists; mem. AMA (Physician's Recognition award 1976), Fleet Res. Assn. (hon.), Assn. Mil. Surgeons U.S., Soc. U.S. Navy Flight Surgeons, Nat. Council Alcoholism. Republican. Roman Catholic. Clubs: Army-Navy Country, Va. Country, Long Beach Yacht, Rotary, UNICO.

RUCCIUS, FREDERICK EDWARD, JR., banker; b. Wyndmoor, Pa., Feb. 29, 1928; s. Frederick Edward and Dorothy Mae (Maust) R.; student Muhlenberg Coll., 1945-46, U. Pa., eves. 1950-56; grad. Stonier Grad. Sch. Banking, Rutgers U., 1962; m. Ruth Louise Lowe, Aug. 13, 1949; children—Frederick Edward III, William L., Ann L., Karen L. Vice pres. Continental Bank, Norristown, Pa., 1948-68; sr. v.p. Bank of Pa., Reading, 1968-74, pres., 1974-78, chmn. bd., chief exec. officer, dir., 1978—; chmn. bd., dir. B-O-P Corp., B-O-P Realty Co. Bd. dirs., vice chmn. Campfire Girls; v.p. United Way Berks County, bd. dirs. Community Gen. Hosp., Greater Berks Devel. Fund, Reading Center City Devel. Fund, Berks County Capital Campaign Rev. Bd.; trustee Reading Mus. Found., Muhlenberg Coll. Bd. Assos.; pres. council Albright Coll. Mem. Reading-Berks C. of C. (pres.), Pa. Bankers Assn. Republican. Lutheran. Clubs: Wyomissing, Iris, Berkshire. Home: 1006 Reading Blvd Wyomissing PA 19610 Office: Bank of Pennsylvania 50 N 5th St Reading PA 19603

RUCKELSHAUS, WILLIAM DOYLE, lawyer, former govt. ofcl.; b. Indpls., July 24, 1932; s. John K. and Marion (Doyle) R.; B.A. cum laude, Princeton, 1957; LL.B., Harvard, 1960; m. Jill Elizabeth Strickland, May 12, 1962; children—Catherine Kiley, Mary Hughes, Jennifer Lea, William Justice, Robin Elizabeth. Admitted to Ind. bar, 1960; atty. firm Ruckelshaus, Bobbitt & O'Connor, Indpls., 1960-68; dep. atty.-gen. Ind., 1960-65; chief counsel office atty.-gen. Ind., 1963-65; minority atty. for Ind. Senate, 1965-67; mem. Ind. Ho. of Reps., 1967-69, maj. leader, 1967-69; asst. atty.-gen. charge civil div. Dept. of Justice, 1969-70; adminstr. EPA, Washington, 1970-73; acting dir. FBI, 1973; dep. atty. gen. U.S., 1973; mem. firm Ruckelshaus, Beveridge, Fairbanks and Diamond, Washington, 1973-75; sr. v.p. Weyerhaeuser Co., Tacoma, 1975—; chmn. Geothermal Kinetics, Inc.; dir. Cummins Engine Co., Inc., Peabody Internat. Corp., Twentieth Century Fund, Nordstrom, Inc. Chmn. bd. Urban Inst.; nominated by Rep. Party for U.S. Senate, Ind., 1968; bd. dirs. Conservation Found. Trustee Pacific Sci. Center Found.; bd. dirs. Am. Paper Inst., Seattle Art Mus.; mem. pub. interest adv. com. med. project Harvard U., also bd. overseers J.F. Kennedy Sch. Govt.; bd. regents Seattle U.; mem. vis. com. Grad. Sch. Pub. Affairs, U. Wash. Served with AUS, 1953-55. Named Outstanding Rep. Legislator, Ind. Ho. of Reps., Working Press, 1967; Outstanding 1st Year Legislator in Ind. Ho. of Reps., Ind. Broadcasters Assn.; Man of Year, Indpls. Jr. C. of C., 1967. Mem. Fed., Am., Ind., D.C., Indpls. bar assns. Clubs: Columbia (Indpls.); Federal City (Washington); Congl. (Md.). Author: Reapportionment—A Continuing Problem, 1963. Home: 1015 Evergreen Pt Rd Medina WA 98039 Office: Weyerhaeuser Co Tacoma WA 98401

RUCKER, RONALD EUGENE, librarian; b. Whittier, Calif., May 25, 1938; s. Eugene Richard and Thelma Inez (Fetterman) R.; A.B., Pomona Coll., 1960; A.M., Harvard, 1963; M.L.S., U. Calif., Berkeley, 1964; m. Nancy Turtle, Aug. 10, 1963; children—Christopher, Steven. Asst. serials librarian Cornell U., Ithaca, N.Y., 1964-66, acting head serials record dept., 1966-67, undergraduate librarian, 1967-76; coll. librarian Middlebury (Vt.) Coll., 1976—; dir. Nelinet, Inc. Mem. Am., Vt. library assns. Democrat. Congregationalist. Home: RD 3 South Munger St Middlebury VT 05753 Office: Middlebury Coll Middlebury VT 05753

RUCKER, TINSLEY WHITE, III, cons.; b. Warrenton, Ga., Dec. 26, 1909; s. Tinsley White Jr. and Elon (Cason) R.; grad. Episcopal Acad., 1927; B.S., Mass. Inst. Tech., 1931; m. Lorol Bowron Rediker, Apr. 7, 1966; stepchildren—John Michael, Diana (Mrs. Slaughter); 1 dau. by previous marriage, Barbara (Mrs. Seaton). Prodn. mgr. G.W. Smith Woodworking Co., 1931-34; engr. Factory Ins. Assn., 1934-37, plant mgr. Mengel Co., 1937-41; v.p. Gen. Plywood Corp., 1941-49; pres., dir. Dixon-Powdermaker Furniture Co., Jacksonville, 1949-79; dir. Rucker Industries, 1966—; cons. Dir., past pres. Asso. Industries Fla. Mem. NAM (past dir.), Nat. Assn. Furniture Mfrs. (dir., past pres.), Jacksonville C. of C. (past v.p.), S.A.R., S.C.V., Sons of Colonial Wars, Sigma Nu. Episcopalian (past sr. warden). Clubs: River, Timuquana Country (Jacksonville); Mountain Brook (Birmingham); Masons, Shriners. Home and office: Beau Rivage 2970 St John's Ave Apt 8E Jacksonville FL 32205

RUCKER, WINFRED RAY, coll. dean; b. Stamford, Tex., Apr. 13, 1920; s. John Lewis and Lou Jeanne (Rae) R.; B.A., Tex. Christian U., 1946, M.A., 1947; Ed. D., Harvard, 1952; m. Norma Ruth Johnston, Jan. 31, 1947. Instr., Tex. Christian U., 1947-49; grad. asst. Harvard, 1949-50; supervising tchr. Genesco (N.Y.) schs., 1950-52; asso. prof. edn. E. Tex. State Coll., Commerce, 1952-56; dir. elementary edn. U. Ariz., 1956-58; dean Nat. Coll. Edn., Evanston, Ill., 1958-61; dean Sch. Edn., E. Tex. State U., 1961-67; dean Grad. Sch. Leadership and Human Behavior, U.S. Internat. U., San Diego, 1967—; curriculum cons. to schools in N.Y., Tex., Ariz., Ill. Mem. Calif. Tchrs. Assn., NEA, Phi Delta Kappa. Author: Curriculum Development in the Elementary School, 1960; co-author Human Values Series of Readers, 1967; Human Values in Education; Personality in Social Process; Value Sharing; Human Values and Natural Science; also articles. Editor: Young People's Science Ency., 1962. Home: 17863 Mirasol Dr San Diego CA 92128

RUCKNAGEL, DONALD LOUIS, physician, educator; b. St. Louis, May 30, 1928; s. Louis H. and Alma M. (Hayden) R.; A.B., Washington U., St. Louis, 1950, M.D., 1954; Ph.D., U. Mich., 1964; m. Lena M. Williams, June 25, 1955; children—Diane Kathleen, Eric Paul. Intern, asst. resident Duke U. Sch. Medicine, 1954-56; hematology fellow dept. medicine U. Pitts., 1956-57; asst. prof. dept. human genetics U. Mich., Ann Arbor, 1964-67, asso. prof., 1967-70, prof., 1970—; vis. lectr. Siriraj Hosp., Bangkok, Thailand, 1966-67; vis. prof. Howard U., Washington, 1973-74; mem. adv. com., sickle cell br. Nat. Heart and Lung Inst. Mem. Ann Arbor City Human Rights Commn., 1971-73, Interfaith Council for Peace, 1967—; mem. med. adv. com. Planned Parenthood of Washtenaw County, 1965-73. Served with NIH, USPHS, 1957-59. Recipient Career Devel. award USPHS, 1959-69, Med. Achievement award SCLC, 1972. Mem. Internat., Am. socs. hematology, Am. Fedn. Clin. Research, Am. Eugenics Soc., Am. Soc. Human Genetics, Sigma Xi, Nu Sigma Nu, Alpha Chi Sigma. Home: 1141 Clair Circle Ann Arbor MI 48103

RUCKS, JOSEPH GIBSON, lawyer; b. Guthrie, Okla., Jan. 7, 1913; s. William Ward and Martha (Gibson) R.; A.B., U. Okla., 1934, LL.B., 1936; m. Mary E. Durand, Mar. 27, 1937; children—Martha Victoria, Charles Durand. Admitted to Okla. bar, 1936, since practiced in Oklahoma City; mem. firm Fowler, Rucks, Baker, Jopling, Gramlich & Mee, 1952-71; mem. firm McAfee, Taft, Mark, Bond, Rucks & Woodruff, 1971—. Pres. Areawide Health Planning Orgn. of Central Okla., 1971-74; mem. Oklahoma City Appeals Rev. Bd., 1965-75; mem., treas. Community Council, 1975-77, v.p., 1978—. Bd. dirs. Okla. State Fair. Chmn. Gov.'s Adv. Council on Capital Expenditures, 1967; mem. town council Nichols Hills, Okla., 1962-65, mayor 1964-65. Served to lt. col. AUS, World War II; ETO. Decorated Bronze Star; Criox de Guerre (France). Fellow Am. Bar Found.; mem. Am., Okla. (bd. govs. 1965-67), Okla. County (pres. 1955, dir. 1977—) bar assns., Okla. Heart Assn. (pres. 1959), Oklahoma City C. of C. (bd. dirs.), Phi Gamma Delta, Phi Delta Phi. Rotarian. Presbyterian (elder). Home: 6705 Avondale Dr Oklahoma City OK 73116 Office: 5th Floor 100 Park Ave Bldg Oklahoma City OK 73102

RUDA, EDWIN, artist; b. N.Y.C., May 15, 1922; M.A., Columbia U., 1949; student Sch. Painting and Sculpture, Mexico City, Mexico, 1949-51; M.F.A., U. Ill., 1956. Exhibited in one-man shows at Globe, Park Pl., Paul Cooper Galleries, all N.Y.C.; exhibited in group shows at Smithsonian Traveling Exhbn., Latin Am., 1966, Systemic Painting Guggenheim Museum, N.Y.C., 1966, Painting Ann. Whitney Mus. Am. Art, N.Y.C., 1969, Two Generations of Color Painting Inst. Contemporary Art, Phila., 1970, Gallery A, Sydney, Australia, 1971; works in pub. collections: State of N.Y. Collection, Albany Mall, Indpls. Mus. Art, Dallas Mus. Fine Art, Allentown (Pa.) Art Mus.; instr. painting U. Tex. at Austin, 1956-59, Sch. Visual Arts, N.Y., 1967-71. Contbr. articles to Art Mag., 1967, Artforum, April, 1968. Co-founder Park Pl. Gallery Art Research. Address: 44 Walker St New York City NY 10013*

RUDD, DALE FREDERICK, chem. engr.; b. Mpls., Mar. 2, 1935; s. Henry G. and Emmy E. (Grip) R.; Ph.D., U. Minn., 1959; m. Sandra Coryell, Aug. 1, 1964; children—Karen, David. Prof. chem. engring. U. Wis., Madison, 1961—; pres. Shanahan Valley Assos., 1979—; cons. Exxon Chem. Co. Am. Soc. Engring. Edn. lectr.; Guggenheim fellow, 1971-72. Mem. Am. Inst. Chem. Engring. (Colburn award 1972), Nat. Acad. Engring. Author: (with Watson) Strategy of Process Engineering, 1968; (with Powers and Siirola) Process Synthesis, 1973; (with Berthouex) Strategy of Pollution Control, 1977. Office: Dept Chem Engring U Wis Madison WI 53706

RUDD, ELDON, congressman; b. Camp Verde, Ariz., July 15, 1920; B.A. in Edn., Ariz. State U., 1947; J.D., U. Ariz., 1949; m. Ann Merritt, 1944; children—Carolyn, Katherine. Admitted to Ariz. bar, 1949, U.S. Supreme Ct., 1953; practice law, Tucson, 1949-50; spl. agt. FBI, 1950-70; mem. Maricopa County (Ariz.) Bd. Suprs., 1972-76; bd. dirs. Ariz.-Mex. Commn., 1972-76; mem. Gov. Ariz. Adv. Commn. Intergovtl. Affairs, 1975-76; mem. 95th Congress, 4th Dist. Ariz. Mem. Scottsdale Sister City Commn., 1973-76. Served as aviator USMCR, 1942-46. Mem. Fed. (past chpt. pres.), Ariz., Maricopa County, Scottsdale bar assns. Republican. Roman Catholic. Address: 1110 Longworth Bldg Washington DC 20515 also 6900 E Camelback Rd Suite 303 Phoenix AZ 85025

RUDD, HUGHES DAY, journalist; b. Wichita, Kans., Sept. 14, 1921; s. Hughes Day and Gladys (Burdett) R.; student U. Mo., 1938-40, U. Minn., 1951-52, Stanford, 1952-55; m. Anna Grenwood, Apr. 10, 1956. With Kansas City (Mo.) Star, 1946-50, Mpls. Tribune, 1950-51; mem. staff CBS News, 1959-79, bur. chief, Moscow, USSR, 1965-66, Central Europe, Bonn, W. Germany, 1966-74, anchorman Morning News, 1974-79; with ABC News, N.Y.C., 1979—. Served with F.A., AUS, 1941-45; ETO. Decorated Silver Star, Purple Heart, Air medal with 6 clusters. Mem. Sigma Alpha Epsilon. Author: My Escape From the CIA and Other Improbable Events, 1966; also numerous articles, stories. Address: care ABC News 1330 Ave of the Americas New York NY 10019

RUDD, PAUL RYAN, actor; b. Boston, May 15, 1940; s. Frank Stanley and Katherine Frances (Ryan) R.; A.B., Fairfield U., 1962; m. Joan Patricia Mannion, Sept. 5, 1965. Stage debut, 1968; appeared with repertory theatres N.Y. Shakespeare Festival, Lincoln Center Repertory, Hartford Stage, Arena Stage, Longwarf Theatre, San Diego Shakespeare Festival, 1968-73; Broadway debut in The Changing Room, 1973; appeared in The National Health, 1974, Ah! Wilderness, 1975, gentleman caller in Glass Menagerie, 1976, Billy Wilson in Streamers, 1976, Henry V in Henry V, 1976, Romeo in Romeo and Juliet, 1977, Charly in Flowers for Algernon, 1978; Scooper in Bosoms and Neglect, 1978; off Broadway appearances include Boys In The Band, 1970, Oliver in DA, 1978; TV debut as Brian Mallory in CBS-TV's Beacon Hill, 1975, followed by John F. Kennedy in NBC-TV's Johnny We Hardly Knew Ye, 1976, Dennisin PBS' End of Summer, 1977, Yankee in BBC/PBS' A Connecticut Yankee in King Arthurs Court, 1978; film debut as Loren Hardeman, Jr. in The Betsy, 1978. Recipient Outer Critics Circle award, 1975-76, Man of Year award Fairfield U., 1977. Mem. Actors Equity Assn., Screen Actors Guild, AFTRA. Home: 145 W 55th St New York NY 10019

RUDD, ROBERT WILLIAM, educator; b. Madisonville, Ky., Nov. 21, 1919; s. Virgil K. and Ethel (Eastwood) R.; student Ohio State U., 1935-36; B.S., U. Ky., 1939; M.S., Iowa State U., 1941; Ph.D., U. Calif., Berkeley, 1952; m. Betty MacGregor, Nov. 24, 1945 (dec.); children—Robert William, Sally MacGregor, Susan Eastwood; m. 2d, Martha Robertson Cheek, Feb. 11, 1971. Asst. prof. to prof. agrl. econs. U. Ky., Lexington, 1948-57, acad. asst. to pres., 1963-64, acting dean Coll. Commerce, 1964-65, prof., chmn. dept. agrl. econs., 1967—; mem. faculty Grad. Sch. Banking, U. Wis., 1963-68; cons. TVA, 1964, 68-69, Nat. Adv. Commn. on Food and Fiber, 1966-67; mem. adv. bd. Aerospace Research Applications Center, Ind. U., 1964-67. Co-chmn. United Community Fund Drive U. Ky., 1967-69; mem. Gov.'s Efficiency Task Force, 1968. Trustee U. Ky., 1968-71. Served from 2d lt. to capt., inf., AUS, 1942-46. Decorated Bronze Star medal, Combat Infantryman's badge. Mem. Am. (editorial council 1958-60), So. (pres. 1968-69) agrl. econs. assns., Assn. So. Agrl. Workers (dir. 1968-70). Home: 663 Tateswood Dr Lexington KY 40502

RUDDICK, J. PERRY, investment banker; b. Montclair, N.J., Mar. 28, 1936; s. Girard Bliss Ruddick and Marcia (Perry) Ruddick Cook; A.B., Princeton U., 1958; M.B.A., Harvard U., 1961; m. Susan Henretty, July 21, 1961; children—Julia A., Pamela M., Girard Bliss. Mgmt. trainee, mem. corporate fin. dept. Smith, Barney & Co., N.Y.C., 1961-63, mem. corporate fin. dept., 1964-65, 2d v.p. investment banking, 1966-67, v.p., dir. investment banking, 1968-69, mgr. corporate fin. dept., 1970-71, sr. v.p., dir., mgr. corporate fin. dept., 1972-73, sr. v.p., dir., mgr. prin. trading and syndicate depts., 1973-76; sr. v.p., dir., mgr. prin. trading and syndicate dept. Smith Barney, Harris Upham & Co., N.Y.C., 1976-77, exec. v.p., sr. adminstrv. officer, 1977—. Mem. Nat. Assn. Securities Dealers, Securities Industry Assn. (past gov.). Clubs: Bond, Econ., Univ. (N.Y.C.); Montclair Golf, Midland Country, Sankaty Head Golf, Siasconset Casino Assn. Office: Smith Barney Harris Upham & Co Inc 1345 Ave of Americas New York NY 10019*

RUDDLE, FRANCIS HUGH, geneticist; b. West New York, N.Y., Aug. 19, 1929; s. Thomas Hugh and Mary Henley (Rodda) R.; B.A., Wayne State U., Detroit, 1953, M.S., 1956; Ph.D., U. Calif., Berkeley, 1960; m. Nancy Marion Hartman, Aug. 1, 1964; children—Kathlyn Gabrielle, Amy Elizabeth. Asst. prof. Yale U., New Haven, 1961-67, asso. prof., 1967-72, prof. biology and human genetics, 1972—, chmn. dept. biology, 1977—; adv. com. Am. Type Culture Collection, 1963-71; planning com. 1st Internat. Congress on Cell Biology, 1975; mem. cell study sect. NIH, 1965-70, chmn. mutant cell lines com., 1972-77. Served with USAAF, 1946-49. NIH postdoctoral fellow U. Glasgow (Scotland), 1960-61. Mem. Nat. Acad. Scis., Am. Acad. Arts and Scis., Conn. Acad. Sci. and Engring., Harvey Soc., Soc. Devel. Biology (pres. 1971-72, trustee 1970-73), AAAS, Am. Soc. Cell Biology, Am. Soc. Human Genetics (dir. 1972-75), Am. Soc. Naturalists, Am. Soc. Zoologists, Genetics Soc. Am., Am. Soc. Biochemistry, Pattern Recognition Soc., Tissue Culture Assn. (dir.), Am. Cancer Soc., Sigma Xi. Editorial bd. Exptl. Cell Research, 1975—, Genetics, 1973—, In Vitro, 1970—, Somatic Cell Genetics, 1975—, Am. Jour. Cell Biology, Biochemistry. Office: Kline Biology Tower Yale U New Haven CT 06520*

RUDDLEY, JOHN, educator; b. N.Y.C., Oct. 29, 1912; s. Anton and Katherine (Glusk) R.; student N.Y. U., 1939, Cooper Union, 1941; B.S., M.A., Columbia, 1954; m. Stella Elizabeth Subisky, Jan. 1, 1938. Architect, exec. radio sta. WOR, also sta. WOR-TV, N.Y.C., 1941-59; adminstr., art therapist Fountain House, N.Y.C., 1959-62; dean Corcoran Sch. Art, Washington, also mem. faculty George Washington U., 1962-65; art edn. cons. Columbia City, Balt., Bklyn. Mus. Art; dir. Westchester Art Workshop, 1965—; also Westchester County supr. art; faculty Pace U., Westchester, Pleasantville, N.Y.; cons. St. Mary's in the Field, Valhalla, N.Y.; lectr. hist. art; art edn. cons. Bklyn. Mus.; cons. N.Y. State Council Arts. Paintings rep. pvt. collections. Trustee Hammond Mus., N. Salem, N.Y.; bd. dirs. White Plains Outdoor Art Festival. Served with AUS, 1942-46. Mem. NEA, Coll. Arts Assn., Am. Craftsmans Council, Am. Soc. Aesthetics, Internat. Soc. Edn. Through Art, Cooper Union Alumni Assn. (bd. govs.), Nat. Art Edn. Assn., Am. Fedn. Art, Westchester Art Soc. (dir.), Asso. Council Arts, Inst. Study Art in Edn., Phi Delta Kappa (pres. Columbia chpt. 1962, coordinator N.Y.C. area 1962—). Clubs: Columbia U.; Arts (Washington); Shell (N.Y.C.). Home: 97-40 62d Dr New York NY 11374 Office: Westchester Arts Workshop White Plains NY 10606 also 2017 I St NW Washington DC. *The uniqueness of the individual, the qualities that make us different one from the other, are natural endowments that are to be treasured. In a world where a mediocrity of "sameness" extends itself everywhere, we must strengthen our individual uniqueness. We can help revitalize the world we live in by developing a creative and unique sense of self through thought, speech and action that is based on the best of man's previous experiences.*

RUDDY, ALBERT STOTLAND, motion picture producer; b. Montreal, Que., Can., Mar. 28, 1934; s. Hy and Ruth (Ruddy) Stotland; B.S. in Architecture, U. So. Cal., 1954. Constrn. supr. Abroe Constrn. Co., Cranford, N.J., 1955-57; systems analyst Systems Devel. Corp., Los Angeles, 1958-59, film producer Universal Studios, Los Angeles, 1960-62, Screen Gems, Los Angeles, 1966-67; pres. Alfran Prodns., Los Angeles, 1965-72, Albert S. Ruddy Prodns., Los Angeles, 1972—; producer film Matilda, 1978. Recipient Acad. award, 1972, Golden Globe award, 1972, 74, David D'Donatello award from Pres. Italy, 1972, Heraldo award Mexican Film Bd., 1972. Mem. Producers Guild Am. (dir. 1973-74), Acad. Motion Picture Arts and Scis., Variety Club S. Cal. Creator: Hogan's Heroes, 1964-71; producer feature films: The Wild Seed, 1965, Little Fauss and Big Halsy, 1968, The Godfather, 1971, The Longest Yard, 1973, Coonskin, 1974. Office: 5451 Marathon St Los Angeles CA 90038*

RUDEL, JULIUS, conductor; b. Vienna, Austria, Mar. 6, 1921; s. Jakob and Josephine (Sonnenblum) R.; student Acad. Music, Vienna; diploma in conducting, Mannes Coll. Music, 1942; hon. doctorates, U. Vt., 1961, U. Mich., 1971, also Pace Coll.; m. Rita Gillis, June 24, 1942; children—Joan, Madeleine, Anthony Jason. Came to U.S., 1938, naturalized, 1944. With N.Y. City Opera, 1943-79, debut, 1944, dir., 1957-79; dir. Third St. Music Sch. Settlement, 1945-52; mus. dir. Chautauqua Opera Assn., 1958-59, Caramoor Festival, Katonah, N.Y., 1964-76, Cin. May Festival, 1971-72, Kennedy Center Performing Arts, 1971-75; music adviser Wolf Trap Farm Park, 1971; condr. Spoleto (Italy) Festival, 1962-63; music dir. Phila. Opera, 1977—, Buffalo Philharmonic Orch., 1979—; debut as condr. Met. Opera, 1978; dir. prodn. Kiss Me Kate, Vienna Opera, Austria, 1956; guest condr. Chgo., Phila., N.Y. Philharmonic, Boston Symphony, Detroit Symphony, Israeli Philharmonic, Paris Opera, other symphonic, operatic orgns. Decorated Croix du Chevalier in arts and letters (France); recipient gold medal Nat. Arts Club, 1958; citation Nat. Assn. Am. Composers and Conductors, 1958, Nat. Fedn. Music Clubs, 1959, Ditson award Columbia, 1959, Page One award in music Newspaper Guild, 1959; hon. insignia for arts and sci. Govt. of Austria, 1961; Handel medal for music City N.Y., 1965; citation Nat. Assn. Negro Musicians, 1965, Nat. Opera Assn., 1971; comdr.'s Cross German Order Merit, 1967; Croix du Chevalier in Arts and Letters (France); hon. lt. Israeli Army, 1969; Julius Rudel award for young condrs. Office: Edgar Vincent Assos 145 E 52d St New York NY 10022

RUDEL, THOMAS RYDER, machine tool exec.; b. Montreal, Que., Can., Apr. 20, 1905 (parents U.S. citizens); s. Clarence Merrill and Anna (Ryder) R.; grad. Lawrenceville Sch. (N.J.), 1925; A.B., Princeton, 1929; m. Doris Taylor, July 3, 1934 (dec. Feb. 1970); one dau., Barbara Susan (Mrs. John K. Wendt); m. 2d, Margaret Murchison, Apr. 3, 1971. With Eberhard Faber Pencil Co., 1932-53, pres., chmn. bd., 1949-52; with Rudel Machinery Co., Ltd., 1938-60, chmn. bd., 1944-60; founder, chmn. bd. Rudel Machinery Co., Inc., 1941—; founder, chmn. bd. Am. SIP Corp., 1950—; chmn. bd. V & O Press Co., Inc.; trustee Lincoln Savs. Bank; dir. Nat. Machine Tool Show Corp., Lynch Corp. Asst. dir. machine tool div. NPA, 1951-52; mem. Dept. Commerce Machine Tool Mission to Japan, 1962, Dept. Commerce Mission to Philippines, 1964, Dept. Commerce Mission to Brazil, 1967, to USSR, 1971, to Peoples Republic China, 1978. Trustee Goucher Coll.; pres. bd. trustees Lawrenceville Sch., 1963-73, Ethel Walker Sch., 1959-72. Mem. Am. Machine Tool Distbr. Assn. (dir., pres. 1953-54), Nat. Machine Tool Builders Assn. (treas., dir. 1969-72, chmn. 1977-78), Newcomen Soc. Episcopalian. Home: 2 Sutton Pl S New York NY 10022 Office: 100 E 42d St New York NY 10017

RUDELIUS, WILLIAM, educator; b. Rockford, Ill., Sept. 2, 1931; s. Carl William and Clarissa Euclid (Davis) R.; B.S. in Mech. Engring., U. Wis., 1953; M.B.A., U. Pa., 1959, Ph.D. in Econs., 1964; m. Jacqueline Urch Dunham, July 3, 1954; children—Robert, Jeanne, Katherine, Kristi. Program engr., missile and space vehicle dept. Gen. Electric Co., Phila., 1956-57, 59-61; sr. research economist North Star Research Inst., Mpls., 1964-66; lectr. U. Minn., Mpls., 1961-64, asst. prof. mktg. Coll. Bus. Adminstrn., 1964, asso. prof., 1966-72, prof., 1972—. Served with USAF, 1954-55. Mem. Am. Mktg. Assn., Am. Inst. for Decision Scis. Author: (with W. Bruce Erickson and William J Bakula, Jr.) An Introduction to Contemporary Business, rev. edit., 1976. Contbr. to Harvard Bus. Rev., Jour. Mktg., Jour. Bus., other profl. publs. Home: 1425 Alpine Pass Minneapolis MN 55416 Office: Coll Bus Adminstrn U Minn 271 19th Ave S Minneapolis MN 55455

RUDENSTINE, NEIL LEON, univ. provost; b. Ossining, N.Y., Jan. 21, 1935; s. Harry and Mae (Esperito) R.; B.A., Princeton, 1956; B.A. (Rhodes Scholar), Oxford, 1959, M.A., 1963; Ph.D., Harvard, 1964; m. Ruth Angelica Zander, Aug. 27, 1960; children—Antonia Margaret, Nicholas David, Sonya. Instr. dept. English, Harvard, Cambridge, Mass., 1964-66, asst. prof., 1966-68; asso. prof. English, dean of students Princeton (N.J.) U., 1968-72, prof. English, dean of coll., 1972-77, provost, 1977—. Trustee Wooster Sch., Danbury, Conn., Coll. Entrance Exam. Bd. Served to 1st lt., arty., AUS, 1959-60. Author: Sidney's Poetic Development, 1967; (with G.S. Rousseau) English Poetic Satire, 1972. Home: 268 Stockton St Princeton NJ 08540

RUDER, DAVID STURTEVANT, lawyer, educator; b. Wausau, Wis., May 25, 1929; s. George Louis and Josephine (Sturtevant) R.; B.A. cum laude, Williams Coll., 1951; J.D. with honors, U. Wis., 1957; children—Victoria Chesley, Julia Larson; m. 2d, Anne Coulter, 1970 (div.); children—David Sturtevant II, John Coulter. Admitted to Wis. bar, 1957, Ill. bar, 1962; of counsel Schiff Hardin & Waite, Chgo., 1971-76; asso. firm Quarles & Brady, Milw., 1957-61; asst. prof. law Northwestern U., Chgo., 1961-63, asso. prof., 1963-65, prof., 1965—, asso. dean, 1965-66; cons. Am. Law Inst. Fed. Securities Code, parts XVII and XVIII; planning dir. Corporate Counsel Inst., 1962-66, 76-77; vis. prof. law U. Pa., Phila., 1971; C.R.B. vis. lectr. Universite de Liege, 1967; faculty Salzburg Seminar, 1976; mem. legal adv. com. to bd. dirs. N.Y. Stock Exchange; mem. com. on profl. responsibility Ill. Supreme Ct.; mem. exec. com. Securities Regulation Inst.; dir. Murray Machinery Co. Served to 1st lt. AUS, 1951-54. Mem. Chgo. (com. chmn.), Am. (mem. council sect. on corp. banking and bus. law 1970-74) bar assns., Am. Law Inst., Order of Coif, Gargoyle Soc., Phi Beta Kappa, Phi Delta Phi, Zeta Psi. Editor-in-chief Williams Coll. Record, 1950-51, U. Wis. Law Rev., 1957; editor Proc. Corp. Counsel Inst. 1962-66; bd. editors Rev. of Securities Regulation. Contbr. articles to legal periodicals. Home: 399 Fullerton Pkwy Chicago IL 60614 Office: 357 E Chicago Ave Chicago IL 60611

RUDER, MELVIN HARVEY, newspaper editor emeritus; b. Manning, N.D., Jan. 19, 1915; s. Moris M. and Rebecca (Friedman) R.; B.A., U. N.D., 1937, M.A., 1941; grad. student Northwestern U., 1940; m. Ruth Bergan, Feb. 10, 1950; 1 dau., Patricia E. Morton. Asst. prof. journalism U. N.D., 1940; indsl. relations specialist Westinghouse Electric Co., Sharon, Pa., 1940-41; pub. relations with Am. Machine & Foundry Co., N.Y.C., 1946; founder, editor Hungry Horse News, Columbia Falls, Mont., 1946-78, editor emeritus, 1978—; dir. emeritus Bank of Columbia Falls. Served to lt. (s.g.) USNR, 1942-45. Recipient Pulitzer prize for gen. local reporting, 1965. Mem. Mont. Press Assn. (pres. 1957). Home: 303 3d Ave E Columbia Falls MT 59912

RUDER, WILLIAM, pub. relations exec.; b. N.Y.C., Oct. 17, 1921; s. Jacob L. and Rose (Rosenberg) R.; B.S.S., City Coll., N.Y., 1942; m. Helen Beatrice Finn, Sept. 21, 1945; children—Robin Ann, Abby, Brian, Michal Ellen, Eric. With Samuel Goldwyn Prodns., 1946-48; chmn. bd. Ruder & Finn, Inc., N.Y.C., 1948-61, 62—, Ruder & Finn Internat., 1957-61; asst. sec. commerce, 1961-62; Tobe lectr. Harvard Grad. Sch. Bus., 1962. Mem. grad. adv. bd. City Coll. N.Y., Baruch Sch. Bus., N.Y.C.; cons. State Dept.; mem. bus. leadership adv. council OEO; bd. dirs. Bus. Com. for Arts, Jewish Bd. Guardians, Chamber Music Soc. Lincoln Center, Asso. Councils Arts, Fund for Peace; exec. com. United Way Am. chmn. bd. trustees Manhattanville Coll., Purchase, N.Y. Served to capt. USAAF, 1941-45. Mem. Public Relations Soc. Am. (gov.), UN Assn. U.S.A. (nat. policy panel dir.). Author: The Businessman's Guide to Washington. Home: 430 E 86th St New York NY 10028 Office: 110 E 59th St New York NY 10022

RUDERMAN, ARMAND PETER, educator; b. N.Y.C., Nov. 19, 1923; s. Louis and Lillian (Prigohzy) R.; S.B., Harvard U., 1943; M.A., 1946, Ph.D., 1947; M.B.A., U. Chgo., 1944; m. Alice Helen Holton, June 17, 1948; children—Ann, Mary, William, John. Instr. econs. Colgate U., 1946-47; asst. prof. S.D. State Coll., 1947-48, Montana State U., 1948-50; statistician Internat. Labour Office, 1950-54; statistician Pan Am. Health Orgn. WHO, Washington, also Latin Am., 1960-62, econ. adviser, 1963-67; prof. health adminstrn. U. Toronto, 1967-75; dean adminstrv. studies Dalhousie U., N.S., 1975—, prof. preventive medicine, 1975—; cons. in field.; coordinator Ont. Jt. Com. on Physicians Compensation, 1973-75; bd. dirs. Oxfam-Can., 1968-74. Fellow Am. Pub. Health Assn., 1963-68. Mem. Canadian Assn. Tchrs. Social and Preventive Medicine (pres. 1977-78), Canadian Pub. Health Assn., Inst. Pub. Adminstrn. Can., Royal Econ. Soc., Halifax Amateur Radio Club, Halifax Canadian Club. Contbr. articles to profl. jours. and books. Home: 29 Fleming Dr Halifax NS B3P 1A8 Canada Office: Dalhousie U Halifax NS B3H 4H6 Canada

RUDERMAN, MALVIN AVRAM, educator, physicist; b. N.Y.C., Mar. 25, 1927; s. Aaron and Hannah (Cohen) R.; A.B., Columbia, 1945; Ph.D., Calif. Inst. Tech., 1951; m. Paula Rosenberg, Aug. 30, 1953; children—Peter, Robert, Nina. Physicist, Radiation Lab., U. Calif. at Berkeley, 1951-52; NSF fellow Columbia, 1952-53, prof. physics, 1969—; mem. faculty physics U. Calif. at Berkeley, 1953-63, prof., 1959-63; prof. N.Y. U., 1963-69. Guggenheim fellow, 1957-58. Mem. Nat. Acad. Sci., Am. Acad. Arts and Scis., Am. Astron. Soc., Am. Phys. Soc. Home: 29 Washington Sq W New York NY 10011

RUDHYAR, DANE, author, composer; b. Paris, France, Mar. 23, 1895; s. Leon and Lucie (Bajaud) R.; Ph.B., U. Paris, 1911; student Paris Conservatoire Music, 1912; m. Malya Contento, June 9, 1930 (div. 1945); m. 2d, Eya Fechin, June 27, 1945 (div. 1954); m. 3d, Gail Tana Whittall, Mar. 27, 1964 (div. 1976); m. 4th, Leyla Rael, Mar. 31, 1977. Came to U.S., 1916, naturalized, 1926. First orchestral performances at festival of abstract dance Met. Opera, N.Y.C., 1917; composed music for Pilgrimage Play, Hollywood, 1920, 22, Surge of Fire, 1925; wrote extensively for piano, orch., also 1975—; wrote music for several modern dancers. Founder Internat. Com. for Humanistic Astrology, 1969. Awarded $1,000 prize for a symphonic poem Los Angeles Philharmonic, 1922, Marjorie Peabody Waite award for music Am. Acad. and Inst. Arts and Letters, 1978. Mem. Internat. Composers Guild, New Music Soc., Am. Composers Alliance. Author: Toward Man, 1929; White Thunder, 1938 (both poetry); Rebirth of Hindu Music, 1928; Art as Release of Power, 1930; Liberation Through Sound, 1931; Astrology of Personality, 1936; New Mansions for New Men, 1937; The Pulse of Life, 1943; The Moon: Cycles of Life, 1945; Modern Man's Conflicts, 1948; Gifts of the Spirit, 1956; Fire Out of the Stone, 1959; The Rhythm of Human Fulfillment, 1966; A Study of Psychological Complexes, 1966; The Lunation Cycle, 1967; The Practice of Astrology, 1968; Triptych, 1968; Birth-Patterns, 1969; The Planetarization of Consciousness, 1970; Directives for New Life, 1971; The Spectrum of Individual Experience, 1972; Rania, 1973; Return from No-Return 1973; An Astrological Mandala, 1973; We Can Begin Again—Together, 1973; The Astrology of America's Destiny, 1974; Occult Preparations for a New Age, 1975; The Sun Is Also a Star (The Galactic Dimension in Astrology), 1975; Culture, Orisis and Creativity, 1977; Beyond Individualism (The Psychology of Transformation), 1978; also articles in mags. Lectr. in Europe, 1960, 62, 63, U.S., twice yearly 1964—; seminars, lectrs. Esalen Inst., Calif., Aureon Inst., N.Y. Address: 3635 Lupine Ave Palo Alto CA 94303. *My "standards" consist in being uncompromisingly true to what I am and what I represent in the world; in being clearly aware of where I stand; in being open and inwardly free; in welcoming all experiences, extracting from them what may deepen and illumine the work for the performance of which I was born.*

RUDI, JOSEPH ODEN (JOE), profl. baseball player; b. Modesto, Calif., Sept. 7, 1946; s. Oden O. and Bessie (Courtney) R.; student Modesto Jr. Coll., Chabot Coll.; m. Sharon Adele Howell, May 9, 1966; children—Michael, Scott, Heather. With Kansas City Athletics, Am. League, 1967, Oakland (Calif.) Athletics, Am. League, 1968-76, Calif. Angels, Am. League, 1977—; played in All-Star games, 1972, 74, 75. Served with USMC. Home: PO Box 98 Laguna Beach CA 92652 Office: care Calif Angels Anaheim Stadium 2000 State College Blvd Anaheim CA 92806*

RUDIN, ALFRED, educator; b. Edmonton, Alta., Can., Feb. 5, 1924; s. Louis and Mary (Wainberg) R.; B.Sc., U. Alta. (Edmonton, Can.), 1949; Ph.D., Northwestern U., 1952; m. Pearl Gold, Aug. 15, 1949; children—Jonathan D., Jeremy R., Joel P. Research chemist Canadian Industries Ltd., McMasterville, Que., 1952-60, research group leader, 1960-64, plastics lab. mgr., Toronto, Ont., 1964-67; asso. prof. chemistry U. Waterloo (Ont., Can.), 1967-69, prof., 1969—. Cons. Served with Can. Army, 1942-45. Mem. Chem. Inst. Can., Am. Chem. Soc., Canadian Soc. Chem. Engring. Patentee in field. Contbr. profl. jours. Home: 211 Stanley Dr Waterloo ON Canada

RUDISILL, RICHARD, mus. curator, educator; b. Butte, Mont., Jan. 17, 1932; s. Darl Cole and Margaret (White) R.; A.A., Sierra Coll., 1950; B.A. in English, Sacramento State Coll., 1952, M.A. in English, 1957; Ph.D. in Am. Studies, U. Minn., 1967. Instr., Am. studies and English, U. Minn. at Mpls., 1959-67, research grantee grad. sch., 1964-65; prof. art U. N.Mex. at Albuquerque, 1968-71; research asso., vis. specialist photog. history Mus. N.Mex., Santa Fe, 1971-73, curator photog. history, 1974—; prof. photog. studies Art Inst. Chgo., 1973-74. Served with AUS, 1953-55. Recipient McKnight Humanities award Am. History, 1967. Nat. Endowment Arts vis. specialist grantee, 1972-73. Democrat. Lutheran. Author: Mirror Image: The Influence of the Daguerreotype on American Society, 1971; Photographers of the New Mexico Territory 1854-1912, 1973. Author articles in photog. history. Address: Museum of New Mexico PO Box 2087 Santa Fe NM 87503

RUDMAN, HERBERT CHARLES, educator; b. N.Y.C., July 29, 1923; s. Abraham and Celia (Factor) R.; B.S., Bradley U., 1947; M.S., U. Ill., 1950, Ed.D., 1954; m. Florence Bromberg, Dec. 22, 1923; 1 dau., Jane Ann. Tchr., asst. to prin. Peoria (Ill.) Bd. Edn., 1946-51; instr. U. Ill., 1951-53; chmn. dept. elementary edn., U.S.C., 1954-56; prof. adminstrn. and higher edn. Mich. State U., East Lansing, 1956—. Served with USAAF, 1942-46. Recipient Outstanding Leadership award Mich. Assn. Elem. Prins., 1972; Ford Found. fellow, USSR, 1958; head U.S. dep. to USSR for U.S. State Dept., 1963-64. Author: (with Truman Kelly, Richard Madden and Eric Gardner) Stanford Achievement Tests, 1964; (with Richard Featherstone) Urban Schooling, 1968; (with Donald J. Leu) Preparation Programs for School Administrators, 1968; (with Frederick King, Herbert Epperly) Concepts in Social Science, 1970; School and State in the USSR, 1967; (with others) Stanford Achievement Tests, 1973; (with Frederick King) Understanding People, 1977, Understanding Communities, 1977, Understanding Regions, 1978; Understanding Our Country, 1979; Understanding Our World, 1979; tests for At Your Best, 1977; Toward Your Future, 1977; Balance In Your Life, 1977. Editor: Measurement in Education, 1979—; contbr. articles to profl. jours. Office: College Education Michigan State U East Lansing MI 48823. *I have, all of my life, valued integrity and truth above all else. Without these two values all relationships—professional and personal—mean little. While I have valued excellence in professional conduct and commitment to professional goals, I have rarely lost perspective concerning my commitment to family and community. While honors, such as this one, are appreciated and valued by me, the greatest honor is that of watching our daughter grow into a fine young woman who, in turn, has developed many of the same values in her professional and personal life, and who now passes them on to her son.*

RUDNER, WILLIAM BARNETT, financial exec.; b. Memphis, June 4, 1920; s. Henry Gordon and Alberta (Isaacs) R.; B.A., U. Pa., 1941; m. Jocelyn Plough, July 27, 1944; children—Patricia Rudner Burnham, Sharon Rudner Eisenberg, Diane Rudner Goldstein. Vice pres. radio Sta. WMPS, Memphis, 1946-54; account exec. Merrill Lynch, Pierce, Fenner & Smith, Memphis, 1955-63; v.p. Union Planters Nat. Bank, Memphis, 1963-71, sr. v.p., 1971-72, exec. v.p., 1972-77; pres. DeSoto Capital Corp., Olive Branch, Miss., 1977—. Mem. Memphis and Shelby County Planning Commn., 1961-63; bd. dirs., treas. Downtown Assn., 1973; v.p. B'nai B'rith Home and Hosp., Memphis, 1969-73, pres., 1974. Served with USNR, 1943-46. Jewish. Clubs: Tenn., Summit, Ridgeway Country, Execs. (pres. 1968-69) (Memphis). Home: 2195 Poplar Ave PH 2 Memphis TN 38104 Office: 9991 Old Hwy 78 Olive Branch MS 38654

RUDNEY, HARRY, biochemist, educator; b. Toronto, Ont., Can., Apr. 14, 1918; s. Joshua and Dina (Gorback) R.; B.A., U. Toronto, 1947, M.A., 1948; Ph.D., Western Res. U., 1952; m. Bernice Dina Snider, June 25, 1946; children—Joel David, Paul Robert. Came to U.S., 1948, naturalized, 1956. Faculty, Western Res. U., Cleve., 1952-67, prof. biochemistry, 1965-67; prof., dir. dept. biol. chemistry U. Cin. Coll. Medicine, 1967—, Andrew Carnegie Found. prof. biol. chemistry, 1967—; vis. prof. Case Inst. Tech., Cleve., 1965-66. Mem. research adv. panel N.E. Ohio Heart Assn., 1966-67; mem. panel metabolic biology NSF, 1968-71; research career award com. NIH, 1969-73; mem. biochemistry test com. Nat. Bd. Med. Examiners, 1974—. Recipient USPHS Research Career award, 1963-67. Am.

Cancer Soc. scholar, 1954-56; NSF Sr. Research fellow U. Amsterdam (Netherlands), 1957. Mem. Am. Soc. Biol. Chemists, Am. Chem. Soc., Am. Soc. Microbiology, Biochem. Soc. (Eng.), Sigma Xi. Mem. editorial bd. Archives of Biochemistry and Biophysics, 1965—, Jour. Biol. Chemistry, 1975—. Contbr. articles profl. jours. Home: 4040 Winding Way Cincinnati OH 45229

RUDNICK, ISADORE, physicist; b. N.Y.C., May 8, 1917; s. Joseph A. and Jennie (Siedlecki) R.; B.A., U. Calif., Los Angeles, 1938, M.A., 1940, Ph.D., 1944; m. Mildred Karasik, Sept. 16. 1939; children—Joseph Alan, Charles Franklin, Deborah Ann, Michael Ira, Daniel Lars. Researcher Duke U., 1942-45; asst. prof. physics Pa. State U., 1945-48; mem. faculty U. Calif., Los Angeles, 1948—, prof. physics, 1958—, Faculty research lectr., 1975-76. Fulbright fellow to Copenhagen, 1957-58, to Israel, 1965; Guggenheim fellow, 1957-58. Mem. Acoustical Soc. Am. (Biennial award 1948, pres. 1969-70. Silver medal 1975), Am. Inst. Physics (governing bd. 1967-69). Office: Physics Dept University of California Los Angeles CA 90024

RUDO, MILTON, mfg. co. exec.; b. Balt., Jan. 17, 1919; s. Saul E. and Bertha (Berkowitz) R.; B.A., Johns Hopkins, 1940; grad. Advanced Mgmt. Program Harvard Bus. Sch., 1964; m. Roslind Mandel, Mar. 27, 1943; children—Stephanie E., Neil D. With Brunswick Corp., Chgo., 1940—, v.p. bowling div., 1957-62, pres. bowling div., 1962-65, 67—, pres. B.C.O. div., 1965-67, v.p. corp., 1962—, pres. Brunswick div., 1972-74, group v.p. charge recreation bus., 1974—. Served to capt. AUS, 1942-45. Recipient Bowling Industry Service award as man of year, 1973. Clubs: Briarwood Country (pres. 1967-68); Metropolitan, Standard (Chgo.); Muirfield Village Golf (Dublin, Ohio). Home: 1777 Balsam Rd Highland Park IL 60035 Office: One Brunswick Plaza Skokie IL 60076

RUDOLF, MAX, symphony and opera condr.; b. Frankfurt-Am-Main, Germany, June 15, 1902; came to U.S., 1940, naturalized, 1946; student Goethe-Gymnasium, Frankfurt, Hoch Conservatory Music, Frankfurt U.; pvt. mus. instrn.; D.Mus. (hon.), Cin. Conservatory Music; L.H.D. (hon.), U. Cin., 1960, Miami U., 1963, Curtis Inst. Music, 1972; D.Mus., Baldwin-Wallace Coll., 1973, Temple U., 1975; m. Liese Ederheimer, Aug. 4, 1927; children—William, Marianne. Asst. condr. Freiburg (Germany) Municipal Opera, 1922-23; condr. Opera State of Hesse, Darmstadt, Germany, 1923-29, German Opera, Prague, 1929-35; guest condr. Gothenburg (Sweden) Orch. Soc., also choral dir. radio concerts Swedish Broadcasting Corp., 1935-40; mem. faculty Central YMCA Coll., Chgo., 1941-43; condr. New Opera Co., N.Y.C., 1944; mem. mus. staff Met. Opera Assn., N.Y.C., 1945-58, artistic adminstr., 1950-58; adminstr. Kathryn Long opera courses Met. Opera, N.Y.C., 1949-58; mus. dir. Cin. May Festival, 1963-70; music dir., condr. Cin. Symphony Orch., 1958-70, world-wide concert tour, 1966; condr. Met. Opera Assn., N.Y.C., 1973-75; mem. faculty Curtis Inst. Music, Phila., 1970-73; tchr. conducting Ford Found. project, Balt., 1962-64, Tanglewood, 1964; Distinguished Service prof. U. Cin., 1966-68; condr. Columbia Records, Book of Month Club Music Appreciation Series, Cetra (Italy), Decca; guest condr. symphony orchs. throughout U.S., Italy; panel mem. Nat. Endowment for Arts, Washington, 1970-73; artistic adviser Dallas Symphony Orch., 1973, N.J. Symphony Orch., 1976-77, Exxon/Art Endowment Condrs. Program, 1977—. Recipient Alice M. Ditson award, 1964. Mem. Pi Kappa Lambda. Author: The Grammar of Conducting, 1950. Home: 220 W Rittenhouse Sq Philadelphia PA 19103. *LIFE. In this confusing make-believe world we preserve our mental health by assuming an attitude which combines realism with friendly skepticism. EDUCATION. Education cannot make anything of anybody, but can serve to open the minds, to advance from cocksure ignorance to thoughtful uncertainty. PERFORMING ARTS. Aren't we lucky, we performers. We are not only permitted to escape from reality in pursuing our daily work, we are even being paid for doing so.*

RUDOLPH, ABRAHAM MORRIS, physician, educator; b. Johannesburg, S.Africa, Feb. 3, 1924; s. Chone and Sarah (Feinstein) R.; M.B.B.Ch. summa cum laude, U. Witwatersrand, Johannesburg, 1946, M.D., 1951; m. Rhona Sax, Nov. 2, 1949; children—Linda, Colin, Jeffrey. Instr., Harvard Med. Sch., 1955-57, asso. pediatrics, 1957-60; asso. cardiologist in charge cardiopulmonary lab. Children's Hosp., Boston, 1955-60; prof. pediatrics, prof. physiology Albert Einstein Coll. Medicine, N.Y.C., 1960-66; dir. pediatric cardiology, vis. pediatrician Bronx Municipal Hosp. Center, N.Y.C., 1960-66; prof. pediatrics U. Calif. San Francisco, 1966—, prof. physiology, 1970—, also Neider prof. pediatric cardiology, prof. obstetrics and gynecology, 1974—; practice medicine, specializing in pediatric cardiology, San Francisco. Mem. cardiovascular study sect. NIH, 1961-65; established investigator Am. Heart Assn., 1958-62; career scientist Health Research Council, City N.Y., 1962-66. Fellow Royal Coll. Physicians (Edinburgh); mem. Royal Coll. Physicians (London), Am. Acad. Pediatrics (E. Mead Johnson award for research in pediatrics 1964, past chmn. sect. on cardiology), Am. Phys. Soc., Soc. for Clin. Investigation, Soc. for Pediatric Research (mem. council 1961-64), N.Y. (dir. 1965—), Am. heart assns. Editorial bd. Pediatrics, 1964-70; asso. editor Circulation Research, 1966-71, Circulation, 1966-72, Pediatric Research, 1972—. Contbr. articles profl. jours. Home: 1125 Clayton St San Francisco CA 94117 Office: Cardiovascular Research Inst Room 1403 HSE U Calif San Francisco CA 94143

RUDOLPH, ARTHUR LOUIS HUGO, mgmt. cons.; b. Stepfershausen, Germany, Nov. 9, 1906; s. Gustav Hugo and Ida (Gerlich) R.; B.S. in Mech. Engring., Coll. Berlin (Germany), 1930; D.Sc. (hon.), Rollins Coll., 1959; m. Martha Therese Kohls, Oct. 3, 1935; 1 dau., Marianne Erika. Came to U.S., 1945, naturalized, 1954. Participated in devel. V2 rocket and predecessors, Germany, 1930-45; with U.S. Govt. in devel. missiles and rockets, 1945-69, asst. dir. systems engring. Office Manned Space Flight, NASA, 1962-63, mgr. Saturn V launch vehicle program Marshall Space Flight Center, Huntsville, Ala., 1963-68; mgmt. cons., 1969—. Cons. missiles and astronautics div. Am. Ordnance Assn., also cons. materials div.; mem. tech. com. Am. Rocket Soc.; nat. chmn. space and electronics symposium I.R.E., 1962. Recipient Exceptional Civilian Service award Dept. Army, 1960; Exceptional Service medal NASA, 1968, Distinguished Service medal, 1969; W. Randolph Lovelace II award Am. Astronautical Soc., 1969; Exceptional membership award German Space Soc., 1969. Fellow Am. Inst. Aeros. and Astronautics (bd. dirs. Huntsville 1964-65; Holger N. Toftoy award Ala. sect. 1968). Patentee in Germany for liquid fueled rocket engines. Home: 5962 Colorview Ct San Jose CA 95120

RUDOLPH, E. GEORGE, lawyer, educator; b. New Richmond, Wis., Jan. 20, 1920; s. Ernest George and Adelaide V. (Burrows) R.; A.B., U. Mich., 1941, J.D., 1943; m. Ruth Anne Casper, Dec. 28, 1946; children—Theresa, Margaret, Martin, Jane, Mary, Sarah, Jack. Admitted to Ill. bar, 1943, Wyo. bar, 1953; mem. faculty U. Wyo. Coll. Law, Laramie, 1947—, prof., 1979—, dean, 1971-79. Served with U.S. Army, 1944-45. Decorated Bronze Star, Mem. Am. Bar Assn., Wyo. State Bar. Democrat. Author: The Wyoming Law of Real Mortgages, 1970. Home: 1628 Ord St Laramie WY 82070 Office: College of Law Laramie WY 82071

RUDOLPH, FREDERICK, educator; b. Balt., June 19, 1920; s. Charles Frederick and Jennie Hill (Swope) R.; B.A., Williams Coll., 1942; M.A., Yale, 1949, Ph.D., 1953; m. Dorothy Dannenbaum, June 18, 1949; children—Marta R. MacDonald, Lisa. Instr. history Williams Coll., 1946-47; asst. instr. Yale, 1949-50; mem. faculty Williams Coll., 1951—, prof., 1961—, Mark Hopkins prof. history, 1964—, chmn. Am. civilization program, 1971—; vis. lectr. history and edn. Harvard, 1960, 61. Mem. commn. plans and objectives Am. Council Edn., 1963-66. Founding mem. Berkshire County Hist. Soc., 1962, v.p., 1962-66, pres., 1966-68, bd. dirs., 1974-76; trustee Hancock-Shaker Community Inc., 1974—, Wyoming Sem., 1976-79. Served to capt. AUS, 1942-46. Guggenheim fellow, 1958-59, 68-69. Mem. Nat. Acad. Edn., Am. Hist. Assn., Am. Studies Assn., Orgn. Am. Historians, AAUP, Phi Beta Kappa (hon.), Sigma Phi, Gargoyle. Democrat. Author: Mark Hopkins and the Log, 1956; The American College and University: A History, 1962; Curriculum: A History of the American Undergraduate Course of Study Since 1636, 1977. Editor: Essays on Education in the Early Republic, 1965. Home: 170 Ide Rd Williamstown MA 01267

RUDOLPH, KARL HENRY, utility exec.; b. Cleve., June 14, 1914; s. Edward H. and Alma (Schmitt) R.; B.B.A., Ohio Wesleyan U., 1936; grad. Advanced Mgmt. Program, Harvard U., 1952; m. Jane Nichols, Apr. 13, 1940; children—Jeffrey W., Stephen E. With Gen. Electric Co., 1936-37, Willard Storage Battery Co., 1937-41, Ernst and Ernst, C.P.A.'s, 1941-42; with Cleve. Electric Illuminating Co., 1942—, exec. v.p., 1964-67, pres., 1967—, chmn. bd., 1977-79; dir. Cleve. Builders Supply Co., Acme-Cleve. Corp., Central Nat. Bank, Cleve., Lubrizol Corp., Splty. Composites Corp., Cleve. Elec. Illuminating Co. Bd. dirs. United Way, Andrews Sch. Girls, Willoughby, Ohio, Med. Mut. Cleve., Greater Cleve. Growth Assn. Mem. Edison Electric Inst., Assn. Edison Illuminating Companies, Newcomen Soc., Phi Beta Kappa, Phi Delta Theta. Club: Union (Cleve.). Home: 3033 Lander Rd Pepper Pike OH 44124 Office: PO Box 5000 Cleveland OH 44101

RUDOLPH, LAVERE CHRISTIAN, library dir.; b. Jasper, Ind., Dec. 24, 1921; s. Joseph Frank and Rose (Stradtner) R.; A.B., DePauw U., 1948; B.D., Louisville Presbyn. Sem., 1951; Ph.D., Yale, 1958; student U. Zurich (Switzerland), 1960; M.L.S., Ind. U., 1968. Ordained to Ministry Presbyn. Ch., 1950; pastor in Ind. and Conn., 1950-54; mem. faculty Louisville Presbyn. Sem., 1954-69, prof. ch. history, 1960-69; lectr. history U. Louisville, 1965-69; rare books bibliographer Van Pelt Library U. Pa.; head tech. services Lilly Library, Ind. U., 1970-78, curator of books, 1978—. Served to capt. USAAF, 1940-46. Mem. Am. Soc. Ch. History, ALA, Assn. Coll. and Research Libraries, Presbyn. Hist. Soc., Phi Beta Kappa. Democrat. Author: Hoosier Zion (Thomas Kuch award; Ind. U. Writers Conf. 1964), 1963; Story of the Church, 1966; Francis Asbury, 1966; Indiana Letters, 1979. Home: 321 E 14th St Apt G-4 Bloomington IN 47401 Office: Lilly Library Ind U Bloomington IN 47405

RUDOLPH, LLOYD IRVING, educator; b. Chgo., Nov. 1, 1927; s. Charles N. and Bertha (Margolin) R.; cadet U.S. Mil. Acad., 1945-46; A.B. magna cum laude, Harvard, 1948, M.P.A., 1950, Ph.D., 1956; m. Susanne Hoeber, July 19, 1952; children—Jenny W., Amelia C., Matthew C.J. Adminstrv. asst. Office Territories, Dept. Interior, 1948; research officer Council Econ. Advisers, 1949; mem. faculty Harvard, 1951-64, asst. prof. govt., Allston Burr sr. tutor Dunster House, 1960-64; asso. prof. polit. sci. U. Chgo., 1964-72, prof. polit. sci. and social scis., 1972—, chmn. Coll. Polit. Sci. program, 1968-70, chmn. divisional master's program social scis., 1973-75; contbr., participant Commn. on Orgn. Govt. for Conduct Fgn. Policy, 1974-75, 1980's Project of Council on Fgn. Relations, 1976—. Bd. overseers com. to visit dept. govt. Harvard, 1975—. Ford Found. fgn. area tng. fellow, India, 1956-57; sr. fellow Fulbright Program, India, 1962-63; Faculty fellow Am. Inst. Indian Studies, India, 1966-67; Fulbright prof., India, 1970-71; NSF grantee, 1973-75; Am. Inst. Indian Studies and Guggenheim fellow, India, 1975-76. Served with AUS, 1954-56. Mem. Am. Polit. Sci. Assn., Am. Soc. Pub. Adminstrn., Assn. Asian Studies. Author: (with Susanne H. Rudolph) The Modernity of Tradition: Political Development in India, 1967, Education and Politics in India: Studies in Organization, Society and Policy, 1972, The Coordination of Complexity in South Asia, 1975; also articles. Home: 4943 S Woodlawn Ave Chicago IL 60615

RUDOLPH, PAUL MARVIN, architect; b. Elkton, Ky., Oct. 23, 1918; s. Keener Lee and Eurie (Stone) R.; B.Arch., Ala. Poly. Inst., 1940; M.Arch., Harvard, 1947; Dr. Arts, Colgate U., 1966; D.F.A. (hon.), Fla. State U., 1970, Southeastern Mass. U., 1970; H.H.D., Auburn U., 1972. Practice residential, comml., instnl. architecture, 1947—; vis. critic archtl. schs. Cornell U., Tulane U., Harvard, Princeton, U. Calif., U. Pa., Ala. Poly. Inst.; chmn. dept. of architecture Yale, 1958-65. Served as lt. USNR, World War II. Recipient Outstanding Young Architect's award Sao Paulo Internat. Competition; first design award Progressive Architecture, 1955; Brunner prize Am. Acad. Arts and Scis., 1958; award of merit AIA., 1949, 59, 62, 64, 1st honors award, 1964, Medal Honor, N.Y. chpt., 1969. Fellow AIA; mem. Nat. Inst. Arts and Letters. Editor spl. edit. L'Architecture d'Aujourdhui, 1950. Contbr. profl., consumer jours. in U.S., Eng., France, Italy, Brazil, Japan.

RUDOLPH, RICHARD CASPER, educator; b. San Francisco, May 21, 1909; s. George Casper and Margaret (Elwood) R.; B.S., U. Calif., 1932, M.A., 1936, Ph.D., 1942; m. Mary Alice Potter, Sept. 8, 1944; children—Richard C., Robert A., Conrad J., Deborah M. Research asso., instr. Chinese, U. Chgo., 1937-40; research asso. Oriental langs. U. Calif. at Berkeley, 1942-43; head Chinese sect. USN lang. sch., U. Colo., 1943-45; asst. prof. Chinese, U. Toronto, 1945-46, asso. prof., acting dir. Sch. Chinese Studies, 1946-47; asst. keeper Far Eastern antiquities Royal Ont. Mus. Archeology, 1945-47; asso. prof., chmn. dept. Oriental langs. U. Calif. at Los Angeles, 1947-52, prof., 1952—, chmn. dept., 1952-62; dir. U. Calif. Study Centre, Chinese U. Hong Kong, 1977-79; research on Chinese archeology Academia Sinica, Formosa, 1959-61. Fulbright research scholar, 1948-49, 59-61; Guggenheim fellow, 1952-53, 59-61; recipient Am. Philos. Soc. grant, 1956. Mem. Far Eastern Assn., Am. Oriental Soc., Am. Archaeol. Inst. Author: Literary Chinese by the Inductive Method (with H. G. Creel, T. C. Chang) 3 vols. 1948, 49, 52; Han Tomb Art of West China: A Collection of First and Second-Century Reliefs, 1951; A Chinese Printing Manual, 1954. Asst. editor Archaeology; asso. editor Monumenta Serica, Jour. Oriental Studies, Hong Kong. Contbr. profl. publs. Home: 437 N Bowling Green Way Los Angeles CA 90049

RUDOLPH, RICHARD HINMAN, electronics co. exec.; b. Marietta, Ohio, Jan. 28, 1921; s. Harold L. and Emaline (Goddard) R.; B.S. in Elec. Engring., Ohio U., 1943; m. Phyllis M. Kilpatrick, Jan. 28, 1945; children—Tawn K., Richard Hinman II, Kevin Lee. With Gen. Electric Co., 1943-56; engaged in ceramic industry, 1956-58; v.p., gen. mgr. semicondr. products div. Motorola Co., 1958-64; pres., dir. GTI Corp., Meadville, Pa., 1964-70; pres., chief exec. officer Dickson Electronics Corp., 1970-74, also dir.; v.p., gen. mgr. components group Siemens Corp., Scottsdale, 1974-77; sec.-treas., v.p. Servi-Supply Co., Inc., Groveport, Ohio, 1977—. Mem. IEEE. Mason. Home: 409 N High St Lancaster OH 43130

RUDOLPH, ROBERT EDMUND, bldg. material co. exec.; b. Indpls., Apr. 5, 1936; s. Carl E. and Eva M. (Moore) R.; B.S., Ind. U., 1963; m. Nancy Distelhorst, Oct. 12, 1957; children—Ann Louise, Kurt Edmund, Stephen Mark. Works controller Am. Steel Foundries, Chgo., 1963-68; mgr. bus. planning ITT Ednl. Services, Indpls., 1968-70; budget coordinator Jim Walter Corp., Tampa, Fla., 1970-71, asst. controller Celotex div., 1971-73; v.p., treas. Celotex Corp., Tampa, 1973—. Served with AUS, 1959-60. Decorated Army Commendation medal. Mem. Planning Execs. Inst. Republican. Methodist. Home: 1884 Oakdale Ln S Clearwater FL 33516 Office: 1500 N Dale Mabry Tampa FL 33607

RUDOLPH, SUSANNE HOEBER, educator; b. Mannheim, Germany, Apr. 3, 1930 (parents Am. citizens); d. Johannes U. and Elfriede (Fischer) Hoeber; A.B., Sarah Lawrence Coll., 1951; M.A., Radcliffe Coll., 1953, Ph.D. in Polit. Sci., 1955; m. Lloyd I. Rudolph, July 19, 1952; children—Jenny W., Amelia C., Matthew C. J. Instr. govt. Harvard, 1957-60, lectr. govt., history and gen. edn., 1960-64; asso. prof. polit. and social scis. U. Chgo., 1964-72, prof., 1972—, chmn. dept. polit. sci., 1976-79 master, social scis. collegiate div., 1973-75, chair dept. polit. sci., 1976-79; cons. Nat. Endowment Humanities. Mem. overseer's vis. coms., grad. schs. of arts and scis. and of gen. edn. Harvard, 1973-77; mem. Bd. Fgn. Scholarships, 1979—. Ford Found. fgn. area tng. fellow, India, 1956-57; sr. fellow Fulbright program, India, 1962-63; faculty fellow Am. Inst. Indian Studies, India, 1966-67; Guggenheim fellow, 1970-71; NSF grantee, 1973-75; Phi Beta Kappa lectr., 1978-79; Nat. Endowment Humanities grantee, 1977-79. Mem. Am. Polit. Sci. Assn. (v.p. 1973-74), Assn. Asian Studies (dir. 1973-75), Author: (with Lloyd I. Rudolph) The Modernity of Tradition: Political Development in India, 1967; Education and Politics in India, 1972, The Coordination of Complexity in South Asia, 1975; also articles. Home: 4943 Woodlawn Ave Chicago IL 60615

RUDOLPH, WALLACE MORTON, univ. adminstr., lawyer; b. Chgo., Sept. 11, 1930; s. Norman Charles and Bertha R.; B.A., U. Chgo., 1950, J.D., 1953; m. Janet L. Gordon, Feb. 14, 1964; children—Alexey, Rebecca, Sarah. Admitted to Ill. bar, 1953, U.S. Ct. Mil. Appeals bar, 1954, U.S. Supreme Ct. bar, 1954, Nebr. bar, 1962, Wash. bar, 1978, others; research asso. Ford Found., 1953-54, Project in Law and Behavior Sci., 1954-55; instr. U. Chgo. Law Sch., 1959; asso. firm Antonow & Fink, Chgo., 1960-61; asst. prof. law U. Nebr., Lincoln, 1961-63, asso. prof., 1963-64, prof., 1965-76; dean, prof. U. Puget Sound Sch. Law, 1976—; mem. Commrs. on Uniform State Law, 1973-77, chmn. spl. com. on corrections, 1975-77; judge Ct. Indsl. Relations, Nebr., 1975-77; mem. Wash. Jud. Council and Com. II, 1976—, Public Employment Relations Commn., Wash., 1977—. Bd. dirs. Nebr. chpt. ACLU, 1965-72; mem. Nebr. Democratic Contact Com., 1973-74, 75-76; chmn. First Congl. Dist. Dem. Party, 1975-76; mem. exec. com. Unitarian Ch., Lincoln, 1965-67. Served with Judge Adv. Gen. Corps, U.S. Army, 1954-57. Mem. AAUP, Soc. Criminology, Am. Bar Assn., Am. Law Inst., Am. Arbitration Assn. Author: Handbook for Correctional Law; contbr. articles to profl. jours.; author Model Criminal Procedure Code, 1975, Model Sentencing and Corrections Act, 1978, Amicus Curiae Brief, Wash. State Supreme Ct., 1979. Office: U Puget Sound Sch Law 8811 S Tacoma Way Tacoma WA 98499

RUDOVSKY, PAUL, cons.; b. N.Y.C., Nov. 22, 1944; s. Samuel and Ruth (Cohen) R.; S.B., M.I.T., 1966; M.S., Grad. Sch. Indsl. Adminstrn., Carnegie-Mellon U., 1968. Unit supr. product devel. controllers office Ford Motor Co., Dearborn, Mich., 1968-70; v.p. Citibank, N.A., N.Y.C., 1970-77; exec. v.p., chief fin. officer Arlen Realty & Devel., Corp., N.Y.C., 1977-79, also dir.; prin. Rudovsky Cons., mgmt. cons., N.Y.C., 1979—. Bd. dirs. Fortune Soc., N.Y.C., 1975-78; mem. exec. com. M.I.T. Alumni Center of N.Y.C., 1976—. Club: Quaker Ridge Golf (Scarsale, N.Y.). Home : 340 E 64th St New York NY 10021. *Continuous excellence takes intelligence, guts and initiative.*

RUDOW, DAVID BARRY, lawyer; b. Balt., Aug. 7, 1934; s. Solomon E. and Mollie E. (Berman) R.; B.S., U. Md., 1956, LL.B., J.D., 1960; m. Vivian Shirley Adelberg, June 11, 1956; children—William, Stephen, Leonard. Field agt. IRS, 1956-60; admitted to Md. bar, 1960, since practiced in Balt.; partner firm Adelberg, Rudow, Hendler & Sameth, 1963—; tchr. income tax courses. Trustee Har Sinai Legacy and Endowment Fund; trustee, past pres. Har Sinai Congregation, also past pres. brotherhood. Mem. Am., Md., Balt. bar assns., Nat. Fedn. Temple Brotherhoods (past mem. nat. bd.). Democrat. Contbr. articles to legal jours. Home: 211 Goodwood Gardens Baltimore MD 21210 Office: 10 Light St Baltimore MD 21202

RUDWALL, JOHN CHARLES, financial exec.; b. Woodstock, Ill., Apr. 23, 1929; s. Harold Louis and Lydia (Berglund) R.; B.S., U. Colo., 1951; postgrad. Northwestern U., 1952-54; m. Nancy Field Spoerri, July 21, 1951 (div. Mar. 1977); children—Thomas Holmes, David Fuller, John Charles, James Field. Staff accountant Lybrand, Ross Bros. & Montgomery, Rockford, Ill., Chgo., 1951-52; mgr. Price Waterhouse & Co., Chgo., 1952-60; sec.-treas., mem. exec. com. L. M. Berry & Co., Dayton, Ohio, 1960-68; vice chmn. finance, dir. Super Food Services, Inc., 1968-69; financial adviser, 1969—. Trustee Loren M. Berry Found. C.P.A., Ill. Mem. Financial Execs. Inst., Am. Inst. C.P.A.'s, Ill. Soc. C.P.A.'s, Kappa Sigma. Club: Dayton Country; Dayton Indoor Tennis (pres.). Home: 109 Oak Knoll Dayton OH 45419 Office: PO Box 24 Dayton OH 45409

RUDY, CHARLES, sculptor; b. York, Pa., Nov. 14, 1904; s. John Horace and Marian Elizabeth (Emig) R.; student Pa. Acad. Fine Arts, 1924-28; m. Lorraine Schwartz, June 13, 1931. Tchr. sculpture Cooper Union, 1931-41; executed sculpture in Fed. bldgs., N.Y. World's Fair, Va. Poly. Inst. War Meml.; rep. collections Pa. Acad. Fine Arts, Brookgreen Gardens, Georgetown, S.C., Met. Mus., N.Y.C., others; executed World War II Meml. for Va. Poly. Inst., portrait bust of John Lloyd Newcomb, pres. U. Va., 1935-47; Sun Seaman's Meml., erected at Marcus Hook, Pa., 1949, war Meml. U. Pa. campus, 1952; carving for Audubon Shrine, Montgomery County, Pa., 1955; seven foot bronze figure Edgar Allen Poe, capitol grounds, Richmond, Va., 1957; meml. tablet of Ormond Rambo for Swedish-Am. Mus., Phila., 1959; sculpture Lehigh County (Pa.) Ct. House, 1964, Pa. Hist. Mus., Harrisburg, 1964; designer Nat. Commemorative Soc. medal, 1967; exhibited one man show York Art Assn., 1976, group show Phila. Mus. Art, 1976; tchr. sculpture Pa. Acad. Fine Arts, Phila.; artist-in-residence, Mich. State Coll. Guggenheim fellow, 1942; winner Bronx Postoffice Competition, 1936; recipient hon. mention. Archtl. League, 1938, Am. Acad. Arts and Letters Award, 1944, Dr. Herbert Howe prize, 1947, Percy M. Owens Meml. prize, Phila., 1971; fellowship, 1st prize Pa. Acad. Fine Arts, 1976, Outstanding Artist award Rutgers Fine Arts Mus., 1976; honored with proclamation of Charles Rudy Day, York, Pa., 1976. Mem. NAD, Nat. Sculpture Soc. (Gold medal 1973). Author: Painters and Sculptors of Modern America; (article) Challenge of Form (Mag. of Art, Apr. 1940). Home and studio: Ottsville PA 18942

RUDY, HERBERT EUGENE, mfg. co. exec.; b. Troy, Ohio, Oct. 21, 1917; s. Harry E. and Elizabeth (Younce) R.; student Ohio State U., 1937-38, Franklin U., Columbus, Ohio, 1939-41; LL.B., John

Marshall Law Sch., Cleve., 1944; postgrad. Case Western Res. U., 1948-50; m. Esther Royer, Sept. 3, 1939; children—Carol Rudy Clear, Diane, Linda. Home loan closer Guarantee Title & Trust Co., Columbus, 1938-42; sr. credit analyst Fed. Res. Bank, Cleve., 1942-44; dir. systems and procedures Weatherhead Co., Cleve., 1944-50; admitted to Ohio bar, 1944; v.p., legal counsel Yale & Towne, Inc., N.Y.C. and Cleve., 1951-65; v.p. mktg. services Eaton, Yale & Towne Inc., Cleve., 1966-68; v.p., treas. Eaton Corp., Cleve., 1968—; pres. Eaton Credit Corp., Cleve., 1963—; dir. Kendale Industries, 1976—. Trustee Huron Rd. Hosp., Cleve., 1973—, Golden Age Centers, 1974—; treas. Republican Fin. Com., Cleve., 1973-76. Clubs: Union, Mayfield Country, Clevelander. Home: 1 Bratenahl Pl Apt 707 Bratenahl OH 44108 Office: 100 Erieview Plaza Room 2400 Cleveland OH 44114

RUDY, LESTER HOWARD, psychiatrist; b. Chgo., Mar. 6, 1918; s. Sol and Mildred (Weinzimmer) R.; B.S., U. Ill., 1939, M.D., 1941; M.S. in Hosp. Adminstrn., Northwestern U., 1957; m. Ruth Jean Schmidt, Nov. 25, 1950; 1 dau., Sharon Ruth. Intern, Cedars of Lebanon Hosp., Los Angeles, 1941-42; resident in psychiatry VA Hosp., Downey, Ill., 1946-48, staff psychiatrist, 1948-52, chief service, 1952-54; supt. Galesburg (Ill.) State Research Hosp., 1954-58; practice medicine specializing in psychiatry, Chgo.; supt. Ill. State Psychiat. Inst., Chgo., 1958-61, dir., 1961—, Ill. Mental Health Insts., Chgo., 1967-75; prof. psychiatry Abraham Lincoln Sch. Medicine U. Ill., 1971—, head dept. psychiatry, 1975—. Chmn. research rev. com. mental health services NIMH, 1972-73; AMA commr. Joint Commn. on Accreditation of Hosps., 1967-75; sr. cons. VA; cons. adv. bd. Chgo., Police Dept.; lectr. dept. psychiatry and neurology Loyola U., 1968-75; mem. Ill. Gov.'s Com. Competency to Stand Trial, 1968. Served to col. AUS, 1942-46. Decorated Bronze Star with two oak leaf clusters; diplomate Am. Bd. Psychiatry and Neurology (exec. dir. 1972—). Fellow Am. Psychiat. Assn. (chmn. ethics com. 1963), Am. Coll. Psychiatrists (charter); mem. Am. Acad. Psychoanalysis (sci. asso.), Ill. Psychiat. Soc. (pres. 1962-63). Contbr. articles to profl. jours. Home: 40 Locust Rd Winnetka IL 60093 Office: 912 S Wood St Chicago IL 60612

RUDY, PETER, educator; b. Buffalo, Apr. 9, 1922; s. Stephen and Tekla (Rudy) R.; B.A., U. Buffalo, 1943, M.A., 1947; Ph.D., Columbia, 1957; m. Hildred Ethel Thau, Sept. 20, 1947; children—George Barrett, Elizabeth. Instr. U. Buffalo, 1946-47, Dartmouth, 1947-48; mem. faculty Northwestern U., 1951-52, 58—, prof., 1969—, chmn. dept. Slavic langs. and lits., 1958-73; asst. prof. Pa. State U., State College, 1952-58. Served with AUS, 1943-46. Mem. Am. Assn. Tchrs. Slavic and East European Langs., Modern Lang. Assn., Phi Beta Kappa. Democrat. Author: Darkness and Light: Three Short Works by Leo Tolstoy, 1965; Russian: A Complete Elementary Course, 1970. Survey editor Modern Lang. Jour., 1959-63. Home: 635 Milburn St Evanston IL 60201

RUDY, RAYMOND BRUCE, JR., food co. exec.; b. Los Angeles, Apr. 24, 1931; s. Raymond Bruce and Wrena Margaret (Higgins) R.; B.S., UCLA, 1953; M.B.A., Xavier U., Cin., 1960; children—Bruce Calvin, Alice Margaret, Barbara Jean. Brand mgr. Procter & Gamble, Cin., 1956-62; product mgr. Hunt-Wesson Foods, Fullerton, Calif., 1962-63; group v.p. Gen. Foods Corp., White Plains, N.Y., 1963-79; pres. Arnold Bakers/Orowert Foods, subs. Continental Grain Co., N.Y.C., 1979—. Served with U.S. Army, 1954-56. Presbyterian. Club: Greenwich Country. Office: 10 Hamilton Ave Greenwich CT 06830

RUDY, RICHARD WILLIAM, ins. co. exec.; b. Salt Lake City, June 6, 1921; s. Ralph Acton and Charlotte (Parker) R.; B.S., U. Calif., Los Angeles, 1943, M.B.A., 1948; m. Anita M. McDonald, Nov. 15, 1958; children—Laura Catherine, Mark. Security analyst Farmers Ins. Group, Inc., Los Angeles, 1948-55, asst. investment mgr., 1955-58, investment dir., 1958-60, asst. treas., 1960-64, v.p., 1964—, treas., 1965—; dir. Mid-Century Ins. Co. Served to lt. USNR, 1943-46. Fellow Fin. Analysts Fedn.; mem. Los Angeles Soc. Fin. Analysts, Soc. Municipal Analysts, Beta Gamma Sigma, Alpha Mu Gamma. Republican. Club: Bond. Home: 2790 Club Dr Los Angeles CA 90064 Office: 4680 Wilshire Blvd Los Angeles CA 90010

RUDY, WILLIS, historian; b. N.Y.C., Jan. 25, 1920; s. Philip and Rose (Handman) R.; B.S.S., Coll. City N.Y., 1939; M.A., Columbia, 1940, Ph.D., 1949; m. Dorothy Lucille Richardson, Jan. 31, 1948; children—Dorothy, Willa. Instr. history coll. City N.Y., 1939-49; instr., lectr. history edn. Harvard, 1949-52, 53, 57, 58; prof. history Mass. State Coll., Worcester, 1953-63; prof. history, Fairleigh Dickinson U., 1963—; research asso. Inst. Higher Edn., Columbia U., 1960. Mem. Am. Hist. Assn., Orgn. Am. Historians, Phi Beta Kappa. Recipient Cromwell medal history and belles lettres Coll. City N.Y., 1939. Unitarian. Author: The College of the City of New York: A History, 1949, reprinted, 1976; (with J.S. Brubacher) Higher Education in Transition, 1958, rev. edit. 1968, 76; The Evolving Liberal Arts Curriculum, 1960; Schools in an Age of Mass Culture, 1965. Editor: (with Peter Sammartino) The Private Urban University, 1966. Home: 161 W Clinton Ave Tenafly NJ 07670 Office: Fairleigh Dickinson Univ Teaneck NJ 07666. *Looking back over the years, I remember of course the many wonderful people I have been privileged to know and especially those closest to me whom I have been able to treasure in love. And I realize also that the study of history has remained for me one of the supreme joys of life, food for the soul. To me one of life's greatest thrills may very well come in the quiet of a research library as one seeks to unravel the threads of a challenging historical problem.*

RUEBHAUSEN, OSCAR MELICK, lawyer; b. N.Y.C., Aug. 28, 1912; s. Oscar and Eleonora J. (Melick) R.; A.B. summa cum laude, Dartmouth, 1934; LL.B. cum laude, Yale, 1937; m. Zelia Krumbhaar Peet, Oct. 31, 1942. Admitted to N.Y. bar, 1938; asso. Debevoise, Stevenson, Plimpton & Page, N.Y.C., 1937-42; partner Debevoise, Plimpton, Lyons & Gates, 1946—; atty. Lend Lease Adminstrn., Washington, 1942-44; gen. counsel OSRD, Washington, 1944-46; counsel Internat. Devel. Adv. Bd., Washington, 1950-51. Dir. Equitable Life Assurance Soc. U.S., Nat. Starch & Chem. Corp.; spl. adviser atomic energy to gov. N.Y. State, 1959; vice chmn. N.Y. State adv. com. on atomic energy, 1959-62; mem. Pres.'s Task Force on Sci. Policy, 1969-70, Pres.'s Sci. Adv. Com. Panel on Chems. and Health, 1970-72; mem. Commn. on Critical Choices for Am., 1973—; chmn. UN Day, N.Y. State, 1962; chmn. Spl. N.Y. Com. on Ins. Holding Cos., 1967-68. Sec., dir. Fund Peaceful Atomic Devel., Inc. 1954-72; dir. Carrie Chapman Catt Meml. Fund, 1948-58; chmn. bd. Bennington Coll., 1957-67; trustee Hudson Inst., Inc., 1961-71, Russell Sage Found., chmn. bd. 1965—; vice chmn. N.Y.C. Univ. Constrn. Fund, 1966-69. Mem. Am., N.Y. State bar assns., Yale Law Sch. Assn. (exec. com. and pres. 1960-62, chmn. 1962-64), Assn. Bar City N.Y., Council Fgn. Relations, Phi Beta Kappa, Sigma Phi Epsilon, Order of Coif. Clubs: Century, River, Coffee House, Hemisphere (N.Y.C.); Bedford (N.Y.) Golf and Tennis. Contbr. articles profl. jours. Home: 450 E 52d St New York City NY 10022 Office: 299 Park Ave New York City NY 10017

RUEDENBERG, KLAUS, educator, theoretical chemist; b. Bielefeld, Germany, Aug. 25, 1920; s. Otto and Meta (Wertheimer) R.; student Montana Coll., Zugerberg, Switzerland, 1938-39; licence es Scis., U. Fribourg (Switzerland), 1944; Ph.D., U. Zurich (Switzerland), 1950; postgrad. U. Chgo., 1948-50; Ph.D. (hon.), U. Basel (Switzerland), 1975; m. Veronika Kutter, Apr. 8, 1948; children—Lucia Meta, Ursula Hedwig, Annette Veronika, Emanuel Klaus. Came to U.S., 1948, naturalized, 1955. Research asso. physics U. Chgo., 1950-55; asst. prof. chemistry, physics Iowa State U., Ames, 1955-60, asso. prof., 1960-62, prof., 1964-78, disting. prof. in sci. and humanities, 1978—, sr. chemist Energy and Mineral Resources Research Inst., 1964—; prof. chemistry Johns Hopkins, Balt., 1962-64; vis. prof. U. Naples (Italy), 1961, Fed. Inst. Tech., Zurich, 1966, 67, Wash. State U. at Pullman, 1970, U. Cal. at Santa Cruz, 1973, U. Bonn (Germany), 1974; lectr. univs., research instns. and sci. symposia, 1953—. Co-founder Ames Center for the Arts, 1966, treas., 1966-71, also bd. dirs. Guggenheim fellow, 1966-67. Fellow Am. Phys. Soc.; mem. A.A.A.S., A.A.U.P., Internat. Acad. for Quantum Molecular Scis., Am. Chem. Soc., A.C.L.U., Sigma Xi, Phi Lambda Upsilon. Presbyn. Author articles in field. Asso. editor Jour. Chem. Physics, 1964-67, Internat. Jour. Quantum Chemistry, Theoretica Chimica Acta, Chem. Physics Letters, 1967—. Home: 2834 Ross Rd Ames IA 50010

RUEDISILI, CHESTER HENRY, univ. dean; b. Hartford, Wis., Jan. 26, 1910; s. Henry A. and Addie (Lehman) R.; B.A., U. Wis., 1933, Ph.D., 1941; m. Jeanette R. Haberman, June 29, 1935; children—Lon, Neal, Todd. Tchr. math., counselor Washington High Sch., Milw., 1934-36; asst. to jr. dean, U. Wis., 1937-41, lectr. psychology, 1941-66, asso. dean letters and sci. 1946—, chmn. honors program, 1963—; mem. faculty Japanese Univ. Insts. Student Personnel Services, 1951-52. Mem. Nat. Collegiate Honors Council Exec. Com., 1968-71, 73-76, pres. 1979-80; pres. Shorewood Hills (Wis.) Sch. Bd., 1958-59. Bd. dirs. Madison United Community Chest, 1954-60. Mem. Am., Midwestern psychol. assns., Am. Coll. Personnel Assn., AAUP, Phi Beta Kappa, Phi Kappa Phi, Phi Eta Sigma, Psi Chi, Alpha Kappa Delta, Phi Delta Kappa, Sigma Chi. Home: 2909 Hunter Hill Madison WI 53705

RUEFLI, TIMOTHY WALTER, educator; b. Torrington, Conn., Oct. 21, 1942; s. Walter Richard and Beatrice Mabel (Chadburn) R.; B.A. cum laude, Wesleyan U., 1964; M.S., Carnegie Inst. Tech., 1967; Ph.D., Carnegie-Mellon U., 1969; m. Mary Jane Connelly, Aug. 28, 1965; children—Christiana Ellen, Chadburn Walter. Instr., Carnegie Inst. Tech., 1966-67; research asso. Rand Corp., 1967-68; asst. prof. Coll. Bus. Adminstrn., U. Tex., Austin, 1968-71, asso. prof., 1971-76, prof., 1976-77, Harkins prof., asso. dir. Inst. Constructive Capitalism, 1977—; vis. prof. U. B.C., 1974-75; prin. Ruefli Cons.; reviewer NSF. Chmn., Mayor's Econ. Task Force, Austin, 1977-78. Ford Found. fellow, 1966-67; McKinsey Found. fellow, 1969. Mem. AAAS, Inst. Mgmt. Scis., Delta Tau Delta. Author: Planning in Decentralized Organizations, 1969; (with others) Horizontal Divestiture of Energy Companies and Alternative Policies, 1976. Home: 7111 Waterline Rd Austin TX 78731 Office: Grad Sch Bus U Tex Austin TX 78712. *It is precisely when I find myself most comfortable with my current intellectual situation that I find it is time to inquire into the possibility of alternative arrangements.*

RUEGAMER, WILLIAM RAYMOND, educator, biochemist; b. Huntington, Ind., Dec. 15, 1922; s. C. Raymond and Edna (Roberts) R.; B.S., Ind. U., 1943; M.S., U. Wis., 1944, Ph.D., 1947; postgrad. U. Colo.; m. Arlene Frankenberg, Apr. 5, 1946. Biochemist, Swift & Co., 1948-49; instr. biophysics U. Colo., 1949-54; asst. dir. Radioisotope Labs., VA Hosp., Syracuse, N.Y., 1954-60; asso. prof. biochemistry State U. N.Y., Syracuse, 1960-67, prof., acting chmn. dept. biochemistry, 1967-68; chmn., prof. dept. biochemistry U. Nebr., Coll. of Medicine, Omaha, 1968—, asso. dean Sch. Allied Health Professions, 1974—; cons. Warner Lambert Pharm. Co., Morris Plains, N.J., 1960-68. Mem. Am. Soc. Biol. Chemists, Am. Thyroid Assn., Am. Soc. Exptl. Biology and Medicine, Am. Inst. Nutrition, Encodrine Soc., Sigma Xi, Phi Sigma, Alpha Chi Sigma. Research and publs. on thyroid metabolism, cholesterol and ground substance metabolism in relation to atherosclerosis. Office: Dept Biochemistry Coll Medicine U Neb Omaha NE 68105

RUEGER, WILLIAM FREDERICK, elec. co. exec., lawyer; b. Bklyn., Dec. 23, 1919; s. William Jacob and Henrietta (Greenhagen) R.; B.A., Bard Coll., 1940; M.A. in Latin and Greek, Columbia, 1941, LL.B. (Harlan Fiske Stone scholar 1946-48), 1948; m. Anna Helen Arrison, Sept. 17, 1949; children—Barbara Anne, Nancy Elizabeth, William Frederick, Sally Patricia. Admitted to N.Y. bar, 1948; asso. firm Hughes, Hubbard & Ewing, N.Y.C., 1948-50; with Sylvania Electric Products Inc. (name now changed to GTE Sylvania Inc.), N.Y.C., 1950—, sr. v.p., gen. counsel, sec., 1961-69, sr. v.p. adminstrn., 1969-76, v.p., gen. counsel GTE Products Corp. subs., 1976—. Bd. mgrs. Meadowbrook Hosp., E. Meadow, N.Y., 1968-71; N.Y. State committeeman 17th A.D., Democratic Party, 1966-68; candidate town council Town of N.Hempstead, N.Y., 1955. Chmn. bd. trustees Bard Coll., Annandale-on-Hudson, 1976—; trustee Westbury Meml. Pub. Library, Nassau County Community Coll.; warden Ch. of Advent, Westbury. Served to 1st lt. USAAF, 1942-45. Mem. Am., Nassau County bar assns., Bar Assn. City N.Y., Phi Beta Kappa. Home: Langley Ln Old Westbury NY 11568 Office: 1 Stamford Forum Stamford CT

RUEGSEGGER, ALCID DEVERE, lawyer; b. Boyne City, Mich., Mar. 5, 1905; s. Ervan A. and Mary J. (Lamoreaux) R.; A.B., Alma Coll., 1926; J.D., U. Mich., 1928; m. Elsa C. Teters, Nov. 17, 1927; 1 dau., Julie Anne. Admitted to Mich. bar, 1928, since practiced in Detroit; mem. firm Dyer, Meek, Ruegsegger & Bullard, and predecessors, 1953—; chief enforcement atty. Detroit dist. office OPA, 1942-44, regional enforcement exec. Cleve. regional office, 1944-47; mem. exec. com. Inst. Continuing Legal Edn., 1960—, speaker 12th ann. Advocacy Inst., 1961; chmn. bd., dir. Kilgore & Hurd, men's furnishings, Detroit. Bd. dirs., treas. Children's Aid Soc., Detroit; bldg. chmn. solicitations United Found., Detroit, 1952-59. Fellow Am. Coll. Trial Lawyers, Am. Bar Found., Internat. Soc. Barristers; mem. Am., Fed., Detroit (chmn. circuit ct. com. 1951-55, spl. com. revision judges salaries 1952-54, dir. 1955-62, treas. 1958-59, sec. 1959-60, pres. 1961-62) bar assns., State Bar Mich. (sec. negligence sect. 1957, vice chmn. 1958, chmn. 1959-60, chmn. ct. adminstrn. com. 1962-64, commr. 1964—, 2d v.p. 1967-68, 1st v.p. 1968-69, pres. 1969-70), Am. Judicature Soc., Nat. Conf. Bar Pres.'s, Nat. Assn. R.R. Trial Lawyers, Mich. R.R. Lawyers Assn. (past pres.), Mich. Assn. Def. Counsel, Delta Theta Phi (bd. govs. Detroit alumni senate 1953—, dean 1953, dist. chancellor 1962—). Clubs: U. Mich. Alumni (pres. 1957-58) (Detroit and Grosse Pointe); Lochmoor Country (Grosse Pointe Woods); Detroit Athletic, Renaissance (Detroit); Nat. Lawyers; Hunter's Creek. Home: 1055 Balfour Rd Grosse Pointe MI 48230 Office: 1 Woodward Ave Detroit MI 48226

RUEHLMANN, EUGENE PETER, lawyer; b. Cin., Feb. 23, 1925; s. John F. and Hattie C. (Mehrckens) R.; B.A., U. Cin., 1948; LL.B., Harvard U., 1950; J.D. (hon.), Xavier U., 1971; m. Virginia Juergens, Aug. 30, 1947; children—Virginia, Peter, Margaret, Andrea, Gregory, James, Mark, Richard. Partner firm Strauss, Troy and Ruehlmann (now Strauss, Troy and Ruehlmann Co, L.P.A.), Cin., 1953—, now pres; vice mayor City of Cin., 1963-67, mayor, 1967-71, mem. City Council, 1959, re-elected 1961, 63, 65, 67, 69, served as chmn. fin. and labor, capital improvements, stadium, public utilities and intergovtl. affairs coms.; chmn. bd. trustees City Retirement System; rep. to Dist. 13 Law Enforcement Agy.; founder Mayor's Housing Coordinating Com.; co-sponsor Citizens' Com. to Improve Local Govt. (Lingle Com.) and Mayor's Prayer Breakfast; pres. Ohio, Ky., Ind. Regional Planning Authority, 1970. Chmn., March of Dimes Campaign, 1973, NCCJ 1974 Ann. Testimonial Dinner; co-chmn. Ohio Republican Fin. Com., Hamilton County Div., 1976, chmn., bd. dirs., 1977; co-chmn. Sch. Levy campaigns, 1977-78; trustee Children's Hosp. Med. Center, St. Francis/St. George Hosp., Inc., Coll. Mt. St. Joseph on the Ohio, Cin. Med. Center Fund; mem. lay bd. advs. St. Xavier High Sch. Served with USMC, 1943-44. Republican. Mem. United Chs. of Christ. Office: 2100 Central Trust Center 201 E Fifth St Cincinnati OH 45202

RUELLAN, ANDREE, artist; b. N.Y.C., Apr. 6, 1905; d. André and Louise (Lambert) Ruellan; student Art Students League, 1920-22; art schs. France and Italy; m. John W. Taylor, May 28, 1929. One-man shows Paris, France, 1925, Weyhe Galleries, N.Y.C., 1928, 31, Maynard Walker Galleries, 1937, 40, Kraushaar Galleries, 1945, 52, 56, 63, Phila. Art Alliance, 1955, S.I. Mus., 1958; nat. exhbns. Carnegie Inst., Whitney Mus., Art Inst. Chgo., Corcoran Gallery, Internat. Expn., San Francisco, Artists for Victory Exhbn., N.Y.C., other cities U.S.; retrospective exhbn. Storm King Art Center, Mountainville, N.Y., 1966, Lehigh U., 1965, Woodstock Artists Assn., 1977; executed murals in Emporia, Va., Lawrenceville, Ga.; rep. Met. Mus., Whitney Mus. Am. Art, N.Y.C., Fogg Mus., Harvard, Phila. Mus., Storm King Art Center, William Rockhill Nelson Mus., Kansas City, Mo., Duncan Phillips Gallery, Washington, Springfield Mus., Norton Gallery, Art Mus., New Britain, Conn., Library of Congress, Ency. Brit., IBM Collections, Art Inst., Zanesville, Ohio, U. Ga., S.I. Mus., Butler Inst., Pa. State U., Lehigh U., Columbia (S.C.) Mus. Art, The Whatcom Mus., Washington, also numerous pvt. collections; guest instr. Pa. State Coll., summer 1957. Recipient 3d prize for painting Charleston, Worcester Mus. Biennial, Jan. 1938; $1,000 grant in arts Am. Acad. and Inst. Arts and Letters, 1945; Pennell medal Pa. Acad., 1945, Medal of Honor and purchase Pepsi-Cola Paintings of the Year, 1948; Dawson Meml. medal Pa. Acad., 1950; Purchase award N.Y. State Fair, 1951; Drawing award Ball State Tchrs. Coll.; Guggenheim fellow, 1950-51. Mem. Woodstock Artists Assn., Art Students League (life), Phila. Watercolor Soc. Home: Shady NY 12479

RUEMMLER, GERD ROBERT, chem. co. exec.; b. Munich, Germany, May 15, 1933; came to U.S., 1975; s. Robert Andreas and Emmy G. R.; student U. Munich, 1952-54; Ph.D., Chem. Faculty, U. Frankfurt (W. Ger.), 1961; m. Eveline C., Oct. 2, 1960; children—Christine, Julia, Corinna. With Hoechst AG, 1962—, mng. dir. Kasei Hoechst, Tokyo, Japan, 1968-72, v.p. Am. Hoechst Corp., Bridgewater, N.J., 1975-78, exec. v.p., 1979—. Office: Route 202/206 Bridgewater NJ 08876

RUENHECK, JEROME B., corp. exec.; b. Aug. 25, 1938; B.S. in Bus. Adminstrn., U. Denver; m. Karen; 3 children. With Burger King Corp., 1969—, div. mgr., 1970-73, exec. v.p., dir. ops., Miami, Fla., 1973—. Mem. exec. bd. S. Fla. council Boy Scouts Am. Served with USMC, 1961-64. Mem. Nat. Restaurant Assn. Office: Burger King Corp 7360 N Kendall Dr Miami FL 33152

RUESCH, JURGEN, psychiatrist, educator; b. Naples, Italy, Nov. 9, 1909; s. Oscar and Vera (Meissner) R.; M.D., U. Zurich (Switzerland), 1935; m. Annemarie Jacobson, Dec. 11, 1937; 1 son, Jeffrey. Came to U.S., 1939, naturalized, 1945. Fellow Rockefeller Found., asst. psychiatry Mass. Gen. Hosp., Boston, 1939-41; research fellow neuropathology Harvard Med. Sch., 1941-43; mem. faculty U. Calif. Sch. Medicine, San Francisco, 1943—, prof. psychiatry, 1956—; research psychiatrist Langley Porter Neuropsychiat. Inst., San Francisco, 1943-58, dir. treatment research center, 1958-64, dir. sect. social psychiatry, 1965-77. Cons. to various fed., state, community, pvt. agys. Diplomate Am. Bd. Psychiatry and Neurology. Fellow Am. Coll. Psychiatrists, Am. Psychiat. Assn. (recipient Hofheimer award 1951); mem. Internat. Fedn. for Med. Psychotherapy (dir. 1964-77), A.M.A., San Francisco County Med. Soc., No. Calif. Psychiat. Soc., Assn. for Research in Nervous and Mental Disease (past v.p.), AAAS, Am. Assn. Social Psychiatry, German Soc. Psychiatry and Neurology (hon.). Author: (with F.L. Wells) Mental Examiners Handbook, 1942; (with G. Bateson) Communication, 1951, rev. edit., 1968; (with W. Kees) Nonverbal Communication, 1956, rev. edit., 1972; Disturbed Communication, 1957, rev. edit., 1972; Therapeutic Communication, 1961, rev. edit., 1973; (with Brodsky, Fischer) Psychiatric Care, 1964; Semiotic Approaches to Human Relations, 1972; Knowledge in Action, 1975. Mem. editorial bd. Psychotherapy and Psychosomatics, 1964—, Communication, 1971—, Archives Gen. Psychiatry, 1961-70, Jour. Nervous and Mental Disease, 1966-71; adv. bd. Internat. Jour. Social Psychiatry (London), Social Psychiatry (Heidelberg). Contbr. articles profl. jours. Address: Langley Porter Inst U Calif San Francisco CA 94143

RUETHER, ROSEMARY RADFORD, theologian; b. St. Paul, Nov. 2, 1936; d. Robert Amstrong and Rebecca Cresap (Ord) Radford; A.B., Scripps Coll., 1958; M.A., Claremont Grad. Sch., 1960, Ph.D., 1965; m. Herman J. Ruether, Aug. 31, 1957; children—Rebecca, David, Mimi. Asso. prof. Howard U., Washington, 1966-76; Georgia Harkness prof. Garrett Sem., Evanston, Ill., 1976—; lectr. Princeton Theol. Sem., 1971, 73; prof. Roman Cath. studies Harvard U., Cambridge, Mass., 1972-73; lectr. Yale Div. Sch., 1973-74. Kent fellow, 1962-65; Danforth fellow, 1960-61. Mem. Soc. Religion in Higher Edn., Am. Theol. Assn., Soc. Arts, Religion and Culture. Author: The Church Against Itself, 1967; Communion is Life Together, 1968; Gregory Nazianzus, Rhetor and Philosopher, 1969; The Radical Kingdom, 1970; Liberation Theology, 1972; Religion and Sexism: Images of Women in the Judeo-Christian Tradition, 1974; Faith and Fratricide, 1974; New Woman/New Earth, 1975; Mary, The Feminine Face of the Church, 1977; The Liberating Bond, 1978; Women of Spirit, 1979; contbg. editor Christianity and Crisis, The Ecumenist; contbr. articles to profl. jours. Home: 1426 Hinman Ave Evanston IL 60201

RUFA, ROBERT HENRY, photographer, artist; b. Bklyn., Jan. 11, 1943; s. Joseph Simon and Alma (Weinbrecht) R.; grad. high sch.; m. Barbara Lee Johnson, June 25, 1971; 1 son, Eric. Tech. editor Tele-Signal Corp., Woodbury, N.Y., 1973; asso. editor Tobacco Leaf mag., Rockville Centre, N.Y., 1973; mem. staff Travel mag., Floral Park, N.Y., 1969-76, mng. editor, 1973-74, editor, 1975-76; artist, photographer, 1976—; mng. editor The Pinehurst Outlook, 1977-78. Served with USAF, 1961-65. Home: Box 477 Pinehurst NC 28374

RUFE, REDDING KANE, hotelier; b. Mpls., June 29, 1930; s. Redding Henry and Dorothy (Liese) R.; B.S. in Hotel Adminstrn., Cornell U., 1952; grad. Program Mgmt. Devel., Harvard U., 1967; m. Marta Judith Kern, May 9, 1959; children—Marta Nicole, Michael Kern. With Inter-Continental Hotels Corp., 1957—, sr. v.p. ops. Far East/Pacific, 1970-72, gen. mgr. Hotel Siam Inter-Continental, 1967-70, pres. Pacific/Asia div., 1973—. Served to 1st lt. USAF, 1952-56. Mem. Assn. Internat. Des Skal Clubs Amicale de Tourisme, Am. Soc. Travel Agts., Pacific Area Travel Assn., Hotel Sales Mgmt. Assn. Internat., Cornell Soc. Hotelmen, Am. C. of C. in Thailand, Thai Hotels Assn., Theta Delta Chi. Lutheran. Clubs: Rotary; Harvard Bus. Sch., Marco Polo (N.Y.C.); de Golf Sotogrande de Espana (LaLinea,

Cadiz, Spain); Royal Bangkok Sports. Address: Hotel Siam Inter-Continental Rama I Rd Bangkok Thailand

RUFF, CHARLES F. C., govt. ofcl.; b. Cleve., Mar. 1, 1939; A.B., Swarthmore Coll., 1960; LL.B., Columbia U., 1963. Instr. law U. Liberia, Monrovia, 1963-65, U. Pa., 1966-67; trial atty., organized crime and racketeering sect., criminal div. U.S. Justice Dept., 1967-70, chief mgmt. and labor sect., criminal div., 1970-72; asso. prof. Georgetown Law Center, 1973-77; acting chief insp. Drug Enforcement Adminstrn., 1975; asst. spl. prosecutor Watergate Spl. Prosecution Force, 1973-75, spl. prosecutor, 1975-77; dep. insp. gen. HEW, 1977—.

RUFF, GEORGE ROBERT, advt. agy. exec.; b. Salt Lake City, Nov. 5, 1918; s. George Alma and Mary (Jensen) R.; A.B. magna cum laude, Brigham Young U., 1943; postgrad. U. Utah, 1946-50; m. Betty Clark, Aug. 28, 1943; children—Alan Robert, Lynn William, Roger Joseph, Robin, Susan. Copywriter, asst. account exec. Stevens & Wallis Advt. Agy., Salt Lake City, 1941-42; account exec. David W. Evans & Assos., advt. agy., Salt Lake City, 1945-53, v.p., 1953-65, sr. v.p., vice chmn. bd., 1960-72, exec. v.p., chmn. exec. com., 1972-74; pres. David W. Evans, Inc., Salt Lake City, 1974—; v.p., dir. Evans Supply, Inc., 1953-73, Evans/Lowe & Stevens, Inc., Atlanta; dir. Evans/Bartholomew, Inc., Denver, Evans/Pacific, Inc., Seattle and Portland, Oreg., David W. Evans/Calif., San Francisco, Evans/Weinberg, Inc., Los Angeles; lectr. communications Brigham Young U., 1965-66; lectr. mktg. U. Utah, 1947-54. Vice chmn. Red Butte dist. Boy Scouts Am., 1964-65; chmn. exec. com. Friends of Brigham Young U. Library, 1963-73; mem. nat. council Brigham Young U., 1978—. Served with USAAF, 1942-45. Decorated Air medal with three oak leaf clusters; recipient Presdl. medal for extraordinary service Brigham Young U., 1969, Meritorious Service award in mass communications, 1977. Mem. Am. Mktg. Assn. (accredited; chpt. pres.), Pub. Relations Soc. Am. (chpt. pres. 1970, chmn. N. Pacific Dist. 1972-73, mem. dist. bd. 1979, del. nat. assembly 1980). Republican. Mem. Ch. of Jesus Christ of Latter-day Saints. Co-chmn. editorial com. The Instructor mag., 1960-71; contbr. articles to profl. jours. Home: 658 17th Ave Salt Lake City UT 84103 Office: 110 Social Hall Ave Salt Lake City UT 84111

RUFFER, DAVID GRAY, coll. pres.; b. Archbold, Ohio, Aug. 25, 1937; s. Lawrence A. and Florence A. (Newcomer) R.; B.S., Defiance Coll., 1959; M.A., Bowling Green State U., 1960; Ph.D., U. Okla., 1964; m. Marilyn Elaine Taylor, Aug. 23, 1958; children—Rochelle Lynne, Robyn Lynne, David Geoffrey. Spl. instr. U. Okla., 1963-64; asst. prof. biology Defiance Coll., 1964-68, asso. prof., 1968-73, faculty dean, 1969-73; provost Elmira (N.Y.) Coll., 1973-78; pres. Albright Coll., Reading, Pa., 1978—; vis. prof. Bowling Green State U., 1966. Mem. Defiance City Bd. Edn., 1969-73, Defiance City Planning Commn., 1969-73, Great Lakes Basin Commn., 1970-73, adv. group Regional Med. Program, 1969-72; mem. exec. com. Hawk Mountain council Boy Scouts Am.; bd. dirs. Reading Hosp. and Med. Center, United Way Berks County. NSF grantee, 1965, 67; Ohio Biol. Survey grantee, 1968-69. Fellow AAAS; mem. Am. Assn. Higher Edn., Animal Behavior Soc., Am. Soc. Mammalogists, Ohio Acad. Sci., Am. Sch. Bds. Assn., Ohio Sch. Bds. Assn. Methodist (trustee). Clubs: Sertoma Internat., Rotary. Author: Exploring and Understanding Mammals, 1971. Contbr. articles to profl. jours. Research evolution of behavior in grasshopper mice and higher edn. Home: 1500 Alsace Rd Reading PA 19604

RUFFI, STEPHEN JOSEPH, mfg. co. exec.; b. McAdoo, Pa., Oct. 25, 1927; s. Stephen John and Stephanie (Severa) R.; B.A., Columbia, 1950, M.S., 1951; m. Audree Eugenia Kuehne, Sept. 12, 1953; children—Andrea, Stephen, Leslie. Sr. accountant Arthur Andersen & Co., N.Y.C., 1951-56; v.p. adminstrn., treas. Emhart Corp., Bloomfield, Conn., 1956-68, v.p. internat., 1968-72, v.p., group exec., 1972—; asso. dir. Conn. Bank & Trust Co.; v.p., group pres. USM Corp., 1976; pres. USM Realty Corp., USM Co. of P.R., USM Italia Co.; dir. USM Argentina, USM France, USM Spain, USMC Internat. Ltd., BUSMC S. Africa, BUSMC Australia, Harmonic Drive Systems, Inc. Bd. dirs. Hartford Symphony Soc. Served with AUS, 1945-46. C.P.A., N.Y. Mem. Am. Inst. C.P.A.'s, Conn. Soc. C.P.A.'s. Home: 93 Westmont West Hartford CT 06117 Office: 426 Colt Hwy Farmington CT 06032 also Elliott St Beverly MA 01915

RUFFIN, ALBERT LESLIE, JR., publishing exec.; b. Greensboro, N.C., Mar. 30, 1926; s. Albert Leslie and Julia Ernestine (West) R.; B.A. cum laude, U. S.C., 1948; M.A., Duke, 1950. English master Longfellow Sch., Bethesda, Md., 1953; actor NBC-TV, Philco-Goodyear Playhouse, N.Y.C., 1954-56; editor TV Guide mag., Miami, 1957-58; editor Smithsonian Instn. Press, Washington, 1959-63, sr. editor, 1964-72, mng. editor, series publs., 1972—. Served to sgt. AUS, 1944-46; ETO. Mem. Sons of Desert, N.Y.C. Baptist. Author: Attacked by a Grizzly, 1965. Home: Chevy Chase MD 20015 Office: Smithsonian Instn Press Arts and Industries Bldg Smithsonian Instn Washington DC 20560

RUFFIN, CLOVIS, fashion designer; b. Clovis, N.Mex.; student Columbia U., Sorbonne, Paris. Organized co. Ruffinwear (now part of Kreisler Group), N.Y.C., 1972; introduced his first at-home wear collection for Keylon Enterprises, Inc. Recipient Coty award, 1973, Crystal Ball award Knitted Textile Assns., 1975. Office: care Ruffinwear 550 Seventh Ave New York NY 10018*

RUFFIN, ROGER SHERMAN, lawyer; b. San Diego, May 18, 1927; s. Roger Sherman and Eula Mae (Prather) R.; B.A. in Econs. with honors and distinction, San Diego State U., 1950; J.D., Stanford U., 1953; m. Beatrice Bright, Jan. 26, 1967; children—Lucia, Margaret, Anthony, Sara. Admitted to Calif. bar, 1954; asso. firm Luce, Forward, Kunzel & Scripps, San Diego, 1954-58; partner firm Reed, Brockway & Ruffin, San Diego, 1958-61; judge San Diego Municipal Ct., 1961-65, presiding judge, 1965; judge Superior Ct. of State of Calif., County of San Diego, 1965-71; individual practice law, San Francisco and San Diego, 1971—; sr. lectr. in philosophy U. Calif., San Diego, 1967-72; mem. faculty Calif. Coll. Trial Judges Earl Warren Legal Center U. Calif., Berkeley, 1968-69, U. Calif. Hastings Coll. Law Center for Trial and Appellate Advocacy, 1977—. Trustee Humanistic Psychology Inst.; chmn. corrections commn. San Diego Community Welfare Council, law and justice task force San Diego Urban Coalition. Served with U.S. Army, 1945-46. Recipient Civil Libertarian of Yr. award San Diego chpt. ACLU, 1971. Mem. San Diego, San Diego County (v.p. dir.), San Francisco (vice chmn. criminal justice adv. council) bar assns., Calif. Attys. for Criminal Justice, San Diego Criminal Def. Lawyers Club (pres.), Lawyers Club San Francisco, Am. Psychology-Law Soc. (v.p. San Diego chpt.). Office: 111 Pine St Suite 1600 San Francisco CA 94111

RUFFING, ANNE ELIZABETH, artist; b. Bklyn.; d. John Paul and Ruth Louise (Price) Frampton; B.S., Cornell U., 1964; postgrad. Drexel Inst. Tech., 1966; m. George W. Ruffing, Mar. 29, 1967; 1 dau., Elizabeth Anne. One-woman exhbns. include: IBM, 1966, Hall of Fame, Goshen, N.Y., 1971; group exhbns. include: Internat. Women's Arts Festival, World Trade Center, N.Y.C., 1975-76, Berkshire Mus., Pittsfield, Mass., 1965, 76, Cooperstown (N.Y.) Mus., 1969; represented in permanent collections: Met. Mus. Art, Bklyn. Mus., Library of Congress, Harvard U., Smithsonian Instn., N.Y. Hist. Soc. Johnston Hist. Mus., Atwater Kent Mus., Albany Inst. History and Art, Boston Public Library. Recipient 1st place Eric Sloane award, 1974; Internat. Women's Year award Internat. Women's Art Festival, 1976. Address: PO Box 125 Bloomington NY 12411

RUFFLE, JOHN FREDERICK, banker; b. Toledo, Mar. 28, 1937; s. Matthew Frederick and Hazel Ruth (Johnson) R.; B.A., Johns Hopkins, 1958; M.B.A., Rutgers, 1963; m. Eleanor Grace Loock, Nov. 19, 1960; children—Donald Alan, William Charles, John Garrett. With Price Waterhouse & Co., N.Y.C., 1958-65, sr. accountant, 1962-65; asst. treas. Internat. Paper Co., N.Y.C., 1965-70; comptroller Morgan Guaranty Trust Co. N.Y., N.Y.C., 1970—. Served with AUS, 1959-60. C.P.A., N.J. Mem. Financial Execs. Inst., Nat. Assn. Accountants, Am. Inst. C.P.A.'s, N.J. Soc. C.P.A.'s. Home: 34 Wynwood Rd Chatham NJ 07928 Office: 23 Wall St New York City NY 10015

RUFFNER, FREDERICK G., JR., publisher; b. Akron, Ohio, Aug. 6, 1926; s. Frederick G. and Olive Mae (Taylor) R.; B.S., Ohio State U., 1950; m. Mary Ann Evans, Oct. 8, 1954; children—Frederic G. III, Peter Evans. Advt. mgr. Jim Robbins Co., Royal Oak, Mich., 1950-52; research mgr. Gen. Detroit Corp., 1953-55; pres. Gale Research Co., Detroit, 1954—. Bd. dirs. Friends of Detroit Pub. Library, 1969—, pres., 1975-76; mem. exec. bd. Detroit council Boy Scouts Am., 1974—, v.p., 1976—; mem. Broward Indsl. Bd., Community Appearance Bd.; pres. Council for Fla. Libraries, 1979—. Served to 1st lt. AUS, 1944-46. Decorated Bronze Star; recipient Centennial award Ohio State U., 1970. Mem. Am. Antiquarian Soc., ALA, Am. Mgmt. Assn., Am. Assn. Mus., Ripon Soc., New River Council (Ft. Lauderdale), Centrum Charette, Detroit Hist. Soc., Bibliog. Soc. Am., Sierra Club, Audubon Soc., Am. Name Soc., Early Am. Industries Assn., Ephemera Soc., Johnny Appleseed Soc., Navy League, Newcomen Soc., Central Bus. Dist. Assn. (dir. 1977—), Nat. Trust for Historic Preservation, Fairfield Heritage Soc., Archives Am. Art, Pvt. Libraries Assn., Friends Ft. Lauderdale Pub. Library, (pres. 1974—), Ohio State U. Club (pres. Detroit club 1958), Soc. Arts and Crafts, Tau Kappa Epsilon. Republican. Methodist. Clubs: Masons, Shrine, Book (Detroit dir. 1967-71), Detroit Athletic, Economic, Detroit (Detroit); Ocean Reef (Key Largo, Fla.); Grosse Pointe Yacht, Le Club International (Ft. Lauderdale); Princeton, Salmagundi, Grolier, Marco Polo (N.Y.C.); Faculty (Ohio State U.). Editor: Ency. of Assns., 1956-68; Code Names Dictionary, 1963; Acronyms and Initialisms Dictionary, 1965. Patentee in graphic arts. Home: 221 Lewiston Rd Grosse Pointe Farms MI 48236 also 4040 Galt Ocean Dr Ft Lauderdale FL 33308 Office: Gale Research Co Book Tower Detroit MI 48226

RUGE, DANIEL AUGUST, neurosurgeon; b. Murdock, Nebr., May 13, 1917; s. August Daniel and Mary Louise R.; B.A., N. Central Coll., Naperville, Ill., 1939, Sc.D., 1971; M.D., Northwestern U., 1945, Ph.D., 1961; m. Greta Piper, June 12, 1942; children—Charlotte, Thomas. Intern, Wesley Meml. Hosp., Chgo., 1945-46, resident, 1949-50; resident Passavant Meml. Hosp., Chgo., 1946-49, VA Hosp., Hines, Ill., 1950-52; practice medicine specializing in neurosurgery, Chgo., 1952-76; prof. surgery Northwestern U., Chgo., 1973-76; professorial lectr. George Washington U., Washington, 1976—; dep. dir. spinal cord injury service VA Central Office, Washington, 1976—. Trustee N. Central Coll., 1960—, chmn. bd., 1974-77. Served to lt. comdr. USN, 1954-56. Recipient service award Northwestern U., 1966; Outstanding Alumnus award N. Central Coll., 1978. Fellow A.C.S.; mem. AMA, Am. Assn. Neurol. Surgeons, Central Surg. Assn., James IV Assn. Surgeons. Presbyterian. Author: Spinal Cord Injuries, 1969; Spinal Disorders: Diagnosis and Treatment, 1977; editor Jour. Am. Paraplegia Soc., 1976—. Home: 3318 N St NW Washington DC 20007 Office: VA Central Office 810 Vermont Ave NW Washington DC 20420

RUGE, NEIL MARSHALL, educator; b. Washington, Dec. 28, 1913; s. Oscar Gustave and Ruth (Jones) R.; student Calif. Inst. Tech., 1931-33; A.B., Stanford, 1935; J.D., U. Calif. at Berkeley, 1938; student Harvard Grad. Sch. Bus. Adminstrn., 1946-47; m. Madeleine Filhol, Jan. 1942 (dec. May 1944); m. 2d, Helga Maria Kley, July 23, 1949; children—Carl, Madeleine. Admitted to Calif. bar, 1938, U.S. Supreme Ct. bar, 1962; practiced law in Tulare, Calif., until 1941; joined the U.S. fgn. service, 1947; assigned Palermo, 1947-49, Casablanca, 1950-55, London, 1956, Cardiff, 1956-58; security and personnel officer State Dept., 1958-62; dep. prin. officer, Munich, 1962-68; 1st sec. Am. embassy, Guatemala, 1968-69; prof. law Calif. State U., Chico, 1969—. Served to maj. AUS, 1941-46; colonel res. Mem. Sierra Club, Phi Beta Kappa. Contbr. articles to profl. jours. Home: 936 Bryant Ave Chico CA 95926 Office: Calif State U Chico CA 95926

RUGGER, GERALD K., ins. co. exec.; b. Buffalo Center, Iowa, Aug. 10, 1916; s. Frederick Ernest and Gertrude (Klein) R.; B.A., U. Iowa, 1936; m. Mary Keefe, June 18, 1938; children—Frederick, Kenneth, Margaret (Mrs. Richard Dunmire), Janet (Mrs. David Martin). Second v.p. group ins. Home Life Ins. Co., N.Y.C., 1957-64, v.p. group ins., 1964-66, sr. v.p., 1966-67, exec. v.p., dir., 1967-69, pres., 1969-78, chmn., chief exec. officer, 1978—; mem. lower Manhattan adv. bd. Chem. Bank N.Y.; trustee Seamen's Bank for Savs., N.Y.C. Fellow Soc. Actuaries; mem. Am. Acad. Actuaries, Life Ins. Council N.Y. (v.p. 1972-73, pres. 1973-74), Hundred Year Assn. N.Y. (pres. 1972-74), Downtown-Lower Manhattan Assn. (bd. govs.), N.Y.C. Chamber Commerce and Industry (bd. govs.), Health Ins. Inst. (bd. dirs. 1973—), Health Ins. Assn. Am. (dir. 1973—). Clubs: Univ., Wall Street, Merchants (N.Y.C.). Home: 26 Rolling Hill Dr Chatham NJ 07928 Office: 253 Broadway New York NY 10007

RUGGIERI, GEORGE DANIEL, marine scientist; b. Phila., Jan. 29, 1925; s. Gervasio and Theresa (DeStefano) R.; B.S., St. Joseph's Coll., Phila., 1948; Ph.D., St. Louis U., 1960. Joined S.J., 1950; ordained priest Roman Catholic Ch., 1962; asst. prof. biology St. Joseph's Coll., 1965-67; coordinator research, research biologist, prin. investigator exptl. embryology Osborn Labs. Marine Scis., N.Y. Aquarium, Bklyn., 1967-70, asst. dir. Osborn Labs. Marine Scis., 1970-72, dir., 1973—, asso. dir. N.Y. Aquarium, 1973-76, dir., 1976—; mem. subcom. on marine resources Mayor's Oceanographic Adv. Com., N.Y.C.; adj. asso. prof. biology Fordham U. Grad. Sch.; adj. asso. prof. biology N.Y. U., 1978—; mem. staff Louis Calder Conservation and Ecology Center, Fordham U., Armonk, N.Y.; research asso. N.Y. Ocean Sci. Lab., N.Y.; co-chmn. Food-Drugs from the Sea Symposiums, 1972, 74; mem. Episcopal Diocesan Commn. on Environment and Ecology, L.I., N.Y.; mem. marine scis. adv. bd. Coral Reef Soc., 1978—; mem. exec. com. Gateway Citizens Com.; bd. dirs. N.Y. Inst. Ocean Resources, St. Josephs Coll., Nat. Theatre Workshop of Handicapped; trustee U. Scranton, Pa., 1970-74, Fordham U., 1978—. Served with AUS, 1943-46. Recipient Alumni Merit award St. Louis U., 1977. Fellow AAAS, N.Y. Acad. Scis., N.Y. Zool. Soc. (editorial adv. bd. Animal Kingdom), Am. Assn. Zool. Parks and Aquariums; mem. Am. Inst. Biol. Scis., Am. Micros. Soc., Am. Soc. Zoologists, Bermuda Biol. Sta. for Research, Hudson River Environ. Soc., Internat. Union Dirs. Zool. Gardens, Soc. Invertebrate Pathology, Harvey Soc., Royal Soc. Medicine, Wildlife Disease Assn., Sigma Xi. Co-author: The Healing Sea, 1978; co-editor: Marine Tech. Soc. Food and Drugs from the Sea Proc., 1974; contbr. sci. articles to profl. jours. Office: New York Aquarium Boardwalk and W 8th St Brooklyn NY 11224

RUGGIERO, FRED F., mfg. co. exec.; b. N.Y.C., Jan. 29, 1929; s. Fred J. and Julia (Astarita) R.; B.S., Queens Coll., 1957; M.B.A., N.Y. U., 1960; m. Isabel, Jan. 11, 1953; children—Fred F., Margaret, Robert, Russell, Christina. Acct., Haskins & Sells, 1957-58; sr. acct. Patterson Ridgeway, 1958-60; asst. controller Ideal Corp., 1960-65; controller Singer Co., 1965-67; controller Ambac Industries Inc., 1968-69, v.p., controller, 1971-75, v.p. fin., 1975-79; v.p. fin. Venus Esterbrook Inc., 1969-71, Automotive group United Technologies Corp., Dearborn, Mich., 1979—. Served with Security Service, USAF, 1948-51. Mem. Nat. Assn. Accts., Inst. Internal Auditors, Am. Mgmt. Assns., Fin. Execs. Inst. Office: Automotive Group United Technologies Corp Dearborn MI

RUGGIERO, JOHN ANTHONY, electronics mfg. co. exec.; b. Boston, Dec. 18, 1935; s. John and Catherine (Myers) R.; B.S.B.A., Boston Coll., 1957, M.B.A., 1962; m. Elva Powers, Sept. 6, 1958; children—Lisa Ann, Kara Jean. Controller, Sylvania Electric Products Co., Woburn, Mass., 1958-63; controller Sanders Assos. Inc., Nashua, N.H., 1963-70, corp. treas., 1974—; dir. Mathew Thornton Health Maintenance Orgn. Served with USAR, 1957-62. Home: Mack Hill Amherst NH 03031 Office: Sanders Assos Inc Daniel Webster Hwy S Nashua NH 03060

RUGGIERO, JOHN SALVATOR, assn. exec.; b. Saranac Lake, N.Y., Apr. 2, 1931; s. Joseph and Santa (Lopresti) R.; B.S. in Pharmacy, St. John's U., 1952; M.S., Duquesne U., 1954; Ph.D. (E. Mead Johnson fellow 1955-57), U. Conn., 1957; m. Marguerite Kathleen Bentivegna, July 4, 1953; children—Judy, John, Mary, Anthony. Grad. asst. Duquesne U., 1952-54, U. Conn., 1954-55; asst. prof. pharmacy Duquesne U., 1957-60, asso. prof., adminstrv. asst. to dean, 1960-61, prof. pharmacy, dean, 1961-71; asst. v.p. sci. and profl. relations Pharm. Mfrs. Assn., 1971—. Fellow Am. Coll. Apothecaries; mem. Am., Md., Montgomery County, D.C. (pres. 1974-75) pharm. assns., Am. Soc. Hosp. Pharmacy, Sigma Xi, Rho Chi, Phi Delta Chi. K.C. (chancellor). Editor: Drug Distribution in Hospitals; Staffing Patterns in Hospital Pharmacy. Home: 910 Brentwood Ln Wheaton MD 20902

RUGGIERO, MATTHEW JOHN, bassoonist; b. Phila., Sept. 18, 1932; s. Pompeo and Theresa (Ciampa) R.; diploma Curtis Inst. Music, 1957; m. Nancy Cirillo, Apr. 2, 1961; children—Eleanor, Claudia, Lisa. Second bassoonist Nat. Symphony Orch., Washington, 1957-60; asst. prin. bassoonist Boston Symphony Orch., 1961—; prin. bassoonist Boston Pops Orch., 1974—; mem. faculty Boston U., 1963—, New Eng. Conservatory Music, 1963—. Served with U.S. Army, 1954-57. Office: Boston Symphony Orch Symphony Hall Boston MA 02115

RUGGLES, RICHARD, educator, economist; b. Columbus, Ohio, June 15, 1916; s. Clyde Orval and Frances (Holmes) R.; A.B., Harvard U., 1939, M.A., 1941, Ph.D., 1942; m. Nancy Dunlap, June 1, 1946; children—Ann Patricia, Catherine Joan, John Steven. Economist, OSS, 1942-46; instr. Harvard U., 1946-47; asst. prof. econs. Yale U., 1947-49, asso. prof., 1949-54, prof., 1954—, chmn. dept. econs., 1959-62; mem. sr. research staff Nat. Bur. Econ. Research, 1966-77. Mem. Econometric Soc. (sec. 1955-70), Conf. Research in Income and Wealth, Internat. Assn. Research in Income and Wealth, Am. Econ. Assn., Am. Statis. Assn. Author: (with Nancy D. Ruggles) National Income Accounting and Income Analysis, 1956; The Design of Economic Accounts, 1970. Mng. editor Rev. Income and Wealth, 1970—. Home: 100 Prospect St New Haven CT 06511

RUGGLES, RICHARD LOUNSBURY, otolaryngologist; b. Cleve., Sept. 7, 1919; s. Charles L. and Phoebe (Otto) R.; student Oberlin Coll., 1941; M.D., Case Western Res. U., 1944; m. Maurine Malster, Jan. 29, 1944; children—Ann, Charles M., Barbara, Maurine, Richard M. Intern, Harper Hosp., Detroit, 1944-45; resident Cleve. Met. Gen. Hosp., 1945-46, 48-49; practice medicine, specializing in otolaryngology, Cleve., 1944—; exec. sec. Am. Laryngol. and Otol. Soc., 1974—; sec.-treas. Centurian Club of Deafness Research Found. Served with M.C., AUS, 1942-48. Mem. Am., Ohio med. assns., Cleve. Acad. Medicine, Am. Acad. Ophthalmology and Otolaryngology, Am. Laryngol. Rhinol. and Otol. Soc., Soc. U. Otolaryngologists, Otosclerosis Study Group, Am. Otol. Soc., Am. Soc. Ophthalmologic and Otolaryngologic Allergy. N.E. Ohio Otolaryngology Club. Contbr. med. articles to profl. jours. Office: 11201 Shaker Blvd Cleveland OH 44104

RUGGLES, RUDY LAMONT, lawyer; b. Phila., Jan. 10, 1909; s. Daniel Emery and A. Leona (Rudy) R.; student U. Cin., 1926-27, Harvard, 1927-31; Harvard scholar, Geneva (Switzerland) Sch. Internat. Studies, 1929; J.D., Boston U., 1934; m. Ruth Cain, Dec. 14, 1935; children—Rudy Lamont, Jean Cain (Mrs. Robert A. Romoser). Admitted to Ill. bar, 1935, U.S. Supreme Ct., 1960; asso. Isham, Lincoln & Beale, Chgo., 1935-42; regional atty. OPA, 1942-43; mem. firm Chadwell, Kayser, Ruggles, McGee & Hastings, Chgo., 1946-75, of counsel, 1976—. Mem. vis. com. humanities div. U. Chgo., 1959-74, mem. citizens bd., 1963—; mem. Chgo. Crime Commn.; mem. nat. bd. Nat. Book Com.; bd. dirs., chmn. legal aid bur. com. United Charities Chgo.; bd. overseers vis. com. to Harvard Coll., 1964-70, Harvard Div. Sch., 1969-75, also mem. standing com. univ. resources; bd. dirs., exec. com. Evanston Hosp., 1965-75; mem. Northwestern U. Assos.; past chmn. lawyers div. Chgo. Crusade of Mercy; trustee Newberry Library, 1964—. Served to lt. USNR, 1944-46. Recipient award distinguished service to profession, community and youth of Am., Monticello Coll., 1959. Fellow Am. Bar Found.; mem. Am., Ill., Chgo., 7th Fed. Circuit bar assns., Am. Soc. Internat. Law, Am. Judicature Soc., Law Club Chgo., Legal Club Chgo., Harvard Alumni Assn. (dir.), Beta Theta Pi, Phi Delta Phi. Clubs: Comml., Econ. (dir., past pres.), Harvard (past pres.), Caxton (past pres.), Chgo. Literary, Chicago (past pres., dir.), Mid-America, Mid-Day (trustee, past pres.), Wayfarers (Chgo.); Glen View (Golf, Ill.); Indian Hill (Winnetka); Grolier (N.Y.C.); Everglades, Lost Tree, Old Port Yacht (Palm Beach, Fla.). Home: 1115 Mohawk Rd Wilmette IL 60091 Office: 8500 Sears Tower 233 S Wacker Dr Chicago IL 60606

RUGOFF, MILTON, editor; b. N.Y.C., Mar. 6, 1913; s. David and Jennie (Joseph) R.; B.A., Columbia, 1933, M.A., 1934, Ph.D., 1940; m. Helen Birkenbaum, Jan. 31, 1937; 1 dau., Kathy. Editor, Alfred A. Knopf, Inc., 1943-47, The Mag., 1947-48, Readers Subscription Book Club, 1953; editor, v.p. Chanticleer Press, N.Y.C., 1948—. Served with AUS, 1943-46. Author: Donne's Imagery, 1940; Penguin Book of World Folk Tales, 1949; The Great Travelers, 1960; Prudery and Passion: Sexuality in Victorian America, 1970; The Wild Places, 1974. Editor: Britannica Ency. American Art, 1973. Office: 424 Madison Ave New York NY 10017

RUHE, C(ARL) H(ENRY) WILLIAM, med. assn. exec.; b. Wilkinsburg, Pa., Dec. 1, 1915; s. Carl and Orra Rebecca (Henderson) R.; B.S., U. Pitts., 1937, M.D., 1940; m. Geraldine McDowell, June 19, 1943 (dec.); m. 2d, Dorothy Mae Duncan, July 12, 1974; children—Barbara Fleming, Nancy Cynthia, David Robert. Intern Western Pa. Hosp., Pitts., 1940-41; instr. physiology and pharmacology U. Pitts., 1941-46, asst. prof., 1946-52, asso. prof., 1952-60, asst. dean sch. medicine, 1954-59, asso. dean, 1959-60; asst. dir. dept. med. edn. AMA, Chgo., 1960-64, asso. dir., 1964-67, dir. div. med. edn., 1967-76, group v.p., 1976, sr. v.p., 1976—. Recipient Philip Hench Distinguished Alumnus award U. Pitts. Med. Alumni Assn., 1975. Mem. Am., Ill. med. assns., Chgo. Med. Soc., Am. Physiol. Soc., AAAS, Soc. for Health and Human Values (pres. 1976-77), Sigma Xi, Phi Rho Sigma. (pres. 1972-76). Presbyterian. Contbr. articles to profl. jours. Home: 240 Timber Ridge LBS Barrington IL 60010 Office: 535 N Dearborn St Chicago IL 60610

RUHE, ROBERT VICTORY, geologist; b. Chicago Heights, Ill., Nov. 7, 1918; s. Henry Frederick and Rose Lenora (Hartmann) R.; B.A., Carleton Coll., Northfield, Minn., 1942; M.S., Iowa State U., 1948; Ph.D., U. Iowa, 1950; m. Barbara Mills, Jan. 9, 1943; children—Robin Ruhe, Jonathan Mills, Deborah. Asst. prof. geology Iowa State U., 1950-51; geomorphologist ECA, Belgian Congo, 1951-52; research geologist Soil Conservation Service, Dept. Agr., Washington, 1953-70; prof. geology, dir. Water Resources Research Center, Ind U., Bloomington, 1970—; vis. prof. Cornell U., 1958, Johns Hopkins U., 1966; adj. prof. Iowa State U., 1963-70; cons. in field. Served to capt. USMC, 1942-46. Nat. research fellow NRC, 1950-51; recipient Book Author award Iowa State U. Press, 1968; Centennial citation Iowa Acad. Scis., 1975. Fellow Geol. Soc. Am. (Kirk Bryan award 1974), AAAS; mem. Internat. Union Quaternary Research (pres. commn. paleopedology 1969-73), Soil Sci. Soc. Am. Author: Geomorphology, 1975; Quaternary Landscapes in Iowa, 1969; also articles. Office: Water Resources Research Center Ind Univ Bloomington IN 47401*

RUHL, ROBERT HENRY, mgmt. cons.; b. Marion, Ohio, Aug. 4, 1906; s. Henry S. and Princess Emily (Mason) R.; student U. Cin., 1924-26; B.S., Ohio State U., 1928; m. Amy C. Nash, July 19, 1947. Indsl. engr. Marion Power Shovel Co., 1928-30, Farrell-Cheek Steel Co., Sandusky, Ohio, 1930-34; chief indsl. engr. Burnside Steel Co., Chgo., 1934-39; sr. partner Stevenson, Jordan & Harrison, mgmt. cons., Chgo., 1939-62; pres. Divco-Wayne Industries, N.Y.C., 1962-68; exec. v.p. Divco-Wayne Corp., 1965-68; pres. Gen. Coach of Can., Neno Valley Coach, Gt. Britain. Presbyterian. Clubs: Lake Shore (Chgo.); Exmoor Country (Highland Park, Ill.); Tamarac Country (Ft. Lauderdale, Fla.). Home: 89 Palm Club Pompano Beach FL 33062

RUHLMAN, TERRELL LOUIS, business exec.; b. Warren, Pa., Nov. 13, 1926; s. Ross L. and Gertrude R.; B.S., Pa. State U., 1949; J.D., George Washington U., 1954; postgrad. Duquesne U. Grad. Bus. Sch., 1966-68; m. Phyllis E., Jan. 15, 1951; children—Robyn D. (Mrs. Jack Dempsey), Randall L., Heather M., Mark A. Admitted to D.C. bar; patent counsel Joy Mfg. Co., Pitts., 1954-59, gen. counsel, 1959-62, asst. to pres., 1962-69, v.p. oilfield ops., Houston, 1969-73; gen. mgr. Reed Tool Co., Houston, 1973-74, pres., chief operating officer, 1974-76, dir., 1975-76; v.p., dir. Baker Internat. Corp., 1975-76, pres. mining group, 1976; pres., chief exec. officer, dir. Ansul Co., Marinette, Wis., 1976—. Served with USAF. Home: RB 167 Riverside Blvd Menominee MI 49858 Office: 1 Stanton St Marinette MI 54143

RUINA, JACK PHILIP, elec. engr.; b. Rypin, Poland, Aug. 19, 1923; s. Michael and Nechuma (Warshaw) R.; came to U.S., 1927; naturalized, 1932; B.E.E., Coll. City N.Y., 1944; M.E.E., Poly. Inst. Bklyn., 1949, D.Elec. Engring., 1951; m. Edith Elster, Oct. 26, 1947; children—Ellen, Andrew, Rachel. Research fellow Microwave Research Inst., Poly. Inst. Bklyn., 1948-50; from instr. to asso. prof. elec. engring. Brown U., 1950-54; research asso. prof. Coordinated Sci. Lab., U. Ill., 1954-59, research prof., 1959-63, prof. elec. engring., 1959-63; prof. elec. engring. Mass. Inst. Tch., 1963—, v.p. for spl. labs., 1966- 70; U.S. observer Antarctica, 1964; on leave to U.S. Govt., 1959-63, as pres. Inst. Def. Analyses, 1964-66; dep. for research to asst. sec. air force, 1959-60; asst. dir. for def. research and engring. Office Sec. Def., 1960-61; dir. Advanced Research Projects Agy., Dept. Def., 1961-63. Mem. Presdl. Sci. Adv. Commn. Panel, 1963-72; sci. adv. bd. USAF, 1964-67; adv. bd. and panels for Dept. Def., HEW, Dept. Transp., ACDA, Office Technology Assessment, NSF, Nat. Security Council, 1963—; gen. adv. com. to ACDA, 1969-74; sr. cons. Office Sci. and Tech. Policy, White House, 1977—; chmn. com. on environ. decision making Nat. Acad. Scis., 1974-77. Dir. Mitre Corp., Flow-Gen. Corp. Recipient Fleming award as one of ten outstanding yound men in govt., 1962. Fellow IEEE, Am. Acad. Arts and Scis., AAAS; mem. Internat. Sci. Radio Union, AAUP, Inst. Strategic Studies, Council Fgn. Relations, Sigma Xi. Home: 28 Hawthorn St Cambridge MA 02138

RUITENBEEK, HENDRIK M., psychoanalyst; b. Leyden, Holland, Feb. 26, 1928; s. Johannes and Marie (de la Court) R.; B.A., U. Leyden, 1948, Ph.D., 1952, LL.D., 1955; tng. in psychoanalysis, Holland and U.S.; came to U.S., 1955, naturalized, 1962. Tchr. existential psychoanalysis N.Y. U., 1963—; pvt. practice psychoanalysis, N.Y.C., 1960—. Fellow Am. Inst. Psychotherapy and Psychoanalysis (supr., mem. faculty, mem. exec. com.); mem. Am. Acad. Psychotherapists, Am. Group Psychotherapy Assn., Am. Otoanalytic Assn., Assn. Applied Psychoanalysis, Am. Psychol. Assn. Author: The Individual and the Crowd: A Study of Identity in America, 2d edit., 1965; Freud and America, 1966; The Male Myth, 1967; The New Group Therapies, 1970; The New Sexuality, 1974; Psychotherapy, 1976; (in Dutch) The Rise and Origin of the Dutch Labour Party, 1955. Editor: Psychoanalysis and Existential Philosophy, 1962; Psychoanalysis and Social Science, 1962; Problem of Homosexuality in Modern Society, 1963; The Dilemma of Organizational Society, 1963; Varieties of Classic Social Theory, 1963; Varieties of Modern Social Theory, 1963; Psychoanalysis and Contemporary American Culture, 1964; Psychoanalysis and Literature, 1964; Varieties of Personality Theory, 1965; The Literary Imagination, 1965; The Creative Imagination, 1965; Heirs to Freud, 1966; Psychoanalysis and Female Sexuality, 1966; Psychoanalysis and Male Sexuality, 1966; The Psychotherapy of Perversions, 1967; Homosexuality and Creative Genius, 1968; Death: Interpretations, 1969; Group Therapy Today, 1969; Sexuality and Identity, 1971; Going Crazy: The Radical Theory of R.D. Laing, 1972; The Analytical Situation: How Patient and Therapist Communicate, 1973; Homosexuality, 1973; Freud As We Knew Him, 1973. Address: 43 Fifth Ave New York City NY 10003

RUIZ, ALDELMO, fgn. service officer; b. Yauco, P.R., June 12, 1923; s. Hipolito and Mercedes (Santiago) R.; B.S., Va. Poly. Inst. and State U., 1949, M.S., 1950; postgrad. spl. courses Fgn. Service Inst., also U. Va., 1969, Indsl. Coll. Armed Forces, 1972, George Washington U., 1971-72; m. Mary T. Lonardelli, July 29, 1949; children—Stella Ann, Michael Linvil. Teaching and research fellow Va. Poly. Inst., 1950; design engr. Washington Suburban San. Commn., Hyattsville, Md.; chief san., utilities depts., asst. mgr., tech. coordinator Thomas B. Bourne Assos., Far East Div., 1955-58; cons. engr. in pvt. practice, 1959-62; san. engr. ERDL, Dept. Army, 1951-52, project engr., 1952-55; chief engr. AID, Taiz, 1962-64; dir. water supply and environ. sanitation dept., YAR, 1964-66, devel. officer, Yemen, 1966-67, chief engring. advisor, Kabul, Afghanistan, 1967-68, gen. engring. officer, Kabul, 1968-71, Indsl. Coll. Armed Forces, 1971-72; interregional engring. coordinator AID, 1972-73; AID affairs officer, Yemen, Sana'a, 1973-74, AID rep., 1974-75, dir. mission, 1975-77; mission dir., El Salvador, San Salvador, 1978-79, Panama City, Panama, 1979—; participant various internat. confs. and seminars. Bd. dirs. Sana Internat. Sch. (Yemen Arab Republic). Served with AUS, 1942-45. Recipient Distinguished Honor award AID, 1966; hon. certificate Yemen Arab Republic, 1977. Registered profl. engr., Del., Md., D.C., Mass., P.R. Fellow ASCE; mem. Am. Water Works Assn., Nat. Soc. Profl. Engrs., Internat. Commn. Irrigation and Drainage, Colegio Ingenieros Arquitectos Agrimensores de P.R. Lion. Contbr. articles to profl. jours. Home: PO Box 299 Yauco PR 00768 Office: US Mission (AID) APO Miami FL 34002. *Fostering modernization in developing nations in their process of social, economic and political development will be a major contribution by the western world industrialized and developed nations toward mankind in the 20th century.*

RUIZ, MANUEL, JR., lawyer; b. Los Angeles, July 25, 1906; s. Manuel and Enriqueta (Gessenius-Arriola) R.; J.D., U. So. Calif., 1930; m. Claudia Scipper, Aug. 5, 1933; 1 dau., Claudia. Internat. lawyer, Los Angeles; mem. U.S. Commn. on Civil Rights, 1971—. Bd. dirs. Mexican Am. Opportunity Found.; hon. bd. dirs. Los Angeles Legal Aid Found.; trustee Mexican Am. Scholarship Found.-Assisting Careers in Law. Recipient Distinguished Service award Los Angeles C. of C.; Lex award Mexican-Am. Bar Assn.; named Distinguished Am., KABC Radio. Author: Mexican-American Legal Heritage in the Southwest. Office: 3859 Franklin Ave Hollywood CA 90027

RUIZ, RAMON EDUARDO, educator; b. La Jolla, Calif., Sept. 9, 1921; s. Ramon and Dolores (Urueta) R.; B.A., San Diego State Coll., 1947; M.A., Claremont Grad. Sch., 1948; Ph.D., U. Calif. at Berkeley, 1954; m. Natalia Marrujo, Oct. 14, 1944; children—Olivia, Maura. Asst. prof. U. Oreg., Eugene, 1955-57, So. Meth. U., Dallas, 1957-58; prof. Smith Coll., Northampton, Mass., 1958-69; prof. Lat. Am. history U. Calif. at San Diego, 1969—, chmn. dept. history, 1971-76, div. humanities, 1972-74; mem. project grant com. Nat. Endowment for Humanities, 1972-73, 75-77, dir. public programs div., 1979—; vis. prof. Sch. Advanced Internat. Studies, Johns Hopkins U., 1979-80; mem. project grant com. Ford Found. Served to lt. USAAF, 1943-46. William Harrison Mills traveling fellow in internat. relations, 1950; John Hay Whitney Found. fellow, 1950; Fulbright fellow, Mex., 1965-66; recipient Am. Philos. Soc. grant in aid, 1959. Mem. Am. Hist. Assn., Conf. Latin Am. History, Phi Beta Kappa, Sigma Delta Pi. Author: Cuba: The Making of A Revolution, 1968; Mexico: The Challenge of Poverty and Illiteracy, 1963; An American in Maximillians's Mexico, 1865-1866, 1959; Interpreting Latin American History, 1970; Labor and the Ambivalent Revolutionaries: Mexico, 1911-23, 1975; The Mexican War: Was It Manifest Destiny?, 1963; The Great Rebellion: Mexico, 1905-1924, 1980. Home: PO Box 1775 Rancho Santa Fe CA 92067 Office: Dept History C-004 Univ Calif San Diego La Jolla CA 92093

RUIZ-DE-CONDE, JUSTINA MALAXECHEVARRIA, ret. educator; b. Madrid, Spain, Nov. 30, 1909; d. Andres de la Peña Ruiz and Prudencia Malaxechevarria; Bachiller, Inst. Cardenal Cisneros, Madrid, 1926; Licenciada en Derecho, Univ. Central, Madrid, 1931; M.A., Radcliffe Coll., 1943, Ph.D., 1945. Came to U.S., 1939, naturalized, 1945. Tchr., Inst. Nacional de Segunda Ensenañza, Valdepeñas, Madrid and Barcelona, 1933-38; practice law, Madrid, 1931-38; instr. Abbott Acad., Andover, Mass., also Middlebury (Vt.) Coll., summers 1939-41; mem. faculty Wellesley Coll., 1941—, prof. Spanish, 1958-75, Helen J. Sanborn prof., 1973-75, emeritus, 1975—, chmn. dept., 1946-52, 54-58, 61-62, 64-69. Mem. New Eng. Assn. Tchrs. Spanish and Portuguese (sec. 1956-57), Modern Lang. Assn. (group sec. 1949-51), AAUW, Phi Beta Kappa, corr. mem. Hispanio Soc. Author: El Amor y el Matrimonio Secreto en los Libros de Caballerias, 1948; Un Pueblo Mexicano, 1949; Antonio Machado y Guiomar, 1964; El cantico americano de Jorge Guillén, 1973. Editor: (with Ada M. Coe) Estudios Hispánicos, Homenaje a Archer M. Huntigton, 1952; (with others) Homenaje a Jorge Guillén, 1978. Home: 75 Grove St Apt 328 Wellesley MA 02181

RUJA, HARRY, educator; b. Paterson, N.J., Feb. 26, 1912; s. Abram Joseph and Sarah Feyge (Skroopka) R.; A.B., U. Calif. at Los Angeles, 1933; M.A., U. Chgo., 1934; Ph.D., Princeton, 1936; M.A., San Diego State U., 1953; m. Rose Leah Rosenberg, Dec. 22, 1940; children—Michele B. (Mrs. Ali M. Hebshi), Ellen Gay (Mrs. Thomas Krause), Nancy Joanna (Mrs. John Terhorst). Instr. philosophy U. Calif. at Los Angeles, 1938; instr. psychology and philosophy Compton Coll., 1939-47; from asst. prof. to prof. philosophy San Diego State U., 1947-79, pres. emeritus, 1979—, chmn. dept., 1959-62, asso. dean curriculum, 1970-71, faculty senate, 1962-64, 72-73, coordinator Jewish studies, 1971-77; vis. prof. philosophy U. Minn., summer 1959, C.W. Post Coll., summer 1965; exchange prof. philosophy Pa. State U., 1964-65. Hillel counselor, 1955-64; bd. dirs. Jewish Community Center of San Diego, 1960-63, v.p., 1961-63. Mem. Am. Philos. Assn., Bertrand Russell Soc. (dir. 1978—), ACLU (pres. San Diego 1957-58, dir. 1959-62, 67-70, mem. bd. So. Calif. chpt. 1959-62), Zionist Orgn. Am. (life, pres. San Diego dist. 1973-75), United Profs. Calif., (v.p. San Diego 1962, sec. 1963, 78-79), Labor Zionist Alliance (pres. local br. 1976-78, 79—). Jewish (pres. congregation 1975-77, chmn. bd. 1977-80). Mem. B'nai B'rith (pres. San Diego 1958, Heartland 1973-74). Author: Psychology for Life, 1955, German edit., 1958; editor: Mortals and Others. Abstractor: Psychol. Abstracts, 1953—. Bd. editors Philosophy and Phenomenol. Research, 1966—; editorial asst. Principles of Physical Realism. Author articles on Bertrand Russell, Zionism, Judaism. Office: Dept Philosophy San Diego State U San Diego CA 92182

RUKEYSER, MERRYLE STANLEY, JR., broadcasting exec.; b. N.Y.C., Apr. 15, 1931; s. Merryle Stanley and Berenice (Simon) R.; student U. Va., 1948-52; m. Phyllis L. Kasha, May 16, 1975; children—Jill Victoria, Patricia Bern. Reporter Albany (N.Y.) Times-Union, 1949, Internat. News Service, N.Y.C., 1951; TV publicist Young & Rubicam, Inc., N.Y.C., 1952-57; with NBC, 1958—, dir. news info., Washington, 1962, v.p. press and publicity, N.Y.C., 1963-72, v.p. corp. info., 1972-74, v.p. pub. info., 1974-77, exec. v.p. pub. info., 1977—. Dir. TV Info. Com. Served with AUS, 1953-54. Mem. Acad. TV Arts and Scis., Internat. Radio and TV Soc., Nat. Press. Club. Home: 275 Central Park W New York City NY 10024 Office: 30 Rockefeller Plaza New York City NY 10020

RUKEYSER, MURIEL, poet; b. N.Y.C., Dec. 15, 1913; d. Lawrence and Myra (Lyons) R.; student Vassar Coll., Columbia U., 1930-32; Litt.D., 1961; 1 son, William L. Author poems, biographies, motion pictures, TV; lectr., tchr.; faculty Sarah Lawrence Coll., 1956-67; bd. dirs. Tchrs.-Writers Collaborative, 1967—. Pres. P.E.N. Am. Center, 1975-76. Recipient Nat. Inst. award, 1942; Swedish Acad. Trans. award, 1968; Copernicus award, 1977; Shelley award, 1977; Guggenheim fellow, 1943; Am. Council Learned Socs. fellow, 1963. Mem. Nat. Inst. Arts and Letters, Soc. Am. Historians. Author: Theory of Flight, 1935; U.S. 1, 1938; A Turning Wind, 1939; Soul and Body of John Brown, 1941; Willard Gibbs, 1942; Beast in View, 1944; The Green Wave, 1948; Orpheus, 1949; The Life of Poetry, 1949; Selected Poems, 1951; One Life, 1957; Body of Waking, 1958; Waterlily Fire, 1962; The Orgy, 1965; The Speed of Darkness, 1968; The Traces of Thomas Hariot, 1971; Breaking Open, 1973; The Gates, 1976; Collected Poems, 1979; (children's books) Come Back Paul, 1955; I Go Out, 1959; Bubbles, 1967; Mazes, 1970; translator: Sun Stone, 1963; Selected Poems of Octavio Paz, 1963; (with Leif Sjoberg) Selected Poems of Gunnar Ekelof, 1967; Brecht's Uncle Eddie's Moustache, 1974. Address: 463 West St New York NY 10014

RUKEYSER, WILLIAM SIMON, mag. editor; b. N.Y.C., June 8, 1939; s. Merryle Stanley and Berenice (Simon) R.; A.B., Princeton U., 1961; student Christ's Coll., Cambridge (Eng.) U., 1962-63; m. Elisabeth Mary Garnett, Nov. 21, 1963; children—Lisa Ellen, James William. Copyreader, Wall St. Jour., 1961-62, staff reporter, Europe, 1963-67; asso. editor Fortune mag., 1967-71, mem. bd. editors, 1971-72; mng. editor Money mag., N.Y.C., 1972—; commentator Good Morning America, ABC-TV, 1978—. Mem. jud. com. Union County (N.J.) Med. Soc., 1977—. Home: 1160 Terrill Rd Scotch Plains NJ 07076 Office: Money Magazine Time and Life Bldg Rockefeller Center New York NY 10020

RULE, ELTON H., broadcasting co. exec.; b. Stockton, Calif., 1917; grad. Sacramento Coll.; m. Betty Louise Bender; children—Cindy Rule Dunne, Christie, James. With ABC, N.Y.C., 1952—, gen. sales mgr. KABC-TV, 1953-60, gen. mgr., 1960-61, v.p., gen. mgr., 1961-68, pres. ABC TV Network, 1968-70, group v.p. Am. Broadcasting Cos. Inc., 1969-72, pres. ABC div., 1970-72, pres., chief operating officer, mem. exec. com. Am. Broadcasting Cos., Inc., 1972—, dir., 1970—; pres. Cal. Broadcasters Assn., 1966-67. Mem. adv. bd. Inst. Sports Medicine and Athletic Trauma, Lenox Hill Hosp., 1973—; adv. com. Will Rogers Hosp. and Research Center, 1974—. Recipient Gold medal award Internat. Radio and TV Soc., 1975, award for outstanding achievement in bus. mgmt. U. So. Calif. Sch. Bus. Adminstrn., 1978. Office: American Broadcasting Companies Inc 1330 Ave of the Americas New York NY 10019

RUMAGGI, LOUIS JACOB, ret. army officer; b. Memphis, Dec. 3, 1900; s. Louis and Garnet (Huntsbarger) R.; student Miami U., Oxford, Ohio, 1917-18; B.S., U.S. Mil. Acad., 1922; B.S. in Civil Engring., U. Calif. at Berkeley, 1927; m. Miriam Louise Tuggle, Mar. 30, 1950; 1 dau., Louise Herron (Mrs. Alan Lyndal Reed). Commd. 2d lt. C.E., U.S. Army, 1922, advanced through grades to maj. gen., 1953; acting chief engr. Army Forces, S.W. Pacific, 1945-46; engr. 8th U.S. Army, Korea, 1952-53; dep. chief engrs. U.S. Army, 1954-55; chief staff 6th U.S. Army, 1955-57; div. engr. N. Central div. Corps Engrs., 1957-59; with Tex. Instruments, Inc., 1959-62. Decorated Legion of Merit with oak leaf cluster, D.S.M.; Ulchi Medal (Korea). Fellow Soc. Am. Mil. Engrs. (life), ASCE (life); mem. SAR (nat. trustee), Mil. Order World Wars, Am. Legion. Clubs: Army and Navy (Washington), Rotary. Home: 6337 Diamond Head Circle Apt B Dallas TX 75225. *All through my life the influences of my Christian mother, the Christian ethic, and the ideals of the United States Military Academy at West Point have tempered my actions and decision. I learned early that any task worth doing was worth doing well and with all the skill and capacity of my being. Every task had to be undertaken faithfully and performed wholeheartedly. Seemingly little things required the same attention as those apparently more important. There was no substitute for honest painstaking attention to all the tasks that came my way.*

RUMBLE, RICHARD EDWARDS, naval officer; b. San Diego, Oct. 26, 1922; s. Cyril Alfred and Eileen Adelle (Loudermilk) R.; B.S.E.E., U.S. Naval Acad., 1944; student Armed Forces Staff Coll., 1958-59, Nat. War Coll., 1966-67; m. Bernice Blease, June 16, 1951; children—Richard Edwards, Rebecca E., Daniel S., Laura A. Enlisted U.S. Navy, 1940, commd. ensign, 1944, advanced thru grades to rear adm., 1972; served on USS Salt Lake City, 1944-45, PTO; with Fighting Squadron 191, 1947-50; stationed at Naval Air Test Center, Patuxent River, Md., 1950-53; pilot, staff various assignments, 1953-60; comdg. officer Attack Squadron 81, 1960-61, comdr. CAW-10 1963-64; various staff assignments, 1964-66; comdr. USS Marias, 1967-68, USS America, 1968-69; chief staff to comdr. 2d Fleet, 1970-72; comdt. First Naval Dist., Boston, comdr. Naval Base, Newport, R.I., 1972-74; comdr. Naval Base Norfolk, comdt. 5th Naval Dist., Norfolk, Va., 1974-76; dep. comdr. to comdr. in chief U.S. Naval Forces, Europe, 1976-78; chief staff to SACLANT, 1978—. Mem. Citizen Advisor Commn., mem. bd. C. of C., Norfolk, Va., 1974-76; mem. bd. Norfolk Acad., 1974-76. Decorated Legion of Merit with gold star, Meritorious Service Medal, Nat. Defense Service Medal with bronze star, Vietnam Service Medal with bronze star, Rep. Vietnam Gallentry Cross. Catholic. Home: 500 Wilder Rd Virginia Beach VA 23451 Office: Chief Staff SACLANT Norfolk VA 12351

RUMBOUGH, STANLEY MADDOX, JR., industrialist; b. N.Y.C., Apr. 25, 1920; s. Stanley Maddox and Elizabeth (Colgate) R.; A.B., Yale, 1942; grad. student bus. adminstrn. N.Y. U., 1947-51; m. Nedenia Hutton, Mar. 23, 1946 (div. Dec. 1966); children—Stanley H., David P. (dec.), Nedenia Colgate; m. Margaretha Wagstrom, Dec. 21, 1967. Vice pres., dir. Willis Air Service, Teterboro, N.J., 1946-47; v.p., dir. White Metal Mfg. Co., Hoboken N.J., 1945-61, pres., 1960-61; pres., dir. Metal Container Corp., 1950-59, Am. Totalisator, Balt., 1956-58; chmn. bd. Extrusion Devel. Corp., 1959-61; co-founder, chmn. bd. Elec. Engring. Ltd., 1960-69; chmn. bd. Wallace Clark & Co., 1962-69; co-founder, dir. Trinidad Flour Mills, Jamaica Flour Mills, 1961-72; dir. Dart Industries, Inc., New Co., Ltd., Internat. Flavors and Fragrances, Comp-U-Card Am., Inc. Spl. asst to sec. commerce, 1953; spl. asst. White House charge exec. br. liaison, 1953-55. Chmn. U.S. Com. for UN, 1957-58; co-founder Citizens for Eisenhower, 1951; vice chmn. Citizens for Eisenhower-Nixon Com., 1952; trustee Young Presidents' Found., 1957-70, pres., 1962-65; bd. dirs. N.Y. World's Fair Corp., 1961-70, Nat. Conf. on Citizenship, 1973—; trustee Library for Presdl. Papers, 1966-70, Internat. House, 1959—, Fgn. Policy Assn., 1961-70, Am. Health Found., 1972-76; bd. dirs. Population Resource Center, 1978—. Served as capt. USMCR, 1942-46. Decorated Air medal (8), D.F.C. (2). Mem. Chief Execs. Forum, World Bus. Council, Zeta Psi. Republican. Clubs: Racquet and Tennis, Internat. Lawn Tennis, Maidstone (East Hampton, N.Y.); Seminole, Bath and Tennis, Sailfish, Everglades (Palm Beach). Home: 318 Caribbean Rd Palm Beach FL 33480 Office: 339 Royal Poinciana Plaza Palm Beach FL 33480

RUMER, RALPH RAYMOND, JR., civil engr., educator; b. Ocean City, N.J., June 22, 1931; s. Ralph Raymond and Anna (Hibbard) R.; BS. in Civil Engring., Duke U., 1953; M.S., Rutgers U., 1959; Sc.D. (ASCE research fellow), M.I.T., 1962; m. Shirley Louise Haynes, Nov. 30, 1953; children—Sherri, Sue, Sandra, Sarah. With Lukens Steel Co., Coatsville, Pa., 1953-54; instr. dept. civil engring. Rutgers U., New Brunswick, N.J., 1956-59; civil engr. U.S. Dept. Agr., New Brunswick summer 1957-59; research asst. Hydrodynamics lab. M.I.T., Boston, 1961-62; asst. prof. dept. civil engring. M.I.T., 1962-63; asso. prof. dept. civil engring. SUNY, Buffalo, 1963-69, prof., 1969-76, 78—, acting head, 1966-67, chmn., 1967-73, dir. Center for Inland Water Resources, 1972-74, acting provost engring. and applied scis., 1974-75; prof., chmn. dept. civil engring. U. Del., Newark, 1976-78; com. mem. Erie County Sewerage and Drainage Agy., N.Y.; mem. Environ. Conservation Adv. Com., Amherst, N.Y.; tech. cons. to govt. and industry in hydraulics, water resources, and environ. engring. Served with U.S. Army, 1954-56. Ford fellow, 1962-63, sr. research fellow Calif. Inst. Tech., 1970-71; lic. prof. engr., N.Y. Mem.

ASCE (dir. Buffalo sect.), Internat. Assn., Hydraulic Research, Am. Geophys. Union, Am. Soc. Engring. Edn., Internat. Assn. Gt. Lakes Research, Sigma Xi, Chi Epsilon. Contbr. research articles in field to profl. jours. Home: 821 Eggert Rd Buffalo NY 14226. *In a sense, I am a composite of those persons that have influenced my life in a positive way.*

RUMER, ROBERT RICHARD, chem. co. exec.; b. St. Louis, Oct. 11, 1922; s. Richard Otto and Margaret Anna (Haver) R.; B.S.Ch.E., Washington U., St. Louis, 1942; postgrad. M.I.T., 1963; m. Shirley Virginia Pemberton, June 9, 1944; children—Susan Meredith, Barbara Ann, Richard Robert, Roger William. With Monsanto Chem. Co., 1942-69, dir. mfg. inorganic and agrl. chem. div., St. Louis, 1959-64, v.p., gen. mgr. agrl. chem. div., 1964-69; exec. v.p. Mobay Chem. Corp., Pitts., 1969—. Served with USN, 1944-46. Mem. Greater Pitts. C. of C., Soc. Plastics Industries. Republican. Presbyterian. Office: Mobay Chem Corp Penn Lincoln Pkwy W Pittsburgh PA 15205

RUMFORD, BEATRIX TYSON, museum ofcl.; b. Balt., June 16, 1939; d. Lewis and Rose (Clymer) R.; B.A., Weslleslev Coll., 1962; M.A., State U. N.Y., Oneonta, 1965. Art research editor D. C. Heath & Co., Boston, 1962-64; research asso. Chgo. Hist. Soc., 1965-67; curator, dept. collections Colonial Williamsburg (Va.), 1967-71; asso. dir. Abby Aldrich Rockefeller Folk Art Collection, Williamsburg, 1971-73, dir., 1973—; cons. Bermuda Nat. Trust, 1973; mem. accession com. Exec. Mansion, Richmond. Mem. Am. Antiquarian Soc., N.Y. State Hist. Assn. (trustee 1975—). Contbr. to Antiques mag., 1969—. Home: Tayloe House Williamsburg VA 23185 Office: Drawer C South England St Williamsburg VA 23185

RUMLER, ROBERT HOKE, assn. exec.; b. Chambersburg, Pa., Apr. 4, 1915; s. Daniel Webster and Jennie (Sellers) R.; B.S., Pa. State U., 1936; m. Frances Jeannette Montgomery, June 7, 1939; children—Craig M., Karen A. Asst. county agt. U. Mo., 1936-37; county agt. Pa. State U., 1937-45; asst. mgr., editor agrl. promotion div. E. I. duPont de Nemours & Co., Inc., Wilmington, Del., 1945-48; asst. exec. sec. Holstein-Friesian Assn. Am., 1948-53, exec. sec., 1953-75, exec. chmn., 1975—; pres. Holstein-Frieslan Services, Inc., 1968—; hon. mem. Holstein-Friesian de Mexico C.A.; dir. Vermont Nat. Bank; mem. U.S./USSR Joint Com. Agrl. Cooperation; v.p. Agrl. Cooperator Council, FAS-U.S. Dept. Agr.; mem. coordinating group Nat. Coop. Dairy Herd Improvement program U.S. Dept. Agr.; mem. agrl. policy adv. com. Multilateral Trade Negotiations. Trustee Eastern States Expn., Asso. Industries Vt. Recipient Disting. award Nat. Dairy Herd Improvement Assn., 1974, mktg. award Nat. Agrl. Mktg. Orgn., 1977; named Disting. Alumnus, Pa. State U., 1978. Mem. Purebred Dairy Cattle Assn. (dir., exec. com.), Nat. Soc. Livestock Record Assns. (past pres., dir.), Am. Dairy Sci. Assn. (Disting. Service award 1977), Nat. Dairy Shrine (Dairy Hall of Fame 1976), Alpha Zeta, Gamma Sigma Delta. Congregationalist (deacon). Clubs: Kiwanis, Masons. Home: 26 Country Hill Brattleboro VT 05301 Office: 1 S Main St Brattleboro VT 05301

RUMMAN, WADI (SALIBA), civil engr.; b. Beit-Jala, Palestine, Sept. 7, 1926; came to U.S., 1948, naturalized, 1959; s. Saliba Y. and Miladeh (Nasrallah) R.; B.S.E., U. Mich., 1949, M.S.E., 1953, Ph.D., 1959; m. Doris E. Reed, Sept. 6, 1955; children—Mary Elaine, Linda Jean. Field engr. Finkbeiner Pettis and Strout, Toledo, 1949; structural engr. Vogt, Ivers, Seaman and Assos., Cin., 1950-51, Gaiffels and Vallet, Inc., Detroit, 1951-52; instr. U. Mich., 1952-59, asst. prof. civil engring., 1959-64, asso. prof., 1964-75, prof., 1975—; cons. on design of reinforced concrete chimneys and other tower structures to industry and other agys. Mem. Am. Concrete Inst. (chmn. com. 307), ASCE, Am. Soc. Engring. Edn., Internat. Assn. Bridge and Structural Engring., Sigma Xi, Chi Epsilon, Phi Kappa Phi. Author: Engineering, 1974. Home: 1945 Peppermill Way Ann Arbor MI 48103 Office: Dept Civil Engring U Mich Ann Arbor MI 48109

RUMMEL, F.C., bus. exec.; b. Port Carbon, Pa., Oct. 21, 1901; s. Fred Charles and Elsie (Lilley) R.; student pub. schs. Port Carbon; m. Mae Irene Rauch, Sept. 1922. Engr. W.G. Parke & Sons, Pottsville, Pa., 1920-22; bond salesman Nat. City Co., N.Y.C., 1922-31, Le Higginson & Co., 1931-32; gen. mgr. Chandler & Co., Phila., 1932-38; pres. Burr & Co., N.Y.C., 1938-48; pres., dir. Spokane Internat. R.R. Co., 1948-59, also chmn. exec. com.; chmn. bd. M.M. Freeman & Co., Phila., 1959-66; chmn. exec. com., chmn. finance com. Royal-McBee Corp., N.Y.C.; chmn. finance com. Gen. Instrument Corp.; limited partner Freeman & Co., N.Y.C.; dir. Royal-Precision Co., Indsl. Devel. Lab., Attelboro, Mass., McBee Co., Athens, Ohio, Gen. Instrument Corp., Elizabeth, N.J., Old Nat. Bank, Spokane, Wash. Gas & Electric Co., Tacoma, Freeman Securities Co., Inc., N.Y.C. Mem. Pa. Soc. Republican. Clubs: Baltusrol Golf (Springfield, N.J.); Bankers, Bond, Econ. (N.Y.C.); Spokane, Country (Spokane); Seignory (Que., Can.); Pottsville (Pa.). Home: 33 Robert Dr Short Hills NJ 07078 Office: 1775 Broadway New York City NY 10019

RUMMEL, ROBERT WILAND, aero. engr.; b. Dakota, Ill., Aug. 4, 1915; s. William Howard and Dora (Ely) R.; m. Marjorie B. Cox, Sept. 30, 1939; children—Linda Kay, Sharon Lee, Marjorie Susan, Robert Wiland, Diana Beth. Stress analyst Hughes Aircraft Co., Burbank, Calif., 1935-36, Lockheed Aircraft Corp., Burbank, 1936; draftsman Aero Engring. Corp., Long Beach, Calif., 1936, Nat. Aircraft Co., Alhambra, Calif., 1936-37; chief engr. Rearwin A/C & Engines, Inc., Kansas City, Kans., 1937-42; chief design engr. Commonwealth A/C, Inc., Kansas City, Kans., 1942-43; v.p. engring. Trans World Airlines, Inc., Kansas City, Mo., 1943-59, v.p. planning and research, 1959-69, v.p. tech. devel., 1969-78; pres. Robert W. Rummel Assos., Inc., Mesa, Ariz., 1978—. Fellow Inst. Aero. Scis., Soc. Automotive Engrs.; mem. Nat. Acad. Engring. Clubs: N.Y. Yacht (N.Y.C.); Saugatuck Harbor Yacht (Westport, Conn.); Masons (32 deg.), Shriners. Home: 1189 Leisure World Mesa AZ 85206 Office: PO Box 7330 Mesa AZ 85206

RUMPF, JOHN LOUIS, civil engr., univ. adminstr.; b. Phila., Feb. 21, 1921; s. Harry L. and Emma S. R.; B.S.C.E., Drexel U., 1943; M.S.C.E., U. Pa., 1954; Ph.D. in Civil Engring. (NSF fellow), Lehigh U., 1960; m. Grace Willis, Apr. 1, 1944 (dec.); children—Jonathan, Christopher; m. 2d Patricia E. Burkitt, June 20, 1970. Structural engr. Belmont Iron Works, Phila., 1946; instr. Drexel U., 1947-50, asst. prof. civil engring., 1950-54, asso. prof., 1954-56, prof., head dept. civil engring., 1960-69; research instr. Fritz Engring. Lab., Lehigh U., 1956-60; dean Coll. Engring. Tech., Temple U., 1969-76; v.p. acad. affairs, 1976—; cons. engr. for bldg. and bridge design and investigations, 1947—. Mem. Lower Moreland Twp. (Pa.) Zoning Bd., 1953-56; mem. Lower Moreland Twp. Sch. Dist. Authority, 1962-70. Served to capt. C.E., U.S. Army, 1943-46. Decorated Army Commendation medal. Named Engr. of Yr., Tech. Socs. of Delaware Valley, 1975. Fellow ASCE; mem. Am. Soc. Engring. Edn., Nat. Soc. Profl. Engrs., Research Council on Riveted and Bolted Structural Joints, Sigma Xi, Tau Beta Pi, Phi Kappa Phi, Chi Epsilon. Club: Engrs. of Phila. (George Washington medal 1979). Author: Plastic Design of Braced Multistory Steel Frames, 1968; research, publs. on structural connections and members, 1956-69. Home: 1213 Red Rambler Rd Rydal PA 19046 Office: Conwell Hall Temple U Philadelphia PA 19122

RUMRILL, CHARLES LEWIS, advt. agy. exec.; b. East Syracuse, N.Y., May 12, 1901; s. Charles Clark and Winifred Churchill) R.; B.S., U. Rochester, 1922; m. Janice Clark, Aug. 21, 1926; children—Janice (Mrs. George Dewire), Charles Clark. Founder Rumrill-Hoyt, Inc., Rochester, N.Y., 1933; dir. Schlegel Corp., Wolfe Publs.; sr. dir. Marine Midland Bank. Trustee Ithaca Coll., Rochester Mus. Assn., Center for Govtl. Research. Recipient outstanding alumnus award U. Rochester, 1955. Mem. Rochester C. of C. (past pres., trustee), Theta Delta Chi (pres. 1941-46). Clubs: Univ. (pres. 1955), Rochester Country, Genesee Valley (Rochester); Univ. (N.Y.C.). Home: 34 Sutherland St Pittsford NY 14534 Office: 1895 Mt Ave Rochester NY 14620

RUMSFELD, DONALD, former govt. ofcl., pharm. co. exec.; b. Chgo., July 9, 1932; s. George Donald and Jeannette (Husted) R.; A.B., Princeton U., 1954; hon. degrees Ill. Coll., Lake Forest Coll., Park Coll.; m. Joyce Pierson, Dec. 27, 1954; children—Valerie Jeanne, Marcy Kay, Donald Nicholas. Adminstrv. asst. U.S. Ho. of Reps., 1958-59; with A.G. Becker & Co., Chgo., 1960-62; mem. 88th-91st congresses from 13th Dist. Ill.; mem. Pres's Cabinet, 1969-73; dir. OEO, 1969-70; dir. Cost of Living Council and counsellor to Pres., 1971-72; U.S. ambassador and permanent rep. to NATO, 1973-74; asst. to Pres., mem. Pres.'s cabinet, 1974-75; sec. Dept. Def., 1975-77; pres., chief exec. officer G.D. Searle & Co., Skokie, Ill., 1977—; dir. Rand Corp., Bendix Corp., Sears Roebuck & Co. Trustee Am. Assembly. Served as naval aviator USN, 1954-57. Recipient Presdl. medal of Freedom. Office: GD Searle & Co PO Box 1045 Skokie IL 60076

RUNALS, CLARENCE RIDER, lawyer; b. Arcade, N.Y., Mar. 27, 1893; s. Leonard Earl and Nellie Gray (Rider) R.; LL.B., U. Buffalo, 1915; LL.D., Niagara U., 1957; m. Edith Ruth Landsheft, Dec. 17, 1919; children—John E., Jane Elizabeth (Mrs. William Mentz Crandall, Jr.), Ruth (Mrs. William Stewart). Admitted to N.Y. bar, 1916; counsel to firm Runals, Broderick, Shoemaker & Rickert and predecessors, Niagara Falls, N.Y., 1951—; mem. hon. adv. bd. Marine Midland Bank. Del. N.Y. State Constl. Conv., 1938; commr. Niagara Frontier State Park, 1955-57. Past pres. Community Chest, Niagara Falls; adv. bd. Salvation Army, Niagara Falls. Recipient citation for meritorious achievement U. Buffalo, 1956. Fellow Am. Coll. Trial Lawyers; mem. N.Y. State (pres. 1957-58, del. ho. of dels. Am. Bar Assn. 1957-62), Niagara County (past pres.), Niagara Falls (past pres.) bar assns., Niagara Falls (N.Y.) C. of C. (past pres.), NCCJ (past Protestant co-chmn. Niagara Falls chpt.). Clubs: Rotary (past pres.), Niagara Falls Country (past pres.), Niagara (past pres.) (Niagara Falls). Home: 151 Buffalo Ave Niagara Falls NY 14303 Office: 256 Third St Niagara Falls NY 14304

RUNCIMAN, ALEXANDER MCINNES, grain co. exec.; b. Invergordon, Rossshire, Scotland, Oct. 8, 1914; s. Alexander and Evelyn (Anderson) R.; came to Can., 1928; m. Marjorie Evelyn Dick, Oct. 8, 1949; children—Dorothy, Catherine. Farmer, Abernethy, Sask., Can., 1934-61; dir. United Grain Growers Ltd., Winnipeg, Man., Can., 1955—, pres., 1961—; dir. Great-West Life Assurance Co., Canadian Pacific, Massey-Ferguson Ltd., Royal Bank Can. Served with Ordnance Corps, Royal Can. Army, 1940-45. Home: 225 Kingsway Ave Winnipeg MB R3M 0G5 Canada Office: United Grain Growers Ltd Box 6600 Winnipeg MB R3C 3A7 Canada

RUNDGREN, TODD, musician, record producer; b. Upper Darby, Pa., June 22, 1948. Mem. musical groups The Nazz, 1967-69, Utopia, 1973—; solo performances, 1970—; record producer Badfinger, Paul Butterfield, Grand Funk, Hall & Oates, New York Dolls, The Band, Patti Smith, others; numerous recs. and compositions include: We Gotta Get You a Woman, Hello It's Me, I Saw the Light, A Dream Goes on Forever, Can We Still be Friends.*

RUNDLES, RALPH WAYNE, educator, physician; b. Urbana, Ill., Sept. 10, 1911; s. Don Cameron and Edith Grace (Hollopeter) R.; A.B., DePauw U., 1933; Ph.D., Cornell U., 1937; M.D., Duke, 1940; m. Mary Alice Cunningham, June 9, 1936 (div.); children—Susanna (Mrs. John Dunn), Charlotte, Ward Frederick; m. 2d, Marguerite S. Grafton, Nov. 28, 1968; 1 dau., Martha Caroline. Successively intern, asst. resident, resident medicine Univ. Hosp., Ann Arbor, Mich., 1940-43; instr. medicine, research asso. Simpson Meml. Inst., U. Mich., 1943-45; mem. faculty dept. medicine Duke Sch. Medicine, 1945—, prof. medicine, 1957—, head hematology and chemotherapy service, 1947—; spl. research neuroanatomy, diabetes, blood diseases, cancer chemotherapy, gout. Chmn. S.E. Cancer Chemotherapy Coop. Study Group, 1956-66. Bd. dirs. Am. Cancer Soc., pres., 1977-78. Mem. Am. (pres. 1966-67), Internat. socs. hematology, Am., Durham-Orange County med. assns., Am. Fedn. Clin. Research, Assn. Am. Physicians, Am. Assn. Cancer Research, Phi Kappa Phi, Alpha Omega Alpha. Contbr. papers in field. Home: 3608 Westover Rd Durham NC 27707

RUNECKLES, VICTOR CHARLES, educator; b. London, Eng., Sept. 2, 1930; s. Ernest Charles and Madeleine Emily Victoria (Every) R.; B.Sc., Imperial Coll., London, 1952, Ph.D., 1955; m. Eileen May Tuck, Aug. 6, 1952; children—Ghislaine Claire, Giles Quentin. Postdoctoral fellow Queen's U., Kingston, Ont., 1955-57; plant biochemist Imperial Tobacco Co., Montreal, Que., 1957-61, asst. research mgr., 1961-65, research mgr., 1965-69; prof., chmn. dept. plant sci. U.B.C., 1969—. Fellow Royal Soc. Arts; life mem. Phytochem. Soc. N.Am.; mem. Agrl. Inst. Can., Air Pollution Control Assn., Canadian Soc. Plant Physiologists (western dir. 1969), A.A.A.S., Canadian Phytopathol. Soc. Editor Recent Advances in Phytochemistry, Vol. 1, 1967—. Home: 5589 University Blvd Vancouver BC Canada Office: Dept Plant Sci U BC Vancouver BC Canada

RUNES, DAGOBERT DAVID, publishing co. exec.; b. Zastavna, Austria-Hungary, Jan. 6, 1902; s. Isadore and Adele (Sussman) R.; came to U.S., 1926, naturalized, 1936; Ph.D., U. Vienna (Austria), 1924; m. Mary Theresa Gronich, Oct. 18, 1936 (dec.); children—Regeen Lenore, Richard Norton; m. 2d, Rose Morse, Apr. 13, 1978. Lectr., free lance writer, 1936-31; dir. Inst. Advanced Edn., N.Y.C., 1931-34; editor Modern Thinker, N.Y.C., 1923-36, Current Digest, N.Y.C., 1936-40; editor-in- chief Philos. Library N.Y., N.Y.C., 1940—, bd. dirs., 1940—. Group comdr. Red Cross Mil. Legion, Vienna, 1918. Mem. Vienna Acad. Soc. Platonica (pres. 1924), Am. Soc. Aesthetics. Jewish. Author: Der Wahre Jesus, 1927; Jordan Lieder, 1948; Letters to My Son, 1949; Spinoza Dictionary, 1951; Of God, the Devil and the Jews, 1952; The Soviet Impact on Society, 1953; Letters to My Daughter, 1954; On the Nature of Man, 1956; A Book of Contemplation, 1957; Dictionary of Judaism, 1958; Letters to My God, 1958; Pictorial History of Philosophy, 1959; Dictionary of Thought, 2d edit., 1965; The Art of Thinking, 1961; Letters to My Teacher, 1961; Lost Legends of Israel, 1961; Despotism: A Pictorial History of Tyranny, 1963; The Disinherited and the Law, 1964; Crosscuts Through History, 1965; The Jew and the Cross, 1965; Treasury of Thought, 1967; The War Against the Jews, 1968; Philosophy for Everyman, 1968; Handbook of Reason, 1972; Let My People Live, 1974; also articles. Home: 44 W 77th St New York NY 10024 Office: 15 E 40th St New York NY 10016

RUNGE, DONALD EDWARD, food wholesaleing co. exec.; b. Milw., Mar. 20, 1938; s. Adam and Helen Teresa (Voss) R.; grad. Spencerian Coll., Milw., 1960; divorced; children—Roland, Richard, Lori. Fin. v.p. Milw. Cheese Co., Waukesha, Wis., 1962-69; pres., dir. Farm House Foods Corp., Milw., 1969—, Midland Gen. Corp., Milw., 1971—; pres. Gen. Food Products Co., Milw., 1966—. Mem. Young Presidents Orgn. Seventhday Adventist. Home: 8005 N Beach Rd Fox Pointe WI 53217 Office: 733 N Van Buren St Milwaukee WI 53202. *I believe there is very little in life that cannot be accomplished if a person truly wants to attain the goal.*

RUNICE, ROBERT E., telephone co. exec.; b. Fargo, N.D., Aug. 20, 1929; s. Elmer M. and Ruth F. (Soule) R.; B.S., N.D. State U., 1951; m. Geraldine Kharas, June 26, 1954; children—Michael R., Christopher E., Paul T., Karen R. With Northwestern Bell Telephone Co., 1945—, sr. v.p., Omaha, 1978—; dir. Nebr. Fed. Savs. and Loan. Treas., Nebr. Meth. Hosp.; mem. Omaha Airport Authority; campaign chmn. United Appeal, 1969. Republican. Episcopalian. Clubs: Rotary, Omaha, Omaha Country. Home: 9512 Valley St Omaha NE 68124 Office: 100 S 19th St Omaha NE 68102

RUNKE, DARRELL M., food co. exec.; b. Mapleton, Minn., July 16, 1919; s. Max E. and Cora (McMahon) R.; B.S. in Chemistry, Mankato (Minn.) State Coll., 1946; m. Phyllis Elsie Wilkens, Mar. 27, 1943; children—Vicky Anne, Kenneth Darrell, Timmy Lee, Sally Jean, Betsy Sue. Tchr., Mapleton Pub. Schs., 1946-48; chemist Central Bi-Products Co., Redwood Falls, Minn., 1948-52; dir. animal nutrition Internat. Milling Co., New Ulm, Minn., 1952-53, sales mgr., 1953-56, sales mgr. formula feeds, Des Moines, 1956-57, Mpls., 1957-61, gen. mgr. formula feeds, 1961-63, v.p. formula feeds, 1963-66, v.p. overseas div., 1966-69, also dir.; group v.p., dir. Internat. Multifoods Corp., Mpls., 1969-74, pres., chief operating officer, 1974—; dir. 1st Nat. Bank Mpls. Served to 1st lt. USAAF, 1941-46; PTO. Mem. Am. (dir. 1965-66, vice chmn. exec. com. sales execs. council 1966), N.W. (dir. 1962-63) feed mfrs. assns. Home: 5637 Interlachen Circle Minneapolis MN 55436 Office: International Multifoods Corp 1200 Multifoods Bldg Minneapolis MN 55402

RUNKLE, LOWE WINFIELD, advt. exec.; b. El Reno, Okla., June 22, 1908; s. Ralph Evans and Clara Leslie (Lowe) R.; B.A., U. Okla., 1930; m. Alice Cornelia Escoe, Dec. 15, 1937; children—Ralph Layton, Kent Evans. Copywriter, Ray K. Glenn Advt., Oklahoma City, 1934-39, v.p., Oklahoma City and Dallas, 1939-46; pres., founder Lowe Runkle Co. (Advt.), Oklahoma City, 1946—, chmn., chief exec. officer, 1973—; dir. Union Bank & Trust Co., Oklahoma City. Chmn., Jud. Nominating Commn. Okla., 1967-73; pres. Met. YMCA Greater Oklahoma City, 1967-70; corp. dir. Presbyn. Hosp., Oklahoma City; mem. nat. bd. govs. Okla. Christian Coll.; trustee Oklahoma City Zool. Trust. Served with USAAF, 1944-45. Recipient Distinguished Service award Oklahoma City Advt. Club, 1952; Outstanding Service award United Fund Greater Oklahoma City, 1960; Silver Medal award Advt. Fedn. Am., 1965; Outstanding Layman award Okla. Bar Assn., 1970; Liberty Bell award Okla. County Bar Assn., 1972. Mem. Am. Judicature Soc. (dir., Herbert Lincoln Harley award 1973), Advt. Mktg. Internat. Network (pres. Am. zone 1965-66), Oklahoma City C. of C. (dir.), Men's Dinner Club Oklahoma City (pres. 1963-66), Alpha Tau Omega, Alpha Delta Sigma. Democrat. Presbyterian (ruling elder). Clubs: Petroleum, Beacon (Oklahoma City); Econ. of Okla. Home: 412 NW 39th St Oklahoma City OK 73118 Office: 1800 Liberty Tower Oklahoma City OK 73102. *Several factors have contributed largely to whatever success I may have enjoyed. First, the basic fundamentals my parents taught me—belief in God, honesty, hard work and a responsibility to those I love. Second, a deep desire to be a good provider for my family. Third, a competitive spirit that was cultivated during my years on the college tennis team. Finally, the luxury of good health and an understanding wife, without which I could have accomplished little.*

RUNNELS, HAROLD LOWELL, congressman; b. Dallas, Mar. 17, 1924; m. Dorothy Gilland, 1944; children—Michael, Phillip, Matt, Eydie. Formerly employed by FBI, Washington, mgr. Magnolia Amusement Co. (Ark.); partner Southland Supply Co., 1952; formed Runnels Mud Co. and RunCo Acidizing & Fracturing Co.; mem. N.Mex. Senate, 1960-70; mem. 92d-96th congresses from 2d Dist. N.Mex. Served with USAAF, World War II. Named Lovington Citizen of Yr., 1971. Mem. Permian Basin Petroleum Assn. (co-founder), Am. Petroleum Inst., C. of C. Democrat. Baptist. Mason. Address: Route 1 Box 157 Aldie VA 22001 Office: 1535 Longworth House Office Bldg Washington DC 20515

RUNNER, MEREDITH NOFTZGER, educator, biologist; b. Schenectady, Jan. 7, 1914; s. C.C. and Gladys G. (Noftzger) R.; student Union Coll., Schenectady, 1932-34; A.B., Ind. U., 1937, Ph.D. (Eigenmann research fellow 1941-42), 1942; m. Helen Falacy, Jan. 31, 1941; children—Carol M., Charles C., Alan S., Marilyn N., Peter L., Suzanne M. Instr., then asst. prof. biology U. Conn., 1942-46; Finney-Howell med. research fellow Jackson Lab., Bar Harbor, Me., 1946-48, research asso., 1948-57, staff scientist, 1957-62; research biologist Roswell Park Meml. Inst., Buffalo, 1955-56; program dir. NSF, 1959-62; prof. biology U. Colo., 1962—, chmn. dept., 1962-63, dir. Inst. for Developmental Biology, 1966-71; spl. research genetic and physiologic mechanisms congenital deformity, reproductive physiology, implantation and intrauterine death. Mem. adv. panel devel. biology NSF, 1962-64; mem. study sect. cell biology NIH, 1964-68, mem. study sect. human embryology and devel., 1969-73; cons. Nat. Inst. Environ. Scis., 1972-73; mem. Exptl. Biology, Breast Cancer Task Force, NIH, 1975-78; prin. investigator research grants NIH, NSF and AEC. Mem. Am. Assn. Anatomists, Am. Soc. Zoologists, Am. Soc. Cell Biology, Genetics Soc. Am., Internat. Inst. Embryology, Internat. Soc. Cell Biology, Soc. Developmental Biology (pres. 1969-70), Teratology Soc. (pres. 1966-67). Author articles in field. Asso. editor Jour. Exptl. Zoology, Jour. Teratology, Bioscience, Anat. Rec., Growth. Home: 715 Willowbrook St Boulder CO 80302

RUNYAN, JOHN WILLIAM, JR., medical educator; b. Memphis, Jan. 23, 1924; s. John William and Lottie (Roberts) R.; A.B., Washington and Lee U., 1943; M.D., Johns Hopkins, 1947; m. Barbara Ruth Zerbe, July 16, 1949; children—John William III, Scott Baylor, Keith Roberts. Intern Johns Hopkins Hosp., 1947-48; asst. to chief resident medicine Albany (N.Y.) Hosp., 1948-50; research fellow Harvard Med. Sch., 1950-53, also Thorndike Meml. Lab., Boston City Hosp.; instr., then asso. prof. medicine Albany Med. Coll., 1953-60; mem. faculty U. Tenn. Med. Sch., 1960—, prof. medicine, 1964—, chief sect. endocrinology, 1963-72, dir. div. health care scis., chmn. dept. community medicine, 1972—; chief med. service John Gaston Hosp., Memphis, 1965-72; cons. endocrinology Memphis VA Hosp., USPHS, 1962—. Served with AUS, 1951-53. Commonwealth Fund fellow, 1950; recipient John D. Rockefeller III Public Service award in health, 1977; diplomate Am. Bd. Internal Medicine (examiner 1967-72). Fellow A.C.P.; mem. Am. Fedn. Clin. Research, Am. Diabetes Assn., AMA, Tenn., Memphis med. socs., Tenn. Diabetes Soc. (pres. 1968-69). Author: Primary Care Guide, 1975. Home: 5496 S Angela Ln Memphis TN 38117

RUNYON, MARVIN TRAVIS, automobile mfg. co. exec.; b. Ft. Worth, Tex., Sept. 16, 1924; s. Marvin T. and Lora Lee (Whittington) R.; B.S., Tex. A&M U., 1948; m. Frances Elizabeth Patton, Aug. 19,

1944; children—Marvin, Elizabeth Anne, Paul, James. Staff mem. mfg. engring. areas assembly plants Ford Motor Co., 1943-60, asst., plant mgr. various assembly plants, 1960-70, mgr. passenger assembly engring. automotive assembly div. gen. office, Dearborn, Mich., 1970-72, gen. mgr. automotive assembly div., 1972-73, v.p. body and assembly ops., 1973-77, v.p. powertrain and chassis ops., 1977-78, v.p. body and assembly ops., 1979—. Served with USAF, 1943-45. Named Outstanding Man of Year Soc. Advancement Mgmt., 1968. Mem. Soc. Automotive Engrs., Inc., Engring. Soc. Detroit. Baptist. Clubs: Oakland Hills Country (Birmingham, Mich.); London (Can.) Hunt and Country. Home: 7229 Creeks Bend Dr West Bloomfield MI 48033 Office: Ford Motor Co Rotunda at Southfield Dearborn MI 48121

RUOFF, ARTHUR LOUIS, physicist; b. Ft. Wayne, Ind., Sept. 17, 1930; s. Louis A. and Wilma (Rall) R.; B.S., Purdue U., 1952; Ph.D., U. Utah, 1955; m. Enid Seaton, Jan. 24, 1954; children—William, Stephen, Rodney, Jeffrey, Kenneth. Asst. prof. materials sci. and engring. Cornell U., 1955-58, asso. prof., 1958-65, prof., 1965—, chmn. dept. materials sci. and engring., 1978—. Pres., Ithaca (N.Y.) Youth Hockey, 1972-73. Named Engr. of Distinction, Engrs. Joint Council, 1970. Fellow Am. Phys. Soc. Author: Introduction to Materials Science, 1972; Materials Science, 1973; Introductory Materials Science, 1973; Concepts of Packaged Courses, 1973. Office: Materials Sci and Engring Bard Hall Cornell U Ithaca NY 14853

RUOTOLO, ROBERT STEVEN, fin. exec.; b. Canton, Ohio, July 23, 1941; s. Nicholas and Mary R.; B.S. cum laude, Fordham U., 1963; M.B.A., Iona Coll., 1971; m. Patricia E. Santorsola, Apr. 25, 1965; children—Robert, Christopher. Sr. auditor Arthur Andersen & Co., N.Y.C., 1963-67; controller Neptune World Wide Moving Co., New Rochelle, N.Y., 1968-75; treas. Norman, Craig & Kummel, Inc., N.Y.C., 1975—. Pres., Briarcliff Manor Little League. Mem. Am. Inst. C.P.A.'s, N.Y. State Soc. C.P.A.'s. Roman Catholic. Home: 157 Washburn Rd Briarcliff Manor NY 10510 Office: 919 3d Ave New York NY 10022

RUPERT, (LYNN) HOOVER, clergyman; b. Madison, N.J., Nov. 3, 1917; s. Lynn Hoover and Hazel L. (Linabary) R.; A.B., Baker U., 1938; A.M., Boston U., 1940, M.Div. cum laude, 1941; student (summers) Garrett Bibl. Inst. and Northwestern U., 1942, Union Theol. Sem., 1943; D.D., Adrian Coll., 1952, Baker U., 1966; L.H.D., Milliken U., 1974; m. Hazel Pearl Senti, June 22, 1941; children—Susan, Elizabeth (Mrs. Warren W. Wright). Ordained to ministry Methodist Ch., 1940; asst. pastor First Meth. Ch., Baldwin, Kans., 1936-38, St. Mark's Meth. Ch., Brookline, Mass., 1938-41; pastor, Thayer-St. Paul, Kans., 1941-43, First Ch., Olathe, Kans., 1943-45; dir. youth dept. Gen. Bd. Edn. Meth. Ch., Nashville, 1945-50; pastor 1st Meth. Ch., Jackson, Mich., 1950-59, 1st United Meth. Ch., Ann Arbor, Mich., 1959-72, 1st United Meth. Ch., Kalamazoo, 1972—; dean Mich. Meth. Pastors Sch., 1959-65; mem. Jud. Council United Meth. Ch., 1968—, sec., 1976—; Lucinda Bidwell Beebe fellow Boston U., 1941. Trustee Bronson Hosp., Adrian Coll.; pres. bd. dirs. Youth For Understanding, Ann Arbor United Fund, YMCA-YWCA. Recipient Distinguished Alumnus award Boston U., 1969. Mem. World Meth. Council, Nat. Council Chs., Mark Twain Soc., Nat. Forensic League, Pi Kappa Delta, Alpha Psi Omega. Mason. Rotarian. Author: Prayer Poems on the Prayer Perfect, 1943; Christ Above All (editor) 1948; Youth and Evangelism, 1948; Youth and Stewardship, rev. 1960; Your Life Counts (editor), 1950; What Methodists Believe, rev. 1959; John Wesley and People Called Methodists, 1953; I Belong, 1954; And Jesus Said, 1960; Enjoy Your Teen-Ager, 1962; A Sense of What is Vital, 1964; The Church in Renewal, 1965; My People are Your People, 1968; Where is thy Sting?, Christian Perspectives On Death, 1969; What's Good about God?, 1970; Woodstock, Main Street and the Garden of Eden, 1971; Some Idiot Raised the Ante, 1975; God Will See You Through, 1976. Writer syndicated weekly mag. column Accent on Living, newspaper series Prayer for Today, newspaper feature Talking to Teens; contbr. to Testament of Faith, 1942, other publs., periodicals and newspapers. Home: 4113 Bronson Blvd Kalamazoo MI 49008 Office: 212 S Park St Kalamazoo MI 49006

RUPERT, JOHN EDWARD, savs. and loan exec.; b. Cleve., Oct. 19, 1927; s. Edward J. and Emma (Levegood) R.; B.A., Cornell U., 1949, LL.B., 1951; certificate Grad. Sch. Savs. & Loan, Ind. U., 1958; m. Virginia Carlson, Oct. 27, 1951; children—Kristen, Karen, David. With Broadview Savs. & Loan Co., Cleve., 1953—, v.p., 1964-74, mng. officer, 1965—, pres., chief exec. officer, 1974—, also dir. Mem. Cleve. Real Estate Bd., 1955—. Mem. Lakewood (Ohio) Bd. Edn., 1973—, pres., 1975—. Vice pres., trustee Lakewood Hosp., 1966-71; trustee Cleve. Orch., WVIZ Ednl. TV; bd. dirs. West Side YMCA; mem. Lakewood Hosp. Found.; mem. Cornell U. Council, 1971—, pres., 1977. Served with USAF, 1951-53. Mem. Cleve. Interfaith Housing Corp. (pres. 1971—), Am. Savs. and Loan Inst. (pres. 1970), Cleve. Real Property Inventory (pres. 1976—), Am., Ohio, Cleve. bar assns., Delta Kappa Epsilon, Phi Delta Phi, Sphinx Head Soc. Clubs: Westwood Country; Union; Cleve. Automobile (trustee), Cleve. Yachting, Cornell (trustee) (Cleve.). Home: 18129 W Clifton Rd Lakewood OH 44107 Office: 4221 Pearl Rd Cleveland OH 44109

RUPP, GEORGE ERIK, univ. dean, clergyman; b. Summit, N.J., Sept. 22, 1942; s. Gustav Wilhelm and Erika (Braunoehler) R.; A.B., Princeton U., 1964; student Ludwig Maximilians U., Munich, Germany, 1962-63; B.D., Yale U., 1967; postgrad. U. Ceylon, Peradeniya, 1969-70; Ph.D., Harvard U., 1972; m. Nancy Katherine Farrar, Aug. 22, 1964; children—Katherine Heather, Stephanie Karin. Ordained to ministry United Presbyterian Ch. U.S.A., 1971; faculty fellow in religion, vice chancellor Johnston Coll., U. Redlands (Calif.), 1971-74; asst. prof. Harvard Div. Sch., Harvard U., Cambridge, Mass., 1974-76, asso. prof., 1976-77, prof., dean Div. Sch., 1979—; prof., dean acad. affairs U. Wis., Green Bay, 1977-79. Danforth Grad. fellow, 1964-71. Mem. Soc. for Values in Higher Edn., Am. Acad. Religion. Author: Christologies and Cultures: Toward a Typology of Religious Worldviews, 1974; Culture Protestantism: German Liberal Theology at the Turn of the Twentieth Century, 1977; Beyond Existentialism and Zen: Religion in a Pluralistic World, 1979; contbr. articles to profl. jours. Home: 44 Francis Ave Cambridge MA 02138 Office: Harvard U Harvard Div Sch Cambridge MA 02138

RUPP, JOHN NORRIS, lawyer; b. Seattle, Mar. 18, 1913; s. Otto Burton and Edith Cornelia (Norris) R.; A.B., U. Wash., 1934, J.D., 1937; m. Elizabeth Milner McElroy, Aug. 31, 1937; children—Joanne (Mrs. H. Terry Tennant), William John, Elizabeth (Mrs. Brian Fulwiler), James McElroy. Admitted to Wash. bar, 1937; law clk. to chief justice Wash. State Supreme Ct., Olympia, 1937-38; atty. McMicken, Rupp & Schweppe, Seattle, 1939-62; v.p., gen. counsel Pacific N.W. Bell Telephone Co., 1962-75; of counsel firm Schweppe, Doolittle, Krug, Tausend & Beezer, Seattle, 1975—. Mem. Wash. State Bd Edn., 1957-67; mem. Seattle Transit Commn., 1957-62, Wash. State Hwy. Commn., 1967-73. Served from ensign to lt. (j.g.), USNR, 1944-46. Decorated Bronze Star. Mem. Am. (ho. dels. 1964-68), Wash. (gov. 1961-63, pres. 1966-67), Seattle (pres. 1956-57) bar assns., U.S., Seattle (gen. counsel 1960-62) chambers commerce, Municipal League of Seattle (pres. 1948-50, trustee 1955-57, 65-67), Order of Coif, Phi Gamma Delta, Phi Delta Phi. Clubs: Rainier, Monday, Harbor, Seattle Yacht. Home: 4100 NE Surber Dr Seattle WA 98105 Office: 1600 Peoples Nat Bank Bldg Seattle WA 98171

RUPP, RALPH RUSSELL, audiologist, educator, author; b. Saginaw, Mich., Apr. 12, 1929; s. Martin Carl and Veronica Marie (Riethmeier) R.; B.A., U. Mich., 1951, M.A., 1952; Ph.D., Wayne State U., 1964; m. Jane M. Buell; children—Richard R., David B. Speech and hearing cons. Detroit Public Schs., 1955-60; exec. dir. Detroit Hearing and Speech Center, 1960-62; asso. in audiology Henry Ford Hosp., Detroit, 1962-65; prof. audiology U. Mich., Ann Arbor, 1965—; cons. St. Joseph Mercy Hosp., Ann Arbor, Ann Arbor VA Hosp., Mott Children's Health Center, Flint, Mich. Pres., Detroit Hearing Center, 1966. Served with Med. Service Corps, U.S. Army, 1953-55. Mem. Am. Speech and Hearing Assn. (Editor's award), Acad. Rehabilitative Audiology (past editor Jour.) Am. Auditory Soc., Mich. Speech and Hearing Assn. (pres. 1954, Disting. Service award, past editor Jour.), Mich. Otolaryngology Soc. Author: (with James Maurer) Hearing and Aging: Tactics for Intervention, 1979; contbr. articles to profl. jours. Home: 1544 Scio Church Rd Ann Arbor MI 48103 Office: 1111 E Catherine St Ann Arbor MI 48109

RUPP, ROBERT GEORGE, mag. editor; b. Aurora, Nebr., Oct. 28, 1918; s. Laurin Everett and Cassie Ellen (Dean) R.; B.Sc., U. Nebr., 1941; postgrad. U. Minn., 1945-46; m. M. Dee Schill, 1942 (dec. 1961); children—Victoria Ann, Robert George II, Lorna Lee Rupp; m. 2d, Matilda Alice Towne, May 26, 1962. News editor Agrl. Extension Service, Iowa State U., Ames, 1946-48; extension news editor Agrl. Extension Service, U. Minn., St. Paul, 1948-50; asso. editor The Farmer mag, St. Paul, 1950-59, mng. editor, 1959-69, editor, 1969—; dir. farms Nat. Safety Council, 1970-76. Chmn. adv. council U. Minn., Crookston, 1971—, vice chmn., Waseca, 1972—, U. Wis., River Falls, 1973-76, Minn. Dept. Edn., 1971—, Minn. Council Coordinating Edn. in Agr., 1974—; mem. Minn. Humanities Commn., 1976—; bd. dirs. Minn. Agrl. Interpretive Center, 1978—. Col., Minn. N.G., ret. Named Hon. State Farmer, Minn. Future Farmers Am., 1952, Hon. Am. Farmer, Nat. Future Farmers Am., 1979; recipient Meritorious Service award 4H Fedn., 1961, Nat. Soil Builders award Nat. Plant Food Council, 1957, Communications award Nat. Assn. Conservations Dists., 1979. Mem. Internat. Fedn. Agrl. Journalists (U.S. dir. 1971—, President's medal 1978), Minn. Assn. Commerce and Industry (v.p. agr. 1972-76), Minn. Agri-Growth Council (bd. dirs. 1973—), Nat. Safety Com., Minn. Safety Council (chmn. agrl. div. 1964—, Meritorious Service award 1966, bd. dirs. 1974—), Am. Agrl. Editors Assn. (past pres.). Club: Rotary. Home: 14906 50th St S Afton MN 55001 Office: 1999 Shepard Rd Saint Paul MN 55116

RUPP, WILLIAM JOHN, architect; b. Phila., Aug. 25, 1927; s. Frank Julius and Sara Viola (Hibbs) R.; B.Arch., U. Fla., 1953; m. Gwendolyn O'Rourke, May 10, 1956; children—Susan Hibbs, Molly O'Rourke, Jason Franz. Draftsman, Paul Rudolph, Architect, Sarasota, Fla., 1953-55; pvt. practice architecture, Sarasota and Naples, Fla., 1956-67; asso. Morris Ketchum, Jr. & Assos., Architects, N.Y.C., 1968-72; mem. firm Callister, Payne & Bischoff, architects and community planners, Amherst, Mass., 1972-75; pvt. practice architecture and planning, 1975—; vis. lectr. U. Mass., 1976-78, asst. prof., 1978—. Served with arty. AUS, 1945-46. Corp. mem. AIA (N.Y. chpt. 1st award for House Design, 1964, N.Y.C. House award 1964). Recipient Archtl. Record award for Housing Design, 1960; Progressive Architecture Design award, 1961. Contbr. articles to jours. Home: 70 N Whitney St Amherst MA 01002 Office: U of Mass Fine Arts Center Amherst MA 01002

RUPPE, PHILIP E., former congressman; b. Laurium, Mich., Sept. 29, 1926; student Central Mich. U., U. Mich., 1944-46; B.A., Yale, 1948; m. Loret Miller; children—Antoinette, Adele, Loretta, Katherine, Mary Speed. Pres., Bosch Brewing Co. to 1965; dir. Houghton Nat. Bank, Comml. Nat. Bank of L'Anse; mem. 90th-95th Congresses from 11th Mich. Dist. Served to lt. (j.g.) USNR, Korean Conflict. Mem. Am. Legion, V.F.W. Republican. K.C., Elk, Eagle, Rotarian. Address: House Office Bldg Washington DC 20515

RUPPEL, GEORGE ROBERT, certified public accountant; b. N.Y.C., Jan. 6, 1911; s. George W. and Cornelia (Klein) R.; grad. St. John's U., 1933; m. Eleanor Holton, Apr. 4, 1941; children—Sandra, Shirley, Lorraine. Chief accountant Am. Agrl. Chem. Co., 1930-36; financial supr. Am. Water Works & Electric Co., 1936-44; v.p., treas., dir. MBS, Inc., 1944-57; v.p., treas. RKO Gen., Inc., 1957-60; treas. Visual Drama, Inc., 1957-60; v.p. finance, dir. Hwy. Trailer Industries, Inc.; v.p., treas. Clinton Engines Corp., 1960-63; pres. Tomahawk Enterprises, Inc., 1963—, Gehar Co., 1963—; financial cons. Treas. RKO Teleradio Found., 1957-60. C.P.A., N.Y. State. Mem. Tax Execs. Inst. (past pres., dir. N.Y. chpt.), Fin. Execs. Inst., N.Y. State Soc. C.P.A.'s, Nat. Assn. Cost Accountants, Nat. Tax Assn. Address: Pound Ridge Rd Bedford Village NY 10506

RUPPENTHAL, KARL M., educator; b. Russell, Kans., Oct. 5, 1917; s. John P. and Viola (Whitaker) R.; A.B., U. Kans., 1939, LL.B., 1941, J.D., 1968; M.B.A., U. Cal. at Berkeley, 1950; Ph.D., Stanford, 1959; m. Irja Alice Autio, May 30, 1942; children—Sara (Mrs. Michael Katz), Stephen, Brian. Reporter Russell County News, 1934-35; owner bookstore and restaurant, 1940-41; pilot TWA, 1942-68; UPS Found. prof., dir. Centre Transp. Studies U. B.C., Vancouver, 1971—; dir. transp. mgmt. program Stanford, 1958-69, dir. European logistics mgmt. program, summers, 1969-71; Ryder prof. transp. U. Miami (Fla.), 1970; dir. Aero Air, Inc., Hazleton Labs., Hazleton Nuclear Sci., Karloid Corp.; cons. Can. Ministry Transport. Mem. Palo Alto (Calif.) City Council, 1953-59. Stanford Sloan fellow; recipient Nathan Burkham award in copywright law; Wilton Park fellow. Mem. Acad. Logistics (founding), Am. Econ. Assn., Indsl. Relations Research Assn., Transp. Research Forum, Canadian Transp. Research Forum, Am. Judicature Soc., Am. Arbitration Assn. (nat. panel). Mason. Club: University. Author: Issues in Transportation Economics; The Air Line Dispatcher in North America; Transportation and Tomorrow; Business Logistics in American Industry; Transportation Subsidies-Nature and Extent; Case Problems in Air Transportation; Regulation, Competition and the Public Interest. Editor Stanford Transp. Series, Logistics and Transp. Rev. Home: 3755 W 2d Ave Vancouver BC V6R 1J8 Canada

RUPPERT, RICHARD DALE, physician, coll. pres.; b. Middletown, Ohio, May 1, 1931; B.S., Ohio State U., 1957, M.D., 1961; m. Elizabeth Ruppert, Aug. 29, 1959; four children. Intern, Presbyn.-St. Luke's Hosp., Chgo., 1961-62; resident Univ. Hosp., Columbus, Ohio, 1962-66; practice medicine, specializing in internal medicine, Columbus, 1966-77, Toledo, 1977—; instr. dept. medicine, div. gastroenterology Ohio State U. Coll. Medicine, 1966-68, asst. prof. medicine, 1968-70, asso. prof., 1970-74, prof., 1974, asst. dean Coll. Medicine, 1970, dir. div. ambulatory medicine, 1970; med. dir. patient service Ohio State U. Hosps., 1972-74; vice chancellor for health affairs Ohio Bd. Regents, 1974-77; pres., prof. medicine Med. Coll. Ohio, Toledo, 1977—. Diplomate Am. Bd. Internal Medicine. Mem. A.C.P., AMA, Am. Fedn. Clin. Research, Am. Soc. Internal Medicine, Am. Assn. Med. Colls., Ohio Med. Assn., Ohio Soc. Internal Medicine (pres.), Alpha Omega Alpha. Home: 2710 Falmouth Dr Toledo OH 43606 Office: C S 10008 Toledo OH 43699

RUSACK, ROBERT CLAFLIN, bishop; b. Worcester, Mass., June 16, 1926; s. Roy Leonard and Dorothy (Claflin) R.; B.A., Hobart Coll., 1946, D.D., 1970; priest-scholar, St. Augustine's Coll., Canterbury, Eng., 1957-58; S.T.D., Gen. Theol. Sem., 1965; m. Janice Morrison Overfield, June 26, 1951; children—Rebecca Morrison, Geoffrey Claflin. Ordained deacon, priest Episcopal Ch., 1951; vicar in Deer Lodge and Philipsburg, Mont., 1951-57; rector in Santa Monica, Calif., 1958-64; suffragan bishop Los Angeles, P.E. Ch., 1964-72, bishop coadjutor of Los Angeles, 1973-74, bishop of Los Angeles, 1974—. Pres., Los Angeles City Mission Soc., 1964—. Bd. dirs. Episcopal Home for Aged, Alhambra, Calif., 1964, Los Angeles Council Alcoholism, 1965—, Neighborhood Youth Assn., 1965—, Seaman's Ch. Inst., San Pedro, Calif., 1964—; bd. dirs., pres. ex officio Gooden Home for Alcoholics; chmn. bd. trustees Bloy Episcopal Sch. Theology, Claremont, Calif.; hon. chmn. bd. Hosp. Good Samaritan, Los Angeles; chmn., trustee Harvard Sch., North Hollywood, Calif.; trustee Ch. Div. Sch. of Pacific, Berkeley, Gen. Theol. Sem., Occidental Coll., Los Angeles; chmn. St. Paul's Cathedral Corp., Los Angeles, 1962—. Clubs: Los Angeles Country, California. Home: 13828 Susnset Blvd Pacific Palisades CA 90272 Office: PO Box 2164 Los Angeles CA 90051 also 1220 W 4th St Los Angeles CA 90051

RUSCH, HAROLD PAUL, scientist; b. Merrill, Wis., July 15, 1908; s. Henry Albert and Olga (Brandenburg) R.; B.A., U. Wis., 1931, M.D., 1933; m. Lenore Robinson, Aug. 6, 1940 (dec. 1978); children—Carolyn Elizabeth, Judith Ann (dec. 1976); m. 2d, Louise Van Wart, Oct. 20, 1979. Intern. Wis. Gen Hosp., Madison, 1933-34; instr. dept. physiology U. Wis., 1934-35, asst. prof. oncology, 1941-43, asso. prof., 1943-45, prof., 1945—, head dept. cancer research, 1940-46; dir. McArdle Lab. for Cancer Research, U. Wis., 1946-72; dir. Wis. Clin. Cancer Center, 1972-78; Bowman Cancer fellow, research asso. in medicine, visiting Am. and European Cancer Labs., 1935-39. Mem. nat. cancer com. NRC, 1954-58, com. on growth, 1949-53; research adv. council Am. Cancer Soc., 1962-65, bd. dirs., 1965—, exec. com., 1970-74, nat. award, 1972, hon. life mem., 1974; mem. Nat. Adv. Cancer Council, 1954-58; mem. Nat. Cancer Adv. Bd., 1972-74; mem. commn. on cancer research Internat. Union Against Cancer, 1954-58; mem. Pres.'s Com. on Heart Disease and Cancer, 1961, U.S. Senate Com. Consultants on Cancer, 1970. Fellow Am. Acad. Arts and Scis.; mem. Am. Assn. Cancer Research (pres. 1953-54), AAAS, Am. Soc. Exptl. Pathology, Soc. Exptl. Biology and Medicine, Madison Geol. Soc. (pres. 1946-47), Sigma Xi, Alpha Omega Alpha, Phi Kappa Phi. Author, contbr. sci. articles. Editor-in-chief Cancer Research jour., 1950-65. Editorial bd. Perspectives in Biology and Medicine, 1959-73. Home: 3511 Sunset Dr Madison WI 53705

RUSCH, HUGH LEONARD, business exec.; b. Reedsville, Wis., May 5, 1902; s. Albert H. and Ernstena (Seybold) R.; B.S. in Elec. Engring., U. Wis., 1923; m. Cynthia Katherine VanTuyl, Aug. 30, 1928, children—Willard, Cynthia, Stephen. Instr. physics U. Wis., 1921-23, Instr. elec. engring., 1923-24; eastern dist. mgr., A.C. Nielsen Co., Chgo., 1924-28, exec. v.p., 1938-46; supr. tech. data Johns-Manville Corp., N.Y.C., 1928-32; v.p., eastern mgr. No. Pump Co., Mpls., 1932-37; v.p., Opinion Research Corp., Princeton, N.J., 1946-66; pres. Hugh Rusch & Assos., Inc., 1967—. Co-chmn. N.J. Gov.'s Fluoridation Commn. Bd. dirs. Insts. of Religion and Health. Recipient Disting. Service award U. Wis., 1959; named Man of Yr. Greater N.Y. Alumni Club U. Wis., 1976. Mem. Pub. Relations Soc. Am., IEEE, Am. Mktg. Assn., Tau Beta Pi, Phi Kappa Phi, Eta Kappa Nu, Alpha Kappa Lambda. Rotarian. Clubs: Univ. (N.Y.); Nassau, Springdale Golf, Old Guard (Princeton); Union League (Chgo.). Contbr. to Readers Digest, Sports Afield, Sci. Am., Elec. World, Forbes Mag., Asbestos Mag., Elec. Engring. Jour., Chem. Engring. Progress, Atlantic Salmon Jour. Inventor patented devices as hydraulic transmission, electrohydraulic motor, graphic recorder for measuring radio and TV listening. Home: Old Turnpike Rd Lambertville NJ 08530 Office: Palmer Sq Bldg 70 Nassau St Princeton NJ 08540

RUSCH, WILLIAM GEORGE, clergyman; b. Dunkirk, N.Y., July 22, 1924; s. Raymond and Isabel (Dufton) R.; A.B magna cum laude, Washington and Jefferson Coll., 1948; M.Div., Western Theol. Sem., 1950; M.Ed., U. Pitts., 1950, Ph.D., 1958; D.Min., Pitts. Theol. Sem., 1975; D.D. (hon.), Grove City (Pa.) Coll., 1968; LL.D., Waynesburg Coll., 1972; L.H.D., Wilson Coll., 1973, Westminster Coll., 1978; Litt.D., Davis and Elkins Coll., 1974, Lafayette Coll., 1975; H.H.D., Washington and Jefferson Coll., 1977; m. Ruth Jeannette Johnson, Aug. 23, 1947; children—Carolyn Louise, Elizabeth Diane, Kathryn Ann, Paul Christopher. Ordained to ministry Presbyn. Ch., 1950; pastor in Tarentum, Pa., 1948-51, Pitts., 1951-54, 2d Presbyn. Ch., Washington, Pa., 1954-60, Ch. of Covenant, Washington, Pa., 1960-67; exec. Synod of Pa., Camp Hill, 1968-72, Synod of Pa.-W.Va., 1972-75, Synod of The Trinity, 1975—. Moderator Washington Presbytery, 1958; chmn. Christian edn. com. Synod Pa., 1960-66, chmn. higher edn. com., 1960-66, moderator, 1966-67; pres. Washington Council Chs., 1967; mem. bd. Christian edn. U.P. Ch., 1967-68, mem. nat. staff, bd. nat. missions, 1968-72; mem. Gen. Assembly Com. on Regional Synod Orgn., 1971-73; mem. council Gen. Assembly of U.P. Ch., 1972-76, mem. churchwide coordinating cabinet, 1972—; co-chmn. Pa. Conf. on Interch. Coop., 1972-76; mem. Pa. Commn. United Ministries in Higher Edn., 1968—; pres. Pa. Council Chs., 1977-78. Chmn. Washington Juvenile Commn., 1966-68. Pres. bd. United Fund Washington, 1962; life trustee Washington and Jefferson Coll., 1957—; chmn. bd. Big Bros. Washington, 1967, Washington Sch. Bd., 1967-68; bd. dirs. Pitts. Theol. Sem., 1971—. Served to 2d lt. USAAF, 1943-46; PTO. Recipient Ch. History prize, also Hebrew prize Western Theol. Sem., 1950; distinguished service citation NAACP, 1968. Mem. Phi Beta Kappa, Beta Theta Pi, Delta Sigma Rho, Eta Sigma Phi, Pi Sigma Alpha. Mason (master 1963, grand chaplain 1971—, grand prelate commandery K.T. Pa. 1973-74). Co-author: The Incomparable Snowden, 1961. Home: 308 Deerfield Rd Camp Hill PA 17011 Office: 3040 Market St Camp Hill PA 17011. *One of the guiding principles that has directed my life has been the thought that we make a living by what we receive, but we make a life by what we give.*

RUSCHA, EDWARD, artist; b. Omaha, Dec. 16, 1937; student Chouinard Art Inst., Los Angeles. Works exhibited Minn. Mus. Art, St. Paul, 1971, La Jolla (Calif.) Mus. Art, 1971, Ill. State U. at Normal, 1971, Hayward Gallery, London, 1971, Buenos Aires, 1971, Albright-Knox Art Gallery, Buffalo, 1976, Stedelijk Mus., Amsterdam, 1976, Ft. Worth Art Mus., 1977, also others; represented in permanent collections including Mus. Modern Art, Los Angeles County Mus. Art, Whitney Mus., Joseph Hirshhorn Collection, Washington, also others; lectr. U. Calif. at Los Angeles, 1969-70. Author: Twenty-Six Gasoline Stations, 1962; Various Small Fires, 1964; Some Los Angeles Apartments, 1965; The Sunset Strip, 1966; Thirty-four Parking Lots, 1967; Royal Road Test, 1967; Business Cards, 1968; Nine Swimming Pools, 1968; Crackers, 1969; Real Estate Opportunities, 1970. Paintings include Standard Station, Amarillo, Tex., 1963, Annie, 1963, Smash, 1963, Electric, 1964. Office: 1024 3/4 N Western Ave Hollywood CA 90029*

RUSCIO, DOMENIC RICHARD, govt. ofcl.; b. Norwood, Mass., Dec. 28, 1946; s. Frank Domenic and Elizabeth Carmella (Raymond) R.; B.S. in Acctg., Bentley Coll., 1968. Budget examiner Office of the

Sec., HEW, Washington, 1968-73; mem. staff U.S. Senate Com. on Appropriations, 1973-77; dep. asst. sec. for edn. resources HEW, Washington, 1977—. Home: 701 6th St NE Washington DC 20002 Office: 200 Independence Ave SW Washington DC 20201

RUSH, ALVIN, entertainment co. exec.; b. N.Y.C., June 24, 1926; s. Max and Sonia (Spetal) R.; B.A., Columbia U., 1949, LL.D., 1952; m. Betty Moyer, Nov. 20, 1950; children—Bruce, Robert, Jeffrey. Admitted to N.Y. State bar; mem. firm Davies, Hardy, Schenck & Soons, N.Y.C., 1952-54; v.p. Music Corp. Am., N.Y.C., 1955-67; exec. v.p. Creative Mgmt. Assos., N.Y.C., 1968-73, NBC, N.Y.C., 1973-78; pres. MCA TV Program Enterprises, Universal City, Calif., 1978—. Served to lt. USN, 1944-46; PTO; 1949-50; Korea. Mem. Am. Bar Assn., Internat. Radio and TV Soc. Home: 24108 Malibu Rd Malibu CA 90265 Office: Universal City Plaza Universal City CA 91608

RUSH, ANDREW WILSON, artist; b. Detroit, Sept. 24, 1931; s. Harvey Ditman and Mary Louise (Stalker) R.; B.F.A. with honors, U. Ill., 1953; M.F.A., U. Iowa, 1958; m. Jean Cochran, Apr., 1957; children—Benjamin, Samuel, Joseph, Margaret; m. 2d, Ann Woodin, Oct., 1978. Asso. prof. art U. Ariz., 1959-69; co-dir. Rockefeller Found. Indian Arts Project, 1960-64; vis. artist, artist-in-residence Ohio State U., 1970, U. Ark., 1972, Colo. Coll., 1973-74; resident mem. Rancho Linda Vista, Community of the Arts, Oracle, Ariz., 1969—; one-man exhbns. include: Carlin Galleries, Fort Worth, 1973, Graphics Gallery, Tucson, 1972, 75; group exhbns. include: World's Fair, N.Y.C., 1964, USIS exhbts. in Europe, Latin Am., 1960-65; represented in permanent collections: Library Congress, Uffizzi Mus., Dallas Mus., Fort Worth Mus., Seattle Mus., Free Library Phila. Served with USMC, 1953-55. Fulbright grantee, 1958-59. Address: Rancho Linda Vista O M Star Rt 2360 Oracle AZ 85623

RUSH, BARBARA, actress; b. Denver, Jan. 4, 1930; d. Roy L. and Marguerite Rush; student U. Calif., Santa Barbara; m. James Gruzalski, Sept. 24, 1970; children—Christopher, Claudie. First stage appearance at age of ten, Loberto Theatre, Santa Barbara, in fantasy Golden Ball; won acting award in coll. for characterization of Birdie (The Little Foxes); scholarship Pasadena Playhouse Theatre Arts Coll.; motion pictures include The First Legion, 1951, Quebec, 1951, Molly, 1950, When Worlds Collide, 1951, Flaming Feather, 1952, Prince of Pirates, 1953, It Came from Outer Space, 1953, Taza Son of Cochise, 1954, Magnificent Obsession, 1956, Black Shield of Falworth, 1957, Captain Lightfoot, 1955, Kiss of Fire, 1955, World In My Corner, 1956, Bigger Than Life, 1957, Oh Men! Oh Women!, 1960, Harry Black and the Tiger, 1958, The Young Philadelphians, 1959, Bramble Bush, 1960, Strangers When We Meet, 1960, Come Blow Your Horn, 1963, Robin and the Seven Hoods, 1964, Hombre, 1967, Airport, 1970, The Man, 1972, Superdad, 1974; numerous theatrical appearances; appeared in TV films Crime Club, 1973, The Last Day, 1975; numerous other TV appearances including Love Boat, Medical Center, Police Story, Streets of San Francisco, Ironside. Office: Internat Creative Mgmt 8899 Beverly Blvd Los Angeles CA 90048*

RUSH, BENJAMIN FRANKLIN, JR., surgeon; b. Honolulu, Jan. 14, 1924; s. Benjamin Franklin and Vera Ried (Marston) R.; student U. Hawaii, 1941-42; B.A., U. Calif., 1944; M.D., Yale U., 1948; m. Norah Hughes Grant, June 15, 1948; children—Stephen Hughes, Christopher Marsten. Intern, asst. resident in surgery Yale U., New Haven, 1948-51; asst. resident, resident in surgery Sloan Kettering Meml. Med. Center, N.Y.C., 1953-57; instr. surgery Johns Hopkins U. Med. Sch., Balt., 1957-59, asst. prof., 1959-62; asso. prof. U. Ky. Coll. Medicine, Lexington, 1962-66, prof., 1966-69; Johnson and Johnson prof. surgery, chmn. dept. surgery Coll. Medicine and Dentistry of N.J.-N.J. Med. Sch., Newark, 1969—, surgeon in chief Coll. Hosp.; cons. USPHS Hosp., Lexington, Ky., St. Barnabas Med. Center, Livingston, N.J., Hackensack (N.J.) Hosp., and others. Pres. Ky. div. Am. Cancer Soc., 1968-69. Served to 1st lt. M.C., U.S. Army, 1951-53. NIH grantee, 1958-79. Fellow A.C.S. (pres. N.J. chpt. 1978); mem. Am. Surg. Assn., Soc. Univ. Surgeons, Am. Assn. Cancer Edn. (pres. 1973), Pan Pacific Surg. Assn. (v.p. 1978—), Southeastern Surg. Congress (mem. nat. council 1978—), N.J. Oncology Soc. (pres. 1978-79), Am. Trauma Soc. (pres. N.J. chpt. 1974-77), Chi Psi, Phi Chi, Alpha Omega Alpha. Democrat. Clubs: Canoe Brook Country (Summit, N.J.), Sawgrass Country (Ponte Verde, Fla.). Editor books in field; contbr. chpts. to med. books. Mem. editorial bd. Am. Jour. Clin. Research, Excerpta Medica, Am. Surgeon, Jour. Surg. Oncology. Home: 51 Rotary Dr Summit NJ 07901 Office: 100 Bergen St Newark NJ 07103

RUSH, FLETCHER GRAY, JR., lawyer; b. Orlando, Fla., Dec. 28, 1917; s. Fletcher Gray and Elizabeth (Knox) R., B.S. in Bus. Adminstrn. with honors, J.D. with honors, U. Fla., 1942; LL.D. (hon.), Fla. So. Coll., 1975; m. Lena Mae Willis, June 6, 1942; children—Margaret Patricia Rush White, Richard Fletcher. Admitted to Fla. bar, 1942; practice in Orlando, 1946—; sr. partner firm Rush, Marshall, Bergstrom & Robison, 1957—. Trustee Lawyers Title Guaranty Fund, 1953-65, chmn. bd., 1962-63, gen. counsel, 1968—; v.p., dir., gen. counsel Orlando Fed. Savs. & Loan Assn., 1955-75; dir. Trust Co. Fla.; mem. jud. nominating council Supreme Ct. Fla., 1972-73 Mem. Orlando Municipal Planning Bd., 1961-63; mem. Orlando Loch Haven Park Bd., 1973—, vice chmn., 1978—; bd. regents State Fla. Colls. and Univs., 1965; trustee Coll. Orlando, 1960-71, Fla. House, Inc., Washington, 1974-76; mem. president's council U. Fla., 1970-75; v.p., exec. com. U. Fla. Found., 1973-75, bd. dirs., 1971-75; bd. dirs. Inst. for Study of Trial, Central Fla. U.; mem. president's council Nat. Meth. Found. Served as officer F.A., AUS, 1942-46; ETO. Recipient Distinguished Service award Stetson U., 1967; Outstanding Alumnus award John Marshall Bar Assn. U. Fla. Coll. Law, 1971; Distinguished Alumnus award U. Fla., 1976. Fellow Am. Coll. Probate Counsel, Am. Coll. Mortgage Attys. (regent 1974-77), Am. Bar Found.; mem. Am. Law Inst., Am. (ho. of dels. 1967—, adv. bd. jour. 1968-71, chmn. standing com. on legislation 1973-75, on lawyers title guaranty funds 1979—), Orange (pres. 1960-61) bar assns., Fla. Bar (bd. govs. 1959-67, pres. 1966-67), Am. Judicature Soc. (dir. 1968, exec. com. 1972, treas. 1973-75, v.p. 1975-77, pres. 1977-79), U. Fla. Law Center Assn. (trustee, exec. com., chmn. bd. trustees 1973-75), Nat. Legal Aid and Defender Assn., Blue Key (pres. Fla. 1941), Phi Kappa Phi, Alpha Tau Omega, Phi Delta Phi. Republican. Methodist (chmn. ch. adminstrv. bd. 1961-63, 75-76, trustee 1968-74, 77—, trustee Fla. Conf., 1973-76). Kiwanian (pres. N. Orlando 1954). Clubs: Country, Univ., Citrus (Orlando). Conbr. articles to legal jours. Home: 508 Lakeview St Orlando FL 32804 Office: 55 E Livingston St Orlando FL 32802

RUSH, JAMES AVERY, JR., oil and gas co. exec.; b. Luxora, Ark., Nov. 22, 1922; s. James Avery and Lois (Chandler) R.; B.A., U. Tex., 1943, LL.B., 1947; m. Dorothy Jane Jenkins, June 9, 1945; children—Dorothy Jo (Mrs. John Mozola), James Avery III, Nancy Chandler, Carol Jane. Admitted to Tex. bar, 1947; with firm Baker, Botts, Andrews & Parish, Houston, 1947-53; with Shamrock Oil & Gas Corp., Amarillo, 1953—, asst. gen. counsel, 1957-61, v.p., gen. counsel, dir., 1961-65, exec. v.p., 1965-67; v.p. finance Diamond Shamrock Corp., Cleve., 1967-69, exec. v.p., 1973—; pres. Diamond Shamrock Oil & Gas Co., 1969; dir. Southwestern Pub. Service Co., Amarillo, Sigmor Corp., San Antonio. Bd. dirs. Amarillo Area Found., Tex. Children's Home Found., 1973—, Tex. Research League, 1973—, Tex. Assn. Taxpayers, Cal Farley's Boys Ranch, Panhandle Producers and Royalty Owners Assn. Served to capt. USAAF, 1943-46, USAF, 1950-52. Mem. Am. Tex., Amarillo (exec. com. 1964—) bar assns., Tex. Mid-Continent Oil and Gas Assn., Nat. Gas Processors Assn., Am. Petroleum Inst., Ind. Petroleum Assn. Am., Chancellors, Order of the Coif, Phi Kappa Psi, Phi Delta Phi. Presbyterian. Clubs: Amarillo, Amarillo Country. Home: 3902 Paramount Amarillo TX 79109 Office: Diamond Shamrock Oil and Gas Co PO Box 631 Amarillo TX 79173

RUSH, KENNETH, lawyer, industrialist, govt. ofcl.; b. Walla Walla, Wash., Jan. 17, 1910; s. David Campbell and Emma Kate (Kidwell) R.; A.B., U. Tenn., 1930; J.D., Yale, 1932; LL.D. (hon.), Tusculum Coll., 1961; m. Jane Gilbert Smith, June 12, 1937; children—George Gilbert (dec.), David (dec.), Malcolm, Cynthia Shepherd (Mrs. Thomas J. Monahan), John Randall, Kenneth. Asso. Chadbourne, Stanchfield & Levy (now Chadbourne, Parke, Whiteside & Wolff) law firm, N.Y.C., 1932-36; asst. prof. Duke U. Law Sch., 1936-37; with Union Carbide Corp., N.Y.C., 1936, 37-69, v.p., 1949-61, exec. v.p., 1961-66, pres., 1966-69, dir., 1958-69, mem. exec. com., 1966-69, chmn. gen. operating com., 1965-69; dir. Bankers Trust Co., 1966-69, Amstar Corp., 1962-69, Bankers Trust N.Y. Corp., 1966-69; U.S. ambassador to Germany, 1969-72, also prin. Am. negotiator Quadripartite Agreement on Berlin; dep. sec. def. U.S., 1972-73; dep. sec. of state, 1973-74, sec. ad interim, 1973; mem. cabinets Presidents Nixon and Ford as counsellor for econ. policy, 1974; ambassador to France, 1974-77; dir. El Paso Co., El Paso Natural Gas Co., El Paso Products Co. Mem. Pres. Johnson's Pub. Adv. Com. U.S. Trade Policy, 1968-69; chmn. Bd. Fgn. Service, 1973-74; mem. Nat. Security Council, 1973-74; chmn. Council Internat. Econ. Policy, Pres.'s Com. East-West Trade Policy, Pres.'s Food Com., Council Wage and Price Stability, Joint Presdl.-Congl. Steering Com. for Conf. on Inflation, all 1974, Atlantic Council, 1978—; chmn. Exec. Council on Fgn. Diplomats, 1977-78; mem. Commn. on Jud. Fellows, U.S. Supreme Ct. Mem. devel. council U. Tenn., 1963—; bd. dirs. Inst. Internat. Edn., 1968-69, Alliance To Save Energy, 1977—; sec.-treas., trustee Grand Central Art Galleries, 1951-69; trustee Taft Sch., 1957-62; bd. govs. Am. Nat. Red Cross, 1972-74; hon. co-chmn. Internat. Found. for Cultural Cooperation and Devel., 1977—; mem. adv. bd. The Citadel, 1977; chmn. personnel com., mem. audit and planning com. Smithsonian Instn. Recipient Distinguished Pub. Service medal Dept. Def., 1972; gold medal French Senate, 1977; decorated Grand Cross Order Merit (Germany), 1972. Mem. Internat. C. of C. (trustee U.S. council 1955-69), Yale Law Sch. Assn. (exec. com. 1952-62), Fgn. Policy Assn. (dir. 1964-69), Council Fgn. Relations, Pilgrims U.S., Phi Beta Kappa. Episcopalian. Clubs: Links, University, Pinnacle (N.Y.C.); Burning Tree (Md.); Chevy Chase (Md.); Pine Valley Golf (Clementon, N.J.); Royal and Ancient Golf (St. Andrews, Scotland); Blind Brook (Port Chester, N.Y.); Ekwanok Country (Manchester, Vt.); U.S. Srs. Golf Assn. Editor, Yale Law Jour., 1930-32. Address: 3147 O St NW Washington DC 20007

RUSH, RICHARD HENRY, financier, writer, lectr.; b. N.Y.C., Mar. 6, 1915; s. Henry Frederick and Bessie (Vreeland) R.; B.A., summa cum laude, Dartmouth, 1937, M.C.S., 1938; M.B.A., Harvard, 1941, D.C.S. (Littauer fellow, Brookings fellow), 1942; m. Julia Ann Halloran, Aug. 15, 1956; 1 dau., Sallie Haywood. Dir. aviation U.S. Bur. Fgn. and Domestic Commerce, 1945-46; chief economist, chmn. planning com. All Am. Aviation (Allegheny Airlines), 1943-45; dir. aircraft div. Nat. Security Resources Bd., 1948-51; Washington rep. to J. Paul Getty, 1951-52; partner Rush & Halloran, finance and ins., 1953-58; pres., chmn. bd. N.Am. Acceptance Corp., Atlanta, also Washington, 1956-59; owner Richard H. Rush Enterprises, Greenwich, Conn., also Washington, 1953-73; prof., chmn. dept. finance and investments Sch. Bus. Adminstrn., Am. U., Washington, 1967-70, 78-79. Trustee, mem. exec. com. Finch Coll., 1968-72. Mem. Am. Marketing Assn. (chmn. nat. com.), Am. Econ. Assn., Am. Statis. Assn., Internat. Platform Assn., AAUP, Phi Beta Kappa, Phi Kappa Phi, Omicron Delta Kappa. Episcopalian. Club: Harvard (N.Y.C.). Author: Trade Barriers in the Food Industry, 1942; Establishing an Aviation Business, 1947; Art as an Investment, 1961; A Strategy of Investing for Higher Return, 1962; The Techniques of Becoming Wealthy, 1963; Antiques as an Investment, 1968; The Wrecking Operation: Phase One, 1972; Investments You Can Live With and Enjoy, 1976; Techniques of Becoming Wealthy, 1977. Contbg. editor Wall St. Transcript, 1971—, Art/Antiques Investment Report, 1973—. Home: Greenwich CT 06830 also Villa Cornaro Piombino Dese (PD) Italy Mailing address: Box 62 Glenville Sta Greenwich CT 06830

RUSHER, WILLIAM ALLEN, publisher; b. Chgo., July 19, 1923; s. Evan Singleton and Verna (Self) R.; A.B., Princeton, 1943; J.D., Harvard, 1948; D.Lit. (hon.), Nathaniel Hawthorne Coll., 1973. Admitted to N.Y. bar, 1949; asso. firm Shearman & Sterling & Wright, N.Y.C., 1948-56; spl. counsel finance com. N.Y. Senate, 1955; asso. counsel internal security subcom. U.S. Senate, 1956-57; pub. Nat. Review mag., N.Y.C., 1957—; dir., v.p. Nat. Review, Inc. Advocate TV program The Advocates, 1970-73; mem. Adv. Task Force on Civil Disorders, 1972. Bd. dirs. Chinese Cultural Center, N.Y.C.; past vice chmn. Am. Conservative Union. Served from 2d lt. to capt., USAAF, 1943-46. Recipient Distinguished Citizen award N.Y. U. Law Sch. Mem. Am. Bar Assn., Nat. News Council, Am.-African Affairs Assn. (past co.-chmn., now dir.). Anglican. Clubs: University (N.Y.C.); Metropolitan (Washington). Author: Special Counsel, 1968; (with Mark Hatfield and Arlie Schardt) Amnesty? 1973; The Making of the New Majority Party, 1975. Columnist, Universal Press Syndicate, 1973—. Home: 30 E 37th St New York NY 10016 Office: 150 E 35th St New York NY 10016

RUSHFORTH, NORMAN BURLEIGH, educator, biologist; b. Blackpool, Eng., Dec. 27, 1932; s. Wilfred and Beatrice Ann (Burley) R.; came to U.S., 1955, naturalized, 1965; B.Sc., Birmingham (Eng.) U., 1954; Dip.Ed., Oxford (Eng.) U., 1955; M.S., Cornell U., 1957, Ph.D., 1961; m. Nancy Marie Edelman, Nov. 27, 1956; children—Alice Marie, Lorna Ann. Postdoctoral fellow Western Res. U., Cleve. (now Case-Western Res. U.), 1961-62, mem. faculty, 1962—, asso. prof. biostatistics, 1971—, chmn. dept. biology, 1970—, prof. biology, 1972—; cons. Nat. Inst. Arthritis, Metabolism and Digestive Diseases, 1968—. Johnson Found. fellow, 1955; Cornell U. sr. fellow, 1959; grantee NIMH, 1965—. Mem. Marine Biol. Lab., Am. Soc. Zoologists. Home: 3002 Meadowbrook St Cleveland OH 44118

RUSHING, JANE GILMORE, writer; b. Pyron, Tex., Nov. 15, 1925; d. Clyde Preston and Mabel Irene (Adams) Gilmore; B.A., Tex. Tech U., 1944, M.A., 1945, Ph.D., 1957; m. James Arthur Rushing, Nov. 29, 1956; 1 son, James Arthur. Reporter, Abilene (Tex.) Reporter-News, 1946-47; tchr. Tex. high schs., 1947-54; instr. U. Tenn., 1957-59; instr. to asst. prof. Tex. Tech U., intermittently, 1959-68; writer, 1960—; novels include: Walnut Grove, 1964; Against the Moon, 1968; Tamzen, 1972; Mary Dove, 1974; The Raincrow, 1977; books include: (with Kline A. Nall) Evolution of a University, Texas Tech's First Fifty Years, 1975. Vassie James Hill fellow of AAUW, 1956-57; recipient Emily Clark Balch prize, 1961; LeBaron R. Barker, Jr., Fiction award, 1975. Mem. Tex. Inst. Letters, Authors Guild, Authors League. Methodist. Home: 3809 39th St Lubbock TX 79413

RUSHING, JOE BOB, ednl. adminstr.; b. Brown County, Tex., May 23, 1921; s. Cordie M. and Vallie P. Rushing; B.A., Howard Payne U., 1946; M.A., East Tex. U., 1949; Ph.D., U. Tex., 1952; m. Elaine Whitis, Dec. 21, 1946; children—Anita Sherron, Cynthia Ann, Robert Scott. Tchr. sci., adminstr. Levelland (Tex.) High Sch., 1946-47, Mt. Pleasant (Tex.) High Sch., 1947-50; teaching fellow U. Tex., 1950-52; dir. adult edn. Wharton Jr. Coll., 1952-54; dean grad. div. Howard Payne U., 1954-58, adminstrv. v.p., 1956-60; pres. Jr. Coll. of Broward County (Fla.), 1960-65; chancellor Tarrant County Jr. Coll. Dist., Ft. Worth, 1969—; mem. Nat. Council on Humanities, 1976-82. Bd. dirs. United Way of Ft. Worth, 1977-78, Country Day Sch., Ft. Worth, 1977, Blue Cross/Blue Shield of Tex., 1979. Served with AUS, 1942-46. Named Boss of Yr., Nat. Secs. Assn., 1971, Educator of Yr., Press Club, 1974; recipient Disting. Alumnus award Howard Payne U., 1976, Disting. Alumnus award East Tex. State U., 1979, Carl Bredt award U. Tex., Austin, 1977; Paul Harris fellow, 1972. Mem. Am. Assn. Community and Jr. Colls. (dir. 1979), Ft. Worth C. of C. (dir. 1977-78), Pi Sigma Alpha, Phi Delta Kappa, Kappa Delta Pi. Baptist. Clubs: Rotary (dist. gov. 1974-75), Ft. Worth. Contbr. articles to profl. jours. Home: 6212 Junea Rd Fort Worth TX 76116 Office: 1400 Electric Service Bldg Fort Worth TX 76102

RUSHING, ROBERT KYGER, lawyer; b. Jackson, Miss., Nov. 19, 1930; s. Edgar and Katherine (Kyger) R.; B.A., U. Miss., 1952, LL.B., 1959; postgrad. Yale U., 1960; m. Sandra Jean McCrowell, Oct. 17, 1969; children—William, Bruce, Robert Kyger, Deborah Jean. Admitted to Miss. bar, 1959; asst. prof. law U. Miss., 1959-60, asso. prof., asst. dean Sch. Law, 1961-63; asso. prof. Washington and Lee U., 1963-69; dean Sch. Law, U. N.D., 1969—, asso. prof., 1969-72, prof., 1972—. Served with U.S. Army, 1952-57. Mem. Am. Law Inst., Nat. Conf. Commrs. Uniform State Laws, State Bar Assn. N.D. (exec. com.), Jud. Council N.D. Presbyterian. Home: PO Box 307 Thompson ND 58278 Office: Sch of Law U ND Grand Forks ND 58202

RUSHNELL, SQUIRE DERRICK, television exec.; b. Adams Center, N.Y., Oct. 31, 1938; s. Reginald Grant and Erica Mifanwy Redwood Sedgemore (Squire) R.; ed. Syracuse U., 1956-60; children—Robin Tracy, Hilary Adair. Disc jockey WOLF, WHEN, WFBL, Syracuse, N.Y., 1958-61, WTRL, Bradenton, Fla., 1961-62; exec. producer Contact, WBZ Radio-TV, Boston, 1962-67; program dir. KYW News-Radio, Phila., 1968; exec. producer Kennedy & Co., WLS-TV, Chgo., 1969-71, program dir. WLS, 1971-73; v.p. programs ABC owned TV stas., N.Y.C., 1973-74, v.p. childrens programs ABC Entertainment, 1974-78, v.p. Good Morning Am. and childrens programs ABC Television Network, N.Y.C., 1978—. Recipient Emmy awards, 1975, 76, 77, 78, 79, TV Critics Circle award, 1976 all for outstanding childrens television programming. Mem. Acad. Television Arts and Scis., Nat. Acad. Arts and Scis., Internat. Radio and Television Soc., Action for Childrens Television (award for outstanding childrens television programming). Office: ABC Entertainment 1330 Ave of the Americas New York NY 10019

RUSHTON, JOHN HENRY, chem. engr.; b. New London, Pa., Nov. 25, 1905; s. Edward Wester and Daisy Rich (Garber) R.; B.S. in Chem. Engring., U. Pa., 1926, M.S., 1929, Ph.D., 1933; m. Ellott May McLellon, Dec. 9, 1933 (dec. 1978); 1 son, Edward Wester, II (dec.); m. 2d Harriet K. Zimmer Scott, 1978. Chem. engr. Royal Electrotype Co., 1926-28; instr. Drexel Inst., 1928, asst. prof. chem. engring., 1929-35; asst. prof. U. Mich., 1935-37; prof., head dept. chem. engring. U. Va., 1937-46, Ill. Inst. Tech., 1946-55; prof. Purdue U., 1955-71, prof. emeritus, 1971—; cons. chem. engring. to petroleum, chem., equipment and mineral cos., 1935—; sec., head office sci. research and devel. U.S. Army, 1942-46; cons., mem. rev. com. Oak Ridge Nat. Labs., 1941-65. Recipient Widsom Soc. award, 1970. Fellow Am. Inst. Chem. Engrs. (Walker award 1952, Founders award 1962, Van Antwerpen award 1979, pres. 1957, treas. 1958-62, adminstr. Design Inst. for Multiphase Processing 1972—); mem. Am. Chem. Soc. (chmn. div. industry and engring. chemistry 1960, citation 1961), Am. Soc. Engring. Edn. Republican. Presbyterian. Clubs: Chemists (N.Y.C.); Univ. (Chgo.); Masons. Author: Oxygen Research, 1942; Process Equipment Design, 1945; contbr. numerous articles in field of mixing, process design cryogenics to profl. jours. Home: 300 Valley St Apt 501 Lafayette IN 47905 Office: CMET Bldg Purdue U West Lafayette IN 47907

RUSHTON, WILLIAM JAMES, life ins. exec.; b. Birmingham, Ala., July 10, 1900; s. James Franklin and Willis (Roberts) R.; B.S., Washington and Lee U., Lexington, Va., 1921; H.H.D., Southwestern at Memphis, 1959; m. Elizabeth Perry, Nov. 24, 1926 (dec. 1972); children—William James III, James. Asst. mgr. Birmingham Ice & Cold Storage Co., 1922-27, v.p., 1927-32, pres. 1932-38, vice chmn. bd., sec., 1938-57; pres. Protective Life Ins. Co., 1937-67, chmn. bd., 1967-76, dir., 1927—; mem. adv. bd. Investment Co. of Am. (Calif.); chmn. bd. Franklin Coal Mining Co., 1927-42; dir. Moore-Handley Hardware Co., 1948-63, 1st Nat Bank Birmingham, 1927-73, Ala. Power Co., 1937-70, Gulf, Mobile & Ohio R.R. Co., 1940-72, Ill. Central Gulf R.R., 1972-74. Vice chmn., life trustee So. Research Inst.; pres. Birmingham council Boy Scouts Am., 1927-30, dir., 1925-55; mem. nat. citizens com. United Community Campaigns Am., 1961-74; dir. Birmingham Community Chest, 1937, v.p., 1942-43, 48-52, exec. com., 1945-56, pres., 1954, now dir. for life; bd. dirs., trustee (life) Birmingham Mus. Art; trustee (life) Children's Hosp.; trustee Agnes Scott Coll., Decatur, Ga., 1935-45; bd. dirs. local chpt. YMCA, local chpt. Salvation Army. Served to col., U.S. Army, World War II. Civilian chief Birmingham Ordnance Dist., U.S. Army, 1946-61. Decorated Legion of Merit; recipient citations Sec. of Army; named to Ala. Acad. Honor, 1975; named to Ala. Acad. Honor, 1975. Mem. Am. Ordnance Assn. (v.p. 1942-64), Nat. Assn. Ice Industries (life dir.; pres. 1936-37), Nat. Assn. Refrigerated Warehouses (pres. 1933-35; mem. Nat. Code Authority), Am. Warehousemen's Assn. (pres. 1935-36), Life Ins. Assn. of Am. (dir. 1955-61), Health Ins. Assn. Am. (dir. 1964-67), Am. Life Conv. (Ala. v.p.), Inst. Life Ins. (dir. 1963-69), Asso. Industries Ala. (dir. 1956-63), Beta Gamma Sigma, Beta Theta Pi, Omicron Delta Kappa, Delta Sigma Rho. Presbyterian (deacon, elder, chmn. trustees; mem. bd. annuities and relief Presbyn. Ch. in U.S. 1959-67). Rotarian (pres. 1952-53). Clubs: Mountain Brook, Birmingham Country, Downtown, The Club, Redstone (Birmingham); Chaparrall (Dallas). Home: 2848 Balmoral Rd Birmingham AL 35223 Office: Protective Life Ins Co Birmingham AL 35202

RUSHTON, WILLIAM JAMES, III, ins. co. exec.; b. Birmingham, Ala., Apr. 23, 1929; s. William James and Elizabeth (Perry) R.; B.A. magna cum laude, Princeton U., 1951; m. LaVona Price, Aug. 19, 1955; children—William James IV, Deakins Ford, Tunstall Perry. Asso. actuary Protective Life Ins. Co., Birmingham, Ala., 1954-59, dir., 1956—, agt., 1959-62, v.p., 1962-63, agy. v.p., 1963-67, pres., 1967—, pres., chief exec. officer, 1969—; dir. Avondale Mills, Moore & Handley Hardware, Ala. Power Co., The Southern Co., First Nat. Bank of Birmingham, Ala. Bancorp., The Economy Co. of Okla. Trustee, So. Research Inst., Children's Hosp., Birmingham So. Coll., Baptist Hosp. Found., Highland Day Sch.; deacon First Presbyn. Ch.; chmn. United Way campaign, 1977; bd. dirs. Birmingham

Coordinating Council Social Agencies, United Appeal, Indsl. Health Council; mem. adv. com. Meyer Found.; adv. bd. Samford U. Sch. Bus.; bd. visitors U. Ala. Coll. Commerce at Tuscaloosa. Served to capt., arty., U.S. Army; Korea. Decorated Bronze Star medal; named to Ala. Acad. of Honors, 1979. Fellow Soc. Actuaries; mem. Am. Council Life Ins. (dir.), Am. Life Conv. (state v.p. 1975), Am. Life Ins. Assn. (Ala. v.p. 1975), Million Dollar Round Table, Birmingham C. of C. (dir.). Clubs: Rotary (dir. 1973-74, treas. 1978-79), Mountain Brook Country, Relay House, Birmingham Country, The Club, Redstone. Home: 2900 Cherokee Rd Birmingham AL 35223 Office: Protective Life Ins Co PO Box 2606 Birmingham AL 35202

RUSHWORTH, ROBERT AITKEN, air force officer, aero. engr.; b. Madison, Maine, Oct. 9, 1924; s. Walter Aitken and Mabel (Tinkham) R.; B.S. in Mech. Engring., U. Maine, 1951; postgrad. in Aero. Engring. USAF Inst. Tech., 1953-54, Nat. War Coll., 1966-67; m. Joyce Butler, June 28, 1947; 1 dau., Cheri. Commd. (beginning rank please) 2d lt. U.S. Air Force, 1944, advanced through grades to maj. gen., 1975; exptl. research pilot, Edwards AFB, Calif., 1956-66; tactical ops. comdr., Vietnam, 1967-69; program mgr. Maverick Missile, Wright-Patterson AFB, Ohio, 1969-70, comdr. 4950th Test Wing, 1971-73, vice comdr. Aero. Systems Div., 1976—; insp. gen. Air Force Systems Command, Andrews AFB, Md., 1973; comdr. Air Force Flight Test Center, Edwards AFB, Calif., 1976. Decorated Legion of Merit, D.F.C., Air medal; recipient Exceptional Service medal NASA, 1965. Fellow Soc. Exptl. Test Pilots (tech. adviser to bd. dirs.); mem. Am. Legion (life), V.F.W. (life), Air Force Assn. Clubs: Wright-Patterson AFB Officers', Wright-Patterson AFB Golf. Home: 440 Metzger Dr Wright-Patterson AFB OH 45433 Office: Aero Systems Div Wright-Patterson AFB OH 45433

RUSK, DEAN, educator, former sec. of state; b. Cherokee County, Ga., Feb. 9, 1909; s. Robert Hugh and Elizabeth (Clotfelter) R.; A.B., Davidson Coll., N.C., 1931; B.S. (Rhodes scholar), St. John's Coll. Oxford (Eng.) U., 1933; M.A., 1934; various hon. degrees; m. Virginia Foisle, June 19, 1937; children—David Patrick, Richard Geary, Margaret Elizabeth. Asso. prof. govt. and dean faculty Mills Coll., 1934-40; asst. chief Div. Internat. Security Affairs, U.S. Dept. State, 1946; spl. asst. sec. of war, 1946-47; dir. Office UN Affairs, U.S. Dept. State, 1947-49; asst. sec. of state, Feb. 1949; dep. under sec. of state, 1949-50; asst. sec. of state for Far Eastern Affairs, 1950-51; pres. Rockefeller Found., 1952-60; sec. of state, Washington, 1961-69; Sibley prof. internat. law Sch. Law, U. Ga., Athens, 1970—. Served with AUS, 1940-46. Recipient Cecil Peace Prize, 1933, Legion of Merit with oak leaf cluster. Mem. Am. Soc. Internat. Law, Phi Beta Kappa. Democrat. Presbyn. Home: 1 Lafayette Sq 620 Hill St Athens GA 30606

RUSK, HOWARD A., physician; b. Brookfield, Mo., Apr. 9, 1901; s. Michael Yost and Augusta Eastin (Shipp) R.; A.B., U. Mo., 1923, LL.D., 1947; M.D., U. Pa., 1925; D.Sc. (hon.), Boston U., 1949, Lehigh U., 1956, Middlebury Coll., 1957, Trinity Coll., 1961, Woman's Med. Coll., 1962, U. Portland, 1969, Hofstra U., 1972, Jersey City State Coll., 1974, Calif. Coll. Podiatric Medicine, 1976, Coll. New Rochelle, 1977, Brandeis U., 1978; LL.D., Westminster Coll., 1950, Hahnemann Med. Coll., 1952, Chungang U., Korea, 1956, L.I. U., 1957, Missouri Valley Coll., 1965; L.H.D. (hon.), Adelphi Coll., 1957; Litt.D., Ithaca Coll., 1961; M.D. (hon.), U. Rennes (France), 1965; D.M.Sc. (hon.), Brown U., 1969; m. Gladys Houx, Oct. 20, 1926; children—Martha (Mrs. Preston Sutphen, Jr.), Howard A., John Michael. Engaged in practice of internal medicine, St. Louis, 1926-42; instr. medicine Washington U., St. Louis, 1929-42; asso. chief of staff St. Luke's Hosp., St. Louis; prof. and chmn. dept. rehab. medicine N.Y. U. Sch. Medicine, 1946—. Cons. in rehab. Baruch Com. secretariat UN, N.Y.C.; chmn. health resources adv. com. ODM, 1950-57, mem. Pub. Health Council, N.Y. Dept. Health. Pres. World Rehab. Fund, dir. Chem. Fund, Inc., Companion Life Ins. Co., Graphic Arts Mut. Ins. Co., IPCO Hosp. Supply Corp.; chmn. pub. policy com. Advt. Council. Trustee U. Pa., 1962-67; bd. dirs. N.Y. Found. Served as col. M.C., chief of convalescent tng. div., Office Air Surgeon, 1943-45; brig. gen. ret. USAF. Decorated D.S.M.; Nat. Medal of Republic Korea; Order Jose Fernandez Madrid (Colombia); officier French Legion of Honor; recipient Dr. C.C. Criss award, 1952; Lasker award Am. Pub. Health Assn., 1952; Research award Am. Pharm. Mfrs. Assn., 1951; Gold medal Nat. Inst. Soc. Sci., 1954, Internat. Benjamin Franklin Soc., 1955, Albert Lasker award for services to physically disabled, 1957, 60, Gold Key award Am. Congress Phys. Medicine and Rehab., 1958, others. Diplomate Am. Bd. Internal Medicine, Am. Bd. Phys. Medicine and Rehab. Fellow A.C.P., Royal Coll. Physicians; mem. N.Y. Acad. Medicine, AMA, Internat. Soc. Welfare of Cripples (pres. 1954), Nat. Assn. Sci. Writers, Phi Beta Kappa, Alpha Omega Alpha, Phi Delta Theta, Nu Sigma Nu. Author: New Hope for the Handicapped (with Eugene J. Taylor), 1949; Living with a Disability, 1953; Rehabilitation Medicine, 1958, 4th edit., 1977; co-author Cardiovascular Rehabilitation, 1958; Rehabilitation of the Cardiovascular Patients, 1958; (autobiography) A World to Care For, 1972; also contbr. med. articles to Ency. Brit., sci. publs. and papers presented before med. assns. Home: 330 E 33d St New York NY 10016 Office: Institute of Rehabilitation Medicine 400 E 34th St New York NY 10016

RUSK, WILLIAM SENER, educator; b. Balt., Sept. 29, 1892; s. George Glanville and Mary Elizabeth (Yeisley) R.; A.B., Princeton U., 1915; A.M., Johns Hopkins U., 1924, Ph.D., 1933; student Am. Acad. in Rome, summer 1925, Ecole du Louvre, Paris, summer 1928, Harvard U., summers 1930-31; m. Evelyn T. Carroll, Aug. 31, 1932. Master Greek and Latin, Boys' Latin Sch., Balt., 1915-18; master English, Gilman Country Sch., Balt., 1918-19; instr. Wells Coll., 1921-25, prof. fine arts, 1928-58, prof. emeritus, 1958—, vis. prof. fine arts, 1961-65; asst. prof. modern art Dartmouth Coll., 1925-28; lectr. fine arts Columbia U., summers 1924, 26, 27, U. Calif. at Los Angeles, summer 1939; vis. prof. fine arts Cornell U., 1959; vis. prof. art U. Richmond, 1965-66; tour dir. Am. Inst. Ednl. Travel, summer 1937. Chmn. Middle Atlantic States Art Conf., 1941-42. Mem. AAUP, Am. Inst. Archaeology, Coll. Art Assn., Am. Soc. Aesthetics, Phi Beta Kappa, Phi Beta Kappa Assos. (Bicentennial fellow). Democrat. Roman Catholic. Clubs: Cloister Inn (Princeton); Princeton (N.Y.C.). Author: Art in Baltimore—Monuments and Memorials, 1924; William Henry Rinehart, Sculptor, 1939; William Thornton, Benjamin H. Latrobe, and Thomas U. Walter and The Classical Influence in Their Work, 1939; Art in its Environment, 1969. Editor: Methods of Teaching the Fine Arts, 1935. Contbg. editor Dictionary of the Arts; contbr. sketches to Thieme-Becker Allgemeines Kûnstlerlexikon, Dictionary of American Biography, others; also articles and reviews. Home: Aurora NY 13026

RUSKIN, JOSEPH RICHARD, actor, dir.; b. Haverhill, Mass., Apr. 14, 1924; s. Ely and Betty Edith (Chaimson) Schlafman; grad. Carnegie Inst. Tech., 1949; 1 dau., Alicia. Founder, Rochester (N.Y.) Arena Theatre, 1949-52; appeared in stage plays on Broadway and Off-Broadway, 1952-58, Houston Alley Theater, 1958; appeared Theatre Group, U. Calif. at Los Angeles, later Mark Taper Forum, 1959-71; dir. Houston Alley, 1965-69; now dir. prodn. and dir. Am. Theatre Arts, Hollywood, Calif.; appeared in films Fall of Legs Diamond, 1959; Magnificent Seven, 1960; Escape from Zahrein, 1963; Robin and the Seven Hoods, 1965; regular performer various TV programs. Served with USNR, 1943-46. Mem. Actors Equity Assn. (western regional v.p., chmn. western adv. bd.), Screen Actors' Guild (dir.). Home: 1560 N Laurel Ave Apt 103 West Hollywood CA 90046

RUSNELL, WESLEY ALLEN, artist; b. Cleve., Nov. 27, 1934; s. James Wesley and Mary (Paul) R.; B.A., San Francisco State Coll., 1961; m. Elizabeth Bradford Willard, Mar. 10, 1967; children—Noel, Ava. Artist-in-residence Roswell (N.Mex.) Mus. and Art Center, 1973-74; affiliated with Group 7, works toured Western Assn. Art Museums, 1966; one-man shows; Stables Gallery, Taos, N.Mex., 1967, Jonson Gallery, U. N.Mex., 1969, Mission Gallery, Taos, 1971, 75, Gallery Contemporary Art, Santa Fe, 1972, Roswell Mus. and Art Center, 1974; exhibited in group shows: Rocky Mountain States Fedn. Art, 1967, N.Mex. Painting Invitational, Santa Fe Fine Arts Mus., 1968, Own Your Own show Denver Art Mus., 1968, 69, N.Mex. Fiesta Biennial, 1969, 71, 11th ann. 8-state exhbn. painting and sculpture Okla. Art Center, 1969, 11th ann. nat. exhbn. prints and drawings Okla. Art Center, 1969, 73d ann. Denver Art Mus., 1971, N.Mex. Fine Arts Biennial, 1973, Museo de Arte e Historica, Ciudad Juarez, Mex., 1973, Abilene (Tex.) Mus. Art, 1974, Wichita Falls (Tex.) Mus. Art, 1974, Beaumont (Tex.) Mus., 1974, Witte Meml. Mus., San Antonio, 1974, Smither Gallery, Dallas, 1974, Comsky Gallery, Beverly Hills, Calif., 1974-75, Kans. State U., Pittsburg, 1975; represented pvt. collections. Recipient Helene Wurlitzer painting prize Taos Art Assn., 1964. Address: 1508 W 7th St Roswell NM 88201

RUSS, JOANNA, writer, educator; b. N.Y.C., Feb. 22, 1937; d. Evarett and Bertha (Zinner) Russ; B.A. in English with high honors, Cornell, U., 1957; M.F.A. in Playwriting and Dramatic Lit., Yale, 1960. Lectr. in English, Cornell U., 1967-70, asst. prof., 1970-72; asst. prof. English, Harpur Coll., State U. N.Y. at Binghamton, 1972-75; asst. prof. English, U. Colo., 1975-77; asso. prof. U. Wash., 1977—. Mem. Modern Lang. Assn., Sci. Fiction Writers Am. (Nebula award for best short story 1972). Author: Picnic on Paradise, 1968; And Chaos Died, 1970; The Female Man, 1975; We Who Are About To, 1977; Kittatinny: A Tale of Magic, 1978; The Two of Them, 1978; also numerous short stories. Address: Dept English GN-30 U Washington Seattle WA 98195

RUSSE, HENRY PAUL, physician, educator; b. Indpls., Feb. 12, 1928; s. Paul Carl and Marie Hubbard (Richart) R.; A.B., Ind. U., 1952, A.B. in Zoology, 1953; M.D. with honors, U. Chgo., 1957; m. Joyce Nadine Swedlund, June 10, 1967; children—Paul, Catherine, Thomas, Sarah. Intern, resident in medicine U. Chgo. Hosps., 1957-61; USPHS fellow in allergy and immunology U. Chgo., U. Chgo., 1961-63; mem. faculty dept. medicine U. Chgo., 1961-68, 76—, prof. medicine, 1976-79, chief gen. medicine, 1964-68, asso. v.p. for med. center U. Chgo. Hosps. and Clinic, 1976-79, chief of staff, 1976-79; chief medicine, chmn. medicine, v.p. medicine Columbus-Cuneo-Cabrini Med. Center, Chgo., 1968-76; asso. clin. prof. Loyola U., 1968-72; asso. prof. medicine Northwestern U., 1972-76; prof. medicine, asso. dean med. sci. and services Rush Med. Coll., asst. v.p. med. services Rush-Presbyn.-St. Luke's Med. Center, Chgo., 1979—. Bd. dirs. Schweppe Found., Chgo. Home for Incurables, Home for Destitute and Crippled Children. Served with U.S. Army, 1949-51. Decorated Bronze Star; Schweppe fellow, 1961-64; USPHS fellow, 1960-62; recipient numerous NIH grants. Fellow A.C.P.; mem. Am. Fedn. Clin. Research, N.Y. Acad. Scis., AAAS, Transplantation Soc., Am. Acad. Allergy, Am. Assn. Immunologists, AMA, Chgo. Soc. Allergy, Ill. Med. Soc., Inst. Medicine Chgo. (pres. 1976-79), Chgo. Soc. Internal Medicine (past pres.). Lutheran. Contbr. articles to profl. jours. Office: Rush-Presbyn-St Luke's Med Center 1753 W Congress Pkwy Chicago IL 60637

RUSSELL, ALBERT RICHARD, assn. exec.; b. Oxford, Miss., Apr. 11, 1915; s. Albert Edgar and Clara Marie (Graves) R.; B.A., U. Miss., 1936, postgrad. law, 1937; m. Sada Frances Norris, Dec. 29, 1961. With Americana Corp., N.Y.C., 1937-39; sec.-mgr. Delta Council, Stoneville, Miss., 1939-41; with Nat. Cotton Council Am., Memphis, 1946—, adminstrv. v.p., 1967-68, exec. v.p., 1969-78, spl. adv. to mgmt., 1978—; exec. v.p. Cotton Council Internat., 1969-78. Bd. dirs. Effective Citizens Orgn., 1963-65; trustee Oscar Johnston Cotton Found., 1969-78. Served as flight navigator USNR, 1942-46. Mem. U. Miss. Hall of Fame, 1937. Mem. Soc. Assn. Execs., Am. Soc. Assn. Execs., A.I.M. (pres. council 1966—), Phi Delta Theta. Club: Summit. Home: Muccaloon Farms Route 5 Oxford MS 38655 Office: 1918 N Parkway Memphis TN 38112

RUSSELL, ALLAN DAVID, corporate lawyer; b. Cleve., May 6, 1924; s. Allan MacGillivray and Marvel (Codling) R.; B.A., Yale U., 1945, LL.B., 1951; m. Lois Anne Robinson, June 12, 1947; children—Lisa Anne, Robinson David, Martha Leslie. Admitted to N.Y. State bar, 1952, Conn. bar, 1956, Mass. bar, 1969, U.S. Supreme Ct. bar, 1977; atty. Sylvania Electric Products, Inc., N.Y.C., 1951-56, div. counsel, Batavia, N.Y., 1956-65, sr. counsel, 1965-71; sec., sr. counsel GTE Sylvania Inc., Stamford, Conn., 1971-76; asst. gen. counsel Gen. Telephone & Electronics Corp., 1976—; sec., dir. Sylvania Entertainment Products Corp., mktg. subs., 1961-67; sec. Wilbur B. Driver Co. Dist. leader Republican party, New Canaan, Conn., 1955-56. Served with USAAF, 1943-46. Mem. Am. Bar Assn., Bar Assn. City N.Y., St. Nicholas Soc., SAR, Soc. Colonial Wars, Yale Alumni Assn. (sec. local chpt. 1953-56), Phi Delta Phi. Home: 75 Olmstead Hill Rd Wilton CT 06897 Office: 1 Stamford Forum Stamford CT 06904

RUSSELL, ALLEN STEVENSON, aluminum co. exec.; b. Bedford, Pa., May 27, 1915; s. Arthur Stainton and Ruth (Stevenson) R.; B.S., Pa. State U., 1936, M.S., 1937, Ph.D., 1941; m. Judith Pauline Sexauer, Apr. 5, 1941. With Aluminum Co. Am., 1940—, asso. dir. research, 1973-74, v.p. Alcoa Labs., Alcoa Center, Pa., 1974-78, v.p. sci. and tech., Pitts., 1978—. Named IR-100 Scientist of Yr., 1979. Fellow Am. Soc. Metals, AIME; mem. Am. Chem. Soc., Dirs. Indsl. Research, Nat. Materials Adv. Bd., Nat. Acad. Engring. (council), Sigma Xi. Republican. Presbyterian. Contbr. articles to profl. jours.; patentee in field. Home: 929 Field Club Rd Pittsburgh PA 15238 Office: 1501 Alcoa Bldg Pittsburgh PA 15219

RUSSELL, BILL, sportscaster, former profl. basketball player and coach; b. Monroe, La., Feb. 12, 1934; grad. San Francisco State Coll., 1956. Player, coach Boston Celtics Profl. Basketball Club, until 1969; sportscaster ABC-TV, 1969—; coach Seattle Supersonics, 1973-77; mem. U.S. Olympic Basketball Team (Gold medal), 1956; appeared in TV series Cowboy in Africa, also commls.; co-host The Superstars, ABC-TV, 1978-79; commentator Sta. KABC-TV, Los Angeles. Author: Second Wind: Memoirs of an Opinionated Man, 1979; weekly columnist Seattle Times. Office: care ABC Sports 1330 Ave of Americas New York NY 10019*

RUSSELL, DAN M., JR., U.S. dist. judge; b. Magee, Miss., Mar. 15, 1913; s. Dan M. and Beulah (Watkins) R.; B.A., U. Miss., 1935, LL.B., 1937; m. Dorothy Tudury, Dec. 27, 1942; children—Ronald Truett, Dorothy Dale, Richard Brian. Admitted to Miss. bar, 1937; practice in Gulfport and Bay St. Louis, Miss.; U.S. judge So. Dist. Miss., 1965—. Dir. So. Savs. & Loan Assn., Gulfport, Miss. Chmn. Hancock (Miss.) Civic Action Assn., 1964—. Democratic presdl. elector, 1964; chmn. Hancock County Election Commn., 1959-64. Served to lt. comdr. USNR, 1941-45. Mem. Miss., Hancock County (v.p. 1964-65) bar assns., Hancock County C. of C. (pres. 1946), Tau Kappa Alpha, Scribblers. Rotarian (pres. Bay St. Louis, Miss. 1946). Home: 321 Main St Bay Saint Louis MS 39520 Office: PO Box 1930 Gulfport MS 39502

RUSSELL, DAVID ALLISON, aero. engr., educator; b. Saint John, N.B., Can., Apr. 25, 1935; s. James Vener and Helen Ringen (Allison) R.; came to U.S., 1954, naturalized, 1967; student U. N.B., Fredericton, 1950-54; B.Mech.Engring., U. So. Calif., 1956; M.Sc. in Aeros., Calif. Inst. Tech., 1957, Ph.D. in Aeros. and Physics, 1961; m. Hazel Anne Garnett, Mar. 22, 1957; children—Karen, Kristen, Kathryn. Sr. scientist Jet Propulsion Lab., Pasadena, Calif., 1961-67; research asso. prof. aeros. and astronautics U. Wash., 1967-70, asso. prof., 1970-74, prof., 1974—, chmn. dept. aeros. and astronautics, 1977—; cons. in field. Mem. Kirkland (Wash.) Planning Commn., 1971-79, chmn., 1977-79; chmn. Kirkland Land Use Policy Plan, 1977-79. NASA grantee, 1969-78; Dept. Def. grantee, 1969-71, 73—. Fellow AIAA (asso.; Pacific N.W. Council 1974-76, Pacific N.W. sect. award for contbns. to aerospace tech. 1972); mem. Am. Phys. Soc. (exec. council div. fluid dynamics 1977-78), Sierra Club, Sigma Xi, Tau Beta Pi, Pi Tau Sigma. Contbr. numerous articles on fluid mechanics and gas physics to profl. jours., especially on shock processes and laser fluid dynamics. Home: 4507 105th St NE Kirkland WA 98033 Office: 206 Guggenheim Hall U Wash FS-10 Seattle WA 98195

RUSSELL, DAVID L(AWSON), psychologist; b. Apr. 1, 1921; B.A. in honors with distinction in Psychology, Wesleyan U., 1942; postgrad. Columbia U., summers 1942, 46; Ph.D. in Psychology, U. Minn., 1953; married; 2 children. Adminstrv. fellow Office Dean of Students, U. Minn., Mpls., 1947, teaching asst. dept. psychology, 1947-48, clin. fellow Student Counseling Bur., 1948-50; dir. student counseling Bowdoin Coll., Brunswick, Maine, 1950-59, instr., 1950-54, asst. prof. psychology, 1954-59; asso. prof. Ohio U., 1959-67, prof., 1967—, asst. chmn. dept. psychology, 1968, chmn., 1969-72; vis. prof. U. N.H., summer 1958; mem. faculty NDEA Counseling and Guidance Inst. at Ohio U., summers 1961, 63, 65, 1966-67; pres. Maine Psychol. Assn., 1956-57; chmn. Maine Bd. Examiners Psychologists, 1959; cons. Div. Undergrad. Edn. in Sci., NSF, 1965, 70, 71; sec. Nat. Council Chairmen Grad. Depts. Psychology, 1971-72. Mem. Superintending Sch. Com., Town of Topsham (Maine), 1953-59, chmn., 1953-54, 56-57, mem. sch. bldg. com., 1953-55, com. chmn., 1953-55; sec. Joint-Com. Maine Sch. Union 46, 1953-59; mem. Topsham Zoning Com., 1956-57. Served to lt. USCGR, 1943-52. Lic. psychologist, Ohio. Mem. Am. Psychol. Assn., Midwestern Psychol. Assn., Ohio Psychol. Assn., Am. Personnel and Guidance Assn., Am. Ednl. Research Assn., Nat. Vocat. Guidance Assn. (profl.), Sigma Xi (pres. Ohio U. chpt. 1972-73), Psi Chi. Author: (with others) Applied Psychology, 1966; contbr. articles to profl. publs. Home: 41 Elmwood Pl Athens OH 45701 Office: Dept Psychology Ohio U Athens OH 45701

RUSSELL, DONALD FRANK, architect; b. Newburyport, Mass., Aug. 7, 1909; s. Frank Foss and Edith Mae (Steer) R.; student Northeastern U., 1927-38, Mass. Inst. Tech., 1928-33; m. Patti Baker; one dau., Linda. Indsl. and archtl. designer with Norman Bel Geddes, 1933-35, with Alfons Bach, 1935-36; also free lance illustrator and oil painter, 1933-36; designer with Steuben Glass, Inc., 1936; in charge design dept. Steuben Glass, Inc. div. Corning Glass Works, 1937-39, subsequently resident architect, now ret.; indsl. and interior designer with Raymond Loewy, 1939—. Serving with U.S. Army Air Force Hdqrs., Washington, 1941—, and designing and illustrating for Tng. Aids Books, Airports and Air Communications layouts. Awarded John Wheelwright 6 yr. scholarship; European tour for Steuben Glass, Inc., as result of design competition, 1937. Home: 6 Tremont St Newburyport MA 01950 Office: 717 Fifth Ave New York City NY 10022

RUSSELL, DONALD GLENN, oil co. exec.; b. Kansas City, Mo., Nov. 24, 1931; s. Virgil G. and Mae (Agey) R.; B.S. in Math. and Physics, Sam Houston State U., 1953; M.S. in Math. and Physics, U. Okla., 1955; m. Norma Jean Robertson, Mar. 21, 1953; children—Karen, Steven. With Shell Oil Co. and subs.'s, 1955—, on spl. assignment Shell Internat. Petroleum Co., London, 1976, v.p. corp. planning, Houston, 1977, v.p. internat. exploration and prodn., pres. Pecten Cos., 1978—. Mem. council Boy Scouts Am. Mem. Soc. Petroleum Engrs. (Cedric K. Ferguson medal 1962, treas. Found. 1977—), Am. Petroleum Inst., AIME, Pi Epsilon Tau. Presbyterian. Clubs: Petroleum of Houston, Champions Golf. Author: (with C. S. Matthews) Pressure Buildup and Flow Tests in Wells. Office: PO Box 205 Houston TX 77001

RUSSELL, DONALD STUART, circuit judge; b. Lafayette Springs, Miss., Feb. 22, 1906; s. Jesse and Lula (Russell) R.; A.B., U. S.C., 1925, LL.B., 1928; student U. Mich., 1929; m. Virginia Utsey, June 15, 1929; children—Donald, Mildred, Scott, John. Admitted to S.C. bar, 1928, practiced in Spartanburg, 1930-42; with Nicholls, Wyche & Byrnes, Nicholls, Wyche & Russell, and Nicholls & Russell, 1930-38; pvt. practice, 1938-42; mem. Price Adjustment Bd., War Dept., Washington, 1942; asst. to dir. econ. stablzn., 1942, asst. to dir. war moblzn., 1943; dep. dir. Office War Moblzn. Reconversion, 1945; asst. sec. state, 1945-47; pres. U. S.C., 1951-57; pvt. law practice, 1957-63; gov. of S.C., 1963-65; U.S. senator from S.C., 1965-66; U.S. dist. judge, 1967-71; U.S. circuit judge, 1971—. Mem. Wriston Com. on Reorgn. Fgn. Service, 1954; trustee emeritus Emory U., Atlanta; trustee Converse Coll., Spartanburg, S.C., Benedict Coll., Columbia, S.C. Served as maj. AUS, 1944; SHAEF, France. Mem. Phi Beta Kappa. Methodist. Home: 716 Otis Blvd Spartanburg SC 29302 Office: Fed Bldg Spartanburg SC 29304

RUSSELL, EDGAR POE, JR., judge; b. Selma, Ala., Dec. 9, 1920; s. Edgar Poe and Sarah Ruth (MacDonald) R.; B.A., U. Ala., 1941, LL.B., 1948; m. Dora Howard Wilkinson, Aug. 7, 1942; children—Mary Russell McKissack, Beth Russell Williams. Admitted to Ala. bar, 1948, practiced in Selma, 1948-69; recorder City of Selma, 1959-69; judge 4th Jud. Circuit of Ala., 1969—. Served with USNR, 1941-45. Mem. Selma and Dallas County C. of C. (pres. 1966-67). Club: Rotary (pres. 1958-59). Home: 108 Russell Dr Selma AL 36701 Office: Dallas County Courthouse Selma AL 36701

RUSSELL, EDWIN F., publisher; b. Elizabeth, N.J., July 15, 1914; s. Lucius T. and Marian (Cronin) R.; student Newark Acad., Lawrenceville (N.J.) Sch., Princeton, 1937; m. Sarah Spencer-Churchill, May 15, 1943 (div. 1966); children—Serena, Consuelo, Alexandra, Jacqueline; m. 2d, Iris Smith, 1967. With Newark Star-Ledger, 1935-47, asso. pub., 1946-47; pub. Harrisburg (Pa.) Patriot, Harrisburg Evening News, 1947-69, Vogue, 1960-64; pres. Patriot-News Co., 1947—, Newhouse Newspapers Metro Suburbia, 1963—; mem. AP. Mem. President's Adv. Com. on U.S.-USSR Relations, 1956-60, mem. bd. Adv. Council, 1965-79; mem. Nat. Commn. on Productivity, 1975—. Chmn., Pa. Citizens for Eisenhower, 1952-56. Served with Brit. Royal Navy on HMS Norfolk, 1940, commd. sub-lt. Royal Naval Coll., 1941; commd. lt. comdr. U.S. Navy, 1943; staff, comdr. naval forces Europe; staff SHAEF, U.S.S. Oklahoma City. Mem. Am. Newspaper Pubs. Assn.,

Delta Sigma Chi. Clubs: Nat. Press (Washington); Pilgrims. Home: Brookville NY 11560 Office: 812 Market St Harrisburg PA 17107 also 485 Lexington Ave New York NY 10017

RUSSELL, FRANCIS, author; b. Boston, Jan. 12, 1910; s. Leo Spotten and Ethel May (Kent) R.; student U. Breslau, Germany, 1931-32; A.B., Bowdoin Coll., 1933; A.M., Harvard U., 1937; m. Sharon Soong, Mar. 5, 1966; 1 dau., Sara. Writer for various Irish, English and Am. publs., 1946—. Served to capt. Can. Army, 1941-46. Recipient Edgar award Mystery Writers Am., 1962. Guggenheim fellow, 1964, 65. Fellow Soc. Am. Historians; mem. Goethe Soc. (dir.), Sandwich Citizens Orgn. (v.p.), Black Watch Assn., Dorchester Hist. Soc. Episcopalian. Club: Harvard (Boston). Author: Three Studies in 20th Century Obscurity, 1954; Tragedy in Dedham, 1962; The Great Interlude, 1964; The World of Dürer, 1967; The Shadow of Blooming Grove, 1968; The Making of the Nation, 1968; The Confident Years, 1969; Forty Years On, 1970; The Horizon Concise History of Germany, 1973; A City in Terror, 1975; The President Makers from Mark Hanna to Joseph P. Kennedy, 1976; Adams: An American Dynasty, 1976. Address: The Lindens Sandwich MA 02563

RUSSELL, FRANCIS GARLAND, JR., banker; b. Columbia, Mo., Nov. 15, 1931; s. Francis Garland and Emily (Joslyn) R.; B.A., U. Chgo., 1951; B.A. with honors in Law, U. Cambridge (Eng.), 1953, M.A., 1961; LL.B., Yale U., 1956; m. Peggy Lee Cowie, May 9, 1967; 1 son, Francis Leland. Admitted to Ill. bar, 1956, Fla. bar, 1957, Mo. bar, 1961; law clk. to Circuit Ct. Judge Warren L. Jones, 1956-57; with Fed. Res. Bank St. Louis, 1960—, sr. v.p., gen. counsel, sec., 1973—. Served to 1st lt. USAF, 1957-60. Home: 3853 Holly Hills Blvd Saint Louis MO 63116 Office: 411 Locust St Saint Louis MO 63102

RUSSELL, FRANK E., newspaper exec.; b. Kokomo, Ind., Dec. 6, 1920; s. Frank E. and Maude (Wiggins) R.; A.B., Evansville Coll., 1942; J.D., Ind. U. 1951; m. Dorothy M. Armstrong, Apr. 30, 1942; children—Linda Carole Russell Atkins, Richard Lee, Frank E. III, Rita Jane Russell Eagle, Julie Beth Russell Smith. Partner, George S. Olive & Co. C.P.A.'s, Indpls., 1947-53; admitted to Ind. bar, 1951; exec. v.p. Spickelmier Industries, Inc., Indpls., 1953-59; bus. mgr. Indpls. Star & News, Indpls., 1959-77; v.p., gen. mgr. Central Newspapers, Inc., 1977-79, pres., 1979—; sec.-treas., dir. Phoenix Newspapers Inc., Indpls. Newspapers, Inc., Muncie Newspapers, Inc.; chmn. adv. bd. Met. Indpls. TV Assos., Inc. Mem. task force on materiality Fin. Accounting Standards Bd. Bd. dirs., treas., v.p., pres., chmn. bd. YMCA, Indpls., 1960-78, 500 Festival Assos., Inc.; treas., bd. dirs. Indpls. Bar Found.; bd. dirs. Winona Meml. Hosp.; mem. adv. bd., sec. Salvation Army; trustee Arthur Jordan Found.; trustee, pres. Benjamin Harrison Found.; treas. Meridian St. United Meth. Ch., 1955-79. Served with USMCR, 1942-45. C.P.A., Ind. Mem. Am., Ind., Indpls. bar assns., Am. Inst. C.P.A.'s, Ind. Assn. C.P.A.'s (past dir.), Tax Execs. Inst. (past pres.), Fin. Execs. Inst., Ind. Assn. Credit Mgmt. (dir., v.p.), Inst. Newspaper Controllers and Fin. Officers (dir., past pres.), Order of Coif, Phi Delta Phi, Sigma Alpha Epsilon. Methodist. Mason (Shriner). Home: 7432 B Lions Head Dr Indianapolis IN 46260 Office: 307 N Pennsylvania St Indianapolis IN 46206

RUSSELL, FRANKLIN ALEXANDER, author; b. Christchurch, New Zealand, Oct. 9, 1926; s. Alexander Grant and Vida (McKay) R.; student Nelson (New Zealand) Coll., 1942; m. Jacqueline Scully, Oct. 1966; 1 son, Alexander. Came to U.S., 1963. Mem. staff New Zealand newspapers, 1947-49, Sydney (Australia) Morning Herald, 1949-50, Asso. Newspapers Ltd., Sydney, 1950-52; free lance Fleet St. papers and mags., London, Eng., Brit. Med. Assn., London, 1952-54, Canadian mags., 1954-63. Guggenheim fellow, 1963-64; Can. Council sr. arts fellow, 1976; recipient award Nat. Assn. Ind. Schs., 1965, Can. Council award, 1967. Author: Watchers at the Pond, 1961; Argen the Gull, 1964; The Secret Islands, 1966; Searchers at the Gulf, 1970; The Sea Has Wings, 1973; Season on the Plain, 1974; The Mountains of America, Wild Creatures, The Secret Life of Animals, 1975; The Audubon Society Book of Wild Birds, 1976; also articles, revs. Address: 16 Fithian Ln East Hampton NY 11932. *There is only one principle of success that makes any sense to me, and that is the capacity to cope with failure.*

RUSSELL, FRED MCFERRIN, journalist, author, lawyer; b. Nashville, Aug. 27, 1906; s. John E. and Mabel Lee (McFerrin) R.; student Vanderbilt U., 1923-27; m. Katherine Wyche Early, Nov. 2, 1933; children—Katherine (Mrs. Earl Beasley), Ellen (Mrs. Robert Sadler), Lee (Mrs. John Brown), Carolyn (Mrs. William Van Derveer). Admitted to Tenn. bar, 1928; atty. Real Estate Title Co., 1928; reporter Nashville Banner, 1929, sports editor, 1930-69, sports dir., 1969—, v.p., 1955—; chmn. honors ct. Nat. Football Found. and Hall of Fame, 1967—; So. chmn. Heisman Trophy Com., 1946—; books include: 50 Years of Vanderbilt Football, 1938; I'll Go Quietly, 1944; I'll Try Anything Twice, 1945; Funny Thing About Sport, 1948; Bury Me in an Old Press Box, 1957; Big Bowl Football, 1963; contbr. to Saturday Eve. Post, 1939-63. A founder Harpeth Hall Sch., 1951, trustee, 1951-55; nat. pres. Vanderbilt Alumni Assn., 1960-61; dir. Children's Regional Med. Center, 1970-72. Recipient Nat. Headliners award, 1936, Grantland Rice award for sports writing, 1955, Jake Wade award, 1966, Coll. Football Centennial award, 1969, writing award Golf Writers Assn. Am., 1972, award for distinguished journalism U.S. Olympic Com., 1976; named to Tenn. Sports Hall of Fame, 1974. Mem. Football Writers Assn. Am. (pres. 1960-61), Sigma Delta Chi, Kappa Sigma, Omicron Delta Kappa. Methodist. Clubs: Belle Meade Country, Cumberland, Univ. (Miami, Fla.); Masons, Shriners. Home: 3804 Brighton Rd Nashville TN 37205 Office: 1100 Broad St Nashville TN 37202. *There is a close affinity between sport and humor, and a sportswriter can provide a good measure of entertainment just by putting into print some of the humor he sees and hears along the way.*

RUSSELL, FREDERICK ARTHUR, engring. educator; b. N.Y.C., Apr. 18, 1915; s. Frederick Clifford and Anna May (Price) R.; B.S. in Elec. Engring., Newark Coll. Engring., 1935, E.E., 1939; M.S., Stevens Inst. Tech., 1941; Sc.D. in Elec. Engring., Columbia, 1953; m. Virginia Jane McCullough, Nov. 1, 1947; children—David Arthur, Jane Searing. Instr., then asst. prof. elec. engring. N.J. Inst. Tech. (formerly Newark Coll. Engring.), 1937-44, mem. faculty, 1945—, prof. elec. engring., 1953—, chmn. dept., 1956-75, Distinguished prof., 1967—, asst. to pres. for instl. research, 1975—; sr. project engr., div. war research Columbia, 1944-45; cons. to industry, 1945—. Bd. dirs. Newark Coll. Engring. Research Found., 1959-65. Chmn. New Providence (N.J.) United Fund drive, 1960. Mem. New Providence Boro Council, 1961-64. Recipient Sr. Sci. Simulation award Electronic Assos., 1966. Fellow IEEE; mem. Am. Soc. Engring. Edn., Sigma Xi, Eta Kappa Nu, Tau Beta Pi. Presbyterian (deacon 1967—). Home: 101 Elkwood Ave New Providence NJ 07974 Office: 323 High St Newark NJ 07102

RUSSELL, GEORGE, corp. exec.; b. Glasgow, Scotland, Mar. 15, 1905; s. James Cowper and Elizabeth Stephen (Chapman) R.; B.S., U. Minn., 1927; LL.D., Strathclyde U. (Scotland); D.Lit., Meharry Med. Coll.; m. Mary Love Rose, Sept. 12, 1936; children—George Russell, Mary-Love (Mrs. William R. Harman). Joined Gen. Motors Corp., N.Y.C., 1927, became asst. treas., 1944; finance mgr. Gen. Motors Overseas Operations, 1949; treas. Gen. Motors Corp., Detroit, 1951, v.p. charge finance, dir., 1956-58, exec. v.p. dir., mem. adminstrn., exec. and finance coms., 1958-67, vice chmn. corp., chmn. finance com., 1967-70, dir., mem. finance and pub. policy coms., 1970-74; dir. S.S. Kresge Co.; adv. dir. Nat. Bank Detroit, 1978—. Trustee Kresge Found., 1970—, Harper-Grace Hosp., Meharry Med. Coll. Clubs: Links, Univ. (N.Y.); Detroit, Bloomfield Hills Country, Yondotega; Lost Tree (Fla.); Everglades, Seminole (Palm Beach, Fla.); Royal and Ancient Golf of St. Andrews (Fife, Scotland). Home: 11741 Lake House Ct Lost Tree Village North Palm Beach FL 33408

RUSSELL, GEORGE ALBERT, coll. adminstr.; b. Bertrand, Mo., July 21, 1921; s. George Albert and Martha (Cramer) R.; B.S. in Elec. Engring., Mass. Inst. Tech., 1947; M.S., U. Ill., 1952, Ph.D. in Physics, 1955; m. Ruth Ann Ashby, Nov. 11, 1944; children—George Albert, Frank Ashby, Ruth Ann, Cramer Anderson. Asso. prof. So. Ill. U., 1960-62; faculty U. Ill., Urbana, 1962—, prof. physics, 1965-77, asso. dir. Materials Research Lab., 1965-67, asso. head physics dept., 1967-70, asso. dean Grad. Coll., 1970-72, dean Grad. Coll., 1972-77, asso. vice chancellor research and devel., 1972-74, vice chancellor research, 1974-77; chancellor U. Mo-Kansas City, 1977—. Cons. Office Naval Research, 1961-76; dir. Microthermal Applications Inc. Vice chmn. Illini Union Bd., 1970; pres. Levis Faculty Center, 1972. Chmn. bd. trustees AUA, 1977. Served with USN, World War II. Mem. Am. Assn. Physics Tchrs., Am. Phys. Soc. Clubs: Champaign Country (pres. 1972); Mission Hills Country, Rockhill Tennis. Home: 5106 Cherry St Kansas City MO 64110 Office: 5100 Rockhill Rd Kansas City MO 64110

RUSSELL, GEORGE ALLEN, composer, musicologist; b. Cin., June 23, 1923; s. Joseph and Bessie (Sledge) R.; student Wilberforce U. High Sch., 1940-43; pupil composition Stephan Volpe, 1949; div.; 1 son, Jock Millgårdh. Formed principles of Lydian Chromatic concept of tonal orgn., 1945-46, published concept, 1953, pvt. tchr. concept, N.Y.C., 1953-68, also confs. and festivals; apptd. mem. faculty New Eng. Conservatory Music, 1969; composer (with Dizzy Gillespie) 1st composition featuring jazz and Latin influences, Cubana-Be, Cubana Bop, presented Carnegie Hall, 1947; performed John F. Kennedy's People to People Music Festival, Washington, 1962, Philharmonic Hall, Lincoln Center, 1963; tour Europe with Newport Jazz Festival, 1964; performed original compostions with large and small European ensembles for radio, TV and new music socs., in Scandinavia, Italy, Sweden, W.Ger., also other parts Europe, 1964-70, also tchr. in Sweden, Norway and Finland; condr. seminars on Lydian Chromatic concept, N.Y.C., 1975; Carnegie Hall performance, 1975; participant 1st White House Jazz Festival, 1978; recs. for RCA Records, Decca, Prestige, Capitol, Atlantic, Columbia, Contemporary, numerous others. Mem. panel Nat. Endowment of Arts, 1975-76. Commd. Brandeis U. to compose maj. jazz work, 1957, Norwegian TV to compose original music for ballet Othello, 1967, Norwegian Cultural Fund to compose 1st choral work Listen to the Silence, 1971, Columbia Recs. to compose Living Time for big band featuring Bill Evans, 1975; recipient Outstanding Composer award Metronome mag., 1958, New Star Composer award Downbeat mag., 1961, Nat. Endowments of Arts award, 1969, 76, Nat. Music award Am. Music Conf., 1976, numerous awards for recs. Guggenheim fellow, 1969, 72; Nat. Endowment for Arts grantee, 1979. Mem. Internat. Soc. Contemporary Music, Norwegian Soc. New Music, Am. Fedn. Musicians. Composer jazz and electronic music. Author papers on Lydian Chromatic concept tonal orgn. Address: 40 Shepard St Cambridge MA 02138

RUSSELL, GLEN ALLAN, chemist, educator; b. Johnsonville, N.Y., Aug. 23, 1925; s. John Allen and Marion (Cottrell) R.; B.S., Rensselaer Poly. Inst., 1947, M.S., 1948; Ph.D., Purdue U., 1951; m. Martha Ellen Havill, June 6, 1953; children—Susan Ann, June Ellen. Research asso. Gen. Electric Research Lab., Schenectady, 1951-58; asso. prof. Iowa State U., Ames, 1958-61, prof., 1961—, distinguished prof. scis. and humanities, 1972—. Mem. adv. panel Petroleum Research Fund, 1964-67; vis. prof. U. Würzburg (Germany), 1966; Reilly lectr. U. Notre Dame, 1966. Guggenheim fellow Centre d'Etude Nucléaires de Grenoble, France, 1972; Alfred P. Sloan Found. fellow, 1959-63; Fulbright-Hayes lectr., 1966. Mem. Am. Chem. Soc. (award in petroleum chemistry 1965, Iowa medal 1971, Midwest award 1974; mem. editorial adv. bd. Jour. Am. Chem. Soc. 1966-76), AAUP, AAAS, Chem. Soc. (London). Research, numerous publs. on directive effects in aliphatic substitutions occurring via free radicals, photochlorination, oxidation, bromination, solvent effects, application of E.S.R. spectroscopy to problems of structure and conformation, mechanism of autoxidation of organic substances in basic solution. Home: 1014 Murray Dr Ames IA 50010

RUSSELL, HAROLD JOHN, mgmt. cons.; b. Sydney, N.S., Can., Jan. 14, 1914; came to U.S., 1921, naturalized, 1945; s. Harold and Gertrude (Croucher) R.; B.A.B.A., Boston U., 1948; B.A. (hon.), Staley Coll., 1958. Pres., Harold Russell Assos., Inc., mgmt. cons. firm which counsels govt. contractors on establishment of affirmative action plans for hiring handicapped workers, Waltham, Mass., 1974—; movie actor: The Best Years of Our Lives, 1946; chmn. Pres.'s Com. on Employment of Handicapped, 1964—; mem. Nat. Council Vocat. Rehab., 1966-68; mem. Mass. Indsl. Accident Rehab. Commn.; mem. adv. council Goodwill Industries Am.; mem. people-to-people com. Handicapped Bd.; mem. adv. council Nat. Easter Seal Soc. Served with paratroopers U.S. Army, 1942-45. Recipient various awards, including being named 1 of 10 Outstanding Young Men, U.S. Jr. C. of C., 1950. Mem. World Vets. Fund (v.p. 1951-64), World Vets. Fedn. (an organizer). Club: AMVETS (nat. comdr. 1949, 50, 60). Author: Victory In My Hands, 1949, transl. in 20 langs.; film for Signal Corps: Diary of a Sargeant, 1945. Home: 44 Dinsmore Ave Framingham MA 01701 Office: 235 Bear Hill Rd Waltham MA 02154

RUSSELL, HAROLD LOUIS, lawyer; b. Abingdon, Va., July 1, 1916; s. Harold L. and Bess (Kinzel) R.; A.B., Hendrix Coll., Conway, Ark., 1937; J.D., Columbia U., 1940; m. Katherine C. Thompson, May 19, 1939 (div. 1968); 1 dau., Katherine T. Russell Wile; m. 2d, Mildred Baggett Roach, Sept. 5, 1970. Admitted to N.Y. State bar, 1941, Ga. bar, 1942, D.C. bar, 1973; practiced in N.Y.C., 1940-41, Atlanta, 1941—; mem. firm Gambrell, Russell, & Forbes, and predecessors, 1941—, partner, 1947—. Mem. council Adminstrv. Conf. U.S., 1968-76. Mem. bd. visitors Columbia Law Sch., 1959—, exec. com., 1978—. Recipient Alumni Fedn. Alumni medal Columbia U., 1965, Distinguished Alumnus award Hendrix Coll., 1969. Mem. Fed. (hon.), Am. (past chmn. pub. utility law sect., past chmn. spl. com. on legal service procedure, past chmn. administrv. law sect.), Ga., Atlanta bar assns., Atlanta Lawyers Club, Atlanta C. of C., Columbia Law Sch. Alumni Assn. (pres. 1972-74), Assn. Bar City N.Y., Am. Judicature Soc., Assn. ICC Practitioners, Am. Coll. Trial Lawyers, Phi Delta Phi. Democrat. Clubs: Capital City, Piedmont Driving (Atlanta). Contbr. articles legal jours. Home: 3999 Parian Ridge Rd NW Atlanta GA 30327 Office: 1st Nat Bank Tower Atlanta GA 30303

RUSSELL, HARVEY CLARENCE, beverage co. exec.; b. Louisville, Apr. 14, 1918; s. Harvey Clarence and Harriet (Tucker) R.; A.B., Ky. State Coll., 1939; postgrad. Ind. U., 1939-41, U. Mich., 1940-41; L.H.D., Livingstone Coll., 1975; m. Jacqueline Denison, July 25, 1958; children—Harvey Denison, John Vance. With W.B. Graham Assos., N.Y.C., 1946-48; sales mgr. Rosa Meta Cosemetics Co., N.Y.C., 1948-50; with Pepsi Cola Co., 1950-69, dir. spl. markets dept., 1957-62, v.p., 1962—, v.p. planning, 1965-69; v.p. community affairs Pepsico., Inc., 1969—. Co-chmn. Nat. Inter-racial Council Bus. Opportunity, N.Y.C., 1963-70, trustee, 1970—; vice chmn. 100 Black Men, 1964-67; mem. N.Y. Gov.'s Com. Welfare Costs, 1964-65; mem. Yonkers Econ. Devel. Commn., 1963-64; adv. council Plans for Progress, 1965-67; mem. adv. council on African affairs U.S. Dept. State, 1967-69, bus. leaders adv. council to OEO, 1967-69; mem. N.Y. State Bd. Social Welfare, 1969—; v.p. Nat. Alliance Businessmen, 1969-70; mem. steering com. on welfare Arden House, 1967-69; mem. Gov.'s Steering Com. on Social Problems, 1969-72, UNA Com. on S.Africa, 1970-72; mem. conf. bd. Pub. Affairs Research Council, 1968—; rep. African-Am. Dialogue, Tunisia, 1970, Lesotho, 1976, Khartoum, 1978; mem. nat. manpower adv. com. U.S. Dept. Labor, 1970-72; mem. exec. bd. N.Y. council Boy Scouts Am., 1966-69, adv. council Region II, 1970-75; mem. Westchester County (N.Y.) Bicentennial Com., 1974—; bd. dirs. Westchester Adoption Service, 1962-69, N.Y. Council Crime and Delinquency, 1962-66, Yonkers Family Service, 1963-65, N.Y. State Communities Aid Assn., 1964—, JOIN, 1964-65, Nat. Safety Council, 1967-69, N.Y. chpt. Nat. Found., 1966-69, Nat. Council on Philanthropy, 1973-78; bd. dirs. Nat. Mcpl. League, 1969—, mem. exec. com., 1970—; trustee Tougaloo Coll., 1966-70; mem. com. econ. studies Brookings Instn., 1972—; mem. bus. adv. council White House Press Corps, 1977; mem. bus. adv. council NAACP, 1973, bd. dirs. Legal Def. Fund, 1974—, Spl. Contbn. Fund, 1975—; bd. dirs. Whitney Young Found., 1974. Served to lt. (j.g.) USCGR, 1942-46. Recipient Achievement award Alpha Kappa Alpha, 1962; Outstanding Achievement award Nat. Assn. Markets Developers, 1963; Distinguished Alumni award Ky. State Coll., 1964; Good Am. award Chgo. Com. 100, 1965; Petergorsky Civic Achievement award N.Y. council Am. Jewish Congress, 1965; Outstanding Citizen award Nat. Mcpl. League, 1978. Mem. Nat. Assn. Study of Afro-American Life and History (exec. bd. 1975), Sigma Pi Phi (nat. pres. 1978—), Alpha Kappa Delta, Kappa Alpha Psi. Home: 9 Alta Vista Dr Yonkers NY 10710 Office: Pspsico Inc Purchase NY 10577

RUSSELL, JAMES ALVIN, JR., coll. pres.; b. Lawrenceville, Va., Dec. 25, 1917; s. Dr. James Alvin and Nellie M. (Pratt) R.; B.A., Oberlin Coll., 1940; B.S., Bradley U., 1941, M.S., 1950; Ed.D., U. Md., 1967; spl. insts. Wayne U., Bradley U., U. Mich., U. Ill., NSF; m. Lottye J. Washington, Dec. 25, 1943; children—Charlotte Justyne, James Alvin III. Prof., dir. div. engring., also prof. edn. div. grad. studies Hampton Inst., 1950-71; pres. St. Paul's Coll., Lawrenceville, 1971—. Pres. Peninsula Council Human Relations, 1961-65. United Negro Coll. Fund fellow, 1966-67. Mem. Am. Soc. Engring. Edn., Am. Assn. Univ. Adminstrs., IEEE, Am. Vocat. Assn., Am. Tech. Edn. Assn., Nat. Assn. Indsl. Tech., Am. Assn. for Higher Edn., Nat. Assn. for Equal Opportunity in Edn., Brunswick C. of C., Sigma Pi Phi, Alpha Kappa Mu, Iota Lambda Sigma, Omega Psi Phi. Home: PO Box 637 Lawrenceville VA 23868

RUSSELL, JAMES WEBSTER, JR., editor, columnist; b. Shreveport, La., Nov. 30, 1921; s. James Webster and Aline (Faulk) R.; B.A., La. State U., 1942; m. Jean Buck, June 29, 1949; children—Nancy Jean, Alicia Eileen. Fla. mgr. Internat. News Service, 1946-51; bur. chief U.P.I., Tallahassee, 1951-52, regional editor, Atlanta, 1953-57; asst. city editor Miami (Fla.) Herald, 1957-58, bus.-fin. editor, 1958—; guest lectr. U. Miami, Fla. Internat. U., Miami-Dade Community Coll. Served with USAAF, 1942-45. Recipient Eagle award Invest-in-Am. Nat. Council, 1976. Decorated Air medal with eleven oak leaf clusters. Mem. Soc. Am. Bus. Writers, Lambda Chi Alpha, Sigma Delta Chi. Republican. Methodist (chmn. ch. council on ministries 1971-72). Contbr. articles to Times of London, N.Y. Times, Gentlemen's Quar., Fla. Trend. Home: 4800 SW 64th Ct Miami FL 33155 Office: 1 Herald Plaza Miami FL 33101

RUSSELL, JANE, motion picture actress; b. Bemidji, Minn., June 21, 1921; d. Roy William and Geraldine (Jacobi) Russell; student Max Reinhardt's Theatrical Workshop, Madame Ouspenskaya's Sch. of Drama, Hollywood; m. Robert Station Waterfield, Apr. 25, 1943 (div. 1967); children—Thomas, Tracy, Robert; m. Roger Barrett, 1967 (dec. 1967); m. 3d, John Calvin Peoples, Jan. 31, 1974. Photographer's model, 1939-40; appeared in motion pictures 1943—, The Outlaw, 1943, Young Widow, 1947, Paleface, 1948, Montana Belle, 1951, His Kind of Woman, 1951, Double Dynamite, 1950, Macao, 1951, Son of Paleface, 1952, Las Vegas Story, 1952, Gentlemen Prefer Blondes, 1953, The French Line, 1954, Underwater, 1955, Gentlemen Marry Brunettes, 1955, The Tall Men, 1955; The Revolt of Mamie Stover, 1957, The Fuzzy Pink Nightgown, 1957, Fate is the Hunter, 1964, Waco, 1966, Born Losers, 1967, Darker Than Amber, 1970; appearances clubs, theatres, TV shows, 1956—; sec.- treas. Russ-Field Corp., 1954-59. Pres. WAIF-Div. Internat. Social Service; adv. com. Los Angeles County Bur. Adoptions. Office: 13527 Leadwell St Van Nuys CA 91405*

RUSSELL, JEFFREY BURTON, historian; b. Fresno, Calif., Aug. 1, 1934; s. Lewis Henry and Ieda Velma (Ogborn) R.; A.B., U. Calif., Berkeley, 1955, A.M., 1957; Ph.D., Emory U., 1960; m. Diana Emily Mansfield, June 30, 1956; children—Jennifer, Mark, William, Penelope. Asst. prof. U. N.Mex., Albuquerque, 1960-61; jr. fellow Soc. of Fellows, Harvard U., Cambridge, Mass., 1961-62; mem. faculty U. Calif., Riverside, 1962-75, prof. dept. history, 1969-75, asso. dean grad. div., 1967-72; dir. Medieval Inst., Michael P. Grace prof. medieval studies U. Notre Dame, South Bend, Ind., 1975-77; dean grad. studies Calif. State U., Sacramento, 1977-79; prof. history U. Calif., Santa Barbara, 1979—. Fulbright fellow, 1959-60; Am. Council Learned Socs. grantee, 1965, 70; Social Sci. Research Council grantee, 1968; Guggenheim fellow, 1968-69; Nat. Endowment for Humanities sr. fellow, 1972-73. Mem. Am. Hist. Assn., Medieval Acad. Am., Medieval Assn. of Pacific, Am. Soc. Ch. History, Am. Acad. Religion, Sierra Club. Author: Dissent and Reform in the Early Middle Ages, 1965; Medieval Civilization, 1968; A History of Medieval Christianity: Prophecy and Order, 1968; Religious Dissent in the Middle Ages, 1971; Witchcraft in the Middle Ages, 1972; The Devil: Perceptions of Evil from Antiquity to Primitive Christianity, 1977; A History of Witchcraft: Sorcerers, Heretics, and Pagans, 1979. contbr. articles in field to profl. jours. Home: 4525 Dartmouth Dr Sacramento CA 95841 Office: Dept History U Calif Santa Barbara CA 93106. *The central concern of my life is the pursuit of a coherent system of truth and understanding through the study of the history of concepts. The most important points of this approach are that the meaning and definition of every human idea and phenomenon can best be understood in terms of their historical traditions; and that the historical approach thus transcends the field of history and becomes the basis of a new epistemology.*

RUSSELL, JOHN, art critic; b. Fleet, Eng., Jan. 22, 1919; s. Isaac James and Harriet Elizabeth (Atkins) R.; came to U.S., 1974; B.A., Magdalen Coll., Oxford (Eng.) U., 1940; m. Rosamond Bernier, 1975. Hon. attache Tate Gallery, London, 1940; with Brit. Ministry Info., London, 1941, intelligence div. Admiralty, London, 1942-46; mem. editorial staff London Sunday Times, 1946-74; art critic N.Y. Times, 1974—. Decorated comdr. Order Brit. Empire; Grand medal of Honor (Austria); officier des Arts et Lettres (France); Frank Jewett Mather award for Art Criticism, Coll. Art Assn., 1979. Author numerous books, including: Shakespeare's Country, 1942;

Switzerland, 1950; Braque, 1959; Erich Kleiber: A Memoir, 1956; Paris, 1960; Max Ernst, 1967; Vuillard, 1971; Francis Bacon, 1971; Seurat, 1965; Henry Moore, 1968; The Meanings of Modern Art, 1975; contbr. Times Lit. Supplement, N.Y. Rev. Books, others. Office: care New York Times 229 W 43d St New York City NY 10036

RUSSELL, JOHN ALBERT, astronomer; b. Ludington, Mich., Mar. 23, 1913; s. Albert James and Orra Emeline (Woodruff) R.; A.B., U. Calif. at Los Angeles, 1935; A.M., U. Calif., 1937, Ph.D., 1943; m. Phyllis Mae Rock, June 13, 1936; children—Carolyn Frances, Stanton James. Grad. teaching asst. U. Calif., 1936-39, instr. astronomy, extension div., 1941; instr. astronomy Pasadena City Coll., 1939-41; Lick Obs. fellow, 1941-42; asst. prof. astronomy U. So. Calif., 1946-49, asso. prof., 1949-56, prof. 1956-78, prof. emeritus, 1978—, head dept., 1946-69, faculty research lectr., 1956-57, chmn. div. phys. scis. and math., 1959-63, asso. dean natural scis. and math., 1963-68; lectr. Griffith Obs. Planetarium, 1953-63; lectr. astronomy course, Beyond the Earth, CBS-TV, 1962, Nat. Ednl. Television, 1963—, Project Universe TV series, 1978. Served as nav. instr. USAAF, 1942-46, U. So. Calif. Assos. Award Teaching Excellence, 1960. Fellow AAAS, Meteoritical Soc. (sec. 1949-58, pres. 1958-62); mem. Am. Astron. Soc., Astron. Soc. Pacific (dir. 1961-63), Inst. Nav. (exec. com. 1949-56), Internat. Astron. Union, Phi Beta Kappa (hon.), Sigma Xi, Phi Kappa Phi. Home: 5654 Coliseum St Los Angeles CA 90016

RUSSELL, JOHN CLIFFORD, ret. fgn. service officer; b. Kewanna, Ind., Oct. 1, 1909; s. Carl Lewis and Arlie (Clifford) R.; B.A., U. N.Mex., 1930, M.A., 1932; Ph.D. (Teaching fellow), Stanford, 1937; postgrad. Vanderbilt U., 1958-59, Bread Loaf Sch. English, summer 1977, 78, 79; m. Eleanor Kemp, Nov. 2, 1933; children—Juliet (Mrs. Peter Pease), John W. Asso. prof. polit. sci. Syracuse U., 1935-42, 46-49; with Budget Office, Dept. War, 1942-43; with U.S. Bur. Budget, 1943-46; dep. adminstrv. sec. UN Conf., San Francisco, 1945; exec. dir. Pres.'s Labor-Mgmt. Conf., 1945; exec. asst. to chief ECA Mission to Greece, 1949-52; chief pub. adminstrn. div. ICA Mission to Philippines, 1952-55; pub. adminstrn. adviser, Egypt, 1955-56; govt. operations adviser, Libya, 1957-58; econ. devel. adviser Vanderbilt U., 1958-59; econ. devel. adviser, Pakistan, 1959; asst. to chief U.S. Weather Bur., 1961-66; urban adviser, Saigon, 1966-68; chief Peoples Self Def. Force Div., MACV, Saigon, 1968-73. Cons. to City of Syracuse, 1937-41, State of N.Y., 1947-49. Recipient ICA Meritorious Service 1955, Dept. Army Achievement award, 1970; Vietnamese Medal of Honor; Peoples Self Def. Force medal 1st class, 1972; Sports medal 1st class, 1973. Mem. Am. Fgn. Service Assn., Am. Polit. Sci. Assn., Am. Soc. Pub. Adminstrn., Sigma Phi Epsilon, Pi Sigma Alpha, Pi Gamma Mu. Republican. Christian Scientist. Clubs: Foreign Service, Sugarbush Golf. Author: Regionalism in New Mexico, 1937; The Budget of the United Nations, 1948; Space Science Aids the Weatherman, 1962. Contbr. articles to profl. jours. Home: 6009 Kirby Rd Bethesda MD 20034 Office: 505 Blackwell Bldg 7758 Wisconsin Ave Bethesda MD 20014

RUSSELL, JOHN JEWETT, food distbn. co. exec.; b. Portland, Maine, Apr. 16, 1927; s. Carl Asa and Ruth Elizabeth (Merrill) R.; A.B., Bowdoin Coll., 1950; m. Hannah Lincoln Talbot, June 18, 1949; children—Nathaniel Merrill, Benjamin Lincoln, Stephen Henry. Treas., Kankakee Water Co. (Ill.), 1950-56; v.p., gen. mgr., dir. Springfield City Water Co. (Mo.), 1957-58; v.p., then exec. v.p., treas., dir. Consumers Water Co., Portland, Maine, 1958-69; sr. v.p., treas., dir. Hannaford Bros. Co., South Portland, Maine, 1969—; dir. Central Maine Power Co., Consumers Water Co.; corporator Portland Savs. Bank. Bd. dirs. Greater Portland Bldg. Fund; corporator Maine Med. Center; mem. adv. com. U. South Maine Sch. Bus.; past pres. Greater Portland United Way; past treas. Episcopal Ch. of St. Mary the Virgin, Falmouth, Maine; mem. Falmouth Town Council, 1968-71, 78-79. Served with USNR, 1945-46. Republican. Clubs: Cumberland, Portland Yacht, Masons. Address: PO Box 1000 Portland ME 04104

RUSSELL, JOHN ST. CLAIR, JR., lawyer; b. Albany, N.Y., Mar. 21, 1917; s. John St. Clair and Hazel (Barbiers) R.; A.B. cum laude, Dartmouth Coll., 1938; LL.B., Yale U., 1941; m. Betty Kixmiller, Sept. 12, 1941; children—Patricia Russell Prager, John St. Clair, David K. Admitted to N.Y. bar, 1942, D.C. bar, 1965; mem. Hale Russell Gray Seaman & Birkett, and predecessors, N.Y.C., 1948—; dir. Brit. Aerospace, Inc., N.Am. Turbine Corp., A. Johnson & Co. Inc., Acoustiguide, Inc.; chmn. KMW-Johnson, Inc. Mem., sec. Irvington (N.Y.) Zoning Bd. Appeals, 1955—; bd. dirs. Phelps Meml. Hosp., Tarrytown. Served to maj. USMCR, 1942-46. Decorated Order of Vasa (Sweden); recipient medal of merit Swedish Red Cross. Mem. Assn. Bar City N.Y., Am. Bar Assn., Phi Beta Kappa, Phi Sigma Kappa. Club: Pinnacle (N.Y.C.). Office: 122 E 42d St New York NY 10017

RUSSELL, JOSIAH COX, historian; b. Richmond, Ind., Sept. 3, 1900; s. Elbert and Lieuetta (Cox) R.; A.B., Earlham Coll., 1922; M.A., Harvard, 1923, Ph.D., 1926; m. Ruth Winslow, Sept. 15, 1924; children—Elbert Winslow, Walter Howard, Joan. Asst. in history Radcliffe Coll., 1923-24, Harvard, 1924-26; asst. prof. Colo. Coll., 1927-29; prof. history and head social sci. dept. N.Mex. Highlands U., 1929-31; instr. to asso. prof. U. N.C., 1931-46; chmn. history dept. U. N.Mex., 1946-53, prof., 1946-65, prof. emeritus, 1965—; prof. Tex. A. and I. U., 1965-71, Piper prof. (hon.), 1971; Fulbright lectr. Univ. Coll., Wales, 1952-53; research grants Guggenheim Found., 1930-31, Am. Council Learned Socs., summers 1933, 34, Social Sci. Research Council, summers 1938, 49, 51, Am. Philos. Soc., 1938-39, 61; fellow Islamic Seminar, Princeton, summer 1935; cons. Fulbright Brit. Empire Prof. Selection, 1955. Chmn. Orange Dist. com. Boy Scouts Am., 1945-46. Fellow Mediaeval Acad. Am.; mem. Am. Hist. Assn. (mem. Pacific Coast council 1964-65), Population Assn. Am., Soc. of Friends, AAUP (state chmn. 1951-52, nat. council 1953-56), Phi Alpha Theta. Author: Dictionary of Writers of Thirteenth Century England, 1936; British Medieval Population, 1948; Late Ancient and Medieval Population, 1958; Medieval Regions and Their Cities, 1972; Twelfth Century Studies, 1978; contbr. chpt. Fontana Economic History of Europe; numerous articles profl. jours. Address: 16 South Wind Circle Saint Augustine FL 32084

RUSSELL, JOYCE ANNE ROGERS, librarian; b. Chgo., Nov. 6, 1920; d. Truman Allen and Mary Louise (Hoelzle) Rogers; student Adelphi Coll., 1937; B.S. in Chemistry, U. Ky., 1942; M.L.S., Rosary Coll., 1967; postgrad. Rutgers U., 1970-71; m. John VanCleve Russell, Dec. 24, 1942; children—Malcolm David, John VanCleve. Research chemist Sherwin Williams Paint Co., Chgo., 1942-45; reference librarian Chicago Heights (Ill.) Pub. Library, 1959-61; librarian Victor Chem. Works, Chicago Heights, 1961-62; lit. chemist Velsicol Chem. Corp., Chgo., 1964-67; chemistry librarian U. Fla., Gainesville, 1967-69, interim asso. prof., 1967-69; librarian Thiokol Chem. Corp., Trenton, N.J., 1969-73; supr. library operations E.R. Squibb Co., Princeton, N.J., 1973—; mem. library adv. commn. Mercer Community Coll., 1979—; adv. asso. Rutgers U. Grad. Sch. Library and Info. Scis., 1978—. Mem. PTA, 1950-66; den mother Cub Scouts, 1952-59. Mem. Spl. Libraries Assn. (sec., dir., v.p., pres. Princeton-Trenton, 1971, 75-80), Am. Chem. Soc. (bus. mgr., sec., dir. Trenton sect. 1969-78), AAUW, Mortar Board, Beta Phi Mu, Sigma Pi Sigma, Chi Delta Phi, Pi Sigma Alpha. Editor Bibliofile, 1967-69; contbr. articles to profl. jours. Home: 343 Berwyn Ave Trenton NJ 08618 Office: PO Box 4000 Princeton NJ 08540

RUSSELL, KEN, film dir.; b. Southampton, Eng., July 3, 1927; s. Henry and Ethel (Smith) R.; student Walthamstow Art Sch., Internat. Ballet Sch.; m. Shirley Kingdon, Feb. 3, 1957; children—Xavier, James, Alexander, Victoria, Toby. Formerly dancer, actor, still photographer; now BBC documentary film maker, feature film dir.; BBC TV documentary films include Elgar, Debussy, Isadora, Delius, Richard Strauss; feature films include French Dressing, 1964, Billion Dollar Brain, 1967, Women in Love, 1909, The Music Lovers, 1970, The Boy Friend, 1971, The Devils, 1971, Savage Messiah, 1972, Mahler, 1975, Tommy, 1975, Lizstomania, 1975; dir., writer film Valentino, 1977. Served with Mcht. Navy, 1945, also RAF. Recipient Screen writers Guild award for TV films Elgar, Debussy, Isadora, Dante's Inferno; Delius award (Merit Scroll); award Guild TV Producers and Dirs., 1966; Desmond Davis award, 1968.*

RUSSELL, KURT VON VOGEL, actor; b. Springfield, Mass., Mar. 17, 1951; s. Bing Oliver and Louise Julia (Crone) R.; student pub. schs.; m. Season Hubley, Mar. 17, 1979. Appeared in numerous Walt Disney films; appeared on television series The Travels of Jamie McPheeters, The New Land, The Quest; starred as Elvis Presley, 1979; profl. baseball player, 1971-73. Served with Calif. Air N.G. Recipient numerous auto racing trophies, 10 baseball awards, 5 acting awards, 1 golf championship. Mem. Profl. Baseball Players Assn., Stuntmans Assn. World championship Class Modified Stock, 1959 Race of Champions, Las Vegas. Office: c/o James McHugh Agy 8150 Beverly Blvd Suite 206 Los Angeles CA 90048

RUSSELL, LAO (MRS. WALTER RUSSELL), philosopher, author, educator; b. Ivinghoe, Buckinghamshire, Eng.; d. Alfred William and Florence (Hills) Cook; naturalized, 1947; ed. pvt. tutors; m. Walter Russell, July 29, 1948. Founder, Walter Russell Found. (now known as U. Sci. and Philosophy), Waynesboro, Va., 1948, mng. dir., 1948—, pres., 1949—; founded Shrine of Beauty known as Swannanoa Palace and Sculpture Gardens, 1948. Founder Man-Woman Equalization League, 1955, Internat. Age of Character Clubs, 1966. Author: God Will Work With You But Not For You (named one of 6 best books of year N.Y. Herald Tribune 1955), 1955; An Eternal Message of Light and Love, 1964; Love-A Scientific and Living Philosophy of Love and Sex, 1966; Why You Cannot Die!-The Continuity of Life-Reincarnation Explained, 1972; (with Walter Russell) One Year Home Study Course in Universal Law, Natural Science and Living Philosophy, 1950, Scientific Answer to Human Relations, 1951; Atomic Suicide?, 1957; The World Crisis-Its Explanation and Solution, 1958, The One-World Purpose-A Plan to Dissolve War By a Power More Mighty than War, 1960. Executed statue (with husband) The Christ of the Blue Ridge, 1948, also colossal model, 1950; presented bronze bust of George Washington (sculptured by husband) to Va. Bicentennial Commn., 1976. Address: Univ Science and Philosophy Swannanoa Waynesboro VA 22980. *Love is the key to all success and eternal happiness, for Love is Cause and is expressed in the inviolate law of Rhythmic Balanced Interchange. This law, in individual and collective action, will ultimately lead to man's fulfillment which is to live the Brotherhood of Man and know Heaven On Earth. Knowing the Source of all things and of my Oneness with the Creator and my fellowman—and all things else—is the secret of my personal success.*

RUSSELL, LEN CYRUS, air force officer; b. Macks Creek, Mo., May 11, 1929; s. James Marion and Delia Hattie (Eidson) R.; student S.W. Mo. State U., 1947-50; B.Gen. Edn., U. Omaha, 1963; m. Edna Ramona Kelso, Jan. 3, 1954; children—Carol, Peggy, David. Served as enlisted man U.S. Air Force, 1950, commd. 2d lt., 1952, advanced through grades to maj. gen.; served on combat tour, Korea, 1952-53; instr. pilot, combat crew, Nellis AFB, Nev., 1954-60, Wheelus Air Base, Libya, 1960-63, Luke AFB, Ariz., 1963-65; mem. Air Staff, Washington, 1966-68; served on combat tour, S.E. Asia, 1968-69; mem. Joint Staff, Pacific Command Hdqrs., 1969-71; dir. ops., vice comdr., wing comdr., 4th Tactical Air Command Fighter Wing, 1971-74; asst. to dep. chief staff for ops. Tactical Air Command, 1974-76; chief of staff Tactical Air Command, 1976-77; dep. chief of staff, plans Hdqrs., U.S. Air Forces in Europe, 1977—. Decorated Legion of Merit with 2 oak leaf clusters, D.F.C., Bronze Star, Air medal with 15 oak leaf clusters. Mem. Air Force Assn. Home: HQ US Air Forces in Europe Box 6254 APO NY 09012 Office: DCS/Plans HQ USAFE APO NY 09012

RUSSELL, LEON, singer, songwriter; b. Lawton, Okla., Apr. 2, 1942. Formed own band at age 14, later on tour with Jerry Lee Lewis; sideman at recording sessions Glen Campbell, Dorsey Burnette, Herb Alpert, others; became exec. Viva record co.; began recording (with Marc Benno) for Mercury Records Smash label, 1968; joined group Friends of Delaney & Bonnie; formed (with Denny Cordell) Shelter Records, broke assn. with firm, 1976; formed Mad Dogs and Englishmen entourage to back Joe Cocker on his Am. tour, 1970; later worked with Bob Dylan and produced some of his records; initiated new label, Paradise Records, 1976. Albums include: Asylum Choir (with Marc Benno), Asylum Choir II (with Benno), Leon Russell, Leon Russell and the Shelter People, Carney, Live, Hank Wilson's Back, Stop All That Jazz, Will O' The Wisp, Wedding Album (with Mary Russell), Life and Love; songs written include: Delta Lady, A Song for You, This Masquerade.

RUSSELL, LEONARD NELSON, educator; b. Coldwater, Mich., Jan. 15, 1922; s. Alger Smith and Marguerite (Snyder) R.; A.B. in Physics, Kalamazoo Coll., 1947; Ph.D. in Nuclear Physics, Ohio State U., 1952; m. Lavon Marcella Woodward, June 28, 1947; children—Linda Carol, Janet Ann. Research physicist Monsanto Chem. Co., Miamisburg, Ohio, 1952-54; from asst. prof. to prof. physics Ohio Wesleyan U., Delaware, 1954—. Served to 1st lt. USAAF, 1943-46. Decorated Purple Heart. Fellow Ohio Acad. Sci. (v.p. sect. 1969-70); mem. Am. Phys. Soc., Sigma Xi. Home: 45 Westgate Dr Delaware OH 43015

RUSSELL, LORIS SHANO, paleontologist, educator; b. Bklyn., Apr. 21, 1904; s. Milan Winslow and Matilda (Shano) R.; B.Sc., U. Alta. (Can.), 1927, LL.D., 1958; M.A., Princeton, 1929, Ph.D., 1930; m. Grace Evelyn LeFeuvre, June 11, 1938. Asst. geologist Geol. Survey Can., Ottawa, Ont., 1930-37; asst. dir. Royal Ont. Museum Palaeontology, Toronto, 1937-45, dir., 1945-50; chief zoologist Nat. Mus. Can., Ottawa, 1950-56, dir., 1956-63; chief biologist Royal Ont. Mus., Toronto, 1963-71, curator emeritus, 1971—; asst. prof. geology U. Toronto, 1937-50, prof., 1964-70, prof. emeritus, 1970—. Served to maj. Royal Can. Corps of Signals, 1942-45, with Royal Can. Corps of Signals Militia, 1945-50. Recipient Festschrift, Royal Ont. Mus., 1976, Can. Silver Jubilee medal, 1978. Fellow Royal Soc. Can. (Willet G. Miller medal 1959), Geol. Soc. Am., Geol. Assn. Can., Can. Mus. Assn., Paleontol. Soc., Ottawa Field-Naturalists' Club; mem. Royal Can. Inst. (pres. 1972-73), Internat. Palaeontol. Assn. (pres. 1972-76), Soc. Vertebrate Paleontology (pres. 1959), Am. Soc. Mammalogists, Am. Malacological Union. Author: (with R. W. Landes) Geology of the Southern Alberta Plains, 1940; A Heritage of Light, 1968; Everyday Life in Colonial Canada, 1973. Contbr. numerous articles on paleontology and geology of western North Am. to profl. jours., also articles on history of crafts and tech. Home: 55 Erskine Ave Apt 1702 Toronto ON M4P 1Y7 Canada Office: Royal Ont Mus 100 Queen's Park Toronto ON M5S 2C6 Canada

RUSSELL, MADELEINE HAAS, former Democratic nat. committeewoman; b. San Francisco, Apr. 2, 1915; d. Charles William and Fannie Marie (Stern) Haas; B.A. magna cum laude, Smith Coll., 1937; children—Alice Cornelia, Charles Phillips, Christine Haas. Translator, Paris, 1938, OWI, San Francisco, 1942-44; research Leon Livingstone Advt. Agy., Calif., 1944-46; dir. Dept. of State Reception Center, San Francisco, 1962-69; Democratic nat. committeewoman from Calif., 1972-76; mem. Dem. Charter Commn., 1973-74; dir. KQED Inc. Bd. dirs. San Francisco Opera Assn.; trustee San Francisco Mus. Art, Brandeis U.; hon. chmn. bd. Bay Area chpt. Am. Friends of Hebrew U.; bd. dirs. Mexican Am. Legal Def. Ednl. Fund, Calif. Center for Research and Edn. in Govt.; treas. Asia Found. Mem. Phi Beta Kappa. Office: Frontier Investment 2 Embarcadero Center San Francisco CA 94106

RUSSELL, MARK, comedian; b. Buffalo, Aug. 23, 1932; s. Marcus Joseph and Marie Elizabeth (Perry) Ruslander; student George Washington U., 1952; m. Alison Kaplan, Dec. 17, 1978; children—Monica, John, Matthew. Polit. comedian; featured performer Shoreham Hotel, Washington, 1961—; prin. Mark Russell Comedy Spls., Public Broadcasting Service, 1975—; lectr., public speaker. Served with USMC, 1953-56. Mem. AFTRA, Am. Fedn. Musicians. Office: 2828 Wisconsin Ave Washington DC 20007

RUSSELL, NIPSEY, comedian; b. Atlanta; grad. U. Cin., 1946. Formerly headlined at Harlem's Small's Paradise, N.Y.C., and The Baby Grand; numerous TV appearances, including Dean Martin Show, Barefoot in the Park, Dean Martin Celebrity Roasts; formerly co-host TV show, Les Crane Show; appeared in movie The Wiz, 1978. Served to capt. AUS, World War II. As co-host of Les Crane Show, became first Black regularly employed as master of ceremonies on nat. TV program. Office: care Norby Walters Assos 1290 Ave of Americas Suite 264 New York NY 10019*

RUSSELL, PAUL FARR, pub. health physician; b. Boston, Aug. 12, 1894; s. Samuel and Sarah (Woodman) R.; A.B., Boston U., 1916; M.D., Cornell U., 1921; M.P.H., Harvard, 1929; Sc.D. (hon.), Colby Coll., 1960; m. Phyllis Additon 1922; children—Christopher Harvey, Theodore Emery. Mem. staff Rockefeller Found., 1923-59; cons. AID, 1957-65, WHO, 1947—; cons. to surg. gen. U.S. Army, 1947-70; vis. prof. Harvard, 1960-63, vis. lectr., 1958-60, 63-67. Commd. lt. col. M.C., U.S. Army, 1942, promoted to col., 1943; assigned chief, tropical disease sect. Office Surgeon Gen., 1942-43; chief malariologist Allied Forces Hdqrs., North African Theater of Operations, U.S. Army, 1943-44; chief malariologist Allied Control Commn., Italy, 1944; chief, div. of parasitology, Army Med. Sch., Washington, 1944-45. Decorated Legion of Merit with oak leaf cluster; Mary Kingsley medalist, Liverpool Sch. Tropical Medicine, 1949, Walter Reed medalist, Am. Soc. Tropical Medicine, Darling medal and prize, WHO, 1957, Cornell Med. Alumni award of Distinction, 1958; named to Collegium Distinguished Alumni Boston U., 1974. Diplomate Am. Bd. Preventive Medicine and Pub. Health. Mem. malaria panel WHO. Fellow AAAS (life), Royal Soc. Tropical Medicine (hon.), mem. Am. Pub. Health Assn.; mem. Am. Soc. Tropical Medicine and Hygiene (LePrince medal 1979), Acad. Nacionale Medicine (Mex.) (hon.), Nat. Malaria Soc. (India) (hon.). Republican. Conglist. Clubs: Cosmos (Washington); Army and Navy (Manila, P.I.); Explorer's (N.Y.). Author: Mans Mastery of Malaria, 1955; several books, 1933—; contbr. to profl. publs. Home: 1900 Lauderdale Dr D-309 Richmond VA 23233

RUSSELL, PAUL SNOWDEN, surgeon, educator; b. Chgo., Jan. 22, 1925; s. Paul Snowden and Carroll (Mason) R.; student Groton (Mass.) Sch., 1939-41; Ph.B., U. Chgo., 1944, B.S., 1945, M.D., 1947; M.A. (hon.), Harvard, 1962; m. Allene Lummis, Sept. 24, 1952; children—Katherine Swift, Paul Snowden, Allene, Laura Rice. Successively surg. intern. asst. resident, resident Mass. Gen. Hosp., 1948-56, asst. surgery, 1957-60, chief gen. surg. services, 1962-69, vis. surgeon, 1969—, chief transplantation unit, 1969—, chmn. com. on research, 1973-76; postdoctoral fellow USPHS, 1954-55; successively teaching fellow, instr., clin. asso. surgery Harvard Med. Sch., 1956-60, John Homans prof. surgery, 1962—; asso. prof. surgery Columbia Coll. Phys. and Surg., 1960-62; asso. attending surgeon Presbyn. Hosp., N.Y.C., 1960-62; asso. vis. surgeon Francis Delafield Hosp., N.Y.C., 1960-62; dir. Warner Lambert Co. Mem. com. tissue transplantation NRC-Nat. Acad. Scis., 1963-71, com. trauma, 1963-68, ad hoc com. to study clin. investigation and edn. in USN, div. med. scis., 1971-73; allergy and immunology study sect. USPHS, 1963-65, chmn. allergy and immunology study sect. B, 1965-67; mem. transplantation and immunology com. Nat. Inst. Allergy and Infectious Diseases, 1967-69, chmn., 1970; mem. com. on cancer immunotherapy Nat. Cancer Inst., 1974—. Trustee Pine Manor Coll., Chestnut Hill, Mass., 1963-76, Groton Sch., 1964—. Served with USAF, 1951-53. Diplomate Am. Bd. Surgery, Am. Bd. Thoracic Surgery. Fellow Royal Soc. Medicine, A.C.S.: mem. Am. Acad. Arts and Scis., Am. Assn. Thoracic Surgery, Assn. Immunologists, N.Y. Acad. Scis., Mass. Med. Soc., New Eng., Boston surg. socs., AAAS, Soc. U. Surgeons, Soc. Exptl. Biology and Medicine, Halsted Soc., Whipple Soc., Internat. Soc. Surgery, Am. Surg. Assn., Transplantation Soc. (pres. 1970), Sigma Xi. Contbr. papers in field. Editorial bd. Archives Surgery, 1963-72, Surgery, 1963-71, Transplantation, 1965—, Annals of Surgery, 1966—, Transplantation Procs., 1966—, Jour. Immunology, 1977—. Home: 32 Lawrence Rd Newton MA 02167 Office: Dept Surgery Mass Gen Hosp Boston MA 02114

RUSSELL, PETER BYROM, chemist; b. Manchester, Eng., Oct. 24, 1918; s. Sydney Arthur and Elsie (Potter) R.; came to U.S., 1947, naturalized, 1959; B.Sc., Victoria U., Manchester, Eng., 1940, M.Sc., 1941, Ph.D., 1945, D.Sc., 1954; m. Joyce Elizabeth Leigh, July 27, 1945; children—Timothy Craig, Pamela Elizabeth Russell Walford. Chem. warfare researcher Brit. Ministry Supply, 1941-43; sr. research chemist Wellcome Research Labs., Tuckahoe, N.Y., 1947-56; acting research dir. Wyeth Labs., Inc., Havant, Eng., 1956-57, West Chester, Pa., 1957-59, dir. research, Radnor, Pa., 1959—; chmn. study group medicinal chemistry U.S. Army Med. Research and Devel. Command, 1973-75. Mem. Am. Chem. Soc. Author publs., patentee in organic and medicinal chemistry. Home: 1708 Sherwood Circle Villanova PA 19085 Office: Wyeth Labs Inc Box 8299 Philadelphia PA 19101

RUSSELL, PETER GARDINER, ins. co. exec.; b. Hartford, Conn., Aug. 14, 1927; s. G. Gardiner and Ruth (Seggerman) R.; B.A., Yale U., 1950; J.D., U. Conn., 1955; m. Elizabeth Stedman, May 19, 1956; children—Laurie, Morgan, Peter, Virginia. Admitted to Conn. bar, 1955; with group div. Aetna Life & Casualty Co., Hartford, 1950-52, fin. div., 1952—, v.p. bond investment dept., 1976—. Trustee, Kingswood Oxford Sch., Stowe-Day Found. Served with U.S. Army, 1946-47. Mem. Conn. Bar Assn., Conn. Hist. Soc. (trustee), Fin. Analysts Fedn. Club: Hartford Golf. Home: 31 Norwood Rd West Hartford CT 06117 Office: Aetna Life & Casualty Co 151 Farmington Ave Hartford CT 06156

RUSSELL, R. DANA, geol. cons.; b. Pomona, Calif., Nov. 15, 1906; s. Henry Edison and Ann Beatrice (Rolph) R.; A.B., Pomona Coll., 1927; Ph.D., U. Cal. at Berkeley, 1931; m. Mary Flower Pugh, June 2, 1933; children—Nancy Beatrice (Mrs. Theodore D. Graves),

Richard Dana. From instr. to asso. prof. geology La. State U., 1931-42; research asso., oceanographer, div. war research U. Calif., 1942-46; from mgr. publs. dept. to sr. cons. geophysics Navy Electronics Lab., 1945-55; mgr. geol. research, then asso. dir. exploration research Marathon Oil Co., 1955-70, cons., 1970-71; ind. cons., 1970—; lectr. Calif. Inst. Tech., 1948, Scripps Instn. Oceanography, 1949-55. Mem. Bikini Sci. Resurvey team, 1947; mem. com. sedimentation NRC, 1932-46; mem. hon. com. Centre de Recherches et d'Etudes Oceanographiques, 1949-72. Recipient commendation meritorious service U.S. Navy, 1947, 55. Fellow Geol. Soc. Am. (chmn. nominating com. 1964, bldg. com. 1969-72, hdqrs. adv. com. 1972-75); mem. Am. Geol. Inst. (dir., pres. 1973), Am. Petroleum Inst., Am. Assn. Petroleum Geologists (chmn. research com. 1956-58, trustees research fund 1960-62), Soc. Econ. Paleontologists and Mineralogists (v.p. 1943, pres. 1948), Am. Inst. Profl. Geologists (pres. 1969). Contbr. to profl. jours., books. Address: 6597 Meadowridge Dr Santa Rosa CA 95405

RUSSELL, R. ROBERT, economist; b. Rock Springs, Wyo., Feb. 17, 1938; s. Ralph Cyril and Elizabeth (Russell) Goddard; B.A., U. Calif., 1961; Ph.D., Harvard U., 1964; m. Judith Lynn Honey, Aug. 14, 1959; children—Jeffrey Robert, Kevin Gregory. Teaching fellow Harvard U., 1963-64; asst. prof., then asso. prof. econs. U. Calif., Santa Barbara, 1964-73; vis. asso. prof. U. Calif., San Diego, 1972-73, asso. prof., 1973-74, prof. econs., 1974—; vis. prof. U. Kans., fall 1975; now dir. Council Wage and Price Stability. Democrat. Contbr. articles to profl. publns. Office: Council Wage and Price Stability 6 Jackson Pl NW Washington DC 20503

RUSSELL, RALSTON, JR., ceramic engr.; b. Pomeroy, Ohio, Nov. 4, 1910; s. Ralston and Helen Brown (Lindsey) R.; B. Ceramic Engring., Ohio State U., 1932, M.Sc., 1933, Ph.D., 1939, Ceramic Engr., 1948; m. Jacqulyn Sue Pace, Nov. 15, 1962. Research and devel. engr. A.C. Spark Plug div. Gen. Motors Corp., Flint, Mich., 1933-37; ceramic engr. Gen. Ceramics and Steatite Corp., Keasbey, N.J., 1937; research engr. Engring. Expt. Sta., Ohio State U., Columbus, 1937-40, prof. ceramic engring., also indsl. cons., 1946—; dir. ceramic research, sect. mgr. research labs. Westinghouse Electric Corp., East Pittsburgh, Pa., 1940-46. Served as sci. cons. Joint Chiefs of Staff in Germany, France, and Eng., 1945. Recipient award of Merit, U.S. Army, 1951; Greaves-Walker award Nat. Inst. Ceramic Engrs., 1970. Registered profl. engr., Ohio, Pa., D.C. Fellow Am. Ceramic Soc. (trustee 1953-56, 74-77, pres. 1975-76, Edward Cramer award 1974), Inst. Ceramics, Ltd.; mem. Ceramic Ednl. Council (pres. 1958-59), Nat. Inst. Ceramic Engrs. (pres. 1950-51), Am. Soc. Metals, ASTM, Varsity O Assn., Ohio State U. Alumni Assn., Brit., Canadian ceramic socs., Keramos (nat. pres. 1968-70, Greaves-Walker Role of Honor award 1975), Nat., Ohio socs. profl. engrs., Pa. Ceramics Assn. (founder), Am. Soc. Engring. Edn., Am. Chem. Soc., AAAS, Ceramic Assn. N.Y., Clay Minerals Soc. (charter), Sigma Xi, Sigma Gamma Epsilon, Phi Delta Theta, Tau Beta Pi, Phi Eta Sigma, Sphinx, Texnikoi. Republican. Episcopalian. Author: The Electrical and Technical Ceramic Industry of Germany, 1947; also tech. papers. Patentee in field. Office: Watts Hall Ohio State U Columbus OH 43210

RUSSELL, RAY, author; b. Chgo., Sept. 4, 1924; s. William James and Margaret (Otto) R.; student Chgo. Conservatory, 1947-48, Goodman Meml. Theater, Chgo., 1949-51; m. Ada Beth Stevens, Sept. 5, 1950; children—Marc Antony, Amanda. Asso. editor Playboy mag., Chgo., 1954-55, exec. editor, 1955-60, contbg. editor, 1968-75; author and screenplay writer, Beverly Hills, Calif., 1961—. Guest lectr. Pasadena City Coll., 1963. Served with USAAF, 1943-46. Recipient Silver Globe for film X Festival Internazionale del Film di Fantascienza, Trieste, Italy, 1963; winner Writers Digest Poetry competition, 1976, Sri Chinmoy Poetry award, 1977. Mem. Writers Guild Am. West. Author: Sardonicus and Other Stories, 1961; The Case Against Satan, 1962 (Catholic Book Club Eng. selection 1963); (play) The Devil's Voice, 1965; The Little Lexicon of Love, 1966; Unholy Trinity, 1967; The Colony, 1969; Sagittarius, 1971; Prince of Darkness, 1971; Incubus, 1976; Holy Horatio, 1976; Princess Pamela, 1979; The Devil's Mirror, 1980; The Book of Hell, 1980; author screenplays: Sardonicus, Zotz (Columbia), 1961; The Soft Sell, 1961, The Other Place, 1966, Murder in Paradise, 1975 (Universal); X, Genghis Khan (A.I.P.), 1963-64; The Florentine Ring (Dominion), 1963; Chamber of Horrors, Warner, 1964; Odd John, Rip Van Winkle (Metro-Goldwyn-Mayer), 1965-66; Incubus (Kings Road), 1976; works transl. into French, German, Spanish, Italian, Portuguese, Danish, Swedish, Japanese. Contbr. short stories, essays, satire, poetry to numerous mags. . *I cannot improve upon Chekhov's words in The Sea Gull: "Everyone writes as he wants to and as he can"—sometimes translated as "Everyone writes in accordance with his desires and capacity."*

RUSSELL, RICHARD DONCASTER, geophysicist, educator; b. Toronto, Ont., Can., Feb. 27, 1929; s. Richard Douglas and Ada Gwennola (Doncaster) R.; B.A., U. Toronto, 1951, M.A., 1952, Ph.D., 1954; m. Virginia Ann Reid Clippingdale, Aug. 11, 1951; children—Linda Jean, Morna Ann, Mary Joyce. Asst. prof. physics U. Toronto, 1956-58, prof., 1962-63; asso. prof. physics U. B.C., Vancouver, 1958-62, prof. geophysics, 1963—, head dept. geophysics, 1968-72, head dept. geophysics and astronomy, 1972-79; sec.-gen. Inter-Union Commn. on Geodynamics, 1976—, bd. govs., 1978—. Fellow Royal Soc. Can.; mem. Am., Canadian geophys. unions, Geol. Assn. Can., Geochem. Soc. Author textbooks. Contbr. articles to profl. jours. Home: 2061 Allison Rd Vancouver BC V6T 1T2 Canada

RUSSELL, RICHARD OLNEY, JR., physician, educator; b. Birmingham, Ala., July 9, 1932; s. Richard Olney and Louise (Taylor) R.; A.B., Vanderbilt U., 1953, M.D., 1956; m. Phyllis Hutchinson, June 15, 1963; children—Scott Richard, Katherine Hutchinson, Meredith Cooper, Stephen Wilbon. Intern, Peter Bent Brigham Hosp., Boston, 1956-57, resident, 1959-60, 63-64; fellow in cardiology Med. Coll. Ala., Birmingham, 1960-62, instr., 1962-63; instr. medicine U. Ala., Birmingham, 1964-65, asst. prof., 1965-70, asso. prof., 1970-73, prof., 1973—. Served to capt. M.C., U.S. Army, 1957-59. NIH Research fellow, 1966-67; diplomate Am. Bd. Internal Medicine. Fellow A.C.P., Am. Coll. Cardiology; mem. Am. Heart Assn. (pres. Ala. affiliate 1975-76), Am. Coll. Chest Physicians. Author: (with Charles Edward Rackley) Hemodynamic Monitoring in a Coronary Intensive Care Unit, 1974, Coronary Artery Disease: Recognition and Management, 1979; (with others) Radiographic Anatomy of the Coronary Arteries: An Atlas, 1976. Home: 4408 Kennesaw Dr Birmingham AL 35212 Office: University Sta Birmingham AL 35294

RUSSELL, ROBERT GILMORE, lawyer; b. Detroit, May 22, 1928; s. William Gilmore and Esther Marion (Redmond) R.; A.B., U. Mich., 1951, J.D., 1953; m. Martha Jones, July 9, 1955; children—Robin, Julie. Admitted to Mich. bar, 1954; atty. firm Kerr, Russell & Weber, and predecessor firms, Detroit, 1953—, partner, 1959—. Instr., Wayne State U. Law Sch., 1954-60. Fellow Am. Coll. Trial Lawyers; mem. Am., Mich., Detroit (dir. 1977—, sec.-treas. 1979) bar assns., Am. Judicature Soc., Internat. Assn. Ins. Counsel, Assn. Def. Trial Counsel Detroit (pres. 1973-74), Barristers, Order of Coif, Mimes, Theta Xi, Phi Delta Phi, Phi Eta Sigma. Clubs: Detroit, Thomas Cooley. Asso. editor: Mich. Law Rev., 1952-53. Home: 879 Sunningdale Dr Grosse Pointe Woods MI 48236 Office: 2100 Detroit Bank & Trust Bldg Detroit MI 48226

RUSSELL, ROBERT HILTON, educator; b. Oak Park, Ill., Dec. 26, 1927; s. Melvin Alvord and Gladys (Hilton) R.; A.B., Knox Coll., 1949; A.M., Harvard U., 1950, Ph.D., 1963; A.M., Dartmouth Coll., 1968; m. June Adele Thayer, Oct. 27, 1956. Instr. Romance langs. and lits. Dartmouth Coll., 1957-61, asst. prof., 1961-63, asso. prof., 1963-67, prof., 1967—; guest lectr. U. Salamanca, 1977, U. Leeds, 1978, Oxford U., 1978. Corporate mem. United Ch. Bd. Homeland Ministries, 1963-69; N.H. del. Gen. Synod, United Ch. Christ, 1973, 75. Mem. Modern Lang. Assn. Am., Asociación Internacional de Hispanistas, Phi Beta Kappa. Democrat. Author: The Christ Figure in Misericordia, 1968; editorial cons. Pergamon Press, Oxford, Eng. Home: 14 Allen St Hanover NH 03755 Office: 344 Dartmouth Hall Hanover NH 03755

RUSSELL, ROBERT WILLIAM, transp. co. exec.; b. Chgo., Apr. 7, 1923; s. William and Ruby (Sanborn) R.; A.B., N. Central Coll., Chgo., 1943; J.D., Northwestern U., 1948; m. Frances Braught, June 25, 1948; children—Robert Scott, Gregory Lee, Barbara Frances, Nancy Marie. Admitted to Ill. bar, 1948; with Chgo. & Northwestern Transp. Co., and predecessor, Chgo., 1948—, v.p. personnel, 1968-75, v.p. personnel and labor relations, 1975-79, sr. v.p. adminstrn., 1979—, dir., 1976—. Past pres. dist. 57, Mt. Prospect (Ill.) Sch. Bd. Served with USAAF, 1943-45. Decorated Air medal. Mem. Am. Bar Assn., Am. Mgmt. Assn., Orgn. Planning Council, Conf. Board, Ill. Bar Assn., Chgo. Bar Assn. Republican. Presbyterian. Clubs: Ill. Athletic, Law (Chgo.); Barrington Bath and Tennis. Office: 400 W Madison St Chicago IL 60606

RUSSELL, STEPHEN, service co. exec.; b. N.Y.C., Mar. 9, 1940; s. Michael and Jennie (Tecklin) Rosentraub; B.A. in Mathematics, Cornell U., 1960, M.B.A. in Finance, 1961; m. Margery Noble; children—Melissa, Stewart. Jonathan. Financial analyst Mobile Internat., N.Y.C., 1961-62; product mgr. Ford Motor Co., Dearborn, Mich., 1962-69; v.p. fin. analysis RCA Corp., N.Y.C., 1969-72; gen. mgr. truck div. Hertz Corp., N.Y.C., 1972-73, exec. v.p. corp., 1973-74; pres., chief operating officer Seatrain Lines, Inc., N.Y.C., 1974—; trustee CI Realty Investors; prin. asso. North Atlantic Freight Conf. Bd. dirs. Dix Hills (N.Y.) Jewish Center. Mem. Mich. Alumni Cornell (chmn. 1968), Pvt. Carrier Conf. (dir.). Home: Mayfair Ln Greenwich CT 06830 Office: Seatrain Lines 1 Chase Manhattan Plaza New York NY 10005

RUSSELL, THOMAS DAMERON, textile mfr.; b. Alexander City, Ala., Oct. 12, 1903; s. Benjamin and Roberta (McDonald) R.; A.B., U. Ala., 1925, LL.D., 1970; m. Julia Walker, Mar. 7, 1929; children—Nancy, Julia, Ann. With Russell Mills, Inc. (name changed to Russell Corp.), Alexander City, 1925—, successively purchasing agt., v.p., pres., 1945-68, chmn., 1968—; pres. Alexander City Mfg. Co. (name changed to Alexander City Bldg. Supply Co.), 1945—; hon. chmn. First Nat. Bank, Alexander City; past dir. First Nat. Bank (Montgomery), Ala. Bankshares, Birmingham. Past mem. Ala. State Docks Commn.; hon. mem. bd. dirs. George Washington Carver Found.; life trustee Samford U., Tuskegee Inst., U. Ala.; trustee So. Research Inst., Birmingham; bd. dirs. Nat. Found., Ala. Safety Council, Julia and Thomas D. Russell Ambulatory Center U. Ala., Birmingham, Ala. Assn. Ind. Colls. Biology bldg. at Stamford U., Birmingham, also library at Alexander City Jr. Coll. named in his honor, also Thomas D. Russell Dormitory Tuskegee (Ala.) Inst.; named to Ala. Hall of Fame. Mem. NAM (past dir.), Ala. Cotton Mfrs. Assn. (past pres.), Nat. Knitwear Mfrs. Assn. (dir.), Am. Textile Mfrs. Assn. (dir.), Newcomen Soc., Ala. Acad. Honor, Chi Phi, Beta Gamma Sigma, Omicron Delta Kappa. Club: Lions. Home: Russwood Alexander City AL 35010 Office: Russell Corp Alexander City AL 35010

RUSSELL, THOMAS FRANK, mfg. co. exec.; b. Detroit, Apr. 7, 1924; s. Frank W. and Agnes V. (Kuhn) R.; student engring. Rutgers U., 1943; B.S. in Accounting, U. Detroit, 1948; m. Ruth H. Costello, June 25, 1949; children—R. Brandon, Scott K. With Fed.-Mogul Corp., Detroit, 1942—, controller, 1959-64, v.p. finance, 1964, v.p., group mgr., pres., 1972-75, chmn. bd., chief exec. officer, 1975—, also dir. Trustee U. Detroit. Served with AUS, 1943-45; ETO. Home: 51 Clairview Rd Grosse Pointe Shores MI 48236 Office: Fed-Mogul Corp PO Box 1966 Detroit MI 48235

RUSSELL, THOMAS NEWTON, lawyer; b. Diamondville, Wyo., Mar. 17, 1918; s. Thomas C. and Cecelia (Sneddon) R.; A.B., Stanford, 1940, LL.B., 1943; m. Margery Emlay, Nov. 10, 1967; children (by previous marriage)—Thomas G., James N. Admitted to Calif. bar, 1943, since practiced in Fresno; mem. firm Thomas, Snell, Jamison, Russell, Williamson & Asperger, 1945—. Mem. Fresno Mall Art Com., 1961-64. Bd. dirs. Internat. Inst., 1945-57, Fresno Arts Center, 1950-61, Fresno YMCA, 1962; bd. govs. Fresno Regional Found., 1968—. Fellow Am. Coll. Probate Counsel; mem. State Bar Calif., Fresno County Bar Assn., Am. Law Inst., Order of Coif, Phi Delta Phi. Sculptor of Trisem in Fulton Mall, Fresno. Home: 1585 W San Madele St Fresno CA 93711 Office: Del Webb Center Fresno CA 93721

RUSSELL, THOMAS SMITH, mfg. co. exec.; b. Van Nuys, Calif., Aug. 20, 1945; s. Clarence J. and Elizabeth S. R.; B.A., Furman U., 1967; M.B.A., U. Conn., 1976; m. Linda Lee Qualman, Sept. 4, 1968; children—Michelle Lyn, Thomas Smith. Mgr. internal fin. Gen. Foods Co., Dover, Del., mgr. domestic fin., White Plains, N.Y., 1967-76; asst. treas. Morton Norwich Products, Inc., Chgo., 1976-78, treas., 1978—; instr. in multinat. bus. fin. U. Conn., 1976. Served to 1st lt. Fin. Corps, U.S. Army, 1967-69. Mem. Beta Gamma Sigma. Congregationalist. Clubs: Tower, Chgo. Athletic (Chgo.). Home: 2960 Colfax Evanston IL 60201 Office: 110 N Wacker Dr Chicago IL 60606*

RUSSELL, THOMAS TRIPLETT, architect; b. Balt., Aug. 21, 1910; s. Stanislaus and Harriet (Triplett) R.; B.A., U. Pa., 1934; M.A., 1935; m. Virginia Triplett, June 7, 1941; 1 dau., Susan (Mrs. John Robert Michael Wojdyla). Architect, Polevitzky & Russell, 1936-42, Weed-Russell-Johnson, 1945-57, T Trip Russell & Assos., 1957-65, Russell, Martinez & Holt, Miami, Fla., 1965—. Pres. Coconut Grove Assn., Miami, 1970-71. Trustee Everglades Sch. for Girls, 1956-60. Served to maj. USAAF, 1943-44. Recipient Burdett Long Meml. prize Archtl. League N.Y., 1952; Merit award Guild Religious Arch., 1968. Fellow AIA (pres. S.Fla. chpt. 1956; chmn. Ford Found. scholarship program 1969-71); mem. Fla. Assn. Architects (award 1966, 68), Am. Arbitration Assn. (nat. panel 1969-71), Sigma Xi. Prin. works include Shelbourne Hotel, Miami Beach, 1940; Am. Embassy, Congo, 1955, Lagos, Nigeria, 1955; Nat. Air Lines, 1956; Four Ambassadors-Intercontinental, 1965; Lindsey Hopkins Vocat. Sch., Miami, 1969; Fla. Regional Office Bldg., Miami, 1976. Home: 4130 Malaga Ave Miami FL 33133 Office: Russell Martinez & Holt 1800 Coral Way Miami FL 33145

RUSSELL, THOMAS WRIGHT, JR., cons.; b. Hartford, Conn., July 19, 1916; s. Thomas Wright and Dorothy (Mason) R.; B.A., Yale U., 1939; student Advanced Mgmt. Program, Harvard U., 1955; m. Mary Ferguson, Feb. 18, 1946; children—Thomas Wright 3d, Jennifer, Sarah. With Am. Brake Shoe Co. (now Abex Corp.), 1945-70, dir., 1966-70, pres., 1968-70, chmn., chief exec. officer, 1970, cons., dir., 1971—; pres., dir. Internat. Execs. Inc., 1973-74; sr. v.p. Haley Assos., Inc., 1974-76, cons., 1977—; dir. Conn. Gen. Ins. Corp., D.C.L., Inc., New Med. Techniques, Inc., Inflight Services Inc., Agrownautics. Mem. Canadian-Am. Com.; pub. mem. Hudson Inst.; mem. bd. Met. Opera Guild. Served from pvt. to capt. AUS, 1941-45; PTO. Mem. Yale Assn. Class Officers (pres. 1955-57), Council Fgn. Relations, Delta Kappa Epsilon. Republican. Presbyterian (elder, trustee). Clubs: Yale, Links, Twentynine, Economic (N.Y.C.); Hay Harbor (Fishers Island); Mount Royal (Montreal). Home: 53 E 66th St New York City NY 10021

RUSSELL, WALLACE ADDISON, coll. dean; b. Windsor, Vt., June 22, 1922; s. Jay Harold and Nina Laura (Thrasher) R.; B.S., U. N.H., 1944, M.A., 1947; Ph.D., U. Iowa, 1949; m. Marjorie Ann Nelson, May 23, 1944; 1 dau., Pamela Jaye. Asst. prof. psychology U. Minn., 1949-55, asso. prof., 1955-59, prof., 1959-72, asso. dean Coll. Liberal Arts, 1971-72; dean Coll. Scis. and Humanities Iowa State U., 1972—, dir. Scis. and Humanities Research Inst., 1972—; guest prof., sr. research grantee Fulbright Commn., U. Wuerzburg, W.Germany, 1957-58. Mem. Commn. on Arts and Scis., Nat. Assn. State U.'s and Land Grant Colls., 1974—, chmn., 1976-78; pres. Council Colls. Arts and Scis, 1978-79. Served with AUS, 1943-46. Decorated Bronze Star, Purple Heart with one oak leaf cluster. Fellow Am. Psychol. Assn.; mem. AAAS, Psychonomic Soc., La Confrérie de la Chaîne des Rôtisseurs, Sigma Xi, Phi Beta Kappa (hon.), Alpha Gamma Rho. Unitarian. Club: Rotary. Author: (with M. Tinker) Introduction to Methods in Experimental Psychology, 3d edit., 1958; editor: Milestones in Motivation, 1970; contbr. articles to profl. jours. Home: 515 Forest Glen Ames IA 50010. *As student, teacher, researcher, administrator, I have spent most of my life in schools. In an easy age for cynicism, I still believe in the potentiality of education to lead man out of strife and ignorance to a more abundant life.*

RUSSELL, WILLIAM BRUCE, ednl. cons.; b. Missoula, Mont., Apr. 15, 1932; s. William Bruce and Mildred Mae (Benedick) R.; B.A., U. Mont., 1954; M.S., U. Colo., 1960; Ed.D. (Tex. scholar), North Tex. State U., 1968; m. Kathryn Ann Rodkey, May 5, 1951; children—Deborah, Mary, William, Caroline, Elizabeth. Tchr., Malta (Mont.) High Sch., 1954-56, Flood Jr. High Sch., Englewood, Colo., 1956-57, Littleton (Colo.) High Sch., 1958-59, Ephrata (Wash.) High Sch., 1960-62; dist. mgr. Hamilton Mgmt. Corp., Denver, 1957-58; div. chmn. Bigbend Community Coll., 1962-66, Dallas County Community Coll., 1966-67; v.p. Yakima Valley Coll., 1968-73, pres., 1973-79; cons. edn., Yakima, Wash., 1979—; participant Acad. Year Inst., U. Colo., 1959-60, NSF Summer Inst., U. Wash., 1961. Mem. NEA, Am. Assn. Community and Jr. Colls., Am. Mensa Soc., Phi Sigma. Republican. Presbyterian. Club: Rotary. Home and Office: 6106 W Walnut St Yakima WA 98908

RUSSELL, WILLIAM FRASER, educator, musician; b. Norwalk, Conn., Sept. 17, 1916; s. William Fraser and Christine Graeme (Smith) R.; B.A., Columbia, 1937; student Middlebury Summer Music Center, 1939-40; M.A. in Teaching English, Harvard, 1939, M.A. in Music, 1946, grad. student, 1945-51; m. Jean Barclay Spence, June 30, 1946; children—John Alexander, Alison Margaret. Master English and music Tabor Acad., Marion, Mass., 1939-41; asst. condr. Harvard Glee Club and Radcliffe Choral Soc., 1947-51, acting condr., 1949-50; condr. Pomona Coll. Choir and Glee Clubs, 1951—, chmn. music dept., 1953—, David J. Baldwin prof., 1959—; condr. Harvard Summer Sch. Chorus, also vis. prof. music, 1961, 64; vis. cons. music Whitman and Occidental colls., 1975, Reed Coll., 1976-77. Served with AUS, 1941-45. Mem. Am., Internat. musicol. socs., Soc. Ethnomusicology, Coll. Music Soc., Soc. Music Liberal Arts Coll. (past pres.), Music Library Assn., Calif. Music Execs. Assn. (past pres.). Home: 382 Blaisdell Dr Claremont CA 91711

RUSSELL, WILLIAM HENRY, coll. dean; b. Bloomington, Ind., May 27, 1923; s. John Dale and Elsie Violet (Hattery) R.; B.A., U. Chgo., 1942, M.A., 1947; Ph.D., U. Wis., 1953; m. Martha Ruth Irons, Sept. 2, 1955; children—Mary Louise, Dale William. Instr. social sci. Woodrow Wilson Jr. Coll., Chgo., 1947-49; asst. prof. history Eureka (Ill.) Coll., 1952-54; prof. history Geneva Coll., Beaver Falls, Pa., 1954—, dean Coll., 1963—. Trustee Carnegie Library, Beaver Falls, 1958-70. Served with USAAC, 1943-46. Presbyterian (elder). Contbr. articles to profl. jours. Home: 3321 5th Ave Beaver Falls PA 15010

RUSSELL, WILLIAM JOSEPH, assn. exec.; b. Boston, Sept. 23, 1941; s. Stanley Whiteside and Helen Rita R.; B.S., Boston Coll., 1963; M.Ed., Northeastern U., 1966; Ph.D., U. Calif., Berkeley, 1971; m. Frances Marie Chapdelaine, June 25, 1967; 1 son, Scott David. Head math. dept. Oceana, Pacifica, Calif., 1966-71; asst. for fed. and profl. affairs Am. Ednl. Research Assn., Washington, 1971-73, dep. exec. officer, 1973-74, exec. officer, 1974—; exec. officer Nat. Council on Measurement in Edn. Mem. Am. Ednl. Research Assn., Phi Delta Kappa. Roman Catholic. Editor Ednl. Researcher, 1979—. Home: 1443 Creekside Ct Vienna VA 22180 Office: 1230 17th St NW Washington DC 20036

RUSSIN, ROBERT ISAIAH, sculptor, educator; b. N.Y.C., Aug. 26, 1914; s. Uriel and Olga (Winnett) R.; B.A., Coll. City N.Y., 1933, M.S., 1935; postgrad. (Inst. fellow) Beaux Arts Inst. Design, 1935-36; m. Adele Mutchnick, May 21, 1937; children—Joseph Mark, Lincoln David, Uriel Robin. One-man shows Tucson Fine Arts Center, 1966, Colorado Springs (Colo.) Fine Arts Center, 1967, Palm Springs (Calif.) Desert Mus., Chas. G. Bowers Meml. Mus., Judah L. Magnes Meml. Mus., Berkeley, Calif.; retrospective one-man exhbn. Nat. Gallery Modern Art, Santo Domingo, Dominican Republic, 1976; sculpture commns. include two 8-foot metal figures Evanston (Ill.) Post Office, 1939, three life-size carved figures Conshohocken (Pa.) Post Office, 1940, Benjamin Franklin Monument campus U. Wyo., 1957, Bust of Lincoln, Lincoln Mus., Washington, 1959 (now in Gettysburg Mus.), Lincoln Monument atop summit Lincoln Hwy. Wyo., 1959, Monumental bas-relief bronze Cheyenne (Wyo.) Fed. Bldg., 1966, two carved wood walls Denver Fed. Bldg., 1966, Monumental Fountain City of Hope Med. Center, Los Angeles, 1966-67, statue Brookhaven (N.Y.) Nat. Lab., 1968, life-size bronze sculpture fountain Pomona Coll., 1969, monumental bronze sculpture Prometheus Natrona County (Wyo.) Pub. Library, Casper, 1974, monumental bronze sculpture Man and Energy Casper C. of C., 1974, 12-foot marble carving plaza of Menorah Med. Center, Kansas City, Mo., 1975, Einstein and Gershwin medals Magnes Meml. Mus., Berkeley, monumental sculpture and fountain Nat. Mus. Art, Santo Domingo, Dominican Republic, 1975, portrait head Charles Bluhdorn, chmn. Gulf & Western, 1975, portrait bust Pres. J. Balaguer of Dominican Republic, 1975, portrait head G. Wilson Knight, Shakespearean actor and scholar, 1975, 2 12-foot bronze figures The Greeting and the Gift for Bicentennial Commn., Cheyenne, Wyo., 1976, monumental marble head of Juan Pablo Duarte liberator Dominican Republic, Santo Domingo, 1976; tchr. sculpture Copper Union Art Inst., N.Y.C., 1944-47; prof. art U. Wyo., Laramie, 1947—, prof., artist-in-residence, 1976—. Recipient awards sec. fine arts U.S. Treasury, 1939, 40, Lincoln medal U.S. Congress, 1959, Alfred G. B. Steel award Pa. Acad. Fine Arts, 1961; Medal of Order of Duarte, Sanchez y Mella (Dominican Republic). Ford Found. fellow, 1953. Mem. Nat. Sculpture Conf. (exec. bd.), Sculptors Guild, Nat.

Sculpture Soc., AIA, AAUP, Coll. Art Internat. Inst. Arts and Letters, Phi Beta Kappa (hon.). Contbr. articles to profl. jours. Home: 716 Ivinson Ave Laramie WY 82070

RUSSO, ALEXANDER PETER, artist, educator; b. Atlantic City, June 11, 1922; s. Peter Joseph and Lillian Mary (Soma) R.; student Pratt Inst., 1940-42, Swarthmore Coll., 1946-47; S.S., Bard Coll., 1947; B.F.A. (Breevort-Eickenmeyer fellow), Columbia U., 1952; postgrad. Acad. Fine Arts, Rome, 1952-54; postgrad. Inst. Advanced Fine Arts, 1977-79; m. Arlene E. Bujese; 1 dau., Eugenie. Instr., New Orleans Acad. Art, 1948-49; asst. prof. art U. Buffalo, 1955-58; instr. in graphic design Parsons Sch. Design, 1958-60; chmn. dept. drawing and painting Corcoran Sch. Art, 1961-70, chmn. faculty, acting dean, 1967-70; lectr., thesis adv. George Washington U., 1961-70; prof., chmn. dept. art Hood Coll., 1970—; one-man shows include: Corcoran Gallery Art, Washington, 1946, 64, Chiurazzi Gallery, Rome, 1953, Cavallino Gallery, Venice, Italy, 1954, U. So. Ill., 1955, Frank Rehn Gallery, N.Y.C., periodic exhbns., 1954-74, Washington Gallery Art, 1963, Franz Bader Gallery, Washington, 1967, Internat. Monetary Fund, Washington, 1968, 79, Agra Gallery, Washington, 1971, Benson Gallery, Bridgehampton, L.I., 1976; group shows include: Salon de la Marne, Paris, 1945, Met. Mus. Art, N.Y.C., 1948, Bordighera Internat., Italy, 1953, 54 (hon. mention), Mus. Modern Art, Madrid, 1953, Sala di Esposizione delle Biblioteca Americano, Rome, 1953, Whitney Mus. Am. Art, N.Y.C., 1960, Mus. Modern Art, N.Y.C., 1969, Guild Hall, East Hampton, N.Y., 1976; represented in permanent collections, including: Albright-Know Gallery, Buffalo, Columbia U., N.Y.C., Delgado Mus. Art, New Orleans, Corcoran Gallery Art, Fiat Automobile Co., Rome, Nat. Collection Smithsonian Inst., Washington, Fed. Ins. Deposit Corp., Washington; cons. in field; Fulbright grantee for painting, research, Rome, 1952-54. Served with USNR, 1942-46. Recipient cert. commendation U.S. Navy, 1974; Guggenheim fellow, 1947-48, 49-50; Edward McDowell fellow, 1956. Home: 519 Culler Ave Frederick MD 21701 Office: Hood Coll Frederick MD 21701 also 14 Oak Hill Ln East Hampton Long Island NY 11937. *Success is an equivocal matter. "Outward success", no doubt, is meaningful and necessary to most people in terms of fulfilling goals or for some similar reason. "Interior success" is more difficult to achieve, for it means the labor of a developing soul, and, more often than not, the relinquishing of what most would consider to be "material success". Whatever I have achieved in the way of outward or material success, therefore, is but a minute reflection of that which I would wish to achieve on the spiritual level. There is a long way to go.*

RUSSO, JAMES RALPH, magazine editor; b. Dumont, N.J., June 3, 1941; s. Ralph Patrick and Anne (Zingg) R.; B.S., Delaware Valley Coll. Sci. and Agr., Doylestown, Pa., 1964; student U. Chgo. Grad. Sch. Bus., 1966-68; m. Janjira Kasemsook, July 5, 1969; children—Jennita, Jaromy. Editor, Putnam Pub. Co., Chgo., 1964-69, Chilton Co., Radnor, Pa., 1969-73, N. Am. Pub. Co., Phila., 1973-76; editor Am. Sch. and Univ. mag., 1973-76, Health Care, 1974-76, Food Engring. mag., 1976—. Mem. security adv. com. Thornbury Twp. (Pa.), 1975. Served with AUS, 1959-61. Recipient John F. Kennedy award Outstanding Citizenship and Academic Achievement, Delaware Valley Coll., 1964; Distinguished Achievement award Ednl. Press Assn. Am., 1975. Mem. Ednl. Press Assn. Am., Inst. Food Technologists, Phila. Inst. Food Technologists (pres.). Home: 14 Grist Mill Rd Glen Mills PA 19342 Office: 134 N 13th St Philadelphia PA 19107

RUSSO, JOSEPH FRANK, coll. pres.; b. Pitts., Jan. 11, 1924; s. Joseph and E. Carmella (Sanseverino) R.; B.A., U. Ariz., 1953; M.A., Ariz. State U., 1961, Ed.D., 1969; m. Jean Montierth, Mar. 26, 1947; children—Joseph Gary, Nancy Louise Russo Cook. From tchr.-coach to prin. Prescott (Ariz.) High Sch., 1953-68; asst. supt. schs., Prescott, 1968; dean student personnel services, then dean instrn. Yavapai Coll., Prescott, 1968-74, pres., 1974—; faculty asso. Ariz. State U., 1960-63, No. Ariz. U., 1972, 73, 78; mem. Ariz. Commn. Post-Secondary Edn., 1976—. Mem. Prescott Charter Rev. Com., 1975; bd. dirs. Prescott Salvation Army, 1970-73. Served with U.S. Army, 1944-46. Far Eastern Studies scholar, 1955; recipient Builder Greater Ariz. award Ariz. Savs. and Loan Assn.-Sta. KTAR, Phoenix, 1967. Mem. Am. Assn. U. Adminstrs., Am. Assn. Higher Edn., Assn. Gov. Bds., Ariz. President's Council, Am. Council Edn., Am. Mgmt. Assn., Phi Delta Kappa. Republican. Roman Catholic. Club: Rotary. Author articles in field. Home: 628 Cypress Dr Prescott AZ 86301 Office: 1100 E Sheldon St Prescott AZ 86301

RUSSO, MARTIN A., congressman; b. Chgo., Jan. 23, 1944; s. Anthony and Lucille R.; B.A., DePaul U., 1965, J.D., 1967; m. Karen Jorgensen; children—Tony, Dan. Admitted to Ill. bar, 1967, U.S. Supreme Ct. bar, 1974, D.C. bar, 1977; law clk. Judge John V. McCormack, Ill. Appellate Ct., 1967-68; asst. state's atty. Cook County (Ill.), 1971-73; practice in Chgo., 1973—; mem. 94th-96th congresses from 3d Dist. Ill., mem. Com. On Ways and Means, Select Com. Aging. Bd. dirs. St. Xavier Coll., Chgo.; mem. Joint Civic Com. of Italian-Ams.; mem. citizens bd. Ill. Masonic Med. Center. Recipient Distinguished Service award Pinta Neri K.C.; named One of Roseland's Ten Outstanding Young Men, Gateway br. Chgo. Jr. Assn. Commerce and Industry, 1968; Man of Year, Chgo. W. Suburban chpt. United Neighbors of Italy Community Orgns., 1975, Chgo. chpt. Magen David Adom, 1977; Outstanding Legis. Leader, Soc. Little Flower, 1975; One of Ten Outstanding Young People, Harvey (Ill.) Jaycees, 1977. Mem. Am., Fed., Ill., D.C., S. Suburban bar assns., Justinian Soc. Lawyers (named Man of Year 1976), Alpha Phi Delta Alumni Assn. Roman Catholic. Clubs: K.C., Elks, Order Sons of Italy. Office: 206 Cannon House Office Bldg Washington DC 20515

RUST, CLINTON ALBERT, hosp. adminstr.; b. Mangum, Okla., Aug. 5, 1934; s. William Albert and Velma Ella (Hill) R.; student Los Angeles Valley Jr. Coll., 1952-54; B.S., U. So. Calif., 1956, M.P.A., 1976; m. JoAnne Johnson, June 19, 1953; children—Robert Lindy, Gary Alan, Sally Anne. Asst. personnel dir. Vegetable Oil Products Co., Wilmington, Calif., 1956-61, asst. to v.p., 1961-66; personnel analyst and recruiter Calif. State Personnel Bd., Los Angeles, Sacramento, 1966-69; personnel analyst Calif. Dept. Mental Hygiene, Sacramento, 1969-70, personnel officer Napa State Hosp., Imola, Calif., 1970-73; asst. hosp. adminstr. Calif. Dept. Health Sonoma State Hosp., Eldridge, Calif., 1973-74, hosp. adminstr. Atascadero State Hosp., 1974-76; exec. dir. Calif. Dept. Developmental Services Camarillo (Calif.) State Hosp., 1976—; mem. psychiat. technician adv. com. Calif. Bd. Vocat. Nurse and Psychiat. Technician Examiners, 1974—; mem. registered nursing adv. bd. Ventura Community Coll., 1978—; mem. health manpower com. Napa Comprehensive Health Planning Council, 1971-73. Mem. allocations com. Ventura County United Way, 1979. Mem. Nat. Assn. Supts. Public Facilities for Mentally Retarded. Repuolican. Club: Masons. Office: PO Box A Camarillo CA 93010

RUST, EDWARD BARRY, ins. exec.; b. Bloomington, Ill., Sept. 5, 1918; s. Adlai H. and Florence Fifer (Barry) R.; A.B. cum laude in Econs., Stanford U., 1940; m. Harriett B. Fuller, Aug. 7, 1940; children—Florence M., Harriet H., Edward B. Asst. sec. State Farm Mut. Automobile Ins. Co., 1942; dir. br. offices, 1946-51, v.p., 1951-58, pres., 1958—; also chief exec. officer, dir., exec. com.; pres., dir. State Farm Life Ins. Co.; pres., dir., exec. com. State Farm Fire & Casualty Co.; pres. State Farm Life & Accident Assurance Co., State Farm County Mut. Ins. Co. Tex., State Farm Gen. Ins. Co.; dir. Gen. Telephone Co. Ill. Trustee Ill. Wesleyan U. Served as lt. USNR, 1943-46. Mem. U.S. C. of C. (dir., pres. 1972-73), Phi Beta Kappa. Home: Rural Route 1 Bloomington IL 61701 Office: One State Farm Plaza Bloomington IL 61701

RUST, JOHN HOWARD, educator; b. Many, La., Sept. 29, 1909; s. Milbern James and Lucile (Osborn) R.; D.V.M., Kans. State U., 1932, D.Sc., 1963; postgrad. Duke U., 1949; Ph.D., U. Chgo., 1956; m. Mary Jo Cortelyou, Sept. 29, 1932; children—Mary Van Zandt (Mrs. J.T. Townsend), Milbern James, John Henry, Joan Helen. Pvt. practice veterinary medicine, Concord, N.H. and Wellesley, Mass., 1932-35; lectr. project dir. Mass. Inst. Tech., 1958-59; prof. pharmacology, head sect. nuclear medicine U. Chgo., 1959-68, prof. pharmacology and radiology, 1968-75, emeritus, 1975—; dir. A.J. Carlson Animal Research Facility, 1967-72. Mem. com. radiation WHO, 1959-78, com. pathol. effects atomic radiation (hematology), NRC, 1957-61; expert com. on safety irradiated foods WHO, 1969; adv. com. on civil def., 1961-68; adv. com. on radioactive waste mgmt., chmn. panel on salt mines, panel on land burial Nat. Acad. Scis., 1968-78, food protection, 1967-72; adv. com. on environ. radiation USPHS, 1965-68; co-chmn. Ill. Commn. on Atomic Energy, 1970-74, Ill. Dept. Pub. Health Council on Radiation Protection, 1970—; mem. Nat. Council on Radiation Protection, 1966—; chmn. life sci. exhibits U.S. del. cons. environ. containment in food Office Tech. Assessment, Atoms for Peace Conf., Geneva, Switzerland, 1958; U.S. Congress, 1978—. Served to col. Vet. Corps, U.S. Army, 1935-58. Mem. AAAS, Soc. Exptl. Biology and Medicine, Am. Soc. Exptl. Pathology, Radiation Research Soc., Am. Vet. Med. Assn., Am. Coll. Vet. Pathologists, Internat. Acad. Pathology, Inst. Medicine Chgo., Sigma Xi, Phi Kappa Phi, Sigma Phi Epsilon. Clubs: Quadrangle (U. Chgo.); Chikaming Country (Lakeside, Mich.); Army and Navy, Cosmos (Washington). Home: 5715 S Kenwood Chicago IL 60637

RUST, STIRLING MURRAY, JR., engring. exec.; b. Lowell, Mass., Apr. 28, 1912; s. Stirling Murray and Mary (Coburn) R.; grad. Shady Side Acad., Pitts., 1930; B.S. in Mech. Engring., Lehigh U., 1934; m. Gladys Over, Oct. 24, 1936 (dec. Dec. 1969); children—Stirling Murray III. James Over, Mary Elizabeth Montgomery, John Mead; m. 2d, Elinor Cowdrey Hill, Aug. 5, 1970; stepchildren—Bruce E. Hill III, Thomas A. Hill, Margot H. Ball. Ret. chmn. Rust Engring. Co. and affiliated cos.; chmn. Woodbridge Co., Birmingham, Ala.; v.p. Birmingham Clay Products Co.; adv. dir. Pitts. Nat. Bank. Trustee Rust Found., Chatham Coll., Lehigh U., Shadyside Hosp., Shady Side Acad. Registered profl. engr., Ariz., Ark., Conn., Fla., Ind., La., Maine, Mass., N.J., Oreg., Pa., Va., Wash. Mem. Chief Execs. Forum, Assn. Iron and Steel Engrs., ASME, Engrs. Soc. Western Pa., Delta Phi, Pi Tau Sigma. Episcopalian. Clubs: Duquesne, Pitts. Golf (Pitts.); Royal Poinciana Golf (Naples, Fla.). Home: Box 457 Monument Rd Orleans MA 02653

RUST, WILLIAM CHARLES, univ. pres., clergyman; b. Butte, Mont., Feb. 18, 1917; s. Harry F. and Rose Elizabeth (Morrow) R.; A.B., DePauw U., 1941; Ph.D., U. So. Calif., 1951; m. Rose Marie Drye, May 30, 1945; children—William Charles, Robert John, Cheryl Lee, Rose Merrianne. Ordained to ministry Methodist Ch., 1945; minister Meth. chs., 1938-42; minister Congl. Ch., 1943-53; prof. humanities, religious edn. and comparative religions U. So. Calif., 1943-46, Iliff Sch. Theology, Denver, 1946-51, U. Denver, 1946-51; pres. U.S. Internat. U. (formerly Cal. Western U.), San Diego, 1952—; moderator TV Univ. series, sta. KFMB-TV, San Diego, 1954-56. Mem. adv. council Am. Arbitration Assn.; bd. govs. Greater San Diego Sci. Fair; bd. dirs. San Diego Symphony Orch., San Diego Urban Coalition, World Affairs Council San Diego. Mem. Phi Delta Kappa. Office: 10455 Pomerado Rd San Diego CA 92131*

RUST, WILLIAM FITZHUGH, JR., broadcasting exec.; b. Cleve., Jan. 27, 1914; s. William Fitzhugh and Mary Elizabeth Lee (Fleming) R.; B.S., Lehigh U., Bethlehem, Pa., 1936; m. Margaret Dole, Feb. 14, 1942; children—Roberta F. (Mrs. Alexander Jeffries), William Fitzhugh III, Richard B.L., Henry L. Engr., Gen. Electric Co., Schenectady, 1936-39, Rust Engring. Co., Pitts., 1939-43; gen. mgr. Granite State Broadcasting Co., Manchester, N.H., 1946-52; pres. Rust Indsl. Co., electronics mfr., Manchester, 1952-60, Rust Communications Group, Rochester, N.Y. and Leesburg, Va., 1961—. Served to lt. USNR, 1943-46. Sr. mem. IEEE; mem. Clear Channel Broadcasters Assn. (dir.), Tau Beta Pi, Delta Phi. Episcopalian. Patentee in field. Home: Yeocomico Leesburg VA 22075 Office: PO Box 1378 Leesburg VA 22075

RUST, WILLIAM JAMES, steel co. exec.; b. Newark, Mar. 21, 1929; s. William G. and Anna (Glavin) R; B.S. in Math. magna cum laude, Boston Coll., 1953; M.B.A. with high distinction, Harvard, 1955; m. Adele M. Laubner, July 29, 1950; 1 dau., Rita Marie. With Nat. Cash Register Co., 1955-68, dir. distbn. and material, 1964-68; v.p., treas. Indian Head, Inc., 1968-72, v.p. planning and fin., 1972-77; v.p. fin. Nat. Steel Co., Pitts., 1977—; dir. Fairfield Communities, Inc., Ark. Pres. Social Health Agy., Dayton, Ohio, 1966-68; chmn. United Fund campaigns, Dayton, 1962-68. Bd. dirs. Good Samaritan Hosp., Dayton, 1965-68. Served with USAAF, 1946-49. Mem. Nat. Assn. Accountants (bd. dirs. Dayton 1960-63), Fin. Execs. Inst. Clubs: Duquesne, Fox Chapel Golf. Home: 117 Haverford Rd Pittsburgh PA 15238 Office: 2800 Grant Bldg Pittsburgh PA 15219

RUSTAGI, JAGDISH SHARAN, educator; b. Sikri, India, Aug. 13, 1923; s. Chhotey Lal and Mora Devi (Rustagi); B.S., Delhi U., 1944, M.S., 1946; Ph.D. (Honors fellow), Stanford U., 1956; m. Kamla Rastogi, June 12, 1949; children—Pradip, Pramod, Madhu. Came to U.S., 1961. Lectr. Hindu Coll., Delhi U., 1946-52; research asst. Stanford U., 1952-55; asst. prof. Carnegie Inst. Tech., 1955-57; asst. prof. Mich. State U., 1957-58; reader Aligarh U., 1958-60; asst. dir. biometrics U. Cin., 1960-63; asso. prof. Ohio State U., 1963-65, prof. math., 1965-70, prof. statistics, 1970—, chmn. dept. stats., 1979—. Fellow Am. Statis. Assn.; mem. Inst. Math. Statistics, Internat. Statistics Inst., Sigma Xi. Research math. statistics, biostatistics, environ. health statistics, ops. research. Home: 6519 Evening St Worthington OH 43085 Office: 1958 Neil Ave Columbus OH 43210

RUSTERHOLZ, KENNETH GEORGE, credit co. exec.; b. Bklyn., July 21, 1928; s. George and Adeline (Weitz) R.; B.B.A., Pace Coll., 1956; m. Joan Martha Sinnott, June 12, 1955; children—Ellen Margaret, Kenneth Paul, Mary Catherine. With Gen. Electric Credit Corp., N.Y.C., 1956—, mgr. corp. placements, 1971-75, v.p., mgr. leasing and indsl. loans, Stamford, Conn., 1975—. Served with AUS, 1966-68. Mem. Assn. Equipment Lessors, Beta Gamma Sigma. Republican. Lutheran. Home: 5288 Madison Ave Trumbull CT 06611 Office: 260 Long Ridge Rd Stamford CT 06902

RUSTGI, MOTI LAL, educator; b. Delhi, India, Sept. 29, 1929; s. Misri Lal and Lakshmi Devi (Rustgi) R.; M.Sc. in Physics, Delhi U., 1951; Ph.D., La. State U., 1957; m. Kamla Rohatgi, Dec. 10, 1952; children—Vinod K., Anil K. Research asso. Yale, 1957-60; NRC postdoctoral fellow, Ottawa, research asso. Harvard, 1960-61; reader Banaras Hind U., 1961-63; asst. prof. U. So. Calif., 1963-64, Yale, 1964-66; asso. prof. State U. N.Y., Buffalo, 1966-68, prof., 1968—; vis. prof. State U. N.Y. at Stony Brook, spring 1973. Fellow Am. Phys. Soc. Home: 75 West Maplemere Buffalo NY 14221 Office: State U NY at Buffalo Physics Dept Buffalo NY 14214

RUSTHOVEN, RICHARD CLARENCE, apparel co. exec.; b. Chgo., July 11, 1940; s. Richard and Henrietta (Iwema) R.: B.A., Calvin Coll., Grand Rapids, Mich., 1962; M.B.A., Mich. State U., 1964; m. Lauralyn Ehrman, Apr. 26, 1975. Buyer, F & R Lazarus, Columbus, Ohio, 1964-69; mgr. br. store Lazarus, Columbus, 1969, div. mdse. mgr., 1970-74; div. mdse. mgr. William H. Block, Indpls., 1974-76; div. mdse. mgr. May D & F, Denver, 1976-77, v.p., gen. mdse. mgr. ready-to-wear, 1977-78; pres. Stix, Baer & Fuller, St. Louis, 1979—. Presbyterian. Office: 601 Washington Ave Saint Louis MO 63101

RUSTICI, CHARLES JOHN, hosp. adminstr.; b. Stonington, Conn., Dec. 30, 1922; s. Michael and Margaret (Sammataro) R.; B.S., Bryant Coll., 1948; certificate data processing Watkins Inst., 1963; m. Patricia Bernice Clemons, June 27, 1953; children—Marc, Craig. Div. controller Nat. Dairy Products Corp., Inc., 1948-63; chief accountant Shaffer Corp., 1963-65; adminstrv. asst. St. Mary and St. Elizabeth Hosp., 1965-70; asso. dir. Harrisburg (Pa.) Hosp., 1970—. Mem. bd. Cath. Bd. Edn., Louisville, 1969-70. Served with AUS. Mem. Nat. Office Mgrs. Assn. (dir. 1955-57), Nat. Assn. Accountants (dir. 1969), Hosp. Financial Mgmt. Assn. (pres. 1968, 73). Home: 503 Springhouse Rd Camp Hill PA 17011 Office: Harrisburg Hosp South Front St Harrisburg PA 17101. *Establish your objective before you attempt to solve the problem; otherwise you'll be attacking the symptom rather than the disease.*

RUSTIN, BAYARD, civil rights activist; b. Westchester, Pa., Mar. 17, 1910; s. Janifer and Julia (Davis) R.; student Wilberforce (Ohio) U., 1930-31, Cheyney (Pa.) State Tchrs. Coll., 1931-33, Coll. City N.Y., 1933-35; LL.D., New Sch. for Social Research, 1968, Brown U., 1972; Litt.D., Montclair State Coll., 1968; hon. degree, Mich. State U. Race relations dir. Fellowship of Reconciliation, 1941-53; field sec. Congress Racial Equality, 1941; exec. sec. War Resisters' League, 1953-55; spl. asst. to Dr. Martin Luther King, Jr., 1955-60; organizer March on Washington for Jobs and Freedom, 1963; pres. A. Philip Randolph Inst., N.Y.C., 1966—. Chmn. Social Democrats U.S.A.; chmn. exec. com. Leadership Conf. on Civil Rights. Bd. dirs. Notre Dame U., Black Ams. to Support Israel Com., League Indsl. Democracy, Internat. Rescue Com., AFL-CIO Labor Studies Center, Alvin Ailey Dance Theater, Coalition for Dem. Majority, Com. on Present Danger, Ams. for Energy Independence, Freedom House. Recipient Eleanor Roosevelt award Trade Union Leadership Council, 1966; Man of Year award Pitts. br. N.A.A.C.P., 1965; Liberty Bell award Howard U. Law Sch., 1967, John Dewey award United Fedn. Tchrs., 1968, Family of Man award Nat. Council Chs., 1969, John F. Kennedy award Nat. Council Jewish Women, 1971, Lyndon Baines Johnson award Urban Coalition, 1974. Mem. UN Assn. (dir.). Mem. Soc. of Friends. Author: Down The Line, 1971; Strategies for Freedom, 1976; also articles. Address: 260 Park Ave S New York NY 10010. *The principle factors which influenced my life are: 1) non-violent tactics; 2) constitutional means; 3) democratic procedures; 4) respect for human personality; 5) a belief that all people are one.*

RUTENBER, CULBERT GEROW, clergyman, educator; b. Grove City, Pa., May 6, 1909; s. Ralph Dudley and Margaret (Gerow) R.; Ph.B., Kenyon Coll., Gambier, Ohio, 1930; B.D., Eastern Baptist Theol. Sem., Phila., 1933, D.D., 1969; M.A., U. Pa., 1937, Ph.D., 1945; D.D., Calif. Bapt. Theol. Sem., Covina, 1958, Georgetown (Ky.) Coll., 1966; m. Duron Sparks, June 28, 1970. Ordained to ministry Bapt. Ch., 1933; pastor in Camden, N.J., 1931-39; mem. faculty Eastern Bapt. Theol. Sem., 1939-59, 74—, prof. philosophy religion and social ethics, 1948-59, prof. philosophy religion, 1974-79, adj. prof., 1979—; prof. philosophy religion Andover Newton Theol. Sch., 1959-69, dir. studies, 1961-63; prof. philosophy religion Am. Bapt. Sem. of the West, Covina, 1969-74; vis. chaplain Stanford, summer 1946; Holland lectr. Southwestern Bapt. Theol. Sem., 1953; Robert Treat Paine Found. lectr., 1954; Gheen lectr., 1963; vis. prof. Episcopal Theol. Sem., Cambridge, Mass., 1963; H. I. Hester lectr. Assn. So. Bapt. Colls. and Schs., 1974; Edwin Stephen Griffiths Meml. lectr. S. Wales Bapt. Coll., Cardiff, Wales, 1975; Chmn. council Christian social progress Am. Bapt. Conv., 1957-58, bd. mgrs. bd. edn. and publ., 1961-67, v.p. conv., 1967-68, pres., 1968-69; mem. Bapt. Joint Com. Pub. Affairs, 1953-58; mem. commn. religious liberty Bapt. World Alliance, 1955—; mem. men's com. Japan Internat. Christian U. Found., 1969—; mem. faith and order commn. So. Calif. Council Chs., 1970-74. Mem. Fellowship of Reconciliation (vice chmn. 1953), Am. Soc. Christian Ethics, Soc. Sci. Study Religion, Am. Philos. Assn., Phi Beta Kappa, Sigma Pi. Author: The Doctrine of the Imitation of God in Plato, 1946; The Dagger and the Cross, 1950; The Price and the Prize, 1953; The Reconciling Gospel, 1960; Peace Keeping and Peace Making, 1968; also articles. Contbr. to Baker's Dictionary of Christian Ethics. Address: Eastern Bapt Theol Sem Lancaster at City Ave Philadelphia PA 19151

RUTENBER, RALPH DUDLEY, JR., educator, author, lectr.; b. Bardonia, N.Y., Aug. 3, 1905; s. Ralph Dudley and Margaret (Gerow) R.; grad. Blackburn Acad., Carlinville, Ill., 1922; A.B., Princeton, 1926; A.M., Columbia, 1940; student Cornell U., 1930; Litt.D., Am. Internat. Coll., 1959; m. Cleminette Downing, Dec. 29, 1932; children—Anne Downing (Mrs. Roger L. Clifton), John Downing. Master in Latin, Choate Sch., 1926-28; head English dept. Wooster Sch., Danbury, Conn., 1928-33, sr. master, 1933-41; headmaster MacDuffie Sch. for Girls, Springfield, Mass., 1941-72, pres., 1975-78; ednl. cons., 1972-75; lectr. edn., lit. and religion; past dir. Community Sch. Religious Edn., Springfield. Past dir. Ind. Schs. Found. of Mass.; former bd. dirs. Ind. Sch. Assn. Mass.; former trustee Springfield Library and Museums, Mental Health and Retardation Area Bd., trustee MacDuffie Sch. Mem. Nat. Assn. Prins. of Schs. for Girls (sec. 1964-66, mem. council, pres. 1971-73), Headmasters Assn., Phi Beta Kappa. Episcopalian. Author: How to Bring Up 2000 Teenagers, 1979; also articles, essays and reviews. Home and office: 334 Maple St Springfield MA 01105. *I try to tell my students that there is no achievement without vigorous effort; that feeling, unbuttressed by hard thinking, is not enough; that a frustration free existence is not possible; that we cannot "drop out" into the world of private sensation; that defeat may be what happens to you, but victory is what you are; that success is measured not by money but by meaning; that hatred, as Fromm says, is 'unlived life"; that joyful response to the needs of others is the answer to our own deepest needs; that the learning process should end not with adaptation but conviction; and that the aim of all education is to develop a certain kind of person with the ability to interpret knowledge in a way which will develop his own character and will have an impact on the lives of others.*

RUTENBERG, CHARLES, constrn. co. exec.; b. Chgo., May 16, 1924; s. Reuben and Mary (Quadow) R; B.A. in Econs., U. Chgo., 1947; m. Isadora Kesselman, Sept. 1, 1947; children—Alan, Laurie, Marc, Pamela. Engaged in retail furniture bus., Chgo., 1948-53; owner Rutenberg Homes, Inc., also Imperial Land Corp., Clearwater Fla., 1955-69; pres., dir. U.S. Home Corp., Clearwater, 1970-73, chmn. bd., chief exec. officer, 1973-75, chmn. bd., 1975-77, chmn. emeritus,

1977—; chmn., pres. Rutenberg Corp., Largo, Fla., 1977—; vice chmn. Orange State Life Ins. Co., Largo. Mem. devel. com. Morton F. Plant Hosp., 1971-73; past pres. Clearwater Symphony Assn.; v.p., bd. dirs. Performing Arts Center and Theatre, Inc., Clearwater; past pres. Clearwater Jewish Welfare Fund; mem. nat. exec. com., chmn. nat. campaign cabinet, region IV, United Jewish Appeal; v.p., trustee Am. Friends Haifa U.; trustee United Israel Appeal; mem. council advisors U. South Fla., Tampa. Served with AUS, 1943-46. Democrat. Jewish. Home: 57 Southwind Dr Belleair Bluffs FL 33540 Office: 2400 W Bay Dr Suite 420 Largo FL 33540

RUTFORD, ROBERT HOXIE, univ. exec.; b. Duluth, Minn., Jan. 26, 1933; s. Skuli and Ruth (Hoxie) R.; B.A., U. Minn., 1954, M.A., 1963, Ph.D., 1969; m. Marjorie Ann, June 19, 1954; children—Gregory, Kristian, Barbara. Football and track coach Hamline U., 1958-62; research fellow U. Minn., 1963-66; asst. prof. geology U. S.D., 1967-70, asso. prof., 1970-72, chmn. dept. geology, 1968-72, chmn. dept. physics, 1971-72; dir. Ross Ice Shelf Project, U. Nebr., Lincoln, 1972-75, vice chancellor for research and grad. studies, prof. geology, 1977—; dir. div. Polar Programs, NSF, Washington, 1975-77. Served to 1st lt. U.S. Army, 1954-56. Recipient Antarctic Service medal, 1964, Distinguished Service award NSF, 1977, Ernie Gunderson award for service to amateur athletics S.D. AAU, 1972. Fellow Geol. Soc. Am.; mem. Antarctican Soc., Arctic Inst. N.Am., Am. Quaternary Assn., Am. Polar Soc., Am. Assn. Higher Edn., Sigma Xi. Lutheran. Home: 7720 N Hazelwood Dr Lincoln NE 68510 Office: Room 411 Adminstrn Bldg U Nebr Lincoln NE 68588

RUTH, FRANKLIN WILLIAM, JR., mfr. metal cutting tools; b. Dayton, Ohio, Oct. 14, 1917; s. Frank William and Florence U. (Iobst) R.; B.A., Pa. State Coll., 1939; m. Pearl Showers, Mar. 23, 1940; children—Betsy Ann (Mrs. Derle M. Snyder), Pamela Jane, Franklin William III. Supr. bookkeeper Pa. Treasury dept., 1942; sr. accountant Main & Co., C.P.A.'s Harrisburg, Pa., 1942-44; chief accounting officer Reiff & Nestor, Co., Lykens, Pa., 1944-46, sec., dir., 1946—, gen. mgr., 1951—, treas., 1965—; sec. dir., gen. mgr. Medco Developing Co. Inc., Lykens, 1955—, treas., 1965—; sec., dir., gen. mgr. Medco Process Inc., Lykens, 1957—, treas., 1965—; dir., sec., mem. exec. com. Miners Bank, Lykens; treas. New Eng. Tap Co. Inc., 1967—, also dir.; dir., mem. exec. com. Capital Blue Cross, Harrisburg. Trustee, Pa. State U., 1956-63; sec., dir. Nestor Charitable Found., 1953—, treas., 1965—; sec., dir. Mary Margaret Nestor Found., 1953—, treas., 1965—; chmn. Upper Dauphin Area Sch. Authority, 1972—. Mem. N.A.M., Nat. Soc. Pub. Accountants, Am. Soc. Tool and Mfg. Engrs. Methodist. Mason (Shriner). Home: 422 S 2d St Lykens PA 17048 Office: Reiff & Nestor Co Reiff and West St Lykens PA 17048

RUTH, JAMES MERLE, lawyer, brewery exec.; b. Milw., Dec. 15, 1920; s. James Joseph and Josephine Ruby (Second) R.; Ph.B., U. Wis., 1947, J.D., 1949; m. Mary Claire Hymel, Sept. 14, 1946; children—Mary Patricia, Joan Eileen, James Robert, Nancy Ann. Admitted to Wis. bar, 1950, Ill. bar, 1964, U.S. Supreme Ct. bar, 1964; partner firm, Ashland, Wis., 1949-58; gen. counsel, sec. St. Croix Corp., Park Falls, Wis., 1959-62; with Libby-McNeill-Libby Co., Chgo., 1963-73, v.p., gen. counsel, sec., 1970-72, v.p. adminstr., 1972-73; sec. Joseph Schlitz Brewing Co., Milw., 1973—; dir. Dunkley Co., C & D Foods, Inc., Geyser Peak Winery, Inc., Florida Groves, Inc., Murphys Products, Inc. Served with U.S. Army, 1942-45. Mem. Am. Bar Assn., Wis. Bar Assn., Ill. Bar Assn., Am. Soc. Corp. Secs. Club: Milw. Athletic. Home: 11427 N Saint James Ln Mequon WI 53092 Office: 235 W Galena St Milwaukee WI 53212

RUTHENBERG, DONALD BURTON, coll. pres.; b. Akron, Ohio, Jan. 7, 1930; s. Kans. Henry Alfred and Delcie May (McDonal) R.; B.A., Baldwin-Wallace Coll., Berea, Ohio, 1953; M.S.T., Iliff Sch. Theology, Denver, 1956; M.A., U. So. Calif., Los Angeles, 1958; Ph.D. in Health Edn., Student Personnel Services, U. Denver, 1961; m. Janet Elizabeth Payne, Aug. 28, 1954; children—Donnel Louise, Charlene Kay, Janet Lynn, Brian Charles, Mark Edward. Asst. prof. sociology, psychology Glendale (Calif.) Coll., 1955-58; dean men Baldwin-Wallace Coll., 1958-61 dean student Dakota Wesleyan U., Mitchell, S.D., 1961-63; asso. dean Ill. Wesleyan U., Bloomington, 1963-68; dir. instl. studies, research Central States Coll. Assn., Bloomington, 1965-68; v.p. student affairs, instl. studies U. Redlands (Calif.), 1968-71; dir. ednl. research, program devel. Ottawa (Kans.) U., 1971-72; pres. Southwestern Coll., Winfield, Kans., 1972—. Active Boy Scouts Am.; exec. bd., vice-chmn. YMCA, Wichita, Kans. Mem. Kans. Cavalry, Winfield C. of C. Rotarian. Home: 110 College St Winfield KS 67156 Office: 100 College St Southwestern Coll Winfield KS 67156

RUTHERFORD, DAVID ROSS, JR., educator; b. Altus, Okla., Mar. 24, 1931; s. David Ross and Jewel (Eley) R.; B.A., U. Okla., 1953, M.A., 1954; Ph.D., Northwestern U., 1958; children—Melissa Kay, David Ross III. With Okla. Cerebral Palsy Inst., 1953-54, Ill. Assn. Crippled, 1955-56; mem. faculty Northwestern U., 1956—, prof. speech pathology, 1964—, chmn. dept. communicative disorders, 1966-78; cons. Center Learning Disorders, Evanston Hosp. Mem. profl. adv. com. United Cerebral Palsy Chgo. Mem. Am., Ill. speech and hearing assns., Am. Acad. Cerebral Palsy and Developmental Medicine. Author: (with H. Westlake) Speech Therapy for the Cerebral Palsied, 1961, Cleft Palate, 1966. Home: 2726 Central St Evanston IL 60201 Office: 2299 Sheridan Rd Evanston IL 60201

RUTHERFORD, F(LOYD) JAMES, govt. adminstr.; b. Stockton, Calif., July 11, 1924; s. James A. and Agnes (Dennison) R.; A.B., U. Calif., Berkeley, 1947; M.A., Stanford U., 1949; Ed.D., Harvard U., 1962; m. Barbara Webster, Oct. 27, 1945; children—Constance, Stephen, Jeffrey, Norman. Tchr. sci., head sci. dept. secondary schs., Calif., 1949-60; sci. cons., dir. sci.-humanities curriculum project San Mateo Union High Sch. Dist., 1961-64; from asst. prof. to asso. prof. edn. Harvard Grad. Sch. Edn., 1964-71, exec. dir. Harvard Project Physics, 1964-71; prof., chmn. sci. edn. dept. N.Y. U., 1971-77, dir. Project City Scis., 1971-77; asst. dir. NSF, Washington, 1977—; cons. in field. Served with USNR, 1943-46. Ford Found. fellow, 1954. Mem. Nat. Sci. Tchrs. Assn. (pres. 1974), AAAS, Am. Assn. Physics Tchrs., Assn. Edn. Tchrs. of Sci., History Sci. Soc., Nat. Sci. Suprs. Assn., Am. Edn. Research Assn. Co-author books in field. Co-producer films: People and Particles, The World of Enrico Fermi, 1968. Home: 2126 Connecticut Ave NW Washington DC 20008 Office: Sci Edn NSF Washington DC 20550

RUTHERFORD, JACK DOW, mfg. co. exec.; b. Greenland, Ark., Oct. 5, 1933; s. James Adolph and Leslie (Williams) R.; grad. Wayne State U., 1954; M.B.A., Mich. State U., 1978; m. Marilyn Pagett, Mar. 26, 1952; children—Barbara, Lori. With Ford Motor Co., 1952-78, plant mgr., Romeo, Mich., to 1978; sr. v.p. agrl. equipment N.Am. ops. Internat. Harvester Co., Chgo., 1978—; bd. dirs. Steiger Corp. Pres. Antwerp Internat. Sch. Bd., 1971-75. Mem. Soc. Automotive Engrs. Methodist. Clubs: Birch Wood Farms Country (Harbor Springs, Mich.); Masons. Office: International Harvester Co 401 N Michigan Ave Chicago IL 60611

RUTHERFORD, JAMES J., holding co. exec.; b. Syracuse, N.Y., Aug. 18, 1929; s. Edward Cooper and Alma Louise (Finster) R.; B.S. in Bus. Adminstrn., Syracuse U., 1962; m. Marilyn Jean Zitzow, June 11, 1955; children—James J., David Mark, Dwight Steven. With Crouse-Hinds Co., Syracuse, 1947-66, mgr. acctg., 1955-57, controller-mgr. Mexican plant, 1959-60, chief fin. officer, 1962-64, v.p., 1964-66; chief exec. officer Financial Execs. Inst., N.Y.C., 1966-69, mgr. dir., 1966-67, sec., 1967-69; exec. v.p. Giffen Industries, Inc., Miami, Fla., 1970-71; v.p. Blount, Inc., Montgomery, Ala., 1971-77, chief fin. officer and treas., 1971-74, group exec. officer, 1974-77; pres., chief exec. officer Rutherford & Assos. Inc., Montgomery, 1977—; dir. Pa. Engring. Corp., 1977—, Birdsboro Corp., Pa., 1978—. Chmn. fin. com. Dalraida United Meth. Ch., 1979—. Mem. Soc. for Advancement Mgmt. (Profl. Mgmt. award 1979, 1st pres. Montgomery area chpt. 1976-77), Am. Mgmt. Assn., Nat. Assn. Accts. (pres. Syracuse chpt. 1963-64, nat. v.p. 1966-67), NAM, Newcomen Soc., Montgomery Mus. of Fine Arts, Beta Alpha Psi. Republican. Methodist. Clubs: Montgomery Country, Capital City, Masons, Shriners.

RUTHERFORD, JAMES WILLIAM, mayor; b. Flint, Mich., Apr. 23, 1925; s. Harry Elwood and Isabelle Rachel (Leake) R.; B.S. in Police Adminstrn., Mich. State U., 1960, M.A., 1964; m. Dorothy Marie Petyak, May 17, 1947 (dec.); children—Marcia Rutherford Atchison, Michelle Marie, Michael James, James Andrew; m. 2d, Betty J. Merrell, 1975. Mem. Flint Police Dept., 1948—, line insp., 1967, chief police, 1967-75; dep. city mgr., City of Flint, 1963, mayor, 1975—; owner Rutherford & Assocs., Cons., Flint; tchr. Flint Community Coll.; guest lectr. in field. Chmn. Flint Anti-poverty Program, 1966; mem. Mich. Police Hall of Fame Com.; vice-chmn. Flint Manpower Devel. Com.; mem. citizens study com. Flint Bd. Edn.; mem. law enforcement adv. com. Ferris (Mich.) State Coll., 1970-71; chmn. Downtown Devel. Authority, Econ. Devel. Commn. Flint; mem. Flint Area Conf. Inc. Served with USNR, 1945-47. Recipient Reverence for Law award, Fraternal Order Eagles, 1968; Golden Deeds award, Flint Exchange Club, 1969; J. Edgar Hoover award, Ridge Homes, 1973. Mem. Internat. (sgt. at arms, chmn. membership com. 1973; named 1 of 10 outstanding police officers 1966), Mich. (dir. 1969), Saginaw Valley, Genessee County (pres.) assns. chiefs police, Pi Alpha, Phi Kappa Phi. Methodist. Club: Masons, K.P., Old Newsboys of Flint. Contbr. for manuals in field. Home: 1713 Chelsea Circle Flint MI 48503 Office: Office of the Mayor City Hall 1101 S Saginaw St Flint MI 48502

RUTHERFORD, JOHN SHERMAN, III (JOHNNY), profl. race car driver; b. Coffeyville, Kans., Mar. 12, 1938; s. John Sherman and Mary Henrietta (Brooks) R.; student Tex. Christian U., 1956; m. Betty Rose Hoyer, July 7, 1963; children—John Sherman, Angela Ann. Profl. race car driver, 1959—; driver super-modified race cars, sprint cars, stock cars, midgets, sports cars, and formula 5000; winner 19 championship car races in U.S. Auto Club: winner Indianapolis 500, 1974, 76, second place, 1975; set new world's record for stock cars, Daytona Beach, Fla., 1963; set record at Indpls. 500, 1973; U.S. Auto Club Nat. Sprint Car Champion, 1965; host TV show The Racers; race commentator NBC; rep. for Car Quest Auto Parts, Central Ind. Oldsmobile Dealers, Minit Lube; mem. championship auto racing teams; appeared in numerous TV commercials; lectr. in field. Hon. state chmn. Am. Cancer Soc., Tex.; bd. dirs. Ft. Worth Kidney Assn.; appeared in TV and radio pub. services messages for Nat. Safety Council, Calif. Hwy. Patrol, U.S. Marines, Muscular Dystrophy Assn. Named Fort Worth Newsmaker of Yr., 1974; Driver of Yr., Sport Mag., 1976; Driver of Yr., Am. Sports Writers and Broadcasters, 1974; recipient Jim Clark award, 1969, Jim Malloy award, 1974, Eddie Sachs award, 1975, Extra Mile award, 1973; chosen for Internat. Race of Champions, 1974, 76, 77, 78, 79. Mem. Fedn. Internat. Automobile, Internat. Motors Sports Assn., Exptl. Aircraft Assn., Warbirds of Am., Confederate Air Force, Internat. Aerobatic Club, League Auto Racing (sec., bd. dirs.), Nat. Rifle Assn. Baptist. Clubs: Lions, Diamond Oaks Country, Shady Oaks Country. . *I am a firm believer in the fact that a person can do anything in this world he or she wants to as long as you have desire. People have to set goals, things to achieve. No one ever remembers who finished second.*

RUTHERFORD, PAUL HARDING, physicist; b. Shipley, Yorkshire, Eng., Jan. 22, 1938; s. Joseph William and Annie (Harding) R.; came to U.S., 1965, naturalized, 1976; B.A., Cambridge (Eng.) U., 1959, M.A., 1963, Ph.D., 1963; m. Audrey Jones Irvine, Oct. 31, 1959; children—Andrea Christine, Julia Irvine. Research asso. Princeton (N.J.) U. Plasma Physics Lab., 1962-63, mem. research staff, 1965-68, research physicist, 1968-71, sr. research physicist, 1971—, head theoretical div., 1972—, dep. asso. dir. for research, 1978—; research asso. U.K. Atomic Energy Authority Culham (Berkshire, Eng.) Lab., 1963-65; lectr. astrophys. scis. Princeton U. Fellow Am. Phys. Soc. Mem. bd. asso. editors Physics of Fluids, 1973-75. Home: 192 Bertrand Dr Princeton NJ 08540 Office: Plasma Physics Lab PO Box 451 Princeton NJ 08540

RUTHRUFF, CLIFFORD NEIL, wholesale grocery exec.; b. Seattle, May 24, 1933; s. Neil Alvin and Katheryn Marie (Andersen) R.; grad. U. Wash., 1960; m. June 12, 1975; children—Jill, Brian, Kim, Eric. Vice-pres. fin. Associated Grocers, Inc., Seattle. Served with USAF, 1950-54. Mem. Wash. C.P.A.'s Soc., Fin. Execs. Inst. Republican. Lutheran. Office: 3301 S Norfolk Seattle WA 98124

RUTKIN, SEYMOUR, architect; b. Weehawken, N.J., Oct. 22, 1927; s. Herman Irving and Dora (Oltarsh) R.; B.S. in Architecture, Ill. Inst. Tech., 1949; certificate arts and architecture, Cooper Union. Apprentice, R.M. Schindler, architect, Los Angeles; one man show projected designs Peter Cooper Gallery, N.Y.C., 1957; presented new shell designs and theories World Conf., San Francisco, 1962, Internat. Congress IASS, Mexico City, 1967, Internat. Colloquim, Madrid, 1969, Internat. Symposium, Beirut, Lebanon, 1971; prin. Works include schs., hotels, 42 story office bldg., dormitories, interiors. Schweinburg scholar Cooper Union; recipient Art in Am.-New Talent USA award, 1959. Asso. mem. Internat. Assn. Shell Structures. Contbr. articles to profl. jours. Address: 445 E 65th St New York NY 10021

RUTLAND, GEORGE PATRICK, banker; b. Tifton, Ga., Sept. 4, 1932; s. George Patrick and Peggy (Roberts) R.; B.B.A., Pace Coll. N.Y., 1961; postgrad. Stonier Sch. of Banking, Rutgers U., 1962-64; m. Dawn Mary O'Neill, Jan. 2, 1954; children—Michael, Kathleen, Dawn, Mary, Thomas. With Citicorp, N.Y.C., 1954-75, sr. v.p. corp. services, 1970-73, exec. v.p. Advance Mortgage subs, 1973-75; sr. v.p. domestic br. adminstrn. Crocker Nat. Bank, San Francisco, 1975—, sr. v.p. ops, 1977-78, exec. v.p., cashier, 1978—. Served with USN, 1950-53. Mem. Los Angeles C. of C., Los Angeles Hdqrs. Assn., Am. Bankers Assn., Bank Adminstrn. Inst. Republican. Roman Catholic. Clubs: Wilshire Country, Jonathan (Los Angeles). Home: 7220 Avenida Altisima Rancho Palos Verdes CA 90274 Office: Crocker National Bank 611 W 6th St Los Angeles CA 90017

RUTLAND, ROBERT ALLEN, educator, historian; b. Okmulgee, Okla., Oct. 1, 1922; s. Stanley Allen and Beatrice (Newman) R.; B.A., U. Okla., 1947; M.A., Cornell U., 1950; Ph.D., Vanderbilt U., 1953; m. Peggy Marchant, Sept. 6, 1947; children—Mary Elizabeth, Nancy Allen. Reporter, U.P., 1947-48; research asso. Hist. Soc. Iowa, 1952-54; mem. faculty U. Calif. at Los Angeles, 1954-60, 61-69; coordinator bicentennial programs Library of Congress, 1969-71; prof. U. Va., 1971—; Fulbright lectr. Innsbruck (Austria) U., 1960-61. Served with AUS, 1943-46. Mem. Orgn. Am. Historians, Am. Antiquarian Soc., Phi Beta Kappa, Kappa Sigma, Sigma Delta Chi. Democrat. Unitarian. Author: Golden Hurricane, 1953; Birth of the Bill of Rights, 1955; George Mason, Reluctant Statesman, 1961; Ordeal of the Constitution (Silver medal Commonwealth Club San Francisco 1967); The Newsmongers, 1973; Madison's Alternatives, 1975; George Mason and the War for Independence, 1976; The Democrats: from Jefferson to Carter, 1979. Editor: Papers of George Mason, 3 vols., 1970, Papers of James Madison, 1971—. Home: 236 Wellington Dr Charlottesville VA 22901

RUTLEDGE, GENE PRESTON, energy consultant; b. Spartanburg, S.C., Dec. 3, 1925; s. Gene Preston and Louise (Inman) R.; student Clemson, 1944-45; B.S., Wofford Coll., 1946, Sc.D. (hon.), 1971; M.S. (Fulton-Sylphon fellow), U. Tenn., 1948; postgrad. Ohio U., 1955, U. Pitts., 1958; m. Mary Louise Orr, Apr. 28, 1950; children—Edward, Preston, Leigh, Erin. Chemist, project engr. Union Carbide Nuclear Co., Oak Ridge, 1948-54; supr. engr. Goodyear Atomic Corp., Waverly, Ohio, 1954- 56; supr. physics, math. Naval Reactors Facility Submarine Project, Westinghouse Electric Corp., Idaho Falls, Idaho, 1956-63, supr. analysis and test, 1963-67; exec. dir. Office Nuclear Energy Devel., Idaho Nuclear Energy Commn., Idaho Falls, 1967-76; energy cons. Alaska Energy Office, Office of Gov., Anchorage, 1976—; research dir., owner Pacific Polar Rims, 1978—; tech. dir. Resource Devel. Council for Alaska, Inc., 1978—; lectr. U. Alaska, 1978—, Alaska Pacific U., 1978—; bd. dirs. Western Interstate Nuclear Compact, 1969-76. Research and thesis adviser U. Idaho. Mem. Am. Chem. Soc., Am. Inst. Chem. Engrs., Am. Nuclear Soc., Sigma Xi. Co-author: (play) D. Boon 1776-War Has Two Sides, 1976; also report Alaska's Energy Resources, 4 vols., 1977; editor: Nuclear Engineering, Par XII. 1965; contbr. papers to profl. jours. Home: 6930 Oakwood Dr Anchorage AK 99507 Office: 447 W 7th St Anchorage AK 99501

RUTLEDGE, HENRY TRENAMAN, former banker; b. Glencoe, Minn., May 27, 1912; s. Henry B. and Eva (Trenaman) R.; grad. Stonier Grad. Sch. Banking; m. Helen Raichert, Oct. 29, 1938; children—Lynn (Mrs. John Swon), Anne. With Northwestern Nat. Bank of Mpls., 1929-65, exec. v.p., 1957-65, also dir.; pres., dir. Northwest Bancorp., Mpls., 1965-71, chmn. bd., chief exec. officer, 1971-77, now ret.; dir. Northwest Bancorp., McQuay-Perfex, Inc., No. States Power Co. Clubs: Minneapolis, Minikahda (Mpls.). Home: 5 Orchard Ln Minneapolis MN 55436 Office: 1150 Northwestern Bank Bldg Minneapolis MN 55402

RUTLEDGE, IVAN CATE, educator; b. White Pine, Tenn., Dec. 24, 1915; s. Wiley B. and Tamsey (Cate) R.; B.A., Carson Newman Coll., 1934; M.A., Duke, 1940, LL.B., 1946; LL.M., Columbia, 1952; m. Carroll Burrage, July 24, 1951; children—Ann Elaine, Thomas Carroll. Tchr. pub. schs., Cleveland, Tenn., 1934-37, Cuthbert, Ga., 1937-39; high sch. prin., 1938-39; jr. examiner Bur. Budget, Washington, 1942-43; admitted to Ga. bar, 1946, Wash. State bar, 1951, Ohio bar, 1966; asst. prof. law Mercer U., 1946-47; asst. prof. law U. Wash., 1947-51, asso. prof., 1951-53, prof., 1953-54; prof. law Ind. U., 1954-63; prof. law Ohio State U., Columbus, 1963—, dean Law Sch., 1965-70. Vis. prof. law U. Ark., George Washington U., U. N.C., U. Queensland. Bd. dirs. Nat. Consumers League, 1958—. Mem. Am., Ohio, Columbus bar assns., Am. Law Inst., Nat. Acad. Arbitrators, Order of Coif, Pi Gamma Mu. Home: 444 Schreyer Pl Columbus OH 43214

RUTLEDGE, JAMES ALBERT, educator; b. Canton, Ohio, Jan. 9, 1917; s. James Alexander and Margaret (Buxton) R.; B.S., Mt. Union Coll., Alliance, Ohio, 1939; M.A., Ohio State U., 1946, Ph.D., 1954; m. Margaret Jane Rohrbacher, June 20, 1941; children—James Paul, David Eric, Robert William, Margaret Jane. Tchr. sci. Gnadenhutten (Ohio) High Sch., 1939-42, Auburn (Ohio) Twp. schs., 1946-47; local exec. head Wayne (Ohio) Twp. Schs., 1947-50; instr. Ohio State U., 1950-53; mem. faculty U. Nebr., 1953-73, prof. secondary edn., 1959-73, asst. dean Grad. Coll., 1968-72, asso. dean, 1972-73; prof. leadership and edn. policy studies, dean Grad. Sch., No. Ill. U., DeKalb, 1974—. Adviser Ednl. Policies Commn., Washington, 1963-66. Mem. grad. council U. Nebr., 1959-64, 66-67. Served to capt. USAAF, 1942-46; PTO. Fellow AAAS (chmn. sect. Q, 1965, pres. acad. conf. 1966, program chmn. acad. conf. 1967, nat. v.p., 1965); mem. Nat. Sci. Tchrs. Assn. (program chmn. 1964, bd. dirs. 1964-68), Nebr. Acad. Scis. (pres. 1960-61, co-dir. vis. scientist program 1959-67, sec. jr. acad. 1953-69), Nat. Soc. for Study Edn., Nat. Assn. Research Sci. Teaching, Am. Ednl. Research Assn., Ill. Acad. Sci., Phi Sigma, Phi Kappa Tau, Phi Delta Kappa. Republican. Methodist. Contbr. articles in field. Office: Altgeld Hall Northern Ill U DeKalb IL 60115

RUTLEDGE, JOHN WILLIAM, watch co. exec.; b. Eureka, Calif., Mar. 12, 1923; s. William Eugene and Ellen Agnes (Jordan) R.; B.S., Northwestern U., 1943; M.B.A., Harvard U., 1947; m. Mary Jo McKinley, Nov. 23, 1951; children—Ellen, John William, Amy. Salesman, Lahey Fargo & Co., 1947-48; asst. controller Lehigh Coal & Navigation Co., 1948-54; sr. v.p., dir. Xerox Corp., Stamford, Conn., 1954-71; sr. v.p. home furnishings group, dir. Magnavox Co., N.Y.C., 1971-73; pres., dir. Bulova Watch Co., N.Y.C., 1973-79; dir. Bankers Nat. Life Ins. Co., Security Ins. Group, Hartford, Conn., Nat. Aviation & Tech. Corp., Orion Capital Corp., K.C.R. Corp., Hartford, Teleresources, Inc., Aladdin Industries, Nashville. Served to lt. USNR. Mem. Sigma Alpha Epsilon. Clubs: Harvard, N.Y. Athletic (N.Y.C.). Home: 127 Dunning Rd New Canaan CT 06840 also 823 S County Rd Palm Beach FL

RUTLEDGE, PHILIP CASTEEN, cons. engr.; b. Champaign, Ill., Feb. 17, 1906; s. George and Rella (Casteen) R.; S.B., Harvard, 1927, Sc.D., 1939; S.M., Mass. Inst. Tech., 1933; D.Eng. (hon.), Purdue U., 1957; m. Dorothy Loomis, June 16, 1934 (dec. 1973); children—John Loomis, Cecily; m. 2d, Catherine P. Brobston, Mar. 29, 1975. Field engr. on constrn., Barney-Ahlers Constrn. Co. N.Y., 1928-29; structural designer, Stone & Webster Engring. Co., Boston, 1929-31; instr. soil mechanics, Grad. Sch. Engring., Harvard, 1933-37; asso. prof. and prof., soil mechanics, Purdue U., 1937-43; prof. civil engring., Tech. Inst. Northwestern U., Evanston, Ill., 1943-52; chmn. dept. civil engring., 1947-52; cons. engr., partner Mueser, Rutledge, Wentworth & Johnston and predecessor firm, N.Y.C., 1952-76. Cons. bd. consultants on airfield pavements, Office Chief of Engrs., U.S. Army, 1943-57; chmn. bd. cons. on earth dams Cal. Dept. Water Resources, 1963-74; tech. asso. Atlantic-Pacific Interoceanic Canal Study Commn., 1965-70; cons. heavy foundations and dams. Treas. Internat. Conf. on Soil Mechanics, Cambridge, Mass., 1936; chmn. Edn. Conf. on Soil Mechanics, Purdue U., 1940; chmn. U.S. Nat. Com. on Soil Mechanics, 1947-48; mem. AEC Plowshare Adv. Com., 1959-71. Mem. Nat. Acad. Engring., ASCE, Am. Inst. Cons. Engrs., Am. Geophys. Inst., The Moles, Boston Soc. C.E., Sigma Xi, Phi Kappa Sigma. Recipient War Dept. Certificate of Appreciation for services during World War II. Congregationalist. Clubs: Harvard, Engineers (N.Y.); Wee Burn (Darien, Conn.). Contbr. tech. articles to Proceedings ASCE. Home: Norfolk CT 06058 also Naples FL 33940

RUTLEDGE, WILLIAM ALVIN, mfg. co. exec.; b. St. Louis, Aug. 16, 1924; s. Alvin T. and Gladys M. (Koupal) R.; B.S.E.E., U. Mo.-Rolla, 1946; hon. degree, U. Mo.-Columbia, 1976; m. Katherine Veronica Krutz, July 1, 1950; children—William Michael, Robert Kevin, Richard Allen, Kimberly Ann. With Gen. Electric Co., Fort Wayne, Ind., 1946-74; group v.p. Emerson Electric Co., St. Louis, 1974-76, exec. v.p. ops., 1976-77, vice chmn., 1977—, also dir. Served with U.S. Army, 1948-49. Patentee in field. Office: 8100 W Florissant Ave Saint Louis MO 63136

RUTSCH, ALEXANDER, painter, sculptor; b. Austria, Aug. 30, 1930; s. Alexander George and Cinaide (Britano) R.; came to U.S., 1968; m. Katherine Stolow, Dec. 7, 1968; children—Alexandra, Vera-Nike, Nina Elizabeth. One-man shows: Galerie Vendome, Belgium, 1965, Austrian Cultural Instn., N.Y.C., 1965, French Cultural Isntn., Vienna, 1951, Galerie Matignon, Paris, 1957; group shows: Grand Palais, Paris, 1966, Salon Aristique Internationale de Sceaux, Paris, 1966, Avanti Galleries, N.Y.C., 1974, 75, represented in permanent collections: Albertina Municipal Mus., Mus. Lower Austria, Vienna, Belvedere, Vienna, Mus. Modern Art, Paris, Queen Fabiola Belgium. Recipient Bronze plaque City of Paris, 1958. Home: 222 Highbrook Ave Pelham NY 10803

RUTSTEIN, DAVID DAVIS, physician, educator; b. Wilkes-Barre, Pa., Feb. 5, 1909; s. Harry and Nellie (Davis) R.; B.S., Harvard U., 1930, M.D., 1934; m. Mazie E. Weissman, Feb. 22, 1935; children—Catherine Ann, David Davis; m. 2d, Ruth E. Rickel, Aug. 11, 1951 (dec. 1978); m. 3d, Beverly Bennett, Nov. 3, 1979. Asst. in bacteriology, research fellow pediatrics Harvard Med. Sch., 1936-47, prof. preventive medicine and head dept., 1947-69, Ridley Watts prof., 1966-75, emeritus, 1975—; Distinguished Physician VA, 1976—; vis. inst. lectr. Mass. Inst. Tech., 1970-71; asst. prof. medicine Albany Med. Coll., 1940-43; asso. vis. physician Bellevue Hosp. 1943-47; cons. preventive medicine Beth Israel Hosp., Boston Hosp. for Women, Mass. Gen. Hosp., Peter Bent Brigham Hosp.; physician Children's Hosp.; cons. physician Mass. Eye and Ear Infirmary; med. cons. pneumonia N.Y. State Dept. Health, Albany, 1937-40, chief cardiac bur., 1940-42, nat. dir. gas protection sect. Office Civilian Def., Washington, 1942-43; dep. commr. health N.Y.C. Dept. Health, 1943-46, dir. bur. labs., 1943-45; med. dir. Am. Heart Assn., Am. Council Rheumatic Fever, N.Y.C., 1946-47; chmn. U.S.-U.K. Coop. Rheumatic Fever Study, 1950-65; chmn. Internat. Conf. Hemolytic Streptococcus in Rheumatic Fever, Internat. Children's Centre, Paris, 1956; chmn. expert com. on rheumatic diseases WHO, Geneva, 1956, mem. expert com. cardiovascular diseases and hypertension, 1958, chmn. expert com. on prevention of rheumatic fever, 1966; corp. vis. com., med. dept. Mass. Inst. Tech., 1964-70; mem. nat. adv. council Peace Corps, 1965-69; com. on interplay of engring. with biology and medicine Nat. Acad. Engring., 1967-73; mem. spl. med. adv. group VA, 1968-73; governing bd. Santé, Centre National de la Recherche Scientifique (CNRS), France. Decorated chevalier Legion of Honor (France); recipient Benjamin Franklin Mag. award, 1957; Jubilee medal Swedish Med. Soc., 1966. Fellow Am. Acad. Arts and Scis. (council); mem. Academie Nationale de Médecine (Paris) (corr.), Royal Soc. Medicine (London), Am. Heart Assn. (v.p., mem. exec. com.; Gold Heart award 1959), Am. Soc. Clin. Investigation, Am. Pub. Health Assn. (governing council), Am. Epidemiol. Soc. (pres. 1966-67), Sigma Xi, Alpha Omega Alpha. Clubs: Aesculapian, St. Botolph (Boston); Confrerie des Chevaliers du Tastevin. Author: Lifetime Health Record, 1958; The Coming Revolution in Medicine, 1967; (with Murray Eden) Engineering and Living Systems, 1970; Blueprint for Medical Care, 1974; also sci. papers. Home: 98 Winthrop St Cambridge MA 02138 Office: 10 Shattuck St Boston MA 02115

RUTSTEIN, DAVID W., lawyer, food co. exec.; b. N.Y.C., July 7, 1944; s. David and Mazie (Weissman) R.; B.A., U. Pa., 1966; J.D. with honors, George Washington U., 1969; m. Rena E. Rutstein, July 19, 1967; children—Sara E., Charles B. Admitted to Pa. bar, 1969, D.C. bar, 1969; dep. atty. gen. Pa., 1969-70; partner firm Danzansky, Dickey, Tydings, Quint & Gordon, Washington, 1970-78; v.p., gen. counsel Giant Food, Inc., Washington, 1978—. Bd. dirs. Washington Hebrew Home for Aged. Mem. Am. Bar Assn., D.C. Bar Assn. Jewish. Home: 7804 Cindy Ln Bethesda MD 20034 Office: Giant Food Inc Box 1804 Washington DC 20013

RUTSTEIN, STANLEY HAROLD, apparel retailing retailing exec.; b. Wilkes-Barre, Pa., July 1, 1941; s. Sydney D. and Bessie H. (Cohen) R.; student Wilkes Coll., 1959-61; grad. Advanced Mgmt. Program, Harvard U., 1975; divorced; children—Wendy Sue, Michael Scott, Lynne Elizabeth. Buyer, Barbara Lynn Stores, Inc., N.Y.C., 1961-63; buyer, then mdsg. mgr. Casual Corner div. U.S. Shoe Corp., Enfield, Conn., 1963-71, pres., 1971-76; pres., cons., dir. U.S. Shoe Corp., Cin., 1976-79; pres. Commonwealth Trading, Inc., Stoughton, Mass., 1979—. Mem. Young Pres.'s Orgn. Home: 5 Edmonds Rd Merriam Close Concord MA 01742 Office: 100 Campanelli Pkwy Stoughton MA 02072

RUTTAN, VERNON WESLEY, educator; b. Alden, Mich., Aug. 16, 1924; s. Ward W. and Marjorie Ann (Chaney) R.; B.A., Yale, 1948; M.A., U. Chgo., 1950, Ph.D., 1952; LL.D. (hon.), Rutgers U., 1978; m. Mabel Mayne Barone, July 30, 1945; children—Lia Marie, Christopher, Alison Elaine, Lore Megan. Economist, TVA, 1951-54; prof. agrl. econs. Purdue U., 1954-63; staff economist President's Council Econ. Advisers, 1961-63; economist Rockefeller Found., 1963-65; head dept. agrl. econs., U. Minn., 1965-70, prof. agrl. and applied econs. and econs., 1978—, dir. Econ. Devel. Center, 1970-73; pres. Agrl. Devel. Council, N.Y.C., 1973-77. Served with AUS, 1943-46. Fellow Am. Acad. Arts and Scis., Am. Agrl. Econs. Assn. (pres. 1971-72; Publ. award 1956, 57, 62, 66, 67, 71); mem. Council on Fgn. Relations. Author: The Economic Demand for Irrigated Acreage, 1965; (with Y. Hayami) Agricultural Development: An International Perspective, 1971; (with Hans Binswanger) Induced Innovation: Technology Institutions and Development, 1978. Home: 2381 Commonwealth Ave Saint Paul MN 55108 Office: U Minn Saint Paul MN 55108

RUTTENBERG, DERALD H., corp. exec.; b. Lafayette, Ind., Feb. 17, 1916; s. Joseph C. and Hattie Ruttenberg; B.A., U. Wis., 1937; LL.B., Yale, 1940; I.A., Harvard, 1943; m. Janet Kadesky, June 16, 1951; children—John Charles, Eric M., Katherine T., Hattie. Chmn. bd. Consol. Foundries and Mfg. Co., 1947-59; chmn. bd., pres. Josam Mfg. Co., 1959-62; chmn. bd. Ill. Iron & Bolt Co. (now Tinicum, Inc.), Chgo., 1961-71; chmn. bd. I-T-E Circuit Breaker Co., 1967-68, chmn. bd. I-T-E Imperial Corp. (merger I-T-E Circuit Breaker Co. and Imperial Eastman Corp.), 1968-73; pres., chief exec. officer Studebaker-Worthington, Inc., 1969-71, chmn., chief exec. officer, 1971—. Bd. dirs. Mt. Sinai Hosp. N.Y. Served with USAAF, 1943-45. Office: 885 2d Ave New York NY 10017

RUTTENBERG, JOSEPH, motion picture photographer; b. Russia, July 4, 1889; s. Frank D. and Miriam (Gelfland) R.; came to U.S., 1893; naturalized, 1910; ed. pub. schs.; m. Rose Wilson, Mar. 25, 1917; 1 dau., Virginia Ruttenberg Silver. News photographer Boston American, 1907-12; dir. photography Fox Films, N.Y.C., 1915-22, Paramount Pictures, N.Y.C., 1928-31, M.G.M. Studios, Los Angeles, 1935, now ret.; cinematographer Waterloo Bridge, The Great Waltz (Acad. award 1938), Gaslight, Mrs. Miniver (Acad. award 1942), Random Harvest, The Great Caruso, Madam Curie, Julius Caesar, Brigadoon, Dr. Jekyl and Mr. Hyde, Somebody Up There Likes Me (Acad. award 1956), Gigi (Acad. award 1958), numerous others. Fellow Soc. Motion Picture and TV Engrs.; mem. Am. Soc. Cinematographers, Acad. Motion Picture Arts and Scis. Home: 132 Spalding Dr Beverly Hills CA 90212

RUTTENBERG, STANLEY HARVEY, economist; b. St. Paul, Mar. 19, 1917; s. Charles and Fannie (Weinstein) R.; student Massanutten Mil. Acad., Woodstock, Va., 1929-33; B.S., U. Pitts., 1937; m. Gertrude Bernstein, Nov. 28, 1940; children—Joel, Ruth, Charles. Asst. to dir. Hull House, Chgo., 1938-39; with CIO, 1937-55, organizer and field rep. in Ohio Valley, Cin., 1937-38, asso. dir. research, Washington, 1939-48, dir. dept. edn. and research, 1948-55; dir. dept. research AFL-CIO, 1955-62; spl. asst. to sec. of labor, 1963-65, manpower adminstr., 1965-69, asst. sec. labor, manpower adminstr., 1966-69; pres. Stanley H. Ruttenberg Assos. Inc., 1969—. Mem. labor com. Nat. Planning Assn.; dir. Nat. Bur. Econ. Res., 1940-41, 48-62; exec. com. U.S. nat. commn. UNESCO, 1948-53, vice chmn., 1952 (spl. adviser to Am. del. 4th and 5th Internat. Confs., 1949, 50); del. to Internat. Labor Orgn. Conf., Geneva, 1952; dir. Resources for the Future, Inc.; pub. mem. Fgn. Service Selection Bd., 1950; mem. Presdl. Price Adv. Com., 1979—. Served as 1st lt. AUS, 1943-46, Okinawa, 1945-46. Mem. Am. Econ. Assn., Am. Statis. Assn., Indsl. Relations Research Assn. (exec. bd. 1953). Author: (with Jocelyn Gutchess) Manpower Challenge of the 1970s: Institutions and Social Change, 1970, The Federal-State Employment Service: A Critique, 1970. Home: 6310 Maiden Ln Bethesda MD 20034 Office: 1211 Connecticut Ave NW Washington DC 20036

RUTTER, FRANCES TOMPSON, publisher; b. Arlington, Mass., Apr. 12, 1920; d. Harold F. and Mildred F. (Wheeler) Tompson; A.B. magna cum laude, Pembroke Coll., Brown U., 1941; postgrad. Mt. Holyoke Coll., 1942-43; m. John H. Ottemiller, Mar. 24, 1943; children—Joan (Mrs. Daniel Cook), John Tompson; m. 2d, William D. Rutter, Oct. 26, 1970. Res. book librarian Brown U., 1941-42; annotator ship's papers John Carter Brown Library, Providence, 1943-44; librarian Sci. Service, Washington, 1944-45; partner Shoe String Press, Hamden, Conn., 1952-58; sec., treas. Shoe String Press, Inc., 1958-68, pres., treas., 1968-80, also dir., 1958—; sec.-treas., dir. Tompson-Malone, Inc., book mfrs., 1967-79; pres., dir. Tompson & Rutter, Inc., 1979—. Vice pres. class 1941 Pembroke Coll., 1967-73, 76—, pres., 1973-76, bequests and trust chmn., 1979—. Mem. Nat. Fedn. Ind. Businesses, Women's Nat. Book Assn., ALA, Yale Library Assos., ACLU (life), Am. Rock Garden Soc. (New Eng. chpt.), Nicholas Brown Soc., Phi Beta Kappa. Congregationalist. Home: PO Box 297 Grantham NH 03753 Office: Greensward Rd Grantham NH 03753

RUTTER, GEORGE WARREN, air force officer; b. San Francisco, May 17, 1927; s. Warren Cressman and Myra (McCoy) R.; B.S., U.S. Mil. Acad., 1948; M.S.E., U. Mich., 1959; m. Virginia Irene Viereck, June 10, 1959; children—Hollis E., Laura K. Joined U.S. Air Force, advanced through grades to maj. gen., 1978; comdr. 366th Tactical Fighter wing, Thailand, 1971-72; dir. maintenance Ogden Air Logistics Center, Hill AFB, Utah, 1973-74; insp. gen. Air Force Logistics Command, Wright-Patterson AFB, Ohio, 1974-75, vice comdr. Air Force Acquisitions-Logistics div., 1975-77; program mgr. electronic systems div. Air Force Systems Command, Hanscom AFB, Mass., 1977—. Decorated Legion of Merit with 2 oak leaf clusters, D.F.C., Air medal with 9 oak leaf clusters. Mem. Am. Def. Preparedness Assn. (pres. Dayton chpt. 1976-77), Soc. Logistics Engrs., Air Force Assn., Am. Forestry Assn. Republican. Episcopalian. Office: ESD/YW Hanscom AFB MA 01731

RUTTER, MARSHALL ANTHONY, lawyer; b. Pottstown, Pa., Oct. 18, 1931; s. Carroll Lennoxx and Dorothy Graham (Tagert) R.; student The Hill Sch., 1946-49, (English-Speaking Union fellow 1949) Radley Coll., 1949-50; B.A., Amherst Coll., 1954; J.D., U. Pa., 1959; m. Virginia Ann Hardy, Jan. 30, 1971; children—Deborah Frances, Gregory Russell, Theodore Thomas. Admitted to Calif. bar, 1960; asso. firm O'Melveny & Meyers, Los Angeles, 1959-65; asso. firm Flint & MacKay, 1965-67, partner, 1967-72; partner Rutter & Ebbert, Los Angeles, 1973—. Pres. Los Angeles Jr. C. of C. Arts Found., 1968. Bd. dirs. Los Angeles Master Chorale Music Assn., 1964—, v.p., 1966-78, pres., 1978—. Served with AUS, 1954-56. Mem. Am., Los Angeles County (various coms. and chmns.) bar assns., State Bar Calif., English-Speaking Union (pres. 1977—). Democrat. Episcopalian (sr. warden 1968-70). Club: University (Los Angeles). Home: 932 Longwood Ave Los Angeles CA 90019 Office: 1900 Ave of Stars Suite 2200 Los Angeles CA 90067

RUTTER, WILLIAM J., scientist, educator; b. Malad City, Idaho, Aug. 28, 1928; s. William H. and Cecelia (Dredge) R.; B.A., Harvard, 1949; M.A., U. Utah, 1950; Ph.D., U. Ill., 1952; m. Jacqueline Waddoups, Aug. 31, 1950 (div. Nov. 1969); children—William Henry II, Cynthia Susan; m. 2d, Virginia Alice Bourke, Oct. 3, 1971. USPHS postdoctoral fellow U. Wis., 1952-54, Nobel Inst., 1954-55; from asst. prof. to prof. biochemistry, dept. chemistry U. Ill., 1955-65; prof. biochemistry U. Wash., 1965-69; Hertzstein prof. biochemistry, chmn. dept. biochemistry and biophysics U. Calif. at San Francisco, 1969—; biochem. cons. Abbott Labs., 1958-75, USPHS Biochemistry and Nutrition Fellowship Panel, 1963-66; Cons. physiol. chemistry study sect. NIH, 1967-71; mem. basic sci. adv. exec. com. Nat. Cystic Fibrosis Research Found., 1969-74, chmn., 1972-74, pres.'s adv. council, 1974-75; exec. com. div. biology and agr. NRC, 1969-72; mem. developmental biology panel NSF, 1971-73; mem. biomed. adv. com. Los Alamos Sci. Lab., 1972-75, pres. Pacific Slope Biochem. Conf., 1972-73; mem. bd. sci. counselors Nat. Inst. Environ. Health Scis., 1976—; mem. adv. com. biology div. Oak Ridge Nat. Lab., 1976—; basic research adv. com. Nat. Found., 1976—; bd. dirs. Keystone Life Sci. Study Center, 1976—. Served with USNR, 1945. Guggenheim fellow, 1962-63. Mem. Am. Soc. Biol. Chemists (treas. 1970-76, mem. editorial bd. jour. 1970-75), Am Soc. Cell Biology, Am. Chem. Soc. (Pfizer award enzyme chemistry 1967), Am. Soc. Developmental Biology (pres. 1975-76). Asso. editor Jour. Exptl. Zoology, 1968-72; editor PAABS Revista, 1971-76, Jour. Cell Biology, Archives Biochemistry and Biophysics, 1978—; editorial bd. various jours. Home: 80 Everson St San Francisco CA 94131

RUTZ, DONALD EDWIN, advt. agency exec.; b. N.Y.C., Sept. 19, 1937; s. Edwin O. and Katherine E. (Merkle) R.; student Lake Forest Coll., 1954-57; B.S. in Econs., Columbia U., 1958; m. Rita M. Creen, Dec. 8, 1962; children—Carey Louise, Laura Ann, Donald Edwin, Robin Lynn. With network ops. dept. CBS, N.Y.C., 1958; broadcast account mgr. Leo Burnett Co., Inc., Chgo., 1959-61; account exec. Clinton E. Frank, Inc., Chgo., 1961-65, v.p., account supr., 1966-70, sr. v.p., 1970-73, exec. v.p., 1973-74, pres., 1974-79, also dir., chm. exec. com.; exec. v.p., partner Garfield-Linn & Co., Chgo., 1979—, also dir. Clubs: Chgo. Athletic, Burnham Park Yacht (Chgo.); Bull Valley Hunt (Woodstock, Ill.); Skokie Country (Glencoe, Ill.). Home: 803 Bluff St Glencoe IL 60022 Office: 875 N Michigan Ave Chicago IL 60611

RUUD, MILLARD HARRINGTON, lawyer, educator; b. Ostrander, Minn., Jan. 7, 1917; s. Mentor L. and Helma M. (Olson) R.; B.S. in Law, U. Minn., 1942, LL.B., 1947; m. Barbara W. Dailey, Aug. 28, 1943; children—Stephen D., Christopher O., Michael L. Admitted to Minn. bar, 1947, Tex. bar, 1956; asst. prof. law U. Kans., 1947-48; asso. prof. U. Tex., 1948-52, prof., 1952-78; asst. exec. dir. Tex. Legis. Council; exec. dir. Assn. Am. Law Schs., Washington, 1973—; mem. Tex. Commn. Uniform State Laws, 1967—; cons. legal edn. Am. Bar Assn., 1968-73; chmn. Law Sch. Admission Council, 1966-69. Mem. Tex., Am. bar assns., Am. Law Inst. Club: Cosmos. Home: 3416 Foothill Terr Austin TX 78731 also 2500 Q St NW Washington DC 20007 Office: One Dupont Circle NW Suite 370 Washington DC 20036

RUVOLO, FELIX, artist; b. N.Y.C., Apr. 28, 1912; s. Celestino and Mary (DeFranco) R.; student Art Inst., Chgo., 1930-33; m. Margaret Stancill, 1947; 1 son, Antonio Felix. Instr., Art. Inst., Chgo., 1944-47; asso. prof. U. Calif. at Berkeley, 1950-59; prof., 1959—, apptd. to Inst. Creative Arts, 1964, 71; represented art exhbns. since 1938; one-man shows: Durand Ruels, N.Y.C., 1947, De Young Mus., San Francisco, 1957, Poindexter Gallery, N.Y.C., 1958, 60, U. So. Calif., 1963, Jason Auer Gallery, San Francisco, 1970. Recipient Kearny Meml. prize Milw. Mus.; Broadus James Clark prize Art. Inst. Chgo., also William and Bertha Clusmann prize, 1942, William Gerstle prize, 1945; Bremer prize San Francisco Mus., 1942; Virginia Biennial (recommended for purchase), 1944; 2d prize Critics Show, Grand Central Galleries, N.Y.C., 1947, Gold medal Palace of Honor, San Francisco; Artist Council prize San Francisco Mus. Art, 1953; prize for painting San Francisco Mus. Art, 1958, 64; 6th ann. prize for drawing Graphics award, 1959, Richmond Art Center; Purchase award San Francisco Hall of Justice, 1967; others. Home: 78 Strathmore Dr Berkeley CA 94705 Office: Kroeber Hall U Calif Berkeley CA

RUZ, ALBERTO LHUILLIER, archeologist; b. Paris, Jan. 27, 1906; s. Alberto Ruz Mas and Luisa Lhuillier Barthelemy; M. Anthrop. Scis., Nat. Sch. Anthropology and History, Mexico D.F., Mex., 1943; D. Anthropology, Nat. Autonoma U. Mex., 1963; m. Celia Gutierrez Ibarra, July 16, 1966; children—Alberto, Jorge, Claudio. Prof., Nat. Sch. Anthropology and History, 1940-44, Nat. U. Mex., 1959-79; chief archeologist Nat. Inst. Anthropology and History, Maya area, 1949-58; dir. Nat. Mus. Anthropology, Mexico City, 1977—. French Govt. grantee, 1945-46. Mem. Sociedad Mexicana de Antropologia, Asociacion de Antropologos Mexicana, Societe des Americauistes (Paris), Societe des Americauistes (Swiss), Am. Anthrop. Assn. Author: Civilization of Ancient Mayas, 1957; costumbres funerarias de los Antiques Mayas, 1968; La Costa de Campeche en los tiempos prehispanicos, 1969; El Templo de Las Inscripciones Palenque, 1973; contbr. numerous articles to profl. jours. Home: 4426 Calzada Desierto Mexico 20 DF Mexico Office: Reforma y Gandhi Mexico DF Mexico

RUZIC, NEIL PIERCE, publisher, scientist, author; b. Chgo., May 12, 1930; s. Joseph Francis and Ida (Pierce) R.; student Loyola at Chgo., 1946-47; B.S. in Journalism, Psychology and Sci., Northwestern U., 1950; m. Carol W. Kalsbeek, Apr. 14, 1950; 1 son, David Neil. Corr., Costa Rica, Latin Am., 1949; writer with various newspapers including Michigan City (Ind.) News-Dispatch, 1950-52; dir. publs. IIT Research Inst., Chgo., 1954-58; founder Indsl. Research Inc., Beverly Shores, Ind., 1958, pres., editor, pub., 1958-73; founder Indsl. Research mag., 1958, and Oceanology mag., 1966; acquired Electro-Tech. mag., 1968; founder Neil Ruzic & Co., Chgo., 1973—; cons. to NASA, 1973-78; founder Island for Sci., Little Stirrup Cay, Bahamas, 1976—. A founder, bd. dirs. Nat. Space Inst. Served with AUS, 1952-54. Mem. IEEE (sr.), Am. Vacuum Soc., Sigma Delta Chi. Author: There's Adventure in Meteorology, 1958; There's Adventure in Civil Engineering, 1958; Stimulus, 1960; The Case for Going to the Moon, 1965; Where the Winds Sleep, 1970; Spinoff 1976, 1976; Island for Science, part 1, 1976, part 2, 1977. Inventor mag. inquiry system, lunar cryostat; patentee device for use on moon. Office: Island for Science Inc PO Box 527 Beverly Shores IN 46301 also Little Stirrup Cay Berry Islands Bahamas. *"Every major invention advances human life more significantly than treaties between nations or other political endeavors. And yet modern invention is anything but profound: it is primarily the combining of existing knowledge with off-the-shelf components."*

RUZICKA, FRANCIS FREDERICK, JR., radiologist, educator; b. Balt., June 30, 1917; s. Francis Frederick and Anne (Kaspar) R.; A.B. cum laude, Holy Cross Coll., Worcester, Mass., 1939; M.D., Johns Hopkins U., Balt., 1943; m. Margaret M. Kernan, May 31, 1941; children—Margaret M., Mary Frances, John F., Francis Frederick III, M. Therese, Joseph T. Intern, Univ. Hosp., Balt., 1943, resident in radiology, 1944-45; fellow Univ. Hosp., Mpls., 1948-49, instr. in radiology, 1949-50; dir. radiology St. Vincents Hosp. and Med. Center, N.Y.C., 1950-73; prof. radiology U. Wis., Madison, 1973-76; prof., chmn. dept. radiology U. Wis. Health Center, 1976—; asso. clin. prof. N.Y. U., 1950-73; acting chmn., clin prof. radiology N.J. Coll., Jersey City, 1964-67; cons. Nat. Acad. Scis., 1975-76. Served with M.C., AUS, 1945-47. Diplomate Am. Bd. Radiology. Fellow Am. Coll. Radiology; mem. Am. Roentgen Ray Soc., Radiol. Soc. N. Am., AMA, Wis. Med. Soc., N.Y. Acad. Scis., Soc. Gastrointestinal Radiology, Soc. Cardiovascular Radiology, Cath. Physicians Guild, N.Y. Roentgen Soc. (past pres.). Editor: With others) Vascular Roentgenology, 1964. Contbr. articles to profl. jours. Home: 5705 Cove Circle Monona WI 53716 Office: 1300 University Ave Madison WI 53706

RYALS, CLYDE DE LOACHE, educator; b. Atlanta, Dec. 19, 1928; s. Chester A. and Ruth C. (de Loache) R.; A.B., Emory U., 1947, M.A., 1949; Ph.D., U. Pa., 1957; m. Hildegard Thun Scheffey Ellerkmann, Sept. 4, 1971. Instr., U. Md., 1956-57; instr. U. Pa., Phila., 1957-60, asst. prof., 1960-64, asso. prof., 1964-69, prof. English, 1969-73, grad. chmn. dept. English, 1969-72; prof. English, Duke U., Durham, N.C., 1973—, chmn. dept. English, 1979—. Guggenheim fellow, 1972-73. Mem. Modern Lang. Assn., Am. Soc. for Aesthetics, Chi Phi. Democrat. Episcopalian. Author: Theme and Symbol in Tennyson's Poetry to 1850, 1964; From the Great Deep, 1967; Browning's Later Poetry, 1871-1889, 1975. Editor: Tennyson's Poems, Chiefly Lyrical, 1966; Mrs. Humphry Ward's Robert Elsmere, 1967; Nineteenth-Century Literary Perspectives, 1974; mem. editorial bd. Victorian Poetry, 1964—, South Atlantic Quar., 1975—. Contbr. articles profl. jours. Home: 1620 University Dr Durham NC 27707

RYAN, ALLAN A., business exec.; b. N.Y.C., July 4, 1903; s. Allan A. and Sarah (Tack) R.; student Canterbury Sch., New Milford, Conn., 1914-20; A.B., Yale, 1924; m. Janet Newbold, Feb. 6, 1929; children—Nancy Anne, Allan A.; m. 2d, Eleanor Barry, Jan. 19, 1937; m. 3d, Priscilla St. George, Aug. 5, 1941; 1 dau., Katherine Delano; m. 4th, Grace M. Amory, Dec. 13, 1950. Mem. N.Y. Curb Exchange, 1924-28, N.Y. Stock Exchange, 1930-32; dir. Royal Typewriter Co., Inc., 1932-54, chmn. bd., 1945-54; chmn. bd., dir. Royal McBee Corp. (merged with Litton Industries 1965), 1954-65; chmn. bd., dir. Kaysam Corp., Inc. (formerly Molded Latex Products, Inc.), 1941—. Mem. N.Y. State Senate from 28th Dist., 1938-42. Served to maj. AUS, 1943-45. Mem. Elihu, Alpha Delta Phi. Roman Catholic. Clubs:

Racquet and Tennis (N.Y.C.); Seminole (Palm Beach, Fla.); Creek (Locust Valley, N.Y.); The Honourable Co. Edinburgh Golfers (Gullane, Scotland). Home: 133 Wells Rd Palm Beach FL 33480

RYAN, CLAUDE, Can. politician; b. Montreal, Que., Can., Jan. 26, 1925; s. Henri-Albert and Blandine (Dorion) R.; student Coll. St. Croix, Montreal, 1937-44, Sch. Social Service, U. Montreal, 1944-46, Pontifical Gregorian U., Rome, 1951-52; m. Madeleine Guay, July 21, 1958; children—Paul, Monique, Therese, Patrice, Andre. Gen. sec. L'Action Catholique Canadienne, 1945-62; with Le Devoir, daily newspaper, Montreal, 1962-78, pub., 1964-78; mng. dir. Imprimerie Populaire Ltd., 1964-78; leader Liberal Party of Que., 1978--; mem. Que. Nat. Assembly from Argentevil, 1979—. Pres., Inst. Can. Edn. des Adultes, 1955-61; Leonard Brockington visitor Queen's U., Kingston, Ont., 1976. Recipient Human Relations award Can. Council Christian and Jews, 1966; named to Can. News Hall of Fame, 1968. Roman Catholic. Office: Que Liberal Party 460 Gilford St Montreal PQ H2J 1N3 Canada

RYAN, CORNELIUS MICHAEL, food and vending co. exec.; b. Chgo., July 25, 1933; s. Cornelius Anthony and Catherine (Hughes) R.; B.S.C., Loyola U., Chgo., 1955; m. Mary J. Murphy. C.P.A., Ill., 1958. With Peat, Marwick, Mitchell & Co., C.P.A.'s, Chgo., 1955-63; with Canteen Corp., Chgo., 1963-79, treas., 1966-73, v.p., 1973-79; v.p., treas. Trans World Corp., 1979—. Served with USNR, 1956-57. Home: 10 Ponderosa Dr Greenwich CT 06830 Office: Trans World Corp 605 3d Ave New York NY 10016

RYAN, CORNELIUS O'BRIEN, lawyer; b. Abilene, Tex., Oct. 15, 1917; s. William Cornelius and Joanna Genevieve (Morris) R.; B.A., Rice U., 1937; LL.B., So. Meth. U., 1940; m. Mary Anne Kelley, Mar. 24, 1942; children—Elisabeth (Mrs. David B. Goldstein), Robert C., Carl E., William E., Joseph W., Mary Louise. Admitted to Tex. Bar, 1940, since practiced in Houston; mem. firm Kelley, Ryan & Merrill, 1951—. Trustee, pres. Burkitt Found., 1963—. Served from ensign to lt. USNR, 1942-46. Mem. Am., Houston bar assns., Tex. State Bar, Am. Judicature Soc., Phi Beta Kappa, Phi Delta Theta, Phi Alpha Delta. Republican. Roman Catholic. Clubs: Houston, Serra (Houston). Home: 1508 Hyde Park Houston TX 77006 Office: 1400 Texas Commerce Bldg Houston TX 77002

RYAN, CORNELIUS THOMAS, investment co. exec.; b. N.Y.C., Nov. 14, 1931; s. John and Margaret (Brady) R.; B.C.S., U. Ottawa, 1953; M.B.A., U. Pa., 1957; m. Ellis Batchelder, Sept. 9, 1961; children—Christopher, Lisa, Cornelia. Asso., Arthur D. Little, Inc., Cambridge, Mass., 1957-63; with Eastman Dillon, Union Securities & Co., N.Y.C., 1963-65; pres. Randolph Computer Corp., Greenwich, Conn., 1965-74; pres. GTE New Ventures Corp., Stamford, Conn., 1974-77; gen. partner Cumberland Investment Group, N.Y.C., 1977-78; pres. AMR Internat., Inc., N.Y.C., 1978—; dir. Centennial Trust. Bd. dirs. Schuster Fund. Served with U.S. Army, 1953-55. Mem. Young Presidents Orgn., Wharton Grad. Sch. Bus. Club N.Y. Home: Gunston Rd Southport CT 06490 Office: AMR Internat Inc 1370 Ave of Americas New York NY 10019

RYAN, DOUGLAS EARL, educator; b. Fredericton, N.B., Can., Jan. 21, 1922; s. Lorne Earl and Goldie Emily (DeLong) R.; B.Sc., U. N.B., 1944; M.A., U. Toronto (Ont., Can.); 1946; Ph.D., D.I.C., U. London, 1951, D.Sc., 1965; m. Nan Pritchard, Aug. 17, 1945; children—Lorne, Michelle, Kelly. Asst. prof. U. N.B., 1946-48; teaching fellow Ill. Inst. Tech., 1948-49; Beaverbrook overseas scholar Imperial Coll., 1949-51, NRC fellow, 1959-60, McLeod prof., 1963; asst. prof. Dalhousie U., Halifax, N.S., Can., 1951-57, asso. prof., 1957-63, chmn. dept. chemistry, 1969-74, dir. Trace Analysis Research Center, 1971, dir. Slowpoke facility, 1976. Recipient Fisher Sci. Lecture award, 1972. Fellow Chem. Inst. Can. Editorial bd. Internat. Jour. Environ. Analytical Chemistry, 1971—, Analytical Chimica Acta, 1973—, Can. Jour. Spectroscopy, 1974—. Contbr. articles to profl. jours. Home: 6095 Coburg Rd Halifax NS Canada

RYAN, FRANCES MARY, educator, lawyer; b. O'Neill, Nebr., Sept. 29, 1920; d. Neil Thomas and Mary Loretta (Gallagher) Ryan; B.A., Briar Cliff Coll., 1942; J.D., Marquette U., 1947; LL.M., U. Mich., 1948. Admitted to Wis. bar, 1947, U.S. Dist. Ct. bar, 1947, U.S. Circuit Ct. of Appeals bar, 1950; individual practice law Milw., 1949-53; asso. firm. Affeldt & Lichtsinn, Milw., 1954; partner firm Lichtsinn, Dede, Anderson & Ryan, Milw., 1960-64, firm Lichtsinn, Dede, Ryan & Haensel, Milw., 1964-73; asso. prof. law Creighton U. Law Sch., Omaha, 1973-76, prof., 1976—; vis. prof. Sch. Law, Temple U., summer 1976; commnr. Milw. County Circuit Ct., 1972-73. Home: Rural Route 73 Chris Lake Lot 65 Omaha NE 68123 Office: Creighton U Sch Law Omaha NE 68178

RYAN, GERALD JOHN, bishop; b. N.Y.C., Aug. 24, 1923; s. Cornelius Joseph and Marian (Hanley) R.; student Cathedral Coll., Bklyn.; M.S.W., Fordham U., 1958; LL.D. (hon.), St. John's U., Bklyn., 1978. Ordained priest, Roman Catholic Ch., 1950; parish priest, 1950-58; dir. Cath. Youth Orgn., 1958-61; dir. Cath. Charities, Rockville Centre (N.Y.) Diocese, 1961-70; pastor St. Raymond's Parish, East Rockaway, N.Y., 1970-77; aux. bishop Diocese of Rockville Centre, 1977—. Pres. bd. visitors Pilgrim State Hosp.; mem. Nassau County Youth Bd., Suffolk County Mental Health Bd. Office: PO Box 33 Brentwood NY 11717*

RYAN, GERARD SPENCER, publisher; b. N.Y.C., June 10, 1926; s. Gerard Aloysius and Helen (Kirwan) R.; B.A., Georgetown U., 1950; m. Barbara Battle, May 3, 1952; children—Jerry, Catherine, Janet, Mary Ellen, Barbara, Elizabeth, David, Peter. Dir. fund raising Georgetown U., 1950-51; sales rep. McGraw Hill Pub. Co., Chgo., 1951-53; mgr. Pitts. Chem. Engring. Dist., 1953-68; sales mgr. Power Mag., N.Y.C., 1968-73; mgr. Elec. Constrn. and Maintenance and Elec. Wholesaling mags., N.Y.C., 1973-74, asso. pub., 1974-75, pub., 1975—. Pres. South Hills Assn. Racial Equality, Pitts., 1966-68. Served with USNR, 1944-46. Mem. Nat. Assn. Indsl. Advertisers (v.p. Pitts. chpt. 1966-68). Democrat. Roman Catholic. Home: 81 Club Rd Upper Montclair NJ 07043 Office: 1221 Ave Americas New York City NY 10020

RYAN, HEWSON ANTHONY, educator; b. New Haven, June 16, 1922; s. James Patrick and Clara Hewson (Sprightly) R.; B.A., Yale U., 1946, M.A., 1948; Ph.D., U. Madrid (Spain), 1950; m. Helene E. Lecko, July 4, 1949; children—Alexander H. (dec.), Anthony H., Anne S. Instr. in Spanish, Yale U., 1947-51, Sterling fellow, 1949; dir. Centro Colombo Americano, Bogota, Colombia, 1951-54; cultural affairs officer Am. embassy, La Paz, Bolivia, 1954-56; info. officer Am. embassy, Santiago, Chile, 1956-58, pub. affairs officer, 1958-61; asst. dir. USIA, Washington, 1961-64, asso. dir., 1964-66, dep. dir., 1966-69; U.S. ambassador to Honduras, 1969-73; diplomat in residence Fletcher Sch. Law and Diplomacy, 1973-74; dep. asst. sec. state Inter-Am. affairs, 1975-77; Murrow prof. pub. diplomacy Fletcher Sch. Law and Diplomacy, 1977—; adviser U.S. del. 5th meeting Fgn. Ministers Americas, 1959; U.S. observer 2d UNESCO Regional Conf. Info., 1960; cons. to UN, 1977—; Chmn. Chilean Fulbright Commn., 1958-61; dir. Nat. Endowment for Humanities Seminar for Journalists, 1978, 79. Served with inf. AUS, 1942-46; ETO. Decorated Bronze Star; Grand Cross of Morazan (Honduras), 1973; recipient Distinguished Service award USIA, 1964. Mem. Council on Fgn. Relations, Fgn. Service Protective Assn. (pres. 1975-77), Am. Soc. New Eng. (v.p. 1978—), Center for Inter-Am. Relations, Pan Am. Soc. New Eng. (v.p. 1978—). Clubs: Overseas Press (N.Y.C.); DACOR (Washington). Contbr. articles to profl. jours. Co-editor texts teaching English as 2d lang. Home: 8 Grove St Winchester MA 01890 Office: Fletcher Sch Law and Diplomacy Medford MA 02155

RYAN, HOWARD CHRIS, state justice; b. Tonica, Ill., June 17, 1916; s. John F. and Sarah (Egger) R.; B.A., U. Ill., 1940, LL.B., J.D., 1942; LL.D. (hon.), John Marshall Law Sch., 1978; m. Helen Cizek, Oct. 16, 1943; children—John F., Elizabeth Ellen, Howard Chris. Admitted to Ill. bar, 1942; practice in Decatur, 1946-47, Peru, 1947-57; asst. state's atty., LaSalle County, 1952-54; county judge, LaSalle County, 1954-57; circuit judge, LaSalle County, 1957-68, chief judge, 1964-68; judge appellate ct. 3d Jud. Dist. Ill., 1968-70; justice Ill. Supreme Ct., 1970—. Served with USAAF, 1942-45. Mem. Am., Ill., LaSalle County bar assns., Am. Judicature Soc., Am. Legion, Phi Alpha Delta. Republican. Methodist. Mason (33 deg.), Elk, Odd Fellow. Home: Box 53 Tonica IL 61370 Office: 111 E Jefferson St Ottawa IL 61350

RYAN, JAMES LEO, state justice; b. Detroit, Nov. 19, 1932; s. Leo Francis and Irene Agnes R.; LL.B., U. Detroit, 1956; LL.D., Madonna Coll., 1976; m. Mary Elizabeth Rogers, Oct. 12, 1957; children—Daniel P., James R., Colleen M., Kathleen A. Justice of peace, Redford Twp., Mich., 1963-66; circuit judge 3d Jud. Circuit Mich., 1966-75; justice Mich. Supreme Ct., 1975—; faculty U. Detroit Sch. Law, Nat. Jud. Coll., Reno, Am. Acad. Jud. Edn., Washington. Bd. dirs. Thomas M. Cooley Law Sch., Lansing, Mich., Donald M. Barton Found., Detroit, U. Detroit Law Sch. Alumni Assn. Served in USN, 1957-60, to comdr. JAGC, Res., 1960—. Mem. Am. Judicature Soc., Am., Detroit bar assns., Naval Res. Lawyers Assn., Nat. Conf. Appellate Ct. Judges, State Bar Mich. Roman Catholic. Club: K.C. Contbr. article to legal jour. Office: care Supreme Ct Mich State Capitol Lansing MI 48024

RYAN, JOHN D., business exec.; b. East St. Louis, Ill., May 17, 1921; s. Michael J. and Mary Elizabeth (Sparn) R.; B.S. in Commerce, St. Louis U., 1943; m. Mary Catherine Kickham, Nov. 3, 1945; children—Michael J., Kathy Ryan Proterra. Midwest mgr. maj. accounts NCR Co., 1946-73; v.p. Wetterau Inc., St. Louis, 1973-74, exec. v.p., 1979—; pres. Wetterau Industries, St. Louis, 1974—. Chmn. lay bd. DePaul U. Community Health Center, 1975—; mem. pres's council St. Louis U., 1975—. Served with USN, 1943-46. Roman Catholic. Clubs: St. Clair Country, Mo. Athletic, Univ. Home: 8 S 79th St Belleville IL 62223 Office: 8920 Pershall Rd Hazelwood MO 63042

RYAN, JOHN RAYMOND, mag. publisher; b. Chgo., Jan. 17, 1928; s. Raymond J. and Ida G. (Weeman) R.; B.S., U. Wis., 1950; postgrad. Northwestern U., evenings 1951-52; m. Joylyn D. Bures, Aug. 12, 1950; children—Jeffrey, John. Advt. rep. VFW mag., 1952-55; advt. rep., then Western advt. mgr. Outdoor Life mag., 1955-64; advt. dir. Elks mag., Chgo., 1964-75, pub., gen. mgr., 1975—. Served with AUS, 1945-47. Club: Elks. Home: 515 Elmwood St Wilmette IL 60091 Office: 425 W Diversey Pkwy Chicago IL 60601

RYAN, JOHN T., JR., business exec.; b. Pitts., Mar. 1, 1912; s. John Thomas and Julia (Brown) R.; B.S., Pa. State Coll., 1934; M.B.A., Harvard, 1936; D.Sc. (hon.), Duquesne U.; LL.D., U. Notre Dame, 1973; m. Irene O'Brien, Aug. 1, 1939; children—John, III, Irene (Mrs. L. Edward Shaw, Jr.), Michael, Daniel, Julia, William. Engr. with Mine Safety Appliances Co., 1936-38, asst. gen. mgr., 1938-40, gen. mgr., 1940-48, exec. v.p. and dir., 1948-53, pres., dir., 1953-63, chmn., 1963—; dir. Allegheny Ludlum Industries, Inc., Internat. Minerals & Chem. Corp., H. J. Heinz Co., Mellon Bank N.A. Mem. exec. com. Allegheny Conf. Community Devel.; vice chmn. Regional Indsl. Devel. Corp.; chmn. Univ. Health Center Pitts.; trustee U. Notre Dame; bd. dirs. Children's Hosp. Pitts., Thomas A. Edison Found. Mem. Am. Mining Congress (dir. mfg. div.), Council on Fgn. Relations, Am. Inst. Mining and Metall. Engrs., ASME, Phi Delta Theta, Tau Beta Pi. Roman Catholic. Knight of Malta. Clubs: Pitts. Golf, Univ., Fox Chapel, Rolling Rock, Duquesne; Union League, Yacht (N.Y.C.); Metropolitan (Washington); Chicago. Home: W Woodland Rd Pittsburgh PA 15232 Office: Mine Safety Appliance Co 600 Penn Center Blvd Pittsburgh PA 15235

RYAN, JOHN WILLIAM, univ. pres.; b. Chgo., Aug. 12, 1929; s. Leonard John and Maxine (Mitchell) R.; B.A., U. Utah, 1951; M.A., Ind. U., 1958, Ph.D., 1959; LL.D. (hon.), U. Notre Dame, 1978; m. D. Patricia Goodday, Mar. 20, 1949; children—Kathleen Elynne Ryan Acker, Kevin Dennis Mitchell, Kerrick Charles Casey. Research analyst Ky. Dept. Revenue, Frankfort, 1954-55; vis. research prof. Ind. U. project at U. Thammasat, Bangkok, Thailand, 1955-57; asst. dir. Inst. Tng. for Public Service, Ind. U., 1957-58; successively asst. prof., asso. prof. polit. sci., asso. dir. Bur. Govt., U. Wis., 1958-62; exec. asst. to pres., sec. of univ. U. Mass., Amherst, 1962-63, chancellor, Boston, 1965-68; v.p. acad. affairs Ariz. State U., 1963-65; v.p., chancellor regional campuses Ind. U., Bloomington, 1968-71; pres. Ind. U., Bloomington, 1971—, also now prof. polit. sci.; dir. Ind. Bell Telephone Co.; chmn. tech. rev. com. Mass. Commn. Aging, 1965-68; mem. Mayor's Com. Minority Housing, Madison, Wis., 1961-62; mem. Nat. Assn. State Univs. and Land Grant Colls. Commn. on Edn. for Bus. Professions, 1976-78, mem. vets. affairs com., 1977—, mem. joint com. on health policy; pres. Newman Found. Ind., 1969-71, bd. dirs., 1969—; mem. regional exec. com. State Tech. Services Act New Eng., 1966-68; pres. Ind. Conf. Higher Edn., 1977-78, mem. exec. com. 1977—; bd. govs. Riley Meml. Assn., 1971—, Public Broadcasting Service, 1973—, bd. dirs. Ind. Center Advanced Research, 1977-80. Am. U. field staff, 1971—, chmn. bd., 1972-77; mem. Ind. Revolutionary Bicentennial Commn., 1972—; chmn. bd. govs. Ind. U. Found.; trustee Coll. St. Thomas, 1975—; bd. vis's. Air U., 1974—; chmn. Air Force Inst. Tech Subcom., 1976—; mem. univ. adv. council Life Ins. Inst.; mem. White River Park Devel. Commn., 1979—; mem. council pres's Midwest Univs. Consortium for Internat. Activities, 1971—, chmn., 1976-78; bd. dirs. Nat. Inst. Campus Ministries, Inc, 1975-78, mem. devel. com.; mem. exec. bd. Commn. on Higher Edn., North Central Assn. Colls. and Secondary Schs., 1976—. Mem. Am. Soc. Public Adminstrn. (pres. Ind. chpt. 1969-70, nat. chpt. 1972-73, nat. council 1970—), Ind. Soc. Chgo. (non-resident v.p. 1976—), Am. Polit. Sci. Assn., Assn. Asian Studies, Am. Council Edn., Am. Judicature Soc., Assn. Am. Univs. (exec. com. 1978—, health edn. com. 1978—), Ind. Soc. N.Y., Ind. Soc. Washington, Nat. Acad. Public Adminstrn., Explorers Club, Adelphia (hon.), Phi Kappa Phi, Phi Alpha Theta, Pi Sigma Alpha, Kappa Sigma. Roman Catholic. Clubs: K.C., Rotary, Elks. Author papers and reports in field. Home: Pres's House Ind U Bloomington IN 47405

RYAN, JOHN WILLIAM, assn. exec.; b. Manchester, N.H., Sept. 16, 1937; s. William Charles and Mary Ann (Marcoux) R.; A.B., St. Anselm's Coll., 1959; M.A., Niagara U., 1960; Ph.D., St. John's U., 1965; m. Carol Jean Battaglia, Sept. 17, 1960; children—James, Kathleen, John, Michael. Asst. prof. history Gannon Coll., Erie, Pa., 1965-66; edn. specialist, div. grad. programs U.S. Office Edn., Washington, 1966-68, regional coordinator, grad. acad. programs, 1968-70; dir. univ. programs Univ. Assos., Inc., Washington, 1970-72; asst. to pres., sec. Council of Grad. Schs. in U.S., Washington, 1972—. Mem. Am. Assn. Higher Edn., Washington Higher Edn. Group (sec. 1970-71). Contbr. articles to profl. jours. Home: 6321 Capella Ave Burke VA 22015 Office: 1 Dupont Circle Suite 310 Washington DC 20036

RYAN, JOHN WILLIAM, univ. adminstr.; b. Chgo., Aug. 12, 1929; s. Leonard John and Maxine (Mitchell) R.; A.B., U. Utah, 1951; M.A., Ind. U., 1954, Ph.D., 1958; Litt.D. (hon.), Coll. of St. Thomas (Minn.); LL.D. (hon.), U. Notre Dame; m. D. Patricia Goodday, Mar. 20, 1949; children—Kathleen Elynne, Kevin Dennis, Kerrick Charles Casey. Research analyst Ky. Dept. Revenue, 1954- 55; vis. research prof. U. Thammasat, Bangkok, Thailand, 1955-57; asst. dir. Inst. Tng. for Pub. Service, Ind. U., 1957-58; successively asst. prof., asso. prof. polit. sci., also asso. dir. Bur. Govt., U. Wis., 1958-62; exec. asst. to pres., sec. of univ. U. Mass., 1962-63, chancellor, 1965-68; v.p. academic affairs Ariz. State U., 1963-65; v.p., chancellor regional campuses Ind. U., 1968-71, pres. Ind. U., 1971—; dir. Ind. Bell Telephone, State Life Ins Co. Bd. govs. Pub. Broadcasting Service, 1973—; bd. dirs. Ind. Newman Found., 1969—; bd. visitors Air U., 1974-77; chmn. bd. dirs. Ind. U. Found., 1972—; trustee Coll. St. Thomas, 1975—. Mem. Am. Soc. Pub. Adminstrn., Ind. Soc. Chgo., Am. Polit. Sci. Assn., Assn. Asian Studies, Adelphia (hon.), Phi Kappa Phi, Phi Alpha Theta, Pi Sigma Alpha, Kappa Sigma (Man of Year 1975). Roman Catholic. Clubs: K.C.; University (N.Y.C., Boston); Cosmos (Washington); Columbia, Athletic (Indpls.). Author papers and reports in field. Home: Presidents House Indiana U Bloomington IN 47401

RYAN, JOHN WILLIAM, JR., constrn. co. exec.; b. N.Y.C., Feb. 6, 1940; s. John William and Josephine R.; B.S.E., Villanova U., 1962; m. Cathy D. Kurtz, July 10, 1976; 1 son, John William III. With John W. Ryan Constrn. Co. Inc., N.Y.C., 1962—, project mgr., estimator, 1962-72, pres., chief exec. officer, 1972—. Vice pres. bd. dirs. Lincoln Hall Sch., Lincolndale, N.Y. Served with Air N.G., 1962-68. Named Gen. Contractor of Yr., N.J. Contractors Assn., 1978. Mem. Am. Arbitration Assn. Republican. Roman Catholic. Clubs: Union League, Sleepy Hollow Country. Office: 41 E 42d St New York NY 10017

RYAN, JOSEPH THOMAS, archbishop; b. Albany, N.Y. Nov. 1, 1913; s. Patrick J. and Agnes (Patterson) R.; B.A., Manhattan Coll., 1935, LL.D., 1966; student St. Joseph's Sem., Yonkers, N.Y., 1939; D.H.L., Siena Coll., 1964. Ordained priest Roman Cath. Ch., 1939; diocesan dir. radio/TV, also diocesan dir. vocations, Albany, 1954-57; chancellor Mil. Ordinariate, 1957-58; nat. sec. Cath. Near East Welfare Assn., also pres. Pontifical Mission for Palestine, 1960-66; archbishop of Anchorage, 1966-75; coadjutor mil. vicar U.S. Armed Forces, 1975—. Served as chaplain USMCR, 1943-46. Named Papal Chamberlain, 1957; knight comdr. Equestrian Order Holy Sepulchre, 1958, comdr. with star, 1960, grand cross, 1966; grand ofcl. Order Independence (Jordan), 1964. Office: 1011 1st Ave New York NY 10022*

RYAN, KENNETH JOHN, physician, educator; b. N.Y.C., Aug. 26, 1926; s. Joseph M. Ryan; student Northwestern U., 1946-48; M.D., Harvard, 1952; m. Marion Elizabeth Kinney, June 8, 1948; children—Alison Leigh, Kenneth John, Christopher Elliot. Intern, then resident internal medicine Mass. Gen. Hosp., Boston, also Columbia-Presbyn. Med. Center, N.Y.C., 1952-54, 56-57; resident obstetrics and gynecology Boston Lying-in Hosp., also Free Hosp. for Women, Brookline, Mass., 1957-60; instr. obstetrics and gynecology Harvard, also dir. Fearing Research Lab., 1960-61; prof. obstetrics and gynecology, dir. dept. Western Res. U. Med. Sch., 1961- 70; prof. reproductive biology, dept. obstetrics and gynecology U. Cal. at San Diego, La Jolla, 1970-73; Kate Macy Ladd prof., chmn. dept. obstetrics and gynecology Harvard Med. Sch., 1973—, dir. Lab. Human Reprodn. and Reproductive Biology, 1974—; chief staff Boston Hosp. for Women, 1973—. Recipient Schering award Harvard Med. Sch., 1951, Soma Weis award, 1952, Bordon award, 1952; Ernst Oppenheimer award, 1964; Max Weinstein award, 1970; fellow Am. Cancer Soc., Mass. Gen. Hosp., 1954-56. Diplomate Am. Bd. Obstetrics and Gynecology. Mem. Am. Coll. Obstetricians and Gynecologists, Am. Soc. Biol. Chemists, Endocrine Soc., Soc. Gynecol. Investigation, Mass. Med. Soc., Am. Soc. Clin. Investigation, Am. Gynecol. Soc., Alpha Omega Alpha. Home: 221 Longwood Ave Boston MA 02115

RYAN, LAWRENCE VINCENT, educator; b. St. Paul, June 22, 1923; s. Thomas Aloysius and Marguerite (Allen) R.; B.A., Coll. St. Thomas, St. Paul, 1944; M.A., Northwestern U., 1946, Ph.D., 1952; m. Patricia Ann Tomsicek, June 23, 1945; children—Katharine Mary, Lawrence Allen, Gregory Paul, Mary Patricia. Instr. English, Coll. St. Thomas, 1946-52; mem. faculty Stanford, 1952—, prof. English, 1963—, prof. humanities, 1970—, Joseph S. Atha prof. humanities, 1977—, dir. grad. program humanities, 1958-67, asso. dean humanities and scis., 1967-70, acting dean, 1974, chmn. humanities spl. programs, 1973—, chmn. adv. bd., 1974-75. Mem. Calif. Adv. Com. English, 1964-67. Served to 1st lt. USMCR, 1943-46; PTO. Decorated Purple Heart with gold star; Guggenheim fellow, 1958; asso. Harvard Renaissance Center, Florence, Italy, 1964; grantee-in-aid Huntington Library, 1953, 56, 72, Am. Philos. Soc., 1957, Am. Council Learned Socs., 1971. Mem. Modern Lang. Assn. (asso. bibliographer 1957-60), Nat. Council Tchrs. English (adv. council 1966-69), Internat. Assn. for Neo-Latin Studies, Renaissance Soc. Am., Dante Soc. Am., Conf. Brit. Studies, Medieval Assn. Pacific, Sierra Club, NAACP. Democrat. Roman Catholic. Author: Roger Ascham, 1963; also articles. Editor: A Science Reader, 1959; Shakespeare's Henry VI, Part One, 1967; Ascham's The Schoolmaster, 1967; co-editor: Neo-Latin News, 1957—. Home: 936 Casanueva Pl Stanford CA 94305

RYAN, LEO ARTHUR, journalist; b. Montreal, Que., Can., June 29, 1937; s. Leo Edward and Madeleine Hectorine (Surveyer) R.; B.A. in History-English, Bishops U., Lennoxville, Que., 1958; M.A. in Slavic Studies magna cum laude, U. Montreal, 1961; m. Nicole Barrette, Jan. 26, 1963; children—Nathalie, Caroline, Nicholas. Reporter, Montreal Star, 1961-62; news editor Africabeams Service of Agence France Presse, 1963-69; spl. freelance European corr., Oise, France, 1970—. Mem. Anglo-Am. Press Assn. of Paris (v.p. 1979). Club: Montreal Badminton and Squash. Contbr. articles to Globe & Mail, Toronto, Ont., Can., Jour. of Commerce, N.Y.C., N.Am. Newspaper Alliance, Winnipeg (Man., Can.) Free Press, Ottawa (Ont.) Jour.; contbr. series of articles on French W. Africa to Globe & Mail, 1972, on Algerian and Portugese economy to Jour. Commerce, 1971, 75; series on Hungary to N.Am. Newspaper Alliance, 1977. Home: 3 du Four Crepy-En-Valois 60800 Oise France Office: 108 rue de Richelieu Paris 2 France

RYAN, LEO VINCENT, univ. dean; b. Waukon, Iowa, Apr. 6, 1927; s. John Joseph and Mary Irene (O'Brien) R.; B.S., Marquette U., 1949; M.B.A., DePaul U., 1954; Ph.D., St. Louis U., 1958; postgrad. Catholic U. Am., 1951-52, Bradley U., 1952-54, Northwestern U., 1950. Joined Order Clerics of St. Viator, 1950; mem. faculty Marquette U., Milw., 1957-65, dir. continuing edn. summer sessions, coordinator evening divs., 1959-65, prof. indsl. mgmt., 1964; prof. mgmt. Loyola U., Chgo., 1965-66, adj. prof. mgmt., 1967-69; dep. dir. Peace Corps, Lagos, Nigeria, 1966-67, dir. Western Nigeria, Ibadan,

1967-68; asst. superior gen. Clerics of St. Viator, Rome, 1968-69, dir. edn. Am. province, Arlington Heights, Ill., 1969-74; pres. St. Viator High Sch., 1972-74; dean Coll. Bus. Adminstrn. U. Notre Dame (Ind.), 1975—; adj. prof. human devel. St. Mary's Coll., Winona, Minn., 1972-74; mem. sch. bd. Archdiocese Chgo., 1972-75; mem. nat. edn. com. U.S. Cath. Conf., 1971-75, mem. exec. com., 1973-75; mem. nat. adv. bd. Benedictine Sisters of Nauvoo, 1973—; vis. prof. U. Ife, Ibadan, 1967-68, Viatorian Sem., Washington, 1961-62, 63-65; dir. 1st Bank Midland-Milw., Haas Assos., Inc., Vilter Mfg. Co., Filbert Corp., Vilter Sales & Service, Vilter Internat., Henricksen & Co., Inc. Mem. Pres.'s Com. on Employment Handicapped, 1959-65, Wis. Gov.'s Com. on Employment Handicapped, 1959-65, Wis. Gov.'s Com. on UN, 1961-64; bd. dirs. Notre Dame Center for Pastoral Liturgy, 1976—; trustee St. Mary of Woods Coll., 1978—. Recipient Freedom award Berlin Commn., 1961; chieftaincy title Asoju Atoaja of Oshogbo, Oba Adenle I, Yorubaland, Nigeria, 1967; Brother Leo V. Ryan award created in his honor Cath. Bus. Edn. Assn., 1962; named Man of Year, Jr. C of C. Milw., 1959, Marquette U. Bus. Adminstrn. Alumni Man of Year, 1974; recipient B'nai B'rith Interfaith award Milw., 1963; Distinguished Alumnus award DePaul U., 1976; Milw. Bd. Realtors travelling fellow, 1964; Nat. Assn. Purchasing Agts. faculty fellow, 1958. Mem. Cath. Bus. Edn. Assn. (nat. pres. 1960-62, nat. exec. bd. 1960-64), Assn. Sch. Bus. Ofcls. (nat. com. chmn. 1965-67), Nat. Nonprofit Mgmt. Assn. (dir.), Am. Assembly Collegiate Schs. Bus. (com. internat. relations), Nat. Assn. Adult Edn. U.S., Am. Fgn. Service Assn., Nat. Cath. Edn. Assn., Soc. Advancement Mgmt., Nigerian Inst. Mgmt., Alpha Sigma Nu, Alpha Kappa Psi (Bronze Disting. Service award 1949, silver Disting. Service award 1958), Beta Gamma Sigma (gov., mem. com. on chpt. ops.), Tau Kappa Epsilon. Home: 1625 Turtle Creek S Dr South Bend IN 46637 Office: Office of Dean Coll Bus Adminstrn U Notre Dame Notre Dame IN 46556

RYAN, LEONARD EAMES, lawyer, pub. affairs cons.; b. Albion, N.Y., July 8, 1930; s. Bernard and Harriet Earle (Fitts) R.; grad. Kent Sch., 1948; A.B., U. Pa., 1954; J.D., N.Y. U., 1962; m. Ann Allen, June 18, 1973; 1 son, Thomas Eames Allen-Ryan. Admitted to D.C., N.Y. bars, 1963, U.S. Ct. of Appeals, D.C., 1963, U.S. Dist. Ct. for So. and Eastern Dists. of N.Y., 1965, U.S. Ct. of Appeals for the second circuit, 1966, U.S. Supreme Ct. bar, 1967; reporter Upper Darby (Pa.) News, 1954; newsman AP, Pitts., Phila., Harrisburg, N.Y.C., 1955-62; reporter, spl. writer on law N.Y. Times, 1962-63; info. adviser corp. hdqrs. IBM, N.Y.C., 1963; atty. firm Perrell, Nielsen & Stephens, N.Y.C., 1964-66; trial atty. Civil Rights Div. Dept. Justice, Washington, 1966-68; asst. to dir. bus. affairs CBS News, N.Y.C., 1968; program officer Office Govt. and Law, Ford Found., N.Y.C., 1968-74; individual practice law and pub. affairs cons., N.Y.C., 1974—; v.p., sec. W.P. Carey & Co., Inc., N.Y.C., 1976—; adminstrv. law judge N.Y. State Div. Human Rights, 1976—; spl. impartial hearing officer Office for Handicapped, N.Y.C. Bd. Edn., 1976—; mem. Indigent Defendants Legal Panel Supreme Ct., N.Y. County, mem. Panel of Attys. under the Criminal Justice Act of 1964, U.S. Dist. Ct. So. Dist. of N.Y., 1975-77; bd. dirs. Community Action for Legal Services Inc. N.Y.C., 1971-77, vice-chmn., 1975-77; co-chmn. Citizens Com. to Save Legal Services, N.Y.C., 1975-76; mem. nat. gas transmission and distribution advisory com. Dept. of Energy, Washington, 1976—. Mem. Am. Arbitration Assn. (mem. panel), Group for Advancement Corrections, Am. Judicature Soc., Nat. Legal Aid and Defender Assn., Assn. Bar City of N.Y. (mem. com. on profl. responsibility 1977-78), N.Y. County Lawyers Assn. (com. on Supreme Ct. 1978—), N.Y. State Bar Assn.; arbitrator Small Claims Ct., N.Y.C., pres. Delta Phi Found., Delta Phi Ednl. Fund. Democrat. Club: St. Elmo, Phila. Author: (with Bernard Ryan Jr.) So You Want to Go Into Journalism, 1963. Contbr. articles to profl. jours. Home: 32 Orange St Brooklyn NY 11201 Office: 689 Fifth Ave New York NY 10022

RYAN, LOUIS FARTHING, lawyer; b. Richmond, Va., Mar. 18, 1947; s. Louis Anthony and Catherine Louise (Farthing) R.; B.S.E., Princeton U., 1969; J.D., U. Va., 1973; m. Prudence Elwell Hartshorn, Sept. 5, 1970. Mgmt. cons. Arthur Andersen & Co., Boston, 1969-70; asso. firm Kaufman and Oberndorfer, Norfolk, Va., 1973-77; sec., in-house counsel Landmark Communications, Inc., Norfolk, 1977—. Bd. dirs. Feldman Chamber Music Soc., 1975-77, Jr. Achievement Tidewater, 1979—; bd. dirs., mem. exec. com. Va. Orch. Group, 1979—; vol. United Way, 1975—; mem. Norfolk Harborfest Com., 1979. Mem. Am. Bar Assn., Va. Bar Assn., Va. State Bar (vice chmn. and mem. bd. govs. bus. law sect.), Norfolk-Portsmouth Bar Assn. Episcopalian. Clubs: Harbor, Norfolk Yacht and Country, Country of Va. Office: 150 W Brambleton Ave Norfolk VA 23501

RYAN, MALCOLM EDWARD, JR., air force officer; b. Pueblo, Colo., Dec. 30, 1927; s. Malcolm Edward and Eileen Gertrude (Gallavan) R.; B.A., U.S. Mil. Acad., 1950; M.S., U. Colo., 1958; grad. Armed Forces Staff Coll., 1965, Indsl. Coll. Armed Forces, 1971; m. Lois Jean MacLean, July 13, 1951; 1 dau., Kathleen Craig Ryan Smith. Commd. 2d lt. USAF, 1950, advanced through grades to maj. gen.; service in Japan, Korea, Eng., Italy and Vietnam; vice comdr. 12th Air Force, Bergstrom AFB, Tex. Decorated D.S.M., Legion of Merit, D.F.C. with 4 oak leaf clusters, Meritorious Service medal, Air medal with 15 oak leaf clusters, Air Force Commendation medal with 2 oak leaf clusters; Gallantry Cross with palm (Republic Vietnam). Mem. Order Daedalians. Home: 2 Sycamore St Bergstrom AFB TX 78743 Office: 12th Air Force Bergstrom AFB TX 78743

RYAN, MARTIN FREDERICK, lawyer; b. Oakland, Calif., Feb. 9, 1938; s. Martin Weston and Viola Marie (Sorenson) R.; A.B., Stanford U., 1960; J.D., U. Ariz., 1963; m. Sarah L. Livingston, Oct. 11, 1963; children—Scott Eric, Stephen Bond. Intern, Dept. Justice, 1962; admitted to Ariz. bar, 1963, since practiced in Douglas; mem. firm Greenwood, Ryan & Herbolich Mem. Douglas Bd. Adjustment, 1966-77; U.S. magistrate, 1978—. Chmn. Cochise County Democratic Party, 1968-70; pres., founding dir. Cochise Coll. Found.; bd. dirs. Ariz. Office Econ. Planning and Devel., 1979—, Ariz. Community Found., 1979—. Heritage scholar Stanford U., 1956-60. Mem. Am., Ariz. (chmn. disciplinary com. 4A 1978—), Cochise County (pres. 1966) bar assns., Ariz. Acad., Stanford U., U. Ariz. alumni assns. Home: 2900 15th St Douglas AZ 85607 Office: 855 Cochise Ave Douglas AZ 85607

RYAN, MICHAEL ALLAN, automotive co. exec.; b. Pontiac, Mich., Aug. 2, 1935; s. Willard James and Lorraine Jane (Steinhelper) R.; B.B.A., Gen. Motors Inst., 1959; M.A., U. Detroit, 1964; m. Mary Pamela Scolaro, Aug. 27, 1955; children—Michael, Timothy, Terrance, Christina. Systems and procedures analyst Gen. Motors Corp., Detroit, 1954-60; fin. program mgr. Vickers, Inc. div. Sperry Rand Co., Troy, Mich., 1960-64; sr. internat. budget coordinator Ford Motor Co., Dearborn, Mich., 1964-68; div. controller Carborundum Co., Niagara Falls, N.Y., 1968-70, group controller abrasive systems, 1970-71, corporate controller, 1971-76; v.p.-fin. Volkswagen Mfgr. Corp. Am., Warren, Mich., 1976—. Home: 2663 Covington Pl Bloomfield Hills MI 48010 Office: 363 W Big Beaver Rd Troy MI 48084

RYAN, MICHAEL BEECHER, govt. ofcl.; b. Chgo., Aug. 20, 1936; s. Walter Joseph and Mary Agnes (Beecher) R.; B.S. in Labor Relations, Manhattan Coll., 1957; J.D., U. Notre Dame, 1964; m. Maria Chantal Wiesman, June 1, 1963; children—Mary, Catherine, Matthew. Admitted to N.Y. bar, 1964; with NLRB, 1964—, sr. trial atty., Peoria (Ill.) region, 1968-74, dep. officer in charge, 1974-78, regional atty., 1978—; exec. v.p. NLRB Union, 1968-69, pres., 1969-71; mem. Peoria Planning Commn., 1977—, chmn., 1979—; adj. prof. labor relations Bradley U., 1972-74; mem. Tri-County Land Use Adv. Com., 1978—. Pres. Catholic Interracial Council Peoria, 1971-72, North Sterling Homeowners Assn., 1973-77. Served with AUS, 1958-61; Korea. Roman Catholic (parish council 1972-75, v.p. 1974-75, parish sch. bd. 1979—). Home: 3718 N Donna Ln Peoria IL 61614 Office: 1600 Savings Tower Center Peoria IL 61602

RYAN, MICHAEL E., newspaper co. exec.; b. N.Y.C., May 30, 1938; s. John J. and Mary K. (Mulligan) R.; B.B.A., St. John's U., Jamaica, N.Y., 1963; J.D., Fordham U., 1967; m. Ellen Todaro, Feb. 10, 1962; children—Michael, Patrick, Maryellen. With N.Y. Times Co., 1956—, asst. controller, 1963-67, corp. atty., 1967-70, asst. sec., 1970-74, sec., corporate counsel, 1974-79, v.p. law, fin., adminstrn., 1979—; dir. Sta. WREG-TV, Memphis, Malbaie Paper Co. (Can.), Family Circle, Inc., Spruce Falls Pulp & Paper Co., Inc. (Can.), Gaspesia Paper Co. (Can.); admitted to N.Y. bar, 1967. Bd. dirs. Fordham U. Law Sch. Served with U.S. Army, 1961-62. Recipient Am. Jurisprudence Corps. award Lawyers Coop. Pub. Co., 1967. Mem. Am. Bar Assn., Assn. Bar City N.Y. Home: 20 Summer St Forest Hills NY 11375 Office: 229 W 43d St New York NY 10036

RYAN, NOLAN, profl. baseball player; b. Refugio, Tex., Jan. 31, 1947; s. Lynn Nolan and Martha (Hancock) R.; student Alvin (Tex.) Jr. Coll., 1966-69; m. Ruth Elsie Holdruff, June 26, 1967. Pitcher N.Y. Mets, N.Y.C., 1966-71, Calif. Angels, 1972-79, Houston Astros, 1979—. Served with AUS, 1967. Holder maj. league record for most strikeouts in one season since 1900; mem. Am. League All-Star Team, 1972, 73, 75, 79. Author: (with Steve Jacobson) Nolan Ryan: Strike-Out King, 1975; (with Bill Libby) Nolan Ryan: The Other Game, 1977; (with Joe Torre) Pitching and Hitting, 1977. Address: care Houston Astros Astrodome PO Box 228 Houston TX 77001*

RYAN, PATRICK GEORGE, ins. co. exec.; b. Milw., May 15, 1937; s. Patrick George and Mary L. Ryan; B.S., Northwestern U., 1959; m. Shirley Ann Welsh, Apr. 16, 1966; children—Patrick G., Robert James Welsh, Corbett Michael. Agt., Penn Mutual Life Ins. Co., 1959-63; ins. broker, 1963-64; dir., pres. Va. Surety Co., Inc., 1969—, Valor Life Ins. Co., 1977—, S.W. Home Life Ins. Co., 1975—, Great Equity Life Ins. Co., 1968—; chmn. bd. Globe Life Ins. Co., 1977-79, dir., 1977—; dir., pres. Geneva Life Ins. Co., 1973—, Dorchester Ins. Co., 1975—, Associated Home Life Ins. Co., 1975—, Pay Ryan & Assos., Inc., 1964—; pres., chmn. bd., dir. Ryan Ins. Group, Inc., 1977—; dir. Cogna Services, Penske Corp. Bd. dirs. Chgo. Boys Clubs; chmn. Cancer Crusade, Am. Cancer Soc., 1980; trustee Rush Presbyn. Med. Center; trustee Northwestern U. Served with USAF, 1959-65. Mem. Young Pres.' Orgn. (chmn. Chgo. chpt. 1979-80), Chgo. Assn. Commerce and Industry (dir.), Better Govt. Assn. (dir.), Better Bus. Bur. (dir.). Clubs: Chgo., Econ., Chgo. Athletic, Tavern, Casino, Chgo. Yacht, Lake Geneva Country (dir.), Arts. Home: 134 Melrose Ave Kenilworth IL 60043 Office: 222 N Dearborn Chicago IL 60601

RYAN, RAYMOND D., steel co. exec.; b. Big Timber, Mont., Feb. 7, 1922; s. Robert Allen and Elsie (Beery) R.; B.A., Mont. State U., 1948; LL.M., N.Y. U., 1949, postgrad. in Comparative Internat. Law, 1950-51; J.D. (hon.), Mont. State U., 1970; m. Eunice Dale Burnett, Jan. 17, 1943; children—Raymond Brant, Brenda Ruth, Ronald Dale. Admitted to Mont. bar, 1948; tax trainee Geneva Steel Co., Provo, Utah, 1949-50; tax supr., asst. comptroller Orinoco Mining Co., Puerto Ordaz, Venezuela, 1950-58; comptroller Oliver Iron Mining Co. div. U.S. Steel Co., Duluth, Minn., 1958-61; v.p. fin. Orinoco Mining Co., Caracas, Venezuela, 1961-68; v.p. U.S. Steel Corp., Pitts., 1968-74, Caracas, 1974-75, v.p., treas., 1975—; asst. instr. N.Y. U., 1948-49. Bd. dirs. Jr. Achievement Western Pa. Served with mil. police AUS, 1943-45; ETO. Mem. Am. Bar Assn., Fin. Execs. Inst. Am. Bankers Assn., Am. Mgmt. Assn., Am. Iron and Steel Inst., Fin. Council Machinery and Allied Products, Pa. C. of C. (dir.), Phi Sigma Kappa, Phi Delta Phi. Clubs: Duquesne (Pitts.); Allegheny Country (Sewickley); Met. (N.Y.C.). Home: Sewickley PA Office: 600 Grant St Pittsburgh PA 15230. *Although luck and ambition have been known to support temporarily many apparently successful careers, true meaningful success is only achieved by hard work, ethical relationships, dedication to duty, and a willingness to accept responsibility.*

RYAN, REGINA CLAIRE (MRS. PAUL DEUTSCHMAN), editor, publisher; b. N.Y.C., June 19, 1938; d. Edward F.X. and Kathryn Regina (Gallagher) R.; B.A., Trinity Coll., 1960; postgrad., New Sch. for Social Research, 1960-61, N.Y. U. Film Sch., 1961, N.Y. U. Grad. Sch. English, 1962-63; m. Paul Deutschman, Apr. 11, 1970. Copywriter trainee, sec. J. Walter Thompson Co., N.Y.C., 1960-64; asst. to mng. editor Alfred A. Knopf, Inc., N.Y.C., 1964-67, editor, 1967-75; editor-in-chief, v.p. Gen. Books div. Macmillan Pub. Co., N.Y.C., 1975-76; pres. Regina Ryan Pub. Enterprises, Inc., N.Y.C., 1976—. Active Larchmont-Mamaroneck (Westchester) Young Republicans, 1960-64; campaign worker, speech writer mayoralty campaign, Larchmont, 1962, 64; mem. Manhattan Women's Polit. Caucus, 1972-74; mem. com. Jimmy Carter Presdl. Campaign. Mem. Women's Forum (dir. 1976-77), Women's Nat. Book Assn., Women's Media Group, Ind. Lit. Agts. Assn., Transp. Alternatives, Internat. Women's Com. for Human Rights, NOW. Democrat. Home and Office: 251 Central Park West New York NY 10024 also Coburn Rd Sherman CT 06784

RYAN, ROBERT S., state ofcl.; b. Columbus, Ohio, July 25, 1922; s. Howard L. and Jennie (McComis) R.; B.S. in Indsl. Engring., Ohio State U., 1947; m. Esther Lee Moore, Mar. 15, 1947; children—Phillip Craig, Lynda Joyce, Lois Jean. Maintenance foreman Internat. Harvester Co., Richmond, Ind., 1947-52; prin. welding engr. Battelle Meml. Inst., Columbus, 1952-55; dir. engring. Columbia Gas System, Columbus, 1955-67, sr. v.p., Pitts., 1967-73; sr. v.p., dir. Columbia Gas Distbn. Cos. in Ohio, Pa., Ky., W.Va., Md., Va., N.Y., 1973-75; dir. Columbia Gas of N.Y., Inc., Columbia Gas of Md., Inc., Columbia Gas Ky., Inc., Columbia Gas Ohio, Inc., Columbia Gas W.Va., Inc., Columbia Gas Va., Inc.; dir. Ohio Energy and Resource Devel. Agy., 1975—, Ohio Dept. Energy, 1976—; mem. Gov.'s Cabinet. Served to capt. AUS, 1944-47. Mem. Am., Pa. (pres., dir.) W.Va. (dir.) gas assns., Am. Mgmt. Assn., Am. Inst. Indsl. Engrs., Nat. C. of C. Methodist. Club: Duquesne (Pitts.). Contbr. articles profl. jours. Home: 6566 Plesenton Dr S Worthington OH 43085 Office: 30 E Broad St Columbus OH 43215

RYAN, STEPHEN JOSEPH, JR., ophthalmologist, educator; b. Honolulu, Mar. 20, 1940; s. S.J. and Mildred Elizabeth (Farrer) F.; A.B., Providence Coll., 1961; M.D., Johns Hopkins U., 1965; m. Anne Christine Mullady, Sept. 25, 1965; 1 dau., Patricia Anne. Intern, Bellevue Hosp., N.Y.C., 1965-66; resident Wilmer Inst. Ophthalmology, Johns Hopkins Hosp., Balt., 1966-69, chief resident, 1969-70; fellow Armed Force Inst. Pathology, Washington, 1970-71; instr. ophthalmology Johns Hopkins U., Balt., 1970-71, asst. prof., 1971-72, asso. prof., 1972-74: prof., chmn. dept. ophthalmology Sch. Medicine, U. So. Calif., Los Angeles, 1974—; chief physician dept. ophthalmology Los Angeles County Gen. Hosp., 1974—; acting head ophthalmology div., dept. surgery Childrens Hosp., Los Angeles, 1975-77: dir. Estelle Doheny Eye Found., Los Angeles, 1977—; ophthalmologist Naval Regional Med Center, Long Beach, Calif., 1975—; mem. advisory panel Calif. Med. Assn., 1974—. Recipient cert. of merit AMA, 1971; Louis B. Mayer Scholar award Research to Prevent Blindness, 1974. Mem. Wilmer Ophthal. Inst. Residents Assn., Am. Acad. Ophthalmology and Otolaryngology (award of Merit 1975), Am., Pan-Am. assn. ophthalmology, Assn. U. Profs. of Ophthalmology, Los Angeles County Soc. Ophthalmology, Calif., Los Angeles County med. assns., Pacific Coast Oto-Ophthal. Soc., Los Angeles County Acad. Medicine, Pan Am. Assn. Microsurgery. Editor: (with M.D. Andrews) A Survey of Ophthalmology—Manual for Medical Students, 1970; (with R.E. Smith) Selected Topics in the Eye in Systemic Disease, 1974. Asso. editor Ophthalmol. Surgery, 1975—; mem. editorial bd. Jour. Ophthalmology, 1976—, Internat. Ophthalmology, 1978—. Contbr. articles in field to med. jours. Office: Estelle Doheny Found Bldg 1355 San Pablo St Los Angeles CA 90033

RYAN, STEPHEN PINTARD, educator; b. Phila., Dec. 8, 1910; s. Thomas J. and Caroline (Shaw) R.; A.B., St. Joseph's Coll., 1932; M.A., U. Pa., 1934; Ph.D., Nat. U. Ireland, 1956; m. Patricia Mary Toye, Aug. 17, 1938. From instr. to prof. English, Xavier U., 1937-57; vis. prof. English, Loyola U., Chgo., 1957-58, U. Coll., Dublin, Ireland, 1958-59; prof. English, U. Scranton, 1960—, chmn. dept., 1964-70. Mem. Modern Lang. Assn., AAUP, Alpha Sigma Nu. Democrat. Roman Catholic. Club: K.C. Contbr. articles to profl. jours. Home: 71 Laurel Dr Scranton PA 18505

RYAN, THOMAS JOSEPH, engring., constrn. co. exec.; b. Bklyn., Dec. 2, 1930; s. Patrick Joseph and Mary Manion (Cunningham) R.; B.B.A., St. John's U., N.Y.C., 1953; M.B.A., N.Y. U., 1963; m. Frances E. Bergen, June 20, 1953; children—Thomas C., Jacqueline, Deirdre B. With M.W. Kellog Co., N.Y.C., 1964-70, Continental Oil Co., N.Y.C., 1970-72; with Pullman Kellogg div. Pullman, Inc., Houston, 1972—, now pres. Served with U.S. Army, 1953-55. Roman Catholic. Home: 851 Silvergate Dr Houston TX 77079 Office: Pullman Kellog 3 Greenway Plaza E Houston TX 77046

RYAN, THOMAS MARTIN, JR., air force officer; b. Detroit, Dec. 10, 1928; s. Thomas Martin and Edith Ann (Hodges) R.; B.A., U. Omaha, 1965; M.S., George Washington U., 1968; m. Gwytha D. Mattox, Oct. 24, 1953; 1 dau., Sherry Ryan Mullen. Commd. 2d lt. U.S. Air Force, 1950, advanced through grades to lt. gen., 1977; asst. dep. chief of staff, logistics Hdqrs. SAC, Offutt AFB, Nebr., 1974-75, dep. chief of staff, logistics, 1975-76; dir. logistics plans and programs Hdqrs. U.S. Air Force, Washington, 1976-77, dep. chief staff systems and logistics, 1977; vice comdr.-in-chief Mil. Airlift Command, Scott AFB, Ill., 1977—. Decorated D.S.M., Legion of Merit, D.F.C., Air medal with 6 oak leaf clusters, Bronze Star medal. Mem. Air Force Assn. Roman Catholic. Home: 200 9th St Scott AFB IL 62225 Office: Mil Airlift Command Scott AFB IL 62225

RYAN, THOMAS PATRICK, JR., mayor Rochester (N.Y.); b. Rochester, Dec. 4, 1928; s. Thomas Patrick and Delia (Mulkeen) R.; B.A., St. Bonaventure U., 1952; LL.B., Syracuse U., 1956; m. Charlotte Carpenter; 1 dau., Mary. Admitted to N.Y. bar, 1956; partner firm Kennedy & Ryan, 1957—; mem. Monroe County (N.Y.) Bd. Suprs., 1962-67; city councilman, Rochester, 1967—, mayor, 1974—. Served in USMC, 1946-48. Mem. Am., N.Y. State, Monroe County bar assns., Phi Alpha Delta. Democrat Office: Office of Mayor City Hall 30 Church St Rochester NY 14614

RYAN, TOM KREUSCH, cartoonist; b. Anderson, Ind., June 6, 1926; s. Francis Gavin Ryan and Mary Katherine (Kreusch) Ryan Smith; student U. Notre Dame, 1945, U. Cin., 1946-47; m. Joanne Faulkner, Dec. 19, 1947; children—Linda, Tim, Dan, Diane. Artist, Del. Engraving Co., Muncie, Ind., 1950-54, Robinson Agy., Muncie, 1954-60; free-lance artist, 1960-65; syndicated cartoonist Tumbleweeds, Lew Little Syndicate 1965—. Named Hon. Old Master, Purdue U., 1978. Mem. Nat. Cartoonist Soc. (Outstanding Cartoonist cert. 1970), Newspaper Comics Council. Roman Catholic. Pub. 10 paperback book compilations of strips, 1970-80.

RYAN, WILLIAM LAWRENCE, journalist; b. N.Y.C., Feb. 28, 1911; s. Bertram Kenneth and Josephine (O'Dwyer) R.; student N.Y. U., 1927-31, Columbia, 1931-32, Am. Inst. Banking, 1932-33; m. Edythe Blasck, July 23, 1939. Reporter, editor N.Y., Conn. newspapers, 1931-43; editor, writer, news analyst, spl. corr. A.P., N.Y.C., 1943-75; mng. editor environ. news features UN Assn. U.S.A., 1975-76; columnist United Feature Syndicate, N.Y.C., 1976—. Mem. Overseas Press Club, Internat. Platform Assn., Silurians. Club: Innis Arden Golf. Author: (with Sam Summerlin) The China Cloud, 1968. Contbr. articles to mags., encys. Home: 31 Richmond Dr Old Greenwich CT 06870 Office: 200 Park Ave New York NY 10017

RYBERG, H(ERMAN) THEODORE, librarian; b. Warren, Pa., Jan. 13, 1927; s. Herman Theodore and Agnes Petrea (Andersen) R.; A.B., Gettysburg (Pa.) Coll., 1955; M.S., Western Res. U., 1957. Head cataloger Rochester (N.Y.) Inst. Tech., 1957-59; asst. dir. libraries U. Buffalo, 1959-60, Syracuse U., 1960-63; prof. library sci., dir. libraries U. Alaska, Fairbanks, 1963-68, 69-80, chmn. exec. com. U. Alaska Press, 1973-79; dean instrnl. services U.S. Fla., Tampa, 1968-69; v.p. Grandview Exploration Co.; sr. partner Amo Assos. Commr., Ballaine Lake subdiv. Fairbanks North Star Borough, 1974-79; mem. Alaska Gov.'s Adv. Council on Libraries. Mem. Internat. Oceanographic Found., Am. Scandinavian Found. Served with USN, 1951-52, U.S. Maritime Service, 1944-47, 52-53. Mem. A.L.A. (intellectual freedom com.), Alaska, Pacific N.W. library assns., No. Libraries Colloquy. Home: PO Box 80529 College Station Fairbanks AK 99708

RYBOLT, ROBERT MARSH, lawyer; b. Cin., Sept. 17, 1913; s. Webster L. and Erma (Marsh) R.; A.B., Ohio Wesleyan U., 1935; J.D., Case Western Res. U., 1938; m. Iris Riley, Jan. 13, 1940; 1 dau., Jane M. Admitted to Ohio bar, 1938, since practiced in Canton; mem. firm Day, Ketterer, Raley, Wright & Rybolt, 1963—. Dir. Central Trust Co. Northeastern Ohio N.A., Ohio Ferro-Alloys Corp., Spartek Inc.; sec., dir. Keener Rubber; sec. Mandrels, Inc. Trustee Canton YMCA, 1952—, pres., 1960-61; trustee Aultman Hosp. Assn., 1965-69; trustee Ohio Wesleyan U., 1961—, chmn. bd., 1976—, univ. counsel, 1970-76; trustee Malone Coll., 1971—, adv. bd. 1963—, chmn., 1968-73. Mem. Am., Ohio, Stark County bar assns., Canton C. of C. (pres. 1956-57), Phi Beta Kappa, Order of Coif, Phi Kappa Psi, Phi Delta Phi. Republican. Methodist (trustee 1970-76). Clubs: Canton Rotary, Canton, Brookside Country (sec. 1962-65), Oakwood Country (pres. 1957-58) (Canton). Home: 3624 Darlington Rd Canton OH 44708 Office: Cleve-Tusc Bldg Canton OH 44702

RYBURN, SAMUEL MCCHESNEY, corp. exec.; b. Morristown, Tenn., Oct. 25, 1914; s. Samuel McChesney and Mary Belle (Whittaker) R.; B.S., U. Ala., 1936; postgrad. U. Vienna (Austria), 1937-38; M.B.A., Boston Coll., 1962; m. Margaret Beverly Huse, June 5, 1943; children—John Huse, Marie DuPlessis. Vice pres. Boston Capital Corp., 1960-72; v.p. Urban Nat. Corp., Boston, 1972-73; v.p. Am. Research and Devel. Co. Boston, 1973-77; pres. Textron Adv. Group Inc., Providence, 1977—. Pres. bd. trustees Charles River Sch., Dover, Mass., 1961-64; trustee Hale Reservation, Boston, 1963-69;

v.p. Dover Found., 1965-67. Served with USN, 1941-45; PTO. Mem. Am. Chem. Soc., Nat. Venture Capital Assn. Roman Catholic. Clubs: Dedham Country and Polo, Marshall St. Hist. Home: 33 Wilsondale St Dover MA 02030 Office: 40 Westminster St Providence RI 02903

RYCKMAN, DEVERE WELLINGTON, cons. environ. engr.; b. South Boardman, Mich., May 27, 1924; s. Seymour Willard and LaVerne Eliza (Jenkins) R.; student U. Maine at Orono, 1941-43; B.S. in Civil Engring., Rensselaer Poly. Inst., 1944; M.S. in Civil Engring., Mich. State U., 1949; Sc.D., Mass. Inst. Tech., 1956; m. Betty Jane Rendall, May 28, 1949; children—Mark, Jill, Stewart. Cons. san. engr. Frank R. Theroux & Assos., East Lansing, Mich., 1946-53; environ. engr., research asst. Mass. Inst. Tech., 1953-56; A.P. Greensfelder prof. environ. engring. Washington U., St. Louis, 1956-69; founder, pres. Ryckman/Edgerley/Tomlinson & Assos., St. Louis, 1956-75; pres., dir. Reta/Nolte & Assos., San Francisco, 1974-76; founder, pres. D.W. Ryckman & Assos., St. Louis, 1975—, also Ryckman's Emergency Action and Cons. Team (REACT); asst. prof. Mich. State U., 1946-53; vis. prof. U. Hawaii, Honolulu, 1962-63; pres., dir. Environ. Triple S Co., St. Louis, 1969-75. Mem., dir. Mo. Gov.'s Sci. Adv. Bd., 1959-66; mem. Washington Architect and Engrs. Pub. Affairs Conf., 1969-75; founder grad. program environ. engring. Washington U. Bd. dirs. Center for Biology, Washington U., 1964-70, Arts and Edn. Fund, St. Louis, 1970-75. Served with USNR, 1944-46. Diplomate Am. Acad. Environ. Engrs. Mem. M.I.T. Alumni (dir. leadership fund 1970-74), Am. Water Works Assn. (Man of Yr. 1965), Engrs. Club St. Louis (award of merit 1970), Cons. Engring. Council U.S. (Grand Conceptor award for excellence in design 1969), Cons. Engrs. Council Mo. (dir. 1971-75, pres. 1973-75), Nat. Soc. Profl. Engrs., Air Pollution Control Assn., ASCE, Water Pollution Control Assn., Sigma Xi, Tau Beta Pi, Chi Epsilon, Lambda Chi Alpha. Republican. Congregationalist (chmn. exec. com., bd. deacons, bd. Christian edn. 1960-72). Clubs: Washington U. Century, Masons, Shriners, Rotary. Contbr. articles to profl. jours. Patentee in field. Address: PO Box 27310 Saint Louis MO 63141

RYCROFT, DONALD CAHILL, ins. co. exec.; b. Chgo., Jan. 3, 1938; s. Ernest C. and Helen C. (Cahill) R.; B.S., Northwestern U., 1960; 1 dau., Deborah. Sales rep. Penn Mut. Life Ins. Co., Chgo., 1960-62; investment analyst Continental Assurance Co., Chgo., 1962-67, asst. treas., 1967-70, treas., 1970-75, v.p., dir. investments, 1973—, also chmn. com. for separate account B; asst. treas. Continental Casualty Co., 1967—; v.p., dir. in investments, 1973—; treas. Valley Forge Life Ins. Co., 1970-75; pres., dir. CNA Income Shares Inc., 1977—; dir. Nat. Industries Fund, ASM Enterprises, Inc., Pine Bluff, Ark., Modern Am. Corp., Dallas. Alumni adviser Phi Delta Theta, Northwestern U., 1965-70. Treas., bd. dirs. Continental Employees Credit Union. Served with U.S. Army, 1961. Chartered financial analyst. Mem. Transp. Securities Club of Chgo. (past pres.), Investment Analysts Soc. Chgo. Clubs: Sunset Ridge Country (Winnetka, Ill.); Univ., Northwestern (Chgo.). Home: 3470 N Lake Shore Dr Chicago IL 60657 Office: CNA Plaza Chicago IL 60685

RYDELL, MARK, motion picture producer, dir.; b. N.Y.C., Mar. 23; s. Sidney and Evelyn Rydell; children—Christopher, Amy. Dir. motion pictures: The Fox, 1968, The Reivers, 1970, Harry and Walter Go to N.Y., 1976, The Rose, 1979; producer, dir. motion pictures: The Cowboys, 1972, Cinderella Liberty, 1974. Bd. dirs. Actors Studio. Mem. Dirs. Guild Am. Office: care Jeff Berg Internat Creative Mgmt 8899 Beverly Blvd Los Angeles CA 90048

RYDER, BERNARD LEROY, chemist, educator; b. Morris, Ill., Apr. 22, 1918; s. George D. and Mae (Hohenshell) R.; B.S., Ill. State Normal U., 1940; M.S., U. Ill., 1947, Ph.D., 1952; m. Ruth Blacker, Aug. 23, 1941; children—Michael, Richard, Mary Ruth. Instr. sci. Mason City (Ill.) High Sch., 1940-42; chemist, supr. E.I. duPont de Nemours & Co., U.S. Rubber Co., 1942-45; instr. sci. Warrensburg (Ill.) High Sch., 1945-46; prof. chemistry Ill. Wesleyan U., 1946-56; prof. chemistry, chmn. dept. phys. sci. Ill. State U., 1956-66, head dept. chemistry, 1966-69, prof. chemistry, 1969—. Mem. Am. Chem. Soc., Ill. Assn. Chemistry Tchrs., Sigma Xi, Kappa Mu Epsilon, Kappa Phi Kappa, Kappa Delta Pi. Home: 1107 N Oak St Normal IL 61761

RYDER, FRANK GLESSNER, educator; b. Mpls., Dec. 23, 1916; s. William and Agnes Crocker (Glessner) R.; B.A., U. Minn., 1937, M.A., 1938; Ph.D., U. Mich., 1950; student U. Heidelberg, 1936; m. Shirley Ruth Sickels, Aug. 21, 1948; children—Elizabeth Gordon, Barbara, Mary. Rackham fellow, instr., research asso. English, U. Mich., 1940-41; instr. German, Dartmouth, 1945-47, asst. prof., 1947-53, prof. German, Japanese and humanities, 1953-63, chmn., 1953-58; prof. German, chmn. dept. Ind. U., Bloomington, 1963-71; Kenan prof. German, U. Va., 1971—; vis. prof. Stanford Advanced German Inst., 1965; vis. prof. U. Wis., 1967-68, U. Hamburg, 1970, Monash U., Melbourne, 1972. Chmn. for N.H., Goethe Bicentennial, 1949. Served as lt. (j.g.) USNR, 1942-45. Recipient Goethe medal, 1970. Am. Council Learned Socs. fellow, 1951; Fund Advancement Edn. faculty fellow, 1955-56; Fulbright sr. scholar, 1972. Mem. Modern Lang. Assn. (exec. council 1968-71), Am. Council German Studies (dir. 1968-71), AAUP, Am. Assn. Tchrs. German (exec. council 1961-64, 72-73), Assn. Depts. Fgn. Langs. (pres. 1971), South Atlantic Modern Lang. Assn (v.p. 1979), Phi Beta Kappa. Author: George Ticknor's Sorrows of Young Werter, 1952; Song of the Nibelungs, 1962; also textbooks in German. Home: Batesville VA 22924

RYDER, GEORGE CONKLIN, editor; b. Bloomington, Ind., June 21, 1920; s. George Conklin and Marvel Louise (Koss) R.; grad. high sch.; m. Shirley Norma Patten, Sept. 10, 1960. Copyboy Indpls. Times (Scripts-Howard) UP-Indpls., 1943; staffer UP, Ft. Wayne and Indpls. burs., 1944; copy deskman Ft. Wayne Jour. Gazette, 1945-46; reporter Ft. Wayne Ind. News Sentinel, 1946-48; house organ editor Internat. Harvesters Publ. Dept., 1949; feature writer Indpsl. Times, 1949-50; asst. editor Hotel and Restaurant Workers, Local 6, N.Y.C., 1950; editorial staff Textile Workers Union Am., 1951-57, United Auto Workers, Detroit, 1958, 61-66, Clothing Workers, 1960; editor Am. Fedn. Govt. Employees, Washington, 1966-74; staff pub. relations dept. United Auto Workers, Detroit, 1974-76, staff community action dept., 1976—, mng. editor Ammunition, 1974-76, editor ReCAP, 1976—. Vice pres. Internat. Labor Press Assn., 1969-74. Democrat. Home: 2234 Hyde Park Dr Detroit MI 48207 Office: 8000 E Jefferson Detroit MI 48214

RYDER, JOHN DOUGLAS, educator, elec. engr.; b. Columbus, Ohio, May 8, 1907; s. John Edwin and Lucy (Rider) R.; B.E.E., Ohio State U., 1928, M.S., 1929; Ph.D., Iowa State U., 1944; D.Eng., Tri-State Coll., 1963; m. Sylvia MacCalla, Sept. 9, 1933; children—Barbara Purves, John MacCalla. With Gen. Electric Co., 1929-31; in charge elec. and electronic product research Bailey Meter Co., Cleve., 1931-41; prof. elec. engring. Iowa State U., Ames, 1941-49, asst. dir. Engring. Expt. Sta., 1947-49; prof., head elec. engring. dept. U. Ill., 1949-54; dean engring. Mich. State U., 1954-68, prof. elec. engring., 1968-72; prof. elec. engring. U. Fla., 1979—. Mem. U.S. AID higher edn. study, Brazil, 1967. Fellow AAAS, IEEE (pres. 1955, editor 1958, 59, 63, 64, v.p. 1974); mem. Am. Soc. Engring. Edn. Rotarian. Author: Electronic Engineering Principles, 1947; Networks, Lines and Fields, 1954; Engineering Electronics, 1967; Electronic Fundamentals and Applications, 1976; Introduction to Circuit Analysis, 1973; Electronic Circuits & Systems, 1976. Home: 1839 SE 12th Ave Ocala FL 32670

RYDER, KENNETH GILMORE, univ. pres.; b. Brockton, Mass., Apr. 30, 1924; s. Russell Gilmore and Etta Coffin (Carr) R.; A.B. (Augustus Howe Buck fellow 1941-46), Boston U., 1946; A.M. (A.H. Buck fellow 1946-48), Harvard U., 1947; L.H.D., Nasson Coll., 1972; m. Virginia Patricia Gagnon, June 29, 1944 (div. July 1975); children—Anne, Jeanne, Bruce; m. C. Teresa Ryan, Aug. 9, 1975; children—Amy, Julie. Instr. history Cambridge Jr. Coll., 1948; instr. history and govt. Northeastern U., 1949-53, asst. prof., 1953-57, asso. prof. history, 1957—, dean of adminstrn., 1958-67, v.p., dean of univ. adminstrn., 1967-71, exec. v.p., 1971-75, pres., 1975—; dir. Shawmut Bank Boston. Past pres. Friends of the Library of Boston U.; trustee Cambridge Jr. Coll., Forsyth Dental Center, Nat. Commn. for Coop. Edn., WGBH Ednl. Found.; mem. adv. council Mass. Gen. Hosp. Sch. Nursing; bd. dirs. Boston br. Nat. Urban Coalition, United Way of Massachusetts Bay. Served to lt. (j.g.) USNR, World War II. Mem. NEA, Am. Hist. Assn., Am. Soc. Engring. Edn., New Eng. Assn. Schs. and Colls., Assn. Ind. Colls. and Univs. Mass. (exec. com.), Boston U. Alumni Assn., Boston U. Coll. Liberal Arts Alumni Soc. (past pres.), PTA (local pres. 1962-63), Phi Beta Kappa, Phi Alpha Theta, Phi Kappa Phi, Kappa Delta Pi, Beta Gamma Sigma. Episcopalian (vestryman). Contbg. author Handbook of College and University Administration, 1970. Office: 360 Huntington Ave Boston MA 02115

RYDER, LOREN LINCOLN, motion picture, TV exec.; b. Pasadena, Calif., Mar. 9, 1900; s. Fred. L. and Lillie (Duncan) R.; B.A., U. Calif. at Berkeley, 1924; m. Isabel Snyder, Aug. 8, 1923; children—Claire Isabel (Mrs. Sherrod C. Swift), Joyce Marrian (Mrs. Judson Vandevere). Research engr. Telephone Co., 1924-25; radio importer Sherman-Clay & Co., San Francisco, 1926-28; sound dir. Paramount Pictures, 1929-45, chief engr., 1945-56; pres. Ryder Sound Services, Inc., Hollywood, Calif., 1948-76, Ryder Magnetic Sales Corp., Hollywood, 1954-79, Sound Mart, Hollywood, 1967-75; v.p., gen. mgr. Nagra Magnetic Recorders, Inc., N.Y.C., 1967—. Served with NDRC, 1945-47. Recipient Motion Picture Acad. awards, 1938, 42, 50, 53. Registered profl. engr., Calif. Fellow Soc. Motion Picture and TV Engrs. (pres. 1947-48); mem. Acad. Motion Picture Arts and Scis. (mem. sound com. 1970—), Nat. Acad. TV Arts and Scis. (sec. 1961-63), Acad. Polit. Sci., Acad. TV Arts and Scis., Audio Engring. Soc., Am. Soc. Cinematographers (asso.), Hollywood C. of C., Tau Kappa Epsilon. Home: 4020 Milaca Pl Sherman Oaks CA 91403 Office: Ryder Magnetic Sales Corp 1147 Vine St Hollywood CA 90038

RYDER, NORMAN BURSTON, educator, statistician; b. Hamilton, Ont., Can., Aug. 24, 1923; s. William George and Jean Burston (Crouchley) R.; B.A., McMaster U., 1944; M.A., U. Toronto, 1946; A.M., Princeton, 1949, Ph.D., 1951; m. Helen Louise Barbour, May 3, 1947; children—Elizabeth Anne R. Anderson, Paul Crouchley. Came to U.S., 1947, naturalized, 1962. Demographer, Canadian Bur. Statistics, Ottawa, Ont., 1950-51; lectr. U. Toronto, 1951-54; demographer Scripps Found., Oxford, Ohio, 1954-56; prof. U. Wis., 1956-71; prof. Princeton, 1971—. Served with Royal Can. Navy, 1943-45. Named to Thorstein Veblen chair in sociology U. Wis., 1970. Fellow Am. Statis. Assn., Am. Acad. Arts and Scis., AAAS; mem. Internat. Population Union, Am. Sociol. Assn., Population Assn. Am. Author: (with C.F. Westoff) Reproduction in the United States: 1965, 1971; The Contraceptive Revolution, 1976. Editor: Am. Sociol. Rev., 1965-69. Contbr. articles to profl. jours. Home: 14 Toth Ln Rocky Hill NJ 08553 Office: Office Population Research 21 Prospect St Princeton NJ 08540

RYDER, ROBERT GUY, educator, univ. dean; b. Newark, July 22, 1934; s. Guy Monsalve and Helen Wrigley (Grimes) R.; B.A. cum laude, Rutgers U., 1957; children—Steven, Rebecca. Research psychologist Family devel. sect. NIMH, Bethesda, Md., 1961-64, chief family devel. sect., 1964-75; pvt. practice psychology, Washington, 1964-75; prof., head dept. child devel. and family relations U. Conn., Storrs, 1975, dean Sch. Home Econs. and Family Studies, 1976—; instr. family and community devel. U. Md., 1973-74. Bd. dirs. Groves Conf. on Marriage and the Family, 1973-76, pres., 1978—. Mem. Am. Assn. Marriage and Family Counselors, Am. Assn. Sex Educators and Counselors, Am. Psychol. Assn., Nat. Council Family Relations, Sigma Xi. Contbr. articles to profl. jours. Home: 28 C Anton Rd Storrs CT 06268

RYDHOLM, RALPH WILLIAMS, advt. agy. exec.; b. Chgo., June 1, 1937; s. Thor Gabriel and Vivian Constance (Williams) R.; B.A., Northwestern U., 1958, postgrad. in bus. adminstrn., 1958-59; m. Jo Anne Beechler, Oct. 5, 1963; children—Kristin, Erik, Julia. Acct. trainee, copywriter Young & Rubicam Advt., Chgo., 1960-63; copywriter Post-Keyes-Gardner Advt., Chgo., 1963, E. H. Weiss Advt., Chgo., 1963-65; copy group head BBDO Advt., Chgo., 1965-66; with J. Walter Thompson Advt., Chgo., 1966—, creative dir., 1969-76, exec. creative dir., 1976—, sr. v.p., 1972—; guest speaker Ad Age Workshop, 1977. Mem. nominating bd. Sta.-WTTW, Channel 11 Public Broadcasting, Chgo. Served with USAFR, 1959-65. Recipient awards, including CLIO, 1973, Internat. Broadcast award Hollywood Radio and TV Soc., 1977, Cannes Film Festival award, 1973, Addy award Women's Ad Clubs, 1979; named One of Top 100 Creative Ad people Ad Daily, 1972. Mem. Chgo. Advt. Club, Chgo. Soc. Communicating Arts, ASCAP, Phi Delta Theta. Club: Saddle and Cycle (Chgo.). Office: 875 N Michigan Ave Chicago IL 60611

RYE, HOWARD HENRY, music educator; b. Ambridge, Pa., Nov. 29, 1917; s. Walter and Isabelle Augusta (Ross) R.; B. Fine Arts in Music, Carnegie Inst. Tech., 1941, B. Fine Arts in Music Edn., 1942; M.A. in Music Edn., Columbia Tchrs. Coll., 1949, Ed.D. in Music Edn., 1952; m. Birdie Solinger Creagh, Jan. 28, 1950. Cellist, Pitts. Symphony Orch., 1938-42, 45-46; instr. instrumental music Midland (Pa.) pub. schs., 1946-48; instr. string instruments Columbia Tchrs. Coll., 1949-53; instr. instrumental music Eastchester Pub. schs., Tuckahoe, N.Y., 1951-53; asst. prof. music Southeastern State Coll., Durant, Okla., 1953-55, asso. prof., head dept., 1955-57; prof. music, head dept. Ill. State U., Normal, 1957-67, prof. music, 1957—; cellist U. String Quartet. Bd. dirs. Bloomington-Normal Symphony Soc., 1958—, pres., 1960-61, personnel chmn., 1964—, also asst. condr. Served with AUS, 1942-45; ETO. Mem. Music Educators Nat. Conf., Music Tchrs. Nat. Assn., Nat., Ill. edn. assns., Nat. Soc. Study Edn., Am. String Tchrs. Assn., Assn. Higher Edn., Phi Mu Alpha. Home: 6 Kent Dr Normal IL 61761

RYE, JOE TERRY, chem. service co. exec.; b. Thaxton, Miss., July 24, 1938; s. Jesse H. and Ophie R. (Rutledge) R.; B.B.A., U. Miss., 1959; m. Gerry R. Murphrey; children—Gregory, Darren, Jonathan. Staff acct. Arthur Andersen & Co., Houston, 1959-65; asst. treas., then sec., treas. AO Industries, Inc., Coral Gables, Fla., 1965-71; v.p. fin., then pres. Duquesne Natural Gas Co., Houston, 1971-73; pres., chief exec. officer S.W. Chem. Services Inc., Houston, 1973—, also dir. parent co. and sub's.; dir., sec.-treas. Iowa-Insul Products, Inc. Active Little League Baseball, Colt League Baseball. C.P.A., Tex., Fla. Mem. Tex. Soc. C.P.A.'s (mem. CPE council Tex. CPE Found., chmn. Houston chpt. CPE council and exec. com.), Am. Inst. C.P.A.'s, Tex. Chem. Council. Republican. Baptist. Office: 2575 Two Shell Plaza Houston TX 77002

RYERSON, JOSEPH LESLIE, electronics engr.; b. Goshen, N.Y., Oct. 20 1918; s. Joseph Leslie and Hazel Knox (Coleman) R.; student Tusculum Coll., Greenville, Tenn., 1936-38; B.A. in Elec. Engring., Clarkson Coll., Potsdam, N.Y., 1941; M.A., Syracuse U., 1954, Ph.D., 1967; m. Gladys Trudell, Feb. 11, 1941; children—Sarah Louise, John David, Elizabeth Ann. Jr. engr. Ward Leonard Electric Co., Mt. Vernon, N.Y., 194146; asst. prof. physics Mohawk Coll., Utica, N.Y., 1946-48, Evansville (Ind.) Coll., 1948-51; elec. engring. cons., Evansville, 1949-51; electronics engr. Rome (N.Y.) Air Devel. Center, 1951-64; tech. asst. dir. SHAPE Tech. Center, The Hague, Netherlands, 1964-67; sci. adviser to dir. devel. Hdqrs. USAF, 1967-69; tech. dir. communications and nav. div. Rome Air Devel. Center, 1969-74, RADC staff, 1974-76, tech. dir. surveillance div., 1976-78; ret., 1978; with Sternlight Assos. and Consultants, Inc., Rome, 1978—. Chmn. metrication panel Dept. Def., 1973—. Recipient Outstanding award USAF, 1962, 72; NATO star, 1967; Golden Knight award Clarkson Coll., 1976; registered profl. engr., Ind. Fellow IEEE, AAAS; mem. Clarkson Coll. Alumni Assn. (pres. Rome-Utica sect. 1960), Nat. PTA, Sigma Xi, Sigma Pi Sigma. Contbr. articles to tech. jours. Home: RD 2 Holland Patent NY 13354 Office: Sternlight Assos and Consultants Inc NY 13440

RYERSON, MARGERY AUSTEN, artist; b. Morristown, N.J., Sept. 15, 1886; d. David Austen and Mary McIlvaine (Brown) R.; A.B., Vassar Coll., 1909; studied at Art Students' League, N.Y.C., and under Robert Henri and Charles W. Hawthorne. Painter, etcher and lithographer; represented by prints in permanent collections: Smithsonian Instn., other museums in U.S. and abroad; paintings in collections: N.J. Hist. Soc., Norfolk (Va.) Mus. Arts and Scis., Abbott Labs., NAD, Vassar Coll., Philbrook Art Center, Tulsa, Frye Mus., Seattle, Va. State Coll., Union Theol. Sem., others. Recipient 1st prize (oil) Hudson Valley Art Assn., 1956, 57, 58; Gold medal for oil portrait Nat. Arts Club, 1957, 62, 69, Silver medal, 1971; Maynard portrait prize NAD, 1959; 1st prize Balt. Water Color Club, 1960; portrait prize (oil) Silvermine Guild, 1960; Hook Meml. award Am. Watercolor Soc.; Talens award N.J. Watercolor Soc., 1963, Winsor and Newton award, 1968; Stevenson prize (oil) Nat. Arts Club, 1967, Grumbacher award, 1972; Clinedinst medal Artists Fellowship, 1971; Holton Meml. watercolor prize Knickerbocker Artists, 1974, prize for graphics, 1978; Dole prize Am. Artists Profl. League, 1973, prize for graphic, 1974; Albany Print Club prize, 1973, N.A., 1959; painter mem. Grand Central Art Galleries. Mem. Am. Watercolor Soc., Balt. Water Color Club, Knickerbocker Artists, Soc. Am. Graphic Artists, Allied Artists Am. (v.p. 1952-53), Audubon Artists (corr. sec. 1958-59). N.J. Water Color Soc., Print Club Albany, Pen and Brush. Contbr. to Art in Am., The Am. Scholar, Am Artist, The Artist, N.Y. Herald Tribune, N.Y. Times Book Rev. Compiler: The Art Spirit, by Robert Henri; co-editor: Hawthorne on Painting; illustrator: Winkie Boo. Home-Studio: Nat Arts Club 15 Gramercy Park New York NY 10003

RYERSON, WILLIAM NEWTON, charitable orgn. exec.; b. Phila., Mar. 9, 1945; s. William Newton and Jean (Hamilton) R.; B.A. magna cum laude (Nat. Merit scholar), Amherst Coll., 1967; M.Phil., Yale, 1970. Founder, dir. state student intern program Population Inst., Washington, 1971-73, dir. youth and student div., 1973-79; founder, chmn. Yale Zero Population Growth; sec., v.p., dir. Zero Population Growth, Inc.; chmn. bd. U.S. Coalition for Population Year; dir. Nat. Orgn. for Nonparents; dir. Internat. Clearinghouse on Adolescent Fertility, Population Inst., 1978-79; dir. devel. Planned Parenthood Southeastern Pa., Phila., 1979—. Recipient Oscar E. Schotte award in biology Amherst Coll., 1967. NASA trainee in biology Yale, 1967-70. Mem. Phi Beta Kappa, Sigma Xi, Psi Upsilon. Episcopalian. Club: Sierra. Contbg. author: The Population Activist's Handbook, 1974. Home: 210 Garrett Ave Swarthmore PA 19081 Office: 1220 Sansom St Philadelphia PA 19107

RYKER, CHARLES EDWIN, aerospace co. exec.; b. Baxter Springs, Kans., Mar. 17, 1920; s. Herbert Earl and Nellie (Sims) R.; student San Diego State Coll., 1937-38; B.S. cum laude, U. So. Calif., 1947; m. Evelyn Maude Fairchild, July 28, 1943; children—Patricia Evelyn, Charles Franklyn. Sr. accountant Arthur Andersen & Co., Los Angeles, 1947-49; auditor Airquipment Co., Burbank, Calif., 1949-50; accounting mgr. Hughes Aircraft Co., Culver City, Calif., 1950-52; with N.Am. Aviation, Inc., Los Angeles, 1952-67, v.p., controller Los Angeles airplane div., 1959-62, asst. corp. controller, asst. corp. treas., 1962-67; controller Rockwell Internat. Corp. (merger N.Am. Aviation, Inc. and Rockwell-Standard Corp.), 1967-73, staff v.p. controller's office Western region, 1973-75, v.p., controller, Pitts., 1975—; dir. N.Am. Aviation Internat., Inc. Served to lt. USNR, 1941-45; PTO. C.P.A., Calif. Mem. Fin. Execs. Inst., Am. Inst. C.P.A.'s, Calif. Soc. C.P.A.'s, Nat. Assn. Accountants, Beta Gamma Sigma, Beta Alpha Psi, Phi Kappa Phi, Chi Phi. Home: 140 Springhouse Ln Pittsburgh PA 15238 Office: 600 Grant St Pittsburgh PA 15219

RYKKEN, WALTER RICHARD, JR., lawyer; b. Rochester, Minn., Aug. 25, 1931; s. Walter R. and A. Theresa (Hildahl) R.; B.A., U. Ariz., 1952, J.D. with distinction, 1960. Admitted to Ariz. bar, 1960, N.Y. bar, 1972; asso. Chandler, Tullar, Udall & Richmond, Tucson, 1960-62; chief city magistrate, Tucson, 1962-64; partner McDonald & Rykken, Tucson, 1965-68; dep. dir. Peace Corps in Venezuela, 1969-70, dir., 1971; spl. asst. to Congressman Paul McCloskey, Washington, 1971; sr. planner Vera Inst. Justice, N.Y.C., 1972; dir. N.Y. Pretrial Services Agy., 1973-74; owner Eclectic Gallery, San Francisco, 1974—; adminstrv. law judge State of Calif., 1975—; lectr. law U. Ariz., 1963-68. Mem. due process of law com. ACLU, 1972-73. Asst. campaign mgr. for senatorial campaign Sen. Barry Goldwater, 1968. Served with USAAF, 1952-57. Mem. Calif. Adminstrv. Law Judges Assn. (v.p. 1977-79), Phi Delta Phi. Home: 1031 Trillium Ln Mill Valley CA 94941 Office 745 Franklin St Room 402 San Francisco CA 94120

RYLAARSDAM, JOHN COERT, educator; b. Lismore, Minn., Nov. 24, 1906; s. Cornelius and Marie (Aarsen) R.; B.A., Hope Coll., 1931; B.D., New Brunswick Theol. Sem., 1938; Ph.D., U. Chgo., 1944; D.D., Central Coll., Pella, Iowa, 1958; m. Harriet Loring Worcester, May 19, 1945; children—John Coert, Katharine Worcester. Instr. Am. Sch. for Boys, 1931-35; ordained to ministry Ref. Ch. in Am., 1941; prof. O.T., New Brunswick Theol. Sem., 1941-45; prof. O.T. theology U. Chgo., 1945-72, prof. emeritus, 1972—; prof. dept. theology Marquette U., Milw., 1971-79, prof. emeritus, 1979—. Mem. Am. Theol. Soc., Soc. Bibl. Lit. Author: Revelation in Jewish Wisdom Literature, 1946; Study of Apocrypha and Pseudspigrapha since Charles, 1947; Exodus, Introduction and Exegesis, 1952; Layman's Bible Commentary, 1964; Transitions in Biblical Studies, 1968. Co-editor Jour. of Religion, 1950-72. Contbr. Peake's Commentary, 1962, Interpreter's Dictionary, 1962, Ency. Brit., 1974. Home: 5544 Kenwood Ave Chicago IL 60637

RYLANCE, GEORGE AUSTIN, fgn. service officer; b. Bisbee, Ariz., Jan. 31, 1918; s. Fred Phillips and Josephine (Laird) R.; A.B., Ariz. State U., 1938; M.A., U. Ariz., 1947; postgrad. U. S.C., 1948-50; m. Vera Rebecca Williams, Nov. 26, 1947; children—Mary Rebecca,

Hollice Helen, Constance Roberta, Teresa Anne. Tchr. elementary sch., Ariz., 1938-41; commd. 2d lt. USAAF, 1942, advanced through grades to lt. col., 1947; ret., 1947; high sch. tchr., Ariz., 1947-51; supt. city schs., Benson, Ariz., 1951-56; entered Fgn. Service USIA, 1956; cultural affairs officer, Caracas, Venezuela, 1956-59, Havana, Cuba, 1959-60, Manila, 1960-62; dep. pub. affairs officer, Buenos Aires, Argentina, 1962-65; asst. dir. for Latin Am., USIA, 1965-68; counsellor for pub. affairs Am. embassy, Mex., 1969-73; counsellor pub. affairs Am. embassy, Madrid, 1973-79; sr. insp. ICA, 1979—. Decorated Air medal with two oak leaf clusters. Mem. Navy League U.S. Clubs: Univ. (Mexico); Nat. Press (Washington); Am. (Madrid). Office: ICA 1750 Pennsylvania Ave NW Washington DC 20547

RYLAND, GLEN LEROY, airline exec.; b. Stockton, Calif., Aug. 10, 1924; s. Hawkesbury Ridgway and Lola Myrle (Stevens) R.; B.S., U. Calif. at Berkeley, 1949; m. Corinne Vere Zurick, June 29, 1947; children—Sally, Gail, Stephen. Purchasing agt. Calif. & Hawaiian Sugar Corp., San Francisco, 1949-51, ins. mgr., 1954-57; mgr. contract, program adminstr. Aerojet-Gen. Corp., Sacramento and Azusa, Calif., 1957-68, controller, chief fin. officer Aerojet Nuclear Systems Co., 1968-71; v.p. fin., chief fin. officer Frontier Airlines, Inc., Denver, 1971-73, exec. v.p., chief operating officer, 1973—, dir., 1971—. Vice chmn. Rancho Cordova Park and Recreation Dist., Calif., 1959-61; mem. Parents of Hearing Handicapped, 1964-71, Alexander Graham Bell Assn.; chmn. LifeWorkshop, Covina, Calif., 1962-64, dir. LifeWorkshop Found., Los Angeles, 1962-64; bd. dirs. Sacramento Hearing Soc., 1964-71, Sacramento Hearing and Speech Center, 1964-71; mem. exec. bd., pres. Denver Area council Boy Scouts Am., 1978-80; campaign chmn. Listen Found., 1978—. Served to lt. col. USAAF, 1942-45, USAF, 1951-54. Mem. Am. Mgmt. Assn., Air Transport Assn. Econ. and Fin. Council (chmn. 1977-78), Assn. Local Transport Airlines, Soaring Soc. Am., Aircraft Owners and Pilots Assn., Phi Kappa Sigma. Republican. Episcopalian. Club: Columbine Country. Home: 3781 S Quebec St Denver CO 80237 Office: 8250 Smith Rd Denver CO 80207

RYLE, JOSEPH DONALD, business exec.; b. Stamford, Conn., Aug. 19, 1911; s. Joseph P. and Vivian (Sander) R.; B.S., N.Y. U., 1933. Pub. relations with Joseph D. Ryle, N.Y.C., 1933-41; dir. pub. relations Am. Overseas Airlines, London, 1946-50, Am. Airlines, N.Y.C., 1950-52; exec. v.p. Fedn. Ry. Progress, Washington, 1953-55, vice chmn., 1955—; pres. Nat. Transit Ads., 1955-57; exec. v.p. pub. relations Thomas J. Deegan Jr., Inc., now dir.; pub. relations cons., N.Y.C.; promotion cons. Met. Mus. Art. Exec. dir. Gov.'s Com. for the Centennial of Thoroughbred Racing at Saratoga; v.p., dir. East Side Settlement House; adv. com. Am. Folk Art Mus.; chmn. emeritus Winter Antiques Show; trustee Hancock (Mass.) Shaker Village. Served with USAAF, 1942-45; dep. to Gen. H. H. Arnold, pub. relations. Decorated Legion of Merit. Mem. Air Transport Assn. (past chmn. pub. relations com.), Newcomen Soc., Irish Georgian Soc. (exec. dir.). Clubs: Nat. Press, Army Navy (Washington); Overseas Press, Wings (N.Y.C.); Squadron A. Home: 455 E 51st St New York City NY 10022 also The Academy Remsenburg NY 11960

RYLES, GERALD FAY, paper co. exec.; b. Walla Walla, Wash., Apr. 3, 1936; s. L. F. and Janie Geraldine (Bassett) R.; B.A., U. Wash., 1958; M.B.A., Harvard U., 1962; m. Ann Jane Birkenmeyer, June 12, 1959; children—Grant, Mark, Kelly. With Gen. Foods Corp., White Plains, N.Y., 1962-65; product mgr. Purex Corp., Ltd., Lakewood, Calif., 1966-68; cons. McKinsey & Co., Inc., Los Angeles, 1968-71; with Fibreboard Corp., San Francisco, 1971-79, v.p., 1973-75, group v.p., 1975-79; exec. v.p. Consol. Fibres, Inc., San Francisco, 1979—. Served with U.S. Army, 1958-59. Mem. Nat. Assn. Recycling Industries, Paperstock Inst., Harvard Bus. Sch. Assn. Republican. Episcopalian. Clubs: Stock Exchange (San Francisco). Home: 106 Amber Valley Dr Orinda CA 94563 Office: 50 California St San Francisco CA 94111

RYMER, S. BRADFORD, JR., appliance mfr.; b. Cleveland, Tenn., May 30, 1915; s. S. Bradford and Clara Ladosky (Gee) R.; grad. Fishburne Mil. Sch., 1933; B.S. in Indsl. Mgmt., Ga. Inst. Tech., 1937; m. Anne Roddye Caudle, Nov. 7, 1942; children—Anita Elise, S. Bradford III. Indsl. engr. Dixie Foundry Co., Inc., Cleveland, Tenn., 1937-40, sec.-treas., dir. prodn., 1940-50, pres., 1950—, now Magic Chef, Inc., Cleveland, Tenn., chmn., 1976—; chmn. Dixie-Narco, Inc., Ranson, W. Va., Gaffers & Sattler, Los Angeles, Johnson Corp., Columbus, Ohio; dir. Navarne Corp. Chattanooga, Coca-Cola Bottling Co., Miami, Standard Coosa Thatcher, Munford Co., Provident Life & Accident Ins. Co., Citizens & So. Nat. Bank, Atlanta. Past pres. Cleveland Asso. Industries. Past trustee Tenn. Wesleyan Coll.; past bd. dirs. Bradley County Meml. Hosp. Civilian flight instr., World War II. Mem. Am. Gas Assn. (past exec. com., dir.), NAM (past dir.), Chief Execs. Forum (pres. 1971, dir.), Gas Appliance Mfrs. Assn. (pres. 1965), Young Pres. Orgn. (past dir., area v.p., chmn. Rebel chpt.), Ga. Tech. Nat. Alumni Assn. (past trustee), Phi Gamma Delta. Methodist (trustee). Home: 1790 Ocoee St NE Cleveland TN 37311. *No man is a success unto himself; for his success has been wrought with the help and talents of many associates.*

RYOR, JOHN, assn. ofcl.; b. Charlotte, Mich., July 30, 1935; s. Noble Beress and Mary Ann (Dwyer) R.; B.A. in Math. and History, Western Mich. U., 1957, M.A. in Math. and Edn., 1963; m. Carol Dollinger, June 21, 1958; children—Kathy, Mary Lynne, Michelle, Lisa, Chuck, Stephanie. Tchr. high sch. math. Springfield High Sch., Battle Creek, Mich., 1959-75; pres. Springfield Edn. Assn., 1964-66, Mich. Edn. Assn., 1972-73, Nat. Council State Edn. Assn., 1973-74, NEA, Washington, 1975-79; bd. dirs. Coalition for Am. Pub. Employees, 1975-79; chief U.S. del. World Confedn. Orgns. Teaching Profession, 1976, 77, 78, 79. Exec. com. Calhoun County (Mich.) Democratic Club, 1973-75. Named Mich. Tchr. of Year, Council Chief State Sch. Officers/Ency. Brit., 1973; recipient Disting. Alumni award Western Mich. U., 1978. Roman Catholic. Address: 1201 16th St NW Washington DC 20036

RYSANEK, LEONIE, soprano; b. Vienna, Austria, Nov. 14, 1926; d. Peter and Josefine (Hoeberth) Rysanek; student Vienna Conservatory, 1947-49; m. Ernst-Ludwig Gausmann, Dec. 23, 1968. First singing engagements include Bayreuth (Sieglinde-Die Walkure), 1951, San Francisco Opera (Senta-Der Fliegende Hollaender), 1956, Metropolitan Opera (Lady Macbeth), 1959; now appears in world's foremost opera houses, N.Y.C., Vienna, Milano, San Francisco, London, Paris (Chrysothemis-Elektra 1973), Berlin (Gioconda 1974), Munich, Hamburg, Budapest, Moscow (Parsifal, 1975), and festivals of Salzburg (Kaiserin-Die Frau Ohne Schatten 1974), Bayreuth, Orange (Salome 1974, Sieglinde-Die Walkuere 1975), Aix en Provence, Athens (Medea 1973), Edinburgh; recordings RCA Victor, Deutsche Grammophon, London Records, EMI and Philips, Kammersangerin of Austria and Bavaria. Recipient Chappel Gold medal of singing, London; Silver Rose Vienna Philharmonic; Austrian Gold Cross 1st class for arts and scis.; San Francisco medal. Hon. mem. Vienna Staatsoper. Home: Altenbeuern Federal Republic of Germany Office: care Herbert H Breslin Inc 119 W 57th St New York NY 10019

RYSCHKEWITSCH, GEORGE EUGENE, educator; b. Frankfurt Am Main, Germany, July 8, 1929; s. Eugene and Else (Hartmann) R.; came to U.S., 1948; B.S., U. Dayton, 1952; Ph.D., Ohio State U., 1955; m. Wunhild Kamm, Aug. 26, 1950; children—Michael George, Peter Eugene, Frances Katherine. Mem. faculty U. Fla., Gainesville, 1956—, asso. prof. chemistry, 1961-65, prof., 1965—. Mem. Am. Chem. Soc. Club: Torch. Author: Chemical Bonding and the Geometry of Molecules, 1963, Italian, Spanish, Japanese translations. Home: 10 SW 41st St Gainesville FL 32601

RYSER, HERBERT JOHN, mathematician, educator; b. Milw., July 28, 1923; s. Fred G. and Edna (Huels) R.; B.A., U. Wis., 1945, M.A., 1947, Ph.D., 1948. Mem. Inst. Advanced Study, Princeton, N.J., 1948-49; mem. faculty Ohio State U., 1949-62, prof., 1956-62; prof. Syracuse U., 1962-67; prof. Calif. Inst. Tech., Pasadena, 1967—. Mem. Math. Assn. Am., Am. Math. Soc. Author: Combinatorial Mathematics, 1963. Editorial bd. Jour. Algebra, 1964-75, Jour. Combinatorial Theory, 1966-75, Linear and Multilinear Algebra, 1973-75. Research on modern algebra, matrix theory, finite geometries, combinatorial math. Office: Dept Math Calif Inst Tech Pasadena CA 91125

RYSER, HUGUES JEAN-PAUL, educator; b. Chaux-de-Fonds, Switzerland, June 11, 1926; came to U.S., 1958, naturalized, 1972; s. Ernest Jacob and Marthe Alice (Zimmermann) R.; M.D., U. Berne (Switzerland), 1953, Dr. Med., 1955; m. Carol Leigh Pierson, June 10, 1961; children—Marc Alain, Jeannine, Eve. Instr. pharmacology Harvard U. Med. Sch., Boston 1960-62, asso. in pharmacology, 1962-64, asst. prof. pharmacology, 1964-69; asso. prof. cell biology and pharmacology U. Md. Med. Sch., Batt., 1969-70, prof., 1970-72; prof. pathology and pharmacology Boston U. Sch. Medicine, 1972—; cons. Zyma-Ciba, Seitzerland, 1969-72; cons. biology dept. Dynapol Corp., Palo Alto, Calif., 1972-79. Recipient Lederle Med. Faculty award, 1964-67; Nat. Cancer Inst. Research Career Devel. award, 1968-69, grantee, 1972—; NIH research grantee, 1961-69. Mem. Am. Histochem. Soc., Am. Assn. Cancer Research, Am. Soc. Cell Biology, Am. Soc. Gen. Physiology, AAAS, Am. Soc. Exptl. Pharmacology and Therapeutics. Contbr. numerous articles to sci. jours. Home: 503 Annursnac Hill Rd Concord MA 01742 Office: 80 E Concord St Boston MA 02118. *My purpose as an educator is to engage in the creative process of making important knowledge exciting.*

RYSKAMP, CHARLES ANDREW, library exec., educator; b. East Grand Rapids, Mich., Oct. 21, 1928; s. Henry Jacob and Flora (DeGraaf) R.; A.B., Calvin Coll., 1950; M.A., Yale, 1951, Ph.D., 1956; postgrad. Pembroke Coll., Cambridge U., 1953-54; Litt.D., Trinity Coll., Hartford, 1975; L.H.D., Union Coll., 1977. Nathan Hale fellow Yale, 1954-55; instr. English, Princeton, 1955-59, asst. prof., 1959-63, asso. prof., 1963-69, curator English and Am. lit. Univ. Library, 1967-69, prof., 1969—; Procter & Gamble faculty fellow, 1958-59, jr. fellow Council of Humanities, 1960-61, John E. Annan preceptor, 1961-64; dir. Pierpont Morgan Library, N.Y.C., 1969—. Adv. bd. Horace Walpole Corr. Yale, Private Papers of James Boswell, Yale; trustee, mem. exec. com. Mus. Broadcasting; trustee Andrew W. Mellon Found., Corning Mus. Glass; bd. advisers Dumbarton Oaks, Gunston Hall; mem. council dept. art and archaeology Columbia; asso. trustee William Blake Trust. Decorated Order St. John of Jerusalem; Bollingen Found. fellow, 1965-67; Guggenheim fellow, 1966-67. Mem. Museums Council N.Y.C. (past v.p.), Keats-Shelley Assn. Am. (v.p.), Master Drawings Assn. (sec.-treas.), Drawing Soc. (nat. com.), Acad. Am. Poets, Assn. Art Mus. Dirs., Modern Lang. Assn. Am. (past chmn. English 8), Friends Princeton Library (council), Cowper Soc., Assn. Internationale de Bibliophilie (com. of honor). Clubs: Johnsonians, Grolier, Pilgrims, Coffee House, Century Assn., Lotos, Round Table (N.Y.C.); Elizabethan (New Haven); Turf, Roxburghe (London). Author: William Cowper of the Inner Temple, Esq., 1959; William Blake, Engraver, 1969. Editor: (with F.A. Pottle) Boswell: The Ominous Years, 1963; The Cast-Away, 1963; Wilde and the Nineties, 1966; William Blake: The Pickering Manuscript, 1972; (with J. King) The Letters and Prose Writings of William Cowper, vol. I, 1979; (with R. Wendorf) The Works of William Collins, 1979; (with J. Baird) The Political Works of William Cowper, vol. I, 1980; others. Editor, Report to the Fellows of the Pierpont Morgan Library, 1969—. Home: 12 Cleveland Ln Princeton NJ 08540 Office: Pierpont Morgan Library 29 E 36th St New York NY 10016

RYSKIND, MORRIE, author, columnist; b. N.Y.C., Oct. 20, 1895; s. Abraham and Ida (Ettelson) R.; B.Litt., Columbia U., 1917; m. Mary House, Dec. 19, 1929; children—Ruth, Allan House. Reporter, N.Y. World, 1917; contbr. Nat. Rev., 1955—; columnist Los Angeles Times Syndicate, 1960-65, Washington Star Syndicate, 1965—; author several sketches for musical Garrick Gaieties, 1925; author plays with George S. Kaufman: Coconuts, 1925, Animal Crackers, 1928, Strike Up the Band, 1930, Of Thee I Sing (Pulitzer prize), 1932, Let 'Em Eat Cake, 1933; alone: Louisiana Purchase, 1940; screenplays include: Coconuts, 1929, Animal Crackers, 1930, A Night at the Opera, 1935, My Man Godfrey, 1936, Stage Door, 1937, Room Service, 1938, Man About Town, 1939, Penny Serenade, 1941, Claudia, 1943, Where Do We Go from Here?, 1943, It's in the Bag, 1945; author: (verse) Unaccustomed As I Am, 1921, Dairy of an Ex-President, 1932. Republican. Jewish. Address: 605 N Hillcrest Rd Beverly Hills CA 90210

RYUN, JAMES RONALD, ret. track athlete; b. Wichita, Kans., Apr. 29, 1947; s. Gerald E. and Wilma (Strutton) R.; B.S., U. Kans., 1970; m. Anne Carol Snider, Jan. 25, 1969; children—Heather, Nathaniel and Andrew (twins), Catharine. Spl. projects dir. for box tops for fun and fitness Post Cereals, White Plains, N.Y., 1974—; free-lance sports photographer, 1966—; profl. track athlete, 1973—; dir. Jim Ryun Distance Running Camps, 1973—. Nat. chmn. Muscular Dystrophy Assn. Love Run, 1980. Named 1 of Ten Top Young Men, Nat. Jr. C. of C., 1970. Mem. AFTRA. Episcopalian. Home: 5415 Vineyard Rd Santa Barbara CA 93111. *In the excitement of today's fast-paced life I would find it difficult to keep a good perspective on priorities in my life, if it were not for one important theme. Jesus is the same, yesterday, today and forever. He provides order, love, wisdom, and understanding simply by asking in prayer. It's worked in my competitive career and is working in my business and family life. And all I have to do is ask.*

RYUS, DAVID DENSLOW, III, publisher, mus. adminstr.; b. Los Angeles, Feb. 8, 1918; s. David Denslow and Sophia Shannon (Dickey) R.; B.A. with distinction, Stanford U., 1939; m. Barry Martin, Apr. 3, 1945 (div., 1953); children—Mimi Bushnell, Peter Rand; m. 2d, Mary Louise Ward, July 26, 1956; 1 son, Michael Denslow. Rep., Wren & Van Allen, Los Angeles, 1939-41; bus. mgr. Time-Life Internat., 1947-56, gen. mgr., 1956-62, mng. dir. Time, Inc., Europe and Africa, 1963-69, dir. internat. pub. subsidiaries, 1969-70; sr. v.p. Sullivan, Stauffer, Colwell & Bayles, N.Y.C., 1971-73; v.p. Am. Mus. Natural History, N.Y.C., 1973—, pub. Natural History mag., 1973—. Served with USNR, 1941-47. Mem. Fedn. Internat. Presse Periodique, Am. Assn. Museums. Republican. Episcopalian. Clubs: River, Links (N.Y.C.); Saville (London); Berkshire (Eng.). Office: Am Mus of Natural History 79th St and Central Park W New York NY 10024

SAAL, HUBERT DANIEL, journalist; b. Bklyn., Feb. 23, 1924; s. Theodore Henry and Mary Rebecca (Valins) S.; student U. Fla., 1941-43; A.B., Yale, 1948; postgrad. Sorbonne, Paris, France, 1948-50, 53-54, Columbia, 1950-51; m. Rollene Waterman (div.); children—Theodora Mathilde, Matthew Adlai, Drusilla Mary. Free-lance writer, Europe, 1948-50, 53-55, N.Y.C., 1955-60; asso. editor Town & Country, 1950-53; instr. U. Miami (Fla.), 1960-64; music and dance editor Newsweek Mag., 1964—. Served with USAAF, 1943-45. Recipient Deems Taylor award, 1974. Fulbright fellow, Paris, 1952-53. Jewish. Home: 35 W 81st St New York City NY 10024 Office: Newsweek 444 Madison Ave New York City NY 10022

SAAR, BETYE (IRENE), artist; b. Los Angeles, July 30, 1926; d. Jefferson Maze and Beatrice Lillian (Parson) Brown; B.A., U. Calif., Los Angeles, 1949; m. Richard W. Saar, Sept. 16, 1952 (div. 1968); children—Lesley Irene, Alison Marie, Tracye Ann. Costume designer Inner City Cultural Center, Los Angeles, also Napa Valley Theatre Co., 1968-73; instr. art Calif. State U., Hayward, 1971, Calif. State U., Northridge, 1973-74, Otis Art Inst., Los Angeles, 1976—; one-woman exhbns. include Monique Knowlton, N.Y.C., 1976, Calif. State U. Gallery, Los Angeles, 1972, Whitney Mus. Art, N.Y.C., 1975, Jan Baum/Iris Silverman, Los Angeles, 1977, 79, Maneville Art Gallery, U. Calif., San Diego, 1979; two-woman exhbn. San Francisco Mus. Modern Art, 1977; group exhbns. include Small Environments, Univ. Galleries, So. Ill. U., 1972, 20th Century Black Am. Art, San Jose (Calif.) Mus., 1976, San Francisco Mus. Modern Art, 1977, Smithsonian Insts., 1977; lectr., free-lance designer for films, 1970—. Grantee Nat. Endowment Arts, 1974. Mem. Women's Caucus Art (nat. adv. bd.), Los Angeles Inst. Contempory Art. Democrat. Home: 8074 Willow Glen Rd Los Angeles CA 90046 Office: 2401 Wilshire Blvd Los Angeles CA 90057

SABAN, LOUIS, football coach; b. Brookfield, Ill., Oct. 13, 1921; s. Nick and Mary (Conkovich) S.; student Ind. U., 1940-43; B.S., Baldwin-Wallace Coll., 1948; M.S., Western Res. U., 1950; m. Lorraine Ann Dahl, Apr. 12, 1947; children—Tom, Barbara, Patricia, Christine. Football coach Case Inst., Cleve., 1950-52, Washington U., St. Louis, 1952-54, Western Ill. U., Macomb, 1957-59; mem. coaching staff Northwestern U., 1954-57, head coach, 1955-57; head coach Boston Patriots, 1960-61; head coach Buffalo Bills, 1962-66, from 1972, v.p. in charge football, from 1972, dir. player personnel, 1961-62; (Am. League champions 1964-65); head football coach U. Md., College Park, 1966-67; gen. mgr., head coach Denver Broncos Football Club, 1967-71; formerly head coach and dir. athletics U. Miami (Fla.); head coach U.S. Mil. Acad., West Point, N.Y., 1979—. Served to 1st lt. OSS, AUS, 1943-46. Named Coach of Year, Am. Football League, 1964, 65; recipient Outstanding Citizen citation, Buffalo, 1964, Distinguished Service award C. of C., Sportsman of Year award Jr. C. of C. Mem. Sigma Chi. Elk. Office: Athletic Dept Mil Acad West Point NY 10996*

SABATELLA, JOSEPH JOHN, artist, coll. dean; b. Chgo., May 5, 1931; s. John Joseph and Mary Rose (Genovese) S.; B.F.A., U. Ill., 1954, M.F.A., 1958; m. Ruth Anne Bernacki, Aug. 16, 1952; children—John J., Steven L., Michael J., Joseph P., Philip A., Thomas F., Mary K., Clarissa L. With Higgins Handcrafted Glass, Chgo., 1954; mgr. Elenhank Designers, Inc., Riverside, Ill., 1958-59; instr. architecture U. Fla., Gainesville, 1959-66, asst. dean Coll. Architecture and Fine Arts, 1966-75, dean Coll. Fine Arts, 1975—; cons. numerous agys. seeking grant funds, 1966—; exhibited one-man shows Atelier Chapman Kelley, Dallas, 1964, Jacksonville Council Arts Festival, 1969; exhibited group shows Fla. Artist Group Annual Show, 1962, 64, 65, Group Gallery, 1963, Issac Delgado Mus. Art, New Orleans, 1963, Atelier Chapman Kelley, 1966, Mint Mus. Art, Charlotte, N.C., 1966, 69, others. Bd. dirs. United Way of Alachua County, Fla., 1976-79. Served to 1st lt. Anti Aircraft Arty., AUS, 1954-56. Recipient numerous awards for art work between 1955-75. Mem. Internat. Council Fine Arts Deans, Acad. Affairs Adminstrs., Fine Arts Commn. of Nat. Assn. Land Grant Colls. and Univs., Phi Kappa Phi, Omicron Delta Kappa, Sigma Lambda Chi. Roman Catholic. Office: Coll Fine Arts U Fla Gainesville FL 32611. *Success, in the truest sense, will probably be achieved by those unafraid to confront the responsibilities associated with decision-making.*

SABATELLA, RAYMOND FRANCIS, JR., banker; b. Southington, Conn., May 18, 1932; s. Raymond Francis and Sabina (Verderame) S.; B.S., U. Conn., 1958, M.A., 1959; postgrad. N.Y. U., 1959-61; m. Joan Marie Stefanik, Oct. 2, 1954; children—Lisa, Nena, Raymond Francis III. Econ. research analyst Chase Manhattan Bank, N.Y.C., 1959-61; research dir., asst. v.p. Hartford Nat. Bank (Conn.), 1961-67, v.p. research and planning, 1967-69; sr. v.p. Colonial Bank & Trust Co., Waterbury, Conn., 1969-71; pres. Raymond Assos., 1971—; chmn., pres. No. Conn. Nat. Bank, Windsor Locks, 1972-78; pres. Danbury (Conn.) Bank & Trust Co., 1978-79; pres. Nat. Trust Bank Fla., 1979—. Treas., Town of Southington, 1967—; chmn. Southington Republican Town Com., 1975-79. Served with U.S. Army, 1951-53. Mem. Nat., Conn. assns. bus. economists, Am. Econ. Assn., UNICO Nat. (pres. Southington chpt. 1965-66), Conn. C. of C. (pres. 1970-71). Republican. Roman Catholic. Elk. Contbr. articles to profl. jours. and newspapers. Home: 35 Glenn Dr Southington CT 06489 Office: 1000 Tyrone Blvd Saint Petersburg FL 33760

SABATINI, FRANK CARMINE, lawyer; b. Chgo., May 24, 1932; s. Carmine and Lisetta (Arguilla) S.; B.S., Kan. U., 1954, LL.B., 1957; m. Alice C. Chandler, Dec. 28, 1955; children—Marcus, Matthew, Michael, Daniel. Admitted to Wis. bar, 1958, Kans. bar, 1957; atty. Allis Chalmers Mfg. Co., Milw., 1958-59; mem. firm Lillard, Eideson, Lewis & Porter, Topeka, 1959-61; partner firm Colmerry, Davis, Bennett & McCure, 1968-69, Sabatini, Waggener, Vincent & Afterborn and predecessor firm, 1969—; mem. Kans. Ho. of Reps., 1969-70. Workman's compensation examiner, 1967; chmn. Legal Aid Soc., 1966-68; instr. Kans. Bankers Assn., 1959-61; chmn. Topeka chpt. March of Dimes, 1961; pres. Hayden Father and Friends, 1974; mem. sch. bd. St. Matthews Grade Sch., Topeka; bd. dirs. St. Francis Hosp., Topeka. Served to 1st lt. U.S. Army, 1957-58. Named Boss of Year, Legal Sec. Assn. Kans., 1972. Mem. Topeka Bar Assn. (exec. com., chmn. ethics com.), Phi Kappa Theta. Club: Topeka Country. Home: 2423 SE 37th St Topeka KS 66605 Office: Law Bldg 1400 Topeka Ave Topeka KS 66612

SABECK, ROBERT V., banker; b. St. Louis, Nov. 6, 1920; s. H.T. and Clara (Mahl) S.; student Phoenix Coll., 1938-40, Pacific Coast Banking Sch., 1960; m. Ruth Mary Enyeart, Aug. 1, 1942; children—Pamela (Mrs. Tom Fitzgerald), Deanne (Mrs. William Hardwick), Debra. With Valley Nat. Bank, Phoenix, 1941—, br. mgr., 1953-60, v.p., 1960-68, v.p., met. div. mgr., 1968-71, sr. v.p., met. div. mgr., 1971-74, sr. v.p., br. adminstr., 1974-77, exec. v.p., br. adminstr., 1977-78, exec. v.p., mgr. systems planning and ops. group, 1978—. Pres., Greater Phoenix United Fund, 1969; pres. Boys' Clubs Phoenix; treas. Beatitudes Campus of Care, 1978. Served with USAAF, 1941-46. Mem. Ariz. Bankers Assn., Am. Inst. Banking, Robert Morris Assn. Republican. Congregationalist (treas.). Kiwanian (pres. 1963). Home: 8033 N 6th St Phoenix AZ 85020 Office: PO Box 71 Phoenix AZ 85001

SABEL, JOHN BURKE, ret. power co. exec., lawyer; b. Huntington, W.Va., Feb. 1, 1909; s. Isaac H. and Minnie (McLaughlin) S.; B.S. in Econs., U. Pa., 1930; LL.D., Fordham U., 1935; student N.Y. U. Law Sch., 1935-36; m. Dale Cooper, Aug. 5, 1936; children—John Burke, Lee Hoover. Student trainee Otis & Co., 1930-31; credit supr. Bank of Manhattan Co., 1931-35, asst. to investment v.p., 1935-37; admitted to N.Y. bar, 1935, W.Va. bar, 1941; spl. investment analyst Adams Express Co., 1937-39; gen. counsel staff SEC, 1939-40; counsel Monongahela Power Co. and subsidiaries, Fairmont, W.Va., 1940-66, sec.-treas., 1966-74. Past chmn. civic, cultural and recreation com. Greater Fairmont Devel. Assn.; co-chmn. cultural com., past pres. Marion County Edn. Council; past pres. Fairmont Concert Assn., Inc. Mem. S.A.R., Internat. Soc. Performing Arts Adminstrs. (past pres., dir.), Alpha Tau Omega. Presbyterian (elder, trustee, treas. and pres. congregation). Rotarian. Club: Economic (Pitts.). Home: Fairmont Farms Fairmont WV 26554

SABELLI, HECTOR CARLOS, psychiatrist, neuropharmacologist; b. Buenos Aires, Argentina, July 25, 1937; s. Antonio and Elena (DiBenedetto) S.; M.D., U. Buenos Aires, 1959, Ph.D., 1961; m. Nora Hojvat, Dec. 22, 1960; children—Martin, Guido. Came to U.S., 1966, naturalized, 1975. Intern, Pecordero Hosp., Buenos Aires, 1959; research fellow Argentine Assn. Advancement Sci., also Argentine Research Council, 1960-62; asst. prof. pharmacology Chgo. Med. Sch., 1962-64; prof., chmn. Inst. Pharmacology, U. Litoral, Rosario, Argentina, 1965-66; prof. pharmacology Chgo. Med. Sch., 1967—, chmn. dept., 1970-75. Mem. AAAS, Am. Soc. Pharmacology and Exptl. Therapeutics, Internat. Soc. Biochem. Pharmacology, Sigma Xi. Editorial bd. Revista Sociedad Argentina de Biologia, 1966—. Contbr. numerous articles to profl. jours. Home: 143 Quincy St Elmhurst IL 60126 Office: Presbyn-St Luke's Hosp Chicago IL 60612

SABERSKY, ROLF HEINRICH, mech. engr.; b. Berlin, Germany, Oct. 20, 1920; s. Fritz and Berta (Eisner) S.; came to U.S., 1938, naturalized, 1944; B.S., Calif. Inst. Tech., 1942, M.S., 1943, Ph.D., 1949; m. Bettina Sofie Schuster, June 16, 1946; children—Carol, Sandra. Devel. engr. Aerojet Gen. Co., 1943-46, regular cons., 1949-70; asst. prof. Calif. Inst. Tech., Pasadena, 1949-55, asso. prof., 1955-61, prof. mech. engring., 1961—; cons. various indsl. orgns. Mem. ASME (Heat Transfer Meml. award 1977), Sigma Xi, Tau Beta Pi. Author: Engineering Thermodynamics, 1957; Fluid Flow, 1971. Hon. mem. editorial bd. Jour. Heat and Mass Transfer, 1973—. Contbr. articles to profl. jours. Home: 1060 Fallen Leaf Rd Arcadia CA 91006 Office: Div Engring and Applied Sci Calif Inst Tech Pasadena CA 91125

SABES, HAROLD, publisher; b. Mpls., Aug. 17, 1912; s. Abraham and Eva (Haskvitz) S.; B.A., U. Minn., 1932; postgrad. Tulane U., 1943, Northwestern U., 1965-66; m. Jessie Winnick, Oct. 11, 1936; children—Earl Martin, Franklin Ellis. Sales and mgmt. positions Brown & Bigelow, Mpls., 1941-51; nat. sales mgr. Esquire, Inc., Chgo., 1951-54; pub. Exec. Rev., also owner Harold Sabes & Assos., Chgo., 1954—; sec., treas. Alert Office Services, Inc., Chgo., 1970—. Mem. Ill. Mfrs. Assn., Indsl. Advertisers Assn., Am. Diabetic Assn., Chgo. Lung Assn. Jewish. Clubs: Masons, Shrine (sec.). Home: 2028 Highland Ave Wilmette IL 60091 Office: 224 S Michigan Ave Chicago IL 60604

SABIN, ALBERT BRUCE, physician, scientist; b. Bialystok, Poland, Aug. 26, 1906; s. Jacob and Tillie (Krugman) S.; B.Sc., M.D., N.Y. U., 1931; recipient 31 hon. degrees from U.S. and fgn. univs.; m. Heloisa Dunshee de Abranches, July 28, 1972; children—Deborah, Amy. Research asso. N.Y. U. Coll. Medicine, 1926-31; house physician Bellevue Hosp., N.Y.C., 1932-33; NRC fellow Lister Inst., London, 1934; mem. sci. staff Rockefeller Inst. for Med. Research, N.Y.C., 1935-39; asso. prof. pediatrics U. Cin. Coll. Medicine and Children's Hosp. Research Found., 1939-43, prof. research pediatrics, 1946-60, Disting. Service prof., 1960-71, Emeritus Disting. Service prof., 1971—; pres. Weizmann Inst. of Sci., Rehovot, Israel, 1970-72, bd. govs., 1965—; cons. U.S. Army, 1941-62; mem. Armed Forces Epidemiological Bd., 1963-69; cons. NIH, USPHS, 1947-73; mem. Nat. Adv. Council Nat. Inst. Allergy and Infectious Diseases, 1965-70; Fogerty scholar Fogarty Internat. Center for Advanced Study in Health Scis., NIH, 1973; mem. adv. com. on med. research Pan Am. Health Orgn., 1973-76; expert cons. Nat. Cancer Inst., 1974; mem. U.S. Army Med. Research and Devel. Adv. Panel, 1974-79; cons. Surgeon Gen., U.S. Army, 1974—; Disting. Research prof. of biomedicine Med. U. S.C., Charleston, 1974—; cons. to asst. sec. for health HEW, 1975-77. Bd. govs. Hebrew U. Jerusalem, 1965—; trustee N.Y. U., 1966-70. Served to lt. col. U.S. Army, 1943-46. Decorated Legion of Merit. Recipient Antonio Feltrinelli prize in med. and surg. sci. Accademia Nazionale dei Lincei, Rome, 1964; Albert Lasker clin. medicine research award, 1965; U.S. nat. medal of sci., 1971; Disting. Civilian Service medal U.S. Army, 1973; gold medal Royal Soc. Health (London), 1969; and many other awards. Mem. Nat. Acad. Scis., Am. Acad. Arts and Scis., Assn. Am. Physicians, Am. Pediatric Soc., Infectious Diseases Soc. Am. (pres. 1969), and many other U.S. and hon. fgn. memberships. Developer of oral polio vaccine. Research in field of poliomyelitis, human viral diseases, toxxplasmosis and human cancer. Author over 300 papers in field. Home: 715 Knotty Pine Rd Charleston SC 29412 Office: Med Univ of SC 171 Ashley Ave Charleston SC 29403

SABIN, ARNOLD LEONARD, coal co. exec.; b. N.Y.C., Mar. 27, 1926; s. Irving and Emma Sabsevitz; student U. of San Carlos, Guatemala City, Guatemala, 1947; B.S. in Bus. Adminstrn., Syracuse (N.Y.) U., 1949; m. Lite Bielenberg, Feb. 16, 1961; 1 dau., Vivien Jill. With Foreston Coal Internat. Inc., and predecessor, N.Y.C., 1950—, treas., 1968—, sec., 1969—; pres., treas. Foreston Equity Holdings Inc.; dir. all companies in Foreston group; guest lectr. N.Y. U., 1975-77. Trustee Lenox Sch., N.Y.C., 1975—; trustee Park Ave. Synagogue, N.Y.C., 1976—; bd. overseers Jewish Theol. Sem. Am., 1979—. Served with USAAF, 1944-45. Mem. Coal Exporters Assn. U.S., Phi Epsilon Pi. Club: 100 (N.Y.C.), (treas. 1972-74, dir. 1972-75, 78—). Home: 200 E 71st St New York NY 10021 Office: 353 Fifth Ave New York NY 10016

SABINE, GORDON ARTHUR, educator, writer; b. Brockton, Mass., Feb. 10, 1917; s. Charles Arthur and Esther (Carey) S.; A.B., U. Wis., 1939, M.A., 1941; Ph.D., U. Minn., 1949; m. Lois Eleanor Freiburg, June 26, 1941 (div. 1973); children—Ellen Jean, Gordon Arthur, Robert Allan, Roger Malcolm. Reporter, Lynchburg (Va.) News, 1931-35; reporter, copy editor Wis. State Jour., 1939-42; contbr. articles to nat. mags. and newspapers, 1938—; corr. United Press Assns., 1946-47; grad. asst. journalism U. Wis., 1939-41; instr., later asst. prof. journalism U. Kans., 1945-47; lectr. journalism U. Minn., 1947-48; asst. prof. U. Oreg., 1948-50, asso. prof., 1950-52, prof. journalism, 1952-55, dean Sch. Journalism, 1950-55; prof. communication arts, dean Coll. Communication Arts, Mich. State U., East Lansing, 1955-60, prof., 1955-72, v.p. for spl. projects, 1960-71; spl. asst. to pres. Ill. State U., 1971-72; dir. Sch. Journalism, U. Iowa, 1972-75; prof. journalism Va. Poly. Inst. and State U., 1975—; dir. Nat. Project in Agrl. Communication, 1960-62, GI Project MEMO, 1969-70; prof.-in-residence Time, Inc., 1951; writer syndicated newspaper column Youthpoll America, 1976-77. Mem. Gov. Commn. Employment Handicapped, 1958-59. Mem. research com. Am. Council Edn. for Journalism, 1951-53. Carnegie Corp. fellow, 1953; FAE-NAEB scholar, TV, 1954; sr. postdoctoral research fellow Am. Coll. Testing Program, 1970-71. Bd. dirs. Oregon Newspaper Pubs. Assn., 1950-55. Served to 1st lt. AUS, Iceland, 1942-45. Mem. Assn. Edn. in Journalism, Assn. Accredited Schs. and Depts. Journalism (pres. 1954-55), Am. Polit. Sci. Assn., Sigma Delta Chi (nat. research com. 1949-51), Omicron Delta Kappa. Author: When You Listen, This is What You Can Hear, 1971; How Students Rate Their Schools and Teachers, 1971; Teachers Tell It Like It Is, Like It Should Be, 1972; The Folks in the Newsroom, 1977. Office: 204 Price House Va Poly Inst and State U Blacksburg VA 24060

SABINS, ROLLAND CLIFFORD, lab. exec.; b. Viroqua, Wis., July 24, 1906; s. Milo S. and Elma (Wall) S.; m. Pearl Louise Sowers, Mar. 17, 1944; children—Todd, James, Capi, Craig, Sherry. Owner, mgr. Sabins Lab., San Diego, 1930—; partner Sabins, Dohrmann & Assos., 1967—; pres., dir. Sabins Industries, Inc., 1975—. Scientist, patentee basic atomic processes and marine corrosion control systems in U.S. and fgn. countries. Club: Admiral's (life). Address: 11917 Orchard Rd Lakeside CA 92040

SABISTON, DAVID COSTON, JR., educator, surgeon; b. Onslow County, N.C., Oct. 4, 1924; s. David Coston and Marie (Jackson) S.; B.S., U. N.C., 1943; M.D., Johns Hopkins, 1947; m. Agnes Barden, Sept. 24, 1955; children—Anne Barden, Agnes Foy, Sarah Coston. Successively intern, asst. resident, chief resident surgery Johns Hopkins Hosp., 1947-53; successively asst. prof., asso. prof., prof. surgery Johns Hopkins Med. Sch., 1955-64, Howard Hughes investigator, 1955-60; Fulbright research scholar U. Oxford (Eng.), 1960; research asso. Hosp. Sick Children, U. London (Eng.), 1961; James B. Duke prof. surgery, chmn. dept. Duke Med. Sch., 1964—, chief of staff Duke U. Hosp. Served to capt., M.C., AUS, 1953-55. Recipient Career Research award NIH, 1962-64; N.C. award in Sci., 1978. Diplomate Am. Bd. Surgery (chmn. 1971-72). Mem. A.C.S. (chmn. bd. govs. 1974-75, regent 1975—), Am. Surg. Assn. (pres. 1977-78), So. Surg. Assn. (sec. 1969-73, pres. 1974-76), Am. Assn. Thoracic Surgery, Soc. Clin. Surgery, Internat. Soc. Cardiovascular Surgery, Soc. Vascular Surgery (v.p. 1967-68), Soc. Univ. Surgeons (pres. 1968-69), Halsted Soc., Surg. Biology Club II, Soc. Thoracic Surgery, Soc. Surgery Alimentary Tract, Soc. Clin. Chairmen (pres. 1974-76), Soc. Thoracic Surgeons Great Britain and Ireland, Phi Beta Kappa, Alpha Omega Alpha. Editor: Christopher Davis Textbook of Surgery; The Biological Basis of Modern Surgical Practice; Gibbon's Surgery of the Chest; chmn. editorial bd. Annals Surgery, Jour. Cardiovascular and Thoracic Surgery, Archives Surgery, World Jour. Surgery. Home: 1528 Pinecrest Rd Durham NC 27706

SABLE, HENRY ZODOC, educator, physician; b. Toronto, Ont., Can., Apr. 1, 1918; s. Zodok and Bertha (Moshkevich) S.; B.A., U. Toronto, 1939, M.D., 1943; M.S., U. Ill., 1947; Ph.D., Washington U., St. Louis, 1950; m. Florence Molien, June 28, 1942; children—Marjorie Rose, Jeremiah Henry. Came to U.S., 1946, naturalized, 1957. Intern, Toronto Western Hosp., 1943; instr. Tufts Coll. Med. Sch., 1950, asst. prof., 1951-53; faculty Case Western Res. U., Cleve., 1953—, asso. prof., 1958-68, prof., 1968—, co-dir. dept. biochemistry, 1969-75, acting dir., 1975-78; vis. prof. U. Geneva, 1959-60; cons. VA Hosp., Cleve., 1964-71; mem. biochemistry test com. Nat. Bd. Med. Examiners, 1974—, chmn., 1977—. Trustee Cleve. Chamber Music Soc., 1962—, treas., 1964-66, v.p., 1969-70, pres., 1970-72. Served to surgeon-lt. comdr. Royal Canadian Navy, 1943-46. Mem. Am. Soc. Biol. Chemistry, Am. Chem. Soc. (chmn. Cleve. sect. 1967—, sec. div. biol. chemistry 1975-78, mem. council 1979—), AAAS. Jewish. Mem. editorial bd. Jour. Biol. Chemistry, 1977—. Home: 2614 Dysart Rd University Heights OH 44118 Office: 2119 Abington Rd Cleveland OH 44106

SABLE, MARTIN HOWARD, educator; b. Haverhill, Mass., Sept. 24, 1924; s. Benjamin and Ida (Saberlinsky) S.; student Northeastern U., 1942-43; A.B., Boston U., 1946, M.A., 1952; Dr. en Letras, Nat. U. Mexico, 1952; M.S. in Library Sci., Simmons Coll., 1959; m. Minna Gibbs, Feb. 5, 1950; children—James S., Charles D. Bibliographer, reference librarian Northeastern U., 1959-63; lang. librarian Calif. State Coll., Los Angeles, 1963-64; asst. research prof. Latin Am. Center, U. Calif. at Los Angeles, 1965-68; asso. prof. Sch. Library and Info. Sci., U. Wis.-Milw., 1968-72, prof., 1972—. Research librarian Harvard, 1962-63. Mem. ALA, Latin Am. Studies Assn., AAUP, Wis. Council Latinamericanists, Pacific Coast Council Latin Am. Studies (editor newsletter 1965-68). Author books, including: A Guide to Latin American Studies I-II, 1967; A Bio-Bibliography of the Kennedy Family, 1969; Latin American Urbanization, 1971; International and Area Studies Librarianship, 1973; The Guerrilla Movement in Latin America since 1950, 1977. Adv. editor Latin Am., Ency. Americana, 1967—. Home: 4518 N Larkin St Milwaukee WI 53211

SABLOFF, JEREMY ARAC, archaeologist; b. N.Y.C., Apr. 16, 1944; s. Louis and Helen (Arac) S.; A.B., U. Pa., 1964; M.A., Ph.D., Harvard U., 1969; m. Paula Lynne Weinberg, May 26, 1968; children—Joshua, Saralinda. Asst. prof., asso. prof. Harvard U., Cambridge, Mass., 1969-76; asso. prof. anthropology U. Utah, Salt Lake City, 1976-77; curator anthropology Utah Mus. Natural History, Salt Lake City, 1976-77; prof. anthropology U. N.Mex., Albuquerque, 1978—. Nat. Geog. Soc. grantee, 1972-74. Fellow Am. Anthrop. Assn., Royal Anthrop Inst.; mem. Soc. Am. Archaeology, Soc. Profl. Archaeologists, AAAS. Author: (with G.R. Willey) A History of American Archaeology, 1974; Excavations at Seibal: Ceramics, 1976; (with C.C. Lamberg-Karlovsky) Ancient Civilizations: The Near East and Mesoamerica, 1979. Editor: (with C.C. Lamberg-Karlovsky) Ancient Civilization and Trade, 1976; American Antiquity, 1977—. Office: U NMex Dept Anthropology Albuquerque NM 87131

SABO, MARTIN OLAV, congressman; b. Crosby, N.D., Feb. 28, 1938; s. Bjorn O. and Klara (Haga) S.; B.A. cum laude, Augsburg Coll., Mpls., 1959; postgrad. U. Minn., 1959-60; m. Sylvia Ann Lee, June 30, 1963; children—Karin, Julie. Mem. Minn. Ho. of Reps. from 57B Dist., 1960-78, Democratic-Farmer-Labor Party minority leader, 1969, 71, speaker, 1973-75, 77-78, chmn. joint legis. coordinating com., 1973, 75, 77; mem. 96th Congress from 5th Minn. Dist.; mem. Nat. Adv. Commn. on Intergovtl. Relations; past pres. Nat. Legis. Conf. Bd. regents Augsburg Coll.; trustee Luth. Deaconess Hosp. Recipient Augsburg Coll. Distinguished Alumni citation; named Man of Yr., Mpls. Jr. C. of C., 1973-74; One of Ten Outstanding Young Men of Yr., Minn. Jr. C. of C., 1974; One of 200 Rising Young Leaders in Am., Time mag., 1974. Mem. Nat. Conf. State Legis. Leaders (past pres.). Home: 3129 E 22d St Minneapolis MN 55406 Office: US Ho of Reps Longworth House Office Bldg Room B-227 Washington DC 20515

SABO, WALTER RICHARD, broadcasting exec.; b. Orange, N.J., Sept. 3, 1952; s. Walter Richard and Gloria (Vagon) S.; B.A. in English and Advt. cum laude, Syracuse U., 1973. Columnist, reporter Worrall Publs., Maplewood, N.J., 1968-70; news exec., air talent Sta.-WCRV, Washington, N.J., 1968-72; editor, writer Syracuse U. Publs. Office, 1972; promotion dir., newsman, talk show host Sta.-WOR-FM, N.Y.C., 1973-74; adminstr. sales promotion, talk show host Sta. WNBC-WNWS, N.Y.C., 1974-76; dir. ABC FM Radio Network, N.Y.C., 1976-78; exec. v.p. FM Radio Group, NBC, Inc., N.Y.C., 1978—; guest lectr. N.Y. U., Syracuse U. Recipient award for broadcasting journalism excellence Sigma Delta Chi, 1972, 1st Pl. award Kodak Mktg. Competition, 1972. Mem. Nat. Arts Club. Home: 241 3d Ave New York NY 10003 Office: 30 Rockefeller Plaza New York NY 10020

SABRA, ABDALHAMID IBRAHIM, historian; b. Egypt, June 8, 1924; B.A., U. Alexandria (Egypt), 1947; Ph.D., U. London, 1955; A.M., Harvard U., 1972; m. Nancy Louise Sutton, June 2, 1955; children—Adam, Peter. Lectr., asso. prof. U. Alexandria; sr. fellow, lectr., reader Warburg Inst., U. London; prof. history of Arabic sci. Harvard U. NSF grantee, Nat. Endowment for Humanities grantee. Mem. History of Sci. Soc., Brit. Soc. for History Sci., Academie Internationale d'Histoire des Sciences. Clubs: The Shop, Harvard U. Author books, including: Omar Khayyam on Difficulties in Euclid's Postulates, 1961; Theories of Light from Descartes to Newton, 1967; Avicenna's Principles of Geometry, 1977; also articles on history of sci. in Islamic middle ages and in 17th-century Europe, especially on optics, geometry, and astronomy; asso. editor: Dictionary of Scientific Biography; mem. bd. Isis, History of Sci. (U.K.), Jour. for History Arabic Sci. (Syria). Home: 37 Woodland Rd Lexington MA 02173 Office: 235 Sci Center Harvard U Cambridge MA 02138*

SABROSKY, CURTIS WILLIAMS, entomologist; b. Sturgis, Mich., Apr. 3, 1910; s. Herman August and Jennie (Curtis) S.; A.B., Kalamazoo Coll., 1931, Sc.D. (hon.), 1966; postgrad. U. Mich.; M.S., Kans. State U., 1933. Mem. faculty Mich. State U. 1936-44, asst. prof. entomology, 1944; research entomologist Dept. Agr., Washington, 1946—, dir. Systematic Entomology Lab., 1967-73. Mem. Internat. Commn. on Zool. Nomenclature, 1963—, mem. council, 1972—, pres., 1977—; mem. Permanent Com. for Internat. Congresses Entomology. 1960—; pres. XV Internat. Congress Entomology, 1976. Recipient Superior Service award U.S. Dept. Agr., 1962, Distinguished Service award Kans. State U., 1965. Fellow Entomol. Soc. Can., AAAS; mem. Assn. Tropical Biology, Am. Inst. Biol. Scis., Entomol. Soc. Am. (hon. mem., life, pres. 1969), Am. (corr. mem.), Kans., Mich. entomol. socs., All Union Entomol. Soc. (hon. fgn.), Soc. Systematic Zoology (pres. 1962), Entomol. Soc. Washington (pres. 1972). Research, numerous publs. on classification and recognition of flies of certain families, zool. nomenclature. Home: 8610 Grant St Bethesda MD 20034 Office: Systematic Entomology I S Dept Agr US Nat Mus Washington DC 20560

SACCIO, LEONARD JOHN, lawyer, former diplomat; b. N.Y.C., Sept. 24, 1911; s. Joseph and Mary (Rallo) S.; B.S.S., Coll. City N.Y., 1932; J.D., Columbia, 1935; m. Churchill Susan Freshman, Oct. 4, 1936; children—Mary A. (Mrs. Raymond E. Gateley), Peter C., Edward A. Admitted to N.Y. bar, 1935, also Conn. bar; asso. firm McLean, Ferris, Ely and Fain, N.Y.C., 1937-38; asst. atty. gen., spl. Kings County investigation, N.Y. State, 1939-42; spl. atty. anti-trust div., war frauds unit, Dept. of Justice, 1942-43; successively gen. counsel, asst. sec., dir. Berger Bros. Co., New Haven, 1943-54; dep. gen. counsel, acting gen. counsel ICA, 1954-56, gen. counsel, 1956-58, dep. dir., 1958-60; econ. minister, Rio de Janeiro, dir. AID Program, Brazil, 1960-62; dep. chief mission Am. embassy, San Salvador, El Salvador, 1962-65; dep. chief mission, Buenos Aires, Argentina, 1965-69; dir. AID Mission to India, 1969-70; U.S. ambassador to Colombia, 1970-73; atty., cons. on fgn. relations, Woodbury, Conn., 1973—; lectr. internat. law, U. Conn. Sch. Law, 1976—. Pros. grand juror, town counsel, justice of peace, Bethlehem, Conn., 1945-54. Selectman, Woodbury, Conn., 1978—, 1st selectman, 1979—. Home: 482 Grassy Hill Rd Woodbury CT 06798 Office: Shore Bldg Main St Woodbury CT 06798

SACCO, IGNATIUS JOSEPH, advt. exec.; b. N.Y.C., Aug. 13, 1920; s. Pellegrino and Rosa (Bongiovi) S.; ed. Coll. City N.Y., 1937-41; m. Hermine Malbin, Jan. 23, 1954; children—Kevin, Joseph. With creative depts. Grey, Y&R, Esty, Bates, NC&K, 1946-65; mng. dir. PKL Ltd., London, 1965-68; pres. Joe Sacco and Friends, N.Y.C., Calif. and London, 1967-72; exec. v.p., creative dir. Moseley Sacco, N.Y.C., 1972-76; pres. Joe Sacco, Inc., N.Y.C., 1976—; dir. Wood Brigdale Ltd., London, Trenear-Harvey Bird & Watson Ltd., London; faculty Sch. Visual Arts, N.Y.C., 1977—. Author: LaGuerre, 1943; (article series) The Risky Life, 1971; co-author: The Negro in American Films, 1949. Home: 311 E 71st St New York NY 10021 Office: 65 E 55th St New York NY 10022

SACHAR, ABRAM LEON, univ. chancellor; b. N.Y.C., N.Y., Feb. 15, 1899; s. Samuel and Sarah (Abramowitz) S.; student Harvard, 1918-19; B.A., M.A., Washington U., St. Louis, 1920, LL.D., 1955; Ph.D., Emmanuel Coll., U. Cambridge (Eng.), 1923; H.H.D. (hon.), Ill. Wesleyan U., 1943, Lowell U., Mass., 1978; Dr. Hebrew Letters, Hebrew Union Coll., 1945; Ed.D. (hon.), R.I. Coll. Edn., 1950, Calvin Coolidge Coll., 1963; Litt. D., Boston U., 1952, Northeastern U., 1960, U. Ill., 1964, Providence Coll., 1965; L.H.D., Boston Coll., 1966; LL.D., U. R.I., 1953, Tufts U., 1955, U. Mass., 1957, Notre Dame U., 1964, Bowdoin Coll., 1964, Brandeis U., 1968, Lafayette Coll., 1968, George Washington U., 1972, Suffolk U., 1973, L.I. U., 1976; D.Sc., Norwich U., 1968; D.H.L., U. Santa Clara, 1968; hon. degree Weizmann Inst. Sci., Rehoveth, Israel, 1969, U. Hartford, 1970; H.H.D., Springfield Coll., 1969; D.Pedagogy, Mercy Coll., N.Y., 1978; m. Thelma Horwitz, June 6, 1926; children—Howard Morley, Edward Joel, David Bernard. Instr. history U. Ill., 1923-29; dir. Hillel Found., U. Ill., 1929-33; nat. dir. B'nai B'rith Hillel Founds. (series of 192 centers on univ. campuses for students), Champaign, Ill., 1933-48, chmn. Nat. Hillel Found. Commn., 1948-55, hon. chmn., 1955—; pres. Brandeis U., Waltham, Mass., 1948-68, chancellor, 1968—; cons. edn. Spl. Commn. on Structure of State Govt., Commonwealth of Mass., 1950; mem. Mass. Com. on Fulbright awards, 1962—; mem. U.S. Adv. Commn. on Internat. Edn. and Cultural Affairs, 1967-72. Trustee Am. ORT Fedn., Am. Jewish Hist. Soc.; bd. govs. Hebrew U.; trustee Palestine Endowment Funds, Inc., Jewish Acad. Arts and Scis., Kennedy Meml. Library, Eleanor Roosevelt Meml. Found.; bd. advisers Nova U., Tugaloo U. Decorated Grosse Verdienstkreuz mit Stern (West Germany), 1969; recipient Spirit of St. Louis award St. Louis U., 1977. Fellow Am. Acad. Arts and Scis.; mem. Phi Beta Kappa. Jewish. Mem. B'nai B'rith. Clubs: Pinebrook, Belmont, Boston (Mass.); Harmonie (N.Y.C.). Author: A History of the Jews, 1929, 5th edit. (Anisfield-Wolf award 1965), Spanish edit. in Chile, 1943, French edit., 1973; Sufferance is the Badge, 1939; The Course of Our Times, 1972, Japanese edit., 3 vols., 1976; A Host at Last, 1977; weekly telecasts Course of Our Times on Nat. Ednl. TV, 1969—; also articles in New Republic, Sat. Rev. Editor and compiler: Religion of a Modern Liberal, 1932. Home: 66 Beaumont Ave Newtonville MA 02160 Office: Brandeis U Waltham MA 02154

SACHAR, EDWARD JOEL, psychiatrist; b. St. Louis, June 23, 1933; s. Abram Leon and Thelma (Horwitz) S.; A.B., Harvard U., 1952; M.D., U. Pa., 1956. Intern Beth Israel Hosp., Boston, 1956-57; resident Mass. Mental Health Center, Boston, 1957-59; asso. in psychiatry Harvard Med. Sch., Boston, 1964-66; asso. prof. psychiatry Albert Einstein Coll. Medicine, Bronx, N.Y., 1966-72, prof. psychiatry, 1972-76, chmn. dept., 1975-76; prof., chmn. dept. psychiatry Columbia U. Coll. Physicians and Surgeons, N.Y.C., 1976—; dir. N.Y. State Psychiat. Inst., 1976—; chmn. program-projects rev. com. NIMH, 1975-77. Served to capt. M.C., U.S. Army, 1959-61. Recipient Anna-Monika Found. prize for research in depression, 1975; USPHS NIMH grantee, 1963—. Mem. Am. Psychosomatic Soc. (sec. treas. 1976), Am. Psychopathol. Assn. (council 1976), Assn. for Research in Nervous and Mental Diseases (trustee 1975—), Am. Psychiat. Assn. (council on research 1976—), Psychiat. Research Soc. (pres. 1975), Am. Coll.

Neuropsychopharmacology. Author: Topics in Psychoendocrinology, 1975; Hormones, Behavior and Psychopathology, 1976. Mem. editorial bd. Ann. Rev. of Medicine, Handbook of Biol. Psychiatry, Psychoneuroendocrinology. Contbr. articles to profl. jours. Home: 945 Fifth Ave New York NY 10021 Office: 722 W 168th St New York NY 10032

SACHAR, HOWARD MORLEY, historian; b. St. Louis, Feb. 10, 1928; s. Abram Leon and Thelma (Horwitz) S.; B.A., Swarthmore Coll., 1947; M.A., Harvard U., 1950, Ph.D., 1953; m. Eliana Steimatzky, July 23, 1963; children—Sharon, Michele, Daniel. Instr. history U. Mass., 1953-54; dir. Hillel Found. UCLA, 1954-57; dir. Hillel Found., Stanford (Calif.) U., 1959-61; dir. Hiatt Inst. in Israel, 1961-64; asso. prof. history George Washington U., Washington, 1964-66, prof., 1966—. Charles Brown fellow, 1957-58; Nat Endowment for Humanities fellow, 1970-71. Mem. Am. Hist. Assn., Am. Jewish Hist. Soc., Phi Beta Kappa. Democrat. Jewish. Author: The Course of Modern Jewish History, 1958; Aliyah, 1961; From the Ends of the Earth, 1964; The Emergence of the Middle East, 1969; Europe Leaves the Middle East, 1972; A History of Israel, 1976; contbr. articles to N.Y. Times Book Rev., New Republic, Commentary, others. Home: 9807 Hillridge Dr Kensington MD 20795 Office: Dept History George Washington U Washington DC 20052

SACHS, ALAN RICHARD, lawyer; b. Balt., Nov. 4, 1944; s. Paul Aaron and Shirley (Lee) S.; A.B., U. Md., 1964, LL.B., 1967; m. Diane C. Dubow, July 17, 1967; children—Kimberly Dee, Ryan Scott. Admitted to Md. bar, 1967, since practiced in Balt.; mem. firm Gordon, Feinblatt, Rothman, Hoffberger & Hollander, 1979—; lectr. law U. Balt. Sch. Law, 1968—, U. Md. Sch. Law, 1978—. Mem. Md. Blue Sky Adv. Commn., 1973-75. Recipient Outstanding Instr. award U. Balt. Sch. Law, 1975. Mem. Am., Md. bar assns., Jr. Bar Assn. Balt., Order of Coif. Mason. Club: Center (Balt.). Co-author: Securities Regulation Forms—Compliance—Practice, 1975; Maryland Corporate Forms-Practice, 1976. Editorial bd. Md. Law Rev., 1964-67. Contbr. articles to legal jours. Home: 5708 Chilham Rd Baltimore MD 21209 Office: Garrett Bldg 233 E Redwood St Baltimore MD 21202

SACHS, ALLAN MAXWELL, physicist, educator; b. N.Y.C., July 13, 1921; s. George M. and Elsa (Shenfield) S.; grad. Horace Mann Sch., 1938; B.A., Harvard, 1942, M.A., 1947. Ph.D., 1949; m. Judith Morrison, Dec. 19, 1949; children—Carolyn, George Morrison, Marjorie. Instr. physics Columbia, N.Y.C., 1949-50, asso., 1950-51, asst. prof., 1951-55, asso. prof., 1955-60, prof., 1960—, chmn. dept. physics, 1967-71, chmn. exec. com. senate, 1971-74. Served to maj. USAAF, 1942-45. Decorated Bronze Star. Fellow Am. Phys. Soc.; mem. Am. Assn. Physics Tchrs., Phi Beta Kappa. Contbr. articles to profl. jours. Research on particle physics. Home: 51 Belden Ave Dobbs Ferry NY 10522 Office: Pupin Lab Columbia New York City NY 10027

SACHS, BENJAMIN K., mfg. co. exec.; b. N.Y.C., Oct. 27, 1930; s. Harry and Augusta (Engel) S.; student Cornell U., 1948-50; B.S. in Indsl. Engring., Columbia, 1952, M.S., 1954; m. Ethel F. Hecht, June 29, 1958; children—David, Leslie, Lawrence. Mgr. planning and control Ketay dept. Norden div. United Aircraft Corp., Commack, N.Y., 1952-60; gen. mgr. Paratron div. Litton Industries, Mt. Vernon, N.Y., 1960-63; dir. reliability and quality assurance Vernitron Corp., Farmingdale, N.Y., 1963-67, sec., 1967-70, sec.-treas., Great Neck, N.Y., 1970-72, v.p., sec., dir., 1972—; dir. Am. Med. Instrument Corp., AST/Servo Systems, Inc., Lafayette Grinding Corp., Lafayette Saw & Knife Corp., Vernitron Elec. Components, Inc., Vernitron Med. Products, Inc., Vernitron Corp. Class chmn. Columbia Engring. Alumni Fund, 1962—; mem. Thomas Egleston Assos., 1967—. Trustee Vernitron Found. Recipient Wendell medal Columbia, 1952. Mem. I.E.E.E., Am. Inst. Indsl. Engrs., Am. Soc. M.E., Am. Soc. Quality Control, Am. Soc. Corporate Secs., Cornell Soc. Engrs., Columbia Engring. Sch. Alumni Assn., Tau Beta Pi, Alpha Pi Mu, Alpha Epsilon Pi. Home: 28 Radcliff Dr Huntington NY 11743 Office: 175 Community Dr Great Neck NY 11021. *Everyone is capable of achieving some of his goals and no one is capable of achieving all of his goals. Personal success lies in identifying one's own rational combination of goals and then working toward their achievement.*

SACHS, BERNICE COHEN (MRS. ALLAN ELI SACHS), physician; b. Passaic, N.J., Sept. 16, 1918; d. Joseph and Rose (Mirelson) Cohen; B.A. with distinction, U. Mich., 1939, M.D. cum laude, 1942; m. Allan Eli Sachs, Dec. 21, 1941; children—Lee William, Robin Beth. Intern, Michael Reese Hosp., Chgo., 1942-43; resident Inst. Psychosomatic and Psychiat. Research and Tng., Chgo., 1945-49; practice medicine in Seattle, specializing in psychiatry and psychosomatic medicine, 1949—; mem. staff Michael Hosp., 1942-49, Group Health Clinic and Hosp., Seattle, 1949—, St. Francis Xavier Cabrini Hosp. Psychiatry Service; chief mental health service Group Health Co-op. Puget Sound, Seattle; chmn. Alcohol and Drug Abuse Commn. Internat. lectr. Bd. dirs. Health and Welfare Council Seattle-King County, 1957-60; exec. com., bd. dirs. Seattle-King County Safety Council, 1960-63; cons. Chgo. Bd. Pub. Health, 1965-66, Med. Womanpower, 1966; mem. Wash. Gov.'s Adv. Com. Youth Opportunities, 1962-65; chmn. children's program com. Jewish Community Center, Seattle, 1955-59; bd. dirs. Western div. Jewish Welfare Bd., 1958-59, past Pres.'s Assembly, 1961-62; ex-officio bd. dirs. Women's Med. Coll. Pa., 1965; v.p. women's div. Jewish Fedn. and Council, 1966-67; mem. women's com. Brandeis U. Recipient Elizabeth Blackwell award, 1979; named Woman of Achievement, Theta Sigma Pi, 1965, Med. Woman of Yr., Am. Med. Women's Assn. 1966. Fellow Soc. Clin. and Exptl. Hypnosis, Acad. Psychosomatic Medicine (exec. council 1973-76, 79—, sec. 1976-78), Am. Group Psychotherapy Assn., AAAS, Am. Soc. Clin. Hypnosis (treas. 1973-76, 1st v.p. 1976-77, pres. 1977, newsletter editor 1978-79), Am. Geriatrics Soc. (founding fellow West div. 1973), Am. Psychiat. Assn. (pres. Seattle chpt. 1976-77, council internat. affairs 1978-79); mem. AMA, Wash., King County (media relations com. 1964-66, 74-76 mental health com. 1967-73, chmn. alcohol and drug abuse) med. socs., Am. Psychiat. Assn. (pres. Seattle chpt. 1976-77), Am. Psychosomatic Soc., Wash. Acad. Clin. Hypnosis (v.p. 1969-70, pres. 1970-73, 75-77, hon. pres. 1977—), Internat. Soc. Hypnosis, Am. (past pres., sponsor Bernice C. Sachs jr. br. U. Wash. Med. Sch.), Seattle (pres. br. 37, 1959-64) med. women's assns., Pan Am. Med. Women's Alliance (corr. sec. 1960-62, v.p. of U.S. 1962-64), Med. Women's Internat. Assn., Soc. Clin. and Exptl. Hypnosis, Council Med. Administrs., Internat. Platform Assn., AAUW, Soroptimist, Puget Sound Group Psychotherapy Soc., Am. Soc. Clin. Hypnosis (fellow research and ednl. found.), Am., Puget Sound group psychotherapy assns., Nat. Council Jewish Women, Intercoll. Assn. Women Students (nat. resources personnel bd.), Hadassah (Myrtle Wreath award 1967), Nat. Forensic League (Ruby Eye of Distinction), B'nai B'rith Women, Women's Am. ORT, Mortar Board (hon.), Phi Beta Kappa, Alpha Omega Alpha, Phi Kappa Phi, Iota Sigma Pi, Alpha Lambda Delta. Clubs: Women's University (Seattle); Glendale Country. Contbr. articles to profl. jours. Home: 13 El Dorado Beach Club Dr Mercer Island WA 98040 Office: 200 15th Ave E Seattle WA 98112

SACHS, GLORIA, designer; b. N.Y.C., Feb. 17, 1927; d. Jacob Harris and Sylvia Wasserman; B.S., Skidmore Coll., 1947; student Cranbrook Acad. Art, 1947, Ferdinand Leger, 1949; m. Irwin Sachs, Mar. 22, 1953; children—Nancy Fairchild, Charles Williard. Fabric designer Hans Knoll and Herman Miller, N.Y.C., 1948-49; apprentice Domus (archtl. mag.), Milan, Italy, 1949-50; with exec. tng. program, fashion coordinator, asst. buyer Bloomingdale's, 1951-56; designer-mfr. pre-teen clothes Red Barn, 1958-60; designer Saks Fifth Ave., 1962-65; pres.-owner-designer Gloria Sachs Designs Ltd., N.Y.C., 1970—. Recipient Saks Fifth Ave Creator award, 1969; Woolknit Design award, 1974, 76. Paintings, sculptures, fabric designs exhibited Pratt Inst., N.Y.C., 1949, Art Alliance Phila., 1950, Art Inst. Chgo., 1950, Mus. Modern Art, N.Y.C., 1951. Mem. Fashion Group (dir.). Office: Gloria Sachs Designs Ltd 550 7th Ave New York NY 10018

SACHS, MORRIS BERNARD, JR., retail clothing mcht.; b. Chgo., May 13, 1933; s. Morris B. and Anna (Baker) S.; B.S., U. Ill., 1954; m. Gail Diane Holsman, Sept. 28, 1958; children—Morris Bernard III, Mark Bernard, Amy Beth. Pres. Morris B. Sachs, Inc., Chgo., 1957-76, also dir.; v.p. Nu-Art, Inc., Chgo. Mem. Neighborhood Redevel. Commn., City Chgo., 1958—, now vice chmn.; dir. State Street Council. Bd. dirs. John Howard Assn., 52 Assn. of Ill.; trustee St. Procopius Coll., Lisle, Ill., Midwest chpt. Nat. Hemophilia Found.; mem. U. Ill. Citizens Com.; mem. Midwest adv. bd. Am. Med. Center; pres., dir. Morris B. Sachs Found., 1957—; citizens bd. Loyola U. Served from 2d lt. to 1st lt. Q.M.C., U.S. Army 1954-56. Named one of ten outstanding young men Chgo. Jr. Assn. Commerce and Industry, 1960. Mem. Internat. Thermographers Assn. (dir.), U. Ill. Commerce Alumni Assn. (dir.), Young Pres.'s Orgn. Clubs: Moose, Garment (N.Y.C.); Lions, Standard (Chgo.); Idlewild Country (Flossmoor, Ill.). Home: 2343 Golfview Ave Flossmoor IL 60422 Office: 6247 W 74th St Chicago IL 60638

SACHS, MURRAY, educator; b. Toronto, Ont., Can., Apr. 10, 1924; s. Thomas and Sarah (Roth) S.; B.A., U. Toronto, 1946; A.M., Columbia, 1947, Ph.D., 1953; m. Miriam Blank, Sept. 14, 1961; children—Deborah Ruth, Aaron Jacob. Came to U.S., 1948, naturalized, 1954. Instr. French, U. Calif. at Berkeley, 1948-50; asst. prof. Romanic langs. Williams Coll., 1954-60; prof. French, Brandeis U., 1960—, chmn. dept. Romance langs. and comparative lit., 1967-71, chmn. grad. program lit. studies, 1975-78. Decorated chevalier Palmes Académiques (France). Mem. Modern Lang. Assn., AAUP, Modern Humanities Research Assn., Assn. Internationale des études Françaises. Author: The Career of Alphonse Daudet, 1965; The French Short Story in the Nineteenth Century: a Critical Anthology, 1969; Anatole France: The Short Stories, 1974. Contbr. to profl. jours. Home: 280 Highland Ave West Newton MA 02165 Office: Brandeis U Waltham MA 02154

SACHS, RAINER KURT, physicist; b. Germany, June 13, 1932; s. George Oscar and Liselotte (Lehmann) S.; came to U.S., 1938, naturalized, 1946; B.S., Mass. Inst. Tech., 1953; Ph.D., Syracuse U., 1958; m. Aug. 20, 1954 (div. June 1978); children—Anna, Elizabeth, Carol, Margaret. Prof. physics and math. U. Calif., Berkeley, 1968—. Served with Signal Corps, U.S. Army, 1959-60. Guggenheim fellow, 1970-71. Mem. Am. Phys. Soc., Am. Astron. Assn., Am. Math. Soc. Author: General Relativity and Cosmology, 1971; (with H. Wu) General Relativity for Mathematicians, 1977. Home: 5300 Shafter St Oakland CA 94618 Office: U Calif Berkeley CA 94720

SACHS, RAYMOND JOSEPH, JR., advt. exec.; b. Orange, N.J., Oct. 11, 1939; s. Raymond Joseph and Monica Ruane (Greeley) S.; A.B., Georgetown U., 1961; J.D., U. Md., 1965; m. Catherine Phoebe Ward, Sept. 19, 1964; children—Catherine Alexandra, Mary Greeley, Anthony Ward. With Van Sant, Dugdale & Co., Inc., Balt., 1963—, sr. v.p., 1976, exec. v.p., 1976—. Home: 4505 Roland Ave Baltimore MD 21210 Office: World Trade Center Baltimore MD 21202

SACHS, ROBERT GREEN, physicist, educator; lab. adminstr.; b. Hagerstown, Md., May 4, 1916; s. Harry Maurice and Anna (Green) S.; Ph.D., Johns Hopkins, 1939; D.Sc. (hon.), Purdue U., 1967, U. Ill., 1977; m. Selma Solomon, Aug. 28, 1941; m. 2d, Jean K. Woolf, Dec. 17, 1950; children—Rebecca, Jennifer, Jeffrey, Judith, Joel; m. 3d, Carolyn L. Wolf, Aug. 21, 1968; stepchildren—Thomas Wolf, Jacqueline Wolf, Katherine Wolf. Research fellow George Washington U., 1939-41; instr. physics Purdue U., 1941-43; on leave as lectr., research fellow U. Calif. at Berkeley, 1941; sect. chief Ballistic Research Lab., Aberdeen (Md.) Proving Ground, 1943-45; dir. theoretical physics div. Argonne Nat. Lab., 1945-47; asso. prof. physics U. Wis., 1947-48, prof., 1948-64; asso. dir. Argonne Nat. Lab., 1964-68; prof. physics U. Chgo., 1964—, dir. Enrico Fermi Inst., 1968-73; dir. Argonne Nat. Lab., 1973-78; Higgins vis. prof. Princeton U., 1955-56; vis. prof. U. Paris, 1959-60, Tohoku U., Japan, 1974; cons. Ballistic Research Labs., 1945-59, Argonne Nat. Lab., 1947-50, 60-64; cons. radiation lab. U. Calif. at Berkeley, 1955-59; adv. panel physics NSF, 1958-61; chmn. elementary particle physics panel Nat. Acad. Scis.; 1969-72; high energy physics adv. panel div. research AEC, 1966-69. Research in theoretical nuclear and atomic physics, terminal ballistics, nuclear power reactors, theoretical particle physics. Vice pres. Midwest Center. Guggenheim fellow, 1959-60. Fellow Am. Acad. Arts and Scis.; mem. Nat. Acad. Scis. (chmn. physics sect. 1977-80), Am. Phys. Soc. (council 1968-71), regional sec. Central States 1964-69), AAAS (v.p., chmn. physics sect. 1970-71), Am. Inst. Physics (mem. governing bd. 1969-71), Phi Beta Kappa, Sigma Xi. Author: Nuclear Theory, 1953. Chief editor: High Energy Nuclear Physics. 1957; editor: National Energy Issues: How Do We Decide?, 1979. Home: 5490 South Shore Dr Chicago IL 60615 Office: Enrico Fermi Inst 5630 Ellis Ave U Chgo Chicago IL 60637

SACHS, SAMUEL, II, museum dir.; b. N.Y.C., Nov. 30, 1935; s. James Henry and Margery (Fay) S.; B.A. cum laude, Harvard, 1957; M.A., N.Y. U., 1962; m. Susan McAllen, Aug. 17, 1957 (div. 1968); children—Katherine, Eleanor; m. 2d, Jerre S. Hollander, Nov. 8, 1969; 1 son, Alexander. Asst. in charge prints and drawings Mpls. Inst. Arts, 1958-60; asst. dir. U. Mich. Mus. of Art, Ann Arbor, 1963-64; chief curator Mpls. Inst. of Arts, 1964-73, dir., 1973—. Trustee Middlesex Sch. Decorated knight 1st class Order North Star (Sweden). Mem. Am. Fedn. Arts (exhbn. com.), Coll. Art Assn., Am. Assn. Museums, Harvard Alumni Assn. (dir.). Clubs: 555; Skylight; Century Assn.; Harvard (pres. 1966). Home: 1786 James Ave S Minneapolis MN 55403 Office: 2400 3d Ave S Minneapolis MN 55404

SACHS, SIDNEY STANLEY, lawyer; b. Washington, Dec. 25, 1916; s. William Michael and Rebecca (Krupsaw) S.; B.A., Am. U., 1937; LL.B., Georgetown U., 1941; m. Betty Kossow, Nov. 20, 1941; children—Ellen (Mrs. Richard Rodin), Susan (Mrs. Richard W. Goldman), Jane, John. Admitted to D.C. bar, 1942, Md. bar, 1949, also U.S. Supreme Ct.; law clk. to judge U.S. Emergency Ct. Appeals, 1943-45; asst. U.S. atty. D.C., 1945-49; practice law, D.C. and Md., 1949—; instr. Washington Coll. Law, Am. U., 1947-52; mem. bd. Inst. Criminal Law and Procedure, Georgetown U., 1955—, chmn. continuing legal edn. adv. bd., 1979—. adv. com. legal intern program, 1965—; mem. Jud. Conf. for D.C., 1958—. Bd. govs. Citizens Communications Center; bd. dirs. D.C. Assn. Mental Health, 1964-66; trustee Pub. Defender Service, 1965-75, Washington Sch. Psychiatry, 1973—; chmn. bd. Hearing, Ednl. Aid and Research Found., 1976—. Fellow Am. Bar Found.; mem. Am. (ho. of dels. 1970—, state del. 1972—), Fed. (sec. com. atomic energy 1950-52), Inter-Am. bar assns., Bar Assn. D.C. (pres. research found. 1959, pres. assn. 1966-67, bd. govs. 1972-75, ACLU. Jewish. Club: Federal City, Burning Tree (Washington). Home: 2717 Daniel Rd Chevy Chase MD 20015 Office: 1620 I St NW Washington DC 20006

SACHS, STEPHEN HOWARD, state atty. gen.; b. Balt., Jan. 31, 1934; s. Leon and Shirley (Blum) S.; A.B., Haverford Coll., 1954; postgrad. New Coll., Oxford, Eng., 1954-55; LL.B., Yale U., 1960; m. Sheila Kleinman, Sept. 4, 1960; children—Elisabeth Leon. Admitted to Md. Ct. Appeals bar, 1960, U.S. Dist. Ct. bar, 1961, 4th Circuit Ct. Appeals bar, 1961, U.S. Supreme Ct. bar, 1965; law clk. U.S. Ct. Appeals, Washington, 1960-61; asst. U.S. atty. for Dist. of Md., 1961-64, U.S. atty., 1967-70; individual practice law, Balt., 1970-78; atty. gen. State of Md., Balt., 1978—; lectr. Md. Sch. of Law. Trustee Enoch Pratt Free Library; bd. dirs. Sinai Hosp., 1969-72, Balt. ARC, 1970-73, Balt. Bar Found., Inc. Served with U.S. Army, 1955-57. Fulbright scholar, 1954-55. Fellow Am. Coll. Trial Lawyers; mem. Am. Bar Assn., Md. State Bar Assn., Balt. Bar Assn., Fed. Bar Assn., Nat. Urban Coalition and Lawyers Com. for Civil Rights Under the Law. Democrat. Jewish. Home: 2426 Brambleton Rd Baltimore MD 21209 Office: 1 S Clavert St Baltimore MD 21202

SACHSE, HARRY RUBENSTEIN, lawyer; b. Baton Rouge, Apr. 1, 1934; s. Victor A. and Janice (Rubenstein) S.; B.A., La. State U., 1955, LL.B., 1957; Diplôme en Droit Compare, U. Paris, 1958; m. Elinor Yudin, Nov. 30, 1975; children—Michael Judah, Marianna Victoria. Admitted to La. bar, 1957, D.C. bar, 1976; partner firm Breazeale, Sachse & Wilson, Baton Rouge, 1958-63; asst., then asso. prof. Tulane U. Law Sch., 1962-68; vis. prof. U. Calif., Davis, also Stanford law schs., 1968-69; asst. gen. counsel AID, Washington, 1969-71; asst. to solicitor gen. U.S., 1971-76; partner firm Sonosky, Chambers & Sachse, Washington, 1976—; adj. prof. U. Va. Law Sch., 1974—. Mem. Am. Law Inst., Order of Coif. Editor-in-chief La. Law Rev., 1956-57. Home: 2934 Newark St NW Washington DC 20008 Office: 2030 M St NW Washington DC 20036

SACHSE, VICTOR A., JR., lawyer; b. Baton Rouge, Sept. 21, 1903; s. Victor A. and Fannye (Bloomenstiel) S.; LL.B., La. State U., 1925; m. Janice Rubenstein, Jan. 2, 1929; children—Victor A. III, Harry R. Admitted to La. bar, 1925, U.S. Supreme Ct. bar, 1934; practiced in Baton Rouge, 1925—; mem. firm Breazeale, Sachse & Wilson; gen. counsel Surplus Property Adminstrn., Washington, 1945-46; dir. Fidelity Nat. Bank. Chmn. prisoner of war adv. com. to sec. of Air Force, 1963-64. Chmn. City-Parish Plan Commn., 1947-48; parish atty., East Baton Rouge, 1949-50. Bd. dirs. Council for a Better La., Found. for Better La., La. Arts and Sci. Center, 1965-67, La. State U. Found. Served to lt. col., AUS, 1942-45. Decorated Legion of Merit. Recipient Brotherhood award NCCJ, 1972. Fellow Am. Coll. Trial Lawyers; mem. Am., La. (bd. govs. 1957-58), Baton Rouge (pres. 1941-42) bar assns., Am., La. (council) law insts., Mil. Order World Wars, Am. Legion, Am. Jewish Com. (mem.-at-large ho. dels.), Order Coif (hon.), Phi Delta Phi. Jewish (pres. congregation 1931, 35). Club: Mason (knight comdr. ct. honor). Home: 370 S Lakeshore Dr Baton Rouge LA 70808 Office: Fidelity Bank Bldg Baton Rouge LA 70801 Died Jan. 1, 1979.

SACHTLEBEN, CARL HENRY, librarian; b. Hoyleton, Ill., June 24, 1919; s. Albert F. and Eleanora (Kasten) S.; A.B., Valparaiso U., 1941; B.S. in L.S., Western Res. U., 1947; postgrad. U. Chgo., 1948-50; M.A., Washington U., St. Louis, 1953; m. Helen E. Rowoldt, July 23, 1942; children—Carl R., Paul L., John R., Philip J., Anita M. Asst. librarian Valparaiso U., 1946-50, dir. libraries, 1964-71; dir. libraries Western Mich. U., Kalamazoo, 1971—; librarian Luth. High Sch., St. Louis, 1950-57; asst. to dir. St. Louis U. Library, 1958-64. Chmn. Midwest Acad. Librarians Conf., 1965-67, Assn. Am. Colls.-Am. Coll. Research Libraries Joint Com. on Library Problems, 1966-68. Served to capt. Transp. Corps, AUS, 1941-46. Mem. Am., Mich. (legis. com. 1978-79) library assns., Am. Coll. Research Libraries (chmn. coll. libraries sect. 1970-71), Mich. Library Consortium (chmn. bd. 1975-77), Luth. Acad. Scholarship, Beta Phi Mu. Democrat. Rotarian. Editor: Mo. Library Assn. Quar., 1959-63. Home: 3413 Leversee Rd Paw Paw MI 49079 Office: Waldo Library Western Mich U Kalamazoo MI 49001

SACK, SYLVAN HANAN, lawyer; b. Phila., Dec. 26, 1932; s. Isidore F. and Mollye (Bellmore) S.; M.S. in Bus. Adminstrn., Pa. State U., 1956; J.D., U. Balt., 1964; m. Ellen L. Foreman, Aug. 13, 1972; children—Reuben H., Sara I. Admitted to Md. bar, 1964, U.S. Tax Ct. bar, 1967, U.S. Supreme Ct. bar, 1970; agt. IRS, Balt., 1956-67; practice in Balt., 1967—. Bd. dirs. Safety First Club of Md., 1972-75, asso. counsel, 1975-78, counsel, 1979—; gov. Md. chpt. Retinitis Pigmentosa Found., 1974-75. Recipient McLeod award Nat. Assn. Accountants, 1975. C.P.A., Md. Mem. Fed. (gov. chpt. 1968—, chmn. bd. govs. 1969-70), Am. (chmn. subcom. sect. taxation 1972-75), Md. bar assns., Am. Trial Lawyers Assn. Contbr. articles to profl. jours. Home: 4420 Wickford Rd Baltimore MD 21210 Office: 2404 St Paul St Baltimore MD 21218

SACKETT, ALBERT MONROE, ret. naval officer; b. Victor, Iowa, June 24, 1920; s. Frank T. and Clara M. (DeMeulenaere) S.; B.A., George Washington U., 1967; m. Patricia A. Soer, Aug. 2, 1947; children—Priscilla, Timothy, Albert, Kirk, David, Julie. Served as enlisted man U.S. Navy, 1937-44; commd. ensign U.S. Navy, 1944, advanced through grades to rear adm., 1972; head Missile Systems Tng. br., chief Naval Personnel, spl. asst. to under sec. Navy, 1962-65; comdr. 6 ships including guided missile cruiser U.S.S. Gridley, 1965-56; comdg. officer Naval Destroyer Sch., Newport, R.I., 1969-70; dir. Officer Distbn. div. Bur. Naval Personnel, 1970-72; chief naval tech. tng. Hdqrs. Naval Air Sta., Memphis, 1972-76; comdt. 9th Naval Dist., comdr. Naval Base, Gt. Lakes, Ill., 1976-77; ret., 1977. Decorated Legion of Merit with gold star, Meritorious Service medal with gold star, Navy Commendation medal with gold star, Bronze Star. Home: 5191 Heatherway Dr Memphis TN 38117

SACKETT, GENE PAUL, psychologist, educator; b. Los Angeles, Feb. 3, 1937; s. Alfred and Ruth (Gold) S.; B.A., U. Calif., Riverside, 1959; Ph.D., Claremont Grad. Sch., 1963; m. Barbara Ann Reese, June 19, 1976; children—Julie Anne, Douglas Philip, Kate Elizabeth. Research asso. psychology U. Wis., Madison, 1963-65, asst. prof., 1965-67, asso. prof., 1967-70; prof. U. Wash., Seattle, 1970—, core staff Regional Primate Research Center, 1970—; asso. dir. Child Devel. and Mental Retardation Center, Seattle, 1975—; instr. NSF Short Course, Central Circuit, 1972, Western Circuit, 1973. Mem. AAAS, Am. Psychol. Assn., Psychonomic Soc., Soc. for Research in Child Devel., Internat. Primatology Soc. Cons. editor Developmental Psychobiology, 1972—; N. Am. editor Biology of Behavior, 1975—. Editor: Observing Behavior, Vols. I and II, 1977. Home: 7020 14th Ave NE Seattle WA 98115 Office: Primate Center University of Washington Seattle WA 98195

SACKETT, LELAND RUSSELL, JR., author, free-lance writer; b. Eugene, Oreg., Mar. 17, 1923; s. Leland Russell and Fannie (McKennon) S.; student Oreg. State U., 1940-43, 45-46; B.S., Northwestern U., 1947, M.S., 1948; m. Carolyn Luttge, Sept. 24,

1966; children—Peter, Scott; children from previous marriage—Dinah, Victoria. Reporter, Oreg. Jour., Portland, 1949-51, Sunday editor, 1951-55; corr. Seattle bur. Time and Life mags., 1955-58; corr. Life mag., Chgo., 1958-61, asso. editor, 1961-62; editor Argus, Seattle, 1962-63; sr. editor, chief of investigative unit Life, N.Y.C., 1963-70; Washington bur. chief Newsday, 1971-72, nat. corr., 1972-75; now author, free-lance writer. Served with USAAF, 1943-45. Mem. Sigma Delta Chi, Sigma Phi Epsilon. Democrat. Unitarian. Home and office: 112 Sylvan Ct Alexandria VA 22304

SACKETT, ROSS DEFOREST, publisher; b. Chgo., Mar. 26, 1930; s. DeForest and Margaret (Ross) S.; B.A., Lawrence Coll., 1951; m. Marvyda Wild, Sept. 1, 1951; children—David, Scott, Cynthia, Amy, Stuart. Trucking supt., salesman Container Corp. Am., Chgo., 1951-57; salesman Prentice-Hall, Inc., Chgo., 1957-59; editor-in-chief Charles Merrill Books, Inc., Columbus, Ohio, 1959-61; gen. mgr., v.p., exec. v.p., dir. Holt, Rinehart & Winston, N.Y.C., 1961-67, pres., dir., 1967-70, chmn. bd., 1970—; pres. CBS Edn. Pub. Group, 1970-72, Ency. Brit. Ednl. Corp., 1972-76; chmn. Angeles Toy Corp.; dir. Ency. Brit. Corp. Mem. Assn. Am. Pubs. (chmn.), Civil War Round Table, Delta Tau Delta, Eta Sigma Phi. Episcopalian. Club: Univ. (N.Y.C.). Home: 246 Spring St Eureka Springs AR 72632 Office: 45 Spring St Eureka Springs AR 72632

SACKETT, WALTER WALLACE, JR., physician, surgeon, former state legislator; b. Bridgeport, Conn., Nov. 20, 1905; s. Walter Wallace and Hermine M. (Archambault) S.; student Harvard, 1922-23; A.B., U. Miami (Fla.), 1932; postgrad. medicine U. Ala., 1932-34; M.D., Rush Med. Coll., Chgo., 1938; m. Sophie Georgeff, Nov. 22, 1972; children by previous marriage—Monica Ann, Walter Wallace III; 1 stepson, Charles A. Dunn; 1 adopted son, John A. (dec.). Instr. anatomy U. Ala., 1934-36, instr. obstetrics, student health physician, 1939-40; prof. anatomy Coll. Mortuary Sci., St. Louis, 1936-37; intern Berwyn (Ill.) Hosp., 1937-38, St. Luke's Hosp., St. Louis, 1938-39; resident Charity Hosp., Natchez, Miss., 1940-41; gen. practice medicine, Miami, Fla., 1941—; mem. Med. Research Found., U. Miami, 1950-53; mem. staff Doctors, Jackson Meml., Variety Children's Dade County (sec. 1962-66), Coral Gables and Baptist hosps. Mem. advisory com. poliomyelitis to surgeon gen. U.S., 1960-61; cons. diabetes and arthritis USPHS, 1961-62; pioneer oral polio vaccine in new borns, 1960-61. Trustee U. Miami, 1961-63. Mem. Fla. Ho. of Reps., 1966-76. Recipient Outstanding Alumni award U. Miami, 1957. Mem. Am. (dir. 1960-63, v.p. 1963-64), Fla. (founder-mem.; pres. 1965), Dade County (pres. 1951-53) acads. gen. practice, Assn. Am. Physicians and Surgeons (Fla. membership chmn.), Am., World, Pan Am. (chmn. N. Am. 1962—), So. (sec., vice chmn., then chmn. gen. practice sect. 1955-58), Fla., Dade County (sec. 1953, pres. 1957, chmn. bd. trustees 1960-61) med. assns., Am. Cancer Soc. (dir. Dade County 1953-60), Am. Soc. Abdominal Surgeons, U. Miami Alumni Assn. (dir. 1957-61, pres. 1959), Coral Gables C. of C., Iron Arrow, Sigma Xi, Phi Chi. Roman Catholic. Moose. Author: Bringing Up Babies, 1962; A Manual on Baby Feeding. Contbr. articles to popular mags., profl. jours Lectr. in field for radio and TV pioneer legislation on death with dignity, 1968-76. Home: 333 University Dr Coral Gables FL 33134 Office: 2500 Coral Way Miami FL 33145

SACKLER, ARTHUR MITCHELL, physician, publisher; b. Bklyn., Aug. 22, 1913; s. Isaac and Sophie S.; B.S., N.Y. U., 1933, M.D., 1937; Sc.D. (hon.), Clark U., 1978; m. Else Jorgensen, 1935; children—Carol Ingrid Master, Elizabeth Ann Smith; m. 2d, Marietta Lutze, 1949; children—Arthur Felix, Denise Marica. House physician and pediatrician Lincoln Hosp., N.Y.C., 1937-39; resident psychiatry Creedmoor State Hosp., Queens Village, L.I., 1944-46; founder, dir. research Creedmoor Inst. Psychobiol. Studies, 1949-54; dir. Labs. for Therapeutic Research, Goldwater Meml. Hosp., N.Y.C., 1957—; chmn. bd. Med. Press, Inc., 1954—; pres. Physicians News Service, Inc., 1955—, Med. Radio and TV Inst., Inc., 1955—; internat. pub. Med. Tribune Newspapers, 1971—. Mem. adv. council dept. art history and archeology Columbia, 1961-74, founder Sackler Labs. Art History and Archeology, 1961, sr. research asso. in anthropology Columbia, 1969-70, research prof. psychiatry N.Y. Med. Coll., 1972—. Asso. chmn. internat. com. research First Internat. Congress Psychiatry, 1950; chmn. internat. task force on world health manpower WHO, 1969—; co-founder Sackler Sch. Medicine, Tel-Aviv. Chmn. Nat. Com. to Save Our Schs. Health, 1971-72; v.p. Internat. Assn. Against Mental Illness, 1975—. Endowed Arthur M. Sackler Gallery at Princeton Mus., also at Met. Mus. Art, N.Y.C., Sackler Collections at Columbia U., Mus. Am. Indian, Bklyn. Mus.; co-endowed Sackler Wing at Met. Mus. Art, 1978. Recipient award advancement med. communications AMA, 1969; Achievement award Heights Colls. Alumni Assn., N.Y. U., 1970; also awards sci. exhbns. Trustee N.Y. Med. Coll., 1968-72; bd. assos. Linus Pauling Inst. Sci. and Medicine, 1974—; co-founder Found. for Nutritional Advancement, 1976; internat. chmn. Am. Pro Deo Council (CIP, Inc.), 1978. Fellow Am. Psychiat. Assn., Am. Geriatrics Soc., Royal Anthrop. Inst. Gt. Britain and Ireland; mem. Internat. Assn. Social Psychiatry (chmn. 1973—), Gerontol. Soc., AAAS, N.Y. Acad. Scis., World Med. Assn. (U.S. com.), Chinese Art Soc. (bd. govs.). Co-author: Great Physiodynamic Therapies, 1956. Editor in chief Jour. Clin. and Exptl. Psychopathology 1950-62. Contbr. articles to numerous jours. Pioneer devel. histamine, sex steroids, biochemotherapies in psychiatry. Office: Goldwater Meml Hosp Franklin D Roosevelt Island New York NY 10044

SACKLER, HOWARD, playwright; b. N.Y.C., 1929; B.A., Bklyn. Coll., 1950; m. Greta Lynn Lungren, 1963; two children. Dir. Caedmon Records, N.Y.C., 1953-68; plays produced in London, San Francisco, Boston and Washington; dir. TV spl. Shakespeare, Soul of an Age, 1964; dir. movies, TV. Grantee Rockefeller Found., 1953, Littauer Found., 1954; recipient Maxwell Anderson award, 1954, Sergei award, 1959, Pulitzer prize, 1969, Drama Critics Circle award, 1969, Tony award, 1969. Author: The Great White Hope; The Pastime of Monsieur Robert; Uriel Acosta; Mr. Welk and Jersey Jim; The Yellow Loves; A Few Inquiries; The Nine O'Clock Mail (also TV), Semmelweiss, 1977; screenplays include Desert Padre, 1950; Killer's Kiss, 1952; Fear and Desire, 1953; A Midsummer Night's Dream, 1961; Bugsy, 1973; Jaws II, 1976. Address: ICM 8899 Beverly Blvd Los Angeles CA 90048*

SACKS, ALBERT MARTIN, lawyer, educator; b. N.Y.C., Aug. 15, 1920; s. Harry and Minnie (Miretsky) S.; B.B.A. magna cum laude, Coll City N.Y., 1940; LL.B. magna cum laude, Harvard, 1948; m. Sadelle R. Rader, Nov. 22, 1945; children—Margery, Janet. Admitted to D.C. bar, 1951, Mass. bar, 1957; law clk. to Judge A.N. Hand, 1948-49, Justice Felix Frankfurter, 1949-50; asso. Covington & Burling, Washington, 1950-52; asst. prof. law Harvard, 1952-55, prof., 1955-69, Dane prof., 1969—, asso. dean, 1968-71, dean, 1971—. Home: 64 Lincoln St Belmont MA 02178 Office: Harvard Law School Cambridge MA 02138

SACKS, HENRY S., publisher; b. Boston, Mar. 10, 1928; s. Joseph I. and Rose (Knellar) S.; student Mass. Coll. Optometry, 1948-52; B.S., Boston U., 1947; m. Theresa M. Martin, Dec. 28, 1950; Asso. editor Benwill Pub. Co., Boston, 1958-62; editor in chief, dir. Computer Design mag., West Concord, Mass., 1962-67; pres., pub., founder Mini-Micro Systems mag., Boston, 1967-77; v.p., pub. Cahners Pub. Co., Boston, 1978—. Served with U.S. Army, 1946-47. Home: 77 Thunder Rd Sudbury MA 01776 Office: 221 Columbus Ave Boston MA 02116

SACKS, HOWARD RAYMOND, lawyer, educator; b. Sioux City, Iowa, Feb. 18, 1921; s. Robert and Bessie (Grueskin) S.; A.B., U. Minn., 1941; LL.B., Yale, 1948; m. Barbara Bevier, Nov. 2, 1952; childrenStephen Alden, David Bevier, Peter Wallace, Susan Miranda. Admitted to Minn. bar, 1948; practiced in Mpls., Washington, 1948-51; with WSB, Dept. Army, 1951-56; prof. law Northwestern U., Evanston, Ill., 1956-67; dean U. Conn. Law Sch., 1967-72, prof. law, 1967—; exec. dir. Nat. Council Legal Clinics, 1960-66; dir. Council Edn. Profl. Responsibility, 1966-67. Mem. Conn. Parole Bd., 1968-74; alt. pub. mem. Conn. Bd. Mediation and Arbitration, 1976—. Served with AUS, 1943-46. Center for Advanced Study in Behavioral Scis. fellow, 1962-63. Contbr. articles to legal periodicals. Home: 51 S Highland St West Hartford CT 06119

SACKS, NORMAN PAUL, educator; b. Phila., Feb. 11, 1914; s. Louis and Pauline (Brody) S.; B.S., Temple U., 1935; M.A., U. Pa., 1937, Ph.D., 1940; m. Miriam Bronstein, Sept. 15, 1943; children—Laurie Ruth, Julie Elizabeth, Robert Neil. Tchr., Phila. high schs., 1936-39; mem. faculty U. Pa., 1938-40, U. Hawaii, 1940-42, Temple U., 1945-46, Oberlin Coll., 1946-61; mem. faculty U. Wis., 1961—, now prof. Spanish and Portuguese, chmn. dept., 1977—, dir. Ibero-Am. Center, 1961-75; vis. summer prof. U. Calif. at Berkeley, 1942, 43, 49, U. So. Calif., 1959, U. Wis., 1960, Harvard, 1964; vis. prof. Western Res. U., fall 1957-58, U. N.Mex., 1959-60; cons. U.S. Office Edn., 1960—. Recipient Distinguished Alumnus award Temple U., 1964, Best Article prize Hispania mag., 1971; Fulbright research fellow, Chile, 1967-68; Am. Philos. Soc. grantee, 1976. Mem. Modern Lang. Assn. (chmn. sects.), Am. Assn. Tchrs. Spanish and Portuguese (pres. 1966), Linguistic Soc. Am., Am. Council Teaching Fgn. Langs., Associacion de Linguistica Filologia de America Latina, AAUP, Programa Interamericano de Linguistica y Ensenanza de Idiomas, Latin Am. Studies Assn. (chmn. nominating and program planning coms.). Author: The Latinity of Dated Documents in the Portuguese Territory, 1941; Spanish for Beginners, 3d edit., 1966; Cuentos de hoy y de ayer, rev. edit., 1965; (with others) Modern Spanish, 3d edit., 1973; also articles, revs. Home: 918 Swarthmore Ct Madison WI 53705

SACKSTEDER, FREDERICK HENRY, fgn. service officer; b. N.Y.C., July 12, 1924; s. Frederick H. and Denise (Dorin) S.; B.A., Amherst Coll., 1947; postgrad. Sch. Advanced Internat. Studies, Washington, 1947; m. Evelyn M. Blickensderfer, Oct. 14, 1977; children by previous marriage—Frederick Henry, III, Timothy W. Asst. to exec. v.p. Internat. Standard Electric Corp., N.Y.C., 1948-49; joined U.S. Fgn. Service, 1950; Kreis resident officer U.S. High Commn. for Germany, 1950-52; vice consul, consul, sec. Am. embassy, Lyon, France, 1952-55, Madrid, 1959-61, Barcelona, Spain, 1962-65, Tunis, Tunisia, 1967-69; internat. relations officer Dept. State, 1955-59; 65-67; mem. U.S. Mission to UN, 1969-72, Internat. Boundary and Water Com., El Paso, Tex., 1972-75; consul gen., Hermosillo, Sonora, Mexico, 1975-79; bd. examiners Fgn. Service, Dept. State, 1979—. Pres., El Paso chpt. UN Assn., 1973-75. Served with USNR, 1943-46. Mem. Fgn. Service Assn., Council for Inter Am. Relations, Polit. Sci. Assn. Club: Hermosillo Country. Home: Apt 7065W 4201 Massachusetts Ave NW Washington DC 20016 Office: 577 Camino Corto Green Valley AZ 85614 also Dept State Washington DC 20520

SACKSTEDER, WILLIAM, educator; b. Muncie, Ind., May 30, 1925; s. Overton, Jr., and May (Krieger) S.; Ph.B., U. Chgo., 1946, M.A., 1949, Ph.D., 1953; m. Margaret Lester, June 14, 1947 (div.); children—Nancy, Alice, James; m. 2d, Elomia Laws, Apr. 28, 1973. Asst. philosophy U. Chgo., 1952-54; instr. Ill. Inst. Tech., 1949-50; instr. philosophy U. Colo., 1952-54, asst. prof., 1954-59, chmn. dept., 1961-63, asso. prof., 1959-65, asso. dean Grad. Sch., 1965-66, prof., 1966—. Mem. Colo. Council Arts and Humanities, 1966-68; v.p. Boulder Assembly Arts and Humanities, 1966-69; dir. Nomad Players, 1970-73, pres., 1971-72. Mem. AAUP, Am. Soc. Aesthetics, Am. Philos. Assn., Mountain Plains Philos. Conf., Assn. Gen. and Liberal Studies, Internat. Philos. Congress, Phi Beta Kappa. Contbr. articles, revs. to profl. jours. Home: 2190 Vassar Dr Boulder CO 80303

SACKTON, FRANK JOSEPH, ret. army officer, univ. dean, lectr.; b. Chgo., Aug. 11, 1912; student Northwestern U., 1936, Yale, 1946; student U. Md., 1951-52, B.S., 1970; grad. Army Inf. Sch., 1940, Command and Gen. Staff Coll., 1942, Armed Forces Staff Coll., 1949, Nat. War Coll., 1954; M.Pub. Adminstrn., Ariz. State U., 1976; m. June Dorothy Raymond, Sept. 21, 1940. Mem. 131st Inf. Regt., Ill. N.G., 1929-40; commd. 2d lt. U.S. Army, 1934, advanced through grades to lt. gen., 1967; brigade plans and ops. officer 33d Inf. Div., PTO, 1941, 33d Div., 1943-45; div. signal officer, 1942-43, div. intelligence officer, 1944, div. plans and ops. officer, 1945; sec. to gen. staff for Gen. MacArthur, Tokyo, 1947-48; bn. comdr. 30th Inf. Regt., 1949-50; mem. spl. staff Dept. Army, 1951; plans and ops. officer Joint Task Force 132, PTO, 1952; comdr. Joint Task Force 7, Marshall Islands, 1953; mem. gen. staff Dept. Army, 1954-55; with Office Sec. Def., 1956; comdr. 18th Inf. Regt., 1957-58; chief staff 1st Inf. Div., 1959; chief army Mil. Mission to Turkey, 1960-62; comdr. XIV Army Corps, 1963; dep. dir. plans Joint Chiefs Staff, 1964-66; army general staff mil. ops., 1966-67; comptroller of the army, 1967-70; ret., 1970; spl. asst. for fed./state relations Gov. Ariz., 1971-75; chmn. Ariz. Programming and Coordinating Com. for Fed. Programs, 1971-75; lectr. Am. Grad. Sch. Internat. Mgmt., 1973-77; vis. asst. prof., lectr. public affairs Ariz. State U., Tempe, 1976-78, dean Coll. Public Programs, 1979—. Mem. Ariz. Steering Com. for Restoration of the State Capitol, 1974-75, Ariz. State Personnel Bd., 1978—. Decorated D.S.M., Silver Star, also Legion of Merit with 4 oak leaf clusters, Bronze Star with 2 oak leaf clusters, Air medal, Army Commendation medal with 1 oak leaf cluster, Combat Inf. badge. Mem. Ariz. Acad. Public Adminstrn., Pi Alpha Alpha (pres. chpt. 1976—). Clubs: Army-Navy (Washington); Arizona (Phoenix). Contbr. articles to mil. jours. Home: 7814 E Northland Dr Scottsdale AZ 85251 Office: College Public Programs Ariz State U Tempe AZ 85281

SADAO, SHOJI, architect; b. Los Angeles, Jan. 2, 1927; s. Riichi and Otatsu (Kodama) S.; B.Arch., Cornell U., 1954; Fulbright scholar, Waseda U., Tokyo, 1956-57; m. Tsuneko Sawada, Apr. 8, 1972. Designer Geodesics, Inc., Raleigh, N.C., 1954-56; job capt. Edison Price, Inc., N.Y.C., 1959-64; v.p. Fuller & Sadao, P.C., Long Island City, N.Y., 1965—; works include Dymaxion World Map, 1954; co-designer U.S. Pavilion at Montreal Expo 67; asso. prof. archtl. design Sch. Architecture and Environ. Design, State U. N.Y. at Buffalo, 1976-77. Served with AUS, 1945-49. Mem. AIA, Japan Soc., World Acad. Art and Sci. Address: 45 E 89th St New York NY 10028

SADDLEMYER, (ELEANOR) ANN, educator; b. Prince Albert, Sask., Can., Nov. 28, 1932; d. Orrin Angus and Elsie Sarah (Ellis) S.; B.A., U. Sask., 1953; M.A., Queen's U., 1956, LL.D., 1977; Ph.D., U. London, 1961. Lectr., Victoria (B.C.) Coll., 1956-57, instr., 1960-62, asst. prof., 1962-65; asso. prof. U. Victoria, 1965-68, prof. English, 1968-71; prof. English, Victoria Coll., U. Toronto, 1971—, dir. Grad. Centre for Study of Drama, 1972-77, sr. fellow Massey Coll., 1975—; Berg prof. N.Y. U., 1975; dir. Theatre Plus, Colin Smythe Pubs. Can. Council scholar, 1958-59, fellow, 1968; Guggenheim fellow, 1968, 77. Fellow Royal Soc. Can.; mem. Internat. Assn. Study Anglo-Irish Lit. (chmn. 1973-76), Assn. Can. Theatre History (pres. 1976-77), Can. Assn. Irish Studies, Humanities Assn., Assn. Can. Univ. Tchrs. English, Can. Assn. Univ. Tchrs., Assn. Can. and Que. Lit. Author: The World of W.B. Yeats, 1965; In Defence of Lady Gregory, Playwright, 1966; Synge and Modern Comedy, 1968; J.M. Synge Plays Books One and Two, 1968; Lady Gregory Plays, 1970; Letters to Molly: Synge to Maire O'Neill, 1971; Letters from Synge to W.B. Yeats and Lady Gregory, 1971; editorial bds. Modern Drama, 1972, English Studies in Can., 1973, Themes in Drama, 1974, Shaw Rev., 1977, Research in the Humanities, 1976, Irish Univ. Rev., 1970: contbr. articles to profl. jours. Home: 297 Watson Ave Oakville ON L6J 3V3 Canada Office: Dept English Victoria Coll U Toronto Toronto ON M5S 1K7 Canada

SADDLER, DONALD EDWARD, choreographer, dancer; b. Van Nuys, Calif., Jan. 24, 1920; s. Elmer Edward and Mary Elizabeth (Roberts) S.; student Los Angeles City Coll., 1939; dance pupil of Carmalita Maracci, Anton Dolin, Anthony Tudor, Madame Anderson Ivantzova. Choreographer for Broadway prodns. Milk and Honey, 1961, Wonderful Town (Antoinette Perry award 1952), 1952, John Murray Anderson's Almanac, 1953, Shangri-La, 1955, Sophie, 1963, We Take the Town, 1963; for Italian musicals Tobia La Candida Spia (Italian Maschera D'Argento 1954), 1954, La Padrona di Raggio di Luna, 1955, Duona Notte Bettina, 1956, L'Andorabile Giulo, 1957, Un Trapezio Per Lisistrata, 1958, Un Manderino Per Teo, 1959; for London musicals Wonderful Town, 1954, When in Rome, 1959; for TV prodns. Bell Telephone Hour, 1959-63, Perry Como Show, 1950, Canzionissima (Rome), 1958; for ballets This Property Condemned, 1959, Winesburg, Ohio, 1959, Dreams of Glory, 1963; for motion pictures April in Paris, 1951, By The Light of the Silvery Moon, 1951, Young at Heart, 1957, Main Attraction, 1963; dir. State Fair Musicales, Dallas, 1957, 59, Carousel Theatre, Farmingham, Mass., 1958, Greek theatre prodn. Wonderful Town, 1958; v.p. Rebekah Harkness Found., asst. artistic dir. Harkness Ballet, 1964-70; now artistic dir. Ballet of Contemporary Art. Office: care Coleman-Rosenberg Agy 667 Madison Ave New York NY 10021*

SADDLER, OWEN LESLIE, TV exec.; b. Wilmington, Del., Nov. 6, 1911; s. Edward and Georgiana (Longacre) S.; B.A., Bucknell U., 1934, M.A., 1935; postgrad. Northwestern U., 1937-38; m. Elizabeth Rankin, Apr. 6, 1940; children—Barbara (Mrs. Bruce Georgi), Owen Leslie, David Rankin; m. 2d, Jocile Butterfield, Apr. 15, 1972. With legal dept. E.I. du Pont de Nemours & Co., Wilmington, 1930-33; reporter Wilmington Jour. Every Evening, 1934; tchr. Warner High Sch., 1936; exec. v.p., dir. May Broadcasting Co., Omaha, Tucson, 1949—; sec. treas., dir. KFAB Broadcasting Co., Omaha, also Bus. Service Co., Omaha and Lincoln, Nebr., 1957—. Mem. affilliates adv. bd. ABC-TV, 1950-53, CBS-TV, 1953-57, NBC-TV 1963-69. Mem. met. bd. YMCA, 1961-64; presdl. councilor Creighton U., Omaha, 1969—; bd. dirs., v.p. Jr. Achievement; v.p., bd. dirs. Lutheran Med. Center, Omaha; bd. regents UCS Citizens Assembly. Recipient Silver medallion Advt. Fedn. Am.-Advt. Assn. West, 1965; named Boss of Year, Nat. Secs. Assn., 1965. Mem. Broadcast Pioneers Am., TV Pioneers Am., Nat. Assn. Broadcasters, Nebr. Broadcasters Assn. (elected to Hall of Fame 1977), Sigma Delta Chi, Alpha Epsilon Rho. Republican. Mem. United Ch. of Christ. Clubs: Happy Hollow Country, Omaha Press, Omaha Skeet, Quad (Omaha). Home: 10533 Shirley St Omaha NE 68124 Office: 10714 Mockingbird Dr Omaha NE 68127

SADE, DONALD STONE, anthropologist; b. Charleston, W.Va., July 17, 1937; s. Samuel and Charolotte Tracy (Stone) S.; grad. N.Y. State Ranger Sch., 1957; student Hamilton Coll., 1957-60; A.B., U. Calif., Berkeley, 1963; Ph.D., U. Calif., Berkeley, 1966; m. Bonita Diane Chepko, Dec. 24, 1971; 1 child, Irony Cuervo del Norte. Instr. anthropology Northwestern U., Evanston, Ill., 1965-66, asst. prof., 1966-70, asso. prof., 1970-75, prof., 1975—; scientist-in-charge Cayo Santiago, U. P.R., 1970-77. NSF grantee, 1967—. Mem. AAAS, Am. Assn. Phys. Anthropologists, Am. Soc. Mammalogists, Animal Behavior Soc. Office: Dept Anthropology Northwestern U Evanston IL 60201. *I have never given undue heed to the opinions of others regarding my work or character.*

SADEK, GEORGE, educator, designer; b. Usti, Czechoslavakia, Oct. 12, 1928; s. Jaroslav and Marie (Soucek) S.; came to U.S., 1953, naturalized, 1955; B.A., Hunter Coll., 1958; M.F.A., Ind. U., 1960; m. Miroslava Zakova, Oct. 22, 1953; 1 dau., Nina Claire. Instr. fine arts Ind. U., 1960-63, asst. prof., 1963-66; prof., head dept. art Cooper Union, N.Y.C., 1966-68, prof., dean Sch. Art and Architecture, 1968—; graphic design cons. Davis, Brody & Assos.; exhibited at Type Dirs. Club N.Y., 1966, 67. Mem. Mayor's Com. on Signs and Communications, N.Y.C., 1968—; visitor to dept. of sch. Mus. Fine Arts, Boston, 1969—. Bd. dirs. Internat. Center for Typographic Arts Served with U.S. Army, 1954-56. Mem. Am. Inst. Graphic Arts (dir.), Coll. Art Assn. Am. (pres. 1976-78), Nat. Assn. Schs. Art (dir. 1969—, chmn. com. on pub. relations). Club: Century Assn. Contbr. articles to profl. jours. Home: 3 Washington Sq Village New York City NY 10012

SADIK, MARVIN SHERWOOD, dir. Nat. Portrait Gallery; b. Springfield, Mass., June 27, 1932; s. Harry Benjamin and Florence (Askinas) S.; A.B. magna cum laude, Harvard, 1954, A.M., 1960. Curatorial asst. Worcester (Mass.) Art Mus., 1955-57; curator Bowdoin (Maine) Coll. Mus. Art, 1961-64, dir., 1964-67; dir. Mus. Art U. Conn. at Storrs, 1967-69, Nat. Portrait Gallery, Washington, 1969—. Mem. adv. bd. Archives of Am. Art, 1970—. Decorated knight Order Dannebrog (Denmark); Harris fellow, 1957-61; Barr fellow, 1957-61. Fellow Pierpont Morgan Library; mem. Am. Assn. Mus. Dirs., Am. Antiquarian Soc., Colonial Soc. Mass. (corr.). Clubs: Century Assn., Grolier. Author: Colonial and Federal Portraits at Bowdoin Coll., 1966; The Drawings of Hyman Bloom, 1968; The Paintings of Charles Hawthorne, 1968; Christian Gullager: Portrait Painter to Federal America, 1976. Editorial bd. Am. Art Jour., 1970—. Home: 2801 New Mexico Ave NW Washington DC 20007 Office: Nat Portrait Gallery 8th and F Sts NW Washington DC 20560

SADIK-KHAN, ORHAN IDRIS, consumer products co. exec.; b. Laghman, Afghanistan, July 3, 1929; s. Alim Jan and Shemsulbenat (Ashrat) Idris; B.A., Am. U. at Cairo, 1948-51; postgrad. Stanford Grad. Sch. Bus., 1951-53; m. Karen Lamond; children—Janette, Alim Jan, Karim, Kadria. Came to U.S., 1951; naturalized, 1965. Dir. tech. research and services Dean Witter & Co., N.Y.C., 1954-61; instl. research Schirmer Atherton & Co., 1961-62, F. Eberstadt, 1962-63; partner charge research Ira Haupt Co., 1963; dir. research N.Y. Securities Co., N.Y.C., 1964-65; v.p. planning Litton Industries, Inc., Beverly Hills, Calif., 1965-67, Hunt Food and Industries, Inc., Fullerton, Calif., 1967-69; v.p. Norton Simon Inc., 1969-73, sr. v.p., 1973—; dir. Omega Fund, Madison Life Ins. Co. Mem. N.Y., Boston socs. security analysts. Clubs: Board Room, Marco Polo (N.Y.C.). Home: 41 Binney Ln Old Grenwich CT 06870 Office: 277 Park Ave New York NY 10017

SADLER, GEORGE MARION, airlines exec.; b. Clarksville, Tenn., Feb. 7, 1911; s. George Marion and Emma Lester (Townsend) S.; A.B., Duke, 1932, M.A., 1933; m. Joy Whitson, Apr. 2, 1936 (dec.

Feb. 1974); children—George Marion (dec.), M. Whitson; m. 2d, Marguerite Bush, Aug. 23, 1976. Tchr. Tenn. secondary schs., 1933-41; with Am. Airlines, Inc., 1941—, gen. mgr., 1959-64, pres., 1964-67, vice chmn. bd. dirs., N.Y.C., 1969—. Dir. Nat. Council on Alcoholism. Served to sgt. USAAF, 1943-45. Mem. Am. Numismatic Soc. (mem. council). Home: 4681 Camino de Oro Tucson AZ 85710 Office: Am Airlines Inc PO Box 61616 Dallas/Fort Worth Airport TX 75261

SADLER, ROBERT EDWARD, ret. air force officer; b. Eagle Grove, Iowa, Sept. 3, 1925; s. Edward Anthony and Elsie June (Sherman) S.; B.S. in Elec. Engring., U. Colo., 1961; postgrad. Air War Coll., 1967, Indsl. Coll. Armed Forces, 1967; m. Kathleen Irene English, Nov. 17, 1951; children—Kathe Sadler Wright, Janet T., Robert E.A., John C., Micheal S., Kathleen T. Served as enlisted man U.S. Army, 1943-45; commd. 2d lt. U.S. Army Air Force, 1945, advanced through grades to maj. gen. U.S. Air Force; served as chief advanced flying tng. Air Force Acad., advanced plans officer Air Force Communication Service, Scott AFB, 1961-66; dir. programs, command control and communications Hdqrs. USAF, Washington, 1967-70; dir. communications-electronics 7th Air Force Vietnam, also comdr. 1964 Communication Group, 1970-71; comdr. No. Communication Area, Griffiss AFB, N.Y., 1971-72; dir. J-6 U.S. Readiness Command, 1972-73; vice comdr. Air Force Communications Service, Richards-Gebaur AFB, Mo., 1974; dep. dir. command control and communication, Hdqrs. USAF, Washington, 1974-75; dir. communication-electronics Joints Chiefs Staff, Washington, 1975-76; dir. plans and programs Def. Communications Agy., Washington, 1976-77; comdr. Air Force Communications Service, Scott AFB, Ill., 1977-79, ret., 1979. Decorated D.S.M., Legion of Merit with 2 oak leaf clusters, Def. Superior Service medal with 1 oak leaf cluster, Meritorious Service medal. Mem. Armed Forces Communications-Electronics Assn. (asso. dir., Medal of Merit 1976, Gold medal 1978, Disting. Service medal). Republican. Roman Catholic. Home: 5013 Canterbury Dr Fort Wayne IN 46815

SADLER, ROBERT LIVINGSTON, banker; b. Beloit, Kans., Dec. 19, 1935; s. D.M. and Retha (Livingston) S.; B.A., Baker U., 1958; M.B.A., Ind. U., 1959; m. Elizabeth Ellen Lewis, July 14, 1957; children—Diane Elizabeth, Julia Ann. Dir. alumni Baker U., Baldwin, Kans., 1957-58; indsl. engr. Colgate Palmolive Co., Louisville, 1959-60, asst. personnel mgr., 1960-64, asst. product mgr., N.Y.C., 1964-65, v.p. personnel, 1965-70, v.p. adminstrv. services, 1970-72; exec. v.p. Old Kent Fin. Corp., Grand Rapids, 1972—; instr. Stonier Grad. Sch. Banking, Rutgers U., 1970-74. Bd. dirs. United Way of Mich., 1973-75; bd. dirs. United Way of Kent County, 1976-79, campaign chmn., 1978, v.p., 1979; bd. dirs., pres. Jr. Achievement, Grand Rapids, 1969-76; trustee, treas. Arts Council, 1970-74; trustee Davenport Coll.; mem. adv. council Ferris State Coll. Recipient Leadership award United Way, 1978, Jr. Achievement, 1978. Mem. Am. Bankers Assn., Am. Inst. Bankers, Sigma Iota Epsilon, Delta Mu Delta. Republican. Methodist. Clubs: Cascade Hills Country (dir.), Univ., Athletic. Office: Old Kent Fin Corp One Vandenberg Center Grand Rapids MI 49503

SADOVE, MAX SAMUEL, physician, educator; b. Balt., Mar. 8, 1914; s. Harry and Rebecca (Must) S.; B.S., Balt. City Coll., 1932; Pharm. B., U. Md., 1937, M.D., 1939; m. Ethel Segall, Apr. 6, 1941; children—Ellen Rose, Alan Michael, Richard Craig. Intern, St. Agnes Hosp., Balt., 1939-40; resident Hines (Ill.) VA Hosp., 1946-47, dir. anesthesiology dept., mem. faculty U. Ill. Coll. Medicine, 1947-71, prof. anesthesiology, 1951-71, chmn. dept., 1949-71; head dept. anesthesiology U. Ill. Research and Ednl. Hosps., 1950-71; dir. anesthesiology West Side VA Hosp., Chgo., 1954-71, cons., 1971—; dir. anesthesiology Hines VA Hosp., 1954-71, cons., 1971—; prof. anesthesiology Rush Med. Coll., Chgo., 1971—; chmn. dept. anesthesiology Presbyn.-St. Luke's Hosp., 1971—; cons. numerous hosps. Chgo. area VA; hon. chmn. dept. anesthesia U. Philippines Coll. Medicine, 1957—. Past mem. Bd. Edn. Oak Park, Ill.; member adv. bd. Chgo. Narcotic Rehab. and Research Center; adviser Med. Council Civil Def., Chgo. Bd. Health; med. lectr. Great Lakes Naval Hosp.; Somner Meml. lectr., 1963. Served to capt. M.C., AUS, 1941-46. Diplomate Am. Bd. Anesthesiologists. Fellow AAAS, Hines Surg. Assn., Soc. U. Profs., Am. Geriatrics Soc., Am. Soc. Anesthesiologists (chmn. sub. com. motion pictures 1958-60), Am. Coll. Clinical Pharmacology and Chemotherapy; mem. Soc. Med. Consultants to Armed Forces, Internat. Coll. Surgeons (vice regent), Chgo. Soc. Anesthesiologists (pres. 1950-51), Walter Reed Soc. (pres. 1954), Am. Soc. Assn. Inhalation Therapists (bd. govs., adv. bd. 1956-57), Am. Coll. Chest Physicians (chmn. sect. resuscitation 1957-59), Am. Fedn. Clin. Research, AMA, Ill. Med. Soc., Chgo. Med. Soc., Ill. Soc. Anesthesiologists (pres. 1963-64, 68-69), Warren H. Cole Soc., Soc. Med. History Chgo., Ill. Soc. Med. Research, Inst. Medicine Chgo., Am. Med. Authors, Am. Dental Soc. of Anesthesiologists (hon.), Flint, Hollywood acads. medicine; corr. fellow Soc. Mexicana de Anesthesiology. Co-author: Recovery Room, 1956; Cardiovascular Collapse in the Operating Room, 1958; Halothane, 1962; Electroencephalography for Anesthesiogists and Surgeons, 1967; also numerous articles. Contbr. to books, cons. editor med. jours. Home: 1021 Lathrop River Forest IL 60305 Office: 1753 W Congress Pkwy Chicago IL 60612

SAEMANN, JESSE CHARLES, JR., educator; b. Adell, Wis., Sept. 16, 1921; s. Jesse Charles and Adelaide Emma (Krumrey) S.; B.S., U. Wis., 1943, M.S., 1950, Ph.D., 1955; m. Evelyn Joyce Isensee, May 23, 1958; children—Lynn, Lauri. Instr. engring. mechanics U. Wis., 1946-55, asst. prof., 1955-57, asso. prof., 1957-61, prof., 1961—; cons. testing of concrete, soils and metals. Served with USNR, 1943-46. Mem. ASCE, Am. Soc. Engring. Edn., Hwy. Research Bd., Internat. Soc. Soil Mechanics and Found. Engring., ASTM, Sigma Xi, Chi Epsilon. Presbyterian. Home: 4421 Waite Ln Madison WI 53711

SAFDIE, MOSHE, architect; b. Haifa, Israel, July 14, 1938; s. Leon Safdie; grad. McGill U., 1961; m. Nina Nusynowicz, Sept. 6, 1959; children—Taal, Oren. With H.P.D. Van Ginkel, architect, Montreal Can., then Louis I. Kahn, Phila.; asso. David, Barott and Boulva, Montreal; in pvt. practice, Montreal; prof. architecture, prof. urban design, dir. urban design program Harvard U. Grad. Sch. Design, 1979—; participated master plan for Expo 67; executed Habitat '67. Recipient Massey medal in architecture; Lt. Gov. Can. Gold medal. Mem. Royal Inst. Can., Province Que. Assn. Architects. Office: 2 Faneuil Hall Marketplace Boston MA 02109

SAFER, JOHN, sculptor; b. Washington, Sept. 6, 1922; s. John M. and Rebecca (Herzmark) S.; A.B., George Washington U., 1947; LL.B., Harvard, 1949; children—Janine Audrey, Thomas Eugene. Investment, mgmt., banking devel. John Safer Properties, Washington, 1951—; chmn. exec. com. Fin. Gen. Bankshares; represented in permanent collections at Balt. Mus. Art, Corcoran Gallery Art, Washington, New York Cultural Center, High Mus. Art, Atlanta, Milw. Art Center, Harvard Law Sch., Phila. Mus. Art, San Francisco Mus. Art, Westmoreland County Mus., Mus. Fine Arts, Caracas, Venezuela, Royal Collection, Madrid. Pub. mem. Fgn. Service Inspection Corps, 1965. Served as 1st lt. USAAF, 1942-46. Clubs: Cosmos, Harvard (Washington); Lyford Cay (Nassau); Mid Ocean (Bermuda). Home: 10401 Grosvenor Pl Rockville MD 20852 Office: 2772 S Randolph St Arlington VA 22206

SAFER, MORLEY, journalist; b. Toronto, Ont., Can., Nov. 8, 1931; s. Max and Anna (Cohn) S.; student U. Western Ont., 1952. Came to U.S., 1964. With Reuters, London, Eng., 1955; corr., producer Canadian Broadcasting Corp., 1955-60, writer, London corr., 1961-64; corr., producer BBC, 1961; Vietnam corr. CBS, 1964-71; co-host 60 Minutes news program CBS-TV, 1971—; writer-corr. news documentary The Second Battle of Britain, 1976. Recipient Polk award L.I.U., 1965, Overseas Press Club award, 1965, 66, Sigma Delta Chi award, 1965, Peabody award, 1965, Paul White award Radio and TV, News Dirs. Assn., 1966. Fellow Royal Coll. Bloviation (Edinburgh). Office: CBS News 524 W 57th St New York NY 10019

SAFF, EDWARD BARRY, mathematician; b. N.Y.C., Jan. 2, 1944; s. Irving H. and Rose (Koslow) S.; B.S. with high honors, Ga. Inst. Tech., 1964; Ph.D., U. Md., 1968; m. Loretta Singer, July 3, 1966; children—Lisa Jill, Tracy Karen. Asst. prof. U. Md., summer 1968; post-doctoral researcher Imperial Coll., London, 1968-69; asst. prof. math. U. South Fla., 1969-71, asso. prof., 1971-76, prof., 1976—, dir. Center for Math. Services, 1978—; sr. vis. fellow Oxford U., spring 1978. Fulbright fellow, 1968-69; NSF grantee, 1970-72; Guggenheim fellow, 1978. Mem. Am. Math. Soc. Author: (with A.D. Snider) Fundamentals of Complex Analysis, 1976. Editor: (with R.S. Varga) Pade and Rational Approximation: Theory and Applications, 1977. Home: 11811 Lipsey Rd Tampa FL 33618 Office: Dept Math Univ of South Fla Tampa FL 33620

SAFFIOTTI, UMBERTO, pathologist; b. Milan, Italy, Jan. 22, 1928; s. Francesco Umberto and Maddalena (Valenzano) S.; came to U.S., 1960, naturalized, 1966; M.D. cum laude, U. Milan, 1951, splty. diploma occupational medicine cum laude, 1957; m. Paola Amman, June 21, 1958; children—Luisa M., Maria Francesca P. Intern, Inst. Pathol. Anatomy, U. Milan, 1951-52; research asst. oncology Chgo. Med. Sch., 1952-54, research asso., 1954-55; asst. to chmn. occupational medicine, chief lab. pathology Inst. Occupational Medicine, U. Milan, 1956-60, fellow Inst. Gen. Pathology, 1957-60; from asst. prof. to prof. oncology Chgo. Med. Sch., 1960-68; mem. staff Nat. Cancer Inst., NIH, Bethesda, Md., 1968—, asso. dir. carcinogenesis, 1968-76, chief lab. exptl. pathology, 1974—; mem. pathology B study sect. NIH, 1964-68; mem. numerous other coms., govt. agy. advisory coms.; mem. Internat. Union Against Cancer cancer prevention com., 1959-66, panel on carcinogenicity, 1963-66; chmn. ad hoc com. evaluation of low levels of environ. carcinogens HEW, 1969-70. Bd. dirs. Rachel Carson Trust, 1976-79. Recipient Career Devel. award NIH, 1965-68; Superior Service Honor award HEW, 1971; Pub. Interest Sci. award Environ. Def. Fund, 1977. Mem. AAAS, Am. Assn. Cancer Research (pres. Chgo. 1966-67), Am. Assn. Pathologists, European Assn. Cancer Research, Italian Soc. Cancerology (corr.), N.Y. Acad. Scis., Permanent Commn. and Internat. Assn. Occupational Health, Soc. Occupational and Environ. Health (councillor 1972-76, v.p. 1976-78, pres. 1978—), Soc. Toxicology, Washington Soc. Pathologists, Sigma Xi. Democrat. Author, co-author sci. articles, reports, co-editor books. Home: 5114 Wissioming Rd Bethesda MD 20016 Office: Bldg 37 Room 3A19 Nat Cancer Inst NIH Bethesda MD 20014

SAFFIR, HERBERT SEYMOUR, cons. civil engr.; b. N.Y.C., Mar. 29, 1917; s. A.L. and Gertrude (Samuels) S.; B.S. in Civil Engring. cum laude, Ga. Inst. Tech., 1940; m. Sarah Young, May 9, 1941; children—Richard Young, Barbara Joan. Civil engr. TVA, Chattanooga, 1940, NACA, Langley Field, Va., 1940-41; structural engr. Ebasco Services, N.Y.C., 1941-43, York & Sawyer & Fred Severud, N.Y.C., 1945; engr. Waddell & Hardesty, Cons. Engrs., N.Y.C., 1945-47; asst. county engr. Dade County, Miami, Fla., 1947-59; cons. engr. Herbert S. Saffir, Coral Gables, Fla., 1959—. Adj. lectr. civil engring. Coll. Engring., U. Miami, 1964—; adviser civil engring. Fla. Internat. U., 1975—; cons. on bldg. codes Govt. Bahamas; cons. on engring. in housing to UN; mem. Am. Nat. Standards Inst. Commn. Bldg. Design Loads; cons. to govt. and industry. Served with AUS, 1943-44. Recipient Outstanding Service award Fla. Profl. Engrs., 1954; Pub. Service award Nat. Weather Service, 1975; named Miami Engr. of Year, 1978; registered profl. engr., Fla., N.Y., Tex., P.R., Miss. Fellow ASCE (past pres. sec.), Fla. Engring. Soc. (award for outstanding tech. achievement 1973); mem. Soc. Am. Mil. Engrs., Am. Concrete Inst., ASTM (mem. com. performance bldg. constrn.), Prestressed Concrete Inst., Colegio de Ingenieros P.R., Am. Meteorol. Soc., Am. Arbitration Assn., Miami, Coral Gables (pres.-elect) chambers commerce, Tau Beta Pi. Author: Housing Construction in Hurricane Prone Areas, 1971; Nature and Extent of Damage by Hurricane Camille, 1975; contbg. author: Wind Effects on Structures, 1976; contbr. articles to profl. jours. Designer Saffir/Simpson hurricane scale. Home: 4818 Alhambra Circle Coral Gables FL 33146 Office: 255 University Dr Coral Gables FL 33134

SAFFMAN, PHILIP G., mathematician; b. Leeds, Eng., Mar. 19, 1931; s. Sam Ralph and Sarah (Rebecca) S.; B.A., Trinity Coll., Cambridge U., 1953, M.A., 1956, Ph.D., 1956; m. Ruth Arion, Sept. 2, 1954; children—Louise J., Mark E., Emma E. Asst. lectr. applied math. Cambridge U., 1958-60; reader in applied math. Kings Coll., London U., 1960-64; prof. fluid mechanics Calif. Inst. Tech., Pasadena, 1964-69, prof. applied math., 1969—; cons. TRW, Inc. Trinity Coll. fellow, 1955-59. Fellow Am. Acad. Arts and Scis. Contbr. articles to profl. jours. Office: 101-50 Firestone Calif Inst Tech Pasadena CA 91125

SAFFORD, ARTHUR RAYMOND, artist; b. Boston, Nov. 5, 1900; s. George H. and Emma (Saben) S.; student Alandale Sch. Art, Boston, 1922-26; spl. student of Ernst L. Major, Mass. Sch. Art, 1927-37; B.A., Calvin Coolidge Coll., 1944, M.A. in Philosophy of Art, 1948; m. Maude E. Durkee, June 16, 1934. One man shows include: Symphony Hall, 1943, Men's City Club, 1944, Copley Soc., 1945, 52, 56, 60 (all Boston), St. Petersburgh (Fla.) Art Assn., 1956, Jordan Marsh Ann., Manchester, Vt., 1957, Springfield (Mass.) Acad. Artists Ann., Copley Soc. Ann., N. Shore Arts Assn. Ann.; prin. works include portrait commns.; faculty Boston U., 1948-56. Pres. North Shore Arts Assn., Gloucester, Mass., 1959-62. Recipient prizes art exhns. Ogonquit, Maine, Jordan Marsh Co., Boston, N. Shore Arts Assn., Springfield Acad. Arts Assn. Mem. Am. Artists Profl. League. Mason. Home and studio: 3 Rocky Neck Ave East Gloucester MA 01930

SAFFT, STUART J., pharm. and chem. co. exec.; b. Bklyn., May 21, 1941; s. Abe and Florence Dorothy (Greenberg) S.; B.S. in Mech. Engring., Swarthmore (Pa.) Coll., 1962; M.B.A. with distinction, Harvard U., 1964; m. Arlene H. Dorfman, June 30, 1963; children—Andrea, Kenneth. With Corning Glass Works (N.Y.), 1964-67; with Sandoz, Inc., East Hanover, N.J., 1967—, dir. corp. planning, 1974-76, dir. data processing, 1976-78, v.p., treas., 1978—. Mem. Fin. Execs. Inst. Office: Sandoz Inc Route 10 East Hanover NJ 07936

SAFIRE, WILLIAM, journalist, author; b. N.Y.C., Dec. 17, 1929; s. Oliver C. and Ida (Panish) S.; student Syracuse U., 1947-49; m. Helene Belmar Julius, Dec. 16, 1962; children—Mark Lindsey, Annabel Victoria. Reporter, N.Y. Herald Tribune Syndicate, 1949-51; corr. WNBC-WNBT, Europe and Middle East, 1951; radio-TV producer WNBC, N.Y.C., 1954-55; v.p. Tex McCrary, Inc., 1955-60; pres. Safire Pub. Relations, Inc., 1960-68; spl. asst. to Pres., Washington, 1969-73; columnist N.Y. Times, Washington, 1973—. Served with AUS, 1952-54. Recipient Pulitzer prize for Disting. Commentary, 1978. Republican. Author: The Relations Explosion, 1963; Plunging into Politics, 1964; Safire's Political Dictionary, 1968, rev. edit., 1972, 78; Before the Fall, 1975; Full Disclosure, 1977. Address: NY Times 1000 Connecticut Ave NW Washington DC 20036

SAFRAN, CLAIRE, writer, editor; b. N.Y.C.; d. Simon and Flora (Rand) Safran; B.A. in English cum laude, Bklyn. Coll., 1951; m. John Milton Williams, June 8, 1958; 1 son, Scott Edward. News editor Photo Dealer mag., 1951-53; asso. editor TV Radio Mirror, 1954-58; mng. editor Photoplay mag., 1958-61; editor TV Radio Mirror, 1961-65, IN mag., 1965-67; asso. editor Family Weekly mag., 1967-68; editor Coronet mag., 1968-71; contbr. to maj. nat. mags., 1972—; contbg. editor Redbook, 1974-77, exec. editor, 1977-78, contbg. editor, 1979—. Recipient Media award Am. Psychol. Found., 1977; Merit award in Journalism, Religious Public Relations Council, 1978. Mem. Am. Soc. Journalists and Authors, Am. Soc. Mag. Editors. Home: 53 Evergreen Ave Westport CT 06880

SAFRAN, HYMAN, printing co. exec.; b. Detroit, Feb. 9, 1913; s. Elias and Freida (Mendelson) S.; student Wayne U., 1929-32; m. Leah Yoffee, July 25, 1937; children—Sharon Elaine, Frederick David, Kenneth Jay, James Allan. Pres., Safran Printing Co., Detroit, 1932-76 (merged into Stecher-Traung-Schmidt Corp. 1976); chmn. bd., chief exec. officer Stecher-Traung-Schmidt Corp., Detroit, 1976—. Pres., Jewish Welfare Fedn., 1964-69, Congregation Shaarey Zedek, 1958-60. Served to lt. USN, 1944-46. Recipient Marshall award Jewish Theol. Sem., 1960; Butzel award Jewish Welfare Fedn., 1970. Mem. Jewish War Vets (post comdr.). Clubs: Knollwood Country (West Bloomfield, Mich.); Wabeek Country (Bloomfield Hills, Mich.); Boca Rio Country (Boca Raton, Fla.). Home: 1873 Wingate Dr Bloomfield Hills MI 48013 Office: Stecher-Traung-Schmidt Corp 3939 Bellevue St Detroit MI 48207

SAFRAN, NADAV, educator; b. Cairo, Aug. 25; s. Joseph and Jeanne (Abadi) S.; came to U.S., 1950, naturalized, 1962; B.A. summa cum laude, Brandeis U., 1954; M.A., Harvard, 1956, Ph.D., 1958; m. Anna Balicka, June 9, 1955; children—Janina, Abigail, Elizabeth. Tchr. govt. and Middle Eastern studies Harvard U., Cambridge, Mass., 1957—, prof., 1967—. Adviser, Am. Jewish Com., Synagogue Council Am., State Dept.; spl. counsel Senate coms. Served as 1st lt. Israel Armed Forces, 1948-49. Recipient Politics prize Brandeis U., 1954, Chase prize, 1958; Sheldon fellow, 1956-57; Guggenheim fellow, 1963-64; Ford fellow, 1968-69. Mem. Phi Beta Kappa. Author: Egypt in Search of Political Community, 1961; The U.S. and Israel, 1963; From War to War, 1969; Israel—The Embattled Ally, 1978. Contbr. articles to profl. jours. Home: 198 Dean Rd Brookline MA 02146

SAGALKIN, SANFORD, lawyer, govt. ofcl.; b. N.Y.C., June 24, 1942; s. Nathan and Blanche (Hoffner) S.; B.A., Queens Coll., 1964; LL.B., Columbia U., 1967; m. Monda E. Fifield, Aug. 25, 1969; children—Nicholas, Amy. Admitted to N.Y. bar, 1967, Alaska bar, 1969; staff atty. N.Y. Mental Health Info. Service, N.Y.C., 1967-69; mem. firm Faulkner, Banfield, Doogan, Gross and Holmes, Juneau, Alaska, 1969-74, firm Ely, Guess & Rudd, Juneau, 1974-75; asst. atty. gen. Atty. Gen.'s Office, State of Alaska, 1975-77; dep. asst. atty. gen. Dept. Justice, Washington, 1977—. Mem. Juneau Parks and Recreation Com., 1972-74. Mem. Alaska Bar Assn., N.Y. State Bar Assn. Democrat. Jewish. Home: 6124 Western Ave Chevy Chase MD 20015 Office: Dept Justice Washington DC 20015

SAGAN, CARL EDWARD, educator, astronomer; b. N.Y.C., Nov. 9, 1934; s. Samuel and Rachel (Gruber) S.; A.B. with gen. and spl. honors, U. Chgo., 1954, B.S., 1955, M.S., 1956, Ph.D., 1960; Sc.D. (hon.), Rensselaer Poly. Inst., 1975, Denison U., 1976, Clarkson Coll. Tech., 1977; D.H.L. (hon.), Skidmore Coll., 1976; children by previous marriage—Dorion Solomon, Jeremy Ethan. Miller research fellow U. Calif. at Berkeley, 1960-62; vis. asst. prof. genetics Stanford Med. Sch., 1962-63; astrophysicist Smithsonian Astrophys. Obs., Cambridge, Mass., 1962-68; lectr., then asst. prof. Harvard, 1962-68; mem. faculty Cornell U., 1968—, prof. astronomy and space scis., 1970—, David Duncan prof. phys. scis., 1976—, dir. Lab. Planetary Studies, 1968—; NSF-Am. Astron. Soc. vis. prof. various colls., 1963-67; Condon lectr., Oreg., 1967-68; Holiday lectr. AAAS, 1970; Vanuxem lectr. Princeton, 1973; Smith lectr. Dartmouth, 1974; Wagner lectr. U. Pa., 1975; Bronowski lectr. U. Toronto, 1975; Philips lectr. Haverford Coll., 1975; Distinguished scholar Am. U., 1976; Danz lectr. U. Wash., 1976; Clark Meml. lectr. U. Tex., 1976; Christmas lectr. Royal Instn., London, 1977. Mem. various adv. groups NASA and Nat. Acad. Scis., 1959—; mem. council Smithsonian Instn., 1975—; vice chmn. working group moon and planets, space orgn. of Internat. Council Sci. Unions, 1968-74; lectr. Apollo flight crews NASA, 1969-72; chmn. U.S. del. joint conf. U.S. Nat. and Soviet Acads. Sci. on Communication with Extraterrestrial Intelligence, 1971; narrator BBC/PBL TV prodn. The Violent Universe, 1969; judge Nat. Book Awards, 1975. Recipient Smith prize Harvard, 1964; NASA medal for exceptional sci. achievement for work on Mars, 1972; Prix Galabert, 1973; John W. Campbell Meml. award, 1974; Klumpke-Roberts prize, 1974; Priestley award, 1975; NASA medal for distinguished pub. service, 1977; Pulitzer prize for Dragons of Eden, 1978; NSF fellow, 1955-60; Sloan research fellow, 1963-67. Fellow AAAS (chmn. astronomy sect. 1975), Am. Inst. Aeros. and Astronautics, Am. Geophys. Union, Am. Astronautical Soc., Brit. Interplanetary Soc.; mem. Am. Phys. Soc., Am. Astron. Soc. (councillor, chmn. div. for planetary scis. 1975-76), Soc. Study Evolution, Genetics Soc. Am., Internat. Astron. Union, Internat. Acad. Astronautics, Sigma Xi. Author: Atmospheres of Mars and Venus, 1961; Planets, 1966; Intelligent Life in the Universe, 1966; Planetary Exploration, 1970; Mars and the Mind of Man, 1973; The Cosmic Connection (Campbell Meml. award best sci. book of year), 1973; Other Worlds, 1975; The Dragons of Eden (Book-of-the-Month Club selection), 1977; Murmurs of Earth: Voyager Interstellar Record; also numerous articles; editor: Icarus: Internat. Jour. Solar System Studies, 1968—; Planetary Atmospheres, 1971; Space Research, 1971; UFOS: A Scientific Debate, 1972; Communication with Extraterrestrial Intelligence, 1973. Research on physics and chemistry of planetary atmospheres and surfaces, origin of life, exobiology, spacecraft observations of planets. Address: Space Sci Bldg Cornell Univ Ithaca NY 14853

SAGAN, JOHN, automobile co. exec.; b. Youngstown, Ohio, Mar. 9, 1921; s. John and Mary (Jubinsky) S.; B.A. in Econs., Ohio Wesleyan U., 1948; M.A., U. Ill., 1949, Ph.D., 1951; m. Margaret Pickett, July 24, 1948; children—John, Linda, Scott. Fellow, Ohio Wesleyan U., 1946-48; scholar, fellow research U. Ill., 1948-51; with Ford Motor Co., 1951—, treas., 1966-69, v.p., treas., 1969—; dir. Ford Motor Credit Co., Ford Internat. Capital Corp., Ford Motor Land Devel. Corp., Transcon Ins. Ltd., Am. Road Ins. Co.; dep. chmn. Fed. Res. Bank Chgo. Trustee Ohio Wesleyan U., 1964—, Com. Econ. Devel. U.S.A., Oakwood Hosp., Dearborn, Mich.; mem. council finance and adminstrn. Detroit conf. United Methodist Ch.; trustee YMCA Found. Detroit. Served with USNR, 1943-46. Mem. Am. Econ. Assn., Fin. Analysts Soc., Conf. Bd. (council fin. execs.), Phi Beta Kappa, Phi Kappa Phi, Delta Sigma Rho. Home: 22149 Long Blvd Dearborn MI 48124 Office: Ford Motor Co American Rd Dearborn MI 48121

SAGAR, WILLIAM CLAYTON, educator; b. Columbus, Ohio, Oct. 17, 1929; s. Herbert Gale and Virginia Agnes (Watkins) S.; B.S., Capital U., 1951; M.S., Ohio State U., 1954; Ph.D., 1958; m. Dorothy Alice Anthony, Feb. 14, 1953; children—Thomas, Victoria, Christina. Research chemist Ethyl Corp., Baton Rouge, 1958-61; asst. prof. Centre Coll., Danville, Ky., 1961-64, asso. prof., 1964-69, prof., 1969—, chmn. div. sci. and math., 1972-79. Mem. Am. Chem. Soc., Sigma Xi. Home: 698 East Dr Danville KY 40422 Office: Centre College Danville KY 40422

SAGE, ANDREW GREGG CURTIN, II, investment banker; b. Bryn Mawr, Pa., Mar. 11, 1926; s. Henry W. and Eleanor (Purviance) S.; m. Sara Wakefield, Sept. 29, 1956; children—Andrew Gregg Curtin III, Sally. Mem. staff DeCoppet & Doremus, odd lot stock house, N.Y.C., 1946-47, Sage & Co., N.Y. Stock Exchange Specialists, N.Y.C., 1947-48; asso. Lehman Bros. Kuhn Loeb, Inc. and predecessor, investment bankers, N.Y.C., 1948-60, gen. partner, 1960-68, pres. 1970-73, vice chmn., 1973-77, mng. dir., 1977—; pres., treas. Sage Land Devel. Co.; dir. Am. Motors Corp., Reeves Bros. Inc., Standard Brands Inc., Italamerica, S.A., Arlen Realty, Inc.; mem. trust adv. bd. U.S.I.F. Real Estate. Bd. dirs. George Jr. Republic. Served with USAAF, 1944-46. Clubs: Piping Rock, Jackson Hole Golf and Tennis; Seminole Golf, Bath and Tennis (Palm Beach, Fla.). Home: 330 S Ocean Blvd Palm Beach FL 33480 also PO Box 1802 Jackson WY 83001 Office: Lehman Bros Kuhn Loeb Inc 1 William St New York NY 10004

SAGE, ANDREW PATRICK, JR., educator; b. Charleston, S.C., Aug. 27, 1933; s. Andrew Patrick and Pearl Louise (Britt) S.; B.S. in Elec. Engring., The Citadel, 1955; S.M., Mass. Inst. Tech., 1956; Ph.D., Purdue U., 1960; m. LaVerne Galhouse, Mar. 3, 1962; children—Theresa Annette, Karen Margaret, Philip Andrew. Instr. elec. engring. Purdue U., 1956-60; asso. prof. U. Ariz., 1960-63; mem. tech. staff Aerospace Corp., Los Angeles, 1963-64; prof. elec. engring. ad nuclear engring. scis. U. Fla., 1964-67; prof., dir. Info. and Control Scis. Center, So. Methodist U., Dallas, 1967-73, head elec. engring. dept., 1973-74; Quarles prof., asso. dean U. Va., Charlottesville, 1974—, chmn. dept. chem. engring., 1974-75, chmn. dept. engring. sci. and systems, 1977—; cons. Martin Marietta, Collins Radio, Atlantic Richfield, Tex. Instruments, LTV Aerospace, Battelle Meml. Inst., NSF; gen. chmn. Internat. Conf. on Systems, Man and Cybernetics, 1974. Recipient Frederick Emmonds Terman award Am. Soc. for Engring. Edn., 1970; M. Barry Carlton award IEEE, 1970. Registered profl. engr., Tex. Fellow IEEE; mem. Inst. Mgmt. Scis., Am. Soc. for Engring. Edn., Sigma Xi, Eta Kappa Nu, Tau Beta Pi. Author: Optimum Systems Control, 1968, 2d edit., 1977; Estimation Theory with Applications to Communications and Control, 1971; System Identification, 1971; An Introduction to Probability and Stochastic Processes, 1973; Methodology for Large Scale Systems, 1977; Systems Engineering: Methodology and Applications, 1977; Linear Systems Control, 1978; contbr. articles to profl. jours.; asso. editor IEEE Transactions on Systems Sci. and Cybernetics, 1968-72, editor IEEE Transactions on Systems, Man and Cybernetics, 1972—; asso. editor Automatica, 1968—; editorial bd. Systems Engring., 1968-72, IEEE Spectrum, 1972-73, Computers and Electrical Engineering, 1972—, Jour. Interdisciplinary Modeling and Simulation, 1976—; editor Elsevier North Holland textbook series in system sci. and engring., Matrix Press textbook series on circuits and systems, 1976—; co-editor-in-chief Jour. Large Scale Systems: Theory and Applications, 1978—; contbr. articles to profl. jours. Home: 303 Ednam Dr Charlottesville VA 22901

SAGE, ROBERT FLOYD, found. exec.; b. Battle Creek, Mich., Dec. 15; s. Charles Floyd and Effa Laurinda (Mooney) S.; student pub. schs., Hillsdale, Mich.; L.H.D. (hon.), Siena Heights Coll., 1973; m. Genevieve Ray Phillips, Nov. 30, 1946; children—Melissa Jane Sage Booth, Anne Elizabeth. Various positions in labor, 1933-42, 46-58; profl. pilot, owner-operator fixed base operation, Marion, Ohio, 1958-68; v.p., dir. Guest House Inc., Lake Orion, Mich., 1968-76, dir., 1963—; pres. Sage Found., Detroit, 1962—; trustee, chmn. student affairs com. Siena Heights Coll., Adrian, Mich., 1969—. Bd. dirs. Catholic Social Service, Adrian, 1976—; mem. Franklyn Two. (Mich.) Planning Commn., 1976-78; mem. Congressman Dave Stockman's Indsl. Adv. Com., 1977—; chmn. com. alcohol studies Mercy Coll., Detroit, 1977, trustee, 1974—; bd. assos. Adrian (Mich.) Coll., 1979—; bd. visitors Mich. Cancer Found., 1979—. Served with USAAF, 1942-46. Recipient Lenawee County Citizen of Yr. award, 1979, Disting. Achievement award Hope Coll., 1979, cert. of recognition Nat. Aborist Assn., 1979; named to Order of Owl, Regis High Sch., N.Y.C., 1978. Republican. Roman Catholic. Office: 2500 Detroit Bank & Trust Bldg Detroit MI. *Be comfortable with yourself and you will be comfortable with most people and on most occasions.*

SAGENDORF, FORREST COWLES (BUD), cartoonist; b. Wenatchee, Wash., Mar. 22, 1915; s. Phillip and Evelyn (Cowles) S.; grad. Santa Monica (Calif.) High Sch., 1934; m. Nadia Crandall, Dec. 17, 1939; children—Martin, Nicki, Bradley. Apprentice, Popeye comic strip King Features Syndicate, N.Y.C., 1932-38, asst. to E.C. Segar, editor, 1939-45, writer, artist Popeye comic strip, 1945—; dir. cartooning course Famous Schs., N.Y.C., 1951-58; lectr. history Am. comics various colls. and univs. Mem. Nat. Cartoonists Soc., Mus. Cartoon Art, Comics Council. Republican. Club: Kiwanis. Author: The Art of Cartooning, 1955; Popeye, The First Fifty Years, 1979. Office: King Features Syndicate 235 E 45th St New York NY 10017

SAGER, CAROLE BAYER, lyricist, singer; b. N.Y.C., Mar. 8, 1947; d. Elias and Anita (Nathan) Bayer; B.S. in Speech and Dramatic Art, N.Y. U., 1967. Lyricist numerous songs, including: Midnight Blue, A Groovy Kind of Love, We Don't Cry Out Loud, You're Moving Out Today, Nobody Does It Better, When I Need You, Come In From the Rain, (all 1977); I'm Coming Home Again, I'd Rather Leave While I'm In Love, Heartbreaker (all 1978); You're the Only One, If You Remember Me, 1979; lyricist (in collaboration with Marvin Hamlisch) Broadway play: They're Playing Our Song, 1979—, Dancin, 1978; also movies: The Spy Who Loved Me, 1977, Ice Castles, 1979; rec. artist, 1977—, including album: Carole Bayer Sager, 1977. Voted Best New Artist in France and Germany, German Record Acad. 1977. Collaborated with numerous composers, including Peter Allen, Marvin Hamlisch, Alice Cooper, Mike MacDonald, Melissa Manchester, Bette Midler, Bruce Roberts, Neil Sedaka. Office: care Chappell Music 810 Seventh Ave New York NY 10019

SAGER, CLIFFORD JULIUS, psychiatrist; b. N.Y.C., Sept. 28, 1916; s. Max and Lena (Lipman) S.; B.S., Pa. State U., 1937; M.D., N.Y. U., 1941; cert. in psychoanalysis, N.Y. Med. Coll., 1949; children—Barbara L., Philip T., Rebecca J., Anthony F. Rotating intern Montefiore Hosp., N.Y.C., 1941-42; resident Bellevue Hosp., N.Y.C., 1942, 46-48; practice medicine specializing in psychiatry, N.Y.C., 1946—; attending psychiatrist Bird S. Coler Hosp., 1960-71; dir. therapeutic services, asso. dean Postgrad. Center Mental Health, 1948-60; vis. psychiatrist, med. bd. Flower and Fifth Ave Hosp., 1960-71, Met. Hosp., 1960-71; dir. psychiat. tng. and edn. N.Y. Med. Coll., 1960-61, clin. dir., 1960-63, asso. prof. psychiatry, 1960-65, prof., 1966-71, dir. partial hosp. programs and family treatment and study unit, 1964-71; clin. prof. psychiatry Mt. Sinai Sch. Medicine, 1971—; attending psychiatrist Mt. Sinai Hosp., 1971—; chief behavioral scis. Gouverneur Hosp.; chief family treatment unit Beth Israel Med. Center, 1970-71, asso. dir. family and group therapy, 1971-74; psychiat. dir. Jewish Family Service, 1974-77; dir. family psychiatry, Jewish Bd. Family and Children's Services. Served as capt. M.C., AUS, 1942-46. Diplomate Am. Bd. Psychiatry and Neurology. Fellow Am. Psychiat. Assn. (life), Am. Orthopsychiat. Assn. (life), Acad. Psychoanalysis, Am. Group Psychotherapy Assn. (pres. 1968-70, dir. 1962—), Soc. Med. Psychoanalysts; mem. AMA, Soc. Med. Psychoanalysts (pres. 1960-61, dir. 1958-62), Am. Soc. Advancement of Psychotherapy (dir. 1954-60), N.Y. Soc. Clin. Psychiatry, Eastern Assn. Sex Therapy (pres. 1976-77). Mem. editorial bd. Am. Jour. Orthopsychiatry, 1960-69, Internat. Jour. Group Psychotherapy, 1968—, Family Process, 1969—, Divorce, 1977—, Comprehensive Rev. Jour. Family and Marriage, 1978—; cons. Sexual Medicine, 1974—; editor: Progress in Group and Family Therapy, 1972; co-editor Jour. Sex and Marital Therapy, 1976—, Jour. Marriage and Family Counseling, 1977—, Internat. Jour. Family Counseling, 1977—; author: Marriage Contracts and Couple Therapy, 1976; Intimate Partners, 1979; co-author: Black Ghetto Family in Therapy, 1970; contbr. articles to profl. jours. Office: 65 E 76th St New York NY 10021

SAGER, DONALD JACK, librarian; b. Milw., Mar. 3, 1938; s. Alfred Herman and Sophia (Sagan) S.; B.S., U. Wis., Milw., 1963; M.S. in L.S., U. Wis., Madison, 1964; m. Irene Lynn Sleeth, June 28, 1969. Sr. documentalist AC Electronics div. Gen. Motors Corp., Milw., 1958-63; teaching asst. U. Wis., Madison, 1963-64; dir. Kingston (N.Y.) Pub. Library, 1964-66, Elyria (Ohio) Pub. Library, 1966-71, Mobile Pub. Library, 1971-75, Pub. Library Columbus and Franklin County, Ohio, 1975-78; commr. Chgo. Pub. Library, 1978—; instr. U. Ala. Grad. Library Sch., summer 1974, Kent (Ohio) State U. Library Sch., fall 1977; chmn. Columbus Area CATV Commn., 1976-78; bd. dirs. OPTIONS: Columbus Adult Career Edn., 1977-78; sec. Ohio Coll. Library Center, 1977-78; bd. dirs. Ill. Regional Library Council; mem. adv. council Ill. State Library; cons. in field. Served with inf. AUS, 1956-58. Mem. Am., Ill., Public (dir.) library assns., Chgo. Library Club, Info. Sci. and Documentation Assn., Internat. Visitors Center, Mus. Contemporary Art. Democrat. Unitarian. Author: Reference: A Programmed Instruction, 1970; Binders, Books and Budgets, 1971; also articles. Home: 6964 N Tonty Ave Chicago IL 60646 Office: 425 N Michigan Ave Chicago IL 60611

SAGER, MEREL SEAMAN, landscape architect; b. Tiffin, Ohio, Sept. 25, 1899; s. Charles Augusta and Lelia (Seaman) S.; B.S., Heidelberg (Ohio) Coll., 1921; M.Landscape Architecture, Harvard U., 1928; m. Evelyn Ruth Rogers, Dec. 9, 1948. Gen. sci. tchr., Van Wert, Ohio, 1923-25; with Nat. Park Service, 1928-66, chief planning div. Nat. Capital Parks, 1945-56; chief landscape architect U.S. Park Service, 1956-66; mem. Com. 100 on Federal City, Washington, 1947-55; mem. Washington Recreational Coordinating Com., 1945-46; chmn. study group Internat. Fedn. Housing and Town Planning, 1952. Served with U.S. Army, 1918, 41-42. Recipient Distinguished Service award Dept. Interior, 1966. Fellow Am. Soc. Landscape Architects (sec. 1961-62, 1st v.p. 1965-67); mem. Internat. Fedn. Landscape Architects. Methodist. Clubs: Kenwood Golf and Country, Masons. Contbr. profl. publs. Address: 3115 S 7th St Arlington VA 22204

SAGER, RICHARD JAMES, food processing co. exec.; b. Maumee, Ohio, Aug. 24, 1925; s. Clarence Admiral and Georgia (Plouck) S.; B.S., Bowling Green State U., 1949; m. Katheryn Jeannette Zelt, Jan. 10, 1947; children—Richard, Michael, Jack, Steven. With Central Soya Co., Inc., Fort Wayne, Ind., 1949—, asst. treas., 1968-70, treas., 1970-76, v.p., treas., sec., 1976—. Served with USAAC, 1943-46. Mem. Financial Execs. Inst. Mem. United Ch. Christ. Home: 3526 Maxim Dr Fort Wayne IN 46805 Office: Central Soya Co Inc 1300 Fort Wayne Bank Bldg Fort Wayne IN 46802

SAGER, ROBERT WILLIAM, educator; b. Lemmon, S.D., Sept. 5, 1915; s. William C. and Alice (Donavan) S.; B.S., U. Wash., 1944, M.S., 1945, Ph.D. (U. fellow 1944-49), 1949; m. Lola Rogers, Dec. 2, 1942; children—William, Barbara, Dorothy, Roberta. Asst. prof. pharmacy U. Pitts., 1949-52, asso. prof., 1952-55, prof., 1955-61, head dept., 1955-61, pharmacist-in-chief health center, 1956-61; prof. pharmacy Oreg. State U. Sch. Pharmacy, 1961—, head dept. pharmacy, 1961—. Mem. Am. Pharm. Assn., AAUP, Sigma Xi, Rho Chi, Kappa Psi. Presbyterian. (elder). Rotarian (past pres. Castle Shannon, Pa.). Home: Route 1 Box 303 D Corvallis OR 97330

SAGER, WILLIAM F., educator, chemist; b. Glencoe, Ill., Jan. 22, 1918; s. Fred Anson and Alta (Stansbury) S.; B.S. in Chemistry, George Washington U., 1939, M.A. in Organic Chemistry, 1941; Ph.D. in Organic Chemistry, Harvard, 1948; m. Marilyn Olga Williams, Dec. 26, 1941; children—Karen Louise (Mrs. Kenneth Keane Dickinson), Judith Lynn (Mrs. Stephen Charles Peyton), Kathryn Gwen (Mrs. Michael Potts). Research chemist The Texas Co., 1941-45; prof. chemistry George Washington U., 1948-65; prof. chemistry, head dept. U. Ill. at Chgo. Circle, 1965—; cons. to govt. and industry, 1952—. Guggenheim fellow, 1954-55. Mem. Am. Chem. Soc., Am. Assn. U. Profs., Sigma Xi, Alpha Chi Sigma. Home: 2145 Thornwood Ave Wilmette IL 60091 Office: Dept Chemistry Univ of Ill at Chicago Circle Chicago IL 60680

SAGERHOLM, JAMES ALVIN, naval officer; b. Uniontown, Pa., Dec. 23, 1927; s. Frithiof Norris and Margaret (Blocker) S.; B.S., U.S. Naval Acad., 1952; m. Margaret Ann Herrlich, June 7, 1952; children—Lisa Marie, Ann Denise, Jeannine Louise, Mark Christian. Commd. ensign U.S. Navy, 1952, advanced through grades to rear adm., 1975; service in Korea, 1952-53, Western Pacific, 1952-63; submarine tng. and service, 1963-71; comdg. officer Naval Intelligence Support Center, 1974-75; dep. dir. naval intelligence, 1975-76; comdr. S. Atlantic Force, U.S. Atlantic Fleet, 1976-78; dir. Office of Program Appraisal, Office of Sec. Navy, Washington, 1978—; comdr. task force 138 during Operation UNITAS, 1976, 77. Decorated Meritorious Service medal; Merito Tamandaré (Brazil). Mem. U.S. Naval Inst., U.S. Naval Acad. Alumni Assn., U.S. Naval Acad. Athletic Assn. Roman Catholic. Clubs: Officers and Faculty (U.S. Naval Acad.); Dorado Beach (P.R.). Home: Maidstone Rectortown VA 22140 Office: Dir Office Program Appraisal Office of Sec Navy Pentagon Washington DC 20350

SAGLE, ROBERT FRANKLIN, lawyer; b. Hagerstown, Md., Dec. 8, 1930; s. Quay Jabez and Anna Florida (Lyon) S.; B.A., George Washington U., 1951, J.D. with honors, 1953; m. Elizabeth Louise Blanchard, Nov. 5, 1960; children—Philip Robert, Leslie Elizabeth. Page, clk. U.S. Congress, Washington, 1947-53; admitted to D.C. bar, 1953; asst. to dep. atty. gen. U.S. Dept. Justice, Washington, 1956-58, 60; asst. U.S. atty. for D.C., 1958; spl. atty. 1st U.S. Dept. of Justice Task Force on Organized Crime, N.Y.C. and Washington, 1958-60; counsel Schenley Industries Inc., distiller, N.Y.C., 1960-62; asso. firm Cooke & Beneman, 1962-68, partner, 1968-70; partner firm Harrison, Lucey & Sagle, Washington, 1970-78, McDermott, Will & Emery, Chgo., Washington and Miami, Fla., 1978—; counsel Bourbon Inst., N.Y.C., 1965-73. Treas., sec. J. Edgar Hoover Found., 1968—; mem. task force for ballot security Republican Nat. Com., 1968, 72, co-chmn., 1976; chmn. laws and regulations com. Distilled Spirits Council U.S., 1978—. Served as 1st lt., JAGC, USAF, 1953-56; Germany. Mem. D.C. Bar, Assn. Bar City N.Y., Bar Assn. D.C., Fed., Am. bar assns., Am. Legion, Phi Delta Phi, Sigma Chi. Episcopalian. Club: Kenwood Country (Bethesda, Md.). Bd. editors George Washington Law Rev., 1952-53. Home: 5207 Bradley Blvd Bethesda MD 20014 Office: 1101 Connecticut Ave NW Washington DC 20036

SAH, CHIH-TANG, educator; b. Peking, China, Nov. 10, 1932; s. Adam Peng-tung and Shushen (Huang) S.; B.S. in Physics, U. Ill., 1953, B.S. in Elec. Engring., 1953; M.S., Stanford, 1954, Ph.D., 1956; Dr. honoris causa, Catholic U. Leuven, 1975; m. Linda Chang, Nov. 29, 1959; children—Dinah, Robert. Research asst. Stanford Electronics Lab., 1954-56, asso., 1956; mem. tech. staff Shockley Semiconductor Lab., 1956-59; with Fairchild Semiconductor Lab., 1959-65, mgr., head physics dept., 1961-65; faculty U. Ill., Urbana, 1962—, prof. elec. engring. and physics, 1963—; NSF Research Initiation Grant Panelist, 1973, Franklin Inst. award on MOS devices, 1975; committeeman Nat. Acad. Scis.-NRC, 1975-78, mem. Honeywell H.W. Sweaft engr.-scientist award com., 1977; cons. Fairchild Semicondr. Corp., 1964-65, Picatinny Arsenal, 1966, Zenith Radio Corp., 1966-69, U. Fla., 1966-78, IBM Corp., 1968-73, Micro-Bit Corp., 1969-78, Teletype Corp., 1971, Indsl. Research Products, inc., 1972-73, Harry Diamond Lab., 1974-75, Am. Micro Systems, Inc., 1975, Jet Propulsion Lab, 1975-78, Honeywell Corp., 1977, Control Data Corp., 1978. Recipient Browder J. Thompson prize IEEE, 1962. Fellow IEEE (fields award com. 1970), Am. Phys. Soc.; mem. Electrochem. Soc., Sigma Xi, Phi Kappa Phi, Tau Beta Pi, Sigma Tau, Pi Mu Epsilon, Eta Kappa Nu, Phi Eta Sigma. Home: 403 Pond Ridge Ln Urbana IL 61801

SAHAKIAN, MABEL MARIE LEWIS (MRS. WILLIAM S. SAHAKIAN), clergywoman, author, educator; b. West Newton, Pa., Mar. 2, 1921; d. Paul Tyson and Blanch Theresa (d'Happart) Lewis; student W.Va. U., 1939-40; A.B., Gordon Coll., 1944; M.Div. (Hester Ann Beebe fellow 1947), Boston U., 1947, postgrad., 1947-49; D.Sc., Curry Coll., 1957; m. William S. Sahakian, Mar. 27, 1945; children—James William, Richard Lewis, Barbara Jacquelyn, Paula Leslie. Ordained to ministry Conglist. Ch., 1953; asso. pastor Riverdale Congl. Ch., Dedham, Mass., 1953-55, pastor, 1967-68, 78—; asso. pastor First Congl. Ch., Chelsea, Mass., 1956-58, Ch. of Christ, Bedford, Mass., 1958-60; lectr. philosophy, speech Northeastern U., Boston, 1960-77, sr. lectr., 1970-77, mem. counseling service, 1963-77; interim minister East Congl. Ch., Milton, Mass., 1966-67, South Congl. Ch., Braintree, Mass., 1968-69, 1st Congl. Ch., Norwood, Mass., 1972-73. Chmn. drive Am. Cancer Soc., Dedham, 1964-65. Mem. Am. Philos. Assn., D.A.R. (regent 1964-67), Mass. Children Am. Revolution (sr. state chaplain 1967-69), Met. Boston Ministerial Assn., Boston Authors Club, Boston Bus. and Profl. Women, Alpha Phi. Author: (with William S. Sahakian) Realms of Philosophy, 1965, 3d edit., 1977; Ideas of the Great Philosophers, 1966; Rousseau as Educator, 1974; John Locke, 1975; Plato, 1977. Home: 49 Eisenhower Circle Wellesley MA 02181 Office: 42 Needham St Dedham MA 02026. *I am committed to the great commandment to love God and my fellow men. This latter involves a good will toward all, practice of the Golden Rule, and treating every person as of infinite intrinsic worth, an end in himself, and not as means to an end. . .I live in the present and always awaken wondering what good news or exciting event the day will bring forth. My first waking thought is always: "This is the day which the Lord hath made. Let us rejoice and be glad in it."*

SAHAKIAN, WILLIAM S(AHAK), author, philosopher, psychologist, educator; b. Boston, Oct. 7, 1921; s. Jacob and Anna (Pakchoian) S.; B.S., Northeastern U., 1944; M.Div., Boston U., 1947, Ph.D., 1951; postgrad. Harvard U., 1948-55; D.Sc., Curry Coll., 1956; m. Mabel Marie Lewis, Mar. 27, 1945; children—James William, Richard Lewis, Barbara Jacquelyn, Paula Leslie. Asso. prof. philosophy and psychology Suffolk U., Boston, chmn. dept. philosophy, 1949-74, prof. philosophy and psychology, 1975—; asst. to pres. Curry Coll., 1954-56; pvt. practice psychotherapy, 1951—; lectr. Northeastern U., 1950-65, Grad. Sch., 1970; lectr. Fisher Sch., 1952, Lasell Coll., 1960-61, Mass. Coll. Pharmacy, 1960-64, Framingham State Coll., 1977-78; mem. Med. Malpractice Tribunal Commonwealth of Mass.; cons. Nat. Assn. Standard Med. Vocabulary. Founder, trustee Boy's Town Mass. Recipient Meritorious Achievement award for psychology. Fellow Am. Psychol. Assn., Am. Assn. Humanistic Psychology, Mass. Psychol. Assn.; mem. Human Factors Soc., Am. Philos. Assn., Boston Med. Library, Britannica Soc., NEA, AAAS, Am. Ontoanlaytic Assn. (award 1970), Assn. for Realistic Philosophy, Philosophy of Edn. Assn., AAUP, N.Y. Acad. Sci., Phi Sigma Tau, Kappa Psi. Rotarian. Author: The Emotive Ethic in Contemporary British and American Philosophy and Psychology, 1951; Systems of Ethics and Value Theory, 1963, rev. edit., 1968; Outline of Philosophers, 1963; Philosophies of Religion, 1965; Realms of Philosophy, 1965, rev. edit., 1974; Psychology of Personality, 1965, rev. edit., 1975, 3d edit., 1977; Ideas of the Great Philosophers, 1966; Psychotherapy and Counseling, 1969, rev. edit., 1976; History of Philosophy, 1968; Psychopathology Today, 1970, rev. edit., 1979; History of Psychology, 1968; Philosophy, 1968; Psychology of Learning, 1970, rev. edit., 1976; Social Psychology, 1972; Ethics: An Introduction to Theories and Problems, 1974; Rousseau as Educator, 1974; Systematic Social Psychology, 1974; History and Systems of Psychology, 1975; John Locke, 1975; Introduction to Psychology of Learning, 1976; Plato, 1977; Philosophies of Life, 1979; History and Systems of Social Psychology, 1980; reviewer Contemporary Psychology, Jour. Group Psychotherapy, Existential Psychiatry, Psychol. Abstracts, Boston Globe, 1965—. Adv. editor in psychology Rand McNally Coll. Pub. Co., 1975—; contbr. chpts. to books; co-editor and contbr.: Logotherapy in Action, 1979; author, adviser test questions Grad. Record Exam. in Psychology. Contbr. to Ency. Brit., Internat. Ency. Neurology, Psychiatry, Psychoanalysis, and Psychology, Collier's Ency., Psycholgia, Am. Psychologist, Jour. Individual Psychology, others, also profl. jours. Home: 49 Eisenhower Circle Box 12 Wellesley MA 02181 Office: Suffolk U 41 Temple St Boston MA 02114. *The recognition and seizing of opportunities as they present themselves are imperative together with the willingness to make instant and creative decisions, notwithstanding the necessary risks involved. Complete confidence in oneself with a committed sense of purpose greatly aids in the realization of one's goals. Valuable lessons can be learned from both enemies and failures. Failures can be transmuted into successes, and enemies can become incisive and inciteful guides to one's success. Do not permit life's setbacks to upset your determination or style of life, but resiliently return to your creative and productive self. A zest derived from the excitement of competition and a joie de vivre enhances a person's opportunity for success, and in turn a joy of living is a concomitant of a sense of achievement and fulfillment.*

SAHL, MORTON LYON, comedian; b. Montreal, Que., Can., May 11, 1927; s. Harry Sahl; student Compton (Calif.) Jr. Coll.; B.S. in City Mgmt. and Engring., U. So. Calif.; m. Sue Babior, June 25, 1955 (div. 1957). Exptl. theater, also writing for little mags., Los Angeles and San Francisco; entertainer Hungry I, San Francisco, 1953—; other night club engagements include Basin Street East and Copacabana, N.Y.C., Chez Paree and Mister Kelley's, Chgo., Crescendo, Los Angeles, Americana, Miami Beach, and Flamingo in Las Vegas; performer radio and TV, including appearances radio show Nightline, Steve

Allen, Jack Paar, Eddie Fisher ABC Comedy News TV shows, also spl. shows Wide Wide World, Acad. Award show; summer monologue appearance, Highland Park, Ill., monologues on long-playing records Verve Records; on Broadway in revue The Next President, 1958; motion pictures include In Love and War, 1958, All the Young Men, 1960; talk show host Sta. WRC, Washington, 1978; author: Heartland, 1976. Served to pvt. USAAF, World War II; editor Elmendorf Field post newspaper, Poop from the Group. Address: care Harcourt Brace Jovanovich Inc 757 3d Ave New York NY 10017*

SAID, EDWARD W., educator; b. Jerusalem, Palestine, Nov. 1, 1935; s. Wadie A. and Hilda (Musa) S.; A.B., Princeton U., 1957; A.M., Harvard U., 1960, Ph.D., 1964; m. Mariam Cortas, Dec. 15, 1970; children—Wadie, Najla. Tutor history and lit. Harvard U., 1961-63; instr. Columbia U., 1963-65, asst. prof. English, 1965-67, asso. prof., 1968-70, prof., 1970-77, Parr prof. English and comparative lit., 1977—; vis. prof. Harvard U., 1974; fellow Center for Advanced Study in Behavioral Scis., Palo Alto, Calif., 1975-76; Christian Gauss lectr. in criticism Princeton U., spring 1977. Social Sci. Research fellow, 1975; Guggenheim fellow, 1972-73. Recipient Lionel Trilling award Columbia U., 1976. Mem. MLA, Assn. Arab Am. U. Grads. (past v.p.), PEN. Author: Joseph Conrad and the Fiction of Autobiography, 1966; Beginnings: Intention and Method, 1975; Orientalism, 1978; The Question of Palestine, 1979. Editor: Literature and Society, 1979. Office: Hamilton Hall Columbia Univ New York NY 10027

SAIDENBERG, DANIEL, cellist, condr.; b. Winnipeg, Man., Can., Oct. 12, 1906; s. Albert and Minnie (Sokoloff) S.; student Paris Conservatory, 1921-22, Julliard Music Found., 1926-30; m. Eleanore Block, Mar. 15, 1933; children—Lawrence Daniel, Robert Paul. Began as concert cellist, 1918; with Phila. Symphony Orch., 1926-29; solo cellist Chgo. Symphony Orch., 1930-36; engaged in chamber music activities, head cello dept. Chgo. Musical Coll., 1933—; condr. small, large groups, 1933—, Cin. Symphony Orch., summer 1936, Chgo. Opera Orch., fall 1937; formed Saidenberg Chamber Orch., 1937, Saidenberg Symphonietta Series, Chgo. and on tour, 1937—; guest condr. Ill. Symphony Orch., 1937, 38, 39; created Saidenberg Little Symphony, 1940; concert series Town Hall, N.Y.C., 1940, 41, 42; condr. Alka Seltzer radio series, NBC; condr. artistic dir. Town Hall Music Forum, N.Y.C., 1943; chief music dept. overseas radio O.W.I., 1944; guest condr. Ballet Theatre, 1945; cellist Coolidge String Quartet, 1944; condr. Saidenberg Little Symphony, N.Y. Times Hall, 1944; guest condr. CBS, 1945, 46, 47, Phila. Orch., 1946; condr. Conn. Symphony Orch., 1947, Concert Hall Soc.; ann. series concerts Town Hall and Kaufman Auditorium, 1948-57; pres. Saidenberg Art Gallery, Inc. Recordings, Saidenberg Little Symphony. Clubs: Cliff Dwellers, Lotos (N.Y.C.). Home: 980 Fifth Ave New York City NY 10021 Office: 1018 Madison Ave New York City NY 10021

SAIDY, ANTHONY FRED, chess master; b. Los Angeles, May 16, 1937; s. Fred Milhem and Marie Delores (Mallouk) S.; B.S., Fordham U., 1958; M.D., Cornell U., 1962; M.P.H., U. Calif. at Los Angeles, 1968. Chess master, 1955—, internat. master, 1969—; Canadian open champion, 1960, Am. open champion, 1967; participant internat. contests, 1956—; intern Wadsworth VA Hosp., Los Angeles, 1962-63; resident internal medicine Ft. Miley VA Hosp., San Francisco, 1965-66; practice medicine specializing in preventive medicine, Los Angeles, 1967-72, 75-80. Served with USPHS, assigned to Peace Corps, 1963-65. Diplomate Am. Bd. Preventive Medicine. Mem. U.S. Chess Fedn. Author: The Battle of Chess Ideas, 1972; co-author: The World of Chess, 1974. Contbr. mag. Chess Life and Rev., 1964—. Address: 336 N Alta Vista Los Angeles CA 90036

SAINI, TEJBHAN SINGH, educator; b. Raiwind, Pakistan, June 17, 1921; s. Puran Singh and Kishan Kaur; B.A. in Econs., Punjab U., Lahore, India, 1941, M.A. in Econs., 1943; Dr. Forestry, Duke, 1958; Ph.D. in Econs., New Sch. Social Research, 1972; m. Betty Ann Stein, Jan. 4, 1962; children—Kiranjit Kaur, Maninder Kaur. Came to U.S., 1954, naturalized, 1957. Lectr. econs. G.N. Tutorial Inst., 1941-42; range forest officer, Punjab, 1945-54; grad. fellow, research asst. Duke, 1954-58; forest economist FAO, Africa, Middle East, Europe, 1962-65; asso. prof., chmn. dept. bus. and econs. Bluffton (Ohio) Coll., 1966-68; prof., chmn. dept. econs. Bloomsburg (Pa.) State Coll., 1968-77, Disting. Teaching prof. econs., 1977—, also dir. Pa. Center for Econ. Edn.; lectr. New Sch. Social Research, 1961-62. Mem. exec. council Internat. Forum Improvement Quality of Life; v.p. Pa. Conf. Economists, 1971-73, pres., 1973-74; bd. dirs. Delaware Valley Area Council on Econ. Edn.; mem. Pa. Gov.'s Econ. Adv. Com., 1975—, Pa. Task Force on Solid Waste Mgmt., 1976-77; bd. dirs. Pa. Center Econ. Edn.; mem., pres. founding exec. bd. central coordinating com. Guru Nanak Edn. Fund, 1977—. Recipient certificate for exceptional acad. service Bloomsburg State Coll., 1974-75, 75-76, certificate for excellence in teaching, 1976-77, 78; Commonwealth teaching fellow, 1978. Mem. Eastern Econ. Assn. (founder, sec.-treas., exec. bd. award 1973-76, pres.-elect 1979-80), Assn. for Indian Econ. Studies (exec. com.), Assn. State Coll. and Univ. Faculties. Author: Distinguished Professors of Pennsylvania, 1979. Founder, mng. editor The Eastern Econ. Jour., 1974-76; editor procs. of several profl. confs.; contbr. articles to profl. jours. Address: #16 W Park St Bloomsburg PA 17816

SAINT, EVA MARIE, actress; b. Newark, July 4, 1924; d. John Merle and Eva Marie (Rice) Saint; B.A., Bowling Green State U., 1946; student Actors Studio, after 1950; m. Jeffery Hayden, Oct. 27, 1951; children—Darrell, Laurette. Appearing in various radio and TV dramatic shows, N.Y.C., 1947—; theater roles include Mr. Roberts, The Trip to Bountiful, 1953; films: On the Waterfront, 1954, Rainbow County, 1955, That Certain Feeling, 1956, A Hatful of Rain, 1957, North by Northwest, 1959, Exodus, 1961, All Fall Down, 1962, 36 Hours, 1963, The Sandpiper, 1964, The Russians Are Coming, 1965, Grand Prix, 1966, The Stalking Moon, Loving, Cancel My Reservation, 1972; TV dramas The Macahans, 1976, Taxi!!, 1978, A Christmas to Remember, 1978. Recipient Outer Circle Critics award, N.Y. Drama Critics award for The Trip to Bountiful, 1953; Acad. Award for best supporting actress in On the Waterfront, 1955. Address: care Phil Gersh Agy 222 N Canon Dr Beverly Hills CA 90210

ST.-AMAND, PIERRE, geophysicist; b. Tacoma, Wash., Feb. 4, 1920; s. Cyrias Z. and Mable (Berg) St.-A.; B.S. in Physics, U. Alaska, 1948; M.S. in Geophysics, Calif. Inst. Tech., 1951, Ph.D. in Geophysics and Geology, 1953; m. Marie Pöss, Dec. 5, 1945; children—Gene, Barbara, Denali, David. Mem., asst. dir. Geophys. Lab., U. Alaska, also head ionospheric and seismologic investigations, 1946-49; physicist U.S. Ordnance Test Sta., China Lake, Calif., 1950-55, head optics br., 1955-58, now head earth planetary scis. div. and head spl. projects office; cons. Calif. Div. Water Resources; fgn. service with ICA as prof. geol. and geophys. Sch. Earth Scis., U. Chile, 1958-60; originator theory rotational displacement Pacific Ocean Basin; cons. Am. Potash & Chem. Co.; v.p., dir. Covillac Corp.; cons. OAS, World Bank; mem. U.S. Army airways communications system Alaska and Can., 1942-46; cons. Chilean and Argentine govts., N.D., S.D., Kern County; mem. Calif. Gov.'s Com. Geol. Hazards; mem. com. magnetic instruments Internat. Union Geodesy and Geophys., 1954-59. Chmn. bd. dirs. Ridgecrest Community Hosp. Recipient certificate of merit OSRD, 1945, USAAF, 1946, letter of commendation USAAF, 1948, Spl. award Philippine Air Force, 1969; Fulbright research fellow, France, 1954-55; Diploma de Honor, Sociedad Geologica de Chile: distinguished civilan service award USN, 1968; L.T.E. Thompson medal, 1973; Thunderbird award Weather Modification Assn., 1974; Distinguished Pub. Service award Fed. Exec. Inst., 1976; decorated knight Mark Twain. Fellow AAAS, Geol. Soc. Am., Earthquake Engr. Research Inst.; mem. Am. Geophys. Union, Weather Modification Assn., Am. Seismol. Soc., Sigma Xi. Club: Rotary. Adv. bd. GeoScience News. Presented papers at profl. meetings. Patentee photometric instrument, weather and ordnance devices. Address: Research Dept Code 382 Naval Weapon Center US Naval Ordnance Test Sta China Lake CA 93555

ST. ANTOINE, THEODORE JOSEPH, lawyer, educator; b. St. Albans, Vt., May 29, 1929; s. Arthur Joseph and Mary Beatrice (Callery) St. A.; A.B. summa cum laude, Fordham U., 1951; J.D., U. Mich., 1954; postgrad. U. London (Eng.), 1957-58; m. Elizabeth Lloyd Frier, Jan. 2, 1960; children—Arthur, Claire, Paul, Sara. Admitted to Mich., Ohio bars, 1954, D.C., U.S. Supreme Ct. bars, 1959; with firms Squire, Sanders & Dempsey, Cleve., 1954, J. Albert Woll, Woll, Mayer & St. Antoine, Washington, 1958-65; faculty U. Mich. Law Sch., Ann Arbor, 1965—, prof. law, 1969—, dean, 1971-78; vis. prof. Duke U. Law Sch., 1978-79; faculty Salzburg (Austria) Seminar in Am. Studies, Summer 1979. Labor arbitrator, 1970—; mem. pub. rev. bd. United Auto Workers, 1973—; mem. Mich. Adv. Employee Relations Com., 1973-74; chmn. Mich. Gov.'s Workmen's Compensation Adv. Commn., 1974-75; com. chmn. NLRB Task Force, 1975-77; pres. Nat. Resource Center for Consumers of Legal Services, 1974-78; trustee Fordham U., 1978—. Served to 1st lt. AUS, 1955-57. Mem. Am. (sec. sect. labor relations law 1969-70, 71-72), Mich. (chmn. sect. labor relations law 1979-80) bar assns., Am. Bar Found., Nat. Acad. Arbitrators, Indsl. Relations Research Assn., Order of Coif, Phi Alpha Delta. Roman Catholic. Co-author: Labor Relations Law: Cases and Materials, 1968, 74, 79. Editor-in-chief Mich. Law Rev., 1953-54; contbr. to various legal jours. Home: 1421 Roxbury Rd Ann Arbor MI 48104 Office: U Mich Law Sch Ann Arbor MI 48109

ST. CLAIR, JAMES DRAPER, lawyer; b. Akron, Ohio, Apr. 14, 1920; s. Clinton Draper and Margaret Joanna (Glenn) St.C.; student Augustana Coll., 1938-39; A.B., U. Ill., 1941; LL.B., Harvard, 1947; LL.D., Gettysburg Coll., 1975; LL.D., New Eng. Sch. Law, 1975; m. Asenath Nestle, Nov. 25, 1944; children—Margaret Nestle, David Scott, Thomas Bruce. Admitted to Mass. bar; asso. Hale & Dorr, Boston, 1947-52, jr. partner, 1952-56, sr. partner, 1956—; spl. counsel to Pres. Richard Nixon, 1974. Lectr. in law Harvard Law Sch.; v.p., dir. Golden Tech., Inc.; asst. counsel to Army, Army-McCarthy Hearings, 1954. Mem. Town Meeting, Wellesley, Mass., 1963-73; gen. counsel United Fund, 1966; mem. Town of Wellesley Adv. Com., 1966-69; mem. steering com. Lawyers Com. for Civil Rights Under Law, 1968-73; mem. adv. com. Mass. Judicial Conf. Com. on Criminal Rules Project, 1972-73. Trustee, bd. dirs. Walker Home for Children, 1951-73. Served to lt. USNR, 1942-45. Mem. Am. (council of litigation sect. 1974—), Boston (council) bar assns., Am. Law Inst., Am. Coll. Trial Lawyers, Practising Law Inst. (nat. adv. council 1967-73), New Eng. Law Inst. (adv. council 1970-71), Order of Coif. Republican. Conglist. Clubs: Brae Burn Country; Eastwood Ho Country. Author: (with others) Assignments in Trial Practice, 1960. Office: 60 State St Boston MA 02109*

ST. CLAIR, JESSE WALTON, JR., banker; b. Phila., Jan. 15, 1930; s. Jesse Walton and Susan Elizabeth (Leath) St. C.; B.A., Coll. of William and Mary, 1951; M.B.A., U. Pa., 1958; postgrad. Harvard, 1968; m. Elizabeth Ann Bartlett, Oct. 6, 1951; children—Jesse Walton III, Susan Elizabeth, Bruce Bartlett, Ann Leath. Trainee, Fed. Res. Bank, Phila., 1955-57; with Girard Trust Bank, Phila., from 1957, asst. treas., 1960-64, asst. v.p., 1964-67, v.p., 1967-70, sr. v.p., 1970-75, exec. v.p., from 1976; now pres., chief exec. officer First Nat. Bank of Allentown (Pa.), also dir. Bd. dirs. Cedarcrest Coll.; trustee endowment fund William and Mary Coll. Served with USNR, 1951-55. Mem. Robert Morris Assos., Am. Inst. Banking, Theta Delta Chi. Republican. Methodist. Clubs: Lehigh Country; Livingston. Home: 8 Bobby Ct Route 1 Guthsville Heights Orefield PA 18069 Office: 1st Nat Bank of Allentown Hamilton at 7th Ave Allentown PA 18101

ST. CLAIR, JOHN WILSON, former banker; b. Indiana, Pa., Oct. 20, 1912; s. John Guerney and Edna (Wilson) St. C.; A.B., Lafayette Coll., 1935; postgrad. U. Pitts., 1937-38, Harvard Grad. Sch., 1944, Rutgers U. Grad. Sch. Banking, 1952; m. Anne Campbell, Sept. 10, 1940; 1 son, John Campbell. Security analyst Lazard Freres, N.Y.C., 1936-38; with Farmers Bank & Trust Co., Indiana, Pa., 1938-41; asst. cashier Mellon Nat. Bank & Trust Co., Pitts., 1950-54; v.p. Schenectady Savs. Bank (N.Y.), 1954-68, sr. v.p., sec., 1968-75, exec. v.p., sec., 1975-78, also trustee. Pres., bd. dirs., trustee YMCA; bd. dirs. Community Chest, ARC. Served to 1st lt. USAAF, 1942-46. Mem. Phi Delta Theta. Presbyterian. Clubs: Mohawk, Mohawk Golf. Home: 1424 Clifton Park Rd Schenectady NY 12309

ST. CLAIR, NELSON LEWIS, JR., hosp. adminstr.; b. Roanoake, Va., Oct. 11, 1935; s. Nelson Lewis and Genevieve (Statom) St. C.; grad. U. Richmond, 1958; M.H.A., Va. Commonwealth U., 1961; m. Patricia Rilee, Dec. 21, 1957; children—Debora Ann, Patrick Lewis, Michael Scott. Adminstrv. resident Norfolk (Va.) Gen. Hosp., 1960-61; asst. adminstr. Riverside Hosp., Newport News, Va., 1961-62, adminstr., 1962-76, exec. v.p., 1976-77, pres., 1977—; chmn. bd. Hosp. Data Center Va., 1969—; dir. Va. Hosp. Service Assn., 1969—, Peninsula Mental Health Clinic, 1971—, Bank Va., 1973—. Preceptor Sch. Hosp. Adminstrn. Med. Coll. Va., Va. Commonwealth U. bd. dirs. Va. Peninsula Indsl. Commn., Tidewater Health Systems Agency; mem. council Peninsula Planning Dist. Commn. Fellow Am. Coll. Hosp. Adminstrs. (Robert S. Hudgens Meml. award 1971); mem. Am., Va. (dir. 1967—), Tidewater hosp. assns. Methodist. Contbr. articles to profl. jours. Home: 208 N Stonehouse Rd Williamsburg VA 23185 Office: Riverside Hospital J Clyde Morris Blvd Newport News VA 23601

ST. CLAIR, RITA ERIKA, interior designer; b. Vienna, Austria; came to U.S., 1940, naturalized, 1946; d. Leo and Josephine Ropschutz; B.F.A., U. Iowa, 1951; m. John N. St. Clair, Sept. 1, 1950; 1 dau., Diane M. Pres. Rita St. Clair Assos., interior design, Balt., 1957—; mem. Mayor N.Y.C. Adv. Council, 1979—, Balt. Council Art and Culture, 1974—; cons. in furniture mfg., lectr. in field; prin. works include Shepperd and Enoch Pratt Hosp., 1970—, Center Stage, 1975, Balt. City Hall, 1976. Recipient Scalamandre award for adaptive reuse Balt. City Hall, 1978, citation for Center Stage, AIA, 1976. Mem. Am. Inst. Interior Designers (treas. 1969), Am. Soc. Interior Designers (pres. 1979). Address: 1009 N Charles St Baltimore MD 21201

ST. CLAIR, THOMAS MCBRYAR, mfg. co. exec.; b. Wilkinsburg, Pa., Sept. 26, 1979; s. Fred C. and Dorothy (Renner) St. C.; A.B., Allegheny Coll., 1957; M.S., M.I.T., 1958; grad. advanced mgmt. program Harvard U.; m. Sarah K. Stewart, Aug. 1, 1959; children—Janet, Susan, Carol. With Koppers Co., Inc., Pitts., 1958—, asst. to gen. mgr. engring. and constrn. div., 1966-69, comptroller and asst. treas., 1969-78, pres. Engineered Metal Products Group, 1978—. Trustee, Allegheny Coll. Mem. Fin. Execs. Inst., Allegheny Coll. Alumni Assn. Presbyterian. Clubs: Duquesne, Univ. Office: 1550 Koppers Bldg Pittsburgh PA 15219

ST. FLORIAN, FRIEDRICH GARTLER, architect, educator; b. Graz, Austria, Dec. 21, 1932; s. Friedrich and Anna Maria (Prassl) G.; came to U.S., 1967, naturalized, 1973; diploma in architecture U. Graz, 1958, M.S. in Architecture, Columbia U., 1962; m. Livia Companella, Jan. 12, 1967; children—Alisia, Ilaria. Instr. architecture Columbia U., N.Y.C., 1962-63; asst. prof. R.I. Sch. Design, Providence, 1963-70, asso. prof., 1974-77, chmn. div. archtl. studies, 1977-78, dean of architecture, 1978—; vis. asso. prof. M.I.T., Cambridge, 1970-71, 74-75; prin. St. Florian/Howes Assos., architects, Providence, 1978—. Recipient Nat. Endowment for Arts award, 1972-73, 76-77, 79; 26th ann. Progressive Architecture Mag. award, 1979; Center for Advanced Visual Studies fellow M.I.T., 1970-77. Mem. AIA. Works exhibited: Nat. Inst. Architects, Rome, 1967, 14th Triennale, Milan, Italy, 1968, Moderna Museet, Stockholm, 1969, Hayden Gallery, M.I.T., 1973, Mus. Modern Art, N.Y.C., 1975, Drawing Center, N.Y.C., 1979, Walker Art Center, Mpls., 1980. Address: RI Sch Design Providence RI 02903

ST. GEORGE, WILLIAM ROSS, naval officer; b. Southport, N.C., Nov. 19, 1924; s. William B. and Ila (Ross) St. G.; B.S., U.S. Naval Acad., 1946; J.D., George Washington U., 1953; m. Emma Louise Bridger, June 10, 1950; children—Victoria Butler, William Ross, Susan Bridger. Commd. ensign U.S. Navy, 1946, advanced through grades to vice adm., 1973; admitted to D.C. bar, 1953, Supreme Ct. U.S., 1964; comdg. officer U.S.S. Josephus Daniels, 1969-70; comdr. Cruiser-Destroyer Flotilla 11, also comdr. Cruiser-Destroyer Flotilla 3, 1973; dep. and chief staff to comdr.-in-chief U.S. Pacific Fleet, 1973-76; comdr. Naval Surface Force, U.S. Pacific Fleet, 1976—. Decorated D.S.M. with oak leaf cluster, Legion of Merit, Bronze Star. Presbyterian. Home: Quarters D NAS North Island San Diego CA 92135 Office: COMNAVSURFPAC San Diego CA 92155

ST. GERMAIN, FERNAND JOSEPH, congressman; b. Blackstone, Mass.; s. Andrew Joseph and Pearl (Talaby) St. G.; Ph.B. in Social Sci., Providence Coll., 1948, LL.D., 1965; LL.B., Boston U., 1955; J.S.D., Suffolk U., 1976; D.C.L. (hon.), Our Lady of Providence Sem., 1968; m. Rachel O'Neill, Aug. 20, 1953; children—Bonnie Laurene, Lisette. Admitted to R.I. bar, 1956; mem. R.I. Ho. of Reps., 1952-60; mem. 87th to 96th Congresses from 1st R.I. Dist., mem. Democratic com. steering and policy, House coms. banking, fin. and urban affairs, govt. ops. Served with AUS, 1949-52. Mem. Am., R.I., Woonsocket, Fed. bar assns., alumni assns. Our Lady of Providence Sem., Providence Coll., Boston U. Law Sch., Am. Legion. Elk. Home: 121 Woodland Rd Woonsocket RI 02895 Office: House Office Bldg Washington DC 20515

ST. JACQUES, RAYMOND, actor; student Yale, also Am. Shakespeare Festival and Ballet Russe. TV appearance in Rawhide. Films include Black Like Me., Mr. Moses, Pawnbroker, The Comedians, Madigan, Up Tight, If He Hollers, Let Him Go, Cool Breeze, The Final Comedown, Come Back Charleston Blue, Book of Numbers, Lost in the Stars, Eyes of Laura Mars. Address: care Contemporary-Korman Artists Ltd Contemporary Artists Bldg 132 Lasky Ave Beverly Hills CA 90212*

SAINT JAMES, SUSAN, actress; b. Los Angeles, Aug. 14, 1946; d. Charles Daniel and Constance (Geiger) Miller; grad. Acad. Sacred Heart, Lake Forest, Ill., 1963. Student Conn. Coll. for Women. Former model; now motion picture actress; films include What's So Bad About Feeling Good?, Jigsaw; P.J.; Where Angels Go...Trouble Follows; Magic Carpet; Outlaw Blues; Love at First Bite; TV appearances on Fame is the Name of the Game, 1967-68, The Name of the Game, 1968-71, also McMillan and Wife, 1971-76, also Ironside, It Takes a Thief, McCloud, Love American Style; also TV movies including Scott Free, Night Cries. Recipient Emmy award, 1969. Home: 2128 N Beverly Glen Blvd Los Angeles CA 90024 Office: care Internat Creative Mgmt 8899 Beverly Blvd Los Angeles CA 90048*

ST. JEAN, JOSEPH, JR., micropaleontologist; b. Tacoma, July 24, 1923; s. Joseph Leger and Rubey Pearl (Berg) St. J.; B.S., Coll. Puget Sound, 1949; M.A., Ind. U., 1953, Ph.D., 1956; m. Elena Mikhailovna Melnikova, Sept. 22, 1971. Field asst., party chief Ind. Geol. Survey, summers 1950-53; instr. Kans. State U., Manhattan, 1951-52; instr., asst. prof. Trinity Coll., Hartford, Conn., 1955-57; faculty U. N.C., Chapel Hill, 1957—, prof. geology, 1966—, gen. coll. advisor, 1979—; peer reviewer NSF, 1966—, profl. jours., 1960—. 2d violinist Durham (N.C.) Symphony Orch., 1977—. Served with Q.M.C., USNR, 1942-45. Grantee, Geol. Soc. Am., 1956-58, AEC, 1958-60, NSF, 1960-62, U. N.C. Faculty Research Council, 1960-62, Soc. Sigma Xi, 1954-56. Mem. Paleontol. Soc., Soc. Econ. Paleontologists and Mineralogists, AAAS, Carolina Geol. Soc., Elisha Mitchell Sci. Soc., Paleontol. Research Instn., N.C. Acad. Scis., Paleontol. Assn. London, Internat. Paleontol. Union, N.Y. Acad. Scis., Sigma Xi. Contbr. sects. to McGraw-Hill Ency. Sci. and Tech., papers to paleontol., biol. jours. Home: Apt 34A Cedar Ct Carrboro NC 27510 Office: Dept Geology U NC Chapel Hill NC 27514. *Every piece of rock, every bit of soil or sediment, every fossil fragment has a story to tell. As we piece together the fascinating history of this everchanging globe, if in the process we discover resources of benefit to mankind, we may justify our professional existence, as well as add partially to our own and society's intellectual development.*

ST JOHN, ADRIAN, II, army officer; b. Ft. Leavenworth, Kans., Nov. 16, 1921; s. Adrian and Marie (McMahon) St. J.; B.S., U.S. Mil. Acad., 1943; M.A., U. Va., 1951; postgrad. Army War Coll., 1960, U. Hawaii, 1963, Am. U., 1977-80; m. Petronella Elizabeth Durham, Jan. 19, 1943; children—Adrian III, Brian. Commd. 2d lt. U.S. Army, 1943, advanced through grades to maj. gen., 1970; company comdg. officer 15th Cav., 1943-45; intelligence staff officer, Berlin, 1945-47; bn. comdg. officer 3d Bn., 31st Inf. Regt., Korea, 1954, comdt. 73d Tank Bn., Korea, 1955; mem. faculty Command and Gen. Staff Coll., Ft. Leavenworth, 1956-59; faculty adviser Iranian Command and Gen. Staff Coll., 1959; S.E. Asia plans officer, G3, USARPAC, 1960-64; assigned long range br. Strategic Div., Orgn. Joint Chiefs of Staff, Washington, 1964-66; Chief Surface P & O Div. J3, USMACV, 1966-67; comdg. officer 14th Armored Cav. Regt., Europe, 1967-69; asst. div. comdr. 4th Armored Div., Europe, 1969-70; chief Strategic Plans and Policy Div. J5, Orgn. Joint Chiefs of Staff, Washington, 1970-71; dir. plans Army Gen. Staff, Washington, 1971-72; comdg. gen. 1st Armored Div., Europe, 1972-74; vice dir. joint staff Joint Chiefs of Staff, 1974-76; ret., 1976; mem. adv. council on internat. security affairs Republican Nat. Com., 1977-79. Decorated D.S.M. with oak leaf cluster, Silver Star, Legion of Merit with 3 oak leaf clusters, Bronze Star with V device, Joint Service Commendation medal, Army Commendation medal with oak leaf cluster; French Crois de Guerre with silver star; Vietnamese Honor Service medal 1st Class; recipient European Comdr. in Chief's Individual Project Partnership award, 1968. Roman Catholic. Home: 2014 Powhatan St Falls Church VA 22043

ST. JOHN, CLEMENT FRANKLIN, ret. army officer; b. Jamestown, Ohio, Feb. 16, 1905; s. Walter and Cora (Sutton) St. J.; B.S., Ohio State U., 1926, M.D., 1928; m. Margaret Evelyn Lackey,

Dec. 25, 1926; 1 dau., Margaret E. (Mrs. Richard P. Layman). Intern, Letterman Gen. Hosp., San Francisco, 1928-29; commd. 1st lt., M.C., U.S. Army, 1930, advanced through grades to maj. gen., 1959; grad. Army Med. Sch., 1930. Med. Field Service Sch., 1931; various assignments, U.S. and C.Z., 1931-42; grad. Command and Gen Staff Coll., 1942; asst. surgeon Western Task Force, 1942; exec. officer later ops. officer 5th Army surgeon, 1943-45; exec. officer 4th Army surgeon, 1945; surgeon 1st Army, 1945, 48-50; exec. officer 1st Army surgeon, 1946-48; grad. Armed Forces Indsl. Coll., 1951; chief med. plans and ops. div. Office Surgeon Gen., 1951-55; dep. surgeon USAREUR, 1955-57; comdg. gen. 9th Hosp. Center, Landstuhl, Germany, 1957-58, Brooke Army Hosp., 1958-59, Walter Reed Army Med. Center, 1959-61; v.p., dir. Med. Center, U. Cin., 1961-70. Decorated Legion of Merit with oak leaf cluster (U.S.); comdr. Royal Order Crown, Medal of Valor (Italy). Fellow A.C.P.; mem. Theta Chi, Nu Sigma Nu. Mason. Home: 23 Belsaw Pl Cincinnati OH 45220. *I have always followed three basic principles that I think are most important. These are: 1. Always delegate responsibilities to the fullest to those who are under your jurisdiction. 2. Don't be concerned whether they are loyal to you, but always make certain you are loyal to them. 3. I have always tried to impress my colleagues that it is so very easy to be kind and pleasant in dealings with others, but it takes time and effort in thinking how to be rude.*

ST. JOHN, JILL, actress; b. Los Angeles, Aug. 19, 1940; father's last name is Oppenheim; attended U. Calif. at Los Angeles; m. Neil Durbin, 1957 (div. 1959); m. 2d, Lance Reventlow, 1960 (div. 1963); m. 3d, Jack Jones, 1967 (div. 1969). Began work at age 6; played part of Sharon Barbour on radio show One Man's Family, for 6 years; by age 16 had appeared in more than 1000 radio shows and 50 TV programs; left U. Calif. at Los Angeles to make film debut in Summer Love, 1957; other movie appearances include: The Lost World, 1960, Who's Minding the Store, Come Blow Your Horn, 1962, Who's Been Sleeping in My Bed?, 1963, The Liquidator, 1965, The Oscar, 1966, Eight on the Lam, 1967, Banning, 1967, Tony Rome, 1967; TV appearances include: Dupont Show of the Month, Bob Hope Chrysler Theatre, Burke's Law, Rogues, Batman, Big Valley; appearances in movies made for TV include: Fame Is the Name of the Game, How I Spent My Summer Vacation, The Spy Killer, Foreign Exchange.*

ST. JOHN, JOHN, food co. exec.; b. Battle Creek, Mich., Aug. 8, 1921; s. Raymond Martin and Hazel (Eastman) St. J.; B.A., Mich. State U., 1943; m. Lorraine Margaret McCarthy, Feb. 27, 1943; 1 dau., Shannon Elaine. With Minute Maid Co., and predecessors, 1949—, fin. v.p., 1963-65, pres., 1965-69; v.p. finance and ops. Citrus Central, Inc., Orlando, Fla., 1969-71, exec. v.p., 1971—; dir. Agfoods, Inc., Flagship Bank of Orlando, Farm Credit Banks Columbia (S.C.), Flagship Banks, Inc., Miami, Fla., Interregional Service Corp., Mpls., Ag-Carriers, Inc., Leesburg, Fla. Past pres., bd. dirs. Central Fla. unit Am. Cancer Soc. Served with USAAF, 1943-46. Episcopalian. Clubs: Winter Park Racquet, Orlando Citrus, Country of Orlando. Home: 910 Pace Ave Maitland FL 32751 Office: PO Box 17774 Orlando FL 32810

ST. JOHN, PHILIP ALAN, educator; b. Lexington, Mass., Feb. 13, 1924; s. Alfred and Gertrude (Cassidy) St. J.; B.S., U. N.H., 1949, M.S., 1951; Ph.D., Harvard, 1956; m. Edmonde Levitan, Sept. 27, 1951; children—Andrea Ellen, Jennifer Lynne. Oceanographer, Am. Mus. Natural History, Bahama Expdn., 1950; fisheries biologist U.S. Fish and Wildlife Service, 1953; successively instr., asst. prof., asst. dean Grad. Sch., Brandeis U., 1956-67; prof. zoology, chmn. dept Butler U., 1967—. Served with USAAF, 1943-46; ETO. Mem. A.A.A.S., Am. Inst. Biol. Scis., Ind. Acad. Sci., A.A.U.P., Sigma Xi, Phi Sigma. Co-author: Chemical Villians: A Biology of Pollution, 1974. Contbr. articles on marine ecology, regeneration physiology, radiation biology, chemotherapy pathogenic organisms to profl. jours. Home: 1557 Brewster Rd Indianapolis IN 46260

ST. JOHN, ROBERT, fgn. corr., writer, lectr.; b. Chgo., Mar. 9, 1902; s. Joseph Matthias and Amy (Archer) St. J.; grad. St. Albans Sch., Sycamore, Ill., 1920; student Trinity Coll., Hartford, Conn., 1920-22; m. Eda Guerrieri, 1926; m. 2d, Ruth Bass, 1965. Reporter, Hartford Courant, then Oak Leaves, Oak Park, Ill., 1922, Chgo. American and Chgo. Daily News, 1923; with brother owned and edited Cicero Tribune, Berwyn Tribune, Riverside Times, all in Ill., 1923-26; mng. editor Rutland (Vt.) News, then city editor Rutland Herald, 1927-29; on the Camden (N.J.) Courier, then cable editor, Phila. Record, 1929-31; city editor, A.P., N.Y. C., 1931-33; farming and free lance writing, Barnstead, N.H., 1933-39; Balkan corr. for A.P., 1939-41; NBC news commentator, London, 1942; NBC commentator, Washington, 1943, N.Y.C., 1944-46; roving corr. NBC-Monitor, 1959-60; fgn. affairs radio commentator Syndicated Broadcast Features, 1960—. Served with USN, 1917-18. Mem. Phi Gamma Delta. Episcopalian. Author: From the Land of Silent People, 1942; It's Always Tomorrow, 1944; The Silent People Speak, 1948; Shalom Means Peace, 1949; Tongue of the Prophets, 1952; This Was My World, 1953; Through Malan's Africa, 1954; Foreign Correspondent, 1957; Ben-Gurion, the Biography of an Extraordinary Man, 1959; The Boss, the biography of Nasser, 1960; Israel; Life World Library, 1961; Builder of Israel, 1961; They Came from Everywhere, 1962; The Man Who Played God (novel), 1963; Roll Jordan Roll, the Life Story of A River and Its People, 1965; Encyclopedia of Broadcasting, 1967; Jews, Justice and Judaism, 1969; Once Around Lightly, 1969; South America More Or Less, 1970; Eban, biography of Israel's foreign minister, 1972. Contbr. articles to numerous mags. Address: care Matson 22 E 40th St New York City NY 10016

ST. JOHN, SEYMOUR, educator; b. New Haven, Feb. 28, 1912; s. George C. and Clara Hitchcock (Seymour) St. J.; student The Choate Sch., 1923-28, 1929-31, The Le Rosey Sch., Rolle, Switzerland, 1928-29; B.A., Yale, 1935; postgrad. Va. Theol. Sem., 1940-41, D.D., 1968; M.A., Columbia, 1946; L.H.D., Tufts Coll. 1951; m. Margaret Gordon Spencer, June 20, 1936; children—Gordon Webb, Margaret Seymour Plater. Ordained priest, Episcopal Ch., 1942; headmaster The Choate Sch., Wallingford, Conn., 1947-73, emeritus, 1973—; minister Christ Meml. Chapel, Jupiter Island, Fla., 1979—. Fellow Pierson Coll. Yale U. Lt. comdr. USNR Res.; active service, 1943-46. Chmn. Conn. State Bd. Healing Arts, 1949-74; mem. Conn. Adv. Council on Nonpub. Sch. Secular Edn. Trustee Athens (Greece) Coll.; hon. trustee Choate Rosemary Hall; past pres. Conn. Found. Ind. Schs.; Nature Conservancy steward Blowing Rock Preserve, Jupiter Island, 1979—. Mem. New Eng. Assn. Colls. and Secondary Schs. (past pres.), Headmasters Assn., English-speaking Union, Council Basic Edn., Nat. Assn. Ind. Schs. (past chmn. bd.), Comparative Edn. Soc., Phi Beta Kappa. Clubs: Jupiter Island (Fla.); Century Assn. (N.Y.C.); Yale; Hobe Sound Yacht (bd. govs.). Contbr. articles to nat. mags. Address: Rural Route 1 Westerly RI 02891

ST. JOHN, SHELDON CURTIS, museum adminstr.; b. Poughkeepsie, N.Y., Sept. 1, 1916; s. Sheldon and Alice S. (Brown) St. J.; B.S., U.S. Naval Acad., 1938; M.B.A., Harvard, 1949; m. Margaret Francis Ralston, July 27, 1940; children—Lani (Mrs. William M. Rakow), Sheldon Curtis. Commd. ensign U.S. Navy, 1938, advanced through grades to capt., 1956; various assignments U.S. and at sea, 1938-60; comdr. officer Naval Supply Depot, Guam, 1960-61; exec. officer Navy supply Center, Oakland, Calif., 1961-64; force supply officer staff Comdr. Naval Forces, Europe, 1964-66; dir. Naval Area Audit Service, San Francisco, 1966-68; mgr. Novitiate Winery, 1968-71; fin. adminstr. San Francisco Museum Art, 1971—. Mem. Def. Supply Assn. (past pres. No. Calif. chpt.), Bay Area Supply Corps Assn. (past pres.). Lion. Home: 150 Blueberry Hill Dr Los Gatos CA 95030 Office: San Francisco Art Musuem Van Ness and McAllister Ave San Francisco CA 94102

ST. JOHNS, RICHARD ROGERS, lawyer, motion picture co. and TV exec.; b. Los Angeles, Jan. 30, 1929; s. Richard Hyland and Adela Rogers St. Johns; B.A., Stanford, 1953, LL.B., 1954; m. Anne Melville, Jan. 30, 1964; children—Kathleen, Tracey, Sean. Admitted to Calif. bar, 1955; asso. firm O'Melveny & Myers, Los Angeles, 1954-63, partner, 1963-68; sr. v.p. Filmways, Inc., Beverly Hills, Calif., N.Y.C., 1968-69, pres., 1969-72; pres. Richard R. St. Johns & Assos., Inc., 1973-76; pres. Film Finance Group Ltd., 1976—; producer or exec. producer Mahalia, 1975, The People That Time Forgot, 1976, Matilda, 1977, Circle of Iron, 1978, Nightwing, 1979, The Wanderers, 1979. Mem. Central Com. Calif. Republican party, 1952-58. Bd. dirs. Constl. Rights Found. Served with AUS, 1946-48. Mem. State Bar Calif., Los Angeles, Beverly Hills bar assns., Los Angeles Copyright Soc., Acad. Motion Picture Arts and Scis., Nat. Council for Humanities. Democrat. Presbyterian. Clubs: N.Y. Athletic (N.Y.C.); Beverly Hills. Home: 10298 Orton Ave Los Angeles CA 90064 Office: care MGM Studios 10202 W Washington Blvd Culver City CA 90230

SAINTE-MARIE, BUFFY, singer, composer; b. Piapot Reserve, Craven, Sask., Can., Feb. 20, 1941; adopted d. Albert C. and Winifred (Kenrick) Saint-M.; B.A. in Philosophy, U. Mass., 1962; m. Dewain Kamaikalani Bugbee, Sept. 16, 1967 (div. 1972); m. 2d, Sheldon Peters Wolfchild, 1975; 1 son, Dakota Starblanket. Appearances at Saladin, Gaslight, Village Gate, Troubedour, also various coffeehouse theatres; concert appearances at Carnegie Hall, 1965, Royal Albert Hall, London, Eng., 1965, N.Y. Philharmonic, 1967, Queen Elizabeth Theatre, Vancouver, Can., 1967, Newport Folk Festival, 1965, 67, Helsinki (Finland) Music Festival, 1967; founder, owner, pres. Gypsy Boy Music Inc. and Caleb Music Inc.; appeared TV shows The Virginian, Bronson; recording artist for Vanguard Recording Soc., MCA and RCA. Adviser Upward Bound. Recipient Billboard award, 1965, Outstanding Artist of the Year award Nat. Assn. of FM Broadcasters, 1975, Premio Roma award from Italy for performance at Sistina Theatre. Founder and major contbr. NIHEWAN Found. for Native Am. Scholarships, founder Native N.American Women's Assn., Creative Native, Inc. mem. AFTRA, Am. Fedn. Musicians. Author, composer, illustrator-The Buffy Sainte-Marie Songbook. Composer of over 300 published songs including It's My Way, Many a Mile, Little Wheel Spin and Spin, Fire and Fleet and Candlelight, I'm Gonna Be a Country Girl Again, Until It's Time for You to Go (ASCAP award), Universal Soldier, Piney Wood Hills, My Country 'Tis of The People You're Dying, Now That the Buffalo's Gone. Address: care Magna Artists Corp 1370 Ave of Americas New York NY 10019*

SAINTE-MARIE, GUY, physician, educator; b. Montreal, Que., Can., May 22, 1928; s. Hubert and Helene (Legault) Sainte-M.; B.A., College Sainte-Marie, 1950; M.D., U. Montreal, 1955; Ph.D., McGill U., Montreal, 1962; m. Marielle Leblanc, July 23, 1955; children—Bernard, Marc, Luc. Nat. Cancer Inst. Can. research fellow McGill U., 1955-58; fellow Centre National de Transfusion Sanguine, Paris, 1958-59, Harvard U., Boston, 1959-61; asst. prof. sr. searcher U. Western Ont. (Can.), London, 1961-64, asso. prof., 1964-66; asso. prof. anatomy U. Montreal, 1966, now prof., chmn. dept. anatomy; asso. Med. Research Council Can., 1966-76. Mem. Am. Soc. Hematology, Internat. Soc. Hematology, Association des Anatomistes du Canada, Am. Assn. Anatomists, Reticulo-endothelial Soc., AAAS, Club de Recherches Cliniques du Quebec, Association des Anatomistes Francais. Office: 2900 Edouard Montpetit Montreal PQ H3C 3J7 Canada*

SAINT-MARTIN, FERNANDE, museum dir.; b. Montreal, Can.; d. Theode and Idelda (Montbriand) Saint-M.; B.A., Ph.B., U. Montreal, 1948, Ph.D., 1973; M.A., McGill U., 1951; m. Guido Molinari, July 1958; children—Guy, Claire. Women's editor La Presse, 1955-60; editor Chatelaine, 1960-72; dir. Musee d'art contemporain, Montreal, 1972-77; prof. art history U., Que., Montreal, 1977—; Recipient Medal of Can., 1967. Mem. Cercles des femmes journalistes (pres. 1957-58), Assn. internationale des critiques d'art, Académie Canadienne-Francaise, Assn. d'esthetique experimentale, Soc. des ecrivains du Que. Author: La litterature et le non-verbal, 1958; Structures de l'espace pictural, 1968; Beckett et l'univers de la fiction, 1968. Home: 3516 Northcliffe St Montreal PQ Canada

ST. PIERRE, GEORGE ROLAND, JR., metallurgist, educator; b. Cambridge, Mass., June 2, 1930; s. George Roland and Rose Ann (Levesque) St. P.; B.S., Mass. Inst. Tech., 1951, Sc. D., 1954; m. Roberta Ann Hansen, July 20, 1956; children—Anne Renee, Jeanne Louise, John David, Thomas George; m. 2d, Mary Elizabeth Adams, Dec. 11, 1976. Supervising research metallurgist Inland Steel Co., 1954-56; mem. faculty Ohio State U., 1956—, prof. metall. engring., 1957—, asso. dean Grad. Sch., 1964-66; cons. in field, 1957—; vis. prof. U. Newcastle, New South Wales, Australia, 1975. Served with USAF, 1956-57. Recipient Milton (Mass.) Sci. prize, 1947; MacQuigg award, 1971; Alumni Disting. Tchr. award, 1978. Fellow Am. Inst. Mining, Metall. and Petroleum Engrs.; mem. Am. Soc. Metals (Bradley Stoughton Outstanding Tchr. award 1961), Am. Soc. Engring. Edn., A.A.U.P., Am. Contract Bridge League (life master), Sigma Xi. Editor: Physical Chemistry of Process Metallurgy, vols. 7 and 8, 1961. Contbr. articles to profl. jours. Home: 3595 Olentangy Blvd Columbus OH 43214 Office: 2041 N College Rd Columbus OH 43210

SAINT-PIERRE, GUY, agri-bus. exec.; b. Windsor Mills, Que., Can., Aug. 3, 1934; s. Armand and Alice (Perra) Saint-P.; B.Applied Sci. in Civil Engring., Laval U., 1957; diploma Imperial Coll., London, 1958; M.Sc., U. London, 1959; m. Francine Garneau, May 4, 1957; children—Marc, Guylaine, Nathalie. Registrar, Corp. Engrs. Que., 1964-66; dir. Irnes Inc., 1966-67; v.p. Acres Que., 1967-70; minister of edn. Govt. Que., 1970-72, of industry and commerce, 1972-76; asst. to pres. John Labatt Ltd., Montreal, 1977-78; pres., chief operating officer Ogilvie Mills Ltd., Montreal, 1978—; dir. Beurrerie Lafrenciere, Popular Industries Ltd., Zymaize Inc., Miron Inc., Laiterie Dallaire Ltd. Bd. dirs. Clin. Research Inst. Montreal. Served as officer C.E., Can. Army, 1959-64. Mem. Montreal Bd. Trade, Engring. Inst. Can., Order Engrs. Que., Council Can. Unity (v.p.), Mil. and Hospitalier Order St. Lazarus Jerusalem. Liberal. Roman Catholic. Clubs: Mt. Royal, St. Denis, Mt. Bruno. Office: 1 Pl Ville Marie Suite 2100 Montreal PQ H3B 2X2 Canada

SAINT-PIERRE, JACQUES, coll. adminstr.; b. Trois Rivières, Que., Can., Aug. 30, 1920; s. Oscar and Lucie (Landreville) St. P.; B.S., U. Montreal, 1948, M.S., 1951; Ph.D., U. N.C., 1954; m. Marguerite Lachaine, July 15, 1947; children—Marc, Guy, Andre, Louis, Francois, Mireille. Mem. faculty U. Montreal, 1947—, prof. stats., 1960—, dir. computing center, 1964-71, v.p. planning, 1971—; cons. statistician, 1954—. Mem. Inst. Math. Stats., Am. Statis. Assn., Biometric Soc., Canadian Ops. Research Soc., Canadian Math. Congress, Canadian Assn. Univ. Tchrs. (pres. 1965-66). Contbr. articles to profl. jours. Home: 1795 Croissant Daviault Duvernay Laval PQ Canada Office: U Montreal Box 6128 Montreal PQ H3C 3J7 Canada

ST. PIERRE, LEON E., chemist; b. Edmonton, Alta., Can., Sept. 1, 1924; s. Joseph Leon and Adele St. Pierre; B.Sc. with honors in Chemistry, U. Alta., 1951; Ph.D. in Chemistry, U. Notre Dame, 1954; m. Pauline E.A. Oel, July 25, 1949; children—Denise L., Jerome P., Noel J., Louis C., Claire G., Martin G. Michele A. Chemist, Gen. Electric Research Lab., Schenectady, 1954-61, mgr. sect. polymer and interface studies, 1962-65; prof. polymer chemistry McGill U., Montreal, Que., Can., 1965—, chmn. dept. chemistry, 1972-76. Served with RCAF, 1944-45, Canadian Inf. Corps, 1945-46. Mem. Chem. Inst. Can., Am. Chem. Soc., Faraday Soc., Soc. Plastics Engrs., AAAS, N.Y. Acad. Sci. Roman Catholic. Co-author: Polyethers, vol. XIII of high polymer series, 1964; contbr. numerous articles to profl. jours.; patentee in field; inventor family of aluminum lubricants. Home: Frelighsburg PQ Canada Office: Dept Chemistry McGill U Otto Maas Chemistry Bldg PO Box 6070 Sta A Montreal PQ H3C 3G1 Canada

ST. PIERRE, RONALD LESLIE, educator; b. Dayton, Ohio, Feb. 2, 1938; s. Leslie Frank and Ruth Eleanor (Rhoten) St.P.; B.S., Ohio U., 1961; M.Sc., Ohio State U., 1962, Ph.D., 1965; m. Joyce A. Guilford, Apr. 1, 1961; children—Michele Christine, David Bryan. Instr. anatomy Ohio State U., Columbus, 1965-67, asst. prof., 1967-69, asso. prof., 1969-72, prof., chmn. dept. anatomy, 1972—, asso. dir. Cancer Research Center, 1974—; vis. research asso. Duke U., 1966-67; cons. Battelle Meml. Inst., Columbus. Chmn. Ohio Gov.'s Com. on Employment of Handicapped, 1970-78; mem. state exec. com. Presdl. Commn. Employ Handicapped, 1970-78, chmn., 1971-72; mem. planning and adv. council White House Conf. on Handicapped Individuals, 1975-78. Recipient Lederle Med. Faculty award, 1968-71; prize for basic research South Atlantic Assn. Obstetricians and Gynecologists, 1960; Outstanding Individual award Ohio Rehab. Assn., 1969; Gov.'s award for community service, 1973. Mem. Am. Assn. Anatomists, Am. Assn. Immunologists, Soc. Exptl. Biology and Medicine, Sigma Xi. Republican. Presbyterian. Contbr. articles to profl. jours. Home: 290 Bryant Ave Worthington OH 43085 Office: Dept Anatomy Ohio State Univ Columbus OH 43210

SAJKOVIC, VLADIMIR, educator; b. Pavlovsk, Russia, Jan. 25, 1912; s. Ivan S. and Lidia I. (Shishkin) S.; B.A., Russkoe Realnoe Uchilische, Terjoki, Finland, 1927-32; postgrad. C.S.R., Ceska Visoka Skola Technicka, 1932-35, U. Helsinki (Finland), 1935-37; M.A., U. Pa., 1949, Ph.D., 1953; m. Miriam Dorcas Taylor, Nov. 22, 1956; children—Tomislav, Marko, Aleksey. Came to U.S., 1946; permanent resident. Instr. Pendle Hill Sch., Wallingford, Pa., 1946-47, U. Pa., 1949-51, U. Kans., 1951-52; from instr. to asso. in Russian, U. Pa., 1953-59; instr. Bryn Mawr Coll., 1954-57; asst. prof. to prof. Mt. Holyoke Coll., 1959-77, prof. emeritus, 1977—, chmn. dept. Russian lang. and literature, 1959-70. Translator, interpreter Immigration and Naturalization Service, Phila., 1948-49; vis. prof. Middlebury Coll., summer 1960, U. Pa., summer 1966. Served with Yugoslav Army, 1940-46; prisoner of war in Germany, 1941-45. Mem. Am. Assn. Tchrs. Slavic and East European Langs., Am. Assn. Advancement Slavic Studies, Soc. Sci. Study Religion, AAUP, Internat. Dostoevsky Soc. Home: 101 College St South Hadley MA 01075. *Basic ideas or standards of conduct: Honesty with oneself first of all-in the light of conscience and in the power of humility. Genuine interest in spiritual freedom and well being of other persons. Primary goal: To be a worthy human being - knowing that deeds and example speak louder than words.*

SAKAI, HIROSHI, lawyer; b. Hawaii, July 2, 1925; A.A., George Washington U., 1948, LL.B., LL.M., 1950. Admitted to D.C. bar, 1950, Hawaii bar, 1951; law clk. Supreme Ct. Hawaii, 1951; dep. city and county atty., 1951-55; individual practice law, Honolulu; dir. City Bank Honolulu, 1974—. Mem. Child and Family Procedure Rules Com., Supreme Ct. Hawaii, 1962—, Standing Com. Rules and Practice and Procedure, 1969; mem. Hawaii Commn. Uniform State Legislation, 1964-74, 76-79, chmn., 1965-66; chmn. Spl. Com. Statutory Survey, Nat. Conf. Commrs. Uniform State Laws, 1969, mem. spl. com. Uniform Land Transactions Code, 1969-74, Uniform Condominium Act, 1976-78. Mem. Am., Hawaii (treas. 1970) bar assns. Author: (with others) Modern Condominium Forms, 1971. Office: 602 City Bank Bldg 810 Richards St Honolulu HI 96813

SAKAMI, WARWICK, educator, biochemist; b. Phila., Nov. 21, 1916; s. Isami and Toraye (Haraguchi) S.; B.A., Swarthmore Coll., 1938; Ph.D., U. Pa., 1944; m. Adalyn Eleanor Berardi, July 17, 1952. Instr. physiol. chemistry Sch. Medicine U. Pa., 1944-46; asst. prof. biochemistry Sch. Medicine, Case Western Res., U., Cleve., 1946-52, asso. prof., 1952-62, prof., 1962—. Mem. Am. Soc. Biol. Chemists, Am. Chem. Soc., Assn. Am. Med. Colls., AAAS, AAUP, N.Y. Acad. Scis., Fedn. Am. Scientists, Sigma Xi. Home: 2700 Edgehill Rd Cleveland Heights OH 44106 Office: 2119 Abington Rd Cleveland OH 44106

SAKIER, GEORGE, industrial designer, artist; N.Y.C.: ed. Pratt Inst. and Columbia. Organized YMCA Sch. of Machine Design; art dir. Paris Vogue, Modes and Manners, Harper's Bazaar, Schenley Distillers Corp.; designer Am. Radiator, Standard Sanitary Corp., Alfred Dunhill, Ltd., Fostoria Glass. Co., and others; works exhibited Met. Mus., Mus. Modern Art, Bklyn. Mus., Pa. Mus., Mus. Beaux Arts, Lausanne, Switzerland; designer Sci. and Edn.; theme exhibits, N.Y. Worlds Fair. Dir. Municipal Art Soc., N.Y.C. Served with Camouflage Div., World War I; research engr. Office Sci. Research and Development, World War II. Fellow Am. Soc. Indsl. Designers (founding mem.). Home: 44 Rue dû Bac Paris 75007 France

SAKS, GENE MICHAEL, actor, dir.; b. N.Y.C., Nov. 8, 1921; s. Morris J. and Beatrix Saks; A.B., Cornell U., 1943; student theatre Dramatic Workshop, N.Y.C., 1946-48, Actors Studio; m. Beatrice Arthur, May 28, 1950; 2 sons. Made profl. debut as Joxer Daly in Juno and the Paycock, 1947, played in The Dog Beneath the Skin, Gas, Henry IV, The Watched Pot, Topaze, The Infernal Machine, Within the Gates, Him, Yes Is for a Very Young Man, Too Many Thumbs, Bourgeois Gentleman, All You Need Is One Good Break, Mister Roberts, Candlelight, The Personal Appearance, The Voice of the Turtle, For Love or Money, Missouri Legend, South Pacific, The Thirteen Clocks, Late Love, Master Builder, The Tender Trap, The Seven Year Itch, Johnny Johnson, The Good Woman of Setzuan, Middle of the Night, The Mistress of the Inn, Howie, A Circle of Wheels, Album Leaves, The Tenth Man, Love and Libel, A Shot in the Dark, A Thousand Clowns, The Prisoner of Second Avenue; dir. (plays) Enter Laughing, Nobody Loves an Albatross, Half a Sixpence, Generation, Mame, A Mother's Kisses, Sheep on The Runway, How The Other Half Loves, Same Time, Next Year, California Suite, I Love My Wife, The Prince of Grand Street; (films) Barefoot in the Park, The Odd Couple, Cactus Flower, Last of the Red Hot Lovers, Mame, The One and Only; TV appearances include Actors Studio Series, 1949, U.S. Steel Hour, Armstrong Circle Theatre, Camera Three, You Are There, Brenner, Bachelor Father, Philco TV Playhouse, Goodyear Playhouse, Kaiser Aluminum Hour, Producers Showcase, Playwrights '55, Playwrights '56. Served to lt. (j.g.) USNR,

World War II; ETO, Mem. A.F.T.R.A., Actors Equity Assn., Screen Actors Guild. Address: care Arthur J Klein 485 Madison Ave New York NY 10022*

SAKURAI, JUN JOHN, educator, physicist; b. Tokyo, Japan, Jan. 31, 1933; s. Yasuemon and Shizue (Ito) S.; came to U.S., 1949; A.B., Harvard, 1955; Ph.D., Cornell U., 1958; m. Noriko Tsunefuji, June 10, 1961; children—Ken, George. Asst. prof. U. Chgo., 1958-62, asso. prof., 1962-64, prof., 1964-70; prof. physics U. Calif. at Los Angeles, 1970—; cons. Argonne Nat. Lab., 1960-69, Nat. Accelerator Lab., 1967-70. Alfred P. Sloan fellow, 1962-66; John S. Guggenheim fellow, 1975-76. Fellow Am. Phys. Soc. Author: Invariance Principles and Elementary Particles, 1964; Advanced Quantum Mechanics, 1966; Currents and Mesons, 1967; contbr. articles to profl. jours. Home: 11223 Cashmere St Los Angeles CA 90049

SAL, DENNIS EDWARD, hosp. adminstr.; b. Detroit, Feb. 9, 1943; m. Edward Joseph and Josephine (Jakuszonak) Szaladzinski; B.B.A., U. Detroit (valedictorian), 1967, M.B.A., 1969; m. Joyce C. Parka, June 20, 1964; children—Carl Anthony, Kristin Beth. Systems supr. Ford Motor Co., Detroit, 1960-66; sr. mgmt. cons. Touche Ross & Co., 1967-69; v.p., dir. ops. Henry Ford Hosp., Detroit, 1969—; mem. faculty bus. adminstrn. Wayne State U. Cons. hosps.; speaker in field. Mem. Hosp. Financial Mgmt. Assn., Am. Mgmt. Assn., Am. Hosp. Assn., Am. Coll. Hosp. Adminstrs., Financial Planning Inst., Alpha Sigma Lambda, Alpha Kappa Psi. Clubs: Western Golf and Country; Oakland Hills Country; Economic (Detroit); Farmington Racquet; Huron Valley Fishing and Tackle; Fairlane. Home: 21635 Beauford Ln Northville MI 48167 Office: 2799 W Brand Blvd Detroit MI 48202

SALAH, ALBERT ANTON, hotel mgmt. co. exec.; b. Jerusalem, May 30, 1936; s. Anton Elias and Mary Mitri (Sabat) S.; came to U.S., 1957, naturalized, 1963; student Amundsen Coll., 1958-60; m. Loretta Joan Wikarski, Feb. 13, 1960; children—Marie, Margaret, Anthony, Catherine. Chief clk. to gen. mgr. Executive House, Chgo., 1960-71; mng. dir. South Shore Country Club, Chgo., 1971-74; v.p., gen. mgr. Ambassador Hotel, Los Angeles, 1974-76; pres. Anthony Mgmt. Internat. Inc., Escondido, Calif., 1976—. Vice pres. Homeowners Assn., Hinsdale, Ill., 1972-73; bd. dirs. rep. hotels in union arbitration, Chgo., San Francisco and Los Angeles; bd. dirs. Los Angeles Tourism and Conv. Bur. Mem. Milbrae C. of C. (dir.). Club: Masons. Home: 1831 Firestone Dr Escondido CA 92026 Office: 333 S Juniper Escondido CA 92025

SALAMUN, PETER JOSEPH, educator; b. La Crosse, Wis., June 12, 1919; s. Peter and Melana (Hardi) S.; B.S., Milw. State Tchrs. Coll., 1941; M.S., U. Wis., 1947, Ph.D., 1950; m. Lorraine Saurman, June 6, 1946; children—Mary Janet, Elizabeth, Charles, William, Edward, David, Lawrence, Katherine. From instr. to asso. prof. biology Wis. State Coll., Milw., 1948-56; mem. faculty U. Wis.-Milw., 1956—, prof. botany, 1960—, chmn. dept., 1960-64, dir. herbarium, 1965—; cons. in field. Trustee Wis. chpt. Nature Conservancy. Served with USAAF, 1941-45. Mem. AAAS, Am. Inst. Biol. Scis., Am. Meteorol. Soc., Am. Soc. Plant Taxonomists, Bot. Soc. Am., Ecol. Soc., Internat. Assn. Plant Taxonomy, Soc. Study Evolution, Wis. Acad. Sci., Arts and Letters, Sigma Xi (pres. Marquette chpt. 1971-72). Home: 5013 N Elkhart Ave Milwaukee WI 53217

SALANS, CARL FREDRIC, lawyer; b. Chicago Heights, Ill., Mar. 13, 1933; s. Leon and Jean (Rudnick) S.; A.B., Harvard, 1954; B.A., Trinity Coll., Cambridge (Eng.) U., 1956, LL.B., 1958, M.A., 1962; J.D., U. Chgo., 1957; m. Edith Motel, Sept. 26, 1956; children—Eric Lee, Marc Robert, Christopher John. Admitted to Ill. bar, 1958, D.C. bar, 1973, U.S. Supreme ct. bar, 1972; admitted in France as conseil juridique; with State Dept., 1959-72, dep. legal adviser, 1966-72; practice law, Paris, 1972—; legal adviser U.S. del. Vietnam Peace Talks, Paris, 1968-71; asso. prof. law George Washington U., 1965-66. Mem. Am. Bar Assn. (chmn. com. East-West trade and investment), Am. Soc. Internat. Law, East-West Trade Council, Am. C. of C. in France (dir. 1977—, chmn. laws and public affairs com.). Home: 13 Ave Bugeaud Paris 16 France Office: 52 Blvd Malesherbes Paris 8 France

SALANT, RICHARD S., broadcasting co. exec.; b. N.Y.C., Apr. 14, 1914; s. Louis and Florence (Aronson) S.; grad. Phillips Exeter Acad., 1931; A.B., Harvard U., 1935, LL.B., 1938. Admitted to N.Y. bar, 1938; atty. U.S. Govt., 1938-43; asso. Rosenman, Goldmark, Colin & Kaye, 1946-48, partner, 1948-52; v.p. CBS, Inc., 1952-61, dir., 1961-68; pres. CBS News, 1961-64, 64-79, v.p. CBS Inc., 1964-66; vice chmn. NBC Inc., 1979—, also dir. Served to lt. comdr., USNR, 1943-46. Office: 30 Rockefeller Plaza New York NY 10020

SALANT, WALTER S., economist; N.Y.C., Oct. 24, 1911; s. Aaron Bennett and Josephine Adele (Scheider) S.; B.S., Harvard, 1933, A.M., 1937, Grad. Sch. Pub. Adminstrn., 1937-38, Ph.D., 1962; postgrad. Cambridge U., Eng., 1933-34; m. Edna Goldstein, Jan. 25, 1939; children—Michael Alan, Stephen Walter. Research, statistics Treasury Dept., 1934-36; research Wall St. firm, 1936; asst. econs. Harvard, 1938; research SEC, 1938-39; mem. sr. staff indsl. econ. div. Office of Sec. Dept. Commerce, 1939-40; head economist research div. OPA and predecessor agencies, 1940-45; econ. adviser to Econ. Stblzn. Dir., 1945-46, Price Decontrol Bd., 1946; economist Council Econ. Advisers, Exec. Office Pres., 1946-52; cons. econ. and finance div. NATO, 1952-53; vis. prof. Stanford, 1954, 69; sr. fellow Brookings Instn., 1954-76, emeritus, 1977—; cons. to sec. of treasury, 1961—; mem. U.S. econ. survey team to Indonesia, 1961; cons. AID, 1963-66. Mem. Univ.-Nat. Bur. Com. Econ. Research, 1956—, mem. exec. com., 1962-74, vice chmn., 1967-74. Mem. Am. Econ. Assn., Royal Econ. Soc., Phi Beta Kappa. Clubs: Cosmos, Harvard (Washington). Author: (with B.N. Vaccara) Import Liberalization and Employment, 1961; (with others) Indonesia: Perspectives and Proposals for U.S. Economic Aid, 1963, The U.S. Balance of Payments in 1968, 1963; International Monetary Arrangements: The Problem of Choice, 1967; Maintaining and Restoring Balance in International Payments, 1966; International Mobility and Movement of Capital, 1972; European Monetary Unification and Its Meaning for the United States, 1973; Worldwide Inflation: Theory and Recent Experience, 1977; The Effects of Increases in Imports on Domestic Employment: A Clarification of Concepts, 1978; bd. editors Am. Econ. Rev., 1956-58; contbr. articles to econs. jours. Home: 2335 California St Washington DC 20008

SALATICH, WILLIAM GEORGE, diversified mfg. co. exec.; b. Chgo., Oct. 25, 1922; s. George and Jenny (Vujnovich) S.; student Northwestern U.; m. Dawn Trbovich, Sept. 20, 1942. With Continental Can Co., 1939-42, Stewart Warner Corp., 1944; with Gillette Safety Razor Co., Chgo., 1947—, from salesman to pres. Toni Co. div., 1964-69, v.p. parent co., 1964-69, exec. v.p., 1969-71, pres. Gillette Co.-N.Am., Boston, 1971—, dir. parent co.; vice chmn. Gillette Co., 1976—; dir. Motorola Corp., New Eng. Mchts. Bank, Boston. Trustee, Mass. Eye-Ear Infirmary; bd. dirs. Curry Coll. Served with AUS, 1942-44. Mem. NAM, Eastern Gas and Fuel Assos. (trustee). Home: 3 Winding River Circle Wellesley Hills MA 02181 Office: Gillette Co Prudential Bldg Boston MA 02199

SALATKA, CHARLES ALEXANDER, archbishop; b. Grand Rapids, Mich., Feb. 26, 1918; s. Charles and Mary (Balun) S.; student St. Joseph's Sem., Grand Rapids, 1932-38; M.A., Cath. U. Am., 1941; J.C.L., Inst. Civil and Canon Law, Rome, Italy, 1948. Instr. St. Joseph's Sem., Grand Rapids, Mich., 1945; ordained priest Roman Catholic Ch., 1945; assigned chancery office Diocese of Grand Rapids, 1948-54, vice chancellor, 1954-61; aux. bishop, 1961, vicar gen., 1961; consecrated bishop, 1962; pastor St. James Parish, Grand Rapids, 1962-68; bishop of Marquette, 1968-77; archbishop of Oklahoma City, 1977—. Mem. Canon Law Soc. Am. Home: 1521 N Hudson St Oklahoma City OK 73103 Office: 4720 N Classen Blvd PO Box 18838 Oklahoma City OK 73154

SALBAING, PIERRE ALCEE, chem. co. exec.; b. Lectoure, France, May 8, 1914; s. Jean and Sylvia (LaForgue) S.; came to Can., 1946, naturalized, 1968; B.A., Caen (France) U., 1931; Engring. Degree, Ecole Polytechnique, Paris, 1937; Naval Architecture Degree, Ecole Genie Maritime, Paris, 1939; m. Genevieve Nehlil, July 18, 1942; children—Michel, Christian, Francois, Patrick. With North Am. dept. Air Liquide, Montreal, Que., Can., 1946—, asst. gen. mgr., 1957-58, gen. mgr., 1958-60; exec. v.p. Canadian Liquid Air Ltd., Montreal, 1960-62, pres., 1962—; pres., chief exec. officer Liquid Air Corp N.Am., San Francisco, 1971—; Man. dir. dir. L'Air Liquide, Paris. Served to lt. comdr. French Navy, 1939-46. Decorated Legion of Honour. Clubs: Canadian (Montreal); St. James, Mt. Royal, St. Denis, Montreal Amateur Athletic Assn. Home: 55 Belvedere Pl Westmount PQ H3Y 1G6 Canada Office: 1 Embarcadero 1975-78) San Francisco CA 94111 also 1155 Sherbrooke W Montreal PQ Canada also 75 Quai d'Orsay 75321 Paris France

SALBER, LEE DOUGLAS, editor; b. Allentown, Pa., May 6, 1944; s. Rudolph and Evelyn M. (Nurnberg) S.; B.S., N.Y. Coll. Forestry, Syracuse U., 1966; M.S., Cornell U., 1968; m. Iris Jane Thornley, Apr. 12, 1969; 1 dau., Susan Ashley. Conservation asst. Nat. Wildlife Fedn., Washington, 1970-72; creative writer N.H. Fish and Game Dept., Concord, 1972-75, chief of info. and edn., 1975-78; editor-in-chief Ducks Unlimited mag., Des Plaines, Ill., 1978—. Served to lt. (j.g.) USNR, 1968-70. Recipient Mead award Mead Paper Co., 1974. Mem. Wildlife Soc., Ducks Unlimited. Methodist. Home: 21 W 704 Glendale St Lake Zurich IL 60047 Office: 3158 River Rd Des Plaines IL 60018

SALCI, LARRY EUGENE, public transit authority exec.; b. Greenville, Mich., Aug. 29, 1946; s. Robert Louis and Margaret C. (Jensen) S.; B.S. in Fin., U. Detroit, 1968; M.B.A., 1975; m. Karen Jean Loncharich, Mar. 21, 1970; children—Jennifer Jean, Brian Robert. Adminstrv. trainee Chrysler Corp., Highland Park, Mich., 1969-70, employment coordinator, 1972-73, budget analyst mfr. div., Detroit, 1973, acctg. supr. axle div., 1973-75; sec. to bd. dirs. Southeastern Mich. Transp. Authority, Detroit, 1975-76, gen. mgr., 1976—. Bd. dirs. Detroit Police Athletic League, 1977-79. Served with U.S. Army, 1970-71. Mem. Am. Mgmt. Assn., Am. Public Transit Assn., Transp. Research Bd., Greater Detroit C. of C. Republican. Roman Catholic. Clubs: Detroit Athletic, Titan, Econ. of Detroit. Home: 2080 Topaz St Troy MI 48090 Office: 660 First National Bldg Detroit MI 48226

SALEM, LEE, editor; b. Orlando, Fla., July 21, 1946; s. Edmund Judson and Rosemary S. (Segars) Callahan; B.A., Park Coll., Parkville, Mo., 1968; M.A., U. Mo., Kansas City, 1972; m. Anita Jo Parker, July 8, 1967; children—Laura Ann, Matthew Aaron. Mng. editor Universal Press Syndicate, Mission, Kans., 1974—; mng. editor syndicate books UPS pub. subs. Andrews & McMeel, Inc. Home: 6319 McGee St Kansas City MO 64113 Office: 6700 Squibb Rd Mission KS 66202

SALEM, SAM, mfg. co. exec.; b. Salonika, Greece, Dec. 28, 1923; s. Israel Samuel and Rebecca (Cassouto) S.; came to U.S., 1946, naturalized, 1959; B.S. in Chem. Engring., Purdue U., 1949, M.S., 1950; m. Shulamith Rachwalski, Dec. 19, 1947; children—Michael Israel, Ronald Elliot, Jonathan David. With Gen. Tire & Rubber Co., 1950—, pres. chem. plastics div., 1962—, v.p. corp., 1966—; dir. Levinson Steel Corp., Papercraft Corp. Recipient Distinguished Alumnus award, Purdue U., 1964. Mem. Am. Chem. Soc., Am. Mgmt. Assn., Mfg. Chemists Assn., Purdue U. Alumni Assn. Patentee in field. Office: Gen Tire and Rubber Co 1 General St Akron OH 44329*

SALGE, HAROLD CONRAD, former life ins. exec.; b. Bristow, Iowa, July 13, 1921; s. Henry William and Ida Emma (Kruse) S.; student Hamilton's Bus. Coll., Mason City, Iowa, 1941-42; m. Helen Louise Trusty, Apr. 16, 1944; children—Robert, Richard, David. With accounting, actuarial, policy service, claims and purchasing depts. Lutheran Mut. Life Ins. Co., Waverly, Iowa, 1942-72, asst. sec., 1961-72, sec., 1972-79; ret., 1979; farm mgr. Mem. Waverly City Council, 1966-74; chmn. Waverly Municipal Utilities Com., 1970-74; mayor pro tem City of Waverly, 1970-74; sec. Bremer County Civil Service Commn.; v.p. Waverly Low Rent Housing. Republican. Lutheran. Home: 112 Sunset Ct Waverly IA 50677

SALHANICK, HILTON AARON, physician, educator; b. Fall River, Mass., Sept. 17, 1924; s. David and Bessie (Silver) S.; A.B., Harvard, 1947, M.A., 1949, Ph.D., 1950; M.D., U. Utah, 1956; m. Catherine Orr, July 8, 1955; children—Beverly, Steven. Intern, St. Louis Maternity Hosp., 1956-57; mem. faculty U. Nebr. Coll. Medicine, 1957-62, asso. prof. obstetrics and gynecology, 1960-62; obstetrician and gynecologist-in-chief Beth Israel Hosp., Boston, 1962-65; obstetrician and gynecologist Boston Hosp. Women, 1965-69, sr. obstetrician and gynecologist, 1970—; prof. obstetrics, gynecology Harvard Med. Sch., 1962—, Frederick L. Hisaw prof. reproductive physiology, 1971—; mem. Harvard Center Population Studies, 1965—; head dept. population scis. Harvard Sch. Pub. Health, 1971-73. Mem. endocrine study sect. NIH, 1961-66, chmn., 1965-66. Fellow Am. Coll. Obstetricians and Gynecologists, N.Y. Acad. Scis.; mem. Soc. Gynecol. Investigation (council 1961-64), AAAS, Am. Chem. Soc., Endocrine Soc., Obstet. Soc. Boston, Sigma Xi. Editorial bd. Jour. Clin. Endocrinology and Metabolism, 1960-67. Home: 87 Colchester St Brookline MA 02146 Office: 665 Huntington Ave Boston MA 02115

SALIBA, JACOB, corp. exec.; b. E. Broughton, Que., Can., June 10, 1913 (parents U.S. citizens); s. Said and Nazira (David) S.; B.S., Boston U., 1941; m. Adla Mudarri, May 31, 1942; children—John, Thomas, Barbara. Sr. supervising engr. Thompson and Lichtner Co., Boston, 1944-49; pres. Kingston Dress Co., Boston, 1949-51, Indsl. & Mgmt. Assos., Inc., Boston, 1951-54; pres., dir. Maine Dress Co., Cornish, 1948-61; exec. v.p., mem. exec. com. Cortland Corp., Inc. (formerly Brockway Motor Co., Inc.), N.Y.C., 1954-59, also dir.; exec. v.p. Sawyer-Tower, Inc., Boston, 1955-56, pres., 1956-59, dir., 1955-60; v.p. Farrington Mfg. Co.; exec. v.p. Farrington Packaging Corp., Farrington Instruments Corp., 1959-61; pres. Northeast Industries, Inc., 1961—, Fanny Farmer Candy Shops, Inc., 1963-66, W.F. Schrafft & Sons Corp., 1967-68; pres. frozen foods div. W. R. Grace & Co., 1966-68; pres. Katy Industries, Inc., 1969—; dir. Mo.-Kans.-Tex. R.R., Bush Universal, Inc., Midland Ins. Co., HMW Industries, Inc., A.M. Castle & Co., Inc. Spl. cons. Air Materiel Command, USAF, Dayton, Ohio, 1942-43; cons. to chief air staff USAF, 1952-54; co-chmn. Air Force Spare Study Group, 1953. Trustee Boston U.; mem. corp. Mass. Gen. Hosp., Mus. Sci. Mem. Soc. Naval Architects and Marine Engrs. Methodist. Clubs: Union League (N.Y.C.); Algonquin (Boston); Bridgton Highlands Country (Bridgton, Maine). Home: 151 Rutledge Rd Belmont MA 02178 Office: 4368 Prudential Center Boston MA 02199

SALIBA, PHILIP E., archbishop; b. Abou-Mizan, Lebanon, 1931; s. Elias Abdallah and Salema (Saliba) S.; came to U.S., 1956, naturalized, 1961; B.A., Wayne State U., 1959; M.Div., St. Vladimir's Sem., N.Y., 1964. Became sub-deacon Antiochian Orthodox Christian Ch. N.Am., 1945-49, ordained deacon, 1949-59, priest, 1959-66, consecrated archbishop, 1966, now primate; chmn. Standing Conf. Am.-Middle Eastern Christian and Moslem Leaders; v.p. Nat. Council Chs. of Christ in U.S.A.; chmn. Orthodox Christian Edn. Commn.; vice chmn. Standing Conf. Canonical Orthodox Bishops in Ams. Trustee St. Valdimir's Orthodox Theol. Sem. Address: 358 Mountain Rd Englewood NJ 07631

SALIGMAN, HARVEY, apparel mfg. co. exec.; b. Phila., July 18, 1938; s. Martin and Lillian (Zitin) S.; B.S., Phila. Coll. Textiles and Sci., 1960; m. Linda Powell, Nov. 25, 1979; children—Martin, Lilli Ann. With Queen Casuals, Inc., Phila., 1960—, v.p., 1966-68, pres., chief exec. officer, 1968—; v.p., dir. Interco Inc., St. Louis. Mem. Young Pres. Orgn., Knitted Outerwear Mfrs. Assn. Phila. (dir.). Clubs: Locust (Phila.); Masons. Office: 10175 Northeast Ave Philadelphia PA 19116

SALIK, JULIAN OSWALD, physician, b. Slavonice, Czechoslovakia, Sept. 17, 1909; s. Maxmillian and Regina (Langer) S.; M.D., Jagiellonian U., Cracow, Poland, 1936; D.M.R.E., Cambridge U., 1939; m. Felicia Bromberg, Aug. 29, 1939. Resident radiology Columbia-Presbyn. Med. Center, 1942-44; practice medicine specializing in radiology, N.Y.C., 1948; chief radiology Halloran VA Hosp., 1948; radiologist-in-chief Sinai Hosp., 1949—; radiologist Johns Hopkins Hosp., 1956—; asst. in radiology Med. Sch. Columbia, 1942-44; asso. prof. radiology Med. Sch. Johns Hopkins, 1958—. Served to maj., M.C., AUS, 1944-47. Diplomate Am. Bd. Radiology. Fellow AMA, N.Y. Acad. Medicine, Am. Coll. Radiology; mem. Am., Brit. roentgen ray socs., Radiol. Soc. N.Am. Contbr. to Vascular Roentgenology, 1964. Contbr. articles to med. jours. Home: 116 W University Pkwy Baltimore MD 21210 Office: Sinai Hosp Belvedere Ave at Greenspring Baltimore MD 21215

SALINGER, JEROME DAVID, author; b. N.Y.C., Jan. 1, 1919; s. Sol and Miriam (Jillich) S.; student Valley Forge Mil. Acad.; student short story writing under Whit Burnett, Columbia; m. Claire Douglas, 1953 (div. 1967); children—Matthew, Peggy. Began writing at age of 15; pub. first story in Story mag., 1940; contbr. stories to Harper's, Sat. Eve. Post, Esquire, Cosmopolitan, New Yorker mags.; story Uncle Wiggly in Connecticut prod. as motion picture My Foolish Heart. Served to sgt. AUS, 1942-46. Author: Catcher in the Rye 1951; Nine Stories, 1953; Franny and Zooey, 1961; Raise High the Roof Beam, Carpenters and Seymour-An Introduction, 1962. Office: care Harold Ober Assos 40 E 49th St New York City NY 10017*

SALINGER, PIERRE EMIL GEORGE, journalist; b. San Francisco, June 14, 1925; s. Herbert and Jehanne (Bietry) S.; B.S., U. San Francisco, 1947; m. Nancy Brook Joy, June 28, 1957; children—Marc, Suzanne, Stephen; m. 2d, Nicole Helene Gilmann, June 18, 1965; 1 son, Gregory. Reporter, night city editor San Francisco Chronicle, 1946-55; guest lectr. journalism Mills Coll., 1950-55; West Coast editor, contbg. editor Collier's mag., 1955-56; investigator select com. to investigate improper activities in labor or mgmt. field U.S. Senate, 1957-59; press sec. to U.S. Senator Kennedy, 1959-60, to Pres. Kennedy, 1961-63, to Pres. Johnson, 1963-64; U.S. Senator from Calif., 1964; v.p. Nat. Gen. Corp., from 1965; v.p. internat. affairs Continental Airlines, Inc. and Continental Air Services, Inc. subsidiary, 1965-68; pres. Gramco Devel. Corp., 1968—; dep. chmn. Gramco (U.K.) Ltd., 1970-71; sr. v.p. AMROP Inc., 1969; Corr. L'Express, Paris, 1973; contbg. corr. ABC for Europe, 1977—, Paris bur. chief, 1979—. Press. officer Calif. Stevenson for Pres. campaign, 1952, Richard Graves for Gov. Calif. campaign, 1954. Trustee Robert F. Kennedy Meml. Found. Served with USNR, World War II. Decorated Legion of Honor (France); Navy and Marine Corps medal. Democrat. Club: Nat. Press (Washington). Author: With Kennedy, 1966; On Instructions of My Government. Editor: A Tribute to John F. Kennedy, 1964; A Tribute to Robert F. Kennedy, 1968; Je Suis un Americain, 1975; La France et le Nouveau Monde, 1976. Address: care ABC Public Relations Office 1330 Ave of Americas New York NY 10019

SALIS, ANDREW EDMOND, elec. engr., educator; b. Boston, Oct. 10, 1915; s. Manuel and Julia (Plunkett) S.; B.S., Auburn (Ala.) U., 1939, M.S., 1940, E.E., 1947; Ph.D., Tex. A. and M. U., 1951; m. Jane Fair Billingsley, Aug. 31, 1941; children—Pat, Tom, Jon. Mem. faculty Tex. A. and M. U., 1940-45, 46-51, asso. prof., 1946-51; with Gen. Dynamics Corp., 1951-59, sr. group engr., 1959; prof. elec. engring. U. Tex., Arlington, 1959—, head dept., 1960, dean engring., 1969—; v.p. Arlington Engring. Cons.; dir. Arlington Research Corp., Constrn. Research Center. Served with USNR, 1945-46. Registered profl. engr., Tex. Mem. Nat., Tex. socs. profl. engrs., IEEE, Tau Beta Pi, Eta Kappa Nu, Sigma Psi. Clubs: Kiwanis, Ft. Worth Petroleum, Ft. Worth Boat. Home: 4105 Shady Valley Ct Arlington TX 76013 Office: Univ Texas Arlington TX 76019

SALISBURY, ARTHUR J., physician, found. adminstr.; b. North Platte, Nebr., June 13, 1924; s. Arthur J. and Katherine Frances (Clark) S.; B.S., Yale U., 1948; M.D., Harvard U., 1952, M.P.H., 1963. Intern, Johns Hopkins Hosp., Balt., 1952-53; resident in pediatrics Children's Hosp. Med. Center, Boston, 1953-55; practice medicine specializing in pediatrics, Boston, 1955-62; med. dir. Mass. Com. on Children and Youth, 1963-70; v.p. med. services Nat. Found.-March of Dimes, White Plains, N.Y., 1970—; clin. asst. prof. pediatrics Cornell U. Med. Center, 1974—. Served with AUS, 1943-46. Diplomate Am. Bd. Pediatrics. Fellow Am. Public Health Assn.; mem. Am. Acad. Pediatrics. Democrat. Episcopalian. Contbr. articles to med. jours. Home: 411 E 57th St Apt 14D New York NY 10022 Office: 1275 Mamaroneck Ave White Plains NY 10605

SALISBURY, FRANK BOYER, educator, plant physiologist; b. Provo, Utah, Aug. 3, 1926; s. Frank M. and Catherine (Boyer) S.; B.S., U. Utah, 1951, M.A., 1952; Ph.D., Calif. Inst. Tech., 1955; m. Lois Marilyn Olson, Sept. 1, 1949; children—Frank Clark, Steven Scott, Michael James, Cynthia Kay, Phillip Boyer, Rebecca Lynn, Blake Charles. Asst. prof. botany Pomona Coll., Claremont, Calif., 1954-55; faculty Colo. State U., Ft. Collins, 1955-66, prof. plant physiology, 1961-66, plant physiologist Expt. Sta., 1961-66; prof. plant physiology Utah State U., Logan, 1966—, head dept. plant sci., 1966-70; tech. rep. plant physiology AEC, Germantown, Md., 1973-74. Trustee Colo. State U. Research Found., 1959-62. Served with USAAF, 1945. NSF sr. postdoctoral fellow, Germany and Austria, 1962-63. Fellow AAAS; mem. Am. Soc. Plant Physiologists, Ecol. Soc. Am., Utah Acad. Sci., Arts and Letters, Am. Inst. Biol. Scis. (governing bd.), Bot. Soc. Am., Sigma Xi, Phi Kappa Phi. Mem. Ch. of Jesus Christ of Latter-day Saints. Author: The Flowering Process, 1963; (with R.V. Parke) Vascular Plants, Form and Function, 2d edit., 1970; Truth by Reason and by Revelation, 1965; (with C. Ross) Plant Physiology,

1969, 2d edit., 1978, The Biology of Flowering, 1971; (with W. Jensen) Botany: An Ecological Approach, 1972; The Utah UFO Display, 1974; The Creation, 1976; (with E. Kormondy, T. Sherman, N. Spratt, and G. McCain) Biology, 1977. Home: 2020 Country Estates North Logan UT 84321 Office: Dept Plant Sci UMC 48 Utah State U Logan UT 84322. *This is an extremely exciting time to live! Science has provided marvelous insight into the cosmos, the earth, and the nature of life. The fact that mankind exists and can contemplate it all cries out that it has purpose and direction. My life is full to overflowing because God's revelation of Himself adds the final capstone to this beautiful structure.*

SALISBURY, HARRISON EVANS, writer; b. Mpls., Nov. 14, 1908; s. Percy Pritchard and Georgiana (Evans) S.; A.B., U. Minn., 1930; LL.D., Macalester Coll., 1967, Ursinus Coll., 1971, Columbia, 1973; L.H.D., Md. Inst., 1967, U. Portland, 1971, Carleton Coll., 1976; D. Journalism, Assumption Coll., 1967; m. Mary Hollis, Apr. 1, 1933 (div.); children—Michael, Stephan; m. 2d, Charlotte Y. Rand, 1964. Reporter, Mpls. Jour., 1928-29; corr. United Press, St. Paul, 1930, later Chgo., Washington and N.Y.C., became London mgr., 1943, Moscow, 1944, fgn. news editor, 1944-48; Moscow corr. N.Y. Times, 1949-54, mem. N.Y. staff, 1954-63; asst. mng. editor, 1964-72, asso. editor, 1972—, editor opposite-editorial page, 1970-73. Recipient Distinguished Achievement medal U. Minn., 1955; Pulitzer prize for internat. corr., 1955; George Polk Meml. award fgn. reporting, 1957, 67; Sigma Delta Chi award fgn. corr., 1958; Overseas Press Club Asian award, 1967; Sydney Hillman award, 1967. Mem. Am. Acad. and Inst. Arts and Letters (pres. 1975-76), Theta Delta Chi, Sigma Delta Chi. Clubs: Century Assn. (N.Y.C.); Nat. Press (Washington). Author: Russia on the Way, 1946; American in Russia, 1955; The Shook Up Generation, 1958; To Moscow and Beyond, 1960; Moscow Journal, 1961; The Northern Palmyra Affair, 1962; A New Russia, 1962; Russia, 1965; Orbit of China, 1967; Behind the Lines-Hanoi, 1967; The Soviet Union-The Fifty Years, 1967; The 900 Days: The Siege of Leningrad, 1969; War Between Russia and China, 1969; The Many Americans Shall Be One, 1971; The Eloquence of Protest (anthology), 1972; To Peking and Beyond, 1973; The Gates of Hell, 1975; Travels Around America, 1976; Black Night, White Snow, 1978; The Unknown War, 1978; Russia in Revolution, 1900-1930, 1978; Without Fear or Favor: The New York Times and Its Times, 1980. Home: Taconic CT 06079 Office: 229 W 43d St New York NY 10036

SALISBURY, KEVIN MAHON, lawyer, mfg. co. exec.; b. Limon, Costa Rica, Oct. 23, 1935; s. Edward Irving and Kathleen Veronica (O'Sullivan) S.; B.A., Holy Cross Coll., 1957; LL.B., U. Pa., 1960; m. Susan J. Amend, Aug. 11, 1962; children—Erin, Marisa, Laney. Admitted to N.Y., D.C. bars; lawyer U.S. Navy, 1960-66; counsel to USN and NATO forces So. Europe, Italy, 1963-66; v.p., gen. counsel, dir. Eltra Corp., N.Y.C., 1966—. Mem. Am. Bar Assn., Assn. Bar City N.Y. Club: Manhasset Bay Yacht. Home: 49 Country Club Dr Port Washington NY 11050 Office: care Eltra Corp 2 Pennsylvania Plaza New York NY 10001

SALISBURY, RICHARD FRANK, anthropologist; b. London, Dec. 8, 1926; s. Thomas and Marjorie Beatrice (Smith) S.; came to Can., 1962, naturalized, 1976; A.B., Cambridge U., 1949, M.A., 1956; M.A., Harvard U., 1955; Ph.D., Australian Nat. U., 1957; m. Mary Elizabeth Roseborough, Aug. 28, 1954; children—Thomas S., John W., Catherine E. Research asso. Harvard Sch. Public Health, Boston, 1955-56; asst. prof. Tufts U., 1956-57; asst. prof. U. Calif. at Berkeley, 1957-62; asso. prof. McGill U., Montreal, Que., Can., 1962-65, prof., 1966—, chmn. dept. sociology social and anthropology, 1966-70, dir. program Anthropology of Devel., 1970—, dir. center developing area studies, 1975-78; vis. prof. U. Papua, New Guinea, 1967; cons. to Adminstr. Papua, 1971, Can. Dept. Agr., 1970, James Bay Devel. Corp., 1971-72, Indians of Que. Assn., 1972-75. Pres. Westmount High Sch. Com., 1974-75; mem. Commn. on Future of Que. Univs., 1977-79. Served with Royal Marines, 1945-48. Fellow Royal Soc. Can., Royal Anthrop. Inst., Am. Anthrop. Assn.; mem. Can. Sociology and Anthropology Assn. (pres. 1969-70), Can. Council Acad. Panel, AAAS, Am. Ethnol. Assn. (pres. 1979-80). Soc. Applied Anthropology, Polynesian Soc. Author: From Stone to Steel, 1962; Structures of Custodial Care, 1962; Behavioral Science Research in New Guinea, 1967; Vunamami, 1969; Development and James Bay, 1972; Not By Bread Alone, 1972; A House Divided, 1978. Home: 451 Strathcona Ave Westmount PQ PQ H3Y 2X2 Canada Office: 3434 McTavish St Montreal PQ H3A 1X9 Canada

SALISBURY, ROBERT HOLT, educator; b. Elmhurst, Ill., Apr. 29, 1930; s. Robert Holt and Beulah (Hammer) S.; A.B., Washington and Lee U., 1951; M.A., U. Ill., 1952, Ph.D., 1955;; m. Rose Marie Cipriani, June 19, 1953; children—Susan Marie, Robert Holt, Matthew Gary. Mem. faculty Washington U., St. Louis, 1955—, prof., 1965—, chmn. dept. polit. sci., 1966-73, dir. Center for Study Pub. Affairs, 1974-77; vis. prof. State U. N.Y. at Buffalo, 1965, So. Ill. U., Edwardsville, 1975; cons. U.S. Conf. Mayors, 1965, Hartford (Conn.) C. of C., 1964, Nat. Sci. Found., 1973. Mem. St. Louis County Charter Commn., 1967, Gov.'s Commn. on Local Govt., 1968-69. Mem. Mo. (pres. 1964-65), Am. (exec. council 1969-71), Midwest (pres. 1977-78) polit. sci. assns., Pi Sigma Alpha. Democrat. Methodist. Author: Interest Groups Politics in America, 1970; American Government (with others), 2d edit., 1965; Governing America, 1973. Contbr. profl. jours. Home: 337 Westgate St University City MO 63130 Office: Dept Polit Sci Washington U St Louis MO 63130

SALK, JONAS EDWARD, physician, scientist; b. N.Y.C., Oct. 28, 1914; s. Daniel B. and Dora (Press) S.; B.S., Coll. City N.Y., 1934, LL.D., 1955; fellow in Chemistry, N.Y. U., 1935-37, exptl. surgery, 1937-38, bacteriology, 1939-40, M.D., 1939, Sc.D., 1955; NRC fellow Sch. Pub. Health, U. Mich., 1942-43, Sc.D., 1955; LL.D., U. Pitts., 1955; Ph.D., Hebrew U., 1959; LL.D., Roosevelt U., 1955; Sc.D., Turin U., 1957, U. Leeds, 1959, Hahnemann Med. Coll., 1959, Franklin and Marshall U., 1960; D.H.L., Yeshiva U., 1959; LL.D., Tuskegee Inst., 1964; m. Donna Lindsay, June 8, 1939; children—Peter Lindsay, Darrell John, Jonathan Daniel; m. 2d, Francoise Gilot, June 29, 1970. Intern Mt. Sinai Hosp., N.Y.C., 1940-42; research fellow epidemiology Sch. Pub. Health, U. Mich., 1943-44, research asso., 1944-46, asst. prof. epidemiology, 1946-47; asso. research prof. bacteriology Sch. Medicine, U. Pitts., 1947-49, dir. virus research lab., 1947-63, research prof. bacteriology, 1949-55, Commonwealth prof. preventive medicine, 1955-57, Commonwealth prof. exptl. medicine, 1957-63; dir. Salk Inst. Biol. Studies, 1963-75, resident fellow, 1963—, founding dir., 1975—; developed vaccine, preventive of poliomyelitis, 1955; cons. epidemic diseases sec. war, 1944-47, sec. army, 1947-54; mem. commn. on influenza Army Epidemiol. Bd., 1944-54, acting dir. commn. on influenza, 1944; mem. expert adv. panel on virus diseases WHO; adj. prof. health scis., depts. psychiatry, community medicine and medicine U. Calif., San Diego, 1970—. Decorated chevalier Legion of Honor (France), officer, 1976; recipient Criss award, 1955, Lasker award, 1956, Gold medal of Congress and presdl. citation, 1955, Howard Ricketts award, 1957, Robert Koch medal, 1963, Mellon Inst. award, 1969; Presdl. medal of Freedom, 1977; Jawaharlal Nehru award for internat. understanding, 1976. Fellow A.A.A.S., Am. Pub. Health Assn.; asso. fellow Am. Acad. Pediatrics (hon.); mem. Am. Coll. Preventive Medicine, Am. Acad. Neurology, Assn. Am. Physicians. Soc. Exptl. Biology and Medicine, Am. Soc. Clin. Investigation, Am. Assn. Immunologists, Am. Epidemiol. Soc., Phi Beta Kappa, Alpha Omega Alpha, Delta Omega. Author: Man Unfolding, 1972; The Survival of the Wisest, 1973. Contbr. sci. articles to jours. Office: Salk Inst Biol Studies PO Box 85800 San Diego CA 92138

SALK, LEE, psychologist; b. N.Y.C., Dec. 27, 1926; s. Daniel Bonn and Dora (Press) S.; student Rutgers U., 1944, U. Louisville, 1946; A.B. in Psychology, U. Mich., 1949, M.A. in Sociology, 1950, Ph.D. in Psychology, 1954; children by previous marriage—Eric, Pia. Asst. in psychology U. Mich., 1948-50, research asst. Research Center Group Dynamics, 1949, instr. in psychology of adjustment Extension Service, 1951-54, clin. psychologist Psychol. Clinic, Inst. Human Adjustment, 1952-53; research asst. Mich. Dept. Mental Health, 1949, research program dir., 1951-52, research cons., 1953-54; researcher Lab. Group Research, 1950; research asso. Wayne U., 1950-51; chief clin. psychologist Pontiac Child Guidance Clinic, 1952; pvt. practice diagnostic cons., 1952-54; clin. psychology intern Detroit Vets. Mental Hygiene Clinic, 1952-53, Dearborn (Mich.) VA Hosp., 1953-54; research asso. dept. psychiatry Allan Meml. Inst. Psychiatry, McGill U., Montreal, Que., Can., 1954-57, instr. Indsl. Relations Centre, 1954-55, McGill Extension Service, 1955, vis. lectr. human relations, 1957-59; pvt. practice diagnosis and psychotherapy, 1954-57; chief psychologist psychiat. cons. service Univ. Settlement House, N.Y.C., 1957-58; instr. sci. methods, resident tng. program, dept. psychiatry City Hosp., Elmhurst, N.Y., 1958-63, clin. dir. deprol research program, 1960; chief psychologist pediatric psychiatry service Lenox Hill Hosp., N.Y., 1962-66, cons. psychologist dept. pediatrics, 1976—; pvt. practice intensive psychotherapy diagnosis and cons., N.Y.C., 1957-66; chief psychologist, child psychiatry service N.Y. Hosp.-Cornell U. Med. Center, N.Y.C., 1966-67, attending psychologist in pediatrics, 1966—, dir. div. pediatric psychology, 1968-76, attending psychologist Payne Whitney Psychiat. Clinic, 1976—; clin. asst. prof. psychology in pediatrics and psychiatry Cornell U. Med. Coll., 1966-67, clin. asso. prof., 1968, clin. prof. psychology in pediatrics, 1971—, clin. prof. psychology in psychiatry, 1976—; asso. research scientist N.Y. U. Coll. Dentistry, 1971-72; lectr. in human devel. and family studies Cornell U. N.Y. State Coll. Human Ecology, 1969-72; adj. prof. Brown U., 1979—; prin. NbC-TV Nightly News Doctor's Office, N.Y.C. and Chgo., 1976—; syndicated on NBC-Radio News and Info. Service, 1975-77; Macklin Meml. lectr. U.S. Naval Med. Hosp., Portsmouth, Va., 1971; Jonas A. Berg Meml. lectr., 1973; invited speaker numerous orgns.; mem. profl. adv. bd. Floating Hosp. (formerly HOPE ship), 1972—, Internat. Childbirth Edn. Assn., 1972—; mem. adv. council, bd. dirs. Postgrad. Center Mental Health, Guanabara, Brazil, 1973—; mem. adv. bd. Found. for Edn. Human Relations, 1976—, Public Action Coalition on Toys, 1976—; mem. nat. adv. council Boys' Clubs Am. Nat. Health Project, 1977—; hon. mem. bd. dirs. Artists Family Theatre Project, Inc., 1977—; bd. dirs. N.Y. State Citizens' Council for Children, Youth and Their Families, 1977—; mem. Head Start Child Abuse and Neglect Prevention Task Force, Agy. for Child Devel., City N.Y., 1978—; mem. nat. adv. council Nat. Orgn. for Non-Parents, 1978—; cons. in field. Served to s/sgt. Armored Forces, World War II. Recipient Key to City and named Ambassador Good Will, City of Chattanooga, 1973; recipient Key to City, City of Indpls., 1974, spl. citation ARC, 1974, Pearl Merrill award, 1974, Nat. Media award hon. mention Am. Psychol. Found., 1977, Hannah G. Solomon award Nat. Council Jewish Women, 1977. Mem. Am. Psychol. Assn. (exec. com. sect. clin. child psychology 1970-72, pres. sect. 1976-77, pres. div. child and youth services 1979-80, Disting. Profl. Contbn. in Clin. Child Psychology award 1978), AAAS, Royal Soc. Medicine, Am. Acad. Psychotherapists, World Fedn. Mental Health, N.Y. Acad. Scis., Soc. Research Child Devel., Soc. Pediatric Psychology (pres. 1970-71, 71-72, Disting. Contbns. award 1977), Harvey Soc., Soc. Psychol. Study Social Issues, Internat. Soc. Polit. Psychology, North Shore Child Guidance Assn. (hon.). Author: (with Rita Kramer) How to Raise a Human Being, 1969; What Every Child Would Like His Parents to Know, 1972; Preparing for Parenthood, 1974; What Every Child Would Like to Know About Divorce, 1978; Dear Dr. Salk, 1979; columnist McCall's Mag., 1972—, Pediatric Annals, 1972-74, Talk to Dr. Salk syndicated newspaper column, 1973-77; contbr. numerous articles to profl. publs.; subject of film features; author audio cassette programs.

SALKEVER, LOUIS ROMOV, univ. adminstr.; b. Phila., Jan. 1, 1914; s. Reuben and Eda (Spector) S.; B.A., U. Pa., 1936; M.A., Am. U., 1950; Ph.D., Cornell U., 1951; L.H.D., Allen U., 1973; m. Edna Tiskowitz, June 26, 1936; children—Stephen G., David S. Newspaper reporter, 1934-36; economist research bur. N.J. Pharm Assn., 1936-37; writer, editor Fed. Writers Project, 1937-38; profl. asst. Pa. Dept. Pub. Assistance, 1938-41; economist, unit chief, sect. chief U.S. Govt., 1941-46; cons., asso. chief Office Case Analysis, Wage Stblzn. Bd., 1951-52; econ. adviser Commerce Dept., Phila., 1954-55; exec. dir. com. labor, civil service and pub. pensions N.Y. State Constl. Conv., 1967; lectr. N.Y. State Sch. Indsl. and Labor Relations, extension div., 1951-71; summer vis. prof. Yale, 1958, Mass. Inst. Tech., 1961, State U. N.Y. at Geneseo, 1962, Cornell U., 1963, State U. N.Y. at Albany, 1965, Brown U., 1966, 68, Union Coll., Schenectady, 1969; vis. prof. Syracuse U., 1961, asso. African Studies Center, 1975—; vis. lectr. econs. Hobart and William Smith Colls., 1948-49; instr., then asst. prof. Sampson Coll., 1946-49; successively research asst., research asso., instr. Sch. Indsl. and Labor Relations, Cornell U., 1949-50; successviely asst. prof., asso. prof., prof., div. chmn. State U. Coll., New Paltz, N.Y., 1950-65; prof. econs., chmn. dept. State U. N.Y. at Albany, 1965-71, v.p. research, dean grad. studies, 1971—; cons. in field, 1951—. Mem. nat. panel Am. Arbitration Assn.; fact-finder, mediator N.Y. Pub. Employment Relations Bd.; panel arbitrators N.Y. State Bd. Mediation; contract arbitrator, 1958—; mem. Nat Commn. Econs. and the Consumer, 1963-66. Bd. dirs. Research Found. State U. N.Y. Served with AUS, 1944-46. Ford fellow, 1958, 61. Mem. Am. Econ. Assn., Indsl. Relations Research Assn., N.Y. State Econ. Assn. (pres. 1966-67), N.Y. State Council Econ. Edn. (chmn. 1968-70), Council Afro-Am. Studies (exec. sec. 1969—), Nat. Council Univ. Research Execs., Eastern Econs. Assn. (exec. bd. 1973—, editor in chief jour. 1973-76), Omicron Delta Epsilon, Phi Kappa Phi. Author: (W.J. Uppal) Africa; Problems in Economic Development, 1972; Wage Structure Theory, 1965; Sub-Saharan Africa: Struggle with the Past, 1964; Essays in Economic Policy, 1958; Personal Income in Philadelphia, A Method of County Income Estimation, 1955; also articles. Editor-in-chief Eastern Econ. Jour., 1974—. Home: 93 Jordan Blvd Delmar NY 12054 Office: State Univ NY at Albany Albany NY 12222

SALKIN, DAVID, physician; b. Khorol, Ukraine, Russia, Aug. 8, 1906; s. Samuel and Eva (Sturman) S.; M.D., U. Toronto, 1929; m. Bess Marguerite Adelman, Sept. 12, 1934; children—Barbara Ruth, Robert David. Came to U.S., 1929, naturalized, 1937. Intern, St. Mary's Hosp., Detroit, 1929; fellow Herman Kiefer Hosp., 1932-33; pathologist Mich. State Sanatorium, Howell, 1933-34; med. dir., supt. Hopemont Sanatorium, W.Va., 1934-48; asst. prof. medicine U. W.Va., 1936-48; chief of staff VA Hosp., San Fernando, Calif., 1948-67, dir. hosp., 1967; dir. VA Hosp., San Fernando, 1967-71; dir. research and edn. La Vina Hosp., Altadena, Calif., 1971—, med. dir., 1971—; asso. clin. prof. medicine U. Calif. at Los Angeles, 1951-61; clin. prof. thoracic disease Loma Linda U., 1960—; clin. prof. medicine Calif. Coll. Medicine, 1963-64, U. So. Calif., 1964—; dir. Calif. Tb and Health Assn. Gold medalist Calif. Thoracic Soc., 1972; recipient commendations and honors: Am. Acad. Tb Physicians, 1958, 62, VA, 1958, Am. Coll. Chest Physicians, 1973, 3d Internat. Coccidioidomycosis Symposium, 1976. Fellow A.C.P.; mem. Am. Coll. Chest Physicians, Am, Trudeau Soc., Am. Therapeutic Soc., Research Soc. Am., AMA, Calif., Los Angeles med. assns., Sigma Xi. Author numerous articles on Tb and chest diseases. Address: La Vina Hosp 3900 N Lincoln Ave Altadena CA 91001

SALKIND, ALVIN J., electrochem. engr., educator, indsl. research exec.; b. N.Y.C., June 12, 1927; s. Samuel M. and Florence (Zins) S.; B.Ch.E., Poly. Inst. N.Y., 1949. M.Ch.E., 1952, D.Ch.E., 1958; postgrad. and mgmt. courses Pa. State U., summer 1965, Harvard U., 1976; m. Marion Ruth Koenig, Nov. 7, 1965; children—Susanne, James. Chem. engr. U.S. Electric Mfg. Co., N.Y.C., 1952-54; sr. scientist Sonotone Corp., Elmsford, N.Y., 1954-56; research asso. Poly. Inst. N.Y., 1956-58, adj. prof. chem. engring., 1960-70; with ESB-Ray OVAC Co., Yardley, Pa., 1958-79, dir. tech., 1971-72, v.p. tech., 1972—, pres. ESB Tech. Co., 1978—; prof., sect. head bioengring. dept. surgery Rutgers U. Med. Sch., 1970—; adj. prof. bioengring. Rutgers U., 1972—, vis. prof. chem. engring., 1979—; dir., cons. various cos., research instns. and govt. orgns. Served with USNR, 1945-46. Recipient Alumnus citation Poly. Inst. N.Y., 1975; registered profl. engr., N.Y., N.J. Fellow Am. Coll. Cardiology, AAAS; mem. Electrochem. Soc. (past chmn. new tech. com., past chmn. battery div.), Assn. Advancement Med. Instrumentation, Am. Inst. Chem. Engrs., Indsl. Research Inst. (edn. com.), Internat. Soc. Electrochemistry, N.Y. Acad. Scis., Sigma Xi, Phi Lambda Upsilon. Author: (with S.U. Falk) Alkaline Storage Batteries, 1969; (with Herbert T. Silverman and Irving F. Miller) Electrochemical Bioscience and Bioengineering, 1973; editor: (with E. Yeager) Techniques of Electrochemistry, 1971, vol. 2, 1973, vol. 3, 1978; contbr. articles to profl. jours. Home: 51 Adams Dr Princeton NJ 08540 Office: PO Box 366 Yardley PA 19067

SALKIND, MILTON, conservatory pres.; b. Wilmington, Del., Feb. 21, 1916; s. Nathan and Rose (Dektor) S.; B.S. in Econs., George Washington U., 1942; B.S. in Music, Juilliard Sch. Music, 1949; m. Peggy Rippé Snyder, Aug. 9, 1948; children—Karen, Mark. Faculty, Lone Mountain Coll., 1962-66; performances of four-hand piano with Peggy Salkind in U.S., Europe, Can. and Mexico; guest artist Bell Telephone Hour, NBC's Recital Hall; appeared on French television; pvt. instr. piano; pres. San Francisco Conservatory Music, 1966—; commd. works for numerous composers. Mem. performing arts panel Calif. Arts Commn.; chmn. arts San Francisco Symphony; mem. music adv. council Young Musicians Found.; mem. music advisory panel Nat. Endowment for the Arts. Served with AUS, 1942-46. Mem. Assn. Independent Conservatories Music (chmn.), Coll. Music Soc. (council), San Francisco Chamber Music Soc. (adv. bd.). Club: Bohemian. Office: 1201 Ortega St San Francisco CA 94122

SALLA, SALVATORE, artist; b. Khosrovabad, Iran, Aug. 3, 1903; s. Abraham and Angele (Tamraz) S.; brought to U.S. 1920; student Justinian Sch. and Coll., Constantinople, Turkey, 1911-14, Freiburg (Switzerland) Coll., 1914-17; Magister Baccalaureus, Royal U., Constantinople, 1920; pupil of Chev. Leonardo De Mango and Antonin Sterba; m. Anna Ursini, July 6, 1926; children—Violet (Mrs. C.G. Koclanes), Irene (Mrs. George Yagjian), Gloria (Mrs. G.A. Durso), Salvatore II; m. 2d, Trudy Bolender. Portait painter 1920—; acquarellist, muralist, marine and landscape painter, art tchr.; exhbt. Art Inst. Chgo., 1929-33, O'Brien Galleries, 1940, Allerton Gallery, 1935-37, Am. Negro expn. at Coliseum, Chgo., 1940, N. Shore Art Assn. Gloucester, Mass., 1946-47; one-man exhbn. Union League Club Chgo., exhbt., taught and gave painting demonstrations; exhbt. Combined Ins. Gallery, 1966-68; executor canvas Multum in Parvo, Ency. Brit.; 24 portraits of Negro celebrities; portraits of Mary Garden, Marion Claire, Hilda Burke, Charles Marshall, Charles Hackett, Herbert Witherspoon, Henry G. Weber, Edward F. Dunne, Otto Kerner, Chief Justice Ill. Edward S. Scheffler, Harry B. Miller, Stephen Adamowski, John C. Lewe, John A. Sbarbaro, William Lindsay, Julius Miner, Hon. William F. Waugh, Their Imperial Majesties Mohamed Reza Pahlavi Aryamehr The Shahanshah and Shahbanou Farah Pahlavi The Empress of Iran, Noble W. Lee, life size portrait Theo Bamberg (known as Okito), also portrait of William Clement Stone, Salla's Magical Masterpiece of the Great Masters; represented in permanent collection Acad. Magical Arts, Hollywood; painted canvas in oil 14 figures depicting Christ's miracle at wedding of Canna; as demonstration, painted portrait in oil of Miss Joy Roberts, May Queen of Randolph-Macon Woman's Coll., Lynchburg, Va., May 1948; painted 16 portraits of G.I. heroes of World War II, residents of Melrose Park, Ill.; executor mural for Grant's Meml. Auditorium. Mem. N. Shore Art Assn., Sanity in Art, Boston Art Club, Soc. Am. Magicians (pres. Chgo. 1968-69), Internat. Brotherhood Magicians, Acad. Magical Arts (life), La Jolla Art Assn. Moose. Clubs: Wizard's, Entertainers and Actors (pres. 1960—). Creator Bobo, hand puppet on stage and TV programs; educator on constructive anatomy and life drawing and painting, Am. Acad. Arts, 1947-67; contbr. to Look at the Art Institute, 1958. Address: 4175 Wabash Ave San Diego CA 92104. *Bitter as it may be the ascendency of recognition through a ladder so high-I surge an eternal gratitude to my parents who sacrificed toward my academic education. And, the untiring encouragement and faith of my dedicated wife, with all the gratifying letters that I occasionally receive from my former art students acknowledging gratefully their refulgent success in their artistic career, all of these have not only been fruitfully rewarding with a comfort to my autumnal years, but also remunerative enough in bringing nostalgic memories with tearful smiles behind my white whiskers and a chuckle to my heart.*

SALLEY, JOHN JONES, univ. adminstr.; b. Richmond, Va., Oct. 29, 1926; s. Thomas Raysor and Kathryn (Josey) S.; D.D.S., Med. Coll. Va., 1951; Ph.D., U. Rochester, 1954; D.Sc., Boston U., 1975; m. Jean Gordon Cunningham, Dec. 21, 1950; children—Katherine Gordon, John Jones, Martha Cunningham. Research fellow U. Rochester, 1951-54; from instr. to prof., chmn. dept. oral pathology Med. Coll. Va., 1954-63; prof. pathology, dean Sch. Dentistry, U. Md., 1963-74; v.p. research and grad. affairs Va. Commonwealth U., Richmond, 1974—; cons. div. research grants NIH, 1962-66; cons. U.S. Naval Dental Sch., Bethesda, Md., 1966—; spl. cons. Nat. Inst. Dental Research, NIH, 1957-64; cons. USPHS Hosp., Balt., 1963-74, U.S. Naval Hosp., Portsmouth, Va., VA Hosp., Balt., 1964-74, dental health div. USPHS; mem. Md. Adv. Council on Comprehensive Health Planning, 1968-74, Nat. Health Council, 1970-71; pres. Am. Assn. Dental Schs., 1971—; sr. program cons. Robert Wood Johnson Found., 1978—. Bd. dirs. Md. div. Am. Cancer Soc., 1963-70, Am. Fund Dental Health. Served with USAAF, 1945-46. Recipient Outstanding Civilian Service medal Dept. Army, 1961, Distinguished Citizenship award State Md., 1974. Fellow AAAS, Am. Coll. Dentists; mem. ADA, Internat. Assn. Dental Research (Novice award 1953), Am. Acad. Oral Pathology, Sigma Xi, Sigma Zeta, Omicron Kappa Upsilon. Episcopalian. Rotarian. Author articles in field. Home: Route 2 Box 118-A Providence Forge VA 23140 Office: 910 W Franklin St Richmond VA 23220

SALMING, BORJE, hockey player; b. Kiruna, Sweden, Apr. 17, 1951; m. Margitta Wendin; children—Anders, Teresa. Mem. Swedish Nat. Jr. Hockey Team, 1967-70, Swedish Nat. Team, 1971-73,

Toronto Maple Leafs Hockey Team, since 1973. Named to All-Star Team World Championships, Moscow, 1973. Address: 60 Carlton St Toronto ON Canada

SALMON, JOHN HEARSEY MCMILLAN, educator, historian; b. Thames, New Zealand, Dec. 2, 1925; s. John Hearsey and Elizabeth (McMillan) S.; M.A., U. New Zealand, 1951; M.Litt., Cambridge (Eng.) U., 1957; Litt.D., Victoria U., 1970; m. Coral Lansbury, Aug. 14, 1968. Came to U.S., 1969. Prof. history U. New S. Wales, Sydney, Australia, 1960-65; prof. history, dean humanities U. Waikato (New Zealand), 1965-69; Marjorie Walter Goodhart prof. history Bryn Mawr Coll., 1969—. Fellow Royal Hist. Soc. Author: The French Religious Wars in English Political Thought, 1959; A History of Goldmining in New Zealand, 1963; Cardinal de Retz, 1969; Society in Crisis - France in The 16th Century, 1975. Editor: The French Wars of Religion, 1967; co-editor Francogallia by François Hotman, 1972. Contbr. to hist. jours. Home: 200 Radnor Chester Rd Villanova PA 19085 Office: Bryn Mawr Coll Bryn Mawr PA 19010

SALMON, JOSEPH THADDEUS, lawyer; b. Auburn, Ala., Nov. 13, 1927; s. William Davis and Helen (Bowman) S.; B.S., Auburn U., 1949; J.D., U. Ala., 1951; m. Mabel Marie Groves, July 7, 1951; children—Joseph Thaddeus, Bruce Groves. Admitted to Ala. bar, 1951; practice in Montgomery, 1953—; gen. counsel Ala. Farm Bur. Mut. Casualty Ins. Co., Inc., Ala. Farm Bur. Mut. Ins. Service, Inc., Federated Guaranty Mut. Ins. Co., Federated Guaranty Life Ins. Co., So. Guaranty Ins. Co. Served with USNR, 1946-47; to 1st lt. USAF, 1951-53. Mem. Am., Ala., Montgomery bar assns., Internat. Assn. Ins. Counsel, Ala. Def. Lawyers Assn., Phi Alpha Delta, Kappa Sigma. Episcopalian. Home: 2731 Lansdowne Dr Montgomery AL 36111 Office: 2108 E South Blvd Montgomery AL 36111

SALMON, LARRY, museum curator; b. Winfield, Kans., May 5, 1945; s. Raymond D. and Thelma E. (Dunbar) S.; B.A. summa cum laude, U. Kans., 1967; M.A., Harvard, 1968. Curatorial asst. City Art Mus., St. Louis, 1968; asst. curator textiles Mus. Fine Arts, Boston, 1968-69, acting curator, 1969-71, curator, 1971—. Mem. Internat. Com. on Museums. Mem. Am. Assn. Museums, Costume Soc. Am. (dir.), Centre International d'Etude des Textiles Anciens (v.p.). Home: 71 Hancock St Boston MA 02114 Office: Museum Fine Arts Boston MA 02115

SALMON, LOUIS, lawyer; b. Mobile, Ala., Aug. 30, 1923; s. Maurice Louis and Wertie (Williams) S.; B.S., U. Ala., 1943, LL.B., 1948; m. Elisabeth Echols Watts, June 11, 1948; children—John Houston, Margaret Elisabeth. Instr. accounting U. Ala., 1946-48; pub. accountant Smith, Dukes & Buckalew, Mobile, 1949-50; admitted to Ala. bar, 1949; practice in Huntsville, 1950—; mem. firm Watts, Salmon, Roberts, Manning & Noojin and predecessor firms, 1950—; dir., gen. counsel 1st Ala. Bank of Huntsville, N.A., v.p., sec., trustee Huntsville Indsl. Assos.; dir. Dunlop Tire and Rubber Co. Mem. exec. com. Ala. Republican Com., 1969-70. Pres., Huntsville Indsl. Expansion Com., 1968-70; v.p., bd. dirs. U. Ala. Huntsville Found.; trustee Randolph Sch. Served to capt. AUS, 1943-46; ETO. Decorated Combat Inf. badge, Purple Heart. Mem. Am., Ala., Huntsville bar assns., Ala. C. of C. (pres., dir.), Farrah Order Jurisprudence, Kappa Alpha, Phi Alpha Delta. Mem. Ch. of Christ. Rotarian. Club: Huntsville Country (past pres.). Home: 2201 Briarcliff Rd SE Huntsville AL 35801 Office: Terry-Hutchens Bldg Huntsville AL 35801

SALMON, PAUL BLAIR, assn. exec.; b. Charleston, Mo., Jan. 10, 1919; s. Joseph Oscar and Miriam Rebecca (Crow) S.; A.B., Whittier (Calif.) Coll., 1941; M.S.Ed. in Sch. Adminstrn., U. So. Calif., 1949, Ed.D., 1957; m. Doris Beryl McKenzie, June 6, 1941; children—Julie (Mrs. Virgil A. Bretz), Thomas Blair, Timothy Mark, Terrell Paul, Sally (Mrs. David Nichols). Elementary sch. tchr. E. Whittier Sch. Dist., 1941-42; marine electrician leadman, concrete shop constructors, National City, Calif., 1942-44; elementary tchr. Los Nietos (Calif.) Sch. Dist., 1946-47; supt. schs. Bloomfield Sch. Dist., Artesia, Calif., 1947-55, Covina (Calif.) Sch. Dist., 1955-60; supt. Covina Valley Unified Sch. Dist., 1960-67, Pasadena (Calif.) Unified Sch. Dist., 1967-68; supt. schs., Sacramento Unified Sch. Dist., 1968-71; exec. dir. Am. Assn. Sch. Adminstrs., Arlington, Va., 1971—; vis. prof. ednl. adminstrn. Calif. State U. at Long Beach, 1950-55, Calif. State U. at Los Angeles, 1963; adj. prof. sch. adminstrn. Claremont Grad. Sch., 1970-71. Pres. Calif. Elementary Sch. Adminstrs. Assn., 1964-65; pres. elect Calif. Assn. Sch. Adminstrs., 1971. Served with USNR, 1944-46. Mem. Am. Assn. Sch. Adminstrs., Va. Assn. Sch. Execs., NEA (life), Phi Delta Kappa. Methodist. Mason. Contbr. to Sch. Mgmt. mag. Home: 9319 Sibelius Dr Vienna VA 22180 Office: 1801 N Moore St Arlington VA 22209

SALMON, SYDNEY ELIAS, oncologist; b. S.I., N.Y., May 8, 1936; s. Herbert M. and Edna W. (Lipsitz) S.; B.A., U. Ariz., 1958; M.D., Washington U., St. Louis, 1962; m. Joan Estelle Tobias, June 1, 1958; children—Howard, Julia, Laura, Stewart, Russell. Intern Strong Meml. Hosp., Rochester, 1962-63, resident, 1963-64; NIH Spl. fellow, 1966-68; asst. prof. medicine, research asso. Cancer Research Inst., U. Calif., San Francisco, 1968-72; asso. prof. medicine, chief sect. hematology/oncology, dept. internal medicine U. Ariz., Tucson, 1972-74, prof. medicine, chief sect. hematology/oncology, 1974—, dir. Cancer Center, 1976—; prin. investigator NIH grants for cancer research, 1971—; mem. bd. sci. counselors, div. cancer treatment Nat. Cancer Inst. Served to lt. comdr. USPHS, 1964-66. Diplomate Am. Bd. Internal Medicine. Mem. Am. Fedn. Clin. Research, Am. Soc. Hematology, Am., Western socs. clin. investigation, AAAS, Am. Soc. Clin. Oncology, Am. Assn. Cancer Research, Leukemia Soc. Am. (dir., mem. sci. adv. bd. 1974-79), Phi Beta Kappa. Contbr. articles to med. jours. Patentee in field. Home: 2121 Camino El Ganado Tucson AZ 85718 Office: Dept Internal Medicine U Ariz Health Scis Center Tucson AZ 85724

SALMON, WALTER JAY, educator; b. N.Y.C., Nov. 16, 1930; s. Clarence S. and Fay (Josephson) S.; student Dartmouth Coll., 1948-49; B.B.A., CCNY, 1952; M.B.A., Harvard U., 1954, D.B.A., 1960; m. Marjorie Swartz, May 31, 1954; children—Elizabeth, Joan, Stephanie. Mem. faculty Harvard Bus. Sch., 1956—, prof., 1967—, Sebastian S. Kresge prof. mktg., 1970—, asso. dean for edn. affairs, 1974-77; dir. Carter Hawley Hale Corp., Zayre Corp., Hannaford Bros., Cole Nat. Corp., Quaker Oats Co., Stride Rite Corp., Cafeterias, Inc. Treas., trustee Decordova Mus. Served with AUS, 1954-56. Author: Product Profitability and Merchandising Decisions, 1965; Cases in Food Distribution, 1964; Problems in Marketing, 1968; Strategy Problems of Mass Retailers and Wholesalers, 1970; co-author: The Super-Store—Strategic Implications for the Seventies, 1972; The Consumer and the Supermarket-1980, 1976. Home: Winter St Lincoln MA 01773 Office: Harvard Bus Sch Soldiers Field Boston MA 02163

SALMON, WESLEY CHARLES, educator; b. Detroit, Aug. 9, 1925; s. Wallis Samuel and Ruth Elizabeth (Springer) S.; student Wayne U., 1943-44; M.A., U. Chgo., 1947; Ph.D., U. Calif. at Los Angeles, 1950; M.A. (hon.), Brown U., 1959; m. Nancy Huston Pilson, Nov. 26, 1949 (div. July 1970); 1 dau., Victoria Anne; m. 2d, Merrilee Hollenkamp, July 26, 1971. Instr., U. Calif., Los Angeles, 1950-51; instr., asst. prof. Wash. State Coll., 1951-54; asst. prof. Northwestern U., 1954-55; asst. prof., asso. prof. Brown U., 1955-63; prof., Hanson prof. history and philosophy of sci. Ind. U., Bloomington, 1963-73; prof. U. Ariz., 1973—; vis. lectr. U. Bristol, 1959; vis. prof. U. Pitts., 1968-69; vis. research prof. Minn. Center for Philosophy of Sci., 1963. Faculty fellow Fund for Advancement Edn., 1953-54. Fellow Am. Acad. Arts and Scis.; mem. Philosophy of Sci. Assn. (v.p. 1968-70, pres. 1971-72, 1st v.p. div. logic, methodology and philosophy of sci. 1979—), Am. Philos. Assn. (mem. exec. com. Western div. 1969-71, pres. Pacific div. 1976-77), Internat. Union of History and Philosophy of Sci. (chmn. U.S. nat. com. 1967-68). Author: Logic, 1963, 2d edition, 1973; Foundations of Scientific Inference, 1967; Statistical Explanation and Statistical Relevance, 1971; Space, Time, and Motion: A Philosophical Introduction, 1975. Editor: Zeno's Paradoxes, 1970; Han's Reichenbach: Logical Empiricist, 1979. Home: 2201 N Norris Tucson AZ 85719

SALMONSON, ROLAND FRANK, accountant; b. Lake Norden, S.D., Aug. 12, 1922; s. Frank Oscar and Laura M. (Thompson) S.; B.B.A., U. Minn., 1948, M.B.A., 1949; Ph.D., U. Mich., 1956; m. Josephine C. Kurz, Aug. 16, 1946; children—Linda Lou, Sherry Lynn, Judy Kay, Lee Frank. Instr., Mich. State U., East Lansing, 1955-56, asst. prof., 1956-59, asso. prof., 1959-63, prof. acctg., 1963—; with Arthur Andersen & Co., Chgo., 1962-63. Served with USN, 1943-46. Recipient Elijah Watt Sells Gold medal, 1962. C.P.A., Ill. Mem. Am. Acctg. Assn. (v.p. 1972-73), Am. Inst. C.P.A.'s (chmn. theory subcom. 1974-75, mem. bd. examiners 1969-75), Mich. Assn. C.P.A.'s Lutheran. Author: Basic Financial Accounting Theory, 1969; Financial Accounting-A Programmed Text, 1978; Managerial Accounting-A Programmed Text, 1978; Accounting: The Language of Business, 1980. Home: 5144 Park Lake Rd East Lansing MI 48823 Office: Eppley Center Mich State U East Lansing MI 48824

SALOMON, MARDOQUEO ISAAC, physician; b. Minsk, Poland, Jan. 26, 1906; s. Joseph S. and Ida (Perkal) S.; Dr. Nat. Sci., U. Brussels, 1929; M.D., U. Geneva, 1933; m. Sofia Lewin, Oct. 21, 1930; children—Ruth Dalila (Mrs. Edward J. King), Hilel-Benami. Came to U.S., 1942, naturalized, 1947. Prof. biology and physiology U. Cochabamba, Bolivia, 1938-42; pvt. practice medicine, Bolivia, 1938-42, LaPaz, 1940-42; now clin. prof. dept. medicine N.Y. Med. Coll.; mem. staff Flower-Fifth Av. Hosp., 1942—, Met. Hosp., N.Y.C., 1942—, Logan Meml. Hosp., 1942—. Bd. dirs. United Israel World Union. Served with Bolivian Army, 1933-35. Recipient Physician's Recognition award 1969. Fellow Am. Coll. Chest Physicians, Am. Coll. Cardiology, Am. Coll. Angiology. Contbr. numerous articles profl. jours. Home: 501 E 79th St New York City NY 10021 Office: 1350 Madison Ave New York City NY 10028

SALOMON, ROBERT STEPHEN, JR., investment banker; b. N.Y.C., Nov. 13, 1936; s. Robert Stephen and Virginia Stern (Steinhardt) S.; B.A., Amherst Coll., 1959; m. Suzanne F. Stern, Dec. 21, 1957; children—Robert Stephen III, Deborah S., James R. Partner, Salomon Bros., N.Y.C., 1975—. Chmn. bd. trustees St. Luke's Sch., New Canaan, Conn.; chmn. bd. trustees FAF Investment Mgmt. Workshop. Mem. N.Y. Soc. Security Analysts. Home: 71 Turner Hill Rd New Canaan CT 06840 Office: One New York Plaza New York NY 10004

SALOMON, ROGER BLAINE, educator; b. Providence, Feb. 26, 1928; s. Henry and Lucia Angell (Capewell) S.; B.A., Harvard, 1950; M.A., U. Calif. at Berkeley, 1951, Ph.D., 1957; m. Elizabeth Helen Lowenstein, June 14, 1950; children—Pamela, Wendy. Instr. Mills Coll., Oakland, Calif., 1955-57; instr., then asst. prof. Yale, 1957-66; mem. faculty Case Western Res. U., 1966—, prof. English, 1969—, chmn. dept., 1974—. Mem. adv. screening com. Am. lit. Sr. Fulbright-Hayes Program, 1973-76, chmn., 1975; mem. grants-in-aid selection com. Am. Council Learned Socs., 1976—. Served to 1st lt. USAF, 1952-53. Morse fellow, 1960-61; Guggenheim fellow, 1972-73. Mem. AAUP, Modern Lang. Assn., Am. Studies Assn., Coll. English Assn. Author: Twain and the Image of History, 1961. Home: 2830 Coventry Rd Shaker Heights OH 44120 Office: Dept English Case Western Res Univ Cleveland OH 44106

SALOMON, ROGER BLAINE, educator; b. Providence, Feb. 26, 1928; s. Henry and Lucia Angell (Capwell) S.; B.A., Harvard U., 1950; M.A., U. Calif., Berkeley, 1951, Ph.D., 1957; m. Elizabeth Lowenstein, June 14, 1950;children—Pamela, Wendy. Instr., Mills Coll., 1955-57; instr. Yale U., 1957-62, asst. prof. English, 1962-66; asso. prof. Case Western Res. U., 1966-69, prof., 1969—, chmn. dept. English, 1974—. Served to 1st lt. USAF, 1952-53. Morse fellow, 1960-61; Guggenheim fellow, 1972-73. Mem. AAUP, MLA, Am. Studies Assn., Phi Beta Kappa. Author: Twain and the Image of History, 1961. Home: 2830 Coventry Shaker Heights OH 44120 Office: Clark Hall Case Western Res U Cleveland OH 44106

SALOMON, WILLIAM ROGER, investment banking exec.; b. N.Y.C., Apr. 2, 1914; s. Percy F. and Elsie (Heiman) S.; ed. King Sch., Stamford, Conn., 1933; m. Virginia Foster, Jan. 7, 1937; children—Peter F., Susan (Mrs. C. Anthony Seiniger). Joined Salomon Bros., N.Y.C., 1933, partner, 1944—, mem. exec. com., 1958, 1st mng. partner, 1963-78; mem. bd. govs. N.Y. Stock Exchange, 1970-72; mem. Downtown Manhattan adv. com. Chase Manhattan Bank, 1969—. Mem. investment policy com. Smithsonian Inst., 1971—; mem. Brit.-N.Am. Com., 1972—. Bd. mgrs. Hosp. for Spl. Surgery, N.Y.C., 1979—; trustee, mem. fin. com. N.Y. U., 1971—; trustee Outward Bound. Served with USAAF, 1945-46. Mem. Securities Industry Assn. (exec. com., governing council, adv. council), Council Fgn. Relations. Clubs: Harmonie, Bond (past pres.), Economic (N.Y.C.); Lyford Cay (Bahamas); Coral Beach and Tennis (Bermuda); Meadow, Nat. Golf Links Am., Shinnecock Hills Golf (Southampton). Home: 550 Park Ave New York NY 10021 Office: 1 New York Plaza New York NY 10004

SALOMONE, A(RCANGELO) WILLIAM, educator, author; b. Guardiagrele, Italy, Aug. 18, 1915, s. Michael and Italia (Scioli) S.; brought to U.S., 1927, naturalized, 1942; B.A., LaSalle Coll., 1938; M.A., U. Pa., 1940, Ph.D. (Social Sci. Research Council fellow), 1943; m. Lina Palmerio, Sept. 13, 1941; 1 dau., Ilia Susan. Instr. history, Italian civilization Haverford Coll., 1942-43; instr. modern European history U. Pa., 1944-45; successively instr., asst. prof., asso. prof., prof. N.Y. U., 1945-62; Wilson prof. modern European and Italian history U. Rochester, 1962—; vis. prof. Columbia, 1961-62, 64. Pres. Am. div. Instituto per le Storia del Risorgimento, 1959-60; cons. in Italian history Collier's Ency. Mem. selection com. Italian government scholarships, Fulbright Italian history fellowships. Recipient Herbert Baxter Adams prize Am. Hist. Assn., 1946. Social Sci. Research Council fellow, 1955-56; Guggenheim fellow, 1951- 52; Nat. Found. for Humanities Sr. fellow, 1967-68. Decorated knight-officer Order Merit Italian Republic, 1960; recipient citation Soc. Italian Hist. Studies, 1967. Mem. Am. Hist. Assn., Renaissance Soc. Am., Assn. European Historians N.Y. (pres. 1970-72), Am. Assn. Tchrs. Italian, Soc. for Italian Hist. Studies (pres.), Am.-Italy Soc., Matteotti Internat. Symposium (pres. 1975). Author: Italian Democracy in the Making, 1945; L'Età Giolittiana, 1949; (with A. Baltzly) Readings in Twentieth-Century European History, 1950; Italy in the Giolittian Era, 1960; Italy from the Risorgimento to Fascism, 1970. Contbr. articles to profl. jours. Home: 320 Chelmsford Rd Rochester NY 14618

SALOUTOS, THEODORE, educator, historian; b. Milw., Aug. 3, 1910; s. Peter and Demetra (Perdikis) S.; B.E., Milw. State Tchrs. Coll., 1933; student U. Wis. Law Sch., summers 1934-36; M. Philosophy, U. Wis., 1938, Ph.D., 1940; m. Florence Louise Schwefel, Sept. 21, 1940; children—Bonita Louise (Mrs. Martin Gilbert), Theodore A. Peter. Tchr., Waukesha (Wis.) Pub. Schs., 1933-36; research asst. history U. Wis., 1937-40, postdoctoral fellow history and agrl. econs., 1940-41, instr. history extension div., 1941-43; vis. lectr. Oberlin Coll., 1943-45; lectr. U. Calif. at Los Angeles, 1945-46, mem. faculty, 1946—, prof. history, 1956—, chmn. dept., 1962—; vis. summer prof. U. Minn., 1947, U. Wis. at Milw., 1962; vis. prof. U. Hawaii, 1968; Fulbright research scholar U. Athens, 1952-53, 66-67; Fulbright lectr. U. Freiburg (W. Germany), 1959-60; Guggenheim fellow, 1966-67; cons., panelist Nat. Endowment Arts and Humanities, 1968-75; mem. nat. adv. bd. Immigration History Research Center, U. Minn., 1973—; cons. Holloman (N.Mex.) AFB, 1958-59. Pres., Mar Vista (Calif.) Democratic Club, 1961-62, Save Cyprus Council So. Calif., 1974-77; mem. Friends of Huntington Library, 1964—. Recipient Disting. Alumnus award U. Wis.-Milw., 1977. Mem. Am. (exec. com. Pacific Coast br. 1962-65). Miss. Valley hist. assns., Agrl. History Soc. (pres. 1965-66), Immigration History Soc. (pres. 1973-76), Bus. History Soc., Econ. History Assn., English Econ. History Soc., Pan Arcadian Fedn., Order Ahepa (chmn. edn. com. 1964-65). Club: Hellenic Univ. So. Calif. (pres. 1961-63, 69-71). Author: (with John D. Hicks) Agricultural Discontent in the Middle West, 1900-1939, 1951; They Remember America, 1956; Farmer Movements in the South, 1865-1933, 1960; The Greeks in the United States, 1964; Twentieth Century Populism, 1964; Farmer Movements in the South, 1964; The Greeks in America, 1967; Populism: Reaction or Reform, 1968. Mem. editorial bd. Agrl. History, 1957—, Jour. Am. History. Home: 3745 Wade St Los Angeles CA 90066

SALPETER, EDWIN ERNEST, educator; b. Vienna, Austria, Dec. 3, 1924; s. Jakob L. and Frieder (Horn) S.; M.S., Sydney U., 1946; Ph.D., Birmingham (Eng.) U., 1948; D.Sc., U. Chgo., 1969; D.Sc., Case-Western Reserve U., 1970; m. Miriam Mark, June 11, 1950; children—Judy Gail, Shelley Ruth. Came to U.S., 1949, naturalized, 1953. Research fellow Birmingham U., 1948-49; faculty Cornell U., Ithaca, N.Y., 1949—, now J.G. White prof. phys. scis.; mem. U.S. Nat. Sci. Bd., 1979—. Mem. AURA bd., 1970-72. Recipient gold medal Royal Astron. Soc., 1973; J.R. Oppenheimer Meml. prize, 1974. Mem. Am. Astron. Soc. (v.p. 1971-73), Am. Philos. Soc., Nat. Acad. Scis., Am. Acad. Arts and Scis., Deutsche Akademie Leopoldina. Author: Quantum Mechanics, 1957, 77. Editorial bd. Astrophys. Jour., 1966-69; asso. editor Rev. Modern Physics, 1971—. Contbr. articles to profl. jours. Home: 116 Westbourne Ln Ithaca NY 14850

SALPETER, MIRIAM M(IRL) MARK, neurobiologist; b. Riga, Latvia, Apr. 8, 1929; came to U.S., 1945, naturalized, 1951; d. Mendel and Beila (Mundel) Mark; B.A. summa cum laude, Hunter Coll., 1950; Ph.D. (Susan Linn Sage fellow), Cornell U., 1953; m. Edwin E. Salpeter, June 11, 1951; children—Judy Gail, Shelley Ruth. Research asso. Cornell U., 1956-57, 58-66, asso. prof. neurobiology and behavior, and applied physics, 1966-72, prof., 1972—; research asso. Western Res. U., 1957-58. Recipient Career Devel. award NIH, 1962-72; Mem. AAAS, Electron Microscope Soc., Am. Soc. Neuroscis., Am. Soc. Cell Biology (exec. council), Phi Beta Kappa, Sigma Xi. Contbr. articles to profl. publs.; editorial bd. Jour. Morphology, 1965-67, Jour. Cell Biology, 1974-77. Home: 116 Westbourne Ln Ithaca NY 14850 Office: Cornell U Ithaca NY 14853

SALSBERG, ARTHUR PHILIP, pub. co. exec.; b. Bklyn., Aug. 28, 1929; s. Solomon William and Rae (Miller) S.; B.B.A., Coll. City N.Y., 1951; m. Rhoda Gelb, Sept. 11, 1960; children—Charles Martin, Solomon William. Mng. editor Ojibway Press, N.Y.C., 1957-64; advt. and promotion mgr. RCA Corp., Harrison, N.J., 1965-67; editor N.Am. Pub. Co., Phila., 1967-70; vice pres., gen. mgr. Lawyers World, Inc., Phila., 1970-72; editorial dir. Ziff-Davis Pub. Co., N.Y.C., 1973—. Mag. and newsletter pub. cons.; electronics instr.; local campaign publicist, speech writer for town mayor, town council, library bd., sch. bd. Publicity chmn. Nassau council Boy Scouts Am., 1975. Served with AUS, 1951-53; Korea. Recipient Indsl. Mktg. Mag. award, 1959. Mem. IEEE (vice-chmn. vehicular communications), Audio Engring. Soc., Radio Club Am., Am. Soc. Mag. Editors. Club: Nassau Sailing. Author: Collier's Ency. Yearbook, 1977, 78, 79; editor: Audio Mag., 1967-70; Lawyers World, 1970-72; Popular Electronics, 1973—; Communications Handbook, 1973—; Electronic Experimenters Handbook, 1973—; Stereo Directory, 1973—; Tape Recorder Directory, 1973—; Citizens Band Handbook, 1976—. Home: 15 Range Dr Merrick NY 11566 Office: 1 Park Ave New York NY 10016

SALSBURY, JASON MELVIN, chem. co. exec.; b. Richmond, Va., June 12, 1920; s. John and Tillie Inez (Berman) S.; B.S., U. Richmond, 1940; M.S., U. Va., 1943, Ph.D., 1945; m. Miriam K. Heller, June 23, 1946; children—David L., Michael H. With Am. Cyanamid Co., 1946—, v.p. research and devel. Formica Corp. div., 1967-72, dir. chem. research div., Wayne, N.J., 1972—. Mem. nat. materials adv. bd. Nat. Acad. Scis., 1977—. Mem. Indsl. Research Inst. (dir. 1972-75, 77—, v.p. 1977, pres. 1979-80), Am. Chem. Soc., Soc. Chem. Industry, Sigma Xi. Patentee in field. Home: 28 Warewoods Rd Saddle River NJ 07458 Office: Am Cyanamid Co Wayne NJ 07470

SALSBURY, STEPHEN MATTHEW, historian, educator; b. Oakland, Calif., Oct. 12, 1931; s. Ralph Thomas and Roma Enola (Connor) S.; A.B., Occidental Coll., 1953; A.M., Harvard U., 1957, Ph.D., 1961. Research asso. Harvard Sch. Bus. Adminstrn., 1961-62; asst. prof. history U. Del., Newark, 1963-68, asso. prof., 1968-70, prof., 1970—, chmn. history dept., 1974-77; prof. economic history U. Sydney (Australia), 1977—, also head dept.; vis. asst. prof. Johns Hopkins, 1967-68; vis. scholar La Trobe U., Melbourne, Australia, 1974; Hunter Baillie fellow St. Andrew's Coll., Sydney. Mem. adv. bd. Eleutherian-Mills-Hagley Found., 1975-78. Served with USAF, 1955-57, 62-63. Mem. Am. Hist. Assn., Econ. History Assn. (chmn. com. research 1976-77), Econ. History Assn. Australia and N.Z., Orgn. Am. Historians, Agrl. History Soc., Hist. Soc. Del., AAUP, Assn. Evolutionary Econs., Phi Beta Kappa, Alpha Tau Omega. Congregationalist. Author: The State, The Investor and the Railroad, 1967; (with Alfred D. Chandler, Jr.) Pierre S. duPont and the Making of the Modern Corporation, 1971; Essays on the History of the American West, 1975. Home: 28 Wahroonga Ave Wahroonga New South Wales Australia 2076 Office: Dept Econ History U Sydney Sydney New South Wales Australia

SALTARELLI, GERALD C., former constrn. materials mfg. co. exec.; b. Bklyn., Mar. 18, 1912; s. Peter E. and Anna (DeStafano) S.; B.S. in Bus. Adminstrn., U. Buffalo, 1935, LL.B., 1938; m. Cora Gentile, Dec. 2, 1938. Admitted to N.Y. State bar, 1939, Mich. bar, 1947; with Houdaille Industries, Inc., Buffalo, 1941-79, sr. v.p., 1958-62, pres., chief exec. officer, 1962-79, chmn., 1964-79, also dir.; pres., dir. Houdaille Industries, Ltd., Houdaille Constrn. Materials, Inc. Home: 2323 Areca Palm Rd Boca Raton FL 33432

SALTER, LEWIS SPENCER, coll. pres.; b. Norman, Okla., Feb. 4, 1926; s. Lewis Spencer and Reaves (Alford) S.; B.S., U. Okla., 1949; M.A., Oxford U. (Eng.), 1953, Ph.D., 1956; m. Mary Anna Morse, June 19, 1950; children—David Reaves, Samuel Allen, John Michael,

Andrew Lewis. Instr. math. U. Md. Overseas Program, Eng., 1952-53; asst. prof., asso. prof., prof. physics Wabash Coll., Crawfordsville, Ind., 1953-67; asso. prof. physics Bandung (Indonesia) Inst. Tech., 1958-60; vis. physicist NRC, Ottawa, Ont., Can., 1963-64; cons. Argonne Nat. Lab., 1965-72; dean Coll., exec. v.p., v.p. acad. affairs Knox Coll., Galesburg, Ill., 1968-78; pres. Wabash Coll., Crawfordsville, 1978—; mem. regional selection coms. for Rhodes scholarships, Woodrow Wilson fellowships, 1957-69; cons. sci. edn., Indonesia, 1972, World Bank sector survey team, 1973. Served to 1st lt., inf. AUS, 1943-46. Recipient award for excellence in teaching Danforth Found., 1967. Mem. Am. Phys. Soc., Am. Assn. Physics Tchrs., Am. Sci. Affiliation, Phi Beta Kappa, Phi Mu Alpha, Sigma Pi Sigma. Democrat. Baptist. Home: 400 E Pike Crawfordsville IN 47933 Office: Wabash Coll Office of Pres Crawfordsville IN 47933

SALTMAN, PAUL DAVID, ednl. adminstr., biologist; b. Los Angeles, Apr. 11, 1928; s. David J. and Sadie (Solotoy) S.; B.S., Calif. Inst. Tech., 1949, Ph.D., 1953; grad. research, Coll. de France, Paris, 1949-50; m. Barbara June Golden, July 3, 1949; children—David Percy, Joshua Fred. From instr. to prof. biology U. So. Calif., 1953-67; vis. prof. U. Copenhagen, 1960-61; prof. biology, provost Revelle Coll. U. Calif. at San Diego, 1967—, vice chancellor academic affairs, 1972—. Named Alumnus of Year Calif. Inst. Tech., 1973. Mem. A.A.A.S., Am. Assn. U. Profs., Am. Chem. Soc., Am. Soc. Biol. Chemists, Am. Soc. Plant Physiology, Fedn. Am. Scientists, Pacific Slope Biochem. Soc., Sigma Xi. Home: 9704 Blackgold Rd LaJolla CA 92037

SALTMARCHE, KENNETH CHARLES, museum ofcl.; b. Cardiff, Wales, Sept. 29, 1920; s. William Hughes and Miriam Mason (Stobbs) S.; immigrated to Can., 1924, naturalized, 1924; hon. grad. fine arts Ont. Coll. Art, Toronto, 1945; student Art Students League, N.Y.C., 1946; LL.D., U. Windsor (Ont.), 1976; m. Judith Ann Davies, Feb. 7, 1948; children—David Hugh and Noel Carter (twins). Curator, Art Gallery Windsor, 1946-59, dir., 1960—; art critic Windsor Daily Star, 1947-74. Sr. Arts fellow Can. Council, 1964-65; recipient Gold medal Mich. Acad. Arts, Letters and Scis., 1969. Mem. Canadian Art Mus. Dirs. Orgn. (pres. 1974-76), Ont. Assn. Art Galleries (pres. 1968-69), Canadian, Am. museums assns. Anglican. Home: 995 Chilver Rd Windsor ON N8Y 2K6 Canada Office: 445 Riverside Dr W Windsor ON N9A 6T8 Canada

SALTON, GERARD, educator; b. Nuremberg, Germany, Mar, 8, 1927; s. Rudolf and Elisabeth (Tuchmann) S.; B.A. magna cum laude, Bklyn. Coll., 1950, M.A., 1952; Ph.D., Harvard, 1958; m. Mary Birnbaum, Aug. 31, 1950; children—Mariann, Peter. Mem. staff computation lab. Harvard, 1952-58, instr., then asst. prof. applied math., 1958-65; prof. computer sci. Cornell U., 1965—, chmn. dept., 1971-77; cons. to industry. Guggenheim fellow, 1963. Fellow AAAS; mem. Assn. Computing Machinery (council 1972-78), Phi Beta Kappa. Author: Automatic Information Organization and Retrieval, 1968; The Smart System-Experiments in Automatic Document Processing, 1971; Dynamic Information and Library Processing, 1975. Editor-in-chief Assn. Computing Machinery Communications, 1966-68, Assn. Computing Machinery Jour., 1969-72; editor Info. Systems, 1974—. Home: 221 Valley Rd Ithaca NY 14850 Office: Upton Hall Cornell U Ithaca NY 14853

SALTSBURG, HOWARD MORTIMER, educator; b. N.Y.C., Sept. 12, 1928; s. Morris and Rose (Siegel) S.; B.S., Coll. City N.Y., 1950; M.A., Boston U., 1951, Ph.D., 1955; m. Iris Beverly Spiegel, Nov. 25, 1951; children—Deborah Ruth, Daniel Martin. Chemist, Gen. Electric Co., Schnectady, Phila., 1955-59; research staff Gulf Gen. Atomic Co., San Diego, 1959-69; prof. chem. engring. and chemistry U. Rochester, 1969—. Vis. lectr. dept. engring. and applied sci. Yale, 1968-69. Dreyfuss Found. Postdoctoral fellow U. Rochester, 1954-55; Alexander Von Humboldt Sr. Scientist award, 1976. Mem. Am. Phys. Soc., Am. Chem. Soc., Am. Vacuum Soc., Am. Inst. Chem. Engrs., Phi Beta Kappa, Sigma Xi. Editor: (with J.N. Smith, Jr., M. Rogers) Fundamentals of Gas Surface Interactions, 1967. Home: 35 Maywood Circle Rochester NY 14618 Office: Dept Chem Engring U Rochester Rochester NY 14618

SALTZER, PAUL, chem. co. exec.; b. N.Y.C., June 12, 1916; s. Zoltan and Margaret (Rosenfeld) S.; B.B.A., Baruch Sch. Bus. Coll. City N.Y., 1939; m. Mildred Wurman, Oct. 31, 1943; children—Susan Sophia, Sandra Zena. Accountant, S.D. Leidesdorf & Co., C.P.A.'s, N.Y.C., 1939-42, 46-54; controller Sonneborn Chem. & Refining Co., N.Y.C., 1954-60; asst. controller, dir. adminstrn. Witco Chem. Corp., N.Y.C., 1960-72, sec., 1972-77, v.p. personnel, 1977—. Served to capt., Finance Dept., AUS, 1942-46. C.P.A., N.Y. Mem. Am. Inst. C.P.A.'s, N.Y. State Soc. C.P.A.'s. Club: B'nai B'rith. Home: 50 Ridgeland Rd Yonkers NY 10710 Office: 277 Park Ave New York City NY 10017. *To become successful in any endeavor one must be happy in what one is doing. Happiness tends towards good will towards others, and coupled with hard work and integrity completes the whole circle to happiness.*

SALTZMAN, ARNOLD ASA, co. exec.; b. N.Y.C., Oct. 1, 1916; s. Irving and Dora (Lieberman) S.; A.B., Columbia U., 1936; m. Joan Roth, Nov. 21, 1942; children—Robert M., Eric F., Marian B. With Premier Knitting Co., Inc., N.Y.C., 1936-63, pres., 1956-63; pres. Premier Corp. Am., N.Y.C., 1959-62; pres., chief exec officer, dir. Seagrave Corp., N.Y.C., 1961—; dir. Bienenfeld Glass Corp., Irving Tanning Co., Debevoise Co., Fentron Archtl. Metals Corp., Maxim Motor Co., Paramount Foam Industries. Head mil. pricing br. OPA, 1941-42; mem. Nat. Indsl. Mblzn. Com., 1940-41, U.S. Procurement Policy Bd., 1942-43, OPS, 1951; mem. staff AID, 1965. Trustee Maimonides Hosp., North Shore Hosp.; chmn. Columbia Coll. Council. Served to lt. USCGR, 1943-45. Office: The Seagrave Corp 350 Fifth Ave New York NY 10001*

SALTZMAN, BARRY, meteorologist, educator; b. N.Y.C., Feb. 26, 1931; s. Benjamin and Bertha (Burmil) S.; B.S., Coll. City N.Y., 1952; S.M., Mass. Inst. Tech., 1954, Ph.D., 1957; M.A. (hon.), Yale, 1968; m. Sheila Eisenberg, June 10, 1962; children—Matthew David, Jennifer Ann. Research staff meteorologist Mass. Inst. Tech., 1957-61; sr. research scientist Travelers Research Center, Inc., Hartford, Conn., 1961-66, research fellow, 1966-68; prof. geophysics Yale, 1968—; dir. grad. studies, Dept. Geology and Geophysics, 1971-74. Fellow Am. Meteorol. Soc.; mem. Conn. Acad. Sci. and Engring., Am. Geophys. Union, A.A.A.S., Royal Meteorol. Soc., Meteorol. Soc. Japan, Phi Beta Kappa, Sigma Xi. Contbr. articles to profl. publs.; editor: Selected Papers on the Theory of Thermal Convection, 1962; Advances in Geophysics, 1977—; asso. editor Jour. Geophys. Research, 1971-74. Home: 9 Forest Glen Dr Woodbridge CT 06525 Office: Dept Geology and Geophysics Yale Univ New Haven CT 06520

SALTZMAN, CHARLES ESKRIDGE, investment banker; b. Zamboanga, Mindanao, Philippines, Sept. 19, 1903; s. Charles McKinley and Mary (Eskridge) S.; student Cornell U., 1920-21; B.S., U.S. Mil. Acad., 1925; B.A., M.A. (Rhodes scholar), Oxford (Eng.) U., 1928; m. Gertrude Lamont, May 2, 1931 (div.); 1 son, Charles McKinley; m. 2d, Cynthia Southall Myrick, Sept. 25, 1947 (div.); children—Cynthia Myrick (Mrs. Warren Motley), Richard Stevens (dec.), Penelope Washburn; m. 3d, Clotilde Knapp McCormick, Sept. 15, 1978. Began civilian career with N.Y. Telephone Co., successively comml. engr., comml. asst. mgr., comml. mgr., directory-prodn. mgr., 1930-35; with N.Y. Stock Exchange, 1935-49, beginning as asst. to exec. v.p., later became sec. and v.p.; asst. sec. of state, 1947-49; partner Henry Sears & Co., 1949-56; under sec. of state for adminstrn., 1954-55; partner Goldman, Sachs & Co., N.Y.C., 1956—. Bd. mgrs. Seamen's Ch. Inst. of N.Y. and N.J., Am. Bible Soc.; bd. dirs. French Inst./Alliance Francaise, Fedn. Protestant Welfare Agys., Milbank Meml. Fund, Am. Council on Germany, Downtown-Lower Manhattan Assn. Served as 2d lt. C.E., U.S. Army, 1925-30; commd. 1st lt., N.Y. N.G., 1930, advanced through grades to lt. col., 1940; on active duty with U.S. Army, 1940-46, serving overseas, 1942-46; brig. gen., 1945; relieved from active duty, 1946; maj. gen. AUS ret. Decorated D.S.M., Legion of Merit (U.S.); Order of Brit. Empire; Croix de Guerre with gold star (France); Cross of Merit with swords (Poland); Bronze medal, grand officer Order of Crown of Italy; War medal (Brazil); comdr. Ouissam Alacuitte (Morocco); knight Order St. John of Jerusalem. Mem. English-Speaking Union U.S. (nat. pres. 1961-66, hon. dir.), Assn. Grads. U.S. Mil. Acad. (hon. trustee, pres. 1974-78), Internat. C. of C. (trustee U.S. council), Soc. Cincinnati (hon.), Kappa Alpha. Methodist. Clubs: University, Union, Century Assn., Recess, River, Pilgrims (N.Y.C.); Met. (Washington). Home: 302 E 62 St New York City NY 10021 Office: 55 Broad St New York City NY 10004

SALTZMAN, ELLIN JANE, fashion exec.; b. N.Y.C., Mar. 14, 1937; d. David R. and Sylvia Sadowsky; B.A., Smith Coll., 1958; m. Renny B. Saltzman, Feb. 7, 1960; children—David Edward, Elizabeth Scott. With Charm mag., 1958-59; asst. editor Mademoiselle mag., N.Y.C., 1959-60; asso. editor Glamour mag., N.Y.C., 1960-68; free lance fashion cons., 1968-75; v.p., corp. fashion dir. Saks Fifth Ave., N.Y.C., 1975—. Mem. Fashion Group (bd. dirs. 1972-75). Club: East Hampton Tennis. Home: 50 E 77th St New York NY 10021 Office: 611 Fifth Ave New York NY 10022

SALTZMAN, HARRY, film producer; b. Can., Oct. 1915. Films include: The Iron Petticoat; Look Back in Anger; The Entertainer; Saturday Night and Sunday Morning; Dr. No; Call Me Bwana; From Russian With Love; Goldfinger; The Ipcress File; Thunderball; Funeral in Berlin; You Only Live Twice; Billion Dollar Brain; Play Dirty; Battle of Britain; On Her Majesty's Secret Service; Diamonds Are Forever; Live and Let Die; The Man with the Golden Gun; Nijinsky. Address: care Mike Beck 729 7th Ave New York City NY 10019

SALTZMAN, IRVING JACKSON, educator; b. Lawrence, Mass., Oct. 21, 1923; s. Harry David and Fannie (Schwartz) S.; B.S., U. Mass., 1944; M.A., Duke, 1945; Ph.D., Johns Hopkins, 1948; m. Dorothy Jeanne Cohen, June 6, 1948; children—Linda Saltzman Anderson, Nancy, Robert, Andrew. Prof. psychology Ind. U., Bloomington, asst. chmn. dept. psychology, 1965-67, acting chmn., 1967, asso. chmn., 1967-69, chmn., 1969—; vis. lectr. psychology and gen. edn. Harvard, 1956-57. NIH grantee, 1956, 1961-63; NIH Spl. Postdoctoral fellow U. Wash., Seattle, 1963-64. Author: Writing Russian Script—A Self-Instructional Program, 1963. Home: 1302 Longwood Dr Bloomington IN 47401

SALTZMAN, JOSEPH, writer, producer, educator; b. Los Angeles, Oct. 28, 1939; s. Morris and Ruth (Weiss) S.; B.A., U. So. Calif., 1961; M.S., Columbia, 1962; m. Barbara Dale Epstein, July 1, 1962; children—Michael Stephen Ulysses, David Charles Laertes. Freelance mag. writer, reporter, 1960—; sr. writer-producer CBS-KNXT TV, Los Angeles, 1964-74; chmn. undergrad. studies, coordinator broadcast journalism sequence Sch. Journalism, U. So. Calif., Los Angeles, 1974—. Recipient A.P. certificates of excellence and merit, 1968, 72, 73, 74, 75, Edward R. Murrow awards for distinguished achievements in broadcast journalism, 1969, 72, Alfred I duPont-Columbia U. award in broadcast journalism, 1973-74, Silver Gavel award Am. Bar Assn., 1973, Ohio State award Am. Exhbn. Ednl. Radio-Television Programs and Inst. for Edn. by Radio-Television Telecommunications Center, 1974, Broadcast Media awards San Francisco State U., 1974, 75; Media award for excellence in communications Am. Cancer Soc., 1976; award for teaching excellence U. So. Calif. Assos., 1977. Seymour Berkson fellow, 1961, Robert E. Sherwood fellow, 1962, alt. Pulitzer traveling fellow, 1962-63. Mem. Radio-Television News Assn. (Golden Mike awards 1969, 71, 73, 75), Nat. Acad. Television Arts and Scis. (regional Emmy awards 1965, 68, 74, 75), Writers Guild Am., Greater Los Angeles Press Club (awards 1968, 74, 75), Columbia U., U. So. Calif. alumni assns., Skull and Dagger, Blue Key, Phi Beta Kappa, Sigma Delta Chi, Pi Sigma Alpha, Alpha Epsilon Rho. Documentaries include: Black on Black, 1968; The Unhappy Hunting Ground, 1971; The Junior High School, 1971; The Very Personal Death of Elizabeth Schell-Holt-Hartford, 1972; Rape, 1972; Why Me?, 1974; contbr. non-fiction to TV Guide, Human Behavior, Los Angeles Times, Newsday, others. Home: 2116 Via Estudillo Palos Verdes Estates CA 90274 Office: Sch Journalism U So Calif University Park Los Angeles CA 90007

SALTZMAN, MAURICE, clothing co. exec.; b. Cleve., May 25, 1918; s. Louis and Yetta (Zachlensky) S.; ed. pub. schs., Cleve.; m. Shirley Rosenberg, Aug. 20, 1944; children—Lorrie Sue, Judy Bea, Terry Ann. Salesman, Lampl Sportswear Co., Cleve., 1937-39; partner Bobbie Brooks, Inc., Cleve., 1939-45, pres., 1945-69, chmn., chief exec. officer, 1969—, also dir.; dir. Multi-Amp Corp., Realty ReFund Trust, Midwestern Nat. Life Ins. Co., Cleve. Chmn. Jewish Welfare drive Cleve., 1956-58, co-chmn. spl. gifts com., 1959; trustee Jewish Community Fedn., Cleve., 1960—; v.p. Temple Emanu El, Cleve., pres. Mt. Sinai Hosp., Cleve., 1976—. Saltsman Hall named for him by Temple Emanu El, 1957; recipient Mfr. of Year award Nat. Assn. Women's and Childrens Apparel Salesmen, 1956. Clubs: Oakwood Country, Beechmont Country (Cleve.); Palm Beach Country (West Palm Beach, Fla.). Office: 3830 Kelley Ave Cleveland OH 44114*

SALTZMAN, PHILIP, television producer; b. Sonora, Mexico, Sept. 19, 1928; brought to U.S., 1929, naturalized, 1948; s. Louis and Vanya (Liberman) S.; B.A., UCLA, 1951, M.A., 1953; m. Caroline Veiller, Jan. 24, 1960; children—Jennifer, Daniel, Anthony. Free lance writer, 1958-68; writer television shows Rifleman, 1961, Perry Mason, 1964, Dr. Kildare, 1964, Fugitive, 1964, Twelve O'Clock High, 1966; producer, writer Felony Squad, 1967-69, F.B.I., 1969-73, Barnaby Jones, 1973-77; producer Attack on Terror, 1975; exec. producer Barnaby Jones, 1978—, A Man Called Sloane, 1979—; pres. Woodruff Prodns., Inc. Mem. Writers Guild Am., West, Caucus for Writers, Producers, Dirs., Acad. Television Arts and Scis. Democrat. Jewish. Office: 1041 N Formosa St Los Angeles CA 90046

SALTZMAN, SIDNEY, educator; b. N.Y.C., Jan. 26, 1926; s. Morris Joseph and Fannie (Grossbaum) S.; student Worcester Poly. Inst., 1943-44; B.S.M.E., Purdue U., 1946; M.S.I.E., Columbia U., 1951; Ph.D., Cornell U., 1963; m. Dolores S. Lehrman, Nov. 23, 1950; children—Matthew Joseph, Nancy Gail. Engr., Combustion Engring., Inc., N.Y.C., 1946-48; asst. to v.p. prodn. Atlas-Ansonia Co., North Haven, Conn., 1948-49; prodn. planner Renwal Mfg. Co., Mineola, N.Y., 1949-51; ops. research and systems analyst Royal McBee Corp., Hartford, Conn. and Port Chester, N.Y., 1953-58; instr. Cornell U., 1958-63, asst. prof. ops. research and indsl. engring., 1963-68, asso. prof. city and regional planning, 1968-71, prof., 1971—, asst. dir. office computer services, 1966-68, chmn. dept. city and regional planning, 1974—; Fulbright-Hays scholar Technion-Israel Inst. Tech., 1965-66; cons. public, pvt. sectors. Served with USN, 1943-46, 51-53. NSF sci. faculty fellow, 1969-70; NATO sci. faculty fellow, 1974; NSF grantee, 1967-68, 73-75; registered profl. engr., N.Y. State. Mem. Inst. Mgmt. Scis., Am. Econs. Assn., Regional Sci. Assn., Peace Sci. Soc., AAUP, Sigma Xi, Phi Kappa Phi. Contbr. articles on mgmt. sci., planning, regional econs., energy and edn. to profl. jours. Office: 106 W Sibley St Ithaca NY 14853

SALTZMAN, WILLIAM, painter; b. Mpls., July 9, 1916; B.S., U. Minn. Asst. dir. U. Minn. Art Gallery, 1946-48; resident artist, also dir. Rochester (Minn.) Art Center, 1948-64; vis. prof. art U. Nebr., Lincoln, 1964; vis. prof. art Macalester Coll., St. Paul, 1967-68, asso. prof. art, 1969-74, prof. art, 1974. Exhbns. include Calif. Palace Legion of Honor, 1945, Minn. State Fair, 1936-41, 46- 58, Mpls. Inst. Art, 1936-41, 59, St. Paul Art Gallery, 1946, 54, 57, Mpls. Women's Club, 1949, 51-58, 62, U. Minn., 1939, San Francisco Mus. Art, 1948, Colorado Springs Fine Arts Center, 1948, Joslyn Art Mus., 1949, 51, 61, 64, Whitney Mus., 1951, Corcoran Gallery Art, 1950, Walker Art Center travelling exhbn., 1950-52, Chgo., 1952, Carnegie Inst., 1952, Chgo. Art Inst., 1947, numerous others; one man exhbns. include Little Gallery, Madison, Wis., Waterloo (Iowa) Art Center, Women's City Club, St. Paul, Luther Coll., Decorah, Iowa, St. Paul Art Center, St. Olaf Coll., Rochester Art Center, 1948-58, 63, Kilbridge-Bradley Art Gallery, Mpls., U. Nebr., 1950, Stephens Coll., 1950, Carlton Coll., 1951, Dayton (Ohio) Art Inst., 1952, Little Studio, N.Y.C., 1960-61, Walker Art Center, 1960, Philbrook Art Center, Tulsa; retrospective Tweed Gallery, U. Minn., 1966, major works include mural Mayo Clinic Bldg., Rochester, Minn., 1953; stained glass windows Temple of Aaron Sanctuary, 1956; mural Northwestern Nat. Bank, Rochester, 1957; stained glass Midwest Fed. Bldg., 1968; copper relief Plymouth Congl. Ch., Lincoln, Nebr., 1968; stained glass Holiday Inn Central, Mpls., 1962, Meditation Chapel at U. Minn., 1965, St. Edward's Parish Ch., Austin, Minn., 1965, chapel at Mpls.-Midwest Fed. Bank Bldg., 1968, Mt. Zion Temple, St. Paul, 1973; brick mural YMCA-YWCA, Rochester, Minn., 1964; copper sculpture B'nai Abraham Synogogue, St. Louis Park, Minn., 1965, Coast to Coast Stores Hdqrs. Bldg., Edina, Minn., 1978; sculpture in lobby Lincoln Gen. Hosp., 1967; copper relief sculpture U. Nebr. New Law Sch. Bldg., 1975, 1st Nat. Bank, Sioux Falls, S.D., 1976, Twin Cities Fed. Bank Bldg., Mpls., 1978, Title Ins. Co., Mpls., 1978. Recipient awards from Mpls. Inst. Art, 1936, Minn. State Fair, 1937, 40, Walker Art Center, 1949, 51; award Guild for Religious Architecture, 1973; award AIA, 1973. Ford Found. grantee, 1966. Mem. Nat. Soc. Mural Painters, Artists Equity Assn., Coll. Art Assn. Address: 5140 Lyndale Ave S Minneapolis MN 55419

SALVADORI, MARIO G., educator; b. Rome, Italy, Mar. 19, 1907; s. Riccardo and Ermelinda (Alatri) S.; D.Civil Engring., U. Rome, 1930, D.Mathematics, 1932; D.Sc. (hon.), Columbia, 1978; 1 son, Vieri R. Asst. to libero docente, theory of structures, U. Rome, 1930-38; cons. engr. Istituto Naz. Calcolo, Rome, 1933-38; time and motion engr. The Lionel Corp., Irvington, N.J., 1939; v.p. Indsl. Products Trading Corp., N.Y.C., 1939-42; from lectr. to James Renwick prof. emeritus civil engring. and prof. emeritus architecture Columbia, 1940—, chmn. div. archtl. technology, 1965-73, chmn. session sci. and tech. U. Bicentennial, 1954; partner Weidlinger Assos., cons. engr., N.Y.C., 1955—; v.p. Advanced Computer Techniques Corp., N.Y.C., 1962-65. Fellow Am. Soc. Mech. Engrs., Am. Soc. C.E. (com. on applied mechanics 1944-50, com. on thin shells, structure div. 1949-52; chmn. com. on math. methods engring. mechanics div. 1952-54); mem. Assembly Internat. Union Theoretical and Applied Mechanics, Sigma Xi, Tau Beta Pi. Fellow N.Y. Acad. Scis. Club: Academic Alpine of Italy. Author: (with K.S. Miller) The Mathematical Solution of Engineering Problems, 1948; (with M.L. Baron) Numerical Methods in Engineering 1952; (with R.J. Schartz) Differential Equations in Engineering Problems, 1954; (with R.A. Heller) Structure in Architecture, 1963; (with John M. McCormick) Numerical Methods in Fortran, 1964; (with M.P. Levy) Structural Design in Architecture, 1967; Mathematics in Architecture, 1968; Statics and Strength of Structures, 1971; also articles in Am., English, and Italian jours. Home: 2 Beekman Pl New York City NY 10022

SALVAGGIO, JOHN EDMOND, physician; b. New Orleans, May 19, 1933; s. Louis and Zenobia Ann (Engman-Riley) S.; B.S., Loyola U., New Orleans, 1954; M.D., La. State U., 1957; m. May 18, 1957; children—John, Garry, Wayne. Intern, Charity Hosp., New Orleans, 1957-58, resident, 1958-60; fellow, instr. Mass. Gen. Hosp. and Harvard U., 1961-63; prof. medicine La. State U., 1964-74; Henderson prof. medicine Tulane U., 1974—; vis. prof. U. Colo., 1972-73; mem. pulmonary diseases adv. com. NIH. Served with USAR, 1959-65. Diplomate Am. Bd. Internal Medicine, Am. Bd. Allergy and Immunology (pres. 1975-78). Mem. AAAS, Am. Fedn. Clin. Research, Am. Acad. Allergy, Soc. Exptl. Biology and Medicine, Am. Assn. Immunologists, Am. Soc. Clin. Investigation, Am. Thoracic Soc. (governing council 1977-79), A.C.P. Contbr. numerous articles to profl. jours. Home: 713 Fairfield St Gretna LA 70053 Office: 1430 Tulane Ave New Orleans LA 70112

SALVAGGIO, TONY JOE, banker; b. Hearne, Tex., Sept. 18, 1931; s. Joe Tony and Bonnie (Piccolo) S.; B.B.A., Tex. A. and M. U., 1956; student Sch. Banking of South, 1963-65; m. Anna Marie Marino, Jan. 29, 1956; children—Annette, Rosemarie. With Fed. Res. Bank Dallas, 1956—, sr. v.p., cashier, 1970—. Served with USN, 1949-53. Roman Catholic. K.C., Kiwanian. Home: 3817 Constitution Dr Dallas TX 75229 Office: 400 S Akard St Dallas TX 75222

SALVESON, MELVIN ERWIN, bus. exec., educator; b. Brea, Calif., Jan. 16, 1919; s. John T. and Elizabeth (Green) S.; B.S., U. Calif. at Berkeley, 1941; M.S., Mass. Inst. Tech., 1947; Ph.D., U. Chgo., 1952; m. Joan Y. Stipek, Aug. 22, 1944; children—Eric C., Kent Erwin. Cons., McKinsey & Co., N.Y.C., 1948-49; asst. prof., dir. mgmt. sci. research U. Calif. at Los Angeles, 1949-54; mgr. advanced data systems Gen. Electric Co., Louisville and N.Y.C., 1954-57; pres. Mgmt. Scis. Corp., Los Angeles, 1957-67; group v.p. Control Data/CEIR, Inc., 1967-68; pres. Electronic Currency Corp. (formerly U.S. Civil Systems Corp.), 1968—; dir. Diversified Earth Scis., Inc., Algeran, Inc., Electronic Currency Corp.; founder Master Charge System, Los Angeles, 1966; chmn. Corporate Strategies Internat.; prof. bus. Pepperdine U.; adj. prof. U. So. Calif.; adviser data processing City of Los Angeles, 1962-64; adviser futures forecasting IBM, 1957-61, strategic systems planning USAF, 1961-67, info systems Calif. Dept. Human Resources, 1972-73, City Los Angeles Automated Urban Data Base, 1962-67; tech. transfer NASA, 1965-70, others. Served to lt. comdr. USNR, 1941-46. Fellow AAAS; mem. Inst. Mgmt. Sci. (founder, past pres.). Republican. Club: Founders (Los Angeles Philharmonic Orch.). Editor: Business Strategy, Planning Rev.; contbr. articles to profl. jours. Home: 1577 N Bundy Dr Los Angeles CA 90049

SALVINO, CARMEN MARIO, profl. bowler; b. Chgo., Nov. 23, 1933; s. Mike and Theresa (DeVito) S.; student pub. schs., Chgo.; m. Virginia Morelli, May 26, 1955; 1 dau., Corinne. Champion numerous bowling competitions, 1961—, latest being Lincoln-Mercury Open, 1973, N.J. Open, 1974, Showboat Invitational, 1975, Pitts. Open,

1975, Quad Cities Open, 1976, Houston Open, 1977; ABC doubles co-champion, 1972; winner Championship Bowling Film, 1963; sanctioned 300 games 5 times; highest 3 games bowled on nat. TV, 846. Named Chgo. All-City Bowling King, 1957; named to Ill. Bowling Assn. Hall of Fame, 1974, Profl. Bowling Assn. Hall of Fame, 1976; named to 1st Team, Bowling Mag. All-America, 1975, 76. Mem. Profl. Bowlers Assn. (charter), Red Cloud Athletic Assn. Address: Chicago IL 60635*

SALVINO, S. M., utility co. exec.; b. Chgo., 1928; B.B.A., U. Wis., 1950; M.B.A., U. Chgo., 1963. Vice pres. accounts Peoples Gas Light & Coke Co., 1950-69, also dir.; with Peoples Gas Co., Chgo., 1969-72, 77—, v.p. planning, controller, now pres., dir.; pres., dir. Natural Gas Pipeline Co. Am., 1973-77; dir. Harper Oil Co., Indsl. Fuel Corp., Uarco Inc., Standard of Am. Fin. Corp., Standard of Am. Life Ins. Co., House of Vision. Office: Peoples Gas Co 122 S Michigan Ave Chicago IL 60603*

SALYARD, ROBERT RUSSEL, corp. exec.; b. York, Nebr., Oct. 25, 1926; s. Floyd E. and Thelma M. (Roberts) S.; B.S., Northwestern U., 1947; M.B.A., Harvard, 1951; m. Ann Biddle Barriger, July 2, 1955; children—Ann Biddle, Elizabeth Thatcher, Margaret Roberts, Robert Russel. Methods engr. Inland Steel Corp., Chgo., 1951-53; prin. Cresap. McCormick & Paget, Chgo., San Francisco, 1953-63; dir. corp. planning Am. Cement Corp., Los Angeles, 1963-64, gen. mgr. L.F. Hickey div., 1964, v.p., asst. gen. mgr. Riverside div., 1964-65, v.p., gen. mgr., 1965, v.p., gen. mgr. Pacific S.W. region, 1965, corporate v.p., 1967-69, sr. v.p., 1969; pres. cement ops., 1969-72; pres., chief exec. officer Fin. Corp. Ariz., also dir., mem. exec. com., 1972-74; exec. v.p., chief operating officer, dir. A.V.C. Corp., Phila., 1975-76, pres., 1976—, also mem. exec. com. dir. Raybestos Manhattan, Inc. Served as ensign U.S. Navy, 1947-49. Mem. Newcomen Soc. N.Am. Clubs: California (Los Angeles); Phila. Country. Home: 209 Booth Ln Haverford PA 19041 Office: PO Box 303 Two Radnor Corporate Center Radnor PA 19087

SALZARULO, LEONARD MICHAEL, educator; b. Montclair, N.J., Oct. 11, 1927; s. Jerry and Mary (Ippolito) S.; B.S., Newark Coll. Engring., 1951, M.S., 1953; postgrad. N.Y.U., 1953-54; Ph.D., Poly. Inst. Bklyn., 1966; m. Maria Grazia Barone, Apr. 24, 1971; 1 dau., Maria. Charge quality control lab. Sun Chem. Corp., Nutley, N.J., 1951-53; instr. chemistry and chem. engring. Newark Coll. Engring., 1953-56, asst. prof. applied mechanics, 1959-60, prof. physics, 1961—, asso. chmn., 1961-73, chmn., 1973—; chem. project engr. S.B. Penick Co., Lyndhurst, N.J., 1956-59; research asso. Poly. Inst. Bklyn., 1960-61; cons. Bendix Corp., 1965-66, Deluxe Reading Corp., 1966. Served with AUS, 1946-47. Registered profl. engr., N.J. Mem. N.Y. Acad. Scis., Am. Soc. Engring. Edn., Am. Chem. Soc., Am. Assn. Physics Tchrs., N.J. Soc. Profl. Engrs., Sigma Xi. Home: 21 The Glen Cedar Grove NJ 07009 Office: 323 High St Newark NJ 07102. *In competition, any victory which is achieved without integrity and due consideration for others must be considered a defeat.*

SALZER, FELIX, author, educator; b. Vienna, Austria, June 13, 1904; s. Max and Helene (Wittgenstein) S.; Ph.D., U. Vienna, 1926; m. Hedi Lemberger-Lindtberg, Sept. 16, 1939. Came to U.S., 1939, naturalized 1945. Prof., dean, chmn. theory dept. Mannes Coll. Music, N.Y.C., 1940-56, 62—; prof. music Queens Coll., 1963—; vis. lectr. U. Calif. at Los Angeles, 1960, Peabody Conservatory Music, 1962, New Sch. Social Research, 1962-63, U. Oreg., summer 1965. Mem. Am. Musicol. Soc. (chmn. N.Y. chpt. 1963-65). Author: Structural Hearing (Tonal Coherence in Music), Vol. I text, Vol. II musical examples and analyses, 2d edit., 1962, German translation, 1960; co-author: Counterpoint in Composition, 1969. Editor: The Music Forum, 4 vols., 1967, 70, 73, 76. Home: 179 E 70th St New York City NY 10021

SALZMAN, DAVID ELLIOT, TV prodn. co. exec.; b. Bklyn., Dec. 1, 1943; s. Benjamin and Rose Harriet (Touby) S.; B.A., Bklyn. Coll., 1965; M.A., Wayne State U., 1967; m. Sonia Camelia Gonsalves, Oct. 19, 1968; children—Daniel Mark, Andrea Jessica, Adam Gabriel. Dir. TV ops. Wayne State U., 1966-67; producer Lou Gordon Program, 1967-70; program mgr. Sta.-WKBD-TV, Detroit, 1970-71; program mgr. Sta.-KDKA-TV, Pitts., 1971-72, gen. mgr., 1973-75; program mgr. Sta.-KYW-TV, Phila., 1972-73; chmn. bd. Group W Prodns., N.Y.C and Los Angeles, 1975—; guest lectr. at schs.; bd. govs. Films of Coll. and Univ. Students. Bd. dirs. Pitts. Civic Light Opera, Am. Blood Bank, Pitts., Hebrew Inst., Pitts., Jewish Community Center, Harrison, N.Y. Recipient local Emmy award, 1972, award Golden Quill, 1971, Golden Gavel, 1971, AP, 1974, Detroit chpt. Am. Women in Radio and TV, 1969. Mem. Acad. TV Arts and Scis., Nat. Assn. TV Program Execs., Am. Mgmt. Assn. Contbr. articles to N.Y. Times, Detroit Free Press, Playboy mag., Variety and numerous communications trade publs. Office: 7800 Beverly Blvd Los Angeles CA 90036

SALZMAN, HERBERT, govt. ofcl.; b. N.Y.C., May 2, 1916; s. William S. and Minnie (Reich) S.; B.A., Yale, 1938; m. Rita Fredricks, May 26, 1947; children—Anthony David, Jeffrey Jonathan. Vice pres. Standard Bag Corp., N.Y.C., 1938-59, pres., 1959-66; asst. adminstr. AID, 1966-71; exec. v.p. Overseas Pvt. Investment Corp., 1971-73, dir., 1973-76; U.S. permanent rep. OECD, Paris, 1976—, ambassador, 1977—; dir. Starwood Corp. Mem. adv. com. on multinat. enterprises Dept. State, 1975—. Bd. dirs. Adlai Stevenson Inst. Internat. Affairs, 1968-75, Kennedy Center Prodns., 1972—; mem. vis. com. Middle East Center, U. Chgo., 1964-70, Center for Internat. Affairs, Harvard, 1975—; vice-chmn. bd. trustees Studio Theatre, John F. Kennedy Center, 1976—. Served to lt. comdr. USNR, 1941-46. Mem. Council Fgn. Relations. Clubs: Federal City, Internat. (Washington); Yale, Harmonie (N.Y.C.). Contbr. chpt. to Global Companies, The Political Economy of World Business (George Ball), 1975. Home: US OECD APO New York NY 09777

SALZMAN, SHELDON ROBERT, tire co. exec.; b. N.Y.C., Jan. 27, 1930; s. Philip and Tess (Goldsmith) S.; B. in Chem. Engring., Pratt Inst., 1951; m. Helen Ann Hemenetz, Jan. 27, 1952; 1 son, David Stewart. With Uniroyal, Inc. (formerly U.S. Rubber Co.), Middlebury, Conn., 1955—, dir. European chem. ops., London, 1972-75, gen. mgr. chems. and polymers, Naugatuck, Conn., 1975-77, pres. chem. div., 1977-79, pres. tire co., Middlebury, 1979—. Served with USAF, 1951, USN, 1951-54. Mem. Soc. Chem. Industry (London), Société Chimie Industrielle, Soc. Plastic Industry, Internat. Inst. Synthetic Rubber Producers, Chem. Mfrs. Assn., Nat. Agrl. Chems. Assn., FAO.

SALZMAN, STANLEY, architect, educator; b. N.Y.C., Feb. 10, 1924; s. Joseph and Regina (Feuerman) S.; student N.Y. U., 1940-42; B.Arch., Harvard, 1945, M.Arch., 1946; m. Susan Stuart Nixdorff, July 31, 1953; children—Sarah-Bly, Brie, Amelia. Designer, Walter Gropius, 1944, Marcel Breuer, 1945-46, Skidmore, Owings & Merrill, 1947; partner William Breger, 1947-55; pvt. practice, 1955-60; with Harold and Judith H. Edelman, N.Y.C., 1960—; prof. architecture Pratt Inst., 1964—, chmn. curriculum Sch. Architecture, 1964-70, coordinator acad. affairs, 1968-70; lectr., mem. adv. bd. N.Y. Sch. Interior Design, 1953—; Hays-Fulbright vis. prof. architecture U. Aarhus, Denmark, 1972; exhibited work in Mus. Modern Art, N.Y.C., 1952, City Art Mus., St. Louis, 1952, Phila. Art Alliance, 1954, Walker Art Center, Mpls., 1954, Bertha Schaefer Gallery, N.Y.C., 1956, Pan-Am. Congress Architects, Havana, Cuba, Meml. Art Gallery, Rochester, N.Y., 1956, U.S. Dept. State Travelling Exhbn. for Display Abroad, 1956, Museo de Art Moderna, Sao Paulo, Brazil, 1956, Bklyn. Mus., 1956, Whitney Mus. Am. Art, N.Y.C., 1962; trustee, dir. edn. Nat. Inst. Archtl. Edn., 1976—. Mem. assn. council Harvard Grad. Sch. Design, 1976—. Recipient Best House in East award House and Garden, 1949, Good Design award Mus. Modern Art, 1952, Brunner award A.I.A., 1960-61, Record House of Year award, 1964, 4th Biennial award for design excellence U.S. Dept. Housing and Urban Devel., 1969, Residential Design award A.I.A., 1969, Albert S. Bard First Honor award for excellence in civic architecture and urban design City Club N.Y., 1969; Charles Hayden scholar, 1940-41, Wheelwright Travelling fellow, 1946, John Simon Guggenheim fellow, 1961. Fellow A.I.A.; mem. Nat. Council Archtl. Registration Bds., Asso. Collegiate School of Arch. Contbr. articles to profl. publs. Home: 193 W 10th St New York NY 10014 Office: 21 West St New York NY 10006

SAM, JOSEPH, univ. dean; b. Gary, Ind., Aug. 15, 1923; s. Andrew and Flora (Toma) S.; student Drake U., 1942-43; B.S., U. S.C., 1948; Ph.D., Kans. U., 1951; m. Frances Adickes, Sept. 11, 1945; children—Sherrie, Joseph A., Suzanne F. Sr. research chemist McNeil Labs., Phila., 1951-54; research group leader Bristol Labs., Syracuse, N.Y., 1955-57; sr. scientist E.I. duPont de Nemours & Co., Inc., 1957-59; faculty U. Miss., 1959—, prof. pharm. chemistry, 1961—, chmn. dept., 1963-69, dir. univ. research, 1968—, dean Grad. Sch., 1968—; Fulbright lectr. Cairo U., 1965-66. Mem. Am. Chem. Soc., Am. Pharm. Assn. (found. research achievement award in pharm. and medicinal chemistry 1968), Sigma Xi, Rho Chi, Phi Lambda Upsilon, Phi Kappa Phi. Home: Box 351 University MS 38677

SAMAHA, FREDERICK JAMES, neurologist; b. N.Y.C., Feb. 6, 1934; A.B., Clark U., 1955; M.D., Tufts U., 1959; m. Claire Ferris, June, 1959; children—Frederick F., Michelle F., James F. Asst. in neurology Mass. Gen. Hosp., Boston, 1965-67; chief of neurology Children's Hosp., Pitts., 1970-76; dir. Children's Muscular Dystrophy Clinics, Pitts., 1974-77; prof., acting chmn. dept. neurology U. Pitts., 1976-77; prof., chmn. dept. neurology U. Cin. Med. Center, 1977—. Mem. Am. Acad. Neurology, Am. Neurol. Assn., Am. Physiol. Soc., Am. Soc. Neurochemistry. Research, numerous publs. on neuromuscular disease. Home: 512 Chisholm Tr Cincinnati OH 45215 Office: U Cin Med Center Dept Neurology 231 Bethesda Ave Cincinnati OH 45267*

SAMBORN, J. WARREN, leasing co. exec.; b. Hollywood, Calif., Dec. 12, 1931; B.A. in Bus. Adminstrn., U. Calif., Berkeley, 1953; M.B.A. in Bus. Adminstrn., Golden Gate U., San Francisco, 1960; m. Patty Sperry, 1955; children—Anne, Amy. Vice pres. Wells Fargo Bank, San Francisco, 1955-69; sr. v.p. finance GATX/ARMCO/Boothe, San Francisco, 1969-72; exec. v.p. GATX Leasing Corp., San Francisco, 1972-74, pres., 1974—. Served with U.S. Army, 1953-55. Club: Orinda (Calif.) Country. Address: 1 Embarcadero Center San Francisco CA 94111

SAMBORSKI, DANIEL JAMES, plant pathologist; b. Hamton, Sask., Can., Aug. 9, 1921; s. William and Elsie S.; B.S.A., U. Sask., 1949, M.Sc., 1951; Ph.D., McGill U., 1955; m. Margaret Isobel Chestnut, Sept. 17, 1951; children—Catherine Lynn, Helen Patricia. Research asso. U. Sask., 1953-56; with Agrl. Can. Research Sta., Winnipeg, Man., 1956—, now sr. scientist. Served with Royal Can. Army, 1941-45. Fellow Royal Soc. Can.; mem. Can. Phytopathological Soc., Can. Soc. Plant Physiology, Am. Phytopathological Soc. Contbr. articles to profl. jours. Home: 63 Brisbane Winnipeg MB R3T 0T1 Canada Office: 195 Dafoe Rd Winnipeg MB R3T 2M9 Canada

SAMELSON, LINCOLN RUSSELL, publisher; b. N.Y.C., Mar. 30, 1926; s. John Sommer and Marjorie (Don) S.; student Columbia, 1944-45; B.S. with honors in Journalism, U. Ill., 1947; m. Marie Janet Schupmann, Nov. 16, 1957; children—Scott Lincoln, Kevin Russell, Quentin Barth, Susan Marie, Timothy Charles, Jeffrey Lincoln. Advt. mgr. Commonwealth Life Ins. Co., Louisville, 1947-48; advt. and promotion mgr. Insulation Mfrs. Corp., Chgo., 1948-54; editor, co-pub. Lake Pub. Co., Lake Forest, Ill., 1954-58; pres., pub. Lake Pub. Corp., Libertyville, Ill., 1958—, pub. Insulation/Circuits, 1958, Plastics Design & Processing, 1961—, Microelectronic Mfg. and Testing, 1978—; mem. conf. on elec. insulation NRC, 1956—; mem. exec. com. Elec.-Electronics Insulation Conf., 1958—, gen. chmn., 1973. Served with USNR, 1943-46. Mem. IEEE, Soc. Plastic Engrs., Soc. Plastics Industry, Power Conversion Products Council, Internat. Soc. Hybrid Microelectronics, ASTM, AAAS, Electrochem. Soc., Bus.-Profl. Advt. Assn. Republican. Lutheran. Clubs: TF (Chgo.); Libertyville Racquet. Home: 920 Hawthorne Ln Libertyville IL 60048 Office: 700 Peterson Rd Libertyville IL 60048

SAMFORD, FRANK PARK, JR., life ins. co. exec.; b. Montgomery, Ala., Jan. 29, 1921; s. Frank Park and Hattie Mae (Noland) S.; student Auburn U., 1937-38; B.A., Yale, 1942; LL.B., U. Ala., 1947; m. Virginia Carolyn Suydam, May 27, 1942; children—Frank Park III, Laura Alice, John Singleton Pitts, Mae Virginia. With Liberty Nat. Life Ins. Co., Birmingham, Ala., 1947—, v.p., 1955-60, pres., 1960—, chmn. bd., 1973—, also dir.; dir. So. Co., South Central Bell Telephone Co., Golden Enterprises, Inc., Ala. Gt. So. R.R., Saunders Leasing System, Inc. Chmn. Life Insurers Conf., 1970; trustee Am. Coll. Life Underwriters. Chmn. Jefferson County United Appeal, 1964; trustee Jefferson County Community Chest, pres. 1965; bd. govs. Indian Springs Sch., Helena, Ala.; trustee Auburn U. Served to lt. (s.g.) USNR, 1942-45. C.L.U. Mem. Alpha Tau Omega, Phi Delta Phi, Berzelius. Presbyterian. Rotarian. Clubs: Birmingham Country, Mountain Brook Country (Birmingham). Home: 3530 Redmont Rd Birmingham AL 35213 Office: PO Box 2612 Birmingham AL 35202

SAMFORD, THOMAS DRAKE, III, lawyer; b. Opelika, Ala., Mar. 4, 1934; s. Thomas Drake and Aileen (Maxwell) S., Jr.; A.B. magna cum laude, Princeton, 1955; J.D., U. Ala., 1961; m. Jacqueline Screws, June 7, 1955; children—Thomas Drake IV, Jacquelyn, Robert Maxwell, Richard Drake. Admitted to Ala. bar, 1961, since practiced in Opelika; partner firm Samford & Samford, 1961—; judge Mcpl. Ct., Opelika, 1961—; mem. Ala. Permanent Jud. Commn., 1979—; lectr., contbr. continuing legal edn. program Ala. State Bar, 1963—, Ala. Law Inst., 1969—, Am. Judicature Soc., 1969—; owner, mng. partner realty, broadcasting, timber and farmer ops.; gen. counsel Auburn U. Chmn. Opelika Downtown Action Com., 1967—. Dir., bd. trustees Opelika Community Chest, 1965-68, pres., 1966-67; bd. dirs. U. Ala. Law Sch. Found., Jr. Achievement Chattahoochee-Lee. Served to capt. USMCR, 1955-58. Recipient John G. Buchanan prize politics, 1955; Farrah, Order Jurisprudence U. Ala., 1956; named one of four Outstanding Young Men in Ala., Jr. C. of C., 1967. Mem. Opelika C. of C. (dir. 1967—, pres. 1968) Am., Lee County (pres. 1965) bar assns., Ala. State Bar, U. Ala. Nat. Alumni Assn. (pres. 1966-67), Phi Beta Kappa, Alpha Tau Omega, Phi Delta Phi, Omicron Delta Kappa. Presbyterian (elder 1974—). Kiwanian (bd. dirs. 1966-67, pres. 1969-70). Editor-in-chief Ala. Law Rev., 1960-61. Home: 805 Ridgewood St Opelika AL 36801 Office: Samford Bldg Ave A Opelika AL 36801

SAMFORD, YETTA GLENN, JR., lawyer; b. Opelika, Ala., June 8, 1923; s. Yetta Glenn and Mary Elizabeth (Denson) S.; B.S., Ala. Poly. Inst., 1947; LL.B., U. Ala., 1949; m. Mary Austill, Sept. 6, 1949; children—Mary Austill Lott, Katherine Park Alford, Yetta Glenn III (dec.). Admitted to Ala. bar, 1949, since practiced in Opelika; mem. firm Samford, Denson, Horsley, Pettey & Martin, and predecessors, 1949—; dir. Liberty Nat. Life Ins. Co., Farmers Nat. Bank Opelika, West Point Pepperell, Inc. Mem. Ala. Senate from Lee and Russell counties, 1958-62. Trustee Mobile Coll., U. Ala. Served to 2d lt. AUS and USAAF, 1943-45. Mem. Ala. C. of C. (bd. dirs.), Phi Delta Phi, Omicron Delta Kappa, Alpha Tau Omega. Republican. Baptist. Mason. Home: 615 Terracewood Opelika AL 36801 Office: Box 2345 Opelika AL 36801

SAMILSON, ROBERT LEBLANG, orthopedic surgeon; b. N.Y.C., Aug. 31, 1923; s. Mortimer Harris and Ette (LeBlang) S.; B.A., Dartmouth Coll., 1943; M.D., N.Y. Med. Coll., 1950; m. June 15, 1947; children—Kathy Ann, Linda Louise, Leslie Carol, Terry Lee. Intern, Mt. Sinai Hosp., N.Y.C., 1950-51; resident in gen. surgery, fellow in phys. medicine Bellevue Hosp., N.Y.C., 1951-53; resident in orthopedic surgery N.Y. Orthopedic Hosp., Columbia-Presbyn. Med. Center, N.Y.C., 1953-56; clin. instr. orthopedic surgery U. Calif., San Francisco, 1957-58, clin. asst. prof., 1958-62, asso. clin. prof., 1963-74, clin. prof., 1974—; practice medicine specializing in orthopedic surgery, San Francisco, 1957—; mem. staffs Children's Hosp., U. Calif. Hosps., Presbyn. Med. Center, Marshall Hale Meml. Hosp.; ABC Traveling fellow, 1963; Hubert Harvey Meml. lectr. Crippled Children's Assn. S. Australia. Diplomate Am. Bd. Orthopedic Surgery (mem. bd. 1975—, chmn. residency rev. com. 1979—). Mem. Am., Western, Latin Am. orthopedic assns., Am. Orthopaedic Foot Soc. (past pres.), Am. Acad. Orthopedic Surgeons, Pediatric Orthopedic Soc., A.C.S., Pan Am. Surg. Soc. Orthopedic Research Soc., Am. Acad. Cerebral Palsy (past pres.), La Societe Internationale de Chirurgie Orthopedique et de Traumatologie, Russell Hibbs Soc., ABC Club. Editor: Orthopaedic Aspects of Cerebral Palsy, 1975. Contbr. to profl. publs. Office: 3838 California St San Francisco CA 94118. *Aristotle has described the virtuous person as one exhibiting courage, temperance and justice. Few achieve true virtue but we may all strive for it. All things worthwhile are difficult to achieve.*

SAMIOS, NICHOLAS PETER, physicist; b. N.Y.C., Mar. 15, 1932; s. Peter and Niki (Vatick) S.; A.B., Columbia U., 1953, Ph.D., 1957; m. Mary Linakis, Jan. 12, 1958; children—Peter, Gregory, Alexandra. Instr. physics Columbia U., N.Y.C., 1956-59; asst. physicist Brookhaven Nat. Lab., Upton, N.Y., 1959-62, asso. physicist, 1962-64, physicist, 1964-68, sr. physicist, 1968—, group leader, 1965-75, chmn. dept. physics, 1975—; adj. prof. Stevens Inst. Tech., 1969-75, Columbia U., 1970—. Fellow Am. Phys. Soc.; mem. Sigma Xi. Contbr. articles in field to profl. jours.; expert field of particle spectroscopy and weak interactions. Office: Dept Physics Brookhaven Nat Lab Upton NY 11973

SAMMARTINO, PETER, univ. chancellor; b. N.Y.C., Aug. 15, 1904; s. Guy and Eva (Amendola) S.; B.S., Coll. City N.Y., 1924; M.A., N.Y. U., 1928, Ph.D., 1931; Sorbonne, U. Paris; Litt.D., L.I. U.; LL.D., U. Liberia, Kyung Hee U.; D.H.L., Fairleigh Dickinson U.; Doct. ès Lettres, U. Zaire; m. Sylvia Scaramelli, Dec. 5, 1933. Tchr. pub. schs., N.Y.C., Townsend Harris High Sch., Coll. City N.Y.; in charge lang. New Coll., Tchrs. Coll., Columbia U.; pres., Fairleigh Dickinson U., Rutherford, N.J., 1942-67; ednl. editor United Am., also Atlantica, La Voix de France. Chmn. Econ. Devel. Participation Pres.'s Commn. on Higher Edn., White House Conf. on Edn., 1956; past pres. N.J. Assn. Colls. and Univs.; bd. chmn. Am. Inst. Italian Studies; past pres. Internat. Assn. Univ. Presidents; v.p. N.J. Constl. Conv.; mem. N.J. Bicentennial Commn.; mem. president's adv. bd. U.S. Peace Corps; mem. bd. fgn. scholarships. Founder, pres. Restore Ellis Island Commn.; mem. bd. Friends of Cuttington Coll.; mem. exec. com. Nat. Italian-Am. Found.; pres. N.Y. Cultural Center, N.Y.C., 1969-76; dir. Tibetan Found., 1969; com. on accreditation and institutional eligibility, Office of Edn., 1971; chmn. N.J. Basic Skills Task Force, 1972. Bd. dirs. Columbus Hosp., Newark; chmn. bd. trustees St. Stephens Sch., Rome; trustee N.J. Hist. Soc., Opera Theater of N.J. Decorated comdr. Order des Palmes Academiques, chevalier Legion of Honor (France); chevalier Order Crown of Italy, grand officer Order of Merit (Italy) grand band Star of Africa (Liberia); chevalier Order of Lion (Iran); comdr. L'Ordre National (Ivory Coast); recipient Silver medal (S.A.R.), Townsend Harris medal, Gold medal U. Bologna, Brotherhood award NCCJ; named N.J. Man of Year, N.J. Advt. Council, 1963; Distinguished alumni award, N.Y. U., 1968; 125th anniversary medal in higher edn., U. City of N.Y. Franklin fellow Royal Soc. Arts. Mem. Alpha Phi Delta (past nat. pres.). Republican. Roman Catholic. Rotarian. Clubs: University (N.Y.C.); Upper Montclair Country, Pot and Kettle, Bar Harbor, Salmagundi, Columbus. Author: Survey of French Literature; Emile Zola; French in Action; Grammaire Simple et Lectures Faciles; Avancons; Il Primo Libro; Il Secondo Libro; Letture Facili; Community College in Action; The President of a Small College; Multiple Campuses; Of Castles and Colleges; I Dreamed a College; History of Higher Education in N.J.; Demanage Higher Education. Home: 140 Ridge Rd Rutherford NJ 07070. *In our twilight years, the thoughts that give my wife and me the greatest glow is our founding and building what is now Fairleigh Dickinson University, for it is in serving others that life becomes meaningful.*

SAMMET, GEORGE, JR., aerospace co. exec.; b. Chgo., Sept. 18, 1919; s. George and Anne (Jeske) S.; B.S., U. Ill., 1940; M.A., George Washington U., 1964; postgrad. U. Pitts., 1965, Command and Gen. Staff Coll., 1955, Armed Forces Staff Coll., 1958, Nat. War Coll., 1963; children—Marianne, (Mrs. Edward C. Chalifoux), Nancy Lee (Mrs. Ben Pfingstag), Celeste K. (Mrs. Charles R. Stevens), George W. Commd. 2d lt. U.S. Army, 1942, advanced through grades to lt. gen., 1975; field arty. officer, Europe, U.S., Japan, 1942-54; dir. instrn. Turkish Arty. Sch. at Polatli, 1955-57; staff officer Office Chief of Research and Devel., Washington, 1959-62, 1964-67, dir. plans, programs, 1969-70; dep. dir. devels. U.S. Army Material Command, Washington, 1967-68; sr. adviser First Republic of Korea Army, Korea, 1968-69; dep. chief of research and devel. Dept. Army, Washington, 1970-73; dep. comdg. gen. for material devel. Army Materiel Command, 1973-77, comdg. gen. Army Devel. and Readiness Command; instr. internat. relations U. Md., Wonju, Korea, 1968-69; ret., 1977; instr. program mgmt. Fla. Inst. Tech., Orlando, 1978-79; with Marietta Aerospace Corp., Orlando, 1978—. Decorated D.S.M., Legion of Merit with two oak leaf clusters, Air medal, Purple Heart, Bronze Star. Home: 8992 Gladin Ct Orlando FL 32811 Office: Martin Marietta Aerospace Corp Orlando FL 32805

SAMMET, JEAN E., computer scientist; b. N.Y.C.; d. Harry and Ruth S.; B.A., Mount Holyoke Coll., Sc.D. (hon.), 1978; M.A., U. Ill. Group leader programming Sperry Gyroscope, Great Neck, N.Y., 1955-58; sect. head, staff cons. programming Sylvania Electric Products, Needham, Mass., 1958-61; with IBM Corp., Cambridge, Mass., 1961—, programming tech. planning mgr., 1968-74, programming lang. tech. mgr. IBM Fed. Systems div., 1974-79, software tech. mgr., 1979—; chmn. history of computing com. Am. Fedn. Info. Processing Socs., 1977-79. Mem. Assn. Computing Machinery (pres. 1974-76), Math. Assn. Am., Nat. Acad. Engring.,

Upsilon Pi Epsilon. Author: Programming Languages: History and Fundamentals, 1969; editor-in-chief Assn. Computing Machinery Computing Revs., 1979—; contbr. articles to profl. jours. Office: IBM Fed Systems Div 10215 Fernwood Rd Bethesda MD 20034

SAMMONS, FRANCIS EDWARD, JR., corp. exec.; b. Evanston, Ill., Nov. 16, 1913; s. Francis E. and Rose (Stokes) S.; student U. Ill.; m. Catharine Strong, July 17, 1943; children—Thomas Edward, Charles Patrick, Timothy Devitt. Vice pres., circulation dir. Street & Smith Publs., Inc., N.Y.C., 1947-52; dir. S-M News Co., N.Y.C., 1949-52; v.p. sales and advt. Bankers Life & Casualty Co., Chgo., 1952-56; v.p. J. Walter Thompson Co., N.Y.C., 1956-60; v.p., dir. publicity and pub. relations Ted Bates & Co., Inc., N.Y.C., 1960-61; partner Fordyce & Dole Assos., Inc., N.Y.C., 1961-64; v.p. mktg. Brown Kauffmann, Inc., Palo Alto, 1965-74; dir. communications Potlatch Corp., San Francisco, 1974—. Served to capt. AUS, 1942-46. Decorated Purple Heart, Bronze Star medal. Mem. Advt. Club San Francisco (dir.), U.S. Golf Assn. Club: Palo Alto Hills Golf and Country. Home: 325 Claremont Way Menlo Park CA 94025 Office: 2 Embarcadero Center San Francisco CA 94111

SAMMONS, JAMES HARRIS, assn. exec.; b. Montgomery, Ala., Mar. 13, 1928; s. Jesse Delmar and Sally Eulalia (Scroggins) S.; B.A., Washington and Lee U., Lexington, Va., 1947; M.D., St. Louis U., 1951; m. JoAnne Halloway, Oct. 14, 1971; children—James Harris, Patricia Sammons Sheets. Intern, Alabama City/County Hosp., Mobile, 1951; gen. practice medicine, Baytown, Tex., 52-74; pres. staff San Jacinto Methodist Hosp., Baytown, 1964, service chief in surgery and obstetrics, 1962-63; mem. faculty Baylor Coll. Medicine, 1972-76, clin. asst. prof. family medicine, 1972-75, vis. asso. prof. family practice, 1975-76; dep. med. examiner Harris County, Tex., 1962-74; exec. v.p. AMA, Chgo., 1974—, chmn. trustees, 1973-74; chmn. Am. Med. Polit. Action Com., 1969-70; pres., chmn. bd. Houston Acad. Medicine. Served with USNR, 1944-45. Mem. Am., So. (asst. councilor 1968-71), Tex. (pres. 1971-72) med. assns., Harris County Med. Soc. (v.p. 1962), Am., Tex., Harris County acads. gen. practice, Am. Soc. Assn. Execs., Am. Med. Soc. Execs., Phi Chi, Kappa Alpha. Club: Economic (Chgo.). Address: AMA 535 N Dearborn St Chicago IL 60610

SAMMONS, JEFFREY LEONARD, educator; b. Cleve., Nov. 9, 1936; s. Harold Leonard and Therese (Herrmann) S.; B.A., Yale, 1958, Ph.D., 1962; m. Christa Ann Smith, Oct. 20, 1967; children—Rebecca Kathryn, Charles Leonard, Harold Hawthorne, Benjamin Gardner. Instr., Brown U., 1961-62, asst. prof., 1963-64; asst. prof. Yale, New Haven, 1964-67, asso. prof., 1967-69, prof., 1969—, chmn. dept. Germanic langs. and lits., 1969-77. Guggenheim fellow, 1972-73; Am. Council Learned Socs. fellow, 1977-78. Mem. MLA, Am. Assn. Tchrs. German, AAUP. Author: Nachtwachen von Bonaventura, 1965; Angelus Silesius, 1967; Heinrich Heine, the Elusive Poet, 1969; Six Essays on the Young German Novel, 1972; Literary Sociology and Practical Criticism, 1977; Heinrich Heine, a Modern Biography, 1979. Home: 211 Highland St New Haven CT 06511

SAMPLE, FREDERICK PALMER, coll. pres.; b. Columbia, Pa., May 22, 1930; s. William Walter and Erna Rebecca (Roye) S.; A.B., Lebanon Valley Coll., 1952; M.Ed., Western Md. Coll., 1956; D.Ed., Pa. State U., 1968; Dr. Pedagogy, Albright Coll., 1968; m. Mary Jane Drager, Aug. 19, 1951; children—Jeffrey Lynn, Roger Lee. Tchr., Annville (Pa.) High Sch., 1952-53; tchr. Red Lion Area (Pa.) High Sch., 1953-57, prin., 1957-59, supervising prin., 1959-64; supt. Manheim Twp. Sch. Dist., Neffsville, Pa., 1964-68; pres. Lebanon Valley Coll., Annville, Pa., 1968—; edn. cons. Bd. dirs. Central Pa. Pub. Broadcasting Corp. Mem. Nat. Assn. Ind. Colls. and Univs., Phi Delta Kappa. Republican. United Methodist. Clubs: Masons, Lebanon Country. Home: RD 2 Annville PA 17003. *Despite failures, difficulties, and disappointments I have tried to find the honorable, responsible, productive, true, and humane solutions to problems and make decisions for progress.*

SAMPLE, GLENN W., coll. exec.; b. Centerville, Ind., July 9, 1912; s. Alfred W. and Thersia Mae (Williamson) S.; B.S. in Agr., Purdue U., 1935, D.Agr. (hon.), 1972; m. Mary Catherine Templin, Oct. 11, 1936; children—Louise M., James A., Joseph T., Elizabeth June. Agrl. editor Purdue U., 1935-44; dir. public relations U. Md., 1944-45; v.p. Ind. Farm Bur., Indpls., 1945-75; pres. Ind. Vocat. Tech. Coll., 1975—; dir. Farmers State Bank; bd. dirs. Channel 20 TV; chmn. bd. Ivy Tech Found. Mem. various Ind. commns. on taxing policy, ednl. structure and policies, 1948-75; active Ind. 4-H Found.; former mem. Ind. Air Pollution Control Bd. Recipient Distinction award Purdue Agrl. Alumni, 1948, Brigham award Am. Agrl. Editors Assn., 1973, Hon. Master Farmer award Prairie Farmer, 1976. Mem. Ind. Farm Bur., Ind. State C. of C., Zionsville C. of C., Ind. Vocat. Edn. Assn., Sigma Delta Chi, Alpha Zeta. Mem. Christian Ch. (Disciples of Christ). Clubs: Columbia, Indpls. Press., Shriners (Indpls.); Univ., Scottish Rite, Masons. Editor Hoosier Farmer Mag., 1945-58. Home: 9090 E SR-334 Zionsville IN 46077 Office: PO Box 1763 Indianapolis IN 46206. *All education is important to sustain our culture and improve ourselves. Without education and training, we would be re-inventing the wheel every generation.*

SAMPLE, JOSEPH SCANLON, broadcasting co. exec.; b. Chgo., Mar. 15, 1923; s. John Glen and Helen (Scanlon) S.; B.A., Yale, 1947; m. Patricia M. Law, Dec. 22, 1942 (div.); children—Michael Scanlon, David Forrest, Patrick Glen; m. 2d, Miriam Tyler Willing, Nov. 19, 1965. Trainee, media analyst, media dir. Dancer-Fitzgerald-Sample, Inc., advt. agy., Chgo., 1947-50, v.p., media dir., 1952-53; pres. Mont. Television Network KTVQ, Billings, KXLF-AM-TV, Butte, Mont., KRTV Great Falls, Mont., KPAX-TV, Missoula, Mont., 1955—; dir. Midland Nat. Bank, Billings, No. Hotel Co. Billings; mem. Mont. adv. bd. Mountain States Tel. & Tel. Mem. Mont. Ednl. Broadcasting Commn.; pres. Billings Bighorns Hockey Club; bd. govs. Western Hockey League. Trustee Rocky Mountain Coll., Billings. Served to 1st lt., OSS, AUS, 1943-46; Intelligence Div. G-2, 5th Army, 1950-52. Mem. Nat. Assn. Broadcasters, Mont. Broadcasters Assn. Clubs: Chicago; Yellowstone Country; Billings Petroleum; Rotary; Port Royal; Hilands Golf. Home: 606 Highland Park Dr Billings MT 59102 Office: 3203 3d Ave N Billings MT 59101

SAMPLE, NATHANIEL WELSHIRE, architect; b. Phila., Apr. 3, 1918; s. Nathaniel Welshire and Evelyn Hope (Aldrich) S.; B.A., Dartmouth Coll., 1940; postgrad. Cornell U., 1941-42; B.Arch., Ill. Inst. Tech., 1946; m. Virginia Louise Bogert, May 19, 1945; children—Peter Nathaniel, Gregory, Deborah, Phoebe, Joan. Archtl. designer Shaw Naess & Murphey, Chgo., 1946-47; designer Weiler & Strang & Assos., Madison, Wis., 1947-51, mgr. project, 1951-58, partner, 1958-62; partner Sample/Mullins, Madison, 1962-67, Sample & Potter, Inc., Madison, 1967—; v.p. Design for Tomorrow, Downtown Rehab., Madison, 1956; lectr. on housing in Europe, Shorewood Coordinating Com.-U. Wis., 1969-70. Pres. Madison chpt. UN Assn., 1965-67. Served with USNR, 1942-45. Fellow AIA (pres. Wis. chpt. 1970). Quaker. Club: Rotary (v.p. local club 1968-69) (Madison). Bldgs. include: Columbus Elementary Sch., 1953 (Wis. chpt. AIA Honor award), own residence, Madison, 1955 (Wis. chpt. AIA Honor award), Children's Treatment Center, Mendota, Wis., 1959 (Wis. chpt. AIA Honor award), remodelling and addition to Chgo. Library, 1970 (1st pl. AIA Nat. competition 1969). Home: 1105 Rutledge St Madison WI 53703 Office: 735 Jenifer St Madison WI 53703

SAMPLE, SEWELL VINCENT, small appliance mfg. co. exec.; b. Los Angeles, Apr. 4, 1928; s. George W. and Harriette J. (Sewell) S.; B.S. in Public Relations, UCLA, 1950; m. Jolyne May Cornes, Jan. 19, 1963; children—Mark, Matthew, Paul, Joanna, John, Elizabeth. Sales rep. Proctor & Gamble, Los Angeles, 1950-51; with Sunbeam Corp. and subs., 1951—, pres., gen. mgr. Sunbeam Mexicana, Mexico City, 1968-71, asst. to chmn. Sunbeam Corp., Chgo., 1971-74, pres. internat. group, Oak Brook, Ill., 1974-78, v.p. Sunbeam Corp., 1976-78, exec. v.p., 1978—, pres. internat. consumer products group, 1978—; dir. Rowenta-Werke, GmbH, Offenbach/Main, W.Ger., Sunbeam Corp., Ltd., Sydney, Australia. Served with USN, 1946-48. Mem. Chgo. Com., Chgo. Council Fgn. Relations. Republican. Episcopalian. Office: 2001 S York Rd Oak Brook IL 60521

SAMPLES, RONALD EUGENE, coal co. exec.; b. Boonville, Ind., Apr. 23, 1926; s. Harold Forest and Hazel Pearl (Grandstaff) S.; student U. Notre Dame, 1944-46; B.S.E.M., N. Mex. Sch. Mines, 1949; m. Virginia Agnes Derr, Feb. 13, 1950; children—Ronald Eugene, II, Rebecca Lee, Thomas Harold, Susan Ann. With Peabody Coal Co., St. Louis, 1949-66, regional chief engr., 1960-66; with Consol. Coal Co., Pitts., 1966-73, 75—, v.p. engring./exploration, 1973, pres., chief operating officer, 1975-77, chmn., chief exec. officer, 1977—; sr. v.p. ops. Amax Coal Co., Indpls., 1973-75, exec. v.p. engring. ops., exploration, purchasing, 1975. Bd. dirs. United Way, Pitts., 1977—, Regional Indsl. Devel. Corp. Southwestern Pa., 1978-79, Allegheny Trails council Boy Scouts Am., 1978-79; mem. sponsoring com. Penn's S.W. Assn., 1978-79; mem. citizen's sponsoring com. Allegheny Conf. on Community Devel., 1978-79; chmn. sect. coal industry, corp. campaign Boys Clubs Am., 1978-80. Served with USN, 1944-46. Registered profl. engr., Ind., Pa., Ky., Mont., N.Mex., Utah; registered profl. land surveyor, Ind., Ky. Mem. Pa. Soc. Profl. Engrs., AIME, Nat. Coal Assn. (dir., chmn. fin. and public relations coms.). Democrat. Clubs: King Coal, St. Clair Country, Duquesne, Renaissance, Laurel Valley Golf, Elks. Home: 3580 Maplevue Dr Bethel Park PA 15102 Office: 1800 Washington Rd Pittsburgh PA 15241

SAMPSON, A(RTHUR) CLARENCE, accountant; b. Lanham, Md., Aug. 2, 1929; s. Arthur Clarence and Bessie Inez (Chafin) S.; B.S., U. Md., 1953; m. Donna May Davis, June 12, 1953; children—Kathryn, Gregory, Laura. Auditor, Arthur Young & Co., Washington, 1956-57, Litton Industries, College Park, Md., 1958-59; with SEC, 1959—, asso. chief acct., Washington, 1969-78, chief acct., 1978—; mem. faculty U. Md., 1959-63. Served with USAF, 1954-56. C.P.A., Md. Mem. Nat. Assn. Accts., Am. Inst. C.P.A.'s, D.C. Inst. C.P.A.'s, Assn. Govt. Accts. Methodist. Club: Lions. Home: 13909 Manchester Rd Upper Marlboro MD 20870 Office: 500 N Capitol Washington DC 20754

SAMPSON, ARTHUR FRANCIS, bus. exec.; b. Fall River, Mass., Oct. 8, 1926; s. Arthur F. and Dora (Couturier) S.; student U. Mass., 1944-45, Sampson Coll., 1947-48; B.S., U. R.I., 1951; m. Blanche Bouffard, Sept. 20, 1947; children—Arthur Francis III, Philip R., Jason E., Matthew S. With Gen. Electric Co., Lynn, Mass., 1951-53, Erie, Pa., 1953-63, mgr. purchasing, 1961-63; dep. sec. procurement Commonwealth of Pa., Harrisburg, 1963-66; sec. adminstrn., budget sec. Gov. Pa. Cabinet, Harrisburg, 1967-69; commr. Fed. Supply Service, commr. Pub. Bldgs. Service, dep. adminstr. for spl. projects GSA, Washington, 1969-72; acting adminstr. GSA, 1972-73, adminstr., 1973-76; pres., chief exec. officer, dir. San-Vel Concrete Corp., Littleton, Mass., 1976-77; pres. SEREC, Inc., Fairfield, Ala., 1978—; bus. cons., 1979—. Mem. White House Regulations and Purchasing Review Bd., 1970—, President's Commn. on Procurement, 1970—, Nat. Capitol Planning Commn., 1970—, President's Adv. Council on Historic Preservation, 1970—, Com. on Ecol. research, 1972—; bd. dirs. Jr. Achievement Met. Washington, 1972—, Prestressed Concrete Inst., Nat. Fire Protection Assn.; mem. D.C. Mayor's Econ. Devel. Com., 1972—. Served with USAAF, 1944-47. Recipient Presdl. citation Soc. Am. Value Engrs., 1969; Synergy III award Soc. Am. Registered Architects, 1972; citation, Engring. News Record, 1972; top ten public works men of the year award, Am. Public Works Assn., 1973. Mem. Nat. Assn. Purchasing Agts., Nat. Assn. Accountants, AIA (hon.), Fed. Govt. Accountants Assn. (hon.). Republican. K.C. Home: 1756 Westwind Way McLean VA 22102 Office: 1730 N Lynn St Suite 400 Arlington VA 22209

SAMPSON, BILL ARTHUR, coll. dean; b. Hermiston, Oreg., Sept. 28, 1918; s. Frank Lester and Rose (Neadeau) S.; B.S., Eastern Oreg. Coll., 1947; M.S., U. Oreg., 1948, Ed.D., 1950; m. Phyllis Ann Harold, Dec. 26, 1948. Elementary tchr., Vale, Oreg., 1939-43, Eugene, Oreg., 1949-50; asst. prof. So. Oreg. Coll., Ashland, 1950-53, asso. prof., 1953-56, prof., 1956—, dean edn., 1967—. Mem. Jackson County Intermediate Edn. Dist. Sch. Bd., 1960-63. Served with AUS, 1943-46. Mem. NEA, Phi Delta Kappa, Kappa Delta Pi. Lion. Home: 668 Leonard St Ashland OR 97520

SAMPSON, DELBERT JOHN, educator; b. Central City, Nebr., Aug. 27, 1911; s. John William and Alfiel (Anderson) S.; A.B., Nebr. Wesleyan Coll., 1935; M.Div., Boston U., 1939, S.T.B., 1939; Ph.D., U. Denver, 1957; m. Mary Etta Dodrill, June 30, 1937; children—John Eugene, Shirley June (Mrs. Michael A. Richards). Tchr. pub. schs. Merrick County, Nebr., 1930-33; ordained to ministry United Methodist Ch., 1937; minister Lewiston-Filley, Nebr., 1939-41, Syracuse, 1941-47, Wymore, Odell, Nebr., 1947-52, Gotherburg, Nebr., 1952-55, Denver, 1955-57; dean men, dir. counseling Nebr. Wesleyan Coll., Lincoln, 1957-62; prof. psychology U. Evansville, 1962-77, chmn. dept., 1962-71. Licensed psychotherapist. Mem. Phi Kappa Phi, Phi Delta Kappa, Psi Chi, Pi Kappa Delta, Phi Kappa Tau. Republican. Methodist. Mason. Home: 1410 Martins Ln Evansville IN 47715

SAMPSON, HAROLD PECK, univ. dean; b. Jefferson, Ohio, June 15, 1925; s. Ernest Anderson and Dora Lucinda (Peck) S.; B.S., Sioux Falls Coll., 1950; M.A., U. S.D., 1953; Ph.D., So. Ill. U., 1966; m. Esther Ruth Rieb, Aug. 12, 1951; children—LuRae Ellen, Douglas Harold. Tchr. high sch., Parkston, S.D., 1950-52, Watertown, S.D., 1952-58; faculty Nebr. Wesleyan U., Lincoln, 1958-66; dean Grad. Sch., Central Mo. State U., Warrensburg, 1966—. Served with AUS, 1943-46. Mem. Pi Kappa Delta, Phi Delta Kappa, Phi Kappa Phi. Baptist. Rotarian. Author: (with Philip Kaye) Preparing Speeches of Substance-The Analysis Method, 1969. Home: 56 High Dr Warrensburg MO 64093

SAMPSON, HAROLD RAY, chem. co. exec.; b. Lincoln, Nebr., May 24, 1918; s. Bert and Ruth (Lederer) S.; B.Sc. in Chem. Engring., U. Nebr., 1941; m. Virginia Maxine Jones, Aug. 16, 1941; children—Candace Anne, Peter G., Jonathan H., Wendy E. With Nat. Starch & Chem. Corp., 1941—, v.p. employee relations, 1964—, also dir. Served to lt. col. AUS, 1942-46; ETO. Home: 1720 Cooper Rd Scotch Plains NJ 07076 Office: 10 Finderne Ave Bridgewater NJ 08876

SAMPSON, HERBERT MARTIN, JR., diversified energy co. exec.; b. Greeley, Nebr., July 23, 1925; s. Herbert Martin and Florence Marie (Harrahill) S.; B.S. in Bus. Adminstrn. cum laude, U. Notre Dame, 1950; m. Adelene V. Coad, Aug. 27, 1949; children—Herbert Martin, III, Steven J., Richard M., Mark C., Laura M., Nancy M. With No. Natural Gas Co., Omaha, 1951—, group v.p. corp. devel., 1979—. Mem. adv. council Coll. Bus. Adminstrn., U. Notre Dame; mem. president's council Creighton U., Omaha; bd. dirs. Father Flanagan's Boys' Home, Boys Town, Nebr. Served with USAAF, World War II. Mem. Ind. Natural Gas Assn., Am. Gas Assn., Mfg. Chemists Assn., Soc. Chem. Industry, Chemists Club N.Y.C. Roman Catholic. Club: Omaha Country. Home: Rural Route 1 Elkhorn NE 68022 Office: 2223 Dodge St Omaha NE 68102

SAMPSON, SIGVED THEODORE, coop. exec.; b. Glenbeulah, Wis., Apr. 17, 1917; s. August and Mabel T. (Omness) S.; B.A., St. Olaf Coll., Northfield, Minn., 1939; m. Elouise Torkelson, July 6, 1946; children—Scott, Donna. Mgr., Milltown Coop. Store, 1939-42, Denmark Coop. Services, Wis., 1946; with Midland Coops, Inc., Mpls., 1946—, dir. mktg., 1964-71, v.p. mktg., 1971-72, pres., 1972—; dir. CF Industries, Inc., Long Grove, Ill., Universal Coops., Inc., Mpls., Interregional Service Co., Mpls., Co-op League, Washington, Twin Ports Grocery Co., Superior, Wis., Nat. Council Farmer Coops., Washington, Nat. Coop. Refinery Assn., McPherson, Kans., Internat. Energy Inc., Tulsa, Energy Co-op, Inc., Long Grove. Mem. St. Anthony Village (Minn.) Bd. Edn., 1961-68, pres., 1965-67. Served with U.S. Army, 1942-45; ETO. Recipient Distinguished Alumnus award St. Olaf Coll., 1976. Mem. Sales Execs. Club Mpls., Mpls. C. of C., Sons of Norway. Lutheran (trustee 1951-58). Club: Mpls. Athletic. Home: 3404 Maplewood Dr Minneapolis MN 55418 Office: 2021 E Hennepin Ave Minneapolis MN 55413. *I believe that man should devote his life to something larger than himself. People are born with wide variations in their capacities to contribute to their fellowman. Those who have been given great talents and abilities should use these gifts to aid those who are less gifted. Personal fortunes have little lasting value. That which we do for others can live on for generations.*

SAMS, HERBERT WILLIAM, consumer product mfg. co. exec.; b. Woolsey, Ga., Sept. 9, 1915; s. Herbert Charles and Vela Grace (Jones) S.; student Ga. Inst. Tech., 1934-38; m. Mary Frances Brooke, Sept. 18, 1937; children—Herbert William, Elizabeth Ann, Robert Brooke. Vice-pres. research and devel. Scripto, Inc., Atlanta, 1965-69, v.p., gen. mgr., 1969-71, pres., chief exec. officer, 1971-74, chmn. bd., 1974—, also dir.; chmn. bd., pres. Vu-Lighter, Inc., 1978—. Mem. Writing Instrument Mfrs. Assn. Republican. Presbyterian. Club: Atlanta Athletic. Patentee in field. Home: 4643 River Ct Duluth GA 30136 Office: 3035 Adriatic Ct Norcross GA 30071

SAMS, W(ILEY) MITCHELL, JR., dermatologist; b. Ann Arbor, Mich., Apr. 15, 1933; s. Wiley Mitchell and Elizabeth (Hastings) S.; B.S., U. Mich., 1955; M.D., Emory U., 1959; m. Marion Ruth Yount, June 7, 1959; children—Robert, Margery, Hunter. Intern, Emory U. Hosp., Atlanta, 1959-60; resident in dermatology Duke U., Durham, N.C., 1960-64; clin. asst. prof. U. Calif., San Francisco, 1964-66; asst., asso. prof. Mayo Grad. Sch. Medicine, Mpls., 1966-72; prof., chmn. dept. dermatology U. Colo., Denver, 1972-76; prof. dermatology U. N.C. Sch. Medicine, Chapel Hill, 1976—, also asst. dir. continuing med. edn. Served to capt. M.C., U.S. Army, 1964-66. NIH research fellow, 1962-64, grantee, 1972. Mem. Am. Acad. Dermatology, Soc. Investigative Dermatology, Am. Dermatol. Assn., So. Med. Assn. Office: Dept Dermatology U NC Sch Medicine Chapel Hill NC 27514

SAMSON, ALVIN, distbg. co. exec.; b. N.Y.C., May 2, 1917; s. Morris and Jennie (Buitekant) S.; m. Ann Carol Furmansky, Aug. 15, 1942; children—Leslie Joan, Marla Adriane. Br. mgr. U.S. Hardware and Paper Co., 1947-51; mdse. mgr. U.S. Servateria, 1951-57; dir. purchasing U.S. Consumer Products, Los Angeles, 1959-64, v.p. ops., 1964-66, pres., 1966-72; pres. U.S. Consumer Products, San Diego, Bakersfield, Las Vegas, Phoenix, 1966-72, Zelman Co., Los Angeles, San Francisco and Las Vegas, 1968-72, Triple A Corp., Los Angeles, 1966-72, U.S. Consumer Products-Wesco Mdse., Los Angeles, 1972-74; v.p. APL Corp., N.Y.C., 1967-74; pres. USCP-WESCO, 1974—. Served with USAAF, 1942-45. Named Man of Year, Housewares Club So. Calif., 1965. Mem. Housewares Club So. Calif. (pres. 1968, bd. govs. 1956-57), Am. Research Merchandisers Inst., Toiletries Merchandisers Assn. Office: 4444 Ayers Ave Los Angeles CA 90023

SAMSON, CHARLES HAROLD, JR., educator, structural engr.; b. Portsmouth, Ohio, July 12, 1924; s. Charles Harold and Gertrude (Morris) S.; B.S. U. Notre Dame, 1947, M.S., 1948; Ph.D., U. Mo., 1953; m. Ruth Aileen Baumbach, Sept. 12, 1947; children—Peggy Aileen, Charles Harold III. Asst. field rep. Loebl, Schlossman and Bennett, architects and engrs., Chgo., 1948- 49; structures engr., Convair Aircraft (now General Dynamics-Fort Worth), Fort Worth, 1951-52, sr. structures engr., 1952-53, sr., project aerodynamics engr., 1956-58, project structures engr., 1958-60; asst. prof. civil engring. U. Notre Dame, 1953-56; office engr. Wilbur H. Gartner & Assos., South Bend, Ind., 1954; grad. lectr. civil engring. So. Meth. U., Dallas, 1952-53, 56-60; prof. structural engring. and mechanics, depts. aerospace and civil engring., Tex. A & M U., College Station, 1960-64, prof., civil engring., 1964— head dept. civil engring., 1964-79; research engr. Tex. Transp. Inst., Tex. A & M U., 1960-62, head structural research dept., 1962-65; pres. S.W. Athletic Conf., 1979—. Served to ensign USNR, 1943-46. Registered profl. engr., Tex., Ind. Fellow ASCE; mem. Am. Concrete Inst., Am. Soc. Engring. Edn., Nat. (past v.p., chmn. profl. engrs. in edn.), Tex. (past pres., past nat. dir.) socs. profl. engrs., Am. Pub. Works Assn., Sigma Xi, Sigma Gamma Tau, Tau Beta Pi, Phi Kappa Phi, Chi Epsilon. Contbr. articles to profl. jours. Home: 2704 Camelot St Bryan TX 77801

SAMTER, MAX, physician, educator; b. Berlin, Germany, Mar. 3, 1908; s. Paul and Claire (Rawicz) S.; student U. Freiburg (Germany), 1926, U. Innsbruck (Austria), 1928; M.D., U. Berlin, 1933; m. Virginia Svarz Ackerman, Oct. 17, 1947; 1 dau., Virginia Claire. Came to U.S., 1937. Intern, resident Medizinische Universitätsklinik der Charité, Berlin, 1931-33; practice medicine, Berlin-Karow, Germany, 1933-37; asst. dispensary physician hematology Johns Hopkins Hosp., 1937-38; guest fellow anatomy U. Pa. Sch. Medicine, 1938-43; research asso. dept. biochemistry U. Ill., Chgo., 1946-47, instr., asst. prof., asso. prof., prof. dept. medicine, 1948-69, prof. medicine Abraham Lincoln Sch. Medicine, 1969—, asso. dean for clin. affairs, 1974-75; chief staff U. Ill. Hosp., 1974-75; dir. Inst. Allergy and Clin. Immunology, Grant Hosp., Chgo., 1975—; cons. in allergy U.S. VA, 1962—. Served to capt. M.C., AUS, 1943-46; ETO. Diplomate Am. Bd. Internal Medicine (past chmn. bd. allergy), Am. Bd. Allergy and Immunology. Mem. A.M.A., A.C.P., Am. Acad. Allergy (past pres.), Internat. Assn. Allergology (past pres.), Sigma Xi, Alpha Omega Alpha. Editor: American Lectures in Allergy, 1950; (with Orec C. Durham) Regional Allergy, 1954; (with Harry L. Alexander) Immunological Diseases, 1965, 71, 78; Excerpts from Classics in Allergy, 1969; (with Charles W. Parker) Hypersensitivity to Drugs, 1972; also articles in field. Home: 645 Sheridan Rd Evanston IL 60202 Office: 551 W Grant Pl Chicago IL 60614

SAMTON, PETER, architect; b. Berlin, Feb. 26, 1935; s. Henry Albert and Margot (Fiegel) S.; B.Arch. (Grunsfeld fellow), Mass. Inst. Tech., 1957; postgrad. (Fulbright fellow) U. Sorbonne, Paris, 1958; m. Emily Samton, Sept. 29, 1963; children—Zach, Noah, Daniel. Designer, Hugh Stubbins & Assos., Boston, 1959-60, Marcel Breuer & Assos., N.Y.C., 1960-61; prin. Samton Assos., Architects, N.Y.C., 1962-63; designer Kelly & Gruzen, N.Y.C., 1963-67, partner, design dir. Gruzen & Partners, 1967—; vis. critic Columbia U., Coll. City N.Y., N.C. State U., Mass. Inst. Tech.; dir. design N.Y.C. Police Hdqrs., New Health Sci. and Service Bldgs., Hebrew Home for Aged, Riverdale, N.Y., Schomburg Plaza, N.Y.C., Genessee Gateway, Rochester, N.Y., Am. Embassy, Moscow, New Community in Iran; panelist architecture and environ. arts N.Y. State Council on Arts, 1979. Fellow AIA (pres. N.Y. chpt. 1978—, co-recipient gold medal 1975). Office: Gruzen and Partners 1700 Broadway New York NY 10019

SAMUCHIN, MICHAEL GEORGE, structural engr., educator; b. Lilienthal, Ger., Mar. 23, 1946; B.Arch., U. Ill., 1969; M.S., Northwestern U., 1971, Ph.D. in Structural Engring., 1972. Teaching asst. dept. civil engring. Northwestern U., Evanston, Ill., 1969-72; instr. Coll. Architecture and Design, Kans. State U., Manhattan, 1972-73; asst. prof. architecture U. Okla., Norman, 1973-76; asso. prof. architecture Ariz. State U., Tempe, 1976-79; prof. archtl. engring. Tenn. State U., Nashville, 1979—, head dept., 1979—; cons. in field. NSF trainee, 1969-72. Mem. Nat. Soc. Profl. Engrs., Tex. Soc. Profl. Engrs., ASCE, Am. Acad. Mechanics, Am. Concrete Inst., Am. Soc. Engring. Edn., Assn. Collegiate Schs. Architecture, AAUP. Contbr. articles to profl. jours. Office: Dept Archtl Engring Tenn State Univ Nashville TN 37203

SAMUEL, ATHANASIUS YESHUE, archbishop; b. Hilwah, Syria, Dec. 25, 1907; s. Sowmey Malkey and Khatoun Malkey (Hido) S.; student St. Mark's Sem., 1923-27, 29-31, Cairo Theol. Coll., 1927-29. Ordained priest Syrian Orthodox Ch. of Antioch, 1932; sec. to Syrian orthodox patriarch of Antioch, 1931-32; father superior St. Mark's Monastery, Jerusalem, 1933-43; patriarchal vicar of Jerusalem, 1943-46, archbishop, 1946-52; patriarchal del. to U.S.A. and Can., 1949-57, archbishop, Hackensack, N.J., 1957—. Decorated by Emperor Haile Selassie I, gold cross and papal medallion Pope Paul VI, cross Knights of St. John of Jerusalem. Mem. World Council Chs., Nat. Council Chs. of Christ in U.S.A. Author: Treasure of Qumran, 1966; Liturgy of St. James, 1967; Rites of Baptism, Holy Matrimony and Burial, 1974. Home and office: 293 Hamilton Pl Hackensack NJ 07601

SAMUEL, DONALD CAROL, investment co. exec.; b. N.Y.C., May 26, 1919; s. Ralph E. and Florence (Weingarten) S.; grad. Fieldston Sch., 1937; student Dartmouth; m. Berelle Katz, Sept. 28, 1947; children—Wendy B., Patricia A., Pamela J. Dist. mgr. Robert Hall Clothes, 1946-47; with Ralph E. Samuel & Co., N.Y.C., 1948-70, partner, 1949-70; exec. partner Neuberger & Berman, N.Y.C., 1970—; asst. treas. Energy Fund, Inc., N.Y.C., 1955-60, pres., 1960—, also dir.; exec. v.p. No Load Mutual Fund Assn., N.Y.C., 1971-75, pres., 1975-78; pres. Neuberger & Berman Mgmt., 1970—; vice chmn. Neuberger & Berman Pension Mgmt., 1976—. dir. Partners Fund. Trustee Jewish Bd. Family and Children's Services; bd. govs. Investment Co. Inst., 1978—; mem. adv. council Columbia U. Sch. Social Work. Served to maj. USAAF, 1941-45. Clubs: Harmonie (N.Y.C.); Century Country (Purchase, N.Y.). Home: 895 Park Ave New York NY 10021 Office: 522 Fifth Ave New York NY 10036

SAMUEL, GERHARD, orch. condr., composer; b. Bonn, Germany, Apr. 20, 1924; s. Arthur and Hilde (Behr) S.; came to U.S., 1939, naturalized, 1943; student violin with Samuel Belov, chamber music with Jacques Gordon (scholarship); B.Mus. cum laude, Eastman Sch. Music, 1945; choral conducting with Hermann Genhart, orch. conducting with Paul White and Howard Hanson, 1945; Mus.B., student of Paul Hindemith (scholarship), Yale, 1947, Mus.M. (Haupt prize), 1947; student Serge Koussevitsky at Tanglewood, Mass., 1945-47, also Boris Goldowsky; Ph.D. (hon.), Cal. Coll. Arts and Crafts. Condr., Ballet Ballads, Music Box Theatre, Broadway, 1947-48; research in France and Italy, condr. concerts Am. contemporary music, Paris, 1948-49; Fulbright grantee for study in Europe, 1949; condr. Accademia Chigiana (1st prize), Siena, Italy, 1949; asso. condr. Mpls. Symphony Orch., 1949-59; condr. Collegium Musicum, Mpls., 1952-59, Mpls. Civic Opera Co., 1954-57; mus. dir. Grand Marais (Minn.) Music Festival, 1957-59, Minn. Centennial Music Festival, 1958, Oakland (Cal.) Symphony Orch., 1959-71; mus. dir., condr. San Francisco Ballet, 1961-70; founder, condr. Cabrillo Music Festival, 1963-68, West Coast New Music Ensemble, 1968-70; condr., mus. dir. Oakland Chamber Orch., 1963-69; asso. condr. Los Angeles Philharmonic, 1970-74; mus. dir., condr. Ojai (Calif.) Festival, 1970-71; artistic dir. Los Angeles Philharmonic Docents; guest condr. Am. Symphony, Lincoln Center, N.Y.C., 1964, Denver Symphony, 1965, San Francisco Spring Opera, 1965, 66, Am. Symphony Orch., 1965, Winnipeg (Can.) Symphony, 1967, Rochester Philharmonic Orch., 1973, Ives-Schoenberg Festival, Washington, 1974; ann. European, Far Eastern and S.Am. concert tours. Exec. com. San Francisco Composers Forum, 1959-62; mem. composers workshop San Francisco Conservatory Music, 1960; condr. concerts on TV, also local opera groups and youth orchs. Prof. music Calif. Inst. Arts, to 1976; dir. orchestral activities and conducting program U. Cin. Conservatory of Music, also condr. Contemporary Ensemble Concert Series, 1976—. lectr. in field. Mem. adv. panel State Dept. Cultural Exchange; mem. music council Young Musicians Found. Rockefeller Found. grantee. Recipient Nat. Endowment for Arts Composition award, 1974-75, Composer's Showcase N.Y. award, 1976, 77, 78. Mem. A.S.C.A.P. Composer numerous works, including In Memoriam D.Q., What of My Music, Into Flight From . . . , Looking at Orpheus Looking, On a Dream, Fortieth Day, Beyond McBean, Au Revoir to Lady R., The Relativity of Icarus, Three Hymns to Apollo, Twelve on Death and No. Recs. with Royal Philharmonic, Am. Symphony Orch., Oakland Symphony. Home: 2355 Fairview Ave Cincinnati OH 45219

SAMUEL, HOWARD DAVID, union ofcl.; b. N.Y.C., Nov. 16, 1924; s. Ralph E. and Florence (Weingarten) S.; B.A., Dartmouth, 1948; m. Ruth H. Zamkin, Apr. 15, 1948; children—Robert H., Donald F., William H. Various positions Amalgamated Clothing and Textile Workers (formerly Amalgamated Clothing Workers Am.), N.Y.C., 1949-60, asst. pres., 1960-64, v.p., 1966-77; dep. under sec. Bur. Internat. Labor Affairs, Dept. Labor, Washington, 1977-79; pres. indsl. union dept. AFL-CIO, Washington, 1979—; v.p. New Sch. for Social Research, N.Y.C., 1964-65; exec. dir. Sidney Hillman Found., N.Y.C., 1951-77; Vice-chmn. N.Y. Urban Coalition, 1969-74; mem. governing bd. Common Cause, 1971-77; sec. Nat. Com. Full Employment, 1975-77; mem. Nat. Manpower Adv. Com., 1969-74; mem. Commn. Population Growth and the Am. Future, 1970-72. Chmn. White Plains Democratic Com., 1960-64, vice-chmn. Westchester County com., 1957-70, alt. del. nat. conv., 1964, mem. Nat. Dem. Charter Revision Com., 1972-73; exec. dir. Nat. Labor Com. McGovern-Shriver, 1972; del. Dem. Conv. on Party Orgn. and Policy, Kansas City, 1974, Nat. Dem. Conv., 1976; trustee Carnegie Corp., 1971-77, Joint Council Econ. Edn., 1971-77; bd. dirs. ACLU, 1966-68. Served with AUS, 1943-46. Mem. Phi Beta Kappa. Author: (with Stephen K. Bailey) Congress at Work, 1952, Government in America, 1957. Editor: Toward a Better America, 1968. Home: 4620 N Park Ave Chevy Chase MD 20015 Office: Indsl Union Dept AFL-CIO 815 16th St Washington DC 20005

SAMUELS, ABRAM, stage equipment mfg. exec.; b. Allentown, Pa., Sept. 15, 1920; s. Irving and Ann (Friedman) S.; B.S., Lehigh U., 1942; auditor philosophy Princeton, 1963-65; m. Harriet Ann Goodman, Sept. 1, 1945; children—Margaret A. Samuels Stine, Katherine E., Sally R. Samuels Slifkin, John A., Dorothy M., Caroline J. Pres. Automatic Devices Co., Allentown, 1946-75, chmn. bd., 1975—; pres. Lehigh Research and Devel. Corp.; dir. Mchts. Nat. Bank of Allentown; past guest lectr. Cedar Crest Coll.; guest lectr. Am. popular music Muhlenberg Coll. Pres., A. Samuels Found.; bd. govs. Civic Little Theatre; bd. assos. Muhlenberg Coll.; past pres. Pa. Soc. for Crippled Children and Adults; past pres., hon. dir. Lehigh County Crippled Children's Soc.; past pres. Lehigh County Humane Soc., Cedar Crest Coll. Assos.; bd. dirs., vice-chmn. Allentown Hosp.; past pres. Lehigh County Hist. Soc.; past bd. dirs. Nat. Soc. for Crippled Children and Adults, Pa. Mental Health Assn., Lehigh County Indsl. Devel. Corp.; past trustee St. Augustine's Coll.; trustee Allentown YWCA. Served with AUS, 1942-46. Recipient Benjamin Rush award Lehigh County Med. Soc., 1956; named Outstanding Young Man of Year, Jr. C. of C., 1955. Mem. ASCAP, Hon. First Defenders, C. of C. (past v.p.), Pa. German Soc. Republican. Jewish. Rotarian (past pres. Allentown, past dist. gov.). Clubs: Princeton (N.Y.C.); Livingston. Home: 142 N Main St Allentown PA 18104 Office: 2121 S 12th St Allentown PA 18103

SAMUELS, ALTA GRANT (MRS. WARREN S. SAMUELS), designer; b. South Orange, N.J., Jan. 20, 1908; d. Charles Crothers and Alta (Packer) Grant; student Wells Coll., 1925-26; B.F.A., U. Pa., 1929; m. Warren S. Samuels, Sept. 2, 1951. Architect, office Charles C. Grant, 1929-31, R. H. Macy & Co., 1931-35; head interior decorating dept. Thalhimer's, Richmond, Va., 1935-41; designer Gibbs & Cox, naval architects, 1941-54; pvt. practice, specializing marine interiors, 1955- -. Recipient Spirit of Achievement award women's div. Albert Einstein Coll. Medicine of Yeshiva U., 1959. Mem. Archtl. League, Soc. Naval Architects, Soc. Women Engrs., Alpha Chi Omega, Mortar Bd. Home: 325 E 41st St New York City NY 10017 also Edificio Doramas 9-G Avenida Escaleritas 68 Las Palmas de Gran Canaria Spain Office: 1860 Broadway New York City NY 10023

SAMUELS, ERNEST, educator, author; b. Chgo., May 19, 1903; s. Albert and Mary (Kaplan) S.; Ph.B., U. Chgo., 1923, J.D., 1926, A.M., 1931, Ph.D., 1942; m. Jayne Porter Newcomer, Aug. 24, 1938; children—Susanna, Jonathan, Elizabeth. Franklyn Bliss Snyder prof. English, Northwestern U., 1942-71, chmn. English dept., 1964-66; Leo S. Bing vis. prof. U. So. Calif., 1966-67; Fulbright lectr. Inter-University Chair in Am. Studies, Belgium, 1958-59; admitted to Ill. bar. Mem. Ill. Commn. of Scholars, 1966-71. Recipient Bancroft award and Parkman award for Henry Adams, 1959, Pulitzer prize in biography, 1965, Friends of Lit. award for Henry Adams, 1965. Guggenheim fellow 1955-56, 71-72. Mem. Nat. Council Tchrs. English (dir. 1956-57), Mass. Hist. Soc. (corr.), Coll. English Assn. (pres. Chgo. area 1957), Am. Studies Assn. (pres. Wis.-No. Ill. chpt. 1960-61), Modern Lang. Assn., Tau Delta Phi. Author: Business English Projects, 1936; The Young Henry Adams, 1948; Henry Adams: The Middle Years, 1958; Henry Adams: The Major Phase, 1964; Bernard Berenson: The Making of a Connoisseur, 1979. Editor: The Education of Henry Adams, 1973; mem. editorial bd. Am. Lit., 1964-71; mem. adv. bd. publ. Adams Papers; asso. editor letters of Henry Adams. Home: 3116 Park Pl Evanston IL 60201

SAMUELS, JOHN STOCKWELL, 3D, financier, mining co. exec.; b. Galveston, Tex., Sept. 15, 1933; s. John Stockwell and Helen Yvonne (Poole) S.; A.B., Tex. A. and M. U., 1954, S.M., 1954; LL.B., Harvard U., 1960; m. Ellen Richards (div. 1979); children—Evelyn, John, Ainlay, Peter A. H. Admitted to N.Y. bar, 1961; chmn. bd. Carbomin Internat., Inc., N.Y.C., 1973. Chmn. bd. City Center Music and Drama, Inc., N.Y.C., N.Y.C. Ballet, N.Y.C. Opera; bd. dirs. Lincoln Center Performing Arts, N.Y.C., Inst. Fine Arts, N.Y.C. Served with U.S. Army, 1954-57. Episcopalian. Clubs: Century; Piping Rock (Locust Valley, L.I.); Meadow, Southampton Bathing Corp. (Southampton, L.I.); Arty. (Galveston); Chgo. Office: PO Box 581 Lenox Hill Sta New York NY 10021

SAMUELS, NORMAN, coll. adminstr.; b. Montreal, Que., Can., Sept. 19, 1939; came to U.S., 1965, naturalized, 1979; s. Moe and Ida Samuels; B.A., McGill U., Montreal, 1958; M.A., Duke U., 1962, Ph.D., 1967; m. Sandra Zelnicker, May 31, 1964; children—David, Rachel, Joseph, Rebecca. Asst. prof. polit. sci. Rutgers U., 1967-70, asso. dean, Newark, 1971-76, dean of coll. Newark Coll., prof. polit. sci., 1976—; planner Medgar Evers Coll., CUNY, 1970-71. Bd. dirs. Jewish Edn. Assn., Newark, 1975-79, Jewish News, Newark, 1975-79, Hebrew Youth Acad., Essex County, N.J., 1975-79, Jewish Community Fedn. N.J., 1978; chmn. acad. div. N.J. United Jewish Appeal, 1976-79. Mem. Am. Polit. Sci. Assn., AAUP, Am. Assn. Coll. Deans. Author: Power and the People. Office: Office of Dean Newark Coll Arts and Sci Rutgers U Newark NJ 07102

SAMUELS, SHELDON WILFRED, labor union ofcl.; b. St. Johnsville, N.Y., Dec. 7, 1929; s. Max and Ethel (Feynman) S.; A.B., U. Chgo., 1951; postgrad., 1951-56; postgrad. State U. N.Y., 1964-66, USPHS Tng. Program, 1960-66; m. Morjean Rogoff, July 6, 1952; children—Charles A., Susan L. Mem. adminstrv. staff U. Chgo., 1952-60; dir. pub. info. Air Pollution Control Bd., N.Y. State Health Dept., 1960-66; pub. health advisor USPHS, Washington, 1967-69; chief field service br. Air Programs Office EPA, Washington, 1970-71; dir. health, safety and environment Indsl. Union Dept. AFL-CIO, Washington, 1971—; adj. prof. State U. N.Y., 1964-66, U. Cin., 1971-73, Mt. Sinai Sch. Medicine, 1973—; past mem. tech. adv. bd. Dept. Commerce, com. on standards ILO; mem. nat. cancer adv. bd. and com. on risk assessment, past mem. com. on cancer control Nat. Cancer Inst.; past mem. task force on research priorities Nat. Inst. Environ. Health Scis.; past mem. com. on regulating chems., com. on food policy and com. on saccharine Nat. Acad. Scis. Trustee, Workers Inst. for Safety and Health. Mem. Soc. Occupational and Environ. Health (founding mem.), Internat. Commn. on Occupational and Environ. Health (co-chmn.), Am. Coll. Toxicology (councilor), Vol. Speakers Program Dept. State, USCG Aux. Contbr. articles on environ. health, environ. and tech. change. Office: 815 16th St NW Washington DC 20006

SAMUELS, STANLEY ARNOLD, lawyer, banker; b. N.Y.C., Aug. 19, 1915; s. Morris Gilbert and Bessie (Krulewich) S.; B.S., Columbia U., 1937; LL.B., N.Y. U., 1940; m. Alice Elting, Oct. 10, 1954; children—Jocelyn, Jonathan M., Carol E. Admitted to N.Y. bar, 1940; with various firms in N.Y.C., 1947-55; counsel, v.p. Mfrs. Hanover Trust Co. Legal Dept., N.Y.C., 1955—; cons. Safe Deposir Assn. Adviser, Rent Clinic, Democratic Party, 1958-62; mem. Dem. Reform Movement N.Y.C., 1958-64. Jewish. Home: 201 W 89th St New York NY 10024 Office: 350 Park Ave New York NY 10022

SAMUELSEN, ROY, bass-baritone; b. Moss, Norway, June 12, 1933; s. Ragnar Andreas and Margaret Olivia (Evensen) S.; came to U.S., 1950, naturalized, 1954; B.S. in Music Edn., Brigham Young U., 1961; Mus.M. in Performance, Ind. U., 1963; diploma Acad. of West, Santa Barbara, Calif., 1960; student voice Joseph Heuler, Lotte Lehmann, Victor Fuchs, Frank St. Leger, Paul Matthen Charles Kullman; m. Mary Lou Thorne, May 25, 1955; children—Eric Roy, Robert Ragnar, Rolf Harold. Sheet metal worker, Utah, 1951-61; performed with Norwegian Opera Co., also opera cos. and in solo recitals throughout U.S.; guest soloist Norwegian Singing Soc. Am. convs., also with Am. orchs.; prof. music Ind. U. Opera Theatre, Bloomington, 1963—; rec. artist. Served with Mil. Police, U.S. Army, 1953-55. Recipient Lotte Lehmann award Acad. of West, 1960; regional winner Met. Opera Auditions, 1960, San Francisco Opera Auditions, 1961. Mem. AAUP, Nat. Assn. Tchrs. of Singing, Am. Guild Mus. Artists. Democrat. Mormon. Home: 2012 Montclair Ave Bloomington IN 47401 Office: Ind U Bloomington IN 47401. *My success in life is a direct reflection upon the standards set by my parents during my early life and by trying to live according to the teachings of my adopted church. These influences, along with my wife's total devotion, have encouraged me and continue to encourage me in my private and professional life.*

SAMUELSON, DERRICK WILLIAM, lawyer; b. Mpls., July 24, 1929; s. Oscar W. and Ruth (Hill) S.; B.S., U.S. Mil. Acad., 1951; LL.B., Harvard U., 1957; m. Diana L. Webster, Aug. 10, 1957; children—David W., Deirdre W. Admitted to N.Y. bar, 1958; asso. firm Lowenstein, Pitcher, Hotchkiss, Amann & Parr, N.Y.C., 1957-60; staff atty. internat. div. Warner-Lambert Pharm. Co., Morris Plains, N.J., 1960-63; counsel internat. div. Olin Mathieson Chem. Corp., N.Y.C., 1964-65; v.p., gen. counsel ITT World Communications Inc., N.Y.C., 1965-70, ITT Asia Pacific, Inc., N.Y.C., 1970—. Pres. Am.-Indonesian C. of C., 1976-79; chmn. Am. ASEAN Trade Council, Inc., 1978—. Served with U.S. Army, 1951-54. Mem. Am., Inter-Am. bar assns., Am. Soc. Internat. Law. Home: 647 Beechwood Ln Smoke Rise NJ 07405 Office: 320 Park Ave New York NY 10022

SAMUELSON, PAUL ANTHONY, economist; b. Gary, Ind., May 15, 1915; s. Frank and Ella (Lipton) S.; B.S., U. Chgo., 1935; M.A., Harvard, 1936, Ph.D. (David A. Wells prize 1941), 1941; hon. degrees: LL.D., U. Chgo., Oberlin Coll., 1961, Boston Coll., 1964, Ind. U. 1966, U. Mich., 1967, Claremont Grad. Sch., 1970, U. N.H., 1971, Keyo U., 1971; D.Sc., East Anglia U., Norwich, Eng., 1966; D.Litt. (hon.), Ripon Coll., 1962, No. Mich. U., 1973; L.H.D., Seton Hall Coll., 1971, Williams Coll., 1971; D.Sc. U. Mass., 1972, U. R.I., 1972; LL.D., Harvard, 1972, Gustavus Adolphus Coll., 1974, U. So. Calif., 1975, U. Pa., 1976, U. Rochester, 1976, Emmanuel Coll., 1977, Stonehill Coll., 1978; Doctorate Honoris Causa, U. Catholique de Louvain (Belgium, 1976; m. Marion Crawford, July 2, 1938 (dec.); children—Jane Kendall, Margaret Wray, William Frank, Robert James, John Crawford, Paul Reid. Prof. econs. Mass. Inst. Tech., 1940—, inst. prof., 1966, mem. staff Radiation Lab., 1944-45; prof. internat. econ. relations Fletcher Sch. Law and Diplomacy, part-time 1945; cons. Nat. Resources Planning Bd., 1941-43, WPB, 1945, U.S. Treasury, 1945-52, 61—, Bur. Budget, 1952, RAND Corp., 1948-75, Fed. Res. Bd., 1965—, council Econ. Advisers, 1960—; econ. adviser to Pres. Kennedy; sr. adviser Brookings Panel on Econ. Activity; mem. spl. commn. on social scis. NSF, 1967—; cons. Joint Econ. Council, Congl. Budget Office; Stamp Meml. lectr., London, 1961; Wicksell lectr., Stockholm, 1962; Franklin lectr., Detroit, 1962; Hoyt vis. fellow Calhoun Coll., Yale, 1962; Carnegie Found. reflective year, 1965-66; John von Neumann lectr. U. Wis., 1971; Gerhard Colm Meml. lectr. New Sch. for Social Research, N.Y.C., 1971; Davidson lectr. U. N.H., 1971; Sultzbacher Meml. lectr. Columbia Law Sch., N.Y.C., 1974; J. Willard Gibbs lectr. Am. Math. Soc., San Francisco, 1974; John Diebold lectr. Harvard, 1976. Chmn. Pres.'s Task Force Maintaining Am. Prosperity, 1964; mem. Nat. Task Force on Econ. Edn., 1960-61; mem. adv. bd. Nat. Commn. Money and Credit, 1958-60. Hon. fellow London Sch. Econs. and Polit. Sci. Guggenheim fellow, 1948-49; Ford Found. research fellow, 1958-59. Recipient John Bates Clark medal Am. Econ. Assn., 1947; Alfred Nobel Meml. prize in econ. sci., 1970; Medal of Honor, U. Evansville (Ill.), 1970; Albert Einstein Commemorative award, 1971; Distinguished Service award Investment Edn. Inst., Nat. Assn. Investment Clubs, 1974. Fellow Brit. Acad. (corr.), Am. Philos. Soc., Econometric Soc. (v.p. 1950, pres. 1951), Am. Econ. Assn. (hon.; pres. 1961); mem. Com. Econ. Devel. (commn. on nat. goals, research adv. bd. 1959-60), Am. Acad. Arts and Scis., Internat. Econ. Assn. (pres. 1966-68, hon. pres.), Nat. Acad. Scis., Phi Beta Kappa, Omicron Delta Kappa (trustee). Author: Foundations of Economic Analysis, 1947; Economics, 1948-80; Readings in Economics, 1955; (with R. Dorfman and R.M. Solow) Linear Programming and Economic Analysis, 1958; Collected Scientific Papers, 4 vols., 1966, 72, 78; co-author numerous other books. Contbr. numerous articles to profl. jours. Columnist for Newsweek. Home: 75 Clairemont Rd Belmont MA 02178

SANASARDO, PAUL SAVIOUR, choreographer, dancer; b. Chgo., Sept. 15, 1928; s. Joseph and Frances (Bonadonna) S.; student in fine arts U. Chgo., Art Inst. Chgo., 1947-51. Dancer, Anna Sokolow Co., N.Y.C.,1953-57; guest artist Pearl Lang Co., N.Y.C., 1958-62; artistic dir., choreographer, dancer Sanasardo Dance Co., N.Y.C., 1963—; guest choreographer Alvin Ailey Dance Theatre, N.Y.C., 1967, Bat-Dor Dance Co., Tel Aviv, 1971-75, Contemporary Dancers, Winnipeg, Man., Can., 1973-74, Gulbenkian Ballet, Lisbon, Portugal, 1974, Sask. Dance Theatre, Saskaton, Sask., Can., 1974, Dancers Co., N.Y.C., 1974-77, Ballet Theatre Contemporain, Angers, France, 1975; artistic dir. Modern Dance Artists, Inc., 1967—, Sch. Modern Dance Saratoga Performing Arts Center, Saratoga Springs, N.Y., 1969-73, Batsheva Dance Co., Tel-Aviv, Israel, 1977-80. Served with U.S. Army, 1950-52. Guggenheim Found. choreography fellow, 1970. Mem. Actors Equity Assn., AFTRA, Am. Guild Mus. Artists, Assn. Am. Dance Cos. Home: RD 1 Box 71-B Fly Creek NY 13337 Office: 59 W 21st St New York City NY 10010

SANAZARO, PAUL JOSEPH, physician, med. adminstr.; b. Sanger, Calif., Sept. 27, 1922; s. Joseph Ugo and Mary (Poggio) S.; A.B. summa cum laude, U. Calif. at Berkeley, 1944; M.D., U. Calif. at San Francisco, 1946; m. Marian V. Moore, July 11, 1974. Intern, San Francisco City and County Hosp., 1946-47; resident medicine U. Calif. Hosp., also VA Hosp., San Francisco, 1947-51; mem. faculty U. Calif. Sch. Medicine, San Francisco, 1950-62, chief gen. med. clinic, 1955-62, asso. prof. medicine, 1959-62; pvt. practice, Berkeley, 1953-55; clin. asso. prof. medicine U. Ill. Coll. Medicine, 1962-67, clin. prof. medicine, 1967-68; dir. Nat. Center for Health Services Research and Devel., HEW 1968-72, asso. dept. adminstr., 1972-73; dir. Pvt. Initiative in P.S.R.O., 1973-76; clin. prof. health care scis. George Washington Sch. Medicine, 1974-75; clin. prof. medicine U. Calif. Sch. Medicine at San Francisco, 1975—; dir. Pvt. Initiative in Quality Assurance, 1978—; dir. div. edn. Assn. Am. Med. Colls., 1962-68; cons. Nat. Commn. Community Health Services, 1963-66; chmn. Health Services Research Study Sect., 1966-68. Served to capt. M.C., AUS, 1951-53. Diplomate Am. Bd. Internal Medicine. Fellow Am. Pub. Health Assn., A.C.P.; mem. Phi Beta Kappa, Alpha Omega Alpha. Presbyn. Co-author: Health Services Research and R & D. Contbr. articles to profl. jours. Home: 1126 Grizzly Peak Blvd Berkeley CA 94708

SANBORN, THEODORE, ins. exec.; b. St. Paul, Jan. 31, 1921; s. Bruce W. and Conradine (Schurmeier) S.; student U. Minn., 1940-43; m. Dorothy Louise Cammack, Jan. 14, 1949; children—Bruce C., David S., Margaret A., Conradine W. Agt., Minn. Mut. Life Ins. Co., St. Paul, 1945-46; agy. supr. Modern Life Ins. Co., 1946-48, v.p., 1948, exec. v.p., 1949-50; chmn., chief exec. officer, dir. North Central Life Ins. Co., St. Paul, 1950—; chmn., pres., chief exec. officer, dir. North Central Cos., St. Paul, 1960—; dir. Am. Nat. Bank. Trustee Hamline U.; past trustee Breck Sch. Served from pvt. to 1st lt., USAAF, 1943-45. Mem. Nat. Consumers Credit Ins. Assn. (past pres.), Chief Execs. Forum, Minn. Execs. Orgn. (past pres.). Presbyterian. (trustee). Home: 13 Manitou Island White Bear Lake MN 55110 Office: 275 E 4th St St Paul MN 55101

SANCES, ANTHONY, JR., educator; b. Chgo., July 13, 1932; s. Anthony G. and Dolores (Duvall) S.; B.S. in Elec. Engring., Am. Inst. Tech., 1953; M.S. in Physics, DePaul U., Chgo., 1959; Ph.D. in Biomed. Engring., Northwestern U., Chgo., 1964; m. Starr Lockhart, Feb. 18, 1965; children—Zachary, Martin, Amy. Project engr. Am. Machine & Foundry, 1953-59; mgr. advanced research dept. Sunbeam Corp., Chgo., 1959-61; asst. prof. Am. Inst. Tech., 1959-60; v.p., dir. research San-Bar Corp., 1960-63; prof., chmn. biomed. engring. Marquette U. and Med. Coll. Wis., Milw., 1964—; biomed. engr. Wood VA Hosp.; cons. various firms. Registered profl. engr., Wis. Founding fellow Soc. Advanced Med. Systems; mem. Biophys. Soc., Instrument Soc. Am., Internat. Soc. for Comprehensive Medicine (nat. adv. bd.), IEEE, Internat. Soc. Electroanesthesia and Electrosleep (v.p.), Neuroelectric Soc. (pres.), N.Y. Acad. Scis., Biomed. Engring. Soc. (dir.), Assn. Advancement Med. Instrumentation Alliance for Engring. in Medicine and Biology (past pres.), Canadian-Am. Med. Dental Assn. (pres.-elect), Internat. Inst. for Med. Electronics and Biol. Engring. (gov.), Soc. for Neurosci., AAUP, Am. Soc. Biomechanics, Am. Soc. Safety Engrs. (asso.), Bioelectromagnetics Soc., Sigma Xi, Eta Kappa Nu, Tau Beta Pi. Adv. bd. Clin. Engring. Newsletter. Contbr. articles to profl. jours. Office: 8700 W Wisconsin St Milwaukee WI 53226

SANCHEZ, ADEL, musician; b. Tampa, Fla., Dec. 18, 1944; s. Alfredo D. and Clemencia M. Sanchez; student Juilliard Sch. Music, 1964-66; m. Janice Kay Patterson, Sept. 20, 1972; children—Christina Mara, Alison Evard. Prin. trumpet Kansas City (Mo.) Philharmonic, 1966-69, Nat. Symphony, Washington, 1969—; soloist Philharmonia Virtuosi, N.Y.C.; mem. faculty Catholic U. Am., 1969—, also U. Mo., U. Wis. Scholarship student Juilliard Sch. Music, 1964-66, Manhattan Sch. Music, 1964, Cin. Conservatory Music, 1961, Interlochen Winter Arts Acad., 1963, Interlochen Music Camp, 1963. Mem. Internat. Trumpet Guild, Am. Fedn. Musicians. Home: 4774 N 25th St Arlington VA 22207 Office: Kennedy Center Performing Arts Washington DC 20566

SANCHEZ, FRANCISCO DEMETRIO, JR., ednl. adminstr.; b. Santa Rosa, N.Mex., Oct. 31, 1926; s. Francisco Demetrio and Candelaria (Gallegos) S.; B.S., U. N.Mex., 1949, M.S., 1954; m. Viola Sanchez, Sept. 17, 1949; children—Francisco D., Donald Edward. With Albuquerque Public Schs., 1949—, dir. new programs, 1968-72, dep. supt. ops., 1972-77, acting supt., 1977, supt., 1977-78, dep. supt., 1978—; mem. Nat. Adv. Council on Extension and Continuing Edn. Mem. budget com. United Way; mem. Albuquerque-Bernalillo County Econ. Opportunity Bd. Served with U.S. Army, 1951-52. Mem. N.Mex. Sch. Adminstrs. Assn., Supts. Assn. Republican. Roman Catholic. Home: 7101 Los Arboles NE Albuquerque NM 87110 Office: PO Box 25704 Albuquerque NM 87125

SANCHEZ, JOSE MARIANO, educator; b. Santa Fe, Nov. 1, 1932; s. Manuel A. and Amalia (Sena) S.; B.S., St. Louis U., 1954, M.A., 1957; Ph.D. (Social Sci. Research Council fellow), U. N.Mex., 1961; m. Carol Mahan, Nov. 17, 1956; children—Clara, Manuel, Maria, Leonora, Rodrigo. Instr. St. Louis U., 1960-62, asst. prof., 1962-65, asso. prof., 1965-69, prof. history, 1969—, chmn. dept., 1971-74. Served with AUS, 1954-56. Mem. Am., Catholic hist. assns. Author: Reform and Reaction: The Politico-Religious Background of the Spanish Civil War, 1964; Anticlericalism: A Brief History, 1972. Co-editor: Great Events from History, 1973. Home: 6235 Pershing St St Louis MO 63130

SANCHEZ, MAURICE, judge; b. Lemitar, N.Mex., May 27, 1912; s. John Francis and Mariana (Miera) S.; A.B., U. N.Mex., 1936; B.S. in Law, Northwestern U., 1937, LL.B., 1939, J.D., 1970; m. Violet Lurba, Mar. 25, 1940; children—Eileen Marie, Philip Charles. Admitted to N.Mex. bar, 1939, since practiced in Albuquerque; apptd. asst. U.S. atty. Dist. N.Mex., 1942, U.S. atty., 1951, by Pres. U.S., 1952, resigned, 1953; judge 2d Jud. Dist. N.Mex., 1973-79. Chmn. N.Mex. Corrections Commn., 1971-73. Chmn. city commn., mayor ex-officio, Albuquerque, 1954-62. Mem. Am., N.Mex. bar assns., Am. Judicature Soc., Phi Kappa Phi, Pi Sigma Alpha, Delta Theta Phi. K.C., Kiwanian (pres. Albuquerque 1969, gov. elect SW dist. 1976-77, gov. 1977-78). Home: 6215 Rio Hondo Dr NE Albuquerque NM 87109

SANCHEZ, RAFAEL CAMILO, physician; b. Tampa, Fla., July 18, 1919; s. Francisco and Catalina (Mateo) S.; B.S., Loyola U., New Orleans, 1940; M.D., La. State U., 1950; m. Sylvia Guitrau, Feb. 21, 1976; children—Stephen Francis, John Thomas, David Lear. Intern, U.S. Marine Hosp., New Orleans, 1950-51; gen. practice medicine, New Orleans, 1951-72; med. educator, dir. continuing med. edn. La. State U., 1963-77; dir. family practice residency program Charity Hosp. of Bogalusa (La.), 1977—. Served with AUS, 1940-46. Diplomate Am. Bd. Family Practice. Mem. Am. Acad. Family Physicians (Thomas W. Johnson award 1978), AMA, So. Med. Assn. Democrat. Roman Catholic. Club: Bogalusa Country. Office: PO Box 459 400 Memphis St Bogalusa LA 70427

SANCHEZ, ROBERT FORTUNE, archbishop; b. Socorro, N.Mex., Mar. 20, 1934; s. Julius C. and Priscilla (Fortune) S.; student Immaculate Heart Sem., Santa Fe, 1954, N.Am. Coll., Gregorian U., Rome, 1960. Ordained priest Roman Cath. Ch., 1959; prof., asst. prin. St. Piux X High Sch., Albuquerque, 1960-68; dir. extension lay vols. Archdiocese Santa Fe, 1965-68, chmn. priest personnel bd., 1968-72, vicar gen., 1972-74, archbishop, 1974—; rep. instl. ministry pastoral care N.Mex. Council Chs., 1968; pres. Archdiocesan Priests Senate, 1973-74; rep. region X, Nat. Fedn. Priests Councils, 1972-73; mem. bd. Am. Bd. Cath. Missions, Cath. Relief Services, Commn. Marriage and Family Life, U.S. Cath. Conf.; chmn. bd. dirs. Mexican Am. Cultural Center; episcopal adviser Theresians Am.; mem. regional com. Nat. Conf. Catholic Bishops, N.Am. Coll., Rome. Mem. U.S. Cath. Conf. (communications com., chmn. ad hoc com. Spanish speaking). Address: 202 Morningside Dr SE Albuquerque NM 87108

SANCHEZ-PEREZ, JESUS MARIA, author, inventor; b. Morata de Tajuna, Madrid, June 30, 1908; s. Jose Augusto and Rosario (Sanchez de Cuevas) S.-P.; came to U.S., 1934, naturalized, 1951; M.D., Madrid U., 1936; m. Maria Ibarguengoytia, Mar. 19, 1953. Fellow, Montreal Neurol. Inst., McGill U., 1934; fellow for research cerebral angiography under Prof. Egas Moniz, Lisbon, Portugal, 1935; lectr. neurol. roentgenology Montreal Neurol. Inst., 1936; practice medicine, Mexico, 1940-46, specializing in neurosurgery, 1936—; lectr. U. So. Calif., Los Angeles County Gen. Hosp., 1946-49; lectr. VA Hosps., Los Angeles, 1947-53; intern Hollywood Presbyn. Hosp., 1951; resident Norwalk (Calif.) State Hosp., 1953. Fellow Lisbon U. Med. Sch., 1935-36. Mem. Radiol. Soc. N.Am. (hon.), Argentina, Mexico, Colombia socs. radiologia, Neuroradiol. Soc. Brazil (hon.). Author: A Doctor's Odyssey, 1973; Babelism, 1974; The Hispanico, 1974; Beliefs and Their Engrammes, 1975; Oppression, Violence and Repression, 1975; Our Sixth Sense, An organic theory of the unknown, 1979; Engrammes of the Universe, Reincarnation, Extra-cerebral Memory, 1979; inventor seriograph cassette changer for automatic serial angiography; inventor stereo-serio radiographic unit for automatically controlled stereoscopic serial angiographic studies of the brain, heart, lungs, kidneys and thoracic and abdominal aorta; inventor policathod X-ray tube for direct stereoscopic magnification in serial angiography; responsible for S-P celular theory to explain organic basis of ESP phenomena. Home: 635 Sierra Leona Mexico 10 DF Mexico

SAND, EDWARD AUSTIN, publishing co. exec.; b. N.Y.C., Apr. 30, 1911; s. Morris and Rose (Schoenfeld) S.; student N.Y. U., 1929-33, Columbia, 1934-35; m. Sarah Ellen Horowitz, Sept. 11, 1912; 1 son, Thomas. Pub.-editor Lit. Workshop, 1933-35; editor Modern Publs., 1936-38; v.p. Simmons-Boardman Pub. Co., 1938-45; pres., dir. Parents Mag. Enterprises, Inc., N.Y.C., 1946—. Office: 52 Vanderbilt Ave New York NY 10017*

SAND, LEONARD B., judge; b. N.Y.C., May 24, 1928; B.S., N.Y. U., 1947; LL.B., Harvard, 1951. Admitted to N.Y. bar, 1953, U.S. Supreme Ct. bar, 1956, D.C. bar, 1969; clk. to dist. ct. judge, N.Y., 1952-53; asst. U.S. atty. So. Dist. N.Y., 1953-54; asst. to U.S. Solictor Gen., 1956-59; mem. firm Robinson, Silverman, Pearce, Aronsohn Sand and Berman, N.Y.C.; judge U.S. Dist. Ct. So. Dist. N.Y., 1978—. Del. N.Y. State Constl. Conv., 1967; v.p., treas. Legal Aid Soc. Fellow Am. Coll. Trial Lawyers; mem. Assn. Bar City N.Y., N.Y. State, Am. bar assns., Fed. Bar Council (pres. elect). Note editor Harvard Law Rev., 1950-51. Office: US Dist Ct Foley Sq New York NY 10007

SAND, PAUL MEINRAD, justice N.D. Supreme Ct.; b. Balta, N.D., Oct. 21, 1914; s. Paul and Clara A. (Vetsch) S.; LL.B., N.D. U., Grandforks, 1941, J.D., 1969; m. Gloria L. Gray, Jan. 15, 1952; 1 dau., Sheila. Admitted to N.D. bar, 1941, U.S. Supreme Ct., 1961; asst. atty. gen. State of N.D., 1949-63, 1st asst. atty. gen., 1963-75; justice N.D. Supreme Ct., Bismarck, 1975—. Served to lt. col. U.S. Army, 1941-47. Mem. Am., N.D. bar assns., Am. Judicature Soc., Order of Coif. Roman Catholic. Clubs: Lions, Elks. Home: 1022 N 8th St Bismarck ND 58501 Office: North Dakota Supreme Ct Bismarck ND 58505

SANDAGE, ALLAN REX, astronomer; b. Iowa City, June 18, 1926; s. Charles Harold and Dorothy (Briggs) S.; A.B., U. Ill., 1948, D.Sc., 1967; Ph.D., Calif. Inst. Tech., 1953; D.Sc., Yale, 1966, U. Chgo., 1967, Miami U., Oxford, Ohio, 1974; LL.D., U. So. Calif., 1971; m. Mary Lois Connelley, June 8, 1959; children—David Allan, John Howard. Astronomer, Mt. Wilson Obs., Palomar Obs., Carnegie Instn., Washington, 1952—; Peyton postdoctoral fellow Princeton U., 1952; asst. astronomer Hale Obs., Santa Barbara, Calif., 1952-56, astronomer, 1956—; vis. lectr. Harvard, 1957; cons. NSF, 1961-64; Sigma Xi nat. lectr., 1966; vis. prof. Mt. Stromlo Obs., Australian Nat. U., 1968-69; mem. astron. expdn. to South Africa, 1958. Mem. permanent organizing com. Solvay Conf. in Physics. Served with USNR, 1944-45. Recipient gold medal Royal Astron. Soc., 1967, Pope Pius XI gold medal Pontifical Acad. Sci., 1966, Rittenhouse medal, 1968, Nat. Medal Sci., 1971. Fulbright-Hayes scholar, 1972. Mem. Am. (Helen Warner prize 1960, Russell prize 1973), Royal (Eddington medal 1963) astron. socs., Astron. Soc. Pacific (Gold medal 1975), Nat. Acad. Scis., Franklin Inst. (Elliott Cresson medal 1973), Phi Beta Kappa, Sigma Xi. Home: 8319 Josard Rd San Gabriel CA 91775 Office: 813 Santa Barbara St Pasadena CA 91101

SANDAGE, CHARLES HAROLD, educator; b. Hatfield, Mo., Aug. 21, 1902; s. Moses and Almatie (Bissell) S.; student Graceland Coll., Lamoni, Iowa, 1921-23; A.B., State U. Iowa, 1926, M.A., 1927, Ph.D., 1931; student U. Ill., 1928; m. Dorothy Briggs, Aug. 5, 1924 (dec. 1970) 1 son, Allan R.; m. 2d, Elizabeth Smith Danner, 1971. Tchr., Dunlap Twp. High Sch., 1923-25; asst. prof. econs. Simpson Coll., Indianola, Iowa, 1927-28: asst. prof. bus. U. Kans., 1928-29; asst., asso. prof. bus. Miami U., Oxford, Ohio, 1929-35, prof. and head dept. mktg., 1937-46; asst. chief, chief, div. transp. and communications Bur. Census, U.S. Dept. Commerce, 1935-37; lectr. advt. U. Pa., 1936-37; prof. advt. U. Ill., 1946—, now emeritus; cons. FCC, 1957-58; lectr. mktg. Evening Coll., U. Cin., 1930-35, 37-39; vis. prof. mktg. U. Calif., 1941; state price officer for Ohio, OPA, 1942; vis. prof. bus. research Harvard, 1943-44; v.p., dir. research Inst. Transit Advt., 1944-45; pres. Farm Research Inst., 1946—; vice chmn. bd., dir. Thomas Jefferson Life Ins. Co., Holding Corp. Am.; dir. Champaign Loan and Bldg. Assn. Mem. Nat. Advt. Rev. Bd. Recipient Advt. gold medal award, 1964. Mem. Am. Mktg. Assn. (dir. 1944-47, 54-56, v.p. 1956-57), Am. Acad. Advt., Am. Assn. Pub. Opinion Research, Phi Beta Kappa, Lambda Delta Sigma, Delta Sigma Pi, Kappa Tau Alpha, Alpha Delta Sigma. Author: Advertising Theory and Practice, 1936, 10th edit. (with V. Fryburger and K. Rotzoll), 1979; Radio Advertising for Retailers, 1945; (contbg. author) Marketing by Manufacturers, 1946, rev., 1951; Changing Perspectives in Marketing, 1951; (monograph) Qualitative Analysis of Radio Listening in Two Illinois Counties, 1948; Building Audiences, 1951; (with V. Fryburger) The Role of Advertising, 1960; The Promise of Advertising, 1961; (with A. Barban) Readings in Advertising and Promotion Strategy, 1968; (with K. Rotzell and J. Haefner) Advertising in Contemporary Society, 1976. Contbr. govt. publs., mag. articles, monographs. Home: 106 W Meadows Urbana IL 61801. *To have the love and compassion of a wife, and work that is highly satisfying.*

SANDBANK, HENRY, photographer, film co. exec.; b. Burg, Germany, Mar. 20, 1932; s. Sylvan and Bella (Spatz) S.; ed. pub. schs.; m. Judith Lebow, July 4, 1952; children—Kenneth, Laura, Lisa, David. Came to U.S., 1939, naturalized, 1950. Partner, Beach & Sandbank, Syracuse, N.Y., 1960-63; pres. Henry Sandbank, Inc., N.Y.C., 1963-78; pres., film dir. Sandbank Films Co., Inc., N.Y.C., 1972—; dir. Vantage Films, 1979—. Instr. Sch. Visual Arts, N.Y.C., 1973-74; lectr. Syracuse U., 1972; cons. Fashion Inst. Tech., 1974—. Served to sgt. AUS, 1952-54; Korea. Recipient Gold Medal awards Art Dirs. and Copywriters Show; Gold medal Film Festival of the Americas; several Clio and Andy awards; Cannes Festival award. Mem. Am. Soc. Mag. Photographers (chmn. exec. com. 1978—), Soc. Photographers in Communications (trustee 1974—, 2d v.p. 1975-76, 1st v.p. 1977, chmn. exec. com. 1979). Home: 24 Nutmeg Dr Greenwich CT 06830 Office: 105 E 16th St New York NY 10003

SANDBERG, KARL C., educator; b. Salt Lake City, Mar. 7, 1931; s. George W. and Ruby (Woodard) S.; B.A., Brigham Young U., 1954, M.A., 1957; Ph.D., U. Wis., 1960; m. Dawn Bennion, June 7, 1954; children—David, Stephanie, Mark, Shireen. Mem. faculty Brigham Young U., Provo, Utah, U. Wis., Duke, U. Ariz., Tucson, U. Colo.; now prof. Macalester Coll., St. Paul, also chmn. dept. linguistics. Served with AUS, 1954-56. Mem. Am. Council Tchrs. Fgn. Lang., Tchrs. of English as Second Lang. Author fgn. lang. textbooks, studies in French 18th Century lit. and poetry. Contbr. articles to profl. jours. Home: 2983 Chatsworth St N St Paul MN 55113

SANDBERG, ROBERT ALEXIS, research orgn. adminstr.; b. Spokane, Sept. 20, 1914; s. Robert A. and Faye P. (Davis) S.; A.B., State Coll. Wash., 1936, A.M., 1937; postgrad. Northwestern U., 1937-38, U. Ill., 1939-41; m. Ruth Margaret Cheatham, Apr. 1, 1934; children—Robert, Howard, William, Douglas. Instr. speech U. Ill., 1939-42; exec. asst. to pres. Wash. State U., 1945-52; v.p. pub. affairs and advt. Kaiser Aluminum and Chem. Corp., Oakland, Calif., 1965-72; sr. v.p. Kaiser Industries, Inc., Oakland, 1972-74; sr. adv. Electric Power Research Inst., Palo Alto, Calif., 1974—. Dir. fund raising Eastern area A.R.C., 1941-45. Trustee Inst. Ednl. Devel.; bd. dirs. Advt. Council. Mem. Pub. Relations Soc., Am. (accreditation bd. 1968—), Newcomen Soc., Sigma Delta Chi. Author: Everyday Business Speech, 1942; Handbook of Public Speaking, 1940; Effective Speaking in Business, 1960. Home: 735 Arroyo Ct Lafayette CA 94549 Office: 3412 Hillview Ave Palo Alto CA 94304

SANDBLOM, ROBERT LELAND, mfg. co. exec.; b. Creston, Iowa, Apr. 9, 1927; s. Edwin Paul and Helen Louisa (Stiles) S.; B.A. with honors, Drake U., 1949; J.D. with distinction, U. Mich., 1952; m. Barbara Frances Reis, July 31, 1953; children—Julie Barbara, Laurie Kay, Robert Paul. Admitted to Iowa bar, 1952; partner firm Herrick, Langdon, Sandblom & Belin, Des Moines, 1952-66; pres. Delavan Corp., West Des Moines, 1966-76, chmn., chief exec. officer, 1976—, also chmn. subsidiaries; dir., chmn. exec. com. Iowa Des Moines Nat. Bank. Dir., pres. Des Moines Area Hosp. Consortium, 1976-78; chmn. Delavan Found.; pres., dir. Iowa Meth. Med. Center, Des Moines; trustee Drake U., Des Moines. Mem. Young Pres.' Orgn. (co-founder Iowa chpt.), Chief Execs. Forum (dir.), Greater Des Moines C. of C. (dir.), World Bus. Council, Nat. Assn. Mfrs., U.S. Indsl. Council (dir.), Iowa State Bar Assn., Iowa Mfrs. Assn. (dir.), Phi Alpha Delta, Sigma Alpha Epsilon. Republican. Methodist. Clubs: Des Moines, Embassy, Wakonda, Masons, Presidents U. Mich. Home: 7023 Bellaire Ave Des Moines IA 50311 Office: 811 4th St West Des Moines IA 50265

SANDBURG, HELGA, author; b. Maywood, Ill., Nov. 24, 1918; d. Carl and Lillian (Steichen) S.; student Mich. State Coll., 1939-40, U. Chgo., 1940; m. George Crile, Jr., Nov. 9, 1963; children by previous marriage—John Carl Steichen, Paula Steichen Polega. Dairy goat breeder, also personal sec. to father, 1944-51; sec. manuscripts div., also for keeper of collections Library of Congress, 1952-56; adminstrv. asst. for papers of Woodrow Wilson, 1958-59; writer, lectr., 1957—. Recipient Va. Quar. Rev. prize for best short story, 1959, Borestone Mountain poetry award, 1962, Poetry award Chgo. Tribune, 1970; 2d prize 7th Ann. Kans. Poetry Contest; grantee Finnish Am. Soc. and Svenska Inst., 1961. Mem. Authors Guild, Poetry Soc. Am., Am. Milk Goat Record Assn., Am.-Scandinavian Found., Nat. Nubian Club, Council Save the Dunes, Am. Luxembourg Soc. Author: (novels) The Wheel of Earth, 1958, Measure My Love, 1959, The Owl's Roost, 1962, The Wizard's Child, 1967; (non-fiction) Sweet Music, A Book of Family Reminiscence and Song, 1963, (with George Crile, Jr.) Above and Below, 1969; (poetry) The Unicorns, 1965, To A New Husband, 1970; (young adult novels) Blueberry, 1963, Gingerbread, 1964; (juveniles) Joel and the Wild Goose, 1963, Bo and the Old Donkey, 1965, Anna and the Baby Buzzard, 1970; (collection of short stories) Children and Lovers: 15 Stories by Helga Sandburg, 1976; (biography) A Great and Glorious Romance: The Story of Carl Sandburg and Lilian Steichen, 1978; also numerous short stories; rep. in collections. Contbr. short stories, poems, articles to popular mags. including New Yorker, Harpers, McCalls, Ladies Home Jour. Address: 2060 Kent Rd Cleveland OH 44106

SANDEFUR, JOSEPH THOMAS, univ. dean; b. Calhoun, Ky., July 24, 1925; s. Dewey Lee and Bessie Ann (Mauzey) S.; A.B., Western Ky. U., 1950; M.A., Ind. U., 1953, Ed.D., 1958; m. Martha Courtney Kelly, Oct. 16, 1948; children—Kelly, Sarah. Prin., Daviess County Pub. Schs., Owensboro, Ky., 1949-58; dir. research, dean Kan. State Tchrs. Coll., Emporia, 1958-71; dean Sch. Edn., Grad. Coll., Western Ky. U., Bowling Green, 1971—. Field reader Bur. Research, U.S. Office Edn., 1968-69. Served with USAAF, 1943-46. Recipient Fulbright-Hayes Travel grants to Colombia, S.Am., 1968, 70. Mem. Assn. Higher Edn., Am. Ednl. Research Assn., NEA, Nat. Assn. Colls. for Tchr. Edn. (pres. 1978), Nat. Assn. for Supervision and Curriculum Devel., Phi Delta Kappa. Contbr. articles profl. jours. Home: 1608 Singletree Lane Bowling Green KY 42101

SANDEL, ARDIS, magazine editor; b. N.Y.C., Oct. 20, 1921; B.A., N.Y. U., 1942, M.A., 1946; m. Michael Sandel, Nov. 15, 1954; 1 dau., Debra Amalie. News editor Front Page weekly, Tel Aviv, 1954-55; editor Macfadden-Bartell, N.Y.C., 1952-53, Fawcett Pub. Co., 1953-54; editor Women's Group, Lady's Circle, Lopez Publs., N.Y.C., 1955—; lectr. profl. writing U. Okla., 1972, 75. Club: Overseas Press of Am. Home: 86-15 Broadway St Elmhurst NY 11373 Office: 23 W 26th St New York NY 10010

SANDEL, THOMAS THEODORE, educator, scientist; b. Dallas, Jan. 2, 1924; s. Joseph Jefferson and Marguerite (Porter) S.; B.A., U. Tex., 1948, M.A., 1950, Ph.D., 1954; m. Katherine Willanne Wetzel, June 21, 1947; children—Martha (Mrs. Ethan Haimo), Thomas, David, Karin. Asst. prof., def. research lab. and dept. psychology U. Tex., Austin, 1952-55; staff mem. research lab. electronics and Lincoln Lab., Mass. Inst. Tech., 1955-64; prof. psychology, dir. psychobiology lab. Washington U., St. Louis, 1964—, chmn. dept., 1969—. Served with USNR and USMCR, 1943-46, USMCR, 1950-51. USPHS postdoctoral fellow, 1955-57. Fellow Acoustical Soc. Am.; mem. AAAS, AAUP, Psychonomic Soc. Contbr. articles to profl. jours. Asso. editor Jour. Acoustical Soc. Am., 1966-71. Home: 6910 Washington Ave St Louis MO 63130

SANDELL, ERNEST BIRGER, analytical chemist, educator; b. Mpls., Feb. 20, 1906; s. John August and Esther (Magnusson) S.; B.S., U. Minn., 1928, M.S. 1929, Ph.D. (DuPont fellow 1931-32), 1932. Instr. div. analytical chemistry sch. chemistry U. Minn., 1932-37, asst. prof., 1937-43, asso. prof., 1943-46, prof., 1946—; vis. prof. Cairo U., 1960. Fellow Am. Mineral. Soc., Geol. Soc. Am.; mem. Am. Chem. Soc., AAAS, Minn. Acad. Sci., Geochem. Soc., Chem. Soc. Gt. Britain (hon.), Sigma Xi, Phi Lambda Upsilon. Author: Textbook of Quantitative Inorganic Analysis, 1936; Colorimetric Determination of Traces of Metals, 3d rev. edit. 1959. Editorial cons. Elsevier Pub. Co., Holland, Interscience, N.Y.C., others. Home: 4424 Victory Ave Minneapolis MN 55412

SANDER, FRANK ERNEST ARNOLD, educator; b. Stuttgart, Germany, July 22, 1927; s. Rudolf and Alice (Epstein) S.; came to U.S., 1940, naturalized, 1946; A.B. in Math. magna cum laude, Harvard, 1949, LL.B. magna cum laude, 1952; m. Emily Bishop Jones, Apr. 26, 1958; children—Alison Bishop, Thomas Harvey, Ernest Ridgway Sander. Admitted to Mass. bar, 1952, also U.S. Supreme Ct.; law clk. to chief judge Magruder, U.S. Ct. Appeals, 1952-53, to Justice Frankfurter, U.S. Supreme Ct., 1953-54; atty. tax div. Dept. Justice, 1954-56; with firm Hill & Barlow, Boston, 1956-59; mem. faculty Harvard Law Sch., 1959—, prof. law, 1962—; spl. fields fed. taxation, family law, welfare law, dispute resolution; mem. Council on Role of Cts.; mem. panels Am. Arbitration Assn., Fed. Mediation and Conciliation Service. Chmn. Council on Legal Edn. Opportunity,

1968-70; cons. Dept. Treasury, 1968. Chmn., Mass. Welfare Adv. Bd., 1975-79; mem. com. civil and polit. rights President's Commn. Status Women, 1962-63; mem. tax mission Internat. Program Taxation to Republic Colombia, 1959; trustee Buckingham Browne and Nichols Sch., 1969-75. Served with AUS, 1946-47. Mem. Am. (spl. com. resolution minor disputes), Mass., Boston bar assns., Phi Beta Kappa. Treas. Harvard Law Rev., 1951-52. Author: (with Foote and Levy) Cases and Materials on Family Law, 2d edit., 1976; (with Gutman) Tax Aspects of Divorce and Separation, 1975; (with Westfall) Readings in Federal Taxation, 1970. Home: 74 Buckingham St Cambridge MA 02138

SANDER, JOHN CARSON, tenor; b. Fairmont, W.Va., Mar. 27, 1946; s. Stephen Joseph and Louise (Janes) S.; B.M., Oberlin U., 1968; M.S. cum laude, Juilliard Sch. Music, 1970; postgrad. Manhattan Sch., 1970-72; m. Carole Louden, June 21, 1969; children—Whitney Ann, John Edward. Appeared with numerous opera cos., symphonies, including Met. Opera Studio, San Francisco Spring and Fall Opera, Barcelona (Spain) Opera, Wexford Festival, Nice (France) Opera; leading artist N.Y.C. Opera, 1975—; tchr. voice. Pres., Rockland County (N.Y.) United Community Services, 1977. Named finalist Met. Opera Awards, 1968, Vercelli Internat. Concurso Competition, 1972; recipient Competition award Nat. Assn. Tchrs. Singing, 1968, awards Inst. Internat. Edn., 1971, Sullivan Found., 1972, Nat. Opera Inst., 1973, Concorso award Treviso (Italy), 1971. Mem. Am. Guild Mus. Artists, Actors Equity U.S., Actors Equity Can., N.W. Bergen County (N.Y.) Bd. Realtors (asso.). Methodist. Home: 26 Sagamore Ave Suffern NY 10901

SANDERLIN, JOHN BOSWELL, aluminum co. exec.; b. Georgetown, Ky., July 2, 1926; s. Jonathan Riddick and Sarah (Boswell) S.; B.S., U. Va., 1950; M.B.A., Harvard, 1952; m. Ann Tefft Hutchinson, June 23, 1951; children—John Kimbrough, George Hutchinson. Mgmt. trainee Citizens Fidelity Bank and Trust Co., Louisville, 1952-54; asst. controller Morton Frozen Foods, Louisville, 1954-56; with aluminum div. Anaconda Co., Louisville, 1957—, v.p. finance, 1967-72, sr. v.p., 1972—; v.p., dir. Anaconda Jamaica Inc., 1970—, Jamaica Alumina Security Co., Ltd.; v.p. Anaconda Internat. Corp.; mem. exec. com. Alumina Partners Jamaica; dir. Alpart Farms (Jamaica) Ltd., Anaconda Ireland Co., Aughinish Alumina Ltd., Alumina Contractors Ltd. Served with USNR, 1944-46. Mem. Fin. Execs. Inst. (dir. Louisville 1962-69). Clubs: Harvard Business of Kentucky (pres. 1964-65); Pendennis, Harmony Landing Country, Filson (Louisville); Harvard (N.Y.C.). Home: 173 Arrowhead Rd Louisville KY 40207 Office: 2700 First National Tower Louisville KY 40201

SANDERS, AARON PERRY, educator; b. Phoenix, Jan. 12, 1924; s. DeWitt and Ruth (Perry) S.; B.S., U. Tex., El Paso, 1950; M.S. (AEC fellow), U. Rochester, 1952; Ph.D., U. N.C., 1964; m. Betty Mae Gelein, Aug. 11, 1944 (div.); children—Merle Anne, Julie Ruth, James DeWitt; m. 2d, Georgia Anne Bullock, Nov. 26, 1972; 1 dau., Kai Marie. Asso. health physicist Brookhaven Nat. Lab., Upton, N.Y. , 1951-53; instr. physics, radiol. safety officer N.C. State Coll., 1953; instr. radiology Duke Med. Center, Durham, N.C., 1953-56, dir. radiosotope lab., 1953-65, asso. in radiology, 1956-57, asst. prof., 1957-64, asso. prof., 1964-65, asso. prof., dir. div. radiobiology, 1965-70, prof., dir. div. radiobiology, 1970—; Fulbright lectr. health physics, Argentina, 1958-59; cons. N.C. Bd. Health, 1961-76; mem. N.C. Radiation Protection Commn., 1976—, chmn., 1978—. Served with USNR, 1942-45. Diplomate Am. Bd. Health Physics. Mem. AAAS, Am. Assn. Physicists in Medicine, Soc. Exptl. Biology and Medicine, Health Physics Soc., Soc. Nuclear Medicine, Biophys. Soc., Radiation Research Soc., Undersea Med Soc., Sigma Xi, Sigma Pi Sigma. Contbr. articles to profl. jours. Address: Box 3164 Duke U Med Center Durham NC 27710. *Each individual has an obligation to himself and society to pursue an education to his maximum capability. This capability should then be used in his career in an effort to contribute to society as much, or more, than he receives. In work and personal relations you must never deny a man the dignity of his work by ridicule or denigration, and you must never use people.*

SANDERS, ANDREW DOMINICK, artist, educator; b. Erie, Pa., Dec. 22, 1918; s. Fred and Anna (Di Placido) S.; grad. Phila. Mus. Sch. Indsl. Art (now Phila. Coll. Art), 1942. Exhibited works N.A.D., 146th-151st Anns., N.Y.C., Audubon Artists, 30th-34th Anns., 1972-75, Mainstreams 72, 73 Marietta Coll., Butler Art Inst., Youngstown, Ohio, 1950-55, 64, 72, 74, Phila. Civic Center Mus., 1975; instr. drawing, painting Ringling Sch. Art, Sarasota, Fla., 1946-59, Columbus (Ohio) Coll., 1960-63. Served with AUS, 1942-45. Recipient Edwards C. Roberts award Conn. Acad. Fine Arts, 1973; certificate of merit N.A.D., 1974, Painters and Sculptors Soc. N.J., 1974. Mem. Audubon Artists. Office: The Art School 18 North Park Row Erie PA 16501

SANDERS, BENJAMIN ELBERT, educator, biochemist; b. Bowersville, Ga., Oct. 19, 1918; s. C. Lamar and Christine (Hogsed) S.; B.S., Wofford Coll., 1939; M.S. in Chemistry, U. Ga., 1942; Ph.D. (Am. Chem. Soc. fellow), Purdue U., 1949; m. Dorothy McIntyre, Sept. 7, 1946; children—Lamar, Marcia Jean. Research biochemist Henry Ford Hosp., Detroit, 1949-51; research asso. Sharp & Dohme Co., West Point, Pa., 1951-53, Merck, Sharp & Dohme Research Labs., West Point, Pa., 1953-58; dir. protein chemistry dept. Merck Inst., West Point, 1958-61; asso. prof. biochemistry State U. N.Y., Buffalo, 1961-67, prof., 1967—, asso. chmn. biochemistry dept., 1966-75. Research collaborator Brookhaven Nat. Lab., 1958-63. Bd. dirs. North Penn YMCA, 1956-61. Served to 1st lt. AUS, 1942-46. Diplomate Am. Bd. Clin. Chemistry. Fellow A.A.A.S.; mem. Am. Chem. Soc., Am. Soc. Biol. Chemists, N.Y. Acad. Scis., Sigma Xi, Phi Lambda Upsilon. Presbyn. Author articles plasma protein isolation and characterization, biochemistry schizophrenia to profl. publs. Patentee in field. Home: 52 Rosedale St Buffalo NY 14226

SANDERS, CARL JULIAN, clergyman; b. Star, N.C., May 18, 1912; s. Hugh T. and Annie Margaret (Crowell) S.; B.A., Wofford Coll., 1933, D.D. (hon.), 1973; B.D., Candler Sch. Theology, 1936; D.D. (hon.), Randolph Mason Coll., 1953, Athens (Ala.) Coll., 1972, Huntingdon Coll., 1975; L.H.D. (hon.), Birmingham-So. Coll., 1977; m. Eleanor Louise Lupo, Sept. 28, 1935; children—Lundi (Mrs. Alan Mansfield), Eleanor (Mrs. Paul T. Kasler). Ordained to ministry Methodist Ch., 1934; pastor, Cheriton, Va., 1936-40, Chase City, Va., 1940-44, Roanoke, Va., 1944-48, Richmond, Va., 1948-55; supt. Petersburg (Va.) Dist., 1955-56, Richmond Dist., 1956-61, Norfolk (Va.) Dist., 1965-71; pastor, Richmond, 1961-65, Arlington, Va., 1971-72; bishop Birmingham (Ala.) Area, 1972—. Pres. com. relief United Meth. Ch., 1972—, v.p. bd. global ministries, 1972—; mem. World Meth. Council, 1971—. Trustee Emory U., 1973—, Carraway Med. Center, Birmingham, 1972—, Athens Coll., 1972—, Huntington Coll., Montgomery, Ala., 1972—, Va. Wesleyan Coll., Norfolk, 1960-72. Mem. Omicron Delta Kappa. Home: 2205 Vestavia Dr Birmingham AL 35216 Office: 6 Office Park Circle Birmingham AL 35223

SANDERS, CHARLES ADDISON, hosp. adminstr., physician; b. Dallas, Feb. 10, 1932; s. Harold Barefoot and May Elizabeth (Forrester) S.; M.D., U. Tex., 1955; m. Elizabeth Ann Chipman, Mar. 6, 1956; children—Elizabeth, Charles Addison, Carlyn, Christopher. Intern, asst. resident Boston City Hosp., 1955-57, chief resident, 1957-58; clin. and research fellow in medicine Mass. Gen. Hosp., Boston, 1958-60, chief cardiac catheterization lab., 1962-72, gen. dir., 1972—, physician, 1973—, program dir. myocardial infarction research unit, 1967-72, program dir. MEDLAB systems, 1969-72. Asso. prof. medicine Harvard, 1969—; lectr. Mass. Inst. Tech., 1973—; dir. Eli Lilly Co., 1st Nat. Boston Corp., New Eng. Life Ins. Co., Mohawk Rubber Co.; mem. vis. com. Sch. Medicine, U. Miami, 1973—; mem. Inst. Medicine, Nat. Acad. Scis.; chmn. Nat. Council Health Care Tech. Bd. dirs. United Way of Mass. Bay; past trustee Mass. Hosp. Assn.; bd. govs. Mass. Tech. Devel. Corp.; dir. Charles Stark Draper Lab., Cambridge, Mass., Avco-Everett Research Lab. Served to capt. M.C., USAF, 1960-62. Mem. Am. Fedn. for Clin. Research, Am., Mass. heart assns., Mass. Med. Soc., A.C.P., Am. Physiol. Soc., Am. Clin. and Climatol. Soc., Am. Coll. Cardiology, Am. Soc. for Clin. Investigation, Soc. Hosp. Adminstrs., Greater Boston C. of C. (dir. 1977—). Unitarian. Club: Harvard. Mem. editorial bd. New Eng. Jour. Medicine, 1969-72. Home: 171 Concord St Wayland MA 01778 Office: Mass Gen Hosp Boston MA 02114

SANDERS, CHARLES LIONEL, educator, mgmt. cons., radio producer; b. Lakeland, Fla., Aug. 10, 1938; s. William A. and Eleather (Jenkins) S.; B.A., Howard U., 1959, M.A., 1961; Ph.D. in Public Adminstrn. (USPHS fellow, Nat. Urban League fellow), N.Y. U., 1972. Adminstrv. dir. St. Luke's Hosp. Center, N.Y.C., 1964-68, v.p., 1974-76; asso. prof., asst. to dean grad. div. Atlanta U., 1970-72; lectr. social work Hunter Coll., N.Y.C., 1970-71, dir. research, adminstrv. cons., 1972-74; scholar-in-residence Inst. Urban Affairs and Research, Howard U., 1976-79, prof. Sch. Social Work, 1979—; sr. asso. Psi Assos., Washington, 1979—; cons. First Nat. City Bank, N.Y.C., 1972, Consol. Edison, N.Y.C., 1973-74, Howard U. Inst. Urban Affairs, 1974-75. Mem. rev. com. Comprehensive Health Planning Bd. Dist. D., N.Y.C., 1974-75, chairperson nat. adv. com. Howard U. Mental Health Research, Devel. Center, 1974—. German Minority Exchange fellow, 1979. Mem. Am. Mgmt. Assn., Nat. Assn. Health Service Execs. (editor newsletter 1972-75), Am. Soc. Pub. Adminstrn. Democrat. Baptist (chmn. budget com. 1973-75). Author: Directory of National Black Organizations, 1972; Black Perceptions of Institutional Racism, 1973; How Black is Big Business, 1977; contbr. articles to profl. jours.; newspaper and radio commentator. Home: 2801 New Mexico Ave NW Washington DC 20007 Office: 1900 L St NW Suite 301 Washington DC 20036

SANDERS, CHARLES LOY, ins. co. exec.; b. Johnstown, Pa., Dec. 23, 1919; s. Charles Loy and Harriet (Shontz) S.; B.A., Princeton, 1941; M.B.A., Harvard, 1943; m. Nancy Jane Cleary, May 1, 1945; children—Judith Lee (Mrs. David Fred Keast), Elizabeth Ann (Mrs. Frank D. Duncan), William Kirby. Accountant, Arthur Andersen & Co., N.Y.C., 1945-50; with Paul Revere Life Ins. Co., Worcester, Mass., 1950—, v.p., 1964, v.p., controller, 1965-68, v.p., controller, treas., 1968—, dir., 1975—; v.p., treas., dir. Paul Revere Variable Annuity Ins. Co., Paul Revere Equity Sales Co., Paul Revere Equity Mgmt. Co., P.R. Realty Corp., P.R. Fin. Corp., P.R. Land Corp.; treas. Paul Revere Investors, Inc. Bd. dirs. Mohegan council Boy Scouts Am., treas. 1955-63, pres., 1964-65; bd. dirs. Worcester Taxpayers Assn., pres. 1970-71; trustee Clark U.; corporator Holden Dist. Hosp. Served to lt. USNR, 1943-45; PTO. Mem. Am. Inst. C.P.A.'s, N.Y. State Soc. C.P.A.'s, Fin. Execs. Inst., Am. Accounting Assn., Nat. Assn. Accountants, Life Office Mgmt. Assn. (past com. chmn.), Phi Beta Kappa. Congregationalist. Mason. Home: 700 Salisbury St Holden MA 01520 Office: 18 Chestnut St Worcester MA 01608

SANDERS, DAVID SCOTT, JR., educator; b. Kellogg, Idaho, June 14, 1926; s. David Scott and Marjorie (Wheat) S.; B.A., U. Calif. at Los Angeles, 1949, M.A., 1953, Ph.D., 1956; m. Mary Frances Finch, Feb. 28, 1948; children—Scott, Bonnie, Peter. Instr. Nordhoff Union High Sch., Ojai, Calif., 1950-52; teaching asst. U. Calif. at Los Angeles, 1953-56; instr. U. Md., 1956-59; asst. prof. Harvey Mudd Coll., 1959-63, asso. prof., 1963-69, prof., 1969-70, 73—, prof., chmn. dept. humanities 1973-77; prof., chmn. dept humanities Clarkson Coll. Tech., Potsdam, N.Y., 1970-73. Served with USNR, 1944-46. Mem. Modern Lang. Assn., Am. Studies Assn., Am. Soc. Engring. Edn. (chmn. liberal studies div. 1970-71). Democrat. Author: John Hersey, 1967. Home: 1630 Rutgers Ct Claremont CA 91711

SANDERS, FREDERICK, meteorologist; b. Detroit, May 17, 1923; s. Frederick William and Dorothy Gail (Martin) S.; B.A., Amherst Coll., 1944; Sc.D., M.I.T., 1954; m. Nancy Seabury Brown, Nov. 30, 1946; children—Christopher Martin, John Arnold, Frederick Duncan. Forecaster, U.S. Weather Bur., N.Y.C., 1947-49; teaching asst. M.I.T., 1949-51, asst. prof. meteorology, 1956-59, asso. prof., 1959-69, prof., 1969—; cons. in field. Served with USAAF, 1942-46. Recipient award for applied research Nat. Weather Assn., 1978; NSF grantee, 1958—; NOAA grantee, 1956-78; Office Naval Research grantee, 1979—; USAF grantee, 1954-78. Fellow Am. Meteorol. Soc.; mem. Royal Meteorol. Soc.. (fgn.). Club: Eastern Yacht (Marblehead, Mass.). Author: (with H.C. Willett) Descriptive Meteorology, 1955; contbr. numerous articles to profl. jours. Home: 9 Flint St Marblehead MA 01945 Office: Room 54-1612 MIT 77 Massachusetts Ave Cambridge MA 02139

SANDERS, GEOFFREY PETER, cabinet mfg. and supply co. exec.; b. London, Eng., July 5, 1920; s. Stanley Singleton and Catherine (Collins) S.; came to U.S., 1921, naturalized, 1946; B.A., Drexel U., 1943; m. Ann Franklin, Oct. 19, 1945; children—Elizabeth Ann (Mrs. James Bullock), Gwendolyn Joy, Geoffrey Franklin, Kenneth Dean. With RCA, 1944-70, exec. v.p. RCA Victor Argentina, Buenos Aires, 1959-62, v.p., treas. RCA Sales Corp., also controller consumer electronics div., treas. RCA Distbg. Corp., Indpls., 1966-69; controller Ducommun, Inc., Los Angeles, 1970-79; pres. Total Living Cabinet Co., San Marcos, Calif. Pres. Ind. Tax Payers Assn., 1969, dir., 1968, 69. Recipient mgr. of improvement award Internat. Work Simplification Inst., 1969. Mem. Fin. Execs. Inst. (treas. Indpls. chpt. 1969, dir. 1968, 69), Theta Chi. Club: Woodland Hills (Calif.) Country (treas., dir. 1975-79, pres. 1977). Home: 7241 Esfera St Carlsbad CA 92008 Office: 1405 Descanso Ave San Marcos CA 92069

SANDERS, HARLAND, food franchising co. exec.; b. nr. Henryville, Ind., Sept. 9, 1890; ed. grammar sch.; m. Claudia Ledington, Nov. 17, 1948; 3 children from previous marriage. Operator gas sta., then restaurant Sanders' Cafe, Corbin, Ky., 1929-56; began franchise operations Ky. Fried Chicken, 1956, owner, 1956-64, now ambassador good will. Active various charities. Named Ky. col., 1936. Recipient Horatio Alger award, 1965. Address: KFC Corp PO Box 32070 Louisville KY 40232

SANDERS, HAROLD BAREFOOT, JR., judge; b. Dallas, Feb. 5, 1925; s. Harold Barefoot and May Elizabeth (Forrester) S.; B.A., U. Tex., 1949, LL.B., 1950; m. Jan Scurlock, June 6, 1952; children—Janet Lea, Martha Kay, Mary Frances, Harold Barefoot III. Admitted to Tex. bar, 1950; asso. firm Storey, Sanders, Sherrill & Armstrong, Dallas, 1950-52; partner firm Sanders & Sanders, 1951-61; U.S. atty. No. Dist. Tex., 1961-65; asst. dep. atty. gen. U.S., 1965-66, asst. atty. gen., 1966-67; legis. counsel to President U.S., 1967-69; partner firm Clark, West, Keller, Sanders & Butler, Dallas, 1969-79; U.S. dist. judge for No. Dist. Tex., Dallas, 1979—. Mem. Tex. Ho. of Reps., 1952-58; Democratic nominee for Congress, 1958, for U.S. Senate, 1972. Served to lt. (j.g.) USNR, World War II. Mem. Am., Fed. (dir. nat. council 1963-66; Distinguished Service award Dallas 1964), Dallas (dir.) bar assns., State Bar Tex., Tex. Ex-Students Assn. (pres. Dallas 1955-56, pres. Washington chpt. 1968-69), Blue Key, Phi Delta Phi, Phi Delta Theta. Methodist. Mason. Club: Chaparral (Dallas). Home: 7326 Malabar Dallas TX 75230 Office: US Courthouse 1100 Commerce St Dallas TX 75242

SANDERS, HOWARD, investment co. exec.; b. Phila., June 30, 1941; s. Louis and Freda (Liss) S.; B.S. in Accounting, Temple U., 1962; M.Accounting, Ohio State U., 1963; m. Dale Rosenberg, Dec. 15, 1963; children—Lee Michael, Kimberly Joy. Accountant, Price, Waterhouse & Co., Phila., 1962-65; asst. prof. accounting Temple U., 1965-72; v.p. Revere Fund, Inc., Phila., 1966-76; pres. Revere Mgmt. Co., Inc., Phila., 1966-72, chmn. bd. Ladies Center of Nebr., Inc., 1976—, Volk Footwear and Findings Co., 1977-78, Mister Plywood Enterprises, Inc., 1970—; pres. Sanders Fin. Mgmt., Inc., Fort Lauderdale, 1972—; chmn. bd. Am. Carpet Backing Distbg. Inc., 1978—; dir. P.K.'s Italian Kitchens. Mem. adv. bd. Phila. Assn. for Retarded Children 1970-72; chmn. bd. Women's Med. Center of Providence, Inc., 1977—, Women's Med. Center of North Jersey, Inc., 1977—, Women's Med. Center of Atlanta, Inc., 1977—, Cherry Hill Women's Center, Inc., 1978—, Metairie Women's Center of New Orleans, Inc. Kaiser Aluminum and Chem. Co. fellow in accounting, 1962-63. C.P.A. Mem. Am., Pa. (award for paper 1961), insts. C.P.A.'s, Phila. Jr. C. of C. (dir. 1966), Nat. Assn. Accountants, B'rith Shalom Assn., Beta Gamma Sigma, Beta Alpha Psi, Tau Epsilon Phi. Contbg. author: How to Start a Mutual Fund, 1970. Home and Office: 9181 NW 24th Ct Fort Lauderdale FL 33322. *My life has been guided by careful attention to words which are rapidly disappearing from the "Dictionary of American Ways." I have concentrated on integrity, prudence, brevity, clarity, ego control and true friendship. In all dealings I insist upon mutual benefit, taking great effort to assure that the opposite party receives a slightly larger gain.*

SANDERS, IRWIN TAYLOR, educator; b. Millersburg, Ky., Jan. 17, 1909; s. Robert Stuart and Lucy (Taylor) S.; student Tenn. Mil. Inst., 1920-25; A.B., Washington and Lee U., 1929; student Theol. Sem., Princeton, 1932-33; Ph.D., Cornell U., 1938; m. Margaret Rydberg, June 23, 1934; children—Gerda S. (Dymsza), Robert Stuart. Instr. American Coll., Sofia, Bulgaria, 1929-32, dean, 1934-37; asst. prof. sociology Ala. Coll., 1938-40; successively asst. prof., asso. prof., prof., head dept. sociology, distinguished univ. prof. U. Ky., 1940-56; lectr. sociology Harvard Sch. Pub. Health, 1958-62; chmn. dept. sociology and anthropology Boston U., 1960-63, 69-72, prof. sociology, 1972—, Univ. lectr., 1973-74, also co-dir. community sociology tng. program; research dir. Assos. Internat. Research, Inc., Cambridge, Mass., 1956-60; asso. dir. Internat. Tng. and Research Program, Ford Found., 1962-66; v.p. Edn. and World Affairs, 1967-69; social science analyst Bur. Agrl. Econ., U.S. Dept. Agr., summer 1943, sr. social scientist Office Fgn. Agrl. Relations, 1943, social sci. Extension Service, summer 1944; agrl. attaché Am. embassy, Belgrade, Yugoslavia, 1945-46; research asso. Harvard, 1952-53. Dir. Roanoke Paint & Glass Co. (Va.), Sanders Bros., Inc., Richmond, Va. Cons. rural welfare division FAO. Bd. dirs. Am. Farm Sch., Thessalonika, Greece, Sofia Am. Schs., Inc., Assn. for Study Southeastern Europe, Bucharest, Rumania; mem. council Polish-Am. Inst. Arts and Scis. Decorated Royal Order of Phoenix (Greece). Mem. Am., So. (pres. 1955-56) sociol. socs., Am. Anthrop. Assn., Rural Sociol. Soc. (pres. 1956-57), Soc. Applied Anthropology, Am. Assn. Advancement Slavic Studies, Bulgarian-Am. Studies Assn., Modern Greek Studies Assn., Société Européone de Culture (Venice), Bulgarian Acad. Scis. (fgn. mem.), Phi Beta Kappa, Omicron Delta Kappa, Kappa Phi Kappa, Delta Sigma Rho, Delta Upsilon. Democrat. Presbyterian. Club: Cornell (N.Y.). Author: Balkan Village, 1949; co-author: Alabama Rural Communities, 1940; Sociological Foundations of Education, 1942; Kentucky: Designs for Her Future, 1944; Farmers of the World, 1945; Making Good Communities Better, 1950; The Community, 1958, 3d edit., 1975; Rainbow in the Rock; People of Rural Greece, 1962; Bridges to Understanding: International Programs at U.S. Colleges and Universities, 1970; Rural Society, 1977. Editor: Societies Around the World, 1953; Collectivization of Agriculture in Eastern Europe, 1958; The Professional School and World Affairs, 1968. Home: 400 School St Wellesley MA 02181 Office: 96 Cummington St Boston MA 02215

SANDERS, JAMES ALVIN, educator, clergyman; b. Memphis, Nov. 28, 1927; s. Robert E. and Sue (Black) S.; B.A. magna cum laude, Vanderbilt U., 1948, B.D. with honors, 1951; student Ecole des Hautes Etudes, U. Paris, 1950-51; Ph.D., Hebrew Union Coll., 1955; D. Litt., Acadia U., 1973; S.T.D., U. Glasgow, 1975; m. Dora Cargille, June 30, 1951; 1 son, Robin David. Ordained teacher Presbyn. Ch., 1955; instr. French, Vanderbilt U., 1948-49; faculty Colgate Rochester Div. Sch., 1954-65; asso. prof., 1957-60, Joseph B. Hoyt prof. O.T. interpretation, 1960-65; prof. O.T., Union Theol. Sem. N.Y.C., 1965-70, Auburn prof. Bibl. studies, 1970-77; adj. prof. Columbia, N.Y.C., 1966-77; Elizabeth Hay Bechtal prof. Bibl. studies Sch. Theology and Grad. Sch., Claremont, Calif., 1977—, ann. prof. Jerusalem Sch. of Am. Schs. Oriental Research, 1961-62; fellow Ecumenical Inst., Jerusalem, 1972-73; Ayer lectr., 1971; Shaffer lectr., 1972; Fondren lectr., 1975; Currie lectr., 1976. Mem. internat. O.T. text critical com. United Bible Socs., 1969—; exec. officer Ancient Bibl. Manuscript Center for Preservation and Research, 1977—. Trustee Am. Schs. Oriental Research, Fulbright grantee, 1950-51; Lefkowitz and Rabinowitz interfaith fellow, 1951-53; Rockefeller fellow, 1953-54; Guggenheim fellow, 1961-62, 72-73. Mem. Soc. Bibl. Lit. and Exegesis (pres. 1977-78), Phi Beta Kappa, Phi Sigma Iota, Theta Chi Beta. Author: Suffering as Divine Discipline in the Old Testament and Post-Biblical Judaism, 1955; The Old Testament in the Cross, 1961; The Psalms Scroll of Qumran Cave 11, 1965; The Dead Sea Psalms Scroll, 1967; Near Eastern Archaeology in the Twentieth Century, 1970; Torah and Canon, 1972, 74; Identite' de la Bible, 1975; God Has a Story Too, 1979; also numerous articles. Mem. editorial bd. Jour. Bibl. Lit., Interpretation, Jour. for Study Judaism. Office: Sch Theology Claremont CA 91711

SANDERS, JOE WILLIAM, chief state justice; b. Pleasant Hill, La., May 31, 1915; s. Oliver Lud and Ozie (Allen) S.; B.A., La. State U., 1935, LL.B., 1938; LL.D., William Mitchell Coll. Law, 1938; m. Marie Sistrunk, Oct. 26, 1940. Admitted to La. bar, 1938; pvt. practice, many, 1938-42, Baton Rouge, 1946-54; judge Family Ct. Parish E. Baton Rouge, 1954-60; asso. justice Supreme Ct. La., 1960-73, chief justice, 1973—. Chmn. E. Baton Rouge Parish Juvenile Commn., 1951-54; chmn. Blue Ridge Tng. Inst. So. Juvenile Ct Judges, 1957, mem. adv. council judges Nat. Council Crime and Delinquency, 1955-75. Mem. La. Ho. of Reps. from Sabine Parish, 1940-44; del. La. Democratic Conv., 1940, Nat. Dem. Conv., 1952. Bd. dirs. Baton Rouge YMCA, 1952-55, 58-61. Served to capt. AUS, 1942-46. Mem. Am., La. bar assns., Conf. Chief Justices, Am. Judicature Soc., La. Jud. Council, La. State U. Found., Am. Legion, Amvets (past post comdr.), V.F.W., Am. Law Inst., Order of Coif, Phi Kappa Phi, Omicron Delta Kappa, Gamma Eta Gamma, Pi Sigma Alpha, Pi Gamma Mu, Theta Xi. Mason, Woodman of World. Home: 1725 S Tamarix Baton Rouge LA 70808 Office: 301 Loyola Ave New Orleans LA 70112

SANDERS, JOHN LASSITER, univ. adminstr.; b. Four Oaks, N.C., June 30, 1927; s. David Hardy and Louie Jane (Lassiter) S.; A.B., U. N.C., Chapel Hill, 1950, J.D., 1954; m. Ann Beal, Aug. 14, 1954; children—Tracy Elizabeth, Jane Nesbit, William Hardy. Admitted to N.C. bar, 1955; law clk. to judge U.S. Ct. Appeals, 1954-55; pvt. practice, Raleigh, 1955-56; mem. faculty Inst. Govt., U. N.C., Chapel Hill, 1956—, dir., 1962-73, 79—, v.p. planning at univ., 1973-78. Served with USNR, 1945-46. Mem. N.C. Bar Assn. Democrat. Baptist. Home: 1107 Sourwood Dr Chapel Hill NC 27514 Office: PO Box 990 Chapel Hill NC 27514

SANDERS, JOHN R., profl. football exec.; b. San Antonio, July 26, 1922; s. Ira William and Johnnie Laurie (Manning) S.; B.A., Occidental Coll., 1949; m. Margaret Jean Werner, July 6, 1946; 2 children. Head football coach North Hollywood (Calif.) High Sch., 1952-58; dir. athletics, football coach U.S. Grant High Sch., Van Nuys, Calif., 1959-63; dir. player personnel Los Angeles Rams, 1964-75, asst. gen. mgr., 1967-75; asst. to pres. San Diego Chargers, 1975, gen. mgr., 1976—. Served with USN, 1943-46. Republican. Baptist. Office: care San Diego Chargers PO Box 20666 San Diego CA 92120*

SANDERS, JOSEPH STANLEY, lawyer; b. Los Angeles, Aug. 9, 1942; s. Hays and Eva (Cook) S.; B.A., Whittier Coll., 1963; B.A., M.A. (Rhodes scholar), Magdalen Coll., Oxford U., 1965; LL.B., Yale, 1968; m. Phyllis Moore, Sept. 2, 1966; children—Edward Moore, Justin Hays. Dir. summer projects Westminster Neighborhood Assn., Los Angeles, 1966-67; dir. pro tem, instr. polit. sci. Yale U. Transitional Year, 1967-68; admitted to Calif. bar, 1969; staff atty. Western Center on Law and Poverty, Los Angeles, 1968-69; exec. dir. Lawyers Com. for Civil Rights Under Law, Los Angeles, 1969-70; asso. law firm Wyman, Bautzer, Finell, Rothman & Kuchel, Beverly Hills, Calif., 1969-71; partner Rosenfeld, Lederer, Jacobs & Sanders, Beverly Hills, 1971-72; partner Sanders & Tisdale, Los Angeles, 1972—. Co-founder Watts Summer Festival, 1966; co-chmn. Whittier Coll. Alumni Fund, 1970-71; mem. Yale Law Alumni Com. on Curriculum Reform, 1970; coordinator Calif. Conf. Black Attys., 1969; chmn. membership drive Dist. 8, Boy Scouts Am., Los Angeles, 1971; mem. Los Angeles World Affairs Council, 1970-74, Com. on Fgn. Affairs, 1971-75. Bd. dirs. West Los Angeles United Way, 1970, Black Arts Council, Econ. Resources Corp.; trustee Center for Law in Pub. Interest, Los Angeles, Whittier Coll. Recipient Ten Outstanding Young Men of Am. award, 1971. Mem. Langston Law Club, Los Angeles County Bar Assn. Mason. Home: 852 S Hauser Ave Los Angeles CA 90036 Office: 5900 Wilshire Blvd Los Angeles CA 90036

SANDERS, LAWRENCE, author; b. Bklyn., 1920; B.A., Wabash Coll., 1940. Staff mem. Macy's Dept. Store, N.Y.C., 1940-43; editor and writer of stories for various mags., editor Mechanix Illus., Sci. and Mechanics, free-lance writer for men's mags., 1946-68; novelist, 1969—; author: The Anderson Tapes, 1970; The Pleasures of Helen, 1971; Love Songs, 1972; The First Deadly Sin, 1973; The Tomorrow File, 1975; The Tangent Objective, 1976; The Marlow Chronicles, 1977; The Second Deadly Sin, 1977; The Tangent Factor, 1978; The Sixth Commandment, 1979. Served as sgt. USMC, 1943-46. Recipient Edgar award Mystery Writers Am., 1970. Office: care GP Putnam's Sons 200 Madison Ave New York NY 10016*

SANDERS, LEONARD MARION, JR., author; b. Denver, Jan. 15, 1929; s. Leonard Marion and Jacqueline (Thomas) S.; student U. Okla., 1946-49, 51, 54, 57; m. Florene Lovette Cooter, Aug. 21, 1956. Mem. staff Enid (Okla.) News-Eagle, 1949; mem. staff Daily Oklahoman, 1950-51; mng. editor Okla. Publisher, 1954; mem. staff Wichita Falls (Tex.) Record-News, 1954-56; mem. staff Norman (Okla.) Transcript, 1957; mem. staff Ft. Worth Star-Telegram, 1958-79, fine arts editor, book page editor, 1964-79. Served with USNR, 1952-53. Mem. Authors Guild, Western Writers of Am., Sci. Fiction Writers Am., Mystery Writers Am., Tex. Inst. Letters. Author: Four-Year Hitch, 1961; The Wooden Horseshoe, 1964; The Seed (pseudonym Dan Thomas), 1968; How Fort Worth Became the Texasmost City, 1973; The Marshal of Stud Horse Flats, 1975; The Hamlet Warning, 1976; The Hamlet Ultimatum, 1979. Home: 4200 Clayton Rd W Fort Worth TX 76116 Office: 400 W 7th St Fort Worth TX 76101

SANDERS, MARLENE, TV corr./producer; b. Cleve., Jan. 10, 1931; d. Mac and Evelyn R. (Fisher) S.; student Ohio State U., 1948-50; m. Jerome Toobin, May 27, 1958; children—Jeff, Mark. Writer, producer Sta. WNEW-TV, N.Y.C., 1955-60, P.M. program Westinghouse Broadcasting Co., N.Y.C., 1961-62; asst. dir. news and public affairs Sta. WNEW, N.Y.C., 1962-64; news corr. ABC, 1964-71, documentary producer, 1971-76; v.p., dir. TV documentaries ABC News, 1976-78; corr./producer CBS Reports, 1978—. Recipient award N.Y. State Broadcasters Assn., 1976, Nat. Press Club, 1976, others. Mem. Am. Women in Radio and TV (Woman of Yr. award 1975, Silver Satellite award 1977), Women in Communications (past pres.), Women's Forum, Assn. Radio and TV Analysts, Sigma Delta Chi. Office: CBS News 524 W 57th St New York NY 10019

SANDERS, MURRAY JONATHAN, physician, med. research inst. exec.; b. Chelsea, Mass., Apr. 11, 1910; s. Louis and Rose (Gould) S.; B.S., Tufts Coll., 1931; student (scholar) Heidelberg (Germany) U., 1929; M.D., U. Chgo., 1936; m. Margaret Weatherly, Dec. 19, 1959; children—Frank Weatherly, Andrea Joan, Murray Jonathan. Asst., Office Coroner Cook County, Chgo., 1936; asst. pathology U. Chgo. Rush Med. Coll., 1936; rotating intern Evanston (Ill.) Gen. Hosp., 1936-38; Oliver Rea scholar Columbia Coll. Phys. and Surg., N.Y.C., 1938-40, instr. bacteriology, 1940-41, asst. prof., 1941-45, asso. prof., 1945-47; prof. bacteriology U. Miami, Coral Gables, Fla., 1948-52; research prof., dir. dept. microbiology U. Miami, South Miami, Fla., 1952-60; med. dir., v.p. Pan Am. Pharms., Inc., Ft. Lauderdale, Fla., 1960-62; founder, med. dir. Sanders Med. Research Found., Delray Beach, Fla., 1971—; cons. pathology N.Y.C. Dept. Hosp., Harlem Hosp., N.Y.C., 1947—; dir. research Variety Children's Hosp., Miami, 1952-53; cons. Nat. Children's Cardiac Hosp., Miami, 1950-55, Blood Plasma Corp. Japan, Osaka, 1950—; hon. med. staff, cons. Guam Meml. Hosp., Agana, 1950-57; chmn. dept. biol. scis. Fla. Atlantic U., 1962-65; med. dir., v.p. Gray Industries, Inc., Gray Research Found. Trustee Palm Beach Atlantic Coll. Served from maj. to lt. col., M.C., AUS, 1940-46; staff officer Gen. MacArthur, 1944-45; cons. Sec. of War, also mem. commn. neurotropic virus disease Bd. Investigation and Control Influenza and Other Epidemic Diseases in Army, 1942-46. Decorated Legion of Merit, D.S.M.; commendation Med. Intelligence Service, Gen. Eisenhower, 1946; nominee medicine Nobel Prize, 1966; mem. Outstanding Citizen Assn., Miami. Fellow Royal Soc. Health (Eng.), AAAS, N.Y. Acad. Scis. (life), N.Y. Acad. Medicine; mem. Am. Assn. Pathologists and Bacteriologists, Soc. Exptl. Biology and Medicine, Am., Fla. pub. health assns., Am. Fedn. Clin. Research, Soc. Am. Bacteriologists, Internat. Soc. Transfusion, Am. Assn. Blood Banks, Tissue Culture Assn., So. Med. Assn., Fla. Acad. Scis., Sociedad Cubana de Salubridad Publica (corr.), Ret. Officers Assn., Sigma Xi. Club: Cosmos (Washington). Editor: Jour. Indsl. Medicine; editor proc. Internat. Symposium Med. and Applied Virology, 1966; editor Modern Concepts, Med. Virology, Oncology and Cytology, 1966. Contbr. articles and chpts. to profl. publs. Home: 3009 Spanish Trail Delray Beach FL 33444 Office: 33 SE 3d St Boca Raton FL 33432

SANDERS, NORMAN O., lawyer; b. Kansas City, Mo., Jan. 22, 1931; s. William O. and Gertrude V. (Devine) S.; B.A., U. Mo., Kansas City, 1958, LL.B., 1958; m. Shirley Ann Stasi, May 9, 1953; children—Debra, Craig, Patrick, Brian, Stacy. Admitted to Mo. bar, 1957; practice in Kansas City, 1957—; asso. firm Popham, Popham, Conway, Sweeny & Fremont, 1957-60, Pew, Taylor, Welch & Sheridan, 1960-61; partner firm Sheridan, Baty, Markey, Sanders & Edwards, 1961-66; sr. partner firm Sheridan, Sanders & Simpson, 1966—; cons., atty. Kansas City Area Transp. Authority, 1971—; legal adviser Kansas City Youth Ct., 1963-69. Pres., De La Salle Ednl. Center, 1972-77, chmn., 1977—; pres. Kansas City Legal Aid and Defender Soc., 1971-72, bd. dirs., 1969—; pres. Bros. Boys Assn., 1964-77; mem. Mayors Prayer Breakfast Com., 1962—, pres., 1971; bd. dirs. U. Mo. at Kansas City Law Found., 1971—, pres., 1975-78; trustee U. Mo., Kansas City, 1975-78. Recipient Lon O. Hocker Trial Lawyer award Mo. Bar, 1965; Outstanding Alumni award De La Salle Alumni Assn., 1972. Mem. U. Mo. at Kansas City Law Sch. Alumni Assn. (pres. 1971), Phi Alpha Delta. Roman Catholic. Club: Kansas City. Home: 9400 Jarboe St Kansas City MO 64114 Office: Sheridan Sanders & Simpson Traders Bank Bldg 1125 Grand Ave Kansas City MO 64114

SANDERS, OLIVER PAUL, univ. adminstr.; b. Caney, Okla., Dec. 26, 1924; s. Ernest Dillon and Effie Anna (Alford) S.; B.A., Southeastern State Coll., 1947; M.S., Okla. State U., 1949, Ph.D., 1956; m. Virginia Lee Frederick, Apr. 1, 1945; children—Stephen Paul, Gina Karin. Asst. prof. Southeastern State Coll., 1949-54; instr. Okla. State U., 1954-56; asso. prof. La. Poly. Inst., 1956-59; prof. Hardin-Simmons U., 1959-62, chmn. math. dept., 1959-62; prof. Appalachian State U., Boone, N.C., 1962—, chmn. math. dept., 1962-65, dean, 1965-68, provost, 1968-70, v.p., from 1970, now prof. math. scis., vice chancellor acad. affairs. Served with AUS, 1943-46. Mem. Math. Assn. Am. Author: Elementary Mathematics: A Logical Approach, 1963. Home: Route 3 Box 337-B Boone NC 28607

SANDERS, PAUL HAMPTON, lawyer, educator, arbitrator; b. Sherman, Tex., Feb. 26, 1909, s. Jewell Richard and Louisa Jane (Gaskill) S.; A.B., Austin Coll., 1931, LL.D., 1960; J.D., Duke, 1934; m. Pauline Cameron, Feb. 23, 1935. Admitted to Tex. bar, 1934, Ga. bar, 1944, N.C. bar, 1946, Tenn. bar, 1951; practiced with Leo Brewer, San Antonio, 1934; asst. to dir. of nat. bar program Am. Bar Assn., Chgo., 1934-36; asst. prof. law Duke U., 1936-40, asso. prof. law, 1940-45, prof. law, 1946—; practiced with firm of Wilson and Sanders, Atlanta, 1946-47; vis. prof. law Sch. Jurisprudence, U. Calif. at Berkeley, 1947-48; prof. law Vanderbilt U., 1948—; regional atty. U.S. Dept. of Labor, 1951-53; prin. mediation officer Nat. War Labor Bd., Washington, 1942, regional atty., hdqrs. Atlanta, 1942-44, regional vice chmn., Atlanta, 1944; regional atty. Nat. Wage Stblzn. Bd., Atlanta, 1946; cons. Fed. Civil Rights Commn., 1958-61; dir. Race Relations Law Reporter, 1955-59; apptd. mem. bd. inquiry, labor disputes in atomic energy installations, Oak Ridge, also Ky.; pub. mem., chmn. Industry Com. on Minimum Wages, Puerto Rico, 1950, 56-58, 60-61, 63, 67, 69, 71, 73, 75, 77; apptd. mem. various Presdl. emergency boards to consider labor disputes. Indsl. relations specialist, 12th Naval Dist., San Francisco, 1944-46; lt. USNR, 1945-53. Mem. Am. Bar Assn. (council mem., sec. labor relations sect. 1949-52), Am. Law Inst. (life), Nat. Acad. Arbitrators (regional chmn. Southeastern states 1968-74), Am. Arbitration Assn. (labor panel), Conf. Personal Fin. Law, Nat. Conf. Jud. Councils, Soc. Profls. in Dispute Resolution, Scholarship Soc. S., Order of Coif, Pi Gamma Mu, Phi Delta Phi. Democrat. Baptist (vice chmn. Christian Life Commn., So. Bapt. Conv. 1953-59). Club: University (Nashville). Asso. editor: Law and Contemporary Problems, 1937-46. Editor symposia on Unauthorized Practice of Law, The Wage and Hour Law, Governmental Tort Liability, Alcoholic Beverage Control, Combating the Loan Shark, Labor in Wartime and Labor Dispute Settlement, all in Law and Contemporary Problems, Duke Univ., 1938-46; also contbr. to Am. Bar Assn. Jour., Law and Contemporary Problems, U. Calif. Law Rev., Vanderbilt Law Rev. Home: 664 Timber Ln Nashville TN 37215. *My primary interests as a law teacher and arbitrator have centered in systematic study of the processes of dispute settlement and conflict resolution, particularly in the labor relations field. This reflects a conviction that building "community" is the essence of civilization and that there needs to be individual and group commitment to understanding and utilizing the arts of peaceful accomodation. Social conflict is as inevitable as change. All too frequently, however, we show that we have not learned to distinguish, and maintain the proper balance, between the productive and counterproductive aspects of such conflict.*

SANDERS, RICHARD KINARD, actor; b. Harrisburg, Pa., Aug. 23, 1940; s. Henry Irvine and Thelma Elizabeth (Williamson) S.; B.F.A., Carnegie Inst. Tech., 1962; postgrad. (Fulbright scholar) London Acad. Music and Dramatic Art, 1962-63. Mem. various acting cos.; Front St., Memphis, Champlain Shakespeare Festival, Vt., Center Stage, Balt., N.Y. Shakespeare Festival, N.Y.C., Chelsea Theater Center, N.Y.C., Mark Taper Forum, Los Angeles, Arena Stage, Washington; appeared on Broadway in Raisin; now regular (Les Nessman) on CBS-TV series WKRP in Cincinnati, also writer, 1978-80; numerous TV appearances; pres. Blood Star, Inc.; vol. Peace Corps, Northeastern Brazil, 1966-69. Recipient Buckeye Newshawk award, 1974-79, Silver Sow award, 1979. Mem. Writers Guild Am., Screen Actors Guild, AFTRA, Actors Equity Assn. Methodist. Address: care Twentieth Century Artists 13273 Ventura Blvd Suite 211 Los Angeles CA 91604 also care WKRP in Cincinnati CBS-TV 7800 Beverly Blvd Los Angeles CA 90036

SANDERS, RONALD, author; b. Union City, N.J., July 7, 1932; s. George Harry and Rose (Rachlin) S.; B.A. summa cum laude, Kenyon Coll., 1954; M.A., Columbia, 1957; m. Beverly Helen Gingold, Mar. 19, 1967. Lectr. history Queens Coll., Flushing, N.Y., 1958-65; asso. editor Midstream mag., N.Y.C., 1965-73, editor, 1973-75. Served with AUS, 1953-55. Fulbright fellow, France, 1960-61; recipient B'nai B'rith Book award, 1970. Jewish. Author: Israel: The View from Masada, 1966; The Downtown Jews, 1969; Reflections on a Tea Pot, 1972; Lost Tribes and Promised Lands, 1978; The Days Grow Short: The Life and Music of Kurt Weill, 1980; co-editor: Socialist Thought: A Documentary History, 1964. Home: 49 W 12th St New York NY 10011

SANDERS, TERRY BENTLEY, JR., chem. co. exec.; b. Memphis, Nov. 18, 1917; s. Terry Bentley and Anna Virginia (Lighter) S.; A.B., Yale, 1939; M.A., Fletcher Sch. Law and Diplomacy, 1940; postgrad. U. Mich., 1951-52; m. Zora Elizabeth Barnes, Apr. 8, 1942; children—Terry, Christie. Vice consul, Colombia, 1940, Puerto de la Cruz, Venezuela, 1941, Managua, Nicaragua, 1942; fgn. service officer, sec. Diplomatic Service, 1942, 3d sec., vice consul, Managua, 1942, Mexico City, Mexico, 1943, London, Eng., 1944; 3d sec., vice consul, Ottawa, Ont., Can., 1946, 2d sec., consul, 1948; consul, Seville, Spain, 1949, Barcelona, Spain, 1950; first sec., Manila, 1952; spl. asst. to asst. sec. of state for pub. affairs, 1954; dep. dir. Office S. Am. Affairs, 1956-58; Nat. War Coll., 1958-59; counselor of embassy, New Delhi, India, 1959, Rangoon, 1960, Rome, Italy, 1961; minister for econ. affairs, dir. AID Mission, Buenos Aires, 1962; minister, polit. adviser Supreme Allied Comdr. Atlantic, also comdr.-in-chief U.S. Forces Atlantic, Norfolk, Va., 1965-68; country dir. Panamanian Affairs, Dept. State, from 1968—; now sr. advisor pub. affairs Pfizer Inc., N.Y.C. Mem. U.S. bus. and industry adv. com. OECD. Mem. Internat. C. of C. (comml. policy com. U.S. council), U.S. C. of C. (panel on fgn. trade policy), Atlantic Council, N.A.M. (mem. internat. econ. policy com.), Phi Beta Kappa. Home: 45 Greenway Terr Princeton NJ 08540 Office: Pfizer Inc 235 E 42d St New York NY 10017

SANDERS, THOMAS ALFRED, JR., banker; b. Winston-Salem, N.C., Jan. 12, 1931; s. Thomas Alfred and Sallie (Lentz) S.; B.S. in Bus. Adminstrn., U. N.C., Chapel Hill, 1953; m. Betty Ruth Smith, Dec. 28, 1950; children—Carl Smith, Steven Adam. Jr. auditor A.M. Pullen Co., Winston-Salem, N.C., 1953-54; mgr. T.A. Sanders Constrn. Co. Winston-Salem, 1954-56; with Wachovia Bank & Trust Co., N.A., also Wachovia Corp., Winston-Salem, 1956—, sr. v.p. finance, 1972—; dir. Lentz Transfer & Storage Co. Mem. Tax Execs. Inst. Presbyterian. Home: 1625 Pembroke Ave Winston-Salem NC 27103 Office: 301 N Main St Winston-Salem NC 27101

SANDERS, W(ILLIAM) EUGENE, JR., physician, educator; b. Frederick, Md., June 25, 1934; s. W(illiam) Eugene and E. Gertrude (Wilburn) S.; A.B., Cornell U., 1956, M.D., 1960; m. Christine Culp, Feb. 22, 1974. Intern, Johns Hopkins Hosp., Balt., 1960-61, resident, 1961-62; instr. medicine Emory U. Sch. Medicine, Atlanta, 1962-64; chief med. resident, instr. U. Fla. Coll. Medicine, Gainesville, 1964-65, asst. prof. medicine and microbiology, 1965-69, asso. prof., 1969-72; prof., chmn. dept. med. microbiology, prof. medicine Creighton U. Sch. Medicine, Omaha, 1972—; cons.-in-research Fla. Dept. Health and Rehab. Services, 1966—. Served as med. officer USPHS, 1962-64. Recipient NIH Research Career Devel. award, 1968-72. John and Mary R. Markle scholar in acad. medicine, 1968-73. Diplomate Am. Bd. Internal Medicine. Mem. Am. Soc. for Microbiology, Infectious Diseases Soc. Am., Soc. for Epidemiol. Research, Am. Lung Assn., Thoracic Soc., N.Y. Acad. Scis., Phi Beta Kappa, Sigma Xi, Phi Kappa Phi. Asso. editor: Am. Jour. of Epidemiology, 1974—. Contbr. sci. articles to profl. jours. Patentee enocin antibiotic. Home: 3000 Farnam St Apt 7C Omaha NE 68131 Office: Creighton U Sch Medicine Omaha NE 68178. *Each day provides more challenges and more opportunities than the preceding. No individual can possibly cope with each of these in any given day. Success depends upon establishing priorities and maintaining them. Fight only those battles and pursue with fervor only those opportunities that improve both one's self and one's fellow man.*

SANDERS, WALTER JEREMIAH, III, electronics co. exec.; b. Chgo., Sept. 12, 1936; s. Walter J. and Kathleen (Finn) S.; B.E.E., U. Ill., 1958; m. Linda Lee Drobman, Nov. 13, 1965; children—Tracy Ellen, Lara Whitney, Alison Ashley. Design engr. Douglas Aircraft Co., Santa Monica, Calif., 1958-59; applications engr. Motorola, Inc., Phoenix, 1959-60, sales engr. 1960-61; with Fairchild Camera & Instrument Co., 1961-69, dir. mktg., Mountain View, Calif., 1961-68, group dir. mktg. worldwide, 1968-69; pres., chmn. bd., chief exec. officer Advanced Micro Devices, Inc., Sunnyvale, Calif., 1969—; dir. Donaldson, Lufkin & Jenrette. Mem. Semicondr. Industry Assn. (co-founder, dir.). Office: 901 Thompson Pl Sunnyvale CA 94086

SANDERS, WILLIAM EVAN, bishop; b. Natchez, Miss., Dec. 25, 1919; s. Walter Richard and Agnes Mortimer (Jones) S.; B.A., Vanderbilt U., 1942; B.D., U. of South, 1945, D.D., 1959; S.T.M., Union Theol. Sem., 1946; m. Kathryn Cowan Schaffer, June 25, 1951; 4 children. Curate St. Paul's Episcopal Ch., Chattanooga, 1945-46; asst. St. Mary's Cathedral, Memphis, 1946-48, dean, 1948-62; bishop coadjutor Tenn., Knoxville, after 1962, now bishop. Address: PO Box 3807 Knoxville TN 37917*

SANDERS, WILLIAM GEORGE, editor; b. Sacramento, Jan. 11, 1932; s. Samuel S. and Alice M. (Trow) S.; student Contra Costa Jr. Coll., 1950-51; B.A. in Journalism, U. Oreg., 1957; postgrad. cinema dept. U. So. Calif., 1962; m. Teresa Helsel, Oct. 20, 1979. Reporter, Roseburg (Oreg.) News-Rev., 1957; group advt. mgr. Montgomery Ward & Co., Oakland, Calif., 1957-61; advt. public relations dir. Jacuzzi Research, Inc., Berkeley, Calif., 1964-65; asst. v.p. corp. communications Airborne Freigh Corp., San Mateo, Calif., 1966-67; sr. editor Motor Trend Mag., Hollywood, Calif., 1967-71; editorial dir. Four Wheeler Mag., Canoga Park, Calif., 1971—. Served with Signal Corps, U.S. Army, 1952-54; Korea. Decorated Bronze Star (U.S.); Singman Rhee citation (Korea); winner Baja 1000 Off Rd. Race for prodn. 4 wheel dr. class, 1973, 4th Pl. Baja 1000, 1979. Mem. Calif. Assn. Four Wheel Dr. Clubs, Specialty Equipment Mfrs. Assn., Am. Automotive Writers and Broadcasters Assn., Chi Psi. Editor automotive sect. World Year Book, 1970, 71. Office: 21216 Vanowen St Canoga Park CA 91303

SANDERS, WILLIAM HUGGINS, lawyer, rancher; b. Springfield, Mo., Nov. 24, 1922; s. J.W. and Helen Pipkin (Huggins) S.; A.B., U. Chgo., 1945; m. Nancy Jane Crane, Dec. 24, 1943; children—Christopher, Cynthia, William Huggins, Dan Crane. Admitted to Mo. bar, since practiced in Kansas City; partner firm Blackwell, Sanders, Matheny, Weary & Lombardi, 1953—. Recipient Lon O. Hocker Meml. Trial Lawyers award Mo. Bar Found., 1957. Clubs: University (Kansas City, Mo.); Lane Recreation Assn. Home: 5322 Mission Woods Rd Shawnee Mission KS 66204 Office: 5 Crown Center Kansas City MO

SANDERSON, BENNETT, lawyer; b. Littleton, Mass., Oct. 31, 1893; s. George Augustus and Annie Sarah (Bennett) S.; grad. Groton (Mass.) Sch., 1912; A.B., Yale, 1916; LL.B., Harvard, 1920; m. Caroline Potter, Oct. 4, 1924; children—Edward Potter (dec.), David, Allen Bennett. Admitted to Mass. bar, 1920; with firm Herrick, Smith, Donald & Farley, Boston, 1920-24; asst. U.S. atty. Mass., 1924-26; U.S. commnr. Mass., 1926-29; partner firm Hale & Sanderson, Boston, 1926-27, Hale, Sanderson, Byrnes & Morton, 1927—. Moderator, Town of Littleton, 1921-24, town counsel, 1938-48; chmn. Littleton Finance Com., 1938-43; pres. Mass. Assn. Town Finance Coms., 1942-43, Littleton Lyceum, 1938; pres. Wachusett council Boy Scouts Am., 1944-46; mem. Mass. Conservation Council, 1944-54. Mem. Littleton Republican Com.; pres. Community Meml. Hosp., Ayer, Mass., 1952-55, exec. com., 1955-65; trustee Social Law Library, Boston, 1947-51, Boston Legal Aid Soc. Served to maj., F.A., U.S. Army, 1917-18. Mem. Mass., Middlesex County (past pres.) bar assns. Episcopalian. Clubs: Boston Yale (past sec.); Appalachian Mountain. Home: 4 Oak Hill Rd Littleton MA 01460 Office: 10 Post Office Sq Boston MA 02109

SANDERSON, DONALD EUGENE, educator; b. Oskaloosa, Iowa, Feb. 4, 1926; s. Arlo Melvin and Laura (Goudy) S.; B.A., Cornell Coll., 1949; M.S., Calif. Inst. Tech., 1951; Ph.D., U. Wis., 1953; m. Carol Mary Shaw, June 24, 1949; children—Robert Charles, Mark Alan, Karen Ann. Instr. Iowa State U., 1953-54, asst. prof., 1954-59, asso. prof., 1959-64, prof., 1964—; vis. lectr. U. Wis. summers, 1959, 1961; vis. asso. prof. Mich. State U., 1962-63. Served with AUS, 1944-46. Mem. Am. Math. Soc., Math. Assn. Am. (vice-chmn. Iowa 1964-65, chmn. 1965-66, gov. 1968-71), AAUP, AAAS, Phi Beta Kappa, Sigma Xi. Presbyterian (elder 1964-67). Home: 1811 Coolidge Dr Ames IA 50010

SANDERSON, EDMUND WHITFORD, paper co. exec.; b. Winchester, Mass., May 6, 1930; s. Edmund W. and Dorothy I. (Graef) S.; B.A., Dartmouth, 1952, M.B.A., 1953; m. Ann Ashley, Feb. 8, 1951; children—Peter, Deborah. With Eliason Refrigerator Co., Hartford, Mich., 1957-60; with Kimberly-Clark Corp., Neenah, Wis., 1960—, asst. to controller, 1963-65, asst. controller pulp and paper div., 1965-66, mgr. adminstrn. Shasta div., Anderson, Calif., 1966-68, financial mgr. internat. group, 1968-70, corp. controller, 1970-72, v.p., controller, 1972-73, v.p., treas., 1973-74, regional v.p. U.S. newsprint and forest products bus. group, 1974-75, v.p., sec., 1975-78, sr. v.p., sec., 1978—. Bd. dirs., treas. Shasta County (Calif.) United Crusade, 1967-68; bd. dirs., pres., treas. Appleton (Wis.) Meml. Hosp., 1971-74, 75—. Served with USNR, 1953-57. Mem. Am. Soc. Corporate Secs. Congregationalist. Home: 1400 Oakcrest Ct Appleton WI 54911 Office: Kimberly Clark Corp Neenah WI 54956

SANDERSON, FRANCIS THAYER, banker; b. Rochester, N.Y., Feb. 13, 1924; s. George and Frances (Church) S.; B.A., Cornell U., 1947, LL.B., 1948; m. Julie Owens, June 10, 1950; children—Katharine, Frances Terry, George Bowie. Admitted to N.Y. bar, 1948, Mass. bar, 1963; trust adminstr. Guaranty Trust Co. N.Y., 1948-49; trust officer Lincoln Rochester Trust Co., Rochester, 1949-62; sr. v.p., sr. trust officer Nat. Shawmut Bank of Boston, 1963-79, exec. v.p., 1979—. Trustee New Eng. Aquarium, New Eng. Deaconess Hosp. Served with Armed Forces, 1942-45; ETO, CBI. Mem. Boston Bar Assn. Club: Union of Boston. Home: 21 Rockridge Rd Wellesley Hills MA 02181 Office: PO Box 2176 Boston MA 02109

SANDERSON, FRED HUGO, fgn. service officer, economist; b. Germany, Apr. 15, 1914; s. Siegfried and Maria (Schulze) S.; Lic.Sc.Econ., U. Geneva (Switzerland), 1935; A.M., Harvard, 1942, Ph.D., 1943; m. Elisabeth Doepfer, Jan. 3, 1938. Came to U.S., 1937, naturalized, 1944. Research asst. Dept. Agr., 1938-42; research asso. com. on research in social scis. Harvard, 1938-43, teaching fellow, 1942-43; economist OSS, 1943-45; chief Central European econ. sect. div. research for Western Europe, Dept. of State, 1946-48, chief Western European econ. br., 1948-52, chief regional econ. staff, 1952-55, asst. chief div., 1955-57, chief div. of research Western Europe, 1957-58; alt. U.S. rep. European Payments Union, 1958-59; dir. finance div. U.S. Mission to OEEC, Paris, 1959-62; chief foodstuffs div. Dept. State, 1963-67, dir. Office Food Policy and Programs, 1967-69, adviser internat. finance, 1970; detailed to Pres.'s Commn. on Internat. Trade and Investment Policy, 1970-71; mem. planning and coordination staff State Dept., 1971-73; fgn. service officer, 1955-73; on leave under Rockefeller Pub. Service award to study econ. effects of European coal and steel community, 1956-57. Cons. to econ. adviser OMGUS, Berlin, 1948; detailed to Pres.'s Materials Policy Commn., 1951 professorial lectr. Sch. Advanced Internat. Studies, Johns Hopkins, 1973—; sr. fellow Brookings Instn., 1974—. Mem. Am. Econ. Assn. Author: Methods of Crop Forecasting (David A. Wells prize), 1954; Japan's Food Prospects and Policies, 1978; (with S. Roy) Food Trends and Prospects in India, 1979. Contbr. to Resources for Freedom, Vol. III, 1952, The Struggle for Democracy in Germany (G. Almond, editor), 1949; Strains in International Finance and Trade, 1974; The Great Food Fumble, 1975. Home: 5017 Westport Rd Chevy Chase MD 20015 Office: Brookings Instn Washington DC 20036

SANDERSON, GLEN CHARLES, wildlife specialist, educator; b. Wayne County, Mo., Jan. 21, 1923; s. Albert Charles and Lillie Bell (Nelson) S.; B.S. in Agr., U. Mo., 1946, M.A. in Zoology, 1949; Ph.D. in Animal Sci., U. Ill., 1961; m. Beverley Carrick, Nov. 26, 1947; children—James William, Laurie Jean. Game biologist Iowa Dept. Conservation, Marion, 1949-55; biologist Ill. Natural History Survey, 1955—; prof. zoology U. Ill., 1965—; adj. prof. So. Ill. U., 1964—. Prin. investor, grantee NIH, 1961-68, U.S. Army, Office Surgeon Gen., 1963. Mem. Am. Soc. Mammalogists, Wildlife Soc., Wildlife Disease Assn., Ill. Acad. Scis., AAAS, Am. Inst. Biol. Scis., Ill. Audubon Soc., Nature Conservancy, Am. Forestry Assn., Wilderness Soc., Nat. Audubon Soc. Methodist. Editor Jour. Wildlife Mgmt., 1971-72. Home: 711 S State St Champaign IL 61820 Office: Ill Natural History Survey Urbana IL 61801

SANDERSON, JAMES RICHARD, naval officer; b. Selma, Calif., Dec. 27, 1925; s. Charles Maxwell and Edith (Wente) S.; student U. Calif., Berkeley, 1943-44, U. Wash., 1944, U. Willamette, 1944-45; grad. USNR Midshipman Sch. at Columbia U., 1945, Nat. War Coll., 1966; student Gen. Line Sch., Monterey, Calif., 1953, Sr. Officers Ship Material Mgmt. Course, Idaho Falls, Idaho, 1979; B.A. in Internat. Affairs, George Washington U., 1968; m. Betty Lee Bradley, Sept. 19, 1947. Served as enlisted man U.S. Naval Res., 1943-45, commd. ensign U.S. Navy, 1946, advanced through grades to rear adm., 1973; gunnery officer U.S.S. Mansfield, 1946-47, U.S.S. Bausell, 1947-48; flight trainee Naval Air Sta., Pensacola, Fla., 1949, Corpus Christi, Tex., 1950; served in Attack Squadron 195, Alameda, Calif., 1950-52; flight instr. Naval Air Sta., Pensacola, 1953-55; served in Attack Squadron 16, 1955-57; air ops. officer on staff Comdr. Carrier Div. Four, U.S.S. Forrestal, 1957-60; ops. officer Attack Squadron 43, Naval Air Sta., Oceana, Va., 1960-62; comdg. officer Attack Squadron 76, 1962-63; comdr. Attack Carrier Air Wing Three in U.S.S. Saratoga, 1963-65; spl. support plans officer, Pacific Area, Strategic Plans and Policy Div., Office of Chief of Naval Ops., Washington, 1966-67, exec. asst. and sr. aide to Dep. Chief Naval Ops., 1967-69; comdg. officer U.S.S. Ranier, 1969-70; dep. chief of staff for ops. and plans U.S. Sixth Fleet, 1970-71; comdg. officer U.S.S. Saratoga, 1971-73; dep. comdr. Naval Striking and Support Forces, So. Europe, Naples, Italy, 1973-76; vice dir. ops. Joint Chiefs of Staff, Washington, 1976-77; asst. dep. chief naval ops. for plans, policy and ops., 1977-79; comdr. Task Force Sixty, U.S. 6th Fleet, 1979—, comdr. Carrier Group Two, 1979—, Battle Force Sixth Fleet, 1979—, Carrier Striking Force So. Region, 1979—. Decorated Legion of Merit with 2 gold stars, D.F.C., Meritorious Service medal, Air medal with 4 gold stars, Navy Commendation medal with combat distinguishing device. Mem. Calif. Alumni Assn., George Washington Alumni Assn., Nat. War Coll. Alumni Assn., Naval Acad. Athletic Assn., Assn. Naval Aviation, Tailhook Assn., Smithsonian Assn., Nat. Eagle Scout Assn., Nat. Skeet Shooting Assn., K.T. Eye Found., Nat. Assn. Investment Clubs, Nat. Wildlife Assn. Clubs: Army Navy Country (Arlington, Va.); Order Daedalians, Masons, Shriners, K.T., Sojourners. Office: COMCARGRU Two FPO NY 09501

SANDERSON, SAMUEL EDWARD, JR., hosp. dir.; b. N.Y.C., Jan. 24, 1927; s. Samuel Edward S.; A.B., Clark U., Worcester, Mass., 1951; M.A., U. Pa., 1956, postgrad., 1956-58; postgrad. Rutgers U., 1972. Secondary sch. tchr., Atlanta, 1951-62; research analyst-cons. Office Research and Stats., Phila. Dept. Health, 1954-58; research cons. Office Mental Health, Pa. Dept. Social Welfare, 1958-62; cons. psychologist USPHS, 1962-64; behavioral scientist, research cons., div. research and evaluation Pa. Dept. Health, 1964-65; behavioral scientist Argyle Pub. Corp., N.Y.C., 1965—; field cons. OEO, 1966-67; dir. div. program research and evaluation Community Devel. Agy., Human Resources Adminstrn., N.Y.C., 1967; dir. Inst. Community Devel., N.Y.C., 1967-68; dir. Office Ednl. Evaluation, N.J. Dept. Edn., 1968-69; asso. prof., chmn. dept. urban studies and community devel. Livingston Coll., Rutgers U., New Brunswick, N.J., 1969-71; adj. asso. prof. SUNY, Purchase, 1971-72, asso. prof., chmn. urban studies, 1974-75; cons. social planner N.Y. State Div. Youth, 1973-74; dep. commr. planning and evaluation N.Y.C. Dept. Mental Health, Mental Retardation and Alcoholism Services, 1974-78; acting exec. dir. Bird S. Coler Hosp. and Home. N.Y.C., 1978—. Served with USNR, 1944-46. Mem. Omega Psi Phi. Roman Catholic. Author papers, reports in field. Office: Bird S Coler Hosp Roosevelt Island New York NY 10044

SANDERSON, WALTON WHITE, banker; b. Washington, Oct. 27, 1938; s. Walton Lemuel and Anna Estelle (White) S.; B.A., U. Md., 1961; m. Beverly Lee Hartle, June 18, 1960; children—Walton White, Kathryn Anne. With Johnston Lemon & Co., investment bankers, Washington, 1961-64; with Nat. Bank Washington, 1964—, pres., 1973—, vice chmn., 1978—, also dir.; dir. Dist. Realty Title Ins. Co., Home Casualty & Surety Co.; mem. Met. Washington Bd. Trade. Washington trustee Fed. City Council. Clubs: Chatterbox, Columbia Country, Rehoboth Beach Yacht and Country, Burning Tree, Shriners. Home: 3527 Hamlet Pl Chevy Chase MD 20015 Office: 619 14th St NW Washington DC 20005

SANDESON, WILLIAM SEYMOUR, cartoonist; b. Mound City, Ill., Dec. 16, 1913; s. William Stephen and Jessie Mae (Mertz) S.; student Chgo. Acad. Fine Arts, 1931-32; m. Ione Wear, June 4, 1938 (dec. 1975); 1 son, William Scott; m. 2d, Ruth Cress, Dec. 31, 1978. Free-lance cartoonist for nat. mags., 1932-37; editorial cartoonist New Orleans Item-Tribune, 1937-41; cartoonist, picture editor and art dir. St. Louis Star-Times, 1941-51; drew daily cartoon feature for Star-Times, Sketching Up With the News; editorial cartoonist Ft. Wayne (Ind.) News-Sentinel, 1951—. Recipient Honor medal Freedoms Found., 1952, 53, 56, George Washington Honor medal, 1954, 55, 57, 58, 59, 60, Disting. Service award, 1961-72, Ind. Sch. Bell award, 1967, Disting. Service awards, 1971-76, prin. cartoon award, 1977, cartoon award, 1978. Mem. Nat. Cartoonist Soc., Assn. Am. Editorial Cartoonists. Congregationalist. Club: Fort Wayne Press (pres. 1965). Home: 119 W Sherwood Terr Fort Wayne IN 46807 Office: Fort Wayne News Sentinel Fort Wayne IN 46802. *Until I'm listed in WHO WAS WHO, I intend to dip my brush in a mixture of self-improvement, stubbornness, and sincere thoughtfulness of my fellow American.*

SANDGREN, CLYDE DAHLMAN, univ. administr.; b. Provo, Utah, Sept. 5, 1910; s. George Edward and Amy Lydia (Swenson) S.; student N.Y. U., 1934; B.S., Brigham Young U., 1937; J.D., St. John's U., 1939; m. Zola Ann Martin, Aug. 25, 1933; children—Vivi-Ann Sandgren Devenport, C. Dee, Gene Edward, Kathleen Elise, Robert Martin, Debbie Jo Sandgren Gagon. Admitted to N.Y. bar, 1940, Utah bar, 1947; partner firm Burroughs & Brown, N.Y.C., 1942-46, Sandgren & Blackham, Provo, 1947-54, Sandgren, Howard & Frazier, Provo, 1954-56; gen. counsel Brigham Young U., 1946-75, v.p., 1961-75, also sec. bd. trustees, 1954-71; vice chancellor Unified Ch. Sch. System, Ch. of Jesus Christ of Latter-day Saints, 1961-65; sec. bd. edn. Ch. of Jesus Christ of Latter-day Saints, 1954-70. Pres. Utah Ednl. TV Found., 1960-64, Council Utah Edn., 1953-54, Intermountain Little Symphony, 1950; mem. exec. com. Nat. Parks council Boy Scouts Am., 1951-53; pres. Brigham Young U. 2d stake Ch. of Jesus Christ of Latter-day Saints, 1961-72, patriarch 2d stake, 1972—. Mem. Provo C. of C. (bd. dirs.), Brigham Young U. Alumni Assn. (pres. 1947-51), Am., N.Y., Utah bar assns. Home: 3535 Canyon Rd Provo UT 84601

SANDGREN, FIND, mech. engr.; b. Copenhagen, June 15, 1922; came to U.S., 1949, naturalized, 1955; s. August Oswald and Marie Charlotte (Peterman) S.; B.S. in Mech. Engring., Copenhagen Teknikum, 1942; postgrad. Poly. Inst. Denmark, 1947; M.B.A., U. Chgo., 1955; m. Jytte Rubak Larsen, Mar. 5, 1949; children—Kim, Eric, Glenn, Karen. Gen. mgr. indsl. automation RCA, Detroit, 1957-59: dir. research and devel. Ideal Industries, Sycamore, Ill., 1959-61, Wabash Inc. (Ind.), 1961-64; exec. v.p., gen. mgr. Midwest Applied Sci. Corp., West Lafayette, Ind., 1964-69; prof. mech. engring. Purdue U., West Lafayette, 1969—, dir. coop. engring. edn., 1969—; propr. Find Sandgren, Cons. to Industry, 1969—. Served with Motorized Arty., Danish Army, 1943. Registered profl. engr., Ill. Mem. IEEE, ASME, Am. Soc. Engring. Edn., Am. Soc. Metals. Home: 314 Wildwood Ln Lafayette IN 47905 Office: Purdue U Potter Bldg West Lafayette IN 47907

SANDGROUND, MARK B., lawyer, restaurateur; b. Boston, June 6, 1932; s. John Henry and Rose (Plotler) S.; B.A., U. Mich., 1952; J.D., U. Va., 1955; D.D. (hon.), U. S. Belgravia, 1974; children—Mark B., Jr., Bruce J. Admitted to D.C. bar, 1955, Va. bar, 1955; since practiced in Washington; partner Sandground, Good & Lewis and predecessors, 1955—; pres. Park Assos., Inc., Washington; dir. Osoñn Gallery, Sigma Centers of Am. Vice chmn. Republican Inaugural Com., 1968, 72. Pres. Friends of the Corcoran Art Gallery, 1968-71; bd. dirs. Psychiat. Inst. Found., 1968—. Club: BFW Internat. Contbr. article to Food, Fat & Fun Jour. Home: 6962 Duncraig Ct McLean VA 22101 Office: 1025 Connecticut Ave NW Suite 911 Washington DC 20036

SANDILANDS, FRANCIS EDWIN PRESCOTT, business exec.; b. Dec. 11, 1913; s. Prescott and Gladys Baird (Murton) S.; M.A., Corpus Christi Coll., Cambridge U., 1938, hon. fellow, 1975; m. Susan Gillian Jackson, 1939; 2 sons. Joined Ocean Accident & Guarantee Corp., Ltd., 1935, mgr., 1955; chief exec. officer Comml. Union Assurance Co., Ltd., London, 1958-72, dir., 1965—, vice chmn., 1968-72, chmn., 1972—; chmn. Royal Trust Co. Can. (U.K.), 1974—, London Salvage Corps, 1962-63, Brit. Ins. Assn., 1965-67; dir. Finance for Industry Ltd., Imperial Chem. Industries Ltd., Kleinwort, Benson, Lonsdale Ltd., Plessey Co. Ltd., Trafalgar House Ltd. Pres. Ins. Inst. London, 1969-70; chmn. Brit. Govt. Com. Inflation Accounting, 1974-75; chmn. Invisible Exports Com., 1976—; mem. Cambridge U. Appointments Bd., 1963-66; treas. Univ. Coll., London, 1973—; gov. Henley Adminstrv. Staff Coll., 1973-77. Bd. dirs. Royal Opera House, Covent Garden; trustee Brit. Mus., 1977. Served to lt. col. Brit. Army, 1939-45; ETO. Decorated comdr. Order Brit. Empire, comdr. Order of Crown of Belgium; created knight, 1976. Address: 53 Cadogan Sq London SW1X OHY England also Thackers Geldeston Nr Beccles Suffolk England

SANDITEN, EDGAR RICHARD, retail co. exec.; b. Okmulgee, Okla., Feb. 1, 1920; s. Herman and Anna (Sanditen) S.; student Western Mil. Acad., 1934-37; B.S. in Bus., Okla. U., 1941; m. Isabel Raffkind, Jan. 26, 1945; children—Linda Caryl, Judith Marie, Ellen Jane, Michael Jay. With Otasco, Inc., Tulsa, 1941—, pres., 1974-77, chmn., chief exec. officer, 1977—; dir. Bank of Okla., Tulsa. Chmn. United Jewish Appeal, Tulsa, 1960; mem. adv. bds. Tulsa YMCA, 1966—; chmn. Tulsa Charity Horse Show, 1969-71; bd. dirs. Tulsa Opera, 1967—, Civic Ballet, 1960-68, Tulsa Econ. Devel. Commn., 1970; bd. dirs. St. John Med. Center, 1973—, chmn., 1979—; pres. Temple Israel, 1968-70. Served with USAAF, 1943-46. Mem. Tulsa Jr. C. of C. (honor award 1943), Tulsa C. of C. (dir. 1977—, v.p. 1978—), Quarter Century Club Automotive Industry. Clubs: Summit (dir. 1971-77), So. Hills Country, Meadowbrook Country (Tulsa). Home: 2140 E 30th St Tulsa OK 74114 Office: PO Box 885 Tulsa OK 74102

SANDLER, BARBARA S., artist; b. N.Y.C.; d. Sidney and Josephine S. One-woman shows include: Danenberg Gallery, N.Y.C., 1973, Gimpel Weitzenhoffer, N.Y.C., 1975, 1st Woman's Bank, N.Y.C., 1975, Southern Newman Gallery, 1978; group shows include: Lehigh U., 1975, Alex Rosenberg Gallery, N.Y.C., 1978; represented in permanent collections: Hirschorn Mus. Collection, Mus. Modern Art, Chgo. Art Mus., Smithsonian Inst., Chase Manhattan Bank; illustrator mags., record covers, book jackets. Elizabeth T. Greenshield Meml. grantee, 1975. Office: 10 W 23d New York NY 10010

SANDLER, CHARLES ROSS, lawyer; b. Buffalo, Dec. 17, 1917; s. Jacob and Ella (Lischner) S.; student Ohio State U., 1935-37; LL.B., U. Buffalo, 1940; m. Gloria Grods, May 8, 1947; children—Alison, Sally. Admitted to N.Y. bar, 1946, since practiced in Buffalo. Pres., Jewish Family Service of Erie County. 1965-67; v.p. United Jewish Fedn. Erie County, 1967; regional atty. N.Y. State Civil Service Employees Assn., 1949—. Pres., Erie County Research and Planning Council, 1973-75; bd. dirs. United Way of Buffalo and Erie County, 1977—. Served from pvt. to lt. col., inf. AUS, 1941-46; ETO (U.S. rep. Inter-Allied Council-Internat. Dist., Vienna, Austria, 1945). Decorated Silver Star medal, Bronze Star medal, Purple Heart, Combat Inf. badge. Mem. N.Y. State, Erie County bar assns., Am., Erie County trial lawyers assns. Home: 95 Lake Ledge Dr Williamsville NY 14221 Office: 120 Delaware Ave Buffalo NY 14202

SANDLER, HERBERT M., savs. and loan assn. exec.; b. N.Y.C., Nov. 16, 1931; s. William B. and Hilda (Schattan) S.; B.S.S., Coll. City N.Y., 1951; J.S.D., Columbia U., 1954; m. Marion Osher, Mar. 26, 1961. Admitted to N.Y. bar, 1956; asst. counsel Waterfront Commn. N.Y. Harbor, 1956-59; partner firm Sandler & Sandler, N.Y.C., 1960-62; pres. Golden West Savs. & Loan Assn., Oakland, Calif., 1963-75; chmn. bd., chief exec. officer World Savs. & Loan Assn., Oakland, 1975—; pres. Golden West Fin. Corp., Oakland, 1963-75, chmn. bd., chief exec. officer, 1975—. Served with AUS, 1954-56. Office: 1970 Broadway Oakland CA 94612

SANDLER, IRVING HARRY, art critic, art historian; b. N.Y.C., July 22, 1925; s. Harry and Anna S.; B.A., Temple U., 1948; M.A., U. Pa., 1950; Ph.D., N.Y. U., 1976; m. Lucy Freeman, Sept. 4, 1958; 1 dau., Catherine Harriet. Instr. in art history N.Y. U., 1960-71; prof. art history SUNY, Purchase, 1971—; art critic N.Y. Post, N.Y.C., 1960-65. Served with USMC, 1943-46. John Simon Guggenheim fellow, 1965; Nat. Endowment for Arts fellow, 1977. Mem. Coll. Art Assn., Internat. Assn. Art Critics. Author: The Triumph of American Painting: A History of Abstract Expressionism, 1970; The New York School: Painters and Sculptors of the Fifties, 1978; Alex Katz, 1979. Home: 100 Bleecker St New York NY 10012 Office: Div Visual Arts SUNY Purchase NY 10577

SANDLER, MARION OSHER, savs. and loan assn. exec.; b. Biddeford, Maine, Oct. 17, 1930; d. Samuel and Leah (Lowe) Osher; B.A., Wellesley Coll., 1952; postgrad. Harvard U.-Radcliffe Coll., 1953; M.B.A., N.Y. U., 1958; m. Herbert M. Sandler, Mar. 26, 1961. Asst. buyer Bloomingdale's, dept. store, N.Y.C., 1953-55; security analyst Dominick & Dominick, N.Y.C., 1955-61; sr. fin. analyst Oppenheimer & Co., N.Y.C., 1961-63; sr. v.p., dir. Golden West Savs. & Loan Assn., Oakland, Calif., 1963-75; vice chmn. bd., co-mng. officer World Savs. and Loan Assn., Oakland, 1975—; sr. v.p., dir. Golden West Fin. Corp., Oakland, 1963-75, vice chmn. bd., co-mng. officer, 1975—; dir. Macy's Calif., 1976—. Mem. Berkeley Bus. Sch. Bd., U. Calif., 1973—. Mem. Phi Beta Kappa, Lambda Alpha, Beta Gamma Sigma. Address: 1970 Broadway Oakland CA 94612

SANDLIN, JOSEPH ERNEST, banker; b. Franklin, Va., Sept. 10, 1919; s. Joseph Fredrick and Rosa (Davis) S.; B.A., Coll. William and Mary, 1943; m. Evelyn Kobcsenski, May 11, 1946; 1 dau., Joan Ellen. With Arthur Andersen & Co., N.Y.C., 1948-53, supervising sr. accountant, 1951-53; controller Amerotron Co., div. Textron, Providence, 1953-63; pres., treas., dir. So. Nat. Corp. also So. Nat. Bank of N.C., and asso. cos., Lumberton, N.C.; dir. Atlantic States Bankcard Assn. Unified Investors Life Ins. Co.; lectr. Advanced Mgmt. Program N.C. Sch. Banking. Pres. N.C. and S.C. councils Boy Scouts Am., 1977-78; pres. Cardinal Health Agy., Inc.; mem. N.C. Treas.'s Com. for Study State Banking Laws. Trustee, treas. Coll. Found. Inc.; pres., chmn. bd. trustees, mem. exec. com. Boys Home, Lake Waccamaw, N.C. Served with USNR, 1943-46. Mem. Am. Inst. C.P.A.'s, N.C. Assn. C.P.A.'s, Am. Bankers Assn., Bankers Adminstrv. Inst. Presbyterian (elder 1975—). Mason (32 deg.). Home: Rt 8 Box 30 Lumberton NC 28358 Office: 500 Chestnut St Lumberton NC 28358

SANDMAIER, PHILIP JAMES, JR., accountant; b. Buffalo, Mar. 21, 1919; s. Philip James and Theresa (Stinely) S.; B.S. maxima cum laude, U. Notre Dame, 1940; m. Antoinette C. Pfeiffer, Oct. 6, 1945; children—Donna M., Marian L., Robert J., Philip R. With Haskins & Sells, C.P.A.'s, 1940—, partner exec. office, N.Y.C., 1958-62, mng. partner, San Diego, 1962-64, mng. partner, Phila. 1964-69, exec. office, N.Y.C., 1969—; dir., treas. Practicing Law Inst., N.Y.C., 1973—, Nat. Bur. Econ. Research, N.Y.C., 1977—. Com. chmn. United Fund, Cleve., 1950-52, United Fund, Newark, 1956-58; vice chmn. United Fund, Phila., 1964-65; lay trustee Villanova U., 1965-69, trustee Asia Soc., N.Y.C., 1971. Served to 2d lt. AUS, 1941-45; ETO. Decorated Bronze Star medal. Mem. Am. Inst. C.P.A.'s, Ohio, N.J., N.Y., Calif., Pa. socs. C.P.A.'s. Home: PO Box 217 Hopewell NJ 08525 Office: 1114 Ave of the Americas New York City NY 10036

SANDMAIER, PHILIP JAMES, JR., accountant; b. Buffalo, Mar. 21, 1919; s. Philip James and Theresa (Stinely) S.; B.S. maxima cum laude, U. Notre Dame, 1940; m. Antoinette C. Pfeiffer, Oct. 6, 1945; children—Donna M., Marian L., Robert J., Philip R. With Haskins & Sells, C.P.A.'s, 1940—, partner exec. office, N.Y.C., 1958-62, mng. partner, San Diego, 1962-64, mng. partner, Phila., 1964-69, exec. office, N.Y.C., 1969—; dir., treas. Practicing Law Inst., N.Y.C., 1973—, Nat. Bur. Econ. Research, N.Y.C., 1977—. Com. chmn. United Fund, Cleve., 1950-52, United Fund, Newark, 1956-58; vice chmn. United Fund, Phila., 1964-65; lay trustee Villanova U., 1965-69, trustee Asia Soc., N.Y.C., 1971. Served to 2d lt. AUS, 1941-45; ETO. Decorated Bronze Star medal. Mem. Am. Inst. C.P.A.'s, Ohio, N.J., N.Y., Calif., Pa. socs. C.P.A.'s. Home: Rolling Hill Rd Skillman NJ 08558 Office: 1114 Ave of the Americas New York City NY 10036

SANDMAN, EDGAR AUGUSTUS, banker; b. Albany, N.Y., Oct. 19, 1919; s. Edgar A. and Miriam V. (Sill) S.; A.B., Union Coll., Schenectady, 1940; LL.B., Albany Law Sch., 1946; m. Margaret M. Dugan, Dec. 28, 1945; children—Paul W., Anne M., James J., Jean M., John M. With First Trust Co. Albany, 1946—, treas., 1954-66, sr. v.p., 1962-66, exec. v.p., 1966-68, pres., 1968-70, also dir.; sr. v.p. finance Bankers Trust N.Y. Corp., 1970-75, exec. v.p., 1975—; dir. Sackman-Gilliland Corp., BT Advisors, Inc., BT Credit Co., Inc., Bankers Trust, Albany. N.Y. State chmn. Found. Comml. Banks, 1967-68; pres. Albany Clearing House Assn., 1956. Pres. Council Community Services Albany Area, 1966-68. Trustee, Albany Law Sch. Served with USAAF, 1942-45. Mem. N.Y. State Bankers Assn. (past chmn. group V). Catholic. Clubs: Fort Orange, Hudson River (Albany). Home: 67 Highfield Rd Harrison NY 10528 Office: 280 Park Ave New York City NY 10017

SANDMEL, SAMUEL, educator, author; b. Dayton, Ohio, Sept. 23, 1911; s. Morris and Rebecca (Lenderman) S.; A.B., U. Mo., 1932; B.H.L., Hebrew Union Coll., 1934; student Duke, 1940-41; Ph.D., Yale, 1949; m. Frances Langsdorf Fox, June 23, 1940; children—Charles, Benjamin, David. Ordained rabbi, 1937; rabbi, Atlanta, 1937-39, Hillel Found., N.C., 1939-42, Hillel Found., Yale, 1946-49; prof. Jewish lit. and thought Vanderbilt U., 1949-52; prof. Bible and Hellenistic lit. Hebrew Union Coll.-Jewish Inst. Religion, 1952-66, Distinguished Service prof. Bible and Hellenistic lit., 1966-79, provost, 1957-66, dir. grad. studies, 1974-76; Helen A. Regenstein prof. religion U. Chgo., 1979—; chmn., exec. com. Frank Weil Inst. Religion and Humanities; hon. vis. prin. Leo Baeck Coll., London, 1968-69; spl. field Hellenistic Jewish lit. and N.T. Served as chaplain USNR, 1942-45. Mem. Soc. Bibl. Lit. (pres. 1961), Central Conf. Am. Rabbis, Phi Beta Kappa. Club: Literary (Cin.). Author: A Jewish Understanding of the New Testament, 1956; Philo's Place in Judaism, 1956; The Genius of Paul, 1958; The Hebrew Scriptures, 1963; We Jews and Jesus, 1965; Herod: Profile of a Tyrant, 1967; We Jews and you Christians, 1967; The First Christian Century in Judaism and Christianity, 1969; The Several Israels, 1971; Two Living Traditions, 1972; The Enjoyment of Scripture, 1972; Alone Atop the Mountain, 1973; A Little Book on Religion, 1975; When a Jew and Christian Marry, 1977. Editor: Old Testament Issues, 1968; Hebrew Union Coll. Ann., 1970-72; Oxford Study edit. New English Bible, 1976; When a Jew and Christian Marry, 1977; Judaism and Christian Beginnings, 1978; Anti-Semitism in the New Testament?, 1978; Philo of Alexandria, 1979. Home: 1642 E 56th St Chicago IL 60637. *Years ago I was unaware as I think I am acutely aware today of the difference between education and wisdom. Surely in a sense they are related, and I am not sure that wisdom is attainable without education. But education and schooling are, of course, not the same. Is education perhaps the amassing of responsible knowledge? Then what is wisdom? Perhaps it is the use of knowledge. Perhaps it is the maturity which experience may supply (or may not). But surely wisdom is something quite beyond either schooling or experience. Can it be taught? No. Can it be caught? Perhaps. But is it not that plus beyond schooling and experience which distills the content of both, and proceeds to transcend them?*

SANDMEYER, ROBERT LEE, economist, univ. adminstr.; b. Evansville, Ind., June 12, 1929; s. Orville G. and Elizabeth (Chandler) S.; B.A., Kans. State U., Ft. Hays, 1956; M.S., Okla. State U., 1958, Ph.D., 1962; m. Loretta Mae Jacobs, Aug. 5, 1950; children—Karen, Bridgit, Barbara, Robert C.; Instr., Kans. State U., Ft. Hays, 1957-58; instr. Iowa State U., 1958-59; asst. prof. econs. Ariz. State U., 1961-62; asst. prof. Okla. State U., 1962-65, asso. prof., 1965-70, prof., dean Coll. Bus. Adminstrn., 1977—; cons. in field; econ. adv. Ariz. Gov.'s Tax Study Com., 1961-62; adv. Okla. Gov.'s Com. on Mental Health, 1963; tax expert Okla. Tax Commn. Served with USN, 1947-51. Mem. So. Econ. Assn., Nat. Tax Assn., Frontiers of Sci. Found. Okla., Mid-Continent Research and Devel. Council, Phi Kappa Phi, Beta Gamma Sigma. Democrat. Roman Catholic. Contbr. articles to profl. publs. Home: 2307 Tanglewood Circle Stillwater OK 74074 Office: Coll Bus Adminstrn Okla State U Stillwater OK 74074

SANDOLOSKI, SANDY MOISE, lawyer; b. Dallas, Nov. 30, 1921; s. Leo Bill and Cora (Weil) S.; LL.B., So. Meth. U., 1949; m. Bernice Madvine, Mar. 12, 1950; children—Lee Robert, Ellen Rae. Admitted to Tex. bar, 1949; practiced in Dallas, 1949—; mem. firms Weinberg & Sandoloski, 1952-73, Weinberg, Sandoloski & McManus, 1973—. Served with USAF, 1941-45. Mason. Optimist (pres. 1961-62). Home: 7322 Azalea St Dallas TX 75230 Office: 1800 Republic Nat Bank Tower Dallas TX 75201

SANDONATO, BARBARA LEE, ballerina; b. Harrison, N.Y., July 22, 1943; d. Frank and Julia (Strino) Sandonato; scholarship student Lorna London Sch. Ballet, 1948-57, Sch. Am. Ballet, 1957-62; m. Aleksej Yudenich, May 8, 1966; children—Ivan Aleksejevich, Aleksandra Aleksejevna. Mem. corps de ballet Radio City Music Hall, N.Y.C., 1960; summer stock Cape Cod Melody Tent, Hyannis, Mass., 1962; mem. Phila. Lyric Opera Ballet, 1961-62; an organizer, prin. dancer Pa. Ballet Co., Phila., 1962-72, 73-77; ballet mistress Opera Co. of Phila., 1978-79; dance faculty Phila. Coll. Performing Arts, 1978—; prin. dancer Nat. Ballet Can., 1972-73; mem. staff Sch. Pa. Ballet, 1962-68; asso. dir. Princeton (N.J.) Ballet, 1979; guest artist Princeton Ballet Co., 1979—; mem. faculty Princeton Ballet Sch., 1979—; guest tchr. Pitts. Ballet Theatre, Pa. Gov. Sch. for Arts, Ocean City Cultural Arts Center, also lectr. colls. and univs.; numerous guest appearance with ballet companies, also TV appearances. Recipient Bronze medal 5th Internat. Ballet competition, Varna, Bulgaria, 1970. Home: 1613 Lawrenceville Rd Lawrenceville NJ 08648 Office: Princeton Ballet 262 Alexander St Princeton NJ 08540. *There must exist a strong desire from within to express an innate feeling of movement through dance coupled with music's inertia and glorious emotional powers. This feeling must be so strong that one can completely relinquish her soul, body and mind to the strenuous and rigorous study of this art through complete dedication.*

SANDOR, GEORGE NASON, mech. engr., educator; b. Budapest, Hungary, Feb. 24, 1912; s. Alexander S. and Maria (Adler) S.; Diploma in Mech. Engring., Poly. U. Budapest, 1934; D. Eng. Sci., Columbia U., 1959; m. Magda Breiner, Dec. 5, 1964; stepchildren—Stephen Gergely, Judith Patricia Gergely (Mrs. J. Peter Vernon). Came to U.S., 1938, naturalized, 1949. Asst. to chief engr. Hungarian Rubber Co., Budapest, 1935-36, mfg. dept. head, 1936-38; design engr. Babcock Printing Press Corp., New London, Conn., 1939-44; v.p., chief engr. H.W. Faeber Corp., N.Y.C., 1944-46; chief engr. Time Inc. Graphic Arts Research Labs., Springdale, Conn., 1946-61; chief engr. Huck Co., Inc., N.Y.C., 1961; asso. prof. mech. engring. Yale, 1961-66; prof. mech. engring. Rensselaer Poly. Inst., Troy, N.Y., 1966-67, Alcoa Found. prof. mech. design, chmn. machines and structures div., 1967-75; research prof. mech. engring. U. Fla., Gainesville, 1976—. instr. engring. U. Conn. Extension, New London and Norwich, 1940-44; lectr. mech. engring. Columbia, 1961-62; dir. Huck Design Corp., Huck Co., Inc., Montvale, N.J., 1964-70; cons. engr., printing equipment and automatic machinery, mech. engring. design, 1961—; cons. NSF Departmental and Instl. Devel. Program, 1970-72; cons. nat. materials adv. bd. Nat. Acad. Scis., 1974; cons. Xerox Corp., Burroughs Corp., Govt. Products div. Pratt & Whitney Aircraft Co., Time Inc., also others, 1961—; dir. and co-dir. NSF, U.S. Army Research Office and NASA sponsored research at Yale U., Rensselaer Poly. Inst. and U. Fla. at Gainesville; chief U.S.A. del. to Internat. Fedn. for Theory Machines and Mechanisms, 1969-75; cons. for materials conservation through design Office Tech. Assessment, Congress U.S., 1977. Registered profl. engr., Fla., N.J., N.Y.; certificate of qualification Nat. Council Engring. Examiners. Fellow ASME (life fellow, Machine Design award 1975); mem. Am. Soc. Engring. Edn., N.Y. Acad. Scis., Nat. Soc. Profl. Engrs., Am. Acad. Mechanics, Flying Engrs. Internat., Sigma Xi, Tau Beta Pi, Pi Tau Sigma. Author: (with others) Mechanical Design and Systems Handbook, 1964; Linkage Design Handbook, 1977. Mem. editorial bd. Jour. of Mechanism, 1966-72, Machine and Mechanism Theory, 1972—. Contbr. articles to profl. jours. Patentee in field. Home: 1719-2D NW 23d Ave Gainesville FL 32605

SANDOR, GYORGY, pianist; b. Budapest, Hungary; s. Ignac and Zsenka (Czipszer) S.; student Liszt Ferenc Conservatory, Budapest, 1927-33; studied piano with Bela Bartok, composition with Zoltan Kodaly; 1 son, Michael. Came to U.S., 1938, naturalized, 1943. Made concert debut, Budapest, 1931; toured Europe, 1931-38; Am. debut Carnegie Hall, N.Y. City, 1939; tour throughout U.S., Mexico, Can., W.I., C.A., S.Am., Europe, Australia, Far East; soloist with major symphony orchs., N.Y.C. Buenos Aires, Rio de Janeiro, London, Berlin, Stockholm; rec. with N.Y. Philharmonic and Phila. orchs., also solo rec.; now dir. doctoral program in performance (piano) U. Mich., Ann Arbor. Recipient Grand Prix du Disque for rec. entire piano repertory of Bela Bartok's works, 1964. Rec. entire solo piano repertory of Prokofiev, 1967, Kodály, 1973. Address: Univ Michigan Ann Arbor MI 48104

SANDOR, THOMAS, biochemist; b. Budapest, Hungary, Nov. 3, 1924; came to Can., 1950, naturalized, 1956; s. Miksa and Iren (Forstner) S.; Dipl. Chem., U. Budapest, 1948; Ph.D., U. Toronto, 1960; m. Vera Varkonyi, July 5, 1949; 1 dau., Catherine-Susanne. Research fellow Inst. A. Fournier, Paris, 1949-50, Hosp. for Sick Children, U. Toronto (Ont.), 1951-56; research biochemist Hotel Dieu Hosp., Montreal, Que., Can., 1956-59; sr. research asso. Hosp. Notre Dame, Montreal, 1959—; research asst. prof. medicine U. Montreal, 1961-67, research asso. prof., 1967-70, research prof., 1970—; hon. prof. McGill U., Montreal, 1969—; career investigator Med. Research Council of Can., 1962—; vis. prof. U. Sheffield (Eng.), 1970-71, 79-80, U. Buenos Aires, 1974; co-prin. Thomas Assos., sci. cons., Montreal, 1969—. Mem. Can. Biochem. Soc., Can. Soc. for Clin. Investigation, Royal Soc. Medicine (Gt. Britain), N.Y. Acad. Scis., Endocrine Soc., Biochem. Soc. (Gt. Britain), Soc. for Endocrinology (Gt. Britain), Am. Soc. Zoologists, European Soc. Comparative Endocrinologists, Am. Fedn. Clin. Research, Order Chemists of Que., Que Hosp. Biochemists Assn. Mem. editorial bd. Gen. and Comparative Endocrinology. Contbr. chpts. on steroid biochemistry to books, articles to profl. jours. Home: 4140 Côte St Catherine Montreal PQ H3T 1E3 Canada Office: 1560 Sherbrooke St E Montreal PQ H2L 4M1 Canada

SANDORFY, CAMILLE, educator; b. Budapest, Hungary, Dec. 9, 1920; came to Can., 1951, naturalized, 1957; s. Kamill and Paula (Fenyes) S.; B.Sc., U. Szeged (Hungary), 1943, Ph.D., 1946; D.Sc., Sorbonne, U. Paris, 1949; m. Rolande Cayla, Aug. 24, 1971. Attache de recherches Centre Nationale de la Recherche Scientifique, Paris, France, 1947-51; postdoctoral fellow Nat. Research Council of Can., 1951-53; asst. prof. chemistry U. Montreal (Que., Can.), 1954-56, asso. prof., 1956-59, prof., 1959—; vis. prof. U. Paris, 1968, 74. Killam Meml. scholar, 1978. Fellow Royal Soc. Can. Author: Les Spectres Electroniques en Chimie Theorique, 1959; Electronic Spectra and Quantum Chemistry, 1964; (with R. Daudel) Semi-empirical Wave-Mechanical Calculatio ns on Polyatomic Molecules, 1971; research, numerous publs. in chemistry. Address: 4612 Stanley Weir Montreal PQ H3W 2C9 Canada

SANDQUIST, OLIVER, architect; b. Chgo., Dec. 9, 1905; s. Axel Sigfrid and Selma Caroline (Fritz) S.; student Wheaton Coll., 1924-25, Armour Inst. Tech. (now Ill. Inst. Tech.), 1927-30; m. Alice Rose Schacht, Sept. 6, 1930; 1 dau., Senny Rose. Owner, Sandquist Co., Chgo., 1931-40; chief designer Skidmore, Owings & Merrill, Chgo., 1941-44; owner Oliver Sandquist, architect, Chgo., 1945-55; partner Samuelson & Sandquist, architects and engrs., Chgo., 1955-63; owner Oliver Sandquist & Assos., architects and engrs., Chgo., 1963—. Bldg. commr. Village of Skokie (Ill.), 1956-58. Recipient award Am. Assn. Sch. Adminstrs. Registered architect. Mem. A.I.A., Soc. Am. Registered Architects (nat. v.p. 1960, Merit award, design citation), Ill. Soc. Architects (dir. 1958-61). Mem. Verdandi Ind. Order Svithiod (chmn. 1968-69, 69-70). Clubs: Architects (pres. 1954-55, dir.) (Chgo.); Evanston Golf. Important works include Thornridge High Sch., Dolton, Ill., numerous others. Home: 4025 Harvard Terr Skokie IL 60076 Office: 4838 Howard St Skokie IL 60077

SANDRICH, JAY H., TV dir.; b. Los Angeles, Feb. 24, 1932; s. Mark R. and Freda (Wirtschafter) S.; B.A., U. Calif. at Los Angeles, 1953; m. Nina Kramer, Feb. 11, 1952 (div.); children—Eric, Tony, Wendy. Producer TV show Get Smart, 1965; dir. TV shows He and She, 1967, Bill Cosby Show, 1969, Mary Tyler Moore show, 1970-77, Soap, 1977-79. Served to 1st lt. Signal Corps, AUS, 1952-55. Mem. Directors Guild Am. (award 1976), Television Acad. Arts and Scis. (Emmy award for comedy directing 1971, 73). Home: 1 Northstar Apt 205 Marina Del Rey CA 90291

SANDRIDGE, SIDNEY EDWIN, coll. pres.; b. nr. Crozert, Va., May 24, 1927; s. Laurie King and Vertie (Batten) S.; A.B., U. Va., 1949; B.D., Candler Sch. Theology, 1951; postgrad. Emory U., 1951-52; Ph.D., Northwestern U., 1959; m. Gladys Brewer, June 15, 1952; children—Jeffrey King, Kim Elizabeth, Sandi Lynn, Jennifer Anne. Ordained to ministry Meth. Ch., 1950; pastor Schuyler (Va.) Meth. Circuit, 1952-56; prof. sociology, dir. of extension Ferrum (Va.) Jr. Coll., 1959-61, v.p., 1961-63, dean, acad. v.p., 1963-65; acad. dean So. Sem. Jr. Coll., Buena Vista, Va., 1965-67, pres., 1967-70; pres. Athens (Ala.) Coll., 1970—. Trustee So. Sem. Jr. Coll. Served with USNR, 1945-46. Va. State 4-H Alumni winner, 1967, Nat. 4-H Alumni winner, 1968. Mem. NEA. Mason, Rotarian. Address: 211 S Beaty St Athens AL 35611*

SANDS, EDITH SYLVIA ABELOFF (MRS. ABRAHAM M. SANDS), educator, author; b. Bklyn.; d. Louis and Jennie (Goldstein) Abeloff; B.A., Adelphi Coll., 1932; M.B.A., Baruch Sch. Bus. Adminstrn., Coll. City N.Y., 1956; Ph.D., N.Y.U., 1961; m. Abraham M. Sands, June 5, 1932; children—Stephanie Lou, John Eliot. Asst. prof. L.I.U., Bklyn., 1961-65, asso. prof., 1965-69, prof., 1969, chmn. dept. finance, 1962-72. Corr. sec. Welfare Council Bklyn. Cancer Com., 1956-58; mem. council Friends of Adelphi Coll. Library, 1955-60; pres. Foster Care Aux., 1959-61. Bd. dirs. Nat. Council Jewish Women, 1935-38, community com. Bklyn. Mus., 1950-52; mem. women's aux. Prospect Heights Hosp., 1954-56, Bklyn. Eye and Ear Hosp., 1950-53; mem. asso. bd. Jewish Child Care Assn., 1959-61; chmn. bd. dirs. Friends Bklyn. Center Libraries L.I. U. Recipient Alumni Achievement award Baruch Alumni Assn. of Coll. City N.Y., 1969; L.I. U. Alumni Assn. award of appreciation, 1978. Mem. AAUW, Am. Econ. Assn., Met. Econ. Assn., Fedn. Woman Shareholders (exec. com.), Econ. History Assn., Am. Finance Assn., Acad. Mgmt., A.I.M., Soc. Advancement Mgmt., Am. Mgmt. Assn., AAUP, N.Y. Soc Security Analysts, Am. Statis. Assn., Financial Mgmt. Assn., Met. Econ. Assn., Beta Gamma Sigma Alumni N.Y. (pres. 1967-70), City Coll. Alumni Assn., N.Y.U. Grad Sch. Bus. Adminstrn. Alumni Assn. (dir. 1968—, treas. 1975-77), Adelphi Coll. Alumnae Assn. (chpt. pres. 1957-59), Nat., N.Y. assns. bus. economists, Money Marketeers N.Y.U. (dir. 1973-75), AAUP, Nat. Economists Club, Beta Gamma Sigma (nat. exec. com. 1972-76), Phi Sigma Sigma. Clubs: Women's City, City College, N.Y. U. Finance (v.p. 1973-75), Money Marketeers, Business Forum, N.Y. U., Princeton in N.Y. (guest mem.). Author: How to Select Executive Personnel, 1963. Contbr. articles to profl. jours. Editor, the Tape, jour. industry studies for investment decisions. Home: 874 Carroll St Brooklyn NY 11215

SANDS, IRA JAY, lawyer, investment and real estate cons.; b. N.Y.C.; B.A., N.Y. U.; J.D., Columbia U., 1944; m. Kiti Reiner; children—Nelson, Tiffany. Admitted to N.Y. bar, 1944, U.S. Supreme Ct., 1966, Mass. bar, 1970, Wis. bar, 1975, Fla. bar, 1977, Ill. bar, 1975, Pa. bar, 1970; practice in N.Y.C., 1944—; mng. partner Korvette Bldg. Assos., N.Y.C., 1957-62; dir., mng. partner First Republic Corp., 1957—, chmn. bd., 1958—, sec., 1960—; partner Velvex Mid-City Parking Center, N.Y.C., 1959-65, Manhattan Parking Assos., 1959; dir., chmn. First Republic Underwriters, Inc., 1958—; pres., dir. Waltham Mgmt. Inc. (Mass.), 1959—; partner Cypress Parking Assos. (Fla.), 1961, Randolph House Co., N.Y.C., 1962-66, Gulf Assos., Fla., 1961-62, Sahara Motel Assos., 1961-66, others; chmn. Waltham Engring. & Research Co., 1959—; gen. partner Allstate Bldg. Co., N.Y.C., 1959—, Fairfax Bldg. Assos. (Mo.), 1958—, Engring. Bldg. Assos. (Ill.), 1958—, Williamsbridge Assos., N.Y.C., 1958—, First Republic Funding Agy., N.Y.C., 1961-66, Atlantic Co. (Fla.), 1961—, Marchwood Realty Co. (Pa.), 1961—, Video Film Center Assos., N.Y.C., 1962—, Imperial Sq. Assos., N.Y.C., 1960—, Ohio Indsl. Assos., 1961—, Pelham Park Assos. (Pa.), 1961—; chmn., dir. Triple P Parking Corp. (Ill.), 1960—, Park Circle Apts., Inc., N.Y.C., 1960—; Home Circle Apts., Inc. (Pa.), 1961—; sec. F.S. Mgmt. Corp., N.Y.C., 1966—; chmn. exec. com., sec., dir. 1st Republic Bldg. Corp., 1962-66; chmn. bd., chmn. exec. com., sec., dir. Div. Sq. Mgmt. Corp., Hempstead, N.Y., 1961—, Nat. Med. Industries, Inc., 1968—, Health Insts. Leasing Corp., 1968—, Am. Med. Computer Corp., 1969—; pres. Med. Contract Supply Corp., 1968—, City Capital Corp. (N.D.), 1978—; real estate cons. Past trustee Baldwin Sch., N.Y.C.; hon. trustee Truman Library. Served as officer AUS, 1942. Harlan Fiske Stone fellow, 1975; named Man of Year, Real Estate Weekly, 1965. Mem. Nat. Real Estate Club, Am. Bar Assn., N.Y. State Bar Assn., Nassau County Bar Assn. (com. fed. cts. and corps.), Nat. Lawyers Club, Fed. Bar Assn., Fed. Bar Council, N.Y. Real Estate Bd., Columbia U. Law Sch. Alumni Assn. (class chmn. 1978), Bldg. Owners and Mgrs. Assn. Clubs: Shriners, Jockey, Mchts., Atrium. Address: 515 Madison Ave New York NY 10022

SANDS, LEO GEORGE, cons. firm exec.; b. Spokane, Wash., Mar. 20, 1912; s. Jacob Herman and Helmi Johanna (Laasanen) S.; student U. Calif., 1933-34; m. Rhea Meuron, May 6, 1944; children—Lee, Craig. Chief airborne electronic engring. and maintenance Sacramento (Calif.) Air Depot, 1942-45; mgr. mktg. Bendix Corp., Towson, Md., 1945-53; adminstr. RCA Corp., Camden, N.J., 1953-54; pres. Sands Tech. Corp., N.Y.C., 1954-76, chmn., 1977; chmn. FCC task force preparing U.S. position on personal-use radio communication at 1979 World Adminstrv. Conf.; mem. personal use radio adv. com. to FCC, 1976-77. Bd. dirs. Santa Barbara (Calif.) Safety Council, 1954-55. Fellow Radio Club Am. (dir.); sr. mem. IEEE (sr. life). Author numerous books on electronics. Editor-in-chief CB Mag., 1965—. Contbr. numerous articles to profl. jours. Home: 7379 Caminito Carlotta San Diego CA 92120

SANDS, LESTER BURTON, univ. chancellor; b. Bklyn., June 10, 1905; s. George and Musette (Bruton) S.; A.B., Stanford U., 1929, M.A., 1933, Ed.D., 1939; m. Carol Brown; children—Anne Musette, Margaret Claire. Vice prin. Haight Sch., Alameda, Calif., 1931-35; coordinator curriculum prin. Palo Alto (Calif.) schs., 1936-40; asso. prof. edn. DePauw U., Greencastle, Ind., 1940-44, coordinator U.S. Naval Flight Sch., 1942-44; dean, chmn. dept. edn. N.Mex. Highlands U., Las Vegas, 1944-46; vis. prof. U. Alaska, Fairbanks, 1973; prof. edn. U. Calif., Santa Barbara, 1946-72; chancellor Laurence U., Santa Barbara, 1974—; Fulbright prof., Peru, 1960-61; cons. in field; cons. AID, Guatemala, 1966, UNESCO, Costa Rica, 1967, U.S. Office Edn., P.R., 1968. Mem. NEA, Philosophy Edn. Assn., History Edn. Soc., Phi Delta Kappa. Club: Rotary. Author: Introduction to Teaching High School, 1949; American Public School Administration, 1952; Audio-Visual Procedures, 1956; History of Education Chart, 1938—. Home: 5446 Rincon Beach Dr Ventura CA 93001 Office: 30 W Mission St Santa Barbara CA 93101

SANDS, MATTHEW LINZEE, educator, physicist; b. Oxford, Mass., Oct. 20, 1919; B.A., Clark U., 1940; M.A., Rice Inst., 1941; Ph.D., Mass. Inst. Tech., 1948; m. Freya Kidner, 1978; children—Michael, Richard, Michelle. Physicist U.S. Naval Ordnance Lab., 1941-43, Los Alamos Sci. Lab., 1943-46; research asso., then asst. prof. physics Mass. Inst. Tech., 1946-50; sr. research fellow, asso. prof., prof. Calif. Inst. Tech., 1950-63; prof. physics, dep. dir. Linear Accelerator Center, Stanford, 1963-69; prof. physics, fellow Kresge Coll., U. Calif. at Santa Cruz, 1969—; vice chancellor for sci., 1969-72; vis. prof. Universite' de Paris-Sud, spring 1976. Mem. Commn. Coll. Physics, 1960-66, chmn., 1964-66; cons. Office Sci. and Tech., ACDA, Inst. Def. Analyses, 1962-67; mem. Pugwash Conf. Sci. and World Affairs, 1960-63. Fulbright scholar, Italy, 1952-53. Fellow Am. Phys. Soc.; mem. Am. Assn. Physics Tchrs., Fedn. Am. Scientists, AAAS. Author: (with W.C. Elmore) Electronics-Experimental Techniques, 1948; (with R.P. Feynman and R.B. Leighton) The Feynman Lectures on Physics, 3 vols., 1965; (with others) Physical Science Today, 1973; also articles. Mem. editorial bd. Il Nuovo Cimento, 1972—. Spl. research electronic instrumentation for nuclear physics, cosmic rays, accelerators, high-energy physics, sci. edn., sci. and public affairs, electron storage rings. Office: Div Natural Science California Santa Cruz CA 95064

SANDS, ROBERT KENNETH, lawyer; b. Worcester, Mass., Aug. 25, 1926; s. John M. and Edith C. (Hammarlund) S.; B.A. cum laude with distinction in Polit. Sci., Ohio State U., 1949; J.D., Yale, 1952. Admitted to Tex. bar, 1952, since practiced in Dallas; pres. firm Sands & Tyler, and predecessors, 1973—. Bd. dirs. Yale Law Sch. Fund, 1974—, mem. exec. com. Yale Law Sch. Assn., 1977—; trustee Timberlawn Psychiat. Research Found., 1974—. Served with USNR, 1944-46. Mem. Am., Dallas bar assns., State Bar Tex., Yale Law Sch. Assn. Dallas (pres. 1966—), Confrerie des Chevaliers du Tastevin, Phi Beta Kappa. Clubs: Dallas, Inwood Racquet (Dallas). Contbr. articles to legal publs. Home: 2912 Hood St Dallas TX 75219 Office: 2030 Republic Nat Bank Tower Dallas TX 75201

SANDS, THOMAS JAHN, army officer; b. Dayton, Ohio, Aug. 2, 1907; s. Jacob Wilford and Florence Estelle (Jahn) S.; B.S., U.S. Mil. Acad., 1929; grad. C.W.S. Sch., 1930; Diplome Superieur with honors, Alliance Francaise, Paris, France, 1933, U. Paris, 1933; grad. F.A. Sch., 1939, Command and Gen. Staff Coll., 1941, Armed Forces Staff Coll., 1947, Nat. War Coll., 1952; m. Renee Ledoux, July 19, 1932; 1 son, Richard J. Commd. 2d lt. F.A., U.S. Army, 1929, advanced through grades to maj. gen., 1952; battery officer, 1929-31; instr. dept. tactics U.S. Mil. Acad., 1932, instr. dept. modern langs., 1933-37, aide-de-camp to supt., 1942; attached Am. embassy, Paris, France, 1932-33; battery officer, then battery comdr., 1938-41; brigade insp., 1941; a.d.c. to comdg. gen. 1st Corps Area, 1941; asst. chief staff G-4, 85th Inf. Div., 1942-43; mem. War Dept. Gen. Staff, assigned Office Asst. Chief Staff G-4, 1943-44; chief C.I., G-2 sect. 12th Army Group, 1944-45, G-2 Div. USFET, 1945-46; staff CIA, Washington, 1946-47; asst. chief staff J-2, Joint Task Force Seven, Pacific Ocean areas, 1947-48; div. arty. comdr. 5th Inf. Div., 1948-50; asst. chief staff G-3, Allied Land Forces, Central Europe (NATO), 1952-55; comdg. gen. III Corps Arty., 1955-57; chief staff Eighth U.S. Army, 1957; comdg. gen. 7th Inf. Div., 1957-58; dep. comdt. Armed Forces Staff Coll., 1958-60; asst. chief of staff SHAPE, 1960-63; army mem. Joint

Strategic Survey Council, 1963-64; chief Army Audit Agy., 1965-66. Decorated D.S.M., Legion of Merit, Bronze Star medal with cluster; officer Order Brit. Empire; chevalier Legion of Honor, Croix de Guerre with 2 palms and 1 gold star (France); Officer Order of Leopold I (Belgium); Order Mil. Merit Taeguk (Korea). Clubs: Century Assn. (N.Y.C.); Army-Navy (Washington). Nat. sr. duelling sword champion, 1935-37, mem. nat. sr. duelling sword championship team, 1934-36; mem. U.S. internat. fencing team Brit.-Am. Match, 1934, Italian-Am. Match, 1934; dept. capt. U.S. Olympic fencing team XI Olympiad, Berlin, Germany, 1936; capt. U.S. internat. fencing team World's Championship, Paris, 1937; finalist World's Individual Duelling Sword Championship, 1937, Fencing Hall of Fame, 1978. Office: care Adjutant General US Army Washington DC 20315

SANDSON, JOHN IVAN, univ. dean; b. Jeannette, Pa., Sept. 20, 1927; s. Abraham and Dora Henrietta (Whitman) S.; B.A., St. Vincent Coll., Latrobe, Pa., 1949; M.D., Washington U., St. Louis, 1953; m. Hannah Elizabeth Ney, June 16, 1957; children—Jennifer Marie, Thomas Andrew. Intern, then resident Columbia Presbyn. Med. Center, N.Y.C., 1953-56; chief resident Bronx Municipal Hosp. Center, 1956-57; from instr. to prof. medicine Albert Einstein Coll. Medicine, 1957-74, med. dir. hosp. of coll., 1969-74; prof. medicine, dean Sch. Medicine, Boston U., 1974—; trustee Univ. Hosp., Boston, Harvard Community Health Plan, Harvard St. Neighborhood Health Center, Boston Med. Library; bd. dirs. Health Planning Council Greater Boston, 1976—; mem. Mass. Health Coordinating Council, 1977—. Served with AUS, 1946-47. Fellow Arthritis Found., 1958-60; career scientist Health Research Council, N.Y.C., 1960-70. Mem. Am. Soc. Clin. Investigation, Assn. Am. Physicians, Council of Deans of Am. Assn. Med. Colls., Am. Rheumatism Assn., New Eng. Rheumatology Soc., Mass. Med. Soc., Mass. Pub. Health Assn. Club: St. Botolph (Boston). Contbr. articles to med. jours.; mem. publs. com. New Eng. Jour. Medicine. Home: 31 Holly Circle Weston MA 02193 Office: 80 E Concord St Boston MA 02118

SANDWEISS, JACK, physicist, educator; b. Chgo., Aug. 19, 1930; s. Charles Ray and Florence (Hymovitz) S.; student UCLA, 1948-50; B.S., U. Calif., Berkeley, 1952, Ph.D., 1957; m. Letha Ann Boeck, Jan. 16, 1956; children—Daniel Howard, Anne Florence, Benjamin Lewis. Research asso. Radiation Lab., U. Calif., Berkeley, 1957; instr. Yale U., New Haven, 1957-59, asst. prof., 1959-62, asso. prof., 1962-64, prof. physics, 1964—, also chmn. dept. physics; cons. Brookhaven Nat. Lab., Fermi Nat. Accelerator Lab. Fellow Am. Phys. Soc. (vice chmn. div. particles and fields 1979); mem. AAAS. Contbr. articles to profl. jours. Home: 248 Ogden St New Haven CT 06511 Office: Sloane Physics Lab Yale U New Haven CT 06520*

SANDWELL, BERNARD DANTON, pub. co. exec.; b. Boston, Jan. 24, 1915; s. Arnold Hugh and Helen (Bower) S.; student Upper Can. Coll., Toronto, 1933-34; B.A. with honours, U. Toronto, 1938; m. Helen Mary Kaufman, June 10, 1939; children—Joan Patricia, Douglas Bernard, Mary Helen. Mgr. coll. and med. books dept. Macmillan Co. Can. Ltd., Toronto, 1939-56, dir. Gen. Pub. Co. Ltd., Toronto, 1957-61; mng. dir. Collier-Macmillan Can. Ltd., Toronto, 1961-64; pres., chmn. bd. Burns & MacEachern Ltd., Toronto, 1964—; chmn. bd. govs. Trent U., Peterborough, Ont., 1971-75; founding trustee Ont. Waterfowl Research Found., Toronto, 1963. Hon. fellow Champlain Coll., Trent U., 1970. Served to capt. Irish Regiment, Canadian Army, 1942-45; ETO. Mem. Book Publishers Assn. Can. (chmn. 1967), Canadian Book Publishers' Council (sec. 1963), Champlain Soc., Ind. Publishers' Assn. (founding, exec. mem.). Clubs: University (Toronto); Caledon Hunt; Chinguacousy Country (Inglewood, Can.). Office: Burns and MacEachern Ltd 62 Railside Rd Don Mills ON M3A 1A6 Canada*

SANDY, GARY, actor; b. Dayton, Ohio, Dec. 25; s. Austin and Dolores Sandy; student Wilmington (Ohio) Coll., Am. Acad. Dramatic Arts, N.Y.C. Off-Broadway appearances include: Romeo and Juliet, The Children's Mass; appeared on Broadway in Saturday, Sunday, Monday; other stage appearances include: Sheba, Cowboy; motion pictures include: Some of My Best Friends Are, Hail to the Chief, The Great Smol Smokey Roadblock; TV films include: The Kansas City Massacre, The Shell Game; formerly regular on TV series As the World Turns, Somerset, The Secret Storm, All That Glitters; star TV series WKRP in Cincinnati, 1978—; other TV appearances include: Movin' On, Harry O, Medical Center, Barnaby Jones, Police Woman, Starsky and Hutch. Office: care MTM Enterprises Inc 4024 Radford Ave Studio City CA 91604*

SANER, REGINALD ANTHONY, poet; b. Morgan County, Ill., Dec. 30, 1931; s. Reginald Anthony and Marie Catherine (Rexroat) S.; B.A., St. Norbert Coll., 1952; M.A., U. Ill., 1956, Ph.D., 1962; m. Anne Costigan, Aug. 16, 1958; children—Timothy, Nicholas. Free lance photographer, 1952-56; asst. prof. English lit. U. Colo., 1962-67, asso. prof., 1967-73, prof., 1973—; author: Climbing into the Roots, 1976; contbr. poetry to lit. jours. Recipient Poetry award Borestone Mountain, 1972, Walt Whitman award for poetry Acad. Am. Poets-Copernicus Soc. Am., 1975; Fulbright scholar, 1960-61; U. Colo. faculty fellow, 1967; Nat. Endowment for Arts fellow, 1976. Mem. Delta Epsilon Sigma. Home: 1925 Vassar Dr Boulder CO 80303

SANFELICI, ARTHUR HUGO, editor-writer; b. Haledon, N.J., May 23, 1934; s. Hugo and Anna (Schilder) S.; attended Lehigh U., 1952-55; m. Betty Louise Van Riper, Aug. 10, 1957; children—Brian Arthur, Amy Elizabeth, Gary Hugh, Bruce Richard. Asso. editor Flying Mag., N.Y.C., 1961-64; mng. editor Am. Aviation Mag., Washington, 1964-68; dist. sales mgr. Gates Learjet Co., N.Y.C., 1969-71; exec. editor Airport World Mag., Westport, Conn., 1971-74; spl. project editor Aircraft Owners & Pilots Assn., Washington, 1974-75, mng. editor Pilot mag., 1975—. Active Boy Scouts Am. Served with USAF, 1955-60. Mem. Aviation and Space Writers Assn. (asst. v.p.), Aircraft Owners and Pilots Assn. Editor, compiler: Yesterday's Wings. Home: 5 Oak Shade Rd Sterling VA 22170 Office: care Aircraft Owners and Pilots Assn 7315 Wisconsin Ave Washington DC 20014

SANFORD, CHARLES LEROY, educator; b. Salem, N.J., Feb. 29, 1920; s. Leroy Benjamin and Anna Mae (Messer) S.; B.A., Middlebury Coll., 1942; M.A., Brown U., 1946; M.A., Harvard U., 1949, Ph.D., 1952; children—Charlotte Messer, Holly. Instr. in Am. lit. Middlebury Coll., 1950-51, vis. lectr., 1954-55; instr. Am. studies Amherst Coll., 1952-54; prof. lang., lit. and communications Rensselaer Poly. Inst., 1955—, Laflin prof. tech. and culture, 1971—, asso. dir. Human Dimensions Center, 1974-78; vis. prof. English Union Coll., 1969; cons. Nat. Endowment for Humanities; vis. lectr. Conf. Automobiles and Urban Design, Berlin, 1978. Bd. dirs. Rensselaer County (N.Y.) Commn. Econ. Opportunity, 1966-68; campaign mgr. 30th N.Y. State Dist. Democrats for McCarthy, 1968. Served with USNR, 1942-45. Fulbright prof., France, 1961-62. Mem. Am. Studies Assn. (editorial bd. Am. Quar. 1966-70), AAUP. Author: Benjamin Franklin and the American Character, 1955; The Quest for Paradise, 1961; Quest for America, 1964; Manifest Destiny, 1974; Automobiles in American Life, 1977; editorial bd. Alternative Futures, 1978; editor: Studies in the Human Dimensions of Science and Technology, 1976—. Home: PO Box 14 Grafton NY 12082 Office: 206 West Hall Rensselaer Polytechnic Inst Troy NY 12181

SANFORD, CHARLES STEADMAN, JR., bank exec.; b. Savannah, Ga., Oct. 8, 1936; s. Charles Steadman and Ann (Lawrence) S.; A.B., U. Ga., 1958; M.B.A., U. Pa., 1961; m. Mary McRitchie, June 19, 1959; children—Ann Whitney, Charles Steadman III. Vice pres. nat. div., account officer Bankers Trust Co., N.Y.C., 1962-68, 1st v.p., asst. to head resources mgmt., 1969-71, exec. v.p., head resources mgmt., 1972—, mem. mgmt. com., 1979—; dir. Balt. Gas & Electric Co. Served with arty. U.S. Army, 1958-59. Mem. Securities Industry Assn., Pub. Securities Assn. (dir.). Home: 19 Bayberry St Bronxville NY 10208 Office: Bankers Trust Co 280 Park Ave New York NY 10017

SANFORD, CHARLES WILSON, educator; b. Allentown, Pa., Aug. 26, 1902; s. Chester Milton and Ella (Stillson) S.; B.S., U. Ill., 1929, M.S., 1930, Ph.D., 1933; m. Mary Marguerite Sharp, June 30, 1923; children—Mary Marguerite (Mrs. James Wayne Davidson), Charles Wilson. Tchr., Ogden (Ill.) Community High Sch., 1923-25, Latrobe (Pa.) High Sch., 1925-28; asst. edn. U. Ill., Champaign, 1929-32, asst. philosophy, 1930-31, prin. Univ. High Sch., 1932-43, instr. edn., 1932-33, asso. edn., 1933-35, asst. prof., 1935-41, asso. prof., 1949, prof., 1949-67, coordinator tchr. edn., 1943-46, asso. dean Coll. Edn., 1949-56, dean admissions, records, 1956-65, univ. dean admissions and records, prof. high edn., 1965—, dean, prof. emeritus, 1967—; chief cons. Study of Comprehensive High Sch. in Mass., 1969-70; lectr. edn. U. Mich., summers, 1939, 46. Dir. Ill. Curriculum Program, 1947-54; mem. Gen. Motors Nat. Scholarship Com., 1957-59, chmn. steering com., 1959; mem. Nat. Adv. Com. Coop. Plan for Guidance and Admissions Ednl. Testing Service, 1963—; pres. annuitants assn. Ill. State Univs. Retirement System, 1973—. Mem. Nat. (past com. chmn.), Ill. (past com. chmn.) assns. secondary sch. prins., Am. Assn. Collegiate Registrars and Admissions Officers, Kappa Delta Pi, Phi Delta Kappa. Presbyn. Author: (with others) Guide to the Study of the Curriculum in the Secondary Schools of Illinois, 1948, The Story in Nineteen Schools, 1950. Editor: Illinois Curriculum Program Series, 1947-54; (with H. C. Hand and W. B. Spalding) The Schools and National Security, 1951; (with others) College Admissions Policies for the 1970s, 1968. Contbr. to Ency. Ednl. Research rev. edit., 1950, Dictionary of Edn., 2d edit., 1959. Contbr. to ednl. jours. Home: 13227 Bonanza Dr Sun City West AZ 85375

SANFORD, DAVID BOYER, magazine editor, author; b. Denver, Mar. 4, 1943; s. Filmore Bowyer and Alice Irene (Peterson) S.; B.A. with honors, U. Denver, 1964; M.S. in Journalism with honors, Columbia, 1965. With New Republic mag., Washington, 1965-76, mng. editor, 1970-76; mng. editor Politics Today (formerly Skeptic), Santa Barbara, Calif., 1976-78, contbg. editor, 1978-79; editorial writer Los Angeles Herald Examiner, 1978-79; mng. editor Harper's mag., N.Y.C., 1979—; syndicated columnist, 1970-71; commentator Canadian Broadcasting Corp., 1967-76. Centennial scholar, 1960-64; N.Y. Newspaper Guild fellow, 1964-65; recipient Sackett Law prize Columbia, 1965, Eckenberg prize, 1965; Gold award N.Y. Art Dirs. Club, 1977. Mem. Authors Guild, White House Corrs. Assn., Phi Beta Kappa. Democrat. Club: Federal City. Author: Who Put the Con in Consumer?, 1972; Me and Ralph, 1976. Editor, co-author: Hot War on the Consumer, 1970. Home: 118 Prospect Park W Brooklyn NY 11215

SANFORD, GEORGE FOSTER, JR., ins. co. exec.; b. Chgo., Apr. 15, 1902; s. G. Foster and Mabel (Clow) s.; grad. Kent Sch., 1924; B.A., U. Pa., 1928; m. Alice Laurie, Dec. 20, 1928; children—G. Foster III, Robert, Richard. With Smyth, Sanford & Gerard, Inc., ins. brokers, 1928—, treas., 1943-69, pres., 1938-69, chmn. bd., 1969—. Mem. Psi Upsilon. Clubs: Wall Street (N.Y.C.); Montclair Golf. Home: 14 Bradford Way Upper Montclair NJ 07043 Office: 68 Williams St New York City NY 10005

SANFORD, ISABEL GWENDOLYN, actress; b. N.Y.C., Aug. 29; d. James Edward and Josephine (Perry) Sanford; ed. pub. schs.; m. William Edward Richmond (dec.); children—Pamela (Mrs. Eddie Ruff), William Eric, Sanford Keith. Stage appearances in Off-Broadway prodns., also in Los Angeles; Broadway appearance in Amen Corner; films appearances include Guess Who's Coming to Dinner, 1968, Pendulum, 1969, Stand Up and Be Counted, 1972, The New Centurions, 1972, Love at First Bite, 1979; TV appearances include Carol Burnett show, Love Am. Style, Bill Cosby show, Tony, Orlando and Dawn, All in the Family, Mod Squad, Bewitched, The Comedy Shop, Supertrain; co-star The Jeffersons, 1974—. Mem. Kwanza Found. Address: care MEW Inc 151 N San Vincente Blvd Beverly Hills CA 90211*

SANFORD, JAMES RICHARD, physicist; b. Zanesville, Ohio, Jan. 29, 1933; s. James C. and Mary W. S.; B.A., Oberlin Coll., 1955; M.S., Yale U., 1957, Ph.D., 1961; m. Mary K. Moyer, June 12, 1956; children—Susan, Elizabeth. Physicist, Brookhaven Nat. Lab., 1962-69; asso. dir. Fermi Nat. Accelerator Lab., Batavia, Ill., 1969-76; asso. dir. Brookhaven Nat. Lab., Upton, N.Y., 1976—, head Isabelle project, 1978—; cons. Dept. Energy. Mem. Am. Phys. Soc., Sigma Xi. Home: PO Box 281 Bellport NY 11713 Office: Brookhaven Nat Lab Upton NY 11973

SANFORD, JOHN BERKSHIRE, JR., investment banker; b. New Orleans, Sept. 25, 1906; s. John Berkshire and Caroline (O'Shaughnessy) S.; B.B.A., Tulane U., 1928; m. Ethel LeGardeur, Dec. 2, 1929; children—Betty (Mrs. Charles B. Molster, Jr.), John Berkshire III, Jane (Mrs. William T. Blessey). With bond dept. Whitney Nat. Bank, New Orleans, 1938—. Treas., dir. Louise S. McGehee Sch., New Orleans. Served to lt. (s.g.) USNR, 1942-45. Mem. Investment Bankers Assn. Am. (bd. govs.), Kappa Alpha. Clubs: Boston, Internat. House (New Orleans). Home: 2100 St Charles Ave New Orleans LA 70140 Office: Whitney Bldg New Orleans LA 70130

SANFORD, NEVITT, psychologist; b. Chatham, Va., May 31, 1909; s. Thomas Ryland and Margaret (Taylor) S.; A.B., U. Richmond (Va.), 1929, Sc.D., 1962; M.A., Columbia U., 1930; Ph.D., Harvard U., 1934; LL.D., Notre Dame U., 1967, Hawaii Loa Coll., 1978; L.H.D., Colgate U., 1968, U. Nev., 1968; m. Christine Dickson, June 15, 1931; children—Elizabeth Sanford Duvenbeck, David, Margaret Sanford Tanous, Robert, Jane, Michael, Mark. Psychologist, Harvard Growth Study Sch. Children, 1935-40; lectr. Mass. Inst. Tech., 1939-40; from asst. prof. to prof. psychology U. Calif. at Berkeley, 1940-60; coordinator Mary Conover Mellon Found., 1952-58; prof. psychology and edn., dir. Inst. Study Human Problems, Stanford U., 1961-69; founder, 1968, since pres. Wright Inst., Berkeley; tchr. Salzburg (Austria) Seminars Am. Studies, 1952; bd. dirs. Social Sci. Research Council, 1960-65; Sloan prof. Menninger Found., 1964. Bd. dirs. ACLU, 1965-68. Served with OSS, World War II. Fellow Center Advanced Study Behavioral Scis., 1960-61; recipient Research Scientist award NIMH, 1969-74; Kurt Lewin Meml. award Soc. Psychol. Study of Social Issues, 1969; award for disting. contbns. Am. Bd. Profl. Psychology, 1978. Mem. Am. (dir. 1957-62, div. pres. 1955, 57), Western (pres. 1971) psychol. assns., Soc. Psychol. Study Social Issues (pres. 1957). Author: Self and Society, 1966; Where Colleges Fail, 1967; Issues in Personality Theory, 1971; co-author: Physique, Personality and Scholarship, 1943; The Authoritarian Personality, 1950; co-editor: Sanctions for Evil, 1971. Author, editor: The American College, 1962. Contbr. articles to profl. jours. Home: 65 Roble Rd Berkeley CA 94705 Office: 2728 Durant Ave Berkeley CA 94704

SANFORD, TERRY, univ. pres., lawyer; b. Laurinburg, N.C., Aug. 20, 1917; s. Cecil and Elizabeth (Martin) S.; A.B., U. N.C., 1939, J.D., 1946; m. Margaret Rose Knight, July 4, 1942; children—Elizabeth Knight, Terry. Asst. dir. Inst. of Govt., U. N.C., 1940-41, 46-48; spl. agt. FBI, 1941-42; admitted to N.C. bar, 1946; practiced in Fayetteville, 1948-60; partner firm Sanford, Adams, McCullough & Beard, 1965—; gov. N.C., 1961-65; pres. Duke U., Durham, N.C., 1969—; public gov. Am. Stock Exchange. Dir. Study of Am. States, Duke, 1965-68; mem. Carnegie Commn. Ednl. TV, 1964-67; pres. Urban Am., Inc., 1968-69; chmn. ITT Internat. Fellowship Com.; pres. Am. Council Young Polit. Leaders; adv. council Pacific Am. Inst., Inc. Sec.-treas. N. C. Port Authority, 1950-53; mem. N.C. Senate, 1953-54; pres. N.C. Young Dem. Clubs, 1949-50; del. Nat. Dem. Conv., 1956, 60, 64, 68, 72; chmn. Nat. Dem. Charter Commn., 1972-74; trustee Cordell Hull Found. Internat. Edn., Nat. Humanities Center; bd. dirs. Children's TV Workshop, 1967-71; trustee Meth. Coll., Howard U.; chmn. So. Regional Edn. Bd., 1961-63. Served to 1st lt. AUS, 1942-46. Mem. Am. Bar Assn., Am. Acad. Polit. and Social Sci., Am. Judicature Soc., Am. Arbitration Assn. (dir.), Nat. Municipal League (v.p.). Methodist. Author: But What About the People?, 1966; Storm Over the States, 1967. Home: 1508 Pinecrest Rd Durham NC 27705

SANFORD, VALERIUS, lawyer; b. Ripley, Tenn., Aug. 25, 1923; s. William Valerius and Mary (Savage) S.; student Va. Mil. Inst., 1940-43; B.A., Vanderbilt U., 1947, LL.B., 1949; m. Betty Bellis, Feb. 27, 1947; children—Mary, Elizabeth, William. Admitted to Tenn. bar, 1949; asso. firm Waring, Walker, Cox & Lewis, Memphis, 1949-50, Clement & Clement, Nashville, 1950-53; individual practice law, Nashville, 1953-59; partner firm Clement, Sanford & Fisher, Nashville, 1959-63, Gullett, Steele, Sanford & Robinson, Nashville, 1963—; chmn. Tenn. Law Revision Commn., 1963-67; sec. Tenn. Bd. Law Examiners, 1979. Served with U.S. Army, 1943-46. Mem. Am. Bar Assn., Tenn. Bar Assn., Nashville Bar Assn., Am. Judicature Soc. (dir. 1966-69), Am. Law Inst. Democrat. Baptist. Office: PO Box 2757 Nashville TN 37219

SANG, ELSIE OLIN (MRS. PHILIP DAVID SANG), hist. documents exhibitor; b. Chgo., Feb. 5, 1906; d. Louis Benjamin and Ida Kalman (Klein) Olin; Litt.D., Lincoln Coll., 1969; Litt.D., Rosary Coll., 1970; D.F.A., North Central Coll., 1972; m. Philip David Sang, Aug. 21, 1923; children—Robert H., Donald G. Co-producer Ann. Philanthropic European Antiques Show at Oak Park Temple, 1963—; exhibited hist. documents and rare manuscripts on human freedom and Am. history at Rutgers U., So. Ill. U., U. Ill., Champaign-Urbana, U. Hawaii, Brandeis U., Knox Coll., Galesburg, Ill., Lincoln U. (Pa.), Newberry Library, Chgo., Ill. State Hist. Library, Springfield, Jewish Theol. Sem., N.Y.C., Chgo. Hist. Soc., No. Ill. U., Rosary Coll., River Forest, Ill., Ga. State Archives, Atlanta, McCormick Place, Chgo., Ill. Inst. Tech., Lincoln (Ill.) Coll., U. Ky., State U. Iowa, North Central Coll., Naperville, Ill., Music Center, Los Angeles, U. Wyo.; co-sponsor Olin-Sang Am. Civlization Center, Brandeis U., Olin-Sang Pavilion, Mt. Sinai Hosp., Chgo., Olin-Sang Hall and Presidential Mus., Lincoln Coll., Olin-Sang Library, Hebrew Union Coll. Bibl. and Archaeol. Sch., Jerusalem, Olin-Sang Camp (Union of Am. Hebrew Congregations), Oconomowoc, Wis., Olin-Sang chair in Leukemia Research, Weizmann Inst. Sci., Rehovot, Israel; co-sponsor Excellence in Teaching ann. awards at various univs. and colls. Trustee Lincoln Coll., 1955-62, Rosary Coll. Recipient Distinguished Service award Lincoln Coll., 1962; co-recipient Nat. Joshua Ben Gamala Gold Medal award for outstanding contbn. to religious and secular edn., 1967; Presdl. medallion Knox Coll., 1972. Fellow U. Ky., 1968. Mem. Ill. Hist. Soc. (v.p.). Club: Standard (Chgo.). Home: 180 E Pearson St Chicago IL 60611

SANGER, HERBERT SHELTON, JR., lawyer, govt. ofcl.; b. Oak Hill, W.Va., Aug. 6, 1936; s. Herbert Shelton and Ethel Dean (Layne) S.; A.B. in English and Polit. Sci., Concord Coll., Athens, W.Va., 1958; LL.B., W.Va. U., Morgantown, 1961; m. Rita Adele Baumgartner, Aug. 20, 1958; children—Charles, Carole, Warren, George. Admitted to W.Va. bar, 1961, Supreme Ct. U.S. bar, 1976, U.S. Ct. Appeals 5th and 6th circuits, 1973, 10th circuit, 1978; staff atty. Office of Gen. Counsel, TVA, Knoxville, 1961-69, asst. gen. counsel power, 1969-72, asso. gen. counsel litigation and power, 1972-73, dep. gen. counsel, 1973-75, gen. counsel, 1975—; asst. prof. law U. Tenn.; Arthur B. Hodges prof. law W.Va. U.; chmn. bd. dirs. TVA Retirement System. Recipient Lawyers Coop award, 1961, Lawyers Title Ins. Co. award, 1961. Mem. Fed., W.Va. bar assns. Baptist. Home: 5100 Malibu Dr Knoxville TN 37918 Office: 400 Commerce Ave E11B33 Knoxville TN 37902

SANGREE, WALTER HINCHMAN, social anthropologist, educator; b. N.Y.C., June 15, 1926; s. Carl Michael and Constance (LaBoiteaux) S.; A.B., Haverford Coll., 1950; M.A., Wesleyan U., 1952; Ph.D. U. Chgo., 1959; m. Mary Lucinda Shaw, June 14, 1952; children—Margaretta Elizabeth, Mary Cora. Asst. prof. anthropology U. Rochester, N.Y., 1957-64, asso. prof., 1964-73, prof., 1973—, chmn. dept. anthropology, 1974-77, Co-clk. Rochester Friends Meeting, 1977—. Fulbright scholar, U.K. and Kenya, 1954-56; NSF research fellow, Nigeria, 1963-65. Mem. AAAS, Am. Anthrop. Assn., Internat. African Inst., Royal Anthropol. Soc. Gt. Britain and Ireland, Sigma Xi. Democrat. Mem. Soc. of Friends. Author: Age, Prayer & Politics in Tiriki, Kenya, 1966. Contbr. articles to profl. jours. Home: 254 Highland Pkwy Rochester NY 14620 Office: Dept Anthropology U Rochester Rochester NY 14627

SANGSTER, WILLIAM MCCOY, educator; b. Austin, Minn., Dec. 9, 1925; s. Earl Yarborough and Margheritta (McCoy) S.; student U.S. Naval Acad., 1944-46; B.S., State U. Iowa, 1947, M.S., 1948, Ph.D. (Grad. fellow), 1964; postgrad. U. Mo., 1949-51; children—William McCoy, Edward Thomas, Sarah Elizabeth. Asst. instr. State U. Iowa, 1948; asst. prof. civil engring U. Mo., Columbia, 1948-55, asso. prof., 1955-61, prof., 1961-67, asso. dir. Engring. Expt. Sta., 1963-67, asso. dean Coll. Engring, 1964-67; prof. civil engring. Ga. Inst. Tech., Atlanta, 1967—, dir. Sch. Civil Engring., 1967-74, dean Coll. Engring., 1974—; engr. Boeing Co., Seattle, summers 1951, 59, 60; dir. research projects USAF, 1952-55, U.S. Bur. Pub. Rds., Mo. Hwy. Dept., 1956-58, Boeing Co., 1959; mem. USIA Mission to India, 1965; cons. Robert L. Reid & Assos., Houston, Orr, Sapp & Wood, Columbia, Henry Fisk, Architect, Iowa City; ednl. cons. to univs. to U.S., Korea, Jordan, Egypt, Lebanon, Israel, Syria, United Arab Emirates, South Africa. Mem. bldg. adv. com. Columbia Sch. Bd., 1961-62; pres. Met. Collegiate Athletic Conf.; chmn. bd. dirs. Franki Found., Boston. Served with USNR, 1944-46. Recipient Mo. honor award for distinguished service in engring., 1975. NSF Sci. Faculty fellow, 1962-63. Diplomate Am. Acad. Environ. Engrs. Fellow ASCE (past pres., past dir., com. chmn., leader exchange group to USSR 1974, 75, Latin Am. 1976, Far East 1978); mem. Am. Soc. Engring. Edn. (dir., past sect. pres.), Engrs. Council Profl. Devel. (dir.), Engrs. Joint Council (dir.), Assn. for Cooperation in Engring., Engring. Socs.

Library (dir.), United Engring. Trustees (dir.), Sigma Xi, Phi Kappa Psi, Tau Beta Pi, Chi Epsilon. Democrat. Methodist. Club: Berkeley Hills Golf (past pres.) (Norcross, Ga.). Home: Apt B-23 LeMans III 2805 Northeast Expressway Atlanta GA 30345

SANGUINETTI, EUGENE F., museum adminstr.; b. Yuma, Ariz., May 12, 1917; s. Eugene F. and Lilah B. (Balsz) S.; B.A., U. Santa Clara, 1939; postgrad. U. Ariz., 1960-62; children by previous marriage—Leslie, Gregory. Instr. in art history U. Ariz., 1960-64; dir. Tucson Mus. and Art Center, 1964-67, Utah Mus. Fine Arts, Salt Lake City, 1967—; adj. prof. art history U. Utah, 1967—; chmn. adv. com. Salt Lake City Bicentennial Center for Arts; mem. Salt Lake City C. of C. Arts Council. Served with USAAF, 1942-44, M.I., U.S. Army, 1944-46. Mem. Am. Assn. Mus's., Western Assn. Art Mus's. (1st v.p.), Coll. Art Assn. Am., Am. Fedn. Arts. Contbr. articles to mus. exhbn. catalogs. Home: 851 E 5th St S Salt Lake City UT 84102 Office: 101 AAC U Utah Salt Lake City UT 84112

SANIK, JOHN, JR., chemist; b. Stamford, Conn., Oct. 2, 1919; s. John and Xenia (Tupick) S.; B.S., U. R.I., 1942, M.S., 1948; Ph.D., Kans. State U., 1951; children—Paul, Lorraine, Gregory, David. Asst. instr. U. R.I., Kingston, 1943-44, Instr., 1946-48; chemist Standard Oil Co. (Ind.), Whiting, Ind., 1951-57; chemist Amoco Chems. Corp., Whiting, 1957-62; asso. prof. Chgo. City Jr. Coll., 1962-63; prof. chemistry SUNY, Oneonta, 1963-69, 76—, dean grad. studies, 1969-76. Sec. Highland (Ind.) Sch. Bd., 1957-59, pres., 1959-62; mem. Highland Recreation Bd., 1959-62. Served with AUS, 1944-46. Mem. Am. Chem. Soc., AAAS, Sigma Xi, Phi Lambda Upsilon, Gamma Sigma Delta. Home: 51 Union St Oneonta NY 13820

SANN, PAUL, newspaperman, author; b. Bklyn., Mar. 7, 1914; s. Harry and Frieda (Spilton) s.; student N.Y. Prep. Sch., 1931; m. Bertha Pullman, July 28, 1934; children—Eleanor, Howard. Copy boy, reporter, night city editor, asst. city editor N.Y. Post, 1931-44, Washington corr., 1945, news editor UN Conf. edit., San Francisco, 1945, city editor, 1948-49, exec. editor, 1949-77; rewrite man N.Y. Jour.-Am., 1944; mng. editor N.Y. Post-Home News, Bronx, 1946-47. Cons. Municipal Housing Authority, Yonkers, N.Y., 1939. Author: (with J.D. Horan) Pictorial History of the Wild West, 1954; the Lawless Decade, 1957; (with Arnold Red Auerbach) Red Auerbach: Winning the Hard Way, 1967; Fads, Follies and Delusions of the American People, 1967; Kill the Dutchman! The Story of Dutch Schultz, 1971; Dead Heat: Love and Money, 1974; The Angry Decade: The Sixties, 1979; American Panorama, 1980; Contbr. to nat. mags.; A Century of Journalism, 1943; More Post Biographies, 1947; These Were Our Years, 1959. Home: 281 W 4th St New York NY 10014

SANNER, ROYCE NORMAN, corp. exec.; b. Lancaster, Minn., Mar. 9, 1931; s. Oscar N. and Clara (Hermanson) S.; B.S., Moorhead State Coll., 1953; LL.B. cum laude, U. Minn., 1961; m. Janice L. Sterne, Dec. 27, 1972; children—Michelle Joy, Craig Allen. Tchr. English, Karlstad (Minn.) High Sch., 1955-57; counsel IDS Life Ins. Co., Mpls., 1961-68, v.p., gen. counsel, 1969-72, exec. v.p., gen. counsel, 1972-77; dir. corporate devel. Investors Diversified Services, Inc., Mpls., 1968-69, v.p., gen. counsel, 1975-78, v.p. Benefit Plans Service Group, 1978—; dir. IDS Life Ins. Co. N.Y., IDS Mktg. Corp., Tower Mortgage Corp. Mem. Citizens League; trustee IDS Realty Trust. Served with arty., U.S. Army, 1953-55. Mem. Am., Minn., Hennepin County, Fed. bar assns., Assn. Life Ins. Counsel. Club: Mpls. Home: 4811 Westminster Rd Minneapolis MN 55435 Office: IDS Tower Minneapolis MN 55402

SANROMA, JESUS MARIA, pianist; b. Carolina, P.R., Nov. 7, 1902; s. José Maria and Maria Torra (de la Riva) S.; grad. New Eng. Conservatory Music, 1920; student of Szumowska (Boston), Cortot (Paris), Schnabel (Berlin); Mus.D. (hon.), Boston Coll., 1949; A.F.D. (hon.), U. P.R., 1950, Mus. D., U. Miami, 1955, New England Conservatory, 1963, World U. of P.R., 1972, Conservatory of Music of P.R., 1972; D.H.L., Catholic U. of Ponce P.R., 1969, St. Peter's Coll., Jersey City, 1973; m. Mercedes Pasarell, Aug. 15, 1934; children—Marisol, Amelia, Mercedes, Natalia. Recital debut, Boston, 1924; orch. debut with Boston Symphony, 1926; recitals in London, Paris, Vienna, Berlin, Madrid, Barcelona, also throughout U.S. and Can.; played at 1st Pan. Am. Chamber Music Festival (Mexico City), Library of Congress Festival, Casal's Festival, P.R., also festivals at Pittsfield, Worcester, Berkshire; Mex., Central and S. Am. tour, summer 1945; mem. faculty New Eng. Conservatory of Music, 1930-40; vis. prof. music U. P.R., summers, 1932-36; now head piano faculty Conservatory Music P.R. Victor Red Seal rec. artist, numerous others. Named Equitem Commendatorem Ordinis Sancti Silvestri Papae by Pope Paul VI, 1977. Mem. Acad. Arts and Scis. P.R., Kappa Gamma Psi; hon. mem. Atenco Puertorriqueno. Roman Catholic. Lion, Rotarian. Home: Cond Garden Hills Tower PH-1 Garden Ct Guaynabo PR 00657 Office: Conservatorio de Musica de PR Hato Rey PR 00931

SANSCHAGRIN, ALBERT, bishop; b. St-Tite, Que., Can., Aug. 5, 1911; s. Henri and Leontine (Chevron) S.; student arts U. Ottawa, 1924-30; oblate scholasticate, Richelieu, Que., 1931-33, Sainte Agathe des Monts, 1933-37. Ordained priest Roman Catholic Ch., 1936; tchr. oblates scholasticate, 1937-39; asst. gen. chaplain Young Christian Workers, Montreal, 1939-47; founder world wide preparation for Marriage Course, 1941; missionary to Chile, 1947-53; superior provincial Oblates of M.I., 1953-57; coadjutor bishop of Amos, Que., 1957-59, apostolic adminstr., 1959-67; bishop of St. Hyacinthe, 1967-79. Pres. Joint Commn. Bishops-Religious, 1968; mem. Episcopal Commn. Missions, 1975. Address: Evêché 1900 Girouard CP 190 St-Hyacinthe PQ J2S 7B4 Canada

SANSOM, RICHARD E., wholesale exec.; b. Jefferson City, Tenn., Nov. 24, 1938; s. Richard E. and Sylvia Margaret (Ball) S.; B.S., U. Tenn., 1961; M.B.A., U. Pa., 1964; m. Claudette Cartwright, Nov. 28, 1970; children—Heather Marie, Charles Richard. Asst. to treas. Sav-A-Stop, Inc., Jacksonville, Fla., 1969-71, asst. treas., 1971-74, treas., 1974—, controller, 1975—, v.p., 1976—; dir. Cherokee Explosives Co. Served with USMC, 1959. Mem. Fin. Execs. Inst. Patentee windage navigation calculator. Home: PO Box 842 Ponte Vedra Beach FL 32082 Office: Sav-A-Stop Inc 2050 Art Museum Dr Jacksonville FL 32207

SANSON, KENNETH DUDLEY, JR., educator; b. Los Angeles, July 26, 1932; s. Kenneth Dudley and Evelyn (Thomas) S.; B.A., Occidental Coll., 1954; M.S., U. So. Calif., 1966. Tenor with Roger Wagner Chorale, 1953-66; mgr. choral dept. Keynote Music Service, Los Angeles, 1962-66; asso. music critic Chgo. Today, 1966-72; mem. faculty Am. Conservatory Music, Chgo., 1970—. Mem. music panel Ill. Arts Council; dir. music Presbyn. Ch. of Western Springs (Ill.), 1974—. Served with AUS, 1956-57. Rockefeller fellow, 1965. Mem. Delta Omicron (hon. patron Psi chpt.). Record reviewer Am. Libraries, 1973-75. Home: 55 W Chestnut St Chicago IL 60610 Office: 116 S Michigan Ave Chicago IL 60603

SAN SOUCIE, ROBERT LOUIS, investment banker; b. Adams, Mass., Apr. 30, 1927; s. Leo Russell and Ora Mae (Sturm) San S.; A.B., U. Mass., 1949; M.A., U. Wis., 1950 Ph.D., 1953; m. Mary Patricia Molm, Sept, 5, 1953; children—Richard Peter, Marc David, Mary Frances. External ballistician U.S. Naval Ordnance Test Sta., China Lake, Calif., 1952; instr., asst. prof. math. U. Oreg., 1953-57; sect. head math. Sylvania Electronic Systems, Buffalo, 1957-58, mgr. communications research devel., 1959, mgr. communications system lab., 1960-61, mgr. systems project lab., 1962, v.p., tech. dir. electronics and space div. Emerson Electric Co., St. Louis, 1962-64, pres., gen. mgr., 1964-67, exec. v.p., 1967-71; pres. DLJ Capital Corp., subsidiary Donaldson, Lufkin & Jenrette, N.Y.C., 1971-75; mng. dir. Mill River Ventures, Ltd., 1975—. Served with USNR, 1945-46; PTO. Mem. Am. Math. Soc., Math. Assn. Am., Am. Rocket Soc., Phi Beta Kappa, Sigma Xi, Phi Kappa Phi. Contbr. articles to profl. jours. Home: 35 Cayuga Way Short Hills NJ 07078 Office: PO Box 156 Short Hills NJ 07078

SANSTEAD, WAYNE GODFREY, educator, lt. gov. N.D.; b. Hot Springs, Ark., Apr. 16, 1935; s. Godrey A. and Clara (Buen) S.; B.A. in Speech and Polit. Sci., St. Olaf Coll., 1957; M.A. in Pub. Address, Northwestern U., 1966; Ed.D., U. N.D., 1974; m. Mary Jane Bober, June 16, 1957; children—Timothy, Jonathan. Tchr., Luverne, Minn., 1959-60; dir. forensics Minot (N.D.) High Sch., 1960-71, tchr. social sci., 1960—; mem. N.D. Ho. of Reps., 1965-70, N.D. Senate, 1971-73; lt. gov. N.D., Bismarck, 1973—. Served with AUS, 1957-59. Coe Family Found. scholar, 1963; Eagleton scholar Rutgers U., 1969; named N.D. Outstanding Freshman Senator, A.P., 1971; Outstanding Young Educator, N.D. Jr. C. of C., 1967; Outstanding Young Man, Minot Jr. C. of C., 1969. Mem. N.D. Edn. Assn., NEA (legis. com. 1969—), Central States Speech Assn., Am. Forensic Assn., Jr. C. of C., Sons of Norway. Democrat. Lutheran (chmn. Western N.D. research and social action com. 1962-68). Elk, Toastmaster. Home: 1114 Keating Dr Bismarck ND 58501 Office: State Capitol Bldg Bismarck ND 58501

SANT, JOHN TALBOT, corp. lawyer; b. Ann Arbor, Mich., Oct. 7, 1932; s. John Francis and Josephine (Williams) S.; A.B., Princeton, 1954; LL.B., Harvard, 1957; m. Almira Steedman Baldwin, Jan. 31, 1959; children—John Talbot, Richard Baldwin, Frank Williams. Admitted to Mo. bar, 1957, since practiced in St. Louis; asso. lawyer firm Thompson, Mitchell, Douglas & Neil, 1958-60; lawyer McDonnell Douglas Corp., 1960-61, asst. sec., 1961-62, sec., 1962-74, corporate v.p., legal sec., 1974-75, corporate v.p., gen. counsel, 1975—, also dir. Mem. Am., St. Louis bar assns. Home: 9 Ridgewood St Louis MO 63124 Office: Box 516 Lambert-St Louis Municipal Airport St Louis MO 63166

SANTANA, CARLOS, guitarist; b. Autlan de Navarro, Mexico, July 20, 1947. Played guitar in Tijuana nightclubs, then moved to San Francisco, late 1960's; recorded with Mike Bloomfield and Al Kooper's Super Session; founder, guitarist rock band Santana, 1966—; appeared at Woodstock Festival, 1969; rec. artist Columbia Records, 1969—; world-wide concert tours with Santana Band; performed and recorded with Buddy Miles, John McLaughlin and Alice Coltrane. Recipient Gold Medal award, 1977. Office: care Bill Graham Prodns 201 11th St San Francisco CA 94103*

SANTANGELI, FRANK, ins. co. exec.; b. Liverpool, Eng., June 20, 1934; s. Louie and Ellen Santangeli; grad. Sch. Slavonic Studies, Cambridge (Eng.) U., 1954; m. Anne Gauge, Dec. 21, 1957; children—Susan, David, Peter. Asst. gen. mgr. for Can., Occidental Life Ins. Co. Calif., 1958-69; with Sun Life Assurance Co. Can., Toronto, 1970—, mgmt. services officer, then corp. sec., 1977-79, v.p. mktg., 1979—. C.L.U., Can., U.S. Mem. Planning Execs. Inst., N.Am. Soc. Corp. Planning. Clubs: York Downs Golf and Country (Toronto), Masons. Home: 56 Coldstream Ave Toronto ON Canada Office: 20 King St W 11th Floor Toronto ON Canada

SANTARELLI, DONALD EUGENE, lawyer; b. Hershey, Pa., July 22, 1937; s. Ambrose and Ercolina (Altobelli) S.; LL.B., U. Va., 1962; m. Anne Constance Dunlap, May 30, 1966; children—Louisa Rush, Alessandro Rush. Admitted to Va. bar, 1962, D.C. bar, 1964; law clk. to judge U.S. Dist. Ct. Western Dist. Va., 1964-65; asst. corp. counsel D.C., 1965; asst. U.S. atty. D.C., 1966-67; counsel U.S. Ho. of Reps. Com. on Judiciary, 1967-68; spl. counsel U.S. Senate Com. on Judiciary, Subcom. on Constl. Rights, 1968; asso. dep. atty. gen. Dept. Justice, Washington, 1969-72, adminstr. Law Enforcement Assistance Adminstrn., 1973-74; partner firm Santarelli and Gimer, Washington, 1974—. Bd. dirs. Corp. Public Broadcasting, 1975—, Nat. Italian Am. Found., 1978—; bd. visitors U. Va., 1970-78; mem. Republican Nat. Com. Council on Gen. Govt., 1978—. Mem. Am. Bar Assn. (council criminal justice sect. 1975—), Am. Judicature Soc. (dir.). Roman Catholic. Club: Farmington Country. Home: 504 Duke St Alexandria VA 22314 Office: 2033 M St NW Suite 700 Washington DC 20036

SANTELLI, T(HOMAS) ROBERT, mfg. co. exec.; b. Pitts., Jan. 20, 1923; s. Joseph Lester and Goldie (Craig) S.; B.S., Westminster Coll., New Wilmington, Pa., 1944; M.S., Purdue U., 1946, Ph.D., 1948; m. A. Irene Treat, June 30, 1945; children—Thomas R., James Craig. Research chemist Gen. Tire & Rubber Co., Akron, Ohio, 1948-49; research asso. Purdue U., 1949-50; sr. research chemist Plaskon div. Allied Chem. Co., Toledo, 1950-54; with Owens-Ill., Inc., 1954—, tech. dir. forest products div., 1965-73, v.p. new product and process devel., Toledo, 1973-74, v.p., dir. research and devel., 1974-78; dir. Pantek, Inc., Mid-Am. Solar Energy Complex, Sunmaster Corp., Andover Controls Corp., Electro Oxide Corp.; gen. mgr. operating com. Nat. Petro Chem. Corp., 1976—, also dir.; v.p., gen. mgr. Energy Products and Ventures Group, 1978—. Div. chmn. Toledo United Way, 1976-78. Fellow AAAS; mem. Am. Chem. Soc. (counsellor), Soc. Plastics Industry, Plastics Inst. Am. (chmn. trustees), Fourdrinier Kraft Bd. Inst., Indsl. Research Inst. (co. rep.), Sigma Xi, Phi Beta Upsilon. Club: Toledo. Patentee silicone compositions for surface treatment glass fibers, plastic blowing processes, foamed plastic articles, plastic container design. Office: PO Box 1035 Toledo OH 43666

SANTELMANN, PAUL WILLIAM, educator; b. Ann Arbor, Mich., Oct. 18, 1926; s. Alfred William and Frances Hazel (Eppens) S.; B.S., U. Md., 1950; M.S., Mich. State U., 1952; Ph.D., Ohio State U., 1954; m. Susanna Porter, Dec. 28, 1950; children—Patricia Santelmann Emerick, Steven, Douglas, Barbara. Asst. prof. agronomy U. Md., 1954-61, asso. prof., 1961-62; asso. prof. agronomy Okla. State U., Stillwater, 1962-65, prof. agronomy, 1965-74, Regents prof. agronomy, 1974-78, head dept. agronomy, 1977—; mem. adv. group on pest mgmt. and research Pres.'s Council on Environ. Quality, 1971-72, mem. USSR pest mgmt. research rev. team, 1974; mem. herbicide study group of adv. com. on hazardous materials EPA, 1972-73; mem. pest control team Nat. Acad. Scis., 1973-74; mem. integrated pest mgmt. rev. team U.S. Dept. Agr., 1976; mem. organizing and policy com. IX Internat. Congress Plant Protection, 1979. Served with U.S. Army, 1944-46. Fellow Weed Sci. Soc. Am. (pres. 1978-79, editor newsletter 1972-75, named outstanding tchr. 1972), Am. Soc. Agronomy; mem. Am. Inst. Biol. Sci. (governing bd. 1979—), Council for Agrl. Sci. and Tech. (dir. 1975-78), So. Weed Sci. Soc. (pres. 1975-76), Intersoc. Consortium for Plant Protection (exec. bd. 1977—). Methodist (treas. ch. 1967—). Contbr. articles to sci. jours. Home: 1101 Lakeridge Dr Stillwater OK 74074

SANTEN, HARRY H(OFFMAN), lawyer; b. Cin., Aug. 29, 1929; s. Herman William and Margaret (Earls) S.; A.B., Georgetown U., 1951; J.D., U. Cin., 1957; m. Ann Hortenstine, Oct. 4, 1958; children—Edward E., Sally Ann, Matthew G. Admitted to Ohio bar, 1957, U.S. Dist. Ct. bar, 1957; co-founding and sr. mem. firm Santen, Santen & Hughes Co., L.P.A., Cin., 1958—, mng. partner, 1966—; dir. Burgoyne Market Research, Natmar, Inc., Champion Screen Co., and other corps.; treas. Legal Aid Soc. Cin. Vice pres. Madeira and Indian Hill (Ohio) Fire Co., 1967-79; chmn. bd. Heart Assn. Southwestern Ohio, 1968-70; pres. Cin. Opera Assn., 1972-76, chmn. bd., 1976-79. Served with U.S. Army, 1950-52. Mem. Cin. Bar Assn., Ohio State Bar Assn. Republican. Roman Catholic. Clubs: Queen City, Camargo. Author Ohio Tax Survey, 1956, 57. Home: 5695 Drake Rd Cincinnati OH 45243 Office: 916 First Nat Bank Bldg Cincinnati OH 45202

SANTERRE, RENAUD GRATIEN, anthropologist, univ. adminstr.; b. Squatteck, Que., Can., Sept. 29, 1936; s. Louis and Adele (Damboise) S.; M.A. in Anthropology, U. Laval (Que.), 1963; Doctorat Ethnologie, U. Paris, 1968; m. Denise Veillette, May 25, 1963 (div.); 1 son, Pierre-Yves. Reporter, Le Droit, Le Soleil, La presse, Ottawa, Quebec, and Montreal, 1958-59, 60-62; asst. prof. anthropology U. Laval, 1968-72, asso. prof., 1972-77, prof., 1977—, dean Faculty Social Scis., 1976—, dir. Journal etudiant Le Carabin de Laval, 1959-60. Pres. Gen. Assn. Students U. Laval, 1961-62. Can. Council Fgn. Area fellow, 1965-68. Mem. Canadian Assn. African Studies, Canadian Ethnology Soc., Canadian Assn. Sociologists, Anthropologists of French Lang., Societe des africanistes. Author: Moslem Pedagogy in Black Africa, 1973. Home: 3297 rue l'Heureux 8 Ste-Foy PQ 61X 1Y7 Canada Office: Faculte des sciences sociales Universite Laval PQ G1K 7P4 Canada

SANTI, MAURICE JOHN, banker; b. N.Y.C., Dec. 12, 1915; s. John E. and Celina M. (Umbdenstock) S.; student Seattle Coll., 1933-35; B.A., U. Wash., 1937, M.B.A., 1939; postgrad. Pacific Coast Banking Sch., 1948-50, Stonier Grad. Sch. Banking Rutgers U., 1958-60; m. Mary E. Sheffield, May 11, 1943; children—Marueen E., John S., Denise M., Robert P., Richard T., Stephen W. Instr. St. Martin's Coll., Lacey, Wash., 1939-41; finance analyst Nat. Resources Planning Bd., 1941-42; with Nat. Bank Commerce (name now Rainier Nat. Bank), Seattle, 1942—, asst. cashier, 1948-50, asst. v.p., 1950-56, v.p., 1957-58, v.p., mgr. central office, 1959-70, sr. v.p., br. adminstr., 1971-74, sr. v.p., mgr. main office region, 1974—. Mem. vis. com. Sch. Social Work U. Wash.; trustee, v.p. Seattle Better Bus. Bur. Clubs: Wash. Athletic, Harbor, Rainier (Seattle). Home: 805 14th Ave E Seattle WA 98112 Office: Rainier Nat Bank PO Box C34028 Seattle WA 98124

SANTI, TINA, corp. exec.; b. Memphis, May 18; d. Clement Alexander and Dale (Pendergrast) S.; B.A., Memphis State U., 1961; hon. Doctorate, St. John's U., 1979; m. William Edward Flaherty, Feb. 22, 1976. Commentator guest interview program Sta. WMC-TV, Memphis, 1960-61; newscaster, commentator Sta. WHER, Memphis, 1961-62; community relations specialist Western Electric Co., N.Y.C., 1964-66; v.p. pub. relations div. Grey Advt., N.Y.C., 1966-72; dep. dir. corporate relations Colgate-Palmolive Co., N.Y.C., 1972-75, dir. corp. relations, 1975-76, corp. v.p., v.p. in charge of communications, 1976—. Gen. chmn. YWCA-N.Y.C., Salute to Women in Business, 1979; chmn. Bus. Council, UN Decade for Women; bd. dirs. Nat. Jr. Achievement, 1978—, Women's Forum, 1979, Girl Scouts U.S., 1979, Nat. Girls Club, 1979—. Named One of 8 Outstanding Women in Bus. and Labor, Women's Equity Action League, 1978; One of N.Y.C.'s Outstanding Women of Achievement, NCCJ, 1978; One of 100 Top Corp. Women, Bus. Week, 1976. Mem. Women Execs. in Pub. Relations, The Exec. Woman (bd. dirs.). Home: 50 E 89th St New York NY 10028 Office: 300 Park Ave New York NY 10022. *Persistence alone is omnipotent.*

SANTILLI, PAUL THOMAS, lawyer; b. Columbus, Ohio, Feb. 10, 1929; s. Paul and Vienna Angela (Ofrenzo) S.; B.S. in Chem. Engring., Ohio State U., 1951, M.S., 1951; LL.B., Capital U., 1960, J.D., 1968; m. Joanne Marie Beer, Feb. 16, 1957. Admitted to Ohio bar, 1960; chem. engr. Battelle Meml. Inst., Columbus, 1953-60, atty., 1960-63, chief counsel, 1968-72, chief counsel, v.p., 1972—; chief counsel Battelle-N.W. Labs., Richland, Wash., 1963-68; dir. Sci. Advances, Inc., Battelle Commons Co. Bd. dirs. Jr. Achievement of Columbus, Inc. Served with USAF, 1951-53. Mem. Am., Ohio, Columbus bar assns., Ohio State U. Alumni Assn., Columbus C. of C., Tau Beta Pi. Kiwanian. Home: 1289 Fountaine Dr Columbus OH 43221 Office: 505 King Ave Columbus OH 43201

SANTINI, JAMES DAVID, Congressman; b. Reno, Aug. 13, 1937; B.S. in Edn., U. Nev., 1959; J.D., U. Calif. at Berkeley, 1962; m. Ann Marie Crane; children—David, Lisa, Kerrie, Lori, Mark, James Danford. Admitted to Calif. bar, 1962, Nev. bar, 1962, Ariz. bar, 1966, U.S. Supreme Ct. bar, 1966; practiced in Las Vegas, 1966-68; dep. dist. atty. Clark County (Nev.), 1968-69, pub. defender, 1968-70; justice of peace, 1970-72; judge Clark County Dist. Ct., 1972-74; mem.-at-large 94th Congress from Nev.; instr. U. Las Vegas, 1967-71; lectr. Nat. Legal Aid and Defender Assn., 1968, Practising Law Inst., 1968-70, Am. Acad. Jud. Edn., 1971-74, Nat. Coll. State Judiciary, 1973; owner, lectr. Nev. Bar Rev., 1970-74. Chmn. So. Nev. chpt. March of Dimes, 1973; bd. dirs., chmn. So. Nev. Mus., 1968-74. Served with AUS, 1963-66. Decorated Order of Merit of Italian Republic; recipient Watchdog of Treasury award Nat. Assn. Businessmen, 1978; named Outstanding Young Man of Year, Nev. Jaycees, 1971. Mem. Nev. Judges Assn. (1st pres. 1971). Democrat. Office: 1007 Longworth House Office Bldg Washington DC 20515

SANTINI, JOHN AMEDEO, educator; b. Detroit, Nov. 4, 1926; s. Amedeo Enrico and Ida Mercurio (LaFata) S.; B.A., U. Chgo., 1948; J.D., Wayne State U., 1953; M.A., U. Mich., 1960; Ed.D., Harvard, 1965; m. Mary Beverly Bergman, Aug. 11, 1956; children—Maria Bettina, Lucia Bianca, John Amedeo. Prodn. engr. Fisher body div. Gen. Motors Corp., 1949-51; admitted to Mich. bar, 1954; pvt. practice, Detroit 1954-56; tchr. elementary and middle grades, St. Clair Shores and Grosse Pointe, Mich., 1956-60; elementary sch. prin., Chagrin Falls, Ohio, 1960-62; curriculum study dir., Brockton, Mass., 1963-64; supt. schs., Farmington, Conn., 1964-66, New Haven, 1966-69; prof. edn., chmn. dept. edn., Conn. Coll., New London, 1969—; lectr. edn. Western Res. U., 1962; vis. prof. edn. adminstrn. U. Bridgeport, 1971; cons. edn. Sarasota (Fla.) County, 1963—, Walpole, Mass., 1964, West Hartford, Conn., 1973. Mem. Corp. Edn. Devel. Center; mem. adv. council Fairfield U. Prep Sch., Conn. State Dept. Edn. Arbitration Panel. Served with USAAF, World War II. Mem. Am. (adv. commn. on youth edn. for citizenship), Mich. bar assns., Am. Judicature Soc., Am. Fedn. Musicians, Am., Conn., New Eng. assns. sch. supts., Nat., Conn., Mich. edn. assns., Nat. Orgn. Legal Problems of Edn., Am. Assn. U. Profs., Conn. Assn. Colls. and Univs. for Tchr. Edn. (pres. 1973-74), Conn. Profs. Ednl. Adminstrn. (pres. 1973-74), Phi Kappa Phi, Phi Delta Kappa. Presbyn. (deacon). Home: Sill Ln Old Lyme CT 06371 Office: Conn Coll New London CT 06320

SANTONI, RONALD ERNEST, educator; b. Arvida, Que., Can., Dec. 19, 1931; s. Fred Albert and Phyllis (Tremaine) S.; B.A., Bishop's U., Lennoxville, Que., 1952; M.A., Brown U., 1954; Ph.D., Boston U., 1961; postgrad. U. Paris (Sorbonne), 1956-57, Yale, 1961-62; m.

Marguerite Ada Kiene, June 25, 1955; children—Christina, Marcia, Andrea, Juanita, Jonathan, Sondra. Asst. prof. philosophy U. Pacific, Stockton, Calif., 1958-61; asst. prof. philosophy Wabash Coll., Crawfordsville, Ind., 1962-64; mem. faculty Denison U., Granville, Ohio, 1964—, prof. philosophy, 1968—, chmn. dept., 1971-73, Maria Theresa Barney chair in philosophy, 1978—. Vice pres. NAACP, Licking County, 1967; mem. Crawfordsville Human Relations Council, 1962-64; mem. nat. exec. com. Episcopal Peace Fellowship, 1968—. Trustee Margaret Hall Sch., Versailles, Ky., 1972-74. Canadian Govt. Overseas fellow, 1956-57; Church Soc. for Coll. Work faculty fellow, 1961-62; Soc. for Religion postdoctoral fellow, 1972—; Yale postdoctoral research fellow, 1961-62, 75; guest fellow Berkeley Coll., Yale, 1975. Mem. Am. Philos. Assn., Internat. Phenomenological Soc., Ch. Soc. for Coll. Work, A.C.L.U., Soc. for Philos. Study Marxism, Fellowship of Reconciliation, War Resisters League; Union of Bi-Nat. Profls. Against Omnicide (v.p. 1978—). Episcopalian. Contbg. author: Current Philosophical Issues, 1966. Editor: Religious Language and the Problem of Religious Knowledge, 1968; co-editor Social and Political Philosophy, 1963. Contbr. numerous articles to profl. jours., also to The Progressive. Home: 500 Burg St Granville OH 43023. *Gratitude for what one has been given, commitment to personal growth and integrity, some "gracious gall," listening to the world's humiliated, and a recognition that success—genuine human success—is a function of grace.*

SANTORA, PHILLIP JOSEPH, feature writer; b. N.Y.C., July 29, 1911; s. Sebastian F. and Rose (Pasquino) s.; student Syracuse U., 1929; B.A., N.Y. U., 1933; postgrad. Sorbonne, Paris; m. Filamena Coletta, July 20, 1939; children—Colette, Elizabeth. Successively copy boy, police reporter, rewriteman, feature writer N.Y. Daily Mirror, 1936-43, 46-54; spl. feature writer N.Y. Daily News, 1954—; prof. Journalism Marymount Coll., Tarrytown, N.Y., 1952-56. Served with Intelligence Corps, AUS, 1943-46. Recipient award for series on Bellevue Hosp., Citizens Budget Commn., 1955; recipient Polk Meml. award for best met. reporting, 1957, award Portestant Council, 1958, Pulitzer prize for internat. reporting, 1959, Page One award for series on Cuban revolution, 1959, Silurian award for best pub. service series on Castro's Cuba, 1960, for series on revolt within Cath. Ch., 1970; recipient V.F.W. award, 1965, 67, Deadline Club award, 1967, award for med. writing, 1962, Internat. Assn. Firefighters and Uniformed Officers award, 1972, Silurian award, Page One award for anti-war article, 1974. Office: 220 E 42d St New York NY 10017*

SANTOS, GEORGE WESLEY, educator, physician; b. Oak Park, Ill., Feb. 3, 1928; s. George and Emma (Gast) S.; S.B., Mass. Inst. Tech., 1951, M.S. in Phys. Biology, 1951; M.D., Johns Hopkins, 1955; m. Joanne Agnes Corrigan, June 7, 1952; children—Susan Elizabeth, George Wesley II, Kelly Anne, Amy Coburn. Intern, Johns Hopkins Hosp., 1955-56, asst. resident, 1958-60; scholar Leukemia Soc., 1961-66; mem. faculty Johns Hopkins Sch. Medicine, 1962—, asso. prof. medicine, 1968-73, prof. oncology and medicine, 1973—; asst. physician in chief Balt. City Hosp., 1963-77; mem. Cancer Clin. Investigative Rev. Com., 1969-73; mem. extramural sci. adv. bd. Meml. Sloan-Kettering Cancer Center, 1977—; mem. Immunology-Epidemiology Spl. Virus Cancer Program, 1969-73; chmn. bone marrow transplant registry A.C.S., 1969-73; mem. Internat. Com. Organ Transplant Registry A.C.S., 1969-73; mem. cell biology-immunology-genetics research evaluation com. VA, 1969-71. Served with USNR, 1956-58. Mem. Am. Assn. Hematology, Transplatation Soc. (counselor 1971-73), Am. Assn. Immunologists, Leukemia Soc. Am. (dir. 1973—), Internat. Soc. Exptl. Hematology (councillor 1973), Am. Assn. Cancer Research, Am. Soc. Clin. Investigation. Asso. editor Cancer Research, 1978—; editorial adv. bd. Jour. Immunopharmacology, 1978—. Home: 13623 Bardon Rd Phoenix MD 21131 Office: Johns Hopkins Hosp Baltimore MD 21205

SANTOS, JOE, actor; b. Bklyn., June 9, 1931; s. Joseph and Rose (Sarno) Minieri; student Fordham U., 1949-50, Miami U., Oxford, Ohio, 1950-51; m. Mary Montero, Mar. 31, 1958; children—Joseph, Perry. Has worked with Warner Bros., Columbia Screen Gems, Metro-Goldwyn-Mayer, Universal Studios; regular TV show The Rockford Files, NBC-TV, 1974—. Served with M.C., AUS, 1952-54. Roman Catholic. Office: care John Crosby and Assos 9046 Sunset Blvd Suite 210 Beverly Hills CA 90210*

SANTRY, ARTHUR JOSEPH, JR., engring. co. exec.; b. Brookline, Mass., Aug. 1, 1918; s. Arthur Joseph and Suzanne (Cawley) S.; B.A., Williams Coll., 1941; LL.B., Harvard, 1948; m. Julia Timmins, June 4, 1955; children—Arthur Joseph III, Suzanne, Peter, Charles, Robert. Admitted to Mass. bar, 1948; partner firm Putnam, Bell, Santry & Ray, Boston, 1948-56; sec. Combustion Engring., Inc., Stamford, Conn., 1956-57, v.p., 1957, vice chmn., 1957, pres., chief exec. officer, vice chmn. exec. com., 1963—, also dir.; dir. AMAX, Inc., Greenwich, Conn., Bristol-Myers Co., N.Y., Jenney Oil Co., Inc., Newton, Mass., N.Am. Reins. Corp., N.Y., N.Am. Reassurance Co., N.Y., Putnam Trust Co. of Greenwich, Conn., Singer Co., N.Y. Served to lt. (s.g.) USNR, 1942-46. Mem. Soc. Naval Architects and Marine Engrs., Navy League U.S., Newcomen Soc. in N.Am., Econ. Club of N.Y. Clubs: Board Room, Links, New York Yacht (N.Y.C.); Seawanhaka Corinthian Yacht (Oyster Bay, N.Y.); Storm Trysail (Larchmont, N.Y.); Country (Brookline, Mass.); Eastern Yacht (Marblehead, Mass.); Indian Harbor Yacht, Field, Round Hill (Greenwich, Conn.); Lyford Cay (Nassau, Bahamas); Royal Bermuda Yacht (Hamilton); Royal Ocean Racing (London, Eng.). Home: 62 Vineyard Ln Greenwich CT 06830 Office: 900 Long Ridge Rd Stamford CT 06902

SANTULLI, THOMAS VINCENT, surgeon; b. N.Y.C., Mar. 16, 1915; s. Frank and Amalia (Avagliano) S.; B.S., Columbia, 1935; M.D., Georgetown U., 1939; m. Dorothy Muriel Beverly, Apr. 10, 1941; children—Thomas Vincent Jr., Robert B. Intern N.Y. Polyclinic Hosp., 1939-41, resident, 1941-44; prof. surgery Columbia, 1967—; chief pediatric surg. service, Babies Hosp., Columbia-Presbyn. Med. Center, N.Y.C., 1955—; attending surgeon Presybn. Hosp., Columbia-Presbyn. Med. Center, 1960—. Mem. Am. Surg. Assn., Am. Pediatric Surg. Assn., A.C.S., British Assn. Pediatric Surgeons, N.Y. Pediatric Surg. Soc. (pres. 1967-69). Office: Babies Hosp 3959 Broadway New York NY 10032

SAPERS, CARL MARTIN, lawyer; b. Boston, July 16, 1932; s. Abraham E. and Anne (Herwitz) S.; A.B., Harvard Coll., 1953; J.D., Harvard U., 1958; m. Judith H. Thompson, Nov. 29, 1959; children—Jonathan Simonds, Rachel Elizabeth, Benjamin Lovell. Admitted to Mass. bar, 1958; asso. firm Hill, Barlow, Goodale & Adams, Boston, 1958-65; partner firm Hill & Barlow, Boston, 1965—; counsel Mass. Crime Commn.; spl. asst. atty. gen. Criminal div. Commonwealth of Mass., 1963-65; vis. sr. lectr. Mass. Inst. Tech., 1972—; spl. cons. Mass. Ethics Commn., 1978-79; mem. com. on legal edn. Supreme Jud. Ct., 1979—. Chmn., Brookline Adv. Com., 1973-75; treas. Citizens Housing and Planning Assn., 1974-75; chmn. Ward 5, Beacon Hill-Back Bay (Boston) Democratic Ward Com., 1960-63; bd. dirs. Boston Archtl. Center, 1970-76, Greater Boston Community Devel., Inc., 1973-75; rep. to bd. trustees Commonwealth Sch., 1976—. Served with U.S. Army, 1953-55. Recipient Allied Professions medal AIA, 1975. Mem. Boston Bar Assn. (council 1970-73, chmn. sect. urban affairs 1971-74), Boston Soc. Architects (hon.). Contbr. to Archtl. Registration Handbook, 1975, Constrn. Industry Handbook, 1978; Dow-Jones Construction Handbook; contbr. articles to constn. industry jours. Home: 26 Chesham Rd Brookline MA 02146 Office: 225 Franklin St Boston MA 02110

SAPERSTEIN, HENRY GAHAGAN, motion picture and TV producer; b. Chgo., 1918; s. Aaron and Beatrice B. (Schilling) S.; student U. Chgo., Ill. Inst. Tech.; children—Richard, Joan, Laurel, Gina, Patricia. Motion picture, TV producer and distbr.; pres. UPA Pictures, Inc., UPA Prodns. of Am., Screen Entertainment Co., Benedict Pictures Corp. Office: 4440 Lakeside Dr Burbank CA 91505

SAPERSTON, HOWARD TRUMAN, SR., lawyer; b. Buffalo, Oct. 30, 1899; s. Willard W. and Julia (Wilson) S.; student Cornell U., 1917; LL.B., Syracuse U., 1921, LL.D. (hon.), 1969; m. Nan Basch, Oct. 5, 1937; children—Howard Truman, Willard B. Admitted to N.Y. bar, 1922, since practiced in Buffalo; mem. firm Saperston, Day & Radler; dir. Woodlets, Inc., Universal Jet, Inc. Mem. Nat. council, mem. exec. com. Buffalo council Boy Scouts Am.; gov. United Jewish Fedn., 1948-51; pres. Community Vol. Service Bur., 1946-47; bd. dirs. United Fund, 1950-68, 1973-74, trustee, 1950—; bd. dirs. Buffalo chpt. ARC, 1948—; gen. chmn. Communtiy Chest-ARC campaign, 1955; v.p. Federated Health Fund Buffalo, 1948-49; mem. adv. bd. Cerebral Palsy Assn. Western N.Y., 1953-68; bd. dirs. Buffalo Tennis Found., 1970-72; mem. exec. bd., co-chmn. Buffalo chpt. NCCJ, 1962-65; v.p. Council Jewish Fedns. and Welfare Funds for N.Y., Ont., 1935-50; bd. dirs. Jr. Achievement of Niagara Frontier, 1960—; pres. United Jewish Fedn., 1952-55, Community Chest, 1956-57; trustee Union of Am. Hebrew Congregations, 1956; pres. Temple Beth Zion, 1953-55; nat. council Joint Def. Appeal; nat. council Am. Jewish Joint Distbn. Com.; del. bd. Community Welfare Council; dir. Western N.Y. Traffic Council; N.Y. State asso. chmn. U.S. Olympic Com., 1976; regent Canisius Coll., 1955-70, trustee, 1970-77; mem. council U. Buffalo, 1957-63; chmn. bd. dirs. Chmns. Club of Erie County Rep. Party 1965-72, pres., 1978—; bd. visitors Syracuse U. Coll. Law, 1960—; mem. deans adv. com. U. Buffalo Coll. Law, 1955-65; bd. dirs. Bradley Sch. Music; pres., 1969-71, trustee Buffalo Gen. Hosp.; mem. adv. com. Children's Hosp., 1962-69; mem. governing com. Buffalo Found., 1960-77, chmn., 1972-75; chmn. United Negro Coll. Fund, 1951-52, gen. chmn., 1953; bd. dirs. Greater Buffalo Devel. Found., 1960-68, Buffalo Urban League, 1942-65, Meals on Wheels, 1978—; mem. devel. bd. U. Buffalo, 1957-62; dir. mem. Presidents' Assos. State U. N.Y. at Buffalo; dir. Jewish Center Buffalo, 1940-43; mem. adv. bd. Camp Lakeland, 1950—; chmn. Erie County Republican Finance Com., 1954-73. Served with U.S. Army, World War I. Named one of 6 outstanding citizens Buffalo Eve. News, 1955; recipient Brotherhood award NCCJ, 1956; President's medal Canisius Coll., 1963; Silver Beaver award Boy Scouts Am., 1964; Nat. award NCCJ, 1966; Distinguished Citizen's award Canisius Coll., 1968. Mem. Am. Judicature Soc., Am., N.Y., Erie County bar assns., Lawyers Club Buffalo, Greater Buffalo Advt. Club (sec.-treas. 1934), 100 Club of Buffalo, Am. Legion, C. of C., Am. Arbitration Assn. (dir. 1960-70), Buffalo Hist. Soc., Buffalo Pub. Library (life), Buffalo Fine Arts Acad. (life), Buffalo Soc. Natural Scis., Grosvenor Soc., Cult White Buffalo, Cornell Spike Shoe Soc., Zeta Beta Tau. Jewish (temple pres., trustee). Mason (Shriner). Asso. editor Cornell U. Daily Sun, 1918. Clubs: Wilmont Country (pres. 1936-38, 43), Buffalo Athletic, Buffalo, Westwood Country (pres. 1948), Cornell, Syracuse, Automobile, 100, Marshall, Saturn (Buffalo); Mid-Day, Capitol Hill. Home: 226 Depew Ave Buffalo NY 14214 Office: Liberty Bank Bldg Buffalo NY 14202

SAPHIER, MICHAEL, indsl. designer; b. N.Y.C. Apr. 10, 1911; s. Louis J. and Sara (Heymann) S.; student N.Y. U., 1928-30, NAD, 1930-31, Art Students League, 1931-32; m. Ruth Zierler, Apr. 6, 1938. Stage designer in N.Y.C. with Henry Dreyfuss, 1930-32, Boris Aaronson, 1932-33; propr. Michael Saphier Assos., graphic and indsl. design, N.Y.C., 1934-43; pres., chmn. bd. Michael Saphier Assos., Inc., office and facilities planning and design, N.Y.C., 1946-62; chmn. bd. Saphier, Lerner, Schindler, Inc., N.Y.C., 1962-74; facilities and office planning cons., 1974—; lectr., tchr. in field; past trustee ednl. found. Nat. Soc. Interior Design. Pres., Am. Child Guidance Found., 1966-72, Fedn. Employment and Guidance Service, 1974-77; trustee Nat. Pollution Control Found., sec. Jewish Child Care Assn.; hon. trustee council regents St. Francis Coll., Bklyn. Served with C.E., U.S. Army, 1943-46. Recipient Good Design award Indsl. Design mag., 1965; Service award Am. Fedn. Jewish Philanthropies, 1969; award of merit Fedn. Employment and Guidance Service, 1977; also several Office of Year awards Adminstrv. Mgmt. Fellow Am. Soc. Interior Designers; mem. Nat. Soc. Interior Design Qualification (past dir.). Jewish. Author: Office Planning and Design (trans. into Spanish), 1974; Planning the New Office, 1978; also articles. Address: 2 Peter Cooper Rd New York NY 10010

SAPIENZA, JOHN THOMAS, lawyer; b. South Orange, N.J., Feb. 26, 1913; s. James C. and Rosalie (Giaimo) S.; A.B., Harvard U., 1934, LL.B., 1937; m. Virginia H. Gignoux, Feb. 12, 1972; children by previous marriage—John Thomas, James K. Admitted to N.Y. bar, 1938, D.C. bar, 1943; law clk. Judge A.N. Hand, N.Y.C., 1937-38, Justice Stanley Reed, Washington, 1938-39; asso. firm Wright, Gordon, Zachry & Parlin, N.Y.C., 1939-41, Covington & Burling, Washington, 1941-48, partner, 1949—; dir. Hiram Walker-Gooderham & Worts Ltd., Hiram Walker & Sons, Inc., Wyman-Gordon Co., Am. Security Bank, N. A., Am. Security Corp. Trustee George Washington U. Served to lt. comdr. USNR, 1943-46. Mem. Am., D.C., Fed., Internat. bar assns., Am. Law Inst., Confrerie des Chevaliers du Tastevin, Phi Beta Kappa. Clubs: Burning Tree, Metropolitan, Internat. (Washington); Farmington Country (Charlottesville, Va.). Home: Apt 204-N Watergate East 2510 Virginia Ave NW Washington DC 20037 Office: Covington & Burling 888 16th St NW Washington DC 20006

SAPINSKY, JOSEPH CHARLES, mag. exec.; b. N.Y.C., Dec. 13, 1923; s. Simon Moses and Janet (Charles) S.; certificate illustration Pratt Inst., 1943, advt. design, 1947; m. Jane Tomney, Oct. 21, 1970; children—Michael Joseph, Jane Anne, Laura Alexandra. Art dir. Today's Living, N.Y. Herald Tribune, N.Y.C., 1960-63; art dir. N.Y. Mag., N.Y.C., 1963-65; asso. art dir., dir. photography Sat. Evening Post, N.Y.C., 1965-67; dir. publs. I.O.S., Geneva, 1967-69; art dir. This Week, N.Y.C., 1969, Jock mag., N.Y.C., 1970; dir. publs. I.I.G., London, 1970; art dir. Woman's Day mag., N.Y.C., 1971—; cons. art dir. Infinity mag., N.Y.C., 1971-73; instr. dept. photography Sch. Visual Arts, N.Y.C. Served with USNR, 1943-46. Recipient numerous art dir. awards. Mem. Am. Soc. Mag. Photographers, Soc. Illustrators, Am. Soc. Mag. Editors, Am. Inst. Graphic Arts, Soc. Publ. Designers, Naval Res. Officers Assn. Home: 76 Bank St New York NY 10014 Office: 1515 Broadway New York NY 10036

SAPIR, PHILIP, govt. ofcl.; b. Ottawa, Ont., Can., Nov. 8, 1916; s. Edward and Florence (Delson) S.; came to U.S., 1925, naturalized, 1942; B.S., Yale, 1938; m. Marjorie V. Peterson, Dec. 11, 1948; children—Carol Nagle Sapir Jawish, James Nagle, Nancy Nagle Sapir Rutledge, Donald Nagle, Susan Nagle, Linda Sapir Bove, Eric. Public health rep., sci. writer USPHS, 1944-48; profl. asst. NRC, 1948-49; with NIMH, USPHS, 1949-67, chief research grants br., 1954-66, chief behavioral scis. research br. extramural research programs, 1966-67; asst. dean Albert Einstein Sch. Medicine, Yeshiva U., N.Y.C., 1967-69, also asst. prof. preventive medicine and community health; asso. dir. Grant Found., N.Y.C., 1969-70, dir., 1970-76, v.p., 1974-76, pres., 1976-78; chief Human Learning and Behavior Br. and spl. asst. to dir. for behavioral and social scis. Nat. Inst. Child Health and Human Devel., NIH, Bethesda, Md., 1979—. Served with AUS, 1945-47. Fellow Am. Orthopsychiat. Assn., Am. Psychiat. Assn. (hon.); mem. AAAS, Soc. Research Child Devel., Sigma Xi. Clubs: Yale (N.Y.C.); Cosmos (Washington). Home: 5208 Pooks Hill Rd Bethesda MD 20014 Office: NIH Bethesda MD 20205

SAPOLSKY, HARVEY MORTON, educator, polit. scientist; b. Haverhill, Mass., Feb. 21, 1939; s. Abraham and Anne Betty (Selig) S.; B.A., Boston U., 1961; M.P.A., Harvard, 1963, Ph.D., 1967; m. Karen P. Stenbo, Aug. 27, 1966. Mem. faculty Mass. Inst. Tech., 1966—, prof. polit. sci., 1977—, dep. dir. Univ. Health Policy Consortium, 1978—, exec. officer dept., 1973-74; vis. prof. U. Mich., 1971-72; cons. to govt. Mem. A.A.A.S. (sec. sect. social and econ. scis. 1968-73), Am. Polit. Sci. Assn. Author: The Polaris System Development, 1972; also articles. Home: 37 Edgemoor Rd Belmont MA 02178 Office: E53-423 Mass Inst Tech Cambridge MA 02139

SAPP, WALTER WILLIAM, lawyer; b. Linton, Ind., Apr. 21, 1930; s. Walter J. and Nona (Stalcup) S.; A.B., Harvard, 1951; J.D., Ind. U., 1957; m. Eva Kaschner, July 10, 1957; children—Karen Elisabeth, Christoph Walter. Admitted to Ind. bar, 1957, N.Y. bar, 1959, Colo. bar, 1966, Tex. bar, 1977; practice in N.Y.C., 1957-60, Paris, France, 1960-63, Colorado Springs, 1966-76; asso. atty. Cahill, Gordon, Reindel & Ohl, N.Y.C., 1957-60, Paris, 1960-63, N.Y.C., 1963-65, partner, 1966; gen. counsel Colo. Interstate Corp., 1966-68, v.p., gen. counsel, 1968-76, sec., 1971-76, sr. v.p., dir., exec. com., 1973-76, exec. v.p., 1975-76; v.p. Coastal States Gas Corp., 1973-76; sr. v.p., gen. counsel Tenneco, Inc., Houston, 1976—. Served to lt. USNR, 1951-54. Mem. Am., N.Y. State bar assns., Assn. Bar City N.Y., Order of Coif. Congregationalist. Club: Coronado. Home: 424 E Friar Tuck Ln Houston TX 77024 Office: Tenneco Bldg PO Box 2511 Houston TX 77001

SAPPENFIELD, CHARLES MADISON, architect, educator; b. Columbia, S.C., Mar. 17, 1930; s. Charles Madison and Elizabeth Olive (Moss) S.; B.Arch., N.C. State Coll., 1956; Postgrad. (Fulbright scholar), Danish Royal Acad., Copenhagen, 1960-61; m. Mary Frances McGowan, Dec. 14, 1963; children—Charles Ross, Sarah Kathleen. Designer-draftsman Pace Assos., Chgo., 1952-53; designer J.B. King, Asheville, N.C., also asst. prof. architecture N.C. State U., 1961-63; pvt. practice architecture, Asheville, 1963-65, also asst. prof. architecture Clemson U., 1963-65; partner Sappenfield, Wiegman, Hall, Asheville, 1966-68; pvt. practice architecture, Muncie, Ind., 1968—, also dean Coll. Architecture and Planning, Ball State U. Cons. in design to Pub. Housing Adminstrn., 1962-65; mem. awards jury Nat. Council Schoolhouse Constrn.; mem. adv. commn. Ind. Planning Services Agy.; mem. screening com. Council for Internat. Exchange Scholars. Dir. Muncie Foresight; mem. Gus Grissom Meml. Com.; mem. Ind. Commn. Aging and Aged. Pres. Asheville Art Mus., 1964-65. Served with AUS, 1953-54. Fellow A.I.A.; mem. Ind. Soc. Architects (pres. 1976), Assn. Collegiate Schs. Architecture, Sigma Phi Epsilon, Alpha Rho Chi, Phi Kappa Phi. Republican. Episcopalian. Home: 2322 Berwyn Rd Muncie IN 47305

SAPPINGTON, LEE EDWARD, retail fast food co. exec.; b. St. Louis, Jan. 30, 1930; s. Edward Folk and Vera Bertha (Reynolds) S.; B.S. in Bus., U. Mo., 1951; m. Dorothy H. Hageman, Nov. 8, 1953; children—Nancy, Robert, Peggy. Controller accounting ops. Standard Brands Inc., N.Y.C., 1970-73; v.p. controller Curtiss Candy Co., Chgo., 1973-74; controller Grand Union Co., Elmwood Park, N.J., 1974-76, treas., 1976-78; chief fin. officer Steak N Shake Inc., Indpls., 1978—. Treas. Ridgewood-Glen Rock council Boy Scouts Am. Served with U.S. Army, 1952-53. Certified internal auditor. Mem. Nat. Assn. Accountants, Delta Sigma Pi, Sigma Phi Epsilon. Address: 245 Raintree Dr Zionsville IL 46077

SAPPINGTON, THOMAS ASBURY, physician, surgeon; b. Sycamore, Ga., May 9, 1913; s. Ernest P. and Nell (Whittle) S.; B.A., Vanderbilt U., 1934, M.D., 1937; m. A. Phyllis Duncan, Aug. 31, 1940; children—Phyllis (Mrs. S. Monte Kellam, Jr.), Kathryn (Mrs. Michael Kellum) Thomas A. Med. examiner for Ga., 1953—; physican Upson County 1956—; clinician Upson County Health Dept., 1956—; preceptor for preceptorship in gen. medicine Med. Coll. Ga., 1971—, also asst. prof. dept. family practice; dir. Ga. Blue Shield. Mem. Upson County Blood Program; mem. panel cancer control USPHS, 1960. Served to lt. col. AUS, 1940-46. Diplomate Am. Bd. Family Practice. Mem. AMA, Upson County (past pres.), 6th Dist. med. socs., Med. Assn. Ga. (named Gen. Practitioner of Yr. 1971), Am. (pres. Ga. chpt. 1970, bd. dirs. 1971—, former mem. commn. edn. 1956-59), Ga. (chmn. edn. com.; plaque for outstanding service as del., Distinguished Service award 1977) acads. gen. practice, S.E. Surg. Congress, So. Med. Assn., V.F.W., Am. Legion. Methodist (steward). Kiwanian, Elk, Mason (Shriner). Home: Canton Pines PO Box 1169 Thomaston GA 30286 Office: 612 W Gordon St Thomaston GA 30286

SARAFIAN, ARMEN, univ. pres.; b. Van Nuys, Calif., Mar. 5, 1920; s. Kevork and Lucy (Gazarian) S.; A.B. magna cum laude, La Verne Coll., 1940, LL.D. (hon.), 1967; M.A., Claremont Grad. U., 1947; Ph.D., U. So. Calif., Los Angeles, 1964; m. Margaret Kirby, 1964; children—William, Winston, Norman, Joy, Madeline. Tchr. public elem. and secondary schs., Calif., 1940-47; tchr. English and Am. history and polit. sci. Pasadena (Calif.) Jr. Coll. Dist., 1947-51; mem. faculty (part-time) various colls. and univs. in Calif., 1947-68; coordinator secondary and jr. coll. edn. Pasadena City Schs., 1951-59; adminstrv. dean for instruction Pasadena City Coll., 1959-65, pres., 1965-76, also supt. Pasadena Area Community Coll. Dist., 1966-76; adj. prof. community coll. adminstrn. U. So. Calif., Los Angeles, 1968-78; pres. La Verna (Calif.) Coll. (name changed to La Verne U. 1978), 1976—; cons. to industry, govt. and bus., 1952—; dir. mgmt. reorgn. of Conn. System of Regional Community Colls., 1974-75; mem. adult and continuing edn. com. for Calif. Community Colls., 1974-75; Delta Epsilon disting. lectr. U. So. Calif., 1973; mem. mgmt. team U. Alaska System, 1977; acad. planning specialist Mary Hardin-Baylor Coll., Belton, Tex., 1974; mem. western regional adv. bd. Coll. Entrance Examination Bd., 1971-75; mgmt. adv. to City of Pasadena Mcpl. Govt., 1972-73. Mem. policy bd. Gt. Plains Nat. Instructional TV Library, 1975-79; founder and mem. exec. com. Pasadena Hall of Sci. Project, 1965-76; founder, adult adv. Pasadena Area Youth Council, 1953-66; mem. St. Luke Hosp. Adv. Bd., 1969-71; Mayor's Com. on Children and Youth, Pasadena, 1960-62; mem. hon. adv. bd. Pasadena Area chpt., ARC, 1956-76; pres. Calif. Conservation Council, 1966-68; mem. nat. adv. council for nurse tng. USPHS, 1967-71; judge Los Angeles Times Scholarship Award Contest, 1974; bd. dirs. Pasadena Urban Coalition, 1973-76; trustee La Verne Coll., 1969-76. Recipient Disting. Community Service award Pasadena Edn. Assn., 1956, Conservation Merit award Calif. Conservation Council, 1960, Meritorious Service award Pasadena City Coll. Faculty Senate, 1960, Ralph Story award Pasadena City Coll. Faculty Assn., 1974, U. So. Calif. Service award, 1974, Recognition award USPHS, 1972, Others award Salvation Army, 1975, Recognition award Pasadena Arts Council, 1976; Named Citizen of the Day, Sierra Madre City Council, 1972. Mem. Calif.

Scholarship Fedn., Calif. Jr. Coll. Assn. (mem. legis. com. 1973-76), Pasadena Area Sch. Trustees Assn. (founder 1966), Pasadena Arts Council, Pasadena Hist. Soc., La Verne C. of C. (pres. 1978-79), Native Sons of the Golden West, Pasadena Council of Parents and Tchrs., Associated Student Body of Pasadena City Coll., Pasadena C. of C. (v.p. 1972), Phi Delta Kappa (Spl. Recognition award 1970). Home: 1046 Ashford St La Verne CA 91750 Office: Office of the President Univ of La Verne 1950 3rd St La Verne CA 91750

SARANDON, SUSAN ABIGAIL, actress; b. N.Y.C., Oct. 4, 1946; d. Phillip Leslie and Lenora Marie (Criscione) Tomalin; B.A. in Drama and English, Cath. U. Am., 1968; m. Chris Sarandon, Sept. 16, 1967. Appeared in motion pictures: Joe, Le Fleur Bleu, Lady Liberty, Loving Molly, The Great Waldo Pepper, The Other Side of Midnight, The Front Page, Dragon Fly, Crash or Checkered Flag, The Last of the Cowboys, Rocky Horror Picture Show, Pretty Baby, King of the Gypsies, Something Short of Paradise, Loving Couples, Atlantic City, USA; TV appearances include: The Last of the Belles, The Rimers of Eldritch, June Moon, The Haunting of Rosilind, The Satan Murders, The Life of Ben Franklin, Owen Marshall, Calucci's Department, and serials A World Apart and Search For Tomorrow; theatre appearances include: An Evening With Richard Nixon, A Stroll In The Air, Albert's Bridge, Private Ear, Public Eye. Mem. AFTRA, Screen Actors Guild, Actors Equity, Acad. Motion Picture Arts and Scis., NOW, Amnesty Internat., ACLU.

SARASIN, RONALD A., congressman; b. Fall River, Mass., Dec. 31, 1934; B.S., U. Conn., 1960, J.D., 1963; 1 son, Michael. Admitted to Conn. bar, 1963; former partner law firm Perelmutter, Sarasin & Cohen; town counsel for Beacon Falls, 1963-72; asst. prof. law New Haven Coll., 1963-66; mem. 93d-95th Congresses from Conn.; mem. Com. on Edn. and Labor, Select Com. on Aging; ranking Republic Subcom. Employment Opportunities, Subcom. Compensation, Health and Safety; mem. Labor Standards Subcom., Republican Policy Com. Mem. Conn. Ho. of Reps., 1968-72, asst. minority leader, 1970-72. Served with USN, 1952-56; Korea. Mem. Am. Trial Lawyers Assn., Am. Arbitration Assn., Am., Conn., New Haven, Naugatuck bar assns., Naugatuck Valley C. of C. Republican. Lion. Home: Beacon Falls CT 06403 Office: 229 Cannon House Office Bldg Washington DC 20515

SARASON, IRWIN GERALD, psychologist, educator; b. Newark, N.J., Sept. 15, 1929; s. Max and Anna S.; B.A., Rutgers U., 1951; M.A., U. Iowa, 1953; Ph.D., Ind. U., 1955; m. Barbara June Ryrholm, Sept. 19, 1953; children—Suzanne, Jane, Donald. Clin psychology intern VA Hosp., West Haven, Conn., 1955-56; asst. prof. psychology U. Wash., Seattle, 1956-59, asso. prof., 1959-65, prof., 1965—; fellow Netherlands Inst. for Advanced Study, 1975-76; vis. prof. Univ. Coll., London, 1971-72. Fellow Am. Psychol. Assn., AAAS; mem. Western Psychol. Assn. (pres. 1978-79), AAUP. Author: (with others) Psychology: The Fontiers of Behavior, 1978; (with B.R. Sarason) Abnormal Psychology: The Problem of Maladaptive Behavior, 3d edit., 1980; Personality: An Objective Approach, 1972. Contbr. articles to prof. jours. Home: 13516 42d Ave NE Seattle WA 98125 Office: Psychology Dept NI-25 Univ of Wash Seattle WA 98195

SARASON, SEYMOUR BERNARD, psychologist, educator, author; b. Bklyn., Jan. 12, 1919; s. Max and Anna (Silverlight) S.; B.A., U. Newark, 1939; M.A., Clark U., 1940, Ph.D., 1942; m. Esther Kroop, May 22, 1943; 1 dau., Julie Carol. Chief psychologist Southbury (Conn.) Tng. Sch., 1942-46; asst. prof. psychology Yale, 1946-49, asso. prof., 1949-55, prof., 1955—, dir. grad. program clin. psychology, 1948-65, dir. psycho-ednl. clinic, dept. psychology, 1963-70. Mem. Am., Eastern, Conn. psychol. assns. Author: Psychological Problems in Mental Deficiency, 1949, rev. edit., 1953, 4th edit. (with Dr John Doris), 1969; The Clinical Interaction, 1954; (with Dr. Thomas Gladwin), Truk: Man in Paradise, 1953; (with Dr. Thomas Gladwin and Richard L. Nasland) Psychological and Cultural Problems in Mental Subnormality, 1958; (with Davidson, Lighthall, Waite and Ruebush) Anxiety in Elementary School Children, 1960; (with Davidson and Blatt) The Preparation of Teachers: An Unstudied Problem in Education, 1962; (with Levine, Goldenberg, Cherlin and Bennett) Psychology in Community Settings, 1966; The Culture of the School and the Problem of Change, 1971; The Creation of Settings and Future Societies, 1972; (with F.K. Grossman and G. Zitnay) The Creation of a Community Setting, 1972; The Psychological Sense of Community: Prospects for a Community Psychology, 1974; Work, Aging, and Social Change, 1977; (with Carroll, Maton, Cohen and Lorentz) Human Services and Resource Networks, 1977; (with John Doris) Educational Handicap, Public Policy and Social History, 1978; (with E. Lorentz) The Challenge of the Resource Exchange Network, 1979. Home: 136 Hartley St North Haven CT 06473 Office: 70 Sachem St New Haven CT 06520

SARAW, ARNOLD F., corp. exec.; b. 1927; B.S. in Bus. Adminstrn., U. Buffalo, 1949; with Flintkote Co., 1949-51; with Jim Walter Corp., 1951—, sec., treas., 1955-71, sr. v.p., 1971—, also dir. Address: 1500 N Dale Mabry Hwy Tampa FL 33607

SARBACHER, ROBERT IRVING, scientist; b. Balt., Sept. 6, 1907; s. Joseph Conrad and Georgiana (Duffy) S.; diploma Balt. Poly. Inst., 1926; student Johns Hopkins, 1928; Sc.B., U. Fla., 1933, E.E., 1951; postgrad. Princeton, 1934; Sc.M., Harvard, 1936, Sc.D., 1939; m. Elizabeth Kampmann Brown, 1954 (div. 1963); 1 dau., Roberta; m. 2d, Betty Lou Spencer (div. 1971); 1 stepdau., Daonn; 1 son, Robert; m. 3d, Mary Frances Phillips Turner, Sept. 1975; 1 stepdau., Mary Frances Turner. Instr. physics and communications engring. Harvard, 1936-40; prof. elec. engring. Ill. Inst. Tech., 1940-42; sci. cons. Navy Dept., Washington, 1942-45; instr. Radcliffe Coll., 1937-39; vis. prof. Harvard, 1941; dean Grad. Sch., Ga. Inst. Tech., 1945-49, chmn. grad. council, mem. adminstrv. council and exec. com., 1945-48; pres., dir. Washington Inst. Tech., 1950—, Nat. Sci. Labs., Inc., 1949-54; pres. Gen. Sci. Corp.; pres., dir. S.W. Union Life Ins. Co., United Fed. Life Ins. Co., United Life Ins. Co., Home Fidelity Life Ins. Co.; dir. research Bowser, Inc., Chgo., Johnson Fare Box Co., Chgo., Gudeman Co., Chgo., Joseph Weidenhoff, Inc., Algona, Iowa, Electrofile Corp., N.Y.C., Briggs Filtration Co., Washington (1949-54); dir. research div. Prosperity Co., Syracuse & N.Y.C.; dir. research Bogue Investment Corp., El Segundo, Calif., 1969—; professorial lectr. George Washington U.; dir. Robert I. Sarbacher & Assos., Atlanta and Washington; cons. scientist, dir. Wedd Labs., Inc., Washington, 1948-49. Sci. cons. guided missiles com. Research and Devel. Bd., Dept. Def. Trustee Ga. Tech. Research Found., 1946-48; instnl. rep. Oak Ridge Inst. Nuclear Studies, 1946-48; mem. adv. council WAA, 1947; bd. dirs. Nat. Patent Council. Recipient citation for edn. institutional program WAA, 1947. Profl. engr., Fla., Washington, 1952. Mem. Am. Acoustical Soc., I.E.E.E., N.E.A., Am. Math. Soc., Harvard Engring. Soc., N.A.M., Am. Soc. Engring. Edn., Soc. Am. Mil. Engrs., A.A.A.S., Am. Phys. Soc., Phi Beta Kappa, Kappa Sigma, Sigma Tau. Clubs: Harvard, Princeton, Lotus (N.Y.C.); University, Engineers, Cosmos (Washington); Author: Hyper and Ultra-High Frequency Engineering, 1944; Research Accrediting at Military Establishments, 1946; Ency. Dictionary for Electronics and Nuclear Engineering, 1955; Biomedical Engineering (in preparation). Sci. library collector. Home: 260 S Ocean Blvd Palm Beach FL 33480 also Yacht Désireé Brazilian Dock Palm Beach FL 33480 Office: 2250 E Imperial Hwy El Segundo CA 90245

SARBANES, PAUL SPYROS, senator; b. Salisbury, Md., Feb. 3, 1933; s. Spyros P. and Matina (Tsigounis) S.; A.B., Princeton, 1954; B.A. (Rhodes scholar), Oxford (Eng.) U., 1957; LL.B., Harvard, 1960; m. Christine Dunbar, June 11, 1960; children—John Peter, Michael Anthony, Janet Matina. Admitted to Md. bar, 1960; law clk. to Judge Morris Soper, 4th Circuit Ct. of Appeals, 1960-61; asso. Piper & Marbury, Balt., 1961-62; adminstrv. asst. Walter W. Heller, chmn. Council Econ. Advisers, 1962-63; exec. dir. Charter Revision Commn., Balt., 1963-64; asso. Venable, Baetjer & Howard, Balt., 1965-70; mem. 92d Congress from 4th Dist. Md., 93d-94th congresses from 3d Dist. Md.; mem. U.S. Senate from Md., 1977—. Mem. Md. Ho. of Dels., 1967-71. Democrat. Greek Orthodox.

SARBER, RAYMOND WILLIAM, assn. exec.; b. Hammond, Ind., Apr. 15, 1916; s. William L. and Lillian May (Mott) S.; A.B., Western Mich. U., 1938; postgrad. U. Mich., 1939-40; M.S., U. Cin., 1941; m. Nilo Pauline Miller, Oct. 9, 1937; children—Nancy Suzanne, Judith Lynn. Instr. bacteriology U. Cin., 1941; asst. prof. bacteriology Cin. Coll. Pharmacy, 1940-42; sci. cons. Clopay Corp., Cin., 1941-43; sr. bacteriologist research div. Parke, Davis & Co., Detroit, 1942-59; mem. Am. Soc. Microbiology (formerly Soc. Am. Bacteriologists), 1941—, councilor, 1954-58, exec. sec., 1959—; exec. sec. Am. Acad. Microbiology, 1968-78; sec. Am. Bd. Med. Microbiology, 1968-74; registrar Nat. Registry Microbiologists, 1968-74; pres. Mich. Soc. Bacteriologists, 1952-53. Dir. Lost Lake Woods Assn., 1954-57; chief biol. def. sect. Detroit office Civilian Def., 1954-60. Regional dir. Nat. Fedn. Young Republicans, 1946-49; chmn. Wayne County (Mich.) Rep. Com., 1946. Mem. AAAS, Nat. Assn. Exposition Mgrs. (dir.), Am. Soc. Assn. Execs., Profl. Conv. Mgmt. Assn., Council Engring. and Sci. Soc. Execs., Mich. Acad. Sci., Sigma Xi. Methodist (lay leader). Mason. Contbr. articles on germicides, Tb chemotherapy, whooping cough, cell culture, poliomyelitis to profl. jours. Home: 2212 Great Falls St Falls Church VA 22046 Office: 1913 I St NW Washington DC 20006

SARBIN, HERSHEL BENJAMIN, publisher, lawyer; b. Massillon, Ohio, Dec. 30, 1924; s. Joseph I. and Sarah Charlotte (Reich) S.; A.B., Western Res. U., 1946; J.D., Harvard, 1950; m. Susan Challman, July 24, 1973; children by previous marriage—Penelope (Mrs. Richard Neubert), Richard, Barbara; 1 stepdau., Caroline Cooley. Admitted to Ill. bar, 1950, N.Y. bar, 1953; asso. firm Lewis and MacDonald, N.Y.C., 1953-58; with Ziff-Davis Pub. Co., 1950—, pub. Popular Photography mag., 1965-66, sr. v.p. co., 1967-74, asso. pub. Travel Weekly, 1967-68, pub., 1969-74, pub. dir., chief exec. officer photog. div., 1968-69, pres. Pub. Transp. and Travel div., 1970-74, pres. Ziff-Davis Pub. Co., 1974-78; exec. v.p. Ziff Corp., 1978—, also dir.; mem. exec. com.; Nat. photography coordinator Pres.'s Council Youth Opportunity, 1968; Fed. commr. Nat. Commn. on New Technol. Uses of Copyrighted Works, 1975-78. Mem. exec. com. Westchester County (N.Y.) Sch. Bd., 1964-66; mem. ethical practices com. N.Y. Sch. Bd. Assn., 1965-68; pres. Hastings-on-Hudson Bd. Edn., 1966-67. Served with AUS, 1946-47. Mem. Am. Bar Assn., Phi Beta Kappa. Clubs: Harvard (N.Y.C.); Ardsley Country (Ardsley-on-Hudson, N.Y.). Author: (with George Chernoff) Photography and the Law, 1958, rev. edit., 1977. Home: North Quaker Hill Rd Pawling NY 12564 Office: 1 Park Ave New York NY 10016

SARD, ROBERT DANIEL, physicist; b. N.Y.C., Aug. 23, 1915; s. Frederick N. and Maria Osipovna (Belloch) S.; S.B. magna cum laude, Harvard U., 1935, A.M., 1940, Ph.D., 1942; postgrad. Cambridge (Eng.) U., 1935-36, Leiden (Netherlands) U., 1936-38; m. Mary Bell Marshall, Sept. 19, 1942; children—David Paul, Frederick Marshall, Hannah Belloch Kapilla. Instr., tutor Harvard U., 1938-42; war research with OSRD, 1942-45; research asso. Mass. Inst. Tech., 1945-46; from asst. prof. to prof. physics Washington U., St. Louis, 1946-61; physicist U. Calif. Lawrence Berkeley Lab., 1959-60; prof. physics U. Ill., Urbana, 1961—; summer visitor Fermi Nat. Accelerator Lab., 1969; vis. scientist CERN, Geneva, also Serpukhov, USSR, 1970-71. Sheldon prize fellow Harvard U., 1935-36, Bayard Cutting fellow, 1939-40; Sr. Fulbright fellow, Manchester, Eng., 1951-52; recipient Army-Navy certificate appreciation, 1947. Fellow Am. Phys. Soc.; mem. Am. Assn. Physics Tchrs., Phi Beta Kappa. Author: Relativistic Mechanics, 1970. Discovered capture of negative muon by proton with emmission of neutron, polarization of cosmic-ray muons. Home: 401 W Nevada St Urbana IL 61801 Office: Physics Dept Univ Ill Urbana IL 61801

SARDI, MAURO ANTHONY, film co. fin. exec.; b. N.Y.C., Apr. 12, 1935; B.B.A., CCNY, 1957, postgrad. in acctg., 1960-62; M.B.A. in Fin., N.Y. U., 1976; m. Virginia R. Spallone, Aug. 14, 1960; 1 dau., Victoria Anne. Supervising sr. acct. Peat, Marwick, Mitchell & Co., N.Y.C., 1958-63; v.p., treas. United Artists TV, Inc., N.Y.C., 1963-76; v.p. adminstrn., controller LIN Broadcasting Corp., N.Y.C., 1976-79; v.p. fin. United Artists Corp., N.Y.C., 1979—; cons. mgmt. decision lab., mem. exec. communications com. N.Y. U. Grad. Sch. Bus. Served with M.C., U.S. Army, 1957. C.P.A., N.Y. State. Mem. Am. Inst. C.P.A.'s, N.Y. State Soc. C.P.A.'s, Fin. Execs. Inst., Data Processing Mgmt. Assn. Office: 729 7th Ave New York NY 10019

SARDI, VINCENT, JR., restaurant exec.; b. N.Y.C., July 23, 1915; s. Vincent Sardi; pre-med. student Columbia U.; m. 2d, Adelle Ramsey; 2 children. Owner, Sardi's restaurant, N.Y.C. Recipient Spl. Tony award for providing the best transient home and haven for show people League N.Y. Theatres and Producers. Office: 234 W 44th St New York NY 10036*

SARETT, LEWIS HASTINGS, chemist; b. Champaign, Ill., Dec. 22, 1917; s. Lew and Margaret (Husted) S.; B.S., Northwestern U., 1939, D.Sc., 1972; Ph.D., Princeton, 1942; m. Mary Adams, Mar. 1, 1944 (div.); children—Mary Nicole, Katharine Wendy; m. 2d, Pamela Thorp, June 28, 1969; children—Will Hastings, Renée MacLeod. With Merck & Co., 1942—, asst. dir. organic and biol. research, 1948-52, dir. dept. med. chemistry, 1952-56, dir. dept. synthetic organic chemistry, 1956-62, exec. dir. fundamental research div., 1962-66, v.p. for basic research, 1966-69; pres. Merck Sharp & Dohme Research Labs., 1969-76, corporate v.p. sci. and tech., 1976—. Cons. chemotherapy of malaria and schistosomiasis Dept. Def., 1967-68; chmn. basic sci. adv. com. Nat. Cystic Fibrosis Research Found., 1966-69; rep. Indsl. Research Inst., 1968—, dir., 1974-77; chmn. vis. com. div. biology Calif. Inst. Tech., 1969-76; mem. indsl. adv. com. U. Calif., San Diego, 1971—; mem. overseers com. Sch. Public Health, Harvard U., 1979—. Trustee Cold Spring Harbor Lab., of Quantitative Biology, 1968-70, Med. Center at Princeton. Recipient Leo Hendrick Baekeland award, 1951, Award of Merit, Northwestern Alumni Assn., 1951, East Union County (N.J.) C. of C. award, 1952, Merck Directors award, 1951, Julius W. Sturmer Meml. Lectr. award, 1959, award Synthetic Organic Chem. Mfrs. Assn., 1964; William Scheele Lectr. award Royal Pharm. Inst., Stockholm, Sweden, 1964, N.J. Patent award N.J. Council Research and Devel., 1966, Nat. Cystic Fibrosis Research Found. award, 1969. Fellow Am. Inst. Chemists (chem. Pioneer award 1972), Soc. Chem. Industry (Perkin medal 1976), Am. Chem. Soc. (award for creative work in synthetic organic chemistry, 1964, Nat. medal Sci. 1975; mem. exec. com. organic chemistry div. 1967-68); mem. Nat. Acad. Scis. Inst. Medicine, Dirs. Indsl. Research, Phi Beta Kappa, Sigma Xi, Phi Eta Sigma, Phi Kappa Psi. Clubs: Princeton; Bedens Brook Country. Editorial bd. Chem. and Engring. News, 1969-71. Contbr. articles to profl. publs. Home: Rolling Hill Rd Skillman NJ 08558 Office: Merck & Co Rahway NJ 07065

SARGEANT, HOWLAND H., internat. radio exec.; b. New Bedford, Mass., July 13, 1911; s. M. Motley and Grace E. (Howland) Sargeant; A.B. summa cum laude, Dartmouth, 1932; A.B. honours sch., Oxford (Eng.) U., 1934, A.M., 1938, B. Litt. (Rhodes scholar), 1940; m. Dorothy Psathas; children—Kimon, Paul. With Fed. Home Loan Bank Bd., 1935-40; editor Fed. Home Loan Bank Rev., 1937-40; exec. sec. NSF of Nat. Acad. Scis., 1940-47; chief div. patent adminstrn. Office Alien Property Custodian, 1942-47; chmn. Tech. Indsl. Intelligence Com., U.S. Joint Chiefs of Staff, 1944-46; dep. asst. sec. of state for pub. affairs, 1947-51, asst. sec. pub. affairs, 1952-53; cons. State Dept. and Ford Found., 1953-54; pres., trustee Radio Liberty Com., Inc., 1954-75; dir. RFE/RL, Inc., 1976—. Pres. Magnesium Devel. Corp., 1945-50. Pres. UNESCO Gen. Conf., Paris, 1951, chmn. U.S. delegations 5th-7th confs. Pres. Dartmouth Alumni Council, 1968-69, mem. advisory com. Dartmouth Inst., 1972—; mem. advisory com. Grad. Sch. Corporate and Polit. Communication Fairfield U., 1968—; mem. Panel Ideas and Polit. Communication in Soviet Union, 1976—. Trustee Freedom House; mem. bd. Internat. Broadcasting, 1974-75. Recipient certificate of appreciation U.S. Army, Superior Service award State Dept. Mem. Assn. Am. Rhodes Scholars, Internat. Radio and TV Execs., Council Fgn. Relations, Am. Fgn. Service Assn., Phi Beta Kappa, Sphinx, Kappa Kappa Kappa. Clubs: West Side Tennis (Forest Hills, N.Y.); Dartmouth College, Century Assn. (N.Y.C.). Author: The Representation of the United States Abroad, 1965; Soviet Propaganda, 1972; contbr. article to profl. jour. Home: 110 Riverside Dr New York City NY 10024 Office: 30 E 42d St New York City NY 10017

SARGEANT, WINTHROP, author, critic, translator; b. San Francisco, Dec. 10, 1903; s. Winthrop and Geneve (Rixford) S.; trained in Europe as musician; m. Jane Smith, Dec. 23, 1955. Violinist, San Francisco Symphony, 1922-24, N.Y. Symphony, 1926-28, N.Y. Philharmonic, 1926-28; music critic Bklyn. Daily Eagle, 1934-36, N.Y. Am., 1936-37; music editor Time mag., 1937-39, gen. writer, 1939-45; sr. writer, roving corr. Life mag., 1945-49; music critic New Yorker mag., 1949-72, record critic, 1972—. Recipient citation for distinguished contbn. to Am. music Nat. Assn. Am. Composers and Conductors. Mem. Am. Oriental Soc. Clubs: Century Assn., Coffee House (N.Y.C.). Author: Jazz: Hot and Hybrid, 1938; Geniuses, Goddesses and People, 1946; Listening to Music, 1958; In Spite of Myself: A Personal Memoir, 1970; Divas: Impressions of Todays Sopranos, 1973; The Bhagavad Gita, An Interlinear Translation from the Sanskrit, 1979; also numerous articles. Contbr. to Ency. Americana; mem. adv. bd. Am. Heritage Dictionary of Am. Lang. Home: Box 88 Salisbury CT 06068 Office: 25 W 43d St New York NY 10036

SARGENT, DICK, actor; b. Carmel, Calif., Apr. 19; s. Elmer Marsden and Ruth (MacNaughton) Cox; student U. Oreg., Stanford U. Appeared in feature films: Hardcore, Private Navy of Sgt. O'Farrell, Love A Little, Live A Little, That Touch of Mink, Ghost and Mr. Chicken, Billie, The Young Runaways, Captain Newman, M.D., For Love Or Money, The Great Imposter, Fluffy, Operation Petticoat, Mardi Gras, Bernardine, Love Me Tender, Great Locomotive Chase, Beast With A Million Eyes, Prisoner of War, TV movies: Wonderful World of Sin, Honeymoon Suite, Melvin Purvis, G-Man, Rich Man, Poor Man, book I, book II, Fantasy Island, Man With The Power; TV series: One Happy Family, Broadside, Tammy Grimes Show, Bewitched; TV series pilot: Home Again, 1979; guest appearances on numerous TV shows; summer stock: Peter Pat, Charlie's Aunt, The Owl and The Pussycat, Born Yesterday, Not With My Daughter; Los Angeles theater: Gog and Magog. Bd. dirs. Yes support group Rancho Los Amis Hosp., Los Angeles County. Recipient Appreciation award Calif. Spl. Olympics. Office: care Belson & Klass Assos 211 S Beverly Dr Beverly Hills CA 90212

SARGENT, FRANCIS W., former state ofcl., newspaper columnist; b. Hamilton, Mass., July 29, 1915; ed. Mass. Inst. Tech.; m. Jessie Fay; children—Fay (Mrs. James W. McLane), Francis W., Jessie (Mrs. Brien J. Flynn). Founder, owner Goose Hummock Shop, Inc., Orleans, Mass.; chmn. Atlantic States Marine Fisheries Commn., 1956-59; chmn. Mass. Water Resources Comm., 1956-59; dir. marine fisheries, commr. Mass. Dept. Natural Resources, 1956-59; exec. dir. U.S. Outdoor Recreation Resources Rev. Com., Washington, 1959-62; chmn. Mass. Dept. Pub. Works, 1965-66; adviser Calif. Park and Recreation Dept., 1964—; lt. gov. Mass., 1967-68, acting gov., 1969-70, gov., 1971-75; New Eng. syndicated newspaper columnist, radio and TV commentator, 1977—. Served to capt. AUS, World War II. Decorated Bronze Star, Purple Heart with oak leaf cluster. Office: 16 Arlington St Boston MA 02116

SARGENT, FREDERICK, II, educator; b. Boston, Jan. 11, 1920; s. Ralph and Elise Hodges (Connor) S.; student Phillips Exeter Acad., 1934-38; S.B., Mass. Inst. Tech., 1942; M.D., Boston U., 1947; m. Anne Virginia Swiedler, Mar. 29, 1968; children—Anne, Peter, Fredericka, Laura. Intern Presbyn. Hosp., Chgo., 1947-48; asst. prof. U. Ill., 1950-55, asso. prof., 1955-59, prof., 1959-67, dir. Center Human Ecology, 1965-67; dean Coll. Environmental Sci., prof. human ecology U. Wis. at Green Bay, 1968-70; provost, prof. human ecology Western Wash. State Coll., Bellingham, 1970-72; prof. human ecology Sch. Pub. Health, U. Tex., Houston, 1972—; cons. in field. Commr. Green Bay Met. Sewage Dist., 1969-70; mem. Wis. Environmental Health Adv. Com., 1969-70, Environmental Health Commn. Comprehensive Health Planning Council, N.W. Wash., 1970-72, environmental health study group Houston-Galveston Area Health Council, 1973. Served with USAF, 1952-54. John Simon Guggenheim fellow, 1957-58; recipient Centennial Alumni award Boston U. Sch. Medicine, 1973. Fellow Am. Public Health Assn. (food and nutrition council), Royal Soc. Health, AAAS, World Acad. Arts and Scis.; mem. Am. Meteorol. Soc. (recipient award 1960), Am. Physiol. Soc., Am. Ecol. Soc. Am., Am. Soc. Clin. Nutrition, Tex. Med. Assn. (chmn. com. on nutrition and food resources 1978—), Internat. Soc. Biometeorology (hon.). Editor: Recent Advances in Bioclimatology, 1954; Human Biometeorology, 1964; Human Ecology, 1974; editorial bd. Bull. Environmental Contamination and Toxicology; regional editor Chemosphere. Contbr. articles to profl. jours. Home: 10722 Cranbrook St Houston TX 77042

SARGENT, JAMES CUNNINGHAM, lawyer; b. New Haven, Feb. 26, 1916; s. Murray and Mary Hale (Cunningham) S.; grad. Taft Sch., 1935; B.A., U. Va., 1938, LL.B., 1940; m. Rebecca Porteous Jackson, Jan. 23, 1943; children—Stephen Denny, James Cunningham, Felicity Hale, Sarah Blanchard. Admitted to N.Y. State bar, 1940, D.C. bar, 1961; with Clarke & Baldwin, N.Y.C., 1940-41; trial atty. Consol. Edison Co. of N.Y., 1941-51; asst. atty. gen., elections fraud bur., State of N.Y., 1948; law asst. appellate div. N.Y. Supreme Ct., 1951-54; asso. atty. Spence & Hotchkiss, N.Y.C., 1954-55; regional adminstr. SEC, N.Y.C., 1955-56, mem. SEC, 1956-60; asst. gen. counsel CIT Finance Corp., N.Y.C., 1960-64; mem. Whitman & Ransom and predecessors, 1964—; guest lectr. corporate securities U. Va. Law Sch., 1958-60, Practicing Law Inst., since 1962—. Served from pvt. to capt. USAAF, 1942-45. Mem. St. Andrew's Soc. N.Y. Bar Assn. City N.Y., N.Y. County Lawyers Assn., Am., Fed., Va.

(hon.) bar assns., Order of Coif, Phi Delta Phi. Episcopalian (vestryman). Clubs: New Haven Lawn; Manhattan, University, Church, Downtown Assn. (N.Y.C.); Capitol Hill (Washington); Farmington (Va.) Country; Watch Hill Yacht (R.I.). Home: 310 E 84th St New York City NY 10028 Office: 522 Fifth Ave New York City NY 10036

SARGENT, JOHN TURNER, publisher; b. Lawrence, N.Y., June 26, 1924; s. Charles and Dagmar (Wetmore) S.; m. Neltje Doubleday, May 16, 1953 (div.); children—Ellen, John Turner. Copywriter, advt. mgr., editor Doubleday & Co., Inc., N.Y.C., 1945-54, gen. mgr. Garden City Books, bus. mgr., dir. Doubleday & Co., Inc., 1955-60, pres., 1961-78, chmn. bd., 1978—, also dir.; dir. Grumman Corp.; trustee East Rivers Savs. Bank. Trustee N.Y. Zool. Soc., N.Y. Pub. Library, Kipsbay Boys Clubs: Knickerbocker, Century Assn., Maidstone. Home: Halsey Ln Watermill NY 11976 Office: 245 Park Ave New York City NY 10017

SARGENT, JOSEPH DANIEL, motion picture, TV dir.; b. Jersey City, July 22, 1925; s. Domenico and Maria (Noviello) Sargente; student theatre arts New Sch. for Social Research, 1946-49; m. Carolyn Nelson, Nov. 22, 1970; children by previous marriage—Athena, Lia. Dir. films: Colosses, The Forbin Project, feature, 1969, Tribes (Outstanding Directorial Achievement award Dirs. Guild Am.), ABC, 1969, Maybe I'll Come Home in the Spring, ABC, 1970, The Man, feature, 1971, White Lightning, feature, 1972, The Marcus-Nelson Murders (Emmy award, Dirs. Guild Am. award), CBS, 1973, Sunshine, CBS, 1973, The Taking of Pelham 1-2-3 (Best Dir. award San Sebastian Film Festival), feature, 1974, Hustling, ABC-TV, 1975, Friendly Persuasion, ABC-TV, 1975, The Night That Panicked America (Fantasy Film Fans Internat. award), ABC-TV, 1975, MacArthur, 1977, Playing for Time, 1979; pres. Joseph Sargent Productions, Inc. Served with U.S. Army, 1943-46. Recipient Best TV Film award Monte Carlo TV Film Festival, 1975 for The Night That Panicked America. Mem. Dirs Guild Am., Screen Actors Guild, AFTRA, Actors Equity Assn. Office: Universal Studios 100 Universal City Plaza Universal City CA 91608

SARGENT, JOSEPH DENNY, stock broker; b. W. Hartford, Conn., Sept. 11, 1929; s. Thomas Denny and Elizabeth (Owen) S.; grad. St. Paul's Sch., Concord, N.H., 1948; B.A., Yale, 1952; m. Mary A. Tennant, June 25, 1955; children—Robert Tennant, Thomas Denny II, Mary Diane, Suzanne Davis. With Conning & Co., mems. N.Y. Stock Exchange, Hartford, 1952—, partner, 1957—, now mng. partner; pres., dir. Fox-Pitt, Kelton, London; chmn. bd., treas. Sherburne Corp.; dir. Beekley Corp., Excess Treaty Holding Corp., Excess Treaty Reins. Corp., Trenwick Ltd., Trenwick Reins. Co. Trustee Wadsworth Atheneum; past trustee Children's Services of Conn.; trustee, chmn. exec. com. Hartford Hosp. Clubs: Hartford, Yale, University, Hartford Golf (Hartford). Home: 25 Colony Rd West Hartford CT 06117 Office: 41 Lewis St Hartford CT 06103

SARGENT, LEON FRANK, lawyer; b. Milw., Jan. 29, 1902; s. Frank H. and Evelyn (Burroughs) S.; A.B., Dartmouth, 1923; LL.B., Yale, 1927; m. Mary I. King, May 28, 1927; children—David B., John K., Elizabeth (Mrs. J.S. Vazifdar). Admitted to Mass. bar, 1927; asso. firm Warner, Stackpole & Bradlee, Boston, 1927-29, Powers and Hall, Boston, 1929-50; partner firm Powers & Hall, Boston 1950—; dir. Am. Core Twine Corp., 1932-52, Turgeons, Inc., 1937—; trustee Winchester Savs. Bank, 1967-75. Trustee Winchester Pub. Library, 1942-57, Alice W. Door Found., 1958—; trustee, sec., treas. Theodore Edson Parker Found., 1970—; v.p., dir Winchester Hosp., 1942-49. Fellow Am. Coll. Trial Lawyers; mem. Am., Mass., Boston bar assns., Phi Delta Phi. Clubs: Winchester Country; Union (Boston). Author articles on med. malpractice. Home: 2 Stevens St Winchester MA 01890 Office: 30 Federal St Boston MA 02110

SARGENT, RALPH MILLARD, educator; b. Austin, Minn., May 10, 1904; s. Charles J. and Katherine (Fox) S.; A.B., Carleton Coll., 1925; Ph.D., Yale, 1931; m. Louise Anderson, June 29, 1929; children—Lydia (Mrs. Hal G. Meyer), Hugh. High sch. tchr., Minn., 1925-26; instr. later asst. prof. Carleton Coll., 1931-34; prof. English, Knox Coll., 1937-41; F.B. Gummere prof. English, Haverford (Pa.) Coll. 1941-70, chmn. dept., 1949-62, editor Haverford Rev., 1942-46, now mem. corp. Chmn. Coll. Conf. on English in Middle Atlantic States, 1947-48; trustee, past pres. Highlands Biol. Sta.; bd. dirs. Henry Found. Bot. Research. Mem. Modern Lang. Assn., Am. Assn. U. Profs. (nat. council 1956-59, nat. com. on orgn. and policy 1960-64), Renaissance Soc. Am. (nat. council 1960-62), Literary Fellowship Phila. (past pres.), Pa. Hort. Soc. (bd. publs.), Bot. Soc. Am., Haverford Arboretum Assn., Haverford Library Assos. (dir., past pres.), Bartram Assn. (dir.), Phila. Art Alliance, Phi Beta Kappa. Democrat. Mem. Soc. Friends. Clubs: Philadelphia Botanical (lectr., past pres.), Franklin Inn (dir.). Author: At the Court of Queen Elizabeth, 1935; Books of the Renaissance, 1952; Shakespeare's As You Like It, 1959. Contbr. to Great Smoky Mountains Wildflowers, 1970, Peter Kalm's Travels into North America, 1972; Biology in the Blue Ridge, 1977; also learned publs. Home: 520 Panmure Rd Haverford PA 19041. *Satisfaction in achievement occurs in the doing, not in external rewards. The full sense of living, with all its pleasure and pain, comes from the constant process of sensitive contacts with the world we live in, employing our talents actively, and continuing warm involvement with people. This intricate process is obviously boundless and inexhaustible.*

SARGENT, WALLACE LESLIE WILLIAM, astronomer, educator; b. Elsham, Eng., Feb. 15, 1935; s. Leslie William and Eleanor (Dennis) S.; B.Sc., Manchester U., 1956, M.Sc., 1957, Ph.D., 1959; m. Anneila Isabel Cassells, Aug. 5, 1964; children—Lindsay Eleanor, Alison Clare. Research fellow Calif. Inst. Tech., 1959-62; sr. research fellow Royal Greenwich Obs., 1962-64; asst. prof. physics U. Calif., San Diego, 1964-66; mem. faculty dept. astronomy Calif. Inst. Tech., Pasadena, 1966—, prof., 1971—, staff mem. Hale Obs. Alfred P. Sloan Found. fellow, 1968-70; recipient Helen B. Warner prize Am. Astron. Soc., 1969. Fellow Am. Acad. Arts and Scis.; mem. Am. Astron. Soc., Royal Astron. Soc., Internat. Astron. Union. Club: Athenaeum (Pasadena). Contbr. articles to profl. jours. Home: 400 S Berkeley Ave Pasadena CA 91107 Office: Astronomy Dept 105-24 Calif Inst Tech Pasadena CA 91125

SARICKS, AMBROSE, educator; b. Wilkes-Barre, Pa., May 12, 1915; s. Ambrose and Barbara (Hauze) S.; B.A., Bucknell U., 1937, M.A., 1941; Ph.D., U. Wis., 1950; m. Reese Pyott, Mar. 4, 1945; children—Christopher Lee, Alison Barbara. Tchr. social studies Muncy Creek (Pa.) Pub. Schs., 1938-39; salesman Liberty Mut. Ins. Co., Bklyn., 1939-40; grad. teaching asst. U. Wis., 1940-42, 46, instr. history, 1946; instr. history Ohio State U., 1947-50; asst. prof. U. Kans., 1950-56, asso. prof., 1956-62, prof., 1962-70, asso. dean Grad. Sch., 1966-70; prof. history, dean Grad. Sch., asso. dean faculties Wichita (Kans.) State U., 1970-72; vice chancellor for acad. affairs U. Kans., Lawrence, 1972-75, prof. history, 1972—. Served with USAAF, 1942-46. Mem. Am. Hist. Assn., Soc. for French Hist. Studies, Soc. for 18th Century Studies, AAUP. Unitarian. Kiwanian. Author: A Bibliography of the Frank E. Melvin Collection of Pamphlets of the French Revolution in the University of Kansas Libraries, 2 vols., 1960; Pierre Samuel DuPont de Nemours, 1965. Home: 2901 Santa Fe Ln Lawrence KS 66044

SARKESIAN, SAM CHARLES, educator, polit. scientist; b. Chgo., Nov. 7, 1927; s. Charles and Khatoon (Babigian) S.; B.A., The Citadel, 1951; M.A., Columbia U., 1962, Ph.D., 1969; certificate in African studies, Syracuse U., 1962; m. Jeannette Minasian, May 7, 1955; children—Gary Charles, Joye Simone, Guy Samuel. Served as enlisted man U.S. Army, 1945-48; commd. 2d lt. U.S. Army, 1951, advanced through grades to lt. col., 1967; served in Germany, Korea, and Vietnam; asst. prof. U.S. Mil. Acad., West Point, N.Y., 1962-66, ret., 1968; mem. faculty Loyola U., Chgo., 1970—, prof. polit. sci., 1974—, chmn. dept., 1974—. Pres. Rosehills Citizens Council, 1971-74; bd. dirs. Edgewater Community Council, 1973-79. Decorated Legion of Merit, Bronze Star medal with 1 oak leaf cluster. Russell Sage Found. grantee, 1970; Army Research Inst. grantee, 1974. Mem. Am. Polit. Sci. Assn., African Studies Assn., Pi Sigma Alpha. Author: The Professional Army in A Changing Society, 1975; (with Krish Nawda) Politics and Power, 1975; (with James Buck) Introduction to Comparative Politics, 1979; editor: The Military-Industrial Complex: A Reassessment, 1971; Revolutionary Guerrila Warfare, 1975; Defenses Policy and the Presidency, 1979. Home: 5948 N Hermitage Ave Chicago IL 60660

SARKISIAN, PAUL, artist; b. Chgo., Aug. 18, 1928; s. Peter and Eugenia (Kazian) S.; student Sch. Art Inst. Chgo., 1945-48, Otis Art Inst., Los Angeles, 1953-54, Mexico City Coll., 1955-56; m. Carol McPhee, Oct. 31, 1958; 1 son, Peter Paul. Exhbns. include: La Jolla Art Center, 1963, Los Angeles County Mus., 1968, Mus. Contemporary Arts, Chgo., 1972, Santa Barbara Mus. Fine Art, 1970, Corcoran Gallery Art, Washington, 1969, San Francisco Mus., 1976, Kunsthaus, Zurich, 1977, Nat. Collection Fine Arts, Washington, 1979, Mus. Contemporary Arts, Houston, 1977, Arts Club, Chgo., 1979; represented in permanent collections: Art Inst. Chgo., Corcoran Gallery Art, Des Moines Art Center, Hirshorn Mus., Washington, Indpls. Mus., Mpls. Mus., Mus. U. Ga., others. Address: Cerrillos NM 87010

SARKOWSKY, HERMAN, bldg. co. exec.; b. Gera, Germany, June 9, 1926; s. Irving and Paula (Goldman) S.; came to U.S., 1935, naturalized, 1943; B.A. in Econs., U. Wash., 1949; m. Faye Mondschein, Aug. 10, 1952; children—Cathy Ann, Steven William. Pres., United Homes Corp., Federal Way, Wash., 1956—; pres., chief exec. officer Levitt & Sons of Cal., Inc.; past pres. Pro Basketball, Inc. owners Portland Trail Blazers; mng. gen. partner Seattle Seahawks profl. football team. Mem. exec. com. Council of Housing Producers. Pres. PONCHO, 1968; bd. dirs. United Arts Council, Seattle Symphony, Seattle Repertory Theatre, Seattle Found. Served with Signal Corps, U.S. Army, 1943-46. Mem. Nat. Assn. Home Builders (life dir., v.p. 1961-62, mem. exec. com.), Tacoma Home Builders (pres. 1957), Nat. Basketball Assn., Zeta Beta Tau. Office: 5305 Lake Washington Blvd Kirkland WA 98033

SARLAT, NOAH, editorial dir.; b. N.Y.C., July 13, 1918; s. Samuel J. and Mary (Rosenstein) S.; B.A., N.Y.U., 1938; m. Eleanor A. Levy, July 23, 1941; children—Laurie, Ivy Syd. Advt. copywriter Alvin Gardner Co., 1939; sales rep. Look mag., 1940-41, writer book dept., 1945-47; free-lance writer, 1947; picture editor Reader's Scope mag., 1947-48, Argosy mag., 1948-50; editorial dir. mags., Stag, For Men Only, Man's World, Male, Men, Sportsman, Action for Men, Adventure Life, Triple-Length Adventure, Men in Action, 1950-77; with Rolat Pub. Corp., pub. Men, True Secrets, Intimate Secrets, Intimate Romances, N.Y.C., 1977—. Served to capt. AUS, 1941-45. Recipient Bronze Star. Jewish. Compiler, editor; Sintown, U.S.A., 1952; America's Cities of Sin, 1952; How I Made a Million, 1955; Combat; Rogues and Lovers, 1956; This is It, 1957; Women With Guns, 1962; War Cry, 1962; Danger Patrol, 1962. Contbr. articles, stories to numerous mags. Home: 263 Maryland Ave Freeport NY 11520 Office: Rolat Pub Corp 667 Madison Ave New York NY 10021. *World War II changed my entire outlook on life. Thrown into a situation where I never knew from minute to minute whether I'd live or die, where basics like food, shelter, a change of clothes became the most important things from day to day, I began to put all of life in a new perspective. Things that used to seem so important and about which I would get all worked up suddenly became insignificant. And even today, in the daily-deadline-pressure kind of work that magazine editing entails, I find myself pulling up short when I find myself getting all worked up and saying to myself, "Are you crazy? It wasn't too many years ago when you didn't know whether you'd live or die - what are you getting so upset about this stupid problem for?" All this day-to-day stuff is just a joke - a way to earn the money I need to maintain my way of life. It sure as hell isn't a matter of life and death - thank God!*

SARLES, PETER MASON, mgmt. cons.; b. N.Y.C., May 29, 1926; s. Van Namee and Ann Edna (McMaster) S.; B.A. E., Rensselaer Poly. Inst., 1951; S.M. (Sloan fellow), Mass. Inst. Tech., 1961; m. Mary Ann Sheehan, Sept. 13, 1952; children—Scott, Wesley. With Westinghouse Electric Corp., 1951-75, gen. mgr. atomic equipment div., Cheswick, Pa., 1962-69, v.p. mfg., Pitts., 1969-70, exec. v.p. major appliances, 1970-71, v.p. planning and service consumer products, 1971-72, div. gen. mgr. gas turbine systems div., 1972-75; v.p., sr. cons. Soltis Assos., Pocopson, Pa., 1975-76; pres. Sarles & Co., Inc., West Chester, Pa., 1976—. Served with USAAF, 1944-46. Mem. Am. Inst. Aero. and Astronautics, Soc. Automotive Engrs. Club: Radley Run Country (West Chester, Pa.). Home: 800 Gen Cornwallis Dr West Chester PA 19380 Office: Sarles & Co Inc PO Box 72 Pocopson PA 19366

SARLES, WILLIAM BOWEN, bacteriologist; b. Viroqua, Wis., Oct. 1, 1906; s. Jesse Eugene and Frances (Bowen) S.; B.S., U. Wis., 1926, M.S., 1927, Ph. D., 1931; postgrad. Iowa State Coll., 1930-31; m. Marion E. Reynolds, Aug. 4, 1927 (dec. Oct. 1973); children—William B., Frank R. Instr. bacteriology Kans. State Coll., 1927-29; grad. fellow bacteriology U. Wis., 1929-30, asst. prof. bacteriology, 1932-36, asso. prof., 1936-43, prof., asst. to pres, 1945-46, prof., coordinator Lake Investigations, 1947-60, prof. bacteriology, 1960-72, prof. emeritus, 1972—, chmn. dept. bacteriology, 1954-68; instr. dairy bacteriology Iowa State Coll., 1930-32; Carnegie vis. prof. bacteriology U. Hawaii, 1959; mem. faculty senate U. Wis., Madison, 1970-72. Served as comdr. USNR, 1943-45. Decorated Legion of Merit (U.S.); Hon. Officer Order Brit. Empire; recipient Carski Found. Distinguished Teaching award, 1972. Fellow AAAS, Am. Acad. Microbiology; mem. Wis. Acad. Sci. Arts and Letters (v.p. scis. 1960-61, pres. 1969-70, hon. life mem.), Soc. for Gen. Microbiology, Soc. Am. Bacteriologists (sec.-treas. 1942-43; rep. NRC 1947-50, pres. N. Central br. 1955), Am. Soc. Limnology and Oceanography, Am. Soc. for Microbiology (chmn. publ. bd. 1961-65, pres. 1966-67, hon. life mem., chief del. internat. congress for microbiology Moscow 1966), Sigma Xi, Phi Kappa Phi, Phi Sigma, Alpha Zeta, Phi Gamma Delta. Author: Microbiology: General and Applied, 1951. Editor: Jour. Bacteriology, 1961-65; trustee Biol. Abstracts, 1954-60. Contbr. articles to profl. jours. Home: 5505 Barton Rd Madison WI 53711

SARNA, NAHUM MATTATHIAS, educator; b. London, Eng., Mar. 27, 1923; s. Jacob and Milly (Horonzick) S.; B.A., U. London, 1944, M.A., 1946; minister's diploma Jews Coll., London, 1947; Ph.D., Dropsie Coll., Phila., 1955; m. Helen Horowitz, Mar. 23, 1947; children—David E. Y., Jonathan D. Came to U.S., 1951, naturalized, 1959. Asst. lectr. Hebrew, Univ. Coll., London, 1946-49; lectr. Gratz Coll., Phila., 1951-57; librarian Jewish Theol. Sem., also asst. prof. Bible Tchrs. Inst., 1957-63, asso. prof. of Bible, 1963-65; asso. prof. Bibl. studies Brandeis U., Waltham, Mass., 1965-67, Dora Golding prof. Bibl. studies, 1967—, chmn. dept. Near Eastern and Judaic studies, 1969-75; vis. prof. Bible, Dropsie Coll., 1967-68. Mem. adv. bd. adult Jewish edn. B'nai B'rth. Asso. trustee Am. Sch. Oriental Research; trustee, mem. exec. com. Boston Hebrew Coll.; acad. adv. council Nat. Found. Jewish Culture. Recipient Jewish Book Ann. award, 1967; Am. Council Learned Socs. fellow, 1971-72. Fellow Royal Asiatic Soc., Am. Acad. Jewish Research; mem. Soc. Bibl. Lit. and Exegesis, Am. Oriental Soc., Israel Exploration Soc., Archons of Colophon, Palestine Exploration Soc. Bibl. Colloquium, Assn. for Jewish Studies (hon. sec.-treas. 1972—). Author: Understanding Genesis, 1966; co-author A New Translation of the Book of Psalms, 1973. Editor, translator Jewish Publ. Soc. Bible, 1966—; editorial bd. Jour. Bibl. Lit., 1973-75, Soc. Bibl. Lit. Monograph Series, 1975—; deptl. editor Ency. Judaica; gen. editor Jewish Publ. Soc. Bible Commentary series, 1974—. Contbr. to Ency. Brit., 1974, also articles to scholarly jours. Home: 35 Everett St Newton Centre MA 02159 Office: Brandeis U Waltham MA 02154

SARNAT, BERNARD GEORGE, plastic surgeon, educator, researcher; b. Chgo., Sept. 1, 1912; s. Isadore M. and Fanny (Sidran) S.; B.S., U. Chgo., 1933, M.D., 1937; M.S., D.D.S., U. Ill., 1940; m. Rhoda Elaine Gerard, Dec. 25, 1941; children—Gerard, Joan. Intern Los Angeles County Gen. Hosp., 1936-37; resident oral and plastic surgery Cook County Hosp., Chgo., 1940-41; asst. to Dr. Marshall Davison, gen. surgery, Chgo., 1942-43; asst. to Drs. Vilray P. Blair and Louis T. Byars, plastic and reconstructive surgery, St. Louis, 1943-46; practice medicine specializing in plastic surgery, Chgo., 1946-56, Beverly Hills, Calif., 1956—; asst. histology U. Ill. Coll. Dentistry, 1937-40, prof., head dept. oral and maxillofacial surgery, 1946-56; asst. dept. surgery Washington U. Sch. Medicine, St. Louis, 1944-46; prof., dir. dept. oral and plastic surgery St. Louis U. Coll. Dentistry, 1945-46; clin. asst. prof. surgery (plastic surgery) U. Ill. Coll. Medicine, 1949-56; adj. prof. oral biology Sch. Dentistry, UCLA, 1969—, mem. Dental Research Inst., 1974—, adj. prof. plastic surgery Sch. Medicine, 1974—; mem. staff, chief plastic surgery, sr. research scientist Cedars-Sinai Med. Center, Los Angeles; cons. in gen., plastic and maxillofacial surgery VA Regional Office, Chgo. until 1956. Co-winner Joseph A. Capps prize for med. research, 1940; recipient Kerbs award for research plastic and reconstructive surgery, 1950, first prize, sr. award Found. Am. Soc. Plastic and Reconstructive Surgeons, 1957; Nat. Achievement award Phi Epsilon Pi, 1964. Diplomate Am. Bd. Plastic Surgery. Fellow A.C.S., AAAS; mem. Calif., Los Angeles med. socs., Am. Soc. Plastic and Reconstructive Surgeons, Plastic Surgery Research Council, Calif. Soc. Plastic Surgeons, Am. Assn. Plastic Surgeons, Beverly Hills Acad. Medicine (pres. 1962-63), Internat. Assn. Craniofacial Biology, Am. Assn. Phys. Anthropologists, Internat. Assn. for Study Dento-Facial Abnormalities (hon.), Sigma Xi, Omicron Kappa Upsilon, Zeta Beta Tau, Phi Delta Epsilon, Alpha Omega. Sr. author (with Dr. Isaac Schour) Oral and Facial Cancer, 2d edit., 1957; (with Dr. Daniel Laskin) Surgery of the Temporomandibular Joint, 1964. Editor: The Temporomandibular Joint, 2d edit., 1964. Contbr. to chpts. textbooks, articles to surg. jours., other publs. Home: 1835 Holmby Los Angeles CA 90025 Office 435 N Roxbury Dr Beverly Hills CA 90210

SARNO, EDWARD FRANCIS, II, coll. pres.; b. Cambridge, Mass., May 22, 1940; s. Edward Francis and Dorothea Agnes (O'Connell) S.; B.S., Boston U., 1961; M.A., Mich. State U., 1963; Ph.D. (fellow), Ohio U., 1966; m. June Marlene Beougher, Jan. 29, 1972; children—Leslie Ann, Edward Francis III. Grad. asst. Mich. State U., 1961-62; instr. speech U. Mass., 1962-64; doctoral teaching fellow, instr. speech Ohio U., Athens, 1965-66, asst. prof. communication, dir. learning resources, 1966-69, asst. dean regional campuses, 1969-70, asso. dean, 1970-73; exec. v.p., prof. communication Milton (Wis.) Coll., 1973-74, pres., 1974—. Dir. Serendipity Systems, Inc. Adminstrv. v.p., bd. dirs. Athens Jr. C. of C., 1968. Recipient Edward P. Morgan award, 1962, Arthur Godfrey award, 1963, Outstanding First Year Jaycee award, 1968; named Man of Year, Boston U. Sch. Pub. Communication, 1961. Mem. Am. Assn. for Higher Edn., Am. Assn. U. Adminstrs., Am. Conf. Acad. Deans, Speech Communications Assn., Nat. Assn. Ednl. Broadcasters, Sigma Delta Chi, Alpha Epsilon Rho. Episcopalian. Rotarian, Kiwanian. Author: The National Radio Conferences, 1969; The Continuing Challenge for Innovation Through Off-Campus Programs, 1969; Tenure Implications for Multi-Campus Institutions, 1971. Adv. bd. The School Law Newsletter, 1971—. Home: 605 Rainbow Dr Lancaster OH 43130

SARNOFF, ALBERT, entertainment co. exec.; b. N.Y.C., July 19, 1925; s. Morris and Clara (Oppenheimer) S.; B.A., Yale U., 1947; m. Nancy Hanak, July 25, 1968; children—Gary, Ken, Doug. Buyer, R.H. Macy & Co., N.Y.C., 1950-52; v.p. sales Pease & Ellman, N.Y.C., 1952-58; pres. Club Razor Blade Mfg. Co., N.J., 1958-62; sr. v.p., treas. Warner Communications Inc., N.Y.C., 1962—; dir. Garden State Nat. Bank, Paramus, N.J. Clubs: Metropolis Country, City Athletic. Office: 75 Rockefeller Plaza New York NY 10019

SARNOFF, STANLEY JAY, physiologist; b. Bklyn., Apr. 5, 1917; s. Jacob and Belle (Roosin) S.; grad. Peddie Sch., 1934; A.B., Princeton, 1938; M.D., Johns Hopkins, 1942; m. Lili Charlotte Dreyfus, Sept. 11, 1948; children—Daniela Martha Sarnoff Bargezi, Robert Burnham Louis. Asst. resident Mass. Gen. Hosp., Boston, 1947; asso. prof. physiology Harvard Sch. Pub. Health, 1948-57; vis. lectr. Howard U. 1957-65; med. dir. Nat. Heart Inst., USPHS, Bethesda, Md., chief lab. cardiovascular physiology NIH, 1954-65; professorial lectr. George Washington U., 1957-64; vis. lectr. Howard U., 1957-65; St. Cyres and Halliburton lectr., London, 1961; chmn. bd., chief exec. officer Survival Tech., Inc., Bethesda, Md., 1969—. Recipient Distinguished Service award Princeton, 1938, 57, Porter travel award, 1950, Jacobs Found. award for meritorious heart research, 1957; Carl J. Wiggers award circulation group Am. Physiol. Soc., 1970; Small Businessman of Year award, Washington, 1973. Mem. Am. Physiol. Soc., Am. Heart Assn., Sigma Xi. Clubs: Princeton, Cosmos (Washington). Editor: Ency. Cardiology, Am. Jour. Cardiology, 1957-65, Am. Jour. Physiology, 1958-66, Jour. Applied Physiology. Home: 7507 Hampden Ln Bethesda MD 20014 Office: Survival Technology Inc 7801 Woodmont Ave Bethesda MD 20014

SARNOFF, THOMAS WARREN, TV exec.; b. N.Y.C., Feb. 23, 1927; s. David and Lizette (Hermant) S.; grad. Phillips Acad., 1939-43; student Princeton, 1943-45; B.S. in Elec. Engring., Stanford, 1948, postgrad. Sch. Bus. Adminstrn., 1948-49; D.H.L., Columbia Coll.; m. Janyce Lundon, May 21, 1955; children—Daniel, Timothy, Cynthia. Engaged in prodn. and sales with ABC, Inc., 1949-51; prodn. Metro-Goldwyn-Mayer, 1951-52; with NBC, 1952—, v.p. prodn. and bus. affairs Pacific div., 1956-60, v.p. adminstrn. West Coast, 1960-62, v.p. charge West Coast, 1962-65, staff exec. v.p. West Coast, 1965-77; pres. NBC Entertainment Corp., 1972-77, Sarnoff Internat. Enterprises, 1977—. Mem. Calif. Commn. for Reform Intermediate and Secondary Edn. Pres., Research Found., St. Joseph Hosp., Burbank, 1965-73, Permanant Charities Com. of Entertainment Industries, 1971-72; nat. trustee Nat. Conf. Christians and Jews. Served with Signal Corps, AUS, World War II. Mem. Acad. TV Arts and Scis. (chmn. trustees 1972-74). Club: Brentwood Country (Los Angeles). Office: Sarnoff Internat Enterprises Inc 4433 Lakeside Dr Burbank CA 91505

SARNOFF, WILLIAM, publishing co. exec.; b. Mt. Vernon, N.Y., May 22, 1929; s. Morris and Clara (Oppenheimer) S.; B.A., Stanford U., 1950; M.B.A., Harvard U., 1952; m. Pam Markus, Dec. 24, 1955; children—Jeffrey, Richard, Nancy. Treas. Club Razor Blade Mfg. Co., Newark, 1955-62; v.p. Warner Communications, Inc., N.Y.C., 1962-75; chmn. Warner Pub., Inc., 1975—. Trustee Horace Mann Sch., Beth Israel Hosp. Served with USAF, 1952-54. Office: 75 Rockefeller Plaza New York NY 10019*

SAROFIM, ADEL FARES, chem. engr.; b. Cairo, Oct. 21, 1934; came to U.S., 1955, naturalized, 1968; s. Fares and Blanche Morcos (Simaika) S.; B.A. with honours, Oxford (Eng.) U., 1955; S.M., M.I.T., 1957, Sc.D., 1962; m. Leticia Borgo, Aug. 5, 1967; 1 son, Marcus. Mem. faculty M.I.T., 1961—, prof. chem. engring., 1972—; vis. prof. Sheffield (Eng.) U., 1971; vis. scientist combustion research lab. Italian Nat. Research Council, U. Naples, 1974; vis. Chevron energy prof. Calif. Inst. Tech., Pasadena, 1979; mem. panel hazardous trace substances Office Sci. and Tech., 1970-72; mem. com. prins. for evaluating chems. in environ. Nat. Acad. Scis., 1972-74; mem. com. health and ecol. effects of increased coal utilization HEW, 1977. Registered profl. engr., Mass. Mem. Am. Inst. Chem. Engrs., Am. Chem. Soc., Combustion Inst., Solar Energy Soc., N.Y. Acad. Sci. Co-author: Radiative Transfer, 1967. Home: 11 Stella Rd Belmont MA 02178 Office: 66-466 Mass Inst Tech Cambridge MA 02139

SAROSDY, LOUIS ROBERT, naval officer; b. Pitts., 1927; B.S., U.S. Naval Acad., 1951; Aero. Engr., Calif. Inst. Tech., Pasadena, 1960; m. Mary Frances Pryor; children—Larry, Maggie, Anne, Amy. Commd. ensign U.S. Navy, 1951, designated naval aviator, 1952, advanced through grades to rear adm., 1978; service in fleet fighter squadrons, air staffs, naval material command, Japan, 1968-70; asst. chief staff material Naval Air Force, U.S. Atlantic Fleet, 1977-78; asst. comdr. logistics/fleet support Naval Air Systems Command, Washington, 1978—. Address: Asst Comdr Logistics/Fleet Support Naval Air Systems Command Dept Navy Washington DC 20361

SAROYAN, WILLIAM, writer; b. Fresno, Calif., Aug. 31, 1908; s. Armenak and Takoohi (Saroyan) S. (of Bitlis, Armenia); ed. public schs., Fresno; m. Carol Marcus, Feb. 1943 (div. Nov. 1949); children—Aram, Lucy. Co-founder Conf. Press, Los Angeles, 1936; dir. Saroyan Theatre, N.Y.C., 1942; writer-in-residence Purdue U., 1961. Author: The Daring Young Man on the Flying Trapeze, 1934; Inhale and Exhale, 1936; Three Times Three, 1936; Little Children, 1937; Love, Here Is My Hat, 1938; The Trouble with Tigers, 1938; Peace, It's Wonderful, 1939; My Name Is Aram, 1940; My Heart's in the Highlands (play, produced by Group Theatre, N.Y.C.), 1939; The Time of Your Life (play, prod. by Theatre Guild, N.Y.C., received Drama Critics Circle Award, also Pulitzer Prize, the latter being rejected; made into film with James Cagney 1948), 1939; Love's Old Sweet Song (play, prod. by Theatre Guild), 1939; The Beautiful People (play, produced and directed by himself in N.Y.C.), 1941; Across the Board on Tomorrow Morning (play, produced by Pasadena (Calif.) Playhouse), 1941; Jim Dandy (play, presented by 60 theatre mems. of Nat. Theatre Conf.), 1941; The Great American Goof (ballet, produced by Ballet Theatre in N.Y.C.), 1940, 41; Saroyan's Fables (old country fables), 1941; Razzle Dazzle (short plays), 1942; (novel and movie) The Human Comedy, 1942; Get Away, Old Man (play, produced by George Abbott), 1944; Dear Baby (stories), 1944; The Adventures of Wesley Jackson (novel), 1946; Jim Dandy, Fat Man in a Famine (play), 1947; The Saroyan Special (selected stories), 1948; Mama, I Love You (novel), 1956; The Whole Voyald (stories), 1956; Papa You're Crazy (novel), 1957; Not Dying (autobiography), 1963; One Day in the Afternoon of the World (novel), 1964; After Thirty Years: The Daring Young Man on the Flying Trapeze, 1964; Short Drive, Sweet Chariot (autobiographical fragment), 1966; Look at Us (photographs by Arthur Rubenstein), 1967; I Used to Believe I Had Forever, Now I'm Not so Sure (stories, essays, plays, poems), 1967; Letters from 74 Rue Taitbout, or Don't Go But If You Must, Say Hello to Everybody (letter-stories), 1969; The Dogs and Two Other Plays (plays), 1969. Dir. moving picture The Good Job, 1942; opened Saroyan Theatre, N.Y.C., with Across the Board on Tomorrow Morning and Talking to You, 1942; The Twin Adventures, 1950; The Assyrian and Other Stories, 1950; Rock Wagram, 1951; Tracy's Tiger, 1951; The Bicycle Rider in Beverly Hills, 1952; The Laughing Matter, 1953; Here Comes/There Goes/You Know Who, 1961; Boys and Girls Together, 1963; Places Where I've Done Time, 1972; The Tooth and My Father, 1974; Sons Come and Go, Mothers Hang in Forever, 1976; Chance Meetings, 1978; Obituaries, 1979. Mem. Nat. Inst. Arts and Letters. Address: care WW Norton and Co Inc 500 Fifth Ave New York NY 10036. *I'm here. I'm 65. I have been all of the intervening years, and I still am all of them, as well as 65 going on 66. I'm watching. I'm ignorant. I used to be angry about this, but thirty years ago I began to see the intelligence of this. It is all right to be ignorant, just so you know it. I have a sense of time, and so I have always sought to use time effectively, especially in writing. I'm interested in everything. I am fascinated by everybody. That's why I'm watching. Living is the only thing. It is an awful pain most of the time, but this compels comedy and dignity.**

SARPKAYA, TURGUT, educator; b. Aydin, Turkey, May 7, 1928; s. Hasip and Huriye (Fetil) S.; came to U.S., 1951, naturalized, 1962; B.S. in Mech. Engring., Tech. U. Istanbul, 1950, M.S., 1951; Ph.D. in Engring. State U. Iowa, 1954; m. Gunel Ataisik, Aug. 26, 1963. Research engr. Mass. Inst. Tech., 1954-55; asst. prof. U. Neb., 1957-59, asso. prof. 1959-62, prof. mech. engring., 1962, distinguished prof., 1962-66; research prof. U. Manchester (Eng.), 1966-67, U. Gottingen (Germany), 1971-72; prof. mech. engring., chmn. dept. U.S. Naval Postgrad. Sch., Monterey, Calif., 1967-71, 72-75, Distinguished prof. mech. engring., 1975—. Cons. aerospace industry, 1967—, petroleum industry, 1976—. Served with C.E., AUS, 1955-57. Fellow Royal Instn. Naval Architects, ASME (Lewis F. Moody award 1967; exec. bd. fluids engring. div., chmn. review com.); mem. ASCE (Collingwood prize 1957), Heat Transfer and Fluid Mechanics Inst. (chmn.), Am. Inst. Aeros. and Astronautics, Internat. Assn. Hydraulics Research, Am. Soc. Engring. Edn. Mem. editorial bd. Zentralblatt fur Mathematik; editor Procs. Heat Transfer and Fluid Mechanics Inst., 1970. Patentee fluidic elements. Home: 25330 Vista del Pinos Carmel CA 93923

SARPY, LEON, lawyer; b. New Orleans, Nov. 25, 1907; s. Henry Leon and Anita Louise (Staigge) S.; A.B., Loyola U., New Orleans, 1928, LL.B., 1931, LL.D. (hon.), 1961; LL.M., Georgetown U., 1932; m. Courtney Dickinson, July 7, 1938 (dec. Mar. 1945); children—Courtney Anne, H. Leon; m. 2d, Eleanor Legier, July 17, 1948; 1 son, John Robert. Admitted to La. bar, 1931; practice in New Orleans, 1932; mem. firm Chaffe, McCall, Phillips, Toler & Sarpy, 1948—; lectr. Loyola U. Law Sch., 1934—; dist. rent atty. OPA, 1942-43; reporter La. Criminal Code, 1942, La. Code Civil Procedure, 1960. Chmn. Civil Service Commn. New Orleans, 1952-63; chmn. civic luncheon for Pres. deGaulle of France, 1960; pres. Asso. Catholic Charities New Orleans, 1953-54; mem. Audubon Park Commn., 1963-70; bd. pres. New Orleans United Fund, 1959-60; bd. dirs. Greater New Orleans Homestead Assn., 1940-77; chmn. adv. bd. Convent Good Shepherd, 1957-58; trustee St. Mary's Dominican Coll., 1963-67; chmn. Community Chest of New Orleans, 1970-73; adv. bd. Loyola U., 1964-72, Tulane Admiralty Inst., 1966—. Mem. La. N.G., 1925-28, USCG Temporary Res., 1944-45. Decorated Legion of Honor (France); named Outstanding Alumnus, Jesuit High Sch., New Orleans, 1964; recipient Brotherhood award Nat. Conf. Christians and Jews, 1964, Gold medal St. Mary's Dominican Coll., 1970; Rex of New Orleans Mardi Gras, 1972. Mem. Am. (ho. dels. 1965-70), La. (pres. 1964-65), New Orleans (pres. 1950-51) bar assns., Am., La. (v.p. 1961—) law insts., Inst. Jud. Adminstrn. (N.Y.), Southwest Legal Found. (chmn. research fellows 1970-72), Order of Coif, Blue Key, Delta Theta Phi. Clubs: Boston, Round Table (pres. 1964-66), Serra (pres. 1960-61) (New Orleans). Contbr. to legal jours. Home: 455 Walnut St New Orleans LA 70118 Office: First Nat Bank Commerce Bldg New Orleans LA 70112

SARRIS, ANDREW GEORGE, film critic; b. Bklyn., Oct. 31, 1928; s. George Andrew and Themis (Katavolos) S.; A.B., Columbia, 1951; m. Molly Clark Haskell, May 31, 1969. Film critic Village Voice, N.Y.C., 1960—; editor-in-chief Cahiers du Cinema in English, instr. Sch. Visual Arts, 1965-67; asst. prof. N.Y. U., 1967-69; asso. prof. films Columbia Sch. Arts, N.Y.C., 1969—. Served with Signal Corps, AUS, 1952-54. Guggenheim fellow, 1969. Mem. Am. Film Inst. (dir.), Soc. Cinema Studies, Nat. Soc. Film Critics, N.Y. Film Critics. Author: The Films of Josef Von Sternberg, 1966; Interviews with Film Directors, 1967; The Film, The American Cinema, both 1968; Confessions of a Cultist, 1970; The Primal Screen, 1973; The John Ford Movie Mystery, 1976; Politics and Cinema, 1978. Home: 19 E 88th St New York City NY 10028 Office: Village Voice 80 University Pl New York City NY 10003. *I keep working toward that last deadline.*

SARRO, RONALD ARMAND, newspaper journalist, editor, author, polit. aide; b. Providence, Aug. 14, 1938; s. Armand G. and Etta (Moretti) S.; student U. Md. at College Park, 1956-58; m. Mary Caramadre, June 4, 1960; children—Ronald Vincent, Anthony Joseph, Jo-Ann, Susan Rose. Reporter, editor U.P.I., Washington, 1960-61; reporter R.I. Jour.-Bull., Providence, 1961-66; met. reporter Washington Star, 1966-69, asst. city editor, 1969, nat. reporter, 1969-74, asst. nat. editor, 1974-76, polit. editor, 1976-77, sr. Congl. reporter, 1977-78; chief writer Office of House Majority Whip, 1979—. Bd. dirs. Md. Media Corp., U. Md., 1974—, lectr. journalism, 1975-78. Active Boy Scouts Am. Recipient Front Page award, 1st prize for local reporting Washington-Balt. Newspaper Guild, 1969. Mem. Washington Press Club (pres. 1974-75), Washington-Balt. Newspaper Guild (dir. 1971-76), Providence Newspaper Guild (pres. 1965-66), Seabrook Little Theater (v.p. 1976-79). Roman Catholic (tchr. religion 1973-76). Author: Are You Safe From Burglars, 1971. Home: 5807 Mentana St New Carrollton MD 20784 Office: Room H-107 US Capitol Washington DC 20515

SARRY, CHRISTINE, ballerina; b. Long Beach, Calif., May 25, 1946; d. John and Beatrice (Thomas) Sarry. With Joffrey Ballet, 1963-64, Am. Ballet Theatre, 1964-68, prin. dancer, 1971-74; leading dancer Am. Ballet Co., 1969-71, Eliot Feld Ballet, 1974—; performer ballets for Agnes DeMille, Anthony Tudor, Jerome Robbins, Eliot Feld; appeared at White House, 1963, 67; U.S. Dept. State tours include Russia, 1963, 66, S. Am., 1964, 76; various tours of N.Am., Orient, Europe; various appearances U.S. nat. TV; tchr. New Ballet Sch., N.Y.C. Office: 890 Broadway New York NY

SARTON, MAY, author, poet; b. Wondelgem, Belgium, May 3, 1912; d. George Alfred Leon and Eleanor Mabel (Elwes) Sarton; brought to U.S., 1916, naturalized, 1924; student Shady Hill Sch., Cambridge, Mass., Inst. Belge de Culture Française, Brussels, 1924-25; grad. Cambridge High and Latin Sch., 1929; Litt.D., Russell Sage Coll., 1959, Clark U., 1975, U. N.H., 1976, Bates Coll., 1976, Colby Coll., 1976, Thomas Starr King Sch. Ministry, 1976. Lectr. poetry U. Chgo., Harvard, U. Iowa, Colo. Coll., Wellesley Coll., Beloit Coll., U. Kans., Denison U., others. Briggs-Copeland instr. composition Harvard, 1950-52. Awarded Golden Rose for poetry, 1945; Edward Bland Meml. prize Poetry Mag., 1945; Alexandrine medal Coll. St. Catherine, 1975. Fellow in poetry Bryn Mawr, 1953-54; Guggenheim Found. fellow, 1954-55. Fellow Am. Acad. Arts and Scis.; mem. N.E. Poetry Soc., Poetry Soc. Am. (Reynolds lyric award 1953). Author: Encounter in April, 1937; The Single Hound, 1938; Inner Landscape (poems), 1939; The Bridge of Years, 1946, The Lion and The Rose (poems), 1948; Shadow of a Man, 1950; A Shower of Summer Days, 1952; The Land of Silence (poems), 1953; Faithful Are the Wounds, 1954; The Birth of a Grandfather, 1957; In Time Like Air, 1957; The Fur Person (fiction), 1957; I Knew a Phoenix, 1959; The Small Room, 1961; Cloud, Stone, Sun, Vine, 1961; Joanna and Ulysses, 1963; Mrs. Stevens Hears the Mermaids Singing, 1965; A Private Mythology (poems), 1966; Miss Pickthorn and Mr. Hare, 1966; As Does New Hampshire (poems), 1967; Plant Dreaming Deep (autobiography), 1968; The Poet and the Donkey, 1969; Kinds of Love, 1970; A Grain of Mustard Seed (poems), 1971; A Durable Fire (poems), 1972; Journal of a Solitude, 1973; As We Are Now, 1973; Collected Poems, 1974; Crucial Conversations (novel), 1975; A World of Light (autobiography), 1976; The House by the Sea, a journal, 1977; A Reckoning (novel), 1978. Home: Box 99 York ME 03909

SARTORELLI, ALAN CLAYTON, educator; b. Chelsea, Mass., Dec. 18, 1931; B.S., New Eng. Coll. Pharmacy Northeastern U., 1953; M.S., Middlebury (Vt.) Coll., 1955; Ph.D., U. Wis., 1958; M.A. (hon.) Yale, 1967; m. Alice C. Anderson, July 7, 1969. Research chemist Samuel Roberts Noble Found., Ardmore, Okla., 1958-60, sr. research chemist, 1960-61; mem. faculty dept. pharmacology Yale Sch. Medicine, 1961—, prof., 1967—, head devel. therapeutics program. Comprehensive Cancer Center, 1974—, chmn. dept. pharmacology, 1977—; Charles B. Smith vis. research prof. Meml. Sloan-Kettering Cancer Center, 1979. Mem. cancer clin. investigation rev. com. Nat. Cancer Inst., 1968-72; mem. instl. research grants com. Am. Cancer Soc., 1971-76; cons. in biochemistry U. Tex. M.D. Anderson Hosp. and Tumor Clinic, Houston, 1970-76; mem. exptl. therapeutics study sect. NIH, 1973-77, mem. working cadre nat. large bowel cancer project, 1973-76; mgmt. cons. to dir. div. cancer treatment Nat. Cancer Inst., 1975-77; mem. council analysis and projection Am. Cancer Soc., 1977—; mem. bd. sci. counselors, div. cancer treatment Nat. Cancer Inst., 1978—; mem. adv. com. Cancer Research Center, Washington U. Sch. Medicine, 1971—; mem. external adv. com. Wis. Clin. Cancer Center, 1978—; mem. sci. adv. com. U. Iowa Cancer Center, 1979—; mem. nat. program com. 13th Internat. Cancer Congress, 1979—; mem. selection com. Bristol-Myers prize in cancer research, 1977—, chmn., 1979—. Fellow N.Y. Acad. Scis.; mem. AAAS, Am. Assn. Cancer Research (dir. 1975-78), Am. Chem. Soc., Am. Soc. Microbiology, Am. Soc. Biol. Chemists, Am. Soc. Cell Biology, Am. Soc. Pharmacology and Exptl. Therapeutics, Biochem. Soc. (London, Eng.). Regional editor Am. Continent Biochem. Pharmacology, 1968—; mem. editorial adv. bd. Cancer Research, 1970-71, asso. editor, 1971—; editorial bd. Internat. Ency. Pharmacology and Therapeutics, 1972—; editor Handbuch der experimentellen Pharmakologie vols. on antineoplastic and immunosuppressive agts.; exec. editor Pharmacology and Therapeutics, 1975—; editorial bd. Seminars in Oncology, 1973—, Chemico-Biol. Interactions, 1975-78, Jour. Medicinal Chemistry, 1977—; adv. bd. Advances in Chemistry Series, ACS Symposium Series, 1977—; editor Am. Chem. Soc. Symposium series on cancer chemotherapy, 1976; contbr. articles to profl. jours. Home: 4 Perkins Rd Woodbridge CT 06525 Office 333 Cedar St New Haven CT 06510

SARTORI, GIOVANNI, polit. scientist; b. Florence, Italy, May 13, 1924; s. Dante and Emilia (Quentin) S.; Ph.D., U. Florence, 1956; m. Giovanna Paterno Castello, Oct. 21, 1969; 1 child, Ilaria. Prof. polit. sci. U. Florence, 1956-76, dean faculty of polit. scis., 1968-71; prof. polit. sci. Stanford U., 1976-79; Albert Schweitzer prof. in the humanities Columbia U., N.Y.C., 1979—; fellow Center Advanced Study Behavioral Scis., 1971-72; sr. fellow Hoover Instn., 1976-79. Guggenheim fellow, 1978-79; Ford Found. fellow, 1979. Mem. Am. Acad. Arts and Scis. Author: Democratic Theory, 1962, 1979; Parties and Party Systems: A Framework for Analysis, 1976; La Politica, 1979. Office: 420 W 118th St New York NY 10027

SARTORI, K. J., corp. exec.; b. Stockton, Calif., Feb. 21, 1911; m. Vivien Clark, May 21, 1934; 1 dau., Jane (Mrs. Kenneth G. Seeborg). Pres., dir. Am. Consumer Industries, 1965—; pres., dir. U.S. Cold Storage of Calif., U.S. Cold Storage of Hawaii, Inc., Container Shipping, Inc.; chmn., dir. Central Calif. Industries, Inc. Chmn. Internat. Assn. Refrigerated Warehouse, 1968-69; bd. govs. The Refrigeration Research Found., pres., 1975-76. Clubs: World Trade (San Francisco); Marco Polo (N.Y.C.); Heritage Golf and Country (Conn.). Home: 501 Bartram Rd Moorestown NJ 08057 Office: 777 Pattison Ave Philadelphia PA 19148

SASAKI, HIDEO, landscape architect, educator; b. Reedley, Calif., Nov. 25, 1919; s. Kaichiro and Kiyome (Agasawara) S.; student U. Calif. at Los Angeles and Berkeley, 1939-41, Central YMCA Coll., Chgo., 1943-44; B.F.A. in Landscape Architecture with highest honors, U. Ill., 1946; M. Landscape Archtecture, Harvard, 1948; m. Kisa Noguchi, Dec. 23, 1951; children—Rin, Ann. Prin. Sasaki Assos., Inc., Watertown, Mass.; faculty U. Ill., 1948-50, 52-53; faculty Harvard Grad. Sch. Design, 1950-52, 53-70, chmn. dept. landscape architecture, 1958-68. Mem. U.S. Commn. Fine Arts, 1962-71; mem. adv. com. arts and architecture John F. Kennedy Meml. Library; mem. U.S. Nat. Arboretum Advisory Council, 1970—. Mem. allied professions medal AIA, 1973. Fellow Am. Soc. Landscape Architecture (medal 1971). Office: 64 Pleasant St Watertown MA 02172

SASENICK, JOSEPH ANTHONY, health care co. exec.; b. Chgo., May 18, 1940; s. Anthony E. and Caroline E. (Smicklas) S.; B.A., DePaul U., 1962; M.A., U. Okla., 1963; m. Barbara Ellen Barr, Aug. 18, 1962; children—Richard Allen, Susan Marie, Michael Joseph. With Miles Labs., Inc., Elkhart, Ind., 1963-70, product mgr. Alka-Seltzer, 1966-68, dir. mktg. grocery products div., 1968-70; with Gillette Corp., Boston, 1970-79, dir. new products/new ventures, personal care div., 1977, v.p. diversified cos. and pres. Jafra Cosmetics Worldwide, 1977-79; corp. v.p. Abbott Labs., North Chicago, 1979, pres. consumer products div., 1979—. Mem. Omicron Delta Epsilon. Clubs: Nashawtuc Country (Concord, Mass.); Tennis and Racquets (Boston); Knollwood (Lake Forest, Ill.). Home: 555 Lakeland Dr Lake Bluff IL 60044 Office: Abbott Park North Chicago IL 60064

SASLOW, DANIEL L., dental supply and equipment co. exec.; b. Chgo., Oct. 28, 1926; s. Joseph J. and Olga E. Saslow; B.S. in Bus. Adminstr., Northwestern U., 1948; m. Fay Finke, Nov. 23, 1949; 1 dau., Lynn Dani. Salesman, Nobilium Products Co., 1948-51; founder, pres. D.L. Saslow Co., Chgo., 1951—. Served with U.S. Army, 1944-45. Mem. Dental Dealers Am. (pres. 1979-80). Home: 175 E Delaware St Chicago IL 60611 Office: DL Saslow Co 500 N Orleans St Chicago IL 60610

SASLOW, GEORGE, psychiatrist, educator; b. N.Y.C., Dec. 5, 1906; s. Abram and Becky (Zinkoff) S.; Sc.B. magna cum laude Washington Sq. Coll. N.Y. U., 1926; postgrad. U. Rochester, 1926-28; Ph.D. in Physiology, N.Y. U., 1931; M.D. cum laude, Harvard, 1940; m. Julia Amy Ipcar, July 28, 1928; children—Michael G., Rondi, Steven, Marguerite. Instr., asst. prof. biology N.Y. U. 1928-37; vis. research asso. physiology Cornell Med. Coll., 1935-36, U. Rochester Sch. Medicine, 1936-37; research asso. physiology Harvard Sch. Pub. Health, 1937-40; neurology-neurosurgery intern Boston City Hosp., 1940-41; resident Worcester State Hosp., 1941-42; chief resident psychiatry Mass. Gen. Hosp., Boston, 1942-43, staff, 1955-57; instr., successively asst., asso. prof., prof. pychiatry Washington U. Sch. Medicine, 1943-55; staff Barnes Hosp., St. Louis, 1943-55; practice of psychiatry, 1943—; clin. prof. psychiatry Harvard, 1955-57; prof. psychiatry U. Oreg. Med. Sch., Portland, 1957-74, head dept., 1957-73, prof. emeritus, 1979—; chief mental health and behavioral sci. edn., chief psychiatry service VA Hosp., Sepulveda, Calif., 1974—; prof. psychiatry in residence UCLA, 1974-79. Fellow Nat. Tng. Labs. Fellow Am. Psychiat. Assn. (life, mem. task force on nomenclature and statistics), Am. Coll. Psychiatrists (charter); mem. AMA, Assn. for Advancement Behavioral Therapy. Home: 16531 Akron St Pacific Palisades CA 90272

SASO, CHARLES FREDERICK, mfg. co. exec.; b. L.I. City, N.Y., Sept. 30, 1916; s. Bounaventure and Mary (DiCarlo) S.; student pub. schs., N.Y.C.; m. Victoria I. Yachinska, July 12, 1948; children—Charles, Paul, Ralph. Mech. draftsman John C. Fisher Co., Long Island City, 1936-41; toolroom supt. Nat. Die and Button Mold Co., N.Y.C., 1941-47; v.p., gen. mgr. Technion Design Corp., N.Y.C., 1947-55; pres., gen. mgr. Duramic Products, Inc., Palisades Park, N.J., 1955—, also dir. Mem. Am. Ceramic Soc., Soc. Mfg. Engrs. Home: 302 Webster Dr New Milford NJ 07646 Office: 426 Commercial Ave Palisades Pk NJ 07650

SASS, DANIEL BENJAMIN, educator; b. Rochester, N.Y., Mar. 28, 1919; s. Julius and Lillian (Gottlieb) S.; A.B. cum laude, U. Rochester, 1949, M.S., 1951; Ph.D., U. Cin., 1959; m. Mary Jane Moler, Aug. 29, 1959; children—Daniel Arthur Julius, Elizabeth Ellen. Asst. prof. geology Alfred (N.Y.) U., 1952-56, asso. prof., prof., 1959—, chmn. dept. geology, 1959-76, coordinator Environ. Studies Program, 1972-78; mus. curator U. Cin., 1956-59; vis. scholar U. Waterloo (Ont., Can.), 1971, U. Coll. Swansea, Wales, U.K., 1965, Inst. Royal des Scis. Naturelles, Brussels, Belgium, 1974. Mem. Appeals Bd., Village of Alfred, 1967; past pres., bd. trustees Paleontology Research Inst., Ithaca, N.Y., 1973-74. Served with M.C., AUS, 1942-45. Fellow Geol. Soc. Am.; mem. Paleontology Soc., AAAS, Electron Microscopy Soc., Nat. Assn. Geology Tchrs., AAUP, Gt. Lakes Assn., Phi Beta Kappa, Sigma Xi, Phi Kappa Phi. Home: 27 High St Alfred NY 14802. *Nullius addictus Jurare in Verba Magistri.*

SASS, LOUIS DEWALD, ret. educator, librarian; b. West Point, Nebr., Sept. 4, 1912; s. Edward Walter and Ann Elizabeth (DeWald) S.; student Juilliard Sch. Music, 1931-33, Harvard, 1946-47; A.B., U. Nebr., 1936, A.M., 1938; B.S., Columbia, 1948, Ph.D. in Philosophy, 1953; m. Hrafnhildur Arnorsson, Dec. 21, 1945 (dec. Jan. 1964); children—Ann Elizabeth, Louis Arnorsson. Grad. asst. philosophy U. Nebr., 1936-41; tchr. math. Holdrege (Neb.) High Sch., 1941-42; library asst. Coll. City N.Y., 1947- 52; lectr., asst. prof. Sch. Librarianship, U. Calif. at Berkeley, 1952-56; dean, prof. Pratt Inst. Library Sch., 1956-68, v.p. acad. affairs, prof., 1968-71, prof., 1971-78, dir. library, 1972-78, asst. provost, 1973-78. Exam. asst. N.Y.C. Bd.

Edn., 1957-60; cons. div. personnel, N.Y.C., 1957-60. Bd. mgrs. Bklyn. Central YMCA, 1956-64. Served to capt. AUS, 1942-46; lt. col. Res. Mem. Assn. Am. Library Schs. (dir. 1957-60), Council Nat. Library Assns. (sec.-treas. 1959-62), ALA, Spl. Libraries Assn., N.Y. Library Assn., Am. Philos. Assn., Mind Assn., AAUP, NEA, Assn. for Higher Edn., Delta Upsilon. Congregationalist. Club: Rembrandt (Bklyn.). Home: 185 Hall St Apt 407 Brooklyn NY 11205

SASSER, JAMES RALPH, U.S. Senator; b. Memphis, Sept. 30, 1936; s. Joseph Ralph and Mary Nell (Gray) S.; B.A., Vanderbilt U., 1958, LL.B., 1961; m. Mary Gorman, Aug. 18, 1962; children—Gray, Elizabeth. Admitted to Tenn. bar, 1961; partner firm Goodpasture, Carpenter, Woods & Sasser, Nashville, 1961-76; mem. U.S. Senate from Tenn., 1976—. Chmn., Tenn. State Dem. Exec. Com., 1973-76; so. vice chmn. Assn. Dem. State Chmn., 1975-76. Served with USMCR, 1958-65. Mem. Am. Bar Assn., NCCJ (dir. Nashville chpt.), UN Assn., Nashville Com. Fgn. Relations, Am. Judicature Soc. Home: 3808 East-West Hwy Chevy Chase MD 20015 Office: 405 Russell Senate Office Bldg Washington DC 20510

SASSO, LOUIS ANTHONY, JR., editor; b. Boston, Jan. 6, 1936; s. Louis Anthony and Josephine (Palladino) S.; B.S. in Edn., Boston Coll., 1957; A.M. in History, Harvard U., 1958; M.S. in L.S., Columbia U., 1962; m. Pamela R. Potter, Aug. 5, 1978. Librarian, Harvard U. Library, Cambridge, Mass., 1962-69; asst. to dir. for personnel Boston Public Library, 1970-77; editor Choice mag., Middletown, Conn., 1978-79. Mem. Soc. for Scholarly Pub. Home: 46 Camp St Middletown CT 06457

SASSON, MICHEL, conductor; b. Alexandria, Egypt, May 18, 1935; s. Albert Mentech and Rosa (Gormezano) S.; premier prix de violon, Conservatoire Nat. de Paris, 1958, premiere medaille chamber music, 1956; artists diploma New Eng. Conservatory, Boston, 1959; m. Doris Posner, Aug. 30, 1959 (div. 1972); children—Pierre, Theodore, Richard; m. 2d, Deborah Ann O'Brien, Sept. 22, 1973. Came to U.S., 1958, naturalized, 1964. First violinist Paris Conservatoire Orch., 1955-58; violinist Boston Symphony, 1959—; music dir.-condr. Boston Civic Symphony, 1969—, Brockton (Mass.) Symphony, 1969—; founder, condr. Newton (Mass.) Symphony, 1967—, also dir.; condr. Boston Ballet Co., 1971—; founder, mus. dir. Boston Esplanade Bach Festival, 1972—; guest condr. Royal Philharmonic Orch., London, 1973; prin. guest condr. Am. Ballet Theater, 1976—. Recipient certificate of appreciation from mayor of Newton, 1970. Jewish religion. Home: 305 Dean Rd Brookline MA 02146 Office: Symphony Hall Boston MA 02115. *Music in all its forms is my life. I hope never to lose my intense curiosity and driving enthusiasm for appreciating and performing the best in symphonic, operatic, balletic, and chamber music.*

SASSOON, VIDAL, hair stylist; b. London, Eng., Jan. 17, 1928; s. Nathan and Betty (Bellin) S.; ed. N.Y. U.; m. Beverly Adams, Feb. 16, 1967; children—Catya, Elan, Eden, David. Founder, chmn. bd. Vidal Sassoon, Inc., beauty treatment products, beauty salons, N.Y.C., Beverly Hills, Chgo., San Francisco, Toronto; tchr. in own schs. in London and Los Angeles lectr. in field. Served with Palmach Israeli Army. Recipient award French Ministry of Culture, award for services rendered Harvard Bus. Sch.; Intercoiffure award Cartier, London, 1978; Hair Artists Internat. fellow. Clubs: Anabelle, Ambassadeurs, Claremont (London, Eng.); Le Club (N.Y.C.). Author: Sorry I Kept You Waiting Madam (autobiography); A Year of Beauty and Health, 1976. Office: 2049 Century Park E Los Angeles CA 90067

SASSOWER, DORIS LIPSON (MRS. GEORGE SASSOWER), lawyer; b. N.Y.C., Sept. 25, 1932; d. Abraham and Rose (Weitz) Lipson; B.A. summa cum laude, Bklyn. Coll., 1954; LL.B. cum laude (Florence Allen scholar), N.Y. U., 1955, J.D., 1968; m. George Sassower, Aug. 24, 1952; children—Elena Ruth, Carey Adina, Lizbeth Avery. Admitted to N.Y. bar, 1955; law asst. chief justice N.J. Supreme Ct., 1956-57; partner firm Sassower & Sassower, N.Y.C., 1955—; lectr. in field; counsel Bus. Council UN Decade for Women, 1977—, Outlook . . . Personal Motivation, Inc., Women's Sports Assn. Trustee, Supreme Ct. Library 9th Jud. Dist., White Plains, N.Y., 1977—. Recipient Disting. Alumna award of honor Bklyn. Coll., 1973; Disting. Woman award Northwood Inst., 1976; named Outstanding Young Woman of Am., State of N.Y., 1969. Fellow Am. Acad. Matrimonial Lawyers, N.Y. Bar Found.; mem. Internat., Am. (steering com. women's rights com., sect. individual rights and responsibilities, family law, litigation), Fed., N.Y. Women's (pres. 1968-69), N.Y. State (jud. selection com. 1972—, legis. com. family law sect. 1974—), Westchester County bar assns., Consular Law Soc., Bklyn. Coll. Alumni Assn. (pres. lawyers group 1963-65, spl. citation for distinguished service 1965, dir. 1965-71), N.Y. U. Law Alumni Assn. (dir. 1974-75), Assn. Bar City N.Y. (chairperson subcom. women in legal profession, subcom. matrimonial law reform), Assn. Trial Lawyers Am., N.Y. State Trial Lawyers Assn. (matrimonial law com.), Nat. Conf. Lawyers and Social Workers (chmn. 1973-74), Profl. Women's Caucus (co-founder, spl. cons. 1970), Profls. Organized for Women's Equal Rights (founder 1970), Nat. Conf. Profl. and Acad. Women (co-organizer 1970), Human Rights for Women, Women's Equity Action League (Econ. Equity award 1978), Am. Judicature Soc., Nat. Assn. Women Lawyers (ofcl. observer to UN 1969-70, legis. com. 1976—), Nat. Council Women (chmn. com. law and suffrage 1977—), Am. Arbitration Assn. (nat. panel arbitrators), Am. Friends of Hebrew U., N.Y. Civil Liberties Union, Assn. Feminist Cons.'s, Women United for UN, Women's Forum, Exec. Women (adv. bd.), Nat. Women's Polit. Caucus, Phi Beta Kappa (pres. N.Y. alumnae 1970-71), Iota Tau Tau (dean N.Y. alumnae chpt. 1956-57). Contbr. articles to profl. jours. Home: 30 Mildred Pkwy New Rochelle NY 10804 Office: Pan Am Bldg 200 Park Ave New York NY 10017. *Such success as I may have attained derives from three things: willpower, hard work, and a career that allowed me to fulfill personally prized values and goals—being of service to society and improving the machinery of our democracy by narrowing the gap between everyday reality and theoretical concepts of liberty, justice, and equality.*

SASSOWER, PHILIP SHELDON, mfg. co. exec.; b. N.Y.C., Nov. 9, 1939; s. Joseph E. and Rebecca A. (Newman) S.; B.S. magna cum laude, Queens Coll., 1961; LL.B. cum laude, Harvard, 1964; m. Susan Barbara Oppenheimer, May 28, 1964; children—Mark, Caroline, Edward. Admitted to N.Y. bar, 1964; rep. Oppenheimer & Co., N.Y.C., 1964-68; pres. founder Sassower, Jacobs & Schneider, Inc., N.Y.C., 1968-72; pres., chief exec. officer Bates Mfg. Co., N.Y.C., 1972—, also dir.; dir. Federated Capital Mgmt. Assos., Inc., N.Y.C., Bates Fabrics, Inc., N.Y.C., Kahn & Feldman, Inc., N.Y.C., Va. Iron Coal and Coke, Roanoke, Avery Coal Co. (Pa.); pres., dir. Arcs Equities Co., N.Y.C., 1972—. Bd. dirs. Fifth Ave. Synagogue Nursery Sch., 1968—, Shaare Zedek Hosp., Jerusalem, 1968—, Anti-Defamation League, 1968—, Manhattan Day Sch., 1968—, Jewish Center of Atlantic Beach, Sutton Pl. Synagogue. Recipient Human Relations award Anti-Defamation League, 1967. Mem. B'nai B'rith (dir. 1967—). Office: 850 3d Ave New York NY 10018*

SATCHLER, GEORGE RAYMOND, physicist; b. London, Eng., June 14, 1926; s. George Cecil and Georgina Lily (Strange) S.; came to U.S., 1959; B.A., Oxford U., 1951, M.A., 1951, D.Phil., 1955; m. Margaret Patricia Gibson, Mar. 27, 1948; children—Patricia Ann, Jacqueline Helen. Research fellow Clarendon Lab., Oxford U., 1954-59, 71; research asso. physics dept. U. Mich., 1956-57; physicist Oak Ridge Nat. Lab., 1959—, asso. dir. physics div., 1967-74, theoretical physics dir., 1974-76, distinguished research staff mem., 1976—. Served with RAF, 1944-48. Corp. research fellow Union Carbide Corp., 1976. Fellow Am. Phys. Soc. (mem. exec. com. nuclear physics div. 1974-75, T.W. Bonner prize 1977. Author: (with D.M. Brink) Angular Momentum, 1962; Introduction to Nuclear Reactions, 1979; contbr. research articles to profl. jours. Home: 973 W Outer Dr Oak Ridge TN 37830 Office: Oak Ridge Nat Lab PO Box X Oak Ridge TN 37830

SATENSTEIN, FRANK, publishing co. exec.; b. N.Y.C., 1924; student Cornell U. Pres., chmn. exec. com., dir. Am. Book-Stratford Press, Inc., now chmn.; pres. Cornwall Press. Home: 150 E 72d St New York City NY 10021 Office: 1212 Ave of Americas New York City NY 10036

SATER, ALEX JOEL, pub., author; b. Birmingham, Ala., June 25, 1921; s. Alex Joel and Edith (Lipsitz) S.; B.A., U. Iowa, 1942; M.A. in Am. Studies, Pa. State U., 1978; m. Denise R. Murphy. Freelance writer, journalist; author: Antiquing with Joel Sater, syndicated column, 1960-70; compilor Antiquing Guides to New Eng., N.Y., Pa., N.J., Mid-Atlantic States, 1965-70; pub., founder Antiques and Auction News, Marietta, Pa., 1967; lectr. antiquities and Am. material culture Franklin and Marshall Coll., Lancaster, Pa.; creator exhbns. of Am. quilts for colls. and ednl. instns. Freelance advt. and pub. relations specialist; cons. in establishing antique shows, markets, businesses; speaker on history and preservation of Am. antiques, architecture, and artifacts. Mem. Columbia (Pa.) Sch. Bd., 1950-56; mem. senate Council for Basic Edn., Washington, 1952-60. Bd. dirs. Pa. Sch. Bd. Assn. Served to lt., USNR, 1942-46; PTO. Mem. Nat. Assn. Paper and Advt. Collectors (pres.). Editor Paper and Advt. Collector; contbr. articles on Am. antiques and artifacts and on pub. edn. to profl. jours., popular mags. Home and office: 225 W Market St Marietta PA 17547

SATERSON, GEORGE, corp. exec.; b. Bklyn., May 14, 1925; s. Constantine and Chresa S.; B.Mech. Engring., CCNY, 1948; m. Athena Galidas, Mar. 6, 1949; children—Constantine, George, Kathryn, Chrysanthe, Anastasia. With U.S. Gypsum Co., 1949-67, S.E. mfg. mgr., Atlanta, to 1967; v.p. mfg. Kimball Systems div. Litton Industries, 1967-71, pres., 1972-76, pres. Sweda Internat., Pine Brook, N.J., 1976—, v.p. Litton Industries, 1977—. Office: 34 Maple Ave Pine Brook NJ 07058

SATHER, JOHN HENRY, biologist, educator, univ. dean; b. Presho, S.D., July 12, 1921; s. Anton and Anna (Imster) S.; B.S., U. Nebr., 1943, Ph.D., 1952; M.A., U. Mo., 1948; m. Shirley M. Johnson, Aug. 21, 1948; children—Kristi, Signe, Ingrid. Research biologist Nebr. Game, Forestation and Parks Commn., Lincoln, 1948-55; prof. biol. scis. Western Ill. U., Macomb, 1955—, dean Grad. Sch., 1964—. Mem. Nat. Wetlands Tech. Council, 1976—; tech. adv. on nat. wetland inventory, 1975—; mem. environ. adv. bd. U.S. Army Chief Engrs., 1978—; pres. Central States Univs. Inc., 1978-79. Edward K. Love fellow, 1946-48. Mem. Wildlife Soc. (pres. Ill. chpt. 1965, v.p. North Central sect. 1967), AAAS, Ecol. Soc. Am., Soc. Mammalogists, Sigma Xi. Research, publs. on life history and ecology of Great Plains muskrat in Nebr., life history and ecology studies of ring-necked pheasant in Nebr., directed radio-telemetry studies of movements of white-tailed deer and muskrats, conducted survey of effects of water level fluctuations of Gt. Lakes upon wildlife populations. Home: 103 Oakland Ln Macomb IL 61455

SATIR, PETER GERALD, cell biologist, educator; b. N.Y.C., July 28, 1936; s. Sidney and Beatrice S.: A.B., Columbia U., 1956; Ph.D., Rockefeller U., 1961; m. Birgit Hegner, Feb. 9, 1962; children—Jakob, Adam. Instr., asst. prof. biology and zoology, U. Chgo., 1961-67; asso. prof. dept. physiology-anatomy U. Calif., Berkeley, 1967-73, prof., 1973-77; prof., chmn. dept. anatomy Albert Einstein Coll. Medicine, N.Y.C., 1977—; dir. Electron Microscope Lab., U. Calif., 1968-75; mem. molecular cytology study sect. NIH, 1975-79. Fellow AAAS; mem. Am. Soc. Cell Biology, Brit. Soc. Cell Biology, Biophys. Soc., Am. Assn. Anatomists, Soc. Protozoology, Soc. Gen. Physiologists, Phi Beta Kappa. Contbr. articles to profl. jours. Office: Dept Anatomy Albert Einstein Coll Medicine Bronx NY 10461

SATO, FRANK SABURO, govt. ofcl.; b. Puyallup, Wash., Mar. 16, 1929; s. Masamori and Masuyo Ishikawa S.; B.A., U. Wash., 1953; postgrad. UCLA, 1962-63; m. June Noriko Matsusawa, June 14, 1953; children—Teresa Lynne, John Robert, Gregory Franklin, Glenn Curtis, Dean Frederick. Mem. staff Moss Adams & Co., C.P.A.'s, 1955; with Office Auditor Gen., U.S. Air Force, Washington, 1955-65; mem. staff Office Sec. Def., Washington, 1965—, dep. asst. sec. def., 1974-79, dir. Def. Audit Service, 1977-79; insp. gen. Dept. Transp., 1979—. Served with USAF, 1953-55. Mem. Assn. Govt. Accts. (nat. pres. elect 1978-79, pres. 1979-80), Am. Inst. C.P.A.'s, Va. Soc. C.P.A.'s, No. Va. Assn. Govt. Accts., Va. Soc. C.P.A.'s, Inst. Internal Auditors, Am. Soc. Mil. Comptrollers, Beta Alpha Psi, Alpha Kappa Psi, Beta Gamma Sigma. Methodist. Clubs: Japanese-Am. Citizens League, Forest Hollow Swim, Synkoa. Home: 4105 Whispering Ln Annandale VA 22003 Office: 400 7th St SW Washington DC 20590

SATO, ROBERT YOICHI, clothing co. exec.; b. Honolulu, Oct. 3, 1917; s. Taichi and Tamiyo (Okamoto) S.; student Keio U., Tokyo, Japan, 1938-41; B.S. in Econs., Wharton Sch., U. Pa., 1943; M.S., Columbia Grad. Sch. Bus., 1944; m. Miyo Hirata, July 16, 1944; children—Janice, Karen, Susan. Research analyst OSS, Washington, 1944-45, Dept. State, Washington, 1945-46; gen. mgr. Sato Clothiers, Ltd., Honolulu, 1946-58, pres., 1958—; sec., dir. Nat. Mortgage & Finance Co., Ltd., Honolulu, 1948—; dir. Dole Corp., 1959-69, Island Ins. Co. Ltd., Nat. Securities & Investment, Inc. (all Honolulu), Office Things, Inc., Dillingham Corp., Am. Security Bank, Honolulu. Mem. Bd. Water supply City and County Honolulu, 1956-71, chmn., 1966-71. Mem. Honolulu-Japanese Jr. (pres. 1950-51), Honolulu (past treas., dir., pres. retail bd.), Honolulu Japanese (pres. 1963) chambers commerce, Pi Sigma Epsilon. Clubs: Rotary (pres. W. Honolulu 1968-69), Waialae Country. Home: 1212 Punahou St 906 Honolulu HI 96826 Office: 1450 Ala Moana Blvd Honolulu HI 96814

SATO, TADASHI, artist; b. Maui, Hawaii, Feb. 6, 1923; student Honolulu Sch. Art, Bklyn. Mus. Art Sch., New Sch. Social Research. Exhbns. include: Guggenheim Mus., 1954, Honolulu Acad. Arts, 1957, Pacific Heritage Exhibit, Los Angeles, 1963, McRoberts and Tunnard, Ltd., London, 1964, White House Festival of Arts, Washington, 1965, Berlin Art Festival, 1967; represented in permanent collections: Albright-Knox Art Gallery, Buffalo, Guggenheim Mus., Whitney Mus. Am. Art, N.Y.C., Honolulu Acad. Arts, Univ. Art Gallery, Tucson; works in Hawaii State Capitol Bldg, State Library Aina Haina, Oahu, State Hosp., Kea-lakekua, Hawaii, Maui-Wailuku War Meml. Gymnasium, Maui. Office: PO Box 476 Lahaina Maui HI 96761

SATOVSKY, ABRAHAM, lawyer; b. Detroit, Oct. 15, 1907; s. Samuel and Stella (Benenson) S.; B.A., U. Mich., 1928, J.D., 1930; m. Toby Nayer, Sept. 4, 1938; children—Sheldon Baer, James Bennett. Admitted to Mich. bar, 1930, also U.S. Supreme Ct. bar; asso. firm William Henry Gallagher, Detroit, 1930-65. Bldg. chmn. lawyers com. United Found. and Torch Dr. Co-chmn. profl. div. Allied Jewish Campaign; adv. council United Synagogue Am.; del. Jewish Community Council Detroit; v.p. Mosies Chetim Orgn. Detroit. Bd. dirs. Detroit Service Group, past chmn. fgn. mission; mem. fund drive com. U. Mich. Law Sch. Recipient Sem. award Jewish Theol. Sem. Am., 1952; citation of merit Jewish Welfare Fedn., Detroit; Jerusalem award State of Israel Bond Orgn. Mem. Am., Mich., Detroit (mem. pub. adv. com. jud. candidates) bar assns., Nat. Fedn. Jewish Men's Clubs (founder and hon. life pres. Gt. Lakes region), Am. Arbitration Assn., Jewish Hist. Soc. Mich. (dir.), Am. Jewish Hist. Soc., Am. Judicature Soc. Jewish (life mem. bd. dirs. congregation; past nat. pres. men's club). Mem. B'nai B'rith (past pres. Detroit). Club: Standard. Home: 22500 Saratoga Dr Southfield MI 48075 also 20379 W Country Club Dr Apt 2334 North Miami Beach FL 33180 Office: 28455 Northwestern Hwy Southfield MI 48034. *With a desire and willingness to improve my profession, my religious beliefs, and help the community, I have devoted a good portion of my time and efforts for those purposes. I, too, have been enriched by the association, have hopefully directed and encouraged others, and hope to continue to do so.*

SATRE, WENDELL JULIAN, utilities exec.; b. Post Falls, Idaho, July 3, 1918; s. Julian J. and Myrtle A. (Clark) S.; B.S. in Elec. Engring., U. Idaho, 1939; m. Jessie E. Stewart, June 1, 1941; children—Janet Elizabeth Satre Tobiska, Clark Wendell, Jeanne Ellen Satre Kanikeberg, Glen Walter. With Wash. Water Power Co., Spokane, 1939—, mgr. constrn., maintenance, 1958-63, exec. asst. to pres., 1963-64, asst. v.p., 1964-65, v.p., dir., 1965, exec. v.p., 1965-71, pres., 1971—, chmn. bd., 1975—; pres., dir. Devel. Assos., Inc., Wash. Irrigation & Devel. Co., Limestone Co., Water Power Improvement Co., Spokane Indsl. Park, Inc.; trustee Fidelity Mut. Savs. Bank. Mem. Gov.'s adv. council Wash. Dept. Commerce and Econ. Devel., 1974—, chmn., 1976—; mem. Wash. Energy Policy Council, 1973-75, Council for Wash.'s Future, 1973—; dir. Wash. Council Econ. Edn., 1973—; co-chmn. Com. of 1000, 1974—; mem. Spokane Little Hoover Commn., 1968-71; past mem. Spokane Area Devel. Council. Bd. dirs. Inland Empire chpt. A.R.C., 1964-69, United Crusade of Spokane County, 1965-67; mem. exec. bd. Inland Empire council Boy Scouts Am., 1974—; past pres. Greater Spokane Music and Allied Arts Festival, 1967; trustee Spokane Symphony Soc., 1966-79; past trustee Whitworth Coll.; adv. bd. Wash. State U. Coll. Engring., 1972—, U. Idaho Coll. Engring., 1972—; pres. Wash. Citizens Com. for Pub. Higher Edn., 1976—; bd. dirs. United for Wash., 1977—; mem. Greater Spokane Community Found., U. Idaho Found. Served to lt. (j.g.), USNR, 1944-46. Mem. Am. (dir. 1976-79, exec. com. 1976-77), Pacific Coast (past pres., past dir.) gas assns., N.W. Electric Light and Power Assn. (past dir., past pres.), Assn. Wash. Gas Utilities (trustee, past pres.), Wash. Council Internat. Trade (v.p. 1973—), Western Environ. Trade Assn. (past 1st v.p., dir. 1973-76), Edison Electric Inst. (dir. 1976-78), NAM (dir. 1974-77), Nat. Assn. Electric Cos. (dir. 1974-77), Spokane C. of C. (v.p., dir., vice chmn. 1978—), Assn. Wash. Bus. (dir. 1971—, exec. com. 1975—, vice chmn. 1978—). Presbyterian (elder). Club: Rotary. Home: W 39 33d Ave Spokane WA 99203 Office: Wash Water Power Co E 1411 Mission Ave Spokane WA 99202

SATTEE, ANDREW L., constrn. co. exec.; b. Trenton, N.J., Oct. 11, 1920; s. Anthony and Civita S.; grad. Wharton Sch., U. Pa., 1944; m. Emily Ozdonsky; 1 son, Drew. Founder, partner Sattee Clayton & Co., pub. accountants, 1944-63; gen. mgr., exec. v.p., dir. Maule Industries, Inc., 1965-76; founder, dir. Burlington Concrete & Asso. Cos., 1954-63. Mem. Fla. Council of 100; mem. exec. bd. South Fla. council Boy Scouts Am. C.P.A., N.J. Mem. Am. Inst. C.P.A.'s. Home: 811 Cordova Rd Ft Lauderdale FL 33316 Office: 100 Biscayne Blvd Miami FL 33132

SATTEN, ROBERT ARNOLD, educator, physicist; b. Chgo., Aug. 4, 1922; s. Frank and Mabel Satten; B.S., U. Chgo., 1944; M.A., U. Calif., Los Angeles, 1947, Ph.D., 1951; m. Erica Semone, Oct. 19, 1946; children—Corey, Glen. Mem. faculty U. Calif. at Los Angeles, 1951—, prof., 1963—, vice chmn. dept. physics, 1968-73; asst. prof. Mass. Inst. Tech., 1952-53. Cons. Argonne (Ill.) Nat. Lab., 1959-72, Hughes Research Labs., Malibu, Calif., 1959-67. Fulbright research scholar, France, 1961-62, Germany, 1969-70; vis. Erskine fellow U. Canterbury, Christchurch, New Zealand, 1971. Fellow Am. Phys. Soc.; mem. Western Spectroscopy Assn. (chmn. 1962), Phi Beta Kappa. Home: 1358 Woodruff Ave Los Angeles CA 90024

SATTERFIELD, CHARLES NELSON, chem. engr., educator; b. Dexter, Mo., Sept. 5, 1921; s. Charles David and Hermine (Weber) S.; B.S. cum laude, Harvard, 1942; M.S., Mass. Inst. Tech., 1943, Sc.D., 1946; m. Anne Pettingell, July 6, 1946; children—Mark Edward, Joye. Asst. prof. chem. engring. Mass. Inst. Tech., Cambridge, 1946-53, asso. prof., 1953-59, prof., 1959—. Lectr. indsl. chemistry Harvard, 1948-57; cons.on rocket propellants Dept. Def., 1952-60; mem. com. chem. kinetics NRC, 1960-66; chmn. ad hoc panel on abatement nitrogen oxide emissions from stationary sources Nat. Acad. Engring., 1970-72; indsl. cons. to major cos. in petroleum, chem., glass and pharm. industries. Registered profl. engr., Mass. Fellow Am. Acad. Arts and Scis.; mem. Am. Chem. Soc., Am. Inst. Chem. Engrs., Sigma Xi, Tau Beta Pi. Co-author: Thermodynamic Charts for Combustion Processes, 1949; Hydrogen Peroxide, 1955 (translated into Russian 1957); Role of Diffusion in Catalysis, 1963; author: Mass Transfer in Heterogeneous Catalysis, 1970 (translated into Russian 1976); Heterogeneous Catalysis in Practice, 1980; also over 90 tech. papers. Mem. editoral adv. bd. Indsl. and Engring. Chemistry, 1966-68, Advances in Chemistry Series, 1971-73. Patentee in field. Home: Tabor Hill Rd South Lincoln MA 01773 Office: Dept Chem Engring Mass Inst Tech Cambridge MA 02139

SATTERFIELD, DAVID EDWARD, III, congressman; b. Richmond, Va., Dec. 2, 1920; s. David Edward, Jr. and Blanche (Kidd) S.; student U. Richmond, 1939-42; LL.B., U. Va., 1948; m. Anne Elizabeth Powell, Dec. 27, 1943; children—David Edward IV, John Bacon. Admitted to Va. bar, 1948, since practiced in Richmond; former partner firm Satterfield, Haw, Anderson, Parkerson & Beazley; asst. U.S. atty. Eastern Dist. Va., 1950-53; councilman, City Richmond, 1954-56; mem. Va. Gen. Assembly from Richmond City, 1960-64; mem. 89th-96th Congresses from 3d Dist. Va. Past. sec.-treas., dir. Richmond Baseball, Inc., The Virginians, A.A.A. baseball club of Internat. League. Trustee U. Richmond, Naval Aviation Mus. Served to lt., pilot, USNR, World War II: PTO; capt. Res. Decorated Purple Heart. Mem. Phi Gamma Delta, Phi Alpha Delta. Democrat. Mason (32 deg., Shriner). Office: 2348 Rayburn House Office Bldg Washington DC 20515*

SATTERFIELD, GREY WILSON, JR., lawyer; b. Oklahoma City, Apr. 9, 1933; s. Grey Wilson and Kathryne (West) S.; B.A., U. Okla., 1955, LL.B., 1959; m. Patricia Pastusek, Aug. 3, 1956; children—Shelley Virginia, Grey Wilson III, Stacey Ann. Admitted to Okla. bar, 1959, since practiced in Oklahoma City; asso. Franklin & Harmon, 1959-61; partner Franklin, Harmon & Satterfield, 1961-69;

sec.-treas. Franklin, Harmon & Satterfield, Inc., 1969—. Spl. lectr. law U. Okla. Coll. Law. Mem. Okla. Sci. and Arts Found. Democratic precinct chmn., 1964-65. Bd. dirs. Okla. County Legal Aid Soc. Served from ensign to lt. (j.g.) USNR, 1955-57. Mem. Okla. (mem. ho. of dels.), Okla. County bar assns., Okla. County Jury Trial Lawyers Assn. (dir.), Res. Officers Assn. (pres. dept. Okla. 1976-77), Navy League, Naval Res. Assn., U. Okla. Coll. Law Assn., Lawyers Club Oklahoma City (pres. 1976), Sigma Alpha Epsilon (trustee Okla. Kappa chpt.), Phi Alpha Delta. Democrat. Methodist. Home: 1706 Elmhurst Ave Oklahoma City OK 73120 Office: 1606 Park/Harvey Center Oklahoma City OK 73102

SATTERFIELD, JOHN CREIGHTON, lawyer; b. Port Gibson, Miss., July 25, 1904; s. Milling Marion and Laura Stevenson (Drake) S.; A.B., Millsaps Coll., 1926; J.D., U. Miss., 1929; LL.D., Mont. State U., 1961, Dalhousie U., 1962; S.J.D., Suffolk U., 1962; m. Ruth Quin, Nov. 13, 1933 (dec.); children—John Creighton, Ellen Drake; m. 2d, Mary Virignia Fly, Sept. 5, 1943; 1 dau., Mary Laura (Mrs. H. Mickey Graham). Admitted to Miss. bar, 1929, since practiced in Jackson; with firm Alexander & Alexander, 1929-35; mem. firm Alexander & Satterfield 1935-43, sr. partner firm Satterfield, Shell, Williams & Buford, 1943-75, Satterfield, Allred & Colbert, 1976—. Mem. Miss. Ho. of Reps., 1928-32, chmn. constn. com., sec. judiciary and ways and means coms., co-author Stansel Hwy. Act. Dir. Hinds County chpt. ARC; state dir. YMCA. Recipient Distinguished Mississippian award U. Miss., 1966. Fellow Am. Bar Found.; mem. Nat. Conf. Commrs. Uniform State Laws, Am. Bar Assn. (gov. 1956-59, pres. 1961-62), Miss. Bar (pres. 1955- 56, past v.p.), Am. Judicature Soc. (dir.), Am. Coll. Probate Counsel (regent 1967—), Scribes, Phi Delta Phi, Beta Theta Pi, Omicron Delta Kappa, Sigma Epsilon. Democrat. Methodist (del. Gen. Conf. 1952, 60, 64, 66, 68, 70, 72, 76, jurisdictional conf., 1952, 56, 60, 64, 66, 68, 70, 72, 76). Clubs: Masons, Shriners. Contbr. articles to legal publs. Home: 242 Ridge Dr Jackson MS 39216 Office: Bankers Trust Plaza Bldg Jackson MS 39205

SATTERFIELD, JOHN ROBERTS, JR., coll. adminstr.; b. Danville, Va., Dec. 4, 1921; s. John Roberts and Sarah Elise (Council) S.; B.A., U. N.C., 1950, Mus.M., 1950, M.A., 1955, Ph.D., 1962; m. Carolyn Keith Talley, Dec. 18, 1948; children—John Roberts, Kenneth Scott, Keith Charles, Jean Council. Instr. music U. N.C., 1953; asst. prof. music Davidson (N.C.) Coll., 1953-60; asso. prof. Fla. Presbyn. Coll., St. Petersburg, 1960-63, prof., 1963-67, prof. humanities and music, 1967-68; v.p. academic affairs, prof. humanities and music Elmira (N.Y.) Coll., 1968-70; asst. dir., academic programs specialist N.C. State Bd. Higher Edn., Raleigh, 1970-72; asst. v.p. academic affairs, dir. Center for Continuing Renewal Higher Edn., dir. Inst. Undergrad. Curricular Reform, U. N.C. Gen. Adminstrn., Chapel Hill, 1972; provost Kalamazoo Coll., 1972-73, provost, exec. v.p., 1973-75; pres. Wagner Coll., S.I., N.Y., 1975—. Bd. dirs. United Meth. City Soc. Served with USAAF, 1942-45. Decorated Bronze Star; recipient Composer's award N.C. Symphony Soc., 1951; Harbison award for Disting. Teaching, Danforth Found., 1965-66. Mem. Empire State Found. Ind. Liberal Arts Colls. (dir.), Melville Soc. Methodist. Clubs: German Soc., Liederkranz (N.Y.C.). Author: Private Higher Education in North Carolina: Conditions and Prospects, 1971; editor: Christopher Tye: The Latin Church Music, 2 vols., 1973. Contbr. articles, short stories and revs. to lit. and profl. jours. Home: 193 Longview Rd Staten Island NY 10301 Office: Wagner Coll Staten Island NY 10301

SATTERLEE, LOWELL DUGGAN, food chemist; b. Duluth, Minn., July 30, 1943; s. Arthur F. and Edna M. (Duggan) S.; B.S., S.D. State U., 1965; M.S., Iowa State U., 1966, Ph.D., 1968; m. Deanna Mae Abel, Sept. 7, 1963; children—Christine Lynne, Melissa Anne, Wendy Marie. Asst. prof. food chemistry Iowa State U., Ames, 1968-69, U. Nebr., Lincoln, 1969-72, asso. prof., 1972-75, prof., 1975—. Recipient Outstanding Tchr. award U. Nebr., 1979; named Outstanding Young Alumnus, Iowa State U., 1977. Mem. Inst. Food Technologists (recipient Samuel Cate Prescott award for Outstanding Young Researcher 1976), Am. Assn. Cereal Chemists, Am. Meat Sci. Assn., Exptl. Aircraft Assn. Methodist. Clubs: Kiwanis, Toastmasters. Patentee in field; contbr. articles to tech. jours.; mem. editorial bd. Jour. Food Biochemistry, 1977—, Jour. Food Processing and Preservation, 1977—. Home: 1200 Beechcraft Rd Rural Route 2 Lincoln NE 68506 Office: Room 20 Filley Hall Univ Nebr Lincoln NE 68583

SATTERLY, JACK, geologist; b. Cambridge, Eng., Sept. 28, 1906; came to Can., 1912; s. John and May Mary Jane (Randall) S.; B.A., U. Toronto (Ont., Can.), 1927, M.A., 1928; Ph.D., U. Cambridge, 1931; postgrad. Princeton U., 1931-32; m. Eileen Sims, Mar. 2, 1935; children—Peter Randall, Elizabeth Hamilton. Geologist, Loangwa Concessions (N.R.) Ltd., No. Rhodesia, 1933-34, Guysborough Mines Ltd., N.S., 1934-35; instr. dept. geology U. Toronto, 1935-36, lectr., 1936-39; asst. dir. Royal Ont. Museum, Toronto, 1936-39, research asso. dept. mineralogy and geology, 1971—; geologist Ont. Dept. Mines, 1939-61, sr. geologist, 1961-67, chief rev. and resources sect., geol. br. Ont. Dept. Mines and No. Affairs, 1967-71. Recipient Centennial medal, 1967; Coleman Gold medal in geology U. Toronto, 1927; Royal Ont. Mus. named Jack Satterly Geochronology Lab., 1977; 1851 Exhbn. Overseas scholar, 1929-30, 30-31. Fellow Geol. Assn. Can., Royal Soc. Can.; mem. Can. Inst. Mining and Metallurgy (life), Mineral. Assn. Can. Author: A Catalogue of the Ontario Localities Represented by the Mineral Collection of the Royal Ontario Museum, 1977.

SATTERTHWAITE, CAMERON B., educator; b. Salem, Ohio, July 26, 1920; s. William David and Mabel (Cameron) S.; B.A., Coll. Wooster, 1942; postgrad. Ohio State U., 1942-44; Ph.D., U. Pitts., 1951; m. Helen Elizabeth Foster, Dec. 23, 1950 (div. July 31, 1979); children—Mark Cameron, Tod Foster, Tracy Lynn, Keith Alan, Craig Evan. Chemist, Manhattan dist. project Monsanto Chem. Co., Dayton, Ohio, 1944-47; research chemist DuPont, Wilmington, Del., 1950-53; researcher, adv. physicist Westinghouse, Pitts., 1953-61; asso. prof. physics U. Ill., Urbana, 1961-63, prof., 1963-79; chmn. dept. physics Va. Commonwealth U., Richmond, 1979—; program dir. NSF, 1975-76. Sch. dir. Monroeville, Pa., 1959-61. Democratic nominee for U.S. Congress, 1966; del. to Dem. Nat. Conv., 1968, 72. Mem. A.A.A.S., Am. Phys. Soc., Fedn. Am. Scientists (chmn. 1968), Ind. Dem. Coalition (chmn. 1969), Com. on Ill. Govt., Sigma Xi. Contbr. articles to profl. jours. Patentee in field. Home: 311 Kensington Ave Richmond VA 23221 Office: Dept Physics Va Commonwealth U Richmond VA 23284

SATTERWHITE, HENRY ALLEN, airline exec., newspaper pub.; b. Fredericksburg, Va., Nov. 1, 1902; s. Charles Emmett and Caroline Thornton (Dommitt) S.; B.S. in Mech. Engring., Va. Poly. Inst., 1926; D.C.S. (hon.), St. Bonaventure U., 1965; m. Margaret Hungiville, Feb. 2, 1940; children—John Henry, Mary Ann. Pub., v.p. Bradford Publs., Inc., Pa., 1943—; dir. Allegheny Airlines, Inc., 1952-78, chmn. bd., 1956-78, chmn. emeritus, 1978—; pres. Condor Corp., Marion Pub. Co.; dir. Top Line Corp., Daily Am. Pub. Co. Pres. Bradford Indsl. Corp., 1951-62, bd. dirs., 1951—; mem. bd. Bradford City Planning Commn., 1959-75; mem. Com. 100, Miami Beach, Fla., 1949—. Chmn. McKean County Democratic Com., 1935-40; mem. Pa. Dem. Com., 1944-59; mem. Pa. Indsl. Devel. Authority, 1974-76. Mem. adv. bd. U. Pitts. Bradford Campus, 1962—; asso. trustee St. Bonaventure U., 1963-74. Mem. Newcomen Soc., Bradford Area C. of C., Pa., Am., newspaper pubs. assns. Club: Nat. Aviation (Washington). Home: 150 Jackson Ave Bradford PA 16701 Office: 43 Main St Bradford PA 16701

SATTERWHITE, WILLIAM THOMAS, gas corp. exec., lawyer; b. Baytown, TX, Dec. 27, 1933; s. Troy Louis and Gertrude Maurine (Hunt) S.; J.D., Baylor U., 1958; m. Neita Faye Erisman, Mar. 2, 1957; children—Susan Maurine, William Thomas, Sharon Louise, Douglas Ross. Admitted to Tex. bar; individual practice law, Ennis, Tex., 1958-66; with Enserch Corp., Dallas, 1966—, now sr. v.p., gen. counsel, mem. all subs. bds. Mem. Tex. Ho. of Reps., 1963-66; chmn. Tex. Bd. Land Surveying, 1979—; mem. Southwestern Legal Found. adv. bds. Internat. Oil and Gas Ednl. Center. Served with AUS. Mem. State Bar of Tex., Am. Bar Assn., Dallas County Bar Assn. Baptist. Office: Enserch Corp 301 S Harwood St Dallas TX 75201

SATTLER, THEODORE HERBERT, physician; b. Tyndall, S.D., Aug. 14, 1914; s. John J. and Paulina (Max) S.; B.A., Yankton (S.D.) Coll., 1937; B.S., U. S.D., Vermillion, 1940; M.D., Northwestern U., 1942, M.S., 1948; m. Isabel Frances Reedy, Aug. 30, 1941; children—Ann Lenore, Susan Elizabeth. Intern, Evanston (Ill.) Gen. Hosp., 1942-43; resident in internal medicine Wesley Meml. Hosp., Chgo., 1946-48; practice medicine specializing in internal medicine, Yankton, 1948—, chmn. dept. medicine Sacred Heart Hosp., Yankton, 1950—; clin. prf. medicine U. S.D., Yankton, 1948-74, prof. internal medicine, 1974—, asst. dean clin. affairs, 1974-76; mem. S.D. Health Service Agy., 1976—; med. dir. S.D. Profl. Standards Orgn., 1977—; mem. S.D. Health Systems Agy., 1975—, S.D. Health Coordination Council, 1976—. Bd. dirs. United Ch. of Christ, Yankton, Yankton Coll., Yankton Carnegie Library, Higher Ednl. Facilities State of S.D.; trustee Mt. Marty Coll., 1977—; mem. adv. com. U. S.D. Sch. Medicine Rural Area Health Edn. Centers Program, 1979—. Served to maj. M.C., U.S. Army, 1943-46. Recipient Alumni Achievement award Yankton Coll., 1974; named Clin. Prof. of Yr., U. S.D., 1969. Diplomate Am. Bd. Internal Medicine. Fellow A.C.P. (gov. S.D. 1964-70); mem. Am., S.D. (pres. 1962) socs. internal medicine, AMA, Am., S.D. (Disting. Service award 1958) heart assns., Am. Diabetes Assn., S.D. (pres. 1973-74), Yankton Dist. med. assns., Sigma Xi. Clubs: Masons, Elks. Contbr. articles to med. jours. Home: 1701 Whiting Dr Yankton SD 57078 Office: 400 Park Ave Yankton SD 57078

SATZ, DAVID MEYER, JR., lawyer; b. N.Y.C., Jan. 14, 1926; s. David Meyer and Marie Jeanne (Lowenberg) S.; A.B., Harvard, 1948; LL.B., U. Pa., 1951; m. Susan Steiner, May 14, 1954; children—Constance Ellen, David James, Jonathan Edward. Admitted to N.J. bar, 1952, also U.S. Supreme Ct.; with firm Lum, Fairlie & Foster, Newark, 1952-54; dep. atty. gen. N.J., 1954-58, 1st asst. atty. gen., 1958-61; U.S. atty. Dist. N.J., 1961-69; partner firm Saiber, Schlesinger, Satz & Goldstein, Newark, 1969—. Chmn. Statewide Com. on Character N.J. Supreme Ct., 1973—. Bd. dirs. N.J. chpt. Am. Jewish Com.; trustee Hosp. Center of Orange, N.J., 1977-78. Served with USAAF, World War II. Mem. Am., Fed., N.J., Essex County bar assns. Club: Harvard (pres. N.J. 1976-77). Home: 283 W End Rd South Orange NJ 07079 Office: Gateway I Newark NJ 07102

SAUCIER, JOHN JAMES, lawyer; b. Calgary, Alta., Can., May 15, 1903; s. Francis Xavier and Anne (Flanagan) S.; B.A., U. Alta., 1924, LL.B., 1926; D.C.L., U. Dallas, 1969; m. Lillian DuBois, June 15, 1933 (dec. July 1973); children—Suzanne (Mrs. D.R. Colter), Mary DuBois (Mrs. Ernest David Dover), Carolyn DuBois (Mrs. Don Ray); m. 2d, Margaret Kayler, May 24, 1974. Called to bar, Alta., 1927, created Queen's counsel; practiced in Calgary, 1927—; counsel Jones, Black & Co., asst. pvt. sec. to prime minister of Can., 1934-35. Recipient Centennial medal, 1967. Mem. Law Soc. Alta. (past pres.), Canadian (past pres.), Calgary bar assns., Calgary C. of C. (past pres.), Alta. Press Council (chmn.). Progressive Conservative. Mem. United Ch. Can. (elder). Club: Ranchmen's (past pres.) (Calgary). Home: 2725 Carleton St SW Calgary AB T2T 3L1 Canada Office: 300 444 7th Ave SW Calgary AB T2P 0X9 Canada

SAUCIER, WALTER JOSEPH, educator; b. Moncla, La., Oct. 5, 1921; s. Louis Edmond and Sidonie (Moncla) S.; B.A., U. Southwestern La., 1942; postgrad. U. Chgo., 1942-43, M.S., 1947, Ph.D., 1951; m. Helen Allie Nobles, May 8, 1943; children—Walter Joseph, Susanne C., Diane H., Janine M., Gerard T., Laurence E. and Loraine A. (twins). Asst., instr. meteorology U. Chgo., 1946-52; from asst. prof. to prof. Tex. A. and M., College Station, 1952-60; prof. U. Okla., Norman, 1960-69, chmn. dept. meteorology, 1965-68; prof. N.C. State U., Raleigh, 1969—; cons. Am. Council Edn., World Book Ency., USAF, U.S. Army, NRC-Nat. Acad. Scis. Trustee Univ. Corp. for Atmospheric Research, 1967-69; bd. dirs. Triangle Univs. Consortium on Air Pollution, 1973—. Served with USAAF, 1942-46. Fellow Am. Meteorol. Soc. (mem. bd. for certification cons. meteorologists 1970-75, chmn. 1971-75; mem. bd. univ. edn. 1976-78), AAAS; mem. Am. Geophys. Union, N.C. Acad. Sci., Sigma Xi. Author: Principles of Meteorological Analysis, 1955. Home: 2000 Hillock Dr Raleigh NC 27612

SAUER, GORDON CHENOWETH, educator, physician; b. Rutland, Ill., Aug. 14, 1921; s. Fred William and Gweneth (Chenoweth) S.; student Northwestern U., 1939-42; B.S., U. Ill., 1943, M.D., 1945; m. Mary Louise Steinhilber, Dec. 28, 1944; children—Elisabeth Ruth, Gordon Chenoweth, Margaret Louise, Amy Kieffer. Intern, Cook County Hosp., Chgo., 1945-46; resident dermatology and syphilology N.Y. U.-Bellevue Med. Center, 1948-51; dermatologist Thompson-Brumm-Knepper Clinic, St. Joseph, Mo., 1951-54; pvt. practice, Kansas City, Mo., 1954—; mem. staff St. Luke's, Research, Kansas City Gen. hosps.; asso. instr. U. Kans., 1951-56, vice chmn. sect. dermatology, 1956-58, asso. clin. prof., 1960-64, clin. prof., 1964—, head sect. dermatology, 1958-70; clin. asso., acting head dermatology sect. U. Mo., 1955-59, cons. dermatology, 1959-67, clin. prof., 1967—; cons. Munson Army Hosp., Ft. Leavenworth, Kans., 1959-68. Mem. dermatology panel, drug efficacy panel Nat. Acad. Sci.-FDA, 1967-69. Bd. dirs. Kansas City Area council Camp Fire Girls Am., 1956-59, Kansas City Lyric Theatre, 1969-74, Kansas City Chamber Choir, 1969-74. Served to sr. asst. surgeon USPHS, 1946-48. Diplomate Am. Bd. Dermatology and Syphilology. Fellow Am. Acad. Dermatology and Syphilology (dir. 1975-79, v.p. 1980); mem. Soc. Investigative Dermatology, AMA, Mo., Jackson County med. socs., Mo. Dermatol. Soc. (pres. 1974-75), Dermatology Found. (trustee 1978—), Am. Ornithol. Union, Wilson Ornithol. Soc., Royal Australasian Ornithologists Union, Soc. Bibliography Natural History, Am. Dermatol. Assn., Alpha Delta Phi, Nu Sigma Nu. Presbyn. Manual of Skin Diseases, 4th edit., 1980; Teen Skin, 1965; John Gould Bird Print Reproductions, 1977. Editor: Kansas City Med. Bull., 1967-69; contbr. articles to profl. jours. Home: 830 W 58th Terr Kansas City MO 64113 Office: 6400 Prospect Ave Kansas City MO 64132

SAUER, HARRY JOHN, JR., engr., educator; b. St. Joseph, Mo., Jan. 27, 1935; s. Harry John and Marie Margaret (Witt) S.; B.S., U. Mo.-Rolla, 1956, M.S., 1958; Ph.D., Kans. State U., 1963; m. Patricia Ann Zbierski, June 9, 1956; children—Harry John, Elizabeth Ann, Carl Andrew, Robert Mark, Katherine Anne, Deborah Elaine, Victoria Lynn, Valerie Joan, Joseph Gerard. Inst. mech. engring. Kans. State U., Manhattan, 1960-62; sr. engr., cons. Midwest Research Inst., Kansas City, Mo., 1963-70; mem. faculty dept. mech. and aerospace engring. U. Mo.-Rolla, 1957—, prof., 1966—; cons. in field; mem. Gov.'s Commn. on Energy Conservation, 1977; mem. Mo. Solar Energy Resource Panel, 1979—. Pres., St. Patrick's Sch. Bd., 1970-72, St. Patrick's Parish Council, 1975-76. Recipient Ralph R. Teetor award Soc. Automotive Engrs., 1968; Hermann F. Spoehrer Meml. award St. Louis chpt. ASHRAE, 1979. Mem. ASME, ASHRAE, Soc. Automotive Engrs., Mo. Acad. Sci., Sigma Xi. Roman Catholic. Co-author: Environmental Control Principles, 1975, 78; contbr. articles to profl. jours. Home: College Hills Rt 4 Rolla MO 65401 Office: Univ of Mo-Rolla Rolla MO 65401

SAUER, JONATHAN DEININGER, educator, plant geographer; b. Ann Arbor, Mich., July 6, 1918; s. Carl Ortwin and Lorena (Schowengerdt) S.; A.B. with honors in History Western Civilization, U. Calif. at Berkeley, 1939; M.A., Washington U., St. Louis, 1948, Ph.D. in Genetics, 1950; m. Hilda Sievers, May 12, 1946; 1 son, Richard Carl. From instr. to prof. botany and geography U. Wis., 1950- 67; prof. geography U. Calif. at Los Angeles, 1967—, dir. Bot. Gardens and Herbarium, 1974—; vis. asso. curator U. Mich. Herbarium, 1955-56; vis. prof. geography La. State U., 1967. Served with USAAF, 1944-46. Mem. Am. Geog. Soc., Brit. Ecol. Soc., Ecol. Soc. Am., Am. Soc. Plant Taxonomists (editorial bd. 1964-67), Soc. Study Evolution (editorial bd. 1964-67), Orgn. for Tropical Studies (course coordinator 1972, bd. dirs. 1978—). Author: Coastal Plant Geography of Mauritius, 1960; Plants and Man on the Seychelles Coast—A Study in Historial Biogeography, 1967; Geographic Reconnaissance of Seashore Vegetation along the Mexican Gulf Coast, 1967. Home: 659 Erskine Dr Pacific Palisades CA 90272 Office: Dept Geography U Calif Los Angeles CA 90024

SAUER, KENNETH, chemist; b. Cleve., June 19, 1931; s. Raymond Harvey and Beatrice Ruth (Hemke) S.; A.B., Oberlin Coll., 1953; M.A., Harvard U., 1954, Ph.D., 1958; m. Marjorie Wright, June 24, 1958; children—Robert, Terence, Rodney, Peter. Asst. prof. Am. U., Beirut, 1957-60; USPHS fellow U. Calif., Berkeley, 1960-63, asst. prof. chemistry, 1963-66, asso. prof., 1966-72, prof., 1972—; faculty sr. scientist Chem. Biodynamics Lab., Lawrence Berkeley Lab., Berkeley, 1963—. Guggenheim Meml. Found. fellow, 1976-77; NSF grantee, 1968, 72, 76. Mem. Am. Chem. Soc., Biophys. Soc., AAAS (fellow 1976—), Am. Soc. Photobiology, Am. Soc. Plant Physiology, AAUP, Phi Beta Kappa, Sigma Xi. Author: (with I. Tinoco, J. Wang) Physical Chemistry, 1977; contbr. numerous articles in field to sci. jours. Office: Dept Chemistry U Calif Berkeley CA 94720

SAUER, LOUIS, architect; b. Forest Park, Ill., June 15, 1928; s. Frank J. and Jeanne (LaFazia) S.; B.S., Ill. Inst. Tech., 1953; regional planning certificate Internat. Sch. City Planning, Venice, Italy, 1956; M.Arch., U. Pa., 1959; m. Elizabeth Mason, June 6, 1956; children—Christopher Giotto, Kathryn Angelica. Archtl. designer Offices Jules Gregory, Lambertville, N.J., Milton Schwartz, Eshbach, Pullinger, Stevens and Bruder, Phila., 1955-61; partner Winchell and Sauer, 1961-62; prin. Louis Sauer, Architect, 1962-67; partner Sauer and Devito, 1967-69; prin. Louis Sauer Assos. Architects, 1969—; founder, partner Peoples Housing Inc., Topanga, Calif., 1971—; instr. archtl. design Drexel Inst. Tech., 1960-65; asso. prof. architecture U. Pa., 1965-67, lectr., 1974-77; vis. lectr. 25 univs.; participant numerous internat. confs.; U.S. rep. Soviet Conf. Mass Housing, Moscow, 1975, U.S. Mission to Lebanon on Policies for Devel. and Reconstrn. Low Income Housing, 1977, U.S. Mission to Portugal for Low Cost Housing Design Criteria, 1978. Registered planner, N.J.; registered architect, Nat. Council Archtl. Registration Bds., Pa., Md. Housing projects include Golf Course Island, Reston, Va., Grundy Towers, Bristol, Pa., Spring Pond Apts., Painted Post, N.Y., Locust St. Townhouses, Penn's Landing Sq., New Market, Phila., Orchard Mews, Fells and Inner Harbor W., Balt., Cincinnatus Concourse, Cin. Recipient numerous awards AIA, including honor awards, Homes for Better Living award, 1965, 71, 74, Pa. Soc. Architects, others. NEA fellow design, 1978. Fellow AIA; mem. Urban Land Inst. Editorial bd. Internat. Jour. Architectural Research, 1974—; contbr. articles to profl. jours. Home: 142 Bethlehem Philadelphia PA 19103

SAUER, RALPH CHARLES, musician; b. Phila., Nov. 8, 1944; s. Ralph Hanna and Florence Sophia (Roller) S.; B.Mus., Eastman Sch. Music, Rochester, N.Y., 1965; m. Linda E. Cowles, May 28, 1966; 1 son, Dietrich Emory. Prin. trombonist Toronto Symphony Orch., 1968-74, CBC, 1969-74, Canadian Opera Co., 1969-74, Los Angeles Philharmonic Assn., 1974—; instr. U. Toronto, 1968-74. Served with U.S. Army, 1966-68. Mem. ASCAP. Editor numerous transcriptions for brass instruments. Home: 4011 Sunswept Dr Studio City CA 91604 Office: 135 N Grand Ave Los Angeles CA 90012

SAUER, WILLIAM GEORGE, physician; b. Cin., July 18, 1915; s. George J. and Ruth J. (Creighton) S.; B.A., U. Cin., 1936, M.B., 1939, M.D., 1940; M.S. in Internal Medicine, U. Minn., 1947; m. Anne McLaughlin, July 29, 1939; children—Nancy (Mrs. E. Brown Crosby), Susan (Mrs. Charles S. Field), Jane (Mrs. John N. Tietjen). Intern, Cin. Gen. Hosp., 1939-40, asst. resident in medicine, 1940-42; fellow medicine Mayo Grad. Sch., U. Minn., 1942-44, 46-47; cons. internal medicine and gastroenterology Mayo Clinic, Rochester, Minn., 1947—; cons. internal medicine and gastroenterology Rochester Methodist Hosp., also St. Mary's Hosp., Rochester, 1947—; instr. medicine Mayo Grad. Sch. Medicine, U. Minn., Rochester, 1947-52, asst. prof., 1952-61, asso. prof., 1961-69, prof. clin. medicine, 1969—, prof. medicine Mayo Med. Sch., 1973—. Bd. dirs. Minn. State Automobile Assn., 1956—, exec. com., 1959—, pres., 1962-66. Bd. govs. Mayo Clinic, 1963-75; trustee Mayo Found., 1965-75. Served with M.C., AUS, 1944-46. Fellow A.C.P.; mem. Am. Gastoent. Assn. (B.B. Vincent Lyon award 1953), AMA, Minn. Soc. Internal Medicine, AAAS, Sigma Xi, Alpha Kappa Kappa, Beta Theta Pi. Club: Rochester Golf and Country. Contbr. articles on internal medicine and gastroenterology to sci. jours., also book chpts. Home: 34 Skyline Dr Rochester MN 55901 Office: Mayo Clinic 200 1st St SW Rochester MN 55901

SAUERS, CLAYTON HENRY, fin. exec.; b. Helena, Mont., Apr. 7, 1926; s. Henry Herman and Elsie Helen (Junkermier) S.; B.S., U. Wash., 1948; M.B.A., Harvard U., 1951; m. Patricia A. Davis, Feb. 3, 1949; children—Gale Elizabeth, Peter Davis. With A. B. Dick Co., Chgo., 1951-79, v.p. fin., 1974-78, exec. v.p. fin., 1978-79; v.p. fin., treas. West Point Pepperell, Inc., West Point, Ga., 1979—. Mem. Arlington Heights (Ill.) Bd. Edn., 1968-72; pres. Prairie Club of Chgo., 1979. Served with USN, 1944-46; PTO. Mem. Fin. Execs. Inst. (pres. Chgo. chpt. 1974). Republican. Christian Scientist. Clubs: Univ. (Chgo.); Chikaming Country (Lakeside, Mich.); Riverside Country (West Point, Ga.). Office: PO Box 71 West Point GA 31833

SAUERTEIG, PAUL JOHN, lawyer; b. Ft. Wayne, Ind., May 9, 1917; s. Otto E. and Clara (Dannecker) S.; A.B., Columbia U., 1939, LL.B., 1942; m. Ruth Hinners Foelber, Sept. 2, 1945; children—Mary Foelber, Ellen Catherine, Paul Otto. Admitted to Ind. bar, 1942; atty. Med. Protective Co., Ft. Wayne, 1946-51; legal counsel Lincoln Nat. Life Ins. Co., Ft. Wayne, 1951-68; v.p., sec. Lincoln Nat. Corp., Ft. Wayne, 1968-77. Chmn. bd. dirs. Lutheran Hosp. of Ft. Wayne,

1972—. Served with AUS, 1942-46. Mem. Am., Ind., Allen County bar assns., Assn. Life Ins. Counsel, Am. Soc. Hosp. Attys. Club: Ft. Wayne Country. Home: 1830 Hawthorne Rd Fort Wayne IN 46804 Office: 222 Utility Bldg Fort Wayne IN 46802

SAUL, B. FRANCIS, II, mortgage banker; b. Washington, Apr. 15, 1932; s. Andrew M. and Ruth Clark (Sheehan) S.; B.S., Villanova U., 1954; LL.B., U. Va., 1957; m. Elizabeth Patricia English, Apr. 30, 1960; children—Sharon Elizabeth, B. Francis, III, Elizabeth Willoughby, Andrew Maquire, II, Patricia English. Admitted to D.C. bar, 1959; with B. F. Saul Co., Chevy Chase, Md., 1957—, asst. v.p., 1959-62, v.p., 1962-65, sr. v.p., 1965-69, pres., 1969—; chmn. B.F. Saul Real Estate Investment Trust, Chevy Chase, Md., 1969—; pres. Chevy Chase Savs. & Loan, Inc., 1969—; chmn. bd. Fin. Gen. Bankshares, Inc.; dir. Garfinckel, Brooks Bros., Miller & Rhoads, Inc. Life trustee Corcoran Gallery Art, Washington; bd. dirs. D.C. Soc. Crippled Children, 1963-75, pres., 1972-75; bd. dirs. D.C. chpt. ARC, 1964—; trustee Suburban Hosp., Bethesda, 1972-76. Decorated knight of Malta (Vatican). Mem. Nat. Assn. Real Estate Trusts (pres. 1973-74), D.C. Mortgage Bankers Assn. (pres. 1968). Republican. Roman Catholic. Clubs: Chevy Chase, Burning Tree (Md.); Met., Alfalfa (Washington); Wianno (Mass.); The Brook (N.Y.C.). Office: 8401 Connecticut Ave Chevy Chase MD 20015

SAUL, GEORGE BRANDON, II, biologist; b. Hartford, Conn., Aug. 8, 1928; s. George Brandon and Dorothy (Ayers) S.; A.B., U. Pa., 1949, A.M., 1950, Ph.D., 1954; m. Sue Grau Williams, Mar. 28, 1953. From instr. to asso. prof. Dartmouth, 1954-67; prof. biology Middlebury (Vt.) Coll., 1967—, chmn. dept., 1968-76, v.p. acad. affairs, 1976-79. Research asso. Calif. Inst. Tech., 1964-65; NSF postdoctoral fellow U. Zurich (Switzerland), 1959-60; vis. scientist Boyce Thompson Inst. for Plant Research, Yonkers, N.Y., 1972-73. Fellow AAAS; mem. Pa. Acad. Sci., Genetics Soc. Am., Am. Genetics Assn., Radiation Research Soc., AAUP, Sigma Xi. Lion. Author papers in field. Home: Munger St RD 3 Middlebury VT 05753

SAUL, RALPH SOUTHEY, fin. co. exec.; b. Bklyn., May 21, 1922; s. Walter Emerson and Helen Douglas (Coutts) S.; B.A., U. Chgo., 1947; LL.B., Yale, 1951; m. Bette Jane Bertschinger, June 16, 1956; children—Robert Southey, Jane Adams. With Am. embassy, Prague, Czechoslovakia, 1947-48; admitted to D.C. bar, 1951, N.Y. bar, 1952; asso. firm Lyeth & Voorhees, N.Y.C., 1951-52; asst. counsel to Gov. N.Y. State, 1952-54; staff atty. RCA, 1954-58; with SEC, 1958-65, dir. div. trading and markets, 1963-65; v.p. corporate devel. Investors Diversified Services, Inc., Mpls., 1965-66; pres. Am. Stock Exchange, N.Y.C., 1966-71; chmn. mgmt. com. First Boston Corp., 1971-74; chmn., chief exec. officer INA Corp., Phila., 1975—; dir. Sun Co., Pennwalt Corp., Compagnie Financière de Suez. Trustee U. Pa. Served with USNR, 1943-46; PTO. Mem. Am. Bar Assn. Clubs: Phila., Union League (Phila.); Merion Golf; Bond, Econ., Links, Board Room (N.Y.C.). Home: 549 Avonwood Rd Haverford PA 19041 Office: INA Corp 1600 Arch St Philadelphia PA 19101

SAUM, BURNELL FRANK, ins. co. exec.; b. Brandon, Nebr., Apr. 16, 1929; s. Harry C. and Opal C. (Coykendall) S.; A.B. in Edn., Nebr. State Tchrs. Coll., Kearney, 1950; m. Mary C. Mason, Aug. 22, 1949; children—Douglas L., Susan K., Bruce F., Linda L., James C., Judy A. Pub. sch. tchr., Lodgepole, Nebr., 1949-53; salesman Ohio Nat. Life Ins. Co., Cin., 1952-55, sales mgmt. positions up to sr. v.p. mktg., 1955-70, exec. v.p., 1971, pres., 1972—, also dir. C.L.U. Mem. Am. Coll. C.L.U.'s. Presbyterian. Club: Kenwood Country. Office: 237 William H Taft Rd Cincinnati OH 45219

SAUNDERS, ARLENE, soprano; b. Cleve. Debut, Milan Opera 1961, has sung with Met. Opera, Phila. Opera, Lyric Opera, Houston Opera, San Francisco Opera, Vienna Staatsoper, Berlin Deutsche Oper, Munich Staatsoper repertoire includes Arabella, Mimi, Marguerita; now with Hamburg State Opera; sang world premieres of Beatrix Cenci, 1971, also Jakobowsky und der Oberst, 1965, Help, Help, The Globolinks, 1968. Recipient Gold medal Vercelli (Italy) voice competition; N.Y.C. Mayor's award, 1962; Kammersängerin, Hamburg, 1967. Address: care Thea Dispeker Artists Rep 59 E 54th St New York NY 10022*

SAUNDERS, BYRON WINTHROP, educator; b. Providence, June 27, 1914; s. Winthrop Henry and Vera (Sweet) S.; B.S. in Elec. Engring., R.I. State Coll., 1937; M.S., Stevens Inst. Tech., 1945; m. Miriam Ellis Wise, Dec. 28, 1942; children—William Clinton, Martha Elizabeth, Carolyn Ellis. With Narragansett Electric Co., 1937-38, Douglas Paton Co., Providence, 1938- 40, RCA, 1940-47; mem. faculty Cornell U., 1947—, prof. indsl. engring., 1956—, chmn. dept., 1963-67, dir. Sch. Indsl. Engring., 1967-75, also dir. continuing edn. in engring., 1971-74, dean faculty, 1974—; Joseph Lucas vis. prof. U. Birmingham (Eng.), 1960-61; cons. in field. Past mem. Ithaca Planning Bd. Trustee St. Lawrence Dist. Unitarian Universalist Assn. Fellow Am. Inst. Indsl. Engrs., mem. ASME, Am. Soc. Engring. Edn., AAAS, Inst. Mgmt. Scis., Tau Kappa Epsilon, Alpha Pi Mu. Unitarian (past pres.). Contbg. editor Materials Handling Handbook. Home: 317 Warren Rd Ithaca NY 14850

SAUNDERS, CHARLES BASKERVILLE, JR., assn. exec.; b. Boston, Dec. 26, 1928; s. Charles Baskerville and Lucy (Carmichael) S.; grad. St. Mark's Sch., 1946; A.B., Princeton, 1950; m. Margaret MacIntire Shafer, Sept. 9, 1950; children—Charles Baskerville III, George Carlton, Margaret Keyser, Lucy C., John R. News reporter, polit. columnist Ogdensburg (N.Y.) Jour., 1950-51; edn. reporter Hartford (Conn.) Times, 1951-53; asst. dir. pub. relations Trinity Coll., Hartford, 1953-55; asst. dir. pub. info. Princeton, 1955-57; legis. asst. Sen. H. Alexander Smith, 85th Congress, 1957-58; asst. to asst. sec. for legislation HEW, 1958-59, asst. to sec. Arthur S. Flemming, 1959-61, dep. asst. sec. for legislation 1969-71; asst. to pres. Brookings Instn., 1961-69; dep. commr. of edn. for external affairs U.S. Office Edn., 1971-72, dep. asst. sec. for edn. HEW, 1973-74; dir. govt. relations Am. Council on Edn., 1975-78, v.p. for govt. relations, 1978—. Mem. Montgomery County Bd. Edn., 1966-70. Trustee Montgomery Coll., 1969-70. Republican. Presbyterian. Author: Brookings Institution: A Fifty-Year History, 1966; Upgrading the American Police, 1970. Home: 7622 Winterberry Pl Bethesda MD 20034 Office: 1 DuPont Circle Washington DC 20036

SAUNDERS, DERO AMES, writer, editor; b. Starkville, Miss., Sept. 27, 1913; s. Madison and Erin (Hearon) S.; A.B., Dartmouth, 1935; A.M., Columbia, 1938; m. Beatrice Nair, May 23, 1936; children—David, Richard. Lectr., lecture mgr., contbr. to various mgs., 1936-42; with Fgn. Econ. Adminstrn., Washington and Cairo, Egypt, 1943-45, chief Middle East div., 1945; asso. editor Fortune mag., 1945-57; v.p. Med. and Pharm. Info. Bur., 1957-59; lectr. Hunter Coll., 1960-61, 67—; asso. editor Forbes mag., 1960-62, sr. editor, 1962-66, exec. editor, 1966—. Pres., Dartmouth Alumni Council, 1970-71. Prin. U.S. civilian rep. Middle East Supply Center, 1945. Clubs: Players (N.Y.C.); Heights Casino (Bklyn.). Contbg. author: Why Do People Buy?, 1953; The Changing American Market, 1954. Editor: The Portable Gibbon, 1952; The Autobiography of Edward Gibbon, 1961. Co-editor: The History of Rome, 1958. Home: 446 W 22d St New York City NY 10011 Office: 60 Fifth Ave New York City NY 10011

SAUNDERS, DORIS EVANS, editor, educator; b. Chgo., Aug. 8, 1921; d. Alvesta Stewart and Thelma (Rice) Evans; B.A., Roosevelt U., 1951; M.S., M.A., Boston U., 1977; m. Vincent E. Saunders, Jr., Oct. 28, 1950 (div. Aug. 1963); children—Ann Camille (Mrs. Charles J. Vivian), Vincent E. III. Sr. library asst. Chgo. Pub. Library, 1942-46, prin. reference librarian, 1946-49; librarian Johnson Pub. Co., 1949-66, dir. book div., 1961-66, 73-77; prof., coordinator print journalism Jackson (Miss.) State U., 1977—; pres. Information Inc., Chgo., 1966-68; dir. community relations Chgo. State Coll., 1968-70; columnist Chgo. Daily Defender, 1966-70, Chgo. Courier, 1970-73; host radio program The Think Tank, 1971-72; writer, producer TV show Our People, 1968-70; staff asso. Office of Chancellor, U. Ill. at Chgo. Circle, 1970-73. Sec. bd. Black Acad. Arts and Letters; bd. dirs. South Side Com. Art Center, Chgo. Mem. NAACP, Soc. Profl. Journalists, Sigma Delta Chi, Nat. Assn. Media Women, Inc., Alpha Gamma Pi. Episcopalian. Co-author: Black Society, 1976. Asso. editor: Negro Digest mag., 1962-66; editor: The Day They Marched, 1963; The Kennedy Years and the Negro, 1964; DuBois: A Pictorial Biography (S.G. DuBois) 1979; compiler, editor: The Negro Handbook, 1966; The Ebony Handbook, 1974. Contbr. to profl. jours., mags. Home: 9718 S Indiana Ave Chicago IL 60628 Office: Dept Mass Communication Jackson State U PO Box 8067 Jackson MS 39217

SAUNDERS, EDWARD A., army officer; b. Manilla, Iowa, Mar. 30, 1925; s. Harry Albert and Clara (Asmus) S.; student Iowa State Coll., 1942-43; B.S., U.S. Mil. Acad., 1946; M.S. in Elec. Engring., Purdue U., 1951; Ph.D., Renssalear Poly. Inst., 1965; m. Lois Jean Riley, Sept. 14, 1946; children—Richard Marvin, Lynn Frances, Lisa Dianne, Michael Scott. Commd. 2d lt. U.S. Army, 1946, advanced through grades to col., 1966; with C.E. Acad., 1951-54; staff officer, Korea, 1954-56; assigned Command and Gen. Staff Coll., 1956-57, research and devel. Def. Atomic Support Agy., 1957-60; mem. faculty U.S. Mil. Acad., 1961—, prof. physics., 1965—, head dept., 1967—. Active local Boy Scouts Am. Mem. Am. Assn. Physics Tchrs., Am. Soc. Engring. Edn., Frontiers in Education, Nat. Sojourners. Presbyn. Mason. Home: 74 Schofield Pl West Point NY 10996

SAUNDERS, ERNEST ERLE, lawyer; b. Bridgeport, Conn., July 18, 1925; s. Erle Freeman and Ora (Jackson) S.; student McGill U., 1942-43, B.A., 1947, B.C.L., 1950; postgrad. Faculte de Droit, Paris, 1950-51; m. Janine Marie Rowe, Aug. 2, 1952; children—Mary, Patricia. Called to Que. bar, 1950; created Queen's counsel, 1968; with firm O'Brien, Hall & Saunders, Montreal, Que., Can., 1951-78, partner, 1962-78; v.p. law and corp. affairs Bell Can., Montreal, 1978—; lectr. Faculty Law McGill U., 1964-68; lectr. Profl. Tng. Sch. Bar of Que., 1969-70, treas. bar, 1967-68. Served to flying officer RCAF, 1943-45. Mem. Can., Que., Montreal bar assns. Clubs: St. James's, Royal Montreal Curling, Royal Montreal Golf (Montreal). Home: 605 Cote St Antoine Rd Westmount PQ Canada Office: Bell Canada 1050 Beaver Hall Hill Montreal PQ Canada

SAUNDERS, HAROLD HENRY, govt. ofcl.; b. Phila., Dec. 27, 1930; s. Harold Manuel and Marian Elizabeth (Weihenmayer) S.; A.B., Princeton U., 1952; Ph.D., Yale U., 1956; m. Barbara Ann McGarrigle, May 4, 1963 (dec. Oct. 1973); children—Catherine Elizabeth, Mark Harril. With CIA, Washington, 1959-61; with NSC, Washington, 1961-74, mem. sr. staff, 1967-74; dep. asst. sec. for Near East and South Asia, Dept. State, Washington, 1974-75, dir. intelligence and research, 1975-78, asst. sec. for Near East and South Asia, 1978—; lectr. in U.S. history George Washington U., 1959-61, 63-65. Ruling elder Lewinsville Presbyn. Ch., McLean, Va., 1971—. Served to 1st lt. USAF, 1956-59. Recipient Pres.'s award for Disting. Fed. Civilian Service, 1979. Mem. Phi Beta Kappa. Home: 2119 Great Falls St Falls Church VA 22043 Office: Dept State Washington DC 20520

SAUNDERS, HARRIS, JR., leasing co. exec.; b. Birmingham, Jan. 26, 1925; s. Harris and Zoe Reed (Black) S.; B.S. in M.E., Ga. Inst. Tech.; m. Jean Rowan, Aug. 9, 1949; children—Sarah Tice, Cynthia Farley, Susan Barry, Nancy, Elizabeth, Rebecca. With Saunders Leasing System, Inc., Birmingham, 1958—, successively exec. v.p., pres., chief exec. officer, also dir.; dir. Trust Nat. Bank, Hudson Thompson Co. Served with U.S. Navy, 1943-45. Mem. Truck Rental and Leasing Assn. (pres.). Office: 301 Office Park Dr Birmingham AL 35223

SAUNDERS, JACK ORVA LESLIE, coll. dean; b. Oshkosh, Nebr., Aug. 9, 1918; s. Floyd Alvin and Gladys (Artlip) S.; B.S., U. Calif. at Los Angeles, 1941; M.Ed., U. Colo., 1950; Ed.D., U. Wyo., 1954; m. Edith Maurine Aldrich, Aug. 15, 1940; children—Stephanie Sue (Mrs. Frank Archer), Jack Orva Leslie. Successively tchr. sci., prin., supt. Garden County (Nebr.) High Sch., 1943-53; asst. prof. Western Wash. Coll., 1954-55; prof., chmn. dept. ednl. psychology, dir. tchr. edn., dir. placement Western N.Mex. U., 1955-62; head. dept. elementary and secondary edn. N.Mex. State U., 1962-68, asst. dean Coll. Edn., 1966-68, dean, 1968—; cons. in field. Served to 1st lt. AUS, 1943-46. Recipient award for outstanding contbns. to edn. N.M. Tchr. Edn. and Profl. Standards Commn., 1962. Mem. N.E.A., Assn. Supervision and Curriculum Devel. (pres. N.M. 1969), Am. Assn. Colls. Tchr. Edn. (liaison rep. N.Mex.), Phi Epsilon Kappa, Alpha Tau Omega, Phi Delta Kappa, Kappa Delta Pi. Rotarian (pres. Oshkosh, Neb. 1950, Silver City, N.M. 1958). Author: (with G.A. Montgomery) Beginners Phonics, 1963; (with others) Helping the Teacher Utilize Aides, 1971; also monographs, articles. Home: 1630 Camino Del Rex Las Cruces NM 88001. *As should be the case, I am a "people" person. After almost thirty years in the profession of education I have found that most people are worth investing one's life in. They do not change fast enough, and they act like human beings, but they do respond favorably to justifiable rewards. In our society, with some values gyrating and with sensationalism being often equated with success, the good teachers and their good students will still constitute the bulwark for our democracy.*

SAUNDERS, JACK PALMER, univ. dean; b. London, Eng., Sept. 11, 1915; s. George Palmer and Jane (Welsh) S.; came to U.S., 1930, naturalized, 1936; B.S., Coll. City of N.Y., 1936; M.S., U. Md., 1949, Ph.D., 1953; m. Margaret Theresa Siebert, Jan. 25, 1942; children—George Palmer, Margaret Catherine. Chemist, R.H. Macy & Co., N.Y.C., 1939-41; pharmacologist Army Med. Labs., Edgewood, Md., 1945-56; pharmacologist NIH, Bethesda, Md., 1956-65, dir. grants div. Nat. Cancer Inst., 1965-74; prof. pharmacology, med. br., dean Grad. Sch., U. Tex., Galveston, 1974—. Served to maj. AUS, 1941-46, 50-53. Recipient Superior Service Honor award HEW, 1972. Fellow AAAS, Am. Acad. Forensic Scis.; mem. Am. Chem. Soc., Am. Soc. for Pharmacology and Exptl. Therapeutics, Soc. Toxicology, Sigma Xi. Democrat. Episcopalian. Club: U. Tex. Faculty (Houston). Contbr. articles to profl. jours. Home: 164 San Fernando Dr Galveston TX 77550

SAUNDERS, JAMES HENRY, chemist; b. Ames, Iowa, May 3, 1923; s. Charles Winston and Irene Dumanie (Peebles) S.; B.S. in Chemistry, U. Ky., 1944; Ph.D. in Organic Chemistry, U. Ill., 1946; m. Mary Prickett Carter, Apr. 13, 1946; children—James Henry, Stephen, Charles Winston, Thomas Dale. Group leader govt. synthetic rubber research program U. Ill., 1946-47; chemist, group leader Monsanto Co., Anniston, Ala., 1947-54; asst. dir. research, then dir. research Mobay Chem. Co., New Martinsville, W.Va. and Pitts., 1955-67; mgr. nylon research Monsanto Textiles Co., Pensacola, Fla., 1968-69, dir. research, 1969-78, dir. polyester research and devel., 1979—; mem. adv. coms. foams and textile functional finishing NRC. Bd. overseers William Penn Coll. Fellow Am. Inst. Chemists; mem. Am. Chem. Soc., N.Y. Acad. Scis., Fiber Soc., AAAS, Phi Beta Kappa, Sigma Xi, Phi Lambda Upsilon, Alpha Chi Sigma, Sigma Alpha Epsilon. Democrat. Presbyterian. Author: (with others) Polyurethanes, Chemistry and Technology, 2 parts, 1962, 64; Careers in Industrial Research and Development, 1974. Co-editor: Plastic Foams, 2 parts, 1972, 73; adv. bd. Jour. Polymer Sci. Patentee in field. Home: 4151 Piedmont Rd Pensacola FL 32503 Office: Monsanto Co PO Box 12830 Pensacola FL 32575

SAUNDERS, JASON LEWIS, educator; b. Boston, Apr. 21, 1922; s. Maurice M. and Ida (Abrams) S.; children—Mitchell A, Rachel T., Dione I. Prof. philosophy U. N.C., 1954-62; prof. philosophy U. Calif. at San Diego, 1962-69, chmn. dept., 1968-69; prof. philosophy CUNY, 1969—, chmn. dept. City Coll. N.Y., 1971-73, also exec. dir. Machiavelli Project. Ford Found. fellow, 1952-53; Matchette Fund fellow, 1953; Pres.'s fellow U. Calif. at San Diego. Author: Renaissance Stoicism-The Philosophy of Justus Lipsius; Greek and Roman Philosophy After Aristotle; Early Stoic Philosophy. Home: 110 Jones Rd Englewood NJ 07631 Office: 33 W 42d St New York NY 10036

SAUNDERS, JOHN ALLEN, writer, cartoonist; b. Lebanon, Ind., Mar. 24, 1899; s. Fred Clark and Nancy Ellen (Jackson) S.; A.B., M.A., Wabash Coll., L.H.D. (hon.), 1963; m. Lois Long, Mar. 27, 1923; children—John Philip, David Allen, Penelope Ellen, Lois Ann. Asst. prof. Romance langs. Wabash Coll., 1927-38; comics editor Pubs. Syndicate, Chgo., 1937-45; continuity writer Field Newspaper Syndicate, Chgo.; co-creator comic strips including Big Chief Wahoo, Steve Roper, Kerry Drake, Mary Worth. Mem. Toledo Bd. Edn., Toledo Library Bd. Mem. Nat. Cartoonists Soc., Newspaper Comics Council, Democrat. Presbyterian. Clubs: Rotary (pres. local chpt.), Players (N.Y.C.), Masons. Playwright Three Taps at Twelve; A Crown on the Hall-Tree; The Big Cough. Contbr. articles and short stories to mags. Home: 4108 River Rd Toledo OH 43614 Office: 717 Security Bldg Toledo OH 43604

SAUNDERS, JOHN ALLEN, cartoonist; b. Lebanon, Ind., Mar. 24, 1899; s. Fred Clark and Nancy Ellen (Jackson) S.; B.A., Wabash Coll., M.A., D.H.L. (hon.); m. Lois L. Long, Mar. 27, 1923; children—John Philip, David Allen, Penelope Ellen, Lois. Asso. prof. romance langs. Wabash Coll., 1920-27; comics editor Pubs. Syndicate, 1927-78; free lance writer, cartoonist, Toledo, 1978—; co-creator Steve Roper, Mary Worth, Kerry Drake, Rex Morgan. Pres., Toledo Bd. Edn. Mem. Newspaper Comics Council (pres.), Nat. Cartoonists Soc. Democrat. Presbyterian. Clubs: Hermes, Players, Masons. Home: 4108 River Rd Toledo OH 43604 Office: 717 Security Bldg Toledo OH 43604*

SAUNDERS, JOHN BAKER, ednl. publishing co. exec.; b. Williamston, N.C., July 23, 1921; s. Joseph Hubbard and Nannie (Smith) S.; A.B., U. N.C., 1943; children—Joseph, John Baker, Henrietta. Gen. editor Scott, Foresman & Co., Chgo., 1952-63; exec. editor Holt, Rinehart & Winston, N.Y.C., 1964-66; v.p. Ency. Brit. Ednl. Corp., Chgo., 1967, L.W. Singer Co., N.Y.C., 1968-69; mgr. export mktg. and devel. Sci. Research Assos., Chgo., 1970—. Trustee Music Center of North Shore, Winnetka, Ill. Served to lt. (j.g.) USNR, 1943-46. Mem. Delta Kappa Epsilon. Democrat. Episcopalian. Clubs: Am. Yacht (Rye, N.Y.); Chgo. Lit.; Yale (N.Y.C.). Home: 570 Sunset Rd Winnetka IL 60093 Office: Sci Research Assos 155 N Wacker Dr Chicago IL 60606

SAUNDERS, JOHN HARVEY, coll. pres.; b. Huntington, W.Va., Feb. 22, 1939; s. George W. and Mary Margueretta (Beckmeyer) S.; A.B., Marshall U., 1961; M.A., Stetson U., 1963; Ph.D., U. Ga., 1966; m. Eve Leah McClatchey, Dec. 18, 1965; children—John McClatchey, Dorothy Penn. Asst. prof. history N.E. La State U., 1966-68; asso. prof. history, asst. dean Coll. Arts and Scis., Marshall U., 1968-71; dean faculty Millsaps Coll., 1971-77; pres. Westminster Coll., Fulton, Mo., 1977—. Mem. Omicron Delta Kappa, Phi Alpha Theta, Sigma Delta Pi, Sigma Alpha Epsilon. Republican. Episcopalian. Clubs: Rotary; Mo. Athletics; St. Louis U. Home: 204 S Westminster St Fulton MO 65251 Office: Westminster Coll Fulton MO 65251

SAUNDERS, JOHN WARREN, JR., biologist, educator; b. Muskogee, Okla., Nov. 12, 1919; s. John Warren and Amanda (Schlattweiler) S.; B.S., U. Okla., 1940, M.S., 1941; Ph.D., Johns Hopkins, 1948; m. Lilyan Clayton, Feb. 27, 1942; children—Sarah Elizabeth (Mrs. Ron Reeder), John Warren III, Margaret Ann (Mrs. Robert Geist), William Michael, Mary Kathryn (Mrs. Thomas Brown). Instr. zoology U. Chgo., 1948-49; mem. faculty Marquette U., 1949-66, prof. biology, 1957-66, chmn. dept., 1958-66; prof. anatomy Sch. Vet. Medicine, U. Pa., 1966-67; prof. biol. scis. State U. N.Y., Albany, 1967—; mem. embryology staff Marine Biol. Lab., Woods Hole, Mass., 1958-63. Mem. Wis. Basic Sci. Bd., pres., 1964-66; mem. adv. com. div. biol. and med. scis. NSF, 1969-71, pres., 1971—. Served to lt. (s.g.) USNR, 1942-46. Mem. Am. Assn. Anatomists, Am. Soc. Cell Biology, Am. Soc. Zoologists (chmn. div. devel. biology 1963, sec. 1964-66), Internat. Inst. Embryology, Soc. Devel. Biology (pres. 1967, exec. com. 1966-68), Soc. Exptl. Biology and Medicine, Phi Beta Kappa, Sigma Xi, Phi Sigma. Author: Animal Morphogenesis, 1968; Patterns and Principles of Animal Devel., 1970. Editorial bd. Jour. Morphology, 1962-64, Developmental Biology, 1958-74, Mechanisms of Aging and Development, 1971—; acting editor in chief Developmental Biology, 1968-69; editorial bd. Jour. Exptl. Zoology, 1968-72. Home: 32 Linda Ct Elsmere NY 12054

SAUNDERS, JOSEPH BENJAMIN, JR., petroleum co. exec.; b. Hillsboro, Tex., July 25, 1901; s. Joseph Benjamin and Irene Imogene (McQuatters) S.; grad. Chillicothe (Mo.) Bus. Coll., 1923; LL.D., Oklahoma City U., 1967; D.Hum., Okla. Christian Coll., 1975; m. Gladys LaVerne Edmondson, Oct. 9, 1926 (dec. Apr. 1966); children—Eleanor Suzanne (Mrs. L.M. Inkley, Jr.), Joseph Benjamin III; m. 2d, Georgia J. Comegys, Mar. 30, 1968 (div. Feb. 1969). Various positions oil industry, 1923-37; partner Triangle Refiners, 1936-46; partner, pres., dir. Triangle Refineries, Inc., Houston, 1946-64, chmn. bd., 1964—; pres., dir. Withers & Wellford Oil Co., Memphis, to 1950; v.p., dir. Transcentral Oil Corp., Chgo., to 1952; v.p., dir., chmn. Triangle Pipeline Co., Shreveport, La., to 1954; chmn. bd. Triangle Realty Co., Houston, to 1972; vice chmn. bd. Kerr-McGee Corp., Oklahoma City, to 1972, now dir. emeritus; chmn. bd. petroleum products terminals in Atlanta, Birmingham, Chattanooga, LaGrange, Mo., Louisville, Mobile, Ala., Nashville, St. Louis, Niceville, Fla., Anniston and Montgomery, Ala., to 1972; dir., mem. exec. com. First State Bank & Trust Co., Oklahoma City, J.R. Butler & Co., Houston. Trustee Oklahoma City U., Oklahoma City Community Found., until 1979; trustee, exec. com., pres., hon. past chmn. Nat. Cowboy Hall Fame; v.p., trustee Mammers Theatre, to 1972; v.p., dir., exec. com. Oklahoma City Symphony Soc.; pres. bd. Okla. Christian Coll. Recipient hon. citations NCCJ, 1972, Oklahoma City Symphony, 1974, Nat. Cowboy Hall of Fame, 1977; named to Okla. Hall of Fame, 1974; Hall of Fame for Gt. Westerners, 1979.

Mem. Oklahoma City C. of C. (v.p., dir.), Am. Petroleum Inst. (life mem. gen. com. 1972—), Nat. Petroleum Refiners Assn., Independent Petroleum Assn. Am. Mason (Shriner, K.T., Legion Honor). Clubs: River Oaks Country, Lakeside Country, Houston, Internat., Petroleum, Coronado (Houston); Petroleum, Beacon (Oklahoma City); Petroleum (Dallas); Seigniory (Que., Can.); Mo. Athletic, St. Louis (St. Louis); Chicago, Chicago Oil Men's; Balboa de Mazatlan (Mexico). Home: 3435 Westheimer Rd Houston TX 77027 Office: PO Box 2944 Houston TX 77001

SAUNDERS, JOSEPH FRANCIS, chemist, govt. ofcl.; b. Mt. Pleasant, Pa., Apr. 2, 1927; B.S., Duquesne U., 1950; M.S., Georgetown U., 1955, Ph.D., 1960; m. Pauline Claire Dugan, Nov. 23, 1950; children—Joseph Francis, William Paul. Asst. to head medicine and dentistry br. Office Naval Research, 1952-57, sci. project officer, 1957-59, asst. head, 1959-60, head medicine and dentistry br., 1960-64; biosatellite program scientist and asst. chief of environ. biology, Office of Space Sci. and Applications, NASA Hdqrs., Washington, 1964-66, chief environ. biology, biosatellite program scientist Office Space Sci. and Applications, 1966-71, chief biology program Office Life Scis., Office Manned Space Flight, 1971-73; coordinator U.S.-USSR cancer research activities Office of Internat. Affairs, Nat. Cancer Inst., NIH, 1973-74, dep. dir., 1974—; organized research program on transplantation of tissues and cryobiology, program for research on indefinite preservation of whole blood at ultra-low temperatures; instr. hematology and lab. techniques Bus. Tng. Coll. of Pitts.; guest scientist Naval Med. Research Inst., 1958-60; mem. several sci. dels. to USSR. Served with USNR, 1945-46, 51-52. Recipient Arthur S. Flemming award in sci., 1962; NASA Group Achievement award, 1974; Dirs. award NIH, 1979. Fellow Am. Inst. Chemists; mem. Am. Chem. Soc., Soc. Cryobiology, Am. Inst. Biol. Scis., Sigma Xi, Alpha Chi Sigma. Author numerous tech. reports. Editor: Bioregenerative Systems, 1968; The Experiments of Biosatellite II, 1971; co-editor Depressed Metabolism, 1969, U.S.A.-USSR Monograph on Methods of Development in New Anticancer Drugs, 1977; editor, narrator movies on biosatellites; mem. editorial bd. Bioscis. Communications, 1975—, Year Book of Cancer, 1976—. Home: 8131 Greeley Blvd Springfield VA 22152 Office: Nat Cancer Inst National Insts Health Bethesda MD 20014. *Certain encounters in a person's career can be unbearably excruciating. But, just like physiologic pain, they become oblivious with time.*

SAUNDERS, RALPH SCOTT, ret. air force officer; b. Roanoke, Va., June 24, 1922; s. Walter Lawrence and Minnie Hammersly (Tibbs) S.; student U. Md., 1950-60, Command and Staff Coll., 1959, Nat. War Coll., 1967; m. Dorris Jean Peeler, June 9, 1945; children—Ralph Scott, James Lawrence, Janice Gayle. Commd. maj. USAF, 1955, advanced through grades to maj. gen., 1971; asst. dep. chief staff ops. Hdqrs. Mil. Airlift Command, Scott AFB, Ill., 1968-70; comdr. 9th Weather Reconnaisance Wing, McClellan AFB, Calif., 1970-71, 60th Mil. Airlift Wing, Travis AFB, Calif., 1972-73, vice comdr. 22d Air Force, 1973; comdr. Aerospace Rescue and Recovery Service, Scott AFB, Ill., 1974-79. Decorated D.S.M., Legion Merit, Bronze Star, D.F.C., Air medal with 12 oak leaf clusters. Mem. Order Daedalians. Home: 8714 Pintail Point San Antonio TX 78239

SAUNDERS, RAYMOND JENNINGS, artist; b. Pitts., Oct. 28; student (Nat. Scholastic scholar) Pa. Acad. Fine Arts, U. Pa., Barnes Found.; B.F.A., Carnegie Inst. Tech., 1960; M.F.A., Calif. Coll. Arts and Crafts. Teaching asst. Calif. Coll. Arts and Crafts, 1960-61; resident Am. Acad. in Rome, 1964-66; art and urban affairs cons. N.Y.C. Bd. Edn. and Human Resources Adminstrn., 1967; vis. artist R.I. Sch. Design, 1968; artist-in-residence, vis. artist and critic at various art schs., univs., 1968—; mem. faculty Calif. State U., Hayward, 1969—, prof., 1971—; show: Terry Dintenfass Gallery, N.Y.C., 1962; represented in permanent collections: Mus. Modern Art, N.Y.C., Whitney Mus. Am. Art, N.Y.C., Phila. Mus. Art. Served with U.S. Army, 1957-59. Recipient Thomas Eakins prize, Schwabacher-Frey award San Francisco Mus. Art Ann., 1961, award Nat. Inst. Arts and Letters, 1963, Prix de Rome, Am. Acad. in Rome, award City of Phila., Atwater Kent award Soc. Four Arts, 1970, Granger Meml. award Pa. Acad. Fine Arts, 1972, Art award KQED, 1975, Guggenheim award, 1976, Nat. Endowment for Arts award, 1977; Cresson European traveling scholar. Subject of profl. articles. Address: 6007 Rock Ridge Blvd Oakland CA 94618*

SAUNDERS, RICHARD HENRY, JR., physician, educator; b. Holland, Va., Feb. 13, 1919; s. Rich-H. and Floy (Simons) S.; B.A., U. Richmond, 1939; M.D., U. Rochester, 1943; m. Betsy Ann Mac-Millan, May 19, 1944; children—Ann MacMillan, Richard Henry III. Instr. medicine Yale, 1949; Damon Runyan fellow New Eng. Center Hosp., Boston, 1949-50; asst. prof. medicine U. Vt., 1950-55, asso. prof., 1955-57; asst. clin. prof. medicine U. Rochester, asso. dir. med. edn. Highland Hosp., Rochester, 1957-60; asso. dean, asst. prof. medicine Cornell U. Med. Coll., 1960-65; asst. attending physician N.Y. Hosp., 1960-65; asst. dir. Nat. Bd. Med. Examiners, 1965-67, asso. dir., 1967-69; asso. dean, asso. prof. medicine U. Mass. Med. Sch., 1969-74, prof. medicine, 1974—, dir. ambulatory care, 1974-77. Served as lt. (j.g.), M.C., USNR, 1945-46. Markle scholar med. sci., 1954-57. Diplomate Am. Bd. Internal Medicine. Fellow Am. Coll. Physicians; mem. AMA, Mass. Med. Soc., Assn. Am. Med. Colls., Am. Fedn. Clin. Research, Sigma Xi. Home: 44 North St Grafton MA 01519 Office: 55 Lake Ave N Worcester MA 01605

SAUNDERS, RICHARD PRESCOTT, educator; b. Somerville, Mass., Aug. 25, 1901; s. Charles Albert and Marion Edna (Prescott) S.; B.S., N.Y. U., 1934, M.A., 1935, Ed.D., 1938; LL.D., Rockford (Ill.) Coll., 1960; m. Dorthy Olton, June 23, 1937; 1 dau., Faith Olton. Real estate exec. Radio-Keith-Orpheum Corp., N.Y.C., 1926-33; instr. evening adult sch. Bklyn. Central YMCA, 1930-32; asst. dir. Inst. Edn., N.Y. U., 1933-34, instr., also dir. off-campus degree credit program, 1934-37; co-founder, 1st pres. New London (Conn.) Jr. Coll. (now Mitchell Coll.), 1938-45; co-founder, 1st pres. Palos Verdes Coll., Rolling Hills, Calif., 1946-51, chmn. bd. trustees, 1951-54, hon. trustee, 1954; board C.A.R.E., 1952-60. Pres. Save the Children Fedn., N.Y.C., 1951-60; pres., chmn. bd. dirs. Futures for Children, Inc., 1960-79, pres. emeritus, hon. bd. dirs., dir. community devel. program, 1979—; asso. exec. sec. Assn. for Higher Edn., 1961-67; exec. dir. Council Advancement Small Colls., 1968. Mem. exec. com. N.E. Jr. Coll. Council, 1940-43; mem. postwar planning commn. Conn. Dept. Edn., 1942-43; bd. dirs. New London YMCA, 1940-43, v.p., 1941-43; mem. bd. edn., New London, 1943; regional dir. bldg. services U.S.O., 1943-45; vice chmn. exec. com. Internat. Union Child Welfare, 1952-58, bd. dirs. U.S. com., 1960-61. Bd. dirs. Instituto Universidad Americano, Medellin, Colombia, Futuro Para la Ninez, Medillin, Colombia; pres. Inst. for Human Resources Devel., 1965-70. Named hon. citizen, Geradmer, France, 1934; decorated officer Order Cedars of Lebanon, 1958; Medal Ville de Calaise, France, 1958; Gold Star of Antioquia (Colombia). Mem. Am. Sociol. Assn., NEA. Mason. Author: Handbook for Village Self-Help Counselors (Spanish and English), 1960, rev. 1966, 70. Contbr. articles to profl. publs. Address: 7617 Comanche Rd NE Albuquerque NM 87110. *I think perhaps the most significant conclusion to which I have come is that man appears to be a deficient entity unless he has an active concern for those less fortunate than himself.*

SAUNDERS, ROBERT MALLOUGH, engring. educator; b. Winnipeg, Man., Can., Sept. 12, 1915; s. Robert and Mabel Grace (Mallough) S.; B.Elec. Engring., U. Minn., 1938, M.S., 1942; D.Engring., Tokyo (Japan) Inst. Tech., 1971; m. Elizabeth Lenander, June 24, 1943. Design engr. Electric Machinery Co., Mpls., part-time 1938-42; teaching asst. elec. engring. U. Minn., 1938-42, instr., 1942-44; faculty U. Calif. at Berkeley, 1946-65, prof. elec. engring., 1957-65, chmn. dept., 1959-63; asst. to chancellor for engring. U. Calif. at Irvine, 1964-65, prof. elec. engring., 1965—, dean Sch. Engring., 1965-73; vis. asso. prof. Mass. Inst. Tech., 1954-55; cons. Gen. Motors Research Lab., Apollo Support Dept., Gen. Electric Co., Aerospace Corp., Rohr Corp. Sec. Nat. Commn. for Elec. Engring. Films, 1962-71; mem. ECPO Engring. Edn. and Accredition Com., 1965-71, chmn., 1969-70, bd. dirs., 1971-75; mem. engring. adv. com. NSF, 1968-71, mem. Sec. Navy's Bd. Edn. and Tng., 1972-78. Bd. visitors U.S. Army Transp. Sch., 1970-73. Served to lt. (j.g.) USNR, 1944-46. Simon fellow engring. Manchester (Eng.) U., 1960. Fellow IEEE (chmn. ednl. activities bd. 1973-74, mem. exec. com., dir. 1973—, v.p. regional activities 1975-76, pres. 1977); mem. Am. Soc. Engring. Edn. (chmn. elec. div. 1965-66), Sigma Xi, Tau Beta Pi, Eta Kappa Nu. Club: Rotary. Co-author: Analysis of Feedback Control Systems, 1956. Contbr. to Ency. Brit., also tech. jours. Home: 2407 Bunya St Newport Beach CA 92660 Office: U Calif Irvine CA 92717

SAUNDERS, ROGER ALFRED, hotel group exec.; b. Boston, Feb. 14, 1929; s. Irving Matthew and Shirley (Brown) S.; A.B., Miami U., 1951; m. Nina Ann Alexander, Oct. 4, 1953; children—Gary, Jeffrey, Todd, Tedd. Vice pres., gen. mgr. Copley Sq. Hotel, Boston, 1952-63; v.p., gen. mgr. Lenox Hotel, Boston, 1963-67; pres. Hotel Mgmt. Assos., Boston/Fla., 1967-77, Hotels of Tradition Inc., Saunders Hotels and Classic Hotels, Ltd., Boston, 1977—; pres., mng. dir. Boston Park Plaza Hotel, 1976—; chmn. Greater Boston Hotel and Restaurant Health and Pension Funds, 1971—; trustee Grove Hall Savs. Bank. Mem. Boston Econ. and Indsl. Commn., 1973—; pres. Back Bay Assn., 1974-76; trustee Freedom Trail Adv. Council, Met. Center, Children's Hosp. and Med. Center, Boston, 1976—; bd. dirs. City of Boston Office of Cultural Affairs, 1977—, Stuart St. Neighborhood Assn., 1977—; bd. advs. Stonehill Coll. Served with Air Force N.G., 1951-54. Recipient Hotel, Restaurant Industry Leadership award of New Eng., 1977, Humanitarian award Nat. Asthma Center and Jewish Nat. Hosp. at Denver, 1979. Mem. Internat. Hotel Assn., Internat. Assn. of SKAL, Am. Hotel/Motel Assn., New Eng. Innkeepers Assn., Mass. Hotel Assn., Boston Hotel Assn., Boston C. of C. (v.p. 1973-78), Chaine des Rotisseurs, Les Amis de Escoffier Soc. Clubs: Longwood Cricket; Badminton and Tennis; Belmont Country; Ft. Hill Tennis (Eastern Point, Gloucester, Mass.). Founder first non-profit N.Am. Hotel Reservation Center. Office: 64 Arlington St Boston MA 02117

SAUNDERS, RUBIE AGNES, editor; b. N.Y.C., Jan. 31, 1929; d. Walter St. Clair and Rubie Gwendolyn (Ford) Saunders; B.A., Hunter Coll. City U. N.Y., 1950. Editorial sec. Parents Mag. Enterprises, Inc., N.Y.C., 1950-51, editorial asst., 1951-53, asst. editor, 1953-54, mng. editor, 1955-60, editor Young Miss mag., 1960-67, editorial dir., 1967—. Bd. dirs. Assn. Neighbors and Friends Hunter Coll. Named to Hunter Coll. Hall Fame, 1972. Author books, including: Calling All Girls Party Book, 1966; Marilyn Morgan, R.N., 1969; Marilyn Morgan's Triumph, 1970; Concise Guide to Baby Sitting, 1972; Concise Guide to Smart Shopping and Consumerism, 1973; Quick and Easy Housekeeping, 1977. Home: 26 Glenwood Ave New Rochelle NY 10801 Office: 52 Vanderbilt Ave New York City NY 10017

SAUNDERS, RUSSELL JOSEPH, mfg. co. exec.; b. San Mateo, Calif., Oct. 4, 1937; s. Russell Lyall and Beatrice Virginia (Clyne) S.; student Stanford, 1955-56, San Mateo Coll., 1956-57, San Jose State Coll., 1957-58, Grad. Sch. Bus. Adminstrn., Harvard U., 1970; m. Carole Marie Luken, Nov. 11, 1978; children—Shelli Marie, Laura Lee. Accountant, Consol. Freightways, Inc., Menlo Park, Calif., 1958-66, dir. budgets, 1966; dir. finance Freighliner Corp., Portland, Oreg., 1966-67, v.p., finance, treas., 1967—, sr. v.p., 1973, also dir.; v.p. finance Diamond Reo Trucks, Inc., Lansing, Mich., 1974-75; sr. v.p., controller Envirotech Corp., Menlo Park, 1975—. dir. Freighliner Canada, Ltd. Mem. Multnomah County Tax Supervising and Conservation Commn., 1973-74. Trustee Oreg. Mus. Sci. and Industry, Portland, 1970—, pres., 1973-74; dir. Found. Oreg. Research and Edn., 1973—. Mem. Planning Execs. Inst. (pres. 1965-66), Stanford Alumni Assn., Harvard Bus. Sch. Alumni Assn., Alpha Eta Sigma. Club: Multnomah Athletic (Portland). Home: 49 Showers Dr Mountain View CA 94040 Office: 3000 Sand Hill Rd Menlo Park CA 94025

SAUNDERS, SALLY LOVE, poet, educator; b. Bryn Mawr, Pa., Jan. 15, 1940; d. Lawrence and Dorothy (Love) Saunders; student Sophia U., Tokyo, Japan, 1963, U. Pa., Columbia; B.S., George Williams Coll., 1965; m. Carter Craigie, May 27, 1967 (dec. Mar. 1974). Poet, 1946—, poems pub. in periodicals including Times Lit. Supplement, N.Y. Times, Christian Sci. Monitor, others; tchr. Shipley Sch., Bryn Mawr, 1962-65, Agnes Irwin Sch., Wynnewood, Pa., 1964-65, Montogmery County Day Sch., Wynnewood, 1962, Miquon (Pa.) Sch., Waldron Acad., Merion, Pa., 1965-66, Phelps Sch., Malvern, Pa., 1965-70, Frankford Friends Sch. Phila., 1965-66, Haverford (Pa.) Sch., 1965-66, Friends Sem. Sch., N.Y.C., 1966-68, Ballard Sch., N.Y.C., 1966-67, Lower Merion Sch., Ardmore, Pa., nights 1967-71, Univ. Settlement House, Phila., 1961-63, Navajo Indian Reservation, Fort Defiance, Ariz., 1963, Young Men's Jewish Youth Center, Chgo., 1964-65, Margaret Fuller Settlement House, Cambridge, Mass., 1958-61; poetry therapist Pa. Hosp. Inst., 1969-74, also drug rehab. house, Phila. Mem. Acad. Am. Poets, Nat. Fedn. State Poetry Socs., Am. Poetry League, Nat. League Am. Pen Women, Poetry Therapy Assn. (v.p.), Avalon Orgn., Authors Guild, Nat. Writers Club, Pen and Brush Club, N.H., Pa. poetry socs., Cath. Poetry Soc. (asso.), Fla. State Poetry Soc. (asso.). Episcopalian. Author: Pauses, 1978. Contbr. poems to newspapers. Pioneer in poetry therapy. Address: 731 Land Title Bldg Broad and Samson Sts Philadelphia PA 19110

SAUNDERS, SAM CUNDIFF, math. statistician; b. Richland, Oreg., Feb. 24, 1931; s. Winston Elmer and Elizabeth Jane (Cundiff) S.; B.S., U. Oreg., 1952; Ph.D., U. Wash., 1956; m. Ruth Ann Lake, Aug. 12, 1954; children—Winston A., Craig S.; 1 adopted dau., Susan L. Mathematician, Boeing Airplane Co., Seattle, 1956-59; sr. scientist Boeing Sci. Research Labs., Seattle, 1961-71; prof. math. Wash. State U., Pullman, 1971—; v.p. Math. Analysis Research Corp., Pullman, 1972—. Fellow Am. Statis. Assn.; mem. Inst. Math. Statistics, Am. Statis. Assn., Math. Assn. Am., Soc. Indsl. and Applied Math. Office: Wash State U Dept Math Pullman WA 99164

SAUNDERS, WARREN PHILLIP, JR., economist, educator; b. Morgantown, W.Va., Sept. 3, 1934; s. Warren Phillip and Thelma Marie (Dotson) S.; B.A., Pa. State U., 1956; M.A., U. Ill., 1957; Ph.D., Mass. Inst. Tech., 1964; m. Nancy Lee Trainor, June 16, 1956; children—Kathleen M., Kevin W., Keith A., Kent T., Kristine A. Instr. econs. Bowdoin Coll., 1961-62; research asso., asst. prof., asso. prof. econs. Carnegie-Mellon U., 1962-70; prof. econs. Ind. U., Bloomington, 1970—, asso. dean arts and scis., 1974-78; cons. Ednl. Testing Service, Agy. for Instructional Television. Recipient Outstanding Teaching award Ind. U. Sr. Class Council, 1974. Mem. Am. Econ. Assn., Indsl. Relations Research Assn., Phi Beta Kappa, Phi Kappa Phi, Phi Eta Sigma, Omicron Delta Kappa. Author: A Framework for Teaching Economics: Basic Concepts, 1977; Resource Manual for Teacher Training Programs in Economics, 1978. Contbr. articles to econ. jours. Home: 2408 Childs Ct Bloomington IN 47401

SAUNDERS, WILLIAM HOWERTON, educator, physician; b. Omaha, Jan. 7, 1920; s. William Howerton and Mabel (Lundgard) S.; B.A., U. Omaha, 1941; M.D., U. Iowa, 1943; m. Louise Stritzinger Skeele, Nov. 28, 1958. Intern U. Tex. Hosp., Galveston, 1944, asst. resident pediatrics, 1945; gen. med. practice, Detroit, 1947-50; resident otolaryngology U. Mich. Hosp., 1950-54; mem. faculty Coll. Medicine, Ohio State U., 1954—, prof. otolaryngology U. Mich. Hosp., 1950-54; mem. faculty Coll. Medicine, Ohio State U., 1954—, prof. otolaryngology, 1958—, chmn. dept., 1961—. Served to capt. AUS, 1945-47. Mem. A.M.A., Am. Laryngol. Assn., A.C.S., Am. Laryngol., Rhinol. and Otol. Soc., Sigma Chi. Home: 3063 Glenrich Pkwy Columbus OH 43221

SAUNDERS, WILLIAM HUNDLEY, JR., chemist, educator; b. Pulaski, Va., Jan. 12, 1926; s. William Hundley and Vivian (Watts) S.; B.S., Coll. William and Mary, 1948; Ph.D., Northwestern U., 1952; m. Nina Velta Plesums, June 25, 1960; children—Anne Michele, Claude William. Research asso. Mass. Inst. Tech., 1951-53; mem. faculty U. Rochester, 1953—, prof. chemistry, 1964—, chmn. dept., 1966-70. Guggenheim fellow, 1960-61, Sloan Found. fellow, 1961-64; NSF sr. postdoctoral fellow, 1970-71. Mem. Am. Chem. Soc., Chem. Soc. (London), Phi Beta Kappa, Sigma Xi, Phi Lambda Upsilon. Author: Ionic Aliphatic Reactions, 1965; (with A.F. Cockerill) Mechanisms of Elimination Reactions, 1973. Contbr. articles to profl. jours. Home: 15 Parkwood Ave Rochester NY 14620

SAUNDERS, WILLIAM LOCKWOOD, fin. cons.; b. Seattle, Dec. 13, 1911; s. William Guy and Elizabeth (Ruggles) S.; B.A., U. Wash., 1948; M.B.A., Northwestern U., 1950; m. Marjorie Allen, Nov. 30, 1945 (dec.); 1 dau., Mary Lee; m. 2d, Margaret Cella, Feb. 13, 1959. Resident mgr. Drumheller Ehrlichman & White, Aberdeen, Wash., 1933-36; with W.L. Saunders, investments, 1936-42; sales mgr. H. Irving Lee & Co., San Jose, Calif., 1946; fin. cons., 1946-48; with A.G. Becker & Co., Inc., Chgo., 1949—, v.p., 1951—, dir., 1960—; pres. Gisholt Machine Co., Madison, Wis., 1963-66, also dir.; chmn. Long Island Tankers, 1958-60; dir. Oregon Am. Lumber Co., 1951-53, Pacific Far East Line, 1957-61, Gilman Engring. & Mfg., 1963, Enterprises Internat., Inc., 1973—. Bd. dirs. John A. Johnson Found. Served to lt. comdr. USNR, 1943-46. Mem. Beta Gamma Sigma, Alpha Sigma Phi. Congregationalist. Clubs: Yacht (Seattle); Bohemian (San Francisco). Home: The Highlands Seattle WA 98177 Office: The Highlands Seattle WA 98133

SAUPE, ALFRED OTTO, physicist, educator; b. Badenweiler, Germany, Feb. 14, 1925; s. Alfred and Luise (Henssler) S.; M.Sc. (Dipl. Phys.), U. Freiburg, Germany, 1955, Dr.rer.nat., 1958; m. Brigitte I. Wiedemann, May 31, 1963; children—Anja Sabine, Welf Alfred, Arne Dennis. DFG Research fellow Phys. Inst. Freiburg, 1958-61; co-worker (with Prof. R. Mecke) Inst. for Phys. Chemistry, Freiburg, 1962; sci. asst. U. Freiburg, 1963-68, dozent phys. chemistry, 1967-70; vis. prof. physics Kent (Ohio) State U., 1968-70, prof. physics, 1970—. Recipient Nernst prize for phys. chemistry Deutsche Bunsengesellschaft, 1974. Contbr. articles to profl. jours. Home: 1958 Brookview Dr Kent OH 44240

SAUSE, GEORGE GABRIEL, coll. dean; b. Souderton, Pa., Sept. 28, 1919; s. George and Maud (Nicholson) S.; B.S., Moravian Coll., 1941; Ph.D., Columbia, 1952; m. Evelyn Gorman, June 23, 1948. Asst. prof. econs. Moravian Coll., Bethlehem, Pa., 1947-48; asst. prof. econs. Lafayette Coll., Easton, Pa., 1950-57, asso. prof. econs., 1957-62, prof. econs., 1962—, head dept., 1970-72, provost, dean faculty, 1972—. Instr. Am. Inst. Banking, Easton, 1954-69; cons. Northampton County Property Reassessment Program, 1956-58, Joint Interim Com. Assessment Practice, State of Cal., 1958, Pa. Bur. Municipal Affairs, 1961-64, Joint Planning Com. Lehigh-Northampton Counties, Pa., 1964-67, Urban Research and Devel. Corp., Bethlehem, Pa., 1971-73; mem. spl. com. tax policies for citizens Housing and Planning Council N.Y., 1959-60. Dist. committeeman Democratic Party, 1954-70, city chmn., 1970-72. Treas. Lehigh-Delaware Devel. Council, 1960-77, exec. bd., 1960—; mem. Easton City Planning Commn., 1962—, vice chmn., 1962-64, 70-71, chmn., 1964-66, 71-73, 77—; trustee Moravian Coll., 1968-70; bd. dirs. Graded Tax League Pa.; academic adv. council Henry George Sch. Social Sci.; trustee, exec. com. Easton United Fund, 1968—. Served with USAAF, 1942-45. Recipient Thomas Roy and Laura Jones award Lafayette Coll., 1958, 62, Comenius Alumni award Moravian Coll., 1975. Mem. Tax Inst. Am. (adv. council 1965-68), Am. Econ. Assn., Nat. Tax Assn. (local nonproperty taxation com. 1972—), Am. Finance Assn., AAUP (chmn. com. faculty participation in univ. govt. 1965-71). Author: Municipal Authorities: The Pennsylvania Experience, 1962; Money, Banking and Economic Activity, 1966. Editorial bd. Jour. Econs. and Sociology, 1963—, Local Taxation, 1970—. Home: 622 W Lafayette St Easton PA 18042

SAUTER, AUGUST, JR., sound control products mfg. co. exec.; b. Phila., Apr. 23, 1942; s. August and Edith Harper (Potts) S.; B.S. in Mech. Engring., Drexel Inst. Tech., 1965; M.E. (NSF trainee), U. Calif. at Berkeley, 1966; m. Susan Darlene Wolf, Aug. 14, 1965; children—Andrew August, Matthew August, Jennifer Susan. Cons. Bolt Beranek & Newman, Inc., Cambridge, Mass., 1966-68; chief engr. Rink Corp. mfrs. sound control products, Hazleton, Pa., 1968-72, nat. sales mgr. Rink div. Lear Siegler, Inc., Tucson, 1972-74; mktg. mgr. Burgess Industries, Dallas, 1974-78; Western region product mgr. Indsl. Acoustics Co., Inc., 1978—. Mem. ASME, ASTM, Acoustical Soc. Am., Am. Soc. Heating, Refrigeration and Air Conditioning Engrs., Pi Tau Sigma, Republican. Lutheran. Patentee in field. Home: 8821 Carmel Circle Westminster CA 92683 Office: 1009 Wilshire Blvd Santa Monica CA 90401

SAUTER, VAN GORDON, communications exec.; b. Middletown, Ohio, Sept. 14, 1935; s. Freeman and Cornelia (Banker) S.; B.A., Ohio U., 1957; M.A., U. Mo., 1959; children—Mark Allen, Jeremy Banker. Reporter, New Bedford (Mass.) Standard-Times, 1959-63; staff writer Detroit Free Press, 1963-67, Chgo. Daily News, 1967-68; news and program dir. WBBM-CBS Radio, Chgo., 1968-71; exec. producer CBS News, radio, 1971; dir. news WBBM-TV, CBS, Chgo., 1972-74, Paris bur. chief CBS News, 1974-76, v.p. program practices CBS TV Network, N.Y.C., 1976-77; v.p., gen. mgr. Sta. KNXT-TV, CBS, Los Angeles, 1977—. Mem. Radio TV News Dirs. Assn., Sigma Delta Chi. Co-author: Nightmare in Detroit, 1968; Fabled Land, Timeless River, Life Along the Mississippi, 1970. Office: 6121 Sunset Blvd Los Angeles CA 90028*

SAUVE, JEANNE, Canadian govt. ofcl.; b. Prud'homme, Sask., Can., Apr. 26, 1922; d. Charles Albert and Anna (Vaillant); grad. U. Ottawa, U. Paris; D.Sc. (hon.), N.B. U., 1974; m. Maurice Sauve, Sept. 24, 1948; 1 son, Jean-Francois. Nat. pres. Jeuness Etudiante Catholique, Montreal, 1942-47; tchr. French, London County Council, 1948-50; asst. to dir. youth sect. UNESCO, Paris, 1951; journalist, broadcaster, 1952-72; bd. dirs. Union des Artistes, Montreal, 1961; v.p. Canadian Inst. on Pub. Affairs, 1962-64, pres., 1964; mem. Canadian Centennial

Commn., 1967; gen. sec. Fedn. des Auteurs et des Artistes du Can., 1966-72; dir. Bushnell Communications Ltd., Ottawa, 1969-72; dir. CKAC Radio Sta., Montreal, 1969-72; mem. Parliament for Montreal, 1972; minister of state in charge of sci. and tech., 1972-74; minister of environment, 1974-75; minister of communications, Ottawa, 1975—. Mem. Liberal Party of Can. Roman Catholic. Home: 281 McDougall St Outremont PQ Canada Office: House of Commons Ottawa ON K1A 0A6 Canada

SAUVE, MAURICE, lawyer, corp. exec.; b. Montreal, Sept. 20, 1923; B.A., U. Montreal, 1944, LL.B., 1948; Ph.D., U. Paris, 1952. Tech. adviser Can. and Cath. Confedn. of Labour, 1952-55; asst. sec. Royal Commn. on Can.'s Econ. Prospects, 1955-58; officer Que. Liberal Party, 1958-62; mem. Can. Parliament for les Iles-de-la-Madeleine, 1962-68; minister of forestry and rural devel. Govt. of Can., 1964-68; with Consol. Bathurst, Inc., Montreal, 1968—, now exec. v.p.; dir. Andres Wines Ltd., Automobiles Renault Can. Ltee, Barclays Can. Ltd., Benson & Hedges (Can.) Ltd., BP Can., Inc., Comml. Life Assurance Co. of Can., Halifax Ins. Co. Home: 281 McDougall Ave Outremont PQ H2V 3P3 Canada Office: 800 Dorchester Blvd W Montreal PQ H3B 1Y9 Canada

SAUVEY, DONALD (ROBERT), musical instrument co. exec.; b. Green Bay, Wis., Mar. 15, 1924; s. Irving and Alice (LaBelle) S.; student Am. TV Lab., 1942-43; cert. electronic tech. Milw. Sch. Engring., 1947; m. Shirley Ann Capelle, Nov. 24, 1949. Sales mgr. Conn Organ Co., Elkhart, Ind., 1960-65; dir. mktg. Electro Music, Pasadena, Calif., 1965-70, v.p., gen. mgr., 1970-73; v.p., gen. mgr. Gulbransen Organ Co. subs. CBS, Chgo., 1973-75; pres., chief exec. officer Hammond Organ Chgo., 1975—; dir. Marmon Co. Mem. businessmen's adv. council Forty-Plus of Chgo., Inc., 1977—. Served with USAAF, 1943-46. Mem. Am. Music Conf. (dir.), Nat. Assn. Music Mchts. Republican. Roman Catholic. Patentee in field. Office: 4200 W Diversey Ave Chicago IL 60639

SAVACOOL, JOHN KENNETH, educator; b. Los Angeles, July 16, 1917; s. James E. and Helen (Braddock) S.; B.A., Williams Coll., 1939; student U. Calif. at Los Angeles, 1941, Sorbonne, Paris, 1947-50; m. Suzanne Lepeytre, Dec. 29, 1965 (dec. 1968); m. 2d, Phebe Cramer, Oct. 1, 1972. Play-reader for Theatre Guild, 1948-52; mem. faculty Williams Coll., Williamstown, Mass., 1952—, prof. French, 1958—. Served with AUS, 1941-45. Decorated Legion of Merit. Mem. Modern Lang. Assn., Am. Assn. Tchrs. French. Co-author: O'Daniel, 1946; Voix du siecle, 1960; Voix du siecle 2, 1966. Adapter; Judith, 1966. Home: 20 Forest Rd Williamstown MA 01267

SAVAGE, CHARLES FRANCIS, lawyer; b. Bklyn., Oct. 2, 1942; s. Charles Lincoln and Frances Regis (Moran) S.; B.A., Columbia, 1963, J.S.D., 1966; m. Maria Ania Bojcun, July 1, 1967; children—Charles F.I., Michael R. Admitted to N.Y. bar, 1966; asso. firm Cadwalader, Wickersham & Taft, N.Y.C., 1966-70; sec., gen. counsel Belco Petroleum Corp., N.Y.C., 1970-75; v.p. planning and devel. Belco Petroleum Corp., N.Y.C., 1975-77, also dir.; v.p., gen. counsel Fla. Gas Co., Winter Park, 1977-78; asst. gen. counsel conservation and solar applications Dept. of Energy, Washington, 1978—. Mem. Am., N.Y., Fla. bar assns., Assn. Bar City N.Y., N.Y. County Lawyers Assn., Fed. Energy Bar. Home: 829 Dolley Madison Blvd McLean VA 22021 Office: 20 Massachusetts Ave NW Washington DC 20585

SAVAGE, EDWARD WARREN, JR., physician; b. Macon, Ga., July 7, 1933; s. Edward Warren and Mildred Eleanor (Goodwin) S.; A.B., Talladega Coll., 1955; postgrad. St. Louis U., 1955; M.D., Meharry Med. Coll., 1960: m. Carole Porter, June 6, 1959; children—Cheryl, Racheal, Edward Warren. Intern, St. Joseph's Hosp., Syracuse, N.Y., 1960-61; resident Kings County Hosp.-State U. N.Y., Bklyn., 1963-67; USPHS fellow in gynecol. cancer State U. N.Y. Downstate Med. Center, Bklyn., 1967-69, asst. instr., 1964-66, instr., 1966-69; dir. gynecologic oncology U. Ill., Chgo., 1970-73, asst. prof., 1969-73, asso. prof., 1973; practice medicine specializing in gynec. cancer, Los Angeles, 1973—; mem. staffs Martin L. King Hosp., St. Francis Hosp., Calif Hosp. Med. Center, Meml. Hosp. Gardena, St. Francis Hosp. of Lynwood, Harbor Gen. Hosp., Cedars-Sinai Med. Center, Dominguiz Valley Hosp., UCLA Hosps. and Clinics: asso. prof. Charles R. Drew Postgrad. Sch. Medicine, 1973—; adj. asso. prof. UCLA Sch. Medicine, 1977. Exec. bd. Los Angeles Community Cancer Control. Served as capt. M.C., USAF, 1961-63. Diplomate Am. Bd. Obstetrics and Gynecology. Fellow A.C.S., Am. Coll. Obstetricians and Gynecologists; mem. Soc. Gynecologic Oncologists, Am., Western Assn. Gynec. Oncologists (pres. 1979-80), Nat., Golden State med. assns., AAUP, Am. Soc. Colposcopy and Cervical Pathology (dir. 1973—), Chgo. Gynecol. Soc., Ill., Los Angeles obstet. and gynecol. socs., Charles R. Drew Med. Soc. Contbr. numerous articles to profl. publs. Office: 12021 S Wilmington Ave Los Angeles CA 90059. *I am the product of two wonderful parents whose support and ideals, inclusive of a strong work ethic, allowed me to be prepared for the several fortuitous opportunities that presented themselves. My hope is that somehow my life will be a positive statement to those who know me.*

SAVAGE, FRANK, corp. exec.; b. Rocky Mount, N.C., July 10, 1938; s. Frank and Grace Vivian (Pitt) S.; B.A., Howard U., 1961; M.A., Sch. Advanced Internat. Studies, Johns Hopkins U., 1964; m. Beryl M. Bowser, July 17, 1961 (div.); children—Eric, Brett, Mark. Officer overseas div. Citibank, N.Y.C., 1964-70; v.p., then pres. Equico Capital Corp., N.Y.C., 1970-73; exec. v.p. TAW Internat. Leasing, N.Y.C., 1973-75; mem. staff of chmn. bd., v.p. Equitable Life Assurance Soc. U.S., N.Y.C., 1975-76, v.p., investment officer, 1976—; dir. Equico Lessors, Inc.; chmn. bd. Freedom Nat. Bank of N.Y. Trustee, Minority Broadcasting Fund; vice chmn. Ops. Crossroads Africa, 1977—; pres. Black Council on Africa, 1977—; trustee YWCA of U.S., 1977—; bd. advisors African-Am. Inst., 1977—; mem. task force White House Conf. on Small Bus., 1978—; trustee Johns Hopkins U., 1977—. Recipient Blackafrica award; Harlem Commonwealth Council Banking award. Presbyterian. Office: 1285 Ave of Americas New York NY 10019

SAVAGE, HENRY, JR., lawyer, author; b. Camden, S.C., Aug. 1, 1903; s. Henry and Helen (Alexander) S.; B.S., U. Va., 1926, LL.B., 1926; L.H.D., U. S.C., 1976, Med. U. S.C., 1976; m. Elizabeth C. Anderson, Aug. 21, 1929 (dec. Apr. 1932); 1 son, William Henry; m. 2d, Elizabeth Clarke Jones, Oct. 7, 1933; children—Carroll J., Elizabeth Hope, Virginia B., Samuel P., Henry III, Helen A. Admitted to S.C. bar, 1926; since practiced in Camden; sr. partner firm Savage, Royall, Kinard, Sheheen & Byars, 1953—; dir. First Fed. Savs. & Loan Assn., Bank S.C.; chmn. bd. S.C. Blue Cross-Blue Shield, Companion Life Ins. Co. Chmn. ednl. survey S.C. Fiscal Survey Commn., 1956, Lynches River Soil Conservation Assn., 1941-45, Kershaw County Forest Protection Assn., 1936-48. Mayor of Camden, 1948-58. Trustee Med. U. S.C., Charleston, 1964-74; mem. adv. council U. S.C. Recipient Charles H. Flory Distinguished Service award for outstanding contbns. to forestry, 1974. Mem. Am. (exec. com. 1958), S.C. (pres. 1955-56) municipal assns., S.C. Hist. Soc. (past curator), S.C. (past pres.), Am. (dir.) forestry assns., Carolina Cup Racing Assn. (vice chmn.), U. S.C. Soc. (pres. 1972-74), Phi Beta Kappa, Phi Sigma Kappa, Phi Delta Phi. Author: America Goes Socialistic, 1933; River of the Carolinas; The Santee, 1956; Seeds of Time; The Background of Southern Thinking, 1959; Lost Heritage, 1970; Discovering America, 1700-1875, 1979. Home: 1707 Lyttleton St Camden SC 29020 Office: 1111 Church St Camden SC 29020

SAVAGE, JAMES FRANCIS, journalist; b. Boston, July 23, 1939; s. James and Hanora (Enright) S.; A.A., Boston U., 1959, B.S., 1961; m. Sharon Kaye Base, May 29, 1965; 1 son, Sean. Reporter, Quincy (Mass.) Patriot Ledger, 1961-63; reporter Miami (Fla.) Herald, 1963-67, investigative reporter, 1967-78, investigations editor, 1978—; investigative reporter Boston Herald Traveler, 1967. Served with AUS, 1962. Recipient Nat. Headliners award, 1969; Fla. Press Assn. award, 1972, George Polk Meml. award for investigative reporting, 1973; Pub. Service award Nat. A.P. Mng. Editors, 1974; award Fla. Soc. Newspaper Editors, 1974, 75. Profl. journalism fellow Stanford, 1974-75. Home: 1004 Orange Isle Fort Lauderdale FL 33315 Office: 1 Herald Plaza Miami FL 33101

SAVAGE, JOHN CHARLES, advt. agy. exec.; b. Bklyn., Jan. 26, 1932; s. John Joseph and Helen Marie (Anderson) S.; B.A., St. John's U., 1953; m. Elizabeth Ann Charles, June 25, 1955; children—Elizabeth, Nancy, Faith, Megan, Dierdre. Account exec. Foote, Cone & Belding, N.Y.C., 1955-62; exec. v.p. Norman, Craig & Kummel, Inc., N.Y.C., 1967-70; pres. NCK Can. Ltd., 1962-70, Norman, Craig & Kummel, Inc., N.Y.C., 1976—; v.p., mktg. dir. Am. Home Products, N.Y.C., 1970-76. Served to capt. USMC, 1953-55. Clubs: Metropolitan, West Side Tennis (N.Y.C.); Royal Can. Military Inst. (Toronto). Office: Norman Craig & Kummel Inc 919 3d Ave New York NY 10022

SAVAGE, JOHN FRANCIS, lawyer; b. Milw., July 23, 1910; s. Patrick J. and Margaret (Keogh) S.; LL.B. cum laude, Marquette U., 1933; m. Dorothy M. Ryan, Sept. 15, 1942; children—John P., Mary Margaret, Thomas R., Katherine Ann. Admitted to Wis. bar, 1933; practice in Milw., 1933-42; spl. agt. FBI, 1942-46; atty. Miller Brewing Co., Milw., 1946-56, gen. counsel, 1956-72, sec., 1957-64, v.p., 1964-66, exec. v.p., 1966-72; pvt. practice law, Milw., 1972—. Pres., Milw. Jr. Bar Assn., 1938-39. Mem. Wis. Corp. Counsel Sect. (past v.p., dir.), Am., Wis., Milw. bar assns., U.S. (chmn. lawyers adv. com. 1968-72), Milw. (pres. 1967—), Wis. (bd. dirs.) brewers assns., Sigma Nu Phi. Roman Catholic. Clubs: Burr Jones Law, Ozaukee Country. Home: 920 W Cedar Ridge Ct Mequon WI 53092 Office: 780 N Water St Milwaukee WI 53202

SAVAGE, JOHN JOSEPH, ins. co. exec.; b. Gary, Ind., Sept. 23, 1915; s John and Dorain (Plese) S.; B.A., Western Res. U., 1937; hon. professorship Golden Gate Coll., San Francisco, 1960; m. Corinne Beck, Nov. 9, 1946; 1 dau., Marcia (Mrs. David T. Rickard). With Nat. Bur. Casualty Underwriters, San Francisco, 1946-65; with United Pacific Ins. Co., Tacoma, 1965—, pres., dir., 1970—, also chief exec. officer; lectr. Golden Gate Coll., 1948-60. Arbitrator, Calif. Surplus Lines Assn., 1959-65; chmn. Hawaii Casualty and Surety Com., 1959-65. Bd. dirs. Tacoma Opera Soc., Salvation Army; trustee Tacoma Gen. Hosp. Served with F.A., AUS, 1942-45. Mem. Tacoma C. of C. (dir.), Am. Assn. U. Profs. Ins. Republican. Elk. Clubs: Tacoma, Tacoma Country and Golf; San Francisco Commerical. Office: 728 St Helens St Tacoma WA 98402*

SAVAGE, ROBERT H., tel. and tel. co. exec.; b. 1916; B.A., Coll. City N.Y., 1937; married. Reporter Wall St. Jour., 1945-50; security analyst Merrill, Lynch, Pierce, Fenner & Smith, 1950-52; sr. security analyst Wood, Struthers & Co., 1952-55; dir. investor relations Chrysler Corp., 1955-64; with Internat. Tel. & Tel. Corp., 1964—, successively, spl. asst. to treas., dir. investor relations treas. dept., dir. investor relations finance and treas. depts., now v.p. investor relations. Office: 320 Park Ave New York NY 10022

SAVAGE, ROBERT HEATH, advt. agy. exec.; b. Chillicothe, Ohio, Nov. 24, 1929; s. Russell Heath and Frances (Hunt) S.; B.A., Principia Coll., 1951; M.B.A., Harvard, 1956; m. Lorna Dale, May 2, 1970. Brand mgr. Procter & Gamble, Cin., 1956-60; sr. v.p., mgmt. supr., dir. Ogilvy & Mather, Inc., N.Y.C., 1960-71; mktg. mgr. personal products div. Lever Bros., N.Y.C., 1971; exec. v.p. Botsford Ketchum, Inc., San Francisco, 1972, pres., 1972-78, chmn., 1978—; pres. KM&G Internat., Inc., 1978—. Served with USMCR, 1951-54. Mem. Am. Assn. Advt. Agys. (chmn. 1975-76), Greater San Francisco C. of C., San Francisco Advt. Club. Clubs: Bankers, Calif. Tennis, Commonwealth. Home: 1 Arroyo Dr Kentfield CA 94904 Office: 55 Union St San Francisco CA 94111

SAVAGE, ROBERT LINCOLN, univ. adminstr.; b. Paulding, Ohio, Mar. 9, 1915; s. Curtis Ray and Mayme (Kennedy) S.; student Ohio No. U., Ada, 1933-34; B.Chem. Engring., Ohio State U., 1938; M.S., Case Inst. Tech., 1942, Ph.D., 1945; m. Thais Nobis, Dec. 30, 1938; children—Linda Lee Savage Mapes, Carol Elizabeth Savage Woods. Research engr. Battelle Meml. Inst., 1938-40, asst. supr., chmn. engr., 1944-48; grad. fellow Case Inst. Tech., Cleve., 1940-44, from asst. prof. to prof. chem. engring., 1948-56; v.p. research N.Am. Coal Corp., Cleve., 1956-64; dir. research sci. and engring. Ohio U., 1964-67, dean Coll. Engring., 1965-67, v.p. research and indsl. liaison, 1967-73, provost, 1969-73, prof. chem. engring., 1973—; on leave as cons. Sch. Engring., MARA Inst. Tech., Selangor, Malaysia, 1973-75. Dir. Bituminous Coal Research, 1958-61; mem. coms. coal chems. and atomic energy Nat. Coal Assn., 1958-62; Cleve. chmn. 9th Nat. Chem. Exposition, 1956; cons. to industry, 1950—. Mem. sci. adv. com. Ohio Bd. Regents, 1965-68; bd. dirs. Athens United Appeal, 1966-71; trustee Willoughby (Ohio) Pub. Library. 1962-64. Recipient Cleve. Chem. Profession certificate of merit, 1957. Registered profl. engr., Ohio. Mem. Am. Chem. Soc. (chmn. Cleve. sect. 1954), Am. Inst. Chem. Engrs., Am. Soc. Engring. Edn., Ohio Acad. Scis., Nat., Ohio socs. profl. engrs., Am. Mgmt. Assn., AAAS, Internat. Assn. for Hydrogen Energy, Nat. Council Univ. Research Adminstrs., Sigma Xi, Alpha Chi Sigma. Presbyn. (chmn. trustees 1951-54, mem. session 1954-57). Rotarian (dir. Athens chpt. 1968—, pres. 1971). Editor: NASA Report on Hydrogen Energy Carrier, 1973. Contbr. articles to profl. jours., chpt. in book. Editor: Adhesion and Adhesives, 1954. Patentee in field. Home: RD 6 Box 86 Coolville Ridge Athens OH 45701

SAVAGE, ROBERT STANLEY, diversified mfg. and service co. exec.; b. Scranton, Pa., Feb. 20, 1928; s. Stanley and Christine (Kozik) S.; S.B. in Chem. Engring., Syracuse (N.Y.) U., 1950; M.B.A., Harvard U., 1957; m. Ann Richardson Shinquin, Sept. 29, 1951; children—Robert, Barbara, Benjamin. With Goodyear Tire & Rubber Co., Akron, Ohio, 1950-69, bus. area dir., 1968-69; sr. v.p. ops. Doric Corp., Oklahoma City, 1969-75; sr. v.p. processing div. Iowa Beef Processors Co., Dakota City, Nebr., 1971-72; exec. v.p., dir. Anta Corp., Oklahoma City, 1975—. Rep., Billerica (Mass.) Town Meeting, 1960-61; active local Boy Scouts Am., 1964—. Served with USNR, 1945-46. Mem. Sigma Chi. Republican. Unitarian-Universalist. Clubs: Rotary, Masons. Home: 2332 NW 119th St Oklahoma City OK 73120 Office: 2400 First Nat Center West Oklahoma City OK 73102

SAVAGE, WALLACE HAMILTON, lawyer; b. Houston, Nov. 21, 1912; s. Homer H. and Mary (Wallace) S.; B.S., U. Va. 1933; J.D., Harvard, 1936; m. Dorothy Harris, Oct. 12, 1940; children—Virginia Wallace (Mrs. A. Lee McAlester), Dorothy Harris. Admitted to Tex., Colo. bars, 1937, practiced in Dallas; now with Lane, Savage, Counts & Winn; dir. Lakewood Bank & Trust Co. Dallas County chmn., nat. vice chmn. Citizens Com. Hoover Report, 1952-54; mem., dir. Citizen's Com. for Reorgn. Exec. Branch of Govt., 1954-59. Mayor pro tem, Dallas, 1947-49, mayor, 1949-51; chmn. Dallas County Democratic Com., 1952-54; chmn. Tex. Dem. Com., 1952-54. Served as comdr. USNR, 1941-45. Univ. fellow U. Colo., 1936- 37. Mem. Am., Dallas bar assns., State Bar Tex., Phi Delta Phi. Episcopalian (past parish chancellor and vestryman). Clubs: Dallas Country, Idlewild, Terpsichorean. Author: A Bait of Perjury, 1970. Home: 5703 Swiss Ave Dallas TX 75214 Office: Lakewood Bank and Trust Co Dallas TX 75214

SAVAGE, WARD KELLY, JR., oil co. exec.; b. Port Neches, Tex., Mar. 4, 1920; s. Ward Kelly and Syble (Woodruff) S.; B.S.Ch.E., U. Tex., 1941; m. Aug. 6, 1945. With Texaco Inc., White Plains, v.p. marine; bd. mgrs. Am. Bur. Shipping; mem. Lloyds Am. Com. Mem. Am. Petroleum Inst. Republican. Presbyterian. Office: 2000 Westchester Ave White Plains NY 10650*

SAVAGE, WARREN FAIRBANK, educator; b. Harvard, Mass., Mar. 10, 1922; s. L. Kingston and Mildred (Fairbank) S.; grad. Lawrence Acad., 1939; B.Chem. Engring., Rensselaer Poly. Inst., 1942, M.Metall. Engring., 1949, Ph.D., 1954; m. Helen Agnes Lambert, Nov. 6, 1943; children—Sharon Anne (Mrs. David P. Mardon), Donald Fairbank. Metall. engr. Adirondack Foundries & Steel Co., Watervliet, N.Y., 1942-44; research fellow Rensselaer Poly. Inst., 1945-48, mem. faculty, 1948—, prof. metall. engring., 1960—, dir. welding research, 1961—; Clarence Jackson honor lectr., 1976; cons. to govt. and industry, 1945—; mem. U.S./USSR Joint Commn. on Welding and Spl. Electrometallurgy, 1975—. Active local Boy Scouts Am. Fellow Am. Soc. Metals (pres. Eastern N.Y. chpt. 1952-53; Tchr. Recognition award Phila. chpt. 1965); hon. life mem. Am. Welding Soc. (Adams Meml. lectr. 1967); mem. Am. Arbitration Bd., Rensselaer Soc. Engrs., (trustee, faculty adviser 1954-64), Sigma Xi, Phi Lambda Upsilon, Tau Beta Pi. Home: RD 2 Averill Park NY 12018 Office: Materials Research Center Rensselaer Poly Inst Troy NY 12181

SAVAGE, WILLIAM WOODROW, educator; b. Onley, Va., Jan. 9, 1914; s. Frank Howard and Florence Elmira (Twyford) S.; A.B., Coll. William and Mary, 1937; M.A., U. Chgo., 1946, Ph.D., 1955; student U. Va., summer 1951; m. Margaret Jane Clarke; children—Earl R., William W. Research editor, div. rural research Fed. Emergency Relief Adminstrn., Richmond, Va., 1935-36; div. mgr. Montgomery Ward & Co., Newport News, Va., 1937-38; statis. worker WPA, Richmond, 1938-39; counselor Va. Consultation Service, Richmond, 1939-42, acting dir., 1942-45; asst. state supr. guidance and consultation services Va. Dept. Edn., 1946-47; dean Longwood Coll., Farmville, Va., 1947-52; project coordinator, asso. dir. Midwest Adminstrn. Center, U. Chgo., 1952-56; dean Sch. Edn., U. S.C., 1956-65, prof. edn., 1956-79, curator Mus. Edn., 1973—. Mem. visitation and appraisal com. Nat. Council for Accreditation Tchr. Edn., 1964-67. Mem. S.C. Assn. Sch. Adminstrs., Palmetto State Tchrs. Assn., Phi Delta Kappa. Methodist. Club: Wardlaw (pres. 1974-75). Author: Interpersonal and Group Relations, 1968. Co-author: Readings in American Education, 1963. Editor Work and Training, monthly Va. Bd. Edn., 1941-47, Administrator's Notebook, monthly Midwest Adminstrn. Center, 1954-56, U. S.C. Edn. Report, 1957-65, 67—; adv. com. Sch. Rev., 1954-56. Contbr. articles to jours. Home: 6316 Eastshore Rd Columbia SC 29206

SAVALAS, TELLY ARISTOTELES, actor; b. Garden City, N.Y., Jan. 21, 1924; s. Nicholas Constantine and Christina (Kapsallis) S.; B.S., Columbia U.; m. 2d, Marilynn Gardner, Oct. 28, 1960; children—Christina, Penelope, Candace; m. 3d, Sally Adams, 1974; 1 son, Nicholas. Asst. dir. Near East, South Asia and Africa, Info. Service, Dept. State, to 1955; sr. dir. news and spl. events dept. ABC, 1955-58, producer Your Voice of America, 1955-58; dir. Stamford (Conn.) Playhouse, 1958-59; debut as actor Bring Home a Baby, Armstrong Circle Theatre, 1959; appeared in numerous motion pictures including Young Savages, 1961, Cape Fear, 1962, Birdman of Alcatraz, 1962, The Man from the Diners Club, 1963, The New Interns, 1964, Genghis Khan, 1965, The Battle of the Bulge, 1965, The Greatest Story Ever Told, 1965, Beau Geste, 1966, The Dirty Dozen, 1967, The Scalphunters, 1968, Buona Sera, Mrs. Campbell, 1968, The Assassination Bureau, 1969, On Her Majesty's Secret Service, 1969, Crooks and Coronets, 1969, MacKenna's Gold, 1969, Kelly's Heroes, 1970, A Town Called Bastard, 1970, Pancho Villa, 1971, Horror Express, 1972, Inside Out, 1975, Diamond Mercenaries, 1975, Killer Force, 1975, Lisa and the Devil, Inside Out, 1976, The House of Exorcism, 1976, Capricorn One, 1978; TV appearances include The Witness (series), 1960-61, The Untouchables, 1961, 77 Sunset Strip, 1963, The Fugitive, 1965, Cimarron Strip, 1967, Garrison's Gorillas, 1967, Combat, 1967, The Marcus-Nelson Murders (TV movie), 1972, Kojak (series), 1973-78, also variety specials, 1976; appeared in TV mini-series The French Atlantic Affair, 1979. Served with AUS, World War II. Recipient Peabody award; Freedom Found. award; Emmy award, 1974. Greek Orthodox. Office: care ICM 40 W 57th St New York NY 10019*

SAVARD, F(RANCIS) G(ERALD) KENNETH, biochemist; b. Quebec, Que., Can., Feb. 26, 1918; s. Joseph Daniel and Isabel Jane (Davis) S.; B.Sc., Laval U., Quebec, 1939, D.Sc., 1946; M.Sc., McGill U., Montreal, Que., 1943; m. Lorraine I. Kelly, 1945; children—Christopher J. K., Julie A. J. Research chemist Ayerst, McKenna & Harrison Ltd., Montreal, 1941-46; research fellow Sloan-Kettering Inst., N.Y.C., 1947-48; asst. staff Cleve. Clinic Research Found., 1948-51; sr. staff scientist Worcester Found. Exptl. Biology, Shrewsbury, Mass., 1951-57; prof. U. Miami Sch. Medicine, 1957-73; investigator Howard Hughes Med. Inst., 1957-69; chmn. dept. biochemistry U. Montreal Sch. Medicine, 1977—; vis. scientist NICHD, 1972-75; cons. in field. Mem. AAAS, Am. Chem. Soc., Endocrine Soc., Am. Assn. Biol. Chemists, Am. Cancer Soc. (adv. bd. 1969-73). Contbr. numerous articles to profl. jours. Office: U Montreal Dept Biochemistry Montreal PQ H3C 3J7 Canada. *The major satisfaction of a scientist and teacher is the respect of his fellow scientists and colleagues.*

SAVARD, PIERRE, historian; b. Quebec City, Que., Can., June 10, 1936; s. Charles-Eugène and Gilberte (Lavallée) S.; Diplôme d'Etudes Supérieures, U. Lyon, France, 1961; Ph.D., U. Laval, Québec, 1965; m. Susan Blue Warder, June 6, 1960; children—Marie, François, Michel. Asst. prof., asso. prof. dept. history U. Laval, 1961-72, sec. dept. history, 1964-67, dir., 1971-72; asso. prof. dept. history U. Ottawa, Ont., 1972-75, prof., 1975—, dir. Research Centre on French Can. Culture, 1973—, dir. U. Ottawa Quar., 1977—; trustee Can. Studies Found.; chmn. Study Group on Arts in French-Speaking Ont., 1976-77; pres. Humanities Research Council Can., 1975-76; dir. Revue d'Histoire de l'Amérique francaise, 1972-75, essay sect. Livres et Auteurs Québecois, 1965-70. Dist. commr. Ottawa Assn. Scouts du Can., 1979—. Recipient Prix Raymond Casgrain, 1967. Can. Council research grantee, 1960-61, 67, 69, 70, 79-80. Fellow Royal Soc. Can.; mem. Canadian Hist. Assn. (v.p. 1979-80), Quebec Hist. Soc., Institut d'Histoire de l'Amérique française, Comité internat. d'historiens et de géographes de langue française (Quebec sect.), Multicultural History Soc. Ont. (trustee), Soc. Profs. Histoire du Quebec (founding pres. 1962-64). Roman Catholic. Author: Jules-Paul Tardivel, la France et les Etats-Unis, 1851-1905, 1967; Le Consulat général de France à

Québec et à Montréal de 1859 à 1914, 1970. Contbr. articles to scholarly jours. and chpts. to books. Office: Dept History U Ottawa Ottawa ON K1N 6N5 Canada

SAVARD, SERGE, hockey player; b. Montreal, Que., Can., Jan. 22, 1946. Hockey player with Montreal Canadiens, 1966—. Winner Conn Smythe trophy, 1969. Office: care Montreal Canadiens 2313 Saint Catherine St W Montreal PQ H3H 1N2 Canada*

SAVARYN, NEIL NICHOLAS, bishop; b. Stary Sambir, Ukraine, May 19, 1905; s. Wasyl and Anna (Sygerych) S.; classical and rhetorical studies, Lavriv, Ukraine, 1924; philos. studies, Dobromyl, 1927; theol. studies, Krystynopil, Ukraine, 1928; Canadian citizen, 1939. Entered Order of St. Basil the Great, 1922; ordained priest, 1931; aux. Bishop Ukrainian Cath. Diocese Toronto, 1943-48; bishop of Edmonton, Alta, Can., 1948—; missionary priest in Mundare, Chipman, St. Michael, Krakiv and Wostok, Alta., 1932—; prof. rhetoric and philosophy Basilian Fathers Monastery, Mundare, 1932—; superior Brasilian Fathers Monastery, 1938—. Address: 6240 Ada Blvd Edmonton AB T5W 4P1 Canada*

SAVAS, EMANUEL S., educator; b. N.Y.C., June 8, 1931; s. John and Olga (Limbos) S.; B.A., U. Chgo., 1951, B.S., 1953; M.A., Columbia U., 1956, Ph.D., 1960; m. Helen Andrew, Dec. 25, 1955; children—Jonathan, Stephen. Control systems cons. IBM, Yorktown Heights and White Plains, N.Y., 1959-65; urban systems mgr., N.Y.C., 1966-67; 1st dep. city adminstr. Office of Mayor of N.Y.C., 1967-72, chmn. Mayor's Urban Action Task Force, 1969-72; prof. public mgmt. Columbia U., N.Y.C., 1972—, dir. Center for Govt. Studies, 1973—, asso. dir. Center for Policy Research, 1973—; cons. NSF, Nat. Bur. Standards, 1973-76, Am. Paper Inst., 1976, Nat. Endowment for Arts, 1979, HUD, others; mem. U.S.-USSR Joint Working Group on Computers in Mgmt., 1972—; mem. voting bd. Blue Cross and Blue Shield Greater N.Y., 1976—. Cons. State Charter Revision Com. for N.Y.C., 1973-75; adv. Com. Econ. Devel., Work in Am. Inst.; bd. dirs. Central Park Community Fund, 1976—. Served with U.S. Army, 1953-54; Korea. Recipient Systems Sci. and Cybernetics award IEEE, 1968; Louis Brownlow award Am. Soc. Public Adminstrn., 1970. Mem. AAAS, Ops. Research Soc. Am., Inst. Mgmt. Scis. (rep. to AAAS 1977—), Urban and Regional Info. Systems Assn., Sigma Xi, Psi Upsilon. Greek Orthodox. Club: City of N.Y. (trustee 1974-77). Author: Computer Control of Industrial Processes, 1965; Organization and Efficiency of Solid Waste Collection, 1977; asso. editor Mgmt. Sci.; editor Alternatives for Delivering Public Services, 1977; editorial bd. Urban Affairs Quar.; contbr. over 50 articles in field to profl. jours. Office: Columbia U New York NY 10027

SAVEDOFF, MALCOLM PAUL, educator; b. N.Y.C., July 4, 1928; s. William Marcus and Celia (Goodman) S.; A.B., Harvard, 1948; M.S., Princeton, 1950, Ph.D., 1951; m. Roberta Rosslyn Lazoff, Aug. 29, 1948; children—Allen Martin, Barbara Elissa, William David. NRC fellow Cal. Inst. Tech., 1951-52; NSF postdoctoral fellow Leiden Obs., 1952-53; mem. faculty U. Rochester, 1953—, prof. astronomy, 1964—, dir. Mees Obs., 1964. Pres., Rochester Bur. Jewish Edn., 1972-74. Alfred P. Sloane fellow, 1956-59; NSF sr. postdoctoral fellow, Leiden, 1964-65. Mem. Am. Astron. Soc., A.A.A.S., Am. Phys. Soc., Royal Astron. Soc., Internat. Astron. Union, Phi Beta Kappa, Sigma Xi. Jewish religion (trustee temple 1967—, chmn. edn. com. 1969-71). Home: 10 Cranston Rd Pittsford NY 14534 Office: Dept Physics and Astronomy Univ Rochester Rochester NY 14627

SAVELL, EDWARD LUPO, lawyer; b. Atlanta, Apr. 29, 1921; s. Leon M. and Lillian (Lupo) S.; B.B.A., Emory U., 1947, LL.B., 1949; m. Bettie Patterson Hoyt, Oct. 11, 1944; 1 dau., Mary Lillian Savell Clarke. Admitted to Ga. bar, 1948; practiced law, Atlanta, 1948-53; partner firm Savell, Williams, Cox and Angel and predecessors, Atlanta, 1953—. Served with USAF, 1942-45; CBI. Fellow Internat. Acad. Trial Lawyers (pres. 1978—, dean of acad. 1976); mem. Atlanta (sec.-treas. 1953-54), Am. bar assns., State Bar Ga., Ga. Def. Lawyers Assn. (v.p.), Internat. Assn. Ins. Counsel, Atlanta Claims Assn., Chi Phi, Phi Delta Phi. Presbyterian. Clubs: Cherokee Town and Country, Commerce, Univ. Yacht, Lawyers of Atlanta. Contbr. articles to legal jours. Home: 4350 E Conway Dr Atlanta GA 30327 Office: 2300 Equitable Bldg 100 Peachtree St Atlanta GA 30303

SAVELLI, ANGELO, artist; b. Pizzo Calabria, Italy, Oct. 30, 1911; s. Giorgio and Maria (Barone) S.; student Ginnasio Vibo Valentia, C.Z., 1928, Maturita Artistica Liceo Artistico, Rome, 1932; diploma Acad. di Belle Arti, Rome, 1936; m. Elizabeth Fisher Friedman, Jan. 10, 1953; 1 stepdau., Ellen; came to U.S., 1954. One man shows include: Galleria Roma, 1941, Galleria Cairola, Genoa, Italy, 1942, Galleria del Naviglio, Milan, Italy, 1947, 54, 61, Centre d'Art Itallienne, Paris, 1952, The Contemporaries, N.Y.C., 1955, Castelli Gallery, N.Y.C., 1958, Galleria del Cavallino, Venice, Italy, 1958, Tweed Gallery, U. Minn., Duluth, Minn., 1960, Peter Deitsch Gallery, N.Y.C., 1962, Art Alliance, Phila., 1963, D'Arcy Galleries, N.Y.C., 1963, XXXII Internat. Biennale, Venice, 1964, Henri Gallery, Washington, 1969, also Peale Galleries, Phila., 1969; group shows include: Quadriennale di Roma, 1943, 49, 60, Biennale of Venice, 1950, 52, 64, Castellie Gallery, 1957, 58, Balt. Mus. Art Gallery, 1957, De Cordova Mus., Lincoln, Mass., 1963, White Chapel Gallery, London, 1963, Musele des Arts Deocratives, Paris, 1963, Bklyn. Mus., 1957, 60, 62, 64, 66, Library of Congress, 1959, 63, 66, U.S.A. Cultural Exchange in 5 Russian Cities, 1963, Whitney Rev., 1965, 66, Whitney Mus. Ann., 1966, Internat. Graphic Show, Lubiana, Yugoslavia, 1964, Janis Gallery, N.Y.C., 1964, Jewish Mus., N.Y.C., 1964, Internat. de Gravure, Tokyo, 1964, Mus. Modern Art, 1966, 67, Galleria Naz. D'Arte Moderna, Rome, Museo Civico, Phila. Mus. Art, 1966, Everson Mus., Syracuse, N.Y., 1972, Weed Mus. Art, Duluth, 1973, Hutchinson Gallery, N.Y.C., 1978, Parsons-Dreyfuss Gallery, N.Y.C., 1978; represented in permanent collections: Torino, Italy, Mus. Modern Art, Cin. Mus. Art, Tweed Gallery, Rosenwald Collection, Nelson Rockefeller Collection, Arnold Maremont Collection, Chrysler Mus., Provincetown, Mass., N.Y. Public Library, Art Mus., Helsinki, Finland, Victoria and Albert Mus., London, Phila. Mus. Art, Nat. Collection Fine Arts, Smithsonian Instn.; instr. Collegio Nazionale, Rome, 1939-40, Liceo Artistico, Rome, 1940, 43, 48, 54, Scarsdale (N.Y.) Workshop, 1957-60, New Sch. Social Research, 1959-65; asso. prof. fine arts Grad. Sch. Fine Arts, U. Pa., 1960—. Fellowship for study in Paris, 1948. Recipient grand prize per L'Incisione, XXXII Venice Biennale, 1964. Office: c/o Max Hutchinson Gallery 127 Greene St New York NY 10012*

SAVILE, DOUGLAS BARTON OSBORNE, mycologist, botanist; b. Dublin, Ireland, July 19, 1909; s. Hugh Osborne and Kathleen Elizabeth (Barton) S.; came to Can., 1928, naturalized, 1930; student Weymouth (Eng.) Coll., 1923-27; Dip. Agr., McGill U., 1930, B.S. in Agr., 1933, M.S., 1934, D.Sc. (hon.), 1978; Ph.D., U. Mich., 1939; m. Constance E. Cole, July 29, 1939; children—Harold Alan, Mary Elizabeth Savile Rhodes. Student asst. Can. Dept. Agr., Ottawa, Ont., 1932-38, asst. plant pathologist, 1939-48, prin. research scientist in mycology, 1967-74, research asso. emeritus, 1974—; cons. tropic-proofing, optical instruments, 1943-45. Served with RCAF, 1941-43. Fellow Arctic Inst. N. Am., AAAS, Royal Soc. Can.; mem. Mycol. Soc. Am., Can. Bot. Assn. (Lawson medal 1977), Soc. Study of Evolution, Am. Soc. Plant Taxonomy, Internat. Assn. Plant Taxonomy, Am. Orinthol. Union, Can. Phytopath. Soc. Author: Collection and Care of Botanical Specimens, 1962; Arctic Adaptations in Plants, 1972, 74; contbr. articles on mycology, botany, bird flight to profl. jours. Home: 357 Hinton Ave S Ottawa ON K1Y 1A6 Canada Office: Biosystematics Research Inst Saunders Bldg Central Exptl Farm Ottawa ON K1A 0C6 Canada

SAVILLE, LLOYD (BLACKSTONE), economist; b. N.Y.C., Oct. 13, 1913; s. Harry Stetson and Sophia Adele (Lloyd) S.; A.B., U. Pa., 1935; A.M., Columbia U., 1936, Ph.D., 1950; m. Eugenia Turk Curtis, July 13, 1932; children—Curtis Lloyd, Lynn Adele. Process control ops. staff mem. Standard Oil Co. N.J., Elizabeth, 1933-42; bus. economist Office Price Adminstrn., Washington, 1942-46; asst. prof. economics Duke U., Durham, N.C., 1946-51, asso. prof., 1959-57, prof., 1957-79, prof. emeritus, 1979—. Served with USNR, 1943-46. Faculty fellow Duke U., 1954-55; Guggenheim fellow, 1959; Fulbright lectr., Turin, Italy, 1959-60; Ford Found. fellow, 1962-63. Mem. Am., So. economic assns., Economic History Assn., Am. Statis. Assn., Royal Economic Soc., AAUP. Democrat. Author: Regional Economic Development in Italy, 1967; contbr. numerous articles to Am. and European economic jours. Home: 1103 Anderson St Durham NC 27705 Office: Dept Economics Duke U Durham NC 27706

SAVILLE, THORNDIKE, JR., hydraulic engr.; b. Balt., Aug. 1, 1925; s. Thorndike and Edith Stedman (Wilson) S.; A.B., Harvard, 1947; M.S., U. Calif. at Berkeley, 1949; m. Janet Foster, Aug. 28, 1950; children—Sarah, Jennifer, Gordon. Research asst. U. Calif. at Berkeley, 1947-49; hydraulic engr. Beach Erosion Bd. and Coastal Engring. Research Center, Ft. Belvoir, Va., 1949—, chief research div., 1964-71, tech. dir., 1971—. Served with USAAF, 1943-46. Fellow AAAS, Wash. Acad. Scis., ASCE; mem. Am. Geophys. Union, Internat. Assn. for Hydraulic Research, Nat. Acad. Engring., Permanent Internat. Assn. Navigation Congresses. Author numerous papers in engring. and sci. lit. Home: 5601 Albia Rd Washington DC 20016 Office: Kingman Bldg Ft Belvoir VA 22060

SAVIN, SAMUEL MARVIN, geologist; b. Boston, Aug. 31, 1940; s. George and Sarah (Lewiton) S.; B.A., Colgate U., 1961; Ph.D., Calif. Inst. Tech., 1967; m. Norma Goulder, Nov. 4, 1978. Asst. prof. earth scis. Case Western Res. U., Cleve., 1967-73, asso. prof., 1973-76, prof., 1976—, dept. chmn., 1977—; industry fellow Marathon Oil Co., Denver, 1976; mem. adv. panel earth scis. NSF, 1978—. Mem. Geol. Soc. Am., Am. Geophys. Union, Clay Minerals Soc. (councillor 1978—), Nat. Assn. Geology Tchrs., No. Ohio Geol. Soc., AAAS. Asso. editor Geochimica et Cosmochimica Acta, 1976-79, Marine Micropaleontology, 1979—; contbr articles to sci. jours. Home: 11430 Cedar Glen Pkwy Cleveland OH 44106 Office: Dept Earth Scis Case Western Res U Cleveland OH 44106

SAVINELLI, EMILIO ALFRED, chem. co. exec.; b. May 7, 1930; s. Alfred and Philomena (Baffino) S.; B.C.E., Manhattan Coll., 1950; M.San. Engring., U. Fla., 1951, Ph.D. in Chemistry, 1955; postgrad. U. Ill., 1956; m. Margaret Brennan; children—Alfred, Catherine, Mary Patricia, Peter, Nina, Steven, Elizabeth, Christopher. Engr., DuPont Co., Wilmington, Del., 1956-60; with Drew Chem. Co., Parsippany, N.J., 1960-62, research dir., 1962-68, div. mgr., v.p., 1968-71, pres., 1971-79; pres. The Perolin Co., Inc., Wilton, Conn., 1979—; dir. Buck Engring. Co. Inc.; lectr., condr. seminars on chemistry of water and waste treatment. Trustee Riverside (N.J.) Hosp., 1977—; trustee Hope House, Dover, N.J., 1977—, pres., 1977-79; bd. mgrs. Family Service of Morris County (N.J.), 1977—, pres., 1977-79. Registered profl. engr., Del. Mem. ASME, Am. Chem. Soc., Am. Mgmt. Assn., Sigma Xi, Alpha Chi Sigma. Club: Mountain Lakes. Contbr. articles on water treatment; patentee in field. Home: 33 Laurel Hill Rd Mountain Lakes NJ 07046 Office: 84 Danbury Rd Wilton CT 06897

SAVINI-BRIONI, GAETANO, high fashion design exec.; b. Terni, Italy, Sept. 10, 1909; s. Godfredo and Viclinda (Mazzola) S.; ed. Tech. Instn., Rome, Italy; m. Eleonora Palombi, Apr. 20, 1940; 1 dau., Gigliola (Mrs. Ettore Perrone). Founder, Brioni Menswear, Rome, 1944, now chmn. Served with Armed Forces, 1931-32. Recipient numerous recognitions and awards. Lion. Home: 156 via Archimede Rome Italy 00197 Office: 79 via Barberini Rome 00186 Italy

SAVIT, CARL HERTZ, geophysicist; b. N.Y.C., July 19, 1922; B.S. with honors, Calif. Inst. Tech., 1942, M.S., 1943, postgrad., 1943-44, 46-48; m. Sandra Kaplan, July 6, 1946; children—Mark, Deborah Savit Pearlman, Judith. Statis. cons. Long Range Meteorology Project, U.S. Air Force, 1943-44; asso. prof. math. San Fernando Valley State Coll., Northridge, Calif., 1959-60; chief math. Western Geophys. Co., Litton Industries, Inc., 1948-60, dir. systems research, 1960-65, v.p. research and devel., 1965-70, sr. v.p. tech., 1971—; asst. for earth, sea, air sci. to U.S. Pres.'s Sci. Adv.; chmn. Interagy Com. for Atmospheric Scis., 1970-71; mem. panel On-Site Inspection Unidentified Seismic Events, 1961; mem. Pres.'s panels on Disposition of Oil Leasing in the Santa Barbara Channel, Offshore Pollution, 1969; mem. U.S. Initiatives in Transp., 1971; mem. U.S. del. to USSR, 1971; mem. Assembly Math. and Phys. Scis., Nat. Acad. Scis./NRC, 1977—; mem. com. on seismology Nat. Acad. Scis./NRC, 1971-75, chmn. 1972-74, mem. U.S. nat. com. on tunneling, 1972-75, chmn. subcom. on tech. data and info., 1972-75, mem. panel on earthquake prediction, 1973-75; dir. Nat. Ocean Industries, Assn., vice chmn. bd., 1973-75, chmn. bd., 1975-76; mem. nat. adv. com. Tex. Marine Biomed. Inst., 1973-78; mem. U.S. Coastal Zone Mgmt. Adv. Com., 1975-78; mem. energy research adv. bd. U.S. Dept. Energy, 1978—, chmn. com. on geothermal energy, 1979—. Served as 2d lt. USAAF, 1944-46. Fellow Geol. Soc. Am.; mem. Assn. Earth Sci. Editor, European Assn. Exploration Geophysicists, Asociacion Mexicana de Geofisicos de Exploracion, Marine Tech. Soc. (Compass award for disting. achievement 1979), Soc. Exploration Geophysicists (named Classic Author of Geophysics 1960, editor jour. 1967-69, pres. 1971-72, chmn. 43d ann. meeting 1973, Kaufman gold medal 1979), Am. Mgmt. Assn. (mem. research and devel. council 1974-76), Internat. Assn. Geophys. Contractors (pres. 1973-75), Sigma Xi. Club: Cosmos (Washington). Contbr. articles to profl. jours. Patentee in field. Address: 13626 Tosca Ln Houston TX 77079. *Life is made up of a set of contests, each with its own rules. Our satisfaction is greatest if we enter only those whose rules give us a chance to win.*

SAVITCH, JESSICA, television news corr.; b. Kennett Square, Pa.; B.S., Ithaca Coll., 1968. Researcher, Sta. WCBS-Newsradio, N.Y.C., 1969-70; with Sta. KHOU-TV, Houston, 1970-72; gen. assignment reporter, anchor Sta. KYW-TV, Phila., 1972-73, weekend anchor, 1973-74, co-anchor Eyewitness News, 1976-77; corr. NBC News, N.Y.C., 1977—, anchor NBC Nightly News, Sunday edit. Recipient Clarion award for documentary, 1974; Broadcast Media Conf. award, Woman in Communications award, 1977. Office: care NBC News 30 Rockefeller Plaza New York NY 10020

SAVITT, SIDNEY ALLAN, chem. engr.; b. Bklyn., Apr. 14, 1920; s. Joseph and Rose (Smerin) S.; B.S., CCNY, 1940; M.Ch.E., Poly. Inst. N.Y., 1945, D.Ch.E., 1948; m. Malvina Meister, Sept. 15, 1946; children—Jill Alison, Brad Marshall, Hope Risa, Wade Manson. Process engr. M.W. Kellogg Co., N.Y.C., 1947-49; tech. dir. Consol. Products Corp., N.Y.C., 1949-53; pres., dir. engring. S. A. Savitt Assos., Clark, N.J., 1953—; lectr. on energy, environ. and pollution control. Pres. YMHA, Union, N.J., 1974; v.p. N.J. Fedn. YMHA's, 1973-75; exec. dir. Am. Inst. City N.Y., 1976—. Registered profl. engr., N.J. Fellow Am. Inst. Chemists, N.Y. Acad. Scis. (vice chmn. engring. 1967-68, chmn. ednl. adv. com. 1969-72, chmn. engring. sect. 1968-70, bd. govs. 1971-73); mem. Am. Inst. Chem. Engrs., ASME, Assn. Cons. Chemists and Chem. Engrs. (council dir. 1978—), Am. Soc. Engring. Edn., N.J. Soc. Profl. Engrs., Am. Chem. Soc., AAAS, Alumni Assn. Poly. Inst. N.Y. (sec. 1979), Sigma Xi, Phi Lambda Upsilon. Clubs: Rotary (Clark); B'nai B'rith (pres. local club 1973) (Linden, N.J.). Contbr. articles to profl. jours.; reviewer for profl. jours.; spl. research in extractive metallurgy of strategic alloys and separation and recovery of precious metals; research and devel. in energy conservation of chem. process plants; designer chem. plants, pilot plants and processes for numerous corps., colls., 1945—. Home: 1050 George St New Brunswick NJ 08901 Office: 287 Central Ave Clark NJ 07066

SAVITZ, GERALD SAMUEL, pharm. co. exec.; b. Easton, Pa.; s. Samuel and Helen (Hoch) S.; Ph.G., Phila. Coll. Pharmacy and Sci., 1934, B.S., 1938; M.D. (Pharmacol), Med. Coll. S.C., 1939; D. Psychiatry, 1975. Med. dir. S.E. Massengill Co., Bristol, Tenn., 1939-42; with Merck & Co., Rahway, N.J., 1942-56, asst. mgr. pharm. div., 1942-46, mgr. pharm. div., 1946-54, asso. dir. marketing, 1954-56; research adminstrn. dir. tech. info. dept. Merck Sharp & Dohme Research Labs., Rahway, N.J. and West Point, Pa., 1956-60; drug and med. cons., N.Y.C., 1960-66; founder Found. Med. Information Mass., 1966-67, also dir.; pres. FMI Drug Data, Inc, N.Y.C., 1967-68, also chmn.; library sci. and pharm. adviser Govt. of Libya, 1968-70; tchr. library sci. govt. of Libya Tripoli & Benghazi, 1968-69; internat. pharm. cons.; exec. dir. Center for Internat. Biomed. Info., N.Y.C., 1971-72, Largo, Fla., 1973-77, Clearwater, Fla., 1977—; affiliate Nat. Inst. Drug Abuse-Dracon Network, 1976; dir. human resource devel. ABILITIES, Inc., Clearwater, 1979; pub., editor Hotline on Am. Drugs, 1972—. Faculty, Phila. Coll. Pharmacy and Sci., 1934-38, econs. and pharmacy Med. Coll. S.C., 1939, U.S. Med. Tng. Acad., St. Petersburg, Fla., 1973—; dir. continuing profl. edn. Med. Edn. Center, St. Petersburg, 1974—; spl. lectr. psychology St. Petersburg Jr. Coll.-Clearwater Campus, 1973—. Ordained to ministry Calvary Grace Ch. and Bible Inst., 1974. Recipient Outstanding Service award, Bur. Medicine & Surgery, U.S. Armed Forces, 1946; Outstanding Service award Libyan Govt., 1969. Fellow Am. Inst. Chemists; mem. Drug Information Assn., Am. Chem. Soc., AAAS, Info. Industry, Inc., Am. Soc. Info. Sci., Library Assn. London, Fedn. Internationale Pharmaceutique-Holland. Author numerous papers in field. Home: PO Box 1538 Largo FL 33540

SAVOCA, CARMEN SALVATORE, opera dir.; b. Bklyn., Sept. 27, 1924; s. Santo and Carlotta (Armena) S.; student Phila. Mus. Acad., 1946-50. Co-founder Tri-Cities Opera Co., Binghamton, N.Y., 1949, stage dir., vocal tchr., 1949—, also bd. dirs.; dir. opera dept. Deerwood Music Center, 1950; stage dir. Garden State Opera, 1951, Scranton Opera, 1953; producer, dir., singer world premiere Myron Fink's Jeremiah, 1962; participant Title Three Tour, 1963-66; stage dir. Elmira Opera, 1963-66; dir., singer, cons. High-Tor Opera Co., 1964-65; stage dir. N.Y.C. Opera, dir. Chautauqua, 1965, Wichita Opera, 1969-72, Oklahoma City Opera, 1973, Ariz. Opera, 1977, Edmonton (Alta., Can.) Opera Assn., 1977; cons. N.Y. State Council on Arts, 1963—. Served with USAAF, 1943-46. Decorated Bronze Star. Mem. Central Opera Service, Opera Am. Home: 79 Main St Binghamton NY 13905 Office: Tri-Cities Opera 315 Clinton St Binghamton NY 13905

SAVOIE, LEONARD NORMAN, transp. co. exec.; b. Manchester, N.H., Aug. 8, 1928; s. Joseph Peter and Angelina (Desmarais) S.; B.S., Queen's U., 1952; M.B.A., U. Detroit, 1955; m. Elsie Anne Berscht, June 9, 1951; children—Deborah Anne, Judith Lynn, Andrew Peter. Indsl. engr. Kelsey-Hayes Can. Ltd., Windsor, Ont., Can., 1952-60; mgmt. cons. P.S. Ross & Partners, Toronto, Ont., 1960-64; pres., gen. mgr. Kelsey-Hayes Can. Ltd., 1964-70; pres., chief exec. officer Algoma Central Ry., Sault Ste. Marie, Ont., 1970—; dir. Can. Gen. Ins. Co., Casualty Co. Can., E-L Fin. Corp. Ltd., Empire Life Ins. Co., Algoma Steel Corp., Ltd., All Canadian-Am. Investments Ltd., Herb Fraser & Assos. United, Thibodeau-Finch Express Ltd., Newaygo Forest Products Ltd. Bd. dirs. United Appeal. Mem. Profl. Engrs. Ont., Engring. Inst. Can., Canadian, Sault Ste. Marie chambers commerce. Clubs: Rotary, Toronto, Toronto Ry., Sault Ste. Marie Golf. Home: 19 Atlas St Sault Ste Marie ON Canada Office: 289 Bay St Sault Ste Marie ON Canada

SAVOIE, ROBERT ELLIS, elec. engr.; b. Port Arthur, Tex., Jan. 15, 1944; s. Rudolph Clifford and Mary Alice (Carney) S.; B.A., Rice U., 1966, B.E.E., 1967; M.E.E. (NSF fellow), Stanford U., 1968, Ph.D., 1972; m. Polly Ann Nash, Apr. 18, 1977; children—Matthew Holmes, Kristin Joy. Research engr. Stanford Research Inst., Menlo Park, Calif., 1971-74; mgr. research and devel. dept. Telesensory Systems, Inc., Palo Alto, Calif., 1974—. NIH, NSF grantee. Mem. IEEE, Optical Soc. Am., Phi Beta Kappa, Tau Beta Pi, Sigma Tau. Patentee signature verification and character recognition devices; prin. investigator OCR-speech output reading machine for blind. Home: 2150 Birch St Palo Alto CA 94306 Office: 3408 Hillview Ave Palo Alto CA 94304

SAVORY, ROGER MERVYN, educator; b. Peterborough, Eng., Jan. 27, 1925; s. Henry and Kathleen (Winterton) S.; B.A. Oxford U., 1950; Ph.D., U. London, 1958; m. Kathleen Mary Plummer, Mar. 27, 1951; children—Jill Elizabeth, Julian Roger. Lectr. Persian, U. London Sch. Oriental and African Studies, 1950-60; asso. prof. Islamic studies, U. Toronto, 1960-65, prof., asso. chmn., 1965-68, prof., 1968—, chmn., 1968-73. Served with Brit. Army, 1943-47. Fellow Royal Soc. Can.; mem. Middle East Studies Assn. North Am. (dir. 1969-71, v.p. 1973), Oxford Soc., Can. Inst. Internat. Affairs, Brit. Inst. Persian Studies, Middle East Studies Assn. North Am., Royal Soc. Can. Anglican. Editorial sec. new edn. Encyclopaedia of Islam, 1954-60. Home: 55 Mason Blvd Toronto ON M5M 3C6 Canada

SAVOY, DOUGLAS EUGENE, explorer, writer; b. Bellingham, Wash., May 11, 1927; s. Lewis Dell and Maymie (Janett) S.; student U. Portland; m. Elvira Clarke, Dec. 5, 1957 (div.); 1 son, Jamil Sean (dec.); m. 2d, Sylvia Ontaneda, July 7, 1971; children—Douglas Eugene, Christopher Sean, Sylvia Jamila. Engaged in newspaper publishing, West Coast, 1949-56; began explorations in jungles east of Andes in Peru to prove his theory that high civilizations of Peru may have had their origin in jungles, 1967; pres., founder Andean Explorers Club, Found., Reno; discoverer lost city of Incas at Vilcabamba Cuzco; discovered numerous ancient cities in Amazonia, including Gran Pajaten, Monte Peruvia, Twelve Cities of the Condors; field dir. Archaeol. Soc. Amazonas; internat. rep. Tourist Soc. Amazonas. Trustee Trust Internat. Community of Christ. Served with AS, USNR, 1944-46. Mem. Geog. Soc. Lima, Authors Guild. Clubs: Explorers (N.Y.C.); Singing River Yacht. Author: Antisuyo, The Search for Lost Cities of the High Amazon, 1970; Vilcabamba, Last City of the Incas, 1970; The Cosolargy Papers, vol. 1, 1970, vol. 2-3, 1972; The Child Christ, 1973; The Decoded New Testament, 1974;

On The Trail of The Feathered Serpent, 1974; Code Book and Community Manual for Overseers, 1975; Prophecies of Jamil, Vol. 1, 1976, Vol. 2, 1976; The Image and The Word, 1976; Project X—The Search For the Secrets of Immortality, 1977; Prophecy to the Races of Man, 1977; Solar Cultures of The Americas, 1977; The Essaei Documents: Secrets of an External Race, 1978; The Lost Gospel of Jesus: Hidden Teachings of Christ, 1978; Prophecy to The Christian Churches, 1978; The Sayings, 1979; Prophecy of The End Times, 1979, numerous others. Contbr. articles on Peruvian cultures to mags., also articles on philosophy and religion. Home: 2025 La Fond Reno NV 89509 Office: 643 Ralston St Reno NV 89503

SAVRIN, LOUIS, lawyer; b. Phila., Jan. 20, 1927; s. William Philip and Anna (Sass) S.; B.S., N.Y. U., 1948; J.D., U. Pa., 1951; m. Barbara J. Schwimmer, Jan. 16, 1954; children—Jonathan Eric, Philip Wade, Daniel Scott. Admitted to N.Y. bar, 1952; atty. tax dept. Arthur Young & Co., C.P.A.'s, N.Y.C., 1951-55; pvt. practice, N.Y.C., 1955—; gen. counsel, sec. Pickwick Internat., Inc., N.Y.C., 1965-77. Mem. sch. bd. Dist. #21, Bklyn., 1962-68. Bd. dirs. Bklyn. Assn. Mental Health. Served with AUS, 1945-46. Mem. N.Y. State Bar Assn., N.Y. County Lawyers Assn., Real Estate Tax Rev. Bar Assn. Mason; mem. B'nai B'rith (pres. lodge 1957-59; named to lodge Hall of Fame 1967). Asso. editor U. Pa. Law Rev., 1949-51. Home: 2354 81st St Brooklyn NY 11214 Office: 60 E 42d St New York NY 10017

SAWABINI, WADI ISSA, dentist; b. Jaffa, Palestine, Jan. 14, 1917; s. Issa J. and Julia C. (Malak) S.; student College des Ecoles Chrétiennes, 1924-32; D.D.S., Am. U. Beirut, 1940; m. Harriet Colgate Abbe Lack, Aug. 6, 1949; children—Wadi' Issa, Frederick Lack, Stuart John, Julia Malak. Grad. study Forsyth Dental Infirmary, 1940-41; intern Med. Center Hosp. Vt. (formerly DeGoesbriand Meml. Hosp.), Burlington, 1941-42, now attending staff; asso. pvt. practice Dr. Charles I. Taggart, 1942-51, pvt. practice, Burlington, Vt., 1951—; instr. oral pathology U. Vt., 1951-58, dir. Sch. Dental Hygiene, 1953-72, asst. prof. oral hygiene Coll. Medicine, 1958—; chief dental staff Mary Fletcher Hosp., 1958-68, asso. prof. dept. allied health scis., 1969-72. Mem. adv. bd. Vt. Pub. Health Dept. Vice pres. bd. dirs. Overlake Day Sch., 1962-63. Fellow Internat. Coll. Dentists (mem. exec. council 1950-54), Am. Coll. Dentists; mem. Vt. (pres. 1956-57, mem. bd. rev.; Distinguished Service award 1972), New Eng., Champlain Valley dental socs., C. of C., Am. Dental Assn., Fedn. Dentaire Internat. Republican. Episcopalian (vestryman). Mason (Shriner). Clubs: Rotary (dir. 1955-56, pres. 1961-62), Ethan Allen (Burlington). Home: 25 South St Burlington VT 05401 Office: 42 Colchester Ave Burlington VT 05401

SAWARD, ERNEST WELTON, physician; b. N.Y.C., Oct. 19, 1914; s. Ernest Welton and Alice Virginia (Knorr) S.; A.B., Colgate U., 1936; M.D., U. Rochester, 1939; m. Carmen Virginia Wagner, Sept. 1, 1938; children—Thomas Welton, Susan Virginia, Lawrence Ernest. Med. house officer Barnes Hosp., St. Louis, 1939-41; resident in medicine Peter Bent Brigham Hosp., Boston, 1941-42; practice internal medicine Permanente Clinic, Portland, Oreg., 1945-70; chief medicine Hanford (Wash.) Engring. Works, 1943-45; med. dir. Permanente Clinic, Kaiser Found. Hosps. and Kaiser Found. Health Plan, Portland, Oreg., 1945-70; prof. social medicine U. Rochester (N.Y.), 1970—, asso. dean for extramural affairs, 1970—; vis. prof. medicine and preventive medicine and community health Stanford U., 1978-79; sr. fellow Center for Advanced Study in Behavioral Scis., Stanford, Calif., 1978-79; mem. exec. com. Community Health Found. Med. Group, Cleve., 1964-70; project dir. Office of Econ. Opportunity Health Project, Kaiser Found., Portland, Oreg., 1966-70; pres. bd. trustees Group Health Found., 1971; chmn. Health Ins. Benefits Adv. Council, 1972-74; chmn. Nat. Profl. Standards Rev. Council, 1973-76, Monroe Community Hosp., 1973-76, N.Y. State Health Adv. Council, 1975-76; 1st vice chmn. Finger Lakes Health Systems Agy., 1975—; chmn. vis. com. to bd. overseers Harvard U. Health Services, 1975—; mem. Nat. Health Ins. Council, HEW, 1977—, N.Y. State Hosp. Rev. and Planning Council, 1976—; mem. bd. medicine Nat. Acad. Scis., 1967-70, mem. council Inst. Medicine, 1970-73; bd. dirs. Kaiser Found. Research Inst., 1967—; chmn. bd. dirs. Group Health Assn. Am., Xerox Center for Health Care Research, 1971-75; mem. tech. bd. Milbank Meml. Fund, 1972—, Health Ins. Plan Greater N.Y., 1972-73, Milbank Meml. Fund Health Soc., 1973-76. Recipient Distinguished Service award Group Health Assn. Am. 1976. Diplomate Am. Bd. Internal Medicine. Mem. AMA, Am. Coll. Chest Physicians, AAAS, Am. Coll. Preventive Medicine, Assn. Tchrs. Preventive Medicine, Royal Soc. Health. Contbr. articles to profl. jours. Home: 134 Stoneleigh Ct Rochester NY 14618 Office: U Rochester 601 Elmwood Ave Rochester NY 14642

SAWHILL, ISABEL VAN DEVANTER, economist; b. Washington, Apr. 2, 1937; d. Winslow B. and Isabel E. Van Devanter; B.A., N.Y. U., 1962, Ph.D., 1968; m. John C. Sawhill, Sept. 13, 1958; 1 son, James W. Policy analyst Office Sec. HEW, 1968-69, Office Mgmt. and Budget, 1969-70; asst. prof. econs. Goucher Coll., Balt., 1969-73, chmn. dept., 1971-73; sr. research asso. Urban Inst., 1973-77, program dir., 1975-77; dir. Nat. Commn. Employment Policy, Washington, 1977—. Mem. Am. Econ. Assn., Phi Beta Kappa. Co-author: Time of Transition: The Growth of Families Headed by Women, 1975; contbr. articles profl. publns. Office: 1522 K St Washington DC 20005

SAWHILL, JOHN CRITTENDEN, govt. ofcl.; b. Cleve., June 12, 1936; B.A., Princeton U., 1958; Ph.D., N.Y. U., 1963. With Merrill Lynch, Pierce, Fenner & Smith, Washington, 1958-60; asso. dean Sch. Bus. Adminstrn., N.Y. U., 1960-63; dir. credit research Comml. Credit Corp., Balt., 1963-65, sr. v.p., 1968-73; sr. asso. McKinsey and Co., mgmt. cons., Washington, 1965-68; asso. dir. Office Mgmt. Natural Resources, Energy and Sci., 1973-74; dep. adminstr., then adminstr. Fed. Energy Adminstrn., 1974; pres. N.Y. U., 1975-79; dep. sec. energy Dept. Energy, 1979—. Address: Office Dep Sec Dept Energy 1000 Independence Ave Washinton DC 20585

SAWIN, ALTON, JR., univ. dean; b. Gardner, Mass., Dec. 16, 1921; s. Alton and Irene H. (Smith) S.; A.B., Norwich U., Northfield, Vt., 1943; student U. Mich., 1947-50, U. N.H., 1953; m. Eugenia Stanford, July 1, 1945; children—Patricia Ann, Margaret Ann, Robert Stanford. Tchr. biology and math., dir. guidance, also admissions officer Tilton (N.H.) Sch., 1945-56; dir. admissions Coll. Liberal Arts, Drew U., 1956-60, dir. admissions, dean students, 1960-66, dean students, 1966—. Instl. rep. Coll. Entrance Exam. Bd., Coll. Scholarship Service, Latin Am. Scholarship Program of Am. Univs., Eastern Assn. Student Fin. Aid Adminstrs. Pres. Madison chpt. Am. Field Service, 1965-68; pres. Madison Jr. Sch. PTA, 1966-67; bd. dirs. Madison Area YMCA, 1974—, v.p., 1975—. Served with AUS, 1943-45; ETO. Decorated D.S.C., Purple Heart. Mem. Assn. Coll. Admissions Counselors (pres. N.J. 1967-68), N.J. Assn. Student Fin. Aid (chmn. certification com. 1977—). Methodist (ofcl. bd. 1958—). Mason, Rotarian. Clubs: Madison (pres. 1967-68), Madison Golf (pres. 1973—). Home: 3 Campus Dr Madison NJ 07940

SAWIN, NANCY CHURCHMAN, educator, artist; b. Wilmington, Del., June 21, 1917; d. Sanford W. and Ellen (Quigley) Sawin; B.A., Principia Coll., 1938; M.A., U. Del., 1940; D.Ed., U. Pa., 1962. With Sanford Sch., Hockessin, Del., 1938-74, dean girls, 1945-62, head sch., 1962-74; coordinator student services U. Del. Div. Continuing Edn., Newark, 1974-77; ednl. cons. DuPont Co., ICI Ams. 1976—. Chmn., Del. State Sci. Fair com., 1962; mem. com. Jr. Sci. and Humanities Symposium, 1962—; mem. English, lang. arts adv. com. State Del., 1965-68; sec., dir. Recreation, Promotion and Service, Inc., 1963—. Exhibited one-person exhbns. Pres. bd. trustees Goldey Beacom Coll., 1973—; bd. dirs. Del. Safety Council, 1964—. mem. Wilmington Savs. Fund Soc. Mem. Headmistress Assn. East, Del. Art Mus., Rehoboth Art League, Middle Atlantic States Assn. Colls. and Secondary Schs. (past pres.), Commn. on Secondary Schs., Red Clay Creek Assn., Internat. Fedn. Women's Hockey Assns. (past pres.), U.S. (past pres.), Del. (past pres.) field hockey assns., Nat. League Am. Pen Women, Delta Kappa Gamma (past pres.), Pi Lambda Theta. Republican. Presbyterian (elder). Club: Quota (pres. Wilmington 1971-73, gov. 10th Dist. 1979-80). Editor: The Eagle, 1961-62; co-pub., illustrator: Delaware Sketch Book; Backroading through Cecil County, Md.; Man-o-War, My Island Home; R.F.D., Countryside Art; Between the Bays. Mem. All-Am. Hockey Team, 1948-59. Address: North Light Studio Route 1 Box 84 Hockessin DE 19707

SAWTELL, STEPHEN M., gas co. exec.; b. St. Paul, Jan. 17, 1931; s. William Amos and Helen Mary (Fiegenbaum) S.; student Northwestern U., 1948-50; B.Sc. in Law, U. Nebr., 1956, J.D., 1957; m. Helen Elizabeth Wencel, June 27, 1956; children—Stephen, Katherine H. Admitted to Neb. bar, 1957; atty. No. Natural Gas Co., Omaha, 1957-59, asst. sec., 1959-72, sec., 1972—, v.p., 1977—. Pres. Omaha Symphony Assn., 1969-71; bd. dirs. Jr. Achievement Omaha, 1961—, pres., 1975; bd. dirs. Omaha Sister City Assn., 1963—, pres., 1974—; mem. Omaha Com. on Fgn. Relations, 1959—, chmn., 1975; mem. adv. council on fine arts, adv. council on Afghanistan studies U. Nebr. at Omaha. Bd. dirs. Western Heritage Soc., Inc., 1978—; bd. dirs. Western Heritage Mus., Omaha, 1978—, v.p., 1979. Served with AUS, 1952-55. Named Omaha's Outstanding Young Man of Year, Omaha Jr. C. of C., 1963. Mem. Am. Soc. Corp. Secs. Conglist. Mason, Rotarian. Clubs: Omaha, Omaha Country Home: 702 Ridgewood Ave Omaha NE 68114 Office: 2223 Dodge St Omaha NE 68102

SAWYER, ALAN REED, author, educator, art cons.; b. Wakefield, Mass., June 18, 1919; s. John B. and Elinor (Clark) S.; B.S. in Geology, Bates Coll., 1941; studied painting Boston Mus. Fine Arts Sch., 1946-48; student Boston U., 1947, 48; M.A. in Art History, Harvard, 1949; D. Fine Arts, Bates Coll., 1969; m. Erika Heininger, November 10, 1945; children—Dana, Diane, Brian, Lynn, Carol. Instr. art dept. Tex. State Coll. for Women, 1949-52, curator of primitive art, 1949-52; asst. to the curator of decorative arts Art Inst. Chgo., 1952-54, asst. curator decorative arts, charge Early Americana, Pre-Columbian art, 1954-56, asso. curator charge primitive art, 1956-58, curator primitive art, 1958-59; dir. Textile Mus., Washington, 1959-71; author, art cons., 1971-74; vis. asso. prof. U. B.C. (Can.), Vancouver, 1974-75, prof., 1975—. Mem. U. Pa. Archeol. Expdn. to Bolivia, 1955; leader of Textile Mus. Archaeol. Expdn. to Peru, 1960; dir. Park Forest (Ill.) Art Center, 1956; group discussion leader Looking at Modern Art, Ford Found., Art Inst. Chgo., 1955-57, lectr. pub. lectures program, U. Chgo.-Art Inst., 1959; curator Master Craftsmen of Ancient Peru exhbn. Guggenheim Mus., 1964-68; adj. prof. art and archeology Columbia, 1968-69; lectr. Smithsonian Assos., 1970-73; guide Smithsonian Archaeol. Tours of Peru and Bolivia, 1973; dir. historic dimension program Norwegian Am. Lines S.S. Vistafjord, 1973. Served as 1st lt., 84th F.A. Bn., 9th Inf. Div., AUS, 1942-46. Decorated Air medal with 2 clusters, Silver Star medal, Purple Heart. Mem. Archeol. Inst. Am., Soc. Am. Archaeology, Inst. Andean Studies. Mason. Author: Handbook of the Nathan Cummings Collection of Ancient Peruvian Art, 1954; Animal Sculpture in Pre-Columbian Art, 1957; Ancient Peruvian Ceramics, 1966; Mastercraftsmen of Ancient Peru, 1968; Ancient Andean Arts, 1975. Home: 1799 W King Edward Ave Vancouver BC Canada Office: Dept Fine Arts University of BC Vancouver BC V6T 1W5 Canada

SAWYER, CHARLES HENRY, educator; b. Andover, Mass., Oct. 20, 1906; s. James Cowan and Mary Pepperrell (Frost) S.; B.A., Yale, 1929, M.A. (hon.), 1947; postgrad. Harvard Law Sch., 1929-30, Harvard Grad. Sch., 1930-32; D.F.A., U. N.H., 1952; D.H.L., Amherst Coll., 1950, Clark U., 1953; m. Katharine Clay, June 28, 1934. Curator, Addison Gallery Am. Art, instr. art and chmn. dept. Phillips Acad., Andover, 1930-40; dir. Worcester (Mass.) Art Mus., 1940-47, Worcester Mus. Sch., 1940-46; prof. (affiliate) fine arts Clark U., Worcester, 1942-47; dir. div. arts, dean Sch. Fine Arts, Yale, 1947-55, master Timothy Dwight Coll., 1947-53, dean Sch. Architecture and Design, 1955-56, prof. history art, 1947-56; prof. art, history of art U. Mich., 1957-75, dir. Univ. Mus. Art, 1957-72; Green Honors prof. Tex. Christian U., Fort Worth, 1973. Mem. Art Commn. Mass., 1942-45; chmn. commn. of fine arts Smithsonian Instn., 1968-71; trustee Corning Mus. of Glass, 1951-76; mem. council U. Notre Dame Art Gallery, 1973—. Served with AUS, 1943-45; asst. sec. Am. Commn. for Protection and Salvage Artistic and Historic Monuments in War Areas, 1945. Mem. Assn. Art Mus. Dirs., Am. Fedn. Arts (trustee 1942-55), Am. Assn. Museums, Am. Acad. Arts and Scis., Am. Antiquarian Soc. Club: Century Assn. (N.Y.). Home: 2 Highland Ln Ann Arbor MI 48104 Office: Dept History of Art Tappan Hall Univ Mich Ann Arbor MI 48109

SAWYER, CHARLES HENRY, anatomist, educator; b. Ludlow, Vt., Jan. 24, 1915; s. John Guy and Edith Mabel (Morgan) S.; B.A., Middlebury Coll., 1937, D.Sc. (h.c.), 1975; student Cambridge U., Eng., 1937-38; Ph.D., Yale, 1941; m. Ruth Eleanor Schaeffer, Aug. 23, 1941; 1 dau., Joan Eleanor. Instr. anatomy Stanford, 1941-44; asso., asst. prof., asso. prof., prof. anatomy Duke U., 1944-51; prof. anatomy U. Calif., Los Angeles, 1951—, chmn. dept., 1955-63, acting chmn., 1968-69, faculty research lectr., 1966-67. Mem. Internat. Brain Research Orgn. (council 1964-68), AAAS, Am. Assn. Anatomists (v.p. 1969-70), Am. Physiol. Soc., Am. Zool. Soc., Neurosci. Soc., Endocrine Soc. (council 1968-70, Koch award 1973), Am. Acad. Arts and Scis., Soc. Exptl. Biology and Medicine, Soc. Study Reprodn. (dir. 1969-71, Hartman award 1977), Internat. Neuroendocrine Soc. (council 1972-76), Hungarian Soc. Endocrinology and Metabolism (hon.), Phi Beta Kappa, Sigma Xi. Editorial bd. Endocrinology, 1955-59, Proc. Soc. Exptl. Biology and Medicine, 1959-63, Am. Jour. Physiology, 1972-75. Author papers on neuroendocrinology. Home: 466 Tuallitan Rd Los Angeles CA 90049

SAWYER, DONALD TURNER, educator, chemist; b. Pomona, Calif., Jan. 10, 1931; s. Donald T. and Lilas (Snider) S.; B.S., U. Calif. at Los Angeles, 1953, Ph.D., 1956; m. Shirley Grace Scott, June 21, 1952; children—Sharon Louise, Robert Scott, Andrew Turner. Mem. faculty U. Calif. at Riverside, 1956—, dir. summer session, 1964-66, asst. to chancellor, 1964-65, prof. chemistry, 1966—, chmn. dept., 1966-70, dean Coll. Phys. Scis., 1970-74. Vis. research fellow Merton Coll., Oxford (Eng.) U., 1970; Faculty Research lectr. U. Calif., Riverside, 1978-79; sci. adviser U.S. FDA, 1975—; mem. grants adv. com. Research Corp., 1978—. Bd. dirs. Riverside Symphony Orch., 1968-74. Guggenheim fellow U. Cambridge (Eng.), 1962-63. Fellow AAAS; mem. Am. Chem. Soc., Sigma Xi, Phi Lambda Upsilon, Alpha Chi Sigma. Author: (with others) Quantitative Analysis, 1958; (with C.N. Reilley) Experiments for Instrumental Methods, 1961; (with J.L. Roberts, Jr.) Experimental Electrochemistry for Chemists, 1974; also research papers. Editor: Electrochemical Studies of Biological Systems, 1977. Mem. adv. bd. chem. analysis series Inter-scis. Pubs., 1965-70; cons. editor analytical chemistry McGraw-Hill Ency. Sci. and Tech., 1961-66; editorial adv. bd. Analytical Chemistry, 1971-74. Office: Dept Chemistry U Calif Riverside CA 92521

SAWYER, ED CURTIS, state senator; b. Glasgow, Mont., Dec. 11, 1926; s. W.C. and Alleen (Robertson) S.; ed. Coyne Elec. Trade Sch.; m. Angie E. Cercone, June 14, 1947; children—Bette Sawyer Newman, Tom, Ed, Dennis, Greg. Owner, operator Cooper City Electric Co., Bisbee, Ariz., 1958-70, Indsl. Electric Service, Safford, Ariz., 1970—; mem. Ariz. Ho. of Reps., 1965-74; mem. Ariz. State Senate, 1974—, pres., 1977-78, chmn. rules com., legis. council. Served with USN, World War II. Mem. Elec. Apparatus Service Assn., Safford C. of C. Democrat. Roman Catholic. Clubs: Am. Legion, Elks. Home: 1274 Hopi PO Box 1033 Safford AZ 85546 Office: 1220 W 8th St Safford AZ 85546

SAWYER, GRANVILLE MONROE, univ. pres.; b. Mobile, Ala., May 9, 1919; s. George F. and Rebecca (Hatcher) S.; A.B., Tenn. A. and I. State Coll., 1947; M.A., U. So. Calif., 1952, Ph.D., 1955; m. Maxine Young, Sept. 18, 1943; children—Patricia Ann, Granville Monroe. Instr., Samuel Huston Coll., Austin, Tex., 1947-52; prof. speech and drama, dean of coll. Huston-Tillotson Coll., Austin, 1952-56; prof. speech and drama, exec. asst. to pres., chmn. interim adminstrv. com. Tenn. A. and I. State U., Nashville, 1956-68, chmn. interim adv. com., 1965-68; pres. Tex. So. U., Houston, 1968—. Dir. MacGregor Park Nat. Bank. Mem. com. on urban affairs Am. Council on Edn.; com. urban affairs Nat. Assn. State Univs. and Land-Grant Colls.; mem. inst. policy com. So. Regional Edn. Bd. Bd. dirs. Nat. Space Hall of Fame, Houston Library Bd.; trustee Houston and Harris County United Fund, So. Assn. Colls. and Schs.; mem. exec. bd. Sam Houston Area council Boy Scouts Am. Served with USAAF, 1942-46. Gen. Edn. Bd. fellow, 1953-54, Meth. Edn. Bd. fellow, 1954. Mem. Houston C. of C. (adv. com. on edn.), Alpha Phi Alpha, Alpha Kappa Mu, Beta Kappa Alpha. Mason. Office: 3201 Wheeler St Houston TX 77004*

SAWYER, HAROLD S., congressman; b. San Francisco, Mar. 21, 1920; s. Harold S. and Agnes (McGugan) S.; B.A., U. Calif., Berkeley, 1940, LL.B., 1943; m. Marcia C. Steketee, Aug. 26, 1944; children—Stephen R., David H., Keary W., Mariya S. Admitted to Calif. bar, 1943, Mich. bar, 1946, practiced in Grand Rapids, 1946-77; mem. firm Warner, Norcross and Judd, 1950-77; mem. 95th-96th Congresses from 5th Mich. Dist.; pros. atty. Kent County (Mich.), 1975-76; v.p., dir. Grand Hotel, Mackinac Island, Mich., 1957-77; legal counsel to Gov. Romney of Mich., 1962; mem. Mich. Law Revision Commn., 1967-76. Pres. bd. dirs. D.A. Blodgett Home for Children, Grand Rapids, 1950-61. Served to lt. (j.g.) USNR, 1941-45. Fellow Internat. Acad. Trial Lawyers (dir. 1964—), Internat. Soc. Barristers, Am. Coll. Trial Lawyers; mem. Am. Law Inst. Home: 11195 Summit Ave Rockford MI 49341 Office: 123 Cannon House Office Bldg Washington DC 20515 also 166 Gerald R Ford Bldg Grand Rapids MI 49503

SAWYER, HELEN ALTON, painter; b. Washington; d. Wells Moses and Kathleen Alton (Bailey) Sawyer; student at Master's School, Dobbs Ferry, 1914-18; studied art with Johansen and Hawthorne; m. Jerry Farnsworth, Aug. 26, 1925. Painter, artist in oil and water color, lithographer; exhibited at principal galleries and museums of U.S. Represented permanent collections numerous museums including Whitney Mus. Am. Art, Pa. Acad., Toledo Mus., Syracuse U. Mus., John Herron Mus., Indpls., Atlanta Mus., Amherst Coll. Mus., Williams Coll. Mus. Art, Chrysler Mus., others, IBM collection, Library of Congress, C. & O. R.R. collections; oil painting Clown Still Life owned Norfolk Mus. Recipient numerous awards, honors. Mem. N.A.D., Nat. Arts Club, Provincetown, Yonkers, Sarasota art assns., Audubon Artists, Nat. Assn. Women Artists. Contbr. articles and verse to jours. Has painted in U.S., Spain, France, Mexico. Home: 3482 Flamingo Sarasota FL 33581

SAWYER, JOHN, profl. football team exec.; s. Charles Sawyer; m. Ruth Sawyer; children—Anne, Elizabeth, Catherine, Mary. Pres., part owner Cin. Bengals Nat. Football League team; pres. J. Sawyer Co., Ohio, Miss., Mont., Wyo. Home: Cincinnati OH Office: J Sawyer Co 8050 Hosbrook Ct Cincinnati OH 45236

SAWYER, JOHN EDWARD, found. officer; b. Worcester, Mass., May 5, 1917; s. William Henry and Dorothy (Winslow) S.; A.B., Williams Coll., 1939; A.M., Harvard, 1941; LL.D., Amherst and Clark Colls., 1961, Wesleyan U., 1962, Yale U., 1974, Williams Coll., 1974; Litt.D., Middlebury Coll., 1964; L.H.D., Hamilton Coll., 1968, Bowdoin Coll., 1973; m. Anne W. Swift, June 28, 1941; children—Katharine, John, Stephen W., William Kent. With Dept. State, 1946; jr. fellow Soc. Fellows, Harvard, 1946-49, asst. prof. econ. history, 1949-53; asso. prof. econ. history Yale, 1953-61; pres. Williams Coll., Williamstown, Mass., 1961-73; v.p. Andrew W. Mellon Found., N.Y.C., 1974, pres., 1975—. Trustee Clark Art Inst., Woods Hole Oceanographic Instn. Served from ensign to lt. USNR, 1942-46; with O.S.S., Washington and overseas, 1942-45. Recipient Bronze Star medal. Fellow Am. Acad. Arts and Scis.; mem. Am. Hist. Assn., Am. Econ. History Assn. (trustee 1956- 60), Am. Econs. Assn., Phi Beta Kappa. Contbr. articles to profl. jours. Office: 140 E 62d St New York City NY 10021

SAWYER, WILBUR HENDERSON, pharmacologist, educator; b. Brisbane, Australia, Mar. 23, 1921 (parents Am. citizens); s. Wilbur Augustus and Margaret Henderson S.; A.B., Harvard U., 1942, M.D., 1945, Ph.D., 1950; m. Marian Gholson Kittredge, Nov. 14, 1942; children—Wilbur Kittredge, Robert Kittredge, Thomas Kittredge, Richard Kittredge. Instr. biology Harvard U., Cambridge, Mass., 1950-53; asst. prof. physiology N.Y. U. Med. Sch., N.Y.C., 1953-57; asso. prof. pharmacology Columbia U. Coll. Physicians and Surgeons, N.Y.C., 1957-64, prof., 1964-78, Gustavus A. Pfeiffer Prof., 1978—. Served to lt. (j.g.) M.C., USN, 1946-48. Recipient Lederle Med. Faculty award N.Y. U., 1955-57; Fulbright-Hays Sr. scholar, 1974; Commonwealth Fund travelling fellow, 1965. Mem. Am. Soc. Zoologists, Am. Physiol. Soc., Soc. Gen. Physiologists, Soc. Exptl. Biology and Medicine, Endocrine Soc., Am. Soc. Pharmacology and Exptl. Therapeutics, Harvey Soc., Soc. Endocrinology, Alpha Omega Alpha. Contbr. articles on exptl. endocrinology, physiology and pharmacology to profl. jours. Home: 12 Warnke Ln Scarsdale NY 10583 Office: 630 W 168th St New York NY 10032

SAWYER, WILLIAM BALLARD HOYT, lawyer; b. Buffalo, Feb. 26, 1916; s. Ansley Wilcox and Esther Lapham (Hoyt) S.; grad. Groton Sch., 1934; B.A., Yale, 1938; LL.B., Harvard, 1941; m. Fannette Horner, Nov. 2, 1943; children—Charles Horner, Sally Ballard, Katherine Ballard. Admitted to N.Y. State bar, 1941; asso. firm Ohlin, Damon, Morey, Sawyer & Moot, and predecessor, Buffalo, 1946-50, partner, 1950—. Pres. Family Service Soc. Buffalo, 1966-69; trustee Park Sch., 1956-68, Family Service Soc., 1956—. Served to lt. comdr. USNR 1942-45. Mem. Am., N.Y. State, Erie County bar assns., Am. Judicature Soc. Home: 48 Lexington Ave Buffalo NY 14222 Office: Liberty Bank Bldg Buffalo NY 14202

SAWYER, WILLIAM DALE, physician, educator; b. Roodhouse, Ill., Dec. 28, 1929; s. Cloyd Howard and Eva Collier (Dale) S.; U. Ill., 1947-50; M.D. cum laude, Washington U., St. Louis, 1954; m. Jane Ann Stewart, Aug. 25, 1951; children—Dale Stewart, Carole Ann. Intern, Washington U., Barnes Hosp., St. Louis, 1954-55, resident, 1957-58, fellow, 1958-60; asst. prof. microbiology Johns Hopkins, 1964-67; prof., chmn. dept. microbiology Rockefeller Found. assigned at Mahidol U., Bangkok, Thailand, 1967-73; prof., chmn. dept. microbiology Ind. U. Sch. Medicine, Indpls., 1973—; adj. prof. biology Ball State U., Muncie, Ind.; cons. U.S. Army Med. Research and Devel. Command, WHO Immunology Centre, Singapore, 1969-73; mem. bd. sci. advisers Armed Forces Inst. Pathology, chmn., 1979-80. Mem. Lobund adv. bd. U. Notre Dame. Served to maj., M.C., AUS, 1955-64. Fellow A.C.P.; mem. Am. Soc. Microbiology (pres. br. 1976—), Sci. Research Soc. Am., Am. Fedn. Clin. Research, Central Soc. for Clin. Research, Infectious Diseases Soc. Am., Soc. Exptl. Biology, Medicine, AAAS, Am. Acad. Microbiology, Am. Assn. Pathologists, Assn. Med. Sch. Microbiology Chairmen (dir.), Assn. Am. Med. Colls. (council acad. socs. 1979—), Phi Beta Kappa, Sigma Xi, Alpha Omega Alpha. Club: Crooked Stick Golf (Carmel, Ind.). Contbr. numerous articles to profl. jours. Home: 5321 Lancelot Dr Indianapolis IN 46208 Office: 1100 W Michigan St Indianapolis IN 46202

SAWYERS, JOHN LAZELLE, physician; b. Centerville, Iowa, July 26, 1925; s. Francis Lazelle and Almira (Baker) S.; A.B., U. Rochester, 1946; M.D., Johns Hopkins U., 1949; m. Julia Edwards, May 25, 1957; children—Charles Lazelle, Al Baker, Julia Edwards. House officer surgery Johns Hopkins Hosp., Balt., 1949-50; asst. resident, resident in surgery Vanderbilt U. Hosp., Nashville, 1953-58; practice medicine specializing in surgery, Nashville, 1958—; surgeon Edwards-Eve Clinic, 1958-60; chief surg. service Nashville Gen. Hosp., 1960-77; surgeon-in-chief St. Thomas Hosp., Nashville, 1977—; prof. surgery Vanderbilt U., Nashville. Bd. dirs. Davidson County unit Am. Cancer Soc. Served from lt. (j.g.) to lt. M.C., USNR, 1950-52. Diplomate Am. Bd. Surgery, Am. Bd. Thoracic Surgery. Fellow A.C.S.; mem. Am. Surg. Assn. Home: 403 Ellendale Dr Nashville TN 37205 Office: St Thomas Hosp PO Box 380 Nashville TN 37202. *Fortunate is the physician who obtains his education in schools that demand high standards of research and education as well as clinical expertise from their faculty. Conscientious, honest, hard work in this environment can pave the way to a successful career.*

SAX, HERBERT, mfg. co. exec.; b. N.Y.C., Nov. 5, 1929; s. Murray and Rose (Rifkin) S.; B.A., Bklyn. Coll., 1950; postgrad. Bernard Baruch Sch. Bus. Adminstrn., 1953-59; m. Carolyn Tambor, Jan. 20, 1952; children—Jeffrey Frank, Edward James. Asst. office mgr. Arrow Metal Products, N.Y.C., 1953-54; accountant Samuel Arlow & Co., N.Y.C., 1954-56, Morris R. Feinsod & Co., N.Y.C., 1956-60; with Ehrenreich Photo-Optical Industries, Inc., Garden City, N.Y., 1960—, v.p. finance, treas., 1972-73, pres., treas., 1973—, also dir. Served with AUS, 1951-53. C.P.A., N.Y. Mem. Am. Inst. C.P.A.'s, N.Y. Soc. C.P.A.'s, Accounting Research Assn. Home: 100 Hickman St Syosset NY 11791 Office: 623 Stewart Ave Garden City NY 11530

SAX, JOSEPH LAWRENCE, educator; b. Chgo., Feb. 3, 1936; s. Benjamin Harry and Mary (Silverman) S.; A.B., Harvard, 1957; J.D., U. Chgo., 1959; m. Eleanor Charlotte Gettes, June 17, 1958; children—Katherine Elaine, Valerie Beth, Anne-Marie. Admitted to D.C. bar, 1960; atty. Dept. Justice, Washington, 1959-60; pvt. practice, Washington, 1960-62; prof. U. Colo. Law Sch., 1962-65; vis. prof. U. Calif. Law Sch., Berkeley, 1965-66; prof. U. Mich. Law Sch., Ann Arbor, 1966—; fellow Center Advanced Study in Behavioral Scis., 1977-78; cons., U.S. Senate Com. on Pub. Works, 1970-71; mem. cons. council Conservation Found., 1969-73; mem. legal adv. com. Pres.'s Council on Environ. Quality, 1970-72; mem. environ. studies bd. Nat. Acad. Sci., 1970-73; mem. Mich. Environ. Rev. Bd., 1973-74. Bd. dirs. Environ. Law Inst., Washington; trustee Center for Law and Social Policy, Washington, Inst. Ecology regional gov. Internat. Council Environmental Law. Served with USAF, 1960. Mem. Fedn. Am. Scientists (nat. council). assembly). Club: Explorers. Author: (with others) Waters and Water Rights, 1967; Water Law, Planning and Policy, 1968; Defending the Environment, 1971. Home: 1220 Fair Oaks St Ann Arbor MI 48104

SAX, STANLEY PAUL, mfg. exec.; b. Cin., Sept. 1, 1925; s. Ben Philip and Goldie (Quitman) S.; A.B., U. Wis., 1948; children—Steven Jay, David Jay; m. 2d, Patricia Moran Leach, June 14, 1970; children—Cathy, Carolyn. Researcher, Market Research Co. Am., Chgo., 1942; instr. U. Wis., 1948; v.p., dir. Am. Buff Co., Detroit, 1948-57, exec. v.p., dir., Chgo., 1957—; pres. Speedway Buff Co.; pres., chmn. bd., dir. J.J. Siefen Co., 1961—, chmn. bd., pres. Sax Abrasive Corp., 1961—, Sax Cal. Corp., 1962—, Klem Chem. Corp., 1963—, Stan Sax Corp., Seco Chems., Inc., 1965—; chmn. bd. Buckingham Products Co., McAleer Mfg. Co., 1968—, Sax Realty Investment Corp., 1967—, Globe Compound Corp., 1971—, Goodison Mfg. Co., 1972—, Ana, Inc., 1974—; partner S & D Leasing Co. Trustee Sax Family Found.; bd. dirs. Met. Soc. Crippled Children and Adults. Served to lt. AUS, 1943-46; to lt. col. Res., 1946—. Recipient Wis. scholar award. Mem. Mil. Order World Wars, Metal Finishing Suppliers Assn. (trustee), Detroit C. of C., Detroit Inst. Arts (patron), Friends of Am. Wing (Founders Soc.), Friends of Henry Ford Mus., Am. Electroplaters Soc., Am. Soc. for Abrasives, Soc. Mil. Engrs., Young President's Orgn., World Bus. Council, Chief Execs. Forum, Amateur Athletic Union, Soc. Die Casting Engrs., Res. Officers Assn., V.F.W., Wis. Alumni Assn., Phi Beta Kappa, Alpha Phi Omega, Phi Kappa Phi, Psi Chi, Phi Eta Sigma. Elk, Rotarian. Clubs: Economic, Renaissance (Detroit); Recess. Contbr. articles to profl. jours. Lender furnishings to diplomatic reception rooms, benefactor fine arts com. Dept. State. Home: 1079 Forest Ln Birmingham MI 48010 Office: 5657 Lauderdale Ave Detroit MI 48209

SAXBE, WILLIAM BART, lawyer, former atty. gen. U.S.; b. Mechanicsburg, Ohio, June 24, 1916; s. Bart Rockwell and Faye Henry (Carey) S.; A.B., Ohio State U., 1940, LL.B., 1948; hon. degrees Central State U., Findlay Coll., Ohio Wesleyan U., Walsh Coll., Capital U., Wilmington Coll., Ohio State U., Bowling Green State U.; m. Ardath Louise Kleinhans, Sept. 14, 1940; children—William Bart, Juliet Louise Saxbe James, Charles Rockwell. Admitted to Ohio bar, 1948; practiced in Mechanicsburg, 1948-55; partner Saxbe, Boyd & Prine, 1955-58; mem. Ohio Gen. Assembly, 1947-48, 49-50, majority leader Ho. Reps., 1951-52, speaker, 1953-54; atty. gen., Ohio, 1957-58, 63-68; partner Dargusch, Saxbe & Dargusch, 1960-63; mem. U.S. Senate from Ohio, 1969-74; atty. gen. U.S., 1974; ambassador to India, 1975-77; partner firm Chester, Saxbe, Hoffman & Wilcox, Columbus, Ohio, 1977—. Served with 107th Cav., AUS, 1940-42, USAAF, 1942-45; col. Res. Mem. Am., Ohio bar assns., Am. Judicature Soc., Chi Phi, Phi Delta Phi. Republican. Episcopalian. Mason. Clubs: University, Columbus Athletic, Columbus, Scioto Country (Columbus); Urbana (Ohio) Country; Burning Tree Country (Bethesda, Md.). Home: Route 2 Mechanicsburg OH 43044 Office: 16 S Main St Mechanicsburg OH 43044

SAXBERG, BORJE OSVALD, educator; b. Helsinki, Finland, Jan. 25, 1928; s. Oskar Valdemar and Martha (Granberg) S.; came to U.S., 1950, naturalized, 1966; B.A., Swedish Sch. Bus. and Econs., 1950; B.S., Oreg. State U., 1952; M.S., U. Ill., 1953, Ph.D., 1958; m. A. Margrete Haug; children—Bo Erland Haug, Bror Valdemar Haug. Teaching asst., instr. U. Ill., 1953-57; prof. dept. mgmt. and orgn. U. Wash., 1957—, asso. dean Bus. Sch., 1967-70, chmn. dept. mgmt. and orgn., 1972-76; cons. in field. Ford Found. fellow, 1960-61. Fellow Soc. Applied Anthropology; mem. Acad. Mgmt., Am. Sociol. Assn. Club: Swedish (Seattle). Author: (with R. Joseph Monsen) The Business World, 1967; (with H.P. Knowles) Personality and Leadership Behavior, 1971; (with R.A. Johnson) Management, Systems and Society, 1976. Home: 4323 NE 44th St Seattle WA 98105 Office: Grad Sch of Bus U Wash Seattle WA 98195

SAXBY, LEWIS WEYBURN, JR., mfg. co. exec.; b. Oak Park, Ill., Dec. 17, 1924; s. Lewis Weyburn and Dorothy Elizabeth (Porter) S.; B.S., U. Calif., Berkeley, 1945; M.B.A., Stanford U., 1948; m. Kathryn Hutchinson, Sept. 7, 1947; children—Steven Lewis, Ann, Jane Porter. With Owens-Corning Fiberglass Corp., Toledo, Ohio, 1964—, operating div. v.p., 1973-79, sr. v.p., 1979—. Nat. bd. dirs. Jr. Achievement, Inc.; bd. dirs. Jr. Achievement Northwestern Ohio, Inc. Served with USNR, 1942-46. Recipient Silver leadership award Jr. Achievement, 1978. Mem. Nat. Insulation Contractors Assn. (sec., bd. dirs.), Alpha Delta Phi. Republican. Presbyterian. Club: Inverness Country. Home: 2021 Orchard Rd Toledo OH 43606 Office: Fiberglass Tower Toledo OH 43659

SAXE, EDWARD LAWRENCE, museum exec.; b. Boston, Jan. 17, 1916; s. William Walter and Cecelia (Franzel) S.; A.B., Harvard U., 1937, M.B.A., 1939; m. Bridget Anthea Gordon, Mar. 2, 1946; children—Andrew Neill Gordon, Christopher Edward Gordon. Spl. insp. U.S. Dept. Justice, 1940-41; asst. to treas. CBS, Inc., 1946-48, exec. asst., 1948-49, controller, 1949-53, v.p., asst. to pres. CBS-TV, 1954-56, v.p. ops., 1956-67, v.p. ops. and engring., 1967-69, pres. CBS-TV Services div., 1969-72; pres. Rapifax Corp., 1973-74, Satellite Holdings, Inc.; chmn., chief exec. Satellite Networks, Inc., 1975-77; dep. dir., gen. mgr. Mus. Modern Art, N.Y.C., 1977—; cons. NSC, 1948-49. Trustee Children's Aid Soc.; bd. dirs. Am. Council for Arts. Served as maj. AUS, 1941-46, attached Brit. 21st Army Group, 1943-44. Decorated Bronze Star, Order Brit. Empire; Croix de Guerre (France and Belgium). Mem. Harvard Bus. Sch. Alumni Assn., 12th Army Group Assn., Nat. CIC Assn., Soc. TV Pioneers. Clubs: Harvard (N.Y.C.); Bucks (London); Harvard (New Canaan). Home: 79 Old Hill Rd Westport CT 06880

SAXE, HARRY CHARLES, civil engr., univ. dean; b. Long Island City, N.Y., Mar. 18, 1920; s. Charles Lawrence and Alice (McGrath) S.; B.C.E., City Coll. N.Y., 1942; M.S.E., U. Fla., 1949; Sc.D., Mass. Inst. Tech., 1952; m. Margaret Veronica Bligh, Nov. 12, 1945; children—Janine Marie, Coreen Marie Saxe Urbina. Grad. asst., instr. civil engring. U. Fla., 1948-50; grad. research asst. civil engring. Mass. Inst. Tech., 1950-52; asso. prof. civil engring. Ga. Inst. Tech., 1950-56; structural engr. Praeger-Kavanagh & Assos., cons. engrs., N.Y.C., 1956-57; asso. prof. Poly. Inst. Bklyn., 1957; U. Cin., 1957-59; prof. civil engring. U. Notre Dame, 1959-69, head dept. 1959-60, 61-65, acting dean Coll. Engring., 1960-61, 66-67, chmn. dept. 1967-69; pres. Inst. Indsl. Research, U. Louisville, 1969-74, prof. civil engring., dean James Breckenridge Speed Sci. Sch., 1969—; spl. research structural engring. and mechanics; NSF sci. faculty fellow Imperial Coll. Sci. and Tech., U. London (Eng.), 1965-66. Cons. USAF Spl. Weapons Center, Albuquerque, 1961-66; mem. Ky. Bd. Registration for Profl. Engrs. and Land Surveyors, 1972—, sec.-treas., 1979—; mem. Ky. Sci. and Tech. Adv. Council, 1970-75; mem. energy research bd. Ky. Dept. Energy, 1976—; mem. exec. bd. INCOME, Inc., 1978—. Served to capt., C.E., AUS and USAAF, 1942-48; ETO. Recipient Notre Dame U. Spl. Service award, 1967. Registered profl. engr., Ga., N.Y., Ind., Ky. Fellow Am. Soc. C.E.; mem. Am. Soc. for Testing and Materials, Internat. Assn. Bridge and Structural Engring., Nat. Council Engring. Examiners, Soc. Am. Mil. Engrs., Am. Soc. Engring. Edn., Newcomen Soc. N.Am., Nat., Ky. socs. profl. engrs., Louisville Engring. and Sci. Socs. Council, Sigma Xi, Tau Beta Pi, Phi Kappa Phi, Chi Epsilon, Sigma Tau, Pi Tau Sigma. Home: 1026 Burning Springs Circle Louisville KY 40223 Office: JB Speed Sci Sch U Louisville Louisville KY 40208

SAXENA, BRIJ B., biochemist, endocrinologist, educator; b. India, July 6, 1930; Ph.D., U. Lucknow (India); D.Sc. (Alexander von Humboldt fellow), U. Muenster (W.Ger.); Ph.D., U. Wis., 1961. Asst. prof. biochemistry U. Lucknow, 1955-57; project asst. U. Wis., Madison, 1959-62; asst. prof. biochemistry N.J. Coll. Medicine. 1962-66; asso. prof. biochemistry and endocrinology Cornell U. Med. Coll., N.Y.C., 1966-74, prof. biochemistry, 1974—, prof. endocrinology, 1972—; mem. nat. com. on ligand assays FDA. Recipient Career Scientist award N.Y.C. Health Research Council; Upjohn research award; Campoz da Paz award. Fellow Royal Soc. Medicine (London); mem. Am. Soc. Biol. Chemists, AAAS, Endocrine Soc., Harvey Soc., N.Y. Acad. Sci., Internat. Soc. Research in Biology of Reproduction, Pacific Coast Fertility Soc., Am. Physiol. Soc., Am. Chem. Soc., Sigma Xi. Mem. editorial bd. Proc. Soc. Exptl. Biology and Medicine, Jour. Immunoassay, Bio-Mathematique, France. contbr. numerous articles to profl. jours. Office: Cornell Univ Medical School 1300 York Ave New York NY 10021

SAXON, DAVID STEPHEN, educator, physicist; b. St. Paul, Feb. 8, 1920; s. Ivan and Rebecca (Moss) S.; B.S., Mass. Inst. Tech., 1941, Ph.D., 1944; L.H.D., Hebrew Union Coll., 1976, U. Judaism, 1977; LL.D., U. S.C., 1978; m. Shirley Goodman, Jan. 6, 1940; children—Margaret Elizabeth, Barbara Susan, Linda Caroline, Catherine Louise, Victoria Jean, Charlotte Mala. Research physicist Radiation Lab., Mass. Inst. Tech., 1943-46, Philips Labs., 1946-47; mem. faculty U. Calif., Los Angeles, 1947-75, prof. physics, 1958-75, chmn. dept., 1963-66, dean phys. scis., 1966-69, exec. vice chancellor, 1968—, univ. provost, 1974-75; pres. U. Calif. at Berkeley, 1975—; vis. scientist Centre d'Etudes Nucléaires, Saclay, France, 1968-69; vis. prof. faculty scis. U. Paris, Orsay, France, 1961-62; cons. to research orgns., 1948—; spl. research theoretical physics, nuclear physics, quantum mechanics, electromagnetic theory, scattering theory. Guggenheim fellow, 1956-57, 61-62; Fulbright grantee, 1961-62. Mem. Am. Phys. Soc., Am. Assn. Physics Tchrs., Am. Inst. Physics, AAUP, Sigma Xi, Sigma Pi Sigma. Author: Elementary Quantum Mechanics, 1968; The Nuclear Independent Particle Model, 1968; Discontinuities in Wave Guides, 1968; Physics for the Liberal Arts Student, 1971. Home: 70 Rincon Rd Kensington CA 94707 Office: President's Office 714 University Hall U Calif Berkeley CA 94720

SAXON, PHILIP DUNHAM, chem. co. exec.; b. N.Y.C., Sept. 6, 1925; s. Olin Glenn and Catherine (Dunham) S.; B.A., Yale U., 1946; LL.B., Harvard U., 1949; m. Barbara Jean Nardozzi, Aug. 30, 1976; children—Philip Dunham, Carolyn Fogg, Janet Barclay, Amy Macomber, Sarah Macomber. Admitted to Conn. bar, 1950, Del. bar, 1960; atty. firm Buck, McCook & Kenyon, Hartford, Conn., 1949-51, OPS, Washington, 1951-52; with Hercules Inc., Wilmington, Del., 1952—, sr. counsel, 1966-68, sec., asst. treas., 1968—. Chmn. bd. trustees Wilmington Coll. Served with USNR, 1943-46. Mem. Am. Soc. Corp. Secs., Stockholder Relations Soc. N.Y., Nat. Conf. Commrs. Uniform State Laws (commr., chmn. Del. commn.), Nat. Investor Relations Inst., Am., Del. bar assns., Del. C. of C. (dir., exec. com. 1976—). Clubs: Wilmington, Wilmington Country, Yale (N.Y.C.). Home: Benge Rd Yorklyn DE 19736 Office: 910 Market St Wilmington DE 19899

SAXTON, MARK, editor, writer; b. Mineola, N.Y., Nov. 28, 1914; s. Eugene Francis and Martha (Plaisted) S.; A.B., Harvard U., 1936; m. Josephine Porter Stocking, June 27, 1940 (dec. 1967); children—Russell Steele, Martha Porter. Newspaper, mag. and radio work, 1936-38; asst. editor Farrar & Rinehart, N.Y.C., 1938-43; asso. editor Rinehart & Co., 1946; exec. editor William Sloane Assos., 1946-50; editor McGraw-Hill Book Co., 1950-52; promotion mgr., editorial adviser Harvard U. Press, Cambridge, Mass., 1952-68; editor-in-chief, dir. Gambit, Inc., Ipswich, Mass., 1968-80. Mem. staff Breadloaf (Vt.) Writers Conf., summers 1947-51, 61. Trustee, v.p. Joseph Collins Found., N.Y.C., 1950—. Served to lt. (j.g.) USNR, 1943-46. Clubs: Century Assn., Harvard (N.Y.C.); St. Botolph (Boston). Author: Danger Road, 1939; The Broken Circle, 1941; The Year of August, 1943; Prepared for Rage, 1947; Paper Chase, 1964; The Islar, 1969; The Two Kingdoms, 1979. Home: 41 E 28 St New York NY 10016

SAYAD, HOMER ELISHA, accountant; b. Rezaieh, Iran, Aug. 15, 1915 (father Am. citizen); s. Elisha E. and Najeeba Mar (Joseph) S.; B.S., U. Nottingham (Eng.), 1937; postgrad. Northwestern U., 1937-39; m. Elizabeth Foster Gentry, May 9, 1963; children—Elisha William Gentry, Helene Elizabeth Todd. Mgr., Deloitte, Plender, Griffiths & Co., Chgo., 1939- 52; resident sr. partner Haskins & Sells, St. Louis, 1954-78; fin. cons. Mark Twain Bancshares, Inc., St. Louis, 1979—. Chmn. profl. div. United Fund Greater St. Louis, 1959-60; pres. Opera Theatre St. Louis, 1963-65; pres. Loretto-Hilton Repertory Theatre, 1971-74, chmn. bd. dirs., 1974-76; chmn. bd. dirs. Greater St. Louis Arts and Edn. Council, pres., 1966-71; trustee William Woods Coll., Fulton, Mo.; bd. dirs. St. Louis Symphony Soc., Columbia (Mo.) Coll., Am. Council for Arts, 1978; bd. commrs. Met. Zool. and Museum Bd., 1972-73; mem. 22d Circuit Jud. Commn., 1974—; mem. adv. bd. Grad. Sch. Acctg., U. Mo., Columbia; bd. dirs. St. Louis Children's Hosp., 1977—; mem. adv. bd. U. Mo., St. Louis. Served with AUS, 1943-46. Mem. Nat. Accounting Assn., Am. Inst. C.P.A.'s, Mo. (past pres.), Ill., N.Y. socs. C.P.A.'s. Clubs: Bellerive Country (past dir.), Noonday (past treas.), Racquet (treas., dir.), St. Louis. Home: 41 Westmoreland Pl Saint Louis MO 63108 Office: 8820 Ladue Rd Saint Louis MO 63104. *To strive constantly for excellence in all undertakings; to be understanding of differences of opinion and thought without sacrifice of principle; to be willing to give of one's self to serve others less fortunate.*

SAYE, ALBERT BERRY, educator; b. Rutledge, Ga., Nov. 29, 1912; s. William Bibb and Suvinnie (Whitten) S.; student Emory U., 1930-32; A.B., U. Ga., 1934, M.A., 1935; diplome de francais, degre superieur U. Dijon (France), 1938; Ph.D., Harvard, 1941; postgrad. Cambridge U., 1939; m. Ruth Kendrick, Dec. 20, 1939. Instr. history U. Ga., 1934-36, asst. prof. history, 1939-41, asst. prof. polit. sci., 1941-43, asso. prof., 1943-47, prof., 1947-57, prof. law and Alumni Found. Distinguished prof. polit. sci., 1957—, Richard B. Russell prof. polit. sci., 1975—. Recipient Lewis H. Beck scholarship, 1936, M.G. Michael research award, 1942. Mem. Internat., Am., So. polit. sci. assns., Ga. Bar Assn., Ga. Hist. Soc., Demosthenian Lit. Soc. Baptist. Author 12 books including American Constitutional Law, 2d edit., 1977; Principles of American Government, 8th edit., 1978; A Constitutional History of Georgia, 1970; Georgia Government and History, 1973. Home: 190 W Lake Pl Athens GA 30606

SAYERS, GALE, educator, ret. profl. football player; b. Wichita, Kans., May 30, 1943; s. Roger Earl and Bernice (Ross) S.; student phys. edn. Kans. U., N.Y. Inst. Finance; m. Ardythe Elaine Bullard, Dec. 1, 1973; children—Gale Lynne, Scott Aaron, Timothy Gale, Gaylon, Guy, Gary. Running back Chgo. Bears Profl. Football Team, 1965-72; then asst. to athletic dir. Kans. U.; now athletic dir. So. Ill. U.; columnist Chgo. Daily News. Co-chmn. legal def. fund sports com. NAACP; co-ordinator Reach-Out program, Chgo.; hon. chmn. Am. Cancer Soc. Commr., Chgo. Park Dist. Recipient numerous award for playing, also holder numerous Nat. Football League records; named to Football Hall of Fame, 1977. Mem. Kappa Alpha Psi. Address: Dept Athletics So Ill U Carbondale IL 62901

SAYERS, GEORGE, endocrinologist; b. Glasgow, Scotland, June 10, 1914; s. George and Elizabeth Clark (Morton) S.; came to U.S., 1929, naturalized, 1938; B.S., Wayne State U., 1934, M.S., 1941; M.S., U. Mich., 1936; Ph.D., Yale, 1943; m. Evelyn Stevens, May 18, 1966; children—William, Tom, Ann, Lynn. Prof., physiology Case Western Res. U., Sch. Medicine, Cleve., 1952-79; adj. prof. physiology and anatomy U. Calif., Berkeley, 1979—. Recipient John Jacob award in pharmacology, 1947. Mem. Endocrine Soc. (Ciba award 1949), Am. Physiol. Soc., Am. Soc. for Pharmacology and Exptl. Therapeutics, AAAS. Contbr. articles to profl. jours. Home: 1441 Campus Dr Berkeley CA 94708 Office: Dept Physiology and Anatomy U Calif Berkeley CA 94720

SAYLES, LEONARD ROBERT, educator; b. Rochester, N.Y., Apr. 30, 1926; s. Robert and Rose (Sklof) S.; B.A. with highest distinction, U. Rochester, 1946; Ph.D. in Econs. and Social Sci., Mass. Inst. Tech., 1950; children—Robert, Emily. Asst. prof. Cornell U., 1950-53, U. Mich., 1953-56; mem. faculty Grad. Sch. Bus. Adminstrn., Columbia, 1956—, prof. bus. adminstrn., 1962—, head div. indsl. relations and orgnl. behavior, 1960-72, dir. M.B.A. program, 1974-75; adviser to adminstr. NASA, 1966-71; cons. to govt. and industry; Distinguished vis. lectr. McGill U., 1974. Recipient awards and prizes Ford Found., Soc. Applied Anthropology, Soc. Psychol. Study Social Issues, McKinsey Found. Mem. Nat. Acad. Pub. Adminstrn., Indsl. Relations Research Assn. (exec. bd. 1970-73), AAAS, Phi Beta Kappa. Author: (with G. Strauss) The Local Union, 1953; Managerial Behavior, 1964; (with G. Strauss) Human Behavior in Organizations, 1966; (with E. Chapple) Measure of Management, 1961; Behavior of Industrial Work Groups, 1958; Individualism and Big Business, 1963; (with W. Dowling) How Managers Motivate, 1971; (with M. Chandler) Managing Large Systems; Organizations for the Future, 1971; (with G. Strauss) Personnel, 3d edit., 1972; Managing Human Resources, 1977; Leadership, 1979. Mem. editorial bd. Human Orgn., 1957-62, Adminstrn. and Soc., 1975—. Home: 19 Birch Ln Dobbs Ferry NY 10522 Office: Uris Hall Columbia U New York City NY 10027

SAYLES, THOMAS DYKE, JR., banker; b. Newton Center, Mass., Jan. 16, 1932; s. Thomas Dyke and Eleanor (Norton) S.; A.B., Dartmouth, 1954; M.A., N.Y. U., 1961; m. Patricia Blake, Dec. 11, 1954; children—Lynn Diane, Richard Norton, Stephen Dyke. With Mfrs. Hanover Trust Co., N.Y.C., 1958-70, v.p., 1966-70, sr. v.p., 1970; dir. Summit & Elizabeth Trust Co., Summit, N.J., 1968—, exec. v.p., chief adminstrn. officer, 1970, chmn., pres., chief exec. officer, 1971—; dir. Oakite Products, Inc. Trustee Overlook Hosp., 1972—. Served to 1st lt. SAC, USAF, 1955-58. Mem. Am. Arbitration Assn., Chatham (N.J.) Jr. C. of C. (dir. 1965). Clubs: Baltusrol (Springfield); Canoe Brook (Summit). Home: 58 Lincoln Ave Chatham NJ 07928 Office: Springfield Ave and Beechwood Rd Summit NJ 07901

SAYPOL, RONALD DIETZ, diversified holding co. exec.; b. N.Y.C., Nov. 12, 1929; s. Irving Howard and Adele (Kaplan) S.; B.A., Dickinson Coll., Carlisle, Pa., 1951; LL.B., Bklyn. Law Sch., 1955; m.

Wendy Saypol; children—Cathy Lynn, Amy Elizabeth, Natasha, Ronald Dietz. Demonstrator, salesman, adminstrv. v.p., v.p. operations Lionel Corp., N.Y.C., 1951-62, pres., 1968—, also chief exec. officer; dir. marketing Ideal Toy Corp., N.Y.C., 1962-63; v.p., exec. v.p. Topper Corp., Elizabeth, N.J., 1963-68; dir. Hardwicke Cos. Inc.; dir., trustee Bulova Systems and Instruments Corp. Fellow Brandeis U., 1965—. Mem. N.Y. State Bar Assn., Mashomack Fish and Game Preserve, Phi Epsilon Pi, Phi Delta Phi. Clubs: L.I. Wyandanch Sportsmen's; Twenty-Nine, Long Island, DeSoto Lake Hunting. Office: 9 W 57th St New York NY 10019

SAYRE, EDWARD VALE, chemist; b. Des Moines, Sept. 8, 1919; s. Edward Agnew and Audrey (Vale) S.; B.S., Iowa State U., 1941; A.M., Columbia U., 1943, Ph.D., 1949; m. Virginia Nelle Rogers, Oct. 20, 1943. Mgr. research sect. Manhattan Dist. project Columbia U., 1942-45; research chemist Eastman Kodak Research Labs., Rochester, N.Y., 1949-52; sr. chemist Brookhaven Nat. Lab., Upton, N.Y., 1952—; dir. research Museum Fine Arts, Boston, 1975-78, sr. scientist, 1978-80; sr. scientist Alexander von Humboldt Found., 1980; vis. lectr. Stevens Inst. Tech., 1955-61; adj. prof. fine arts Inst. Fine Arts, N.Y. U., 1960-74; distinguished vis. prof. Am. U. Cairo, 1970; Regents prof. U. Calif., Irvine, 1972; mem. sci. advisory council Winterthur Mus. Guggenheim fellow, 1969. Fellow Internat., Am. insts. for conservation hist. and artistic works; mem. Am. Chem. Soc. Contbr. numerous articles on research to profl. jours.; asso. editor Archaeometry, 1969—, Art and Archaeology Tech. Abstracts, 1970—, Jour. Archaeol. Sci., 1971-77. Home: 5 Titus Ln Bellport NY 11713 Office: Upton NY 11973

SAYRE, ELEANOR AXSON, museum curator; b. Phila., Mar. 26, 1916; d. Francis B. and Jessie W. (Wilson) Sayre; A.B., Bryn Mawr Coll., 1938; postgrad. fine arts, Harvard, 1938-40. Curatorial asst. Yale Art Gallery, 1940-41, Lyman Allyn Mus., New London, Conn., 1942, R.I. Sch. Design Mus. Art, 1942-45; mem. staff Boston Mus. Fine Arts, 1945—, curator prints and drawings, 1967—; tchr. print seminars Harvard, 1969, 70, 72, 78. Mem. internat. adv. com. Keepers Pub. Collections Graphic Arts. Trustee Print Council Am. Grantee Am. Philos. Soc., Ford Found. Decorated Lazo de Dama, Order Isabel la Catolica. Mem. Hispanic Soc. Am. (corr.); Real Academia de Bellas Artes de San Fernando (corr.). Contbr. to museum publs. Author notes and commentary: Late Caprichos by Goya, Fragments from a Series, 1971. Co-author: Rembrandt: Experimental Etcher, 1969; Albrecht Dürer: Master Printmaker, 1971; The Changing Image: Prints by Francisco Goya, 1974. Editor: A Christmas Book, 1966. Office: Museum Fine Arts Huntington Av Boston MA 02115

SAYRE, FRANCIS BOWES, JR., clergyman; b. Washington, Jan. 17, 1915; s. Francis Bowes and Jessie Woodrow (Wilson) S.; A.B. cum laude, Williams Coll., 1937, D.D. (hon.), 1963; M.Div., Episcopal Theol. Sch., Cambridge, Mass., 1940; L.H.D. (hon.), Wooster Coll., 1956; D.D. (hon.), Va. Theol. Sch., 1957, Wesleyan U., Conn., 1958, Hobart Coll., 1966; S.T.D., Queen's U., Belfast, 1966; Litt.D. (hon.), Lehigh U., Ursinus Coll., 1973; m. Harriet Taft Hart, June 8, 1946; children—Jessie Wilson, Thomas Hart, Harriet Brownson, Francis Nevin. Ordained to ministry Episcopal Ch., 1940; asst. minister Christ Ch., Cambridge, 1940-42; indsl. chaplain Diocese of Ohio, Cleve., 1946-51; rector St. Paul's Ch., East Cleveland, Ohio, 1947-51; dean Washington Cathedral, 1951-78; asso. dir. Woodrow Wilson Internat. Center for Scholars, Washington, 1978-79. Chmn. bd. Detroit Indsl. Mission, 1956-68; chmn. U.S. Com. for Refugees, 1958-61; mem. Pres.'s Com. on Equal Employment Opportunity, 1961-65; chmn. Woodrow Wilson Meml. Commn., 1962-68; mem. adv. com. Bishop of Armed Forces, 1972-78. Bd. govs. Nat. Space Inst.; bd. dirs. Presbyn. Ministers Fund. Served as chaplain USNR, 1942-46. Recipient Clergyman of Year award Religious Heritage Am., 1976; Distinguished Pub. Service medal NASA, 1977. Mem. Sigma Phi.

SAYRE, ROBERT H., elec. and mining mfg. co. exec.; b. Marion, Ind., Mar. 5, 1922; s. Virgil H. and Ruth M. (Kraut) S.; B.S. in Mech. Engring., Purdue U., 1943; postgrad. Northwestern U., 1947-48, Ind. U., 1948-49; m. Jane Leah Clesi, Oct. 5, 1957; children—Robert H., Eric David, Michael Brian. Br. mgr. Kawneer Co., Dallas, 1950-51; v.p. Wax Novelty Co., Dallas, 1951-52; sales engr. Kaiser Aluminum, Dallas, 1952-54, br. mgr., New Orleans, 1954-58, Houston, 1958-60; dist. mgr. Ohio Brass Co., Denver, 1961—; pres. Bow Mar South, Inc., 1967-68. Served to lt. USNR, 1943-46; PTO. Registered profl. engr., Ind., Colo. Mem. Rocky Mountain Elec. League, Northwest Electric Light and Power Assn., Colo. Mining Assn., Rocky Mountain Coal Mining Inst., Wyo. Mining Assn., Am. Mining Congress, IEEE, Kappa Sigma. Elk, Kiwanian. Clubs: Denver Athletic, Pinehurst Country. Republican. Home: 5800 Wood Sorrel Dr Littleton CO 80123 Office: 5401 S Prince St Littleton CO 80120

SAYRE, ROBERT MARION, ambassador; b. Hillsboro, Oreg., Aug. 18, 1924; s. William Octavius and Mary (Brozka) S.; B.A. summa cum laude, Willamette U., 1949; J.D. cum laude (Alexander Welborn Weddell Peace prize 1956), George Washington U., 1956; M.A., Stanford, 1960; LL.D., Willamette U., 1965; m. Elora Amanda Moyhihan, Dec. 29, 1951; children—Marian Amanda, Robert Marion, Daniel Humphrey. Joined U.S. Fgn. Service, 1949; econ. adviser on Latin Am., 1950-52, mil. adviser, 1952-57; officer charge inter-Am. security affairs, 1955-57; chief polit. sect. embassy, Lima, Peru, 1958-59; fin. attache embassy, Havana, Cuba, 1960; exec. sec. Task Force Latin Am., State Dept., 1961, officer charge Mexican affairs, 1961-63, dep. dir. Office Caribbean and Mexican Affairs, 1963-64, dir., Office Mexican Affairs, 1964; sr. staff mem. White House, 1964-65; dep. asst. sec. Bur. Inter-Am. Affairs, Dept. State, 1965-67; acting asst. sec. State, 1968—; U.S. ambassador to Uruguay, 1968-69; U.S. ambassador to Panama, 1969-74; sr. insp. Dept. State, 1974-75, insp. gen., 1975-78; ambassador to Brazil, 1978—; admitted to D.C. bar, 1956, U.S. Supreme Ct., 1962. Served to capt. AUS, World War II; col. Res. ret. Recipient Outstanding Employee award Dept. State, 1952, Superior Honor awards, 1964, 75, Disting. Honor award, 1978. Mem. Blue Key, Phi Delta Theta, Phi Eta Sigma, Tau Kappa Alpha. Methodist. Rotarian. Home: 3714 Bent Branch Rd Falls Church VA 22041 Office: Am Embassy Brasilia APO Miami 34030

SAYRE, THOMAS HENRY, lawyer, ret. utilities exec.; b. Scottown, Ohio, Sept. 15, 1904; s. John Wilson and Frances (Marks) S.; LL.B., N.Y. U., 1942; postgrad. Harvard U., 1957; m. Margaret Edwards Lothrop, June 26, 1926. With Appalachian Power Co. and predecessor cos., 1922-36; admitted to N.Y. bar, 1942; practiced in N.Y.C., to 1977; with Am. Electric Power Service Corp., 1936-69, asst. chief counsel, 1954-67, v.p., chief counsel and sec., 1967-69; past sec. Appalachian Power Co., Beach Bottom Power Co., Inc., Captina Operating Co., Cardinal Operating Co., Central Appalachian Coal Co., Central Coal Co., Central Ohio Coal Co., Central Operating Co., Franklin Real Estate Co., Ind. Franklin Realty Inc., Ind. & Mich. Electric Co., Kanawha Valley Power Co., Ky. Power Co., Kingsport Power Co., Mich. Gas & Electric Co., Mich. Gas Exploration Co., Ohio Power Co., South Bend Mfg. Co., Twin Br. R.R. Co., W.Va. Power Co., Wheeling Electric Co.; past dir. Am. Electric Power Service Corp., Central Appalachian Coal Co., Central Ohio Coal Co., Franklin Real Estate Co., Ind. Franklin Realty, Inc., W.Va. Power Co. Mem. Am. Bar Assn., Pilgrims of U.S., Phi Delta Phi, Theta Sigma Lambda. Republican. Baptist. Club: Masons. Home: 105 Wildwood Ave Beckley WV 25801

SAZEGAR, MORTEZA, artist; b. Tehran, Iran, Nov. 11, 1933; s. Hassan Ali and Zahra (Frootan) S.; B.A., U. Tex., El Paso, 1955, B.S., 1956; postgrad. Baylor U. Coll. Medicine, 1956-57, Cornell U., 1958-59; m. Patricia Jean Kaurich, July 13, 1959. One man exhibitions include: Poindexter Gallery, N.Y.C., 1964, 67, 69, 71, 73, 75, 77; group exhibitions include: Detroit Inst. Arts, 1965, Chgo. Art Inst., 1965, Univ. Art Mus., U. Tex., Austin, 1965, 72, Whitney Mus. Am. Art, 1970, Cleve. Mus. Art, 1972, Corcoran Gallery Art, Washington, 1973, Tyler Sch. Art, Temple U., Phila., 1979; represented in permanent collections: Whitney Mus. Am. Art, N.Y.C., San Francisco Mus. Modern Art, Riverside Mus., N.Y.C., U. Mass., Amherst, Corcoran Gallery Art, Prudential Ins. Corp. Am., Mus. Contemporary Art, Tehran, Iran. Mem. Artists Equity Assn. Democrat. Address: Rural Route 1 Cochranville PA 19330

SCAASI, ARNOLD MARTIN, fashion designer; b. Montreal, Que., Can.; s. Samuel and Elizabeth (Seigler) Isaacs; came to U.S., 1955; student Cotnoir Capponi Sch. Haute Design, Montreal, 1953, Chambre Syndicale de la Haute Couture Parisienne, Paris, 1954. Apprentice, House of Paquin, Paris, 1954; asst. Charles James, N.Y.C., 1955; pres. Arnold Scaasi, Inc., N.Y.C., 1957—. Recipient Winnie award Coty Fashion Critics, 1958; 1 Today award NBC TV, 1959; Neiman-Marcus award, 1959; Chgo. Gold Coast Fashion award, 1961. Office: 681 Fifth Ave New York NY 10022

SCAGGS, HOWARD IRWIN, savs. and loan assn. exec., lawyer; b. Balt., July 4, 1921; s. Howard Irwin and Margaret Anna (Mitchell) S.; LL.B., U. Balt., 1941; m. Grace Briscoe Brawner, Aug. 16, 1941; children—Howard Irwin III, Gordon B., Robert Mark. Clk.-teller Am. Nat. Bldg. & Loan Assn., Balt., 1945-61, pres., 1961—, chmn. bd., 1968—; pvt. law practice, 1948—; vice chmn., dir. Fed. Home Loan Bank Atlanta, 1973-78; past mem. adv. council Fed. Home Loan Bank Bd., Washington. Mem. policy com., center for met. planning and research Johns Hopkins U. Chmn., Commn. Forests and Parks Md., 1963-68. Chmn. bd. Neighborhood Housing Services Balt., Inc., 1974-78; mem. Balt. Conv. Center Com., Md. Gov.'s Salary Commn. Served with AUS, 1943; served to lt. USNR, 1943-46. Mem. U.S. (chmn. urban affairs com.), Md. (past dir.) savs. and loan leagues, Citizens Planning and Housing Assn., Real Estate Bd. Greater Balt., Advt. Club Balt. (past pres.), C. of C. Met. Balt. (past dir.), Sigma Delta Kappa. Democrat. Episcopalian. Home: 309 Ivy Church Rd Timonium MD 21093 Office: Am Nat Bldg & Loan Assn Lexington and Liberty Sts Baltimore MD 21201

SCAGGS, WILLIAM ROYCE (BOZ), musician; b. Ohio, June 8, 1944; student U. Wis. at Madison; m. Carmella Scaggs; children—Oscar, Austin. With Steve Miller's band The Marksmen, then his Ardells band (also under name Fabulous Night Train); formed own rhythm-and-blues band The Wigs; rejoined Steve Miller in 1967, made 2 albums: Children of the Future and Sailor; solo albums include: Boz, Boz Scaggs, Moments, Boz Scaggs and Band, My Time, 1972, Slow Dancer, Silk Degrees, 1976, Down Two Then Left, 1977. Winner Grammy award Best Rhythm and Blues Song for Lowdown, 1976. Office: care Irv Azoff Front Line Mgmt 8380 Melrose Ave Suite 307 Los Angeles CA 90069

SCAGLIONE, ALDO DOMENICO, educator; b. Turin, Italy, Jan. 10, 1925; s. Teodoro and Angela (Grasso) S.; D.Modern Letters, U. Torino, 1948; m. Jeanne Mathilde Daman, June 28, 1952. Came to U.S., 1951, naturalized, 1958. Lectr., U. Toulouse, France, 1949-51; instr. Italian, U. Chgo., 1951-52; mem. faculty U. Calif. at Berkeley, 1952-68, prof. Italian and comparative lit., 1963-68, chmn. dept. Italian, 1963-65; W.R. Kenan prof. Romance langs., comparative lit. U. N.C., Chapel Hill, N.C., 1968—; vis. prof. Romance langs. Yale, 1965-66; vis. prof. comparative lit. Grad. Center, City U. N.Y., 1971-72. Asso., Columbia U. Renaissance Seminar. Chmn. Berkeley campus campaign Woodrow Wilson Nat. Found., 1964-65. Served with Italian Liberation Army, 1944-45. Decorated Knight Order of Merit (Italy). Fulbright fellow, 1951; Guggenheim fellow, 1958; Newberry Library sr. resident fellow, Chgo., 1965; fellow Southeastern Inst. for Medieval and Renaissance Studies, 1968, Cini Found. Program in Medieval and Renaissance Culture, 1973, German Acad. Exchange, W.Ger., 1977; fellow Rockefeller Found. Conf. and Study Center, Bellagio, Italy, 1978. Mem. Renaissance Soc. N. Calif. (pres. 1962-63), Modern Lang. Assn., Renaissance Soc. Am., Dante Soc. Am., Am. Assn. Tchrs. Italian, Medieval Acad. Am., Am. Comparative Lit. Assn. Author: Nature and Love in the Late Middle Ages, 1963; Ars Grammatica, 1970; The Classical Theory of Composition, 1972; also articles. Editor: (M.M. Boiardo) Orlando Innamorato, Amorum Libri, 2 vols., rev. edit., 1963; Francis Petrarch, Six Centuries Later: A Symposium, 1975; Ariosto 1974 in America, 1976; Series L'Interprete and Speculum Artium, Longo Editore, Ravenna, 1976—; Italian Culture, 1978—; gen. editor Romance Notes and N.C. Studies in Romance Langs. and Lits., 1971-75; asso. editor Romance Philology, 1963—, N.C. Studies in Comparative Literature, 1968—, Studies in Philology, 1969—, Amsterdam Studies in the History of Linguistics, 1973—. U.S. corr. Studi Francesi, 1961—. Home: Route 4 Box 539 Chapel Hill NC 27514

SCAGLIONE, FRANK, community coll. pres.; b. Tampa, Fla., May 13, 1933; s. Alex and Josephine (Traina) S.; B.S., U. Tampa, 1956; M.Ed., U. Miss., 1962; m. Evelyn Pyle, Aug. 10, 1956; children—Dale, David, Dana. Tchr., then dean boys Madison Jr. High Sch., 1956-62; asst. prin. Jefferson High Sch., 1962-65; asst. prin., then prin. Leto Comprehensive High Sch., 1965-72; exec. v.p. Hillsborough Community Coll., Tampa, 1973-77, pres., 1977—; asso. mem. Fla. com. United Negro Coll. Fund. Bd. dirs. Tampa United Way, Tampa Sports Club. Mem. Community Coll. Council Pres., Greater Tampa C. of C., So. Assn. Colls. and Schs., Fla. Assn. Secondary Sch. Prins. (dist. dir.), Nat. Assn. Schs. (sec. Western conf.). Roman Catholic. Office: 39 Columbia Dr Tampa FL 33606

SCAIFE, RICHARD MELLON, publishing co. exec.; b. Pitts., July 3, 1932; s. Alan Magee and Sarah (Mellon) S.; student Yale, 1950-51; B.A., U. Pitts., 1957; m. Frances Louise Gilmore, July 14, 1956; children—Jennie, David. Research asso. Mellon Inst. Indsl. Research, Pitts., 1953-57; coordinator Gulf Oil Corp., Pitts., 1957-58; v.p., gov. T. Mellon and Sons, Pitts. 1961-70; owner, pub., chmn. bd. Tribune Rev. Pub. Co., Greensburg, Pa., 1970—; pub., dir. City Communications, Inc., 1976—; dir. Sierra Pub. Co. and affiliates, Sacramento, Parax Corp., Lansing, Mich., Air Tool Parts & Service Co. Mem. Allegheny Conf. Community Devel.; mem. adv. bd. Hoover Instn. War, Revolution and Peace, Center for Strategic and Internat. Studies, 1968-76; mem. pres.'s bd. Pepperdine Coll. Trustee Deerfield Acad., Carnegie Inst., Brandywine Conservancy, Chadds Ford, Pa.; trustee, vice chmn. Sarah Scaife Found.; trustee, chmn. Allegheny Found.; bd. dirs. Pitts. Zool. Soc., 1962-75, Goodwill Industries Pitts., 1975—; v.p., bd. dirs. Western Pa. Hosp.; bd. dirs. Preservation Action, Pitts. History and Landmarks Found., Pennsylvanians for Effective Govt.; bd. regents Pepperdine U., 1976—; mem. Pitts. Zool. Park Commn., 1975—. Mem. Hist. Soc. Western Pa. (trustee). Republican. Clubs: Duquesne (Pitts.); Rolling Rock, Laurel Valley Golf (Ligonier, Pa.). Office: 525 William Penn Pl Pittsburgh PA 15219

SCALAPINO, ROBERT ANTHONY, educator; b. Leavenworth, Kans., Oct. 19, 1919; s. Anthony and Beulah (Stephenson) S.; A.B., Santa Barbara Coll., 1940; M.A., Harvard, 1943, Ph.D., 1948, LL.D., 1976; m. Dee Jessen, Aug. 23, 1941; children—Diane (Mrs. Barry Jablon), Sharon Leslie, Lynne Ann (Mrs. Clyde Thompson). Instr., Harvard, 1948-49; asst. prof. U. Calif. at Berkeley, 1949-51, asso. prof., 1951-56, prof., 1956-76, Robson research prof. govt., 1976—, chmn. dept. polit. sci., 1962-65, dir. Inst. East Asian Studies, 1976—; chmn. Am. adv. com. U.S.-Japan Transl. Service Center, Tokyo, 1979—; cons. Rockefeller Found., 1957-62, Rockefeller Brothers Fund, 1957-58, Ford Found., 1958-61, RAND Corp., 1961-69; chmn. adv. com. internat. studies Hoover Instn., Stanford U., 1976—; mem. nat. adv. bd. Council on Learning, 1978—; mem. internat. research council Center Strategic and Internat. Studies, Georgetown U., 1977—; prin. Am. acad. adv. U.S. Congress and Japanese Diet, 1979—; vis. com. fgn. policy studies Brookings Instn., 1976—; mem. Am. com. U.S.-Japan Culture Center, 1979—; mem. several adv. panels; cons. World Affairs Council, San Francisco, 1952-54; founder, 1st chmn. Nat. Com. on U.S.-China Relations, 1966—; mem. adv. bd. U.S.-China Trade Council, 1974—. Bd. govs. Inst. Current World Affairs, N.Y., 1962-76; adv. com. Japan Found., 1972-75. Bd. dirs. Freedom House, N.Y.C., 1976—. Served from ensign to lt. (j.g.), USNR, 1943-46; PTO. Social Sci. Research Council fellow, 1952-53; Carnegie Found. grantee, 1951, Rockefeller Found. grantee, 1956-59; Guggenheim fellow, 1965-66; Nat. Endowment for Humanities grantee, 1978-81; Luce Found. grantee, 1977-82. Fellow Am. Acad. Arts and Scis.; mem. Atlantic Council U.S., Am., Western polit. sci. assns., Asian Assn. (asso. mem. China council 1976—), UN Assn. (policy studies com. 1970—), Fgn. Policy Assn., Council on Fgn. Relations (scholarship com.). Author: Democracy and the Party Movement in Prewar Japan, 1953; Parties and Politics in Contemporary Japan, 1962; North Korea Today, 1964; The Communist Revolution in Asia, 1965; The Japanese Communist Party, 1920-66, 1967; (with Chong Sik Lee) Communism in Korea, 2 vols., 1972 (Woodrow Wilson award Am. Polit. Sci. Assn. 1974); American-Japanese Relations in a Changing Era, 1972; Asia and the Major Powers, 1972; Asia and the Road Ahead, 1975. Editor: Asian Survey, 1962—; editor, contbr. Elites in the People's Republic of China, 1972; The Foreign Policy of Modern Japan, 1977; editorial bd. Jour. Asian Politics, Orbis, China Quar., Contemporary China, Strategic Rev., Comparative Strategy, Internat. Security, Freedom At Issue. Home: 2850 Buena Vista Way Berkeley CA 94708

SCALERA, RALPH FRANCIS, lawyer; b. Midland, Pa., June 28, 1930; s. Dominic J. and Josephine R. (D'Angelo) S.; A.B., Harvard, 1952; LL.B., U. Pa., 1955; m. Janet Ruth Roosa, Nov. 19, 1960; 1 dau., Amy Marie. Admitted to Pa. bar, 1958; mem. firm Buchanan, Wallover & Barrickman, Beaver, Pa., 1958-59; asst. U.S. atty. Western Dist. Pa., Pitts., 1959-61; mem. firm Wallover, Barrickman & Scalera, Beaver, 1961-64; judge Ct. of Common Pleas, Beaver County, 1964-70, pres. judge, 1966-70; partner Wallover, Barrickman, Scalera, Reed & Steff, Beaver, 1970-71; judge U.S. Dist. Ct., Western Dist. Pa., Pitts., 1971-76; partner firm Thorp, Reed & Armstrong, Pitts., 1976—. Mem. Beaver Planning Commn., 1966-68; chmn. planning council S.E. region Pa. Crime Commn., 1969-70; chmn. Pa. Conf. on Cts., 1969; co-chmn. Pa., Nat. Citizens Com. on Revenue Sharing, 1971; mem. Beaver Community Improvement Assn., 1968-74; mem. Pa. Gov.'s Council on Human Services, 1968-69; Beaver County chmn. Arthritis and Rheumatism Found., 1961-62; Republican candidate lt. gov., Pa., 1970. Bd. dirs. McGuire Meml. Home Retarded Children, 1964-74, Merrick Art Gallery Assos., 1971-74, Gateway Rehab. Center, 1971-74, Catholic Social Service Agy. Beaver County, 1964-72, Beaver County Rehab. Center, 1971-72; bd. mgmt. Golden Triangle YMCA, 1975—; chmn. devel. fund drive Med. Center of Beaver County, 1977. Served with AUS, 1955-57. Named Outstanding Young Man of Pa., Pa. Jr. C. of C., 1964. Mem. Am., Pa., Beaver County bar assns. Republican. Roman Catholic. K.C. Clubs: Harvard-Yale-Princeton of Pitts.; Beaver Valley Country; Harvard of Western Pa. (pres. 1976-77). Home: River Rd Beaver PA 15009 Office: 2900 Grant Bldg Pittsburgh PA 15219

SCALES, HAROLD EDWARD, savs. and loan assn. exec.; b. N.Y.C., Aug. 3, 1920; s. Harold Edward and Beatrice Lottie (Crane) S.; B.B.A., U. Wis., 1949; m. Doreen Evelyn Steinhauer, Nov. 14, 1943. With Anchor Savs. & Loan Assn., Madison, Wis., 1950—, v.p., treas., 1952-71, pres., chief exec. officer, 1971—, chmn. bd., 1979—, also dir.; mem. Gov. Wis. Council Econ. Devel. Past treas. Wis. Jaycees; campaign chmn. United Way of Dane County, 1979. Served with USNR, 1942-45. Recipient Pat O'Dea Sportsmanship award Madison Pen and Mike Club. Mem. Financial Controllers Soc. (past dist. gov.), Wis. Savs. and Loan League (past pres.), U. Wis. Alumni Assn. (past pres.). Clubs: Blackhawk Country (past pres.), Rotary, Madison, Elks, Shriners. Home: 5026 Milward Dr Madison WI 53711 Office: PO Box 7933 25 W Main St Madison WI 53707

SCALES, JAMES RALPH, univ. pres.; b. Jay, Okla., May 27, 1919; s. John Grover and Katie (Whitley) S.; B.A., Okla. Baptist U., 1939; M.A., U. Okla., 1941, Ph.D., 1949; postgrad. U. Chgo., 1945-47, U. London, 1958; LL.D., Alderson Broaddus Coll., 1971, Duke U., 1976; Litt.D., No. Mich. U., 1972; m. Elizabeth Ann Randel, August 4, 1944; children—Laura (dec.), Ann Catherine. Reporter, Miami (Okla.) News Record, 1934-35, Shawnee (Okla.) News-Star, 1935-36; instr. Okla. Baptist U., Shawnee, 1940-42, asst. prof., 1946-47, asso. prof., 1947-51, prof. history, govt., 1951-61, v.p., 1950-53, exec. v.p., 1953-61, pres., 1961-65; dean arts and scis. Okla. State U., Stillwater, 1965-67; pres. Wake Forest U., Winston-Salem, N.C., 1967—; founder Cimarron Rev., 1967—. Mem. Pres.'s Com. Edn. Beyond High Sch., 1957; mem. adv. com. U.S. Army Command and Gen. Staff Coll., Ft. Leavenworth, Kans., 1969-72, chmn., 1971-72; mem. U.S. del. UNESCO, 1978—. Mem. Okla. del. Democratic Nat. Conv., 1956; trustee Belmont Abbey Coll., 1977—. Served as officer USNR, 1942-45. Mem. Am. Hist. Assn., Am. Polit. Sci. Assn., Am. Assn. U. Profs., So. Assn. Bapt. Colls. (pres. 1969-70), N.C. Assn. Ind. Colls. (pres. 1969-71), Winston-Salem C. of C. (dir.), Phi Beta Kappa, Omicron Delta Kappa, Phi Eta Sigma. Baptist (deacon). Rotarian. Clubs: University (N.Y.C.); Bay Hill Golf and Country (Orlando, Fla.); Cape Fear (Wilmington, N.C.). Address: President's Home Wake Forest U Winston-Salem NC 27109

SCALI, JOHN ALFRED, journalist; b. Canton, Ohio, Apr. 27, 1918; s. Paul M. and Lucy (Leone) S.; B.S. in Journalism, Boston U., 1942; m. Helen Lauinger Glock, Aug. 30, 1945 (div. 1973); children—Donna Claire, Paula, Carla; m. 2d, Denise St. Germain, Mar. 4, 1973. Reporter, Boston Herald, 1942, Boston bur. U.P., 1942-43; with A.P., 1944-61, war corr., ETO, 1944, then diplomatic corr., and with Washington Bur., 1945-61; diplomatic corr. ABC News, Washington, 1961-71; spl. cons. for fgn. affairs to Pres. U.S., 1971-73; U.S. ambassador to UN, N.Y.C., 1973-75; sr. corr. ABC News, Washington, 1975—. Recipient Journalism award U. So. Cal., 1964, spl. award Washington chpt. Nat. Acad. Arts and Scis., 1964, Man of Year award in journalism Boston U., 1965, spl. award Overseas Press Clubs, 1965; John Scali award created by Washington chpt. A.F.T.R.A., 1964. Mem. A.F.T.R.A., Sigma Delta Chi. Clubs: Nat. Press (Washington). Office: 1124 Connecticut Ave NW Washington DC 20036

SCALIA, ANTONIN, lawyer, educator; b. Trenton, N.J., Mar. 11, 1936; s. S. Eugene and Catherine Louise (Panaro) S.; A.B., Georgetown U., 1957; student U. Fribourg, Switzerland, 1955-56; LL.B., Harvard, 1960; m. Maureen McCarthy, Sept. 10, 1960;

children—Ann Forrest, Eugene, John Francis, Catherine Elisabeth, Mary Clare, Paul David, Matthew, Christopher James. Admitted to Ohio bar, 1962, Va. bar, 1970; asso. Jones, Day, Cockley & Reavis, Cleve., 1961-67; asso. prof. U. Va. Law Sch., 1967-70, prof., 1970-74; gen. counsel Office Telecommunications Policy, Exec. Office of Pres., 1971-72; chmn. Adminstrv. Conf. U.S., Washington, 1972-74; asst. atty. gen. U.S., Office Legal Counsel, Justice Dept., 1974-77; vis. prof. Georgetown Law Center, 1977; vis. scholar Am. Enterprise Inst., 1977; prof. Law Sch., U. Chgo., 1977—; cons. CSC, 1969, 77, FCC, 1977, FTC, 1978. Bd. dirs. Nat. Inst. for Consumer Justice, 1972-73, Center for Adminstrv. Justice, 1972-74; adv. council for legal policy studies Am. Enterprise Inst., 1978—. Sheldon fellow Harvard, 1960-61. Mem. Am. Bar Assn. (council, sect. adminstrv. law 1974-77). Club: Cosmos (Washington). Co-editor Regulation mag., 1979—. Home: 5725 S Woodlawn Ave Chicago IL 60637 Office: U Chgo Law Sch 1111 E 60th St Chicago IL 60637

SCALLEN, THOMAS KAINE, advt. exec.; b. Mpls., Aug. 14, 1925; s. Raymond A. and Lenore (Kaine) S.; grad. St. Thomas Coll.; B.A., LL.B., U. Denver; m. Mary Semsch, Sept., 1947; children—Thomas, Sheila, Patrick, Eileen, Timothy and Maureen (twins). Admitted to Minn. bar; asst. atty. gen. State of Minn., 1950-55; gen. practice law, 1955-57; pres. Med. Investment Corp., 1957—; pres., exec. producer Shipstads and Johnson Ice Follies and Holiday on Ice. dir. Northwest Sports Enterprises, Ltd., Vancouver, B.C., Can., Advance Machine Tool, Mpls.; chmn. bd. Blaine-Thompson Co., Inc., N.Y.C. Mem. Young Presidents Orgn. Served with AUS. Clubs: University (St. Paul, Mpls.); Rochester (Minn.) Golf and Country; Edina (Minn.) Country; Athletic (Mpls.). Home: 5329 Grand Ave South Minneapolis MN 55419 Office: 2200 Foshay Tower Minneapolis MN 55402

SCAMMON, RICHARD MONTGOMERY, polit. scientist; b. Mpls., July 17, 1915; s. Richard Everingham and Julia (Simms) S.; A.B., U. Minn., 1935; A.M., U. Mich., 1938; m. Mary Stark Allen. Feb. 20, 1952; 1 dau., Anne Valerie. Research sec., radio office U. Chgo., 1939-41; dep. mil. gov., Kreis Mergentheim, Wuerttemberg, 1945; polit. officer, Land Wuerttemberg-Baden, 1945-46; chief, polit. activities br., civil adminstrn. div., Office Mil. Govt. for Germany (U.S.), 1946-48, chief, div. research for Western Europe, Dept. of State, 1948-55; dir. Elections Research Center, 1955-61, 65—; dir. Bur. Census, Dept. Commerce, 1961-65. Chmn. U.S. delegation observe elections in USSR, 1958; chmn. Pres.'s Commn. Registration and Voting Participation, 1963; mem. OAS electoral mission to Dominican Republic, 1966; chmn. U.S. Select Commn. Western Hemisphere Immigration, 1966-68; pres. Nat. Council on Pub. Polls, 1969-70; mem. Pres.'s Commn. on Fed. Statistics, 1970-71; mem. U.S. delegation Gen. Assembly UN, 1973. Mem. Am. Polit. Sci. Assn., Am. Acad. Polit. and Social Sci., Acad. Polit. Sci., Canadian Polit. Sci. Assn. Clubs: Cosmos (Washington); Reform (London). Co-author: This U.S.A.; The Real Majority. Editor: America Votes, vols. 1-13; America at the Polls. Home: 5508 Greystone St Chevy Chase MD 20015 Office: 1619 Massachusetts Ave NW Washington DC 20036

SCANDALIOS, JOHN GEORGE, geneticist; b. Nisyros Isle, Greece, Nov. 1, 1934 (parents Am. citizens); s. George John and Calliope (Broujos) S.; B.A., U. Va., 1957; M.S., Adelphi U., 1962; Ph.D., U. Hawaii, 1965; m. Penelope Anne Lawrence, Jan. 18, 1961; children—Artemis Christina, Melissa Joan, Nikki Eleni. Asso. in bacterial genetics Cold Spring Harbor Labs., 1960-62; NIH postdoctoral fellow U. Hawaii Med. Sch., 1965; asst. prof. Mich. State U., East Lansing, 1965-70, asso. prof., 1970-72; prof., head dept. biology U. S.C., Columbia, 1973-75; prof., head dept. genetics N.C. State U., Raleigh, 1975—; vis. prof. genetics U. Calif., Davis, 1969; vis. prof. OAS, Argentina, Chile and Brazil, 1972. Served with USAF, 1957. Alexander von Humboldt travel fellow, 1976; mem. exchange program NAS, US/USSR, Mem. Genetics Soc. Am., Am. Soc. Human Genetics, Am. Genetic Assn., AAAS, Soc. Devel. Biology (dir.), Am. Inst. Biol. Scis., Am. Soc. Plant Pathologists, Sigma Xi. Greek Orthodox. Author: Physiological Genetics, 1979. Editor: Developmental Genetics; co-editor: Isozymes, 4 vols., 1975; Monographs in Developmental Biology, 1968—. Office: Dept Genetics NC State U PO Box 5487 Raleigh NC 27650

SCANDLING, WILLIAM FREDRIC, food service exec.; b. Rochester, N.Y., June 17, 1922; s. Fredric D. and Helen T. (Moran) S.; A.B., Hobart Coll., 1949, LL.D. (hon.), 1967; m. Margaret Warner, Apr. 19, 1949; 1 son, Michael. Founding partner ALS, Geneva, N.Y., 1948, inc. as Saga Adminstrv. Corp., 1957, moved to Menlo Park, Calif., 1962, name changed to Saga Corp., 1974, officer, dir., 1957—, pres., 1968-78, now founder dir.; dir. Empire Broadcasting Corp. Chmn. bd. trustees Hobart Coll., William Smith Coll.; mem. nat. council Salk Inst. Served with USAAF, 1943-45. Home: 38 Barry Ln Atherton CA 94025 Office: 1 Saga Ln Menlo Park CA 94025

SCANGA, ITALO, sculptor; b. Lago, Calabria, Italy, June 6, 1932; s. Giuseppe and Serafina (Ziccarelli) S.; came to U.S., 1947; student Soc. Arts and Crafts, Detroit, 1951-53; B.A., Mich. State U., 1960, M.A., 1961. Mem. faculty U. Wis., Madison, 1961-64, Brown U., Providence, summers 1964, 66, R.I. Sch. Design, Providence, 1964-66, Pa. State U., University Park, 1966-67; asso. prof. sculpture Tyler Sch. Art, Temple U., Phila., 1967-78, U. Calif., San Diego, 1976-77, 78—; sculpture exhibited 23 one-man shows, 81 group exhbns.; univ. lectr.; work pub. in Arts Yearbrook of Contemporary Sculpture, 1965, Avalanch Mag., 1973, Artforum, 1975, Interfunktionen, Art in Am., 1975-78, SoHo News, 1975, Phila. Three Centuries of Am. Art Catalogue, 1976, Glass Art Mag., 1976, Artforum, 1977-79; work included in pvt. collections. Served with U.S. Army, 1953-55. Recipient best in show Milw. Art Center, 1963; Howard Found. grantee, 1970; Cassandra grantee, 1972; Nat. Endowment for Arts grantee, 1973. Mem. Nat. Coll. Art Assn., AAUP. Home and office: 6717 Vista Del Mar La Jolla CA 92037

SCANLAN, EUGENE RICHARD, hotel exec.; b. N.Y.C., Mar. 3, 1923; s. William Francis and Lillian Mary (McGarrett) S.; student pub. schs., Nanuet, N.Y., Pearl River, N.Y.; m. Anne Veronica Kenny, Oct. 16, 1952; children—Daniel Charles, Patricia Anne. With Waldorf-Astoria, N.Y.C., 1942-54, 61—, exec. chef, 1961-66, dir. food and beverage, 1966-71, v.p., dir. food and beverage, 1971-74, v.p., mgr., 1974—; exec. chef Fontainebleau Hotel, Miami Beach, Fla., 1954-61; hon. trustee Culinary Inst. Am.; mem. permanent com. Les Amis d'Escoffier Soc. of N.Y., Inc.; bailli honoraire de N.Y., Confrerie de la Chaine des Rotisseurs. Mem. Cardinals' Com. of Laity, N.Y.C.; bd. dirs. Mission of Immaculate Virgin, Mt. Loretto, S.I. Recipient Escoffier plaque Les Amis d'Escoffier, 1966, Grand prize Salon of Culinary Arts of Societe Culinaire Philanthropique, 1965, only Gold medal and diplome d'honneur, Societe des Cuisiniers de Paris, 1964, Chef of Yr. award Hotel Dept. N.Y. City Community Coll., 1963. Mem. Am. Culinary Fedn., N.Y. Hotel and Motel Assn, Assn. Master Knights Sovereign Mil. Order Malta in U.S.A. Malta. Chef for only meals partaken of by His Holiness, Pope Paul VI on N.Y.C. visit, 1965. Office: Waldorf-Astoria 301 Park Ave New York NY 10022

SCANLAN, JAMES PATRICK, educator; b. Chgo., Feb. 22, 1927; s. Gilbert Francis and Helen (Meyers) S.; B.A., U. Chgo., 1948, M.A. in Philosophy, 1950, Ph.D., 1956; postgrad. Georgetown U., summer 1959, U. Calif. at Berkeley, 1960-61, Moscow (USSR) State U., 1964-65, 69; m. Marilyn A. Morrison, June 12, 1948. Research fellow Inst. Philos. Research, San Francisco, 1953-55; Ford fellow instr. humanities Case Inst. Tech., 1955-56; from instr. to asso. prof. philosophy Goucher Coll., 1956-68; prof. philosophy, chmn. Slavic and Soviet area studies U. Kans., 1968-70; prof. philosophy Ohio State U., Columbus, 1971—; vis. prof. Acad. Scis. USSR, Moscow, 1978. Served with USMCR, 1945-46. Mem. Am. Philos. Assn., Am. Assn. Advancement Slavic Studies, Central Slavic Conf. (pres. 1970), Phi Beta Kappa. Editor, translator (Peter Lavrov) Historical Letters, 1967, (Michael Gershenzon) A History of Young Russia, 1974. Co-editor Russian Philosophy, 3 vols., 3d edit., 1976, Marxism and Religion in Eastern Europe, 1976; Editor: American Bibliography of Slavic and East European Studies, 1970-72, 74. Home: 113 E Beck St Columbus OH 43206

SCANLAN, JOHN J., Roman Catholic Bishop; b. Ireland, May 24, 1906; s. Peter and Katherine (Coleman) Scanlan; student Christian Brothers Schs., Cork, Ireland, 1918-23, Nat. U. of Ireland, Dublin, 1923-24, All Hallows Coll., Dublin, 1923-30, U. Calif., 1930-31. Came to U.S., 1930, naturalized, 1937. Ordained priest, Roman Cath. Ch., 1930; pastor St. Thomas More Ch., San Francisco, 1950-54; aux. bishop, Honolulu, 1954-68, bishop of Honolulu, 1968—. Dir. San Francisco Archdiocesan Council Cath. Men, 1952-54. Office: 1184 Bishop St Honolulu HI 96813*

SCANLON, CHARLES FRANKLIN, lawyer; b. Portland, Maine, Nov. 13, 1906; s. Daniel A. and Bertha (Cowan) S.; A.B., Holy Cross Coll., 1928; LL.B., U. Mich., 1931; m. Elizabeth L. Powell, Nov. 17, 1934; children—Patricia (Mrs. Thomas F. McCarthy), Timothy F., Michael C., Terence E., Lawrence J. Admitted to Ohio bar, 1932, since practiced in Akron; sr. partner firm Buckingham, Doolittle & Burroughs, 1965—; spl. hearing officer Office U.S. Atty., 1952. Dir. N. Akron Savs. Assn. Vice pres. St. Sebastian conf. St. Vincent DePaul Soc., 1951—. Served with AUS, 1944. Fellow Am. Coll. Trial Lawyers; mem. Am. Judicature Soc., Am., Ohio, Akron bar assns., Phi Alpha Delta. Home: 266 Dorchester Rd Akron OH 44313 Office: Cascade Plaza Akron OH 44308

SCANLON, CHARLES JOSEPH, bus. exec.; b. Chgo., July 14, 1915; s. Charles J. and Mary J. (Clark) S.; student Northwestern U.; grad. Rutgers U. Grad. Sch. Banking, 1949; LL.D., North Central Coll., 1963; D.B.A., Western Mich. U., 1964; m. Margaret Hemmens, May 14, 1938; children—Barbara J. (Mrs. Stephen Brodt), Lisbeth C. (Mrs. Kent Fairfield). With Fed. Res. Bank Chgo., 1933-70, chief examiner, 1955-59, 1st v.p., 1959-62, pres., 1962-70; v.p. Gen. Motors Corp., N.Y.C., 1970—; dir. Gen. Motors Acceptance Corp., Motors Ins. Corp., United Student Aid Funds, Inc., First Nat. Co., Storm Lake, Iowa. Lectr. Inter-Agy. Bank Examination Sch., 1953-57, Grad. Sch. Banking U. Wis.; banking cons. Republic Liberia, 1961. Trustee Buena Vista Coll., Com. Econ. Devel., Citizens Budget Commn., Alfred P. Sloan Found., Roosevelt Hosp. Episcopalian. Clubs: Economic, Commercial, Bankers, Executives, Union League (Chgo.). Home: 4 Orchard Dr Chappaqua NY 10514 Office: 767 Fifth Ave New York NY 10022

SCANLON, EDWARD LEO, vehicle rental and leasing co. exec.; b. Woonsocket, R.I., Mar. 18, 1934; s. Edward Leo and Elizabeth Ann (Hagarty) S.; B.S. in Bus. Mgmt., Providence Coll., 1955; postgrad. Rutgers U. Sch. Bus., 1958-60, 65-66; m. Andree LeJeune, June 20, 1959; children—Kristin Anne, Paul Damien. With RCA, 1960-77, dir. labor relations, N.Y.C., 1972, div. v.p. indsl. relations, 1972-77; exec. v.p. indsl. relations Hertz Corp., N.Y.C., 1977—, also dir. subsidiaries; mem. faculty U. Maine, Active Urban League, Youth Program N.Y.C. Served with U.S. Army, 1955-57. Clubs: Lions, Kiwanis. Office: 660 Madison Ave New York NY 10021

SCANLON, GEORGE FRANCIS, JR., ins. co. exec.; b. Bridgeport, Conn., Dec. 25, 1929; s. George Francis and Mary Ellen (Reardon) S.; B.S., Villanova U., 1951; M.B.A., U. Pa., 1953; m. Jane MacKenzie, Oct. 12, 1956; children—John, James, Christine, Thomas. Field salesman John Hancock Mut. Life Ins. Co., Boston, 1955-60, hdqrs. salesman, 1960-68; v.p. John Hancock Distbrs. Co., Boston, 1968-70, pres., 1970—, also dir.; dir. John Hancock Advisers Inc. Served with U.S. Army, 1953-55. Mem. Nat. Assn. Securities Dealers. Roman Catholic. Home: 4 Ivy Ct South Weymouth MA 02190 Office: John Hancock Distbrs Co John Hancock Pl Boston MA 02116

SCANLON, JANE CRONIN (MRS. JOSEPH C. SCANLON), educator; b. N.Y.C., July 17, 1922; d. John Timothy and Janet Smiley (Murphy) Cronin; student Highland Park Jr. Coll., 1939-41; B.S., Wayne State U., 1943; M.A., U. Mich., 1945, Ph.D., 1949; m. Joseph C. Scanlon, Mar. 5, 1953; children—Justin, Mari, Emer, Edmund. Mathematician, Air Force Cambridge Research Center, 1951-54; instr. Wheaton Coll., Norton, Mass., 1954-55; asst. prof. Poly. Inst. Bklyn., 1957-58, asso. prof., 1958-60, prof., 1960-65; prof. math. Rutgers U., 1965—; cons. Singer-Kearfott Div., Naval Research Lab. Office Naval Research Fellow Princeton, 1948-49, Horace H. Rockham Postdoctoral fellow U. Mich., 1950-51, Rutgers Research Council fellow, 1968-69, 72-73. Mem. Am. Math. Soc., Soc. for Indsl. and Applied Math., Internat. Soc. Chronobiology, Soc. Math. Biology. Author: Fixed Points and Topological Degree in Nonlinear Analysis, 1964; Advanced Calculus, 1967. Home: 110 Valentine St Highland Park NJ 08904 Office: Dept Math Rutgers U New Brunswick NJ 08903

SCANLON, PETER REDMOND, accountant; b. N.Y.C., Feb. 18, 1931; s. John Thomas and Loretta Dolores (Ryan) S.; B.B.A. in Accounting, Iona Coll., 1952; m. Mary Jane E. Condon, Mar. 7, 1953; children—Peter, Barbara, Mark, Brian, Janet. Mem. profl. staff Coopers & Lybrand, N.Y.C., 1956-66, partner, 1966—, vice chmn., mem. exec. com. Bd. dirs. Miserecordia Hosp., Coopers & Lybrand Found.; bd. dirs., mem. bus. adv. bd. Religion in Am. Life. Served to lt. USN, 1952-56. Decorated Knight of Malta; recipient Arthur A. Loftus award Iona Coll., 1974. C.P.A., N.Y. Mem. Am. Inst. C.P.A.'s, N.Y. State Soc. C.P.A.'s, Am. Mining Congress. Roman Catholic. Clubs: N.Y. Athletic; Marco Polo; Ridgewood Country. Home: 19 Blue Spruce Dr Upper Sadle River NJ 07458 Office: 1251 Ave of Americas New York NY 10020

SCANLON, ROBERT GILBERT, state ofcl.; b. North Braddock, Pa., Apr. 15, 1933; s. Eugene Francis and Catherine Ann (Klagus) S.; B.S. in Elementary Edn., Duquesne U., 1954, M.A. in Adminstrn., 1956; Ed.D. in Elementary Edn., U. Pitts., 1966; m. Charlotte Ann Makar, June 19, 1954; children—Karen, Robin, James, Mark, Kevin, Christine. Tchr., Churchill Borough Elementary Sch., Pitts., 1954-59; elementary adminstr. Orchard Hill Elementary Sch., Leetonia, O., 1959-62; dir. elementary edn. City of Middletown (N.Y.), 1962-66; adminstr. Oakleaf Elementary Sch., Pitts., 1964-66; program dir. individualizing learning program Research for Better Schs., Inc., Phila., 1966-72, exec. dir., 1972-79; sec. of edn. Commonwealth of Pa., 1979—. Cons., U.S. Navy Tng. Command, 1973—; cons. Greater Phila. Movement, 1973—; cons. OECD, 1974—. Bd. dirs. Counselor Films, Inc. Phila., 1974—; trustee Council for Ednl. Devel. and Research, Washington, 1973—, chmn., 1974. Mem. Am. Ednl. Research Assn. (mem. profl. liaison com. 1975—), Assn. Supervision and Curriculum Devel., Am. Assn. Sch. Adminstrs., Assn. Ednl. Data Systems, Soc. Applied Learning Tech., Am. Mgmt. Assn., Am. Fedn. Information Processing Socs. Roman Catholic. Contbr. several chpts. in books, also several articles in field to profl. jours. Editorial bd. Jour. Applied Tech., 1974—. Home: 1489 Graeme Way Warminster PA 18974 Office: 1700 Market St Philadelphia PA 19103

SCANLON, THOMAS MICHAEL, lawyer; b. Indpls., Apr. 20, 1909; s. John H. and Anna C. (Ferriter) S.; A.B., Butler U., 1932; LL.B., Ind. U., 1935; m. Grace L. Barnett, July 10, 1937; children—Thomas M., Christopher G. Admitted to Ind. bar, 1935; asso. Noel, Hickam, Boyd & Armstrong, Indpls., 1935-40, partner Barnes, Hickam, Pantzer & Boyd, 1940—. Sec.-treas. Ind. State Bd. Law Examiners, 1942-43, 47-52. Bd. dirs. Ind. State Symphony Orch.; trustee, lectr. Butler U. Served as lt. comdr. USNR, 1943-46. Fellow Am. Bar Found.; mem. Am. (chmn. sect. antitrust law 1973-74), Fed., Ind. (pres. 1955-56), Indpls. bar assns., Bar Assn. 7th Fed. Circuit (pres. 1956-57), Am. Coll. Trial Lawyers, Delta Tau Delta, Phi Delta Phi. Clubs: Lawyers of Indianapolis (pres. 1964-65), Woodstock, Players (Indpls.). Co-author: Preparation for Trial. Home: 9570 Copley Dr Indianapolis IN 46260 Office: Merchants Bank Bldg Indianapolis IN 46204

SCANLON, THOMAS MICHAEL, JR., philosopher, educator; b. Indpls., June 28, 1940; s. Thomas Michael and Grace Louise (Barnett) S.; A.B., Princeton U., 1962; Ph.D., Harvard U., 1968; m. Lucy Welliver, June 12, 1965; children—Sarah, Jessica. Asst. prof. philosophy Princeton U., 1966-72, asso. prof., 1972-77, prof., 1977—. Fulbright fellow, 1962-63; Nat. Endowment Humanities fellow, 1975-76. Mem. Am. Philos. Assn., Am. Assn. Polit. and Legal Philosophy, Conf. Study of Polit. Thought, AAUP. Asso. editor Philosophy and Public Affairs, 1971—. Office: Dept Philosophy Princeton Univ Princeton NJ 08544

SCANNELL, DALE PAUL, univ. dean; b. Iowa City, Mar. 3, 1929; s. Paul A. and Florence (Fieseler) S.; B.A., U. Iowa, 1951, M.A., 1955, Ph.D., 1957; m. Joan Patricia Swanson, Feb. 9, 1952; children—Steven, Jeffrey, Susan, Janet. Tchr., Iowa City High Sch., 1950-51, 53-57; acting asst. prof. edn. U. Calif. at Berkeley, 1958-59; asst. prof. U. Kans., 1959-62, asso. prof., 1962-64, prof., 1964-67, asso. dean Grad. Sch., 1963-67; prof. edn. U. Iowa, 1967-69; dean Sch. Edn. U. Kans., 1969—. Served to lt. USAF, 1951-53. Mem. AAUP, Am. Ednl. Research Assn., Nat. Council Measurements in Edn., Lawrence C. of C., Phi Delta Kappa. Congregationalist. Kiwanian. Author: (with others) Tests of Academic Progress, 2d edit., 1971; Tests of Achievement and Proficiency, Form 2, 1978; (with A.J. Edwards) Educational Psychology, 1968; (with V.H. Noll) Introduction to Educational Measurement, 4th edit., 1979; (with V.H. Noll and Rachel Noll) Introductory Readings in Educational Measurement, 1972; (with D.B. Tracy) Testing and Measurement in the Classroom, 1975. Home: 2618 Orchard Ln Lawrence KS 66044

SCANNELL, FRANCIS XAVIER, librarian; b. Boston, Dec. 15, 1917; s. William James and Helen Gertrude (Ahern) S.; grad. Roxbury Latin Sch., 1938; A.B., Harvard, 1942; B.S., Columbia, 1943; m. Mary R. Donovan, Dec. 28, 1946; children—Chris, Joel, Elizabeth, Martha. Reference librarian Boston Pub. Library, 1943-46; gen. reference librarian Detroit Pub. Library, 1946-48, asst. chief reference, 1948-53; head reader services Mich. State Library, Lansing, 1953-65, reference librarian Mich. State U., 1965-68, state librarian Mich., 1968—. Mem. library adv. com. Sch. Librarianship Western Mich. U., Kalamazoo, 1968—; del. White House Conf. on Libraries, 1979. Recipient library service citation Mich. Constl. Conv., 1961. Mem. Mich. Library Assn., A.L.A., U. Mich. Library Sci. Alumni Assn. (hon.). Author: (pamphlet) Michigan Novelists, 1964. Home: 3627 Colchester Rd Lansing MI 48906 Office: 735 E Michigan Ave Lansing MI 48913

SCANTLAND, DONALD MAURICE, wholesale co. exec.; b. Richmond, Ind., Aug. 29, 1931; s. Elbert Jacobs and Naomi (Elleman) S.; A.B. (Naval ROTC scholar), Harvard, 1953; postgrad. U. Mich., 1956-57, Western Res. U., 1957-60; m. Dolores Joan Deubreau, Jan. 17, 1959; children—Douglas, Philip, Donald. Asst. controller Bowman Products Co., then Bowman Products div. Asso. Spring Corp., Cleve., 1960-67; group controller Bowman distbn. Barnes Group Inc., Cleve., 1967—. Mem. Nat. Assn. Accountants, YMCA. Republican. Methodist. Home: 269 S Park Dr Aurora OH 44202 Office: 28300 Euclid Ave Cleveland OH 44092

SCARBOROUGH, CHARLES BISHOP, III, broadcast journalist, author; b. Pitts., Nov. 4, 1943; s. Charles Bishop and Esther Francis (Campbell) S.; B.S., U. So. Miss., 1969; m. Linda Anne Gross, Dec. 14, 1972; 1 son, Charles Bishop, IV. Prodn. mgr. Sta.-WLOX-TV, Biloxi, Miss., 1966-68; reporter, anchorman Sta.-WDAM-TV, Hattiesburg, Miss., 1968-69; reporter, anchorman, mng. editor Sta.-WAGA-TV, Atlanta, 1969-72; reporter, anchorman Sta.-WNAC-TV, Boston, 1972-74, NBC News, N.Y.C., 1974—; author novel: Stryker, 1978. Served with USAF, 1961-65. Recipient awards for journalism AP (6), 1969-72, Emmy awards (4), 1974-79, Aviation/Space Writers Assn., 1977, 78. Office: 30 Rockefeller Plaza New York NY 10020

SCARBOROUGH, ROBERT BOWMAN, ins. co. exec.; b. Charleston, S.C., June 28; s. Yancey Wilcox and Lillie (Thomas) S.; A.B., The Citadel, 1950; m. Elizabeth Adelia Martin, Jan. 10, 1953; children—Robert B., Wallace B. Agt., Cosmopolitan Life Ins. Co., Charleston, 1950-53, spl. agt., Charleston, 1954; sec.-treas. Atlantic Coast Life Ins. Co., Charleston, 1955—; mem. S.C. Ho. of Reps., 1963-64, 65-66, 67-68, chmn. Charleston Ho. Delegation, 1967-68; mem. S.C. Senate, 1968-72; chmn. Ho. and Senate Delegation, 1969-72. Mem. S.C. Tricentennial Commn., 1969-71. Pres.'s Traffic Safety Com., 1956, S.C. Safety Com., 1963; mem. S.C. Hwy. Commn., 1974—; mem. S.C. Drug Abuse Commn., 1969-73; active A.R.C. 1954—, chpt. chmn., Charleston, 1958-59, chmn. S. Atlantic blood adv. com., 1960-63, nat. bd. govs., 1966-69; active United Fund, 1954—, chmn. West Ashley (S.C.) bus. group, 1956, chmn. higher edn. div., 1971, gen. chmn., 1973; chmn. Cancer Soc. Crusade, Charleston, 1952, bd. dirs., 1956-59; pres. Coastal Carolina Fair, 1957-61, sec., 1962-74; bd. dirs. Salvation Army, Charleston, 1961-67; bd. dirs. YMCA, 1973-75, treas., 1974; mem. S.C. Democratic Exec. Com., 1968-73; mem. sch. bd. Trident Acad., 1975-77. Served to capt. S.C. N.G., 1950-57. Recipient Distinguished Service award Charleston Jr. C. of C., 1962; named Man of the Year Exchange Club Charleston, 1955, 58, 59. Mem. S.C.V., Hibernian Soc., S.C. Assn. Life Ins. Cos. (v.p. 1974), Charleston C. of C. (v.p. 1962, 64-75, pres. 1977), Internat. Platform Assn., Nat. Sojourners, Alliance Francaise de Charleston, Charleston Navy League (pres. 1962-64), English Speaking Union, Nat. Ry. Hist. Soc. Assn., Citadel Men (pres. 1968). Episcopalian (jr. warden 1962, 75). Mason (32 deg., Shriner). Clubs: Charleston Country, Exchange of Charleston (S.C. pres. 1960, nat. bd. dirs. 1962-68, nat. v.p. 1968, pres. 1969). Home: 26 Broughton Rd Charleston SC 29407 Office: 149 Wentworth St Charleston SC 29401

SCARBOROUGH, ROBERT HENRY, JR., coast guard officer; b. Hawkinsville, Ga., Mar. 12, 1923; s. Robert Henry and Janet Augusta (Burton) S.; B.B.A., U. Hawaii, 1969, M.B.A., 1971; M.S., George Washington U., 1971; grad. U.S. Mcht. Marine Acad., 1944, Armed Forces Staff Coll., 1963, Nat. War Coll., 1971; m. Walterene Brant, July 1, 1946; children—Robert Henry, James Burton. Commd. lt. (j.g.)

U.S. Coast Guard, 1949, advanced through grades to vice adm., 1978; chief Office of Ops., 1974-75, chief of staff U.S. Coast Guard, 1975-77; comdr. 9th Coast Guard Dist., 1977-78; vice comdt. U.S. Coast Guard, Washington, 1978—. Served with USNR, 1942-49. Decorated Legion of Merit. Mem. Armed Forces Relief and Benefit Assn. (vice chmn.), Beta Gamma Sigma. Office: 400 7th St SW Washington DC 20590. *I live each day as though I'm going to have to live with myself for the rest of my life.*

SCARBROUGH, CLEVE KNOX, JR., museum ofcl.; b. Florence, Ala., July 17, 1939; s. Cleve Knox and Emma Lee (Matheny) S.; B.S., U. No. Ala., 1962; M.A., U. Iowa, 1967; m. Sharon K. Smith, Sept. 9, 1972. Asst. prof. art history U. Tenn., 1967-69; dir. Mint Mus. Art, Charlotte, N.C., 1969-76, Hunter Mus. Art, Chattanooga, 1976—; pres. N.C. Museum Council, 1976; bd. mem., adv. com. Tenn. Arts Commn., 1976-77, chmn. visual arts com., 1978-80; mem. Chattanooga Landmark Com., City Planning Bd. Bd. dirs. Chattanooga Conv. and Visitors Bur., 1977—. Served with USN, 1962-64. Mem. Am. Assn. Museums, Southeastern Mus. Conf. (council 1976—). Club: Rotary. Compiler, editor North Carolinians Collect, 1970; Pre Columbian Art of the Americas, 1971; Graphics by Four Modern Swiss Sculptors, 1972; British Paintings from the North Carolina Museum, 1973; Mint Museum, Montain Landscapes by Swiss Artists, 1976. Office: Hunter Museum of Art 10 Bluff View Chattanooga TN 37403

SCARBROUGH, W. CARL, labor union ofcl.; b. Chester County, Tenn., May 31, 1935; s. Joseph Frank and Genretta (Skinner) S.; grad. high sch.; m. Faye Emerson, June 20, 1952; children—Vicki, Carla. Pres. local 282 United Furniture Workers Am., AFL-CIO, 1963-70, internat. v.p. So. region, 1964-70, internat. sec.-treas., 1970-74, internat. pres., 1974—; editor Furniture Workers Press, 1974—. Office: 700 Broadway New York NY 10003*

SCARF, FREDERICK LEONARD, physicist; b. Phila., July 25, 1930; s. Louis Harris and Lena (Elkman) S.; A.B., Temple U., Phila., 1951; Ph.D., Mass. Inst. Tech., 1955; m. Mimi Florence Levin, Aug. 30, 1953; children—Elizabeth Anna, Robert Henry, Daniel Albert. Research asso. Mass. Inst. Tech., 1955-56; asst. prof., then asso. prof. physics U. Wash., Seattle, 1956-62; mgr. space sci. dept. TRW Def. and Space Systems Group, Redondo Beach, Calif., 1962—; cons. mission planning NASA; chmn. panel internat. magnetosphere study Nat. Acad. Scis. Mass. Inst. Tech. overseas fellow, summer 1955; NSF postdoctoral fellow, 1958-59. Fellow Am. Geophys. Union; mem. Internat. Radio Sci. Union (chmn. commn. IV, 1972-75). Contbr. profl. publs. Home: 3676 Crownridge Dr Sherman Oaks CA 91403 Office: TRW DSSG 1 Space Park Redondo Beach CA 90278

SCARF, HERBERT ELY, educator, economist; b. Phila., July 25, 1930; s. Louis Harris and Lena (Elkman) S.; A.B., Temple U., 1951; Ph.D. in Math., Princeton U., 1954; L.H.D., U. Chgo., 1978; m. Margaret Klein, June 28, 1953; children—Martha, Elizabeth, Susan. Mathematician, Rand Corp., 1954-57; asst. prof. statistics Stanford, 1957-60, asso. prof., 1960-63; prof. econs. Yale, 1963—. Stanley Resor prof. econ., 1970-79, Sterling prof. econs., 1979—, dir. div. social scis., 1971-72, 73-74; dir. Cowles Found. Yale, 1967-71. Trustee Urban Inst., Washington, 1973—. Recipient Lancaster prize Ops. Research Soc. Am., 1974. Fellow Center-Advanced Study Behavioral Scis., 1962. Fellow Econometric Soc., Am. Acad. Arts and Scis.; mem. Nat. Acad. Scis. Author: (with Arrow and Karlin) Studies in the Mathematical Theory of Inventory and Production, 1958. Studies in Applied Probability and Management Science, 1962; (with Gilford and Shelly) Multistage Inventory Models and Techniques, 1963; (with T. Hansen) The Computation of Economic Equilibria, 1973. Home: 88 Blake Rd Hamden CT 06517 Office: Dept Economics Yale Univ New Haven CT 06520

SCARFF, DONALD DOUGLAS, elec. mfg. co. exec.; b. Pitts., May 8, 1919; s. Thomas Douglas and Dorothy (Wyeth) S.; B.S. in Elec. Engring., Mass. Inst. Tech., 1941; m. Marie Louise Stafford, June 27, 1942; children—Douglas Stafford, Anne Wyeth (Mrs. Thaanum). With Gen. Electric Co., 1941—, gen. mgr. large lamp dept., 1960-62, gen. mgr. lamp div., 1962-67, v.p., 1964—, gen. mgr. consumer electronics div., 1967-68, group exec. of consumer products group, N.Y.C., 1968-71, regional v.p. Atlantic region, Phila., 1971—. Mem. Tau Beta Pi, Eta Kappa Nu, Alpha Tau Omega. Clubs: Phila. Country, Duquesne, Union League (Phila.); Ekwanok Country; University (Washington). Home: 2401 Pennsylvania Ave Apt 5A4 Philadelphia PA 19130 Office: 3 Penn Center Plaza Philadelphia PA 19102

SCARFF, S. THOMAS, sculptor; b. Mt. Pleasant, Iowa, Jan. 5, 1942; s. Larry V. and Mary Margaret (Ewart) S.; diploma Sch. of Art Inst. Chgo., 1960-64; m. Signe Varco, July 16, 1970; children—Siena, Seaton. One-man shows: Live From Chgo. Gallery, 1969-70, Ox Box Sch. Art, Saugatuck, Mich., 1972, One Ill. Center, Chgo., 1972-73, Electric Gallery, Toronto, Ont., Can., 1973, U. Wis., Eau Claire, 1973, St. Mary's Coll., Notre Dame, Ind., 1974, U. Wis., Waukesha, 1975, Fragments of A Light Year, Mus. Sci. and Industry, Chgo. (Chgo. Internat. Film Festival Bronze Hugo 1976, Chgo. Art award 1977), 1976, Gilman Gallery, Chgo., 1977; group shows: Nelson Atkins Gallery Fine Arts, Kansas City, Mo., 1963, 66, Art Inst. Chgo., 1965, 66, 68, Hyde Park Art Center, Chgo., 1971, Reese Paley Gallery, N.Y.C., 1971, Dobrick Gallery, Chgo., 1975, Northwestern U., 1975, Sch. of Art Inst. of Chgo., 1976, Evanston (Ill.) Art Center, 1977, Chgo. Pub. Library Cultural Center, 1977; represented in pvt. collections; sculptures include: Sky Diamond Landing, 1975, 100 Ft. Sculpture, 1977; dir. Senses, Inc., multimedia concept group, 1976—, pres., 1976-77. Founder, organizer Blood Network, Chgo., 1969-72. Recipient award for Body of Work Over Year 1976-77, Chgo. Art Awards, 1977; Sch. of Art Inst. Chgo. travelling fellow, 1964; Nat. Endowment for Arts grantee, 1974; Ill. Arts Council grantee, 1974. Mem. Sculptors' Group (charter). Dir. motion pictures: Blood Networks, 1971; End One Way, 1974; Sky Diamond Landing, 1976; subject of numerous articles in newspapers, mags. Studio: 1544 N Sedgwick St Chicago IL 60610

SCARLETT, JOHN DONALD, univ. adminstr., lawyer; b. Reading, Pa., Aug. 23, 1923; s. Clarence A. and Mossie A. (Ritzman) S.; B.A. magna cum laude, Catawba Coll., 1948; LL.B., Harvard U., 1951; m. Sharon L. Richards, June 21, 1970; children—Randy, Holly, Sean. Admitted to N.Y. bar, 1952, N.C. bar, 1960, S.D. bar, 1964, Iowa bar, 1975; asso. firm Lundgren, Lincoln & Peterson, N.Y.C., 1951-53; asst. dir. Inst. Govt., U. N.C., Chapel Hill, 1953-54; asst. prof. law Ohio No. Law Sch., 1954-55; asst. prof. Wake Forest Law Sch., 1955-58, asso. prof., 1958-62, prof., 1962-63, dean, 1979—; dean U. S.D. Law Sch., Vermillion, 1963-68, Drake U. Law Sch., 1968-79; mem. S.D. Jud. Council, 1963-69; chmn. Iowa Crime Commn., 1971-78; mem. adv. bd. CRENLO Corp., 1977-78. Served with U.S. Army, 1943-45. Decorated Purple Heart; Congressional fellow, 1960-61. Office: Wake Forest Law Sch Winston-Salem NC 27109

SCARNE, JOHN, game co. exec.; b. Steubenville, Ohio, Mar. 4, 1903; s. Fiorangelo and Maria (Tamburro) S.; student pub. schs., Guttenberg, N.J.; m. Steffi Kearney, 1956; 1 son, John Teeko. Magician, stage, screen and television; pres. John Scarne Games, Inc., North Bergen, N.J., 1950—; gaming cons. Hilton Hotels Internat. Cons. to U.S. Armed Forces, 1941-45. Named Man of Year for Police Chiefs of U.S., 1960. Author: Scarne on Dice, 1945; Scarne on Cards, 1950; Scarne on Card Tricks, 1950; Scarne on Magic Tricks, 1952; Scarne's New Complete Guide to Gambling, 1962; The Odds Against Me, 1967; Scarne's Encyclopedia of Games, 1973; The Mafia Conspiracy, 1976; Scarne's Guide to Casino Gambling; Scarne's Guide to Modern Poker. Contbr. to World Book Ency., 1970, Ency. Brit., 1975. Office: 4319 Meadowview Ave North Bergen NJ 07047

SCARPITTI, FRANK ROLAND, educator; b. Butler, Pa., Nov. 12, 1936; s. Frank and Geneva (Costanza) S.; B.A., Cleve. State U., 1958; M.A., Ohio State U., 1959, Ph.D., 1962; m. Ellen Louise Canfield, Sept. 5, 1959; children—Susan, Jeffrey. Research asso. Ohio State U. Psychiat. Inst., Columbus, 1961-63; asst. prof. Rutgers U., 1963-67; asso. prof. sociology U. Del., 1967-69, prof., 1969—, chmn. dept., 1969—; cons. state and fed. govts. Bd. dirs. Joint Commn. on Criminology and Criminal Justice Edn. and Standards, 1977—. Recipient Hofheimer prize for research Am. Psychiat. Assn., 1967; mem. Danforth Found. asso. program. Mem. Am. Sociol. Assn., Eastern Sociol. Soc., Am. Soc. Criminology (v.p. 1978-79, pres.-elect 1979-80, pres. 1980-81), Soc. Study of Social Problems, AAUP, Alpha Kappa Delta, Phi Kappa Phi, Omicron Delta Kappa. Author: Schizophrenics in the Community, 1967; Combatting Social Problems, 1967; Youth and Drugs, 1970; Group Interaction as Therapy, 1974; Social Problems, 1974, 77, 80; Deviance: Action, Reaction, Interaction, 1975; Women, Crime and Justice, 1980; The Young Drug User, 1980. Contbr. articles to profl. jours. Home: 104 Radcliffe Dr Newark DE 19711

SCARRY, RICHARD MCCLURE, author, illustrator; b. Boston, June 5, 1919; s. John James and Mary Louise Barbara (McClure) S.; student Boston Mus. Sch., 1939-42; m. Patricia Murphy, Sept. 11, 1948; 1 son, Richard. Writer, illustrator children's books, 1947—; pres. Best Book Club Ever, Random House, Inc., N.Y.C., 1975—. Served with AUS, 1942-46. Recipient Edgar Allen Poe Spl. award Mystery Writers of Am., 1976. Mem. Authors Guild New York. Club: Gstaad (Switzerland) Yacht. Author: Best Word Book Ever, Busy, Busy World, 1965, Storybook Dictionary, 1966, Cars and Trucks and Things That Go, 1974, Busiest People Ever, 1976, Best Make-It Book Ever, 1977, Postman Pig, 1978; Best First Book Ever, 1979. Home: Schwyzerhus Gstaad Switzerland

SCARTON, BENNIE, JR., editor; b. Bretz, W.Va., July 7, 1936; s. Bennie and Leona Genevieve (Holipski) S.; B.S., W.Va. U., 1959; m. Ramona Matlick, Dec. 26, 1959; children—Tamara, Kyra. Reporter-photographer, asso. editor, news editor Jour. Messenger, Manassas, Va., 1959-73, mng. editor, 1973—. Mem. A.P. Com. Performance, 1974—. Chmn. pub. relations Prince William United Way, 1974—, Prince William Boy Scouts, 1972; mem. Manassas Centennial Com., 1973; ofcl. photographer Prince William County Fair, 1960-77. Served with USAF, 1954-55. Recipient Safety Writing Spl. award Am. Trucking Assn., 1969, Alfred P. Sloan award for distinguished pub. service in hwy. safety, 1970, Achievement award Va. Travel Council, 1971, Elijah Parish Lovejoy award for courage in journalism, 1973, First prize for newspaper promotion Nat. Newspaper Contests, 1974, Distinguished Service award Manassas Jr. C. of C., 1964. Roman Catholic. Moose. Club: Sudley Tennis and Swim. Contbr. articles to profl. jours. Home: 8926 Virginia Ave Manassas VA 22110 Office: 9009 Church St Manassas VA 22110

SCAVULLO, FRANCESCO, photographer; b. Staten Island, N.Y., Jan. 16, 1929; s. Angelo and Margaret (Pavis) S.; student pub. schs., N.Y.C.; m. Carol McCallson, 1952. Apprentice photographer with Horst at Vogue Studio, N.Y.C., 1945-48; propr. Scavullo Studio, N.Y.C., 1948—; photographer Seventeen mag., 1948-50, Town and Country mag., 1950, Harper's Bazaar mag., 1960, Cosmopolitan mag., 1965—, Vogue mag., 1970; represented in permanent collection Met. Mus. Art. Recipient Photograph of Year award, 1977; recipient numerous awards advt. art dirs. clubs. Mem. Dirs. Guild Am. Roman Catholic. Author: Scavullo on Beauty, 1976; Scavullo Men, 1977. Home: 212 E 63d St New York NY 10021

SCHAAF, C(ARL) HART, former UN ofcl., cons., writer; b. Ft. Wayne, Ind., Jan. 14, 1912; s. Albert H. and Bertha May (Hart) S.; student U. Montpellier (France), 1930-31, U. Stockholm (Sweden), 1937-39; B.A., U. Mich., 1935, Ph.D., (Horace H. Rackham fellow), 1940; m. Barbara Joan Crook, Nov. 22, 1945; children—Albert H., Timothy H. Instr. polit. sci. Coll. City N.Y., summer 1940; asso. prof. pub. adminstrn. Richmond div. Coll. William and Mary, 1940-42; state rationing adminstr. for Va., U.S. OPA, 1942-43; asst. dep. dir. gen., also chief supply for Europe UNRRA, 1944-47; asso. prof. adminstrn. Sch. Bus. and Pub. Adminstrn. Cornell U., 1947-49; dep. exec. sec. UN Econ. Commn. for Asia and Far East, 1949-54; mem. UN Tech. Assistance Survey Mission to Indonesia, 1950; spl. adviser to UN sec. gen. on relief and support civilian population Korea, 1950-51; resident rep. in Israel UN Tech. Assistance Bd., 1954-57, resident rep. in Phillippines, 1957-59; co-chmn. Seminar on Devel. and Adminstrn. Internat. River Basin U. B.C., 1961; exec. agt. Com. Coordination Investigations Lower Mekong Basin UN Econ. Commn. for Asia and Far East, Bangkok, Thailand, 1959-69; resident rep. UN Devel. Program, Sri Lanka and Republic of Maldives, 1969-74; dep. exec. dir. ops. UN Fund for Population Activities, N.Y.C., 1974-77; writer, cons. Mem. Mekong Advisory Com. Bd., 1969-72. Recipient (with Mekong Com.) Ramon Magsaysay award for internat. understanding, 1966, Outstanding Achievement award U. Mich., 1966. Mem. Am. Polit. Sci. Assn., Soc. Internat. Devel. Author: (play) Partition, 1948; (with Russell H. Fifield) The Lower Mekong: Challenge to Cooperation in Southeast Asia, 1963. Contbr. articles to tech. and academic jours. Home: 3525 Twin Branches Dr Silver Spring MD 20906

SCHAAF, JAMES HOWARD, football club exec.; b. Erie, Pa., May 22, 1938; s. Raymond and Marion Coletta S.; B.S. in Econs. U. Notre Dame, 1959; m. Julia Kay Brockmeier, Feb. 2, 1963; children—Jill Marie, James Michae. Stockbroker, A.C. Allyn & Co., 1960-61; traveling sec., public relations dir. Kansas City Athletics Baseball Club, 1961-66; public relations dir. Kansas City Chiefs Football Club, 1966-68, asst. gen. mgr., public relations dir., 1969-74, v.p., asst. gen. mgr., 1974-78, v.p., gen. mgr., 1978—. Mem. Kansas City Sports Commn.; bd. dirs., v.p. St. Mary's Hosp. Served with U.S. Army, 1959. Mem. Greater Kansas City C. of C. Club: Kansas City. Office: 1 Arrowhead Dr Kansas City MO 64129

SCHAAL, RICHARD VICTOR, actor, dir., writer; b. Chgo., May 5, 1928; s. Victor Cornilius and Margaret Semple (Waddell) S.; student Morgan Park Jr. Coll., 1950-51, Wilson Jr. Coll., 1951, Ray Vogue Sch. Comml. Art, 1951-52, Inst. Design, Chgo., 1952-53, Northwestern U. Sch. Journalism, 1953, Ill. Inst. Tech., 1954; m. Lois Haddick, Aug. 2, 1952; 1 dau., Wendy; m. 2d, Valerie Harper, Dec. 13, 1965. Comml. artist W.L. Stensgaard Co., Chgo., 1953-55; indsl. designer Edward Hines Lumber Co., Chgo., 1955-58; owner, operator bldg. and design co., Crete, Ill., 1958-60; mem. co. Second City, Chgo., 1960-63; appeared on Broadway: Little Murders, Story Theatre, Harry Noon and Night, Same Time Next Year; star TV show: Please Stand By, 1978—; other TV appearances include: Phyllis, Rhoda, Mary Tyler Moore Show, Bob Newhart Show, Rockford Files, Police Woman, Harry O; appeared in films: The Russians are Coming, The Russians are Coming, Americathon; pres. My Space Inc., Los Angeles; instr. dept. psychology U. So. Calif. Active hunger project Am. Youth Found. Served with USMC, 1946-48. Mem. Screen Actors Guild, Actors Equity, AFTRA, Dirs. Guild, Writers Guild, Acad. TV Arts and Scis. Home: 10570 Lindbrook Dr Los Angeles CA 90024 Office: 9200 Sunset Blvd Suite 905 Los Angeles CA 90069. *I know that life is all about satisfaction, and satisfaction is produced by acknowledging that things and people are the way the are and the way they are not. This is the definition of love. This is the path I have finally been able to choose and I'm satisfied.*

SCHABER, GORDON DUANE, law sch. dean; b. Ashley, N.D., Nov. 22, 1927; s. Ronald and Esther (Schatz) S.; A.B. with distinction, Sacramento State Coll., 1949; J.D. with honors, U. Calif. at San Francisco, 1952; LL.D., McGeorge Sch. Law, 1961. Admitted to Calif. bar, 1953; practice in Sacramento, 1953—; mem. firm Schaber & Cecchettini, Sacramento, 1953-65; prof. McGeorge Coll. of Law (now McGeorge Sch. Law of U. Pacific), Sacramento, 1953—, asst. dean, 1956, dean, 1957—; lectr. Calif. Bar Rev. Course, 1967-72; presiding judge Superior Ct. Sacramento County, 1964-70. Mem. Calif. Bd. Control, 1962-64; chmn. Greater Sacramento Plan Com., 1970; cons. on establishment Sch. Law at U. Puget Sound, 1970-71; cons. study on jud. workload Jud. Council Calif., 1971-72; mem. Adv. Com. to Chief Justice Calif. on Superior Ct. Mgmt., 1971; cons. vehicle theft study Calif. Hwy. Patrol, 1972; panelist Sacramento Bee Crime Prevention Program, 1971-76; mem. adv. com. to Calif. Office Econ. Opportunity, Calif. Legal Services Expt., 1972; vice chmn. Calif. Ednl. Facilities Authority, 1978—; bd. dirs. Nat. Center Adminstrv. Justice, 1978 Chmn., Sacramento County Democratic Central Com., 1960-64; mem. Dem. State Central Com., 1960-64, 74—. Named Sacramento County Young Man of Year, 1963; Outstanding Contbr. Law award Am. Trial Lawyers Assn., 1965; Trial Judge of Year, Calif. Trial Lawyers Assn., 1969; grantee Law Enforcement Assistance Adminstrn. and Office Calif. Criminal Justice Planning, 1974. Fellow Am. Bar Assn. (vice chmn. council sect. legal edn. and admissions to bar 1975-79, adv. com. pres.-elect on competence of lawyers continuing edn. 1978); mem. Sacramento Bar Assn. (v.p. 1970), State Bar Calif. (mem. com. legislation 1969—, spl. com. appellate cts. 1970-72, long range adv. planning com. 1972—; vice chmn. com. law sch. edn. 1973 chmn. 1974; mem. commn. to study bar examination processes 1976—), Am. Judicature Soc., Order of Coif. Author: Contracts in a Nutshell. Home: 937 Piedmont Dr Sacramento CA 95822 Office: U of Pacific McGeorge Sch of Law Sacramento CA 95817

SCHACHER, JOHN FREDRICK, educator; b. Jamestown, N.D., July 17, 1928; s. William and Rachel Cecile (Hummel) S.; B.S., N.D. State U., 1953; M.S., Tulane U., 1955, Ph.D., 1960; m. Dolores Ann Polack, July 6, 1952; children—Eric, Susan, David. Research asso. N.D. Inst. Regional Studies, 1952-53; mem. faculty U. Malaya, Singapore, 1956-58: asst. prof. med. scis., tropical health dept. Am. U., Beirut, Lebanon, 1960-66, asso. prof., 1966-69; asso. prof. Sch. Pub. Health, UCLA, 1969-72, prof. infectious and tropical diseases, 1972—; mem. sci. tech. advisory com. WHO, 1974—, mem. expert com., 1973—. Served with U.S. Army, 1947-49. Fellow Zool. Soc. London; mem. Am. (council 1974-77), Brit. socs. parasitology, Malaysian Soc. Parasitology, Am. Soc. Tropical Medicine and Hygiene, Royal Soc. Tropical Medicine and Hygiene (sec. Calif.), N.Y. Acad. Sci., AAAS, Internat. Filariasis Assn. (sec. gen. 1969-79), So. Calif. Parasitologists (pres. 1974-75). Contbr. articles to profl. jours. Home: 3120 Castle Heights Ave Los Angeles CA 90034 Office: Sch Public Health U Calif Los Angeles CA 90024

SCHACHMAN, HOWARD KAPNEK, molecular biologist, educator; b. Phila., Dec. 5, 1918; s. Morris H. and Rose (Kapnek) S.; B.S. in Chem. Engring., Mass. Inst. Tech., 1939; Ph.D. in Phys. Chemistry, Princeton, 1948; D.Sc. (hon.), Northwestern U., 1974; m. Ethel H. Lazarus, Oct. 20, 1945; children—Marc, David. Fellow NIH, 1946-48; instr., asst. prof. U. Calif. at Berkeley, 1948-54, asso. prof. biochemistry, 1954-59, prof. biochemistry and molecular biology, 1959—, chmn. dept. molecular biology, dir. virus lab., 1969-76. Served from ensign to lt., USNR, 1945-47. Guggenheim Meml. fellow, 1956. Recipient John Scott award, 1964, Warren Triennial prize Mass. Gen. Hosp., 1965. Mem. Nat. Acad. Sci., Am. Chem. Soc. (recipient award in Chem. Instrumentation 1962, Calif. sec. award 1958), AAAS, Am. Soc. Biol. Chemists, Am. Acad. Arts and Scis., Sigma Xi. Author: Ultracentrifugation in Biochemistry, 1959. Office: Molecular Biology and Virus Lab U Calif Berkeley CA 94720

SCHACHT, HENRY BREWER, diesel engine mfg. co. exec.; b. Erie, Pa., Oct. 16, 1934; s. Henry Blass and Virginia (Brewer) S.; B.S., Yale, 1956; M.B.A., Harvard, 1962; m. Nancy Godfrey, Aug. 27, 1960; children—James, Laura, Jane, Mary. Sales trainee Am. Brake Shoe Co., N.Y.C., 1956-57; investment mgr. Irwin Mgmt. Co., Columbus, Ind., 1962-64; v.p. finance Cummins Engine Co., Inc., Columbus, 1964-66, v.p., central area mgr. internat., London, Eng., 1966-67, group v.p. internat. and subsidiaries, 1967-69, pres., Columbus, 1969-77, chmn., 1977—; dir. CBS. Mem. Com. Econ. Devel., Urban Inst., Western Hwy. Inst.; adv. com. Yale Sch. Orgn. and Mgmt.; mem. Trilateral Commn.; trustee Rockefeller Found. Served with USNR, 1957-60. Mem. Conf. Bd., Council Fgn. Relations, Mgmt. Execs. Soc., Tau Beta Pi. Republican. Home: 4300 N Riverside Dr Columbus IN 47201 Office: 1000 5th St Columbus IN 47201

SCHACHT, HENRY MEVIS, pub. relations exec.; b. Pasadena, Calif., Feb. 28, 1916; s. Henry and Amelia (Claussen) S.; B.A., U. Calif. at Berkeley, 1936; m. Mary Joan Turnbull, Dec. 30, 1937; children—Henry John, Linda Joan. Info. specialist U. Calif. at Berkeley, 1936-42; dir. agr. NBC, San Francisco, 1942-59, ABC, San Francisco, 1959-60; agrl. columnist San Francisco Chronicle, 1959—; dir. agrl. info. U. Calif., 1961-65; v.p. corp. relations, corp. sec. Calif. Canners & Growers, San Francisco, 1965—; freelance writer, 1936—; cons. radio-TV to FAO of UN, Cairo, 1963, Mexico City, 1965, Tokyo, 1966; dir. Calif. Co. for Internat. Trade, Parrott Ranch Co. Pres., U.S. Fruit Export Council, 1972-75. Mem. Pub. Relations Soc. Am., Pub. Relations Roundtable San Francisco, Nat. Assn. Farm Broadcasters, Agrl. Relations Council, Nat. Canners Assn. (dir. 1966—). Home: 60 Hiller Dr Oakland CA 94618 Office: Ferry Bldg San Francisco CA 94106

SCHACHTEL, HYMAN JUDAH, rabbi; b. London, Eng., May 24, 1907; s. Barnard and Janie (Spector) S.; came to U.S., 1914, naturalized, 1921; B.A., U. Cin., 1928; B.H., Rabbi, Hebrew Union Coll., 1931; postgrad. Columbia Tchrs. Coll., 1933-37; Ed.D., Ed.D., U. Houston, 1948 D.D., Hebrew Union Coll., 1958; D.H.L., Southwestern U., 1955; m. Barbara H. Levin, Oct. 15, 1941; children—Bernard, Ann Mollie. Ordained rabbi, 1931; rabbi West End Synagogue, N.Y.C. 1931-43; chief rabbi Temple Beth Israel, Houston, 1943—; tchr. philosophy U. Houston, 1950-55; lectr. theology, history, philosophy St. Mary's Cath. Sem., Houston; adj. prof. religion Inst. Religion, 1973—; lectr. Judaism, U. Houston, 1974—, U. St. Thomas, 1973—. Chmn. subcom. edn. Gov.'s Commn. Human Relations, 1970—; pres. Tex. Kallah Rabbis, 1962, Houston Rabbinical Assn., 1960; mem. exec. bd. Central Conf. Am. Rabbis, 1965-67, v.p., sec.-treas. Southwest region 1966—; chaplain Variety Club, Houston, 1955—, Houston Fire Dept., 1964—; delivered inaugural prayer for Pres. Lyndon Johnson, 1965; v.p. N.Y. Bd. Rabbis, 1942-43; exec. com. Houston Met. Ministries. Pres., Harris

County Mental Health Assn., 1960; mem. bd. Houston Symphony Soc., 1955—, San Harris County Mental Health Assn., 1960; mem. bd. Houston Symphony Soc., 1955—, San Jacinto council Girl Scouts, 1962—, Houston Heart Assn., 1964—, Houston Crime Commn., 1962-65; mem. nat. planning bd., trustee United Fund Harris County, 1965—; bd. overseers Hebrew Fund Harris County, 1965—; bd. overseers Hebrew Union Coll.-Jewish Inst. Religion, 1961-65; trustee Houston Salvation Army, Houston chpt. ARC, Inst. Religion, Houston, DePelchin Faith Home, Houston, Harris County Mental Health Assn. Recipient Coronat medal St. Edward's U., Austin Tex., 1963, award NCCJ, 1975, Human Relations award Houston chpt. Am. Jewish Com., 1975, Humanitarian award B'nai B'rith, Houston, 1975, Disting. Alumnus award U. Houston, 1977. Mem. Tex. Philos. Soc., Phi Delta Kappa, Phi Epsilon Pi (hon.). Kiwanian. Author: Real Enjoyment of Living, 1954; The Life You Want to Live, 1956; The Shadowed Valley, 1964; Aspects of Jewish Homiletics, 1964; How to Meet The Challenge of Life and Death, 1974. Home: 2527 Glenhaven St Houston TX 77025 Office: 5600 N Braeswood Houston TX 77096. *This is the wisdom for the successful life-to work hard but not to expect too much; to love but not to deem it inviolable; to dream but not to rage at the rude awakening; to believe in God but not to rebel and blaspheme if our prayers are unanswered; to live on as righteous men and women but not to deny the righteous life when the inevitable sorrows overtake us; to be gazing upward, ever upward with such eager intensity that the light of our own eyes lends color and radiance to the world around us, so that we can go forward undaunted and faithful, unafraid and confident, meeting successfully whatever betide. If it be skies of sunshine, to enjoy them deeply, knowing how unusually blessed we are. And if it be skies of clouds, to find even in the clouds the rainbow of promise.*

SCHACHTER, ALBERT, educator; b. Winnipeg, Man., Can., Aug. 23, 1932; s. Harry and Rebecca (Raskin) S.; B.A. with honors in Classics, McGill U., 1955; D.Phil., Oxford U., 1968; m. June Hoysager, Aug. 11, 1960. Lectr. classics McGill U., Montreal, Que., Can., 1959-64, asst. prof., 1964-68, asso. prof., 1968-71, prof., 1972—, chmn. dept. classics, 1970-74. Arthur Sims scholar, 1956-59; grantee Can. Council, 1958-60, 66, 71-73, 75, Ford Found., 1968-72; Commonwealth Study grantee Inst. Classical Studies, London, 1965-66. Mem. Am. Philol. Assn., Archaeol. Inst. Am., Audio-Visual Lang. Assn. (U.K.), Classical Assn. Can., Hellenic Soc., Joint Assn. Classical Tchrs. (U.K.), Societe des Etudes Grecques et Latines du Que. (exec. council 1977—). Club: Faculty (McGill U.). Author: (with C.D. Ellis) Ancient Greek; A Structural Programme, 1973; McGill Greek Project Stage 2.1, 1974. Gen. editor: Teiresias: A Review and Continuing Bibliography of Boiotian Studies, 1971—. Home: 5559 Borden Ave Montreal PQ H4V 2T7 Canada

SCHACHTER, JACK JULIUS, accountant; b. Boston, Oct. 29, 1905; s. Carl and Rebecca (Gordon) S.; student pub. schs., bus. coll.; m. Lillian Cohen, June 8, 1930; children—Robert Allen Schachter, Joan Carol (Mrs. Theodore G. Goldfarb). Chief accountant, credit mgr. Ferro Steel Products Co., 1928-31; pub. accountant, 1931—, also tax cons.; treas. All Purpose Spreader Co., Elyria, Ohio, 1948-54; asst. treas. Plas Constrn. Co., Elyria, 1948-56; sr. partner Katz, Schachter & Krause (formerly known as Res. Audit Co.), Cleve., 1931—; dir. Tyroler Metals, Inc., E.C. Andrews Co., Bettcher Mfg. Co. (all Cleve.), Blaw Knox Co., Pitts. Mem. Citizens League of Cleve., Newcomen Soc. Am., Internat. Platform Assn. K.P. (past chancellor). Mason (32 deg.). Club: Temple of Cleveland (pres. 1949-50). Home: 2585 Buckhurst Dr Beachwood OH 44122 Office: 5001 Mayfield Rd Lyndhurst OH 44124

SCHACHTER, OSCAR, lawyer, educator; b. N.Y.C., June 19, 1915; s. Max and Fannie (Javits) S.; B.S.S., Coll. City N.Y., 1936; J.D., Columbia, 1939; m. Mollie Miller, Aug. 9, 1936; children—Judith (Mrs. John Modell), Ellen (Mrs. John P. Leventhal). Editor-in-chief Columbia Law Rev., 1938-39; admitted to N.Y. bar, 1939; in law practice, N.Y.C., 1939-40; atty. U.S. Dept. of Labor, Washington, 1940; chief nat. defense sect., law dept. FCC, 1941; sect. of law com. and adviser on internat. communications Bd. of War Communications, 1941-42; prin., divisional asst. U.S. Dept. State (adviser on wartime econ. controls and on European liberated areas), 1942-43; asst. gen. counsel UNRRA, 1944-46; drafting officer UNRRA council sessions, 1944-45, legal adv. UNRRA del. to USSR and Poland, 1945; legal counselor UN, 1946-52, dir. gen. legal div., 1952-66; dep. exec. dir., dir. studies UN Inst. for Tng. and Research, 1966-75; lectr. law Yale U. Law Sch., 1955-71; Carnegie lectr. Hague Acad. Internat. Law, 1963; Rosenthal lectr. Northwestern U. Law Sch., 1974; prof. law Columbia U. Law Sch. and Faculty Internat. Affairs, 1975—. Chmn. legal com. UN Maritime Conf., 1948; legal cons. UNESCO, 1948; past dir. Gen. Legal Div. of UN; served as legal adviser various internat. confs. and UN councils and coms.; sec. legal adv. com. UN Atomic Energy Commn., 1946-47; vice chmn. Internat. Investment Law Conf., 1958; exec. sec. Internat. Arbitration Conf., 1958. Bd. dirs. Internat. Peace Acad.; governing council Inst. Internat. Orgn., Sussex (Eng.) U. Fellow World Acad. Art and Sci.; mem. Am. Soc. Internat. Law (pres. 1968-70, hon. v.p., mem. exec. council), Council on Fgn. Relations, Inst. de Droit Internat., Internat. Law Assn., Internat. Astronautical Acad., Com. to Study Orgn. of Peace, Assn. Bar City N.Y. (chmn. com. on internat. human rights 1977—), Phi Beta Kappa. Club: Chaos (N.Y.). Author: Relation of Law, Politics and Action in the U.N., 1964; Sharing The World's Resources, 1977. Co-author: Across the Space Frontier, 1952; Toward Wider Acceptance of UN Treaties, 1971. Contbr. articles, monographs on internat. law, internat. instns., legal philosophy, human rights, internat. peace and security, internat. resources. Editor-in-chief: Am. Jour. Internat. Law, 1978—; editorial bd. Earth Law Jour., Marine Policy (Eng.). Home: 36 Sutton Pl S New York NY 10022 Office: Columbia U Law Sch New York NY 10027

SCHACK, MARIO LAWRENCE, architect; b. Germany, Apr. 3, 1929; s. Jack and Erica (Sormane) S.; came to U.S., 1939, naturalized, 1944; Diploma Architecture, Swiss Fed. Inst. Tech., 1960; M.Arch. in Urban Design, Harvard U., 1961; m. Romilda A. Foti, Aug. 12, 1956; children—Lawrence Eric, Nina Francesca. Asso. architect Sert, Jackson, Gourley, Cambridge, Mass.; v.p., prin. RTKL Assos., Inc., 1965-78; asst. prof. architecture Cornell U., 1963-65, prof., chmn. dept. architecture, 1975—; prin. Marks, Cooke, Schack, Thomas, Inc., Balt., 1978—; mem. faculty U. Md., 1969-73; vis. critic, lectr. various univs. Served with U.S. Army, 1951-54. Mem. AIA, Md. Soc. Architects (pres. 1973-74), Am. Inst. Planners (asso.). Prin. projects with RTKL, Inc. include: St. Mary's Convent, Annapolis, Md., 1966, Southwestern High Sch., Balt., 1966, U. Md. Balt. Campus Library, Catonsville, 1967, Charles Center South, Balt., 580 Devel., Cin., Queensgate Housing, Cin., St. Elizabeth Hosp., Covington, Ky. Office: Sibley Hall Dept Architecture Cornell U Ithaca NY 14850 also 219 W Joppa Rd Baltimore MD 21204

SCHAD, THEODORE GEORGE, JR., food co. exec.; b. N.Y.C., Mar. 4, 1927; s. Theodore George and Helen (Tennyson) S.; student Va. Mil. Inst., 1944-45; B.S. in Bus. and Econs., Ill. Inst. Tech., 1950, M.S. in Bus. and Econs., 1951; m. Karma Rose Cundell, Mar. 21, 1957; children—Roberta, Theodore George, Olive Schad Smith, Peter Tennyson. Vice pres. mktg. Great Western Savs. Co., Los Angeles, 1961-63; prin., nat. dir. mktg. and econs. cons. Peat, Marwick, Mitchell, N.Y.C., 1964-71; chmn. bd., pres., chief exec. officer Lou Ana Foods, Inc., Lou Ana Industries, Inc., Lou Ana Industries Internat., Opelousas, La., 1971—; instr. mktg. and econs. U. Calif., Los Angeles, Riverside, U. So. Calif., Los Angeles State Coll. Pres., Assn. Parents Retarded Children, Mamaroneck, N.Y., 1970-71; bd. dirs. Council for Better La., Baton Rouge, 1975—, U.S. Indsl. Council, 1979—; trustee Va. Mil. Inst. Found., 1978—. Mem. Am. Mktg. Assn. (pres. So. Calif. chpt. 1961-62, dir. 1962-63). Republican. Methodist. Office: Lou Ana Foods PO Box 591 Opelousas LA 70570. *Too often we don't acknowledge enough that much of our success in life is due to the support of our wives and our associates. My late wife was a tower of strength. I cannot possibly express my gratitude for her support in all my endeavors. Her faith in me never wavered.*

SCHAEBERLE, ROBERT MARTIN, food co. exec.; b. Newark, Jan. 2, 1923; s. Frederick M. and Bertha M. (Thieleman) S.; A.B., Dartmouth, 1944; m. Barbara J. Slockbower, Aug. 15, 1945. With Nabisco, Inc., 1946—, asst. to pres., 1962, v.p., 1962-65, exec. v.p., 1966-68, pres., 1968-73, chmn., chief exec. officer, 1973—, also dir.; dir. Libby-Owens Ford Co., Prudential Life Ins. Co. Served to lt. comdr. USNR, World War II. Mem. Fin. Execs. Inst. Office: River Rd East Hanover NJ 07936

SCHAEDLER, RUSSELL WILLIAM, physician, educator; b. Hatfield, Pa., Dec. 17, 1927; s. Robert and Sophia Louise (Enz) S.; B.S., Ursinus Coll., 1949; M.D., Jefferson Med. Coll., 1953. Intern, Jefferson Med. Coll. Hosp., Thomas Jefferson U., Phila., 1953-54, prof., chmn. dept. microbiology, 1968—; asst. Rockefeller Inst. for Med. Research, asst. physician Hosp. of Rockefeller Inst., 1954-57, asst. prof. Rockefeller Inst., resident asso. physician, 1957-62, asso. prof., physician to Hosp., 1962-67; asso. mem. Armed Forces Epidemiology Bd., Enteric Commn., 1967-72; mem. bacteriology and mycology study sect. NIH, 1970-71, chmn., 1973-74; mem. and chmn. NIH bacteriology and mycology AHR study sect., 1978—. Bd. dirs. Cardeza Found. Served with U.S. Army, 1946-47. Mem. Am. Assn. Immunologists, Am. Soc. Microbiology, Am. Gastroent. Assn., Infectious Disease Soc. Am., Coll. Physicians Phila., Harvey Soc., AAAS, J. Aitken Meigs Med. Assn., N.Y. Tb. and Health Assn. (dir. 1965-68), Sigma Xi, Alpha Omega Alpha. Clubs: Vesper; Sydenham Coterie. Mem. editorial bd. Jour. Bacteriology, 1965-69, Jour. Infection and Immunity, 1970-72; contbr. articles to sci. jours. Research in anaerobes and microecology of the gut. Home: 320 Delancey St Philadelphia PA 19106 Office: 1020 Locust St Philadelphia PA 19107

SCHAEFER, ADOLPH (OSCAR), JR., advt. agy. exec.; b. Phila., May 21, 1932; s. Adolph Oscar and Jessie Rae (Brooks) S.; B.S. in Econs., Wharton Sch. U. Pa., 1954; m. Elizabeth Stewart Howie, June 16, 1972; children by previous marriage—Jeffrey S., Andrew C.; step-children—Deborah H., Scott S. With drug products div. Procter & Gamble, Cin., 1954-56; mfrs. rep. Towle & Son Co., Phila., 1956-61; partner Rockett & Schaefer, advt., Phila., 1961-63; v.p. Eldridge Co., Phila., 1963-64; pres. Schaefer Advt. Inc., Valley Forge, Pa., 1964—. Mem. alumni bd. mgrs. Episcopal Acad., 1969-73. Served with U.S. Army, 1954-56. Mem. Bus. and Profl. Advt. Assn., Phi Gamma Delta. Club: Aronimink Golf. Mem. editorial adv. bd. Pa. Gazette, U. Pa., 1970—. Home: 137 Jaffrey Rd Malvern PA 19355 Office: Valley Forge PA 19482

SCHAEFER, ANDRE, hotel exec.; b. Exch Sue Alzeite, Luxembourg, Dec. 1, 1931; s. George and Lilia (De'Gregori) S.; B. Commerce and Econs., Comml. Coll., Worms-Rhine, Germany, 1952; M. Commerce, U. Heidelberg (Germany), 1954; m. Marianne, Dec. 17, 1955; 1 son, Robert J. Sales exec. tng., nat. sales office Palmer House, Chgo., 1965; asst. dir. sales, then dir. sales and account exec. Netherland Hilton and Terrace Hilton, Cin., 1965-69; dir. sales Pitts. Hilton, 1969-70, Statler Hilton, Boston, 1970-71; resident mgr. Omaha Hilton, 1971-74; gen. mgr. Univ. Hilton, Los Angeles, 1974-77; gen. mgr. Anchorage Westward Hilton, 1977—; bd. dirs. Anchorage Conv. Bur.; instr. in sales mgmt. Allegheny Coll., 1969-70. Mem. Alaska C. of C., Anchorage C. of C., Chaine Des Rotisseurs (chargé de missions), Alaska Visitors Assn., Downtown Mcht. Assn. Roman Catholic. Club: Skal Internat. Home and Office: Anchorage Westward Hilton PO Box 520 Anchorage AK 99510

SCHAEFER, ARTHUR JOSEPH, ret. univ. adminstr.; b. Chgo., Mar. 20, 1913; s. William Joseph and Elizabeth (Kostlevy) S.; Ph.B., DePaul U., 1934; postgrad. U. Chgo., 1935-40; m. Virginia Hayden, Aug. 20, 1940; (dec. July, 1965); children—Martha, Michael, Mark, Laura Mary, Sarah, Christopher, Jonathan, Margaret, Mary Honora; m. 2d, Rosemary Lind Sullivan, July 30, 1966; children—Theresa, Timothy, Kevin, Mary Eileen Sullivan Schaefer. Mem. faculty DePaul U., Chgo., 1935-42, dir. pub. relations, 1946-55, v.p. for devel. and pub. relations, 1955-79, emeritus, 1979—; dir. Arlington Heights Fed. Savs. & Loan Assn. Mem. Pub. Relations Clinic Chgo., pres., 1957. Chmn. Cana Conf. of Chgo., 1953-54; pres. Chgo. Soc. Fund-Raising Execs, 1962-63. Trustee Marmion Mil. Acad. Served to lt. (s.g.) USNR, 1943-46. Mem. Council Advancement and Support Edn. (pres. 1961-62). Roman Catholic. Home: 318 S Prospect Ave Park Ridge IL 60068 Office: DePaul U 25 E Jackson Blvd Chicago IL 60604

SCHAEFER, CARL FELLMAN, artist; b. Hanover, Ont., Can., Apr. 30, 1903; s. John Daniel and Mamie (Fellman) S.; student Ont. Coll. Art, Toronto, 1921-24; student of lithography with Ray Nash, Dartmouth, 1940-41; D.Litt., U. Waterloo, 1976; m. Lily Anne Evers, Mar. 17, 1927; children—Mark, Paul. Free-lance artist, 1924-29; instr. Central Tech. Sch., Toronto, 1930; dir. art Hart House, U. Toronto, 1934-40, Art Center, Art Gallery Toronto, 1935-37; dir. art Trinity Coll. Sch., Port Hope, Ont., 1936-40, 46-48; instr. Queen's U., Kingston, 1945-60; instr. Ont. Coll. Art, 1948, dir., 1956-68, chmn. emeritus, 1968-69, fellow, 1976; instr. Schneider Sch. Fine Arts, Actinolite, Ont., 1967—; prin. works include St. Ann's Ch., Toronto, 1923; stage sets, 1927; Claridge Apts. and Concourse Bldg., 1928-29; assisted Emannuel Hahn, Sculptor, 1926; display designer T. Eaton Co., 1929; assisted Charles Comfort with mural for N. Am. Life Ins. Co., 1932; commnd. series of paintings for Can. Packers. Hon. mem. sr. common room Trinity Coll., U. Toronto, 1974—. Served as flight lt., ofcl. artist, RCAF, 1943-46. Guggenheim fellow (1st Canadian), 1940; recipient Queen Elizabeth II Coronation medal, 1953, Can. Centennial medal, 1967, Can. Silver Jubilee Elizabeth II medal, 1978; mem. Order of Can. Fellow Royal Soc. Arts (London), Ont. Coll. Art; mem. Can. Group Painters (charter), Can. Soc. Graphic Arts (charter), Can. Soc. Painters in Watercolour (charter mem.; pres. 1938-40); life fellow Internat. Inst. Arts and Letters; asso. Royal Canadian Acad. Arts, 1949, academician, 1964, companion, 1972. Address: 157 St Clements Ave Toronto ON M4R IHI Canada. *All art is abstract and I am forever impelled to express myself through the use of symbols to identify myself with the humanism and the intimacy of the world of nature. Art must have organic structure and meaning and it must grow as it were out of and according to the laws of nature to be expressed with a communicable sympathy.*

SCHAEFER, CARL GEORGE LEWIS, writer, pub. relations and advt. exec.; b. Cleve., Sept. 2; s. George S. and Margaret (Freyberg) S.; A.B., U. Calif. at Los Angeles, 1931; m. Virginia Clark, Sept. 2, 1938; 1 dau., Susan Diane (Mrs. Cedric Francis). Free-lance mag. writer, 1931; reporter Hollywood (Calif.) Citizen-News, 1931-35; with Warner Bros.-Seven Arts, Burbank, Calif., 1935-71, dir. internat. relations, 1962-71; owner Carl Schaefer Enterprises, Hollywood, 1971— bur. chief movie/TV mktg. Movie News, S'pore, Antena, B.A., 1975—. Mem. internat. com. Acad. Motion Picture Arts and Scis., 1940—; chmn. internat. Hollywood Museum, 1964. Vice chmn. Hollywood-Wilshire council Boy Scouts Am., 1957-58; mem. Mayor Los Angeles Council Internat. Visitors, 1964—; mem. interview bd. Los Angeles Police Dept., 1965—. Mng. dir. Internat. Festival Adv. Council, 1971—. Served with AUS, World War II; ETO. Decorated Huesped de Honor (Mexico); Legion of Honor (France); Ordine al Merito (Italy); l'Ordre de la Courrenne (Belgium). Mem. Am. Soc. French Legion of Honor, Assn. Motion Picture and TV Producers (chmn. internat. co. 1967-68, 69-70), Internat. Press Photo-Journalists (hon.), Fgn. Trade Assn. So. Calif. (past pres., chmn. bd.), Brit.-Am. (dir.), Los Angeles chambers commerce, Western Publs. Assn., Am. Bus. Press (coordinator Hollywood Reporter internat. poster competition 1971—, exec. com. ShoWest 1978—), Blue Key, Sigma Alpha Epsilon, Alpha Delta Sigma. Republican. Methodist. Mason (Shriner). Clubs: Press, Brit. United Services (Los Angeles). Address: 3320 Bennett Dr Hollywood CA 90068. *When I lose my imagination, I'll be more than happy to cash in the chips whatever—and slink off.*

SCHAEFER, CLARENCE HAROLD, pen co. exec.; b. Petersburg, Ohio, Apr. 17, 1920; s. Delmer Leroy and Lillie Idella (Sitler) S.; student Youngstown Coll., 1940-41; B.C.S., Golden Gate U., 1955; m. Lucille Marie Potter, May 5, 1942; children—Karen Lynn Schaefer Awad, Mark Daryl. Sr. accountant Marchant Calculators, Inc., Oakland, Calif., 1945-49; chief accountant SCM Corp., N.Y.C., 1950-54, controller, 1955-63, v.p. fin. and adminstrn., 1964-68; v.p. corp. devel. Parker Pen Co., Janesville, Wis., 1969-70, treas., 1971, v.p. fin., treas., 1972—. Mem. adv. com. Public Expenditure Survey of Wis. Served with USN, 1941-45. Mem. Fin. Execs. Inst. (dir. and treas. Milw. chpt.). Home: 2421 Chickasaw Dr Janesville WI 53545 Office: 219 E Court St Janesville WI 53545

SCHAEFER, EDWARD JOHN, electric co. exec.; b. Balt., July 10, 1901; s. Michael and Elizabeth (Plantholt) S.; B.Elec. Engring., Johns Hopkins, 1923; D.Engring. (hon.), Ind. Inst. Tech.; m. Hildegarde H. Hormel, Dec. 25, 1928; children—Patricia, Diane Dorothy. With Franklin Electric Co., Bluffton, Inc., 1944—, chmn. bd., 1947—; chmn. bd. Franklin Electric of Can., Ltd., Strathroy, Franklin Electric Europa Gmbh, Wittlich, West Germany; dir. Oil Dynamics, Inc., Tulsa, Franklin Electric (Australia) Pty., Ltd., Dandenong, Victoria, First Nat. Bank, Bluffton, Ind. Trustee Ind. Inst. Tech.; fellow of bd. trustees Johns Hopkins U. Recipient Coffin award Gen. Electric Co., 1937. Fellow Am. Inst. E.E.; mem. Tau Beta Pi. Clubs: Ft. Wayne Engineers, Ft. Wayne Country. Patentee elec. and mech. devices. Home: Rural Route 5 Box 30 Bluffton IN 46714 Office: Franklin Electric Co Bluffton IN 46714

SCHAEFER, FRANK, author; b. Newburg, N.Y., Oct. 25, 1936; s. Francis Henry and Mary Elizabeth (Hutchinson) S.; B.A., Tex. A&I U., 1963; M.A. in Drama, Trinity U., 1968; m. Jerelyn Kay Williams; 1 son, Frank. Author numerous books with Kerry Newcomb (under pseudonyms) including: Raven (Shana Carrol), 1978; Love's Wildest Fires (Christina Savage), 1978; Matanza (Peter Gentry), 1979; Pandora Man, 1979. Served with U.S. Navy, 1956-59. Home: Dallas TX Office: care Aaron Priest Literary Agy 150 E 35th St New York NY 10016

SCHAEFER, GEORGE LOUIS, producer-dir.; b. Wallingford, Conn., Dec. 16, 1920; s. Louis and Elsie (Otterbein) S.; A.B. magna cum laude, Lafayette Coll., 1941; student Yale Drama Sch., 1942; D.Litt., Lafayette Coll., 1963; D.H.L., Coker Coll., 1973; m. Mildred Trares, Feb. 5, 1954. Producer-dir. TV series, Hallmark Hall of Fame, 1955-68; dir. Broadway prodns. G.I. Hamlet, 1945, Man and Superman, 1947, The Linden Tree, 1948, The Heiress (revival), 1949, Idiot's Delight (revival), 1950, Southwest Corner, 1955, The Apple Cart, 1956, The Body Beautiful, 1958, Write Me a Murder, 1961, The Great Indoors, 1966, The Last of Mrs. Lincoln, 1972; co-producer The Teahouse of the August Moon, 1953 (also in London); artistic dir. N.Y.C. Center Theatre Co., 1949-52; dir. Dallas State Fair Musicals, 1952-58; dir., co-produced Zenda for Los Angeles Civic Light Opera Co., 1963; produced To Broadway with Love, at the Music Hall N.Y. World's Fair, 1964; pres. Compass Prodns., Inc., 1959—; producer-dir. Do Not Go Gentle into That Good Night, TV, 1967, A War of Children, TV, 1972, Sandburg's Lincoln series, TV, 1974-76, In This House of Brede, TV, 1975, Truman at Potsdam, Amelia Earhart, 1976, Our Town, 1977, First You Cry, Orchard Children, 1978, Blind Ambition, Mayflower, 1979; dir. films Generation, Macbeth, Pendulum, Doctors' Wives, Once Upon a Scoundrel, An Enemy of the People. Recipient Emmy awards for Show of Year, 1960, 61, for best dir., 1959, 61, for best single dramatic show, 1968, 73, Dir. of Year award Radio-TV Daily, 1957, 60, 63, 65; Dirs. Guild Am. TV award, 1961, 64, 67, 68, Dinneen award Nat. Cath. Theatre Conf., 1964. Mem. Dirs. Guild Am. (v.p. 1961-79, pres. 1979-81), Phi Beta Kappa. Club: Players (N.Y.C.). Home: 1040 Woodland Dr Beverly Hills CA 90210 Office: 1801 Ave of Stars Los Angeles CA 90067

SCHAEFER, GORDON E., brewing co. exec.; b. 1932; B.S., Marquette U., 1956; C.P.A.; married. With Peat, Marwick, Mitchell & Co., 1955-59; controller Wells Badger Corp., 1960-63, Polaris Corp., 1963-65; treas. Pabst Brewing Co., 1965-72, v.p. adminstrn., 1972-75, v.p. ops., 1975-76, exec. v.p. ops., 1976—, also dir. Address: 917 W Juneau Ave Milwaukee WI 53201

SCHAEFER, HENRY FREDERICK, III, chemist; b. Grand Rapids, Mich., June 8, 1944; s. Henry Frederick and Janice Christine (Troust) S.; S.B., M.I.T., 1966; Ph.D., Stanford U., 1969; m. Karen Regine Rasmussen, Sept. 2, 1966; children—Charlotte Ann, Pierre Edward. Faculty chemistry U. Calif., Berkeley, 1969—; faculty sr. scientist Lawrence Berkeley Lab., 1972—; Wilfred T. Doherty prof. U. Tex., Austin, also dir. Inst. for Theoretical Chemistry. Alfred P. Sloan fellow, 1972-74; John S. Guggenheim fellow, 1976-77. Mem. Am. Chem. Soc. (Pure Chemistry award 1979), Am. Phys. Soc., Sigma Xi, Phi Lambda Upsilon. Evangelical Christian. Author: The Electronic Structure of Atoms and Molecules, 1972; Modern Theoretical Chemistry, 1977. Office: 3-237 Welch Hall Dept Chemistry U Tex Austin TX 78712

SCHAEFER, HERWIN, ret. educator; b. Bonn, Germany, Feb. 4, 1916; s. Joseph and Mary (Luke) S.; came to U.S., 1937, naturalized, 1941; A.B., U. Chgo., 1939, M.A., 1941; Ph.D., Harvard, 1944; m. Hildegarde Hinchman, June 12, 1940; children—Louisa (Mrs. Robert Ertl); Christopher, Andrew. Asst. curator Mus. Art, Providence, 1945-47, Mus. Modern Art, N.Y.C., 1947-49; dir. State Dept. exhbn. program, Germany, 1951-55; prof. history design U. Calif., Berkeley, 1956-79, humanities research prof., 1966-67. Grantee Graham Found. Advanced Studies Fine Arts, 1966. Mem. Coll. Art Assn. Author: World Furniture, 1965; Nineteenth Century Modern, The Functional Tradition in Victorian Design, 1970; also articles.

SCHAEFER, JACK WARNER, writer; b. Cleve., Nov. 19, 1907; s. Carl Walter and Minnie Luella (Hively) S.; A.B., Oberlin Coll., 1929; postgrad. Columbia U., 1929-30; m. Eugenia Hammond Ives, Aug. 26,

1931 (div. Dec. 1948); children—Carl Walter, Christopher Pomery, Susan Hammond, Jonathan Ives; m. 2d, Louise Wilhide Deans, 1949. Reporter and office man U.P., 1930-31; asst. dir. edn. Conn. State Reformatory, 1931-38; asso. editor New Haven Jour. Courier, 1932-39, editor, 1939-42; editorial writer Balt. Sun, 1942-44; asso. editor Norfolk Virginian-Pilot, 1944-48; editor The Shoreliner, 1949; asso. Lindsay Advt. Co., New Haven, 1949; editor and pub. Theatre News, 1935-40, The Movies, 1939-41. Author: (novel) Shane, 1949; (novel) First Blood, 1953; (short stories) The Big Range, 1953; (novel) The Canyon, 1953 (short stories) The Pioneers, 1954; (novel) Company of Cowards, 1957; The Kean Land and Other Stories, published 1959; Old Ramon, 1960; (short stories) The Plainsmen, 1963; (novel) Monte Walsh, 1963; The Great Endurance Horse Race, 1963; Stubby Pringle's Christmas, 1964, Heroes Without Glory, 1965; Collected Stories, 1966; Mavericks, 1967; New Mexico, 1967; Collected Short Novels, 1967; An American Bestiary, 1975; Conversations with a Pocket Gopher . . . and Other Outspoken Neighbors, 1978; also stories in nat. mags. Home: 905 Camino Ranchitos Santa Fe NM 87501

SCHAEFER, JOHN PAUL, univ. pres.; b. N.Y.C., Sept. 17, 1934; s. Conrad and Meta (Rekelkamm) S.; B.S., Poly. Inst. Bklyn., 1955; Ph.D. in Chemistry, U. Ill., 1958; fellow Calif. Inst. Tech., 1958-59; m. Helen Marie Schwarz, May 18, 1958; children—Ann Marie, Susan Margaret. Asst. prof. U. Calif. at Berkeley, 1959-60; mem. faculty U. Ariz., 1960—, prof. chemistry, head dept., 1968-70, dean Coll. Liberal Arts, 1970-71, pres., 1971—; dir. Home Fed. Savs.; cons. to industry. Bd. commrs. Navajo Health Authority; bd. govs. U.S.-Israel Binat. Sci. Found., 1972-77; bd. dirs. Research Corp. Mem. Nat., Tucson (pres. 1961-65), Audubon socs., Am. Chem. Soc., Ariz. Acad., AAAS, Nature Conservancy, Sigma Xi, Phi Lambda Upsilon, Phi Kappa Phi. Home: 7401 E Kenyon Dr Tucson AZ 85710

SCHAEFER, RAYMOND HERMAN, metall. engr.; b. Lynn, Mass., Apr. 14, 1911; s. Gustave and Hattie (Telchmeier) S.; B.S., Carnegie Inst. Tech., 1934; m. Amy F. Dodge, Sept. 1934; children—Cris Hayden, Sandra Noel, Susan Finlay, Laurie Dodge. Metallurgist Internat. Nickel Co., 1934-40, Am. Manganese Steel Div., 1940-43; chief metallurgist Am. Brake Shoe Co. (now Abex Corp.), 1943-45, dir. research and devel., 1945-51, v.p., 1951-68; asst. to v.p. Internat. Nickel Co., Inc., N.Y.C., 1969-70, dir. product research and devel., 1970-71, v.p. research and devel., 1972-73, asst. v.p. Internat. Nickel Co. Can., Ltd., 1973-74, asst. to pres., 1974-76; cons. Inco Ltd., 1976—. Mem. Am. Inst. Mining and Metall. Engrs., Am. Soc. Metals Am. Foundrymens Soc., Delta Upsilon. Clubs: University (N.Y.C.); Heritage Village Country (Southbury, Conn.). Home: 1024A New Wheeler Rd Heritage Village Southbury CT 06488 Office: One New York Plaza New York City NY 10004

SCHAEFER, ROBERT ELLSWORTH, advt. exec.; b. Rochester, N.Y., Dec. 9, 1927; s. Ellsworth J. and Irene (Pugsley) S.; B.S., Fla. State U., 1950, M.S., 1951; m. Marion Thompson, Sept. 29, 1956; 1 dau., Elizabeth Suzanne. Instr. marketing Sch. Bus., Fla. State U., 1951-52; asst. prof. advt. and marketing Ga. State U., 1952-57; gen. mgr. staff Rich's, Inc., dept. store, Atlanta, 1952-53; with Tucker Wayne & Co., Atlanta, 1953—, pres., 1965—, chmn. bd., chief exec. officer, 1978—; chmn. bd., chief exec. officer Quadrant Corp., 1978—. Bd. dirs. Atlanta Boys Club, 1962. Served with USN, 1943-46; ETO, PTO. Mem. Am. Mktg. Assn. (pres. Atanta 1961-62), Lambda Chi Alpha. Republican. Baptist. Clubs: Capital City, Peachtree Golf, Commerce (Atlanta). Home: 3435 Woodhaven Rd NW Atlanta GA 30327 Office: 2700 Peachtree Center Bldg Atlanta GA 30303

SCHAEFER, ROBERT JOSEPH, educator; b. Cin., Aug. 29, 1917; s. Albert John and Elizabeth (Forsting) S.; B.A., Columbia, 1940, M.A., Tchrs. Coll., 1948, Ph.D., 1951; m. Eileen Slattery, Sept. 15, 1942; children—Steven Albert, Robert Emmett, Eric Forsting. Tchr. history Middletown (N.Y.) High Sch., 1945-46, Juilliard Sch. Music, 1946, Horace-Mann-Lincoln Schs., N.Y.C., 1948-49, Columbia Tchrs. Coll., 1948-49; instr., supr. student teaching social studies Columbia Tchrs. Coll., 1947-48, dean, 1963-75, prof., chmn. dept. ednl. adminstrn., 1975—; chmn. history dept. Oneonta (N.Y.) State Tchrs. Coll., 1946-47; faculty arts and scis., also Grad. Sch. Edn. Harvard, dir. master in arts teaching program, 1949-52; asst. dean Harvard Grad. Sch. Edn., Harvard, 1952-55; prof. edn., chmn. dept. Washington U., St. Louis, 1955-56, dir. Grad. Inst. Edn., 1956-63. Served with USNR, World War II. Mem. Am. Assn. Colls. Tchr. Edn. (chmn. com. studies), Nat. Council Accreditation Tchr. Edn. (chmn. visitation teams), Nat. Council Social Studies, Am. Edn. Research Assn., Assn. Supervision and Curriculum Devel., Assn. Higher Edn., Kappa Delta Pi, Phi Delta Kappa. Author: The School as a Center of Inquiry, 1967. Home: 16 Northwood Ave Demarest NJ 07627 Office: 212 Main Hall Tchrs Coll Columbia U 525 W 120th St New York NY 10027

SCHAEFER, ROBERT WAYNE, banker; b. Balt., Feb. 28, 1934; s. Roland Elmer and Lillian (Reid) S.; student Balt. City Coll., 1949-51; B.S. in Accounting, U. Balt., 1955; M.B.A. in Finance, Loyola Coll., 1971; m. Elaine Lennon, May 18, 1963; children—Linda, Karen. With First Nat. Bank of Md., Balt., 1951-55, 59—, comptroller, 1961—, v.p., 1965-69, sr. v.p., 1969-73, exec. v.p., 1973—; instr. accounting N.C. State Coll., 1956-58; instr. accounting, econs., taxes, credit Balt. chpt. Am. Inst. Banking, 1960-66; dir. Devel. Credit Corp. Md. Mem. Balt. City Sch. Bd., 1973-75. Bd. dirs., treas. Balt. Area United Fund, 1964—; former bd. dirs. Balt. council Boy Scouts Am., Balt. chpt. ARC, Md. Gen. Hosp., Boys Latin Sch., Balt. City Aquarium; trustee, pres. Wesley Home for Aged. Served to 1st lt. USMCR, 1956-58. C.P.A., Md. Mem. Nat. Assn. Bank Auditors and Comptrollers (past pres., dir. Balt. chpt.), Md. C.P.A. Assn., Fin. Execs. Inst., Am. Mgmt. Assn., U. Balt. Alumni Assn. (dir. 1972—). Republican. Methodist (bd. dirs., mem. finance com.). Mason. Club: Valley Country (Towson, Md.). Home: 5903 Meadowood Rd Baltimore MD 21212 Office: First Nat Bank Light and Redwood Sts Baltimore MD 21202

SCHAEFER, THEODORE PETER, educator; b. Gnadenthal, Man., Can., July 22, 1933; s. Paul Jacob and Margarethe (Wiebe) S.; B.S. with Honors, U. Man., 1954, M.S., 1955; Ph.D. (Shell scholar), Oxford (Eng.) U., 1958; m. Nicola Caroline Sewell, Dec. 26, 1960; children—Catherine, Dominic, Benjamin. Prof. chemistry U. Man., Winnipeg, Can., 1958—; researcher NRC, Ottawa, Can., 1959, 62, Nat. Phys. Lab., Teddington, U.K., 1960, 65, Argonne Nat. Lab., Chgo., 1967, 68; sr. fellow, mem. grants com. NRC, Ottawa. Fellow Chem. Inst. Can. (Noranda award 1973), Royal Soc. Can. Contbr. articles on nuclear magnetic resonance to sci. jours. Home: 210 Oak St Winnipeg MB R3M 3R4 Canada Office: Dept Chemistry U Man Winnipeg MB R3T 2N2 Canada. *Persistence can sometimes emulate perspicacity.*

SCHAEFER, VINCENT JOSEPH, research physicist; b. Schenectady, July 4, 1906; s. Peter A. and Rose A. (Holtslag) S.; student Union Coll.; grad. Davey Inst. of Tree Surgery, 1928; Sc.D. (hon.), U. Notre Dame, 1948; H.L.D. (hon.), Siena Coll., 1975; m. Lois K. Perret, July 26, 1935; children—Susan, Katherine Rose, James Michael. Grad. Gen. Electric Apprentice System, 1926; research asst. to Dr. Irving Langmuir, Gen. Electric Research Lab., 1933-38, research asso., 1938-54; dir. research Munitalp Found., Inc., 1954-59, cons. in N.Am., 1959-64; prof. State U. N.Y. at Albany, also research prof. Atmospheric Scis. Research Center; dir. Nat. Scis. Inst.; cons. on mech. tech. to mfg. cos.; distinguished lectr. sci. SUNY Coll. Edn., Albany, 1959-60; mem. sci. adv. bd. U. Nev. System, 1961-78. Trustee Inst. Man and Sci., Mohonk Trust. Recipient Losey award Inst. Aero. Scis., 1953, award Am. Meteorol. Soc., 1957, spl. citation, 1976. Fellow AAAS, Rochester Mus. Arts and Scis., Am. Meteorol. Soc.; mem. Ecol. Soc., Am. Geophys. Union, Am. Chem. Soc., N.Y. Archaeol. Assn., Wilderness Soc., Friends of Forest Preserve, Royal Meteorol. Soc., Nat. Speleol. Soc., Soc. Am. Archeology, Sigma Xi. Roman Catholic. Clubs: Mohawk Valley Hiking, Schenectady Wintersports. Discoverer of cloud seeding methods. Contbr. to sci. jours. Home: RFD 3 Schermerhorn Rd Schenectady NY 12306 Office: Atmospheric Scis Research Center 100 Fuller Rd Albany NY 12203

SCHAEFER, W(ILLIAM) STANLEY, pub. co. exec.; b. Adams, N.Y., Mar. 31, 1907; s. William and Katherine (Lehman) S.; A.B. (State N.Y. scholar), Cornell U., 1931, student Law Sch., 1929-31; m. Marthe Marschall, Feb. 16, 1934; children—Ann (Mrs. Donald Pease), Katherine. Mgr., Cornell U. Press, 1931-40, dir., 1940-43; mgr. Comstock Pub. Co., 1931-43; Univ. pub. Cornell U., 1940-43; v.p. W.H. Freeman & Co., San Francisco, 1949-62, pres., 1962-69, 71-73, chmn., 1962—, chief exec. officer, 1962-73, editor-in-chief, 1962-69, 71-73; dir. W.H. Freeman & Co., Ltd., Reading, Eng. Clubs: Cornell of N.Y., Players (N.Y.C.); Cercle de l'Union (San Francisco). Home: 418 Yerba Santa Ave Los Altos CA 94022 Office: 660 Market St San Francisco CA 94104. *Throughout my career in educational publishing my efforts have been directed toward improving the quality of education in colleges and universities.*

SCHAEFER, WILLIAM DAVID, educator; b. Dighton, Mass., May 11, 1928; s. Louis and Elsie (Otterbein) S.; B.A., N.Y.U., 1957; M.S., U. Wis., 1958, Ph.D., 1962; m. Josephine Lamprecht, Aug. 8, 1958; 1 dau., Kimberly. Mem. faculty UCLA, 1962—, prof. English, 1970—, chmn. dept., 1969-71, exec. vice chancellor, 1978—. Served with AUS, 1954-56. Fulbright fellow, Eng., 1961-62. Mem. Modern Lang. Assn. (exec. dir. 1971-78). Author: James (BV) Thomson: Beyond The City, 1965; Speedy Extinction of Evil and Misery, 1967; also articles. Office: U Calif Los Angeles CA 90024

SCHAEFER, WILLIAM DONALD, mayor Balt.; b. Balt., Nov. 2, 1921; s. William Henry and Tululu (Skipper) S.; LL.B., U. Balt., 1943, LL.M., 1952, LL.D. (hon.), 1976; J.D. (hon.), Loyola Coll., 1976. Admitted to Md. bar, 1943; practiced in Balt., 1943—; mem. Balt. City Council, 1955-67, pres., 1967-71; mayor City of Balt., 1971—. Served with AUS, 1942-45. Recipient numerous awards, including 1st ann. Civic Statesmanship award Citizens Planning and Housing Assn., Jefferson award for outstanding public service, 1979, Outstanding Leadership in Devel. and Support of Citizen Volunteerism, U.S. Conf. Mayors, 1979; named Alumni of Yr., U. Balt., 1971; Man of Yr., Jewish Nat. Fund, 1972. Mem. Nat. League Cities (dir.), Md. Assn. Counties, Md. Mcpl. League, Balt. Bar Assn., Citizens Planning and Housing Assn. Balt., Nat. Hist. Soc., Balt. Ecol. Soc., Md. Ret. Officers Assn., Balt. Assn. Retarded Citizens, Md. Acad. Scis., VFW, Navy League U.S., Am. Pub. Works Assn., Am. Inst. Banking (hon.), Am. Public Works Assn., AIA (hon. mem. Balt. chpt.), Md. Law Enforcement Officers, Md 4-H Club. Democrat. Club: Rotary (Balt.). Office: 250 City Hall 100 Holliday St Baltimore MD 21202

SCHAEFER, WILLIAM GOERMAN, JR., lawyer; b. Kansas City, Mo., June 16, 1941; s. William Goerman and Ava Dean (Hamilton) S.; B.A., U. Kans., 1963; J.D., Harvard U., 1966; m. Sharon Saylor, Dec. 21, 1963; children—James, Kristen. Admitted to Ill. bar, 1966, D.C. bar, 1978; partner firm Sidley & Austin, Chgo. and Washington, 1966-74, 78—; v.p., gen. counsel DeKalb AgResearch, Inc. (Ill.), 1974-77. Mem. Am., D.C., Chgo. bar assns. Office: Sidley & Austin 1730 Pennsylvania Ave Washington DC 20006

SCHAEFFER, FRANCIS AUGUST, clergyman, author, found. adminstr.; b. Phila., Jan. 30, 1912; s. Francis August and Bessie W. (Williamson) S.; A.B. magna cum laude, Hampden-Sydney Coll., 1935; B.D., Faith Theol. Sem., Phila., 1938; LL.D., Gordon Coll., Wenham, Mass., 1971; m. Edith Rachel Seville, July 6, 1935; children—Janet Priscilla, Susan Jane, Deborah Ann, Francis August. Ordained to ministry Ref. Presbyn. Ch. (Evang. Synod), 1938; pastor chs. in Pa. and Mo., 1938-48; pres. L'Abri Fellowship Found., Huemoz, Switzerland, 1955—; author: 21 books, 1968—, latest being: Art and The Bible, 1973; (with Mrs. Schaeffer) Everybody Can Know, 1973; No Little People, 1974; Two Contents, Two Realities, 1974; Joshua and The Flow of Biblical History, 1975; No Final Conflict, 1975; How Should We Then Live?, 1976; (with C. Everett Koop) Whatever Happened to the Human Race?, 1979; narrator documentary films How Should We Then Live?, Whatever Happened to the Human Race?. Home: Chalet Chardonnet 1885 Chesieres Switzerland Office: Chalet les Melezes 1861 Huemoz Switzerland

SCHAEFFER, HENRI BELLA (MRS. THEMIS DE VITIS), artist; b. N.Y.C.; d. Leon and Luba (Tchelitchew) Schaeffer; student Columbia; studied Art Alliance Francaise, Paris, Academie L'Hote, Paris, Grand Chaumier, Paris; pupil William A. Mackay, 1935-38; certificate Fashion Inst. Tech., 1961; m. Themis De Vitis, Oct. 1947. One-man shows include Artists Gallery, 1941, 49, 51, 53, Mayorga Gallery, N.Y.C., 1964-65, Hollis F. Price Library, Le Moyne Coll., Memphis, 1966, Saranac Lake (N.Y.) Community Gallery, 1970, Saranac Lake Pub. Library, 1970; exhibited in numerous group shows in U.S. and fgn. countries, including Salon C'automne, Paris, 1938, Salon des Tulleries, Paris, 1938, Met. Mus. Artists for Victory, N.Y.C., 1942, Graphic Gala, Artists Gallery, 1955, Art U.S.A., 1958, Butler Inst. Am. Art, Youngstown, Ohio, 1958, Masilion (Ohio) Mus., 1958, Ashtabula (Ohio) Art Centre, 1958, Artists Gallery Group, 1958, 59, Painters and Sculptors of N.J. exhbn., Newark Mus., 1960, anns. Am. Assn. Women Artists, Fla. Internat. Art Exhbn. (honorable mention 1960), Acad. Arts and Letters, 1961, Nat. Assn. of Women Artists at N.A.D. Galleries, 1960, 62, 63, 68, 69, Nat. Assn. of Women Artists Print and Drawing exhbn. at Pen and Brush, 1962, Chateau De Napoule, Cannes, 1965, Cognac Mus., 1965, 66, Internat. Womens Salon, Cannes, 1966, Spring Arts Festival Ednl. and Cultural Trust Fund of Elec. Industry, 1970, 71; in traveling show oils, U.S., 1963-65, other nat. shows; represented in permanent collections Fla. So. Coll., Alfred Khourl collection Va. Mus. Fine Arts, Richmond, Butler Inst. Am. Art, Youngstown, Ohio, Le Moyne Coll., Norfolk Mus. Arts and Scis., Hollis Price Library, numerous pvt. collections; participant World Affairs Conv., Boulder, Colo. Chmn. Helen West Heller Meml. Com., 1956. Trustee Dorothy Yepez Art Gallery, Saranac, N.Y. Recipient Marcia Brady Tucker prize, Medal of Honor, Nat. Assn. Women Artists at N.A.D., 1962. Mem. Nat. Assn. Women Artists (oil jury 1963-65), Artists Equity Assn. (exec. bd. N.Y. Chpt. 1954—, dir., 1956-57; chmn. nat. welfare commn. 1954-59, nat. bd. 1954-55, dir.-at-large 1956-58, nat. sec., 1961-63, 63-65, nat. exec. com., nat. dir. 1960—, observer 4th Congress Internat. Assn. Art, 1963, del. to U.S. com., 1964—; rep. hearings and U.S. nat. art legislation 1964—; chmn. grants and fellowships fine arts 1963—, mem. spl. congress com.; mem. art legislation com. Nat. Historic Shrines Found., Inc. (adv. council arts). Author poetry. Address: 111 Bank St New York NY 10014

SCHAEFFER, LEONARD DAVID, govt. ofcl.; b. Chgo., July 28, 1945; s. David and Sarah (Levin) S.; B.A., Princeton U., 1969; m. Pamela Sidford, Aug. 11, 1968; children—David, Jacqueline. Mgmt. cons. Arthur Anderson & Co., 1969-73; dep. dir. Ill. Dept. Mental Health and Devel. Disabilities, Springfield, 1973-75; dir. Ill. Bur. of the Budget, Springfield, 1975-76; v.p. Citibank, N.Y.C., 1976-78; asst. sec. for mgmt. and budget HEW, Washington, 1978; adminstr. Health Care Financing Adminstrn., Washington, 1978—; mem. HEW Sec.'s Select Panel on Child Health, mem. Nat. Council on Health Care Tech., 1979. Chmn. Ill. Capital Devel. Bd., 1975; mem. Ill. Data Info. Systems Commn., 1973-76, Ill. Sch. Problems Commn., 1975-76, Ill. Bldg. Authority, 1975-76. Mem. Am. Soc. Public Adminstrn., Am. Public Health Assn., Assn. Mental Health Adminstrs., Data Processing Mgmt. Assn. Club: Princeton. Office: Room 5006 330 C St SW Washington DC 20201

SCHAEFFER, OLIVER ADAM, educator; b. Fleetwood, Pa., Feb. 20, 1919; s. Charles Boyd and Mary Kaufman (Heffner) S.; B.S., Pa. State U., 1941; M.S., U. Mich., 1942; Ph.D., Harvard, 1946; m. Alice Viola Long, Oct. 21, 1944; children—Mary, Oliver, Nancy, George, Clare, Alice. Analytical chemist TVA, Wilson Dam, Ala., 1942-44; postdoctoral research asso. Harvard, 1946-47; asso. chemist Brookhaven Nat. Lab., Upton, N.Y., 1947-60, sr. chemist, 1960-65; prof. earth and space scis. State U. N.Y., Stony Brook, 1965—, chmn. dept., 1965-71; vis. scientist Max-Planck-Institut für Kernphysik, Heidelberg, Germany, 1961-62, 71-72, 74—; vis. prof. U. Heidelberg, Germany, 1971-72, 74—. Trustee U. Space Research Assn., 1969-78. Recipient Boris Pregel prize N.Y. Acad. Scis., 1954; research grantee NASA, 1967—, NSF, 1979—, AEC, 1965-75. Mem. AAAS, Am. Geophys. Union, Meteoritical Soc., Am. Chem. Soc., Am. Astron. Soc., Auswärtiges mitgleid der Max-Planck-Gesellschaft zur Forderung der Wissenschaften. Editor: Potassium Argon Dating, 1966; asso. editor Jour. Geophys. Research, 1965-67, Modern Geology, 1970—. Research on cosmochemistry, ages of lunar rocks, history of cosmic rays, marine chemistry. Home: 16 Childs Ln Box 1075 Setauket NY 11733 Office: Dept Earth and Space Scis State U NY Stony Brook NY 11794

SCHAEFFER, WENDELL GORDON, educator; b. Waverly, Ill., Nov. 5, 1917; s. Samuel Carlyle and Minnie Pearl (Morton) S.; B.S., U. So. Calif., 1939; M.A., U. Calif., Berkeley, 1946, Ph.D., 1949; m. Luella Pauline Elmes, Nov. 24, 1939; children—Thomas Leslie, Wendy Elizabeth Schaeffer Brandeau. Asst. prof. history, polit. sci. U. Fla., 1948-50; publs. dir., hdqrs. supr., chief of party in El Salvador and Puerto Rico, resident rep. in Burma, Pub. Adminstrn. Service, Chgo., 1950-59; asso. prof. pub. affairs, prof. pub., internat. affairs, asst. dean, asso. dean U. Pitts., 1959-66, dean faculties in Ecuador, 1963-66; pres. Govtl. Affairs Inst., Washington, 1966-69, chmn., 1968-70; Herman Brown prof. polit. sci. Tex. Christian U., Ft. Worth, 1969—, chmn. dept., 1969-76, dir. grad. program in pub. affairs and adminstrn., 1974-76; cons. UN on local govt. in Latin Am., 1959, 68; program evaluator Brazil mission U.S. AID, 1969-70, cons. program devel. Colombia mission, 1974; cons. UN on adminstrn. regional devel. programs, 1971—, spl. missions Venezuela, 1971-72, Japan, 1972, Panama, 1974-75, 78, Chile, 1976; cons. Met. Miami Municipal Bd., 1954; mem. Three-Man Commn. to Review Program Tech. Cooperation of OAS, 1962. Dir. Pre-Conv. Constl. Studies for Alaska Statehood Commn., 1955. Served to 2d lt. USAAF, World War II. Fulbright-Hays scholar Nat. Chung Hsing U., Taiwan, 1976-77. Mem. Am. Polit. Sci. Assn., Am. Soc. Pub. Adminstrn. (pres. North Tex. chpt. 1972-73, chmn. sect. internat. and comparative adminstrn. 1976-77, nat. council 1976-79), Am. Consortium for Internat. Pub. Adminstrn. (sec. 1978—), Nat. Assn. Schs. Public Affairs and Adminstrn. (chmn. com. on internat. and comparative adminstrn. 1977—), Nat. Acad. Pub. Adminstrn., Soc. for Internat. Devel., Phi Beta Kappa. Presbyn. Clubs: Century II, Colonial Country (Fort Worth). Author: (with Donald Worcester) The Growth and Culture of Latin America, 1956, 2 vols., rev. 1970; Modernizing Government Revenue Administration, 1961; Public Policy: An International Perspective, 1977. Home: 2621 Hartwood Dr Fort Worth TX 76109 Office: Tex Christian U Fort Worth TX 76129

SCHAEFLER, LEON, lawyer; b. N.Y.C., July 2, 1903; s. Morris I. and Kate (Eckstein) S.; student N.Y.U., 1920-21; LL.B., Fordham U., 1924; m. Gertrude Herbert, June 10, 1927; children—Roberta, Kathryn. Admitted to N.Y. bar, 1925, since practiced in that state; gen. counsel, Fifth Av. Bank, N.Y.C., 1936-48; atty. Bank of N.Y., midtown offices; sr. partner firm Finch & Schaefler, specializing in surrogate and banking law. Fellow (hon.) Am. Coll. Probate Counsel (pres. 1959-61, dir., 1957-62); mem. Fordham Law Alumni Assn. (dir. 1955-58). Clubs: Ocean Beach; Sky (N.Y.C.). Author articles on estate and banking practice. Home: 36 Sutton Pl New York NY 10022 also Chez Fleurs Elberon NJ 07740 Office: 36 W 44th St New York NY 10036

SCHAFER, ALICE TURNER, mathematician; b. Richmond, Va., June 18, 1915; d. John H. and Cleon (Dermott) Turner; A.B., U. Richmond, 1936, D.Sc., 1964; M.S., U. Chgo., 1940, Ph.D. (fellow), 1942; m. Richard Donald Schafer, Sept. 8, 1942; children—John Dickerson, Richard Stone. Tchr., Glen Allen (Va.) High Sch., 1936-39; instr. math. Con. Coll., New London, 1942-44, asst. prof., 1954-57, asso. prof., 1957-61, prof., 1961-62; prof. math. Wellesley Coll., 1962—, Helen Day Gould prof. math., 1969—; instr. U. Mich., Ann Arbor, 1945-46; lectr. Douglass Coll., New Brunswick, N.J., 1946-48; asst. prof. Swarthmore (Pa.) Coll., 1948-51, Drexel Inst. Tech. Phila., 1951-53; mathematician Johns Hopkins Applied Physics Lab., Silver Spring, Md., 1945; Recipient Distinguished Alumna award Westhampton Coll., 1977; NSF Sci. Faculty fellow Inst. Advanced Study, Princeton, N.J., 1958-59. Mem. Am. Math. Soc. (chmn. joint com. with Math. Assn. Am., Soc. Indsl. and Applied Math. com. on women 1975—), Math. Assn. Am., AAUP, Assn. for Women in Math. (pres. 1973-75), Phi Beta Kappa, Sigma Xi, Sigma Delta Epsilon. Contbr. articles to math. jours. Office: Dept Math Wellesley Coll Wellesley MA 02181

SCHAFER, EDWARD HETZEL, educator, author; b. Seattle, Aug. 23, 1913; s. Edward Hetzel and Lillian (Moorehead) S.; A.B. in Anthropology, U. Calif., Berkeley, 1938, Ph.D. in Oriental Langs., 1947; M.A., U. Hawaii, 1940; postgrad. Harvard U., 1940-41; m. Phyllis Brooks, Sept. 7, 1971; children from previous marriage—Tamlyn, Julian, Kevin. Lectr. in Oriental langs. U. Calif., Berkeley, 1947, asst. prof. Oriental langs., 1947-53, asso. prof., 1953-58, prof., 1958-69, Agassiz prof. Oriental langs. and lit., 1969—. Served with USNR, 1941-46. Decorated Bronze Star; Guggenheim fellow, 1953-54, 68-69. Mem. Am. Oriental Soc. (past pres.), Medieval Soc. Am. Author: The Empire of Min, 1954; Tu Wan's Stone Catalogue of Cloudy Forest, 1961; The Golden Peaches of Samarkand, 1963; Ancient China, 1967; The Vermilion Bird, 1967; Shore of Pearls, 1970; The Divine Woman, 1973; Pacing the Void, 1977. Editor: Jour. Am. Oriental Soc., 1958-64. Contbr. articles to profl. jours. Home: 60 Avis Rd Berkeley CA 94707 Office: Dept Oriental Langs Univ of Calif Berkeley CA 94720

SCHAFER, ELDON (GUY), coll. adminstr.; b. Molalla, Oreg., Feb. 27, 1922; s. Guy F. and Lillian (Mitts) S.; B.A., Pomona Coll., 1948; M.A., Claremont Grad. Sch., 1960, Ph.D., 1965; m. Lucy Jane Brokaw, Sept. 10, 1947; 1 son, Kenneth. Tchr., Capistrano High Sch.,

1950-52; dir. athletics Puente High Sch., 1953-54; instr.-coach Pomona Coll., 1954-55; dist. supt. Capistrano Union High Sch. Dist., San Juan Capistrano, Calif., 1957-65; asso. dean instrn. Riverside City Coll., 1966-67; pres. Linn-Benton Community Coll., 1967-70, Lane Community Coll. 1970—. Bd. dirs. ARC, Eugene, Oreg., LWV, Eugene; pres. Oregon Trail council Boy Scouts Am., 1976-78. Served with U.S. Army, 1942-46. Inducted into Helms Athletic Hall of Fame, Los Angeles, 1971. Mem. N.W. Assn. Schs. and Colls. (commn. on colls.), Am. Assn. Community and Jr. Colls. (chmn. panel on assn. vitality 1977-78, vice chmn. bd. dirs. 1978-79), League for Innovation in Community Coll. (pres. 1977-78), N.W. Assn. Community and Jr. Colls. (pres. 1977-78), Oreg. Community Coll. Assembly (rep. to Oreg. Ednl. Coordinating Commn. 1974-77), Oreg. Community Coll. Assn. (chmn. 1974), Eugene Area C. of C. (dir.). Club: Rotary (Eugene). Home: 2230 Hideaway Ct Eugene OR 97401 Office: 4000 E 30th St Eugene OR 97405

SCHAFER, JOHN HENRY, lawyer; b. Montclair, N.J., Oct 28, 1926; s. John H. and Helen Willard (Robbins) S.; A.B., Williams Coll., 1948; M.A., Sch. Advanced Internat. Studies, 1950; LL.B., U. Va., 1954; m. Edith T. Nalle, Dec. 30, 1961; children—Alison T., John R., Nancy C. Admitted to U.S. Supreme Ct., 1958; asso. firm Covington & Burling, Washington, 1954-63, partner, 1963—; lectr. U. Va. Law Sch.; mem. exec. bd. Lawyers Com. for Civil Rights Under Law. Mem. exec. bd. Jackson Lab., Bar Harbor, Maine. Served with U.S. Navy, 1944-46. Mem. Am. Bar Assn., Am. Law Inst., Order of Coif. Democrat. Episcopalian. Clubs: Met., Chevy Chase, Federal City, 1925 F St. Home: 1530 30th St NW Washington DC 20007 Office: 888 16th St NW Washington DC 20006

SCHAFER, LOTHAR, chemist, educator; b. Dusseldorf, W. Ger., May 5, 1939; s. Ernst Rudolf and Sybilla (Nolden) S.; diploma in chemistry U. Munich (Germany), 1962, Ph.D. in Chemistry, 1965; m. Gabriele Maria Brand, Apr. 9, 1965; children—Nicole, Nathalie. Came to U.S., 1967, naturalized, 1978. Research asso. Ind. U., 1967-68; asst. prof. dept. chemistry U. Ark., Fayetteville, 1968-72, asso. prof., 1972-75, prof., 1975—; vis. prof. Yukawa Hall, U. Kyoto (Japan), 1976; NATO fellow U. Oslo (Norway), 1965-67. Recipient Disting. Faculty award U. Ark. Alumni Assn., 1977; Dreyfus Found. grantee, 1971. Mem. Am. Chem. Soc., Chem. Soc. Eng., AAUP. Contbr. articles on chemistry to sci. jours. Home: 828 Skyline Dr Fayetteville AR 72701

SCHAFER, R. MURRAY, composer, author, educator; b. Sarnia, Ont., Can., July 18, 1933; s. Harold J. and Belle (Rose) S.; studied piano with Alberto Guerrero, theory and composition with John Weinzweig at Royal Conservatory of Music, Toronto, Ont., 1950-55; studied with Peter Racine Fricker, Eng., 1958; m. Phyllis Mailing, Feb. 2, 1960. Worked as free-lance journalist and broadcaster, Eng. and Europe, 1956-60; founder, organizer Ten Centuries Concerts, 1961, first pres., 1961-62; artist-in-residnce Meml. U., St. John's, Nfld., Can., 1963-65; resident in music Communication Centre, Simon Fraser U., Burnaby, Vancouver, B.C., Can., from 1965; composer for opera and orch., also of chamber, vocal, choral, electronic music; compositions include: Concerto for Harpsichord and Eight Wind Instruments, Minnelieder, In Memoriam: Alberto Guerrero, Canzoni for Prisoners, Statement in Blue, Threnody, Requiems for the Party-Girl, Gita, Epitaph for Moonlight, From the Tibetan Book of the Dead, Divan i Shams: Tabriz, In Search of Zoroaster, Okeanos, Tehillah; lectr. in field. Recipient Fromm Found. award, 1968, Can. Music Council medal, 1972, Leger prize, 1978. Mem. Can. League Composers. Publs. include: British Composers in Interview, Composer in the Classroom, Ear Cleaning, The New Soundscape, When Words Sing, The Book of Noise, The Public of the Music Theatre: Louis Riel-a Case Study, E.T.A. Hoffmann and Music, European Sound Diary, Five Village Soundscapes in Europe, The Tuning of the World, The Vancouver Soundscape; contbr. numerous articles to nat. and internat. jours.*

SCHAFER, RAYMOND MURRAY, composer, author; b. Sarnia, Ont., Can., July 18, 1933; s. Harold J. and Belle (Rose) S.; L.R.S.M., Royal Coll. and Royal Acad. Music (London), 1954; m. Jean C. Reed, Sept. 18, 1975. Artist in residence Meml. U. Nfld., 1963-65; prof. communications studies Simon Fraser U., Burnaby, B.C., Can., 1965-75; composer, author. Recipient Arts award Can. Council, 1968-69, Fromm Music Found. award, 1969, Serge Koussevitzky Music Found. award, 1969, Can. Music Council medal, 1972; Guggenheim fellow, 1976. Mem. Broadcast Music Inc. (Can.), Can. Music Council, Phi Mu Alpha. Sinfonia. Author: British Composers in Interview, 1963; The Composer in the Classroom, 1965; Ear Cleaning, 1967; The New Soundscape, 1969; The Book of Noise, 1970; When Words Sing, 1970; The Rhinoceros in the Classroom, 1974; E.T.A. Hoffmann and Music, 1975; Creative Music Education, 1976; The Tuning of the World, 1977. Composer various works including: Music for the Morning of the World, 1972; From the Tibetan Book of the Dead, 1968; String Quartet, 1970; Miniwanka, 1973; Son of Heldenleben, 1968. Commns. from various orgns. including Fromm Found., Serge Koussevitzky Found., Can. Broadcasting Co. Address: Rural Route #5 Bancroft ON Canada

SCHAFER, RICHARD DONALD, mathematician, educator; b. Buffalo, Feb. 25, 1918; s. Edward J. and Ruth (Stone) S.; B.A., U. Buffalo, 1938, M.A., 1940; Ph.D., U. Chgo., 1942; m. Alice E. Turner, Sept. 8, 1942; children—John Dickerson, Richard Stone. Instr. mathematics U. Mich., 1945-46; mem. Inst. Advanced Study, Princeton, N.J., 1946-48; asst. prof. mathematics U. Pa., 1948-53; prof., head dept. math. U. Conn., 1953-59; prof., dep. head dept. math. Mass. Inst. Tech., 1959-68, prof. math., 1959—; mem. Sci. Manpower Com., 1959-63. Served to lt. USNR, 1942-45. NSF sr. postdoctoral fellow, 1958-59. Mem. Am. Math. Soc. (asso. sec. 1955-58), Math. Assn. Am. (vis. lectr. 1957-58, chmn. Northeastern sect. 1971), Phi Beta Kappa, Sigma Xi. Research in nonassociative algebras, principally Lie, Jordan and alternative. Home: 60 Spring Valley Rd Belmont MA 02178 Office: Mass Inst Tech Cambridge MA 02139

SCHAFER-ESCAMILLA, HENRY JOSE, marine scientist, univ. dean; b. Mexico City, June 5, 1927; s. Felix Anton and Mercedes (Escamilla) S.; B.S., Ia. State U., 1951; M.S., U. Miami, Coral Gables, Fla., 1961, Ph.D., 1964; m. Shirley Elaine Jackson, Sept. 28, 1951; children—Rebecca Lyn, Henry Steven, John Christopher, Erik Drew. Co-pres. E. Escamilla & Co., Guatemala, C.A., 1951-58; prof. Instituto Tecnologico y de Estudios Superiores de Monterrey, 1963-64, chmn. dept. marine and food scis., 1964-67, dean Sch. Marine and Food Scis., dir. gen. Guaymas campus, 1967—. Convener physiology sect. World Sci. Conf. on Biology and Culture of Shrimps and Prawns, Mexico City, 1967; co-chmn. Agr. in the Ams., Sci. and Man in the Ams. Symposium, Mexico City, 1973. Hon. mem. Comite Mexicano de Ingenierir de los Recursos Oceanicos. Mem. World Mariculture Soc. (dir. 1973—), Gulf and Caribbean Fisheries Inst., Marine Tech. Soc. Rotarian. Home: Colonia Lomas de Miramar Guaymas Sonora Mexico Office: PO Box 484 Guaymas Sonora Mexico

SCHAFFER, DAVID IRVING, lawyer, vehicle rental co. exec.; b. N.Y.C., Oct. 17, 1935; s. Frank and Edith (Montlack) S.; B.A., U. Pa., 1956; LL.B., Harvard, 1959; m. Lois Ann Warshauer, June 16, 1957; children—Susan Edith, Eric Michael. Admitted to N.Y. bar, 1960; practice in N.Y.C., 1960-66, Garden City, N.Y., 1966-77, N.Y.C., 1977—; asso. firm Shearman & Sterling, N.Y.C., 1960-65; sec., counsel Yale Express System, Inc., N.Y.C., 1965-66; corporate counsel Avis Rent A Car System, Inc., Garden City, 1966-68, gen. counsel, sec., 1968—, v.p., 1971-75, sr. v.p., 1975—. Mem. exec. bd. PTA, Pub. Sch. 26, Queens, N.Y., 1969-72. Great Neck South Sr. High Sch. PTA, 1975—. Trustee Legal Aid Soc. Nassau County. Served with AUS, 1959-60. Mem. Am., N.Y., Nassau County bar assns., Assn. Bar City N.Y., Conf. Am. Renting and Leasing Assns. Home: 31 Amherst Rd Great Neck Estates NY 11021 Office: Avis Inc 1114 Ave of Americas New York NY 10036

SCHAFFER, DONALD L., ins. co. exec., lawyer; b. Charleston, W.Va., July 1, 1923; s. Philip F. and Irma (Williams) S.; B.A., W.Va. U., 1947; LL.B., 1949; m. Phyllis J. Holmes, Aug. 22, 1944; children—Steven G., Jeffrey H., Susan B. Admitted to W.Va. bar, 1949, Ill. bar, 1958; atty. Litton, Fisher & Schaffer, Charleston, 1949-57; asst. gen. counsel Allstate Ins. Cos., Skokie, Ill., 1957-61, v.p., gen. atty. Northbrook, Ill., 1961-72, v.p., sec., gen. counsel, 1972-77, sr. v.p., sec., gen. counsel, 1977—, also dir.; dir. Northbrook Ins. Co. Mem. Jud. Council W.Va., 1956-60; Ill. Crusade chmn. Am. Cancer Soc., 1963-64; bd. govs. Ins. Inst. Hwy. Safety, 1961—, chmn., 1968-69; bd. govs. Ill. Ins. Info. Service, 1963—, pres., 1965, 73; v.p. Allstate Found., 1962—. Served with inf. U.S. Army, 1942-46. Mem. Am., W.Va. (certificate of merit 1960), Chgo. bar assns., Internat. Assn. Ins. Law, Nat. Assn. Ind. Insurers (gov. 1972—). Clubs: Nat. Lawyers (Washington); Mid-Am., Metropolitan (Chgo.); Westmoreland Country (Wilmette, Ill.); Ironwood Country (Palm Desert, Calif.). Methodist. Home: 2658 Sheridan Rd Evanston IL 60201 Office: Allstate Plaza Northbrook IL 60022

SCHAFFER, EDMUND JOHN, business exec.; b. N.Y.C., July 28, 1925; B.S. in Indsl. Engring., Syracuse U., 1950; m. Muriel Spiro, Aug. 22, 1948; children—Diane, Elaine Schaffer Frankel. Sr. staff indsl. engr. Carborundum Co., Niagara Falls, N.Y., 1952-60; mgr. mfg. Ford Motor Co., Detroit, 1952-60; sr. indsl. engr. ITT, N.Y.C., 1960-69, v.p., dir. worldwide indsl. engring. and mfg., 1969—. Served with USN, 1943-47. Home: 63 Slope Dr Short Hills NJ 07078

SCHAFFER, FRANKLIN EDWIN, advt. exec.; b. New Rochelle, N.Y., Jan. 1, 1924; s. Franklin Pierce and Isabel Cornell (Young) S.; A.B. summa cum laude, Princeton, 1945; m. Diane Wormser, Mar. 17, 1951; children—Quentin Munro, Darcy Diane, Jocelyn Grant. Account exec. Fred Eldean Orgn., N.Y.C., 1947-49; with G. Munro Hubbard, pub. relations, N.Y.C., 1949-54; with Doremus & Co., N.Y.C., 1954—, pres., 1967—, chmn. bd., 1973—, also dir. Chmn., Nat. Princeton Alumni Council, 1979—; dir. Citizens for Eisenhower, Rye, N.Y., 1951-52; trustee Greenwich (Conn.) Library; bd. dirs. Greenwich Hosp., 1976—. Served with F.A., U.S. Army, 1942-45. Mem. Public Relations Soc. Am., Am. Assn. Advt. Agys. (gov. N.Y. council 1973-74, dir.-at-large 1975—), Phi Beta Kappa, Sigma Xi. Republican. Congregationalist. Clubs: Field, Belle Haven (Greenwich); Recess, Brook, Princeton (N.Y.C.). Home: Butternut Hollow Rd Greenwich CT 06830 Office: 120 Broadway New York NY 10005

SCHAFFER, ROSE NUSSBAUM, artist; b. Newark; d. Adolph and Carrie (Kolber) Nussbaum; student N.Y. U., 1919-20, Art Students League, 1931-34, Pratt Graphic Center, 1958; pvt. study with Bernard Karfiol, Morris Davidson, Sol Wilson, Antonio Frasconi, Seong Moy; m. Jacob Schaffer, June 4, 1923; children—Judith Schaffer Howard, Ruth Ann. Exhibited various one-woman shows N.Y.C., including Barzansky Galleries; group shows Nat. Acad., Audubon Artists, Nat. Assn. Women Artists, ACA Gallery, N.Y.C., Argent Gallery, N.Y.C., Library of Congress, Washington, Smithsonian Instn., Washington, Montclair Mus., Newark Mus., Jersey City Mus., Delgado Mus., New Orleans, Boston Mus., Wichita Mus., Bklyn. Mus., Rochester Meml. Gallery, Conn. Acad., Cape Cod Gallery, Provincetown Gallery, Albany Print Club, Henry Clews Found., Napoule, France, Casino Municipal, Cannes, France; represented in permanent collections Smithsonian Instn., Montclair (N.J.) Mus., Tenn. Fine Arts Center, Nashville, Art Assn. Richmond (Ind.), Chryster Mus., Norfolk, Va., Rutgers Coll. Mus., Springfield (Mass.) Art Mus., J.F. Kennedy Library, Newark and West Orange (N.J.) Libraries, Daus. of Israel, Pleasant Valley Home, West Orange, Burpee Art Mus., Rockford, Ill., others. Vice pres. Newart sect. Nat. Council Jewish Women, 1945; founder Essex unit Nat. Assn. Retarded Children, 1948; founder, sec. Occupational Center Essex County, 1950-69; founder Curative Workshop (now N.J. Rehab. Bur.), Newark, 1923; pres. Sisterhood Temple Israel, South Orange, N.J. Recipient Ida Wells Stroud award Am. Artists Profl. League, 1951, award Painters and Sculptors Soc. N.J., 1956, Ross Gallery, 1932, Art Center of Oranges, 1947, Terry Nat., 1935, Short Hills at Mall, 1969, Seton Hall U., 1956, New Haven Paint and Print Club, 1958, South Orange-Maplewood Gallery, 1958, L. Bamberger & Co., 1960, purchase award Art for Overlook Hosp., 1961, 62. Mem. Am. Fedn. Arts, Art Students League, Nat. Assn. Women Artists, Artists Equity, United Order True Sisters (pres. 1931). Address: Rossmoor 119A Old Nassau Rd Jamesburg NJ 08831

SCHAFFER, STANLEY G., utility exec.; b. 1919; B.S. in Mech. Engring., Pa. State U., 1941; m. Dorothy Henrietta Stambaugh, Apr. 13, 1941; children—Barbara Lee (Mrs. Gilbert W. Moore, Jr.), Eugenia Louise (Mrs. Regis R. Boyle). With Duquesne Light Co., 1941, exec. v.p., 1967-68, pres., dir., 1968—; dir. 1st Fed. Savs. & Loan Assn. Pitts. Exec. bd. E. Central Area Reliability Coordination Agreement; engring. exec. com. Central Area Power Coordination, mem. sustaining fund Pitts. Symphony Soc.; bd. dirs. Welding Research Council; bd. visitors Grad. Sch. Bus., U. Pitts.; trustee Pa. State U. Recipient Distinguished Alumnus award Pa. State U., 1972. Fellow ASME; mem. Engrs. Soc. Western Pa., Am. Nuclear Soc. (corporate rep.), Nat., Pa. socs. profl. engrs., Pa. State Alumni Assn. (exec. bd.), Tau Beta Pi, Sigma Tau, Pi Tau Sigma. Methodist. Club: Duquesne (Pitts.). Address: 435 6th Ave Pittsburgh PA 15219

SCHAFFER, WILLIAM GRAY, lawyer; b. Phila., Jan. 3, 1942; s. Lester J. and Marian H. S.; B.A., Yale U., 1964, LL.B., 1967; m. Janice Ellen Cooper; children—Timothy, Alexandra. Admitted to D.C. bar, 1968, Pa. bar, 1973, Calif. bar, 1976; staff atty. Public Defender Service D.C., 1970-73, Communications Satellite Corp., 1967-70; partner firm Schaffer, Perazich and Kolker, Washington, 1973-74; tng. dir. Public Defender Service D.C., 1974-77; dep. asst. atty. gen. civil div. Dept. Justice, 1977—; asst. professorial lectr. in law George Washington U., 1972-74. Office: US Dept Justice Washington DC 20530

SCHAFFNER, CHARLES ETZEL, educator; b. N.Y.C., July 21, 1919; s. Louis C. and Christina (Etzel) S.; B.C.E., Cooper Union, 1941, C.E., 1952; M.C.E., Bklyn. Poly. Inst., 1944; B.S.S.E., U. Ill., 1945, N.Y. U.; m. Olga T. Stroedecke, Feb. 13, 1943; children—Charles Etzel II, Linda Jean. Jr. engr. Moran Proctor, Freeman & Mueser, N.Y.C., 1941; instr. Cooper Union, 1941-44; mem. faculty Bklyn. Poly. Inst., 1946-70, prof. engring., 1957-70, adj. prof., 1970-72, asst. dean, 1954-57, asso. dean, 1957-58, dean, dir. planning, 1958-62, v.p. adminstrn., 1962-70; v.p. Syska & Hennessy, Inc., 1970-73, sr. v.p., 1973-76, exec. v.p., 1976—, also dir. Chmn. nat. adv. bd. Summer Inst. Young Engring. Tchrs., 1959-63; mem. adv. panel NSF, 1960—; chmn. exec. bd. N.Y.C. Bldg. Code Project, 1962-66; mem. panel 421.00 adv. to bldg. research div. Inst. Applied Tech., Nat. Bur. Standards, 1966-69; mem. bldg., constrn. adv. council Dept. Bldgs. City N.Y., 1966—; mem. bldg. research adv. bd. NRC, 1972-79, vice chmn., 1973-77 chmn., 1977-78; chmn. Mayor's Bldg. and Constrn. Adv. Council, 1971-73; exec. dir. Mayor's Fire Safety Com., 1971-73; mem. N.Y.C. Constrn. Industry Advisory Council, 1973—; v.p., bd. dirs. N.Y. Bldg. Congress, 1967-71, sec., 1971—, chmn. govtl. affairs com., 1977-78, pres., 1979—. Commr. edn. dist. Locust Valley, N.Y., 1956-59, pres., 1958-59; commr. edn., pres. Central Dist. 3, Oyster Bay, N.Y., 1959-63. Trustee Coopel Union, 1975-78. Served with AUS, 1944-46. Named Outstanding Alumnus, Cooper Union, 1966, Distinguished Alumnus award Poly. Alumni Assn., Alumnus of Year, 1972. Mem. N.Y. Bldg. Congress (bd. govs.), Operation Democracy, ASCE (Civil Engr. of Year 1969), ASTM, Am. Arbitration Assn. (bd. arbitrators), Am. Soc. Engring. Edn. (v.p., gen. council 1965-67, v.p. fin. 1974-77, bd. dirs. 1965-67, 74-77, pres. 1979-80), Nat. Inst. Bldg. Scis. (exec. com. consultative council 1978—), Engrs. Joint Council (dir. 1976-79), Am. Assn. Engring. Socs. (bd. govs. 1979—), Am. Concrete Inst., N.Y. State Sch. Bds. Assn., N.Y. State Soc. Profl. Engrs. (bd. dirs. Nassau County chpt., Engr. of Year, Kings County chpt. 1968), Cooper Union Alumni Assn. (pres. 1973), Tau Beta Pi, Chi Epsilon, Omega Delta Phi. Clubs: Municipal, Seaview, Nassau. Contbr. articles profl. jours. Home: Linden Farms Rd Locust Valley NY 11560 Office: 11 W 42d St New York NY 10036

SCHAFFNER, FENTON, physician, educator; b. Chgo., Dec. 8, 1920; s. Samuel and Rose (Cannon) S.; B.S., U. Chgo., 1941, M.D., 1943; M.S. in Pathology, Northwestern U., 1947; children—Roberta, John, Andrea, Marjorie.Intern, asst. resident medicine Jackson Meml. Hosp., Miami, Fla., 1944-45; resident medicine Woodlawn Hosp., 1947,attending physician, co-chmn. dept. medicine, 1950-58; asso. attending physician Cook County Hosp., Chgo., 1955-58; asst. pathology Northwestern U.,1949-53, instr. medicine, 1955-58; asso. in medicine Columbia Coll. Phys. and Surg.,N.Y.C., 1958-62, asst. prof. pathology, 1963-66; asso. prof. medicine Mt. Sinai Sch. Medicine, City U. N.Y., N.Y.C., 1966-68 prof. pathology, 1967—, prof. medicine, 1968—, George Baehr prof. medicine, 1973—, acting chmn. dept. medicine, 1972-74; staff Mt. Sinai Hosp., 1958—, attending physician, 1967—. Panel mem. NRC-Nat. Acad. Scis. Drug Efficacy Study, 1968-69. Served to lt. (j.g.) USNR, 1945-46, lt. comdr., 1953-54. Diplomate Am. Bd. Internal Medicine. Fellow A.C.P. (bd. govs,), mem. Am. Assn. Study Liver Diseases (sec. 1958-72, pres. 1976-77), Am Gastroenterol. Assn. (chmn. research com. 1968-70). Author; editor several books and numerous papers in field. Co-editor: Progress in Liver Disease, vols.1-6, 1962—. Editorial bd. Med. Letter, 1966—, Gastroenterology, 1966-71, Digestion, 1968—. Home: 500 E 77th St New York NY 10021 Office: Mt Sinai Sch Medicine 1 Gustave Levy Plaza New York NY 10029

SCHAFFNER, FRANKLIN JAMES, dir., producer; b. Tokyo, Japan, May 30, 1922; s. Paul Franklin and Sarah (Swords) S.; A.B., Franklin and Marshall Coll., 1942; m. Helen Jean Gilchrist, Apr. 17, 1948; children—Jenny, Kate. TV dir. Studio One, 1948-51, 52-56, Ford Theater, 1951-52, Person to Person with Edward R. Murrow, 1956-58, Playhouse 90, 1958-60; producer, dir. Kaiser Aluminum Hour, 1958, Dupont Show of Week, 1963-65; dir. plays including Twelve Angry Men, 1955, also Caine Mutiny Court Martial, World's Greatest Robbery, The Army Game, Cruel Day; dir. Broadway play Advise and Consent, 1960 (recipient Best Direction award Variety Critics Poll); dir. movies including The Stripper, 1963, Best Man, 1964 (recipient diploma Kalrovy Vary Festival 1964), War Lord, 1965, Double Man, 1966, Planet of the Apes, 1968, Patton (Dirs. Guild Am. award, Acad. Motion Picture Arts and Scis. Oscar 1971), Nicholas and Alexandra, 1972, Papillon, 1973, Islands in the Stream, 1976, The Boys From Brazil, 1978; pres. Gilchrist Prodns., 1962-68, Franklin Schaffner Prodns., Beverly Hills, Calif., 1969—. Served to lt. USNR, 1942-46. Recipient Emmy awards, 1954, 55, 62, Sylvania award, 1953, 54; recipient Trustee award for documentary Tour of the White House, Am. Acad. TV Arts and Scis., 1962. Mem. Dirs. Guild Am. (nat. bd. dirs. 1960-61, 62-63, 64-65, 73-74), Nat. Acad. TV Arts and Scis., Acad. Motion Pictures Arts and Scis., Phi Beta Kappa. Clubs: Players (N.Y.C.); Riviera Tennis (Los Angeles); Waramaug Country (New Preston, Conn.); Reform (London). Address: care of Exec Business Mgmt 132 S Rodeo St Beverly Hills CA 90212*

SCHAFFNER, MARLOWE HARLAN, physician; b. Salem, Oreg., Feb. 10, 1922; s. Damon Clifford and Lucille Nirene (Perry) S.; B.A., Walla Walla Coll., 1944; M.D., Loma Linda U., 1945; diploma Institut de Medicine Tropicale, Antwerp, Belguim, 1954; M.P.H., UCLA, 1966; m. Dorothy Dye Schaffner, Mar. 21, 1943; children—Ronald, Rita, Richard, Roberta. Intern, White Meml. Hosp., 1946, resident in surgery, 1959; practice medicine specializing in family practice, Cottage Grove, Oreg., 1948-53; med. dir. Songa Hosp., Zaire, 1953-62; med. sec. Trans-Africa Div. Seventh-day Adventists, Salisbury, Rhodesia, 1962-68; pres. Kettering Med. Center, Dayton, Ohio, 1969-79; asst. prof. health adminstrn. Loma Linda U., 1971—, asso. prof. family medicine 1979—, v.p. for med. affairs, 1979—; pres. Cox Heart Inst., 1972-76. Participant U.S. Air Force Nat. Security Conf., 1978. Served as capt. U.S. Army, 1946-48. Named Honored Alumnus of Yr., Loma Linda U., 1962. Mem. Calif. Med. Assn., AMA, Am. Coll. Hosp. Adminstrs., Am. Coll. Emergency Physicians, Seventh-day Adventist Hosp. Assn. (pres. 1978-79), Dayton C. of C. Club: Rotary (Dayton). Author: (with Dorothy Schaffner) Highways to Health and Happiness, 1967; Health for Leaders, 1968. Office: Loma Linda U Loma Linda CA 92354

SCHAFFNER, ROBERT MICHAEL, govt. ofcl.; b. Bklyn., Jan. 30, 1915; s. Arthur G. and Helen (Von Holleuffer) S.; B.S., Poly Inst. Bklyn., 1936; M.S., W.Va. U., 1939; Ph.D., U. Pitts., 1941; m. Blanche Wharton, June 1, 1940; children—Val, Pam, Todd. Chem. engr. A. Hess & Co., N.Y.C., 1936-37; teaching asst. W.Va. U., 1937-39; instr. chem. engring. U. Pitts., 1939-41; chem. engr. Standard Oil Co. (Ind.), 1941-43; dir. research Guardite Corp., Miner Labs., Chgo., 1943-44; chem. engr. Libby McNeill & Libby, 1945-48, asst. to v.p. prodn., 1949-53, plant mgr., 1953, asst. gen. supt. Eastern div., 1954-57, v.p. research and quality control, 1957-70; asso. dir. for tech. Bur. Foods, FDA, Washington, 1971—. Mem. Inst. Food Tech., Assn. Food and Drug Assn., Am. Chem. Soc., Am. Inst. Chem. Engrs., Lambda Chi Alpha, Phi Lambda Upsilon. Author tech. articles. Holder patents on food dehydration. Home: 6629 Van Winkle Dr Falls Church VA 22044 Office: FDA 200 C St SW Washington DC 20204

SCHAFLER, NORMAN I., corp. exec.; b. N.Y.C., 1917; grad. Pratt Inst., Bklyn.; m. Rubelle Sanders; children—Julie, Richard. Sales engr. Atlantic Heat and Power Co., N.Y.C., 1938-40; pres. Continental Heat and Power Co., N.Y.C., 1940-42; v.p. Consol. Diesel Electric Corp., Mt. Vernon, N.Y., 1942-49, pres., Stamford, Conn., 1949-64; chmn. bd., chief exec. officer, dir. Condec Corp., 1964—; dir. United Aircraft Products Corp., Fidelity Trust Co., Bangor Punta Corp. Trustee Congregation Rodeph Sholom, Stamford Hosp.; bd. visitors Pratt Inst. Mem. Chief Execs. Forum, World Bus. Council, Econ. Club, Tower Fellows. Clubs: Birchwood Country, City Athletic, Harmonie, Lotos, Manhattan, Saugatuck Harbor Yacht, Metropolis Country. Home: 944 Fifth Ave New York NY 10021 also 22 Bluewater Hill Westport CT 06880 Office: Condec Corp Boston Post Rd Old Greenwich CT 06870

SCHAIE, KLAUS WARNER, educator; b. Stettin, Germany, Feb. 1, 1928; s. Sally and Lottie Louise (Gabriel) S.; A.A., City Coll. San Francisco, 1951; B.A., U. Calif. at Berkeley, 1952; M.S., U. Wash., 1953, Ph.D., 1956; m. Coloma John Harrison, Aug. 9, 1953 (div.); 1 son, Stephan Harrison; m. 2d, Joyce Kathleen Parr, July 4, 1974 (div.); 1 son, Christopher Parr. Psychology trainee Western State Hosp., Ft. Steilacoom, Wash., 1956-57; postdoctoral fellow med. psychology Washington U. Sch. Medicine, St. Louis, 1956-57; asst. prof., asso. prof. psychology U. Nebr., 1957-64; vis. prof. U. of Saar, Germany, 1960-61; vis. research asso. prof. U. Wash., 1963-64; asso. prof., prof., chmn. dept. psychology W.Va. U., Morgantown, 1964-73, acting dir., dir. Human Resources Research Inst., 1965-68; prof. psychology, dir. Gerontology Research Inst., Ethel Percy Andrus gerontology center U. So. Calif., Los Angeles, 1973—. Vis. prof. U. Bern (Switzerland), 1970-71, Macquarrie U., Australia, 1976, U. Trier (Ger.), 1979-80; cons. psychology VA, 1961—. Mem. developmental behavioral scis. study sect. NIH, 1970-74; mem. community mental health rev. com. W.Va. Dept. Mental Health, 1968-73. NIH research grantee, 1963-65, 69—; Fulbright lectr., 1961. Fellow Am. Psychol. Assn., Gerontol. Soc.; mem. Psychometric Soc., AAUP, Western Psychol. Assn., Soc. for Research in Child Devel., Sigma Xi. Author: Color and Personality, 1964. Editor: Theories and Methods of Research on Aging, 1968; Life-Span Developmental Psychology: Personality and Socialization, 1973; Developmental Human Behavior Genetics, 1975; Handbook of the Psychology of Aging, 1977. Contbr. articles to profl. jours. Home: 1085 Armada Dr Pasadena CA 91103

SCHALEBEN, ARVILLE, newspaper editor, writer, educator; b. Brown County, Minn., Jan. 25, 1907; s. Wilhelm and Lina (Helling) S.; B.A., U. Minn., 1929; m. Ida Androvandi, Sept. 14, 1935; children—Joy (Mrs. Lewis), Susan (Mrs. Wilson), Mary (Mrs. Totero), Will. With Milw. Journal, 1929-72, asst. city editor, then city editor, 1936-46, asst. mng. editor, 1946-59, mng. editor, 1959-62, exec. editor, 1962-66, asso. editor, 1966-72; v.p. The Jour. Co., 1962-68, dir., 1960-72; editor-in-residence U. Wis., Madison, 1972—, also vis. prof.; vis. prof. Medill Sch. Journalism, Northwestern U., 1972—; Riley prof. journalism Ind. U., Bloomington, 1972; lectr. U. Wis., Milw., 1976-77. Pres., Androvandi, Ltd., Milw. Dir. Fox Point (Wis.) Sch. Bd., 1942-48; mem. President's Com. for Handicapped, 1950-58; chmn. Nicolet High Sch. bldg. com., 1953. Named Wis. Journalist of Year, Soc. Profl. Journalists, 1975; recipient Honor al Merito award N.Am. Assn. of Venezuela. Mem. Wis. Asso. Press (pres.), Asso. Press Mng. Editors Assn. (dir.; chmn. news research com. 1965, mem. media competition com., new methods com., com. future newspapers), Am. Newspaper Pubs. Assn. (mem. news research center steering com. 1964-72), Am. Soc. Newspaper Editors (co-chmn. edn. com., mem. research com., com. edn. for journalism, com. minorities), Sigma Delta Chi (chmn. Wis. 1958, mem. prof. goals com.). Conglist. (past mem. bldg. com.). Clubs: Milw. Press (pres. 1936-39, pres. Found. 1975—); Ozaukee Country (Mequon, Wis.); Makai Golf and Tennis (Princeville, Hanalei, Hawaii). Author: Your Future in Journalism. Editorial bd. This Week mag. Home: 8254 N Gray Log Ln Fox Point WI 53217 Office: 333 W State St Milwaukee WI 53203 also Vilas Communications Hall U Wis-Madison Madison WI 53706. *In our good earth's eternity, not one among us is more enduring than the least among us unless he lives to lengthen mankind's future.*

SCHALK, WILLI, advt. agy. exec.; b. Aschaffenburg, Germany, Mar. 7, 1940; came to U.S., 1978; m. Gerdi Goehler; children—Silke, Sven. Product mgr. Enka Glanzstoff AG, Wuppertal, Germany, 1959-63, mktg. mgr., 1963-66; mng. partner Spl. Team Advt. Agy., Duesseldorf, Germany, 1967-70, TEAM/BBDO Group of Cos., Duesseldorf, 1969—; exec. v.p., gen. mgr. internat. ops BBDO Internat., Inc., N.Y.C., 1978—, also dir. Mem. Industrie Club (Duesseldorf). Home: 860 UN Plaza New York NY 10017 Office: 383 Madison Ave New York NY 10017

SCHALL, RICHARD LANGLEY, retail co. exec.; b. Mpls., Oct. 27, 1929; s. Richard Cannon and Ilyvon (Langley) S.; B.A., Macalester Coll., 1951; children—David, Caryn, Janet, Diane. With Gen. Mills, Inc., Mpls., 1952-69, fin. v.p., controller, 1967-69; exec. v.p., dir. Metro-Goldwyn-Mayer, Inc., 1969-70; pres., chief exec. officer, dir. Josten's, Inc., Mpls., 1970-71, chmn. bd., chief exec. officer, 1971; v.p., controller Dayton-Hudson Corp., Mpls., 1972-73, sr. v.p., 1973-74, sr. v.p. adminstrn., 1974-75, exec. v.p., 1975—, vice chmn. bd., 1977—; dir. Medtronic, Inc., 1st Nat. Bank Mpls., Econs. Lab. Bd. dirs. Mpls. YMCA, Upper Midwest Council; trustee Mpls. Soc. Fine Arts; trustee Macalester Coll., St. Paul, chmn., 1979-80. Served with AUS, 1951-52. Mem. Fin. Execs. Inst., U.S. C. of C., U.S. Lawn Tennis Assn. Office: 777 Nicollet Mall Minneapolis MN 55402

SCHALLER, HARRY WARREN, banker; b. Storm Lake, Iowa, Jan. 25, 1905; s. George Jacob and Eloise (Warren) S.; B.S., Columbia, 1926; m. Janet E. Young, June 18, 1930; children—Margaret Annette (Mrs. Robert Kitchen), Carolyn J. (Mrs. John K. Hopley), George H. With Citizens First Nat. Bank, Storm Lake, 1926—, v.p., 1931-33, pres., 1934-74, chmn., 1975—; also dir.; dir. Fed. Res. Bank Chgo., 1963-69, Iowa Public Service 1965-68; pres., dir. Schaller Co., 1961—; chmn. First Nat. Co., 1971—, Citizens Credit Corp., 1969—, First Leasing Co., 1973—. Mem. Iowa Devel. Commn., 1949-53. Served to maj. USAAF, 1942-45. Decorated Air medal with cluster, Bronze Star. Mem. Am. (exec. council 1935-37), Iowa (pres. 1948-49) bankers assns., Phi Sigma Kappa, Beta Gamma Sigma. Republican. Presbyn. Mason, Elk, Rotarian. Club: Union League (Chgo.). Home: 1 South Shore Storm Lake IA 50588 Office: Citizens First Nat Bank E 5th and Lake Sts Storm Lake IA 50588

SCHALLER, WARREN EDWARD, educator; b. Wauwatosa, Wis., Dec. 25, 1931; s. Adolph Frederick and Jean (Cox) S.; B.S., U. Wis., LaCrosse, 1953; M.S., Ind. U., 1956, D.Health and Safety, 1959; Sc.D. (hon.), Ricker Coll., Houlton, Maine, 1977; m. Judith Ann Arnet, Aug. 30, 1952; children—Jean Elizabeth, John Frederick. Elementary and secondary sch. tchr., Madison, Wis., 1956-58; mem. faculty Ball State U., Muncie, Ind., 1959—, prof. physiology and health sci. 1966—, chmn. dept. physiology and health sci., 1965—; cons. allied health scis. McGovern Allergy Clinic, Houston, 1974—; v.p. Delaware County (Ind.) Safety Council, 1965; bd. dirs. Delaware County Tb Assn., 1975—. Served with U.S. Army, 1953-55. WHO fellow, 1971. Mem. Am. Sch. Health Assn. (pres. 1976-77; Distinguished Service award 1976), Am. Pub. Health Assn., Assn. Advancement Health Edn., Am. Coll. Health Assn., Soc. Pub. Health Educators, Royal Soc. Health, Eta Sigma Gamma (co-founder 1967, pres. 1967—, distinguished service award 1977), Phi Delta Kappa, Phi Epsilon Kappa. Republican. Lutheran. Club: Masons. Author: Your Health Today, 1965; Critical Issues in Health, 1967; The School Health Program, 1975; Health, Quackery and the Consumer, 1976; Alcohol, Tobacco and Drugs, 1977. Home: 1010 N Tyrone Dr Muncie IN 47304 Office: 2000 University Ave Muncie IN 47306

SCHALLERT, WILLIAM JOSEPH, actor; b. Los Angeles, July 6, 1922; s. Edwin Francis and Elza Emily (Baumgarten) S.; B.A., U. Calif. at Los Angeles, 1946; postgrad. Sanford Meisner, 1963-65; m. Rosemarie Diann Waggner, Feb. 26, 1949; children—William Joseph, Edwin G., Mark M., Brendan C. Co-founder, owner Circle Theatre, Hollywood, Calif., 1947-50; appeared in motion pictures, TV, stage, radio, 1950—; movies include Lonely are the Brave, Heat of the Night, Charlie Varrick; starred in TV series Patty Duke Show, 1963-66, Nancy Drew Mysteries, 1977-78, Little Women, 1979; starred as judge in stage play and film The Trial of the Catonsville Nine, N.Y.C., Los Angeles, 1971 (Obie award 1971); starred in TV series appeared in TV movies Ike, Blind Ambition, 1979. Mem. Permanent Charities Com. Entertainment Industry, 1975—; trustee Motion Picture and TV Fund, 1975—. Served with AUS, 1942-44, USAAF, 1944-45. Recipient Los Angeles Drama Critics nomination, 1972; Fulbright fellow Brit. Repertory Theatre, 1952-53. Mem. Acad. Motion Picture Arts and Scis. (gov. 1977-79, chmn. Margaret Herrick Library com. 1979—), ASCAP, Screen Actors Guild (pres. 1979—, trustee Found. 1979—). Office: Freedman Kinzelberg and Broder 1801 Ave of Stars Suite 911 Los Angeles CA 90067

SCHALLY, ANDREW VICTOR, med. research scientist; b. Poland, Nov. 30, 1926; s. Casimir Peter and Maria (Lacka) S.; B.Sc., McGill U. (Can.), 1955, Ph.D. in Biochemistry, 1957; 8 hon. doctorates; children—Karen, Gordon; m. 2d, Ana Maria Comaru, Aug. 1975. Came to U.S., 1957. Research asst. biochemistry Nat. Inst. Med. Research, London, 1949-52, dept. psychiatry, McGill U., Montreal, Que., 1952-57; research asso., asst. prof. physiology and biochemistry Coll. Medicine, Baylor U., Houston, 1957-62; chief endocrine and polypeptide labs. VA Hosp., New Orleans, 1962—; asso. prof. Sch. Medicine, Tulane U., New Orleans, 1962-67, prof., 1967—; sr. med. investigator VA, 1973—. Recipient Dir.'s award for outstanding med. research VA Hosp., New Orleans, 1968; Van Meter prize Am. Thyroid Assn., 1969; Ayerst-Squibb award Endocrine Soc., 1970; William S. Middletown award VA, 1970; Ch. Mickle award U. Toronto, 1974; Gairdner Internat. award, 1974; Borden award Assn. Am. Med. Colls. and Borden Co. Found., 1975; Lasker Basic Research award, 1975; co-recipient Nobel prize for medicine, 1977. USPHS sr. research fellow, 1961-62. Mem. Endocrine Soc., Am. Physiol. Soc., Soc. Biol. Chemists, Am. Chem. Soc., AAAS, Soc. Exptl. Biol. Medicine, Internat. Soc. Research Biology Reprodn., Soc. Study Reprodn., Soc. Internat. Brain Research Orgn., Mexican Acad. Medicine, Am. Soc. Animal Sci., Endocrine Soc. Madrid, Sigma Xi, others. Author several books; contbr. articles to profl. jours. Home: 5025 Kawanee Ave Metairie LA 70002 Office: 1601 Perdido St New Orleans LA 70140

SCHANBERG, SYDNEY HILLEL, journalist; b. Clinton, Mass., Jan. 17, 1934; s. Louis and Freda (Feinberg) S.; B.A., Harvard U., 1955; m. Janice Leah Sakofsky, Oct. 22, 1967; children—Jessica, Rebecca. Joined N.Y. Times, 1959, became reporter, 1960, bur. chief, Albany, N.Y., 1967-69, chief bur., New Delhi, India, 1969-73, S.E. Asia corr., Singapore, 1973-75, met. editor, 1977—. Served with AUS, 1956-58. Recipient Page One award for fgn. reporting Newspaper Guild N.Y., 1972; George Polk Meml. award for fgn. reporting, 1972, spl. award for coverage fall of Phnom Penh, 1975; Overseas Press Club award for fgn. reporting, 1972, for fgn. photography, 1974, Bob Considine Meml. award, 1975; Pulitzer prize, 1975; Front Page award Newspaper Guild; Sigma Delta Chi award for distinguished service in journalism. Address: care NY Times 229 W 43d St New York City NY 10036

SCHANCK, FRANCIS RABER, investment banker; b. Los Angeles, Oct. 22, 1907; s. Francis Raber and Florence Ethel (Carr) S.; student Stanford, 1926-29; m. Kathryn Sterling Short, June 10, 1933; children—Jordan Thomas, Susan, Peter Carr. Successively with E.A. Pierce & Co., Anderson & Fox Co., also C.F. Childs & Co., 1927-30; office and dept. mgr. First Boston Corp., Portland, Ore., San Francisco, Los Angeles and Chgo., 1930-42, 46-48; dept. mgr., partner Bacon, Whipple & Co., Chgo., 1948-62, mng. partner, 1962-76, sr. partner, 1977—; chmn. bd. Bank of Hinsdale (Ill.); dir. Empire Gas Corp. Past mem. sch. edn. Community Consol. Sch. Dist. 181 and High Sch. Dist. 86, DuPage-Cook County, Ill. Past trustee Village Hinsdale, Ill. Served to comdr. USNR, World War II; PTO. Mem. Investment Bankers Assn. Am. (chmn. central states group 1962-63, nat. bd. govs., v.p. 1964-65, 1st v.p. 1966-67, pres. 1967-68), Municipal Bond Club Chgo. (past pres.), Security Industry Assn. (chmn. governing council 1972), Bond Club Chgo. (past pres.), Zeta Psi. Clubs: Chicago, Commercial, Union League, Attic (Chgo.); Hinsdale Golf (Ill.); Links (N.Y.C.). Home: 537 Pamela Circle Hinsdale IL 60521 Office: 135 S LaSalle St Chicago IL 60603. *I have used the following definition in making personal and business decisions: Truth-the highest degree of probability which withstands all presently known scientific tests. My belief is that all enterprises should conduct themselves as if they expect to exist in perpetuity. While most aspects of life are subject to constant change, there are a few immutable, essential character traits found in all worthy entities-individuals, businesses and governments. Most important among these characteristics are integrity, productivity, thrift, and humility.*

SCHANCK, JORDAN THOMAS, mfg. co. exec.; b. Portland, Oreg., Feb. 5, 1931; s. Francis Raber and Kathryn (Short) S.; B.A., Dartmouth, 1952; m. Barbara Burgoyne, Apr. 27, 1957; children—Karen, William, Rebecca. With Signode Corp., Chgo., 1954—, gen. sales mgr. Paslode div., 1959-64, dir. sales, 1964-66, asst. to pres., 1966-68, dir. corporate planning, 1969, v.p. corporate planning, 1970-71, exec. v.p., dir., 1972-73, pres., 1974, chief exec. officer, 1975, mem. exec. com., 1973—; dir. Amsted Industries, Chgo., Am. Nat. Bank and Trust Co., Chgo., Maytag Co., Newton, Iowa, Lindberg Corp., Chgo. Bd. govs. United Republican Fund Ill., 1974—; bd. dirs. John Crerar Library, Chgo., Lyric Opera Guild, Chgo.; pres. York Woods Community Assn., 1971; mem. adv. bd. YMCA of Met. Chgo., Drug Abuse Council Ill.; past mem. bd. dirs. United Charities of Chgo.; trustee, former chmn. George Williams Coll.; bd. govs. Soc. for Environ. Awareness, Downers Grove, Ill. Served with AUS, 1952-54. Mem. Chgo. Assn. Commerce and Industry (dir.), Dartmouth Alumni Assn. Chgo. (past dir.). Presbyn. Clubs: Hinsdale (Ill.) Golf; Economics, Chicago, Commonwealth, Comml., Plaza (Chgo.). Home: 38 Croydon Ln Oak Brook IL 60521 Office: 3600 W Lake St Glenview IL 60025

SCHANES, STEVEN ELI, employee benefits cons.; b. Newark, Jan. 7, 1924; s. Isadore J. and Lillian (Lubman) S.; A.B. cum laude, State Tchrs. Coll., Montclair, N.J., 1943; Ph.D. in Internat. and Constl. Law, Cornell U., 1948; m. Christine Marie Marra, June 11, 1947; children—Christine Elise, Paul Anthony, Laura Marie, Steven Joseph, William David. Instr. govt. Boston U., 1948-49; research analyst N.J. C. of C., 1949-52; instr. govt. Rutgers U., 1950-51; adminstrv. sec. N.J. Bur. Pub. Employee Pensions, 1952-55; dir. N.J. Div. Pensions, 1955-58; v.p. Martin E. Segal & Co., pension and ins. consultants, N.Y.C., 1958-69; v.p. Nat. Assn. State Social Security Adminstrs., 1956-57, pres., 1957-58; asso. prof. polit. sci. and history Seton Hall U., 1964-66; acad. dean, chmn. div. econs. and bus. adminstrn., prof. polit. sci. U. San Diego, 1966-69; dir. office program planning U.S. Dept. Commerce, Washington, 1969-70, spl. asst. to sec. for policy devel., 1970-71; asst. dir. Nat. Marine Fisheries Service, Washington, 1971-74; asst. to chmn. Nat. Adv. Commn. on Oceans and Atmosphere, Washington, 1972; dir. policy, office coastal zone mgmt. Nat. Oceanic and Atmospheric Adminstrn., Washington, 1972-73; U.S. commr. Inter-Am. Tropical Tuna Commn., 1972-74; exec. dir. U.S. Pension Benefit Guaranty Corp., Washington, 1974-76; exec. dir. Soc. Profl. Benefit Adminstrs., 1977-79, cons., 1979—; pres. Schanes Assos., San Diego and Washington, 1976—; adj. prof. govt. Am. U., 1975; bd. dirs. Nat. Employee Benefits Inst., 1977—; bd. dirs. Assn. Pvt. Pension and Welfare Funds, 1977-79, chmn. com. nat. health care, 1976-79; mem. govt. affairs com., nat. health ins. com. Internat. Found. Employee Benefits. Mem. Bd. Edn., Nutley, N.J., 1953-55, N.J. Council on Aging, 1956-58; bd. dirs. San Francisco Home Health Services; mem. Health Systems Agy., San Diego. Served to 1st lt. USAAF, 1943-45; ETO. Decorated Air medal with 4 oak leaf clusters. Named Employee Benefits Man of Year, Pension World, 1976. Mem. Am. Polit. Sci. Assn., Govt. Research Assn., Western Govtl. Research Assn., Municipal Finance Officers Assn., Am. Pub. Adminstrn. Soc., N.J. Patrolmens Benevolent Assn., N.J. Firemens Mut. Benevolent Assn., Am. Arbitration Assn. (nat. labor panel), Am. Civil Liberties Union, Am. Mgmt. Assn., Gulf and Caribbean Fisheries Inst. Author: Internation Cooperation in Civil Aviation, 1945-47, 1948; Benefits of Major Public Employee Retirement Systems, 1963. Home and office: 4884 San Joaquin Dr San Diego CA 92109

SCHANK, STANLEY COX, cytogeneticist; b. Fallon, Nev., Oct. 31, 1932; s. LeRoy Christian and Prudence Verona (Cox) S.; B.S., Utah State U., Logan, 1954; Ph.D., U. Calif., Davis, 1961; m. Sandra Richards, Mar. 12, 1954; children—Colleen Schank McGrath, David S., Gary S., Linda, Rodney W. Mem. faculty U. Fla., Gainesville, 1961—, prof. genetics and plant breeding, 1972—; cons. IRI Research Inst. and IICA, Brazil, 1966, 79; vis. prof., scientist Commonwealth Sci. and Indsl. Research Orgn., Brisbane, Australia, 1971, 78; vis. research prof. Empressa Brasileira de Pesquisa Agropecuaria, Brazil, 1973-75; co-dir., investigator AID grants. Adult leader N. Fla. council Boy Scouts Am., 1975-77. Served with U.S. Army, 1955-57. Mem. Am. Soc. Agronomy, Crop Sci. Soc. Am., Canadian Genetics Soc., Fla. Soil and Crop Sci. Soc., Am. Genetic Assn., Gamma Sigma Delta, Phi Kappa Phi, Phi Sigma. Author articles, monograph. Home: 60 NW 44th St Gainesville FL 32607 Office: 2189 McCarty Hall Dept Agronomy U Fla Gainesville FL 32611

SCHANNEN, RICHARD HAROLD, lawyer, ins. co. exec.; b. Ft. Wayne, Ind., Mar. 3, 1917; s. William H. and Anna (Braun) S.; B.S., Ind. U., 1939; LL.B., Harvard U., 1942; m. Ruth E. Garrison, Oct. 5, 1946; children—William H., Doris L. Admitted to Ind. bar, 1942, Mass. bar, 1950; mem. firm Barnes, Hickam, Pantzer & Boyd, Indpls., 1942; atty. Med. Protective Co., Ft. Wayne, 1946-50; v.p., sec., gen. counsel Am. Mut. Liability Ins. Co., Wakefield, Mass., 1950—. Served to lt. USNR, 1942-46. Mem. Am.. Mass. bar assns. Home: 7 Grey Ln Lynnfield MA 01940 Office: Am Mut Liability Ins Co Wakefield MA 01880

SCHAPERY, RICHARD ALLAN, educator; b. Duluth, Minn., Mar. 3, 1935; s. Aaron and Nellie (Slovut) S.; B.S. in Mech. Engring. with high distinction, Wayne State U., 1957; M.S., Calif. Inst. Tech., 1958, Ph.D. in Aeros., 1962; m. Mable Etta Burns, June 14, 1957; 1 son, Phillip Randal. Mem. faculty Purdue U., Lafayette, Ind., 1962-69; prof. civil and aerospace engring. Tex. A. and M. U., College Station, 1969—, dir. Mechanics and Materials Research Center, 1972—. Cons. industry, govt. Recipient machinery's award for design; Disting. Achievement award for research Tex. A&M U.; formerly Gen. Motors Corp. fellow, Woodrow Wilson fellow, Douglas Aircraft fellow; past Purdue XL grantee. Mem. Am. Inst. Aeros. and Astronautics, Sigma Xi, Omicron Delta Kappa, Tau Beta Pi. Contbr. to profl. jours. and books. Home: 1205 Brook Hollow Bryan TX 77801 Office: Dept Civil Engring Tex A and M Univ College Station TX 77843

SCHAPIRO, DONALD, lawyer; b. N.Y.C., Aug. 8, 1925; s. John Max and Lydia (Chaitkin) S.; A.B., Yale, 1944, LL.B., 1949; m. Ruth Ellen Goldman, June 29, 1952; children—Jane G., Robert A. Admitted to N.Y. bar, 1949; asso. Paul, Weiss, Rifkind, Wharton & Garrison, N.Y.C., 1949-51; asst. chief counsel U.S. Ho. of Reps. subcom. ways and means com. on adminstrn. revenue laws, Washington, 1951-52; asso. Barrett, Smith, Schapiro, Simon & Armstrong, N.Y.C., 1952-55, partner, 1955—. Gen. partner Waterside Redevel. Co.; dir. Whitney Communications Corp. Vis. lectr. law Yale Law Sch., 1949-78, instr. law and econs., 1945-49. Mem. Order of Coif, Phi Beta Kappa, Phi Delta Phi. Home: 1035 Fifth Ave New York NY 10028 Office: 26 Broadway New York NY 10004

SCHAPIRO, MORRIS A., investment banker; b. Shavly, Lithuania, Apr. 9, 1903; s. Nathan M. and Fanny (Adelman) S.; came to U.S., 1907, naturalized, 1914; B.A., Columbia U., 1923, Engr. Mines, 1925; m. Alma Binion Cahn, Mar. 28, 1929; children—Linda S. Collins, Daniel E. Engr., geologist Am. Metal Co., 1925-27; security analyst Hoit, Rose & Troster, 1927-31; partner firm Monahan, Schapiro & Co., 1931-39; pres. M.A. Schapiro & Co., Inc., N.Y.C., 1939—, 2d Dist. Securities Co., Inc., N.Y.C., 1939-79; chmn. adv. com. N.Y. State Joint Legis. Com. to Revise Banking Law, 1957-60. Mem. Am. Inst. Mining and Metall. Engrs. (hon.), N.Y. Soc. Security Analysts, Securities Industry Assn. Am. Club: Columbia (N.Y.C.). Contbr. articles on banking to profl. jours. Home: 910 Fifth Ave New York NY 10021 Office: 1 Chase Manhattan Plaza New York NY 10005

SCHAPIRO, NATHAN, chain store exec., lawyer; b. Sassow, Poland, Aug. 3, 1921 (parents Am. citizens); s. Jacob and Betty (Kohl) S.; Ph.B., U. Wis., 1946, LL.D., 1949; m. Mildred Hillman, July 3, 1954; children—Charles Jay, Karen Mala. Admitted to Wis. bar, 1949, since practiced in Milw.; gen. counsel, v.p., sec. Kohl Corp., 1967—; dir. various Kohl Food Stores entities. Pres., Milw. chpt. Am. Jewish Congress, 1963-69, mem. nat. governing body, 1965-68; bd. dirs. Milw. Jewish Council. Served with USAAF, 1942-45. Decorated Air medal with 2 oak leaf clusters, D.F.C. with 2 oak leaf clusters. Mem. Wis. Fedn. Mchts. (dir.). Home: 5347 N Santa Monica Blvd Milwaukee WI 53217 Office: 11100 W Burleigh St Milwaukee WI 53222

SCHARADIN, HARRY LINWOOD, equipment mfg. corp. exec.; b. Orwigsburg, Pa., Aug. 10, 1922; s. Garson Johnathon and Emma Ruth (Frantz) S.; grad. Reading Bus. Inst., 1941; m. Fern Mayetta Troutman, Jan. 11, 1945; children—Lynne Ann, Scott Alyn. With Acco Industries Inc. (formerly Am. Chain & Cable Co., Inc.), 1941—, div. controller, office mgr., Reading, Pa., 1958-61, staff asst. to corp. controller, Bridgeport, Conn., 1961-63, asst. corp. controller, 1963-67, corp. controller, 1967-77, treas., 1977—. Treas. Kate Sterling Bunnell Scholarship Fund, 1966—. Mem. Nat. Assn. Accts., Controllers Inst. Republican. Congregationalist. Home: 161 Old Spring Rd Stratford CT 06497 Office: Acco Industries Inc 929 Connecticut Ave Bridgeport CT 06602

SCHARF, WALTER, composer, condr., arranger; b. N.Y.C.; grad. N.Y. U.; postgrad. (scholar) Walter Damrosch Inst.; studied music (scholar) European conservatories; m. Betty King, 1935; children—Allen, Susan. Formerly night club accompanist, then became pianist and arranger for big-name bands, including Vincent Lopez and Rudy Vallee; first Hollywood film credits with Sweet Music, Warner Bros., 1935; with Warner Bros., 1935-36, 20th Century-Fox, 1936-40, Paramount Studios, 1941-42; music head Republic Pictures, 1942-46; for many years was arranger-condr. for Phil Harris-Alice Faye Hour, radio; condr. Kate Smith's premier performance of God Bless America at Hollywood Bowl; composer/arranger for numerous films, including: Alexander's

Ragtime Band, Hearts Divided, On The Avenue, Rose of Washington Square, Tin Pan Alley, Birth of The Blues, Holiday Inn (including orchestration of White Christmas), Star Spangled Rhythm, Dakota, I've Always Loved You, Casbah, City Across The River, Bundle of Joy, Take One False Step, The Saxon Charm, Red Canyon, Sierra, Two Tickets to Broadway, Hans Christian Andersen, Three Violent People, The Joker Is Wild, Pocketful of Miracles, Where Love Has Gone, My Six Loves, Pendulum, If It's Tuesday It Must Be Belgium, Cheyenne Social Club, Willy Wonka and The Chocolate Factory, Ben, Walking Tall films, Funny Girl, also 9 Dean Martin and Jerry Lewis films and 7 Jerry Lewis films; composer, arranger and condr. for Jacques Cousteau TV spls., including: The Tragedy of the Red Salmon (Emmy award 1971), Beneath The Frozen World (Emmy award 1974), A Sound of Dolphins (Nat. Acad. TV Arts and Scis. spl. citation 1974); other TV credits include Nat. Geog. spls., Shirley Temple's Storybook Theater, Killy: Le Superman, Mr. Magoo's Christmas Carol, Uncle Sam Magoo, several George Plimpton spls., Hallmark Hall of Fame's A Storm in Summer, The Dangerous Christmas of Red Riding Hood, and numerous episodes of TV series, including Mission: Impossible, Ben Casey, Slattery's People; composer musical shows C'est La Vie and Maybe That's Your Problem; composer opera based on Norman Corwin's The Plot to Overthrow Christmas; composed The Legend of The Living Sea Symphony, ofcl. music of Cousteau's Museum of the Living Sea aboard Queen Mary, Long Beach, Calif., and Wilderness Trail album for Nat. Geog. Soc., first symphonic work: The Israeli Suite; songs include: (lyrics by Don Black) Ben (Golden Globe award 1973); music cons. U. Wyo. Mem. Motion Picture Acad. (past dir. music br.), Nat. Acad. TV Arts and Scis. (past mem. blue ribbon panel). Office: care Shefrin Co Public Relations PO Box 48559 Los Angeles CA 90048

SCHARFFENBERGER, GEORGE THOMAS, diversified industry exec.; b. Hollis, N.Y., May 22, 1919; s. George L. and Martha L. (Watson) S.; B.S., Columbia, 1940; m. Marion Agnes Nelson, July 17, 1948; children—Ann Marie, George Thomas, John Edward, Thomas James, James Nelson, Joan Ellen. With Arthur Andersen & Co., 1940-43; with Internat. Tel. & Tel. Corp., subsidiaries and divs., 1943-59, successively gen. auditor, asst. comptroller, comptroller, asst. to pres., 1943-53, v.p., 1953-55; pres. Kellogg Switchboard & Supply Co. (div.), Chgo., 1955-59, also dir.; pres., dir. Westrex Corp.; v.p. Litton Industries, Inc., 1959-62, sr. v.p., 1962-66, dir.; exec. v.p. Litton Systems, Inc., 1961-66; chmn., dir. City Investing Co., N.Y.C., 1966—, chief exec. officer, 1966—; dir. IC Industries, Chgo., Litton Industries, Inc., Beverly Hills, Calif., Earle M. Jorgensen Co., Los Angeles. Trustee U. So. Cal. Served with AUS, World War II. Mem. Financial Execs. Inst., Met. Mus. Art. Clubs: California (Los Angeles); Brook (N.Y.C.). Home: 4 Appaloosa Ln Rolling Hills CA 90274 Office: 767 Fifth Ave New York NY 10022 also 9100 Wilshire Blvd Beverly Hills CA 90212

SCHARINGER, DALE HERBERT, educator; b. Sheboygan, Wis., Nov. 20, 1934; s. Herbert C. and Frances (Fleming) S.; B.Ed., Wis. State U., Whitewater, 1957; M.B.A., Ind. U., 1958, D.B.A., 1964; m. Carole Donna Porter, June 15, 1957; children—Anne Elisabeth, Steven Dale. Jr. accountant Henkel, Pattison & Co., C.P.A.'s, Wis., 1960-61; teaching asst. Ind. U., 1961-64; instr. Spencerian Coll., Milw., 1961; prof. mgmt. and finance, asst. dean Coll. Bus. and Econs., Wis. State U., Whitewater, 1966-67, acting dean Sch. Bus. and Econs., 1967-68, asso. dean, 1968-76, chmn. finance and bus. law dept., 1973-75, prof. mgmt., 1976—. Served with AUS, 1958-60. Mem. Acad. Mgmt., Midwest Bus. Adminstrn. Assn., Soc. Advancement Mgmt. (council ind. mgrs. Milw. chpt.), Am. Soc. for Personnel Adminstrn., Blackhawk Personnel Assn. (pres. 1972-73), Phi Delta Kappa (pres. 1956-57), Delta Pi Epsilon (pres. 1963-64), Pi Omega Pi, Beta Gamma Sigma. Contbr. articles to profl. jours. Home: 407 S Douglas Court Whitewater WI 53190

SCHARPER, PHILIP JENKINS, editor; b. Balt., Sept. 15, 1919; s. William Albert and Marie Louise (Griffin) S.; A.B., Georgetown U., 1943, Ph.L., 1944, M.A. in Edn., 1945; M.A. in English, Fordham U., 1947; Litt.D., Loyola Coll., 1966, Mt. Mary Coll., 1966, St. Joseph's Coll., 1975; m. Sarah J. Moormann, June 11, 1949; children—Grail, Philip, Katherine, Alice, David, Bede. Instr. English, Xavier U., Cin., 1948-50; asst. prof. English Fordham U., 1950-55; asso. editor The Commonweal, 1956-57; editor-in-chief Sheed & Ward, Inc., N.Y.C., 1957-70, v.p., 1962-70; editor-in-chief Orbis Books, Maryknoll, N.Y., 1970—. Adviser Nat. Fedn. Catholic Coll. Students Program on Pluralism, 1960-61; del. Nat. Conf. Race and Religion, 1962. Bd. dirs. Manhattan region Nat. Conf. Christians and Jews, Nat. Com. Support Pub. Schs.; nat. adv. com. Cath. Council Civil Liberties. Trustee John XXIII Inst., St. Xavier Coll., Chgo. Recipient Xavier award Xavier U., 1961, Kelley award Loyola High Sch., Balt., 1963; Edith Stein award, N.Y.; recipient fellowship for visit to Israel, Jewish Theol. Sem. Mem. Religious Edn. Assn. U.S. and Can. (pres. 1963-64; chmn. 1964-70), Am. Benedictine Acad. Author: Meet the American Catholic, 1969; also TV scripts. Editor: American Catholics: A Protestant-Jewish View, 1959; Torah and Gospel, 1966; The Radical Bible, 1972; The Patriot's Bible, 1975. Contbg. author: Catholics and Vietnam, 1968. Home: 1623 Newfield Ave Stamford CT 06905 Office: Orbis Books Maryknoll NY 10545

SCHARRER, BERTA VOGEL, biologist, educator; b. Munich, Germany, Dec. 1, 1906; d. Karl Phillip and Johanna (Greis) Vogel; came to U.S., 1937, naturalized, 1944; Ph.D., U. Munich, 1930; M.D. honoris causa, U. Giessen (W.Ger.), 1976; Sc.D. (hon.), Northwestern U., 1977, U. N.C., 1978; m. Ernst Albert Scharrer, Mar 1, 1934 (dec. 1965). Research asso. Research Inst. Psychiatry, Munich, 1931-34, Neurol. Inst., Frankfurt-am-Main, Germany, 1934-37, dept. anatomy U. Chgo., 1937-38, Rockefeller Inst. Med. Research, N.Y.C., 1938-40; sr. instr., fellow dept. anatomy Western Res U., Cleve., 1940-46; Guggenheim fellow dept. anatomy U. Colo. Sch. Medicine, Denver, 1947-48, USPHS spl. research fellow, 1948-50, asst. prof. research, 1950-55; prof. anatomy Albert Einstein Coll. Medicine, N.Y.C., from 1955, now prof. emeritus, acting chmn., 1965-66, 74-77; researcher comparative neuroendocrinology, neurosecretion, fine structure neuroglandular elements, neurotrophic factors in tumor growth. Recipient Kraepelin Gold medal, 1978. Mem. Nat. Acad. Scis., Am. Acad. Arts and Scis., Deutsche Akademie der Naturforscher Leopoldina, Royal Netherlands Acad. Arts and Scis. (fgn.), Internat. Soc. Neuroendocrinology, Internat. Brain Research Orgn., NRC (com. brain scis.), Endocrine Soc. Co-editor: Cell and Tissue Research, 1957; editorial bd. Jour. Gen. Comparative Endocrinology, 1968—, Biol. Bull. Home: 1240 Neill Ave Bronx NY 10461 Office: 1300 Morris Park Ave Bronx NY 10461

SCHARY, DORE, motion picture producer, playwright, city ofcl.; b. Newark, Aug. 31, 1905; s. Herman Hugo and Belle (Drachler) S.; ed. Central High Sch., Newark; L.H.D. (hon.), Coll. Pacific, 1951, Wilberforce U.; D.F.A. (hon.), Lincoln Coll., 1960; m. Miriam Svet, Mar. 5, 1932; children—Jill, Joy, Jeb. Dir. Little Theatre; actor, playwright, publicity and newspaper work, 1926-32; with Columbia, Paramount, Warner Bros. as writer of 35 screen plays, 1933-37; writer Metro-Goldwyn-Mayer studios, 1938-41, exec. producer, 1941-46; producer David O. Selznick, 1943-46; exec. v.p. in charge prodn. RKO Studios, 1947-48; exec. v.p. in charge prodn. and studio operations M-G-M Studios, Culver City, Calif., 1948-56, became head ind. producer, 1956—; past chief exec. officer Theatrevision, Inc., also pres. Schary Prodns. Commr. cultural affairs, City N.Y. Mem. Citizens Crusade Against Poverty, Pres.'s Com.-Nat. Citizens Commn., Nat. Adv. Com. Farm Labor, Nat. Com. Immigration. Fellow, trustee Eleanor Roosevelt Meml. Found. Recipient Acad. award for story Boys Town; Antoinette Perry award for Sunrise at Campobello, 1958. Mem. Author's League, Screen Writers Guild, Producers Guild, Acad. Motion Picture Arts and Scis., Dramatists Guild Fund (pres.), Anti-Defamation League (nat. chmn. 1963-69, now hon. chmn.). Democrat. Mem. B'nai B'rith. Author: Boys Town; Edison the Man; Young Tom Edison; Case History of A Movie; For Special Occasions, 1962; (with Sinclair Lewis) Storm in the West, 1963; (autobiography) Heyday, 1979. Exec. producer films Joe Smith, American, Journey for Margaret, Bataan, Lassie Come Home, Lost Angel. Producer films Spiral Staircase, I'll Be Seeing You, The Farmer's Daughter, The Bachelor and the Bobby-Soxer, Till the End of Time, Battleground, The Next Voice You Hear, Go For Broke, Plymouth Adventure, Dream Wife, Take the High Ground, Bad Day at Black Rock, The Last Hunt, Designing Woman; writer, co-producer Sunrise at Campobello, 1958; co-producer, dir. A Majority of One, 1959; writer, dir., co-producer The Highest Tree, 1959, The Devils Advocate, 1960; writer, producer motion picture Sunrise at Campobello, 1960; co-producer, dir. The Unsinkable Molly Brown, 1960, Something About a Soldier, 1962, The Zulu and The Zayda, 1965; producer, dir., writer motion picture Act One, 1963; producer, dir., playwright One By One, 1964; playwright Brightower, 1970; producer, co-playwright Herzl, 1976. Office: 50 Sutton Pl S New York NY 10022

SCHATZ, ALBERT GERARD, judge; b. Omaha, Aug. 4, 1921; s. Albert A. and Elizabeth C. (Howland) S.; A.B., Nebr. U., 1943; LL.B., Creighton U., 1948; m. Mary Jean Murray, Feb. 14, 1944; children—Gregory M., Thomas G., Philip H., Mary C., Ann L., Jane E. Admitted to Nebr. bar, 1948; law clk. to judge Ct. Appeals for 8th Circuit, Omaha, 1948-50; partner firm Gross, Welch, Vinardi, Kauffman & Schatz, Omaha, 1950-73; judge U.S. Dist. Ct. for Nebr., Omaha, 1973—. Served to capt. USMCR, 1943-46. Mem. Am., Omaha, Nebr. State bar assns., Am. Coll. Trial Lawyers, Am. Judicature Soc., Sierra Internat., Omaha Press Club, Sigma Nu. Republican. Roman Catholic. Rotarian. Club: Omaha Country. Home: 9929 Broadmoor Rd Omaha NE 68114 Office: PO Box 607 Omaha NE 68101

SCHATZ, ARTHUR HERSCHEL, lawyer; b. Hartford, Conn., Dec. 31, 1918; s. Nathan A. and Dora (Goldberg) S.; A.B., Cornell U., 1940, J.D., 1942; m. Cecil Ruskay, Feb. 11, 1945; children—Ellen Levine, Robert F., Daniel N. Admitted to Conn. bar, 1942, Fed. Ct., 1946; sr. partner Schatz & Schatz, Hartford, 1945-78, Schatz & Schatz, Ribicoff & Kotkin, Hartford, 1978—; trial counsel, cons. in forensic sci.; lectr. Cornell Law Sch., 1959-72, U. Conn., 1959-72, New Eng. Law Inst., 1960-76; faculty Law Sci. Inst., U. Tex.; del. Internat. Congress on Forensic Sci., 1960, 63, 66, 69, 72, 75, 78, v.p., gen. counsel, 1975-78; del. Congress Internat. Assn. Traffic Accident Medicine, 1963, 66, 69, 72, 75; mem. Conn. Commn. on Medicolegal Investigations, 1969—, vice chmn., 1972-79. Mem. council Cornell U., 1970-77; trustee Forensic Sci. Found., 1969-72, Law-Sci. Found Am.; trustee, v.p., gen. counsel Internat. Reference Orgn. in Forensic Medicine, 1969—. Fellow Am. Acad. Forensic Scis. (chmn. jurisprudence sect., mem. exec. council, 1959-71, sec.-treas. 1969-71); mem. Brit. Acad. Forensic Scis., Am. Assn. Automotive Medicine, Cornell Law Assn. (exec. com. 1958-62), Am., Conn., Hartford County bar assns., New Eng. Law Inst. (exec. com. 1960-76), Soc. Med. Jurisprudence. Home: 33 Juniper Rd Bloomfield CT 06002 Office: 1 Financial Plaza Hartford CT 06103

SCHATZ, EDWARD RALPH, ednl. adminstr.; b. St. Marys, Pa., Nov. 28, 1921; s. Ralph George and Thecla (Marshall) S.; B.S., Carnegie Inst. Tech., 1942, M.S., 1943, D.Sc., 1949; m. Virginia Louise Wright, Aug. 5, 1948; children—Eleanor Louise, George Edward. Asst. engr. Metall. Lab., U. Chgo., 1944, Los Alamos (Calif.) Sci. Lab., 1944-46; mem. faculty and staff Carnegie-Mellon U., Pitts., 1946—, prof. elec. engring., 1961—, dean research, 1961-64, v.p. acad. affairs, 1964-72, acting pres., 1972, v.p. acad. affairs, provost, 1973—. Dir. MPC Corp., Pitts., First Fed. Savs. and Loan Assn. Pitts., Penn Group Health Plan, Pitts. Mem. sci and research adv. group Regional Indsl. Devel. Corp. Mem. Pitts. Bd. Pub. Edn., 1974-76; trustee Western Pa. Sch. for Deaf., Pitts. Recipient Carnegie Teaching award, 1952. Sr. mem. IEEE; mem. Am. Soc. Engring. Edn., Tau Beta Pi, Eta Kappa Nu, Omicron Delta Kappa. Editor: Transition Metal Compounds, 1964. Home: 4752 Bayard St Pittsburgh PA 15213

SCHATZ, IRWIN JACOB, physician; b. St. Boniface, Man., Can., Oct. 16, 1931; s. Jacob and Reva S.; came to U.S., 1956, naturalized, 1966; student U. Man. (Can.), Winnipeg, 1951, M.D. with honors, 1956; m. Barbara Jane Binder, Nov. 12, 1967; children—Jacob, Edward, Stephen and Brian (twins). Intern, Vancouver (B.C.) Gen. Hosp., 1955-56; resident Hammersmith Hosp., U. London, 1957, Mayo Clinic, Rochester, Minn., 1958-61; head sec. peripheral vascular disease Henry Ford Hosp., Detroit, 1961-68; asso. prof. medicine Wayne State U., 1968-71, chief sect. cardiovascular disease, 1969-71; asso. prof., asso. dir. sect. cardiology U. Mich., 1972-73, prof. internal medicine, 1973-75; prof. medicine, chmn. dept. medicine John A. Burns Sch. Medicine, U. Hawaii, 1975—. Diplomate Am. Bd. Internal Medicine. Fellow A.C.P., Am. Coll. Cardiology, Am. Coll. Chest Physicians; mem. Am. Heart Assn. (fellow councils on cardiology and circulation), Am. Fedn. Clin. Research, Assn. Profs. Medicine, Hawaii Heart Assn., Mich. Heart Assn., Hawaii Med. Library. Jewish. Contbr. numerous articles to med. jours. Home: 4983 Kolohala St Honolulu HI 96816 Office: 1356 Lusitana St Honolulu HI 96813

SCHATZ, S. MICHAEL, lawyer; b. Hartford, Conn., May 28, 1921; s. Nathan Arthur and Dora (Goldberg) S.; A.B., Cornell U., 1941, LL.B., 1942; m. Norma Hirshon, Oct. 28, 1945; children—Andrew M., Debra J., Nathan A., Donald N. Admitted to Conn. bar, N.Y. bar also U.S. Fed. Cts. and U.S. Treasury Dept.; asso., jr. partner, then sr. partner Schatz & Schatz, Ribicoff & Kotkin, Hartford, 1946—; gen. counsel Conn. Vet. Assn., Tobacco Distbrs. Assn. Conn., Conn. State Dental Assn., Outdoor Advt. Assn. Conn. Dir. Sage-Allen & Co., Inc., Edward Balf Co., Hartford, Dunham-Bush, Inc., West Hartford, Conn. Bank and Trust Co., West Hartford, Atlantic Carton Corp., Norwich, Ripley Co., Inc., Middletown, Conn., Griese Advt. Co., West Hartford; partner B.L. McTeague & Co., Hartford. Mem. council Cornell U., exec. com. Law Sch. Bd. dirs. Hartford chpt. ARC, 1960-62, St. Francis Hosp. Assn., Conn. Dental Service, Inc., Friends of Sch. Dental Medicine, U. Conn.; corporate mem. Saint Francis Hosp., Hartford Pub. Library, Mt. Sinai Hosp., Hartford. Served to lt. USNR, 1942-46. Mem. Am., N.Y. State, Hartford County bar assns., State Bar Assn. Conn. (pres. jr. bar sect. 1951, exec. com., asst. sec.-treas. 1956-57, sec. 1957-59), Order Coif, Phi Beta Kappa, Phi Kappa Phi. Editor-in-chief Cornell Law Quar. Home: 156 Waterville Rd Avon CT 06001 Office: One Financial Plaza Hartford CT 06103

SCHAUB, JAMES HAMILTON, engring. educator; b. Moundsville, W.Va., Jan. 27, 1925; s. Carroll Franklin and Lilian Hoyle (Hutchison) S.; student George Washington U., 1942-43; B.S. in Civil Engring., Va. Poly. Inst., 1948; S.M. in Civil Engring., Harvard, 1949; Ph.D., Purdue U., 1960; m. Malinda Katherine Bailey, June 15, 1948. Soils engr. Ore. Hwy. Dept., 1949-50, 51-52; lab. dir. Palmer and Baker, Inc., Mobile, 1952-55; asst. prof. civil engring. Va. Poly. Inst., 1955-58; instr., research engr. Purdue U., 1958-60; prof. civil engring., chmn. dept. W.Va. U., 1960-67, asso. dean engring., 1967-69; prof. civil engring., chmn. dept. U. Fla. at Gainesville, 1969—, NSF faculty fellow, 1975-76, affiliate prof. dept. history, 1977—; acad. visitor dept. history of sci. and tech. Imperial Coll., U. London, 1975-76; cons. engr. to state, fed. and pvt. agys. and cos., 1960—. Served with inf. AUS, 1943-46, with C.E., 1950-51; ETO, Korea. Registered profl. engr., Va., Fla. Fellow ASCE (named Engr. of Year, Fla. sect. 1974); mem. Am. Soc. Engring. Edn., Nat. Soc. Profl. Engrs., Hwy. Research Bd., Am. Pub. Works Assn., Sigma Xi, Tau Beta Pi, Chi Epsilon, Phi Kappa Phi, Kappa Sigma. Episcopalian. Author tech. papers. Home: 4401 NW 15th Pl Gainesville FL 32605

SCHAUDER, FREDERICK FRANCIS, indsl. products co. exec.; b. N.Y.C., July 25, 1938; s. Frederick Francis and Emma Gertrude (Ames) S.; B.B.A., Manhattan Coll., 1962; m. Pauline Linda King, Nov. 4, 1962; children—Frederick, Nancy, Paul, Jennifer. With Arthur Andersen & Co., C.P.A.'s, 1962-73, audit mgr., 1968-73; asst. corp. controller Cerro Corp., N.Y.C., 1973-74; corp. controller M. Lowenstein & Sons, N.Y.C., 1975; sr. v.p. fin. and adminstrn. Engelhard Industries, Iselin, N.J., 1976—. C.P.A., N.Y. Mem. Am. Inst. C.P.A.'s, N.Y. State Soc. C.P.A.'s, N.Y. State Assn. C.P.A. Candidates (pres. 1968). Republican. Roman Catholic. Home: 26 Eliot Ln Stamford CT 06903 Office: 70 Wood Ave S Iselin NJ 08830

SCHAUER, WILBERT EDWARD, JR., mfg. co. exec.; b. Milw., Oct. 28, 1926; s. Wilbert Edward and Gertrude (Nickel) S.; B.B.A., U. Wis., 1949, M.B.A., 1950, J.D., 1950; m. Genevieve Stone, June 23, 1951; children—Jeffrey Edward, Constance Emily, Gregory Wilbert, Martha Ann, Jennifer Caroline. Admitted to Wis. bar, 1950; accountant Pub. Service Commn. Wis., 1950-52; with Rexnord, Inc., Milw., 1952—, v.p. finance, treas., 1968-76, v.p. fin. and law, 1977-78, exec. v.p. fin. and adminstrn., 1978—. Alderman, Brookfield, Wis., 1958-68, pres. Common Council, 1966-68. Clubs: Milwaukee; Westmoor Country (Brookfield). Home: 16100 Choctaw Trail Brookfield WI 53005 Office: 3500 First Wis Center Milwaukee WI 53202

SCHAUFELE, WILLIAM EVERETT, JR., fgn. service officer, ambassador; b. Lakewood, Ohio, Dec. 7, 1923; s. William Elias and Lillian (Bergen) S.; B.A., Yale, 1948; M.Internat. Affairs, Columbia, 1950; m. Heather Moon, Feb. 1, 1950; children—Steven William, Peter Henry. Joined U.S. Fgn. Service, 1950; resident officer, Pfaffenhefen an der Ilm, Germany, 1950-52, Augsburg, Germany, 1952; vice consul, Dusseldorf, Germany, 1952-53, Munich, Germany, 1953-56; assigned State Dept., 1956-59; consul, Casablanca, Morocco, 1959-63; consul, prin. officer, Bukavu, Republic Congo, 1963-64; officer charge Congo affairs State Dept., 1964-65, dep. dir. Central African affairs, 1965-67, country dir. Central West African affairs, 1967-69; ambassador to Upper Volta, 1969-71; sr. adviser to U.S. permanent rep. to UN, N.Y.C., 1971-73; U.S. dep. rep. UN Security Council, 1973-75; insp. gen. U.S. Fgn. Service, Washington, 1975, asst. sec. state for African affairs, 1975-77; ambassador to Poland, 1977—. Mem. adv. council Sch. Internat. Affairs, Columbia. Trustee, INTERALP. Served with AUS, 1943-46; ETO. Office: US Embassy Vjazdowskie 29/31 Warsaw Poland*

SCHAUFUSS, PETER, ballet dancer; b. Copenhagen, Denmark, Apr. 26, 1949; s. Frank and Mona (Vangsaa) Schaufuss; student Royal Danish Ballet Sch. Joined Royal Danish Ballet, 1965, now appears as guest performer with company; guest dancer Nat. Ballet Can., Zagreb Ballet, London Festival Ballet, Pitts. Ballet, Frankfurt Ballet, San Francisco Ballet; prin. dancer N.Y. City Ballet, 1974-77; dancer Nat. Ballet of Can., 1977—. created role in George Balanchine's Steadfast Tin Soldier, 1975. Recipient Silver medal Moscow competition, 1973. *

SCHAUMBERG, WILLIAM LLOYD, banker; b. Lincoln, Nebr., May 4, 1923; s. Edward George and Claire Elizabeth (Barentsen) S.; B.S., U. Nebr., 1947, LL.B., 1949; m. Patricia Louise Ward, Sept. 4, 1948; children—DeeAnn, W. Ward, Denise Lynn, Kirstin. Admitted to Nebr. bar, 1949, Oreg. bar, 1953; dep. county atty. Lancaster County (Nebr.), 1949-51; v.p. 1st Nat. Bank of Oreg., Portland, 1952-69, Columbia Mgmt. Co., Portland, Oreg., 1970-73; exec. v.p., mgr. trust div. Rainier Nat. Bank, Seattle, 1973—; dir. Pacific Securities Depository Trust Co., Inc., San Francisco. Served with U.S. Army, 1943-46, 51-52. Mem. Oreg. Bar Assn., Corp. Trustees Assn. Wash., Seattle Estate Planning Council. Republican. Episcopalian. Clubs: Rainier, Broadmoor Golf. Home: 8520 SE 80th St Mercer Island WA 98040 Office: 1 Rainier Sq Seattle WA 98124

SCHAUMBURG, FRANK DAVID, environ. engr.; b. Watseka, Ill., Jan. 15, 1938; s. Frank L. and Helen K. (Voigt) S.; B.S.C.E., Ariz. State U., 1961; M.S.C.E., Purdue U., Ph.D., 1966; m. Judith Charlene Ebeling, Aug. 21, 1960; children—Susan Annette, Cynthia Elise. Research engr. B.C. (Can.) Research Council, Vancouver, 1966; asst. prof., asso. prof., prof. environ. engring. Oreg. State U., 1967—, head dept. civil engring., 1972—; cons. to govt., industry. Served with C.E., U.S. Army, 1961-62. Registered profl. engr. Mem. ASCE, Water Pollution Control Fedn., Associated Gen. Contractors, Izaak Walton League. Author: Judgement Reserved - A Landmark Environmental Case, 1976. Office: Apperson Hall 206 Oregon State U Corvallis OR 97331

SCHAUS, FREDERICK A., univ. basketball coach; b. Newark, Ohio, June 30, 1925; s. George L. and Jessie M. (Dusthiemer) S.; B.S., W. Va., U., 1949, M.S., 1954; m. Barbara Jean Scherr, May 6, 1950; children—John William, James Robert. Profl. basketball player Ft. Wayne Pistons, 1949-53, N.Y. Knickerbockers, 1953-54; head basketball coach W. Va. U., 1954-60, Los Angeles Lakers, 1960-69; gen. mgr. Los Angeles Lakers, 1969-72; head basketball coach Purdue U., West Lafayette, 1972—. Mem. Sigma Chi. Office: Purdue University West Lafayette IN 47907*

SCHAUT, QUENTIN LEMAR, clergyman, educator; b. St. Marys, Pa., Dec. 9, 1900; s. Joseph J. and Caroline (Kuntz) S.; grad. St. Vincent Prep. Sch., Latrobe, Pa., 1918; A.B., St. Vincent Coll., 1923, L.H.D. (hon.), 1966; M.A., St. Vincent Sem., 1927; M.A., Harvard, 1936; LL.D. (hon.), St. Francis Coll., Loretto, Pa., 1960. Professed as Benedictine Monk, 1921, ordained priest Roman Cath. Ch., 1927; prefect St. Vincent Prep. Sch., 1921-23, instr. English, 1927-29, 31-34; prefect St. Vincent Coll., 1925-28, acting dean, 1928, instr. English, 1939-47, asso. prof., 1947-49, prof., 1949-62, chmn. dept. English, 1951-55, v.p., 1954-55, pres., 1955-62, pres. emeritus, 1966—; rector Penn State Cath. Center, Pa. State U., University Park, 1962—; master of novices of St. Vincent Archabbey, 1944-50, spiritual dir. St. Vincent Sem., 1951-54. Founder, v.p. Latrobe Civic Music Assn.; founder, v.p. Western Pa. Intercollegiate Athletic Conf.; exec. com. Pa. Found. Independent Colls., 1959. Recipient Charles Dexter scholarship for study and travel in Eng., Harvard, summer 1938. Mem. Coll. English Assn., Modern Lang. Assn., Am. Benedictine Acad. (exec. sec. 1947-57). Author articles, reviews. Asso. editor The American Benedictine Review, 1960-67. Home: 531 W Fairmount Ave State College PA 16801 Office: Chapel Bldg University Park PA 16802

SCHAWLOW, ARTHUR LEONARD, educator, physicist; b. Mt. Vernon, N.Y., May 5, 1921; s. Arthur and Helen (Mason) S.; B.A., U. Toronto, 1941, M.A., 1942, Ph.D., 1949, LL.D. (hon.), 1970; D.Sc. (hon.), U. Ghent, Belgium, 1968, U. Bradford (Eng.), 1970; m. Aurelia Keith Townes, May 19, 1951; children—Arthur Keith, Helen Aurelia, Edith Ellen. Postdoctoral fellow, research asso. Columbia, 1949-51, vis. asso. prof., 1960; research physicist Bell Telephone Labs., 1951-61, cons., 1961-62; prof. physics Stanford, 1961—, now J.G. Jackson-C.J. Wood prof. physics, exec. head dept., 1966-70, acting chmn. dept., 1973-74. Recipient Ballantine medal Franklin Inst., 1962, Thomas Young medal and prize Inst. Physics and Phys. Soc., London, Eng., 1963; named Calif. Scientist of Year, 1973, Marconi Internat. fellow, 1977. Fellow Am. Acad. Arts and Scis., Am. Phys. Soc. (council 1966-70, chmn. div. electron and atomic physics 1974, v.p. 1980), Optical Soc. Am. (dir.-at-large 1966-68, pres. 1975, Frederick Ives medal 1976); mem. Nat. Acad. Scis., IEEE (Liebmann prize 1964), AAAS (chmn. physics sect. 1979). Author: (with C.H. Townes) Microwave Spectroscopy, 1955. Co-inventor (with C.H. Townes) optical Maser on laser, 1958. Home: 849 Esplanada Way Stanford CA 94305

SCHECHNER, RICHARD, theatre producer and dir.; b. Newark, Aug. 23, 1934; s. Sheridan and Selma Sophia (Schwartz) S.; B.A., Cornell U., 1956; postgrad. Johns Hopkins U., 1957; M.A., State U. Iowa, 1958; Ph.D., Tulane U., 1962; m. Joan MacIntosh, Apr. 4, 1970 (div. 1979); 1 son, Samuel. Asst. prof. theatre Tulane U., 1962-66, asso. prof., 1966-67; prof. drama N.Y. U., 1967—; co-founder, co-dir. New Orleans Group, 1964-67; founder, co-dir. Performance Group, N.Y.C., 1978—; co-pres., dir. Wooster Group, Inc., N.Y.C., 1978—; dir. Oedipus, 1977. Served with AUS, 1958-60. Am. Council Learned Socs. grantee, 1964; Ford Found. grantee, 1968; John D. Rockefeller 3d Fund grantee, 1971-72; Guggenheim fellow, 1976; Fulbright fellow, 1976. Author: Public Domain, 1968; Environmental Theater, 1973; (with others) Theatres, Spaces, Environments, 1975; Essays in Performance Theory, 1977; editor: Dionysus in 69, 1970; co-editor: Free Southern Theater, 1968, Ritual, Play, and Performance, 1976. Editor Drama Rev., Tulane Drama Rev., 1962-69; dir.: Dionysus in 69, 1968, Makbeth, 1969, Commune, 1970, The Tooth of Crime, 1972, Mother Courage, 1975, The Marilyn Project, 1975, Oedipus, 1977, Cops, 1978, The Balcony, 1979. Home: Room 300 South Bldg New York U Washington Sq New York NY 10003 Office: Performing Garage 33 Wooster St New York NY 10013

SCHECHNER, SHERIDAN, savs. and loan assn. exec.; b. Newark, Jan. 4, 1905; s. Samuel and Fannie (Scheps) S.; B.C.S., N.Y.U., 1925; m. Selma Schwarz, Nov. 15, 1927; children—David, Arthur, Richard, William. With Schechner Agy., 1925-60; pres. Barton Savs. & Loan Assn., Newark, 1960-77, chmn., chief exec. officer, 1978—; adv. bd. First Jersey Nat. Bank. Bd. overseers Jewish Theol. Sem. Home: 4 Walnut Ct South Orange NJ 07079 Office: 1166 Raymond Blvd Newark NJ 07102

SCHECHTER, ABEL ALAN, public relations cons.; b. Central Falls, R.I., Aug. 10, 1907; s. George and Celia (Riven) S.; grad. Boston U., 1929; m. Fritzi B. Breger, July 24, 1941. Reporter Providence (R.I.) Jour., N.Y. World, A.P., Internat. News Service; dir. news NBC, N.Y.C., 1932-42; pub. relations cons. War Dept., 1941; v.p. MBS, 1945-50; v.p. Crowell Collier Pub. Co., 1950-51; 1st exec. producer Today show NBC, 1951-52; chmn. A.A. Schechter Assos., Inc., pub. relations, 1952—. Served as lt. col. USAAF, Washington, 1942-43, in charge radio and press communications for war corrs. at G.H.Q., Southwest Pacific area, 1943-45. Decorated Legion of Merit. Mem. Sigma Delta Chi. Clubs: Overseas Press (N.Y.); Dutch Treat, Nat. Press (Washington). Author: Go Ahead Garrison, 1940; I Live On Air (with Edward Anthony), 1941. Home: 229 E 79th St New York NY 10021 Office: 633 3d Ave New York NY 10017

SCHECHTER, EDMUND, govt. ofcl.; b. Vienna, Austria, Apr. 22, 1908; s. David and Anny (Hermann) S.; Ph.D., U. Vienna, 1933; m. Gerda Marjorie Frankley, Apr. 4, 1958; 1 son, Peter David. Came to U.S., 1940, naturalized, 1946. Fgn. service officer, 1947-71; served posts in Bonn, Munich and Berlin, Germany, 1947-54, Washington, 1954-58, Rome, Italy, 1958-64, La Paz, Bolivia, 1964-66; counselor embassy, Caracas, Venezuela, 1967-71; staff Presdl. Study Commn. on Internat. Radio Broadcasting, Washington, 1972—. Exec. sec. Venezuelan-U.S. Symposium, Fletcher Sch. Law and Diplomacy, Tufts U., Medford, Mass., 1974-75; cons. USIA, 1971-76. Served with Psychol. Warfare div. SHAEF, London, 1943-45. Recipient Meritorious Service award USIA, 1965. Mem. Fgn. Service Assn. Address: 4301 Massachusetts Ave NW Washington DC 20016

SCHECHTER, MARTIN, educator, mathematician; b. Phila., Mar. 10, 1930; s. Joshua and Rose (Shames) S.; B.S., City Coll. N.Y., 1953; M.S., N.Y.U., 1955, Ph.D., 1957; m. Naomi Deborah Kirzner, Dec. 23, 1957; children—Sharon Libby, Arthur Irving, Isaac David, Raphael Morris. Mem. faculty N.Y.U., 1958-66, prof. math., 1965-66; prof. math. Belfer Grad. Sch. Sci., Yeshiva U., 1965—, chmn. dept., 1965-69; mem. Inst. Advanced Study, Princeton, N.J., 1965-66; vis. asso. prof. U. Chgo., 1961; vis. prof. Hebrew U., 1973. NSF sr. postdoctoral fellow, 1965-66. Mem. Am. Math. Soc., Assn. Orthodox Jewish Scientists, Phi Beta Kappa, Pi Mu Epsilon. Author: (with L. Bers and F. John) Partial Differential Equations, 1964; Principles of Functional Analysis, 1971; Spectra of Partial Differential Operators, 1971; Modern Methods in Partial Differential Equations, 1977; also over 100 research articles. Home: 1677 51st St Brooklyn NY 11204 Office: Belfer Grad Sch Sci 186 St and Amsterdam Ave New York City NY 10033

SCHECHTER, ROBERT SAMUEL, chem. engr., educator; b. Houston, Feb. 26, 1929; s. Morris Samuel and Helen Ruth Schechter; B.S. in Chem. Engring., Tex. A. and M. U., 1950; Ph.D. in Chem. Engring., U. Minn., 1956; m. Mary Ethel Rosenberg, Feb. 15, 1953; children—Richard Martin, Alan Lawrence, Geoffrey Louis. Asst. prof. chem. engring. U. Tex. at Austin, 1956-60, asso. prof., 1960-63, prof., 1963—, adminstrv. dir. Center Statis. Mechs. and Thermodynamics, 1968-72, chmn. dept. chem. engring., 1970-73, chmn. petroleum engring., 1975—, E. J. Cockrell, Jr. prof. chem. and petroleum engring., 1975—; cons. in field. Vis. prof. U. Edinburgh (Scotland), 1965-66; Distinguished vis. prof. U. Kan., spring 1968; vis. prof. U. Brussels (Belgium), 1969. Served to 1st lt. Chem. Corps, AUS, 1951-53. Recipient Outstanding Teaching award U. Tex., 1969, Outstanding Paper award, 1973, Katz lectr., 1979; registered profl. engr., Tex. Mem. Am. Inst. Chem. Engrs., Am. Chem. Soc., Soc. Petroleum Engrs., Nat. Acad. Engrs., Sigma Xi, Tau Beta Pi. Author: Variational Method in Engineering, 1967; (with G.S.G. Beveridge) Optimization—Theory and Practice, 1970; Adventures in Fortran Programming, 1975. Contbr. numerous articles to profl. jours. Developer methods of measuring surface viscosity and ultra low inter-facial tensions; discoverer instability of thermal diffusion. Home: 4700 Ridge Oak Dr Austin TX 78731

SCHECTER, HARRY, TV-radio sales exec.; b. Poland, May 14, 1912; s. Louis and Sarah (Frankfort) S.; brought to U.S., 1918; student high schs., N.Y.C.; m. Evelyn Kasdan, Jan. 19, 1941; children—Carol Helene, Edward Leslie. Radio and electronic components dealer, 1933-44; wholesale salesman Motorola, Inc., N.Y.C., 1944-48, sales mgr., 1948-50, gen. sales mgr., 1950-53, regional mgr., Chgo., 1956, gen. mgr. Motorola div. Warren-Connolly Co., N.Y.C., 1957; gen. mgr. CBS-Columbia Distbg. Corp., 1953, v.p. charge nat. sales, 1953-56; merchandising asst. to v.p., dir. sales Zenith Radio Corp., Chgo., 1958; pres., gen. mgr. Zenith Radio Corp. of N.Y., 1958—, also dir.; pres., gen. mgr. Zenith Radio Corp. N.J. Dir. Better Bus. Bur. Met. N.Y., 1968—. Home: 248 Oakwood Ave Cedarhurst NY 11516 Office: 666 Fifth Ave New York City NY 10019

SCHEEL, PAUL JOSEPH, ins. co. exec.; b. Balt., Nov. 15, 1933; s. Joseph A. and Julia S.; B.S. in Math., Loyola Coll., Balt., 1959; m. Beverly Ann Mitchell, June 1, 1957; children—Mary Clare, Paul Joseph. With U.S. Fidelity and Guaranty Co., Balt., 1959—, asso. actuary, 1971, v.p., sr. actuary, 1971-78, exec. v.p., 1978—, also dir. affiliates Fidelity and Guaranty Ins. Underwriters, Inc., Fidelity and Guaranty Ins. Co., Thomas Jefferson Life Ins. Co., Fidelity Ins. Co. Can. Served with U.S. Army, 1953-55. Fellow Casualty Actuarial Soc.; mem. Am. Acad. Actuaries, Internat. Actuarial Assn. Roman Catholic. Home: 8506 Pleasant Plains Rd Towson MD 21204 Office: 100 Light St Baltimore MD 21202

SCHEELE, PAUL DRAKE, hosp. supply corp. exec.; b. Elgin, Ill., Aug. 6, 1922; s. Arthur R. and Helen M. (Christiansen) S.; B.A., Coe Coll., 1944; M.B.A., Harvard, 1947. With Am. Hosp. Supply Corp., 1947—, pres. Harleco div., Phila., 1966-68, group v.p., 1968-70, exec. v.p., also pres. internat. group, Evanston, Ill., 1970-74, v.p., asst. to chmn. bd., 1974—. Trustee Coe Coll. Served with inf. AUS, 1943-46. Mem. Tau Kappa Epsilon, Pi Delta Epsilon. Clubs: Harvard Bus. Sch., Economic (Chgo.). Home: 900 N Lake Shore Dr Chicago IL 60611 Office: 1740 Ridge Ave Evanston IL 60204

SCHEELER, CHARLES, constrn. co. exec.; b. Balt., June 20, 1925; s. George F. and Catherine Louise (Seward) S.; B.S., U. Md., 1948, LL.B., 1952; m. Mary Katherine Scarborough, Aug. 22, 1953; children—Charles P., George D., Donald C. Admitted to Md. bar; with C. J. Langenfelder & Son., Inc., Balt., 1949—, exec. v.p., treas., 1974-77, pres., chief exec. officer, 1977—; dir. Rosedale Fed. Savs. & Loan Assn., Equitable Trust Co., Equitable Bancorp. Served with USN, 1943-46; PTO. C.P.A., Md. Mem. Md. Assn. C.P.A.'s., Am. Inst. C.P.A.'s. Office: 8427 Pulaski Hwy Baltimore MD 21237

SCHEELER, JAMES ARTHUR, architect; b. Pontiac, Ill., Dec. 20, 1927; s. Aman B. and Jane (Steele) S.; B.S. with highest honors, U. Ill., 1951, M.S., 1952; postgrad. U. Liverpool, 1952-53; m. Barbara Jean Lloyd, Sept. 2, 1950; children—James Erich, Carl Aman, Orissa Jane Elizabeth. Grad. asst. U. Ill., Urbana, 1950-52; draftsman-designer Lundeen & Hilfinger, Bloomington, Ill., 1952-53; designer Skidmore, Owings & Merrill, Chgo., 1955-59; partner Richardson, Severns, Scheeler & Assos., Inc., Champaign, Ill., 1959-65, v.p., treas., 1965-71; vice-chmn. bd., dir. Prodn. Systems for Architects and Engrs., Inc., 1973—. vis. critic U. Ill., 1959-60. Mem. Plan Commn., Champaign, 1966—, chmn., 1969-71; mem. Champaign County Regional Planning Commn., 1967-71. Served with USN, 1946-47. Recipient various archtl. awards. Francis J. Plym fellow, 1953-54, Fulbright fellow, 1953. Fellow AIA (treas. Central Ill. chpt. 1967-68, sec. 1968-69, pres. 1970-71; nat. dep. exec. v.p. 1971-76, pres. corp. 1974-78, exec. v.p. 1977-78, program devel. group exec. 1976—); mem. Ill. Arts Council (archtl. adv. bd. 1966-71), Montessori Soc. Champaign-Urbana (dir. 1964-66), Gargoyle, Scarab, Phi Kappa Phi, Lambda Chi Alpha. Episcopalian. Address: 11179 Saffold Way Reston VA 22090

SCHEER, ALAN AUSTIN, physician; b. N.Y.C., May 12, 1923; s. Henry Morris and Helen (Levy) S.; student Lafayette Coll., 1941-43; M.D., N.Y.C., 1946; m. Lucille Diamond, Dec. 17, 1950; children—Joanne, Robert. Intern, resident otolaryngology Morrisania City Hosp., N.Y.C.,; resident tng. otolaryngology Bromx Eye and Ear Hosp., Presbyn. Hosp., N.Y.C.; practice, N.Y.C., 1949—; now dir. otolaryngology Polycine Hosp. and Postgrad. Med. Sch.; mem. staff Manhattan Eye and Ear Hosp., Queens Gen. Hosp.; dir. N.Y. Found. Otologic Research, 1962—; spl. research surg. rehab. hard hearing; devel. plastic replacement prothesis, 1957; pioneer in stapedectomy technique; established postgrad. courses otologic surgery N.Y. Poly. Hosp., 1959. Trustee Lafayette Coll., N.Y. U. Club: Brae Burn. Home: Brae Burn Dr Purchase NY 10577 Office: 920 Park Ave New York City NY 10021

SCHEER, CARL, profl. basketball team exec.; b. 1936; A.B., Middlebury Coll., 1958; LL.B., U. Miami, 1960; m. Marsha Scheer; children—Bobby, Lauren. Admitted to N.C. bar, 1962; practiced in Greensboro, 1960-69; asst. to commr. Nat. Basketball Assn., N.Y.C., 1969-71; gen. mgr. Buffalo Braves Nat. Basketball Assn., 1971; pres., gen. mgr. Carolina Cougars, Am. Basketball Assn., Greensboro, 1971-74, Denver Nuggets, Nat. Basketball Assn., 1974—. past announcer U. Miami, Guilford Coll. Office: Denver Nuggets PO Box 4286 Denver CO 80204*

SCHEER, JULIAN WEISEL, author, mfg. co. exec.; b. Richmond, Va., Feb. 20, 1926; s. George Fabian and Hilda (Knopf) S.; A.B., U. N.C., 1950; m. Suzanne Fugler Huggan, Oct. 9, 1965; one dau., Hilary Susannah Scheer; children (by previous marriage)—Susan, David Scott, George Grey. Reporter, Mid-Va. Publs., Richmond, 1939-43; pres. Scheer Syndicate, Chapel Hill, N.C., 1947-53; asst. dir. sports information U. N.C., 1949-53; columnist-reporter Charlotte (N.C.) News, 1953-62; free-lance writer for nat. publs., 1945—; tchr. eve. div. Queens Coll., 1959; asst. adminstr. pub. affairs NASA, 1962-71; partner Sullivan, Murray & Scheer, Washington, 1971-76; sr. v.p. corp. affairs LTV Corp., Dallas, 1976—; dir. Eastern Airlines. Bd. advs. Goodwill Industries; trustee Dermatology Found. Served with U.S. Mcht. Marine, 1943-46, with USNR, 1946-53. Mem. Sigma Delta Chi, Pi Lambda Phi. Clubs: Algonquin Soc., University, City Tavern (Washington). Author: Tweetsie: The Blue Ridge Stemwinder, 1958; Choo-Choo; The Charlie Justice Story, 1958; First Into Outer Space, 1959; Rain Makes Appleauce, 1964; Upside Down Day, 1968. Home: Route 2 Box 24 Catlett VA 22019 Office: 1155 15th St NW Washington DC 20005

SCHEER, MILTON DAVID, phys. chemist; b. N.Y.C., Dec. 22, 1922; s. Abraham and Lena (Brauner) S.; B.S., CCNY, 1943; M.S., N.Y. U., 1947, Ph.D., 1951; m. Emily Hirsch, June 23, 1945; children—Jessica, Richard Mark, Julia Rachel. Chemist, Bd. Econ. Warfare, Guatemala, C. Am., 1943-44; research asst. N.Y. U., 1947-50; combustion scientist U.S. Naval Air Rocket Test Sta., Dover, N.J., 1959-60; phys. chemist U.S. Bur. Mines, Pitts., 1952-55; research scientist Gen. Electric Co., Cin., 1955-58; phys. chemist Nat. Bur. Standards, Washington, 1958-68, chief photochemistry sect., 1968-70, chief phys. chemistry div., 1970-77, dir. Center for Thermodynamics and Molecular Sci., Nat. Measurement Lab., 1977—; vis. prof. Grad. Sch. Georgetown U., 1962-63. Served with USNR, 1944-46. Fellow Am. Inst. Chemists, AAAS; mem. Am. Chem. Soc., Am. Phys. Soc. Contbr. 60 articles to profl. jours. Home: 811 N Belgrade Rd Silver Spring MD 20902 Office: Bldg 22 Nat Bur Standards Washington DC 20234

SCHEER, STUART CHARLES, fgn. service officer; b. N.Y.C., Mar. 1, 1935; s. Harry S. and Ray (Edelstein) S.; B.S., Coll. City N.Y., 1956; M.D., Tufts U., 1960; USPHS fellow, Cornell U., 1965-67; m. Dagnija Miske, Oct. 23, 1965; children—Jennifer Alexandra, Nicholas Stuart. Joined Dept. State, 1967; med. attache, Rio de Janeiro, 1968-71, Addis Ababa, Ethiopia, 1971-73, chief med. services Dept. State, Washington, 1973-75; attache, Tunis, Tunisia, 1975, Bangkok, 1978—. Served as capt. USAF, 1963-65. Office: care Office of Med Services Dept State Washington DC 20520

SCHEERENBERGER, RICHARD CHARLES, sch. rehab. supt.; b. Milw., Feb. 17, 1930; s. Matt H. and Senta (Estergard) S.; B.S., U. Wis.-Milw., 1951; M.Ed., Marquette U., 1954; Ph.D., U. Wis.-Madison, 1963; m. Emilie Berg, Aug. 14, 1954; children—Dana Louise, Matthew Andrew. Tchr., So. Wis. Colony and Tng. Sch., Union Grove, 1951-54; dir. spl. edn. Minot (N.D.) Pub. Schs., 1954-57; prin. No. Wis. Colony and Tng. Sch., Chippewa Falls, 1957-61; dir. documentation service Am. Assn. Mental Deficiency, Columbus, Ohio, 1963-65; asst. dir. Ill. Div. Mental Retardation, Springfield, 1965-69; dir. Central Wis. Center for Developmentally Disabled, Madison, 1969—; asso. prof. Western Ill. U., Macomb, 1967-69; lectr. U. Wis.-Madison, 1967—, Wis. State Coll., Eau Claire, 1960-61, U. Wis., Whitewater, 1972. Fellow Am. Assn. Mental Deficiency (pres.); mem. Council Exceptional Children, Internat. Congress Sci. Study Mental Retardation, Am. Psychol. Assn., Nat. Assn. Supts. Pub. Residential Facilities for Mentally Retarded (pres. 1973, 74), Wis. Assn. Mental Deficiency (past pres.), Phi Delta Kappa. Editor: Mental Retardation Abstracts, 1961-63; Mental Retardation in Illinois, 1967-69; asso. editor Mental Retardation, 1963—; book rev. editor Am. Jour. Mental Deficiency, 1967-71. Author books; contbr. articles to books and profl. jours. Home: 5205 Comanche Way Madison WI 53704 Office: 317 Knutson Dr Madison WI 53704

SCHEERER, ROBERT JOSEPH, performing arts producer, dir.; b. Santa Barbara, Calif., Dec. 28, 1928; s. Albert Joseph and Bernice (Mount) S.; grad. high sch.; children—Amanda, Evan. Dancer, actor, Universal Pictures, Hollywood, Calif., 1941-42; dancer, actor in Lend An Ear, Broadway, 1948, Dance Me A Song, 1949, Top Banana, 1951, Boy Friend, 1954; dir. TV shows including Andy Williams Show, 1962 (recipient Emmy for best show), Danny Kaye Show, 1964-65, Shirley MacLaine: If They Could See Me Now (nominee Emmy for best dir.), 1974, Danny Kaye's Look In at the Met (recipient Emmy for best show), 1975; producer TV shows: Danny Kaye Show, 1965-66, Frank Sinatra & Ella & Jobim, 1968; producer/dir. TV shows: Barbra Streisand: A Happening in Central Park, 1968 (nominee Emmy for best dir.), First Peggy Fleming Spl., 1969; dir. films: Adam at 6:00 A.M., 1972, World's Greatest Athlete (Disney Studios), 1973, Moneyball, 1979. Served with AUS, 1951-53. Recipient Emmy for Best Dir. for Danny Kaye Series, 1963-64, Single Musical Number award with Group One Atlanta Film Festival, 1968. Home: 818 S Gretna Green Way W Los Angeles CA 90049

SCHEETZ, SISTER MARY JOELLEN, coll. pres.; b. Lafayette, Ind., May 20, 1926; d. Joseph Albert and Ellen Isabelle (Fitzgerald) Scheetz; A.B., St. Francis Coll., 1956; M.A., U. Notre Dame, 1964; Ph.D., U. Mich., 1970. Tchr. English, Bishop Luers High Sch., Fort Wayne, Ind., 1965-67; acad. dean St. Francis Coll., Fort Wayne, 1967-68, pres., 1970—. Mem. Delta Epsilon Sigma. Address: 2701 Spring St Fort Wayne IN 46808

SCHEFFER, ROBERT PAUL, educator; b. Newton, N.C., Jan. 26, 1920; s. Paul and Mary Alice (Shuford) S.; student U. Tenn., 1938-41; B.S., N.C. State Coll. (name later changed to N.C. State U.), 1947, M.S., 1949; Ph.D., U. Wis. at Madison, 1952; m. Beulah J. Spoolman, June 12, 1951; children—Thomas Jay, Mary Karen. Research asso. U. Wis., 1952-53; asst. prof. botany Mich. State U., East Lansing, 1953-58, asso. prof., 1958-63, prof., 1963—. Guest investigator Rockefeller U., N.Y.C., 1960-61; cons. in regulatory biology NSF, 1965-68; participant in numerous internat. symposia; mem. Am. Phytopathology Council, 1965-66. Served with USAAF, 1941-45. NSF grantee, 1958—; NIH fellow, 1960; Dept. Agr. grantee, 1978—. Fellow Am. Phytopathology Soc. (asso. editor jour. 1972-75); mem. Am. Soc. Plant Physiologists, AAUP. Home: 912 Gainsborough East Lansing MI 48823 Office: Dept of Botany Mich State U East Lansing MI 48824

SCHEFFER, WALTER FRANCIS, educator; b. Humbird, Wis., Mar. 16, 1921; s. Frank John and Clara (Fassbender) S.; B.S., Wis. State U., Eau Claire, 1943; M.S., U. Wis., 1947, Ph.D., 1955; m. Barbara Anne Moore, Nov. 10, 1945; children—Paula Jean, Nicole Marie, David John, Claudia Marie. Prin., Hiles High Sch., Wis., 1943; instr. U. Wis. Extension div., 1946-47; instr. to prof. U. Okla., Norman, 1951—, chmn. dept. polit. sci., 1962-67, dir. Grad. Program in Pub. Adminstrn., 1966—, Regents prof. polit. sci., 1978—, asst. dir. Bur. Govt. Research, 1958, acting dir., summer 1968; asst. prof. U. Tulsa, summer 1954; cons. Bur. Pub. Rds. Dept. Commerce, Washington, 1957. Mem. urban policy conf. Brookings Instn., 1963. Served with USAAF 1943-45. Mem. Am., Okla. (past pres.), S.W. polit. sci. assns., Am. Soc. Pub. Adminstrn. (pres. Okla. chpt., nat. council), Nat. Assn. Schs. Pub. Affairs and Adminstrn., Nat. Municipal League, AAUP, Kappa Delta Pi. Author: Energy Impacts on Public Policy and Administration, 1974; also articles. Author: General Revenue Sharing and Decentralization, 1976. Mem. editorial bd., past pres. Midwest Review of Public Administration, 1966—; editor, contbr. General Revenue Sharing and Decentralization, 1976. Home: 807 Elmwood Dr Norman OK 73069

SCHEFFLER, ISRAEL, philosopher, educator; b. N.Y.C., Nov. 25, 1923; s. Leon and Ethel (Grünberg) S.; B.A., Bklyn. Coll., 1945, M.A., 1948; M.H.L., Jewish Theol. Sem., 1949; Ph.D. (Ford fellow 1951), U. Pa., 1952; A.M. (hon.), Harvard, 1959; m. Rosalind Zuckerbrod, June 26, 1949; children—Samuel, Laurie. Mem. faculty Harvard, 1952—, prof. edn., 1961-62, prof. edn. and philosophy, 1962-64, Victor S. Thomas prof. edn. and philosophy, 1964—, hon. research fellow in cognitive studies, 1965-66. Fellow Center for Advanced Study in Behavioral Scis., 1972-73. Guggenheim fellow, 1958-59, 72-73; NSF grantee, 1962, 65. Mem. Am. Acad. Arts and Scis., Am. Philos. Assn., Aristotelian Soc., Philosophy Edn. Soc., Nat. Acad. Edn. (charter). Philosophy of Sci. Assn. (pres. 1973-75). Author: The Language of Education, 1960; The Anatomy of Inquiry, 1963; Conditions of Knowledge, 1965; Science and Subjectivity, 1967; Reason and Teaching, 1973; Four Pragmatists, 1974; Beyond the Letter, 1979; editor: Philosophy and Education, 1958, 66; (with R.S. Rudner) Logic and Art, 1972. Contbr. articles to profl. jours. Office: Emerson Hall Harvard U Cambridge MA 02138

SCHEFTNER, GEROLD, dental radiology equipment mktg. co. exec.; b. Milw., June 1, 1937; s. Arthur Joseph and Alice Agnes (Gregory) S.; student Milw. Bus. Inst., 1953, Great Lakes Naval Acad. Sch. Dental-Med. Surgery, USAF, 1955-56, USAF Inst., 1959, Marquette U., 1959-60; div.; children—Mark A., Mary L., Scot P., Michael D. Territorial rep. Mossey-Otto Co., Milw., 1960-63; with Den-Tal-Ez Mfg. Co., Des Moines, 1963—, dir. fgn. affairs, 1969-71, dir. Far Eastern affairs, 1971-72, exec. dir. internat. sales/mktg., 1973, v.p., gen. mgr. internat. ops., 1974—, also corp. dir., 1969—, chmn. bd. Den-Tal-Ez Ltd., Gt. Britain, 1974—; pres. Gen. Electric X-Ray Div. Consultants for Mktg., Seven Seas Ltd., Lyss, Switzerland subs. Bd. dirs. Dist. Export Council of Iowa, 1976-77; mem. Lake Panorama (Iowa) Devel. Assn., 1972-73; chmn. World Trade Council Iowa, 1976-77; adv. bd. bldg. program St. Charles Boys Home, Milw., 1963.

Served with USAF, 1955-59. Recipient Presdl. Mgr. of Year award Den-Tal-Ez Co., 1967, Lectr. award Faculdade de Odontologia, U. Ribeirao Preto, Brazil, 1974. Mem. Am. Dental Trade Assn., Am. Dental Mfrs. Assn., Hong Kong Dental Trade Assn. (hon.), Internat. Platform Assn., Greater Des Moines C. of C. (dir. 1976-77. Republican. Lion. Research in devel. equipment and apparatus for dental therapy. Office: PO Box 414 Milwaukee WI 53201. *Live enthusiastically, expand your natural attributes, be truthful and sincere, assume responsibility, respect authority, live for today, but improve tomorrow-pray consistently and confidently, love and be loved.*

SCHEIBE, FRED KARL, educator, author, artist; b. Kiel, Germany, Dec. 2, 1911; s. Karl Johannes and Anna Katharine (Kreutzfeldt) S.; student Coll. City N.Y., 1932-34, Fordham U., 1934-35, Bklyn. Law Sch., 1935-36, L.I.U., 1936-37; B.A., Clark U., 1938; postgrad. Boston U., 1938-39; M.A., U. Pa., 1941; postgrad U. Wis., 1942; Ph.D., U. Cin., 1954; m. Rosalie Robertson, June 9, 1956 (div. July 1964); m. 2d, Margaret Stucki, June 25, 1966; children—Sean, Wilfred; stepchildren—Hans, Ann. Tchr. high sch., 1945-46; faculty Sampson Coll., 1946-47; asso. prof. German, Western Coll. for Women, 1947-51; tchr. English, Universidad Nacional de Mexico, 1952; Taft teaching fellow U. Cin., 1952-54; lectr. German, Bklyn. Coll., spring 1955; prof. modern langs. Alderson-Broaddus Coll., 1955-57; head German dept. Thiel Coll., 1957-61; prof., chmn. dept. modern and ancient langs., asso. editor rev. Emory and Henry Coll., 1961-64; prof. modern langs., editor rev. Hartwick Coll., Oneonta, N.Y., 1964-71; chmn. dept. fgn. langs. Shelton Coll., Cape Canaveral, Fla., 1971-74. Vice pres. for acad. affairs Freedom U., Fla.; executed murals for Langenheim Meml. Library, water tank, Abingdon, Va.; exhibited paintings, Stuttgart, Germany, 1963. Served with AUS, 1942-44. Recipient Gold medal Associazione di Cultura Letteraria e Scientifica, Genoa, Italy, 1949; named knight Sovereign Order St. John Jerusalem. Mem. Modern Lang. Assn. Am., U. Profs. for Acad. Order, Am. Assn. Tchrs. German, Archaeol. Inst. Am., W.Va. Hist. Soc., South Atlantic Modern Lang. Assn., Sigma Iota, Delta Phi Alpha. Rotarian, Mason (32 deg., Shriner). Author: Dem Licht Entgegen, 1941; Wiskonsin Erlebnis, 1942; Isle of Tears, 1942; Life and Poetry, 1942; Lost Souls, 1944; Rubinrot, 1944; Reflections, 1948; All, Erde und Mensch, 1950; Union of Fools, 1953; Walther von der Vogelweide-Troubadour of the Middle Ages, 1968. Lit. editor Christian Educator. Home: 1915 Sherwood Dr Tallahassee FL 32303. *I achieved my present success because I work hard. I believe in a power higher than I am. I respect my fellowman and I like to make my family happy.*

SCHEIBEL, ARNOLD BERNARD, educator, psychiat. researcher; b. N.Y.C., Jan. 18, 1923; s. William and Ethel (Greenberg) S.; B.A., Columbia, 1944, M.D., 1946; M.S., U. Ill., 1952; m. Madge Mila Ragland, Mar. 3, 1950 (dec. Jan. 1977). Intern Mt. Sinai Hosp., N.Y.C., 1946-47; resident psychiatry Barnes and McMillan Hosp., St. Louis, 1947-48, Ill. Neuropsychiat. Inst., Chgo., 1950-52; asst. prof. psychiatry and anatomy U. Tenn. Med. Sch., 1952-53, asso. prof., 1953-55; asso. prof. U. Calif. at Los Angeles Med. Center, 1955-67, prof. psychiatry and anatomy, 1967—, mem. Brain Research Inst., 1960—; cons. VA hosps., Los Angeles, 1956—. Served with AUS, 1943-46; from lt. to capt. M.C., AUS, 1948-50. Guggenheim fellow (with wife), 1953-54, 59. Mem. AAAS, Am. Psychiat. Assn., Am. Neurol. Assn., Soc. Neurosci., Psychiat. Research Assn., Am. EEG Assn., Am. Assn. Anatomists, Soc. Biol. Psychiatry, Am. Acad. Neurology, So. Calif. Psychiat. Assn. Contbr. numerous articles to tech. jours, chpts. to books. Editorial bd. Brain Research, 1967—, Developmental Psychobiology, 1968—, Internat. Jour. Neurosci., 1969—, Jour. Biol. Psychiatry, 1968—. Home: 16231 Morrison St Encino CA 91316 Office: U Calif at Los Angeles Los Angeles CA 90024. *Intense personal tragedy can embitter life and choke off further personal creativity. It may also offer the opportunity to open new doors in the discovery of self. I am more aware than ever of my good fortune in having the opportunity to teach, to continue investigative work in the structure and function of the brain, and to give love and care to those who need it. I am more than ever convinced that loving and being loved is the greatest good that we can know, the state in which we most nearly fulfill our roles as human beings.*

SCHEIBEL, KENNETH MAYNARD, newspaperman; b. Campbell, Nebr., May 17, 1920; s. G. Alfred and Rachel Christine (Koch) S.; student George Washington U., 1938-41; B.A., U. Va., 1947, M.A., 1949; m. Helen Schmitt, May 14, 1955 (div. Sept. 1977); children—Victor Warren, William Becker (foster sons), Kenneth, Sally. Mag. salesman Periodical Publishers' Service Bur., Inc., 1935-38; reporter Internat. News Service, Washington, 1940-41; reporter Wall Street Jour., Washington, 1949-51; Washington corr. Gannett Newspapers, 1951-63; syndicated columnist N.Am. Newspaper Alliance, 1963-64; chief of Washington bur. Donrey Media Group, 1964-67; founder, bur. chief Washington Bur. News, 1967—; founder nat. syndicated column Washington Farm Beat, 1970—. Washington corr. Wis. State Jour., 1963-66, LaCrosse (Wis.) Tribune, 1963-66, Billings (Mont.) Gazette, 1964-71, V.I. Network, 1966-67, Moline (Ill.) Daily Dispatch, 1967-68, Drovers' Jour., 1967-68, Newport News (Va.) Daily Press & Times Herald, 1969-71, Packer Pub. Co., 1964—, Gasoline Retailer, 1966-67, Okla., Farmer Stockman; congl. corr. F-D-C Reports, 1975—; covered nat. polit. convs., campaigns. Served from pvt. to capt. AUS, 1941-46; 755th Tank Bn., Europe, N. Africa, Italy, 1942-45. Decorated Croix de Guerre (France). Mem. Izaak Walton League Am., White House Corrs. Assn., Sigma Chi. Presbyn. Club: Nat. Press (financial sec., gov. 1969-73, vice chmn. bd. 1971, dir. Nat. Press Bldg. Corp. 1973, v.p., pres. club and bldg. corp. 1974) (Washington). Congl. broadcast interviewer. Contbr. nat. mags., newspaper syndicates. Home: 1325 18th St NW Washington DC 20036 Office: Nat Press Bldg Washington DC 20045. *The greatest sins are timidity and self indulgence, the greatest virtue is to love. Live each day, don't fret about yesterday or tomorrow. Enjoy the senses, learn from others, and never forget that both love and hate are returned.*

SCHEIBNER, EDWIN JOSEPH, educator, physicist; b. Newark, June 2, 1919; s. Henry Aloysius and Jennie Marie (Dreher) S.; B.S., Ga. Inst. Tech., 1950; M.S., Ill. Inst. Tech., 1952, Ph.D., 1955; m. Jacquelyn King Crymes, Feb. 16, 1946; children—Beverly Anne, Michael Joseph. Mem. tech. staff Bell Telephone Labs., Murray Hill, N.J., 1955-59; mem. staff Ga. Inst. Tech., Atlanta, 1959—, research prof. physics, 1962-75, prof. physics, 1975—, chief phys. scis. div. Engring. Expt. Sta., 1962-72, dir. Bioengring. Center, 1969-72, prin. research scientist Systems and Techniques Lab., 1979—; cons. AEC, 1966-70. Served with Signal Corps, AUS, 1940-46. Mem. AAAS, Am. Vacuum Soc., Am. Phys. Soc., Sigma Xi. Pioneer work with auger spectroscopy technique; research on radar systems. Patentee in surface field. Home: 430 Amberidge Trail Atlanta GA 30328

SCHEID, FRANCIS, educator; b. Plymouth, Mass., Sept. 24, 1920; s. John and Rose (Bergdoll) S.; B.S., Boston U., 1942, M.A., 1943; Ph.D., Mass. Inst. Tech., 1948; m. Barbara Paty, June 2, 1944; children—Betsy, Lisa, Sarah. Mem. faculty Boston U., 1948—, prof. math., 1960—, chmn. dept., 1956-68; cons. astronautics Mass. Inst. Tech., 1953-61; TV lectr. WGBH-TV, Boston, 1958—; TV, kinescope lectures U.S. Navy and Harvard Commn. Extension Courses. Fulbright lectr. Rangoon (Burma) U., 1961-62. Mem. AAAS, Math. Assn. Am., Am. Math. Soc., Soc. Indsl. and Applied Math., Inst. Mgmt. Scis., Nat. Council Tchrs. Math. (speakers panel), Soc. South Pole, N.Y. Acad. Scis., U.S. Golf Assn. (handicap com.). Author: Elements of Finite Mathematics, 1962; The Game of Numbers, 1965; Theory and Problems of Numerical Analysis, 1967; Theory and Problems of Computer Science, 1969; also articles in field. Research and publs. on problem accurate golf handicapping and course rating. Home: Elm St Kingston MA 02364 Office: Math Dept Boston U Boston MA 02115

SCHEID, VERNON EDWARD, geologist, educator; b. Balt., Sept. 5, 1906; s. Charles (Christian) and Blanche McLenny (Donaldson) S.; A.B., Johns Hopkins, 1928, Ph.D., 1946; M.S., U. Idaho, 1940; m. Martha Frances Helm, Aug. 17, 1934; children—Donald Edward, Margaret Kathryn. Instr. geology Johns Hopkins, 1931-34, summers 1932, 34; asst. geologist Ark. Geol. Survey, summer 1931; geol. field asst. U.S. Geol. Survey, Idaho and Colo., summers 1929, 30, 35, 36; geologist ore deposits, Ida., summers 1940, 41; geologist Strategic Minerals Investigations, Mont., Idaho and Wash., 1942-47; asst. geologist Ida. Bur. Mines and Geology, summer 1938; part-time mineralogist, 1938-39; instr. U. Idaho, 1934-38, asst. prof., 1938-42, prof. geology, head dept. geology-geography, 1947-51; dean Mackay Sch. Mines, prof. mineral sci. U. Nev., 1951-72, prof. mineral econs., 1973—, dir. Nev. Bur. Mines and Nev. Mining Analytical Lab., 1951-72; organizer, chmn., dir. Nev. Oil and Gas Conservation Commn., 1953-72; co-author Nev. Oil and Gas Conservation Law, 1953. Asst. leader Econ. Geol. Excursion, 16th Internat. Geol. Congress, Wash., 1933; collaborator in seismology for Idaho, U.S. Coast and Geodetic Survey, 1939-42, 1947; mem. numerous Nev. Gov.'s adv. councils on mining, natural resources, maps, water energy, 1951—; del. Internat. Geol. Congress, Mexico, 1956, Czechoslovakia, 1968, Can., 1972, Australia, 1976; mining engring. geology cons. fgn. countries UN, 1973—, also pvt. industry. Registered profl. engr., Nev.; registered geologist, Calif. Fellow Geol. Soc. Am., A.A.A.S.; mem. Nat. Soc. Profl. Engrs., Am. Geophys. Union, Am. Inst. Mining, Metall. and Petroleum Engrs. (Pacific S.W. chmn. indsl. minerals div. 1956-58, gen. chmn. div. conf. 1957, chmn. Nev. sect. 1965), Mineral Soc. Am., Assn. Geoscientists for Internat. Devel., Assn. Am. State Geologists, Soc. Econ. Geologists, Sigma Xi, Phi Kappa Phi, Sigma Gamma Epsilon, Sigma Tau, Tau Beta Pi. Rotarian. Author: (reports) Mineral Deposits of Ark., Mont., Idaho and Wash.; Economic Geology; Ceramic and High-Alumina Clay; Industrial Minerals and Rocks; Groundwater; Engineering Geology; Mineral Resources; Mineral Economics. Address: Mackay School of Mines U Nevada Reno NV 89557

SCHEIDE, RICHARD GILSON, bank exec.; b. Hartford, Conn., May 14, 1929; s. Philip W. and Virginia R. (Gilson) S.; B.A., U. Va., 1952; m. Geraldine A. Pierre, June 14, 1952; children—William C., Robert G., Susan R. Vice pres. trust Conn. Bank and Trust Co., Hartford, 1956-72, United Calif. Bank, Los Angeles, 1972-76; exec. v.p., mgr. trust div. New Eng. Mchts. Nat. Bank, Boston, 1976—; dir. Balfour Co., Attleboro, Mass., New Eng. Enterprise Capital Corp., Boston. Bd. dirs. Mass. Taxpayers Found., Inc., Boston; trustee Wheaton Coll., Norton Mass., Fruitlands Mus., Harvard, Mass.; sec./treas., trustee Am. Coll. Greece, Athens. Served with USMC, 1952-54. Mem. Mass. Bankers Assn. (exec. com.). Republican. Congregationalist. Club: Dedham Country and Polo. Office: 28 State St Boston MA 02106

SCHEIDE, WILLIAM HURD, musicologist; b. Phila., Jan. 6, 1914; s. John Hinsdale and Harriet Eliza (Hurd) S.; A.B., Princeton U., 1936; A.M., Columbia U., 1940; Mus. D. (hon.), Coll. Wooster, 1961; m. 2d Gertrude B. Kennedy, June 19, 1971; children—Louise Scheide Marshall, Barbara Scheide Breger, John R. Asst. dept. music Cornell U., 1940-41, instr., 1941-42; organizer, dir. Bach Aria Group, 1946-80; gov. City Center Music and Drama; trustee Westminster Choir Coll. Trustee Princeton Theol. Sem.; mem. exec. com., dir. NAACP Legal Def. Fund. Fellow (life) Pierpont Morgan Library; mem. Neue Bachgesellschaft, Grolier Club, Internat. Assn. Bibliophiles, New Bach Soc. (dir. Am. chpt.). Republican. Presbyterian. Clubs: Princeton of N.Y., Nassau. Author Princeton Sem. pamphlet: J.S. Bach as a Biblical Interpreter, 1952; contbr. articles to Bachjahrbuch, 1959, 61, 62, 76. Home: 133 Library Pl Princeton NJ 08540

SCHEIDEL, THOMAS MAYNARD, educator; b. Columbus, Nebr., July 24, 1931; s. Ralph Maynard and Helen Margaret (Beierle) S.; B.A., Willamette U., Salem, Oreg., 1953; M.A., U. Wash., 1955, Ph.D., 1958; m. Frances Emily Smith, Sept. 4, 1953; children—Susan Jane, Thomas Parker. Instr., asst. prof. U. Wash., 1958-60; asst. prof. speech communication Cornell U., Ithaca, N.Y., 1960-63; asso. prof. U. Ill., 1963-69; prof. U. Wis., Madison, 1969-76; prof., chmn. dept. speech communication U. Wash., Seattle, 1976—. Mem. Speech Communication Assn., Internat. Communication Assn. Author: Persuasive Speaking, 1967; Speech Communication and Human Interaction, 1972, 2d edit., 1976; (with Laura Crowell) Discussing and Deciding, 1979. Home: 5736 60th Ave NE Seattle WA 98105 Office: 107 Parrington Hall Dept Speech Communication Univ of Wash Seattle WA 98195

SCHEIDER, ROY RICHARD, actor; b. Orange, N.J., Nov. 10, 1935; s. Roy Bernhard and Anna (Crosson) S.; B.A. in History, Franklin and Marshall Coll., 1955; m. Cynthia Eddenfield Bebout, Nov. 8, 1962; 1 dau., Maximillia. Broadway appearances include Chinese Prime Minister, 1963, Betrayal, 1979; off-Broadway appearances include The Alchemist, 1964, Serjeant Musgrave's Dance, 1967, Stephen D., 1968; TV appearances on Hallmark Hall Fame, N.Y. Police Dept., Secret Storm; films include Paper Lion, 1968, Star, 1968, Stilleto, 1969, Puzzle of a Downfall Child, 1970, French Connection, 1971, The Outside Man, 1973, The Seven-Ups, 1973, Jaws, 1975, Marathon Man, 1976, Sheila Levine is Dead and Living in New York, 1975, Sorcerer, 1977, Jaws 2, 1978, The Last Embrace, 1979, All That Jazz, 1979. Chmn. Am. Actors Com., N.Y.C., 1967—. Recipient Obie award, 1968. Mem. Actors Equity (councilor), AFTRA, Screen Actors Guild.*

SCHEIE, HAROLD GLENDON, ophthalmologist; b. Brookings, S.D., Mar. 24, 1909; s. Lars T. and Ella Mae (Ware) S.; B.S., U. Minn., 1931, M.D., 1935; D.Sc., U. Pa., 1940, LL.D. (hon.), 1978; D.Med.Sci. (hon.), Villanova U., 1968; one son by previous marriage, Harold Glendon; m. 2d, Mary Ann Tallman, Nov. 1, 1951; children—Eric Glendon, Nancy Ware. Intern U. Pa. Hosp., 1935-37; instr. ophthalmology U. Pa., 1940-45, asst. prof., 1945-49, asso. prof., 1949-53, prof., 1953-60, prof. grad. sch., 1956-75, Norris and deSchweinitz prof., chmn. dept. ophthalmology U. Pa., 1960-75, emeritus prof. ophthalmology, 1977—; chief Phila. Gen. Hosp., Children's Hosp. Phila., 1960-75; founding dir. Scheie Eye Inst., 1977—; pvt. practice medicine limited to diseases of eye, 1940—; dir. Scheie Eye Inst., Presbyn.-U. Pa. Med. Center, 1972-77; lectr. ophthalmology U.S. Naval Hosp., Phila., 1967. Mem. adv. council Res. Affairs to Surgeon Gen.'s adv. panel Med. Scis. to Sec. Def.; cons. Chronic Disease Program USPHS; civilian cons. Ocular Research Unit, Walter Reed Army Hosp. and Med. Center, mem. spl. med. adv. group VA, 1951-59; adv. bd. Internat. Eye Found.; trustee Nat. Med. Found. for Eye Care, Minn. Med. Found.; mem. nat. com. MEDICO; mem. nat. adv. com. Eye-Bank for Sight Restoration; bd. dirs. Nat. Soc. Prevention Blindness, Inc., 1968—, exec. com., 1970—, v.p., 1972-73; mem. panel experts Impartial Med. Test Plan, State Pa. Trustee Episcopal Acad. Served as maj. M.C., AUS, 1942-46, col. M.C., U.S. Army Res., 1950-54, brig. gen. Res. ret., 1964. Decorated Order Brit. Empire; Legion of Merit (U.S.); recipient Howe award in ophthalmology A.M.A., 1964; Horatio Alger award, 1974, gold medal Internat. Glaucoma Congress, 1978, Super Achiever award Juvenile Diabetes Found., 1979, numerous other profl. awards. Diplomate Am. Bd. Ophthalmology (mem. bd.). Fellow A.C.S. (regent 1964-72); mem. A.M.A. (rep. at large sect. ophthalmology), Pa., Phila. County (Strittmatter award 1976) med. socs., Am. Assn. Ophtalmology (3d v.p. 1970), Am. Ophthal. Soc. (mem. council 1965-70, pres. council 1970), Central Ill. Soc. Ophthalmology and Otolaryngology, Am. Acad. Ophthalmology and Otolaryngology (1st v.p. 1960-61), Ophthalmic Club Phila., A.A.A.S., Res. Officers Assn., Guild Prescription Opticians Am., Med. Club Phila., Assn. Research Ophthalmology, Pan-Pacific Surg. Assn., Australian Coll. Ophtalmologists, Soc. Consultants Armed Forces, Coll. Physicians Phila. (chmn. finance com. 1964-65, v.p. 1958-59), John Morgan Soc., Assn. Mil. Surgs. U.S., Assn. U.S. Army (certificate appreciation 1964), Pa. Acad. Ophthalmology and Otolaryngology (pres. 1968), Explorers Club, English-Speaking Union, Academia Ophthalmologica Internationalis, Kungligo Vetenskaps-och Vitterhats-Samhallet i Goteborg, Am. Med. Writers Assn., Assn. U. Profs. Ophthalmology, Benjamin Franklin Assos. of U. Pa., Deutsche Ophthalmologische Gesellschaft, John Archer Soc., Jules Gonin Soc., Minn. Alumni Assn., Ophthal. Soc. U.K., Pacific Coast Oto-Ophthal. Soc. (hon.), Pan-Am. Ophthal. Soc., Pa. Med. Soc., Soc. for Contemporary Ophthalmology (bd. govs. 1970, Disting. Service award 1974), Soc. Mil. Ophthalmologists, World Med. Assn., Physiol. Soc. Phila., Sigma Xi, Phi Rho Sigma, Alpha Omega Alpha. Clubs: Union League, British Officers, Philadelphia Country (Phila.), Penn, Variety, Army-Navy, Capitol Hill, Faculty (U. Pa.), Marines' Memorial, Merion Golf, Seaview Country. Author: Surgery of the Eye (with M. Weiner), 1952; A History of Ophthalmology at the University of Pa., 1965; (with Daniel M. Albert) Textbook of Ophthalmology, 9th edit., 1976; mem. editorial bd. Archives of Ophthalmology, 1954-64, Contemporary Surgery, 1971—, Jour. Pediatric Ophthalmology, Med. Communications, Inc., Boston, 1968—. Contbr. over 200 publs. in field. Home: 1820 Rittenhouse Sq Philadelphia PA 19103 Office: Scheie Eye Inst 51 N 39th St Philadelphia PA 19104

SCHEIFELE, STUART, mfg. co. exec.; b. Royal Oak, Mich., Nov. 8, 1934; s. Webster and Lucille Sayre (Porter) S.; B.B.A., U. Mich., Ann Arbor, 1956, M.B.A., 1957; m. Elizabeth Ann Schemm, July 5, 1958; children—Wendy Sayre, Heidi Ann. Staff accountant Arthur Andersen & Co., Detroit, 1957-59, sr. accountant, 1959-62, audit mgr., Sydney, Australia, 1963-66, Detroit, 1966-67; adminstrv. mgr. William C. Roney & Co., Detroit, 1967-68; v.p. Kirsch Co., Sturgis, Mich., 1968, v.p., treas., 1969, group v.p., 1970-72, exec. v.p., chief fin. officer, 1972—; dir. 1st Nat. Bank of Sturgis. Bd. dirs., regional v.p. Jr. Achievement, 1973—; bd. dirs. United Fund, 1974. Served with Air NG, 1957-63. C.P.A. Mem. Sturgis C. of C. (dir.), Am. Inst. C.P.A.'s, Mich. Assn. C.P.A.'s, Nat. Investor Relations Inst., Chi Psi. Clubs: Klinger Lake Country, Elks. Home: 500 Michigaan St Sturgis MI 49091 Office: 309 N Prospect St Sturgis MI 49091

SCHEIFLY, JOHN EDWARD, tax lawyer; b. Mexico, Mo., Aug. 25, 1925; s. Luke Clauser and Isabella (Sprankle) S.; Sc.B., Brown U., 1945; J.D., Washington and Lee U., 1948; m. Patricia Ann Lenhart, Dec. 27, 1947; children—John Edward, Jan Ellen. Admitted to Calif., W. Va. bars; practiced law, Los Angeles, 1953—; mem. firm Baker, Scheifly & Porter, Huntington, W. Va., 1949-53, McClean, Salisbury, Petty & McClean, Los Angeles, 1953-57, Willis, Butler, Scheifly, Leydorf & Grant, predecessor firms, Los Angeles, 1958—; lectr. tax law U. So. Calif., 1960-74. Served to lt. USNR, 1943-46, 51-53. Mem. Los Angeles County (chmn. tax. sect. 1965-66), Am. (mem. council sect. taxation 1974-77) bar assns., State Bar Calif. Clubs: Jonathan (Los Angeles); Hacienda Golf (LaHabra, Calif.). Author, lectr. fed. tax matters profl. publs., insts. Home: 9441 Friendly Woods Lane Whittier CA 90605 Office: 606 S Olive St Los Angeles CA 90014

SCHEIG, HENRY FREDERICK, fraternal ins. soc. exec.; b. Warren, Ohio, June 14, 1924; s. Henry F. and Martha J. (Zivitz) S.; B.A. in Math., U. Iowa, 1947, M.S., 1949; LL.D., Valparaiso (Ind.) U., 1976; m. Mary Beardsley, June 8, 1946; children—Kathryn C., William B. Asst. sec. Lincoln Nat. Life Ins. Co., 1949-54; with Aid Assn. for Lutherans, Appleton, Wis., 1954—, actuary, 1958-68, sr. v.p., then exec. v.p., 1964-72, pres., 1972—; dir. H.C. Prange Co. Exec. bd. Bay Lakes Council Boy Scouts Am., 1976—; bd. dirs. Outagamie County Health Center, 1977—. Served with USAAF, 1943-46. Fellow Soc. Actuaries, Fraternal Actuarial Assn. (pres. 1961-62); mem. Am. Acad. Actuaries (dir. 1971-74), Internat. Actuarial Assn., Wis. Actuaries Club, Wis. Ins. Club, Life Office Mgmt. Assn. (dir. 1974-77), Nat. Fraternal Congress Am. (exec. com. 1971-76, pres. 1974-75, pres. gen. sessions program commn. 1969-71), Fox Cities C. of C. and Industry (dir. 1975-77). Lutheran. Club: North Shore Country (Menasha, Wis.). Address: 4321 N Ballard Rd Appleton WI 54919

SCHEIMER, LOUIS, TV producer; b. Pitts., Oct. 19, 1928; s. Sam and Lena (Kessler) S.; B.F.A., Carnegie Inst. Tech., 1952; m. Jay Wucher, Dec. 29, 1953; children—Lane, Erika. With various animation studios, 1955-62; founder, 1962, since pres. Filmation Studios, Reseda, Calif.; TV productions include Fat Albert, 1972, Star Trek animated, 1973, Space Academy, 1977, Isis, 1975, Tarzan animated, 1976. Recipient Emmy award Nat. Acad. TV Arts and Scis. for Star Trek animated, 1974; Christopher award, 1972; Ohio State U. award. Mem. Nat. Acad. TV Arts and Scis. Jewish. Home: 18918 La Montana Pl Tarzana CA 91356 Office: 18107 Sherman Way Reseda CA 91335

SCHEIN, EDGAR HENRY, educator; b. Zurich, Switzerland, Mar. 5, 1928; s. Marcel and Hilde (Schoenbeck) S.; came to U.S., 1939, naturalized, 1944; Ph.B., U. Chgo., 1946, B.A., 1947; B.A., Stanford, 1948, M.A., 1949; Ph.D., Harvard, 1953; m. Mary Louise Lodmell, July 28, 1956; children—Louisa, Elizabeth, Peter. Teaching asst. statistics Stanford, 1947-49; teaching asst. social psychology Harvard, 1949-52; research psychologist, neuropsychiatry div. Walter Reed Army Inst. Research, also chief social psychology sect., 1952-56; mem. faculty Mass. Inst. Tech., 1956—, prof. orgnl. psychology and mgmt., 1964—, chmn. orgn. studies group Sloan Sch. Mgmt., 1972—, Sloan Fellows prof. mgmt., 1978—; mem. bd., exec. com. Nat. Tng. Labs., 1962-64; cons. to govt. and industry, 1956—. Served to capt. AUS, 1950-56. Recipient Aux. Research award Social Sci. Research Council, 1958. Mem. Am. Psychol. Assn., Am. Sociol. Assn., Phi Beta Kappa, Sigma Xi. Research in orgnl. psychology, adult socialization, career devel. Author books and articles in field. Home: 1 Parkway Terr Cambridge MA 02138

SCHEIN, HARVEY L., communications co. exec.; b. N.Y.C., Sept. 15, 1927; s. Morris and Matilda (Feld) S.; A.B., N.Y. U., 1949; LL.B., Harvard, 1952; m. Joy Carol Gitlin, Dec. 11, 1963; children—Mark David, Justin Harris. Admitted to N.Y. bar, 1953; asso. firm Roseman, Colin, Kaye, Petschek & Freund, N.Y.C., 1952-58; gen. atty. Columbia records div. CBS, also asst. sec. CBS, 1958-60, div. v.p. internat., 1961-67, pres. CBS Internat. div., 1968-71, pres. CBS

Columbia Group, 1971-72; pres., chief exec. officer Sony Corp. Am., 1972-77, chmn., 1977-78; exec. v.p. Warner Communications Inc., 1978—; pres. Warner Plays, Inc., 1978—. Vice pres., bd. dirs. Internat. Fedn. Phonographic Industries, 1969-73; mem. Marconi Internat. Fellowship Council; mem. adv. council Partners of the Americas; asst. sec. Franklin D. Roosevelt Found., 1952-58. Served with USNR, 1945. Mem. Phi Beta Kappa. Editor: Harvard Law Rev., 1951-52. Home: 800 Park Ave New York NY 10021 Office: 9 W 57th St New York NY 10019

SCHEIN, JEROME DANIEL, educator; b. Mpls., May 27, 1923; s. Adolph and Jeanette Adele (Green) S.; B.A., U. Minn., 1946, M.A., 1947, Ph.D., 1958; children—Carole Dianne (Mrs. Robert Owens), Raleigh Helene (Mrs. Robert Rudnik). Instr. U. Wis., 1958-59; asso. prof. Fla. State U., 1959-60; prof. Gallaudet Coll., Washington, 1960-68; dean Coll. Edn., U. Cin., 1968-70; prof. deafness rehab. N.Y. U., 1970—, dir. Deafness Research & Tng. Center, 1970—; cons. U.S. Office Edn., 1966—. Dir. Nat. Census of Deaf Population, 1969-73; chmn. social commn. World Congress of Deaf, 1975—. Bd. dirs., pres. N.Y. Soc. for Deaf. Recipient Boyce R. Williams award Profl. Rehab. Workers with Adult Deaf, Internat. Solidarity Merit award World Fedn. of Deaf, 1975, Samuelson award N.Y. League for Hard of Hearing, 1975. Fellow Am. Psychol. Assn. (div. 22); mem. Nat. Assn. Deaf (chmn. research com. 1966—), Am. Speech and Hearing Assn., Nat. Rehab. Assn. AAUP. Author: The Deaf Community: Studies in Social Psychology of Deafness, 1968; The Deaf Population of the United States, 1974; For Parents of Deaf Children, 1978. Editor: Deafness, Speech and Hearing Abstracts, 1961-66. Home: 100 Bleecker St New York NY 10012

SCHEIN, PHILIP SAMUEL, physician; b. Asbury Park, N.J., May 10, 1939; s. Irving and Henrietta (Setzer) S.; A.B., Rutgers U., 1961; M.D., SUNY, Syracuse, 1965; m. Dorothy Rosenfeld, May 28, 1967; children—Deborah, Andrew. Intern, Beth Israel Hosp., Boston, 1966-68, resident, 1968-69, 70-71; sr. house officer Radcliffe Infirmary, Oxford, Eng., 1969-70; instr. medicine Harvard U., 1970-71; sr. investigator Nat. Cancer Inst., Bethesda, Md., 1971-74; head clin. pharm. sect. Nat. Cancer Inst., 1973-74; dir. div. med. oncology Georgetown U. Hosp. and Cancer Center, 1974—; cons. oncology Walter Reed Gen. Hosp., Washington, 1971—, Clin. Center, NIH, 1971—; asso. prof. medicine and pharmacology Georgetown U., 1974-77, prof., 1977—; mem. Nat. Pancreatic Cancer Project, 1974-79; chmn. Gastrointestinal Tumor Study Group, 1974—, FDA adv. com. on oncology drugs, 1979—. Diplomate Am. Bd. Internal Medicine (chmn. med. oncology com. 1980—). Fellow Royal Soc. Medicine, A.C.P.; mem. Royal Coll. Physicians London, Am. Soc. Clin. Oncology, Am. Assn. Cancer Research, Am. Soc. Hematology, Alpha Omega Alpha. Club: Cosmos. Research on mechanisms in action of cancer chemotherapy drugs, prediction and prevention drug toxicity, treatment malignant and hematologic diseases; editorial bd. Seminars in Oncology, Cancer Chemotherapy and Pharmacology. Home: 6212 Robinwood Rd Bethesda MD 20034 Office: Div Med Oncology Georgetown U Hosp Washington DC 20007

SCHEINBERG, LABE CHARLES, physician, educator; b. Memphis, Dec. 11, 1925; s. Jacob and Ardie (Cohen) S.; A.B., U. N.C., 1945; M.D., U. Tenn., 1948; m. Louise Goldman, Jan. 6, 1952; children—Susan, David, Ellen, Amy. Intern Wesley Meml. Hosp., Chgo., 1949; resident psychiatry Elgin (Ill.) State Hosp., 1950; resident, asst. neurology Neurol. Inst. N.Y., 1952-56; mem. faculty Albert Einstein Coll. Medicine, 1956—, prof. neurology, asst. dean, 1968-69, asso. dean, 1969-70, dean, 1970-72, dir. neurology Hosp., 1966-73; dir. dept. neurology and psychiatry St. Barnabas Hosp., Bronx, N.Y., 1974-79. Served as capt. M.C., USAF, 1951-52. Fellow Am. Acad. Neurology; mem. Am. Neurol. Assn., Am. Assn. Neuro-pathology, Am. Soc. Exptl. Pathology, Phi Beta Kappa, Alpha Omega Alpha. Cons. editor N.Y. Acad. Scis., 1964. Home: 9 Oak Ln Scarsdale NY 10583 Office: 1300 Morris Park Ave Bronx NY 10461

SCHEINBERG, PERITZ, neurologist; b. Miami, Fla., Dec. 21, 1920; s. Mendel and Esther Dobrisch (Asch) S.; A.B. in Chemistry, Emory U., 1941, M.D., 1944; m. Chantal D'Adesky, Mar. 12, 1971; children—Philip Asch, Richard David, Marissa. Intern, Grady Hosp., Atlanta, 1944-45; resident in internal medicine and neurology Grady Hosp. and Duke U. Hosp., 1946-50; research asst. prof. physiology U. Miami Med. Research Unit, Miami, Fla., 1950-53, asso. prof. neurology, 1955-57, prof. neurology, 1957—, chmn. dept. neurology U. Miami Sch. Medicine, 1961—. Served with M.C., USNR, 1945-46, 53-55. Diplomate Am. Bd. Internal Medicine, Am. Bd. Psychiatry and Neurology. Fellow A.C.P., Am. Acad. Neurology; mem. Am. Neurol. Assn. (pres. elect), Assn. Univ. Profs. Neurology (pres. 1977-78), Am. Heart Assn., Nat. Multiple Sclerosis Soc. (mem. med. adv. bd.). Democrat. Jewish. Author, editor books in field. Contbr. articles to profl. jours. Office: 1501 NW 9th Ave Miami FL 33136

SCHEINER, SAMUEL, architect; b. Hicksville, N.Y., Nov. 10, 1911; s. Morris and Dora (Brienes) S.; B.S. in Arch., U. Mich., 1935; m. Marjorie June Israel, Apr. 11, 1939; children—Susan (Mrs. Martin S. Goldstein), Robert Michael. Mem. firm C.E. Kern, Architect, Freeport, N.Y., 1935-37, Edward Kline, Great Neck, N.Y., 1937-41; architect Navy Ordinance Plant, Aerial Products, Inc., 1941-45; practice architecture in Massapequa, N.Y., 1945—, partner firm Scheiner & Swit, 1952-78; ret., 1978; adj. asso. prof. architecture N.Y. Inst. Tech. at Old Westbury, 1969—. Cons. architect Archtl. Barriers Com. Nassau County, 1970, Assn. for Better Conditions for Disables, Inc., 1971; spl. cons. for Mitchel Park Sports Complex, Nassau County, 1973-74. Chmn. Merrick-North Merrick (N.Y.) Planning Commn., 1949-51, Citizen's Adv. Com. Urban Renewal, Town of Hempstead, N.Y., 1965-69; mem. Boynton Beach (Fla.) Code Enforcement Bd. Named Man of Year, Merrick C. of C., 1968. Registered architect, Fla. Mem. AIA (past pres. L.I. chpt.), N.Y. Assn. Architects (v.p. 1969-71), Tau Sigma Delta. Rotarian (past pres. Merrick). Prin. works include animal shelter, Oyster Bay, N.Y., 1955, Merrick (N.Y.) Pub. Library, 1960, Suburban Temple, Wantagh, N.Y., 1962, golf club house, Hempstead, N.Y., 1966, Security Nat. Bank, N. Massapequa, N.Y., 1966, facilities for handicapped at state parks, L.I., 1968-70. Home and Office: Los Mangos Box 47-8 Boynton Beach FL 33435. *I have tried to see myself as others see me, to be honest with myself and with others in my personal and professional affairs, and to have compassion and respect for the feelings of others.*

SCHEINFELD, JAMES DAVID, business service exec.; b. Milw., Nov. 11, 1926; s. Aaron and Sylvia (Rosenberg) S.; B.A. in Econs. magna cum laude, U. Wis., 1949; m. Mary Kathleen McGrew, Dec. 29, 1974; children by previous marriage—John Stephen, Nancy Ellen, Robert Alan. With Manpower, Inc., 1948-78, salesman, Chgo., 1949-51, br. mgr., 1951-53, nat. sales mgr., Milw., 1953-56, dir. sales, corp. sec., 1956-59, v.p. sales, 1959-62, v.p. marketing, 1962-65, exec. v.p., 1965-70, exec. v.p., chief ops. officer, 1970-76, v.p. spl. projects, 1976-78, cons., 1978—, dir., 1959-76, mem. exec. com.; v.p. Transpersonnel, Inc., Any Task, Inc.; exec. v.p., dir. Manpower Argentina, Manpower Europe, Manpower Ltd. (U.K.), Manpower Australia, Manpower Japan, Manpower Germany GmbH, Manpower Norway, Manpower Denmark, Manpower Venezuela, 1966-76; pres. Aide Services, Inc., Tampa, Fla., 1976—; pres., chief exec. officer Travway Internat., Inc., 1976—; dir. Heritage Bank of Whitefish Bay, Nat. Assn. Temporary Services, 1969-77. Chmn., Cancer Crusade Milw. County, 1970. Bd. dirs. Better Bus. Bur. Milw., Am. Cancer Soc. Milw., U. Wis.-Milw. Found., 1977—. Served with USNR, 1944-46. Mem. Am. Mgmt. Assn., Sales Promotion Execs. Assn. (1st pres. Milw. chpt. 1965), Nat. Assn. Temporary Services (pres. 1975-76), Hickory Assn. (v.p. 1978-79). Rotarian. Clubs: Milwaukee Athletic, University (Milw.). Contbr. articles to profl. jours. Home: 7210 N Beach Dr Milwaukee WI 53217 Office: Suite 310 152 W Wisconsin Ave Milwaukee WI 53203. *I do not often walk or look back where my footprints are. I prefer to walk that part of the beach I have never walked before. I am a person who thinks more about tomorrow than yesterday . . . more about what can be done than what has been done . . . more about challenges than accomplishments. Looking back is helpful only if I can find a sign to help me in my future.*

SCHELL, BRAXTON, lawyer; b. Raleigh, N.C., Feb. 24, 1924; s. Marshall H. and Margaret (Newson) S.; student N.C. State Coll., 1942-43; B.S., U. N.C., 1948, J.D. with honors, 1951; m. Ann Cooper Knight, Mar. 30, 1951; children—Braxton, Richard Knight, James Gray. Admitted to N.C. bar, 1951, since practiced in Greensboro; asso. Smith, Moore, Smith, Schell & Hunter, Greensboro, 1951—, partner, 1956—. Gen. counsel, dir. TexFi Industries, Inc.; dir. Rex Plastics Inc., Dillard Paper Co. Chmn. Special Liason Tax Com. Southeastern Region, 1960-61; bd. dirs. N.C. Outward Bound Sch., 1975—, chmn., 1977—; trustee Outward Bound, Inc., 1978—. Served with USAAF, 1942-45. Fellow Am. Bar Found.; mem. Am., N.C. bar assns., Order of Coif, Phi Beta Kappa. Presbyn. Club: Greensboro Country (pres. 1971-72). Asso. editor: N.C. Law Rev., 1950-51. Home: 2200 Carlisle Rd Greensboro NC 27408 Office: NCNB Bldg Greensboro NC 27402

SCHELL, JOHN LE ROY, pub. relations exec.; b. Mpls., June 30, 1919; s. Arvid and Svea (Johnson) S.; student U. Minn., 1938-41; m. Marjorie Eddy, Oct. 19, 1950. Joined N. Am. Newspaper Alliance, N.Y.C., 1946, editor, 1951-55, exec. v.p., asst. to chmn. bd., 1953-55, promotion dir. Bell Syndicate, Inc., Asso. Newspapers, Inc., Consol. Newspaper, McClure Newspaper Syndicate, 1952-55; dir. pub. relations Gen. Foods Co., 1955-62; pub. relations cons., 1962-65; v.p., dir. pub. relations Armour & Co., 1965-70; in charge N.Am., Neilson McCarthy Internat., 1971--. Chmn. pub. relations com. 5th Internat. Food Conf. and Exhbn., 1960-62. Served as lt., fighter pilot USN, 1941-46. Decorated D.F.C. with gold star, Air medal with 2 gold stars. Mem. Pub. Relations Soc. Am. Clubs: Bagatelle, Dutch Treat, Lake Shore. Home: 142 E 71st St New York NY 10021 also 311 Broadway Saltaire NY 11706

SCHELL, JOSEPH OTIS, educator, clergyman; b. Port Huron, Mich., May 30, 1914; s. Otis D. and Marie (Trese) S.; A.B., Loyola U., Chgo., 1936, A.M., 1941; Ph.L., W. Baden (Ind.) Coll., 1938, S.T.L., 1945; student U. Toronto, 1938-39. Joined Soc. of Jesus, 1931, ordained priest Roman Catholic Ch., 1944; instr. philosophy John Carroll U., Cleve., 1946-50, asst. prof., 1950-53, chmn. dept. philosophy, 1950-64, asso. prof., 1953-59, headmaster residence halls, 1959-64, prof. philosophy, 1959—, dean Coll. Arts and Scis., 1964-67, univ. pres., 1967-70, coordinator religious affairs, 1971—, hon. trustee, 1974—. Mem. Cleve. Commn. Heigher Edn. Vice chmn. univ. and colls. div. United Appeal Greater Cleve., 1968-70; mem. Greater Cleve. Growth Assn., Urban Coalition of Cleve.; mem. adv. bd. Greater Cleve. Safety Council. Trustee U. Detroit, Lake Erie Opera Theatre, Cleve. Internat. Program for Youth Leaders, regional office NCCJ, Cleve.; mem. adv. bd. Martha Holden Jennings Found. Mem. Am. Cath., Jesuit philos. assns., Jesuit, Nat. Cath. ednl. assns., Assn. Higher Edn., Ohio Coll. Assn. (exec. com. 1970—), Cath., Jesuit campus ministry assns., Nat. Assn. Coll. and Univ. Chaplains. Address: John Carroll U Cleveland OH 44118

SCHELL, MAXIMILIAN, actor; b. Vienna, Austria, Dec. 8, 1930; s. Hermann Ferdinand and Margarethe (Noe von Nordberg) S.; student Humanistiches Gymnasium, Basel, Switzerland, Freies Gymanasium, Zûrich, Switzerland, also univs. Zûrich, Basel and Munich. Various appearances on stage in Switzerland and Germany, 1952-55; German film debut in Children, Mothers and the General, 1955, Am. Film debut in Young Lions, 1957; on Broadway stage in Interlock, 1958; prin. roles in films Judgment at Nuremberg, 1961, Five Finger Exercise, 1961, Reluctant Saint, 1962, Condemned of Altona, 1962, Topkapi, 1964, Return From the Ashes, 1965; The Deadly Affair, 1966, Counterpoint, 1966, The Castle, 1968, Simon Bolivar, 1969, First Love, 1970, Pope Joan, 1971, Paulina, 1880, 1971, The Man in The Glass Booth, 1974, The Odessa File, 1974, Assassination, 1975, The Iron Cross, 1976, A Bridge Too Far, 1976, Julia, 1976, The Black Hole, 1979; stage roles in Hamlet, Prince of Homburg, Mannerhouse, Don Carlos, Durrell's Sappho, A Patroit for Me, London, Eng., 1965, Broadway, 1969, The Twins of Venice, 1966, Old Times Vienna, 1972; producer, dir. The Pedestrian, 1973, End of the Game, 1975; producer Ansichten eines Clowns, 1975; stage dir. Hamburg State Theatre, All For the Best, Vienna, 1966, Hamlet, Munich, 1968, Pygmalion, Dusseldorf, 1970, La Traviata, 1975, Tales from the Vienna Woods, London, 1977. Served as corporal in Swiss Army, 1948-49. Nominated Critics award (Broadway), 1958, Academy award, 1970, Golden Globe award, 1976; recipient N.Y. Critics award, 1961, Golden Globe award, 1961, Acad. award, 1961, Silver Shell award, 1970, 75, Bund es film preis (Germany), 1970; Chgo. Film Critics award, 1973, Golden Globe award, 1974, nominated for Oscar, 1974 (all for film The Pedestrian). Office: JCM 8899 Beverly Blvd Los Angeles CA

SCHELL, ORVILLE HICKOK, JR., lawyer; b. New Rochelle, N.Y., July 11, 1908; s. Dr. Orville Hickok and Marea (Martin) S.; grad. Lawrenceville Sch., 1926; A.B., Yale, 1930; LL.B., Harvard, 1933; m. Marjorie Elizabeth Bertha, June 29, 1935 (div. 1970); children—Suzanne Elizabeth (Mrs. John Pearce), Orville Hickok III, Jonathan Edward; m. 2d, Elinor Sterling Johnson, June 20, 1970; children—Christopher Sterling, Andrew John, Peter O.H. Admitted to N.Y. bar, 1934; asso. lawyer Hughes, Schurman & Dwight, 1933-37, Hughes, Richards, Hubbard & Ewing, 1937-40, Hughes, Hubbard & Ewing, 1941-42, partner, 1942—, now Hughes, Hubbard & Reed. Sec., asst.-treas., dir. J. Stirling Getchell, Inc., advt. agy., 1940-41; exec. compensation com., dir. Merck & Co., Inc.; dir. W. O. Hickok Mfg. Co.; chief counsel bur. ordnance Navy Dept., 1945-46; chmn. N.Y. Lawyers for the Pub. Interest, 1977—. Bd. dirs. Regional Plan Assn., N.Y., 1955-64, New York Urban Coalition, 1974—, Council on Pub. Interest Law, 1974—, NAACP Legal Def. and Ednl. Fund, 1975—, N.Y.C. Ballet, 1975—; pres., bd. dirs. Union Settlement Assn., 1971-73; chmn. N.Y. State Moreland Commn., 1975—; co-chmn. joint com. for study N.Y. State narcotics laws of Assn. Bar City N.Y. and Drug Abuse Council; co-chmn. Com. for Pub. Justice, 1977—; chmn. N.Y. Lawyers for Public Interest, 1977; mem. com. character and fitness appellate div. 1st Dept. N.Y. State Supreme Ct.; mem. Zoning Bd., Town of Redding (Conn.), 1979. Trustee, vice chmn. Vassar Coll., 1963-73; trustee Town Sch., N.Y.C., 1977—, South St. Seaport Mus., 1977—; bd. dirs., vice chmn. U.S. Citizens Helsinki Watch, 1978—. Served as It. USNR, 1943-45. Mem. Am. Bar Assn., Assn. Bar City N.Y. (pres. 1972-74), N.Y. State Bar Assn. Clubs: Downtown Assn., Yale, Century Assn. (N.Y.C.); Wilton (Conn.) Riding. Home: 200 E 66th St New York NY 10021 also Giles Hill Rd Redding Ridge CT 06875 Office: 1 Wall St New York NY 10005

SCHELLENGER, JAMES KNOX POLK, investment co. exec.; b. Cape May, N.J., Sept. 14, 1919; s. Henry E. and Edythe (Dellett) S.; B.S. in Econs., U. Pa., 1941, J.D., 1947; m. Ann H. Fussell, Dec. 11, 1948; children—Suzanne F. (Mrs. James G. Williamson), James Knox Polk III, Elizabeth Dellett, Henry Ewen, Georgeann Dock. Admitted to Pa. bar, 1948; practice in Phila., 1948-53; with Delaware Fund, Inc., Phila., 1954—, exec. v.p., 1965-71, pres., 1971-76, chmn. bd., 1977—, also dir.; with Decatur Income Fund, Inc., Phila., 1956—, exec. v.p., 1965-71, pres., 1971-76, chmn. bd., 1977—, also dir.; with Del Mgmt. Co., Inc., Phila., 1955—, exec. v.p., 1965-71, pres., 1971—, also dir.; exec. v.p. Delta Trend Fund, Inc., Phila., 1968-71, pres., 1971-77, chmn. bd., 1977—, also dir.; exec. v.p. Delchester Bond Fund, Inc., Phila., 1970-71, pres., 1971-77, chmn. bd., 1977—, also dir.; pres. Delaware Investment Advisers, Inc., Phila., 1972—, chmn. bd., 1975—, also dir.; chmn. bd. DMC Tax Free Income Trust-Pa., 1977—, also dir.; partner Del. Co., Phila., 1954—. chmn. bd., dir. Del. Cash Res., 1978. Served to lt. USNR, 1942-46. Mem. Am., Phila. bar assns., Phila. Fin. Analysts, U. Pa. Alumni Assn., Navy League, Investment Co. Inst., Nat. Assn. Security Dealers. Clubs: Lawyers, Racquet, Union League (Phila.); Varsity (U. Pa.); Waynesboro Country (Paoli, Pa.). Home: 421 Timber Ln Devon PA 19333 Office: 7 Penn Center Plaza Philadelphia PA 19103

SCHELLING, JOHN PAUL, engring. and contracting co. exec.; b. Chgo., Aug. 24, 1924; s. Lawrence C. and Hattie (LaBonete) S.; student St. Mary's Coll., Winona, Minn., 1942-43, U. Ill., 1946-47; J.D., Loyola U., Chgo., 1950; postgrad. U. Chgo., 1954-55; m. V. Jacqueline Davis, Aug. 27, 1945; children—Lawrence, Donna Schelling Carson, Gloria. Asso. firm McMahon & Plunkett, Chgo., 1950-51; mem. indsl. relations staff Union Asbestos & Rubber Co., Chgo., 1951-56; fin. mgr. Land-Air, Inc. subs. Dynalectron Corp., Chgo., 1956-60; sec. Dynalectron Corp., McLean, Va., 1960-65, v.p., 1962-71, v.p., gen. counsel, 1972-76, sr. v.p. fin. and adminstrn. group, 1977—; admitted to Ill. bar, 1959. Bd. dirs., v.p. Potomac Hills Citizens Assn., McLean, 1963-64; organizer, mem. bd. dirs., v.p. Highland Swim Club, McLean, Va., 1964-67. Served in USNR, 1943-46. Mem. D.C., Ill. bar assns., Am. Mgmt. Assn., Delta Theta Phi. Home: 1442 Cola Dr McLean VA 22101 Office: 1313 Dolley Madison Blvd McLean VA 22101

SCHELLING, THOMAS CROMBIE, educator, economist; b. Oakland, Calif., Apr. 14, 1921; s. John M. and Zelda M. (Ayres) S.; A.B., U. Calif. at Berkeley, 1943; Ph.D., Harvard, 1951; m. Corinne T. Saposs, Sept, 13, 1947; children—Andrew, Thomas, Daniel, Robert. Economist for U.S. Govt. in Copenhagen, Paris, Washington, 1948-53; prof. econs. Yale, 1953-58, Harvard, 1958—; sr. staff mem. RAND Corp., 1958-59; chmn. research adv. bd. Com. for Econ. Devel., 1978—; mem. assembly of behavioral and social scis. NRC-Nat. Acad. Scis., 1978—. Recipient Frank E. Seidman Disting. award in polit. economy, 1977. Fellow Am. Acad. Arts and Scis.; mem. Am. Econs. Assn. Author: National Income Behavior, 1951; International Economics, 1958; The Strategy of Conflict, 1960; Arms and Influence, 1966; Micromotives and Macrobehavior, 1978; co-author: Strategy and Arms Control, 1961. Home: 20 Oakland St Lexington MA 02173

SCHELSKE, CLAIRE L., limnologist; b. Fayetteville, Ark., Apr. 1, 1932; s. Theodore J. and Ida S. S.; A.B., Kans. State Tchrs. Coll., Emporia, 1955, M.S., 1956; Ph.D., U. Mich., 1961; m. Betty Breukelman, June 2, 1957; children—Cynthia, John, Steven. Teaching and research asst. dept. biology Kans. State Tchrs. Coll., 1952-55, vis. instr., summer 1960; teaching fellow dept. zoology U. Mich., 1955-57, asst. prof. radiol. health dept. environ. health Sch. Public Health, asst. research limnologist Gt. Lakes Research Div., Inst. Sci. and Tech., 1967-68, asso. research limnologist, 1969-71, research limnologist, 1971—, asst. dir. Gt. Lakes Research Div., 1970-72, acting dir., 1973-76, asso. prof. limnology, dept. atmospheric and oceanic sci., 1976—, asso. prof. natural resources Sch. Natural Resources, 1976—; research fellow Inst. Fisheries Research, Mich. Dept. Conservation, 1957-60; research asso. U. Ga. Marine Inst., 1960-62; fishery biologist, supervisory fishery biologist, chief Estuarine Ecology Program, Bur. Comml. Fisheries, Radiobiol. Lab., Beaufort, N.C., 1962-66; adj. asst. prof. dept. zoology N.C. State U., Raleigh, 1964-66; tech. asst. Office Sci. and Tech., Exec. Office of Pres., Washington, 1966-67; mem. bd., research adv. bd. Internat. Joint Commn.: mem. NRC ocean scis. bd. site rev. team for Gt. Lakes Environ. Research Lab., NOAA, 1976; cons. Ill. Atty. Gen., 1977—, WAPORA, Inc., Washington, 1977—, UNESCO. NSF travel grantee to 18th Limnol. Congress, Leningrad, 1971; research grantee NSF, 1976-79, EPA, 1973—, Dept. Energy, 1969—. Fellow AAAS, Am. Inst. Fishery Research Biologists (dist. dir. South-Central Gt. Lakes Dist. 1977—); mem. Am. Soc. Limnology and Oceanography (sec. 1976—), Ecol. Soc. Am. (asso. editor 1972-75), Internat. Assn. Gt. Lakes Research (editorial bd. 1970-73, chmn. 20th Conf. 1977), Internat. Ecol. Soc., Phycological Soc. Am., Societas Internationalis Limnologiae. Author: (with J.C. Roth) Limnological Survey of Lakes Michigan, Superior, Huron and Erie, 1973. Home: 1439 Glastonbury Rd Ann Arbor MI 48103 Office: Gt Lakes Research Div U Mich Ann Arbor MI 48109

SCHENCK, FREDERICK A., govt. ofcl.; b. Trenton, May 12, 1928; s. Frederick A. and Alwilda M. (McLain) S.; student Howard U., 1948-50; B.S., Rider Coll., 1958, M.A., 1976; m. Quinta Chapman, Jan. 25, 1974. With N.J. Dept. Community Affairs, 1967-72; dir. youth and family services div. N.J. Dept. Instns. and Agys., 1972-74; dep. dir. adminstrn. purchase and property div. N.J. Treasury Dept., 1974-77; secretarial rep. Fed. Region II, Dept. Commerce, 1977-78, dep. under sec. Dept. Commerce, 1978—. Mem. adv. bd. Rider Coll. Program for Adminstrs.; mem. N.J. State Disciplinary Rev. Bd. Served with USNR, 1946-48. Mem. Am. Soc. Public Adminstrn. Presbyterian. Clubs: 100 Black Men of N.Y., Sundowners. Home: 569 Sanderling Ct Secaucus NJ 07094 Office: US Dept Commerce 14th and Constitution NW Washington DC 20230

SCHENCK, RICHARD ELWOOD, savs. and loan assn. exec.; b. Dayton, Ohio, Dec. 31, 1924; s. Paul David and Rachel L (Loy) S.; student U. Shrivenham (Eng.), 1945-46; m. Lois E. Forrest, Apr. 6, 1946; children—Sue Anne (Mrs. Lyle T. Storlie), Robert Forrest; m. Teresa Pederson. With Gem City Savs. Assn., Dayton, 1947-68, v.p., 1964-68; pres., dir. First Savs. Assn., Saginaw, Mich., 1968—, chmn. bd., 1977—. Past v.p., campaign chmn. United Way Saginaw County; chmn. Saginaw Gen. Hosp.; trustee Harvey Randall Wickes Found.; past met. chmn. Tri-County Nat. Alliance Businessmen. Mem. Republican 300 Club. Served with AUS, 1943-46. Mem. Greater Saginaw C. of C. (past pres.), U.S. Savs. and Loan League, Am. Savs. & Loan Inst., Golf Assn. Mich. Lutheran. Clubs: Saginaw City (past dir., pres.), Country (Saginaw). Home: 4250 Hilray St Saginaw MI 48603 Office: 124 S Jefferson Ave Saginaw MI 48607

SCHENE, ARTHUR V., electronics co. exec.; b. N.Y.C., July 22, 1916; s. Henry W. and Genevieve (Larkin) S.; B.B.A., Coll. City N.Y., 1946; C.P.A., N.Y., 1950; m. Margaret Deegan, Nov. 22, 1940; children—Carol Ann, Edward. Auditor, Scovell Wellington & Co., C.P.A.'s, N.Y.C., 1946-50; treas., controller Airtron Inc., Linden, N.J., 1950-58; v.p., controller Raytheon Co., Lexington, Mass., 1958—. Lectr. Bentley Coll., Waltham, Mass., 1975—. Mem. Fin.

Execs. Inst. (pres. Boston chpt. 1970-71). Home: RFD 1 Harvard MA 01451 Office: Raytheon Co Lexington MA 02173

SCHENK, BOYD FREDERICK, food co. exec.; b. Providence, Utah, July 23, 1922; s. Frederick Lyman and Mabel (Reddish) S.; student U. Utah, 1942, U. Ida., 1940-43, also exec. program, Columbia, 1961; m. June Verlee Hansen, Aug 21, 1942; children—Sandra Lee, Greg F., Brent J., Julie, Peggy. With Pet Inc., 1947—, pres. frozen foods div., 1963-65, corp. v.p., 1964—, corp. group v.p., 1965—, exec. v.p. operations, 1968—, pres., chief exec. officer, 1969—, chmn. bd., 1975—, chmn. exec. com., 1969-75; dir. 1st Nat. Bank St. Louis, Laclede Gas Co., St. Louis, Ill. Power Co., Decatur, IC Industries, Inc., Chgo., A.E. Staley Mfg. Co., Decatur. Mem. exec. bd. St. Louis Area council Boy Scouts Am.; mem. Civic Progress, St. Louis; mem. devel. council Mo. Cancer Research Center; mem. vis. com. Washington U., St. Louis; mem. bd. assos. Gettysburg (Pa.) Coll. Trustee Nutrition Found., N.Y.C. Served with inf. AUS, World War II. Mem. Grocery Mfrs. Am. (dir.), Conf. Bd., Municipal Theatre Assn. (St. Louis). Office: Pet Plaza 400 S 4th St St Louis MO 63166

SCHENK, PETER JOSEPH, telecommunications co. exec.; b. Vienna, Austria, Aug. 10, 1920; s. Joseph and Ilse (Petersen) von Schenk; came to U.S., 1932, naturalized, 1937; A.B. in Physics, Lafayette Coll., 1941; Sc.D. (hon.), Coll. Advanced Sci., Canaan, N.H., 1961; m. Norma B. Otis, Mar. 28, 1941 (div. 1960); children—Peter Joseph, Steven George and Robert Henry (twins); m. 2d, Hazel Regina Holmes, Apr. 8, 1961; 1 dau., Andrea Mary. Instr. physics Lafayette Coll., 1941; product planning mgr., mil. electronic equipment, then marketing mgr. def. electronic equipment Gen. Electric Co., 1954-58; asst. to pres. Raytheon Co., 1958-60; exec. v.p. Mitre Corp., 1960-62; mgr. partner Peter J. Schenk & Co., Arlington, Va., 1962-64; v.p. govt. communications systems Western Union Telegraph Co., Arlington, 1964-72, group v.p. pub. services group, McLean, Va., 1972-73; pres. Telcom, Inc., Vienna, Va., 1973-77, chmn., 1977-78; pres. Vt. Toy Farm Inc., 1978—; cons. electronics panel Air Force Sci. Adv. Bd., 1956-62. Trustee Aerospace Edn. Found., 1960—, Coll. Advanced Sci., 1960-63, Air Force Hist. Found., 1959-63, Air Force Acad. Found., 1958-62; nat. council Boy Scouts Am., 1964—; mem. mil. sci. vis. com. Harvard, 1960-64. Served to lt. col. AUS, and USAF, 1941-54; col. Res. Sr. mem. I.E.E.E.; mem. Armed Forces Communications and Electronics Assn. (pres. Washington 1962-64, nat. dir. 1966—), Air Force Assn. (nat pres. 1957-59, nat. dir. 1955-57, 60—). Home: RFD 1 Box 84A Jericho VT 05465 Office: 66 Chapin Rd Essex Junction VT 05452

SCHENK, QUENTIN FREDERICK, educator; b. Fort Madison, Iowa, Aug. 25, 1922; s. Fred Edward John and Ida (Sabrowsky) S.; B.A., Willamette U., 1948; M.S., U. Wis., 1950, M.S. in Social Work, 1953, Ph.D., 1953; m. Patricia J. Kelley, Aug. 6, 1946 (div. Apr. 1970); children—Fred W. (dec. Jan. 1972), Patricia, Karl, Martha; m. 2d, Emmy Lou Willson, May 23, 1970. Asst. prof. social work U. Wis.-Madison, 1953-55, prof., chmn. extension social work, 1961-63, prof., former dean Sch. Social Welfare, Milw., 1963—; asso. prof. U. Mo., 1955-61; project specialist Ford Found., 1968-71. Spl. cons. on urban mission in Africa, United Presbyn. Ch., 1971—, World Council Chs., 1971—; adviser to Haile Sellassie I U., Addis Ababa, Ethiopia, 1968-71. Alderman, City of Cedarburg (Wis.), 1974—; mem. Wis. Historic Preservation Negotiating Bd. Served as pilot USNR, 1942-46. Decorated Air medal with 3 gold stars. Mem. AAUP, Nat. Trust for Historic Preservation, Am. Sociol. Assn., Council on Social Work Edn., Aircraft Owners and Pilots Assn. Author: (with Emmy Lou Schenk) Pulling Up Roots, 1978; Welfare and Society, 1980; contbr. articles, bulls., reports to profl. lit. Home: Box 2335 W61 N 439 Washington Ave Cedarburg WI 53012 Office: Sch Social Welfare U Wis Milwaukee WI 53201

SCHENKEL, CHRIS, sportscaster; grad. Purdue U., 1943, Litt. D. (hon.); H.H.D. (hon.), Ball State U., 1977; m. Fran Paige; children—Christiana, Ted, Johnny. Sportscaster, ABC, anchorman coverage of 1968 Olympic Games, Mexico City, 1972 Olympic Games, Munich, W. Ger., play-by-play commentator 1976 Winter and Summer Olympic Games, sportscaster Profl. Bowlers Tour, ABC's Wide World of Sports, also worked on many sports spls. Served with U.S. Army. Recipient George Foster Peabody award, 1968; Disting. Service award Billiard and Bowling Inst. Am., 1974; Presdl. Gold medal U. Detroit, 1978; inducted into Profl. Bowling Assn.'s Hall of Fame, 1976. Office: care ABC Sports 1330 Ave of Americas New York NY 10019*

SCHENKEL, JAMES MILTON, ret. ins. co. exec.; b. Bklyn., Aug. 19, 1913; s. Elbert Stevens and Rebecca Cornelia (Ballagh) S.; B.A. magna cum laude, Colgate U., 1934; m. Elizabeth I. Johnston, May 18, 1946; children—James Parkhill, Mary Elizabeth, Margaret Schenkel Watson. With Met. Life Ins. Co., 1934-36; with Home Life Ins. Co., N.Y.C., 1936-78, asso. actuary, 1960-67, actuary, 1968-72, 2d v.p., actuary, 1972-78. Served to lt. USNR, 1942-46. Fellow Soc. Actuaries; mem. Am. Acad. Actuaries, Internat. Actuarial Assn., Empire State Soc. SAR. Clubs: Vero Beach Country; Moorings Golf; Skytop (Pa.). Home: 5000 N A-1-A Apt 540 Vero Beach FL 32960

SCHENKER, ALEXANDER MARIAN, educator; b. Cracow, Poland, Dec. 20, 1924; s. Oskar and Gizela (Szaminski) S.; student Stalinabad Pedagogical Inst., 1943-46, U. Paris, 1947-48; M.A., Yale, 1950, Ph.D., 1953; m. Krystyna Czajka, Oct. 15, 1970; children—Alfred R., Michael J., Catherine I. Came to U.S., 1946, naturalized, 1952. Asst. in instrn. Yale, New Haven, 1950-52, instr., 1952-56, asst. prof., 1956-63, asso. prof., 1963-67, prof. Slavic linguistics, 1967—; vis. prof. Slavic linguistics U. Cal., Berkeley, 1969-70. Mem. Linguistic Soc. Am., Modern Lang. Assn., Internat. Linguistic Assn., Conn. Acad. Arts and Scis., Polish Inst. Arts/Scis., Am. Assn. Tchrs. Slavic and E. European. Langs., Am. Assn. Advancement Slavic Studies. Author: Polish Declension, 1964; Beginning Polish, Vol. I, 1966, Vol. II, 1967; Fifteen Modern Polish Short Stories, 1970. Home: 145 Deepwood Dr Hamden CT 06517 Office: Hall Grad Studies Yale New Haven CT 06520

SCHENKER, ERIC, univ. dean, economist; b. Vienna, Austria, Feb. 24, 1931; s. Adolph and Olga (Strauss) S.; came to U.S., 1939, naturalized, 1945; B.B.A., City Coll. N.Y., 1952; M.S., U. Tenn., 1955; Ph.D., U. Fla., 1957; m. Virginia Martha Wick, Apr. 14, 1963; children—David, Richard, Robert. Asst. prof. Mich. State U., 1957-59; mem. faculty U. Wis.-Milw., 1959—, prof. econs., 1965—, dean Sch. Bus. Adminstrn., 1976—, dir. Urban Research Center, 1974-76, asso. dir. Center Great Lakes Studies, 1967-74, sr. scientist, 1974—, asso. dean Coll. Letters and Scis., 1963-69; cons. in field. Sr. mem. Milw. Bd. Harbor Commrs., 1960-72, chmn., 1965-68; chmn. panel on future port requirements of U.S., Maritime Transp. Research Bd., Nat. Acad. Scis., 1973-76; mem. pilotage adv. bd. to U.S. sec. transp., 1972-75. Served with AUS, 1952-54. Mem. Am., So. econs. assns., Phi Kappa Phi. Author: The Port of Milwaukee: An Economic Review, 1967; co-author Port Planning and Development as Related to Problems of U.S. Ports and the U.S. Coastal Environment, 1974; The Great Lakes Transportation System, 1976; Port Development in the United States, 1976; Maritime Labor Organizations on the Great Lakes-St. Lawrence Seaway System, 1978; also monographs and articles. Home: 2254 W Dunwood Rd Milwaukee WI 53209

SCHENKKAN, ROBERT FREDERIC, TV sta. exec.; b. N.Y.C., Mar. 4, 1917; s. Joseph and Flora (Vander Zyl) S.; A.B., U. Va., 1941; postgrad. U. N.C., 1941-42, M.A. in Drama, 1947; m. Jean McKenzie, Aug. 26, 1944; children—Pieter, Dirk, Robert, Gerard. Mgr. WUNC-TV, Chapel Hill, N.C., 1954-55; pres., gen. mgr. KLRN-TV, Austin, Tex., 1964—; dir. Communication Center, also prof. radio-TV-film U. Tex., 1964-77; 1955-77; dir. Tex. Knowledge Network, 1962—, KMFA-FM; chmn. bd. mgrs., bd. dirs. Pub. Broadcasting Service, 1973-74, chmn. pro tem bd. dirs.; communications cons.; cons. rural satellite program AID, 1979—; chmn. Nat. Ednl. TV Affiliates Council, 1969; cons. AID, El Salvador, 1967, World Bank, Colombia, 1968, Latin Am. Satellite Study, Stanford Research Inst., 1968, Dept. State, Yugoslavia, 1969, Indonesia, 1974, Acad. Ednl. Devel., Internat. Network Study, 1975, European Program Decision Study, Pub. Broadcasting System, Ford Found., 1976-77. Vice pres. Arts Council Austin, 1969-70; pres. Austin High Sch. PTA, 1970-71; chmn. U. Tex. United Fund Drive, 1968-69; bd. dirs. Austin Symphony, 1956-57, Austin Ballet Soc., 1958-62, Recs. for the Blind. Served with USNR, 1942-46, comdr. Res. ret. Rockefeller Found. grantee, 1941-42; Fulbright grantee, 1969, 72; Ford Found. grantee, 1970, 76. Mem. Nat. Assn. Ednl. Broadcasters (vice chmn. 1968), So. Ednl. Communications Assn. (dir. 1971—, chmn. planning com. 1971—, mem. exec. com. 1971—). Author: (with Kai Jurgensen) Plays of Henrik Ibsen, a translation, 1948; also plays for ch. Home: 1804 Robin Hood Trail Austin TX 78703 Office: PO Box 7158 Austin TX 78712

SCHENKMAN, ALFRED SEYMOUR, publishing co. exec.; b. New Market, N.J., Sept. 27, 1919; s. Max and Rae Edith (Kuntz) S.; B.S., Rutgers U., 1940; M.S., U. Minn., 1941; B.D., U. Chgo., 1943; postgrad. Harvard, 1947-49; m. Pamela Wrinch, Sept. 13, 1966 (dec. Dec. 1975). Traveled in Europe, India and Far East, 1950-57; editor Orient Review, Calcutta, India, 1954-56; editor Rinehart & Co., N.Y.C., 1957-60, Addison Wesley Pub. Co., Reading, Mass., 1960-61; pres. Schenkman Pub. Co., Inc., Cambridge, Mass., 1961—. Served with AUS, 1945-46. Mem. A.A.U.P. Home: 46 Shepard St Cambridge MA 02138 Office: 3 Mt Auburn Pl Cambridge MA 02138

SCHEPMAN, BERNE ADAIR, mfg. co. exec.; b. near Bushton, Kans., Dec. 23, 1926; s. William F. and Caroline (Mai) S.; B.S. in Chem. Engring., Northwestern U., 1950; m. Grace J. Koepchen, June 21, 1952; children—Ruth Evelyn, Stephen Brian, Carolyn Lydia. Chem. engr. Esso Standard Oil Co., Linden, N.J., 1950-53; with Eimco Corp., 1953-69, exec. v.p., 1961-64, pres., 1964-69; pres., dir. Envirotech Corp., Menlo Park, Calif., 1969—. Served with USNR, 1944-46. Mem. Am. Inst. C.E., Am. Inst. Mining and Metall. Engrs., Water Pollution Control Fedn., Tau Beta Pi. Lutheran. Office: 3000 Sand Hill Rd Menlo Park CA 94025

SCHEPS, CLARENCE, univ. adminstr.; b. Houston, Jan. 16, 1915; s. Benjamin and Libbie (Solman) S.; B.A., Rice Inst., 1935; M.S., Columbia, 1936; Ph.D., La. State U., 1943; m. Mary E. Brown, Aug. 28, 1939; children—Philip, Edward. Instr. accounting La. State U., 1936-41; supr. finance La. Dept. Edn., 1941-46; comptroller U. Miss., 1946-47; exec. asst. to pres. Tulane U., 1947-48, comptroller, 1948-57, v.p., 1957-66, exec. v.p., 1966-79, v.p. for bus., 1979—. Mem. Orleans Parish School Bd., 1950-56, pres., 1952-55. Gen. chmn. United Fund Campaign Greater New Orleans, 1958; vice chmn. New Orleans A.R.C., 1958-60, chmn., 1966-68; pres. Southeastern La. council Girl Scouts U.S.A., 1962-65. Mem. exec. com. Nat. Fedn. Coll. and Univ. Bus. Officer Assns., 1959, dir., 1952—; mem. commn. on adminstrn. affairs Am. Council on Edn., 1973-77; mem. council on fed. relations Assn. Am. Univs., 1969—. Bd. dirs. Internat. House New Orleans, 1969-74, New Orleans chpt. NCCJ, Nat. Center for Higher Edn. Mgmt. Systems, 1976-79. Mem. So. (pres. 1959), Nat. (v.p. 1963-65, pres. 1965-67) assns. coll. and univ. bus. officers. Author: Accounting for Colleges and Universities, 1949, rev. edit. (with E.E. Davidson), 1978. Home: 6321 Freret St New Orleans LA 70118

SCHER, ALLEN MYRON, scientist, educator; b. Boston, Apr. 17, 1921; s. Emmanuel and Celia (Richmond) S.; B.A., Yale, 1942, Ph.D., 1951; m. Maryonda Edmonstone, Aug. 31, 1952; children—Celia, John. Mem. faculty dept. physiology and biophysics U. Wash. Sch. Medicine, Seattle, 1950—, prof., 1962—; George E. Brown meml. lectr. Am. Heart Assn., 1976. Mem. computer research study sect. NIH, 1963-67, mem. cardiovascular study sect., 1967-71. Mem. Am. Physiol. Soc. (exec. com. circulation group 1972-76), Biophys. Soc., Biomed. Engring. Soc. (dir. 1970-73). Contbg. author: Physiology and Biophysics, 20th edit., 1975. Mem. editorial bds. jours. in field. Research and publs. on pathway of elec. activity in heart, origin of electrocardiogram, control of heart stroke output, control system analysis of pressure control. Office: Dept Physiology and Biophysics U Wash Sch Medicine Seattle WA 98195

SCHERAGA, HAROLD ABRAHAM, phys. chemist; b. Bklyn., Oct. 18, 1921; s. Samuel and Etta (Goldberg) S.; B.S., Coll. City N.Y., 1941; A.M., Duke, 1942, Ph.D., 1946, Sc.D. (hon.), 1961; m. Miriam Kurnow, June 20, 1943; children—Judith Anne, Deborah Ruth, Daniel Michael. Teaching, research asst. Duke, 1941-46; fellow Harvard Med. Sch., 1946-47; instr. chemistry Cornell U., 1947-50, asst. prof., 1950-53, asso. prof., 1953-58, prof., 1958—, Todd prof. chemistry, 1965—, chmn. dept., 1960-67; vis. asso. biochemist Brookhaven Nat. Lab., summers 1950, 51, cons. biology dept., 1950-56; vis. lectr. div. protein chemistry Wool Research Labs., Melbourne, Australia, 1959; vis. prof. Soc. for Promotion Sci., Japan, Aug. 1977; mem. tech. adv. panel Xerox Corp., 1969-71, 74-79. Mem. biochemistry tng. com. NIH, 1963-65, mem. research career award com. NIGMS, 1967-71; commn. molecular biophysics Internat. Union for Pure and Applied Biophysics, 1965-69, mem. commn. macromolecular biophysics, 1969-75, pres., 1972-75, mem. commn. subcellular and macromolecular biophysics, 1975—; adv. panel molecular biology NSF, 1960-62; Welch Found. lectr., 1962, Harvey lectr., 1968, Gallagher lectr., 1968, Lemieux lectr., 1973, Hill lectr., 1976. Co-chmn. Gordon Conf. on Proteins, 1963; mem. council Gordon Research Confs., 1969-71. Mem. Ithaca Bd. Edn., 1958-59. Bd. govs. Weizmann Inst., Israel, 1970—. Mem. staff Naval Research Lab. Project, Air Force OSRD Project World War II. Fulbright, Guggenheim fellow Carlsberg Lab., Denmark, 1956-57, Weizmann Inst., Israel, 1963; NIH Spl. fellow Weizmann Inst., 1970; recipient Townsend Harris medal Coll. City N.Y., 1970, chemistry alumni sci. achievement award, 1977. Fellow AAAS; mem. Nat. Acad. Scis., Faraday Soc., Am. Chem. Soc. (chmn. Cornell sect. 1955-56, mem. exec. com. div. biol. chemistry 1966-69, vice chmn. div. biol. chemistry, 1970, chmn. div. biol. chemistry, 1971, Eli Lilly award 1957, Nichols medal 1974, Kendall award 1978), Am. Soc. Biol. Chemists, Biophys. Soc. (council 1967-70), Am. Acad. Arts and Scis., Phi Beta Kappa, Sigma Xi, Phi Lambda Upsilon. Author: Protein Structure; Theory of Helix-Coil Transitions in Biopolymers. Co-editor: Molecular Biology, 1961—. Mem. editorial bd. Physiol. Chemistry and Physics, 1969-75, Mechanochemistry and Motility, 1970—, Thrombosis Research, 1972-76, Biophys. Jour., 1973-75, Macromolecules, 1973—, Computers and Chemistry, 1974—, Internat. Jour. Peptide and Protein Research, 1978—; corr. PAABS Revista, 1971-75; editorial adv. bd. Biopolymers, 1963—, Biochemistry, 1969-74. Home: 212 Homestead Terr Ithaca NY 14850

SCHERER, GORDON HARRY, lawyer, former congressman; b. Cin., Dec. 26, 1906; s. John E. and Minnie (Kuehnle) S.; student U. Cin.; LL.B., Salmon P. Chase Coll. Law, 1929; LL.D., Institutum Divi Thomae, 1961; m. Virginia E. Mottern, Feb. 18, 1933; children—Gordon Mottern, Suzanne Virginia (Mrs. John C. Louiso). Admitted to Ohio bar, 1929, since practiced in Cin.; asst. pros. atty. Hamilton County, Ohio, 1933-41; dir. safety City of Cin., 1943-44; mem. planning commn., Cin., 1946-47, city council, 1945-49; mem. 83d-87th Congresses, 1st Dist. Ohio, mem. Un-Am. activities com. mem. U.S. nat. commn. UNESCO, 1970—, U.S. mem. exec. bd., Paris, France, 1974—; U.S. rep. to UN, 1972-73. Dir. Universal Guaranty Life Ins. Co. of Ohio; chmn. bd. Gentile Bros. Co.; sec., dir. Dorman Products, Inc.; pres. bd. trustees Cin. So. Ry. Mem. Ohio Supreme Ct. Bd. Commrs. on Grievances and Discipline, 1970-75. Mem. bd. visitors USAF Acad., Colorado Springs, Colo., 1971-73. Chmn. Republican Party of Hamilton County, 1962-68; mem. Ohio Rep. State Central and Exec. Coms., 1964-70; mem. bd. elections Hamilton County. Trustee Ams. for Constl. Action; Recipient Patriotic Service awards Coalition Am. Patriotic Socs., Am. Legion, D.A.R. Distinguished Service award Negro Citizens Cin. Mem. Am., Ohio, Cin. bar assns., Order of Curia, Phi Alpha Delta. Mason (33 deg.). Home: Highland Towers Cincinnati OH 45202 Office: Carew Tower Cincinnati OH 45202

SCHERER, LEE RICHARD, JR., govt. ofcl.; b. Charleston, S.C., Sept. 20, 1919; s. Lee Richard and Sara Mae (Getsinger) S.; B.S. in Elec. Engring., Naval Acad., 1942; B.S. in Aero. Engring., U.S. Naval Postgrad. Sch., 1949; M.S. in Aero. Engring., Calif. Inst. Tech., 1950; D.Aerospace Engring. (hon.); m. Betty Jean Hemsky, Feb. 21, 1944; children—Candace (Mrs. William Bane Hunt), William, Michael, Tracy. Commd. ensign U.S. Navy, 1942, advanced through grades to capt., 1962; program mgr. lunar orbiter NASA Hdqrs., Washington, 1962-67, dir. Apollo Lunar Exploration Office, 1967-71; dir. Flight Research Center, Edwards, Calif., 1971-74; dir. John F. Kennedy Space Center, Fla., 1975—. Recipient Exceptional Service award NASA, 1967, Exceptional Sci. Achievement award, 1969, Distinguished Service award, 1974. Mem. Sigma Xi, Tau Beta Pi. Office: John F Kennedy Space Center NASA Kennedy Space Center FL 32899

SCHERER, OTTO ERNEST, service co. exec.; b. Palmyra, Wis., July 15, 1915; s. Otto Ernest and Mae (Downey) S.; B.S. in Accounting magna cum laude, U. Notre Dame, 1938; m. Agnes Rita Cahalan, June 30, 1942; children—Mary Ann Scherer Crutchlow, Thomas, Margaret Scherer Hickman. Accountant Studebaker Corp., South Bend, Ind., 1938-41; spl. agt. FBI, 1941-46; chief accountant, controller, Blessings Corp., N.Y.C., 1946-50, treas., 1950-68, v.p., 1968-70, exec. v.p., 1970, pres., 1970-76, vice-chmn., 1976-77, chmn., 1977—, also dir. and dir. subs. cos. Mem. Bd. Edn., Englewood, N.J., 1954-58. C.P.A., Ind. Mem. Am. Inst. C.P.A.'s, Fin. Execs. Inst. Republican. Roman Catholic. Elk. Home: 79 Pine St Closter NJ 07624 Office: 45 Knightsbridge Rd Piscataway NJ 08854

SCHERER, RAYMOND LEWIS, communications corp. exec.; b. Ft. Wayne, Ind., June 7, 1919; s. Arnold F. and Eleanor M. (Vonderau) S.; A.B., Valparaiso U., 1942; M.A., U. Chgo., 1947; m. Barbara Hetzner, Dec. 28, 1950; children—Nancy, David. Bus. dept. Ft. Wayne Jour.-Gazette, 1940-41, gen. assignment reporter, feature writer, 1942, 47; news editor NBC, Washington, 1947-49, broadcaster Pentagon, Congl. news, 1949-52, White House corr., 1952-69, London (Eng.) corr., 1969-73, Washington corr., 1973-75; v.p. RCA Corp., Washington, 1975—. Served to lt. (s.g.) U.S. Naval Res., 1942-46. Mem. Sigma Delta Chi. Clubs: Cosmos, Federal City, Nat. Press, F Street, Carlton, Internat., George Town (Washington); Garrick (London). Home: 3550 Springland Ln NW Washington DC 20008 Office: RCA Corp 1800 K St NW Suite 810 Washington DC 20006

SCHERER, ROBERT W., utility exec.; b. 1925; B.S., Yale, 1946; LL.B., Emory U., 1950; married. With Ga. Power Co., Atlanta, 1946—, v.p., div. mgr. Rome div., 1965-69, exec. v.p., 1969-75, pres., 1975—, chief exec. officer, 1978—, also dir.; dir. So. Co., So. Co. Services, Inc., Southeastern Elec. Exchange, So. Electric Generating Co. Office: 270 Peachtree St NW Atlanta GA 30303

SCHERER, WILLIAM FRANKLIN, physician, microbiologist; b. Buffalo, Aug. 2, 1925; s. William F. and Helen (Seymour) S.; M.D., U. Rochester, 1947; m. Janice Spicer, Aug. 10, 1946; children—Judith, John, Robert. Intern internal medicine Barnes Hosp., St. Louis, 1947-48; intern pathology Strong Meml. Hosp., Rochester, 1948-49; asst. resident internal medicine Vanderbilt U. Hosp., 1949-50; from instr. to prof. microbiology U. Minn., 1950-62; prof. microbiology Cornell U. Med. Coll., N.Y.C. 1962—, chmn. dept., 1962—; dir. com. viral infection Armed Forced Epidemiology Bd., 1965-72; chmn. bd. sci. counsellors Nat. Inst. Allergy and Infectious Disease, 1966-68. Recipient Theobald Smith award A.A.A.S., 1959; NRC fellow, 1950-51; Markle scholar, 1953-55, 57-60. Mem. Soc. Exptl. Biology, Soc. Tropical Medicine, Assn. Bacteriologists and Pathologists, Assn. Immunologists, Am. Acad. Microbiology, Epidemiological Soc., Soc. Cell Biology, Soc. Microbiology, Infectious Disease Soc. Discoverer of poliovirus growth in HeLa human cancer cells. Home: 6 Sherman Ave Bronxville NY 10708 Office: 1300 York Ave New York City NY 10021

SCHERICH, EDWARD BAPTISTE, diversified co. exec.; b. Inland, Nebr., Dec. 3, 1923; s. Clarence H. and Clara E. (Baptiste) S.; B.B.A., Tulane U., 1948; m. Hyacinth Rau, Aug. 11, 1945; children—Carol, Eileen, John. Accountant, Colo. Milling & Elevator Co., Denver, 1948-50; accountant, office mgr. Southdown, Inc., New Orleans, 1950-55, controller, 1955-69; v.p. finance, sec., treas. Southdown Sugars Inc., New Orleans, 1970-73; v.p., sec., treas. Southdown Land Co., New Orleans, 1971-75; sec.-treas. Southdown, Inc., Houston, 1975-78, v.p., sec., 1979—. Served in USNR, 1943-45. Mem. Beta Gamma Sigma. Office: 2200 Two Allen Center Houston TX 77002

SCHERK, PETER, educator; b. Berlin, Germany, Sept. 2, 1910; s. Alfred and Lea Scherk; student Berlin U.; Ph.D., Goettingen (Germany) U., 1935; m. Eva Goldsmith, Apr. 25, 1946; children—John, Michael, Margaret. Came to Can., 1943. Fellow Yale, 1940-41; asst. Ind. U., Bloomington, 1941-43; from instr. to prof. U. Sask., Saskatoon, Can., 1943-59; prof. math. U. Toronto (Ont., Can.), 1959—; vis. prof. U. Pa., 1956-57, U. Colo., summers 1952, 59, 62, U. B.C., Vancouver, 1965, U. Freiburg (Germany), 1970. NRC postdoctoral fellow, 1967-68. Fellow Royal Soc. Can.; mem. Am. Math. Soc., Canadian Math. Congress. Editor Bull. Canadian Math. Congress, 1958-62, Canadian Jour. Math., 1962-67. Contbr. articles to profl. jours. Home: 247 Yonge Blvd Toronto ON Canada Office: Dept Math Univ Toronto Toronto ON Canada

SCHERMAN, THOMAS, orch. condr.; b. N.Y.C., Feb. 12, 1917; s. Harry and Bernardine (Kielty) S.; grad. Columbia, 1937; student Mannes Sch. Music, Juilliard Sch. Music; student conducting with Max Rudolf, Carl Bamberger, piano with Isabelle Vengerova, composition and theory with Hans Wiesse. Asst. to Otto Klemperer, chamber orch. New Sch. Social Research, N.Y.C., 1940-41; orginator radio program Let's Go to the Opera, also condr. radio sta. WQXR, 1946; asst. condr. Opera Nacional, Mexico City, summer 1947;

founder, mus. dir., condr. Little Orchestra Soc., N.Y.C., 1947—, toured with Little Orchestra, U. S. and Can., 1951—, tour of the Far East, 1959; nat. tours, 1960-76; cons. various local Little Symphonies. Condr. concerts Vienna Symphony, BBC, London Symphony, Berlin Symphony, Hamburg Symphony, Dubrovnik Festival, also Orchestre de la Suisse Romande, Switzerland, summers 1950-51; condr. concerts Lewisohn Stadium, N.Y.C. 1954—; guest condr. St. Louis, Denver, San Francisco, Kansas City, 1954-60, Israel Philharmonia, 1960, Jacksonville, Fla., 1969. Served as capt. S.C., AUS, 1941-46. Recipient Medal for Excellence, Columbia, 1952, Peabody Award citation Nat. Assn. Am. Composers and Condrs., 1954, Peabody Award, 1957, award Nat. Fedn. Music Clubs, 1958, Gold Medal of Honor, Nat. Arts Club, 1960, decorated chevalier de l'Ordre des Arts et des Lettres (France), Cavaliere Ufficiale dell' Ordine Al Merito della Repubblica, Italiana (Italy).

SCHERMAN, WILLIAM HARRIS, pub. co. exec., cons.; b. N.Y.C., Aug. 11, 1913; s. William S. and Celia (Harris) S.; A.B. magna cum laude, Dartmouth, 1934; m. Alice E. Rowland, Sept. 8, 1935 (div. Mar. 1957); children—Betsy (Mrs. Richard Smith), Rowland, Thomas, David; m. 2d, Germaine Ganteaume, Feb. 19, 1961; children—Daniel, Timothy. With Schwab and Beatty, advt., 1934-43, Simon and Schuster, 1943-45; advt. promotion mgr. Time mag., 1945-50; asst. circulation dir. Time, Inc., 1950-52; asst. promotion dir. Life mag., 1952-54; promotion mgr. Sports Illustrated, 1954-61; promotion mgr. Life mag., 1961-63; v.p., promotion dir. Newsweek mag., 1963-79. Founding mem. Mag. Promotion Group, 1950. Mem. Dartmouth Alumni Council, 1962-65. Mem. Delta Kappa Epsilon. Clubs: Dartmouth of N.Y. Home: 71 Hardscrabble Rd Bernardsville NJ 07924 Office: 444 Madison Ave New York NY 10022

SCHERMERHORN, KENNETH DEWITT, orch. condr.; b. Schenectady, Nov. 20, 1929; s. Willis and Charlotte (Raes) S.; Artists diploma New Eng. Conservatory Music, 1950; Mus.D., Ripon Coll., 1973; m. Carol Neblett, Dec. 1973; 1 son, Stefan Gerrit; children (by previous marriage)—Erica Louise, Veronica Lynn. Music dir. Am. Ballet Theatre, 1956-65, N.J. Symphony, 1962-68, Milw. Symphony, 1968—; asst. condr. N.Y. Philharmonic, 1959-60. Bd. dirs. Nat. Endowment for the Arts. Served with AUS, 1951-55. Office: 929 N Water St Milwaukee WI 53202

SCHERR, LAWRENCE, physician, educator; b. N.Y.C., Nov. 6, 1928; s. Harry and Sophia (Schwartz) S.; A.B., Cornell U., 1950, M.D., 1957; m. Peggy L. Binenkorb, June 13, 1954; children—Cynthia E., Robert W. Intern, Cornell Med. div. Bellevue Hosp. and Meml. Center, 1957-58, asst. resident, 1958-59, research fellow cardiorenal lab., 1959-60, chief resident, 1960-61, co-dir. cardiorenal lab., 1961-62, asst. vis. physician, 1961-63, asso. vis. physician, 1963-65, dir. cardiology and renal unit, 1963-67, asso. dir., 1964-67, vis. physician, 1966-68; physician to out-patients N.Y. Hosp., 1961-63, asst. attending physician, 1963-66, asso. attending physician, 1966-71, attending physician, 1971—; asst. attending physician Meml. Sloan-Kettering Cancer Center, 1962-71, cons., 1971—; cons. St. Francis Hosp., 1973—; dir. dept. medicine North Shore Univ. Hosp., 1967—, dir. acad. affairs, 1969—; asst. in medicine Cornell U. Med. Coll., 1958-59, research fellow N.Y. Heart Assn., 1959-60, instr. medicine, 1960-63, asst. prof., 1963-66, asso. prof., 1966-71, prof., 1971—, asso. dean, 1969—; career scientist Health Research Council, N.Y.C., 1962-66; teaching scholar Am. Heart Assn., 1966-67. Pres. N.Y. State Bd. Medicine, 1974-75; bd. dirs. Nat. Bd. Med. Examiners, 1976—. Served to lt. USNR, 1950-53. Diplomate Am. Bd. Internal Medicine. Fellow A.C.P. (gov. Downstate N.Y. region II), Am. Heart Assn. (fellow council on clin. cardiology), Nassau Acad. Medicine (trustee); mem. Am. Fedn. Clin. Research, Harvey Soc., AMA, N.Y., Nassau County med. socs., Assn. Am. Med. Colls. Contbr. articles to profl. jours. Home: 93 Hendrickson St Haworth NJ 07641 Office: North Shore Univ Hosp Manhasset NY 11030

SCHERSTEN, H. DONALD, mgmt. cons.; b. Titusville, Pa., Nov. 6, 1919; s. H.J. and Clara (Brown) S.; B.S., Temple U., 1941; postgrad. Tulsa U., 1946-48, Columbia U., 1955; m. Katherine Conley; 1 dau. by previous marriage, Sandra S. Hotard. With Creole Petroleum Corp. (affiliate Exxon Corp.), 1948-69, successively dist. field chief accountant Cabimas, Venezuela, coordinator procedures, fin. statements and audits, asst. controller, 1951-62, controller, Caracas, 1962-69; gen. auditor Exxon Corp., N.Y.C., 1969-74, coordinator math., computers, systems, 1975-76; pres. H. Donald Schersten & Assos., Mgmt. Cons., Sarasota, Fla., 1977—. Pres. council Am. Ch. Caracas, 1960. Served to 1st lt. AUS, 1942-45. Mem. Am. Petroleum Inst. (chmn. audit com. 1974-76), Inst. Internal Auditors (cert.), U.S. Power Squadron, USCG Aux. Clubs: Internat. Safari, Toastmasters (past pres. Caracas chpt.); Los Rancheros Deep Sea Fishing. Home: 454 Partridge Circle Bird Key Sarasota FL 33577

SCHETZ, JOSEPH ALFRED, educator; b. Orange, N.J., Oct. 19, 1936; s. Alfred John and Teresa (Zappa) S.; B.S., Webb Inst. Naval Architecture, 1958; M.S., M.A., Ph.D., Princeton; m. Katherine Frances Giorgianni, Jan. 31, 1959; children—Holly, Joseph, Katherine, John. Sr. scientist Gen. Applied Sci. Lab., Westbury, N.Y., 1961-64; asso. prof. aerospace engring. U. Md., 1964-69; prof. aerospace and ocean engring., chmn. dept. Va. Poly. Inst. and State U., 1969—; cons. Applied Physics Lab., Johns Hopkins, 1964—, Atlantic Research Corp., Alexandria, Va., 1966-72; guest prof. Inst. for Theoretical Gas Dynamics, Aachen, Germany, summer 1970. Religious edn. tchr. St. John's Roman Catholic Ch., Colesville, Md., 1965-69; prin. High Sch. Religion, St. Mary's Roman Cath. Ch., Blacksburg, Va., 1970-71. Republican precinct chmn. Montgomery County, Md., 1965-69, mem. Rep. Exec. Com., 1973—; faculty adviser Va. Poly. Inst. Rep. Club, 1973-76. Asso. fellow Am. Inst. Aero. and Astronautics (asso. editor jour. 1975-77, mem. publs. com. 1978—); mem. ASME, Wind Energy Soc. Am., Soc. Naval Architects and Marine Engrs., Sigma Gamma Tau. Contbr. articles in field. Home: 607 Rainbow Ridge Dr Blacksburg VA 24060

SCHEU, EDWARD MAGNUS, JR., business exec.; b. Buffalo, Nov. 8, 1924; s. Edward Magnus and Marguerite (Stone) S.; B.A. in Bus. Adminstrn., Dartmouth, 1949; grad. advanced mgmt. course, U. Pitts., 1954; m. Mary Potter, Dec. 31, 1949; children—Jenny Potter, Edward Grosvenor, Robert Nichols. With sales, purchasing, mfg. and planning depts. Scott Paper Co., 1949-57; asst. to group v.p. Diamond Nat. Corp., 1957-58, pres. Diamond Match div., 1958-60; v.p. devel. Thomas J. Lipton, Inc., 1960-62, v.p., dir., 1962-64; pres., dir. Good Humor Corp., 1962-64; pres. New Eng. Services Co., Stratton Mountain, Vt., 1965—; pres., chief exec. officer Atkins & Merrill, Inc., Lebanon, N.H., 1965-74, chmn. bd., chief exec. officer, 1974-79, also dir.; pres., chief exec. officer, dir. Luminescent Systems Inc.; gen. partner LSI Holdings Ltd., Lebanon; dir. Sage Labs., Inc., Natick, Mass. Clubs: Dartmouth (N.Y.C.) Stratton Mountain Country; Cruising of Am.; Hanover Country. Home: 3 N Balch St Hanover NH 03755 Office: Etna Rd Lebanon NH 03766

SCHEU, WILLIAM EDWARD, savs. and loan assn. exec.; b. Chippawa, Ont., Can., Oct. 18, 1916 (parents Am. citizens); s. Edwin and Harriet (Pearson) S.; student Rochester (N.Y.) Bus. Inst., 1938; grad. Am. Savs. and Loan Inst., 1952, Ind. U. Grad. Sch. Savs. and Loan, 1958; m. Mary-Elizabeth Schroedel, Oct. 26, 1946; 1 dau., Ann Pearson. With First Fed. Savs. and Loan Assn., Rochester, 1940—, v.p., 1958-64, chief mortgage officer, 1962-64, exec. v.p., 1962-64, pres., 1964-77, chief exec. officer, 1968—, chmn. bd., 1977—. Mem. thesis rev. com. Ind. U. Grad. Sch. Savs. and Loan, 1959—, counselor on faculty, 1959; bd. dirs. Fed. Home Loan Bank Bd. of N.Y., 1976—. Mem. finance com. Salvation Army. Served with AUS, 1940-45. Decorated Bronze Star. Mem. U.S. (past pres., dir. Rochester), Monroe County (past. pres., dir.) savs. and loan leagues, Alumni Assn. Ind. U. Grad. Sch. Savs. and Loan (past bd. dirs.), Rochester C. of C. (trustee 1972—), VFW, Am. Legion. Presbyn. (trustee). Clubs: Rotary, Oak Hill Country. Home: 8 Oak Manor Ln Pittsford NY 14534 Office: One First Fed Plaza Rochester NY 14614

SCHEUCH, RICHARD, economist; b. N.Y.C., July 15, 1921; s. William Allen and Marjorie (Tuller) S.; A.B., Princeton U., 1942, M.A., 1948, Ph.D., 1952; m. Fayette Van Alstyne Smith, Sept. 1, 1948; children—Evelyn Scheuch Lord, W. Allen. Asst. in econs., Princeton U., 1946-50; mem. faculty dept. econs. Trinity Coll., Hartford, Conn., 1950—, G. Fox and Co. prof. econs., 1967—; dir. Phoenix Capital Fund, Phoenix Fund. Trustee Wenner-Gren Found., Kingswood-Oxford Sch.; bd. dirs. Symphony Soc. Greater Hartford. Served with USNR, 1942-46. Woodrow Wilson fellow, 1946-47. Mem. Am. Econ. Assn., Indsl. Relations Research Assn., Internat. Indsl. Relations Assn., Soc. Profls. in Disputes Resolution. Unitarian. Clubs: Hartford Golf; Hyannis Port Yacht; Princeton (N.Y.C). Home: 54 Westwood Rd West Hartford CT 06117 Office: Trinity Coll Hartford CT 06106

SCHEUER, JAMES HAAS, congressman; b. N.Y.C., Feb. 6, 1920; s. S(imon) H. and Helen (Rose) S.; A.B., Swarthmore Coll., 1942; LL.B., Columbia, 1948; I.A., Harvard, 1943; m. Emily Malino, Mar. 21, 1948; children—Laura Lee, Elizabeth Helen, James H(aas), John William. Admitted to N.Y. bar, 1949; economist FEA, 1945-46; mem. legal staff OPA, 1951-52; chmn. housing adv. council N.Y. State Commn. Against Discrimination, 1955-64; mem. N.Y. State Task Force Middle Income Housing; cons. Pres. Kennedy and White House Staff on housing and human rights problems, 1960-64; pres. Renewal and Devel. Corp.; lectr. in field, 1950—; mem. 89th-92d congresses from 21st Dist. N.Y., 94th-96th congresses from 11th Dist. N.Y.; also writer, lectr. Del. UN Conf. Housing, Human Rights, City Planning and Urban Renewal in Europe and Far East, 1958, 60, 61, 62, also member Internat. seminars in field; pres. Citizens Housing and Planning Council N.Y.C., 1958-61; exec. bd. Citizens Union N.Y.C., 1950-64; bd. dirs. Nat. Housing Conf., 1958—, pres., 1972-74. Pres. N.Y. chpt. Am. Jewish Com., 1960; chmn. exec. com. Met. council Am. Jewish Congress, 1964. Served with USAAF, 1943-45. Recipient 1st Walter White Meml. award Nat. Com. Against Discrimination in Housing, 1956, 1st Human Relations award Urban League Greater N.Y., 1962. Mem. Bar Assn. City N.Y., Civil Rights Leadership Conf. Democrat. Author numerous articles in field. Home: 3525 Woodley Rd NW Washington DC 20016 Office: 2402 Rayburn House Office Bldg Washington DC 20515

SCHEUER, PAUL JOSEF, educator; b. Heilbronn, Germany, May 25, 1915; s. Albert and Emma (Neu) S.; came to U.S., 1938, naturalized, 1944; B.S., Northeastern U., 1943; M.A., Harvard, 1947, Ph.D., 1950; m. Alice Elizabeth Dash, Sept. 5, 1950; children—Elizabeth E., Deborah A., David A.L., Jonathan L.L. Asst. prof. U. Hawaii, Honolulu, 1950-55, asso. prof., 1955-61, prof. chemistry, 1961—, chmn. dept., 1959-62; vis. prof. U. Copenhagen, 1977; J.F. Toole lectr. U. N.B., 1977. Served with AUS, 1944-46. Mem. Am., Swiss chem. socs., Chem. Soc. (London), AAAS, Sigma Xi, Phi Kappa Phi. Author: Chemistry of Marine Natural Products, 1973. Editor: Marine Natural Products: Chemical and Biological Perspectives, Vol. 1, 2, 1978. Research in molecular structure natural products from marine organisms, terrestrial plants. Home: 3271 Melemele Pl Honolulu HI 96822

SCHEUER, SIDNEY HENRY, internat. trade exec.; b. N.Y.C., July 17, 1893; s. Henry and Sarah (Schiff) S.; m. Linda Ullman, Nov. 18, 1920; children—Robert, Thomas, James. Sr. partner Scheuer & Co., N.Y.C., 1930—; chmn. Textexes Internat., Inc., Scheuer Assos., Inc., Scheuer Cons., Inc., Intertex Internat., Inc.; econ. fin. cons. to industry and social instns.; speaker, discussion leader seminars on internat. relations and East-West trade Johns Hopkins, Columbia, N.Y.U., Am. Mgmt. Assn., 1960, 65-66. Exec. dir. Fgn. Econ. Adminstrn., 1942-45; exec. v.p. U.S. Comml. Corp., R.F.C., 1944-45; mem. U.S. delegation to Inter-Am. Conf. on Problems War and Peace, Mexico City, 1945; founder Nat. Com. For Effective Congress, 1948, chmn., 1955—; chmn. Textile Mission to Occupied Germany, 1947; mem. Econ. Mission to Japan, Korea, 1948; del White House Conf. on Export Expansion, 1963. Bd. govs. Ethical Culture Schs. N.Y. Served to capt. Q.M.C., U.S. Army, World War I. Mem. Ethical Culture Soc. N.Y. (trustee, past pres.), Internat. Humanist and Ethical Union (treas.). Home: Horseshoe Hill Rd Pound Ridge NY 10576 Office: 270 Madison Ave New York NY 10016

SCHEVILL, JAMES ERWIN, poet, playwright; b. Berkeley, Calif., June 10, 1920; s. Rudolph and Margaret (Erwin) S.; B.S., Harvard, 1942; m. Margot Helmuth, Aug. 2, 1966; children (by previous marriage)—Deborah, Susanna. Mem. faculty San Francisco State Coll., 1959—, dir. Poetry Center, 1961-67, prof. English, 1968—; prof. Brown U., 1969—. Served with AUS, 1942-46. Recipient Performance prize Nat. Theatre Competition, 1945; fellow Fund Advancement Edn., 1953-54; 2d prize Phelan Biography Competition, 1954, 2d prize Phelan Drama Competition, 1958; Fromm Found. commn., 1959; Ford Found. grantee, 1960-61; Rockefeller fellow, 1964; Roadstead Found. award, 1966; Gov.'s Award in Arts, R.I., 1975. Author: Tensions (poems), 1947; The American Fantasies (poems), 1951; Sherwood Anderson: His Life and Work (biography), 1951; High Sinners, Low Angels (musical play), 1953; The Right to Greet (poems), 1956; The Roaring Market and the Silent Tomb (biography), 1956; The Bloody Tenet (verse play; commd. Nat. Council Chs. and Central Congl. Ch., Providence 1954), 1957; Selected Poems, 1959; The Cid, 1961; Private Dooms and Public Destinations (poems), 1945-69; Voices of Mass. and Capital A (play for voices; commd. Nat. Council Chs.), 1962; The Stalingrad Elegies, 1964; The Black President and Other Plays, 1965; The Buddhist Car, 1968 Violence and Glory; Poems, 1962-68, 1969; Lovecraft's Follies (play), 1970; Breakout: In Search of New Theatrical Environments, 1973; The Buddhist Car and Other Characters (poems), 1973; Pursuing Elegy: A Poem about Haiti, 1974; (play) Cathedral of Ice, 1975; The Arena of Ants (novel), 1977; The Mayan Poems, 1978. Home: 17 Keene St Providence RI 02906

SCHEVING, LAWRENCE EINAR, scientist, educator; b. Hensel, N.D., Oct. 20, 1920; s. Einar L. and Mary (Brown) S.; B.S. in Biology, DePaul U., 1949, M.S. in Zoology, 1950; Ph.D., Loyola U. Chgo., 1957; m. Virginia M. Krumdick, Aug. 6, 1949; children—Lawrence, Mary, John, Jennifer, Patricia (dec.). Mem. faculty Lewis Coll., Lockport, Ill., 1950-57, successively instr., asst. prof., asso. prof. and head dept. biol. sci., 1950-57; prof. anatomy Chgo. Med. Sch., 1957-67, La. State U. Med. Sch., New Orleans, 1967-70; prof. anatomy U. Ark. Coll. Med., Little Rock, 1970-74, Rebsamen prof. anat. sci., 1974—; mem. breast cancer task force Nat. Cancer Inst. Served to capt. AUS, 1940-45; Col. Res. Decorated Bronze Star medal, Meritorious Service medal; recipient Research award, Chgo. Med. Sch. Bd. Dirs., 1962, Most Helpful Prof. award La. State U., 1968; named Prof. Year, Student Council Chgo. Med. Sch., 1964; recipient Golden Apple award student body U. Ark. Med. Sch., 1972; Alexander von Humboldt Sr. Scientist award German govt., 1973; others. Mem. Am. Assn. Anatomists, Am. Soc. Zoologists, Internat. Soc. Am. Soc. Photobiology, Internat. Soc. Chronobiology (hon. mem., sec.-treas.), So. Assn. Anatomists (past councillor), AAAS, Sigma Xi (chpt. pres. 1964-65). Roman Catholic. Author: Chronobiology. Contbr. numerous chpts. to books, articles in field of chronobiology and other biol. areas to profl. jours. Editorial bd. Internat. Jour. of Chronobiology, Chronobiologia. Home: 1 Redcoat Ln Little Rock AR 72207

SCHEWEL, STANFORD, lawyer; b. Lynchburg, Va., June 1, 1918; s. Abraham M. and Anna R. (Temko) S.; LL.B., Washington and Lee U., 1940. Admitted to Va. bar, 1939, N.Y. bar, 1947; atty. O.P.A., Washington, 1941-42; asso. firm Davis, Polk, Wardwell, Sunderland & Kiendl, N.Y.C., 1940, 46-50, with Neil P. Cullom, 1950-56; practiced in N.Y.C., 1956—. Vice consul, econ. analyst, U.S. Diplomatic Service, financial attaché, U.S. Consulate Gen., Amsterdam, The Netherlands, 1945-46. Cons. Hoover Commn., 1948. Trustee Bar Harbor Music Festival. Served as cpl. AUS, 1941; with OSS, Egypt, Ehtiopia, Palestine, 1942-45. Clubs: Harmonie (gov.), City (N.Y.C.). Author: The Development of Governmental Powers in the United States, 1948. Home: 333 E 34th St New York NY 10016 Office: 500 Fifth Ave New York NY 10036

SCHICK, THOMAS ANDREW, hosp. pub. relations exec.; b. Hamilton, Ohio, Oct. 22, 1940; s. Carl Edwin and Lucille Joan (Wittman) S.; B.A., Loyola U., Chgo., 1963, M.A., 1966; Ph.L., Bellarmine Sch. Theology, North Aurora, Ill., 1965; postgrad. U. Cin., 1967-69; m. Ida JoAnn Critelli, Apr. 6, 1968; children—Michele Maria, Michael Montague. Instr. philosophy St. Mary's Coll., Notre Dame, Ind., 1966-67, Xavier U., Cin., 1967-69; asst. editor St. Anthony Messenger mag., Cin., 1968-70; asso. communications specialist Armco Steel Corp., Middletown, Ohio, 1970-71; mem. pub. relations staff Gen. Motors Corp., Detroit, 1972-73; editor Am. Iron and Steel Inst., Washington, 1973-74, mgr. news and info., 1974-76; dir. pub. relations Glenmary Sisters, Cin., 1976-77; dir. community relations and devel. Mercy Hosp., Hamilton, 1977—. Chmn. bd. trustees Birthright of Cincinnati, 1971-72. Recipient 1st pl. award Ohio Editors contest, 1970. Mem. Pub. Relations Soc. Am., Am. Soc. for Hosp. Pub. Relations, S.W. Ohio Pub. Relations for Health (pres. 1979). Roman Catholic. Club: Rotary. Author: (with Ida J. Critelli) Unmarried and Pregnant: What Now?, 1977. Home: 153 Junefield Ave Cincinnati OH 45218 Office: 116 Dayton St Hamilton OH 45011

SCHICKEL, RICHARD, writer; b. Milw., Feb. 10, 1933; s. Edward J. and Helen (Hendricks) S.; B.S., U. Wis., 1955; m. Julia Whedon, Mar. 11, 1961; children—Erika Tracy, Jessica Avery. Sr. editor Look mag., 1957-60, Show mag., 1960-63; self-employed, 1963—; film critic Life mag., 1965-72; critic Time mag., 1973—. Cons. Rockefeller Bros. Fund, 1964, Rockefeller Found., 1965; lectr. in history art Yale, 1972, 76. Guggenheim fellow, 1964. Mem. Nat. Soc. Film Critics, N.Y. Film Critics. Author: The World of Carnegie Hall, 1960; The Stars, 1962; movies: The History of an Art and an Institution, 1964; The Gentle knight, 1964; The Disney Version, 1968; The World of Goya, 1968; Second Sight: Notes on Some Movies, 1972; His Picture in the Papers, 1974; Harold Lloyd: The Shape of Laughter, 1974; The Men Who Made the Movies, 1975; The World of Tennis, 1975; The Fairbanks Album, 1975; Another I, Another You, 1978; co-author: Lena, 1965; The Platinum Years, 1974. Co-editor: Film 67-68, 1968. Producer, dir., writer TV series The Men Who Made the Movies, 1973; producer-writer TV spl. Life Goes to the Movies, 1976; producer, writer, dir. Funny Business, 1978, Into the Morning: Willa Cather's America, 1978, The Horror Show, 1979. Address: 311 E 83d St New York NY 10028

SCHICKELE, PETER, composer; b. Ames, Iowa, July 17, 1935; s. Rainer W. and Elizabeth (Wilcox) S.; B.A., Swarthmore Coll., 1957; M.S., Julliard Sch. Music, 1960; m. Susan Sindall, Oct. 27, 1962; children—Karla, Matthew. Composer-in-residence Los Angeles High Sch. under Ford Found. grant, 1960-61; faculty Swarthmore Coll., 1961-62, Juilliard Sch. Music, 1961-65, Aspen Festival Music, Colo., 1963; composer scores for films The Crazy Quilt, 1965, Funny Man, 1967, Silent Running, 1972, also several non-theatrical and TV films; arranger for Joan Baez albums Noel, Joan, Baptism; composer mus. score for Film at Tex. pavilion of Hemisfair, San Antonio, 1968; TV appearances include Camera Three, CBS, Profile on the Arts, WNBC-TV, N.Y.C., Bach 'N' Roll, WNDT, 13 Stars for 13, WNDT, Dick Cavett Show, Mike Douglas Show, David Frost Show, ABC Comedy News; comedian; recorded P.D.Q. Bach On The Air, 1968, The Wurst of P.D.Q. Bach, other comedy albums; mem. The Open Window, chamber-rock trio, 1967-71, also composer and lyricist for Oh Calcutta; composer numerous works for orch., chorus, piano, chamber music, band, organ, voice and instruments, 1953—. Recipient Gershwin Meml. award, 1959, Elizabeth Tow Newman Contemporary Music award, 1964. Mem. ASCAP. Author: The Definitive Biography of P.D.Q. Bach. Address: care Vanguard Records 71 W 23d St New York NY 10010*

SCHIEBLER, GEROLD LUDWIG, physician, educator; b. Hamburg, Pa., June 20, 1928; s. Alwin Robert and Charlotte Elizabeth (Schmoele) S.; B.S., Franklin and Marshall Coll., 1950; M.D., Harvard 1954; m. Audrey Jean Lincourt, Jan. 8, 1954; children—Mark, Marcella, Kristen, Bettina, Wanda, Michele. Intern pediatrics and internal medicine Mass. Gen. Hosp., Boston, 1954-55, resident, 1955-56; resident, pediatrics U. Minn. Hosp., Mpls., 1956-57, fellow pediatric cardiology, 1957-58, research fellow, 1958-59; research fellow sect. physiology Mayo Clinic and Mayo Found., 1959-60; asst. prof. pediatric cardiology U. Fla., 1960-63, asso. prof., 1963-66, prof., 1966—, chmn. dept. pediatrics, 1968—. Dir., Div. Children's Med. Services, State of Fla., 1973-74. Mem. Am. Acad. Pediatrics, Fla. Pediatric Soc. (exec. com.), Fla. Heart Assn. (past pres.), AAAS, Soc. Pediatric Research (emeritus), Fla. Med. Assn. (editor jour.), Am. Coll. Cardiology, Phi Beta Kappa, Alpha Omega Alpha. Author: (with L.P. Elliott) The X-ray Diagnosis of Congenital Cardiac Disease in Infants, Children and Adults, 1979; (with L.J. Krovetz and I.H. Gessner) Handbook of Pediatric Cardiology, 2d edit., 1979. Home: 2115 NW 15th Ave Gainesville FL 32605

SCHIEDER, JOSEPH EUGENE, clergyman; b. Buffalo, Sept. 23, 1908; s. Robert and Mary Loretto (Quinn) S.; B.A., Niagara U., 1931; M.A. St. Bonaventure U., 1935; Ph.D., U. Ottawa, Ont., Can., 1943; LL.D., St. Vincent's Coll., 1951; Litt.D. (hon.) Seaton Hall U., 1954; L.H.D. (hon.), LaSalle Coll., 1956. Ordained priest Roman Catholic Ch., 1935; dir. Youth Retreats Diocese of Buffalo, 1939-48; diocesan dir. Confraternity of Christian Doctrine, Buffalo, 1941-48; dir. youth bur. Buffalo Police Dept., 1942-48; nat. dir. Cath. Youth Am., Washington, 1948-61, also dir. youth dept. Nat. Cath. Welfare Conf., Washington; apptd. Papal Chamberlain, 1950, Domestic Prelate, 1953, Prothonatary Apostolic, 1968; pastor St. Andrew's Ch., Buffalo, 1963-76; founder, 1st dir. St. Andrew's Montessori Sch., 1973; mem. Mental Health Bd., 1968—; dean theology Marymount Coll., Arlington, Va., 1961-63; diocesan consultor, 1969—; regional coordinator Diocese of Buffalo, procurator diocesan properties, 1977—; founder Nat. Cath. Youth Week; chmn. Permanent Com.

Pub. Decency, Buffalo, 1941-48; diocesan dir. financial drive Diocese of Buffalo, 1971; mem. White House Conf. Children and Youth, 1950; adviser on Youth Spl. Mission to Germany USAF, 1952, Spl. Mission to Tokyo, Japan for UNESCO, 1953; adviser on youth U.S. Sec. Labor, 1951-60; adviser on fitness of youth to Pres. Eisenhower, 1955-60; chmn. task force founding Stella Niagara Ednl. Parks, Niagara Falls, N.Y.; mem. exec. bd. Cantalician Center, Buffalo; mem. adv. bd. A.R.C., Kenmore Mercy Hosp.; mem. ho. of dels. United Way, 1973—, vice chmn., 1975; bd. dirs. Oral Sch., Ft. Lauderdale, Fla., 1977; vice chmn. Bicentennial Celebration; bd. trustees Erie County Library Assn., 1979—; bd. fin. Diocese of Buffalo, 1979—. Served as adviser to Cath. chief chaplain, USAF, 1953, chief chaplain, AUS, 1954. Founder, past bd. dirs. various Cath. youth assns.; bd. founders St. Andrew's Country Day Sch. Recipient award Christian Bros., 1947, Mayor of Rome, Italy, 1950, Archdiocese of Hartford, Conn., 1954, De la Salle medal Manhattan Coll., 1958, Padre Youth award for U.S., 1961, Star Solidarity from Pres. Italy, 1969; Bishop McNulty Meml. award, 1973; Pres.'s medal St. John's Coll., Washington, 1973; also awards dioceses, Charleston, S.C., Wichita, Kans.; Man of Yr. award Town of Tonawanda, 1977. K.C. (4 deg.). Clubs: University (Washington); Niagara Falls Country; Park Country, Saturn (Buffalo); Tower (Ft. Lauderdale, Fla.). Author: Talks to Parents, 1954; Spiritual Lifts for Youth, 1956. Editor of Youth mag., 1949-61. Address: 72 Somersby Ct Buffalo NY 14221. *Zeal for my position and my vocation, accompanied by hard labor, has contributed much to whatever success I have attained. Love of people and sincerity and the spirit of sacrifice where others are concerned has added to my happiness in life. My faith in God has made difficult undertakings much easier.*

SCHIEFFELIN, WILLIAM JAY, III, business exec.; b. N.Y.C., Feb. 9, 1922; s. William Jay, Jr., and Annette (Markoe) S.; grad. Groton (Mass.) Sch., 1941; B.A., Yale, 1945; m. Joy Williams Proctor, June 19, 1947; children—Hope Williams, Peter Jay, Timothy Proctor, Andrew Lawrence, Michael Markoe. With Schieffelin & Co., N.Y.C., 1948—, v.p. charge pharm. labs. div., 1949-62, chmn., chief exec. officer, 1962—; chmn. Almay, Inc., N.Y.C.; dir. Baccarat, Inc., N.Y.C., Centennial Ins. Co.; trustee East River Savings Bank, Atlantic Mut. Ins. Co. Bd. dirs. Drug. Chem. and Allied Trades Assn., 1955—, pres., 1961-62; bd. dirs. Econ. Devel. Council N.Y., 1974—; mem. exec. com. Nat. Assn. Alcoholic Beverage Importers, Inc.; adv. bd. La Maison Francaise; adv. com. European Inst. Bus. Adminstrn.; past dir. N.Y. Bd. Trade, 1955-63. Trustee Tuskegee Inst. Served to capt., 612th F.A. Bn. (Pack), AUS, 1942-46; CBI. Decorated chevalier Ordre National du Mérite (France); knight Order of Merit of Republic of Italy. Mem. Am. Pharm. Assn. (life), Am.-Italy Soc. (dir.), Hundred Year Assn. N.Y. (past pres.), N.Y. Offshore Power Boat Racing Assn. (hon. life), N.Y. Importers and Distillers Assn. (mem. importers adv. com. 1974—), Commerce and Industry Assn. N.Y. (past chmn.), N.Y. Chamber Commerce and Industry (exec. com.), French C. of C. of U.S. (exec. v.p.), Brit.-Am. C. of C. (dir. 1971—), Commanderie de Bordeaux (comdr. 1966), Pilgrims U.S., Beta Theta Pi (past pres. Phi Chi chpt.), Clubs: New York Yacht, Yale, Union (N.Y.C.). Office: 30 Cooper Sq New York NY 10003

SCHIEFFER, BOB, broadcast journalist; b. Austin, Tex.; B.A. in Journalism, Tex. Christian U.; m. Patricia Penrose; children—Susan, Sharon. Reporter, Ft. Worth Star-Telegram; news anchorman Sta. WBAP-TV, Dallas-Ft. Worth; with CBS News, 1969—, Pentagon corr., 1970-74, anchorman CBS Sunday Night News, 1973-74, White House corr., 1974-79, anchorman Sunday edit. CBS Evening News, 1976, then Saturday edit., anchorman Monday-through-Friday edits. Morning, 1979—, also participant CBS news spls. and spl. reports, including Peace and the Pentagon, 1974, Watergate-The White House Transcripts, 1974, The Mysterious Alert, 1974, 1976 Democratic Nat. Conv., 1976 Republican Nat. Conv., Campaign '72, and mem. Emmy award-winning team CBS Evening News with Walter Cronkite, 1971. Recipient various awards Sigma Delta Chi, Tex. Associated Broadcasters, AP Mng. Editors. Office: care CBS News 51 W 52d St New York NY 10019*

SCHIELE, GEORGE WARREN, pub.; b. Phila., Aug. 2, 1931; s. Paul Ellsworth and Emma Adele (Gilliam) S.; student Carson Long Inst., 1949; B.S., U. Pa., 1954; m. Joan Ann Burga de Cisneros, Nov. 18, 1961; children—Caroline A.A., Warren S.C., Erick P.G. Dir. public relations Triangle Stas., Phila., 1956-57; advt. mgr. Magness Corp., Wilmington, Del., 1958-59; nat. sales mgr. Broadcast Advertisers Reports, N.Y.C., 1959-61; pres. Broadcast Billing Corp., N.Y.C., 1961-63; gen. mgr. Mailbag Internat., Inc., Stamford, Conn., 1963-64, pres., 1965—, dir., 1967—: pres. George Warren Schiele Advt., 1976—, MII Sers., Inc., 1974—; pub. Young Once mag., Stamford; chmn. 13/21 Corp., Stamford, 1976—; past dir. R.H. Carlson Inc., Greenwich, Conn., NSM Inc., Chgo. lectr. N.Y. U., City Coll. N.Y., Am. Mgmt. Assn., Am. Mktg. Assn. Bd. dirs. Greenwich Transit Dist., 1975—, Community Concert Assn., 1977-79. Served with USAF, 1954-56. Clubs: Pinnacle, City (N.Y.C.). Contbr. articles to Harvard Bus. Rev., N.Y. Times profl. jours. Home: 19 Hill Rd Greenwich CT 06830 Office: 2777 Summer St Stamford CT 06905

SCHIER, DONALD STEPHEN, educator; b. Ft. Madison, Iowa, Sept. 10, 1914; s. Francis and Marcella (Kenny) S.; B.A., State U. Iowa, 1936, M.A., Columbia, 1937, Ph.D., 1941. Mem. faculty State Tchrs. Coll., Bemidji, Minn., 1939-41, 41-42, Ill. Inst. Tech., 1946; mem. faculty Carleton Coll., Northfield, Minn., 1946—, prof. French, 1953—; vis. prof. U. Wis., 1964-65. Mem. selection com. Young Scholar Program, Nat. Found. Arts and Humanities, 1966-67. Served to capt. AUS, 1942-46. Mem. Modern Lang. Assn., Am. Assn. Tchrs. French, AAUP, Midwest Modern Lang. Assn. Author: Louis-Bertrand Castel, 1942. Editor: (with Scott Elledge) The Continental Model, 1960, 2d edit., 1970; (Bertrand de Fontenelle) Nouveaux Dialogues des morts, 1965, rev. edit., 1974; translator: Letter on Italian Music (Charles de Brosses), 1978. Home: 717 E 2d St Northfield MN 55057

SCHIER, ERNEST LEONARD, journalist; b. N.Y.C.; student public schs., N.Y.C. Asst. film and drama critic Washington Post, 1941-43; columnist, drama critic Washington Times Herald, 1946-54; asso. dir. Arena Stage Press, Washington, 1954-55; theater and film critic, columnist Phila. Bull., 1958—; dir. Nat. Critics Inst., O'Neill Theater Center. Mem. Am. Theatre Critics Assn. (co-founder, first chmn., mem. exec. bd.). Home: 2601 Parkway Philadelphia PA 19130 Office: Phila Bull 30th and Market Sts Philadelphia PA 19101

SCHIER, RICHARD FRANCIS, educator; b. Ft. Madison, Iowa, Mar. 23, 1922; s. Frank Stephen and Marcella Eleanor (Kenny) S.; A.B., U. Iowa, 1946, M.A., 1947; Ph.D., U. Calif. at Los Angeles, 1951. Instr. dept. polit. sci. U. Akron, 1947-48; edn. adviser U.S. Dept. Def., Germany and Eng., 1951-53; asst. prof. Franklin and Marshall Coll., 1953-56, asso. prof., 1957-64, prof., 1964—, chmn. dept. govt., 1969-72. Pa. polit. analyst ABC-TV, 1966—; dep. supt. pub. instrn. Commonwealth of Pa., 1960-61; chief of staff task force on higher edn. Gov.'s Com. on Edn., 1960-61; legislative asst. to Senator Joseph S. Clark, 1965. Chmn. Commonwealth Compensation Commn., 1971-72. Served with F.A., AUS, 1943-46. Mem. Am., Pa. (pres. 1962-63) polit. sci. assns., AAUP (mem. com. on coll. and univ. govt. 1969-72). Author: (with Sidney Wise) The Presidential Office, 1968, Studies on Congress, 1969. Asso. nat. affairs editor USA-Today, 1974—. Home: 2326 Middlegreen Ct Lancaster PA 17601

SCHIERHOLZ, WILLIAM FRANCIS, JR., chem. co. exec.; b. St. Louis, Oct. 14, 1921; s. William Francis and Florence Cecelia (Wuensch) S.; B.S. in Engring. Adminstrn., Washington U., St. Louis, 1943; m. Joan Flavin, Sept. 7, 1947; children—Margaret Ann, John W., William Francis, III. Vice pres., gen. mgr. Fuel Oil of St. Louis, 1949-55; pres. Chemtech Industries, Inc., St. Louis, 1956—, Affiliated Chem. Group, Ltd., Bermuda; dir. St. Louis Fed. Savs. & Loan Assn. Chmn., Mo. State Com. Reponsible Consumerism, 1977-78; mem. adv. bd. INROADS, also chmn.; bd. dirs. Jr. Achievement of Miss. Valley. Served to capt. USAAF, 1943-46. Mem. U.S., Mo. (dir., exec. com.) chambers commerce, St. Louis Regional Commerce and Growth Assn. (dir., exec. com.) Am. Assn. Indsl. Mgmt. (pres. 1976, dir.), Mfg. Chemists Assn., NAM, Presidents Assn, Chem. Industry Council Greater St. Louis (pres. 1970), Backstoppers, Affiliated Chem. Group (pres. 1966), Beta Theta Pi (pres. alumni assn. 1967). Clubs: Stadium, Univ., Mo. Athletic, Rotary (v.p. chpt. 1972—), Forest Hills Country (St. Louis). Home: 1151 Westmoor Pl Saint Louis MO 63131 Office: 9909 Clayton Rd Saint Louis MO 63124

SCHIERING, HARRY CALVIN, banker; b. Danville, Ill., Aug. 5, 1924; s. Harry C. and Esther (Betscher) S.; student Fenn Coll., 1942-43; B.B.S., Miami U., Oxford, Ohio, 1948; grad. Stonier Sch. Banking, 1967; m. Geraldine J. Oldham, Mar. 4, 1950; 1 dau., Sally L. Asst. bank examiner Fed. Res. Bank Cleve., 1948-51; asst. auditor Nat. City Bank, Cleve., 1951-54; asst. cashier Broward Nat. Bank, Ft. Lauderdale, Fla., 1954-62; gen. auditor Fed. Res. Bank Atlanta, 1963—; chmn. steering com. Conf. of Gen. Auditors, FRS, 1970-71, 77. Served to sgt., 3d Inf., AUS, 1943-45. Decorated Purple Heart, Bronze Star medal. Mem. Bank Adminstrn. Inst. (pres. Atlanta chpt. 1971-72), Inst. Internal Auditors (certified), Sigma Alpha Epsilon. Christian Scientist (exec. bd. 1968-71, First Reader 1971-74). Home: 609 Pinetree Dr Decatur GA 30030 Office: 104 Marietta St NW Atlanta GA 30303

SCHIERL, PAUL JULIUS, paper co. exec., lawyer; b. Neenah, Wis., Mar. 28, 1935; s. Julius Michael and Erna (Landig) S.; B.S. in Polit. Sci., U. Notre Dame, 1957, LL.B., 1961; m. Rosemary Clare Harte, Nov. 24, 1960; children—Michael, Kathryn, Susan, David, Daniel. Mem. firm Wickham, Borgelt, Skogstad & Powell, attys., Milw., 1961-64; with Fort Howard Paper Co., Green Bay, Wis., 1964—, sec., gen. counsel, 1967-74, pres., chief exec. officer, 1974—; dir. Marine Corp. Pres. Fort Howard Paper Found. Inc., also dir. Served with AUS. Mem. Am. Bar Assn., State Bar Wis. Clubs: Union League of Chicago, University of Chicago. Home: 144 Gwynn St Green Bay WI 54301 Office: PO Box 130 Green Bay WI 54305

SCHIESSLER, ROBERT WALTER, corp. exec.; b. Honesdale, Pa., Oct. 2, 1918; s. Walter A. and Josephine (Herzog) S.; B.S., Pa. State U., 1939, Ph.D., 1944; M.S., McGill U., 1941; m. Betty Hartman, June 5, 1939; children—Lynn Alice, Dale Ann; m. 2d, Florence Cutler, Aug. 16, 1968. Research chemist Gen. Electric Co., Schenectady, 1941; from instr. to asso. Prof. chemistry and dir. Am. Petroleum Inst. Research Pa. State U., 1942-55; chemistry and physics cons., 1946-55; tech. dir. Central Research div. Mobil Oil Co., Paulsboro and Princeton, N.J., 1950-60, mgr. central research div., asst. gen. mgr. research dept., 1960-62, gen. mgr. research dept., 1962-67, v.p. research Mobil Research & Devel. Corp., 1967-68; chmn., pres. Indsl. Reactor Labs., Inc., 1966-67; mgr. long-range planning Mobil Oil Corp., 1968-72, gen. mgr. real estate and land devel., 1972—; chmn. Mobil Land Devel. Corp., 1972—; dir. Mei Foo Investments Ltd., Hong Kong. Chmn. bd. trustees Gordon Research Conf., Inc., 1957; mem. bd. Am. Chem. Soc. Petroleum Research Fund, 1955-59, 60-63. Research chemist Canadian govt., 1940-41. Recipient award in petroleum chemistry Am. Chem. Soc., 1953; named outstanding young man State Coll. of Pa., Jr. C. of C., 1952; recipient Wisdom award, 1970. Fellow Am. Inst. Chemists, AAAS (v.p. for chemistry, chmn. chemistry sect. 1960); mem. Am. Chem. Soc., Urban Land Inst., AAUP, Sigma Xi, Phi Lambda Upsilon, Phi Eta Sigma. Co-Author: Chemistry of Petroleum Hydrocarbons, 1954. Discoverer method for prodn. super-explosive used by U.S. and Can., World War II. Home: 1500 Palisade Ave Fort Lee NJ 07024 Office: 150 E 42d St New York NY 10017

SCHIEVE, GEORGE ROBERT, state ofcl.; b. Dollar Bay, Mich., Jan. 14, 1920; s. Ferdinand A. and Margaret T. (Greenslade) S.; B.A., Mich. State U., 1942; M.P.A., U. Mich., 1961; postgrad. Cornell U., 1960; m. Dorothy Wilson, Apr. 14, 1945; children—J. Ronald, Mary M. (Mrs. Steven Wilber), E. Jane (Mrs. Gerald Provencal). Asst. bus. exec. Ypsilanti (Mich.) State Hosp., 1946-55, adminstrv. officer, 1955-65; adminstrv. officer Plymouth State Home and Tng. Sch., Northville, Mich., 1965-72; dir. finance Ariz. Dept. Mental Retardation, 1972-73, dir. dept., 1973; supt. Muscatatuck State Hosp. and Tng. Center, Butlerville, Ind., 1973-75; dep. commr. adminstrn. Ind. Dept. Mental Health, Indpls., 1975—. Served to capt. AUS, 1943-46; ETO. Charter fellow Am. Assn. Mental Health Adminstrs.; mem. Am. Soc. Mental Health Adminstrs., Am. Assn. Mental Deficiency, Nat. Assn. Supts. Pub. Residential Facilities. Club: Prestwick Country. Home: 496 Cobblestone Pl Plainfield IN 46168 Office: 5 Indiana Sq Indianapolis IN 46204

SCHIFF, HAROLD IRVIN, chemist, educator; b. Kitchener, Ont., Can., June 24, 1923; s. Jacob and Lena (Bierstock) S.; B.A., U. Toronto, 1945, M.A., 1946, Ph.D., 1948; m. Daphne Line, Dec. 30, 1948; children—Jack Michael, Sherry Lyn. Postdoctoral fellow NRC, Ottawa, Ont., Can., 1948-50; asst. prof. chemistry McGill U., Montreal, Que., Can., 1950-54, asso. prof., 1954-60, prof., 1960-64, dir. Upper Atmosphere Chemistry Group, 1955-64; prof. chemistry York U., Downsview, Ont., Can., 1964—, dept. chmn., 1965-67, dean sci. faculty, 1965-73; dir. Scintrex, Ltd.; chmn. U.S. Nat. Acad. Scis. Panel on Stratospheric Transport and Chemistry, 1978—; mem. adv. com. to Can. govt. on stratospheric pollution, 1972—; mem. adv. com. FAA High Altitude Pollution Program; mem. Internat. Ozone Commn. Recipient Best Paper award U.S. Dept. Commerce, 1968; grantee NRC (Can.), NASA, FAA. Fellow Royal Soc. Can., Chem. Inst. Can.; mem. Am. Geophys. Union. Author: The Ozone War, 1978; editor: Aeronomy of the Stratosphere and Mesosphere, 1974; contbr. chpts. to Physics and Chemistry of Upper Atmospheres, 1972, Atmospheres of Earth and Planets, 1974. Patentee in field. Home: 60 Donwoods Dr Toronto ON M4N 2G5 Canada Office: York U Downsview ON M3J 1P3 Canada

SCHIFF, HERBERT HAROLD, shoe co. exec.; b. Columbus, Ohio, Oct. 6, 1916; s. Robert W. and Rebecca (Lurie) S.; grad. Peddie Sch., 1934; B.B.S., U. Pa., 1938; m. Betty Topkis, June 19, 1938; children—Suzanne (Mrs. Murray Gallant), Patricia (Mrs. Richard Hershorin), Jane Ann (Mrs. Douglas J. Fleckner). With SCOA Industries Inc. (formerly Shoe Corp. Am.), Columbus, 1938—, salesman, 1938, asst. mgr., 1939-41, mgr., 1941-45, asst. merchandise mgr., 1945-46, v.p.-merchandise mgr., 1946-60, v.p. charge coordination, 1960-62, exec. v.p., 1962-65, pres., 1965-68, chmn. bd., chief exec. officer, 1968; dir. Ohio Nat. Bank, Columbus. Bd. dirs., vice chmn., mem. exec. com. Am. Retail Fedn.; bd. dirs. Ohio Retail Mchts., Jewish Center, Heritage House, Hillel of Ohio State U., United HIAS, Council Jewish Fedns. and Welfare Funds, Inc.; mem. adv. council Grad. Sch. Adminstrn., Capital U.; trustee, past pres. United Jewish Fund and Council; trustee United Israel Appeal, United Jewish Appeal, Peddie Sch.; fellow, mem. exec. com. Brandeis U.; exec. com., adminstrv. com., resources devel. com., bd. dirs. Am. Jewish Joint Distbn. Com.; nat. exec. bd. Am. Jewish Com. Recipient 28th ann. award T. Kenyon Holly/Two-Ten Assn., 1976, Spirit of Life award City of Hope, 1977, Milton Weill Human Relations award Am. Jewish Com., 1979, Patriots award U.S. Savs. Bonds Campaign, 1979, Israel Prime Minister's medal, 1979. Mem. Vol. Footwear Retailers Assn. (active hon. dir.), Nat. Footwear Mfg. Assn. (past dir.), Am. Footwear Industries Assn. (past dir.), Nat. Council Fgn. Policy Assn., Pres.'s Assn., Newcomen Soc. N.Am. Jewish religion. Mem. B'nai B'rith. Clubs: Winding Hollow Country, President's of Ohio State U., Ohio State U. Faculty, Athletic (Columbus); Standard (Chgo.); Long Boat Key Golf, University (Sarasota, Fla.). Home: 1620 E Broad St Columbus OH 43203 Office: 155 E Broad St Columbus OH 43215

SCHIFF, JEROME ARNOLD, biologist, educator; b. Bklyn., Feb. 20, 1931; s. Charles K. and Molly (Weinberg) S.; B.A. in Biology and Chemistry, Bklyn. Coll., 1952; Ph.D. in Botany and Biochemistry, U. Pa., 1956. Predoctoral fellow USPHS, 1954-56; fellow Brookhaven Nat. Labs., summer 1956; research asso. biology Brandeis U., Waltham, Mass., 1956-57, mem. faculty, 1957—, prof. biology, 1966—, chmn. dept., 1972-75, Abraham and Etta Goodman chair biology, 1974—, dir. Inst. for Photobiology of Cells and Organelles, 1975—; summer instr. Exptl. Marine Botany, Woods Hole, Mass., 1971, sr. investigator, 1972-74, dir. programs, 1974—. Cons. NSF, 1965-68; vis. prof. Tel Aviv U., 1972, Hebrew U., 1972, Weizmann Inst., Israel, 1977. Mem. biology grant rev. program U.S.-Israel Binat. Sci. Found., 1974. Carnegie Found. fellow Stanford, 1962-63. Recipient Distinguished Alumni award Bklyn. Coll., 1972. Fellow Am. Acad. Arts and Scis., A.A.A.s.; mem. Soc. Developmental Biology (sec. 1964-66, exec. com.), Am. Soc. Biol. Chemists, Am. Soc. Plant Physiologists (exec. com. 1972—), Biophys. Soc., Canadian Soc. Plant Physiologists, Internat. Phycological Soc., Phycological Soc. Am., Soc. Cell Biology, Soc. Gen. Microbiology, Soc. Protozoologists, Am. Soc. for Microbiology, Internat. Soc. of Developmental Biologists, Brit. Phycological Soc., Am. Soc. Photobiology, Bot. Soc. Am., Sigma Xi. Editorial bd. Developmental Biology, 1971-74; editorial bd. Plant Sci. Letters, 1972-78, asso. editor, 1978—; asst. editor Ann. Revs. Plant Physiology, 1964-69, adv. editor, 1969—; mem. editorial com. Ann. Rev. Plant Physiology, 1974—. Research in metabolism of protista, sulfate reduction by plants and microorganisms, pathway of biosynthesis of chlorophylls, carotenoids and anthocyanins, chloroplast devel., replication and function particularly in Euglena. Home: 37 Harland Rd Waltham MA 02154 Office: Inst for Photobiology of Cells and Organelles Brandeis Univ Waltham MA 02154

SCHIFF, SAUL BEN, shoe co. exec.; b. Massaque, Lithuania, Apr. 15, 1898; s. Efraim and Sara (Touff) S.; B.A., U. Cin., 1921; m. Mollie Shapiro, Nov. 6, 1927; children—Barbara Joy (Mrs. Richard Passloff), Carole Ann (Mrs. James A. Straus), Simone Janet (Mrs. Roger W. Englander). Officer, dir. Shoe Corp. Am., Columbus, Ohio, 1940-62; pres., dir. A.S. Beck Shoe Corp., N.Y.C., 1947-68; dir. Allied Foods, Inc. Chmn. shoe retail div. Greater N.Y. Fund, 1958, 64, 65; chmn. shoe industry campaign United Jewish Appeal, 1950-53; chmn. shoe div. Nat. Fund for Med. Edn., 1961-62. Trustee Jewish Home and Hosp. for Aged, 1951-72; co-founder Albert Einstein Coll. Medicine; sponsor Herbert H. Lehman Inst. Ethics; bd. dirs. Am. Friends Hebrew Inst. Recipient Louis Marshall award Jewish Theol. Sem. Am., 1960. Mem. Soc. Hon. Alumni Hebrew U. Jerusalem, Navy League U.S. Clubs: Economic (N.Y.C.); Winding Hollow (Columbus, Ohio). Home: 60 Park Rd Scarsdale NY 10583

SCHIFFER, JOHN PAUL, physicist; b. Budapest, Hungary, Nov. 22, 1930; s. Ernest and Elisabeth (Tornai) S.; came to U.S., 1947, naturalized, 1953; A.B., Oberlin Coll., 1951; M.S., Yale, 1952, Ph.D., 1954; m. Marianne Tsuk, June 28, 1960; children—Celia Anne, Peter Ernest. Research asso. Rice Inst., Houston, 1954-56; asst. physicist Argonne (Ill.) Nat. Lab., 1956-59, asso. physicist, 1960-63, sr. physicist, 1964—, asso. dir. physics div., 1964-79, dir. physics div., 1979—; prof. physics U. Chgo., 1968—; vis. asso. prof. Princeton, 1964; vis. prof. U. Rochester (N.Y.), 1967-68; mem. adv. coms. nuclear physics Nat. Acad. Scis. Recipient Alexander V. Humboldt Found. sr. U.S. scientist award, 1973-74; Guggenheim fellow, 1959-60. Fellow Am. Phys. Soc. (chmn. div. nuclear physics 1975-76, Tom W. Bonner prize 1976). Editor: Comments on Nuclear and Particle Physics, 1971-75; asso. editor Revs. Modern Physics, 1972-77; editor Physics Letters, 1978—. Contbr. articles on nuclear structure physics and nuclear reactions to phys. jours. and books. Office: Physics Division Argonne Nat Lab Argonne IL 60439

SCHIFFRIN, ANDRE, publisher; b. Paris, France, June 12, 1935; s. Jacques and Simone (Heymann) S.; came to U.S., 1941; B.A. summa cum laude, Yale, 1957; M.A. with 1st class honours, Cambridge (Eng.) U., 1959; m. Maria Elena de la Iglesia, June 14, 1961; children—Anya, Natalia. With New American Library, 1959-63; with Pantheon Books, Inc., N.Y.C., 1962—, editor, editor-in-chief, mng. dir., 1969—; vis. fellow Davenport Coll., 1977-79; vis. lectr. Yale U., 1977, 79. Mem. council Smithsonian Instn., 1969—; mem. N.Y. Council for Humanities, 1978—; bd. dirs. N.Y. Civil Liberties Union; mem. Freedom To Pub. Com. Mellon fellow Clare Coll., 1957, hon. scholar, 1959; Fulbright travel grantee, 1958-59. Mem. Assn. Am. Pubs. Contbr. articles to profl. jours., N.Y. Times Book Review, Nation, New Republic; editorial bd. Civil Liberties Review. Home: 250 W 94th St New York NY 10025 Office: 201 E 50th St New York NY 10022

SCHIFMAN, BEN BYLAH, former newspaper editor; b. Kansas City, Mo., Apr. 20, 1913; s. Aron and Celia (Sambursky) S.; student Am. Inst. Banking, 1935-36; m. Mary Lapin, June 5, 1937; children—Stanley, Elinor (Mrs. Paul N. Gershon), William. Copy editor, fin. writer U.P., 1930-34; mem. staff Kansas City (Mo.) Star, 1934-79, asst. treas., 1961-66, treas., 1966-79, fin. editor, 1955-78; pension trustee investment mgr. Kansas City Star Co., 1961-79, dir., 1967-79, also fin. v.p.; dir. GMK Assos., Inc., Topsy's Internat., Inc. Area dir. Boy Scouts Am., 1950—; bd. dirs. Jr. Achievement Greater Kansas City, 1959-65. Recipient Loeb award U. Conn., 1962. Mem. Soc. Am. Bus. Writers (pres. 1966-67), Kansas City Press Soc., Kansas City Soc. Fin. Analysts, Sigma Delta Chi. Jewish (trustee congregation). Home: 2108 W 70th St Mission Hills KS 66208 Office: 1729 Grand Ave Kansas City MO 64108

SCHIFRIN, LALO BORIS, composer; b. Buenos Aires, Argentina, June 21, 1932; student Juan Carlos Paz and Olivier Messiaen. Argentinian rep. Internat. Jazz Festival, Paris, 1955; formed own jazz group; composer for stage, modern dance, TV; arranger for Xavier Cugat; with Dizzy Gillespie's band, 1962; film and TV composer, Hollywood, Calif., 1964—; compositions: (for ballet) Jazz Faust, 1963; (for orch.) Suite for Trumpet and Brass Orchestra, Tunisian Fantasy; (jazz) Gillespiana, Jazz Suite on Mass Texts, Dionysos; theme for TV series Mission: Impossible; film scores include: The Cincinnati Kid, 1965, Cool Hand Luke, 1967, The Fox, 1968, Magnum Force, 1973, The Four Musketeers, 1975, The Eagle Has Landed, 1977, Voyage of the Damned, 1976, Rollercoaster, 1977, Day of the Animals, 1977, Special Delivery, 1977, Telefon, 1977, The

Cat From Outer Space, 1978, The Manitou, 1978, Nunzio, 1978, Return From Witch Mountain, 1978, Boulevard Nights, 1979; score for TV movie Brenda Starr, 1976, for dramatic spl. Foster and Laurie, 1975, TV movie Starsky and Hutch (also TV series). Winner Grammy award (2) for Mission: Impossible. Office: care Acad Motion Picture Arts and Scis 8949 Wilshire Blvd Beverly Hills CA 90211

SCHILD, ALBERT, educator, mathematician; b. Hessdorf, Germany, Mar. 3, 1920; s. Josef and Sara (Wolf) S.; B.A., U. Toronto, 1946, M.A., U. Pa., 1948, Ph.D., 1950; m. Clara Shekter, Dec. 29, 1946; children—Hannah, Ruth, Rebecca, Chava, Judith, Brocha, Naomi Batsheva. Came to U.S. 1946, naturalized, 1959. Asst. instr. math. dept. U. Pa., 1946-50; from instr. to asso. prof. math. Temple U., 1950-62, prof., 1962—, chmn. dept., 1963-79. Lectr., NSF: cons.; exec. v.p. Talmudical Yeshiva, Phila. Mem. Am. Math. Soc., Math. Assn. Am., Soc. for Indsl. and Applied Math., Nat. Council Tchrs. Math. Home: 4940 N 9th St Philadelphia PA 19141

SCHILDKRAUT, JOSEPH JACOB, psychiatrist; b. Bklyn., Jan. 21, 1934; s. Simon and Shirley (Schwartz) S.; A.B. summa cum laude, Harvard U., 1955, M.D. cum laude, 1959; m. Elizabeth Rose Beilenson, May 22, 1966; children—Peter Jeremy, Michael John. Intern medicine U. Calif. Hosp., San Francisco, 1959-60; resident in psychiatry Mass. Mental Health Center, Boston, 1960-63; dir. neuropsychopharmacology lab., sr. psychiatrist, 1967—; research psychiatrist NIMH, Bethesda, Md., 1963-67, cons., 1967-68; asst. prof. psychiatry Harvard Med. Sch., Boston, 1967-70, asso. prof., 1970-74, prof., 1974—. Served as surgeon USPHS, 1963-65. Recipient Anna-Monika Found. prize, 1967, Hofheimer award Am. Psychiat. Assn., 1971, hon. mention award, 1968; McCurdy-Rinkel prize No. New Eng. Dist. br. Am. Psychiat. Assn., 1969; William C. Menninger award A.C.P., 1978. Mem. World Psychiat. Assn. (sec. sect. biol. psychiatry 1972-77), Psychiat. Research Soc., Am. Coll. Neuropsychopharmacology, Am. Psychiat. Assn., Am. Psychosomatic Soc., AAAS, Soc. Biol. Psychiatry, N.Y. Acad. Scis., Am. Psychopath. Assn., Am. Coll. Psychiatrists, Am. Soc. Pharmacology and Exptl. Therapeutics, Am. Soc. Neurochemistry, Group Without a Name, Assn. for Research in Nervous and Mental Disease, Collegium Internationale Neuropsychopharmacolgicum, Phi Beta Kappa. Author: Neuropsychopharmacology and the Affective Disorders, 1970. Mem. editorial bd. Psychophysiology, 1968-74, Jour. Psychiat. Research, 1968—, Psychopharmacology, 1970—, Sleep Reviews, 1972—, Communications in Psychopharmacology Communications, 1974—, Psychotherapy and Psychosomatics, 1974—, Research Communications in Psychology, Psychiatry and Behavior, 1976—. Contbr. articles to profl. jours. Home: 35 Jefferson Rd Chestnut Hill MA 02167 Office: Massachusetts Mental Health Center 74 Fenwood Rd Boston MA 02115

SCHILLER, ALFRED GEORGE, veterinarian, educator; b. Irma, Wis., Dec. 5, 1918; s. Adam and Bertha Schiller; D.V.M., Mich. State U., 1943; M.S., U. Ill., Urbana, 1957; m. Carolyn Schiller, Apr. 14, 1944; children—James, Charles. Practice vet. medicine specializing in small animals, Mpls., 1947-52; mem. faculty Coll. Vet. Medicine, U. Ill., 1952—, also acting head dept. vet. clin. medicine, 1976-78, acting asso. dean coll., 1978-79, acting dir. Lab. Animal Care, 1979—. Served with Vet. Corps, AUS, 1944-47. Recipient Service awards Ill. Alumni, 1971, Ill. State Vet., 1972, Disting. Alumni award Coll. Vet. Medicine, Mich. State U., 1978. Mem. Am. Animal Hosp. Assn., Am., Ill. State vet. med. assns., Am. Coll. Vet. Surgeons (pres. 1972, chmn. bd. regents 1973, exec. sec. 1975—), Sigma Xi, Alpha Psi, Phi Zeta. Home: 405 Park Ln Champaign IL 61820 Office: Small Animal Clinic U Ill Urbana IL 61801

SCHILLER, EVERETT LYLE, educator, parasitologist; b. Marshfield, Wis., Aug. 31, 1917; s. Gustave H. and Ethel (Stringham) S.; B.S., U. Wis., 1949, M.S., 1950; Sc.D. in Parasitology, 1958; m. Ive Lorraine Williams, Oct. 13, 1945; 1 dau., Pamela Lee. Asst. parasitologist U. Wis., 1949-50; parasitologist Arctic Health Research Center, USPHS, Alaska, 1950-55; instr. zoology Anchorage Community Coll., 1955; supr., instr. diagnostic parasitology lab. Johns Hopkins Hosp., 1956-61; mem. faculty Johns Hopkins Sch. Hygiene and Pub. Health, 1957—, prof. pathobiology, 1965—. Mem. ad hoc study group parasitic diseases U.S. Army Med. Research and Devel. Adv. Panel, 1973—; mem. expert adv. panel on parasitic diseases WHO, 1975—. Bd. dirs. Gorgas Meml. Inst. Tropical and Preventive Medicine, 1972—; trustee Balt. Zool. Soc., 1972—. Served to 2d lt. USAAF, 1941-46. Recipient J.N. Chowdhuri award Calcutta (India) Sch. Tropical Medicine, 1969. Mem. Am. Soc. Parasitologists (Henry Baldwin Ward award 1964, chmn. nominating com. 1966, chmn. awards com. 1966, chmn. com. spl. awards 1972-73), Helminthological Soc. Washington (sec. 1963-64), Soc. Hygiene (pres. Johns Hopkins U. 1967-68). Asst. editor jour. Parasitology, 1961-62; asso. editor Am. jour. Epidemiology, 1964—; mem. editorial com. parasitological revs. Exptl. Parasitology, 1965—; bd. reviewers Transactions Am. Micros. Soc., 1968; mem. editorial bd. Proc. of Helminthological Soc. Washington, 1976—. Home: 517 Charles Ave Towson MD 21204 Office: 615 N Wolfe St Baltimore MD 21205

SCHILLER, HERBERT I., educator, social scientist; b. N.Y.C., Nov. 5, 1919; s. Benjamin Franklin and Gertrude (Perner) S.; B.S.S., Coll. City N.Y., 1940; M.A., Columbia, 1941; Ph.D., N.Y. U., 1960; m. Anita Rosenbaum, Nov. 5, 1946; children—Daniel T., P. Zachary. Teaching fellow Coll. City N.Y., 1940-41, lectr. econs., 1949-59; economist U.S. Govt., 1941-42, 46-48; mem. faculty Pratt Inst., Bklyn., 1950-63, prof. econs., chmn. dept. social studies, 1962-63; research asso. prof. Bur. Econ. and Bus. Research, U. Ill. at Urbana, 1963-65, research prof., 1965-70; prof. communications U. Calif. at San Diego, 1970—; lectr. Bklyn. Acad. Music, 1961-66; vis. fellow Inst. Policy Studies, Wash., 1968; vis. prof. U. Amsterdam (Netherlands), 1973-74; Thord-Gray vis. lectr. U. Stockholm, 1978; vis. prof. communications Hunter Coll., City U. N.Y., 1978-79. Served with AUS, 1942-45; MTO. Mem. AAAS, Internat. Assn. Mass Communication Research (v.p.), AAUP (sec. Ill. U.), Phi Beta Kappa. Author: Mass Communications and American Empire, 1969; Superstate: Readings in the Military-Industrial Complex, 1970; The Mind Managers, 1973; Communication and Cultural Domination, 1976. Editor: Quar. Rev. Econs. and Bus., 1963-70; National Sovereignty and International Communication, 1979. Home: 7109 Monte Vista La Jolla CA 92037 Office: Univ Calif San Diego La Jolla CA 92093

SCHILLER, MILTON S., lawyer; b. Boston, Mar. 18, 1914; s. Louis B. and Augusta (Goldberg) S.; A.B. cum laude, Harvard, 1935, LL.B., 1938; m. Muriel Wilson, Mar. 7, 1943; children—Dorothy Ellen (Mrs. Frederic Barton Askin), Leslie Ann (Mrs. Stanley H. Cohen). Admitted to Mass. bar, 1938, to Md. bar, 1945; practice in Boston, 1938-41, Balt., 1945—; asso. firm Slater & Goldman, Boston, 1938-41; with U.S. Dept. Justice, Boston, N.Y.C., 1942-43; with Tax Ct. U.S., Washington, 1943-45; partner Weinberg & Green, 1945—. Mem. Md. Capital Dept Affordability Com., 1941—; mem. adv. council Md. Bd. Pub. Works for Administering Higher Edn. Facilities Act, 1963—; mem. Greater Balt. Commn.; treas. Asso. Jewish Charities of Balt.; bd. dirs., exec. com., planning council Center Club, Balt., Inc. Mem. Am., Md., Balt. bar assns. Clubs: Suburban Baltimore County, Banyan Country (Palm Beach, Fla.). Home: 1 Slade Ave Pikesville MD 21208 Office: 10 Light St Baltimore MD 21202

SCHILLER, PIETER JON, chem. co. exec.; b. Orange, N.J., Jan. 14, 1938; s. John Fasel and Helen Roff (Roberts) S.; B.A. in Econs. with honors, Middlebury (Vt.) Coll., 1960; M.B.A., N.Y. U., 1966; m. Elizabeth Ann Williams, Nov. 20, 1965; children—Cathryn Ann, Suzanne Elizabeth. Fin. analyst Merck & Co., Inc., N.Y.C., 1960-61; fin. analyst, asst. div. controller, dir. auditing, then asst. controller Allied Chem. Corp., N.Y.C. and Morristown, N.J., 1961-75, treas., 1975-79, v.p. planning and devel., 1979—; mem. adv. bd. Chatham Trust Co. (N.J.). Chmn. trustees Newark Boys Chorus Sch., 1976-78, pres. bd., 1974-76; trustee Colonial Symphony Soc., 1978—; chmn. allocations com. United Way of Morris County, 1974-79, v.p., bd. dirs., mem. exec. com., 1979—. Mem. Fin. Execs. Inst. Home: 15 Cross Gates Rd Madison NJ 07940 Office: PO Box 1219R Columbia Rd and Park Ave Morristown NJ 07960

SCHILLER, ROBERT (BOB) ACHILLE, TV producer and writer; b. San Francisco, Nov. 8, 1918; s. Roland E. and Lucille (Block) S.; B.A. in Econs., UCLA, 1939; m. Joyce Harris, July 20, 1947 (dec. 1965) children—Thomas, James; m. 2d, Sabrina Scharf, May 25, 1968; children—Abigail, Sarah. Writer radio shows, including Duffy's Tavern, Jimmy Durante, Ozzie and Harriet and December Bride, 1946-50; TV writer: Danny Thomas Hour, Ed Wynn Show, 1950-53, That's My Boy, 1954, I Love Lucy, 1955-57 (Writers Guild award 1955), The Lucille Ball-Desi Arnaz Hour, 1957-60, The Lucy Show, 1962-64, The Red Skelton Hour, 1964-67, Carol Burnett, 1968, Flip Wilson Show, 1968-71 (Emmy award 1971, Peabody award 1970), All in The Family, 1977— (Emmy award 1978, Writers Guild award 1978, Peabody award 1978); creator and writer TV show: The Ann Sothern Show, 1958; producer and writer TV shows: The Good Guys, 1968, Maude, 1972-76 (Writers Guild award 1974, Population Inst. award 1975); creator, writer, producer TV show: All's Fair, 1976-77. Served with U.S. Army, 1941-46; ETO. Mem. Writers Guild Am., AFTRA. Democrat. Club: Riviera Golf and Country. Author play: (with Bob Weiskopf) So Long Stanley, 1979. Home: 1661 Casale Rd Pacific Palisades CA 90272 Office: CBS TV City 7800 Beverly Blvd Los Angeles CA 90036

SCHILLING, CHARLES HENRY, army officer, educator; b. Louisville, June 3, 1918; s. Henry M. and Caroline (Ravenscroft) S.; B.S., U.S. Mil. Acad., 1941; M.S. in Civil Engring., U. Cal. at Berkeley, 1947; Ph.D., Rensselaer Poly. Inst., 1959; m. Martha Hunter Wall, Sept. 2, 1945; children—Carolyn Hunter, Charles Henry, Mary Kathryn, Stephen Thomas, Robert Herschel. Commd. 2d lt. U.S. Army, 1941, advanced through grades to col., 1955; served with engr. troops, 1941-43; bn. comdr. 284th Engr. Bn., 1943-44, 165th Engr. Combat Bn., XV Corps, ETO, 1944-45, 831st and 862d Engr. Aviation Bns., Germany, 1947-50; instr., then asso. prof. mil. art and engring. U.S. Mil. Acad., 1951-55, prof. mil. art and engring., 1956-69, head dept., 1963-69, prof. engring., head dept., 1969—, chmn. acad. computer com., 1960—, mem. chapel bd., 1962-63, 69—. Area engr., Iceland, 1955-56; vis. prof. chem. and metall. engring. U. Mich., summer 1965; vis. prof. Inst. Statistics and Dynamics U. Stuttgart (W. Germany), 1968-69; mem. computer graphics task force, waterways expt. sta. C.E., 1974—. Pres. bd. edn. West Point elementary schs., 1960-63. Registered profl. engr., N.Y. Decorated Legion of Merit, Bronze Star, Croix de Guerre with silver star (France). Mem. Soc. Am. Mil. Engrs., Am. Soc. Engring. Edn. (computers in edn. div.), Assn. Grads. U.S. Mil. Acad. (trustee 1959-62), Tech. Council on Computer Practices (on state-of-art computer tech.), ASCE (chmn. subcom. on spl. topics 1973-75), Sigma Xi. Co-author: Application of Matrix Methods, in Structural Theory, 1969. Contbg. author: History of Public Works in the United States, 1974. Contbr. to encys. Home: Quarters 70 USMA West Point NY 10996

SCHILLING, JOHN ALBERT, surgeon; b. Kansas City, Mo., Nov. 5, 1917; s. Carl Fielding and Lottie Lee (Henderson) S.; A.B. with honors, Dartmouth Coll., 1937; M.D., Harvard U., 1941; m. Lucy West, June 8, 1957 (dec.); children—Christine Henderson, Katharine Ann, Jolyon David, John Jay; m. 2d, Helen R. Spelbrink, May 28, 1979. Intern, then resident in surgery Roosevelt Hosp., N.Y.C., 1941-44; mem. faculty U. Rochester (N.Y.) Med. Sch., 1945-53, asst. prof. surgery, 1955-56; prof. surgery, head dept. U. Okla. Med. Sch., 1956-74; prof. surgery U. Wash. Med. Sch., Seattle, 1974—, chmn. dept., 1975—; mem. bd. sci. counselors Nat. Cancer Inst., also mem. diagnosis subcom. breast cancer task force; chmn. adv. com. to surgeon gen. on metabolism of trauma Army Med. Research and Devel. Command; mem. surgery study sect., div. research grants NIH; chief surgery USAF Sch. Aviation Medicine; cons. Surgeon Gen. USAF, 1959-75. Served to maj. M.C., USAF, 1953-55. Grantee Army Office Surgeon Gen., 1956—. Diplomate Am. Bd. Surgery (chmn. 1969). Mem. A.C.S. (bd. govs., chmn. com. surg. edn. in med. schs.), Am., So., Western, Pan-Pacific, N. Pacific, Pacific Coast surg. assns., Soc. Univ. Surgeons, Am. Assn. Surgery Trauma, Surg. Biology Club, Am. Physiol. Soc., Soc. Surg. Chmn., Am. Trauma Soc., Seattle Surg. Soc., Soc. Exptl. Pathology, Soc. Surgery Alimentary Tract, Alpha Omega Alpha. Clubs: Explorers (N.Y.C.); Yacht, University (Seattle). Author articles, chpts. in books, abstracts, reports. Editorial bd. Annals Surgery, Am. Jour. Surgery. Home: 9807 Lake Washington Blvd NE Bellevue WA 98004 Office: Dept Surgery (RF-25) Univ Wash Medical Sch Seattle WA 98195

SCHILLING, PHILIP ALAN, editor, author; b. Ft. Wayne, Ind., Oct. 2, 1940; s. Irvin Earl and Lois Leora (Summers) S.; B.A., Northwestern U., 1962; M.S., U. Wis., 1964. Faculty, Nicolet High Sch., Glendale, Wis., 1967-68; free lance writer, Madison, Wis., 1968-70; mng. editor Cycle mag. Ziff-Davis Pub. Co., N.Y.C., 1970-72, exec. editor, N.Y.C. and Westlake Village, Calif., 1972-79, editor-in-chief, 1979—. U. Wis. fellow in history, 1962-63. Mem. Phi Beta Kappa. Author: The Motorcycle World, 1974; Motorcycles, 1975; 77. Am. editor: Motor Cycle Racing Guide, 1974. Home: 1634 Fordham Ave Thousand Oaks CA 91360 Office: 780-A Lakefield Rd Westlake Village CA 91361

SCHILLING, RALPH FRANKLIN, univ. pres.; b. Morris, Okla., July 5, 1921; s. R. F. and Mattie E. (Crume) S.; Ed.D., Tex. Tech U., 1957; M. Ed., Okla. U., 1950; B.A., Oklahoma City U., 1948; m. Mary Katherine Brooks, Jan. 19, 1942; 1 son, Ralph Franklin. Instr., asst. coach Oklahoma City U., 1947-50; high sch. prin., Crosbyton, Tex., 1950-52, Littlefield, Tex., 1952-54; supt. schs., Littlefield, 1954-60; pres. Pan Am. U., Edinburg, Tex., 1960—. Chmn. adv. bd. Littlefield Salvation Army, 1959. Named Littlefield Man of Year, 1958. Mem. NEA (life), Tex. PTA (life), Tex. Assn. Coll. Tchrs. (life), Am. Assn. Sch. Adminstrs., Tex. Tchrs. Assn., Tex. Adminstrs. Assn., Phi Delta Kappa. Methodist (past chmn. stewards). Rotarian (pres. Littlefield 1959-60). Home: Box 232 Edinburg TX 78539

SCHILLING, RICHARD ROBERT, JR., lawyer, diversified holding co. exec.; b. N.Y.C., Jan. 26, 1926; s. Richard Robert and Mae Frances (Walsh) S.; A.B., Fordham Coll., 1947; LL.B., Columbia, 1949; m. Joan Marie Edmonds, July 1, 1961; children—Mia, Richard Robert III, Andrew. Admitted to N.Y. State bar, 1949; asso. firm Saxe, Bacon & OShea, N.Y.C., 1949-56, partner, 1956-64; partner firm Burns, Kennedy, Schilling & O'Shea, N.Y.C., 1964—; v.p. Lionel Corp., N.Y.C., 1961-73, exec. v.p., 1973—, also dir.; dir. Megadata Computer & Communications Corp. Served with USAAF, 1944-45. Mem. Am., N.Y. State bar assns., Assn. Bar City of N.Y. Democrat. Roman Catholic. Clubs: Univ., N.Y. Athletic (N.Y.C.); Montauk (Bklyn.); Spring Lake Bath and Tennis. Home: 321 Garfield Pl Brooklyn NY 11215 Office: Lionel Corp 9 W 57th St New York NY 10019 also 598 Madison Ave New York NY 10022

SCHILLING, ROBERT FREDERICK, physician, educator; b. Adell, Wis., Jan. 19, 1919; s. Edgar F. and Lillian (Bollard) S.; B.S., U. Wis., 1940, M.D., 1943; m. Mariam Alan Hansen, Feb. 2, 1946 (dec.); children—Carla, Robert Frederick, Fredericka, Richard, Anne; m. 2d, Marilyn Carbon Johnsrud, July 14, 1973. Intern Phila. Gen. Hosp., 1943; resident dept. medicine U. Wis., Madison, 1946-48, asst. prof. medicine, 1951-56, asso. prof., 1956-62, prof., 1962—, USPHS research prof., 1963-64, chmn. dept. medicine, 1964-71. Research fellow, asst. in medicine Thorndike Meml. Lab., Harvard, 1949, 50; Commonwealth Fund vis. scholar U. London, 1959. Served to lt. (s.g.), M.C., USNR, 1944-46. Mem. Assn. Am. Physicians, Am. Soc. Clin. Investigation, Central Soc. Clin. Research, Soc. Exptl. Biology and Medicine, Phi Beta Kappa, Alpha Omega Alpha. Home: 4153 Mandan Crescent Madison WI 53711

SCHILLING, SYLVESTER PAUL, clergyman, educator; b. Cumberland, Md., Feb. 7, 1904; s. Sylvester and Ida Christina (Weber) S.; B.S., St. John's Coll., Annapolis, Md., 1923; A.M., Boston U., 1927, S.T.B., 1929, Ph.D., 1934; student Harvard, 1929-30, U. Berlin, 1930-31; m. Mary Elizabeth Albright, June 18, 1930; children—Robert Albright, Paula Carol (Mrs. Bruce E. Foreman). Ordained to ministry Methodist Ch., 1930; pastor, Vienna, Va., 1932-33; asst. pastor Mt. Vernon Place, Balt., 1933-36; pastor, Prince Frederick, Md., 1936-40, Brookland, Washington, 1940-45; prof. systematic theology and philosophy of religion Westminster Theol. Sem., Md., 1945-53; prof. systematic theology Boston U. Sch. Theology, 1953-69, acting dean, 1961-62, chmn. div. theol. studies Grad. Sch., 1954-69, prof. emeritus, 1969—; theol. lectr. Lowell Inst., 1968; vis. prof. systematic theology Union Theol. Sem., Manila, Philippines, 1969-70, Evang. Theol. Sem., Naperville, Ill., 1973-74; vis. prof. philos. theology Wesley Theol. Sem., Washington, 1970-73; vis. prof. systematic theology Andover Newton Theol. Sch., Newton Centre, Mass., 1978-80; theologian in residence Fla. So. Coll., Lakeland, 1977-78. Pres. bd. edn. Balt. Conf. Meth. Ch., 1948-53. Fellow Soc. for Values in Higher Edn.; mem. Am. Theol. Soc. (pres. 1968-69), ACLU, Am. Philos. Assn., Fellowship of Reconcilation, Am. Acad. Religion. Author: (with others) The Responsible Student, 1957; Isaiah Speaks, 1958; Methodism and Society in Theological Perspective, 1960; Contemporary Continental Theologians, 1966; God in an Age of Atheism, 1969; God Incognito, 1974; God and Human Anguish, 1977. Contbr. Church and Social Responsibility, 1953; Christian Mission in Theological Perspective, 1967; Theological Perspectives of Stewardship, 1969; Dynamic Interpersonalism for Ministry, 1973. Home: 219 Holly Point Rd Centerville MA 02632

SCHILLING, WARNER ROLLER, polit. scientist, educator; b. Glendale, Calif., May 23, 1925; s. Jule Frederick and Pauline Frances de Berri (Warner) S.; A.B., Yale, 1949, M.A., 1951, Ph.D., 1954; m. Jane Pierce Metzger, Jan. 27, 1951; children—Jonathan, Frederick. Research fellow Center Internat. Studies, Princeton U., 1953-54; asst. prof. internat. relations Mass. Inst. Tech., 1957-58; mem. faculty Columbia, 1954—, prof. govt., 1967-73, James T. Shotwell prof. internat. relations, 1973—; dir. Inst. War and Peace Studies, 1976—; cons., occasional lectr. in field. Served with USAAF, 1944-46. Guggenheim fellow, 1964-65; resident fellow Bellagio Study and Conf. Center, 1975. Mem. Internat. Inst. Strategic Studies, Council Fgn. Relations. Clubs: Faculty House (Columbia); Leonia Democratic. Co-author: Strategy, Politics and Defense Budgets, 1962; European Security and the Atlantic System, 1973; American Arms and a Changing Europe, 1973. Contbr. numerous articles to jours. Home: 496 Park Ave Leonia NJ 07605 Office: 420 W 118th St New York NY 10027

SCHILPP, PAUL ARTHUR, philosopher, editor, clergyman; b. Dillenburg, Hessen-Nassau, Germany, Feb. 6, 1897; s. Hermann and Emilie (Dittmar) S.; came to U.S., 1913, naturalized, 1926; student Humanistic Gymnasium Bayreuth, Bavaria, 1907-13; A.B., Baldwin-Wallace Coll., Berea, O., 1916, Litt.D., 1946; student Columbia, summers 1916, 17, Drew Theol. Sem., 1916-17; M.A., Northwestern U., 1922; B.D., Garrett Theol. Sem., 1922; auditor U. Munich, summer 1928; Ph.D., Stanford, 1936; L.H.D., Springfield (Mass.) Coll., 1963, Kent State U., 1975; m. Louise Gruenholz, Sept. 16, 1918; children—Erna Emilie (Mrs. Bimson), Marjorie Elizabeth (Mrs. Goodere), Robert Warner, Walter Norman; m. 2d, Madelon Golden, July 27, 1950; children—Erich Andrew, Margot Marlene. Ordained to ministry Methodist Ch., 1918; pastor Calvary Ch., Terre Haute, Ind., 1918-21; prof. psychology and religious edn. Coll. Puget Sound, 1922-23; asso. prof. philosophy, acting head dept. Coll. of Pacific, 1923-24, prof. philosophy, 1924-34, 2d chmn. Sch. Social Scis., 1930-34, asso. prof. German lang. and lit., 1935-36; lectr. philosophy Northwestern U., 1936-37, asso. prof. philosophy, 1937-50, prof., 1950-65, prof. emeritus, 1965—; disting. research prof. So. Ill. U., 1965-80, prof. emeritus, 1980—. Mendenhall Found. lectr. DePauw U., 1938; Tully C. Knoles Found. lectr. Coll. Pacific, 1954; Watumull Found. research fellow U. Calcutta, other univs. in India, 1950-51; Ingraham lectr. philosophy and religion Colby Coll., spring 1957; Grady Gammage Meml. lectr. Ariz. State U., 1963; U.S. participant Kant Workshop, U. Cologne, Germany, 1963. Ofcl. rep. Dept. State, 3d Pakistan Philos. Congress, 1956. Mem. No. Ill. Conf., United Meth. Ch. Recipient Distinguished Service medal Phi Beta Kappa Assn. Chgo., 1974. Mem. Am. Philos. Assn. (past pres. western div.), other fgn., nat., state profl. and philos. assns. and orgns. Author numerous works in field of philosophy, 1928—, latest being: Human Nature and Progress, 1954; The Crisis in Science and Education, 1963; Kant's Pre-Critical Ethics, 1966, 77; contbg. author: This is My Faith (S.G. Cole), 1956; New Frontiers of Christianity (R.C. Raughley), 1962; In Albert Schweitzer's Realms (A. A. Roback), 1962; Religion Ponders Science (E.P. Booth), 1964; The World of Philosophy, 1965; The Critique of War (Robert Ginsberg), 1969; Value and Valuation (J.W. Davis), 1972; 15 vols. Library of Living Philosophers; Vol. IX The Philosophy of Karl Jaspers, 1958; Vol. X Philosophy of C.D. Broad, 1959; Vol. XI Philosophy of Rudolf Carnap, 1964; La Etica Precritica de Kant, 1966; Vol. XII, Philosophy of Martin Buber, 1967; Vol. XIII Philosophy of C. I. Lewis, 1968; Vol. XIV, Philosophy of Karl Popper, (2 vols.) 1974; Philosophy of Brand Blanshard, 2 vols., 1979, 80; editor: Albert Einstein: Autobiographical Notes, 1979; contbg. editor Dictionary of Philosophy, Kantstudien. Asso. editor Existential Psychiatry, Religious Humanism. Contbr. articles. to philos. jours. Cons. philosophy to Ency. Brit. Home: 9 Hillcrest Dr Carbondale IL 62901 Office: Dept Philosophy So Ill U Carbondale IL 62901. *All my life I have believed that no man is greater than the causes he espouses and to which he is dedicated and no cause is greater than the improvement of humanity in all areas. Humanity is in danger of succumbing to thoughtless emotionalism, unwilling to pay the price of serious thinking. Love, I believe, is more powerful than hate, and ideas are still the most effective weapons.*

SCHIMBERG, LEWIS, lawyer; b. Chgo., Sept. 4, 1904; Ph.B., U. Chgo.; LL.B., Harvard. Admitted to Ill. bar, 1928; mem. firm Aaron, Aaron, Schimberg & Hess. Mem. Am., Ill., Chgo. bar assns. Address: 1040 Lake Shore Dr Chicago IL 60611

SCHIMKE, ROBERT TOD, educator, biochemist; b. Spokane, Wash., Oct. 25, 1932; s. Tolbert Daniel and Marion (Evans) S.; A.B., Stanford, 1954, M.D., 1958; m. Faith Fagan, July 5, 1952 (dec. 1958); children—Steven R., Caroline E.; m. 2d, Ruth Buddington, Feb. 6, 1959; children—Cynthia E., Allison R.; m. 3d, Mary Content, June 16, 1973 (dec. 1975); m. 4th, Hope Raymond, June 25, 1977. Intern, asst. resident medicine Mass. Gen. Hosp., Boston, 1958-60; commd. officer Lab. Biochemical Pharmacology sect. on pharmacology Nat. Insts. Arthritis and Metabolic Diseases, 1960-63, med. officer internal medicine research, 1963-65, chief sect. biochem. regulation, 1965-66; asso. prof. pharmacology and biology dept. pharmacology Stanford, 1966-69, prof., 1969-73, chmn. dept., 1970-73, prof. biology, 1973—, chmn. dept. biol. sci., 1978—, dir. med. scientist tng. program, 1969-75. Mem. molecular biol. study sect. NIH, 1970-74, nat. adv. council on aging, 1978—; mem. adv. panel on nucleic acid and protein synthesis Am Cancer Soc., 1971-75, Nat. Acad. Scis., 1976, Am. Acad. Arts and Scis., 1977. Recipient Chas. Pfizer award Am. Chem. Soc., 1969; Boris Pregal award N.Y. Acad. Scis., 1974; named Outstanding Young Scientist of Year, Md. Acad. Sci., 1964. Mem. Am. Soc. Biol. Chemists, Phi Beta Kappa, Alpha Omega Alpha. Mem. editorial bd. Jour. Biol. Chemistry, 1968-72, asso. editor, 1975—; editorial bd. Molecular Pharmacology, 1969-72; exec. editor Archives Biochem. Biophysics, 1973-75. Home: 639 Arastradero Rd Palo Alto CA 94306 Office: Dept Biological Scis Stanford U Stanford CA 94305

SCHIMMEL, ANNEMARIE BRIGITTE, educator; b. Erfurt, Germany, Apr. 7, 1922; d. Paul Wilhelm and Anna (Ulfers) S.; came to U.S., 1967; Dr.phil., Berlin U., 1941; Dr.phil. habil Marburg U., 1946, Dr.sc. rel., 1951; M.A., Harvard U., 1970; D.Litt. (hon.), U. Sind, 1975, Quaid-i Azam U., 1976, U. Peshawar, 1978. Translator; German Foreign Office, 1941-45; asst. prof. Islamic studies Marburg U., 1946-53, asso. prof., 1953; prof. history of religion Ankara U., 1954; asso. prof. Islamic studies Bonn U., 1961-68; lectr. Indo-Muslim studies Harvard, 1967-70, prof., 1970—. Mem. Am. Inst. Pakistan Studies, German-Iranian Assn., Middle East Studies Assn., Assn. for Study of Religion, Deutsche Morgenländische Gesellschaft, Brit. Oriental Soc., Royal Dutch Acad. Scis. (fgn.). Lutheran. Author books including: Mystical Dimensions of Islam, 1975; contbr. articles to profl. jours. Office: 6 Divinity Ave Cambridge MA 02138

SCHIMMEL, CAROLINE FEAREY, assn. exec.; b. N.Y.C., June 2, 1944; d. John Lawrence and Mary Lavell (White) Fearey; A.B., U. Pa., 1967; M.L.S., Columbia U., 1976; m. Stuart Barr Schimmel, Apr. 14, 1977. Cataloguer, appraiser rare books Sotheby Parke Bernet, N.Y.C., 1968-70; asst. editor Limited Editions Club, N.Y.C. and Avon, Conn., 1970-73; exec. sec. Bibliog. Soc. Am., N.Y.C., 1969—; researcher Am. Book Prices Current, N.Y.C., 1978—. Mem. ALA, Corredentia Soc., Citizens Union, N.Y. Bot. Garden, Guild Book Workers, NOW. Club: Grolier. Co-editor: Thomas W. Streeter Collection, Vols. 5-7, 1968-70; John Fass: Printer, 1978; Aucassin and Nicolette: A Bibliography, 1976. Home: 2 Beekman Pl New York NY 10022 Office: PO Box 397 Grand Central Station New York NY 10017

SCHIMMEL, PAUL REINHARD, biochemist, biophysicist; b. Hartford, Conn., Aug. 4, 1940; s. Alfred E. and Doris (Hudson) S.; A.B., Ohio Wesleyan U., 1962; postgrad. Tufts U. Sch. Medicine, 1962-63, Mass. Inst. Tech., 1963-65, Cornell U., 1965-66, Stanford U., 1966-67, U. Calif., Santa Barbara, 1975-76; Ph.D., Mass. Inst. Tech., 1966; m. Judith F. Ritz, Dec. 30, 1961; children—Kirsten, Katherine. Asst. prof. biology and chemistry Mass. Inst. Tech., 1967-71, asso. prof., 1971-76, prof. biochemistry and biophysics, 1976—; mem. NIH Study Sect. Physiol. Chemistry, 1975-79. Alfred P. Sloan fellow, 1970-72. Mem. Am. Chem. Soc. (Pfizer award in enzyme chemistry 1978), Am. Soc. Biol. Chemists, Biophys. Soc. Contbr. numerous articles to profl. jours.; editorial bd. Archives Biochemistry, Biophysics, 1976—, Nucleic Acids Research, 1977—, Jour. Biol. Chemistry, 1977—, Biopolymers, 1978—. Office: Dept Biology Mass Inst Tech Cambridge MA 02139

SCHIMMEL, STUART BARR, investment exec.; b. N.Y.C., Apr. 16, 1925; s. Michael and Lenore (Barr) S.; B.Mgmt. Engring., Rensselaer Poly. Inst., 1948; M.B.A., Columbia U., 1949; m. 2d, Caroline Fearey, Apr. 14, 1977; children—Bruce Andrew, Paul Gordon, Amy Diane. Partner, Michael Schimmel & Co., C.P.A.'s, N.Y.C., 1949-66, Consol. Investing Co., N.Y.C., 1949—. Served with AUS, 1944-46. C.P.A., N.Y. Mem. Am. Inst. C.P.A.'s, N.Y. State Soc. C.P.A.'s, Manuscript Soc. (past pres.), Bibliog. Soc. Am. (pres. 1976-77). Clubs: Grolier, City Athletic (N.Y.C.). Home: 2 Beekman Pl New York NY 10022 Office: 510 Fifth Ave New York NY 10036

SCHINDERLE, ROBERT FRANK, hosp. adminstr.; b. Mayville, Wis., Aug. 3, 1923; B.S., Marquette U., 1949; M.S., Northwestern U., 1959; m. Elizabeth, June 23, 1949; children—David, Gary, Mary, Brian. Asst. office mgr. Western Leather Co., Milw., 1949-51; mgr. bus. office St. Francis Hosp., Peoria, Ill., 1951-55; credit mgr. Mercy Hosp., Chgo., 1955-59, asst. to adminstr., 1957-58, controller, 1958-59, asst. adminstr., 1959-65; asst. adminstr. St. Joseph Hosp., Joliet, Ill., 1965-70, asso. adminstr., 1970-71, adminstr., 1971-76, exec. dir., 1976—; chmn. Areawide Hosp. Emergency Services Council. Bd. dirs. Region IX Health Systems Agy. Served with U.S. Army, 1942-46; ETO. Fellow Am. Coll. Hosp. Adminstrs.; mem. Am. Hosp. Assn., Ill. Hosp. Assn. (chmn. 1975-76), Catholic Hosp. Assn. (dir.), Ill. Cath. Hosp. Assn. (chmn. 1972-73). Roman Catholic. Clubs: Rotary, Elks. Office: 333 N Madison St Joliet IL 60435

SCHINDLER, ALBERT ISADORE, physicist; b. Pitts., June 24, 1927; s. Jonas and Esther (Nass) S.; B.S., Carnegie Inst. Tech., 1947, M.S., 1948, D.Sc., 1950; m. Phyllis Irene Liberman, June 17, 1951; children—Janet Mae, Jerald Scott, Ellen Susan. Research asst. Carnegie Inst. Tech., Pitts., 1947-50, research physicist, 1950-51; supervisory research physicist Naval Research Lab., Washington, 1951—, asso. dir. research for materials and radiation scis., 1975—. Recipient E.O. Hulburt award Naval Research Lab., 1956, Nat. Capitol award for applied sci., 1962; Pure Sci. award Naval Research Lab.-Sci. Research Soc. Am., 1965; award Washington Acad. Scis., 1965; USN Disting. Achievement in Sci. award, 1975. Fellow Am. Phys. Soc.; mem. Sigma Xi. (dir.). Home: 1012 Crest Park Dr Silver Spring MD 20903 Office: Code 6000 Naval Research Lab 4555 Overlook Ave SW Washington DC 20375*

SCHINDLER, ALEXANDER MOSHE, clergyman, orgn. exec.; b. Munich, Germany, Oct. 4, 1925; s. Eliezer and Sali (Hoyda) S.; B.Social Sci., Coll. City N.Y., 1950; B.Hebrew Letters, Hebrew Union Coll., 1951, M.Hebrew Letters, 1953, Rabbi, 1953, D.D. (hon.), 1977; m. Rhea Rosenblum, Sept. 29, 1956; children—Elisa Ruth, Debra Lee, Joshua Michael, Judith Rachel, Jonathan David. Asst. rabbi Temple Emanuel, Worcester, Mass., 1953-56, asso., rabbi, 1956-59; dir. New Eng. council Union Am. Hebrew Congregations, 1959-63, nat. dir. edn., 1963-67, v.p., 1967-72; pres.-elect, 1972, pres., 1973—. Mem. exec. bd. Conf. Presidents of Maj. Am. Jewish Orgns., 1967—, chmn., 1976-78; exec. bd. Hebrew Union Coll./Jewish Inst. Religion, 1967—; mem. exec. bd. Meml. Found. Jewish Culture, 1967—; mem. exec. com. Am. sect. World Zionist Orgn., 1973—. Served with AUS, 1944-46. Decorated Bronze Star, Purple Heart; recipient Solomon Bublick prize Hebrew U. Jerusalem, 1978; Townsend Harris medal CCNY, 1979. Mem. Am. Assn. Jewish Edn. (exec. bd. 1963—), Central Conf. Am. Rabbis (exec. bd. 1967—), World Union for Progressive Judaism (governing bd. 1967—). Author: From Discrimination to Extermination, 1950. Lit. editor CCAR Jour., 1959-63; founding editor Dimensions, Reform Judaism's quar. religious thought, 1966—; editor Reform Judaism's graded text book series, 1963-67. Home: 6 River Ln Westport CT 06880 Office: 838 Fifth Ave New York City NY 10021. *To live life fully, clinging to its many gifts with all my might—and then, paradoxically, to let go when life compels us to surrender what it gave.*

SCHINDLER, ALFRED, former business exec.; b. St. Louis, Mo.; s. Frank and Bertha (Lovack) S.; ed. univs. and bus. schs., St. Louis, Mo.; m. Katherine Stolz, Oct. 25, 1922. Sales mgr. Ralston Purina Co., St. Louis, Mo., 1917-42. Mem. Nat. Civilian Defense Com., 1941; spl. asst. to sec. of commerce, chief cons. div., Defense Plant Corp., 1942-43; under sec. of commerce, Dept. Commerce, Washington, 1945-46. Bd. dirs. Com. for Econ. Devel. St. Louis, Mo., 1943-44. Chmn. exec. com. Nat. Distbn. Council, Dept. Commerce, Washington, D.C., 1947-48; chmn. bd. Nat. Fedn. Sales Execs., 1948-49; trustee, mem. exec. com. Nat. Council for Community Improvement, Washington, 1948-51. Office: 4233 Sulphur Ave St Louis MO 63109

SCHINDLER, CLAYTON MOSS, educator; b. East Palestine, Ohio, Aug. 22, 1912; s. Emil Adam and Eva (Moss) S.; B.A., Mt. Union Coll., 1934; student Northwestern U., 1937; M.S. in Edn., U. So. Calif., 1946; Ph.D., Ohio State U., 1950; m. Winona German, Aug. 22, 1937. Caseworker, Fed. Emergency Relief Adminstrn., 1934-35; tchr. English and speech, high sch., East Palestine, 1935-37, Shelby, 1937-39, Canton, Ohio, 1939-46; dir. Canton br. Kent State U., 1946-50, dir. extension and spl. activities, 1950-56, asso. dean Coll. Edn., 1956-58, dean, 1958-71; dean Coll. Profl. Studies, George Mason U., Fairfax, Va., 1971-78, prof. edn., 1978—. Mem. NEA, Nat. Forensic League (nat. dir. 1944- 48, nat. tournament chmn. 1948), Northeastern Ohio Tchrs. Assn., Canton Edn. Assn. (pres. 1946), Phi Delta Kappa, Kappa Delta Pi. Office: Robinson Hall George Mason U Fairfax VA 22030

SCHINDLER, WILLIAM STANLEY, pub. relations exec.; b. Detroit, Jan. 4, 1933; s. William Henry and Katherine (Schilling) S.; student Wayne State U., 1950-53. Copywriter, motion picture writer-dir., writer, pub. relations exec.; sr. v.p., dir. pub. relations Campbell-Ewald Co., Detroit, 1959—; v.p. Sandusky Pub. Co. (Mich.). Past mem. Detroit Hist. Commn., vice chmn. Detroit CSC; past mem. Detroit Fire Commn.; past pres. Detroit Hist. Soc.; pres. Hist. Soc. Mich. Served with U.S. Army, 1954-56. Decorated Commendation Medal with pendant. Mem. Pub. Relations Soc. Am. (counselors sect., Detroit chpt.), Adcraft Club of Detroit, Detroit Press Club, Sons of Whiskey Rebellion. Clubs: Recess; University, Detroit Athletic, Prismatic; Box 12. Editor: Progress Report-New Detroit, Inc., 1969. Home: 1247 Navarre Pl Detroit MI 48224 Office: 3044 W Grand Blvd Detroit MI 48202

SCHINE, GERARD DAVID, entertainment co. exec.; b. Gloversville, N.Y., Sept. 11, 1927; s. J. Myer and Hildegarde (Feldman) S.; grad. Fessenden Sch., West Newton, Mass., 1941, Phillips Acad., Andover, Mass., 1945; A.B., Harvard, 1949; m. Anna Kristina Hillevi (Rombin), 1957; children—Anna Vidette Angela, Jonathan Mark, Alexander Kevin, Frederick Berndt, Benjamin Axel, William Lance. Pres., gen. mgr. Schine Hotels, 1950-63; exec. v.p. Schine Enterprises, 1952-57, pres., 1957-63; pres. Ski Dek Corp., 1961-67, David Schine & Co., Inc., Mgmt. Internat., Inc., Auto Inns Am., Inc., 1963-72, Ambassador Hotel Co. Los Angeles, 1960-63, 64-67; exec. producer The French Connection, 1971; writer, producer, dir. That's Action!, 1977; now pres. David Schine & Co. Inc., Schine Music, Myhil Music, Schine Prodns., Los Angeles. Adviser, spl. asst. atty.-gen. U.S. charge subversive activities, 1952, assisted investigation Communist infiltration into UN; chief cons. Senate Permanent Subcom. on Investigations, Com. on Govt. Operations, Jan. to Nov. 1953; directed investigation of Internat. Information Adminstrn., also Voice of America, Dept. State, 1953; mem. Los Angeles Citizens Com. for 1960 Democratic Conv. Trustee Hotel Industry Devel. Fund; past dir. Symphony Club of Miami, Community Concert Assn. Miami Beach, Fla.; past chmn. adv. bd. Conv. Bur., Miami Beach; mem. citizens adv. com. Hotel Employees Med. Plan; past dir. Com. 1000 for Variety Children's Hosp.; past dir. Greater Miami Philharmonic Soc., Inc.; nat. bd. trustees City of Hope; past chmn. Miami Beach Com. Opera Guild; trustee Hope for Hearing Found. Served as lt. Army Transport Service, 1946-47; pvt. AUS, 1953-55. Mem. Young Presidents' Orgn. Am. (founding mem.), Nat. Bus. Aircraft Assn., Aircraft Owners and Pilots Assn., A.I.M. (pres.'s council), So. Fla. Hotel and Motel Assn. (founding pres.), Dade County (Fla.) Devel. Com. Clubs: Lotos; Harvard (N.Y.C.). Author articles and pamphlets. Home: 626 S Hudson Ave Los Angeles CA 90005

SCHINE, LEONARD ALBERT, lawyer; b. Bridgeport, Conn., Jan. 20, 1917; B.S., U. Vt., 1938; J.D., U. Conn., 1941; m. Lois V. Gildersleeve, Dec. 20, 1951; children—Leslie, Daniel, Lindsay, Lauren, Edward. Admitted to names of bars and dates of admission) Conn. bar, 1942, U.S. Dist. Ct. bar, 1950, U.S. Tax Ct. bar, 1952, U.S. Supreme Ct. bar, 1955, U.S. Circuit Ct. bar, 1965; sr. partner firm Schine, Julianelle, Karp & Bozelko, P.C., Westport, Conn., 1947—; gen. counsel Natural Sci. for Youth Found.; gen. counsel, dir., mem. exec. com., univ. sec. Sacred Heart U.; dir. State Nat. Bank of Conn. Asso. Bd.; dir., gen. counsel All State Venture Capital Corp. Presdl. commr. Nat. Commn. Air Quality; founder, bd. dirs. Aspetuck Land Trust Inc., Westport, Conn.; trustee, chmn. fin. com. Fairfield (Conn.) Country Day Sch.; trustee YMCA, Westport; Conn. del. Regional Plan Assn. Served with U.S. Army, 1944-45; ETO. Mem. Am. Judicature Soc., Am. Bar Assn., Conn. Bar Assn. (chmn. legal aid 1952-53, mem. exec. com. antitrust sect. 1965—), Am. Trial Lawyers Assn. Clubs: Patterson-Fairfield County, Landmark. Office: 830 Post Rd E Westport CT 06880

SCHINELLER, RICHARD JOHN, computer mfg. co. exec.; b. N.Y.C., Aug. 6, 1934; s. Howard John and Marion Theresa (Maxwell) S.; student West Chester Coll., U. Md.; m. Eileen Gianelli, Dec. 1, 1956; children—Richard John, William, Diane, Elena, Erik. Vice pres. Leasco, Gt. Neck, N.Y., 1968-70, Potter Instrument Co., N.Y.C., 1970-72; pres. Sorbus, Inc., King of Prussia, Pa., 1972-75; exec. v.p. U.S. ops. Mgmt. Assistance, Inc., N.Y.C., 1975—; chmn. Basic/Four, Wordstream Corp., Sorbus Inc. Served in USAF, 1952-56. Mem. Am. Mgmt. Assn. Roman Catholic. Club: Bronxville (N.Y.) Field. Home: 129 White Plains Rd Bronxville NY 10708 Office: 300 E 44th St New York City NY 10017

SCHINK, CLIFFORD ERNEST, mgmt. cons.; b. Dawson, Yukon Ter., Can., Dec. 29, 1902; s. Ernest F. and Augusta (Maron) S.; A.B., Stanford, 1926, M.B.A., 1928; m. Esther Abrams, Sept. 15, 1930; children—David R., Peter N., Christopher E., Mary A. With Calif. and Hawaiian Sugar Refining Corp., Ltd., San Francisco, 1928-68, successively various clerical positions, controller, asst. treas., 1928-34, treas., 1934-68, v.p., 1937-68; sr. asso. Case & Co., mgmt. consultants, 1968-69; sr. asso. Beeson & Assos., mgmt. consultants, 1969—. Cons. prof. Finance Grad. Sch. Bus. Stanford, 1935-60; adv. council Dept. Nutritional Scis. U. Calif.; vol. exec. Ministere du Commerce Morocco, 1972, Sugar Devel. Corp., Tanzania, 1974. Pres., bd. trustees Castilleja Sch. Found. Mem. Calif. Mfrs. Assn. (pres. 1958-59), Soc. Advancement Mgmt., Phi Beta Kappa. Home: 300 Santa Rita Ave Palo Alto CA 94301 Office: 800 Welch Rd Palo Alto CA 93405

SCHINKEL, KENNETH CALVIN, profl. hockey player; b. Jansen, Sask., Can., Nov. 27, 1932. Right wing N.Y. Rangers, 1959-64, 66-67, Pitts. Penguins (both Nat. Hockey League teams), from 1967; now pro scout Pitts. Penguins. Address: care Pittsburgh Penguins Civic Arena Gate No 7 Pittsburgh PA 15219

SCHIRBER, MARTIN EDWARD, clergyman, educator; b. Herreid, S.D., June 23, 1907; s. Frank William and Claudia (Meagher) S.; A.B., St. John's U., 1931; Ph.D., Harvard, 1940. Entered Benedictine Order, 1929, ordained priest Roman Catholic Ch., 1935; prof. econs., St. John's U., 1939-79, prof. emeritus, 1979—, dean coll., 1943-52; dir. rural life schs., Nat. Cath. Rural Life Conf., 1941-46; v.p. Am. Benedictine Acad., 1943-57, pres., 1957-62. Mem. Am. Econ. Assn., Cath. Econ. Assn., Am. Cath. Sociol. Soc. Contbr. articles to profl. publs. Home: St John's Abbey Collegeville MN 56321

SCHIRMER, HENRY WILLIAM, architect; b. St. Joseph, Mo., Dec. 8, 1922; s. Henry William and Asta (Hansen) S.; A.S., St. Joseph Jr. Coll., 1942; B.Arch. Design, U. Mich., 1949; m. Jane Irene Krueger; children—Andrew Lewis, Monica Sue, Daniel F. Carr. With Eugene Meier, St. Joseph, 1939, Neville Sharp & Simon, Kansas City, Mo., 1946, 49, Ramey & Himes, Wichita, Kans., 1950-57; partner Schaefer & Schirmer, Wichita, 1957-60, Schaefer, Schirmer & Eflin, Wichita, 1960-72, Schaefer, Schirmer & Assos., P.A., 1972-76; prin. Henry W. Schirmer, cons. to architects, 1976—; works include Wichita Pub. Library, Burn Center at U. Kans. Med. Center, Allen County Community Jr. Coll., Iola, Kans., Rainbow Mental Health Center, Kansas City, Kans., Capitol Area Plaza Project, Topeka. Pres. East Br. YMCA, 1954—; dir. Wichita YMCA, 1956-73. Served with C.E., AUS, World War II; ETO. Decorated Purple Heart. Mem. AIA (past pres. Kans. chpt., seminar leader, chmn. nat. com. on office mgmt. 1976, dir. 1979—, nat. documents com. 1978, chmn. nat. com. on project mgmt. 1977), Tau Sigma Delta. Lutheran. Editor: Profile/Archtl. Firms/The AIA, 1978, 79; contbr. to AIA Handbook. Home: 3033 Lydia St Apt 207 Topeka KS 66614 Office: 3715 SW 29th St Topeka KS 66614. *An architect must always look toward the future. If he does not, it is absolutely impossible for him to be progressively creative; and if he is not, he does not deserve the title. To look to, and design for, the future, one must be lovingly familiar with the past and the present. And when that is not so, mediocrity reigns supreme. I cannot be content with anything less than excellence accomplished through an ethical process.*

SCHIRMER, HOWARD AUGUST, JR., civil engr.; b. Oakland, Calif., Apr. 21, 1942; s. Howard August and Amy (Freuler) S.; B.S., U. Calif., Berkeley, 1964, M.S., 1965; m. Leslie May Mecum, Jan. 29, 1965; children—Christine Nani, Amy Kiana, Patricia Leolani. Engr. in tng. materials and research dept. Calif. Div. Hwys., Sacramento, 1960-64; engring. analyst Dames & Moore, San Francisco, 1964-65, asst. staff engr., 1965-69, chief engr., 1969-72, asso., Honolulu, 1972-75, partner, mng. prin. in charge, 1975—, regional mgr. Pacific Far East and Australia, 1978—; chmn. geotech. engring. com. Am. Cons. Engrs. Council, 1976-78; past chmn. adv. com. for engring. tech. Honolulu Community Coll. Chmn. engring. sect., mem. budget com. Aloha United Way, 1974; first aid instr. ARC, 1971—; mem. Maunalua Triangle Assn. Registered profl. engr., Hawaii, Guam; certified ski proficiency instr. Nat. Ski Patrol System. Mem. ASCE (Edmund Friedman Young Engr. award for profl. achievement 1974, pres. Hawaii sect.), Cons. Engrs. Council Hawaii (pres.), Engring. Assn. Hawaii, Internat. Soc. Soil Mechanics and Found. Engring., Am. Public Works Assn. (sec. 1978, dir. 1979-80), Soc. Am. Mil. Engrs., Structural Engrs. Assn. Hawaii, Chi Epsilon, Sigma Phi Epsilon. Republican. Episcopalian. Clubs: Outrigger Canoe; Ski Assn. Hawaii. Important works include Aloha Stadium, Honolulu Municipal Office Bldg., Honolulu Internat. Airport Expansion, AFDM Berthing Wharf, Pearl Harbor. Founder, Mauna Kea Ski Patrol, 1969. Home: 79 Makaweli St Honolulu HI 96825 Office: 1144 10th Ave Honolulu HI 96816

SCHIRRA, WALTER MARTY, JR., corp. exec.; b. Hackensack, N.J., Mar. 12, 1923; s. Walter Marty and Florence (Leach) S.; student Newark Coll. Engring., 1940-42; B.S., U.S. Naval Acad., 1945; D. Astronautics (hon.), Lafayette Coll., U. So. Calif., New Eng. Coll.; m. Josephine Cook Fraser, Feb. 23, 1946; children—Walter Marty III, Suzanne Karen. Commd. ensign U.S. Navy, 1945, advanced through grades to capt., 1965; designated naval aviator, 1948; service aboard battle cruiser Alaska, 1945-46; mem. staff 7th Fleet, 1946-48; assigned Fighter Squadron 71, 1948-51; exchange pilot 154th USAF Fighter Bomber Squadron, 1951; engaged in devel. Sidewinder missile, China Lake, Calif., 1952-54; project pilot F7U-3 Cutlass, also instr. pilot F7U-3 Cutlass and FJ3 Fury, 1954-56; operations officer Fighter Squadron 124, U.S.S. Lexington, 1956-57; assigned Naval Air Safety Officer Sch., 1957, Naval Air Test Center, 1958-59; engaged in suitability devel. work F4H, 1958-59; joined Project Mercury, man-in-space, NASA, 1959; pilot spacecraft Sigma 7 in 6 orbital flights, Oct. 1962; in charge operations and tng. Astronaut Office, 1964-69, command pilot Gemini 6 which made rendezvous with target, Gemini 7, Dec. 1965, comdr. 11 day flight Apollo 7, 1968, ret., 1969; pres. Regency Investors, Inc., Denver, 1969-70; chmn., chief exec. officer ECCO Corp., Englewood, Colo., 1970-73; chmn. Sernco, Inc., 1973-74; with Johns-Manville Corp., Denver, 1974-77; v.p. devel. Goodwin Cos., Inc., Littleton, Colo., 1977—; ind. cons., 1979—; dir. Rocky Mountain Airlines, Advt. Unltd., Mankato, Minn. Mem. media adv. com. U.S. Navy Recruiting; internat. sponsor Project Concern, Inc.; mem. adv. bd./council U.S. Nat. Parks; Belgian consul for Colo. and N.Mex. Decorated D.F.C., Air medal (2), Navy D.S.M.; recipient Distinguished Service medal (2), also Exceptional Service medal NASA. Fellow Am. Astronautical Soc., Soc. Exptl. Test Pilots; mem. Am. Inst. Aeros. and Astronautics, Am. Fighter Pilots Assn. (v.p.). Office: 5 DTC Pkwy Englewood CO 80111

SCHISGAL, MURRAY, playwright; b. N.Y.C., Nov. 25, 1926; s. Abraham and Irene (Sperling) S.; LL.B., Bklyn. Law Sch., 1953; B.A., New Sch. Social Research, 1959; m. Reene Schapiro, June 29, 1958; children—Jane, Zachary. Author: The Typists and The Tiger, London, Eng., 1960, N.Y.C., 1963 (pub. 1963); Ducks and Lovers, London, 1961; Knit One, Purl Two, Boston, 1963; Luv (pub. Best Plays of 1964-65), London, 1963, N.Y.C., 1964 (pub. 1964); Fragments, Windows and other plays (pub. 1965); The Love Song of Barney Kempinski (original TV play), 1966; Fragments (off-Broadway), 1967, The Basement (off-Broadway), 1967; (Broadway) Jimmy Shine, 1968 (pub. 1969), The Chinese, N.Y.C., 1970 (pub. in Best Short Plays of the World Theatre 1973), Dr. Fish, N.Y.C., 1970, An American Millionaire, 1974, All Over Town (pub. Best Plays 1974-75), 1974, screenplay The Tiger Makes Out, 1967; The Pushcart Peddlers (produced off-Broadway), 1979; (novel) Days and Nights of a French Horn Player, 1980. Recipient Vernon Rice award outstanding achievement Off—Broadway Theatre, 1963; Outer Circle award outstanding Theatre, 1963; Outer Circle award outstanding playwright, 1963.

SCHKADE, LAWRENCE LOUIS, educator; b. Port Arthur, Tex., July 31, 1930; s. Henry W. and Henrietta A. (Leschber) S.; B.B.A., Lamar U., 1956; M.B.A., La. State U., 1957, Ph.D. (Sperry and Hutchinson fellow), 1961; m. Paula Locke, Sept. 1, 1977; children—David, Paul. Asst. dean of student life Lamar U., Beaumont, Tex., 1957-59; asst. prof. mgmt. U. Southwestern La., Lafayette, La., 1960-61; asst. prof. mgmt. and statistics La. State U., Baton Rouge, 1961-63; asso. prof. bus. statistics, computer sci. and mgmt. U. Tex. at Austin, 1963-67; Ford Found. prof. mgmt. Instituto Tecnologico de Monterrey (Mexico), 1966-67; prof. bus. adminstr. North Tex. State U., Denton, 1967-69, vis. prof. bus. adminstrn., 1972-73; asso. dean, prof. bus. adminstrn. U. Tex. at Arlington, 1969-72, acting dean Grad. Sch., prof. bus. adminstrn. and urban studies, 1973—. Dir. Ecology Control, Inc., Houston. Cons. editor South-Western Pub. Co., 1969—. Served with USAF, 1948-52. Recipient Distinguished Scholar award Am. Assembly Coll. Schs. Bus.-Beta Gamma Sigma. Ford Found. grantee, 1962, 65, Ford Found. fellow, 1966-67. Fellow AAAS, Am. Inst. Decision Scis. (pres. 1976-77); mem. Am. Statis. Assn., Ops. Research Soc. Am., Soc. for Gen. Systems Research (coordinator Southwestern region 1971-72), Inst. Mgmt. Scis., Alpha Iota Delta (nat. v.p. 1972-73), Alpha Tau Omega, Beta Gamma Sigma, Delta Sigma Pi, Upsilon Pi Epsilon, Omicron Delta Kappa, Phi Kappa Phi, Sigma Iota Epsilon. Author: Vectors and Matrices, 1964; Statistical Methods for Business Decisions, 1969; Statistical Analysis for Administrative Decision, 1974. Editor Gen. Systems Bull., 1969-73; asso. editor Social Sci. Quar., 1963-64, Decision Scis., 1973—; cons. editor Ark. Bus. and Econ. Rev., 1973—. Home: 5102 Tremont St Dallas TX 75214

SCHLACK, ALOIS LEO, JR., engring. mechanic scientist; b. Eagle River, Wis., June 24, 1934; s. Alois Leo and Helen Catherine (Hoppe) S.; B.S. in Applied Math. and Mechs., U. Wis., 1956, Ph.D. in Engring. Mechs. (Coll. Engring. research fellow), 1961; m. Sally Ann Dussault, June 22, 1957; children—David, Steven, Mary Sue, James. Research engr. Ford Motor Co., Dearborn, Mich., 1957; engr. Baker Mfg. Co., Evansville, Wis., 1957-60, also dir., cons.; instr. dept. engring. mechs. U. Wis., Madison, 1960-61, asst. prof., 1961-64, asso. prof., 1964-68, prof., 1968—, dept. chmn., 1974—. Recipient Outstanding Tchr. awards, 1972—. Mem. Am. Inst. Aeros. and Astronautics, Am. Soc. Engring. Edn., Assn. Chairmen Depts. Mechs. Roman Catholic. Contbr. tech. articles to profl. jours. Home: 6005 Midwood Ave Monona WI 53716 Office: Dept Engring Mechanics U Wis 2350 Engring Bldg 1415 Johnson Dr Madison WI 53706

SCHLAFLY, HUBERT JOSEPH, JR., communications co. exec.; b. St. Louis, Aug. 14, 1919; s. Hubert J. and Mary Ross (Parker) S.; B.S. in Elec. Engring., U. Notre Dame, 1941; postgrad. Syracuse U. extension, 1946-47; m. Leona Martin, June 12, 1944. Electronics engr. Gen. Electric Co., Schenectady, 1941-44, Syracuse, 1946-47; project engr. Radiation Lab., Mass., Inst. Tech., 1944-45; dir. TV research 20th Century Fox Film Corp., N.Y.C., 1947-51; a founder Teleprompter Corp., N.Y.C., 1951, v.p., dir., 1951-74, pres., 1971-72, exec. v.p. tech. devel., 1972-74; communications cons., 1974; chmn. exec. com. Am. Trans-Communications Inc., Greenwich, Conn., 1975—; pres. Transponder Corp., Greenwich, 1977—; industry coordinator, chmn. exec. com., cable tech. adv. com. FCC, 1972-75; adviser com. telecommunications Nat. Acad. Engring.; adviser Sloan Commn. Cable Communications; mem. engring. adv. council U. Notre Dame, 1977—; lectr. in field. Recipient Engring. Honor award U. Notre Dame, 1976. Fellow Soc. Motion Picture and TV Engrs.; sr. mem. IEEE (Delmer Ports award 1979); mem. Nat. Cable TV Assn. (chmn. standards com. 1965-69, chmn. domestic satellite com. 1971-73, chmn. future services com. 1972, outstanding tech. achievements award 1974), Electronic Industries Assn. (chmn. broadband cable sect. 1971-73). Roman Catholic. Club: Milbrook Country. Author: The Real World of Technological Evolution; Your Personal Genie in the Cable; Computer in the Living Room. Patentee in field. Office: 34 Putnam Ave Greenwich CT 06830 Home: 27 Orchard Dr Greenwich CT 06830

SCHLAFLY, PHYLLIS STEWART, author, lawyer; b. St. Louis, Aug. 15, 1924; d. John Bruce and Odile (Dodge) Stewart; B.A., Washington U., St. Louis, 1944, J.D., 1978; M.A., Radcliffe Coll., 1945; LL.D., Niagara U., 1976; m. Fred Schlafly, Oct. 20, 1949; children—John F., Bruce S., Roger S., Phyllis Liza, Andrew L., Anne V. Author, pub. Phyllis Schlafly Report, 1967—; broadcaster Spectrum, CBS Radio Network, 1973-78; nat. chmn. Stop ERA, 1972—; commentator Matters of Opinion radio sta. WBBM, Chgo., 1973-75; syndicated columnist Copley News Service, 1976—; admitted to Ill. bar, 1979. Del. Republican Nat. Conv., 1956, 64, 68, alt., 1960; pres. Ill. Fedn. Rep. Women, 1960-64; 1st v.p. Nat. Fedn. Rep. Women, 1964-67; mem. Ill. Commn. on Status of Women, 1975—; pres. Eagle Forum, 1975—. Recipient 9 Honor awards Freedoms Found.; Brotherhood award NCCJ, 1975; named Woman of Achievement in Pub. Affairs, St. Louis Globe-Democrat, 1963. Mem. D.A.R. (nat. chmn. Am. history 1965-68, nat. chmn. bicentennial com. 1967-70, nat. chmn. nat. def. 1977—), Am., Ill. bar assns., Phi Beta Kappa, Pi Sigma Alpha. Author: A Choice Not an Echo, 1964; The Gravediggers, 1964; Strike From Space, 1965; Safe Not Sorry, 1967; The Betrayers, 1968; Mindszenty The Man, 1972; Kissinger on the Couch, 1975; Ambush at Vladivostok, 1976; The Power of the Positive Woman, 1977. Address: 68 Fairmount Alton IL 62002

SCHLAGEL, RICHARD HAROLD, educator; b. Springfield, Mass., Nov. 22, 1925; s. Harold Mustrom and Emily Habel (Dutton) S.; B.S., Springfield Coll., 1949; M.A., Boston U., 1952, Ph.D. (Borden Parker Bowne fellow), 1955; m. Josephine Weaver Regar, Apr. 7, 1962. Instr., Coll. of Wooster (O.), 1954-55; instr. Clark U., Worcester, Mass., 1955-56; asst. prof. George Washington U., Washington, 1956-61, asso. prof., 1961-68, prof. philosophy, 1968—, chmn. dept. philosophy, 1964-70. Served with USAAF, 1943-45. Mem. Am. Philos. Assn. (Eastern div.), Am. Assn. U. Profs., Washington Philosophy Club (pres. 1965-66). Home: 2737 Devonshire Pl NW Washington DC 20008

SCHLAGETER, ROBERT, ins. co. exec.; b. N.Y.C., Dec. 6, 1917; s. John and Jeanette (Gastmeyer) S.; B.B.A. cum laude, St. John's U., N.Y.C., 1944; m. Dorothy Ann Golden, Nov., 1941; children—Jeanne, Robert, Susan, Jane. With Equitable Life Assurance Soc. U.S., N.Y.C., 1935—, v.p., 1969-74, sr. v.p., 1974-77, exec. v.p., 1977—; pres., dir. Planters Redevel. Corp.; trustee Equitable Life Mortgage and Realty Investors; pres. Main-Evansville Corp.; dir. N.Y. Real Estate Bd.; mem. advisory bd. N.Y. U. Real Estate Inst. Trustee, vice chmn. bd. trustees Ladycliff Coll.; mem. N.Y. Mayor's Midtown Citizen's Com. Mem. Thirty Fourth St. Midtown Assn. (pres. 1967-69, dir.), Ave. of Americas Assn. (dir.), Constrn. Users Council (policy com.), Bldg. Owners', Mgrs'. Assn., Urban Land Inst., N.Y. Bldg. Congress. Clubs: Cherry Valley Country, Malibu Beach. Home: 181 Stewart Ave Garden City NY 11530 Office: 1285 Ave of the Americas New York City NY 10019

SCHLAIFER, CHARLES, advt. exec.; b. Omaha, July 1, 1909; s. Abraham S.; privately ed.; Litt.D. (hon.), John F. Kennedy Coll., 1969; m. Evelyn Chaikin, June 10, 1934; children—Arlene Lois Silk, Roberta Semer. Newspaper reporter, Omaha, 1926-29; advt. dir. Publix Tri-States Theatres, Nebr., Iowa, 1929-37; mng. dir. United Artists Theatres, San Francisco, 1937-42; nat. advt. cons. United Artists Producers, 1937-42; nat. advt. mgr. 20th Century-Fox Film Corp., N.Y.C., 1942-45, v.p. charge advt. and pub. relations, 1945-49; pres. Charles Schlaifer & Co., Inc., N.Y.C., Los Angeles, 1949—; vis. prof. New Sch. Social Research; expert witness U.S. Congl. and Senatorial coms. on mental health, 1949—. Mem. Pres.'s Com. Employment Handicapped, 1960—; founder, co-chmn. Nat. Mental Health Com., 1949-57; mem. nat. mental health adv. council Surgeon Gen. U.S., 1950-54; sec.-treas. Joint Commn. Mental Illness and Health, 1955-61; vice chmn. Found. Child Mental Welfare, 1963; mem. Gov.'s Youth Council State N.Y.; chmn. N.Y. State Mental Hygiene Facilities Improvement Corp., 1963—, White House Conf. Children, 1970; sec.-treas., bd. dirs. Joint Commn. Mental Health Children; chmn. N.Y. State Facilities Devel. Corp., 1973; mem. adv. council NIMH, 1976—; bd. dirs. Hillside Hosp., League Sch. For Seriously Disturbed Children, Menninger Found. Recipient Social Conscience award Karen Horney Clinic, 1972. Hon. fellow Postgrad. Center Mental Health. Fellow Am. Psychiat. Assn. (hon.), Brit. Royal Soc. Health (hon.), Am. Orthopsychiat. Assn. (hon.); mem. Motion Picture Pioneers, Acad. for Motion Picture Arts and Scis. Clubs: Variety, Harmonie, AKC, Racquet. Co-author: Action for Mental Health, 1961. Contbr. articles psychiat. jours. Home: 150 E 69th St New York NY 10021 Office: 150 E 58th St New York NY 10022 also 6430 Sunset Blvd Los Angeles CA 90028

SCHLANG, JOSEPH, business exec.; b. N.Y.C., Feb. 24, 1911; s. Alexander and Blanche (Cohen) S.; B.C.S., N.Y. U., 1931; m. Bernice S. Breitbart, June 8, 1944; 1 son, Stuart Alexander. Organized firm of Schlang Bros. & Co., real estate, N.Y.C., 1934, since partner of firm; mgr. 80, 89, 67 and 41 Broad St., 100 Gold St., 132 Nassau St., 30 Pine St., 67 Wall St., 15 Moore St., 27 William St., and others; owner bldg. material co. of Candee, Smith & Howland Co., 1944-55; dir., part owner Fork Lift Truck Rental Corp., Bond Indsl. Maintenance Corp., 1956-57; owner 271 Central Park West, 1958-59; ltd. partner 975 Park Ave., 1957-60, 1165 Park Av., 1957-60, Majidot Realty Corp., 1958—, 67 Wall St. Co., 1957—, 80 Broad St. Mortgage, 1956-61, 1036 Park Ave. Assos., 1960-61; ltd. partner N.Y. Stock Exchange firm Kalb, Voorhis & Co., 1958—; pres. Schlang Manuscript Co., Inc., 1965—; pres. Internat. Opera Co., 1969—, Opera Gems, Inc., 1971—, Opera Presentations, Inc., 1972—; producer, sponsor, panelist weekly radio programs Opera Stars of Tomorrow, 100 and More Ways to Improve New York City, WNYC, 1973—; asso. pub. Graphic History Jewish Heritage, 1963, The Bible and Modern Medicine, 1963. Asst. treas. Downtown Hosp., 1945-47; nat. council N.Y. Met. Opera, 1960—, 1st patron, 1962; bd. dirs. Bklyn. Lyric Opera Co., 1972—; life mem. Concert Artists Guild, 1972—; sponsor N.Y. City Opera, 1962-63; patron Cultural Film Club, Palm Beach, Fla., Bicentennial Exhibits, Palm Beach, Civic Opera Palm Beaches, Greater Miami Opera Guild, Norton Gallery of Art, Hist. Assn. Palm Beaches Round Table Palm Beach, Soc. Four Arts, Lighthouse Gallery Art and Mus.; founder, 1st chmn. bus. Com. for Arts of Palm Beach County, 1979—; mem. pres.'s council Council of Civic Opera of Palm Beach, 1979—; adviser Library of Presdl. Papers, 1966-70; cons. Mayor's Cultural Com., Yonkers, 1972—, Mamaroneck, 1972-73; sec., dir. Kehillah of N.Y.C. (Jewish community); sec., treas. Synagogue Council Am., 1953-57, mem. exec. com., dir., 1947-67; pres. Schlang Found., Inc., Broad St. Found., Inc., Barclay Found., Inc., Joseph Schlang Found., Inc.; treas. Elias Cohen Found., Inc., Found. For a Graphic History Jewish Lit., Inc., E.A. Cohen Inst. Jewish Edn.; dir. bd. review and conciliation in Jewish Schs.; trustee Cong. Kehilath Jeshurun N.Y., 1957-77. Founder Albert Einstein Coll. Medicine, Technion Inst. Medicine, Technion Inst. in Israel. Recipient award Am. Jewish Lit. Found., 1960; Statesman award Synagogue Council Am., 1964; proclamations for presentation of free opera festivals from Gov. N.Y. and mayors of 9 cities; certificate of appreciation Mayor N.Y.C., 1974; proclamations County Exec. Nassau and mayors N.Y.C., Mamaroneck, Yonkers for Verdi Festival Periods, 1974. Mem. U.S. and N.Y. Power Squadron, N.Y. Real Estate Bd., Nat. Assn. Real Estate Boards, Manuscript Soc. Am., Nat. Assn. Owners, Mgrs. and Builders. Republican. Jewish Orthodox (mem. exec. com. dir. Union Orthodox Jewish Congregation Am.). Clubs: Town, 100 (co-founder 1938, v.p. 1970-72, pres. 1972-74), Lancers (v.p., pres. 1960—), City, Colonial Yacht, Palm Beach Poinciana. Author: (booklet) Survey of the Financial District of New York City, 1940; Financial District of New York City, 1956; also numerous newspaper and mag. articles. Home: 35 E 84th St New York City NY 10028 also Palm Beach Towers 44 Cocoanut Row Palm Beach FL Office: 75 Maiden Ln New York City NY 10038

SCHLANGER, ARNOLD GEOFFREY, textile co. exec.; b. Bklyn., July 5, 1942; s. Emanuel David and Edna (Stark) S.; A.B. cum laude, U. Rochester, 1964; J.D. (Nat. Honor scholar), U. Chgo., 1967; m. Barbara Joan Goldberg, Sept. 12, 1971; children—Alison Gail, Andrew Ryan; 1 dau. by previous marriage, Laura Ellen. Admitted to N.Y. bar, 1968; asso. Parker, Chapin, Flattau & Klimpl, N.Y.C., 1967-70; sec., gen. counsel, dir. Nat. Spinning Co., Inc., N.Y.C., 1970—; dir. Dye Masters, Inc., Long Beach, Calif., Network Computing Corp., Carlotte, N.C. Sec., lawyers com. Am. Policy Towards Viet Nam, 1970—. Mem. exec. bd., treas., coordinator N.Y. State Lawyers for McGovern, 1971-72; co-chmn. Lawyers for Ramsey Clark for U.S. Senate, 1974, 76. Mem. N.Y. State Bar Assn., Lawyers Assn. of Textile Industry, Am. Arbitration Assn. (panelist). Home: 207 E 74th St New York NY 10021 Office: 183 Madison Ave New York NY 10016

SCHLANGER, SEYMOUR OSCAR, geologist, educator; b. N.Y.C., Sept. 12, 1927; s. Carl Joseph and Pauline (Eisenstein) S.; B.Sc., Rutgers U., 1950, M.Sc. in Geology, 1951; Ph.D., in Geology and Oceanography, Johns Hopkins, 1959; m. Sarah Huber Wimsatt, Sept. 12, 1953; children—Stephanie Ann, Sarah Helen; m. 2d, Sandra Margot von Valtier, Jan. 12, 1973; children—Steven E., William J. Research asst. Rutgers U., 1950-51; geologist U.S. Geol. Survey, 1951-59, 61-62; prof. Petroleo Brasileiro, Brazil, 1959-61; mem. faculty U. Calif. at Riverside, 1962-75; vis. prof. Tohoku (Japan) U., 1965-66, Swiss Fed. Inst. Tech., 1969; prof. U. Leiden (Netherlands), 1975-77, U. Hawaii, Honolulu, 1977—; cons. in field, 1968—; U. Calif. del. XXIII Internat. Geol. Congress, Prague, 1968; participant, co-chief scientist Legs XVII, XXXIII, XVXI Deep Sea Drilling Project, 1971, 73, 78; cons. U.S.-Japan marine geology panel U.S. Dept. Interior, 1971—. Served with USNR, 1945-46. Guggenheim fellow, 1969-70. Fellow Geol. Soc. Am.; mem. Am. Assn. Petroleum Geologists, Internat. Assn. Sedimentologists (treas. 1975-77), Soc. Econ. Mineralogists and Paleontologists, Sigma Xi. Research in sedimentary petrology, marine geology. Address: Hawaii Inst Geophysics U Hawaii Honolulu HI

SCHLARETZKI, WALTER ERNEST, educator; b. Dallas City, Ill., Feb. 7, 1920; s. Walter and Anna Faye (Taylor) S.; A.B., Monmouth Coll., 1941; A.M., U. Ill., 1942; postgrad. Chgo. Theol. Sem., 1942-44; Ph.D., Cornell U., 1948; m. Eleanor Frances Campbell, Dec. 26, 1948. Asst. prof. Okla. A. and M. Coll., Stillwater, 1948-51, asso. prof., 1951-53; asst. prof. U. Md., 1953-60, asso. prof., 1960-64, prof., 1964—, chmn. dept. philosophy, 1963-72. Vis. asst. prof. Cornell U., 1950-51; vis. asso. prof. U. Ill., 1957-58. Served with USNR, 1944-46. Faculty fellow Fund Advancement Edn., 1955-56. Mem. Am. Philos. Assn. Home: 11534 Highview Ave Silver Spring MD 20902 Office: U Md College Park MD 20742

SCHLATTER, RICHARD, educator; b. Fostoria, Ohio, Mar. 3, 1912; s. Daniel and Bessie (Bulger) S.; B.A., Harvard U., 1934; B.Litt., Oxford (Eng.) U. 1936; D.Phil., 1938; L.H.D., Rutgers U., 1973; m. Suzanne Wynmalen, Dec. 21, 1940; children—Daniel, Heidi, Lance. Rhodes scholar, 1934-37; asst. prof. history Harvard, 1937-46; prof. history Rutgers U., 1946—, chmn. history dept., 1957-60, provost, v.p., 1962-72, univ. prof., 1972—; Fulbright prof., Eng., 1950; vis. prof. history Princeton, 1954-55, dir. Ford Humanities project, 1959-65; exec. dir. XIV Internat. Congress Hist. Scis., 1973-75. Dir. S. and H. Found. lectureship program, 1976—; mem. Fulbright selection com., 1976—. Ford fellow, 1955-56. Mem. Am. Hist. Assn., Phi Beta Kappa (dir. bicentennial fellowship program 1973—, Ralph Waldo Emerson award com. 1975—). Clubs: Harvard, Century Assn. (N.Y.C.). Author: Social Ideas of Religious Leaders, 1940; Private Property, 1950; Puritan Politics, 1957; Hobbes's Thucydides, 1975. Home: Neshanic Station NJ 08853 Office: Rutgers The State U NJ New Brunswick NJ 08903

SCHLATTER, WILLIAM JOSEPH, educator; b. Brookings, S.D., Nov. 25, 1912; s. Charles Fordemwalt and Lora Elta (Nusbaum) S.; A.B. in Philosophy, U. Ill., 1933, A.M. in Econs., 1934, B.S. in Banking and Finance, 1935, Ph.D. in Econs., 1947; postgrad. U. Wis., 1934, U. Calif. at Berkeley, 1937-38; m. Kathryn Maxine Dawson, Dec. 26, 1936; children—Barbara Walts, Roger Thomas, Ann Singer, Kathryn (Mrs. John Christian). Instr. accounting Geneva Coll., Beaver Falls, Pa., 1935-37; instr. econs. Yale, 1938-44; supervising accountant OPA Regional Office, Chgo., 1944-46; asst. prof. accounting U. Mich., 1946-48, asso. prof., 1948-51, prof., 1951-67, asso. dean Sch. Bus. Adminstrn., 1958-60, asst. to v.p. acad. affairs, 1965-67; prof. control and finance Istituto Post- Universitario per lo Studio dell' Organizzazione Aziendale, Turin, Italy, 1955-56; dean Faculty Bus., McMaster U., Hamilton, Ont., Can., 1967-73, prof. accounting, 1967—, chmn. dept., 1976—. C.P.A., Ill. Mem. Am. Assn. C.P.A.'s, Nat. Assn. Accountants, Fin. Execs. Inst., Am. Econ. Assn., AAAS, Phi Beta Kappa, Beta Gamma Sigma, Beta Alpha Psi. Mem. United Ch. Can. Author: (with C.F. Schlatter) Cost Accounting, 1957; (with George Husband) Introductory Accounting, 1949. Editorial bd. Cost and Management, 1967—. Home: 44 Cait Ct Ancaster ON Canada Office: Faculty Bus McMaster U Hamilton ON Canada

SCHLECHTE, WALTER AUGUST, banker; b. Tawas, Mich., June 16, 1909; s. Martin H. and Ida (Waack) S.; grad. Rutgers U. Grad. Sch. Banking, 1937; m. Dorothea Johnson, Sept. 22, 1934; children—Thomas W., John V., Anne Louise. Pres. Old Nat. Bank, Evansville, Ind., 1953-66, chmn., 1966—; pres. Peoples Bank & Trust Co., Mt. Vernon, Ind., 1955-66, chmn., 1966—. Bd. dirs. Evansville's Future, Inc., Evansville Indsl. Found., Inc.; trustee U. Evansville. Mem. Am., Ind. (past pres.) bankers assns. Presbyn. Rotarian (past pres. Evansville). Clubs: Western Hills Country (Mt. Vernon); Oak Meadow Golf and Tennis; Evansville Country. Home: 1315 E Chandler Ave Evansville IN 47714 Office: 420 Main St Evansville IN 47708

SCHLECHTEN, ALBERT WILBUR, metallurgist; b. Bozeman, Mont., Nov. 28, 1914; s. Albert and Clara (Schmidt) S.; B.S., Mont. Sch. of Mines, 1937; D.Sc., Mass. Inst. Tech., 1940; m. Eleanor L. Rodgers, Aug. 23, 1941; children—Mark, Carol, Jean, Eric, Brian. Asst. prof. metallurgy U. Minn., 1940-42; asst. research engr. Anaconda Copper Mining Co. (Mont.), 1941; asso. prof. mining engring. Oreg. State Coll., 1942-44; metallurgist U.S. Bur. Mines (devel. ductile zirconium metal), Albany, Oreg., 1944-46; prof. and chmn. dept. metall. engring. Mo. Sch. Mines and Metallurgy, Rolla, 1946-63; prof., head dept. metall. engring. Colo. Sch. Mines, Golden, 1963-68, dir. inst. for extractive metallugy, 1964—, v.p. for acad. affairs, 1968-71, Alcoa prof. metallurgy, 1971-75; cons. metallurgist, 1964—. Fulbright lectr., Australia, 1966. Mem. Am. Inst. M.E. (bd. dirs.), Am. Soc. Metals, ASEE Am. Foundrymen's Soc., Sigma Xi, Sigma Phi Epsilon, Theta Tau. Episcopalian. Contbr. articles to tech. jours. Departmental editor Ency. Brit. Home: 1904 Pinal Rd Golden CO 80401

SCHLEGEL, DAVID EDWARD, plant pathologist, educator; b. Fresno, Calif., Sept. 3, 1927; s. Edward and Lydia (Denny) S.; B.S., Oreg. State U., 1950; Ph.D., U. Calif. at Berkeley, 1954; m. Betty Carolyn Adkins, Sept. 12, 1948; children—Marsha Elaine, Linda Elise, Mark David, Susan Eileen. Faculty dept. plant pathology U. Calif. at Berkeley, 1953—, prof. plant pathology, plant pathologist, chmn. dept., 1970-76, asso. dean research Coll. Natural Resources, 1976-79, dean, 1979—, Miller prof., 1966-67. Asso. dir. project on pest mgmt. and environ. protection AID, 1973—. Served with USNR, 1945-46. NIH grantee, 1960-73; NSF grantee, 1974-76. Mem. Am. Phytopath. Soc., Am. Inst. Biol. Sci., Soc. Gen. Microbiology (U.K.), Sigma Xi. Research on plant virus replication, structure function relationships, comparative virology. Home: 3995 Paseo Grande Moraga CA 94556 Office: Coll Natural Resources U Calif at Berkeley Berkeley CA 94720

SCHLEGEL, EDWARD JOHN, machinery mfr.; b. Peoria, Ill., Apr. 7, 1922; s. Edward John and Anna (Endres) S.; B.S. in Bus. Adminstrn., Bradley U., Peoria, 1947; m. Teresa A. Radosevich, Apr. 17, 1948; children—Christine, Susan. With Caterpillar Tractor Co., Peoria, 1947—, treas., 1962-66, mng. dir. Caterpillar of Australia, 1966-70, chmn. Caterpillar Mitsubishi, Ltd., Japan, 1970-73, v.p., Peoria, 1973-75, exec. v.p., 1975—; dir. Univ. Nat. Bank of Peoria, Caterpillar Tractor Co., Peoria, NCR Corp., Dayton, Ohio. Dir. Japan-Am. Soc. Chgo.; trustee Meth. Med. Center of Ill., Bradley U.; vice chmn. bd. dirs. Overseas Devel. Council. Served with Signal Corps, AUS, 1943-46. Club: Country of Peoria. Office: 100 NE Adams St Peoria IL 61629

SCHLEGEL, RICHARD, physicist, educator; b. Davenport, Iowa, Aug. 29, 1913; s. Richard and Mayme (Hansen) S.; A.B., U. Chgo., 1935; M.A., U. Iowa, 1936; postgrad. U. Colo., 1940-41; Ph.D., U. Ill., 1943; m. Frances Stanley McKee, June 26, 1946; children—Thomas H., Catherine M. Lectr., Mus. Sci. and Industry, Chgo., 1938-40; asso. physicist Metall. Lab., U. Chgo., 1941-43; instr. physics Princeton, 1945-48; faculty Mich. State U., East Lansing, 1948—, prof. physics, 1957—, acting head dept. physics, 1955-56; vis. prof. U. Calif., Berkeley, summer 1959. Vis. asso. Cavendish Lab., Cambridge, Eng., 1954-55, 68-69, 75-76; affiliate History and Philosophy of Sci. Group, Cambridge, Eng., 1961-62. Fellow Am. Phys. Soc. Author: Time and the Physical World, 1961; Completeness in Science, 1967; Inquiry Into Science, 1971. Research on Lorentz transformations and quantum theory, cosmology, cultural and religious implications of modern physics, limits of sci. Home: 660 Stoddard Ave East Lansing MI 48823

SCHLEGEL, ROBERT PHILIP, mfg. co. exec.; b. Columbus, Ohio, May 23, 1929; s. Edward Paul and Sylvia Elizabeth (Kahler) S.; B.Sc., Capital U., Columbus, 1951; grad. Advanced Mgmt. Program, Harvard U., 1972; m. Mary Lou Peters, June 15, 1952; children—Debra Lynn, Edward Paul, Dana Sue. With Ames Co., Elkhart, Ind., 1952—, pres., 1971—; partner Peters-Schlegel Co., Columbus, 1966—; sr. v.p. profl. products group Miles Labs., Inc.; dir. Miles-Sankyo Ltd., Tokyo, Ames-Yissum, Jerusalem, Scripps-Miles Inc., San Diego. Mem. exec. com. Canadian Diabetic Assn., 1963;

treas. Elkhart County Young Republican Club, 1965-66. Club: Crystal Lake (Mich.) Yacht. Office: 1127 Myrtle St Elkhart IN 46514

SCHLEGEL, WALTER LOTHAR, JR., lawyer; b. Chgo., Apr. 21, 1916; s. Walter Lothar and Eva Minnette (Pearce) S.; student Wright Jr. Coll., 1934-36; LL.B., Chgo.-Kent Coll. Law, 1939; B.A. in History, U. Chgo., 1941; grad. exec. devel. program Ind. U., 1956; m. Grace May Dramdahl, Aug. 25, 1950; children—Walter Lothar, III, Frank Pearce, Jean Marie Schlegel Bigger. Admitted to bar; with Amsted Industries, 1941-44, 46—, asst. sec. and chief patent atty., 1959-73, gen. counsel and chief patent atty., 1973-75, gen. counsel, 1975—. Served with AUS, 1944-46. Mem. Am. Bar Assn., Am. Patent Law Assn., Patent Law Assn. Chgo., Lutheran. Clubs: Chgo. Athletic Assn.; Elks (Wheaton-Glen Ellyn, Ill.). Home: 1 S 311 Edgewood Walk West Chicago IL 60185 Office: 3700 Prudential Plaza Chicago IL 60601

SCHLEI, NORBERT ANTHONY, lawyer; b. Dayton, Ohio, June 14, 1929; s. William Frank and Norma (Lindsley) S.; B.A., Ohio State U., 1950; LL.B. magna cum laude, Yale U., 1956; m. Jane Moore, 1950 (div. 1964); children—Anne, William, Andrew; m. 2d, Barbara Lindemann, Mar. 7, 1965; children—Bradford, Graham, Norbert L., Norma. Admitted to Ohio bar, 1956, Calif. bar, 1958, D.C. bar, 1963; law clerk U.S. Justice Harlan, 1956-57; practice in Los Angeles, 1957-62, 67—; asst. atty. gen. U.S., Washington, 1962-66; mem. firm Hughes Hubbard & Reed, 1972—. George H. Leatherbee lectr. Harvard U. Grad. Sch. Bus. Adminstrn., 1961; lectr. law U. So. Calif. Sch. Law, 1961-62. Democratic candidate for Calif. Assembly, 1962, for Cal. sec. of state, 1966. Served to lt. (j.g.) USNR, 1950-53. Recipient Benjamin N. Cardozo prize Yale U., 1954, Edward S. Robbins meml. prize, 1956. Mem. Am., Calif., Los Angeles, Fed. bar assns., Am. Judicature Soc., Am. Soc. Internat. Law, Order of Coif, Phi Alpha Delta, Phi Kappa Sigma, Phi Eta Sigma. Author: McDougal & Associates, Studies in World Public Order (co-recipient annual award Am. Soc. Internat. Law, 1962), 1961; State Regulation of Corporate Financial Practices: The California Experience, 1962; also articles. Editor-in-chief Yale Law Jour., 1955-56. Office: 515 S Flower St Los Angeles CA 90071 also One Wall St New York NY 10005

SCHLEIDER, HENRY I., fin. co. exec.; b. Bklyn., June 5, 1923; s. Sidney and Dora (Weissman) S.; B.B.A., Coll. City N.Y., 1950; m. Muriel Stern, Sept. 11, 1949; 1 dau., Dorothy Anne. Accountant, Charles M. Riedell & Co., C.P.A.'s, 1950-59; treas., controller H.C. Bohack Co., Inc., N.Y.C., 1959-66; dir., v.p., treas. Bohack Realty Corp., 1962-66; v.p. finance Cunningham Drug Stores, Inc., 1967-70; v.p., treas. Crowley, Milner & Co., dept. store chain, 1970-78; controller Alpha X Corp., Bloomfield Hills, Mich., 1978—. Served with AUS, 1943-46. Mem. Financial Execs. Inst., Am. Mgmt. Assn., Nat. Assn. Accountants. Home: 5579 Swanlake Dr West Bloomfield MI 48033 Office: PO Box 86 Bloomfield Hills MI 48013

SCHLEIFER, ARTHUR, JR., educator; b. N.Y.C., June 18, 1931; s. Arthur and Miriam (Fishel), S.; A.B., Yale U., 1952; M.B.A., Harvard U., 1954, D.B.A., 1961; m. Yvette Roman, Sept. 21, 1961; children—Caroline Ann, Arthur, David Roman. Asst. prof. Amos Tuck Sch. Bus. Adminstrn., Dartmouth Coll., Hanover, N.H., 1957, asso. prof., to 1964; research asst. Harvard Bus. Sch., Cambridge, Mass., 1954, research asso., 1957, asso. prof., 1964, now prof.; cons. in field. Mem. Am. Statis. Assn., Sigma Xi. Author: (with J.G. Kemeny, J.L. Snell, G.L. Thompson) Finite Mathematics with Business Applications, 1962, 72; (with J. Bracken) Tables for Normal Sampling with Unknown Variance, 1964. Home: 25 Farlow Rd Newton MA 02158 Office: Harvard Bus Sch Boston MA 02163

SCHLEIN, PETER ELI, physicist, educator; b. N.Y.C., Nov. 18, 1932; s. Irving and Ann (Seigal) S.; B.S., Union Coll., 1954; postgrad. Northwestern U., 1954-55, 56-58, Ph.D., 1959; postgrad. Swiss Fed. Inst. Tech., Zurich, 1955-56; m. Lisa Rosenfarb, Nov. 25, 1962; children—Oren, Ilana. Research asso. Northwestern U., 1958-59, U. Chgo. 1959, Johns Hopkins, 1959-61; research asso. U. Calif. at Los Angeles, 1961-62, asst. prof., 1962-65, asso. prof., 1965-68, prof., 1968—; vis. physicist Saclay, Paris, France, 1963-64, CERN, Geneva, 1969-70. Guggenheim fellow, 1969-70. Fellow Am. Phys. Soc. Contbr. research articles in high energy physics to tech. jours. Home: 3230 Kelton Ave Los Angeles CA 90034 Office: Physics Dept U Calif Los Angeles CA 90024

SCHLENDER, WILLIAM ELMER, educator; b. Sawyer, Mich., Oct. 28, 1920; s. Gustav A. and Marie (Zindler) S.; A.B., Valparaiso U., 1941; M.B.A., U. Denver, 1947; Ph.D., Ohio State U., 1955; m. Lela R. Pullen, June 9, 1956. With U.S. Rubber Co., 1941-43, 46; asst. prof., asso. prof. bus. adminstrn. Bowling Green State U., 1947-53; asst. prof. bus. orgn., prof. Ohio State U., 1954-65, asst. dean, 1959-62, asso. dean Coll. Commerce and Adminstrn., 1962-63; prof. mgmt. U. Tex., 1965-68, chmn. dept., 1966-68; dean Cleve. State U. Coll. Bus. Adminstrn., 1968-75, prof. mgmt., 1975-76; Internat. Luth. Laymen's League prof. bus. ethics Valparaiso (Ind.) U., 1976—; vis. asso. prof. mgmt. Columbia, 1957-58; cons. in field. Mem. Gov.'s Adv. Council Internat. Trade. Bd. govs. Internat. Ins. Seminars. Served with AUS, 1943-45. Decorated Bronze Star. Fellow Acad. Mgmt.; mem. Indsl. Relations Research Assn., Inst. Mgmt. Scis., Am. Mgmt. Assn., Am. Acad. Polit. and Social Scis., Nat. Council Small Bus. Mgmt. Devel., Assn. Ohio Commodores, Tau Kappa Epsilon, Beta Gamma Sigma, Sigma Iota Epsilon, Phi Delta Phi, Alpha Kappa Psi, Phi Kappa Phi. Rotarian. Author: (with M.J. Jucius) Elements of Managerial Action, 3d edit., 1973; (with others) Management in Perspective: Selected Readings, 1965. Editor: Management in a Dynamic Society, 1965. Contbr. articles to profl. jours. Home: 205 Sturdy Rd Apt 21 Valparaiso IN 46383. *I resolved long ago that where I worked and what I did would be guided not by prestige considerations, but by the answers to three questions: (1) Will my work allow me to grow by discovering and developing my capabilities? (2) Will it make a significant contribution to my profession and to the community? (3) Will I enjoy doing it? My career, and my personal philosophy, have these underlying guidelines.*

SCHLENGER, JACQUES THOMPSON, lawyer; b. Balt., Oct. 11, 1927; s. Leo B. and Martha E. (Thompson) S.; B.S., U. Va., 1948; LL.B., Yale U., 1951; m. Suzanne Johnson, July 1, 1951; children—Lynda Sue, Martha Jaye, Kirsten. Admitted to D.C. bar, 1951, Md. bar, 1951, U.S. Tax Ct., U.S. Supreme Ct., 1955; asso. firm M. Quinn Shaughnessey, Washington, D.C., 1950-52; spl. atty. interpretative div. Office of Chief Counsel, IRS, Washington, 1952-55; individual practice law, Balt., 1955-63; partner firm Schlenger & Steinmann, Balt., 1963; partner firm Venable, Baetjer & Howard, Balt., 1963-79, mng. partner, 1979—; dir. Merry-Go-Round Enterprises, CHC Corp.; mem. fin. com. Broventure Co. Inc; lectr. tax, corporate taxation. Former counsel, mem. bd. dirs. Citizens' Planning and Housing Assn.; bd. dirs. Md. Children's Aide and Family Service Soc.; chmn. Balt. County Revenue Authority, Port Study Com., Greater Balt. Com.; trustee, v.p. Bryn Mawr Sch. Mem. Am. Law Inst., Am. Bar Assn., Fed. Bar Assn., Md. Bar Assn. (chmn. tax sect. 1969-70), Balt. City Bar (sec. ethics com. 1955-56), Am. Judicature Soc. (tax adv. group, editorial adv. bd.), Md. Hist. Soc. (counsel). Clubs: Yale (N.Y.C.); Nat. Lawyers; Balt. Bibliophiles, Center (Towson, Md.); Maryland. Contbr. articles to legal jours. Home: 408 Fox Chapel Dr Lutherville MD 21093 Office: 1800 Two Hopkins Plaza Baltimore MD 21201

SCHLESINGER, ARTHUR (MEIER), JR., writer, educator; b. Columbus, Ohio, Oct. 15, 1917; s. Arthur M. and Elizabeth (Bancroft) S.; A.B. summa cum laude, Harvard U., 1938, mem. Soc. of Fellows, 1939-42; postgrad. (Henry fellow) Cambridge (Eng.) U., 1938-39; hon. degrees: D Muhlenberg Coll., 1950, Bethany Coll., 1956, U. New Brunswick, 1960, New Sch. Social Research, 1966, Tusculum Coll., 1966, R.I. Coll., 1969, Aquinas Coll., 1971, Western New Eng. Coll., 1974, Ripon Coll., 1976, Iona Coll., 1977, Utah State U., 1978, U. Louisville, 1978; m. Marian Cannon, 1940 (div. 1970); children—Stephen Cannon, Katharine Kinderman, Christina, Andrew Bancroft. m. 2d, Alexandra Emmet, July 9, 1971; 1 son, Robert Emmet Kennedy. With OWI, 1942-43, OSS, 1943-45; asso. prof. history Harvard U., 1946-54, prof., 1954-61; vis. fellow Inst. Advanced Study, Princeton, N.J., 1966; Schweitzer prof. humanities City U. N.Y., 1966—. Mem. jury Cannes Film Festival, 1964; Mem. Adlai E. Stevenson campaign staff, 1952, 56; spl. asst. to Pres. of U.S., 1961-64. Trustee Twentieth Century Fund, Robert F. Kennedy Meml.; bd. dirs. John F. Kennedy Library, Harry S. Truman Library Ins. Served with AUS, 1945. Recipient Pulitzer prize for History, 1946, Francis Parkman prize, 1957, Bancroft prize, 1958, Pulitzer prize for biography, 1966, Nat. Book award, 1966, 79, Nat. Inst. Arts and Letters Gold Medal for History, 1967. Mem. Mass. Hist. Soc., Colonial Soc. Mass., Am. Hist. Assn., Orgn. Am. Historians, Soc. Am. Historians, Nat. Inst. Arts and Letters, ACLU, Council on Fgn. Relations Americans Dem. Action (nat. chmn. 1953-54), Assn. Study Afro-Am. Life and History, Phi Beta Kappa. Democrat. Unitarian. Club: Century. Author: Orestes A. Brownson, 1939; The Age of Jackson, 1945; The Vital Center, 1949; The General and the President (with R. H. Rovere), 1951; The Crisis of the Old Order, 1957; The Coming of the New Deal, 1958; The Politics of Upheaval, 1960; Kennedy or Nixon, 1960; The Politics of Hope, 1963; A Thousand Days, 1965; The Bitter Heritage, 1967; The Crisis of Confidence, 1969; The Imperial Presidency, 1973; Robert Kennedy and His Times, 1978. Contbr. articles to mags. and newspapers; film reviewer Show mag., 1962-64, Vogue, 1967-72, Saturday Rev., 1977—. Office: 33 W 42d St New York City NY 10036

SCHLESINGER, EDWARD BRUCE, neurol. surgeon; b. Pitts., Sept. 6, 1913; s. Samuel B. and Sara Marie (Schlesinger) S.; B.A., U. Pa., 1934, M.D., 1938; m. Mary Eddy, Nov. 1941; children—Jane, Mary, Ralph, Prudence. Mem. faculty Columbia Coll. Phys. and Surg., N.Y.C., 1946—, prof. clin. neurol. surgery, 1964—, Byron Stookey prof., chmn. dept. neurol. surgery, 1973—; dir. neurol. surgery Columbia Presbyn. Hosp., 1973—, pres. med. bd., 1976—. Diplomate Am. Bd. Neurosurgey. Fellow N.Y. Acad. Scis.; mem. Harvey Cushing Soc., Harvey Soc., AAAS, Assn. Research in Nervous and Mental Disease, Neurosurg. Soc. Am. (pres. 1970-71), Soc. Neurol. Surgeons, Am. Assn. Surgery of Trauma, Am. Rheumatism Soc., Am. Coll. Clin. Pharmacology and Chemotherapy, AMA, Eastern Assn. Electroencephalographers, Sigma Xi. Research, publs. on uses, effects of curare in neuromsucualr disease, lesions of central nervous system, localization of brain tumors using radioactive tagged isotopes. Home: Closter Dock Rd Alpine NJ 07620 Office: 710 W 168th St New York NY 10032

SCHLESINGER, JAMES RODNEY, former govt. ofcl.; b. N.Y.C., Feb. 15, 1929; s. Julius and Rhea (Rogen) S.; A.B. summa cum laude, Harvard, 1950, A.M., 1952, Ph.D., 1956; m. Rachel Mellinger, June 19, 1954; children—Cora K., Charles L., Ann R., William F., Emily, Thomas S., Clara, James Rodney. Asst. prof., then asso. prof. U. Va., 1955-63; sr. staff mem. RAND Corp., 1963-67 dir. strategic studies, 1967-69; asst. dir. Bur. of Budget, 1969, acting dep. dir., 1969-70, asst. dir. Office Mgmt. and Budget, 1970-71; chmn. AEC, 1971-73; dir. CIA, Feb.-July 1973; U.S. sec. def., 1973-75; asst. to Pres., 1977; sec. Dept. Energy, 1977-79; staff Center for Strategic and Internat. Studies, Georgetown U., 1979—; sr. adv. Lehman Bros. Kuhn Loeb, Inc., 1979—; vis. scholar Johns Hopkins Sch. Advanced Internat. Studies, 1976-77; cons. in field. Mem. bd. assos. Fgn. Policy Research Inst., U. Pa., 1962-63. Frederick Sheldon prize fellow Harvard, 1950-51. Mem. Am. Econ. Assn., Phi Beta Kappa. Republican. Lutheran. Author: The Political Economy of National Security, 1960. Co-author: Issues in Defense Economics, 1967. Asso. editor Jour. Finance, 1964-65. Home: 3601 N 26th St Arlington VA 22207 Office: Center Strategic and Internat Studies Georgetown U 1800 K St NW Washington DC 20006

SCHLESINGER, JOHN RICHARD, film and theatre dir.; b. London, Eng., Feb. 16, 1926; s. Bernard Edward and Winifred Henrietta (Regensburg) S.; B.A., Balliol Coll., Oxford U., 1950. Dir., B.B.C. Television, 1958-60; dir. feature films including: A Kind of Loving, 1962, (recipient Golden Bear award Berlin Film Festival), Billy Liar, 1963, Darling (recipient N.Y. Critics award), 1965, Far From the Madding Crowd, 1966, Midnight Cowboy (recipient Academy award), 1968, Sunday Bloody Sunday, 1970, Day of the Locust, 1974, Marathon Man, 1976, Yanks, 1979; dir. plays Royal Shakespeare Co. including: Days in the Trees, 1966, I and Albert, 1972; dir. plays Nat. Theatre: Heartbreak House, 1974, Julius Caesar, 1977, asso. dir. Nat. Theatre, London, 1973—. Served with Royal Engrs., 1944-48. Office: care of Michael Oliver Berger Oliver & Co 40 Piccadilly London WI England*

SCHLESINGER, JOSEPH ABRAHAM, polit. scientist; b. Boston, Jan. 4, 1922; s. Monroe Jacob and Millie (Romansky) S.; A.B., U. Chgo., 1942; A.M., Harvard U., 1947; Ph.D., Yale U., 1955; m. Mildred Saks, Sept. 9, 1951; children—Elizabeth Hannah, Jacob Monroe. Instr. Boston U., 1947-49; teaching fellow Wesleyan U., Middletown, Conn., 1952-53; mem. faculty Mich. State U., East Lansing, 1953—, prof. polit. sci., 1963—; vis. prof. U. Calif., Berkeley, 1964-65. Del. Ingham County (Mich.) Democratic Conv., 1966-68. Served with AUS, 1943-45. Cowles fellow, 1950-51; Block fellow, 1951-52; grantee Social Sci. Research Council, 1955-57, 68-69; recipient Distinguished Faculty award Mich. State U., 1976. Mem. Am., Midwest (v.p. 1969-70), So. polit. sci. assns., Mich. Conf. Polit. Scientists, Acad. Polit. Sci. Democrat. Jewish. Club: University. Author: How They Became Governor, 1957; Ambition and Politics: Political Careers in the United States, 1966; also articles. Home: 930 Roxburgh Ave East Lansing MI 48823 Office: Dept Polit Sci Mich State Univ East Lansing MI 48824

SCHLESINGER, LEE HAROLD, physician, univ. ofcl.; b. Pitts., May 9, 1905; s. Maurice and Rose (Braun) S.; B.S., U. Pitts., 1927; M.D., N.Y. U., 1931; m. Gertrude Mary Coggins, Nov. 15, 1935; children—Mary Ann (Mrs. John C. Cram), Patricia. Intern, resident U. Pitts. Hosps., 1931-34; pvt. practice, Pitts., 1933-38; asst. chief medicine Hines (Ill.) VA Hosp., 1938-42; clin. dir. Newington (Conn.) VA Hosp., 1946, White River (Vt.) VA Hosp., 1946-52; dir. VA Hosp., Clarksburg, W.Va., 1952-53, VA Hosp., Westside, Chgo., 1953-58; area med. dir. VA, Columbus, Ohio and Washington, 1958-63; dir. VA Hosp., Hines, 1963-73, ret. Vis. lectr. hosp. adminstrn. U. Chgo., 1964-68; asst. prof. medicine Stritch Sch. Medicine, Loyola U., 1966-79, emeritus, 1979—, asso. dean, 1971-78. Mem. coordinating com. Loyola Med. Center, 1963-73; mem. Adv. Council for Comprehensive State Health Planning, 1970-73. Mem. Western Suburban Planning Council, 1964-73. Served to col. M.C., USAAF. Decorated Purple Heart, Bronze Star. Fellow Am. Coll. Hosp. Adminstrs.; fellow Inst. Medicine Chgo.; mem. Chgo. Heart Assn., Am. Legion, VFW, DAV. Home: 3 Oak Brook Club Dr Oak Brook IL 60521

SCHLESINGER, ROBERT WALTER, microbiologist; b. Hamburg, Germany, Mar. 27, 1913; s. Emil and Flora (Srelitz) S.; student U. Hamburg Med. Sch., 1931-34; M.D., U. Basel (Switzerland), 1937; m. Adeline P. Sacks, Jan. 7, 1942; children—Robert, Ann. Came to U.S., 1938, naturalized, 1943. Guest Investigator Inst. Bacteriology and Hygiene, U. Basel, 1937-38; intern Beekman Hosp., N.Y.C., Stamford (Conn.) Hosp., 1938-40; fellow, asst. pathology and bacteriology Rockefeller Inst., N.Y.C., 1940-46; asso. research prof. pathology, head virus research lab. U. Pitts. Sch. Medicine, 1946-47; asso. mem., div. infectious diseases Pub. Health Research Inst., City of N.Y., Inc., 1947-55; prof., dir. dept. microbiology St. Louis U. Sch. Medicine, 1955-63; prof., chmn. dept. microbiology, Rutgers Med. Sch., Coll. Medicine and Dentistry N.J., Piscataway, also acting dean. Cons., Sec. War, 1946; mem. virology study sect. NIH; mem. adv. com. Nat. Cancer Inst.; mem. cell biology and virology adv. com. Am. Cancer Soc. Served as capt. M.C., AUS, 1944-46. Guggenheim fellow, 1972-73. Mem. Am. Acad. Microbiology, Am. Assn. Immunologists, Am. Soc. Microbiology, Am. Soc. Cancer Research, AAAS, N.Y. Acad. Scis., Sigma Xi. Editor: Virology. Contbr. articles to sci. jours. Home: 802 East Meadow Dr Bound Brook NJ 08805 Office: Rutgers Med Sch Piscataway NJ 08854

SCHLESINGER, RUDOLF BERTHOLD, lawyer, educator; b. Munich, Germany, Oct. 11, 1909 (father U.S. citizen); s. Morris and Emma (Aufhauser) S.; Dr.Jur. summa cum laude, U. Munich, 1933; LL.B., Columbia, 1942; m. Ruth Hirschland, Sept. 4, 1942; children—Steven, June, Fay. Law sec. to Chief Judge Irving Lehman, N.Y. Ct. Appeals, 1942-43; confidential law sec. Judges N.Y. Ct. Appeals, 1943- 44; asso. Milbank, Tweed, Hope & Hadley, N.Y.C., 1944-48; asso. prof. Cornell U., 1948-51, prof., 1951-75, William N. Cromwell prof. internat. and comparative law, 1956-75; prof. Hastings Coll. Law, U. Calif., 1975—, vis. prof., 1974. Cons. N.Y. State Law Rev. Commn., 1949—; mem. adv. com. internat. rules of jud. procedure, 1959-66; vis. prof. Columbia, 1952, Salzburg Seminar, 1964; Charles Inglis Thomson distinguished vis. prof. U. Colo., summer 1976. Trustee Cornell U., 1961-66; Carnegie Corp. Reflective year fellowship, 1962-63. Mem. Am. Law Inst., Am. Bar Assn., Internat. Acad. Comparative Law, Phi Beta Kappa, Order of Coif. Author: Cases, Text and Materials on Comparative Law, 2d edit., 1959, 3d edit., 1970, Updating Manual, 1978; Formation of Contracts: A Study of the Common Core of Legal Systems, 2 vols., 1968, others. Editor-in-chief Columbia Law Rev., 1941-42; bd. editors Am. Jour. Comparative Law. Author articles legal topics. Home: 2601 Vallejo St San Francisco CA 94123

SCHLESINGER, STEPHEN LYONS, found. exec.; b. N.Y.C., July 24, 1940; s. Nathan and Gertrude (Lyons) S.; B.A., Williams Coll., 1962; student U. Paris, 1960-61; M.A. in French, Columbia U., 1964; m. Barbara Bernthal, Feb. 17, 1963; children—Adam Lyons, Lauren Elizabeth. Lectr. in French, Hunter Coll., 1963-64, Columbia U., summers 1963-64; adminstrv. asst. John Simon Guggenheim Meml. Found., N.Y.C., 1965-67, asst. sec., 1967-70, asso. sec., 1970-73, sec., 1973—. Woodrow Wilson fellow, 1962-63. Office: 90 Park Ave New York NY 10016

SCHLESINGER, THEODORE, business exec.; b. N.Y.C., Oct. 27, 1908; s. Albert and Cornelia (Friedman) S.; A.B., City Coll. of N.Y., 1928; LL.D., Fordham U., 1931; m. Alma Ehrlich, Jan. 17, 1935; children—Albert E., Donald E. With Allied Stores Corp., 1929—, asst. to pres., 1939-45, v.p., 1945-59, pres., chief exec. officer, 1959-69, chmn. bd., chief exec. officer, 1970-72, chmn. exec. com., 1972-74; trustee Mut. Life N.Y. Home and office: 580 Yardarm Ln Longboat Key FL 33548

SCHLEUSENER, RICHARD AUGUST, coll. pres.; b. Oxford, Nebr., May 6, 1926; s. August William and Katherine Charlotte (Albrecht) S.; B.S., U. Nebr., 1949; M.S., Kans. State U., 1956; Ph.D., Colo. State U., 1958; postgrad. Mass. Inst. Tech., 1951-52; m. Elaine Emma Wilhelm, June 12, 1949; children—Kathryn Jeanne Schleusener Hanna, Richard Dennis, Rand Lee, Debra Sue, Jeffrey Thomas. Research engr. Colo. State U., 1958-64; dir. Inst. Atmospheric Sci., prof., head dept. meteorology S.D. Sch. Mines and Tech., Rapid City, 1965-74, v.p., dean engring., 1974-75, acting pres., 1975-76, pres., 1976—. Cons. weather modification Interior Dept., 1964—, U.S. Forest Service, 1966—, UNESCO, 1971—, also pvt. firms. Served with USAF, 1950-55. Mem. Am. Meteorol. Soc., Am. Geophys. Union, ASCE, Sigma Xi, Beta Sigma Psi. Lutheran. Clubs: Rotary, Cosmopolitan Internat. (Rapid City). Contbr. articles to tech. jours. Home: 315 S Berry Pine Rd Rapid City SD 57701

SCHLEYER, PAUL VON RAGUÉ, educator; b. Cleve., Feb. 27, 1930; s. Charles Ernest and Hulda Betty (Kamphausen) S.; A.B. Princeton, 1951; M.A., Harvard, 1956, Ph.D., 1957; Dr. Honoris Causa, U. Lyon (France), 1971; m. Ingeborg Venema, Dec. 29, 1969; children by previous marriage—Betti, Laura, Karen. Instr., Princeton, 1954-58, asst. prof., 1958-63. asso. prof., 1963-65, prof., 1965-69, Eugene Higgins prof. chemistry, 1969-76; prof. ordinarius, inst. dir. U. Erlangen-Nuremberg, W.Ger., 1976—; sr. fellow U. So. Calif., 1978—; vis. U. Colo., 1963, U. Würzburg (Germany), 1967, U. Mich., 1969, U. Munich (Germany), 1969, Carnegie Mellon U., 1969, Kyoto (Japan) U., 1970, U. Münster (Germany), 1971, U. Geneva (Switzerland), 1972, U. Groningen (Netherlands), 1972-73, U. Jerusalem (Israel), 1973, U. Paris (France), 1973, U. Louvain (Belgium), 1974, U. Regensburg, W.Ger., 1975, Case Western Res. U., 1976-77, U. Western Ont., 1978, Carnegie-Mellon U., 1977-78, U. Copenhagen (Denmark), 1979; cons. to industry, 1955—. Mem. rev. com. NIH, 1967-70. Recipient Von Humboldt sr. scientist award U. Munich, 1974-75. A.P. Sloan research fellow, 1962-66; Fulbright fellow, also Guggenheim fellow U. Munich, 1965. Editorial bd. Chem. Revs., 1969-72, Jour. Am. Chem. Soc., 1970—. Co-editor: (series) Carbonium Ions, vol. 1, 1968, vol. 2, 1970, vol. 3, 1972, vol. 4, 1973, vol. 5, 1977. Contbr. numerous research articles to tech. jours. Home: Deer Run Farm Rural Delivery 2 Box 169 Buckmanville Rd Newtown PA 18940 also Rathsberger Strasse 31 8520 Erlangen Federal Republic Germany Office: Inst Organic Chemistry U Erlangen-Nuremberg Henkestrasse 42 8520 Erlangen Federal Republic Germany also Hydrocarbon Inst U So Calif Los Angeles CA 90007

SCHLEZINGER, JULIUS, lawyer; B.A., Ohio State U., 1934, J.D. cum laude, 1935. Admitted to Ohio bar, 1935, U.S. Supreme Ct. bar, 1942, D.C. bar, 1947, Md. bar, 1960; atty. Rural Electrification Adminstrn., 1935-37, NLRB, 1937-39, U.S. Dept. Labor, 1939-43; with U.S. Mil. Govt., Germany, 1945-46; chief Claims Br. and Legal Brs., Office Alien Property, U.S. Dept. Justice, 1946-53; formerly partner firm Pehle, Luxford, Riemer, Schlezinger & Naiden, Washington; now mem. firm Morgan, Lewis & Bockius, Washington. Dir. Knoll Pharm. Co., Knoll Fine Chems., Inc. Served with U.S. Army, 1943-45; ETO. Mem. Order of Coif. Office: 1800 M St NW Washington DC 20036

SCHLICKAU, GEORGE HANS, cattle breeder, profl. cattlemen's assns. exec.; b. Haven, Kans., Nov. 2, 1922; s. Albert Rudulph and Florence Elsabe (Wittorff) S.; grad. high sch.; m. Lois Marie Ritthaler, Apr. 26, 1955; children—Bruce Alan, Susan Marie, James Darwin, Nancy Ann. Breeder registered Schlickau Hereford cattle, Haven, 1943—; pres. Reno County (Kans.) Hereford Assn., 1947-56, treas., 1956-58; dir. Reno County Cattleman's Assn., 1970-74, sec., 1970-71, treas., 1974; dir. Kans. Hereford Assn., 1955-71, v.p., 1959, pres. 1960, 61; county committeeman Kans. Livestock Assn., 1960-75, bd. dirs., 1976—; bd. dirs. Am. Hereford Assn., 1969-75, v.p., 1973-74, pres., 1974-75; bd. dirs. Am. Nat. Cattleman's Assn., 1974-76. Host ann. judging sch. and contest for Future Farmers Am. and 4-H youth, 1940—; dir. Kans. Nat. Jr. Livestock Show, 1973—; dir. Haven State Bank, 1962—; bd. dirs. Equus Beds Groundwater Mgmt. Dist. 2, 1975—. Beef leader Haven 4-H Club, 1947-67; mem. Haven High Sch. Bd., 1962-65, clk., 1964-65; mem. agrl. adv. com. Hutchinson (Kans.) Community Jr. Coll., Kans., 1974—; adv. Am. Jr. Hereford Assn., 1977—. Recipient Am. Farmer Degree award Future Farmers Am., 1942; Reno County Outstanding Young Farmer award Hutchinson Jaycees, 1959; Kans. Hereford Herdsman of the Year award High Plains Jour., 1960; Soil Conservation award Kans. Bankers Assn., 1968; Hon. State Farmer Degree award Future Farmers Am., 1972; Kans. Hereford Breeder of Yr., 1976; Portrait Gallery Outstanding Livestock Breeder award Kans. State U. Block and Bridle Club, 1978. Mem. Kans. Wheat Growers Assn., Kans. Farm Bur., Haven Industries, Inc., Kansas City (Kans.) Hereford Club, Kans. State U. Block and Bridle Club (hon. mem.), Haven Booster Club (sec. 1952-53, pres. 1954-56), Future Farmers Am. (mem. adv. com. Haven chpt. 1971—). Lutheran. (mem. sch. bd. 1967-70, chmn. 1969-70; chmn. ch. bd. 8 yrs., elder 1977-79). Contbr. articles in field to profl. jours. Exhibitor, also winner numerous awards at major cattle shows across country. Guest speaker, judge at numerous Hereford cattle events across country. Home: Route 2 Haven KS 67543

SCHLINGER, EVERT IRVING, entomologist; b. Los Angeles, Apr. 17, 1928; s. William M. and Julia (Gleason) S.; B.S., U. Calif., Berkeley, 1950; Ph.D., U. Calif., Davis, 1957; m. Audrey Darlene Sirois, June 8, 1957; children—Evert Irving, Mathew J., Jane Ann, Brian Thomas. Profl. insect collector Peruvian Expdn., Calif. Acad. Sci., 1954-55; jr. entomologist U. Calif., Riverside, 1956-57, asst. entomologist, 1957-62, asso. entomologist, asso. prof. entomology, 1962-67, prof. entomology, entomologist, 1967-69, chmn. dept., 1968-69; prof. div. entomology U. Calif., Berkeley, 1969—, chmn. div. entomology, 1975-76, chmn. dept. entomol. scis., 1976-79. Guggenheim fellow, 1966-67. Fellow AAAS, Calif. Acad. Sci., Entomol. Soc. Chile; mem. entomol. and ecol. socs., Nature Conservancy (dir. N. Calif. chpt. 1974-76). Author, asst. editor: Biological Control of Insect Pests and Weeds, 1964; author: (with F.R. Cole) Flies of Western North America, 1969; chmn. editorial bd. Jour. Econ. Entomology, 1967. Home: 3151 Diablo View Rd Lafayette CA 94549 Office: Dept Entomol Sci U Calif Berkeley CA 94720

SCHLINK, FREDERICK JOHN, mech. engr., physicist, consumers orgn. exec.; b. Peoria, Ill., Oct. 26, 1891; s. Valentine Louis and Margaret (Brutcher) S.; B.S., U. of Ill., 1912, M.E., 1917; married. Asso. physicist and tech. asst. to dir. U.S. Bur. Standards, 1913-19; physicist in charge of instruments-control dept. Firestone Tire & Rubber Co., Akron, O., 1919-20; mech. engr., physicist, Western Electric Co. (now Bell Telephone Labs.), N.Y.C., 1920-22; asst. sec. Am. Standards Assn., 1922-31; tech. dir., editor in chief Consumers' Research, non-profit orgn. supplying information on tests of products for ultimate consumers, Washington, N.J., 1929—, pres., 1931—; vis. prof. econs. of consumption U. Tenn., 1950; lectr. econs. consumption, other subjects. Mem. consumer adv. council and bd. dirs. conf. tech. users consumer products Underwriters Labs. Recipient U. Ill. Disting. Grad. in Mech. Engring. award, 1969; Alumni Honor Medal award for distinguished service in engring., 1971; Edward Longstreth medal Franklin Inst. Fellow Am. Phys. Soc., AAAS, ASME, Franklin Inst. (life); mem. Am. Inst. Physics, IEEE, Am. Econ. Assn., Am. Nat. Standards Assn. (dir.), Sigma Xi. Co-author: Your Money's Worth, 1927; One Hundred Million Guinea Pigs, 1933; Meat Three Times a Day, 1946; Don't You Believe It, 1966. Author: Eat, Drink and Be Wary, 1935. Contbr. numerous papers to tech., scientific, econ. and gen. jours. and to bulls. Nat. Bur. Standards and Consumers' Research. Home: RD 4 Washington NJ 07882 Office: care Consumers' Research Inc Washington NJ 07882

SCHLOEGEL, GEORGE ANTHONY, banker; b. Gulfport, Miss., June 17, 1940; s. Joseph A. and Nancy (Betrucci) S.; B.S., La. State U., 1962; grad. various bank mgmt. courses; m. Peggy Jay Harry, Mar. 14, 1959; children—Matthew, Mellisa, Mark, Michael. With Hancock Bank, Gulfport, 1956-59, 62—, exec. v.p., 1978—; with Whitney Nat. Bank, New Orleans, 1960-62. Pres. Gulfport Mcpl. Separate Sch. Dist., 1971-76, St. James Roman Catholic Ch. Parish Council, Golfport, 1972-74, Handsboro Preservation Soc., 1978-80; adv. bd. Gulfport Salvation Army, 1963-76; pres. Harrison County Assn. Retarded Citizens, 1963-65, Gulfport United Fund, 1974, Harbor Sq. Commn., 1978-80, Cheshire Home, Gulfport, 1978-80, Miss. Gulf Coast Jr. Coll. Found., 1978-80; dist. commr. Boy Scouts Am., 1970-74; chmn. Miss USA Pageant, 1979-80. Mem. Army N.G., 1954-62. Recipient Pine Burr Dist. Scouting award, 1974. Mem. Am. Bankers Assn., Am. Inst. Banking, Bank Mktg. Assn., Miss. Bankers Assn., U.S. Jaycees (v.p. 1969-70; Clayton Frost Meml. award 1969), Miss. Jaycees (pres. 1968-69; Outstanding Young Man award 1965), Gulfport Jaycees (pres. 1965; Disting. Service award 1965) Krewe of Baachus Carnival Orgn. Club: Gulfport Yacht (vice commodore). Home: 800 Commerce St Gulfport MS 39501 Office: 2400 14th St Gulfport MS 39501

SCHLOERB, PAUL RICHARD, educator, surgeon; b. Buffalo, Oct. 22, 1919; s. Herman George and Vera (Gross) S.; A.B., Harvard, 1941; M.D., U. Rochester, 1944; m. Louise M. Grimmer, Feb. 25, 1950; children—Ronald G., Patricia J., Marilyn A., Dorothy E., Paul Richard. Intern, U. Rochester Med. Sch., 1944-45, asst. resident, 1947-48, instr. surgery, 1952; research fellow, resident Peter Bent Brigham Hosp., Boston, 1948-52; mem. faculty U. Kans. Med. Center, Kansas City, 1952-79, prof. surgery, 1964-79, dean for research, 1972-79; prof. surgery U. Rochester (N.Y.) Med Center, 1979—; surgeon Strong Meml. Hosp., 1979—. Served to lt. (j.g.), M.C., USNR, 1944-45, to lt., 1953-55. Mem. Am. Surg. Assn., Soc. U. Surgeons, A.C.S., AAAS, Am. Physiol. Soc., Internat. Soc. Surgery, Central Surg. Assn., Am. Assn. Cancer Research, AMA, Sigma Xi. Contbr. articles to profl. jours. Office: U Rochester Med Center Dept Surgery 601 Elmwood Ave Rochester NY 14642

SCHLOM, JEFFREY BERT, scientist; b. N.Y.C., June 22, 1942; s. David and Anna (Klein) S.; B.S. (Pres.'s Scholar), Ohio State U., 1964; M.S., Adelphia U., 1966; Ph.D., Rutgers U., 1969; m. Myra Kesselman; children—Amy Melissa, Steven Michael. Instr., Columbia Coll. Phys. and Surg., 1969-71, asst. prof., 1971-73; chmn. breast cancer virus segment Nat Cancer Inst., NIH, Bethesda, Md., 1973-76, head tumor virus detection sect. 1976—; prof. George Washington U., Washington, 1975—. Recipient Dir.'s award NIH, 1977. Mem. AAAS, Harvey Soc., N.Y. Acad. Scis. Contbr. articles to profl. jours. Home: 404 Victoria Ct NW Vienna VA 22180 Office: Bodg 37 Room 1B19 Nat Cancer Inst NIH Bethesda MD 20014

SCHLOSS, MILTON JOSEPH, food co. exec.; b. Louisville, Nov. 15, 1913; s. Milton Joseph and Matilda (Kahn) S.; B.A., U. Mich., 1934; J.D., U. Cin., 1937; m. Mary Louise Telker, Mar. 19, 1941; children—Milton Joseph, Bert J., James D. With Kahn's and Co., Cin., 1929—, dept. supr., 1937-46, v.p., 1946-48, pres., 1948-78, chmn., 1978—; exec. v.p., dir. Consol. Foods Corp.; dir. Ohio Nat. Life Ins. Co. Pres. Citizens Sch. Com., 1962, Cin. Citizens Police Assn., 1966; chmn. Cin. Pub. Recreation Study, 1967. Served to capt. AUS, 1942-46; ETO. Decorated Bronze Star medal. Mem. Am. Meat Inst. (dir.), Cin. C. of C. (dir.), Order of Coif, Phi Epsilon Pi. Mem. B'nai B'rith. Home: 975 Marion Ave Cincinnati OH 45229 Office: 3241 Spring Grove Ave Cincinnati OH 45225

SCHLOSSER, GEORGE MCGARRAUGH, lawyer; b. Sioux Falls, S.D., Sept. 17, 1907; s. Arthur Rolland and Edna (McGarraugh) S.; student Carleton Coll., 1924-25; A.B., Yankton Coll., 1929, LL.D. (hon.), 1979; J.D., U. S. D., 1933; m. Florence Hohf, Apr. 26, 1928; children—Paul Douglas, Carolyn Ruth (Mrs. Arthur Duetsch). Admitted to S.D. bar, 1933, Ill. bar, 1943; practice of law, Brookings, S.D., 1933-43; with McBride, Baker, Wienke & Schlosser and predecessor firms, Chgo., 1943—; dir. 1st Nat. Bank Hinsdale (Ill.); exec. sec. Window Shade Mfrs. Assn. Pres., Village of Clarendon Hills, Ill., 1965-69. Trustee Yankton Coll., chmn. bd. trustees, 1976—. Mem. Am., Ill., DuPage County, Chgo. bar assns., State Bar S.D., Oak Brook Assn. Commerce and Industry (pres. 1978-79), Beta Theta Pi. Republican. Presbyn. Mason (32 deg., Shriner). Clubs: Executives, Tower (Chgo.); Hinsdale (Ill.) Golf (pres. 1965). Home: 322 Harris Ave Clarendon Hills IL 60514 Office: Oak Brook Executive Plaza Oak Brook IL 60521

SCHLOSSER, HERBERT S., broadcasting co. exec.; b. Atlantic City, Apr. 21, 1926; s. Abraham and Anna (Olesker) S.; A.B. summa cum laude, Princeton, 1948; LL.B., Yale, 1951; m. Judith P. Gassner, July 8, 1951; children—Lynn C., Eric M. Admitted to N.Y. bar, 1952; asso. firm Wickes, Riddell, Bloomer, Jacobi & McGuire, N.Y.C., 1951-54, Phillips, Nizer, Benjamin, Krim & Ballon, N.Y.C., 1954-57; with NBC, 1957-78, v.p., gen. mgr. subsidiary Calif. Nat. Prodns., Inc., 1960-61, dir. talent and program adminstrn., 1961-62, v.p. talent and program adminstrn., 1962-66, v.p. programs, West Coast NBC, 1966-72, exec. v.p. NBC-TV, 1972-73, pres., 1973-74, pres. NBC, Inc., 1974-78, chief exec. officer, 1977-78; exec. v.p. RCA, 1978—. Trustee, Internat. Radio and Television Found., 1972—; bd. govs. Ford's Theatre Soc.; trustee Nat. Urban League. Served with USNR, 1944-46. Recipient Humanitarian award NCCJ, 1974, Gold Brotherhood award, 1978. Mem. Assn. Bar City N.Y., Am., N.Y. State bar assns., Council on Fgn. Relations, Acad. Television Arts and Scis., Advt. Council (dir.), Yale Law Sch. Assn., Phi Beta Kappa (pres. alumni assn. So. Calif. 1970-72), Internat. Radio and Television Soc. (trustee 1973-74), Hollywood Radio and TV Soc. (trustee 1970-72). Club: Princeton (N.Y.). Office: RCA 30 Rockefeller Plaza New York NY 10020*

SCHLOTFELDT, ROZELLA MAY, educator; b. DeWitt, Iowa, June 29, 1914; d. John W. and Clara C. (Doering) Schlotfeldt; B.S., State U. Iowa, 1935; M.S., U. Chgo., 1947, Ph.D., 1956; D.Sc. (hon.), Georgetown U., 1972; L.H.D. (hon.), Med. U. S.C., 1976. Staff nurse State U. Ia., VA Hosp., 1935-39; instr., supr. maternity nursing State U. Ia., 1939-44; asst. prof. U. Colo. Sch. Nursing, 1947-48; asst., then asso. prof. Wayne State U. Coll. Nursing, 1948-55, prof., asso. dean Coll. Nursing, 1957-60; dean Frances Payne Bolton Sch. Nursing, Case Western Res. U., 1960-72, prof., 1960—. Spl. cons. Surgeon Gen.'s Adv. Group on Nursing, 1961-63; mem. nursing research study sect. USPHS, 1962-66; mem. Nat. League for Nursing-USPHS Com. on Nursing Edn. Facilities, 1962-64; mem. com. on health goals Cleve. Health Council, 1961-66; mem. Cleve. Health Planning and Devel. Commn., 1969-72; adv. com. div. nursing W.K. Kellog Found., 1959-67; v.p. Ohio Bd. Nursing Edn. and Nurse Registration, 1970-71, pres., 1971-72; mem. Nat. Health Services Research Tng. Com., 1970-71; mem. supply and edn. panel Health Manpower Com., 1966-67, rev. com. Nurse Tng. Act, 1967-68; bd. visitors Duke U. Med. Center, 1968-70; mem. council, exec. com. Inst. Medicine of Nat. Acad. Scis., 1971-75; mem. nat. adv. health services council Health Services and Mental Health Adminstrn., 1971-75; mem. def. adv. com. on women in services Dept. Def., 1972-75; bd. mem., treas. Nursing Home Adv. and Research Council, 1975—; mem. adv. panel Health Services Research Commn. on Human Resources, Nat. Acad. Sci., 1977—; cons. Walter Reed Army Inst.; adv. council on nursing U.S. VA, 1965-69, chmn., 1966-69. Served to 1st lt. Army Nurse Corps, 1944-46. Recipient Distinguished Service award U. Iowa, 1973. Fellow Am. Acad. Nursing (v.p. 1975-77), Nat. League Nursing; mem. Am. Nurses Assn. (chmn. commn. on nurse edn. 1967-70, mem. com. for studying credentials 1976—), Sigma Theta Tau (nat. v.p. 1948-50), Pi Lambda Theta. Mem. editorial bd. Nursing Forum; editorial adv. bd. Health Care Dimensions, 1973—. Contbr. numerous articles to profl. jours. Home: 1111 Carver Rd Cleveland Heights OH 44112 Office: 2121 Abington Rd Cleveland OH 44106

SCHLOTTERBECK, WALTER ALBERT, mfg. co. lawyer; b. N.Y.C., Dec. 22, 1926; s. Albert Gottlob and Maria Louise (Fritz) S.; A.B., Columbia U., 1949, LL.B., 1952; m. Pauline Elizabeth Hoerz, Sept. 2, 1951; children—Susan, Thomas, Paul. Admitted to N.Y. bar, 1953; counsel Gen. Electric Co., various locations, 1952—, v.p., corp. counsel, N.Y.C., 1970—, sec., 1975-76, gen. counsel, 1976—, sr. v.p., 1977—. Served with USNR, 1944-46. Home: 752 Town House Rd Fairfield CT 06430 Office: Fairfield CT 06431

SCHLUETER, JOHN F., assn. exec.; b. Chgo., June 30, 1920; s. Walter and Matilda (Van Volkenburg) S.; B.S., Mich. State U., 1943, M.A., 1948; m. Betty Jeanne Gibson, Apr. 7, 1945; children—Cathy Lynn, John Kirk. Placement dir. Mich. State U., 1946-53; mem. indsl. relations staff Ford Motor Co., 1953-58; with Pacific Fin. Corp., 1958-63, R.R. Donnelly & Sons, 1963-66, Nat. Bank of N.Am., 1966-73; exec. dir. Assn. Exec. Recruiting Cons., Inc., N.Y.C., 1973—. Nat. pres. Leukemia Soc. Am., Inc., 1973-74. Served with USNR, 1943-45. Mem. Am. Soc. Assn. Execs. Club: University (N.Y.C.). Home: 18-05 215th St New York NY 11360 Office: 30 Rockefeller Plaza New York NY 10020*

SCHLUSSEL, MARK EDWARD, lawyer; b. Detroit, Dec. 14, 1940; s. Irving Wolf and Marilyn (Dorman) S.; B.A., Wayne State U., 1962; J.D., U. Mich., 1965; m. Rose Lynn Meckler, Aug. 11, 1963. Admitted to Mich. bar, 1966; law clk. Chief Judge T. John Lesinski, Mich. Ct. of Appeals, 1965-66; mem. firm Sugar, Schwartz & Silver, Detroit, 1966-68; partner Schlussel, Lifton, Simon, Rands, Kaufman, Lesinski & Jackier, Southfield, Mich., 1968—. City councilman, Southfield, 1972-73. Mem. edn. cultural commn. Jewish Welfare Fedn. Met. Detroit, 1971—, bd. dirs., 1973—; pres. Fedn. Towers, 1976—; bd. dirs. Msgr. Clement Kern Hosp. for Spl. Surgery; pres. Jewish Nat. Fund Detroit, 1975-78; bd. govs. Jewish Welfare Fedn. Detroit, 1976—. Mem. Am., Detroit bar assns., Tau Epsilon Rho. Jewish (pres. congregation). Clubs: Standard (Detroit); Knollwood Country. Office: 29201 Telegraph Rd Southfield MI 48075

SCHLUTER, FREDRIC EDWARD, mgmt. cons.; b. N.Y.C., May 31, 1900; s. Christian L. and Anna (Von Thaden) S.; B.S., Columbia, 1922; m. Charlotte Mueller, Sept. 6, 1924 (div. 1948); children—Fredric, William, John, Peter; m. 2d, Dorothy Miskell, 1951. With Internat. News Service, Berlin, 1922; safety engr. Hamlin & Co., 1923; with Minsch, Monel & Co., Inc., investments, N.Y.C., 1923-25; pres., dir. Schluter & Co., Inc., investments, N.Y.C., 1925-35; pres. Androscoggin Pulp Co., South Windham, Maine, 1931-34; chmn., dir. Thermoid Co., automotive and indsl. rubber and asbestos products, 1934-52; chmn. Brager-Eisenberg, Inc., 1939-56; pres. Thermoid Mgrs. Group, Inc., 1957—. Rep. N.J. council State Chambers Commerce; industry mem. Nat. Labor Bd. Phila., 1944-48. N.J. del. Republican Nat. Conv., 1944, asst. chmn. Rep. Nat. Conv., 1948, 52. Pres., trustee Trenton Gen. Hosp.; nat. dir. Boys Club Am.; bd. mgrs. Rutgers U. Coll. Agr., 1940-58; mem. pres.'s council Brigham Young U., Provo, Utah, 1977—. Served with USNR, 1918. Recipient Columbia Alumni Service award, 1935; Silver medallion Boys' Clubs Am., 1956; Distinguished Am. award Del. Valley chpt. Nat. Football Found. Hall of Fame, 1969. Mem. N.J. Agrl. Soc., AIM (pres.'s council). Mem. Ch. of Jesus Christ of Latter-day Saints (high priest N.J. stake). Mason. Clubs: Salmagundi, Univ., Columbia (N.Y.C.); Princeton Golf (N.J.). Home: 340 Knob Hill Blvd Boca Raton FL 33431

SCHMALZER, VICTOR DAVID, publishing co. exec.; b. Queens Village, N.Y., Oct. 28, 1941; s. Peter and Anna M. (Burmeister) S.; A.B., Harvard U., 1963; m. Emily Ann van den Bergh, Aug. 26, 1967; children—Sigrid Ann, Peter Nils. Project mgr., mgr. contracts and royalties Litton Ednl. Pub., Inc., 1963-72; bus. and sales mgr., gen. mgr. Liveright Pub. Corp., N.Y.C., 1972-74; gen. mgr. W.W. Norton & Co., Inc., 1974-76, sec., 1976—. Home: Middle Rd Brentwood NH 03833 Office: 500 Fifth Ave New York City NY 10036

SCHMALZRIED, MARVIN EUGENE, diversified drug co. exec.; b. Dighton, Kans., Nov. 11, 1924; s. Carl D. and Marie M. (Bahm) S.; B.B.A., Northwestern U., 1949; LL.B., U. Conn., 1955; m. Jean Landino, Nov. 27, 1946; children—Darlene, Candace, Cynthia, Derek, Valerie, Rebecca. Accountant, Webster, Blanchard & Willard, C.P.A.'s, Hartford, Conn., 1950-55; admitted to Conn. bar, 1955; controller, asst. treas. J.B. Williams Co., Glastonbury, Conn., 1955-57; treas., sec. Curtis 1000, Inc., Atlanta, 1957-61; asst. to pres. Am. Home Products Corp., New York City, 1961-63, comptroller, 1964-67, v.p., 1967-72, sr. v.p., 1972—. Deacon, 1st Congl. Ch., Darien, Conn. Recipient Gold medal Conn. Soc. C.P.A.'s 1953. C.P.A., Conn. Mem. Am. Inst. C.P.A.'s, Am. Bar Assn., Fin. Execs. Inst., Old Greenwich Friday Evening Reading Soc. (pres.). Club: Darien Country. Home: 10 Duffy's-Lane Darien CT 06820 Office: 685 3d Ave New York City NY 10017

SCHMEIDLER, GERTRUDE RAFFEL, educator; b. Long Branch, N.J., June 15, 1912; d. Harry B. and Clare (Holzman) Raffel; B.A., magna cum laude, Smith Coll., 1932; M.A., Clark U., 1933; Ph.D., Harvard U., 1935, D. honoris causa, 1977; m. Robert Schmeidler, Aug. 27, 1937; children—James, Richard, Emilie, Katherine. Research asst. Found. for Neuro-Endocrine Research, Worcester, Mass., 1932-33; instr. Monmouth Coll., Long Branch, N.J., 1935-37; research asst. Harvard U., 1941-45; with City Coll. City Univ. N.Y., 1945—, prof. dept. psychology, 1963—. Recipient McDougall award, 1964. Fellow AAAS, Am. Psychol. Assn., Soc. for Psychol. Study for Social Issues; Eastern Psychol. Assn., Parapsychol. Assn. (pres. 1958, 71), Am. Soc. Psychical Research v.p. 1971—), Soc. Psychical Research, AAUP, Theta Assos., Phi Beta Kappa, Sigma Xi. Author: ESP and Personality Patterns, 1958; Extrasensory Perception, 1969; Parapsychology: Its Relation to Physics, Biology, Psychology and Psychiatry, 1976. Contbr. articles to profl. jours. Home: 17 Kent Ave Hastings on Hudson NY 10706 Office: Dept Psychology City Coll of New York Convent Ave and 138th St New York NY 10031

SCHMELING, GARETH, educator; b. Algoma, Wis., May 28, 1940; B.A., Northwestern Coll., 1963; M.A. (Knapp fellow), U. Wis., 1964, Ph.D. (Knapp travelling grantee 1965-66, Univ. fellow 1967-68), 1968; married. Asst. prof. classics U. Va., 1968-70; asso. prof. U. Fla., 1970-74, prof., 1974—, chmn. classics, 1974—, chmn. humanities, 1974-76, dir. Center for Studies in Humanities, 1978—, prin. investigator Humanities Perspectives on Professions, 1975—; panelist, research div. Nat. Endowment for Humanities. Named 1 of 5 Tchrs. of Yr. for Arts and Scis., U. Fla., 1973; recipient Rome prize Am. Acad., 1977-78; U. Va. faculty fellow, summer 1969, summer 1970; U. Fla. fellow, summer 1971, summer 1974; Nat. Endowment for Humanities fellow, 1973-74; Am. Council Learned Socs. summer fellow, 1974; Am. Philos. Soc. grantee, 1970, 71, 72, 77-78; U. Fla. grantee, 1977-78; Mem. Am. Philol. Assn., Am. Classical League, Vergilian Soc., Classical Assn. of Middle West and South (sec.-treas. 1975—). Translator and author introduction: Cornelius Nepos: Lives of Famous Men, 1971, author: Petronius' Satyricon, 1971; Ovid's The Art of Love, 1972; Chariton and the Rise of Ancient Fiction, 1974; Homer's the Odyssey, 1974; A Bibliography of Petronius, 1977; contbr. numerous articles, revs. to profl. jours.; editor Newsletter Petronian Soc., 1970—; editorial com. U. Fla. Press Humanities Monographs, 1978—. Home: 320 NW 30th St Gainesville FL 32607 Office: Dept Classics U Fla Gainesville FL 32611

SCHMELLER, KURT RICHARD, coll. pres.; b. Johnson City, N.Y., June 28, 1937; s. Rudolph and Liska (Bergmann) S.; A.B., Bates Coll., Lewiston, Me., 1959; M.A. in History, Princeton, 1961, Ph.D., 1962; m. Beata Sowka, Apr. 24, 1965; children—Rudolph, Sylvie-Marie, Jesse Paul. Mem. faculty Wis. State U., Stevens Point, 1962-67, asso. prof. history, 1966-67, asst. to pres., 1964-67; pres. Queensborough Community Coll., Bayside, N.Y., 1967—; dir. Bayside Fed. Savs. & Loan Assn. Mem. exec. bd. Queens Council Boy Scouts Am. Bd. dirs. Council Higher Ednl. Instns. N.Y.C. Bd. dirs. Queens Symphony Orch., Research Found. City U. N.Y.; trustee Proposed Queens Med. Sch. Devel. Corp. Woodrow Wilson fellow, 1959; Danforth fellow, 1959; Philip Rollins fellow, 1961-62. Mem. Am. Assn. for Higher Edn., Am. Hist. Assn., Soc. Religion Higher Edn., Phi Beta Kappa. Club: Princeton (N.Y.C.). Author: The Course of Europe Since Waterloo, 1968. Home: 51 Town Path Glen Cove NY 11542

SCHMELTZER, EDWARD, lawyer; b. N.Y.C., Aug. 22, 1923; s. Harry A. and Julia (Hoffman) S.; B.A., Hunter Coll., 1950; M.A., Columbia, 1951; J.D., George Washington U., 1954; m. Elizabeth Ann Cooper, June 19, 1949; children—Henry Cooper, Elizabeth Sabine. Admitted to D.C. bar, 1954, also U.S. Supreme Ct.; economist PHA, 1951-53; econ. cons., 1953-54; trial atty. Fed. Maritime Bd. Maritime Adminstrn., 1955-60; dir. bur. domestic regulation Fed. Maritime Commn., 1961-66, mng. dir., 1966-69; partner Morgan, Lewis & Bockius, 1969-76, Schmeltzer, Aptaker & Sheppard, 1976—. U.S. rep. 12th Diplomatic Conf. on Internat. Maritime Law, Brussels, 1967, 13th Diplomatic Conf., Brussels, 1968. Served with USAAF, 1943-46. Recipient Fed. Maritime Commn. Distinguished Service award, 1969. Mem. Maritime Adminstrv. Bar Assn. (pres. 1971-73). Mem. adv. bd. editors Jour. Maritime Law and Commerce. Contbr. articles to profl. jours. Home: 10412 Buckboard Pl Potomac MD 20854 Office: 1800 Massachusetts Ave NW Washington DC 20036

SCHMERTZ, HERBERT, oil co. exec.; b. Yonkers, N.Y., Mar. 22, 1930; s. Max and Hetty (Frank) S.; A.B., Union Coll., 1952, LL.D. (hon.), 1977; LL.B., Columbia U., 1955; children—Anthony, Lexy. Admitted to N.Y. State bar, 1958; with Am. Arbitration Assn., N.Y.C., 1955-61; gen. counsel, asst. to dir. Fedn. Mediation and

Conciliation Service, N.Y.C., 1961-66; with Mobil Oil Corp., N.Y.C., 1966—, pres. Mobil Shipping and Transp. Co., 1973-74, v.p. public affairs Mobil Oil Corp., 1974—, also dir. and dir. Mobil Corp.; mem. adv. council Aspen Inst. Humanistic Studies. Bd. dirs. Mcpl. Art Soc., N.Y.C. Served with CIC, U.S. Army, 1955-57. Democrat. Jewish. Clubs: Fed. City, Internat. (Washington); Pinnacle (N.Y.C.). Author: Takeover, 1980. Office: 150 E 42d St New York NY 10017

SCHMERTZ, MILDRED FLOYD, editor; b. Pitts., Mar. 29, 1925; d. Robert Watson and Mildred Patricia (Floyd) S.; B.Arch., Carnegie Mellon U., 1947; M.F.A., Yale U., 1957. Archtl. designer John Schurko, Architect, Pitts., 1947-55; asso. editor Archtl. Record, N.Y.C., 1957-65, sr. editor, 1965—; vis. lectr. Yale Sch. Architecture, 1979—. Bd. mgrs. Jr. League, City of N.Y., 1964-65. Fellow AIA; mem. Archtl. League N.Y. Club: Yale (N.Y.C.). Editor, contbr.: Campus Planning and Design; Office Building Design; Open Space for People. Home: 310 E 46th St New York NY 10017 Office: 1221 Ave of Americas New York NY 10020

SCHMICK, WILLIAM FREDERICK, JR., newspaper exec.; b. Balt., Dec. 3, 1913; s. William Frederick and Nancy M. (Reindollar) S.; A.B., Princeton U., 1936; m. Mary E. Novak, Apr. 17, 1939; children—Elizabeth A., William Frederick, Mary J., John E. With A.S. Abell Co., publishers Balt. Sun papers and owners Sta. WMAR-TV, Balt., 1938—, exec. v.p., 1953-60, pres., 1960—. Clubs: Md., Elkridge (Balt.). Office: care AS Abell Co 501 N Calvert St Baltimore MD 21203*

SCHMID, BERNARD FRANCIS, lawyer; b. Little Falls, Minn., Feb. 24, 1914; s. Joseph A. and Catherine (Thome) S.; student S.D. Sch. Mines, 1931-33; LL.B., Columbus U., Washington, 1937; m. Pearl L. Carroll, Nov. 11, 1934; children—Darlene Jo, Carol Marie, Kathleen Rose, Robert Anthony. With S.D. Hwy. Commn., Rapid City, 1933-34; accountant, adminstr. HOLC, Washington, 1934-40; economist, adminstr. OPA, Washington, 1941-46; bus. and trade relations Nat. Housing Agy., Washington., 1946-47; budget examiner Bur. of Budget, Washington, 1947-54; dep. adminstrv. asst. atty. gen. Dept. Justice, Washington, 1954-56; mng. dir. ICC, Washington, 1956-69; now prin. asso. Exec. Mgmt. Service, Inc., Arlington, Va. Mem. D.C. Bar Assn. K.C. Home: 14000 Castle Blvd Silver Spring MD 20904 Office: 2201 Wilson Blvd Arlington VA 22201

SCHMID, HELLMUT HEINRICH, educator; b. Dresden, Germany, Sept. 12, 1914; s. Kurt Rudolf and Dora Hedwig (Meissner) S.; Ph.D., Tech. U. Dresden, 1941; D.Engring. Scis. (hon.), Rheinisch Friedrich-Wilhelm U., Bonn, Germany, 1971; m. Ilse Hieby, Oct. 7, 1949; 1 dau., Monica Ilse. Came to U.S., 1945, naturalized, 1955. Chief geodetic sect. U.S. Army, Ft. Bliss, Tex., 1945-50; supr. research geodesist BRL, Aberdeen Proving Ground, Md., 1950-62; sci. adviser GIMRADA, Ft. Belvoir, Va., 1962-63; dir. geodetic research and devel. lab. Nat. Ocean Survey, Nat. Oceanic and Atmospheric Adminstrn., Rockville, Md., 1963-74; prof. photogrammetry Eidg Technische Hochschule, Zurich, Switzerland, 1974—. Recipient Colbert medal, 1965, Gold medal Commerce Dept., 1966, Brock award Internat. Soc. Photogrammetry, 1968. Fellow Am. Geophys. Union; mem. Am. Soc. Photogrammetry, Soc. Am. Mil. Engrs., Bavarian Acad. Scis. (corr. mem. math. and natural scis. class), German Geodetic Commn. (corr. mem.). Office: Inst for Geodesy and Photogrammetry ETH-Zurich Hönggerberg (HIL) Einsteinstrasse 8093 Zurich Switzerland

SCHMID, JOHN HENRY, mfg. co. exec.; b. Erie, Pa., Dec. 19, 1913; s. Frank J. and Edna S. (Smith) S.; B.Chemistry, Cornell U., Ithaca, N.Y., 1935, Chem. Engr., 1936; m. Margery S. St. Lawrence, Sept. 14, 1940; children—Margery (Mrs. Donald W. Wilson), John Henry. Indsl. engr. E. I. duPont deNemours Inc., Wilmington, Del., 1936-39; v.p. product devel. Zurn Industries Inc., Erie, 1939—. Cons. in liability litigation. Mem. Pa. Gov.'s Sci. Adv. Com., 1971—; mem. Great Lakes Commn., 1973-75, Erie County Solid Waste Authority, 1974-76; chmn. Millcreek Twp. (Pa.) Water Authority, 1974—. Corporator Hamot Med. Center. Mem. Am. Inst. Chem. Engrs., Am. Water Works Assn., Water Pollution Control Fedn. Republican. Presbyn. Club: Kahkwa. Patentee in field. Home: 402 Wilkins Rd Erie PA 16505 Office: One Zurn Pl Erie PA 16512

SCHMID, JOHN SAMUEL, lawyer; b. Newark, May 26, 1928; s. John and Meta (Pfenninger) S.; A.B., Princeton, 1952; LL.B., U. Pa., 1956; m. Barbara Jones, Dec. 8, 1956; children—William, Nancy, John. Admitted to N.Y. State bar, 1957, D.C. bar, 1977; asso. firm Thacher, Proffitt, Prizer, Crawley & Wood, N.Y.C., 1956-59; partner firm Glendening & Schmid, Washington, 1961—. Served with AUS, 1946-48. Mem. Am., Fed. Energy, N.Y. State, D.C. bar assns., Nat. Lawyers Club, Sigma Xi. Home: 6621 Lybrook Ct Bethesda MD 20034 Office: 1750 Pennsylvania Ave NW Washington DC 20006

SCHMID, LEOPOLD, hotel exec.; b. Vienna, Austria, June 8, 1928; s. Joseph and Anna (Schneider) S.; student Hotel and Restaurant Sch., Vienna, 1942-45; m. Yvonne Berube, Aug. 6, 1955; 1 dau., Marie-Carmen. Positions with numerous hotels, Switzerland, Holland, South Am., 1945-54; restaurant mgr. Rest Hill Bros., Montreal, 1954-60; food and beverage controller Queen Elizabeth Hotel and Hotel La Salle, Montreal, 1960-64; restaurant mgr. T. Eaton Co., Montreal, 1963-64; food and beverage mgr. Le Chateau Champlain, Montreal, 1964-67; dir. food and beverage services Can. Pacific Hotel system, Montreal, 1967-68, mgr. Airport restaurant, Vancouver Internat. Airport, 1968-70, mgr. catering services Can. Pacific Air, 1971-72, food and beverage dir. Royal York Hotel, CP-Hotels, 1972-73, gen. mgr. Can. Pacific Hotels, Acapulco, Mexico, 1973-74; regional dir. hotel ops., gen. mgr. Ramada Inn, Toronto, 1974-75, regional dir. France and Switzerland Ramada Inns Europe, Paris, 1975-76; exec. dir. restaurants div. Can. Pacific Hotels, 1976-77; gen. mgr. CP-Hamburg (W. Ger.) Plaza, 1977-79, Le Chateau Frontenac, Quebec, 1979—. Roman Catholic. Office: 1 Rue des Carrieres Quebec PQ G1R 4P5 Canada

SCHMID, RUDI RUDOLF, physician; b. Switzerland, May 2, 1922; s. Rudolf and Bertha (Schiesser) S.; B.S., U. Zurich, 1941, M.D., 1947; Ph.D., U. Minn., 1954; m. Sonja D. Wild, Sept. 17, 1949; children—Isabelle S., Peter R. Came to U.S., 1948, naturalized, 1954. Intern U. Calif. Med. Center, San Francisco, 1948-49; resident medicine U. Minn., 1949-52, instr., 1952-54; research fellow biochemistry Columbia, 1954-55; investigator Nat. Insts. Health, Bethesda, Md., 1955-57; asso. medicine Harvard, 1957-59, asst. prof., 1959-62; prof. medicine U. Chgo., 1962-66, U. Calif., San Francisco, 1966—. Cons. U.S. Army Surgeon Gen., USPHS, VA. Served with Swiss Army, 1943-45. Fellow A.C.P., N.Y. Acad. Scis.; mem. Nat. Acad. Scis., Assn. Am. Physicians, Am. Soc. Clin. Investigation, Am. Soc. Biol. Chemists, Am. Soc. Exptl. Pathology, Am. Soc. Hematology, Am. Gastroenterol. Assn., Am. Assn. Study Liver Disease (pres. 1965), Internat. Assn. Study Liver (pres.-elect 1978), Leopoldina. Mem. editorial bd. Jour. Clin. Investigation, 1965-70, Jour. Lab. and Clin. Medicine, 1964-70, Blood, 1962-75, Gastroenterology, 1965-70, Jour. Investigative Dermatology, 1968-72, Annals Internal Medicine, 1975-79, Proc. Soc. Exptl. Biology and Medicine, 1976—; research in metabolism of hemoglobin, heme, prophyrins, bile pigments and liver. Home: 211 Woodland Rd Kentfield CA 94904 Office: University of California Med Center San Francisco CA 94143

SCHMID, WILFRIED, educator; b. Hamburg, Germany, May 28, 1943; s. Wolfgang and Kathe (Erfling) S.; came to U.S., 1960; B.A., Princeton, 1964; M.A., U. Calif. at Berkeley, 1966, Ph.D., 1967. Asst. prof. math. U. Calif. at Berkeley, 1967-70; prof. math. Columbia U., 1970-78, Harvard U., 1978—; vis. mem. Inst. for Advanced Study, Princeton, 1969-70, 75-76; vis. prof. U. Bonn, 1973-74. Contbr. articles to profl. jours. Home: Stonehedge Lincoln MA 01773 Office: Dept Math Harvard University Cambridge MA 02138

SCHMID, WILLIAM JACOB, lawyer; b. Cin., May 18, 1911; s. Henry M. and Cora (Schaefer) S.; LL.B., U. Cin., 1934; m. Virginia Haller, Sept. 12, 1936; children—Linda Ann (Mrs. Gordon C. Sine), David H. Admitted to Ohio bar, 1934; practiced in Cin., 1934-43, 46-47; spl. agt. FBI, 1943-46; chief asst. pros. atty. Hamilton County (Ohio), 1947-56; sr. v.p., gen. counsel Ohio Nat. Life Ins. Co., Cin., 1956-76, dir., 1973-76; mem. firm Drew & Ward, Cin., 1976—. Bd. mgmt. YMCA. Mem. Am., Ohio bar assns., Assn. Life Ins. Counsel, Cin. C. of C., Soc. Former Agts. FBI, Pi Kappa Alpha, Phi Alpha Delta. Republican. Presbyn. (elder, trustee, deacon). Mason, Kiwanian. Clubs: Torch, Miami View Golf (Cin.). Home: 3139 Northgate Dr Cincinnati OH 45211 Office: Drew & Ward 2302 Central Trust Bank Tower Cincinnati OH 45202

SCHMIDHAUSER, JOHN RICHARD, educator; b. N.Y.C., Jan. 3, 1922; s. Richard J. and Gertrude (Grabinger) S.; B.A. with honors, U. Del., 1949; M.A., U. Va., 1952, Ph.D., 1954; m. Thelma Lorraine Ficker, June 9, 1952; children—Steven, Paul, Thomas, John C., Martha, Sarah, Susan. Instr., U. Va., 1952-54; prof. constl. law U. Iowa, 1954-64, prof. polit. sci., 1967-73; prof. polit. sci. U. So. Calif., 1973—; mem. 89th Congress 1st dist. Iowa. Sr. fellow law and behavorial scis. U. Chgo., 1959-60; research fellow Research Inst. on Jud. Process, Social Sci. Research Council, 1958; lectr. on problems gerontology. Chmn. Citizens Action Com. for Fair Representation in Iowa Legislature, 1961; chmn. Johnson County Democratic Central Com., 1961-64; del. Iowa Dem. Convs., 1956, 58, 60, 62; dist. chmn. Operation Support Presidents Kennedy and Johnson, 1961—. Served with USNR, 1941-45; PTO. Mem. Iowa City Mgr. Assn. (bd. reps. 1956-59, chmn. handbook revision 1958), Internat., Am., Midwestern, Western polit. sci. assns., AAUP (sec.-treas. State U. Iowa 1958-59; mem. com. on relationship fed. and state govt. to higher edn.), Humanities Soc., Isaak Walton League, Raven Soc., Phi Beta Kappa, Phi Kappa Phi. Unitarian (chmn. Men's Club 1960-61). Author: The Role of Supreme Court as Final Arbiter in Federal-State Relations, 1789-1957, 1958; The Supreme Court; Its Politics, Personalities and Procedures, 1960; Constitutional Law in the Political Process, 1963; (with Berg) The Supreme Court and Congress, 1972; (with Berg and Hahn) American Political Institutions and Corruption, 1976; Whaling in Japan-U.S. Relations, 1978; Judges and Justices, 1979; also numerous articles in jours. Home: 136 W 64th Pl Inglewood CA 90302

SCHMIDT, ADOLPH WILLIAM, ret. ambassador; b. McKeesport, Pa., Sept. 13, 1904; s. Adolph and Louise (Schmidt) S.; A.B., Princeton, 1926; M.B.A., Harvard, 1929; certificates U. Dijon, U. Berlin and U. Paris (Sorbonne), 1926-27; LL.D., U. Pitts, 1954, U. N.B., 1973, Princeton U., 1977; L.H.D., Chatham Coll., 1965; m. Helen Sedgeley Mellon, June 27, 1936; children—Helen (Mrs. William F. Claire) Thomas M. Officer Mellon Nat. Bank and affiliated orgns. Pitts., 1929-42; chmn. bd., dir. Columbia Radiator Co., McKeesport, 1939-42; mem. exec. com., dir. Pitts. Coal Co., 1940-44; v.p., gov. T. Mellon & Sons, Pitts., 1946-69; trustee A.W. Mellon Edul. and Charitable Trust, pres., 1954-65; trustee Old Dominion Found., 1941-69, Carnegie Inst., 1965—; ambassador to Can., Ottawa, Ont., 1969-74. U.S. del. Conf. on North Atlantic Community, Bruges, Belgium, 1957, Atlantic Congress, London, Eng., 1959, Atlantic Conv. NATO Nations, Paris, France, 1962; adviser to U.S. delegation Econ. Commn. for Europe, Geneva, Switzerland, 1967; bd. govs. Atlantic Inst., Paris; bd. dirs. Atlantic Council U.S., Washington. Co-founder Pitts. Playhouse, 1934, Pitts. Symphony, 1937; 1st chmn. Three Rivers Arts Festival, 1960; pres., chmn. Allegheny Conf. on Community Devel., Pitts., 1956-61; vice chmn. Urban Redevel. Authority, 1954-59; 1st chmn. Southwestern Pa. Regional Planning Commn.; mem. bus. and internat. coms. Nat. Planning Assn., 1955-69; mem. Can.-Am. Com., 1974—; chmn. Pa. State Planning Bd., 1955-68; dir. Population Crisis Com., Washington, 1965-69, Environmental Fund, Washington, 1973—. Mem. bd. visitors and govs. St. Johns Coll., Annapolis, Md. and Santa Fe, N.Mex., also chmn., 1956, 62; mem. grad. council Princeton U. Served from capt. to lt. col. U.S. Army, 1942-46, with OSS in Africa and Europe, Allied Control Commn., Berlin. Awarded Bronze Star, Two Battle Stars; Benjamin Rush award Allegheny Co. Med. Soc., 1950, David Glick award World Affairs Council, 1965. Mem. Council Fgn. Relations, Mil. Order World Wars. Republican. Presbyn. Clubs: Links, Anglers (N.Y.C.); Duquesne, Pittsburgh Golf (Pitts.); Laurel Valley Golf, Rolling Rock (Ligonier, Pa.); Metropolitan (Washington). Home: RD 4 Ligonier PA 15658

SCHMIDT, ALEXANDER MACKAY, univ. adminstr.; b. Jamestown, N.D., Jan. 26, 1930; s. Theodore G. and Marion W. (MacKay) S.; B.S., Northwestern U., 1951; M.D., U. Utah, 1955; m. Patricia Ann White, June 27, 1952; children—Susan Jane, Sarah Ann. Intern medicine U. Utah Affiliated Hosps., 1955-56, resident, 1958-60; research fellow cardiology U. Utah Coll. Medicine, 1960-62, from instr. medicine to asst. dean, 1962-68, dir. planning Cardiovascular Research and Tng. Center, 1966-67; chief continuing edn. and tng. br. Div. Regional Med. Programs, NIH, 1967-68; exec. asso. dean, asso. prof. medicine U. Ill. Coll. Medicine, 1969-70; dean, prof. medicine Abraham Lincoln Sch. Medicine, U. Ill., 1970-73; commr. FDA, HEW, Washington, 1972-76; vice chancellor health services U. Ill., Chgo., 1977—; co-chmn. rev. com., div. regional med. programs Health Services and Mental Health Adminstrn., 1970—. Trustee Food and Drug Law Inst., 1974—. Served with AUS, 1956-58; ETO. Markle scholar academic medicine, 1966; named Best Tchr., Class of 1968 U. Utah; recipient Distinguished Service medal USPHS, 1976, HEW, 1976. Mem. Am. Fedn. Clin. Research, Am., Utah thoracic socs., AMA, Utah Med. Soc., AAAS, Am., Utah socs. internal medicine, N.Y. Acad. Sci., Alpha Omega Alpha. Contbr. articles to profl. jours. Home: 1424 Bonnie Brae River Forest IL 60305 Office: 1737 W Polk St Chicago IL 60612

SCHMIDT, BENNO CHARLES, business exec.; b. Abilene, Tex., 1913; B.A., U. Tex., 1936, LL.B., 1936; LL.D. (honoris causa), Columbia; L.H.D., N.Y. Med. Coll.; m. Nancy Montgomery Fleischmann; children—Benno, Ralph, Thomas (dec.), John and William (twins). Mem. law faculty U. Tex., 1936-40; Thayer teaching fellow Harvard Law Sch., 1940-41; with Office Gen. Counsel, WPB, Washington, 1941-42; gen. counsel Office Fgn. Liquidation Commn., Dept. State, Washington, 1945-46; now mng. partner J.H. Whitney & Co., N.Y.C.; chmn. bd. Freeport Minerals; dir. numerous bus. enterprises with holdings in U.S., Australia, New Zealand and Western Europe including Schlumberger Ltd., Memorex, CBS Inc. Chmn., Pres.'s Cancer Panel; mem. Pres.'s Biomed. Research Panel, 1975-76; pres. Am. Australian Assn.; chmn. Bedford-Stuyvesant Devel. & Services Corp., Fund for City N.Y., 1968-77, Roosevelt Island Devel. Corp., 1969-76; pres. Thomas Payne Schmidt Found.; chmn. bd. Meml. Hosp. for Cancer and Allied Diseases; vice chmn. bd. Meml. Sloan-Kettering Cancer Center; trustee Whitney Mus. Am. Art; trustee Carnegie Found. for Internat. Peace; mem. chancellor's council U. Tex. Served to col. AUS, 1942-45. Decorated Legion of Merit, Bronze Star, Legion d'Honneur, Croix de Guerre with palms, French Medal Merit; named Distinguished Alumnus, U. Tex., 1969; recipient certificate of award Am. Assn. for Cancer Research, 1971; Clement Cleveland award for distinguished service in crusade to control cancer. N.Y.C. div. Am. Cancer Soc., 1972, Nat. award for distinguished service, 1974; Papanicolaou award for distinguished service to cancer control, 1974; James Ewing Soc. Ann. award for outstanding contributions in fight against cancer, 1975, Alfred P. Sloan, Jr. Meml. award N.Y.C. div. Am. Cancer Soc., 1977, Stanley P. Reimann medal The Fox Chase Cancer Center, 1977, medal of the City of Rotterdam, 1977, NIH Dir.'s award, 1978. Hon. mem. Alpha Omega Alpha. Home: New York NY Office: 630 Fifth Ave New York NY 10020

SCHMIDT, BLAINE GALEN, educator; b. Belleville, Ill., Aug. 7, 1916; s. Henry Galen and Anna (Wolter) S.; B.S. in Bus. Adminstrn., Washington U., St. Louis, 1938, M.S. in Bus. Adminstrn., 1940; Ph.D. in Econs., St. Louis U., 1953; m. Adele Eunice Groene, Sept. 3, 1938; children—Richard G., Prudence C. Market research analyst E.I. duPont De Nemours, Wilmington, Del., 1953-59; prof. bus. adminstrn. U. Del., 1959—, chmn. dept., 1967-72, promotion coordinator M.B.A. program; cons. in field. Mem. Del. Gov.'s Adv. Com. Employment Hard Core Unemployables; mem. econ. devel. com. Greater Wilmington Devel. Council, col. Res. ret. Bd. dirs. Bur. Econ. and Research U. Del., Del. Heart Assn. Served with AUS, World War II. Decorated Bronze Star. Mem. Am. Mktg. Assn., Acad. Mgmt., Sales and Mktg. Execs. Internat., Purchasing Agts. Assn., Eastern Indsl. Advertisers, Beta Gamma Sigma. Contbr. articles to profl. jours., indsl. studies; research on shopping center mall locations and fast food restaurants. Home: 16 Georgian Circle Newark DE 19711

SCHMIDT, CARL FREDERIC, educator, pharmacologist, physiologist; b. Lebanon, Pa., July 29, 1893; s. Jacob Charles and Mary Ellen (Greth) S.; A.B., Lebanon Valley Coll., 1914, D.Sc., (hon.), 1955; M.D., U. Pa., 1918, Sc.D. (hon.), 1965; D.S.M., Charles U., Prague, 1963; m. Elizabeth Viola Gruber, June 24, 1920; children—Carl F., Barbara Elizabeth. Intern, Hosp. U. Pa., 1918-19; instr. in pharmacology, U. Pa., 1919-22, asst. prof., 1924-29, asso. prof., 1929-31, prof. pharmacology U. Pa. Med. Sch., 1931-59, emeritus prof. pharmacology, 1959—, Dental Sch., 1949-52; asso. in pharmacology, Peking (China) Union Med. Coll., 1922-24; guest lectr., Portland (Oreg.) Med. Soc., U. Oreg. Med. Sch., 1943; Mary Scott Newbold lectr., Coll. Physicians Phila., 1943; Commonwealth vis. prof., U. Louisville, 1946; Harvey lectr., N.Y., 1949, ann. lectr. in pharmacology, U. London, 1949; Henry Lower lectr., Cleve., 1949; Hachmeister Meml. lectr., Georgetown U., 1951; Graves lectr. Ind. U., 1954; chmn. adv. com. Life Ins. Research Fund, 1954-55; cons. surgeon gen. U.S. Army and VA; vis. prof. U. Philippines, 1955; research dir. U.S. Naval Aerospace, Med. Research Dept., Naval Air Devel. Center, Johnsville, 1962-69; clin. prof. pharmacology U. South Fla. Coll. Medicine, 1970—. Mem. Unitarian Med. Mission to Germany, 1948. Served as 1st lt., Med. Res. Corps, U.S. Army, 1918-25. Chmn. pharmacology study sect., USPHS, 1947-51, mem. phsyiology study sec., 1947-48; chmn. Internat. Fellowships Com., 1963-64; mem. drug research bd. Nat. Acad. Sci., 1963-69. Mem. NRC, 1947-50 (sec., subcom. on oxygen and anoxia, 1941-45)- Chmn. panel on physiology, Research and Devel. Bd., 1948-50. Chmn. subpanel on med. aspects of chem. warfare, 1948-50. Mem. adv. panel on physiology, Office Naval Research, 1947-52. Mem. Internat. Union Physiol. Scis. (v.p. pres. sect. pharmacology 1959-65, pres. 1965-66, hon. pres., 1966—), Am. Heart Assn., Am. Soc. for Pharmacology (v.p. 1940-42, pres., 1948-50), Am. Physiology Soc., Soc. Exptl. Biology and Medicine, Assn. Am. Physicians, AAAS, Physiology Soc. of Phila., Penn Valley Assn. (pres. 1944-46), Nat. Acad. Scis., Am. Acad. of Arts and Sci., Aerospace Medical Assn., Alpha Omega Alpha, Sigma Xi.; hon. mem. Pharmacol. Soc., Argentine Med. Assn., other assns., faculties. Club: Merion Cricket (Haverford, Pa.). Mng. editor Jour. Pharmacol. and Exptl. Therapeutics, 1940-42; asso. editor Chem. Abstracts, 1942-48; mng. editor Circulation Research, 1958-62. Contbr. articles in med. publs. on respiration, cerebral and coronary circulation, action of Chinese drugs; kidney function, aerospace pharmacology to profl. jours. Home: 15462 Gulf Blvd Madeira Beach FL 33708

SCHMIDT, CHARLES WILSON, paper mfg. co. exec.; b. N.Y.C., Mar. 18, 1928; s. William Charles and Anita (Wilson) S.; grad. Deerfield Acad., 1945; A.B., Williams Coll., 1948; postgrad. Carnegie Inst. Tech., 1950; grad. Advanced Mgmt. Program, Harvard U., 1973; m. Martha Moore, Dec. 29, 1951; children—Anne, Martha, William, Heidi. Apprentice, S.D. Warren Co. div. Scott Paper Corp., Westbrooke, Maine, 1948, salesman, N.Y.C., 1950-52, dist. sales mgr., Rochester, N.Y., 1962-66, dist. sales mgr. West Coast, 1956-59, dist. sales mgr., Phila., 1963-67, dist. sales mgr., N.Y.C., 1967-69, asst. sales mgr., Boston, 1969, v.p. mktg. and sales, 1969-72, pres., 1972—, also sr. v.p. parent co., 1975—; dir. Boston Safe Deposit and Trust Co. Mem. Recreation Commn., Irvington, N.Y., 1964-67. Trustee, v.p. U. Maine. Pulp and Paper Found.; bd. dirs. New Eng. Colls. Fund; mem. corp. Mass. Gen. Hosp. Mem. Am. Paper Inst. (exec. com. printing-writing div., chmn. 1977-78), Sales Assn. of Paper Industry (pres. 1973-74), New Eng. Paper Trade Assn. (pres.), Gargoyle Alumni Assn. (past pres.), Deerfield Acad. Alumni Assn. (pres., trustee 1974-75), Alpha Delta Phi. Clubs: Ardsley Country (past gov.) (Irvington, N.Y.); Williams of N.Y. (past gov.), (N.Y.C.); Weston (Mass.) Golf; Royal Cork Yacht (Ireland); Vineyard Haven Yacht; Pine Valley Golf. Home: 63 Claypit Hill Rd Wayland MA 01778 Office: 225 Franklin St Boston MA 02101

SCHMIDT, CHAUNCEY EVERETT, banker; b. Oxford, Ia., June 7, 1931; s. Walter Frederick and Vilda (Saxton) S.; B.S., U.S. Naval Acad., 1953; M.B.A., Harvard, 1959; m. Anne Garrett McWilliams, Mar. 3, 1954; children—Carla, Julia, Chauncey Everett. With First Nat. Bank Chgo., 1959-75, v.p., gen. mgr. br., London, Eng., 1965-68, v.p. for Europe, Middle East, Africa, 1968-69, sr. v.p., Chgo., 1969-72, exec. v.p., 1972, vice chmn. bd., 1973, pres., 1974-75; chmn. bd., pres., chief exec. officer, dir. Bank of Calif. N.A., San Francisco, 1976—, BanCal Tri-State Corp., 1976—; dir. Amfac, Inc., Honolulu; mem. adv. council Fed. Res. Bd.; mem. Adv. Council Japan-U.S. Econ. Relations; adv. bd. Pacific Rim Bankers Program. Exec. bd. San Francisco Bay Area council Boy Scouts Am.; council Stanford Research Inst.; bd. dirs. Bay Area Council; bd. govs. San Francisco Symphony Assn. Served with USAF, 1953-56. Mem. Assn. Res. City Bankers (dir.), Am. Bankers Assn., Internat. Monetary Conf., Calif. Bankers Clearing House Assn. (dir.), Calif. Roundtable (dir.), San Francisco C. of C. (dir.), Japan-Calif. Assn. Clubs: Comml. (Chgo.); Bankers (San Francisco. Home: 234 Albion Ave Woodside CA 94062 Office: 400 California St San Francisco CA 94104

SCHMIDT, CHRISTIAN GEORGE, hosp. supply co. exec.; b. Dysart, Iowa, May 9, 1911; s. Charles W. and Elma (Blexrud) S.; B.S.C., State U. Iowa, 1934, M.A., 1935; m. Artis Arlene Fenley, Mar. 21, 1945 (dec. Oct. 1969); children—Christian George, Charles

Walter; m. 2d, Julia A. Popovich Williams, Apr. 3, 1971. Head freshman coach State U. Iowa, 1935-37; sales rep. match and paper goods Diamond Match Co., 1937-40; with Am. Hosp. Supply Corp., 1940—, group v.p., 1964-68, exec. v.p., 1968—, chmn. exec. com., 1970, also dir. corp. and dir. and officer subsidiaries; dir. Kemper Fin. Services, Inc., Instrumentation Labs. Served to lt. comdr. USNR, 1943-45. Mem. Scientific Apparatus Makers Assn. (dir.), Delta Upsilon. Home: 900 Pontiac Rd Wilmette IL 60091 Office: 1740 Ridge Ave Evanston IL 60204

SCHMIDT, CYRIL JAMES, librarian; b. Flint, Mich., June 27, 1939; s. Cyril August and Elizabeth Josephine Schmidt; B.A., Catholic U. Am., 1962; M.S. in L.S., Columbia U., 1963; Ph.D., Fla. State U., 1974; m. Martha Joe Meadows, May 22, 1965; children—Susan, Emily. Asst. bus. and industry dept. Flint Pub. Library, 1963-65; reference librarian Gen. Motors Inst., Flint, 1965; asso. librarian S.W. Tex. State U., San Marcos, 1965-67; head undergrad. libraries, asst. prof. Ohio State U., 1967-70; dir. libraries SUNY, Albany, 1972-79, also mem. faculty Sch. Library and Info. Sci.; univ. librarian Brown U., Providence, 1979—; cons. in field. Fellow Library Services Act, 1962-63, Higher Edn. Act, 1970-72. Mem. AAUP, ALA, Am. Soc. Info. Sci., ACLU, Am. Mgmt. Assn., Pi Sigma Alpha, Beta Phi Mu. Author papers in field. Home: 31 Benefit St Providence RI 02904 Office: Brown U Box A Providence RI 02912

SCHMIDT, DELBERT RUEBEN, ins. co. exec.; b. Lyndhurst, Wis., July 20, 1915; s. Fred H. and Bertha (Voelz) S.; student Lawrence Coll., 1933-35; Ph.B., U. Wis., 1938; m. Dorothy Helbing, Oct. 14, 1944 (div. Aug. 73); children—Deede (Mrs. Robert Wyatt), Debra (Mrs. Jay Vander Wort), Steven; m. 2d, Mary Parker, Mar. 9, 1974. With Employers Mut. Liability Ins. Co. Wis., 1938—, auditor, Mpls., 1938-44, audit mgr., San Francisco, 1944-57, br. mgr., San Francisco, 1957-60, resident v.p., Albany, N.Y., 1960-63, resident v.p., Wausau, Wis., 1963-66, asst. v.p. br. operations, Wausau, 1966-68, v.p. br. operations, Wausau, 1968-70, sr. v.p. field operations, Wausau, 1970—. Bd. dirs. YMCA, 1966-71; trustee nat. summer camp handicapped children, 1973—. C.P.A., Wis. Mason (Shriner), Rotarian (pres., dir. 1970-71). Home: 1205 Forest Hill Rd Wausau WI 54401 Office: 2000 Westwood Dr Wausau WI 54401

SCHMIDT, DOUGLAS WOCHER, scenery designer; b. Cin., Oct. 4, 1942; s. Robert Wocher and Amy Jean (Murdoch) S.; student Sch. Fine and Applied Arts, Boston U., 1961-64. Designer, stage mgr., gopher Monmouth (Maine) Repertory Theatre, summer 1961; asst. to designer Ming Cho Lee, N.Y.C., 1964-67; scenery designer La Boheme, Julliard Opera Theatre, N.Y.C., 1966, Broadway show Paris Is Out, 1970; resident designer Repertory Theatre of Lincoln Center, 1969-73; designer Broadway shows Grease, 1972—, Veronica's Room, 1973, Over Here, 1974, Three Penny Opera, 1976, Runaways, 1978; now freelance designer represented by works in various U.S. opera reps. and on Broadway by They're Playing Our Song, a musical by Neil Simon, Marvin Hamlish and Carol Bayer Sager, Imperial Theatre, N.Y.C.; lectr. New York Center for Field Studies; bd. dirs. Studio and Forum of Stage Design, Inc., N.Y.C. Recipient N.Y. Drama Desk awards for Enemies, 1973, Over Here!, 1974, Veronica's Room, 1974, Obie award for The Crazy Locomotive, 1977, Joseph Maharahm Design awards for Agamemnon, 1977, Mem. Am. Soc. Interior Designers, United Scenic Artists Local Union 829. Office: 325 W 89th St New York NY 10024. *I am guided more and more by the need to become involved in projects that will provide the satisfaction of intimate creative collaboration and, hoepfully, insight and personal growth through that interaction.*

SCHMIDT, (ORVAL) (FREDERICK) FRED, editor; b. Lone Wolf, Okla., Sept. 17, 1922; s. Otto Frederick and Mabel Marie (Johnson) S.; student U. Okla., 1941-42, Chgo. Sch. Photography, 1947-48; m. Eleanor Minerva Austin, Jan. 15, 1949; 1 son, Frederick Curtis. Asst. photographer Frank Lewis, Inc., Chgo., 1949; photographer, color technician James Israel Studio, Mt. Vernon, O., 1949-55; adminstrv. asst. to asso. editor to mng. editor Profl. Photographers Am., Inc., Milw., 1955-66, Des Plaines, Ill., 1966-74; editor Photomethods, N.Y.C., 1974—; tchr. photojournalism Milw. Area Tech. Coll., 1965-66, mem. adv. bd., 1972-74; lectr. No. Ill. U., 1968-73; sec. Profl. Photographers Ohio, 1954-55; photog. cons. L.I. Hist. Soc. Bd. advisers Chgo. Internat. Film Festival, 1967-75. Served with USCGR, 1942-46. Recipient Nat. award Profl. Photographers Am., 1964. Mem. Cameracraftsmen Am., Am. Soc. Photographers, Soc. Photog. Scientists and Engrs., Royal Photog. Soc., Am. Soc. Bus. Press Editors (v.p. 1970-71, dir. 1976-79). Republican. Club: Chgo. Press. Co-author: Opportunities in Photography, 1978. Home: 138 Joralemon St Brooklyn Heights NY 11201 Office: 1 Park Ave New York NY 10016

SCHMIDT, FRED HENRY, educator; b. Detroit, Sept. 12, 1915; s. Hugo W. and Maude (Schmidt) S.; B.S. in Engring., U. Mich., 1937; M.A., U. Buffalo, 1940; Ph.D., U. Cal. at Berkeley, 1945; m. Margaret Cresswell, Sept. 5, 1939; children—Karla, Kurt. Engr., Am. Tel. & Tel. Co., Denver, 1937-39; physicist Manhattan Project, Berkeley, Oak Ridge and Los Alamos, 1942-45, Radiation Lab., U. Cal. at Berkeley, 1945-46; mem. faculty U. Wash., Seattle, 1946—, prof. physics, 1956—. Guggenheim fellow, Amsterdam, Geneva, 1956-57; NSF Postdoctoral fellow, Geneva, 1963-64. Fellow Am. Phys. Soc.; mem. Sigma Xi. Author: (with others) The Energy Controversy: The Fight Over Nuclear Power, 1976. Contbr. articles to physics jours. Research on nuclear physics. Home: 7300 57th Ave NE Seattle WA 98115

SCHMIDT, HAROLD EUGENE, land co. exec.; b. Cedar Rapids, Iowa, Oct. 12, 1925; s. Alfons W. and Lillie (Schlegel) S.; B.S. in Civil Engring., U. Iowa, 1949; M.S. in San. Engring., Mass. Inst. Tech., 1953; m. Lucy Hermann, Apr. 13, 1957; children—Harold, Sandra. Research and devel. engr. Chgo. Pump Co., 1949-51; engr. A.B. Kononoff, Miami, Fla., 1956-58; with Gen. Devel. Corp., Miami, 1958—, v.p. utilities, asst. v.p. operations, 1967-72, v.p., 1972—, v.p. community div., 1973—; pres. Gen. Devel. Utilities Inc., 1972—; dir. Port Charllote Bank (Fla.). Served to capt. USAF, 1951-56. Mem. Am. Water Works Assn., Water Pollution Control Fedn., Sigma Xi, Chi Epsilon. Home: 641 W 53d St Hialeah FL 33012 Office: 1111 S Bayshore Dr Miami FL 33131

SCHMIDT, HAROLD ROBERT, lawyer; b. Braddock, Pa., Sept. 4, 1913; s. Abraham I. and Gustella (Frankle) S.; A.B., U. Mich., 1934; LL.B., U. Pitts., 1937; m. Bernice V. Williams, June 24, 1941; children—Barbara N. (Mrs. Emerson M. Wickwire), Edward C., Gordon W. Admitted to Pa. bar, 1937, since practiced Pitts.; sr. partner charge litigation Rose, Schmidt, Dixon, Hasley, Whyte & Hardesty, and predecessors, 1946—. Co-chmn. Lawyers Non-Partisan Com. to Secure Additional Judges for Ct. Common Pleas Allegheny County, 1963; chmn. Com. to Modernize Jury Selection Procedures, Allegheny County, 1965; permanent mem. Jud. Conf. of 3d Circuit; former govt. appeal agt. local bd. 19 Selective Service System, Pitts.; mem. grievance com. U.S. Dist. Ct. for Western Dist. Pa.; panel participant 1st Internat. Med.-Legal Seminar Pitts. Inst. Legal Medicine, U. Rome, 1965, lectr. 3d seminar, U. London Med. Coll., 1967; adj. prof. antitrust law So. Meth. U., July, 1979; lectr. in field. Chmn. exec. com. Pitts. chpt. Am. Jewish Com.; emeritus bd. dirs. ann. giving fund U. Pitts., bd. visitors Sch. Law, 1978—; mem. Ft. Pitt Mus. Assos., law sch. ann. fund leadership com. U. Mich.; mem. Gov.'s Trial Ct. Nominating Commn. of Allegheny County (Pa.), 1979. Served to capt. AUS, World War II. Fellow Internat. Acad. Trial Lawyers; mem. World Assn. Lawyers (founder, life mem.), Am. Bar Assn. (vice chmn. civil practice and procedure com. sect. antitrust law 1978—), Pa., Allegheny County bar assns., Supreme Ct. Hist. Soc., Nat. Assn. R.R. Trial Counsel, Judge Adv. Gen. Assn., Acad. Trial Lawyers Allegheny County (past pres.), U. Pitts. Law Sch. Alumni Assn. (past pres.), Am. Law Inst., World Peace through Law Center, Am. Judicature Soc., Internat. Soc. Barristers (past gov.), Soc. Mining Law Antiquarians, Pa. Inst. Legal Medicine, Pa. Def. Inst., Def. Research Inst., Res. Officers Assn. U.S., Pa. Soc., Order of Coif, Phi Beta Kappa, Phi Kappa Psi, Phi Eta Sigma. Mason. Clubs: University Michigan (past pres.); Downtown (past pres.); Concordia. Author: Handbook and Guide to the Federal Coal Mine Health and Safety Act of 1969 and Related State Statutes, 1970. Editor-in-chief U. Pitts. Law Rev., 1936-37. Home: 5419 Northumberland St Pittsburgh PA 15217 Office: Oliver Bldg Pittsburgh PA 15222

SCHMIDT, HARVEY LESTER, artist, writer, composer; b. Dallas, Sept. 12, 1929; s. Emmanuel Carl and Edna (Wieting) S.; B.F.A., U. Tex., 1952. Graphic artist on staff NBC TV, 1955-58; free-lance artist, 1958—; illustrations appearing in Life, Look, Esquire, Fortune, Sports Illustrated, The Lamp, Harpers' Bazaar and Seventeen mags.; co-author: The In and Out Book, 1959; illustrator The Mighty Ones, 1959; composer music for Ben Bagley's Shoestring, 1957, Julius Monk's Upstairs At the Downstairs, 1956-60, The Fantasticks (composer award 1961), 1960; composer Broadway mus. 110 in the Shade, 1963, I Do I Do (Tony award 1967), 1966, Celebration 1969; composer mus. play Colette, 1970; painter, composer for art film: A Texas Romance, 1909, 1964; composer film score Bad Company, 1972; composer ballet music for Texas Fourth for Agnes de Mille's Heritage Dance Theatre, 1973; composer Portfolio Revue for N.Y. theatre, 1974, Philemon, 1975, The Bone Room, 1975. Served with AUS, 1953-55. Recipient gold medal N.Y. Soc. Illustrators, 1959, 60, 63; recipient Vernon Rice award, 1961. Mem. ASCAP (outstanding country-western song award 1970), Dramatists Guild. Methodist. Co-author: The Worry Book, 1962. Address: 313 W 74th St New York NY 10023. *Symmetry and beauty.**

SCHMIDT, HELEN LAUBACH, orgn. exec.; b. Phila., Nov. 21, 1917; d. Harvey Augustus and Henrietta Jeroma (Mehler) Laubach; C.L.U., The Am. Coll., 1955; divorced; 1 dau., Annette (Mrs. Frederick H. Crotchfelt III). Sec. bus. law dept. Wharton Sch., U. Pa., 1935-43; mem. The Am. Coll., Bryn Mawr, Pa., 1949—, exec. asst. to pres., corp. sec., 1969—. Mem. Am. Soc. Chartered Life Underwriters. Co-author: Insurance Courses in Colleges and Universities Outside the United States, 1960, 77; CLU Profile, 1969. Home: 432 W Montgomery Ave Haverford PA 19041 Office: 270 Bryn Mawr Ave Bryn Mawr PA 19010

SCHMIDT, HELMUT JOACHIM, finance co. exec.; b. Frankfurt, Germany, May 9, 1922; s. William S. and Erica F. Schmidt; came to U.S., 1924, naturalized, 1929; attended Wis. State Coll., Marquette U., U. Colo., Okla. A. and M. Coll., U. Notre Dame, U. Ga., DePauw U., U. Wis.; B.A., U. Wis., 1948; m. Shirley Louise Blagrave, Dec. 15, 1962. With Transamerica Financial Corp., Los Angeles, 1948—, pres., chief exec. officer, after 1972, now vice-chmn. Served to lt. (j.g.) USNR, 1943-46. *

SCHMIDT, HERMAN J., former oil co. exec.; b. Davenport, Ia., Feb. 26, 1917; s. Herman and Lillian (Beard) S.; A.B., U. Ia., 1938; J.D., Harvard U., 1941; m. Eileen Carpenter, Dec. 20, 1967; children—Paul David and Sarah Louise. Admitted to N.Y. bar, 1943; with Cravath, Swaine & Moore, 1941-44, 47-51; tax counsel Socony Mobil Oil Co., Inc. (co. name now Mobil Corp.); N.Y.C., 1951-55, adminstrv. asst. to gen. counsel, 1955, asso. gen. counsel, 1955-56, gen. counsel, 1956-59, dir., 1957-78, exec. v.p., 1959-74, vice chmn., 1974-78; pres. Mobil Internat. Oil Co., 1959-63; dir. C.I.T. Fin. Corp., H.J. Heinz Co., NL Industries Inc., Kaiser Cement Corp., MAPCO Inc. Chmn. bd. trustees Am. Enterprise Inst.; hon. life trustee U. Iowa Found. Served as 1st lt. Mil. Intelligence Corps., AUS, 1944-47. Mem. Harvard Law Rev. Assn., Phi Beta Kappa, Phi Gamma Delta. Club: Blind Brook (Port Chester, N.Y.).

SCHMIDT, HUGO, educator; b. Vienna, Austria, Jan. 24, 1929; s. Johann and Maria (Schuster) S.; came to U.S., 1951, naturalized, 1956; student U. Vienna, 1949-51, Bard Coll., 1951-52; Ph.D., Columbia, 1959. Instr., Columbia, 1954-59; asst. prof., then asso. prof. Bryn Mawr Coll., 1959-67; prof. German lit. U. Colo., 1967—, chmn. dept., 1968-72; vis. prof. U. Pa., spring 1963. Chmn. and/or mem. coms. Ednl. Testing Service, Princeton, N.J., 1959—. Mem. Am. Assn. Tchrs. German, Modern Lang. Assn., Colo. Mountain Club, Rocky Mountain Rescue Group. Author: Nikolaus Lenau, 1971. Editor: (with Eric Bentley) Bertolt Brecht, Manual of Piety, 1966. Book rev. editor Modern Lang. Jour., 1970—; adv. editor Oxford U. Press, 1961-68. Home: 2950 Bixby St Boulder CO 80303

SCHMIDT, JAKOB EDWARD, medical and medicolegal lexicographer, physician, author, inventor; b. Riga, Livonia, Latvia, June 16, 1906 (came to U.S. 1924, naturalized 1929); s. Michael E. and Rachel I. (Goldman) S.; grad. Balt. City Coll., 1929; Ph.G., U. Md., 1932, B.S. in Pharmacy, 1935, M.D., 1937; postgrad., 1939. Intern, Sinai Hosp., Balt.; engaged in pvt. med. practice, Balt., 1940-53; resident, Charlestown, Ind., 1953—; indsl. physician Ind. Ordnance Works, 1953-54; med., paramed., and medicolegal lexicographer, 1950—; columnist What's the Good Word (Balt. Sun); Sharpen Your Tongue (Am. Mercury); The Medical Lexicographer (Modern Medicine); Medical Semantics (Medical Science); Underworld English (Police); Medical Vocabulary Builder (Trauma); English Word Power and Culture (Charlestown Courier), also Understanding Med. Talk. Asso. med. editor, Trauma, 1959—; editor Medical Dictionary, 1959—; compiler 50,000-word vocabulary test, 1956; numerous articles in med. jours., lay press, Esquire, Playboy, others; contbr. articles to press services U.P.I., N.A.N.A., others; cons. JAMA (Jour. AMA); cons., med. and medicolegal terminology; also cons. in med. lexicography, med. tradenames and trademarks; pres. Sculptural Arts Jewelers, 1973—, Med. Sculpture Art Co., 1974—. Mem. revision com. U.S. Pharmacopeia XI. Mem. Am. Dialect Soc., Nat. Hist. Soc., Am. Name Soc., Am. Med. Writers' Assn., Internat. Soc. Gen. Semantics, AMA, Med. and Chirurgical Faculty of Md., Balt. City Med. Soc., Nat. Assn. Standard Med. Vocabulary (chmn. 1961-64), Nat. Soc. Lit. and Arts, Smithsonian Instn., Owl Club, Rho Chi. Inventor iodine-pentoxide-shunt method and apparatus for detection of carbon monoxide in oxygen, atmosphere, and medicinal gases; shock-proof electric fuse; magnetic needle finger ring; prosthetic papilla mammae; mammary hammock cum indwelling mammillary surrogates; cosmetic mammillary simulators; discovered effect of cesium and related metals on oxidation of organic matter in lakes, ponds and drinking water; the TV eye phenomenon; others. Recipient Owl gold medal Balt. City Coll., 1929; Rho Chi gold key U. Md. Sch. Pharmacy, 1932; gold medal for excellence in all subjects, 1932; certificate of honor U. Md. Sch. Medicine, 1937; award and citation Am. Med. Writers' Assn., N.Y. Met. chpt., 1959. Author: Terminology of Sex and Related Emotions, 1954; Medical Terms Defined for the Layman, 1957; Reversicon, A Physician's Medical Word Finder, 1958; Medical Discoveries, Who and When, 1959; Dictionary of Medical Slang and Related Expressions, 1959; Narcotics, Lingo and Lore, 1959; Libido, Scientific, Lay, and Slang Terminology, 1960; Baby Name Finder—The Romance of Names, 1961; Attorneys' Dictionary of Medicine, 1962, 14th edit.; 1978, 15th edit., 1979; Attorneys' Medical Word Finder, 1964; One Thousand Elegant Phrases, 1965; Supplement to Attorneys' Dictionary of Medicine and Word Finder, 1966, ann. revision, 1967—, also The Medical Lexicographer, 1966; Cyclopedic Lexicon of Sex Terminology, 1967; Police Medical Dictionary, 1968; Practical Nurse's Medical Dictionary, 1968; Paramedical Dictionary, 1969, 2d edit., 1973; Structural Units of Medical and Biological Terms, 1969; English Word Power for Physicians, 1971; English Idioms and Americanisms, 1972; English Speech for Foreign Students, 1973; Textbook of Medical Terminology, 1972; Visual Aids for Paramedical Vocabulary, 1973; Analyzer of Medical-Biological Words, 1973; Index of Medical-Paramedical Vocabulary, 1974; Diccionario para Auxiliares de la Medicina, 1976. Home: Monroe nr Park St Charlestown IN 47111 Office: 934 Monroe St Charlestown IN 47111

SCHMIDT, JAMES CRAIG, savs. and loan exec.; b. Peoria, Ill., Sept. 27, 1927; s. Walter Henry and Clara (Wolfenbarger) S.; student Ill. Wesleyan U., 1945, 48-50, Ph.B. in Bus. Adminstrn., 1952; postgrad. U. Ill. Coll. Law, 1950-52; J.D., DePaul U., 1953; m. Jerrie Louise Bond, Dec. 6, 1958; children—Julie, Sandra, Suzanne. Spl. agt. Fidelity & Deposit Co., Chgo., 1956-58; with Home Fed. Savs. & Loan Assn., San Diego, 1958-67; asst. sec. bus. and transp. State of Calif., 1967-69; exec. v.p., mng. officer, dir. San Diego Fed. Savs. & Loan Assn., 1969—; pres. Calif. Gen. Mortgage Co., 1969—; vice chmn. Fin. Scene, Inc., 1978—. Pres., Conf. Fed. Savs. and Loans of Calif., 1974-75. Mem. Calif. Toll Bridge Authority, 1969-74; mem. Calif. State Transp. Bd., 1972-78; past pres. SEED, Inc. San Diego; past chmn. San Diego Bal. Commn. Task Force; exec. com. San Diego Holiday Bowl; bd. dirs. Aztec Athletic Found. Served with USN, 1945-48. Mem. Calif., Ill. bar assns., San Diego C. of C. (dir.), Sigma Chi, Phi Delta Phi. Clubs: Rancho Las Palmas Country; San Diego Country, San Diego Rotary. Office: 600 B St San Diego CA 92183

SCHMIDT, JOHN JOSEPH, holding co. exec.; b. Chgo., Jan. 13, 1928; s. William Fred and Mildred C. (Petrone) S.; B.S., DePaul U., 1951; J.D., Loyola U., Chgo., 1955; m. Gail Bormann, Oct. 8, 1955; children—Cathleen M., Karen B., Linda G. Admitted to Ill. bar, 1955; trial atty. The Atchison, Topeka and Santa Fe Ry., Chgo., 1955-69, asst. v.p. exec. dept., 1969-73; v.p. Santa Fe Industries, Inc., Chgo., 1969-73, exec. v.p., 1973-78, pres., 1978—, also dir.; dir. The Atchison, Topeka and Santa Fe Ry., Santa Fe Natural Resources, Inc., Santa Fe Pipelines, Inc., Harris Trust & Savs. Bank, Harris Bankcorp, Inc. Mem. Zoning Bd. Appeals, Planning Commn., Village of Burr Ridge, Ill., 1973—. Served with U.S. Army, 1945-47. Mem. Am., Ill., Chgo. bar assns., Soc. Trial Lawyers (past dir.), Ill. Def. Council (past pres.), Nat. Assn. R.R. Trial Counsel (past pres.). Clubs: Chgo. Athletic, Chgo. Economic. Home: 6401 County Line Burr Ridge IL 60521 Office: 224 S Michigan Ave Chicago IL 60604

SCHMIDT, JOHN RICHARD, educator; b. Madison, Wis., July 3, 1929; s. Oscar John and Alma Theodora (Ula) S.; B.S., U. Wis., 1951, M.S., 1953; Ph.D., U. Minn., 1960; m. Rosemary Pigorsch, Oct. 7, 1951; children—Janet, Deborah, Allen. Asst. prof. agrl. econs. U. Wis., Madison, 1956-61, asso. prof. agrl. econs., 1961-65, prof., 1965—, chmn. dept. agrl. econs., 1966-70. Farm mgmt. cons. Am. Farm Bur. Fedn., Chgo., 1962; cons. Banco de Mexico, 1972—, IBRD (World Bank), 1973—, Agrl. Devel. Bank Iran, 1974-76. Bd. dirs. U. Wis. Credit Union, 1968-77, pres., 1969-75. Served with AUS, 1953-54. Mem. Am. Agrl. Econs. Assn., Western Farm Econs. Assn., Wis. Soc. Farm Mgrs. and Rural Appraisers, Delta Theta Sigma (nat. sec. 1962-64), Gamma Sigma Delta (pres. Wis. chpt. 1975). Lutheran (mem. ch. council 1967-69, 72-75, pres. 1974-75, mem. Wis.-Upper Mich. Synod Sem. com. 1972-75) Rotarian. Contbr. articles to tech. jours., also monographs, bulls. Home: 106 Frigate Dr Madison WI 53705

SCHMIDT, JOSEPH WILLIAM, JR., educator; b. Balt., Feb. 11, 1937; s. Joseph William and Lillian (Deen) S.; B.S., Loyola U., Balt., 1960; M.S., Pa. State U., 1962; Ph.D., W.Va. U., 1968; m. Mary Joan Hamilton, Sept. 9, 1961; children—Suzanne Carol, Joseph William III, Patricia Lynn, George Kurt, Catherine Joan. Asst. prof. indsl. engring. Va. Poly. Inst. and State U., Blacksburg, 1968-71, asso. prof., 1971-74, prof., 1975—; v.p. CBM Inc., cons., Cleve., 1974-75. Mem. Am. Inst. Indsl. Engrs., Inst. Mgmt. Sci., Simulation Councils Inc., Am. Soc. Engring. Edn. Author: Simulation and Analysis of Industiral Systems, 1970; Mathematical Foundations for Management Sci. and Systems Analysis, 1974; Analysis of Queueing Systems, 1975; contbr. articles to profl. jours. Home: 2805 Heritage Ln Blacksburg VA 24060 Office: Dept Indsl Engring and Ops Research Va Poly Inst and State U Blacksburg VA 24060

SCHMIDT, JULIUS, sculptor; b. Stamford, Conn., June 2, 1923; s. Louis Frank and Susie (Koment) S.; student Okla. A. and M. Coll., 1950-51; B.F.A., Cranbrook Acad. Art, 1952, M.F.A., 1955; student Ossip Zadkine (Paris), 1953, Accademia di Belle Arti (Florence, Italy), 1954; m. Carolyn Marsha Wolf (div.); children—Ania J., Ianos. Chmn. sculpture dept. Kansas City Art Inst., 1954-59, R.I. Sch. Design, 1959-60, U. Calif. at Berkeley, 1961-62, Cranbrook Acad. Art, 1962-70, U. Iowa, Iowa City, 1970—; 21 one-man shows, 1953—; exhibited Allen Meml. Art Mus., Oberlin, Ohio, 1958, Arts Club of Chgo. and Milw. Art Center, 1958, Art Inst. of Chgo., Mus. Modern Art, N.Y.C., 1960, Whitney Mus., 1960-63, Gallerie Claude Bernard, Paris, 1960, Guggenheim Mus., 1962, San Francisco Mus. Art, 1962, Phila. Art Alliance, 1963, Battersea Park, London, 1963, Sao Paolo Bienal, Brazil, 1963, White House Festival of Arts, Washington, 1965, Bienale Middleheim, Belgium, 1971; represented in permanent collections Nelson Gallery-Atkins Mus., Kansas City, Mo., Art Inst. Chgo., Mus. Modern Art, N.Y.C., Mus. U. Nebr., Whitney Mus. Am. Art, N.Y.C., Krannert Art Mus., Urbana, Ill., Washington, U., Walker Art Center, Mpls., Albright-Knox Mus., Buffalo, Detroit Inst. Art, U. Calif. Art Mus., Cranbrook Acad. Art, Mich., Princeton Mus. Art, several others. Served with USNR, World War II. Guggenheim fellow, 1963-64. Address: Dept Art University of Iowa Iowa City IA 52242

SCHMIDT, KLAUS FRANZ, advt. agency exec.; b. Dessau, Germany, May 25, 1928; s. Franz and Elfriede (Klamroth) S.; came to U.S., 1951, naturalized, 1957; student Coll. Journalism, Aachen, Germany, 1947-48, Sch. Design and Printing, Bochum, Germany, 1948-50; B.A., Wayne State U., 1956; m. Gisela Garbrecht, June 19, 1954; children—Dagmar, Ena. Printer, compositor, 1948-56; type dir. Mogul Williams & Saylor, N.Y.C., 1956-59, Doyle Dane Bernbach Co., N.Y.C., 1959-61; type dir. Young & Rubicam Inc., N.Y.C., 1961-68, v.p., dir. print ops., 1968-75, dir. creative support, 1975—; co-organizer Vision congresses Internat. Center for Communications Arts and Scis., N.Y.C., 1965, 67, 69, 77; chmn. bd. trustees Internat. Center for Typographic Arts, N.Y.C., 1969-70. Recipient Typomundus award Internat. Center for Typographic Arts, Internat. Book Exhbn. award, Leipzig, Germany, 1965. Mem. Print Advt. Assn. (chmn. N.Y. chpt. 1969-71, nat. sr. v.p., 1971-75), Am. Assn. Advt. Agencies (chmn. subcom. on phototypography 1969-75), Gravure Tech. Assn. (chmn. customer relations com. 1970-72), N.Y. Type Dirs. Club (recipient awards 1962, 64-66, 68, 69), N.Y. Art Dirs.

Club, Advt. Prodn. Club (chmn. tech. com. 1969-70). Am. editor Der Druckspiegel, Stuttgart, Germany, 1957-64; contbg. editor Print mag., N.Y.C., 1968—. Home: 549 Munroe Ave North Tarrytown NY 10591 Office: 285 Madison Ave New York NY 10017

SCHMIDT, MAARTEN, educator, astronomer; b. Groningen, The Netherlands, Dec. 28, 1929 (came to U.S. 1959); s. Wilhelm and Antje (Haringhuizen) S.; B.Sc., U. Groningen, 1949; Ph.D., Leiden (The Netherlands) U., 1956; Sc.D., Yale, 1966; m. Cornelia Johanna Tom, Sept. 16, 1955; children—Elizabeth Tjimkje, Maryke Antje, Anne Wilhelmina. Sci. officer Leiden (The Netherlands) Obs., 1953-59; postdoctoral Carnegie fellow Mt. Wilson Obs., Pasadena, Calif., 1956-58; mem. faculty Calif. Inst. Tech., 1959—, prof. astronomy, 1964—, exec. officer for astronomy, 1972-75, chmn. div. physics, math. and astronomy, 1975-78. Mem. staff Hale Obs., 1959—, dir., 1978—; Russell lectr. Am. Astron. Soc., 1978. Co-winner Calif. Scientist of Year award, 1964. Fellow Am. Acad. Arts and Scis. (Rumford award 1968); mem. Am. Astron. Soc. (Helen B. Warner prize 1964), Nat. Acad. Scis. (fgn. asso.), Internat. Astron. Union, Royal Astron. Soc. (asso.) Spl. research dynamics of our galaxy, star formation, radio galaxies, quasi-stellar radio sources. Office: 813 Santa Barbara St Pasadena CA 91109

SCHMIDT, MICHAEL JACK, baseball player; b. Dayton, Ohio, Sept. 27, 1949; B.A. in Bus. Adminstrn., Ohio U., Athens. With Phila. Phillies, 1972—; Nat. League Player in All-Star Game, 1974, 76, 77.*

SCHMIDT, MILTON OTTO, educator; b. Milw., Nov. 7, 1910; s. Otto George and Louise (Schmidt) S.; B.S., U. Wis., 1938, M.S., 1941; Ph.D., U. Ill., 1950; m. Vita R. Rasmussen, Nov. 26, 1936; children—Kathleen Garvin, Sally Simmons, Mark, Pamela. Instr. civil engring. Carnegie Inst. Tech., 1941-44; asst. prof., asso. prof. civil engring. U. Ill., Urbana, 1946-52, prof. civil engring., 1952-74, prof. emeritus, 1974—. Served to lt. USNR, 1944-46. NSF Sci. Faculty fellow, 1959-60. Fellow ASCE. Author: (with H.W. Rayner) Elementary Surveying, 4th edit., 1963; Surveying-Elementary and Advanced, 1957; Fundamentals of Surveying, 1969, 2d edit., 1978. Home: 2304 Galen Dr Champaign IL 61820

SCHMIDT, PAUL FELIX, scientist; b. Narva, Estonia, Aug. 20, 1916; s. Paul Rhoderich and Olga Peraskeva (Kuznetsov) S.; B.S., Inst. Tech., Tallinn, Estonia, 1938; M.S., U. Königsberg (Germany), 1945; Ph.D., U. Heidelberg (West Germany), 1951; m. Eva Luise Kohn, Oct. 14, 1944; children—E. Regine Schmidt Magacs, A. Irene. Came to U.S., 1952, naturalized, 1957. Chemist, Leimen Cement Works, Baden, Germany, 1945-48; research asso. Temple U., Phila., 1952-54; sect. mgr. research div. Philco Corp., Phila., 1954-59; sect. mgr. research labs. Westinghouse Electric Corp., Pitts., 1959-64; mem. tech. staff Bell Telephone Labs., Inc., Allentown, Pa., 1964—. Served with German Air Force, 1940-45. Mem. Electrochem. Soc., Am. Phys. Soc., IEEE, Am. Chem. Soc., various chess clubs. Chess player, 1935-43; champion of Estonia, 1936, Germany, 1941; recipient 1st prizes in internat. tournaments, Tallinn, 1935, Pärnu, Estonia, 1937, Cracow, Poland, 1941. Author: Schachmeister denken, 1949. Research and publs. on anodic oxidation of semiconductors, radiation effects in insulators, mechanism of electrolytic rectification, neutron activation analysis. Home: 429 N Broad St Allentown PA 18104 Office: Bell Telephone Labs Inc Allentown PA 18103

SCHMIDT, RALPH LEOPOLD WILLIAM, univ. dean; b. Hampton, Nebr., Nov. 28, 1919; s. Constantine Martin and Leonore Elisabeth (Lenz) S.; B.A., York (Nebr.) Coll., 1941; M.A., U. Nebr., 1951, Ph.D., 1951; m. Dolores Grotelueschen, July 4, 1945; children—Constance Marie Schmidt Raggio, Elizabeth Anne. Prin., St. Paul (Nebr.) High Sch., 1946-47; supt. Shickley (Nebr.) High Sch., 1947-49; off campus class organizer U. Nebr., 1949-51; asst. prof. edn. Baylor U., 1951-54; asso. prof. edn. La. State U., Baton Rouge, 1954-59, prof. edn., 1959-65, prof. edn., dean Univ. Coll., 1965—. Bd. dirs. Girl Scouts U.S.A. Served to capt. AUS, 1941-46, to col. Res., 1946-73. Mem. Assn. for Continuing Higher Edn., Res. Officers Assn., NEA, La. Assn. Educators, Nat. Soc. for Study Edn., Smithsonian Instn., Nat. Geog. Soc., Am. Legion, Phi Delta Kappa, Kappa Delta Pi, Phi Kappa Phi, Alpha Sigma Lambda. Presbyterian. Clubs: Capital City Kiwanis of Baton Rouge (sec., 2d v.p., 1st v.p., pres., chmn. pub. and bus. affairs com.), Kiwanis of La. State U. (pres.). Contbr. articles to profl. jours. Home: 568 Magnolia Wood Ave Baton Rouge LA 70808 Office: Univ Coll 150 Himes Hall La State U Baton Rouge LA 70803

SCHMIDT, RICHARD MARTEN, JR., lawyer; b. Winfield, Kans., Aug. 2, 1924; s. Richard M. and Ida (Marten) S.; A.B., U. Denver, 1945, J.D., 1948; m. Ann Downing, Jan. 2, 1948; children—Eric, Gregory, Rolf (dec.), Heidi. Admitted to Colo. bar, 1948; D.C. bar, 1968; dep. dist. atty. City and County of Denver, 1949-50; mem. firm McComb, Zarlengo, Mott & Schmidt, Denver, 1950-54; partner firm Schmidt & Van Cise, and predecessor, Denver, 1954-65; 65; gen. counsel USIA 1965-68; partner firm Cohn and Marks, Washington, 1969—; counsel spl. agrl. investing subcom. U.S. Senate, 1959-60. Mem. Gov.'s Council Local Govt., Colo., 1963-64; chmn. Mayor's Jud. Adv. Com., Denver, 1963-64, Gov.'s Supreme Ct. Nominating Com., 1964-65; mem. Gov.'s Oil Shale Adv. Com., 1963-65; mem. Colo. Commn. on Higher Edn., 1965. Trustee U. Denver. Mem. Am. (chmn. standing com. on assn. communications 1969-73), Colo. (gov.), Denver (pres. 1963-64), D.C. bar assns. Episcopalian. Clubs: Denver Law (pres. 1955-56), Denver Press; Federal City, International, Nat. Press (Washington). Home: 115 5th St SE Washington DC 20003 Office: Cohn and Marks 1333 New Hampshire Ave NW Washington DC 20036

SCHMIDT, RICHARD PENROSE, univ. pres.; b. Akron, Ohio, July 27, 1921; s. Richard Homer and Frances Angeline (Speakman) S.; student Miami U., Oxford, O., 1939-40; B.S., Kent State U., 1953; M.D., U. Louisville, 1945; m. Betty Corrine Heminger, June 5, 1943; children—Victoria Frances, Richard Penrose. Asst. prof. U. Wash., 1954-58; asso. prof. U. Fla., 1958-61, prof., 1961-70, head div. neurology, 1958-61, chmn. dept. medicine, 1962-65, asso. dean, 1965-70, dean, v.p. for acad. affairs State U. N.Y. Upstate Med. Center, 1970-75, acting pres., 1974-75, pres., 1975—; on leave as acting pres. SUNY, Stony Brook, 1979—; mem. nat. adv. neurol. disease and stroke council Nat. Inst. Neurol. Diseases and Stroke, NIH, 1970-74. Served to capt. AUS, 1946-48. Fellow A.C.P.; mem. Am. Epilepsy Soc. (pres. 1964, trustee William G. Lennox Fund 1969-74), Brazilian Acad. Neurology (hon.), Puerto Rican Soc. Psychiatry and Neurology (hon.), Am. Acad. Neurology (pres. 1967-69), Am. Electroencephalographic Soc., Am. Neurol. Assn., Assn. for Research in Nervous and Mental Diseases, Sigma Xi (hon.), Alpha Omega Alpha. Author: (with B.J. Wilder) Epilepsy, 1968; also articles. Home: 2 Johns Hollow Rd Setauket NY 11733 Office: State U NY Stony Brook NY 11794

SCHMIDT, ROBERT A., brewery exec.; b. Tumwater, Wash., Mar. 3, 1915; s. Adolph D. and Winnifred (Lang) S.; student Wash. State U., U.S. Brewers Acad.; m. Jeannette Mikkelsen, Nov. 20, 1937; children—Robert A., Jennifer (Mrs. Thomas R. Ingham, Jr.), Frank C. With Olympia Brewing Co. (Wash.), 1934-77, asst. brewmaster, 1938-41, brewmaster, 1941-47, asst. supt., 1947-50, dir., 1950—, supt., 1951-53, v.p. charge prodn., 1953-63, pres., 1963-77, chmn., chief exec. officer, 1974-77; ret., 1977; dir. Seattle-1st Nat. Bank, Olympia Fed. Savs. & Loan Assn. Bd. dirs. Olympia-Tumwater Found. Mem. Master Brewers Assn. Am. (past pres. N.W. dist.), Beta Theta Pi. Elk. Home: PO Box 4066 Tumwater WA 98501 also 5047-B Cooper Point Rd NW Olympia WA 98502

SCHMIDT, ROBERT LOUIS, assn. exec.; b. Evanston, Ill., May 24, 1939; s. Theo George and Margaret W. (Bruning) S.; student U. Notre Dame, 1957-58; B.S., U. So. Calif., 1961; M.S. in Internat. Bus., Am. U., 1969; J.D., Georgetown U., 1972; m. Patricia Godfrey, Sept. 18, 1965; children—Mary Margaret, Laura, Christian, Angela. Asst. to chmn., spl. asst. to treas. Dem. Nat. Com., Washington, 1961-64; dir. pub. affairs ITT, Washington, 1964-74; admitted to Va. bar, 1973, D.C. bar, 1974; counsel Washington Ambassadors, World Football League franchise, 1973-74; individual practice law, Washington, 1974-75; pres. Nat. Cable TV Assn., Washington, 1975—. Mem. nat. advisory bd. Lombardi Center Cancer Research, Georgetown U.; exec. dir. Vince Lombardi Meml. Golf and Tennis Tournament, 1970—; chmn. bd. So Others Might Eat, 1973—; pres. Washington chpt. Nat. Football Hall of Fame, 1978; treas., bd. dirs. Am. Council Young Polit. Leaders. Mem. Am., D.C., Va. bar assns., Naval Res. Assn., U. So. Calif. Football Alumni Assn., Ducks Unlimited, Delta Theta Phi. Democrat. Roman Catholic. Club: University (Washington). Home: 7641 Burford Dr McLean VA 22101 Office: 918 16th St NW Washington DC 20006

SCHMIDT, TERRY LANE, congl. and govt. health liaison co. exec.; b. Chgo., Nov. 28, 1943; s. LeRoy C. and Eunice P. Schmidt; B.S., Bowling Green State U., 1965; M.B.A. in Health Care Adminstrn., George Washington U., 1971; children—Christie Anne, Terry Lane II. Resident in hosp. adminstrn. U. Pitts. Med. Center, VA Hosp., Pitts., 1968-69; adminstrv. asst. Mt. Sinai Med. Center, N.Y.C., 1969-70; asst. dir. Health Facilities Planning Council of Met. Washington, 1970-71; asst. dir. dept. govtl. relations A.M.A., Washington, 1971-74; pres. Terry L. Schmidt Assos., Inc., rep. in health, Washington, 1974—; pres. Washington Actions on Health, 1975-78; partner Washington Council Medicine and Health, 1979—. Lectr. dept. health care adminstrn. George Washington U., 1969-71, asst. prof., 1971—; asst. prof. Nat. Naval Sch. Health Care Adminstrn., 1971—; mem. faculty CSC Legis. Insts., 1972—, Am. Assn. State Colls. and Univs. Health Tng. Insts.; mem. adv. com. on ambulatory care standards Joint Commn. on Accreditation of Hosps., 1971-72. Bd. dirs. Nat. Eye Found., 1976-78. Fellow Am. Pub. Health Assn.; mem. Am. Hosp. Assn., Assn. Am. Med. Colls., Am. Assn. for Health Planning, Hosp. Fin. Mgmt. Assn., Alpha Phi Omega (pres. Bowling Green alumni chpt. 1967-70, sec.-treas. alumni assn. 1968-71). Clubs: George Washington University; Nat. Democratic (life); Nat. Republican (life); Capitol Hill. Author: Congress and Health: An Introduction to the Legislative Process and the Key Participants, 1976; A Directory of Federal Health Resources and Services for the Disadvantaged, 1976. Mem. editorial adv. bd. Nation's Health, 1971-73. Contbr. numerous articles to profl. jours. Home: 7000 Western Ave Chevy Chase MD 20015 Office: 1747 Pennsylvania Ave Washington DC 20006

SCHMIDT, THOMAS CARSON, state ofcl.; b. York, Pa., Oct. 15, 1930; s. George Small and Josephine Foot (Reifnider) S.; A.B., Princeton U., 1952; M.Div., Va. Sem., 1955; Ph.D., in Policy Scis., State U. N.Y., 1971; m. Lucy Carter Searby, Aug. 21, 1954; children—Peter, Lucy, Thomas. Ordained to ministry, Episcopalian Ch., 1955; rector St. Albans Ch., Bogota, Columbia, 1955-58; asst. St. James, New London, Conn., 1958-61; rector St. Andrew's, Longmeadow, Mass., 1961-68, on leave serving Diocese Zululand-Swaziland, South Africa, 1965-66; mgmt. cons., 1968-71; asst. commr. edn. State of R.I., Providence, 1971-73, commr. edn., 1975—; mem. R.I. Gov.'s Policy and Program Rev. Staff, Providence, 1973—; mgmt. cons. to nat. and fgn. firms; mem. Met. regional bd. advs. R.I. Hosp. Trust Nat. Bank; dir. Sheepscot Island Co., Georgetown, Maine. Chmn. manpower task force R.I. Health Sci. Edn. Council, 1973—, mem. exec. bd., 1973—. Mem. Internat. Soc. Ednl. Planners (treas. 1973—), Internat. Assn. Applied Social Scientists, Council Chief State Sch. Officers (chmn. legis. com.), State Higher Edn. Exec. Officers Assn. (legis. com.), Am. Assn. State Colls. and Univs. (legis. com.), SUNY Buffalo Alumni Assn. (dir.). Club: Barrington (R.I.) Yacht. Home: 28 Benefit St Providence RI 02904 Office: 199 Promenade St Providence RI 02908

SCHMIDT, WILLIAM HENRY, JR., writer; b. N.Y.C., Jan. 8. 1915; s. William Henry and Kathryn (Carroll) S.; B.A., U. Calif. at Los Angeles, 1936; m. Celia Carey, Dec. 12, 1958; 1 dau., Catherine Louise (Mrs. Gregory Dinoto). Tng. specialist Lockheed Aircraft Corp., Burbank, Cal., 1940-46, mgmt. trainer, 1948-50, dir. stockholder relations and corporate publs., 1957-70; tng. supr. Los Angeles County Civil Service Dept., Los Angeles, 1947-48; editor, tng. mgr. Hughes Aircraft Culver City, Calif., 1951-56; spl. asst. to sec. Dept. Labor, Washington, 1970-73; asst. to chmn. bd. Lockheed Aircraft Corp., 1973-76, dir. corp. publs., 1976—. Mem. Pub. Relations Soc. Am. Home: 995 S Orange Grove Pasadena CA 91105 Office: Lockheed Aircraft Corp PO Box 551 Burbank CA 91520

SCHMIDT, WILSON EMERSON, educator, economist; b. Madison, Wis., Mar. 22, 1927; s. Emerson Peter and Gertrude (Wilson) S.; B.S., U. Md., 1947; M.A., U. Pitts, 1948; Ph.D., U. Va., 1952; m. Eleanor Butt Parker, Dec. 26, 1950; children—Eric Emerson, Carl Wilson, Orrin Edward. Lectr., U. Pitts., 1948; mem. staff Bur. Population and Econ. Research, U. Va., Charlottesville, 1948-49, instr., 1949-50; from instr. to prof. George Washington U., Washington, 1950-66; prof. econs. Va. Poly. Inst. and State U., Blacksburg, 1966—, head dept., 1966-77; vis. prof. Sch. Advanced Internat. Studies, Johns Hopkins, 1960; prof. Bologna (Italy) Center, 1963-65; cons. in field, 1952—. Dep. asst. sec. U.S. Treasury, 1970-72. Mem. Am. Econ. Assn., Nat. Assn. Bus. Economists, Mont Pelerin Soc., Beta Gamma Sigma. Club: Cosmos (Washington). Author: (with J.N. Behrman) International Economics, 1957, Spanish edit., 1963. Home: 1514 Palmer Dr Blacksburg VA 24060

SCHMIDT-NIELSEN, BODIL MIMI (MRS. ROGER G. CHAGNON), physiologist; b. Copenhagen, Denmark, Nov. 3, 1918 (came to U.S. 1946, naturalized 1952); d. August and Marie (Jorgensen) Krogh; D.D.S., U. Copenhagen, 1941, D.Odont., 1946, Ph.D., 1955; m. Knut Schmidt-Nielsen, Sept. 20, 1939 (div. Feb. 1966); children—Astrid, Bent, Bodil; m. 2d, Roger G. Chagnon, Oct. 1968. Faculty, Duke, Durham, N.C., 1952-64; prof. biology Case Western Res. U., Cleve., 1964-71, chmn. dept., 1970-71, adj. prof., 1971—; trustee Mt. Desert Island (Maine) Biol. Lab., research scientist 1971—, exec. com., 1978—, v.p., 1979—, dep. dir., 1979—; adj. prof. Brown U., Providence, 1972—. Mem. tng. grant com. NIGMS, 1967-71. Trustee Coll. of Atlantic, Bar Harbor, Maine, 1972—. Recipient Career award NIH, 1962. John Simon Guggenheim Meml. fellow, 1952-53; Bowditch lectr., 1958; Jacobaeus lectr., 1974. Fellow N.Y. Acad. Scis., AAAS (del. council 1977-79), Am. Acad. Arts and Scis.; mem. Am. Physiol. Soc. (council 1971-77, pres. 1975-76), Soc. Exptl. Biology and Medicine (council 1969-71). Editor: Urea and the Kidney, 1970; asso. editor Am. Jour. Physiology: Regulatory, Integrative and Comparative Physiology; research, publs. on biochemistry of saliva, water metabolism of desert animals, comparative kidney physiology, comparative physiology of excretory organs. Home: Salsbury Cove ME 04672 Office: Mt Desert Island Biol Lab Salsbury Cove ME 04672

SCHMIDT-NIELSEN, KNUT, educator, physiologist; b. Norway, Sept. 24, 1915; s. Sigval and Signe Torborg (Sturzen-Becker) Schmidt-N.; Mag. Scient., U. Copenhagen, 1941, Dr. Phil., 1946. Came to U.S., 1946, naturalized, 1952. Research fellow Carlsberg Labs., Copenhagen, 1941-44, U. Copenhagen, 1944-46; research asso. zoology Swarthmore (Pa.) Coll., 1946-48; docent U. Oslo (Norway), 1947-49; research asso. physiology Stanford, 1948-49; asst. prof. Coll. Medicine, U. Cin., 1949-52; prof. physiology Duke, Durham, N.C., 1952—, James B. Duke prof. physiology, 1963—; Harvey Soc. lectr., 1962; Regents' lectr. U. Calif. at Davis, 1963; Brody Meml. lectr. U. Mo., 1962; Hans Gadow lectr. Cambridge (Eng.) U., 1971; vis. Agassiz prof. Harvard 1972. Mem. panel environmental biology NSF, 1957-61; mem. sci. adv. com. New Eng. Regional Primate Center, 1962-66; mem. nat. adv. bd. physiol. research lab. Scripps Instn. Oceanography, U. Calif. at San Diego, 1963-69, chmn., 1968-69; pres. organizing com. 1st Internat. Conf. on Comparative Physiology, 1972—; mem. U.S. nat. com. Internat. Union Physiol. Scis., 1966-78, vice chmn., 1969-78; mem. subcom. on environmental physiology U.S. nat. com. Internat. Biol. Programme, 1965-67; mem. com. on research utilization uncommon animals, div. biology and agr. Nat. Acad. Scis., 1966-68; mem. animal resources adv. com. NIH, 1968; mem. adv. bd. Bio-Med. Scis., Inc., 1973-74. Guggenheim fellow, 1953-54; grantee Office Naval Research, 1952-54, 58-61, UNCESCO 1953-54, Office Q.M. Gen., 1953-54, Office Surgeon Gen., 1953-54, NIH, 1955—, NSF, 1957-61, 59-60, 60-61, 61-63; recipient Research Career award USPHS, 1964. Fellow N.Y. Acad. Sci., A.A.A.S., Am. Acad. Arts and Scis.; mem. Nat. Acad. Scis., N.C. Acad. Sci. (Poteat award 1957), Am. Physiol. Soc., Am. Soc. Zoologists (chmn. div. comparative physiology 1964), Soc. Exptl. Biology, Harvey Soc. (hon.), Royal Danish Acad., Académie des Sciences (France) (fgn. asso.), Royal Norwegian Soc. Arts and Sci., Norwegian Acad. Scis. Author: Animal Physiology, 3d. edit., 1970; The Physiology of Desert Animals; Physiological Problems of Heat and Water, 1964; How Animals Work, 1972; Animal Physiology; Adaptation and Environment, 1975, 2d edit., 1979. Sect. editor Am. Jour. Physiology, 1961-64, 70-76, Jour. Applied Physiology, 1961-64, 70-76; editorial bd. Jour. Cellular and Comparative Physiology, 1961-66, Physiol. Zoology, 1959-70, Am. Jour. Physiology, 1971-76, Jour. Applied Physiology, 1971-76, Jour. Exptl. Biology, 1975-79; cons. editor: Annals of Arid Zone, 1962—; hon. editorial adv. bd. Comparative Biochemistry and Physiology, 1962-63. Contbr. articles to sci. publs. Chief scientist Scripps Instn. Amazon expdn., 1967. Office: Dept Zoology Duke Univ Durham NC 27706

SCHMIEDER, FRANK JOSEPH, bus. exec.; b. Granite City, Ill., June 26, 1941; s. Frank John and Ione Mina (Scheller) S.; B.S. (Nat. Merit scholar, State Assembly scholar), U. Ill., 1963, M.A., 1964; postgrad. (U. Ill. grad. research fellow) Mass. Inst. Tech., 1966; m. Anne Loraine Murray, Aug. 26, 1961; children—Kevin Frank, Craig Michael. Asst. to v.p. indsl. relations Cummins Engine Co., Columbus, Ind., 1964-66, mgr. corp. devel. systems, 1966-68; dir. corp. planning Samsonite Co., Denver, 1969-71, v.p. finance, 1971-73; v.p., treas. Fairchild Camera & Instrument Corp., Mountain View, Calif., 1973-76; v.p. adminstrn. Peterson, Howell & Heather Inc., Hunt Valley, Md., 1976-79, sr. v.p., chief fin. officer, 1979—; pres., dir. Vail Restaurant & Food Services, 1973—. Spl. cons. on econs. and efficiency to Gov. Colo., 1968. Bd. dirs. Retarded Children Unltd., 1969-71. Mem. Nat. Assn. Accountants (award of merit 1971), Am. Econ. Assn., Inst. Mgmt. Sci. Republican. Roman Catholic. Author: Application of Game Theory to Collective Bargaining, 1965. Home: 495 Padonia Rd W Cockeysville MD 21030 Office: PO Box 2174 Baltimore MD 21203

SCHMIEL, EDGAR HERMAN, office products mfg. co. exec., lawyer; b. Lotts Creek, Iowa, Sept. 1, 1921; s. William and Eugenia (Fuerstenau) S.; B.A., Cornell Coll., Mt. Vernon, Iowa, 1943; LL.B., U. Mich., Ann Arbor, 1949; m. Marjorie Ruth Littell, Dec. 21, 1947; 1 dau., Mary Aileen. Admitted to Wis. bar, 1949, Ill. bar, 1966; atty. Marathon Corp., Neenah, Wis., 1951-57; gen. atty. Marathon div. Am. Can Co., Neenah, 1957-66; v.p., gen. counsel, sec. A. B. Dick Co., Chgo., 1966—. Served with USNR, 1943-46. Mem. Am., Ill. State bar assns., State Bar Wis. Lutheran. Home: 1831 E Mission Hills Rd Northbrook IL 60062 Office: 5700 W Touhy Ave Chicago IL 60648

SCHMIT, LUCIEN ANDRÉ, JR., structural engr.; b. N.Y.C., May 5, 1928; s. Lucien Alexander and Eleanor Jessie (Donley) S.; B.S., M.I.T., 1949, M.S., 1950; m. Eleanor Constance Trabish, June 24, 1951; 1 son, Lucien Alexander, III. Structures engr. Grumman Aircraft Co., Bethpage, N.Y., 1951-53; research engr., aeroelastic and structures lab. M.I.T., 1954-58; asst. prof. engring. Case Inst. Tech., 1958-60, asso. prof., 1961-63, prof., 1964-70; prof. engring. and applied sci. UCLA, 1970—; mem. sci. adv. bd. USAF, Fellow ASCE (Walter L. Huber Civil Engring. Research prize 1970), AIAA (asso., Design Lecture award 1977, Structures, Structural Dynamics and Materials award 1979); mem. ASME, Sigma Xi. Contbr. numerous articles on analysis and synthesis of structural systems, finite element methods, design of fiber composite components to profl. jours. Home: 712 El Medio Ave Pacific Palisades CA 90272 Office: 6731K Boelter Hall UCLA Los Angeles CA 90024

SCHMIT, TIMOTHY BRUCE, musician; b. Sacramento; attended Sacramento State Coll. Bass player with musical groups the New Breed, Poco, then Eagles, 1977—; session musician for Gene Clark, Steely Dan, Richie Furay. Office: care Front Line Mgmt 8380 Melrose Ave Los Angeles CA 90069*

SCHMITT, EDWARD HENRY, fast food chain exec.; b. Chgo., Aug. 26, 1925; s. Henry Peter and Anne (Kemp) S.; B.S., DePaul U., 1952; m. Marie Clare Collins, Aug. 23, 1952; children—Edward Henry, Richard C. Self-employed, 1952-64; with McDonald's Corp., Oak Brook, Ill., 1964—, exec. v.p., chief operating officer, 1970-77, pres., chief adminstrv. officer, 1977—, also dir. Served to 1st lt. AUS. Decorated Purple Heart, Silver Star, Bronze Star, Croix de Guerre, Presdl. Citation. Club: Aurora (Ill.) Country. Office: 1 McDonald's Plaza Oak Brook IL 60521*

SCHMITT, FRANCIS OTTO, educator, neuroscientist; b. St. Louis, Mo., Nov. 23, 1903; s. Otto Franz and Clara Elizabeth (Senniger) S.; A.B., Washington U., St. Louis, 1924, Ph.D., 1927; postgrad. (NRC fellow), U. Calif., 1927-28, U. Coll., London, 1928, Kaiser Wilhelm Inst. Berlin-Dahlem, 1928-29; D.Sc., Johns Hopkins, 1950, Washington U., 1952, U. Chgo., 1957, Valparaiso U., 1959, Mich. State U., 1968, N.Y. State Med. Coll., 1971; M.D. honoris causa, U. Gothenburg, Sweden, 1964; LL.D. honoris causa, Wittenberg U., 1966, Juniata Coll., 1968; m. Barbara Hecker, June 18, 1927 (dec.); children—David (dec.), Robert Hecker, Marion. Asst. prof. zoology, Washington U., St. Louis, 1929-34, asso. prof., 1934-38, prof., 1938-44, head dept., 1940-41; prof. biology Mass. Inst. Tech., 1941, head dept. biology, 1942-55, inst. prof., 1955-69, emeritus, 1969—, chmn. Neuroscis. Research Found., Inc., 1962—, chmn. neuroscis. research program, 1962-74, found. scientist, neuroscis. research program, 1974—. Mem. Nat. Adv. Health Council, USPHS, 1959-63, Nat. Adv. Gen. Med. Scis. Council, 1969-71; mem. Nat. Acad.

Scis.-NRC Com. on Neurobiology, 1945, Com. on Growth, 1946-50, Com. on Radiation Cataracts, 1949-53, Com. on Atherosclerosis, 1953-54, Biol. Council, 1954-56; chmn. NIH study sect. on biophysics and biophys. chemistry, 1954-58, other study programs; mem. bd. scientific counselors NINCDS, NIH, 1976-79; mem. fellowships for basic research com. Alfred P. Sloan Found., 1971-78; bd. sci. cons. Sloan-Kettering Inst. Cancer Research, 1963-72; bd. sci. adv. com. New Eng. Aquarium, 1967—; nat. adv. council Marine Biomed. Inst., U. Tex. Med. Br., Galveston, 1973—. Trustee, Mass. Gen. Hosp., 1947—; bd. dirs. Hall-Mercer Hosp.; vis. com. Harvard Div. Sch., 1964-68. Recipient Alsop award Am. Leather Chem. Assn., 1947, Lasker award Am. Pub. Health Assn., 1956, T. Duckett Jones Meml. award Helen Hay Whitney Found., 1963. Fellow Am. Acad. Arts and Scis. (council 1950-52, 64-65), AAAS, N.Y. Acad. Scis.; mem. Soc. Gen. Physiologists, Histochem. Soc., Am. Philos. Soc. (council 1964-66, v.p. 1972-75), Am. Physiol. Soc., Am. Soc. Zoologists, Soc. Exptl. Biology and Medicine, Soc. Growth and Devel. (treas. 1945-46, pres. 1947), Am. Leather Chem. Assn., Soc. for Neuroscience, Neurochemistry Soc., Internat. Neurochemistry Soc., Biophys. Soc. (councilor), Electron Microscope Soc. Am. (dir. 1944-47, pres. 1949), Soc. Philomathique de Paris, Nat. Acad. Scis., Swedish Royal Acad. Scis., Phi Beta Kappa, Sigma Xi. Mem. editorial bd. Quar. Rev. Biology, 1961—, Brain Research, 1966—, Jour. Mechanochemistry and Cell Motility, 1971—, Annual Rev. Biophysics and Bioengring., 1970-73. Home: 72 Byron Rd Weston MA 02193 Office: 165 Allandale St Boston MA 02130

SCHMITT, GEORGE FREDERICK, JR., chem. engr.; b. Louisville, Nov. 3, 1939; s. George Frederick and Jane Limbird (Hurst) S.; B.S., U. Louisville, 1962, M.S., 1963; M.B.A., Ohio State U., 1966; m. Ann Cheatham, July 31, 1965; 2 children. Materials research engr. USAF Materials Lab., Wright Patterson AFB, O., 1966—. Guest lectr. U. Dayton, 1970, Catholic U., 1973, U. Mich., 1975. Mem. Kettering (Ohio) Civic Band, 1965—; chmn. Affiliate Socs. Council of Dayton, 1972—. Served to 1st lt. USAF, 1963-66. Named Fed. Profl. Employee of Year, Dayton, 1972, One of Ten Outstanding Engrs., Engrs. Week, 1975. Mem. Am. Chem. Soc., Am. Inst. Aeros. and Astronautics, ASTM (rec. sec. 1972—, chmn. com. on erosion and wear 1975-79, chmn. com. on erosion and wear 1976-79, 2d nat. v.p. 1979—), Affiliate Socs. Council Dayton (chmn. 1978-79), Fedn. Socs. for Paint Tech., Soc. for Advancement Materials and Process Engrs. (Best Paper award 1973, nat. sec. 1975—, nat. membership chmn. 1977-79), Am. Inst. Chem. Engrs. Republican. Mem. United Ch. of Christ. Contbr. articles profl. jours. Home: 1500 Wardmier Dr Dayton OH 45459 Office: USAF Materials Lab MBE Wright Patterson Air Force Base OH 45433

SCHMITT, GEORGE HERBERT, hosp. adminstr.; b. Dallas, Dec. 16, 1939; s. Herbert S. and Regina T. (King) S.; A.B., Cardinal Glennon Coll., St. Louis, 1961; postgrad. Kenrick Sem., St. Louis, 1961-63; M.H.A., U. Minn., 1967; D.Sc. (hon.), Maryville Coll., St. Louis, 1978; m. Sue Ann Klein, Jan. 29, 1966; children—George Michael, Kristin Sue (dec.), Joseph Christopher. Gen. accountant Ameron Corp., St. Louis, 1965-66; asst. dir. Stanford Med. Center, Palo Alto, Cal., 1966-68; asso. adminstr., dir. planning and devel. St. Joseph Infirmary, Louisville, 1968-70, exec. dir., 1970-74; pres., chief exec. officer Forbes Health System, Pitts., 1974—. Guest lectr., preceptor U. Minn., Duke U., Northwestern U., Ohio State U., U. Pitts. Bd. dirs. Pa. Med. Care Found., Hosp. Council Western Pa. Mem. Am. Pub. Health Assn., Am. Coll. Hosp. Adminstrs., Pa. Hosp. Assn., Nat. Assn. Hosp. Planning. Home: 2 Deer Spring Ln Pittsburgh PA 15238 Office: 500 Finley St Pittsburgh PA 15206

SCHMITT, HARRISON HAGAN, U.S. senator; b. Santa Rita, N.Mex., July 3, 1935; s. Harrison A. and Ethel (Hagan) S.; B.A., Calif. Inst. Tech., 1957; postgrad. (Fulbright fellow) U. Oslo, 1957-58; Ph.D. (NSF fellow), Harvard U., 1964. Geologist U.S Geol. Survey, 1964-65; astronaut NASA from 1965, lunar module pilot Apollo 17, Dec. 1972, spl. asst. to adminstr., 1974, asst. adminstr. Office Energy Programs, 1974; mem. U.S. Senate from N.Mex. Recipient MSC Superior Achievement award, 1970, Disting. Service medal NASA, 1973. Office: 248 Russell Senate Office Bldg Washington DC 20510

SCHMITT, HENRY JOSEPH, publisher; b. Wahpeton, N.D., Aug. 11, 1909; s. Peter and Mary (Ridder) S.; student St. John's Parochial Sch., Wahpeton, N.D., 1915-24, Coll. of Science, Wahpeton, 1924-27; m. Viola Oyhus, Jan. 1, 1937; 1 son, Peter Oyhus. Advt. solicitor Aberdeen (S.D.) American News, 1928-30, Grand Forks (N.D.) Herald, 1930-32; Aberdeen American News, 1932-35, St. Paul (Minn.) Daily News, 1935-36, Duluth (Minn.) Herald, 1936, 37, Ridder-Johns, Inc., N.Y. City, 1937-38; chmn. bd. Aberdeen News Co., 1939—; dir., v.p. Grand Forks (N.D.) Herald, 1956—; dir. Boulder Pub., Inc. (Colo.). Served with AUS World War II. Mem. Am. Soc. Newspaper Editors, U.S. C. of C. (dir. 1970—, v.p. 1971), Am. Legion, Sigma Delta Chi, Beta Gamma Sigma. Roman Catholic. Elk. Clubs: Moccasin Creek Country. Home: 1415 N Washington Aberdeen SD 57401 Office: 124 S 2d St Aberdeen SD 57401

SCHMITT, JOHN ARVID, JR., educator; b. Buffalo, July 30, 1925; s. John Arvid and Emily Virginia (Norvell) S.; B.S. in Zoology, U. Mich., 1949; M.S. in Botany, 1950, Ph.D. in Botany and Mycology, 1954; m. Alyce L. Ridinger, Sept. 6, 1947; children—Mark R., Holly L. Prof., head biology dept. Findlay (Ohio) Coll., 1953-54; asst. prof. biology U. Miss., Oxford, 1954-55; instr. botany and plant pathology Ohio State U., Columbus, 1955-57 asst. prof. botany and plant pathology, 1957-62, asso. prof. botany, 1962-69, prof., 1969—, also chmn. dept. botany, 1969-74, head gen. biology sect. Coll. Biol. Scis., 1979—; cons. Ericksen, Mackenroth & Arbuthnot, Inc., Allergy Labs. of Ohio. Served with USNR, 1943-45. Fellow Ohio Acad. Sci.; mem. Mycol. Soc. Am., Bot. Soc. Am., Internat. Soc. Human and Animal Mycology, Med. Mycol. Soc. Ams., Am. Inst. Biol. Scis., Am. Soc. Microbiology, Cin.-Dayton-Indpls.-Columbus Soc. for Coatings Tech. Research on mycology and ecology of Candida albicans, Aureobasidium pullulans. Home: 4477 Lauraland Dr E Columbus OH 43214

SCHMITT, KARL MICHAEL, polit. scientist; b. Louisville, Ky., July 22, 1922; s. Edward Peter and Mary Ann (Iula) S.; B.A., Cath. U. Am., 1947, M.A., 1949; Ph.D., U. Pa., 1954; m. Grace Bernadette Leary, June 18, 1949; children—Karl, Edward, Barbara, William, Michael. Teaching asst. U. Pa., 1948-50; instr. history Niagara U., 1950-54, asst. prof., 1954-55; research analyst U.S. Dept. State, 1955-58; asst. prof. dept. govt. U. Tex., 1958-63, asso. prof., 1963-66, prof., 1966—, chairperson, 1975—; vis. prof. U. Calif., Los Angeles summer 1959, Nat. War Coll., 1970-71; cons. Dept. of State, 1962-70. Served with U.S. Army, 1943-45. Decorated Purple Heart. Mem. So. Polit. Sci. Assn., Conf. Latin Am. History, S.W. Council Latin Am. Studies, Am., Tex. (pres. 1976-77) Cath. hist. assns. Roman Catholic. Author: Communism in Mexico; A Study in Political Frustration, 1965; Mexico and the United States, 1821-1973: Conflict and Coexistence, 1974; and others. Contbr. articles to profl. jours. Home: 2603 Pinewood Terr Austin TX 78757 Office: Dept Govt U Tex Austin TX 78712

SCHMITT, ROLAND WALTER, mfg. co. exec.; b. Seguin, Tex., July 24, 1923; s. Walter L. and Myrtle F. (Caldwell) S.; B.A. in Math., U. Tex., 1947, B.S. in Physics, 1947, M.A. in Physics, 1948; Ph.D., Rice U., 1951; m. Claire Freeman Kunz, Sept. 19, 1957; children—Lorenz Allen, Brian Walter, Alice Elizabeth, Henry Caldwell. With Gen. Electric Co., 1951—, research and devel. mgr. phys. sci. and engring. Gen. Electric Corp. Research and Devel., Schenectady, 1967-74, research and devel. mgr. energy sci. and engring., 1974-78, v.p. corp. research and devel., 1978—; mem. energy research adv. bd. Dept. Energy; bd. dirs. N.Y. State Sci. and Tech. Found. Bd. govs. Albany Med. Center Hosp.; trustee Schenectady Savs. Bank; bd. dirs. Sunnyview Hosp. and Rehab. Center. Served with USAAF, 1943-46. Fellow Am. Phys. Soc.; mem. Am. Inst. Physics (chmn. com. on corp. assos.), Nat. Acad. Engring., IEEE, AAAS, Am. Nuclear Soc., Am. Mgmt. Assn. Office: PO Box 8 Schenectady NY 12301

SCHMITT, ROMAN AUGUSTINE, educator; b. Johnsburg, Ill., Nov. 13, 1925; s. Joseph S. and Mary (Freund) S.; student Ill. Coll., 1946-48; M.S., U. Chgo., 1950, Ph.D., 1953; m. Jean Marie Vertovec, Dec. 28, 1954; children—Joseph, Mary, Peter, Katherine. Instr., U. Ill., Champaign, 1953-56; with Gen. Atomic Co., San Diego, 1956-66; faculty dept. chemistry Chemistry and Radiation Center, Oreg. State U., Corvallis, 1966—; mem. faculty U. San Diego, 1959. Mem. Am. Chem. Soc., Geochem. Soc., Meteoretical Soc. Research and publs. on photodisintegration and fission uranium and thorium, recoiling atoms in solids, various Szilard-Chalmers reactions, trace elements determined in meteorites, terrestrial and lunar matter; application technique of neutron activation for multielement analysis. Home: 1830 Hawthorne Pl Corvallis OR 97330

SCHMITTER, CHARLES HARRY, electronics mfg. co. exec., lawyer; b. Paterson, N.J., Feb. 4, 1928; s. Charles and Jennie (Schoe) S.; A.B. magna cum laude, Rutgers U., 1948; J.D., Columbia, 1953; m. Margaret Ann Roose, Oct. 24, 1964. Admitted to N.Y. bar, 1956, Mich. bar, 1960; asso. atty. firm Cravath, Swaine & Moore, N.Y.C., 1955-59; asst. sec. Ford Motor Co., 1959-64; corp. sec. Sperry Rand Corp., N.Y.C., 1964—. Served with AUS, 1953-55. Mem. Am. Bar Assn., Am. Soc. Corp. Secretaries, Phi Alpha Delta, Theta Chi. Club: Rockefeller Center Luncheon (N.Y.C.). Home: 420 E 51st St New York City NY 10022 Office: 1290 Ave of Americas New York City NY 10019

SCHMITZ, DENNIS MATHEW, educator; b. Dubuque, Iowa, Aug. 11, 1937; s. Anthony Peter and Roselyn S.; B.A., Loras Coll., 1959; M.A., U. Chgo., 1961; m. Loretta D'Agostino, Aug. 20, 1960; children—Anne, Sara, Martha, Paul, Matthew. Instr. in English, Ill. Inst. Tech., Chgo., 1961-62, U. Wis., Milw., 1962-66; asst. prof. Calif. State U., Sacramento, 1966-69, asso. prof., 1969-74, prof., 1974—, poet-in-residence, 1966—. Recipient Discovery award Poetry Center, N.Y.C., 1968; winner First Book Competition, Follett Pub. Co., 1969; NEA fellow, 1976-77; Guggenheim fellow, 1978-79. Mem. PEN, Associated Writing Programs. Roman Catholic. Author: We Weep for Our Strangeness, 1969; Double Exposures, 1971; Goodwill, Inc., 1976. Office: Calif State U 6000 Jay St English Dept Sacramento CA 95819

SCHMITZ, EUGENIA EVANGELINE, educator; b. Grand Rapids, Mich.; d. Joseph A. and Eugenia (Newhouse) Schmitz; A.B., Western Mich. U.; B.S., Coll. St. Catherine; A.M., U. Mich., Ph.D., 1966. Br. librarian Grand Rapids Pub. Library; librarian Creston High Sch., Grand Rapids, Sr. High Sch., Benton Harbor, Mich.; lectr. dept. library sci. U. Mich., 1963-67, asst. prof., 1967-68; asst. prof. library sci. U. Wis. at Oshkosh, 1968-70, asso. prof., 1970-75, prof., 1975—, chmn. dept. library sci., 1968—. Mem. ALA, Wis. Library Assn., Phi Beta Kappa, Phi Kappa Phi, Beta Phi Mu, Pi Lambda Theta, Sigma Pi Epsilon. Contbr. book revs. to Best Sellers. Home: 1220 Maricopa Dr Oshkosh WI 54901

SCHMITZ, PAUL P., fraternal orgn. exec.; b. Aurora, Ill., Apr. 30, 1902; grad. Mayo Coll. Commerce, Chgo.; m. Nan Schmitz; 1 son, Paul P. Former chmn. bd. Aurora Fed. Savs. & Loan Assn.; dir. Mchts. Nat. Bank of Aurora. Past dir. gen. Loyal Order of Moose, Mooseheart, Ill.; now mem. supreme council. Home: Aurora IL Office: 1951 Kensington Pl Aurora IL 60506

SCHMULLER, ANGELO AARON, publishing co. exec., author; b. Lakovich-Minsk, Poland, May 27, 1910 (came to U.S. 1923, naturalized 1947); s. Joseph and Rachel (Muraskin) S.; student Coll. City N.Y., 1933; m. Sara Riba, June 30, 1940; children—David, Joseph. Owner Parthenon Pub. Co., Bklyn., 1962—. Mem. Poetry Soc. Am. Author: Man in the Mirror, 1945; Moments of Meditation, 1953; Treblinka Grass, 1957; Crossing the Borderland, 1959; Legend of his Lyre, 1960; Tokens of Devotion, 1966; While Man Exists. 1970; Triumphalis, 1973; Eternal Meanings 1976, 1975; Going Steady, 1976. Editor: The Muse Anthology, 1962; The Singing Muse Anthology, 1963; Parthenon Poetry Anthology, 1978. Contbr. to numerous periodicals, lit. mags., poetry arthologies. Address: 9227 Kaufman Pl Brooklyn NY 11236

SCHMULTS, EDWARD CHARLES, lawyer; b. Paterson, N.J., Feb. 6, 1931; s. Edward M. and Mildred (Moore) S.; B.S., Yale, 1953; LL.B., Harvard, 1958; m. Diane E. Beers, Apr. 23, 1960; children—Alison C., Edward M., Robert C. Admitted to N.Y. State bar, 1959, D.C. bar, 1974; asso. firm White & Case, N.Y.C., 1958-65, partner, 1965-73; gen. counsel Treasury Dept., Washington, 1973-74, under sec., 1974-75; dep. counsel to Pres. U.S., 1975-76; partner firm White & Case, N.Y.C., 1977—. Lectr. securities laws. Served with USMCR, 1953-55. Mem. Am., N.Y. State, Fed. bar assns., Assn. Bar City N.Y., Adminstrv. Conf. U.S. (council 1977—). Club: Sakonnet Golf (Little Compton, R.I.). Home: 68 Pheasant Ln Greenwich CT 06830 Office: 14 Wall St New York City NY 10005

SCHNABEL, KARL ULRICH, pianist; b. Berlin, Germany, Aug. 6, 1909; came to U.S. 1938, naturalized 1944; s. Artur and Therese (Behr) S.; student State Acad. Music, Berlin, 1922-28; m. Helen Fogel, Nov. 22, 1939; 1 dau., Ann. Concert debut, Berlin, 1925; recitals, broadcasts, soloist with orchestra in Germany, Austria, Eng., 1927-32; dir. motion picture, 1932; concert tours, Britain, France, Italy, Holland, Austria, Denmark, Poland, USSR, Switzerland, Sweden, Norway, 1933-39, 1947—, Australia, New Zealand, 1971—; debut, N.Y., 1937; 1st Am. tour, 1937, S.Am., 1951; piano duo appearances with wife, 1939-41, 47—; faculty Dalcroze Sch. Music, N.Y., 1938—; internat. summer classes, Tremezzo, Lake Como, Italy, 1947—; master courses Bryanston Summer Music Sch., 1948, Teresópolis, Brazil, 1951, São Paulo, 1952, U. Bahia, 1955, Coll. Holy Names, Oakland, Calif., 1966, 68, Mannes Coll. Music, N.Y.C., 1966-67, 70, 72, 74, 76, 79, Immaculate Heart Coll., Los Angeles, 1967-68, U. Wis., 1968, U. Calif. at Los Angeles, 1969, U. Calif. at Riverside, 1970, 71, 73, 74, 79, Merritt Coll., Oakland, Calif., 1970-79, Pacific Union Coll., Angwin, Calif., 1970, U. Utah, 1970, 76, Brigham Young U., Provo, Utah, 1971, 76, Hamline U., St. Paul, 1971, Royal Conservatory, Toronto, 1976-79, San Francisco State U., 1978. Author: Modern Technique of the Pedal, 1954. Home: 305 West End Ave New York NY 10023

SCHNABEL, TRUMAN GROSS, physician; b. Phila., Jan., 5, 1919; s. Truman Gross and Heldegarde (Rohner) S.; student Bowdoin Coll., 1936-37; B.S., Yale U., 1940; M.D., U. Pa., 1943; m. Mary Hyatt, Sept. 13, 1947; children—Ann, Daniel, Paul, Brooke. Intern, resident in medicine Hosp. of U. Pa., Phila., 1944-49, mem. faculty U. Med. Sch., 1948—, C. Mahlon Kline prof. medicine, 1973—, staff physician dept. medicine, 1952—. Served to maj. M.C., AUS, 1944-46. Hon. fellow Royal Coll. Physicians of Ireland; Am. Heart Assn. fellow, 1949-52; Markle scholar med. scis., 1952-57; diplomate Am. Bd. Internal Medicine (sec.-treas. 1971-72), Nat. Bd. Med. Examiners. Mem. A.C.P. (gov. Eastern Pa. 1962-68, regent 1968-73, 75-76, pres. 1974-75), Am. Clin. and Climatol. Soc. (v.p. 1968-69), Council Med. Splty. Socs. (pres. 1975-78), Am. Soc. for Clin. Investigation, Assn. Am. Physicians, Liaison Com. for Grad. Med. Edn. (chmn. 1979), Am. Bd. Family Practice Dirs., Am. Bd. Med. Spltys., Alpha Omega Alpha, Sigma Psi. Author: (with Marion Laffey Fox) Patient's Guide to Medical Testing, 1979; profl. jours. Office: Room 191 Gibson Bldg Hosp of U Pa 34th and Spruce Sts Philadelphia PA 19104

SCHNACKE, ROBERT HOWARD, judge; b. San Francisco, Oct. 8, 1913; s. Carl H. and Elfriede A. (Hanschen) S.; student U. Calif. at Berkeley, 1930-32; J.D., Hastings Coll. of Law, 1938; m. June Doris Borina, Sept. 7, 1956. Admitted to Cal. bar, 1938; practiced in San Francisco 1938-42, 51-53, 59-68; dep. commr. div. corps. State Calif., San Francisco, 1947-51; chief criminal div. Office U.S. Atty., San Francisco, 1953-58; U.S. atty. No. Dist. Calif., San Francisco, 1958-59; judge Superior Ct., San Francisco, 1968-70; judge U.S. Dist. Ct., No. Dist. Calif., San Francisco, 1970—. Chmn. uniform rules of evidence com. 9th Circuit Jud. Conf., 1963-76. Pres. Guide Dogs for Blind, 1959-62. Bd. dirs. Fed. Jud. Center, 1975-79; mem. Jud. Panel on Multidist. Litigation, 1979—. Served with AUS, 1942-46. Mem. Calif. Hist. Soc., Fed., San Francisco bar assns., Am. Judicature Soc. Mason. Club: Burlingame Country. Home: Hillsborough CA 94010 Office: US Dist Ct No Dist Cal Box 36060 Fed Office Bldg San Francisco CA 94102

SCHNACKENBERG, ROY, artist; b. Chgo., Jan. 14, 1934; s. Elmer J. and Hazel (Bard) S.; B.F.A., Miami U., Oxford, Ohio, 1956. One man shows include Joachim Gallery, Chgo., 1962, Main St. Galleries, Chgo., 1963, 64, 66, 68-69; Michael Wyman Gallery, Chgo., 1972, Esther Robles Gallery, Los Angeles, 1973; group exhbns. include print and drawing biennial Art Inst. Chgo., 1961, Chgo. and Vicinity Show Art Inst. Chgo., 1961, 62, 64, 66-69, 73, 78, Soc. Contemporary Art, Art Inst. Chgo., 1962, 70, New Horizons in Sculpture, Chgo., 1962, 2d ann. art dealers show, N.Y.C., 1963, Ill. Biennial Show, Champaign, 1965, 67, Twelve Chgo. Artists, Walker Mus., Mpls., 1965, also Milw., 1965. Selected Painter, Mulvane Art Center, Topeka, 1965, 50 States of Art Exhibit, Burpee Mus., Rockford, Ill., Recent Aquisitions Exhbn., Whitney Mus., 1967, also ann. exhbn. painting and sculpture, 1967, 68-69, 69-70. No. Ill. U. group exhbn., Normal, 1968-69, Western Ill. U. show, Macomb, 1968-69, Ill. Arts council traveling Sculpture exhbn., 1968-69, Des Moines Art Center exhbn., New Am. Realists, Konsthallen, Gotenborg, Sweden, 1970, The Art of Playboy World Tour, Milan, 1971, Dept. Interior Bicentennial Exhbn., Corcoran Gallery, Washington, nat. tour, 1976, 200 Years of Illustration, N.Y. Hist. Soc., Zriny-Hayes Gallery, Chgo., 1978; executed mural Crucible, S. Chgo. Savs. Bank, 1977, S.E. Savs. & Loan, 1979; represented in permanent collections Whitney Mus. Am. Art, N.Y.C., Art Inst. Chgo., Mus. Contemporary Art, Chgo., Burpee Art Mus., Rockford, Ill., others. Recipient Joseph R. Shapiro award New Horizons in Sculpture, Chgo., 1962; Slobe award, 1964, Viehler award, 1965, Logan medal, 1973 Municipal award, 1974 (all Art Inst. Chgo.); recipient purchase prize Burpee Mus., 1965, Copley Found. award N.Y.C., 1967. Served with AUS, 1956-58. Address: 1919 N Orchard Chicago IL 60614

SCHNADER, DONALD DIXON, banker; b. Balt., Mar. 28, 1935; s. William Alexander and Doris Ada (Dixon) S.; high sch. diploma Balt. Poly. Inst., 1954. Mgmt. trainee Provident Savs. Bank, Balt., 1956-57, asst. mgr., 1957-62, mgr., 1962-69, auditor, 1969—. Mem. Bank Adminstrn. Inst., Inst. Internal Auditors (cert. internal auditor), Am. Guild Organists, Balt. Poly. Inst. Alumni Assn. (dir. 1978—, treas. 1979-80). Lutheran. Home: 2920 Shirey Ave Baltimore MD 21214 Office: 240 N Howard St Baltimore MD 21201

SCHNADIG, LAWRENCE K., furniture co. exec.; b. Chgo., Apr. 24, 1908; s. Jacob L. and Lillie (Reach) S.; Wharton Sch. of Fin., U. Pa., 1930; m. Dorothy Dottenheim, Apr. 12, 1936; children—J. Larence, Richard H., Susan Schnadig Belgrad. Various positions Pullman Couch Co., 1930-53, pres., 1947-53; pres., owner, Internat. Furniture Co. and Karpen Furniture Co., Chgo., after 1953; now chmn. bd. Schnadig Corp. parent co. of Internat. Furniture Co., Karpen Furniture Co. and Internat. Table Co., Chgo.; bd. govs. Am. Furniture Mart. Trustee Ill. Children's Home and Aid Soc.; mem. various Ill. child care coms.; bd. dirs. U. Chgo. Sch. Social Service Adminstrn., NCCJ. Named Furniture Man of Yr., Am. Furniture Mart; recipient Brotherhood award NCCJ, Home Furnishings Div. award Jewish United Fund, Friend of the Child award, Child Care Assn. Ill., 1979. Mem. Nat. Assn. Furniture Mfrs., Chgo. Tennis Assn. Clubs: Lake Shore Country, Ridge and Valley Tennis. Home: 235 Prospect Ave Highland Park IL 60035 Office: 4820 W Belmont Ave Chicago IL 60641

SCHNAIBERG, ALLAN, sociologist; b. Montreal, Que., Can., Aug. 20, 1939; s. Harry and Belle (Katzoff) S.; came to U.S., 1964; B.S., McGill U., 1960; M.A., U. Mich., 1964, Ph.D., 1968; m. Elayne Reva Bond, Dec. 16, 1962; children—Lynn Renee, Jill Ann. Analytical chemist Can. Nat. Rys., Montreal, 1960-61; materials and process engr. Canadair, Ltd., Montreal, 1961-63; asso. dir. West Malaysian Family Survey, Kuala Lumpur, 1966-67; prof. sociology Northwestern U., Evanston, Ill., 1969—, chmn. dept. sociology, 1976-79. Population Council fellow, 1967-68; Nat. Inst. Child Health and Human Devel. research grantee, 1970-72. Mem. Am. Sociol. Assn., Population Assn. Am., Soc. for Study Social Problems (chmn. environ. problems div. 1978-80, mem. C. Wright Mills com. 1979), AAAS, Monthly Rev. Assos. Author: The Environment: From Surplus to Scarcity, 1980. Home: 855 Hinman Apt 108 Evanston IL 60202 Office: 1834 Sheridan Rd Evanston IL 60201. *Learn conventional wisdom, but be prepared to challenge it at all times. What most people agree upon is often wrong, though they won't welcome you bringing this to their attention*

SCHNAITMAN, WILLIAM KENNETH, finance co. exec.; b. Talbot County, Md., May 12, 1926; s. William and Catherine Almeda (Cheezum) S.; student Strayer Bus. Sch., Balt., 1943; m. Beverly June Marshall, July 13, 1963. Clk., Comml. Credit Co., Balt., 1946-70, asst. sec., 1970-72, treas., 1972-76, dir. cash mgmt., 1976—. Served with AUS, 1944-46; ETO. Home: 2301 Pentland Dr Baltimore MD 21234 Office: 300 St Paul Pl Baltimore MD 21202

SCHNAITTER, ALLENE FLORA, librarian; b. Sandusky, Ohio, Nov. 19, 1921; d. Edward Cornelius and Winifred Harriet (Platt) S.; A.B., U. Mich., 1949, A.M.L.S., 1952; Ph.D., Ind. U., 1972. Asst. current serials acquisition order dept. U. Mich. Library, 1949-52; sci. and music librarian Antioch Coll., 1953-54; asst. head Order Dept. U. Mich. Law Library, 1954-61; head order dept. U. Mo. Library, Columbia, 1961-67; H.E.A. fellow Ind. U. Grad. Library Sch., 1967-70; asst. dir. learning resources center Govs. State U., Park Forest South, Ill., 1970-73, dir., 1974-76; dir. of libraries Wash. State U., Pullman, 1976—. Mem. Am., Ill., Wash., Pacific N.W. library assns., AAUW. Home: PO Box 2337 CS Pullman WA 99163 Office:

Univ Library Wash State U Pullman WA 99164. *Reaching out for change and taking advantage of opportunities for personal and professional growth are two attributes which have helped me achieve my goals. It is extremely important not to become stale or rigid, but to keep open to new ideas and challenges.*

SCHNALL, HERBERT KENNETH, publishing co. exec.; b. Bklyn., July 28, 1928; s. Maurice and Sadye R. Schnall; m. Annabel Helpern, Apr. 5, 1952; children—Linda, Steven. Staff accountant S.D. Leiderdorf & Co., N.Y.C., 1951-52; sr. accountant Peat Marwick, Mitchell & Co., N.Y.C., 1954-57; controller Parents Mag. Enterprises, N.Y.C., 1957-67; pres. New Am. Library, N.Y.C., 1967—. Served to 1st lt. USAF, 1952-54. C.P.A., N.Y. Mem. Am. Inst. C.P.A.'s, Assn. Am. Publishers (chmn. mass market paperback div. 1974-75). Jewish. Home: 41-27 Matule Dr Fair Lawn NJ 07410 Office: 1633 Broadway New York NY 10019

SCHNEEMANN, CAROLEE, performing artist, filmmaker, writer; b. Pa., Oct. 12, 1939; B.A., Bard Coll., 1960; M.F.A., U. Ill., 1961. Originated Kinetic Theater, 1962; with Judson Dance Theater, 1962-66; performance works, film showings throughout U.S. and Europe; erotic film Fuses, 1964-68 (Spl. Jury Selection Cannes 1968); most recent films: Acts of Perception, 1973, Kitch's Last Meal, 1973-78, ABC-We Print Anything-In the Cards, 1976-77; video tapes: Up To and Including Her Limits, 1974-77, Interior Scroll, 1975, ABC-We Print Anything—In The Cards, 1976-77, Homerunmuse, 1977; books: Part Of A Body House Book, 1972, Cezanne, She Was A Great Painter, 1974, ABC-We Print Anything-In The Cards, 1977, More Than Meat Joy, Complete Performance Works and Selected Writings, 1978. Creative Artists Public Service Program fellow, 1978-79; N.Y. State Council on Arts grantee, 1968; Nat. Endowment for Arts grantee, 1974, 77-78. Mem. Feminist Writers Guild, Woman's Salon.

SCHNEEWIND, JEROME BORGES, coll. adminstr.; b. Mt. Vernon, N.Y., May 17, 1930; s. Jerome John and Charlotte (Borges) S.; B.A., Cornell U., 1951; M.A., Princeton U., 1953, Ph.D., 1957; m. Elizabeth G.R. Hughes, Feb. 23, 1963; children—Sarah, Rachel, Hannah. Instr. philosophy U. Chgo., 1957-60, Princeton, 1960-61; asst. prof. Yale U., 1961-63; asso. prof. philosophy U. Pitts., 1964-68, prof., 1968-75, dean Coll. Arts and Scis., 1969-73; v.p., provost Hunter Coll. City U. N.Y., 1975—; philosophy adviser Ency. Americana, 1967—. Mem. adv. bd. in sci. tech. and values program Nat. Endowment for Humanities, 1975-78. Served with Signal Corps, AUS, 1954-56. Mellon post-doctoral fellow, 1963-64; Guggenheim fellow, 1967-68; Am. Council Learned Socs. grantee, 1973; Nat. Endowment Humanities sr. fellow, 1974. Mem. Am. Philos. Assn. (exec. com. Eastern div. 1964-67, chmn. com. on teaching philosophy 1973-78). Author: Backgrounds of English Victorian Literature, 1970; Sidgwick's Ethics and Victorian Moral Philosophy, 1977. Editorial bd. Victorian Studies, 1968-75, The Monist, 1969-76, Am. Philosophy Quar., 1975—, Philos. Studies, 1975-78. Contbr. articles on 19th century Brit. moral thought, ethics and sociobiology to publs. Office: Hunter Coll 695 Park Ave New York City NY 10021

SCHNEIDEMAN, ROBERT IVAN, educator; b. Bay City, Mich., June 23, 1926; s. Louis Abraham and Frances (Koss) S.; B.S., Northwestern U., 1948, M.A., 1949, Ph.D., 1956; m. Joyce Mary Butson, Mar. 19, 1966. Instr. dramatic prodn. Northwestern U., Evanston, Ill., 1953-56, asst. prof., 1957-62, asso. prof., 1963-67, prof., 1968—, chmn. theatre dept., 1968-71. Adv. bd. World Center For Shakespeare Studies, 1972. Mem. drama adv. bd. Hull House, Chgo., 1964-66; advisor to Mayor's Com., Chgo., 1963-64. Mem. Am. Ednl. Theatre Assn. (exec. sec. 1961-64, certificate of service 1964). Mem. advisory editorial bd. Themes in Drama. Home: 1500 Oak Ave Apt 2F Evanston IL 60201

SCHNEIDER, ALAN, theatre dir. Dir. Beckett, including Waiting for Godot, 1956, Endgame, 1958, Happy Days, 1961; Albee's Who's Afraid of Virginia Woolf?, 1962, Tiny Alice, 1964; Beckett's Play, 1964; dir. Albee's A Delicate Balance, 1966; Anderson's You Know I Can't Hear You When the Water's Running, 1967; Pinter's Dumbwaiter and The Collection, 1962, The Birthday Party, 1967; Albee's Box and Quotations from Chairman Mao Tse-Tung, 1968; Anderson's I Never Sang For My Father, 1968, Inquest, 1970; Edward Bond's Saved, 1970; Michael Weller's Moonchildren, 1971; Gunter Grass' Uptight, 1972; E.A. Whitehead's Foursome, 1972; Beckett's Not I, 1972; Elie Wiesel's The Madness of God, 1974; Preston Jones' The Last Meeting of the Knights of the White Magnolia, 1975, Texas Trilogy, 1976; Beckett's That Time, Footfalls, 1976; Weller's Loose Ends, 1979; dir. Theater Center, Juilliard Sch., 1976-79; prof. drama U. Calif., San Diego, 1979—. Recipient Antoinette Perry (Tony) award, 1962; Off-Broadway (Obie) award, 1962. Home: 41 Gingerbread Ln East Hampton NY 11937

SCHNEIDER, ALEXANDER, violinist; b. Vilna, Russia, Oct. 21, 1908; s. Isak and Chasia (Dainowski) S.; student violin Vilna Conservatory, Frankfurt Conservatory; studied with E. Malkin, Adolph Rebner, Carl Flesch (Berlin), Pablo Casals (Prades, France); D.F.A., New Sch. for Social Research, 1965. Came to the U.S., 1932, naturalized. Concertmaster Symphony Orch. Frankfurt, later State Opera and Symphony Orch. Saarbrücken, also Hamburg; traveled extensively with own string quartet, Germany; with Budapest String Quartet toured Europe, N. Africa, East Indies, Australia, U.S., 1938-50, U.S., S.Am., 1955—; founder Albeneri Trio, chamber music concerts U.S. and Can., 1944; with Ralph Kirkpatrick formed Sonata Ensemble, 1944; also mem. N.Y. Quartet for Piano and Strings, concerts with Eugene Istomin; condr. concerts Dumbarton Oaks Chamber Music Orch., 1944—; former mem. faculty U. Wash., Mills Coll., Royal Conservatory of Toronto; prof. State U. N.Y., Buffalo; organized Schneider Quartet, 1952; presented series chamber music concerts N.Y. theaters-in-the round; organized, participated outdoor chamber music concerts Washington Sq., N.Y.C., 1953, 54, also South Mountain, Pittsfield, Mass.; with pianist Mieczyslaw Horszowski performed series sonata concerts, 1955, 56; orchestra, choral midnight Christmas Eve concert Carnegie Hall, 1955—; mus. dir., founder New Sch. Concerts, N.Y.C., 1956; organized (with others) Israel Music Festival, 1960-61; guest condr. Boston Philharmonic, St. Louis Symphony, Israel Philharmonic, Los Angeles Philharmonic, Orch. French Nat. Radio and TV, Paris, Lincoln Center Mozart Festival, N.Y.C., Met. Mus. Art; also dir. Interlochen (Mich.) Acad., Christmas String Seminar, N.Y.C. asst. mus. dir. Casals Festival, San Juan P.R., participant ann. Casals Festivals, France, Marlboro Music Festival, Marlboro, Vt.; music dir. N.Y. String Orch. and Wind Ensemble. Mem. exec. bd. Fromm Music Found. Recipient Elizabeth Sprague Coolidge medal for eminent services to chamber music, 1945; Mayor's Scroll of Appreciation, N.Y.C., 1959. 1st violinist to present all of Bach unaccompanied violin pieces in concert series, N.Y.C. Address: Frank Salomon Assos Suite 4C 201 W 54th St New York NY 10019. *For me, my purpose is to get young people to learn how to make music. When you make music, it has to come from your heart, from your soul, or it has no meaning. It's an extraordinary experience when I see the results. They produce a sound a professional orchestra couldn't-a love of music. For me it's better than any Christmas vacation.**

SCHNEIDER, ALFRED REUBEN, TV exec.; b. Bklyn., Apr. 25, 1926; s. Sol. and Lena (Schneider) S.; B.A., Hamilton Coll., 1949; LL.B., Harvard, 1952; m. Jane Harris, July 26, 1953; children—Leland, Jeffrey, Elizabeth. Admitted to N.Y. bar, 1952; legal dept. Am. Broadcasting-Paramount Theatres, Inc., 1952-54, asst. to exec. v.p. Am. Broadcasting Cos., Inc., 1962-72, v.p., 1972—, asst. dir. bus. affairs ABC TV Network, 1955, v.p. in charge adminstrn., 1960-62, v.p., asst. to exec. v.p. Am. Broadcasting Co., 1962-72; asst. to dir. bus. affairs CBS TV Network, 1955-58, exec. asst. to pres., 1958-59. Bd. dirs., exec. com. nat. council Better Bus. Burs., Inc. Mem. Nat. Assn. Broadcasters (sr., television code review bd.), Internat. Radio and Television Soc. (gov.), Phi Beta Kappa. Home: 65 Shore Dr Larchmont NY 10538 Office: 1330 Ave of Americas New York NY 10019

SCHNEIDER, ARTHUR PAUL, video tape editor; b. Rochester, N.Y., Jan. 26, 1930; s. Mendell Phillip and Frieda (Bland) S.; student U. So. Calif., 1953; m. Helen Deloise Thompson, June 5, 1954; children—Robert Paul, Lori Ann. With NBC, 1951-68, film editor, 1953-60, film and tape editor all Bob Hope shows, 1960-67, supr. kinescope and video tape editors, 1966-67, video tape editor all Laugh-In series, 1967-68; a developer double system method of editing video tape, 1958; pres. Burbank (Calif.) Film Editing, Inc., 1968-72, Electronic Video Industries Inc., 1977—; supr. video tape editing Consol. Film Industries Inc., Hollywood, Calif., 1972—; video tape editor TV series Sonny & Cher, 1973, Sonny Comedy Revue, 1974, Tony Orlando and Dawn, 1974, Hudson Bros. (summer), 1974, Dean Martin Series, 1975-76, Mickey Mouse Club Series, Walt Disney Prodns., 1976, Redd Foxx Series, 1977, Comedy Shop Series, 1978-79; post prodn. cons., lectr., author. Recipient Broadcast Preceptor award San Francisco State U., 1975; named hon. Ky. Col. Mem. Nat. Acad. Television Arts and Scis. (Emmy award for video tape editing 1966, 68, 73, gov. 1977-80), Am. Cinema Editors, Soc. Motion Picture and Television Engrs., Delta Kappa Alpha (life). Home: 27044 Helmond Dr Agoura CA 91301 Office: 2800 W Olive Ave Burbank CA 91505

SCHNEIDER, CARL GLENDON, former air force officer, bus. exec.; b. Ralls, Tex., Mar. 6, 1928; s. Carl Watson and Laura Kerlin S.; B.S., Ariz. State U., 1964; M.S., George Washington U., 1967; m. Elaine Eliason, Dec. 24, 1954; children—Robert, Debra. Enlisted in USAF, 1946; advanced through grades from pvt. to maj. gen., 1978; comdr. Moody AFB, Ga., 1970-71; asst. chief of staff UN Command, Korea, 1971-74; comdr. Air Logistics Center, Oklahoma City, 1976-77; chief of staff Air Force Logistics Command, Wright-Patterson AFB, Ohio, 1977-78; ret., 1978; dir. 3 cos. Mem. Republican Nat. Com., 1979—. Decorated D.F.C. Republican. Methodist. Clubs: Rotary, Execs., Internat., Ben Franklin. Home: 3129 S Orm Tempe AZ 85282 Office: 201 E Southern Tempe AZ 85282. *I believe each person should set goals in eight areas: career, family, financial, physical, spiritual, social, mental, and recreational.*

SCHNEIDER, CARL WILLIAM, lawyer: b. Phila., Apr. 27, 1932; s. Nathan J. and Eleanor (Milgram) S.; B.A., Cornell U., 1953; LL.M. magna cum laude, U. Pa., 1956; m. Mary Ellen Baylinson, Mar. 3, 1957; children—Eric M., Mark A., Adam D., Cara L. Admitted to Pa. bar, 1957: clk. U.S. Ct. Appeals for 3d Circuit, Phila., 1956-57; sr. clk. U.S. Supreme Ct., Washington, 1957-58; mem. firm Wolf, Block, Schorr & Solis-Cohen, Phila., 1958—, partner, 1965—; spl. adv. div. corp. fin. SEC, Washington, 1964; lectr. securities law U. Pa., 1968-70, vis. asso. prof., 1978-80, acting dir. Center for Study Fin. Instns., 1978-80; adv. bd. N.Y. U. Law Sch. Securities Inst.; b. editors and advs. Rev. of Securities Regulation. Mem. Am., Fed., Pa., Phila. (co-chmn. com. on securities regulation 1967-70) bar assns. Author: SEC Consequences of Corporate Acquisitions, 1971; editorial adv. bd. Securities Regulation Law Jour.: contbr. articles to profl. jours. Office: Wolf Block et al 12th Floor Packard Bldg Philadelphia PA 19102

SCHNEIDER, CHARLES I., newspaper exec.; b. Chgo., Apr. 6, 1923; s. Samuel Hiram and Eva (Smith) S.; B.S., Northwestern U., 1944; m. Barbara Anne Krause, Oct. 27, 1963; children—Susan, Charles I. Jr., Kim, Karen, Traci. Pres., Curtis-Electro Lighting Corp., Chgo., 1954-62, Jefferson Electronics, Inc., Santa Barbara, Calif., 1962-64; pres. 3 subsidiaries, v.p., asst. to pres. Am. Bldg. Maintenance Industries, Los Angeles, 1964-66; group v.p. Times Mirror Co., Los Angeles, 1966—; dir. Denoyer-Geppert Co., Chgo., Denoyer-Geppert Audio Visuals, Inc., N.Y.C., Jeppesen Sanderson, Inc., Denver, Pickett Industries, Irvine, Calif., Plan Hold Corp., Irvine, H.M. Gousha Co., San Jose, Cal., Chartpak, Inc., Leeds, Mass., M. Grumbacher, N.Y.C., Graphic Controls Corp., Buffalo, Regional Airports Improvement Corp. Bd. regents Northwestern U., Evanston, Ill.; pres. bd. trustees Reiss-Davis Child Study Center, Los Angeles; trustee Scripps Coll.; bd. dirs. Los Angeles council Girl Scouts U.S.A., Music Center Operating Co. of Los Angeles County; pres. bd. govs. Performing Arts Council; bd. visitors U. Calif. at Los Angeles Grad. Sch. Edn. Served with AUS, 1942-44. Mem. Chief Execs. Forum (dir.), Confrerie de la Chaine des Rotisseurs. Clubs: Racquet, University (Los Angeles); Standard (Chgo.). Home: 522 N Beverly Dr Beverly Hills CA 90210 Office: Times Mirror Sq Los Angeles CA 90053. *An individual's growth and success as a manager are in direct proportion to his or her ability to develop and orchestrate able, capable people.*

SCHNEIDER, DAVID MURRAY, educator, anthropologist; b. N.Y.C., Nov. 11, 1918; B.S., Cornell U., 1940, M.A., 1941; Ph.D., Harvard, 1949. Field trips to Yap Island, Trust Terr. Pacific, 1947-48, Mescalero Apache, N.Mex., 1955-58; lectr. London Sch. Econs., 1949-51; asst. prof. Harvard, 1951-55; prof. anthropology U. Calif. at Berkeley, 1956-60; prof. anthropology U. Chgo., 1960—, now William B. Ogden disting. service prof. anthropology, chmn. dept. anthropology, 1963-66. Cons. behavioral sci. study sect., NIH, 1960-64; mem. com. personnel Social Sci. Research Council, 1960-62, bd. dirs., 1971-73; rep. Am. Anthrop. Assn. to div. anthrop. and psychol. NRC-Nat. Acad. Scis., 1962-64; dir. Founds. Fund Research Psychiatry, 1963-66. Fellow Center Advanced Study in Behavioral Scis., 1955-56, 66-67. Fellow Am. Anthropology Assn. (exec. bd. 1968-70), Am. Acad. Arts and Scis., Royal Anthrop. Inst. Great Britain; mem. Assn. Social Anthropologists Commonwealth. Author: (with Homans) Marriage, Authority and Final Causes, 1955; (with Gough) Matrilineal Kinship, 1961; American Kinship, 1968; (with Smith) Class Differences and Sex Role in American Kinship and Family Structure, 1973; (with Cottrell) The American Kin Universe, 1975. Office: Dept Anthropology University of Chicago 1126 E 59th St Chicago IL 60637

SCHNEIDER, DAVID TAYLOR, ambassador; b. Cin., Nov. 20, 1922; s. Ben Ross and Jean (Taylor) S.; B.A., Yale U., 1947; m. Ann Theresa Scannell, June 3, 1950; children—Jean, Andrea, David. With U.S. State Dept., 1950—, minister, Rawalpindi, Pakistan, 1967-68, country dir. for India, Ceylon, Nepal and Maldives, Washington, 1969-73, minister-counsellor, dep. chief mission Am. embassy, New Delhi, 1973-77; ambassador to Bangladesh, Dacca, 1978—. Served with USAF, 1943-45. Chmn. editorial bd. Fgn. Service Jour., 1969-70. Office: Am Embassy Adamjee Court Bldg 5th Floor Montijheel Commercial Area GPO Box 323 Ramna Dacca Bangladesh

SCHNEIDER, DONALD FREDERIC, banker; b. N.Y.C., Nov. 12, 1939; s. Charles and Lillian (Anton) S.; B.S., Lehigh U., 1961; M.B.A., N.Y. U., 1968; m. Mary Patricia McCafferty, Sept. 7, 1963; children—Laurie, John. Mgmt. trainee Marine Midland Bank, N.Y.C., 1961-65, asst. sec., 1965-68, asst. v.p., 1968-69, v.p., 1969—v.p. 1st Nat. Bank Chgo., 1979—; mem. corp. trust activities com. Am. Bankers Assn. Mem. Am. Soc. Corporate Secs., Stock Transfer Assn. Home: 399 N Valley Rd Barrington IL 60010 Office: One 1st Nat Plaza Chicago IL 60670

SCHNEIDER, ERWIN HENRY, educator, musician; b. St. Louis, Feb. 17, 1920; s. Erwin Louis and Anna Marie (Busse) S.; B.S., N.W. Mo. State Coll., 1942; M.S., U. Kans., 1946, Ph.D., 1956; m. Jenila Marie Adkins, Nov. 29, 1941; 1 dau., Nila Marie. Instr. music U. Kans., 1946-47; asso. prof. music Western State Coll., Gunnison, Colo., 1948-49; prof., head dept. art and music edn. U. Tenn., Knoxville, 1949-60; prof. music Ohio State U., Columbus, 1961-69, acting dir. Sch. Music, 1964-65, head div. music edn., 1965-69; prof., head dept. music edn. U. Iowa, Iowa City, 1969—. Mem. Nat. Assn. Music Therapy (pres. 1964-65, editor Bull., Yearbooks), Am. Psychol. Assn., Am. Ednl. Research Assn., AAAS, Music Tchrs. Nat. Assn., Music Educators Nat. Conf., Phi Delta Kappa, Phi Mu Alpha, Phi Kappa Lambda. Home: 1004 17th Ave Coralville IA 52240 Office: Dept Music U Iowa Iowa City IA 52240

SCHNEIDER, F. RUSSELL, ins. co. exec.; b. Barkhamsted, Conn., May 8, 1920; s. Frank E. and Susan (Russell) S.; A.B., Wesleyan U., Middletown, Conn., 1940; m. Barbara M. Carey, Oct. 27, 1949; children—Robert E., William D., Marjorie A., Kathleen J., Edward T., Patricia G. With Met. Life Ins. Co., 1940-47; with Conn. Gen. Life Ins. Co., Hartford, 1947—, actuary, 1956—, v.p., 1964-73, sr. v.p., 1973-76, exec. v.p., 1976—; adv. bd. Hartford Nat. Bank and Trust Co. Served to capt. USAAF, 1942-46. Fellow Soc. Actuaries; mem. Phi Beta Kappa. Office: 900 Cottage Grove Rd Hartford CT 06115

SCHNEIDER, FREDERICK H., banker; grad. U. Pa., 1939; LL.B., St. John's U., 1947. Trustee, Roosevelt Savs. Bank, Bklyn., 1951—, v.p., 1963-67, pres., 1967—; dir. Instl. Securities Corp., 1968-74, 78—, INSTLCORP, 1968-74, Savs. Banks Retirement System, 1973-74, Savs. Banks Trust Co., 1973-74, Drayton Co. Ltd., 1972-75; mem. Nassau adv. bd. Mfrs. Hanover Trust, 1971—. Mayor, Village of Garden City, 1969-71, trustee, 1963-69; bd. dirs. Ottilie Home for Children, 1952-77, pres., 1961-63. Served with USNR, World War II. Mem. Savs. Bank Assn. N.Y. State (pres. 1973-74, dir.), Nat. Assn. Mut. Savs. Banks (dir. 1973—), L.I. Assn. (dir. 1975—), Garden City C. of C., Nassau Bar Assn. Clubs: Rotary (dir. 1967—), Masons. Address: 1122 Franklin Ave Garden City NY 11530

SCHNEIDER, HAROLD K., educator; b. Aberdeen. S.D., Aug. 24, 1925; s. Frank X. and Bernice (Anderson) S.; B.A., Macalester Coll., 1946; postgrad. Seabury-Western Theol. Sem., 1946-48; Ph.D., Northwestern U., 1953; m. Carol Snyder, Sept. 11, 1948; children—Ann Elizabeth, Amy, Jane, Caroline, David Paul. Mem. faculty Lawrence U., Appleton, Wis., 1953-70, prof., 1966-70; prof. anthropology Ind. U., Bloomington, 1970—. Anthrop. field worker, Pokot, Kenya, 1951-52, Nyaturu, Tanzania, 1959-60. Ind. U. rep. Council Rural Devel., Midwest Univs. Consortium Internat. Activities; mem. nomad commn. Internat. Union Anthrop. and Ethnol. Scis. First vice chmn. Outagamie County (Wis.) Democratic Com., 1967-68, 69-70; mem. Wis. Democratic Reform Commn., 1970. Fulbright fellow, 1951-52; NSF Grantee, 1959-60, 66-67. Fellow Am. Anthrop. Assn., AAAS, Current Anthropology; mem. Central States Anthrop. Soc. (pres. 1965-66, dir. 1977—). Clubs: Four Winds Yacht, Monroe County Saddle. Author: (with E.E. Leclair) Economic Anthropology, 1968; The Wahi Wanyaturu, 1970; Economic Man, 1974; Livestock and Equality in East Africa. Home: 7839 S Zikes Rd Bloomington IN 47401

SCHNEIDER, HERBERT WILLIAM, architect; b. Elmwood Park, Ill., July 6, 1930; s. August F. and Nettie (Dormert) S.; B.Arch., U. Ill., 1955; m. Sonja Irene Rogne, Feb. 4, 1953; children—Susan Lee, Mark Herbert, Karen Lynn. Project capt. Bricker & Busby Architects, Phoenix, 1957-59; partner Busby Assos., Architects, Phoenix, 1959-67, Busby, Crosier & Schneider, Architects, Phoenix, 1967-69; office and constrn. mgr. Rossman & Assos., Phoenix, 1969-72; partner Rossman & Partners, Architects, Phoenix, 1972—; archtl. cons. Ariz. State Community Coll. Bd., 1971—; guest lectr. Ariz. State U. Mem. Phoenix Fire Safety Adv. Bd., 1972—; chmn. Santa Rita Project, Maricopa County Young Rupublican League, 1965-67. Served with C.E., U.S. Army, 1955-57. Fellow AIA (pres. Central Ariz. chpt. 1971), Ariz. Soc. Arhcitects (v.p. 1972). Presbyterian. Archtl. works of partnership include: Student Union and Dining Hall facility No. Ariz. U., Flagstaff, 1970, Coll. Bus. Adminstrn. Bldg., 1972; South Mountain High Sch. Auditorium, Phoenix, 1972, Communications Arts and Channel 8 TV Studios, Ariz. State U., Tempe, 1973, Thunderbird High Sch., Glendale, Ariz., 1973, Greenway High Sch., Glendale, 1974, State of Ariz. Mental Retardation Tng. Facility, Phoenix, 1974, McClintock High Sch. Auditorium, Tempe, 1976, Show Low (Ariz.) High Sch. Auditorium, 1977, No. Ariz. U. Ensphere, 1977, North Campus, Agua Fria Union High Sch. Dist., Litchfield Park, Ariz., 1979. Home: 3528 W Campbell Ave Phoenix AZ 85019 Office: 4601 E McDowell Rd Phoenix AZ 85008

SCHNEIDER, HOWARD, lawyer; b. N.Y.C., Mar. 21, 1935; s. Abraham and Lena (Pincus) S.; A.B., Cornell U., 1956, J.D. with distinction, 1959; m. Anne Evelyn Gorfinkle, Aug. 29, 1966; children—Andrea Rose, Jeffrey Winston. Admitted to N.Y. State bar, 1960, D.C. bar, 1976; asso. atty. Stroock & Stroock & Lavan, N.Y.C., 1959-69; partner, 1969-75; gen. counsel Commodity Futures Trading Commn., Washington, 1975-77; partner firm Rosenman Colin Freund Lewis & Cohen, N.Y.C., 1977—. Vice pres. Nassau County Legal Aid Soc., 1972-75. Asso. trustee Long Island Jewish-Hillside Med. Center, 1973-75; trustee, gen. counsel, sec. Children's Med. Center of N.Y. Fund, 1970-75; v.p. Ednl. Alliance (settlement house), 1968-75, 77—. Mem. Am. Bar Assn. (com. on commodity regulation 1976—), Assn. Bar City N.Y. (mem. grievance com. 1969-72, 73-74, ethics com. 1974-75, com. on commodity regulation 1976—), N.Y. State Bar Assn. (mem. spl. com. on availability legal services 1971-75). Mason. Club: Harmonie (N.Y.C.). Home: 830 Park Ave New York NY 10021 Office: 575 Madison Ave New York NY 10022

SCHNEIDER, HOWARD A., cartoonist; b. N.Y.C., Apr. 24, 1930; s. Joseph I. and Lilliad Davis S.; A.A., N.Y. State Inst. Applied Arts and Scis.; children—Evan, Peter. Partner advt. agy., N.Y.C., 1951-54; art dir. Guild Films N.Y.C., 1954-59; creator studio cards Norcross, N.Y.C., 1961-64; creator, cartoonist syndicated comic strip Eek and Meek, 1964—. Served with U.S. Army, 1948-49. Mem. Newspaper Comics Council (mem. exec. com.), Nat. Cartoonists Soc., Outer Cape Environ. Assn. (pres.). Author: The World is no Place for Children, 1960; The Deceivers, 1961; Mom's The Word, 1968. Office: care Newspaper Enterprise Assn Inc 230 Park Ave New York NY 10017

SCHNEIDER, JAMES GORDON, savs. and loan exec.; b. Kankakee, Ill., Aug. 24, 1925; s. William Albert and Dorothy (Marlow) S.; student Milligan Coll., 1943-44, Duke, 1944; B.A., State U. Ia., 1948, J.D., 1953; m. Phyllis C. Jordan, Aug. 12, 1950; children—Holly M., Scott J., Thomas M. Instr., Colls. Commerce and

Law, State U. Ia., 1952-53; admitted to Ia. bar, 1953, Mo. bar, 1954, Ill. bar, 1955; contract atty. C.G.W. R.R., Kansas City, 1953-54; from loan officer to v.p. Kankakee Fed. Savs. and Loan Assn., 1954-61, pres., 1961—, dir., 1955—; dir. Fed. Home Loan Bank, Chgo., 1967-70, 79—; dir. Kankakee County Title & Trust Co. Past pres. Fed. Savs. and Loan Council Ill.; vice chmn. Council of Mut. Savs. Instns. Vice pres. Kankakee Indsl. Devel. Assn., 1965—, Central Parking Corp., 1963—, Kankakee Devel. Corp., 1963—. Pres. Riverside Hosp., Kankakee, 1959-71, trustee, 1972—; pres. Riverside Hosp. Found., 1972—; trustee Savs. Assns. Retirement Fund, 1972-77, Rockford Coll., 1978—; treas. Council on Abandoned Mil. Posts, 1972-76; trustee Kankakee YMCA; chmn. Kankakee County Bicentennial Commn., 1975-77; alt. del. Republican Nat. Conv., 1976. Served to lt. USNR, 1943-46, 50-52. Mem. Am. Legion, VFW, Order of Coif, Chgo. Westerners, Phi Delta Phi, Alpha Tau Omega, Sigma Pi Sigma. Anglican. Elk, Kiwanian. Clubs: Kankakee Country; University (Chgo.). Author: The Ballad of Otto Mears. Home: 888 Cobb Blvd Kankakee IL 60901 Office: 310 S Schuyler Ave PO Box 552 Kankakee IL 60901

SCHNEIDER, JOHN ARNOLD, cons.; b. Chgo., Dec. 4, 1926; s. Arnold George and Anna (Wagner) S.; B.S., U. Notre Dame, 1948; m. Elizabeth C. Simpson, Oct. 20, 1951; children—Richard Ward, William Arnold, Elizabeth Anne. Exec. assignments with CBS-TV in Chgo. and N.Y.C., 1950-58; v.p., gen. mgr. sta. WCAU-TV, Phila., 1958-64, sta. WCBS-TV, N.Y.C., 1964-65; pres. CBS TV Network, 1965-66; pres. CBS/Broadcast Group, 1966-69, 71-77; exec. v.p. CBS, Inc., 1969-71, sr. v.p., from 1977; now pres., chief exec. officer Warner Amex Satellite Entertainment Corp. Trustee, mem. exec. com. U. Notre Dame; vice chmn. Am. Film Inst.; trustee Com. for Econ. Devel. Served with USNR, 1943-46. Roman Catholic. Clubs: Philadelphia Country; Indian Harbor Yacht. Home: Indian Harbor Greenwich CT 06830 Office: Warner Amex Satellite Entertainment Corp 1211 Ave of Americas New York NY 10036

SCHNEIDER, JOHN HOKE, govt. ofcl.; b. Eau Claire, Wis., Sept. 29, 1931; B.S. in Chemistry, U. Wis., Madison, 1953, M.S. in Exptl. Oncology, 1955, Ph.D., 1958; married; 2 children. Research asst. McArdle Meml. Lab., U. Wis., 1953-58; asst. prof. biochemistry Am. U. Beirut, 1958-61; asst. prof. biochemistry Vanderbilt U. Med. Sch., 1961-62; editor-in-chief Biol. Abstracts, Phila., 1962-63; trainee grants assos. tng. program NIH, Bethesda, Md., 1963-64, sci. and program info. specialist, then sci. and tech. info. officer Nat. Cancer Inst., 1964—, dir. internat. cancer research data bank program, 1973—. Recipient Quality Increase award NIH, 1971, Spl. Achievement award, 1978. Mem. Am. Soc. Info. Sci. (chpt. pres. 1972-73), AAAS, Am. Assn. Cancer Research, Phi Beta Kappa, Sigma Xi (chpt. pres. 1960-61). Author numerous papers in field. Address: Nat Cancer Inst Blair Bldg Room 114 8300 Colesville Rd Silver Spring MD 20910

SCHNEIDER, KENNETH ALBERT, pathologist; b. Joliet, Ill., Apr. 30, 1933; s. Harry Carl and Edna Lorraine (Sumbaum) S.; B.A., Northwestern U., 1955, M.A., 1959, M.D., 1959; m. Nancy Ann Dankes, Sept. 16, 1955; children—Della, Dale, Dwight. Intern, Northwestern Meml. Hosp., Chgo., 1959-60, resident in pathology, 1960-64; asso. pathologist Wesley Meml. Hosp., Chgo., 1964-69, acting dir. labs., 1968-69; dir. clin. chemistry Northwestern U. Med. Sch., Chgo., 1969-74, asso. prof. pathology, 1974-76; dir. hosp. labs., prof. pathology Duke U. Med. Center, Durham, N.C., 1976—; chmn. Gov.'s Task Force on Blood Banking, Ill., 1973-76; dir. clin. labs. Lakeside VA Hosp., Chgo., 1974-76; prin. investigator hypertension detection and follow-up program Nat. Heart Lung and Blood Inst., 1972—. Mem. Am. Assn. Blood Banks, Am. Soc. Clin. Pathologists (dep. commr. for ednl. materials 1968-73). Lutheran. Producer dir. audiovisual ednl. series for med. lab edn. Home: Route 6 Box 148 Chapel Hill NC 27514 Office: Duke U Med Center Box 3712 Durham NC 27710

SCHNEIDER, LOUIS, educator; b. Vienna, Austria, Mar. 22, 1915 (came to U.S. 1921, naturalized 1927); s. Gustave and Frieda (Salz) S.; came to U.S., 1921, naturalized, 1927; B.A., Coll. City N.Y., 1935; M.A., Columbia, 1938, Ph.D., 1947; m. 2d, Josephine A. Sundine, Jan. 3, 1956; one dau., Valerie S.; children by previous marriage—David S., Dana A. Tutor sociology Brooklyn Coll., 1937-43; labor economist WPB, 1943-45; economist OPA, 1945-47; asst. prof. sociology Colgate U., 1947-49; asso. prof. sociology Purdue U., Lafayette, Ind., 1949-54, prof., 1954-59; prof. sociology U. Ill. at Urbana, 1960-67, head dept., 1960-64; prof. sociology U. Tex., Austin, 1967—; vis. prof. Dartmouth, 1959-60. Fellow Center Advanced Study Behavioral Scis., 1954-55. Fellow Am. Sociol. Assn.; mem. Ohio Valley Sociol. Soc. (pres. 1959-60), Phi Beta Kappa. Author: (with Ogle and Wiley) Power, Order and the Economy, 1954; (with S. M. Dornbusch) Popular Religion, 1958; Sociological Approach To Religion, 1970; The Sociological Way of Looking at the World, 1975; Classical Theories of Social Change, 1976. Editor: Problems of Economics and Sociology (by Carl Menger), 1963; The Scottish Moralists on Human Nature and Society, 1967; editor, contbr. Religion, Culture and Society, 1964; (with C.M. Bonjean) The Idea of Culture in the Social Sciences, 1973; (with C.M. Bonjean and R. Lineberry) Social Science in America, 1976. Asso. editor Am. Sociol. Rev., 1958-61. Contbr. articles to profl. jours. Home: 7905 Havenwood Dr Austin TX 78759

SCHNEIDER, MARK LEWIS, govt. ofcl.; b. Newark, N.J., Dec. 31, 1941; s. Benjamin and Ruth (Kobran) S.; A.B. in Journalism with honors, U. Calif., Berkeley, 1963; M.A. in Polit. Sci., San Jose State Coll., 1965; m. Susan Gilbert, June 20, 1965; children—Aaron Mitchell, Miriam Beth. Reporter UPI, San Francisco, 1963-64; reporter San Francisco Call Bull., 1965; vol. Peace Corps, El Salvador, 1966-68; reporter Washington News Call Bull., 1969-70; mem. staff U.S. Senate Judiciary Subcom., 1970-71; legis. asst. Sen. Edward M. Kennedy, 1971-77; mem. U.S. Senate del. N.Atlantic Assembly, 1971-73; dep. asst. sec. for human rights Dept. State, Washington, 1977—; mem. del. UN Human Rights Commn., 1979; mem. del. UN Gen. Assembly, 1978; lectr. Kennedy Inst. Politics, Harvard U., 1976. Fulbright fellow, 1976. Recipient F.W. Richardson award Calif. Press Assn., 1963. Mem. Am. Polit. Sci. Assn., Latin Am. Studies Assn., Sigma Delta Chi. Democrat. Jewish. Home: 815 Independence Ave SE Washington DC 20003 Office: Room 7802 Dept of State Washington DC 20520

SCHNEIDER, RICHARD COY, physician, educator; b. Newark, May 29, 1913; s. Louis and Elizabeth (Coy) S.; B.A., Dartmouth, 1935; M.D., U. Pa., 1939; M.S., U. Mich., 1948; m. Madeleine T. Thomas, Feb. 12, 1943. Intern, Newark City Hosp., 1939-41; resident pathology Cleve. City Hosp., 1941-42; resident gen. surgery City of Detroit Receiving Hosp., 1942-43; resident neurosurgery U. Mich., 1946-48; practice medicine specializing in neurosurgery, Cleve., 1948-50; asst. prof. neurosurgery U. Mich., Ann Arbor, 1950-52, asso. prof., 1952-62, prof. neurosurgery, 1962-69, head sect. neurosurgery Med. Center, 1969—; 1st E. Latunde Odeku Meml. lectr. U. Ibadan (Nigeria), 1976; honored guest Congress Neurol. Surgeons, 1978. Mem. Council Med. Splty. Socs., 1974-76. Served to capt. M.C., AUS, 1943-46; ETO. Diplomate Am. Bd. Neurol. Surgery (vice chmn. 1970-72). Named Man of Year Culver Mil. Acad., 1970. Mem. A.C.S., Neurosurg. Soc. Am. (v.p.), Am. Acad. Neurol. Surg., Am. Assn. Neurol. Surgeons (pres. 1974, dir. 1970—), World Fedn. Neurosurg. Socs. (rep., sec., v.p. 1977—), Aerospace Med. Assn., Am. Epilepsy Soc., Assn. Research on Mental Disease, Am. Soc. for Surgery of Trauma, Phi Kappa Psi, Nu Sigma Nu. Author: (with others) Correlative Neurosurgery, 1969; Surgery of the Cranial Nerves, 1973; Head and Neck Injuries in Football, 1973. Patentee pneumatic helmet. Home: 2110 Hill St Ann Arbor MI 48104

SCHNEIDER, ROBERT JULES, food co. exec.; b. N.Y.C., Mar. 16, 1928; s. Christian W. and Rose (Geile) S.; B.S. in Commerce, St. Louis U., 1952, LL.B., 1952; m. Doris Jeanne Gruner, July 5, 1952; children—Anne M., Joan E., Carolyn M., Susan L., Robert C. Admitted to Mo. bar, 1952; adminstrv. asst. to v.p. Sohio Pipe Line Co., St. Louis, 1955-60; house counsel Huttig Sash & Door Co., St. Louis, 1960-62; sec., corp. counsel Wetterau, Inc., Hazelwood, Mo., 1962-73, v.p., gen. counsel, sec., 1973-78, 1st v.p., gen. counsel, sec., 1978—, also sec. and counsel subsidiaries. Served to 1st lt. USAF, 1952-54. Mem. Mo. Bar, St. Louis Bar Assn. Home: 12336 Borcherding Lane Des Peres MO 63131 Office: 8920 Pershall Rd Hazlewood MO 63042

SCHNEIDER, RONALD MILTON, educator; b. Mpls., Sept. 29, 1932; s. Howard Edward and Mildred Elizabeth (Davis) S.; B.S., Northwestern U., 1954; M.A., Princeton, 1956, Ph.D., 1958; m. Anita Dolores Lombana, June 15, 1954; children—Ronald Milton, Carol Jean, Diana Marie. Intelligence research specialist State Dept., Washington, 1957-63; vis. asso. prof. Columbia, 1963-66; asso. prof., 1966-69; prof. polit. sci. Queens Coll., City U., Flushing, N.Y., 1969—, chmn., 1974-75, chmn. Latin Am. area studies, 1979—. Research asst. Fgn. Policy Research Inst. U. Pa., 1956-57; vis. lectr. George Washington U., Washington, 1959-60; vis. asso. prof. Cath. U. Am., Washington, 1963; vis. lectr. U. Pa., 1970, N.Y. U., 1974. Social Sci. Research Council fellow, 1953; Fulbright-Hays faculty fellow, 1966-67. Mem. Am. Polit. Sci. Assn., Acad. Polit. Sci., Latin Am. Studies Assn., Am. Acad. Polit. and Social Sci., Inter-Univ. Seminar on Armed Forces and Soc., Inter-Am. Assn. for Democracy and Freedom, Center Inter-Am. Relations, Phi Beta Kappa, Delta Phi Epsilon. Methodist. Author: Communism in Guatemala, 1944-54, 1958; An Atlas of Latin American Affairs, 1965; Brazil Election Fact Book, 1965; Latin American Panorama, 1966; The Political System of Brazil, 1971; Brazil, Foreign Policy of a Future World Power, 1977; Brazil: An Introduction, 1980. Home: 36 E Glen Ave Ridgewood NJ 07450 Office: Dept Polit Sci Queens Coll Flushing NY 11367

SCHNEIDER, ROY LESTER, territorial ofcl., oncological surgeon; b. St. Thomas, V.I.; s. Aluvis and Winifred (Degnoff) S.; B.S., Howard U., 1961, M.D., 1965. Intern, Freedmen's Hosp.-Howard U., Washington, 1965-66; resident Howard U., 1968-71, Chief resident in surgery, instr. in surgery and radiotherapy, Howard U., 1971-72, asst. prof. surgery, 1973-75, asso. prof., 1975-77, asso. dir. Cancer Research Center, 1973-77, vice chmn. dept. oncology, 1973-77; commr. health U.S. V.I., St. Thomas, 1977—; cons. in field; U.S. del. Pan Am. Health Orgn., 1977; vice chmn. profl. edn. com., trustee D.C. chpt. Am. Cancer Soc., 1975; guest lectr. Internat. Radiotherapy Conf., Venezuela, 1971. Served to capt. M.C., U.S. Army, 1966-68; Vietnam. Decorated Bronze Star; diplomate Am. Bd. Surgery. Fellow A.C.S., Internat. Coll. Surgeons; mem. Soc. Head and Neck Surgeons, Soc. Surg. Oncology, Soc. Acad. Surgeons, Soc. Surgery Alimentary Tract, Internat. Coll. Digestive Tract Surgery. Contbr. numerous articles on cancer to profl. jours.; author Howard U. Cancer Man., 1976; co-inventor Howard U. applicator for cancer of the cervix, 1971. Home: PO Box 22 Saint Thomas VI 00801 Office: PO Box 7309 Dept Health Saint Thomas VI 00801

SCHNEIDER, STEPHEN HENRY, climatologist; b. N.Y.C., Feb. 11, 1945; s. Samuel and Doris C. (Swarte) S.; B.S., Columbia U., 1966, M.S., 1967, Ph.D., 1971; m. Cheryl Kay Hunter, Aug. 19, 1978. Nat. Acad. Scis., NRC postdoctoral research asso. Goddard Inst. Space Studies NASA, N.Y.C., 1971-72; fellow advanced study program Nat. Center Atmospheric Research, Boulder, Colo., 1972-73, scientist, dep. head climate project, 1973-78, acting leader climate sensitivity group, 1978—; affiliate prof. U. Corp. Atmospheric Research Lamont-Doherty Geol. Obs., Columbia U.; mem. Carter-Mondale Sci. Policy Task Force, 1976—; mem. internat. sci. coms. climatic change, energy, food and pub. policy; expert witness congl. coms. Author: (with Lynne E. Mesirow) The Genesis Strategy: Climate and Global Survival, 1976; also sci. and popular articles on theory of climate, influence of climate on soc., relation of climatic change to world food, population, and environ. policy issues. Editor: Climatic Change, 1976—. Office: Nat Center Atmospheric Research Box 3000 Boulder CO 80307

SCHNEIDER, VERNON EARL, educator; b. Cosby, Mo., Sept. 26, 1925; s. Alfred Jacob and Elsie Louise (Mandler) S.; B.S. in Agrl. Journalism, U. Mo., 1950; M.S. in Agrl. Econs., Purdue U., 1960; Ph.D. in Agrl. Econs., Ore. State U., 1962; m. Nancy Jo Van Ginkel, Sept. 4, 1954; children—David, Kirk, Mark, Jonathan, Elizabeth. Editor Successful Farming, 1950-58; asso. prof. U. Wis.-Madison, 1962-66; dir. Agrl. Research Center Stanford Research Inst., Los Angeles, 1966-68; prof. Sch. Bus. U. Cal. at Los Angeles, 1968-69; pres. Am. Inst. Coop., Washington, 1969-73; Distinguished prof. in agrl. coop. Dept. Agrl. Econs. Tex. A. and M. U., College Station, 1973—. Bd. dirs. Agrl. Coop. Devel. Internat., Washington, 1959-73, Vol. Devel. Coop, Washington, 1970-74, Am. Country Life Assn., Sioux Falls, S.D., Coop. Edn. and Tng., Madison, Wis., Am. Inst. Cooperation, Washington, 1975—, Coop. Found., St. Paul, 1972—. Served with USNR, 1943-46. Recipient Am. Seed Trade Assn. Profl. Writers award, 1957. Mem. Am. Agrl. Econ. Assn., Am. Mgmt. Assn., Internat. Assn. Agrl. Econs. Office: Dept Agrl Econs Texas A and M University College Station TX 77843

SCHNEIDER, WILLIAM CHARLES, govt. ofcl.; b. N.Y.C., Dec. 24, 1923; s. Charles J. and Margaret (Stoeffler) S.; B.S., Mass. Inst. Tech., 1949; M.S., U. Va., 1952; D.Engring., Catholic U., 1976; m. Rose Ann Vasco, Oct. 4, 1964; children—Catherine M., Jeanne M., Robert J., Robert Sherer. Research scientist NACA Langley Research Center, Hampton, Va., 1949-55; asst. br. head Air-to-Air Missiles Bur. Aeros., Washington, 1955-60; dir. space vehicles USN Bur. Weapons, Washington, 1960-61; dir. space systems Internat. Tel. & Tel., Nutley, N.J., 1961-63; dep. dir. Gemini program Office Manned Space Flight NASA Hdqrs., Washington, 1963-65, dir., dep. dir. operations, mission dir. Gemini program, 1965-66, dir. Apollo applications missions, 1966-67, Apollo Mission dir., 1967-68, dir. Skylab program, 1968-74, dep. asso. adminstr. for space transp. systems, 1974-78, asso. adminstr. for space tracking and data systems, 1978—. Mem. bd. visitors Cath. U. Served with USNR, 1942-46. Recipient Exceptional Service medal NASA, 1965, Distinguished Service medal, 1968-73; Astronautics Engr. award, 1974; Robert J. Collier trophy, 1974; Apollo Group Achievement award, 1969; Am. Astronautical Soc. Space Flight award, 1974. Fellow Am. Inst. Aeros. and Astronautics (asso.), Am. Astronautical Soc. (v.p.). Home: 11801 Clintwood Pl Silver Spring MD 20902 Office: NASA Hdqrs (Code M-1) Washington DC

SCHNEIDER, WILLIAM GEORGE, research orgn. exec.; b. Wolseley, Sask., Can., June 1, 1915; s. Michael and Phillipina (Krauschaar) S.; B.Sc., U. Sask., 1937, M.Sc., 1939, D.Sc., 1969; Ph.D., McGill U., 1941, D.Sc., 1970; D.Sc. (hon.) York U., 1966, Meml. U., 1968, McMaster U., 1969, Laval U., 1969, Moncton U., 1969, U. N.B., 1970, U. Montreal, 1970, Acadia U., 1976, U. Regina, 1976, Ottawa U., 1978; LL.D., U. Alta., 1968, Laurentian U., 1968; m. Jean Purves, Sept. 2, 1940; children—Judith Schneider Connolly, Joanne. Head phys. chemistry sect., div. chemistry NRC Can., Ottawa, Ont., 1946-63, dir. div. pure chemistry, 1963-65, v.p., 1965-67, pres., 1967—. Decorated Order of Can., 1977. Fellow Royal Soc. London, Royal Soc. Can. (Henry Marshall Tory medal), Chem. Inst. Can. (medal 1969, Montreal medal 1973). Author: (with J.A. Pople, H.J. Bernstein) High Resolution Nuclear Magnetic Resonance, 1959. Contbr. articles to profl. jours. Office: National Research Council Canada Ottawa ON K1A 0R6 Canada

SCHNEIDERMAN, HOWARD ALLEN, educator, zoologist; b. N.Y.C., Feb. 9, 1927; s. Louis and Anna (Center) S.; A.B., Swarthmore Coll., 1948; M.A. in Zoology, Harvard, 1949, Ph.D. in Physiology, 1952; D.Sc., La Salle Coll., 1975; m. Audrey MacLeod, Sept. 16, 1951; children—Anne Mercedes, John Howard. AEC predoctoral fellow Harvard, 1949-52, Univ. Research fellow, 1952-53; asst. prof. zoology, then asso. prof. Cornell U., 1953-61; prof. biology, chmn. dept. Case Western Reserve U., Cleve., 1961-66, Jared Potter Kirtland Distinguished prof. biology, 1966-69, co-dir. devel. biology center, 1961-69; prof. biol. sci., dean sch., dir. Center Pathobiology, U. Calif., Irvine, 1969-79, chmn. dept. developmental and cell biology, 1969-75; v.p. research and devel. Monsanto Co., St. Louis, 1979—; cons. Gen. Med. Sci. Inst., Nat. Inst. Child Health and Devel., NIH, 1961-79; instr. invertebrate zoology Marine Biol. Lab., Woods Hole, Mass., 1956-58, trustee, mem. exec. com., 1966-72, spl. research, devel., genetics, insect hormones, and insect physiology. Adv. commr. Marshall Scholarship Commn., 1973-77, chmn., 1976-77. Served with USNR, 1945-46. NSF sr. fellow Cambridge (Eng.) U., 1959-60. Fellow AAAS, N.Y. Acad. Scis.; mem. Nat. Acad. Sci. (assembly life scis. 1975—), Am. Acad. Arts and Scis., Soc. Exptl. Biology (Eng.), Am. Soc. Zoologists, Entomol. Soc. Am., Lepidopterist Soc., Corp. Marine Biol Lab., Am. Soc. Naturalists, Soc. for Development Biology (pres. 1965-66), Genetics Soc. Am., AAUP, Am. Inst. Biol. Scis., Am. Soc. Cell Biology, Japanese Soc. Development at Biology, Phi Beta Kappa, Sigma Xi. Editorial bd. Roux' Archives Developmental Biology, Biologica Bull; Jour. Chem Ecology, Current Topics in Devel. Biology, Devel. Genetics; Results and Problems of Cell Differentiation. Address: Dept Research and Devel Monsanto Co 800 N Linderberg Blvd Saint Louis MO 63166

SCHNEIDERMAN, IRWIN, lawyer; b. N.Y.C., May 28, 1923; s. Meyer and Bessie (Klein) S.; B.A. Bklyn. Coll., 1943; LL.B. cum laude, Harvard, 1948; m. Roberta Haig, Nov. 28, 1966; 1 son, Eric T. Admitted to N.Y. bar, 1949, D.C. bar, 1952, since practiced in N.Y.C.; asso. Cahill Gordon & Reindel, 1948-59, partner, 1959—; dir. Continental Telephone Corp.; dir. Seaboard World Airlines. Served to lt. (j.g.) USNR, 1943-46. Mem. Am., N.Y. State bar assns., Assn. Bar City N.Y. Clubs: Harvard, Wings. Home: 203 E 72d St New York NY 10021 Office: 80 Pine St New York NY 10005

SCHNEIDERS, GREGORY STEPHEN, polit. cons., educator, former mem. Presdl. staff; b. Detroit, Apr. 15, 1947; s. Alexander Aloysius and Glen E. (Ogle) S.; A.B., Georgetown U., 1978; m. Marie Hartnett, Dec. 31, 1976. Restaurant entrepreneur, Washington, 1969-75; adminstrv. asst. Carter for Pres. campaign, 1975-76; dir. White House Projects, Washington, 1977; dep. asst. to Pres. for communications, 1978-79; faculty Georgetown U., 1979—; polit. cons. Home: 311 N Oxford St Arlington VA 22203

SCHNEIDMAN, HAROLD M., dermatologist; b. Mpls., Mar. 28, 1924; s. Morris and Freda (Palay) S.; B.S., U. Minn., 1946, M.B., 1947, M.D., 1948; m. Shirley Goldstep, Mar. 7, 1965; children—Marla Matte, Marc Robert. Intern, U. Okla. Hosps., Oklahoma City, 1947-48; resident Michael Reese Hosp., Chgo., 1949-50, U. Chgo., 1950-51, Stanford U., 1954-56; practice medicine specializing in dermatology, San Francisco, 1956—; mem. staff Presbyn. Hosp. Pacific Med. Center, San Francisco, 1959—, chmn. dept. dermatology, 1960—; mem. staffs Children's Hosp., San Francisco, Mt. Zion Hosp.; clin. prof. dermatology Sch. Medicine, Stanford U., 1967—. Served as capt. U.S. Army, 1952-54. Mem. Am. Acad. Dermatology, Pan Am. Med. Assn. (dir.), San Francisco Dermatol. Soc. (pres. 1965-66). Contbr. articles to med. publs. Home: 124 25th Ave San Francisco CA 94121 Office: 490 Post St San Francisco CA 94102

SCHNELL, GEORGE ADAM, educator, geographer; b. Phila., July 13, 1931; s. Earl Blackwood and Emily (Bernheimer) S.; B.S., State Coll., West Chester, Pa., 1958; M.S., Pa. State U., 1960, Ph.D., 1965; postdoctoral study Ohio State U., summer 1965; m. Mary Lou Williams, June 21, 1958; children—David Adam, Douglas Powell, Thomas Earl. Asst. prof. State U. Coll., New Paltz, N.Y., 1962-65, asso. prof., 1965-68, prof., chmn. dept. geography, 1968—; vis. asso. prof. U. Hawaii, summer 1966; cons. community action programming, 1965. Served with AUS, 1952-54. Mem. Assn. Am. Geographers, Nat. Council Geog. Edn., Pa. Council for Geog. Edn., Pa. Acad. Sci. Mem. Reformed Ch. (elder). Author: (with K. E. Corey, others) The Local Community: A Handbook for Teachers, 1971; contbg. author: The World's Population, Problems of Growth, 1972; West Virginia and Appalachia: Selected Readings, 1977. Editor: (with G.J. Demko and H.M. Rose) Population Geography: A Reader, 1970. Contbr articles to profl. jours. and books. Home: 1 N Manheim Blvd New Paltz NY 12561

SCHNEPS, JACK, educator; b. N.Y.C., Aug. 18, 1929; s. Elias and Rose (Rephen) S.; B.A., N.Y. U., 1951; M.S., U. Wis., 1953, Ph.D., 1956; m. Lucia DeMarchi, Mar. 11, 1960; children—Loredana, Melissa, Leila. Asst. prof. physics Tufts U., 1956-60, asso. prof., 1960-63, prof., 1963—; vis. scientist European Orgn. Nuclear Research, Geneva, Switzerland, 1965-66; lectr. Internat. Sch. Elementary Particle Physics, Yugoslavia, 1968; vis. research fellow Univ. Coll., London, Eng., 1973-74. NSF postdoctoral fellow U. Padua (Italy), 1958-59. Fellow Am. Phys. Soc.; mem. European Phys. Soc., AAUP, Phi Beta Kappa, Sigma Xi. Contbg. author: Methods in Subnuclear Physics, Vol. IV, 1970. Contbr. articles to profl. jours. Home: 3 Foxcroft Rd Winchester MA 01890 Office: Dept Physics Tufts U Medford MA 02155

SCHNERING, PHILIP BLESSED, investment banker; b. Detroit, Dec. 26, 1917; s. Otto Young and Dorothy (Russell) S.; B.A., U. Chgo., 1939; m. Ruth Scott, June 10, 1940; children—Sally, Sandra, Philip S., Judith, Wendy. Salesman, retail crew worker, factory trainee Curtiss Candy Co., Chgo., 1938-40, salesman supvr., 1940, dist. field mgr., 1941-43, asst. to pres., 1943-48, v.p., div. sales mgr., 1948-53, exec. v.p., 1953-58; dir. comml. devel. McCormick & Co., Inc., Balt., 1958-64; exec. v.p. Farboil Co., Balt., 1965-66; pres. Bowen Co., Balt., 1966-72; investment banker, 1973—; chmn. bd. Curtiss Breeding Service, Cary, Ill. Vice pres. Balt. Boy Scouts Am.; past pres., dir. Balt. Council Camp Fire Girls; chmn. nat. bd., dir. finance com. Nat. Camp Fire Girls; trustee Nat. Council Crime and Delinquency; chmn. Md. Commn. Crime and Delinquency. Asso. trustee Northwestern U. Mem. Am. Mgmt. Assn., Soc. Am. Archaeology. Clubs: Antique Auto; Baltimore Yacht; Green Spring Valley Hunt. Home: Hillside Rd Stevenson MD 21153 Office: Box 61 Stevenson MD 21153

SCHNITTKER, JOHN ALVIN, agrl. bus. exec.; b. Nashville, Kans., Sept. 22, 1924; s. John and Theodora (Steffan) S.; B.S., Kans. State U., 1950, M.S., 1954; Ph.D., Iowa State U., 1956. Staff, Council of Economic Advisers, 1958-59; staff economist Dept. Agr., 1961-64, dir. agrl. econs., 1964-65, undersec. agr., 1965-69; pres. Schnittker Assos., Washington, 1972—. Served with inf. AUS, 1951-52; Korea. Mem. Am. Agr. Econ. Assn., Am. Econ. Assn. Office: Schnittker Assos 1339 Wisconsin Ave NW Washington DC 20007

SCHNITTMANN, SACHA STANISLAV ALEXANDER, archtl. sculptor; b. N.Y.C., Sept. 1, 1913; s. Maximilian and Rosalie S.; student Cooper Union, N.Y.C., 1929-30, Nat. Acad. Design, 1930-33, Beaux Arts Inst. Design, 1931-36, Leonardo da Vinci Sch. Fine Arts, 1934-36, Sorbonne, Am. Acad., Rome, Am. U., Beirut; studied under Attillio Piccirilli, Alexander Sambougnac, Philip Snowden, Charles Keck, Robert Aitken; m. Mary Frances Clarke, June 17, 1937 (div.); children—Pamela Clarke, Darwin Howard; m. 2d, Carole Cathey, May 14, 1962; 1 dau., Leslie Cathey. Taught sculpture Beaux Arts Atelier, Hollis, L.I., art dir. Ifta Sculptura, N.Y.C. (did series of 16 busts for Pan-Am. Soc.), 1936; prof. creative sculpture and anatomy Maryville Coll. and Fontbonne Coll., St. Louis, 1942-49; dir. Ark. State Capitol Mus. Fine Arts, Fine Arts Commn. State of Ark., State Hall of Sculpture, 1950-64; dir. Triton Museum Art, San Jose, 1965-66; pvt. practice as archtl. and meml. sculptor; condr. weekly radio commentary; feature writer, art critic Ark. Democrat; sculptor for petroleum exhibit N.Y. World's Fair, 1938; commd. to execute Am. Legion Monument Meml. Plaza, St. Louis (unveiled 1942); designed The Rigger a 65 ft. high figure in bronze; 68 ft. high giraffe for Griffeth Park, also overlife-size hippopotamus, Morganhorse; over-life-size monument in bronze King Kamehameha, Hawaii, Heroic portrait bust of Dr. Martin Luther King, Jr., also meml. portrait, 18-foot abstract bronze sculpture Chaconne, San Antonio Shopping Center, 1974, others; also numerous monuments throughout U.S.; other works include 263 portrait busts, meml. portraits, bronze statues; designer 6 granite panels UN Bldg., fountains for Embarcadero Center, San Francisco; commd. to design 25 foot bronze monument of Elvis Presley, Hilton Las Vegas, 1978. Vice pres., bd. dirs. Ark. State Symphony Assn. Recipient Kemper award, Kansas City Art Inst., 1942, Nelson Rockhill Mus. purchase award Kansas City Art Inst., Jr. League award St. Louis City Art Mus., Soc. Independent Artists award (detail of Goethe Monument), Savage award, 1944, McMillan award for Am. sculpture, 1945, Am. Prize Winners award, 1946, Fraser gold medal for sculpture, 1937, award for figure of Lenin cast in steel Moscow State U., 1938, Allied Artists award for sculpture, 1941, Carnegie gold medal for sculpture Nat. Prize Winners, Chgo., exhibited Chgo., Art Soc. of Art Inst. Chgo., 1946. Mem. Medalic Arts Soc., Am. Artists Assn., Artists Assn. Am., Soc. Independent Artists, Russian Sculpture Soc. (hon. life), Ecole des Beaux Artes (Paris, France, hon. life), Am. Inst. Archtl. Sculpture, Beaux Arts Inst. Design N.Y., Nat. Soc. Archtl. Sculptors, Am. Acad. Sci., Am. Fedn. Arts, Western Assn. Art Museums, Nat. Acad. Author: Anatomy and Dissection, 1939; Plastic Histology, 1940; Anatomy for Artists, 1943; Creative Designs, 1951; Architectural Sculpture, 1951; Sculpture, Sculptors and their Social Significance, 1952. Contbr. numerous articles on archtl. sculpture to profl. publs. Office: 915 Commercial St Suite 3 San Jose CA 95112. *Among other things art is, to me, an expression of my essential urge to record creatively a dynamic moment in the drama of life itself. Aside from the early and fundamental disciplines necessarily experienced in the course of my development-the adventurous, creative, personal experimentation; studio exercises; my attempts to assert my individuality; my early dreams of immortality, etc.-yet always, when a completed work was to be presented to and viewed by the general public, I set forth that which represented my very best efforts in the form of a personal, formal and comprehensive statement-never revealing those many hours of doubt, exultation, critical analysis, and adventurous experimentation which preceded It-so that the public may view and comprehend my meaning at a glance.*•

SCHNITZER, BRUCE WILLIAM, corp. exec.; b. New Orleans, May 5, 1944; s. Fred J. and Inetta (Abdnor) S.; B.A., U. Tex., 1966, M.B.A., 1967; m. Dec. 8, 1973; 1 dau., Annabel Bradford. Asst. treas. Morgan Guaranty Trust Co., N.Y.C., 1967-71, asst. v.p., 1971-72, v.p., head merger and acquisition group, 1972-77; v.p., chief fin. officer Marsh & McLennan Cos., Inc., N.Y.C., 1977—, also dir.; dir. William M. Mercer, Inc., Marsh & McLennan Mgmt. Co., Am. Overseas Mgmt. Corp., Guy Carpenter & Co., Am. Overseas Reinsurance Co., Tower Hill Ins. Co., Menasha Corp. Trustee Doctor's Hosp. Served with U.S. Army, 1967. Mem. Fin. Execs. Inst. Episcopalian. Clubs: Union League (N.Y.C.); Creek (Locust Valley, N.Y.). Office: 1221 Ave of the Americas New York NY 10020

SCHNITZER, HOWARD JOEL, educator, physicist; b. Newark, Nov. 12, 1934; s. Albert and Helen (Ehrlich) S.; B.S. in Mech. Engring., Newark Coll. Engring., 1955; Ph.D. in Physics, U. Rochester, 1960; m. Phoebe Kazdin, May 22, 1966; children—Mark Jacob, Elizabeth Karen. Postdoctoral research asso. U. Rochester, 1960-61; mem. faculty Brandeis U., Waltham, Mass., 1961—, prof. physics, 1968—. Vis. prof. Rockefeller U., 1969-70; hon. research asso. Harvard, 1974, 76-80. Sloan fellow, 1965-67. Fellow Am. Phys. Soc.; mem. Sigma Xi. Asso. editor: Phys. Rev. Letters, 1978—. Home: 397 Highland St Newtonville MA 02160 Office: Dept Physics Brandeis Univ Waltham MA 02154

SCHNITZER, MARTIN COLBY, educator; b. Wilmette, Ill., Aug. 20, 1925; s. Leon Wendell and Homera Almeda (Portman) S.; student U. of South, 1944-46; B.A., U. Ala., 1949, M.B.A, 1951; Ph.D., U. Fla., 1960; m. Joan Hammet Brown, June 30, 1951; children—Melanie, Meredith, Marcy. Asst. prof. bus. U. Ark., Fayetteville, 1955-58; asst. prof. U. Fla., Gainesville, 1958-60; prof. econs. Va. Poly. Inst. and State U., Blacksburg, 1964—. Mem. Va. Gov's Adv. Bd. of Economists, 1978—; mem. adv. bd. to U.S. Sec. of Commerce, 1970-72; mem. U.S. East-West Trade Commn., 1974-75; mem. Va. Indsl. Facilities Financing Commn., 1974-76; mem. Fulbright Selection Com., 1976. Ford Found. grantee, 1962-63; Am. Philos. Soc. grantee, 1963-64. Episcopalian. Author: The Economy of Sweden, 1970; Comparative Economic Systems, 1971; Readings in Public Finance and Pulic Policy, 1972; East and West Germany: A Comparative Economic Analysis; Income Distribution, 1975; Contemporary Government and Bus. Relations, 1978. Editor: Va. Social Sci. Jour., 1964-68. Home: 606 Rainbow Ridge Blacksburg VA 24060

SCHNOBRICH, ROGER WILLIAM, lawyer; b. New Ulm, Minn., Dec. 21, 1929; s. Arthur G. and Amanda (Reinhart) S.; B.B.A. with distinction, U. Minn., 1952, LL.B., 1954; m. Angeline Ann Schmitz, Jan. 21, 1961; children—Julie Ann, Jennifer Lynn, Kathryn Mary, Karen Lee. Accountant, Touche, Ross, & Co., C.P.A.'s, Mpls., summers 1951-53; admitted to Minn. bar, 1956, since practiced in Mpls.; mem. firm Popham, Haik, Schnobrich, Kaufman & Doty, Ltd., 1960—; parttime instr. law William Mitchell Coll. Law, St. Paul, 1961-64. Served with AUS, 1954-56. Mem. Am., Minn., Hennepin County bar assns., Order of Coif, Phi Delta Phi, Beta Gamma Sigma, Beta Alpha Psi, Roman Cath. K.C. Club: Mpls. Athletic. Mem. editorial bd. Minn. Law Rev., 1953-54. Home: 5910 Kenneth Way Golden Valley MN 55422 Office: 4344 IDS Center Minneapolis MN 55402

SCHNOES, ROBERT FREDERICK, business exec.; b. Mt. Lebanon, Pa., Apr. 4, 1926; s. Sebastian J. and Henrietta C. (Schertler) S.; B.S. in Indsl. Mgmt., U. Pitts. 1949; m. Dolores K. Hewston, Aug. 13, 1949; children—Carolyn S. Schnoes Black, Christine P. Schnoes Rost, Nancy E. Schnoes Anderson, Judith A. With Midwest sales div. Autographic Register Co., Hoboken, N.J., 1949-50; with quality control dept. Fisher Body div. Gen. Motors Corp., Pitts., 1950-51; successively buyer, supervisory buyer, asst. purchasing agt., asst. to surface ship project mgr. Bettis Atomic Power div. Westinghouse Electric Corp., Pitts., 1951-59; dir. material and facilities Am. Standard Mil. Products Div., Norwood, Mass., 1959-62; exec. v.p. Hamill Mfg. Co., Monroeville, Pa., 1962-63; gen. mgr. aero. research instrument dept. Am. Standard Corp., Chgo., 1963-65, pres. controls div., 1965-68; pres. Dresser Indsl. Valve & Instrument div. Dresser Industries, Inc., Stratford, Conn., 1968-70, pres. Indsl. Spltys. group, Stratford, 1970-71, v.p. ops. Dresser Industries, Inc., Dallas, 1971-74, sr. v.p. ops. office of pres., 1975-77; pres., chief operating officer, dir. IC Industries, Inc., Chgo., 1977—; dir. Pet, Inc., Lincoln Fin., Inc., Am. Nat. Bank & Trust Co. Chgo., Abex Corp., Ill. Central Gulf R.R., Midas Internat. Corp., Pepsi-Cola Gen. Bottlers. Mem. Council on Grad. Sch. Bus., U. Chgo. Served with USNR, 1944-46. Mem. Engring. Soc. Detroit, Chgo. Assn. Commerce and Industry (dir.), Orchtl. Assn. Chgo., N.W. Univ. Assos. Club: Mid-Am., Chicago, Executives (Chgo.). Home: 2 Golf Ln Winnetka IL 60093 Office: One Illinois Center 111 E Wacker Dr Chicago IL 60601

SCHNORE, LEO F., educator, sociologist; b. Elyria, Ohio, Jan. 10, 1927; s. Leo Francis and Mildred Elizabeth (Kraus) S.; A.B. in Sociology cum laude, Miami U., Oxford, Ohio, 1950; M.A., U. Mich., 1951, Ph.D., 1955; m. Elinor Carole Schick, Sept. 9, 1950 (div. 1968); children—Carol, Barbara; m. 2d, Julie R. Kraft, Oct. 31, 1969 (div. 1971); 1 son, Aaron F. Instr., asst. prof. sociology and anthropology Brown U., Providence, R.I., 1954-56; asst. prof. Mich. State U., 1956-57; asst. prof. sociology and biostatistics U. Cal. at Berkeley, 1957-59; asso. prof. sociology and urban and regional planning U. Wis., Madison, 1959-62, prof., 1962—. Cons. NSF, 1963-64; dir. Social Sci. Research Council, 1964-67, treas., 1965. Center for Advanced Study in Behavioral Scis. fellow, 1971-72; Guggenheim fellow, 1974-75. Served with AUS, 1945-46. Mem. Population Assn. Am. (dir. 1964-66), Am. Sociol. Assn., Sociol. Research Assn. Author: The Urban Scene: Human Ecology and Demography, 1965; Class and Race in Cities and Suburbs, 1972. Editor: (with P.M. Hauser) The Study of Urbanization, 1965; (with Henry Fagin) Urban Research and Policy Planning, 1967; Social Science and the City, 1968; The New Urban History-Quantitative Studies by American Historians, 1975. Home: 3208 Bluff St Apt 3 Madison WI 53705

SCHNUR, JEROME, television producer, dir.; b. N.Y.C., July 30, 1923; s. Irving I. and Frances (Buchsbaum) S.; grad. Carnegie Inst. Tech., 1944. Asso. producer feature films, until 1950; dir., producer network television, 1950—, pres. Jerome Schnur Productions, Inc., N.Y.C., 1963—, producer, dir. numerous TV shows, including PBS specials The Joffrey Ballet, The American Ballet Theatre, over a dozen music and ballet specials for CBS-TV; cons. in field; spl. lectr. television film dept. U. Miami. Served with USAAF, 1943-46. Recipient Peabody award, 1970; Emmy citation, 1971; Ohio State award, 1975, others. Mem. Acad. Motion Picture Arts and Scis., Acad. Television Arts and Scis., Dirs. Guild Am. Address: 135 Central Park W New York NY 10023

SCHOBER, FRANK JOSE, JR., nat. guard officer; b. Los Angeles, Nov. 17, 1933; s. Frank Jose and Mildred A. (Lucien) S.; B.S. summa cum laude, Santa Clara (Calif.) U., 1946; M.P.A., Harvard U., 1962; grad. Command and Gen. Staff Coll., 1971, Army War Coll., 1974; m. Gale Rogers, July 14, 1974; children—Christopher, Wakefield. Commd. 2d lt. U.S. Army, 1956, advanced through grades to maj. gen., 1975; comdr. units in Europe, U.S. and Vietnam; asst. prof. history U.S. Mil. Acad., 1964-67; ret., 1975; maj. gen., comdg. gen. Calif. N.G., also adj. gen. Calif., 1975—; dir. Calif. Drought Emergency Task Force, 1977—; adviser Saudi Arabia Ministry Def. and Aviation, 1968-69; mem. Army Strategic Studies Inst., 1973-75. Mem. energy adv. bd. Coll. Engring., Northrup U., Los Angeles, 1977—. Decorated Legion of Merit, Bronze Star, Meritorious Service medal; Cross Gallantry with palm (Vietnam). Mem. Assn. U.S. Army, N.G. Assn., Newcomen Soc. N.Am., Air Force Assn., Navy League, VFW. Catholic. Club: Commonwealth (San Francisco). Co-author: War College Energy Study, 1974; author: The Middle East: Averting Armageddon, 1975; editor: Middle East Readings, 1966. Author poetry. Office: 2829 Watt Ave Sacramento CA 95821

SCHOBER, GLENN E., educator; b. Mpls., July 1, 1938; s. Wayne and Frieda (Ponath) S.; B.S., U. Minn., 1960, Ph.D., 1965; m. Madrean Rod, Apr. 2, 1966; children—Kristi Vicki. Asst. prof. U. Calif., San Diego, 1965-66; with dept. math. Ind. U., Bloomington, 1966—, prof., 1976—; vis. prof. ETH, Zurich, Switzerland, 1972, U. Md., 1973-74, U. N.C., 1976. Mem. Am. Math. Soc. Home: 2204 Fairmount Ct Bloomington IN 47401 Office: Dept Math Ind U Bloomington IN 47405

SCHOBER, MARSHALL, steel co. exec.; b. Monroeville, N.J., Jan. 23, 1925; s. Frank and Josephine (McNeill) S.; B.S., Mass. Inst. Tech., 1943; m. Tina E. Anderson, June 14, 1947; children—Stephen Scott, Robert Gunnar, Tina Joanne. Engr., DeLaval Steam Turbine Co., 1946-48; buyer Am. Viscose Corp., 1948-50; with Latrobe Steel Co. (Pa.), 1950—, pres., 1971—; dir. Vulcan, Inc. Served with USNR, 1943-46. Mem. Am. Iron and Steel Inst. Methodist. Office: 2626 Ligonier St Latrobe PA 15650•

SCHOBERL, ANTHONY DENIS, banker; b. N.Y.C., Aug. 22, 1915; s. John Joseph and Anna (Hadjinetz) S.; certificate Am. Inst. Banking, 1944; student Columbia U. Sch. Gen. Studies, 1947-50; m. Ellen Mary Reeve, Apr. 30, 1938; children—Anthony Denis, Mariana (Mrs. John Dubnowski), Barbara (Mrs. Jeffrey Buck), Peter. Clk., First Nat. City Bank, N.Y.C., 1935-38; head cashier McGinnis Restaurant, Inc., 1938-41; asst. v.p. Clinton Trust Co., 1941-58; sec. First State Bank of Union, N.J., 1958-63; pres. Franklin State Bank, Somerset, N.J., 1963-76, vice chmn., 1976—; dir. Ideal Mut. Ins. Co. N.Y., Citizens Bank N.A. Chmn. bd. commrs. New Brunswick Housing and Redevel. Authority; pres., bd. dirs. Easter Seal Soc. N.J. Chmn. lay bd. trustees Georgian Ct. Coll.; trustee, treas., chmn. fin. com. Rutgers Community Health Plan, New Brunswick; trustee Rutgers Prep. Sch., Somerset, 1975-78, St. Peter's Med. Center, George St. Playhouse (both New Brunswick), Franklin Arts Council. Served with USMCR; PTO. Named Citizen of Yr., Franklin Twp. Lions, 1978; recipient medal State of Israel Bonds, 1977. Mem. N.J. Bankers Assn. (chmn. 1978-79), Franklin Twp. C. of C. (past pres., named Man of Year 1969, Citizen of Yr. 1977). K.C. (4 deg.). Home: 1050 George St New Brunswick NJ 08901 Office: 630 Franklin Blvd Somerset NJ 08873. *Without question, open honesty and compassion leads to the most pleasant form of success.*

SCHOECK, HELMUT, educator, author; b. Graz, Austria, July 3, 1922; s. Stephan J. and Anna (Heigl) S.; student U. Munich Med. Sch., 1941-45, U. Tuebingen, 1946-50; Dr. Phil., 1948; postdoctoral fellow sociology Yale, 1953-54; m. Margaret Weiler, June 24, 1947; children—Natalia, Raymond, Stephanie. Came to U.S., 1950, naturalized, 1956. Asst. dept. philosophy U. Munich, 1943-45; asst. to script dir. Radio Stuttgart, 1946; prof. social sci. Fairmont (W.Va.) State Coll., 1950-53; asst. prof. sociology Emory U., 1954-56, asso. prof. sociology, 1956-65; prof., dir. Inst. Sociology, U. Mainz, 1965—; vis. prof. Am. studies U. Erlangen-Nürnberg, 1964. Dir. Interdisciplinary Symposium on Culture Contact in Underdeveloped Countries, Emory U., 1957; dir. symposium on Scientism and the Study of Man, 1958, on Relativism and the Study of Man, 1959, on effects psychiatric theories modern society, 1960, on pvt. sector versus pub. sector, 1961. Fellow Am. Anthrop. Assn., Am. Sociol. Assn.; mem. Mont Pelerin Soc. Author: Nietzsches Philosophie des Menschlich-Alizumenschlichen, 1948; Religionssoziologie (trans.), 1951; Soziologie, 1952; USA: Motive und Strukturen, 1958; Was Heisst politisch unmoeglich, 1959; Umgang mit Völkern: Amerikaner, 1961; Die Soziologie und die Gesellschaften, 1964; Der Neid: Eine Theorie der Gesellschaft, 1966; Envy: A Theory of Social Behavior, New York-London, 1969, Italian edit., 1974; Soziologisches Wörterbuch, 1969, Spanish edit., 1973; La Envidia, Buenos Aires, 1970; 1st Leistung unanstaendig, 1971; Entwicklungshilfe, 1972; Vorsicht Schreibtischtaeter, 1972; Die Lust am schlechten Gewissen, 1973; Umverteilung als Klassenkampf, 1974; L'Invidia e la Società, 1974; Geschichte der Soziologie, 1974; Das Geschäft mit dem Pessimismus, 1975; Schülermanipulation, 1976; Vermogensdeling—Aspect van Klassenstrijd?, 1977; Historia de la Sociologia, 1977; Das Recht auf Ungleichheit, 1979; columnist Internat. Med. Tribune, 1977—; also articles in field. Editor: Foreign Aid Reexamined, 1958, Central Planning and Neomercantilism, 1964, others. Home: Haideweg 30 Wiesbaden-Sonnenberg West Germany Office: U Mainz 6500 Mainz Federal Republic of Germany

SCHOECK, RICHARD JOSEPH, educator; b. N.Y.C., Oct. 10, 1920; s. Gustav J. and Frances M. (Kuntz) S.; M.A., Princeton U., 1949, Ph.D., 1949; m. Reta R. Haberer, 1945 (div. 1977); children—Eric R., Christine C., Jennifer A.; m. 2d, Megan S. Lloyd, Feb. 19, 1977. Instr. English, Cornell U., 1949-55; asst. prof., then asso. prof. U. Notre Dame, 1955-61; prof. English, U. Toronto, 1961-71, head dept. English, St. Michael's Coll., 1965-70; prof. vernacular lit. Pontifical Inst. Mediaeval Studies, Toronto, 1964-71; dir. research activities Folger Shakespeare Library also dir. Folger Inst. Renaissance and 18th Century Studies, 1970-74; adj. prof. English, Cath. U. Am., 1972 prof. English, medieval and renaissance studies U. Md., 1974-75; prof. English and humanities U. Colo., Boulder, 1972—, chmn. dept. integrated studies, 1976—; Vincent J. Flynn Chair of Letters, Coll. St. Thomas, 1960; vis. prof. Princeton U., 1964; cons. Nat. Endowment Humanities; bd. dirs. Natural Law Inst., U. Notre Dame. Served with AUS, 1940-46. Fellow Assn. Advancement Edn., 1952-53, Yale U., 1959-60, Can. Council, 1967-68, Guggenheim Found., 1968-69; grantee UNESCO, Am. Council Learned Socs., U. Toronto, U. Colo., Brit. Council. Fellow Royal Soc. Can., Royal Hist. Soc.; mem. Internat. Assn. Neo-Latin Studies (pres. 1976-79), Modern Lang. Assn. Am., Mediaeval Acad. Am., Renaissance Soc. Am., Selden Soc., PEN, Canadian Humanities Assn., Rocky Mountain Conf. Brit. Studies, Internat. Assn. U. Profs. English, Assn. Canadian Studies in U.S., Author: The Achievement of Thomas More, 1976; also numerous articles, papers, revs. Editor: Delehaye's Legends of the Saints, 1961; Editing 16th Century Texts, 1966; (Roger Ascham) The Scholemaster, 1966; Shakespeare Quar., 1972-74; gen. editor: The Confutation of Tyndale, 3 vols., 1973; co-editor: Voices of Literature, 2 vols., 1964, 66; Chaucer Criticism, 2 vols., 1960, 61; Style, Rhetoric and Rhythm: Essays by M.W. Croll, 1966; former gen. editor Patterns of Literary Criticism; spl. editor Canada vol. Rev. Nat. Literatures, 1977, mem. editorial bds. profl. jours. Home: 4628 Tanglewood Trail Boulder CO 80301 Office: Dept Integrated Studies Univ Colo Boulder CO 80309. *More than a thousand years ago Bede summed up what are for me the principles of my professional career: I have always thought it fitting to learn and to teach and to write.*

SCHOELKOPF, DEAN HAROLD, editor; b. St. Cloud, Minn., July 4, 1932; s. Harold L. and Anne S.; B.A. magna cum laude, U. Minn., 1954, M.A., 1959. City editor Mpls. Tribune, 1954-63; nat. and fgn. editor Chgo. Daily News, 1963-66; cons. Econ. Devel. Adminstrn., 1966; White House corr. USIA, 1967; editor The Paper, Oshkosh, Wis., 1968-70; editor-in-chief Ency. Brit. Book of Yr., Brit. Yearbook of Sci., Compton Yearbook, Chgo., 1970-72; asst. mng. editor Detroit Free Press, 1972; editor KNT News Wire, v.p. KNT News Services, Inc., Washington, 1972—. Served to 1st lt. USAF, 1955-56. Decorated Air Force Commendation medal; recipient Page One award Twin Cities News Guild, 1957, 60, News award Ill. AP, UPI, 1963-64, Stick of Type award Chgo. News Guild, 1964; Seymour Berkson Fgn. Assignment grantee, 1961. Mem. Sigma Delta Chi (Public Service award 1963), Kappa Tau Alpha. Club: Nat. Press (Washington). Home: 2500 Virginia Ave NW Washington DC 20037 Office: 1195 Nat Press Bldg Washington DC 20045

SCHOEN, HERBERT PAUL, ins. co. cons. and dir.; b. Glens Falls, N.Y., June 30, 1913; A.B., Harvard, 1935, LL.B., 1938; m. Jeanne Ball; children—Susan Jeanne (Mrs. Joseph B. Sappington), Stephen George, James Herbert. Admitted to N.Y. bar, Conn. bar; atty., Glen Falls Ins. Co., 1939-42, div. war research Columbia, 1942-43; with Hartford Ins. Group, 1946—, now cons. and dir. past chmn. Hartford Fire Ins. Co. and Subs. cos. of Hartford Ins. Group; dir Conn. Bank & Trust Co., Ins. Assn. Conn., Greater Hartford Corp. Corporator Inst. Living, Hartford Hosp., St. Francis Hosp.; trustee Conn. Pub. Expenditure Council, Am. Inst. for Property and Liability Underwriters, Ins. Inst. Am.; bd. dirs. St. Francis Hosp., YMCA of Greater Hartford, World Affairs Center Hartford, Hartford Stage Co., Hartford Inst. Criminal and Social Justice; civilian aide to sec. army for Conn.; chmn. Conn. Gaming Policy Bd., Citizens' Com. for Effective Govt., Inc.; mem. nat. corps. com. United Negro Coll. Fund. Served to lt. comdr. UNSR, 1943-46. Home: 1083 Farmington Ave West Hartford CT 06107 Office: Hartford Plaza Hartford CT 06115

SCHOEN, MAX HOWARD, dentist, educator; b. N.Y.C., Feb. 4, 1922; s. Adolph and Ella (Grossman) S.; B.S., U. So. Calif., 1943, D.D.S., 1943; M.P.H., U. Calif., Los Angeles, 1962, D.P.H., 1969; m. Beatrice Mildred Hoch, Feb. 5, 1950; children—Steven Charles, Karen Ruth. Practice dentistry, Los Angeles, 1947-54; founding partner group dental practice, So. Los Angeles, 1954—; vis. prof. Sch. Dental Medicine, U. Conn., 1972; prof., dean pro-tem, asso. dean Sch. Dental Medicine, State U. N.Y., Stony Brook, 1973-76; prof., chmn. sect. preventive dentistry and pub. health U. Calif. Sch. Dentistry, Los Angeles, 1976—; mem. Com. for Nat. Health Ins.; chmn. dental adv. bd. Headstart, Los Angeles, 1966; cons. in field. Served to capt. Dental Corps, U.S. Army, 1943-46. Diplomate Am. Bd. Dental Pub. Health. Fellow Am. Pub. Health Assn.; mem. Inst. Medicine, Am. Dental Assn., Am. Assn. Pub. Health Dentists, Fedn. Dentaire Internat., Am. Assn. Dental Schs., Group Health Assn. Am. Author papers in field. Home: 5818 Sherbourne Dr Los Angeles CA 90056 Office: Sch Dentistry Univ Calif Los Angeles CA 90024

SCHOEN, WILLIAM JACK, brewing co. exec.; b. Los Angeles, Aug. 2, 1935; s. Jack Conrad and Kathryn Mabel (Stegmayer) S.; B.S. in Fin. magna cum laude, U. So. Calif., 1960, M.B.A., 1963; m. Sharon Ann Barto, Oct. 1, 1966; children—Kathryn Lynn, Karen Anne, Kristine Lea, William Jack. Mktg. mgr. Anchor Hocking Glass Co., 1964-68; v.p. sales and mktg. Obear-Nester Glass Co., 1968-71; pres. Pierce Glass Co., Port Allegheny, Pa., 1971-73; pres., chief exec.

officer, dir. F.&M. Schaefer Brewing Co., N.Y.C., 1973—. Served with USMC, 1953-56; Korea. Mem. U.S. Brewers Assn. (exec. bd.), Young Pres. Orgn., Am. Mgmt. Assn., Mfrs. Assn., Blackstonian Soc., Alpha Kappa Psi, Alpha Gamma Sigma, Phi Kappa Phi. Republican. Lutheran. Clubs: Union League (N.Y.C.); Greenwich Country. Contbr. to indsl. publns. Home: 108 Birch Ln Greenwich CT 06830 Office: 3 Park Ave New York NY 10016

SCHOENBACH, SOL ISRAEL, musician; b. N.Y.C., Mar. 15, 1915; s. Abraham and Anna (Hochmeyer) S.; diploma in bassoon Juilliard Sch. Music, 1936; B.A. cum laude, N.Y. U., 1939; Mus.D., Curtis Inst. Music, 1969, Temple U., 1971; m. Bertha Karp, July 2, 1939; 1 son, Peter. Staff bassoonist CBS Orch., 1932-37; solo bassoonist Phila. Orch., 1937-57; instr. bassoon Curtis Inst. Music, Phila., 1943-77; an organizer Phila. Woodwind Quintet, 1950, mem., 1950-66; exec. dir. Settlement Music Sch., Phila., 1957—; participant Festival Two Worlds, Spoleto, Italy, Stratford Festival (Can.), Bach Festival, Bethlehem, Pa., Ventnor (N.J.) Festival, Marlboro Festival, New Coll. Festival, Fla. Mem. Commonwealth Pa. Council Arts, 1966-72. Dir. Presser Co. Served with AUS, 1944-46. Recipient Hartmann Kuhn award Phila. Orch., 1943-53, Music award Phila. Fine Arts Festival, 1962, Netzky award B'nai B'rith Vocational Service, 1969; Phila. award, 1976; Distinguished Merit award Phila. Art Alliance, 1976; Celebrations and Fulfillment award Am. Found. for Sci. of Creative Intelligence; Young Audiences award Edn. to Youth, 1977. Mem. Phi Beta Kappa. Home: 1810 Rittenhouse Sq Philadelphia PA 19103

SCHOENBAUM, ALEX, restaurant chain exec.; b. Richmond, Va., Aug. 8, 1915; s. Emil Boris and Goldie (Masinter) S.; B.S., Ohio State U., 1939; m. Betty Frank, Apr. 14, 1940; children—Raymond, Jeffry, Joann, Emily. Founder, Shoney's, Inc., and predecessor, Nashville, 1947, chmn. bd., 1971-76, sr. chmn. bd., 1976—; pres. Blvd. Recreation Center, Venture Bowling Corp., Blvd. Realty Corp.; dir. Kanawha Drug Corp.; mem. exec. com. Adams, Scott & Conway, a Nat. Ins. Co. Co-originator Roy Rogers Roast Beef Shoppes. Bd. dirs. Federated Jewish Charities W.Va., 1962—, pres., 1965-69; chmn. Charleston (W.Va.) Urban Renewal; past fund raising chmn. Buckskin council Boy Scouts Am.; chmn. fund drive Heart Assn., 1974-75; bd. dirs. Jewish Community Council, Jr. Achievement Kanawha Valley, Kiskimenetas Springs Prep. Sch.; trustee U. Charleston; chmn. Cancer Soc., Charleston, 1973; exec. com. Boys' Club; fin. com. Kanawha Pastoral Counseling Center; past fund-raising chmn., now mem. Bronco Junction Asmatic Camp, Charleston; bd. overseers N.Y. U. Sch. Food Service Mgmt.; chmn. big gifts Jewish Community Center; chmn. advanced gifts United Jewish Appeal, Sarasota, Fla., 1977; mem. bd. Sarasota Jewish Council, 1977—; a founder Com. of 100; past chmn. Indsl. Devel. Greater Charleston Area. Named to All-Am. Football Team, 1937, 38; Schoenbaum med. research fellowship established City of Hope Med. Center, Calif., 1977. Mem. Nat., W.Va. (past pres.) restaurant assns., W.Va. Bowling Proprs. Assn. (past pres.), Internat. Foodservice Mfrs. Assn., Internat. Food Service Council, Charleston C. of C. (past chmn. indsl. devel.), Zeta Beta Tau. Democrat. Jewish. Clubs: Rotary, President's of Ohio State U., Ohio State Varsity O, Country of Sarasota, B'nai B'rith. Home: 4902 Kanawha Ave SE Charleston WV 25304 also 8710 Midnight Pass Rd Sarasota FL 33581 Office: 312 21st St Charleston WV 25312

SCHOENBAUM, SAMUEL, educator; b. N.Y.C., Mar. 6, 1927; s. Abraham and Sarah (Altschuler) S.; B.A., Bklyn. Coll., 1947; M.A., Columbia, 1949, Ph.D., 1953; m. Marilyn Turk, June 10, 1946. Mem. faculty Northwestern U., 1953-75, Franklyn Bliss Snyder prof. English Lit., 1971-75; distinguished prof. English, U. City N.Y., 1975-76; distinguished prof. Renaissance lit. U. Md., 1976—; vis. prof. King's Coll., London, 1961, U. Chgo., 1964, 65, Columbia, 1966, U. Wash., 1968. Mem. adv. com. Internat. Shakespeare Conf., 1972—; exec. bd. Shakespeare Quar.; mem. Shakespeare Variorum Com.; trustee Folger Shakespeare Library; trustee Shakespeare Assn. Am., 1976-79. Guggenheim fellow, 1956-57, 69-70; Nat. Endowment Humanities Sr. fellowship, 1973-74; recipient Huntington Library grant, 1959, 67; Newberry Library grant, 1958; recipient Friends of Lit. non-fiction award for Shakespeare's Lives, 1970. Mem. Modern Language Assn. Am. Author: Internal Evidence and Elizabethan Dramatic Authorship, 1966; Shakespeare's Lives, 1970; William Shakespeare: A Documentary Life (Distinguished Service award Soc. Midland Authors 1976), 1975; William Shakespeare: A Compact Documentary Life, 1977; William Shakespeare: The Globe and the World, 1979; editor: (with K. Muir) A New Companion to Shakespeare Studies, 1971; Renaissance Drama, 1964-73. Home: 333 Maryland Ave NE Washington DC 20002

SCHOENBERG, HARRY WECHSLER, urologist, ednl. adminstr.; b. N.Y.C., July 27, 1927; s. Herman B. and Esther (Wechsler) S.; student U.S. Naval Acad., 1945-47; B.S., Yale U., 1948; M.D., U. Pa., Phila., 1952; children—Mark, Jennifer, Richard. Gen. rotating intern Hosp. U. Pa., Phila., 1952-53, asst. resident in surgery, 1953-54, 57-58, Harrison Dept. Surg. Research fellow, 1953-54, 57-58, asst. resident in urology, 1958-59, sr. resident in urology, 1959-60; asst. instr. surgery U. Pa., Phila., 1953-54, 57-58, asst. instr. urology, 1958-59, instr. urology, 1959-60; asst. prof. urology Hosp. U. Pa., Sch. Medicine U. Pa., 1963-65, asso. prof. urology, 1965-69, prof. urology, 1969-72; asst. urologist Grad. Hosp. U. Pa., 1960-72; cons. urology VA Hosp., Phila., 1961-72, Valley Forge Hosp., Phoenixville, Pa., 1963-72; cons. surgeon urology, Pa. Hosp., Phila., 1968-72; asst. surgeon div. urology Children's Hosp. Phila., 1967-70, sr. surgeon, 1970-72; prof., chmn. dept. urology St. Louis U. Sch. Medicine, 1972-76; prof., chmn. sect. urology U. Chgo. Pritzker Sch. Medicine, 1976—. Served as officer M.C., U.S. Army, 1954-56. Diplomate Am. Bd. Surgery, Am. Bd. Urology. Fellow A.C.S. Contbr. articles to med. jours. Office: Univ Chicago Hospitals Clinics Box 403 950 E 59th St Chicago IL 60637

SCHOENBORN, EDWIN AUGUST, banker; b. N.Y.C., Oct. 20, 1917; s. William Edward and Catherine (Beck) S.; B.S., N.Y. U., 1940; student Columbia, 1940-41, Harvard, 1970; m. Ione Clarisse Stasek, Oct. 3, 1943; children—Dale, Elaine. With Irving Trust Co., N.Y.C., 1941—, asst. sec., 1950-51, asst. v.p., 1951-57, v.p., 1957-71, sr. v.p., 1971-74, exec. v.p., 1974— sr. exec. v.p., 1978—. Served to capt. USAAF, 1942-46. Home: 29 Pleasant Manor Dr Thornwood NY 10594 Office: 1 Wall St New York NY 10015

SCHOENBRUNN, LEE ERNST, hotel exec.; b. Milw., Nov. 12, 1914; s. Robert Brierly and Frances (Ertl) S.; student St. Mary's Coll., Winona, Minn., 1932-36; B.S., Cornell U., 1940; student Northwestern U., 1953-55; m. Laura Elizabeth Reince, Aug. 21, 1939. Pres., gen. mgr. Student Agencies, Ithaca, N.Y., 1937-40; asst. mgr. Lake Placid Club, 1939; mgr. Haverford (Pa.) Court Hotel, 1940-42, Indiana Hotel, Ft. Wayne, 1942, Bannock Hotel, Pocatello, Idaho, 1942; owner Swoboda Hotel, Sturgeon Bay, Wis., 1942-47; mgr. Rumely Hotel, LaPorte, Ind., 1947; mgr. Association Island Gen. Electric Co., 1947-50; successively asst. mgr., asst. to pres., resident mgr., gen. mgr. Drake Hotel, Chgo., 1949-61; mgr. The La Qunita Hotel, Calif., 1961-62; gen. mgr. Chase Park Plaza Hotel, St. Louis, 1962—; v.p. Koplar Enterprises, including Chase Park Plaza Hotel, Lodge Four Seasons, KPLR-TV, Land of Fifth Season; dir. Continental Connector Corp., M & R Investment Inc. (Dunes Hotel and Casino, Las Vegas). Trustee St. Louis Jr. Coll. Hotel Sch.; chmn. Midwest Internat. Hotel Expn., Chgo., 1955-56; adv. bd. Inst. Labor Relations, Loyola U., Chgo., 1955-56; bd. commrs. St. Louis Conv. Center. Served as ensign USNR, 1942-43. Named Mo. Hotelman of Yr., 1978. Mem. Nat. Cornell Soc. Hotelmen (pres. 1955-56), Cornell Alumni Assn. (dir. 1955-56), Greater Chgo. Hotel Assn. (pres. 1960-61, chmn. bd. 1961). Mo. Hotel and Motel Assn. (v.p.), Ark., Mo. (v.p.), Kans., Okla. St. Louis (v.p.) hotel assns. Club: Cornell (gov. 1953-56). Address: 212 N Kingshighway St Louis MO 63108

SCHOENEMAN, RICHARD HOWARD, air force officer; b. Rochester, N.Y., Mar. 11, 1926; s. Howard George and Mary Thelma (Campbell) S.; B.S., U.S. Mil. Acad., 1949; postgrad. Nat. War Coll., 1967-68; M.S., George Washington U., 1968; m. Margaret Cooney, June 23, 1953; children—Curt Michael, Paul Joseph, John Patrick, James Steven, Kay Marie, Lisa Barbara. Commd. 2d lt. USAF, 1949, advanced through grades to maj. gen., 1975; tactical fighter squadron comdr., Spangdahlem, Germany, 1964-67; dir. operations 49th Tactical Fighter Wing, Holloman AFB, N.M., 1968-71; comdr. 12th Tactical Fighter Wing, Phu Cat Air Base, Vietnam, 1971; comdr. Task Force Alpha, Royal Thai AFB, Nakhon Phanom, Thailand, 1971-72; asst. dep. chief of staff for operations Hdqrs. Pacific Air Forces, Hawaii, 1972-74, insp. gen., 1974-75; comdr. 21st NORAD region 21st Air Div., Hancock Field, N.Y., 1975-77; comdt. Air War Coll., 1977-79; ret., 1979. Decorated Legion of Merit, D.F.C. with oak leaf cluster, Air medal with 9 oak leaf clusters, Meritorious Service medal. Home: 1508 Royal Palm Dr Niceville FL 32578

SCHOENER, EDGAR CHAPMAN, utility co. exec.; b. N.Y.C., Dec. 17, 1917; s. Charles P. and Alice M. (Warren) S.; B.B.A., Coll. City N.Y., 1947; J.D., Rutgers U., 1956; m. Anne C. Speight, Apr. 18, 1958; children—Edgar Chapman, Randi, Susan. Staff accountant Arthur Andersen & Co., N.Y.C., 1952-56; asst. comptroller Charles Bruning Co. Inc., 1956-58; sec., treas. Jersey Central Power & Light Co., Morristown, 1964—; v.p., dir. Utilities Employees Credit Union, Reading, Pa., 1964—. Served as officer inf. AUS, 1941-46. C.P.A., N.Y. Mem. Am. Inst. C.P.A.'s, N.Y. State Soc. C.P.A.'s. Home: 19 Calumet Rd Mt Fern Randolph NJ 07801 Office: Jersey Central Power & Light Co Madison Ave at Punch Bowl Rd Morristown NJ 07960

SCHOENER, JASON, artist, educator; b. Cleve., May 17, 1919; s. Harry and Ida C. (Fink) S.; diploma Cleve. Inst. Art, 1941; B.S., Western Res. U., 1941; postgrad. Art Students League N.Y., 1946-47; M.A., Columbia U., 1949; m. Catharine Virginia Worley, Aug. 17, 1951. Instr. sculpture, ceramics Munson-Williams Proctor Inst., Utica, N.Y., 1949-53; vis. lectr. art Mills Coll., Oakland, Calif., 1962-63; vis. prof. art Athens Tech. Inst. (Greece), 1964-65; prof. fine art, dean advanced studies Calif. Coll. Arts and Crafts, Oakland, 1953—; represented in permanent collections: Calif. Palace of Legion of Honor, Whitney Mus. Am. Art, Cleve. Mus. Art, Columbus (Ohio) Fine Arts Gallery, Nat. Mus. Art, Trinidad-Tobago, Athens Tech. Inst., Syracuse U., U. Maine, Bowdoin Coll. Bd. dirs. Center for Visual Arts, Oakland, Calif.; trustee Calif. Coll. Arts and Crafts. Served with USNR, 1944-46. Mem. AAUP, Art Students League N.Y., Coll. Art Assn. Am., Phila. Watercolor Club. Democrat. Congregationalist. Home: 74 Ross Circle Oakland CA 94618 Office: Calif Coll Arts and Crafts Broadway at College Age Oakland CA 94618. *I have always had a great interest in natural beauty. As a painter, I desire to convey to others by visual means all that I feel about nature and beauty. I experience the moods of nature with much joy and excitement. Secondly, I love beauty-that which is visually joyful to me. It is to me a positive concept, and from nature's beauty I seek inspiration for my painting.*

SCHOENFEIN, ROBERT A., advt. co. exec.; b. N.Y.C., Feb. 19, 1937; s. Benjamin P. and Elizabeth (Weiss) S.; B.A., Union Coll., 1958; M.S., Columbia U., 1959; m. Sandra Feldman, June 10, 1959; children—Liza, Karen. Staff asst. Grey Advt., Inc., N.Y.C., 1965-66, v.p., account supr., 1969-73, sr. v.p., mgmt. supr., 1973-78, exec. v.p., mgmt. rep., 1978—. Club: City Athletic (N.Y.C.). Home: 142 E 71st St New York NY 10021 Office: 777 3d Ave New York NY 10017

SCHOENFELD, HANNS-MARTIN WALTER, educator; b. Leipzig, Germany, July 12, 1928 (came to U.S. 1962, naturalized 1968); s. Alwin and Lisbeth (Kirbach) S.; Diplom Kaufmann, U. Hamburg (Germany), 1952, Dr.rer.pol., 1954; Habilitation (Ph.D.), U. Braunschweig (Germany), 1966; m. Margit Frese, Aug. 10, 1956; 1 dau., Gabriele. Practice pub. accounting, Hamburg, 1948-54; bus. cons. in Europe, 1958-62; faculty accountancy U. Ill., Urbana, 1962—, prof. accounting, bus. adminstrn., 1967—, Weldon Powell prof. accounting, 1976. Served with German Army, 1944-45. Mem. Am. Accounting Assn. (chmn. internat. sect.), Acad. Accounting Historians (v.p. 1976-77, pres. 1978-79), Acad. Internat. Bus., German Profs. Bus. Adminstrn., German Assn. Indsl. Engring., Beta Gamma Sigma, Beta Alpha Psi. Author numerous books including: (with W. Sommer) Management Dictionary 2 vols., 4th edit., 1971; Cost Accounting, 3 vols., 7 edit., 1974-75; Management Development, 1967; Cost Terminology and Cost Theory, 1974. Editorial bd. Mgmt. Internat. Rev. 1969—. Home: 1014 Devonshire Dr Champaign IL 61820 Office: 211 Commerce W Univ Ill Urbana IL 61801

SCHOENHERR, WALTER JOSEPH, bishop; b. Detroit, Feb. 28, 1920; s. Alex M. and Ida (Schmitz) S.; student Sacred Heart Sem., Detroit, 1935-42, Mt. St. Mary's Sem., Norwood, Ohio, 1942-44, S.S. Cyril and Methodius Sem., Orchard Lake, Mich., 1944-45. Ordained priest Roman Catholic Ch., 1945; asst. pastor Detroit Parishes of St. Davids, St. Leos, St. Roses, Presentation and St. Bedes, Southfield, Mich., 1959-61; pastor St. Aloysius Parish, Detroit, 1961-65, Blessed Sacrament Cathedral, 1965-68; aux. bishop of Detroit, 1968—; appointed to serve South region Archdiocese of Detroit, 1977—; mem. Permanent Diaconate and Pastoral Ministry to Correctional Instns.; mem. Archidocesan Liturgical Commn.; founding chaplain De LaSalle council K.C. Served with Mich. N.G., 1952-67. Home: 11350 Reeck Rd Southgate MI 48195 Office: 1234 Washington Blvd Detroit MI 48226

SCHOENING, ROGER WARREN, art dir.; b. Mpls., Oct. 3, 1928; s. Herbert Frederick and Alvilda Marie (Engh) S.; B.A., St. Olaf Coll., Northfield, Minn., 1950; certificate Parsons Sch. Design, N.Y.C., 1952-55; m. Carol Ann Erickson, October 31, 1964; children—Roger J.H., Julie A.S. Asst. to art dir. Mademoiselle magazine, 1959-61, art dir., 1961—; art dir. Vogue mag., 1977—. Served with AUS, 1950-52; Korea. Recipient Art Directors award, 1962. Home: 47 King St New York City NY 10014 Office: 350 Madison Ave New York City NY 10017

SCHOENLEB, EDWIN CHRISTIAN, fast food restaurant chain exec.; b. Portsmouth, Ohio, Apr. 10, 1934; s. Edwin Aquilla and Elaine (Gibson) S.; B.A. magna cum laude, Kenyon Coll., 1956; grad. exec. program, Dartmouth Coll., 1975; m. Joanne Adams, Nov. 28, 1955; children—Patricia, Barbara, William, E. Christian. Brand mgr. Procter & Gamble, 1956-62; brand mgr. Pet Milk, 1962-63; v.p., account supr. Needham, Harper & Steers, Chgo., 1963-67; dir. merchandising Am. Motors, Detroit, 1968-70; group product mgr. Gallo Wine, Modesto, Calif., 1970-72; v.p. mktg. Burger King Corp., Miami, Fla., 1972-77, exec. v.p., dir. mktg., 1978—. Pres., Royal Palm Civic Assn., 1976-77; trustee Fla. Internat. U., 1978—; dir. sta. WPBT, Ednl. TV, 1977—; dir. Miami Sch. Vol. Program, 19/8—. Mem. Premium Mktg. Assn. Am. (dir. 1976-79), Assn. Nat. Advertisers, Phi Beta Kappa. Republican. Methodist. Club: Calusa Country. Home: 14540 SW 79th Ave Miami FL 33158 Office: 7360 N Kendall Dr Miami FL 33156

SCHOENTHAL, VAL L., ret. lawyer; b. Sioux City, Iowa, July 16, 1924; s. Lynn O. and Bess (Crane) S.; student Grinnell Coll., 1941-42; B.S.C., U. Iowa, 1947; J.D., Harvard, 1950; m. Grace Irene Goodwin, Jan. 1, 1948; children—Daniel, Henry, Valerie, Audrey. Admitted to Iowa bar, 1950, D.C. bar, 1968; sr. partner Thoma, Schoenthal, Davis, Hockenberg & Wine, Des Moines, 1950-78, of counsel, 1978-79; lectr. labor law Drake U., Des Moines, 1958-60. Pres., Am. Family Forum, 1960-62, Greater Des Moines United Way, 1968, Iowa Children's Home Soc., 1961, U.S. Assn. for Children with Learning Disabilities, 1972; founder, pres. Iowa Assn. for Children with Learning Disabilities, 1968—. Served with USAAF, 1943-45. Mem. Iowa Civil Liberties Union (dir. 1955-72, vice chmn. 1960-64), UN Assn. (1st v.p. Iowa div. 1969), Am., Iowa bar assns., Indsl. Relations and Research Assn., Beta Sigma Rho, Order of Artus. Contbr. articles to profl. publs. Home: 5105 Waterbury Rd Des Moines IA 50312. *Whether you believe a challenge can be met or not—you are probably right.*

SCHOEP, ARTHUR PAUL, musician, educator; b. Orange City, Iowa, Dec. 13, 1920; s. Arie Anton and Lena (DeMey) S.; B.F.A. summa cum laude, U. S.D., 1942; Mus.M., performer's certificate in voice Eastman Sch. Music, 1944-46; student U. Amsterdam, 1950-51, Amsterdam Conservatory Music, 1950-51, Royal U. Utrecht (Netherlands), 1950-51; artist diploma New Eng. Conservatory Music, 1946-48; D.Mus. A. (Univ. fellow), U. Colo., 1962; m. Donna Mae Swainey, June 8, 1957; 1 son, Laurence Dale. Instr. North Tex. State Coll., 1948-50; head voice dept. Tyler (Tex.) Jr. Coll., 1951-53; mem. faculty opera dept. New Eng. Conservatory Music, 1955-58; asst. prof. U. Tenn., 1958-60; research fellow U. Colo., 1961-62; asso. prof. Colo. Woman's Coll., Denver, 1962-67; prof. music North Tex. State U., Denton, 1967—; artistic dir. Denver Lyric Theatre, 1961-67; stage dir. Omaha Civic Opera, 1965; asso. dir. Oglebay Inst. Opera Workshop, Wheeling, W.Va., 1954—; dir. voice and opera div. Centre Continuing Edn. Summer Sch. Arts, Elliott Lake, Ont., Can., 1966-76; adminstr., mem. faculty opera dept. Berkshire Music Center, Tanglewood, Lenox, Mass., 1955-61; leading roles in opera, U.S. and Europe, 1945—; founder, dir., adminstr., mem. faculty summer opera workshops throughout U.S. Served as 2d lt. USAR, 1942-44. Fulbright scholar, 1950-51. Mem. Nat. Assn. Tchrs. Singing, Am. Guild Mus. Artists, Nat. Opera Assn. (pres. 1972-73), Actors Equity, Phi Mu Alpha, Pi Kappa Lambda, Alpha Tau Omega. Co-author: Word by Word Translations of Songs and Arias, II-Italian, 1972; Bringing Soprano Arias to Life, 1973. Contbg. editor Opera Canada, 1975—. Contbr. articles to profl. jours. Home: 1705 Emery Dr Denton TX 76201. *My father, a humble Dutch immigrant baker whose formal education stopped at the age of thirteen, was a self-taught amateur musician who instilled in me the secure knowledge that music constantly challenged the intellect, deeply moved the emotions, and ennobled the soul of man. If I have succeeded in passing this philosophy on to others—to audiences as a performer, and to students as a teacher—then I will be satisfied that I have done my work well.*

SCHOETTGER, THEODORE LEO, city ofcl.; b. Burton, Nebr., Sept. 2, 1920; s. Frederick and Louise Cecelia (Gierau) S.; B.S. in Bus. Adminstrn. with Distinction, U. Nebr., 1948; m. Kathlyn Marguerite Hughey, June 3, 1943; children—Gregory Paul, Julie Anne. Sr. accountant Haskins & Sells, Los Angeles, 1948-55; controller Beckman Instruments, Inc., Fullerton, Calif., 1955-58, corporate chief accountant, 1958-60; treas. Documnun Inc., Los Angeles, 1960-77; fin. dir. City of Orange (Calif.), 1977—. Mem. finance com., treas., bd. dirs. Childrens Hosp. Served to lt. USNR, 1942-45. C.P.A., Calif. Mem. Calif. Soc. C.P.A.'s (nat. dir., v.p., past pres. Los Angeles chpt.), Fin. Execs. Inst., Municipal Fin. Officers Assn., Beta Gamma Sigma, Alpha Kappa Psi. Methodist. Clubs: Jonathan, Town Hall. Home: 9626 Shellyfield Rd Downey CA 90240 Office: 300 E Chapman Ave Orange CA 92666

SCHOFIELD, JACK H., bus. exec.; b. Charleston, W.Va., June 18, 1923; s. George H. and Ethyl M. (Farrell) S.; B.S. in Engring., George Washington U., 1951; grad. Advanced Mgmt. Program, Harvard U., 1964; m. Doris Jean Wagner, June 16, 1947; children—Jack H. II, Barbara Jean. Engr., York (Pa.) div. Borg Warner Corp., 1951-57; group v.p. U.S.M. Corp., Boston, 1957-68; gen. mgr. chain div. ACCO Co., York, 1969-71; exec. v.p. Loctite Corp., Newington, Conn., 1971—. Mem. Simsbury (Conn.) Republican Town Com.; 1st pres. Lower Naugatuck Valley C. of C., 1964-65; mem. Shelton (Conn.) Sch. Bd., 1964-65, Simsbury Water Pollution Control Authority. Served with USNR, 1942-44, U.S. Mcht. Marine, 1944-45, USMCR, 1946-48. Named Ky. col.; registered profl. engr., Pa. Methodist. Clubs: Capitol Hill, Rotary, Shriners. Office: 705 N Mountain Rd Newington CT 06111

SCHOFIELD, PAUL MICHAEL, fin. co. exec.; b. Wilmington, Del., Mar. 30, 1937; s. John Edward and Sabina A. (Clarke) S.; B.S., LaSalle Coll., Phila., 1960; postgrad. U. Del., 1963-64; m. Carol Ann Hane, July 11, 1964; children—Paul Michael, Andrew Clarke, Dennis Charles. With Sears Roebuck Acceptance Corp., Wilmington, 1961—, asst. v.p., 1973-74, treas., 1974—. Active local United Fund, Boys Club. Mem. Del. Fin. Assn. (treas. 1976). Democrat. Roman Catholic. Club: Irish Culture Del. (dir. 1977, 79). Home: 2014 Delaware Ave Wilmington DE 19806 Office: 1 Customs House Sq Wilmington DE 19899

SCHOFIELD, ROBERT EDWIN, educator; b. Milford, Neb., June 1, 1923; s. Charles Edwin and Nora May (Fullerton) S.; A.B., Princeton, 1944; M.S., U. Minn., 1948; Ph.D., Harvard, 1955; m. Mary-Peale Smith, June 20, 1959; 1 son, Charles Stockton Peale. Research asst. Fercleve Corp. and Clinton Labs., Oak Ridge, 1944-46; research asso. Knolls Atomic Power Lab., Gen. Electric Co., 1948-51; asst. prof., then asso. prof. history U. Kans., Lawrence, 1955-60; mem. faculty Case Western Res. U., Cleve., 1960-79, prof. history of sci., 1963-72, Lynn Thorndike prof. history of sci., 1972-79; prof. history Iowa State U., Ames, 1979—, dir. grad. program history tech. and sci., 1979—; mem. Inst. Advanced Study, 1967-68, 74-75; Sigma Xi nat. lectr., 1978-80. Served with AUS, 1945-46. Fulbright fellow, 1953-54; Guggenheim fellow, 1959-60, 67-68. Mem. Am. Phys. Soc., History of Sci. Soc., Soc. History Tech., Midwest Junto History of Sci., Royal Soc. Arts, Am. Soc. 18th Century Studies, Acad. Internat. d'Histoire des Scis. (corr.). Author: The Lunar Society of Birmingham, 1963; Scientific Autobiography of Joseph Priestley: Selected Scientific Correspondence, 1966; Mechanism and Materialism: British Natural Philosophy in an Age of Reason, 1970. Home: 3209 Woodland St Ames IA 50010 Office: Ross Hall Iowa State U Ames IA 50011

SCHOFIELD, WILLIAM, educator, psychologist; b. Springfield, Mass., Apr. 19, 1921; s. William and Angie Mae (St. John) S.; B.S., Springfield Coll., 1942; M.A., U. Minn., 1946, Ph.D., 1948; m. Geraldine Bryan, Jan. 11, 1946; children—Bryan St. John, Gwen Star. Instr., U. Minn., Mpls., 1947-48, asst. prof., 1948-51, asso. prof., 1951-59, prof. psychology, 1959—; vis. prof. U. Wash., 1960, U.

Colo., 1965. Cons. VA Hosp., Mpls., child study dept. Mpls. Pub. Schs.; examiner, instr. USCG Aux., 1968—; mem. adv. council VA, 1970-75. Mem. med. policy adv. com. Dept. Pub. Welfare Minn., 1960-68; mem. mental health services research rev. com. NIMH, 1969-73; bd. dirs. Profl. Exam. Service, 1976—. Served with USAAF, 1943-46. Diplomate Am. Bd. Profl. Psychology. Fellow Am. Psychol. Assn. (com. on health ins. 1968-71, membership com. 1968-71, sec.-treas. clin. div. 1969-72, chmn. task force on health research 1973-75, chmn. sect. health research div. psychologists in pub. service 1977); mem. Midwestern, Minn. (chmn. ethics com.) psychol. assns., AAAS, AAUP, Assn. Am. Med. Colls. (chmn. com. on measurement of personality 1970-74), Sigma Xi, Pi Gamma Mu. Club: St. Croix Yacht. Author: Psychotherapy: The Purchase of Friendship, 1964. Contbr. articles to profl. jours. Home: 1441 E River Rd Minneapolis MN 55414 Office: Box 393 University Hosps Minneapolis MN 55455

SCHOGGEN, PHIL (HOWARD), psychologist; b. Tulsa, Aug. 28, 1923; s. Walter B. and Emma F. S.; A.B. in Psychology, Park Coll., 1946; M.S., U. Kans., Lawrence, 1951, Ph.D. in Psychology, 1954; m. Maxine F. Spoor, June 28, 1944; children—Leida, Christopher, Ann, Susan. Asst. prof. psychology U. Oreg., 1957-62, asso. prof., 1962-66; prof., chmn. dept. psychology George Peabody Coll., 1966-75; prof. York U., Toronto, Ont., Can., 1975-77; prof. human devel. and family studies, chmn. dept. N.Y. State Coll. Human Ecology, Cornell U., 1977—. Served with USNR, 1944-46, 50-51. Mem. Am. Psychol. Assn., Soc. Research in Child Devel., AAAS, Sigma Xi. Author: (with R. G. Barker) Qualities of Community Life, 1973. Office: Dept Human Devel and Family Studies Cornell U Ithaca NY 14853

SCHOGT, HENRY GILIUS, educator; b. Amsterdam, Netherlands, May 24, 1927; s. Johannes Herman and Ida Jacoba (Van Rijn) S.; B.A. in French, U. Amsterdam, 1947, B.A. in Russian, 1948, M.A. in Russian, 1951, M.A. cum laude in French, 1952; m. Corrie Frenkel, Apr. 2, 1955; children—Barbara, Philibert Johannes, Elida. Docent Russian, U. Groningen (Netherlands) 1953-63; sr. lectr. French, U. Utrecht (Netherlands), 1954-63; master asst. gen. linguistics U. Paris, 1963-64; vis. lectr. Russian and French, Princeton U., 1964-66; prof. French and linguistics U. Toronto (Ont., Can.), 1966—. Fellow Royal Soc. Can.; mem. Société de linguitique de Paris, Can. Linguistic Assn. Author books including: Les causes de la double issue de e fermé tonique libre en français, 1960; Le système verbal du français contemporain, 1968; Sémantique synchronique, synonymie, homonymie, polysémie, 1976; (with Pierre Léon and Edward Burstynsky) La phonologie, 1977. Home: 47 Turner Rd Toronto ON M6G 3H7 Canada Office: Dept French Univ Toronto Toronto ON M5S 1A1 Canada. *My ideas and goals in life are closely connected with the ideals of a socialist system of distribution of wealth and of individual responsibility towards one's fellow human beings and towards society.*

SCHOLANDER, PER FREDRIK, physiologist, educator; b. Orebro, Sweden, Nov. 29, 1905; s. Torkel F. and Agnethe (Faye-Hansen) S.; M.D., U. Oslo, 1932, Ph.D., 1934; D.Sc., U. Alaska, 1973, U. Uppsala, 1977; m. Susan Irving, June 20, 1951. Came to U.S., 1939, naturalized, 1945. Research fellow physiology U. Oslo, 1932-39; research asso. zoology Swarthmore Coll., 1939-43, research biologist, 1946-49; research fellow biol. chemistry Harvard Med. Sch., 1949-51; physiologist Woods Hole Oceanographic Inst., 1952-55; prof. physiology, dir. Inst. Zoophysiology, U. Oslo, 1955-58; prof. physiology Scripps Instn. Oceanography, U. Calif., 1958—, dir. Physiol. Research Lab., 1963-70; research asso. in zoology U. Wash., Seattle, 1972—; Harvey lectr., 1962, NIH lectr., 1972. Served to maj. USAAF, 1943-46. Decorated Legion of Merit, Soldier's medal; recipient Nansen prize, Oslo, 1979; Rockefeller fellow, 1939-41; John Simon Guggenheim fellow, 1969. Mem. Nat., Norwegian, Royal Swedish acads. scis., Am. Philos. Soc., Am. Acad. Arts and Scis., Arctic Inst. N.Am., Am. Physiol. Soc., Marine Biol. Lab. Assn., AAAS, Soc. Gen. Physiologists, Sigma Xi. Clubs: Cosmos (Washington); Explorers (N.Y.C.). Author: (with others) Osmosis and Tensile Solvent, 1976. Home: 8374 Paseo del Ocaso La Jolla CA 92037 also 5508 NE 180th St Seattle WA 98155

SCHOLDER, FRITZ, artist; b. Breckenridge, Minn., Oct. 6, 1937; s. Fritz William and Ella Mae (Haney) S.; student Wis. State Coll., 1956-57; A.A., Sacramento City Coll., 1958; B.A., Sacramento State Coll., 1960; M.F.A., U. Ariz.; m. Peggy Stephenson, June 28, 1958 (div. Mar. 1966); 1 son, Fritz VI; m. 2d, Romona Attenberger, July 30, 1966. Exhibited one man shows: Crocker Art Gallery, Sacramento, 1959, Coll. Santa Fe, 1967, Roswell (N.Mex.) Art Center, 1969, Esther Bear Gallery, Santa Barbara, Calif., 1971, Tally Richards Gallery Contemporary Art, Taos, N.Mex., 1971, 73, 75, 78, 79, Elaine Horwitch Gallery, Scottsdale, Ariz., 1972-79, St. John's Coll., Santa Fe, 1972, Cordier & Ekstrom, N.Y.C., 1972, 74, 76, 78, Gimpel & Weitzenhoffer, N.Y.C., 1977, Graphics 1 and 2, Boston, 1977, Smith Andersen Gallery, Palo Alto, Calif., 1979; group shows: Carnegie Art Inst., Butler Inst. Am. Art, Calif. Palace of Legion of Honor, Houston Mus. Fine Arts, Dallas Mus. Fine Arts, San Francisco Mus. Art, Denver Art Mus., Fort Worth Art Center, Basel Art 5, Linden Mus., Stuttgart, Philbrook Art Center, Oakland Art Mus., Tucson Art Center, N.Mex. Art Mus., Edinburgh Art Festival, Museo de Bellas Artes, Buenos Aires, Biblioteca Nacional, Santiago, Chile, Mus. voor Land-en-Volkenkunder, Rotterdam, Amerika Haus, Berlin Festival, Center for Arts of Indian Am., Washington, Yellowstone Art Center, Nat. Mus. Modern Art, Tokyo, Nat. Mus. Modern Art, Kyoto, Japan, also other fgn. and Am. shows; Smithsonian tour Bucharest, Berlin, London, Ankara, Madrid, Belgrade, Athens, 1972-73; represented in permanent collections: Mus. Modern Art, N.Y.C., Art Inst. Chgo., Center Culturel Americain, Paris, Art Gallery Toronto, NEA, Houston Mus. Fine Arts, Boston Fine Arts Mus., Milw. Art Mus., Portland (Oreg.) Art Mus., Dallas Mus. Fine Arts, Bur. Indian Affairs, Mus. N.Mex., Smithsonian Instn., Bklyn. Mus., Phoenix Art Mus., San Diego Fine Arts Gallery, Okla. Art Center, Brigham Young U., Heard Mus., Phoenix, Bibliotheque Nat., Paris, San Francisco Mus. Art, others; teaching asst. art Univ. Ariz. 1962-64; instr. art history, advanced painting Inst. Am. Indian Arts, 1964-69; artist in residence Dartmouth Coll., 1973. Recipient Ford Found. Purchase award, 1962; 1st prize W.Va. Centennial Exhibition, 1963; purchase prize 13th S.W. Print Drawing Show, 1963; John Hay Whitney fellow, 1962-63; Hallmark purchase award, 1965; 1st prize Scottsdale Indian Nat., 1966; Grand prize Washington Biennial Indian Show, 1967; Grand prize Scottsdale Indian Nat., 1969; jurors award S.W. Fine Arts Biennial, 1970, 71, 72; prize in painting Am. Acad. and Inst. Arts and Letters, 1977. Included in Politics in Art; American Indian Painters; Indian Voices; Indians Today, Indian Painters and White Patrons; The Vincent Price Treasury of American Art; Scholder/Indians; The World of the American Indian; Kein Platz für Wilde Menschen, Art and Indian Individuals, Fritz Scholder Lithographs; Song from the Earth; Anpao; An American Indian Odyssey; Ency. of Artists of the American West; Many Smokes, Many Moons; Weg ohne Mokassins; Indian Kitsch: Photographs by Fritz Scholder. Subject of PBS film Fritz Scholder, 1976. Home: Galisteo NM 87540 also 118 Cattletrack Rd Scottsdale AZ 85251. *I Believe in Art, Love, and Magic.*

SCHOLER, WALTER, JR., architect; b. Indpls., Apr. 11, 1915; s. Walter and Alice (Caster) S.; B.S. in Civil Engring., Purdue U., 1937; m. Mary P. Bass, Oct. 26, 1952; 1 dau., Susan. With Walter Scholer, architect, Lafayette, Ind., 1937-41; partner Walter Scholer & Assos., architects, Lafayette, 1945-63, pres., 1963—; dir. Purdue Nat. Bank, Lafayette. Mem. Ind. Bd. Registration for Architects, 1969-78, chmn., 1971, 73. Mem. lay adv. bd. St. Elizabeth Hosp., Lafayette, 1959-72; mem. Tippecanoe Area Plan Commn. Lafayette, 1968-74, pres. 1973-74. Served to maj. AUS, 1941-45. Fellow AIA (dir. 1964-67), Ind. Soc. Architects (pres. 1962-63). Prin. works include bldgs. at Purdue U., Lafayette, Ball State U., Muncie, Wabash Coll., Crawfordsville, Franklin Coll. (all Ind.). Home: PO Box 808 1908 Sweetbriar Ct Lafayette IN 47905 Office: US Hwy 231 South in Wea-Ton PO Box 808 Lafayette IN 47902. *My life has been devoted to architecture and improving architectural services. Architects begin by committing themselves to total involvement with their clients. A stimulating inter-action of ideas is established, and we respond to the clients' challenges of our creative skills and imagination.*

SCHOLES, SAMUEL RAY, JR., educator, chemist; b. Pitts., June 5, 1915; s. Samuel Ray and Lois E. (Boren) S.; B.S., Alfred U., 1937; Ph.D., Yale, 1940; m. Doris Emily Hann, Oct. 28, 1944; children—Susan, Jean Ann. Mem. faculty Alfred (N.Y.) U., 1940-41, 46—, prof. Chemistry, 1958—, chmn. dept., 1958-70; mem. faculty Tufts Coll., Medford, Mass., 1941-46. Mem. Am. Chem. Soc., Am. Assn. U. Profs., Sigma Xi. Research in determined dissociation constants for bicarbonate ions at temperatures from 0 deg. to 55 deg. C using reversible cells. Home: 45 W University St Alfred NY 14802

SCHOLTES, ROBERT MARTIN, civil engr.; educator; b. Biloxi, Miss., May 28, 1928; s. Leo Martin and Marguerite (Stroeker) S.; B.S., Miss. State U., 1951, M.S., 1956; Ph.D., Ga. Inst. Tech., 1964; m. Hilda L. Beck, Jan. 1, 1954; children—Sharon Rae, Cynthia Joan, Sandra Ann, Robert Beck. Mem. faculty Miss State U., State Coll., 1951—, prof. civil engring., 1963—, head dept. 1966—; cons. engr., 1956—. Registered profl. engr., Miss. Mem. Nat., Miss. socs. profl. engrs., Am. Soc. Engring. Edn., Am. Soc. C.E., Sigma Xi, Phi Kappa Phi. Chi Epsilon, Tau Beta Pi. Presbyn. Home: 108 Briarwood Dr Starkville MS 39759 Office: Drawer CE Mississippi State MS 39762

SCHOLTZ, ELIZABETH, bot. garden adminstr.; b. Pretoria, South Africa, Apr. 29, 1921; d. Tielman Johannes and Vera Vogel (Roux) Roos-Scholtz; B.Sc., Witwatersrand U., 1941; D.H.L., Pace U., 1974. Came to U.S., 1960, naturalized, 1978. Technician, South African Inst. Med. Research, Johannesburg, 1942-44; technician dept. medicine, Johannesburg and Pretoria gen. hosps., 1944-46; with Groote Schuur Hosp., Capetown, as technician charge student labs., 1948-52, technician charge hematology lab., 1952-60; mem. staff Bklyn. Bot. Garden, 1960—, asso. curator instrn., 1964-71, acting dir., 1972-73, dir., 1973—; trustee Independence Savs. Bank. Bd. dirs. Bklyn. Ednl. and Cultural Alliance. Fellow Yamins Blood Lab., Harvard, 1957-58. Mem. Am. Hort. Soc., Am. Assn. Bot. Gardens and Arboreta (dir. 1976-79), Am. Bonsai Soc. (dir. 1972-79). Clubs: Brooklyn Heights Casino, Cosmopolitan. Home: 115 Henry St Brooklyn NY 11201 Office: 1000 Washington Ave Brooklyn NY 11225

SCHOLZ, CHRISTOPHER HENRY, seismologist; b. Pasadena, Calif., Feb. 25, 1943; s. Joseph George and Elizabeth (Ochsner) S.; B.S., U. Nev., 1964; Ph.D., M.I.T., 1967; m. Paula Hanna, May 19, 1962; children—Erich Frederich, Adrienne Louise. Research fellow Calif. Inst. Tech., Pasadena, 1967-68; research asso. Lamont-Doherty Geol. Obs., Columbia U., N.Y.C., 1968-70, sr. research asso., 1970—, asso. prof. geology, 1971-75, prof., 1975—. A.P. Sloan fellow, 1975-77. Mem. Am. Geophys. Union, Seismol. Soc. Am. Contbr. articles on earthquakes, deformation of the earth, mech. properties of rock to profl. jours. Office: Lamont-Doherty Geol Obs Palisades NY 10964

SCHOMAKER, VERNER, chemist; b. Nehawka, Nebr., June 22, 1914; s. Edwin Henry and Anna (Heesch) S.; B.S., U. Nebr., 1934, M.S., 1935; Ph.D., Calif. Inst. Tech., 1938; m. Judith Rooke, Sept. 9, 1944; children—David Rooke, Eric Alan, Peter Edwin. George Ellery Hale fellow Calif., Inst. Tech., Pasadena, 1938-40, sr. fellow in chem. research, 1940-45, asst. prof., 1945-46, asso. prof., 1946-50, prof. chemistry, 1950-58; with Union Carbide Research Inst., 1958-65, asst. dir., 1959-63, asso. dir., 1963-65; prof. chemistry U. Wash., Seattle, 1965—, chmn. dept., 1965-70. John Simon Guggenheim Meml. Found. fellow, 1947-48. Recipient Am. Chem. Soc. award in pure chemistry, 1950. Fellow AAAS, N.Y. Acad. Scis.; mem. Am. Chem. Soc., Am. Crystallographic Assn. (pres. 1961-62), Sigma Xi, Phi Lambda Upsilon, Pi Mu Epsilon, Sigma Tau, Alpha Chi Sigma. Contbr. articles on molecular structure to chem. jours. Home: 13224 42d Ave NE Seattle WA 98125

SCHOMER, HOWARD, clergyman, ch. exec.; b. Chgo., June 9, 1915; s. Frank Michael and Daisy (Aline) S.; B.S. summa cum laude, Harvard, 1937, postgrad. 1939-40; student Chgo. Theol. Sem., 1938-39, 40-41, D.D., 1954; LL.D., Olivet Coll., 1966; m. Elsie Pauline Swenson, Mar. 23, 1942; children—Karine, Mark, Paul, Ellen. Ordained to ministry United Ch. of Christ, 1941; student pastor, Fitzwilliam, N.H., Oak Park, Ill.; asst. dean U. Chgo. Chapel.; counsellor Am. history Harvard; civilian pub. service Am. Friends Service Com., 1940-45; Am. Bd. Mission fellow to churches of Europe, le Chambon-sur-Lignon, France, 1946-55; history tchr., work camp dir. Coll. Cevenol, founder internat. conf. center Accueil Fraternel, Permanent Conf. Protestant Chs. in Latin Countries of Europe; asst. to rapporteur UN Commn. on Human Rights, also to pres. UN Econ. and Social Council, 1947-48; inter-church aid sec. for Europe, World Council Chs., Geneva, Switzerland, 1955-58; pres., prof. ch. history Chgo. Theol. Sem., 1959-66; exec. dir. dept. specialized ministries Div. Overseas Ministries, Nat. Council Chs., N.Y.C., 1967-70; world issues sec. United Ch. Bd. World Ministries, 1971—; Indochina liaison officer World Council of Chs., 1970-71; United Ch. of Christ officer for social responsibility in investments, 1972—. Pres., Internat. Fellowship of Reconciliation, 1959-63, v.p., 1963-65; participant 1st-3d assemblies World Council Chs., Amsterdam, 1948, Evanston, 1954, New Delhi, 1961; delegated observer Vatican Council II, 1963; treas. Am. Friends Coll. Cevenol.; mem. exec. com. Interfaith Center for Corp. Responsibility, 1973—; chmn. exec. com. Freedom of Faith - A Christian Com. for Religious Rights, 1978—. Past co-chmn. Chgo. Com. for Sane Nuclear Policy; bd. dirs. World Conf. on Religion and Peace, 1974—; former trustee Am. Waldensian Aid Soc. Mem. Wider Quaker Fellowship, Fellowship Reconciliation, Am. Civil Liberties Union, Phi Beta Kappa. Club: Harvard (N.Y.C.). Translator: The Prayer of the Church Universal (Marc Boegner), 1954. Editor: The Oppression of Protestants in Spain, 1955; The Role of Transnational Business in Mass Economic Development, 1975. editor-at-large Christian Century, 1959-70. Contbr. articles to religious and interdisciplinary publs. Home: 13 Fairmount Upper Montclair NJ 07043 Office: 475 Riverside Dr New York NY 10027

SCHÖN, DONALD ALAN, educator; b. Boston, Sept. 19, 1930; s. Marcus David Henry and Ann (Mason) S.; student Conservatoire Nationale de Paris, 1950; B.A., Yale U., 1951; M.A. (Woodrow Wilson fellow), Harvard U., 1952, Ph.D. in Philosophy, 1955; m. Dec. 20, 1952; children—Ellen, Andrew, Elizabeth, Susan. Sr. staff mem. Arthur D. Little, Inc., Cambridge, Mass., 1957-63; dir. Inst. for Applied Tech., Nat. Bur. Standards, Washington, 1963-66; pres. Orgn. for Social and Tech. Innovation, Cambridge, 1966-72; Ford prof. urban studies and planning, div. for ednl. research M.I.T., 1972—; bd. dirs. Ednl. Devel. Center, Newton, Mass., Community Systems Found., Ann Arbor, Mich.; Reith lectr. BBC, Eng., 1970; Cecil Green disting. vis. prof. U. B.C. (Can.), 1979. Served with U.S. Army, 1955-57. Recipient 1st prize Conservatoire Nationale de Paris, 1950. Mem. Commn. on Sociotech. Systems, Nat. Acad. Scis. Jewish. Author books, including: (with Chris Argyris) Theory In Practice, 1974, Organizational Learning, 1978; contbr. numerous articles to profl. jours. Office: MIT Bldg 9 Room 517 Cambridge MA 02138

SCHONBERG, HAROLD C., music critic, columnist; b. N.Y.C., Nov. 29, 1915; s. David and Minnie (Kirsch) S.; A.B. cum laude, Bklyn. Coll., 1937; A.M., N.Y. U., 1938; Litt.D., Temple U., 1964; L.H.D., Grinnell Coll., 1967; m. Rosalyn Krokover, Nov. 28, 1942; m. 2d, Helene Cornell, May 10, 1975. Asso. editor Am. Music Lover, 1939-41; contbr. editor Mus. Digest, 1946-48; music critic N.Y. Sun, 1946-50; contbg. editor, record columnist Mus. Courier, 1948-52; music and record critic N.Y. Times, 1950-60, sr. music critic, 1960-; columnist on The Gramophone of London, 1948-60; illustrator of his own articles with caricatures. Served as 1st lt. Airborne Signal Corps, AUS, 1942-46. Recipient Pulitzer prize for criticism, 1971. Clubs: Manhattan Chess; Century Assn. Author: The Guide to Long-Playing Records; Chamber and Solo Instrument Music, 1955; The Collector's Chopin and Schumann, 1959; The Great Pianists, 1963; The Great Conductors, 1967; Lives of The Great Composers, 1970; Grandmasters of Chess, 1973. Contbg. editor Internat. Cyclopedia of Music and Musicians. Home: 118 Riverside Dr New York NY 10024 Office: New York Times Times Square New York NY 10036

SCHONFELD, FABIAN, rabbi; b. Poland, Dec. 14, 1923; s. Samuel and Manja (Oksenhendler) S.; came to U.S., 1950; naturalized, 1955; B.A., U. London, 1945; grad. Yeshiva U., 1952; m. Charlotte Jakobovits, 1944 (dec. Aug. 1959); m. 2d, Ruth Leifer, Nov. 7, 1961; several children. Ordained rabbi, 1952; rabbi Young Israel Synagogue Kew Gardens, Flushing, N.Y., 1951—; lectr. Judaic studies Yeshiva U., 1970—; mem. bds. edn. Jewish day schs. Recipient awards United Jewish Appeal, 1958, Fedn. Jewish Philanthropy, 1969. Mem. Rabbinical Council Am. (past pres.), Rabbinic Alumni Yeshiva U., Council Young Israel Rabbis, Queens Rabbinical Assn. Democrat. Contbr. articles to religious jours. Home: 70-41 153d St Flushing NY 11367 Office: 150-05 70 Rd Flushing NY 11361

SCHONK, ROBERT MARTIN, banker; b. Norfolk, Va., May 13, 1925; s. Martin Luther and Marie Elizabeth (Hardee) S.; B.S. in Econs., U. Pa., 1949, M.B.A., 1950; grad. Stonier Grad. Sch. Banking, Rutgers U., 1960; m. Jean Bolling White, July 17, 1948; children—Robert Martin, Stuart Randolph, John Bolling, Rebecca Meade. Staff accountant Waller & Woodhouse, Norfolk, Va., 1950-52, Paul E. Cofer, Norfolk, 1952; with Va. Nat. Bank, Norfolk, 1952—, sr. v.p., 1961-70, corp. exec. officer, 1970—; treas. Va. Nat. Bankshares, Inc., 1971—; mem. faculty Va.-Md. Bankers Sch., Inst. Mgmt., Old Dominion U., 1965-71. Treas. Feldman Chamber Music Soc., 1962-77; bd. dirs. Hosp. Data Center Va., 1966-74; chmn. rate rev. bd. Va. Hosp. Assn., 1973-75; chmn. bd. Norfolk United Communities Fund, 1976-77, mem. exec. com., 1975-78; bd. dirs. Eastern Va. Health System Agy., 1977—. Served with USAAF, 1943-45. Mem. Bank Adminstrn. Inst., Va. Bankers Assn., Am. Inst. C.P.A.'s. Episcopalian. Club: Harbor (Norfolk). Home: 7410 Shirland Ave Norfolk VA 23505 Office: 1 Commercial Pl Norfolk VA 23510

SCHONWALD, GARY ALAN, lawyer; b. Elizabeth, N.J., Mar. 28, 1942; s. Walter and Helen (Hirschmann) S.; A.B., Columbia U., 1964, J.D., 1967; m. Elizabeth Bernstein, July 3, 1966; children—Matthew H., Carrie L. Admitted to N.Y. bar, 1967, since practiced in N.Y.C.; partner firm Law Offices of Gary A. Schonwald, 1978—; sec. Gen. Felt Industries, Inc., Clarkson Labs., Inc., Michaele Vollbracht and Co. Ltd.; asst. sec. Knoll Internat., Inc. Mem. Am., N.Y. State, Fla., N.Y.C. bar assns., Ferrari Club Am., Vintage Sports Car Club, Ltd. Democrat. Jewish. Home: 250 Cabrini Blvd New York City NY 10033 Office: 919 3d Ave 11th Floor New York NY 10022

SCHOOLAR, JOSEPH CLAYTON, pharmacologist, psychiatrist; b. Marks, Miss., Feb. 28, 1928; s. Adrien Taylor and Leah (Covington) S.; A.B. (Univ. Faculty scholar), U. Tenn., 1950, M.S., 1952; Ph.D. (Merck scholar), U. Chgo. 1957, M.D. (Merck scholar), 1960; m. Betty Peck, Nov. 2, 1960; children—Johnathan Covington, Cynthia Jane, Geoffrey Michael, Catherine Elizabeth, Adrian Carson. Chief sect. drug abuse research Tex. Research Inst. Mental Scis., Houston, 1966-72, chief div. clin. research, 1967-69, chief clin. and sociol. research div., 1969-72, asst. dir. inst., 1968-72, dir., 1972—; prof. pharmacology Baylor Coll. Medicine, 1974—, prof. psychiatry, 1975—; chmn. central office research rev. com. Tex. Dept. Mental Health and Mental Retardation, 1975—; mem. drug abuse tng. rev. com. Nat. Inst. Drug Abuse, HEW, 1974-79. Recipient Eugen Kahn award Baylor Coll. Medicine, 1963. Diplomate Am. Bd. Psychiatry and Neurology. Fellow Am. Psychiat. Assn., Am. Coll. Psychiatrists; mem. Am. Soc. Clin. Pharmacology and Therapeutics, Am. Coll. Neuropsychopharmacology, Soc. Neurosci., Am. Acad. Clin. Toxicology, Internat. Council on Alcohol and Addictions, AAAS, Tex. Med. Assn. (chmn. spl. com. on alcoholism and drug abuse 1976—), Sigma Xi. Episcopalian. Editor: (with C.M. Gaitz) Research and the Psychiatric Patient, 1975; (with J.L. Claghorn) The Kinetics of Psychiatric Drugs, 1979. Home: 222 Sunset Blvd Houston TX 77005 Office: 1300 Moursund Ave Houston TX 77030*

SCHOOLEY, ALLEN HEATEN, govt. scientist; b. Terril, Iowa, Dec. 16, 1909; s. Alfred Heaten and Bertha Hope (Allen) S., B.S. in Elec. Engring., Iowa State U., 1931; M.S. in Elec. Engring., Purdue U., 1932, D.Eng., 1966; m. Meriel Mercedes Vestrem, Sept. 10, 1938; children—Robert Allen, Jean (Mrs. S.W. Freeman), Mary Elena. Electronic engr. RCA, 1936-40; with U.S. Naval Research Lab., 1940—, supt. electronics div., 1954-56, asso. dir. research 1957-67, sr. research scientist, 1967—; resident adviser to Brazilian Navy, Rio de Janeiro, 1956-57; research scientist NATO Anti-Submarine Submarine Warfare Research Center, La Spezia, Italy, 1963-65; lectr. Geophysical Inst., U. Bergen (Norway), 1965. Mem. U.S. Navy Undersea Warfare Research and Devel. Planning Council, 1959-63, U.S. nat. com. Union Radio Sci. Internat., 1958-78. Decorated Knight Ordem do Merito Naval (Brazil); recipient Distinguished Civilian Service award U.S. Navy, 1946; Marston Gold medal Ia. State U., 1974, Profl. Achievement Citation, 1969; Honor Iowan award Buena Vista Coll., 1966. Registered profl. engr., D.C. Fellow IEEE (Harry Diamond Meml. prize 1963, Distinguished Service award Washington sect. 1963; chmn. Washington sect. 1957-58), AAAS, Washington Acad. Scis.; mem. Am. Meteorol. Soc., Internat. Assn. Phys. Scis. Ocean; Marine Tech. Soc., Internat. Oceanographic Found., Am. Geophys. Union, Sci. Research Soc. Am., Am. Inst. Physics, Washington Philos. Soc., Armed Forces Electronics and Communications Assn., Sci. Research Soc. Am. (Applied Sci. award 1971), Am. Assn. Physics Tchrs., U.S. Naval Inst., Sigma Xi, Phi Kappa Phi, Theta Xi. Contbr. articles on interdisciplinary fields electronics, optics, oceanography, fluid dynamics, research mgmt. to profl. jours. Patentee in field. Home: 6113 Cloud Dr Springfield VA 22150 Office: US Naval Research Lab Washington DC 20375

SCHOOLEY, CHARLES EARL, cons.; b. Archie, Mo., Sept. 18, 1905; s. Charles Elias and Virginia Maria (Bone) S.; B.S. in Elec. Engring., U. Mo., 1928; m. Dorothy S. Alexander, Apr. 29, 1934 (dec. 1965); 1 dau., Dorothy Virginia; m. Dolores Harter, Apr. 1966. With Ozark Utilities Co., Bolivar Telephone Co., Mo. Pacific R.R.; transmission engr. long lines dept. Am. Tel. & Tel. Co., St. Louis, Kansas City, N.Y.C., 1927-44, co-axial carrier engr., elec. coordination engr., N.Y.C., 1944-48, div. engr., Washington, 1948-49, facility engr., engr. transmission, comml. devel. engr., 1949-51, toll dialing engr., plant extension engr., system planning engr., operating and engring. dep., 1951-53, asst. chief engr., dir. customer products planning, 1956-57; chief engr. So. Bell Tel. & Tel. Co., Atlanta, 1953-55; v.p. operations, dir. Ind. bell Telephone Co., Indpls., 1958-59; dir. operations, mem. bd. long lines dept., Am. Tel. & Tel. Co., N.Y., 1959-66; dir., v.p. Transpacific Communications Co., Transocean Cable Ship Co., Eastern Tel. & Tel. Co., 1960-66; v.p., treas., dir. Eds, Inc., Sharon, Conn., 1970—. Recipient Disting. Service to Engring. medal U. Mo., 1960; registered profl. engr., Ga. Fellow IEEE; mem. Ga. Engring. Soc., Delta Upsilon (bd. dirs. 1962-70), Eta Kappa Nu. Club: Sharon Country. Address: Wingspread Sharon CT 06069

SCHOOLEY, ELMER WAYNE, artist, educator; b. Lawrence, Kans., Feb. 20, 1916; s. Sparks Sylvester and Nella (Winey) S.; B.F.A., U. Colo., 1938; M.A., State U. Iowa, 1942; m. Gertrude Lucille Rogers, Sept. 2, 1942; children—David, Edwin, John, Theodore. Grade sch. tchr., Lafayette, Colo., 1940-41; instr. N.Mex. State Tchrs. Coll., Silver City, 1946-47; prof. dept. arts and crafts N.Mex. Highlands U., Las Vegas, 1947-77; paintings represented in permanent collections U. Okla. Art Mus., Mus. N.Mex., Roswell (N.Mex.) Mus., Hallmark Collection, Kansas City (Mo.) Mus. Modern Art; print rep. permanent collections Met. Mus., Bklyn. Art Mus., Library of Congress, Dallas Art Mus., Wichita Art Assn., Mus. N.Mex. Served to capt. AUS, 1942-46. Democrat. Mem. Soc. of Friends. Home: Route 1 Box 245 Roswell NM 88201. *I'd rather be here than somewhere else.*

SCHOON, RICHARD GEORGE, assn. exec.; b. Fonda, Iowa, Oct. 15, 1932; s. George Rolf and Anna Schoon; B.A., Buena Vista Coll., 1955; m. Catherine R. Karr, Aug. 3, 1952; children—Richard J., Stephanie C. Coach, tchr., 1955-59; C. of C. exec., Bemidji, Minn., Aberdeen, S.D., Missoula, Mont., Duluth, Minn. and St. Louis, 1959-73, chief exec. officer Greater Providence C. of C., 1973—; trustee, officer R.I. Credit Bur., 1974—. Treas., Providence Found., 1974—, Providence Conv. and Visitors Bur., 1975—; bd. dirs. Opportunities Industrialization Center, 1975—, Scandanavian Home for Aged, 1978—. Mem. Am. C. of C. Execs. (vice chmn. bd. 1978, chmn. mgmt. standards task force 1977). Republican. Lutheran. Home: 385 Country View Dr Warwick RI 02886 Office: Greater Providence C of C 10 Dorrance St Providence RI 02903

SCHOONOVER, JEAN WAY, pub. relations counselor; b. Richfield Springs, N.Y., Sept. 22, 1920; d. Walter Denslow and Hilda (Greenawalt) Way; A.B., Cornell U., 1941; student N.Y. State U. Library Sch., Albany, 1941-42; m. Raymond E. Schoonover, Oct. 28, 1950; children—Katherine Way, Charles Daniel, James Alan. Tchr. English, librarian Castleton High Sch., Castleton-on-Hudson, N.Y., 1941-43; reporter Food Field Reporter, N.Y.C., 1944-46, news editor, 1948-49; with Dudley-Anderson-Yutzy Pub. Relations, Inc., and predecessor, N.Y.C., 1949—, pres., 1970—; mem. com. bds. Better Bus. Bur. N.Y.C., Universidad Boricua; mem. program com., panel moderator 7th Pub. Relations World Congress, Boston, 1976; exec. com. Public Relations Seminar. Trustee, Cornell U., and exec. com. Cornell U. Alumni Council; bd. dirs. Am. Nat. Metric Council. Named Advt. Woman of Year, Am. Advt. Fedn., 1972; recipient Matrix award N.Y. Women in Communications, 1976. Mem. Women Execs. in Pub. Relations N.Y.C. (pres.-elect), Advt. Women N.Y., Am., N.Y. (pres.) pub. relations socs. Home: 25 Stuyvesant St New York NY 10003 Office: 40 W 57th St New York NY 10019

SCHOPF, JAMES WILLIAM, paleobiologist, educator; b. Urbana, Ill., Sept. 27, 1941; s. James Morton and Esther Julie (Nissen) S.; A.B., with high honors, Oberlin Coll., 1963; A.M., Harvard U., 1965, Ph.D. (Harvard fellow, NSF fellow), 1968; m. Julie Morgan, Aug. 7, 1965; 1 son, James Christopher. Research chemist NASA, Ames Research Center, Calif., 1967, mem. lunar sample preliminary exam. team Manned Spacecraft Center, Tex., 1968-71; asst. prof. dept. geology U. Calif., Los Angeles, 1968-70, asso. prof., 1970-73, prof., 1973—, mem. Inst. Evolutionary and Environ. Biology, 1970—, mem. Inst. Geophysics and Planetary Physics, 1973—; vis. lectr. Am. Inst. Biol. Scis. Vis. Biologists Program, 1969-72. Bd. dirs. Brentwood Glen (Calif.) Assn., 1972—. Recipient N.Y. Bot. Garden award Bot. Soc. Am., 1966, Group Achievement award NASA, 1969, Outstanding Paper award Jour. Paleontology, 1971, Charles Schuchert award Paleontol. Soc., 1974; John Simon Guggenheim fellow, 1973; U.S. Nat. Acad. Scis. exchange scientist USSR, 1975. Mem. numerous sci. assns. Contbr. articles to profl. jours.; mem. editorial bd. Origins of Life, 1973—, Precambrian Research, 1973—, Evolutionary Theory, 1973—, U. Calif. Press, 1973—, Paleobiology, 1974—. Home: 11433 Chenault St Los Angeles CA 90049 Office: Dept of Geology U of Calif Los Angeles CA 90024

SCHOPLER, ERIC, educator, psychologist; b. Furth, Germany, Feb. 8, 1927; s. Ernest H. and Erna (Oppenheimer) S.; came to U.S., 1938, naturalized, 1943; A.B., U. Chgo., 1949, M.A. (USPHS fellow), 1955, Ph.D. (NIMH fellow), 1964; children by previous marriage—Susan, Robert, Thomas; m. 2d, Margaret B. Dunham, Apr. 8, 1972. Research asso. Treatment and Research Center for Childhood Schizophrenia, Chgo., 1960-64; prof. psychology, dir. research devel., child research project Sch. Medicine, U. N.C., Chapel Hill, 1964—, dir. childhood psychosis project; dir. N.C. Ednl. Program for Autistic Children. Served with AUS, 1945-47. Recipient Gold Achievement award Am. Psychiat. Assn. Mem. Nat. Soc. for Autistic Children (chmn. profl. adv. bd. 1972-75). Editor Jour. of Autism and Developmental Disorders; mem. editorial bd. Schizophrenia Bull. Home: Route 1 Box 182B Chapel Hill NC 27514

SCHOR, MANNY, marketing and distbn. co. exec.; b. Cleve., Dec. 9, 1918; s. William and Rebecca (Wallack) S.; B.Sc. in Journalism, Ohio State U., 1940; M.A., U. Minn., 1948; m. Marjorie Lewis, Feb. 18, 1943; children—Edward L., Jo A., Matthew D. Reporter, Cleve. Press, 1940-46; instr. Sch. Journalism, Ohio State U., 1947-49; with Curtis Industries, Inc., Eastlake, Ohio, 1950-75, pres., 1965-75; pres., chief exec. officer Curtis Noll Corp., Eastlake, 1975-78, chief exec. officer, 1978—, also dir.; v.p. Congoleum Corp., 1978—. Served with USAAF, 1941-45. Home: 3295 Green Rd Beachwood OH 44122 Office: 34959 Curtis Blvd Eastlake OH 44094

SCHOR, STANLEY SIDNEY, educator; b. Phila., Mar. 3, 1922; s. Joseph and Dorothy (Abrams) S.; A.B., U. Pa., 1943, A.M., 1950, Ph.D., 1952; certificate U. Cin., 1944; m. Irene Sternberg, June 19, 1949; children—Mark, Robin, Randi. Instr. U. Pa., 1950-53, asst. prof. statistics, 1953-58, asso. prof. statistics, 1958-64, dir. Nat. Periodic Health Exam. Research Group, 1958-64; dir. dept. biostatistics A.M.A., Chgo., 1964-66; prof. biostatistics Chgo. Med. Sch., 1964-66; prof., chmn. dept. biometrics Temple U. Med. Sch., 1966-75, adj. prof., 1975—; vis. prof. Tel Aviv U., 1973-74, Med. Coll. Pa., 1979—; exec. dir. Cbards, Merck Sharp & Dohme, West Point, Pa., 1975—; clin. prof. Hahnemann Med. Sch., 1975—. Cons. in field. Served with AUS, 1943-46. Fellow Am. Public Health Assn., Am. Statis. Assn., Phila. Coll. Physicians; mem. Biometric Soc., AAUP, Royal Soc. Health, Pi Gamma Mu. Author: Fundamentals of Biostatistics, 1968. Editorial staff Chest, 1966—, Jour. Trauma, 1955—, Jour. AMA, 1964—. Contbr. articles to profl. jours. Home: 536 Cedar Dr Lafayette Hill PA 19444 Office: West Point PA 19486

SCHORK, JOHN EDWARD, environmental mgmt. co. exec.; b. South Amboy, N.J., Mar. 4, 1923; s. John and Florence (Gerwert) S.; B.S., Mo. Sch. Mines and Metallurgy, 1947; postgrad. mgmt. Harvard Bus. Sch., 1962; m. Claudine Rosemary Hanby, Sept. 23, 1945; children—Evelyn, John W., Robert. Asst. metallurgist U.S. Metals Refining, Cartaret, N.J., 1947-49; asst. plant supt. Hudson Smelting & Refining, Newark, 1949-54, plant supt., 1954-56; with Research-Cottrell, Inc., Bound Brook, N.J., 1956—, pres., 1964-68, chmn. bd., pres., 1968—, also dir.; dir. 1st Nat. Bank Central Jersey, Bound Brook, Oxy-Catalyst, W. Chester, Pa., Research-Cotrel Canada, Toronto, Research Corp., N.Y.C.; mem. listed co. adv. com. Am. Stock Exchange. Mem. bd. edn. Bedminster Twp., N.J., 1956-62, pres., 1959-62; mem. Bedminster Twp. Com., 1963-66. Served with A.C., USMCR, 1942-45. Decorated D.F.C., Air medal. Mem. Am. Soc. Mining, Metall. and Petroleum Engrs., Am. Inst. Mining Engrs., Am. Mgmt. Assn., Air Pollution Control Assn., Nat. Indsl. Pollution Control Council (process and systems engring. sub council). Clubs: Raritan Valley Country (Somerville, N.J.); Fiddler's Elbow Country (Bedminster); Club de Golf (Sotogrande, Spain). Home: RD 2 Ridge Rd Lebanon NJ 08833 Office: PO Box 750 Bound Brook NJ 08805

SCHORK, RUDOLPH JOSEPH, JR., philologist; b. Balt., Apr. 17, 1933; s. Rudolph Joseph and Helen (Marcks) S.; A.B. summa cum laude, Coll. of Holy Cross, Worcester, Mass., 1955; D.Phil. (Woodrow Wilson fellow 1955, Fulbright scholar 1955-57), Exeter Coll., Oxford (Eng.) U., 1957; m. Jeanne Marie Delay, July 12, 1956; 1 dau., Heidi Anna. Instr., then asst. prof. John Carroll U., Cleve., 1957-60; successively asst. prof., asso. prof., chmn. dept. classics Georgetown U., 1960-66; asso. prof., then prof. U. Minn., 1966-72; dir. Nat. Humanities Series, Princeton, N.J., 1972-73; vis. prof. U. Cin., 1973-74; prof., chmn. dept. classics Bklyn. Coll., City U. N.Y., 1974-75; prof., chmn. dept. classics U. Mass., Boston, 1975—. Cons., Nat. Humanities Faculty, 1971—. Mem. Am. Philol. Assn. Democrat. Roman Catholic. Contbr. articles to profl. jours. Home: 62 Crest Rd Wellesley MA 02181

SCHORLING, HORACE OREN, univ. adminstr.; b. Indpls., Aug. 26, 1912; s. Frank John and Ida May (Taylor) S.; A.B., San Jose State Coll., 1939; M.S., Oreg. State Coll., 1946, Ed.D., 1950; m. Thea S. Frisbie, Mar. 23, 1940; children—Barbara, Gayden, Douglas; m. 2d, Dorothy Jean Klyver. High sch. tchr., Santa Maria, Calif., 1939-41; prof. Fresno State Coll., 1941-51, head div. fine and practical arts, 1951-57, dean Sch. Profl. Studies, 1965-70, prof. indsl. arts, head div. applied arts, chmn. indsl. arts dept., acting acad. v.p., 1970-71, exec. v.p., 71-77, exec. dir. Internat. Inst. Housing Tech., 1971-77, exec. v.p. emeritus, 1977—, prof. indsl. arts and tech., 1977—. Recipient USAF Outstanding Service citation, 1970. Mem. U.S. Mission to Korea on Edn., 1948. Mem. Western Coll. Assn. (chmn. survey team 1953, 55, 75), Am. Vocat. Assn., Am. Indsl. Arts Assn., Phi Kappa Phi, Epsilon Pi Tau, Phi Delta Kappa, Kappa Delta Pi. Conglist. Club: Engineers. Home: 4817 E San Gabriel Fresno CA 93726

SCHORR, ALAN EDWARD, librarian; b. N.Y.C., Jan. 7, 1945; s. Herbert and Regina (Fingerman) S.; B.A., City U. N.Y., 1966; M.A., Syracuse U., 1967; postgrad. U. Iowa, 1967-71; M.L.S., U. Tex., 1973; m. Debra Genner, June 11, 1967; 1 son, Zebediah. Tchr., research asst. dept. history U. Iowa, 1967-70; govt. publs. and map librarian, asst. prof. Elmer E. Rasmuson Library, U. Alaska, Fairbanks, 1973-78; asst. prof., dir. library U. Alaska, Juneau, 1978—; free lance indexer and bibliographer: mem. Alaska Ednl. Del. to People's Republic China, 1975. Mem. Auke Bay (Alaska) Vol. Fire Dept. Mem. ALA (reference and subscription books rev. com. 1975—, reference and adult services div. publs. com. 1975-77, Mudge citation commn. 1977-79, governing council 1977-81), Alaska (exec. bd. 1974-75, nominating com. 1977-79), Pacific N.W. (rep. publs. com. 1973-75) library assns., Assn. Coll. and Research Libraries (publ. com. 1976-80), Spl. Libraries Assn. (asso. editor geography and map div. bull. 1975-76), Am. Polar Soc. Club: Explorers N.Y. Author: Alaska Place Names, 1974; Directory of Special Libraries in Alaska, 1975; Government Reference Books, 1974-75, 76; Government Reference Books, 1976-77, 78; Government Documents in the Library Literature, 1909-1974, 1976; ALA RSBRC Manual, 1979; editor The Sourdough, 1974-75; book reviewer, columnist Southeast Alaska Empire, 1979—; contbr. articles to profl. jours. Home: Box 944 Auke Bay AK 99821 Office: U Alaska Univ Library PO Box 1447 Juneau AK 99802

SCHORR, ALVIN LOUIS, social worker; b. N.Y.C., Apr. 13, 1921; s. Louis and Tillie (Godiner) S.; B.S.S., City Coll. N.Y., 1941; M.S.W., Washington U., St. Louis, 1943; D.H.L., Adelphi U., 1975; m. Ann Girson, Aug. 21, 1948; children—Jessica Lee, Kenneth L., Wendy Lauren. With Family Service No. Va., 1956-58; family life specialist Office Commnr. Social Security, 1958-62; vis. prof. London (Eng.) Sch. Econs., 1962-63; acting chief long range research Social Security Adminstrn., 1962-63; dir. research and planning Office Econ. Opportunity, 1965-66; dep. asst. sec. Dept. Health, Edn. and Welfare, 1967-69; prof. social policy, dir. income maintenance project Brandeis U., 1969-70; dean Grad. Sch. Social Work, N.Y.U., 1970-73; gen. dir. Community Service Soc. N.Y., 1973-77; vis. prof. Cath. U. Am., 1977-79; Leonard W. Mayo prof. Case Western Res. U., 1979—; Fulbright sr. research scholar, 1962-63; recipient Distinguished Service in Social Welfare award Washington U. Alumni Assn., 1969. Mem. Phi Beta Kappa. Author: Filial Responsibility in the Modern American Family, 1961; Slums and Social Insecurity, 1963; Social Services and Social Security in France, 1964; Poor Kids, 1966; Explorations in Social Policy, 1968; Children and Decent People, 1974; Jubilee for Our Times, 1977. Home: 45 Gramercy Park N New York NY 10010

SCHORR, DANIEL LOUIS, journalist, author, lectr.; b. N.Y.C., Aug. 31, 1916; s. Louis and Tillie (Godiner) S.; B.S.S., Coll. City N.Y., 1939; m. Lisbeth Bamberger, 1967; children—Jonathan, Lisa. Asst. editor Jewish Telegraphic Agy., 1934-41; news editor ANETA (Netherlands) News Agy. in N.Y., 1941-48; free-lance corr. N.Y. Times, Christian Sci. Monitor, London Daily Mail, 1948-53; Washington corr. CBS News, also spl. assignments Latin Am. and Europe, 1953-55, reopened CBS Moscow Bur., 1955, roving assignments U.S. and Europe, 1958-60, chief CBS News Bur., Germany, Central Europe, 1960-66, Washington corr. CBS, 1966-76; Regents prof. U. Calif., Berkeley, 1977; columnist Des Moines Register, Tribune Syndicate; commentator Nat. Public Radio and Ind. TV, 1979; sr. Washington corr. Cable News Network, 1980—. Decorated Officer Orange Nassau (Netherlands), 1955; Grand Cross of Merit (Fed. Republic Germany); recipient citations of excellence for radio-TV reporting from Soviet Union, Overseas Press Club, 1956, award for best TV interpretation fgn. news, 1963; Emmy awards for coverage of Watergate scandal, 1972, 73, 74, ACLU and other awards for pub. suppressed House intelligence report. Mem. Am. Fedn. Radio-TV Artists, Council on Fgn. Relations N.Y.C. Author: Don't Get Sick in America!, 1971; Clearing the Air, 1977. . *To be a reporter has been, for me, not only a profession, but an attitude and a way of life. It meant to be inquisitive and critical about all institutions—including the institution of the Press in which I worked.*

SCHORR, LISBETH BAMBERGER, child health advocate; b. Munich, Germany, Jan. 20, 1931; d. Fred S. and Lotte (Krafft) Bamberger; B.A. with highest honors, U. Calif. at Berkeley, 1952; m. Daniel L. Schorr, Jan. 8, 1967; children—Jonathan, Lisa. Med. care cons. U.A.W. and Community Health Assn., Detroit, 1956-58; asst. dir. Dept. Social Security AFL-CIO, Washington, 1958-65; chief program planning Office for Health Affairs, OEO, Washington, 1967, acting chief CAP Health Services, 1965-66; cons. Children's Defense Fund, Washington, 1973—; scholar-in-residence Inst. of Medicine, 1979—; chmn. Select Panel on Promotion Child Health, 1979—; public mem. Am. Bd. Pediatrics, 1978—; vice chmn. bd. dirs. Found. for Child Devel., 1976—. Mem. Inst. Medicine, Nat. Acad. Scis. (mem. council 1975-78), Phi Beta Kappa. Home: 3113 Woodley Rd NW Washington DC 20008 Office: Children's Defense Fund 1520 New Hampshire Ave NW Washington DC

SCHORR, MARVIN GERALD, diversified tech., constrn. and broadcasting co. exec.; b. N.Y.C., Mar. 10, 1925; s. Samuel and Fannie (Smolen) S.; B.S., Yale U., 1944, M.S., 1947, Ph.D. in Physics and Electronics, 1949; m. Rosalie Yorshis, Dec. 22, 1957; children—Eric Douglas, Susan Ellen. Research asst., instr. Yale U., 1946-47; project dir. physics and electronics div. Tracerlab, Inc., 1940-51; spl. cons. USAF, 1951-52; exec. v.p., treas. Tech. Ops., Inc., Boston, 1951-62, pres., chief exec. officer, 1962—, also dir. Trustee New Eng. Deaconess Hosp., Boston, Park Sch., Brookline, Mass.; chmn. bd. govs. Mass. Tech. Devel. Corp., Boston; trustee, exec. com. Pierce Coll., Athens, Greece. Served with AUS, 1944-46. Mem. Am. Phys. Soc., IEEE, Ops. Research Soc. Am., AAAS, World Bus. Council, Chief Exec. Forum, Sigma Xi. Clubs: Cosmos (Washington); Explorers, Yale (N.Y.C.); Harvard, Yale, St. Botolph, Union (Boston). Contbr. tech. jours. Home: 330 Beacon St Boston MA 02116 Office: 1 Beacon St 31st Floor Boston MA 02108

SCHORRE, LOUIS CHARLES, JR., artist; b. Cuero, Tex., Mar. 9, 1925; s. Louis Charles and Anna (Barthlome) S.; B.F.A., U. Tex., 1948; student Southwestern U., 1943-44; m. Margaret Phipps Storm, July 17, 1948; children—Alice Ann Schorre Stultz, Martha Schorre Swart, Robin Elisabeth Schorre Carameros. Instr. art Mus. Fine Arts, Houston, 1950-55; prof. Sch. Architecture, Rice U., 1962-72; one-man shows Dubose Gallery, Houston, David B. Findlay Galleries, N.Y.C.; paintings and drawings in numerous publs. also pvt. and corp. collections throughout U.S. Author, editor, art dir.: Life Class, 1968 (gold medals in N.Y.C. and abroad; author: Drawings and Notes, 1975. Served with USMCR, 1943-46. Home: 12115 Broken Bough Dr Houston TX 77024 Studio: 2406 Tangley Rd Houston TX 77005. *I am influenced by almost everything that is happening . . . therefore I am touched by the romance of history, the excitement and depression of now and the anticipation of what is to be. I am motivated by love received and given . . . hopefully I am still a child.*

SCHORSKE, CARL EMIL, educator; b. N.Y.C., Mar. 15, 1915; s. Theodore A. and Gertrude (Goldschmidt) S.; A.B., Columbia, 1936; M.A., Harvard, 1937, Ph.D., 1950; D.Litt., Wesleyan U., 1967; m. Elizabeth Gilbert Rorke, June 14, 1941; children—Carl Theodore, Anne (Mrs. J. L. Edwards), Stephen James, John Simon, Richard. Prof. history Wesleyan U., Middletown, Conn., 1946-60; prof. history U. Calif. at Berkeley, 1960-69; prof. history Princeton, 1969—. Served to lt. (j.g.) USNR, 1943-46, OSS, 1941-46. Mem. Am. Acad. Arts and Scis., Am. Hist. Assn. (council 1964-68), Center Advanced Study Behavioral Sci., Inst. Advanced Study. Author: (with Hoyt Price) The Problem of Germany, 1947; German Social Democracy 1905-17, 1955; Fin-de-Siecle Vienna, 1979. Home: 106 Winant Rd Princeton NJ 08540

SCHOTLAND, ROY ARNOLD, lawyer, educator; b. Newark, N.J., Mar. 18, 1933; s. Joseph J. and Thelma S. S.; A.B., Columbia Coll., 1954; LL.B., Harvard U., 1960; m. Sara Deutch, Mar. 29, 1969; children—Rebecca, Joseph. Admitted to N.Y. State bar, 1964; research asst. Paul Freund, Harvard U. Law Sch., 1960-61; clk. Justice William J. Brennan, U.S. Supreme Ct., 1961-62; prof. U. Va. Law Sch., 1964-68; prof. law Georgetown U., Washington, 1968—. Mem. Am. Law Inst. Democrat. Jewish. Office: 600 New Jersey Ave NW Washington DC 20001

SCHOTT, ELIHU, airline exec.; b. N.Y.C., Oct. 14, 1914; s. David L. and Rose (Ward) S.; B.A., Bklyn. Coll., 1934; LL.B., Columbia U., 1938; m. Marian Goldstein, June 15, 1941; children—Penelope, Heather Florence. Atty., SEC, also, Dept. Justice, Washington, 1938-44; asso. various law firms, N.Y.C., 1944-50; successively v.p. law, asso. gen. counsel, v.p. regulatory affairs, sr. v.p. internat. and regulatory services Pan Am. World Airways, N.Y.C., 1951—. Office: Pan Am World Airways Inc Pan Am Bldg New York City NY 10017

SCHOTTELKOTTE, JAMES EDWARD, editor; b. Cin., June 24, 1930; s. Albert William and Venetta (Mentrup) S.; B.S. in History, Xavier U., 1952; m. Shirley Ann Kraft, June 8, 1957; children—David, Kathleen, Stephen, Julia Marie. With Cin. Enquirer, 1948—, exec. sports editor, 1967-68, sports editor, 1968-76, mng. editor, 1976—. Served with AUS, 1953-54. Club: Cincinnati. Home: 6313 Elkwater Ct Cincinnati OH 45211 Office: 617 Vine St Cincinnati OH 45202

SCHOTTERS, BERNARD WILLIAM, ret. business exec.; b. Indpls., Dec. 26, 1908; s. Frank J. and Elizabeth (Neuhardt) S.; J.D., Ind. U., 1935; m. Virginia J. Hubbard, May 25, 1935; children—Sally J., Bernard William II. With Indpls. Power & Light Co., 1926-74, pres., 1967-71, chmn. bd., chief exec. officer, 1971-74, mem. exec. com., now ret. Past pres. Indpls. Better Bus. Bur. Served to lt. col. USMCR, World War II. Mem. Ind., Indpls. bar assns., Indpls. C. of C., Sigma Delta Kappa, Am. Legion. Mem. Christian Ch. (33 deg.). Mason (Shriner). Clubs: Rotary, Indpls. Athletic, Columbia, Indpls. Country, Meridian Hills Country (Indpls.). Home: 737 Kessler Blvd W Dr Indianapolis IN 46208

SCHOTTLAND, CHARLES IRWIN, educator; b. Chgo., Oct. 29, 1906; s. Harry and Millie (Lustberg) S. A.B., U. Calif. at Los Angeles, 1927; postgrad. N.Y. Sch. Social Work, 1928-29, U. So. Calif. Law Sch., 1929-33; D.H.L., Boston U., 1969; LL.D., Western Mich. U., 1970; D.H., Centro Escolar U., Manila, Philippines, 1970, Washington U., 1976; LL.D., Emerson Coll., 1972, Brandeis U., 1972; m. Edna Lilyan Greenberg, June 7, 1931; children—Richard R., Mary Elizabeth (dec.). Dir. Modern Social Center, Los Angeles, 1929-33; admitted to Calif. bar, 1933; adminstr. Calif. Relief Adminstrn., 1933-36; exec. dir. Fedn. Jewish Welfare Orgns., Los Angeles, 1936-41; asst. to chief, children's bur. Dept. Labor, 1941-42; asst. dir. UNRRA for Germany, 1945; practice law, Los Angeles, 1948-50; dir. Calif. Dept. Social Welfare; 1950-54; lectr. U. Calif. at Los Angeles, 1949-54; commr. social security HEW, 1954-59; dean Florence Heller Grad. Sch. for Advanced Studies in Social Welfare, Brandeis U., 1959-70; pres. Brandeis U., Waltham, Mass., 1970-72, prof., 1972—; dir. Boston Five Cents Savs. Bank. Pres. Internat. Council Social

Welfare, 1968-72, chmn. U.S. com., 1961-66; mem. com. social security experts Internat. Labor Office, 1956-59; prin. adviser U.S. delegation UN Social Commn., 1955, 57; mem. adv. bd. Dept. Social Welfare, Commonwealth of Mass., 1964; mem.-at-large Nat. Social Welfare Assembly, 1964-71; mem. task force on financing community health services and facilities Nat. Commn. on Community Health, 1964; mem. Citizens Crusade Against Poverty, 1964; cons. pub. health service Nat. Inst. Mental Health, 1964, chmn. research consultants com., 1973—; chmn. subcom. on retirement income Nat. Council on Aging, 1964; chmn. task force on social services HEW, 1968; mem. pub. health services Nat. Adv. Mental Health Council, 1968-72; mem. Milbank Commn. on Pub. Health, 1972-76. Bd. dirs. Big Brothers Assn. Los Angeles, 1945—, Nat. Big Bros. Assn., 1975—. Served from maj. to lt. col. AUS, 1942-45; ETO. Decorated by govts. of France, Czechoslovakia, Holland, Greece, Poland; recipient Koshland award Calif. Conf., Social Work, 1954. Mem. Am. Pub. Welfare Assn., Nat. Assn. Social Workers (chmn. div. social policy and action 1962-66, pres.-elect 1966-67, pres. 1967-68), Nat. Conf. Social Welfare (pres. 1953, 59-60), Am. Pub. Welfare Assn. (dir.), Calif. State Bar, Am. Legion, Mil. Order World Wars, Mil. Govt. Assn., Zeta Beta Tau, Pi Sigma Alpha, Pi Kappa Delta. Author: The Social Security Program in the United States, 1963; The Welfare State, 1967. Home: 61 Fairgreen Pl Chestnut Hill MA 02167 Office: Brandeis Univ Waltham MA 02154

SCHOTTSTAEDT, WILLIAM WALTER, physician, educator; b. Fresno, Calif., Mar. 28, 1917; s. W.E. Richard and Marjorie (Wall) S.; student Fresno State Coll., 1933-35; A.B., U. Calif., 1937, M.D., 1948; Mus.B., U. Mich., 1940, Mus. M., 1941; m. Mary Frances Gardner, Dec. 27, 1947; children—Margaret, William, Elinor, Louise. Intern, U. Calif. Hosp., San Francisco, 1948-49, resident, 1949-51; resident in psychosomatic medicine N.Y. Hosp., 1951-53; practice medicine, specializing in internal medicine; asst. prof. U. Okla. Med. Sch., 1953-56, asso. prof., 1956-60, prof., chmn. dept. preventive medicine and pub. health, 1960-67, dean Sch. Health, 1968-73, adminstrv. officer Sch. Health-Related Professions, 1967-70; prof. U. Tex. Med. Br., Galveston, 1974—, now asso. dean continuing med. edn. Mem. Health Planning Council Okla., 1968—, Nat. Adv. Public Health Tng. Council, 1972. Served with M.C., AUS, 1942-45; CBI, Middle East. Mem. Health Services Mental Health Adminstrn. (health services research tng. com. 1968, research scientist award com. 1970), AMA, Am. Pub. Health Assn., Assn. Tchrs. Preventive Medicine (press. 1965), Am. Psychosomatic Soc. (council 1964), Am. Clin. and Climatol. Assn. Author: Psychophysiological Approach to Medical Practice, 1960. Home: 2501 Gerol Dr Galveston TX 77550

SCHOWALTER, WILLIAM RAYMOND, educator; b. Milw., Dec. 15, 1929; s. Raymond Philip and Martha (Kowalke) S.; B.S., U. Wis., 1951; postgrad. Inst. Paper Chemistry, 1951-52; M.S., U. Ill., 1953, Ph.D., 1957; m. Jane Ruth Gregg, Aug. 22, 1953; children—Katherine Ruth, Mary Patricia, David Gregg. Asst. prof. dept. chem. engring. Princeton U., 1957-63, asso. prof., 1963-66, prof., 1966—, acting chmn. dept. chem. engring., 1971, chmn. dept. chem. engring., 1978—, asso. dean Sch. Engring. and Applied Sci., 1972-77; Sherman Fairchild Distinguished scholar Calif. Inst. Tech., 1977-78; vis. fellow U. Salford (Eng.), 1974; vis. sr. fellow Sci. Research Council, U. Cambridge, Eng., 1970; cons. to chem. and petroleum cos.; mem. editorial adv. bd. McGraw-Hill Pub. Co., 1964—. Co-chmn. Internat. Seminar for Heat and Mass Transfer, 1970. Served with AUS, 1953-55. Recipient Lectureship award Chem. Engring. div. Am. Soc. Engring. Edn., 1971. Mem. Am. Inst. Chem. Engrs., Am. Chem. Soc., Soc. of Rheology (exec. com. 1977—), Sigma Xi, Tau Beta Pi, Phi Lambda Upsilon, Phi Eta Sigma. Author: Mechanics of Non-Newtonian Fluids, 1978; mem. editorial com. Ann. Rev. Fluid Mechanics, 1974—; editorial bd. Internat. Jour. Chem. Engring., 1974—, Indsl. and Engring. Chemistry Fundamentals, 1975-78, Jour. Non-Newtonian Fluid Mechanics, 1976—. Contbr. articles to profl. jours. Home: 106 Crestview Dr Princeton NJ 08540

SCHRADER, BERNARD WILLIAM, lawyer; b. San Angelo, Tex., May 13, 1926; s. William and Charity A. S.; B.S., U. Corpus Christi, 1950; J.D., U. Tex., 1956; m. Barbara Ann Freeman, Dec. 18, 1950; children—Brenda Ann Schrader Keller, Beverly Kaye Schrader Nault. Admitted to Tex. bar, 1955, U.S. Supreme Ct. bar, 1977; airport mgr. City of Corpus Christi (Tex.), 1946-53, airport coordinator, 1957-61; gen. practice law, Corpus Christi, 1961-64; sr. v.p. Coastal States Gas Corp., Houston, 1964—. Served with USAAF, 1943-45. Named Disting. Alumni, U. Corpus Christi, 1966. Home: 17315 Queenslake Dr Cypress TX 77429 Office: Coastal States Gas Corp Nine Greenway Plaza Houston TX 77046

SCHRADER, GEORGE ALFRED, JR., educator, philosopher; b. English, Ind., May 30, 1917; s. George A. and Elizabeth (Wheatley) S.; A.B., Park Coll., 1939; B.D., Yale, 1942, Ph.D., 1945; student U. Heidelberg (Germany), 1952-53, U. Munich (Germany), 1957-58; m. Norma Lucille Rogers, Jan. 26, 1966; children—Alfred III, Ann; stepchildren—Diana, Nancy, Barbara, Judith. Mem. faculty Trinity U., 1944-47, Colgate U., 1947-48; mem. faculty Yale, 1948—, prof. philosophy, 1961—, chmn. dept., 1963-70, master Branford Coll., 1959-66. Panelist Nat. Endowment for Humanities, 1968-72, Bd. dirs. New Haven Redevel. Agy., 1962-66, Day Hill Prospect Sch., 1963-68. Morse fellow Yale, 1952-53; St. Fulbright research fellow, 1957-58; Kent fellow, 1943—. Mem. Am. Philos. Assn. (exec. com. 1969-73), Am. Psychol. Assn., Metaphys. Soc. Am. Soc. Phenomenology and Existential Philosophy (exec. com. 1964-67). Author: Existential Philosophy: Kierkegaard to Merleau Ponty, 1968; also articles. Mem. editorial bd. Kantstudien, Am. Philos. Quar., Idealistic Studies, Northwestern Studies in Existential Philosophy. Home: 307 St Ronan St New Haven CT 06511

SCHRADER, GEORGE ROBERT, city ofcl.; b. Olivet, Kans., Feb. 16, 1931; s. Ellis George and Jane Ann (Ewbank) S.; A.B., Baker U., 1953; M.P.A., U. Kans., 1955; cert. program for urban execs. M.I.T., 1969; m. Mary Elizabeth Rogers, Aug. 8, 1954; 1 dau., Janise Kaye. Adminstrv. asst.-planner City of San Angelo (Tex.), 1954-55, adminstrv. asst. to city mgr., 1955-57; city mgr. City of Ennis (Tex.), 1957-59; city mgr. City of Mesquite (Tex.), 1959-66; asst. city mgr. City of Dallas, 1966-72, city mgr., 1972—; lectr. Nat. Fire Mgmt. Sch., So. Meth. U., 1970-78; mem. Dallas Assembly; mem. adv. com. U.S. Comptroller of Currency. Bd. dirs. Baker U., Circle Ten council Boy Scouts Am., United Way of Met. Dallas, Dallas County Assn. for Blind. Named 1 of 5 Outstanding Young Texans, Tex. Jaycees, 1965, Public Adminstr. of Yr., North Tex. chpt. Am. Soc. Public Adminstrn., 1976; recipient citation for disting. service Baker U., 1972, citation of honor Tex. Soc. Architects, 1974. Mem. North Tex. City Mgmt. Assn. (pres. 1976), Tex. City Mgmt. Assn. (pres. 1976), Internat. City Mgmt. Assn. (v.p. 1975-77, pres. 1979-80, Mgmt. Innovation award 1974, 78, 79), Nat. Acad. Public Adminstrn., Dallas Alliance, Pi Sigma Alpha. Methodist. Club: Salesmanship (Dallas). Office: 4E S City Hall Dallas TX 75201

SCHRADER, HARRY CHRISTIAN, JR., naval officer; b. Sheboygan, Wis., Aug. 4, 1932; s. Harry Christian and Edna Flora (Stubbe) S.; B.S., U.S. Naval Acad., 1955; M.S., U.S. Naval Postgrad. Sch., 1963; m. Carol Joan Gossman, June 23, 1956; 1 dau., Mary Clare. Commd. ensign U.S. Navy, 1955, advanced through grades to rear adm., 1979; comdr. U.S.S. Tawasa, 1963-64, U.S.S. A. Hamilton, 1970-72, U.S.S. Jackson, 1972-73, U.S.S. Gilmore, 1973-75, U.S.S. Long Beach, 1975-78; dir. MLSF Amphibious, Mine Warfare and Advanced Vehicles div. Office Naval Ops., Washington, 1978—. Mem. Am. Def. Preparedness Assn., Sigma Xi. Office: OP-37 US Navy Dept Pentagon Washington DC 20350

SCHRADER, LEE FREDERICK, agrl. economist; b. Okawville, Ill., Mar. 11, 1933; s. Fred and Alma (Koenemann) S.; B.S., U. Ill., 1955; M.S., Mich. State U., 1958; Ph.D., U. Calif., Berkeley, 1961; m. Martha Ellen Kohl, Dec. 27, 1958; children—Mark, Katherine, Amanda. Buyer, Lever Bros. Co., N.Y.C., 1961-64; economist Armour & Co., Chgo., 1965-66; mem. faculty Sch. Agr., Purdue U., West Lafayette, Ind., 1966—, prof. agrl. econs., 1971—. Served with U.S. Army, 1955-57. Mem. Agrl Agrl. Econs. Assn. Author: (with R.A. Goldberg) Farmers' Cooperatives and Federal Income Taxes, 1975. Home: 711 Carrolton West Lafayette IN 47906 Office: Dept Agrl Econs Purdue Univ West Lafayette IN 47907

SCHRADER, MARTIN HARRY, publisher; b. Queens, N.Y., Nov. 26, 1925; s. Harry F. and Ida (Spiess) S.; B.A., Queens Coll., 1946; m. Cecelia Sofer, July 7, 1957; children—Howard, Daniel, Esther. Vice pres. Alfred Auerbach & Co., 1950-60; dir. mktg. House Beautiful mag., N.Y.C., 1960-65, pub. spl. publs. div., 1965-69; pub. Town and Country mag., N.Y.C., 1969-77, Harpers Bazaar, 1977—; lectr. merchandising Fairleigh Dickenson U., 1958-61, Parsons Sch. Design, 1976—. Mem. nat. adv. bd. Salk Inst., La Jolla, Calif., 1970—. Bd. govs. Coty Fashion Critics Awards. Recipient Human Relations award Am. Jewish Com., 1979. Mem. U.S. Lawn Tennis Assn. (umpire's com. 1961—). Jewish (trustee temple 1965—). Office: Harpers Bazaar 717 Fifth Ave New York NY 10022

SCHRAG, ADELE FRISBIE, educator; b. Cynthiana, Ky., May 7, 1921; d. Shirley Ledyard and Edna Kate (Ford) S.; B.S., Temple U., 1942; M.A., N.Y. U., 1944, Ph.D., 1961; m. William Albert Schrag, Apr. 6, 1963; 1 stepdau., Marie Carol. Tchr. Manor Twp. High Sch., Millersville, Pa., 1942-43, Downingtown (Pa.) Sr. High Sch., 1943-50; instr., asst. prof. Temple U. Sch. Bus. and Pub. Administrn., Phila., 1950-60; prof. bus. edn. and vocat. edn. Coll. Edn., 1960—; vis. lectr. N.Y. U.; cons. Phila. Community Coll., 1967—. Recipient Profl. Panhellenic award, 1963; Kensington High Sch. Alumnae award, 1972. Mem. Soc. Automation in Bus. Edn. (pres. 1969-73, dir. 1974), Bus. Edn. Certification Council, Phi Gamma Nu (nat. treas. 1952-54, nat. sec. 1954-56), Delta Pi Epsilon (policy commn. for bus. and econ. edn. 1975-78), Editor: Business Education for the Automated Office, 1964. Author: (with Estelle L. Popham and Wanda Blockhus) A Teaching-Learning System for Business Education, 1975. Contbr. articles to profl. jours. Home: 305 Longfield Rd Philadelphia PA 19118 Office: Ritter Hall Annex Philadelphia PA 19122

SCHRAG, CALVIN ORVILLE, educator: b. Marion, S.D., May 4, 1928; s. John J. and Katherine (Miller) S.; B.A., Bethel Coll., Newton, Kan., 1950; B.D., Yale, 1953; postgrad. U. Heidelberg (Germany), 1954-55, Oxford (Eng.) U., 1955; Ph.D., Harvard, 1957; m. Virginia Marie Fields, Aug. 8, 1964; 1 dau., Heather Sue. Teaching fellow Harvard, 1956-57; faculty Purdue U., Lafayette, Ind., 1957—, prof. philosophy, 1964—. Vis. lectr. U. Ill., 1959-60; vis. asso. prof. Northwestern U., 1962-63; vis. prof. philosophy Ind. U., 1967-68; cons. editor Northwestern U. Press. Fulbright fellow, 1954-55; Nat. Found. Humanities and Arts grantee, 1967; Guggenheim fellow, 1965-66; Am. Council Learned Socs. grant-in-aid, 1974. Mem. Metaphys. Soc. N.Am. (chmn. program com. 1979-80), Soc. Phenomenology and Existential Philosophy (exec. sec. 1977-80), Am., Ind. (past pres.) philos. assns. Author: Existence and Freedom, 1961; Experience and Being, 1969. Co-editor: Patterns of the Life-World, 1970; Radical Reflection and the Origin of the Human Sciences, 1980; Man and World, quar., 1967—. Home: 1315 N Grant St West Lafayette IN 47906 Office: Dept Philosophy Purdue U Lafayette IN 47907

SCHRAG, EDWARD A., JR., lawyer; b. Milw., Mar. 27, 1932; s. Edward A. and Mabel Lena (Baumbach) S.; B.S. in Econs., U. Pa., 1954; J.D., Harvard, 1960; m. Leslie Jean Israel, June 19, 1954; children—Amelia Marie, Katherine Allison, Edward A. III. Admitted to Ohio bar, 1961; asso., then firm partner Vorys, Sater, Seymour & Pease, Columbus, 1960—. Sec. Ranco Inc.; trustee Lake of the Woods Water Co. Mem. Downtown Area Com., 1970-74. Served to lt. (j.g.) USNR, 1954-57. Mem. Am., Ohio, Columbus bar assns., Columbus Area C. of C., Navy League, Alpha Tau Omega, Beta Gamma Sigma, Phi Sigma Alpha, Pi Gamma Mu. Episcopalian. Kiwanian. Clubs: Crichton, Ohio State U. Pres.'s, University. Home: 9400 White Oak Ln Westerville OH 43081 Office: 52 E Gay St Columbus OH 43215

SCHRAG, KARL, painter; b. Karlsruhe, Germany, Dec. 7, 1912; s. Hugo and Bella (Sulzberger) S.; art student, Geneva, Switzerland, 1930, Ecole Nationale Superieure des Beaux Arts, Paris, 1931-35; studied with Lucien Simon, Roger Bissiere; student Art Student's League of New York, and also student Atelier 17, New York; m. Ilse Szamatolski, June 12, 1945; children—Peter, Katherine. Came to U.S., 1938, naturalized, 1944. Paintings and prints exhibited Art Inst. Chgo., Boston Mus. Fine Arts, Met. Mus. Art, Mus. Modern Art, Whitney Mus. Am. Art, Mus. Modern Art, Paris, Tate Gallery, London Nat. Inst. Arts, Stockholm, others; one-man shows, Brussels, 1938, U.S. Nat. Mus., 1945, Kraushaar Galleries, 1947, 50, 52, 56, 59, 62, 64, 66, 68, 70, 74, 77, 79, Phila. Art Alliance, 1952, U. Ala., 1948, Maine U., 1953, 58, Wagner Coll., S.I., N.Y., 1955, Asso. Am. Artists, 1971, Nat. Collection Fine Arts, 1972; represented in 53 pub. collections, including Mus. Modern Art, Whitney Mus. Am. Art, Solomon R. Guggenheim Mus., Met. Mus. Art, Nat. Gallery, Washington, Bibliotheque Nationale, Paris, Library of Congress, N.Y. Pub. Library, Phila. Mus., Cleve. Mus., Bklyn. Mus., others. Tchr. Bklyn Coll., 1953, Cooper Union, 1954-68. Recipient award Bklyn. Mus. Print ann., 1947, 50; purchase award Bradley U., 1952, Erickson prize Soc. Am. Graphic Artists, 1962, 64, 67, 77, Lea prize Phila. Print Club, 1954; Am. Colorprint Soc., 1958, 60, 63, 64; awarded retrospective traveling exhbn. by Ford Found., 1959; Ford Found. fellowship Tamarind Lithography Workshop, 1963; grant Nat. Inst. Arts and Letters, 1966, Childe Hassam Purchase Fund award Am. Acad. Arts and Letters, 1969, 73, 77. Mem. Art Students League N.Y., Artists Equity, Assn. Am. Graphic Artists. Home: 127 E 95th St New York NY 10028

SCHRAG, PETER, editor, writer; b. Karlsruhe, Germany, July 24, 1931; s. Otto and Judith (Haas) S.; came to U.S., 1941, naturalized, 1953; A.B. cum laude, Amherst Coll., 1953; m. Melissa Jane Mowrer, June 9, 1953 (div. 1969); children—Mitzi, Erin Andrew; m. 2d, Diane Divoky, May 24, 1969; children—David Divoky, Benaiah Divoky. Reporter, El Paso (Tex.) Herald Post, 1953-55; asst. sec., asst. dir. publs. Amherst Coll., 1955-66, instr. Am. Studies, 1960-64; asso. edn. editor Sat. Rev., 1966-68, exec. editor, 1968-69; editor Change mag., 1969-70; editor at large Saturday Rev., 1969-72; contbg. editor Saturday Review/Education, 1972-73; editorial adv. bd. The Columbia Forum, 1972-75; editorial bd. Social Policy, 1971—; contbg. editor More, 1974—; editorial page editor Sacramento Bee, 1978—. Vis. lectr. U. Mass. Sch. Edn., 1970-72; fellow in profl. journalism Stanford U., Palo Alto, Calif., 1973-74; lectr. U. Calif. at Berkeley, 1974—. Mem. adv. com. Student Rights Project, N.Y. Civil Liberties Union, 1970-72; mem. Com. Study History, 1958-72. Trustee Emma Willard Sch., 1967-69; bd. dirs. Park Sch., Oakland, Calif., 1976-77. Guggenheim fellow, 1971-72; Nat. Endowment for Arts fellow, 1976—. Author: Voices in the Classroom, 1965; Village School Downtown, 1967; Out of Place in America, 1971; The Decline of the Wasp, 1972; The End of the American Future, 1973; Test of Loyalty, 1974; (with Diane Divoky) The Myth of the Hyperactive Child, 1975; Mind Control, 1978. Contbr. articles to Atlantic, Harper's, N.Y. Times, N.Y. Rev. Books, Playboy, also others. Home: 648 College St Woodland CA 95695 Office: Sacramento Bee 21st and Q Sts Sacramento CA 95813

SCHRAGE, PAUL DANIEL, fast food co. exec.; b. Chgo., Feb. 25, 1935; s. William and Rose Marie (Bruell) S.; B.A., U. Ill., 1957, M.S. in Advt., 1959; m. Janet Carolyn Sievers, June 15, 1957; children—Paul Daniel, Gordon Clark. Media buyer Young & Rubicam, advt., Chgo., 1959-61; brand mgr. Quaker Oats Co., Chgo., 1961-65; salesman This Week mag., Chgo., 1965-66; asso. media dir. D'Arcy Advt., Chgo., 1966-67; exec. v.p., chief mktg. officer McDonald's Corp., Oak Brook, Ill., 1967—; dir. Luth. Mut. Life Ins. Co. Mem. president's council Valparaiso (Ind.) U. Lutheran. Club: Medinah (Ill.) Country. Office: 1 McDonald's Plaza Oak Brook IL 60521

SCHRAM, LLOYD WILLIAM, univ. dean; b. Ray, N.D., Mar. 27, 1912; s. John Michael and Mayme (Ericson) S.; B.A., U. Wash., 1934, J.D., 1937, Ph.D., 1955; LL.M., Harvard, 1938; m. Annette Joan Isham, Dec. 28, 1938; children—Deanne (Mrs. James D. McBride), Brent Hunter. Admitted to Wash. bar, 1939; asst. counsel Wash. Tax Commn., 1939; mem. staff and faculty U. Wash., 1940—, dir. pub. services and univ. relations, 1960-64, dean continuing edn., 1964-76, dean emeritus, 1976—, project dir. Demonstration Center for Continuing Edn., 1976—; cons. in field, 1950—. Mem. Wash. Adv. Council Community Service Problems, 1966; asso. mem. adv. council Wash. Tech. Services Program, 1966—; mem. com. contests and awards Alexander Hamilton Bicentennial Commn., 1956-57; nat. selection com., leadership tng. awards program Fund Adult Edn., 1957-58; guest Republic W. Germany, 1966. Adv. council USPHS Hosp., Seattle, 1966—; trustee Seattle World Affairs Council, 1955, exec. com.; bd. dirs. Seattle-King County chpt. A.R.C., 1960-66, 68—, vice chmn., 1966, 72, chmn., 1975-78; bd. dirs. Center Study Liberal Edn. Adults, 1956-59, chmn., 1959; mem. Washington Commn. for Humanities, 1972—, vice chmn., 1973, chmn., 1974; adv. com. Planning and Community Affairs, 1972; Wash. State Select Commn. for Non-traditional Study, 1972; exec. bd. Seattle 2000 Commn., 1972—. Fellow Fund Adult Edn., 1954. Mem. Am. Assn. UN (trustee Seattle 1955-57), Nat. Univ. Extension Assn. (exec. com. 1951-56, pres. 1955, Julius M. Nolte award 1976), Seattle Bar Assn., Am. Soc. Pub. Adminstrn., Am. Acad. Polit. and Social Sci., Phi Delta Phi, Pi Sigma Alpha. Psi Upsilon. Home: 5528 55th Ave NE Seattle WA 98105

SCHRAM, MARTIN JAY, journalist; b. Chgo., Sept. 15, 1942; s. Marlo Joseph and Charleene Janice (Fidler) S.; B.A., U. Fla., 1964; m. Patricia Stewart Morgan, May 23, 1964; children—Kenneth Marlo, David Morgan. Reporter The Miami (Fla.) News, 1964-65; reporter Newsday, Garden City, N.Y., 1965-67, mem. Washington bur., 1967-69, White House corr., 1969-73, chief Washington bur., sr. editor paper, 1973-79; writer on the presidency Washington Post, 1979—. Recipient James Wright Brown Meml. award Sigma Delta Chi, 1965. Clubs: Nat. Press, Federal City (Washington). Author: Running for President, A Journal of the Carter Campaign, 1976; Running for President: 1976, The Carter Campaign, 1977. Home: 6309 E Halbert Rd Bethesda MD 20034 Office: 1150 15 St NW Washington DC 20071

SCHRAM, WILLIAM CLARENCE, clergyman; b. Cin., July 26, 1921; s. Lauren and Katharine (Kreidler) S.; B.A., Williams Coll., 1943; B.D., Union Theol. Sem., N.Y.C., 1949; D.D. (hon.) Westminster Coll., 1959; m. Elizabeth Case, Sept. 6, 1947; children—William Case, Robert Lauren, Thomas Hastings. Ordained to ministry Presbyn. Ch., 1949; minister in Port Jefferson, N.Y., 1949-53; sec. adult program bd. Christian edn. Presbyn. Ch. U.S.A., 1953-59; sec. consolidations com. Presbyn. Ch. U.S.A. and United Presbyn. Ch. N.Am., 1957-59; minister Huguenot Meml. Presbyn. Ch., Pelham, N.Y., 1959-73, Westminster Presbyn Ch., Dayton, O., 1974—. Asst. to state clk. Gen. Assembly United Presbyn. Ch. U.S.A., 1961-67; moderator Hudson River Presbytery, 1972. Emeritus bd. dirs. Union Theol. Sem., McCormick Theol. Sem., Chgo.; bd. dirs. Goodwill Industries, Children's Med. Center; trustee Davis and Elkins Coll., United Presbyn. Ch. in U.S.A.; pres. Dayton Met. Chs. United, 1976-78. Served with USAAF, 1942-45. Mem. Chi Psi. Home: 211 Northview Rd Dayton OH 45419 Office: Westminster Presbyn Church 125 N Wilkinson St Dayton OH 45402

SCHRAMEK, JOHN MANNING (JACK), mfg. co. exec.; b. Lansing, Mich., June 25, 1936; s. John James and Gertrude Teresa (Manning) S.; B.S. cum laude in Math., Mich. State U., 1957; m. Kathleen Ann Welsh, Nov. 24, 1961; children—John Welsh, Angela, Nancy. Various positions in fin. Ford Motor Co., 1958-68; various positions in fin. Rockwell Internat. Corp., 1968-74, v.p., controller Collins Radio Group, Dallas, 1974-76, v.p., controller electronics ops., Dallas, 1976-78, staff v.p. fin. planning and analysis, Pitts., 1978—. Republican. Roman Catholic. Home: 105 Royston Rd Fox Chapel PA 15238 Office: Rockwell Internat Corp 600 Grant St Pittsburgh PA 15219

SCHRAMEK, TOMAS, ballet dancer; b. Bratislava, Czechoslovakia, Sept. 11, 1944; s. Hans and Valeria (Neudorfer) S.; immigrated to Can., 1968, naturalized, 1973; grad. Acad. Mus. and Theatre Arts, Bratislava, 1968. Mem. Sluk, Slovakia folk dance ensemble, 1959-68, prin. dancer, 1964-68; dancer Nat. Ballet Can., 1969-71, soloist, 1971-73, prin. dancer, 1973—; mem. faculty, guest tchr. Nat. Ballet Sch., Lois Smith Sch. Dance, Toronto. Mem. Actors Equity Assn., Assn. Can. TV and Radio Artists. Home: 17 Metcalfe St Toronto ON M4X 1R5 Canada Office: 157 King St E Toronto ON M5C 169 Canada

SCHRAMM, DAVID NORMAN, educator, astrophysicist; b. St. Louis, Oct. 25, 1945; s. Marvin and Betty (Math) S.; S.B. in Physics, M.I.T., 1967; Ph.D. in Physics, Calif. Inst. Tech., 1971; m. Melinda Holzhauer, 1963; children—Cary, Brett. Research fellow in physics Calif. Inst. Tech., Pasadena, 1971-72; asst. prof. astronomy and physics U. Tex. at Austin, 1972-74; asso. prof. astronomy, astrophysics and physics Enrico Fermi Inst. and the Coll., U. Chgo., 1974-77, prof., 1977—, acting chmn. dept. astronomy and astrophysics, 1977, chmn., 1978—; cons., lectr. Adler Planetarium; organizer numerous sci. confs. Recipient Robert J. Trumpler award Astron. Soc. Pacific, 1974, Gravity Research Found. awards, 1974, 75, 76. Fellow Am. Phys. Soc.; mem. Am. Astron. Soc. (Helen B. Warner prize 1978, sec.-treas. planetary sci. div. 1979-81, exec. com. high energy astrophysics div. 1977-79), Astron. Soc. Pacific, Meteoritical Soc., Internat. Astron. Union, Am. Alpine Club, Austrian Alpine Club, Sigma Xi. Club: Quadrangle. Contbr. numerous articles to profl. jours.; co-editor: Explosive Nucleosynthesis, 1973; editor: Supernovae, 1977; asso. editor Am. Jour. Physics, 1978—; co-editor Phys. Cosmology; editorial rev. Ann. Revs. Nuclear and Particle Sci., 1976-80; co-author: Advanced States of Stellar

Evolution, 1977. Home: 4923 S Kimbark St Chicago IL 60615 Office: Astronomy and Astrophysics Center Univ Chicago 5640 S Ellis Ave Chicago IL 60637. *One can learn new information about the universe if one does not allow oneself to be bound by the traditional boundaries of various disciplines but instead synthesizes.*

SCHRAMM, GEORGE JOSEPH, tobacco co. exec.; b. Bklyn., June 21, 1916; s. John Charles and Marie (Grimpel) S.; student St. Johns U., 1939-42, N.Y. U. Grad. Sch. Bus Adminstrn., 1949-56; m. Mary Josephine Lernihan, Jan. 16, 1943; children—Gregory J., Jacquelyn M., Mary T. Asst. to treas. Austin Nichols Co., 1936-41; with Am. Brands, Inc., 1941—, v.p., controller, 1968-71, exec. v.p., 1971—, also dir.; dir. Am. Tobacco Internat. Corp., James Beam Distilling Co., Acme Visible Records, Inc., Swingline, Inc., Gallaher Ltd., Master Lock Co., Andrew Jergens Co., Duffy-Mott Co., Inc., Sunshine Biscuits, Inc., Acushnet Co., Wilson Jones Co., Franklin Life Ins. Co. Served with AUS, 1942-46. Decorated Bronze Star, Commendation medal. Mem. Financial Execs. Inst., N.Y. C. of C. Home: 15 Bighorn Dr Wayne NJ 07470 Office: 245 Park Ave New York NY 10017

SCHRAMM, JAMES SIEGMUND, ret. business exec; b. Burlington, Iowa, Feb. 4, 1904; s. Frank Edgar and Carrie Ash (Higgason) S.; student Amherst Coll., 1923-24, L.H.D., 1961; LL.D., Coe Coll., 1954; D.F.A., Grinell Coll., 1972; m. Dorothy Daniell, Sept. 26, 1931; children—Sieglinde Schramm Martin, Kristina Schramm Doughty. Joined J. S. Schramm Co., Burlington, 1924, exec. v.p., 1946-62; dir. Burlington Bank & Trust Co. Republican fin. chmn. Iowa, 1950-51, state chmn., mem. Rep. Nat. Com. Iowa, 1952-54; trustee Parsons Coll., Fairfield, Iowa, 1953-58; exec. v.p. Com. for Nat. Trade Policy, 1952-53; mem. U.S. Trade Mission to Japan, 1959, France, 1960; mem. bd. com. Internat. Trade Orgn., 1950-51; pres. Am. Fedn. Arts, 1956-58, trustee, exec. com.; past pres., trustee, chmn. acquisition and exhbn. com. Des Moines Art Center; chmn. Amherst Coll. adv. com. on contemporary art; mem. adv. council Iowa Econ. Studies Council; bd. mem. Iowa Mental Health Soc., 1950-52; chmn. Iowa Arts Council, 1966-68; mem. adv. com. John F. Kennedy Center Co. Performing Arts; trustee Chgo. Mus. Contemporary Art, 1967-70; hon. chmn. Amherst Coll. Friends Art; assisted in re-orgn. U.S. Office Civilian Def., 1942; mem. SBA adv. council, 1954-56. Served as lt. col., AUS, 1942-45; assisted in establishing controlled materials plan Army Service Forces. Recipient Legion of Merit; Distinguished Service award U. Iowa, 1971. Benjamin Franklin fellow Royall Soc. Arts; mem. Nat. Retail Mchts. Assn., Nat. Planning Assn. (nat. council, bus. com. 1955), Alpha Delta Phi. Presbyterian (elder). Clubs: Collectors Am., Des Moines; Century Assn. (N.Y.C.). Home: 2700 S Main St Burlington IA 52601

SCHRAMM, JOHN CLARENDON, found. exec.; b. Tarrytown, N.Y., July 5, 1908; s. Emil and Vera Victoria (Ormsby) S.; A.B., Columbia, 1929, A.M., 1943, student, 1945-46; m. Loraine Tonjes, Sept. 18, 1936; children—Judith Jane (Mrs. William K. Waterston), Linda (Mrs. Donald Bergquist), Ellen Christie (Mrs. Sherwin C. Day). Asst. to merchandising mgr. N.Y. Edison Co. 1929; asst. chief of program supply NBC, N.Y.C., 1929-33; radio announcer WOR, WNEW, WBNX, N.Y.C., 1933-35; program dir. WOV, N.Y.C., 1935-41; radio stage coordinator for Met. Opera Broadcast, seasons 1942-44; asst. ednl. dir., prodn. dir. Blue Network, Radio City, 1942-44; instr. in charge of radio prodn. and workshop Queens Coll., 1943; radio dir. Christian Herald Mag., 1944; radio dir. and alternate moderator Wake Up America radio forum, 1944-47; tchr. English, Patchogue (L.I.) High Sch., 1947-48; asst. prof. speech radio U. Fla., 1948-49; mng. dir. Calvin K. Kazanjian Econs. Found., Inc., 1949-50, mng. trustee, 1950—; spl. lectr. econs. So. Conn. State Coll., New Haven, 1973, 74, 77, 78; chmn. consortium on gen. systems edn. S.C. State Coll., New Haven. Trustee Conn. Joint Council on Econ. Edn. Mem. Am. Econ. Assn. Acad. Polit. and Social Soc., Acad. Polit. Sci., Soc. for Gen. Systems Research. Episcopalian. Address: RD 2 West Redding CT 06896

SCHRAMM, TEXAS E., football club ofcl.; b. Los Angeles, June 20, 1920. Publicity dir., then gen. mgr. Los Angeles Rams, 1947-57; asst. dir. sports CBS, 1957-60; gen. mgr. Dallas Cowboys, 1960—, pres., 1966—. Office: Dallas Cowboys 6116 N Central Expressway Dallas TX 75206*

SCHRANK, AULINE RAYMOND, educator, physiologist; b. Hamilton, Tex., Aug. 15, 1915; s. Herman and Emma Hulda (Schrank) S.; B.A., S.W. Tex. State Coll., San Marcos, 1937; Ph.D., U. Tex., 1942; m. Dorris Parke, Sept. 5, 1942; children—Kenton Parke, Karon. Mem. faculty U. Tex., 1939—, prof. zoology, 1959—, chmn. dept. 1963-70, asso. dean Coll. Natural Scis., 1971-72, acting dean, 1972-74, 76-77, asso. dean, 1974-76, dean, 1977—. Mem. Biophys. Soc., Soc. Gen. Physiologists, Am., Scandinavian socs. plant physiologists, Tex. Acad. Scis., Sigma Xi, Alpha Chi. Home: 2502 Tower Dr Austin TX 78703

SCHRANZ, VERN CYRIL, ret. mfg. exec.; b. Moorhead, Minn., Aug. 29, 1914; s. Pierre J. and Bennedikke (Opgrande) S.; B.E., Moorhead State Coll., 1936; M.A., U. Minn., 1940; m. Lenore Helen Allen, Aug. 2, 1941 (dec. Jan. 1978); children—Michael, Peter, Kathryn, Thomas; m. 2d, Mary Helena Purkey Pressler, July 29, 1978. Tchr., coach, West Fargo, N.D., 1936-38; teaching asst. U. Minn., 1938-41; prin. high sch. Litchfield, Minn., 1941-44; asst. dir. owner relations Studebaker Corp., South Bend, 1944-49, asst. dir. sales tng., 1949-54; with Ball Corp., Muncie, Ind., 1954-79, dir. pub. relations, 1963-66, dir. marketing services and pub. relations, 1966-68, adminstrv. asst. to pres. and dir. pub. relations, 1968-69, corp. sec., dir. pub. relations, 1969-79. State chmn. youth activities program K.C., 1948-51; dir. Delaware County United Fund 1969-73; vice chmn. Muncie Human Rights Commn., 1968-74; dir. Delaware County Assn. for Crippled, 1957-60, Family Counseling Service, 1961-64, Newman Found., Ball State U., 1967-75, Ind. Environ. Quality Control, Inc., 1969—, Ind. Council for Econ. Edn., 1973—; chmn. center for econ. edn. Ball State U., 1974-78. Recipient community services award Muncie Jr. C. of C., 1970, Distinguished Alumnus award Moorhead State Coll., 1974. Mem. Ind. (chmn. edn. com. 1969-78), Ill., Muncie chambers commerce NAM, Glass Container Mfrs. Inst., Ind. Mfrs. Assn., Am. Soc. Corporate Secs. Republican. Roman Catholic. K.C. Clubs: Delaware Country, Muncie Tennis, Catalina Swim (Muncie). Home: 1003 N Bittersweet St Muncie IN 47304

SCHRAUT, KENNETH CHARLES, mathematician, educator; b. Hillsboro, Ill., May 19, 1913; s. Charles Frederick and Theresa (Panska) S.; A.B. with honors, U. Ill., 1936; M.A., U. Cin., 1938, Ph.D., 1940; m. Virginia Haury, Feb. 5, 1952; 1 dau., Marilyn Schraut Szorc. Vis. instr. U. Notre Dame, 1940; instr. dept. math. U. Dayton (Ohio), 1940-41, asst. prof., 1941-44, asso. prof., 1944-48, prof., 1948-72, chmn. dept. math., 1954-72, Distinguished Service prof., 1972—, project dir. U. Dayton Research Center, 1951-54; vis. lectr. Grad. Sch., Ohio State U., 1946-49; acting prof. Grad. Sch., U. Cin., 1958-60. Dir. NSF Math Inst., Ponce, P.R., 1959, Catholic U. P.R., U. Dayton, 1961-66, 72. Mem. Am. Math. Soc., Math. Assn. Am., Am. Soc. Engring. Edn. (vice chmn. math. sect. 1966-67, chmn. 1967-68, 78-79, mem. exec. com. 1969-73, 76, program chmn. 1977-78), Sigma Xi, Pi Mu Epsilon. Home: 412 Marchester Dr Dayton OH 45429 Office: Dept Math Univ Dayton Dayton OH 45469

SCHREIBER, ARTHUR ADOLPHUS, transp. exec.; b. Canton, Ohio, Nov. 12, 1927; s. Valentine Adolphus and Nora (Harrison) S.; B.S. in Psychology, Westminster Coll., New Wilmington, Pa., 1951; postgrad. Kent State U., 1951-52; m. Alice Virginia Vogel, June 19, 1953 (dec. July 1975); children—Amy Jo, Mark Arthur. News dir. Sta. KYW, Cleve., 1960; news dir. Sta. WCFL, Chgo., 1965; chief Nat. and Fgn. News Service Group W Washington News Bur., 1965-67; asst. gen. mgr. sta. KYW Radio, Phila., 1967-69; asst. gen. mgr. sta. KFWB Radio, Los Angeles, 1969, gen. mgr., 1969-77; pres. commuter Transp. Services, Inc., 1977—, commuter Computer Van Pool, Inc., 1977—; faculty U. So. Calif. Mem. communication arts and sci. adv. council Pepperdine U. Mem. Mayor Bradley's Energy Policy Com.; bd. dirs. YMCA; mem. Para-Transit Adv. Commn. Named Young Man of Year Zanesville, Ohio, 1959, Parma Heights, Ohio, 1963, Alumnus of Year Westminster Coll.; recipient Good Samaritan award Ch. of Jesus Christ of Latter-day Saints, 1975, Outstanding Contbns. recognition Los Angeles Pub. Schs., 1975, 77. Mem. Nat. Assn. Van Pool Operators, Nat. Press Club, Town Hall Calif., Hollywood Radio, TV Soc., NAACP, Hollywood Leadership Council, Sigma Delta Chi (dir.). Office: 3440 Wilshire Blvd Suite 610 Los Angeles CA 90010

SCHREIBER, FLORA RHETA, theatre arts and speech specialist, author; b. N.Y.C., Apr. 24, 1918; d. William and Esther (Aaronson) Schreiber; B.S., Columbia U., 1938, M.A., 1939; certificate Central Sch. Speech Tng. and Dramatic Art, U. London, 1937, N.Y. U. Radio Workship, 1942. Instr. speech and dramatic art Bklyn. Coll., 1944-46; creator-producer Bklyn. Coll. Radio Forum, Sta. WYNC, N.Y.C., 1944-46; drama critic Players mag., 1941-46; instr. Exeter Coll., U. S.W., Eng., 1937; asst. prof. Adelphi Coll., Garden City, N.Y., 1947-53, dir. radio-TV div. Center Creative Arts, 1948-51; lectr. New Sch. Social Research, 1952-76; prof. English and speech John Jay Coll. Criminal Justice, City U. N.Y., 1974—, dir. publs., 1966—, asst. to pres., 1969—. Cornelia Otis Skinner scholar, 1937. Mem. AAUW, AAUP, Speech, Assn. Am., ANTA, Speech Assn. Eastern States, Soc. Journalists and Authors (past v.p.), Authors League Am., PEN. Club: Overseas Press. Author: William Schuman, 1954; Your Child's Speech, 1956; Jobs with a Future in Law Enforcement, 1970; Sybil, 1973, paperback edit., 1974, fgn. edits., 1974-76; also short stories plays, opera libretti and art songs. Contbr. nat. mags. including Cosmopolitan, Reader's Digest, Good Housekeeping, The Freeman, Redbook, Mademoiselle, Am. Mercury, N.Y. Times, Quar. of Film, Radio, and TV, Family Weekly, Today's Health, Woman's Day, others. Columnist Sci. Digest, 1966-72, Bell McClure, United Features; feature writer N.Y. Times Spl. Features. Producer radio forum on Community Theater for NBC, 1949; numerous radio and TV appearances in U.S. and Eng.; lectr. Home: 32 Gramercy Park S New York NY 10003 Office: John Jay College of Criminal Justice 444 W 56th St New York NY 10019. *I consider myself a humanist who puts standards of humanism in the philosophical, the aesthetic and the daily sense, above external criteria. Within this framework, quality is more important than quantity. Paradoxically, the cultivation of a garden of quality has sometimes produced what, in quantitative terms, is commonly called success.*

SCHREIBER, FRED JAMES, JR., mgmt. cons.; b. Cleve., Apr. 13, 1922; s. Fred Jacob and Arline (Rueter) S.; B.S., Case Inst. Tech., 1947; M.S., U. Pitts., 1951; m. Leann Frances Balog, June 14, 1947; children—Fred James III, Jody Lee, Janet Lynn, Robert Glenn. Analyst comml. research U.S. Steel Co., Pitts., 1947-48; mgr. comml. research Nat. Tube Co., 1949-53; dir. comml. research Townsend Co., Beaver Falls, Pa., 1953-56; asso. Robert Heller & Assos., Cleve., 1956-62, v.p., 1962-63; pres., dir. Allen, Hartman & Schreiber, Cleve., 1963-65; v.p. corporate planning and mgmt. services Central Nat. Bank, Cleve., 1966-68; sr. v.p. Marine Midland Trust of Western N.Y., Buffalo, 1968-73, exec. v.p., 1973-74; exec. v.p. Marine Midland Bank Inc., Buffalo, 1974-76; v.p. Lamalie Assos., Atlanta, 1976—. Served with AUS, 1943-46. Decorated Purple Heart. Mem. Bank Marketing Assn., S.M.E., Newcomen Soc., Tau Beta Pi, Theta Tau, Phi Delta Theta. Republican. Roman Catholic. Club: Univ. (N.Y.C.). Home: 5455 Trowbridge Dr Atlanta GA 30338 Office: Tower Place 3340 Peachtree Rd NE Atlanta GA 30326

SCHREIBER, GEORGE ARTHUR, utility co. exec.; b. Ellwood City, Pa., June 1, 1919; s. George Leroy and Christene (McGinley) S; student U. N.Mex., 1936-38; A.B. in Econs., U. Notre Dame, 1941; m. Mary Taylor Cook, Apr. 16, 1944; children—Peter F., George Arthur, Mary T. With Pub. Service Co. of N.Mex., 1949—, pres., 1966-75, chmn. bd., 1975—; dir. Pub. Service Co. N.Mex. Served as lt. comdr. USNR, 1942-46. Mem. Albuquerque C. of C. (dir. 1954-60), Sigma Chi. Club: Albuquerque Country. Home: 6 Tennis Ct La Luz NW Albuquerque NM 87120 Office: PO Box 2267 Silver Ave SW Albuquerque NM 87103

SCHREIBER, GEORGE RICHARD, assn. exec.; b. Ironton, Ohio, July 4, 1922; s. George Joseph and Marie Frances (Heitzman) S.; A.B., St. Joseph's Coll., Rensselaer, Ind., 1943, L.H.D., 1974; M.A., U. Chgo., 1944; m. Veva Jeanette Hopkins, May 14, 1945; children—Susan (Mrs. Arlan Shorey), George, Ellen (Mrs. Norman Hodge). Exec. editor Billboard mag., 1945-60; editor, pub. Vend mag., 1946-66; editorial dir. Billboard Publs., 1966-70; pres., chief exec. officer Nat. Automatic Mdsg. Assn., Chgo., 1970—; mem. staff and faculty U. Chgo., 1944-46. Chmn. Glenview (Ill.) Plan Commn., 1962-64, mayor, 1964-67; chmn. Region 1, Chgo. Area Transp. Study Group, 1962-63; bd. dirs. Rockefeller Meml. Chapel, U. Chgo., 1944-45; trustee St. Joseph's Coll., 1964—, chmn., 1970-76, chmn. exec. com., 1978—. Recipient Jesse H. Neal award for editorial achievement, 1964. Mem. Am. Bus. Press (editorial bd.), Assn. Econs. Council, Am. Soc. Assn. Execs. Clubs: Tavern, Internat. (Chgo.). Author: Verses from the River Country, 1941; What Makes News, 1943; Automatic Selling, 1954; A Concise History of Vending in the U.S.A., 1965; The Bobby Baker Affair—How to Make Millions in Washington, 1964. Home: 735 Ravine Ave Lake Bluff IL 60044 Office: 7 S Dearborn St Chicago IL 60603

SCHREIBER, LE ANNE, journalist; b. Evanston, Ill., Aug. 4, 1945; d. Newton Bartholemew and Beatrice (Meyer) S.; B.A. in English (Wsodrow Wilson fellow), Rice U., 1967; M.A. in English, Stanford U., 1968; postgrad. in English (Harvard Prize fellow) Harvard U., 1969-74. Teaching fellow English dept. Harvard U., 1971-74: staff writer Time mag., N.Y.C., 1974-76; editor-in-chief womenSports Mag., N.Y.C., 1976-78; asst. editor sports dept. N.Y. Times, N.Y.C., 1978, sports editor, 1978—. Recipient Helen Rogers Reid award N.Y. League Bus. and Profl. Women, 1979. Office: 229 W 43d St New York NY 10023

SCHREIBER, MARTIN JAMES, ins. co. exec.; b. Milw., Apr. 8, 1939; s. Martin Eugene and Emeline (Kurz) S.; B.S., Valparaiso U.; LL.B., Marquette U.; postgrad. urban affairs, U. Wis.; m. Elaine Ruth Thaney, June 3, 1961; children—Martin, Matthew, Katherine, Kristine. Admitted to Wis. bar; mem. Wis. Senate, 1962-69; chmn. Democratic caucus, 1967-69; lt. gov. Wis., 1971-77, gov., 1977-79; v.p. Sentry Ins. Co., Stevens Point, Wis., 1979—. Wis. nursing home ombudsman; chmn. Gov.'s Council for Consumer Affairs, 1972-77; chmn. Wis. Ins. Laws Revision Com.; chmn. Wis. Am. Revolution Bicentennial Commn.; mem. Interstate Cooperation Commn. Mem. Wis. Assn. Mental Health, 1967-68, Bd. dirs. Community Tng. and Devel. Corp., Wonderful Wis. Found. Mem. Nat. Conf. Lt. Govs. (chmn. 1972), Wis. Community Care Orgn., Wis. Acad. Scis., Arts and Letters, Milw. Bar Assn. Lutheran. Office: State Capitol Bldg Madison WI 53702

SCHREIBER, MELVYN HIRSH, radiologist; b. Galveston, Tex., May 28, 1931; s. Edward and Sue S.; M.D., U. Tex. Med. Br., Galveston, 1955; m. Laurentina; children—William, Diane, Karen, Lori. Intern, U. Tex. Med. Br., Galveston, 1955-56, resident, 1956-59, asst. prof. radiology, 1961-64, asso. prof., 1964-67, prof., 1967—, chmn. dept. radiology, 1976—. Served as capt. M.C., U.S. Army, 1959-61. Markie Found. scholar, 1963-68. Diplomate Am. Bd. Radiology. Fellow Am. Coll. Radiology, A.C.P.; mem. Assn. Univ. Radiologists (pres. 1974-75). Author: (with Robert N. Cooley) Radiology of the Heart and Great Vessels, 1978. Office: U Tex Med Br Radiology Dept Galveston TX 77550

SCHREIBER, RICHARD WILLIAM, educator; b. Lawrence, Mass., Apr. 4, 1917; s. William and Rose Anne (Thibodeau) S.; B.S., U. N.H., 1951, M.S., 1952; Ph.D., U. Wis., 1956; m. Joan Winslow Moody, Nov. 25, 1948; 1 son, Kurt Winslow. Instr. biology U. Wis., Green Bay, 1955-57; asst. prof. botany U. N.H., Durham, 1957-63, asso. prof., 1963-66, prof., 1966—, chmn. exec. com. botany dept., 1969-72. Bd. dirs. N.H. br. A.C.L.U. Served with AUS, 1942-45; MTO. Mem. AAUP (chpt. pres. 1970-71), Am. Soc. Cell Biology, Bot. Soc. Am., AAAS, N.Y. Acad. Scis., Am. Soc. Plant Physiologists. Contbr. articles to sci. jours. Home: Cherry Ln Box 70A RFD 2 Dover NH 03820 Office: Botany Dept Nesmith Hall U NH Durham NH 03824

SCHREIBER, SIDNEY M., justice N.J. Supreme Ct.; b. N.Y.C., Nov. 18, 1914; B.A., Yale U., 1936, LL.B., 1939; m. Ruth Butt; 1 dau., Florence. Admitted to N.J. bar, 1939; practiced law; judge N.J. Superior Ct., 1972-75; asso. justice N.J. Supreme Ct., 1975—; atty. U.S. Retirement Bd., SEC; dir. War Crimes Rev. sect. Judge Adv.'s Office Third Army. Del. Constl. Conv., 1966; mem. Union County (N.J.) Park Commn. Served as lt. U.S. Army, 1943-46. Mem. Am. Bar Assn. Office: 520 Broad St Newark NJ 07102*

SCHREIER, JOHN FRANK, labor union exec.; b. Cleve., Oct. 24, 1905; s. Frank Michael and Katherine (Bauman) S.; student Chgo. Tech. Coll., 1924; Spencerian Bus. Coll., 1926; m. Elizabeth Ethel May, May 27, 1933; children—Jeanne (Mrs. Kelly B. Heffner, Jr.) and Joyce (Mrs. Kenneth E. Roberts) (twins), John Frank. Sec., Arch Metal Workers AFL, 1933-37; AFL staff rep. Ohio-Ill.-Ind.-Ia.-N.Y., 1936-53, area dir., Buffalo, 1946-53, dir. Mich., 1953-56; asst. nat. dir. AFL-CIO North Central States, 1956-66, dir. Mich., 1966-67, dir. Region XI Mich.-Wis., 1968—, asst. dir. Region 1, 1974—, mem. exec. bd. Mich. State AFL-CIO council, mem. labor adv. com., Inst. Labor and Indsl. Relations, Wayne State U. and U. Mich.; v.p. labor prodns. Video I, Inc., Oak Park, Mich., 1979—. Chmn., AFL Optical Council, 1944-50, v.p. Labors Internat. Hall of Fame. Mem. bd. N.Y. State, Ams. for Dem. Action, 1948-53. Trustee Cleve. Metal Trades Council (AFL); mem. exec. bd. Labor's Com. to Combat Intolerance Buffalo. Mem. Assn. Registered Pharmacists (past local bus. mgr.). Home: 10770 Blaine Rd Brighton MI 48116 Office: 10160 W Nine Mile Rd Oak Park MI 48237

SCHREINER, ALBERT WILLIAM, physician, educator; b. Cin., Feb. 15, 1926; s. Albert William and Ruth Mary (Neuer) S.; B.S., U. Cin., 1947, M.D., 1949; m. Jean Tellstrom, Dec. 12, 1953; 1 son, David William. Clin. investigator VA Hosp., Cin., 1957-59; chief med. service, 1959-68; dir. dept. internal medicine Christ Hosp., Cin., 1968—; mem. faculty U. Cin. Coll. Medicine, 1955—, asso. prof. medicine, 1962-67, prof. internal medicine, 1967—; attending physician Cin. Gen. Hosp., 1957—, Christ Hosp., Cin., 1968—, Holmes Hosp., 1962—; cons. VA Hosp., Cin., cons. to med. dir., Ohio Nat. Life Ins., Co. Bd. dirs., chmn. health com. Community Action Commn., 1968-70; trustee Drake Meml. Hosp., 1975—. Served with AUS, 1953-55. Diplomate Am. Bd. Internal Medicine. Fellow A.C.P.; mem. N.Y. Acad. Scis., Am. Fedn. Clin. Research, Ohio Med. Assn., Ohio Soc. Internal Med. (trustee), Phi Beta Kappa, Sigma Xi. Roman Catholic. Contbr. articles tech. jours. Home: 8525 Given St Cincinnati OH 45243 Office: 2139 Auburn St Cincinnati OH 45219

SCHREINER, ALEXANDER, organist; b. Nuremberg, Germany, July 31, 1901; s. John Christian and Margarethe (Schwemmer) S.; came to U.S., 1912, naturalized, 1920; studied music with John J. McClellan, Salt Lake City, Louis Vierne, Charles Marie Widor, Henri Libert, Paris; A.B., U. Utah, 1942; Ph.D., 1954, L.H.D. (hon.), 1968, D.F.A. (hon.), 1974, Mus.D. (hon.), 1978; m. Margaret Lyman, 1927; children—Richard Lyman, John Christian, Gretchen, Julianne. Organist, The Tabernacle, Salt Lake City, 1924—; organist, lectr. in music U. Calif., Los Angeles, 1930-39; organist, dir. Wilshire Boulevard Temple, Los Angeles, 1936-39; organ broadcasting over nat. network, Salt Lake Tabernacle, 1929—. Ann. transcontinental recital tours, 1943-65. Decorated cross Order of Merit 1st class (West Germany). Fellow Am. Guild Organists (dean Los Angeles chpt. 1937-39); mem. Phi Beta Kappa, Phi Kappa Phi. Republican. Mormon. Club: Timpanogos. Composer, compiler and author: Organ Voluntaries, 1937; author Organ Voluntaries, Vol II, 1945. Home: 1283 E South Temple St Salt Lake City UT 84102

SCHREUDER, GERARD FRITZ, educator; b. Medan, Indonesia, Apr. 4, 1937; s. Evert Jan and Wilma S.; came to U.S., 1964, naturalized, 1976; Master in Forestry, Wageningen Coll., 1960; M.S. in Stats., N.C. State U., 1967; Ph.D. in Econs., Yale U., 1968; m. Ally van Buuren, July 18, 1961; children—Astrid Brigitte, John Gerard. Asst. expert Inter-Am. Inst. for Agrl. Scis., Turrialba, Costa Rica, 1961-64; lectr. stats. and aerial photos Yale U., New Haven, 1967-68, asst. prof., 1968-70; asso. prof. U. Wash. Coll. Forest Resources, Seattle, 1971-75, prof., 1975—, dir. Resources Mgmt. Research Center. NSF grantee, 1972-76. Mem. AAAS, Netherlands Inst. Agrl. Engrs., Am. Econ. Assn., Phi Kappa Phi. Contbr. articles to profl. jours. Home: 2956 74th Ave SE Mercer Island WA 98040 Office: Coll Forest Resources U Wash Seattle WA 98195

SCHREY, JACK WILLIAM, mfg. co. exec.; b. Columbus, Nebr., Mar. 7, 1916; s. Albert O. and Catherine (Borgwardt) S.; B.S. in Accounting, U. Kan., 1937; m. Theda J. Dickerhoof, Dec. 30, 1940; children—Patricia A. (Mrs. Rehn Nelson), Susan L. (Mrs. Rich Bigler), Laurie J. (Mrs. Charles Roth), Janis I. (Mrs. Charles Ford). Plant auditor Firestone Tire & Rubber Co., Akron, Ohio, 1937-42, cost accountant, Des Moines, 1947-48; internal auditor Magnavox Co., Ft. Wayne, Ind., 1948-53, asst. controller, 1953-61, controller, 1961—, v.p., 1963-71, sr. v.p., dir., 1971—; pres. Magnavox Govt. & Indsl. Electronics Co., 1975—; dir. Ft. Wayne Nat. Bank. Gen. campaign chmn. United Fund, 1973; chmn. Ind. Sci. Edn. Found., 1969—. Lay bd. advisers St. Francis Coll.; bd. dirs. United Way, Jr. Achievement; trustee Ind. Inst. Tech., YMCA; bd. advisers Ind. U.-Purdue U., Ft. Wayne. Served from 2d lt. to capt. USAAF, 1942-45. Decorated Bronze Star; recipient Silver Knight award Magnavox Mgmt. Club, 1966, Toastmasters Internat. award for communications and leadership, 1973. Mem. Nat. Assn. Accountants (past pres.), Am. Ordnance Assn., Am. Inst. Mgmt., Fin. Execs. Inst.

Yale U., 1979—; lectr. profl., acad., bus., univ., govt. and citizen groups. Jewish. Author: The Judiciary Committees, 1975; contbr. articles, revs. to profl. and popular publs. Home: 1056 Whitney Ave Hamden CT 06517 Office: Yale Law Sch 401 A Yale Sta New Haven CT 06520

SCHUCK, VICTORIA, coll. pres.; b. Oklahoma City, Mar. 16, 1909; d. Anthony B. and Anna (Priebe) Schuck; A.B. with great distinction, Stanford, 1930, M.A., 1931, Ph.D., 1937, Univ. fellow Stanford, 1931-33, teaching asst. 1934-35, acting instr., 1935-36, instr., 1936-37; asst. prof. Fla. State Coll. Women, 1937-40; mem. faculty Mt. Holyoke Coll., 1940-77, prof. polit. sci., 1950-77; pres. Mt. Vernon Coll., Washington, 1977—; vis. lectr. Smith Coll., 1948-49; vis. prof. Stanford, summer 1952; guest scholar Brookings Instn., 1967-68, summers 68, 70 Prin. program analyst, planning for local bds. OPA, 1942-44; cons. Office Temporary Controls, 1945-47; mem. internat. secretariat UN Conf. San Francisco, 1945; mem. Mass. Commn. Interstate Coop., 1957-60; mem. U. Mass. Bldg. Authority, 1960-68; Mass. adv. com. U.S. Commn. Civil Rights, 1962—. Mem. President's Commn. Registration and Voting Participation, 1963; mem. Berkshire Community Coll. Planning Com., 1964-68, Greenfield Community Coll. Planning Com., 1965-68, Mass. Bd. Higher Edn., 1976-77; mem. Town of South Hadley Planning Bd., 1959-67, chmn., 1961-67. Trustee U. Mass., 1958-65. Grantee Hayes Found., 1951-52, Asia Soc., 1971-72. Mem. Am. (sec. 1959-60, v.p. 1970-71), New Eng. (pres. 1950-51), Northeastern (pres. 1972-73) polit. sci. assns., AAUW (pres. Mass. 1946-50, nat. chmn. legislative program com., bd. dirs. 1965-69), Am. Soc. Pub. Adminstrn., AAUP (pres. Mt. Holyoke 1962-64), Internat. Polit. Sci. Assn., Assn. Asian Studies, Phi Beta Kappa, Chi Omega, Mortar Bd. (hon.). Club: Cosmopolitan (N.Y.C.). Regional editor Ency. Brit., 1958-61. Contbr. articles to profl. jours. Home: Mount Vernon Coll Washington DC 20007

SCHUDEL, HANSJOERG, export-import co. exec.; b. Wald, Switzerland, Sept. 27, 1937; s. Rene and Alice S.; ed. Coll. Bus. Adminstrn., Zurich, Switzerland. With Byk-Gulden, Konstanz, Germany, Sao Paulo, Brazil and Hicksville, N.Y., 1962-69; pres., dir. Stinnes Corp., N.Y.C., 1971—; vice chmn. bd. Cockerill-Stinnes Steel Corp., N.Y.C., 1973—; chmn. bd. CBC Industries Inc., Los Angeles, Stinnes Industries Inc., N.Y.C., Richard Bros. Punch Co., Detroit, Goldberg-Emerman Corp., Elk Grove Village, Ill., F & S Alloys & Minerals Corp., N.Y.C., Diesel Engine and Fabricating Co., Houston, Mine Equipment Co., Mt. Vernon, Ill., Center Service and Equipment Co.; vice chmn. bd. Precision Nat. Corp., Mt. Vernon, Ill., REMEX, Mex.; dir. Rheuus Transport Internat. Corp., N.Y.C., Stinnes Oil & Chem. Co., Houston, Stinnes Coal Co., N.Y.C. Mem. Swiss Soc. N.Y., Presidents Assn. Home: 40 Pond Hill Rd Chappaqua NY 10514 Office: 750 3d Ave New York NY 10017

SCHUDT, WILLIAM ARTHUR, JR., broadcasting cons.; b. Bklyn., Jan. 18, 1906; s. William A. and Mary (Curry) S.; student pub. schs., m. Eugenia Marie Richards, Mar. 3, 1949; 1 dau., Alicia Marie. Radio columnist N.Y. Telegram, 1926; dir. publicity A-H. Grebe Co., radio sta. WABC, 1928; condr. newspaper editor radio feature Bill Schudt's Going To Press, C.B.S., 1929-33, apptd. gen. mgr. WBT, Charlotte, N.C., 1933-38, gen. mgr. WKRC, Cin., 1938-40, gen. mgr. transcription div. Columbia Records, 1940-42, Eastern mgr. sta. relations, 1942-48, dir., 1948-51, nat. dir. sta. relations, 1951-53, v.p. in charge sta. relations C.B.S. Radio 1953-58, v.p. in charge affiliate relations CBS Radio, 1958-66, cons., 1966—. Mem. Broadcast Pioneers. Home: 640 W Carl Ave Baldwin NY 11510

SCHUE, JOHN RICHARD, educator; b. Gaylord, Minn., Feb. 6, 1932; s. George P. and Alma (Uecker) S.; A.B., Macalester Coll., 1953; Ph.D., Mass. Inst. Tech., 1959; m. Barbara James, Sept. 4, 1957; children—Martha, Daniel, Stephen, Paul. Instr., Mass. Inst. Tech., 1957-59; asst. prof. Oberlin (Ohio) Coll., 1959-62; asso. prof. Macalester Coll., St. Paul, 1962-68, prof. math., 1968—; NSF sci. faculty fellow Dartmouth, 1968-69. Mem. Math. Assn. Am., Am. Math. Soc., Am. Assn. U. Profs., Phi Beta Kappa, Sigma Xi. Mem. United Ch. Home: 1512 Goodrich Ave St Paul MN 55105

SCHUELE, DONALD EDWARD, educator; b. Cleve., June 16, 1934; s. Edward and Mildred (Matousek) S.; B.S., John Carroll U., Cleve., 1956, M.S., 1957; Ph.D., Case Inst. Tech., 1962; m. Clare Ann Kirchner, Sept. 5, 1956; children—Donna, Karen, Melanie, Judy, Rachel, Ruth. Instr. physics and math. John Carroll U., 1956-59; part-time instr. physics Case Inst. Tech., 1959-62, successively instr., asst. prof., asso. prof., 1962-70; mem. tech. staff Bell Telephone Labs., 1970-72; asso. prof. physics Case Western Res. U., 1972-74, prof., 1974—, dean undergrad. coll., 1973-76, chmn. dept. physics, 1976-78, vice dean Case Inst. Tech., 1978; cons. in field. Mem. adv. bd. St. Charles Borromeo Sch., 1970-72; bd. overseers St. Mary's Sem. NSF Faculty fellow, 1961-63. Mem. Am. Phys. Soc., Am. Assn. Physics Tchrs., Ohio Acad. Sci., Newman Apostolate, Sigma Xi, Alpha Sigma Nu. Republican. Roman Catholic. Contbr. articles to profl. jours. Co-editor Critical Revs. in Solid State Scis., 1969—. Patentee in field. Home: 4892 Countryside Lane Lyndhurst OH 44124 Office: 10900 Euclid Ave Cleveland OH 44106

SCHUELKE, LANG DAVID, educator; b. Manistee, Mich., Sept. 11, 1939; s. Alfred Alvin and Eva (Lange) S.; B.S., Northwestern U., 1961; M.A., U. Ill., 1964; Ph.D., Purdue U., 1969; m. Judith Mercedes Wheeler, Aug. 26, 1961; children—Susan Rosemary, Martin Robert, Jennifer Lynn, Melinda Eva Jane. Asst. prof. Purdue U., Hammond, Ind., 1969-70; acting dir. communication, dir. acad. devel. prof. Governors State U., Park Forest, Ill., 1970-72; prof., dir. lab. for research in sci. communication U. Minn., St. Paul, 1972—; cons. to industry, profl. assns. Mem. Am. Arbitration Assn., Internat. Communication Assn., Speech Communication Assn., AAAS, IEEE, Gamma Sigma Delta, Sigma Delta Chi. Democrat. Episcopalian. Author: Innovation, Communication and the Management of Technology Transfer, 1977; co-author: Classroom Communication: The Role of Communication in Teaching and Learning; co-editor: Career Communication: Directions for the Seventies, 1972. Home: 1 Lily Pond Rd Saint Paul MN 55110

SCHUENKE, DONALD JOHN, ins. co. exec.; b. Milw., Jan. 12, 1929; s. Ray H. and Josephine P. (Maciolek) S.; Ph.B., Marquette U., 1950, LL.B., 1958; m. Joyce A. Wetzel, July 19, 1952; children—Ann, Thomas, Mary. Admitted to Wis. bar, 1958; spl. agt. Nat. Life of Vt., 1958-59; real estate rep. Standard Oil Co. of Ind., Milw., 1959-63; atty. Northwestern Mut. Life Ins. Co., Milw., 1963-65, asst. gen. counsel, 1965-74, v.p., gen. counsel, sec., 1974-76, sr. v.p. investments, 1976—; chmn., pres., trustee Northwestern Mut. Life Mortgage and Realty Investors. Bd. dirs. Milw. Symphony Orch., U. Wis.-Milw. Found., Curative Workshop, St. Camillus Health Center, Sacred Heart Sch. Theology; mem. adv. bd. YWCA of Milw. Mem. Wis. Bar Assn., Am. Council Life Ins., Urban Land Inst., Marquette U. Law Sch. Alumni Assn. (bd. dirs.). Home: 7733 W Wisconsin Ave Wauwatosa WI 53213 Office: Northwestern Mut Life Ins Co 720 E Wisconsin Ave Milwaukee WI 53202

SCHUERCH, CONRAD, educator, chemist; b. Boston, Aug. 2, 1918; s. Conrad and Emma Melanie (Steinmuller) S.; B.S., Mass. Inst. Tech., 1940, Ph.D., 1947; m. Margaret Childs Pratt, June 26, 1948; children—Barbara Merle, Conrad, William Edward, Peter Henry. With McGill U., 1947-49; mem. faculty State U. N.Y. Coll. Environmental Sci. Forestry, Syracuse 1949—, prof. chemistry, 1956—, chmn. dept., 1956-72, SUNY disting. prof., 1978. Served to 1st lt. USAAF, 1943-45. Decorated Air medal with 3 oak leaf clusters, D.F.C., Purple Heart; Harold Hibbert Meml. fellow McGill U., 1948-49; Guggenheim fellow, 1959-60. Mem. Am. Chem. Soc. (chmn. Syracuse sect. 1962, chmn. cellulose, paper and textile div. 1977, Anselm Payen award 1972, Syracuse sect. award 1973), AAAS, TAPPI. Research synthetic and natural polymers, carbohydrate and wood chemistry. Home: 125 Concord Pl Syracuse NY 13210

SCHUESSLER, KARL FREDERICK, sociologist, educator; b. Quincy, Ill., Feb. 15, 1915; s. Hugo and Elsa (Westerbeck) S.; B.A., Evansville (Ind.) Coll., 1936; M.A., U. Chgo., 1939; Ph.D., Ind. U., 1947; m. Lucille Smith, June 27, 1946; children—Thomas Brian. Sociologist, Ill. State Prison, 1938; tchr. Highland Park (Ill). High Sch., 1939-40; instr. Vanderbilt U., 1946-47; mem. faculty Ind. U., 1947—, prof. sociology, 1960-76, Distinguished prof. sociology, 1976—, chmn. dept., 1961-69; research cons. Thammasat U., Bangkok, Thailand, 1963; vis. prof. U. Calif., Los Angeles, 1957, U. Calif., Berkeley 1965-66, U. Wash., 1967. Mem. adv. panel sociology NSF, 1962-63; mem. behavioral sect. NIH, 1964-68; mem. social sci. research study sect. Nat. Inst. Mental Health, 1968-69, social sci. tng. study sect., 1969-73; mem. NRC, 1970—. Served to lt. USNR, 1942-46. Mem. Am. Sociol. Assn., Am. Statis. Assn. Author: (with J.H. Mueller) Statistical Reasoning in Sociology, 1961; Social Research Methods; Analyzing Social Data, 1971; (with H. Costner) Statistical Reasoning in Sociology, 3d edit., 1977; also numerous articles. Editor: (with Cohen and Lindesmith) The Sutherland Papers, 1956; (with E.H. Sutherland) On Analyzing Crime, 1972; (with Demerath and Larsen) Public Policy and Sociology, 1975. Editor Am. Sociol. Rev., 1969-71, Sociol. Methodology, 1977—. Home: 1820 E Hunter St Bloomington IN 47401

SCHUETTE, OSWALD FRANCIS, educator; b. Washington, Aug. 20, 1921; s. Oswald Frances and Mary (Moran) S.; B.S., Georgetown U., 1943; Ph.D., Yale, 1949; m. Kathryn E. Cronin, June 7, 1947; children—Patrick Thomas, Mary Kathryn, Elizabeth Anne. Asso. prof. physics Coll. William and Mary, 1948-53; Fulbright research prof. physics Max Planck Inst. for Chemistry, 1953-54; sci. liaison officer U.S. Naval Forces, Germany, 1954-58; mem. staff Nat. Acad. Scis., Washington, 1958- 60; dep. spl. asst. for space Office Sec. Def., Washington, 1961-63; prof., chmn. physics dept. U. S.C., 1963—. Mem. council Oak Ridge Asso. Univs.; trustee Univs. Research Assn. Inc. Served to lt. USNR, 1944-46. Mem. Am. Phys. Soc., S.C. Acad. Sci. (pres.), AAUP, Sigma Xi. Home: 4979 Quail Ln Columbia SC 29206

SCHUETTE, PAUL WILLIAM, motivational services co. exec.; b. Rock Springs, Wis., Feb. 24, 1916; s. Paul Walter and Martha (Vorlop) S.; Ph.B., U. Wis., 1937, J.D., 1939; m. Enid Iva Warzyn, June 16, 1940; children—Kathryn Dawn, Robert Wade. Admitted to Wis. bar, 1939, N.J. bar, 1947, Ohio bar, 1957; grad. asst. U. Wis. Law Sch., 1939-40; atty. Nat. Union Radio Corp., Newark, 1940-46, asst. sec., 1943-46, sec., 1946; sec. Security Banknote Co., N.Y.C., 1947-53; sec. John B. Moore Corp., N.J., 1952-56, dir., 1952-78; counsel TRW, Inc., Cleve., 1956-60, sec., 1960-70; chmn. bd., treas. Mont Chalet, Inc., 1964—; pres. Success Dynamics, Inc., 1970—, Relaxalot Corp., 1971—, Imagination Assos., Inc., 1971—, Alpha Center, Inc., 1977—, Ch. of Inner Wisdom, 1978—; sec.-treas. Good-All Electric Mfg. Co., 1960-63; sec. Milam Electric Mfg. Co., 1960-64, Ramsey Corp., 1960-70. Served to lt. (j.g.) USNR, 1944-46. Mem. Wis. Bar Assn., Am. Soc. Corp. Secs., Soc. Am. Magicians, Internat. Brotherhood Magicians, Cleve. Magicians Club, Assn. to Advance Ethical Hypnosis, Internat. Platform Assn., Internat. Soc. for Profl. Hypnosis, Phi Beta Kappa, Order of Coif, Phi Delta Phi. Home: 25205 Chatworth Dr Euclid OH 44117 Office: 2633 State Route 59 Suite E Ravenna OH 44266

SCHUFLE, JOSEPH ALBERT, educator; b. Akron, Ohio, Dec. 21, 1917; s. Albert Bernard and Daisy Susanna (Frick) S.; B.S., U. Akron, 1938, M.S., 1942; Ph.D., Western Res. U., 1948; m. Lois Carolyn Mytholar, May 31, 1942; children—Joseph Albert and Jean Ann (twins). Chemist, City of Akron, 1939-42; instr. math Western Res. U., 1946-47; asst. prof. to prof. chemistry N.Mex. Inst. Mining and Tech., Socorro, 1948-64; vis. prof. chemistry Univ. Coll., Dublin, 1961-62; prof. chemistry N.Mex. Highlands U., Las Vegas, 1964—; vis. scholar hist. sci. Uppsala (Sweden) U., 1977; Pres., bd. dirs. Westminster Found. Synod of N.Mex., 1960-70. Served from 2d lt. to capt. C.W.S., AUS, 1942-46. Fellow A.A.A.S. (pres. S.W. Rocky Mountain div. 1974), Am. Inst. Chemists, Inst. Chemistry Ireland, N.Mex. Acad. Sci. (Ann. award for outstanding contbns. to sci. 1972); mem. Am. Chem. Soc., History of Sci. Soc., ACLU, AAUP, Sigma Xi. Presbyterian. Author: Bergman's Dissertation on Elective Attractions, 1968; Preparing the Way, 1970; D'Elhuyar and 18th Century New Granada (transl. from Spanish), 1976; Vaquero to Dominie, 1978; (biography) Torbern Bergman, 1979; contbg. author: Aridity and Man, 1963; Teaching of History of Chemistry, 1971. Home: 1301 8th St Las Vegas NM 87701

SCHUH, G(EORGE) EDWARD, agrl. economist; b. Indpls., Sept. 13, 1930; s. George Edward and Viola (Lentz) S.; B.S. in Agrl. Edn., Purdue U., 1952; M.S., Mich. State U., 1954, M.A. in Econs., U. Chgo., 1958, Ph.D., 1961; m. Maria Ignez, May 23, 1965; children—Audrey, Susan, Tanya. From instr. to prof. agrl. econs. Purdue U., 1959-79, dir. Center for Public Policy and Public Affairs, 1977-78; dep. undersec. for internat. affairs and commodity programs Dept. Agr., Washington, 1978-79; prof. agrl. and applied econs., head dept., 1979—; program adv. Ford Found., 1966-72; sr. staff economist Pres.'s Council Econ. Adv's., 1974-75; dir. Nat. Bur. Econ. Research, 1977—; hon. prof. Fed. U. Vicosa (Brazil), 1965; mem. policy adv. com. Econs. Inst., Boulder, Colo., 1979—. Served with U.S. Army, 1954-56. Fellow Am. Acad. Arts and Scis.; mem. Am. Agrl. Econs. Assn. (Thesis award 1962, Published Research award 1971, Article award 1975, Policy award 1979, dir. 1977-80), Internat. Assn. Agrl. Econs., Am. Econ. Assn., Brazilian Soc. Agrl. Economists. Author, editor profl. books; contbr. numerous articles to profl. publs. Office: 231 Classroom Office Bldg 1994 Buford Ave U Minn Saint Paul MN 55108

SCHUKNECHT, HAROLD FREDERICK, physician, educator; b. Chancellor, S.D., Feb. 10, 1917; s. J.G. and Dena (Weeldreyer) S.; student U. S.D., 1934-36; B.S., S.D. Sch. Med. Scis., 1938; M.D., U. Chgo., 1940; M.S. (hon.) Harvard, 1961; D.Sc. (hon.) U. S.D., 1972; m. Anne Bodle, June 30, 1941; children—Judith, James, Intern, Mercy Hosp., Des Moines, 1940-41; resident U. Chgo. Clinics, 1946-49; asst. prof. otology U. Chgo., 1949-53; asso. surgeon Henry Ford Hosp., Detroit, 1953-61; chief otolaryngology Mass Eye and Ear Infirmary, 1961—; Walter A. LeCompte prof. otology, prof. laryngology Harvard Med. Sch., 1961—; spl. research pathology ear and physiology hearing. Recipient Achievement award Deafness Research Found., Beltone award. Diplomate Am. Bd. Otolaryngology. Fellow Acoustical Soc. Am., Royal Coll. Surgeons (Glasgow) (hon.); mem. A.M.A., Am. Acad. Ophthalmology and Otolaryngology, Am. Triolgical Soc., Am. Otol. Soc., Mass., Suffolk County med. socs., New Eng. Otolaryn. Soc., Soc. Univ. Otolaryngologists, Collegium ORL Amicitiae Sacrum, Deutsche Akademie der Naturforscher Leopoldina, Am. Council Otolaryngology, Am. Neurotology Soc., Assn. for Research in Otolaryngology, Sigma Xi; hon. mem. Royal Soc. Medicine, Phila. Laryngol. Soc., S.D. Acad. Ophthalmology and Otolaryngology, Royal Soc. Medicine (London) (hon.), also otolaryn. socs. in South Africa, Panama, Australia, Nicaragua, Japan, Egypt. Home: 263 Highland St Weston MA 02193 Office: 243 Charles St Boston MA 02114

SCHULBERG, BUDD, author; b. N.Y.C., Mar. 27, 1914; s. Benjamin P. and Adeline (Jaffe) S.; student Deerfield Acad., 1931-32; A.B., cum laude Dartmouth, 1936, LL.D., 1960; m. Virginia Ray, July 23, 1936; 1 dau., Victoria; m. 2d, Victoria Anderson, Feb. 17, 1943; children—Stephen, David; m. 3d, Geraldine Brooks, July 12, 1964; m. 4th, Betsy Anne Langman, June 9, 1979; Screen writer, Hollywood, 1936-39; short stories, articles leading nat. mags. and anthologies, dir. Douglass House Watts Writers Workshop. Bd. dirs. Westminster Neighborhood Assn., Watts, Inner City Cultural Center, Los Angeles; founder Frederick Douglass Creative Arts Center, N.Y.C., 1971; mem. nat. adv. commn. on black participation John F. Kennedy Center for Performing Arts; trustee Humanitas Prize. Served as lt. (j.g.) USNR, 1943-46, assigned to O.S.S. Awarded Army Commendation Ribbon for gathering photog. evidence of war crimes for Nuremberg Trial, 1945-46; recipient Susie Humanitarian award B'nai B'rith, Image award NAACP, Journalism award Dartmouth Coll., Merit award Lotos Club. Mem. Dramatists Guild, ASCAP, Authors Guild N.Y.C. (mem. council), ACLU, Writers Guild West, P.E.N., Sphinx (Dartmouth), Phi Beta Kappa. Author: What Makes Sammy Run (co-author libretto for the Broadway musical 1964), 1941; The Harder They Fall, 1947; The Disenchanted, 1950 (selected one of 3 outstanding works of fiction for 1950 by A.L.A. and nat. book critics); Some Faces In The Crowd (vol. short stories), 1953; On the Waterfront (screenplay, N.Y. critics award, Fgn. Correspondents Award, Screen Writers Guild award, Acad. Award best story and screenplay, Venice Festival award), 1954, Waterfront (novel) (Christopher award), 1955; (screen adaptation) The Harder They Fall, 1955; A Face In The Crowd (screenplay; German Film Critics award), 1957; Wind Across the Everglades; The Disenchanted (Broadway play 1958-59); From the Ashes Voices of Watts, 1967; Sanctuary V, 1969; The Four Seasons of Success, 1972; Loser and Still Champion: Muhammed Ali, 1973; (with Geraldine Brooks) Swan Watch, 1975. Contbr. to Sports Illustrated, Life, N.Y. Times Book Rev., Esquire, Newsday Syndicate, Los Angeles Times Book Rev., Playboy. Home: Westhampton Beach NY 11978 Office: care Alyss Dorese 41 W 82d St New York NY 10024

SCHULER, ROBERT HUGO, educator, chemist; b. Buffalo, Jan. 4, 1926; s. Robert H. and Mary J. (Mayer) S.; B.S., Canisius Coll., Buffalo, 1946; Ph.D., U. Notre Dame, 1949; m. Florence J. Forrest, June 18, 1952; children—Mary A., Margaret A., Carol A., Robert E., Thomas C. Asst. prof. chemistry Canisius Coll., 1949-53; asso. chemist, then chemist Brookhaven Nat. Lab., 1953-56; staff fellow, dir. radiation research lab. Mellon Inst., 1956-76, mem. adv. bd., 1962-76; prof. chemistry, dir. radiation research lab. Carnegie-Mellon U., 1967-76; prof. chemistry U. Notre Dame (Ind.), 1976—, dir. Radiation Lab., 1976—. Fellow AAAS; mem. Am. Chem. Soc., Am. Phys. Soc., Chem. Soc., Radiation Research Soc. (pres. 1975-76), Sigma Xi. Club: Cosmos. Author articles in field. Office: Radiation Lab U Notre Dame Notre Dame IN 46556

SCHULHOF, MICHAEL PETER, office products mfg. co. exec.; b. N.Y.C., Nov. 30, 1942; s. Rudolph B. and Hannelore (Buck) S.; B.A., Grinnell Coll., 1964; M.Sc., Cornell U., 1967; Ph.D. (NSF fellow), Brandeis U., 1970; m. Paola Nissim, Apr. 17, 1969; children—David Kenneth, Jonathan Nissim. Research fellow Brookhaven Nat. Lab., Upton, N.Y., 1969-71; asst. to v.p. mfg. CBS Records, CBS Inc., N.Y.C., 1971-73; gen. mgr. bus. products div. Sony Corp., N.Y.C., 1973-77, v.p., 1977-78, sr. v.p., 1978—; pres. Sony Industries, Inc., 1978—; dir. Sony Corp. Lic. comml. pilot. Am. Mem. Am. Phys. Soc. (dir. 1978), Computer and Bus. Equipment Mfrs. Assn. (dir.), Am. Radio Relay League, Aircraft Owners and Pilots Assn., Guggenheim Mus., Whitney Mus. Club: Fenway Golf. Contbr. articles to profl. jours. Office: 9 W 57th St New York NY 10019

SCHULL, WILLIAM JACKSON, educator; b. Louisiana, Mo., Mar. 17, 1922; s. Eugene and Gertrude (Davenport) S.; B.S., Marquette U., 1946, M.S., 1947; Ph.D., Ohio State U., 1949; m. Victoria Margaret Novak, Sept. 7, 1946. Head dept. genetics Atomic Bomb Casualty Commn., Japan, 1949-51; from jr. geneticist to asso. geneticist Inst. Human Biology, U. Mich., 1951-56, mem. faculty univ., 1956-72, prof. human genetics, 1962-72; prof. population genetics, dir. Center for Demographic and Population Genetics, U. Tex. Health Sci. Center, Houston, 1972—; permanent dir. Radiation Effects Research Found., Hiroshima, Japan, 1978—; vis. prof. U. Chgo., 1963; vis. fellow Australian Nat. U., 1969; Deutsche Forschungs-gemeinschaft vis. prof. U. Heidelberg (Germany), 1970, U. Chile, Santiago, 1975; cons. to govt., 1951—. Panel experts WHO, 1958—. Served with AUS, 1943-46. Decorated Bronze Star; recipient Centennial award Ohio State U., 1970. Mem. Genetics Soc. Am., Am. Soc. Human Genetics, Inst. Math. Statistics, A.A.A.S., Am. Assn. Phys. Anthropologists, Teratology Soc., Soc. Biology, Soc. Epidemol. Research, Chilean, Japanese, Peruvian socs. human genetics (hon.), Soc. Human Biologists, Sigma Xi, Phi Sigma. Co-author 4 books; editor 3 books; author numerous papers. Home: 1600 Holcombe Blvd Houston TX 77025

SCHULLER, GORDON JOSEPH, naval officer; b. Cleve., Aug. 3, 1927; s. Carl George and Ruth Mary (Gordon) S.; B.S., U.S. Naval Acad., 1951; M.S. in Mgmt., U.S. Naval Postgrad. Sch., 1964; M.S. in Internat. Affairs, George Washington U., 1971; grad. Nat. War Coll., 1971; m. Anita F. Faustini, June 4, 1951; children—Jeffrey G., Ronald C., Donna, Laura, Richard. Commd. ensign U.S. Navy, 1951, advanced through grades to rear adm., 1975; head readiness and tng. div., comdr. Fleet Air Wings Pacific, 1968-70; politico/mil. adviser to sec. def., 1971-73; comd. Patrol Wing 2, 1973-75; comdr. Patrol and Reconnaissance Force, 7th Fleet, comdr. Task Force 72, comdr. Patrol Wing 1, 1975-77; comdr. Fleet Air Western Pacific, 1976-77, dir. Interam. region Office Asst. Sec. Def. for Internat. Security Affairs, Washington, 1977—. Roman Catholic. Home: Fairfax VA 22030 Office: The Pentagon Washington DC 20301

SCHULLER, GRETE, sculptress; b. Vienna, Austria, Apr. 26, 1900; d. Alexander and Stefanie (Hellman) Schoenberger; ed. Vienna Lyceum, Art Sch., Austria, Art Students League, N.Y.C., 1946, Sculpture Center, N.Y.C., 1947-51; m. Alexander Fritz Schuller, Nov. 14, 1926; children—Susan Afroyim, Maximilian. One-woman shows Sculpture Center, 1958, A.F.I. Gallery, N.Y.C., 1963, ROKO Gallery, N.Y.C., 1966; exhibited many group shows throughout U.S.; represented permanent collections Norfolk (Va.) Mus. Arts and Scis., Am. Mus. of Natural History, N.Y.C., Museum Sci., Boston. Recipient many prizes design and sculpture. Mem. Nat. Sculpture Soc., Allied Artists Am., Am. Mus. Natural History, Audubon Artists, Nat. Assn. Women Artists, Sculptors League, Catherine Lorrilard Wolfe Art Club. Home: 8 Barstow Rd #7G Great Neck NY 11021. *I tried to give permanence to the fleeting beauty which excited me in* *nature. I never let my creative energies stagnate and this helped overcome the hardships of life.*

SCHULLER, GUNTHER, composer; b. N.Y.C., Nov. 22, 1925; s. Arthur E. and Elsie (Bernartz) S.; student St. Thomas Choir Sch., N.Y.C., also Manhattan Sch. Music; Mus. D.D., Northeastern U., 1967; Mus.D., U. Ill., 1968, Colby Coll., 1969, Williams 1974; m. Marjorie Black, June 8, 1948; children—Edwin Gunther, George Alexander. Appeared as boy soprano St. Thomas Choir at age 12; French horn player Ballet Theatre, then first horn player, Cin. Symphony Orch.; solo French horn Met. Opera Orch., 1945-59; tchr. Manhattan Sch. Music, 1950-63; premiere of Symphony for Brass and Percussion, Cin., 1950, Salzburg Festival, 1957; premiere Dramatic Overture, N.Y. Philharmonic, 1956; premiere String Quartet, Contemporary Arts Festival, U. Ill., 1957, Concertino for Jazz Quartet and Orch., Balt. Symphony Orch., 1959, Seven Studies on Themes of Paul Klee, Ford Found. commn., Minn. Symphony, 1959, Spectra, N.Y. Philharmonic, 1960, Music for Brass Quintet, Coolidge Found. commn., Library of Congress, 1961; Triplum, N.Y. Philharmonic commd. Lincoln Center, 1967; Aphorisms for Flute and String Trio commd. Carlton Coll. Centennial, 1967; Fanfare for St. Louis, St. Louis Symphony, 1968; Museum Piece commd. Boston Mus. Fine Arts and Boston Symphony, 1970; head composition dept. Tanglewood, 1965—; pres. New Eng. Conservatory of Music, 1967-77; artistic dir. Berkshire Music Center, Tanglewood, 1969—; Recipient creative arts award 1960; Deems Taylor award ASCAP, 1970; Alice M. Ditson Conducting award, 1970; Rodgers and Hammerstein award 1971; Guggenheim grantee, 1962, 63. Mem. Nat. Inst. Arts and Letters, Am. Acad. Arts and Scis. Composer: Quartet for Four Double Bass, 1947; Fantasy for Unaccompanied Cello, 1951; Recitative and Rondo for Violin and Piano, 1953; Music for Violin, Piano and Percussion, 1957; Contours, 1958; Woodwind Quintet, 1958; Six Renaissance Lyrics, 1962; The Visitation (opera), 1966; Fisherman and His Wife (opera), 1970; The Power Within Us, 1972; Four Soundscapes, 1974; Concerto No. 2 for Orch., 1975; Horn Concerto No. 2, 1975; Violin Concerto, 1976; Concerto Number 2 for Orch., 1976; author: Early Jazz: Its Roots and Development, 1968. Address: 167 Dudley Rd Newton Centre MA 02159*

SCHULLER, ROBERT HAROLD, clergyman, author; b. Alton, Iowa, Sept. 16, 1926; s. Anthony and Jennie (Beltman) S.; B.A., Hope Coll., 1947, D.D., 1973; B.D., Western Theol. Sem., 1950; LL.D., Azusa Pacific Coll., 1970, Pepperdine U., 1976; Litt.D., Barrington Coll., 1977; m. Arvella DeHaan, June 15, 1950; children—Sheila, Robert, Jeanne, Carol, Gretchen. Ordained to ministry Reformed Ch. in Am., 1950; pastor Ivanhoe Ref. Ch., Chgo., 1950-55; founder, sr. pastor Garden Grove (Calif.) Community Ch., 1955—. Founder, pres. Hour of Power TV Ministry, Garden Grove, 1970—; founder, dir. Robert H. Schuller Inst. for Successful Ch. Leadership, Garden Grove, 1970—; chmn. nat. religious sponsor program Religion in Am. Life, N.Y.C., 1975—. Bd. dirs. Religion in Am. Life; pres. bd. dirs. Christian Counseling Service; founder Robert H. Schuller Corr. Center for Possibility Thinkers, 1976. Recipient Distinguished Alumnus award Hope Coll., 1970, Prin. award Freedoms Found., 1974; named Headliner of Year in Religion, Orange County, 1977, Clergyman of Year, Religious Heritage Am., 1977. Mem. Religious Guild Architects (hon.). Rotarian. Author: God's Way to the Good Life, 1963; Your Future Is Your Friend, 1964; Move Ahead with Possibility Thinking, 1967; Self Love, the Dynamic Force of Success, 1969; Power Ideas for a Happy Family, 1972; The Greatest Possibility Thinker That Ever Lived, 1973; Turn Your Scars into Stars, 1973; You Can Become the Person You Want To Be, 1973; Your Church Has Real Possibilities, 1974; Love or Loneliness—You Decide, 1974; Positive Prayers for Power-Filled Living, 1976; Keep on Believing, 1976; Reach Out for New Life, 1977; Peace of Mind Through Possibility Thinking, 1977; Turning Your Stress Into Strength, 1978; Daily Power Thoughts, 1978; co-author: The Courage of Carol, 1978. Office: 12141 Lewis St Garden Grove CA 92640

SCHULLIAN, DOROTHY MAY, librarian, historian; b. Lakewood, Ohio, May 19, 1906; d. Joseph Gustave and Louise (Knippel) Schullian; A.B., Western Res. U., 1927; Ph.D. U. Chgo., 1931; m. Howard Bernhardt Adelmann, July 6, 1978. Fellow Am. Acad., Rome 1931-34; instr. ancient langs. Albion Coll., 1939-44; asst. curator, curator, asst. chief, then chief history medicine div. Nat. Library of Medicine, Cleve., 1944-61; curator History of Sci. Collections, Cornell U. Library, 1961-72; Garrison lectr. Am. Assn. History Medicine. Fellow Internat. Acad. History of Med.; mem. Am. Assn. History Medicine, History of Sci. Soc., Bibliog. Soc. Am., Am. Philol. Assn., Mediaeval Acad. Am., Am. Classical League, Classical Assn. of the Atlantic States, Phi Beta Kappa. Methodist. Author: (with Marbury B. Ogle) Rodulfi Tortarii Carmina, 1933; (with Max Schoen) Music and Medicine, 1948; (with Francis E. Sommer) Catalogue of Incunabula and Manuscripts, 1950; (with Luigi Belloni) Carlo Francesco Cogrossi, New Theory of the Contagious Disease Among Oxen, 1953, Tortellii de Medicina et Medicis, Iac Bartholoti de Antiquitate Medicinae, 1954; Alessandro Benedetti, Diaria de bello Carolino, with Latin text, English translation, commentary, 1967; The Baglivi Correspondence from the library of Sir William Osler, 1974. Editor: Notes and Events in Jour. of History of Medicine and Allied Scis., 1952—. Contbr. articles to profl. periodicals. Home: 400 Triphammer Rd Apt L-1 Cayuga Heights Ithaca NY 14850

SCHULMAN, IRVING, physician, educator; b. N.Y.C., Feb. 17, 1922; s. Louis and Minnie (Lowen) S.; B.A., N.Y. U., 1942, M.D., 1945; m. Naomi Zion, May 28, 1950; children—Margaret, John. Intern Queens Gen. Hosp., N.Y.C., 1945-46; resident Bellevue Hosp., N.Y.C., 1948-50; practice medicine, specializing in pediatrics; asso. prof. pediatrics Cornell U. Med. Sch., 1950-58; prof. Med. Sch., Northwestern U., 1958-61; prof., head dept. pediatrics U. Ill. Coll. Medicine, Chgo., 1961-72; chief pediatrics U. Ill. Hosp., 1961-72; prof., chmn. dept. pediatrics Stanford (Calif.) Sch. Medicine, also pediatrician-in-chief Stanford U. Hosp., 1972—. Mem. research com. Chgo. Heart Assn., 1961-72, Leukemia Research Soc., 1967—; mem. med. adv. bd. Nat. Hemophilia Fdn., 1963-78; cons. NIH, 1961-67. Served to capt. M.C., AUS, 1946-48. Recipient Mead-Johnson award for pediatrc research Am. Acad. Pediatrics, 1960. Mem. Am. Acad. Pediatrics, Am. Pediatric Soc., Soc. Pediatric Research Am. Soc. For Clin. Investigation, Phi Beta Kappa. Editor-in-chief Advances in Pediatrics, 1969-76. Contbr. articles to profl. jours. Home: 836 Mayfield Ave Stanford CA 94305

SCHULMAN, IVAN ALBERT, educator; b. N.Y.C., Oct. 4, 1931; s. Isadore and Elizabeth (Raskin) S.; B.A. summa cum laude, Bklyn. Coll., 1953; fellow U. Nacional Autonoma de Mexico, 1952; M.A., U. Calif. at Los Angeles, 1954, Ph.D., 1959; m. Evelyn Picon Garfield, Nov. 17, 1979; children—David, Rosalind, Paul. Mem. faculty Washington U., St. Louis, 1959-70, prof. Spanish, 1964-68, prof. Spanish Am. lit., 1968-70, chmn. dept. Romance langs., 1965-69, dir. grad. studies Romance langs. dept., 1969-70; prof. Spanish Am. lit., chmn. Romance langs. State U. N.Y. at Stony Brook, 1970-71, chmn. dept. Hispanic lang. and lit., 1971-73; grad. research prof. Latin Am. lit. U. Fla., 1973—, dir. Center for Latin Am. Studies, 1977—; pres. Instituto Internacional de Literatura Iberoamericana, 1975-77, v.p., 1977-79; cons., Ednl. Testing Service, 1965—. Vice pres., sec. Jose Marti Found., Los Angeles, 1968-74, pres., 1974-76. U. Calif. fellow, 1957-58; Social Sci. Research Council grantee, 1960-61, 68-69, 74; Guggenheim fellow, 1968-69; Columbia U. Latin Am. seminar scholar, 1971—. Author: Simbolo y color en la obra de Jose Marti, 2d edit., 1970; Esquema ideologico de Jose Marti, 1961; Genesis del modernismo: Marti, Najera, Silva, Casal, 2d edit., 1968; Coloquio sobre la novela hispanoamericana, 1967; Marti, Dario y el modernismo, 1969; Marti, Casal y el modernismo, 1969; El modernismo hispanoamericano, 1969; Versos libres de Jose Marti, 1970; Autobiografia de un esclavo de Juan Francisco Manzano, 1975; (with Vernon A. Chamberlin) La Revista Ilustrada de Nueva York: History, Anthology and Index of Literary Selections, 1976. Mem. editorial bd. Duquesne Hispanic Rev., 1962—, Nueva Narrativa Hispanoamericana, 1971—, Problemas de Literatura, 1972—, Jour. Spanish Studies: Twentieth Century, 1973, Estudios Cubanos, 1974—, Revista de Estudios Hispanicos, 1976—, Latin American Lore, 1978—. Home: Route 1 Box 68W Saint Augustine FL 32084

SCHULMAN, JEROME LEWIS, child psychiatrist; b. N.Y.C., Nov. 15, 1925; s. Jacob and Pauline (Lewis) S.; B.A., U. Rochester, 1945; M.D., L.I. Coll., 1949; children—Ellen, Martha. Intern, Jewish Hosp., Bklyn., 1949-50; resident pediatrics Jewish Hosp., Bklyn., 1950-51, 53-54; resident psychiatry Johns Hopkins Hosp., 1954-57; instr., mem. faculty Northwestern U. Med. Sch., 1957—, prof. pediatrics, psychiatry and neurology, 1965—; head div. child psychiatry Children's Meml. Hosp., Chgo., 1957—. Served to ensign U.S. Pediatrics, Am. Bd. Psychiatry, Am. Bd. Psychiatry in Child Psychiatry. Fellow Am. Acad. Pediatrics; mem. Am. Psychiat. Assn., Am. Assn. Mental Deficiency, Soc. Biol. Psychiatry, Midwest Soc. Pediatric Research, Am. Pediatric Soc. Author: Therapeutic Dialogue, 1964; Brain Damage and Behavior, 1965; Psychologic Responsibility of Children to Hospitals and Illness, 1965; Learning to Letter, 1965; Management of Emotional Illness in Pediatric Practice, 1967; also chpts. yearbooks, films, papers. Home: 1910 W North Ave Chicago IL 60622 Office: 2300 Children's Plaza Chicago IL 60614

SCHULMAN, JOSEPH DANIEL, physician, geneticist; b. Bklyn., Dec. 20, 1941; s. Max and Miriam (Grossman) S.; B.A., Bklyn. Coll., 1961; M.D., Harvard U., 1966; m. Carol Ann Brimberg, June 14, 1964; children—Erica N., Julie K. Intern, resident in pediatrics Mass. Gen. Hosp., Boston, 1966-68; clin. asso. Nat. Inst. Arthritis and Metabolic Diseases, 1968-70; resident in obstetrics and fellow in pediatrics N.Y. Hosp.-Cornell Med. Center, 1970-73; Gilbert and Nat. Found. fellow Cambridge (Eng.) U., 1973-74; head sect. human biochem. genetics Nat. Inst. Child Health and Human Devel., NIH, Bethesda, Md., 1974—; prof. obstetrics and pediatrics George Washington U., 1975—. Served with USPHS, 1968-70. Diplomate Am. Bd. Pediatrics, Am. Bd. Ob-Gyn. Fellow Am. Coll. Obstetricians and Gynecologists; mem. Soc. Pediatric Research, Soc. Gynecologic Investigation, Am. Soc. Human Genetics, Phi Beta Kappa, Sigma Xi. Clubs: Harvard, Cosmos. Author 2 books; contbr. articles to med. jours. Home: 9207 Aldershot Dr Bethesda MD 20034 Office: Room 13N 260 Bldg 10 NIH Bethesda MD 20205

SCHULMAN, ROBERT ARNOLD, lawyer; b. N.Y.C., Feb. 16, 1916; s. Isadore Alexander and Adele (Wyzanski) S.; A.B., Columbia, 1935, LL.B., 1938; m. Betty Menderson, Sept. 5, 1945; children—John Arthur, Barbara Ann Crum, Michael Ted. Admitted to N.Y. bar, 1939, D.C. bar, 1947; atty. Office Chief Counsel, IRS, 1942-44, spl. asst. to chief counsel, 1944-47; partner firm Wenchel, Schulman & Manning, Washington, 1947-78, firm Williams & Connolly, Washington, 1978—. Mem. Am., D.C. bar assns., Zeta Beta Tau. Club: Princeton Univ. Office: Hill Bldg 839 17th St NW Washington DC 20006

SCHULMAN, SAMUEL, profl. basketball team exec.; b. N.Y.C., Apr. 10, 1910; S.; B.A., U. N.Y., 1932; M.B.A., Harvard, 1934; m. Sylvia Leibel, 1942; children-Susan (Mrs. Edward Begley), Patricia. Pres., George McKibbin & Sons, N.Y.C., 1935-60; partner Exec. Car Leasing, 1948-60; pres. Mission Pak, Los Angeles, 1961-69; v.p. Peninsula Savs. & Loan Assn., San Mateo, Calif., 1963-68; pres. Seattle SuperSonics. Established Grad. Inst. in Book Pub. at N.Y.U. Trustee Brandeis U., City of Hope, Cedars of Sinai. Clubs: Hillcrest Country (Los Angeles), Tamarisk Country (Palm Springs, Calif.). Office: care Seattle SuperSonics 419 Occidental St Seattle WA 98104*

SCHULMAN, SIDNEY, neurologist, educator; b. Chgo., Mar. 1, 1923; s. Samuel E. and Ethel (Miller) S.; B.S., U. Chgo., 1944, M.D., 1946; m. Mary Jean Diamond, June 17, 1945; children—Samuel E., Patricia, Daniel. Asst. prof. neurology U. Chgo., 1952-57, asso. prof., 1957-65, prof., 1965-75, Ellen C. Manning prof., div. biol. scis., 1975—. Served with M.C., AUS, 1947-49. Mem. Am. Neurol. Assn., U. Chgo. Med. Alumni Assn. (pres. 1968-69), Chgo. Neurol. Soc. (pres. 1964-65). Home: 5000 East End Ave Chicago IL 60615 Office: U Chgo Culver Hall 1025 E 57th St Chicago IL 60637

SCHULTE, DAVID MICHAEL, mfg. co. exec.; b. N.Y.C., Nov. 12, 1946; s. Irving and Ruth (Stein) S.; B.A., Williams Coll., 1968; postgrad. (John E. Moody scholar) Exeter Coll., Oxford (Eng.) U., 1968-69; J.D., Yale U., 1972; m. Nancy Fisher, June 30, 1968; children—Michael B., Katherine F. Admitted to D.C. bar, 1973; law clk. to Mr. Justice Stewart, U.S. Supreme Ct., 1972-73; spl. asst. to pres. N.W. Industries, Inc., Chgo., 1973-75, v.p. corp. devel., 1975-79, exec. v.p., 1979—; dir. Manpower Demonstration Research Corp., N.Y.C. Bd. dirs. Chgo. Child Care Soc. Mem. Washington Bar Assn. Editor-in-chief Yale Law Jour., 1971-72. Office: 6300 Sears Tower Chicago IL 60606

SCHULTE, HENRY FRANK, univ. dean; b. Lincoln, Nebr., Sept. 24, 1924; s. Henry F. and Neva Irene (Arnold) S.; A.B., McGill U., 1951; M.S., Columbia, 1952; Ph.D., U. Ill., 1966; m. Irene Nef, May 12, 1951; children—Nancy, Susanne. Editor-corr. U.P.I., London, 1954-56, mgr., Spain, 1956-62; asso. prof. journalism Pa. State U., 1965-69; chmn. newspaper dept. Syracuse (N.Y.) U., 1969-72, dean Newhouse Sch. Pub. Communications, 1972—; cons. Nat. Endowment for Arts; dir. WCNY-TV/FM; external U. W.I., 1975-78; cons. external degree program U. State N.Y.; chmn. Jesse H. Neal awards judging Am. Bus. Press. Served with AUS, 1945-46. Mem. Internat. Press Inst., Inter-Am. Press Assn., Soc. Profl. Journalists, Women in Communications, Assn. for Edn. in Journalism, N.Y. State Soc. Newspaper Editors (exec. sec. 1969-73), Assn. Educators in Journalism/Am. Newspaper Publishers Assn. (regional liaison officer), Overseas Press Club. Author: The Spanish Press, 1470-1966: Print, Power and Politics, 1968. Editor, pub. Mingote's World, 1957. Home: 8332 Vassar Dr Manlius NY 13104 Office: 215 University Pl Syracuse NY 13210

SCHULTE, RAINER, poet, critic, playwright, educator; b. Germany, July 8, 1937; s. Hans and Hedwig (Keller) S.; M.A., U. Mainz (Germany), 1962; Ph.D. in Comparative Lit., U. Mich., 1965. Prof. comparative lit. Ohio U., 1965-75, U. Tex. at Dallas, 1975—. Fulbright scholar. Author: (poetry) The Suicide at the Piano, 1969, The Other Side of the Word, 1978. Editor-in-chief Mundus Artium: A Jour. of Internat. Lit. and Arts; editor Giant Talk: An Anthology of Third World Writing, 1975, Needle Off Center: A Multi-Media Show, 1973; editor: Translation Rev. Home: 605 W Lamar St McKinney TX 75069 Office: U of Tex at Dallas Box 688 Richardson TX 75080

SCHULTES, RICHARD EVANS, botanist, museum exec., educator; b. Boston, Jan. 12, 1915; s. Otto Richard and Maude Beatrice (Bagley) S.; A.B., Harvard, 1937, A.M., 1938, Ph.D., 1941; M.H. (hon.), Universidad Nacional de Colombia, Bogotá, 1953; m. Dorothy Crawford McNeil, Mar. 26, 1959; children—Richard Evans II, Neil Parker and Alexandra Ames (twins). Plant explorer, NRC fellow Harvard Bot. Mus., Cambridge, Mass., 1941-42, research asso., 1942-53, curator Orchid Herbarium of Oakes Ames, 1953-58, curator econ. botany, 1958—, exec. dir., 1967-70, dir., 1970—; Guggenheim Found. fellow, collaborator U.S. Dept. Agr., Amazon of Colombia, 1942-43; plant explorer in South Am. Bur. Plant Industry, 1944-54; prof. biology Harvard, 1970-72, Paul C. Mangelsdorf prof. natural scis., 1973—; adj. prof. pharmacognosy U. Ill., Chgo., 1975—; Hubert Humphrey vis. prof. Macalaster Coll., 1979; field agt. Rubber Devel. Corp. of U.S. Govt., in S.Am., 1943-44; collaborator Instituto Agronômico Norte, Belem, Brazil, 1948-50; hon. prof. Universidad Nacional de Colombia, 1953—, prof. econ. botany, 1963; bot. cons. Smith, Kline & French Co., Phila., 1957-67; mem. NIH Adv. Panel, 1964; mem. selection com. for Latin Am. Guggenheim Found., 1964—; chmn. on-site visit U. Hawaii Natural Products Grant NIH, 1966, 67; Laura L. Barnes Annual lectr. Morris Arboretum, Phila., 1969; Koch lectr. Rho Chi Soc., Pitts., 1971, Chgo., 1974; vis. prof. econ. botany, plants in relation to man's progress Jardín Botánico, Medellín, Colombia, 1973; Cecil and Ida H. Green Vis. Lectr. U. B.C., Vancouver, Can., 1974; mem. adv. bd. Fitz Hugh Ludlow Library, San Francisco, 1974—; mem. governing bd. Amazonas 2000, Bogotá; asso. in ethnobotany Museo del Oro, Bogota, 1974—; chmn. NRC panels, 1974, 75; mem. NRC Workshop on Natural Products, Sri Lanka, 1975; participant numerous sems., congresses, meetings. Decorated Orden de la Victoria Regia in recognition of work in Amazon Colombian Govt., 1969. Fellow Am. Acad. Arts, Scis., Am. Coll. Neuropsychopharmacology; mem. Nat. Acad. Sci., Linnean Soc., Academia Colombiana de Ciencias Exactas, Fisico-Quimicas y Naturales, Instituto Ecuatoriano de Ciencias Naturales, Sociedad Cientifica Antonio Alzate (Mexico), Argentine Acad. Scis., Am. Orchid Soc. (life hon.), Pan Am. Soc. New Eng. (gov.), Asociación de Amigos de Jardines Botánicos (life), Soc. Econ. Botany (organizer annual meeting 1961, Disting. Botanist of Yr. 1979), New Eng. Bot. Club (pres. 1954-60), Internat. Assn. Plant Taxonomy, Am. Soc. Pharmacognosy, Phytochem. Soc. N.Am., Sociedad Colombiana de Orquideologia, Assn. Tropical Biology, Asociación Colombiana de Ingenieros Agrónomos, Sociedad Cubana de Botánica, Explorer's Club, Sigma Xi (pres. Harvard chpt. 1971-72), Beta Nu chpt. Phi Sigma (first hon.). Unitarian (vestryman Kings Chapel 1974-76). Author: (with P. A. Vestal) Economic Botany of the Kiowa Indians, 1941; Native Orchids of Trinidad and Tobago, 1960; (with A. F. Hill) Plants and Human Affairs, 1960, rev. edit., 1968; (with A. S. Pease) Generic Names of Orchids—their Origin and Meaning, 1963; (with A. Hofmann) The Botany and Chemistry of Hallucinogens, 1973, rev. edit., 1980, Plants of the Gods, 1979; Plant Hallucinogens, 1976; contbg. author: Ency. Biol. Scis., 1961; Ency. Brit., 1966; Ency. Biochemistry, 1967; McGraw-Hill Yearbook Sci., Tech., 1971; author numerous Harvard Bot. Mus. leaflets. Asst. editor Chronica Botanica, 1947-52; editor Bot. Mus. Leaflets, 1957—; editor Econ. Botany, 1962-79; mem. editorial bd. Lloydia, 1965-76, Altered States of Consciousness, 1973—, Jour. Psychedelic Drugs, 1974—; mem. adv. bd. Cannabis Rx, Jour. Cannabis Research, 1973—, Horticulture, 1976-78, Jour. Ethnopharmacology, 1978—. Contbr. numerous articles to profl. jours. Home: 78 Larchmont Rd Melrose MA 02176 Office: Bot Museum Harvard U Cambridge MA 02138

SCHULTZ, ANDREW SCHULTZ, JR., educator; b. Harrisburg, Pa., Aug. 14, 1913; s. Andrew S. and Ada S. (DeHaven) S.; student Phillips (Andover) Acad. 1928-32; B.S., Cornell U., 1936, Ph.D., 1941; m. Mary S. Mory, Sept. 2, 1939; children—Susan Tapscott, Andrew M. Installer, N.J. Bell Telephone Co., 1936-37; instr. Sibley Sch. Mech. Engring., Coll. Engring. Cornell U., 1937-41, asst. prof., 1941-46, asso. prof., 1946-50, prof., head dept. indsl. and engring. adminstrn., 1950-62, dean Coll. Engring., 1963-72, acting dean, 1978, Spencer T. Olin prof. engring., 1973—; v.p. Logistics Mgmt. Inst., Wash., 1962-63, now chmn. bd. trustees. Dir. Lexington Growth Fund, Lexington Research Fund, Sl Handling Systems, Inc., Chgo. Pneumatic Tool Co., Inc., Zurn Industries. Bd. dirs. Engring. Council Profl. Devel., 1968-73. Served as lt. col. AUS, 1941-46, indsl. service ammunition div. Office Chief Ordnance. Fellow Am. Inst. Indsl. Engrs. (dir. research 1955-62); mem. Operation Research Soc. Am., Inst. Mgmt. Sci., Am. Soc. Engring. Edn., Triangle, Tau Beta Pi, Pi Tau Sigma, Phi Gamma Delta. Home: 631 Highland Rd Ithaca NY 14850

SCHULTZ, ARTHUR LEROY, coll. pres.; b. Johnstown, Pa., June 14, 1928; s. Elmer A.R. and Alice (Flegal) S.; B.A., Otterbein Coll., 1949, LL.D., 1970; B.D., United Theol. Sem., 1952; M.Ed., U. Pitts., 1955, Ph.D., 1964; LL.D., Phila. Coll. Osteopathy, 1966; D.D., Albright Coll., 1977; m. Mildred Louise Stouffer, Nov. 29, 1947; children—Thomas Arthur, Rebecca Louise. Ordained to ministry United Methodist Ch., 1952; pastor in Dayton, Ohio, 1949-52, Pitts., 1952-56; dir. pub. relations Otterbein Coll., 1956-65; pres. Albright Coll., Reading, Pa., 1965-77, Ashland (Ohio) Coll., 1977—; vice chmn. Found. Ind. Colls. Pa., 1971-72; exec. com. sec.-treas. Pa. Assn. Colls. and Univs., 1968—, sec.-treas., 1971-73, v.p., 1973-74, pres., 1974-75. Pres. Pa.. Council Alcohol Problems, 1970-74; v.p. Daniel Boone council Boy Scouts Am., 1966—. Bd. dirs. Schuykill Valley area chpt. Americans Competitive Enterprise System, 1967—; trustee Wyoming Sem., Kingston, R.I. Named Outstanding Young Man of Year, Westerville, Ohio, 1959. Mem. Newcomen Soc., Ashland C. of C., Tall Cedars of Lebanon, Phi Alpha Theta, Alpha Phi Omega. Republican. Mason (32, K.T., Shriner), Rotarian (dist. gov. 1965-66). Clubs: Torch, Ashland Country. Office: Office of Pres Ashland College 401 College Ave Ashland OH 44805

SCHULTZ, ARTHUR WARREN, advt. exec.; b. N.Y.C., Jan. 13, 1922; s. Milton Warren and Genevieve (Dann) S.; grad. U. Chgo.; m. Elizabeth Carroll Mahan, Apr. 23, 1949; children—Arthur Warren, John Carroll (dec.), Julia Hollingsworth. With Foote, Cone & Belding Communications, Chgo., 1948—, v.p., 1957-63, sr. v.p., dir., 1963-69, gen. mgr., Chgo. office, 1967-71 exec. v.p., 1969, chmn. bd., 1970—; dir. Paxall, Inc. Bd. dirs. Lyric Opera Chgo., 1967-77; trustee U. Chgo., 1977—, Chgo. Public TV, 1978—, Lake Front Gardens, 1978—; trustee Art Inst. Chgo., 1975—, YWCA 1962-74, Chgo. Council on Fgn. Relations, 1977—; mem. bus. adv. council Urban League Chgo., 1971—; bd. dirs. Better Bus. Bur., 1970-78, Community Fund, 1966-67, Chgo. Crime Commn., 1965-71; pres. Cook County Sch. Nursing, 1963-64, Welfare Council Met. Chgo., 1965-67. Served to 1st lt. USAAF, 1943-45. Mem. Am. Assn. Advt. Agys. (dir. 1968-71, 74-76, chmn. Chgo. council 1964-65, chmn. central region 1970-71), Delta Kappa Epsilon. Clubs: Chicago, Racquet, Economic, Executives, Commercial, Commonwealth, Old Elm; Barrington Hills Country. Home: Route 2 Meadow Hill Rd Barrington IL 60010 Office: 401 N Michigan Ave Chicago IL 60611

SCHULTZ, CARL HERBERT, retail chain exec.; b. Chgo., Jan. 9, 1925; s. Herbert V. and Olga (Swanson) S.; B.S. in Gen. Engring., Iowa State U., 1948; m. Helen Ann Stevesson, June 6, 1948; children—Mark Carl, Julia Ann. With Schultz Bros. Co., 1948—, mdse. mgr. and store planner, Chgo., 1962-70, v.p., Lake Zurich, Ill., 1968-72, pres., 1972—; pres. Ill. Schultz Bros. Co., Ind. Schultz Bros.

Co., Iowa Schultz Bros. Co., Wis. Schultz Bros. Co. Mem. Lake Bluff (Ill.) Zoning Bd. Appeals, 1976—, chmn., 1978—. Served with U.S. Army, 1944-46. Mem. Lake Zurich Indsl. Council (sec. 1976), Assn. Gen. Mdse. Chains (dir. 1975—). Presbyterian. Club: Bath and Tennis (Lake Bluff). Home: 701 Center St Lake Bluff IL 60044 Office: 800 N Church St Lake Zurich IL 60047

SCHULTZ, CLAIRE KELLY (MRS. WALLACE L. SCHULTZ), educator; b. York, Pa., Nov. 17, 1924; d. Joseph Z. and Mary (Ross) Kelly; B.S., Juniata Coll., 1944; postgrad. U. Pa., 1945-47; M.S. in L.S., Drexel Inst. Tech., 1952; m. Wallace L. Schultz, June 28, 1945; children—Gawain, Gareth, Mary Lou, Wallace II, Peter. Librarian, research asso. Wistar Inst. Anatomy and Biology, Phila., 1946-49; librarian Sharp & Dohme (became Merck, Sharp & Dohme), Phila., 1949-58; systems analyst Remington Rand Univac div. Sperry Rand Corp., Phila., 1958-61; research asso. Inst. Advancement Med. Communication, 1961-70; vis. asso. prof. Sch. Info. Sci. Drexel Inst., Phila., 1962-70; free-lance cons. on info. sci., 1970-72; prof. info. sci. Med. Coll. Pa., Phila., 1972—, dir. libraries, 1972—; cons. to acad., indsl. and service orgns. Leader Cub Scouts, 1955-57. Mem. Assn. Computing Machinery, Am. Soc. for Info. Sci. (pres. 1962), Am. Chem. Soc., Nat. P.T.A., Spl. Libraries Assn. (chmn. pharm. sect. 1954-55), AAAS. Editor: H.P. Luhn, Pioneer in Information Science, 1978; editor, compiler: Thesaurus of Information Science Terminology, 3d edit., 1978; contbr. articles to profl. jours. Home: Line Lexington PA Office: Med Coll of Pa Philadelphia PA 19129

SCHULTZ, ERICH RICHARD WILLIAM, librarian, archivist; b. Rankin, Ont., Can., June 1, 1930; s. William Henry and Martha Frieda (Geelhaar) S.; B.A., U. Western Ont., Waterloo Coll., 1951, B.D., 1957; Th.M., U. Toronto, 1958, B.L.S., 1959. Ordained to ministry, Lutheran Ch. Am., 1954; pastor St. Paul's Luth. Ch., Ellice Twp., Ont., Can., 1954-56; librarian Waterloo Luth. Sem., Ont., Can., 1959-60, lectr., 1959-70; librarian, archivist Wilfrid Laurier U., Ont., 1960—; archivist Eastern Can. Synod, Luth. Ch. Am., 1961—. Mem. Am. Theol. Library Assn. (v.p. 1975-76, pres. 1976-77), Ont. Library Assn. (pres. 1968-69), Inst. Profl. Librarians Ont. (pres. 1969-70), Canadian Library Assn., Canadian Assn. Coll. and Univ. Libraries, Ont. Council Libraries (chmn. 1978-80), Luth. Hist. Conf., Luth. Soc. for Worship, Music and the Arts. Home: 235 Erb St E Waterloo ON N2J 1M9 Canada Office: Wilfrid Laurier U Library Waterloo ON N2L 3C5 Canada

SCHULTZ, ERWIN GILBERT, assn. exec.; b. Atkinson, Nebr., Jan. 27, 1929; s. Paul Theodore and Sara Josephine (McCreath) S.; B.A., U. Nebr., 1952; m. Mary Ann Segelberg, Apr. 7, 1956; children—Kathy Jo, Bradley J., Lynne M., Patricia S. Exec. sec. Omaha Jr. C. of C., 1955-56; adminstrv. asst. Omaha C. of C., 1956-59; exec. v.p. Fargo (N.D.) C. of C., 1959-66; pres. Greater Syracuse (N.Y.) C. of C., 1966—; dir., mem. investment com. Blue Cross Central N.Y.; past pres. N.Y. State C. of C. Execs. Assn., N.D. C. of C. Execs. Assn.; pres. Mid-Atlantic C. of C. Execs., 1975-76; Mem. exec. com., bd. regents Inst. Orgn. Mgmt., U. Colo., 1962-66; bd. regents Inst. Orgn. Mgmt., U. Del., 1972—; mem. Syracuse Indsl. Devel. Agy.; mem. steering com. Empire State Games; former mem. bd. dirs. Urban League Onondage County, Syracuse Community Housing Devel. Corp.; bd. dirs. Community Cable TV, Syracuse Econ. Devel. Corp., Downtown Com. of Syracuse, Onondaga Indsl. Devel. Corp.; chmn. Mayor's Pvt. Industry Council, CETA. Served with AUS, 1952-55. Mem. Am. C. of C. Execs. Assn. (dir. 1976—), Greater Syracuse C. of C. (pres. econ. devel. corp.). Clubs: Masons, Shriners. Home: 4528 Henneberry Rd Manlius NY 13104 Office: 1500 1 MONY Plaza Syracuse NY 13202

SCHULTZ, FRANKLIN M., lawyer; b. Cin., June 16, 1917; s. Max and Goldie (Wise) S.; B.A., Yale U., 1939, LL.B., 1942; m. Jean Carol Barnett, Apr. 5, 1946; children—William B., John M., Katherine, Caroline. Admitted to Ohio bar, 1947, D.C. bar, 1954, U.S. Supreme Ct. bar, 1954; atty. Fed. Power Commn., 1946-47; asso. prof. Ind. U. Sch. Law, Bloomington, 1947-53; mem. firm Purcell & Nelson, Washington, 1953—, partner firm, 1957—; lectr. George Washington U. Law Sch., 1958-59; vis. prof. U. Va. Law Sch., 1975; mem. ednl. appeal bd. Office of Edn., HEW, 1974—. Served to capt. AUS, 1942-46. Decorated Bronze stars. Mem. Am. Bar Assn. (mem. council adminstrv. law sect. 1966-69, chmn., 1970-71, del. ho. of dels. 1972-74), D.C. Bar (gen. counsel 1977-79, mem. legal ethics com. 1976—), Am. Law Inst., Am. Bar Found. Contbr. articles to profl. jours. Home: 1953 Martha's Rd Alexandria VA 22307 Office: 1776 F St NW Washington DC 20006

SCHULTZ, FREDERICK HENRY, govt. ofcl.; b. Jacksonville, Fla., Jan. 16, 1929; s. Clifford G. and Mae (Wangler) S.; B.A., Princeton U., 1951; postgrad. U. Fla. Sch. Law, 1954-56; m. Nancy Reilly, Aug., 1951; children—Catherine G., Frederick H., Clifford G., John Reilly. With Barnett Nat. Bank, Jacksonville, 1956-57; owner, operator investment firm, from 1957; mem. Fla. Ho. of Reps., 1963-70, speaker of the house, 1968-70; chmn. bd. Barnett Investment Services, Inc., dir. Barnett Banks of Fla., to 1979; vice chmn. bd. govs. Fed. Res. System, Washington, 1979—. Served to lt. U.S. Army, 1952-54. Decorated Bronze Star, Korean Service medal, UN medal. Roman Catholic. Office: Fed Res System Office of Vice Chmn 20th and Constitution Ave NW Washington DC 20551*

SCHULTZ, GEORGE LA VIE, toiletries co. exec.; b. N.Y.C., May 10, 1917; s. William L. and Mabel LaVie S.; B.S., Princeton, 1940; m. Margaret E. Fraser, June 21, 1941; children—Margaret E., Katherine L., Marilyn G., Elizabeth F. With Shulton, Inc., Clifton, N.J. 1936—, v.p., dir., 1942-50, pres., chief exec. officer, 1950-71, chmn. bd., 1971—; dir. Am. Cyanamid Co. Episcopalian. Clubs: John's Island; Montclair Golf. Home: 171 Oldchester Rd Essex Fells NJ 07021 Office: Shulton Inc Clifton NJ 07015

SCHULTZ, GEORGE STEPHEN, clergyman; b. Holland, Ind., Mar. 28, 1916; s. George Stephen and Stella Marie (Sealing) S.; B.A., Capital U., 1937; postgrad. Julliard Sch. Music, 1939; B.D., Evang. Lutheran Theol. Sem., 1940; postgrad. Ohio State U., 1942; LL.D., Wartburg Coll., 1954; D.D., Luther Coll., 1967; m. Mary Elizabeth Kauper, June 21, 1940; children—Gretchen Elizabeth, John Stephen, Douglas Richard. Reporter, Columbus (Ohio) Dispatch, 1937-40; tchr. singing, singer Capital U. Conservatory Music, Columbus, 1940-42; pub. relations Capital U., 1942-45; asst. dir. stewardship and fin. Am. Luth. Ch., Columbus, 1945-50, dir., 1950-60, exec. sec., bd. trustees, Mpls., 1961—; tchr. homiletics Evang. Luth. Theol. Sem., Columbus, 1949-50; bd. dirs. Ministers Life and Casualty Union, 1969—. Mem. Luth. Council of U.S.A. (pres.), Luth. World Fedn. (dir. U.S.A. nat. com.). Home: 5511 Hansen Rd Edina MN 55436 Office: 422 S 5th St Minneapolis MN 55415

SCHULTZ, JAMES CLEMENT, lawyer; b. Council Bluffs, Iowa, Nov. 24, 1934; s. John William and Lillian Ruth (Clement) S.; B.S., U. Nebr., 1956; J.D. with honors, George Washington U., 1961; m. Nancy Jean Dixon, May 29, 1969; children—James Vincent, Erica Ruth. Minority counsel Senate Anti-trust Subcom. of Judiciary Com., 1965-68; trial atty. antitrust div. U.S. Dept. Justice, 1969-70; asst. gen. counsel U.S. Dept. Transp., 1971-74; chief counsel Nat. Hwy. Traffic Safety Adminstrn., 1975; gen. counsel CAB, Washington, 1976-77; now sr. v.p., gen. counsel Trailways, Inc., Dallas. Served with AUS, 1957-58. Home: 9511 Hollow Way Rd Dallas TX 75220 Office: 1500 Jackson St Dallas TX 75201

SCHULTZ, JEROME SAMSON, biochem. engr.; b. Bklyn., June 25, 1933; s. Henry Herman and Sally Schultz; B.S. in Chem. Engring., Columbia U., 1954, M.S., 1956; Ph.D. in Biochemistry, U. Wis., 1958; m. Jane Paula Schwartz, Sept. 1, 1955; children—Daniel Stuart, Judith Susan, Kathryn Ann. Group leader biochem. research Lederle Labs., N.Y.C., 1958-64; asst. prof. dept. chem. engring. U. Mich., Ann Arbor, 1964-67, asso. prof., 1967-70, prof., 1970—, chmn. dept., 1977—. NIH research career devel. awardee, 1970-75. Mem. Am. Chem. Soc. (past chmn. microbial chemistry div.), Am. Inst. Chem. Engrs. (past chmn. food and bioengring. div.), Am. Soc. Artifical Internal Organs, AAAS, Sigma Xi, Phi Lambda Upsilon, Tau Beta Pi. Contbr. articles to profl. jours. Patentee in field. Home: 2743 Antietam Dr Ann Arbor MI 48105 Office: Dept Chem Engring Univ of Mich Ann Arbor MI 48109

SCHULTZ, LESLIE P., ins. co. exec.; b. Lake Mills, Wis., Sept. 8, 1918; B.A., U. Wis., 1940, M.B.A., 1950. Spl. agt. Northwestern Mut., 1938-43; mgr. Midwest div. Union Mut. Life, 1946-54; exec. v.p., dir. Independence Life, 1954-65; pres., dir. Bankers Security Life Ins. Soc., 1965-75, chmn., chief exec. officer, 1976—; chmn., pres., dir. United Services Equities, Inc., 1970—; pres., chief exec. officer, dir. United Services Life Ins. Co., 1968—, United Services Gen. Life Co., 1970—, Asso. Ins. Cos., Inc. (formerly Asso. Life Cos., Inc.), 1972—, Gen. Services Life Ins. Co., 1975—; sr. v.p. Internat. Bank, 1974—; sr. v.p., dir. Nat. Indsl. Credit Corp., 1972-78; dir. Foster Wheeler Corp., 1st Reins. Co. Hartford, Hawkeye-Security Ins. Co., United Security Ins. Co., Northeastern Ins. Co., Fin. Security Group, Inc., Internat. Risks, Inc., IB Credit Corp., Indsl. Agy., Inc., Indsl. Broker, Inc.; mem. adv. bd. Am. Security Bank, Washington. Bd. dirs. Heart Assn. No. Va. Heart Assn., 1967-75, pres., 1974; bd. govs. Internat. Ins. Seminars, 1967—. C.L.U., C.P.C.U. Mem. Gen. Agts. and Mgrs. Conf. Mason. Club: Big Ten (past pres. Los Angeles). Office: 1701 Pennsylvania Ave NW Washington DC 20006

SCHULTZ, MAXWELL I., business exec.; b. Worcester, Mass., July 4, 1910; s. Philip H. and Eva (Nadel) S.; student Dartmouth; B.S., U. Pa., 1931; m. Estelle Bernstein, June 6, 1933; children—Philip Gary, Arlene Carol, Eva Lynn. Exec. v.p. Willmark Service System, Inc., 1931-43, Willmark Research Corp., 1936-43; mem. exec. com. Norwalk Lock Co., 1944-45; exec. v.p., asst. to pres. Adam Hat Stores, Inc., 1946-47, pres., dir., 1947-; pres., dir. Mountain Paper Products Corp., Bellows Falls, Vt., 1962—; bus. cons., 1948—; lectr. U. Pa., 1939—, Northwestern U., Babson Inst.; guest speaker numerous trade group meetings. Mem. Am., N.Y. marketing assns., Muscular Dystrophy Assn. (trustee, mem. exec. com.), Pi Gamma Mu. Clubs: Beach Point, City Athletic. Author: How to Satisfy Customers and Win More Sales; G.G.I. Dynamic Key to Sales Success; co-author: Selling Knacks; Turn on the Green Lights in Your Life. Contbr. various trade publs. Created, developed unique method of measuring standards of selling and efficiency. Home: 29 Brite Ave Scarsdale NY 10583 Office: 50 Rockefeller Plaza New York City NY 10020. *To bring yourself to the threshold of life's most dynamic and rewarding experience, make up your mind to become a positive personality, to discipline and train yourself to grow and to develop into the complete person you were intended to be. In this way, one of life's precious secrets for personal happiness will unfold-be one with God-give of yourself and share with others.*

SCHULTZ, MICHAEL, stage and film dir.; b. Milw., Nov. 10, 1938; s. Leo and Katherine Frances (Leslie) Schultz; ed. U. Wis., Marquette U.; m. Lauren Jones. Dir. stage plays Waiting for Godot, 1966, Song of the Lusitanian Bogey (Negro Ensemble Co., N.Y.C., 1968 and London, 1968), Kongi's Harvest, God Is a (Guess What?), Does A Tiger Wear a Necktie (Broadway debut), The Reckoning, 1969, Every Night When the Sun Goes Down, 1969, works of new playwrights at Eugene O'Neill Meml. Theatre, 1969, Operation Sidewinder, Dream on Monkey Mountain, 1970, Woyzeck, 1970, The Three Sisters, 1973, Thoughts, 1973, The Poison Tree, 1973, What the Winesellers Buy, 1974; dir. films including To Be Young, Gifted and Black, 1971, Cooley High, 1975, Car Wash, 1976, Greased Lightning, 1977, Which Way Is Up?, 1977, Sgt. Pepper's Lonely Hearts Club Band, 1978; Scavenger Hunt, 1979.

SCHULTZ, MILTON JOHN, JR., naval officer; b. Salina, Kans., Oct. 14, 1926; s. Milton John and Vera Matilda (Pehrson) S.; B.S., U.S. Naval Acad., 1950; postgrad. George Washington U., 1963, U.S. Naval Postgrad. Sch., 1956, U.S. Naval War Coll., 1962; m. Mary Jane Strowig, June 2, 1950; children—Linda Rae Schultz Vining, Milton J., Mary C., Peter M., Edith Elaine. Commd. ensign U.S. Navy, 1950, advanced through grades to rear adm., 1978; exec. officer USS England, 1964-66; comdg. officer USS Richard L. Page, 1967-69; mem. staff Office of Chief of Naval Ops., 1957-58; 1969-71, dir. naval communications, 1976-78; dep. dir. C3 Systems, Orgn. Joint Chiefs of Staff, Washington, 1979—. Pres. congregation Redeemer Luth. Ch., McLean, Va., 1979-80. Decorated Legion of Merit. Mem. Naval Inst., U.S. Naval Acad. Alumni Assn., Armed Forces Communications Assn. Clubs: Masons, Kiwanis. Office: Orgn of Joint Chiefs of Staff Washington DC

SCHULTZ, PHILIP, poet, lectr.; b. Rochester, N.Y., Jan. 6, 1945; s. Samuel B. and Lillian (Bernstein) S.; student U. Louisville, 1963-65, San Francisco State U., 1965-67; B.A. in English Lit., U. Iowa, 1968, M.F.A. in Poetry, 1971. Various clerical positions Dept. Social Services, San Francisco, 1969-70; writer-in-residence Kalamazoo Coll., 1971-72; lectr. in poetry Newton (Mass.) Coll. of Sacred Heart, 1973-74; lectr. in writing U. Mass., Boston, 1973-75; tchr. poetry elem. schs. in Mich., 1971-72, Mass., 1974-75, N.Y., 1977—; lectr. in creative writing N.Y. U., N.Y.C., 1978—. Author: (poems) Like Wings (Am. Acad.-Inst. of Arts and Letters award 1979), 1978; contbr. numerous poems to lit. jours. and mags. including New Yorker, The Nation, Am. Review, Poetry, The Kenyon Review; contbr. short stories to lit. jours. Recipient Kansas City Star Poetry award 1971, Discovery-Nation Poetry award 1976; N.Y. State Council for the Arts fellow, 1976. Mem. Poetry Soc. Am., PEN, Poets and Writers. Democrat. Jewish. Office: New York Univ Dept of English 19 University Place New York NY 10003 also Russell & Volkening 551 Fifth Ave New York NY 10017. *I write rather slowly as I believe that the art of good writing takes place in the art of revision, which, if taxing, often enough provides me with the time to discover what I am truly trying to express. I place clarity and precision above all else in my work, and if these are the modes of expression, honesty of feeling is the substance and goal. I choose to write about only those things which I feel most passionate about; the particular circumstances of my life.*

SCHULTZ, RICHARD CARLTON, plastic surgeon; b. Grosse Pointe, Mich., Nov. 19, 1927; s. Herbert H. and Carmen (Huebner) S.; student U. Mich., 1946-49; M.D., Wayne State U., 1953; m. Pauline Zimmermann, Oct. 8, 1955; children—Richard, Lisa, Alexandra, Jennifer. Intern, Harper Hosp., Detroit, 1953-54, resident in gen. surgery, 1954-55; resident in gen. surgery U.S. Army Hosp., Ft. Carson, Colo., 1955-57; resident in plastic surgery St. Luke's Hosp., Chgo., 1957-58, U. Ill. Hosp., Chgo., 1958-59, VA Hosp., Hines, Ill., 1959-60; practice medicine specializing in plastic surgery, Park Ridge, Ill., 1961—; clin. asst. prof. surgery U. Ill. Coll. Medicine, 1966-70, asso. prof. surgery, 1970-76, prof., 1976—, head div. plastic surgery, 1970—; pres. med. staff Lutheran Gen. Hosp., Park Ridge, 1977-79. Mem. sch. bd., Lake Zurich, Ill., 1966—, pres., 1966-72; pres. Chgo. Found. for Plastic Surgery, 1966—. Served to capt. M.C., AUS, 1955-57. Recipient research award Found. Am. Soc. Plastic and Reconstructive Surgery, 1964-65, Robert H. Ivy award, 1969, Disting. Sci. Achievement award Wayne U. Coll. Medicine Alumni, 1975; Fulbright scholar to U. Uppsala, Sweden, 1960-61. Diplomate Am. Bd. Plastic Surgery. Fellow A.C.S.; mem. Am. Assn. Plastic Surgeons, Midwestern Assn. Plastic Surgeons (pres. 1978-79), Am. Assn. Automotive Medicine (pres. 1970-71). Author: Facial Injuries, 1970, 2d edit., 1977; Maxillo-Facial Injuries from Vehicle Accidents, 1975; Outpatient Surgery, 1979. Home: 21150 N Middleton Dr Kildeer IL 60047 Office: 1600 Dempster St Park Ridge IL 60068. *The quality of life is made up of many things but in the end it settles to what is really important to each individual. Improvement in the concept of oneself will always enhance the quality of life. We are conditioned to do this throughout life by the growth possible through education. For many it can also be enhanced by improving their physical appearance. In a way it amounts to changing the inside from the outside.*

SCHULTZ, RICHARD DALE, univ. adminstr.; b. Grinnell, Iowa, Sept. 5, 1929; s. August Henry and Marjorie Ruth (Turner) S.; B.S., Central Coll., Pella, Iowa, 1950; M.A., U. Iowa, 1964; m. Jacquilyn Lu Duistermars, June 26, 1949; children—Robert Dale, William Joel, Kim Marie. Head basketball coach, athletic dir. Humboldt (Iowa) High Sch., 1950-60; freshman basketball coach U. Iowa, Iowa City, 1960-62, head baseball coach, asso. basketball coach, 1962-70, head basketball coach, 1970-74, asst. v.p., 1974-76; dir. athletics and phys. edn. Cornell U., Ithaca, N.Y., 1976—; dir. Arwen Instrument Co., 3 Crosses Ranch; organizer Iowa Steel Mill, Inc. Mem. nat. staff, mem. bd. Fellowship of Christian Athletes, 1974; chmn. Multiple Sclerosis, 1974-75. Recipient Distinguished Alumni award Central Coll., Pella, 1970. Mem. Baseball Coaches Assn., Nat. Assn. Coll. Basketball Coaches. Lion. Author: A Course of Study for the Coaching of Baseball, 1964; The Theory and Techniques of Coaching Basketball, 1970. Contbr. articles to mags. Home: 3 Highgate Circle Ithaca NY 14850

SCHULTZ, RICHARD DEWYL, zoo adminstr.; b. Jefferson City, Mo., Jan. 19, 1917; s. Carl Frederick and Molly Mabel (Cruzen) S.; B.S. in Bus. Adminstrn., Washington U., St. Louis, 1938; M.B.A., U. Chgo., 1943; m. Jean Crowder, June 18, 1959. Accountant, Price Waterhouse & Co., C.P.A.'s, St. Louis, 1938-56; controller Petrolite Corp., St. Louis, 1956-64, fin. v.p., 1964-72, dir., 1969-72; dir. fin. St. Louis Zool. Park, 1973-75, dir., 1975—. C.P.A., Mo. Mem. Internat. Union Dirs. of Zool. Gardens, Am. Assn. Zool. Parks and Aquariums, Fin. Execs. Inst., Am. Inst. C.P.A.'s, Explorers Club, Beta Gamma Sigma, Phi Delta Theta. Episcopalian. Club: University (St. Louis). Home: 425 Breezewood Dr Ballwin MO 63011 Office: St Louis Zool Park Forest Park Saint Louis MO 63110

SCHULTZ, RICHARD OTTO, ophthalmologist; b. RacRacine, Wis., Mar. 19, 1930; s. Henry Arthur and Josephine (Wagoner) S.; B.A., U. Wis., 1950, M.S., 1954; M.D., Albany Med. Coll., 1956; M.Sc., U. Iowa, 1960; m. Jane Davidson, Aug. 2, 1952; children—Henry Reid, Richard Paul, Karen Jo. Intern, Univ. Hosps., Iowa City, Iowa, 1956-57, resident in opthalmology, 1957-60; chief ophthalmology sect. div. Indian health USPHS, Phoenix, 1960-63; practice medicine specializing in ophthalmology, Phoenix, 1963; NIH spl. fellow in ophthalmic microbiology U. Calif., San Francisco, 1963-64, clin. asso. 1963-64, research asso., 1963-64; asso. prof., chmn. dept. ophthalmology Marquette U. Sch. Medicine (now Med. Coll. Wis.), Milw., 1964-68, prof., chmn., 1968—; dir. Eye Inst., dir. ophthalmology Milw. County Med. Complex, Milw.; cons. Wood VA, Milw. Children's, Columbia, Luth., St. Mary's hosps. (all Milw.). Served with USPHS, 1960-63. Diplomate Am. Bd. Ophthalmology. Fellow Am. Acad. Ophthalmology, ACS, Am. Ophthal. Soc., (bd. govs.), Soc. Eye Surgeons; mem. Royal Soc. Medicine, Assn. Univ. Profs. Ophthalmology (trustee), pres. 1978)., Nat. Acad. Scis., AMA, Council Med. Splty. Socs., Am., Milw. ophthalmol. socs., Assn. Research Vision and Ophthalmology, Assn. Am. Med. Colls., N.Y. Acad. Scis., Research to Prevent Blindness, Oxford Ophthalmol. Congress (Eng.), Pan Am. Assn. Ophthalmology, State Med. Soc. Wis., Wis. Soc. Prevention Blindness, Med. Soc. Milw. County, Milw. Acad. Medicine. Contbr. articles to profl. jours. Home: 690 Meadow Ln Elm Grove WI 53122 Office: 8700 W Wisconsin Ave Milwaukee WI 53226

SCHULTZ, RONALD GLEN, univ. adminstr.; b. Hammond, Ind., Nov. 15, 1931; s. Arnold C. and Minnie (Schultz) S.; B.S., Valparaiso U., 1953; M.S., Northwestern U., 1954; Ph.D., U. Pitts., 1959; m. Eunice L. Rossey, Sept. 1, 1956; children—Kathy Lynn, David Glen, Dean Richard. Instr., U. Pitts., 1954-56, asst. prof., 1956-61, asso. prof., 1961-68; sr. engr. U.S. Steel Research Lab., Monroeville, Pa., 1961-64; prof., chmn. elec. engring. dept., acting dean Coll. Grad. Studies, Cleve. State U., 1968-72, dean grad. studies, 1972-75, asso. v.p. academic affairs, 1975—; cons. to industry, 1954-—, to legal firms and ins. cos., 1966—. Mem. I.E.E.E., Am. Soc. Engring. Edn., Sigma Xi, Theta Chi, Eta Kappa Nu. Lutheran. Patentee in field. Home: 589 Welshire Dr Bay Village OH 44140 Office: Cleve State U East 24th and Euclid Cleveland OH 44115

SCHULTZ, SAMUEL JACOB, clergyman, educator; b. Mountain Lake, Minn., June 9, 1914;; s. David D. and Anna (Eitzen) S.; A.A., Bethel Coll., 1938; B.A., John Fletcher Coll., 1940; B.D., Faith Theol. Sem., 1944; M.S.T., Harvard, 1945, Th.D., 1949; m. Eyla June Tolliver, June 17, 1943; children—Linda Sue, David Carl. Ordained to ministry Christian and Missionary Alliance Ch., 1944; pastor First Meth. Ch., Pine River, Minn., 1940-41, Waldo Congl. Ch., Brockton, Mass., 1944-45, Evang. Bapt. Ch., Belmont, Mass., 1945-47; prof. Gordon Coll., Boston, 1946-47, Bethel Coll. and Sem., St. Paul, 1947-49, St. Paul Bible Inst., 1948-49; prof. Wheaton (Ill.) Coll., 1949—, Samuel Robinson prof. Bible and theology, 1955-80, chmn. Bible and philosophy dept., 1957-63, chmn. div. Bibl. edn. and philosophy, 1963-67, chmn. div. Bibl. studies, 1972-79; interim supply pastor Bible Ch. Winnetka, Ill., 1951, 60; resident supply pastor South Shore Bapt. Ch., Hingham, Mass., 1958-59. Mem. bd. edn. Bethel Coll. and Sem., 1960-65. Bd. dirs. Inst. in Basic Youth Conflicts, 1965—. N.Y. U. study grantee, Israel, summer 1966; Wheaton Coll. Alumni research grantee, 1958. Mem. Soc. Bibl. Lit., Evang. Theol. Soc. (editor Jour. 1962-75), Near East Archaeol. Soc. (sec., dir.), Wheaton Coll. Scholastic Honors Soc., Phi Sigma Tau. Author: The Old Testament Speaks, 1960; Law and History, 1964; The Prophets Speak, 1968; Deuteronomy-Gospel of Love, 1971; The Gospel of Moses, 1974. Home: 18 Lois Ln Lexington MA 02173

SCHULTZ, SIGRID (LILLIAN), newspaper corr.; b. Chgo., 1893; d. Herman and Hedwig (Jaskewitz) Schultz; Diplôme de Certificat d'Etudes Supérieures; student Sorbonne, Paris, 1913, Berlin U., 1916. Asst. corr. Chgo. Tribune, Berlin, 1919; corr.-in-chief Central Europe, 1925-41; broadcasting for MBS, 1939-41; also war corr. Chgo. Tribune, McCalls Mag., MBS; corr., Bonn, Germany, 1952-53; now free lance news corr. Clubs: Overseas Press (bd. govs.); Pen. Author: Germany Will Try It Again, 1944. Editor: Overseas Press Club

Cookbook, 1962. Contbr. articles to nat. mags., lectr. Home: 35 Elm St Westport CT 06880

SCHULTZ, STANLEY GEORGE, physiologist, educator; b. Bayonne, N.J., Oct. 26, 1931; s. Aaron and Sylvia (Kaplan) S.; A.B. summa cum laude, Columbia, 1952; M.D., N.Y. U., 1956; m. Harriet Taran, Dec. 25, 1960; children—Jeffery, Kenneth. Intern, Bellevue Hosp., N.Y.C., 1956-57, resident, 1957-59; research asso. in biophysics Harvard, 1959-62, instr. biophysics, 1964-67; asso. prof. physiology U. Pitts., 1967-70, prof. physiology, 1970—, prof., chmn. dept. physiology U. Tex. Med. Sch., Houston, 1979—; cons. USPHS, NIH, 1970—; mem. physiology test com. Nat. Bd. Med. Examiners, 1974-79, chmn., 1976-79. Served to capt. M.C., USAF, 1962-64. Recipient Research Career award NIH, 1969—; overseas fellow Churchill Coll., Cambridge U., 1975-76. Mem. Am. Heart Assn. (established investigator 1964-69), Am. Physiol. Soc., AAAS, Biophysical Soc., Soc. for Gen. Physiologists, Internat. Cell. Research Orgn., Internat. Union Physiol. Scis. (chmn. internat. com. gastro intestinal physiology 1977—), Phi Beta Kappa, Alpha Omega Alpha. Editor Am. Jour. of Physiology, Jour. Applied Physiology, 1971-75, Physiol. Revs., 1979—; mem. editorial bd. Jour. Gen. Physiology, 1969—; editorial bd. Ann. Revs. Physiology, 1974—, asso. editor, 1977—; editorial bd. Current Topics in Membranes and Transport, 1975—, Jour. Membrane Biology, 1977—. Contbr. articles to profl. jours. Home: 4955 Heatherglen Dr Houston TX 77096

SCHULTZ, THEODORE JOHN, acoustical cons.; b. Jefferson City, Mo., Aug. 16, 1922; s. Otto Theodore and Juliaetta (Zeitz) S.; student Eastman Sch. Music, 1940-41, U. Mo., 1941-43, U. Tex., 1943-44; S.M., Harvard U., 1947, Ph.D., 1954. Instr., U.S. Naval Acad., 1944-46; research physicist Naval Research Lab., 1947-48; instr. Harvard U., 1948-53, research fellow in acoustics, 1953-55; asst. chief acoustics sect. Douglas Aircraft Co., Santa Monica, Calif., 1956-60; cons. in electronics and acoustics, 1950-60; with Bolt Beranek and Newman, Inc., Cambridge, Mass., 1960—, prin. scientist, 1966—. Fellow Acoustical Soc. Am. (Silver medal in archtl. acoustics 1976), Inst. Acoustics (Gt. Britain). Author: Community Noise Ratings, 1972. Home: 7 Rutland Sq Boston MA 02118 Office: 50 Moulton St Cambridge MA 02138

SCHULTZ, THEODORE WILLIAM, ret. educator, economist; b. Arlington, S.D., Apr. 30, 1902; s. Henry Edward and Anna Elizabeth (Weiss) S.; grad. Sch. of Agr., Brookings, S.D., 1924; B.S., S.D. State Coll., 1927, D.Sc. (hon.), 1959; M.S., U. Wis., 1928, Ph.D., 1930; LL.D., Grinnell Coll. 1949, Mich. State U., in 1962, U. Ill., 1968, U. Wis., 1968; m. Esther Florence Werth; children—Elaine, Margaret, T. Paul. Mem. faculty La. State Coll., Ames, 1930-43, prof., head dept. econs. and sociology, 1934-43; prof. econs. U. Chgo., 1943-72, chmn. dept. econs., 1946-61. Charles L. Hutchinson Distinguished Service prof., 1952-72, now emeritus. Econ. adviser, occasional cons. Com. Econ. Devel., U.S. Dept. Agr., Dept. of State Fed. Res. Bd., various congl. coms., U.S. Dept. of Commerce, FAO, U.S. Dept. of Def. (in Germany 1948), Fgn. Econ. Adminstrn. (in U.K. and Germany 1945), Internat. Bank for Reconstrn. and Development, Resources for the Future, Twentieth Century Fund, Nat. Farm Inst., and others. Dir. Nat. Bur. Econ. Research, 1949-67; research dir. Studies of Tech. Assistance in Latin Am., also bd. mem. Nat. Planning Assn.; chmn. Am. Famine Mission to India, 1946; studies of agrl. developments in central Europe and Russia, 1929, Scandinavian countries and Scotland, 1936, Brazil, Uruguay and Argentina, 1941, Western Europe, 1955; research fellow Center Advanced Study in Behavioral Sci., 1956-57. Recipient Nobel Prize in Econs., 1979. Fellow Am. Acad. Arts and Scis., Am. Farm Econs. Assn., Nat. Acad. Scis.; mem. Am. Farm Assn., Am. Econ. Assn. (pres. 1960, Walker medal 1972), Royal Econ. Soc., Am. Philos. Soc., also others. Author: Redirecting Farm Policy, 1943; Food for the World, 1945; Agriculture in an Unstable Economy, 1945; Production and Welfare in Agriculture, 1950; The Economic Organization of Agriculture, 1953; Economic Test in Latin America, 1956; Transforming Traditional Agriculture, 1964; The Economic Value of Education, 1963; Economic Crises in World Agriculture, 1965; Economic Growth and Agriculture, 1968; Investment in Human Capital; The Role of Education And of Research, 1971; Human Resources, 1972; Economics of the Family: Marriage, Children, and Human Capital, 1975. Co-author: Measures for Economic Development of Under-Developed Countries, 1951. Editor Jour. of Farm Economics, 1939-42. Contbr. articles to profl. jours. Home: 5620 Kimbark Ave Chicago IL 60637

SCHULTZE, CHARLES LOUIS, economist; b. Alexandria, Va., Dec. 12, 1924; s. Richard Lee and Nora Woolls (Baggett) S.; A.B., Georgetown U., 1948, M.A., 1950; Ph.D., U. Md., 1960; m. Rita Irene Hertzog, Sept. 6, 1947; children—Karen M., Kevin C., Helen L., Kathleen, Carol, Mary. Mem. staff President's Council Econ. Advisers, 1952-58; asso. prof. econs. Ind. U., 1959-61; prof. econs. U. Md., 1961; asst. dir. U.S. Bur of Budget, 1962-65, dir., 1965-67; sr. fellow Brookings Instn. 1968-76; chmn. Pres.'s Council Econ. Advisers, Washington, 1977—. Served with AUS, 1943-46; ETO. Decorated Purple Heart, Bronze Star. Mem. Am. Econ. Assn., Royal Econ. Soc. Author: Recent Inflation in the United States, 1959; The Politics and Economics of Public Spending, 1969; (with others) Setting National Priorities: The 1974 Budget; The Public Use of Private Interest, 1977. Home: 5826 Nevada Ave NW Washington DC 20015

SCHULZ, CHARLES MONROE, cartoonist; b. Mpls., Nov. 26, 1922; s. Carl and Dena (Halverson) S.; L.H.D. (hon.), Anderson Coll., 1963; m. Joyce Halverson, Apr. 18, 1949; children—Meredith, Charles Monroe, Craig, Amy, Jill. Cartoonist, St. Paul Pioneer Press, Sat. Eve. Post, 1948-49; created syndicated comic strip Peanuts, 1950. Recipient Outstanding Cartoonist award Nat. Cartoonist Soc., 1956; Emmy award for children's program A Charlie Brown Christmas, CBS cartoon spl., 1966. Collected cartoons pub. in book form: Peanuts, 1952; More Peanuts, 1954; Good Grief, More Peanuts, 1956; Good Ol' Charlie Brown; Snoopy; You're Out of Your Mind Charlie Brown; But We Love You Charlie Brown; Peanuts Revisited; Go Fly a Kite Charlie Brown; Peanuts Every Sunday; You Can Do It, Charlie Brown, Happiness is a Warm Puppy, 1962; Love is Walking Hand in Hand, 1965; A Charlie Brown Christmas, 1965; You Need Help, Charlie Brown, 1966; Charlie Brown's All-Stars, 1966; You've Had It Charlie Brown, 1969; The Snoopy Festival, 1974; also author, illustrator Snoopy and the Red Baron, 1966; Snoopy and His Sopwith Camel, 1969; The Snoopy Come Home Movie Book, 1972; also The Charlie Brown Dictionary. Office: care Fawcett World 1515 Broadway New York NY 10036*

SCHULZ, HOWARD NEFF, assn. exec.; b. Gary, Ind., June 18, 1919; s. Raymond Neff and Clara (Bell) S.; B.S., Western Ill. U., 1941; postgrad. Purdue U., 1941, Lehigh U., 1942, Northwestern U., 1948-51; m. Julia L. Porter, Feb. 21, 1942; children—Janet Lynn (Mrs. William King), Peggy Jo (Mrs. David Hayes), Gail Ellen (Mrs. Thomas Robinson). Indsl. hygienist Abbott Labs., North Chicago, Ill., 1946-57; asst. dir. dept. environ. health AMA, Chgo., 1957-66; exec. dir. Am. Occupational Med. Assn., Chgo., 1966—, Am. Acad. Occupational Medicine, 1977—; sec. Occupational Health Inst., 1972—. Served with USAAF, 1943-46. Mem. Am. Indsl. Hygiene Assn., Am. Chem. Soc., Health Physics Soc., AAAS, Am. Soc. Assn. Execs., Am. Assn. Med. Soc. Execs. Home: 125 S O'Plaine Rd Gurnee IL 60031 Office: 150 N Wacker Dr Chicago IL 60606

SCHULZ, JUERGEN, educator, art historian; b. Kiel, Germany, Aug. 18, 1927; s. Johannes and Ilse (Lebenbaum) S.; came to U.S., 1938, naturalized, 1944; B.A., U. Calif. at Berkeley, 1950; Ph.D., Courtauld Inst. Art, London, 1958; children (by previous marriage)—Christoph (dec.), Ursula, Catherine; m. Anne Markham, June 17, 1968; 1 son, Jeremy. From instr. to asso. prof. history art U. Calif. at Berkeley, 1958-68, curator Renaissance art Univ. Art Mus., 1964-68; prof. history art Brown U., Providence, 1968—, chmn. art dept., 1968-72. Served with AUS, 1945-47. Decorated Ordine della Stella della Solidarietà Italiana. S.H. Kress Found. fellow, 1965; Guggenheim fellow, 1966-67; mem. Inst. for Advanced Study, 1972-73; Nat. Endowment for Humanities fellow, 1972-73, 78-79. Mem. Coll. Art Assn., Renaissance Soc. Am., Soc. Archtl. Historians, Nat. Com. for History Art, Verein zur Erhaltung des Kunsthistorischen Insts. (Florence, Italy). Author: Venetian Painted Ceilings of the Renaissance, 1968; Printed Plans and Panoramic Views of Venice, 1970. Contbr. articles to profl. jours. Home: 192 Bowen St Providence RI 02906

SCHULZ, MILFORD DAVID, physician; b. Sister Bay, Wis., Dec. 12, 1909; s. William George and Anna Friedarika Wilhelmina (Lucht) S.; B.A., North Central Coll., 1931; M.D., Northwestern U., 1936; m. E. Marie Brandt, July 3, 1937; 1 dau., M. Catherine. Intern, West Suburban Hosp., Oak Park, Ill., 1935-36; fellow in radiology Northwestern U., 1936-39; asst. radiologist Collis P. Huntington Hosp., Harvard Cancer Commn., 1940-41; mem. faculty dept. radiation therapy Harvard Med. Sch., 1942-76, prof., 1970-76, prof. prof. emeritus, 1976—; radiotherapist Mass. Gen. Hosp., 1942-76, sr. cons., 1976—; cons. Mass. Eye and Ear Infirmary, Mt. Auburn Hosp., Mass. Dept. Health. Bd. dirs. Mass. div., Am. Cancer Soc., also past pres. Recipient Bronze medal Am. Cancer Soc., 1970. Mem. AMA, Am. Radium Soc. (past pres., Gold medal 1974), Am. Soc. Therapeutic Radiologists (past pres.), New Eng. Cancer Soc. (past pres.), New Eng. Roentgen Ray Soc. (past pres.), Am. Soc. Clin. Oncologists, New Eng. Soc. Radiation Oncologists (past pres.), Mass. Med. Soc., Am. Coll. Radiology (past chancellor), Am. Roentgen Ray Soc., Radiol. Soc. N. Am. Contbr. articles to profl. jours. Home: 50 Bow Rd Belmont MA 02178 Office: Mass Gen Hosp Boston MA 02114

SCHULZ, ROBERT L(UDWIG), business exec.; b. N.Y.C., Sept. 17, 1907; s. Carl and Alice (Zallveis) S.; m. Dorothy E. Cost, Oct. 28, 1943; children—Karen Elizabeth, Carl Frederick, Carol Roberta. Indsl. traffic mgr., Chgo., 1938-42; transp. cons. War Dept., 1942; commd. capt. Transp. Corps, U.S. Army, 1942, advanced through ranks to brig. gen., 1962; a.d.c. Gen. Dwight D. Eisenhower, 1947-52; mil. aide Pres. U.S., 1953-61; exec. asst. to former Pres. Eisenhower, 1961-69; spl. asst. to Pres. for liaison with former presidents, Washington, 1969-73. Dir. Capitol Hill Assos. Decorated Legion Merit. Mem. Am. Soc. Traffic and Transp., Traffic Club Chgo. Club: DACOR (Washington). Home: 2834 Young Dr Oakton VA 22124 Office: 218 N Lee St Alexandria VA 22314

SCHULZ, RUDOLPH WALTER, univ. dean; b. Chgo., Aug. 10, 1930; s. Walter Adolph and Minna Louise (Burmeister) S.; B.S., Northwestern U., 1954, Ph.D., 1958; M.A., Stanford, 1955; m. Charlotte Helen Adams, Sept. 8, 1956; children—Stephanie Sue, Kyle Scott. Lectr., research asso. Northwestern U., 1956-58, instr., 1958-59; asst. prof. psychology Carnegie-Mellon U., 1959-60; asst. prof. U. Iowa, 1960-64, asso. prof., 1964-66, prof., 1966—, prof., chmn. dept., 1970-73, dean for advanced studies, 1976—; cons. in field, mem. NSF fellowship selection panel, 1962-68; NSF vis. scientist, 1962-76. Served with USNR, 1950-52. Decorated Air medal. Old Gold research fellow U. Iowa, 1963; NSF research grantee, 1964-76. Fellow Am. Psychol. Assn., AAAS (mem. council 1974-75); mem. Psychonomic Soc., Midwestern Psychol. Assn. (sec.-treas. 1973-76, pres. 1978), Iowa Acad. Sci., Sigma Xi. Cons. editor Jour. Exptl. Psychology, 1962-74, Jour. Verbal Learning and Verbal Behavior, 1964-74, Contemporary Psychology, 1970—, editor Psychonomic Science, 1971-72, Memory and Cognition, 1972-76. Contbr. articles to profl. jours. Home: Route 6 River Heights Iowa City IA 52240

SCHULZ, VALDYN, retail exec.; b. 1929; married. With Red Owl Stores, Inc., 1959-73; exec. v.p. Nat. Tea Co., Rosemont, Ill., 1973-76, pres., chief exec. officer, 1976—. Office: Nat Tea Co 9701 W Higgins Rd Rosemont IL 60018*

SCHULZE, ARTHUR ROBERT, JR., food co. exec.; b. LaCrosse, Wis., Jan. 31, 1931; s. Arthur Robert and Elizabeth Margaret (Showers) S.; B.A., Carleton Coll., Northfield, Minn., 1952; M.B.A. with distinction, Harvard U., 1958; m. Joan M. Hanifan, June 25, 1955; children—Brett, Mark, David, Anne. With Procter & Gamble Co., Cin., 1959-62, product mgr., 1961-62; with Gen. Mills, Inc., Mpls., 1962—, v.p., gen. mgr. Golden Valley div., 1970-73, group v.p. consumer foods, 1973—. Trustee Carleton Coll.; bd. dirs. United Way Mpls. Served with AUS, 1953-56. Recipient Merit award Mpls. United Way. Mem. NAM, Cereal Inst. (exec. com., bd. dirs.), Food Protein Council (dir.), Civic League Mpls. Republican. Clubs: Harvard Bus. Sch., Interlachen Country. Home: 14 Paddock Rd Edina MN 55436 Office: 9200 Wayzata Blvd Minneapolis MN 55440

SCHULZE, ERWIN EMIL, mfg. co. exec., lawyer; b. Davenport, Iowa, May 4, 1925; s. Erwin F. and Hazel (Sorensen) S.; B.A., De Pauw U., 1947; LL.B., Yale, 1950; m. Jean E. Steele, June 21, 1952; children—Suzanne Schulze Walker, William Steele, Donna Wilson, Stephen Johnson. Admitted to Ill. bar, 1950, since practiced in Chgo.; partner firm Rooks, Pitts, Fullagar & Poust, and predecessor firms, 1950-67, counsel, 1967—; exec. v.p., treas., dir. Standard Alliance Industries, Inc., now pres., dir.; gen. counsel Standard Forgings Corp., Chgo., 1963-65, exec. v.p., 1965-67; treas., dir. Transue & Williams Steel Forging Corp., Alliance, Ohio, 1965-66; dir. Ill. State Bank Chgo., 1968—, Danly Machine Corp., 1974—, AAR Corp., 1977—; mem. com. on specialist assignment and evaluation Midwest Stock Exchange, bd. govs., 1979—. Mem. Adv. Council Zoning, Chgo., 1955-57; bd. visitors De Pauw U., 1979—; co-chmn. Joint Com. Codify Ill. Family Law, 1958-61; mem. Mayor Chgo. Adv. Council Juvenile Delinquency, 1958-62; v.p., dir. Midwestern Air Pollution Prevention Assn., 1958-72, chmn. legal com., 1960-63. Vice pres., dir. Chgo. Tennis Assn., 1964-71; sec., dir. Chgo. Tennis Patrons, 1960-74; chmn. men's ranking com. U.S. Lawn and Tennis Assn., 1961-71. Served as lt. (j.g.) USNR, 1943-46; PTO. Mem. Am., Ill., Chgo. bar assns., Legal Club Chgo., Econ. Club Chgo., Phi Beta Kappa. Presbyterian (deacon, elder trustee). Clubs: Knollwood, Lake Bluff Racquet; Chicago, Chicago Golf (Chgo.). Home: St Mary's Rd Route 1 Box 64-A Libertyville IL 60048 Office: 1211 W 22d St Oak Brook IL 60521

SCHULZE, FRANZ, JR., educator, art critic; b. Uniontown, Pa., Jan. 30, 1927; s. Franz and Anna E. (Krimmel) S.; student Northwestern U., 1943; Ph.B., U. Chgo., 1945; B.F.A., Sch. Art Inst. Chgo., 1949, M.F.A., 1950; postgrad. Acad. Fine Arts, Munich, Germany, 1956-57; m. Marianne Gaw, June 24, 1961; children—F. C. Matthew, Lukas. Instr. art Purdue U., 1950-52; chmn. dept. art Lake Forest (Ill.) Coll., 1952-58, artist-in-residence, 1958-61, prof. art, 1961—, Hollender prof. art, 1974—. Art critic Chgo. Daily News, 1962-78, Chgo. Sun-Times, 1978—; contbg. editor Art News, 1958-64, 73—, Inland Architect, 1975—; Chgo. corr. in art Christian Sci. Monitor, 1958-62, Art in Am., 1965-73, Art Internat., 1966-67; art and architecture critic The Chicagoan, 1973-74. Mem. vis. com. dept. art U. Chgo., 1974—. Recipient Harbison award for teaching Danforth Found. of St. Louis, 1971; Adenauer fellow, 1956-57; Ford Found. fellow 1964-65; Graham Found. for Advanced Studies in the Fine Arts fellow, 1971; recipient Distinguished Service award Chgo. Phi Beta Kappa Soc., 1972. Mem. Coll. Art Assn., Am. Assn. U. Profs., Archives Am. Art, Lovis Corinth Meml. Found., S.M. Koffler Found. Author: Art, Architecture and Civilization, 1969, Fantastic Images: Chicago Art Since 1945, 1972; 100 Years of Chicago Architecture; Stealing Is My Game. Office: Dept Art Lake Forest Coll Lake Forest IL 60045

SCHULZE, RICHARD CARL, marine corps officer; b. Oakland Calif., May 7, 1929; s. Carl Max and Geniveve Ann (King) S.; B.A. in History, Stanford U., 1954; grad. Marine Corps. Command and Staff Coll., 1966, Indsl. Coll. Armed Forces, 1971; M.S. in Public Adminstrn., George Washington U., 1971; m. Sally Ann Sutton, July 21, 1951; children—Jeffrey, Carl. Served as enlisted man U.S. Marine Corps, 1950-51, commd. 2d lt., 1951, advanced through grades to maj. gen., 1978; inf. officer, Korea, 1952, Vietnam, 1968-69; in various command and staff positions, Hawaii, 1966-68, Okinawa, 1961-62, Calif., 1953-61, Washington, 1969-73, Va., 1962-66, 73-75; aide to Sec. of Navy, Washington, 1971-73, dir. personnel procurement, also dir. manpower plans and policy USMC, 1975-78; comdg. gen. Marine Corps Recruit Depot, San Diego, 1978-79; insp. gen. USMC, Washington, 1979—; lectr. in field. Mem. exec. council Boy Scouts Am., YMCA, Salvation Army, USO, United Way, (all San Diego), 1978-79; active Big Bros., Washington, USO, 1973-75. Decorated Silver Star, Legion of Merit (two). Mem. Marine Corps Assn., Smithsonian Assos., Stanford Alumni Assn., Assn. Indsl. Coll. Armed Forces. Contbr. numerous articles to Marine Corps Gazette. Home: 1600 S Eads St Arlington VA 22202 Office: HQMC Washington DC 20380

SCHULZE, RICHARD TAYLOR, congressman; b. Phila., Aug. 7, 1929; s. John L. and Grace (Taylor) S.; student U. Houston, 1948, 50, Villanova U., 1952, Temple U., 1968; m. Nancy Lockwood, May 14, 1955; children—Karen, Richard Taylor, Michael, Linda. Propr. Home Appliance Center, Paoli, Pa., 1950—; register of wills, clk. Orphans Ct., Chester County, 1967-69; mem. Pa. Ho. of Reps. from 157th Dist., 1969-74, sec. ways and means com., 1973-74, sec. bus. and commerce com., 1973-74; mem. 94th-96th Congresses from 5th Pa. dist. Pres. Upper Main Line Jr. C. of C., 1956; scoutmaster local Boy Scouts Am., 1954, chmn. Chester County council Philmont Com., 1956, chmn. advancement com. Conestoga Dist., 1957; chmn. Paoli Meml. Hosp. Day, 1970; chmn. Tredyffrin Twp. Republican Com., 1966; pres. Upper Main Line Young Rep. Club, 1963, Chester County Fedn. Rep. Clubs, 1965; mem. Pa. Young Reps., 1965; chmn. nominating com. Pa. Young Rep. Biennial Conv., 1966; exec. com. Chester County Rep. Com., 1965, campaign chmn., 1964, 66, 69, 70. Served with U.S. Army, 1951-53. Recipient Scoutmaster Key award Boy Scouts Am., 1957, Dist. Merit award, 1958; Retail Promotion of Year award Nat. Elec. Mfrs. Assn., 1965; Distinguished Merchant award Gen. Electric Co., 1967, 68; named Outstanding Jaycee of Year, Upper Main Line chpt. Jr. C. of C., 1955. Mem. Paoli Bus. Assn. (past v.p., dir.), Hillside Sch. PTA (charter), Great Valley Jr. C. of C., Archaeol. Inst. Am., Great Valley Assn., Register of Wills Assn. Pa., Am. Legion, Circus Saints and Sinners, Green Valleys Assn. Presbyn. Clubs: Masons, Maxwell Football (Phila.). Home: 525 Morris Ln Berwyn PA 19312 Office: 432 Cannon House Office Bldg Washington DC 20515

SCHULZE, ROBERT OSCAR, univ. dean; b. Springfield, Ill., Aug. 6, 1922; s. Walter O. and Lydia I. (Schorr) S.; A.B., U. Mich., 1947, Ph.D., 1956; M.A., Columbia U., 1952; m. Suzanne Sims, Oct. 23, 1948; children—Peter Compton, Elizabeth Sinclair. Asst. personnel mgr. Sandia Lab., Albuquerque, 1947-50; teaching fellow sociology U. Mich., 1951-55; instr. sociology Brown U., 1955-57, asst. prof., 1957-61, asso. prof., 1961-66, prof., 1966-70, asst. dean coll., 1959-64, dean, 1964-68; exec. dir. Thomas J. Watson Found., 1968-72; prof. sociology, dean Coll. Arts and Scis., U. No. Colo., Greeley, 1972—. Faculty research fellow Social Sci. Research Council, 1963-64. Chmn. family and children's div., mem. bd. R.I. Council Community Services, 1961-63; bd. dirs. Colo. Humanities Program, 1975-79. Served to warrant officer AUS, 1943-46. Mem. Vachel Lindsay Assn. (co-founder), ACLU. Democrat. Contbr. articles to profl. publs. Home: 1814 Reservoir Rd Greeley CO 80631

SCHUMACHER, BERTHOLD WALTER, physicist, engr.; b. Karlsruhe, Germany, Apr. 15, 1921; s. Ernst Walter and Luise Alvine (Hofmann) S.; came to U.S., 1966, naturalized, 1976; diploma in physics U. Stuttgart (Germany), 1950, Dr. rer.—nat., 1953; m. Maja M. Gruen, Nov. 14, 1955; children—Reinhard, Thomas. Design and devel. engr. Electronics and X-Ray Equipment Laboratorium Prof. Dr. Berthold, Wildbad, Germany, 1953-54; research fellow Ont. Research Found., Toronto, Can., 1954-58, dir. dept. physics, 1958-66; mgr. high power electron beams Westinghouse Research Labs., Pitts., 1966-76; prin. engr. advanced welding, engrng. and research staff Ford Motor Co., Dearborn, Mich., 1977—. Mem. Am. Phys. Soc., N.Y. Acad. Scis., German Soc. Engrs., Inst. Physics, Eng., German phys. socs. Research in areas of electron beam physics, analytical electron probes, electron beam welding in air, X-ray spectroscopy, vacuum systems engrng. patentee in field. Office: Ford Motor Co 24500 Glendale Ave Detroit MI 48239

SCHUMACHER, CARL J., JR., lawyer, educator; b. New Orleans, Sept. 17, 1926; s. Carl J. and Katherine (Bagnetto) S.; B.A., Tulane U., 1947, LL.B., 1950, M.C.L., 1959; m. Leila Flournoy, Sept. 7, 1952; children—Carl David, Steven Stone, Katherine Holliday, Robert Priestley, Gerald Flourney. Admitted to La. bar, 1950; mem. firm Schumacher Law Corp., New Orleans; lectr. Tulane U. Law Sch., La. State U. Law Sch.; chmn. adv. com. New Orleans Juvenile Ct., 1954-57. Democratic candidate for U.S. Senate, 1980. Served to ensign USNR, World War II. Fellow Am. Coll. Trial Lawyers; mem. Am., La., New Orleans bar assns., Internat. Assn. Ins. Counsel, Maritime Law Assn. U.S. Kappa Delta Phi, Phi Delta Phi, Kappa Sigma. Democrat. Roman Catholic. Clubs: New Orleans Athletic, New Orleans Lawn Tennis, Alhambra, Zulu. Home: Convent LA also 1123 Nashville Ave New Orleans LA 70115 1106 Arabella St New Orleans LA 70115

SCHUMACHER, FREDERICK CARL, former ins. co. exec.; b. St. Louis, Sept. 5, 1911; s. John Charles Robert and Edna Eugenia (Hanausky) S.; A.B., Washington U., St. Louis, 1932; LL.D., Westminster Coll., 1973; m. Althea Fuqua Hickey, Nov. 4, 1936; children—Nancy S. (Mrs. John D. Dennis), Frederick Carl Jr. With Merc. Ins. Agy., St. Louis, 1933-72, dir., 1966-72, chmn. bd., 1970-72; with Hickey-Mitchell Co., 1937-76, former chmn. bd., dir., pres.; dir. Nat. Home Life Assurance Co., 1945-73, sr. v.p., 1966-69; chmn. bd., dir. Nat. Bonding & Accident Ins. Co., 1967—, former pres.; former dir. Nat. Liberty Corp., Commerce Bank of St. Louis, Nationwide Corp., Pacific Life Ins. Co., Nat. Services, Inc., Nat. Casualty Co.,

Mich. Life Ins. Co., Gulf Atlantic Life Ins. Co. Alderman, Clayton, Mo., 1953-54; mem. Charter Commn., Clayton, 1955; mem. Citizens Com. for State Reorgn., 1973; mem. 22d Circuit Jud. Commn., 1975—; treas. Mo. Republicans Unlimited, 1959-62. Life trustee, former chmn. bd. Westminster Coll.; trustee Edgewood Children's Center; former bd. dirs. and pres. Child Guidance and Evaluation Clinic, Family and Childrens Service Agy., Health and Welfare Council, St. Louis Council on Alcoholism; past bd. dirs. St. Louis Country Day Sch., St. Louis Community Sch. Council, Girls' Home; former sec., bd. dirs. St. Lukes Hosp.; bd. dirs. Hickey-Schumacher Found. Served to lt. comdr. USNR, 1942-45; ETO, PTO. Mem. Sigma Chi. Presbyterian (former pres. bd. deacons, pres. bd. trustees, clk. of session Ladue Chapel). Clubs: University, Bogey (St. Louis); Belvedere (past pres.), Belvedere Golf (pres.) (Charlevoix, Mich.); Riomar Bay Yacht, John's Island (Vero Beach, Fla.). Home: 625 S Skinker Blvd Saint Louis MO 63105 Office: 4242 Lindell Blvd Saint Louis MO 63108

SCHUMACHER, GEBHARD FRIEDERICH BERNHARD, obstetrician and gynecologist; b. Osnabrueck, W. Ger., June 13, 1924; s. Kaspar and Magarete (Pommer) S.; came to U.S., 1962; M.D., U. Goettingen and Tuebingen, 1951; Sc.D. equivalent in obstetrics and gynecology, U. Tuebingen, 1962; m. Anne Rose Zanker, Oct. 24, 1958; children—Michael A., Marc M. Intern, U. Tuebingen Med. Sch., 1951-52; tng. biochemistry Max Planck Inst. Biochemistry, Tuebingen, 1952-53; tng. biochemistry and immunology Max Planck Inst. Virus Research, 1953-54; resident in obstetrics and gynecology U. Tuebingen, 1954-59, tng. internal medicine, 1959, asst. scientist in obstetrics and gynecology and biochem. research, 1959-62, dozent in obstetrics and gynecology, 1964-65; research asso. immunology Inst. Tb Research, U. Ill. Coll. Medicine, 1962-63; research asso., asst. prof. obstetrics and gynecology U. Chgo., 1963-64; asso. prof. obstetrics and gynecology, asst. prof. biochemistry Albany Med. Coll. of Union U., 1965-67; research physician, div. labs. and research N.Y. State Dept. Health, Albany, 1965-67; asso. prof. obstetrics and gynecology U. Chgo.-Chgo. Lying-In Hosp., 1967-71, chief sect. reproductive biology, 1971—, prof., 1973—, mem. interdepartmental com. immunology Div. Biol. Scis., 1974--; cons. WHO, Nat. Inst. Health, other nat. and internat. orgns. Fellow Am. Coll. Obstetricians and Gynecologists; mem. Soc. Gynecologic Investigation, Am. Fertility Soc., Soc. Study of Reprodn., Am. Acad. Reproductive Medicine, Am. Soc. Cytology, Am. Assn. Pathologists, N.Y. Acad. Scis., Deutsche Gesellschaft fur Gynakologie und Geburtshilfe, Gesellschaft für Biologische Chemie, Gesellschaft fuer Immunologie, Deutsche Gesellschaft für Bluttransfusion, Gesellschaft Deutscher Naturforscher und Arzte. Contbr. articles to profl. jours. Home: 557 Hamilton Wood Homewood IL 60430 Office: 5841 S Maryland Ave Chicago IL 60637

SCHUMACHER, JOSEPH CHARLES, chem. engr.; b. Peru, Ill., Sept. 15, 1911; s. Joseph F. and Josephine (Mattes) S.; student U. Ill., 1928-30; A.B., U. So. Calif., 1946; m. Theresa I. Flynn, Jan. 28, 1933; children—John Christian, Kathleen (Mrs. Eugene Hoffmann), Stephen Joseph, Paul. Research chemist, prodn. supr. Carus Chem. Co., LaSalle, Ill., 1931-40; research and devel. Fine Chems., Inc., Los Angeles, 1940-41; co-founder Western Electro-chem. Co., Los Angeles, 1941, dir., 1941-54, v.p. dir. research, 1941-54; dir. research Am. Potash & Chem. Corp., 1954-56, v.p. research, 1956-67; v.p. AFN, Inc., 1956-67, Kerr-McGee Chem. Corp., 1967-69; pres. J.C. Schumacher Co., 1971-74, chmn., 1974—. Trustee Whittier Coll., 1968-77. Recipient Honors award U. So. Calif. Chemistry Alumni Soc., 1962. Registered profl. chem. engr., Calif. Mem. Los Angeles World Affairs Council, N.Y. Mus. Modern Art, Nat. Geographic Soc., Electrochem. Soc., Am. Chem. Soc., Sigma Xi, Phi Kappa Theta. Roman Catholic. Clubs: Los Angeles Country; Jonathan. Regional editor of Electrochemical Soc. Jour., 1953-59. Contbr. articles profl. jours., co-author, editor Perchlorates. Mem. adv. editorial bd. Research Management, 1963-69. Numerous patents on chem. products, processes and apparatus. Home: 2220 Ave of Stars West Tower Los Angeles CA 90067 Office: 580 Airport Rd Oceanside CA 92054

SCHUMACHER, ROBERT KENT, lawyer; b. Omaha, Nov. 29, 1924; s. William Alfred and Doris (Scroggin) S.; S.B. in Elec. Engring., Mass. Inst. Tech., 1947; J.D., Harvard, 1950; m. Margaret Clary Stocks, Dec. 23, 1949; children—Doris Ann, Richard Wendell, John William. Admitted to Okla. bar, 1952, Ill. bar, 1961; sec. patent atty., mgr. legal and patents Well Surveys, Inc., Tulsa, 1950-61; practice in Chgo., 1961—; partner firm Fitch, Even, Tabin & Luedeka, 1963—. Served with AUS, 1944-46. Mem. Am., Chgo. bar assns., Am. Patent Law Assn., Patent Law Assn. Chgo., Sigma Xi. Home: 911 Euclid Ave Winnetka IL 60093 Office: 135 S LaSalle St Chicago IL 60603

SCHUMAN, DANIEL GERALD, indsl. co. exec.; b. N.Y.C., Sept. 12, 1916; s. Jacob A. and Bessie (Hyman) S.; B.S. in Engring., Calif. Inst. Tech., 1937; M.B.A. with distinction, Harvard, 1941; m. Jacquelyne May, Oct. 25, 1942; children—Joel Leslie, Craig Alan, Meredith Ann. Mgr. mgmt. adv. services Price Waterhouse & Co., N.Y.C, 1946-52; v.p., controller Stromberg Carlson Co., Rochester, N.Y., 1952-59; v.p. finance Bausch & Lomb, Rochester, 1959-67, exec. v.p. finance and adminstrn., 1967-71, chmn. bd., 1971—, pres., 1978—, also dir.; dir. Security Trust Co., Rochester, Utica Mut. Ins. Co. (N.Y.). Dir. N.Y. State Energy Research and Devel. Authority. Served to lt. comdr. USNR, 1942-46. Mem. Fin. Execs. Inst., Am. Mgmt. Assn. Clubs: Genesee Valley, Irondequoit Country (Rochester). Home: 22 Berkeley St Rochester NY 14607 Office: Lincoln First Tower Rochester NY 14601

SCHUMAN, EDWIN Z., steel co. exec.; b. Hartford, Conn., Sept. 3, 1929; s. Leon and Rhea Schuman; B.E. in Civil Engring., Yale U., 1951, M.E. in Structural Engring., 1952; m. Virginia Ruth Stauffer, Aug. 3, 1969; children—Lisa Gallun, Eric M., Linda J., Karen D. Roberta L., Darryl F. Stress analyst Chance-Vought Aircraft div. United Aircraft, Dallas, 1952-53; field engr. Stone & Webster Engring. Corp., Newark, 1956-57; with Levinson Steel Co., Pitts., 1957—, exec. v.p., 1967-75, pres., chief operating officer, 1975—, also dir.; pres., dir. Auxier-Scott Supply Co. Served with Civil Engring. Corps., USN, 1953-56; lt. comdr. Res. ret. Mem. Tri-State Structural Steel Fabricators Assn. (pres.), Am. Inst. Steel Constrn. (dir.), Duquesne Golf Assn., Tau Beta Pi. Club: Standard (Pitts.). Home: 615 Aljo Dr Pittsburgh PA 15241 Office: Levinson Steel Co S 20th and Wharton Sts Pittsburgh PA 15203

SCHUMAN, FREDERICK LEWIS, author, educator; b. Chgo., Feb. 22, 1904; s. August and Ella (Schulze) S.; Ph.B., U. Chgo., 1924, Ph.D., 1927; m. Lily Caroline Abell, June 23, 1930 (dec. 1977); children—Karl (dec.), Donald Robert, Marcia Lenore Armstrong. Instr. polit. sci. U. Chgo., 1927-32, asst. prof., 1932-36; prof. polit. sci. Williams Coll., Williamstown, Mass., 1936-38, Woodrow Wilson prof. govt., 1938-68, Woodrow Wilson prof. govt. emeritus, 1968—; prof. polit. sci. Portland (Oreg.) State U., 1968—; vis. prof. Harvard Summer Sch., 1938, U. Calif., 1939, 55, Cornell U., 1944, Columbia, 1946, U. Chgo., 1956, Central Wash. Coll., 1959, Portland State Coll., 1961, Stanford, 1963, others. Polit. analyst, for broadcast intelligence service. Fellow Social Sci. Research Council, 1929-30; fellow Am. Acad. Polit. and Social Sci., 1933, Found. for World Govt., 1950-51. Mem. Am. Polit. Sci. Assn., Am. Soc. Internat. Law, Am. Anthrop. Assn., Civil Liberties Union, Phi Beta Kappa. Author several books including: Soviet Politics, 1946; The Commonwealth of Man, 1952; Russia Since 1917, 1957; International Politics, 7th edit., 1969; Government in the Soviet Union, 1961; The Cold War: Retrospect and Prospect, 1962. Contbr. to mags. Home: 1717 SW Park Apt 1009 Portland OR 97201

SCHUMAN, HOWARD, educator; b. Cin., Mar. 16, 1928; s. Robert A. and Esther (Bohn) S.; student U. Chgo., 1947-48; A.B., Antioch Coll., 1953; M.S. in Psychology, Trinity U., 1956; Ph.D. in Sociology, Harvard, 1961; m. Josephine Miles, Sept. 1, 1951; children—Marc, Elisabeth, David. Research asso. Harvard, 1961-64; asst. prof. U. Mich., Ann Arbor, 1964-67, asso. prof., 1967-71, prof. sociology, 1971—, chmn. dept., 1970-73, dir. Detroit Area Study, 1965-71, faculty asso. Survey Research Center, 1967-74, program dir. Survey Research Center, 1974—. Mem. Am. Sociol. Soc., Am. Assn. for Pub. Opinion Research. Editor: Social Psychology Quar. Home: 1306 Kensington St Ann Arbor MI 48104

SCHUMAN, LEONARD MICHAEL, physician, educator; b. Cleve., Mar. 4, 1913; s. Morris and Rebecca (Lazarowitz) S.; A.B., Oberlin Coll., 1934; M.Sc. (fellow hygiene and bacteriology), Western Res. U., 1939, M.D., 1940; fellow nutrition Hillman Hosp., Birmingham, Ala., Vanderbilt U., 1946; m. Marie Romich, Oct. 30, 1954; children by previous marriage—Lowell, Judith. Intern U.S. Marine Hosp., Chgo., 1940-41; asst. epidemiologist Ill. Dept. Pub. Health, 1941-42, dist. health supt., 1943, asst. chief div. local health adminstrn., 1943-45, chief div. venereal disease control, 1947-50, dep. dir. div. preventive medicine, 1950-54; dir. S.E. Nutrition Research unit USPHS, 1945-47; epidemiologist Korean cold injury research team U.S. Dept. Def., 1951-53; asso. prof. U. Minn. Med. Sch., 1954-58, prof. epidemiology, 1958—. Cons. air pollution med. program Communicable Disease Center USPHS, Minn. Dept. Health; cons. pediatrics Hennepin County Gen. Hosp.; mem. nat. adv. coms. on gamma globulin prophylaxis in poliomyelitis, polio vaccine field trials, also tech. adv. com. polio vaccine evaluation U. Mich.; sec. Nat. Subcom. Epidemic Intelligence; mem. nat. cancer control com. Nat. Cancer Inst., chmn. panel epidemiology and biometry, 1961-62, cons., 1958—; cons. div. radiol. health USPHS, 1961-69, cons. to chronic disease div., 1964-72, adv. com. on bio-effects radiation, 1966-69, task force on smoking and health, 1967-68, nat. adv. urban and indsl. health council, 1968-69; accident prevention research study sect. NIH, 1963-66; cons. tng. program in epidemiology U.S. Dept. Agr., 1961—; mem. Surgeon Gen.'s Adv. Com. Smoking and Health, 1962-64; field studies bd. Nat. Adv. Cancer Council, 1961-62; chmn. Conf. Chronic Disease Tng. Program Dirs., 1960-72; mem. Nat. Leukemia Study Com., 1959-63; mem. adv. com. on health protection and disease prevention to sec. health, edn. and welfare, 1969-71; mem. Nat. Adv. Environmental Control Council, 1969-71; mem. Cancer Research Center rev. com. NIH, 1971-75; collaborative researcher Norwegian Cancer Registry, Oslo; cons. to WHO, Peru, 1967, India, 1971, Montserrat, 1973; vis. lectr. U. Valle Med. Sch., Cali, Colombia, 1975; AID cons., Ban-dung, Indonesia, 1977; mem. steering com. AID World Research Needs in Nutrition. Served as sr. surgeon USPHS, 1941-47, med. dir. USPHS Res., 1951-77. Diplomate Am. Bd. Preventive Medicine. Mem. A.M.A., Royal Soc. Health, Pub. Health Cancer Assn., Middle States, Am. (governing council, 1964-70, chmn. infectious disease monograph subcom. 1961-68, chmn. subcom. drugs 1964-65, chmn. epidemiology sect. 1967, chmn. program area com. communicable diseases 1966-70, mem. tech. devel. bd. 1966-70), Ill., Minn. pub. health assns., Internat. Epidemiological Soc., Internat. Soc. Cardiology, Internat. Soc. Thrombosis and Hemostasis, Am. Heart Assn. (fellow council epidemiology 1965), Am. Thoracic Soc., Am. Coll. Preventive Med. (chmn. council research), Am. Epidemiology Soc., N.Y. Acad. Scis., Assn. Tchrs. Preventive Medicine, Am. Venereal Disease Assn., Am. Assn. Pub. Health Physicians, Assn. Mil. Surgeons U.S., AAAS, Soc. for Epidemiologic Research, Phi Beta Kappa, Sigma Xi, Alpha Omega Alpha, Phi Zeta Soc. Contbr. sci. papers to profl. lit. Discovered (with Dr. Thomas Lowry) silo-fillers' disease. Home: 17 Merilane S Edina MN 55436 Office: Health Scis-Unit A Bldg U Minn Minneapolis MN 55455

SCHUMAN, STANTON, lawyer; b. Chgo., Jan. 28, 1915; s. Isidore and Ida (Schiff) S.; A.B., U. Mich., 1937, J.D., 1939; m. Marie Friedlander, Feb. 10, 1940; children—Samuel, David, Joseph, Sarah. Admitted to Ill. bar, 1939, since practiced in Chgo.; sr. partner firm Foss, Schuman & Drake, 1950—; lectr. Am. Law Inst., Ill. Continuing Bar Edn.; dir. Opelika Mfg. Corp., Midwest Iron Works, Inc., Bank North Shore. Commr., Glencoe (Ill.) Park Dist., 1965, pres., 1971. Served with AUS, 1942-45. Recipient Silver Beaver award Boy Scouts Am., 1960. Mem. Am., Ill., Chgo. (bd. govs. 1976-78) bar assns. Republican. Jewish. Club: City (past pres.) (Chgo.). Contbr. articles to legal jours. Home: 262 Maple Hill Glencoe IL 60022 Office: 11 S LaSalle St Chicago IL 60603

SCHUMAN, WILLIAM HOWARD, composer, adminstr., educator; b. N.Y.C., Aug. 4, 1910; B.S., Columbia, 1935, M.A., 1937, Mus. D., 1954; pvt. study Max Persin, Charles Haubiel and Roy Harris; Mus.D., Chgo. Mus. Coll., 1946, U. Wis., 1949, Phila. Conservatory Music, 1952, Cin. Coll. Music, 1953, Hartt Coll. Music, 1956, Allegheny Coll., 1961, N.Y. U., 1962, Oberlin Coll., 1963, U. R.I., 1965, Peabody Conservatory, 1971, U. Rochester, 1972; A.F.D., Adelphi Coll., 1963, Northwestern U., 1963, U. N.Mex., 1964, State U. N.Y., 1974; LL.D., Bates Coll., 1966; L.H.D., Colgate U., 1960, Brandeis U., 1962, Dartmouth Coll., 1962, Fordham U., 1967, Ashland Coll., 1970; m. Frances Prince, Mar. 27, 1936; children—Anthony William, Andrea Frances Weiss. Dir. chorus, mem. faculty Sarah Lawrence Coll., Bronxville, N.Y., 1935-45; dir. publs. G. Schirmer, Inc., N.Y.C., 1944-45; spl. publs. cons., 1945-51; pres. Julliard Sch. Music, N.Y.C., 1945-62, pres. emeritus, 1962—; pres. Lincoln Center Performing Arts, N.Y.C., 1962-69, emeritus, 1969—; mem. adv. com. cultural info. USIA; vice chmn. U.S. delegation UNESCO Internat. Conf. Artists, Venice, Italy, 1952; chmn. bd. judges Student Composers Awards of Broadcast Music, Inc.; mem. Nat. Ednl. TV Bd.; music panel Nat. Endowment for Arts; adv. com. N.C. Sch. Arts. Dir. Koussevitzky Music Found., Walter W. Naumburg Found., Composers Forum; chmn. MacDowell Colony, Chamber Music Soc. and Film Soc. Lincoln Center. Recipient numerous awards including 1st Town Hall-League of Composers award, 1940, N.Y. Critics Circle award, 1941-42, award of Merit Nat. Assn. Am. Composers and Condrs., 1941-42, 1st Pulitzer prize for music, 1943, award Nat. Inst. Arts and Letters, 1944, N.Y. Critics Circle award, 1950-51, Columbia U. Bicentennial Anniversary medal, 1957, 1st Brandeis U. Creative Arts award in music, 1957, Citation of Merit State U. N.Y., 1963, Gold Medal Honor for music, Nat. Arts Club, 1964, Ann. Composer's Award, Lancaster Symphony Orch., 1965, Brandeis medal for distinguished service to higher edn., 1965, certificate of Merit Sigma Alpha Iota, 1967, Concert Artists Guild award, 1967. Guggenheim fellow, 1939-41. Fellow Nat. Inst. Arts and Letters, Am. Acad. and Inst. Arts and Letters; mem. Royal Acad. Music (hon.), others. Clubs: Century, Lotos (N.Y.C.). Prin. compositions include: (orchestral works) 10 symphonies, Am. Festival Overture, Circus Overture, Concerto for Piano and Orchestra, Concerto for Violin and Orchestra, Prayer in Time of War, Credendum, New England Triptych, The Earth is Born, A Song of Orpheus, Concerto on Old English Rounds, The Young Dead Soldiers, Orchestra Song, To Thee Old Cause, In Praise of Shahn; (choral works) cantatas include: This is Our Time, Requiescat, Holiday Song, A Free Song, numerous shorter works such as Prelude for Voice, Five Rounds on Famous Words, Carols of Death; (band works) Newsreel, George Washington Bridge, Chester, When Jesus Wept; (chamber music) 4 string quartets, Quartettino for Four Bassoons, Amaryllis' Variations for String Trio; In Sweet Music; (solo piano) Three Score Set, Three Piano Moods, Voyage; (for dance) Undertow, Night Journey, Judith, Theatre for a Voyage, The Witch of Endor; (scores for films) The Earth is Born, Steeltown; (opera) The Mighty Casey; (recs.) Symphonies No. III-IX, Credendum, New England Triptych, Undertow, Judith, Chester, George Washington Bridge, String Quartets Number III, IV, Voyage, Variations on Am., Dedication Fanfare, Evocation-To Thee Old Cause. Prin. commns. include Elizabeth Sprague Coolidge Found. in Library of Congress, The Koussevitzky Music Found., Inc., Dallas Symphony League, Louisville Philharmonic, Ballet Theatre, U.S. Nat. Commn. for UNESCO through Dept. of State, Andre Kostelanetz, Samuel Dushkin, St. Lawrence U., Ford Found., Chamber Music Soc. Lincoln Center, N.Y. Philharmonic (3), Boston Symphony Orch., Broadcast Music, Inc. Address: Richmond Hill Rd Greenwich CT 06830

SCHUMANN, FREDERICK JOHN, lawyer; b. Talmadge, Mich., Oct. 19, 1904; s. Winfred M. and Edith (Cross) S.; B.A., U. Mich., 1926, J.D., 1927; m. Clara Helm, June 29, 1931; 1 dau., Linda Diane (Mrs. Hubert J. Ostrowski). Admitted to Mich. bar, 1927, since practiced in Detroit; partner firm Helm, Schumann & Miller and predecessor, 1957—. Dir. Barton Malow Co., White Chapel Meml. Assn. Pres., Harsen's Island-St. Clair Flats Assn., Mich., 1949-50. Mem. State Bar Mich. (chmn. com. unauthorized practice law), Detroit, Am. bar assns., Order of Coif. Unitarian. Home: 836 Harcourt Rd Grosse Pointe MI 48230 Office: City Nat Bank Bldg Detroit MI 48226

SCHUMANN, JOHN SAMUEL, accountant; b. Camden, N.J., May 30, 1914; s. John and Anna E. (Stilwill) S.; B.S. Temple U., 1935; m. Lettie W. Tyree, Mar. 27, 1937; children—Robert J., Eileen M. With Haskins & Sells, C.P.A.'s, 1936-43, 44-74, mem. firm, 1948-74, charge Los Angeles office, 1961-64, N.Y.C. office, 1967-71, charge U.S. operations, 1971-74; asst. to comptroller Bell Aircraft Corp., 1943-44. Bd. dirs., mem. finance com. YMCA Greater N.Y., 1965-76, treas., 1966-70, chmn. finance com., 1970-75, chmn. bd., 1973-76; bd. dirs. nat. council YMCA, 1975-79; bd. dirs. YMCA of San Diego County, 1976—, treas., 1977-78, chmn. fin. com., 1977-79. C.P.A., N.Y., other states. Mem. Am. Inst. C.P.A.'s, Am. Ordnance Assn. (1st v.p. Los Angeles, 1963-64, v.p., bd. dirs. N.Y.C. 1965-76, mem. nat. council 1965-69, sec., treas. N.Y. chpt. 1968-71), Nat. Assn. Accountants, Am. Accounting Assn., Beta Gamma Sigma. Home: 5976 Germaine Ln La Jolla CA 92037 Office: 1114 Ave of Americas New York NY 10036

SCHUMER, WILLIAM, surgeon, educator; b. Chgo., June 29, 1926; s. Solomon and Gussie (Gross) S.; M.B., Chgo. Med. Sch., 1949, M.D., 1950; M.S., U. Ill., 1966; children—Scott, Fern. Intern, Mt. Sinai Hosp. Med. Center, Chgo., 1949-50, resident, 1950-54; asst. prof. surgery Chgo. Med. Sch., 1959-65, asst. prof. cardiovascular research, 1964-65; attending surgeon, then asst. chief surgery Mt. Sinai Hosp., Chgo., 1962-65; attending surgeon Hines (Ill.) VA Hosp., 1960-63, VA West Side Hosp., Chgo., 1963-64; dir. surg. service U. Calif. at Davis, Sacramento County Med. Center, 1965-67; chief surg. service VA West Side Hosp., 1967-75; mem. faculty Abraham Lincoln Sch. Medicine, U. Ill., Chgo., 1967-75, prof. surgery, 1969-75; prof. biol. chemistry Grad. Coll., U. Ill. Med. Center, Chgo., 1974-75; mem. staff U. Ill. Hosp., 1967-75; prof. surgery, chmn. dept. Univ. Health Scis./Chgo. Med. Sch., North Chicago Ill., 1975—; chief surg. service North Chicago VA Med. Center, 1975-79, attending surgeon, 1979—; prof. biochemistry U. Health Scis. Chgo. Med. Sch., 1977—. Mem. numerous coms. VA. Named Clin. Educator of Year, Chgo. Med. Sch., 1962, recipient Distinguished Alumnus award, 1974; recipient Honors Achievement award Angiology Research Found., 1965; named Fed. Outstanding Profl. Employee of Year, 1970; recipient numerous awards for sci. exhibits and films. Diplomate Am. Bd. Surgery. Mem. AAAS, Am. Assn. Surgery of Trauma, AAUP, A.C.S., AMA, Am. Physiol. Soc., Assn. Am. Med. Colls., Assn. VA Surgeons (pres. 1976), Central Soc. Clin. Research, Central, Midwest, Ill. surg. socs., Chgo. Ill. State Med. Soc., Shock Soc. (pres. 1978-79), Collegium Internat. Chirurgiae Digestivae, Digestive Disease Found., Inst. Medicine Chgo., Lake County Med. Soc., N.Y. Acad. Scis., Reticuloendothelial Soc., Soc. Internat. de Chirurgie, Soc. Surgery Alimentary Tract, Soc. Critical Care Medicine, Internat. Fedn. Surg. Colls., Soc. U. Surgeons, Soc. U. Chairmen, Warren H. Cole Soc., Alumni Assn. U. Ill., Lake County Med. Soc. Alumni Assn. Chgo. Med. Sch. (pres. Chgo. chpt.), Sigma Xi, Alpha Omega Alpha. Author numerous articles, chpts. in books. Co-editor: Corticosteroids in the Treatment of Shock, 1970; The Treatment of Shock: Principles and Practice, 1974; Advances in Shock Research, Vol. 2, 1979; editor Circulatory Shock, Comprehensive Therapy; mem. editorial bd. Critical Care Medicine.

SCHUMM, JOSEPH JAMES, JR., retail trade exec.; b. Bklyn., Aug. 13, 1944; s. Joseph James and Dorothy (Glaze) S.; A.B., Georgetown U., 1966; J.D., Fordham U., 1969; m. Carol L. Bishop, July 6, 1968; children—David K., Julie A., Laura M., James J. Admitted to N.Y. bar, 1969; asso. firm Gould & Wilkie, N.Y.C., 1969-71; asst. sec. Asso. Dry Goods Corp., N.Y.C., 1971, corp. sec., 1971-76, v.p., sec., corp. counsel, 1976—. Mem. Fordham Alumni Assn., Am. Bar Assn. Home: 19 Grouse Ln Lloyd Harbor NY 11743 Office: 417 Fifth Ave New York NY 10016

SCHUMM, STANLEY ALFRED, geologist, educator; b. Kearny, N.J., Feb. 22, 1927; s. Alfred Henry and Mary Elizabeth (Murdock) S.; B.A., Upsala Coll., 1950; Ph.D., Columbia U., 1955; m. Ethel Patricia Radli, Sept. 3, 1950; children—Brian Murdock, Mary Theresa, Christine Ann. Research geologist U.S. Geol. Survey, Denver, 1955-67; prof. geology Colo. State U., Ft. Collins, 1967—, acting asso. dean, 1973-74; vis. prof. U. Calif., Berkeley, 1959-60, U. Witwatersrand, South Africa, 1975; fellow U. Sydney (Australia), 1964-65; vice chmn. U.S. Nat. Com. Quaternary Research, 1967-70, 75—; dist. vis. scientist U. Tex., 1970; vis. lectr. numerous univs. in U.S.; vis. scientist, N.Z., Europe, Can., Venezuela, Brazil, Polish Acad. Sci., 1969; cons. to govt. agys., engring. firms; prin. geomorphologist, dir. Water Engring. Tech., Shreveport, La. and Ft. Collins; prin. investigator research projects NSF, 1969—, Colo. Agrl. Expt. Sta., 1970—, Army Research Office, 1970—, Office Water Research and Tech., 1974—, Nat. Park Service, 1975-77, Fed. Hwy. Adminstrn., 1978—. Served with USNR, 1944-45. Fellow Geol. Soc. Am. (asso. editor 1973-75, vice chmn. geomorphology div. 1978-79, chmn. 1979—, Kirk Bryan award 1979); mem. Am. Geophys. Union (Horton award 1958, asso. editor 1973-75), ASCE, Internat. Geog. Union, Assn. Am. Geographers, Internat. Assn. Quaternary Research, Am. Quaternary Assn. (councilor). Author: The Fluvial System, 1977; editor: United States Contribution to Quaternary Research, 1969; River Morphology, 1972; Slope Morphology, 1973; Drainage Basin Morphology, 1977; contbr. chpts. to sci. books, articles to profl. jours. Home: 1308 Rollingwood Ln Fort Collins CO 80523 Office: Dept Earth Resources Colo State U Fort Collins CO 80525

SCHUPACK, MARK BARRY, educator, economist; b. New Britain, Conn., July 11, 1931; s. Edward and Betty (Saltzman) S.; B.S., Mass. Inst. Tech., 1953; M.A., Princeton, 1958, Ph.D., 1960; m. Helaine Marcus, Feb. 1, 1952; children—Andrew, Roberta. Engr., Sylvania Electric Products, Inc., Mill Hall, Pa., 1953-54; instr. Brown U., 1959-60, asst. prof., 1960-65, asso. prof., 1965-70, prof., 1970—, chmn. dept. econs., 1969-74, asso. dean faculty, 1978—; cons. RAND Corp., Santa Monica, Calif., 1963-66; vis. scholar Mass. Inst. Tech., 1974-75; cons. U.S. Dept. of Transp., 1976. Mem. R.I. Consumers Council, 1966—. Served to 1st lt. USAF, 1954-56. Mem. Am. Econ. Assn., Econometric Soc. Author: (with P. Taft and M. Brennan) Economics of Age, 1967. Home: 475 Lloyd Ave Providence RI 02906

SCHUR, LEON MILTON, educator, economist; b. Milw., Jan. 11, 1923; s. Ben and Bertha (Stein) S.; student U. Wis., 1941-43, Dartmouth, 1943-44; B.A., U. Wis., 1946, Ph.D., 1955; m. Edith Laiken, Sept. 4, 1949; children—Julie Miriam, Claudia Laiken, Amy Ruth. From instr. to prof. econs. La. State U., 1954-64; prof. econs., dir. Center Econ. Edn., U. Wis.-Milw., 1964—, acting chancellor, 1979-80; vis. prof. Tulane U., 1961, U. Wis., 1962. Dir. Univ. Nat. Bank. Cons. comml. banks in La., Miss. and Wis., 1960—, Cal. Dept. Edn., 1966, Am. Assn. Colls. Tchr. Edn., 1970; participant President U.S. Conf. Fiscal and Monetary Policy, 1962; dir. Wis. Council Econ. Edn., 1964—. Served from seaman to lt. (j.g.), USNR, 1943-46. Mem. Am. Econ. Assn., Am. Finance Assn., Am. Assn. U. Profs., Phi Eta Sigma, Beta Gamma Sigma. Jewish. Contbr. articles to profl. jours. Home: 173 W Suburban Dr Milwaukee WI 53217

SCHURE, ALEXANDER, coll. pres.; b. Can., Aug. 4, 1921; s. Harry Joshua and Bessie (Ginsberg) S.; A.S.T. in Elec. Engring., Pratt Inst., 1943; B.S., Coll. City N.Y., 1947; M.A., N.Y. U., 1948, Ph.D., 1950, Ed.D., 1953; D.Engring. Sci., Nova U., N.Y. Inst. Tech., 1976; LL.D., Boca Raton Coll., 1975; m. Dorothy Rubin, Dec. 8, 1943; children—Barbara, Matthew, Louis, Jonathan. Asst. dir. Melville Radio Insts., N.Y.C., 1945-46; pres. Crescent Sch. Radio and Televison, Bklyn., 1946-53, Crescent Electronics Corp., N.Y.C., 1952-55, N.Y. Tech. Inst., Bklyn., 1953-55, N.Y. Inst. Tech., 1955—; chancellor Nova U.; dir. Seversky Electronatom Corp., N.Y.C. Cons. N.Y. State Dept. Edn., U.S. Office Edn.; mem. Regents Regional Coordinating Council for Post-Secondary Edn. in N.Y.C., 1973—, Nassau County Consortia on Higher Edn., L.I., 1971—, Alfred P. Sloan Found. adv. com. for expanding minority opportunities in engring., 1974; rep. to Nat. Assn. State Adv. Council, 1975—; mem. steering com. L.I. Regional Adv. Council, 1974— Pres. bd. dirs. L.I. Ednl. TV Council, Garden City; bd. dirs. Council Higher Ednl. Instns., N.Y.C., 1973-74. Served with Signal Corps, AUS, 1942-45. Mem. I.E.E.E., N.Y. Acad. Sci., Am. Inst. Engring. Edn., N.E.A., Electronic Industries Assn. (chmn. task force curriculum devel.), Phi Delta Kappa, Delta Mu Delta. Author and-or editor textbooks. Designer automatic teaching machine. Patentee in field. Office: NY Inst Tech Old Westbury Campus Old Westbury NY 11568. *The world is an ever changing, ever challenging reality, filled with opportunities for individual fulfillment and success. A positive philosophy toward life does much to make the realization of individual potential an actuality.*

SCHUREMAN, JEPTHA WADE, lawyer; b. Detroit, Apr. 2, 1920; s. Jeptha Wade and Rose Luella (Williams) S.; J.D., Detroit Coll. Law, 1942. Admitted to Mich. bar, 1942, since practiced in Detroit; lectr. U. Detroit, 1953-67; mem. firm Schureman, Frakes, Glass & Wulfmeier, Detroit. Mem. com. visitors Wayne State U. Law Sch., 1960—. Bd. dirs. Art Centre Hosp., Detroit; trustee Detroit Coll. Law. Served with USAF, 1942-46. Fellow Am. Bar Assn. Found., Am. Coll. Trial Lawyers, Am. Judicature Soc.; mem. State Bar Mich., Detroit Bar Assn. (dir., pres. 1970-71), Hundred Club Detroit, Thomas M. Cooley Club. Episcopalian. Clubs: Country of Detroit, Detroit Athletic. Home: 1009 Cadieux Rd Grosse Pointe Park MI 48230 Office: Suite 3333 Renaissance Center Detroit MI 48243

SCHURMAN, DONALD GLENN, aluminum corp. exec.; b. Pitts., June 13, 1933; s. Andrew Matthew and Mary Ann (Plavan) S.; B.B.A., M. Litt., U. Pitts., 1950-54; m. Barbara Jean Burby, Oct. 20, 1962; children—Lonnette, Kathleen, William, Marianne. With Lybrand, Ross Bros. & Montgomery, Pitts., 1954-59, U.S. Steel Corp., Pitts., 1959-62, The Chesapeake & Ohio Ry., Cleve., 1962-65; asst. to v.p. and controller Liquid Carbonic div. Gen. Dynamics Corp., Chgo., 1965-66; treas. Alcan Aluminum Corp., Cleve., 1966—, v.p., 1975—. Served with AUS, 1956-58. C.P.A., Pa., Ohio. Home: 1112 E Dartmoor Ave Seven Hills OH 44131 Office: 100 Erieview Plaza Cleveland OH 44114

SCHURMAN, JOSEPH RATHBORNE, lawyer; b. N.Y.C., Jan. 5, 1924; student Cornell U., 1941-43, U. Minn., 1944; J.D., Harvard U., 1949. Admitted to N.Y. bar, 1949, Md. bar, 1961; individual practice law, Rochester, N.Y., 1949-56; atty. Dept. Army, 1956-58; atty. NSF, 1958-69; gen. counsel Nat. Endowment for Humanities, Washington, 1969—; sec. Nat. Council on Humanities, 1969—; cons. Commn. on Govt. Procurement, 1970-72. Mem. Fed. Bar Assn. Home: 17 Hesketh St Chevy Chase MD 20015 Office: 806 15th St NW Washington DC 20506

SCHURR, GARMOND GAYLORD, coatings chemist; b. Almont, N.D., Sept. 7, 1918; s. Edward and Florence (Ostering) S.; B.S. in Chemistry, N.D. State U., 1940; m. Ida S. Todd, May 22, 1945; children—Beverly, Michael, Richard, Kathleen. With Sherwin-Williams Co., 1946—, dir. Research Center, Chgo., 1974—. Mem. Ill. Dist. 218 Sch. Bd., 1960-67. Served with Chem. Warfare Service, AUS, 1940-46. Mem. AAAS, Am. Chem. Soc., Am. Soc. Quality Control, ASTM, Nat. Assn. Corrosion Engrs., Fed. Soc. Coatings Tech. Republican. Author papers on house paints, durability, intercoat peeling, mech. testing. Home: 6220 W 127th Pl Palos Heights IL 60463 Office: 10909 S Cottage Grove Ave Chicago IL 60628

SCHURZ, FRANKLIN D., newspaper exec.; b. South Bend, Ind., Mar. 8, 1898; s. John Giles and Grace (Dunn) S.; A.B., Harvard, 1920, M.B.A., 1921; LL.D., Ind. U., U. Notre Dame, St. Mary's Coll.; m. Martha Montgomery, Sept. 11, 1929; children—Franklin D., James M., Scott Clark, Mary. Jr. asso. Food Research Inst., Stanford, 1922-23; accountant, 1924-25; with South Bend Tribune, 1925-76, v.p., 1929-46; mgr. sta. WSBT, South Bend, 1936-46; sec.-treas., bus. mgr. South Bend Tribune, 1946-54, gen. mgr., 1954-64, editor, pub. 1954-72, pres., 1957-75, chmn. bd., 1975-76; chmn. bd. Schurz Communications, Inc., 1976—, also dir. Past pres. Inland Daily Press Assn.; past 1st v.p. A.P.; mem. bd. Am. Newspaper Pubs. Assn., 1952-60. Mem. adv. council arts and letters, hon. trustee U. Notre Dame (Ind). Recipient U. Minn. award distinguished service in journalism, 1959. C.P.A., Calif. Mem. Am. Inst. C.P.A.'s, Am. Soc. Newspaper Editors, Ind. Acad., Ind. Journalism Hall Fame, Sigma Delta Chi. Mason, Rotarian, Kiwanian. Clubs: South Bend Press, Morris Park Country (South Bend). Home: 1418 E Wayne St South Bend IN 46615 Office: 225 W Colfax Ave South Bend IN 46626

SCHUSSHEIM, MORTON JOEL, economist; b. Cleve., Nov. 5, 1924; s. Elmer and Sylvia (Sprung) S.; A.B., Western Res. U., 1947; M.Econs., M.P.A., Harvard U., 1949, Ph.D. in Econs., 1952; m. Hanna Levine, June 18, 1950; children—Elizabeth, Rowen, Amy, Charles. Research asso. Harvard, 1950-52; economist Cleve. Planning Commn., 1952-55; cons., dir. research N.Y. State Rent Commn., 1955-59; dep. dir. area devel. Com. Econ. Devel., 1959-61; asst. adminstr. program policy HHFA, 1961-66; dir. Office Program Policy, Dept. Housing and Urban Devel., 1966; prof. city planning U. Pa., Phila., 1966-73; sr. specialist in housing Library Congress, Washington, 1973—; adj. prof. city planning Howard U., 1976—; lectr. econs., urban problems Western Res. U., 1953-55, Columbia, 1956-57, N.Y. U., 1957-58. Staff sec. Better Housing Assn. Cleve., 1946; mem. U.S. cultural exchange mission on city planning to USSR, 1965; mem. bldg. research adv. bd. Nat. Acad. Scis., 1962-68; mem. Phila. Housing Adv. Service Corp., 1968-73. Mem. Mass. bd. Ams. for Democratic Action, 1950. Served with AUS, 1943-46. Mem. Lambda Alpha. Author: (with William L.C. Wheaton) The Cost of Municipal Services in Residential Areas, 1955; High Rent Housing and Rent Control in New York City, 1958; Prospects for Rehabilitation, 1960; Toward a New Housing Policy, 1969; The Modest Commitment to Cities, 1974. Office: Library of Congress Congressional Research Service Washington DC 20540

SCHUST, RALPH HENRY, bakery exec.; b. Saginaw, Mich., May 27, 1904; s. Edward and Della (Edelmann) S.; grad. Culver (Ind.) Mil. Acad., 1923; m. Hannah L. Sovereign, 1932 (dec. Jan. 1973); children—Penelope (Mrs. David M. Merrill), Deborah (Mrs. Deborah S. Harding), Antonia (Mrs. Peter S. Zegras); m. Juliana Everist Haire, 1974. Sales mgr. Schust Co., Saginaw, 1920-37; asst. gen. mgr. sales mgr. Schust Bakery of Loose-Wiles Biscuit Co., Saginaw, 1937-42; mgr., sales mgr. Loose-Wiles Biscuit Co., 1942-43; v.p. Sunshine Biscuit, Inc. subs. Am. Brands Inc., N.Y.C., 1943-60, dir., 1947-69, v.p., dir. sales, 1969—; with Office Price Emergency Prepardness, Washington, 1970-71; cons. marketing, sales. Clubs: Saginaw; Detroit Athletic; Creek (Locust Valley, N.Y.); Union League (N.Y.C.); Balboa (Mazatlan, Mex.); Ponte Vedra (Ponte Vedra Beach, Fla.). Address: 7810 Westmoreland Dr Sarasota FL 33580

SCHUSTER, GARY FRANCIS, newspaper exec.; b. Detroit, Jan. 26, 1942; s. Dwayne Alger and Mary Elizabeth (Cullen) S.; B.S. in Journalism/Psychology, Wayne State U., 1966; m. Barbara Anne Leopold, Aug. 30, 1968; children—Rory Anne, Reid Patrick. Gen. assignment reporter Royal Oak (Mich.) Tribune, 1966-68; gen. assignment reporter Detroit News, 1968-70, state capital corr., 1970-74, bur. chief, Lansing, 1974-75, chief asst. city editor, Detroit, 1975-76, city editor, 1976-77, news editor, 1977-78, Washington Bur. chief, 1978—. Recipient UPI award for investigative reporting in Mich., 1975. Mem. Nat. Press Club. Roman Catholic. Club: Univ. Office: Detroit News 511 National Press Bldg Washington DC 20045

SCHUSTER, HERMAN FREDERICK, utility cons.; b. Hope, Kans., Nov. 8, 1908; s. John William and LuElla (Taylor) S.; student Kans. Wesleyan U., Salina, 1927-29, Washburn U., 1946-47, 62-63; m. Henrietta Catherine Bates, Jan. 30, 1936; children—Mary Gayle Weddle, Jean Ann Ford. Comptroller, Kans. Power & Light Co., Topeka, 1962-72, v.p. corp. services, 1972; utility cons., 1972—. Served to brig. gen. AUS, 1941-45, 59-61. Decorated Bronze Star with oak leaf cluster; Croix de Guerre with star (France). Mem. Mil. Order World Wars (past pres.), N.G. Assn. Kans. (past pres.). Baptist. Home: PO Box 785 Siloam Springs AR 72761

SCHUSTER, JOSEPH LAWRENCE, educator; b. Teague, Tex., May 21, 1932; s. Michael and Anna (Schaefer) S.; Asso. Sci., Tapleton State Coll., 1952; B.S., Tex. A. and M. U., 1954, Ph.D., 1962; M.S., Colo. State U., 1959; m. Sylvia A. Needham, Sept. 7, 1957; children—David, Stanley, James, Suzanne. With Wildlife Habitat Research, U.S. Forest Service, Nacogdoches, Tex., 1961-64; asst. prof. Tex. Tech. U., Lubbock, 1964-67, asso. prof., 1967-69, prof., 1969-72, chmn. range and wildlife dept., 1969-72; prof., head dept. range sci. Tex. A and M U., College Station, 1972—. Served with AUS, 1954-57. Mem. Soc. Range Mgmt. (chmn. Tex. sect. 1969, Outstanding Rangeman of Yr. award 1975), Soil Conservation Soc. Am. (pres. So. Plains chpt. 1964, 65), Wildlife Soc. (pres. Tex. chpt. 1973), Weed Sci. Soc., Southwest Assn. Naturalists, Sigma Xi, Alpha Zeta. Home: 1006 Esther Blvd Bryan TX 77801

SCHUSTER, SEYMOUR, mathematician, educator; b. Bronx, N.Y., July 31, 1926; s. Oscar and Goldie (Smilowitz) S.; B.A., Pa. State U., 1947; A.M., Columbia U., 1948; Ph.D., Pa. State U., 1953; postgrad. (fellow) U. Toronto, 1952-53; m. Marilyn Weinberg, May 2, 1954; children—Paul Samuel, Eve Elizabeth. Instr., Pa. State U., 1950-52; instr. Poly. Inst. Bklyn., 1953-54, asst. prof., 1954-56, asso. prof. 1956-58; vis. asso. prof. Carleton Coll., Northfield, Minn., 1958-59, asso. prof., 1959-63, prof. math., 1968—, chmn. dept., 1973-76; vis. asso. prof. U. N.C., Chapel Hill, 1961; research asso. math. dept. U. Minn., Mpls., 1962-63, asso. prof. 1963-65, asso. prof. Minn. Math Center, 1965-68, dir. coll. geometry project, 1964-74, dir. Acad. Year Inst. for Coll. Tchrs., 1966-67, NSF Faculty fellow, 1970-71; vis. scholar U. Calif., Santa Barbara, 1970-71; guest scholar Western Mich. U., 1976. Served with USNR, 1944-46. Recipient Honor award Am. Film Festival, 1967, Golden Eagle award Cine Film Festival, 1967, 68. Mem. Math. Assn. Am., Am. Math. Soc., Nat. Council Tchrs. Math., Canadian Math. Soc., Sigma Xi, Pi Mu Epsilon. Author: (with K. O. May) Undergraduate Research in Mathematics, 1961; Elementary Vector Geometry, 1962; (with P.C. Rosenbloom) Prelude to Analysis, 1966; also research articles on geometry, graph theory, and analysis. Cons. editor Xerox Pub. Co., 1962-71; asso. editor Am. Math. Monthly, 1969—, Indian Jour. Math. Edn., 1976—. Co-producer 12 films on geometry. Home: 316 E Summer St Northfield MN 55057

SCHUTT, WALTER EUGENE, lawyer; b. Cleve., July 27, 1917; s. Erle Minchin and Elizabeth (Eastman) S.; A.B., Miami U., Oxford, Ohio, 1939; J.D., U. Cin., 1948; m. Dorothy Louise Gilbert, Apr. 18, 1942; children—Gretchen Sue, Stephen David, Elizabeth Ann, Robert Barclay. Admitted to Ohio bar, 1948, since practiced in Wilmington. City solicitor, Wilmington, 1950-53; mem. Wilmington Bd. Edn., 1958-65; chmn. Clinton County chpt. A.R.C., 1951-53; Wilmington chmn. Cin. Symphony Orch. Area Artists Series, 1969-71. Trustee Wilmington Coll., 1962-74, sec., 1966-74; trustee Quaker Hill Found., Richmond, Ind., 1970-75. Served to 1st lt. USAAF, 1943-46. Decorated D.F.C.; recipient Distinguished Service award Wilmington Jr. C. of C., 1953. Mem. Am. (arms control and disarmament com.), Ohio, Clinton County (past pres.) bar assns., World Peace Through Law Center. Mem. Soc. of Friends (presiding clk. Friends United Meeting). Rotarian. Home: 81 Columbus St Wilmington OH 45177 Office: Thorne Bldg 36 1/2 N South St Wilmington OH 45177. *A rooted belief in God as the Father of mankind. That from this source certain ethical principles, qualities for living, flow-among which are justice, mercy, and love. . . Correspondingly, a belief in basic adherence to man's law as his social compact. That not to adhere means departure from that fellowship and mutual support of one's kind necessary to life. That within this form we are to have life, in abundance; provided our own willingness to seek, to work, to find it. And to do so, thereby to seek the star, remembering however that it is only through the step by daily step succession that it is attained.*

SCHUTTA, HENRY SZCZESNY, educator, neurologist; b. Gdansk, Poland, Sept. 15, 1928; s. Jakub and Janina (Zerbst) S.; came to U.S., 1962, naturalized, 1967; M.B., B.S., U. Sydney (Australia), 1955, M.D., 1968; m. Henryka Kosmal, Apr. 29, 1950; children—Katharine, Mark, Caroline. Jr. resident, then sr. resident St. Vincent's Hosp., Sydney, 1956-58; acad. registrar, house physician Nat. Hosp. Nervous Diseases, London, 1958-62; neurologist Pa. Hosp., Phila., 1962-73; asso. prof. neurology U. Pa. Med. Sch., 1963-73; prof. neurology, chmn. dept. State U. N.Y. Downstate Med. Center, Bklyn., 1973—; cons. VA, L.I. Coll. and Kingsbrook Jewish hosps. Research on bilirubin encephalopathy, cerebral edema, degeneration and regeneration of muscle. Home: 17 Mohegan Rd Larchmont NY 10538 Office: 450 Clarkson Ave Brooklyn NY 11203

SCHUTTE, CHARLES FREDERICK, lawyer; b. Honolulu, May 29, 1921; s. Charles Frederick and Genevieve (Murphy) S.; B.A., U. Hawaii, 1943, M.A., 1947; J.D., Columbia U., 1950; m. Kathleen McCall, Nov. 5, 1942. Admitted to N.Y. bar, 1950, Hawaii bar, 1953; lectr. govt. U. Hawaii, 1947, 52-53; asso. firm Root, Ballantine, Harlan, Bushby & Palmer, N.Y.C., 1950-51; asso. firm Smith, Wild, Beebe & Cades (name changed to Cades Schutte Fleming & Wright), Honolulu, 1952-53, partner, 1954—. Dir. First Hawaiian Bank, Theo. H. Davies & Co. Ltd.; chmn. Hawaiian Western Steel Ltd. Served to capt. AUS, 1942-46. Decorated Bronze Star. Fellow Am. Bar Found.; mem. Am., Hawaii (pres. 1976) bar assns., Assn. Bar City N.Y. Clubs: Pacific (pres. 1970-71), Oahu Country (Honolulu). Home: 931 Maunawili Circle Kailua HI 96734 Office: 1000 Bishop St Honolulu HI 96813

SCHUTTE, GILES W., mail order co. exec.; b. Erie, Pa., Dec. 5, 1931; B.A. in Bus. Adminstrn., Pa. State U., 1954; m. Joan G. Todaro, June 12, 1954; children—Sharon, Anna. Vice pres., treas. New Process Co., Warren, Pa., 1974—, also dir.; dir. Pa. Bank and Trust Co. Bd. dirs. Warren Gen. Hosp. Served with USCG, 1955-58. C.P.A., Pa. Mem. Am., Pa. insts. C.P.A.'s. Home: 7 Quaker Ct Warren PA 16365 Office: 220 Hickory St Warren PA 16366

SCHUTTE, THOMAS FREDERICK, coll. pres.; b. Rochester, N.Y., Dec. 19, 1935; A.B., Valparaiso (Ind.) U., 1957; M.B.A., Ind. U., 1958; D.B.A., U. Colo., 1963; m. Tess Lansing; children—Douglas Lindsley, David Lansing. Dir. freshman's men's residence center Valparaiso U., 1959-60, instr. econs., 1958-60; instr. Sch. Bus., U. Colo., 1960-63; part-time lectr. grad. div. Wharton Sch., U. Pa., 1964-66, asso. prof. mktg., 1972-75, asst. dean, 1973-75; project dir., research asso. Mktg. Sci. Inst., Phila., 1963-66; pres. Phila. Coll. Art, 1975—; chmn. various task forces, lectr., cons. in field. Pub. trustee Greater Phila. Cultural Alliance, 1974—; trustee Pa. Ballet Co., 1975—; bd. dirs. Prints in Progress, 1977—, Union Ind. Colls. Art, 1975—; mem. East Coast Art Colls. Consortium, 1976—. Recipient Anvil award Wharton Grad. Assn.; Most Outstanding Teaching award Wharton Eve. Div. Mem. Am. Mktg. Assn., Beta Gamma Sigma, Gamma Theta Epsilon, Sigma Iota Epsilon. Co-author: Brand Policies and Practices, 1966, Brand Policy Determination, 1967. Editor: A Directory for Graduate Education in Marketing, 1968; An Uneasy Coalition: Design and Corporate America, 1975. Contbr. profl. publs. Office: Phila Coll Art Broad and Spruce Sts Philadelphia PA 19102*

SCHUTTE, WILLIAM METCALF, educator; b. New Haven, May 9, 1919; s. Louis Henry and Anna (Metcalf) S.; grad. Hotchkiss Sch., 1937; B.A., Yale, 1941, M.A., 1947, Ph.D., 1954; m. Susan Roberts McDowell, May 15, 1943 (dec. Sept. 1965); children—Scott, Kirk, Kim; m. 2d, Anne Cole Jacobson, Dec. 21, 1967. Mem. faculty Carnegie Inst. Tech., 1947-60, asso. prof. English, 1955, asst. to pres., 1956-60; mem. faculty Lawrence U., 1960—, Lucia R. Briggs prof. English, 1965—, dir. London Center, 1975-76; faculty fellow Newberry Library Seminar Asso. Colls. Midwest, Chgo., 1969-71; cons. in communications. Bd. govs. Attic Theatre, Appleton, 1961-66, pres., 1963-66. Served with AUS, 1941-45. Recipient Carnegie Corp. Teaching award Carnegie Inst. Tech., 1954. Mem. Am. Assn. U. Profs., Modern Lang. Assn. Am., Renaissance Soc. Am., Wis. Hist. Soc., Shakespeare Assn. Am. Author: Joyce and Shakespeare: A Study in the Meaning of Ulysses, 1957; (with E.R. Steinberg) Communication in Business and Industry, 1960; Personal Integrity, 1961; Twentieth Century Interpretations of Joyce's A Portrait of the Artist as a Young Man, 1968. Contbr. articles to profl. jours. Home: 4 Brokaw Pl Appleton WI 54911

SCHUTZ, HERBERT DIETRICH, publishing co. exec.; b. Munich, Germany, July 16, 1922; s. Anton Friedrich and Maria Hedwig (Gross) S.; came to U.S., 1924, naturalized, 1930; B.S., Harvard, 1944; m. Betty Prescott, July 20, 1946; children—Prescott, Peter, Jeffrey, Elizabeth; m. 2d, Suzanne Cameron, Mar. 22, 1971; children—Leslie, Suzanne. Partner, New York Graphic Soc., Ltd., Greenwich, Conn., 1946-66, pres., editor-in-chief, 1966—; v.p. Time, Inc., 1966—, Alva Mus. Replicas, Inc.; chmn. bd. trustees Art Barn, Greenwich, Conn. Trustee Silvermine Guild Artists, Inc., New Canaan, Conn., 1977—. Served to 1st lt. USMCR, 1943-46. Mem. Assn. Am. Pubs., N.Y. Graphic Soc. and Alva Museum Replicas (vice chmn. 1977). Clubs: Harvard (N.Y.C.); Belle Haven (Greenwich, Conn.). Home: The Barn Dewart Rd Greenwich CT 06830 Office: 140 Greenwich Ave Greenwich CT 06830

SCHUTZ, JOHN ADOLPH, univ. dean, historian; b. Los Angeles, Apr. 10, 1919; s. Adolph J. and Augusta K. (Glicker) S.; A.A., Bakersfield Coll., 1940; B.A., U. Calif., Los Angeles, 1942, M.A., 1943, Ph.D., 1945. Asst. prof. history Calif. Inst. Tech., Pasadena, 1945-53; asso. prof. history Whittier (Calif.) Coll., 1953-56, prof., 1956-65; prof. Am. history U. So. Calif., Los Angeles, 1965—, chmn. dept. history, 1974-76, dean social scis. and communication, 1976—. Nat. Endowment for Humanities grantee, 1971; Sr. Faculty grantee, 1971-74. Mem. Am. Hist. Assn. (pres. Pacific Coast br. 1972-73), Am. Studies Assn. (pres. 1974-75), Mass. Hist. Soc. (corr.), New. Eng. Hist. Geneal. Soc. (council 1979—). Author: William Shirley: King's Governor of Massachusetts, 1961; Peter Oliver's Origin and Progress of the American Rebellion, 1967; The Promise of America, 1970; The American Republic, 1978. Home: 1100 White Knoll Los Angeles CA 90012 Office: U So Calif Los Angeles CA 90007

SCHUTZ, RICHARD EDWARD, research exec.; b. Long Beach, Calif., May 6, 1929; s. Marvin Edward and Caroline Elizabeth (Jones) S.; B.A., U. Calif. at Los Angeles, 1951, M.A., 1953, Ph.D., Columbia U., 1957; m. Iris May Horsefield, June 24, 1951; children—Jerrold, Charles, Stephen, Jody. Test editor World Book Co., 1955-57; prof. ednl. psychology, dir. testing service Ariz. State U., 1957-66; exec. dir. SWRL Ednl. Research and Devel., Los Alamitos, Calif., 1966—. Mem. research and devel. com. Ednl. Testing Service, Calif. Commn. Ednl. Measurement and Evaluation, 1972-75; trustee Council for Ednl. Devel. and Research, 1978—, chairperson elect, 1979. Served to 1st lt. USAF, 1951-53. Fellow ednl. measurement Am. Ednl. Research Assn., 1955-56. Fellow Am. Psychol. Assn.; mem. Am. Ednl. Research Assn. (v.p. 1976-77), Psychometric Soc., Nat. Council Measurement in Edn. (pres. 1972), Soc. Research Child Devel., Psychonomic Soc., Phi Beta Kappa, Sigma Xi, Phi Kappa Phi, Phi Delta Kappa. Contbr. articles in field to profl. jours. Editor Jour. Ednl. Measurement, 1964-68, Ednl. Researcher, 1972-77, Am. Ednl. Research Jour., 1978—. Home: 259 Claiborne Pl Long Beach CA 90807 Office: 4665 Lampson Ave Los Alamitos CA 90720

SCHUYLER, DANIEL MERRICK, lawyer, educator; b. Oconomowoc, Wis., July 26, 1912; s. Daniel J. and Fannie Sybil (Moorhouse) S.; A.B. summa cum laude, Dartmouth, 1934; J.D., Northwestern U., 1937; m. Claribel Seaman, June 15, 1935; children—Daniel M., Sheila Gordon. Admitted to Ill. bar, 1937, U.S. Supreme Ct. bar, 1942, Wis. bar, 1943; tchr. constl. history Chgo. Latin Sch., 1935-37; asso. Schuyler & Hennessy, attys., 1937-42, partner, 1948; partner Schuyler, Richert & Stough, 1948-58, Schuyler, Stough & Morris, Chgo., 1958-76, Schuyler, Ballard & Cowen, 1976—; treas., later sec. and controller B-W Superchargers, Inc., div. Borg-Warner Corp., Milw., 1942-46; lectr. trusts, real property, future interests Northwestern U. Sch. Law, 1946-50, asso. prof. law 1950-52, prof., 1952—. Republican nominee for judge Cook County Circuit Ct., 1958. Bd. dirs. United Cerebral Palsy Greater Chgo.; bd. mgrs. Mary Bartelme Homes. Fellow Am. Bar Found.; mem. Chgo. Estate Planning Council (past pres., Distinguished Service award 1977), Am. Coll. Probate Counsel (past pres.), Internat. Acad. Estate and Trust Law, Am. (past mem. ho. dels., past chmn. sect. real property, probate trust law), Chgo. (past chmn. coms. on trust law and post-admission edn., past bd. mgrs.), Ill. (past chmn. real estate and legal edn. sects., past bd. govs.), Wis. bar assns., Am. Judicature Soc., Phi Beta Kappa, Order of Coif, Phi Kappa Psi. Clubs: Legal, Law, Chicago, University, Executive (Chgo.). Author: (with Homer F. Carey) Illinois Law of Future Interests, 1941, supplement, 1954; (with William M. McGovern, Jr.) Illinois Trust and Will Manual, 1970, supplements, 1972, 74, 76, 77. Contbr. to profl. jours. Home: 324 Cumnor Rd Kenilworth IL 60043 Office: 100 W Monroe St Chicago IL 60603

SCHUYLER, PHILIP, artist, ednl. adminstr.; b. Marshfield, Oreg., Dec. 4, 1913; s. Benjamin Griffin and Lillian (Fox) S.; student Art Students League N.Y., 1946-50, Los Angeles State Coll., 1963-64, U. Oreg. Grad. Sch., 1964; diplomate of fine arts U. Santa Clara, 1968; m. Joyce Biddle Casaroli, June 24, 1960. Art dir. Republic Pictures, 1935; staff artist Boston Herald, 1937, Phila. Inquirer, 1945; chmn. art dept. Coll. Steubenville (Ohio), 1950-52; instr. art dept. UCLA, 1959-60; vis. Disting. prof. U. Houston, 1954-55; vis. prof. Munich (W. Ger.) Acad. Fine Arts, 1964; chmn. fine arts, artist in residence U. Santa Clara, 1967—; exhibited in 1-man shows, including: Palacio de Bellas Artes, Mexico City, 1954, Palace of Fine Arts, San Francisco, 1967, U. Santa Clara, 1969, Oakland (Calif.), Meml. Hall, 1970, U.S. Mil. Acad., 1971; exhibited in group shows, including: Farragil Gallery, N.Y.C., 1951, Art Alliance, Phila., 1954, George Fox Coll., Newburg, Oreg., 1978; represented in permanent collections; Met. Mus. Art, Nat. Palace of Mexico, Mexico City, Nat. Steel Co., Pitts., U.S. Mil. Acad. permanent archives, Smithsonian Instn., Washington, also pvt. collections; works include: ofcl. portrait of Pres. Ruiz Cortines of Mexico, Mexican Ballet, 30-piece series on Vietnam War. Served to capt. U.S. Army, 1940-46. Recipient Nat. prize for Am. Motors entry Brand Names Found., 1962; art works named Nat. Treasures of Republic of Mexico, of U.S. Fellow Montalvo Center of Arts; mem. Art Students League, Mil. Order World Wars, Assn. U.S. Army. Office: Schuyler Edits 6 Surfside Ct Newport Beach CA 92663

SCHUYLER, ROB RENE, lawyer; b. Larchmont, N.Y., Aug. 13, 1932; s. William and Margaret (Sternbergh) S.; student U. Paris (France), 1950-52; B.A., U. So. Calif., 1955; J.D., U. Mich., 1958; m. Odette E. Sagardoy, Feb. 21, 1959; children—Marc Philip, Clifford Robert, Paul Frederic. Admitted to Calif. bar, 1958; dep. city atty., Los Angeles, 1958-61; practice law, Los Angeles, 1961-73; partner firm Mihaly, Schuyler & Burton, P.C., Los Angeles, 1973—. Mem. Calif., Wilshire (gov., pres. 1973), Los Angeles County (chmn. sect. internat. law 1973-74) bar assns., Acacia, Delta Theta Phi. Mason (Shriner). Office: 1801 Century Park E Los Angeles CA 90067

SCHUYLER, ROBERT LEN, forest products co. exec.; b. Burwell, Nebr., Mar. 4, 1936; s. Norman S. and Alva M. (Hoppes) S.; B.S., U. Nebr., 1958; M.B.A., Harvard U., 1960; m. Mary Carol Huston, June 13, 1958; children—Kylie Anne, Nina Leigh, Melynn Kae, Gwyer Lenn. Asst. to treas. Potlatch Forests, Inc., Lewiston, Idaho, 1962-64, dir. corp. planning, San Francisco, 1964-66; mgr. fin. analysis Weyerhaeuser Co., Tacoma, 1966-68, mgr. investment evaluation dept., 1968-70, v.p. fin. and planning, 1970-72, sr. v.p. fin. and planning, 1972—. Mem. Council Fin. Execs., Fin. Execs. Inst., Fin. Mgmt. Assn., Rhododendron Species Found., Assos. Harvard Bus. Sch. (dir.). Club: Anglers (N.Y.C.). Home: 12101 Gravelly Lake Dr SW Tacoma WA 98499 Office: Weyerhaeuser Co Tacoma WA 98477

SCHWAB, BERNARD, library adminstr.; b. Bklyn., Nov. 25, 1920; s. Morris and Bessie (Potash) S.; B.Social Sci., Coll. City N.Y., 1943; B.L.S., Pratt Inst., 1947; m. Mona Fay Shapiro, June 1, 1947; children—Joel Martin, Richard Burton, William Eric, Lael Carol. Sub-librarian Bklyn. Pub. Library, 1946; supr. central circulation D.C. Pub. Library, 1947-51, chief bus. and econs. div., 1950-52, service expediter, 1951-52, acting chief acquisitions dept., 1952, chief extension dept., 1953; asst. city librarian Madison (Wis.) Pub. Library, 1954-57, dir., 1957—; instr. extension div. U. Wis., 1959-65; vis. lectr. Library Sch., 1968-72. Pres. Madison Area Library Council, 1970-72, 77; mem. Wis. Library Law Revision Com., 1970, 77-78; mem. Wis. Council for Library Devel., 1970-76, chmn., 1973-74. Served with AUS, 1943-46. Mem. Am. (council 1960-64), Wis. (v.p. 1965-66, pres. 1966-67; named Librarian of Year 1970) library assns., Mcpl. Execs. Madison (pres. 1977-78). Home: 3211 Stevens St Madison WI 53705 Office: 201 W Mifflin St Madison WI 53703

SCHWAB, HERMANN CASPAR, banker; b. N.Y.C., Jan. 8, 1920; s. Hermann Caspar and Ruth (Bliss) S.; grad. St. Marks Sch., 1937, Yale, 1941; m. C. Meteer Shanks, July 5, 1955; children—Henry R., Lesley Schwab Forman, Margery Schwab Weekes, Stuart Taylor, George Bliss, Katharine Lambard. With Hanover Bank, 1941-44, 46-55, asst. sec., 1949-53, asst. v.p., 1953-55; partner Dick & Merle Smith, 1956; v.p. Empire Trust Co., 1957-66, sr. v.p., 1965-66; with Bank of N.Y., 1966-67; sr. v.p. Schroder Trust Co., N.Y.C., 1967-73, dir., 1970-73; pres., dir. Cheapside Dollar Fund Ltd., N.Y.C., 1970—; sr. v.p. Schroder Naess & Thomas, N.Y.C., 1973—. Mayor, Oyster Bay Cove, N.Y. Trustee, vice chmn., treas. St. Lukes Hosp. Center. Served to 2d lt., inf., AUS, 1943-46. Clubs: Piping Rock (Locust Valley, N.Y.); The Brook, Turf and Field (N.Y.C.); Seawanhaka Corinthian Yacht (Oyster Bay). Home: Box 34 North Hempstead Turnpike Oyster Bay NY 11771 Office: 1 State St New York NY 10015

SCHWAB, JOHN JOSEPH, psychiatrist, educator; b. Cumberland, Md., Feb. 10, 1923; s. Joseph L. and Eleanor (Cadden) S.; B.S., U. Ky., 1946; M.D., U. Louisville, 1946; M.S. in Physiology (Med. fellow), U. Ill., 1949; postgrad. Duke, 1951-52, U. Fla., 1959-61; m. Ruby Baxter, Apr. 4, 1945; 1 dau., Mary Eleanor. Intern Phila. Gen. Hosp., 1947-48; resident medicine Louisville Gen. Hosp., 1949-50; resident psychiatry U. Fla. Hosp., 1959-61; internist, psychosomaticist Holzer Clinic, Galipolis, Ohio, 1954-59; Nat. Inst. Mental Health Career tchr. U. Fla., 1962-64, mem. faculty, 1961-73, prof. psychiatry and medicine, Gainesville, 1967-73, dir. cons. liaison program, 1964-67; chief consultation service, Gainesville, 1961-64; prof., chmn. dept. psychiatry and behavioral scis. Sch. Medicine, U. Louisville, 1974—. Chmn. epidemiologic studies rev. com. Center for Epidemiologic Studies, NIMH, 1973-75, cons. psychiatry br., 1975—. Diplomate Nat. Bd. Med. Examiners. Fellow Am. Coll. Psychiatrists (regent 1977—), Internat. Assn. Social Psychiatry, A.A.A.S., Am. Psychiat. Assn. (chmn. council on research and devel. 1974-75); mem. A.M.A., Psychosomatic Soc., Acad. Psychosomatic Medicine (exec. 1965—, pres. 1970-71), Found thanatology So., Jefferson County med. assns., Ky. Psychiat. Assn., Am. Assn. Social Psychiatry (pres. 1971-73), Alpha Omega Alpha. Author: The Handbook for the Psychiatric Consulation, 1968, also articles; co-author: Sociocultural Roots of Mental Illness: An Epidemiologic Survey, 1978, Social Order and Mental Health, 1979. Asso. editor Psychosomatics, 1965—. Co-editor: Man For Humanity: On Concordance V. Discord in Human Behavior, 1972; Social Psychiatry, Vol. 1, 1974; The Psychiatric Examination, 1974. Research on applicability of psychiat. concepts to gen. medicine, sociocultural aspects of mental illness; establishing guidelines for identification and mgmt. of med. patients whose illnesses are complicated by emotional stress; epidemiology of mental illness. Home: 6217 Innes Trace Louisville KY 40222

SCHWAB, JOSEPH JACKSON, educator; b. Columbus, Miss., Feb. 2, 1909; s. Samuel Buchsbaum and Hortense (Jackson) S.; Ph.B., U. Chgo., 1930, S.M., 1936, Ph.D., 1938; m. Rosamond Martin McGill, Sept. 13, 1932; 1 dau., Jill. Research asso. Columbia, 1936-37; asst. biology U. Chgo., 1934-36, instr., 1937-39, asst. prof., 1940-44, asso. prof., 1945-48, prof. biol. scis., prof. edn., 1949—, William Rainey Harper prof. natural scis., 1950, chmn. natural scis. The College 1945-51; Inglis lectr. Harvard, 1960. Recipient teaching award U. Chgo., 1945, 65; fellow Center Advanced Study in Behavioral Scis., 1958-59; Guggenheim fellow, 1971-72; vis. fellow Center Study Democratic Instns., 1973—. Mem. Genetics Soc. Am., Sigma Xi. Author: College Curriculum and Student Protest, Teaching of Science as Enquiry, Science, Curriculum and Liberal Education. Editor, author: Biology Tchrs.'s Handbook. Contbr. articles to profl., popular publs. Home: 151 Santa Elena Ln Santa Barbara CA 93108

SCHWAB, WILLIAM SAMUEL, lawyer; b. Columbus, Miss., Aug. 14, 1911; s. Samuel B. and Hortense (Jackson) S.; B.A., U. Wis., 1932; LL.B., Harvard, 1937; m. Frances Platz, Dec. 11, 1938; children—Jeril, Richard. Admitted to Ill. bar, 1937, since practiced in Chgo. Dir. Colt Industries, Inc.; dir., mem. exec. com. Old Orchard Bank & Trust Co. Mem. Am., Chgo. bar assns., Chgo. Law Inst. Clubs: Briarwood Country; Harvard (Chgo.). Home: 365 Iris Ln Highland Park IL 60035 Office: 180 N LaSalle St Chicago IL 60602

SCHWABE, ARTHUR DAVID, physician, educator; b. Varel, Germany, Feb. 1, 1924; s. Curt and Frieda (Roseno) S.; came to U.S., 1938, naturalized, 1943; M.D., U. Chgo., 1956. Intern U. Calif. at Los Angeles Med. Center, 1956-57, asst. resident, then asso. resident medicine, 1957-59, chief resident medicine, 1960-61, USPHS fellow gastroenterology, 1959-60, now mem. staff; chief gastroenterology Harbor Gen. Hosp., Torrance, Calif., 1962-67, now cons.; cons. Wadsworth VA Center, Los Angeles, Sepulveda (Calif.) VA Hosp.; mem. faculty U. Calif. at Los Angeles Med. Sch., 1961—, asst. prof. medicine, 1962-67, asso. prof., 1967-71, prof., 1971—, chief div. gastroenterology, 1967—, vice chmn. dept. medicine, 1971-74. Served with AUS, 1943-46. Recipient Golden Apple award sr. class U. Calif. at Los Angeles, 1967, 70, Outstanding Tchr. award U. Calif. at Los Angeles Med. House Staff, 1968, 78, Disting. Teaching award U. Calif. at Los Angeles, 1971; Edward F. Kraft scholar, 1951; Ambrose and Gladys Bowyer fellow medicine, 1958-59. Fellow A.C.P.; mem. Am. Fedn. Clin. Research, Am. Gastroenterol. Assn., Los Angeles Soc. Internal Medicine, N.Y. Acad. Sci., So. Calif. Soc. Gastroenterology (pres. 1969), Western Soc. Clin. Research, Western Gut Club (chmn. 1969-70), Alpha Omega Alpha. Contbr. articles to profl. jours. Office: 10833 LeConte St Los Angeles CA 90024

SCHWABE, CALVIN WALTER, educator, veterinarian; b. Newark, Mar. 15, 1927; s. Calvin Walter and Marie Catherine (Hassfeld) S.; B.S., Va. Poly. Inst., 1948; M.S., U. Hawaii, 1950; D.V.M., Auburn U., 1954; M.P.H., Harvard, 1955, Sc.D., 1956; m. Gwendolyn Joyce Thompson, June 7, 1951; children—Catherine Marie, Christopher Lawrence. From asso. prof. to prof. parasitology and epidemiology, chmn. dept. tropical health, and asst. dir. Sch. Pub. Health of Am. U. of Beirut, 1956-66; mem. Secretariat of WHO, Geneva, 1964-66; prof. epidemiology Sch. Vet. Medicine, also Sch. Medicine, U. Calif. at Davis, 1966—, chmn. dept. epidemiology and preventive medicine Sch. Vet. Medicine, 1966-70, asso. dean, 1970-71; cons. WHO, UN Environ. Program, FAO, NIH, Pan Am. Health Orgn., Nat. Acad. Scis.; univ. lectr. U. Sask.; Fulbright fellow U. Coll. of E. Africa, Cambridge (Eng.) U.; Srinivasan Meml. lectr. U. Madras; Spivik lectr. comparative medicine U. Minn.; Franklin lectr. scis. and humanities Auburn U. Fellow Am. Pub. Health Assn.; mem. Am. Vet. Med. Assn., Am. Soc. Tropical Medicine and Hygiene. Democrat. Mem. Soc. of Friends. Author: Veterinary Medicine and Human Health, 1969; What Should a Veterinarian Do?, 1972; Epidemiology in Veterinary Practice, 1977; Cattle, Priests and Progress in Medicine, 1978; also articles. Home: 849 A St Davis CA 95616

SCHWACHA, GEORGE, artist; b. Newark, Oct. 2, 1908; s. George and Bertha (Poppele) S.; student Art Students League; m. Ruth J. Hunt, 1954; children—Barbara Schwacha Fraccio, Keith, Martin. Pres. Art Centre of Oranges, 1966—, Art Centre of N.J., 1977—; works exhibited Denver Art Mus., Pa. Acad. Fine Arts, Art Inst. Chgo., NAD; represented permanent collections Albany Inst. History and Art, Montgomery (Ala.) Mus., Montclair (N.J.) Art Mus., Newark Mus., Fla. So. Coll., Butler Art Inst., Youngstown, Ohio, Delgado Mus., New Orleans, Norfolk Mus., Washington County Mus., U. Maine Art Gallery. Past pres. Art Centre of Oranges, 1975-76; treas. Art Centre N.J. Recipient medal State Exhbn., Montclair Art Mus., 1937; medal of honor Ala. Water Color Soc., 1954, Nat. Soc. Painters in Casein, 1956; 1st prize Washington Water Color Soc., 1955; 1st oil prize Montclair Art Mus., 1963; numerous others. Mem. Audubon Artists (past pres.), Am. Water Color Soc., Am. Artists Profl. League (pres.), Phila. Water Color Club. Home: 4 Hugenot St East Hanover NJ 07936 Office: 273 Glenwood Ave Bloomfield NJ 07003

SCHWADA, JOHN, univ. pres.; b. Tyrone, Okla., Sept. 23, 1919; s. William and Grace (Foster) S.; B.S., N.E. Mo. State Coll., 1941; M.A., U. Mo., 1947; Ph.D., U. Tex., 1951; m. Wilma Ruth Webster, May 24, 1947; children—John Webster, Ann. Teaching fellow U. Tex., 1947-50; prof. polit. sci. U. Mo., Columbia, 1951-71, chancellor, 1964-71; pres. Ariz. State U., Tempe, 1971—. Comptroller, budget dir. State of Mo., 1958-61; bd. fellows Am. Grad. Sch. Internat. Mgmt.; bd. dirs. Pub. Broadcasting Service; mem. Ariz. State Bd. Edn., 1975-79. Served to capt. AC, AUS, 1942-46. Rotarian. Home: 2400 S College Ave Tempe AZ 85282

SCHWAIT, ALLEN LOUIS, lawyer; b. Phila., Aug. 18, 1937; s. Albert and Dora M. (Lieberman) S.; B.S. in Econs., U. Pa., 1959; LL.B., U. Md., 1963; m. Lois Crandall, Sept. 3, 1961; children—Anne Elizabeth, Adam Michael. Admitted to Md. bar, 1964; law clk. to Hon. Edward S. Northrup, U.S. dist. judge Md., 1963-64; trial atty. Tax Div., Dept. Justice, 1964-67; partner Garbis & Schwait, Balt., 1968—. Lectr., U. Md. Sch. Law, 1973—. Mem. Charter Rev. Commn., Balt., 1973—; chmn. Mayor's Citizens Crime Com., 1974—. Mem. Balt. Assn. Tax Counsel (pres. 1971-72), Am., Balt., Fed. (pres. 1974—), Md. (bd. govs.) bar assns., Am. Jewish Com. Author: (with Garbis) Tax Refund Litigation, 1971, Tax Practice, 1974. Home: 2221 Arden Rd Baltimore MD 21209 Office: 1001 Keyser Bldg Baltimore MD 21202

SCHWALJE, JOSEPH LOUIS, engring. cons.; b. Metuchen, N.J., Nov. 30, 1922; s. John D. and Theresa (Moor) S.; B.S., Cornell U., 1944; M.S. (NSF fellow), Rutgers U., 1949; postgrad. Stevens Inst. Tech., summers 1960, 63; m. Helen M. Meloy, Jan. 6, 1945; children—Peter, Paula, Jeffrey, James. Application engr. steam power div. Worthington Corp., Harrison, N.J., 1946-47; instr., asst. prof. mech. engring. Rutgers U., 1947-51; sr. project engr. Merck & Co., Rahway, N.J., 1951-53; asso. prof. Pratt Inst., Bklyn., 1953-62, prof., chmn. mech. engring., 1963-71, dean Coll. Engring., 1972-75; owner Joseph L. Schwalje Assos., engr. cons., 1954—. Mem. exec. com., power press and forging sect. Nat. Safety Council, 1978—. Served to lt. (j.g.) C.E., USNR, 1943-46. Mem. ASME (chmn. region II mech. engring. dept. heads com. 1969-71), Am. Soc. Engring. Edn., AAUP, Tau Beta Pi, Pi Tau Sigma. Author: Elements of Engineering Materials, 1955. Home: 43 Oak Hills Rd Edison NJ 08817 Office: Coll Engring Pratt Inst Brooklyn NY 11205 also Joseph Schwalje Assos 38 Edgewood Rd Edison NJ 08817

SCHWAN, HERMAN PAUL, educator, research scientist; b. Aachen, Germany, Aug. 7, 1915; s. Wilheim and Meta (Pattberg) S.; student U. Goettingen, 1934-37; Ph.D., U. Frankfurt, 1940; Doctor habil. in physics and biophysics, 1946; m. Anne Marie DelBorello, June 15, 1949; children—Barbara, Margaret, Steven, Carol, Cathryn. Came to U.S., 1947; naturalized, 1952. Research scientist, prof. Kaiser Wilheim Inst. Biophysics, 1937-47, asst. dir., 1945-47; research sci. USN, 1947-50; prof. elec. engring., prof. elec. engring. in phys. medicine, asso. prof. phys. medicine U. Pa., Phila., 1950—, dir. electromed. div., 1952—, chmn. biomed. engring., 1961-73, program dir. biomed. engr. tng. program, 1960-77; vis. prof. U. Calif. at Berkeley, 1956, U. of Frankfurt (Germany), 1962; lectr. Johns Hopkins U., 1962-67. Fgn. sci. mem. Max Planck Soc. Adv. Research, Germany, 1962—; cons. NIH, 1962—; chmn. nat. and internat. meetings biomed. engring. and biophysics, 1959-61, 1965; mem. nat. adv. council environmental health HEW, 1969-71; mem. Nat. Acad. Scis.-NRC coms., 1968-77; mem. Nat. Acad. Engring., 1975—. Recipient Citizenship award, Phila., 1952, 1st prize Am. Inst. E.E., 1953, Achievement award Phila. Inst. E.E. and Electronics, 1963, Rajewsky prize for biophysics, 1974. Fellow Inst. Elec. Engrs. and Electronics (Morlock award 1967, chmn. and vice chmn. nat. profl. group biomed. engring. 1955, 62-68), AAAS; mem. Am. Standards Assn. (chmn. com. 1961-64), Am. Phys. Soc., Biophys. Soc. (publicity com., council, constrn. com.) Soc. for Cryobiology, Internat. Fedn. Med., and Biol. Engring., Biomed. Engring. Soc. (dir.), Sigma Xi, Eta Kappa Nu. Co-author: Advances in Medical and Biological Physics, 1957; Therapeutic Heat, 1958; Physical Techniques in Medicine and Biology, 1963. Editor: Biol. Engring., 1969. Mem. editorial bd. Biophys. Zeitschrift, Phys. Med. Biology, Transactions Biomed. Engring., Jour. Med. Electronics and Biol. Engring., Nonionizing Radiation, Environ. Biophysics. Contbr. articles to profl. jours. Home: 99 Kynlyn Rd Radnor PA 19087 also 162 59th St Avalon NJ 08202 Office: Dept Bioengring D2 U Pa Philadelphia PA 19104

SCHWANN, WILLIAM, publisher, musician; b. Salem, Ill., May 13, 1913; s. Henry W. and Effie A. (Garthwait) S.; student Louisville Conservatory Music, 1930-31; A.B., U. Louisville, 1935, D.Mus. (hon.), 1969; postgrad. Boston U. Sch. Music, 1935-36, Harvard, 1937-38; m. Aire-Maija Kutvonen, June 1, 1959. Organist, choir dir. Louisville chs., 1930-35; organ, piano tchr., organist, choir dir., Boston area, 1935-50; music revs. Boston Herald, Boston Transcript, others, 1937-39; owner Record Shop, Cambridge, Mass., 1939-53; organ concerts, broadcasts, 1930-40; compiler, pub. 1st Long Playing Record Catalog, 1949, now known as monthly Schwann-1 Record and Tape Guide; compiler, pub. Artist Listing LP Catalog, semi-ann. Schwann-2 Record and Tape Guide, Schwann Children's Rec. Catalog, Basic Rec. Library, Basic Jazz Record Library, 1953—; pres., treas. W. Schwann, Inc., 1957-77; pres., chief exec. officer ABC Schwann Publications, Inc., 1976—. Mem. staff radiation lab. Mass. Inst. Tech., 1944-45. Trustee Marlboro Sch. Music, Boston Ballet Co.; bd. dirs. Greater Boston Youth Symphony Orch., Longy Sch. Music, Cambridge Soc. Early Music; bd. visitors Boston U. Sch. Music, vis. com. Harvard Coll. Dept. Music. Life mem. Nat. Audubon Soc., Nat Parks and Conservation Assn., New Eng. Wild Flower Preservation Soc., Save-the-Redwoods League, Soc. for Protection N.H. Forests, Am. Forestry Assn., Trustees of Reservations, Wilderness Soc., Izaak Walton League, Nature Conservancy, Appalachian Mountain Club, Sierra Club. Clubs: St. Botolph, Harvard of Boston, Harvard Mus. Assn. Editor: White House Record Library Catalog (listing 2,000 RIAA record collection presented to White House), 1973. Home: Old Winter Rd Lincoln MA 01773 Office: 137 Newbury St Boston MA 02116

SCHWANTNER, JOSEPH, composer; b. Chgo., Mar. 22, 1943; B.Mus., Chgo. Conservatory Coll.; M.Mus., Northwestern U., 1966, D.Mus., 1968; m. Janet Elaine Rossate; 2 children. Teaching fellow Northwestern U., 1966-68; mem. faculty Chgo. Conservatory Coll., 1967-68; asst. prof. Pacific Lutheran U., 1968-69, Ball State U., 1969-70; asst. prof., then asso. prof. Eastman Sch. Music, U. Rochester, 1970—; compositions include: Sinfonia Brevis, Pastorale for Winds, Nonet, Diaphonia Intervallum, Entropy, Chronicon, Enchiridion, August Canticle, Consortium, In Aeternum, Modis Caelestis, Shadows, Canticle for the Evening Bells, Elixir, Aftertones of Infinity (Pulitzer prize for music 1979). Recipient Faricy award, 1965, BMI Student award, 1965, 66, 67, Bearns prize Columbia U., 1967, Nat. Inst. Arts and Letters Charles Ives scholar, 1970; N.Y. State Council on Arts Creative Arts Public Service grantee, 1973. Office: Eastman Sch Music 26 Gibbs St Rochester NY 14604*

SCHWANZ, H(ERMAN) LEE, publishing co. exec.; b. Lorimor, Iowa, Apr. 29, 1923; s. Arthur I. and Elva Rae (Caffery) S.; B.S. in Agrl. Journalism, Iowa State U., 1947; m. Kathleen J. Boland, Sept. 1, 1947; children—Michael L., Leslie Anne Schwanz Satran, Stephen E., Susan E. Farm editor Cedar Rapids (Iowa) Gazette, 1947-50; asso. editor Country Gentleman mag. Curtis Pub. Co., Phila., 1950-55; editor, pub. Agrl. Pubs., Milw., 1955-70; pres., pub. Market Communications, Milw., 1970—. Bd. dirs. Lancer-Sparton Scholarship Found. Served with 90th inf. div. AUS, 1943-46. Decorated Silver Star. Mem. Sigma Delta Chi. Republican. Methodist. Clubs: Milw. Press, Westmoor Country. Editor Farmer's Digest, 1970—; asso. editor Nat. Wildlife. Home: 2645 Maple Hill Ln Brookfield WI 53005 Office: 225 E Michigan Milwaukee WI 53202

SCHWARTING, ARTHUR ERNEST, univ. dean; b. Waubay, S.D., June 8, 1917; s. John Ernest and Johanna Martha (Boelte) S.; B.S., S.D. State U., 1940; Ph.D., Ohio State U., 1943; m. Roberta L. Mitchell, June 14, 1941; children—Jon Michael, Stephen Arthur (dec.), Gerald Allen. Instr., U. Nebr., 1943-45, asst. prof., 1945-49; asso. prof. U. Conn., Storrs, 1949-53, prof. pharmacognosy, 1953—, dean Sch. Pharmacy, 1970—; vis. prof. U. Munich, 1968-69. Mem. Mansfield (Conn.) Bd. Edn., 1965-70. Bd. dirs. Am. Found. Pharm. Edn., 1974—. Recipient Research Achievement award Am. Pharm. Assn. Found., 1964; U. Conn. Alumni Assn. award for faculty excellence, 1965; Centennial Achievement award Ohio State U., 1970. Fellow AAAS; mem. Am. Assn. Colls. Pharmacy (pres. 1971-72, pres. council deans 1977-78), Am. Pharm. Assn., Am. Soc.

Pharmacognosy, Sigma Xi, Phi Lambda Upsilon, Phi Kappa Phi, Rho Chi. Lutheran. Club: Willimantic Country. Author: (with others) Introduction to Chromatography, 1968. Editor: Lloydia, Jour. Natural Products, 1960-76. Research and publs. on chemistry and biochemistry of natural drug products. Home: 18 Ledgewood Dr Storrs CT 06268

SCHWARTZ, ABBA PHILIP, lawyer; b. Balt., Apr. 17, 1916; s. Harry and Fannie (Berman) S.; B.S. in Fgn. Service, Georgetown U., 1936; LL.B., Harvard, 1939. Admitted to D.C. bar, 1940; ofcl. Intergovtl. Com. on Refugees, London, Eng., 1946-47; reparations dir. UN Internat. Refugee Orgn., Geneva, Switzerland, 1947-49; partner law firm, Washington, 1949-62; adminstr., asst. sec. Bur. Security and Consular Affairs, State Dept., 1962-66; practice law, Washington, 1967—. U.S. rep. 18th Session, Council Intergovtl. Com. on European Migration, Geneva, 1962, 20th-24th sessions, 1963-65; U.S. del., vice chmn. 20th Internat. Conf. Red Cross, Vienna, Austria, 1965; spl. asst. to sec. def. on prisoners of war in Vietnam, Washington, 1967—. Bd. govs. ARC, 1963-66. Served with U.S. Mcht. Marines, 1942-44; to lt. USNR, 1944-46. Decorated Order Orange Nassau (Netherlands). Mem. Am., Fed., D.C. bar assns., PEN. Clubs: Reform (London); Nat. Capital Democratic; Harvard (N.Y.C.). Author: The Open Society, 1968, paperback, 1969. Contbr. articles on immigration and refugees to periodicals. Address: 3306 R St NW Washington DC 20007 also 166 E 63d St New York NY 10021

SCHWARTZ, ABRAHAM, educator; b. N.Y.C., June 13, 1916; s. Nathan and Lena (Swoff) S.; B.S.S., Coll. City N.Y., 1936; M.S., Mass. Inst. Tech., 1937, Ph.D., 1939; m. Sylvia Paymer, June 16, 1940; children—Ina Barbara (Mrs. Lewis Heafitz), Susan Doris (Mrs. Lewis Steinberg), Margery Helen (Mrs. Gerald Goldman). Research asst. Inst. Advanced Study, Princeton, 1939-41; instr., then asst. prof. Pa. State U., 1941-48; mem. faculty Coll. City N.Y., 1948—, prof. math., 1966—, chmn. dept., 1964-66, dean Sch. Gen. Studies, 1966-70, provost, 1970-71. Bd. mgrs. N.J. YMCA, 1959—, pres., 1972—. Mem. Math. Assn. Am. (bd. govs. 1966-69), Am. Math. Soc., Phi Beta Kappa, Sigma Xi. Author: Analytic Geometry and Calculus, 3d edit., 1974. Home: 321 Windsor Rd Englewood NJ 07631 Office: City Coll New York City NY 10031

SCHWARTZ, ALAN E., lawyer; b. Detroit, Dec. 21, 1925; s. Maurice H. and Sophia (Welkowitz) S.; student Western Mich. Coll., 1944-45, Harvard Bus. Sch., 1945; B.A. with distinction, U. Mich., 1947; LL.B. magna cum laude, Harvard, 1950; m. Marianne Shapero, Aug. 24, 1950; children—Marc Alan, Kurt Nathan, Ruth Anne. Admitted to N.Y. bar, 1951, Mich. bar, 1952; asso. Kelley, Drye & Warren, N.Y.C., 1950-52; mem. Honigman, Miller, Schwartz & Cohn, Detroit, 1952—, now sr. mem. Spl. asst. counsel N.Y. State Crime Commission, 1951; chmn. exec. com. Cunningham Drug Stores, Inc., 1969; dir. Mich. Bell Telephone Co., Burroughs Corp., Detroit Edison Co., Core Industries Inc., Handleman Co., Howell Industries, Inc., Pulte Home Corp., Detroitbank Corp., Cunningham Drug Stores, Inc., Bendix Corp., Fisher Corp. Vice pres., mem. exec. com. Detroit Symphony Orch.; pres. United Found.; bd. dirs. March of Dimes, United Found., Detroit Renaissance, Mich. Cancer Found., Detroit Econ. Growth Corp., New Detroit, Oakland U., Met. Fund, Jewish Welfare Fedn. Detroit; hon. trustee Kalamazoo Coll.; trustee Harper-Grace Hosp., Detroit Grand Opera Assn. Interlochen Arts Acad., Cranbrook Sch. Served as ensign Supply Corps, USNR, 1945-46. Mem. Am., N.Y., Mich. bar assns. Clubs: Franklin Hills Country; Detroit, Standard City, Detroit, Economic (dir.), Renaissance (Detroit). Medical Expert Testmony. Editor Harvard Law Rev., 1950. Home: 4120 Echo Rd Bloomfield Hills MI 48013 Office: 1st Nat Bldg Detroit MI 48226

SCHWARTZ, ALFRED, univ. adminstr.; b. Chgo., Jan. 8, 1922; s. Isadore and Lena (Ziff) S.; B.Ed., Chgo. Tchrs. Coll., 1944; M.A. in Polit. Sci., U. Chgo., 1946, Ph.D. in Ednl. Adminstrn., 1949; m. Delle Weiss, Aug. 26, 1945; children—Reid Mitchell, Karen Ruth. Tchr., Chgo. pub. schs., 1944-45; contact officer VA, 1946; instr. U. Chgo. Lab. Sch., 1946-50; asso. prof. edn. Drake U., 1950-56; asso. prof. edn. U. Del., also exec. sec. Del. Sch. Study Council, 1956-58; dean Univ. Coll., prof. Coll. Edn., Drake U., 1958—, dean Coll. Edn., 1964—, acting v.p. acad. adminstrn., 1969—; adv. Iowa Dept. Pub. Instrn. Mem. Gov.'s Commn. State-Local Relations. Mem. Iowa Adult Edn. Assn. (pres.), Iowa Assn. Colls. for Tchr. Edn. (pres.), Am. Assn. Sch. Asminstrs., AAAS, Adult Edn. Assn. Am., Am. Ednl. Research Assn., Nat. Soc. Study Edn., Mo. Valley Adult Edn. Assn. (pres.), Nat. Conf. Profs. Ednl. Adminstrn., Nat., Iowa edn. assns., Phi Delta Kappa, Kappa Delta Pi. Author: (with Harian L. Hagman) Administration in Profile for School Executives, 1954; (with Stuart Tiedeman) Evaluating Student Progress, 1957; (with Willard Fox) Managerial Guide for School Principals, 1965. Home: 4044 Beaver Ave Des Moines IA 50310

SCHWARTZ, ALFRED LOWIN, lawyer; b. N.Y.C., May 15, 1930; s. Louis L. and Martha (Lowin) S.; A.B., N.Y.U., 1950; LL.B., Columbia, 1953; m. Renee Adrienne Gerstler, July 30, 1955; children—Carolyn Susan, Deborah Jane. Admitted to N.Y. bar, 1953; legal draftsman Columbia U. Legislative Drafting Research Fund, 1955-59; atty. ABC, 1959-65; asst. gen. counsel Metromedia, Inc., N.Y.C., 1965-68, gen. atty., 1968-69, gen. counsel, 1969—, v.p., 1969-74, sr. v.p., 1974—; v.p., dir. Metromedia Producers Corp., Ice Capades, Inc., Harlem Globetrotters, Inc., Figi's Inc. Served to 1st lt. USAF, 1953-55; former capt. Res. Mem. Assn. Bar City N.Y. Home: 211 Central Park W New York NY 10024 Office: 1 Harmon Plaza Secaucus NJ 07094

SCHWARTZ, ARNOLD, pharmacologist; b. Bronx, N.Y., Mar. 1, 1929; s. Saul and Ray Schwartz; B.Sc. in Pharmacy cum laude, L.I. U., 1951; M.Sc., Ohio State U., Columbus, 1957; Ph.D., SUNY, Bklyn., 1960; m. Ina Price, Dec. 23, 1956; children—Tracy, Stacy. Mem. faculty Baylor Coll. Medicine, 1962-77, prof. pharmacology, 1968-72, head div. myocardial biology, 1972-77; Edward Wendland prof. materia medica and therapeutics U. Cin. Med. Center, 1977—, chmn. dept. pharmacology and cell biophysics, 1977—; mem. rev. panels Nat. Heart, Lung and Blood Inst. and Am. Heart Assn., 1970—; pres. Internat. Study Group Research in Cardiac Metabolism, 1976-77. Served with USAF, 1952-56. Fellow NIH, 1960-62, recipient Career Devel. award, 1965-72; Josiah Macy scholar Oxford U., 1979. Fellow Am. Coll. Cardiology, N.Y. Acad. Sci. Author articles in field; mem. editorial bds. profl. jours.; editor Methods in Pharmacology Series. Office: 231 Bethesda Ave Room 5006 Cincinnati OH 45267. *The need to discover is of paramount importance.*

SCHWARTZ, ARTHUR HARRY, judge; b. N.Y.C., Nov. 18, 1903; s. Louis and Ida (Rothstein) S.; A.B., Columbia, 1923, LL.B., 1926; m. Dorothy Blaine, Aug. 5, 1928 (dec. 1956); children—Anne, Lois; m. 2d, Betty Sapro, Feb. 14, 1958. Asst. dept. govt. Columbia, 1922-25; asst. U.S. atty. So. Dist. N.Y., 1926-33, chief asst. charge prohibition div., 1931-33; counsel N.Y. State Joint Legislative Com. Legislative Practices, 1944-46; Republican campaign mgr. N.Y. State, 1944; counsel N.Y. State Republican Com., 1944—; counsel Temp. Commn. Need for a State U., 1946-48, N.Y. Temp. Commn. on Coordination State Activities, 1948-59, to Rep. State Campaign mgr., 1948-52; apptd. justice N.Y. State Supreme Ct., 1952; mem. com. on character and fitness 1st Jud. Dept., 1948—, vice chmn., 1977—; lectr. law Pace Inst. Accountancy, 1928-35; mem. law firm Schwartz, Burns, Lesser & Jacoby, N.Y.C.; disting. lectr. law Pace Law Sch., White Plains, N.Y., 1979. Mem. N.Y. State Law Revision Commn., 1960-74, N.Y. State Commn. Jud. and Legislative Salaries, 1972-74. Mem. N.Y. County Rep. Com.; chmn. N.Y. State Bd. Elections, 1974-76. Recipient James Gordon Bennett prize, 1921; J. Winthrop Chanier Hist. prize, 1923 (both of Columbia Coll.); Columbia Alumni medal, 1957; fellow Brandeis U. Mem. Columbia Law Alumni Assn., Nat. Legal Aid Assn., Municipal Art Soc., Am. Coll. Trial Lawyers, Am. Judicature Soc., Civil Liberties Union, Fed., Am., N.Y. bar assns., Columbia Coll. Alumni Assn., N.Y. County Lawyers Assn. (past pres.), Legal Aid Soc. N.Y. (past dir.), Assn. Bar City N.Y. (past v.p.), Soc. Am. Magicians, Phi Beta Kappa Assos. Club: Friars, Univ. Editor-in-chief Columbia Law Rev., 1925-26; bd. editors N.Y. Law Jour., 1976—. Home: 3 Deerfoot Ln Dobbs Ferry NY 10522 Office: 445 Park Ave New York NY 10022

SCHWARTZ, AUBREY EARL, artist; b. N.Y.C., Jan. 13, 1928; s. Louis and Clara S.; student Art Students League, Bklyn. Mus. Art Sch. One-man shows: Grippi Gallery, N.Y.C., 1958, Art U.S.A., N.Y. Coliseum, N.Y.C., 1959, Contemporary Graphic Art, U.S. State Dept., 1959; group shows include: Whitney Mus. Am. Art, N.Y.C., 1957: represented in permanent collections: Nat. Gallery Art, Washington, Bklyn. Mus. Art, Phila. Mus. Art, Library Congress, Washington, Art Inst. Chgo.; asso. prof. art Harpur Coll., SUNY, Binghamton, 1969--. Recipient 1st prize for graphic art Boston Arts Festival, 1960; Guggenheim fellow, 1958-60; Tamarind fellow, 1960. Home: 104 S Main St Afton NY 13730 Office: Harpur Coll SUNY Binghamton NY 13901

SCHWARTZ, BERNARD, educator, lawyer; b. N.Y.C., Aug. 25, 1923; s. Isidore and Ethel (Levenson) S.; B.S.S., Coll. City N.Y., 1944; LL.B., N.Y.U., 1944; LL.M., Harvard, 1945; Ph.D., Cambridge U., 1947, LL.D., 1956; Doctorat d'Universite, U. Paris, 1963; m. Aileen Haas, Apr. 18, 1950; 1 son, Brian Michael. Admitted to N.Y. bar, 1945; mem. law faculty N.Y.U., 1947—, Edwin D. Webb prof. law, 1967—. Cons. Hoover Commn., 1955; chief counsel, staff dir. spl. subcom. legislative oversight U.S. Ho. Reps., 1957-58. Bd. dirs. Center Adminstrv. Justice, 1973—. Mem. Am. Bar Assn., Assn. Bar City N.Y. Author: French Adminstrative Law and the Common Law World, 1954; The Supreme Court, 1957; The Professor and the Commissions, 1959; Introduction to American Administrative Law, 1962; The Reins of Power, 1963; Commentary on the Constitution of the U.S., 5 vols., 1963-68; The Roots of Freedom, 1967; Legal Control of Government, 1972; Constitutional Law: A Textbook, 1972, 2d edit., 1979; The Law in America, 1974; Administrative Law, 1976; The Great Rights of Mankind, 1977. Home: 60 Sutton Pl S New York NY 10022

SCHWARTZ, BERNARD, physician b. Toronto, Can., Nov. 12, 1927; s. Samuel and Gertrude (Levinsky) S.; M.D., U. Toronto, 1951; M.S., State U. Ia., 1953, Ph.D., 1959; children—Lawrence Frederick, Karen Lynne, Jennifer Carla. Intern U. Hosps., State U. Iowa, 1951-52, resident ophthalmology, 1951-54; research fellow U. Iowa, 1954-58; asst. prof. to asso. prof. Downstate Med. Center fo State U. N.Y., 1958-68; prof. ophthalmology, chmn. dept. Tufts U., 1968—; ophthalmologist in chief New Eng. Med. Center. Dir. Mass. Soc. Prevention of Blindness. Fellow Am. Acad. Ophthalmology and Otolaryngology, A.C.S.; mem. Am. Soc. Cell Biology, Assn. Research in Ophthalmology, Assn. Am. Med. Colls., Assn. U. Profs. Ophthalmology, New Eng. Ophthalmol. Soc., N.Y. Acad. Medicine, N.Y. Acad. Scis., Tissue Culture Assn., Soc. Franciase D'Ophthalmologie, Sigma Xi. Author: Corticosteroids and the Eye; Decision-Making in the Diagnosis and Therapy of the Glaucomas; Syphilis and the Eye. Editor in chief of Survey of Ophthalmology, 1968—. Contbr. articles to profl. jours. Home: 19 Nash Ln Weston MA 02193 Office: 171 Harrison Ave Boston MA 02111

SCHWARTZ, BERNARD LEON, electronics co. exec.; b. N.Y.C., Dec. 13, 1925; s. Harry and Hannah (Forman) S.; B.B.A., Coll. City N.Y., 1948; m. Irene Zanderer, June 17, 1950; children—Karen Marcia, Fran Andrea. Sr. partner Schnee, Hauer & Schwartz, N.Y.C, 1948-62; sr. v.p. APL Corp., Great Neck, N.Y., 1962-68, dir., 1959—; dir. Reliance Group, Inc., N.Y.C., 1961—, chmn. exec. com., pres., 1968-72; chmn. bd., pres., dir. Loral Corp., N.Y.C., 1972—; dir. Reliance Group Inc., Commonwealth Land Title Ins. Co., Reliance Ins. Cos. Served with USAAF, 1943-45. Home: 944 Fifth Ave New York NY 10021 Office: 600 3d Ave New York NY 10016

SCHWARTZ, BERTRAM, utility exec.; b. Bklyn., Sept. 22, 1930; s. Jack and Rae (Becker) S.; B.S., Lafayette Coll., Easton, Pa., 1952; M.S., Columbia U., 1953; m. Isabel Shapiro, Dec. 14, 1969; children—Rachel Lisa, Adam Gabriel. With U.S. AEC, 1953-65, chief chem. processing, 1962-65; asst. to pres. Nuclear Materials and Equipment Corp., Apollo, Pa., 1965-68; with Consol. Edison Co., N.Y.C., 1968—, v.p., 1971-75, sr. v.p., 1975—; lectr. in field. Named Outstanding Young Engr., AEC, 1963, recipient Superior Performance award, 1964. Jewish. Home: 5 Warren Pl Armonk NY 10504 Office: 4 Irving Pl New York NY 10003

SCHWARTZ, BRIAN BENJAMIN, coll. dean; b. N.Y.C., Apr. 15, 1938; s. David and Frieda (Streigold) S.; student Cooper Union, 1955-57; B.S. in Physics, CCNY, 1959; Ph.D. in Physics, Brown U., 1963; m. Teri Geller, Jan. 28, 1961; children—Robin, Adam. Mem. faculty Rutgers - The State U., New Brunswick, N.J., 1963-65; with Francis Bitter Nat. Magnet Lab., M.I.T., 1965-77, leader theoretical physics group, magnet lab., 1970-77, asso. prof. physics dept., 1969-73; dean Sch. of Sci., dean of research, prof. physics Bklyn. Coll. of City U. N.Y., Bklyn., 1977—; cons. in field; dir. NATO Advanced Study Insts., 1973, 76, 80. Fellow Am. Phys. Soc. (mem. council 1973-77, chmn. forum on physics and society 1979-80); mem. AAAS, N.Y. Acad. Scis., Sigma Xi. Jewish. Author: Scientific Manpower, 1971; Superconducting Machines and Devices, 1974; Superconductor Applications, SQUID's and Machines, 1977; Solids and Plasmas in High Magnetic Fields, 1979. Home: 301 E 47th St Apt 6A New York NY 10017 Office: Bklyn Coll Brooklyn NY 11210

SCHWARTZ, CARL EDWARD, painter, printmaker; b. Detroit, Sept. 20, 1935; s. Carl and Verna (Steiner) S.; B.F.A., Art Inst. Chgo. Sch.-U. Chgo., 1957; m. Kay Joyce Hofmann, June 18, 1955; children—Dawn Ellen, Cari Leigh. One-man shows include: South Bend (Ind.) Art Center, Feingarten Gallery, Chgo., 1960, Bernard Horwich Center, Chgo., Covenant Club, Chgo., Barat Coll., Chgo. Public Library, Alverno Coll., 1020 Art Center, Rosenberg Gallery, Peoria (Ill.) Art Guild, 1977; numerous group shows include: 9th Ann. Michigana Exhbt., Detroit (Cloetingh and Deman award), 1959, Hyde Park Art Center, Chgo. (5th Ann. Jury Exhbn. prize), 1960, Spectrum Exhbn. '63, Chgo. (1st prize), New Horizons Exhbt., Chgo. (Joseph Shapiro award), 1960, Nat. Design Center, Chgo. (New Horizons in Painting 1st prize), 1965, 3d Ann. Chgo. Arts Competition (1st prize), 1962, Union League Club, Chgo. (2d prize), 1967, N. Shore Art League Ann. Drawing and Print Show, Chgo. (1st prize), 1965, Artists Guild Chgo. (prize), 1965, McCormack Pl., Chgo. (1st prize), 1965, Detroit Art Inst. (Commonwealth prize), 1965, Park Forest (Ill.) Art Exhbn. (Best of Show), 1969, 14th Ann. Virginia Beach (Va.) Show (Best of Show), 1969, Suburban Fine Arts Center, Highland Park, Ill. (prize), 1970, 15th Ann. Virginia Beach Show (prize), 1970, 32d Ann. Artists Guild, Chgo. (2d prize), 1970, N. Shore Art League Print and Drawing Show (prize), 1970, 16th Ann. Virginia Beach Show (2d prize), 1971, Ill. State Fair (prize), 1972, Artists Guild Chgo. (1st prize), 1972, 17th Ann. Virginia Beach Exhbt. (1st prize), 1972, Artists Guild 50th Fine Art Exhbn., Chgo. (prize), 1973, Dickinson State U. (prize), 1973, N. Shore Art League Print Exhbn. (prize), 1973, Lakehurst Exhbt. (prize), 1974, Union League Art Exhbt. (1st prize), 1974, Artists Guild Fine Arts Exhbn. (best of Show), 1974, Bluegrass Painting Exhbn., Louisville (award), 1975, Union League Art Exhbn. (prize), 1976; represented in permanent collections: Brit. Mus., London, Smithsonian Inst., Washington, Art Inst. Chgo.; tchr. art N. Shore Art League, Suburban Fine Arts Center, Deerpath Art League. Home: 4228 N Hazel St Chicago IL 60613

SCHWARTZ, CHARLES, JR., judge; b. New Orleans, Aug. 20, 1922; s. Charles and Sophie (Hess) S.; B.A., Tulane U., 1943, J.D., 1947; m. Patricia May, Aug. 31, 1950; children—Priscilla May, John Putney. Admitted to La. bar, 1947; practiced in New Orleans, until 1976; partner firm Little, Schwartz & Dussom, 1970-76; dist. counsel Gulf Coast dist. U.S. Maritime Adminstrn., 1953-62; U.S. dist. judge Eastern Dist. La., New Orleans, 1976—; lectr. Tulane U. Law Sch.; lectr. continuing law insts. Pres. New Orleans unit Am. Cancer Soc., 1956-57; v.p., chmn. budget com. United Fund Greater New Orleans Area, 1959-61, trustee, 1963-65; pres. Cancer Assn. Greater New Orleans, 1972-73, United Cancer Council, 1971-73; mem. com. on grants to agencies Community Chest, 1965—; men's adv. com. League Women Voters, 1966-68; chmn. com. admissions of program devel. and coordination com. United Way Greater New Orleans, 1974-76; mem. comml. panel Am. Arbitration Assn., 1974-76; bd. dirs. Willow Wood Home, 1979—; trustee Metairie Park Country Day Sch., 1977—; mem. La. Republican Central Com., 1961-76; mem. Orleans Parish Rep. Exec. Com., 1960-74, chmn., 1965-75; mem. Jefferson Parish Rep. Exec. Com., 1975-76; del. Rep. Nat. Conv., 1960, 64, 68. Served to 2d lt. AUS, 1943-46; maj. U.S. Army Res. ret. Mem. Am., La., New Orleans bar assns., Am. Judicature Soc., Fgn. Relations Assn. New Orleans (past dir.). Club: Lakewood Country (dir. 1967—, pres. 1975-77). Address: US Dist Ct US Courthouse 500 Camp St New Orleans LA 70130

SCHWARTZ, CHARLES FREDERICK, economist; b. Balt., May 2, 1916; s. Charles Herzog and Cora (Miller) S.; B.A., U. Va., 1936, M.A., 1937, Ph.D., 1939; postgrad. Va. Poly. Inst., 1937-38, Georgetown U., 1941-42; m. Marika Rupis, June 7, 1941; children—Mary Louise (Mrs. W. David Solomon), Charles Anthony. Instr. rural econs. U. Va., 1939-41; economist nat. income div. Office Bus. Econs., U.S. Dept. Commerce, 1941-51, asst. chief, 1951-56, asst. dir. Office Bus. Econs., 1956-59; chief N.Am. div. Western Hemisphere Dept., IMF, 1959-62, asst. dir., 1962-66, dep. dir. research dept., 1966-79, dir. adjustment studies, 1979—. Recipient gold medal for exceptional service Dept. Commerce, 1951. Mem. Internat. Assn. Research in Income and Wealth, Conf. on Research Income and Wealth, Am. Econ. Assn., Am. Statis. Assn., Phi Beta Kappa, Alpha Kappa Psi, Theta Delta Chi. Author articles on nat. income, internat. finance. Home: 7504 Honeywell Ln Bethesda MD 20014 Office: IMF 19th and H Sts Washington DC 20431

SCHWARTZ, DAVID, judge; b. N.Y.C., July 7, 1916; s. Hyman and Nettie (Strauss) S.; A.B. cum laude, N.Y. U., 1936; LL.B. magna cum laude, Harvard U., 1939; m. Louisa Van Wezel, June 15, 1968; children by previous marriage—Jonathan, Joanna M. Admitted to N.Y. bar, 1940, D.C. bar, 1965, U.S. Supreme Ct. bar, 1946, U.S. Ct. Claims bar, 1954; practice law with firm Karelsen & Karelsen, N.Y.C., 1939-40; spl. asst. to atty. gen. Dept. Justice, Washington, 1941-42, chief trial atty. antitrust and enemy property div., 1945-56; law clk. to Justice Stanley Reed, 1942-43; legal adviser Greece and Balkan missions UNRRA and predecessor Dept. State, 1943-45; counsel Devel. & Resources Corp., N.Y.C., 1956-57; partner firm Stroock & Stroock & Lavan, N.Y.C., 1957-68; trial judge U.S. Ct. Claims, Washington, 1968—; adj. prof. law Georgetown U., 1954-55; adj. asst. prof. N.Y. U. law sch., 1957-68; vis. prof. U. Wis. at Madison Law Sch., summers 1976, 78, U. San Diego Law Sch., summers 1977, 79. Recipient John D. Rockefeller III Pub. Service award, 1955. Mem. Am., D.C., Fed. bar assns., Assn. Bar City N.Y. Democrat. Jewish. Author: (with S.B. Jacoby) Government Litigation-Cases and Notes, 1963; Litigation with the Federal Government, 1970. Office: US Ct Claims 717 Madison Pl NW Washington DC 20005

SCHWARTZ, DONALD, univ. chancellor; b. Scarsdale, N.Y., Dec. 27, 1927; s. Harry A. and Ethel Schwartz; B.S., U. Mo., 1949; M.S., Mont. State U., 1951; Ph.D., Pa. State U., 1955; m. Lois Schwartz, Sept. 8, 1948; children—Leanne, Mark W., Scott B., Bradley F. Program dir. NSF, 1966-68; asso. dean Grad. Sch., Memphis State U., 1968-70; dean advanced studies Fla. Atlantic U., Boca Raton, 1970-71; v.p., acting pres. State U. N.Y., Buffalo, 1971-74; chancellor Ind. U.-Purdue U., Ft. Wayne, Ind., 1974-78, U. Colo., Colorado Springs, 1978—; cons. in field. Served with USCG, 1945. Research fellow AEC, 1953-55; N.Y. State fellow, 1947-48. Mem. Am. Chem. Soc., AAAS, Sigma Xi, Phi Lambda Upsilon, Phi Delta Kappa. Clubs: Rotary, Country of Colo., Shriners. Author papers structure of coal and organo-titanium compounds, also on higher edn. Home: 21 Sanford Rd Colorado Springs CO 80906 Office: U of Colo Cragmor Rd Colorado Springs CO 80907. *Each can become all that he or she is capable of being through education, hard work and compassion for other human beings. This I believe!*

SCHWARTZ, DONALD EDWARD, lawyer, educator; b. Bklyn., Aug. 21, 1930; s. Harry and Esther (Goldman) S.; A.B., Union Coll., 1952; LL.B., Harvard U., 1955; LL.M., N.Y. U., 1966; m. Ann Roberta Sher, June 23, 1968; children—Pamela Bonnie, Abigail Jane. Admitted to N.Y. bar, 1956, D.C. bar, 1960; mem. staff Office of Opinion Writing, SEC, 1957-59; counsel, sec. Columbia Fin. Corp., Washington, 1959-61; asso. firm Brinsmade & Schafrann, N.Y.C., 1961-62, partner, 1962-64; asso. firm Hill, Betts, Yamaoka, Freehill and Longcope, N.Y.C., 1964-66; of counsel firm Williams & Connolly; mem. faculty Georgetown U. Law Center, Washington, 1966—, prof., 1969—, asso. dean, 1979—; vis. prof. N.Y. U. Law Sch., 1973-74; dir., cons. Bur. of Nat. Affairs, Inc., Washington; mem. legal adv. com. N.Y. Stock Exchange; dir. Project on Corp. Responsibility, Inc.; dir. Center for Auto Safety. Served with U.S. Army, 1955-57. Mem. Am. Bar Assn. (com. on corp. laws, com. on fed. regulation of securities), Fed. Bar Assn. (mem. exec. council of fed. securities law com.), Assn. Bar City N.Y., Am. Law Inst. Democrat. Jewish. Author, editor books on corp. law. Contbr. articles to profl. jours. Office: 600 New Jersey Ave NW Washington DC 20001

SCHWARTZ, DOUGLAS WRIGHT, archaeologist, anthropologist; b. Erie, Pa., July 29, 1929; s. Harry and Vernon Kelsey (Schaaf) S.; B.A., U. Ky., 1950; Ph.D., Yale U., 1955; m. Rita Jaunita Hartley, Oct. 4, 1950; children—Steven, Susan, Kelsey. Pres., Sch. Am. Research, Santa Fe; dir. Sena Plaza Corp. Pres. Witter Bynner Found. for Poetry, Inc.; mem. Public Broadcasting Assos. Adv. Bd.; vice chmn. Harvard U. Overseer's Com. on Peabody Mus.; trustee Jane Goodall African Wildlife Research Center; mem. council Nat. Park Service Adv. Bd. Mem. Am. Soc. Am. Archaeology (past pres.). Clubs: Kiva, Harvard, Century. Archeol. research No. Rio Grande area, N.Mex., Grand

Canyon, Ariz., Ky., So. Italy; author: Conceptions of Kentucky Prehistory. Office: PO Box 2188 Santa Fe NM 87501

SCHWARTZ, EDWARD ARTHUR, digital equipment mfr.; b. Boston, Sept. 27, 1937; s. Abe and Sophie (Gottheim) S.; A.B., Oberlin Coll., 1959; LL.B., Boston Coll., 1962; postgrad. Am. U., 1958-59, Northeastern U., 1970; m. Alice Chester, Aug. 30, 1959; children—Eric Allen, Jeffrey Michael. Admitted to Conn. bar, 1962, Mass. bar, 1965; legal intern Office Atty. Gen., Commonwealth of Mass., 1961; asso. Schatz & Schatz, Hartford, Conn., 1962-65, Cohn, Reimer & Pollack, Boston, 1965-67; v.p., gen. counsel, sec. Digital Equipment Corp., Maynard, Mass., 1967—; dir. Stanmar, Inc. Dir. Boston Aid to The Blind. Mem. Am., Mass., Boston bar assns. Editor Boston Coll. Indsl. and Comml. Law Rev., 1960-62, Ann. Survey Mass. Law, 1960-62. Home: 133 Tudor Rd Needham MA 02192 Office: 146 Main St Maynard MA 01754

SCHWARTZ, EDWARD J., judge. Judge, Mcpl. Ct. and Superior Ct., San Diego, judge U.S. Dist. Ct. for So. Dist. Calif., now chief judge. Office: US Courthouse Room 1 940 Front St San Diego CA 92189*

SCHWARTZ, FRANKLIN DAVID, physician, educator; b. Balt., May 16, 1933; s. George Henry and Anna (Snyder) S.; B.S. cum laude, U. Md., 1953, M.D. summa cum laude, 1957; m. Harriet Joan Mohline, May 25, 1972; children—Michael Howard, Ellen Sue. Intern, U. Hosp., Balt., 1957-58, asst. resident in medicine, 1958-60; USPHS research fellow U. Md., 1960-61; practice medicine specializing in nephrology, Balt., 1975-60, Washington, 1960-64, Chgo., 1964—; asso. dir. sect. nephrology U. Ill. Hosp., Chgo., 1970-71, acting chief, 1971-72, asso. chief, 1972—, attending physician, 1972—; attending physician St. Joseph Hosp., Chgo., 1971—, dir. sect. nephrology, 1971—; adj. physician Rush-Presbyn.-St. Luke's Med. Center, 1964-65, asst. attending physician, 1965-67, asso. attending physician, 1967-70, dir. hemodialysis unit, 1968-70, cons. physician in medicine, 1970-71; asso. chief sect. nephrology Columbus-Cuneo Cabrini Med. Center, 1971—; asst. prof. medicine Abraham Lincoln Sch. Medicine, Chgo., 1964-69, asso. prof., 1969-75, clin. prof., 1975-76, prof. clin. medicine, 1976—; cons. staff Ill. Masonic Med. Center, Augustana Hosp., Martha Washington Hosp., Ravenswood Hosp., N.W. Community Hosp., Ill. Central Hosp.; mem. renal disease adv. com. Ill. Dept. Pub. Health, 1972—; mem. sci. adv. bd. Kidney Found. Ill., 1972—; co.-dir. hepatitis project Walter Reed Army Inst. Research, 1962; cons. physician VA West Side Hosp., Chgo., 1972—. Diplomate Am. Bd. Internal Medicine. Mem. Ill., Chgo. med. socs., Am., Ill., Chgo. socs. internal medicine, A.C.P., Internat. Soc. Nephrology, Am. Soc. Nephrology, Am. Fedn. Clin. Research, AMA, Sigma Xi. Contbr. articles to med. jours., chpts. to med. books. Home: 1110 N Lake Shore Dr Chicago IL 60611 Office: 450 E Ohio St Chicago IL 60611

SCHWARTZ, FREDERIC N., business exec.; b. Springfield, Mass., Dec. 3, 1906; s. Michael J. and Regina (Burdick) S.; A.B., Syracuse U., 1931, LL.D., 1963; m. Eleanor Haley, 1935. Chmn. bd., pres. Bristol-Myers Co., until 1965, chmn. bd., 1965-66, chmn. exec. com., 1967-71. Served as lt. col. AUS, 1942-45. Decorated Legion of Merit, 1945. Mem. Delta Kappa Epsilon. Clubs: River, University (N.Y.C.). Home: 435 E 52d St New York NY 10022 Office: 345 Park Ave New York NY 10022

SCHWARTZ, HAROLD, investment co. exec.; b. N.Y.C., Oct. 27, 1920; s. Max and Toby (Hornstein) S.; student U. Mo., 1938-40; B.A., N.Y. U., 1946; m. Leatrice Kornhauser, Sept. 17, 1948 (div. Nov. 1972); children—Peter, William; m. 2d, Penelope Carnahan Welcher, Dec. 7, 1972; children—Margaret, Hilary. Mag. editor Street & Smith, N.Y.C., 1946-48; v.p., editorial dir. Juvenile div. Parents Mag. Enterprises, N.Y.C., 1949-67; co-founder Greenwood Press, Inc., Westport, Conn., 1967, pres., 1967-72; founder Blue Hill Trading Co., North Brooklin, Maine, 1972, pres., 1972—. Served with USAAF, 1942-46. Home: Blue Hill Rd South Penobscot ME 04476

SCHWARTZ, HARRY, journalist; b. N.Y.C., Sept. 10, 1919; s. Sam and Rose (Schnell) S.; B.A., Columbia U., 1940, M.A., 1941, Ph.D., 1943; m. Ruth E. Blumner, June 8, 1941; children—William Daniel, John Leonard, Robert Steven. Economist, War Prodn. Bd., 1942-43, Office Strategic Services, 1944-46; asst. prof. econs. Syracuse U., 1946-48, asso. prof., 1948-51, prof., 1951-53; editorial bd. N.Y. Times, N.Y.C., 1951-79; Disting. prof. SUNY, New Paltz, 1967-79; vis. prof. med. econs. Coll. Physicians and Surgeons, Columbia U., 1974, 78-79. Served with U.S. Army, 1943-45. Mem. Council Fgn. Relations, Century Assn. Jewish. Author books, including: Russia's Soviet Economy, 1949; China, 1966; Prague's 200 Days, 1968; The Case for American Medicine, 1972; contbr. numerous articles to profl. jours., newspapers. Home: 50 Argyle Rd Scarsdale NY 10583 Office: Dept Surgery Coll Physicians and Surgeons Columbia U New York NY 10032

SCHWARTZ, HARRY KANE, govt. ofcl.; b. Phila., Apr. 20, 1934; s. M. Murray and Minne G. (Schoenfeld) S.; B.A. summa cum laude, Harvard Coll., 1955; Fulbright fellow Worcester Coll., Oxford U., 1955-56; LL.B. magna cum laude, U. Pa., 1959; m. Marinda Kelley, June 20, 1961; children—Anthony Clark, Amanda Lyle. Admitted to Pa. bar, 1960, D.C. bar, 1961, U.S. Supreme Ct. bar, 1965; law clk. U.S. Ct. of Appeals, Washington, 1960-61; asst. U.S. atty., 1961-62; atty. SEC, 1962-63; legis. asst. U.S. Sen. Joseph S. Clark, 1963-66; counsel U.S. Senate Subcom. on Employment, Manpower and Poverty, 1966-68; partner firm Dechert Price & Rhoads, 1969-76; asst. sec. for legislation and intergovtl. relations HUD, Washington, 1977-78; staff adv. domestic policy staff White House, 1978—. Dir., Phila. Urban Coalition, 1974-76; nat. task force dir. Carter-Mondale Campaign, 1976. Served with Army N.G., 1961-65. Fellow, Salzburg Seminar in Am. Studies, 1964. Mem. Am., Pa., Phila. bar assns., Order of Coif, Phi Beta Kappa. Democrat. Jewish. Office: White House Washington DC

SCHWARTZ, HARVEY SELMAN, cosmetics co. exec.; b. Paterson, N.J., Sept. 21, 1926; s. Alex and Diana (Slotkin) S.; B.A., Ohio State U., 1949; m. Elaine Mishler, June 24, 1950; children—Shelly Dale, Sherrie Lee. With Revlon Inc., 1950—, sr. v.p. toiletries, N.Y.C., 1970-76, exec. v.p. Group II, 1976-78, pres. Group II-Beauty Care Div., 1979—. Served with USN. Jewish. Club: Masons. Home: 30 Manor Rd Harrington Park NJ 07640 Office: 767 Fifth Ave New York NY 10022*

SCHWARTZ, HENRY GERARD, educator, surgeon; b. N.Y.C.; Mar. 11, 1909; s. Nathan Theodore and Marie (Zagat) S.; A.B., Princeton, 1928; M.D., Johns Hopkins, 1932; m. Edith Courtenay Robinson, Sept. 13, 1934; children—Henry G., Michael R., Richard H. Denison fellow with Prof. O. Forester, Breslau, Germany, 1931; surg. house officer Johns Hopkins Hosp., 1932-33; NRC fellow Harvard Med. Sch., 1933-35, instr. anatomy, 1935-36; fellow neurol. surgery Washington U. Med. Sch., St. Louis, 1936-37, instr., asst. prof., asso. prof. neurol. surgery, 1937-46, prof., 1946—; acting surgeon-in-chief Barnes and Allied hosps., 1965-67; chief neurosurgeon Barnes, St. Louis Children's hosps.; cons. neurosurgeon St. Louis City, Jewish, Los Alamos (N.M.) hosps.; cons. to surgeon gen. USPHS. to surgeon gen. U.S. Army. Mem. subcom. neurosurgery NRC; del. World Fedn. Neurosurgery. Served with AUS, 1942-45. Recipient ofcl. citation and commendation Brit. Army; decorated Legion of Merit; recipient Harvey Cushing medal, 1979. Diplomate Am. Bd. Neurol. Surgery (chmn. 1968-70). Fellow A.C.S. (adv. council on neurosurgery 1950, 60, v.p. 1972-73); mem. Soc. Neurol. Surgeons (pres. 1968-69), Am. Acad. Neurol. Surgery (pres. 1951-52), Harvey Cushing Soc. (pres. 1967-68), Assn. Research Nervous and Mental Disease, Central Neuropsychiat. Assn. Am. Assn. Anatomists, So. Neurosurg. Soc. (pres. 1953-54), Soc. Med. Cons. to Armed Forces, Am. Surg. Assn. (v.p. 1975-76), Soc. de Neuro-Chirurgie de Langue Francaise, Excelsior Surg. Soc., Johns Hopkins Soc. Scholars, Soc. Internat. de Chirugie. Mem. editorial bd. Jour. Neurosurgery (chmn. 1967-69), editor, 1975—. Home: 2 Briar Oak St Ladue MO 63132 Office: Barnes Hospital Plaza St Louis MO 63110

SCHWARTZ, HERBERT CHARLES, physician, educator; b. New Haven, May 8, 1926; s. Simon and Bertha (Golemba) S.; student Alma Coll., 1944-45, Ill. Inst. Tech., 1945-46; A.B., Yale, 1948; M.D., State U. N.Y., Bklyn., 1952; m. Carolyn Jex, June 15, 1958; children—Michael Scott, Rebecca Ann, Sara Leslie. Intern VA Hosp., also Grace New Haven Hosp., 1952-53; resident Kings County Hosp., 1953-54, Stanford Hosp., 1954-55; clin. and research fellow hematology U. Utah Med. Sch., 1955-57, research fellow biochemistry, 1957-58, research instr. medicine, 1958-60; asst. prof. pediatrics Stanford Med. Sch., 1960-63, asso. prof., 1963-68, prof., 1968—, chmn. dept., 1970-71. Mem. Am. Fedn. Clin. Research, Western Soc. Clin. Research, Soc. Pediatric Research, Western Soc. Pediatric Research, Am. Soc. Clin. Investigation, Am. Pediatric Soc., Am. Soc. Hematology. Office: Dept Pediatrics Stanford Univ Stanford CA 94305

SCHWARTZ, HOWARD ARTHUR, advt. agy. exec.; b. N.Y.C., July 20, 1916; s. Nathan and Vera (Rosovsky) S.; student Coll. City N.Y., 1932-35; m. Arline Goldberg, Mar. 9, 1941; children—Nancy, Susan, Barbara, Joan. Chmn. bd. Beacon Mktg. Asso., N.Y.C.; pres. Amherst Prodns., Inc., N.Y.C. Served to lt. Ordnance Corps, AUS, 1942-45. Home: 6 Hidden Hill Westport CT Office: Beacon Advertising Asso Inc 15 W 44th St New York NY 10036

SCHWARTZ, IRVING DONN, architect; b. Chgo., June 11, 1927; s. Simon S. and Rose P. (Pilot) S.; B.S., U. Ill., 1949, B.S. in Architecture, 1965, M.S. in Architecture, 1972; children—Charles, Linda. Chief standard cost and indsl. engring. Lanzit Corrugated Box Co., Chgo., 1950-53; pres. Kaufman, Inc., Champaign, Ill., 1953-60; v.p. Hart Mirro Plate Co., Grand Rapids, Mich., 1953-60; asso. Richardson, Severns, Scheeler & Assos., Inc., Champaign, 1960-71; pres. IDS, Inc., Champaign, 1971—; prof. architecture Grad. Sch. Architecture, U. Ill., 1976—; cons. in field. Mem. Champaign County Devel. Council; mem. Model Community Coordinating Council, Champaign; co-chmn. bldg. com. Mercy Hosp.; bd. frat. affairs U. Ill.; bd. dirs. United Fund. Served to 2d lt. U.S. Army, 1945-47. Recipient archtl. design research award, graphic design citation Progressive Architecture mag., 1974; registered architect, Ill., Ind., Fla., D.C. Fellow Am. Soc. Interior Designers (treas. 1976, nat. pres. 1978); mem. AIA, Nat. Council Archtl. Registration Bds., Nat. Council Interior Design Qualifications (dir.). Club: Standard (Chgo.). Home: 3108 S 1st St Rd Champaign IL 61820 Office: 821 S Neil St Champaign IL 61820

SCHWARTZ, IRVING LEON, scientist, educator; b. Cedarhurst, N.Y., Dec. 25, 1918; s. Abraham and Rose (Doniger) S.; A.B., Columbia 1939; M.D., N.Y.U., 1943; m. Felice T. Nierenberg, Jan. 12, 1946; children—Cornelia Ann, Albert Anthony, James Oliver. Intern, asst. resident Bellevue Hosp., N.Y.C., 1943-44, 46-47; NIH fellow physiology N.Y.U. Coll. Medicine, 1947-50; Am. Physiol. Soc. Porter fellow, also Gibbs meml. fellow in clin. sci. Rockefeller Inst., N.Y.C., 1950-51, Am. Heart Assn. fellow, 1951-52; asst., then asso. Rockefeller Inst., 1952-58; asst. physician, asso. physician Rockefeller Inst. Hosp., 1950-58; sr. scientist Brookhaven Nat. Lab., Upton, L.I., N.Y., 1958-61, attending physician Brookhaven Nat. Lab. Hosp., 1958—; research collaborator Brookhaven Nat. Lab., 1961—; Joseph Eichberg prof. physiology, dir. dept. U. Cincinnati Coll. Medicine, 1961-65; dean grad. faculties Mt. Sinai Med. and Grad. Schs., 1965—; prof. physiology and biophysics, chmn. dept. Mt. Sinai Med. and Grad. Schs. City U. N.Y., 1968—; exec. officer biomed. scis. doctoral program, City U. N.Y., 1969-72, Dr. Harold and Golden Lamport disting. prof., 1979—. Pres. Life Scis. Found., 1962—. Served from 1st lt. to capt., M.C., AUS, 1944-46. Diplomate Am. Bd. Internal Medicine. Fellow A.C.P.; mem. Am. Physiol. Soc., Soc. Exptl. Biology and Medicine, Am. Soc. Clin. Investigation, Am. Fedn. Clin. Research, Biophys. Soc., Endocrine Soc., Harvey Soc., Soc. for Neurosci., Am. Heart Assn., John Jay Assos. Columbia Coll., AAAS, N.Y. Acad. Sci., Sigma Xi, Alpha Omega Alpha. Contbr. articles to sci. publs. Home: 1120 Fifth Ave New York NY 10028 also 9 Thorn Hedge Rd Bellport NY 11713 Office: Mount Sinai Med and Grad Schs City U NY 100th St and Fifth Ave New York NY 10029 also Med Research Center Brookhaven Nat Lab Upton NY 11973

SCHWARTZ, JACK THEODORE, publisher, chain store exec.; b. N.Y.C., Aug. 24, 1914; s. Nathan and Vera Ida (Rosovsky) S.; student Columbia Coll., 1932-34; m. Pearl Tarnower, May 20, 1941; children—Harriet (Mrs. Tod Johnson), Deborah (Mrs. Gary Raizes). Founder, pres. Syndicate Mags., Inc., N.Y.C., 1939—; founder, pres. Beacon Advt. Assos., Inc., 1950-76; mng. partner Beacon Mktg. Consultants, 1959—; pub. Better Nutrition, Today's Living, Art Material Trade News; chmn. Gold Key Furniture Warehouse Showrooms, Van Nuys, Calif. Trustee, mem. exec. com. Lesley Coll., Cambridge, Mass. Served to 1st lt. AUS, 1943-45. Club: Hampshire Country (Mamaroneck, N.Y.). Home: 27 Highwood Ave Larchmont NY 10538 Office: 6 E 43d St New York NY 10017. *I feel that the luckiest decision I ever made was the one to balance my business and family lives. I program my family time as carefully as my business time and make sure that my family is never cheated. This, for me, has made for contentment and happiness at home, allowing me to approach my business hours with full concentration and energy.*

SCHWARTZ, JAMES H., neurobiologist; b. N.Y.C., Apr. 20, 1932; s. Milton A. and Marjorie A. (Bloom) S.; A.B., Columbia U., 1954; M.D., N.Y. U., 1959; Ph.D., Rockefeller U., 1964; m. Frances Messik, June 30, 1963; children—Peter Joseph, Margaret Clare. Asst. prof. microbiology N.Y. U. Sch. Medicine, 1964-67, asso. prof., 1967-72, prof., 1972-74; asso. mem. Public Health Research Inst. of City of N.Y., 1969-74; prof. physiology Columbia U. Coll. Physicians and Surgeons, 1974-76, prof. physiology and neurology, 1976—; cons. Nat. Inst. Neurol. and Communicative Disorders and Stroke. Bd. dirs. Hewbrew Free Loan Soc., 1976—. Recipient Selman A. Waksman lectureship award Theobald Smith Soc., 1968. Mem. Am. Soc. Biol. Chemists, Harvey Soc., Soc. Neurosci., AAAS, Am. Soc. Neurochemistry, Sigma Xi. Mem. editorial bd. Brain Research, 1974—. Contbr. articles to profl. jours. Office: 630 W 168th St New York NY 10032

SCHWARTZ, JEFFREY, chemist, educator; b. N.Y.C., Jan. 3, 1945; s. Gabriel and Sara S.; S.B. in Organic Chemistry, M.I.T., 1966; Ph.D., Stanford U., 1970; m. Laraine Mittleman, Apr. 19, 1970. Asst. prof. chemistry Princeton U., 1970-75, asso. prof., prof., 1978—. NSF fellow, 1970; NIH fellow, 1970; Alfred P. Sloan fellow, 1976-79. Mem. Am. Chem. Soc., Chem. Soc. London, Sigma Xi, Phi Lambda Upsilon. Contbr. articles to profl. jours. Home: 55 Locust Ln Princeton NJ 08540 Office: Dept Chemistry Princeton NJ 08544

SCHWARTZ, JOHN THOMAS, publishing exec.; b. Marinette, Wis., June 29, 1921; s. Edwin R. and Margaret (Sundet) S.; B.B.A., U. Minn., 1943, M.A., 1948; m. Elinore G. Tufte, Sept. 3, 1957; 1 dau., Jennifer. Dir. Colo. Asso. U. Press, Boulder, 1969—. Served as lt. USNR, 1943-45. Home: 360 Norton St Boulder CO 80303 Office: Univ Colo 1424 15th St Boulder CO 80309

SCHWARTZ, JOSEPH, educator; b. Milw., Apr. 9, 1925; s. Alfred George and Mary (Brandt) S.; B.A., Marquette U., 1946, M.A., 1947; Ph.D., U. Wis., 1952; m. Joan Jackson, Aug. 28, 1954; 1 son, Adam. Teaching asst. Marquette U., Milw., 1946-47, instr., 1947-48, 50-54, asst. prof., 1954-59, asso. prof., 1959-64, prof., 1964—, chmn. dept. English, 1963-75; teaching fellow U. Wis., 1948-50. Chmn. region X Woodrow Wilson Nat. Fellowship Found., 1967-73; pres. bd. edn. Archdiocese of Milw., 1977-79. Recipient Distinguished Alumni award Marquette U. Sch. Speech, 1967, Nicolas Salgo Outstanding Tchr. award Marquette U., 1974. Ford Found. grantee, 1956, Am. Council Learned Socs. grantee, 1972, HEW grantee, 1966, 67. Mem. Modern Lang. Assn., Nat. Council Tchrs. English (nat. dir. 1965-68), Cath. Renascence Soc. (bd. dirs. 1968—, pres. 1976-77), Midwest Modern Lang. Assn. (exec. com. 1973-76), Alpha Sigma Mu (hon.). Republican. Roman Catholic. Author: A Reader for Writers, 3d edit., 1971; Perspectives on Language, 1963; Province of Rhetoric, 1965; Poetry: Meaning and Form, 1969; Hart Crane: A Critical Bibliography, 1970; Hart Crane: A Descriptive Bibliography, 1972; Exposition, 2d edit., 1971. Editor Renascence mag. Home: 8516 W Mequon Rd 112 N Mequon WI 53092 Office: Dept English Marquette U Milwaukee WI 53233

SCHWARTZ, JULES JACOB, educator; b. Phila., Apr. 9, 1932; s. Harry J. and Marion E. (Friedmann) S.; B.M.E., U. Del., 1953, M.B.A., 1963; D.B.A. (fellow), Harvard, 1973; m. Sandra Leigh Burgoon, Dec. 18, 1971. Engr. Westinghouse Electric Co., Phila., 1953; program mgr. Thiokol Chem. Corp., 1957-69; asso. prof., asst. dean Wharton Sch., U. Pa., 1973-77; dean Sch. Mgmt. Boston U., 1977—; dir. Bergen-Paterson Pipesupport Corp., Infinetics Inc., Hart, Whitley & Co.; gov. Boston Stock Exchange; cons. Xerox, Internat. Tel. & Tel., Getty Oil, Phila. Nat. Bank, AT&T, New Eng. Telephone Co., A.D. Little, Fischer-Porter Corp.; receiver U.S. Dist. Ct. (Delaware), 1969—. Served to lt. col. U.S. Army, 1953-57. Recipient Gen. J. Ernest Smith prize. Chrysler fellow. Mem. ASME, Am. Inst. Aeros. and Astronautics, Nat. Soc. Profl. Engrs., Tau Beta Pi, Beta Gamma Sigma, Phi Kappa Phi. Clubs: Harvard (N.Y.C. and Boston); Army-Navy (Washington). Author: The Decision to Innovate, Profit Opportunities in Put and Call Options, Corporate Policy. Patentee in field. Home: 96 Radcliffe Rd Belmont MA 02178 Office: Sch Mgmt Boston U Boston MA 02215

SCHWARTZ, KENNETH MARTIN, lawyer; b. Cleve.; Sept. 7, 1916; s. Sam and Justine Yetta (Rothschild) S.; B.B.A., Western Res. U., 1941; LL.B., Southwestern U., 1950; m. Helen Louise Smith, Sept. 24, 1941; Spl. agt. IRS, 1945-47; partner Commodore Dress Suit Rental, Cleve., 1947-49; admitted to Calif. bar, 1951, U.S. Supreme Ct. bar, 1962; atty. NLRB, 1957-59; mem. firm Arnold, Smith & Schwartz, Los Angeles, 1959; sr. partner Schwartz, Steinsapir Dohrmann & Krepack, Los Angeles, 1970—. Served with AUS, 1941-45, 50-55; PTO. Mem. faculty Practicing Law Inst., N.Y. Law Jour. Mem. Am. Bar Assn. (labor law sect., vice chmn. Los Angeles labor law com. 1974). Contbr. articles to Practising Law Inst. seminar booklets. Home: 141 S Linden Dr Apt 203 Beverly Hills CA 90212 Office: 2 Century Plaza 2049 Century Park E Los Angeles CA 90067

SCHWARTZ, KESSEL, educator; b. Kansas City, Mo., Mar. 19, 1920; s. Henry and Dora (Tanenbaum) S.; B.A., U. Mo., 1940, M.A., 1941; Ph.D., Columbia, 1953; m. Barbara Lewin, Apr. 3, 1947; children—Joseph David, Deborah, Edward, Michael. Asst. instr. U. Mo., 1940-42; dir. cultural centers in Nicaragua, Ecuador, cultural observer in Costa Rica, State Dept., 1946-48; instr. Hofstra, Hamilton, Colby colls., 1948-53; asst. prof. U. Vt., 1953-57; asso. prof., then prof. modern langs., chmn. dept. U. Ark., 1957-62; prof. modern langs. U. Miami (Fla.), 1962—, chmn. dept., 1962-64, 74—, dir. grad. studies, 1964-65; vis. prof. U. N.C., Chapel Hill, 1966-67. Served with AUS, 1942-46. Mem. Modern Lang. Assn. (group sec. 1964, group chmn. 1965, chmn. nominating com. for modern Spanish lit. 1966-68), Am. Assn. Tchrs. Spanish and Portuguese (chmn. Penisular lit. sect. 1972), S. Atlantic Modern Lang. Assn., Phi Beta Kappa, Phi Sigma Iota, Sigma Delta Pi, Pi Delta Phi, Delta Phi Alpha. Author: The Ecuadorian Novel, 1953; An Introduction to Modern Spanish Literature, 1967; The Meaning of Existence in Contemporary Hispanic Literature, 1969; Vicente Aleixandre, 1970; Juan Goytisolo, 1970; A New History of Spanish American Fiction (named Outstanding Acad. Book of Year, Am. Assn. Coll. and Research Librarians), 1972; co-author: A New History of Spanish Literature, 1961, A New Anthology of Spanish Literature, 1968. Asso. editor Hispania; editorial adv. bd. Anales de la Novela de Posguerra. Contbr. numerous articles to profl. jours., chpts. to books, ency. Home: 6400 Maynada Coral Gables FL 33146. *If men loved one another sufficiently, we might not need our legal systems. Given our imperfect nature as human beings, we must believe in some higher goals to give meaning to our lives but be ever vigilant that in the pursuit of success we do not infringe upon the happiness of others or confuse the means with the end.*

SCHWARTZ, LEON, educator; b. Boston, Aug. 22, 1922; s. Charles and Celia (Emer) S.; student Providence Coll., 1939-41; B.A., U. Calif. at Los Angeles, 1948; certificat de phonetique U. Paris, 1949; M.A, U. So. Cal., 1950, Ph.D., 1962; m. Jeanne Gurtat, Mar. 31, 1949; children—Eric Alan, Claire Marie. Tchr. English, Spanish, Latin Redlands (Calif.) Jr. High Sch., 1951-54; tchr. Spanish, French, high sch., 1954-59; prof. French Calif. State U. at Los Angeles, 1959—, chmn. dept. fgn. langs. and lit., 1970-73. Served as 2d lt. USAAF, 1942-45. Decorated Air medal with 5 oak leaf clusters; recipient Outstanding Prof. award Calif. State U. at Los Angeles, 1976. Mem. Am. Assn. Tchrs. French, Modern and Classical Lang. Assn. So. Calif., Western Soc. 18th Century Studies, Am. Soc. 18th Century Studies, Phi Beta Kappa, Phi Kappa Phi, Pi Delta Phi, Sigma Delta Pi, Alpha Mu Gamma. Office: Dept Fgn Langs and Literatures Calif State U Los Angeles CA 90032

SCHWARTZ, LILLIAN FELDMAN, artist, filmmaker; b. Cin., July 13, 1927; d. Jacob and Katie (Green) Feldman; diploma U. Cin. Coll. Nursing and Health, 1957; m. Jack James Schwartz, Dec. 22, 1946; children—Jeffrey Hugh, Laurens Robert. Nurse, Cin. Gen. Hosp., 1947; head supr. premature nursery St. Louis Maternity Hosp., 1947-48; resident visitor Bell Labs., Murray Hill, N.J., 1969—; artist-in-resident Channel 13 WNET-TV, N.Y.C., 1974, 76; cons. artist IBM Corp., Watson Research Lab., Yorktown Heights, N.Y.; vis. mem. picture processing dept. Computer Sci. U. Md., College Park, 1975—; vis. mem. Stevens Inst. Tech., 1976—; artist-in-residence Rutgers U., 1977-78; one-woman shows of sculpture and paintings include Columbia U., 1967, 68, Rabin & Krueger Gallery, Newark, 1968; films shown at Met. Mus., N.Y.C.,

Franklin Inst., Phila., 1972, U. Toronto, 1972, Am. Embassy, London, 1972, Los Angeles County Mus., Corcoran Gallery, Washington, 1972, Whitney Mus., N.Y.C., 1973, IBM, Zurich, 1973, IBM, Sydney, Australia, 1974; retrospective exhbn. Cinématèque Française, 1980; numerous group shows in U.S., Sweden, Eng., Amsterdam, Brazil, Can., Scotland, Australia, Germany, France, Switzerland; represented in permanent collections at Mus. Modern Art, N.Y.C., Moderna Mus., Stockholm, Newark Mus., Smithsonian Instn., Washington, Stedelijk Mus., Amsterdam, also Columbia U., IBM, AT&T, numerous others; also pvt. collections; guest Lectr. Princeton U., Columbia U., Yale U., Rockefeller U. Recipient numerous art and film awards; Nat. Endowment for Arts grantee, 1977; grantee Corp. Pub. Broadcasting, 1979. Mem. Am. Watercolor Soc., Am. Film Inst., Ind. Video and Filmmakers Assn., Soc. Motion Picture TV Engrs., Artists Equity, Academia Italia delle Arti. Contbr. chpts. to books. Address: 524 Ridge Rd Watchung NJ 07060

SCHWARTZ, LLOYD MARVIN, newspaper corr.; b. Bklyn., Mar. 6, 1923; s. Philip and Celia W. Schwartz; B.A., N.Y. U., 1944; m. Doris Grossman, May 19, 1946; children—Ellen, Philip, Laura. N.Y. U. corr. N.Y. Times, 1942-44; news editor, writer Trade Union Courier, 1943-44; reporter Lima (Ohio) News, 1945; reporter, White House corr. Fairchild Publs., Washington, 1945-65, Washington bur. chief, 1965—, Congressional corr. Fairchild News Service, 1977—, panelist, news broadcaster Voice of Am., AFL-CIO, Fairchild Broadcast News and WJR-Detroit, 1960—; cons. Research Inst. Am. Mem. White House Corrs. Assn., Senate and Ho. of Reps. News Galleries, Am. Philatelic Soc., Soc. Philatelic Ams., African Violet Soc. Am. Democrat. Jewish. Club: Nat. Press (Washington). Home: 1905 Courtland Rd Alexandria VA 22306 Office: US Senate Press Gallery US Capitol Washington DC 20510

SCHWARTZ, LOU, editor; b. N.Y.C., Jan. 14, 1932; s. Harry Milton and Beatrice (Skelton) S.; B.A., Syracuse U. Sch. Journalism, 1953; children—David, Jill. Various editing positions Newsday Inc. (N.Y.), 1957-70, mng. editor, 1970—. Served to lt. (j.g.) USN, 1953-57. Recipient 1st Place Lifestyle Journalism award J.C. Penney-U. Mo., 1966. Mem. Am. Assn. Sunday and Mag. Editors (pres. 1978), AP Mng. Editors Assn. (dir.), Am. Soc. Newspaper Editors. Home: 94 Prospect Rd Centerport NY 11721 Office: Newday Inc Newsday LI NY 11747

SCHWARTZ, LOUIS BROWN, lawyer, educator; b. Phila., Feb. 22, 1913; s. Samuel and Rose (Brown) S.; B.S. in Econs., U. Pa., 1932, J.D., 1935; m. Berta Wilson, Mar. 29, 1937 (div. 1954); children—Johanna, Victoria; m. 2d, Miriam Robbins Humboldt, Sept. 16, 1964. Admitted to Pa. bar, 1935, U.S. Supreme Ct. bar, 1942; atty. SEC, Washington, 1935-39; chief gen. crimes and spl. projects sect. Dept. Justice, 1939-43, chief judgment and enforcement sect. antitrust div., 1945-46, also mem. inter-departmental coms. on war crimes and status-of-forces treaties; prof. law U. Pa. Law Sch., 1946—, Benjamin Franklin prof., 1964—. Vis. prof. Harvard, Columbia, U. Calif. at Berkeley, Cambridge (Eng.) U.; Ford vis. Am. prof. Inst. Advanced Legal Studies, U. London (Eng.), 1974. Mem. Atty. Gen.'s Nat. Com. Study Antitrust Laws, 1954-55, Pa. Gov.'s Commn. on Penal and Correctional Affairs, 1956-60; adv. commn. Revision Pa. Penal Code, 1963-68; mem. White House Lawyers' Com. Civil Rights Through Law, 1963—; nat. adv. council Nat. Defender Project, 1964-69; dir. Nat. Commn. on Reform of Fed. Criminal Laws, 1968-71; cons. FTC, Dept. Justice, other agencies. Served as lt. (j.g.) USNR, 1944-45. Mem. Ams. Democratic Action (nat. bd.), Am. Law Inst. (adv. com. pre-arraignment code), Order of Coif. Author: Free Enterprise and Economic Organization, 1959, 4th edit., 1972, 5th edit. (with John J. Flynn) titled Antitrust and Regulatory Alternatives, 1977; (with Herbert Wechsler) Model Penal Code of American Law Institute; Le Système Pénal des Etats-Unis, 1964; Law Enforcement Handbook for Police, 1970, 2d edit., 1979; Proposed Federal Criminal Code (with Comments and Working Papers), 1971. Contbr. numerous articles to profl. jours. Home: 510 Woodland Terr Philadelphia PA 19104

SCHWARTZ, LYNNE SHARON, writer; b. N.Y.C., Mar. 19, 1939; d. Jacob M. and Sarah (Slatus) Sharon; B.A., Barnard Coll., 1959; M.A. (Woodrow Wilson Nat. fellow), Bryn Mawr Coll., 1961; postgrad. N.Y. U., 1967-72; m. Harry Schwartz, Dec. 22, 1957; children—Rachel Eve, Miranda Ruth. Asso. editor The Writer mag., Boston, 1961-63; editorial dir. Calliope Records, spoken records, Boston, 1962-64; pub. relations writer Operation Open City N.Y. Urban League, N.Y.C., 1965-67; freelance writer, 1972—; contbr. short fiction, revs., poetry and satire to lit. and popular mags., including New Republic, Nation, Ms., Redbook, Ont. Rev.; freelance editor, translator; adj. lectr. English, Hunter Coll., 1971-77. Recipient James Henle award for prose Vanguard Press, 1974-75. Fiction selected for inclusion The Pushcart Prize III: Best of the Small Presses; The Best American Short Stories, 1978; O. Henry Prize Stories, 1979. Address: 547 Riverside Dr New York NY 10027

SCHWARTZ, MARVIN, lawyer; b. Phila., Nov. 3, 1922; s. Abe and Freda (Newman) S.; LL.B., U. Pa., 1949; m. Joyce Ellen Sidner, Sept. 7, 1947; children—John Burkhart, Daniel Bruce, Pamela Louise. Admitted to Pa. bar, 1950, N.Y. bar, 1951, D.C. bar, 1955; law sec. to judge U.S. Ct. Appeals, 3d Circuit, Phila., 1949-50, Mr. Justice Burton of Supreme Ct. U.S., Washington, 1950-51; asso. firm Sullivan & Cromwell, N.Y.C., 1951-60, partner, 1960—. Served with Signal Corps, U.S. Army, 1943-46. Mem. Am. Coll. Trial Lawyers (vice chmn. com. on Rule 23 and multidist. litigation, chmn. Downstate N.Y. com.), Am. Law Inst., N.Y. Bar Assn., Pa. Bar Assn., D.C. Bar Assn. Democrat. Jewish. Clubs: Univ., City Midday (N.Y.C.). Home: 25 Sutton Pl S New York NY 10022 Office: 125 Broad St New York NY 10004

SCHWARTZ, MELVIN, educator, physicist; b. N.Y.C., Nov. 2, 1932; s. Harry and Hannah (Shulman) S.; A.B., Columbia U., 1953, Ph.D., 1958; m. Marilyn Fenster, Nov. 25, 1953; children—David N., Diane R., Betty Lynn. Asso. physicist Brookhaven Nat. Lab., 1956-58; mem. faculty Columbia U., 1958-66, prof. physics, 1963-66; prof. physics Stanford U., 1966—. Pres. Digital Pathways, Inc. Bd. govs. Weizmann Inst. Sci. Guggenheim fellow, 1968. Fellow Am. Phys. Soc. (Hughes award 1964); mem. Nat. Acad. Scis. Discoverer muon neutrino, 1962. Home: 770 Funston Ave San Francisco CA 94118 Office: Physics Dept Stanford U Stanford CA 94305

SCHWARTZ, MICHAEL AVERILL, univ. adminstr., pharm. scientist; b. N.Y.C., Aug. 4, 1930; B.S. in Pharmacy, Bklyn. Coll. Pharmacy, 1952; M.S. in Pharmacy, Columbia U., 1956; Ph.D. in Pharmacy (Am. Found. Pharm. Edn. Fellow), U. Wis., 1959; m. Marilyn Etttinger, Nov. 24, 1954; children—Lori, Sharon. Sr. research scientist Bristol Labs., Syracuse, N.Y., 1959-63; asst. prof. pharmaceutics SUNY, Buffalo, 1963-65, asso. prof., 1965-70, prof., 1970-78, asst. dean Sch. Pharmacy, 1966-70, dean, 1970-76; dean Coll. Pharmacy, prof. pharmaceutics U. Fla., 1978—; mem. U.S. Herbal Pharmacology Del. to People's Republic of China, 1974; cons. to Pharm. industry. Served with Med. Service Corps, U.S. Army, 1952-54. Lic. pharmacist, N.Y., Ill. Fellow AAAS, Acad. Pharm. Scis. (chmn. com. hon. membership 1972-75); mem. Am. Pharm. Assn., Am. Chem. Soc., Am. Soc. Hosp. Pharmacists, Am. Assn. Colls. Pharmacy, Fla. Pharm. Assn., Fla. Soc. Hosp. Pharmacists, Gainesville (Fla.) C. of C., Sigma Xi, Rho Chi. Contbr. numerous articles to profl. publs. Home: 1615 NW 27th Terr Gainesville FL 32605 Office: U Fla Box J-4 JHMHC Gainesville FL 32610

SCHWARTZ, MICHAEL ROBINSON, hosp. adminstr.; b. St. Louis, Mar. 18, 1940; s. Henry G. and Edith C. (Robinson) S.; B.A., Dartmouth Coll., 1962; M.H.A., U. Minn., 1964; m. Virginia Abbott, Sept. 29, 1962; children—Christine, Richard. Asst. in adminstrn. Shands Teaching Hosp, Gainesville, Fla., 1966-67, asst. dir., 1967-68, asso. dir., 1968-73; asso. adminstr. St. Joseph Mercy Hosp., Pontiac, Mich., 1973-76, pres., adminstr., 1976—; asst. prof. hosp. adminstrn. U. Fla., 1967-73; pres. Sisters of Mercy Health Corp. Eastern Mich. Regional Bd., 1976-79; bd. dirs. Lourdes Nursing Home, 1973—, pres., 1975; bd. dirs. Oakland Livingston Human Service Agy., Mercy Sch. Nursing, United Way-Pontiac/North Oakland; bd. dirs. Oakland Health Edn. Program, 1977—, treas., 1978; mem. Blue Cross/Blue Shield Reimbursement Rev. Com.; mem. Greater Detroit Area Hosp. Council coms.; mem. Oakland County Emergency Med. Services; mem. Comprehensive Health Planning Council Emergency Med. Services/Emergency Dept. Coordination Commn. Served with U.S. Army, 1964-66. Mem. Mich. Hosp. Assn. (vice chmn. task force on multi-hosp. arrangements 1979—), Am. Coll. Hosp. Adminstrs. Home: 4517 Wagon Wheel Birmingham MI 48010 Office: 900 Woodward Ave Pontiac MI 48053

SCHWARTZ, MILTON LEWIS, fed. judge; b. Oakland, Calif., Jan. 20, 1920; s. Colman and Selma (Lavenson) S.; A.B., U. Calif. at Berkeley, 1941, J.D., 1948; m. Barbara Ann Moore, May 15, 1942; children—Dirk L., Tracy Ann, Damon M., Brooke. Admitted to Calif. bar, 1949; research asst. 3d Dist. Ct. Appeal, Sacramento, 1948; dep. dist. atty., 1949-51; practice in Sacramento, 1951-79; partner McDonough, Holland, Schwartz & Allen, 1953-79; U.S. dist. judge Eastern Dist. Calif., 1979—; prof. law McGeorge Coll. Law, Sacramento, 1952-55. Mem. Com. Bar Examiners Calif., 1971-75. Pres. Bd. Edn. Sacramento City Sch. Dist., 1961; v.p. Calif. Bd. Edn., 1967-68. Trustee Sutterville Heights Sch. Dist. Served to maj. 40th Inf. Div., AUS, 1942-46; PTO. Fellow Am. Coll. Trial Lawyers; mem. State Bar Calif., Am. Bar Assn., Am. Bd. Trial Advocates. Home: 501 Elmhurst Circle Sacramento CA 95825 Office: US Courthouse 650 Capitol Mall Sacramento CA 95814

SCHWARTZ, MISCHA, educator; b. N.Y.C., Sept. 21, 1926; s. Isaiah and Bessie (Weinstein) S.; B.E.E., Cooper Union, 1947; M.E.E., Poly. Inst. Bklyn., 1949; Ph.D. in Applied Physics (Sperry Gyroscope grad. scholar), Harvard U., 1951; m. Lillian Mitchnick, June 23, 1957 (div.); 1 son, David; m. 2d, Charlotte F. Berney, July 12, 1970. Project engr. Sperry Gyroscope Co., 1947-52; mem. faculty Poly. Inst. Bklyn., 1952-74, prof. elec. engring., 1959-74, head dept., 1961-65; prof. elec. engring. and computer sci. Columbia, 1974—. Part-time tchr. Coll. City N.Y., 1952, Adelphi Coll., 1951-52; cons. radiation physicist Montefiore Hosp., N.Y.C., 1954-56; cons. to industry, 1956—; vis. prof. systems sci. dept. U. Calif. at Los Angeles, 1964, dept. elec. engring. and computer sci. Columbia, 1973-74. Served with AUS, 1944-46. NSF sci. faculty fellow, 1965-66; recipient Distinguished Visitor award Australian-Am. Ednl. Found., 1975. Fellow IEEE (gov. Communications Soc., chmn. adminstrv. com. profl. group info. theory 1964-65, dir. 1978—), AAAS; mem. AAUP (chpt. pres. 1970-72), Sigma Xi, Tau Beta Pi, Eta Kappa Nu. Author: Information Transmission, Modulation and Noise, 2d edit., 1970; (with L. Shaw) Signal Processing, 1975; Computer Communication Network Design and Analysis, 1977. Editor, contbr. Communication Systems and Techniques, 1966. Home: 66 Maple Dr Great Neck NY 11021 Office: Dept Elec Engring and Computer Sci Columbia Univ New York NY 10027

SCHWARTZ, MURRAY LOUIS, lawyer, educator; b. Phila., Oct. 27, 1920; s. Harry and Isabelle (Friedman) S.; B.S., Pa. State U., 1942; LL.B., U. Pa., 1949; LL.D. (hon.), Lewis and Clark Coll., 1977; m. Audrey James, Feb. 12, 1950; children—Deborah, Jonathan, Daniel. Admitted to Pa. bar, 1950, also U.S. Supreme Ct.; chemist Standard Oil Ind., Whiting, 1942-44; law clk. Fred M. Vinson, Chief Justice U.S, 1949-51; asso. firm Shea, Greenman, Gardner & McConnaughey, Washington, 1951-53; spl. asst. to U.S. atty. gen. Office Solicitor Gen., 1953-54; 1st dept. city solicitor City Phila., 1954-56; asso. firm Dilworth, Paxson, Kalish & Green, Phila., 1956-58; prof. law Law Sch., U. Calif. at Los Angeles, 1958—, dean, 1969-75; cons. Presdl. Panel on Mental Retardation, 1961-62, Rand Corp., 1962-68, Ford Found., 1964-65, 68-69, Presdl. Task Force War Against Poverty, 1964; reporter Joint Legislative Com. Revision Calif. Penal Code, 1964-68; vice chmn. group legal services com. Calif. State Bar, 1961-64, vice-chmn. bd. legal specialization, 1972-75. Served to lt. (j.g.) USNR, 1944-46. Author: Professional Responsibility and the Administration of Criminal Justice, 1961; (with J.C.N. Paul) Federal Censorship: Obscenity in the Mail, 1961; (with W. Cohen and D. Sobul) The Bill of Rights: A Source Book for Teachers, 1966; (with K.L. Karst and A.J. Schwartz) The Evolution of Law in the Barrios of Caracas, 1973; Law and the American Future, 1976; contbr. articles to profl. jours. Home: 1339 Marinette Rd Pacific Palisades CA 90272 Office: Sch Law U Calif Los Angeles CA 90024

SCHWARTZ, NEENA BETTY, endocrinologist; b. Balt., Dec. 10, 1926; d. Paul Howard and Pauline (Shulman) Schwartz; A.B., Goucher Coll., 1948; M.S., Northwestern U., 1950, Ph.D., 1953. From instr. to prof. U. Ill. Coll. Medicine, Chgo., 1953-72, asst. dean for faculty, 1968-70; prof. physiology Northwestern U. Med. Sch., Chgo., 1973-74; Deering prof. Northwestern U., Evanston, Ill., 1974—, chmn. dept. biol. scis., 1974-78. NIH research grantee, 1955—. Mem. Endocrine Soc. (v.p. 1970-71, mem. council 1979—), Soc. for Study of Reprodn. (dir. 1975-77, exec. v.p. 1976-77, pres. 1977-78), Assn. Women in Sci. (pres. 1972-73), Am. Physiol. Soc., Phi Beta Kappa. Contbr. chpts. to books, articles to profl. jours. Home: 1215 Chancellor St Evanston IL 60201

SCHWARTZ, RICHARD DERECKTOR, educator; sociologist; b. Newark, Apr. 26, 1925; s. Selig and Tillie (Derecktor) S.; B.A., Yale U., 1947, Ph.D. in Sociology, 1952; LL.D. (hon.), Am. Internat. Coll., 1977; m. Emilie Zane Rosenbaum, June 30, 1946; children—David, Margaret Jane, Deborah. Research fellow Inst. Human Relations, Yale, 1951-54, instr., asst. prof. sociology and law, 1953-61; faculty Northwestern U., Evanston, 1961-71, prof. sociology, 1964-71, prof. sociology and law, 1966-71, dir. Council Intersocietal Studies, 1965-70, co-dir. law and social sci. program, 1967-70; dean, provost Faculty of Law and Jurisprudence, State U. N.Y. at Buffalo, 1971-76; Ernest I. White prof. law Syracuse U., 1977—. Research cons. Nat. Council Juvenile Ct. Judges, 1961-68; lecture tour for U.S. embassy, India, 1968; adviser Ill. Council on Criminal Defendants, 1968-69, U.S. Dept. Justice, 1977—; cons. U.S. Dept. Transp., 1968-69, Nat. Conf. Commrs. on Uniform State Laws, 1968-70; mem. com. law enforcement and criminal justice Nat. Acad. Sci., 1975—; fellowship referee Russell Sage Found., 1970-77, Nat. Endowment for Humanities, 1972-77, NSF, 1978—. Mem. bd. edn., Orange, Conn., 1954-61; bd. dirs. Transitional Living Ser. Greater Syracuse, 1977—. Served with USNR, 1943-45. Mem. Am. Sociol. Assn., AAAS, Law and Soc. Assn. (pres. 1972-75). Jewish. Author with others: Criminal Law, 1974, Unobstrusive Measures, 1966, Society and the Legal Order, 1970. Editor: Law and Soc. Rev., 1966-69. Home: 15 Clarmar Rd Fayetteville NY 13066 Office: Coll Law Syracuse U Syracuse NY 13210. *I believe that we could create a better way of life if we structured society to encourage-rather than to penalize-altruism. Although I have not yet contributed much toward achieving such a society, the effort to do so has been satisfying.*

SCHWARTZ, RICHARD JAY, apparel co. exec.; b. N.Y.C., Dec. 29, 1938; s. David and Irene (Krugman) S.; B.A., Cornell U., 1960; m. Sheila Hunter Wood, Dec. 6, 1970; children—John Stephen, Jennifer Beth. With Jonathan Logan, Inc., N.Y.C., 1960—, exec. v.p., 1961-64, pres., chief exec. officer, 1964—, chmn. bd., 1977—; dir. Simplicity Pattern Co., Inc. Mem. pres.'s council Brandeis U.; chmn. gen. campaign Fedn. Jewish Philanthropies N.Y., 1969-70; mem. council Cornell U., Wofford Coll. Assos. Bd. dirs. Mt. Sinai Med. Center, N.Y.C., Internat. Ladies Garment Workers Union Pension Fund; trustee Nat. Urban League, Riverdale Sch. Mem. Cornell U. Alumni Assn. Clubs: Sleepy Hollow Country, City Athletic, Cornell of N.Y., Century Country. Office: Jonathan Logan Inc 50 Terminal Rd Secaucus NJ 07094*

SCHWARTZ, ROBERT, automotive mfg. co. exec.; b. Atlantic City, N.J., Mar. 9, 1939; s. Robert A. and Irene (Davis) S.; B.S., Drexel U., 1961; M.B.A., Wash. State U., 1962; m. Judith H. Amole, Apr. 30, 1961. With Ford Motor Co., 1964-70; dist. mgr. Simplicity Mfg., Port Washington, Wis., 1970-71; zone mgr. Am. Motors Corp., Boston, 1971-72, N.Y.C., 1972-74, dir. sales ops., Boston, 1975, regional mgr., 1975-76, gen. mgr. U.S. sales, 1976—, pres. Am. Motors Sales Corp., Detroit, 1978—. Mem. Republican Nat. Com. Mem. Soc. Automotive Engrs. Home: 6061 Eastmoor Birmingham MI 48010 also Ocean City NJ Office: 27777 Franklin Rd Southfield MI 48034

SCHWARTZ, ROBERT GEORGE, ins. co. exec.; b. Czechoslovakia, Mar. 27, 1928; s. George and Frances (Antoni) S.; came to U.S., 1929, naturalized, 1935; B.A., Pa. State U., 1949; M.B.A., N.Y. U., 1956; m. Caroline Bachurski, Oct. 12, 1952; children—Joanne, Tracy, Robert G. With Met. Life Ins. Co., N.Y.C., 1949—, v.p. securities, 1968-70, v.p., 1970-75, sr. v.p., 1975-78, exec. v.p., 1979—; dir. Potlatch Corp., San Francisco, Lowe's Cos., Inc., North Wilkesboro, N.C., Kaiser Cement Corp., Oakland, Calif. Served with AUS, 1950-52. Mem. Alpha Chi Rho. Clubs: Treasurers, Seaview Country, Springdale Country. Office: 1 Madison Ave New York NY 10010

SCHWARTZ, ROBERT NASH, pub. relations exec.; b. Chgo., Mar. 6, 1917; s. Jacob and Sarah (Nerush) S.; B.A. cum laude, U. Ill., 1940; m. Judith Goldman, June 3, 1940; children—Frances, James. Reporter, Champaign (Ill.) News-Gazette, 1941-42; reporter, editor St. Louis Post-Dispatch, 1942-43; writer, editor N.Y. Times Sunday dept., 1943-46; editorial writer Chgo. Sun, 1946; bur. mgr., sci. editor Internat. News Service, Chgo., 1947-51; with Manning, Selvage & Lee, N.Y.C., 1957—, sr. v.p., 1967-71, vice chmn. bd., 1971-73, pres., 1973-78, pres., chief exec. officer, 1978—. Mem. Nat. Assn. Sci. Writers, Pub. Relations Soc. Am., Phi Beta Kappa. Clubs: Univ., Chemists (N.Y.C.). Home: 33 W 93d St New York NY 10025 Office: 99 Park Ave New York City NY 10016

SCHWARTZ, SAMUEL, oil co. exec.; b. Moose Jaw, Sask., Can., Nov. 12, 1927; came to U.S., 1951, naturalized, 1965; s. Benjamin and Rose (Becker) S.; B.A., U. Sask., 1948, B.Comm., 1950; M.B.A., Harvard U., 1953; m. Margaret Patterson, Feb. 20, 1956; children—Michael R., Thomas R., David C., Janet C. Research asso. Harvard U., 1953-57; with Conoco Inc., 1957—, sr. v.p. coordinating and planning, Stamford, Conn., 1974-75, sr. v.p. corp. planning, 1975-78, sr. v.p. adminstrv., 1978—; dir. Hudson's Bay Oil and Gas Co. Ltd., Consol. Coal Co.; mem. coordinating subcom. Nat. Petroleum Council's Study of U.S. Energy Outlook, 1970-72. Bd. dirs. U. Conn. Found., 1974—, Inst. for the Future, 1975—. Mem. Am. Petroleum Assn. Home: 941 Ponus Ridge Rd New Canaan CT 06840 Office: Conoco Inc High Ridge Park Stamford CT 06904

SCHWARTZ, SEYMOUR I., surgeon; b. N.Y.C., Jan. 22, 1928; s. Samuel and Martha (Paull) S.; B.A., U. Wis., 1947; postgrad. Syracuse Coll. Medicine, 1946-48; M.D., N.Y. U., 1950; m. Ruth Wainer-Schwartz, June 18, 1949; children—Richard Earl, Kenneth Alan, David Brian. Intern in surgery U. Rochester, 1950-51, asst. resident in surgery, 1951-52, chief resident, 1956-57, asst. prof. surgery, 1959-63, asso. prof., 1963-67, prof. surgery, sr. surgeon, 1967—; vice chmn. Am. Bd. Surgery; mem. adv. bd. Monroe Community Coll. Served with USNR, 1952-54. Recipient Acrel medal Swedish Surg. Assn., 1975. Fellow A.C.S. (vice-chmn. surg. forum, chmn. undergrad. edn.); mem. Am., Pan Pacific surg. assns., Am. Assn. Study of Liver Diseases, Am. Assn. Thoracic Surgery, Soc. Vascular Surgery, Internat. Soc. Surgery, Am Gastroenterol. Assn., Soc. Surgery of Alimentary Tract, Soc. Clin. Surgery, So. Surg. Assn., AMA, Brazilian Coll. Surgeons (hon.), Soc. Univ. Surgeons. Jewish. Clubs: Cosmos (Washington), Grolier (N.Y.C.). Editor-in-chief Principles of Surgery, Year Book of Surgery, 1971—, Contemporary Surgery; asso. editor Jour. Surgical Research, 1971—, others. Contbr. chpts. to med. textbooks, articles to profl. jours. Home: 18 Lake Lacoma Dr Pittsford NY 14534 Office: Dept Surgery U Rochester 601 Elmwood Ave Rochester NY 14642

SCHWARTZ, STEPHEN LAWRENCE, composer/lyricist; b. N.Y.C., Mar. 6, 1948; s. Stanley Leonard and Sheila Lorna (Siegel) S.; student Juillard Sch. Music, 1960-64; B.F.A., Carnegie Inst. Tech., 1968; m. Carole Ann Piasecki, June 6, 1969; children—Scott Lawrence, Jessica Lauren. Composer/lyricist title song for Butterflies Are Free, 1969; composer music and new lyrics for Godspell, 1971; author (with Leonard Bernstein) English texts for Leonard Bernstein's Mass, 1971; music and lyrics for Pippin, 1972, The Baker's Wife, 1976; songs for The Magic Show, 1974; author: (juvenile) The Perfect Peach, 1977; four songs, adaptation and direction Working, 1978. Recipient Grammy award (2), 1971; Drama Desk award (3), 1971 (2), 1978; Trendsetter award Billboard, 1971; award Nat. Theatre Arts Conf., 1971. Mem. ASCAP, Dramatists Guild, Nat. Acad. Rec. Arts and Scis. Address: care Paramuse Assos 1414 Ave Americas New York NY 10019

SCHWARTZ, STEVEN OTTO, physician, educator; b. Hungary, July 6, 1911; s. Otto and Henrietta (Lemberger) S.; came to U.S., 1923, naturalized, 1929; B.S., Northwestern, 1932, M.S., 1935, M.D., 1936; m. Ruth Deimel, Apr. 24, 1942; children—Kay, Ann, James. Intern Michael Reese Hosp., Chgo., 1935-37, asso. hematology, chief hematology clinic Mandel Clinic, 1938-50; research asso. hematology Beth Israel Hosp., Boston, 1937-38, also Charlton research fellow medicine Med. Sch., Tufts Coll.; attending hematologist Cook County Hosp., Chgo., 1939-68, dir. hematology dept., 1942-68; dir. dept. hematology Hektoen Inst., 1945-68; cons. hematologist Columbus, Ill. Masonic, Mother Cabrini hosps., Chgo., Chgo. State Hosp., 1941-49, Highland Park (Ill.) Hosp., 1950—; sr. attending physician Northwestern Meml. Hosp.; asso. medicine Mt. Sinai Hosp., 1948-51; prof. internal medicine Cook County Grad. Sch., 1939-68; asst. prof. medicine U. Ill., 1942-47; prof. hematology Chgo. Med. Sch., 1947-55; asso. prof. medicine Northwestern U. Med. Sch., 1955-59, prof. medicine, 1959-79, prof. emeritus, 1979—. Diplomate Am. Bd. Internal Medicine. Fellow Acad. Internat. Medicine, A.C.P., AAAS, AMA; mem. Am. Assn. Cancer Research, Am. Fedn. Clin. Research, Soc. Exptl. Biology and Medicine, Central Soc. Clin. Research, Chgo. Soc. Internal Medicine, Inst. Medicine Chgo., Am. Geriatrics Soc.,

Pan Am. Med. Assn., Internat. Soc. Hematology (charter), Am., European (corr.) socs. hematology, Sigma Xi. Mason. Author: Hematology in Practice. Asst. editor blood Jour. Hematology, 1946-50. Contbr. numerous articles to profl. jour. Home: 2185 Linden Ave Highland Park IL 60035 Office: 645 N Michigan Ave Chicago IL 60611

SCHWARTZ, STUART CARL, elec. engr.; b. N.Y.C., July 12, 1939; s. Charles M. and Rose (Greenberg) S.; B.S. in Aero. Engring., Mass. Inst. Tech., 1961, M.S. in Aero. Engring., 1961; Ph.D., U. Mich., 1966; m. Miriam Jane Loewengart, June 11, 1961; children—Julie, Alan. Research engr. Jet Propulsion Lab., Pasadena, Calif., 1961-62; asst. prof. dept. elec. engring. and computer sci. Princeton (N.J.) U., 1966-70, asso. prof., 1970-76, prof., 1976—, asso. dean Sch. Engring. and Applied Sci., 1977—; vis. asso. prof. (John Simon Guggenheim Meml. fellow) dept. elec. engring. The Technion, Haifa, Israel, 1972-73. Mem. IEEE, Inst. Math. Statistics, Soc. Indsl. and Applied Math. (editor Jour. Applied Math., 1970-76), Sigma Xi, Sigma Gamma Tau, Phi Kappa Phi, Eta Kappa Nu. Office: Dept Elec Engring Princeton U Princeton NJ 08540

SCHWARTZ, THEODORE B., physician, educator; b. Phila., Feb. 14, 1918; s. William F. and Fanny (Farkas) S.; B.S., Franklin and Marshall Coll., 1939; M.D., Johns Hopkins, 1943; m. Genevieve Etta Bangs, Jan. 9, 1948; children—Richard, Steven, Michael, David, Jonathan, Thomas. Intern Osler Clinic, Johns Hopkins Hosp., 1943-44; asst. resident medicine Salt Lake City Gen. Hosp., 1946-47, resident medicine, 1947-48; fellow medicine Duke Med. Sch., 1948-50, asso. medicine, asst. prof. medicine, 1950-55; dir. sect. endocrinology and metabolism Rush-Presbyn.-St. Luke's Med. Center, Chgo., 1955—, attending physician, 1960—; chmn. dept. medicine Rush-Presbyn.-St. Lukes's Med. Center, 1970; cons. endocrinology Hines (Ill.) VA Hosp., 1956-71, Great Lakes Naval Hosp., 1960-74; prof. medicine U. Ill. Coll. Medicine, 1960-71; prof., chmn. dept. medicine Rush Med. Coll., 1971—. Mem. Am. Bd. Med. Specialities, 1972—. Served with M.C., AUS, 1944-46. Decorated Bronze Star. Diplomate Am. Bd. Internal Medicine (bd. govs., 1970-78, sec.-treas., 1976-78). Fellow A.C.P. (mem. publs. com. 1973-78); mem. Assn. Program Dirs. Internal Medicine (councilor 1978), Am. Fedn. Clin. Research, Am. Diabetes Assn., Diabetes Assn. Greater Chgo. (bd. dirs.), Am. Soc. Clin. Investigation, Am. Thyroid Assn., Endocrine Soc., Central Clin. Research Club, Central Soc. Clin. Research, Chgo. Soc. Internal Medicine (pres. 1966-67), Phi Beta Kappa, Alpha Omega Alpha. Contbr. articles to profl. jours. Editor: Yearbook of Endocrinology, 1964—. Home: 1637 Judson Ave Evanston IL 60201 Office: 1753 W Congress Pkwy Chicago IL 60612

SCHWARTZ, THOMAS D., box bd. co. exec., lawyer; b. Carbondale, Ill., Apr. 1, 1932; s. Walker and Mabel (Smith) S.; B.A., So. Ill. U., 1956; J.D., U. Chgo., 1961; m. Kathryn Ann Hooker, Mar. 16, 1957; children—Patricia Ann, Thomas Andrew. Admitted to Ill. bar, 1961; lectr. bus. law and govt., asst. legal counsel So. Ill. U., Carbondale, 1961-62; practice law, Carbondale, 1962-63; trust officer, v.p. First Nat. Bank & Trust Co., Mt. Vernon, Ill., 1963-65; asst. to pres. Alton Box Board Co. (Ill.), 1965-66, corp. sec., 1966—, v.p. adminstrn., 1978—; dir. First Nat. Bank & Trust, Carbondale. Bd. dirs. St. Anthony's Hosp., Alton, Ill.; bd. dirs. First Presbyn. Ch., Alton, 1970-76, chmn., 1972-76; bd. dirs. Pride, Inc., Jr. Achievement, pres., 1979-80. Served with AUS, 1956-58. Mem. Am., Ill., Madison County, St. Louis bar assns., Southwestern Ill. Indsl. Assn. (dir., chmn. 1974), Ill. Mfg. Assn. (dir., chmn. So. div. 1977—). Home: 1402 D Adrian Dr Godfrey IL 62035 Office: 401 Alton St Alton IL 62002

SCHWARTZ, VICTOR ELLIOT, lawyer, educator; b. N.Y.C., July 3, 1940; A.B. summa cum laude, Boston U., 1962; J.D. magna cum laude, Columbia U., 1965. Admitted to N.Y. bar, 1965, Ohio bar, 1974; law clk. to judge So. Dist. N.Y., 1965-67; from asst. to asso. prof. law U. Cin., 1967-72, prof., 1972-79, acting dean, 1973-74; vis. prof. U. Va. Law Sch., 1970-71; adj. prof. law Am. U., 1980—; chmn. Fed. Interagy. task Force on Products Liability, 1976; chmn. Dept of Commerce Task Force on Product Liability and Accident Compensation, 1977—. Chmn. stewardship com. Fairlington United Methodist Ch., 1980. Recipient Sec. of Commerce award for disting. service. Mem. Am. Bar Assn. (chmn. faculty-liaison com. negligence, ins. and compensation sect.), Am. Law Inst., Phi Beta Kappa. Author: Comparative Negligence, 1974; (with Prosser and Wade) Cases and Materials on Torts, 1976; How to Prepare For the Multi-State Bar Examination, 1977; editor Columbia Law Rev., 1965; prin. draftsman Model Uniform Product Liability Act. Office: US Dept Commerce Office of Sec Room 5027 Washington DC 20330. *I believe that people's attitudes regarding achievement are better than is generally thought to be the case. Time and again I have seen that people's self-interest can be made to work in the interest of others; if you appeal to the best in people they usually respond.*

SCHWARTZ, WILLIAM, lawyer, educator; b. Providence, May 6, 1933; s. Morris Victor and Martha (Glassman) S.; A.A., Boston U., 1952; J.D. magna cum laude, Boston U., 1955, M.A., 1960; postgrad. Harvard Law Sch., 1955-56; m. Bernice Konigsberg, Jan. 13, 1957; children—Alan Gershon, Robin Libby. Admitted to Mass. bar, 1962; prof. law Boston U., 1955—, Fletcher prof. law, 1968-70, Roscoe Pound prof. law, 1970-73; of counsel firm Swartz & Swartz, Boston, 1973—; mem. faculty Frances Glessner Lee Inst., Harvard Med. Sch., Nat. Coll. Probate Judges, 1970, 77, 78, 79; gen. dir. Assn. Trial Lawyers Am., 1968-73; reporter New Eng. Trial Judges Conf., 1965-67; participant Nat. Met. Cts. Conf., 1968; dir. Mass. Probate Study, 1976—; dir. Sperry and Hutchinson Co., UST Fin. Planning Corp. Bd. dirs. Kerry Found.; trustee Hebrew Coll., 1975—; rep. Office Public Info., UN, 1968-73; chmn. legal adv. panel Nat. Commn. Med. Malpractice, 1972-73; examiner of titles Commonwealth of Mass., 1964—; spl. counsel Mass. Bay Transp. Authority, 1979—. Recipient Homer Albers award Boston U., 1955, John Ordronaux prize 1955; Disting. Service award Religious Zionists Am., 1977. Mem. Am. Bar Assn., Am. Law Inst., Mass. Trial Lawyers Assn. Author: Future Interests and Estate Planning, 1965, 77; Comparative Negligence, 1970; A Products Liability Primer, 1970; Civil Trial Practice Manual, 1972; New Vistas in Litigation, 1973; Massachusetts Pleading and Practice, 1974—, others. Note editor Boston U. Law Rev., 1954-55; property editor Annual Survey of Mass. Law, 1960—. Contbr. articles to legal jours. Home: 990 Centre St Newton MA 02159 Office: 10 Marshall St Boston MA 02108. *I have been guided by the maxim: Ideals are like stars. You cannot touch them with your hands, but like the seafaring man, if you choose them as your guide and follow them, you will reach your destiny."*

SCHWARTZ, WILLIAM B., JR., ambassador; b. Atlanta, Nov. 14, 1921; s. William B. and Ruth (Kuhn) S.; B.S., U. N.C., 1942; m. Sonia Weinberg, Dec. 3, 1942; children—William B., Arthur Jay, Robert C. Various positions, to v.p. Nat. Service Industries, Atlanta, 1945-68; pres. Weine Investment Corp., Atlanta, 1969-77; ambassador to Bahamas, 1977—; bd. dirs. Weine Investment Corp., 1950—. Mem. pres.'s council Brandeis U., 1966—; trustee, past chmn. Atlanta chapt. Am. Jewish Com.; mem. Chatham Valley Found.; bd. dirs. Met. Atlanta Rapid Transit Authority, 1969-76, vice chmn., 1971-73; bd. dirs. Big Bros. Atlanta; bd. dirs. Atlanta Jewish Welfare Fedn.; mem. Pres.'s Council Oglethorp U.; bd. dirs. Jewish Home for the Aged; chmn. bd. visitors Emory U., 1966-74. Served with USN, 1942-45. Recipient Man of Yr. award Am. Jewish Com., 1972. Clubs: Standard, Commerce (Atlanta); East Hill, Lyford Cay (Nassau); B'nai Brith, Masons, Shriners. Home: 35 Valley Rd Atlanta GA 30305 also Longboat Key FL

SCHWARTZ, WILLIAM BENJAMIN, educator, physician; b. Montgomery, Ala., May 16, 1922; s. William Benjamin and Molly (Vendruff) S.; M.D., Duke, 1945; m. Carol Levine, June 25, 1950; children—Eric A., Kenneth B., Laurie A. Intern, then asst. resident medicine U. Chgo. Clinics, 1945-46; asst. medicine Peter Bent Brigham Hosp., Boston, also research fellow medicine Harvard Med. Sch., 1948-50; fellow medicine Children's Hosp., Boston, 1949-50; mem. faculty Tufts U. Sch. Medicine, 1950—, prof. medicine, 1958—, Endicott prof., 1975-76, Vannevar Bush Univ. prof., 1976—, chmn. dept. medicine, 1971-76; mem. staff New Eng. Center Hosps., 1950—, sr. physician, chief renal service, 1959-71, physician-in-chief, 1971-76. Established investigator Am. Heart Assn., 1956-61; chmn. gen. medicine study sect. NIH, 1965-69; mem. sci. adv. bd. USAF, 1965-68; mem. sci. adv. bd. Nat. Kidney Found., 1968—, chmn., 1970—; mem. tng. com. Nat. Heart Inst., 1969-70; chmn. health policy adv. bd. Rand Corp., 1970—; prin. adviser health scis. program Rand Corp., 1977—. Markle scholar med. scis., 1950-55. Diplomate Am. Bd. Internal Medicine (mem. test com. nephrology). Mem. Inst. Medicine, Nat. Acad. Scis., Am. Soc. Nephrology (pres. 1974-75), Acad. Arts and Scis., A.C.P., Am. Fedn. Clin. Research, Am. Physiol. Soc., Am. Soc. Clin. Investigation, Assn. Am. Physicians, Phi Beta Kappa, Sigma Xi, Alpha Omega Alpha. Author numerous articles in field. Home: 51 Montvale Rd Newton Center MA 02159 Office: 136 Harrison Ave Boston MA 02111

SCHWARTZMAN, ALAN, architect; b. Balt., Aug. 16, 1923; s. Isidore A. and Ida (Berman) S.; B.E., Johns Hopkins, 1943; M.Arch., Pratt Inst.; postgrad. Écoles des Beaux Arts Americaines, Fontainebleau, France, 1950; m. Ruth Michel, Apr. 18, 1953; children—Eric Guy, Paul Jacques. Draftsman-designer Daniel Schwartzman, Architect, 1946-48, asso., 1956-59; architect-engr. U.S. Dept. Def., S.W. France, 1950-51; partner K.G. Belt & Assos., Paris, France, 1951-54; pvt. practice architecture, N.Y.C., 1959-65; partner Davis, Brody & Assos., N.Y.C., 1965—; prof. Sch. Architecture, Cooper Union, N.Y.C., 1960—. Sec. N.Y. State Bd. Examiners of Architects, 1963-68; mem. vis. com. Nat. Archtl. Accrediting Bd., 1969, 71; mem. advisory bd. Sch. Architecture Pratt Inst., 1977—. Served with CEC, USNR, 1943-46. Recipient various archtl. awards. Fellow AIA (chmn. com. on environ. edn., firm award 1975, medal of honor N.Y. chpt., Louis Sullivan award 1977); mem. N.Y. State Assn. Architects (chmn. edn. law com., com. fellows). Editor: Contemporary Copper, 1966. Prin. works include U.S. Pavilion Expo '70 Japan, Joseph Ellicott Complex, State U. N.Y., Amherst Campus, Sci. Complex, State U. N.Y. at Binghamton, Waterside Houses, Estee Lauder Plant, Riverbend Houses. Home: 20 W 77th St New York NY 10024 Office: 130 E 59th St New York NY 10022

SCHWARTZMAN, DAVID, educator, economist; b. Montreal, Que., Can., Apr. 22, 1924; s. Joseph and Jeannette (Zurick) S.; B.A., McGill U., 1945; postgrad. U. Minn., 1945-46; Ph.D., U. Calif. at Berkeley, 1953; m. Gertrude Schneiderman, June 17, 1951; children—Michael, Jason, Paul. Came to U.S., 1954, naturalized, 1964. Lectr., McGill U., 1948-51; economist Dominion Bur. Statistics, 1951-53 economist United 5c to $1.00 Stores, Can., 1953-54; instr. Columbia, 1954-58; asst. prof. N.Y. U., 1958-60; asso. prof. New Sch. for Social Research, N.Y.C., 1960-64, prof., 1964—, chmn. dept. econs., 1966-69, 76; mem. staff Nat. Bur. Econ. Research, 1963-69; prof. environ. medicine and community health state U. N.Y. Downstate Med. Center, part-time 1969-70. Cons. Royal Commn. on Farm Machinery, Ottawa, Can. 1968-70, U.S. Bur. Census, 1973, anti-trust div. U.S. Dept. Justice, 1973, U.S. Council on Wage and Price Stability, Exec. Office of Pres., 1975-76; adj. mem. Com. on Trade Regulation, N.Y. County Lawyers' Assn., 1976—. Bd. advisors Inst. Health Economics and Social Studies, 1976—. Mem. Am. Econ. Assn., Am. Statis. Assn. Author: Oligopoly in the Farm Machine Industry, 1970; Decline of Service in Retail Trade, 1971; The Expected Return from Pharmaceutical Research, 1975; Innovation in the Pharmaceutical Industry, 1976; contbr. articles to profl. jours. Home: 285 Central Park W New York NY 10024

SCHWARZ, DANIEL TRACY, singer; b. N.Y.C., Nov. 13, 1938; s. Hamilton David and Constance Lorraine (Harrigan) S.; B.S., Millersville (Pa.) State Coll., 1972; m. Eloise Jeandrevin King, Dec. 20, 1963; children—Robert Jeandrevin, Sally Ann, Peter Hamilton; stepchildren—Clyde Cottingham Smith, Mark Vanderveer Smith. Mem. Strange Creek Singers; mem. New Lost City Ramblers, from 1962; now mem. Tracy's Family Band; toured Europe and U.S.; numerous recs. Served with AUS, 1960-62. Address: Rural Delivery 1 Brodbecks PA 17308. *My motto has always been: "I may be finished, but I'm not done yet."*

SCHWARZ, FREDERIC GEORGE, mineral and chem. co. exec.; b. N.Y.C., Feb. 22, 1926; s. Gottlob David and Luise (Nagel) S.; B.B.A., Manhattan Coll., 1951; M.B.A., N.Y. U., 1955; m. Ingeborg Wieland, Sept. 19, 1953; children—Tracey Ingrid, Leslie Ann. Credit analyst Chase Manhattan Bank N.A., N.Y.C., 1951-56, adminstrv. asst., 1956-57, asst. treas., 1958-62, asst. v.p., 1962, v.p., 1967-71; v.p. Englehard Minerals & Chems. Corp., N.Y.C., 1971—, treas., 1973—. Served with U.S. Army, 1944-46. Home: 11 Seneca Rd Scarsdale NY 10583 Office: 1221 Ave of the Americas New York City NY 10020

SCHWARZ, FREDERICK AUGUST OTTO, JR., lawyer; b. N.Y.C., Apr. 20, 1935; s. Frederick A.O. and Mary Delafield (DuBois) D.; B.A., Harvard U., 1957, LL.B., 1960; m. Marian Lapsley, June 19, 1959; children—Frederick A.O., Adair L., Eliza Ladd. Admitted to N.Y. State bar, 1961; U.S. Supreme Ct. bar, 1973; law clk. to chief judge U.S. Ct. of Appeals, 2d Circuit, 1960-61; asst. commr. for law revision Govt. of No. Nigeria, 1961-62; asso. firm Cravath, Swaine & Moore, N.Y.C., 1963-68, partner firm, 1969-75, 76—; chief counsel Senate Select Com. on Intelligence, 1975-76; dir. F.A.O. Schwarz. Chmn. Fund for the City of N.Y., 1977—; pres. Vera Inst. Justice, 1978—; mem. Harvard Bd. Overseers, 1977—; trustee Experiment in Internat. Living, 1965—; bd. dirs. Manhattan Bowery Corp., 1970—, Lawyers for the Public Interest, 1976—; trustee Legal Action Center, 1973—, N.Y.C. Criminal Justice Agy., 1977—, Town Sch., 1972—, Am. Com. on Africa, 1965-79, Milton Acad., 1960's. Mem. Am. Law Inst., Am. Bar Assn., Assn. Bar of City of N.Y., Council Fgn. Relations. Author: Nigeria, The Tribes, The Nation, or the Race, 1966. Contbr. articles to profl. jours. Home: 610 West End Ave New York NY 10024 Office: Cravath Swaine & Moore 1 Chase Manhattan Plaza New York NY 10005

SCHWARZ, GERARD RALPH, musician; b. Weehawken, N.J., Aug. 19, 1947; s. John and Gerta (Weiss) S.; B.S., Juilliard Sch., 1972; m. Lillo Way, Aug. 21, 1972; children—Alysandra, Daniel. Trumpet player Am. Symphony Orch., 1965-72, Am. Brass Quintet, 1965-73, N.Y. Philharmonic, 1973-77; condr. Erick Hawkins Dance Co., 1966-70, Eliot Feld Ballet, 1976—; trumpet player, guest condr. Aspen Music Festival, 1969-75, bd. dirs., 1973-75; music dir., condr. Waterloo Festival, 1976—, Chamber Symphony (N.Y.), 1977—, Los Angeles Chamber Orch., 1978—, White Mountains (N.H.) Music Festival, 1978; mem. faculty Juilliard Sch., 1975—, Mannes Coll. Music, 1973—, Montclair State Coll., 1975—; rec. artist Columbia, Nonesuch, Vox, MMO, Destro records; guest condr., performer numerous orchs. Bd. dirs. Naumberg Found., 1975—. Recipient award for concert artists Ford Found., 1973; Record of Year award for cornet favorites Streo Rev., 1975. Mem. Am. Musicol. Soc. Jewish. Composer, Greenhouse Dance Co., Lillo Way. Editor early music edits. Asso. Music Publishers, 1975—. Address: 167 Upper Mountain Ave Montclair NJ 07042

SCHWARZ, GERHART STEVEN, radiologist; b. Vienna, Austria, June 19, 1912; s. Gottwald and Charlotte (Hiller) S.; student Vienna Inst. Tech., 1931-32, U. Vienna Med. Sch., 1932-38; M.D., U. Basle (Switzerland), 1939; m. Gertrude Aschner, Aug. 22, 1942; children—Doris Audrey, Marion Janet, Richard Michael. Came to U.S., 1939, naturalized, 1944. Intern, Michael Reese Hosp., Chgo., 1939-41; resident radiology U. Chgo. Clinics, 1942-44; instr. roentgenology U. Chgo., 1945-46; dir. radiology Clifton Springs (N.Y.) Sanitarium and Clinic, 1946-50; asst. attending radiology Columbia-Presbyn. Med. Center, N.Y.C., 1950-60, dir. radiology Squier Urol. Clinic, 1960-64; chief radiol. service Bird S. Coler Hosp., N.Y.C., 1964-70; dir. radiology N.Y. Eye and Ear Infirmary, 1971—; vis. physician Met. Hosp., 1964—; attending Flower Hosp., 1964—; cons. Prospect Hosp., 1964—; asst. prof. Columbia Coll. Phys. and Surg., 1952-64; prof. radiology N.Y. Med. Coll., 1964-70, clin. prof., 1971—; vis. asso. dept. history medicine Albert Einstein Coll. Medicine. Vice chmn. subcom. U.S. Standards Inst., 1967-73, mem., 1974—. Recipient Siemens prize elecromed. research Siemens-Reiniger-Veifa Werke, 1936; Col. Martin award for Teaching, 1974. Fellow N.Y. Acad. Medicine, Am. Coll. Radiology; mem. N.Y. Acad. Scis., N.Y. Acad. Medicine (past chmn. sect. history medicine), AMA, Am. Roentgen Ray Soc. (Merritt award 1968), Radiol. Soc. N.Am., Interam. Coll. Radiology, Pirquet Soc. Clin. Medicine (past pres.), Virchow-Pirquet Med. Soc. (pres. 1978—). Author: Unit-Step Radiography, 1961; (with Golthamer) Radiographic Atlas of The Human Skull, 1965; (with Powsner) Alphabetical Index of Roentgendiagnoses and Procedures, 1966. Editor-in-chief: Procs. Virchow-Pirquet Med. Soc., 1976—. Patentee in field. Home: 31 Inverness Rd New Rochelle NY 10804 Office: 310 E 14th St New York NY 10003. *As to life in general: my prescription is to do a juggling act of wearing rose colored glasses and taking them off. The former makes life enjoyable by blinding us to injustices, inequities and mismanagement. The latter helps to face the truth squarely. To do too much of one, makes one a coward. To do too much of the other, an unhappy frustrated rebel. As to Medicine: the old rule "Foremost, avoid doing harm" should be amplified by "Don't rock the boat" to reduce unnecessary medical hyperactivism.*

SCHWARZ, HELMUT JULIUS, educator, physicist; b. Wuppertal, West Germany, Nov. 20, 1915; s. Gottlieb and Maria (Platte) S.; Ph.D., U. Bonn (West Germany), 1940; m. Ruth Else Mengel, Aug. 12, 1950; children—Yorck-Wedigo Michael, Arno (dec. 1976). Asst. prof. U. Bonn, 1940; mem. staff high frequency research German Air Force Ministry, 1944-45; dr. Pvt. Inst. Phys. Scis., Wuppertal, 1945-49; mem. faculty Centro Brasileiro de Pesquisas Fisicas, Rio de Janeiro, 1950-54; prof. applied physics U. Rio de Janerio, 1951-57; mem. faculty Centro Tecnico de Aeros., San Jose dos Campos, Sao Paulo, Brazil 1955-57; dir. projects phys. electronics RCA, 1957-60; mem. sr. staff United Aircraft Corp., 1960-63; prof. physics Rensselaer Poly. Inst., 1963—. Cons. to industry, 1963—; prof. titular visitante U. Brasilia, 1974-75, prof. titular do quadro, 1975—; mem. U.S. liaison for U.S.-Japan Coop. Sci. Program, 1972—. with German Air Force, 1940-42. Recipient I.R. 100 award, 1969; Technol. award NASA, 1970, award for invention, 1972. Fellow Inst. Physics; mem. European, Am., German, Brazilian phys. socs., Am. Vacuum Soc., Internat. Orgn. Vacuum Sci. and Tech. (a founder), Electron Microscopy Soc. Am., IEEE, N.Y. Acad. Scis. (A. Cressey Morrison award 1970), Sci. Research Soc. Am., AAAS, Sigma Xi. Club: Explorers (fellow). Author: (with R. Jaeckel) High Vacuum Techniques, 1950. Co-editor Tech. Proc. of Laser Interaction and Related Plasma Phenomena, 1971, 72, 74, 77. Pioneer prodn. ultra-high vacuum by ionization, 1938-40; organizer, editor biannual workshop on Laser Interaction and Related Plasma Phenomena, 1969—. First observation Kapitza-Dirac effect, 1965, nonlinear effects in laser produced plasmas from solid targets, 1966, modulation of electron beam at optical frequencies, 1969. Home: 49 Carver Circle Simsbury CT 06070 Office: Rensselaer Poly Inst Dept Physics Troy NY 12181

SCHWARZ, HENRY MARSHALL, banker; b. N.Y.C., Nov. 5, 1936; s. Frederick A.O. and Mary D. (DuBois) S.; grad. Milton Acad., 1954; A.B., Harvard, 1958, M.B.A., 1961; m. 1962 (div. 1975); children—James Marshall, Serena Reed; m. 2d, J. Rae Paige, 1978. With Morgan Stanley & Co., N.Y.C., 1961-67; with U.S. Trust Co. N.Y., N.Y.C., 1967—, exec. v.p., trustee, 1977—; dir. F.A.O. Schwarz, Gen. Agr. Corp. Trustee Tchrs. Coll., Columbia U.; bd. dirs. Camille and Henry Dreyfus Found.; mem. adv. bd. Salvation Army Greater N.Y. Office: 45 Wall St New York City NY 10005

SCHWARZ, JOSEPH EDMUND, artist; b. Hartford, Conn., May 13, 1929; s. Jules and Dora (Sklarinsky) S.; B.F.A., Ohio Wesleyan U., 1950; M.F.A., U. Ill., 1952; Ph.D., Ohio State U., 1957; m. Jean Bunker Chalmers, Jan. 29, 1951; children— David Bunker, Dina Ruth, Jonathan Chalmers, Adam Jules; m. 2d, Sarah Rollings, Oct. 21, 1971. Exhibited group shows Butler Art Inst. Annual, 1949-55, Southeastern Annual, Atlanta, 1957, 59-61, 66-67, Chrysler Show, Provincetown, Mass., 1958, Hunter Gallery Annual, Chattanooga, 1960-62, 67, Whitney Annual, N.Y.C., 1958, Montgomery Mus.; represented pub. art collections Butler Art Inst., Atlanta High Mus., Ball State U., Temple Beth Israel, Hartford, LaGrange Coll. U. Ga. Sch. Law; instr. Ohio State U., 1952-57; asso. prof. U. Ga., 1957-68; prof., dir. grad. studies Va. Commonwealth U., 1968-73; prof. U. Maine at Machias, 1973-74; prof. Auburn U., Montgomery, Ala., 1977—, head dept. art and music, 1977—. Home: Edgemont Ave W Montgomery AL 36105 Office: Dept Art and Music Auburn U Montgomery AL 36117. *As a humanist and as a painter, my life's goal is to be actually what I hope I am, that is to realize myself, to develop fully whatever it is that makes my life unique. I want my paintings to be records of my ideas and values, and if it should be that my being and my work have specialty, then I would hope that others would find there compassion and passion, a witnessing of human joy and pain and, finally, affirmation of the beauty of man and of human life.*

SCHWARZ, JOSEPHINE LINDEMAN, ballet co. dir.; b. Dayton, Ohio, Apr. 8, 1908; d. Joseph and Hannah (Lindeman) Schwarz; D.F.A. (hon.), U. Dayton, 1974. Profl. dancer Adolph Bolm's Ballet Intime, 1925-27, Ravinia Opera Ballet, Chgo., 1925-27; European study and performances, 1929-30; founder Schwarz Sch. Dance, Dayton, 1927, dir., 1927-78; mem. Weidman Theatre Dance Co., 1934-37; founder, 1937, since dir. Exptl. Group for Young Dancers (now Dayton Ballet); guest tchr., lectr., choreographer Hunter Coll., N.Y.C., YM-YWHA, N.Y.C., also regional dance companies in Cleve., Phila., Indpls., Houston; pres. N.E. Regional Ballet Assn., 1961; chmn. dance adv. panel Ohio Arts Council, 1967-70; founder, program dir. Nat. Craft Choreography Confs., 1968-70; dance advisory panels Nat. Endowment for Arts, 1975-78, also Ohio Arts Council, 1975-78. Mem. Assn. Am. Dance Cos. (bd. 1967-68), Nat. Assn. Regional Ballet (bd. dirs. 1970-75), Am. Dance Guild, Com.

Research in Dance, Friends Dayton Ballet, Dayton Art Inst. Jewish. Author articles. Home: 454 Dayton Towers Dr Dayton OH 45410 Office: 140 N Main St Dayton OH 45402. *There are no short cuts.*

SCHWARZ, M. ROY, univ. adminstr., physician; b. American Falls, Idaho, July 30, 1936; B.A., Pacific Luth. U., 1959; M.D., U. Wash., 1963; m. Thelma Constance Nygaard, June 9, 1958; children—Ryan, Tanna Berit. Fellow in anatomy U. Wash., 1960-61, instr. in biol. structure, 1963-64, asst. prof. biol. structure, 1965-68, asso. prof., 1968-73, prof., 1973-79, asst. dean, 1968-70, asso. dean, dir. WAMI (Wash./Alaska/Mont./Idaho) program, 1970-79, asso. dean academic affairs, 1973-79; prof. dept. anatomy, dean Sch. Medicine, U. Colo., 1979—; lectr. in anatomy McGill U., Montreal, Que., Can., 1964-65; dir. Exptl. Communication Satellite Program, 1974—. Bd. regents Pacific Luth. U., 1971—. Named Outstanding Grad. U. Wash. Sch. Medicine, 1963, Alumnus of Year Pacific Luth. U., 1970; recipient R. H. Williams research award U. Wash., 1963, Blue and Gold award Mont. State U., 1975, Disting. Alumnus award Pacific Luth. U., 1979. Fellow Calif. Luth. Coll.; mem. Am. Assn. Anatomists, Reticuloendothelial Soc., Am. Assn. Immunologists, Danforth Assos., Alpha Omega Alpha. Contbr. numerous articles to sci., ednl. jours.; editor Proc. Sixth Leucocyte Culture Conf., 1971. Home: 5950 E 6th Ave Denver CO 80220 Office: 4200 E 9th Ave Denver CO 80262

SCHWARZ, MICHAEL JAY, lawyer; b. Bklyn., Aug. 15, 1935; s. Sigmund and Minnie (Schneider) S.; B.A., Johns Hopkins U., 1957; LL.B., U. Md., 1960; m. Diane Penny Ulman, Aug. 14, 1963; 1 son, Stefan. Admitted to Md. bar, 1961, since practiced in Balt.; partner firm Fleischmann, Needle, Ehudin and Schwarz, 1970. C.P.A., Md. Home: 6208 Sareva Dr Baltimore MD 21209 Office: 705 One Charles Center Baltimore MD 21201

SCHWARZ, RALPH JACQUES, univ. dean; b. Hamburg, Germany, June 13, 1922; s. Simon J. and Anna (Schoendorff) S.; naturalized, 1944; B.S., Columbia, 1943, M.S., 1944, Ph.D., 1949; postgrad. Poly. Inst. Bklyn., 1944-45, N.Y. U., 1946-47; m. Irene Lassally, Sept. 9, 1951; children—Ronald Paul, Sylvia Anne. Mem. faculty Columbia, 1943—, prof. elec. engring., 1958—, chmn. dept., 1958-65, 71-72, asso. dean acad. affairs Faculty Engring. and Applied Sci., 1972-75, acting dean, 1975-76, vice dean, Thayer Lindsley prof., 1976—, mem. staff Electronics Research Lab., 1951-62; cons. systems analysis, communications and noise theory, 1945—; vis. asso. prof. U. Calif. at Los Angeles, 1956; adviser Inst. Internat. Edn., 1952—; vis. scientist IBM Research Center, 1969-70. Bd. dirs. Armstrong Meml. Research Found. Registered profl. engr., N.Y. Fellow IEEE (chmn. circuit theory group 1963-65); mem. Soc. Indsl. and Applied Math., Pattern Recognition Soc., Am. Soc. Engring. Edn., AAAS, Sigma Xi, Tau Beta Pi, Pi Mu Epsilon, Eta Kappa Nu. Club: Faculty House (Columbia). Author: (with M.G. Salvadori) Differential Equations in Engineering Problems, 1954; (with B. Friedland) Linear Systems, 1965. Home: 33 Wood Ln New Rochelle NY 10804 Office: Columbia U New York NY 10027

SCHWARZ, RICHARD WILLIAM, educator; b. Wataga, Ill., Sept. 11, 1925; s. George William and Mildred (Imschweiler) S.; B.A., Andrews U., 1949; M.S., U. Ill., 1953; M.A., U. Mich., 1959, Ph.D., 1964; m. Joyce Frances Anderson, June 11, 1950; children—Constance Kay, Richard Paul, Dwight Luther. Tchr.-librarian Broadview Acad., La Grange, Ill., 1949-53, Adelphian Acad., Holly, Mich., 1953-55; instr. history Andrews U., 1955-58, asst. librarian, 1955-56, acting librarian, 1956-58, asst. prof., 1958-63, asso. prof., 1963-68, prof., 1968—, acting chmn. dept. history and polit. sci., 1964-66, chmn., 1966-77, v.p. for acad. adminstrn., 1977—; vis. instr. Mich. State U., 1967; book reviewer Library Jour., 1957—. Del. Berrien County Republican Conv., 1966, 68, 74. Served with USNR, 1944-46. Mem. Am. Hist. Assn., Phi Beta Kappa, Phi Alpha Theta. Republican. Seventh-day Adventist (editor HIstorians' Newsletter 1967-72). Author: John Harvey Kellogg, M.D., 1970; Lightbearers to the Remnants, 1979. Bd. editors Studies in Adventist History, 1971—; cons. editor Adventist Heritage. Home: 229 N Maplewood Dr Berrien Springs MI 49103

SCHWARZ, SANFORD, mag. pub.; b. N.Y.C., Feb. 28, 1920; m. Francis Riley, 1952; m. 2d, Charlotte Voelker, Mar. 31, 1977. Advt. dir. Mag. Mgmt. Co., N.Y.C., 1946-52; salesman, then advt. dir. Hillman Periodicals, Inc., N.Y.C., 1952-57; advt. sales exec. Ideal Pub. Corp., N.Y.C., 1957-62; pres. Sanford Schwarz & Co., Inc., N.Y.C., 1962—, Sterling's Maga., Inc., N.Y.C., 1974—; sec., dir. Pebble Resorts, Inc., 1973—. Mem. pub. affairs com. Cancer Care Inc. and Nat. Cancer Found., Inc., 1976—. Served with USAAF, 1941-45. Mem. Euthanasia Ednl. Council (dir. 1971-74, adviser 1974—), Soc. for Right to Die (dir. 1974—). Clubs: Players, Friars (N.Y.C.). Home: 452 W 20th St New York NY 10011 also 113 Louse Point Rd East Hampton NY 11937 Office: 355 Lexington Ave New York NY 10017

SCHWARZER, WILLIAM W., fed. judge; b. Berlin, Apr. 30, 1925; s. John F. and Edith M. (Daniel) S.; came to U.S., 1938, naturalized, 1944; A.B. cum laude, U. So. Calif., 1948; LL.B. cum laude, Harvard U., 1951; m. Anne Halbersleben, Feb. 2, 1951; children—Jane Elizabeth, Andrew William. Admitted to Calif. bar, 1953, U.S. Supreme Ct. bar, 1967; teaching fellow Harvard U. Law Sch., 1951-52; asso. firm McCutchen, Doyle, Brown & Enersen, San Francisco, 1952-60, partner, 1960-76; U.S. dist. judge for No. Dist. Calif., San Francisco, 1976—; counsel Pres.'s Commn. on CIA Activities Within the U.S., 1975; mem. faculty Nat. Coll. Trial Advocacy, 1979. Trustee World Affairs Council No. Calif., 1961—; bd. dirs. William Babcock Meml. Endowment, San Rafael, Calif., 1962-78; pres. bd. trustees Marin Country Day Sch., 1963-66; chmn. Marin County Aviation Commn., 1969-76. Served with Intelligence, U.S. Army, 1943-46. Fellow Am. Coll. Trial Lawyers; mem. Am., San Francisco bar assns., State Bar Calif. Clubs: Bohemian, Mt. Tam Racquet. Contbr. articles to legal publs., aviation jours. Office: 450 Golden Gate Ave San Francisco CA 94102

SCHWARZKOPF, ELISABETH, soprano; b. Jarotschin, Posen; d. Fredrich and Elizabeth (Frohlich) Schwarzkopf; student pvt. schs., Hochschule for Musik, Berlin; studied with Maria Ivogun; D.Mus. (hon.), Cambridge (Eng.) U.; m. Walter Legge. Debut Stadtische Opera, Berlin, Staatsoper, Vienna, 1946-48, Covent Garden, London, 1948-50, Am. opera debut San Francisco, 1955; appeared with La Scala, Milan, 1948-63, Met. Opera, N.Y.C., 1964-65; appeared festivals, Salzburg, Bayreuth, others; concert singer specializing in German art songs, classical oratorio; prin. roles include Marschallin, Flordiligi, Contessa Almaviva, Donna Elvira, Mimi, Liu, Pamina, others. Decorated Ordre of Dannebrog (Denmark), Grosses Verdienst Kreuz (E. Ger.); recipient Lilli Lehmann medal, Salzburg; first Orfeo D'Oro Mantova; academician Societa Nazionale di Santa Cecilia (Rome); Golden Star of City of Vienna. Mem. Swedish Acad. Arts and Scis. Address: care Musical Advisers Establishment PO Box 583 9490 Vaduz Lichtenstein*

SCHWARZSCHILD, MARTIN, educator, astronomer; b. Potsdam, Germany, May 31, 1912; s. Karl and Else (Rosenbach) S.; Ph.D., U. Goettingen, 1935; D.Sc. (hon.), Swarthmore Coll., 1960, Columbia U., 1973; m. Barbara Cherry, Aug. 24, 1945. Came to U.S., 1937, naturalized, 1942. Research fellow Inst. Astrophysics, Oslo (Norway) U., 1936-37, Harvard U. Obs., 1937-40; lectr., later asst. prof. Rutherfurd Obs., Columbia U., 1940-47; prof. Princeton U., 1947-50, Higgins prof. astronomy, 1950-79. Served to 1st lt. AUS, 1942-45. Recipient Dannie Heineman prize Akademie der Wissenschaften zu Goettingen (Germany), 1967; Albert A. Michelson award Case Western Res. U., 1967; Newcomb Cleveland prize AAAS, 1957; Rittenhouse Silver medal, 1966; Prix Janssen, Société astronomique de France, 1970. Fellow Am. Acad. Arts and Scis.; mem. Internat. Astron. Union (v.p. 1964-70), Akademie der Naturforscher Leopoldina, Royal Astron. Soc. (asso.; Gold medal 1969, Eddington medal 1963), Royal Astron. Soc. Can. (hon.), Am. Astron. Soc. (pres. 1970-72), Nat. Acad. Scis. (Henry Draper medal 1961), Soc. Royale des Sciences de Liege (corr.), Royal Netherlands (fgn.), Royal Danish (fgn.), Norwegian acads. sci. and letters, Astron. Soc. Pacific (Bruce medal 1965), Sigma Xi. Author: Structure and Evolution of the Stars. Home: 12 Ober Rd Princeton NJ 08540

SCHWARZSCHILD, WILLIAM HARRY, JR., banker; b. Richmond, Va., Sept. 19, 1903; s. William Harry and Rosalie (Held) S.; A.B., U. Va., 1923; M.B.A., Harvard, 1925; m. Kathryn Emsheimer, Sept. 6, 1945; children—Kathrin, William Harry. With J. & W. Seligman & Co., 1926-30; v.p. Central Nat. Bank, 1931-41, exec. v.p., 1945-49, pres., 1949-71, chmn. bd., 1967-73, 76-78, also dir.; chmn. bd. Schwarzchild Bros. Inc., Central Nat. Corp., 1971-73, 76—; dir., mem. exec. com. Commonwealth Banks, Inc., 1978—, Central Nat. Bank, Central-Fidelity Banks, Inc. Chmn. Va. Bd. Vocational Rehab., 1964-73; chmn. gen. fund drive, Henrico, Richmond, Chesterfield, A.R.C., 1952. Trustee Richmond Meml. Hosp. Served to lt. comdr. USNR, 1942-45. Decorated Bronze Star. Mem. Richmond C. of C. (pres. 1955-57), Am. Inst. Banking, Phi Beta Kappa. Clubs: Commonwealth, Jefferson Lakeside, Fishing Bay Yacht; Westwood Racquet. Home: 210 Overlook Rd Richmond VA 23229 Office: 219 E Broad St Richmond VA 23219

SCHWARZWALDER, JOHN CARL, educator, TV exec.; b. Columbus, Ohio, June 21, 1917; s. S. John and Alice (Enright) S.; A.B., Ohio State U., 1937; Mus.M., U. Mich., 1940, A.M., 1941; Ed.D., U. Houston, 1953; m. Ruth Marie Dierker, July 10, 1945; children—Joan Dierdre, Raymond John. Asso. dir. Wall Sch. of Music, Asso. Republic Prodns., 1946-48; became prof. U. Houston, 1948, chmn. radio-TV dept., 1950; pioneer mgr. nation's first ednl. TV sta.; became mgr. radio sta. KUHF, 1950, KUHT-TV, 1953; gen. mgr. KTCA-TV, St. Paul, 1956-76, KTCI-TV, 1965-76; trustee Twin City Area ETV Corp., 1975-78, exec. cons., 1976—; mgr. KOKH-TV, Oklahoma City, 1977-78, mgr. Denton (Tex.) Channel Two Found., 1977—; pres. ETV Assos., Inc.; dir. Midwest ETV, Inc.; Gt. Plains Nat. TV Library; cons. Tex. Humanities Com.; former bd. dirs. Am. Heart Assn., Minn. Humanities com., Afro-Am. Music Assn., Council State Ednl. TV Commns.; former pres. Minn. Planning Commn. Served to maj. AUS, 1941-46. Mem. Nat. Assn. Better Radio-TV (dir.), Nat. Assn. Ednl. TV (sec.-treas.), Nat. Assn. Ednl. Broadcasters, Nat. Assn. for Better Broadcasts, Phi Mu Alpha, Kappa Phi Kappa, Alpha Epsilon Rho. Democrat. Episcopalian. Rotarian. Clubs: University (St. Paul); Lakeview (Austin). Author: ETV in Controversy: We Caught Spies; numerous articles on pub. TV. Home: 1700 Timberwood Dr Austin TX 78741 Office: 313 First State Bank Bldg Denton TX 76201. *Running with the pack is the way to a safe life. Standing against the pack is the way to a valuable life.*

SCHWEBEL, MILTON, psychologist, educator; b. Troy, N.Y., May 11, 1914; s. Frank and Sarah (Oxenhandler) S.; A.B., Union Coll., 1934; M.A., SUNY at Albany, 1936; Ph.D., Columbia U., 1949; certificate in psychotherapy Postgrad. Center for Mental Health, 1958; m. Bernice Lois Davison, Sept. 3, 1939; children—Andrew I., Robert S. Tchr. high schs. upstate N.Y., 1936-39; counselor Nat. Youth Adminstrn., White Plains, N.Y., 1939-41; employment counselor N.Y. State Employment Service, 1941-43; labor market analyst War Manpower Commn., 1943; psychometrist Coll. City N.Y., 1946; dir. guidance, asst. prof. psychology, chmn. philosophy-psychology dept. Mohawk Coll., 1946-48; asst. prof. psychology Champlain Coll., 1948-49; asst. to prof. edn. N.Y. U., 1949-67, chmn. dept. guidance and personnel adminstrn., 1964-66, asso. dean, 1965-67; dean, prof. edn. Grad. Sch. Edn., Rutgers U., New Brunswick, N.J., 1967-77, prof. Grad. Sch. Applied and Profl. Psychology, 1977—; vis. prof. U. So. Calif., summer 1953, U. Hawaii, summer 1965; lectr. psychologist Postgrad. Center for Mental Health, 1958-60; cons. NIMH, 1963-66, U.S. Office Edn., 1968-72, Hadassah-Wizo Research Inst., Israel, 1968-69, India, 1975, Rumania and Cypress, 1978, VA, 1978; pvt. cons. psychologist and psychotherapist, 1953—. Trustee, Edn. Law Center, 1973—, Nat. Com. Employment Youth, Nat. Child Labor Com., 1967-75, Union Exptl. Colls. and Univs., 1976-78, Opera Theatre N.J., 1979—; chmn. adv. com. Nat. Com. Edn. Migrant Children, 1970-75, exec. bd. Inst. and Mus. Fantasy and Play, 1977—; bd. dirs. Breast Disease Assn. Am., 1976—; v.p. Nat. Orgn. for Migrant Children, 1976—. Served with AUS, 1943-46; ETO. Postdoctoral fellow Postgrad. Center for Mental Health, 1954-56; Met. Applied Research Council fellow, 1970. Diplomate Am. Bd. Examiners Profl. Psychology; licensed psychologist, N.Y., N.J. Fellow Am. Psychol. Assn., Am. Orthopsychiatry Assn., Soc. Psychol. Study Social Issues; mem. Am. Personnel and Guidance Assn. (past pres. N.Y.), AAAS, AAUP, Jean Piaget Soc. (trustee), Am. Ednl. Research Assn., N.Y. Acad. Scis. Author: The Interests of Pharmacists, 1951; (with Ella Harris) Health Counseling, 1951; Resistance to Learning, 1963; Who Can Be Educated, 1968; (with Andrew, Bernice and Carol Schwebel) Student Teacher's Manual, 1979; (film) (with Bernice Schwebel) Why Some Children Don't Learn, 1962. Editor: Behavioral Science and Human Survival, 1965; (with Jane Raph) Piaget in the Classroom, 1973. Rev. editor: Am. Jour. Orthopsychiatry, 1963-71; mem. editorial bd. Jour. Contemporary Psychotherapy, 1965-73, Jour. Counseling Psychology, 1966-75; mem. editorial com. Jour. Social Issues, 1965-70; editorial bd. N.Y. U. Edn. Quar., 1969-71, 73—, Rev. of Edn., 1974—; editorial advisory bd. Change in Higher Edn., 1969-74. Home: 1050 George St New Brunswick NJ 08901

SCHWEBEL, STEPHEN MYRON, govt. ofcl., lawyer; b. N.Y.C., Mar. 10, 1929; s. Victor and Pauline (Pfeffer) S.; B.A. magna cum laude with highest honors in Govt., Harvard, 1950; Frank Knox Meml. fellow, Trinity Coll., Cambridge (Eng.) U. 1950-51; LL.B., Yale, 1954; m. Louise I.N. Killander, Aug. 2, 1972; children—Jennifer Pauline Anna, Anna Nina Cecilia. Admitted to N.Y. bar, 1955, U.S. Supreme Ct. bar, 1965, D.C. bar, 1976; dir. UN hdqrs. office World Fedn. UN Assns., 1950-53; lectr. Am. fgn. policy univs. in India for State Dept., 1952; research, drafting asst. to Trygve Lie in writing In the Cause of Peace, 1953; legal asso. White & Case, N.Y.C., 1954-59; vis. lectr. internat. law Cambridge U., 1957; asst. prof. law Harvard Law Sch., 1959- 61; asst. legal adviser for UN affairs State Dept., 1961-66; spl. asst. to asst. sec. state internat. orgn. affairs, 1966-67; exec. dir., exec. v.p. Am. Soc. Internat. Law, 1967-73; dep. legal adviser State Dept., 1974—. Prof. internat. law Sch. Advanced Internat. Studies, Johns Hopkins, Washington, 1967, Edward B. Burling prof. internat. law and orgn., 1973—. Dept. State's spl. rep. Micronesian claims, 1966-71; cons. Dept. State, 1967-73, U.S. ACDA, 1970-73; legal adviser U.S. del. 16th-20th and 4th Spl. Gen. Assemblies UN; asso. rep. U.S. before Internat. Ct. Justice, 1962; U.S. rep., chmn. U.S. delegation to 1st session UN Spl. Com on Principles Internat. Law concerning friendly relations and cooperation among states, Mexico City, 1964; U.S. rep. on adv. com. UN Program Assistance in Teaching, Study, Dissemination and Wider Appreciation Internat. Law, 1966-74; U.S. counsel Franco-Am. Air Arbitration, 1978; vis. lectr. Dag Hammarskjold Inst., Uppsala, Sweden, 1967; vis. prof. internat. law Australian Nat. U., Canberra, 1969; U.S. rep., chmn. delegation 3d session UN Spl. Com. on Question Defining Aggression, Geneva, 1970; Carnegie lectr. Hague Acad. Internat. Law, 1972; counselor internat. law U.S. Dept. State, 1973; U.S. rep., chmn. delegation 2d and 4th sessions UNCTAD Working Group on Charter Econ. Rights and Duties of States, Geneva, 1973, Mexico City, 1974; U.S. alt. rep. UN Econ. and Social Council, Geneva, 1974; legal adviser U.S. del. Conf. Internat. Econ. Coop., Paris, 1975; mem. Internat. Law Commn., UN, Geneva, 1977—, spl. rapporteur internat. Watercourses, 1977—, chmn. drafting com., 1978—. Mem. exec. com. Commn. Study Orgn. Peace, 1948-61; adv. joint com. law internat. transactions Am. Law Inst. and Am. Bar Assn., 1959-61; cons. USN War Coll., Newport, R.I., 1967; lectr. USN War Coll., Newport, 1966-68, Nat. War Coll., 1970-77; nat. chmn. Collegiate Council for UN, 1948-50; pres. Internat. Student Movement for UN, 1950-51; mem. advisory bd. Center for Oceans Law and Policy, U. Va., 1975—; vice chmn. Sec. State's Advisory Com. Pvt. Internat. Law, 1978—. Mem. Am. Law Inst., Washington Inst. Fgn. Affairs, Internat. Law Assn. (past Am. br. chmn. com. on charter UN, exec. com. Am. br. 1968-74), Am. Bar Assn., Am. Soc. Internat. Law (chmn. com. library 1961-62, mem. exec. council 1967—), Council Fgn. Relations, Brit. Inst. Internat. and Comparative Law, Am. Fgn. Service Assn., Inter-Am. Inst. Internat. Legal Studies (asso.), Phi Beta Kappa. Clubs: Athenaeum (London); Cosmos (Washington); Harvard (N.Y.C.). Author: The Secretary-General of the United Nations, 1952. Editor: The Effectiveness of International Decisions, 1971. Editorial bd. Am. Jour. Internat. Law, 1967—; chmn. editorial advisory com. Internat. Legal Materials, 1967-73; advisory bd. Law and Policy in Internat. advisory 1968—. Home: 1917 23d St NW Washington DC 20008 Office: State Dept Washington DC 20510

SCHWEBER, SILVAN SAMUEL, educator; b. Strasbourg, France, Apr. 10, 1928; s. David and Dora (Edelman) S.; came to U.S., 1942, naturalized, 1951; B.S., Coll. City N.Y., 1947; M.S., U. Pa., 1959; Ph.D. (Proctor fellow), Princeton, 1952; m. Myrna Tapper, June 21, 1951 (div. Feb. 1965); m. 2d, Miriam Fields, June 14, 1965; 1 dau., Simone Aviva. Instr., Princeton U., 1951-52; mem. Inst. Advanced Studies, Princeton, N.J., 1955; faculty Brandeis U., Waltham, Mass., 1955—, prof. physics, 1961—, chmn. dept., 1958-61, 64-65, 74-76, chmn. Sch. Sci., 1963-64, 79-80; vis. prof. M.I.T., 1961-62, 69-70; Distinguished vis. prof. Hebrew U., Jerusalem, 1971-72; vis. fellow Harvard, 1976-78. NSF postdoctoral fellow Cornell U., 1952-54; sr. postdoctoral fellow Carnegie Inst. Tech., 1955. Mem. Am. Phys. Soc., AAAS, Am. Math. Soc., History of Sci. Soc., Phi Beta Kappa, Sigma Xi. Author: Quantum Field Theory, 2d edit., 1961. Home: 22 Turning Mill Rd Lexington MA 02173 Office: Dept Physics Brandeis U Waltham MA 02154

SCHWED, PETER, editor-publisher, author; b. N.Y.C., Jan. 18, 1911; s. Frederick and Bertie (Stiefel) S.; grad. Lawrenceville (N.J.) Sch., 1928; student Princeton, 1929-32; m. Antonia Sanxay Holding, Mar. 6, 1947; children—Katharine Holding (Mrs. Eric F. Wood), Peter Gregory, Laura Sanxay, Roger Eaton. Asst. v.p. Provident Loan Soc. N.Y., 1932-42; with Simon & Schuster, Inc., N.Y.C., 1946—, v.p., exec. editor, 1957-62, exec. v.p., 1962-66, pub. trade books, 1966-72, chmn. editorial bd., 1972—, dir., 1966-72. Trustee Lawrenceville Sch., 1968-72. Served to capt. F.A., AUS, World War II. Decorated Bronze Star, Purple Heart. Mem. Authors Guild, P.E.N. Democrat. Clubs: Century Assn., Princeton (N.Y.C.). Author: Sinister Tennis, 1975; God Bless Pawnbrokers, 1975; The Serve and the Overhead Smash, 1976; Hanging in There, 1977; (with Nancy Lopez) The Education of a Woman Golfer, 1979. Compiler: The Cook Charts, 1949. Editor: (with H.W. Wind) Great Stories From the World of Sports, 1958; (with Allison Danzig) The Fireside Book of Tennis, 1972. Contbr. articles to periodicals. Home: 151 W 86th St New York NY 10024 Office: 1230 Ave of Americas New York NY 10020. *I suppose my guiding principle has been to face up to problems and difficult situations as immediately as I can, even if taking more time to think about them might have resulted in better ideas and actions. But an honest, un-Machiavellian handling of matters, without putting them off while brooding about them, has always struck me as effective when I do it, and appealing when others do. I try to carry this principle through with everyone, from my wife and children, through my office associates, to community affairs. It gives me a reputation ranging from bluntness to rudeness with those whose favorite I may not be, but one of respect and admiration with those about whom I care.*

SCHWEDLER, WILLIAM A., artist; b. Chgo., Mar. 22, 1942; S. Arthur Clarence and Katheryn (Wille) s.; B.F.A., Art Inst. Chgo., 1964; M.F.A., Pratt Inst., Bklyn., 1966. One-man shows: U. R.I., 1969, Pa. State U., 1969, Pyramid Gallery, Washington, 1970, Kornblee Gallery, N.Y.C., 1972, Phyllis Kind Gallery, Chgo., 1973, Andrew Crispo Gallery, N.Y.C., 1975, Alessandra Gallery, N.Y.C., 1976; group shows include: Whitney Mus., N.Y.C., 1970, 72, Art Inst. Chgo., 1972, Indpls. Mus., 1972, Andrew Crispo Gallery, 1973, Alessandra Gallery, 1975; represented in permanent collections: Art Inst. Chgo., Phila. Mus., Whitney Mus., Hirshhorn Mus., Washington, M.I.T. Address: 52 White St New York NY 10013

SCHWEGLER, RAYMOND ALLEN, physician, educator; b. Ottawa, Kans., July 26, 1907; s. Raymond Alfred and Eula Lee (Dunn) S.; A.B., U. Kans., 1926; B.M., U. Minn., 1930, M.D., 1931, Ph.D., 1936; m. Alice J. Wilson, July 1, 1935; children—Raymond Allen, Charles Edwards, David Wilson. Fellow in obstetrics and gynecology U. Minn., Mpls., 1931-34, intern U. Minn. Hosps., Mpls., 1930-31, resident, 1931-35, instr., 1934-35; practice medicine specializing in obstetrics and gynecology, Lawrence, Kans., 1935-42, 46-56; staff physician, cons. in obstetrics and gynecology U. Kans. Student Health Service, Watkins Meml. Hosp., Lawrence, 1958-65, 73—, dir. student health service, 1965-73; instr. obstetrics and gynecology U. Kans., 1935-42, asso., 1946-57, clin. prof., 1957—. Mem. Douglas County Bd. Health, 1969—. Bd. dirs. Watkins Meml. Hosp. Served from capt. to lt. col. M.C., AUS, 1942-46. Fellow A.C.S., Am. Coll. Health Assn., Am. Coll. Obstetrics and Gynecology, Am., Central assns. obstetricians and gynecologists; mem. Kans., Douglas County med. assns., AMA, Sigma Xi, Alpha Omega Alpha, Phi Beta Pi, Alpha Chi Sigma, Phi Sigma. Republican. Episcopalian. Mason (32 deg.). Home: 1504 University Dr Lawrence KS 66044 Office: U Kans Watkins Meml Hosp Lawrence KS 66044

SCHWEGMANN, JACK CARL, aluminum co. exec.; b. Denver, Nov. 4, 1925; s. Leo Benjamin and Agness (Skene) S.; B.S., Tulane U., 1948; M.S., U. Okla., 1950; Ph.D., La. State U., 1953; grad. mgmt. program U. Calif. at Berkeley, 1970; m. Thomas Nanette Taylor, Dec. 27, 1947; children—Gerard Bruce, Michael Carl. With Kaiser Aluminum & Chem. Corp., Oakland, Calif., 1953—, dir. environ. services, metals div., 1967-68, dir. environ. services all corporate divs., 1968—. Served with USAAF, 1944-46. Mem. Research Soc. Am., Am. Inst. Biol. Scientists, AAAS, N.Y. Acad. Scis., Am. Phytopath. Soc., Air Pollution Control Assn., Sigma Xi. Club: Ballena Bay Yacht

(Alameda). Contbr. articles to profl. jours. Home: 2001 Sandcreek Way Alameda CA 94501 Office: 300 Lakeside Dr Oakland CA 94604

SCHWEICKART, RUSSELL L., astronaut, govt. ofcl.; b. Neptune, N.J., Oct. 25, 1935; s. George L. Schweickart; B.S. in Aero. Engring., Mass. Inst. Tech., 1956, M.S. in Aeros. and Astronautics, 1963; m. Clare Grantham Whitfield; children—Vicki Louise, Russell and Randolph (twins), Elin Ashley, Diana Croom. Former research scientist Mass. Inst. Tech. Exptl. Astronomy Lab.; astronaut NASA Manned Spacecraft Center, Houston, lunar module pilot Apollo 9, 1969, dir. user affairs Office of Applications, NASA; now chmn. Calif. Energy Commn.; exec. interchange assignment as asst. for sci. and tech. to gov. State of Calif. Served as pilot USAF, 1956-60, 61. Capt., Mass. Air N.G. Recipient Distinguished Service medal NASA, 1970, De La Vaulx medal FAI, 1970, Spl. Trustees award Nat. Acad. TV Arts and Scis., 1969. Fellow Am. Astronautical Soc.; mem. Soc. Exptl. Test Pilots, AIAA, Sigma Xi. Club: Explorers. Office: 1111 Howe Ave Sacramento CA 95825

SCHWEIKER, MALCOLM ALDERFER, tile co. exec.; b. Skippack, Pa., Feb. 27, 1895; s. George W. and Alice M. (Alderfer) S.; student Williamson Free Sch. Mech. Trades; LL.B., Ursinus Coll.; m. Blanche R. Schultz, Apr. 1920; children—Malcolm Alderfer (dec. World War II), Richard Schultz, Sylvia Schultz (Mrs. William E. Strasburg). Chmn. bd. Am. Olean Tile Co., 1960—; cons. Nat. Gypsum Co., Dallas. Mem. SAR. Republican. Mason. Home: Worcester PA 19490 Office: 1000 Cannon Ave Lansdale PA 19446

SCHWEIKER, RICHARD SCHULTZ, U.S. senator; b. Norristown, Pa., June 1, 1926; s. Malcolm Alderfer and Blanche (Schultz) S.; B.A., Pa. State U., 1950; LL.D. (hon.) Ursinus Coll., 1963, Pa. Med. Coll., 1972, Dickinson Coll., 1972, LaSalle Coll., 1973, Albright Coll., 1973; D.P.S. (hon.), Temple U., 1970; L.H.D., Pa. Coll. Podiatric Medicine, 1973; D.C.L., Widener Coll., 1973; m. Claire Joan Coleman, Sept. 10, 1955; children—Malcolm C., Lani, Kyle, Richard Schultz, Lara Kristi. Bus. exec., 1950-60; mem. 87th-90th Congresses, 13th Dist. Pa., mem. house armed services and govt. ops. coms.; U.S. senator from Pa., 1969—, mem. Appropriations com., Rules and Adminstrn. com., ranking mem. Labor-HEW subcom., ranking mem. Health and Human Resources com. Hon. mem. nat. council Boy Scouts Am.; Bd. dirs. Schwenkfelder Library. Alternate del. Nat. Republican Conv., 1952, 56, del., 1972. Served with USNR, World War II. Named Outstanding Young Man Pa., Jr. C. of C., 1960; recipient Liberty Bell award Pa. Jr. Bar Assn., 1965, JFK Council, K.C. appreciation award, 1966, Bringer of Light award Jewish Nat. Fund, 1971, Daroff Humanitarian award Anti-Defamation League, B'nai B'rith, 1971, Distinguished Alumnus award Pa. State U., 1970, Nat. Soc. Prevention Blindness award, 1974, Dr. Charles H. Best award Am. Diabetes Assn., 1974, Humanitarian award Juvenile Diabetes Found., 1974, Nat. Assn. Mental Health award, 1974, SER award, 1974, Opportunities Industrialization Centers Key award, 1974; Israel Prime Minister's medal, 1974. Mem. V.F.W. (life), Anthrasilicosis League Pa. (hon.), Am. Legion, Navy League, S.A.R., Pa. Soc., Amvets (life), Phi Beta Kappa. Lion, Rotarian (hon.), Kiwanian (hon.), Slumbering Groundhog Lodge (hon.) (Qarryville, Pa.). Office: Senate Office Bldg Washington DC 20510 also 2001 Fed Office Bldg Pittsburgh PA 15222 also 600 Arch St Philadelphia PA 19106 also Fed Office Bldg PO Box 493 Fed Sq Sta Harrisburg PA 17108

SCHWEIKERT, NORMAN CARL, musician; b. Los Angeles, Oct. 8, 1937; s. Carl Albert and Hilda (Meade) S.; Mus.B., performer's certificate in horn, Eastman Sch. Music, 1961; m. Sally Hardin Haizlip, July 22, 1961; 1 son, Eric Carl. Successively 4th, 2d and 3d horn with Rochester Philharmonic, Civic and Eastman-Rochester symphonies, 1955-62, 64-66; instr. horn, mem. Interlochen (Mich.) Arts Quintet, Interlochen Arts Acad., 1966-71; 1st horn Rochester Chamber Orch., 1965-66, Midland (Mich.) Symphony Orch., 1969-71; 1st horn, soloist Northwestern Mich. Symphony Orch., 1966-71, Chgo. Little Symphony, tours 1967, 68; asst. 1st horn, soloist Chgo. Symphony Orch., 1971-75, 2d horn, 1975—; appearances with Eastman Chamber Orch., Rochester Bach Festival, Aspen Festival Orch., Moravian Music Festival, Alaska Festival, Peninsula Music Festival, Rochester Brass Quintet, Canterbury Wind Quintet, Westchester Brass Quintet, Eastman Wind Ensemble; soloist New Japan Philharmonic horn instr. Nat. Music Camp, Interlochen, 1967; teaching asso. Northwestern U., 1973-75, asso. prof. (part-time), 1975—; curator Leland B. Greenleaf Collection Mus. Instruments, Interlochen, 1970-71; rec. artist for Mercury, Columbia, Everest, C.R.I., Capitol. Mark Ednl., London-Decca, DGG, RCA Victor records; recitals, also lecture demonstrations. Served with AUS, 1962-64. Recipient certificate of merit City Chgo., 1971. Mem. Galpin Soc., Internat. Horn Soc. (chmn. organizing com., sec.-treas. 1970-72, mem. adv. council 1972-76), Am. Mus. Instrument Soc., Phi Mu Alpha Sinfonia (life alumni mem.), Pi Kappa Lambda. Contbr. articles to profl. jours. Home: 1340 Golf Ave Highland Park IL 60035 Office: care Chicago Symphony Orch 220 S Michigan Ave Chicago IL 60604

SCHWEIKHER, PAUL, architect; b. Denver, July 28, 1903; s. Frederick and Elisabeth Ann (Williams) S.; student U. Colo., 1921-22; B.F.A. (fellow), Yale U., 1929, M.A. (hon.), 1953; m. Dorothy Miller, Dec. 17, 1923; 1 son, Paul. Practicing architect, 1933—; partner Schweikher & Elting, 1945-53; co-founder Chgo. Workshops, 1933-35; archtl. works exhibited Mus. Modern Art, N.Y.C., Renaissance Soc., U. Chgo., Carnegie Inst. Tech., Akron (Ohio) Art Inst., galleries U. Minn., U. Ill., U. Kans., Yale, Princeton, Ariz. State U., Carnegie Inst. Mus. Fine Arts; vis. critic architecture Yale, 1947, 50-53, chmn. architecture, 1953-56; head dept. architecture Carnegie-Mellon U., 1956-68, now prof. emeritus architecture; vis. prof. Princeton U., 1960-61; vis. critic architecture U. Kans., 1950; lectr. Syracuse U., 1951; 2 one-man exhbns. Harvard, 1968, Yale, 1968. Mem. U. Ill. Conf. Archtl. Edn., 1949; mem. panel Sch. Planning Conf., Nat. Art Edn. Assn., N.Y.C., 1951; mem. Conf. on Edn. in Architecture and the Fine Arts, Carnegie Inst. tech., 1953; mem. jury architecture Fulbright awards Inst. Internat. Edn., 1953-54, fellowships Am. Acad. Rome, 1955; mem. Pitts. Planning Commn., 1961-64. Mem. adv. council Sch. Architecture, Princeton, 1961-69. Served to lt. comdr. USNR, 1942-45. Registered Nat. Council Archtl. Registration Bds., also in 14 states. Recipient Ford Found. research grant in theater design, 1960-61. Mem. Art Inst. Chgo. (life), Chi Psi. Club: Arts (Chgo.). Contbr. articles to profl. publs. Address: Rural Route High Tor Sedona AZ 86336

SCHWEIKLE, CARL FREDERICK, steel co. exec.; b. Williamsport, Pa., June 30, 1928; s. Carl F. and Grace (Stewart) S.; B.S., Bucknell U., 1954; m. Barbara Ann Fite, Apr. 21, 1951; children—Gail, Brett. With Arthur Young & Co., C.P.A.'s, Phila., 1954-57; with Carpenter Tech. Corp., Reading, Pa., 1957—, v.p., 1975—; dir. Nat. Central Bank, Lancaster, Pa. Bd. dirs. Reading Hosp. and Med. Center, Berks County Conservancy. Served with USMC, 1946-48, 50-51. C.P.A., Pa. Mem. Am., Pa. insts. C.P.A.'s, Fin. Execs. Inst., Am. Iron and Steel Inst. (com. accounting, taxation and ins.), Reading-Berks County C. of C. Methodist (fin. com. 1971, audit com. 1971—). Club: Green Valley Country (Reading). Home: 2405 Bresler Dr Reading PA 19609 Office: 101 W Bern St Reading PA 19603

SCHWEITZ, ROBERT EDWIN, journalist; b. Cleve., June 19, 1923; s. Samuel Bernard and Mae (Novick) S.; B.S., Ohio U., 1949; m. Joan Lenore Elswit, Aug. 15, 1948; children—Jonathan, Susan. Photographer, Ellis Studios, Cleve., 1941-43; Sunday editor Mansfield (Ohio) News-Jour., 1949-52; corr. UP, Cleve. Press, 1949-52; asso. editor Civic Edn. Service, Washington, 1952-57; mng. editor Army, Navy, Air Force Register, Washington, 1957-62; def. corr. Army, Navy, Air Force Times, 1962-71; exec. editor Army Times Pub. Co., 1971-73, v.p., editorial dir., 1973—; exec. editor Jour. Newspapers, Inc., Springfield, Va., 1971-73, editorial dir., 1973—. Served with USAAF, 1943-45; ETO. Decorated Air medal with 8 oak leaf clusters. Clubs: Nat. Press (Washington); Army Navy Country (Arlington, Va.). Author newspaper, mag. articles. Home: 3808 Haynsworth Pl Fairfax VA 22031 Office: 475 School St SW Washington DC 20024

SCHWEITZER, GEORGE KEENE, educator; b. Poplar Bluff, Mo., Dec. 5, 1924; s. Francis John and Ruth Elizabeth (Keene) S.; B.A., Central Coll., 1945, Sc.D., 1964; M.S., U. Ill., 1946; M.A. (Faculty fellow 1958-60), Columbia, 1959; Ph.D. in Chemistry, U. Ill., 1948; Ph.D. in Philosophy, N.Y.U., 1964; m. Verna Lee Pratt, June 4, 1948; children—Ruth Anne, Deborah Keene, Eric George. Asst., Central Coll., 1943-45; fellow U. Ill., 1946-48; asst. prof. chemistry U. Tenn., 1948-52, asso. prof., 1952-58, prof., 1960-69, Alumni Distinguished prof. 1970—; cons to Monsanto Co., Proctor & Gamble, Am. Cyanamid Co., AEC, U.S. Army, Massengill; lectr. colls. and univs. Adv. bd. Va. Intermont Coll. Mem. Am. Chem. Soc., Am. Philos. Assn., History Sci. Soc., Phi Beta Kappa, Sigma Xi. Author: Radioactive Tracer Techniques, 1950; The Doctorate, 1966; also articles. Home: 7914 Gleason Rd C-1136 Knoxville TN 37919

SCHWEITZER, GERTRUDE, artist; b. N.Y.C. One-man shows Montclair (N.J.) Art Mus., Washington Water Color Club, Cayuga Mus. History and Art, Auburn, N.Y., Potsdam Gallery Art, Currier Gallery Art, Manchester, N.H., Bevier Gallery, Rochester (N.Y.) Inst. Tech., Erie (Pa.) Pub. Mus., Cortland Library, N.Y.C., Norton Gallery and Sch. Art, West Palm Beach, Fla., Galerie Charpentier, Paris (1st Am.), Hanover Gallery, London, Gallery L'Obelisco, Rome, Galleria Al Cavallion, Venice, Italy, Galleria Il Naviglio, Milan, Italy, High Mus., Atlanta, Worth Av. Gallery, Palm Beach, Fla., Fla. So. Coll., Lakeland, Witte Meml. Mus., San Antonio, Phila. Art Alliance, Hokin Gallery, Palm Beach, Pratt Manhattan Center, N.Y.C., New Britain (Mus.) Am. Art; exhibited Corcoran Gallery, Washington, Art Inst. Chgo., R.I. Sch. Design, Denver Art Mus., Sarasota Art Mus., NAD, N.Y.C., Audubon Soc., N.Y.C., Los Angeles County Fair, U. Minn., U. Ill., Ball State Tchrs. Coll., Muncie, Ind., Newark Art Club, Mus. Art, Santa Fe, N.Mex., Mus. Legion of Honor, San Francisco, Menina, Sicily, 200 Years Am. Watercolors Met. Mus. Art, N.Y.C.; represented in permanent collections Albi Mus., France, Bklyn. Mus., Toledo Mus., Met. Mus. Art, N.Y.C., Walker Art Mus. of Bowdoin Coll., Whitney Mus. of Am. Art, N.Y.C., Mus. of Palm Beaches and Norton Gallery and Sch. Art, West Palm Beach, Montclair Art Mus., Witte Meml. Mus., San Antonio, Atlanta Art Assn. Galleries, Chgo. Art Inst., Mus. Modern Art, Paris, Albi (France) Mus., Hackley Art Gallery, Muskegon, Mich., Davenport (Iowa) Municipal Art Gallery, Canajoharie (N.Y.) Library and Art Gallery, Rochester (N.Y.) Meml. Art Gallery, New Britain Mus. Am. Art, NAD, Neuberger Mus. State U. N.Y., Soc. of Four Arts, Palm Beach, Fla., Mus. N.Mex., also numerous pvt. collections. Served as chmn. arts and skills corps N.Y. chpt. ARC, Ft. Jay Regional Hosp., Governor's Island, N.Y., World War II. Recipient Am. Water Color Soc. medal; Am. Artists Profl. League medal for water color State of N.J.; Phila. Water Color prize Pa. Acad. Fine Arts, 1st prize Norton Gallery and Sch. Art, Soc. Four Arts, Grand Nat. Exhbn., Miami, Fla.; 1st prize, best woman painter N.J. State Exhbn.; N.Y. State award Am. Artists Profl. League, Nat. Arts Club; also Pauline Wick award; 1st prize, medal award Seton Hall U.; 1st Grumbacher Purchase award Audubon 17th Ann. Exhbn., Crumbacher award 27th Ann. Exhbn.; Honor Roll award Am. Artist Profl. League; 27th Ann. N.J. State Exhbn. Eleanor S. Higgins award; Alumni medal Pratt Inst. Mem. Am. Water Color Soc., Fla. Artists Group, Soc. Four Arts (award), Audubon Soc., N.J. Water Color and Sculpture Soc. Home: Stone Hill Farm Colts Neck NJ 07722 also Palm Beach FL 33480

SCHWEITZER, H. GEORGE, lawyer; b. Erie, Pa., Mar. 12, 1927; s. George Herman and Louise Ida (Gove) S.; A.B. in Econs., Tufts Coll., 1949; J.D., George Washington U., 1956; m. Deborah E. Steere, Dec. 22, 1961; children—Hilary Louise, Stacey Gove, Gillian Aldrich. Spl. agt. Gt. Am. Indemnity Co., 1949-56; admitted to D.C. bar, 1956, since practiced in Washington; sr. partner firm Schweitzer & Rabil, and predecessor, 1976—. Served with USNR, 1944-46. Mem. Am., D.C. bar assns., State Bar Va., Am. Judicature Soc., Theta Delta Chi, Delta Theta Phi. Clubs: Congl. Country, Lawyers. Address: 1750 K St NW Washington DC 20006

SCHWEITZER, PETER ALLEN, mktg. exec.; b. Chgo., Aug. 31, 1939; s. John Jacob and Ellen Mae (Boughton) S.; B.A., U. Mich., 1961; M.B.A., Western Mich. U., 1967; m. Nadeen Peterson, Dec. 31, 1977; children by previous marriage—Mark, Cynthia, Jenifer, Samatha. With Post div. Gen. Foods Corp., Battle Creek, Mich., 1961-69; v.p. Grey Advt. Co., N.Y.C., 1969-75; with Walter Thompson Co., N.Y.C., 1975-79, sr. v.p., account dir., 1976-79; sr. v.p. mktg. Burger King Corp., Miami, Fla., 1979—. Club: N.Y. Yacht. Home: 15 W 81st St New York NY 10024

SCHWEITZER, PIERRE-PAUL, banker; b. Strasbourg, France, May 29, 1912; s. Paul and Emma (Munch) S.; grad. univs. Strasbourg and Paris, Ecole Libre des Sciences Politiques; LL.D., Yale U., 1966, Harvard U., 1966, Leeds (Eng.) U., N.Y. U., 1968, George Washington U., 1972, U. Wales, 1972, Williams Coll., 1973; m. Catherine Hatt, Aug. 7, 1941; children—Louis, Juliette. Insp. Finance French Treasury, 1936-47; alternate exec. dir. for France, IMF, 1947-48; sec. gen. Interministerial Com. European Econ. Coop., 1948-49; fin. attache embassy, Washington, 1949-53; dir. treasury Ministry Finance, 1953-60; dep. gov. Bank of France, 1960-63; mng. dir. IMF, 1963-73 also chmn. exec. bd.; hon. inspecteur général des finances, 1974; chmn. bd. Bank Am. Internat. S.A. Luxembourg, 1974-77, Bank Petrofigaz, Paris, 1974-79, Compagnie de Participations et d'Investissements Holding S.A. Luxembourg, 1975—, Société Financière Internationale de Participations, Paris, 1976, Compagnie Monégasque de Banque, Monaco, 1978—; advisory dir. Unilever N.V. Rotterdam; mem. supervisory bd. Robeco Group, Rotterdam, Netherlands. Decorated grand officer Legion of Honour, Croix de Guerre, Medaille de la Resistance. Mem. Am. Philos. Soc. Home: 19 rue de Valois 75001 Paris France Office: Petrofigaz 49 Ave de l'Opéra 75002 Paris France

SCHWEMM, JOHN BUTLER, printing co. exec., lawyer; b. Barrington, Ill., May 18, 1934; s. Earl M. and Eunice (Butler) S.; A.B., Amherst Coll., 1956; J.D., U. Mich., 1959; m. Nancy Lea Prickett, Sept. 7, 1956; children—Catherine Ann, Karen Elizabeth. Admitted to Ill. bar, 1959; with Sidley & Austin, Chgo., 1959-65; with legal dept. R.R. Donnelley & Sons Co., Chgo., 1965-69, gen. counsel, 1969-75, v.p., 1971—, dir. Mattoon Mfg. div., 1975-76, group v.p., 1976—. Bd. dirs. Chgo. Crime Commn., 1970-75; zoning bd. appeals Downers Grove Ill., 1964-66, bd. edn. Downers Grove, 1965-71, plan commn. Downers Grove, 1973-75. Mem. Am., Ill., Chgo. bar assns., Legal Club Chgo., Law Club Chgo., Order of Coif, Phi Beta Kappa. Clubs: Chicago, University (Chgo.); Hinsdale (Ill.) Golf. Home: 2 Turvey Ln Downers Grove IL 60515 Office: 2223 King Dr Chicago IL 60616

SCHWEND, FRED SEATON, petroleum cons.; b. Dallas, Dec. 31, 1916; s. John Monroe and Verna (Seaton) S.; B.S. in Chem. Engring., U. Tex., 1939; advanced mgmt. program Harvard, 1951; m. Lucille Caroline Selby, Dec. 23, 1939; children—Pamela, Susan, Fred, Cathy, Selby. Process engr. Phillips Petroleum Co., 1939-44; prodn. mgr. RFC, Office Rubber Reserve, 1945-46; v.p. Warren Petroleum Corp., Tulsa, 1947-60, sr. v.p., dir., 1960, exec. v.p., chief exec. officer, dir. until 1966; sr. v.p. Gulf Oil Corp., Pitts., 1966-68; pres. Gulf Oil Co.-U.S., Houston, 1968-73, chmn., 1973-75; petroleum cons., 1975—. Clubs: Garden of Gods (Colorado Springs); River Oaks Country, Petroleum, Ramada (Houston). Home: 28 Sugar Berry Circle Houston TX 77024 Office: Suite 1325 1980 1100 S Post Oak Rd Houston TX 77056

SCHWENDEMAN, J(OSEPH) R(AYMOND), geographer; b. Waterford, Ohio, May 11, 1897; s. Francis John and Margaret (Tornes) S.; B.S., Ohio U., 1926; A.M., Clarke U., 1927, Ph.D., 1941; student U. Minn., 1927-28; m. Eithnea O'Donnell, Oct. 12, 1921; children—Elaine, Marion, Gerald, Joseph, Francis, Beth Ann. Part-time instr. U. of Minn., 1927-28; head dept. geography State Tchrs. Coll., Moorhead, Minn., 1928-44; prof. and head dept. geog., U. of Ky., 1944-67, emeritus, 1967—; cons., distinguished prof. geography Eastern Ky. U., Richmond, 1967—; vis. lectr. summers, Columbia, 1927, State Tchrs. Coll., Spearfish, S.D., 1928, Ohio U., 1941, St. John's U., Collegeville, Minn., 1943; worked on preparation of land use suitability maps, atlas and state base maps for state of Ky. Served as instr. USAAC, State Tchrs. Coll., Moorehead, 1943, Recipient citation Am. Assn. Geographers, 1967. Fellow Nat. Council Geography Tchrs.; mem. Cath. Commn. on Intellectual and Cultural Affairs, Ky. Econ. Devel. Bd., Assn. Am. Geographers, AAUP, Ky. Acad. Sci. Roman Catholic. Club: Kiwanis. Author publs. in field; compiler (with Irwin Sanders) Societies Around the World, 2 vols., 1948; rev. 1956; Geography of Kentucky, 5th edit., 1980. Editor, pub. Directory of Coll. Geography of U.S., Vols. 1-18, 1949-67, co-editor Vols., 19-30, 1967—. Filmstrips and manuals: (6) Kentucky: Its Geography and Resources, rev., 1979; Historical Geography of Kentucky Environment and Resource Use, with manual, 1979. Contbr. chpt. Lower Ohio Valley, Regional Geography of North American Mid-west, 1956; World Political Geography; revised geog. section Lincoln Library, 1952 edition. Holder patents and copyrights. Directed student travel groups in Europe, Canada, United States, Mexico; organized and conducted expdn. for study of weather on volcano Orizaba, Mexico, 1949. Inventor Geomatic World Map Projection, 1963. Home: 3512 Greentree Dr Lexington KY 40502. *Personal discipline is the best insurance for a long life of pleasant living.*

SCHWENKE, THOMAS GLENN, lawyer, business exec.; b. Lincoln, Nebr., Oct. 7, 1943; s. Emmett Anthony and Helen Irene (Grimes) S.; A.B., U. Nebr., 1965; J.D. cum laude, Northwestern U., 1968; m. Karen Jane Hansen, Aug. 13, 1966; children—Jonathan Thomas, Margaret Ellen. Admitted to N.Y. State bar, 1969; asso. atty. firm Breed, Abbott & Morgan, N.Y.C., 1968-71; partner firm Schwenke & Devine, N.Y.C., 1971-78; individual practice, 1978—; exec. v.p. Wind Baron Corp. Mem. Am. (mem. sect. corp., banking and bus. law 1975—), N.Y. State bar assns., Assn. Bar City N.Y. (mem. com. profl. and judicial ethics 1973—), Phi Delta Phi, Kappa Sigma. Club: Apawamis (Rye, N.Y.). Home: 1076 Boston Post Rd Rye NY 10580 Office: 15 Elm Pl Rye NY 10580

SCHWENN, LEE WILLIAM, med. center exec.; b. Morrisonville, Wis., Dec. 23, 1925; s. LeRoy William and Vivian Mae (Kramer) S.; B.S., U. Wis., 1948; M.P.H., U. N.C., 1956; m. Glenna Edith Mehne, Jan. 16, 1947; 1 son, William Lee. Tchr. pub. schs., Appleton, Wis., 1948-52; teaching cons. Wis. Health Dept., 1952-53; adminstrv. asst. Madison (Wis.) Health Dept., 1953-57; adminstrv. cons. U.S. Children's Bur., Atlanta Regional Office, 1957-58; adminstr. USPHS, Washington, 1958-66; asso. dir. D.C. Dept. Health, 1966-70, D.C. Dept. Human Resources, 1970-71; exec. v.p. Maimonides Med. Center, Bklyn., 1971—. Recipient Distinguished Pub. Service award D.C. Govt., 1970. Mem. Am. Pub. Health Assn., Am. Acad. Health Adminstrs., Delta Omega. Home: 8 Jeffrey Ln Princeton Junction NJ 08550 Office: 4802 10th Ave Brooklyn NY 11219

SCHWEPPE, ALFRED JOHN, lawyer; b. Brown County, Minn., Mar. 29, 1895; s. Fred Herman and Alwina (Poehler) S.; A.B., Northwestern Coll., Watertown, Wis., 1915; A.B., U. Wis., 1916, M.A., 1917; LL.B., U. Minn., 1922; m. Dorothy Lawrence Greene, June 30, 1922; children—Elizabeth Lawrence, Warren Greene. Part-time instr. in English, U. Wis., 1916-17; tchr. English, New Trier High Sch., Kenilworth, Ill., 1917-18, 1919; part-time instr. in English, U. Minn., 1919-22; admitted to Wash. State bar, 1922; with firm Tanner & Garvin, Seattle, 1922-24; partner firm Long & Schweppe, Seattle, 1924-26; lectr. law U. Wash., 1923-26; dean law sch., also prof. constl. law, 1926-30; partner firm McMicken, Rupp & Schweppe, 1930-62, Schweppe, Reiter, Doolittle & Krug, 1962-66, Schweppe, Doolittle, Krug, Tausend, Beezer & Bieierle, Seattle, 1967—; mem. State Bar Commn., 1933, State Liquor Adv. Commn., 1933, Code Compilation and Revision Com., 1941; exec. sec. Wash. Jud. Council, 1930-57; chmn. Seattle Crime Prevention Commn., 1968-71; mem. Forward Thrust. Served in USN, World War I. Mem. Seattle (exec. sec. 1930-33), Wash. (exec. sec. 1930-33, pres. 1954-55), Alaska, Am. (chmn. com. jud. councils 1938-39, mem. ho. dels. 1948-60, 66-68, mem. com. peace and law 1948-59, 66—, chmn. 1959-58, chmn. com. on bill of rights 1959, 61-64, vice chmn. sect. individual rights 1966—, bd. editors jour. 1949-71, council legal edn. 1949) bar assns., Am. Judicature Soc. (dir. 1949), Iron Wedge, Order of Coif, Phi Delta Phi. Republican. Clubs: Rainier, Seattle Golf, Seattle Tennis. Author: Simkins' Federal Practice, 1934, rev. edit., 1938; West's U.S. Court of Appeals Forms, 1952, 64; contbr. numerous articles to legal and other jours. Office: 1600 Peoples Nat Bank Bldg Seattle WA 98171*

SCHWEPPE, ALFRED JOHN, lawyer; b. Brown County, Minn., Mar. 29, 1895; s. Fred Herman and Alwina (Poehler) S.; A.B., Northwestern Coll., Watertown, Wis., 1915; A.B., U. Wis., 1916, M.A., 1917; LL.B., U. Minn., 1922; m. Dorothy Lawrence Greene, June 30, 1922; children—Elizabeth Lawrence, Warren Greene. Part-time instr. in English, U. Wis., 1916-17; tchr. English, New Trier High Sch., Kenilworth, Ill., 1917-18, 1919; part-time instr. in English, U. Minn., 1919-22; admitted to Wash. State bar, 1922; with firm Tanner & Garvin, Seattle, 1922-24; partner firm Long & Schweppe, Seattle, 1924-26; lectr. law U. Wash., 1923-26, dean law sch., also prof. constl. law, 1926-30; partner firm McMicken, Rupp & Schweppe, 1930-62, Schweppe, Reiter, Doolittle & Krug, 1962-66, Schweppe, Doolittle, Krug, Tausend, Beezer & Bieierle, Seattle, 1967—; mem. State Bar Commn., 1933, State Liquor Adv. Commn., 1933, Code Compilation and Revision Com., 1941; exec. sec. Wash. Jud. Council, 1930-57; chmn. Seattle Crime Prevention Commn., 1968-71; mem. Forward Thrust. Served in USN, World War I. Mem. Seattle (exec. sec. 1930-33), Wash. (exec. sec. 1930-33, pres. 1954-55), Alaska, Am. (chmn. com. jud. councils 1938-39, mem. ho. dels. 1948-60, 66-68, mem. com. peace and law 1948-59, 66—, chmn.

1949-58, chmn. com. on bill of rights 1959, 61-64, vice chmn. sect. individual rights 1966—, bd. editors jour. 1949-71, council legal edn. 1949) bar assns., Am. Judicature Soc. (dir. 1949), Iron Wedge, Order of Coif, Phi Delta Phi. Republican. Clubs: Rainier, Seattle Golf, Seattle Tennis. Author: Simkins' Federal Practice, 1934, rev. edit., 1938; West's U.S. Court of Appeals Forms, 1952, 64; contbr. numerous articles to legal and other jours. Home: 1220 Boren Ave Seattle WA 98101 Office: 1600 Peoples Nat Bank Bldg Seattle WA 98171

SCHWER, GEORGE ALBERT, lawyer; b. Sandusky, Ohio, Dec. 6, 1907; s. George Alfred and Emelia (Ferbach) S.; J.D., Ohio State U., 1930; m. Louise Wuerdeman, Nov. 2, 1932 (dec. May 1978); 1 dau., Louise Anne Rymsha. Admitted to Ohio bar, 1930, since practiced in Springfield; U.S. commr., 1931-42; spl. agt. FBI, 1942-44; mem. bd. commrs. on grievances and discipline Supreme Ct. Ohio, 1957-63, chmn., 1962. Fellow Am., Ohio bar assn. founds; mem. Ohio (past mem. exec. com.), Springfield bar assns., Springfield Area C. of C. (dir., past pres.). Home: 21 E Home Rd Springfield OH 45504 Office: 304 M & M Bldg Springfield OH 45502

SCHWERDT, CARLTON EVERETT, educator, virologist; b. N.Y.C., Jan. 2, 1917; s. Charles Herman and Theresia (Rabe) S.; A.B., Stanford U., 1939, Ph.D., 1946; m. Patricia Buffum Ruth, June 9, 1945; children—Christopher Buffum, Elizabeth Ann, Karen Louise. Asst. prof. biochemistry Johns Hopkins Sch. Hygiene and Pub. Health, 1947-50; research biochemistry Virus Lab., U. Calif. at Berkeley, 1950-56; mem. faculty Stanford U. Sch. Medicine, 1956—, prof. virology, 1961—. Fellow N.Y. Acad. Scis., AAAS; mem. Soc. Exptl. Biology and Medicine (bd. editors proc. 1956-60), Am. Soc. Biol. Chemists, Am. Chem. Soc. Research animal virus purification, chem. and phys. and biol. characterization, polio viruses, pox viruses and rhino viruses; crystallized polio virus with Dr. F.L. Schaffer, 1955. Home: 835 La Jennifer Way Palo Alto CA 94306 Office: Dept Med Microbiology Stanford Univ Stanford CA 94305

SCHWERIN, HORACE S., marketing research exec.; b. N.Y.C., Jan. 18, 1914; s. Paul and Rose (Lewis) S.; B.S., Lafayette Coll., 1935; M.A., Kings Coll., London (Eng.) U., 1936; M.S., U. Paris (France), 1937; m. Lorraine Roth, June 14, 1941 (div. Dec. 1969); children—Barbara, Bruce; m. 2d, Enid May Highton, Apr. 28, 1973. Gen. mgr., research dir., cons. N.Y. advt. agys., 1936-41; pres. Research Analysts, Inc., 1946; chmn. bd. Schwerin Research Corp., N.Y.C., Toronto, London, Hamburg, to 1968; chmn., pres. Horace Schwerin & Assos., Englewood Cliffs, N.J., 1968-72; dir. marketing devel. Campbell Soup Co., 1972—, v.p. market planning Canned Food div., 1977—. Mem. Am. Marketing Assn., Market Research Council. Methodist. Clubs: Metropolitan, Canadian (N.Y.C.). Author articles, booklets on market research. Home: 5-D Toll Gate of Moorestown Moorestown NJ 08057 Office: Campbell Soup Co Campbell Pl Camden NJ 08101

SCHWERT, GEORGE WILLIAM, educator, biochemist; b. Denver, Jan. 27, 1919; s. George William and Agnes (Alford) S.; B.A., summa cum laude, Carleton Coll., 1940; Ph.D., U. Minn., 1943; m. Margaret Houlton, June 25, 1943 (dec. 1975); children—George William, Janet Margaret; m. 2d, Jean Coplin, Nov. 23, 1979. Asst. div. agrl. biochemistry U. Minn., 1941-42, part-time instr., 1942-43; research biochemist Sharp & Dohme, Inc., 1943-44; instr., research asso. biochemistry Duke Sch. Medicine, 1946-48, asst. prof., 1948-52, asso. prof., 1952-57, prof., 1957-59; prof., dept. biochemistry Coll. Medicine, U. Ky., 1959—, dept. chmn., 1959-75; cons., NIH, 1958-62. Mem. biochemistry panel Wooldridge com. Office Sci. and Tech., 1964. Served from ensign to lt. (j.g.), USNR, 1944-46. Mem. Am. Soc. Biol. Chemists, Am. Chem. Soc., AAAS, AAUP, Biochem. Soc. (Gt. Britain), Phi Beta Kappa, Sigma Xi, Phi Lambda Upsilon. Editorial bd. Jour. Biol. Chemistry, 1965-69, 72-77. Contbr. articles to profl. jours. Home: 3316 Braemer Dr Lexington KY 40502

SCHWERTFEGER, FLOYD EDWARD, glass mfg. co. exec.; b. Norfolk, Nebr., May 8, 1915; s. Max Edward and Gladys Olive (Fricke) S.; student Midland Coll., Fremont, Nebr., 1932-33; m. Betty Jane Sanders, June 14, 1938; children—Louise Ann (Mrs. John Jaqua), Robert Edward, Betsy Jane (Mrs. Gareth Davis), Sandra Sue (Mrs. Paul Ansted), Virginia Marie (Mrs. Jerry Steer). With Libbey-Owens-Ford Glass Co., 1936—, mgr. mfg. Eastern plants, co. prodn. mgr., 1961-63, v.p., 1963-70, v.p. glass mfg. operations, 1970-72, v.p., gen. mgr. glass operations, 1972—, also dir., exec. v.p. and pres. glass div., 1975—. Mem. Toledo C. of C. Methodist. Mason (Shriner). Clubs: Toledo, Belmont Country. Home: Eagle Point Colony Rossford OH 43460 Office: 811 Madison Ave Toledo OH 43624

SCHWETMAN, HERBERT DEWITT, educator, physicist; b. Waco, Tex., Aug. 1, 1911; s. Henry William and Camilla Alice (Henderson) S.; B.A., Baylor U., 1932; M.A., U. Tex., 1937, Ph.D., 1952; M.S., Harvard, 1934; m. Mary Jean Knight, July 29, 1939; children—Herbert Dewitt, John William, Rosemary. Tchr. pub. schs., Brucevill-Eddy, Tex., also Waco, 1933-41; instr. electrons, research asso. Harvard, 1941-47; asso. prof. physics Baylor U., 1947-52, prof., chmn. dept., 1952—; sr. nuclear engr., nuclear analysis group Convair, Ft. Worth. Fellow AAAS, Tex. Acad. Sci.; mem. AAUP, Am. Assn. Physics Tchrs. (pres. Tex. br.), Am. Phys. Soc., Am. Inst. Physics, Am. Inst. Radio Engrs., Am. Assn. Coll. Profs., Sigma Xi, Sigma Pi Sigma. Baptist. Contbr. articles on analogue computers to jours. Home: 519 Edgewood Waco TX 76708

SCHWIEBERT, LESLIE NORDEAN, hotel exec.; b. Boise, Idaho, Feb. 8, 1923; s. Ernest George and Emma (Norden) S.; B.A. in Accounting, U. Wash., 1947; children—Margaret Leslie, Elizabeth Anne. Exec. asst. mgr. Schimmel Hotels, Omaha, 1951-53; food and beverage mgr. Eppley Hotels, Omaha, 1953-55, French Lick Sheraton Hotel (Ind.), 1955-59; catering dir. Sheraton-Park Hotel, Washington, 1959-66, resident mgr., 1966-67, v.p., mng. dir., 1967—. Pres. Idaho State Soc., 1968-69; mem. Washington Mayor's Econ. Devel. Com., 1970. Served with USN, 1943-45. Mem. Hotel Assn. Washington (pres. 1970-71, dir. 1968—), Washington Area Conv. and Visitors Assn. (dir.), Am. Hotel and Motel Assn., Zeta Psi. Clubs: Columbia Country (Chevy Chase, Md.); Kiwanis. Home: 2660 Woodley Rd NW Washington DC 20008 Office: Sheraton-Park Hotel 2660 Woodley Rd NW Washington DC 20008

SCHWIER, FREDERICK WARREN, mfg. co. exec.; b. Ft. Wayne, Ind., Sept. 28, 1923; s. Frederick G. and Louise (Kohte) S.; student Mich. State U., 1948-51, Advanced Mgmt. Program, Harvard U., 1978; m. Jean Stadeker, Nov. 7, 1973; children by previous marriage—Frederick D., Francella L. With Aeroquip Corp., Jackson, Mich., 1951—, v.p., gen. mgr. AMB div., 1972-74, exec. v.p., 1974-76, pres., 1976—; exec. v.p. Libbey-Owens-Ford Co., Toledo, 1979—; pres. Aeroquip Corp., 1979—; dir. Nat. Bank Jackson. Chmn. keystone div. United Way campaign, Jackson, 1977; bd. dirs. Jackson Found. Served with C.E., AUS, 1943-46. Mem. Greater Jackson C. of C. (dir. 1977-79), Am. Ordnance Assn., Am. Mgmt. Assn., Mich. Mfrs. Assn. Methodist. Clubs: Jackson Country, Town, Racquet (Jackson). Home: 1052 S Brown St Jackson MI 49203 Office: 811 Madison Ave Toledo OH 43695

SCHWILCK, GENE LEROY, found. adminstr.; b. Corydon, Iowa, Dec. 2, 1925; s. Gerald Alfred and Hazel (Woods) S.; A.B., Knox Coll., 1948; M.S., U. Wis., 1949; Ed.D., Ind. U., 1956; m. Sara Celeste Anderson, June 11, 1950; children—Carol, Cathy. Dir. guidance Park Prep. Sch., Indpls., 1949-55; prin., asst. supt. North Central High Sch., Indpls., 1959-62; supt. Oak Park (Ill.) and River Forest High Sch., 1963-67; v.p. Danforth Found., St. Louis, 1967-73, pres., 1973—; pub. speaker, 1957—. Mem. Council on Edn.; mem. testing com. Coll. Entrance Exam Bd., 1965—; mem. Commn. Equal Edn., Mo. Arts and Edn. Bd., Gov. Mo. Commn. Edn.; sch. bd. Mark Twain and Lakeside schs. Trustee Nat. Merit Scholarship Corp., Ednl. Records Bur., YMCA Bd.; bd. dirs. Resource Devel. Center, Assn. Community Coll. Trustees, Found. Center, Nat. Council on Philanthropy. Served with USAAF, World War II. Recipient Alumni Achievement award Knox Coll., 1965. Mem. Am. Psychol. Assn., Nat. Assn. Secondary Sch. Prins., Nat. Vocat. Guidance Assn., Assn. Supervision and Curriculum Devel., Am. Assn. Sch. Adminstrs., C. of C., Headmasters Assn., Nat. Council Philanthropy, St. Louis Met. Assn. Philanthropy (pres.), Phi Beta Kappa, Delta Sigma Rho, Phi Delta Kappa. Methodist. Contbr. articles ednl. publs. Home: 77 Webster Woods Webster Groves MO 63119 Office: 222 S Central Ave St Louis MO 63105

SCHWIMMER, DAVID, physician; b. Gödényháza, Hungary, Dec. 8, 1913; s. George and Laura (Green) S.; came to U.S., 1921; B.S. cum laude, Lafayette Coll., 1935; M.D., N.Y. U., 1939; M.Med. Sci., N.Y. Med. Coll., 1944; m. Gertrude Alpha Dounn, Nov. 12, 1939; children—Betty Laura, Georgia, Mark Ian. Intern Met. Hosp., N.Y.C., 1939-41, resident, 1942-44; practice medicine specializing in internal medicine, N.Y.C., 1944—; attending physician Flower Fifth Av. Hosp., pres. med. bd., 1970-71; attending physician Met., Bird S. Coler, Doctors, Manhattan Eye, Ear and Throat, St. Luke's, Lenox Hill hosps.; mem. faculty N.Y. Med. Coll., 1944—, clin. prof. medicine, 1966—; cons. internist Monmouth Med. Center, Long Branch, N.J., 1950—. Research fellow, N.Y. Med. Coll., 1944-51, fellow internal medicine, 1941-44. Diplomate Am. Bd. Internal Medicine. Fellow A.C.P., N.Y. Acad. Medicine, N.Y. Acad. Scis., Am. Coll. Angiology, N.Y. Cardiol. Soc.; mem. Endocrine Soc., Harvey Soc., AAAS, AAUP, Am. Soc. Internal Medicine, Royal Soc. Medicine (affiliate), Alpha Omega Alpha. Author: (with Morton Schwimmer) Role of Algae and Plankton in Medicine, 1955. Contbr. profl. jours. Patentee on facial tissue box with self-contained disposal unit for used tissues. Home: 764 Carrol Pl Teaneck NJ 07666 Office: 239 E 79th St New York NY 10021

SCHWIMMER, SAMUEL HAROLD, fin. exec.; b. N.Y.C., Sept. 20, 1948; s. Herman and Fany S.; student in computer sci. (N.Y. State scholar) Pratt Inst., 1969; B.S. with honors, M'Kor Coll., 1970; M.B.A., L.I. U., 1975; m. Hanna Grunfeld, June 18, 1969; children—Sima, Ari, Risa, Pearl. Project mgr. Mobil Oil Corp., 1969-73; corp. officer Citibank, 1973-77; v.p. ops./document processing Am. Express Co., N.Y.C., 1977—; pres. All-Consumer Products Inc., also dir.; cons. Pres., Agudath Israel, 1977-78. Recipient Community Service award, 1978. Mem. Am. Mgmt. Assn. Democrat. Editor Tech. Perspective, 1975-77. Office: 125 Broad St New York NY 10004

SCHWIMMER, WALTER, TV producer; b. Chgo., May 25, 1903; s. Jacob H. and Hermina (Brandt) S.; B.S., Northwestern U., 1924; L.H.D., Lincoln Coll., 1968; m. Daisy Seltzer, Feb. 10, 1927 (dec. Mar. 1945); children—Philip and Bettina Schwimmer; m. 2d, Faye Drucker, Aug. 1, 1958; children—Marcy, Fred. Partner, Schwimmer & Scott, advt., Chgo., 1933-48; pres. Walter Schwimmer, Inc., Chgo., 1948-67; pres. Television Bus., Inc., 1968—; originator for TV, Championship Bowling, 1954, All-Star Golf, 1956, Championship Bridge, 1959, Let's Go to the Races, 1963; creator World Series of Golf, 1962, Nobel Prize Awards program, 1964; Wall St. Jour. Bus. Report, 1979; chmn., TV lectr. series Roosevelt U., Chgo., 1964-67; exec. producer TV spl. I Remember Ill., 1968. Named Man of Year, Acad. TV Arts and Scis., 1964; recipient award Nat. Assn. for Better Radio and TV, 1964. Mem. Nat. Acad. TV Arts and Scis., Phi Epsilon Pi. Clubs: Tavern, Standard (Chgo.); Palm Bay (Miami, Fla.). Author: What Have You Done for Me Lately?, 1957; It Happened on Rush Street, 1971. Home: 1040 Lake Shore Dr Chicago IL 60611 Office: Television Business Inc 400 N Michigan Ave Chicago IL 60611. *Never underestimate the importance of good taste and good manners. If I had to name the most important word in the language, the word would be integrity.*

SCHWINDEN, TED, lt. gov. Mont.; b. Wolf Point, Mont., Aug. 31, 1925; s. Michael James and Mary (Preble) S.; student Mont. Sch. Mines, 1946-47; B.A., U. Mont., 1949, M.A., 1950; postgrad. U. Minn., 1950-54; m. B. Jean Christianson, Dec. 21, 1946; children—Mike, Chrys, Dore. Owner-operator grain farm, Roosevelt County, Mont., 1954—; land commr. State of Mont., 1969-76, lt. gov., 1977—; mem. U.S. Wheat Trade Mission to Asia, 1968. Chmn., Mont. Bicentennial Adv. Council, 1973-76; mem. Mont. Ho. of Reps., 1959, 61, Legis. Council, 1959-61, Wolf Point Sch. Bd., 1966-69, Pub. Employees Retirement System Bd., 1969-74. Served with inf., AUS, 1943-46. Decorated Combat Inf. badge. Mem. Mont. Grain Growers (pres. 1965-67), Western Wheat Assos. (dir.). Democrat. Lutheran. Clubs: Masons; Elks. Home: 1335 Highland St Helena MT 59601 Office: Capitol Sta Helena MT 59601

SCHWING, CHARLES EDWARD, architect; b. Plaquemine, La., Nov. 21, 1929; s. Calvin Kendrick and Mary Howard (Slack) S.; student La. State U., 1947-51; B.S., Ga. Inst. Tech., 1953, B.Architecture, 1954; 3e Assessit de'Architecture, Ecole Des Beaux-Arts; m. Cynthia Benjamin, June 14, 1952 (div. 1967); children—Calvin Kendick III, Therra Cynthia; m. 2d, Geraldine Fleniken Hofmann, Dec. 27, 1969; 1 stepson, Steven Blake. Field insp. Bodman, Murrell and Smith, Baton Rouge, 1954-55; asso. architect Post & Harelson, Baton Rouge, 1955-59; partner Hughes and Schwing, Baton Rouge, 1959-61; owner Charles E. Schwing, Baton Rouge, 1961-69, Charles E. Schwing & Assos., Baton Rouge, 1969—; v.p. Schwing Inc. Fellow AIA (treas., exec. com., dir., planning com., chmn. finance com. 1976-77; treas., exec. com., dir., finance com. research corp. 1976-77; treas., dir. found. 1976-77, v.p. 1978, pres. elect 1979), La. Architect Assn. (sec.-treas. 1971, v.p. 1972, pres. 1973), C. of C., La. State U. Alumni Fedn., Ga. Tech. Alumni Club, Sigma Alpha Epsilon. Episcopalian. Elk. Clubs: Baton Rouge Country, City. Home: 8655 Jefferson Hwy No 12 Stone's Throw Baton Rouge LA 70809 Office: 721 Government St Baton Rouge LA 70802

SCHWINGER, JULIAN, educator, physicist; b. N.Y.C., Feb. 12, 1918; s. Benjamin and Belle (Rosenfeld) S.; A.B., Columbia, 1936, Ph.D., 1939, D.Sc., 1966; D.Sc. (hon.), Purdue U., 1961, Harvard, 1962, Brandeis U., 1973, Gustavus Adolphus Coll., 1975; LL.D., City Coll. N.Y., 1972; m. Clarice Carrol, 1947. NRC fellow, 1939-40; research asso. U. Calif. at Berkeley, 1940-41; instr., then asst. prof. Purdue U., 1941-43; staff mem. Radiation Lab., Mass. Inst. Tech., 1943-46; staff Metall. Lab., U. Chgo., 1943; asso. prof. Harvard, 1945-47, prof., 1947-72, Higgins prof. physics, 1966-72; prof. physics U. Calif. at Los Angeles, 1972—. Mem. bd. sponsors Bull. Atomic Sci.; sponsor Fedn. Am. Scientists; J.W. Gibbs hon. lectr. Am. Math. Soc., 1960. Recipient C. L. Mayer nature of light award, 1949, univ. medal Columbia, 1951, 1st Einstein prize award, 1951; Nat. Medal of Sci. award for physics, 1964; co-recipient Nobel prize in Physics, 1965; Guggenheim fellow, 1970. Mem. Nat. Acad. Scis., Am. Acad. Arts and Scis., Am. Phys. Soc., Civil Liberties Union, A.A.A.S., N.Y. Acad. Scis. Author: Particles and Sources, 1969; (with D. Saxon) Discontinuities in Wave Guides, 1968; Particles, Sources and Fields, 1970, Vol. II, 1973; Quantum Kinematics and Dynamics, 1970. Editor: Quantum Electrodynamics, 1958. Office: Dept Physics U Calif Los Angeles CA 90024*

SCHWINGHAMER, ROBERT JOHN, materials engr.; b. Jasper, Ind., Mar. 12, 1928; s. Robert J. and Eustella (Uebelhor) S.; B.S. in Elec. Engring., Purdue U., 1950; postgrad. U. Ala., Auburn U., U. Mich.; M.S., M.I.T., 1968; m. Constance Gramelspacher, Sept. 16, 1950; children—Bettye Lee, Denise, Antoinette, Robyn. Lead product engr. Sylvania Co., 1950-57; supervisory research engr. Army Ballistic Missile Agy., Dept. Army, 1957-60; sec. br. and div. chief NASA, Marshall Space Flight Center, Huntsville, Ala., 1960-73, dir. Materials and Processes Lab., 1973—. Asso. fellow AIAA. Contbr. articles to profl. jours. Patentee in field. Office: Materials and Processes Lab NASA Marshall Space Flight Center AL 35812

SCHWOEBEL, WILLIAM SYLVESTER, bus. exec.; b. Pitts, May 29, 1912; s. William L. and Anna (Cotter) S.; student U. Pitts.; grad. Advanced Mgmt. Program, Harvard; m. Georgina E. Connell, Dec. 25, 1946 (dec.); m. 2d, Martha L. Bremer, Dec. 10, 1955; children—Ann, Mary. Auditor, Nat. Steel Products Co., Houston, 1939-42; asst. comptroller Nat. Steel Corp., Pitts., 1954-56, controller, 1956-64, v.p., controller, 1964-69, v.p. fin. 1969-72, sr. v.p. fin., 1972-78; chmn. corporate ins. Reins. Co. Ltd., Bermuda, 1978—; vice chmn. Nat. Underground Storage, Inc., Butler, Pa., 1978—. Served to 1st lt. USAAF, 1942-46. Mem. Fin. Execs. Inst., Am. Iron and Steel Inst., Soc. Fin. Analysts, AIM. Clubs: Duquesne, St. Clair Country, Rolling Rock. Home: 737 Pinoak Rd Pittsburgh PA 15243 Office: Grant Bldg Pittsburgh PA 15219

SCIFRES, ROBERT E., corp. exec.; b. Lafayette, Ind., Dec. 5, 1917; s. Clarence Edgar and Bertha Mae (McCord) S.; B.S.E.E., Purdue U., 1938; M.B.A., M.I.T., 1950; m. Claire O'Brien, Sept. 12, 1969; chldren by previous marriage—Linda, Caryl, Cynthia, Dianne, Robert, Michael. With Nat. Gypsum Co., 1942—, plant mgr., Shoals, Ind., 1954-56, prodn. mgr. coastal Gypsum plants, 1956-64, v.p. mfg. Huron Cement div., 1964-67, gen. mgr. Kansas Army Ammunition plant, 1967-70, v.p., asst. to chmn. bd., Buffalo, 1970-71, dir., corp. group v.p., 1972-77, vice chmn. bd., 1977, chmn., chief exec. officer, 1977—; dir. Republic Nat. Bank of Dallas, Mem. Tex. Research League (dir.), Tex. Assn. Bus., Dallas Citizens Council, Dallas C. of C., Conf. Bd. Home: 7103 Spanky Br Dallas TX 75248 Office: 4100 1st International Bldg Dallas TX 75270

SCISSON, SIDNEY E., corp. exec., engr.; b. Danville, Ark., Feb. 4, 1917; s. Eugene and Arvie (Keathley) S.; student Ark. Tech. U., 1934-36; B.S. in Gen. Engring., Okla. State U., 1939; m. Betti Shumaker, Sept. 8, 1942; children—Jane Scisson Grimshaw, Judith Scisson Moore. Civil engr. U.S. C.E., Tulsa, 1939-42; civil engr. Pate Engring. Co., Tulsa, 1945-48; a founder and with Fenix & Scisson, Inc., engring. and constrn. services for govt. and industry, Tulsa, 1948—, formerly pres., now chmn. bd.; dir. Bank of Okla., Atlas Life Ins. Co. Treas.-pres. Tulsa Civic Ballet, 1965. Served with USNR, 1942-45. Named Disting. Alumnus, Okla. State U., Stillwater, Ark. Tech. U., Russellville; registered profl. engr., Ill., Ky., Ohio, Okla., R.I. Mem. Nat. Acad. Engring., AIME, ASCE, Okla. Soc. Civil Engrs., Nat. Soc. Profl. Engrs., Okla. Soc. Profl. Engrs., Am. Gas Assn., Natural Gas Processors Assn., Associated Gen. Contractors Am. Clubs: So. Hills Country; Tulsa, Summit (Tulsa). Home: 2835 E 58th St Tulsa OK 74112 Office: 1401 S Boulder Tulsa OK 74119

SCOBIE, JAMES RALSTON, educator; b. Valparaiso, Chile, June 16, 1929 (parents Am. citizens); s. Jordan Ralston and Freda Otela (Johnson) S.; A.B., Princeton U., 1950; M.A., Harvard U., 1951, Ph.D., 1954; m. Patricia Pearson Beauchamp, Nov. 1, 1957 (dec. 1965); children—William Ralston, Clare Beauchamp; m. 2d, Ingrid Ellen Winther, June 14, 1967; children—Kirsten Winther, Bruce Robert. Instr. history U. Calif. at Berkeley, 1957-59, asst. prof., 1959-62, 63-64; vis. scholar Columbia U., 1962-63; asso. prof. Ind. U., Bloomington, 1964-65, prof. history, 1965-77, dir. Latin Am. studies, 1965-68, chmn. dept. history, 1970-74; prof. history U. Calif. at San Diego, 1977—. Mem. Inst. for Advanced Studies, 1974-75. U.S. nat. rep. History Commn., Pan Am. Inst. Geography and History, 1973-78; Latin Am. adv. com. Council Internat. Exchange of Scholars, 1976-79. Served to 1st lt. AUS, 1954-57. Doherty fellow, 1952-53, OAS fellow, 1959-60, Social Sci. Research Council fellow, 1959-60, 68-69, Rockefeller Found. vis. scholar Columbia, 1962-63; Guggenheim fellow, 1967-68; research grantee Nat. Endowment for Humanities, 1974-76. Mem. Am. Hist. Assn. (mem. Beveridge prize com. 1973-75), Latin Am. Studies Assn., Conf. Latin Am. History (chmn. 1977-78), Phi Beta Kappa. Author: Correspondencia Mitre-Elizalde, 1960; Argentina: A City and a Nation, 1964, 2d edit., 1971; La lucha por la consolidacion de la nacionalidad argentina, 1852-1862, 1964; Three Years in California: William Perkins' Journal of Life at Sonora, 1849-1852, 1964; Revolution on the Pampas: A Social History of Argentine Wheat, 1860-1910, 1964; Buenos Aires: Plaza to Suburb, 1870-1910, 1974. Contbg. and adv. editor Handbook of Latin American Studies, 1966—; adv. editor Latin American Research Rev., 1967-69, 79—; bd. editors Hispanic Am. Hist. Rev., 1966-72, 77—. Office: Dept History U Calif at San Diego La Jolla CA 92093

SCOFIELD, GORDON LLOYD, mech. engr.; b. Huron, S.D., Sept. 29, 1925; s. Perry Lee and Zella (Reese) S.; B.M.E., Purdue U., 1946; M.M.E., U. Mo., Rolla, 1949; Ph.D. in M.E., U. Okla., 1968; m. Nancy Lou Cooney, Dec. 27, 1947; children—Cathy Lynn, Terrence Lee. Instr. mech. engring. S.D. State Coll., Brookings, 1946-47; successively grad. asst., instr., asst. prof., asso. prof., prof. U. Mo., Rolla, 1947-69; prof., head mech. engring.-engring. mechs. dept. Mich. Technol. U., Houghton, 1969—; cons. U.S. Naval Ordnance Test Sta., China Lake, Calif., 1956-71; bd. dirs. Engring. Council Profl. Devel., 1974-76; cons. to industry. Served with USNR, 1943-46. NSF sci. faculty fellow, 1966-67; recipient alumni achievement award U. Mo., Rolla, 1975. Mem. Soc. Automotive Engrs. (pres. 1977), ASME, Am. Soc. Engring. Edn., Am. Inst. Aeros. and Astronautics, Sigma Xi, Tau Beta Pi, Pi Tau Sigma, Phi Kappa Phi. Club: Rotary. Home: 402 Vivian St Houghton MI 49931 Office: Mich Technol U Houghton MI 49931. *Satisfaction comes from sharing achievements. By acknowledging and sharing the importance of others in our success it is possible to accomplish more that is worth remembering.*

SCOFIELD, HENRY HARLAND, dentist; b. Chgo., Mar. 3, 1918; s. Henry Harland and Theresa Mary (McMullin) S.; B.S., Loyola U., 1942, D.D.S., 1945; M.S. in Pathology, Georgetown U., 1952; m. Patricia Jane Doyle, Nov. 24, 1945; 1 dau., Kathleen Ann. Commd. ensign U.S. Navy, 1942, advanced through grades to capt., 1961; dir. Oral Histopathology Center, Naval Grad. Dental Sch., Nat. Naval Med. Center, Bethesda, Md., 1957-63, 66-72; chief dental and oral pathology div. Armed Forces Inst. Pathology, Washington, 1963-66; ret., 1972; asso. prof. oral pathology Georgetown U., 1972-76, prof., chmn. dept. oral pathology, 1976—; cons. Council on Dental Edn.,

Am. Dental Assn. Decorated Navy Meritorious Service medal, Army Commendation medal. Diplomate Am. Bd. Oral Pathology (bd. dirs. 1967, sec.-treas., 1975—). Fellow Am. Coll. Dentists, Am. Acad. Oral Pathology. Contbr. chpts. to textbooks, articles to profl. jours. Home: 10418 Democracy Ln Potomac MD 20854 Office: Sch Dentistry Georgetown U Washington DC 20007

SCOFIELD, MILTON N., lawyer; b. N.Y.C., Aug. 7, 1911; s. Elias and Celia (Neinken) Socolof; A.B., Columbia U., 1932, LL.B. (editor Law Rev.), 1935; m. Nanette Eisler, Sept. 5, 1945; children—Elizabeth M., Anthony L. Admitted to N.Y. bar, 1935; asso. N.Y.C. Law Revision Commn., 1935; with firm Stroock & Stroock, N.Y.C., 1942, 43-45; partner firm Stroock & Stroock & Lavan, 1945—; chief counsel food rationing div. OPA, 1942; cons. rationing to sec. war, 1943; police magistrate, Scarsdale, N.Y., 1961-62. Mem. Am. Bar Assn., Assn. Bar City N.Y., N.Y. County Law Assn. Home: 30 E 62d St New York NY 10021 Office: 61 Broadway New York NY 10006

SCOLES, EUGENE FRANCIS, educator; b. Shelby, Iowa, June 12, 1921; s. Sam S. and Nola Elizabeth (Leslie) S.; A.B., U. Iowa, 1943, J.D., 1945; LL.M., Harvard U., 1949; J.S.D., Columbia U., 1955; m. R. Helen Glawson, Sept. 6, 1942; children—Kathleen E., Janene H. Admitted to Iowa bar, 1945, Ill. bar, 1946; asso. prof. law Northeastern U. Law Sch., 1946-49; prof. law U. Fla. Coll. Law, 1949-56, U. Ill. Coll. Law at Champaign, 1956-68; vis. prof. law U. Khartoum (Sudan), 1964-65; dean U. Oreg. Law Sch., 1968-74, prof. law, 1968—. Reporter, Uniform Probate Code, 1965—; commr. on uniform state laws, 1971—. Fellow Am. Bar Found.; mem. Am., Ill., Lane County bar assns., Am. Law Inst., Soc. Pub. Tchrs. Law, Assn. Am. Law Schs. (pres. 1978). Order of Coif. Author: (with others) Illinois Annotations to the Restatement of Trusts, 2d edit., 1961; (with H.F. Goodrich) Conflict of Laws, 4th edit., 1964; (with E. C. Halbach, Jr.) Problems and Materials on Decedents' Estate and Trusts, 2d edit., 1973; (with R.J. Weintraub) Cases and Materials on Conflict of Laws, 2d edit., 1972; (with E.C. Halbach, Jr.) Problems and Materials on Future Interests, 1977. Home: 1931 Kimberly Dr Eugene OR 97405

SCOLLARD, PATRICK JOHN, ins. co. exec.; b. Chgo., Apr. 20, 1937; s. Patrick J. and Kathleen (Cooney) S.; B.S. in Econs., Marquette U., 1959; grad. sr. exec. devel. program Mass. Inst. Tech., 1976; m. Gloria Ann Carroll, July 1, 1961; children—Kevin, Maureen, Daniel, Thomas, Brian. With Equitable Life Assurance Soc. U.S., N.Y.C., 1962-79, mgmt. trainee, 1962-64, advanced systems analyst, 1964-65, mgr. profl. placement, 1965-67, mgr. salary adminstrn., 1967-68, dir. compensation, 1968-69, asst. v.p., 1969-71, v.p., personnel dir., 1971-75, v.p. adminstrv. services, 1975-78, v.p. corporate adminstrv. and employee sers., 1978—, chmn. benefits com., chmn. savs. bond drive, 1977; sr. v.p. Chem. N.Y. Corp., 1979—. Bd. dirs. Nat. Manpower Inst.; mem. adv. bd. Manhattan Coll., Marquette U.; chmn. task force on compensation N.Y. Mayor's Bus. Adv. Group; guest lectr. in field. Served with USN, 1959-62. Mem. Nat. Assn. Securities Dealers, Am. Mgmt. Assn., Am. Soc. Personnel Adminstrn., Am. Assembly Collegiate Schs. Bus., N.Y. Personnel Mgmt. Assn. Office: 20 Pine St New York NY 10005

SCOMMEGNA, ANTONIO, physician, educator; b. Barletta, Italy, Aug. 26, 1931; s. Francesco Paola and Antonietta (Maresca) S.; B.A., State Lyceum A. Casardi, Barletta, 1947; M.D., U. Bari (Italy), 1953; m. Lillian F. Sinkiewicz, May 3, 1958; children—Paola, Frank, Roger. Came to U.S., 1954, naturalized, 1960. Rotating intern New Eng. Hosp., Boston, 1954-55; resident obstetrics and gynecology Michael Reese Hosp. and Med. Center, Chgo., 1956-59, fellow dept. research human reprodn., 1960-61, research asso., 1961; fellow steroid tng. program Worcester Found. Exptl. Biology, also Clark U., Shrewsbury, Mass., 1964-65; asso. prof. obstetrics and gynecology Chgo. Med. Sch., 1965-69; mem. staff Michael Reese Hosp. and Med. Center, 1961—, attending physician obstetrics and gynecology, 1961—, dir. sect. gynecologic endocrinology, 1965—, dir. ambulatory care obstetrics and gynecology Mandel Clinic, 1968-69, chmn. dept., 1969—, trustee, 1977—; prof. dept. obstetrics and gynecology Pritzker Sch. Medicine, U. Chgo., 1969—. Fulbright fellow, 1954-55. Diplomate Am. Bd. Obstetrics and Gynecology, also sub-bd. endocrinology and reprodn. Fellow Am. Coll. Obstetricians and Gynecologists, Endocrine Soc., Chgo. Inst. Medicine, N.Y. Acad. Scis.; mem. A.M.A., Ill., Chgo. med. socs., Am. Fertility Soc., Chgo. Gynecol. Soc. (sec. 1976—), Soc. Study Reprodn., A.A.A.S., Soc. for Gynecologic Investigation. Author numerous articles in field. Home: 1837 Ellendale Dr Northbrook IL 60062 Office: Michael Reese Hosp 29th St and Ellis Ave Chicago IL 60616

SCOPPETTONE, SANDRA VALERIE, writer; b. Morristown, N.J., June 1, 1936; d. Casimiro Radames and Helen Katherine (Greis) S. Picture books: Suzuki Beane, 1961; Bang Bang You're Dead, 1968; novels: Trying Hard to Hear You, 1974; The Late Great Me, 1976; Some Unknown Person, 1977; Happy Endings Are All Alike, 1978, Such Nice People, 1980. Ludwig Vogelstein grantee, 1974; recipient Eugene O'Neill award, 1972. Home: 131 Prince St New York NY 10012

SCORDELIS, ALEXANDER COSTICAS, civil engr., educator; b. San Francisco, Sept. 27, 1923; s. Philip Kostas and Vasilica (Zois) S.; B.S., U. Calif., Berkeley, 1948; M.S., M.I.T., 1949; m. Georgia Gumas, May 9, 1948; children—Byron, Karen. Structural designer Pacific Gas & Electric Co., San Francisco, 1948; engr. Bechtel Corp., San Francisco, summer 1951, 52, 53, 54; instr. civil engring. U. Calif., Berkeley, 1949-50, asst. prof., 1951-56, asso. prof., 1957-61, prof., 1962—, asst. dean Coll. Engring., 1962-65, vice chmn. div. structural engring, structural mechanics, 1970-73; cons. engring. firms, govt. agys. Served to capt., C.E., U.S. Army, 1943-46; ETO. Decorated Bronze Star, Purple Heart; recipient Western Electric award Am. Soc. Engring. Edn., 1978; Axion award Hellenic Am. Profl. Soc., 1979; registered profl. engr., Calif. Fellow ASCE (Moissieff award 1976), Am. Concrete Inst.; mem. Internat. Assn. Shell and Spatial Structures, Structural Engrs. Assn. Calif., Nat. Acad. Engring. Contbr. articles on analysis and design of complex structural systems, reinforced and prestressed concrete shell and bridge structures to profl. jours. Home: 724 Gelston Pl El Cerrito CA 94530 Office: 729 Davis Hall U Calif Berkeley CA 94720

SCORSESE, MARTIN, film dir., writer; b. Flushing, L.I., N.Y., Nov. 17, 1942; s. Charles and Catherine (Cappa) S.; B.S. in Film Communications, N.Y.U., 1964, M.A. in Film Communications, 1966; m. Laraine Marie Brennan, May 15, 1965; 1 dau., Catherine Terese Glinora Sophia; m. 2d, Julia Cameron; 1 dau., Domenica Elizabeth; m. 3d, Isabella Rossellini, Sept. 29, 1979. Faculty asst., instr. film dept. N.Y.U., 1963-66; instr. film N.Y. U., 1968-70; dir.-writer What's a Nice Girl Like You Doing in a Place Like This?, 1963, It's Not Just You, Murray, 1964, Who's That Knocking At My Door, 1968, The Big Shave, 1967, 68; dir. play The Act, 1977-78; dir.-writer documentaries; supervising editor, asst. dir. Woodstock, 1970; asso. producer, post prodn. supr. Medicine Ball Caravan, 1971, Box Car Bertha, 1972, Mean Streets, 1973; dir. Alice Doesn't Live Here Anymore, 1974, Taxi Driver, 1976, New York, New York, 1977; actor film Cannonball, 1976; actor, dir. film The Last Waltz, 1978. Recipient Edward L. Kingsley Found. award, 1963, 64, 1st prize Rosenthal Found. awards Soc. Cinemetologists, 1964, 1st prize Screen Producer's Guild, 1965, Brown U. Film Festival, 1965, also others. Office: care United Artists 10202 W Washington Blvd Culver City CA 90230*

SCOTESE, PETER G., textile co. exec.; b. Phila., Mar. 13, 1920; s. Peter and Caroline (Mangino) S.; grad. U. Pa., 1942; postgrad. Harvard U., 1960; m. Mildred Marie Heintz, Jan. 24, 1942; children—Jane (Mrs. Raymond Joseph Carey III), James Peter. Sec., accountant A. Greenfield & Co., Phila., 1937-46; terr. salesman, Eastern regional sales mgr., gen. sales mgr. Indian Head Mills, N.Y.C., 1947-54, v.p., gen. mgr. finished goods div., 1954-63; chmn. bd. Milw. Boston Store div. Federated Dept. Stores, Inc., 1963-69; v.p. Federated Dept. Stores, Inc., 1964-69; pres., dir. Springs Mills, Inc., N.Y.C., 1969—, vice-chmn., 1975—, chief exec. officer, 1976—; dir. Armstrong Rubber Co., New Haven, Cooper Industries, Inc., Houston Bell & Howell Co., Chgo. Co-chmn. NAB-JOBS Program, Milw., 1967-68. Trustee Fashion Inst. Tech., N.Y.C.; vice chmn. bus. adv. com. Met. Mus. Art, N.Y.C.; nat. trustee Boys Clubs Am. Served to 1st lt. AUS, 1942-46. Decorated Bronze Star medal, Purple Heart with oak leaf cluster; recipient Alumni award of merit Girard Coll. High Sch., Phila., 1968, Community Service award Wis. Allied Constrn. Employers Assn., 1968. Mem. Am. Mgmt. Assn. (chmn. exec. com., past dir., gen. mgmt. planning council, exec. com., v.p. at large), Am. Fedn. Art, Mus. Modern Art. Clubs: Harvard, N.Y. Yacht, (N.Y.C.); DeVon Yacht (East Hampton, L.I.); Nat. Golf Links (Southhampton, L.I.); Lyford Cay (New Providence, Bahamas). Contbr. chpt. to handbook, articles to mags. and profl. jours. Office: 205 N White St Fort Mill SC 29715

SCOTFORD, DAVID MATTESON, geologist, educator; b. Cleve., Jan. 7, 1921; s. John Ryland and Mable (Matteson) S.; A.B., Dartmouth Coll., 1946; student U. Chgo., 1946-47; Ph.D., Johns Hopkins U., 1950; m. Patricia Taaffe, Sept. 9, 1947; children—Barbara Lynn, David Carlton, Nancy Ellen, Laura Ann. Geologist, N.Y. Geol. Survey, 1946; asst. prof. geology Miami U., Oxford, Ohio, 1950-55, asso. prof., 1955-60, prof., chmn. dept., 1960—; geol. cons. Bear Creek Mining Co., summer 1955; research cons. Shell Devel. Co., summers 1958-60; Fulbright lectr. grantee Ege U., Turkey, 1964-65; research M.T.A., Inst., Ankara, 1965. Del. Internat. Geol. Congress, Copenhagen, 1960, head delegation New Delhi, 1964. Served to 1st lt. USAAF, 1942-45. Research grantee mineral. study Am. Chem. Soc., 1961-63, 69. Fellow Ohio Acad. Sci. (v.p. 1974), Geol. Soc. Am. (mgmt. bd. 1977-80), Mineral. Soc. Am.; mem. AAAS, Sigma Xi. Research on metamorphic petrology. Home: 1029 Cedar Dr Oxford OH 45056

SCOTT, ALASTAIR IAN, educator; b. Glasgow, Scotland, Apr. 10, 1928; s. William and Nell (Newton) S.; B.Sc., Glasgow U., 1949, Ph.D., 1952, D.Sc., 1964; M.A. (hon.), Yale U., 1968; m. Elizabeth Wilson Walters, Mar. 4, 1950; children—William Stewart, Ann Walker. Came to U.S., 1968. Lectr. organic chemistry Glasgow U., 1957-62; prof. U. B.C., Vancouver, 1962-65, Sussex (Eng.) U., 1965-68, Yale, 1968-77; Distinguished prof. Tex. A. and M. U., 1977—; cons. in field. Fellow Royal Soc.; mem. Am. Chem. Soc. (Ernest Guenther award 1976), The Chem. Soc. (Corday-Morgan medal 1964), Biochem. Soc., Swiss Chem. Soc. Author: Interpretations of Ultraviolet Spectra of Natural Products, 1964. Contbr. articles to profl. jours. Office: Chemistry Dept Tex A and M U College Station TX 77843

SCOTT, ALEXANDER ROBINSON, engring. assn. exec.; b. Elizabeth, N.J., June 15, 1941; s. Marvin Chester and Jane (Robinson) S.; B.A. in History, Va. Mil. Inst., 1963; M.A. in Personnel and Counseling Psychology, Rutgers U., 1965; m. Angela Jean Kendall, July 17, 1971; children—Alexander Robinson, Jennifer Angela. Sales mgr. Hilton Hotels, 1967-70; meetings mgr. Am. Inst. Mining Engrs., N.Y.C., 1971-73, exec. dir. Metall. Soc., 1973—. Served with U.S. Army, 1965-67. Decorated Bronze Star. Mem. Am. Soc. Assn. Execs. Republican. Baptist. Home: 107 Staghorn Dr Sewickley PA 15143 Office: PO Box 430 Warrendale PA 15086

SCOTT, ANDREW EDINGTON, educator; b. Newport-on-Tay, Scotland, Apr. 27, 1919; s. John Colville and Edith (Mathers) S.; came to Can., 1950, naturalized, 1955; B.Sc. in Chemistry with honours, U. St. Andrews (Scotland), 1950, Ph.D., 1959; m. Vivien Nelson Weekes, July 27, 1946; 1 dau., Vivien Edith Nelson. Research fellow Ont. Research Found., Toronto, 1950-53, research chemist, 1959-60; research chemist Electric Reduction Co. Can. Ltd., Toronto, 1953-55; lectr. U. Bristol (Eng.), 1960-62; mem. faculty U. Western Ont., London, 1963—, prof. chemistry, head dept., 1965-66, dean Faculty Sci., 1966-79, bd. govs. univ., 1974-78, prof. emeritus, 1979—. Served to capt. Brit. Army, 1939-46. Fellow Canadian Inst. Chemistry. Presbyterian. Club: Univ. (London). Author, patentee in field. Home: 451 Westmount Dr London ON N6K 1X4 Canada Office: Faculty Sci U Western Ont London ON N6A 5B7 Canada

SCOTT, ANTHONY DALTON, economist, educator; b. Vancouver, B.C., Can., Aug. 2, 1923; s. Sydney Dunn and Edith (Dalton) S.; B.A., U. B.C., 1947; M.A. (Univ. scholar), Harvard U., 1949; Ph.D. (Univ. scholar), London Sch. Econs., 1953; m. Barbara Wilson, Dec. 13, 1953; children—Nicholas, Margot. Asst. lectr. London Sch. Econs., 1950; mem. faculty dept. econs. U. B.C., Vancouver, 1953—, prof., 1961—; mem. Royal Commn. on Can.'s Econ. Prospects, 1955-57; commr. Internat. Joint Commn., 1967-71; mem. nat. adv. councilon water resources research, 1966-71; del., cons. Orgn. for Econ. Cooperation and Devel., Paris, 1971-75. Served with Can. Army, 1943-45. Can. Council sr. research fellow, 1959-60; Lilly faculty fellow, 1964-65; Killam fellow, Can. Council, 1972, 74. Fellow Royal Soc. Can.; mem. Am. Econ. Assn. (exec. com. 1966-70), Can. Polit. Sci. Assn. (pres. 1966-67), Am. Assn. Environ. Economists (bd. officers 1975-78, v.p. 1978—), Law of Sea Inst. (exec. bd. 1978—). Author: Natural Resources: The Economics of Conservation, 1955, 2d edit., 1973; (with Albert Breton) The Economic Constitution of Federal States, 1978; contbr. articles to profl. jours.; bd. editors Jour. Environ. Econs. and Mgmt., 1973—, Land Econs., 1969-75, Western Econ. Jour., 1968-71. Office: Dept Econs Univ of BC Vancouver BC Canada

SCOTT, ARNOLD DUANE, investment co. exec.; b. Troy, W.Va., Dec. 16, 1942; s. Russell P. and Geraldine (White) S.; B.A., Alderson-Broaddus Coll., Philippi, W.Va., 1964; LL.B., Rutgers U., 1967; m. Ruth Marie Cottignoli, June 6, 1964; 1 son, Arnold Duane. Admitted to N.J. bar, 1968, D.C. bar, 1968; asso. atty. firm Carpenter, Bennett & Morrissey, Newark, 1968-69; sr. v.p., gen. counsel, sec. Mass. Fin. Services, Boston, 1969—; sec. Mass. Investors Trust. Served with USAF, 1967. Mem. Am., Fed., Boston, D.C. bar assns. Republican. Episcopalian. Address: 200 Berkeley St Boston MA 02116

SCOTT, ARTHUR FERDINAND, chemist, educator; b. Coytesville, N.J., Aug. 14, 1898; s. George John and Carrie (Kerwien) S.; B.S., Colby Coll., 1919, D.Sc. (hon.), 1964; A.M., Harvard, 1921, Ph.D., 1924; student U. Munich, 1922-23; D.Sc. (hon.), Reed Coll., 1973; m. Vera Prásilova, Mar. 19, 1925; children—Kytja (Mrs. John Kemph), Nadia Scott Autrey, Dascha S. Nicholl. Asst. prof. chemistry Reed Coll., Portland, Oreg., 1923-26, prof. chemistry, 1937—, past chmn. dept., past acting pres. coll.; instr. in analytical chemistry Rice Inst., Houston, 1926-37; past dir. Reed Reactor Project; past head spl. projects sci. edn. NSF, Washington, 1962-64. Past chmn. Oreg. Nuclear Devel. Coordinating Com.; past acting pres. Oreg. Grad. Center. Bd. dirs. Learning Resource Center. Served in O.T.C., Plattsburg, N.Y., summer 1918; assigned S.A.T.C., for duration World War I. Recipient award Mfg. Chemists Assn., 1957; Am. Chem. Soc. Petroleum Research Fund study grantee, 1958; Sci. Apparatus Mfrs. award Am. Chem. Soc., 1960; citation Oreg. Acad. Sci., 1962. Mem. Am. Chem. Soc. (ex-councillor), Phi Beta Kappa, Sigma Xi. Editor: Survey of Progress in Chemistry, Vol. 1, 1963, Vol. 2, 1964, Vol. 3, 1966, Vol. 4, 1968, Vol. 5, 1970, Vol. 6, 1973, Vol. 7, 1976, Vol. 8, 1977; contbr. papers to chem. jours. Home: 6608 SE 32d St Portland OR 97202 Office: Reed Coll Portland OR 97202

SCOTT, CAMPBELL, artist; b. Milngavie, Scotland, Oct. 5, 1930; s. Robert and Catherine S.; apprentice woodcarver, Glasgow, Scotland, 1946-51; student Royal Acad. Art, Copenhagen, 1965-66; studies with S.W. Hayter, Paris, 1966. Exhbns. include: 1st Biennial Internat. Graphics, Krakow, Poland, 1966, 1st Brit. Internat. Print Biennale, Eng., 1969, traveling exhbn. Nat. Gallery Can., Ottawa, 1969, 4th Am. Biennial Engraving, Santiago, Chile, Can. Embassy, Washington, 1971, Pratt Inst., N.Y.C., 1971; represented in permanent collections: Brit. Mus., Bibliotheque Nat., Paris, Scottish Nat. Gallery Modern Art, Montreal Mus. Art, Victoria and Albert Mus., London; commd. works include: bronze sculpture Public Library Niagara Falls, Can., wood sculpture Public Library, St. Catharines, Can. Mem. Print and Drawing Council Can. Address: 89 Byron Niagara on the Lake ON L0S 1J0 Canada

SCOTT, CHARLES RAY, fed. judge; b. Adel, Iowa, Jan. 13, 1904; s. Walter E. and Elma (Harrington) S.; J.D., Valparaiso U., 1924; m. Exie Smith, June 17, 1933 (dec. Nov. 1942); children—Barbara Exie Scott Majure, William, Charlene Scott Edwards; m. 2d, Grace Kathryn Stephens, Mar. 21, 1947. Admitted to Ind. bar, 1925, Fla. bar, 1926; asso. and partner Fleming, Hamilton, Diver & Jones, and Fleming, Jones, Scott & Botts, 1926-55; sr. mem. Fleming, Scott & Botts, 1955-57, Scott & Cox, 1957-60; circuit judge 4th Jud. Circuit, 1960-66; U.S. dist. judge Middle Dist. Fla., 1966-76, sr. judge, 1976—; mem. Fla. Bd. Law Examiners, 1954-55; mem. bd. govs. Fla. bar, 1958-61. Fellow Am. Coll. Trial Lawyers; mem. SAR. Presbyterian (elder). Clubs: Masons, Shriners, Jesters; San Jose Country; Nat. Lawyers (Washington); River; Ponte Vedra; Seminole. Home: 829 Mapleton Terr Jacksonville FL 32207 Office: 307 US Courthouse and Post Office Bldg PO Box 660 Jacksonville FL 32201

SCOTT, CHARLES ROSS, business exec.; b. El Paso, Tex., Mar. 2, 1928; s. Patrick H. and Ruth (Ross) S., B.J., U. Tex., 1949; m. Katherine A. Anderson, Aug. 7, 1964; children—Patrick W., Kelly D. Exec. v.p. Southwestern Investors, Inc., Dallas, 1954-55; Southwestern regional mgr. Hugh W. Long & Co., Inc., Elizabeth, N.J., 1955-57; pres. Parker, Ford & Co., Inc., investment bankers, Dallas, 1957-62; pres., chief exec. officer Roberts, Scott & Co., Inc., mems. N.Y. Stock Exchange, San Diego, 1962-70; pres. Intermark Inc., La Jolla, Calif., 1970—; dir. Greater San Diego Sports Assn., pres., 1977; dir. Atlas Hotels, Inc., Topaz Inc., Mission Investment Trust. past mem. Am., N.Y., Pacific Coast stock exchanges, Chgo. Bd. Trade. Vice pres., dir. San Diego Kiwanis Club Found.; asst. treas., former dir. COMBO II. Bd. dirs. Children's Hosp., San Diego, San Diego YMCA, San Diego United Fund, Operation Highline. Mem. San Diego Stock and Bond Club (past pres., dir.), Young Presidents' Orgn. (chmn. 1975-76), San Diego C. of C. (dir.), Holiday Bowl Game Assn. (dir.), Navy League (past dir. San Diego), Alpha Delta Sigma (past pres.). Presbyterian. Club: La Jolla Country (past pres.). Home: 7185 Fairway Rd La Jolla CA 92037 Office: Suite 210 Prospect Center Bldg La Jolla CA 92037

SCOTT, CHARLES WALDO, surgeon; b. Atlanta, Apr. 22, 1916; s. Charles Waldo and Eva Beatrice (Price) S.; B.S., Howard U., 1936, M.S., 1937; M.D., U. Mich., 1941; m. Mae Ernestine Hamlin, July 5, 1942; children—Charles Waldo, Robert Cortez, Jon Llewyn, Valerie Lynn. Intern, resident in surgery Cleve. City Hosp., 1941-44; resident in thoracic surgery Freedmen's Hosp., 1944-45; asst. in thoracic surgery Howard U. Med. Sch., 1945-46, instr. gen. surgery, 1946-48; practice medicine specializing in surgery, Newport News, Va., 1948—; mem. staff Whittaker Meml., Hampton Gen., Mary Immaculate hosps. Mem. Newport News Sch. Bd., 1952-58, 62-66; mem. exec. bd. Peninsula Community Planning Council, 1953-63; bd. dirs. Va. Council on Human Relations, 1955-60; vestryman St. Augustine's Episcopal Ch., 1956-60; chmn. Newport News Econ. Opportunity Com., 1966-67; bd. visitors Va. State Coll., 1964-69, Norfolk State Coll., 1969-75; bd. dirs. Hampton Roads chpt. ARC. Mem. Nat. Med. Assn., Peninsula, Old Dominion med. socs., A.C.S., Omega Psi Phi, Sigma Pi Phi. Home: 914 Shore Dr Newport News VA 23607 Office: 2010 27th St Newport News VA 23607

SCOTT, CHARLEY, univ. ofcl.; b. Meridian, Miss., June 10, 1923; s. James Jack and Alice (Adams) S.; B.S., Miss. State U., 1944; M.S., Ga. Inst. Tech., 1950; Ph.D., Purdue U., 1953; postgrad. U. Mich., 1962-63, Harvard U., 1976; m. Uldine McDonald, Apr. 5, 1947; children—David Keith, Joseph Leigh. Instr. Miss. State U., 1946-47, asst. prof., 1949-51, asso. prof., 1953-56, thermodynamicist Materials Research Center, 1961-63, prof. mech. engring. 1956-63; asst. dean grad. sch. U. Ala., Tuscaloosa, 1963-68, dir. instrn., Huntsville, 1963-66, asso. dean Grad Sch., 1968-72, dean, 1972-76, asst. acad. v.p., 1973-76, asso. acad. v.p., 1976—, prof. mech. engring., 1963-66, 69—, acting dean Grad. Sch. Library Service, 1970-71, acting dir. univ. libraries, 1973; dir. acad. affairs, dir. div. engring. U. Ala. in Huntsville, 1966-68, dir. div. grad. progams, 1968-69, prof. mech. engring., 1966-69; instr. W.Va. U., Morgantown, 1947-48, Meridian Jr. Coll., Miss., 1947; asst. engr. Manhattan Project, Oak Ridge, 1944-46; research engr. Army Ballistic Missle Agy., Huntsville, 1957, 58. Mem. planning com. Tenn. Valley Edn. Center, 1966; v.p. Conf. So. Grad. Schs., 1973-74, pres., 1974-75; mem. exec. com. Southeastern Conf. Intercollegiate Athletics, 1974-77; v.p. Nat. Collegiate Athletic Assn., 1976—, chmn. div. I, 1978—. Bd. dirs. Community Council Huntsville Madison County, 1964-69, Community Council Tuscaloosa County, 1975-77; chmn. edn. div. United Fund of Tuscaloosa County, 1976-77. Served with AUS, 1945-46. Fellow ASME (past state and regional officer); mem. Sigma Xi, Tau Beta Pi, Phi Kappa Phi, Omicron Delta Kappa, Pi Tau Sigma, Sigma Pi Sigma. Home: PO Box 1336 University AL 35486. *I try to recognize that each person is much like a snowflake. Each is present in life an instant in the totality of time. In that instant each must grasp as much of what has happened, use it as a base, and make contributions to the improvement of civilization. Otherwise, a person might as well not have existed.*

SCOTT, DAVID BYTOVETZSKI, dentist, govt. ofcl.; b. Providence, May 8, 1919; A.B., Brown U., 1939; D.D.S., U. Md., 1943; M.S., U. Rochester, 1944; Sc.D. (hon.), Med. and Dental Coll. N.J., 1979; married; 3 children. Staff, Nat. Inst. Dental Research, NIH, Bethesda, Md., 1944-56, chief lab. histology and pathology, 1956-65, dir. Inst., 1976—; faculty Case Western Res. U., Cleve., 1965-76, Thomas J. Hill Distinguished prof. phys. biology Sch. Dentistry, prof. anatomy Sch. Medicine, 1965-76, dean Sch. Dentistry, 1969-76. Mem. ADA, Am. Acad. Forensic Sci., Electron Micros. Soc. Am., Internat., Am. colls. dentists, Internat. Assn. Dental Research, Royal Soc. Medicine (hon.). Recipient Arthur S. Flemming award, 1955; award for Research in Mineralization, Internat. Assn. Dental Research, 1968; Research Achievement award Mass. Dental Soc., 1978; Fred Birnberg Dental Research medal Columbia U., 1978. Office: Nat Inst Dental Research NIH 9000 Rockville Pike Bethesda MD 20014

SCOTT, DAVID C., mfg. co. exec.; b. Akron, Ohio, 1915; grad. U. Ky., 1940, D.Sc. (hon.), 1971. Owner engring. cons. firm Inst. Tech. Research, 1942; exec. Gen. Electric Co., 1945-63, mgr. power tube plant, Schenectady, 1954-60, gen. mgr. cathode ray tube dept., Syracuse, N.Y., 1960-63; v.p. group exec. Colt Industries Inc., 1963-65, exec. v.p., dir., 1965-68; pres. Allis-Chalmers Corp., Milw., 1968-69, chmn. bd., pres., chief exec. officer, 1969—; dir. Am. Can Co., First Wis. Corp., Harris Corp., Humana, Inc., Martin Marietta Corp., Martin Marietta Aluminum Co., Royal Crown Cos., Travelers Corp.; dir., chmn. Siemens-Allis. Mem. adv. council Coll. Engring., U. Ky.; chmn. U.S. sect. Egypt-U.S. Bus. Council; vice chmn. U.S. sect. Sudan-U.S. Bus. Council; bd. dirs. U.S.-USSR Trade and Econ. Council; trustee, mem. The Conf. Bd.; founding mem. Rockefeller U. Council. Mem. C. of C. of U.S. (internat. policy com.), U. Ky. Alumni Assn. (chmn. devel. council). Home: 2100 W Dean Rd River Hills WI 53217 Office: 1205 S 70th St Milwaukee WI 53214

SCOTT, DAVID JANVIER, advt. writer; b. Ft. Huachuca, Ariz., Jan. 8, 1923; s. John F. Reynolds and Mary Newbold (Janvier) S.; A.B. in Architecture, Princeton U., 1947. Exec. v.p. Ogilvy & Mather Inc., N.Y.C., 1976—. Served to capt. U.S. Army, 1942-45, 50-52. Home: 80 Stockton St Princeton NJ 08540 Office: 2 E 48th St New York NY 10017

SCOTT, DAVID R., former astronaut, bus. exec.; b. San Antonio, June 6, 1932; s. Rom. W. Scott; student U. Mich.; B.S., U.S. Mil. Acad., 1594; M.S. in Aeros. and Astronautics, Mass. Inst. Tech., 1962; grad. Air Force Aerospace Research Pilot Sch., Edwards AFB, Calif., 1963; D.Astronautical Sci. (hon.), U. Mich., 1971; m. Ann Lurton Ott; children—Tracy Lee, William Douglas. Joined USAF, 1954, advanced through grades to col.; former dir. NASA Dryden Flight Research Center, Edwards, Calif.; astronaut on flights of Gemini VIII, Mar. 1966, Apollo IX, Mar. 1969, Apollo XV, July 1971; now partner Scott Preyss Assos., technol. cons. firm, Lancaster, Calif. Decorated DFC, DSM; recipient Distinguished Service medal, Exceptional Service medal NASA; Superior Achievement award Manned Spacecraft Center, 1970; Spl. Trustees award Nat. Acad. Television Arts and Scis., 1969, Robert J. Collier award, 1971. Fellow Am. Astronautical Soc.; asso. fellow Am. Inst. Aeros. and Astronautics (Astronautics award 1966); mem. Soc. Exptl. Test Pilots, Sigma Xi, Tau Beta Pi, Sigma Gamma Tau. Office: Scott Preyss Assos 213 E Ave M Lancaster CA 93534*

SCOTT, DONALD ALBERT, educator; b. Campville, N.Y., Nov. 20, 1917; s. Roy C. and Luella (Morgan) S.; A.B., Cornell Coll., 1939; M.S., U. Ariz., 1941; Ph.D., U. Iowa, 1952; m. Dorothy J. LeMahieu, June 22, 1946; children—Mary Jennifer, Rebecca Suzanne. Instr. U. Ariz., 1941-42, Cornell Coll., 1942-43, 46-49; asst. prof. Washington and Jefferson Coll., 1951-54; asso. prof., chmn. dept. Drew U., 1954-57, prof., 1957—, chmn., 1957-71; vis. scholar UCLA, 1960-61. NSF Sci. Faculty fellow, 1960-61. Mem. AAUP, AAAS, Middle Atlantic Assn. Liberal Arts Chem. Tchrs. (pres. 1971), Nat. Sci. Tchrs. Assn., Am. Chem. Soc., Sigma Xi, Phi Lambda Upsilon. Methodist. Author: Textbook for General Chemistry; Laboratory Manual for General Chemistry; Laboratory Manual for Organic Chemistry. Research on natural products, stereochemistry and organic reaction mechanisms. Home: 42 Glenwild Rd Madison NJ 07940

SCOTT, DONALD ALLISON, lawyer; b. Phila., Oct. 7, 1929; s. Garfield and Grace Louise (Nevin) S.; A.B., Princeton U., 1951; J.D., Harvard U., 1956; m. Jeanne Marie Cooper, June 25, 1955; children—Allison Cooper, Andrew Garfield, John Wallace, Lindsay Nevin. Admitted to Pa. bar, 1958; law clk. Judge Learned Hand, U.S. Ct. Appeals, 2d Circuit, 1956-57; asso. firm Morgan, Lewis & Bockius, Phila., 1957-64, partner firm, 1964—; dir., lectr. Pa. Bar Inst. Served with USNR, 1951-53. Mem. Am. Bar Assn., Pa. Bar Assn., Phila. Bar Assn., Am. Law Inst. Republican. Presbyterian. Clubs: Phila. Cricket, Merion Cricket, Union League. Home: 714 W Mt Airy Ave Philadelphia PA 19119 Office: 123 S Broad St Philadelphia PA 19109

SCOTT, DONALD HUNT, assn. exec.; b. Bloomfield, N.J., Oct. 22, 1916; s. Benjamin and Janet (McAlpine) S.; B.S., Rutgers U., 1948; LL.D., Bloomfield Coll., 1969; m. Ruth M. Keating, Dec. 13, 1942; children—Donald Hunt, Dale Heather. Exec. various positions AT&T, N.Y.C., 1935-46; entrepreneur, Bloomfield, 1946-59; mgr. pub. affairs Am. Cyanamid Co., Wayne, N.J., 1959-71; pres. N.J. C. of C., Newark, 1971—. Councilman, Bloomfield, 1948-49, mayor, 1950-60; chmn. bd. trustees Bloomfield Coll., 1960-74. Served to maj. USAAF, 1942-46. Home: 59 Winding Ln Bloomfield NJ 07003 Office: 5 Commerce St Newark NJ 07102

SCOTT, DONALD JOHN, librarian; b. Florence, Cape Breton, N.S., Can., July 17, 1940; s. William Lawson and Jessie Elizabeth (Grainger) S.; B.A., Mt. Allison U., 1963; B.L.S., McGill U., 1964; m. Jeanette Anne Poole, July 16, 1966; children—Peter William, Jeffrey Michael. Asst. librarian Confedn. Centre Library, Charlottetown, P.E.I., Can., 1964-66; asst. dir. NERLS, Kirkland Lake, Ont., Can., 1966-68; librarian Econ. Improvement Corp., Charlottetown, 1968-69; librarian Confedn. Centre Library, Charlottetown, 1969-70; provincial librarian P.E.I. Dept. Edn., Charlottetown, 1970—. Mem. Atlantic Provinces Library Assn., (past pres.), Can. Library Assn. Mem. United Ch. Can. Contbr. articles to profl. jours. Home: Tea Hill Crescent Charlottetown Rural Route 1 PE CIA 7J6 Canada Office: University Ave Charlottetown PE CIA 7N9 Canada

SCOTT, DONALD RECTOR, educator; b. Hagaman, N.Y., May 21, 1905; s. Charles Willard and Jessie Catherine (Rector) S.; A.B., Gettysburg Coll., 1928; M.A., Syracuse U., 1937; Ph.D., Cornell U., 1947; m. Vivian Ellis, Aug. 6, 1949; 1 son, David Nelson. Tchr., sch. adminstr. N.Y. State pub. schs., 1932-45; research N.Y. State Dept. Edn., 1945-47; mem. faculty edn. Iowa State Tchrs. Coll., 1947-54; tech. dir. edn. Inst. Inter-Am. Affairs, Quito, Ecuador, 1950-52; edn. adviser Egyptian-Am. rural improvement service ICA, Cairo, Egypt, 1954-56; provincial chief educationist (Cyrenaica), ICA, Benghazi, Libya, 1956-58; secondary edn. specialist ICA, Washington, 1958-60; chief ednl. adviser, Mogadiscia, Somalia, 1960-62; dep. chief ednl. advisor Addis Ababa, Ethiopia, 1962-63; dep. chief edn. adviser, Blantyre, Malawi, 1963-65; secondary and higher edn. adviser Tegucigalpa, Honduras, 1965-68; edn. cons., lectr., 1968—; internat. edn. cons. So. Ill. U., 1970-75; vis. lectr. sociology Am. U. Cairo, 1955-56. Mem. N.Y. State Com. Sch. Dist. Reorgn., 1943-47; chmn. Iowa com. White House Conf. Children and Youth, 1950; ICA rep. White House Conf. on Children and Youth, 1960; mem. Calif. Republican State Central Com. Recipient Meritorious Service citation ICA, 1960. Mem. Fgn. Service Assn., DACOR, Phi Kappa Phi, Phi Delta Kappa, Lambda Chi Alpha. Club: Dacor House (Washington). Mason, Kiwanian. Author: Implementing the Educational Program in Intermediate Districts; co-author The Intermediate District in N.Y. State. Home: Route 2 Box 1232 Smith River CA 95567

SCOTT, DONALD STRONG, educator; b. Edmonton, Alta., Can., Dec. 17, 1922; s. Robert James and Clara Regina (Allen) S.; B.Sc., U. Alta., 1944, M.Sc., 1946; Ph.D., U. Ill., 1949; m. Dorothy Phyllis Hensel, May 17, 1945; children—Garry Alexander Donald, Jillian Demaris Clare. Petroleum engr. Imperial Oil Ltd., N.W.T., Can., 1944-45; research engr. Nat. Research Council Can., Ottawa, Ont., 1946-47; asst. prof. U. B.C., Vancouver, 1949-55, asso. prof., 1955-64; prof., chmn. dept. chem. engring. U. Waterloo (Ont.), 1964-69, dean Engring., 1969-70, prof., 1970—. Shell vis. prof. U. Cambridge (Eng.), 1963-64; Sci. Research Council sr. fellow U.K., 1971; recipient Centennial medal Canada, 1967; Silver Jubilee medal, 1977. Registered profl. engr. Ont. Fellow Chem. Inst. Can., Am. Inst. Chem. Engrs.; mem. Canadian Soc. Chem. Engrs. (pres., 1971-72), Am. Chem. Soc., Am. Inst. Mining and Metall. Engrs., Sigma Xi, Delta Upsilon. Author: Cocurrent Gas-Liquid Flow, 1970; The Technical Entrepreneur, 1979; editorial bd. Canadian Jour. Chem. Engrs., 1966-74. Contbr. articles to profl. jours. Home: 382 Arden Pl Waterloo ON Canada

SCOTT, EDGAR, investment broker; b. Am. Embassy, Paris, France, Jan. 11, 1899; s. Edgar and Mary Howard (Sturgis) S.; student Groton Sch.; A.B. cum laude, Harvard U., 1920, grad. study playwriting, 1920-22; m. Helen Hope Montgomery, Sept. 20, 1923; children—Edgar, Robert Montgomery. Newspaper reporter, freelance writer, 1925-28; founder, mem. Janney Montgomery Scott Inc., and predecessor (mems. N.Y. Stock Exchange), Phila. and N.Y.C., 1929—. Gov. N.Y. Stock Exchange, 1940-45; pres. Phila. Stock Exchange, 1942-46; gov. Phila.-Baltimore Exchange, 1932-51. Mem. bd. commrs. Radnor Twp., Delaware Co., Pa., 1934-48, pres. bd., 1946-47. Dir. Independence Found., Phila., 1955-76; hon. dir. Bryn Mawr Hosp.; past dir., past pres. World Affairs Council Phila.; bd. dirs. Edwin Forrest Home, 1949-58, pres., 1958-75. Clubs: Philadelphia, Merion Cricket, Racquet, Urban (Phila.); The Brook, River (N.Y.C.). Author: How to Lay a Nest Egg, Financial Facts of Life for the Average Girl, 1950. Home: 245 Abraham's Ln Villanova PA 19085 Office: 5 Penn Center Plaza Philadelphia PA 19103 also 26 Broadway New York NY 10004

SCOTT, EDWARD WALTER, clergyman; b. Edmonton, Alta., Can., Apr. 30, 1919; B.A., U. B.C.; L.Th., Theol. Coll., Vancouver, 1942; m. Isabel Florence Brannan; children—Maureen (Mrs. Peter Harris), Patricia Anne (Mrs. Paul Robinson), Douglas, Elizabeth Jean. Rector, St. Peters, Seal Cove, Prince Rupert, B.C., 1942-45; gen. sec. Student Christian Movement, U. Man., 1945-49; also part-time lectr. St. Johns Coll.; rector Ch. of St. John the Baptist, Fort Garry, 1949-55, St. Jude's, Winnipeg, 1955-60; named dir. social service and priest-dir. Indian work Diocese of Ruperts Land, 1960; helped establish first Indian-Metis Friendship Center; joined staff Ch.'s nat. hdqrs., Toronto, 1964; consecrated bishop of Kootenay, 1966; primate Anglican Ch. of Can., 1971—; moderator central com. World Council Chs., 1975—. Address: 600 Jarvis St Toronto ON M4Y 2J6 Canada

SCOTT, EDWARD WILLIAM, JR., govt. ofcl.; b. Panama City, Panama, May 25, 1938; s. Edward William and Janice Gertrude (Grimison) S.; B.A., Mich. State U. (univ. scholar 1957-60), 1959, M.A., 1963; B.A., Oxford (Eng.) U., 1962; children—Edward William, Heather Yolanda Deirdre. Personnel specialist Panama Canal Co., 1962-64, staff asst. to dir. personnel, 1964-66; personnel officer IRS, Detroit, 1966-68; staff personnel mgmt. specialist U.S. Dept. Justice, Washington, 1968-69, chief personnel systems and evaluation sect., 1970-72, dir. Office Mgmt. Programs, 1972-74, asso. dep. commr. planning and evaluation U.S. Immigration and Naturalization Service, 1974-75, dep. asst. atty. gen. adminstrn., 1972-75; asst. sec. for adminstrn. Transp. Dept., 1977—. Pres., U.S. Dept. Justice Fed. Credit Union, 1970-73. Recipient Presdl. Mgmt. Improvement certificate, 1971; Spl. Commendation award Dept. Justice, 1973, also Spl. Achievement award, 1976, William A. Jump Meml. award, 1974. Mem. Phi Eta Sigma, Phi Kappa Phi. Democrat.

SCOTT, FRANK LAURENCE, oil well drilling equipment co. fin. exec.; b. Tex., July 27, 1915; s. Willie Gifford and Mary (Danek) S.; grad. in accounting U. Houston, 1934-38; m. Florine Elizabeth Bean, July 3, 1936; children—Sheila Rae, Frank Laurence. With Baker Internat. Corp., Orange, Calif., 1937—, mgr. materials and purchases, 1950-63, treas., 1964—, v.p., 1978—. Served with USCG, 1943-49. Home: 724 Arbolado Dr Fullerton CA 92635 Office: PO Box 5500 Orange CA 92667

SCOTT, FREDERICK ISADORE, JR., editor, business exec.; b. Balt., Oct. 27, 1927; s. Frederick Isadore and Rebecca Esther (Waller) S.; B.E. in Chem. Engring., Johns Hopkins, 1950; M.S. in Mgmt. Engring., Newark Coll. Engring., 1956; m. Viola Fowlkes, Feb. 4, 1949. Chem. process engr. in research and devel. RCA, Harrison, N.J., 1951-59; with Kearfott div. Gen. Precision Aerospace, Little Falls, N.J., 1960-62; asst. sales mgr. Isotopes, Inc., Westwood, N.J., 1964-66; mgr. capacitor sect. Wellington Electronics, Inc., Englewood, N.J., 1967-68; owner F.I. Scott & Assos., med. equipment, Montclair, N.J., 1968—; editor instrumentation publ. Am. tech. product mktg. and editorial services, Check, Va., 1968—. Served with AUS, 1946-47. Mem. Am. Chem. Soc. (sr.), I.E.E.E. (editor newsletter No. N.J. sect. 1957-58, chmn. publs. com. 1958-59). Home: Route 1 Box 51-B Check VA 24072 Office: PO Box 86 Check VA 24072. *Perhaps the most significant aspect of my life is a long-felt realization that each person is ultimately responsible for his or her condition in life. Application of this principle continually requires that the individual assess a failure in such a way as to determine how his or her actions might have avoided it or, if unavoidable, how its recurrence can be obviated. Accepting responsibility in this manner can, I believe, lead the way toward a society based on a federation of autonomous individuals delegating authority to units of government when appropriate but clearly retaining the capability to recall that delegated authority should it be abused.*

SCOTT, GARY KUPER, educator; b. Jefferson City, Mo., Jan. 3, 1933; s. Ralph Elmer and Lillian Rachel (Kuper) S.; A.A., Jefferson City Jr. Coll., 1953; B.Ed., Western Wash. State Coll., 1960, M.Ed., 1962; Ph.D., U. Minn., 1965; m. Paddy Joyce Hanna, June 13, 1958; children—Tina Marie, Lisa René, Corey Kuper. Dir. student counseling center Minot (N.D.) State Coll., 1965-67; faculty, head dept. psychology Lincoln U., Jefferson City, 1967-77, chmn. dept. edn. and psychology, 1979—. Pres., Cole County Mental Health Assn., 1969-70. Bd. dirs. YMCA. Mem. Cole County Democratic Com., 1968-70. Mem. Am., Mo. psychol. assns. Club: Rotary. Home: 1002 Roseridge Circle Jefferson City MO 65101

SCOTT, GEORGE CAMPBELL, actor, dir.; b. Wise, Va., Oct. 18, 1927; student U. Mo., 1950; m. Trish Van Devere, 1972. Actor stock cos., 1950-57; N.Y.C. debut as Richard III, Shakespeare Festival, 1957; stage appearances include: As You Like It, 1958, Children of Darkness, 1958, Antony and Cleopatra, 1959, Merchant of Venice, 1960, 62, The Wall, 1960, Desire Under the Elms, 1963, Plaza Suite, 1968, Uncle Vanya, 1973, Andersonville Trial, 1959, Comes a Day, 1958; co-founder Theatre of Mich. Co., Inc., 1961, produced Great Day in the Morning, 1962; dir., played title role General Seeger, 1962; dir. All God's Chillun Got Wings, 1975; actor, dir. Death of a Salesman, 1975, Sly Fox, 1976; films include: The Hanging Tree, 1959, Anatomy of a Murder, 1959, The Hustler, 1961, The List of Adrian Messenger, 1963, Dr. Strangelove, 1964, The Bible, 1966, Flim-Flam Man, 1967, Patton, 1970, The Hospital, 1971, The Last Run, 1971, They Might Be Giants, 1971, The New Centurions, 1972, The Day of the Dolphin, 1973, Oklahoma Crude, 1973, Jane Eyre, The Hindenburg, 1975, Beauty and the Beast, 1976, Islands in the Stream, 1977, Crossed Swords, 1978, Movie, Movie, 1978, Hardcore, 1979; actor, dir. Rage, 1972; dir., actor, producer The Savage is Loose, 1974; TV appearances include: Kraft Mystery Theater, Omnibus, Playhouse 90, Play of Week, Hallmark Hall of Fame, others; dir. The Andersonville Trial (Emmy award); star TV series East Side/West Side, 1963. Served with USMC, 1945-49. Recipient Clarence Derwent award, 1958; Vernon Rice award, 1958; Theatre World award, 1958; Obie award Village Voice, 1958, 63; Golden Globe, 1970; refused Oscar for film Patton, 1971; Emmy for The Price, 1971. Mem. Actors Equity Assn., Screen Actors Guild, AFTRA, Dirs. Guild Am., Soc. Stage Dirs. and Choreographers. Address: care Jane Deacy Agy 119 E 54th St New York City NY 10022*

SCOTT, GEORGE ERNEST, publisher; b. Detroit, Sept. 12, 1924; s. George Ernest and Ruth Janet (Moffett) S.; student U. Detroit, 1946-47, Woodbury Coll., Los Angeles, 1947-48; m. Lois Aurlie Brown, Mar. 28, 1953. With advt. prodn. dept. D.P. Brother Advt., Detroit, 1947-49, Ruthrauff & Ryan Advt., Detroit, 1950-51; advt. account exec. Betteridge & Co. Advt., Detroit, 1951-53; founder, 1954, pub., pres. Scott Advt. & Pub. Co., Livonia, Mich.; owner, pub. Ceramic Arts & Crafts mag., 1955—, Ceramic Teaching Projects and Trade News, quar., 1965—. Served with USNR, 1942-46. Mem. Nat. Ceramic Mfrs. Assn. (past dir.), Mich. Ceramic Dealers Assn. (past pres.). Club: Coral Ridge Country (Ft. Lauderdale, Fla.). Home: 3251 W Shore Dr Orchard Lake MI 48033

SCOTT, GEORGE MATTHEW, judge; b. Clark, N.J., Sept. 14, 1922; s. Francis Patrick and Harriet Ann (O'Donnell) S.; B.S., U. Minn.; J.D., William Mitchell Coll. Law; m. Joyce E. Hughes, July 26, 1947; children—Dan, Neil, Brian, George Matthew, Sheila. Admitted to Minn. bar; practice law, 1951-55; dep. atty. gen. State of Minn., 1955; atty. Hennepin County, Mpls., 1955-73; justice Minn. Supreme Ct., St. Paul, 1973—. Trustee William Mitchell Coll. Del. Democratic Nat. Conv., 1960; campaign chmn. Hubert H. Humphrey for Senator, 1960. Served with AUS, 1942-45. Mem. Am., Minn. bar assns., Nat. Dist. Atty's. Assn. (pres. 1964-65), Am. Legion. Roman Catholic. Club: Optimists. Contbr. articles to profl. jours. Office: 228 Minnesota State Capitol Saint Paul MN 55155*

SCOTT, GEORGE TAYLOR, scientist, educator; b. Stillwater, N.Y., Sept. 10, 1914; s. Robert Winfield and Helen Denison (Taylor) S.; B.S., Union Coll., 1938; A.M., Harvard, 1941, Ph.D., 1943; m. Elsie Mae Welling, Oct. 16, 1943; children—Helen Ann, Georganne Elsie. Austin teaching fellow Harvard, 1940-43; instr. zoology Oberlin Coll., 1943-45, asst. prof., 1945-49, asso. prof., 1949-52, prof., 1952—, chmn. dept. biology, 1956-67; asso. scientist Woods Hole Oceanographic Inst., 1954-59. Trustee Bermuda Biol. Sta. for Research, 1955—, pres., 1967-77; trustee Marine Biol. Lab., 1956-73. Fellow AAAS, Ohio, N.Y. acads. sci.; mem. Am. Soc. Zoologists, Soc. Gen. Physiologists, AAUP, Corp. Marine Biol. Lab., Sigma Xi, Theta Nu Epsilon, Gamma Alpha. Contbr. articles to profl. jours. Home: 111 Forest St Oberlin OH 44074

SCOTT, GERALD EDWARDS, fin. cons.; b. W.Va., Nov. 8, 1925; s. W. E. and M. M. Scott; B.B.A., Fenn Coll., 1951; LL.B. magna cum laude, Cleve.-Marshall Law Sch., 1955; m. Emelia I. Krakowiecki, Apr. 17, 1945; children—Gerald Edwards, Deborah Jo. Admitted to Ohio bar; cost. acct., budget dir. Reliance Electric Co., Cleve., 1951-53; public acct. Peat Marwick Mitchell, Haskin & Sells, Cleve., 1953-55; controller subs. Curtis(-Wright Corp., Cleve., 1955-60; individual practice law, practice acctg., Cleve., 1955-60; v.p. fin. Microdot, Inc., Conn., 1960-70, 75-78; practice law, cons. bus., Canton, Ohio, 1970-74; cons. fin. Ingredient Tech. Corp., N.Y.C., 1978—; dir., cons. R.U.R. Industries, Northeast, Pa.; partner Scott-Webb and Assos., Cons., Holmes Beach, Fla. Served in USAAF, 1943-46. C.P.A., Ohio. Mem. Stark County Bar Assn., Am. Inst. C.P.A.'s. Office: 245 Park Ave New York NY 10003

SCOTT, HAROLD BARTLETT, JR., bus. exec.; b. Tarrytown, N.Y., July 11, 1917; s. Harold Bartlett and Mabel (Brace) S.; attended Yale U., 1939; m. Jane Russell, Sept., 1974; children—Jane, Susan, Judy, Audrey, Anne, Harold Bartlett. Vice pres. internat. Charles Pfizer & Co., 1949-52; pres. Harold B. Scott, Inc., 1953-69, now chmn. bd., N.Y.C.; dir. Bur. Internat. Commerce, Dept. Commerce, 1969-71, asst. sec. for domestic and internat. bus., 1971-72; pres. U.S.-USSR Trade and Econ. Council, 1973-78; now chmn. bd., dir. Syracuse Supply Co. (N.Y.); dir. A-T-O, Givaudan, Houbigant. Bd. dirs. U.S.-USSR Trade and Econ. Council. Served with USN, 1942-45. Mem. Council Fgn. Relations, Fgn. Policy Assn., Pilgrim Soc. Clubs: Univ., N.Y.C., Union, Yale (N.Y.C.); Everglades (Palm Beach, Fla.). Office: 675 Third Ave New York NY 10017

SCOTT, HENRY L., concert pianist-humorist; b. Tivoli on Hudson, N.Y., Jan. 20, 1908; s. Walter and Mary Wigram (Keeney) S.; student Syracuse (N.Y.) U., class 1930; L.H.D., Bard Coll., Annandale, N.Y., 1964; m. Mary Bell Bard, Aug. 28, 1938; children—Barbara Bell, Henry Lawrence. Teaching and radio, screen, stage and TV work, 1931-41; concert work throughout U.S., 1939—; debut Town Hall, 1941, Carnegie Hall, 1945-46; 27 transcontinental concert tours, Carnegie Hall, N.Y.C. (2), Town Hall, N.Y.C. (2), Detroit Town Hall, Kansas City Town Hall, West Point Mil. Academy (12), Akron Concert Course, Fine Arts Series, Worcester, U. Minn. (8), U. Tex. (3), U. Notre Dame (2), Miss Porters Sch., Conn. (2), St. Mark's Sch., Southborough, Mass. (5), So. Ill. U. (10), USAF Acad., 1960, Mt. Mary Coll., Milw., Emanuel Missionary Coll., Mich., Pacific Union Coll., Calif., U. So. Calif., Amherst (Mass.) U., Dartmouth, Purdue U., U. N.C., U. Oreg., Med. Coll. Va., Union Coll., Lincoln, Nebr., U. N.Mex., others, also Woman's Inst., Knoxville Friday Morning Musicales, Syracuse, Meml. Auditorium, Lowell, Mass., Eaton Auditorium, Toronto, Met. Opera House, N.Y.C., U. Wash., U. Utah, U. Fla. (3), U. Ga., Artists Series, San Diego, U. N.C. (3), North-Western State Coll. (7), 6th tour Can., 1966-67, Hawaiian Islands, Saudi Arabia, 1963; guest artist various orchs. and symphonies; indsl. concerts for General Electric Co., Eastman Kodak, IBM Corp., others, 1958-61; pioneer concert humor; now presenting humorous and ednl. lecture recitals in schs., colls., univs. and concert halls; head Henry Scott Sch. Modern Piano, N.Y.C.; mem. faculty Champlin Sch., 1940-42; pres., chmn. bd. Solo Theater of Am. Corp., 1948; producer, star, Concerto for Fun, 1949; introduced Fun at the Philharmonic, 1952; asst. to pres. Bard Coll., Annandale-on-Hudson, 1966; guest appearance TV show Be Our Guest, 1960. Mem. bd. trustees Bard Coll., Annandale, N.Y., 1953-63, Crow Hill Sch., Rhinebeck, N.Y., 1969—, Charleston Symphony Orch., 1971-75; trustee Charleston Concert Assn., 1971-78, pres., 1979—; founder, chmn. Stockholder Advocate Found., 1975—, Stockholder Adv. Assn., Inc., 1976—; investment adv. Johnson Lane Space and Smith, 1978—. Mem. Am. Platform Guild, S.A.R., English Speaking Union (pres. Charleston 1977—), Internat. Platform Assn., Hudson River Conservation Soc., Nat. Trust Historic Preservation, Rhinebeck, Dutchess County hist. socs., Navy League Charleston, Charleston Preservation Soc. Republican. Episcopalian. Clubs: Carolina Yacht Charleston Tennis, Charleston, Old Town (Charleston); Beach House (pres. 1979-80) (Sullivan's Island, S.C.); Town Hall, University, (N.Y.C.); Edgewood (bd. govs. 1961-63, v.p. 1962-63) (Tivoli, N.Y.); Sea Island Yacht. Inventor Technic Mittens for piano practice. Composer: Musical Racetrack, The Little Upright Piano, The Christmas Party, Clavichord Joe. Home: 34 Smith St Charleston SC 29401. *Fulfillment in life comes from serving and giving. My most frequent prayer is "Lord help me to be a better husband, father and friend."*

SCOTT, HENRY WILLIAM, JR., educator, surgeon; b. Graham, N.C., Aug. 22, 1916; s. Henry William and Claire (Turner) S.; A.B., U. N.C., 1937; M.D., Harvard, 1941; D.Sc., U. Aberdeen, 1976; m. Mary Louisa Vanamee, Oct. 17, 1942; children—Henry William III, Mary Elizabeth, Virginia Wright, Patricia Vanamee. Intern Peter Bent Brigham, Children's hosps., Boston, 1941-43, resident surgery Children's Hosp., 1943-45; Harvey Cushing fellow neurosurgery, 1945-46, resident surgeon Johns Hopkins Hosp., 1946-47; from instr. to asso. prof. surgery Johns Hopkins Med. Sch., 1947-51; prof. surgery, head dept. Vanderbilt U. Sch. Medicine, 1952—, dir. surg. scis., 1975—; surgeon in chief Vanderbilt U. Hosp., 1952—; clin. prof. surgery Meharry Med. Sch., 1970—. Mem. surg. study sect. USPHS, 1961-65, chmn., 1966-70; cons. USPHS. Diplomate Am. Bd. Surgery (mem. bd. 1956-62, vice chmn. 1961-62). Fellow A.C.S. (gov. 1965-67, treas. 1967-72, regent 1972-75, pres. 1975-76, pres. Tenn. chpt. 1968-69), Royal Australasian Coll. Surgeons (hon.), Swedish Surg. Soc. (hon.); mem. Am. Gastroent. Soc., Soc. Vascular Surgery, Am. Assn. Thoracic Surgery, Internat. Soc. Surgery (sec. N.Am. chpt. 1967-74, v.p. 1979), Internat. Surg. Group, Am. Geriatrics Soc., Am. (treas. 1958-65, pres. 1973-74), So. (pres. 1976-77) surg. assns., Nashville Surg. Soc. (pres. 1964), Soc. U. Surgeons (pres. 1960-61), Soc. Clin. Surgery (pres. 1970-72), Internat. Soc. Cardiovascular Surgery, Soc. Surgery Alimentary Tract (pres. 1970-71), Pan Pacific Surg. Assn. (pres. 1980— Surg. Biology Club, AMA, So. Med. Assn., Halsted Soc. (pres. 1968-70), Am. Trauma Soc., James IV Surg. Assn. (v.p. 1978-79), Phi Beta Kappa, Phi Delta Theta, Nu Sigma Nu, Alpha Omega Alpha. Clubs: Belle Meade Country; Nashville; La Mirador Country; Mont Pelerin; Lac Léman (Switzerland). Editorial bd. Current Problems in Surgery. Home: 1050 Tyne Blvd Nashville TN 37220 Office: Vanderbilt U Hosp Nashville TN 37203

SCOTT, HOMER VERNON, tax and business cons.; b. Elizabethtown, Ky., Feb. 3, 1902; s. Evan Bailey and Effie Agnes (Franklin) S.; ed. pub. schs.; m. Anita Perazzi, Feb. 15, 1922 (div. 1944); children—Homer Vernon, Patricia (Mrs. Elmer Jones), Jean (Mrs. William R. Sims); m. 2d, Susan Hughey, Mar. 8, 1946. Dir. finance Calif. C. of C., 1926-39, Cal. Festival Assn., 1934-39; brought Max Reinhardt to U.S., staged Midsummer Night's Dream in Hollywood, 1934; financial cons. Ohio C. of C., 1939-44, Ind. C. of C., 1941-50, E. Tex. C. of C., 1940-43; organizer Nat. Tax. Equality Assn., 1943, pres., 1962-75, chmn. adv. com., 1975—; organized Nat. Asso. Businessmen, 1946, v.p., 1959-67, pres., 1968-75, chmn. adv. com., 1975—; prin. H. Vernon Scott, cons., Washington, 1971—. Served with U.S. Navy, 1918-20. Club: Eldorado Country (Calif.). Home: 76-421 Fairway Dr Indian Wells CA 92260 Office: 1000 Connecticut Ave NW Washington DC 20036

SCOTT, HUGH, former U.S. senator; b. Fredericksburg, Va., Nov. 11, 1900; s. Hugh D. and Jane Lee (Lewis) S.; A.B., Randolph-Macon Coll., 1919, LL.D., 1955; student U. Pa., 1917; LL.B., U. Va., 1922; L.H.D., La Salle U., 1955; LL.D., Dickinson Coll., 1959, Temple U., 1959, Ursinus Coll., 1960, Phila. Textile Inst., 1960, Washington and Jefferson Coll., 1961, Lebanon Valley Coll., 1962, Lincoln U., 1963, Westminster Coll., 1964, U. Pa., 1966, Waynesburg Coll., 1966, Franklin and Marshall Coll., 1966, Lehigh U., 1968, Albright Coll., 1969, Hanover Coll., 1969, Hahnemann Med. Coll. and Hosp., 1969, Gettysburg Coll., 1970, Drexel U., 1970, Lafayette U., 1971, Dropsie U., 1971, York Coll. of Pa., 1972, William Jewell Coll., 1976; D.Pub. Adminstrn., Suffolk U., 1959; Litt.D., Phila. Coll. Osteopathy, 1960; D.Sc., Delaware Valley Coll., 1963; D.C.L., Susquehanna U., 1966, Union Coll., 1967; L.H.D., Thomas Jefferson U., 1970, Hebrew Union Coll., 1973; m. Marian Huntington Chase, Apr. 12, 1924; 1 dau., Marian Scott Concannon. Admitted to Va. bar, 1921, Pa. bar, 1922; practiced in Phila.; counsel firm Obermayer, Rebmann, Maxwell & Hippel; asst. dist. atty., Philadelphia County, 1926-41; mem. 77th-78th, 79th-85th congresses, 6th Dist. Pa., mem. policy com.; mem. U.S. Senate from Pa., 1959-77, Republican minority leader, 1969-77, mem. coms. on fgn. relations, judiciary, rules, adminstrn., minority policy com. Civil War Centennial Commn.; vice chmn. Senate Commn. Art and Antiquities. Vice chmn. U.S. del. Interparliamentary Union. Mem. bd. visitors Naval Acad., 1948, U. Va., 1971-79; bd. regents Smithsonian Instn., chmn. com. Freer Gallery; bd. regents USCG Acad., 1963; chmn. bd. visitors Mcht. Marine Acad., 1959; bd. dirs. Georgetown Center Strategic Studies; trustee Randolph-Macon Coll.; mem. Oriental art com. Phila. Museum Art; chmn. Youth for Understanding; mem. Bd. Fgn. Scholarships, 1977-79. Chmn., Rep. Nat. Com., 1948-49; chmn. regional orgn. com. Eisenhower campaign, 1952, chmn. Eisenhower hdqrs. com., mem. rules com., 1954, gen. counsel Nat. Com., 1955-60. Served in U.S. Navy, World War II; from lt. to capt. USNR. Recipient Annual Fgn. Trade award Phila. Fgn. Traders Assn., 1944, Greater Phila. mag. 50th Ann. award, Pa. Assn. Broadcasters' award, 1963, also numerous Man of the Year awards chambers commerce, service, press, vets. orgns.; Distinguished Pennsylvanian of Yr. award Pa. Soc., 1973; decorated comdr. Royal Order of Phoenix (Greece); grand cross Order of El Quetzal (Guatemala), Order of Merit 1st Class (Korea). Hon. fellow Am. Bar Found.; mem. Am., Pa., Phila. bar assns., Am. Legion, VFW, Amvets, Friendly Sons St. Patrick, Pa. Soc. (N.Y.), Chinese Art Soc. Am., S.R., Alpha Chi Rho (nat. pres. 1942-46), Phi Beta Kappa, Tau Kappa Alpha, Phi Alpha Delta, Alpha Zeta. Episcopalian. Clubs: Cricket (Phila.); Lions (Germantown); Kiwanis (hon.). Author: Scott on Bailments, 1931; How to Go into Politics, 1949; The Golden Age of Chinese Art: The Lively T'ang Dynasty, 1967; Come To The Party, 1968; How To Run for Public Office and Win, 1968; (co-author) Politics, U.S.A., 1960. Home: 3014 Woodland Dr NW Washington DC also 765 Germantown Pike Lafayette Hills PA Office: 2011 I St NW Suite 500 Washington DC 20006

SCOTT, IRA OSCAR, JR., orgn. adminstr.; b. Winfield, Kans., Dec. 13, 1918; s. Ira Oscar and Kathryn (Haney) S.; A.B., U. Kans., 1940, M.A. in Polit. Sci., 1941; M.A. in Econs., Harvard, 1951, Ph.D., 1953; m. Rethel Richmond, May 16, 1964; children—Christine Stephanie, Ira Oscar III. Instr. U. Kans., 1947-49; teaching fellow, then instr. Harvard, 1949-55; asst. prof., then asso. prof. U. Minn., 1955-57; asso. prof. N.Y. U., 1957-58, Columbia, 1958-66; prof., dean Arthur T. Roth Grad. Sch. Bus. Adminstrn., 1966-70; pres. Savs. Banks Assn. N.Y. State, N.Y.C., 1970—; Fulbright prof. U. Uppsala (Sweden), 1960-61, Johns Hopkins Bologna (Italy) Center, 1964-65; cons. in field, 1951—. Served with USAAF, 1942-46. Guggenheim fellow, 1960-61; NSF grantee, 1964-65; Merrill Found. Advancement Financial Knowledge grantee, 1956-57. Mem. Am. Assn. U. Profs., Am. Econ. Assn., Am. Finance Assn., Nat. Assn. Bus. Economists, Phi Beta Kappa. Author: Government Securities Market, 1965; European Capital Markets, 1968; also articles. Home: 5 Bowden Ln Glen Head NY 11545 Office: Savings Bank Assn NY State 200 Park Ave New York NY 10017

SCOTT, IRENE FEAGIN, U.S. judge; b. Union Springs, Ala., Oct. 6, 1912; d. Arthur H. and Irene (Peach) Feagin; A.B., U. Ala., 1932, LL.B., 1936, LL.D., 1978; LL.M., Catholic U. Am., 1939; m. Thomas Jefferson Scott, Dec. 27, 1939; children—Thomas Jefferson, Irene (Mrs. Franklin L. Carroll III). Law librarian U. Ala. Law Sch., 1932-34; admitted to Ala. bar, 1936; atty. Office Chief Counsel, Internal Revenue Service, 1937-50, mem. excess profits tax council, 1950-52, spl. asst. to head appeals div. Office Chief Counsel, 1952-59, staff asst. to chief counsel, 1959-60; judge U.S. Tax Ct., 1960—. Mem. Ala. Bar, Am., Fed., D.C. (hon.) bar assns., Nat. Assn. Women Lawyers, Nat. Lawyers Club, Kappa Delta, Kappa Beta Pi. Office: US Tax Ct 400 2d St NW Washington DC 20217

SCOTT, ISADORE MEYER, energy co. exec.; b. Wilcoe, W.Va., Nov. 21, 1912; s. David and Libby (Roston) S.; A.B., W.Va. U., 1934, M.A., 1938; J.D., Washington and Lee U., 1937; m. Joan Rosenwald, Feb. 14, 1943; children—Betsy Scott Kleeblatt, Peggy, Jonathan D. Admitted to Va. bar, 1937; practiced law, Richmond, Va., 1937-38; v.p. Lee I. Robinson Hosiery Mills. Phila., 1938-42; with Winner Mfg. Co., Inc., Trenton, 1947-61, v.p., 1947-51, pres., 1951-61; chmn. bd. Tri-Instl. Facilities, Inc., Phila., 1962-78; chmn. bd. TOSCO Corp., Los Angeles, 1978—, also dir.; dir. Am. Stores Co., Girard Bank and Co., Sci. Am., Inc., Starwood Corp., Western Sav. Fund Soc. Phila., Univ. City Assos., Inc. Bd. dirs. S.E. Pa. chpt. ARC; dir. Internat. Rescue Com.; bd. dirs., mem. exec. com. Greater Phila. Partnership, Phila. Mus. Art, Univ. City Sci. Center, Phila.; mem. Phila. Com. Fgn. Relations; trustee Washington and Lee U.; asso. trustee U. Pa. Served with inf. U.S. Army, 1942-46; NATOUSA, ETO. Decorated Legion of Merit, Silver Star, Purple Heart, Bronze Star (U.S.); Crown of Italy; medal of merit (Czechoslovakia); Mentioned-in-dispatches (Eng.). Mem. Phila. Bar Assn., Va. State Bar, Phi Beta Kappa, Omicron Delta Kappa. Republican. Jewish. Clubs: Union League, Phila., Gulph Mills Golf, Philmont Country, Anglers of Phila., Masons. Home: 1050 Dale Rd Meadowbrook PA 19046 Office: 3236 PSFS Bldg 12 S 12th St Philadelphia PA 19107

SCOTT, JACK ALAN, community coll. pres.; b. Sweetwater, Tex., Aug. 24, 1933; s. William Hopkins and Ethelda (Cravy) S.; B.A., Abilene Christian U., Abilene, Tex., 1954; M.Div., Yale U., 1962; M.A. (Danforth Found. Tchr.'s grantee 1966-68), Claremont (Calif.) Grad. Sch., 1967, Ph.D. (Haynes Found. fellow 1969), 1970; m. Lacreta Isbell, Sept. 2, 1954; children—Sharon Mitchell, Sheila, Amy Schones, Gregory, Adam. Asso. prof. history and religion, then provost and dean Pepperdine U., Los Angeles, 1962-73, bd. regents, 1975—; dean instr. Orange Coast Coll., Costa Mesa, Calif., 1973-78; pres. Cypress (Calif.) Coll., 1978—. Bd. dirs., v.p. Orange County chpt. Am. Heart Assn., 1979—; mem. Calif. Employment Services Bd., 1972-75, Calif. Commn. Crime Control and Violence Prevention, 1980—, Orange County Industry-Edn. Council. Recipient Am. History prize Soc. Colonial Dames, 1968. Mem. Am. Assn. Higher Edn., Am. Hist. Assn., Assn. Calif. Community Coll. Adminstrs. Democrat. Club: Cypress Rotary. Editor: An Annotated Edition of Witherspoon's Lectures on Moral Philosophy, 1979. Home: 1084 Corona Ln Costa Mesa CA 92626 Office: 9200 Valley View St Cypress CA 90630

SCOTT, JAMES CAMPBELL, educator; b. Mt. Holly, N.J., Dec. 2, 1936; s. Parry Mason and Augusta Butterworth (Campbell) S.; B.A., Williams Coll., 1958; Ph.D., Yale U., 1967; m. Louise Glover Goehring, Sept. 2, 1961; children—Mia Louise, Aaron Parry, Noah Raymond. Asst. prof. polit. sci. U. Wis., 1968-70, asso. prof., 1970-72, prof., 1972-76; prof. Yale U., 1976—. Nat. Endowment for the Humanities grantee, 1975; NSF grantee, 1973-74. Mem. Am. Polit. Sci. Assn., Asian Studies Assn., Com. Concerned Asian Scholars. Quaker. Author: Political Ideology in Malaysia, 1968; Comparative Political Corruption, 1971; Moral Economy of the Peasant, 1976. Home: Maiden Ln Durham CT 06422 Office: Dept Polit Sci Yale U New Haven CT 06520

SCOTT, JAMES HERNANDEZ, naval officer; b. Jasper, Ala., Jan. 1, 1927; s. Winfield A. and Olga Louise (Hernandez) S.; B.S., U.S. Naval Acad., 1949; postgrad. U.S. Navy Postgrad. Sch., 1957-58, Naval War Coll., 1966-67; m. Nina Jean Seevers, Oct. 25, 1952; children—Nina Jean Scott Mulkey, James Hernandez, Marguerite Louise. Commd. ensign, U.S. Navy, 1949, advanced through grades to rear adm., 1975; flight tng., 1949-51; designated naval aviator, 1950; exchange pilot to Royal Navy, 1953-54; various squadron assignments, 1951-53, 61-66; naval air tng. instr., 1954-57; with Office of Chief of Naval Ops., 1967-68, 70-72; comdr. Airwing 21, 1969-70; comdg. officer U.S.S. Butte, 1972-73; staff comdr. Naval Air Atlantic, 1973-74; comdg. officer U.S.S. Forrestal, 1974-75; comdr. Tactical Wings Atlantic, Virginia Beach, Va., 1975-77; comdr. Iberian Atlantic area, Oeiras, Portugal, 1977—. Decorated Legion of Merit (3), D.F.C., Bronze Star, 5 Air Medals, 2 Navy Commendation Medals, Meritorious Unit Commendation, others. Mem. Assn. Naval Aviation, U.S. Naval Acad. Alumni Assn., U.S. Naval Inst., Naval Res. Assn., Nat. Trust for Hist. Preservation. Methodist. Home: Alto da Luz Av de Sintra Abuxarda Cascais Portugal Office: Commander Iberian Atlantic Area APO New York NY 09678

SCOTT, JAMES WHITE, journalist; b. Lebanon, Kans., Feb. 22, 1926; s. James Malcolm and Bernice (White) S.; B.J., U. Kans., 1950; m. Sammy Peete, June 9, 1950; children—James Peete, Thomas Whiteford, Edward English. Reporter, Kansas City (Mo.) Times, 1950-54; editorial writer Kansas City (Mo.) Star, 1954—, nat. affairs writer, arts and entertainment cons. editor, 1968-77; editor editorial pages Star and Times, 1977—. Served with AUS, 1944-46; ETO. Mem. Sigma Delta Chi, Delta Upsilon. Episcopalian. Home: 5337 Mission Rd Shawnee Mission KS 66205 Office: Kansas City Star Kansas City MO 64108

SCOTT, JEROME HAYES, banker; b. Kensington, Kans., Oct. 26, 1922; s. Jerome Hawthorne and Edith Weeks (Hayes) S.; B.S. in Econs., U. Pa., 1943; m. Elizabeth Ess, Apr. 22, 1950; children—Deborah, Jerome, Elizabeth, Barbara, Robert. Automotive dealer, Kansas City, Mo., 1947-67; pres. Jerry Scott, Inc., Kansas City, Mo., Scott Leasing Co., Kansas City, Mo., 1957-67; pres. United Mo. Bank of Kansas City, 1971—; sec., dir. United Mo. Bancshares, Inc., Kansas City, 1969—. Treas. bd. govs. Kansas City Art Inst.; past pres. Kansas City area council Boy Scouts of Am., 1971-72; dir. Kansas City Mayor's Corps of Progress. Bd. dirs. Kansas City Mus. History and Sci., Heart of Am. United Way, Heart of Am. council Boy Scouts Am.; treas. bd. govs. Am. Royal Assn.; bd. govs. Friends of Art. Served with USNR. Mem. C. of C. of Greater Kansas City (treas., dir.). Clubs: River, Kansas City Country, Kansas City, Saddle and Sirloin (Kansas City, Mo.). Office: 10th & Grand Sts Kansas City MO 64141*

SCOTT, JESSIE M., govt. ofcl.; b. Wilkes-Barre, Pa.; d. Chester A. and Eva M. (Snyder) S.; nursing diploma Wilkes-Barre Gen. Hosp. Sch. Nursing, 1936; B.S., U. Pa., 1943; M.A., Columbia U., 1949; D.Sc., Boston U., 1975, U. Nebr., 1975, Tex. Christian U., 1976, Rush U., 1976, U. N.C., 1976, Ball State U., 1978; L.H.D., Southeastern Mass. U., 1972, Coll. Misericordia, 1977; LL.D., Russell Sage Coll., 1979, Thomas Jefferson U., 1979. Former instr. Jefferson Med. Coll., U. Pa., Phila., St. Luke's Hosp., N.Y.C.; past ednl. dir. Mt. Sinai Hosp., Phila.; commd. officer USPHS, 1955, advanced through grades to rear adm., successively nurse cons., dep. chief, now dir. div. nursing; dir. Bur. Health Manpower, Health Resources Adminstrn. (formerly NIH); asst. surgeon gen. USPHS. Bd. dirs. COGFNS, Phila.; bd. overseers U. Pa. Recipient Meritorious service medal, D.S.M., USPHS; Sesquicentennial award Ind. U. Sch. Nursing; Mary Adelaide Nutting award; R. Louise McManus award Columbia U.; U. Evansville medal of Honor; Distinguished Alumni award U. Pa.; Florence Nightingale medal State U. N.Y. Mem. Am. (honorary recognition), Pa. (past asst. exec. sec. Phila., award for distinguished service to nursing) nurses assns., Internat. Council Nurses (chmn. profl. services com.), Nat. League Nursing (chmn., mem. awards com., rep. to joint com. Am. Hosp. Assn.), Am. Pub. Health Assn. (spl. bd. trustees com. on nursing), Commd. Officers Assn. (exec. com.), History Nursing Archives Assn. Boston U., Western Soc. Research in Nursing, Sigma Theta Tau (hon). Home: PO Box 501 McLean VA 22101 Office: 3700 East West Hwy Hyattsville MD 20782

SCOTT, JOAN WALLACH, historian; b. Bklyn., Dec. 18, 1941; d. Samuel and Lottie (Tannenbaum) Wallach; B.A., Brandeis U., 1962; M.A., U. Wis., Madison, 1964, Ph.D., 1969; m. Donald M. Scott, Jan. 30, 1965; children—Anthony Oliver, Elizabeth Rose. Asst. prof. history U. Ill., Chgo., 1970-72; asst. prof. Northwestern U., 1972-74; asso. prof. U. N.C., Chapel Hill, 1974-77, prof., 1977-80; Nancy Duke Lewis prof. history Brown U., 1980—; dir. Nat. Endowment for Humanities Summer Seminar for Coll. Tchrs., 1977; mem. Inst. for Advanced Study, Princeton, N.J., 1978-79, Social Sci. Research Council research tng. fellow, 1966-68; Nat. Endowment for Humanities fellow, 1975-76. Mem. Am. Hist. Assn. (chmn. com. on women historians 1978—), Social Sci. History Assn., Soc. French Hist. Studies. Author: The Glassworkers of Carmaux, 1974 (Am. Hist. Assn. Herbert Baxter Adams prize 1974), (with Louise Tilly) Women Work and Family, 1978. Office: Dept History Brown U Providence RI 02912

SCOTT, JOHN ALDEN, newspaper found. exec.; b. Litchfield, Conn., Mar. 11, 1916; s. Alden John and Jennie Eugenia (Wheeler) S.; A.B., U. Notre Dame, 1938; postgrad. Ind. U., Purdue U.; m. Patricia Jean Myers, Dec. 1, 1945; children—Sally Jean (Mrs. Larry Ogden), Susan Jane (Mrs. Jerry Burns), Steven Carl, John A. With South Bend (Ind.) Tribune, 1950, Elkhart (Ind.) Truth, 1957-62; pub. Lafayette (Ind.) Jour. and Courier, 1962-70, Olympia (Wash.) Olympian and Bellingham (Wash.) Herald, 1969-70; chief exec., pub. Honolulu Star Bull., 1972-76; pres. Gannett Newspaper Found., Rochester, N.Y., 1976—. Mayor of South Bend, 1952-56. Served as officer USMCR, 1941-45; brig. gen. Res. (ret.). Decorated Silver Star, Bronze Star, Purple Heart, Named Young Man of Year in South Bend, Jr. Assn. Commerce, 1949. Mem. Sigma Delta Chi. Mason (Shriner), Rotarian. Home: 673 S Atlantic Ave Cocoa Beach FL 32931 Office: One Lincoln First Sq Rochester NY 14604

SCOTT, JOHN DILWORTH, mgmt. co. exec.; b. Pitts., June 23, 1911; s. John Dilworth and Clara (Moedinger) S.; student N.Y. U., 1930, U. Pitts., 1931; m. Jean Frances McIlwain, Apr. 1937 (dec. Mar. 1974); children—Jean Claire, Elizabeth, John Charles; m. 2d, Virginia Williams Swanson, July 20, 1974. With H.J. Heinz Co., Pitts., 1932-74, beginning as salesman, successively supr., br. mgr., sales promotion mgr., hotel and restaurant sales mgr., chain store sales mgr., 1932-54, gen. sales mgr., 1954-74, v.p., 1956-74; pres. J. and D. Assos., Dunedin, Fla., 1974—; pres., dir. Point Chautauqua Land Co. Pres., Point Chautaugua Assn. Presbyterian. Mason (Shriner). Clubs: Chautauqua Golf; Dunedin Country. Home: 2301 Harrison Dr Dunedin FL 33528

SCOTT, JOHN EDWARD, librarian; b. Washington, Ga., Aug. 12, 1920; s. John Edward and Martha Heard (Williams) S.; A.B., Morehouse Coll., 1948; B.L.S., Atlanta U., 1949; M.L.S., U. Ill., 1955; m. Dorris Louise Webb, Jan 28, 1948; children—Patricia Louise, Clifford Allen, Martha Ellen. Librarian, Kans. Tech. Inst., Topeka, 1949-55; circulation librarian Va. State Coll., Petersburg, 1955-56; asst. reference librarian U. Kans., 1956-57; dir. library resources W. Va. State Coll., 1957—. Served with USNR, 1942-46. Mem. AAUP, ALA (councilor 1964—, chmn. coll. libraries sect. 1969-70), Southeastern (treas. 1979—), W.Va. (chmn coll. library sect. 1958-60, pres. 1961-62) library assns., Tri-State Assn. Coll. and Research Libraries, Middle Atlantic Regional Library Fedn. (exec. bd.), Kappa Delta Pi, Beta Phi Mu, Alpha Phi Alpha. Home: PO Box 303 Institute WV 25112

SCOTT, JOHN IRVING ELIAS, educator; b. Jamaica, B.W.I.; s. Joseph N. and Harriet (Dawkins) S.; came to U.S., 1920, naturalized, 1932; A.B., Lincoln (Pa.) U., 1927; A.M., Wittenberg Coll., Springfield, Ohio, 1937; Ph.D., U. Pitts., 1942; m. Helen R. Timms; children—Irvlen, J. Irving E., Jr. Dean, Fla. Meml. Coll., 1927-29; prin. pub. sch., Jacksonville, Fla., 1929-44; dean Wiley Coll., Marshall, Tex., 1944-48; dean instrn. Alcorn Coll., 1948-50; prof. edn. Grad. Sch., dir. ednl. extension service (S.C.) State A. and M. Coll., 1950-53; dir. Negro edn. Jacksonville and Duval County, 1953-60; asst. dir. edn. Duval County, 1960-65, dir. spl. projects, 1965—; dir. tchr. tng. program Fla. Normal Coll., summers 1937, 38; extension work Bethune-Cookman Coll., Daytona Beach, Fla., 1933-35; extension classes Hampton (Va.) Inst., 1942-44, Albany State Coll. Summer Sch., 1943, Fla. A. and M. Coll., 1943-44; pres. Citizens Investment Corp. Mem. Nat. Tchrs. Research Assn. (founder, pres.), A.R.C., Boy Scouts Am., Fla., Tex. tchrs. assns., N.E.A. (dept. elementary prins.), Am. Acad. Polit. and Social Sci., Am. Tchrs. Assn. (commn. teaching profession), Doctoral Assn. U. Pitts., Beta Kappa Chi, Alpha Kappa Mu, Phi Beta Sigma. Mason. Author: Living With Others, 1939; Chemistry Through Life Situation Method; Best Fields for Small Investment; Professional Functions of Negro Principals in State of Florida in Relation to Status; An Educational Point of View; Negro Students and Their Colleges, 1949; Finding My Way, 1949; Research in Negro Colleges; Foreign Students in Negro Colleges and Universities; Guide to Thesis Writing; Education of Negroes above the Master's Degree; Honorary Degrees Conferred by Negro Colleges; Getting the Most Out of High School; The Education of Black People in Florida, 1974; other publs. in field of edn. Editor-in-chief The Negro Educational Rev. Home: 7236 Richardson Rd Jacksonville FL 32209 Office: 2307 Myrtle Ave Jacksonville FL 32209

SCOTT, JOHN PAUL, scientist, educator, author; b. Kansas City, Mo., Dec. 17, 1909; s. John William and Vivian (Armstrong) S.; B.A., U. Wyo., 1930; B.A. (Rhodes scholar 1930-32), Lincoln Coll., Oxford (Eng.) U., 1932; Ph.D., U. Chgo., 1935; m. Sarah Fisher, June 18, 1933 (d. Sept. 1978); children—Jean Scott Franck, Vivian Scott Hixson, John, David; m. 2d, Mary-Vesta Marston, June 30, 1979. Asst. in zoology U. Chgo., 1932-35; mem. faculty Wabash Coll., 1935-45, prof. zoology, 1942-45, chmn. dept., 1935-45; chmn. div. behavior studies Roscoe B. Jackson Meml. Lab., Bar Harbor, Maine, 1945-58, trustee, 1946-49, sr. staff scientist, 1958-65; research prof. psychology Bowling Green (Ohio) U., 1965—, Ohio Regent's prof., 1968—, dir. Center Research Social Behavior; prof. biopsychology U. Chgo., 1958. Mem. Maine Bd. Psychol. Examiners, 1956-59. Recipient Jordan prize Ind. Acad. Sci., 1947, Distinguished Alumnus award U. Wyo., 1976. Fellow Center Advanced Study in Behavioral Scis., 1963-64. Fellow Am. Psychol. Assn., Animal Behavior Soc., N.Y. Zool. Soc., A.A.A.S.; mem. Maine Psychol. Assn. (pres.

1953-54), Am. Soc. Zoologists, Am. Eugenics Soc. (v.p. 1963), Ecol. Soc. Am. (chmn. sect. animal behavior and sociobiology 1957-58), Internat. Soc. for Developmental Psychobiology (pres. 1972-73), Internat. Soc. for Research on Aggression (pres. 1973-74), Genetics Soc. Am., Behavior Genetics Assn. (pres. 1975-76), Phi Beta Kappa, Sigma Xi. Author: Animal Behavior, 1958, 72; Aggression, 1958, 75; (with John L. Fuller) Genetics and the Social Behavior of the Dog, 1965; Early Experience and the Organization of Behavior, 1968; (with C.J. Pfaffenberger) Guide Dogs for the Blind, 1976; also sci. articles, chpts. in books. Editor: (with Sarah F. Scott) Social Control and Social Change, 1971; (with Basil Eleftheriou) The Physiology of Aggression and Defeat, 1971; (with Edward Senay) Separation and Depression, 1972; Critical Periods, 1978. Office: Dept Psychology Bowling Green State U Bowling Green OH 43402

SCOTT, JOHN WINFIELD, JR., lawyer, educator; b. Fayetteville, Ark., Apr. 27, 1922; s. John Winfield and Lucile (Davidson) S.; B.S., Auburn U., 1943; LL.B., Harvard U., 1947, LL.M., 1951; children—Madeleine Davidson, Caroline Garrett, John Winfield. Faculty asst. Harvard Law Sch., 1949-51; admitted to Ala. bar, 1948, D.C. bar, 1954, N.Y. bar, 1957; atty. U.S. Treasury Dept., 1951-53; individual practice law, Birmingham, Ala., 1947-49, Washington, 1953-56, N.Y.C., 1956-62; asso. prof. U. N.C. Chapel Hill, 1962-64, prof., 1964-72, Graham Kenan prof. law, 1972—. Bd. dirs. N.C. Sch. of Arts Found., 1966-77, Sarah Graham Kenan Found., 1965-77; trustee N.C. Symphony, 1966-71, Louisburg Coll., 1967—. Served with AUS, 1943-44. Mem. Am. Bar Assn., D.C. Bar Assn. Democrat. Presbyterian. Club: Country of N.C. Author: Federal Income Taxation of Corporate Reorganizations and Divisions, 1972. Mem. bd. editors Tax Mgmt. Home: 2308 Honeysuckle Rd Chapel Hill NC 27514 Office: Univ of NC Chapel Hill NC 27514

SCOTT, JONATHAN LAVON, grocery chain exec.; b. Nampa, Idaho, Feb. 2, 1930; s. Buell Bonnie and Jewel Pearl (Horn) S.; B.A. magna cum laude, Coll. Idaho, 1951; grad. Advanced Mgmt. Program, Harvard U., 1951; m. Barbara Jean Albertson, May 28, 1952 (div. Mar. 1962); children—Joseph Buell, Anthony Robert (dec.); m. 2d, Dolores Hormechea, Dec. 21, 1963; children—Richard Teles, Daniel. With Western Enterprises, Inc., 1952-53; with Albertson's Inc., Boise, Idaho, 1953-75, vice chmn. bd., chief exec. officer, 1972-75; vice chmn. bd. Gt. Atlantic & Pacific Tea Co., Inc., Montvale, N.J., 1975, chmn. bd., chief exec. officer, 1975—; dir. Morrison-Knudsen Co., Bendix Corp. Trustee Com. Econ. Devel.; bd. dirs. Boys Clubs Am., United Way Tri-State; chmn. Retail Foods Industry U.S. Indsl. Payroll Savs. campaign, 1978; trustee Coll. Idaho. Served to 1st lt. USAF, 1953-54. Mem. Young Pres. Orgn., Econ. Club, N.Y.C. Clubs: Harvard, Sky, Arid (N.Y.C.). Home: 86 Cider Hill Upper Saddle River NJ 07458 Office: 2 Paragon Dr Montvale NJ 07645

SCOTT, JOSEPH VERNON, automotive aftermarket exec.; b. Scranton, Pa., Jan. 23, 1926; s. Joseph V. and Teresa (Gallagher) S.; Marine Engr., Pa. Maritime Acad., 1944-45; B.S., U. Pa., 1950; postgrad. with honors in Bus. Adminstrn., Wayne U., 1950-51; m. Mary Kay Feran, June 26, 1954; children—Joseph V., James D., Michael E., Catherine A., Teresa R., Mary Pat. Quality engring. mgr. Ford Motor Co., Kansas City Aircraft Plant (Mo.), 1951-54; planning, engring. mgr. Ford Motor Co., Dearborn, Mich., 1954-60; pres., dir. Chamberlain Mfg. Corp., Elmhurst, Ill., 1960-68, now dir.; pres., dir. Echlin Mfg. Co., Branford, Conn., McHenry, Ill., 1968—; dir. Motive Equipment Mfrs. Assn., 1976—, Mfrs. Council Nat. Automobile Parts Assn. Served as lt. USNR, 1945-46. Mem Tau Beta Pi, Sigma Tau. Home: 1180 South Shore Dr Crystal Lake IL 60014 Office: 1600 Industrial Dr McHenry IL 60050

SCOTT, KENNETH ELSNER, educator; b. Webster, Mass., May 18, 1926; s. Henry Anderson and Amanda (Elsner) S.; B.S. in Mech. Engring., Worcester Poly. Inst., 1948, M.S., 1954; m. Elizabeth Ann Oldham, June 21, 1952; children—Kenneth Elsner, Cynthia Lynne, Jeffrey Alan, Donald Leighton. Mem. faculty Worcester Poly. Inst., 1948—, prof. mech. engring., 1966—, George I. Alden prof. engring., 1971-75, inst. dir. audio-visual devel., 1971-74, dir. instructional TV, 1974—. Mem. bd. health, Holden, Mass., 1963-70. Served with AUS, 1944-46. Recipient Trustees' award for Outstanding Tchr. of Year, 1971; Western Electric Fund award New Eng. sect. Am. Soc. Engring. Edn., 1972. Registered profl. engr., Mass. Mem. ASME (exec. com. Worcester sect. 1952-57, sec.-treas. 1955-56, chmn. 1956-57, region I chmn. profl. divs. com. 1957-59, chmn. agenda, audit, budget and nominating com. Worcester 1957-58, chmn. symposium lubrication Worcester sect. 1957-58, chmn. Adm. Earle award com. 1958-59, chmn. devel. com. 1960-61), Am. Soc. Engring. Edn. (sec.-treas. New Eng.), Sigma Xi, Pi Tau Sigma, Tau Beta Pi. Home: 30 Brentwood Dr Holden MA 01520 Office: Worcester Polytech Inst Worcester MA 01609

SCOTT, KENNETH EUGENE, lawyer, educator; b. Western Springs, Ill., Nov. 21, 1928; s. Kenneth L. and Bernice (Albright) S.; B.A., Coll. William and Mary, 1949; M.A., Princeton, 1953; LL.B., Stanford, 1956; m. Viviane H. May, Sept. 22, 1956; children—Clifton, Jeffrey, Linda. Admitted to N.Y. bar, 1957, Calif. bar, 1957, D.C. bar, 1967; practice in N.Y.C., 1956-59, Los Angeles, 1959-61; asso. firm Sullivan & Cromwell, 1956-59, Musick, Peeler & Garrett, Los Angeles, 1959-60; chief dep. savs. and loan commr. State of Calif., 1961-63; gen. counsel Fed. Home Loan Bank Bd., Washington, 1963-67; law prof. Stanford Law Sch., 1968—. Mem. Am., Calif. bar assns., Phi Beta Kappa, Order of Coif, Pi Kappa Alpha, Omicron Delta Kappa. Co-author: Retail Banking in the Electronic Age, 1977. Home: 60 Bear Gulch Dr Portola Valley CA 94025 Office: Stanford Law Sch Stanford CA 94305

SCOTT, LESLIE WRIGHT, univ. ofcl.; b. Chgo., July 25, 1913; s. Charles O. and Charlotte (Wright) S.; A.B., Mich. State U., 1935; m. Ellen Meyer, June 6 1942; children—William, Leslie Ann, Mary Ellen, Timothy. Dir. Kellogg Center for Continuing Edn., Mich. State U., 1950-56, dir. Sch. Hotel and Restaurant Mgmt., 1947-55, dean continuing edn., 1955-56; v.p. Fred Harvey, Chgo., 1956-60, pres., 1960-72, vice chmn. Fred Harvey, Inc., 1970-72; v.p. for devel., prof. hotel, restaurant and instl. mgmt. Mich. State U., East Lansing, 1972—; dir. Canteen Corp., Win Schulers, Inc., Yellowstone Park Co. Bd. dirs. St. Lawrence Hosp., Lansing, Lansing Symphony; pres. Mich. State U. Found., 1976—. Served to lt. USNR, 1942-46. Mem. Nat. Restaurant Assn. (past pres.). Episcopalian. Clubs: Hinsdale Golf; Chicago; University (Mich. State U.); Rotary, Country of Lansing, City of Lansing. Contbr. articles trade jours. Home: 839 Wildwood East Lansing MI 48823

SCOTT, LEWIS PENNINGTON, III, pediatric cardiologist; b. Atlantic City, Feb. 24, 1927; s. Lewis Pennington and Florence Emily (Fisher) S.; student Brown U., 1947-51; M.D., Jefferson Med. Coll., 1954; m. Ethel Jefferies, June 21, 1952; children—Lewis Pennington, Jeffrey, Emily, Timothy. Intern, U.S. Naval Hosp., Phila., 1954-55, resident in pediatrics, 1955-57; chief pediatrics U.S. Naval Hosp., Bremerton, Wash., 1957-59; fellow in pediatric cardiology Boston Children's Hosp., 1959-61; chief pediatric cardiology U.S. Naval Hosp., Bethesda, Md., 1961-64, Children's Hosp. Nat. Med. Center, Washington, 1964—; prof. pediatrics George Washington U. Med. Center, 1964—. Served with USN, 1954-64. Diplomate Am. Bd. Pediatrics. Fellow Am. Coll. Cardiology, Am. Acad. Pediatrics; mem. Am. Heart Assn., Alpha Omega Alpha. Republican. Episcopalian. Club: Congressional Country. Contbr. numerous articles to med. jours. Office: 111 Michigan Ave NW Washington DC 20010

SCOTT, LIZABETH VIRGINIA, actress; b. Scranton, Pa.; d. John and Mary (Pennock) Matso; ed. Marywood Sem., Marywood Coll., Alviene Sch. Theatre. Actress numerous films, including You Came Along, 1947, The Strange Love of Martha Ivers, Dead Reckoning, Desert Fury, Variety Girl, I Walk Alone, Pitfall, Two of a Kind, Scared Stiff, Bad for Each Other, Silver Lode, Loving You, Pulp, also numerous TV films. Office: PO Box 5522 Beverly Hills CA 90210. *I believe primarily that one must be enveloped and bound by God's laws. One must have unwavering faith in one's talent and proceed toward one's goals with idealism, fervent desire, abundant tenacity, overwhelming love, and extraordinary enthusiasm.*

SCOTT, LOIS AURLIE BROWN, publisher; b. Hamilton, Ont., Can., Mar. 13, 1918; d. Roy Abbott and Alice Thurza (Fletcher) Brown; came to U.S., 1931, naturalized, 1936; student Detroit Bus. Inst., 1951-52; m. Robert Wilson Brown, 1936; m. George Ernest Scott, Mar. 28, 1953; 1 son by previous marriage—Robert George Brown. Owner, sec.-treas. Scott Advt. & Pub. Co., Livonia, Mich., 1954—; editor, pub. Ceramic Arts and Crafts, 1955—, Ceramic Teaching Projects, 1964—, Hobby Arts and Crafts, 1972-74. Mem. Mich. Potters Guild, Am. Crafts Council, Nat. Ceramic Mfrs. Assn., Mich. China Painting and Tchrs. Assn., Mich. Ceramic Dealers Assn., Goldcoast Needlearts Guild, Embroiderers Guild Am., Mich. Weavers Guild, Mich. League Handweavers, Mich. Handspinners Guild. Club: Coral Ridge Country (Ft. Lauderdale, Fla.). Editor: The Fundamentals of Hobby Ceramics (Bill Thompson), 1975; The Basics of China Painting (Bill Thompson), 1976; The Techniques of Hobby Ceramics (Thompson), 1977; China Painting with Bill Thompson, 1978. Home: 3251 West Shore Dr Orchard Lake MI 48033

SCOTT, LOUIS EDWARD, advt. agy. exec.; b. Waterbury, Conn., June 17, 1923; s. Louis Arthur and Ellen (Eckert) S.; B.S., U. Calif. at Berkeley, 1944; m. Phyllis Corrine Denker, Jan. 27, 1942; children—Susan Louise, Eric Richard, Jane Lynn. Sr. account exec. McCarty Co., advt., Los Angeles, 1946-50; with Foote, Cone & Belding, Los Angeles, 1950—, v.p., 1956, gen. mgr., 1959, became sr. v.p., 1963, dir., 1961—, chmn. exec. com., 1970—, chmn. ops. com., pres. Foote, Cone & Belding/Honig, 1975—; dir. Ador Corp. Chmn. publicity com. Los Angeles Community Chest, 1960; patron mem. Los Angeles YMCA; mem. Freedoms Found.; chmn. So. Calif. advisory bd. Advt. Council, mem. exec. advisory bd. Art Center Coll. Design. Served with U.S. Maritime Service, also USNR, World War II. Named Western Advt. Man of Year, 1972. Mem. Am. Assn. Advt. Agys. (dir., past chmn. Western region), Los Angeles Advt. Club (dir.), Calif., Los Angeles chambers commerce, Los Angeles World Affairs Council. Clubs: Balboa Bay, California, Town Hall, Wilshire Country, Newport Harbor Yacht, Santa Ana Country, La Quinta Country. Home: 2561 Circle Dr Newport Beach CA 92660 also 49835 Adelito Dr La Quinta CA 92253 Office: 2727 W 6th St Los Angeles CA 90057

SCOTT, MARIANNE FLORENCE, librarian, univ. library adminstr., educator; b. Toronto, Ont., Can., Dec. 4, 1928; d. Merle Redvers and Florence Ethel (Hutton) Scott; B.A., McGill U., Montreal, Que., Can., 1949, B.L.S., 1952. Asst. librarian Bank of Montreal, 1952-55; law librarian McGill U., 1955-73, law area librarian, 1973-75, dir. libraries, 1975—, lectr. legal bibliography faculty of law, 1964-75. Mem. Internat. (dir. 1974-77), Am., Can. (pres. 1963-69, exec. bd. 1973-75) assns. law libraries, Que. Library Assn. (pres. 1961-62), Corp. Profl. Librarians of Que. (v.p. 1975-76), Can. Assn. Research Libraries (pres. 1978-79, past pres. 1979-80). Co-founder, editor Index to Can. Legal Periodical Lit., 1963—. Contbr. articles to profl. jours. Home: 3848 Melrose Ave Montreal PQ H4A 2S2 Canada Office: 3459 McTavish St Montreal PQ H3A 1Y1 Canada

SCOTT, MARTHA ELLEN, actress; b. Jamesport, Mo.; d. Walter Alva and Letha (McKinley) Scott; B.A., teachers certificate U. Mich.; m. Carleton Alsop, Sept. 1940 (div. July 1946); 1 son, Scott Alsop; m. 2d, Mel Powell, July 23, 1946; children—Mary Mark, Kathleen Ellen. Actress on stage in Soldiers Wife, 1944, Remarkable Mr. Pennypacker, 1954, Our Town, 1938 (picture 1940), 49th Cousin, 1960, Never Too Late, 1964-65; motion pictures include Cheers for Miss Bishop, 1941, One Foot in Heaven, 1943, Desperate Hours, 1954, Ten Commandments, 1956, Sayonora, 1957, Ben Hur, 1959, Airport, 1975, Turning Point, 1977; has made numerous TV appearances; co-founder, Plumstead Playhouse, Inc. 1968; opened Am. Bicentennial Theater at Kennedy Center in Skin of Our Teeth, 1975; co-producer First Monday in October, Kennedy Center and Broadway, 1978. Mem. ANTA West, Delta Gamma. Office: Artists Agy 190 N Canon Dr Beverly Hills CA 90210

SCOTT, MICHAEL JAMES FOLEY, film producer-dir.; b. Winnipeg, Man., Can., Nov. 29, 1942; s. John Gorrie and Dehlia Helen (Foley) S.; student U. Man., 1962; radio and TV arts diploma Ryerson Poly. Inst., 1966; m. Oaria Antonina Kiperchuk, June 19, 1976. With Nat. Film Bd. Can., 1967—, dir., 1968-76, producer, 1975-76, exec. producer Prairie region, Winnipeg, 1976—; films include: Station 10, 1972; Recess, 1967; That's The Price, 1969; Small Smoke at Blaze Creek, 1970; Whistling Smith, 1974; For Gentlemen Only, 1976; One Man, 1977; Red Dress, 1979. Recipient Canadian Film awards, Am. Film award; awards festivals Berlin, Melbourne and Sidney, Australia, Washington, San Francisco, Cannes, France, Oberhausen, W.Ger., Krakow, Poland, Los Angeles. Home: 84 Queenston St Winnipeg MB Canada Office: 674 St James St Winnipeg MB Canada

SCOTT, MILTON LEONARD, educator; b. Tempe, Ariz., Feb. 21, 1915; s. Squire Milton and Ione Frances (Greenleaf) S.; A.B., U. Calif., Berkeley, 1937; Ph.D., Cornell U., 1945; m. Dorothy Marie Jaeger, July 1, 1938; children—Grace Ione Scott Saroka, June Marie Scott Kopald. Vitamin chemist Coop. G.L.F. Mills, Inc., Buffalo, 1937-42; research asso. Cornell U., Ithaca, N.Y., 1945-46, asst. prof. dept. poultry sci., 1946-48, asso. prof., 1948-53, prof., 1953—, Jacob Gould Schurman prof. nutrition, 1976—, chmn. dept. poultry sci., 1976—; cons., lectr. in field. Scoutmaster, Louis Fuertes Council Boy Scouts Am., 1938-50. Recipient awards Am. Feed Mfrs. Assn., 1952, Distillers Feed Research Council, 1964, Calcium Carbonate Co., 1966, N.Y. Farmer's, 1971, D.W. Brooks Lectr., 1978; research award Nat. Turkey Fedn., 1958; nutrition award Pioneer in Poultry, 1977; Borden award Inst. Nutrition, 1977. Fellow AAAS, Poultry Sci. Assn. (Borden award 1965); mem. Am. Inst. Nutrition, Soc. Exptl. Biology and Medicine, Am. Chem. Soc., Am. Soc. Biol. Chemists, World's Poultry Sci. Assn., Sigma Xi, Phi Kappa Phi. Republican. Presbyterian. Clubs: Rotary Internat., Statler, Tower, Yacht, Country. Author: (with M.C. Nesheim, R.J. Young) Nutrition of the Chicken, 1976; contbr. chpts.: Diseases of Poultry, 1978, Organic Selenium Compounds: Their Chemistry and Biology, 1973, The Fat-Soluble Vitamins, 1978. Home: 1581 Taughannock Blvd Trumansburg NY 14886 Office: Dept Poultry Sci 200 Rice Hall Cornell U Ithaca NY 14853

SCOTT, NATHAN ALEXANDER, JR., clergyman, educator; b. Cleve., Apr. 24, 1925; s. Nathan Alexander and Maggie (Martin) S.; student Wayne State U., 1940-41; A.B., U. Mich., 1944; B.D., Union Theol. Sem., 1946; Ph.D., Columbia, 1949; Litt.D., Ripon Coll., 1965, Denison U., 1976; L.H.D., Wittenberg U., 1965, Fed. City Coll., 1976; D.D., Phila. Div. Sch., 1967; S.T.D., Gen. Theol. Sem., 1968; Litt.D., St. Mary's Coll., Notre Dame, 1969; m. Charlotte Hanley, Dec. 21, 1946; children—Nathan Alexander III, Leslie Kristin. Ordained to ministry Protestant Episcopal Ch. as deacon, priest, 1960; dean chapel Va. Union U., Richmond, 1946-47; instr. humanities Howard U., Washington, 1948-50, asst. prof., 1950-53, asso. prof., 1953-55, dir. gen. edn. program in humanities, 1953-55; asst. prof. theology and lit. Div. Sch., U. Chgo., 1955-58, asso. prof., 1958-64, prof., 1964-72, Shailer Mathews prof., 1972-76; canon theologian Cathedral of St. James, Chgo., 1966-76; Commonwealth prof. religious studies, prof. English U. Va., Charlottesville, 1976—. Bd. dirs. Soc. for Arts, Religion and Culture; trustee Seabury-Western Theol. Sem., 1970-75. Fellow Sch. Letters, Ind. U., 1965-73. Fellow Am. Acad. Arts and Scis.; mem. Soc. for Values in Higher Edn. (Kent fellow), Am. Philos. Assn., MLA, Am. Acad. Religion, Chgo. Hist. Soc. Author: Rehearsals of Discomposure: Alienation and Reconciliation in Modern Literature, 1952; The Tragic Vision and the Christian Faith, 1957; Modern Literature and the Religious Frontier, 1958; Albert Camus, 1962; Reinhold Niebuhr, 1963; The New Orpheus: Essays toward a Christian Poetic, 1964; The Climate of Faith in Modern Literature, 1964; Samuel Beckett, 1965; Forms of Extremity in the Modern Novel, 1965; Four Ways of Modern Poetry, 1965; Man in the Modern Theatre, 1965; The Broken Center: Studies in the Theological Horizon of Modern Literature, 1966; Ernest Hemingway, 1966; The Modern Vision of Death, 1967; Adversity and Grace: Studies in Recent American Literature, 1968; Craters of the Spirit: Studies in the Modern Novel, 1968; Negative Capability: Studies in the New Literature and the Religious Situation, 1969; The Unquiet Vision: Mirrors of Man in Existentialism, 1969; The Wild Prayer of Longing: Poetry and The Sacred, 1971; Nathanael West, 1971; Three American Moralists: Mailer, Bellow, Trilling, 1973; The Poetry of Civic Virtue: Eliot, Malraux, Auden, 1976; Mirrors of Manin Existentialism, 1978. Bd. cons. Jour. of Religion; advisory editor Notre Dame Eng. Jour., also Modernist Studies. Home: 1419 Hilltop Rd Charlottesville VA 22903

SCOTT, NAUMAN S., judge; b. New Roads, La., June 15, 1916; s. Nauman Steele and Sidonie (Provosty) Scott; A.B., Amherst Coll., 1938; LL.B., Tulane U., 1941; m. Blanche Hammond, Jan. 8, 1942; children—Ashley, Nauman S. III, John W., Arthur Hammond. Admitted to La. bar, 1942, practiced in Alexandria; chief judge U.S. Dist. Ct. for La., Western dist., Alexandria, 1970—; mem. jud. council La. Supreme Ct., 1961-70. Chmn. local United Fund, local unit ARC; bd. dirs. La. Assn. for Mental Health, Vocat. and Rehab. Center. Served to 1st lt., 1942-45. Mem. Am., La. (nominating com.), Alexandria (pres. 1965-66) bar assns., Alexandria C. of C., Young Men's Bus. Assn. Republican. Roman Catholic. Club: Kiwanis.*

SCOTT, RACHEL ANN, free-lance writer; b. Shenandoah, Iowa, Apr. 20, 1947; d. Duane Clarence and Elizabeth Ann (Clark) Scott; B.S., Kans. State U., 1969. Reporter, Winston-Salem (N.C.) Jour., 1969; free-lance writer, Washington, 1970-71, Brownsville, Md., 1972-74; reporter Balt. Sun, 1974; dir. health and safety Ill. Indsl. Commn., 1974-75; free-lance writer, Washington, 1975-76, 77—; writer-editor cons. Occupational Safety & Health Adminstrn., Dept. Labor, 1978-79; public info. specialist EPA, 1979—; reporter, editor Environ. Action mag., 1977; reporter news series WRC-TV News Center, Washington. Recipient Mademoiselle award, 1974; silversmith, 1977-78. Ford Found. grantee, 1972-73; Abelard Found. grantee, 1972; Fund Investigative Journalism grantee, 1970, 72, 75. Author: Muscle and Blood, 1974. Research on environment indsl. safety. Address: care Paul Reynolds Agy 12 E 41st St New York NY 10017

SCOTT, RALPH C., physician, educator; b. Bethel, Ohio, June 7, 1921; s. John Carey and Leona (Laycock) S.; B.S., U. Cin., 1942, M.D., 1945; m. Rosemary Ann Schultz, June 26, 1945; children—Susan Ann, Barbara Lynne, Marianne. Intern Univ. Hosps., U. Iowa, 1945-46; resident, asst. dept. pathology U. Cin. Coll. Medicine, 1948-49, fellow internal medicine, 1949-53, fellow cardiology, 1953-57, mem. faculty, 1950—, prof. medicine, 1968—; staff clinics Cin. Gen. Hosp., 1950-75, clinician in internal medicine, 1952-75, dir. cardiac clinics, 1965-75, attending physician med. service, 1958—; staff VA Hosp., Cin., 1954—, cons., 1961—; attending physician Med. Service, Christian R. Holmes Hosp., Cin., 1957—; attending staff USAF Hosp., Wright Patterson AFB, 1960—; staff Good Samaritan Hosp., Cin., 1961—, cons., 1967—; staff Jewish Hosp., Cin., 1957—, cons., 1968—; cons. Children's Hosp., Cin., 1968—; attending physician Providence Hosp., Cin., 1971—. Served from 1st lt. to capt., AUS, 1946-48. Nat. Heart Inst. grantee, 1964-68, 67-74, 76—. Diplomate Am. Bd. Internal Medicine (subspecialty cardiovascular disease). Fellow A.C.P. Am. Coll. Cardiology, Am. Coll. Chest Physicians; mem. AMA, Ohio State Med. Assn., Cin. Acad. Medicine, Central Soc. Clin. Research, Am. Heart Assn. (fellow council clin. cardiology), Cin. Soc. Internal Medicine, Heart Assn. Southwestern Ohio, Am. Fedn. for Clin. Research, Internat. Cardiovascular Soc., Sigma Xi, Alpha Omega Alpha, Phi Eta Sigma, Phi Chi. Contbr. articles to med. jours. Editorial bd. Am. Heart Jour., 1967-79, Jour. Electrocardiology, 1967—; editor Electrocardiographic-Pathologic Conf., Jour. Electrocardiology, 1967—, Clin. Cardiology and Diabetes, 1980. Home: 2955 Alpine Terr Cincinnati OH 45208 Office: Room 7157 Med Scis Bldg Univ Cincinnati Med Center 231 Bethesda Ave Cincinnati OH 45267

SCOTT, RALPH MASON, physician, educator; b. Leemont, Va., Nov. 23, 1921; s. Benjamin Thomas and Marion Hazel (Mason) S.; B.A., U. Va., 1947; M.D., Med. Coll., Va., 1946-50; m. Alice Latine Francisco, Dec. 21, 1946; children—Susan Taylor, Ralph Mason, John Thomas. Intern Robert Packer Hosp., Sayre, Pa., 1953-54, resident, 1954-57, dir. radiation therapy and nuclear medicine sect., 1957-59; asst. prof. radiology U. Chgo. Med. Sch., 1959-60; asso. prof. radiology, dir. radiation therapy and radioisotopes U. Louisville Med. Sch., 1960-64, prof., dir. radiation therapy, 1964-77; prof., chmn. dept. therapeutic radiology U. Md. Sch. Medicine, 1977—; dir. radiation therapy program div. cancer research resources and centers Nat. Cancer Inst. (on leave from U. Louisville), 1976-77. Pres. Ky. div. Am. Cancer Soc., 1972-73. Served to lt. (j.g.) USNR, 1943-46. Fellow Christie Hosp. and Holt Radium Inst., Manchester, Eng., 1956-57. Diplomate Am. Bd. Radiology (trustee 1965-76, treas., 1969-70, v.p. 1970-72, pres. 1972-74). Mem. Am. Roentgen-Ray Soc. (exec. council 1968—, chmn. exec. council 1972-73), AMA, Am. Coll. R1diology (vice chmn. commn. on cancer 1968-69), Am. Radium Soc., Am. Soc. Therapeutic Radiologists, Assn. U. Radiologists, Radiol. Soc. N.Am., Pi Kappa Alpha, Phi Chi. Office: Dept Therapeutic Radiology U Md Sch Medicine Baltimore MD 21201

SCOTT, RICHARD A(LAN), retail drug chain exec.; b. Berkeley, Calif., May 2, 1935; s. Alan R. and Jessie W. Scott; B.S., U. Calif., Berkeley, 1961; m. Alice L. McCrudden, Aug. 13, 1966; children—Kelly, Kristin. With Longs Drug Stores, Inc., Walnut Creek, Calif., 1971—, sr. v.p., 1976-77, exec. v.p., 1977—, also dir.;

chmn. Good Govt. Council-Longs Drugs. Served with USAF, 1953-57. Mem. Calif. Retailers Assn. (dir., chmn. chain drug com.). Republican. Home: 917 Kirkcrest Rd Alamo CA 94507 Office: 141 N Civic Dr Walnut Creek CA 94596

SCOTT, ROBERT COOPER, banker; b. Dallas, Nov. 19, 1930; s. John Oliver and Ella (Tindell) S.; A.A., U. Tex., Arlington, 1956; B.B.A., North Tex. State U., Denton, 1957; M.B.A., So. Methodist U., 1960; grad. Am. Inst. Banking, 1967; postgrad. U. Wis., 1967-69, U. Mich., 1968; m. Patsy Lou Raburn, Apr. 25, 1958; children—Gina Michelle, Robert Keith. Pub. accountant Alford, Meroney & Co., 1957; cost estimator Chance Vought, 1958; cost accountant Republic Nat. Bank, Dallas, 1959-64, sr. v.p., controller, 1965—; sr. v.p., treas. Republic of Tex. Corp., 1974—; v.p., dir. Republic Money-Order Inc.; dir. Livingston, Inc., Medipark, Inc., Republic Computer Corp. Mem. adv. bd. Christian Schs., Inc.; bd. dirs. Richardson Symphony Orch. Served with USAF, 1951-55. Mem. Planning Execs. Inst. (past pres. Dallas chpt.), Am. Inst. C.P.A.'s, Tex. Soc. C.P.A.'s, Bank Adminstrn. Inst., Financial Execs. Inst. Mem. Ch. of Christ (elder). Clubs: Dallas Athletic, Brookhaven Country (Dallas). Home: 6840 Dartbrook Dr Dallas TX 75240 Office: Ervay and Pacific Sts Dallas TX 75222

SCOTT, ROBERT FREDERICK, utility co. exec.; b. Biddeford, Maine, Aug. 31, 1929; s. Harry Albert and Caroline Gertrude (McCarthy) S.; B.S.B.A., U. N.H., 1953; M.B.A., U. Maine, 1969; children—Bradley David, Gregory James, Cynthia Ann, William Alan, John Frederick. With Central Maine Power Co., Augusta, 1953—, sr. v.p. customer services and rates, also dir.; dir. Maine Yankee Atomic Power Co., Union Water Power Co.; v.p., dir. Central Securities Corp., Cumberland Securities Corp.; corporator First Consumer Savs. Bank. Active United Fund, Indsl. Devel. Corp. Served with U.S. Army, 1947-49. Mem. Augusta C. of C., New Eng. Council (chmn. Maine chpt.), New Eng. Council for Econ. Devel. (dir.). Club: Rotary (pres. Sanford, Maine). Office: Central Maine Power Co Edison Dr Augusta ME 04336*

SCOTT, ROBERT LANE, educator, chemist; b. Santa Rosa, Calif., Mar. 20, 1922; s. Horace Albert and Maurine (Lane) S.; S.B., Harvard, 1942; M.A., Princeton, 1944, Ph.D., 1945; m. Elizabeth Sewall Hunter, May 27, 1944; children—Joanna Ingersoll, Jonathan Armat, David St. Clair, Janet Hamilton. Sci. staff Los Alamos Lab., 1945-46; Frank B. Jewett fellow U. Calif. at Berkeley, 1946-48, faculty U. Calif. at Los Angeles, 1948—, prof. chemistry, 1960—, chmn. dept., 1970-75. Guggenheim fellow, 1955; NSF sr. fellow, 1961-62; Fulbright lectr., 1968-69. Mem. Am. Chem. Soc., Am. Phys. Soc., AAAS, Chem. Soc. (London), Sigma Xi. Author: (with J.H. Hildebrand) Solubility of Nonelectrolytes, 3d edit., 1950, rev., 1964; Regular Solutions, 1962; (with others) Regular and Related Solutions, 1970. Contbr. articles to profl. jours. Home: 11128 Montana Ave Los Angeles CA 90049

SCOTT, ROBERT MONTGOMERY, lawyer; b. Bryn Mawr, Pa., May 22, 1929; s. Edgar and Helen Hope (Montgomery) S.; Groton Sch. (Mass.), 1942-47; A.B., Harvard, 1951; LL.B., U. Pa., 1954; m. H. Gay Elliot, June 30, 1951; children—Hope Tyler, Janet Pauling, Elliot Montgomery. Atty. firm Montgomery McCracken Walker & Rhoads, Phila., 1954-69, 73—; spl. asst. to U.S. Ambassador to Ct. of St. James, London, Eng., 1969-73; dir. Fidelcor, Inc., Fidelity Bank, Phila. Pres. Acad. of Music, Phila.; v.p. Phila. Mus. Art; chmn. Royal Oak Found., Inst. Cancer Research, Fox Chase, Pa.; trustee U. Pa., Lankenau Hosp.; bd. dirs. Phila. Orch. Assn., Independence Found., Glyndebourne Assn. Am., English-Speaking Union. Recipient Superior Honor award Dept. State, 1973. Fellow Am. Bar Found.; mem. Am., Pa., Phila., Fed. bar assns. Republican. Clubs: Philadelphia, Union League, Knickerbocker; White's, Radnor Hunt, American (London). Home: Church Rd Wayne PA 19087 Office: 3 Parkway Philadelphia PA 19102

SCOTT, ROBERT TIMOTHY, interpretative center ofcl.; b. Duluth, Minn., Feb. 18, 1927; s. Frederick George and Alice Ethel (Shean) S.; A.A., Duluth Jr. Coll., 1949; m. Patricia Joan Spehar, Sept. 22, 1951; children—John, Mary Jo (Mrs. John W. Nickila), Robert Timothy, Theresa, Patrick. Accountant, Erie Mining Co., Hoyt Lakes, Minn., 1952-61; mgr. Aguar, Jyring, Whitman, Moser, architects and planners, Duluth, 1961-73; cons. Architects Four, Duluth, 1973-74; dir. Iron Range Interpretative Center, history of people and industry, Chisholm, Minn., 1974—. Chmn. Gt. Lakes Commn., 1971—. Councilman, Hoyt Lakes, 1955-61. Served with USNR, 1945-46. Mem. Am. Soc. Planning Ofcls., Am. Inst. Planners, Nat. Hist. Soc. Clubs: Kiwanis, K.C. Home: 401 5th Ave NE Chisholm MN 55719 Office: Box 392 Chisholm MN 55719

SCOTT, ROBERT VERNON, ret. govt. ofcl.; b. Clarksburg, W.Va., June 29, 1921; s. Emory Lee and Lula Marie (Pople) S.; B.C.S., Columbus U., 1948; postgrad. Johns Hopkins U., 1962; m. Opal Louise Wentz, Aug. 16, 1942; children—Susan Scott Kraft, Barbara Scott Hotvedt, Robert, Catherine Scott McElrath. Accountant, field supr. Dept. Agr., Washington, 1940-42, 46-50; supervisory accounting GAO, Washington, 1950-54, 54-59; chief fin. audit and control CSC, 1952-54; controller AID, Washington and Seoul, Korea, 1960-62, Vientiane, Laos, 1963-65, Ankara, Turkey, 1966-72, Saigon, Vietnam, 1972-73, Bangkok, Thailand, 1973, ret.; cons. fin. mgmt. Served with USNR, 1942-45. Named Ky. Col., 1965. Presbyterian (elder, stated clk.). Home: 26 Hemingway Circle Savannah GA 31411

SCOTT, RODERIC MACDONALD, optical co. exec.; b. Sandusky, Ohio, Apr. 9, 1916; s. William Charles and Margaret Carol (Scott) S.; B.S. in Physics, Case Sch. Applied Sci., 1938; M.A., Harvard U., 1939, Ph.D. in Astronomy, 1945; m. Joyce Ris Komanec, Dec. 22, 1938; children—Roderic MacDonald, Jeffrey Anderson, Dane Chapman. Instr. physics Vanderbilt U., 1941; research asso. Harvard U., 1942-45; research physicist Sharples Corp., Phila., 1946-48; with Perkin Elmer Corp., 1948—, v.p., 1965—, chief scientist, 1965-69, tech. dir. optical tech. div., Danbury, Conn., 1969-76, prin. scientist, 1976—. Bd. dirs. Perkin Fund. Fellow Optical Soc. Am. (dir.; David Richardson medal 1973, 76); mem. U.S. Nat. Com. Internat. Commn. Optics (v.p. 1970-72), Phys. Soc., Soc. Photogrammetry, Soc. Photo-Optical Engrs. (dir., exec. v.p. 1975-76; George W. Goddard award 1977). Home: 240 Chestnut Hill Rd Stamford CT 06903 Office: Perkin-Elmer Corp 100 Wooster Heights Rd Danbury CT 06810

SCOTT, ROLAND BOYD, pediatrician; b. Houston, Apr. 18, 1909; s. Ernest John and Cordie (Clark) S.; B.S., Howard U., 1931, M.D., 1934; Gen. Edn. Bd. fellow U. Chgo., 1936-39; m. Sarah Rosetta Weaver, June 24, 1935 (dec.); children—Roland Boyd, Venice Rosetta, Estelle Irene. Faculty, Howard U., Washington, 1937—, prof. pediatrics, 1952-77, distinguished prof. pediatrics and child health, 1977—, chmn. dept. pediatrics, 1945-73, dir. Center for Sickle Cell Anemia, 1973—; chief pediatrician Freedmen's Hosp., 1947-73; professorial lectr. in child health and devel. George Washington U. Sch. Medicine, 1971—; staff Children's Hosp., Providence Hosp., Columbia Hosp., D.C. Gen. Hosp., Washington Hosp. Center; cons. in pediatrics to NIH, hosps. Mem. com. Pub. Health Adv. Council, 1964—, U.S. Children's Bur., 1964—; mem. Nat. Com. for Children and Youth. Recipient Sci. and Community award Medico-Chirurgical Med. Soc. D.C., 1971, Community Service award Med. Soc. D.C., 1972, award for contbns. to sickle cell research Delta Sigma Theta, 1973, 34 years Dedicated and Distinguished Service award in pediatrics dept. pediatrics Howard U., 1973, Faculty award for excellence in research, 1974, certificate of appreciation Sickle Cell Anemia Research and Edn., 1977; Mead Johnson award D.C. chpt. Am. Acad. Pediatrics, 1978; Percy L. Julian award We Do Care, Chgo., 1979. Diplomate Nat. Bd. Med. Examiners, Am. Bd. Pediatrics. Mem. AMA, Am. Pediatric Soc., Soc. Pediatric Research, Am. Acad. Allergy (v.p. 1966-67), Am. Acad. Pediatrics (mem. com. on children with handicaps, cons. head start program), Am. Fedn. Clin. Research, Nat. Med. Assn. (Distinguished Service medal 1966), AAAS, Internat. Corr. Soc. Allergists, Assn. Ambulatory Pediatric Services, AAUP, Internat. Congress Pediatrics, Am. Coll. Allergists (Distinguished Service award 1977), Can. Sickle Cell Soc. (hon. life), Phi Beta Kappa, Sigma Xi (Percy L. Julian award Howard U. chpt. 1977), Kappa Pi, Beta Kappa Chi, Alpha Omega Alpha, others. Author: (with Althea D. Kessler) Sickle Cell Anemia and Your Child; (with C.G. Uy) Guidelines For Care of Patients With Sickle Cell Disease. Mem. editorial bd. Clin. Pediatrics, 1962—, Jour. Nat. Med. Assn., 1978; cons. editor Medical Aspects of Human Sexuality; editorial bd. Annals of Allergy, 1977. Research, publs. on sickle cell anemia, growth and devel. of infants and children, allergy in children. Home: 1723 Shepherd St NW Washington DC 20011 Office: 1114 Girard St NW Washington DC 20009

SCOTT, SPENCER, savs. and loan assn. exec.; b. Hutchinson, Kans., Aug. 13, 1922; married; 2 children. With Hutchinson State Bank, 1939-41; acct., head office trust dept. Security First Nat. Bank, Los Angeles, 1941-42; with Fidelity Fed. Savs. and Loan Assn., Glendale, Calif., 1946—, exec. v.p., 1968-70, pres., 1970—, chmn. bd., 1974—, also dir. Chmn. CSC, Glendale, 1972-78; gen. chmn. fin. devel. program Los Angeles Heart Inst. at St. Vincent's Med. Center. Served with USAAF, World War II. Mem. Calif. Savs. and Loan League, U.S. League Savs. Assns., Conf. Fed. Savs. and Loan Assns., Nat. Savs. and Loan League. Clubs: Jonathan (Los Angeles); Verdugo, Oakmont Country (Glendale); Annandale Golf (Pasadena, Calif.). Office: 600 N Brand Blvd PO Box 1631 Glendale CA 91209

SCOTT, STANLEY SOUTHALL, co. exec.; b. Bolivar, Tenn., July 2, 1933; s. Lewis Augustus and Clinora Neely (Hamer) S.; student U. Kans., Lawrence, 1951-53; B.S. in Journalism, Lincoln U., Jefferson City, Mo., 1959; m. Bettye L. Lovejoy, Dec. 23, 1962; children—Kenneth Earl, Susan Lovejoy, Stanley Southall II. Editor, gen. mgr. Memphis World, 1960-61; gen. assignment news reporter, copy editor, editorial writer Atlanta Daily World, 1961-64; gen. assignment news reporter U.P.I., N.Y.C., 1964-66; asst. dir. pub. relations NAACP, N.Y.C., 1966-67; radio newsman Westinghouse Broadcasting Corp., N.Y.C., 1967-71; asst. to dir. communications exec. br. White House, Washington, 1971-73, spl. asst. to pres., 1973-75; asst. adminstr. AID, 1975-77; asst. dir. corp. relations Philip Morris, Inc., N.Y.C., 1977, dir. corp. pub. affairs, 1977—; lectr. journalism Columbia, New Sch., N.Y.C. Served with U.S. Army, 1954-56. Recipient Russwurm award for excellence in radio news reporting, 1967, Silurians award, 1965, Pulitzer nomination for Malcolm X coverage, 1965, Wisemens award for series on police-minority community confrontation in Atlanta, 1961. Mem. AFTRA, New York Reporters Assn., NAACP, Huntington Civic Assn. Republican. Congregationalist. Home: 20 Birch Ln Dobbs Ferry NY 10522

SCOTT, TASSO HAROLD, lawyer; b. Natoma, Kans., Jan. 25, 1905; s. Paul Dawson and Sadie Velzetta (Kroh) S.; A.B., U. Colo., 1931; M.S. in Fgn. Service, Georgetown U., 1933; J.D., George Washington U., 1940; m. Kathryn M. Terhune, Dec. 5, 1942; children—Watson T., Thomas Harold, Douglas Bennett. Legislative adviser U.S. Senator Adams of Colo., 1934-41; admitted to D.C. bar, 1940, also U.S. Supreme Ct.; atty. FTC, 1941-60, charge radio, TV and periodical advt., 1957-58; asso. commr. Indian Claims Commn., 1960-68; mem. law firm Rhyne & Rhyne, 1969-76; of counsel to Paul M. Niebell, 1976-79. Mem. D.C., Fed. bar assns., Colo. State Soc. (past pres.), Am. Judicature Soc., Inter-Am., Am. bar assns., World Assn. Judges, World Peace through Law Center, St. Andrews Soc., Phi Kappa Tau. Mason (Shriner, Jester). Methodist. Clubs: National Lawyers (Washington); Kenwood Golf and Country (Chevy Chase, Md.); Optimist. Author articles, reports in field. Home: 9615 Hillridge Dr Kensington MD 20795 Office: 910 17th St NW Washington DC 20006

SCOTT, THEODORE R., lawyer; b. Mount Vernon, Ill., Dec. 7, 1924; s. Theodore R. and Beulah (Flannigan) S.; A.B., U. Ill., 1947; J.D., 1949; m. Virginia Scott, June 1, 1947; children—Anne, Sarah, Daniel, Barbara. Admitted to Ill. bar, 1950; law clk. to judge U.S. Ct. Appeals, 1949-51; since practiced in Chgo.; asso. firm Spalding Glass, 1951-53, Loftus, Lucas & Hammand, 1953-58, Ooms, McDougall, Williams & Hersh, 1958-60; partner firm McDougall, Hersh & Scott, 1960—. Served to 2d lt. USAAF, 1943-45. Decorated Air medal. Fellow Am. Coll. Trial Lawyers. mem. Am., Ill., Chgo., 7th Circuit bar assns., Legal Club Chgo., Law Club Chgo., Patent Law Assn. Chgo. (past pres.), Phi Beta Kappa. Club: Union League (Chgo.); Exmoor Country (Highland Park, Ill.). Home: 1569 Woodvale Ave Deerfield IL 60015 Office: 135 S LaSalle St Chicago IL 60603

SCOTT, THOMAS FREDERICK MCNAIR, physician; b. Inchbare, Scotland, June 18, 1901; s. Robert F. McNair and Alice (Nystrom) S.; B.A., Cambridge U., 1923, M.A., 1928, M.D., 1938; m. Mary Dwight Baker, July 18, 1936; children—Robert McNair, Carolyn Dwight. Came to U.S., 1938, naturalized, 1941. Asst. physician in charge children's diseases St. Georges Hosp., London, Eng., 1936-38; asst. physician Queens Hosp. for Children, 1936-38; prof. pediatrics Temple U. Med. Sch., Phila., 1938-40; research prof. pediatrics U. Pa. Med. Sch., 1940-66, prof. pediatrics, 1966-69, emeritus prof., 1969—; dir. research dept. Children's Hosp. of Phila., 1940-66, sr. physician, 1940-69, emeritus sr. physician, 1969—; prof. pediatrics Hahnemann Med. Coll. and Hosp., Phila., 1974—, dir. ambulatory pediatric edn., 1974—, co-dir. pediatric ambulatory services, 1975—. Fellow Royal Coll. Physicians (London), Am. Acad. Pediatrics, Coll. Physicians Phila.; mem. Royal Coll. Surgeons (Eng.), Soc. Clin. Investigation, Am. Pediatric Soc., Soc. Pediatric Research; hon. mem. Brit. Pediatric Assn., Pediatric Assn. Guatemala. Home: 426 S 26th St Philadelphia PA 19146 Office: Dept Pediatrics 230 N Broad St Philadelphia PA 19102

SCOTT, THOMAS WRIGHT, composer, instrumentalist, arranger; b. Los Angeles, May 19, 1948; s. Nathan George and Margery (Wright) S.; student U. So. Calif., 1966-67. Instrumentalist on saxes, woodwinds, lyricon; rec. artist; arranger and performer on numerous albums, including with Paul McCartney, George Harrison, Ringo Starr, Barbra Streisand, Carole King, Rod Stewart, Aretha Franklin, Joni Mitchell (as leader of L.A. Express), Steely Dan, Quincy Jones, Ravi Shankar; composer background music for TV shows: Dan August, Cannon, Barnaby Jones, Streets of San Francisco, Baretta; composer theme music for TV show Starsky and Hutch; composer for motion pictures: Conquest of The Planet of The Apes, 1973, Uptown Saturday Night, 1974, Americathon, 1979; vis. prof. music U. Utah, 1971, Westminster Coll., 1975; clinician Capitol U., Columbus, Ohio, 1973-77. Mem. Am. Fedn. Musicians, Nat. Acad. Rec. Arts and Scis. (dir. Los Angeles chpt. 1971-72, Grammy award 1974, chpt. Most Valuable Player 1973, 74, 75, 77), Composers and Lyricists Guild Am. (exec. bd. 1972-73, 80-81). Office: care Paul Cheslaw Mgmt 1137 2d St Suite 101 Santa Monica CA 90403

SCOTT, TOM BURKETT, JR., savs. and loan assn. exec.; b. Pasadena, Calif., Oct. 16, 1922; s. Tom Burkett and Lola Olive (Emery) S.; B.A., Millsaps Coll., 1943; LL.B., U. Miss., 1948; m. Laura Elizabeth Hewes, May 28, 1946; children—Sharon Scott Rhoden, Deborah Scott Helgeson, Tom Burkett III, Charles Christopher IV. Asst. clk. Miss. Ho. of Reps., 1948; partner firm Scott, Barbour & Scott, Jackson, Miss., 1949-77; pres., chief exec. officer Unifirst Fed. Savs. & Loan Assn., Jackson, 1962—; dir. Guarantee Nat. Bank, Standard Life Ins. Co., S. Central Bell Telephone Co. Bd. dirs. Jackson Redevel. Authority, 1974—, United Student Aid Funds, 1978—, Miss. Econ. Council, Boys' Club of Jackson, Boy Scouts Am.; bd. dirs., mem. exec. com. Sch. Pictures, Inc., 1971—; past pres. Jackson Symphony Orch. Served to capt. USAAF, 1943-46. Decorated Air medal with 3 oak leaf clusters. Mem. Internat. Bar Assn., Am. Bar Assn., Miss. Bar Assn., Student Loan Mktg. Assn. (dir. 1973-77), U.S. C. of C. (dir., mem. exec. com. 1973—), Jackson C. of C. (pres. 1966), Savs. and Loan Found. (chmn. bd.), U.S. League Savs. Assns. (past pres.), Internat. Union Savings Assns. (v.p.), Newcomen Soc. N. Am., Kappa Alpha. Episcopalian. Clubs: Hundred, Jackson Country, River Hills, Univ., Capital City, Jackson Kiwanis (past pres.). Home: 2505 Eastover Dr Jackson MS 39211 Office: 525 E Capitol St Jackson MS 39205*

SCOTT, TOM KECK, botanist, educator; b. St. Louis, Aug. 4, 1931; s. George Drake and Mary Ann (Keck) S.; B.A., Pomona (Calif.) Coll., 1954; M.A., Stanford 1959, Ph.D., 1961; m. Harriet Isabel Warner, Aug. 19, 1953; children—David Seymour, Stephen Arthur, John Warner, Cynthia Keck. Research asso. Princeton, 1961-63; asst. prof., then asso. prof. biology Oberlin (Ohio) Coll., 1963-69; mem. faculty U. N.C., Chapel Hill, 1969—, prof. botany, 1972—, chmn. biology curriculum, 1970-75, chmn. dept. botany, 1972—; vis. research prof. U. Nottingham (Eng.), 1967-68; Fulbright lectr. Ege U., Izmir, Turkey, 1972-73. Served with AUS, 1954-56. Danforth asso., 1974; NATO grantee, 1978. Fellow AAAS; mem. Am. Inst. Biol. Scis., Am. Soc. Plant Physiologists (trustee), Bot. Soc. Am., Ohio Acad. Scis., Scandinavian Soc. Plant Physiology, Soc. Gen. Physiologists, Assn. Southeastern Biologists, Internat. Plant Growth Substance Assn., Plant Growth Regulator Working Group, Sigma Xi. Author: Plant Regulation and World Agriculture, 1979. Research on characteristics of growth devel. and hormone translocation in higher plants. Home: 1711 Audubon Rd Chapel Hill NC 27514 Office: Dept Botany Coker Hall 010 A U NC Chapel Hill NC 27514

SCOTT, VERNE HARRY, educator; b. Salem, Oreg., June 19, 1924; s. Harry W. and Lois M. (Tyler) S.; student Willamette U., 1942-44; B.S. in Civil Engring., U. Mich., 1945, M.S., 1948; Ph.D. in Engring. (NSF Faculty fellow), Colo. State U., 1959; m. Dorothy J. Forshee; children—Patricia M., David F., Jane A. Faculty dept. land, air and water resources and civil engring. depts. U. Calif. at Davis, 1948—, prof. water sci. and civil engring., 1965—, chmn. dept. water sci. and engring., 1964-71, dir. campuswide work-learn program, 1972—; cons. to industry, state and fed. agys. Mem. Davis Park and Recreation Commn., 1969-75. Served with USNR, 1943-46. Mem. ASCE, Am. Soc. Engring. Edn., Sigma Xi, Sigma Alpha Epsilon. Contbr. articles to profl. jours., Ency. Americana. Home: 646 Elmwood Dr Davis CA 95616

SCOTT, WALLACE M., JR., diversified industry exec.; b. 1926; student N.D. State Tchrs. Coll., Ky. State Tchrs. Coll.; B.B.A., U. Utah, 1947. Sr. internal auditor U.S. Steel Co., 1948-62; corporate audit mgr. Montgomery Ward Co., 1962-65; mgr. accounting, bus. equipment div. Litton Industries, 1965; controller Eastex Packaging, Inc., 1966-67; controller Weyerhauser Co., Tacoma, Wash. 1967-70; pres., chief exec. officer MSL Industries, Lincolnwood, Ill., 1970—. Served with USNR, 1943-46. Office: 7373 N Lincoln Ave Lincolnwood IL 60646

SCOTT, WALTER, JR., food corp. exec.; b. Balt., July 24, 1925; s. Walter and Margaret Katherine (Pfeiffer) S.; A.B. Duke U., 1945; M.B.A. with distinction, Harvard U., 1949; m. Barbara Main, 1945 (dec. 1964); children—Stephen Walter, Susan Marjorie, Cynthia Margaret, Christopher Main; m. 2d, Mary Joan Braun, 1966. Advt. mgr. Quaker Oats Co., Chgo.; v.p. mktg. J.H. Filbert, Inc., Balt., then pres., chief exec. officer; div. gen. mgr. Central Soya Co., Ft. Wayne, Ind.; now exec. v.p. Fairmont Foods Co., Chgo.; lectr. Presidents Assn., Am. Mgmt. Assn. Served with USNR, 1943-46. Mem. Assn. for Dressings and Sauces (past v.p.), Nat. Assn. Margarine Mfrs. (past chmn. bd.), Milk Industry Found. (dir.), Internat. Assn. Ice Cream Mfrs. Republican. Episcopalian. Club: Baltimore Country. Home: 17W726 Butterfield Rd Oakbrook Terrace IL 60181 Office: Fairmont Foods Co 1111 E Touhy Ave Des Plaines IL 60018

SCOTT, WALTER BRUCE, electronics mfg. co. exec.; b. Chgo., Sept. 18, 1915; s. William and Agnes (Valentine) S.; student Northwestern Mil. and Naval Acad.; B.S., Drake U., 1937; postgrad. Northwestern U., 1938-42; m. Lucile Alice Pilmer, June 1, 1940 (dec. July 1968); children—Walter, Susan, William, Douglas; m. 2d, Beverly E. Lilly, June 14, 1969. Staff gen. mgr. Am. Can Co., 1937-42; asst. to v.p. J.I. Case Co., 1942-46; v.p. mfg., dir. Motorola, Inc., Chgo., 1946—; dir. C.F.S. Continental Corp. Pres. Thacher Woods council Boy Scouts; chmn. fund raising com. for new coll. bus. Drake U.; vice chmn. fin. advisory bd. to pres. Drake U., now trustee; pres., bd. mem., chmn. exec. com. Gottlieb Hosp. Mem. Am. Mgmt. Assn. (trustee, v.p. mfg. council), Alpha Tau Omega, Delta Sigma Pi. Presbyterian. (chmn. bldg. com., elder). Club: Oak Park (Ill.) Country. Home: 346 Island View Ln Lake Barrington Shores Barrington IL 60010 Office: 1303 E Algonquin Rd Schaumburg IL 60196

SCOTT, WALTER COKE, sugar co. exec., lawyer; b. Norfolk, Va., July 20, 1919; s. Walter Coke and Rosemary (White) S.; B.S., Hampden-Sydney Coll., 1939; J.D., U. Va., 1948; m. Virginia Kemper Millard, May 14, 1949; children—Mary Lyman, Roberta Coke, Alexander McRae, Buford Coke. Admitted to Va. bar, 1947, Ga. bar, 1954; atty. U.S. Dept. Justice, Jacksonville, Fla., 1948; commerce atty. S.A.L. Ry., Norfolk, 1948-54; commerce counsel, gen. solicitor Central of Ga. Ry., Savannah, 1954-60, v.p., 1960-62, dir., 1960—; partner law firm Hitch, Miller & Beckmann, Savannah, 1956-60; sr. v.p., sec. Savannah Foods & Industries, Inc. (formerly Savannah Sugar Refining Corp.), 1962-72, exec. v.p., mem. exec. com., 1972—, also dir.; exec. v.p., sec., mem. exec. com. dir. Everglades Sugar Refinery, Inc., Clewiston, Fla.; sec., mem. exec. com., dir. The Jim Dandy Co., Birmingham, Ala., 1968—; dir. Savannah Bank & Trust Co., Transales Corp., Dixie Terminal Co., Savannah. Pres., chmn. exec. com. Historic Savannah Found., 1963-64; bd. dirs. United Community Services, 1965-68, pres., 1967; gen. chmn. United Community Appeal, 1966; mem. Chatham-Savannah Met. Planning Commn., 1963-68; trustee, chmn. finance com. Telfair Acad. Arts and Scis., 1964-67; trustee, vice chmn. Savannah Country Day Sch., 1967-69, chmn., 1970-72. Bd. dirs., chmn. finance com. Savannah Speech and Hearing Center, 1967-70; bd. dirs. Savannah chpt. ARC, Savannah Symphony Soc., Inc. Mem. U.S. C. of C., Va. State Bar, ICC Practitioners Assn., Ga. State Bar, St. Andrews Soc., Savannah Benevolent Assn., Kappa Sigma, Omicron Delta Kappa, Phi Alpha Delta, Chi Beta Phi, Pi Delta Epsilon. Episcopalian (past vestryman, sr. warden). Rotarian. Clubs: Chatham, Oglethorpe, Savannah Golf. Home: 56 E 54th St Savannah GA 31405 Office: Savannah Bank Bldg Savannah GA 31401

SCOTT, WALTER DECKER, cons., ret. broadcasting exec.; b. Kansas City, Mo., Mar. 2, 1915; s. Robert Marshall and Ellen (Pearson) S.; student Washington U.; B.J., U. Mo., 1936; m. Arline Stenz, Oct. 5, 1940; children—Shelley (Mrs. Diedrick S. Cassel), Valerie (Mrs. Miguel Miro-Quesada). With NBC, Inc., N.Y.C., 1937-72, successively radio and TV sales exec., v.p. charge TV sales, exec. v.p., pres. TV network div., pres., 1966, chmn., chief exec. officer; ret., 1972. Mem. Pres.'s Com. on Employment of Handicapped; mem. nat. adv. bd. Salk Inst. Trustee Community Hosp. of Monterey Peninsula, Carmel, Calif., Amon Carter Mus. Western Art, Ft. Worth; bd. dirs. Green Meadows, Inc. Mem. Advt. Council (hon. dir.). Clubs: Cypress Point Pebble Beach, Calif.); Carmel Valley Golf (Carmel); Old Capital (Monterey, Calif.). Home and office: 7020 Valley Greens Dr Carmel CA 93923

SCOTT, WALTER DILL, food co. exec.; b. Chgo., Oct. 27, 1931; s. John Marcy and Mary Louise (Gent) S.; student Williams Coll., 1949-51; B.S., Northwestern U., 1953; M.S., Columbia, 1958; m. Barbara Ann Stein, Sept. 9, 1961; children—Timothy Walter, David Frederick, Gordon Charles. Cons. Booz, Allen & Hamilton, N.Y.C., 1956-58; asso. Glore, Forgan & Co., N.Y.C., 1958-63, partner, Chgo., 1963-65; partner Lehman Bros., Chgo., 1965-72, sr. partner, 1972-73, also dir.; asso. dir. econs. and govt. Office Mgmt. and Budget, Washington, 1973-75; sr. v.p. internat. and fin. Pillsbury Co., Mpls., 1975-78, exec. v.p., 1978—, also dir.; dir. Seven Funds of Investors Group. Mem. adv. council Northwestern U. Grad. Sch. Mgmt.; mem. bd. overseers Coll. and Grad. Sch. Bus. Adminstrn., U. Minn.; mem. adv. commn. CAB, 1975; bd. dirs. Nat. Fgn. Trade Council; trustee Mpls. Soc. Fine Arts. Served to lt. (j.g.) USN, 1953-56. Clubs: Woodhill; Minneapolis. Home: 2520 Cedar Ridge Rd Wayzata MN 55391 Office: 608 2d Ave S Minneapolis MN 55402

SCOTT, WILL, automotive exec.; b. Cleve., Aug. 22, 1921; s. Clarence W. and Nelle M. S.; A.B., U. Mich., 1943, M.B.A., 1947; m. Barbara De Fries, Aug. 22, 1943; children—Linda, Sarah, Patricia, William, David. With Ford Motor Co., Dearborn, Mich., 1948—, corporate planning, 1968-71, v.p. product planning, 1971, v.p. North Am. govtl. relations, 1972—. Served with USN, 1943-46. Mem. Hwy. Users Fedn., Automotive Safety Found., Citizen's Research Council, Soc. Automotive Engrs. Methodist. Clubs: Bloomfield Hills Country, Detroit Athletic, Renaissance; Birmingham (Mich.) Athletic. Home: 783 Hupp Cross Rd Birmingham MI 48010 Office: Ford Motor Co The American Rd Dearborn MI 48121

SCOTT, WILLARD PHILIP, lawyer, co. exec.; b. Columbus, Ohio, Jan. 8, 1909; s. Wirt Stanley and Mabel Lynne (Rond) S.; A.B. with honors, Ohio State U., 1930; LL.B. (dean's scholar), Columbia, 1933; m. Lucille Westrom, June 27, 1936; children—Robert W., David W., Anne L. Admitted to N.Y. bar, 1934, D.C. bar, 1934; partner Olver & Donnally, N.Y.C., 1938-65. Dir. Am. Potash & Chem. Corp., 1951—, v.p., 1955-68, vice chmn. bd., 1968—; v.p., gen. counsel Kerr-McGee Corp., 1968-73, v.p. finance, 1973-75, sr. v.p., 1973-75, cons., 1975—; gen. counsel Nat. Assn. Mut. Savs. Banks and Savs. Banks Assn. N.Y., 1945-60; counsel bondholders coms. r.r. reorgn. C. & N.-W. Ry., Soo Line, Alton, B. & M. R.R., C., M., St. P. & P. Ry., Fla. East Coast, Central N.J., D. & H. R.R.; dir. 1st Nat. Bank & Trust Co. of Oklahoma City, Transocean Drilling Co. Ltd., Bikita Minerals Ltd. Trustee, Scarsdale, N.Y., 1951-55, police commr., acting mayor, 1953-55, mayor, 1955-57, mem. bd. appeals, 1957-68. Bd. dirs. Oklahoma City Allied Arts Found., Oklahoma City Symphony Soc.; trustee Okla. Sci. and Arts Found.; bd. advisers Mercy Hosp. Fellow Am. Bar Found., Southwestern Legal Found. Mem. Internat. (patron), Am. (commn. on corporate laws 1947—, chmn. sect. corporate banking and bus. law 1960-61, ho. of dels. 1961-62, chmn. com. ednl. programs), N.Y., D.C., Okla. bar assns., Am. Law Inst., Assn. Bar City N.Y., Phi Beta Kappa, Phi Kappa Sigma, Phi Delta Phi, Phi Alpha Theta, Pi Sigma Alpha. Republican. Presbyn. Clubs: Union League, Madison Square Garden (N.Y.C.); Metropolitan (Washington); Scarsdale Golf; Oklahoma City Golf and Country, Beacon, Whitehall (Oklahoma City). Editor: Business Lawyer, 1958-59. Contbr. articles on corporate law to profl. jours. Home: 01812 Drury Ln Oklahoma City OK 73116 Office: Kerr-McGee Bldg Oklahoma City OK 73102

SCOTT, WILLIAM CAMPBELL, lawyer, bus. exec.; b. Lexington, Ky., Nov. 2, 1906; s. William Campbell and Katherine (Shelby) S.; A.B., U. Ky., 1926, LL.B., 1929; LL.M. (research fellow), Columbia, 1942; m. Anne Hodgson, Sept. 12, 1929; children—Anne McKinney, Katherine S. (Mrs. A.W. Allen), Adelaide S. (Mrs. Bruce Franklin). Admitted to N.Y. bar, 1931; practiced in N.Y.C., 1931-76; asso. firm Satterlee & Stephens and predecessor, 1930-39, partner, 1939-71, of counsel, 1971-76; vice chmn. bd. Am. Cystoscope Makers, Inc.; dir. Am. Latex Corp., Wappler Instrument Co. Inc. Trustee Wappler Found. Mem. Am., Ky. bar assns., Order of Coif, Kappa Alpha, Phi Delta Phi. Republican. Mason. Clubs: University (N.Y.C.); Heritage Village Country. Author: Practical Federalism, 1942; also articles. Home: 561-B Heritage Village Southbury CT 06488 Office: 300 Stillwater Ave Stamford CT 06902

SCOTT, WILLIAM CLEMENT, III, corp. exec.; b. N.Y.C., Apr. 25, 1934; s. William Clement and Susan L. (Cameron) S.; A.B., Coll. William and Mary, Williamsburg, Va., 1956; m. Lise Campbell, Nov. 23, 1966; 1 son, David. Self-employed, 1956-64; v.p. Booz-Allen & Hamilton, N.Y.C., 1964-69; group v.p., Cordura Corp., Los Angeles, 1969-72; exec. v.p. Western Pacific Industries, N.Y.C., 1972-76, pres., chief operating officer, 1976—, also dir.; pres. Veeder Industries Inc., 1975—. Republican. Episcopalian. Clubs: Union League, Racquet and Tennis (N.Y.C.); Coral Beach (Bermuda). Office: 345 Park Ave New York NY 10022

SCOTT, WILLIAM JOHN, lawyer, atty. gen. Ill.; b. Chgo., Nov. 11, 1926; s. William Earl and Edith (Swanson) S.; student Bucknell U., 1945, U. Pa., 1946; J.D., Kent Coll. Law, Chgo., 1950; m. Dorothy Lorraine Johnson, May 27, 1950 (div. Sept. 1970); children—Elizabeth Anne, William G. Admitted to Ill. bar, 1950; practiced in Chgo., 1950-51, 67-69; with LaSalle Nat. Bank, Chgo., 1951-53, Am. Nat. Bank & Trust Co., Chgo., 1953-58; v.p. Nat. Blvd. Bank Chgo., 1959-62; spl. asst. U.S. atty., 1959; pres. Holiday Travel House, 1959—; treas. State of Ill., 1963-67, atty. gen., 1969—. Trustee MacMurray Coll., Jacksonville, Ill., 1963-67. Served with USNR, 1945-46. Mem. Am., Fed., Ill., Chgo. bar assns. Presbyterian. Home: 520 S 2d Springfield IL 62701 Office: 500 S 2d St Springfield IL 62701

SCOTT, WILLIAM LLOYD, lawyer, former senator; b. Williamsburg, Va., July 1, 1915; s. William David and Nora Bell (Ingram) S.; J.D., George Washington U., 1938, LL.M., 1939; m. Ruth Inez Huffman, Feb. 5, 1940; children—Gail Ann (Mrs. Charles Eldred), William Lloyd, Paul Alvin. Admitted to Va. bar; trial atty. Dept. Justice, 1942-60; spl. asst. to solicitor Dept. Interior, 1960-61; practiced in Fairfax, Va., 1961-66, Springfield, Va., 1979—; mem. 90th-92d congresses 8th dist. Va.; mem. U.S. Senate from Va., 1973-79, mem. armed services and judiciary coms. Mem. Va. Republican Central Com., 1964-68; del. Rep. Nat. Conv., 1968, 72, 76. Served with AUS, World War II. Mem. Va., Fairfax County bar assns., Am. Legion, 40 and 8, Sigma Nu Phi (past chancellor). Methodist. Lion, Mason (33 deg., Shriner). Home: 3930 W Ox Rd Fairfax County VA 22030 Office: 6417 Loisdale Rd Springfield VA 22150

SCOTT, WILLIAM RICHARD, sociologist, educator; b. Parsons, Kans., Dec. 18, 1932; s. Charles Hogue and Hildegarde (Hewit) S.; student Parsons Jr. Coll., 1950-52; A.B., U. Kans., 1954, M.A. (Woodrow Wilson fellow), 1955; Ph.D. (Social Sci. Research Council fellow), U. Chgo., 1961; m. Joy Lee Whitney, Aug. 14, 1955; children—Jennifer Ann, Elliot Whitney, Sydney Brooke. Asst. prof. sociology Stanford, 1960-65, asso. prof., 1965-69, vice chmn. dept. sociology, 1968-72, prof. sociology, 1969—, chmn. dept. sociology, 1972-75; Edmund P. Learned Distinguished vis. prof. bus. adminstrn. U. Kans., 1970-71; vis. sr. scientist Nat. Center Health Services Research, 1975-76. Mem. health services research study sect., sci. adv. bd. HEW, 1968-72, dir. orgns. research tng. program, 1972—; mem. com. on human value issues in health care Nat. Acad. Scis., 1972, mem. Inst. Medicine, 1975—, mem. steering com. med. injury compensation study Inst. Medicine, 1976—, mem. panel on productivity statistics com. on nat. statistics, 1977-78. Chmn. bd. United Campus Christian Ministry, Stanford, 1968-70. Fellow Am. Sociol. Assn. (pres. sect. on sociology of orgns. and occupations 1970-71); mem. Sociol. Research Assn., Phi Beta Kappa. Presbyterian (deacon 1973-77, elder 1977—). Author: (with O.D. Duncan and others) Metropolis and Region, 1960; (with Peter M. Blau) Formal Organizations, 1962; Social Processes and Social Structures, 1970; (with Sanford M. Dornbusch) Evaluation and the Exercise of Authority, 1975. Asso. editor Pacific Sociol. Rev., 1964-67, Adminstrv. Sci. Quar., 1965-68, Am. Jour. Sociology, 1965-68, Am. Sociol. Rev., 1968-69, Med. Care, 1970-71. Editor: (with Edmund H. Volkart) Medical Care, 1966. Home: 940 Lathrop Pl Stanford CA 94305

SCOTT, WILTON ELEGE, geologist, petroleum co. exec.; b. Elgin, Tex., Jan. 3, 1913; s. Samuel S. and Clara (Schuerman) S.; B.A. in Geology, U. Tex., 1936; m. Loradean Allen, 1942; children—Sherman, Susan Scott Simons, Sarah. Geologist, Standard Oil Co. of N.J., Venezuela, S.Am., 1936-38; geologist Cities Service in Hobbs, N.Mex., 1938-44; chief geologist Buffalo Oil Co., Dallas, 1944-54, v.p., Midland, Tex., 1954-55; oil and gas exploration mgr. Tenneco, Inc., Houston, 1955-56, exec. v.p., 1970-73, vice chmn. bd., 1974, pres., 1974-77, chief exec. officer, 1974-78, chmn. bd., 1975-78; sr. v.p. Tenneco Oil Co., 1960-61, pres., 1961-70; dir. Republic of Tex. Corp. Mem. Am. Assn. Petroleum Geologists, Houston C. of C. Home: 107 Glynn Way Dr Houston TX 77056 Office: PO Box 2511 Houston TX 77001

SCOTTO, RENATA, soprano; b. Savona, Italy, Feb. 24, 1935; studied under Ghirardini, Merlino and Mercedes Llopart, Accademia Musicale Savonese, Conservatory Giuseppe Verdi, Milan; m. Lorenzo Anselmi. Debut in La Traviata, Teatro Nuevo, Milan, 1954, then joined La Scala Opera Co.; appeared with Met. Opera, N.Y.C., 1965, Concert Garden, Hamburg State Opera, Vienna State Opera, Nat. Theatre Munich, San Francisco Opera, Chgo. Lyric Opera; roles include La Sonnambula, I Puritani, L'Elisir d'amore, Lucia di Lammermoor, La Boheme, Turandot, Otello (Verdi), Trovatore, Vespri Siciliani, Le Prophete, Madama Butterfly, Adriana Lecouvreur, Norma, Tosca, Manon Lescaut, Ballo in Maschera. Address: care Robert J Lombardo 30 W 60th St New York NY 10023

SCOVIL, SAMUEL KINGSTON, mining co. exec.; b. Cleve., June 15, 1923; s. R. Malcolm and Dorothy Lee (Brown) S.; B.S., Yale, 1945; grad. Advanced Mgmt. Program, Harvard, 1962; m. Barbara C. Baker, May 22, 1944; children—Emily, Malcolm (dec.), Samuel, Alexander. With Republic Steel Corp., 1947-50; with Cleve.-Cliffs Iron Co., 1950—, mgr. sales, 1960-63, v.p. sales, 1963-69, sr. v.p. sales, 1970-72, sr. v.p., 1972-74, pres., 1974—, chief exec. officer, 1976—, also dir.; dir. Eaton Corp., Hill Acme Co., Nat. City Bank Cleve. Trustee, Univ. Sch., Cleve., Cleve. Clinic Found. Home: Gates Mills OH 44040 Office: Union Commerce Bldg Cleveland OH 44115

SCOVILLE, HERBERT, JR., author, cons.; b. N.Y.C., Mar. 16, 1915; s. Herbert and Orlena (Zabriskie) S.; B.S., Yale, 1937; Ph.D., U. Rochester, 1942; postgrad U. Cambridge (Eng.), 1937-39; m. Ann Curtiss, June 26, 1937; children—Anthony Church, Thomas Welch, Nicholas Zabriskie, Mary Curtiss. Sr. scientist Los Alamos contract AEC, Washington, 1946-48; tech. dir. armed forces spl. weapons project Dept. Def., Washington, 1948-55; dep. dir. sci. and tech. CIA, Washington, 1955-63; asst. dir. sci. and tech. ACDA, Washington, 1963-69; dir. arms control program Carnegie Endowment for Internat. Peace, Washington, 1969-71; cons. arms control program Carnegie Endowment, 1971—, adv. com. nuclear safeguards AEC, 1970-72, ACDA, 1969-73; pres. Arms Control Assn. Chmn. U.S. del., NATO Disarmament Experts Meetings, 1966-68; mem. sci. adv. bd. Air Force, 1955-62; Pres.'s Sci. adv. com. cons., 1957-63; chmn. SALT II Group, Council on Fgn. Relations, 1972-78. Bd. dirs. Pub. Welfare Found., Washington, 1971. Mem. AAAS (council), Sigma Xi. Clubs: Century (N.Y.C.); Cosmos (Washington). Author: (with R. Osborn) Missile Madness, 1970. Contbr. articles to profl. jours., chpts. to books). Address: 6400 Georgetown Pike McLean VA 22101

SCOVILLE, JAMES GRIFFIN, economist; b. Amarillo, Tex., Mar. 19, 1940; s. Orlin James and Carol Howe (Griffin) S.; B.A., Oberlin Coll., 1961; M.A., Harvard U., 1963, Ph.D., 1965; m. Judith Ann Nelson, June 12, 1962; 1 son, Nathan James. Economist, ILO, Geneva, 1965-66; instr. econs. Harvard U., Cambridge, Mass., 1964-65, asst. prof., 1966-69; asso. prof. econs. and labor and indsl. relations U. Ill., Urbana, 1969-75, prof., 1975-80; prof. indsl. relations, dir. Indsl. Relations Center, U. Minn., Mpls., 1980—; cons. ILO, World Bank, U.S. Dept. Labor. Mem. Am. Econ. Assn., Indsl. Relations Research Assn. Author: The Job Content of the US Economy, 1940-70, 1969; Perspectives on Poverty and Income Distribution, 1971; Manpower and Occupational Analysis: Concepts and Measurements, 1972; (with A. Sturmthal) The International Labor Movement in Transition, 1973. Home: 4849 Girard Ave S Minneapolis MN 55409 Office: 537 Bus Adminstrn Bldg 271 19th Ave S Minneapolis MN 55455

SCOVILLE, JOYCE MAXINE, civic worker; b. Garrison, Kans., July 20, 1917; d. Benjamin Joseph and Letha Leola (Thornburgh) Boyle; student Kans. U., 1934-36; m. Raymond W. Scoville, May 24, 1936; 1 dau., Sharon Lead Scoville Ellis. Tchr., Atichison and Leavenworth County (Kans.) schs., 1935-40; substitute tchr. Kansas City (Kans.) Schs., 1950-56; adult edn. lectr. Kansas City (Kans.) Schs., 1956-66, tchr. parent and family life classes, 1956-66; active PTA's, 1965-68, v.p. region V Nat. Congress Parents and Tchrs., 1965-68, chmn. Joint Conf. Nat. PTA and OEO, Home Sch. Cooperation for Disadvantaged, 1966-68; observer Pres. Johnson's Conf. on Edn. for Disadvantaged, Washington, 1966; mem. Kans. State Bd. Edn., 1964-68, Kans. Bd. Vocat. Edn., 1963-69; mem. Kansas City (Kans.) Bd. Edn., 1966—, v.p., 1967-71, pres., 1971-75; trustee Kansas City (Kans.) Public Library, 1961—. Mem. adminstrv. bd. Trinity Meth. Ch., Kansas City, Kans., 1960-74, pres. Women's Soc. Christian Service, 1970-74. Recipient Matrix award Theta Sigma Phi, 1961; Disting. Jayhawker award Gov. Kans., 1963; Honor award Soroptimist Club, 1972; named Woman of Yr., Kansas City Bus. and Profl. Women, 1974. Mem. ALA, Am. Library Trustee Assn. (pres. 1976-77), Kans. Library Assn., Friends of Philharmonic, Grinter Pl. Friends, Nat. PTA, Kans. State PTA, Delta Kappa Gamma (hon.). Club: MacDowell Music. Contbr. monthly articles to Kansas Parent Tchr., 1960-63.

SCOWCROFT, BRENT, air force officer; b. Ogden, Utah, Mar. 19, 1925; s. James and Lucile (Ballantyne) S.; B.S., U.S. Mil. Acad., 1947; M.A., Columbia U., 1953, Ph.D., 1967; postgrad. Georgetown U., 1958; m. Marian Horner, Sept. 17, 1951; 1 dau., Karen. Commd. 2d lt., USAAF, 1947, advanced through grades to lt. gen., USAF, 1974; asst. prof. dept. social sci. U.S. Mil. Acad., 1953-57; asst. air attache Am. embassy, Belgrade, Yugoslavia, 1959-61, asso. prof. dept. polit. sci. U.S. Air Force Acad., Colo., 1962-63, prof., head dept., 1963-64; mem. staff long range planning div. Office Dep. Chief Staff Plans and Ops., Washington, 1964-67; assigned Nat. War Coll., 1967-68; staff asst. Western Hemisphere region Office Asst. Sec. Def. Internat. Security Affairs, Washington, 1968-69; dep. asst. dir. plans for nat. security matters office Dep. Chief Staff Plans and Ops., 1969-70; spl. asst. to dir. Joint Staff, Joint Chiefs of Staff, 1970-71; mil. asst. to Pres., 1972-73; dep. asst. to Pres. for nat. security affairs, 1973-75, asst. to Pres. for nat. security affairs, 1975-77; mem. Pres.'s Gen. Adv. Com. on Arms Control, 1977—; dir. Atlantic Council U.S. Bd. visitors U.S. Air Force Acad., 1977—. Decorated D.S.M. with two oak leaf clusters, Legion of Merit with oak leaf cluster, Air Force Commendation medal, D.S.M., Dept. Def., Nat. Security medal. Mem. Council Fgn. Relations, Am. Polit. Sci. Assn., Acad. Polit. Sci. Mem. Ch. Jesus Christ of Latter-day Saints. Office: 1825 I St NW Washington DC 20006

SCRANTON, WILLIAM MAXWELL, mfg. co. exec.; b. Scranton, Pa., Mar. 1, 1921; s. William Henry and Dorothy (Bessell) S.; B.S. in Engring., Princeton, 1942; M.B.A., Harvard, 1948; m. Andrea Orne Abbott, Sept. 24, 1949; children—John Selden and Nancy Orne (Mrs. Don J. Sporburg) (twins), James Maxwell, Sarah Abbott. With Pratt & Whitney Aircraft div. United Aircraft Crop., East Hartford, Conn., 1942-46, 48-50; with MPB Corp., Keene, N.H., 1950-77, exec. v.p., 1953-62, pres., 1962-77, dir., 1959-76; pres., dir. Beede Elec. Instrument Co. Inc., 1977—; dir. Indian Head Nat. Bank of Keene, Internat. Packings Corp., Pub. Service Co. N.H., OK Tool Co., Inc., Summa Four, Inc. Home: RFD 2 Hurricane Rd Keene NH 03431 Office: S Main St Penacook NH 03303

SCRANTON, WILLIAM W., III, state ofcl.; b. Scranton, Pa., July 20, 1947; s. William W. and Mary Lowe (Chamberlin) S.; B.A., Yale U., 1969; m. Coral Vange, Dec. 20, 1973; 1 dau., Elizabeth Brook. Editor, Mountain Eagle, Mountain Top, Pa., 1969-70; pres., mng. editor Greenstreet News Co., Dallas, Pa., 1971-72; field dir. Pa. Republican State Com., 1976; v.p., bd. dirs. Sauquoit Industries, 1977-7 8; lt. gov. Commonwealth of Pa., 1979—; mem. World Plan Exec. Council, 1973-76. Bd. dirs. Metro Action Inc., Scranton, UN Assn. Greater Scranton. Republican. Episcopalian. Office: 200 Main Capitol Harrisburg PA 17120

SCRANTON, WILLIAM WARREN, former ambassador to UN, former gov. Pa.; b. Madison, Conn. July 19, 1917; s. Worthington and Marion Margery (Warren) S.; B.A., Yale, 1939, LL.B., 1946; hon. degrees 32 colls. and univs.; m. Mary Lowe Chamberlin, July 6, 1942; children—Susan, William Worthington, Joseph Curtis, Peter Kip. Admitted to Pa. bar, 1946; joined firm O'Malley, Harris, Harris & Warren, Scranton, 1947; v.p. Internat. Textbook Co., Scranton, 1949-52; pres. Scranton-Lackawanna Trust Co., 1954-56; chmn. bd., dir. Northeastern Pa. Broadcasting Co., 1952-59; spl. asst. to U.S. sec. of state, 1959-60; mem. 87th Congress, 10th Dist. Pa.; gov. State of Pa., 1963-67; chmn. bd. Nat. Liberty Corp., 1969-71; mem. Pres.'s Price Commn., 1971-72, Pres.'s Gen. Adv. Com. on Arms Control and Disarmament, 1969-76, Pres.'s Commn. on Nat. Agenda for the Eighties, 1979; cons. to Pres., 1974-76; ambassador to UN, 1976-77; dir. IBM Corp., N.Y. Times, Scott Paper Co., Bethlehem Steel, Cummins Engines, Am. Express; past chmn. bd. Northeastern Nat. Bank of Pa., 1973-76. Vice chmn. Pres.'s Panel for Riot Torn Areas, 1967; U.S. ambassador, chmn. U.S. delegation INTELSAT, 1969; chmn. Pres.'s Commn. on Campus Unrest, 1970. Chmn., Nat. Conf. on Govt., 1974-76; chmn. Urban Inst., 1974-76; mem. exec. com. Trilateral Commn. (Japan, N.Am. and European Community). Served as capt. USAAF, 1941-45. Office: Northeastern Bank Scranton PA 18503

SCREVANE, PAUL ROGERS, bus. exec.; b. Woodcliffe, N.J., Aug. 1914; s. Joseph and Anne (Reardon) S.; student Miss. State Coll.; m. Bridie McKessey, 1942; children—Paul Owen, Sara Anne, Christopher, Brian. Employee, N.Y.C. Dept. sanitation, 1936-53, dir. operations, 1953-57, commr., 1957-61; dep. mayor, N.Y.C., 1961; pres. council, N.Y.C., 1962-65; coordinator anti-poverty program, N.Y.C., 1964; chmn., pres. N.Y.C. Off-Track Betting Corp., 1974-78; pres. Fed. Metal Maintenance Inc.; vice chmn. bd. Arcade Maintenance Corp. trustee Jamaica Savs. Bank; dir. Air Pollution Control Corp. Pres. Catholic Interracial Council, 1975. Chmn. bd. N.Y.C. U.S.O.; Trustee Hall Sci., N.Y. Served to maj. F.A., AUS, 1941-45; ETO; col. Res. ret. Decorated Silver Star, Bronze Star (2); recipient decorations govts. Greece and Italy; named knight Order Merit (Italy). Mem. Am. Pub. Works Assn. (pres. 1964). Democrat. Home: 52-35 241st St Douglaston New York City NY 11362 Office: 152 W 52d St New York City NY 10019

SCRIBNER, CHARLES, JR., publisher; b. Quogue, N.Y., July 13, 1921; s. Charles and Vera Gordon (Bloodgood) S.; student St. Paul's Sch., 1939; A.B., Princeton, 1943; m. Dorothy Joan Sunderland, July 16, 1949; children—Charles, Blair Sund, John. Advt. mgr. Charles Scribner's Sons, 1946-48, v.p., 1948-50, pres., 1952-77, chmn., 1977—. Pres., Am. Book Pubs. Council, 1966-68. Trustee Princeton, 1969-79, Princeton U. Press. Served as lt. USNR, 1943-46, 50-52. Clubs: Racquet and Tennis, University, Church (N.Y.C.); Nassau (Princeton, N.J.). Home: 211 E 70th St New York NY 10021 Office: 597 Fifth Ave New York NY 10017

SCRIBNER, FRED CLARK, JR., lawyer; b. Bath, Maine, Feb. 14, 1908; s. Fred Clark and Emma Amelia (Cheltra) A.; A.B., Dartmouth, 1930, LL.D., 1959; LL.B., Harvard, 1933; LL.D., U. Maine, 1958, Colby Coll., 1959, Bowdoin Coll., 1959, U. Vt., 1960; m. Barbara Curtis Merrill, Aug. 24, 1935; children—Fred Clark, Curtis Merrill, Charles Dewey. Admitted to Maine, Mass. bars, 1933, D.C. bar, 1961; asso. Cook, Hutchinson, Pierce, and Connell, Portland, Maine, 1933-35, partner, 1935-55; partner Pierce, Atwood, Scribner, Allen, Smith and Lancaster, Portland, 1961—, Scribner, Hall, Thornburg & Thompson, Washington, 1961—; chmn. bd. Coordinated Apparel, Inc.; dir., gen. counsel, v.p., treas. Bates Mfg. Co., Lewiston, Me., 1946-55; gen. counsel Dept. Treasury, 1955-57, asst. sec. treasury, 1957, under sec., 1957-61; dir. Sentinel Group Funds, Inc. Mem. Am. Bd. Arbitration; mem. commr.'s adv. com. on exempt orgns. Internal Revenue Service; chmn. ad hoc adv. group on presdl. vote for P.R. Mem. nat. council Boy Scouts Am. (Silver Beaver award; mem. exec. com. Region I); pres. Maine Constl. Commn., 1963-64; chmn. Portland Republican City Com., 1936-40; chmn. Maine Council Young Rep. Clubs, 1938-40; mem. Maine Rep. State Com., 1940-50 (chmn. exec. com. 1944-50); Rep. nat. committeeman from Maine, 1948-56; del. Rep. Nat. Conv., 1940, 44, 56, 60, 64, 68, counsel Rep.

Nat. Com., 1952-55, 61-73; gen. counsel arrangements com. Nat. Conv., 1956-72; Presdl. elector, 1976; bd. dirs. Maine Med. Center, Portland, Am. Council Capitol Formation, Am. Council for Nationalities Service; former pres. bd. trustees Bradford Coll., Haverhill, Mass.; trustee Cardigan Mountain Sch., Canaan, N.H. Recipient Alexander Hamilton award, Dartmouth Alumni Council award, 1971. Mem. Am., Fed., Maine, Cumberland County bar assns., Am. Law Inst., Newcomen Soc. in N.Am. (clk.), Phi Beta Kappa, Delta Sigma Rho, Alpha Chi Rho. Episcopalian. (mem. standing com. Diocesan Council, chancellor Diocese of Maine; del. Gen. Conv. P.E. Ch., 1943, 46, 52, 61, 64, 67, 69, 70, 73, 76, 79). Mason (33 deg.). Clubs: Capitol Hill (Washington); Portland, Woodfords, Kiwanis. Home: 335 Foreside Rd Falmouth Foreside ME 04105 Office: 10th Floor One Monument Sq Portland ME 04101 also 1875 Eye St NW Washington DC 20006

SCRIBNER, GILBERT HILTON, JR., real estate broker; b. Milw., June 1, 1918; s. Gilbert Hilton and Nancy (Van Dyke) S.; B.S., Yale, 1939; m. Helen Shoemaker, Mar. 22, 1941; children—Helen Eaton (Mrs. Gregory E. Euston), Nancy Van Dyke (Mrs. David W. Clarke, Jr.), William Van Dyke, II. Pres. Scribner & Co., 1962-77, chmn., 1977—; dir. Abbott Labs., No. Trust Co., Quaker Oats Co., Gen. Electric Co., No. Trust Corp.; trustee Northwestern Mut. Life Mortgage & Realty Investors. Pres. Civic Fedn. 1955-57; mem. Chgo. Pub. Bldgs. Com., 1967-71. Trustee Northwestern U.; bd. dirs. Mid-Am. chpt. A.R.C., 1952-57, 67-72; chmn. adv. com. to bd. commrs. Forest Preserve Dist. Cook County, Ill. Chmn. Ill. Commn. for Constnl. Revision, 1958-61. Bd. dirs. Northwestern Meml. Hosp. Served as lt. comdr. USNR, 1941-45. Mem. Chgo. Hist. Soc. (trustee 1946-78). Republican. Episcopalian. Clubs: Chicago, Mid-Day, Commercial (Chgo.); Indian Hill (Winnetka); Links (N.Y.C.); Shoreacres (Lake Bluff, Ill.); Old Elm (Highland Park, Ill.). Home: 17 Meadowview Dr Northfield IL 60093 Office: One First Nat Plaza Chicago IL 60603

SCRIBNER, LOUIE LORRAINE, architect; b. Raleigh, N.C., Aug. 25, 1906; s. Walter Brevort and Katherine (Mason) S.; student U. Va., 1925-30; m. Virginia Bell Stainback, Sept. 4, 1937; children—Louie Lorraine Jr., Willard Mason. Mem. archtl. firm Stainback & Scribner, Charlottesville, Va., 1949—, sr. partner, 1965—. Dir. Nat. Bank & Trust, Charlottesville. Mem. Charlottesville City Council, 1957-66, mayor, 1960-62; chmn. Charlottesville City Planning Commn., 1959-77; chmn. City-County Indsl. Commn., 1977—. Bd. dirs. Va. Archtl. Ednl. Found. Served with AUS, 1943-45. Fellow AIA; mem. Theta Chi, Alpha Rho Chi. Democrat. Baptist (trustee 1977—). Kiwanian. Home: 712 Lyons Ct Ln Charlottesville VA 22901 Office: Nat Bank Bldg E Main St Charlottesville VA 22902

SCRIGGINS, LARRY PALMER, lawyer; b. Englewood, N.J., Nov. 27, 1936; s. Thomas Dalby and M. Patricia (Fowler) S.; A.B., Middlebury Coll., 1958; J.D., U. Chgo., 1961; m. M. Ann Boyer, Dec. 26, 1959 (div. 1976); children—Elizabeth J., Thomas P.; m. 2d, Victoria J. Rossetti, Feb. 17, 1979. Admitted to Md. bar, 1962; law clk. to chief judge Ct. of Appeals of Md., 1962; asso. firm Piper & Marbury, Balt., 1962-69, partner, 1969—; reporter Commn. on Revision of Md. Corp. Laws, 1965-66. Mem. Am. Bar Assn. (mem. council sect. corp., banking and bus. law 1972-77), Md. State Bar Assn. (chmn. council sect. corp., banking and bus. law 1977-78), Am. Law Inst., Am. Judicature Soc., Internat. Bar Assn. Home: 13 E Eager St Baltimore MD 21202 Office: 1100 Charles Center S 36 S Charles St Baltimore MD 21201

SCRIMENTI, ADOLPH ROBERT, architect; b. Bklyn., Jan. 21, 1913; s. Matthew and Maria (DiPolito) S.; diploma Pratt Inst. Sch. Arch., 1934; postgrad. Beaux Arts Inst. Design-Atelier-Fletcher-Moore, 1934-37; m. Rachel R. Rush, Dec. 6, 1945; children—Janet R., Michael B. Designer, asst. to architect H. Hurwit, N.Y.C., 1934-39; asso. architect Office Chief of Engrs., U.S. Dept. War, Washington, 1939-42; partner J.C. Van Nuys & Assos., 1945-57, Tectonic Assos., 1950-54 (both Somerville, N.J.); sr. partner Scrimenti, Swackhamer & Perantoni, Somerville, 1957-73, Scrimenti, Shive, Spinelli and Perontoni, Somerville, 1973—. Mem. N.J. Comm. to Make Bldgs. Useable to Physically Handicapped, 1960-64; mem. N.J. Bd. Architects on Licensing, 1965-72, pres, 1969-71. Mem. com. arch. Commn. to Study Arts in N.J., 1964-67; mem., chmn. Parking Authority, 1957-61, Improvement Commn., 1960-66 (both Somerville). Served with C.E., AUS, 1942-45; ETO. Decorated Bronze Star; recipient Architect of the Year Bronze plaque State of N.J., 1970, Citizen of the Year Bronze plaque N.J. Jewish Community Centers, 1968, Architect of Year Bronze Plaque award N.J. Subcontractors Assn., 1974, also various archtl. awards. Fellow A.I.A. (treas. N.J. chpt. 1957-58, v.p. 1959-60, pres. 1961-62 nat. and regional dir. 1974-78; mem. Nat. Inst. Archtl. Edn. (trustee 1972-78), Am. Assn. Sch. Adminstrs., N.J., Central N.J. (pres. 1957-58) socs. architects, Water Pollution Fedn. Club: Pratt Architectural (Bklyn.). Prin. works include Hillsborough (N.J.) Sch., 1951; Hanover Park (N.J.) Regional High Sch.,1957; Meditation Chapel, Trenton State Coll., 1962; Lab. Sch. and Child Study Clinic, Newark State Coll., 1966, Fine Arts-Theatre Arts bldg., 1971; Somerset County Coll., 1976. Home: 308 Altamont Pl Somerville NJ 08876 Office: 350 Grove St Somerville NJ 08876

SCRIMSHAW, NEVIN STEWART, educator; b. Milw., Jan. 20, 1918; s. Stewart and Harriet Fernwood (Smith) S.; B.A., Ohio Wesleyan U., 1938, D.Pub. Service (hon.), 1961; M.A., Harvard, 1939, Ph.D., 1941, M.P.H., 1959; M.D., U. Rochester, 1945; Ph.D. (hon.), U. Tokushima, 1979; m. Mary Ware Goodrich, Aug. 26, 1941; children—Susan March Norman Stewart, Nevin Baker, Steven Ware, Nathaniel Lewis. Teaching fellow comparative anatomy Harvard, 1939-41; instr. embryology and comparative anatomy Ohio Wesleyan U., 1941-42; postdoctoral fellow nutrition and endocrinology U. Rochester, 1942-43, Rockefeller Found. postdoctoral fellow, 1946-47, Merck-NRC fellow, 1947- 49; rotating intern Gorgas Hosp., C.Z., 1945-46; asst. resident physician obstetrics and gynecology Strong Meml., Genesee hosps., Rochester, N.Y., 1948-49; cons. nutrition Pan Am. San. Bur., Office for Ams. WHO, 1948-49, chief nutrition sect., 1949-53, regional nutrition adviser, 1953-58; dir. Inst. Nutrition C. Am., Panama, Guatemala, 1949-61, cons. dir., 1961-65, cons., 1965—; vis. lectr. pub. tropical health Harvard U., 1968—; adj. prof. pub. health nutrition Columbia, 1959-61, vis. lectr., 1961-66; head dept. nutrition and food sci. Mass. Inst. Tech., 1961-79, Inst. prof., 1979—. Mem. coms. NIH, NRC, govt. depts.; sci. adv. com. Nutrition Found., 1960-68, Williams-Waterman Fund and Williams-Waterman Program Com. Research Corp., 1962-75; bd. govs. Pan. Am. Soc. New Eng., 1962-70; chmn. malnutrition panel U.S.-Japan Coop. Med. Sci. Program, 1964-74, mem. U.S. delegation of joint com., 1974—; chmn. internat. centers com. NIH, 1965-69; cons. med. and natural scis. program Rockefeller Found., 1966-71, trustee, 1971—; mem. adv. com. med. research WHO, 1971—, chmn., 1973-78, mem. expert adv. council on nutrition, 1975—; sr. adviser World Hunger Programme UN U., 1975—; mem. coms., del. confs. WHO, FAO, UNICEF, others. Trustee Am. Freedom from Hunger Found. Served with AUS, 1942-45. Recipient Mead-Johnson prize Rochester Acad. Medicine, 1947; Joseph Goldberger award AMA, 1969; Univ. alumni citation U. Rochester, 1969; 1st James R. Killian, Jr. Faculty Achievement award Mass. Inst. Tech., 1972; Bolton L. Corson medal Franklin Inst., 1976; medal of Honor, Fundacion F. Cvenca Villoro, Spain, 1978; decorated Order Rodolfo Robles (Guatemala), 1961. Diplomate Nat. Bd. Med. Examiners, Am. Bd. Nutrition (sec.-treas. 1965-69). Fellow Am. Pub. Health Assn. (chmn. food and nutrition sect. 1962-63, mem. council 1966—, award for excellence 1974), Royal Soc. Health, Am. Acad. Arts and Scis. (chmn. com. nutrition 1975—), Am. Coll. Preventive Medicine, Council on Fgn. Relations, Internat. Epidemiol. Assn.; mem. Am. Inst. Nutrition (Osborne-Mendel award 1960, Elvehjem award 1976), Nat. Acad. Scis. (mem. inst. medicine), Am. Soc. Clin. Nutrition (McCollum award 1975), Am. Physiol. Soc., Am. Chem. Soc., Inst. Food Technologists (Internat. award 1969), Am. Soc. Tropical Medicine and Hygiene, Genetics Soc. Am., Mass. Pub. Health Assn., Assn. Pediatrica de Guatemala (hon.), Assn. Medica Nacional de Panama (hon.), Royal Soc. Scis. Uppsala (Sweden), Czechoslovak Soc. for Gastroenterology and Nutrition (corr.), Asociacion Argentina de Nutricion y Dietologia (hon.), AAAS, Am. Epidemiological Soc., Biometrics Soc., Asociacion de Nutricionistas y Dietistas de Centro Am. y Panama (hon.), Sociedad Latino-americana de Nutrición, Internat. Union Nutritional Scis. (pres. 1978—), Group European Nutritionists (corr.), Phi Beta Kappa, Sigma Xi (nat. lectr. 1971-72), Omicron Delta Kappa, Gamma Alpha, Phi Tau Sigma. Delta Omega, numerous others. Unitarian. Club: Cosmos (Washington). Author: (with Carl E. Taylor, John E. Gordon) Interactions of Nutrition and Infection, 1968. Editor: (with John E. Gordon) Proceedings of the International Conference on Malnutrition, Learning and Behavior, 1967; Malnutrition, Learning and Behavior, 1968; (with A.M. Altschul) Amino Acid Fortification of Protein Foods, 1971; (with A. Berg, D.L. Call) Nutrition, National Development and Planning, 1973; (with Steven R. Tamenbaum and Bruce R. Stillings) The Economics, Marketing, and Technology of Fish Protein Concentrate, 1974; (with M. Behar) Nutrition and Agricultural Development: Significance and Potential for the Tropics, 1976; (with others) Single-Cell Protein: Safety for Animal and Human Feeding, 1979; editorial bd. Am. Jour. Physiology, Jour., Jour. Applied Physiology, Procs. Nat. Acad. Scis.; contbr. articles to profl. jours. Home: 285 Commonwealth Ave Boston MA 02215 Office: Dept Nutrition and Food Sci Mass Inst Tech Cambridge MA 02139

SCRIPPS, CHARLES EDWARD, newspaper publisher; b. San Diego, Jan. 27, 1920; s. Robert Paine and Margaret Lou (Culbertson) S.; student Coll. William and Mary, 1938-40, Pomona Coll., 1940-41; m. Louann Copeland, June 28, 1941 (div. July 1947); m. 2d, Lois Anne MacKay, Oct. 14, 1949; children—Charles Edward, Marilyn Joy, Eaton Mackay, Julia Osborne. Reporter Cleve. Press, 1941; successor-trustee Edward W. Scripps Trust, 1945, chmn. bd. trustees, 1948—, v.p., dir. E.W. Scripps Co., 1946—, chmn. bd., 1953—; dir. various Scripps-Howard newspapers and affiliated enterprises, The First Nat. Bank Cin. Pres., Community Improvement Corp. of Cin. Trustee Freedoms Found.; mem. Scripps Clinic and Research Found.; trustee Webb Sch. Enlisted in USCG, 1942, commd. ensign, USCGR, 1944, advanced to lt. (j.g.), 1945; inactive duty, 1946-72. Mem. CAP, Theta Delta Chi. Home: 10 Grandin Ln Cincinnati OH 45208 Office: 1100 Central Trust Tower Cincinnati OH 45202

SCRIPPS, EDWARD WYLLIS, newspaper publisher; b. San Diego, May 21, 1909; s. James G. and Josephine (Stedem) S.; student Pomona Coll.; m. Betty Jeanne Knight McDonnell, Jan. 31, 1950; children—Edward Wyllis III, Barry Howard. Chmn. bd. Scripps League of Newspapers, 1931—. Mem. Inter-Am. Press Assn. (dir., pres. tech. center). Clubs: St. Francis Yacht, Villa Taverna (San Francisco); Rainier (Seattle), Corinthian Yacht (Belvedere); Lyford Cay (Nassau, Bahamas). Home: Eagle Hill Star Route 1 Box 16B Charlottesville VA 22901 also PO Box N7776 Lyford Cay Club Nassau Bahamas Office: 400 El Camino Real San Mateo CA 94401

SCRIVEN, L. E(DWARD), (II), engring. scientist, educator; b. Battle Creek, Mich., Nov. 4, 1931; s. L. Edward and Esther Mabel (Davis) S.; B.S., U. Calif., Berkeley, 1952; M.Ch.E., U. Del., 1954, Ph.D., 1956; m. Dorene Bates Hayes, June 19, 1952; children—Ellen Dorene, Teresa Ann, Mark Hayes. Research engr. Shell Devel. Co., Emeryville, Calif., 1956-59; asst. prof. chem. engring. and fluid mechanics U. Minn., Mpls., 1959-62, asso. prof., 1962-66, prof., 1966—, asso. dept. head, 1975-78; cons. in field; sci. asso. Jet Propulsion Lab., Pasadena, Calif.; tech. expert UN Indsl. Devel. Orgn., Vienna. Recipient Gold medal U. Calif., Berkeley, 1952; Disting. Teaching award U. Minn., 1966; Chem. Engring. award Am. Soc. Engring. Edn., 1968; A.M. Rutherford award, 1979; Guggenheim fellow, 1969-70. Mem. Am. Inst. Chem. Engrs. (mem. nat. program com. 1964-69, Colburn award 1960, Walker award 1977), Am. Phys. Soc., Soc. Petroleum Engrs., Gordon Research Confs., Chem. Soc. (Faraday div.), Nat. Acad. Engring. Editor: Physicochemical Hydrodynamics (V.G. Levich), 1962; asso. editor Jour. Fluid Mechanics, 1970-75; research in capillarity and fluid mechanics, porous media, cold-stage electron microscopy, microstructured fluids and interfaces, origins of pattern and form, computer-aided subdomain methods.

SCRIVEN, L. EDWARD, internat. mgmt. and marketing exec.; b. Spokane, Wash., Sept. 8, 1905; s. Burt J. and Lurenda (Tharp) S.; student U. Wash., 1923-26, Wash. State U., 1926-27, Columbia, 1928-29; m. Esther Davis, Nov. 23, 1927; children—L. Edward II, Marc Coleman, Stephen Arthur, Jacqueline Harriet; m. 2d Marguerite Guard, Dec. 30, 1953. With Kellogg Co., Battle Creek, Mich., 1932-34, Lord & Thomas, also Batten, Barten, Durstine & Osborn, advt., 1934-38; v.p. A.C. Nielsen Co., Chgo., also mng. dir. A.C. Nielson Co., Ltd., London and Oxford, Eng., 1938-41; asst. dep. dir. WPB, and predecessors, 1941-43; Western mgr. McKinsey- Kearney Co., San Francisco, 1943-45; gen. mgr. Niagara Duplicator Co., San Francisco, 1945-48; dir. mktg. Rainier Brewing Co., San Francisco, 1948-49; owner pres. L.E. Scriven Co., Washington, 1949-53; chief engr.-adminstrn. cons. gaseous diffusion project AEC, Portsmouth, Ohio, 1953-54; v.p. A.J. Wood & Co., Phila., 1954-56; mng. dir. Am. Assos. for Mgmt. Devel., Helsinki, Finland, 1956-59; prin. Wallace Clark & Co., mgmt. engr., N.Y.C., 1960-61: dir. Bur. Internat. Bus. Operation, Dept. Commerce, 1961-63, acting nat. export coordinator U.S., 1963-64; gen. mgr. devel. and sales World Trade Center, Port of New York Authority, 1964-73; sr. adviser on export expansion to Govt. of Vietnam, AID, Saigon, 1973-74, dir. tng. Vietnamese internat. trade specialists, 1974-75. Mgmt. adviser to sr. execs. Council Internat. Progress Mgmt. in Finland, Sweden and Norway, 1956-59; adviser Finnish Found. Productivity Research, 1956-59; initiated first Advanced Mgmt. Tng. Program for sr. execs. in Finland, 1957; guest lectr. U.S., fgn. univs. Dir. Inter-racial Bus. Council. Decorated comdr. Order of the Lion (Finland); recipient of citation Finnish Found. Productivity Research, 1959, Silver medal and citation Govt. of Vietnam, 1974. Mem. Am. Marketing Assn. (founder-charter), Market Research Council, Am. Statis. Assn., Soc. Advancement Mgmt., Am. Mgmt. Assn., Council Internat. Progress in Mgmt. (dir.), UN Assn., Soc. Internat. Devel. Rotarian. Club: Union League (N.Y.C.). Address: 401 S Palm Ave Sarasota FL 33577

SCRIVER, CHARLES ROBERT, physician; b. Montreal, Que., Can., Nov. 7, 1930; s. Walter deM. and Jessie (Boyd) S.; B.A. cum laude, McGill U., Montreal, 1951, M.D.C.M. cum laude, 1955; m. E.K. Peirce, Sept. 8, 1956; children—Dorothy, Peter, Julie, Paul. Intern, Royal Victoria Hosp., Montreal, 1955-56; resident Royal Victoria and Montreal Children's hosps., 1956-57, Children's Med. Center, Boston, 1957-58; McLaughlin travelling fellow Univ. Coll., London, 1958-60; chief resident pediatrics Montreal Children's Hosp., 1960-61; asst. prof. pediatrics McGill U., 1961. now prof. genetics Human Genetics Center, prof. biology Faculty of Sci., prof. pediatrics Faculty of Medicine. Recipient Wood Gold medal McGill U., 1955, Borden award Nutrition Soc. Can., 1969, Gairdner Internat. award Gairdner Found., 1979; Markle scholar, 1962-67; Med. Research Council Can. asso., 1968—. Fellow Royal Soc. Can.; mem. Can. Soc. Clin. Investigation (pres. 1974-75, G. Malcolm Brown award 1979), Soc. Pediatric Research (pres. 1975-76), Am. Soc. Human Genetics (dir. 1971-74, William Allen award 1978), Am. Soc. Clin. Investigation, Brit. Pediatric Assn. (hon.; 50th Anniversary lectr. 1978), Soc. Francaise de Pediat (hon.), Am. Acad. Pediatrics (Mead Johnson award 1968, Borden award 1973). Co-author: Amino Acid Metabolism and Its Disorders, 1973; research, 256 publs. in field. Office: Montreal Children's Hosp Research Inst 2300 Tupper St Montreal PQ H3H 1P3 Canada

SCRUGGS, EARL EUGENE, entertainer; b. Cleveland County, N.C., Jan. 6, 1924; s. George Elam and Georgia Lula (Ruppe) S.; m. Anne Louise Certain, Apr. 18, 1948; children—Gary Eugene, Randy Lynn, Steven Earl. Banjo player, 1945—; formed Earl Scruggs Revue, 1969—; major performances include Carnegie Hall, N.Y.C., Wembley Festival, London, Eng., Washington Moratorium for Peace, 1969, also rock festivals, coll. concerts U.S. and Can.; TV appearances include NET-TV Spl. Earl Scruggs: His Family and Friends, 1971, Midnight Spl., NBC-Harper Valley U.S.A. Spl., NBC Country Music Awards Show, Phil Donahue Show, Mike Douglas Show, Austin City Limits, 1977; rec. artist, Columbia Records, 1950—; star movie Banjo Man, 1975; made music score for movie Where The Lilies Bloom. Recipient Grammy award, 1969; Broadcast Music, Inc. award for instrumental Foggy Mountain Breakdown, 1969; named Artist of Year, Hi-Fi Inst., 1975; numerous other awards. Author: Earl Scruggs and the 5-String Banjo, 1968.

SCRUGGS, JOHN DUDLEY, landscape architect; b. Flemingsburg, Ky., May 3, 1911; B.A., Berea Coll., 1933; M.L.A., Harvard, 1938. Landscape architect Associated Architects, Lexington, Ky., 1938-40, Harland Bartholomew and Assos., 1941-42; co-founder, v.p. Scruggs and Hammond, Inc., Landscape Architects and Planning Cons., Lexington, Columbus, Ohio and Peoria, Ill., 1946—; pres. Ky. Bd. Registration for Landscape Architects; vis. critic U. Ky., Harvard. Served with AUS, 1942-46. Fellow Am. Soc. Landscape Architects (chmn. com. on pub. relations 1953-63, chmn. com. on biographies of fellows 1976—), AIA. Clubs: Lafayette, Harvard. Home: Ash Grove Pike Route 5 Nicholasville KY 40356 Office: 239 N Broadway Lexington KY 40508

SCUDDER, GEOFFREY G(EORGE) E(DGAR), zoologist: b. Fawkham, Kent, Eng., Mar. 18, 1934; s. George T. A. and Eva L. (Chapman) S.; came to Can., 1958, naturalized, 1973; B.Sc. in Zoology with honors, U. Wales, 1955; D. Phil., U. Oxford (Eng.), 1958; m. Jacqueline Howard, Apr. 7, 1958; 1 dau., Nicola Claire. Instr. in zoology U. B.C. (Can.), Vancouver, 1958-60, asst. prof. zoology, 1960-64, asso. prof., 1964-68, prof., 1968—, head dept. zoology, 1976—: vis. prof. Imperial Coll., London U., 1964-65; exchange scientist NRC Can.-Soviet Acad. Scis., 1965; vis. scientist Wau (Papua New Guinea) Ecology Inst., 1972. Recipient Master Tchr. award U. B.C., 1976; award Royal Soc. and Nuffield Found. Commonwealth Bursary, 1964: NRC Can. grantee, 1959-78; Nat. Scis. and Engring. Research Council Can. grantee, 1979—. Fellow Royal Soc. Can., Entomol. Soc. Can. (Gold medal 1975); mem. Soc. Study Evolution, Can. Soc. Zoology, Systematics Assn. Gt. Britain, Internat. Assn. Theoretical and Applied Limnology, Freshwater Biol. Assn. Gt. Britain, Royal Entomol. Soc. London, Entomol. Soc. B.C., Pacific Sci. Assn., Western Soc. Naturalists. Contbr. articles on entomology, zoology and limnology to profl. jours. Office: Dept Zoology U BC Vancouver BC V6T 1W5 Canada

SCUDDER, RICHARD B., paper co. exec.; b. Newark, May 13, 1913; s. Edward W. and Katherine (Hollifield) S.; A.B., Princeton, 1935; m. Elizabeth A. Shibley, June 24, 1944; children—Elizabeth H. (Mrs. Philip Difani), Charles A., Carolyn (Mrs. Peter M. Miller), Jean. Reporter, Newark News, 1935-37, v.p., 1941-51, pub., 1951-72; reporter Boston Herald, 1937-38; pres. Hollifield, Inc.; chmn. bd. Garden State Paper Co.; v.p. Newark Broadcasting Corp., Garden State Fibre Co. of Calif.; dir. Midlantic Bank; mem. Nat. Adv. Com. on Indsl. Innovation, 1978—. Trustee Riverview Hosp., Frost Valley YMCA; v.p., bd. dirs. Paper Mill Playhouse, Millburn, N.J.; pres. Duryea Found. Served from pvt. to maj. AUS, 1941-45. Decorated Bronze Star; recipient TAPPI award, 1971; Nat. Recycling award Nat. Assn. Secondary Materials Industries, 1972; Nat. Resource Recovery Man of Year award, 1978; Papermaker of Year award Paper Trade Jour., 1978. Clubs: Rumson Country, Seabright Beach, Seabright Lawn Tennis and Cricket, Essex; Adirondack League. Home: Brown's Dock Rd Navesink NJ 07752 Office: Park 80 Plaza East Saddle Brook NJ 07662

SCUDDER, THAYER, anthropologist, educator; b. New Haven, Aug. 4, 1930; s. Townsend III and Virginia (Boody) S.; grad. Phillips Exeter Acad., 1948; A.B., Harvard, 1952, Ph.D., 1960; postgrad. Yale, 1953-54, London Sch. Econs., 1960-61; m. Mary Eliza Drinker, Aug. 26, 1950; children—Mary Eliza, Alice Thayer. Research officer Rhodes-Livingstone Inst., No. Rhodesia, 1956-57, sr. research officer, 1962-63; asst. prof. Am. U., Cairo, 1961-62; research fellow Center Middle East Studies, Harvard, 1963-64; asst. prof. Calif. Inst. Tech., Pasadena, 1964-66, asso. prof., 1966-69, prof. anthropology, 1969—; dir. Inst. for Devel. Anthropology, Binghamton, N.Y., 1976—; cons. UN Devel. Program, FAO, IBRD, WHO, Navajo Tribal Council, AID. Mem. Am. Anthrop. Assn., Soc. Applied Anthropology, Am. Alpine Club. Author: The Ecology of the Gwembe Tonga, 1962. Office: 228-77 Calif Inst Tech Pasadena CA 91125

SCUDDER, TOWNSEND, III, writer, educator; b. Glenwood, L.I., N.Y., Aug. 27, 1900; s. Townsend and Mary Dannat (Thayer) S.; B.A., Yale, 1923, Ph.D., 1933; m. Virginia Louise Boody, June 23, 1923; children—Townsend, Thayer. With book editorial dept. Doubleday, Page & Co., 1923; editorial work Rockefeller Found., 1924; with English dept. Yale, 1924-31; asst. prof. English, Swarthmore Coll., 1931-40; asso. prof., 1940-43, on leave, 1943-48, prof., 1943-53; exec. dir. Center for Information on Am., Washington, Conn., 1951-56, pres., 1956—. Trustee Middlesex Coll. Guggenheim fellow, 1943-44; asso. fellow Timothy Dwight Coll., Yale. Mem. Phi Beta Kappa. Club: Coffee House (N.Y.). Author: The Lonely Wayfaring Man, Emerson and Some Englishmen, 1935; Jane Welsh Carlyle, 1939; Concord; American Town, 1947. Contbr. chpt. on Henry David Thoreau to The Literary History of the United States, 1948; various essays, revs. to profl. lit. Editor: Letters of Jane Welsh Carlyle to Joseph Neuberg, 1931. Home: Woodbury CT 06798 Office: Center for Information on America Washington CT 06793

SCULFORT, MAURICE CHARLES, advt. agy. exec.; b. N.Y.C., Oct. 26, 1925; s. Edward and Marcelle (Bonnier) S.; student N.Y. U., 1946-50; m. Helen A. Yankow, July 3, 1964; children—Raymond J., Jack T. Sales, Sears Roebuck & Co., 1946; advt. Donahue & Coe, 1947; with Compton Advt., Inc., N.Y.C., 1947—, v.p., 1959-69, sr. v.p., 1969—. Active Boy Scouts Am., YMCA. Served with USNR, 1943-46; PTO, ETO, MTO. Republican. Contbr. articles to profl.

publs. Home: Stony Ford Rd RD 2 Box 124 Middletown NY 10940 Office: 625 Madison Ave New York City NY 10022

SCULLION, WILLIAM JOSEPH, energy co. exec.; b. Paterson, N.J., Aug. 30, 1932; s. William Joseph and Catherine (Fendt) S.; student Marietta Coll., 1953; B.S. magna cum laude, Seton Hall U., 1959; m. Phyllis Bell, Jan. 3, 1954; children—Patricia, Sharon, Colleen, William Joseph, Catherine. Tax mgr. Coopers & Lybrand, C.P.A.'s, N.Y.C., 1960-67; div. audit mgr. Uniroyal, Inc., N.Y.C., 1968-69; comptroller, v.p. ITT World Directories, Inc., Brussels, Belgium, after 1970, pres., chief operating officer, N.Y.C., to 1977, now group gen. mgr. Energy Resources Group, ITT, N.Y.C. Served with AUS, 1954-55. Mem. Am. Inst. C.P.A.'s, N.J. Soc. C.P.A.'s. Office: ITT Energy Resources Group 320 Park Ave New York NY 10022

SCULLION, WILLIAM JOSEPH, publishing co. exec.; b. Paterson, N.J., Aug. 30, 1932; s. William Joseph and Catherine (Fendt) S.; student Marietta Coll., 1953; B.S. magna cum laude, Seton Hall U., 1959; m. Phyllis Bell, Jan. 3, 1954; children—Patricia, Sharon, Colleen, William Joseph, Catherine. Tax mgr. Coopers & Lybrand, C.P.A.'s, N.Y.C., 1960-67; div. audit mgr. Uniroyal, Inc., N.Y.C., 1968-69; comptroller, v.p. ITT World Directories, Inc., Brussels, Belgium, after 1970, now pres., chief operating officer, N.Y.C. Served with AUS, 1954-55. Mem. Am. Inst. C.P.A.'s, N.J. Soc. C.P.A.'s. Office: ITT World Directories Inc 320 Park Ave New York NY 10022

SCULLY, DAVID WILLIAMS, mfg. co. exec.; b. Bryn Mawr, Pa., Oct. 23, 1927; s. Charles Alison and Elizabeth Good (Williams) S.; grad. St. Paul's Sch., 1945; B.A., Yale, 1950; LL.B., Harvard, 1958; m. Sarah Ives, July 28, 1962; children—Vaughan Merrick, Amos Appleton, Patrick Williams. Media researcher Compton Advt., N.Y.C., 1950-51; intelligence officer CIA, 1951-55; admitted to Pa. bar, 1959; atty. Pepper Hamilton & Scheetz, Phila., 1958-62; v.p. trust dept. First Nat. City Bank, N.Y.C., 1962-68, Princeton Bank & Trust Co. (N.J.), 1968-69; sr. v.p. trust dept. Fidelity Bank, Phila., 1969-77; pres. Eastern Fire Equipment, Portland, Maine, 1978—. Served with USNR, 1946; with AUS, 1954-55. Democrat. Episcopalian. Club: Philadelphia. Home: 85 Foreside Rd Cumberland Foreside ME 04110

SCULLY, FRANCIS JOSEPH, publishing co. exec.; b. Phila., June 12, 1925; s. Francis Joseph and Mary Veronica (Soren) S.; B.S. in Bus. Adminstrn. and Accounting, La Salle Coll., 1949; postgrad. N.Y. U. Sch. Bus., 1959; m. Mary E. O'Connor, Oct. 29, 1949 (div.); children—Susan, Brian, Maura, Sharon, Frances Anne. With Kurnit, Geller Asso. Advt., N.Y.C., 1962-64; v.p. Norman, Craig and Kummel, N.Y.C., 1964-66; dir. advt. and mdsg. Hertz Corp., N.Y.C., 1966-69; pres. Standard Reference Library, Inc., N.Y.C., 1969-71; pres., chief exec. officer, also dir. Funk & Wagnalls, Inc., N.Y.C., 1971-73; pres., dir. Marshall Cavendish Corp., 1977—. Served with AUS, 1943-46. Decorated Purple Heart, Combat Inf. badge. Mem. Phila. Art Dirs. Club, Am. Inst. Graphic Arts. Club: N.Y. Athletic. Office: 575 Lexington Ave New York NY 10022*

SCULLY, JOHN CARROLL, life ins. co. exec.; b. Springfield, Mass., Mar. 16, 1932; s. James and Frances (Carroll) S.; B.A., Holy Cross Coll., 1953; C.L.U., Boston U., 1963; postgrad. Dartmouth Inst., 1977; m. Barbara A. Fougere, Sept. 7, 1953; children—Kathleen, Margaret, John, James, Patricia, Mary Ellen, Susan. With John Hancock Mut. Life Ins. Co., 1953—, gen. agent, Indpls., 1966-75, sr. v.p. agency dept., Boston, 1975—; chmn. bd. H.F. Cluthe Co., 1975—; dir. Hanseco Ins. Co., J.H. Distbrs. Bd. dirs. Greater Boston YMCA, 1975—; trustee Ins. Inst., Northeastern U. Served with U.S. Army, 1954-56. Mem. Am. Coll. Life Underwriters, Nat. Assn. Life Underwriters (v.p. Ind. 1973-75), Gen. Agents and Mgrs. Assn. (past pres. Indpls., Nat. Mgmt. award 1973, 74, 75). Roman Catholic. Clubs: Wellesley, K. C. Home: 67 Maugus Ave Wellesley Hills MA 02181 Office: John Hancock Pl T-21 Boston MA 02117

SCULLY, JOHN THOMAS, obstetrician, gynecologist; b. N.Y.C., Mar. 11, 1931; s. John Thomas and Mildred Frances (Dunstrop) S.; B.S., Georgetown U., 1952; M.D., U. Mex., 1959; m. Donna Eckardt, July 29, 1977; children—John, Helen Mary, Thomas, Nora, James, Sara, Jason Bishop. Intern, Nassau Hosp., 1959-60, resident, 1960-63; practice medicine specializing in Ob-Gyn, 1963—; dir. dept. Ob-Gyn, St. Peter's Med. Center, 1971-76; clin. prof. Ob-Gyn, Rutgers U. Med. Sch., 1971—. Diplomate Am. Bd. Ob-Gyn. Fellow A.C.S., Am. Coll. Obstetrics and Gynecology; mem. N.J. Med. Soc., Middlesex County Med. Soc., N.J. Ob-Gyn Soc., N.J. Right to Life (charter). Republican. Roman Catholic. Office: 23 Duke St New Brunswick NJ 08901

SCULLY, THOMAS FRANCIS, coll. adminstr.; b. Chgo., Oct. 2, 1928; s. Benedict William and Lucille S.; A.B., DePaul U., 1949; M.B.A. U. Chgo., 1961; children—Thomas F., Mary Ellen. Div. mgr. Jewel Tea Co., Inc., Chgo., 1949-65; mgr. stores program PPG Industries, Pitts., 1965-70; v.p. dental products Litton Industries, Toledo, 1970-73; pres. Bradford Schs., Ft. Wayne, Ind., 1973-77; pres. Ind. Inst. Tech., Ft. Wayne, 1977—; v.p. Ednl. Cons. Served with U.S. Army, 1950-52. Mem. AAUP. Roman Catholic. Clubs; Pine Valley Country, Summit, Rotary. Home: 11307 Kings Crossing Fort Wayne IN 46825 Office: 1600 E Washington Fort Wayne IN 46803

SCULLY, VINCENT EDWARD, sports broadcaster; b. Bronx, N.Y., Nov. 29, 1927; s. Vincent Aloysius and Bridget (Freehill) S.; B.A., Fordham U., 1949; m. Sandra Hunt, Nov. 11, 1973; children—Michael, Kevin, Todd, Erin, Kelly, Catherine Anne. Sports announcer Bklyn. Dodgers Profl. Baseball Team, 1950-57, Los Angeles Dodgers Profl. Baseball Team, 1957—, CBS-TV, 1975—. Served with USNR, 1944-45. Recipient TV award Look mag., 1959; named Sportscaster of Year in Calif., 1959, 60, 63, 69, 71, 73-75; Nat. Sportscaster of Year, 1966, 78; named to Fordham U. Hall of Fame, 1976. Mem. AFTRA, Screen Actors Guild, Catholic Actors, TV Acad. Arts and Scis. Roman Cath. Clubs: Lambs (N.Y.C.); Bel Air Country, Beach. Address: CBS-TV 51 W 52d St New York NY 10019*

SCURLOCK, ARCH CHILTON, chem. engr.; b. Beaumont, Tex., Jan. 29, 1920; s. Marvin and Mary (Chilton) S.; B.S. in Chem. Engring., U. Tex., 1941, A.B. in Physics, 1941; M.S., Mass. Inst. Tech., 1943, Sc.D., 1948; spl. course meteorology U. Chgo., 1944; m. Maurine Spurbeck, Nov. 27, 1945 (div.); children—Arch, Susan, Marvin Curtis; m. 2d, Nancy Morrison Yonick, Nov. 16, 1962; children—Mary, Nancy, Margaret Ann. Research asso. chem. engring. dept. Mass. Inst. Tech., 1946-48; asst. dir. chemistry Engring. Research Assos., 1948-49; pres. Atlantic Research Corp., Alexandria, Va., 1949-62, chmn. bd., 1962-65, dir., 1959-67; pres., dir. Research Industries Inc., Alexandria, 1968—; chmn. TransTechnology Corp.; dir. Halifax Engring. Corp., Com-Dev, Inc. Served to lt. (s.g.) USNR, 1943-46. Mem. Am. Inst. Chem. Engrs., Am. Chem. Soc., Am. Inst. Aero. Scis., Am. Phys. Soc., Am. Meteorol. Soc., Am. Rocket Soc., Am. Ordnance Assn., Combustion Inst., Phi Beta Kappa, Sigma Xi, Tau Beta Pi. Clubs: University (Washington); Belle Haven Country, Army Navy Country (Va.); Mid-Ocean (Tuckers Town, Bermuda); Jonathan (Los Angeles). Home: 1753 Army Navy Dr Arlington VA 22202 Office: 123 N Pitt St Alexandria VA 22314

SCURLOCK, EDDY CLARK, oil co. exec.; b. Newton, Tex., Jan. 13, 1905; s. R.W. and Ella (Clark) S.; L.H.D., Southwestern U.; D.B.A., Limestone Coll.; m. Elizabeth Belschner, July 17, 1927; 1 dau., Laura Lee (Mrs. Jack Sawtelle Blanton). Founder Scurlock Oil Co., 1936; founder Eddy Refining Co., 1946, now chmn. bd., chief exec. officer; adv. dir. Tex. Commerce Bank, Chem. Bank & Trust. Trustee Baylor Coll. Medicine, Meth. Hosp., Lon Morris Coll., Inst. Religion; bd. dirs. Tex. Med. Center, Inc., Rice U. Assos., Salvation Army, Turner Found. Recipient City of Hope humanitarian award, 1966; Ann. Brotherhood award NCCJ, 1968; Religious Heritage Am. Businessman of Year, 1970; Disting. Service award Tex. Mid-Continent Oil and Gas Assn., 1977; Torch of Liberty award Anti-Defamation League, B'nai B'rith, 1979. Mem. Am. Petroleum Inst. Methodist. (bd. stewards). Clubs: River Oaks Country; Petroleum; Houston; El Dorado Country (Palm Springs, Calif.). Home: 3739 Knollwood Dr Houston TX 77019 Office: 1800 Houston Club Bldg Houston TX 77002

SCURLOCK, ROBERT, air force officer; b. San Diego, Feb. 16, 1928; s. Robert Ingersoll and Phoebe Elizabeth (Cook) S.; B.S., Ohio State U., 1954; M.B.A., U. So. Calif., 1961; M.S., George Washington U., 1967; m. Elizabeth Mabelle Rakich, July 6, 1949; children—Bradley Wright, Cecelia Alexandra. Commd. officer U.S. Air Force, 1948, advanced through grades to maj. gen., 1977; jet. fighter pilot, Korea, 1951-53; test pilot, 1954-60; procurement officer, logistics assignments, U.S., Lebanon, Spain, 1954-74; dep. chief of staff procurement Logistics Command, 1975; F-15 program dir., Wright Patterson AFB, Ohio, 1976-78; dir. budget Hdqrs. U.S. Air Force, Washington, 1978—; mem. faculty Air War Coll., 1967-69. Decorated D.F.C., Legion of Merit. Mem. Air Force Assn., Nat. Soc. Mil. Comptrollers, Beta Gamma Sigma. Home: 2755 Brant St San Diego CA 92103 Office: Hqrs USAF The Pentagon Washington DC 20330

SCURO, JOSEPH EUGENE, publisher; b. Jersey City, July 11, 1921; s. James A. and Mary C. (DeCaro) S.; B.S., St. Peters Coll., 1950; m. Phyllis M. Amato, Apr. 7, 1945; children—Joseph Eugene, Vincent P. Asst. comptroller Trust Co. of N.J., 1941-44; accountant, credit mgr., controller Dodd, Mead & Co., Inc., N.Y.C., 1944-66, treas., 1966-73, dir., 1970—, v.p., treas., 1973-76, exec. v.p., treas., 1976—, v.p., dir. Dodd, Mead & Co. (Can.), Ltd. Pres., Bergenfield Bd. Edn., 1976-79. Mem. N.Y. Credit Financial Mgmt. Assn., Assn. Am. Pubs. (chmn. ins. com.). Clubs: Elks (past exalted ruler Jersey City); Unico Nat. (Bergenfield). Home: 20 Dalton Pl Bergenfield NJ 07621 Office: 79 Madison Ave New York NY 10016

SEABERG, DOROTHY I., educator; b. Clark, S.D., Dec. 22, 1917; B.A. in Christian Edn. magna cum laude, Wheaton Coll., 1951; M.Ed. in Elementary Edn., Nat. Coll. Edn., 1957; Ed.D., in Adminstrn. and Supervision of Elementary Edn., Wayne State U., 1961. Tchr. 4th grade Sch. Dist. 64, Park Ridge, Ill., 1955-57; instr. Wayne State U., 1957-61; asst. prof. U. Pacific, 1961-64; prof. edn. No. Ill. U., 1964—. Mem. Am. Assn. Supervision and Curriculum Devel., NEA, Future's Soc., Nat. Council Social Studies, Assn. for Tchr. Educators, Ill. Assn. for Tchr. Educators, Delta Kappa Gamma, Pi Lambda Theta. Author: The Four Faces of Teaching: The Role of the Teacher in Humanizing Education, 1974. Specialist in social studies edn. elementary curriculum, ednl. psychology. Home: 105 Pooler Ave DeKalb IL 60115 Office: 162H Gabel Graham Hall No Ill U DeKalb IL 60115

SEABORG, GLENN THEODORE, educator; b. Ishpeming, Mich., Apr. 19, 1912; s. H. Theodore and Selma (Erickson) S.; A.B., U. Calif. at Los Angeles, 1934; Ph.D., U. Calif. at Berkeley, 1937; numerous hon. degrees including: LL.D., U. Mich., 1958, Rutgers U., 1970; D.Sc., Northwestern U., 1954, U. Notre Dame, 1961, John Carroll U., Duquesne U., 1968, Ind. State U., 1969, U. Utah, 1970, Rockford Coll., 1975, Kent State U., 1975; L.H.D., No. Mich. Coll., 1962; D.P.S., George Washington U., 1962; D.P.A., U. Puget Sound, 1963; Litt.D., Lafayette Coll., 1966; D.Eng., Mich. Technol. U., 1970; Sc.D., U. Bucharest, 1971, Manhattan Coll., 1976; m. Helen Griggs, June 6, 1942; children—Peter, Lynne (Mrs. William B. Cobb), David, Stephen, John Eric, Dianne. Research chemist U. Calif. at Berkeley, 1937-39, instr. dept. chemistry, 1939-41, asst. prof., 1941-45, prof., 1945-71, univ. prof., 1971— (leave of absence 1942-46, 61-71), dir. nuclear chem. research, 1946-58, 72-75, asso. dir. Lawrence Berkeley Lab., 1954-61, 71—, chancellor Univ., 1958-61; sect. chief metall. lab. U. Chgo., 1942-46; chmn. AEC, 1961-71, gen. adv. com., 1946-50; research nuclear chemistry and physics, transuranium elements. Co-discoverer elements 94-102, and 106: plutonium, 1940, americium, 1944-45, curium, 1944, berkelium, 1949, californium, 1950, einsteinium, 1952, fermium, 1953, mendelevium, 1955, nobelium, 1958, element 106, 1974; co-discoverer nuclear energy isotopes Pu-239, U-233, Np-237, other isotopes including I-131, Fe-59, Te-99m, Co-60; originator actinide concept for placing heaviest elements in periodic system. Chmn. bd. Kevex Corp., Burlingame, Calif., 1972—; dir. Geomet, Inc., Dreyfus 3d Century Fund. Mem. Pres.'s Sci. Adv. Com., 1959-61; mem. nat. sci. bd. NSF, 1960-61; mem. Pres.'s Com. on Equal Employment Opportunity, 1961-65, Fed. Radiation Council, 1961-69, Nat. Aeros. and Space Council, 1961-71, Fed. Council Sci. and Tech., 1961-71, Nat. Com. Am.'s Goals and Resources, 1962-64, Pres.'s Com. Manpower, 1964-69, Nat. Council Marine Resources and Engring. Devel., 1966-71; chmn. Chem. Edn. Material Study, 1959-74, Nat. Programming Council for Pub. TV, 1970-72; dir. Ednl. TV and Radio Center, Ann Arbor, Mich., 1958-64, 67-70; pres. 4th UN Internat. Conf. Peaceful Uses Atomic Energy, Geneva, Switzerland, 1971, also chmn. U.S. del., 1964, 71; U.S. rep. 5th-15th gen. confs. IAEC, chmn., 1961-71; chmn. U.S. del. to USSR for signing Memorandum Cooperation Field Utilization Atomic Energy Peaceful Purposes, 1963; mem. U.S. del. for signing Limited Test Ban Treaty, 1963; mem. commn. on humanities Am. Council Learned Socs., 1962-65; mem. sci. adv. bd. Robert A. Welch Found., 1957—. Trustee Pacific Sci. Center Found., 1962-77; trustee Sci. Service, 1965—, pres., 1966—; trustee Am.-Scandinavian Found., 1968—, Ednl. Broadcasting Corp., 1970-72; trustee Swedish Council Am., 1976—, chmn. bd. dirs., 1978—; bd. dirs. World Future Soc., 1969—, Calif. Council for Environ. and Econ. Balance, 1974—; bd. govs. Am. Swedish Hist. Found., 1972-75. Named 1 of Am.'s 10 outstanding young men Jr. C. of C., 1947; recipient John Ericsson Gold medal Am. Soc. Swedish Engrs., 1948; Nobel Prize for Chemistry (with E.M. McMillan), 1951; John Scott award and medal City of Phila., 1953; Perkin medal Am. sect. Soc. Chem. Industry, 1957; U.S. AEC Enrico Fermi award, 1959; Joseph Priestley Meml. award Dickinson Coll., 1960; Sci. and Engring. award Fedn. Engring. Socs., Drexel Inst. Tech., Phila., 1962; named Swedish Am. of Year, Vasa Order of Am., 1962; Franklin medal Franklin Inst., 1963; 1st Spirit of St. Louis award, 1964; Leif Erikson Found. award, 1964; Washington award Western Soc. Engrs., 1965; Arches of Sci. award Pacific Sci. Center, 1968; Internat. Platform Assn. award, 1969; Prometheus award Nat. Elec. Mfrs. Assn., 1969; Nuclear Pioneer award Soc. Nuclear Medicine, 1971; Oliver Townsend award Atomic Indsl. Forum, 1971; Distinguished Honor award U.S. Dept. State, 1971, Golden Plate award Am. Acad. Achievement, 1972; decorated officeur Legion of Honor (France); Daniel Webster medal, 1976. Fellow Am. Phys. Soc., Am. Inst. Chemists (Pioneer award 1968, Gold medal award 1973), Chem. Soc. London (hon.), Royal Soc. Edinburgh (hon.), Am. Nuclear Soc., Calif., N.Y., Washington acads. scis., A.A.A.S. (pres. 1972, chmn. bd. 1973), Royal Soc. Arts (Eng.); mem. Am. Chem. Soc. (award in pure chemistry 1947, William H. Nichols medal N.Y. sect. 1948, Charles L. Parsons award 1964, Gibbs medal chgo. sect. 1966, Madison Marshall award No. Ala. sect. 1972, Priestley medal 1979, pres. 1976), Am. Philos. Soc., Royal Swedish Acad. Engring. Scis., Am. Nat., Argentine Nat., Bavarian, Polish, Royal Swedish, USSR acads. scis., Royal Acad. Exact, Phys. and Natural Scis. Spain (acad. fgn. corr.), Soc. Nuclear Medicine (hon.), Deutsche Akademie der Naturforscher Leopoldina (East Germany), Nat. Acad. Pub. Adminstrn., Phi Beta Kappa, Sigma Xi, Pi Mu Epsilon, Alpha Chi Sigma (John R. Kuebler award 1978), Phi Lambda Upsilon (hon.). Clubs: Bohemian (San Francisco); Chemists (N.Y.C.); Cosmos, University (Washington); Faculty (Berkeley). Author: (with Joseph J. Katz) The Actinide Elements, 1954; (with Joseph J. Katz) The Chemistry of the Actinide Elements, 1957; The Transuranium Elements, 1958; (with E.G. Valens) Elements of the Universe, 1958 (winner Thomas Alva Edison Found. award); Man-Made Transuranium Elements, 1963; (with D.M. Wilkes) Education and the Atom, 1964; (with E.K. Hyde, I. Perlman) Nuclear Properties of the Heavy Elements, 1964; (with others) Oppenheimer, 1969; (with W.R. Corliss) Man and Atom, 1971; Nuclear Milestones, 1972; editor: Transuranium Elements: Products of Modern Alchemy, 1978; asso. editor Jour. Chem. Physics, 1948-50; editorial adv. bd. Jour. Inorganic and Nuclear Chemistry, 1954—, Indsl. Research, Inc., 1967-75; adv. bd. Chem. and Engring. News, 1957-59; editorial bd. Jour. Am. Chem. Soc., 1950-59, Ency. Chem. Tech., 1975—; mem. hon. editorial adv. bd. Internat. Ency. Phys. Chemistry and Chem. Physics, 1957—; mem. panel Golden Picture Ency. for Children, 1957-61; mem. cons. and adv. bd. Funk and Wagnells Universal Standard Ency., 1957-61; mem. Am. Heritage Dictionary Panel Usage Cons., 1964—; contbr. articles to profl. jours. Home: 1154 Glen Rd Lafayette CA 94549 Office: Lawrence Berkeley Lab U Calif Berkeley CA 94720

SEABORN, ROBERT LOWDER, archbishop; b. Toronto, Ont., Can., July 9, 1911; s. Richard and Muriel (Reid) S.; B.A., U. Toronto, 1932, M.A., 1934; B.D., Trinity Coll., Toronto, 1938, D.D., 1948; D.C.L., Bishop's U., Lennoxville, Que., Can., 1962; LL.D., Meml. U., St. Johns, Nfld., Can., 1972; m. Mary Elizabeth Gilchrist, Jan. 29, 1938; children—Richard, Robert, Jane Seaborn Hachey, Alan, Michael. Ordained priest Anglican Ch. of Can., 1935, consecrated bishop, 1958; asst. curate ch., Toronto, 1934-36, 37-41; rector ch., Cobourg, Ont., 1941-48, St. Mary's Ch., Kerrisdale, Vancouver, B.C., Can., 1957-58; dean, rector Holy Trinity Cathedral, Quebec, Can., 1948-57; asst. bishop Diocese of Nfld., 1958-65, bishop, 1965-75; archbishop Eccles. Province Can., 1975—; bishop Eastern Nfld. and Labrador, 1976—. Served as chaplain Can. Army, 1942-45. Decorated Croix de Guerre (France). Author: Faith in Our Time, 1963. Home: 67 Portugal Cove Rd Saint John's NF A1B 2M2 Canada Office: 19 King's Bridge Rd Saint John's NF A1C 3K4 Canada

SEABROOK, JOHN MARTIN, corp. exec., engr.; b. Seabrook, N.J., Apr. 16, 1917; s. Charles Franklin and Norma Dale (Ivins) S.; B.S. in Chem. Engring., Princeton, 1939; LL.D. (hon.), Gettysburg Coll., 1974; m. Anne Schlaudecker, Apr. 5, 1939 (div. 1951); children—Carol Ormsby (Mrs. Jacques P. Boulanger), Elizabeth Anne (Mrs. Jonathan G. Leatham); m. 2d, Elizabeth Toomey, 1956; children—John Martin, Bruce Cameron. Engr., Deerfield Packing Corp., 1939-41; v.p. Seabrook Farms Co., 1941-50, exec. v.p., 1950-54, dir., 1941-59, pres., 1954-59, chief exec. officer, 1955-59; cons. IU Internat. Corp., Wilmington, 1959, v.p., 1960-65, dir., 1963—, pres., 1965-73, 74-78, chief exec., 1967—, chmn. bd., 1969—; pres., dir. Cumberland Automobile & Truck Co., 1954-59, Cumberland Warehouse Corp., 1954-59, Salem Farms Corp. (N.J.), 1948—; dir. Frick Co., Waynesboro, Pa., 1959-69, chmn., 1959-68; chmn., dir. S.W. Fabricating & Welding Co., Inc., Houston, 1964-68; chmn. Divcon, Inc., Houston, 1967-69, dir., 1967-71; pres., dir. Internat. Utilities Overseas Capital Corp., Wilmington, Del., 1966—, chmn., 1970—; v.p. Gen. Waterworks Corp., Phila., 1959-66, dir., 1963-71; pres., 1966-68, chmn., 1968-71; chmn., dir. GWC Inc., Phila., 1971-73; pres. Brown Bros. Contractors, Inc., Phila., 1960, dir., 1960-67, chmn., 1965-67; pres. Am. Portable Irrigation Co., Eugene, Oreg., 1961, dir., 1961-68, chmn., 1966-68; chmn. Gotaas-Larsen Shipping Corp., 1979; dir. Amvit Corp., Cleve., 1962-69, chmn., 1964-68; dir. N.J. Bell Telephone Co., Canadian Utilities, Ltd., Edmonton, C. Brewer & Co. Ltd., Hawaii, South Jersey Gas Co., Folsom, N.J., South Jersey Industries, Inc., Folsom, Consol.-Bathurst Ltd., Montreal, Lenox, Inc. Mem. N.J. Migrant Labor Bd., 1945-67, chmn., 1955-67; mem. N.J. Bd. Higher Edn., 1967-70, Pres.'s Air Quality Adv. Bd., 1968-70; bd. dirs. Brandywine Conservancy, Inc., 1972—; trustee Eisenhower Exchange Fellowships, 1974—. Registered profl. engr., N.J., Del. Mem. Phi Beta Kappa. Clubs: Racquet and Tennis (N.Y.C.); The Philadelphia, Racquet (Phila.); Buck's (London, Eng.); Wilmington (Del.); Toronto (Ont.) Home: R D 1 Griscom Rd Salem NJ 08079 Office: 11 West Ave Woodstown NJ 08098 also 1500 Walnut St Philadelphia PA 19102

SEABURY, JOHN WARD, business exec.; b. Oak Park, Ill., Dec. 1, 1921; s. Charles Ward and Louise (Lovett) S.; grad. Choate Sch., 1940; B.S. in Indsl. Adminstrn. and Engring., Yale, 1943; m. Charlene Adrienne Brown, Feb. 23, 1946; children—Deborah S. Holloway, Charles Ward II, David Grant. With Marsh & McLennan, Inc., Chgo., 1946-76, asst. v.p., 1952-56, v.p., 1956-76; pres. Hanover Securities Co., 1966—; exec. dir. Seabury Found. Trustee Berea Coll., Ch. Home (Episcopal) Chgo., Chgo. Zool. Soc., Seabury-Western Theol. Sem., Evanston, Ill., Lyric Opera Chgo. Served to lt. (j.g.) USNR, 1943-46. Mem. Chgo. Art Inst., Chgo. Hist. Soc., Chgo. Zool. Soc., Field Mus. Natural History, Shedd Aquarium Soc. Chgo., Orchestral Soc. Chgo., Chi Phi. Republican. Episcopalian. Clubs: Crystal Lake Yacht, Crystal Downs Country (Frankfort, Mich.); Tower, University, Yale, Economic (Chgo.); Indian Hill (Winnetka). Home: 936 Sunset Rd Winnetka IL 60093 Office: 208 S La Salle St Chicago IL 60604. *There is no limit to the amount of good a man can do if he does not care who gets the credit.*

SEABURY, PAUL, educator; b. Hempstead, N.Y., May 6, 1923; s. Adam Alden and Maude (Harris) S.; B.A. magna cum laude, Swarthmore Coll., 1946; Ph.D. in Govt., Columbia, 1953; m. Marie-Anne Phelps, June 3, 1950; children—David Phelps, John Huntington. Lectr., instr. Columbia, 1947-53; guest lectr. Free Univ., Berlin, Germany, 1951; faculty U. Calif., Berkeley, 1953-65, prof. polit. sci., 1963-65, asst. dean Coll. Letters and Sci., 1963-64, vice chmn. dept. polit. sci., 1964-65; prof. govt., provost U. Calif., Santa Cruz, 1966-67; prof. govt. U. Calif., Berkeley, 1967—, chmn. faculty Coll. of Letters and Sci., 1967-69. Vis. research scholar Center Internat. Affairs, Harvard, 1965-66, Royal Inst. Internat. Affairs, London, 1972-73. Chmn. nat. exec. com. Ams. for Democratic Action, 1961-62, nat. vice chmn, 1963-65; cons. State Dept., 1963-70, vice chmn. Bd. Fgn. Scholarships, 1967-71; mem., vice chmn. Univ. Centers for Rational Alternatives, 1970—; exec. com. Internat. Council on Future of Univ., 1971—; vis. fellow Hoover Instn., 1978-79. Mem. Harriman fgn. policy task force Democratic Nat. Com., 1974-76. Bd. dirs. Freedom House, League for Indsl. Democracy, 1974—. Guggenheim fellow, 1961-62. Mem. Am. Polit. Sci. Assn., Council Fgn. Relations, Pumpkin Papers Irregulars (founding mem., dir. 1978—), Phi Beta Kappa. Democrat. Anglican. Author: Wilhelmstrasse: A Study of German Diplomacy Under the Nazi Regime, 1954; Power, Freedom and Diplomacy (Bancroft prize

1964), 1963; The Balance of Power, 1965; The Rise and Decline of the Cold War, 1967; The Game of Croquet, 1968; (with Aaron Wildavsky) U.S. Foreign Policy: Perspectives and Proposals, 1969; The Foreign Policy of the United States of America, 1972; (with Friedland and Wildavsky) The Great Detente Disaster, 1975. Editor: Universities in the Western World, 1975. Home: 600 Alvarado Rd Berkeley CA 94705

SEACREST, JOSEPH RUSHTON, publishing exec.; b. Lincoln, Nebr., Feb. 3, 1920; s. Joe W. Seacrest; grad. cum laude Phillips Acad., Exeter, N.H., 1938; B.S., Yale, 1942; J.D., U. Nebr., 1949; m. Beatrice H. Costello, May 21, 1944; children—Eric, Theodore, Gary, Kent, Shawn. Admitted to Nebr. bar; editor Lincoln Jour.; pres. State Jour. Co.; chmn. bd., exec. v.p. Jour. Star Printing Co.; sec.-treas. Western Pub. Co., Star-Herald Publishing Co. Pub. consumer mem., mem. exec. com. Nebr. Blue Cross-Blue Shield; past mem. Nat. Hwy. Safety Adv. Com. Past mem. dirs. Nebraskaland Found. Served with USNR, World War II. Mem. Am., Nebr. (joint press-bar free press-free trial com.) bar assns., Nebr. Press Assn., Am. Soc. Newspaper Editors, Am. Newspaper Pub. Assn., Lincoln C. of C. (past v.p., dir.), Sigma Delta Chi (freedom of information com.). Home: 1725 S 33d St Lincoln NE 68506 Office: 926 P St Lincoln NE 68508

SEADER, JUNIOR DEVERE, educator; b. San Francisco, Aug. 16, 1927; s. George Joseph and Eva (Burbank) S.; B.S., U. Calif. at Berkeley, 1949, M.S., 1950; Ph.D., U. Wis., 1952; m. Sylvia Bowen, Aug. 11, 1961; children—Steven Frederick, Clayton Mitchell, Gregory Randolph, Donald Jeffrey, Suzanne Marie, Robert Clark, Kathleen Michelle, Jennifer Anne. Instr. chem. engring. U. Wis., 1951-52; group supr. chem. process design Chevron Research Corp., Richmond, Calif., 1952-57, group supr. engring. research, 1957-59; instr. chem. engring. U. Calif. at Berkeley, 1954-59; prin. scientist heat transfer and fluid dynamics research Rocketdyne div. N.Am. Aviation, Canoga Park, Calif., 1959-65, sr. tech. specialist, summer 1967; prof. chem. engring. U. Idaho, 1965-66; prof. chem. engring., adj. prof. material sci. and engring. U. Utah, 1966—, chmn. dept. chem. engring., 1975-78; tech. cons.; trustee CACHE Corp., Cambridge, Mass. Served with USNR, 1945-46. Recipient Distinguished Teaching award U. Utah, 1975. Mem. Am. Inst. Chem. Engrs., Am. Inst. Aeros. and Astronautics, Sigma Xi, Phi Lambda Upsilon. Author 2 books. Contbr. articles to profl. jours. Heat transfer research connected with the development of rocket engines associated with the Apollo and Space Shuttle projects, 1960-65; research on polymer and fabric flammability, coal hydrogenation, tar sands, process synthesis, 1969—. Home: 3786 View Crest Dr Salt Lake City UT 84117

SEAGER, DANIEL ALBERT, univ. librarian; b. Jacksonville, Fla., Jan. 1, 1920; s. Harry James and Albertina Adeline (Klarer) S.; A.A., St. John's Coll., Winfield, Kans., 1941; A.B., Okla. Bapt. U., 1948; B.A. in L.S., U. Okla., 1950, M.A., 1953; postgrad. Colo. State Coll. (now U. No. Colo.), 1956-59; m. Helen Ruthe Medearis, Mar. 6, 1943; children—Mary Adele, Susan Kathleen, Dana Ruthe. Head librarian, prof. English, Southwest Coll., Bolivar, Mo., 1949-53; head librarian, asst. prof. library sci., chmn. dept. Ouachita U., Arkadelphia, Ark., 1953-56; head librarian, head library sci. edn., asso. prof. library sci. U. No. Colo., Greeley, 1956-66, dir. library services, 1966-71, coordinator library research and devel., 1971—, chief bibliographer/editor library publns., cons., instr. ednl. media program, 1968-71; cons. Ency. Brit. ultramicrofiche project, 1967-69; lectr. in field. Mem. book adv. council Edn. for Freedom Found.; mem. Com. library standards Colo. pub. schs., 1960-62; mem. exec. bd. Rocky Mountain Bibliog. Center Research, 1959-60, 65-74, sec., 1961-63; sec. Colo. Council Librarians State-Operated Instns., 1966, chm., 1968-70. Mem. exec. bd. Weld County Assn. Mental Health, 1966, mem. library com., 1969; mem. Colo. Civil Service Examining Bd., 1961—. Served with AUS, 1942-45. Recipient several citations of merit profl. orgns. Fellow Intercontinental Biog. Assn.; mem. Am. (library recruitment com. 1957—), Nat., Colo. assns. higher edn., United Profs. for Acad. Order Nat. Hist. Soc., Am., Colo. (cons.) assns. sch. librarians, Spl. Libraries Assn., A.L.A. (region recruitment rep. 1958—), Utah, Kans., Wyo., Nebr., N.D., S.D., Nev., Mountain Plains (treas. 1959-63, exec. sec. 1963—, archivist 1974—, President's Spl. award, 15 Years Service award) Colo. (auditor), Tex., Southwestern, Ill., Calif., Cath., Mich., Ohio, N.Y., Pa., Midcontinent Med. library assns., Library Automation Research and Cons. Assn., Intercollegiate Studies Inst., Marquis Biog. Soc., Am. Security Council, Alumni Assn. U. No. Colo., Black Silent Majority Com. (hon.), Colo. Council Higher Edn., Assn. Coll. and Reference Libraries, Colo. Hist. Soc., Assn. Research Libraries, Colo. Audiovisual Assn., Air Force Assn., Internat. Platform Assn., Acad. Polit. Sci. Columbia, Nat. Geog. Soc., Weld County Assn. Mental Health (mem. bd., chmn. library com.), Am. Judicature Soc., A.A.U.P., Am. Numis. Assn., Am. Sci. Affiliation, Council on Consumer Information, Smithsonian Assos., Chem. Abstracts Service Panel, Audubon Nature Program, Forest History Soc., Journalism Edn. Assn., Greeley Numis. Club, Greeley C. of C., Phi Delta Kappa. Mem. Christian Ch. (deacon, elder). Clubs: Nat. Travel, Civitan (lt. gov. Mountain Plains dist. 1960-62), Knife and Fork; Republican, Republican Congressional (Washington). Contbr. articles to profl. jours. Home: 1230 24th Ave Greeley CO 80631

SEAGER, ROBERT, II, educator; b. Nanking, China, Sept. 12, 1924; s. Warren Armstrong and Helen (Hales) S.; B.A., Rutgers U., 1948; M.A., Columbia, 1949; Ph.D., Ohio State U., 1956; m. Caroline Parrish, Aug. 14, 1945. From instr. to asso. prof. history Denison U., 1949-61; asst. prof., asso. prof. history U.S. Naval Acad., 1961-67; prof. history, head dept. U. Me., 1967-70; prof. history, dean of coll. Washington Coll., Chestertown, Md., 1970-72; prof. history, v.p. for acad. affairs U. Balt., 1972-77; prof. history U. Ky., Lexington, 1977—, editor papers of Henry Clay, 1977—. Served with U.S. Mcht. Marine, 1943-46. Mem. So. Hist. Assn., Orgn. Am. Historians. Democrat. Episcopalian. Author: And Tyler Too, 1963; America's Major Wars, 1973; Letters and Papers of Alfred Thayer Mahan, 1975; Alfred Thayer Mahan: The Man and His Letters, 1977. Contbr. articles and papers to profl. jours. Home: 543 Boonesboro Ave Lexington KY 40508 Office: Dept History U Ky Lexington KY 40506

SEAGONDOLLAR, LEWIS WORTH, educator; b. Hoisington, Kans., Sept. 30, 1920; s. Fred Lewis and Bessie Estelle (Smilie) S.; A.B., Emporia State Tchrs. Coll., 1941; Ph.M., U. Wis., 1943, Ph.D., 1948; m. Winifred Elizabeth Varner, Sept. 5, 1942; children—Bryan Worth, Laurel Jane, Mark Winston. Mem. faculty U. Kans., Lawrence, 1947-65, prof. physics, 1960-65; prof. physics N.C. State U., Raleigh, 1965—, chmn. dept., 1965-75; cons. Los Alamos Sci. Lab., summer, 1959, Hanford Lab., Richland, Wash., 1962-65. Recipient Distinguished Teaching award N.C. State U., 1969-70, Distinguished Alumni award Kans. State Tchrs. Coll., 1971. Fellow Am. Phys. Soc. (sec. Southeastern sect. 1968—, regional sect. 1969—), A.A.A.S.; mem. Am. Assn. Physics Tchrs., Soc. Physics Students, Sigma Xi, Sigma Pi Sigma (pres. 1962-68). Contbr. articles to profl. jours. Home: Box 177 Route 8 Raleigh NC 27612

SEAGRAM, JOSEPH EDWARD FROWDE, distilleries exec.; s. Edward Frowde and Edna Irvine (MacLachlan) S. Chmn., Canbar Products Ltd.; hon. chmn. Joseph E. Seagram & Sons, Ltd., 1937—; hon. dir. Seagram Co. Ltd. Home: 50 Albert St Waterloo ON N2L 3S2 Canada Office: Box 635 Waterloo ON N2J 4B8 Canada

SEAL, JOHN RIDLEY, govt. ofcl.; b. W.Va., Mar. 10, 1912; s. Gordon S. and Inez A. (Crump) S.; M.D., U. Va., 1937; m. Frances C. Shackelford, Jan. 7, 1937. Intern, Strong Meml. Hosp., Rochester, N.Y., 1937-38; fellow in pathology U. Va. Sch. Medicine, 1938-40; resident in medicine N.Y. Hosp., N.Y.C., 1940-42; commd. lt. (j.g.) U.S. Navy, 1942, advanced through grades to capt., 1957; officer in charge Naval Med. Research Unit 4, Great Lakes, Ill., 1946-54; dir. communicable disease div. Bur. Medicine and Surgery Navy Dept., Washington, 1954-58; comdg. officer Naval Med. Research Unit 3, Cairo, Ill., 1958-61, Naval Med. Research Inst., Bethesda, Md., 1961-65, ret., 1965; asso. dir. intramural research Nat. Inst. Allergy and Infectious Diseases NIH, Bethesda, 1965-70, sci. dir., 1970-75, dep. dir. Nat. Inst. Allergy and Infectious Disease, 1975—. Recipient Superior Service award HEW, 1968, Distinguished Service award, 1972; Stitt award Assn. Mil. Surgeons U.S., 1954, Founders medal, 1963, 68. Fellow A.C.P.; mem. Infectious Disease Soc., Am. Epidemiol. Soc., AAAS, N.Y. Acad. Scis., Am. Soc. Tropical Medicine and Hygiene. Research, publs. in field. Home: 4517 Cumberland Ave Bethesda MD 20015 Office: Nat Inst Allergy and Infectious Diseases NIH 9000 Rockville Pike Bldg 31 Room 7A03 Bethesda MD 20205

SEALS, DANNY WAYLAND, entertainer, singer; b. McCamey, Tex., Feb. 8, 1948; s. Eugene Wayland and Sue Louella (Taylor) S.; student pub. schs., Dallas; m. Andrea Gilbert, Aug. 9, 1975; children—Jimmy, Jeremy, Holly Mae. Saxophone player in local groups with partner John Coley, 1963-69; formed duo England Dan and John Ford Coley, 1969; toured worldwide until 1976; recording star, 1976—; appeared on numerous television shows; albums include England Dan and John Ford Coley, 1971, Fables, 1973, I Hear the Music, 1976, Nights Are Forever, 1976, Dowdy Ferry Road, 1977, Some Things Don't Come Easy, 1978, Dr. Heckle and Mr. Jive, 1979, The Best of England Dan and John Ford Coley, 1979. Recipient Gold single record, 1976, Gold album, 1976. Bahai. Home: 918 Santa Hidalga Solana Beach CA 92075 Office: 10100 Santa Monica Blvd Suite 1095 Los Angeles CA 90067. *When the world is unified in the heart, all major ills will disappear.*

SEALS, JAMES, musician; b. Sidney, Tex. Mem. group The Champs, had hit single Tequila; then mem. group The Dawnbreakers; duo with Dash Crofts as Seals & Crofts; albums include: Seals & Crofts I & II, Year of Sunday, Summer Breeze, Diamond Girl, I'll Play for You, Greatest Hits, Get Closer, Sudan Village, Takin It Easy. Office: care Day 5 Prodns 216 Chatsworth Dr San Fernando CA 91340*

SEALS, WOODROW, U.S. dist. judge; b. Bogalusa, La., Dec. 23, 1917; s. Charles Bradley and Ruby (Hughey) S.; LL.B., U. Tex., 1949; m. Sarah Elizabeth Newman, June 1, 1942; 1 son, Bradley Newman. Admitted to Tex. bar, 1949; U.S. atty. So. Dist. Tex., 1961-66; U.S. dist. judge, 1966—. Del. gen. conf. United Meth. Ch. Served to lt. col. USAF. Home: 1510 Lehman St Houston TX 77018 Office: U S Courthouse Houston TX 77208

SEALY, ALBERT HENRY, lawyer; b. Columbus, Ohio, Oct. 23, 1917; s. Albert H. and Lillian E. (Stock) S.; B.A. summa cum laude, Ohio State U., 1938; LL.B. (J.D.), Harvard, 1941; m. Flora Kinkel, Aug. 23, 1947; children—Catherine Ann, Thomas P., Joan Deborah. Admitted to N.Y. bar, 1942, Ohio bar, 1955; with firm Simpson, Thacher & Bartlett, N.Y.C., 1941-43, 46-55, firm Smith and Schnacke, Dayton, Ohio, 1955—; sec. Mead Corp., 1964-75; dir. Chemineer, Inc., Danis Industries Corp. Mem. Ohio Ho. of Reps., 1966-68. Chmn. Ohioans for Fair Taxation, 1972—, Ohio Inst. on Pub. Finance, 1973—; chmn. bd. trustees Wright State U., 1977—. Served to lt. USNR, 1943-46. Mem. Am., Ohio (chmn. corp. law com.), N.Y. State, Dayton bar assns., Bar Assn. City N.Y., Phi Beta Kappa, Sigma Chi. Clubs: Dayton Country, Dayton City, Dayton Racquet, Columbus Athletic. Contbr. articles to profl. jours. Home: 236 W Schantz Ave Dayton OH 45409 Office: 2000 Courthouse Plaza NE Dayton OH 45402

SEALY, TOM, lawyer; b. Santa Anna, Tex., Feb. 18, 1909; s. Thomas Richard and Elizabeth (Harper) S.; LL.B., U. Tex., 1931; m. Mary Velma McCord, Jan. 16, 1936; 1 dau., Nancy. Admitted to Tex. bar, 1931; practice in Midland, 1935—; mem. firm Stubbeman, McRae, Sealy, Laughlin & Browder, 1936—. Dir. Midland Nat. Bank; past dir. First Savs. and Loan Assn., Tex. Land & Mortgage Co. (Midland). Past mem. city council, Midland. Past chmn. bd. regents U. Tex., past. chmn. devel. bd.; mem., former chmn. coordinating bd. Tex. Coll. and U. System; past trustee Tex. Presbyn. Found., Presbyn.-Austin Theol. Sem.; trustee Southwestern Legal Found.; past chmn., dir. Tex. Research League; pres. U. Texas Law Sch. Found. Served to lt. col. USAAF, World War II. Recipient Distinguished Alumnus award U. Tex., 1966; Outstanding Alumnus award U. Tex. Law Sch., 1970. Fellow Am., Tex. bar founds.; mem. Midland C. of C. (past pres.), Tex. Assn. Def. Counsel (past pres.), Am. Bar Assn., State Bar of Tex., Internat. Assn. Ins. Counsel, Am. Assn. Petroleum Landmen (hon.), Phi Delta Phi (hon.). Presbyn. Clubs: Midland Petroleum (past pres.), Midland Country; Austin, Headliners (Austin); Chaparral (Dallas); Century II (Ft. Worth); St. Anthony (San Antonio). Home: 915 Harvard St Midland TX 79701 Office: Midland Savings Bldg Midland TX 79701

SEALY, WILL CAMP, physician; b. Roberta, Ga., Nov. 16, 1912; s. Hugh Key and Marjorie Parkie (Camp) S.; B.S., Emory U., 1933, M.D., 1936; m. Jacqueline Womble, May 1, 1965; children—Leigh, Marjorie, Neil, Brian, Jacqueline, Karen. Intern, resident in surgery Duke U. Med. Center, 1926-42, mem. faculty, 1946—, prof. thoracic surgery, 1956—; vis. prof. U. Toulouse (France), U. Ky., U. Ga., N.Y. Hosp., Cornell U., Med. Coll. Va., U. Iowa, U. Mich., Coll. Phys. and Surgeons Columbia U.; chmn. research rev. com. for thoracic surgery surg. study sect. NIH, 1975-77. Served to lt. col. U.S. Army, 1942-46. Decorated Bronze Star medal; diplomate Am. Bd. Thoracic Surgery (dir. 1971-77). Fellow A.C.S.; mem. Societe de Chirurgie Thoracique et Cardiovasculaire de Longue Francaise, Soc. Univ. Surgeons, Am. Surg. Assn., So. Surg. Assn., So. Thoracic Surg. Assn. (pres. 1965), N.C. Surg. Assn. (pres. 1975-76), Durham Orange County Med. Soc. (pres. 1975-76), Am. Assn. Thoracic Surgery, Soc. Thoracic Surgeons (pres. 1970-71), Soc. Vascular Surgeons, Democrat. Methodist. Club: Hope Valley Country. Author: Surgery of the Oesophagus, 1959. Devised successful operation for correction of Wolff-Parkinson White Sndyrome; introduced use of moderate and deep hypothermia with cardiopulmonary bypass. Contbr. articles to profl. jours. Home: 2232 Cranford Rd Durham NC 27706 Office: Box 3093 Duke U Med Center Durham NC 27710

SEAMAN, ALFRED JARVIS, advt. agy. exec.; b. Hempstead, L.I., N.Y., Sept. 17, 1912; s. Alfred J. and Ellen (Delaney) S.; B.S., Columbia U., 1935; m. Mary M. Schill, Sept. 26, 1937 (dec. June 1975); children—Marilyn (Mrs. John Olen Pickett, Jr.), Susan, Barry, Deborah; m. 2d, Honor S. Mellor, July 16, 1977. Account exec. Fuller & Smith & Ross, Inc., N.Y.C., 1937-41; partner Knight & Gilbert. Inc., Boston, 1941-43; with Compton Advt., Inc., N.Y.C., 1946-59, exec. v.p., creative dir., dir., 1954-59; vice chmn. bd., chmn. exec. com. SSC & B, Inc., 1959-60, pres., 1960-79, chmn., chief exec. officer, 1979—, chmn. ops. com. SSC & B-Lintas Internat.; dir. Interpublic Group of Cos., Inc. Mem. adv. council, pres. ednl. found. Am. Assn. Advt. Agys.; bd. dirs., chmn. campaign rev. com. Advt. Council. Trustee, mayor Village Upper Brookville; co-chmn. exec. com. Samuel Waxman Cancer Research Fund. Served as lt. USNR, 1943-46. Clubs: Creek (pres.), Piping Rock, Beaver Dam (Locust Valley, L.I.); Racquet and Tennis, Links (N.Y.C.); Jupiter Island (Fla.); Mid-Ocean (Bermuda). Home: Wolver Hollow Rd Upper Brookville Oyster Bay NY 11771 Office: 1 Dag Hammarskjold Plaza New York NY 10017

SEAMAN, EDWIN, ins. co. exec.; b. N.Y.C., June 11, 1926; s. John Edwin and Edith (Petterson) S.; B.S., Stanford, 1950; m. Grace Louise Rexroth, June 18, 1951; children—Jonathan, Matthew, David. Sr. accountant Price Waterhouse & Co., San Francisco, 1951-57; sr. auditor, asst. controller Gen. Ins. Co. of Am., 1957-62; asst. treas. Transamerica Corp., 1962; controller, v.p., Transamerica Ins. Co., Los Angeles, 1962-65, exec. v.p., 1965-71, pres., 1971—, also dir.; chmn. bd. Premier Ins. Co.; dir., chmn. Wolverine Ins. Co., Riverside Ins. Co.; dir. Can. Surety Countywide Ins. Co.; Olympic Ins. Co., Mt. Beacon Ins. Co., Marathon Ins. Co., Occidental Life Ins. Co. Calif. Served with USNR, 1943-45. C.P.A.

SEAMAN, IRVING, JR., banker; b. Milw., July 14, 1923; s. Irving and Anne (Douglas S.; B.A., Yale, 1944; m. June Carry, June 24, 1950; children—Peter Stewart, Marion Carry, Irving Osborne, Anne Douglas. With Continental Ill. Nat. Bank & Trust Co., Chgo., 1947-61, v.p., 1959-61; pres., chief exec. officer, dir. Nat. Boulevard Bank, Chgo., 1961-65, chmn. exec. com., chief exec. officer, dir., 1966-76; vice chmn. bd., dir. Sears Bank and Trust Co., Chgo., 1976-77, pres., chief operating officer, dir., 1977—; exec. v.p., asst. sec., dir. Midland Bancorp. Inc.; dir. Abbott Labs., William Wrigley Jr. Co., Inc. Mem. Northwestern U. Assos.; life mem. bd. dirs. Lake Forest Hosp.; bd. dirs. Better Bus. Bur. of Met. Chgo., Inc.; bd. dirs. United Way of Met. Chgo., pres., 1979. Served to lt. (j.g.) USNR, World War II. Clubs: Commonwealth, Metropolitan, Economic, Chicago, Casino, Commercial, Racquet, Bankers (Chgo); Onwentsia, Winter (Lake Forest); Old Elm (Ft. Sheridan, Ill.; Shoreacres (Lake Bluff, Ill.); Augusta (Ga.) Nat. Golf; Sawgrass (Fla.); Ponte Vedra (Fla.). Home: 946 N Elm Tree Rd Lake Forest IL 60045 Office: Sears Tower Chicago IL 60606

SEAMAN, ROBERT LEE, copper co. exec.; b. Long Island, N.Y., Mar. 29, 1942; s. Farrand Robert and Leona (Hicks) S.; B.A., Harvard U., 1963; LL.B., U. Va., 1966; m. Carolyn Holmes Hopgood, July 23, 1966; children—Elizabeth, Jennifer, Rebecca. Admitted to N.Y., Va. bars, 1966; law clk. to U.S. dist. judge, 1966-68; lectr. U. Va. Grad. Sch. Bus. Adminstrn., 1967-68; asso. firm Brown, Wood, Ivey, Mitchell & Petty, N.Y.C., 1968-74; officer Phelps Dodge Corp., N.Y.C., 1974—, corp. sec., from 1976; lectr. in field. Bd. trustees Friends Acad., Locust Valley, N.Y., from 1975. Home: 14 Beach Dr Hungtington NY 11743 Office: 300 Park Ave New York NY 10022

SEAMAN, WILLIAM BERNARD, physician; b. Chgo., Jan. 5, 1917; s. Benjamin and Dorothy E. Seaman; student U. Mich., 1934-37; M.D., Harvard, 1941; m. Veryl Swick, February 26, 1944; children—Cheryl Dorothy, William David. Intern Billings Hosp., U. Chgo., 1941-42; asst. radiology Yale U. Sch. Medicine, 1947-48, instr., 1948-49; instr. radiology Washington U. Sch. Medicine, St. Louis, 1949-51, asso. prof., 1951-55, prof., 1955-56; prof. radiology, chmn. dept. Coll. Phys. and Surg., Columbia, 1956—; dir. radiology service, trustee Presbyn. Hosp., N.Y.C. Served as maj. USAAF, 1942-46; flight surgeon. Diplomate Am. Bd. Radiology. Mem. A.M.A., Radiol. Soc. N.A., Am. Roentgen Ray Soc. (pres. 1973-74), Am. Coll. Radiology, Radiation Research Soc., Assn. U. Radiologists (pres. 1955-56), N.Y. Roentgen Soc. (pres. 1961-62), N.Y. Gastroent. Soc. (pres. 1965-66), Soc. Chmn. Academic Radiology Depts. (pres. 1967-68). Presbyn. Home: 47 Depeyster Tenafly NJ 07670 Office: 622 W 168th St New York City NY 10032

SEAMAN, WILLIAM CASPER, news photographer; b. Grand Island, Nebr., Jan. 19, 1925; s. William H. and Minnie (Cords) S.; grad. high sch.; m. Ruth Witwer, Feb. 14, 1945; 1 son, Lawrence William. Photographer, Leschinsky Studio, Grand Island; news photographer Mpls. Star & Tribune, 1945—. Recipient Pulitzer prize, 1959; also awards Nat. Headliners Club, Nat. Press Photographers Assn., Inland Daily Press Assn., Kent State U., Mo. U., Local Page One, State A.P. contest; Silver Anniversary award Honeywell Photog. Products, 1975. Mem. Nat. Press Photographers Assn., Sigma Delta Chi. Home: 8206 S Virginia Circle Minneapolis MN 55426 Office: 425 Portland Ave Minneapolis MN 55488

SEAMANS, FRANK L., lawyer; b. Canton, Ill.; A.B., U. Ill., 1935; LL.B., Harvard 1938. Admitted to Pa. bar, 1939; now partner firm Eckert, Seamans, Cherin & Mellott, Pitts. Mem. Am., Pa., Allegheny County bar assns. Home: 820 Osage Rd Pittsburgh PA 15243 Office: Eckert Seamans Cherin & Mellott 600 Grant St Pittsburgh PA 15219

SEAMANS, JAMES MCGEERY, oil co. exec.; b. Casper, Wyo., Dec. 27, 1922; s. Walter Louis and Irene Alberta (McGeery) S.; B.S. in Chem. Engring., U. Wyo., 1950; m. Wyoma Lou Osborn, July 10, 1944; children—Sandra K., Linda Sue, Carol Ann. With Texaco Inc., 1950—, asst. gen. mgr. refining for U.S., Houston, 1972-77, gen. mgr. refining U.S., 1978, v.p. petroleum products dept. U.S., 1978—; dir. Coltexo Corp. Served with armored inf. U.S. Army, 1941-46. Mem. Am. Inst. Chem. Engrs., Houston C. of C. Republican. Methodist. Clubs: Texaco Country, Houston. Home: 13718 Apple Tree Houston TX 77079 Office: 1111 Rusk Ave Houston TX 77002*

SEAMANS, ROBERT CHANNING, JR., educator; b. Salem, Mass., Oct. 30, 1918; s. Robert Channing and Pauline (Bosson) S.; B.S., Harvard, 1939; M.S., Mass. Inst. Tech., 1942, Sc.D., 1951; grad. exec. program bus. adminstrn. Columbia, 1959; D.Sc., Rollins Coll., 1962, N.Y.U., 1967; D.Eng., Norwich Acad., 1971, Notre Dame U., 1974, Rensselaer Poly. Inst., 1974, U. Wyo., 1975, George Washington U., 1975, Lehigh U., 1976; m. Eugenia Merrill, June 13, 1942; children—Katherine (Mrs. Louis Padulo), Robert Channing III, Joseph, May (Mrs. Eugene Baldwin III), Daniel M. With Mass. Inst. Tech., 1941-55, successively instr. dept. aero. engring., staff engr. instrumentation lab., asst. prof., project leader instrumentation lab., asso. prof., 1941-50, chief engr. Project Meteor, 1950-55, dir. flight control lab., 1953-55; mgr. airborne systems lab., chief systems engr. airborne systems dept. RCA, 1955-58, chief engr. missile electronics and controls div., 1958-60; asso. adminstr. NASA, 1960-65, dep. adminstr., 1965-68, cons., 1968-69; vis. prof. Mass. Inst. Tech., 1968, Hunsaker prof., 1968-69; sec. air force, 1969-73; pres. Nat. Acad. Engring., 1973-74; adminstr. ERDA, Washington, 1974-77; Henry R. Luce prof. environment and pub. policy Mass. Inst. Tech., Cambridge, 1977—, dean Sch. Engring., 1978—; dir. Air Products Corp., Charles Stark Draper Lab., Inc., Combustion Engring. Inc., Eli Lilly and Co., Johnny Appleseed's Inc., Mass. Tech. Devel. Corp.; trustee Aerospace Corp.; mem. sci. adv. bd. USAF, 1957-62, asso. adviser, 1963-67. Bd. overseers Harvard, 1968-74; trustee Mus. of Sci., Boston, Sea Edn. Assn., Nat. Geog. Soc., USAF Hist. Found., Carnegie Inst., Nat. Fund Minority Engring. Students; bd. dirs. Alliance to Save Energy. Recipient Naval Ordnance Devel. award, 1945; Godfrey L. Cabot award Aero Club New Eng., 1965;

Distinguished Service medal NASA, 1965, 69; Robert H. Goddard Meml. trophy, 1968; Distinguished Pub. Service medal Dept. Def., 1973, Exceptional Civilian Service award Dept. Air Force, 1973, Gen. Thomas D. White U.S. Air Force Space Trophy, 1973, Ralph Coats Roe medal ASME, 1977, Achievement award Nat. Soc. Profl. Engrs. Fellow Am. Acad. Arts and Scis., Am. Astron. Soc., IEEE, Am. Inst. Aeros. and Astronautics (hon., Lawrence Sperry award 1951); mem. Internat. Acad. Astronautics, Am. Soc. Pub. Adminstrn., Nat. Acad. Engring., AAAS, Air Force Acad. Found., Fgn. Policy Assn., Am. Geophys. Union, Smithsonian Instn., Conf. Bd. (sr. exec. council), Am. Ordnance Assn., Nat. Space Club, Council on Fgn. Relations, Sigma Xi. Clubs: Harvard (Boston); Manchester (Mass.) Yacht; Essex County (Mass.); Chevy Chase, Cosmos, Federal City (Washington). Office: 1-206 Mass Inst Tech Cambridge MA 02139

SEAMANS, WILLIAM, television-radio journalist; b. Providence, July 8, 1925; s. William and Mary S.; A.B., Brown U., 1949; M.Sc., Columbia U., 1952; m. Jane Kingsbury, Sept. 15, 1951; children—Laurie, Jonathan, Adam. Freelance journalist, 1952-53; journalist CBS News, 1953-63; corr., bur. chief ABC News, Tel Aviv, Israel, 1963—. Served with inf., AUS, 1942-45. Recipient Emmy award for best local news program, 1960-61. CBS News fellow Columbia U., 1961-62. Mem. Writers Guild Am., Nat. Acad. Television Arts and Scis., Overseas Press Club Am. (award for best radio reporting invasion of Cyprus, 1974, award for best fgn. affairs documentary Yitzhak Rabin biography 1975), Fgn. Corrs. Assn. in Israel. Office: ABC News 53 Petach Tikva Rd Tel Aviv Israel

SEAR, MOREY LEONARD, judge; b. New Orleans, Feb. 26. 1929; s. William and Yetty (Streiffer) S.; J.D., Tulane U., 1950; m. Lee Edrehi, May 26, 1951; children—William Sear II, Jane Lee. Admitted to La. bar, 1950; asst. dist. atty. Parish Orleans, 1952-55; individual practice law, New Orleans, 1955-71; spl. counsel New Orleans Aviation Bd., 1956-60; U.S. magistrate Eastern Dist. La., 1971-76; judge U.S. Dist. Ct. Eastern Dist. La., 1976—; mem. faculty Fed. Jud. Center, Washington, 1971—, Tulane U. Coll. Law. Founding dir. River Oaks Pvt. Psychiat. Hosp., 1968; pres. Congregation Temple Sinai, 1977—; bd. govs. Tulane Med. Center, 1976—; bd. dirs. Tulane Med. Center Hosp., 1976—. Mem. Am., New Orleans, La. bar assns. Home: 475 Jewel St New Orleans LA 70130 Office: 500 Camp St New Orleans LA 70130

SEARCY, ALAN WINN, chemist, educator; b. Covina, Calif., Oct. 12, 1925; s. Claude Winn and Esther (Scofield) S.; A.B., Pomona Coll., 1946; Ph.D., U. Calif. at Berkeley, 1950; m. Gail Vaught, Oct. 30, 1945; children—Gay, William, Anne. Faculty, Purdue U., 1949-54, asst. prof. chemistry, 1950-54; faculty U. Calif. at Berkeley, 1954—, prof., 1958—, prof. materials sci., 1960—, asso. div. head inorganic materials div. Lawrence Radiation Lab., 1961-64, asst. to chancellor, 1963-64, vice-chancellor, 1964-67, chmn. faculty Coll. Engring., 1969-70, Miller research prof., 1970-71, acting chmn. dept. materials sci. and engring., 1973. Fulbright lectr. phys. chemistry Inst. Physics, Bariloche, Argentina, 1960; cons. Gen. Motors Tech. Center, 1956-64, Union Carbide, 1956-72, Gen. Atomic, 1957-72. Mem. com. high temperature chemistry NRC, 1961-70. Served with AUS, 1944-46. Guggenheim fellow, 1967-68. Fellow Am. Ceramic Soc.; mem. Am. Chem. Soc., A.A.A.S., Phi Beta Kappa, Sigma Xi. Editor: (with D.V. Ragone, U. Colombo) Chemical and Mechanical Behavior of Inorganic Materials, 1970. Editorial adv. bd. High Temperature High Pressure, 1969—, High Temperature Sci., 1969—, Advances in High Temperature Chemistry, 1971—. Contbr. numerous articles to profl. jours. Home: 24 Northampton Berkeley CA 94707

SEARCY, ALBERT WYNNE, lawyer, judge; b. Brenham, Tex., Nov. 29, 1909; s. William Williams and Nina Kasson (Jones) S.; B.A., Tex. U., 1930, postgrad. Law Sch., 1930-31; LL.B., Cumberland U., 1932; m. Marie Ferne Rodman, Nov. 6, 1938; children—Edith (Mrs. Edith Wisehart), Albert Rodman, Ina (Mrs. Roy O. Ragsdale). Admitted to Tex. bar, 1932; practiced in Corpus Christi, 1932-43, Junction, 1943—; mcpl. judge City of Junction, 1979—; owner ins. agy., Junction, 1946—; county atty. Kimble County, 1949-72. Mem. Sigma Delta Kappa, Beta Theta Pi. Democrat. Presbyn. (elder 1938-41, 47-50, deacon 1958-41, 44-47). Lion (charter mem., pres. 1946-47, 68-69). Home: Kerrville Star Route Junction TX 76849 Office: 1411 Main St PO Box 21 Junction TX 76849

SEARER, R. FLOYD, lawyer; b. Kokomo, Ind., Feb. 26, 1905; s. Clarence A. and Alice (Herr) S.; A.B., U. Notre Dame, 1928, J.D., 1930; m. Marguerite Westphal, Sept. 5, 1932; children—Russell F. (dec.), Susan M. Admitted to Ind. bar, 1930; mem. legal dept. Assos. Investment Co., South Bend, Ind., 1931-32; v.p., trust officer First Bank & Trust Co., South Bend, 1932-47; partner firm May, Searer, Oberfell & Helling, South Bend, 1948—. Dir. Peoples First Fed. Savs. and Loan Assn., South Bend. Past pres. St. Joseph County Bd. Aviation Commrs., local Community Fund, March of Dimes, Crippled Children's Soc. Mem. Am., Ind., St. Joseph County (past pres.) bar assns. Mason (33 deg.). Home: 219 Swanson Circle South Bend IN 46615 Office: C of C Bldg South Bend IN 46601

SEARLE, CAMPBELL LEACH, educator; b. Winnipeg, Man., Can., July 24, 1926; s. Stewart Augustus and Sally Elisabeth (Appleyard) S.; B.Sc., Queen's U., Kingston, Ont., 1947; S.M., Mass. Inst. Tech., 1951; m. Eleanor Whittlesey Reed, Feb. 28, 1953; children—Catherine, Susan, Sally, Reed. Mem. faculty Mass. Inst. Tech., 1957-74, prof., 1968-74; prof. elec. engring. and psychology Queen's U., 1974—; dir. Fed. Industries. Mem. IEEE, AAAS. Co-author: Electronic Principles, 1968. Office: MIT Cambridge MA 02139

SEARLE, DANIEL CROW, med. and health services co. exec.; b. Evanston, Ill., May 6, 1926; s. John Gideon and Frances Louise (Crow) S.; B.S., Yale, 1950; M.B.A., Harvard, 1952; m. Dain Depew Fuller, Sept. 2, 1950; children—Anne Searle Meers, Daniel Gideon, Michael Dain. With G.D. Searle & Co., Chgo., 1938—, successively staff asst. to v.p. charge finance and mfg., asst. sec., sec., 1952-59, v.p., 1961-63, exec. v.p., 1963-66, pres., chief ops. officer 1966-70, pres., chief exec. officer, 1970-72, chmn. exec. com., 1972—, chmn. bd., 1977—, dir., 1964—; dir. Atlanta/LaSalle Corp., Chgo., Harris Trust & Savs. Bank, Chgo., Utilities Inc., Maynard Oil Co., Jim Walter Corp. Bd. dirs. Evanston Hosp.; trustee Northwestern U., Com. for Econ. Devel., Better Govt. Assn.; mem. exec. com. Yale Devel. Bd.; mem. at large Yale Alumni Bd.; bd. dirs. Pharm. Mfrs. Assn. Found. Served with USNR, World War II. Mem. Pharm. Mfrs. Assn. (dir.). Republican. Episcopalian (vestry). Clubs: Glen View (Golf, Ill.); Indian Hill (Winnetka, Ill.); Shoreacres (Lake Bluff, Ill.); Chicago, Chicago Commonwealth, Mid-America (Chgo.); Seminole Golf; Augusta Nat. Golf; Old Elm (Highland Park, Ill.); Jupiter Island (Fla.). Home: 33 Woodley Rd Winnetka IL 60093 Office: PO Box 1045 Skokie IL 60076

SEARLE, JOHN ROGERS, philosopher, educator; b. Denver, July 31, 1932; s. George W. and Hester (Beck) S.; student U. Wis., 1949-52; B.A. 1st class honors (Rhodes scholar), U. Oxford (Eng.), 1955, M.A., 1959, D.Phil., 1959; m. Dagmar Carboch, Dec. 24, 1958; children—Thomas R., Mark R. Lectr., Christ Ch., Oxford, 1956-59; prof. philosophy U. Calif., Berkeley, 1959—, chmn. dept. philosophy, 1973-75, spl. asst. to chancellor, 1965-67. Vis. prof. U. Mich., 1961-62, U. Wash., 1963, Brasenose Coll., Oxford, 1967-68, State U. N.Y. Buffalo, 1971, U. Oslo, 1971; regular panelist World Press weekly program Nat. Ednl. Television Network, 1970-77, moderator, 1972-74; sec.-treas. Hanzell Vineyards Ltd. Mem. Am. Council Edn. Com. on Campus Tension, 1969-70, Presdl. Adv. Group on Campus Unrest, 1970. Mem. vis. com. for linguistics and philosophy Mass. Inst. Tech., 1971-77. Bd. dirs. No. Calif. chpt. ACLU, 1968-71, Council on Philos. Studies, 1975—, Am. Council Learned Socs., 1979—; trustee Nat. Humanities Center, 1975—. Guggenheim fellow, 1975-76. Mem. Aristotelian Soc., Am. Philos Assn., Am. Acad. Arts and Scis. Author: Speech Acts, 1969; The Campus War, 1971; Expression and Meaning, 1979. Editor: Philosophy of Language, 1970. Contbr. articles to profl. jours. Home: 1900 Yosemite Rd Berkeley CA 94707

SEARLE, PHILIP FORD, banker; b. Kansas City, Mo., July 23, 1924; s. Albert Addison and Edith (Thompson) S.; A.B., Cornell U., 1949; grad. Stonier Grad. Sch. Banking, Rutgers U., 1957, 64; m. Jean Adair Hanneman, Nov. 22, 1950; 1 son, Charles Randolph. With Geneva Savs. and Trust Co. (O.), 1949-60, pres., 1959-60; pres., sr. trust officer Northeastern Ohio Nat. Bank, Ashtabula, 1960-69, also dir.; pres., chief exec. officer BancOhio Corp., Columbus, 1969-75, also dir.; chmn., chief exec. officer Flagship Banks, Inc., Miami Beach, Fla., 1975—, also dir.; dir. MidContinent Telephone Corp.; former mem. faculty Ohio Sch. Banking, Ohio U., 1959-70, Nat. Trust Sch., Northwestern U., 1965-68. Past chmn. bd. regents Stonier Grad. Sch. Banking, Rutgers U., 1974-76, past mem. faculty; Christmas seal chmn. State of Fla., 1977-78; mem. South Fla. Coordinating Council; bd. dirs. Greater Miami Opera Assn., 1976—. Served to capt. AUS, 1943-46, 51-52. Decorated Bronze Star; named Outstanding Citizens in Ashtabula County, 1967. Mem. Am. (past dir., governing council), Fla. (dir. 1979-80), Ohio (pres. 1970-71) bankers assns., Assn. Bank Holding Cos. (govt. relations com.), Fla. Assn. Registered Bank Holding Cos. (pres. 1979-80), Fla. Council 100, Fla. C. of C. (dir. 1978—), Phi Kappa Tau. Clubs: Miami; Riviera Country (Coral Gables, Fla.). Co-author: The Management of a Trust Department, 1967. Mem. editorial adv. bd. Issues in Bank Regulation, 1978. Office: 1111 Lincoln Rd Mall Miami Beach FL 33139

SEARLE, RODNEY NEWELL, ins. agt., farmer, state legislator; b. Camden, N.J., July 17, 1920; s. William Albert and Ruby Marie (Barrus) S.; B.A., Mankato State U., 1960; m. Janette Elizabeth Christie, May 17, 1940; children—Rodney Newell, Linda Jennison, Alan John. Prodn. coordinator Johnson & Johnson, New Brunswick, N.J., 1940-47; farmer, Waseca, Minn., 1947—; spl. agt. John Hancock Mut. Ins. Co., Waseca, Minn., 1961—; mem. Minn. Ho. of Reps., St. Paul, 1957—, speaker of the house, 1979—. Lay reader St. John's Episcopal Ch., 1952—. Named Minn. State Tree Farmer of Yr., 1978. Mem. Am. Tree Farm System, Nat. Conf. State Legislators. Republican. Clubs: Masons, Rotary (pres. club 1968) (Waseca, Minn.). Office: Room 390 State Office Bldg Saint Paul MN 55155

SEARLE, RONALD, artist; b. Cambridge, Eng., Mar. 3, 1920; s. William James and Nellie (Hunt) S.; ed. Cambridge Sch. Art; m. Monica Koenig, 1967. First pub. work appeared in Cambridge Daily News, 1935-39; one-man exhbns. include Leicester Galleries, London, 1948, 50, 54, 57, Kraushaar Gallery, N.Y.C., 1959, Blanchini Gallery, N.Y.C., 1963, city museums Bremen, Hannover, Dusseldorf, Stuttgart, Berlin, 1965, 3d Biennale Tolentino, Italy, 1965, Galerie Pro Arte, Delmenhorst, Germany, Mus. Art, Bremerhaven, Germany, Galerie Münsterberg, Basle, Switzerland, Galerie Pribaut, Amsterdam, Holland, Wolfgang-Gurlitt Mus., Linz, Austria, Galerie La Pochade, Paris 1966-71, Art Alliance Gallery, Phila., 1967, Galerie Garlitt, Munich, 1967-76, Grosvenor Gallery, London, 1968, Galerie Obere Zaune, Zurich, 1968, Galerie Hauswedell, Baden-Baden, 1968, Galerie Brumme, Frankfurt, 1969, Kunsthallen, Södertälje, Sweden, 1969, Rizzoli Gallery, N.Y.C., 1969, Kunsthalle, Konstanz, 1970, Würzburg, 1970, Galerie Welz, Salzburg, 1971, Galerie Rivolta, Lausanne, 1972, Galerie Gaëton, Geneva, 1972, Bibliothèque Nationale, Paris, 1973, Galerie Würthle, Vienna, 1973, Kulterhaus Graz, Austria, 1973, 79, Galerie Rivolta, Lausanne, 1974, 78, Galerie l'Angle Aigu, Brussels, 1974, 77, Galerie Carmen Casse', Paris, 1975-77, Staatliche Museen Preussicher Kulturbesitz, Berlin, 1976, others; contbr. to nat. publs., 1946—; theatre artist Punch, 1949-61; created series of cartoons on fictitious girls sch., 1941, became film series Belles of St. Trinian's, 1954, Blue Murder at St. Trinian's 1957, The Pure Hell of St. Trinian's, 1960, The Great St. Trinian's Train Robbery, 1965); films designs include John Gilpin (Brit. Film Inst.), 1951, On the Twelfth Day, 1954 (nominated Acad. award), Energetically Yours, 1957; The Kings Breakfast, 1963; Those Magnificient Men in Their Flying Machines, 1965; Monte Carlo or Bust, 1969, Scrooge, 1970; Dick Deadeye, or Duty Done, 1975. Recipient medal Art Dirs. Club Los Angeles, 1959, Art Dirs. Mem. Club Phila., Pa., 1959, gold medal 3d Biennale, Tolentino, Italy, 1965, Prix de la Critique Belge, 1968, medaille de la ville d'Avignon, 1971, Prix de l' Humour S.P.H. Festival d' Avignon, 1971, Prix de l' Humour Noir "Grandville," France, 1971, Prix Internationale Charles Huard, France, 1972. Club: The Garrick (London). Author: (pub. in U.S.) The Female Approach, 1954; Merry England, 1957; (with Kaye Webb) Paris Sketchbook, 1958, The St. Trinian's Story, 1959, Refugees, 1960; (with Alex Atkinson) The Big City, 1958, U.S.A. for Beginners, 1959, Russia for Beginners, 1960, Escape from the Amazon., 1964; Which Way Did He Go? 1962; From Frozen North to Filthy Lucre, 1964; Those Magnificient Men in Their Flying Machines, 1965; (with Heinz Huber) Haven't We Met Before Somewhere? 1966; Searle's Cats, 1968; The Square Egg, 1969; Hello—Where Did All the People Go?, 1970; (with Kildare Dobbs) The Great Fur Opera, 1970; The Addict, 1971; More Cats, 1975; Zoodiac, 1978; Ronald Searle Album, 1979; contbr. to New Yorker. Home: care Hope Leresche and Sayle 11 Jubilee Pl London SW 3-3TE England Office: care John Locke Studio 15 E 76th St New York NY 10021

SEARLE, WILLIAM LOUIS, med. and health services exec.; b. Evanston, Ill., Mar. 4, 1928; s. John G. and Frances (Crow) S.; B.A., U. Mich., 1951; postgrad. Harvard, 1969; m. Sally Burnett, Dec. 4, 1953; children—Marion Scott, Elizabeth Burnett, Louise Crow. With G. D. Searle & Co., Chgo., 1956—, v.p. marketing, 1965-68, v.p., gen. mgr., 1968-70, sr. v.p., gen. mgr., 1970-72, chmn. bd., 1972-77, vice chmn., from 1977, now chmn. adminstrv. com., also dir.; dir. Nat. Blvd. Bank. Bd. dirs. Field Mus., Childrens Meml. Hosp., Lake Forest Country Day Sch. Served with Chem. Corps, AUS, 1951. Clubs: Chicago, Chicago Commonwealth, Executives, Commercial, Mid-America, Onwantsia, Shoreacres (Chgo.). Office: PO Box 1045 Skokie IL 60076*

SEARLES, DEWITT RICHARD, investment firm exec., ret. air force officer; b. Birmingham, Ala., Aug. 7, 1920; s. DeWitt Richard and Miriam (Hostetler) S.; student Coll. William and Mary, 1939-41; B.A., U. Md., 1949; M.A., George Washington U., 1964; grad. Army Command and Gen. Staff Sch., Ft. Leavenworth, Kans., 1945, USAF Command and Gen. Staff Coll., Maxwell AFB, Ala., 1956, Nat. War Coll., Washington, 1964; m. Barbara Elizabeth Brown, Jan. 28, 1949; children—Ann Hampton, DeWitt Richard III, Elizabeth Alison. Commd. 2d lt. USAAF, 1942, advanced through grades to maj. gen. USAF, 1971; fighter pilot and squadron comdr., New Guinea and Philippines, 1943-45; comdr. 81st Tactical Fighter Wing, Eng., 1965-67; insp. gen. Tactical Air Command, Va., 1967-69; comdr. 327th Air Dir., Taiwan, Republic of China, 1969-71; dep. comdr. 7/13 Air Force, Udorn AFB, Thailand, 1971-72; dep. insp. gen. Hdqrs. USAF, Washington, 1972-74, ret.; account exec. Merrill Lynch, Pierce, Fenner & Smith, Washington, 1974—. Decorated D.S.M. with 2 oak leaf clusters, Legion of Merit with oak leaf cluster, D.F.C., Air medal with 7 oak leaf clusters. Home: 1605 Dunterry Pl McLean VA 22101 Office: 8320 Old Court House Rd Vienna VA 22180

SEARLS, FREDERICK TAYLOR, lawyer; b. San Francisco, July 8, 1912; s. Robert McMurray and Gertrude (Taylor) S.; B.A., Stanford, 1933; J.D., Harvard, 1936; m. Dorothy Bates; children—David C., Catherine P. (Mrs. E. Owen Clark), Carol T. (Mrs. John Hilliard). Admitted to Calif. bar, 1936; with Pacific Gas & Electric Co., San Francisco, 1936-74, gen. atty., 1955-70, v.p., gen. counsel, 1970-74; partner Debevoise & Liberman, Washington, 1975—. Served to lt. col. USAF, 1942-46. Mem. Am., D.C. bar assns., Calif. State Bar, Fed. Energy Bar Assn. Office: 1200 17th St NW Washington DC 20036

SEARS, ARTHUR, JR., electric co. exec.; b. Pitts., July 1, 1928; s. James Arthur and Matilda (Hardy) S.; student U. Wis., 1951; B.A., U. Pitts., 1954; m. Bettie Jean Virgis, Sept. 21, 1957 (div. Oct. 1977); children—Norma Jean, Arthur III, Galana, Jory, Ryan. Reporter, Norfolk (Va.) Jour. and Guide, 1954-57; reporter Cleve. Call and Post, 1957-58, Cin. dist. mgr.-editor, 1958-59; asso. editor Jet mag., 1959-64; N.Y. editor Jet mag., asso. editor Ebony mag., 1964-66; asso. dir. pub. relations dept. Nat. Urban League, N.Y.C., 1966-67; staff reporter Wall St. Jour., N.Y. Bur., 1967-69; cons. bus. environment studies dept. Gen. Electric Co., N.Y.C., 1969-72, cons. corporate ednl. communications, Fairfield, Conn., 1972-76, mgr. pub. affairs Export Sales and Services div., N.Y.C., 1976—; summer lectr. journalism Plainfield (N.J.) High Sch., 1970, Middlesex (N.J.) Coll., 1971, Rutgers U., 1972. Mem. Mayor's Adv. Com. on Econ. Devel., Plainfield, 1970-72; Webelo Cub Scout leader, Plainfield, 1969-72. Bd. dirs. Plainfield Library Bd., 1970-72, Plainfield Area United Fund, 1971-73. Served with C.E., AUS, 1950-52. Recipient Meyer Berger award for journalism Grad. Sch. Journalism, Columbia, 1970. Mem. Alpha Phi Alpha. Baptist. Contbr. chpt. to Malcolm X: A Man and His Times, 1968. Home: Lancaster Hotel 22 E 38th St Room 334 New York NY 10016 Office: 570 Lexington Ave New York NY 10022. *Focus on your profession, your love. The fame and glory will automatically follow.*

SEARS, BARNABAS FRANCIS, lawyer; b. Webster, S.D., Nov. 13, 1902; student St. Thomas Coll., St. Paul; LL.B., Georgetown U., 1926, LL.D., 1971; LL.D., John Marshall Law Sch., 1971, William Mitchell Coll. Law, 1972. Admitted to Ill. bar, 1926; practice in Chgo., 1942—; now partner Boodell, Sears, Giambalvo, Sugrue & Crowley. Named Chicagoan of Year, Chgo. Jr. C. of C., 1971. Mem. Am. (ho. dels. 1952-75, chmn. 1968-70, standing com. on fed. judiciary 1959-68), Ill. (past mem. council, chmn. sect. on jud. compensation, selection and tenure 1962—, pres. 1957-58), Kane County, Aurora, Chgo. bar assns., Soc. Trial Lawyers of Chgo., Am. Law Inst., Am. Judicature Soc., Am. Coll. Trial Lawyers (bd. regents 1961-65, pres. 1970-71; award Courageous Advocacy 1975), Internat. Acad. Trial Lawyers. Clubs: Chgo. Athletic Assn. Home: 505 N Lake Shore Dr Chicago IL 60611 Office: One IBM Plaza Suite 2650 Chicago IL 60611. *My principle endeavor has been to maintain my dignity and integrity as a lawyer, my duty of fidelity to my clients and their causes, and to uphold and maintain the traditions of an ancient and honorable profession.*

SEARS, BRADFORD GEORGE, landscape architect; b. Philmont, N.Y., June 21, 1915; s. Russell Lockwood and Alla (Scutt) Sears; B.S., N.Y. State Coll. Forestry, 1939, M.S., 1948; m. Ruth Ellen Fox, July 5, 1936; children—Bradford Alan, Brian Scutt, Patricia Ruth. With State U. N.Y., Syracuse, 1941-76, prof. landscape architecture, 1950-76, dean landscape architecture, 1968-76, dean emeritus, 1976—; pvt. practice landscape architecture, 1945—; mem. bd. landscape architecture N.Y. State Dept. Edn., 1967-79. Fellow Am. Soc. Landscape Architects; mem. Am. Soc. Landscape Architects (past pres. N.Y. Upstate chpt.), Am. Camping Assn. Contbr. articles to profl. jours. Methodist. Address: 116 Wellwood Dr Fayetteville NY 13066

SEARS, DON WALTER, lawyer, educator; b. Chillicothe, Ohio, Oct. 18, 1921; s. Walter D. and Blanche (Compton) S.; B.S., Ohio State U., 1946, J.D., 1948; m. Eve Willey, Feb. 14, 1946; children—Stephanie, Lance, Don, Kathleen, Shannon. Admitted to Ohio bar, 1949; asso. Effler, Eastman, Stichter & Smith, Toledo, 1949-50; asst. prof. law U. Colo., 1950-52, asso. prof., 1952-55, prof., 1955—, dean Sch. of Law, 1968-73. Dir. Colo. Rural Legal Services, 1969-72. Mem. Colo. adv. commn. U.S. Civil Rights Commn., 1962-75, Fed. Mediation and Conciliation Service, 1959—. Served with AUS, 1943-46; ETO. Recipient Stearns award U. Colo. 1967, Univ. Recognition medal, 1975, Faculty Humanist award, 1979. Mem. Nat. Acad. Arbitrators, Colo. (exec. com., bd. govs.), Boulder County (past pres.) bar assns., Urban League Colo. (bd. dirs.), Order of Coif (exec. com.). Author: (with F.P. Storke) Colorado Security Law Treatise, 1955. Co-editor: The American Law of Mining, 1960; The Employment Relation and the Law, 1957; Labor Relations and the Law, 3d edit., 1965; (with D. Wollett) Collective Bargaining in the Public Sector, 1972. Asso. editor: The Developing Labor Law, The Board, The Courts and The National Labor Relations Act, 1971. Contbr. articles to profl. jours. Home: 504 Geneva Ave Boulder CO 80302

SEARS, EARL WAYNE, trade orgn. exec.; b. Brownfield, Tex., June 29, 1927; s. Kelly and Era Atwood (McLeroy) S.; Tex. Technol. U.; m. Gwendolyn Y. Moor, June 28, 1949; children—Cathy Gwen, Robert E., David D., Kristie Ann. Head, Dept. Vocat. Agr., Lamesa, Tex., 1948-52; field rep. Nat. Cotton Council, Lubbock, Tex., 1952-54, supr. S.W. area, Dallas, 1954-65, asst. to exec. v.p., Memphis, 1971-75, adminstrv. v.p., 1975-77, exec. v.p., 1978—; product mgr. Hesston Corp. (Kans.), 1965-68, mktg. mgr., 1969-71. Served with N.G. Mem. Am. Soc. Assn. Execs., AIM. Home: 2174 Thornwood St Memphis TN 38117 Office: Nat Cotton Council PO Box 12285 1918 N Parkway Memphis TN 38112

SEARS, ERNEST ROBERT, geneticist, educator; b. Bethel, Oreg., Oct. 15, 1910; s. Jacob Perlonzo and Ada Estella (McKee) S.; B.S., Oreg. State Agrl. Coll., 1932; A.M. Harvard, 1934, Ph.D., 1936; D.Sc., Goettingen U.; m. Caroline F. Elchorn, July 5, 1936; 1 son, Michael Allan; m. 2d, Lotti Maria Steinitz, June 16, 1950; children—John, Barbara, Kathleen. Agt., Dept. Agr., 1936-41, geneticist, 1941—; research asso. U. Mo., Columbia, 1937-63, prof., 1963—, Fulbright research fellow, Germany, 1958. Recipient Stevenson award for research in agronomy, 1951, Hoblitzelle award for research in agrl. sci., 1958, Distinguished Service award Oreg. State Agrl. Coll., 1973. Fellow Agronomy Soc. Am., AAAS, Indian Soc. Genetics and Plant Breeding (hon.), Japanese Genetics Soc. (hon.); mem. Am. Acad. Arts and Scis., Nat. Acad. Scis., Bot. Soc. Am., Genetics Soc. Am. (pres. 1978-79), Am. Soc. Naturalists, Genetics Soc. Can. (Excellence award 1977), Am. Inst. Biol. Scis., Am. Assn. Cereal Chemists (hon.), Sigma Xi (chpt. research award 1970), Phi Kappa Phi, Alpha Zeta, Gamma Sigma Delta (Distinguished Service award 1958), Alpha Gamma Rho. Contbr. articles to tech. jours. Home: 2009 Mob Hill Columbia MO 65201

SEARS, GORDON MORTIMER, pub. relations exec.; b. Bristol, Tenn., June 25, 1923; s. Harold M. and Kythe (McClellan) S.; B.A. in Journalism, Emory U., 1943; m. Mabel C. Waddell, Aug. 28, 1948; children—Kythe, Patricia, Elizabeth. With S.E. div. United Press, 1947-51; account exec. Carl Byoir & Assos., Inc., N.Y.C., 1952-60; dir. pub. relations Kern County Land Co., San Francisco, 1960-64; v.p. T.J. Ross and Assos., Inc., N.Y.C., 1964-69, exec. v.p., 1969-71, pres., 1971-78, pres., chief exec. officer, 1978—. Served to capt. USMCR, 1943-46, 51-52. Mem. Pub. Relations Soc. Am., Pub. Relations Seminar, World Trade Club, Calif. Pacific Basin Council, Soc. Profl. Journalists. Republican. Episcopalian. Clubs: Pinnacle (N.Y.C.); Commerce (Atlanta); Patterson (Fairfield, Conn.). Office: 405 Lexington Ave New York NY 10017

SEARS, JAMES PATRICK, mfg. co. exec.; b. Springfield, Mass., July 12, 1929; s. Patrick James and Mary Irene (Murphy) S.; B.S., Am. Internat. Coll., 1954; m. Jane Lucille McIntyre, Apr. 30, 1955; children—Maureen, Ann, Teresa, Catherine, Gregory. With Arthur Young & Co., N.Y.C., 1954-68, prin., 1964-68; group dir. finance Am. Standard, Inc., N.Y.C., 1968-70, controller, 1970—, v.p., 1973-76, v.p. corp. devel., 1976—, also officer, dir. subsidiaries. Served with AUS, 1948-52. Decorated Bronze Star. C.P.A., N.Y., D.C. Mem. N.Y. Soc. C.P.A.'s, Am. Inst. C.P.A.'s. Roman Catholic. Lion. Clubs: Chemists (N.Y.C.); Wykagyl Country (New Rochelle). Home: 27 Siebrecht Pl New Rochelle NY 10804 Office: American Standard Inc 40 W 40th St New York City NY 10018

SEARS, JOHN PATRICK, lawyer; b. Syracuse, N.Y., July 3, 1940; s. James Louis and Helen Mary (Fitzgerald) S.; B.S., Notre Dame U., 1960; LL.B., J.D., Georgetown U., 1963; m. Carol Jean Osborne, Aug. 25, 1962; children—James Louis, Ellen Margaret, Amy Elizabeth. Admitted to N.Y. bar, 1963; clk. N.Y. Ct. Appeals, 1962-65; asso. firm Nixon, Mudge, Rose, Guthrie, Alexander & Mitchell, 1965-66; mem. staff Richard M. Nixon, 1966-69, dep. counsel to Pres. Nixon, 1969-70; partner Gadsby & Hannah, Washington, 1970-75, Baskin & Sears, Washington, 1977—; mgr. Ronald Reagan's Presdl. Campaign, 1975-76, 79-80. Fellow Kennedy Inst. Politics, Harvard, 1970. Home: 7718 Falstaff Ct McLean VA 22101 Office: 818 Connecticut Ave Washington DC 20006

SEARS, JOHN RAYMOND, JR., savs. and loan exec.; b. Norfolk, Va., June 15, 1921; s. John Raymond and Ethel (Towe) S.; B.S., U. N.C., 1944; J.D., U. Va., 1949; m. Lillian Jean Barnacascel, Jan. 14, 1951; children—Jane Towe, John Raymond III. Admitted to Va. bar, 1949; mem. firm Sears, Jackson & Willis, Norfolk, 1950-58; chmn. bd., pres. Home Fed. Savs. & Loan Assn., Norfolk, 1958—; pres. Cavalier Service Corp., 1971—, Naut. Adventures, Inc., Capitol Desk Co.; adv. bd. Va. Nat. Bank; v.p., dir. Greater Norfolk Corp. Chmn. Citizens Adv. Com. to Mayor, 1944-45; mem. City Planning Commn., 1945-46; chmn. Va. Mass Transp. Study Commn., 1968-75, Va. state del., 1966-72; mem. State Bd. Accountancy, 1970-73, Va. Independence Bicentennial Commn., 1970—; vice chmn. Tidewater Transp. Dist. Commn., 1973—; mem. Va. Gov.'s Council on Transp., 1976; dean Hampton Roads Consular Corps.; past chmn. bd. Old Dominion U. Ednl. Found., also bd. visitors, vice rector univ.; bd. dirs. Norfolk Gen. Hosp., Tidewater Health Found., Southeastern Tidewater Occupational Industrialization Center. Served to lt. USNR, 1944-46, 50-51. Decorated officer Order of Crown (Belgium). Hon. Belgian consul. Mem. U.S. (past dir.), Va. (past pres.) savs. and loan leagues, Va. Assn. Public Transit Ofcls. (pres.), Am. Sail Tng. Assn. (dir.), Sigma Nu. Methodist. Mason. Club: Sertoma (Norfolk). Home: 1320 Harmott Ave Norfolk VA 23509 Office: 700 Boush St Norfolk VA 23510

SEARS, LESLIE RAY, JR., financial cons.; b. Weymouth, Mass., Jan. 18, 1928; s. Leslie Ray and Harriett (Thurston) S.; B.S. in Bus. Adminstrn., Boston U., 1950; M.B.A., Harvard U., 1960; grad. Indsl. Coll. Armed Forces, 1968; m. Claire Lavina Sanders, Mar. 19, 1951; children—Leslie Ray, III, Marilyn Jean Sears Leal, Pamela Marie. Entered U.S. Army, 1951, advanced through grades to maj. gen.; exec.-asst. sec. Dept. Army, Washington, 1969-70; asst. dir. army budget, 1970-71, comptroller, 1972-76; ret., 1976; cons. in municipal finance Robert Stubbs Inc., Fla., 1976—; realtor asso. Tourtelot Real Estate, Fla. Decorated D.S.M., Legion of Merit. Mem. Am. Soc. Mil. Comptrollers (pres. 1975; life). Republican. Methodist. Clubs: Bath and Yacht, Harvard Bus. Sch. of Washington and of Fla. Author, pub. The Future of Pleasure Boating, 1960. Home: 820 115th Ave Treasure Island FL 33706

SEARS, PAUL BIGELOW, ecologist, educator; b. Bucyrus, Ohio, Dec. 17, 1891; s. Rufus Victor and Sallie (Harris) S.; B.Sc., Ohio Wesleyan U., 1913, A.B., 1914, D.Sc., 1937; A.M., U. Nebr., 1915, LL.D., 1957; Ph.D., U. Chgo., 1922; D.Sc., Oberlin Coll., 1958; Litt.D., Marietta Coll., 1951; LL.D., U. Ark., 1957, Wayne State U., 1959; m. Marjorie Lea McCutcheon, June 22, 1917; children—Paul McCutcheon, Catherine Louise, Sallie Harris. Instr. botany Ohio State U., 1915-17, 18-19; asst. prof., then asso. prof. U. Nebr., 1919-28; prof. botany, chmn. dept. U. Okla., 1928-38, Oberlin Coll., 1938-50; chmn. conservation program Yale, 1950-60; vis. prof. U. Louisville, 1957, 61, U. Hawaii, 1960-61, Carleton Coll., 1962, Wake Forest Coll., 1962-63, U. So. Ill., 1965. Mem. Ohio Conservation Commn., 1946-52; mem. plowshare adv. com. AEC, 1962-72; mem. Nat. Sci. Bd., 1958-62; mem. bd. Pacific Tropical Bot. Garden, 1964-70. Dir. Va.-Carolina Chem. Co., 1956-60; dir. Crawford County Nat. Bank, 1945-62, hon. dir., 1970—. Served with U.S. Army, 1917-18. Recipient Book of Month award, 1936; Conservation medal Garden Club Am., 1952; Bromfield medal, 1958; Ettinger award, 1963; Daly medal Am. Geog. Soc., 1970; Alumni award Ohio State U., 1971, U. Chgo., 1972; Browning award, 1972; Distinguished Service award Am. Inst. Biol. Scis., 1976. Guggenheim fellow, 1958. Mem. A.A.A.S. (pres. 1956), Am. Acad. Arts and Scis., Am. Soc. Naturalists (pres. 1959), Bot. Soc. Am. (named Eminent Botanist 1956). Ecol. Soc. Am. (pres. 1948; named Eminent Ecologist 1956), Nat. Audubon Soc. (hon. pres. 1970—), Phi Beta Kappa, Sigma Xi (nat. lectr. 1956), Delta Tau Delta. Author: Deserts on the March, 1935; This is Our World, 1937; Who Are These Americans?, 1939; Life and Environment, 1939; Charles Darwin, 1950; Where There is Life, 1962; The Living Landscape, 1966; Lands Beyond the Forest, 1969; co-author: Wild Wealth, 1971. Contbr. numerous articles on ecology, conservation and climatic history to profl. jours. and other periodicals. Home: 17 Las Milpas Taos NM 87571. *The teacher teaches not only what he knows, but more profoundly what he is. As in other activities of our society, his art is degraded by any delusion that it can be mass-produced.*

SEARS, ROBERT NEEDHAM, petroleum co. exec.; b. N.Y.C., Oct. 1, 1915; s. John Septimus and Florence Augusta (Scholes) S.; B.A., U. Utah, 1936, Fuels Engr. (hon.), 1967; M.B.A., Harvard, 1938; m. Peggy Broomfield, Dec. 1, 1941; children—Robert Needham, Mary Jane, Sally. Refinery, sales positions Inland Empire Refineries, Spokane, Wash., 1938-42; asst. to pres. Wasatch Oil Co., Salt Lake City, 1946-48; asst. to exec. staff Phillips Petroleum Co., Bartlesville, Okla., 1948-60, sec., 1960-62, v.p., 1962-74, sr. v.p., 1974-79, also dir.; pres. Phillips Investment Co., Phillips Petroleum Internat. Investment Co.; dir. Zions Utah Bancorp.; Petroleum cons. Dept. Interior, 1954-56, sec. and asst. to chmn. Mil. Petroleum Adv. Bd., 1948-51, 54-60; mem. Fgn. Petroleum Study Com., 1964-73; dir. Joint Operating Staff West (NATO) representing U.S. Govt. and FEA. Chmn. nat. adv. council U. Utah, 1970-72; chmn. nat. adv. council Brigham Young U. Coll. Bus., 1972-76; mem. nat. adv. council Utah Symphony Orch.; commr. Accrediting Commn. for Bus. Schs., 1970-74. Chmn. bd. dirs. Radio New York Worldwide (WREM); trustee Am. Indian Inst., 1977—; mem. Utah Air Travel Commn., 1979—; active Boy Scouts Am. Served to lt. (s.g.) USNR, 1943-46. Recipient award for outstanding achievement in bus., 1956, Distinguished Alumni award, 1974 (both U. Utah); Jessie R. Knight award for indsl. citizenship Brigham Young U., 1972. Mem. Beta Theta Pi, Alpha Kappa Psi. Mem. Ch. of Jesus Christ Latter-day Saints (regional rep. 1967-72, spl. cons. communications dept. 1976—). Clubs: Kiwanis; Canoe Brook Country (Short Hills, N.J.); River, Recess, Lochinvar (N.Y.C.); Bloomington Country (St. George, Utah). Home: PO Box 985 Saint George UT 84770

SEARS, ROBERT RICHARDSON, educator; b. Palo Alto, Calif., Aug. 31, 1908; s. Jesse Brundage and Stella Louise (Richardson) S.; A.B., Stanford, 1929, Ph.D., Yale, 1932; m. Pauline Kirkpatrick Snedden, June 25, 1932; children—David O'Keefe, Nancy Louise. Instr. psychology U. Ill., 1932-35, asso., 1935-36; research asst. prof. Inst. Human Relations, Yale, 1936-37, asst. prof. psychology, 1937-42, asso. prof., 1942; prof. child psychology, dir. U. Iowa Child Welfare Research Sta., 1942-49; prof. edn. and child psychology, dir. lab. human devel. Harvard Grad. Sch. Edn., 1949-53; prof. psychology, head dept. Stanford, 1953-61, dean Sch. Humanities and Sci., 1961-70, David Starr Jordan prof. psychology, 1970—; lectr. psychology Wesleyan U., Conn., spring 1937; vis. asst. prof. Stanford, summer 1941. Trustee, Center Advanced Study Behavioral Scis., 1953-75, fellow, 1968-69. Mem. Am. Philos. Soc., Am. Acad. Arts and Scis., Am. (pres. 1950-51), Western (pres. 1964) psychol. assns., Soc. Research Child Devel. (editor monographs 1971-75, pres. 1973-75), NRC (chmn. com. child devel. 1947-50, div. anthropology and psychology 1945-48), Social Sci. Research Council (vice chmn. bd. dirs. 1950-53), Sigma Xi. Author: (with others) Frustration and Aggression, 1939; Objective Studies of Psychoanalytic Concepts 1943; (with others) Patterns of Child Rearing, 1958; (with others) Identification and Child Rearing, 1965. Contbr. tech. articles to psychol. jours. Office: Dept Psychology Stanford U Stanford CA 94305

SEARS, WALTER EDWIN, pub. co. exec.; b. Long Beach, Calif., Oct. 8, 1924; s. Roy and Hazel (Livingston) S.; A.B. cum laude in Anthropology, Harvard, 1950; postgrad. U. N.M., 1950-51, U. Calif., 1951; m. Jean MacDonald, Sept. 6, 1948; children—Robin, Scott, Cynthia. Asst. editor G. & C. Merriam Co., Springfield, Mass., 1951-55; field rep. McGraw Hill Book Co., Ann Arbor, Mich., 1956-59; sci. editor, editor-in-chief Harper & Row, N.Y.C., 1960-69; v.p. Holden-Day, Inc., 1969-73; dir. U. Mich. Press, Ann Arbor, 1974—. Served with USNR, 1943-46. Clubs: Hasty Pudding (Harvard); Harvard (N.Y.C.). Home: 3629 Chatham Way Ann Arbor MI 48105 Office: 839 Greene St Ann Arbor MI 48106

SEARS, WILLIAM GRAY (WILL), lawyer; b. Houston, Oct. 18, 1910; s. William Gray and Betty Bringhurst (Gaines) S.; student Rice U., 1927-29; J.D., South Tex. Coll. Law, 1935; m. Maurine Rawlings, Sept. 14, 1935; children—Betty (Mrs. Warren A. Munson), William Gray III (dec.), Charles R. Admitted to Tex. bar, 1935; atty. Fed. Land Bank of Houston, 1935-38; asst. city atty., Houston, 1938-40, 1st asst. city atty., 1946-48, city atty., 1948-56; partner firm Hofheinz, Sears, James & Burns, Houston, 1956-61, Sears & Burns, Houston, 1962—. Trustee, Retina Research Found. Served to maj., AUS, 1940-46. Decorated Purple Heart with oak leaf cluster; recipient certificate of Meritorious Service SSS, 1970. Fellow Tex. Bar Found. (life); mem. Am., Fed., Houston bar assns., Am. Judicature Soc., Nat. Inst. Municipal Law Officers, Tex. State Bar, Am., Southwestern hist. assns., Philos. Soc. Tex., Nat. Trust Hist. Preservation, Am. Heritage Assn., Ret. Officers Assn., Disabled Officers Assn., Mil. Order Purple Heart, Delta Theta Phi (scholarship key). Clubs: University, Plaza (Houston). Home: 22 Knipp Rd Houston TX 77024 Office: 2 Houston Center Houston TX 77002

SEARS, WILLIAM REES, engr., educator; b. Mpls., Mar. 1, 1913; s. William Everett and Gertrude (Rees) S.; B.S. in Aero. Engring., U. Minn., 1934; Ph.D., Calif. Inst. Tech., 1938; m. Mabel Jeannette Rhodes, Mar. 20, 1936; children—David William, Susan Carol. Asst. prof. Calif. Inst. Tech., 1939-41; chief aerodynamics Northrop Aircraft, Inc., 1941-46; dir. Grad. Sch. Aero. Engring., Cornell U., Ithaca, N.Y., 1946-63, dir. Center Applied Math., 1963-67, J.L. Given prof. engring., 1962-74; prof. aerospace and mech. engring. U. Ariz., Tucson, 1974—. Cons. aerodynamics. Recipient Distinguished Alumnus award U. Minn., 1950; Vincent Bendix award Am. Soc. Engring. Edn., 1965, Prandtl Ring, Deutsche Gesellschaft für Luft-und Raumfahrt, 1974; Von Karman lectr. Am. Inst. Aeros. and Astronautics, 1968; F.W. Lanchester lectr. Royal Aero. Soc., 1973. Recipient Von Karman medal AGARD, NATO, 1977. Fellow Internat. Acad. Astronautics, Am. Acad. Arts and Scis., Am. Inst. Aeros. and Astronautics (hon.; G. Edward Pendray award 1975); mem. Nat. Acad. Engring., Nat. Acad. Engring. Mexico (fgn.), Nat. Acad. Scis., Sigma Xi. Author: The Airplane and its Components, 1941. Editor: Jet Propulsion and High-Speed Aerodynamics, vol. VI, 1954; Jour. Aerospace Scis., 1956-63, Ann. Revs. of Fluid Mechanics, Vol. I. Home: 6560 Skyway Rd Tucson AZ 85718 Office: Aerospace and Mech Engring Dept U Ariz Tucson AZ 85721

SEARS, WILLIAM ROBERT, cons.; b. N.Y.C., Mar. 5, 1920; s. Isaac and Bertha (Jay) S.; B.A., Yale U., 1946; M.A. in Internat. Econs. (Melville Jacoby fellow 1950-51), Stanford U., 1951; m. Alice Hart, Apr. 24, 1942; children—Richard Collier, Beth Susan, Catherine Jill. Fgn. fin. editor UPI, N.Y.C., 1945-50; mgr. sales and promotion Sylvania Electric Co., San Francisco, 1951-60; mgr. mktg. services Philco Corp., Palo Alto, Calif., 1960-63; mng. partner Sears & Co., Mgmt. Cons., San Francisco and San Mateo, Calif., 1964—; vis. lectr. U. San Francisco, 1958-59, U. Santa Clara, 1960-61. Served with AUS, 1942-45. Mem. Sales and Mktg. Execs. Assn., IEEE, Mensa. Clubs: Press, Yale of No. Calif. (San Francisco); Stanford. Address: 3187 Greenoak St San Mateo CA 94403. *I now understand what Aristotle intended when he posed a question that has challenged me too: "Why am I here; what's my purpose?" A lifetime of endeavor teaches me one's purposes is to seize every opportunity to reach one's own full potential in whatever path the striving leads me.*

SEASE, GENE ELWOOD, univ. pres.; b. Portage, Pa., June 28,, 1931; s. Grover Chauncey and Clara Mae (Over) S.; A.B., Juniata Coll., 1952; B.D., Pitts. Theol. Sem., 1956, Th.M., 1959; Ph.D., U. Pitts., 1965, M.Ed., 1958; LL.D., U. Evansville, 1972, Butler U., 1972; Litt.D., Ind. State U., 1974; m. Joanne D. Cherry, July 20, 1952; children—David Gene, Daniel Elwood, Cheryl Joanne. Ordained to ministry United Methodist Ch., 1956; pastor Grace United Meth. Ch., Wilkinsburg, Pitts., 1952-63; conf. dir., supt. Western Pa. Conf. United Meth. Ch., Pitts., 1963-68; lectr. grad. faculty U. Pitts., 1965-68; mem. staff Ind. Central U., Indpls., 1968—, asst. to pres., 1968-69, pres.-elect., 1969-70, pres., 1970—; dir. Indpls. Life Ins. Co., Mchts. Nat. Bank and Trust Co., WYFI Channel 20. Pres. Greater Indpls. Progress Com., 1972—; pres. Marion County Sheriff's Merit Bd.; mem. Ind. Scholarship Commn., 1970—. Trustee United Theol. Sem.; bd. dirs. Indpls. Conv. Bur., Ind. Law Enforcement Tng. Acad., 500 Festival, Crossroads council Boy Scouts Am., Community Hosp. Indpls., St. Francis Hosp., Mem. Internat. Platform Assn., English Speaking Union, Ind. Schoolmen's Club, Phi Delta Kappa, Alpha Phi Omega, Alpha Psi Omega. Mason (33 deg., Shriner), Kiwanian. Club: Columbia (Indpls.). Author: Christian Word Book, 1968; also numerous articles. Home: 4001 Otterbein Ave Indianapolis IN 46227

SEASONGOOD, MURRAY, lawyer, former mayor; b. Cin., Oct. 27, 1878; s. Alfred and Emily (Fechheimer) S.; A.B., Harvard, 1900, A.M., 1901, LL.B., 1903; LL.D., Marietta Coll., 1950, N.Y. U., 1951, Miami U., 1963, U. Cin., 1964; L.H.D., Hebrew Union Coll. Jewish Inst. Religion, 1962; LL.D., Wilmington Coll., 1963; m. Agnes Senior, Nov. 28, 1912; 1 dau., Janet (Mrs. Herbert Hoffheimer, Jr.). Admitted to Ohio bar, 1903; practiced law, Cin.; mem. Paxton & Seasongood; part time prof. U. Cin. Coll. Law, 1925-59, now prof. emeritus; vis. prof. law Harvard, 1947-48, Godkin lectr., 1932; radio and TV speaker on govt., law and art. Mayor, Cin., 1926-30, chmn. City Planning Commn. Former pres. Cin. Legal Aid Soc., Nat. Municipal League; v.p. Nat. Civil Service League; hon. v.p. Nat. Legal Aid Assn.; mem. Pres.'s Housing Conf., 1932; security cons. to personnel Clearance Security Bd., U.S. AEC, 1954-59; mem. adv. com. rules criminal procedure U.S. Supreme Ct., 1941-44, Ohio Commn. Code Revision, 1945-49; former pres. Hamilton County Good Govt. League; former mem. Hamilton County Charter Commn.; former pres. Nat. Assn. Legal Aid Orgns.; mem. U.S. Civil Service Commn. Loyalty Rev. Bd., 1947-53, Ohio Turnpike Commn., 1949-52, Task Force on Personnel Adminstrn., Ohio Program Commn. 1950-51; mem. Ohio Commn. for Blind, 1915-26. Mem. overseers com. to visit Harvard Dept. Govt.; trustee, v.p. Clovernook Home and Sch. Blind, Cin., also v.p. Mem. Nat. Municipal League (former pres., life mem. council), Am. Law Inst., Am. (ho. of dels., chmn. standing com. on civil service, 1949-53, former chmn. municipal law sect.), Cin. (past pres.) bar assns., Harvard Law Sch. Assn. Cin. (1st pres., gov.), English-Speaking Union (dir. Cin. br.), Phi Beta Kappa (past v.p. Cin. chpt., life sec., treas. Class of 1903 Harvard Law Sch.), Delta Upsilon. Republican. Clubs: Harvard (past pres.), University (past v.p.), Literary (past pres.), Travel, Print and Drawing, Queen City, Cincinnati Art (life asso.) (Cin.); Harvard Faculty (Cambridge); Harvard (N.Y.C.). Author: Local Government in the United States: A Challenge and an Opportunity, 1933; Cases on the Law of Municipal Corporations, 3d edit., 1953; Selections From Speeches: 1900-1959 of Murray Seasongood, 1960. Contbr. articles to various publs., Ency. Americana, Evidence. Home: 2850 Grandin Hollow Ln Cincinnati OH 45208 Office: Central Trust Tower Cincinnati OH 45202

SEATH, JOHN, communications co. exec.; b. Edinburgh, Scotland, Oct. 25, 1914; s. John and Elizabeth A. (Sutherland) S.; came to U.S., 1915, naturalized, 1918; B.B.A. cum laude, Coll. City N.Y., 1948; m. Rose A. Featherstone, June 17, 1939; children—John, Ellaine A. Mgr., Milton M. Bernard, C.P.A., N.Y.C., 1946-55; tax mgr. Gen. Dynamics Corp., N.Y.C., 1955-59, Budd Co., Phila., 1959-61; asst. v.p., dir. taxes ITT, 1961-64, v.p., 1964-73, dir. taxes, 1964-79, sr. v.p., 1973-79. Served with AUS, 1943-46. C.P.A., N.Y. Mem. Am. Inst. C.P.A.'s, Tax Execs. Inst., Fin. Execs. Inst. (tax com.), Tax Found., Tax Inst., NAM (tax com.), Nat. Fgn. Trade Council (tax com.), Internat. Fiscal Assn., Machinery and Allied Products Assn. (tax com.). Republican. Presbyterian. Clubs: Knickerbocker Country (Tenafly, N.J.); Englewood. Died Feb. 15, 1979. Home: 150 Brayton St Englewood NJ 07631

SEATON, KENNETH DUNCAN, savs. and loan assn. exec.; b. Hancock, Mich., Dec. 18, 1929; s. Donald Wylie and Mary Lucille (Finlayson) S.; B.S. in Civil Engring., Mich. Tech. U., 1951; student U.S. Savs. and Loan Grad. Sch. Ind. U., 1962; m. Lois Isaac, July 27, 1952; children—Timothy, Kim, Mary, Shelby, Shannon. Constrn. engr. Mich. State Hwy. Dept., 1951-52; civil engr. Jones & Laughlin Steel Corp., Virginia and Calumet, Minn., 1956-57; with Detroit & No. Savs. & Loan Assn., Hancock, Mich., 1957—, asst. v.p., 1958-60, sr. v.p., 1960-63, exec. v.p., 1963-68, pres., 1968—, chmn. bd., 1973—; bd. dirs. Fed. Home Loan Bank Bd. Indpls., 1978—. Pres. Copper Country Indsl. Devel. Council; chmn. bd. trustees Suomi Coll., Hancock; trustee Hancock Pub. Schs. Served as aviator USNR, 1952-55. Mem. U.S., Mich. (legislative com.) savs. and loan leagues, Mich. (dir.), Houghton-Hancock (pres. 1964-65) chambers commerce. Lutheran. Home: 400 Lakeview Dr Hancock MI 49930 Office: 400 Quincy St Hancock MI 49930

SEATON, ROBERT FINLAYSON, savs. and loan exec.; b. Hancock, Mich., Nov. 28, 1930; s. Donald W. and Mary Lucille (Finlayson) S.; B.S., Mich. Technol. U., 1952; M.B.A., Stanford, 1956; postgrad. Ind. U., 1966, U. So. Calif., 1973; m. Helen Jean Robarts, Apr. 18, 1954; children—Scott, Sandy. Asst. sec. Palo Alto Mut. Savs. & Loan Assn. (Calif.), 1956-60; asst. v.p. Pioneer Investors Savs. & Loan Assn., 1960-63; v.p. 1st Western Savs. & Loan Assn., Las Vegas, Nev., 1963-67; v.p., sec. Fed. Home Loan Bank, Cin., 1967-72; pres., chief exec. officer Second Fed. Savs. & Loan Assn., Cleve., 1973, Cardinal Fed. Savs. & Loan Assn., Cleve., 1974—. Mem. adv. bd. Cleve. Safety Council, 1973—; treas., trustee Center for Human Services, Cleve.; treas. Garfield Meml. Ch.; trustee Better Bus. Bur.; asso. v.p. United Way Services. Served to lt. USNR, 1952-54. Mem. Western Res. Hist. Soc., Nat. Trust for Hist. Preservation, Northeastern Ohio Savs. and Loan League (mem. exec. com.), Ohio League Savs. Assns. (exec. com.), Inst. Fin. Edn. Republican. Methodist. Clubs: Country, Bankers Cin.; Union of Cleve., Cleve. Athletic. Home: 16 Pepper Creek Dr Pepper Pike OH 44124 Office: 333 Euclid Ave Cleveland OH 44114

SEATON, WILLIAM RUSSELL, oil co. exec.; b. Ashland, Ky., Jan. 2, 1928; s. Edward William and Virginia (Russell) S.; B.S., Yale, 1949; m. Suzanne Webb, Aug. 9, 1950; children—Katherine Graham Seaton James, Suzanne Elizabeth Seaton Beach, Mildred Webb Seaton Grizzle, Edward William II. Trainee, Ashland Oil, Inc. (Ky.), 1949, trainee personnel dept., 1950, jr. engr. personnel dept., 1950, adminstrv. asst. personnel, 1951-52, asst. ins. mgr., 1953-55, ins. mgr., 1955-60, exec. asst., 1960-67, v.p., 1967, adminstrv. v.p., 1968, dir., 1969—, sr. v.p., chief adminstrv. officer, 1970-72, vice chmn., 1972—. Nat. committeeman Ky. Young Republican Party, 1956-60. Mem. Ashland Area C. of C. (chmn. air transp. com. 1965-68), Chi Psi. Home: 409 Country Club Dr Ashland KY 41101 Office: 1409 Winchester Ave Ashland KY 41101

SEATZ, LLOYD FRANK, educator; b. Winchester, Idaho, June 2, 1919; s. William Frank and Emma (Hyder) S.; B.S., U. Idaho, 1940; M.S., U. Tenn., 1941; Ph.D., N.C. State U., 1949; m. Dorothy Jane Whittle, Aug. 12, 1949; 1 son, William Lloyd. Asst. prof. agronomy U. Tenn., 1947-49, asso. prof., 1949-55, on leave as agronomist and asst. br. chief soils and fertilizer research br. TVA, 1953-55; prof. agronomy U. Tenn., 1955—, head dept., 1961—, Clyde B. Austin distinguished prof. agr., 1968—. Mem. Bikini Sci. Resurvey Team, 1947; dir. So. Appalachian Sci. Fair, Inc. Served with AUS, 1942-46. Fellow Am. Soc. Agronomy (pres. So. sect.), Soil Sci. Soc. Am., mem. Am. Soc. Agronomy, Internat. Soc. Soil Sci., Sigma Xi, Phi Eta Sigma, Alpha Zeta, Omicron Delta Kappa, Phi Kappa Phi, Gamma Sigma Delta, Delta Chi. Contbr. articles to sci. jours., chpts. in books. Home: 9729 Tunbridge Ln Knoxville TN 37922 Office: PO Box 1071 Univ Tennessee Knoxville TN 37901

SEAVER, JAY JOHN, consulting engr.; b. Ypsilanti, Mich., Jan. 6, 1885; S. John Smith and Tracey (Geis) S.; B.M.E., U. Mich., 1912; D. Engring., Eastern Mich. U., 1967; m. Hallie Phelps, Sept. 11, 1917 (dec. 1951); children—Roberta Marie, James Phelps; m. 2d, Virginia P. Tegarden, July 1, 1965. Successively draftsman, supt. gen. supt. and v.p. Arthur G. McKee & Co., engineers, Cleve., 1912-28; pres. Pulaski Foundry & Mfg. Corp. (Va.), 1923-28, Pulaski Engring. Works, 1924-28; v.p., dir. H.A. Brassert & Co., Chgo., engrs., 1928-40; with Day & Zimmermann, Inc., engrs., Phila., 1941-46, as constrn. engr., Iowa Ordnance Plant, Burlington, then cons. engr. blast furnace and coke plant, Provo, Utah, cons. engr. blast furnace plant, Duluth, Minn., blast furnace and steel plant, Monclova, Coahuila, Mexico, 1941-43, v.p. Chgo. office, 1943-46; organizer, mgr. Jay J. Seaver Engrs., Chgo., 1946; pres., dir. Asso. Plastics Cos., Inc., 1951-52. Mem. Am., Brit. iron and steel insts., Eastern, Western blast furnace and coke assns., Inst. Iron and Steel Engrs., Am. Inst. Mining and Metall. Engrs., S.A.R., Order Founders and Patriots Am. (Ill. gov. 1952-55). Clubs: South Shore Country, Acacia, Union League, Michigan; Adventures. Republican. Patentee in field. Home: 102-A Paseo Quinta Green Valley AZ 85614

SEAVER, PHILIP HENRY, engring. and constrn. co. exec.; b. Ridgewood, N.J., July 2, 1920; s. John Eliot and Helen Elizabeth (Benson) S.; B.Chem. Engring., Cornell U., 1943; grad. Advanced Mgmt. Program, Harvard U., 1964; m. Anne Lillian Laskowy, Apr. 12, 1947; children—John Benson, Scott Hall. Process engr. E.B. Badger & Sons Co., Boston, 1943-44, 46-51; with Badger Co., Inc., Cambridge, Mass., 1951—, v.p., 1965-68, exec. v.p., 1968-77, pres., chief operating officer, 1977—, also dir.; officer, dir. various subsidiaries Badger Co., Inc. Mem. corp. Morgan Meml. Goodwill Industries, Mus. Sci., Boston. Served to lt. (j.g.) USNR, World War II. Registered profl. engr., Mass. Mem. Am. Inst. Chem. Engrs., Nat. Soc. Profl. Engrs., Soc. Chem. Industry, Phi Kappa Sigma. Republican. Conglist. Clubs: Harvard, Algonquin, Cornell (Boston); Chemists (N.Y.C.); Eastern Yacht (Marblehead). Patentee in field. Home: 16 Harbor Ave Marblehead MA 01945 Office: 1 Broadway Cambridge MA 02142

SEAVER, RICHARD CARLTON, oil field equipment co. exec., lawyer; b. Los Angeles, June 10, 1922; s. Byron D. and Mary Louise (Schmidt) S.; B.A., Pomona Coll., 1946; J.D., U. Calif. at Berkeley, 1949; m. Joan Tierney Sutherland, Nov. 10, 1971; children (by previous marriage)—Richard Carlton, Christopher T., Patrick T., Victoria, Martha. Admitted to Calif. bar, 1950, since practiced in Los Angeles; asso. Thelen, Marrin, Johnson & Bridges, 1950-57; sec., counsel Hydril Co., 1957-64, pres., 1964—; dir. Republic Corp., DeAnza Land & Leisure Corp. Pres., bd. dirs. Seaver Inst.; bd. dirs. Episcopal Ch. Found.; bd. govs. Los Angeles County Mus. Natural History; treas., bd. dirs. Hosp. of Good Samaritan; trustee Episcopal Diocesan Investment Trust, Doheny Eye Found., Pomona Coll.; v.p., trustee Harvard Sch.; mem. bd. Pepperdine U., Seaver Coll., Malibu, Calif. Served to capt., inf., AUS, 1942-46; PTO. Decorated Bronze Star medal with oak leaf cluster. Mem. Am., Calif., Los Angeles County bar assns. Republican. Episcopalian. Clubs: St. Francis Yacht, Los Angeles Country, Los Angeles Yacht, California (Los Angeles); Newport Harbor Yacht (Balboa). Home: 149 S Bristol Ave Los Angeles CA 90049 also 8 Bay Island Balboa CA 92661 Office: 714 W Olympic Blvd Los Angeles CA 90015

SEAVER, TOM (GEORGE THOMAS), profl. baseball player; b. Fresno, Calif., Nov. 17, 1944; s. Charles H. and Betty Lee (Cline) S.; student Fresno City Coll., 1964, U. So. Calif., 1965-68; m. Nancy Lynn McIntyre, June 9, 1966; children—Sarah, Anne Elizabeth. Pitcher, Jacksonville (Fla.) Suns, 1966, N.Y. Mets, 1967-77, Cin. Reds, 1977—. Served with USMCR, 1963. Recipient Cy Young award Nat. League, 1969, 73, 75; named Rookie of Yr., Baseball Writers Assn. Am., 1967; named Nat. League Pitcher of Yr., Sporting News, 1969, 73, 75; mem. Nat. League All-Star Team, 1969-73, 75-78. Office: care Cincinnati Reds 100 Riverfront Stadium Cincinnati OH 45202*

SEAVITT, KARL L(OUIS), utility co. exec.; b. Ecorse, Mich., Aug. 21, 1919; s. Louis A. and Hazel M. (Cook) S.; J.D., Detroit Coll. Law, 1942; m. Margaret L. Thomas, Nov. 11, 1943; children—Perry, James, Karl L., Margaret, P. Kevin. Admitted to Mich. bar, 1946; practiced law, Allen Park, Mich., 1946-55; atty., asst. sec. Mich. Consol. Gas Co., Detroit, 1955-73, sec., gen. atty., 1973—; atty. City of Allen Park, 1950-55. Served with Security Intelligence Corps, U.S. Army, 1942-46. Mem. Am. Bar Assn., Am. Judicature Soc., Am. Gas Assn., Mich. Bar Assn., Detroit Bar Assn. Roman Catholic. Club: Detroit Econ. Home: 14892 Dasher Allen Park MI 48101 Office: 1 Woodward Detroit MI 48226

SEAWELL, DONALD RAY, lawyer, publisher, producer; b. Jonesboro, N.C., Aug. 1, 1912; s. A.A.F. and Bertha (Smith) S.; A.B., U. N.C., 1933, J.D., 1936; L.H.D., U. No. Colo., 1978; m. Eugenia Rawls, Apr. 5, 1941; children—Brook (Mrs. Joseph Speidel), Donald Brockman. Admitted to N.C. bar, 1936, N.Y. bar, 1947; with SEC, 1939-41, 45-47, Dept. Justice, 1942-43; pres., chmn. bd., pub., dir. Denver Post; pres., chmn. bd., dir. Gravure West, Los Angeles; dir. Swan Prodns., London, Eng.; of counsel firm Bernstein, Seawell & Kove, N.Y.C., 1975—; partner Bonfils-Seawell Enterprises, N.Y.C.; dir. Newspaper Advt. Bur. Chmn. bd. ANTA, 1965—; mem. theatre panel Nat. Council Arts; trustee Am. Acad. Dramatic Arts, 1967—, Hofstra U., 1968-69, Central City Opera Assn., Denver Symphony; bd. dirs., chmn. exec. com. Air Force Acad. Found., Nat. Ints. Outdoor Drama, Walter Hampden Meml. Library, Hammond Mus. pres. Helen G. Bonfils Found., Frederick G. Bonfils Found.; chmn. bd. Bonfils Theatre, Denver Center Performing Arts; pres. Denver Opera Found.; chmn., pres., mem. founding bd. Civilian/Mil. Inst. Served with AUS, World War II. Clubs: Bucks (London); Players, Dutch Treat (N.Y.C.); Denver Country, Denver, Cherry Hills Country, Mile High (Denver); Garden of Gods (Colorado Springs, Colo.). Home: 1000 Grant St Denver CO 80203 Office: Denver Post 650 15th St Denver CO 80202

SEAWELL, WILLIAM THOMAS, airline exec.; b. Pine Bluff, Ark., Jan. 27, 1918; s. George Marion and Harriet (Aldridge) S.; B.S., U.S. Mil. Acad., 1941; J.D., Harvard, 1949; m. Judith Alexander, June 12, 1941; children—Alexander Brooke, Anne Seawell Robinson. Commd. 2d lt. U.S. Army, 1941, advanced through grades to brig. gen. USAF, 1959; comdr. 401st Bombardment Group, ETO, World War II; comdr. 11th Bomb Wing SAC, 1953-54; dep. comdr. 7th Air Div., 1954-55; mil. asst. to sec. USAF, 1958-59, to dep. sec. def., 1959-61; comdt. cadets U.S. Air Force Acad., 1961-63; ret., 1963; v.p. operations and engring. Air Transport Assn. Am., Washington, 1963-65; sr. v.p. operations Am. Airlines, N.Y.C., 1965-68; pres. Rolls Royce Aero Engines Inc. U.S. subsidiary Rolls Royce, Ltd., 1968-71; pres., chief operating officer Pan Am. World Airways Inc., N.Y.C., 1971-72, chmn. bd., pres., chief exec. officer, 1972-75, chmn. bd., chief exec. officer, 1976—; dir. Cluett, Peabody & Co., Inc., The Lehman Corp., J. Ray McDermott & Co. Inc., McGraw Hill, Inc. Decorated Silver Star, D.F.C. with three oak leaf clusters, Air medal with three oak leaf clusters; Croix de Guerre with palm (France). Clubs: Chevy Chase, Metropolitan (Washington); River, Sky, Wings (N.Y.C.). Office: Pan Am World Airways 200 Park Ave New York NY 10017

SEAY, EDWARD WARD, coll. pres.; b. Rockvale, Tenn., Nov. 20, 1910; s. Harvey Weakly and Mary Elizabeth (Peeler) S.; B.S., George Peabody Coll. Tchrs., 1934, M.A., 1935; postgrad. Scarritt Coll. for Christian Workers; Pd.D., W. Va. Wesleyan Coll., 1951; LL.D., Tenn. Wesleyan Coll., 1958, Centenary Coll., 1976; m. Helen Harriet Welch, Apr. 12, 1941; 1 son, Robert Edward. Tchr. English, Elba (Ala.) High Sch., 1935-36; asso. headmaster, master English, Morgan Sch. for Boys, Tenn., 1936-37; dean instrn. Pfeiffer (N.C.) Jr. Coll., 1937-39; pres. Wood Jr. Coll., Miss., 1939-43; dir. admissions, asso. prof. econs. Knox Coll., Ill., 1943-48; pres. Centenary Coll. Women, Hackettstown, N.J., 1948-76; ret., 1976. Former v.p. N.J. Coll. Fund Assn.; past bd. dirs. N.J. Assn. Colls. and Univs.; past pres. Nat. Assn. Schs. and Colls. Methodist Ch. Past mem. Univ. Senate of the Methodist Ch. Past trustee Morristown Preparatory Sch., Santiago (Chile) Coll., Alumnae Adv. Centre, Inc. (former). Mem. Am. Acad. Polit. and Social Sci., Am. Econ. Assn., N.E.A., Middle States Assn. Colls. and Secondary Schs. (former commr. instns. higher edn.), Nat. Commn. on Accrediting, N.J. Scholarship Commn., N.J. Jr. Coll. Assn., Phi Theta Kappa, Pi Gamma Mu, Phi Delta Kappa. Methodist. Clubs: Rotary; University. Contbr. articles to profl. jours. Home: 1336 Ben Franklin Dr Sarasota FL 33577

SEAY, WILLIAM H., ins. co. exec.; b. 1919; B.B.A., U. Tex., 1941. Partner, Henry, Seay & Black, 1948-57; v.p. Universal Life & Accident Ins. Co., Dallas, 1958-61, pres., 1961-68; exec. v.p. Southwestern Life Ins. Co., 1968-69, pres., 1969-73, chief exec. officer, 1969—, chmn., 1973—, also dir.; dir. Guardian Savs. & Loan Assn., Dallas, Southwestern Investors, Inc., Tex. Life Conv., Dallas, Mem. nat. adv. council Religious Heritage Am. Served to capt. AUS, 1942-46. Office: PO Box 2699 Dallas TX 75221*

SEBALD, JOSEPH FRANCIS, heat transfer equipment co. exec.; b. Pitts., May 24, 1906; s. Joseph Henry and Cornelia Margarette (Biedermann) S.; B.S. in Mech. Engring., Va. Poly. Inst. and State U., 1928; M.S., Stevens Inst. Tech., 1953, postgrad., 1953-56; m. Dorothy Elizabeth Davis, Nov. 23, 1932. With Worthington Corp., Harrison, N.J., 1928-70, chief engr., 1955-62, sr. cons. engr., 1962-70; organizer Heat Power Products Corp., Bloomfield, N.J., 1966, pres., 1966—, cons. engr., 1966—; instr. mech. engring. Rutgers U., 1941-46. Fellow ASME (John C. Vaaler Top Honors award 1968, Engring. Leadership award Met. sect. 1968, Codes and Standards medal 1979, v.p. 1968-71); mem. Soc. Naval Architects and Marine Engrs. (life), Nat. Soc. Profl. Engrs., Essex County Soc. Profl. Engrs., Montclair Soc. Engrs., Tau Beta Pi (life). Republican. Clubs: Highland Lakes (N.J.) Country; Engrs. Patentee in field of heat exchangers. Home and Office: 9 Haines Dr Bloomfield NJ 07003

SEBASTIAN, REX ARDEN, mfg. co. exec.; b. Robinson, Ill., Sept. 16, 1929; s. Dean and Rhea (Gideon) S.; B.S., Purdue U., 1951; M.B.A., Ind. U., 1952; m. Dorothy Lynne Bryson, Sept. 1, 1951; children—Steven Bryson, Annie Laurie, David Rex, Lisa Gay, Amy Lynne. Gen. prodn. foreman Procter & Gamble, Cin., 1952; with Cummins Engine Co., Inc., Columbus, Ind., 1955-60; mng. dir. Shotts Co., Lanarkshire, Scotland, 1960-63, v.p. internat., Columbus, 1963-64, London, 1964-66; v.p. internat. ops. Dresser Industries, Inc., Dallas, 1966-71, v.p. ops. office of pres., 1971-74, sr. v.p. ops. office of pres., 1975—. Served to lt. (s.g.) USNR, 1952-55. Mem. Dallas C. of C., Am. Mgmt. Assn., Machinery and Allied Products Inst., Nat. Fgn. Trade Council, Nat. Indsl. Council Bd., Sigma Phi Epsilon. Republican. Presbyterian. Home: 4526 Dorset Rd Dallas TX 75229 Office: Dresser Bldg PO Box 718 Dallas TX 75221

SEBELIUS, KEITH GEORGE, congressman; b. Almena, Kans., Sept. 10, 1916; s. Carl Elstrom and Minnie (Peak) S.; A.B., Ft. Hays (Kans.) State U., 1941; J.D., George Washington U., 1939; m. Bette A. Roberts, Mar. 5, 1949; children—Keith Gary, Ralph Douglas. Admitted to Kans., D.C., U.S. Supreme Ct. bars; with Bur. Printing and Engraving, 1936-40; jr. examiner ICC, 1940-41; spl. agt. investigation div. CSC, 1941; practiced in Norton, Kans., 1946—; atty. Norton County, 1947-53; mayor, Almena, 1949-51, city atty., 1953-69, councilman, 1947-49; mem. Kans. Senate from 38th Dist., 1962-68; mem. 91st-96th congresses 1st Dist. Kans. Pres. Norton County Fair Bd., 1957. Chmn. Kans. Republican Vets. Club, 1968-70. Served from pvt. to maj. AUS, 1941-45, 51-52. Mem. Ft. Hays State U. Alumni Assn. (pres. 1954), Am. Legion (comdr. Kans. 1955-56), Norton C. of C. (pres. 1958-59), Farm Bur. Methodist. Lion (pres. Norton 1953), Mason (33 deg.), Odd Fellow. Home: 602 W Wilberforce St Norton KS 67654 Office: Longworth House Office Bldg Washington DC 20515

SEBENTHALL, ELIZABETH ROBERTA, author; b. Eau Claire, Wis., Jan. 6, 1917; d. Robert Graham and Laura Rose (Cote) Sebenthall. Recipient Nat. Endowment for the Arts award, 1970. Author numerous novels including: If the Shroud Fits, 1969; The Cold Ones, 1972; The Bronze Claws, 1972; (poetry) Acquainted with a Chance of Bobcats, 1969, Anatomy of December, 1978. Home: 104 Thompson St Mount Horeb WI 53572

SEBEOK, THOMAS ALBERT, educator; b. Budapest, Hungary, Nov. 9, 1920; s. Dezso and Veronica (Perlman) S.; came to U.S., 1937, naturalized, 1944; B.A., U. Chgo., 1941; M.A., Princeton, 1943, Ph.D., 1945; m. Eleanor Lawton, Sept. 1947; 1 dau., Veronica C.; m. 2d, Jean Umiker, Oct. 1972; children—Jessica A., Erica L. Mem. faculty Ind. U., Bloomington, 1943—, Distinguished prof. linguistics, 1967—, prof. anthropology, prof. Uralic and Altaic studies, fellow Folklore Inst., mem. Russian and East European Inst., chmn. Research Center for Lang. and Semiotic Studies, chmn. Grad. Program in Semantic Studies. Mem.-at-large Nat. Acad. Scis.-NRC, also mem. various coms.; lectr. European, Can. and Asian acads. and univs.; vis. prof. U. Mich., 1945, 58, U. P.R., 1949, U. N.Mex., 1953, U. Ariz., 1958-59, U. Vienna, 1963, U. Besançon, 1965, U. Hamburg, 1966, U. Bucharest, 1967, 69, U. Ill., 1968, U. Colo., 1969, Stanford, 1971, U. South Fla., 1972; Linguistic Soc. Am. prof., 1975; cons. Ford Found., Guggenheim Found., Wenner-Gren Found. for Anthrop. Research, U.S. Office Edn., NSF, fellowship div. Nat. Acad. Scis., Can. Council; panel mem. for linguistics Nat. Endowment for Humanities, 1966-67; mem. U.S. del. to permanent council Internat. Union Anthrop. and Ethnol. Scis., 1970-73; U.S. del. Comité International Permanent des Linguistes, 1972—; mem. internat. sci. council Royaumont Center for Sci. of Man, 1973—; exchange prof. Nat. Acad. Scis.-USSR Acad. Scis., 1973. Mem. vis. com. Harvard U., 1973, Simon Fraser U., 1975, Georgetown U., 1977, Vanderbilt U., 1977-78. Fellow John Simon Guggenheim Meml. Found., 1958-59, Center for Advanced Study in Behavioral Scis., 1960-61, 66-67, 71; Fulbright grantee, Germany, 1966, 71, Italy, 1969, 71; NSF sr. postdoctoral fellow, 1966-67. Fellow Am. Anthrop. Assn., Am. Folklore Soc., A.A.A.S., also fgn. linguistic socs.; mem. Internat. Assn. Semiotic Studies (editor-in-chief 1968—, exec. com. 1969—), Linguistic Soc. Am. (sec.-treas. 1969-73, v.p. 1974, pres. 1975; asso. dir. Linguistic Inst. 1958, 75, dir. 1964), Central States Anthrop. Soc. (pres. 1956), Am. Assn. Machine Translation and Computational Linguistics (exec. bd. 1964-66), Animal Behavior Soc. (exec. bd. 1968—), Semiotic Soc. Am. (sec.-treas. 1975, exec. dir. 1976—), Sigma Xi. Clubs: Cosmos (Washington); University (Chgo.); Princeton, Explorers (N.Y.C.); Internat. House (Tokyo). Editor-in-chief Semiotica, 1968—; Current Trends in Linguistics, 1963—; Approaches to Semiotics, 1968-74; editor: Studies in Semiotics, 1974—; gen. editor Advances in Semiotics, 1974—. Contbr. numerous articles to profl. jours. Home: 1104 Covenanter Dr Bloomington IN 47401

SEBES, JOSEPH SCHOBERT, educator; b. Nagypall, Baranya M. Hungary, Aug. 18, 1915; s. Joseph and Catherine (Kungl) Schobert; came to U.S., 1950, naturalized, 1956; grad. Pius X. Gymnasium, Pecs, Hungary, 1934; licentiate Gregorian U. Rome, 1947; Ph.D., Harvard U., 1958; Ph.D. (hon.), Georgetown U., 1976. Joined Soc. of Jesus, 1934; asst. prof. Asian history Georgetown U., Washington, 1958-65, regent Edmund A. Walsh Sch. Fgn. Service and Bus. Adminstrn., 1961-64, dean Sch. Bus., 1964-66, dean Sch. Fgn. Service, 1966-68, prof. Asian history, 1968—. Fellow, Woodrow Wilson Internat. Center for Scholars, 1976-77. Mem. Nat. Com. for U.S.-China Relations, Am. Fgn. Service Assn., Toho Gakkai (Inst. Eastern Cultures), Tokyo, Am. Hist. Assn., Assn. Asian Studies, Am. Oriental Soc. Roman Catholic. Author: The Jesuits and the Sino-Russian Treaty of Nerchinsk 1689, 1961; The Diary of Thomas Pereira, S.J., 1962. Home: Jesuit Community Georgetown U Washington DC 20057 Office: Dept History Georgetown U Washington DC 20057

SEBESTA, CHARLES JOSEPH, JR., dist. atty.; b. Bryan, Tex., Sept. 16, 1940; s. Charles J. and Dolores (Vance) S.; B.A. in History and Govt., Tex. A. and M. U., 1962; J.D., Baylor U., 1966; m. Jane McKenzie, May 13, 1972. Admitted to Tex. bar, 1966, since practiced in Caldwell; city atty. Somerville, Tex., 1969-70; county judge Burleson County Ct., Caldwell, 1971-75; dist. atty. 21st Jud. Dist. Tex., 1975—; registrar local bd. 85, Tex. SSS, Giddings, 1968-73; rancher Hereford cattle, Somerville, 1957—. Mem. adv. bd. Tex. Com. for Pub. Edn., 1971-74; bd. dirs. Brazos Valley Devel. Council, 1972-76, Big 8 Resource, Conservation and Devel. Project Area, 1972-76; bd. dirs. Ednl. Service Center, region VI, Huntsville, Tex., 1969—, chmn., 1973-74; bd. dirs. Tex. Arts Alliance, 1978—. Served with Transp. Corps, AUS, 1963-65; maj. Res. Named Outstanding Young Men Am., Caldwell C. of C., 1972. Mem. East Tex. C. of C. (dir. 1972-75). Mason, Rotarian (pres. 1970-71). Home: 309 Buck St Caldwell TX 77836 Office: PO Box 58 Caldwell TX 77836

SEBOK, GYORGY, educator, pianist; b. Szeged, Hungary, Nov. 2, 1922; s. Vilmos and Klara (Krausz) S.; ed. Franz Liszt Acad. Music, Budapest, Hungary; m. Eva Mandel, Jan. 29, 1957. Came to U.S., 1962. First pub. appearance, 1936; concerts throughout Europe, N.Am., Japan, Africa, 1957—; rec. artist for Erato, Mercury, Philips records; prof. piano Bela Bartok Conservatory, Budapest, 1949-56, Ind. U., Bloomington, 1962—. Recipient Internat. prize Berlin, Germany, 1951; Liszt prize Budapest, 1952; Grand Prix du Disque, Paris, France, 1958. Home: 1724 Circle Dr Bloomington IN 47401

SEBOLD, RUSSELL PERRY, III, educator, author; b. Dayton, Ohio, Aug. 20, 1928; s. Russell Perry and Mary (Kiger) S.; student U. Chgo., 1945-47; B.A., Ind. U., 1949; M.A. (Woodrow Wilson fellow), Princeton, 1951, Ph.D., 1953; m. Jane Norvell Hale, Nov. 24, 1955; children—Mary Norvell, Alice Hale. Instr. Spanish, Duke, 1955-56; instr. Spanish U. Wis., 1956-58, asst. prof., 1958-62, asso. prof., 1962-66; prof. Spanish, chmn. dept. fgn. langs. and lits. U. Md., 1966-68; prof. Spanish, U. Pa., 1968—, chmn. dept. Romance langs., 1968-78. Adv. Council Soc. Ibero-Am. Enlightenment, 1968—, treas., 1969—; steering com. Am. Soc. for Eighteenth Century Studies, 1970—. Served with AUS, 1953-55. Guggenheim fellow, 1962-63; Am. Philos. Soc. grantee, 1971, 76; Am. Council Learned Socs. fellow, 1979-80. Mem. Am. Assn. Tchrs. Spanish and Portuguese, Am. Assn. Tchrs. French, Modern Lang. Assn. Am., Center 18th Century Studies (Oviedo, Spain), Phi Beta Kappa, Phi Gamma Delta, Sigma Delta Pi; corr. mem. Hispanic Soc. Am. Episcopalian. Author: Tomas de Iriarte: poeta de rapto racional, 1961; El rapto de la mente, 1970; Colonel Don Jose Cadalso, 1970; Cadalso: el primer romántico europeo de España, 1974; Novela y autobiografía en la Vida de Torres Villarroel, 1975. Author, editor: Fray Gerundio de Campazas (Jose Francisco de Isla), 4 vols., 1960-64; Visiones y visitas de Torres con don Francisco de Quevedo por la Corte (Diego de Torres Villarroel), 1966; Numancia destruida (Ignacio Lopez de Ayala) 1971; Poética (Ignacio de Luzán), 1977; Comedias (Tomás de Iriarte), 1978. Gen. editor Hispanic Rev. Contbr. articles to profl. jours. Home: 16 Flintshire Rd Malvern PA 19355 Office: U Pa Philadelphia PA 19104

SEBRELL, WILLIAM HENRY, JR., physician; b. Portsmouth, Va., Sept. 11, 1901; s. William Henry and Mildred J. (Overton) S.; M.D., U. Va., 1925; postgrad. George Washington U., 1928-30; grad. USPHS Officers Sch., 1926; Sc.D., Alfred U., 1955, Rutgers U., 1956; m. Margaret Shirley Bruffey, June 16, 1926 (dec. 1945); children—Betty Clark, William Henry; m. 2d, Eloise Hopkins Glover, May 13, 1950 (dec. 1973); 1 step-son, Page Glover; m. 3d, Helena Braddock Lemp, Sept. 29, 1978. Intern Marine Hosp., New Orleans, 1925-26; commd. officer USPHS, 1925, advanced through grades to asst. surgeon gen., 1950; various assignments, 1926-43; chief div. physiology, 1943-48; dir. Exptl. Biology and Medicine Inst., 1947-50, NIH, 1950-55; instnl. research grants Am. Cancer Soc., 1955-57, research cons., 1955-57; dir. inst. human nutrition Columbia, 1957-70, Robert R. Williams prof. nutrition, 1961-70, prof. emeritus, 1970—; med. dir. Weight Watchers Internat., 1972—; exec. dir. Weight Watchers Internat. Found., 1971—. Past chmn. Williams-Waterman Fund Research Corp.; past dir. Nat. Health Council; nutrition cons. St. Luke's Hosp.; past mem. or mem. internat. commns. on health, nutrition, 1935—; mem. Food and Nutrition Bd. (exec. com. 1956-70), NRC, Nat. Vitamin Found. (pres. 1955); chmn. protein adv. group UNICEF, WHO, FAO, 1964. Recipient Mead Johnson prize, 1940; Research medal So. Med. Assn., 1946, Legion of Merit, 1946; Joseph Goldberger award A.M.A., 1952; Distinguished Service award Food and Nutrition Council Greater N.Y., 1968. Fellow A.C.P., Am. Pub. Health Assn., AAAS, Am. Inst. Nutrition (pres. 1955); mem. Am. Soc. Clin. Nutrition (Conrad Elvehjem 1968, pres. 1963), Internat. Union Nutrition Scis. (chmn. U.S. nat. com. 1963, chmn. com. recommended dietary allowances 1968), fgn., nat. and local med. and profl. assns. or orgns., Phi Beta Kappa, Sigma Xi, Alpha Omega Alpha, Phi Tau Sigma. Episcopalian. Clubs: Cosmos (Washington); Century, N.Y. Yacht (N.Y.C.); Ocean Reef; Manhasset Bay Yacht. Contbr. numerous articles to med. jours., texts. Home: 812 Briny Ave Pompano Beach FL 33062 Office: PO Box 2597 Pompano Beach FL 33062

SECKLER, STANLEY GEORGE, physician, educator; b. Bklyn., Feb. 22, 1929; s. Benjamin David and Fannie (Shaefer) S.; B.A. magna cum laude, Syracuse U., 1951; M.D., Tulane U. Med. Sch., 1955; m. Clare Daub, Sept. 5, 1954; children—Philip, Victoria, Mark, Jonathan, Benjamin. Intern Mt. Sinai Hosp., N.Y.C., 1955-56, resident, 1956-59; chief dept. medicine Greepoint Hosp., N.Y.C., 1962-64; dir. dept. medicine City Hosp. Center, N.Y.C., 1964—, pres. med. bd., 1975-78; prof. clin. medicine Mt. Sinai Sch. Medicine, City U. N.Y., also attending physician Mt. Sinai Hosp., 1968—. Served to capt. USAF, 1960-62. Diplomate Am. Bd. Internal Medicine. Fellow A.C.P., N.Y. Acad. Medicine; mem. A.A.A.S., Assn. Am. Med. Colls., Tulane Med. Sch. Alumni Assn. (dir.), Phi Beta Kappa, Alpha Omega Alpha. Contbg. editor Med. Jour. Contbr. articles to med. jours., also chpt. textbook. Home: 500 West St Harrison NY 10528 Office: 79-01 Broadway Elmhurst NY 11373. *I concern myself with only those things that I can influence and try to accept those things*

I cannot change. I make a sharp distinction between knowledge and wisdom. Knowledge I utilize to tell me what I can do; wisdom I depend on to tell me what I should do.

SECONDARI, HELEN JEAN ROGERS, producer, dir.; b. Fond du lac, Wis.; d. William Martin and Helen Mary (O'Grady) Rogers; A.B. magna cum laude, Catholic U. Am., 1951; M.A., Radcliffe Coll., 1955; m. John H. Secondari, July 1, 1961; children—John Gerry, Linda Helen. Teaching fellow govt. Harvard, 1957-59; producer Washington Bur., ABC News, 1959-61; producer documentary spls. ABC, 1961-68; producer, exec. John H. Secondari Prodns., Ltd., N.Y.C., 1968-74; pres. Secondari Prodns. Ltd., also Secondari Prodn. Learning Films, Ltd., N.Y.C., 1974—. Bd. visitors dept. history Columbia, 1975—; mem. Commn. Religion and Arts in Am. President's Council Children and Youth. Recipient George Peabody award, 1964, 66, Golden Mike award, 1961, Page One award, 1962, Christopher award, 1969; named Woman of Year in TV, 1962, Dir. of Year, 1963; recipient awards Nat. Acad. TV Arts and Scis., NEA, Ohio State U. Mem. Am. Council Edn., Am. Women in Radio and TV, Dirs. Guild Am. Home: 1148 Fifth Ave New York NY 10028

SECOR, PHILIP BRUCE, coll. pres.; b. Mt. Kisco, N.Y., Dec. 12, 1931; s. Allen B. and E. Winifred (Eible) S.; A.B., Drew U., 1953; M.A., Duke, 1958, Ph.D., 1959; m. Anne Louise Smith, May 15, 1955; children—Nanette Elizabeth, David Hallock, Catherine Paulding. Teaching fellow polit. sci. Duke, 1956-57, James B. Duke fellow, 1957, instr. polit. sci., 1958, exec. sec. Lilly Endowment research program Christianity and politics, 1958-59; asst. prof. Dickinson Coll., 1959-63, dir. religious affairs, 1961-62, asst. dean coll., 1962; asst. prof. Davidson Coll., 1963-65, asso. prof., 1966-67; asso. prof. polit. sci. Muhlenberg Coll., 1967-74, dean coll., 1967-74; pres. Cornell Coll., Mt. Vernon, Iowa, 1974—; chmn. Iowa Assn. Ind. Colls. and Univs., 1978-79, Iowa Coll. Found., 1980-81; mem. Iowa Coordinating Council for Postsecondary Edn., 1979-81. Bd. commrs. Allentown Housing Authority, 1970-72; bd. dirs. Allentown Sch. Dist., 1971-74, Planned Parenthood Assn. Lehigh County, 1969-72. Fellow Soc. for Values in Higher Edn.; mem. Am. Polit. Sci. Assn., Am. Assn. Advancement Slavic Studies. Contbr. articles, revs. to periodicals. Home: President's House Cornell College Mount Vernon IA 52314

SECORD, LLOYD CALVIN, cons. mech. engr.; b. St. Thomas, Ont., Can., Aug. 28, 1923; s. Cortlandt Lionel and Eleanor Louva (Ward) S.; B.Sc. in Mech. Engring. with honors, Queen's U., Kingston, Ont., 1945; m. Lillian Gordon Mutrie, Sept. 14, 1944; 1 son, Timothy Scott. Design engr. Turbo Research, 1945-46; chief design engr. A. V. Roe (Can.) Ltd., Ont., 1946-53; asso. DSMA ATCON Ltd., and predecessors, Toronto, Ont., 1953-56, prin., v.p., 1956-78, pres., 1978—; mem. Sci. Council Can., 1972-75. Recipient Gold medal Queen's U., 1945. Fellow Can. Aeros. and Space Inst., Engring. Inst. Can.; mem. Soc. Automotive Engrs., Assn. Profl. Engrs. Ont., Assn. Cons. Engrs. Can., Can. Nuclear Assn. (pres. 1969-70, dir. 1963—). Presbyterian. Clubs: Ont., St. George's Golf and Country, Can. Author: What's Ahead in Canada's Nuclear Future?, 1970; (with J. H. White) In Orbit Servicing of Spacecraft, 1972; patentee in field. Home: 413 The Kingsway Islington ON M9A 3W1 Canada Office: 4195 Dundas St W Toronto ON M8X 1Y4 Canada

SECREST, FRED GILBERT, automobile co. exec.; b. Lakewood, Ohio, Aug. 25, 1922; s. Fred Miller and Mary (Gilbert) S.; B.A. summa cum laude, Ohio State U., 1943; M.B.A., Harvard, 1947; m. Stephanie Jenkins, July 29, 1944; children—Stephen, William, Daniel, Marion, Fritz. Mem. staff Harvard Bus. Sch., 1947-48; with Ford Motor Co., 1948—, gen. asst. controller, 1960-62, controller, 1962-73, v.p., 1965-73, exec. v.p., 1973—. Mem. bd. control Mich. Technol. U., 1959-67; trustee Alma Coll., 1975—. Served with AUS, 1943-46. Mem. Fin. Execs. Inst., Motor Vehicle Mfrs. Assn., Phi Beta Kappa, Beta Gamma Sigma, Sigma Chi. Presbyterian. Clubs: Dearborn Country; Walloon Lake Country. Home: 374 River Ln Dearborn MI 48124 Office: Ford Motor Co American Rd Dearborn MI 48121

SECREST, JOHN CARY, automotive co. exec.; b. Lakewood, Ohio, June 11, 1922; s. Paul E. and Charlene (Cary) S.; B.A., Ohio Wesleyan U., 1946; M.B.A., Harvard, 1948; m. Harriet Louise Porter, Oct. 31, 1954; children—Paul Porter, Jeffrey Adams, Carol Ann. Vice pres., gen. mgr. appliance div. Am. Motors Corp., Detroit, 1964-65, v.p. finance, 1965-68, v.p. corporate staffs, 1968-72, group v.p. staff and internat., 1972—, also dir.; cons. Bracken, Secrest Tompkins, 1979. Vice chmn. Mich. campaign United Negro Coll. Fund; bd. dirs., chmn. exec. com. Meadow Brook Theatre and Music Festival; bd. dirs. Boys' Club Met. Detroit; past mem. bd. dirs. S.E. Mich. Jr. Achievement; asso. Ohio Wesleyan U. Served with USAAF, AUS, 1943-46. Mem. Internat. Road Fedn. (dir., exec. com.), Ohio Wesleyan U. Alumni Assn. (past pres. Detroit). Clubs: Orchard Lake Country; Birmingham Athletic; Harvard Bus. Sch. (past dir.) (Detroit). Home: 923 Waddington St Birmingham MI 48009 Office: Am Motors Corp 27777 Franklin Rd Southfield MI 48034

SECTER, DAVID IRVING, motion picture, theater and television writer, producer and dir.; b. Brandon, Man., Can., Mar. 24, 1943; s. Joseph and Gwendolyn Arnetta (Feinstein) S.; student U. Man., 1960-62; B.A. with honors, U. Toronto (Ont., Can.), 1965. Pres., Varsity Films, Toronto, 1966-69, Secter Films, 1969-75, Total Impact, N.Y.C., 1973—, Movie Buff Ltd., N.Y.C., 1975—; creative dir., chmn. bd. Entermedia, Inc., N.Y.C., 1977—; writer, producer, dir. Winter Kept Us Warm, 1965; writer book, lyrics, producer Off-Broadway musical Get Thee to Canterbury, 1969-70; producer, dir. The Offering (100 Flowers), 1966, The Harrowing Tale of the Haunted Lighthouse, 1971; writer, producer, dir. Getting Together (What A Way to Live!), 1973-75, Splice of Life, 1973-75; creator Family Jam, 1978, Am. Mavericks, 1979, Hey Zeus!, 1979. Recipient Spl. Jury prize Montreal (Que., Can.) Film Festival, 1966, Spl. award Cinestud, Amsterdam (Holland), 1967. Home: 231 2d Ave New York NY 10003 Office: 189 2d Ave New York NY 10003

SECUNDA, (HOLLAND) ARTHUR, artist; b. Jersey City, Nov. 12, 1927; s. Leo Konstantinovich and Catherine (Volkovitzky) S.; student N.Y. U., 1946, Art Students League N.Y., 1947-48; pvt. study with Ossip Zadkine, Paris, France, 1949; m. Gladys Bullis, Mar. 5, 1956 (div. Feb. 1974); 1 son, David Abraham. Art critic Beverly Hills (Calif.) Times, 1959-61; asso. editor Artforum Mag., 1962-64; art tchr. U. Calif. at Los Angeles, Pasadena Art Mus., Long Beach (Calif.) State Coll., Otis Art Inst., Los Angeles. Curator edn. Santa Barbara Art Mus., 1957-58; guest curator Long Beach Art Mus., 1970; organizer traveling exhibits; artist Center Mag., Center Study Democratic Instns., 1969-75; exhibited numerous one-man shows U.S. and abroad; represented in numerous pub. collections, museums and univs. Tamarind fellow, 1969, 73. Mem. Artists Equity. Address: PO Box 6363 Beverly Hills CA 90212

SECUNDA, EUGENE, advt. agy. exec.; b. Bklyn., June 15, 1934; s. Sholom and Betty (Almer) S.; comml. degree N.Y. Inst. Photography, 1955; B.S., N.Y. U. Sch. Bus., 1956; M.S., Boston U., 1962; m. Shirley Carol Frummer, Sept. 23, 1961; children—Ruthanne, Andrew. News editor Sta.-WBMS, Boston, 1956-57; reporter New London (Conn.) Daily Day, 1958-59; publicist various Broadway shows, 1959-62; sr. publicist 20th Century Fox Film Corp., N.Y.C., 1962-65; with J. Walter Thompson Co., N.Y.C., 1965—, dir. corp. and public affairs, 1974-78, sr. v.p., dir. entertainment group, 1977—; asst. prof. advt. N.Y. U., 1972—; guest lectr. FBI Acad. Served with USAR, 1957-63. Mem. Assn. Theatrical Press Agts. and Mgrs., Am. Mktg. Assn., Screen Publicists Guild, Am. Advt. Fedn. (conv. planning com.), Mcpl. Arts Soc., Sales Exec. Club., Broadway Assn. Contbr. articles to Broadcasting Mag., Mktg. Communications Mag. Office: J Walter Thompson Co 420 Lexington Ave New York NY 10019

SEDAKA, NEIL, singer, songwriter; b. Mar. 13, 1939; s. Mac and Eleanor (Appel) S.; student Juilliard Sch. Music; m. Leba Margaret Strassberg, Sept. 11, 1962; children—Dara Felice, Marc Charles. Composer numerous popular songs, including: Stupid Cupid, Calendar Girl, Oh, Carol, Stairway to Heaven, Happy Birthday Sweet Sixteen, Laughter in the Rain, Bad Blood, Love Will Keep Us Together, Lonely Night (Angel Face), Breaking Up Is Hard to Do; solo performer throughout U.S. and Great Britain, 1959—; appeared in NBC-TV Special, 1976; recorded numerous albums including Sedaka's Back, The Hungry Years, Steppin' Out, A Song, All You Need Is the Music. Recipient numerous gold records and industry awards. Mem. AGVA, Am. Fedn. Musicians, AFTRA. Address: 1370 Ave of Americas New York NY 10019

SEDELMAIER, JOHN JOSEF, film dir., cinematographer; b. Orrville, Ohio, May 31, 1933; s. Josef Heinrich and Anne Isabel (Baughman) S.; B.F.A., Art Inst. Chgo.-U. Chgo., 1955; m. Barbara Jean Frank, June 6, 1965; children—John Josef, Nancy Rachel, Adam Frederich. Art dir., Young and Rubicam, Chgo., 1955-61; art dir., asso. creative dir. Clinton E. Frank, Chgo., 1961-64; art dir., producer J. Walter Thompson, Chgo., 1964-67; pres. Sedelmaier Film Productions, Chgo., 1967—. Recipient Golden ducat Mannheim Film Festival, 1968; Golden Gate award San Francisco Film Festival, 1969; Gold hugo Chgo. Film Festival, 1976; Golden Lion, Cannes Film Festival, 1972. Office: 610 Fairbanks Ct Chicago IL 60611

SEDELOW, SALLY ANN YEATES, educator; b. Greenfield, Iowa, Aug. 10, 1931; d. J.H. and Bessie M. (Williams) Yeates; B.A. with high distinction, U. Iowa, 1953; M.A., Mt. Holyoke Coll., 1956; Ph.D., Bryn Mawr Coll., 1960; m. Walter Alfred Sedelow, Jr., June 14, 1958. Instr. English, Smith Coll., 1959-60; asst. prof. English lit. Parsons Coll., 1960-61; asst. prof. Rockford (Ill.) Coll., 1961-62; human factors scientist System Devel. Corp., 1962-64; cons., 1964-67; asst. prof. English, St. Louis U., 1964-66; asso. prof. English and computer and information sci. U. N.C. at Chapel Hill, 1966-70; prof. computer sci. and linguistics U. Kans., 1970—, asso. dean Coll. Liberal Arts and Scis., 1979—. Disting. vis. scholar Va. Poly. Inst., 1970; Philips Fund lectr. Haverford Coll., 1970, 74; Sigma Xi lectr. Mt. Holyoke Coll., 1970; NSF Inst. Computer Sci. in Behavior Sci. lectr. U. Colo., summer 1973; cons. Coll. Human Ecology, Mich. State U., 1973; English Lit. Symposium lectr. Bryn Mawr Grad. Sch., 1975. program dir. techniques and systems program and intelligent systems program div. math. and computer scis. NSF, 1974-77; pres. Taos Book Shop, Inc., N.Mex., 1975—. Mem. adv. panel NSF Instl. Computing Scis. Sect., 1968; field reader HEW, 1966—; cons. Coordinated Sci. Lab., U. Ill., 1969; vis. scientist Assn. Computing Machinery, NSF Vis. Scientist Program, 1969-70; prin. investigator research contracts Office Naval Research, 1964-74, NSF, 1971-73; chmn. investigative com. V, World Shakespeare Congress, 1971; mem. com. on information tech. Am. Council Learned Socs., 1970-74; mem. research adv. panel Nat. Endowment for Humanities, 1973-75, 76-77; mem. adv. com. computing NSF, 1972-74; mem. Fulbright Computer Sci. Screening Com., 1973-77, chmn., 1976-77; mem. U.S. del. U.S.-USSR Sci. Exchange Program in Natural Lang. Processing, 1978. Recipient Burge and Fowler awards U. Iowa, also non-resident scholar, 1956-57; fellow English, Bryn Mawr Coll., 1957-58. Mem. Assn. Computing Machinery (chmn. spl. interest group 1968-70), Linguistic Soc. Am., Modern Lang. Assn. (chmn. conf. computing devices 1965, chmn. group on computing and lit. 1978, Am. Soc. Information Sci., Mass. Soc. Mayflower Descs., Denison Soc., Mortar Bd., Phi Beta Kappa, Delta Delta Delta. Club: Woman's Nat. Dem. (Washington). Contbr. author: The Computer and Literary Style, 1966; Automated Language Processing, 1967; The Analysis of Communication Content, 1969; Current Trends in Stylistics, 1972; Procs. World Shakespeare Congress, 1973; Procs. Nat. Computer Conf., 1976; contbg. author, co-editor: Computers and Language Research: Formal Methods, 1979. Co-author: Language Research and the Computer, 1972. Gen. editor Computer Studies Humanities and Verbal Behavior, 1967-75. Home: 1401 Engel Rd Lawrence KS 66044 Office: Coll Liberal Arts and Scis U Kans Lawrence KS 66045

SEDELOW, WALTER ALFRED, JR., educator; b. Ludlow, Mass., Apr. 17, 1928; s. Walter Alfred and Una M. (Roberts) S.; B.A. summa cum laude, Amherst Coll., 1947; M.A., Harvard 1951, Ph.D., 1957; m. Sally Ann Yeates, June 14, 1958. Master, Milton (Mass.) Acad., 1947-48; instr. history Williams Coll., 1948-50; instr., then asst. prof. history Amherst Coll., 1954-56, 57-60; asso. prof. history and sociology, chmn. dept. sociology Parsons (Iowa) Coll., 1960-61; Jane Addams asso. prof. sociology and history, chmn. dept. sociology Rockford (Ill.) Coll., 1961-62; human factors scientist System Devel. Corp., 1962-64; asso. prof. sociology, chmn. dept. sociology and anthropology, dir. health orgn. research program St. Louis U., 1964-66; mem. faculty U. N.C., 1966-70, research asso. Inst. Research Social Scis., 1966-68, asso. prof. sociology and information sci., 1966-68, dean Sch. Library Sci., 1967-70, prof. sociology, computer and information sci., 1968-70; prof. sociology and computer sci., mem. com. for program in history and philosophy of sci. U. Kans., Lawrence, 1970—, also faculty in Soviet and East European studies, 1979—; cons. in field, 1964—; dir. networking-for-sci. program, staff asso. for computers and soc., div. math. and computer scis. NSF, 1974-77; v.p. Taos Book Shop, Inc. (N.Mex.), 1975—. Mem. com. information tech. Am. Council Learned Socs., 1968-70; mem. evaluation panel project INTREX, NSF, 1968; cons. Coordinated Sci. Lab., U. Ill., 1969; prin. investigator NASA project, 1968-70, Office of Edn. project, 1968-70, NSF project, 1971-73; vis. scientist NSF/Assn. for Computing Machinery Vis. Scientist Program, 1969-70; mem. adv. panel Western Behavioral Scis. Inst., NSF Sci. Communication Project, La Jolla, Calif., 1976-77; cons. Coll. Human Ecology, Mich. State U., 1973; lectr. NSF Summer Inst., Computers in Behavioral Sci., U. Colo., 1973; mem. adv. panel, alternative approaches to mgmt. and financing univ. computer centers project (NSF), Denver Research Inst., U. Denver, 1971-74; mem. adv. panel (computer applications) Nat. Endowment for Humanities, 1975—; mem. oversight com., tech. assessment program Battelle Lab., 1975-76; mem. Fulbright Sr. Scientist Selection Com. (Computer Sci.), 1976-80, chmn., 1979-80; cons. biotech. resources NIH, 1978—; cons., lectr. Ketron, Inc., Barcelona, N.Y.C. and Washington, 1978—. Trustee Internat. Social Sci. Inst., Santa Barbara, Cal., 1966—; trustee, mem. corp. Porter-Phelps-Huntington Found., 1957-60. Served to 1st lt. USAF, 1952-54; capt. Res., 1956-68. Recipient Woods prize, Travis prize Amherst Coll., 1948; Charles Smith scholar Harvard, 1951-52; Henry P. Field fellow, 1956-57; Amherst Meml. fellow, 1956-57; fellow interdisciplinary studies Menninger Found., 1977—. Fellow Am. Sociol. Assn.; mem. Assn. Computing Machinery, Soc. Gen. Systems Research, Human Factors Soc., AAAS, Am. Hist. Assn., Assn. Computational Linguistics, Soc. for History Tech., Phi Beta Kappa. Club: Cosmos (Washington). Author: Bibliography for a Science of Language, 1976; co-author: Language Research and the Computer, 1972; contbg. author to The Computer and Literary Style, 1966, Automated Language Processing, 1967, The Analysis of Communication Content, 1969; Computer Applications in Medical Care, 1978; editor, contbg. author: Computers and Language Research: Formal Methods, 1979; also articles, chpts. to books. Asso. editor Social Forces, 1966-70; bd. editors Computer Studies in Humanities and Verbal Behavior, 1966-75; series editor Free Press, 1968-70; bd. editors Hist. Abstracts, 1973—. Home: 1401 Engel Rd Lawrence KS 66044 Office: Dept Computer Sci U Kans Lawrence KS 66045 also The Menninger Found Topeka KS 66601

SEDER, ARTHUR RAYMOND, JR., utility exec.; b. Oak Park, Ill., Apr. 20, 1920; s. Arthur Raymond and Mary Aline (Grantham) S.; student U. Minn., 1938-39; B.S.L., Northwestern U., 1946, LL.B., 1947; m. Marion Frances Heltzel, Feb. 28, 1942; children—James A., Susan J., Elizabeth A. Admitted to Ill. bar, 1948, Mich. bar, 1961; law clk. Supreme Ct. Justice Vinson, 1948-50, mem. firm Sidley & Austin. Chgo., 1950-72; pres., Am. Natural Resources Co., Detroit, 1973-76, chmn., chief exec. officer, dir., 1976—, also dir. certain subsidiaries; dir. Nat. Bank Detroit, Burroughs Corp., Kimberly-Clark Corp. Bd. dirs. Detroit Symphony Orchestra, Detroit Grand Opera; trustee St. John Hosp., Detroit, Northwestern U., Evanston, Ill. Mem. Am., Ill., Mich. bar assns. Clubs: Links (N.Y.C.); Detroit, Detroit Athletic, Country of Detroit. Home: 96 Vendome Grosse Pointe Farms MI 48236 Office: 1 Woodward Ave Detroit MI 48226

SEDERBAUM, WILLIAM, marketing exec.; b. N.Y.C., Dec. 22, 1914; s. Harry and Sarah (Steingart) S.; B.S., N.Y.U., 1936, M.A., 1943; m. Harriet Warschauer, Aug. 29, 1940; children—Arthur David, Caroline Joan. Asso. Sigmund Pines Co., 1935-38, also tchr. N.Y.C. pub. schs., 1935-39; pub. accountant, restaurant propr., 1939-41; v.p. Schenley Distillers Co., N.Y.C., 1941-61; pres. Distbrs. New Eng., 1956-61, Melrose Distillers Co., 1957-59, Park & Tilford Distillers Co., 1959-61; exec. v.p. Meade & Co., 1961-62; v.p., marketing dir. J. T. S. Brown Distillers Co., 1962-65; marketing cons., 1965-67; exec. v.p., gen. mgr. Fulton Distbg. Co., 1967-77; asst. gen. mgr. Am. Distbrs. Fla., 1977—. Mem. Eleanor Roosevelt Cancer Com., U.S. Olympic Games Com.; exec. com. Fedn. Jewish Charities, March of Dimes; bd. dirs. Jacksonville Urban League, 1975—; mem. Com. of 100. Recipient Arch award N.Y. U. Mem. Jacksonville Wholesale Liquor Assn. (pres. 1970-76), Jacksonville Symphony Assn., Jacksonville Civic Music Assn., Jacksonville C. of C. (econ. edn. com., airline service com.), Kappa Phi Kappa. Jewish. (chmn. bd. trustees, pres. men's club). Clubs: River, Carriage (N.Y.C.); Beauclerc Country; N.Y. University; Playboy; Key; Deerwood. Home: 4305 Plaza Gate Ln S Jacksonville FL 32217 Office: 6867 Stuart Ln Jacksonville FL 32205. *Live life the way it should be-not the way it is.*

SEDGWICK, ELLERY, JR., mfg. co. exec.; b. Boston, Oct. 28, 1908; s. Ellery and Mabel (Cabot) S.; student Milton Acad., 1927-28, Harvard, 1929-34; m. Elizabeth Wade, May 5, 1940; children—Ellery, Irene, Walter, Theodore. Asst. bank examiner Fed. Res. Bank of Cleve., 1934-35; various positions, including v.p. Nat. City Bank of Cleve., 1935-40, 45-52; pres. Medusa Corp., 1952-65, chmn., chief exec. officer, 1965—, chmn. exec. com., 1976-79; dir. Medusa Corp., Oglebay Norton Co., Cleveland Trust Co.; trustee First Union Real Estate Equity & Mortgage Investments. Trustee Univ. Hosps.; trustee, hon. mem. bd. govs. Case-Western Res. U.; trustee Lake View Cemetery Assn.; trustee Hawken Sch., Com. Econ. Devel. (hon.). Home: Woodstock Rd Gates Mills OH 44040 Office: Medusa Bldg 3000 Monticello Blvd Cleveland Heights OH 44118

SEDGWICK, WALLACE ERNEST, lawyer; b. Mexico City, Sept. 23, 1908; s. Allan Ernest and Gertrude Jeannette (Post) S.; A.B., U. Calif. at Berkeley, 1930; LL.B., Southwestern U., 1936; m. Lucine Arau, July 11, 1954; children—Jeannette, Lynn, Nancy. Spl. agt., then dist. mgr. State Compensation Ins. Fund, Long Beach, Calif., 1930-37; admitted to Calif. bar, 1937; claims mgr. Gen. Ins. Co. Am.. San Francisco, 1937-43; partner firm Keith, Creede & Sedgwick, San Francisco, 1945-58; sr. partner firm Sedgwick, Detert, Moran & Arnold, San Francisco, 1958—. Fellow Am. Coll. Trial Lawyers, Am. Bar Found.; mem. Am., San Francisco bar assns., State Bar Calif., Internat. Assn. Ins. Counsel (pres. 1965-66), Def. Counsel Inst., Def. Research Inst. Inc. (dir. 1964-67), Big C Soc., Phi Kappa Psi. Clubs: Commonwealth, World Trade, Olympic (San Francisco); Orinda (Calif.) Country. Contbr. articles legal publs. Home: 2259 Gladwin Dr Walnut Creek CA 94596 Office: 111 Pine St San Francisco CA 94111

SEDLACEK, FRANK THOMAS, savs. and loan assn. exec.; b. Chgo., Feb. 11, 1912; s. Frank and Mary (Cizek) S.; ed. Morton Jr. Coll.; LL.B., Chgo.-Kent Coll. Law, 1934, LL.M., 1935; m. Adeline A. Talman, June 5, 1943; children—F. Thomas, Wesley E. Admitted to Ill. bar, 1934; pvt. practice law, 1934-51; pres. Olympic Savs. & Loan Assn., Berwyn, Ill., 1951—. Mem. Ill. Savs. and Loan League (pres. 1964-65), Cook County Council Insured Savs. and Loan Assns. (pres. 1958-59), Am., Ill., W. Suburban bar assns., Bohemian Lawyers Assn. Chgo. (pres. 1947). Elk, Mason. Home: 7 Baybrook Ct Oak Brook IL 60521 Office: 6201 W Cermak Rd Berwyn IL 60402

SEDLIN, ELIAS DAVID, physician, orthopedic researcher, educator; b. N.Y.C., Jan. 21, 1932; s. Arnold Boris and Sonia Davidovna (Lipschitz) S.; B.S. in Biology, U. Ala., 1951; M.D., Tulane U., 1955; D.Med. Sci., U. Gothenburg (Sweden), 1966; m. Barbara Sue Zidell, July 9, 1960; children— Faith Avril, Adrian Intern Mobile (Ala.) Gen. Hosp., 1955-56; resident Charity Hosp., New Orleans, 1956-57; chief resident Bronx (N.Y.) Municipal Hosp., 1959-60; sr. resident Henry Ford Hosp., Detroit, 1960-61, research asso., emergency room lectr., 1961-63, NIH fellow, 1963-64; jr. attending physician Detroit Receiving Hosp., 1962-63; spl. NIH fellow dept. orthopedic surgery Sahlgrenska Sjukhuset, Gothenburg, 1964-66; asst. prof. dept. orthopaedic surgery Albert Einstein Coll. Medicine, 1966-69, asso. prof., 1969-75, prof., 1975—, dir. orthopaedic surgery, 1969—. Served to capt. AUS, 1957-59. Fulbright scholar, 1962; NSF postdoctoral fellow, 1964; recipient P.D. McGehee award Mobile Gen. Hosp., 1956; Ludvic Hektoen gold medal A.M.A., 1963; Nicholas Andry award Assn. Bone and Joint Surgeons, 1964. Diplomate Am. Bd. Orthopedic Surgery. Fellow A.C.S., Am. Acad. Orthopaedic Surgeons, A.A.A.S.; mem. Orthopedic Research Soc., Phi Beta Kappa. Contbr. to multiple symposia, profl. meetings; also articles to profl. jours. 1185 Park Ave New York City NY 10028 Office: Dept Orthopaedic Surgery Albert Einstein Coll Medicine Bronx New York City NY 10461

SEDWICK, (BENJAMIN) FRANK, educator; b. Balt., Apr. 7, 1924; s. Benjamin Frank and Louise (Lambert) S.; A.B., Duke, 1945; M.A., Stanford, 1947; Ph.D., U. So. Cal., 1953; m. Alice Elvira Magdeburger, June 4, 1949; children—Eric, Lyn, Coralie, Daniel. Instr. Spanish, U. Md., College Park, 1947-49; asst. prof. Spanish and Italian, U.S. Naval Acad., 1951-53; asst. prof. Spanish, U. Wis.-Milw., 1953-58; prof. Spanish and Italian, Ohio Wesleyan U., Delaware, 1958-63; prof. Spanish, head dept. fgn. langs., Rollins Coll., Winter Park, Fla., 1963—, dir. overseas programs, 1963—. Served to lt. USNR, 1942-46; PTO. Author: The Tragedy of Manuel Azaña and the Fate of the Spanish Republic, 1963; A History of the Useless-Precaution Plot in Spanish and French Literature, 1964; El otro and Raquel encadenada, 1960; La forja de los sueños, 1960; La gloria de don Ramiro, 1966; Selecciones de Madariaga, 1969; Conversation in Spanish (also co-author French, Italian, English and German edits.), 2d edit., 1975; Conversaciones con madrileños, 1973. Contbr. articles to profl. jours., mags. Home: 2033 Cove Trail Maitland FL 32751

SEDWICK, ROBERT CURTIS, univ. adminstr.; b. Pitts., June 27, 1926; s. Hyram Jobe and Anna Grace (Silver) S.; B.S., U.S. Coast Guard Acad., 1949; M.E.A., George Washington U., 1960, D.B.A., 1964; m. Elizabeth Angeline King, Dec. 28, 1947; children—Robert Curtis, Elizabeth Ann. Staff engr. Emerson Research Labs., Silver Spring, Md., 1956-57; plant mgr. Polytronics, Inc., Rockville, Md., 1958; chief engring. adminstr. Allis Chalmers Nuclear Power Dept., Washington, 1959-62; sr. contracts adminstr., negotiator Johns Hopkins Applied Physics Lab., Silver Spring, 1963-65; dir. Tidewater Center, George Washington U., 1965-76; dean Coll. Bus. Adminstrn. Fairleigh Dickinson U., Teaneck, N.J., 1976—; dir. Adminstrv. Research Assos., 1966—. Served with USCG, 1945-56. Mem. Am. Mgmt. Assn. Presbyterian. Author: Interaction: Interpersonal Relationships in Organizations, 1974; People Motivation and Work, 1975. Home: 185 Prospect Ave Hackensack NJ 07601 Office: 1000 River Rd Teaneck NJ 07666

SEE, HAROLD WENTZ, educator; b. Lenox, Iowa, Feb. 21, 1920; s. Otis Andrew and Martha Margaret (Koenemann) S.; B.S., N.E. Mo. State U., 1943; M.A., Northwestern, 1945; Ed.D., Ind. U., 1951; m. Helen Louise Davidson, Jan. 16, 1942; 1 dau., Barbara Louise Shoemaker. Tchr. pub. schs. Mo., 1940-42; edn. specialist U.S. Office Edn., Chgo., 1942; asst. to pres., dir. Grad. Center, Evansville (Ind.) U., 1945-49; research dir. cost effect study State of Ind., Bloomington, 1949-50; asso. prof. U. Cin., 1950-55; exec. v.p. So. Ill. U., Edwardsville, 1955-61; edn. officer AID, Kabul, Afghanistan, 1961-64; v.p. acad. service and research U. Bridgeport (Conn.), 1964-70; chief edn. planning Ford Found., Bangkok, Thailand, 1970-72; William Benton prof. internat. and higher edn. U. Bridgeport, 1973—, acting dean Coll. Edn. Chmn. resource com. Master Plan for Conn. Higher Edn., 1973; exec. dir. P.R. and Internat. Programs, 1976—; mem. Conn. adv. com. Edn. and Profl. Act, 1968-70; research dir. Model Cities Program, Bridgeport, 1968-69; cons. Nat. Air Space Agy., Washington, 1964-68; exec. dir. Southwestern Ill. Council Higher Edn., 1955-61. Chmn. bd. dirs. Am. Internat. Sch., Afghanistan, 1961-64. Served with USNR, 1942-45. Recipient Distinguished Service award NASA, 1972; Fulbright lectr., Rangoon, Burma, 1954-55; Ford travel award, 1972. Mem. Conn. Conf. Ind. Colls. (pres. 1968-70), Fedn. State Assns. Ind. Colls. and Univs. (dir. 1968-70), Phi Delta Kappa, Kappa Delta Pi. Methodist. Author: Dictionary of Education, Statistics and Measurements and Evaluation, 1955; Handbook for College and University Administrators, 1970; Systems Analysis in Planning, 1971. Home: 150 Lindamir Ln Fairfield CT 06430 Office: Dept Education Univ Bridgeport Bridgeport CT 06602

SEEBASS, ALFRED RICHARD, III, aerospace engr., educator; b. Denver, Mar. 27, 1936; s. Alfred Richard and Marie Estelle (Wright) S.; B.S.E. magna cum laude, Princeton, 1958, M.S.E. (Guggenheim fellow), 1961; Ph.D. (Woodrow Wilson fellow), Cornell U., 1962; m. Nancy Jane Palm, June 20, 1958; children—Erik Peter, Scott Gregory. Asst. prof. Cornell U., 1962-64, asso. prof., 1964-72, prof., 1972-75, asso. dean, 1972-75; prof. aerospace and mech. engring., prof. math. U. Ariz., Tucson, 1975—; cons. in field. Mem. coms. Nat. Acad. Sci., NRC, NASA, Dept. Transp., 1970—; mem. Aeros. and Space Engring. Bd., Air Force Studies Bd.; grant investigator NASA, Office Naval Research, Air Force Office Sci. Research, 1966—. Fellow Am. Inst. Aeros. and Astronautics (asso.); mem. AAAS, AAUP, Soc. Indsl. and Applied Math., Sigma Xi, Tau Beta Pi. Editor: Sonic Boom Research, 1967; Nonlinear Waves, 1974; editorial bd. Ann. Rev. Fluid Mechanics, Phys. Fluids. Contbg. author: Handbook of Applied Mathematics, 1974. Contbr. articles to profl. jours. Home: 6715 N Camino Padre Isidoro Tucson AZ 85718

SEEBOHM, PAUL MINOR, physician, educator; b. Cin., Jan. 13, 1916; s. John Savage and Alma Sophia (Marker) S.; student Oberlin Coll., 1934-36; B.A., U. Cin., 1938, M.D., 1941; m. Dorothy Eberhart, July 13, 1942; 1 dau., Karen. Intern Wis. Gen. Hosp., Madison, 1941-42; resident Cin. Gen. Hosp., 1946-48, R.A. Cooke Inst. Allergy, Roosevelt Hosp., N.Y.C., 1948-49; mem. faculty U. Iowa Coll. Medicine, Iowa City, 1949—, prof. internal medicine, 1959—, dir. allergy sect., 1949-70, exec. asso. dean Coll. Medicine, 1970—; cons. VA Hosp., Iowa City, 1952—; mem. Iowa Bd. Health, 1971—, pres., 1976—; mem. spl. med. adv. group VA, 1972-76; mem. allergy and immunology research com. NIH, 1973-76; mem. med. assistance adv. council State Iowa, 1970—, regional adv. group Iowa Regional Med. Program, 1972—; chmn. allergenic extract rev. panel FDA, 1974—. Bd. dirs. Health Planning Council Iowa, 1970-72, Iowa Health Systems Agy., 1976—. Served as maj. USAAF, 1942-46. Diplomate Nat. Bd. Med. Examiners, Am. Bd. Internal Medicine (chmn. bd. allergy and immunology 1967-69), Am. Bd. Allergy and Immunology. Fellow A.C.P., Am. Acad. Allergy (pres. 1966 Distinguished Service award 1974); mem. A.M.A. (sec. allergy sect. council 1971—, ho. dels. 1978—), Central Soc. Clin. Research, Iowa Med. Soc. (pres. 1979-80), Iowa Clin. Soc. Internal Medicine (Internist of Yr. award 1976), Sigma Xi, Alpha Omega Alpha. Mem. editorial bd. Jour. Allergy and Immunology, 1966-70. Home: 1908 Glendale Rd Iowa City IA 52240

SEEBURG, NOEL MARSHALL, JR., mfg. co. exec.; b. Chgo., Jan. 7, 1924; s. Noel Marshall and Alice Greenfield (Van Sands) S.; grad. Phillips Andover Acad., 1942; A.B. magna cum laude, Harvard, 1946, J.D. cum laude, 1952; m. Alice Ann Neville, Apr. 5, 1949; children—Lucy Van Sands, Karin Neville, Alice Dudley. Admitted to Ill. bar, 1952; with firm Sidley & Austin, Chgo., 1952; sec., dir. J.P. Seeburg Corp., Chgo., 1952-53, v.p., 1954; pres. N. Marshall Seeburg & Sons, Inc., Chgo., 1958—; pres., chmn. NMS Industries, Chgo., 1968—; chmn. U.S. Axle Co., Pottstown, Pa., 1968—, Gilchrist Vending, Ltd., Toronto, 1965-68, Herter's Inc., Waseca, Minn.; pres. Seeburg Enterprises, Inc., Chgo., 1971—, J.A. Olson Co., Winona, Miss., 1972—. Trustee Seeburg Found. Served to capt., inf., AUS, 1943-46. Decorated Bronze Star with oak leaf cluster, Combat Inf. badge. Mem. Phi Beta Kappa. Republican. Episcopalian. Clubs: Iroquois, Hasty Pudding (Harvard); Harvard (N.Y.C.); Tavern, Swedish, Chicago, Chicago Yacht, Casino, Saddle and Cycle (pres. 1967) (Chgo.). Home: 501 King St Beaufort SC 29902 Office: 230 N Michigan Ave Chicago IL 60601

SEED, HARRY BOLTON, educator; b. Bolton, Eng., Aug. 19, 1922; s. Arthur Bolton and Annie (Wood) S.; B.Sc. in Engring., Kings Coll., London U., 1944, Ph.D., 1947; S.M., Harvard, 1948; m. Muriel Johnson Evans, Dec. 29, 1953; children—Raymond Bolton, Jacqueline Carol. Came to U.S., 1947, naturalized, 1966. Asst. lectr. King's Coll., 1945-47; instr. Harvard, 1948-49; found. engr. Thomas Worcester Inc., Boston, 1949-50; mem. faculty U. Calif. at Berkeley, 1950—, prof. civil engring., 1960—; cons. U.S. Bur. Reclamation, 1965—, sec. interior, 1966—, NASA, 1966-68, AEC, 1973—, C.E., U.S. Army, 1967—, Calif. Dept. Water Resources, 1963—, U.S. Navy, 1972, also engring. cos.; mem. adv. com. on reactor safeguards Nuclear Regulatory Commn., 1973—; mem. Calif. Seismic Safety Commn., Presdl. Panel on Safety Fed. Dams. Recipient Croes medal ASCE, 1960, 62, 72, Middlebrooks award, 1958, 64, 66, 71, Wellington prize, 1968, Rowland prize, 1961, Research prize, 1962, Terzaghi lectr., 1967, Norman medal, 1968, 77, Karl Terzaghi award, 1973, Vincent Bendix award, 1976. Mem. ASCE, Earthquake Engring. Research Inst., Hwy. Research Bd., Nat. Acad. Engring., Seismol. Soc. Am., U.S. Com. on Large Dams, Structural Engrs. Assn. Calif. Home: 138 Whitethorn Dr Moraga CA 94556

SEEDS, ASA ELMORE, obstetrician, gynecologist; b. Balt., Apr. 5, 1934; s. Asas Elmore S.; A.B., Stanford U., 1955, M.D., 1958; m. Sheila Ellen Gocke, Oct. 28, 1960; children—William Asa, John Thomas, James Robert. Intern, U. Oreg. Hosp., 1958-59; resident in ob-gyn. Johns Hopkins U., 1959-64; practice medicine specializing in ob-gyn., Cin.; fellow dept. ob-gyn. Johns Hopkins U. Sch. Medicine, 1964-66, asst. prof., 1966-69, dir. Toxemia Clinic, 1967-71, asso. prof., 1969-71; prof. dept. ob-gyn. Georgetown U. Sch. Medicine, 1971-72; prof. depts. ob-gyn. and physiology, dir. Minn. Center for Perinatal Care and Obstet. Service, Univ. Hosp., U. Minn. Med. Sch., 1972-75; prof., chmn. dept. ob-gyn. U. Cin. Sch. Medicine, 1975—; cons. Nat. Inst. Child Health and Devel., NIH, 1973-76. Recipient NIH Career Devel. award, 1968-71. Diplomate Am. Bd. Obstetrics and Gynecology (examiner 1973—). Mem. Am. Coll. Obstetricians and Gynecologists (editorial bd. Jour. Ob-Gyn.), Perinatal Research Soc., Soc. for Gynecologic Investigation, Am. Assn. Obstetricians and Gynecologists, Central Assn. Obstetricians and Gynecologists. Contbr. articles to med. jours. Home: 7628 Lakewater Dr Cincinnati OH 45242 Office: Dept Obstetrics and Gynecology Room 4415 U Cin Med Center Cincinnati OH 45267*

SEEFELDT, JOHN ASMUS, city ofcl.; b. Plymouth, Wis., Jan. 23, 1922; s. Walter and Rola (Asmus) S.; grad. high sch.; m. Eleanor Newby, Jan. 23, 1943; children—J. Allan, Jane Ann. Formerly with Milw. City Harbor Commn.; chmn. Wis. Council Gt. Lakes Ports; port dir., Green Bay, Wis.; dir. Badger State Mut. Casualty Ins. Co. Chmn. Great Lakes Task Force, 1973-74; adviser Great Lakes Commn.; vice chmn. Gt. Lakes Task Force, 1978-79. Councilman, Ascension Luth. Ch., Green Bay. Served with USNR. Mem. Internat. Assn. Great Lakes Ports (dir.). Home: 452 Floral Dr Green Bay WI 54301. *My prime goal in life is to do my level best in my chosen field and to treat all people as I would like to be treated and, hopefully, to be a friend to all.*

SEEGAL, HERBERT LEONARD, dept. store exec.; b. Brookline, Mass., Aug. 13, 1915; s. Morris and Rose (Beerman) S.; A.B., U. Mich., 1937; m. Dorothy Goldstein, June 27, 1941 (div. June 1954); children—Jane Laura, Norma Ann. With R.H. White's, Boston, 1937-41; with Thalhimer's, Richmond, Va., 1941-53, v.p. charge gen. merchandising, 1949-53; sr. v.p. merchandising, dir. Macy's N.Y., N.Y.C., 1953-62; pres. Bamberger's N.J., Newark, 1962-71; dir. R.H. Macy & Co., Inc., 1965—, vice chmn. bd., 1971-72, pres., 1972—; dir. Midlantic Nat. Bank, N.J. Bell Telephone Co. Trustee Tobe lectures retailing distbn. Harvard Bus. Sch. Mem. N.J. Econ. Stblzn. Bd.; mem. econ. stblzn. com., regional office Fed. Emergency Mgmt. Agy.; mem. mchts. council N.Y. U. Clubs: City Athletic, Princeton (N.Y.C.); Century Country (Purchase, N.Y.); Two Hundred (trustee Newark). Home: 128 Central Park S New York NY 10019 Office: 151 W 34th St New York NY 10001

SEEGAL, SAMUEL MELBOURNE, medical assn. exec.; b. Chelsea, Mass., May 18, 1902; s. Morris and Rose (Beerman) S.; B.S., Mass. Inst. Tech., 1922; M.A., Harvard, 1923; m. Martha Paula Lewenberg, June 8, 1933; children—Paula Ann, Joan Lois, John Franklin. Statistician, economist Office of Herbert Hoover, Sec. of Commerce, Washington, 1923-24; statistician Wm. Filene's Sons Co., Boston, 1924-25, asst. to v.p., 1925-31, asst. to v.p., asst. to mdse. mgr., 1931-41, mdse. mgr., v.p., dir., mem. mgmt. bd., 1941-46, asst. gen. mgr., mem. exec. com., 1946-58, exec. v.p., mem. exec. com., 1958-62; dir. Asso. Merchandising Corp., N.Y.C., 1952-62; instr. retail buying and mdsg. Evening Coll. Commerce, Boston U., 1935-44; mem. nat. bd. Am. Cancer Soc., N.Y.C., 1968—, sec., 1971—, del., dir., 1968—, mem. exec. com., 1968—, research and clin. investigative com., com. to advance worldwide fight against cancer, 1969—, co-chmn. spl. projects com., 1970-72, mem. survey com., 1972—, chmn. intra-mural research com., 1972—, v.p. Mass. div., 1962—, chmn. exec. com., 1960—, dir., 1948—. Mem. survey com., tech. devel. program Mass. Inst. Tech., 1960-62. Trustee Asso. Jewish Philanthropies, Boston, 1953-63; bd. dirs. Faulkner Hosp., Boston, 1952-71. Recipient Medalle de L'Ordre du Merite Comml. (France). Mem. Am. Inst. Arbitration, Sigma Alpha Mu. Jewish reform religion. Clubs: Belmont Country (bd. govs. 1959-61, pres., 1960-61); Rockport Country; Harvard (Boston). Home: 4 Channing Rd Brookline MA 02146 Office: Am Cancer Soc Inc 219 E 42d St New York City NY 10017

SEEGER, MICHAEL, musician, lectr.; b. N.Y.C., Aug. 15, 1933; s. Charles Louis and Ruth Porter (Crawford) S.; m. Marjorie L. Ostrow, Dec. 20, 1960 (div. 1968) children—Kim, Arley, Jeremy; m. 2d, Alice L. Gerrard, Aug. 16, 1970. Founding mem. New Lost City Ramblers, 1958-79, Strange Creek Singers, 1968-76; performs So. traditional music solo, with wife Alice and sister Peggy at concerts, folk festivals or folk song clubs, U.S., Canada, Eng., Scotland, Holland, Belgium, Switzerland, Germany, Denmark, Sweden, Australia, N.Z., Japan, Finland; also numerous record albums including field collections from traditional folk musicians; cons. major folk festivals in N. Am., 1960—; guest lectr. English dept. U. Calif., Fresno, 1974. Mem. jazz/folk/ethnic music sect. Nat. Endowment for Arts, 1973-77; judge Nat. Hollerin' Contest, Spivey Corners, N.C., 1975, Nat. Yodeling Contest, Kerrville, Tex., 1975. Trustee Newport (R.I.) Folk Festival, 1963-71, John Edwards Meml. Found., U. Calif. at Los Angeles, 1962—; bd. dirs. Nat. Folk Festival, Washington, 1972-78, Smithsonian Am. Folklife Company, 1970-76, So. Folk Cultural Revival Project, Atlanta, 1973—, Am. Old Time Music Festival, 1975. Recipient 1st prize banjo category Galax Va. Old Time Fiddlers Conv., 1958, Tenn. Valley Old Time Fiddlers Conv., 1975. Home: Garrett Park MD 20766

SEEGER, MURRAY, journalist. Formerly Moscow and Washington corr. for Los Angeles Times, corr. Bonn Bur., 1975-78, economics corr., Brussels, Belgium, 1978—. Office: Los Angeles Times International Press Center Blvd Charlemagne 1 1040 Brussels Belgium

SEEGER, PETE, folk singer, composer; b. N.Y.C., May 3, 1919; s. Charles Louis and Constance de Clyver (Edson) S.; student Harvard U., 1936-38; m. Toshi Aline Ohta, July 20, 1943; children—Daniel Adams, Mika Salter, Tinya. Assisted curator Archive of Am. Folk Song, Library of Congress, recorded songs remote areas, appeared Lomax CBS radio program; an organizer Almanac Singers, 1940, toured U.S. with group, 1940-41; teamed with Woody Guthrie; toured South and Southwest, Mexico, collaborated on writing labor and anti-Fascist songs, sang on overseas broadcasts OWI; became nat. dir. People's Songs, Inc., 1945; performed motion picture film To Hear My Banjo Play, 1946; appeared in revival of folk play Dark of the Moon, Los Angeles Repertory Theatre; toured U.S. with Progressive Party candidate Henry Wallace, 1948; with others organized the Weavers, 1948, appeared nat. radio and TV shows, night clubs and theaters, rec. for Decca, 1949-52, Folkways, 1953-75, Columbia, 1961-73; appearances Town Hall, Carnegie Hall, numberous colls., also Can. and Eng.; concert series Am. Folk Music and Origins, Columbia U. Inst. Arts and Scis., 1954-55; appeared Nat. Folk Festival, St. Louis; assisted orgn. Newport (R.I.) Folk Festivals; recorded numerous albums for Folkways, Columbia, other recording cos.; albums include Am. Favorite Ballads, 4 vols., Frontier Ballads, 3 vols., also children's songs, Civil War songs, indsl. ballads, African freedom songs, instructional records for banjo and guitar; songwriter Where Have All the Flowers Gone, 1961, If I Had a Hammer (in collaboration with Lee Hays) Kisses Sweeter than Wine (in collaboration with Weavers), Turn, Turn, Turn, 1959; TV series Rainbow Quest, 1965; prod. ednl. short subjects Folklore Research Films; with family on global singing tour, including 24 countries, 1963-64; appeared in film Tell Me That You Love Me, Junie Moon, 1970. Chmn. bd. Hudson River Sloop Restoration, Inc., 1967-70. Recipient Paul Robeson award Actors Equity Assn., 1977. Club: Sloop (Beacon, N.Y.). Author: American Favorite Ballads, 1961; The Bells of Rhymney, 1964; How To Play The Five-String Banjo; Henscratches and Flyspecks, 1973; The Incompleat Folksinger, 1973; (with Charles Seeger) The Foolish Frog, 1973. Editorial staff Sing Out mag.; contbr. articles to numerous music publs. Home: Dutchess Junction Beacon NY 12508 Office: care Harold Leventhal 250 W 57th St New York City NY 10019

SEEGERS, WALTER HENRY, educator; b. Fayette County, Iowa, Jan. 4, 1910; s. William and Mary (Wente) S.; B.A., U. Iowa, 1931, M.S., 1932, Ph.D., 1934; D.Sc., Wartburg Coll., 1953; M.D. (hon.), Justus Liebig U., Germany, 1974; D.Sc. (hon.), Med. Coll. Ohio, 1978; m. Lillian Entz, Dec. 31, 1935; 1 dau., Dorothy Margaret. Research fellow U. Iowa, 1931-34, research asso., 1934-35, 37-42; research asso. Antioch Coll., 1936-37; research Parke, Davis & Co., Detroit, 1942-45; asso. prof. physiology Wayne State U. Coll. Medicine, 1945-46, prof., head dept. physiology, 1946-48, prof. physiology and pharmacology, 1948—, William D. Traitel prof. hematology, 1965—, chmn. symposium on blood, 1950-68, dir. Thrombosis Specialized Center of Research, 1972-77; prof. physiology U. Detroit, 1946-51; vis. prof. Baylor U., 1950, 52, U. Uruguay, summer, 1957; vis. scientist, lectr., Rio de Janeiro, 1963; hon. mem. faculty medicine U. Chile; lectr., exhibitor med., chem., indsl. sci. subjects; NSC vis. chair prof. Nat. Taiwan U., 1975. Mem. health research facilities sci. rev. com. NIH, USPHS, 1966-70; chmn. subcom. blood coagulation NRC, 1950-53, chmn. panel on blood coagulation, 1953-57; mem. Internat. Com. on Hemostasis and Thrombosis, 1954—; Detroit Mayor's Com. Rehab. Narcotic Addicts, 1961-73; mem. sci. adv. bd. A.R.C., 1969-72. Bd. regents Wartburg Coll., 1966—; mem. bd. Center for Health Edn., 1961—, pres., 1969. Co-recipient Ward Burdick award Am. Soc. Clin. Pathologists, 1940, James F. Mitchell Found. Internat. award for heart and vascular research, 1969; recipient Commonwealth Fund Spl. award, 1957, Mayo Clinic Vis. Faculty Certificate, 1964, Distinguished Service award Lutheran Brotherhood Ins. Soc., 1967, Acad. Achievement award Probus Club, 1963, Research award Wayne chpt. Sigma Xi, 1957, Distinguished Service certificate Wartburg Alumni Assn., 1959, Faculty Service award Wayne State U. Alumni, 1971, Wisdom award honor Wisdom Soc., 1970, Mich. Minuteman Gov.'s award, 1973; H.P. Smith award Am. Soc. Clin. Pathologists, 1978. Fellow N.Y. Acad. Scis.; mem. A.A.A.S., Am. Inst. Chemists, Am. Soc. Hematology, Am. Heart Assn., Am. Chem. Soc., Am. Soc. Biol. Chemists, Soc. Exptl. Biology and Medicine, European Soc. Hematology (hon.), Am., Detroit (pres. 1948) Canadian physiol. socs., Mich. Acad. Sci., Harvey Soc., Chilean Soc. for Transfusion and Hematology (hon.), Am. Coll. Clin. Pharmacology and Chemotherapy, Engring. Soc. Detroit, N.Y. Acad. Scis. (hon. life), Med. Soc. Turkey (hon.), Hematology Soc. Turkey (hon.), Mexican Soc. Hematology (hon.), Société Internationale Europeenne d'Hematologie (corr.), Phi Beta Kappa (hon.), Sigma Xi, Alpha Omega Alpha, Phi Lambda Upsilon, Alpha Chi Sigma, Phi Beta Pi (hon.). Lutheran. Club: Torch (Detroit). Author: Prothrombin, 1962; (with E.A. Sharp) Hemostatic Agents, 1948; (with J.M. Dorsey) Living Consciously: The Science of Self, 1959; (with Shirley A. Johnson) Physiology of Hemostasis and Thrombosis, 1967; Prothrombin in Enzymology, Thrombosis and Hemophilia, 1967; Blood Clotting Enzymology, 1967. Contbr. The Enzymes; also articles to sci. jours. Mem. editorial bd. Am. Jour. Applied Physiology, 1956-63, Am. Jour. Physiology, 1956-63, Circulation Research, 1954-64, Preparative Biochemistry, 1970—, Thrombosis Research, 1972. Research on nutrition and reproductive biology; isolation of enzymes from blood; formulated theory blood coagulation based on study of properties of purified components; introduced thrombin as hemostatic agt.; contbd. to understanding biochem. abnormalities in hemophilia. Home: 406 Barclay Rd Grosse Pointe Farms MI 48236

SEEGMILLER, JARVIS EDWIN, physician, biochemist, educator; b. St. George, Utah, June 22, 1920; s. Edwin Dee and Eleanor (Jarvis) S.; student Dixie Jr. Coll., 1938-40; A.B., U. Utah, 1942; M.D., U. Chgo., 1948; m. Roberta Eads, Nov. 1, 1950; children—Susan Dale, Robert, Lisa, Richard. Research asso. Thorndike Meml. Lab., Harvard Med. Sch., Boston City Hosp., 1951-52; vis. investigator Pub. Health Research Inst., N.Y.C., 1952-54; biochemist Nat. Inst. Arthritis and Metabolic Diseases, NIH, Bethesda, Md., 1949-51, clin. investigator, 1954-64, chief sect. on human biochem. genetics, 1965-69; prof. rheumatology, human biochem. genetics, U. Calif. at San Diego, 1969—; vis. scientist U. Coll. Hosp., London, Eng., 1964-65, Basel (Switzerland) Inst. for Immunology, 1975-76, Sir William Dunn Sch. Pathology, Oxford (Eng.) U., 1976. Mem. Nat. Acad. Scis. Office: U Calif San Diego Sch Medicine PO Box 109 La Jolla CA 92096

SEEGMILLER, RAY REUBEN, corp. exec.; b. Dysart, Iowa, May 15, 1935; s. Reuben Jacob and Lula Fern (Gragy) S.; B.S.B.A., Drake U., 1957; m. Nancy Louise Schilz, July 27, 1958; children—Jane Rae, Anna Carla. Acct., Arthur Anderson & Co., Chgo., 1957-61; div. controller S.W. Forest Industries, Phoenix, 1961-63; asst. controller Allison Steel Mfg. Co., Phoenix, 1963-68; with Marathon Mfg. Co., Houston, 1969—, now exec. v.p. Mem. Am. Inst. C.P.A.'s, Fin. Execs. Inst. Office: 600 Jefferson Houston TX 77002

SEEGRABER, FRANK JOSEPH, librarian; b. Boston, Oct. 8, 1916; s. Andrew and Emma (Herr) S.; A.B., Holy Cross Coll., 1938; B.S. in L.S., Columbia, 1943; spl. grad. student, Harvard, 1953; m. Edith Walker, June 24, 1944; children—Barbara, Frank Joseph, Jean, Rita, Claire, Richard, Loretta, Carol, John, Paul. Spl. library asst. Littauer Center, Harvard, 1939; asst. gen. reference dept. Boston Pub. Library, 1939-41; grad. asst. Columbia Coll. Library, 1941-42; asst. periodicals dept. N.Y. Pub. Library, 1942-43; inventory supr. Holtzer-Cabot Electric Co., Boston, 1944-47; ednl. counselor Grolier Soc., 1947; asst. Kirstein Bus. Library, Boston, 1948; reference librarian Boston Coll. Library, 1948-58; librarian Merrimack Coll., N. Andover, Mass., 1958-65; asst. librarian U. Mass. Boston br., 1965-68; librarian Coll. Bus. Adminstrn., Boston Coll., 1968-69, librarian Sch. Mgmt., 1969-75, spl. collections librarian, 1975—; lectr. bibliography Boston Coll., 1955-58; lectr. library sci. Northeastern U., 1966-75; sr. lectr., cons., 1975—. Mem. Area Planning Council, 1968-69. Mem. Am., New Eng. (bibl. com.), Mass. (chmn. edn. com.) library assns., New Eng. Tech. Services Librarians (vice chmn. 1961-62, chmn. 1962-63, exec. com. 1963-65, archivist 1968—), Spl. Libraries Assn. (chmn. ednl. com. Boston 1955-56), bibliog. socs. Am., U. Va. Catholic. K.C. Home: 79 Winthrop Av Wollaston MA 02170 Office: Bapst Library Boston Coll Chestnut Hill MA 02167. *While love of books is essential,* *it alone does not warrant prediction of a successful library career. Misers love money, but who wants them as tellers or bank managers? Love of people, and a desire to help, should come first, after which, given his special interests, one decides that he can best accomplish this within a library context. The concept of the librarian as both generalist and teacher has dominated my attitude from the beginning. After 39 years, I still recommend this approach.*

SEELER, ROBERT STANLEY, transp. corp. exec.; b. Chgo., June 19, 1935; s. Ferdinand T. and Helen (Brostowski) S.; B.S., U. Ill., 1959; M.B.A., U. Chgo., 1972; m. Charmaine Pasternak, Nov. 21, 1956; children—Robert, Kathy. Tax cons. Ernst & Whinney, Chgo., 1960-64; mgr. acctg. Indsl. Nucleonics, Columbus, Ohio, 1964-68; controller furniture div. All Steel, Inc., Aurora, Ill., 1968-75; corp. controller Allied Van Lines, Inc., Broadview, Ill., 1975-76, v.p. fin., 1976—, corp. dir. subs. bds., 1977—. Served with USN, 1954-56. C.P.A., Ill. Mem. Am. Inst. C.P.A.s, Fin. Execs. Inst., Chgo. Tax Club. Roman Catholic. Office: Allied Van Lines Inc 25th St and Roosevelt Rd Broadview IL 60153

SEELEY, HARRY WILBUR, JR., educator; b. Bridgeport, Conn., Mar. 5, 1917; s. Harry W. and Genevieve (Quinlan) S.; B.S., U. Conn., 1941, M.S., 1942; Ph.D., Cornell U., 1947; m. Margaret Johnson, Dec. 21, 1940; children—Gail (Mrs. Michael Fox), Beth (Mrs. Frank Shuck), Carol. Mem. faculty Cornell U., 1947—, prof. bacteriology, 1955—, chmn. sect. microbiology, 1964-68, prof.-in-charge microbiology, 1974-77, acting chmn. dept. microbiology, 1977-78. Guggenheim fellow, 1958. Mem. Soc. Gen. Microbiology, Am. Soc. Microbiology, Am. Acad. Microbiology, Soc. Applied Bacteriology, Internat. Oceanographic Found., AAAS, Am. Inst. Biol. Scientists, AAUP, Sigma Xi, Phi Kappa Phi. Author: Microbes in Action, 1962, 2d edit., 1972; Microbes and Man, 1974. Home: Park Ln Jacksonville NY 14854 Office: Stocking Hall Cornell Univ Ithaca NY 14853

SEELEY, JOHN GEORGE, educator; b. North Bergen, N.J., Dec. 21, 1915; s. Howard Wilson and Lillian (Fiedler) S.; B.S., Rutgers U., 1937, M.S., 1940; Ph.D., Cornell U., 1948; m. Catherine L. Cook, May 28, 1938; children—Catherine Ann, David John, Daniel Henry, George Bingham, Thomas Dyer. Research asst. N.J. Agrl. Exptl. Sta., 1937-40, foreman ornamental gardens, 1940-41; instr. floriculture Cornell U., 1941-43, 45-48, asst. prof., 1948-49, prof., 1956—, head dept. floriculture, 1956-70; asst. agronomist Bur. Plant Industry, U.S. Dept. Agr., 1943-44; chemist Wright Aero. Corp., Paterson, N.J., 1944-45; prof. floriculture Pa. State U., 1949-56. Recipient Leonard H. Vaughan award Am. Soc. Hort. Sci., 1950; Found. for Floriculture Research award, 1965. Fellow Am. Soc. Hort. Sci.; mem. Am. Acad. Florists (hon.), Soc. Am. Florists (named to Hall of Fame 1979), Am. Hort. Soc., Internat. Soc. for Hort. Sci., A.A.A.S., Am. Carnation Soc., Am. Orchid Soc., N.Y., Pa. flower growers assns., Sigma Xi, Phi Kappa Phi, Alpha Zeta, Pi Alpha Xi (pres. 1951-53), Epsilon Sigma Phi. Presbyn. Rotarian (dist. gov. 1973-74). Home: 1344 Ellis Hollow Rd RD 2 Ithaca NY 14850

SEELEY, JOHN RONALD, social scientist, educator; b. London, Eng., Feb. 21, 1913; came to U.S., 1940; A.B. with honors in Sociology, U. Chgo., 1942, postgrad., 1945-46; Ph.D., Internat. Coll., 1975; m. Margaret Mary DeRocher, June 19, 1943; children—Michael John, David Andrew, Ronald James, Peter Clair. Research asst social scis. U. Chgo., 1945-46, instr., 1946-47; field research dir. Ohio Mental Health Study, Ohio State U., 1946; exec. officer Canadian Mental Health Assn., 1947-48; clin. tchr. psychiatry U. Toronto, 1948-59, asso., 1950-53, 57-64, asso. prof. sociology, 1950-53, dir. Forest Hill Village Project, 1948-53; exec. dir. Community Surveys, Inc., Indpls., 1953-56; research dir. Alcoholism Research Found. Ont., 1957-60, cons., 1960-62; co-founder, prof. sociology, also tutor York U., Toronto, 1960-63, chmn. dept., asst. to pres., 1962; prin. research asso., com. space efforts and soc. Am. Acad. Arts and Scis., summer 1962; sociologist med. dept. Mass. Inst. Tech., 1963-66; Jacob Ziskind vis. prof. sociology Brandeis U., 1963-64, Klutznick prof. sociology, 1965-66, chmn. dept., 1965-66; fellow Center Advanced Study Behavioral Scis., 1964-65; dean, program dir., permanent sr. fellow Center Study Democratic Instns., Santa Barbara, Calif., 1966-69; McCuaig lectr. Queen's U., 1961; Helmsley lectr. Brandeis U., 1962, Distinguished Visitor, 1973; cons. in field, 1950—; cons., supr. So. Calif. Counseling Center, Los Angeles, Santa Barbara, 1969—; cons. Ednl. Research Center; Mass. Inst. Tech., summer 1969; adj. prof. Union for Experimenting Colls. and Univs., 1970—, Univ. Without Walls, 1970—; sr. partner, v.p. Communications Assos., Santa Barbara, Los Angeles and Watts, 1969-72; cons., supr. So. Calif. Counseling Center, Santa Barbara and Los Angeles, 1969—; sr. v.p. Comma, Inc., 1973-76; facilitator Free U. of Isla Vista, 1970-71; asso. Sci. Analysis Corp., San Francisco and Santa Barbara, 1971-73; co-project dir. Documentation and Evaluation Exptl. Projects in Schs., Berkeley, 1971-73; adj. prof. Union Research and Experimentation in Higher Edn., Undergrad. and Grad. schs., 1970—; prof. critical studies Calif. Inst. Arts, 1970-72; lectr. dept. pub. health, dept. city and regional planning U. Calif. at Berkeley, 1972-74; research sociologist dept. psychiatry UCLA, 1973-74, cons. Neuropsychiat. Inst., 1973; tutor, asso. dean faculty Internat. Coll., Los Angeles, 1973—; prof. psychiatry (social) Charles R. Drew Postgrad. Med. Sch. and Martin Luther King Gen. Hosp., Los Angeles, 1974—; lectr. Sch. Social Welfare, UCLA, 1974-76; cons. Fanon Research and Devel. Center, 1975—. Mem. sci. adv. commn. Canadian Peace Research Inst., 1969—, dir., 1973-75; com. environ. determinants mental health NIMH, 1954-68; chmn. bd. Council Study Mankind, 1965-67; mem. advisory bd. planning seminar Peace Corps, 1964-67; mem. Social Sci. Teaching Council, 1964-67; adv. bd. Maurice Falk Med. Fund., 1965-79; research adv. bd. Nat. Assn. Retarded Children, 1961-71; adv. com. psychiat. tng. program Fernald State Sch., 1965-66; nat. adv. council Operation Upward Bound, 1968-72; mem. Students Evaluate Teaching, Fullerton (Calif.) State Coll.; mem. internat. adv. bd. Alcoholism and Drug Addiction Research Found., Toronto; mem. adv. bd. Child Study Assn. Am., Edn. Through Communication, Council Study Mankind; hon. bd. dirs. Calif. Black Commn. Alcoholism; mem. Minority Access to Research Careers NIH; cons. to Can. Privy Council Staff, other Can. and Ont. govt. depts. Trustee Earthmind (Calif. and Colo.); hon. trustee Free Sch., Los Angeles; bd. dirs. Found. Research in Psychoanalysis, Internat. Coll., Internat. Univ. Center Postgrad. Studies, Dubrovnik, Yogoslavia. Served to staff capt. Canadian Army, 1942-45. Center for Humanities fellow Wesleyan U., Middletown, Conn., 1974. Fellow AAAS, Am. Sociol. Assn., Am. Assn. Humanistic Psychology, Center for Advanced Study in Behavioral Scis.; sci. asso. Acad. Psychoanalysis; mem. Internat. Assn. Social Psychiatry, AAUP, NAACP, Soc. Study Social Problems, Soc. for Integration Whole Person (charter), Phi Beta Kappa. Author: The Pulhems Dictionary: A Manual for Military Manpower Classification, 1944; (with others) Crestwood Heights: A Study of the Culture of Suburban Life, 1956; (with others) Community Chest: A Case Study in Philanthropy, 1957; (with Mark Keller) The Alcohol Language, 1958; (with others) Liver Cirrhosis Mortality as a Means to Measure the Prevalence of Alcoholism, 1960; The Americanization of the Unconscious: Collected Essays in Social Psychiatry, 1967; also numerous articles, revs., papers, reports, chpts. in books. Editor: Mental Health Problems of the Forty-Eight States, 1950; formerly editor: New Critics Press; sometime asso. editor Am. Sociol. Rev., Social Problems; cons. editor Indian Sociol. Bull., Jour. Applied Behavioral Sci., 1966-68; contbg. editor Psychiatry and Social Sci. Rev., Renewal and Critique in Social Theory, Theory and Society; editorial referee Quar. Jour. Studies in Alcohol; editorial bd. Ency. Child Care, Canadian Welfare, Internat. Ency. Social Scis., Internat. Jour. Social Psychiatry. Home: 2339 Amherst Ave Los Angeles CA 90064. *I have tried to understand. I have tried to understand in order to change. I have had to change in order to understand. It has been very rewarding - and very costly. Pain and joy have been nicely proportioned and inextricably intertwined. That is the nature of life. The life-task is to say 'yes"-and then live it.*

SEELEY, ROBERT THOMAS, educator; b. Bryn Mawr, Pa., Feb. 26, 1932; s. Harold Thomas and Marguerite (Dauchy) S.; B.S., Haverford Coll., 1953; student U. Amsterdam (Netherlands), 1953-54; Ph.D., Mass. Inst. Tech., 1958; m. Charlotte Bass, June 22, 1958; children—Joseph Thomas, Marguerite Rachel, Lauren Francesca, Karl Harold. Instr., then asst. prof. Harvey Mudd Coll., 1958-61; with Mathematisch Centrum, Amsterdam, 1961-62; mem. faculty Brandeis U., Waltham, Mass., 1962-72, prof. math., 1967-72; prof. U. Mass., Boston, 1972—. Author: An Introduction to Fourier Series, 1966; Calculus of One Variable, 1968; Calculus of Several Variables, 1970. Address: Math Dept U Mass Boston MA 02125

SEELIG, GERARD LEO, diversified co. exec.; b. Schluchtern, Germany, June 15, 1926; s. Herman and Bella (Bach) S.; came to U.S., 1934, naturalized, 1943; B.E.E., Ohio State U., 1948; M.S. in Indsl. Mgmt., N.Y. U., 1954; m. Lorraine Peters, June 28, 1953; children—Tina Lynn, Robert Mark and Carol Ann (twins). Electronics engr. Martin Corp., Balt., 1948-50; sr. engr. Fairchild Aircraft Co., Farmingdale, N.Y., 1950-54; program mgr. RCA, Moorestown, N.J., 1954-59, Van Nuys, Calif., 1959-61; div. mgr. Missile & Space Co. div. Lockheed Aircraft Corp., Van Nuys, 1961-63, v.p., gen. mgr. Lockheed Electronics div., Los Angeles, 1963-68; exec. v.p. Lockheed Electronics Co., Inc., Plainfield, N.J., 1968-69, pres., 1969-71; group exec., exec. asst. to office of pres. ITT, N.Y.C., 1971-72, corporate v.p., 1972-79, sr. v.p., 1979—; mem. Ohio Bd. Profl. Engrs. and Surveyors, 1953—. Served with AUS, 1944-46. Registered profl. engr., Ohio. Fellow Am. Inst. Aeros. and Astronautics (asso.); mem. Western Electronics Mfrs. Assn. (dir.), Electronic Industries Assn. (bd. govs. 1976—), Am. Mgmt. Assn., IEEE (sr.). Office: 320 Park Ave New York NY 10022

SEELIG, RICHARD PAUL, diversified mfg. and service corp. exec.; b. Berlin, Germany, Dec. 23, 1913; M.E., Inst. Tech. Berlin, 1936; postgrad. Pratt Inst., also N.Y.U., 1937; Came to U.S., 1936, naturalized, 1940. Draftsman, Loucks & Norling Studios, N.Y.C., 1937; chief engr. Powder Metallurgy Corp., Long Island City, 1937-46; v.p. Am. Electro Metal Corp., Yonkers, N.Y., 1946-52; exec. v.p. Chromalloy Am. Corp., N.Y.C., 1952-60, pres., 1960-71, vice chmn. bd., 1971-78; officer, dir. several wholly and partially owned subsidiaries including Valley Line (Barge) Co., St. Louis, 1970—; dir. Mohawk Sintered Alloys, Inc., Cobleskill, N.Y. Bd. dirs. Westchester br. NCCJ; trustee Nyack (N.Y.) Hosp., St. Thomas Aquinas Coll. Mem. Am. Inst. Mining, Metall. and Petroleum Engrs., Am. Soc. Metals, ASME, Soc. Automotive Engrs., Am. Inst. Aeros. and Astronautics. Patentee powder metallurgy and diffusion coatings. Rotarian. Clubs: Internat. Execs., Wings (N.Y.C.). Home: 2 Mayfair Rd Elmsford NY 10523 Office: 169 Western Hwy West Nyack NY 10994

SEELY, LYMAN E., banker; b. Woodburn, Oreg., 1917; ed. Oreg. State Coll., 1938. Vice chmn. bd., dir. First Nat. Bank Oreg., Portland; chmn., dir. VISA, U.S.A., VISA Internat.; dir. Williamette Industries, Inc. Trustee Reed Coll., Oreg. State U. Found. Home: Route 2 Box 764 Aurora OR 97002 Office: PO Box 3131 Portland OR 97208

SEELYE, TALCOTT WILLIAMS, U.S. ambassador; b. Beirut, Lebanon, Mar. 6, 1922 (parents Am. citizens); s. Laurens Hickok and Kate (Chambers) S.; B.A., Amherst Coll., 1947, LL.D., 1974; student George Washington U., 1948; m. Joan Hazeltine, Mar. 4, 1950; children—Lauren, Ammanda, Talcott Williams, Kate. Tchr. Deerfield (Mass.) Acad., 1947-48; analyst div. research Near East State Dept., 1948-49; joined U.S. Fgn. Service, 1950; resident officer High Commn. for Germany, 1950-52; assigned Amman, Jordan, 1952-54, Beirut, 1955-56, Kuwait, 1956-60, Office Near East Affairs, State Dept., 1960-64, Nat. War Coll., 1964-65, Jidda, Saudi Arbia, 1965-68; country dir. Arabian N. region State Dept., 1968-72; ambassador to Tunisia, 1972-75; dep. asst. sec. Bur. African Affairs, Dept. State, 1976-77; ambassador to Syria, 1978—; spl. Presdl. emissary to Lebanon, June-July, 1976. Mem. nat. adv. council Hampshire Coll., Amherst, Mass. Served to capt. AUS, 1943-46. Mem. Midle East Inst., Am. Fgn. Service Assn., Phi Beta Kappa, Alpha Delta Phi. Club: Kenwood Golf and Country (Washington). Home: 5510 Pembroke Rd Bethesda MD 20034 Office: Dept State Damascus Washington DC 20520

SEEMAN, MELVIN, sociologist; b. Balt., Feb. 5, 1918; s. Morris and Sophie (Hirschman) S.; B.A., Johns Hopkins U., 1944; Ph.D., Ohio State U., 1947; m. Alice Ruth Zerbola, June 30, 1944; children—Teresa E., Paul D. Asst. prof. sociology Ohio State U., 1947-52, asso. prof., 1953-59; prof. UCLA, 1959—, chmn. dept. sociology, 1977—. Mem. Am. Sociol. Assn. Home: 21532 Paseo Serra Malibu CA 90265 Office: Dept Sociology UCLA 405 Hilgard Los Angeles CA 90024

SEEMANN, ERNEST ALBRIGHT, publishing co. exec.; b. Leipzig, Germany, Oct. 18, 1929; s. Erich Winrich Albrecht and Käte Renate (Wipper) S.; grad. in Classical Langs., Sch. St. Thomas, Leipzig, 1945; m. Eola Semple Hamlett, Aug. 6, 1965; children—Eric Alexander, Ernest Arthur. Came to U.S., 1959, naturalized, 1964. Editor, corp. exec. Verlagsanstalt Hermann Klemm, book pubs., Freiburg, Germany, 1955-59; dir. U. Ala. Press, 1962-66, U. Miami (Fla.) Press, 1967-74; pres. E.A. Seemann Pub., Inc., Miami, 1974—. Mem. Assn. Am. Pubs., Schlaraffia Amerika (Miami chpt.). Episcopalian. Rotarian. Home: 14701 SW 84th Ct Miami FL 33158 Office: PO Box K Miami FL 33156

SEEVERS, CHARLES JUNIOR, assn. exec., psychologist; b. Seward, Nebr., May 13, 1925; s. Ferdinand Carl and Hilda Anna (Schultz) S.; A.A., St. John's Coll., 1945; B.A., Concordia Sem., St. Louis, 1949; M.S. magna cum laude, St. Francis Coll., Ft. Wayne, Ind., 1965, postgrad., 1966; Ph.D., U. Notre Dame, 1970; m. Florine Marie Viets, June 5, 1949; children—Steven, Roger, Sandra, Jane. Ordained to ministry Lutheran Ch., 1949; asst. pastor Immanuel Luth. Ch., Balt., 1949-50; pastor St. Paul's Luth. Ch., Kingsville, Md., 1950-57, Bethlehem Luth. Ch., Richmond, Va., 1957-63; sr. pastor Zion Luth. Ch., Ft. Wayne, 1963-66; exec. dir. Assn. for Disabled of Elkhart County (Ind.), 1966—; adj. prof. psychology and spl. edn. Ind. U., South Bend, 1972-76; cons. Kans. Developmental Disabilities Div., 1972—; cons. Accreditation Council for Facilities for the Mentally Retarded, Chgo., 1972—; cons. on assessment of developmentally disabled in various states, 1974—, Leicester, Eng., 1974-75; mem. Ind. Gov.'s Planning and Adv. Bd. for Mental Retardation and Other Developmental Disabilities, 1973-78, chmn., 1976-78; mem. No. Ind. Health Systems Agy. Central Sub-Area Adv. Council, 1976-78, vice chmn., 1977-78. Chmn., United Way Execs., Elkhart, 1971-73; bd. dirs. Mill Neck Manor Sch. for the Deaf, L.I., N.Y., 1950-57; charter mem. Area Vocat. Edn. Adv. Bd., 1973-76; mem. state adv. bd. Prevention: To Be Born Well Curriculum Project, 1977—; mem. residential services and facilities com. Nat. Assn. Retarded Citizens, 1973-78. Recipient United Way Exec. of Yr. award, 1979: Eli Lilly fellow in religion and mental health Ind. U. Med. Center, Indpls., 1964-65. Recipient Liberty Bell award Elkhart Bar Assn., 1974. Mem. Nat. Conf. Execs. of Assns. for Retarded Children (chmn. 1974-75), Am. Psychol. Assn., Am. Assn. Mental Deficiency, Am. Soc. Assn. Execs., Luth. Acad. for Scholarship, Internat. Acad. Preventive Medicine, United Cerebral Palsy Am., Epilepsy Found. Am., Nat. Soc. Autistic Children, Phi Delta Kappa, Elkhart C. of C. (bd. dirs. 1974-76). Club: Rotary. Contbr. articles to profl. publs. Home: 1744 Canterbury Dr Elkhart IN 46514 Office: PO Box 398 Bristol IN 46507. *I believe I am a uniquely individual child of God, born to fulfill a purpose for which God continues to give me life each new day. We are joined together in a common effort to fulfill the purpose for which each of us is given life.*

SEEVERS, GARY LEONARD, commodities broker; b. Jonesville, Mich., May 24, 1937; s. Leonard William and Hattie Elizabeth (Mundy) S.; B.S., Mich. State U., 1959, M.S., 1966, Ph.D., 1968; m. Marian Rose Rice, Oct. 4, 1957 (div. Dec. 1979); children—Gary, Bonnie, Sharon, Donna. Mem. faculty Oreg. State U., 1968-70; mem. sr. staff President's Council Econ. Advisers, Washington, 1970-72, spl. asst. to chmn., 1972-73, mem. council, 1973-75; mem. Commodity Futures Trading Commn., 1975-79, vice chmn., acting chmn., 1978-79; v.p. commodities dept. Goldman, Sachs & Co., N.Y.C., 1979—. Office: Goldman Sachs & Co 55 Broad St New York NY 10004

SEGAL, BERNARD GERARD, lawyer; b. N.Y.C., June 11, 1907; s. Samuel I. and Rose (Cantor) S.; A.B., U. Pa., 1928, LL.B., 1931, Gowen fellow Law Sch., 1931-32, LL.D., 1969; LL.D., Franklin and Marshall Coll., 1953, Temple U., 1954, Dropsie U., 1966; J.S.D., Suffolk U., 1969; D.H.L., Hebrew Union Coll., 1970; LL.D., Jewish Theol. Sem. Am., 1977, Vt. Law Sch., 1978; m. Geraldine Rosenbaum, Oct. 22, 1933; children—Loretta Joan (Mrs. Bruce A. Cohen), Richard Murry. Instr. polit. sci. Wharton Sch., U. Pa., 1928-32, instr. pub. finance Grad. Sch., 1934-35, coach univ., freshman debating teams, 1928-32; lectr. U. Pa. Law Sch., 1931-35, 45-47; instr. grad. bus., govt., debating Am. Inst. Banking, 1936-39; lectr. law Franklin and Marshall Coll., 1937-38; admitted to Pa. bar, 1932; legal asst. Am. Law Inst., 1932-33; Am. reporter on contracts Internat. Congress of Law, The Hague, 1932; dep. atty. gen., 1932-35, drafted dept. banking code, banking code, bldg. and loan code, 1933, milk control law, 1934; mem. firm Schnader, Harrison, Segal & Lewis, Phila., 1936—, chmn., 1968—; chmn. Commn. Jud. and Congl. Salaries, U.S. Govt., 1953-55; mem. Bd. Law Examiners, Phila., 1940-46; mem. council World Peace Through Law Center, 1973—, also confs., Athens, 1963, Geneva, 1963-67, U.S., 1965, Thailand, 1969, chmn. demonstration trial, Belgrade, Yugoslavia, 1971, also chmn. com. on internat. communications, world chmn. World Law Day, Madrid, 1979; chmn. bd. dirs. Council Legal Edn. Opportunities, 1968-71; co-chmn. Lawyers Com. for Civil Rights Under Law, 1963-65; adv. Commn. Commitment, Detention and Discharge of Prisoners, 1953-55; mem. Atty. Gen.'s Nat. Com. to Study Antitrust Laws, 1953-55; exec. com. Atty. Gen.'s Nat. Conf. on Court Congestion, 1958-61; chmn. jud. nominating commn. Commonwealth of Pa., 1964-65; mem. Appellate Ct. Nominating Commn., 1973-76; standing com. on rules of practice and procedure Jud. Conf. U.S., 1959-76. Mem. Medico bd. Care, Inc., 1961-76; mem. Nat. Citizens Com. on Community Relations, 1964—; adv. com. U.S. mission UN, 1967-68; adv. panel internat. law U.S. Dept. State, 1967—; mem. Adminstrv. Conf. U.S., 1968-74; mem. nat. adv. com. on legal services, 1968-74, chmn. exec. com. Office Econ. Opportunity, 1971-74; mem. U.S. Commn. on Revision Fed. Ct. Appellate System, 1974-75; mem. Jud. Council Pa., 1968-71; mem. U.S. Commn. on Exec., Legis. and Jud. Salaries, 1976—. Mem. Commn. on Anti-Poverty Program for Phila., 1967-71; Life trustee emeritus, exec. bd. trustees U. Pa., also bd. overseers Law Sch., joint bd. Annenberg Sch. Communications, bd. overseers, fellow Faculty Arts and Scis.; bd. govs. emeritus, past v.p., past treas. Dropsie U.; chmn. bd. Council for Advancement Legal Edn., 1972—; hon. bd. govs. Hebrew U. Jerusalem; trustee Chapel of Four Chaplains; trustee, exec. com. Albert Einstein Med. Center; bd. dirs. NAACP Legal Def. and Ednl. Fund, Found. Fed. Bar Assn. Recipient World Lawyer award World Peace Through Law Center, 1975. Fellow Am. Coll. Trial Lawyers (bd. regents 1956-65, pres. 1964-65, ex-officio mem. 1965—), Inst. Jud. Adminstrn. (bd. fellows), Am. Bar Found. (life fellow, pres. 1976-78); mem. Fedn. Jewish Agys. Greater Phila. (life mem., exec. com., dir.), Phila. (chancellor 1952, 53), Pa. (1st pres. Pa. Jr. Bar Assn. (now young lawyers sect.; past exec. com.), Am. (chmn. standing com. fed. judiciary 1956-62, chmn. standing com., jud. selection, tenure and compensation 1963-68, pres. 1969-70, Gold medal 1976), Inter-Am., Internat., Fed. (nat. council) bar assns., Assn. Bar City N.Y., Am. Arbitration Assn. (dir., past exec. com.), Am. Law Inst. (treas. 1955-68, 2d v.p. 1968-76, 1st v.p. 1976—), Am. Judicature Soc. (chmn. bd. 1958-61, dir. 1970—); council legal edn. for profl. responsibility, dir. 1972—), Fed. Jud. Conf. 3d Circuit (life), World Assn. Lawyers (pres. for Ams. 1976—), Nat. Conf. Bar Pres., Taxpayers Forum Pa. (past pres.), Juristic Soc., Brandeis Lawyers Soc. (gov.), Allied Jewish Appeal (hon. pres.; former pres., chmn. bd.), Legal Aid Soc. Phila. (dir.), United Way (dir.), Selden Soc. Eng., Jewish League Israel (nat. bd.), Jewish Pub. Soc. Am. (past v.p., trustee, exec. com.), Jewish Family Service (hon. dir.), Order of Coif, Tau Epsilon Rho, Delta Sigma Rho. Republican. Jewish. Clubs: Socialegal, Locust, Nat. Lawyers (dir.), Internat. Variety, Pen and Pencil; Faculty (U. Pa.); Union League, Metropolitan (Washington); Atrium (N.Y.). Editor-in-chief Pennsylvania Banking Building and Loan Law, 3 vols., 1941. Contbr. articles to law reviews, other legal publs. Editor: The Belgrade Spaceship Trial, 1972. Mem. internat. hon. bd. Ency. Judaica. Home: The Philadelphian 2401 Pennsylvania Ave Philadelphia PA 19130 Office: 1719 Bldg Philadelphia PA 19102

SEGAL, BERNARD LOUIS, physician; b. Montreal, Que., Can., Feb. 13, 1929; s. Irving and Fay (Schecter) S.; B.Sc. cum laude, McGill U., 1950, post-grad., 1950-51, M.D., C.M. high standing, 1955; m. Idaiane Fischman, Feb. 17, 1963; 1 dau., Jody Segal. Came to U.S., 1961, naturalized, 1966. Intern, Jewish Gen Hosp., Montreal, 1955-56; resident Balt. City Hosp., 1956-57, Beth Israel Hosp., Boston, 1957-58, Georgetown Med. Center, Washington, 1958-59, St. George's Hosp., London, Eng., 1959-61; practice medicine specializing in internal medicine and cardiology, Phila., 1961—; prof., sr. attending physician medicine Hahnemann Med. Coll., Phila., 1964—, dir. William Likoff Cardiovascular Inst. Diplomate Am. Bd. Internal Medicine. Fellow A.C.P., Am. Coll. Cardiology (chmn. scholar-trainee com.; trustee 1969-71), Am. Coll. Chest Physicians; mem. N.Y. Acad. Scis., Alpha Omega Alpha. Author: Auscultation of the Heart, 1965. Editor: Theory and Practice of Auscultation, 1964; Engineering in the Practice of Medicine, 1966; Your Heart, 1972; Arteriosclerosis and Coronary Heart Disease, 1972. Editorial bd. Am. Jour. Cardiology, 1970—, Clin. Echocardiography, 1978. Contbr. more than 200 articles on cardiology to med. jours. Home: 1156 Red Rose Ln Villanova PA 19085 Office: 1320 Race St Philadelphia PA 19102

SEGAL, CHARLES PAUL, classics scholar, educator; b. Boston, Mar. 19, 1936; s. Robert and Gladys (Barsky) S.; A.B. summa cum laude, Harvard U., 1957, Ph.D., 1961; postgrad. (Fulbright scholar), Am. Sch. Classical Studies, Athens, Greece, 1957-58; m. Esther Hawley Rogers, Dec. 20, 1961; children—Joshua Hawley, Thaddeus Gabriel. Teaching fellow, classics tutor Harvard U., 1959-61, instr., 1963-64; asst. prof. classics U. Pa., Phila., 1964-65, asso. prof., 1965-67, chmn. grad. studies classics, 1967; asso. prof. Brown U., Providence, 1968-70, prof., 1970—, prof. classics and comparative lit., 1978—, chmn. classics, 1978—; jr. fellow Center for Hellenic Studies, 1967-68; vis. prof., prof.-in-charge Intercollegiate Center for Classical Studies, Rome, 1970-72; vis. prof. Brandeis U., 1974; vis. dir. studies Ecole Hautes Etudes, Paris, 1975-76; Fulbright exchange lectr. U. Melbourne (Australia), 1978; vis. prof. Greek, Columbia U., 1979; participant 1st Soviet/Am. Semiotics Colloquium, Am. Council Learned Socs./USSR Acad. Scis., 1979; cons. in field; mem. jury Classical Sch., Am. Acad. Rome, 1972-74. Am. Council Learned Soc. fellow, 1975; Nat. Endowment for Humanities grantee, 1977. Recipient Prix de Rome, Am. Acad. in Rome, 1961-63. Mem. Am. Philol. Assn., Classical Assn. New Eng., Virgilian Soc., Internat. Ovid Soc. Author: Landscape in Ovid's Metamorphoses, 1969; The Theme of the Mutilation of Corpse in the Iliad, 1971. Contbr. articles to profl. jours., books and encys. Home: 245 Brook St Providence RI 02906 Office: Box 1935 Brown U Providence RI 02912

SEGAL, D. ROBERT, pub. co. exec.; b. Oshkosh, Wis., Oct. 30, 1920; s. Morris Henry and Ida (Belond) S.; m. Kathryn McKenzie; children—Jonathan McKenzie, Janet Elizabeth. Currently pres. Freedom Newspapers, Inc., Santa Ana, Calif., pub. Gastonia (N.C.) Gazette, pres. Kinston (N.C.) Free-Press, New Bern (N.C.) Sun Jour., Burlington (N.C.) Times-News, Jacksonville (N.C.) Daily News, Freedom Newspapers of N.Y. Trustee, Children's Hosp of Orange County (Calif.). Served with USAAF, 1942-45. Office: 1055 N Main Suite 901 Santa Ana CA 92711

SEGAL, ERICH, educator, author; b. Bklyn., June 16, 1937; s. Samuel Michael and Cynthia (Shapiro) S.; A.B., Harvard U., 1958, A.M., 1959, Ph.D., 1965; m. Karen Ilona Marianne James, June 10, 1975. Vis. lectr. Yale U., 1964-65, asst. prof., 1965-68, asso. prof. classics and comparative lit., 1968-73; vis. prof. Classical philology U. Munich (Germany), 1973; vis. prof. classics Princeton U., 1974-75, Tel Aviv U., spring 1976; vis. prof. comparative lit. Dartmouth Coll., fall 1976, 77; vis. fellow Wolfson Coll., Oxford U., 1978, 79; author, narrator TV spl. The Ancient Games, 1972, Mourning Becomes Electra, 1978; TV commentator Olympics, 1972, 76, 80; host Mourning Becomes Electra, Pub. Broadcasting System, 1978; author: (novels) Love Story, 1970, Fairy Tale, 1973, Oliver's Story, 1977, Man, Woman and Child, 1980; (book and lyrics) Sing Muse, 1961-62; (play) Odyssey, 1974; (screenplays) Yellow Submarine, The Games, Love Story (Golden Globe award), R.P.M., Oliver's Story, Consenting Adults; also articles revs.; editor: Euripides: A Collection of Critical Essays, 1968; Roman Laughter: The Comedy of Plautus, 1968; editor, translator: Plautus: Three Comedies, 1969; Problems in Plautus, 1979; The Birth of Comedy, 1980. Office: Room 1106 119 W 57th St New York NY 10019*

SEGAL, GEORGE, actor. Appeared in films Who's Afraid of Virginia Woolf?, The Quiller Memorandum, King Rat, Bye Bye Braverman, No Way to Treat a Lady, Loving, The Owl and the Pussycat, Where's Poppa?, Born To Win, The Hot Rock, A Touch of Class, Blume in Love, The Terminal Man, California Split, Russian Roulette, Blackbird, Duchess and Dirt Water Fox, Fun with Dick and Jane, others. Office: care Wallin Simon Black & Co 1350 6th Ave New York NY 10019

SEGAL, GEORGE, sculptor; b. N.Y.C., Nov. 26, 1924; s. Jacob and Sophie (Gerstenfeld) S.; B.S. in Art Edn., N.Y. U., 1950; M.F.A., Rutgers U., 1963, Ph.D. in Fine Art (hon.), 1970; m. Helen Steinberg, Apr. 7, 1946; children—Jeffrey, Rena. One man shows include Hansa Gallery, N.Y.C., 1956-59, Rutgers U., 1958, 63, Green Gallery, N.Y.C., 1960-62, 64, Sonnabend Gallery, Paris, France, 1963, Schmela Gallery Dusseldorf, 1963, Janis Gallery, N.Y.C., 1965, 67, 68, 70, 71, 73-74, 77, Mus. Contemporary Art, Chgo., 1968, Galerie Speyer, Paris, 1969, 71, Princeton U., 1969, Western Gallery Western Wash. State Coll., 1970, Onnasch Galerie, Cologne, 1971, also European mus. tour, 1971-73, U. Wis., Milw., 1973, Onnasch Galerie, Switzerland, 1974, Andre Emmerich, Zurich, 1975, Dartmouth Coll., 1975, Inst. Contemporary Art, 1976, Nina Freudenheim Gallery, Buffalo, 1976, Art Assn. Newport (R.I.), 1976, Suzette Schochet Gallery, 1976, Santa Barbara Mus. Art, 1976, Whitney Mus. Am. Art, N.Y.C., 1979 (retrospective); group shows include Sao Paulo Bienal, Janis Gallery, Jewish Mus., N.Y.C., Carnegie Internat., Whitney Mus.; represented in permanent collections including Mus. Modern Art, Whitney Mus., Mint Mus., Charlotte, N.C., Albright-Knox Mus., Mus. Modern Art, Stockholm, Sweden, numerous others. Recipient award Walter H. Gutman Found., 1962. Office: care Sidney Janis Gallery 6 W 57th St New York NY 10019*

SEGAL, HARRY LOUIS, physician; b. Phila., Jan. 13, 1900; s. Morris and Bertha (Adams) S.; B.S. in Medicine magna cum laude, Syracuse U., 1922, M.D., 1924; postgrad. U. Vienna Med. Clinics, 1928-29; m. Evelyn Edith Buff, Aug. 26, 1935. Intern pathology Michael Reese Hosp., Chgo., 1924-25, intern, 1925-26, resident medicine, 1926-27; fellow in research Nelson Morris Inst., Chgo., 1927-28; instr. medicine U. Rochester Sch. Med. and Dentistry, 1932-49, asso. in medicine, 1949-51, asst. prof., 1951-56, asso. prof. medicine, 1956-60, clin. prof., 1960-65, prof., 1965-70, prof. emeritus, 1970—; practice medicine, specializing in internal medicine and gastroenterology, Rochester, 1929—; dir. gastrointestinal tng. program Strong Meml. Hosp., 1959-67, dir. gastroenterology sect., 1959-65; physician in chief Genesee Hosp., 1955-67, head gastrointestinal unit, 1967-70, coordinator med. edn., 1955-65, 71-73; cons. internal medicine Rochester Gen. Hosp.; vis. prof. medicine U. Lagos Med. Sch., 1962-63, 64, 70, 72, 73, external examiner, 1967, vis. prof., acting chmn. dept. medicine, 1968, 70, 72, 73, dir. Gastrointestinal Research Project, established 1946. Co-recipient Schindler award Am. Gastroscopic Soc., 1959; recipient Centennial award Syracuse U., 1970; Alumni citation U. Rochester, 1973. Diplomate Am. Bd. Internal Medicine (subsplty. gastro-enterology). Fellow A.C.P., A.M.A.; mem. AAUP, Assn. Am. Med. Colls., Am. Gastroent. Assn., Rochester Acad. Medicine (award 1938 Award of Merit 1956, Albert D. Kaiser award, 1959), Am. Soc. Gastointestinal Endoscopy, Am. Psychosomatic soc., N.Y. Acad. Scis., Am. Heart Assn., A.A.A.S., West African Soc. Gastroenterology (hon.), Sigma Xi, Alpha Omega Alpha. Contbr. chpts. Fundamentals of Nutrition, 1940, Ion Exchanges in Organic and Biochemistry, 1956, Gastroenterologic Medicine, 1969; also articles to med. jours. Co-developer gastroscopic color photographic system; originator tubeless gastric analysis with cation exchange resins. Home: 30 Stoneham Rd Rochester NY 14625 Office: 220 Alexander St Rochester NY 14607

SEGAL, IRVING EZRA, educator; b. N.Y.C., Sept. 13, 1918; s. Aaron and Fannie (Weinstein) S.; A.B., Princeton, 1937; Ph.D., Yale, 1940; m. Osa Skotting, Feb. 15, 1955; children—William, Andrew, Karen B. Instr., Harvard, 1941; research asst. Princeton, 1941-42, asso., 1942-43; asst. to O. Veblen, Inst. for Advanced Study, 1945-46, asst. prof. U. Chgo., 1948-53, asso. prof., 1953-57, prof., 1957-60; prof. Mass. Inst. Tech., Cambridge, 1960—; vis. asso. prof. Columbia, 1953-54; vis. fellow Insts. Math. and Theoretical Physics, Copenhagen, 1958-59; vis. prof. Sorbonne, Paris, France, 1965, U. Lund (Sweden), 1971, Coll. de France, 1977. Served with AUS, 1943-45. Guggenheim fellow, 1947, 51-52, 67-68. Mem. Am. Math. Soc., Am. Phys. Soc., Am. Acad. Arts and Sci., Royal Danish Acad. Scis., Am. Astron. Soc., Soc. Indsl. and Applied Math., Nat. Acad. Sci. Author: Mathematical Problems of Relativistic Physics, 1963; (with R.A. Kunze) Integrals and Operators, 1968; Mathematical Cosmology and Extragalactic Astronomy, 1976. Editor: (with W.T. Martin) Analysis in Function Space, 1964; (with Roe Goodman) Mathematical Theory of Elementary Particles, 1966. Contbr. articles to profl. jours. Home: 25 Moon Hill Rd Lexington MA 02173

SEGAL, IRVING RANDALL, lawyer; b. Allentown, Pa., Oct. 15, 1914; s. Samuel I. and Rose (Kantor) S.; B.A., U. Pa., 1935; LL.B., 1938; m. Eleanor F. Smolens, Dec. 26, 1943; children—Betsy A., Kathy J., Robert J. Admitted to Pa. bar, 1938; instr. polit. sci. U. Pa., 1938-42; law clk. Ct. Common Pleas No. 4, Philadelphia County, 1938-39; asso. firm Schnader, Harrison, Segal & Lewis, Phila., 1939-49, partner 1949—. Permanent mem. Jud. Conf. 3d Circuit U.S. Ct. Appeals; regional rationing atty. OPA, 1942; v.p. Nat. Kidney Disease Found., 1954-59, hon. life del., 1959-64; pres. Nephrosis Found., Phila., 1953-56; bd. mgrs. Woman's Hosp. Phila., 1957-64, v.p., 1962-63; bd. Jewish Edn., Phila., 1948-72; trustee YM and WYHA, Phila., 1954-58. Served to capt. Judge Adv. Gen. Dept., AUS, 1942-46. Decorated Mil. Commendation medal. Fellow Am. Coll. Trial Lawyers (regent 1976-79, sec. 1979-80); mem. Am. Bar Assn., Pa. Bar Assn., Phila. Bar Assn., Am. Law Inst., Am. Bar Found., Phila. Bar Found., Am. Judicature Soc., Phila. Socialegal Club, World Peace Through Law, Internat. Law and Social Legislation, Am. Acad. Polit. and Social Sci., Fed. Bar Assn., Internat. Bar Assn., Order of Coif, Phi Beta Kappa, Pi Gamma Mu (pres. 1934-35), Delta Sigma Rho. Jewish (dir., v.p. temple). Clubs: Midday, Phila. Lawyers, Art Alliance, Peale, Philobiblon, Locust. Home: 250 S 17th St Philadelphia PA 19103 Office: Packard Bldg Philadelphia PA 19102

SEGAL, JACK, mathematician; b. Phila., May 9, 1934; s. Morris and Rose (Novin) S.; B.S., U. Miami, 1955, M.S., 1957; Ph.D., U. Ga., 1960; m. Arlene Stern, Dec. 18, 1955; children—Gregory, Sharon. Instr. mathematics U. Wash., Seattle, 1960-61, asst. prof., 1961-65, asso. prof., 1965-70, prof., 1970—, chmn. dept., 1975-78. NSF postdoctoral fellow Inst. Advanced Study, Princeton, N.J., 1963-64; Fulbright fellow U. Zagreb, Yugoslavia, 1969-70. Mem. Am. Math. Soc. Author: Shape Theory Notes, 1978. Home: 8711 25th Pl NE Seattle WA 98115 Office: Dept Mathematics U Washington Seattle WA 98195

SEGAL, JONATHAN BRUCE, editor; b. N.Y.C., May 12, 1946; s. Clement and Florence Lillian (Miller) S.; B.A., Washington Coll., 1966; m. Haidi Kuhn, June 30, 1974. Writer, editor N.Y. Times, N.Y.C., 1966-73; editor Quadrangle/N.Y. Times Book Co., N.Y.C., 1974-76; sr. editor Simon & Schuster, N.Y.C., 1976—. Democrat. Jewish. Contbr. articles to popular jours. Home: 115 E 9th St Apt 12E New York City NY 10003 Office: Simon & Schuster 1230 Ave of Americas New York City NY 10020

SEGAL, LORE, writer; b. Vienna, Austria, Mar. 8, 1928; d. Ignatz and Franzi (Stern) Groszmann; B.A. in English with honors, Bedford Coll., U. London (Eng.), 1948; m. David I. Segal, Nov. 3, 1960 (dec.); children—Beatrice Ann, Jacob Paul. Came to U.S., 1951, naturalized, 1956. Prof. writing div. Sch. Arts, Columbia, also Princeton, Sarah Lawrence Coll., Bennington Coll.; prof. writing U. Ill. at Chgo. Circle. Guggenheim fellow, 1965-66; Council on Arts and Humanities grantee, 1968-69; Artists Public Service grantee, 1970-71; CAPS grantee, 1975. Author: Other People's Houses, 1964; (with W.D. Snodgrass) Gallows Songs, 1968; (novel) Lucinella, 1976. (children's books) Tell Me A Mitzi, All the Way Home, 1973, The Juniper Tree and Other Tales from Grimm, 1973, Tell Me a Trudy, 1977. Contbr. short stories, articles to Commentary, Sat. Eve. Post, Audience, Epoch, New Yorker, New Republic, Partison Rev., New Am. Rev., N.Y. Times Book Rev. Address: 280 Riverside Dr New York NY 10025

SEGAL, MARTIN, economist, educator; b. Warsaw, Poland, Feb. 5, 1921; s. Jacob and Sarah (Rabinowicz) S.; B.A., Queens Coll., 1948; M.A., Harvard, 1950, Ph.D., 1953; m. Ruth Berkowicz, June 26, 1945; children—Naomi, Jonathan. Came to U.S., 1940, naturalized, 1943. Instr. Harvard, 1953-56; economist N.Y. Met. Region Study, N.Y.C., 1956-57; asst. prof. Williams Coll., Williamstown, Mass., 1957-58; prof. econs. Dartmouth, 1958—; sr. economist Council Econ. Advisers, Washington 1965-66. Ofcl. econ. br. ILO, Geneva, Switzerland, 1968-69; cons. Senate Subcom. on Antitrust, 1955, U.S. Dept. Commerce, 1963-64, A.I.D., 1971-72. Served with AUS, 1942-46. Named Alumnus of Year, Queens Coll., 1962. Mem. Am. Econ. Assn., Indsl. Relations Research Assn., Phi Beta Kappa (hon.). Author: Wages in the Metropolis, 1960; The Rise of the United Association, 1970; Government Pay Policies in Ceylon, 1971. Contbr. articles to profl. jours. Home: 5 Fairview Ave Hanover NH 03755

SEGAL, MORTON, pub. relations co. exec.; b. Bklyn., Mar. 3, 1931; s. Louis and Regina (Zucker) S.; B.A., Kenyon Coll., Gambier, Ohio, 1953; M.F.A., Columbia U., 1955; divorced; children—Erica Leslie, Peter Stephen, Karen Leigh, Matthew Justin. With Max Eisen Publicity, N.Y.C., 1956-57; producer, gen. mgr. Broadway and Off-Broadway prodns., 1957-61; asst. publicity mgr. Paramoutn Pictures, 1961-63; dir. publicity and pub. relations 20th Century-Fox, 1963-65; exec. asst. to v.p. advt. and publicity MGM, 1965-69, dir. advt. pub. relations, 1969-72; partner Allan, Ingersoll, Segal & Henry, 1973-75, ICPR Pub. Relations, Los Angeles, 1975—; dir., exec. com. Computer Transp. Services, Inc., 1974—. Served with AUS, 1953-55. Mem. Pub. Relations Soc. Am. (Silver Anvil award 1976, 77, 79), Acad. Motion Picture Arts and Scis., Los Angeles C. of C. Democrat. Address: 9255 Sunset Blvd Los Angeles CA 90069

SEGAL, ROBERT MANDAL, lawyer; b. Worcester, Mass., Mar. 21, 1915; s. Abe C. and Bella (Perry) S.; A.B., Amherst Coll., 1936; postgrad. in econs. U. Chgo., 1936-38; LL.B., J.D., Harvard U., 1942; m. Sharlee M. Segal, June 17, 1941; children—Terry P., Ellen J. Huvelle. Asst. to pres. R.R. Emergency Bd., Washington, 1938; economist U.S. Steel Corp., Pitts., N.Y., 1938-39; economist WPB, 1940-41; admitted to Mass. bar, 1942; N.E. counsel Am. Fedn. of TV and Radio Artists, 1948—; counsel Mass. State Labor Council AFL-CIO, 1955—; N.E. counsel Screen Actors Guild, 1955—; sr. partner Segal, Roitman & Coleman, Boston, 1972—; lectr. labor law Harvard Bus. Sch., 1960—, collective bargaining and law Boston Coll. Law Sch., 1973-77; dir. Newton Coop. Bank, 1960—. Pres., Jewish Community Council of Boston, 1969-71; bd. dirs. United Jewish Appeal, 1971—; mem. alumni Council Law Sch., Harvard U., 1954-57, vice chmn. fund drive, 1967-71; chmn. Mass. Bar-Press Com. of Mass., 1967-70; v.p. Mass. Continuing Legal Edn.-N.E. Law Inst., 1974—; mem. Mass. Edn. Compact Council Mass., 1968—; mem. adv. bd. Mass. Civil Liberties Union, 1958-76, Mayor's Minority Housing Boston, 1963-68, Mayor's Minimum Employment Commn., 1969—; mem. adv. com. on Mass. Prepaid Legal Services, 1978—. Served with U.S. Army, 1943-45. Brookings Instn. fellow, 1938. Fellow Am. Bar Found.; mem. Am. (mem. ho. of dels. 1957, chmn. labor relations law council 1954, mem. Consortium 1974-79, dir. Prepaid Legal Service Inst. 1975—), Mass., Boston (exec. council 1960-63, co-chmn. labor relations com. 1960—) bar assns., Indsl. Labor Relations Assn., Am. Judicature Soc., Mass. Civic League, Am. Law Inst., Am. Econ. Assn., Ams. for Dem. Action (chmn. Mass. 1964), Phi Beta Kappa, Delta Sigma Rho. Contbr. articles to profl. jours. Home: 153 Chestnut Circle Lincoln MA 01773 Office: 11 Beacon St Boston MA 02108

SEGAL, SHELDON JEROME, biologist, found. ofcl., educator; b. N.Y.C., Mar. 15, 1926; s. Morris M. and Florence (Bogan) S.; B.A., Dartmouth, 1947; postgrad. U. Geneva, 1947-48; M.S., State U. Ia., 1951, Ph.D., 1952; m. Harriet Ellen Feinberg, May 22, 1961; children—Amy Robin, Jennifer Ann, Laura Jane. Asst. prof. State U. Iowa, 1953-56; asst. med. dir. Population Council, Rockefeller U., N.Y.C., 1956-63, med. dir., 1963-78, v.p., 1969-76, sr. v.p., 1976-78, affiliate univ., 1956-76, adj. prof., 1977—; dir. population scis. Rockefeller Found., 1978—; lectr. Columbia U., 1959-61; mem. Marine Biol. Lab., Woods Hole, Mass.; cons. World Bank, WHO, NIH, Ford Found., Indian Govt., UN, Office Sci. and Tech., 1976-77, UN Fund Population Affairs, 1979; mem. com. on contraceptive tech. Nat. Acad. Scis., 1977—; mem. adv. com. on human reproduction FDA; cons. to dir. Nat. Inst. Child Health and Human Devel., 1978—; mem. adv. subgroup on human reprodn. European Med. Research Councils, 1978—; mem. task force on conception, reprodn., parturition, contraception and sexual differentiation NIH; Sigma Xi lectr. U. Idaho, 1976; lectr. World Congress on Gynecology and Obstetrics, 1976; vis. prof. All-India Inst. Med. Sci., New Delhi. Served to lt. (j.g.) USNR, 1943-45. Recipient Honor award Innsbruck U., Austria; hon. citation Pres. of India, 1978; invited lectr. Chinese Acad. Scis., 1977. Fellow AAAS; mem. Internat. Soc. for Study Reprodn. (pres. 1968-72), Am. Fertility Soc. (hon. v.p. 1975-76, Upjohn lectr.), The Endocrine Soc., Am. Assn. Anatomists, Internat. Inst. Embryology, Am. Soc. Zoologists, Population Assn. Am., Council on Fgn. Relations. Co-editor 6 books. Contbr. numerous articles to profl. jours. Home: 9 Topland Rd Hartsdale NY 10530 Office: Rockefeller Found 1133 Ave of Americas New York NY 10036

SEGALL, ARTHUR A., lawyer; b. N.Y.C., Sept. 29, 1905; s. Jacob W. and Clara (Holzman) S.; student Dartmouth; LL.B., U. Mich., 1928; m. Natalie Freed, Jan. 12, 1933; children—Matthew A., Ann Thomas. Admitted to N.Y. bar, 1930; asst. corp. counsel, then chief div. taxes Law Dept., N.Y.C., 1939-43; spl. dept. commr. investigation City of N.Y.C., 1944; now mem. firm Hess, Segall, Guterman, Pelz & Steiner, N.Y.C. Trustee Lexington Sch. for Deaf. Mem. Assn. Bar City N.Y. (chmn. municipal affairs com. 1963), New York County Lawyers Assn. Home: 860 Fifth Ave New York City NY 10021 Office: 230 Park Ave New York City NY 10017

SEGALL, HAROLD ABRAHAM, lawyer; b. N.Y.C., May 22, 1918; s. Morris and Mildred (Borkan) S.; B.A. with distinction, Cornell U., 1938; LL.B. cum laude, Yale, 1941; m. Edith S. Besser, Jan. 27, 1952; children—Mark E., Grant D., Bruce K. Admitted to N.Y. bar, 1941; practiced in N.Y.C., 1946—; asso. mem. firm Gilbert, Segall & Young and predecessors, 1946-49, partner, 1949—; dir. Oneita Knitting Mills; vis. lectr. Yale Law Sch., 1974-75. Mem. council State U. N.Y. at Purchase, 1974—. Counsel United Republican Finance Com., N.Y. State, 1955-61, Rep. City Com., N.Y.C., 1961, Nat. Rep. Citizens Com., 1962, Keating for Senator Com., 1964, Eisenhower 75th Birthday Com., 1965, Friends of the Gov. Wilson Team, 1974, Gov.'s Club, N.Y., 1965-75. Served to maj. AUS, World War II; ETO, PTO. Recipient Edgar M. Cullen prize, 1939. Mem. Am. Bar Assn., Bar City N.Y. (com. on trademark and unfair competition 1967-69, chmn. subcom. legislation 1968-69), Jewish Community Center, Order of Coif, Phi Beta Kappa, Phi Kappa Phi, Phi Sigma Delta. Clubs: Yale, (N.Y.C.); Elmwood Country (gov. 1966-70, 73-75). Author: (with R.B. Kelley) Estate Planning for the Corporate Executive, 1971; Representing the Seller of a Closely-Held Business, 1973 (with J.A. Arouh) How to Prepare Legal Opinions, 1979. Editor: Yale Law Jour., 1939. Contbr. articles to profl. jours. Home: Woodlands Rd Harrison NY 10528 Office: 430 Park Ave New York NY 10022

SEGALL, JOEL, coll. pres.; b. Bridgeport, Conn., Mar. 2, 1923; s. Irving and Jennie (Krawitz) S.; M.B.A., U. Chgo., 1948, A.M., 1952, Ph.D., 1956; LL.D. (hon.), U. Bridgeport, 1979; m. Joan Downey, June 29, 1958; children—Jennifer, Patricia. Asst. prof., then asso. prof. fin. U. Chgo., from 1952, prof., to 1973; dep. asst. sec. Dept. Treasury, Washington, 1970-72; dep. undersec. Dept. Labor, Washington, 1972-77; pres. Bernard M. Baruch Coll., 1977—; bd. mgrs., mem. exec. com., mem. fin. com. Coffee, Sugar and Cocoa Exchange; bd. dirs. Thomson McKinnon Nat. Govt. Securities Reinvestment Program, Inc, Internat. Center Econ. Policy Studies. Served with USAAF, 1942-45. Recipient Exceptional Service award Dept. Treasury, 1972; Personal award Sec. Labor, 1974. Editor Jour. Fin., 1957-60. Office: 17 Lexington Ave New York NY 10010

SEGALL, MAURICE, retail co. exec.; b. Joliette, Que., Can., May 16, 1929; s. Jack and Adela (Segall) S.; B.Econs., McGill U., Montreal, Que., 1950; M.Econs., Columbia U., 1952; Hudson Bay Co. fellow London Sch. Econs., 1953-54; m. Sarah Ostrousky, Nov. 25, 1951; children—Elizabeth, Eric, Peter. Came to U.S., 1962. Economist, Canadian Fed. Govt., 1951-55; chief economist, dir. research planning and orgn. Steinbergs Ltd. of Montreal, 1955-62; dir. ops. treasury stores J.C. Penney Co., N.Y.C., 1962-70, dir. treasury stores, 1970-71; sr. v.p. Am. Express Co., N.Y.C., 1971, gen. mgr. credit card div., 1971-74; pres. Am. Express Co./Credit Card Div., 1974-78; pres., chief exec. officer Zayre Corp., Framingham, Mass., 1978—; pres. Am. Express Reservations, Inc., 1971. Club: Canadian (N.Y.C.); Sands Point Bath and Tennis. Office: Zayre Corp Framingham MA 01701*

SEGAR, WILLIAM ELIAS, physician, educator; b. Indpls., Dec. 16, 1923; s. Louis H. and Beatrice (Felsenthal) S.; B.S., Ind. U., 1944, M.D., 1947; m. Julie Anne Feld, July 17, 1954; children—Douglas Scott, Jeffrey Lewis. Intern Ind. U. Med. Center, 1947-48; resident pediatrics U. Ill. Hosps., 1948-49, Ind. U. Med. Center, 1949-51, fellow pediatrics, instr. pediatrics Yale Sch. Medicine, 1951-53; mem. faculty Ind. U. Sch. Medicine, 1955-67, prof. pediatrics, 1963-67; prof. pediatrics Mayo Clinic and Mayo Grad. Sch. Medicine, 1967-70; prof. pediatrics U. Wis. Med. Sch., Madison, 1970—, chmn. dept., 1975—. Served to capt. M.C., AUS, 1953-55. Diplomate Am. Bd. Pediatrics. Mem. Am. Pediatric Soc., Soc. Pediatric Research, Midwest Soc. Pediatric Research (pres. 1966-67), Central Soc. Clin. Investigation, Am. Fedn. Clin. Research, A.A.A.S., Am. Soc. Nephrology, Sigma Xi. Contbr. articles to med. jours. Home: 3975 Plymouth Circle Madison WI 53705

SEGELIN, BERNARD, motion picture co. exec.; b. Rochester, N.Y., Sept. 25, 1921; s. David and Mae (Levine) S.; B.A., U. Mich., 1944; LL.B., N.Y. U., 1948; m. Ziona Stalowitz, Mar. 19, 1950; 1 dau., Amy. Admitted to N.Y. bar, 1949, Cal. bar, 1971; asso. Phillips, Nizer, Benjamin & Krim, N.Y.C., 1949-52, Schwartz & Frohlich, N.Y.C., 1952-56; with Metro-Goldwyn-Mayer, Inc., Culver City, Calif., 1956—, sec., 1970—. Served with USAAF, 1943-46. Mem. State Bar

Calif. Home: 523 Cashmere Terr Los Angeles CA 90049 Office: 10202 W Washington Blvd Culver City CA 90230

SEGELSTEIN, IRWIN, broadcasting co. exec.; student CCNY; m. Bernice Segelstein; children—Emily, James. With Benton & Bowles, 1947-65; v.p. programs CBS-TV, 1965-70, v.p. program adminstrn., 1970-73, pres. CBS Records, 1973-76; exec. v.p. programs NBC-TV, 1976-77, exec. v.p. program planning, 1977-78, exec. v.p. broadcasting, 1978—. Office: care NBC Press Dept 30 Rockefeller Plaza New York NY 10020*

SEGER, BOB, musician; b. Ann Arbor, Mich. Recorded 4 albums for Capitol Records, then recorded Smokin O.P.'s with duo Teegarden and Van Winkle for Warner Bros., also 2 other albums; currently rec. for Capitol Records and touring with own back-up group The Silver Bullet Band; albums include: Live Bullet, Night Moves, Beautiful Loser, Stranger in Town. Office: care Punch Enterprises 567 Purdy St Birmingham MI 48009

SEGERSTEN, ROBERT HAGY, investment banker, lawyer; b. Boston, June 24, 1941; s. Wendell C. and Claire H. S.; A.B., Bates Coll., 1963; J.D., Boston U., 1970; m. Marie E. Makinen, Feb. 13, 1965; children—Amanda Beth, Vanessa Bryce. Admitted to Mass. bar, 1970; asso. firm Nessen & Csaplar, Boston, 1970-75; v.p. March Co., Boston, 1975-77; pres. March-Eton Corp., Concord, Mass., 1977—; partner firm Nessen, Goodwin & Segersten, Concord, 1977—; bd. advisers Continental Resources Corp., Washington; adj. prof. real estate law Bentley Coll. Officer, bd. dirs. Friends of The Jimmy Fund, Boston. Served to lt. USN, 1963-67. Mem. Boston Bar Assn., ACLU. Democrat. Episcopalian. Home: 71 Montview St West Roxbury MA 02132 Office: 81 Middle St Concord MA 01742

SEGGERMAN, HARRY GURNEY ATHA, investment co. exec.; b. N.Y.C., Aug. 15, 1927; s. Kenneth and Sarah (Atha) S.; A.B., Princeton U., 1950; m. Anne Crellin, Apr. 14, 1951; children—Patricia, Henry, Marianne, Yvonne, Suzanne, John. With Dominick & Dominick, N.Y.C., 1951-56; internat. investment specialist Capital Research Co., Los Angeles, 1957-62; with Japan Fund, Inc., N.Y.C., 1962-68, pres., 1967-68; v.p. Fidelity Mgmt. and Research Co., Boston, 1968—; vice chmn. Fidelity Pacific Fund S.A.; dir. Fidelity World Fund, Fidelity Far East Fund. Mem. fin. com. Huxley Inst. Biosocial Research. Served with USNR, 1945-46. Mem. N.Y. Soc. Security Analysts. Home: 5060 Congress St Fairfield CT 06430 Office: 82 Devonshire St Boston MA 02109

SEGHI, PHILLIP DOMENIC, profl. baseball team exec.; b. Cedar Point, Ill., 1918; student Northwestern U., 1931-34. Former infielder profl. baseball teams; mgr. minor league teams Pitts. Pirates, 1946-48; with Cleve. Indians Am. League baseball team, 1949-55, 71—, mgr. minor league teams Fargo-Moorhead, Green Bay, 1949-55, v.p., dir. player personnel, 1971-72, v.p., gen. mgr., 1973—; scout Cin. Reds, 1956-58, farm dir., 1958-68; farm dir. Oakland A's, 1968-71. Address: care Cleveland Indians Cleveland Stadium Cleveland OH 44114*

SEGOVIA, ANDRES, guitarist; b. Linares, Spain, Feb. 18, 1894; specialized in study guitar Granada Mus. Inst.; D.Mus. (hon.), Oxford U., 1972; m. Emilia, 1962; 1 son; 2 children (by former marriage). Started playing guitar at age 10; debut in Granada, Spain, 1909; toured in Europe and South Am.; made N.Y. debut, Town Hall, 1928; has appeared in recitals throughout U.S.; has taught at Santiago de Compostela, Acad. Chigi, Sienna, U. Calif., Berkeley, other schs.; adapted works of Bach, Haydn, and Mozart. Recipient Grammy award, 1958; Gold medal for meritorious work, Spain, 1967. Mem. Royal Acad. Fine Arts (Spain). Address: care ICA Artists Ltd 40 W 57th St New York NY 10019*

SEGRÈ, EMILIO, physicist, educator; b. Tivoli, Rome, Italy, Feb. 1, 1905; s. Giuseppe and Amelia (Treves) S.; Ph.D., U. Rome, 1928; Dr. honoris causa, U. Palermo (Italy), Gustavus Adolphus Coll., St. Peter, Minn., Tel Aviv U. (Israel), Hebrew Union Coll., Los Angeles; m. Elfriede Spiro, Feb. 2, 1936 (dec. Oct. 1970); children—Claudio, Amelia, Fausta; m. 2d, Rosa Mines, Feb. 12, 1972. Came to U.S., 1938, naturalized, 1944. Asst. prof. U. Rome, 1932-36; dir. physics lab. U. Palermo (Italy), 1936-38; research asst. U. Calif. at Berkeley, 1938-43, prof. physics, 1945-72, emeritus, 1972—, group leader Los Alamos Sci. Lab., 1943-46; hon. prof. S. Marcos U., Lima; vis. prof. U. Ill., Purdue U.; prof. physics U. Rome, 1974-75. Recipient Hofmann medal German Chem. Soc., Cannizzaro medal Accad. Lincei; Nobel prize in physics, 1959; decorated great cross merit Republic of Italy; Rockefeller Found. fellow, 1930-31; Guggenheim fellow, 1959; Fulbright fellow. Fellow Am. Phys. Soc.; mem. Nat. Acad. Scis., Am. Philos. Soc., Am. Acad. Arts and Scis., Heidelberg Akademie Wissenschaften, European Phys. Soc., Acad. Scis. Peru, Soc. Progress of Sci. (Uruguay), Società Italiana di fisica, Accad. Naz. Lincei (Italy), Indian Acad. Scis. Bangalore, others. Co-discoverer slow neutrons, elements technetium, astatine, plutonium and the antiproton. Home: 3802 Quail Ridge Rd Lafayette CA 94549 Office: Dept Physics U of California Berkeley CA 94720

SEGUIN, ROBERT-LIONEL, ethnologist; b. Rigaud, Que., Can., Mar. 7, 1920; s. Omer and Jeanne S.; Lic. Soc. Scis., U. Montreal (Que.), 1951; Dip. in History, U. Laval (Que.), 1957, Dr. Letters and History, 1964; Dr. Letters and Human Scis., Sorbonne, U. Paris, 1972; m. Huguette, Servant, Oct., 1957. Prof. ethnology U. Que., Trois-Rivières, also dir. Center Documentation in Traditional Civilization. Recipient Gov.-Gen. of Can. prize, 1967, Broquette-Gonin prize Acad. francaise, 1967, France-Que. prize Assn. France-Que., Paris, 1973, Duvernay prize Soc. St. Jean Baptiste, Montreal, 1975. Mem. Royal Soc. Can., Societe des Dix (Que.), Societe d'ethnologie francaise (Paris). Roman Catholic. Author books, including: La Civilisation traditionnelle de l'habitant aux 17e et 18e Siècles, 1967; La Vie libertine en Nouvelle-France au XVIIe Siècle, 1972; L'Esprit révolutionnaire dans l'art québécois, 1973; La Sorcellerie au Québec du XVII au XIXe Siècle, 1978. Research, numerous publs. on folk civilization of Que., 1955—. Home: 440 Grande-Ligne Rigaud comte Vaudreuil PQ J0P LP0 Canada Office: Pavillon Michel-Sarrazin Universite du Que Trois-Rivieres PQ Canada

SEIB, CHARLES BACH, journalist; b. Kingston, N.Y., Aug. 22, 1919; s. Charles Bach and Elizabeth (Meyer) S.; B.A., Lehigh U., 1941; m. Shirley Jane Mayer, Oct. 1, 1945; children—Philip, Caroline. Reporter, Allentown (Pa.) Chronicle, 1942-44, A.P., 1944-45; deskman Phila. Record, 1945-46; reporter I.N.S., 1946-52; asst. bur. chief Gannett News Service, Washington, 1952-54; with Washington Star, 1954-74, mng. editor, 1968-74; asso. editor, ombudsman Washington Post, 1974-79; columnist The News Business, 1974-79. Club: Federal City (Washington). Author: The Woods, 1971. Home: 3750 Oliver St NW Washington DC 20015 Office: 1150 15th St NW Washington DC 20071

SEIBERLICH, CARL JOSEPH, naval officer; b. Jenkintown, Pa., July 4, 1921; s. Charles A. and Helen (Dolan) S.; B.S., U.S. Mcht. Marine Acad., 1943; grad. Armed Forces Staff Coll., 1959; m. Trudy Germi, May 29, 1952; children—Eric P., Heidi M., Curt A. Commd. ensign U.S. Navy, 1943, advanced through grades to rear adm., 1971; designated naval aviator, 1947; carrier ops. Heavier-than-Air, Lighter-than-Air and helicopters; comdg. officer Airship ZPM-1, 1949, Air Anti-Submarine Squadron 26, 1961, U.S.S. Salamonie, 1967, U.S.S. Hornet, 1969; dir. recovery astronauts Apollo 11 and 12 lunar missions, 1969, comdr. anti-submarine warfare group 3 Flagship U.S.S. Ticonderoga, 1971; comdr. task force 74, Viet Nam Ops., 1972; asst. dep. chief naval ops. for air warfare Navy Dept., 1975-77; dep. chief naval personnel, 1977-78; comdr. Naval Mil. Personnel Command, 1978—. Active Boy Scouts Am. Decorated Legion of Merit (5), Air medal; recipient Harmon Internat. trophy for devel. 1st variable depth towed sonar, 1951. Mem. Am. Inst. Aeros. and Astronautics, U.S. Naval Inst., U.S. Naval Sailing Assn. (commodore 1979), Am. Angus Assn., Order Daedalians, Tailhook Assn., Navy Helicopter Assn., U.S. Mcht. Marine Acad. Alumni Assn., Assn. Naval Aviation, Am. Legion, Delta Sigma Pi. Clubs: N.Y. Yacht, Nat. Space. Home: Seagate Farm 1510 Loudoun Dr Haymarket VA 22069 Office: Comdr Naval Mil Personnel Command Navy Dept Washington DC 20370. *Maintain a clear set of moral values, prepare yourself professionally, maintain phys. fitness, persevere as you move toward your goal. Value personal relationships. Never give less than your best; never accept less than the best. Don't trade on the accomplishments of yesterday. Have fun and at times pause and admire the flowers.*

SEIBERLING, JOHN F., congressman; b. Akron, Ohio, Sept. 8, 1918; s. J. Frederick and Henrietta (Buckler) S.; A.B., Harvard, 1941; LL.B., Columbia, 1949; m. Elizabeth Pope Behr, June 4, 1949; children—John B., David P., Stephen M. Admitted to N.Y. bar, 1950, Ohio bar, 1955; asso. mem. firm Donovan, Leisure, Newton, Lumbard & Irvine, N.Y.C., 1949-53; atty. Goodyear Tire & Rubber Co., Akron, 1954-71; mem. 92d-96th Congresses from 14th Ohio Dist.; mem. com. on interior and insular affairs, chmn. subcom. on public lands, com. on judiciary, mem. Democratic steering and policy com. Served to maj. AUS, 1942-46. Mem. Akron Bar Assn. Mem. United Ch. of Christ. Office: 2 S Main St Akron OH 44308 also 1225 Longworth House Office Bldg Washington DC 20515

SEIBERT, DONALD VINCENT, retail chain exec.; b. Hamilton, Ohio, Aug. 17, 1923; s. Carl F. and Minnie L. (Wells) S.; student U. Cin., 1942, D.C.S. (hon.), 1975; LL.D. (hon.), Nyack Coll., 1974; m. Verna S. Stone, Aug. 24, 1945. Store ops. J. C. Penney Co., Inc., N.Y.C., 1947-56, store mgr., 1957-58, dist. mgr., 1959-62, corporate exec., 1963-73, chmn., chief exec. officer, 1974—; dir. Continental Group Inc., Citicorp/Citibank, Sperry-Rand Corp. Bd. dirs. United Way Am.; trustee Nyack Coll.; chmn. bd. advisors to dean Coll. Bus. Adminstrn., U. Cin. Served with USAAF, 1942-46. Mem. Nat. Retail Mchts. Assn. (chmn. exec. com.), Bus. Council, Bus. Roundtable (policy com.), N.Y. Chamber Commerce and Industry (dir.), Econ. Devel. Council of N.Y.C. (dir.), Nat. Minority Purchasing Council (dir.), Catalyst (chmn.). Mem. Christian and Missionary Alliance. Club: Econ. (N.Y.C.). Office: 1301 Ave of Americas New York City NY 10019

SEIBERT, RUSSELL JACOB, botanist; b. Shiloh Valley, Ill., Aug. 14, 1914; s. Erwin W. and Helen A. (Renner) S.; A.B., Washington U., St. Louis, 1937, M.S., 1938, Ph.D., 1947; m. Isabelle L. Pring, Dec. 26, 1942; children—Michael, Donna, Lisa. With U.S. Dept. Agr., 1940-50, botanist-geneticist, Haiti, 1941-42, Peru, 1943-46, Costa Rica, 1947-49; dir. Los Angeles State and County Arboretum, Arcadia, Calif., 1950-55, Longwood Gardens, Kennett Square, Pa., 1955-79; curator tropical horticulture Marie Selby Bot. Garden, Sarasota, Fla., 1979—; adj. prof. bot. garden mgmt. U. Del., 1967-79; head dept. arboreta and bot. gardens Los Angeles County, 1952-55. Am. del. Internat. Soc. Hort. Sci., 1960-70; chmn. Am. Hort. Council-U.S.A. hort. exhbn., 1960 floriade, Rotterdam, Holland; v.p. XVII Internat. Hort. Congress, 1966; chmn. Am. Hort. Film Festival, 1964-69. Recipient Frank N. Meyer Meml. medal Am. Genetic Soc., 1966, Arthur Hoyt Scott Garden and Horticulture medal Swarthmore Coll., 1975, Distinguished Service award Hort. Soc. N.Y., 1969. Mem. Am. Hort. Soc. (pres. 1964-65, Liberty Hyde Bailey medal 1975), AAAS, Am. Inst. Biol. Scis., Sigma Xi, Phi Sigma, Gamma Sigma Delta. Rotarian. Home: 1613 Caribbean Dr Sarasota FL 33581 Office: Marie Selby Botanical Garden Sarasota FL 33577

SEIBERT, WILSON ADRIANCE, JR., advt. exec.; b. Bklyn., May 2, 1927; s. Wilson Adriance and Helen (Martens) S.; B.A., Wesleyan U., 1950; M.A., U. Wis., 1951; m. Susan C. Hughes, Sept. 27, 1952; children—Dena, Sara, Susan, Andrew. With J. Walter Thompson Co., N.Y.C., 1951—, v.p., 1960-65, creative supr., 1965-67, sr. v.p., 1967—, exec. creative dir., 1978—; dir. Lane Bryant, Inc., 1978—. Nat. chmn. Wesleyan U. Alumni Fund, 1971-73; mem. Mayor's Expert Com. on Health, N.Y.C.; bd. dirs. Am. Lung Assn. Served with USNR, 1943-45. Mem. Skull and Serpent Soc., Teatown Soc. (dir.), N.Y. Advt. Club, Delta Kappa Epsilon. Presbyterian (elder). Clubs: Yale, Meeting, Inc. (pres. 1967) (N.Y.C.). Home: Quakerbridge Rd Croton-on-Hudson NY 10520 Office: 420 Lexington Ave New York City NY 10017

SEIBOLD, FREDERICK CARL, JR., oil co. exec.; b. Madison, Wis., May 5, 1927; s. Frederick Carl and Florence (Corsaw) S.; A.B., U. Wis., 1949, LL.B., 1956; A.M., Harvard, 1956; m. Eleanor Stoddard, May 25, 1957; children—Mark S., Emilia. Admitted to N.Y. bar, 1956; with firm Sullivan & Cromwell, N.Y.C., 1956-65; with Mobil Corp., 1965—, sr. asst. treas., 1972—. Trustee Allen-Stevenson Sch. Served with USNR, 1945-46, 52-53. Mem. Am. Mgmt. Assn. (internat. council), Am., N.Y., Wis. bar assns., Am. Soc. Internat. Law, Japan Soc., Council Fgn. Relations, Phi Beta Kappa, Phi Kappa Phi. Home: 434 E 87th St New York City NY 10028 Office: 150 E 42d St New York City NY 10017

SEIBOLD, MARTIN, hotel exec.; b. Vilseck, Germany, May 22, 1926; s. Andreas and Anna S.; came to U.S., 1959; student Interpreter Sch. Ratisbona, Regensburg, Bavaria, 1948, Hotel Sch. Bad Reichenhall (W. Ger.), 1951; B.A., Ednl. Inst. of Am. Hotel-Motel Assn., Columbia U., 1974; m. Clara Samayoa, May 22, 1960; children—Vivian, Andres. Asst. mgr. food and beverage Hotel Inter-Continental, Ponce, P.R., 1966, exec. asst. mgr., 1967; exec. asst. mgr. Hotel Tequendama, Bogota, Colombia, 1968-69; gen. mgr. Hotel El Prado Inter-Continental, Barranquilla, Colombia, 1969-71; gen. mgr. Inter-Continental Medellin (Colombia), 1971-73, Hotel Ivoire Inter-Continental, Abidjan, Ivory Coast, 1973-76, Rose Hall Inter-Continental Hotel and Country Club, Montego Bay, Jamaica, 1976-78; gen. mgr. Hotel Inter-Continental Miami (Fla.) and regional dir. ops. Inter-Continental Hotels-Jamaica, 1978—; mem. adv. bd. City of Miami. Decorated officer Nat. Order (Ivory Coast); gt. officer Order of Temple; comdr. Order St. Eugene de Trebizone. Mem. Greater Miami C. of C. (trustee), Greater Miami Hotel and Motel Assn. (dir.), Fla. Hotel and Motel Assn., Internat. Food Service Execs. Assn., Internat. Hotel Sales Mgmt. Execs. Assn., Confrerie de la Chaine des Rotisseurs (officer Maitre de Table), Vereinigung Ehemaliger Hotel Fachschuler Bad Reichenhall, Am. Soc. Travel Agts. (allied). Clubs: Calusa Country; Bankers, Skal (Miami). Home and Office: Hotel Inter-Continental Miami 801 S Bayshore Dr Miami FL 33131

SEID, HERMAN, lawyer; b. Bklyn., Aug. 14, 1902; s. Joseph and Ida (Niedelmann) S.; student Stevens Inst. Tech., 1918-21; LL.B., Bklyn. Law Sch., 1924; children—John, Richard. Admitted to bars N.Y., Pa., Supreme Ct. U.S.; practice corporate, patent and internat. law. Counsel Carrier Corp., Syracuse, N.Y., 1929—, Aerofin Corp., Lynchburg, Va., 1935—, also cos. in Europe, Japan, S.Am.; pres. River Co. Del.; chmn. SEID Internat. S.A., Brussels; SEID Internat. A/S Denmark. Bd. dirs. Northeastern (Dental) Dispensary, N.Y. Vice pres. Assn. Bds. Edn. of Conn., 1942-47; pres. Met. Com. for Religious Liberty, N.Y., 1951-53; deacon Unitarian Ch. All Souls, N.Y.C.; chmn. East Side Forum, N.Y., 1953-56. Mem. N.A.M. (patents com., spl. rep. India and Caracas), Am. Soc. Corporate Secs. (chmn. stock exchange com. 1960), Internat. Assn. for Protection Indsl. Property, Am., N.Y. Patent Law Assn. (chmn. fgn. patents com. 1967), Am. Patent Law Assn. Unitarian. Mason. Clubs: Squadron A, Talk (N.Y.C.); Pettipaug Yacht (Essex); Black Hall (Old Lyme, Conn.). Contbr. legal jours. Home: River Rd Essex CT 06426 also Sanibel FL 33957 Office: 1075 Park Ave New York NY 10028. *Courage to disagree with a client may in the short run threaten a lawyer's pocketbook, but in the long run it builds a sound reputation with commensurate monetary reward.*

SEID, RICHARD, univ. adminstr., lawyer; b. N.Y.C., Dec. 7, 1933; s. Benjamin and Augusta (Lerner) S.; B.A., U. Mich., 1955; LL.B., N.Y. U., 1959; m. Florence Murray Harvey, Aug. 24, 1971; children—Jerome, Leonora. Admitted to N.Y. bar, 1960, Mass. bar, 1968, Mich. bar, 1973; legal asst. Atty. Gen. State of N.Y., 1959-60; practiced law, Glen Cove, N.Y., N.Y.C., Boston and Detroit, 1961-66; OEO atty. in charge Long Beach office Nassau County (N.Y.) Law Services, 1966-68; OEO sr. atty. Boston Legal Assistance Project, 1968-70; OEO asso. gen. counsel, dir. ops for community action Legal Services Agy. for N.Y.C., 1970-72; asst. prof. law U. Detroit, 1972-74, asso. prof., 1975-77, acting dean Law Sch., 1975-76, dean, prof., 1977—; bd. dirs. Legis. Commn. on Cts. Mem. Nat. Legal Aid and Defenders Assn., Am. Bar Assn., Detroit Bar Assn., State Bar Mich., Am. Judicature Soc. Jewish. Home: 19494 Suffolk St Detroit MI 48203 Office: 651 E Jefferson Ave Detroit MI 48226

SEID, RUTH (JO SINCLAIR, PSEUDONYM), author; b. Bklyn., July 1, 1913; d. Nathan and Ida Seid; grad. John Hay High Sch., Cleve. Various clerical jobs, publicity work, 1943-46; asst. dir. publicity dept. Greater Cleve. chpt. A.R.C., 1945-46. Author: Wasteland, 1946; Sing at My Wake, 1951; The Long Moment (play), 1951; The Changelings, 1955; Anna Teller, 1960. Short stories anthologies: Theme and Variation in the Short Story, 1938; Of the People, 1942; America in Literature, 1944; This Way to Unity, 1945; Social Insight Through Short Stories, 1946; Cross Section, 1947; This Land, These People, 1950. Contbr. short story to anthologies A Treasury of American Jewish Stories, 1958; The American Judaism Reader, 1967; Tales of Our People, 1969. Contbr. mags. including American Judaism, Esquire, Coronet, Glamour, Harper's, Sat. Eve. Post, Cosmopolitan, American, Liberty, Readers Digest. Recipient Harper's Prize novel award, 1946; 2d prize nat. TV competition Fund for Republic, 1956; Ann. Fiction award Jewish Book Council Am., 1956; ann. award Ohioana Library, 1956, 61; Brotherhood Week certificate of recognition NCCJ, 1956; Lit. award Cleve. Arts prize, 1961; Wolpaw Play Writing grant Jewish Community Centers, Cleve., 1969. Mem. Authors League Am., P.E.N. Jo Sinclair collection in Mugar Meml. Library, Boston U. Home: 1021 Wellington Rd Jenkintown PA 19046

SEIDEL, ARTHUR HARRIS, lawyer; b. N.Y.C., May 25, 1923; s. Philip and Pearl (Geller) S.; B.S., CCNY, 1942; A.M., U. Mich., 1943; J.D. with honors, George Washington U., 1949; m. Raquel Eliovich, Aug. 21, 1949; children—Stephen A., Paul B., Mary Beth. Admitted to D.C. bar, 1949, Pa. bar, 1956, N.Y. bar, 1955; atty. patent dept. Gulf Oil Corp., Washington and Pitts., 1947-52; individual practice law, 1952-64; sr. partner firm Seidel & Gonda, 1964-78; pres. firm Seidel, Gonda, Goldhammer & Panitch, P.C., Phila., 1978—; lectr. in intellectual property Temple U., 1973—, Am. Law Inst. Mem. Am. Bar Assn., Pa. Bar Assn., Phila. Bar Assn., Am. Patent Law Assn. Editor George Washington Law Rev., 1949; author: (with others) Trademark Practice, 2 vols., 1963; Monographs on Patent Law and Practice, 3d edit., 1976; Trademarks and Copyrights, 3d edit., 1976; (with Ronald L. Panitch) Trade Secrets and Employment Agreements, 1973; also articles. Home: 904 Centennial Rd Narberth PA 19072 Office: 600 Three Penn Center Plaza Philadelphia PA 19102. *My entire professional career has been devoted to the question of innovation, patents for inventions, trademarks for new businesses and copyrights for new writings. I have seen the United States go from the world's leader in technology and business to the lesser role which it occupies today.*

SEIDEN, HENRY, advt. agy. exec.; b. Bklyn., Sept. 6, 1928; s. Jack S. and Shirley (Berkowitz) S.; B.A., Bklyn. Coll., 1949; M.B.A., Coll. City N.Y., 1954; m. Helena Ruth Zaldin, Sept. 10, 1949; children—Laurie Ann, Matthew Ian. Trainee, Ben Sackheim Advt. Agy., 1949-51; nat. promotion mgr. N.Y. Post Corp., 1951-53; promotion mgr. Crowell-Collier Pub. Co., Inc., 1953-54; copy group head Batten, Barton, Durstine & Osborn, Inc., 1954-60; v.p., creative dir. Keyes, Madden & Jones, 1960-61; sr. v.p., asso. creative dir. McCann-Marschalk, Inc., 1961-65, chmn. plans bd., 1964-65; creative dir., dir., prin. Hicks & Greist, Inc., N.Y.C., 1965—, sr. v.p., 1965-74, exec. v.p., 1974—. Guest lectr. Bernard M. Baruch Sch. Bus. and Pub. Adminstrn., Coll. City N.Y., 1962—, Baruch Coll., Coll. City N.Y., 1969—, New Sch. Social Scis., 1968, 72, 73, Sch. Visual Arts, 1979, 80—; cons. pub. relations and communication to mayor of New Rochelle, N.Y., 1959—, also marketing dept. Ohio State U. Cons. to pres. N.Y.C. City Council, 1972-73, to Postmaster Gen. U.S., 1972-74; communications adviser to Police Commr. N.Y.C., 1973—. Vice commr. Little League of New Rochelle. Bd. dirs. Police Res. Assn. N.Y.C., 1973—; bd. dirs., exec. v.p. N.Y.'s Finest Found., 1975—. Recipient award Four Freedoms Found., 1959, Printers Ink, 1960, promotion award Editor and Publisher, 1955, Am. TV Commls. Festival award, 1963-69, Effie award Am. Marketing Assn., 1969, 70, award Art Directors Club N.Y., 1963-70, award Am. Inst. Graphic Arts, 1963, Starch award, 1969; spl. award graphic art lodge B'nai B'rith Greater N.Y., 1971. Mem. A.I.M. (asso.), Nat. Acad. TV Arts and Scis., Advt. Club N.Y. (exec. judge Andy awards; award 1963-65), Advt. Writers Assn. N.Y. (Gold Key award for best newspaper and mag. advts. 1962-64), Copy Club (co-chmn. awards com.; Gold Key award for best TV comml. 1969), Alpha Phi Omega. Author: Advertising Pure and Simple, 1976. Contbg. editor Madison Av. mag., 1966—; guest columnist N.Y. Times, 1972. Home: 12 Winchcombe Way Scarsdale NY 10583 Office: 522 Fifth Ave New York NY 10036. *Be yourself but don't take yourself too seriously.*

SEIDENBAUM, ART DAVID, journalist; b. Bronx, N.Y., May 4, 1930; s. William G. and Lida (Aretsky) S.; B.S., Northwestern U., 1951; postgrad., Harvard U., 1951-52; children—Kyle Scott, Kerry Kai. Reporter, Life mag., N.Y.C., 1955-59, corr., Los Angeles, 1959-61; W. Coast bur. chief, contbg. editor Saturday Evening Post, Los Angeles, 1961-62; columnist Los Angeles Times, 1962-78, editor book review sect., 1978—; moderator City Watcher's KCET ednl. TV. Served to lt. (j.g.) USNR, 1952-55. Contbr. to various popular mags. Office: Los Angeles Times Times Mirror Co Times Mirror Sq Los Angeles CA 90053

SEIDENSTICKER, EDWARD GEORGE, educator; b. Castle Rock, Colo., Feb. 11, 1921; s. Edward George and Mary Elizabeth (Dillon) S.; B.A., U. Colo., 1942; M.A., Columbia U., 1947; postgrad. Harvard U., 1947-48. With U.S. Fgn. Service, Dept. State, Japan, 1947-50; mem. faculty Stanford U., 1962-66, prof., 1964-66; prof. dept. Far Eastern langs. and lit. U. Mich., Ann Arbor, 1966-77; prof. Japanese, Columbia U., 1977—. Served with USMCR, 1942-46. Decorated Order of Rising Sun (Japan); recipient Nat. Book award, 1970; citation Japanese Ministry Edn., 1971. Mem. Am. Oriental Soc., Assn. for Asian Studies. Author: Kafu The Scribbler, 1965; Japan, 1961. Translator: (by Murasaki Shikibu) The Tale of Genji, 1976. Home: 445 Riverside Dr New York NY 10027 Office: 407 Kent Hall Columbia U New York NY 10027. *"Make yourself a routine and stick to it," said my childhood piano teacher when I went off to college. I have never had, as some people seem to have, great plans for my future; but if a person has a serious routine and sticks resolutely with it, something is bound to get accomplished.*

SEIDL, ANTHONY EMANUEL, educator; b. Almont, N.D., Dec. 1, 1919; s. Frank Joseph and Ludmilla Philomena (Braxmeyer) S.; B.A., U. Portland, 1947, M. Ed., 1956; Ph.D., U. Notre Dame, 1964; m. Betty Jean Spieth, Feb. 1, 1945; children—Suzanne Seidl Griffin, Mary Louise Seidl Kinney, Deborah Seidl Sipe. Elizabeth. Bus. mgr., tchr., coach Central Cath. High Sch., Portland, Oreg., 1951-61; tchr. James Lick High Sch., San Jose, Calif., 1961-62; asst. prof. U. Notre Dame, 1964-66; asst. prof., dir. summer session, provost, prof., now prof. emeritus U. San Francisco, 1966—; cons. Acad. Ednl. Devel., 1963—. Bd. dirs. Holy Names Coll. Served with USNR, 1942-46. Author: Management of Resources in Catholic Schools, 1968; Long Range Planning for Catholic Schools, 1969. Contbr. articles to profl. jours. Home: 3348 Terra Linda Dr Santa Rosa CA 95404 Office: 2130 Fulton St San Francisco CA 94117

SEIDL, ROBERT JOSEPH, paper co. exec.; b. Menominee, Mich., Aug. 15, 1915; s. Michael Gabriel and Mary Catherine (Maihafer) S.; B.S. in Chem. Engring., U. Wis., 1940; m. Gwen Bryce, Dec. 7, 1941; children—Lynn Elizabeth, Robert Bryce, David Richard. Chem. engr. Jos. E. Seagram Co., Louisville, 1940-41; chief chemist Merrimac Paper Co., Lawrence, Mass., 1940-41; asst. chief pulp and paper div. Forest Products Lab., U.S. Forest Service, Madison, Wis., 1941-57; dir. research, mgr. Chems. div., v.p. research Simpson Timber Co., Seattle, 1957-73; v.p., mgr. mfg., pres., dir. Simpson Paper Co., San Francisco, 1973—. Mem. adv. bd. U. Wash., Wash. State U. Fellow TAPPI (past dir., chmn. publs. com.); mem. Forest Products Research Soc. (past dir.). Club: Wash. Athletic. Contbr. articles on forest products to profl. jours. Home: 2200 Pacific Ave San Francisco CA 94115 Office: 1 Post St San Francisco CA 94104

SEIDLER, DORIS, artist; b. London, Nov. 26, 1912; m. Bernard Seidler, Sept. 5, 1935; 1 son, David. Exhbns. include: Bkyn. Mus. Bi-Ann., Vancouver Internat. Print Exhbns., Honolulu Acad. Arts, Pa. Acad. Fine Arts, Phila., Soc. Am. Graphic Artists, Associated Am. Artists Gallery, 1971, Jewish Mus., N.Y.C., Bklyn. Mus., 1978; represented in permanent collections: Library of Congress, Smithsonian Inst., Washington, Phila. Mus. Art, Bklyn. Mus., Seattle Mus. Art. Mem. Soc. Am. Graphic Artists (rec. sec. 1964-71), Artists Equity. Address: 14 Stoner Ave Great Neck NY 11021

SEIDLER, I. MARSHALL, lawyer; b. Balt., Dec. 23, 1934; s. Joseph and Celia (Klayman) S.; B.S., U. Md., 1958, J.D., 1959; m. Leah Eve Gaponoff, Dec. 19, 1959; children—Samuel, Adam, Shari. Admitted to Md. bar, 1959, Md. Ct. Appeals bar, U.S. Dist. Ct. Md., U.S. Ct. Appeals for 4th circuit, U.S. Supreme Ct. bar; atty. Legal Aid Bur., Balt., 1959-60; practice law, Balt., 1960—; partner firm Eccleston, Seidler & Miller, Balt., 1967—. Vice pres. Fallstaff Middle Sch., Balt., 1973-75; pres. Wellwood Little League, Balt., 1974; treas. Pikesville Sr. High Sch. Parent-Tchr.-Student Assn., 1979—. Recipient Safety award Gov. Md., 1960. Mem. Am. Bar Assn., Md. Bar Assn., Balt. City Bar Assn., Cheswolde Neighborhood Assn. (v.p. 1971-74). Home: 3407 Janellen Dr Pikesville MD 21208 Office: 110 E Lexington St Baltimore MD 21202

SEIDLIN, JOSEPH, educator; b. Pavlograd, Russia, May 23, 1892; s. Moses and Katherine (Smith) S.; B.S., Columbia, 1915, A.M., 1916, Ph.D., 1931; D.Sc., Alfred U., 1965; m. Ada Becker, Dec. 22, 1917; 1 son, John Woodrow. Instr. math. and sci. Rhodes Sch., N.Y.C., 1915-17, chmn. dept., 1917-18; head dept. math. Lincoln Sch., 1919-20; asso. prof. Alfred U., 1920-24, prof. math., 1924-37, chmn. dept. edn., dir. tchr. edn., 1937-65, dir. grad. div., 1938, dean Grad. Sch., 1947-62, acting dean Coll. Liberal Arts, 1959-60; established Central Inst. Math., U. Concepción (Chile), summer 1959; teaching cons. State U. N.Y., Agrl. and Tech. Coll., Alfred, 1966—; cons. Am. Assn. Jr. Colls., 1969—. Seidlin Hall at Alfred U. named in his honor, 1974. Fellow A.A.A.S.; mem. N.E.A., Assn. Sch. Adminstrs., A.A.U.P., Math. Soc., Math. Assn., Council Tchrs. Maths., Nat. Inst. Tchr. Placement Assn. (past pres.), Sigma Xi, Pi Gamma Mu, Phi Delta Kappa; hon. mem. Eastern Assn. Deans. Author: A Brief Course in Elementary Mathematics for College Students, 1926; A Critical Study of the Teaching of College Mathematics, 1931; (with Freilich and Shanholt) Spherical Trigonometry, 1943. Asso. editor Mathematics mag., 1934-62. Contbr. numerous articles to profl. jours. Home: 37 S Main St Alfred NY 14802

SEIDLIN, OSKAR, educator, author; b. Koenigshuette, Feb. 17, 1911; s. Heinrich and Johanna (Seidler) Koplowitz; student univs. Freiburg, Berlin and Frankfurt/Main, 1929-33; Ph.D. summa cum laude, U. Basel (Switzerland), 1935; postgrad. U. Lausanne (Switzerland), 1935-38; D.H.L., U. Mich., 1969. Came to U.S., 1938, naturalized, 1942. Asst. prof. Smith Coll., 1939-46; mem. faculty Ohio State U., Columbus, 1946-72, prof. German lit., 1950-66, Regents prof., 1966-72; prof. German lit. Ind. U., Bloomington, 1972-74, Distinguished Service prof., 1974—. Vis. prof. German Summer Sch., Middlebury (Vt.) Coll., U. Wash., 1949; lectr. Am., Swiss and W. German univs., 1954—; guest Fed. Republic Germany, 1956; Ford prof. in residence Free U. Berlin, 1959. Served to 2d lt. AUS, 1942-46. Recipient Distinguished Teaching award Ohio State U., 1960, Eichendorff medal Eichendorff Mus., Wangen, 1961; Golden Goethe medal Goethe Inst., Munich, Germany, 1963; named Tchr. of Year, Ohio State U., 1967; recipient prize for Germanic studies abroad German Acad. Lang. and Lit., 1968; Wisdom award of honor, 1970, Eichendorff medal Eichendorff Soc., Würzburg, 1974, Kulturpreis, Nordrhein Westfalen, 1975. Guggenheim fellow, 1963, 77. Mem. Akademie der Wissenschaften (Göttingen), Modern Lang. Assn. (1st v.p. 1965), Am. Assn. Tchrs. German, Internat. Humanities Research Assn., Internat. Germanisten Verband, Internat. Kleist Gesellschaft, Freies Deutsches Hochstift, Phi Beta Kappa (chpt. pres. 1965). Author: Essays in German and Comparative Literature, 2d edit., 1966; An Outline History of German Literature (with others), 1950; Von Goethe zu Thomas Mann, 2d edit, 1969; Versuche ueber Eichendorff, 1965, 2d edit., 1978; Klassische und moderne Klassiker, 1972; Der Briefwechsel Arthur Schnitzler-Otto Brahm, 1975; Der Theaterkritiker Otto Brahm, 1978; Von erwachendem Bewusstein und vom Sündenfall, 1979; also numerous articles. Co-editor jour. Arcadia, 1966-73, German Quar., 1972-77, Mich. Germanic Studies, 1975—, Festschrift: Herkommen und Erneuerung, Essays für Oskar Seidlin, 1976. Office: German Dept Indiana U Bloomington IN 47401

SEIDLITZ, GEORGE RICHARDS, chem. co. exec.; b. Kansas City, Jan. 25, 1918; s. Charles N. and Alice (Richards) S.; A.B., Cornell U., 1939; m. Amelia Brown, Apr. 19, 1941; children—Alison, Courtenay, Katharine. With Seidlitz Paint & Varnish Co., Kansas City, 1938-60, pres., 1954-60; pres. ConChemCo., Inc., Kansas City, 1960-70, dir., chmn. bd., 1970-71; pres., dir. Napko Corp., Fremont, Calif., 1971—; sr. v.p., dir. Napko Corp., Houston, 1971—. Served to lt. comdr. USNR, 1940-46. Decorated Bronze Star medal with cluster. Home: 18 Rinconada Circle Belmont CA 94002 Office: PO Box 1910 Fremont CA 94538

SEIDMAN, BERT, union ofcl.; b. N.Y.C., Sept. 22, 1919; s. Nathan H. and Jeannette S. (Kaplan) S.; B.A., U. Wis., 1938; M.A., 1941; m. Annabel Henry, Apr. 16, 1948; children—Margaret, Joan, Elizabeth. With AFL-CIO, Washington, 1948—, European econ. rep., 1962-66, dir. dept. social security, 1966—. Mem. U.S. worker del. ILO, 1958-75, bd. govs., 1972-75; mem. Fed. Hosp. Council, 1968-70, Fed. Adv. Council Employment Security, 1969-71, Adv. Council on Social Security, 1969-71, 78-79, Health Ins. Benefits Adv. Council, 1970-76, Task Force on Skilled Nursing Homes, 1969, adv. council Employee Retirement Income Security Act of 1974, 1975—, Nat. Commn. on Unemployment Compensation. Pres. Fairfax County Com. Human Relations, 1959-62, 70, No. Va. Fair Housing, 1967-70; mem. Fairfax County Health Care Adv. Bd. Trustee Group Health Assn., 1970—. Mem. Indsl. Relations Research Assn. (trustee 1970-73). Home: 6200 Wilson Blvd Falls Church VA 22044 Office: 815 16th St NW Washington DC 20006

SEIDMAN, HAROLD, educator; b. Bklyn., July 2, 1911; s. Joseph A. and Rebecca J. (Duchowney) S.; A.B. summa cum laude, Brown U., 1934, A.M., 1935; Ph.D., Yale, 1940. Dir. div. coordination, research N.Y.C. Dept. Investigation, 1938-43; with U.S. Bur. Budget, Washington, 1943-68, asst. dir. mgmt. and orgn., 1964-68; scholar-in-residence Nat. Acad. Pub. Adminstrn., Washington, 1968-71; research fellow Leeds U., 1971; vis. prof. polit. sci. U. Conn., 1971-72, prof., 1973—. Mem. Commn. Application Fed. Laws to Guam, 1950-51; mem. Adminstrv. Conf. U.S., 1961-62; lectr. George Washington U., 1953, U. So. Calif., 1962; cons. Colombia, 1950, UN, 1953, 59, 66, Guatemala 1957, Turkey, 1961, P.R., 1970, Econ. Com. for Africa, 1969, Panama Canal, 1975, Iran, 1977-78; vis. prof. Syracuse (N.Y.) U., 1969; vis. prof. politics U. Leeds (Eng.), 1972-75; fed. coordinator Alaska and Hawaii transitions to statehood; cons. senate com. on govt. OPS, 1973. Ford Found. grantee. Mem. Am. Soc. Pub. Adminstrn., Am. Polit. Sci. Assn., Nat. Acad. Pub. Adminstrn., Phi Beta Kappa. Club: Cosmos (Washington). Author: Politics, Position and Power, 3d edit., 1980. Contbr. to Ency. Brit., 1959; also articles. Home: Dept Polit Sci Univ Conn Storrs CT 06268

SEIDMAN, JACOB STEWART, accountant; b. N.Y.C., Sept. 8, 1901; s. Louis and Fanny (Goldfarb) S.; B.C.S. magna cum laude, N.Y. U., 1921, B.S. cum laude, 1928; J.D. cum laude, Fordham U., 1924; LL.M. cum laude, St. Lawrence U., 1925; m. Jan Sherman, Dec. 29, 1950. Founding partner Seidman & Seidman, C.P.A.'s, 1921-41, 45—. Del. N.Y. State to Nat. Tax Assn. convs., 1926-29; accounting cons. appropriations com. U.S. Ho. Reps., 1948, 50; mem. exec. com. N.Y. Bd. Trade, 1957—; adv. com. comptroller N.Y. State, 1956-59; acad. council Advanced Tng. Center of Internal Revenue Service, 1952-54; mem. accounting task force Hoover Commn., 1953; former chmn. Council Accountancy State U. N.Y.; head U.S. exchange mission on accountancy to Soviet Union; counsultor taxation adv. bd. Pace Coll.; mem. adv. council Joint Legislative Com. on N.Y. State's Commerce, Econ. Devel. and Tourism; mem. N.Y. State Atty. Gen.'s Adv. Com. on Theatrical Financing and Practices; chmn. com. on econs. Bd. Standards and Planning for Living Theatre. Treas., trustee Am. Acad. Dramatic Arts; bd. dirs. Nat. Parkinson Found., New Dramatists Com., Albert Gallatin Asso. of N.Y. U.; life trustee N.Y. U.; trustee Hosp. Joint Diseases; vice chmn. disaster relief com. N.Y.C. chpt. A.R.C., 1948; adv. com., law com. Fedn. Jewish Philanthropies. Served from lt. comdr. to capt., USNR, World War II. Recipient John T. Madden meml. award N.Y.U., 1955; named hon. fellow in accounting L.I. U., 1956; recipient award for outstanding service to advancement of human rights, Joint Def. Appeal, 1956; N.Y. U. Alumni Meritorious Service award, 1962. C.P.A., N.Y. State. Mem. Am. Inst. C.P.A.'s (pres. 1959-60; chmn. tax com., mem. council, exec. com.; named Accountant of Year 1956, past mem. accounting prins. bd.), N.Y. State Soc. C.P.A.'s (past pres.; award of the year 1956), Soc. Bus. Adv. Professions, Am. Accounting Assn., Nat. Assn. Cost Accountants, Nat. Security Indsl. Assn., N.Y. U. Commerce Alumni Fedn. (pres.), N.Y. Alumni Fedn. (exec. com.), N.Y. U. Finance Club (pres. 1961), Navy League U.S., ANTA (dir. Greater New York chpt.), Alpha Epsilon Pi, Beta Gamma Sigma (dir.; hon.), Alpha Beta Psi (hon.), Delta Mu Delta (hon.), Sphinx Club, Arch and Square. Clubs: Economic, Accountants (N.Y.C.). Author: Seidman's Legislative History; Federal Income and Excess Profits Tax Laws, 4 vols. Contbr. newspapers, profl. jours., theatrical mags. Tax columnist N.Y. Herald Tribune, 1936-57; tax contbr. N.Y. Times, 1959—. Home: 2 E 67th St New York NY 10021 Office: 15 Columbus Circle New York NY 10023

SEIDMAN, LEWIS WILLIAM, mfg. co. exec.; b. Grand Rapids, Mich., Apr. 29, 1921; s. Frank E. and Esther (Lubetsky) S.; A.B., Dartmouth Coll., 1943; LL.B., Harvard U., 1948; M.B.A., U. Mich., 1949; m. Sarah Berry, Mar. 3, 1944; children—Thomas, Tracy, Sarah, Carrie, Meg, Robin. Spl. asst. fin. affairs to gov. of Mich., 1963-66; nat. mng. partner Seidman & Seidman, C.P.A.'s, N.Y.C., 1969-74; asst. for econ. affairs to Pres. Gerald R. Ford, 1974-77; sr. v.p., dir. Phelps Dodge Corp., N.Y.C., 1977—; dir. Gt. Sky Land & Devel. Co., Am. Seating Co.; chmn. Detroit br. Fed. Res. Bank Chgo., 1970; spl. adv. Aspen Inst.; mem. bd. fgn. scholars Dept. State. Nat. chmn., trustee Youth for Understanding, 1973-75. Served to lt. USNR, 1942-46. Decorated Bronze Star. Mem. Am. Instn. C.P.A.'s, Mich. Bar Assn., D.C. Bar Assn. Clubs: Chevy Chase (Md.); Univ. (N.Y.C. and Washington). Admitted to Mich. bar, 1949, D.C. bar, 1977. Home: 8 E 67th St New York NY 10021 Office: 300 Park Ave New York NY 10022

SEIDNER, FREDERIC JAY, pub. relations co. exec.; b. Chgo., Mar. 4, 1931; s. Leo and Jewel (Sachs) S.; B.J., U. Mo., 1953; m. Eloise Ann Albert, Dec. 26, 1960; children—Allen P., Cary D., Loren A. Editorial writer pub. relations dept. Ill. Bell Telephone Co., 1956-57; with Pub. Relations Bd., Inc., Chgo., 1957—, exec. v.p., 1969—. Mem. Chgo. area council Boy Scouts Am., 1958-66, North Shore council, 1967-77; mem. adv. bd. Evanston Theatre Co., 1976—; bd. dirs. Mt. Sinai Hosp. Med. Center, Chgo., 1961-77. Served to 1st lt. USAF, 1954-56. Mem. Pub. Relations Soc. Am., Sigma Delta Chi. Home: 1116 Mulford St Evanston IL 60202 Office: 150 E Huron St Chicago IL 60611

SEIFERHELD, DAVID FROEHLICH, textile co. cons.; b. N.Y.C., Sept. 20, 1904; s. Sigmund and Gertrude (Froehlich) S.; B.A., Yale, 1926; m. Elizabeth S. Deutsch, Oct. 28, 1929; 1 son, James D.; m. 2d, Helene Danforth Coler Jackson, Aug. 19, 1955; m. 3d, Jeanne Lucienne Longuet, Oct. 13, 1964. With N. Erlanger, Blumgart & Co., Inc., 1926—, dir., 1932—, v.p., 1937-43, pres., 1943-59, chmn. exec. com., 1959-69, now cons. Adviser, cons. NRA, 1933; dir. Youth Builders, Inc., 1939-42; founder, treas. Internat. Coordination Council, 1939; dir., treas. Shortwave Research, Inc., 1940-42; treas., dir. Emergency Rescue Com., 1940-44; dir. Internat. Rescue Com., 1945-59; with OSS, 1942-43; dir. Overseas News Agy., 1944-45; cons. OPA, 1946-47, OPS, 1951. Bd. dirs. Wiltwyck Sch. for Boys, 1960-69. Home: L'Escarel Chemin de Noailles 06130 Grasse France

SEIFERT, GEORGE, educator; b. Jena, Germany, Mar. 4, 1921; s. Max and Frieda (Ranft) S.; came to U.S., 1926, naturalized, 1932; B.A., N.Y. State Coll. Tchrs., 1942; M.A., Cornell U., 1948, Ph.D., 1950; m. Bertha E. Scheffel, Feb. 5, 1948; children—Curt, Edward. Asst. prof. U. Nebr., 1950-55; asst. prof. Iowa State U., Ames, 1955-56, asso. prof., 1956-62, prof. math., 1962—, acting chmn. dept., 1964-66; research Inst. Applied Scis., Balt., 1959-60; faculty improvement leave Brown U., 1970. Served with USNR, 1943-46. Mem. Am. Math. Soc., Math. Assn. Am., Soc. for Indsl. and Applied Math., AAUP, Sigma Xi, Phi Kappa Phi. Contbr. articles to profl. jours. Home: 2526 Kellogg Ave Ames IA 50010

SEIFERT, LEE ROE, banker; b. Mobile, Ala., Feb. 13, 1917; s. William Ross and Esther Adele (McAuley) S.; student Spring Hill Coll., 1934-36; m. Dorothy Marie Goodman, July 16, 1942; children—Lee Roe, Gail (Mrs. Mathew J. Dick), William Ross II. With First Nat. Bank Mobile, 1937—, v.p., 1955-68, sr. v.p., 1968-74, exec. v.p., 1974—; dir. Oppenheimer Intercontinental Corp., Panama. Hon. consul, Republic of Korea, 1972—; chmn. Consular Corps of Mobile. Mem. cons. com. on forestry research Auburn U., 1963—; mem. adv. bd. Coll. Bus., U. Montevallo (Ala.); pres. Mobile Port Traffic Rate Bur., 1968-72, bd. dirs., 1968—. Served to 2d lt. USAAF, 1942-45. Mem. Regional (chmn. 1969-74) Export Expansion Council, Mobile Area C. of C., Internat. Trade Club (pres. 1972-74, dir. 1966—), Bankers' Assn. Fgn. Trade (sec. 1964-65, dir. 1965-67), Mobile Traffic and Transp. Club, World Trade Club Greater New Orleans, Internat. House of New Orleans, Ala. World Trade Assn. (dir. 1977—). Episcopalian. Clubs: Propeller of United States, Touchdown, Bienville, Athelstan, Country (Mobile). Home: PO Box 283 Point Clear AL 36564 Office: 31 N Royal St PO Box 1467 Mobile AL 36621

SEIFERT, RALPH LOUIS (EDWIN), ret. educator; b. Posey County, Ind., Feb. 4, 1914; s. Daniel Frederick and Elfrieda Caroline (Ehrhardt) S.; A.B., U. Evansville, 1934; M.A., U. Ill., 1935, Ph.D., 1937; m. Catherine Ford Dyer, June 18, 1938; 1 son, Ralph Louis. Instr. U. Ill., 1937-38; instr. to prof. Alma Coll., 1938-44; research chemist Respiration Lab., U. Chgo., summer 1942, Metall. Lab., 1944-46; asso. prof. Carleton Coll., 1946-49; asso. prof. Ind. U., 1949-66, prof. chemistry, 1966-77, prof. emeritus, 1977—; cons. Argonne (Ill.) Nat. Lab., 1946-68, research chemist, summers, 1948, 49, 55. Fellow A.A.A.S.; mem. Am. Chem. Soc., Electrochem. Soc., Chem. Soc., Ind. Acad. Sci., Sigma Xi, Phi Lambda Upsilon, Alpha Chi Sigma. Author: (with F.T. Gucker) Physical Chemistry, 1966. Editorial bd. Jour. Phys. Chemistry, 1968-72. Research thermodynamic and electrochem. properties of substances at high temperatures. Home: 907 S Manor Rd Bloomington IN 47401

SEIFERT, THOMAS LLOYD, lawyer; b. Boston, June 6, 1940; s. Ralph Frederick and Hazel Belle (Harrington) S.; B.S. cum laude, Ind. U., 1962, J.D. cum laude, 1965; m. Ann Cecelia Berg, June 19, 1965. Admitted to Ill. bar, 1965, Ind. bar, 1965, N.Y. State bar, 1979; asso. law firm Keck, Cushman, Mahin & Cate, Chgo., 1965-67; atty. Essex Group, Inc., Ft. Wayne, Ind., 1967-70; atty. Standard Oil Co. (Ind.), Chgo., 1970-73; asso. gen. counsel, asst. sec. Canteen Corp., Chgo., 1973-75; sec., legal counsel The Marmon Group, Inc. and predecessor cos., Chgo., 1975-78; v.p., gen. counsel, sec. Hanson Industries, Inc., N.Y.C., 1978—. Mem. Am. Soc. Corp. Secs., Am. (mem. labor, bus. and anti-trust coms.), N.Y. State, Ill., Chgo. bar assns., Phi Delta Phi, Order of Coif, Beta Gamma Sigma. Note editor Ind. Law Jour., 1964-65. Home: 800 Fifth Ave New York NY 10021 Office: 430 Park Ave New York NY 10022

SEIFERT, WILLIAM WALTHER, educator; b. Troy, N.Y., Feb. 22, 1920; s. Harry Herman and Alice (Turner) S.; B.E.E., Rensselaer Poly. Inst., 1941; M.S., Mass. Inst. Tech., 1947, D.Sc., 1951; m. Sylvia Campbell, Oct. 7, 1943 (dec. Sept. 1949); children—Linda Lee, Charles William; m. 2d, Doris Patterson, May 10, 1950 (dec. June 1979); children—Robert Patterson, Camilla Walther (dec. Aug. 1959), Janet Elder. Instr., Rensselaer Poly. Inst., 1941-44; mem. staff and faculty Mass. Inst. Tech., 1944—, prof. elec. engring., 1965—, asst. dean engring., 1962-68, dir. project transport, 1964-70, asso. dir. Commodity Transp. and Econ. Devel. Lab., 1970-72, prof. engring. and elec. engring., 1968-74, prof. civil engring., 1974-78, sr. lectr. civil engring., 1978—, dir. Sahel-Sudano project, 1973-75; pres. Devel. Analysis Assos., Inc., Cambridge, Mass., 1975—. Mem. IEEE (sr.), Am. Soc. Engring. Edn. Author: (with C.W. Steeg, Jr.) Control Systems Engineering, 1960; (with B.A. Schriever) Air Transportation 1975 and Beyond, 1968; (with M.A. Bakr and M.A. Kettani) Energy and Development: A Case Study, 1973. Editorial adv. bd., chmn. sci. and tech. com. World Book Ency., 1963-69. Home: 7 Longfellow Rd Wellesley Hills MA 02181 Office: 675 Massachusetts Ave Cambridge MA 02139

SEIFERTH, SOLIS, architect; b. New Orleans, Feb. 13, 1895; s. Herman Joshua and Cecelia (Cohen) S.; B.Arch., Tulane U., 1915; m. Helen B. Stern, Feb. 7, 1923; 1 dau., Celia (Mrs. Robert J. Kornfeld). Ind. practice architecture, New Orleans, 1920—; prin. works include La. State Capitol, Baton Rouge, 1930, bldgs. La State U., 1932-59, Southeastern La. Coll., 1934-38, Southwestern La. U., 1935-38, Charity Hosp., New Orleans, 1938, Touro Infirmary, New Orleans, 1938-61, IBM bldg., New Orleans, 1956, also schs., hotels, stores, residences; chief archtl. supr. for La. FHA, 1934-36. Pres. La. Bd. Archtl. Examiners, 1930-38; pres. Nat. Council Archtl. Registration Bds., 1945-48; chmn. zoning and major st. plan-coms. New Orleans City Planning and Zoning Commn., 1923-30; mem. New Orleans Vieux Carre Commn., 1966-72. Pres. New Orleans Cultural Centre Commn., 1961-71; pres. Jewish Children's Home, New Orleans, 1950-58, trustee trust funds, 1960—; sec., trustee Newman Sch., New Orleans, 1940-60; trustee F.P. Keyes Found., 1970—; bd. dirs. Friends Tulane U. Library. Served to capt. U.S. Army, 1917-19; to maj. AUS, 1942-45. Fellow A.I.A. (pres. New Orleans 1928-30, 58-60, Faget award 1973); mem. Am. Geog. Soc., Soc. Archtl. Historians, La. Architects Assn., La. Landmarks Soc. (dir.), Nat. Trust Historic Preservation, La. Engring. Soc., La. Hist. Soc., La. Hist. Assn. Home: 1838 Jefferson Ave New Orleans LA 70115

SEIFRIED, DEAN BARDON, utility exec.; b. Clarkstown, N.Y., May 10, 1914; s. Harold Edward and Sophie Madeline (Bardon) S.; B.S. in Elec. Engring., Cooper Union, 1936, M.S., 1968; m. Janet M. Blauvelt, Apr. 4, 1942; children—Linda L., Wendy A., Bruce B. From cadet engr. to chief engr. Rockland Gas Co., Spring Valley, N.Y., 1937-52; with Orange and Rockland Utilities, Inc., and predecessor, Spring Valley, 1952—, exec. v.p., 1969-70, pres., 1970—, chief exec. officer, 1976—, also of subsidiaries; trustee Savs. Bank Rockland County; dir. Bankers Trust Hudson Valley, Palisades Geophys. Research Inst., N.Y. Power Pool. Pres. Clarkstown Central Schs., 1949-63. Registered profl. engr., N.Y., N.J., N.H. Republican. Clubs: University (N.Y.C.); Tuxedo Park (N.Y.). Home: 77 Circuit Rd Tuxedo Park NY 10987 Office: 1 Blue Hill Plaza Pearl River NY 10965

SEIGEL, STUART EVAN, lawyer; b. N.Y.C., Mar. 25, 1933; s. Philip Herman and Betty Sarah (Leventhal) S.; B.S., N.Y. U., 1953; LL.B., N.Y. U., 1957; LL.M. in Taxation, Georgetown U., 1960; m. Joyce Roberta Meyers, Aug. 11, 1957; children—Charles Meyers, Lee Bennett, Suzanne Marcie. Admitted to N.Y. bar, 1958, D.C. bar, 1958; atty. Office Chief Counsel, IRS, Washington, 1957-65; atty. Office Tax Legis. Counsel, Dept. Treasury, Washington, 1965-69, asso. tax legis. counsel, 1968-69; partner firm Cohen and Uretz, Washington, 1969-77; chief counsel IRS, Washington, 1977-79; partner firm Williams and Connolly, Washington, 1979—; lectr. George Washington U. Sch. Law, 1970-73; adj. prof. law Antioch Sch. Law, 1973-76. Mem. Am. Bar Assn., Fed. Bar Assn., Am. Judicature Soc. Club: Federal City (Washington). Office: 839 17th St NW Washington DC 20006

SEIGENTHALER, JOHN LAWRENCE, newspaper publisher; b. Nashville, July 27, 1927; s. John and Mary (Brew) S.; student Peabody Coll.; Nieman fellow, Harvard; m. Dolores Watson, Jan. 3, 1955; 1 son, John Michael. Staff corr. Nashville Tennessean, 1949-60, editor, 1962-72, pub., 1973—, pres., 1979—; adminstv. asst. to atty. gen. U.S., 1961; dir. Tennessean Newspapers, Inc.; dir. German-Marshall Fund, 1978—. Mem. U.S. Adv. Commn. Information, 1962-64, Pres.'s Jud. Nominating Commn., 1978-79. Mem. Am. Soc. Newspaper Editors, Sigma Delta Chi. Home: Vaughn Rd Route 5 Nashville TN 37215 Office: 1100 Broadway Nashville TN 37202

SEIGLE, JOHN WILLIAM, army officer; b. Cin., May 21, 1929; s. Harry and Cordelia Love (Nicholson) S.; B.S., U.S. Mil. Acad., 1953; M.P.A., Harvard U., 1960, Ph.D., 1967; m. Marilyn Anne Johnson, July 15, 1955; children—Sally, John, Gregory. Commd. 2d lt. U.S. Army, 1953, advanced through grades to maj. gen., 1977; coordinator Army Studies, Washington, 1969-71; pres. Combat Arms Tng. Bd., 1972-73; comdr. 2d armored cav. regt., Germany, 1973-74, dep. def. adv. U.S. Mission to NATO, Brussels, 1975-77; dep. chief of staff for tng. Hdqrs. U.S. Army Tng. and Doctrine Command, Fort Monroe, Va., 1977—; asst. prof. social scis. U.S. Mil. Acad., 1961-65. Decorated Silver Star, Legion of Merit, D.F.C., Bronze Star, Purple Heart. Mem. Council Fgn. Relations, Internat. Inst. Strategic Studies. Home: 37 Fenwick Rd Fort Monroe VA 23651 Office: Dep Chief of Staff for Tng US Army Tng and Doctrine Command Fort Monroe VA 23651

SEIGNIOUS, GEORGE MARION, II, govt. ofcl., former coll. pres., ret. army officer; b. Orangeburg, S.C., June 21, 1921; s. Francis Pelmoin and Mary (Robottom) S.; B.S., The Citadel, 1938-42, D.Mil.Sci., 1973; grad. Armor Sch., 1947-48, Brit. Joint Services Staff Coll., 1955-56, Nat. War Coll., 1961; D.Humanities, Lander Coll., 1976; m. Lavinia Anne Ficken, Apr. 5, 1947 (dec. Dec. 1975); 1 stepson, Richard P. Padgett; children—Pamela A., George Marion III, Mollie Kent; m. 2d, Doretta Louise Fleischmann, June 26, 1977; stepchildren—Charles Fleischmann, Melanie Fleischmann. Commd. 2d lt. U.S. Army, 1942, advanced through grades to lt. gen., 1971; comdg. officer 44th Tank Bn., 1951-52; asst. exec. sec. Joint Chiefs of Staff, 1952-55; tng. adviser, Spain, 1956-57; exec. to sec. army, 1957-60; comdg. officer 11th Cav., chief staff 3d Armored Div., Germany, 1961-65; dir. policy planning Office Sec. Def., 1966; asst. comdr. 2d Inf. Div., Korea, 1966-67; dep. dir. plans and policy Joint Chiefs of Staff, 1967; mil. adviser Paris (France) Peace Talks, 1968; comdg. gen. 3d Inf. Div., Germany, 1969; U.S. comdr., Berlin, Germany, 1970-71; dep. chief U.S. Mission, Berlin, 1970-71; dep. asst. sec. def. charge mil. assistance and sales, 1971; dir. Def. Security Assistance Agy., 1971-72; dir. joint staff Orgn. Joint Chiefs Staff, 1972-74; pres. The Citadel, Charleston, S.C., 1972-79; del. at large SALT talks, Geneva, 1977-79; dir. U.S. Arms Control Agy., 1979—; dir. So. Bank and Trust Co., So. Bancorp., Inc. Chmn. Frankenwald dist. Boy Scouts Am., Germany, 1969-70; exec. bd. Transatlantic Boy Scout Council, 1970-71; bd. dirs. North Atlantic Girl Scouts, 1969-71, Trident United Way, Inc., 1976—. Decorated D.S.M. with 2 oak leaf clusters, Silver Star, Bronze Star with 2 oak leaf clusters, Legion of Merit with 3 oak leaf clusters. Mem. Charleston Trident C. of C. (dir.). Episcopalian. Club: European Rod and Gun (v.p. 1963-64). Home: 1555 35 St NW Washington DC 20451 Office: 320 21 St NW Washington DC 20451

SEIKEL, OLIVER EDWARD, lawyer; b. Akron, Ohio, July 6, 1937; s. Herman William and Josephine Marie (Weaver) S.; B.S., Mass. Inst. Tech., 1959; J.D., U. Mich., 1962; postgrad. (fellow) U. Hamburg, 1962-63. Admitted to Ohio bar, 1963; asso. firm Falsgraf, Reidy, Shoup & Ault, Cleve., 1963-68, partner firm, 1969-71; legal mgr. internat. ops. Midland-Ross Corp., Cleve., 1971-73; individual practice law, Cleve., 1974-78; partner firm Seikel & Stinson, Cleve., 1978—; sec. Bearings, Inc., and subsidiaries, Cleve., Midland Steel Products Co., Forest City Foundries Co., MIDSCO, Inc., Cleve.; asst. sec. Perinold Corp. Trustee Our Lady of the Wayside Home, Avon, Ohio, 1969—, Gilmour Acad., Gates Mills, Ohio, 1970—, Cath. Charities Corp., Cleve., 1975—. Mem. Am., Ohio, Greater Cleve. bar assns., Delta Theta Phi. Roman Catholic. Clubs: Cleve. Athletic, Cleve. Yachting, Cleve. City, Cleve. Playhouse, Rotary (Cleve.). Home: 283 Yacht Club Dr Rocky River OH 44116 Office: 2130 Illuminating Bldg 55 Public Sq Cleveland OH 44113

SEILER, LEWIS P., dept. store exec.; b. Louisville, Feb. 12, 1906; s. John A. and Alice (Gray) S.; A.B., Cornell, 1928; m. Elizabeth Engelhard, Oct. 4, 1930. Vice pres. J. N. Adams & Co., Buffalo, 1938-44; v.p. Stewart & Co., Balt., 1944-49, pres., 1949—; v.p. Asso. Dry Goods Corp., 1952-57, dir., regional exec. v.p., 1957—; pres. Stewart Dry Goods Corp., Louisville-Lexington, Ky., 1957-59; pres. Asso. Dry Goods Corp., N.Y.C., 1959-67, chief exec. officer, 1963, chmn. bd., 1967—, also dir.; adv. dir. Chem. Bank, Lehman Corp., N.Y.C.; dir. emeritus Black & Decker Mfg. Co., Balt., One William St. Fund. Home: 1230 Seaspray Ave Delray Beach FL 33444

SEILER, ROBERT EDWARD, accountant, educator; b. Ft. Worth, Oct. 12, 1925; s. Ralph G. and Willie B. (Smith) S.; B.C.S., Tex. Christian U., 1949, M.B.A., 1951; Ph.D., U. Ala., 1953; m. Norma E. Allen, Aug. 30, 1948; children—Suzanne, Robert, Glenn, Richard. Asst. prof. acctg. Miami U., Oxford, Ohio, 1953-65; asso. prof. U. Tex., 1965; prof. Stanford (Calif.) U., 1965-67; prof. U. Houston, 1967—, chmn. dept. acctg., 1975-77. Served with USNR, 1942-46. Recipient Thurston award Inst. Internal Auditors, 1959, Pool award, 1972; Ford Found. fellow, 1963; C.P.A., Tex. Mem. Am. Inst. C.P.A.'s, Tex. Soc. C.P.A.'s, Fin. Execs. Inst., Am. Acctg. Assn., Beta Gamma Sigma, Beta Alpha Psi. Author: Managerial Accounting, 3d edit., 1980; Administration of Research and Development, 1963; Elementary Accounting, 2d edit., 1974; also articles. Home: 134 Plantation St Houston TX 77024 Office: 210B Heyne U Houston Houston TX 77004

SEILER, ROBERT ELDRIDGE, state justice; b. Kansas City, Kans., Dec. 5, 1912; s. Walter Albert and Maude Virginia (Eldridge) S.; A.B., U. Mo., 1933, LL.B., 1935; m. Faye Poore, Apr. 2, 1942; children—Sunny (Mrs. Frederick F. Dupree), Lu (Mrs. David Fahrland), Robert Poore. Admitted to Mo. bar, 1934; practiced in Joplin, Mo., 1935-66; city atty. of Joplin, 1950-54; judge Supreme Ct. Mo., 1967—, chief justice, 1975-77. Sec. Joplin Home Rule Charter Commn., 1953-54; mem. Mo. Bd. Law Examiners, 1948-65, sec., 1950-63, pres., 1963-65. Fellow Am. Coll. Trial Lawyers; mem. Am., Jasper County, Kansas City bar assns., Am. Judicature Soc., Inst. Jud. Adminstrn., Mo. Bar, Mo. Law Sch. Alumni Assn., Nat. Conf. Bar Examiners (chmn. 1967-68), Order of Coif, Kappa Sigma. Club: Jefferson City Country. Office: Supreme Ct Bldg Jefferson City MO 65101

SEILS, WILLIAM GEORGE, lawyer; b. Chgo., Aug. 9, 1935; s. Harry H. and Hazel C. (Sullivan) S.; A.B., J.D., U. Mich., 1959; m. Evelyn E. Oliver, Sept. 8, 1956; children—Elizabeth Ann, Ellen Carol, Eileen Alison. Admitted to Ill. bar, 1959, since practiced in Chgo.; partner firm Arvey, Hodes & Costello & Burman, 1968—. Mem. Ill. Bar Assn., Order of Coif, Tau Epsilon Rho. Contbr. articles to profl. jours. Asst. editor Mich. Law Rev., 1958-59. Office: 180 N LaSalle St Chicago IL 60601

SEINFELD, JOHN HERSH, educator; b. Elmira, N.Y., Aug. 3, 1942; s. Ben B. and Minna (Johnson) S.; B.S., U. Rochester (N.Y.), 1964; Ph.D., Princeton, 1967. Asst. prof. chem. engring. Calif. Inst. Tech., Pasadena, 1967-70, asso. prof., 1970-74, exec. officer for chem. engring., 1973—, prof., 1974—; Allan P. Colburn meml. lectr. U. Del., 1976; Camille and Henry Dreyfus Found. lectr. M.I.T., 1979; cons. Standard Oil of Calif., Systems Applications Inc.; mem. research screening com. Calif. Air Resources Bd.; mem. sci. adv. bd. EPA; mem. adv. com. office space and terrestial applications NASA. Recipient Donald P. Eckman award Am. Automatic Control Council, 1970; Curtis W. McGraw Research award Am. Soc. Engring. Edn., 1976; Allan P. Colburn award Am. Inst. Chem. Engrs., 1976; Camille and Henry Dreyfus Found. Tchr. Scholar grantee, 1972. Mem. Am. Inst. Chem. Engrs., Am. Soc. Engring. Edn., Air Pollution Control Assn., Am. Chem. Soc., Soc. Petroleum Engrs., Sigma Xi, Tau Beta Pi. Author: (with Leon Lapidus) Numerical Solution of Ordinary Differential Equations, 1971; Mathematical Methods in Chemical Engineering, Vol. III; Process Modeling, Estimation and Identification, 1974; Air Pollution: Physical and Chemical Fundamentals, 1975. Asso. editor Chem. Engring. Communications, 1973—; editorial bds. Environ. Sci., Tech., 1973-76, Computers, Chem. Engring., 1974-76, Jour. Colloid and Interface Sci., 1978—; asso. editor Atmospheric and Environment, 1976—. Home: 960 San Pasqual Apt 210 Pasadena CA 91106 Office: Dept of Chem Engring Calif Inst of Tech Pasadena CA 91125

SEINSHEIMER, JOSEPH FELLMAN, JR., ins. co. exec.; b. Galveston, Tex., Aug. 25, 1913; s. Joseph Fellman and Irma (Kraus) S.; grad. Mercersburg Acad., 1932; B.B.A., Tulane U., 1936; m. Jessie Lee Gould, July 19, 1938; children—Joseph Fellman III, Virginia Lee, Robert L. Pres., dir. Am. Indemnity Fin. Corp., Galveston, 1973—, Am. Indemnity Co., Galveston, 1951—, Am. Fire & Indemnity Co., 1951—, Tex. Gen. Indemnity Co., 1951—, Am. Computing Co., 1970—, Am. Fin. Co. of Galveston, 1951—, U.S. Securities Corp., 1951—; dir. Galveston Corp., U.S. Nat. Bank of Galveston, U.S. Nat. Bancshares, Inc., Tex. Fibreglas Products, Inc. Served with USCGR, 1942-45. Clubs: Galveston Arty., Bob Smith Yacht. Home: 4809 Woodrow Ave Galveston TX 77550 Office: Am Indemnity Co 1 American Indemnity Plaza Galveston TX 77550

SEIREG, ALI A(BDEL HAY), mech. engr.; b. Egypt, Oct. 26, 1927; came to U.S., 1951, naturalized, 1960; s. Abdel Hay and Aisha S.; B.Sc. M.E., U. Cairo, 1948; Ph.D., U. Wis., 1954; m. Shirley Marachowsky, Dec. 24, 1954; children—Mirette Elizabeth, Pamela Aisha. Lectr., Cairo U., 1954-56; staff adv. engr. Falk Corp., Milw., 1956-59; asso. prof. theoretical and applied mechanics Marquette U., 1959-64, prof., 1964-65; prof. mech. engring. U. Wis., Madison, 1965—; cons. industry, ednl. and govt. agys.; chmn. U.S. council Internat. Fedn. Theory of Machines, 1974—; co-chmn. 5th World Congress of Theory of Machines, 1979. Mem. ASME (Richards Meml. award 1973, Machine Design award 1978, chmn. div. design engring. 1977-78, chmn. computer tech. 1978-81, mem. policy bd. communications 1978—, mem. policy bd. gen. engring. 1979—, chmn. Century II Internat. Computer Tech. Conf. 1980), Am. Soc. Engring. Edn. (George Westinghouse award 1970), Soc. Exptl. Stress Analysis, Am. Gear Mfg. Assn. (E. P. Connell award 1974), Automation Research Council. Author: Mechanical Systems Analysis, 1969; contbr. numerous articles to profl. jours. Home: 219 DuRose Terr Madison WI 53705 Office: 1513 University Ave Madison WI 53706. *I have always tried my best to look beyond what I hear, to think beyond what I see, to give more than I receive, and to do good as its own reward.*

SEITZ, COLLINS JACQUES, judge; b. Wilmington, Del., June 20, 1914; s. George Hilary and Margaret Jane (Collins) S.; A.B., U. Del., 1937, LL.D., 1962; LL.B., U. Va., 1940; LL.D., Widener Coll., 1975; m. Virginia Anne Day; children—Virginia Anne, Collins Jacques, Mark, Stephen. Admitted to Del. bar, 1940; vice chancellor Del., 1946, chancellor, 1951-66; judge U.S. Ct. Appeals, 3d Circuit, 1966—, chief judge, 1971—. Recipient James J. Hoey award, 1954; award NCCJ, 1957; Pro Ecclesia et Pontifice (papal award), 1965. Mem. Am., Del. bar assns. Democrat. Roman Catholic. Club: Wilmington. Office: Federal Bldg 844 King St Wilmington DE 19801

SEITZ, FREDERICK, univ. pres. emeritus; b. San Francisco, July 4, 1911; s. Frederick and Emily Charlotte (Hofman) S.; A.B., Leland Stanford Jr. U., 1932; Ph.D., Princeton U., 1934; Doctorate Hon. Causa, U. Ghent, 1957; D.Sc., U. Reading, 1960, Rensselaer Poly. Inst., 1961, Marquette U., 1963, Carnegie Inst. Tech., 1963, Case Inst. Tech., 1964, Princeton U., 1964, Northwestern U., 1965, U. Del., 1966, Poly. Inst. Bklyn., 1967, U. Mich., 1967, U. Utah, 1968, Brown U., 1968, Duquesne U., 1968, St. Louis U., 1969, Nebr. Wesleyan U., 1970, U. Ill., 1972; LL.D., Lehigh U., 1966, U. Notre Dame, 1962, Mich. State U., 1965, Ill. Inst. Tech., 1968, N.Y. U., 1969; L.H.D., Davis and Elkins Coll., 1970; m. Elizabeth K. Marshall, May 18, 1935. Instr. physics U. Rochester, 1935-36, asst. prof., 1936-37; physicist research labs. Gen. Electric Co., 1937-39; asst. prof. Randal Morgan Lab. Physics, U. Pa., 1939-41, asso. prof., 1941-42; prof. physics, head dept. Carnegie Inst. Tech., Pitts., 1942-49; prof. physics U. Ill., 1949-57, head dept., 1957-64, dir. control systems lab., 1951-52, dean Grad. Coll., v.p. research, 1964-65; exec. pres. Nat. Acad. Scis., 1962-69; pres. Rockefeller U., N.Y.C., 1968-78; trustee Ogden Corp., 1977—; dir. tng. program Clinton Labs., Oak Ridge, 1946-47. Chmn. Naval Research Adv. Com., 1960-62; vice chmn. Def. Sci. Bd., 1961-62, chmn., 1964-68; sci. adviser NATO, 1959-60; mem. nat. advisory com. Marine Biomed. Inst. U. Tex., Galveston, 1975-77; mem. adv. group White House Conf. Anticipated Advances in Sci. and Tech., 1975-76; mem. advisory bd. Desert Research Inst., 1975—, Center Strategic and Internat. Studies, 1975—; mem. Nat. Cancer Advisory Bd., 1976—. Dir. Akzona Inc., Tex. Instruments Inc. Trustee Rockefeller Found., 1964-77, Princeton U., 1968-72, Lehigh U., 1970—, Research Corp., 1966—, Inst. Internat. Edn., 1971—, Woodrow Wilson Nat. Fellowship Found., 1972—, Internat. Commn. Nutrition, 1973—, Univ. Corp. Atmospheric Research, Am. Museum Natural History, 1975—; trustee John Simon Guggenheim Meml. Found., 1973—, chmn. bd., 1976—; mem. Belgian Am. Edn. Found. Recipient Franklin medal Franklin Inst. Phila., 1965; Hoover medal Stanford U., 1968; Nat. Medal of Sci., 1973; James Madison award Princeton U., 1978. Fellow Am. Phys. Soc. (pres. 1961); mem. Nat. Acad. Scis., Am. Acad. Arts and Scis., Am. Inst. Mining, Metall. and Petroleum Engrs., Am. Philos. Soc., Am. Inst. Physics (chmn. governing bd. 1954-59), Inst. for Def. Analysis, Finnish Acad. Sci. and Letters (fgn. mem.), Phi Beta Kappa Assos. Author: Modern Theory of Solids, 1940; The Physics of Metals, 1943; Solid State Physics, 1955. Address: Rockefeller U 66th St and York Ave New York NY 10021

SEITZ, HOWARD ALEXANDER, lawyer; b. Bklyn., Nov. 14, 1907; s. Louis A. and Elizabeth A. (Ternan) S.; A.B., Fordham U., 1930; LL.B., Columbia, 1933; m. Mary V. Cunningham, Sept. 7, 1933; children—Mary Virginia (Mrs. Edward M. Gallagher), Howard G. Admitted to N.Y. bar, 1934, Fla. bar, 1978; practiced in N.Y.C., 1934—; mem. firm Paul, Weiss, Rifkind, Wharton & Garrison, 1943-78, counsel, 1978—; instr. St. John's U. Sch. Law, 1953-57; dir. Cullman Ventures, Inc., Allied Graphic Arts, Inc. Chmn. Cardinal's Task Force on Aging, 1977—; bd. mgrs. Lincoln Hall; trustee Aquinas Fund, Coll. Mt. St. Vincent; bd. dirs. Bklyn. Bur. Community Service, Community Council Greater N.Y., Inner City Scholarship Fund, Inc. Decorated knight of Malta, knight Holy Sepulchre. Mem. Am., N.Y. State bar assns., Fla. bar, Assn. Bar City N.Y., Cath. Lawyers Guild Bklyn. (past pres.), Emerald Assn. L.I. Roman Catholic. Clubs: Metropolitan (N.Y.C.); Westhampton Country (Westhampton Beach, N.Y.); Nat. Golf Links Am., Lost Tree. Home: 1088 Park Ave New York NY 10028 Office: 345 Park Ave New York NY 10022

SEITZ, NICHOLAS JOSEPH, mag. editor; b. Topeka, Kans., Jan. 30, 1939; s. Frank Joseph and Lydia Natalie (Clerico) S.; B.A., U. Okla., 1966; m. Velma Jean Pfannenstiel, Sept. 12, 1959; children—Bradley Joseph, Gregory Joseph. Sports editor Manhattan (Kans.) Mercury, 1960-62, Norman (Okla.) Transcript, 1962-64, Okla. Jour., Oklahoma City, 1964-67; mem. staff Golf Digest mag., Norwalk, Conn., 1967—, editor, 1973—; syndicated golf instrn. and commentary CBS Radio Network. Bd. dirs. World Golf Hall of Fame, 1974—. Named Okla. Sports Writer of Year, Nat. Sportswriters and Sportscasters Assn., 1965; winner contests Nat. Basketball Writers Assn., Golf Writers Assn. Author: (with Dave Hill) Teed Off, 1977; Superstars of Golf, 1978. Contbr. articles to profl. jours. Home: 36 Hunt St Rowayton CT 06853 Office: 495 Westport Ave Norwalk CT 06856

SEITZ, REYNOLDS C., lawyer; b. Chgo., Nov. 30, 1909; s. J. Charles and Gertrude L. (Reynolds) S.; A.B., U. Norte Dame, 1929; A.M., Northwestern U., 1932; J.D., Creighton U., 1935; postgrad. law U. Chgo., U. Northwestern, in edn. Northwestern U., Ind. U., summers 1939-41; m. Anne T. Rouse, Aug. 29, 1939; children—Eileen, Kathleen, Dianne, Louise. Instr. English and debate Evanson (Ill.) High Sch., 1930-32; instr. speech and debate Creighton U., 1934-36, prof. law, 1938-41; asst. to supt. pub. schs., Omaha, 1936-38, St. Louis, 1941; sr. atty. NLRB, Washington, 1941-42; labor relations atty. Montgomery Ward & Co., Chgo., 1943; dir. advt. promotion and market research Chgo. Daily News, 1943-47, editor, staff writer, 1947-53; lectr. law for the journalist Northwestern U., Evanston, 1947-50, on labor law dept. econs., 1947-53, dir. Chgo. div. Northwestern-Medill Sch. Journalism, also asso. prof. journalism, asso. prof. pub. relations, asso. prof. law for journalist, asso. prof. Sch. Law, 1950-53; dean Marquette U. Law Sch., Milw., 1953-66, prof. law, 1953—. Mem. Am. Acad. Polit. and Social Sci., Nat. Orgn. on Legal Problems in Edn. (pres. 1958-60, editor-in-chief sch. law Reporter), Am., Nebr., Wis. bar assns., Nat. Acad. Arbitrators, Am. Arbitration Assn., Soc. Profls. in Dispute Resolution, Phi Delta Kappa. Co-author: 1971 Yearbook Sch. Law; contbr. articles to law revs., profl. jours. Home: 5274 N Santa Monica Blvd Milwaukee WI 53217

SEIXAS, FRANK ARCHIBALD, physician; b. N.Y.C., Oct. 5, 1919; s. Archibald Sousa and Ethel Miriam (Isaacs) S.; B.A., Cornell U., 1939; M.A., Columbia, 1940, M.D., 1951; postgrad. Rutgers U., 1966, Am. Coll. Physicians, 1970; m. Judith Sartorius, Sept. 29, 1946; children—Peter, Abigail (Mrs. Mark Horowitz), Noah. Intern, Montefiore Hosp., Bronx, N.Y., 1951-52; resident Roosevelt Hosp., N.Y.C., 1952-54; fellow in psychiatry Mt. Sinai Hosp., 1954-55; practice medicine, specializing in internal medicine, N.Y.C., 1955—; mem. staff N.Y. Cardiac Center, Yonkers, 1956-65, Roosevelt Hosp., 1955—, N.Y. Hosp., 1955—; clin. asst. prof. medicine Cornell U. Med. Coll., 1966—, clin. asso. prof. pub. health, 1975—; med. dir. Nat. Council on Alcoholism, 1968-78, Norwood Hosp. Comprehensive Alcoholism Program, 1979—; adminstr. Support Program for Alcoholism Research-NCA, 1973-78; med. dir. ACCEPT, 1965-70; rep. to UN and Pan-Am. Health Orgn. for ICAA, 1966—. Chmn. bd. Shipping Digest, to 1978; sec., bd. dirs. Nat. Alliance on Shaping Safer Cities, 1973-75; bd. dirs. New York Assn. for New Ams., Lower East Side Service Center, Westchester Council on Alcoholism; mem. adv. council on alcoholism Dept. Mental Health and Mental Retardation Services of N.Y.C. Served to lt. comdr. USNR, 1940-45. Diplomate Am. Bd. Internal Medicine. Fellow A.C.P., Hastings Inst.; mem. Pan Am. Med. Assn. (v.p. alcoholism div. Western Hemisphere), S.A.R. Clubs: Princeton U., Cornell U. Med. Faculty, Cornell (N.Y.C.). Editor-in-chief Physicians Alcohol Newsletter of A.M.S.A., 1965-78; editor Annals of N.Y. Acad. Scis., Vols. 178, 197, 215, 233, 252, 1968—, Alcoholism Clin. and Exptl. Research, 1977—, Currents in Alcoholism, 1977-79. Home: 24 Morrill Rd Norwood MA 02062

SEJNOST, RICHARD LEONARD, hosp. supt.; b. Kansas City, May 11, 1926; s. Frank Joseph and Louise Anna (Frish) S.; student U. Calif. at Los Angeles, 1945-46; B.A., Park Coll., Parkville, Mo., 1948; M.S. in Hosp. Adminstrn., Northwestern U., 1950; m. Beverly Ann Henderson, June 3, 1950; children—Patricia, Thomas, Todd, Martha. With Harper Hosp., Detroit, 1950—, adminstr., v.p., 1966—; sr. v.p. Harper-Grace Hosps.; non-resident lectr. U. Mich. Cons. Dept. Health Edn. and Welfare, Assn. Am. Med. Colls.; adv. com. Nat. Acad. Sci., mem. assn. services commn. Greater Detroit Area Hosp. Council, 1968-76; trustee Mich. chpt. ARC. Mem. planning commn. village Beverly Hills (Mich.), 1966-76. Served with USNR, 1943-46. Fellow Am. Coll. Hosp. Adminstrs.; mem. Am. (chmn. com. edn.), Mich. (trustee, exec. com., chmn. bd.) hosp. assns., Soc. Health Service Adminstrs., Tri-State Hosp. Assembly (dir. 1970-76). Presbyn. (deacon). Rotarian. Club: Detroit Athletic. Home: 31115 Pickwick Ln Birmingham MI 48009 Office: 3990 John R Detroit MI 48201

SEKLER, EDUARD FRANZ, architect, educator; b. Vienna, Austria, Sept. 30, 1920; s. Eduard Jakob and Elisabeth (Demmel) S.; Dipl. Ing., Tech. U., Vienna, 1945; student Sch. Planning and Regional Research, London, Eng., 1947; Ph.D., Warburg Inst., London U., 1948; A.M. (hon.), Harvard, 1960; m. Mary Patricia May, July 20, 1962. Came to U.S., 1955; Partner archtl. firm Prehsler and Sekler, Vienna, 1945—; teaching asst., lectr. faculty architecture Tech. U., Vienna, 1945-54; vis. prof. architecture Harvard, 1954-56, asso. prof., 1956-60, prof., 1960—, Osgood Hooker prof. visual arts, 1970—; coordinator studies Carpenter Center Visual Arts, 1962-65, dir., 1966-76, chmn. dept. visual and environmental studies, 1968-70; principal works include restoration church, Leopoldsberg, nr. Vienna, 1950, urban redevel. Alt Erdberg, 1956, Austrian Cultural Inst., N.Y.C., 1962, several housing schemes, Vienna, 1948-68, Telephone Exchange, Vienna, 1970; expert mem. internat. com. hist. monuments UNESCO, 1951-54, UNESCO adviser to planning dept. Govt. Nepal, 1972; cons. Historic Monuments Office, Vienna, 1975; head UNESCO team for masterplan for Conservation Cultural Heritage of

Kathmandu Valley, 1975; UNESCO cons. masterplan for Sukothai Hist. Park, Thailand, 1978. Mem. Cambridge Arts Council. Bd. dirs. Archtl. Heritage, Inc., 1969-75. Decorated Cross of Honor for Scis. and Art, Austrian Republic; Guggenheim fellow, 1961-62, 62-63. Fellow Am. Acad. Arts and Scis.; mem. Internat. Council Monuments and Sites, Soc. Archtl. Historians (dir. 1963-66, 70-73), Archtl. Assn. London, Austrian Chamber Architects, Royal Town Planning Inst. (hon. corr. mem. London), Signet Soc. Author: Point-houses in European Housing, 1952; Wren and his Place in European Architecture, 1956; Proportion, a Measure of Order, 1965; Historic Urban Spaces I-IV, 1962-71; (with others) Kathmandu Valley, The Preservation of Physical Environment and Cultural Heritage, 2 vols., 1975; Le Corbusier at Work: The Genesis of the Carpenter Center for the Visual Arts, 1977. Home: 21 Gibson St Cambridge MA 02138

SEKULER, ROBERT WILLIAM, scientist, educator; b. Elizabeth, N.J., May 7, 1939; s. Sidney and Marian (Siegel) S.; A.B., Brandeis U., 1960; Sc.M., Brown U., 1963, Ph.D., 1964; postgrad. (NIH postdoctoral fellow) M.I.T., 1964-65; m. Susan Pamela Nemser, June 25, 1961; children—Stacia, Allison, Erica. Prof. psychology Northwestern U., Evanston, Ill., 1973—, chmn. dept., 1975—, prof. ophthalmology Med. Sch., 1978—; cons. NSF, NIH, AAAS; mem. NRC Working Group on Visual Function and Aging. Grantee, Nat. Inst. Neurol Diseases and Stroke, U.S. Air Force, NSF, Nat. Eye Inst., Nat. Inst. Aging; U.S. Navy, U.S. Army contractor. Fellow Optical Soc. Am.; mem. Assn. Research in Vision and Ophthalmology, Psychonomic Soc., Soc. Neurosci., Human Factors Soc. Editor: Perception and Psychophysics, 1971—; Jour. Exptl. Psychology, 1973-74; Vision Research Jour., 1974-79; Optics Letters, 1977—; Am. Jour. Psychology, 1979—; Sensory Processes, 1979—; contbr. Handbook of Sensory Physiology, Handbook of Perception, other sci. jours. Office: Cresap Neurosci Lab Northwestern Univ Evanston IL 60201

SELANDER, ROBERT KEITH, biologist; b. Garfield, Utah, July 21, 1927; s. Clyde Service and Genevieve Selander; B.S., U. Utah, 1950, M.S., 1951; Ph.D. in Zoology (Thompson Meml. fellow 1952, NSF fellow 1953, Univ. fellow 1955), U. Calif., Berkeley, 1956; m. Bonnie Jean Slater, Sept. 21, 1952; children—David Martin, Jennifer Jean. Instr., U. Tex., Austin, 1956-58, asst. prof. zoology, 1959-63, asso. prof., 1964-67, prof., 1968-74; prof. biology U. Rochester, 1974—, chmn. dept. biology, 1976-78; research fellow Am. Mus. Natural History, 1961; Guggenheim fellow U. Calif., Berkeley, 1965; Herbert W. Rand fellow Marine Biol. Lab., Woods Hole, Mass., summer 1971. Served with U.S. Army, 1946. Recipient Walker prize Mus. Sci., Boston, 1969, Painton award Cooper Ornithol. Soc., 1970; co-recipient Elliott Coues award Am. Ornithol. Soc., 1975; NSF grantee, 1956—; NIH grantee, 1968—; NATO grantee, 1977-78. Fellow Am. Ornithologists' Union, AAAS mem.; Am. Inst. Biol. Scis., Am. Soc. Human Genetics, Am. Soc. Mammalogists, Am. Soc. Naturalists, Animal Behavior Soc., Genetics Soc. Am., Soc. Study Evolution (pres. 1976), Soc. Systematic Zoology (editorial bd. 1973-76), Phi Beta Kappa. Contbr. numerous articles to profl. publs.; asso. editor Evolution, 1972-74; editorial bd. Evolutionary Theory, 1973—. Home: 47 S Ridge Trail Fairport NY 14450 Office: U Rochester Dept Biology Rochester NY 14627

SELBY, CECILY CANNAN, educator, scientist, corp. exec.; b. London, Feb. 4, 1927; d. Keith and Catherine Anne Cannan; A.B. cum laude, Radcliffe Coll., 1946; Ph.D. in Phys. Biology, Mass. Inst. Tech., 1950; m. Henry M. Selby, Aug. 11, 1951 (div. 1979); children—Norman, William, Russell. Teaching asst. in biology Mass. Inst. Tech., 1948-49; adminstrv. head virus study sect. Sloan-Kettering Inst., N.Y.C., 1949-50, asst. mem. inst., 1950-55; research asso. Sloan-Kettering div. Cornell U. Med. Coll., N.Y.C., 1953-55, also instr. microscopic anatomy, 1955-57; tchr. sci. Lenox Sch., N.Y.C., 1957-58, headmistress, 1959-72; nat. exec. dir. Girl Scouts U.S.A., N.Y.C., 1972-75; mem. speakers program Edison Electric Inst., 1976—; adv. com. Simmons Coll. Grad. Mgmt. Program, 1977-78; mem. Com. for Corp. Support of Pvt. Univs., 1977—; spl. asst. acad. planning N.C. Sch. Sci. and Math., 1979—; cons. U.S. Dept. Commerce, 1976-77; dir. Avon Products Inc., RCA, NBC, Loehmanns Inc.; pres. Am. Energy Ind., 1976. Founder, chmn. N.Y. Ind. Schs. Opportunity Project, 1968-72; mem. invitational workshops Aspen Inst., 1973, 75, 77, 79. Trustee Mass. Inst. Tech., Bklyn. Law Sch., Radcliffe Coll., Women's Forum N.Y. Mem. Headmistresses of East (hon. mem.; pres. 1970-72), Cum Laude Soc. (past chpt. pres., dist. regent), Sigma Xi. Contbr. articles to profl. jours., chpt. to book. Clubs: Cosmopolitan (N.Y.C.); Women's Forum N.Y.; Westhampton Country (gov. 1969-75). Office: 45 Sutton Pl S New York NY 10022

SELBY, HENRY ANDERSON, anthropologist; b. Toronto, Ont., Can., Sept. 2, 1934; s. David Longland and Katherine Elizabeth (Anderson) S.; came to U.S., 1961; B.A., Toronto U., 1955; M.A., London U., 1961; Ph.D., Stanford U., 1966; m. Lucy Reed Garretson, Aug. 20, 1960; children—Washington Gardner, Mary Theadosia, Thomas Henry Longland. Asso. prof. Temple U., Phila., 1972-77; asso. prof. U. Tex., Austin, 1966-72, prof., chmn. dept. anthropology, 1977—; cons. U.S., Mexican govts. Served as midshipman Royal Can. Navy, 1951-54. Fellow Am. Anthrop. Assn.; mem. CIBOLA, Sigma Xi, Kappa Alpha. Author books, articles on Mexican ethnology, contemporary problems in rural farming communities, urban popular (poor) settlements. Home: 2000 Sharon Ln Austin TX 78703 Office: Burdine Hall 336B U Tex Austin TX 78712

SELBY, HUBERT, JR., writer; b. Bklyn., July 23, 1928; s. Hubert and Adalin (Layne) S.; student public schs., N.Y.C.; m. Suzanne Shaw, Dec. 26, 1969; children—Rachel, William. Author: Last Exit to Brooklyn, 1964, The Room, 1971, The Demon, 1976, Requiem for a Dream, 1978. Served with U.S. Mcht. Marine, 1944-46. Mem. Writers Guild Am., Authors Guild.

SELBY, JOHN DOUGLAS, utility exec.; b. Odebolt, Iowa, Oct. 12, 1921; s. John Hanna and Della Anna (Nelson) S.; B.S. in Gen. Engring., Iowa State U., 1946; postgrad. in advanced mgmt. Harvard U. Bus. Sch., 1971; m. Marion Elizabeth Harrison, Oct. 23, 1944; children—Elizabeth Selby Beckingham, Marcia Selby Cubeck, John Douglas, Michael Paul. Mem. staff light mil. electronics dept. Gen. Electric Co., Utica, N.Y., 1965-67, aerospace electronics dept., 1967-71, nuclear energy dept., San Jose, Calif., 1971-75; pres., chief exec. officer Consumers Power Co., Jackson, Mich., 1975—, chmn., 1979—; dir. No. Mich. Exploration Co., Plateau Resources Ltd.; dir., officer Mich. Gas Storage Co. Bd. dirs. Atomic Indsl. Forum, 1979; bd. dirs. Inst. Nuclear Power Ops. Served with USN 1942-46. Mem. ASME, Profl. Engrs. Assn., Edison Electric Inst. (dir., mem. com. on nuclear power), Detroit Econ. Club, Mich., Greater Jackson chambers of commerce. Republican. Clubs: Jackson Country, Jackson Town. Home: 1739 Probert Rd Jackson MI 49203 Office: 212 W Michigan Ave Jackson MI 49201

SELBY, JOHN EDWARD, coll. dean; b. Boston, Jan. 1, 1929; s. Paul Norman and Nora A. (Keane) S.; A.B., Harvard, 1950; M.A., Brown U., 1951, Ph.D. in History, 1955; m. Mary Theresa Tierney, June 26, 1954; children—Hilary, Holly, Jonathan, Christopher. Instr., then asst. prof. U. Oreg., Eugene, 1955-61; asst. dir. research Colonial Williamsburg Found., 1961-66; mem. faculty Coll. William and Mary, 1966—, prof. history, 1970—, grad. dean arts and scis., 1968—. Mem. Am. Hist. Assn. Book rev. editor William and Mary Quar., 1966-70, 71—, acting editor, 1970-71. Home: Duke of Gloucester St Williamsburg VA 23195

SELBY, JOHN RODNEY, fastener co. exec.; b. Des Moines, Aug. 20, 1929; s. Rodney Q. and Lucille M. (Weiker) S.; B.S. in Indsl. Engring., Iowa State U., 1956; m. Sheila; children—John, Sara, Rodney, Beth, Robert, Peter. Indsl. engr. Lennox Industries, Marshalltown, Iowa, 1950-57; v.p. Europe, The Trane Co., LaCrosse, Wis., 1957-68; v.p. mfg. Emerson Electric Co., St. Louis, 1968-69; pres. U.S. Motors div. Emerson Electric Co., Milford, Conn., 1969-71; pres., chief exec. officer SPS Techs., Inc., Jenkintown, Pa., 1971—; dir. Fidelity Mut. Life Ins. Co., Rorer Group, Inc. Served with Air N.G., 1949-51. Fisher Found. scholar, 1954-56. Mem. World Affairs Council Phila. (dir.), Gamma Epsilon Sigma, Phi Gamma Delta. Home: Box 246 Lahaska PA 18931 Office: Benson E Jenkintown PA 19046

SELBY, RICHARD ROY, economist; b. Oakland, Calif., Mar. 6, 1926; s. Richard Roy and Jennie Rose (Young) S.; A.B., Tufts Coll., 1947; M.A., Fletcher Sch. Law and Diplomacy, 1948; student U. Calif. at Berkeley, 1959-60; m. Roberta Alice Hess; children—Cynthia Woods, Richard Roy IV, Robin Alice; m. 2d, Mary M. Glenn; children—Leigh Hays, Anne Hale, Lynn Marie. Instr. econs. New Eng. Coll., Henniker, N.H., 1948-50; joined U.S. Fgn. Service, 1950; vice consul, Stuttgart, Germany, 1950-52; 3d sec., Saigon, Vietnam, 1953-54; with Exec. Secretariat, State Dept., 1954-56; consul, Budapest, Hungary, 1956-58; with Bur. European Affairs, State Dept., 1958-62; 1st sec. embassy, Warsaw, Poland, 1962-64; assigned State Dept., 1965-66; sr. economist IMF, 1966—; adviser to gov., Central Bank of Afghanistan, 1968-71, European office, Paris, 1973-77, exchange and trade relations dept., Washington, 1977—. Served with USNR, 1944-46. Mem. Am. Fgn. Service Assn., Am. Econ. Assn. Address: 9409 Falls Bridge Ln Potomac MD 20854

SELBY, ROGER LOWELL, museum ofcl.; b. Phila., July 4, 1933; s. Willard Lowell and Margaret Anne (Gray) S.; A.B., U. Md., 1960; postgrad. Claremont Grad. Sch., 1960-61, Ind. U., 1963-65; m. Claudia Engel, Oct. 23, 1974; 1 dau., Christine. Curator edn. Nat. Gallery Art, Washington, 1961-62, Corcoran Gallery Art, Washington, 1965-68; head edn. Wadsworth Atheneum, Hartford, 1968-74; dir. Winnipeg (Man., Can.) Art Gallery, 1974—; instr. Corcoran Sch. Art, 1965-68, Hartford Art Sch., 1969-71. Served with U.S. Army, 1953-55. Asst., gen. fellow Claremont Grad. Sch., 1960-61; asst. Ind. U., 1963-65. Mem. Assn. Art Mus. Dirs., Canadian Art Mus. Dirs. Orgn., Mus. Dirs. Assn. Can. Home: 134 Wellington Crescent Winnipeg MB R3M 0A9 Canada Office: 300 Memorial Blvd Winnipeg MB R3C 1V1 Canada. *Elements of Success: A stubborn dedication towards a goal, nourished by life's varied experiences, coupled with exhaustive thought; a fortunate set of circumstances; the realization that nothing is accomplished alone; and the resolved question—why are we here in the first place?*

SELCHOW, ROGER HOFFMAN, painter, sculptor; b. Greenwich, Conn., Feb. 13, 1911; s. Paul Hoffman and Alice Allen (Mills) S.; student Grand Central Sch. Art, N.Y.C., 1931-33, Columbia U., 1947-48, Dong Kingman, N.Y.C., 1947-48, Xavier Gonzalez, Wellfleet, Mass., 1949—, Andre Lhote, Fernand Leger and Academie de la Grande Chaumiere, Paris, 1949-53, Instituto Statale d'Arte, Florence, Italy, 1950-51; One-man shows include: Galerie Arnaud, Paris, 1953, 54, Delacorte Gallery, N.Y.C., 1956, Newman Gallery Contemporary Art, Phila., 1960, Galerie d'Art du Faubourg, Paris, 1961, Angeleski Gallery, N.Y.C., 1962; group shows include: Galerie Parnass, Wuppertal, Ger., 1953, Galerie Arnaud, Paris, 1954, Internat. Collage Show, Rose Fried Gallery, N.Y.C., 1956, Musee des Beaux-Arts, Liege, Belgium, 1965; represented in permanent collections: Musee des Beaux-Arts, Liege, Wadsworth Atheneum, Hartford, Conn., N.Y. U. Art Collection, Bklyn. Mus., Met. Mus. Art, N.Y.C., Loch Haven Art Center, Orlando, Fla., Sheldon Swope Art Mus. and Ind. State Coll., Terre Haute, Witherspoon Art Gallery, Greensboro, N.C., Ark. Art Center, Little Rock, Bruce Mus., Greenwich, Wichita (Kans.) Art Mus., also numerous pvt. collections; dir. Atelier du Vieux Vaison, Vaison-La-Romaine, France, 1953-60. Served with USNR, 1942-45. Recipient 2 1st Place medals Grand Central Sch. Art, 1933, several 1st Place awards Greenwich Art Soc., 1954. Contbr. hist. articles and comments to Greenwich newspapers. Home: London Terr Gardens 415 W 23d St Apt 9-F New York NY 10011

SELDEN, ALBERT W., theatrical producer; b. N.Y.C., Oct. 20, 1922; s. Lynde and Muriel (Wiggin) S.; B.A., Yale, 1943; m. Jean Beaven, Dec. 22, 1942 (div. Feb. 1960); 3 sons, 2 daus.; m. 2d, Carlye Rogerson; 2 sons, 2 daus. Began theatrical career at Yale; musician and composer; wrote score for Broadway revue Small Wonder, also many TV spls.; produced Broadway plays Body Beautiful, His and Hers, The Grey-Eyed People, Man of La Mancha (Tony award, Critics award 1965); founder, producer, mng. dir. Conn. Landmark Goodspeed Opera House, East Haddam, Conn., 1962—; producer Hallelujah, Baby (Tony award 1968), Portrait of a Queen, Come Summer, Irene (all N.Y.). Served to 1st lt. AUS, 1942-45. Decorated Bronze Star. Mem. Dramatists Guild, A.S.C.A.P., League N.Y. Theatres. Address: 246 W 44th St New York NY 10036*

SELDEN, DAVID SEELEY, labor union ofcl.; b. Grand Haven, Mich., June 6, 1914; s. Arthur Willis and Florence (Seeley) S.; A.B., Mich. State Normal Coll., 1936; M.A., Wayne State U., 1940; m. Isabel L. Igel, 1932 (div. 1945); 1 dau., Christine Hamor; m. 2d, Dolores Velez, 1946 (div. 1956); 1 dau., Denise Dolores; m. 3d, Bernice Cohen, May 12, 1956; 1 son, John. Social studies tchr. Salina Jr. High Sch., Dearborn, Mich., 1936; tchr. Oak Hill (Fla.) Sch., 1947, Montrose, N.Y., 1948; field rep. Am. Fedn. Tchrs., 1949-53, dir. orgn., N.Y.C., 1964, asst. to pres., 1964-68, pres., 1968—; ednl. cons. Mem. ad hoc com. on edn. Commn. on Intergovtl. Relations, 1972—. Served with USNR, 1943-46. Mem. Nat. Inst. Edn., Phi Delta Kappa. Contbr. articles on edn., labor and social reform to mags., chpts. to books. Home: 1403 Sutherland Ave Kalamazoo MI 49007

SELDEN, JOSEPH WIXSON, indsl. cons.; b. Englewood, N.J., Aug. 21, 1916; s. Joseph Phillip and Ella Louise (King) S.; student Wayne State U., 1932-35; B.S. in Indsl. Engring., Pa. State U., 1938; m. Ellen L. Howe, June 30, 1939; children—Marcia Selden Niles, Joseph Cass. Sales engr. Goodyear Tire & Rubber Co., Akron, Ohio, 1938-41, prodn. supt., Phoenix, 1942-46, Chgo., 1946-48; v.p. new product devel. Minn. Mining & Mfg. Co., St. Paul, 1948-68; pres. indsl. and marine divs. N. Rockwell Corp., Pitts., 1968-71, staff v.p. corporate devel., 1971; v.p., group exec. CCI Corp., Tulsa, 1971-73; pres. Sands Measurement Corp., Dallas, 1973-74; cons., Tulsa, 1974—. Mem. Anthony Wayne Soc., Tau Beta Pi, Sigma Tau, Alpha Sigma Phi. Republican. Clubs: Univ., So. Hills (Tulsa); Duquesne (Pitts.). Home: 5819 S Evanston Ct Tulsa OK 74105

SELDEN, RICHARD THOMAS, educator, economist; b. Pontiac, Mich., Mar. 31, 1922; s. Arthur Willis and Florence L. (Seeley) S.; B.A., U. Chgo., 1948, Ph.D., 1954; M.A., Columbia, 1949; m. Martha Mathiasen, Mar. 21, 1953; children—Phoebe Serena, Thomas Mathiasen. Instr. U. Mass., Amherst, 1949-50; mem. faculty Vanderbilt U., Nashville, 1952-59, asso. prof., 1955-59; research asso. Nat. Bur. Econ. Research, N.Y.C., 1958-59; asso. prof. banking Columbia, 1959-63; economist 1st Nat. City Bank, N.Y.C., 1962-63; prof. econs. Cornell U., 1963-69; Carter Glass prof. econs. U. Va., 1969—, chmn. dept., 1972-79. Mem. adv. council banking and financial research com. Am. Bankers Assn., 1964-67; U. Va. rep. on univs. Nat. Bur. Com. for Econ. Research, 1969-79. Guggenheim fellow, 1965; Fulbright Advanced Research scholar, Brussels, Belgium, 1964-65; Ford Found. faculty fellow Cornell U., 1968-69. Mem. Am., So. econ. assns., Am. Finance Assn. Author: The Postwar Rise in the Velocity of Money, 1962; Trends and Cycles in the Commercial Paper Market, 1963; (with George R. Morrison) Time Deposit Growth and the Employment of Bank Funds, 1965. Contbr. articles to profl. jours. Home: Box 3 Ivy VA 22945

SELDEN, WILLIAM KIRKPATRICK, ednl. cons.; b. Oil City, Pa., Nov. 11, 1911; s. Edwin van D. and Cornelia Fuller (Earp) S.; A.B., Princeton U., 1934; LL.D., Carthage Coll., 1954; Litt.D., Jacksonville U., 1964; m. Virginia Barr, June 25, 1938; children—Edwin van Deusen, Joseph Barr. Asst. to faculty dean, coll. dean Princeton U., 1934-37; clk. Eastman Kodak Co., Rochester, N.Y., 1937-38; asst. dir. admissions, admissions officer, asst. coll. dean Brown U., Providence, 1938-43, asst. to pres., 1943-45; asst. dean students, dir. admissions Northwestern U., Evanston, Ill., 1945-52, univ. recorder, 1952-53; pres. Ill. Coll., 1953-55; exec. dir. Nat. Commn. on Accrediting, 1955-65; v.p. The Am. Assembly, 1965-66; Ednl. specialist in India, U.S. Dept. State, 1965; adv. com. on nursing edn. facilities USPHS, 1964-65; cons. N.J. Dept. Edn., 1966-67; chmn. Spl. Com. on Status of Podiatry Edn., 1960-61; dir. Va. Gov.'s Com. on Nursing, 1967-69; cons., dir. projects numerous profl. assns. and orgns. Ford Found. travel and study grantee, 1960; exec. com. Coll. Entrance Exam. Bd., 1953; mem. Gov.'s Commn. Higher Edn. Ill., 1954-55; grad. council Princeton U., 1954-56; mem. ednl. adv. council NAM, 1954-58; adv. com. Presbyn. Bd. Christian Edn., 1959-63; exec. com. Episcopal Ch. Soc. for Ch. Work, 1962-66, pres., 1964-66; vice chmn. St. John's Orphanage Assn., 1960-65; chmn. adv. com. CIT Fin. Found., 1960-65; past pres. vol. bur. Providence Civilian Def. Council; mem. bd. Vets. Info. Center, Bur. Handicapped; chmn. citizens adv. com. long-range planning Princeton Regional Schs., 1970-71; bd. acad. advisors U.S. Marine Corps Schs., Quantico, 1969-70; dir. health scis. research project New Eng. Bd. Higher Edn., 1974-75; chmn. podiatry edn. feasibility study So. Regional Edn. Bd., 1976-77; trustee Profl. Exam. Service, 1974-76; chmn. adv. com. health programs Ednl. Testing Service, 1976—; chmn. spl. higher edn. com. ADA, 1978-79; exec. dir. Nat. Bd. Podiatry Examiners, 1978—; mem. com. for study credentialing in nursing Am. Nurses Assn., 1976-79; mem. council on optometric edn. Am. Optometric Assn., 1977—; mem. com. on edn. for allied health professions AMA, 1969-70, dir. study accreditation selected health edn. programs, 1971-72. Mem. bd. Evanston YMCA; mem. borough council, Princeton, 1976-79; judge Miss Am. Pageant, 1951; co-chmn. Princeton Joint Mcpl. Consolidation Study Commn., 1978-79; mem. adv. panel ROTC affairs, Dept. Def., 1950-53. Recipient Recognition awards Nat. Assn. Schs. Art, 1967, Princeton class of 1934, 1971, Am. Podiatry Assn., 1961, 76. Mem. Council Social Work Agys., Fund Advancement Edn. (cons. 1953), Am. Council Edn. (sec. com. on civil def. and higher edn. 1952), Assn. Naval ROTC Colls. (sec.-treas., 1948-53). Episcopalian. Clubs: Cap and Gown, Pretty Brook Tennis, Springdale Golf (Princeton); Cosmos (Washington). Author: Accreditation—A Struggle Over Standards in Higher Edn., 1960; contbr. articles to profl. jours. Home: 58 Westcott Rd Princeton NJ 08540

SELDES, GEORGE, writer; b. Alliance, N.J., Nov. 16, 1890; s. George Sergius and Anna (Saphro) S.; prep. edn., high sch., Vineland, N.J., and East Liberty Acad., Pitts.; student Harvard, 1912-13; m. Helen Larkin Wiesman. Reporter, Pitts. Leader, 1909-10; night editor Pitts. Post, 1910-16; mng. editor Pulitzer's Weekly, N.Y.C., 1916; war corr. with AEF, 1917-18; head Berlin bur. Chgo. Tribune, 1920-25, Rome bur., 1925; war corr. French campaign in Syria, 1926-27, N.Y. Post in Spain, 1936-37; author, 1928—; editor weekly newsletter In Fact, 1940-50. Democrat. Author numerous books including: Facts and Fascism, 1943; 1000 Americans, 1947; The People Don't Know, 1949; Tell the Truth and Run, 1953; The Great Quotations, 1960; Never Tire of Protesting, 1968; Even the Gods Cannot Change History, 1976. Address: RFD 1 Box 127 Windsor VT 05089

SELDES, MARIAN, actress; b. N.Y.C.; d. Gilbert and Alice (Hall) S.; grad. Neighborhood Playhouse, N.Y.C., 1947; m. Julian Claman, Nov. 3, 1953 (div.); 1 dau., Katharine. Appeared with Cambridge (Mass.) Summer Theatre, 1945, Boston Summer Theatre, 1946, St. Michael's Playhouse, Winooski, Vt., 1947-48, Bermudiana Theatre, Hamilton, Bermuda, 1951, Elitch Gardens Theatre, Denver, 1953; Broadway appearances include Medea, 1947, Crime and Punishment, 1948, That Lady, 1949, Tower Beyond Tragedy, 1950, The High Ground, 1951, Come of Age, 1952, Ondine, 1954, The Chalk Garden, 1955, The Wall, 1960, A Gift of Time, 1962, The Milk Train Doesn't Stop Here Any More, 1964, Tiny Alice, 1965, A Delicate Balance (Tony award for best supporting actress), 1967, Before You Go, 1968, Father's Day (Drama Desk award), 1971, Mendicants of Evening (Martha Graham Co.), 1973, Equus, 1974-77; The Merchant, 1977; Deathtrap, 1978; off-Broadway appearances include Diff'rent, 1961, The Ginger Man (Obie award), 1963, All Women Are One, 1964, Juana LaLoca, 1965, Three Sisters, 1969; Am. Shakespeare Festival, Stratford, Conn., Mercy Street, Am. Place Theater, N.Y.C., 1969, Isadora Duncan (Obie award), 1976, Other People, Berkshire Theatre Festival, 1969, The Celebration, Hedgerow Theater, Pa., 1971, Remember Me, Lakewood Theatre, Skowhegan, Maine; engaged in nat. tour Medea, 1947, U.S. entry Berlin Festival, 1951; motion picture appearances include Mr. Lincoln, The Lonely Night, A Light in the Forest, The Big Fisherman, The Greatest Story Ever Told; numerous appearances in TV dramatic shows; mem. faculty drama and dance div. Juilliard Sch. Lincoln Center, N.Y.C., 1969—. Bd. dirs. Neighborhood Playhouse, The Acting Co., nat. repertory theatre. Author: The Bright Lights, 1978. Home: 125 E 57th St New York NY 10022

SELECMAN, CHARLES EDWARD, business exec.; b. Dallas, Sept. 17, 1928; s. Frank A. and Eloise (Olive) S.; B.A., So. Meth. U., 1950; m. Nan Harton Nash, May 11, 1951 (div. 1975); children—Mary Lucinda, Nan Elizabeth, Amy Eloise; m. 2d, Judith Wallace Pollard, Feb. 6, 1976. Bus. mgmt. clk. Buick Motor div. Gen. Motor Corp., Dallas, 1951-52; personnel dept. Chance Vought Aircraft, Inc. Dallas, 1952-56; div. personnel mgr. Axelson div. U.S. Industries, Inc., Longview, Tex., 1956-64, div. v.p. marketing, 1964-66, div. exec. v.p., 1966-67, div. pres., 1967, corp. v.p., N.Y.C., 1967-68, corp. exec. v.p., 1968-70, pres., 1970-73, vice chmn., chief exec. officer, 1973, also dir.; owner Charles E. Selecman & Assos., 1974-75; pres., chief exec. officer E.T. Barwick Industries, Inc., 1975-78; partner Marshalsea Texas Partners, Dallas, 1978—. Mem. Sigma Alpha Epsilon. Home: 3433 Southwestern Blvd Dallas TX 75225 Office: Univ Tower Dallas TX 75206

SELESKY, HAROLD F., banker; b. N.Y.C., Aug. 1, 1913; s. Joseph F. and Mae (O'Neal) S.; B.S. in Econs., U. Pa., 1934; m. Bernice Evelyn Deacon (dec. 1966); 1 son, Donald Bryant; m. 2d, Helen Theresa McGirr, Aug. 9, 1967. With U.S. Dept. Agr., 1934-35; with Chem. Bank, N.Y.C., 1935-78, sr. v.p., 1968—, chmn. loan policy com., 1976-78, exec. v.p., 1976-78; ret., 1978; past dir. Cuban Am. Nickel Co., Chemlease Inc., Chemlease Worldwide Inc., Chem. Realty Corp. Pres. bd. Haworth (N.J.) Community Chest, 1958; chmn. matching gifts program U. Pa., 1972-74. Served to maj., inf., AUS, 1942-46. Decorated Bronze Star. Mem. Credit Research Found., Robert Morris Assos., Tau Kappa Epsilon. Congregationalist. Club: Wharton Bus. N.Y. Home: 83 Morris Ave Haworth NJ 07641 also Lake Simcoe Rural Route 4 Barrie ON L4M 4S6 Canada

SELEY, JASON, sculptor, educator; b. Newark, May 20, 1919; s. Simon M. and Leah (Kridel) S.; B.A., Cornell U., 1940; student Art Students League, 1943-45, Ecole des Beaux-Arts, Paris, 1949-50; m. Clara Kalnitsky, Feb. 27, 1942. One-man shows include: Le Centre D'Art, Port-Au-Prince, Haiti, 1946, 48, 49, Am. Brit. Art Center, N.Y.C., 1947, 48, Associated Am. Artists Gallery, N.Y.C., 1955, Barone Gallery, N.Y.C., 1960, Kornblee Gallery, N.Y.C., 1962, 64, 67, 69, White Mus., Cornell U., 1965, Dartmouth Coll., 1968, Amerika Haus, Berlin, 1971, Colgate U., 1974, Louis K. Meisel Gallery, N.Y.C., 1974, 78, Emerson Mus., Syracuse, N.Y., 1977; group shows: Mus. Modern Art, 1961, 62, 63, 65, Guggenheim Mus., 1962, Whitney Mus., 1952, 53, 62, 64, 67, 69; represented in permanent collections: Trenton (N.J.) Mus., Newark Mus., Dartmouth Coll., Mus. Modern Art, Whitney Mus., Chase-Manhattan Bank, Everson Mus., Syracuse, Nat. Gallery, Ottawa, Can., Art Gallery Ont., Toronto, Casper (Wyo.) Coll., State U. N.Y.-Fredonia, St. Lawrence U., Inst. Internat. Edn., N.Y.C., Empire State Plaza, Albany, N.Y.; asso. prof. fine arts Hofstra U., Hempstead, N.Y., 1963-65; asso. prof., artist-in-residence Sch. Edn., N.Y. U., 1965-67; artist-in-residence Dartmouth Coll., 1968; prof. art Cornell U., 1968—, chmn. dept. Coll. Architecture, Art and Planning, 1968-73; artist-in-residence Berliner Kunstler programm Deutscher Akademischer Austauschdienst, 1970-71. Fulbright scholar, 1949-50. Mem. Coll. Art Assn., AAUP, Art Students League. Home: 209 Hudson St Ithaca NY 14850

SELF, DAVID WILSON, church ofcl.; b. Leighton, Ala., Oct. 10, 1919; s. James T. and Lucy (Childers) S.; B.S., U. Ala., 1942, M.A., 1946; Ed.D., Columbia, 1965; m. Helen Frances Huckabee, Mar. 15, 1944; children—Carol Ann, Jane, Frances (Mrs. Earle Drennen), James. Tchr., athletic coach Brookwood (Ala.) High Sch., 1946-47; asst. prin. Greenville (Ala.) High Sch., 1947-49, prin., 1950-55; prin. Frisco City (Ala.) Sch., 1949-50; supt. Butler County schs., Greenville, 1955-58; supt. Phenix City (Ala.) schs., 1958-65; asso. prof. Sch. Adminstrn., U. Ala., 1965-69; mem. Methodist Ch., 1927—; conf. dir. Meth. Men, 1957-64; mem. gen. bd. edn., 1962-68; sec. div. local ch., 1964-68; vice chmn. Ala.-W. Fla. bd. lay activities, 1964-68; chmn. conf. bd. edn., 1964-68; gen. sec. gen. bd. laity United Meth. Ch., 1968-72, asso. gen. sec. div. lay life and work, bd. discipleship, 1972—; mem. gen. and jurisdictional confs., 1964, 66. Served with USNR, 1942-45. Decorated Air medal. Mem. N.E.A. (life), Phi Delta Kappa, Pi Kappa Phi. Rotarian (past pres.), Lion (past pres.). Home: 1303 Toddington Dr Murfreesboro TN 37130 Office: Box 840 Nashville TN 37202

SELF, EDWIN FORBES, editor, publisher; b. Dundee, Scotland, June 15, 1920; s. Robert Henry and Agnes (Dick) S.; A.B. Magna cum laude with distinction in Polit. Sci., Dartmouth, 1942; m. Dorothy McCloskey, Nov. 1, 1942; children—Joan, Robert; m. 2d, Gloria Eileen Winke Wade, Aug. 18, 1951; children—Winke, Carey. Advertising manager La Jolla, (Calif.) Light, 1946; pub. North Shores Sentinel, Pacific Beach, Calif., 1947-48; bus. manager Frontier Magazine, Los Angeles, 1949-55; editor, publisher San Diego Magazine, 1948—; publisher cons. for San Francisco mag.; pub. cons. Washingtonian Mag. Mem. La Jolla Museum Art. Recipient Telesu award, Am. Inst. Planners, San Diego, 1963, Pub. Info. award Calif. A.I.A., 1970. Mem. San Diego C. of C., Phi Beta Kappa, Delta Tau Delta, Sigma Delta Chi. Clubs: La Jolla Country, Tennis. Home: La Jolla CA 92037 Office: 3254 Rosecrans St San Diego CA 92110

SELF, JAMES CUTHBERT, textile co. exec.; b. Greenwood, S.C., Oct. 19, 1919; s. James Cuthbert and Lura (Mathews) S.; The Citadel, B.S. in Bus. Adminstrn., LL.D., 1961; Dr. Industry (hon.), Lander Coll., 1964; LL.D., U. S.C., 1973; H.H.D., Erskine Coll., 1975; m. Virginia Turner, Jan. 24, 1942; children—James Cuthbert, Virginia Preston, William Mathews, Sally Elizabeth. With Greenwood Mills, Inc., 1935—, asst. treas., 1943-49, treas., 1949-55, pres., 1955—; dir. S.C. Nat. Bank. Pres. Self Found., Greenwood; trustee Duke Endowment, Charlotte, N.C.; life mem. bd. trustees Clemson (S.C.) U. Served from 2d lt. to maj. AUS, 1941-46. Mem. S.C. Textile Mfrs. Assn. Columbia, Greenwood C. of C., Am. Textile Mfrs. Inst., N.Y. Cotton Exchange. Methodist. Clubs: Rotary (Greenwood); Metropolitan (N.Y.C.). Home: 1 S Cedar Dr Greenwood SC 29646 Office: Greenwood Mills Inc Drawer 1017 Greenwood SC 29646

SELF, MARGARET CABELL, author; b. Cin., Feb. 12, 1902; d. Hartwell and Margaret Polk (Logan) Cabell; student Chatham Hall, 1915-17, N.Y. Sch. Applied Design for Women, 1917-19; m. Sydney Baldwin Self, June 11, 1921; children—Sydney Baldwin, Shirley (Mrs. John O. Brotherhood, Jr.), Hartwell C., Virginia (Mrs. Harris Bucklin). Portrait artist, 1923-38; author specialty, tech., children's and travel books related to horses, also lectr. relating to subjects; cons. Ecole Equestre do San Miguel; musician mem. Chamber Orch., of San Miguel, Mexico; editor Block Island Times (R.I.), 1970—. Founder, commandant New Canaan Mounted Troop, Jr. Cavalry Am. Mem. Authors Guild, Am. Chamber Music Assn., No Friends of Music. Author: Teaching the Young to Ride, 1935; Red Clay Country, 1936; Horses, Their Selection, Care and Handling, 1943; Those Smith Kids, 1945; The Horseman's Encyclopedia, 1945; Fun on Horseback, 1945; Ponies on Parade, 1945; Chitter Chat Stories, 1946; A Treasury of Horse Stories, 1946; Come Away, 1948; Riding Simplified, 1948; Horseman's Companion, 1949; Horsemastership, 1953; Irish Adventure, 1954; The American Horse Show, 1958; Riding and Hunting Simplified, 1959; Jumping Simplified, 1959; Riding with Mariles, 1960; The How and Why of Horses, 1961; Horses of the World, 1961; Complete Book of Horses and Ponies; Riding Step by Step; The Happy Year; Horses of Today; The Shaggy Little Burro of San Miguel, 1965; The Horseman's Almanac, 1966; Henrietta, 1966; At the Horseshow with Margaret Cabell Self, 1966; In Ireland with Margaret Cabell Self 1967; The Morgan Horse in Pictures, 1967; Susan and Jane Learn to Ride, 1967; The Quarter Horse in Pictures; Sky Rocket, The Story of a Little Bay Horse, 1970; The Hunter In Pictures, 1971; The Young Rider and His First Pony, 1969; How to Buy the Right Horse, 1972; The Nature of the Horse, 1973; The Problem Horse and the Problem Rider, 1976. Home: Block Island RI 02807 also San Miguel de Allende GTO Mexico. *To achieve happiness and success in life one must have a goal. One must work continuously to make this goal come true, never losing sight of it, nor giving up when opportunities fail to appear, never being led away into paths which lead elsewhere. Many satisfactions come to the person who seeks to understand and develop all facets of his goal.*

SELF, RAYMOND WEAVER, bus. exec.; s. Arlie M. and Dora Elizabeth (McCombs) S.; student Massey Bus. Coll., 1934-45; cert. in acctg. U. Ala., 1952; cert. Birmingham So. Coll., 1961; m. Alma M., July 12, 1938; 1 dau., Mary Elizabeth Self Nelson. Display mgr. S.H. Kress & Co., 1936-38; with Ala. By-Products Corp., Birmingham, 1938—, v.p., controller, 1969, v.p. fin., controller, 1970-79, v.p. fin., treas., 1979—. Served with USNR, 1943-46. Mem. Nat. Assn. Accts. (pres. Birmingham chpt. 1962-63, Lybrand award for publ.), Fin. Exec. Inst., Am. Acctg. Assn. Methodist. Clubs: Masons, Vestavia Country, Civitan (dir. 1967-70). Home: 3333 Pembrooke Ln Hoover AL Office: Ala By-Products Corp PO Box 10246 Birmingham AL 35202

SELFRIDGE, GEORGE DEVER, dentist, ret. naval officer; b. Pitman, N.J., Sept. 24, 1924; s. William John and Edith (Gorman) S.; student Gettysburg Coll., 1942-43, Muhlenburg Coll., 1943-45; D.D.S., U. Buffalo, 1947; M.A., George Washington U., 1974; m. Ruth Motisher, 1948; children—Pamela Ruth, Kimberly Dawn, Cheryl Beth. Commd. lt. (j.g.) U.S. Navy, 1948, advanced through grades to rear adm., 1973; intern Naval Dental Sch., Bethesda, Md., 1948-49, Naval Hosp., St. Albans, N.Y., 1949-50; various dental positions, 1951-64; sr. dental officer U.S.S. Cadmus, 1964-65, U.S.S. Vulcan, 1965-66, Service Force, 1964-66, Submarine Force, Atlantic Fleet, 1967-69; asst. dir. grad. edn. Navy Grad. Dental Sch., Bethesda, 1969-72, comdg. officer, 1973-76; dep. exec. officer Norfolk (Va.) Navy Dental Clinic, 1972-73, ret., 1976; dean Dental Sch., Washington U., St. Louis, 1976—; dir. dental services Barnes Hosp., St. Louis, 1976—, Children's Hosp., St. Louis, 1976—; mem. adv. bd. VA Hosp., St. Louis, 1976—; mem. exec. council Central Regional Testing Service, 1976—; mem. adv. com. St. Louis Jr. Coll. Dist., 1976—. Decorated Legion of Merit, Commendation medal. Mem. Am. Dental Assn., Am. Coll. Dentists, Internat. Coll. Dentists, Am. Acad. Gen. Dentists, Am. Acad. Operative Dentistry, Am. Mil. Surgeons U.S., Navy Gold Foil Club. Republican. Contbr. articles to med. jours. Home: 14545 Foxham Ct Chesterfield MO 63017 Office: Sch Dental Medicine Washington U St Louis MO 63110

SELIG, ALLAN H. (BUD), profl. baseball team exec.; b. Milw., July 30, 1934; s. Ben and Marie Selig; grad. U. Wis. at Madison, 1956. With Selig Ford, West Allis, Wis., 1959—, pres., 1966—; part owner Milw. Braves became Atlanta Braves 1965), 1963-65; co-founder Teams, Inc., 1964; co-founder Milw. Brewers Am. League baseball team, 1965, owner, pres., 1970—. Served with U.S. Army, 1956-58. Address: care Milwaukee Brewers Milwaukee County Stadium Milwaukee WI 53214*

SELIG, JOHN SAMUEL, lawyer; b. Chgo., Nov. 3, 1939; s. Leonard L. and Elsie E. (Jacobs) S.; student Tulane U., 1957-60, Tulane Sch. Law, 1960-61; LL.B., U. Ark., 1963; postgrad. N.Y. U. Sch. Law, 1964-65; m. Lynda Ann Solomon, June 9, 1962; children—Leah Elizabeth, Michael John. Admitted to Ark. bar, 1963; asso. firm Chowning, Mitchell, Hamilton & Burrow, Little Rock, 1967-70, partner, 1970-71; trust officer Worthen Bank & Trust Co., Little Rock, 1971; securities commr. State of Ark., Little Rock, 1971-74; v.p., gen. counsel 1st Ark. Bankstock Corp., Little Rock, 1974-77; partner firm Williams, Selig & Sayre, Little Rock, 1977-79, firm Mitchell, Williams, Gill & Selig, Little Rock, 1980—. Bd. dirs. St. Vincent Infirmary, St. Vincent Devel. Found.; v.p. Temple B'nai Israel; panel chmn. United Way Priorities and Allocation Com. Served with U.S. Army, 1964-67. Mem. Am. Bar Assn., Ark. Bar Assn., Pulaski County Bar Assn., Am. Law Inst. Home: 3 Gibson Dr Little Rock AR 72207 Office: 1500 Worthen Bldg Little Rock AR 72201

SELIG, KARL-LUDWIG, educator; b. Wiesbaden, Germany, Aug. 14, 1926; s. Lucian and Erna (Reiss) S.; naturalized, 1948; B.A., Ohio State U., 1946, M.A., 1947; student U. Rome (Italy), 1949-50; Ph.D., U. Tex., 1955. Asst. prof. Romance langs. and lit. Johns Hopkins, 1954-58; asso. prof. U. N.C., 1958-61, U. Minn., 1961-63; vis. prof. U. Tex., 1963-64, prof. Romance langs. and lit., 1964-65; Hinchliff prof. Spanish lit. Cornell U., 1965-69, dir. grad. studies in Romance lit., 1966-69; prof. Spanish lit. Columbia 1969—. Vis. prof. U. Munich (Germany), 1963, 64, U. Berlin (Germany), 1967; cons. prof. Ohio State U., 1967-69; vis. lectr. U. Zulia, Maracaibo, Venezuela, 1968; dir. summer seminar Nat. Endowment for Humanities, 1975, cons., 1975-77; vis. scholar Ga. U. System, 1977. Mem. com. grants-in-aid Am. Council Learned Socs., 1969-73. Fulbright fellow, Rome, 1949-50, research scholar, Utrecht, Netherlands, 1958-59; Newberry Library fellow, 1958; Folger Shakespeare Library fellow, 1959, 63; spl. fellow Belgian Am. Ednl. Found., 1960, 61; sr. fellow Mediaeval and Renaissance Inst., Duke U., 1978; fellow Herzog August Bibliothek Wolfenbüttel, W. Ger., 1979. Recipient Mark Van Doren award Columbia, 1974. Mem. Modern Lang. Assn. Am. (sec., then chmn. Romance sect. 1965-66, chmn. comparative lit. 1973), Am. Assn. Tchrs. Spanish and Portuguese, Am. Assn. Teachers Italian, Mediaeval Acad. Am., Renaissance So. Am., Modern Humanities Research Assn., Internat. Assn. Hispanists, Am. Comparative Lit. Assn., Coll. Art Assn., Acad. Lit. Studies, Phi Beta Kappa (ho.). Author: The Library of Vincencio Juan de Lastanosa, Patron of Gracián, Geneva, 1960; also numerous articles, revs. Editor: (Thomas Blundeville) of Councils and Counselors, 1963; (with A. G. Hatcher) Studia Philologica et Litteraria in Honorem L. Spitzer, 1958; (with J. E. Keller) Essays in Honor of N. B. Adams, 1966; asso. editor Modern Lang. Notes, 1955-58; mng. editor Romance Notes, 1959-61; editor U. N.C. Studies in Comparative Lit., 1959-61; editor Bull. Comediantes, 1959-64, asso. editor, 1964-68, 79—; co-editor Yearbook of Comparative Lit., Vol. IX, 1960; editorial bd. Colección Támesis (London), 1962-79, Romanic Rev., 1969—, Teaching Lang. Through Lit., 1978—; asso. editor Hispania 1969-74, Ky. Romance Quar., 1973—; gen. editor Revista Hispánica Moderna, 1971—; mem. nat. adv. bd. Modern Lang. Assn. Internat. Bibliography, 1978—. Editorial bd. Yale Italian Studies, 1976—. Home: 30 E 37th St New York NY 10016

SELIGER, CHARLES, artist; b. N.Y.C., June 3, 1926; s. George Zekowski and Hortense Seliger; ed. by pvt. art instrn., also WPA Sch., 1940; m. Ruth Lewin, June 20, 1948 (dec. May 1975); children—Robert, Mark; m. 2d, Lenore Klebanow, 1975. One man shows include Peggy Guggenheim Gallery, N.Y.C., 1945-46, Carlebach Gallery, 1948, DeYoung Meml. Mus., San Francisco, 1949, Whitney Mus. ann., 1949-57, Willard Gallery, N.Y.C., 1951, 53, 55, 57, 61, 62, 66, 68, Seligman Gallery, Seattle, 1955, 58, 65, Nassau Community Coll., N.Y.C., 1965, Wooster Community Art Center, Conn., 1969, Andrew Crispo Gallery, 1973, 75, 76, 78, also Mus. Modern Art, Hayden Calhoun Gallery, Dallas, others; exhibited in Norlyst Gallery, N.Y.C., 1942, 67 Gallery, N.Y.C., 1943, David Porter Gallery, Washington, 1945, Four Arts Club, Palm Beach, Fla., 1946, Va. Mus. Fine Arts, 1946, U. Iowa, 1946, Salon des Realites Nouvelle, Paris, France, 1948, Bklyn. Mus., 1949, Cornell U., 1951, Art Inst. Chgo., 1961, 64, Syracuse Mus. Fine Arts, 1953, Nebr. Art Assn., 1953, Am. Acad. Arts & Letters, 1965, 67, 68, Smithsonian Inst., 1968, many others. works in permanent collections Addison Gallery, Andover, Mass., Munson Williams Proctor Mus., Utica, N.Y., Guggenheim Mus., Whitney Mus., Mus. Modern Art, Chgo. Art Inst., Newark Mus. Art, Iowa State U., Municipal Art Mus., The Hague, Holland, Tel Aviv Mus., Balt. Mus. Art, Joseph H. Hirshhorn Found., others, also numerous pvt. collections; artist, 1960—; v.p. design Comml. Decal, Inc., Mt. Vernon; Home: 10 Lenox Ave Mt Vernon NY 10552 Office: 650 S Columbus Ave Mt Vernon NY 10550

SELIGER, HOWARD H., educator; b. Bklyn., Dec. 4, 1924; s. Morton and Essie (Datz) S.; B.S., Coll. City N.Y., 1943; M.S., Purdue U., 1948; Ph.D., U. Md., 1954; m. Beatrice Semel, Jan. 15, 1944; children—Carol Ann, Susan Diane. Supervisory physicist Nat. Bur. Standards, Washington, 1948-60; asso. prof. biology McCollum Pratt Inst., Johns Hopkins, Balt., 1962-68, prof. biology, 1968—, radiation safety officer, 1962—. Pres. Radiation Instrument Co., 1952-62. Mem. environmental research guidance com. Md. Acad. Sci.; spl. research devel. bonsai in artificial environment. Served to 1st lt. USAAF, 1943-46. Guggenheim fellow, 1958-59; recipient Meritorious Service award Dept. Commerce, 1958. Fellow Am. Phys. Soc. Author: (with W.D. McElroy) Light, Physical and Biological Action, 1965; Ecology of Bioluminescent Bays; Phytoplankton Ecology. Home: 1805 W Rogers Ave Baltimore MD 21209

SELIGMAN, DANIEL, editor; b. N.Y.C., Sept. 25, 1924; s. Irving and Clare (O'Brien) S.; student Rutgers U., 1941-42; A.B., N.Y. U., 1946; m. Mary Gale Sherburn, May 23, 1953; children—Nora, William Paul. Editorial asst. New Leader, 1946; asst. editor Am. Mercury, 1946-50; asso. editor Fortune, 1950-59, editorial bd., 1959-66, asst. mng. editor, 1966-69, exec. editor, 1970-77, asso. mng. editor, 1977—; sr. staff editor all Time, Inc., Publs., 1969-70. Home: 190 E 72d St New York City NY 10021 Office: Time and Life Bldg New York City NY 10020

SELIGMANN, ALBERT LOUIS, fgn. service officer; b. N.Y.C., May 26, 1925; s. Louis Washington and Florence (Judson) S.; A.B., Columbia U., 1943, M.Internat. Affairs, 1949; m. Barbara Beller, June 27, 1948; children—Susan Lynn, Linda Jane, Ann Louise, Wendy Lee. With Office Intelligence Research, Dept. State, 1949- 55; assigned lang. sch., Tokyo, 1955-56; consul, Kobe-Osaka, Japan, 1956-59; 2d sec. embassy, Tokyo, 1959-62; 1st sec. embassy, Bangkok, Thailand, 1962-65; assigned Dept. State, 1965-67, dep. dir. Office Research and Analysis for E. Asia and Pacific, 1966-67; spl. asst. to dir. policy planning staff Office Internat. Security Affairs, Dept. Def., Washington, 1967-68, dep. dir., 1969; mem. planning and coordinating staff Dept. State, Washington, 1969-71; dep. polit. adviser U.S. Mission, Berlin, 1971-74, polit. adviser, 1974-75; mem. sr. seminar in fgn. policy Dept. State, Washington, 1975-76; counselor for polit. affairs Am. embassy, Tokyo, 1976—. Served to 1st lt. AUS, 1943-47. Mem. Am. Fgn. Service Assn., Internat. House Japan. Contbr. articles to profl. jours. Home: 7407 Recard Ln Alexandria VA 22307 Office: Am Embassy Tokyo Japan

SELIGMANN, JAMES FREDERICK, lit. agt.; b. Cedarhurst, L.I., N.Y., July 30, 1918; s. Arthur Walter and Hortense (Firuski) S.; B.A., Coll. City N.Y.; M.A., N.Y. U., 1960; m. Ursula Buchholz, Feb. 19, 1948. Editorial asst. Random House, Inc., N.Y.C., 1947; book sales rep. Sterling Pub. Co., N.Y.C., 1949-51, also sales mgr.; book sales rep. Holiday House, Ind., William R. Scott, Inc., Pantheon Books, Inc., Arco Pub. Co., Inc., N.Y.C., 1949-51; lit. agt. 1960—; pres. James F. Seligmann, Inc., N.Y.C., 1960-68; partner Seligmann & Collier, N.Y.C., 1968-75; propr. James Seligmann Agy., 1976—. Vol. for Stevenson, 1952; mem. Stevensonian Democratic Club (name changed to East Midtown Reform Dem. Club), 1953-68; mem. Gramercy-Stuyvesant Ind. Democrats, 1973—. Served with AUS, 1942-45. Mem. Soc. Authors' Reps. Author: How to Be Happy Though Drafted, 1951. Composer: Once I Saw A Little Man, 1969. Home: 601 E 20th St New York NY 10010 Office: 280 Madison Ave New York NY 10016

SELIGMANN, WERNER, architect, univ. dean; b. Osnabrück, Germany, Mar. 30, 1930; s. Fritz and Charlotte Louise (Czermin) S.; came to U.S., 1949, naturalized, 1955; B.Arch., Cornell U., 1954; student Technische Hochschule Braunschweig (Germany), 1958-59; m. Jean Lois Liberman, Aug. 29, 1954; children—Raphael John, Sabina Charlotte. Mem. faculty U. Tex., 1956-58, Eidgenössische Technische Hochschule, Zürich, 1959-61, Cornell U., 1961-74, Harvard Grad. Sch. Design, 1974-76; prof. architecture, dean Sch. Architecture, Syracuse (N.Y.) U., 1976—; prin. firm Werner Seligmann and Assos., 1961—; prin. works include scattered site housing, Ithaca, N.Y., 1972, adminstrn. bldg., Willard, N.Y., 1971, Sci. Bldg. II, State U. N.Y., Cortland, 1967, Beth David Synagogue, Binghamton, N.Y., 1963. AIA grantee, 1966. Office: Sch Architecture Slocum Hall Syracuse Univ Syracuse NY 13210

SELIGSON, ROBERT ALLEN, lawyer; b. Far Rockaway, N.Y., Nov. 12, 1932; s. Sidney C. and Lillian (Colvin) S.; A.B., Brown U., 1954; J.D., U. Calif., Berkeley, 1957; m. Marlene Kameny, Jan. 26, 1957; children—Linda, Amy, David. Admitted to Calif. bar, 1957; clk. to presiding justice Calif. Appellate Ct., 1957-58; pvt. practice, San Francisco, 1958—; propr. Robert A. Seligson, Inc., 1973—; asso. prof. Hastings Coll. Law, San Francisco, 1969-75; adv. com. project Calif. Cts. of Appeal, Nat. Center State Cts.; co-chmn. Chief Justice's Com. to Study Appellate Practices and Procedures, 1977—. Mem. State Bar Calif. (chmn. spl. com. appellate cts. 1972-74), Calif. Acad. Appellate Lawyers (pres. 1977-78), Bar Assn. San Francisco (dir. 1965, 70-72, chmn. com. appellate cts. 1975-77), Phi Beta Kappa. Jewish. Contbr. articles to legal publs. Home: 6 King Ave Piedmont CA 94611 Office: 300 Montgomery St San Francisco CA 94104

SELIKOFF, IRVING JOHN, physician; b. Bklyn., Jan. 15, 1915; s. Abraham and Tilli (Katz) S.; B.S., Columbia, 1935; M.D., Anderson Coll. Medicine, U. Melbourne (Australia), 1941; Sc.D. (hon.), Tufts U., 1976, Bucknell U., 1979; m. Celia Shiffrin, Feb. 4, 1946. Intern, Newark Beth Israel Hosp., 1943-44; asst. morbid anatomy Mt. Sinai Hosp., N.Y.C., 1941, now attending physician community medicine; prof. medicine and community medicine Mt. Sinai Sch. Medicine, City U. N.Y., prof. and chmn. div. environmental medicine, dir. environmental scis. lab.; resident Sea View Hosp., N.Y.C., 1944-46; research in treatment Tb, 1945; with Dr. Edward H. Robitzek introduced isoniazid and iproniazid, chemotherapy of Tb, 1951-52; cons. medicine Barnert Meml. Hosp., Paterson, N.J.; mem. Nat. Cancer Adv. Bd., 1979—. Recipient Lasker award in Medicine 1955; Ann. Research award Am. Cancer Soc., 1976; Edwards medal Welsh Nat. Sch. Medicine, 1977. Diplomate Am. Bd. Preventive Medicine. Fellow Am. Pub. Health Assn., Am. Coll. Chest Physicians (pres. N.J. chpt. 1954-55); mem. N.Y. Pub. Health Assn. (Haven Emerson award 1975), N.Y. Acad. Scis. (pres. 1969-70, bd. govs. 1970—, Poiley award and medal 1974), AMA, N.J., Passaic County med. socs., Inst. Medicine Nat. Acad. Scis., Soc. Occupational and Environ. Health (pres. 1973-74), Am. Coll. Toxicology (v.p. 1979). Author: The Management of Tuberculosis, 1956; Biological Effects of Asbestos, 1965; Toxicity of Vinyl Chloride and Polyvinyl Chloride; (with D.H.K. Lee) Asbestos and Disease, 1978; also articles profl. jours. Sr. asso. editor Mt. Sinai Jour. Medicine, N.Y.C.; editor-in-chief Environ. Research, Am. Jour. Occupational Medicine. Office: Mount Sinai Med Center 10 E 102d St New York NY 10029

SELIN, IVAN, computer services co. exec.; b. N.Y.C., Mar. 11, 1937; s. Saul and Freda (Kuhlman) Selicoff; B.E., Yale U., 1957, M.E., 1958, Ph.D., 1960; Dr. es Sciences, U. Paris, 1962; m. Nina Cantor, June 8, 1957; children—Douglas, Jessica. Research engr. Rand Corp., Santa Monica, Calif., 1960-65; systems analyst Dept. Def., Washington, 1965-67, dep. asst. sec. def., 1967-69, acting asst. sec. for systems analysis, 1969-70; founder, chief exec. Am. Mgmt. Systems, Inc., Arlington, Va., 1970—; cons. to govt.; lectr. UCLA, 1961-63. Trustee Nat. Cathedral Sch., Washington; bd. dirs. Tennis Patrons Assn., Washington. Decorated Disting. Civilian Service medal; Fulbright scholar, 1959-60; Ford Found. grantee, 1952-54. Mem. Council Fgn. Relations, UN Assn., IEEE (editor Trans. on Ifo. Theory 1960-65),

Tau Beta Pi. Club: Yale. Author: Detection Theory, 1964; contbr. articles to profl. jours. Home: 2905 32d St NW Washington DC 20008 Office: 1515 Wilson Blvd Arlington VA 22209

SELKIRK, JAMES KIRKWOOD, biochemist; b. N.Y.C., Dec. 3, 1938; s. James Kirkwood and Doris (Schuler) S.; B.S., Syracuse (N.Y.) U., 1964; Ph.D., Upstate Med. Center, Syracuse, 1969; m. Carole Ann Bozzone, Sept. 16, 1961; children—James Kirkwood, David Edward. Postdoctoral fellow McArdle Lab. Cancer Research, U. Wis., Madison, 1969-72; staff fellow Nat. Cancer Inst., NIH, Bethesda, Md., 1972-74, sr. staff fellow, 1974-75; unit leader chem. carcinogenesis, biology div. Oak Ridge Nat. Lab., 1975—; lectr. U. Tenn.-Oak Ridge Biomed. Grad. Sch.; mem. breast cancer task force NIH, 1979—. Served with AUS, 1959-61. Mem. AAAS, N.Y. Acad. Scis., Am. Assn. Cancer Research, Sigma Xi, Alpha Chi Sigma. Author research articles, chpts. in books; editorial bd. Carcinogenesis, 1979—. Home: 106 Norway Ln Oak Ridge TN 37830 Office: Biology Div Box Y Oak Ridge Nat Lab Oak Ridge TN 37830

SELKURT, EWALD ERDMAN, physiologist, educator; b. Edmonton, Alta., Can., Mar. 13, 1914; s. Ephraim and Amanda Olga (Stirle) S.; B.A., U. Wis., 1937, M.A., 1939, Ph.D., 1941; m. Ruth Marion Gesley, June 21, 1941; children—Claire Elaine, Sylvia Anne. Instr. physiology N.Y. U. Sch. Medicine, 1941-44; sr. instr. Western Res. U. Sch. Medicine, Cleve., 1944-46, asst. prof., 1946-49, asso. prof., 1949-58; prof., chmn. dept. physiology Ind. U. Sch. Medicine, Indpls., 1958—, Distinguished prof., 1976—; Centennial vis. prof. physiology Ohio State U. Sch. Medicine, 1970; mem. Josiah Macey Conf. on Kidney, 1949-53, Conf. Shock and Circulatory Homeostasis, 1949-53; mem. subcom. on shock Com. Med. Scis., NRC, 1953-57; mem. cardiovascular study sect. Nat. Heart Inst., NIH, 1963-68; panel mem. evaluation of sci. faculty fellowships NSF, 1963-64; mem. kidney council Unitarian Service Com., Germany, 1954. Active Indpls. Symphonic Chorus. NSF fellow, Göttingen, W.Ger., 1964-65. Mem. Am. Soc. Nephrology, AAUP, Am. Heart Assn., Am. Physiol. Soc. (council 1971-74, pres. elect 1975), Harvey Soc., Assn. Chmn. Depts. Physiology (councilor 1967-70, pres. 1971-72, Service award 1979), Soc. Exptl. Biology and Medicine (council 1978—), Phi Beta Kappa, Sigma Xi, Phi Sigma, Gamma Alpha, Pi Kappa Delta. Lutheran. Club: Singer's (Cleve.). Author: Textbook of Physiology, 1963; Basic Physiology for Health Sciences, 1975; cons. editor Am. Jour. Physiology and Jour. Applied Physiology, 1963-67, 70-73, Am. Heart Jour., 1966—, procs. Soc. Exptl. Biology and Medicine, 1967—, Circulatory Shock, 1974—. Editorial com. Ann. Rev. Physiology, 1965-69. Home: 3269 W 42d St Indianapolis IN 46208

SELL, EDWARD SCOTT, JR., lawyer; b. Athens, Ga., Mar. 13, 1917; s. Edward Scott and Nettie Ruth (Whatley) S.; A.B., U. Ga., 1937; J.D. cum laude, U. Ga., 1939; m. Mary Deupree Eckford, Sept. 14, 1940; 1 son, Edward Scott. Admitted to Ga. bar, 1938; partner firm Lewis & Sell, 1940-55, Lane & Sell, 1955-56, Sell & Comer, Macon, Ga., 1955-69, Sell, Comer & Popper, Macon, 1969—; city atty. Macon, 1947-53; atty. Macon-Bibb County Planning & Zoning Commn., 1953-65; county atty. Bibb County (Ga.), 1965—; lectr. law Mercer U., 1958-60. Trustee Wesleyan Coll., Macon, 1973—. Served with U.S. Army, 1942-46. Decorated Bronze Star, Army Commendation medal. Fellow Am. Bar Found.; mem. State Bar Ga. (bd. govs. 1947-50), Macon Bar Assn. (past pres.), Phi Beta Kappa, Phi Kappa Phi, Phi Delta Phi, Macon Circuit Bar Assn. (past pres.). Clubs: Lions, Atlanta City, Shriners, Masons. Home: 1644 Hawthorne Rd Macon GA 31211 Office: PO Box 1014 Macon GA 31202

SELL, KENNETH WALTER, govt. adminstr., pediatrician; b. Valley City, N.D., Apr. 29, 1931; s. Walter Robert and Patricia Haldora (Gottskalkson) S.; B.A., U. N.D., 1953, B.S., 1954; M.D., Harvard U., 1956; Ph.D., Cambridge (Eng.) U., 1968; m. Dec. 20, 1950; children—Gregory, Thomas, Barbette, Susan. Commd. capt. M.C., U.S. Navy, 1956; intern Nat. Naval Med. Center, Bethesda, Md., 1956-57; resident, pediatrician, 1956-65, dir. Navy tissue bank, 1965-70, chmn. dept. clin. and exptl. immunology, 1970-74, inst. comdg. officer, 1974-77; ret., 1977; sci. dir. Nat. Inst. Allergy and Infectious Diseases, Bethesda, 1977—; clin. prof. pediatrics Georgetown U. Trustee, Christ Lutheran Ch., Bethesda. Decorated Legion of Merit. Diplomate Am. Bd. Pediatrics. Fellow Am. Acad. Pediatrics, Am. Acad. Pathology; mem. AMA, Brit. Soc. Immunology, Tissue Culture Assn., Soc. Cryobiology, Transplantation Soc., Am. Assn. Immunologists, Soc. Exptl. Hematology, Am. Assn. Tissue Banks (pres.), Am. Coll. Pathology, Am. Soc. Microbiology, Phi Beta Kappa, Sigma Xi, Phi Beta Pi. Editor: Tissue Banking for Transplantation, 1976. Home: 12311 Old Canal Rd Rockville MD 20854 Office: NIH Nat Inst Allergy and Infectious Diseases Bldg 5/137 Bethesda MD 20205

SELL, WILLIAM EDWARD, educator, lawyer; b. Hanover, Pa., Jan. 1, 1923; s. Henry A. and Blanche M. (Newman) S.; A.B., Washington and Jefferson Coll., 1944, L.H.D., 1973; J.D., Yale U., 1947; LL.D., Dickinson Sch. Law, 1968; m. Cordelia I. Fulton, Aug. 20, 1949; 1 son, Jeffrey Edward. Mem. faculty U. Pitts. Law Sch., 1947-51, 53—, prof. law, 1954—, asso. dean Law Sch., 1957-62, dean, 1966-77, Distinguished Service prof. law, 1977—; admitted to D.C. bar, 1951, Pa. bar, 1952; practice in Pitts., 1952—; of counsel firm Meyer, Unkovic & Scott, Pitts.; atty. U.S. Steel Corp., 1951-53; vis. prof. U. Mich. Law Sch., 1957; past pres. Pa. Bar Inst. Pres. bd. dirs. St. Clair Meml. Hosp. Served with USAAF, World War II. Mem. Am., Pa., Allegheny County bar assns., Assn. Am. Law Schs., Am. Law Inst., Phi Beta Kappa, Order of Coif, Pi Delta Epsilon, Phi Gamma Delta, Phi Delta Phi, Omicron Delta Kappa. Presbyterian (elder, deacon). Club: Masons. Author: Fundamentals of Accounting Lawyers, 1960; Pennsylvania Business Corporations, 2 vols., 1969; Sell on Agency, 1975; also articles; editor: Pennsylvania Keystone Lawyers Desk Library. Home: 106 Seneca Dr Pittsburgh PA 15228

SELLA, GEORGE JOHN, JR., chem. co. exec.; b. West New York, N.J., Sept. 29, 1928; s. George John and Angelina (Dominoni) S.; B.S., Princeton U., 1950; M.B.A., Harvard U., 1952; m. Janet May Auf-der Heide, May 14, 1955; children—George Caldwell, Jaime Ann, Lorie Jean, Michael Joseph. With Am. Cyanamid Co., Wayne, N.J., 1954—, pres. Europe/Mideast/African div., 1976, corp. v.p., 1977, sr. v.p., 1977-78, vice chmn., 1978—. Served with USAF, 1952-54. Mem. Am. Chem. Soc., Am. Inst. Chem. Engrs. Office: Am Cyanamid Co Berdan Ave Wayne NJ 07470

SELLE, ELAINE LOUISE BABCOCK, pub. co. exec.; b. Hartford, Conn., Dec. 3, 1925; d. Herbert Bruce and Caroline (Dorsheimer) Babcock; stepdau. Constance (Lytle) Babcock; student Mary Washington Coll., 1942-43; A.B., Wellesley Coll., 1946; M.S., Boston U., 1970; m. Henry Frederick Selle, July 26, 1964 (div. 1974); children—Steven Foskin, Dorothy Foskin. Art cataloguer Fogg Mus., Cambridge, Mass., 1947-50; editorial asst. Beacon Press, Boston, 1950-51; art editor Ginn & Co. Publs., Boston, 1952; art editor McLean-Hunter Publs., Toronto, Ont., Can., 1956-58; tech. writer RCA, Bedford, Mass., 1960-61; tech. editor Tech. Ops. Inc., Burlington, Mass., 1962-63; asst. editor Jour. Neurosurgery, Hanover, N.H., 1966-74; dir. div. pub. Dartmouth Printing Co., Hanover, 1974—. Pub. relations cons. Montshire Mus. Sci., Squam Lakes Sci. Center. Founder Women's Info. Service Inc., 1971, also pub. relations cons., dir. Bd. dirs. N.H. Frontiers in Adoption Inc.; trustee Montshire Mus. Sci. Mem. AAUW (pres. div. 1972-74, dir. div.), Soc. Tech. Communication (sr. mem.; dir.), Ednl. Press Assn., Council Biology Editors (publs. com.), Women in Communication, Soc. Scholarly Publishing, Pub. Relations Soc. Am., New Eng. Women's Press Assn., Assn. Sci. Jours., Press Club of Boston. Club: Wellesley. Contbr. articles to newspapers, mags. Home: 7 Claflin Circle Hanover NH 03755 Office: Dartmouth Printing Co Hanover NH 03755

SELLECK, ROBERT W., soft drink bottling co. exec.; b. 1921; ed. Flint Jr. Coll.; married. Salesman, Coca-Cola Co., Inc., 1941-52; propr. R.W. Selleck Distbg. Co., 1953-56; mktg. mgr. Pepsi-Cola Gen. Bottlers, Inc., Chgo., 1956, v.p. sales, 1956-59, sr. v.p. mktg., 1959-68, exec. v.p. mktg., mem. exec. com., mem. finance com., 1968-70, sr. exec. v.p., chief. operating officer, mem. exec. com., mem. finance com., 1970-72, pres., chief operating officer, 1972-75, pres., chief exec. officer, 1975—, also mem. exec. com., dir.; dir. Bubble Up Co., Midas Internat. Corp., IC Products Co. div IC Industries, Tollway Arlington Nat. Bank. Served with AUS, 1942-45. Office: 1745 N Kolmar Ave Chicago IL 60639

SELLERS, CHARLES, educator; b. Charlotte, N.C., Sept. 9, 1923; s. Charles Grier and Irene (Templeton) S.; A.B., Harvard, 1947; Ph.D., U. N.C., 1950; children—Charles Grier, Janet Smart, Steen Harold. Instr., U. Md., 1950-51; asst. prof. Princeton, 1951-58; mem. faculty U. Calif. at Berkeley, 1958—, prof. history, 1960—. Served with AUS, 1943-46. Fellow Center Advanced Studies Behavioral Scis., 1960-61; Guggenheim fellow, 1963-64. Mem. Phi Beta Kappa. Author: James K. Polk, vol. 1, 1958, Vol. 11, 1966 (Bancroft prize). Address: Dept History U Calif Berkeley CA 94720

SELLERS, GEORGE H., corp. ofcl.; b. Winnipeg, Man., Can., Apr. 19, 1914; s. Henry Eugene and Irene (Maulson) S.; student Ridley Coll., U. Man.; m. Margaret Anne Aikens, Sept. 26, 1936; children—David Henry, Margaret Anne, Joan Irene. Pres. Sellers, Dickson Securities, Ltd., Riverwood Investments Ltd., Regent Trust Co.; dir. Bank of Montreal, Radar Internat. Investments Ltd., Greater Winnipeg Gas Co., Can. Malting Co., Ltd., Royal Trust Co., Heritage Craftsmen Inc., Grain Ins. Brokers Ltd. Bd. dirs. Ridley Coll., Man. Centennial Corp. Served to col. RCAF, 1934-45. Decorated Air Force Cross, France and Germany Star, Order of St. John. Mem. Man. Forestry Assn. (dir.), RCAF Assn. (grand pres. 1972-75). Home: Riverbend Farm PO Box 129 Headingley MB R0H 0J0 Canada Office: 2210 One Lombard Pl Winnipeg MB R3BOX3 Canada

SELLERS, JAMES EARL, theol. ethicist; b. Lucedale, Miss., Nov. 1, 1926; s. Lucius Earl and Grace (McVicar) S.; B.E.E., Ga. Inst. Tech., 1947; M.S., Fla. State U., 1954; Ph.D. (Kent fellow), Vanderbilt U., 1958. Asst. prof. Christian ethics and theology Vanderbilt Div. Sch., Nashville, 1958-61, asso. prof., 1961-64, prof., 1964-71, dean Div. Sch., 1964-67; David Rice prof. ethics Rice U., Houston, 1971—. Served to lt. USNR, 1944-54. Recipient Danforth award for research in France, 1966. Mem. Soc. for Values in Higher Edn., L'Alliance Française, AAUP. Author: The Outsider and the Word of God, 1961; The South and Christian Ethics, 1962; Theological Ethics, 1966; Public Ethics, 1970; Warming Fires, 1975. Editor-at-large The Christian Century, 1971—; contbr. articles to New Theology No. 1, Lifeboat Ethics, Ethical Issues in Am. Life. Home: 2601 S Braeswood St Houston TX 77025 Office: Dept Religious Studies Rice U Houston TX 77001. *After more than twenty years of teaching ethics to university students and churchmen, I have concluded that neither "morality" nor "religion" is as basic as the American tradition of justice. If we would rescue the oppressed here or elsewhere, indeed, if we would redeem mankind, we should begin by affirming life with dignity, liberty, and the right of all to the pursuit of happiness, the disadvantaged as well as the advantaged.*

SELLERS, JAMES MCBRAYER, mil. acad. pres., educator; b. Lexington, Mo., June 20, 1895; s. Sandford and Lucia Valentine (Rogers) S.; A.B., U. Chgo., 1917; m. Rebekah Hall Evans, Dec. 28, 1925; children—Stephen Wentworth, James McBrayer, Frederick Evans. Asst. comdt. and instr. Wentworth Mil. Acad., Lexington, Mo., 1920-24, comdt., 1924-30, exec. officer, 1930-35, supt., 1935-60, pres., 1967—. Served from 2d lt. to capt., 6th Regt., USMC, 1917-20. Decorated D.S.C., Navy Cross with 2 silver star citations, Purple Heart; Croix de Guerre. Mem. Mil. Schs. Assn. (past pres.), Phi Beta Kappa, Sigma Xi. Beta Theta Pi, Presbyn. Mason (K.T., grand comdr. 1951-52; grand master 1953-54). Address: Wentworth Mil Acad Lexington MO 64067

SELLERS, RICHARD MORGAN, ins. co. exec.; b. Beeville, Tex., Aug. 14, 1913; s. Richard and Lena Lee (Morgan) S.; A.B., So. Methodist U., 1934; M.A., U. Mich., 1936; m. Lucille Marshall, Mar. 22, 1941; 1 son, R. Marshall. With Commonwealth Life Ins. Co., Louisville, 1936-62, 70-78, pres., 1970-73, vice chmn. bd., 1973-78, now dir.; sr. v.p. U.S. Life Ins. Co., N.Y.C., 1962-70. Bd. dirs. Louisville Philharmonic Soc., Greater Louisville Fund for Arts, 2d Presbyn. Ch., Macauley Theatre. Mem. Soc. Actuaries, Louisville Area C. of C. Clubs: Louisville Country, Wynn Stay; Princeton, Cavendish, Regency Whist (N.Y.C.). Contbr. articles to profl. jours. Home: 2 Glen Arden Rd Glenview KY 40025

SELLERS, ROBERT VERNON, oil co. exec.; b. Bartlesville, Okla., Mar. 26, 1927; s. C. Vernon and Helen (Weeks) S.; B.S. in Mech. Engring., U. Kans., 1948; grad. Advanced Mgmt. Program, Harvard, 1967; m. Anna Marie Hughes, Feb. 11, 1950; children—Barbara (Mrs. E.W. Bredemeier Jr.), Patricia (Mrs. D.M. Wheeler), Scott, John. Service engr. Dowell, Inc., 1949-50; various positions in transp. and supply, corporate planning and finance Cities Service Co., 1951-69, v.p. finance, 1969-71, dir., mem. exec. com., 1969—, vice chmn. bd., 1971-72, chmn. bd., chief exec. officer, chmn. exec. com., 1972—, chmn. finance com., 1973—; dir. John Hancock Mut. Life Ins. Co. Asst. to dir. prodn. div. Petroleum Adminstrn. Def., 1951-52. Mem. adv. bd. Sch. Bus., U. Kans.; trustee U. Tulsa; chmn. nat. adv. council Salvation Army; bd. dirs. So. Growth Policies Bd.; trustee Kans. U. Endowment Assn. Served with USNR, 1945-46. Mem. Financial Execs. Inst., Am. Petroleum Inst. (dir., exec. com.), Internat. C. of C. (trustee U.S. council), Conf. Bd., Com. Econ. Devel. (trustee), Met. Tulsa C. of C., Nat. Petroleum Council, Sigma Chi, Tau Beta Pi. Clubs: Tulsa, Summit, So. Hills Country (Tulsa); Internat. (Washington); Pipe Liners; Board Room, Economic, Nat. Golf Links Am. Home: 2131 E 29 St Tulsa OK 74114 Office: Box 300 Tulsa OK 74102

SELLEW, FRANCIS BERNARD, architect; b. Natick, Mass., July 23, 1913; s. Francis Leo and Rose (McManus) S.; B.Arch., Mass. Inst. Tech., 1935, M.Arch., 1940. Architect, Newport News, Va., 1938-42, Panama Canal, 1942-43, Washington, 1943; architect firm Coolidge, Shepley, Bulfinch & Abbott, Boston, 1946-48, The Architects Collaborative, Cambridge, Mass., 1948-50; partner firm Smith & Sellew (name changed to Sellew, Doherty & Sheskey, Inc.), Boston, 1950—. Mem. Boston Mayor's Blue Ribbon Panel for N. Harvard St. Urban Renewal, 1966; permanent mem. Rotch Travelling Scholarship. Trustee Wediko Children's Services, Inc., Boston. Served with USNR, 1943-46. Fellow A.I.A.; mem. Boston Soc. Architects (chmn. honors and awards com. 1969—, sec. 1960-65, v.p. 1965-67), Mass. Assn. Architects (pres. 1963-65). Club: St. Botolph (Boston). Home: 28 Wellesley Ave Wellesley MA 02181 Office: 1200 Hancock St Quincy MA 02169

SELLIN, THEODORE, fgn. ser. officer; b. Phila., June 17, 1928; s. Thorsten and Amy (Anderson) S.; student U. Uppsala (Sweden), 1946-48; B.A., U. Pa., 1951, M.A., 1952; m. Taru Jarvi, July 10, 1965; 1 son, Derek. Commd. fgn. ser. officer Dept. State, 1952; vice consul, Copenhagen, 1952-56; research analyst Dept. State, Washington, 1956-58; program officer Office Internat. Confs., 1965-67; acad. tng. U. Ind., 1958-59; 2d sec., Helsinki, Finland, 1959-64; 1st sec., labor-polit. officer, Oslo, Norway, 1967-71; 1st sec., polit. officer, Helsinki, 1971-73; polar affairs officer State Dept., 1975; now consul gen., Goteborg, Sweden. Office: US Consulate Gen Sodra Hamngatan 53 Box 428 Goteborg Sweden

SELLINGER, FRANCIS JOHN, brewing co. exec.; b. Phila., July 8, 1914; s. Frank and L. Caroline (Wiseman) S.; B.S., St. Joseph's Coll., 1936; postgrad. Drexel Inst., 1936-37, E.A. Siebel Inst. Tech., Chgo., 1928; m. Helen Brown, Feb. 22, 1941; children—Frank, Mary, Joseph, Helen, Dorothy, John, Patricia, Elizabeth, James. Chief chemist, asst. brewmaster Esslinger Brewing Co., Phila., 1936-41; chief chemist, purchasing agt. Hudepohl Brewing Co., Cin., 1941-46; asst. to gen. mgr. August Wagner Breweries, Columbus, Ohio, 1946-50; owner, pres. Hi-State Beverage Co., 1950-52; supt. packaging, purchasing agt. Burger Brewing Co., 1952, v.p., gen. mgr., 1956-64; with Anheuser-Busch Inc., St. Louis, 1964-77, v.p. engring., 1966-74, group v.p., 1974-76, exec. v.p. mgmt. and industry affairs, 1976-77; pres. Joseph Schlitz Brewing Co., Milw., 1977—, dir., 1979—; dir. Marine Nat. Exchange Bank, Milw., 1979—. Mem. Master Brewers Assn. Am. Clubs: Milw. Athletic, Milw. Country. Office: 235 W Galena St Milwaukee WI 53201

SELLINGER, FRANK J., brewing co. exec.; b. Phila., 1914; B.S., St. Joseph's Coll., 1936; married. Exec. v.p. mgmt. and industry affairs Anheuser-Bush, Inc., 1964-77; pres. Joseph Schlitz Brewing Co., Milw., 1977—. Office: Joseph Schlitz Brewing Co 235 W Galena St PO Box 614 Milwaukee WI 53201

SELLINGER, JOSEPH ANTHONY, coll. pres.; b. Phila., Jan. 17, 1921; s. Frank and L. Caroline (Wiseman) S.; Ph.L., Spring Hill Coll., 1945, B.S. in Chemistry, 1945; student theology Weston Coll., 1948-49, Woodstock Coll., 1949-50; S.T.L., Facultes St. Albert, Louvain, Belgium, 1952. Entered Soc. of Jesus, 1938; ordained priest, Roman Cath. Ch., 1951; asso. dean Coll. Art and Scis., Georgetown U., 1955-57, dean, 1957-64, sec. corp., dir. 1957-64; pres., rector Loyola Coll., Balt., 1964—. Mem. Am. Council on Edn. (vice chmn.), Assn. for Higher Edn., Middle States Assn., Nat. Cath. Ednl. Assn., Cath. Theol. Soc., Assn. Am. Colls., Phi Beta Kappa (hon.). Address: Loyola College 4501 N Charles St Baltimore MD 21210*

SELLON, JOHN A., reins. co. exec.; b. London, Eng., May 20, 1910; s. Ernest M. and Barbara Ann (Porter) S.; ed. Choate Sch., Princeton; m. Emily Boenke, Sept. 22, 1931; children—Peter J., Michael, Jeffrey B. With Lloyds, London, 1930-31, Nat. Surety Corp., 1931-32; joined Am. Reins. Co. N.Y.C., 1932; now pres. Cuisenaire Co. Am., Learning Games, Inc., S & B Brokerage Service Corp.; partner Municipal Issuers Service Co., Sellon Assos. Home: Hillandale Rd Port Chester NY 10573 Office: PO Box 820C North White Plains NY 10603

SELLON, WILLIAM ARTHUR, coll. dean; b. Elk River, Minn., June 6, 1922; s. Earl Robert and Clara (Golisch) S.; B.S., Stout State U., 1943; Ed.M., Okla. U., 1946; Ed.D., Bradley U., 1950; m. Roberta Hardin, May 30, 1947; children—Michael, Patricia, Kristi, Teresa, Mary, Jon. Instr. ind. edn. U. Okla., Norman, 1946-48; asst. prof. Bradley U., Peoria, Ill., 1949-54; asst. prof. Ohio U., Athens, 1954-56; prof., dean grad. studies Bemidji (Minn.) State U., 1956—; vis. lectr. W.Va. U., Morganton, 1956; cons. James F. Lincoln Arc Welding Found., Cleve., 1954-70. Pres. Beltrami County Hist. Soc., 1970-74. Served with USNR, 1944-46. Mem. Am. Council Indsl. Tchr. Edn., Am. Indsl. Arts Assn., Am. Legion, Izaak Walton League, Epsilon Pi Tau. Author: Industrial Arts Arc Welding, 1956; (with John Mathews) A Basic Manual of Instruction, 1958; Arc Welded Projects, 1959. Contbr. articles to profl. jours., mags. Home: 315 Norwood Dr Bemidji MN 56601

SELLS, ROBERT LEE, educator; b. Lancaster, Ohio, Oct. 14, 1925; s. Robert L. and Elizabeth (Fosnaugh) S.; B.S. in Mech. Engring., U. Mich., 1948; Ph.D. in Physics, U. Notre Dame, 1953; m. Patricia Vail Converse, July 3, 1947; children—Robert L., Cynthia Vail. Asst. prof., then asso. prof. Rutgers U., New Brunswick, N.J., 1953-63; prof. physics, chmn. dept. State U. N.Y. at Geneseo, 1963—, Distinguished Teaching prof., 1973—. Commr. on Coll. Physics, 1966-70. Served with USNR, 1943-47. Recipient Centennial Sci. award U. Notre Dame, 1965. Mem. Am. Assn. Physics Tchrs. (Distinguished Service citation 1969), Am. Phys. Soc., Am. Assn. U. Profs. Author: (with R.T. Weidner) Elementary Classical Physics, 2 vols. 1965; (with R.T. Weidner) Elementary Modern Physics, 2d edit., 1968; (with R.T. Weidner) Elementary Physics—Classical and Modern, 1975. Home: 4771 Resevoir Rd Geneseo NY 14454

SELLS, SAUL B., psychologist, educator; b. N.Y.C., Jan. 13, 1913; s. Maxwell I. and Dora B. Sells; A.B., Bklyn. Coll., 1933; Ph.D., Columbia U., 1936; m. Helen Frances Roberts, July 2, 1939. Research asst., then instr. psychology Columbia U., 1936-39; research asso. spl. projects N.Y.C. Bd. Edn., 1939-42; lectr. ednl. psychology Grad. Sch. Edn., Bklyn. Coll., 1939-42; chief statistician, head div. statis. standards, dep. dir. consumers goods div. OPA, 1942-46; asst. to pres. A.B. Frank Co., San Antonio, 1946-48; prof., head dept. med. psychology USAF Sch. Aviation Medicine, Randolph AFB, Tex., 1948-58; prof., then research prof. psychology, dir. Inst. Behavioral Research, Tex. Christian U., 1958—; vis. prof. U. Tex. at Austin, 1950-51; cons. in field, 1948—; pres. Psychology Press, Inc., 1962-68; cons. WHO, 1976; participant Internat. Conf. Drug Abuse, Geneva, 1976, Rome, 1977, Lisbon, 1977, NATO Symposium on Man in Isolation and Enclosed Space, Rome, 1969, 3d Banff Conf. on Theoretical Psychology, 1972. Bd. dirs. Bexar County Mental Health Assn., 1950-57; bd. dirs. Tarrant County Heart Assn., 1969—, chmn. bd., 1975. Recipient Longacre award Aerospace Med. Assn., 1956, commendation for meritorious civilian service USAF, 1957, Pacesetter award Nat. Inst. Drug Abuse, 1978. Fellow Am. Psychol. Assn. (pres. div. mil. psychology 1970), AAAS, Aerospace Med. Assn. (Longacre award 1956); mem. Am. Astronautical Soc. (sr. mem.; dir. S.W. br.), Am. Statis. Assn., Am. Ednl. Research Assn., Psychometric Soc., NEA, Soc. Psychol. Study Social Issues, Southwestern Psychol. Assn. (pres. 1963), Soc. Multivariate Exptl. Psychology (pres. 1964), Sigma Xi (pres. RESA br. San Antonio 1956). Author: Essentials of Psychology, 1962; Bioelectronics Abstracts, Vol. I, 1961, Vol 2, 1963; (with others) Social Adjustment and Personality Development in Children, 1972; also articles, monographs; editor: (with C.A. Berry) Human Factors in Jet and Space Travel, 1961; Stimulus Determinants of Behavior, 1964; The Definition and Measurement of Mental Health, 1969; Effectiveness of Drug Abuse Treatments, 2 vols., 1974, with D.D. Simpson, 3 vols., 1976; (with others) Human Functioning in Longitudinal Perspective: Studies of Normal and Psychopathological Populations, 1979; mng. editor, asso. editor Multivariate Behavioral Research, Vol. 1, 1966; editor Behavioral Science Monographs, 1971—; cons. editor in field, 1955—. Home: 3850 Overton Park Dr W Fort Worth TX 76109

SELLSTROM, ALBERT DONALD, educator; b. Elgin, Tex., Sept. 25, 1926; s. Albert and Amelia Pauline (Nelson) S.; student Tex. Christian U., 1944-45; B.A., U. Tex. at Austin, 1947, M.A., 1949; postgrad. (Fulbright fellow) Universite de Bordeaux (France), 1949-50; M.A., Princeton, 1953, Ph.D., 1956; m. Eleanor Wood McCleary, Jan. 31, 1958; children—Peter Wiley, Eric Augustus, Margaret Nelson, Oren McCleary. Instr. French, Princeton, 1954-58; asst. prof. U. Tex. at Austin, 1958-61, asso. prof., 1961-67, prof., 1967—, chmn. dept. French, Italian, 1972-78. Served with USNR, 1944-46. Decorated Palmes academiques (France), 1975. Mem. Modern Lang. Assn. Am., South-Central Modern Lang. Assn., Am. Assn. Tchrs. French, A.A.U.P., Phi Beta Kappa. Editor: Le Cid (Corneille), 1967. Contbr. articles on 17th-century French lit. to profl. jours. Home: 2617 Pecos St Austin TX 78703 Office: Dept of French and Italian U of Tex Austin TX 78712

SELONICK, JAMES BENNETT, dept. store exec.; b. N.Y.C., July 6, 1925; s. Stanley E. and Cecile R. (Rosenblum) S.; A.B., U. Cin., 1948, LL.B., 1949; m. Peggy Frieder, Nov. 19, 1949; children—Ellen, James, William. Admitted to Ohio bar, 1949, U.S. Dist. Ct. bar, 1949; asso. firm Harmon Colston, Goldsmith & Hoadley, 1949-52; asso. co. counsel, asst. mgr. real estate Federated Dept. Stores, Cin., 1952-61; exec. v.p. Simon Enterprises, Inc., Reston, Va., 1961-64, v.p., 1964-65, exec. v.p., 1965-68; v.p. Mugar Group, Boston, 1968-70; v.p. property devel. Federated Dept. Stores, 1970-73, sr. v.p., 1973—; pres. Federated Stores Realty, Inc., 1973-78, chmn. bd., chief exec. officer, 1978—. Treas. Rockdale Temple, Cin., 1975—. Served with USNR, 1942-45. Mem. Internat. Council Shopping Centers (dir., exec. com.), Cin. Improvement Corp. (dir.). Club: La Santaville Country. Home: 2600 Handasyde Ave Cincinnati OH 45208 Office: 222 W 7th St Cincinnati OH 45202

SELOVE, WALTER, physicist; b. Chgo., Sept. 11, 1921; s. Abe and Rose (Feld) S.; B.S., U. Chgo., 1942, Ph.D. (NRC fellow), 1949; m. Fay Ajzenberg, Dec. 18, 1955. Asst. instr. U. Chgo., 1942-43; staff mem. Mass. Inst. Tech. Radiation Lab., 1943-45; physicist Argonne Nat. Lab., 1947-50; instr. Harvard U., 1950-52, asst. prof., 1952-56; asso. prof. U. Pa., Phila., 1957-61, prof. physics, 1961—; staff mem. Livermore Lab., 1953-54; cons. Joint Congl. Com. on Atomic Energy, 1957-62. NSF sr. postdoctoral fellow, 1956-57, Guggenheim fellow, 1971-72. Fellow Am. Phys. Soc.; mem. Fedn. Am. Scientists (chmn. radiation hazards com. 1957, vice chmn. fedn. 1958), Phi Beta Kappa, Sigma Xi. Pioneer fast neutron chopper for neutron spectroscopy, F meson, scattering of proton constituents at high energy. Office: Physics Dept U Pa Philadelphia PA 19104

SELSAM, MILICENT ELLIS, author; b. Bklyn.; d. Israel and Ida (Abrams) Ellis; A.B., Bklyn. Coll., 1932; M.A., Columbia U., 1934; m. Howard Selsam, Sept. 1, 1936; 1 son, Robert. Author, editor numerous books, including: Stars, Mosquitoes and Crocodiles; The American Travels of Alexander von Humboldt (Gold Medal award Boys Club Am.), 1962; Let's Get Turtles, 1965; (with J. Bronowski) Biography of an Atom (Thomas A. Edison award), 1965; Animals as Parents, 1965; Penny's Animals and How He Put Them in Order (Boys Club Am. jr. book award), 1966; How to Be a Nature Detective, 1966; When an Animal Grows, 1966; Bug That Laid the Golden Eggs, 1967; How Animals Tell Time, 1967; Milkweed, 1967; Questions and Answers About Ants, 1967; Maple Tree, 1968; The Tiger, 1969; Peanut, 1969; Hidden Animals, 1969; The Tomato and Other Fruit Vegetables, 1970; Egg to Chick, 1970; The Carrot and Other Root Vegetables, 1971; Vegetables from Stems and Leaves, 1972; More Potatoes, 1972; How Puppies Grow, 1972; Is This a Baby Dinosaur, 1972; A First Look at Leaves, 1972; A First Look at Fish, 1972; A First Look at Mammals, 1973; The Apple and Other Fruits, 1973; Questions and Answers about Horses, 1973; A First Look at Birds, 1974; Bulbs, Corms and Such, 1974; A First Look at Insects, 1975; A First Look at Snakes, Lizards and Other Reptiles, 1975; Harlequin Moth, 1975; How Kittens Grow, 1975; A First Look at Frogs, Toads and Salamanders, 1976; Animals of the Sea, 1976; Popcorn, 1976; The Amazing Dandelion, 1977; A First Look at Flowers, 1977; Land of the Giant Tortoise, 1977; Up, Down and Around, 1977; Sea Monsters of Long Ago, 1977; Mimosa, 1978; A First Look at the World of Plants, 1978; A First Look at Animals with Backbones, 1978; Tyrannosaurus Rex, 1978; Play with Plants rev., 1978; A First Look at Monkeys and Apes, 1979; A First Look at Sharks, 1979; How Animals Live Together, 2d edit., 1979; (adult) The Don't Throw It Grow It Book of Houseplants, 1977; juvenile sci. editor Walker and Co. Pubs. Recipient Eva L. Gordon award Am. Nature Study Soc., 1964; Four-Leaf Clover award Lucky Book Club, 1973. Mem. Am. Nature Study Soc., Authors Guild. Home: 100 W 94th St New York NY 10025 Office: 720 Fifth Ave New York NY 10019. *I have a scientific world view and I hope to inspire my young readers to have the same. I feel that the lives of young people will be richer and fuller if they become and stay curious about the world around them. To this end, I try to stimulate the mind, arouse the curiosity and fire the imagination of young people.*

SELTZER, LEO, filmmaker, educator; b. Montreal, Que., Can., Mar. 13, 1913; s. Boris and Atalia S.; B.A., U. Mass., 1979; m. E. Basil, Apr. 15, 1941 (div. 1950); children—Janzie, John; m. 2d, D. Ransohoff, 1951 (div. 1963). Producer, dir. over 60 documentary, informational, theatrical and TV films, 1931—, including: First Steps, UN Div. Social Affairs (Acad. award for best documentary 1948), 1947, Fate of a Child, 1949, For the Living, 1952, Conquest of Aging, 1958, All the Years, 1959, Jacqueline Kennedy's Asian Journey, 1962, Progress through Freedom (pres. Kennedy's visit to Mex.), 1962, The American Commitment, 1963, Report on Acupuncture, 1977; dir.-producer Nat. Film Bd. Can., 1941; chief cons. visual aids City of N.Y.; 1941-42; producer N.Y.C. Mcpl. Film and TV Unit WNYC, 1949-50; faculty Columbia U., 1954-60, CCNY, 1949-55, Phila. Coll. Art, 1955-56, New Sch. Social Research, 1949-51, 79, N.Y. U., 1966—; dir. audio-visual therapy program N.Y. U. Med. Center, 1970-76; instr. film prodn. workshop Sch. Visual Arts, 1969—; asst. prof. performing and creative arts Coll. S.I., CUNY, 1977-78, prof. film Bklyn. Coll., 1978—; pres. Leo Seltzer Assos., Inc., N.Y.C., 1950—; lectr. in field; film biographer to White House for Pres. Kennedy, 1962; exec. producer Quadrant Communications, Inc., 1973-75. Served as 1st lt. Signal Corps., U.S. Army, 1943-46; officer-in-charge Film and Equipment Depot, ETO. Recipient Silver medals Venice Film Festival, 1945, 63; 7 citations Cannes and Edinburgh Film Festivals, 1948-63, Freedom's Found. award, 1953, Golden Reel award Scholastic Mag., 1955, Robert Flaherty award CCNY, 1956, Silver medal Atlanta Internat. Film Festival, 1977. Mem. Dirs. Guild Am. Films are in Nat. Archives, Library of Congress; photographs are in Houston Museum Fine Arts collection, Nat. Gallery Can., Visual Studies Workshop, Rochester, N.Y.; research on Early Am. social documentary films; reconstn. 6 Am. Social Documentary Films of 1930's for Mus. Modern Art Collection, 1976-77. Home and Office: 368 E 69th St New York NY 10021

SELTZER, LEON EUGENE, publisher; b. Auburn, Maine, Aug. 14, 1918; s. Samuel and Sadye (Shapiro) S.; A.B., Columbia U., 1940; J.D., Stanford U., 1974; m. Lenore Chafetz, Mar. 14, 1948; children—Deborah, Janet, Marcia. Asst. editor Columbia U. Press, 1939-41, editor, 1946-52, sales promotion mgr., 1952-56; dir. Stanford U. Press, 1956—; asst. editor Columbia Ency., 1946-50; editor Columbia Lippincott Gazetteer of the World, 1946-52; admitted to Calif., bar, 1974; scholar-in-residence Center for Advanced Study in Behavioral Scis., 1975-76. Vice pres. Santa Clara County Bd. Edn., 1966-71. Served from pvt. to maj. C.E., AUS, 1941-46; PTO. Guggenheim fellow, 1975-76. Mem. Assn. Am. Univ. Presses (pres. 1968-69). Contbr. short stories, articles and verse to nat. mags.; author: Exemptions and Fair Use in Copyright, 1977. Home: 459 Traverso Ave Los Altos CA 94022 Office: Stanford U Press Stanford CA 94305

SELTZER, LEON ZEE, coll. dean; b. Chgo., Apr. 17, 1914; s. Karel and Gussie (Lidovsky) S.; Ph.C., U. Ill., 1934; B.S. in Aero. Engring. (Gemmel, Donovan Sheehan Aero. scholar) U. Mich., 1940; m. Mary Jane Kehoe, June 17, 1940; 1 son, Thomas Lee. Design criteria engr. Douglas Aircraft Co., Santa Monica, Calif., 1940-41; specialist in theoretical and applied aerodynamics; organizer dept. aero. engring., prof., chmn. dept. Va. Poly Inst., Blacksburg, 1941-47; prof., chmn. dept. aero-space engring. W.Va. U., 1949-63, aero. engr. Engring. Expt. Sta., W.Va. U.; dean Parks Coll. Aero. Tech., St. Louis U., 1963—; mem. Nat. Pvt. Flying Safety Panel; mem. sci. adv. group, cons. U.S. Army Aviation Systems Command. Chmn. bd. W.Va. U. YMCA; chmn. aviation com. St. Louis Regional Commerce and Growth Assn.; bd. dirs. S.W. Civic Meml. Airport Assn. Registered profl. engr., Mo. Fellow Am. Inst. Aeros. and Astronautics (asso., vice chmn. St. Louis, Civic award); mem. Army Aviation Assn. Am. (hon.), Am. Helicopter Soc., Am. Soc. Engring. Edn. (gen. council; chmn. aerospace engring. div.), Nat. (chmn. engring. preparation com.), Mo., W.Va. (dir.) socs. profl. engrs., Am. Inst. Plant Engrs., Air Force Assn., Nat. Aerospace Edn. Assn., Aircraft Owners and Pilots Assn., Soc. Automotive Engrs. (v.p. St. Louis sect.), Conf. Jesuit Schs. Engring. (v.p.), Univ. Aviation Assn., Cahokia (Ill.) C. of C. (v.p.), East St. Louis C. of C. (dir.), Assn. U.S. Army (dir. St. Louis sect.), Sigma Xi, Sigma Gamma Tau (nat. pres. 1964-67), Pi Mu Epsilon, Alpha Eta Rho, Tau Beta Pi, Gamma Alpha Rho, Pi Tau Sigma, Sigma Gamma Tau (nat. pres.). Clubs: Normandie Golf; Engrs. (St. Louis); Norwood Hills Country (dir.). Author tech. papers. Licensed airplane pilot. Home: 8021 Orlando Dr Clayton MO 63105 Office: Parks Coll Saint Louis U Cahokia IL 62206

SELTZER, PHYLLIS ESTELLE, artist, printmaker; b. Detroit, May 17, 1928; d. Max and Lillian (Weiss) Finkelstein; B.F.A., U. Iowa, 1949, M.F.A., 1952; postgrad. U. Mich., 1953-55, Case Western Res. U., Cleve., 1966-70; m. Gerard Seltzer, May 30, 1953; children—Kim, Hiram. Faculty, U. Iowa, 1950-52, U. Mich., Ann Arbor, 1954-55, Case Western Res. U., Cleve., 1966-70; program coordinator arts and humanities Cleve. State U., 1969-71, Lake Erie Coll., Painesville, Ohio, 1970-72; art interior designer Dalton, VanDijk, Johnson, Cleve., 1973-74; pvt. practice as designer, Cleve., 1975—; group shows include: Phila. Print Show, 1952, Dayton Art Mus., 1952, Cleve. Mus. Art, 1952, Walker Mus., 1961, Massilion (Ohio) Mus., 1973, Asso. Am. Artists, N.Y.C., 1975, 79, Cleve. Area Arts Council, 1975-76, Cleve. Mus., 1973, 74, Bklyn. Print Show, 1975, Minn. Mus. Art, 1975, Georgetown (Ky.) Coll., 1979, Mitchell Mus., Mt. Vernon, Ill., 1979. Sec., Edgewater Homeowners Assn., Cleve., 1976—. Tiffany fellow, 1952; Cleve. Health Dept. award, 1975. Mem. Am. Soc. Aesthetics, New Orgn. Visual Arts Cleve. (v.p. 1974). Designer poster Cleve. Bicentennial, 1975. Home: 11225 Harborview Dr Cleveland OH 44102 Studio: 1400 W 10th St Cleveland OH 44113. *I am guided mainly by a need to make a visual contribution to society that adds another dimension to our American way of life so that we grow by seeing it and therefore further enhance our manner of living.*

SELTZER, RONALD, retail co. exec.; b. Boston, Nov. 16, 1931; s. Harold and Molly (Scheinberg) S.; B.B.A., Boston U., 1953; m. Leila Podell, Feb. 24, 1957; children—Marjory, Michael, Barbara, Janet. Asst. employment mgr. Gilchrist Co., Boston, 1956-59; personnel mgr. Bamberger's, Plainfield, N.J., 1959-61, employment and employee relations mgr., Newark, 1961-66, v.p., store mgr., Newark, 1966-67, dir. sales promotion, Newark, 1967-70, sr. v.p., dir. stores, Newark, 1970-71, exec. v.p., 1971-73, dir., 1969—; chmn. bd. R.H. Macy, N.Y.C., 1973—; exec. v.p. ops. Macy N.Y., 1979—. Trustee Urban Coalition, N.J. Safety Council Inc., Garden State Ballet. Served with USNR, 1950-53, AUS, 1953-55. Mem. Greater Newark C. of C. (dir. 1970—, mem. tax task force, 1970—). Home: 278 Garfield Ave Oakhurst NJ 07755 Office: 151 W 34th St New York NY 10001

SELVIN, PAUL PHILLIP, lawyer; b. Hartford, Conn., July 23, 1917; s. Meyer J. and Molly (Podorowsky) S.; A.B. magna cum laude, Harvard, 1939; LL.B. cum laude, U. Conn., 1949; m. Marian Glater, Oct. 25, 1946; children—Molly, Peter. Admitted to Calif. bar, 1950; practice law, specializing in trial and appellate law, Los Angeles, 1951—; partner Selvin Weiner, 1962—. Teaching fellow, acting asst. prof. law Stanford U. Law Sch., 1949-51; prof., lectr. Loyola U. Law Sch., Los Angeles, 1953—; lectr. Continuing Edn. of Bar, intermittently, 1961—. Served with AUS, 1942-46. Mem. Am. Arbitration Assn. (arbitrator), Am. Civil Liberties Union, State Bar Calif., Los Angeles, Beverly Hills bar assns., Calif. Acad. Appellate Lawyers (pres. 1978-79), Phi Beta Kappa. Club: Harvard of So. Calif. Contbr. articles to legal jours., short stories to lit. mags. Home: 11556 Coolidge Pl Los Angeles CA 90066 Office: 1900 Ave of the Stars Los Angeles CA 90067

SELWYN, DONALD, researcher, inventor, adminstr.; b. N.Y.C., Jan. 31, 1936; s. Gerald Selwyn and Ethel (Waxman) Selwyn Moss; B.E.E., Dallas State, 1965, Ph.D. (hon.), 1972; B.A., Thomas A. Edison Coll. N.J., 1976; m. Delia Nemec, Mar. 11, 1956; children—Laurie, Gerald, Marcia. Service engr. Bendix Aviation, Teterboro, N.J., 1956-59; service mgr. Bogue Electric Mfg. Co., Paterson, N.J., 1959; proposal engr. advanced design group Curtiss-Wright Corp., East Paterson, N.J., 1960-64; ind. bioengr., rehab. engring. cons., N.Y.C., 1964-67; pres. bd. trustees, exec. tech. and tng. dir. Nat. Inst. for Rehab. Engring., Butler, N.J., 1967—. Cons. N.Y. State Office Vocat. Rehab., 1964—, Pres.'s Com. on Employment of Handicapped, 1966—, also numerous state rehab. agys., health depts., vol. groups, agys. for handicapped in fgn. countries. Trustee Nat. Inst. for Rehab. Engring. Rehab. Research Center Trust. Recipient Humanitarian award U.S. Ho. of Reps., 1972, Bicentennial Pub. Service award, 1975; named knight Malta, 1973. Mem. Am. Acad. Consultants, I.E.E.E. (sr.), Soc. Tech. Writers and Pubs. (sr.), Nat. Rehab. Assn., N.Y. Acad. Scis., Mensa. Contbr. articles on amateur radio, rehab. of severely and totally disabled to profl., gen. mags.; developer or co-developer field-expander glasses for hemianopsia, tunnel and monocular vision, electronic speech clarifiers, electronically guided wheelchairs, off-road vehicles and cars for quadriplegics, others; patentee indsl., mil. and handicapped rehab. inventions. Home: 238 Poplar Ave Pompton Lakes NJ 07442

SELYE, HANS, physician; b. Vienna, Austria, Jan. 26, 1907; s. Hugo and Maria Felicitas (Langbank) S.; student Coll. Benedictine Fathers, Komárom, Hungary, 1916-24; med. student German U., Prague, 1924-25, 27-29, U. Paris, 1925-26, U. Rome, 1926-27; M.D., German U., Prague, 1929, Ph.D., 1931; D.Sc., McGill U., 1942; hon. degree U. Windsor, 1955, Cath. U. Chile, 1956, Hahnemann Med. Coll. and Hosp., 1962, U. San Carlos, 1959, Nat. U. Argentina, 1950, U. Montevideo, 1956, Westfälische Wilhelms Universität, 1966, U. Cagliari (Italy), 1967, Karl-Franzens U., 1967, J.E. Purkyne U., Brno, 1969, U. Guelph, 1973, Laval U., 1975, Phila. Coll., 1975, Hebrew U. Jerusalem, 1977, U. Haifa, Toronto, 1978, U. Alta., 1978; m. Louise Drevet, Oct. 5, 1978; children—Catherine Michel, Jean, Marie, André. Asst. in exptl. pathology, histology lab. German U., 1929-31; Rockefeller research fellow dept. biochem. hygiene Johns Hopkins U., 1931; research fellow dept. biochemistry McGill U., Montreal, Que., Can., 1932-33, lectr. biochemistry, 1933-34, asst. prof. biochemistry, 1934-37, asst prof. histology, 1937-41, asso. prof. histology, 1941-45; prof., dir. Inst. Exptl. Medicine and Surgery, U. Montreal, 1945-76, prof. emeritus, 1977—; pres. Internat. Inst. of Stress, 1976—; pres. Hans Selye Found., 1979; expert cons. to Surgeon Gen., U.S. Army, 1947-57. Recipient Casgrain and Charbonneau prize, 1946; Gordon Wilson medal, 1948; Heberden medal, 1950; medal Academia Medico Fisica Fiorentina, 1950; Henderson Gold medal Am. Geriatrics Soc., 1964; medal Swedish Med. Soc., 1965; Canadian Centennial medal, 1967; companion Order of Can., 1968; gold medal Rudolf Virchow, 1970; commemorative plate Paul D. White symposium Am. Coll. Cardiology, 1971; Harry G. Armstrong lectr. Aerospace Med. Assn., 1972; Grieve Meml. lectr. Canadian Assn. Orthodontists, 1972; Starr medal Canadian Med. Assn., 1972; Prix de l'Oeuvre Scientifique, Assn. medecins langue française Can., 1974; Distinguished Service award Am. Soc. Abdominal Surgeons, 1974; Killam prize, 1974; Kittay award, 1976; Order of Flag (Hungary), 1977; Queen's Silver Jubilee medal Can., 1977; Achievement in Life award Ency. Brit., 1977; medal U. Calcutta, 1979; other honors and awards. Fellow Royal Soc. (Can.), N.Y. Acad. Scis., AAAS, Pan Am. Med. Assn. (N.Am. chmn. sect. endocrinology); hon. fellow Alpha Ency. (Montreal), Acad. Pharm. Scis., Société medicale polonaise; mem. Ohio Hungarian Soc.; hon. and corr. mem. fgn., nat., state and local profl. med. assns. and orgns., in both gen. and spl. fields. Author several specialized med. books including: Annual Reports on Stress, 1951-56; The Story of the Adaptation Syndrome, 1952; The Stress of Life, 1956; The Chemical Prevention of Cardiac Necroses, 1958; Calciphylaxis, 1962; From Dream to Discovery, 1964; The Mast Cells, 1965; Thrombohemorrhagic Phenomena, 1966; In Vivo, 1967; Anaphylactoid Edema, 1968; Experimental Cardiovascular Diseases, 1970; Hormones and Resistance, 1971; Stress Without Distress, 1974; Stress in Health and Disease, 1976; The Stress of Life, 2d edit., 1976; The Stress of My Life (Can. Authors Assn. Lit. award), 1977, 2d edit., 1979; Selye's Guide to Stress Research, Vol. 1, 1979; editor (with others) Cancer, Stress and Death, 1979; editorial bd. Ars Medici (Belgium), Experimentelle Chirurgie (Germany), Am. Jour. Clin. Hypnosis, Internat. Jour. Neuropsychiatry, others; author philosophy of altruistic egoism to cope with stress. Home: 659 Milton St Montreal PQ Canada Office: U Montreal PO Box 6128 Montreal PQ H3C 3J7 Canada. *Essentially this is an admission of selfish motivation although, one must add, it is selfishness positively directed toward accumulating the most valuable and permanent capital of all: goodwill and love, which are the proof of doing something useful to others. This idea has helped me to overcome any complexes or guilt feelings I might have developed over the years, for surely no one can condemn an egoism which manifests itself in an insatiable drive to "earn one's neighbor's love".*

SELZ, PETER HOWARD, educator; b. Munich, Germany, Mar. 27, 1919; s. Eugene and Edith Selz; student Columbia, U. Paris; M.A., U. Chgo., 1949, Ph.D., 1954; D.F.A., Calif. Coll. Arts and Crafts, 1967; m. Thalia Cheronis, June 10, 1948 (div. 1965); children—Tanya Nicole Eugenia, Diana Gabrielle Hamlin. Came to U.S., 1936, naturalized, 1942. Instr. U. Chgo., 1951-56; asst. prof. art history, head art edn. dept. Inst. Design, Ill. Inst. Tech., Chgo., 1949-55; chmn. art dept., dir. art gallery Pomona Coll., 1955-58; curator dept. painting and sculpture exhbns. Mus. Modern Art, 1958-65; dir. univ. art mus. U. Calif. at Berkeley, 1965-73, prof. history of art, 1965—; Zaks prof. Hebrew U., Jerusalem, 1976. Mem. pres.'s council on art and architecture Yale, 1971-76. Served with OSS, AUS, 1941-46. Decorated Order of Merit (Fed. Republic Germany); Fulbright grantee, Paris, 1949-50; fellow Belgian-Am. Ednl. Found.; sr. fellow Nat. Endowment for Humanities, 1972. Mem. Coll. Art Assn. Am. (dir. 1959-64, 67-71), Am. Assn. U. Profs., Internat. Art Critics Assn. Author: German Expressionist Painting, 1957; New Images of Man, 1959; Art Nouveau, 1960; Mark Rothko, 1961; Fifteen Polish Painters, 1961; The Art of Jean Dubuffet, 1962; Emil Nolde, 1963; Max Beckmann, 1964; Alberto Giacometti, 1965; Directions in Kinetic Sculpture, 1966; Funk, 1967; Hardd Paris, 1972; Ferdinand Hodler, 1972; Sam Francis, 1975; The American Presidency in Political Cartoons, 1976. Editor: Art in Am., 1967—, Art Quar., 1969—. Contbr. articles to art publs. Office: Dept Art History U Calif Berkeley CA 94720

SELZER, CHARLES LOUIS, supt. schs.; b. Homestead, Iowa, Dec. 21, 1914; s. Louis Carl and Caroline (Shoup) S.; B.A. cum laude, Coe Coll., 1935; M.A., State U. Iowa, 1950, postgrad., 1951—; m. Louise Kippenhan, Mar. 9, 1935; 1 dau., Patricia Madelyn (Mrs. Robert Carstensen). Tchr., prin., coach Amana (Iowa) High Sch., 1935-50; supt. Amana Community Schs., 1950—; guest lectr. U. Iowa, summer 1977, 78, 79; dir. Amana Telephone Co., Amana Woolens, Inc. Former justice of peace Iowa County; mem. Iowa County Crime Commn. Pres. Amana Community Chest, 1951-53; mem. adv. bd. Kirkwood Coll., Amana Service Co.; mem. Iowa County Soc. Aging; mem. Area X Grant Wood Spl. Edn. Bd., also mem. Amana Travel Council; mem. Amana Hist. Landmark Charter and Constn. Commn., 1977—. Mem. Am., Iowa assns. sch. adminstrs., NEA, Iowa Edn. Assn., Amana Young Men's Bur. (hon. past pres.), Iowa Poweshiek County Supts. Assn., Sr. Supts. Iowa, Joint County Area X Supts. Assn. (legis. com.), Iowa Benton Supts. Assn. (legis. com.), Amana Soc. (dir.), Iowa Peace Officers Assn., Amana Hist. Soc., Nat. Notary Assn., Amana Men's Chorus, Iowa County Hist. Soc. (pres. 1965-67), Iowa County Schoolmasters Assn. (past pres.), Amana Landmark Soc. (mem. constn. com.), Phi Beta Kappa. Mem. Amana Ch. Soc. (trustee, elder, pres. 1971—). Elk, Mason (32 deg., Shriner), El Kahir. Clubs: Homestead Welfare (past pres., sec.), Cedar Rapids Toastmasters (hon.). Translator Amana documents and testimonies; author Amana coop. edn. plan. Home: Homestead IA 52236 Office: Middle IA 52307

SELZNICK, IRENE MAYER, theatrical producer; b. N.Y.C., Apr. 2, 1910; d. Louis B. and Margaret (Shenberg) Mayer; ed. pub. schs. Brookline, Mass., Hollywood (Calif.) Sch. Girls; m. David O. Selznick, Apr. 29, 1930 (div. Jan. 1948); children—Lewis Jeffrey, Daniel Mayer. With Selznick-Internat. Pictures, Inc., Culver City, Calif., 1936-40, Vanguard Films, Calif., N.Y.C., 1941-49; mng. dir. Irene M. Selznick Co., N.Y.C., 1946—; produced Tennessee Williams' A Street Car Named Desire, N.Y.C., 1947, London, Oct. 1949, John von Druten's Bell, Book and Candle, 1950, George Tabori's Flight Into Egypt, 1952, Enid Bagnold's, The Chalk Garden, N.Y.C., 1955, London, 1956; The Last Joke, London, 1960, Graham Greene's The Complaisant Lover, N.Y.C., 1961. Former juvenile probation officer, Los Angeles. Home: Hotel Pierre New York NY 10021

SEMANS, TRUMAN THOMAS, investment banker; b. Balt., Oct. 27, 1927; s. William Ritchie and Ann Roberts (Thomas) S.; A.B. in History, Princeton, 1949; student U. Va. Law Sch., 1949-50; m. Nellie McEvoy Merrick, Dec. 14, 1961; children—Truman Thomas, William Merrick. With Robert Garrett & Sons, Inc., Balt., 1960—, gen. partner, 1957-64, pres., chief exec. officer, 1964-67, vice chmn. bd., 1967, chmn. exec. com., 1970, chmn. bd., 1973; partner Alex. Brown & Sons, Balt., 1974—; dir. P.J. McEvoy & Co., Balt. &

Annapolis R.R. Co., Easco Corp. Mem. exchange panels of arbitrators N.Y. Stock Exchange. Mem. finance com. Loyola Coll., Balt. Bd. dirs. So. Md. Soc., Md. Hist. Soc.; chmn. Mercy Hosp., Balt. Served with USNR, 1944-46. Mem. Investment Bankers Assn., Soc. Colonial Wars. Clubs: Ivy (Princeton) (former gov.); Green Spring Valley Hunt (former gov.) (Garrison, Md.); Maryland (bd. govs.) (Balt.); Brook (N.Y.C.). Home: Owings Mills MD 21153 Office: Alex Brown & Sons 135 E Baltimore St Baltimore MD 21203

SEMARK, PHILIP NORMAN, ballet company dir.; b. Rawalpindi, India, Dec. 17, 1945, naturalized U.S. citizen, 1979; s. Alec Edward and Marjorie Lillian (Phillips) S.; B.Laws, U. Birmingham, 1967. With Spillers Ltd., London, 1967-70; mgmt. trainee Brit. Consulate-Gen., N.Y.C., 1970-72; asst. to consul comml. H.I. Enterprises, Inc., N.Y.C., 1972-75; gen. mgr. San Francisco Ballet, 1975—; pres. Performing Art Services, San Francisco; dir. Hosp. Audiences, Inc., San Francisco. Mem. dance adv. panel Calif. Arts Council. Mem. Calif. Confederation of the Arts, Assn. Am. Dance Companies. Democrat. Club: Commonwealth of Calif. Home: 1150 Union St San Francisco CA 94109 Office: 378-18th Ave San Francisco CA 94121

SEMBER, MICHAEL DANIEL, mag. pub.; b. Cleve., Nov. 28, 1928; s. Michael Stephen and Barbara Ann (Hozuda) S.; B.S., U. Pitts., 1951; m. Constance Chase, Feb. 3, 1951; children—Michael David, Patricia Ann, Paul Scott. Advt. mgr. graphics div. Rockweel Mfg. Co., 1953-55; account exec. Ladd, Southward, Bentley, Inc., advt. agy., 1955-60; account supr. Reach, McClinton, Inc., 1960-64; pub. Maclean-Hunter Pub. Co., Chgo., 1965—. Served with AUS. Mem. Printers Guild Chgo. (pres. 1965), Am. Bus. Press, Chgo. Bus. Publs. Assn., Printing Industries Am., U.S. Profl. Tennis Assn. Clubs: Lansing Country, Holiday Tennis. Home: 17511 Bernadine St Lansing IL 60438 Office: 300 W Adams St Chicago IL 60606

SEMEL, TERRY STEVEN, motion picture co. exec.; b. N.Y.C., Feb. 24, 1943; s. Ben and Mildred (Wenig) S.; B.S. in Acctg., L.I. U., 1964; postgrad. in market research CCNY, 1966-67; m. Jane Bovingdon, Aug. 24, 1977; 1 son, Eric Scott. Domestic sales mgr. C.B.S.-Cinema Center Films, Studio City, Calif., 1970-72; v.p., gen. mgr. Walt Disney's Buena Vista, Burbank, Calif., 1972-75; pres. W.B. Distbn. Corp., Burbank, 1975-78; exec. v.p., chief operating officer Warner Bros. Inc., Burbank, 1979—. Office: 4000 Warner Blvd Burbank CA 91522

SEMKOW, JERZY GEORG, conductor; b. Radomsko, Poland, Oct. 12, 1928; s. Aleksander and Waleria (Sienczak) S.; came to U.S., 1975; student U. Cracow (Poland), 1946-50; grad. Leningrad Mus. Conservatoire (USSR), 1951-55. Asst. condr. Leningrad Philharmonic Orch., 1954-56, Bolshoi Opera and Ballet Theater, Moscow, 1956-58; artistic dir., prin. condr. Warsaw (Poland) Nat. Opera, 1959-62; permanent condr. Danish Royal Opera, Copenhagen, 1966—; music dir., prin. condr. St. Louis Symphony Orch., 1975-79; music dir. Orchestra Sinfonica della RAI, Rome, 1979—; guest condr. Vienna (Austria) Symphony Orch., Suisse Romande Orch., Orchestre de Paris, London Philharmonic, Madrid Symphony Orch., orchs. in Berlin, Milan, Italy, and others in Europe, also N.Y. Philharmonic, Boston Symphony, Chgo. Symphony, Cleve. Symphony Orch. and others in U.S.; condr. at numerous festivals. Decorated Great Order Commandoria Polonia Restituta; recipient Polish Radio award, 1965. Mem. Respighi Soc. Bologne (hon.). Recorded 1st complete rendition of the original Mussorgsky version of opera Boris Godunov with Polish Nat. Radio and TV Orch., recording honored with 5 internat. awards: Polish Nat. Radio and TV ann. Award of First Degree, Deutschen Schallplatten Preis (Ger.), Premio Discográfico Italiano (Italy), Grand Prix des Discophilles (France), nominated for Grammy award in category Best Opera Recording (U.S.). Address: care Mazzonis Orchestra Sinfonica della RAI Foro Italico Roma Italia

SEMLER, BERNARD HENRY, health care co. exec.; b. Winona, Minn., Apr. 20, 1917; s. Henry John and Helen Catherine (Schneider) S.; B.S. summa cum laude, St. Mary's Coll., Winona, 1938; m. Mary Ann Fitzgerald, Mar. 30, 1940; children—Sharon Ann, Thomas B., Bruce E. With Scovell Wellington & Co., C.P.A.'s, Chgo., 1941-49; asst. controller Johnson & Johnson, 1949-55; successively gen. controller, v.p. and controller, exec. v.p. Freeman Shoe Corp., Beloit, Wis., 1955-60; v.p. finance Hunt Foods and Industries, Inc., Fullerton, Calif., 1960-68; v.p., treas. Norton Simon, Inc., 1968-69; v.p. finance Abbott Lab., North Chicago, Ill., 1969-74, exec. v.p. finance, 1974—, also dir.; dir. First Nat. Bank Lake Forest (Ill.). Bd. dirs. Lake Forest Hosp. C.P.A., Ill. Mem. Nat. Assn. Accountants (nat. v.p. 1959-60, 1st pres. Raritan Valley chpt. 1955), Am. Mgmt. Assn., Am. Inst. C.P.A.'s (mem., past chmn. steering com. fin. sect.), Pharm. Mfrs. Assn. Home: 125 Blackthorn Ln Lake Forest IL 60045 Office: Abbott Park North Chicago IL 60064

SEMLER, DEAN RUSSELL, food co. exec.; b. East St. Louis, Ill., Mar. 25, 1929; s. Ray Russell and Margaret Mildred (Swindler) S.; student Dyke Spencerian Bus. Coll., 1947-48, Akron U., 1950-56; m. Mary Ann Millhoff, Feb. 10, 1961; 1 son, James R. From cost accountant to controller Ohio Match Co., Wadsworth, O., 1948-61; accounting analyst Hunt-Wesson Foods, Inc., Fullerton, Cal., 1962-63, accounting mgr., 1961-68, controller, 1969-74, v.p., controller, 1975—. Mem. Nat. Assn. Accountants. Home: 106 Demmer Dr Placentia CA 92670 Office: 1645 W Valencia St Fullerton CA 92634

SEMMEL, BERNARD, historian, educator; b. N.Y.C., July 23, 1928; s. Samuel and Tillie (Beer) S.; B.A., CCNY, 1947; M.A., Columbia U., 1951, Ph.D., 1955; postgrad. London Sch. Econs., 1959-60; m. Maxine Loraine Guse, Mar. 19, 1955; 1 son, Stuart Mill. With Nat. Citizens Commn. for Pub. Schs. and Council for Fin. Aid to Edn., N.Y.C., 1951-55; asst. prof. history Park Coll., Parkville, Mo., 1956-60; mem. faculty SUNY, Stony Brook, 1960—, prof. history, 1964—, chmn. dept., 1966-69; vis. prof. Columbia U., 1966-67, asso., seminar in social and polit. thought, 1968—; fellow Lehrman Inst., 1974-76. Rockefeller Found. fellow, 1959-60; Am. Council Learned Socs. fellow, 1964-65; Guggenheim fellow, 1967-68, 74-75. Fellow Royal Hist. Soc.; mem. Am. Hist. Assn., Econ. History Soc., Conf. Brit. Studies, U.S. Strategic Inst., Phi Beta Kappa. Author: Imperialism and Social Reform, 1960; Jamaican Blood and Victorian Conscience, 1963; The Rise of Free Trade Imperialism, 1970; The Methodist Revolution, 1973; editor: Occasional Papers of T.R. Malthus, 1963; editor, translator Halevy's The Birth of Methodism in England, 1971; editor Jour. Brit. Studies, 1969-74. Home: Box 1162 6 Woodbine Ave Stony Brook NY 11790 Office: Dept History State U NY Stony Brook NY 11794

SEMMELHACK, MARTIN F(REDRICK), chemist; b. Appleton, Wis., Nov. 19, 1941; s. Fred A. and Evelyn S. (Shreve) S.; B.S., U. Wis., 1963; A.M., Harvard U., 1965, Ph.D., 1967; m. Carol S. Lee, June 9, 1973. NIH postdoctoral fellow Stanford U., 1967-68; asst. prof. chemistry Cornell U., 1968-73, asso. prof., 1974-76, prof., 1976-78; prof. Princeton U., 1978—; cons. BASF Corp., W.Ger., 1979. Alfred P. Sloan fellow, 1973-75; Camille and Henry Dreyfuss fellow, 1973-78; J.S. Guggenheim Found. fellow, 1978-79. Mem. Am. Chem. Soc., Chem. Soc. (London). Editorial adv. bd. Jour. Organic Chemistry, Organic Syntheses; research, numerous publs. in organic synthesis. Home: 236 Cherry Hill Rd Princeton NJ 08540 Office: Frick Lab Princeton NJ 08540

SEMON, WARREN LLOYD, educator; b. Boise, Ida., Jan. 17, 1921; s. August and Viola Lorreta (Eastman) S.; student Hobart Coll., 1940-43; S.B., U. Chgo., 1944; M.A., Harvard, 1949, Ph.D., 1954; m. Ruth Valerie Swift, Dec. 1, 1945; children—Warren Lloyd, Nolan David, Jonathan Richard, Sue Anne. Lectr. applied math. Harvard, 1956-61, asst. dir. computation lab., 1954-61; head applied math. dept. Sperry Rand Research Center, Sudbury, Mass., 1961-64; mgr. computation and analysis lab. Burroughs Research Center, Paoli, Pa., 1964-67; prof. computer sci. Syracuse (N.Y.) U., 1967—, dir. system and information sci., 1968-76, dean Sch. Computer and Info. Sci., 1976—; cons. USAF, 1957, NSA, 1957, Lockheed Electronics Corp., 1967, Monsanto Co., 1972. Served to 1st lt. USAAF, 1943-46; MTO. Fellow IEEE; mem. Assn. Computing Machinery, Math. Assn. Am., IEEE Computer Soc. (chmn. publs. com. 1972-74, bd. govs. 1973-74, editor-in-chief 1975-76), Sigma Xi. Contbr. profl. jours. Home: 12 Pebble Hill Rd N DeWitt NY 13214 Office: Link Hall Syracuse U Syracuse NY 13210

SEMONOFF, RALPH PERLOW, lawyer; b. Providence, May 6, 1918; s. Judah C. and Lucy (Perlow) S.; A.B., Brown U., 1939; LL.B., Harvard U., 1947; m. Hinda M. Pritsker, Oct. 25, 1942; children—Susan A. Semonoff Sagar, Ellen M. Semonoff Silberman, Judith W. Admitted to R.I. bar, 1947; partner firm Semonoff & Semonoff, Providence, 1947-60, Levy, Goodman, Semonoff & Gorin, Providence, 1961—; mem. R.I. Gov.'s Commn. on Jud. Selection, 1977—. Pres., Urban League R.I., 1957-59, Citizens League Pawtucket (R.I.), 1961-63, Jewish Family and Children's Service R.I., 1974-77; trustee Miriam Hosp., Providence, 1971—, vice chmn. bd., 1979—. Served with U.S. Army, 1941-46. Mem. Am. Bar Assn., R.I. Bar Assn. (pres. 1978-79), Pawtucket Bar Assn. (pres. 1963), Am. Law Inst., New Eng. Bar Assn. (dir. 1979—). Home: 40 Lowden St Pawtucket RI 02860 Office: 40 Westminster St Providence RI 02903

SEMPLE, ROBERT BAYLOR, corp. exec.; b. St. Louis, Aug. 18, 1910; s. Nathaniel Meacon and Margery (Ferriss) S.; B.S., Mass. Inst. Tech., 1932, M.S., 1933; m. Isabelle Ashby Neer, June 15, 1933; children—Robert B. Jr., Lloyd A., Elizabeth H., William T. and Nathaniel M. (twins). Research chemist Monsanto Chem. Co., 1933-35, pilot plant group leader, mgr. interim mfg. dept., 1935-39, asst. dir., gen. devel. dept., 1939-42, mgr. petroleum chem. sales, 1942-44, dir. gen. devel. dept., 1944-49; pres. Wyandotte Chem. Corp. (Mich.), 1949-70; pres. BASF Wyandotte Corp., 1970-71, chmn. bd., 1971—; dir. Nat. Detroit Corp., Nat. Bank Detroit, Atlantic Mut. Ins. Co., Am. Natural Resources Co.; trustee Chrysler Corp., Centennial Ins. Co. Sr. mem. Conf. Bd. Pres., bd. dirs. Detroit Symphony Orch.; emeritus trustee Harper-Grace Hosps., Detroit, Citizens Research Council Mich.; life mem. corp. Mass. Inst. Tech. Mem. Detroit C. of C. (past dir.), Com. Econ. Devel. (trustee), Mfg. Chemists' Assn., Am. Inst. Chem. Engrs., Am. Chem. Soc., Soc. Chem. Industry. Episcopalian. Clubs: Links, Twenty Nine, Sky (N.Y.C.); Detroit, Detroit Athletic; Yondotega; Grosse Pointe, Country (Grosse Pointe, Mich.); Country (St. Louis); Bohemian (San Francisco); Metropolitan (Washington). Home: 33 Beacon Hill Grosse Pointe Farms MI 48236 Office: Box 111 Wyandotte MI 48192

SEMPLE, T. DARRINGTON, JR., reins. co. exec., lawyer; b. N.Y.C., Jan. 9, 1926; s. T. Darrington and Eola (Strait) S.; A.B., U. Ala., 1950, J.D., 1951; m. Florence Bibb Evans, June 20, 1953; children—Emily, Sarah-Ellen. Admitted to Ala. bar, 1951, N.Y. bar, 1952; trial counsel Aetna Life & Casualty Co., N.Y.C., 1952-55; asst. counsel Waterfront Commn. N.Y. Harbor, 1955-58; counsel Arabian Am. Oil Co., 1958-62; asso. sec. Am. Reins. Co., N.Y.C., 1962-63, sec., 1963—, resident counsel, 1975—. Served with USAAF, 1944-45. Mem. Am. Judicature Soc., Am. Soc. Internat. Law, Internat., Am., N.Y., Ala. bar assns., Am. Fgn. Law Assn., N.Y. County Lawyers Assn., Internat. Law Assn., Assn. Bar City N.Y. Office: 91 Liberty St New York City NY 10006

SEMROD, T. JOSEPH, banker; b. Oklahoma City, Dec. 13, 1936; s. L.J. and Theda Jo (Hummel) S.; B.A. in Polit. Sci., U. Okla., 1958, LL.B., 1963; m. Janice Lee Wood, June 1, 1968; children—Ronald, Catherine, Christopher, Elizabeth. With Liberty Nat. Bank, Oklahoma City, 1963—, v.p., 1967-69, sr. v.p., 1969-71, exec. v.p., 1971-73, pres., 1973—; pres. Liberty Nat. Corp., Oklahoma City, 1976—; admitted to Okla. bar, 1963; faculty Grad. Banking Sch., So. Meth. U., 1976—, Am. Bankers Assn. Comml. Lending Sch. and Nat. Comml. Lending Grad. Sch., 1973—. Trustee, mem. exec. com. Nat. Urban League; chmn. Oklahoma City met. area Nat. Alliance for Bus.; mem. Oklahoma County adv. bd. Legal Aid Western Okla., Inc.; lay adv. bd. St. Anthony Hosp., Oklahoma City; bd. dirs. Appeals Rev. Bd. Oklahoma City, Inc.; former bd. dirs. ARC, YMCA, Salvation Army, Touchstone Sch. Served to 1st lt. U.S. Army, 1958-60. Mem. Am. Bankers Assn., Am. Bar Assn., Assn. Res. City Bankers, Nat. Alliance Businessmen, Young Pres.'s Orgn., Oklahoma City C. of C. (dir.), Okla. Bankers Assn. (past dir.). Democrat. Roman Catholic. Clubs: Oklahoma City Golf and Country, Petroleum. Office: PO Box 25848 Oklahoma City OK 73125

SEMROW, HARRY H., county ofcl.; b. Chgo., Aug. 19, 1915; ed. pub. and parochial schs., Chgo.; student Am. Conservatory Music; children—Harry, Quandee. Chmn., Semrow Products Co., Chgo.; postmaster, Chgo., 1961-66; Cook County commr., 1966-70; mem. Cook County Bd. Appeals, 1970—. Mem. Ill. Ho. of Reps., 1956-60. Democrat. Clubs: Ill. Athletic, Chgo. Yacht (Chgo.). Home: 7131 N Caldwell #124 Chicago IL 60646

SENCER, DAVID JUDSON, physician; b. Grand Rapids, Mich., Nov. 10, 1924; s. Martin J. and Helen (Furniss) S.; student Wesleyan U., Middletown, Conn., 1942-44; M.D., U. Mich., 1951; M.P.H., Harvard, 1958; m. Jane P. Blood, Aug. 25, 1951; children—Susan, Ann, Stephen. Intern Univ. Hosp., Ann Arbor, Mich., 1951-52, resident, 1952-54; med. officer USPHS, 1955-60, asst. chief, 1960-62, dep. chief, 1962-66, dir. Center for Disease Control, Atlanta, 1966-77; sr. v.p. med. and sci. affairs Becton, Dickinson & Co., Paramus, N.J., 1977—; prof. Emory U. Sch. Medicine; prof. medicine Coll. Medicine and Dentistry N.J.; vis. lectr. Harvard Sch. Pub. Health; cons. WHO. Served with USNR, 1944-46; to asst. surgeon gen. USPHS, 1955—. Recipient Meritorious Service award USPHS, 1968, Distinguished Service award, 1976. Diplomate Am. Bd. Preventive Medicine. Fellow Am. Pub. Health Assn. (award for excellence 1976); mem. AMA, Am. Tropical Medicine Soc., Am. Thoracic Soc. Home: 950 Hillcrest Rd Ridgewood NJ 07450 Office: Becton Dickinson & Co Paramus NJ 07652

SENDAK, MAURICE BERNARD, writer, illustrator; b. Bklyn., June 10, 1928; s. Philip and Sadie (Schindler) S.; student Art Students League, N.Y.C., 1949-51. Writer, illustrator children's books, 1951—; one-man show Gallery Sch. Visual Arts, N.Y.C., 1964, Ashmolean Mus., Oxford, 1975, Am. Cultural Center, Paris, 1978. Author, illustrator: Kenny's Window, 1956; Very Far Away, 1957; The Sign on Rosie's Door, 1960; The Nutshell Library, 1963; Where The Wild Things Are (Caldecott medal 1964), 1963; illustrator: A Hole is to Dig, 1952; A Very Special House, 1954; I'll Be You and You Be Me, 1954; Charlotte and the White Horse, 1955; What Do You Say, Dear?, 1959; The Moonjumpers, 1960; Little Bear's Visit, 1962; Schoolmaster Whackwell's Wonderful Sons, 1962; Mr. Rabbit and the Lovely Present, 1963; The Griffin and the Minor Canon, 1963; Nikolenka's Childhood, 1963; The Bat-Poet, 1964; Lullabies and Night Songs, 1965; Hector Protector and As I Went Over the Water, 1965; Zlateh the Goat, 1966; Higglety Pigglety Pop, Or There Must Be More to Life, 1967; In the Night Kitchen, 1970; illustrator The Animal Family, 1965; In The Night Kitchen Coloring Book, 1971; Pictures By Maurice Sendak, 1971; The Juniper Tree and Other Tales from Grimm, 1973; writer, dir., lyricist TV animated spl. Really Rosie, 1975. Recipient Hans Christian Andersen Illustrators award (first American), 1970. Address: 200 Chestnut Hill Rd Ridgefield CT 06877

SENDAK, THEODORE LORRAINE, atty. gen. Ind.; b. Chgo., Mar. 16, 1918; s. Jack and Annette (Frankel) S.; A.B. in Polit. Sci., Harvard U., 1940; LL.B., J.D., Valparaiso U., 1958; m. Tennessee Elisabeth Read, Sept. 13, 1942; children—Theodore Tipton, Timothy Read, Cynthia Louise. Chief editorial writer Hammond (Ind.) Times, 1940-41; pub. relations dir. Ind. Dept. Vets. Affairs, 1946-48; gen. mgr. Gary (Ind.) Electric Co., 1949-59; admitted to Ind. bar, 1959, since practiced in Crown Point; atty.-gen. Ind., 1969—. Mem. adv. bd. Salvation Army, 1970—; mem. nat. adv. bd. Ams. for Effective Law Enforcement; chmn. Lake County (Ind.) Republican Party, 1962-70, 1st Congl. Dist. Com. Ind., 1962-66; state committeeman and mem. exec. com., 1962-70; del. Rep. Nat. Conv., 1964. Served with AUS, 1941-46; PTO; col. Res. Recipient award Freedom Found., 1973, 77. Mem. Am., 7th Circuit, Ind., Crown Point-Lowell (pres. 1963-64) bar assns., Nat. Assn. Attys. Gen. (chmn. Midwest conf. 1971-72, v.p. 1975-76, nat. pres. 1977-78), Am. Legion, Demolay Legion of Honor, Nat. Sojourners. Methodist. Clubs: Masons, Elks, Press (Indpls.); Youche Country. Home: PO Box 359 Crown Point IN 46307 Office: State House Indianapolis IN 46204. *If this country is to regain and maintain faith and confidence in its form of government, and in its leaders, and to progress accordingly, the first thing we must do is to restore the word "responsibility" to the working vocabulary of every man and woman, and every teenager who seeks the rights of manhood and womanhood.*

SENDLER, DAVID ALAN, mag. editor; b. White Plains, N.Y., Dec. 12, 1938; s. Morris and Rose S.; B.A., Dartmouth Coll., 1960; M.S., Columbia U., 1961; m. Emily Shimm, Oct. 12, 1965; 2 children. Asso. editor Sport mag., 1964-65; with Pageant mag., 1965-71, exec. editor, 1969-71; editor Today's Health, 1971-74; sr. editor Parade, N.Y.C., 1974-75; articles editor Ladies Home Jour., 1975-76; mng. editor TV Guide mag., Radnor, Pa., 1976-79, exec. editor, 1979—. Served with U.S. Army, 1961-63. Clubs: Pa. Soc., Dartmouth (Phila.). Contbr. articles to numerous nat. mags. Office: 250 King of Prussia Rd Radnor PA 19088

SENECAL, VANCE EVAN, chem. mfg. co. exec., chem. engr.; b. Phillipston, Pa., Aug. 16, 1921; s. Leon V. and Ruth E. (Stevens) S.; B.S. in Edn., Slippery Rock State Coll., 1943; B.S. Chem. Engring., Carnegie Inst. Tech., 1947, M.S. Chem. Engring., 1948, Ph.D. in Chem. Engring., 1951; m. Marian J. Cramer, Jan. 27, 1945; children—Vance R., David E., Keith E., Scott C. With E.I. duPont de Nemours & Co., Inc., Wilmington, Del., 1951—, lab. dir. engring. dept. research and devel., now mgr. engring. research. Served with AC, USN, 1943-45. Registered profl. engr., Del. Mem. Am. Inst. Chem. Engrs., Am. Chem. Soc., Sigma Xi, Tau Beta Pi, Theta Tau. Republican. Home: 1309 Grayson Rd Welshire Wilmington DE 19803 Office: E I duPont de Nemours & Co Inc Engring Dept Louviers Wilmington DE 19898

SENER, JOSEPH WARD, investment banker; b. Balt., June 13, 1901; s. Beverley T. and Susie Helen (Griffin) S.; grad. pub. schs.; m. Clara Adele Hodshon, Aug. 28, 1925; children—Joseph Ward, Richard Beverley, Robert N.H. Clk., Mackubin, Goodrich & Co., 1917-20; mgr. trading dept. Mackubin, Legg & Co., 1921-40; gen. partner Legg & Co., Balt., 1941-62, mng. partner, 1962—; chmn. exec. com. emeritus Legg Mason Wood Walker Inc., Allied N.Y. and Am. stock exchanges. Past pres. Community Chest Balt. Mem. Nat. Security Traders Assn. (past pres.), Investment Bankers Assn. (former gov.). Clubs: Maryland, Mchts. (past pres. dir.), Johns Hopkins Center (Balt.). Home: 4 Bishop's Rd Baltimore MD 21218 Office: 7 E Redwood St Baltimore MD 21203

SENER, JOSEPH WARD, JR., securities co. exec.; b. Balt., June 30, 1926; s. Joseph Ward and Clara (Hodshon) S.; A.B., Haverford (Pa.) Coll., 1950; diploma Inst. Investment Banking, U. Pa., 1954; m. 2d, Jean Eisenbrandt-Johnston, Feb. 6, 1971; children by previous marriage—J. TenEyck, Beverley T., Joseph Ward, III. With John C. Legg & Co., Inc., Balt., 1950-70, gen. partner, 1961-70; exec. v.p., dir. Legg, Mason & Co., Inc., Balt., 1970-72; vice chmn. bd. dirs., chief adminstrv. officer Legg Mason Wood Walker, Inc., Balt., 1976—; dir. Orchard Capital Mgmt., Inc. Trustee Boys' Latin Sch., Balt.; bd. dirs. Arthritis Found. Md., Children's Fresh Air Soc. Served with USAAF, 1944-46. Mem. Nat. Assn. Securities Dealers (past dist. chmn.), Balt. Security Analysts Soc. (past pres.). Republican. Episcopalian. Clubs: Maryland, Bond (pres. 1966), Merchants (gov.) (Balt.). Office: 7E Redwood St Baltimore MD 21202

SENGSTACKE, JOHN HERMAN HENRY, pub. co. exec.; b. Savannah, Ga., Nov. 25, 1912; s. Herman Alexander and Rosa Mae (Davis) S.; B.S., Hampton (Va.) Inst., 1933; postgrad. Ohio State U., 1933; children—Robert Abbott, Lewis Willis. With Robert S. Abbott Pub. Co., publishers Chgo. Defender, Tri-State Defender, 1934—, v.p., gen. mgr., 1934-40, pres., gen. mgr., 1940—; chmn. bd. Mich. Chronicle (Detroit), Louisville Defender; pres. Tri-State Defender, Defender Publs., Amalgamated Pubs., Inc.; pub. Daily Defender; pres. Sengstacke Enterprises, Inc., Sengstacke Publs., Pitts. Courier Newspaper Chain; dir. Ill. Fed. Savs. & Loan Assn., Golden State Mut. Life Ins. Co. Mem. exec. bd. Nat. Alliance Businessmen; bd. govs. USO; mem. Ill. Sesquicentennial Commn., Pres.'s Com. on Equal Opportunity in Armed Services; mem. pub. affairs adv. com. Air Force Acad.; trustee Bethune-Cookman Coll., Daytona Beach, Fla., Hampton Inst.; bd. dirs. Washington Park YMCA; chmn. bd. Provident Hosp. Recipient Two Friends award Nat. Urban League, 1950; Hampton Alumni award, 1954; 1st Mass. Media award Am. Jewish Com. Mem. Negro Newspaper Pubs. Assn. (founder), Nat. (founder, pres.), Am. newspaper pubs. assns., Am. Soc. Newspaper Editors (dir.). Congregationalist. Clubs: Royal Order of Snakes, Masons, Elks, Rotary, Econs., Chgo. Press. Address: 2400 S Michigan Ave Chicago IL 60616

SENHAUSER, DONALD A(LBERT), pathologist; b. Dover, Ohio, Jan. 30, 1927; s. Albert Carl and Maude Anne (Snyder) S.; student U. Chgo., 1944-45; B.S., Columbia U., 1947, M.D., 1951; grad. with honors U.S. Naval Sch. Aviation Medicine, 1953; m. Helen Brown, July 22, 1961; children—William, Norman. Intern, Roosevelt Hosp., N.Y.C., 1951-52; resident Columbia-Presbyn. Hosp., N.Y.C., 1955-56, Cleve. Clinic, 1956-60; instr. in pathology Columbia U., 1955-56; fellow in immuno-pathology Middlesex Hosp. Med. Sch., London, 1960-61; mem. dept. pathology Cleve. Clinic Found., 1961-63; asso. prof. pathology U. Mo., 1963-65, prof., asst. dean Sch. Medicine, 1969-70, dir. teaching labs., 1968-70, prof., vice-chmn. dept. pathology, 1965-75; prof. pathology, chmn. dept. pathology, Ohio State U. Coll. Medicine, 1975—, prof. Sch. Allied Med.

Professions, 1975—; dir. labs. Ohio State U. Hosps., 1975—; bd. dirs. Columbia area chpt. ARC, 1978—; cons. in field; WHO-AMA Vietnam med. edn. project mem. U. Saigon Med. Sch., 1967-72; vis. scientist HEW, 1972-73; acting dir. Central Ohio Regional Blood Center, 1976-79. Served as capt. M.C., USNR, 1944-45, 52-55; China, Korea. Recipient Lower award Bunts Ednl. Found., 1960; diplomate Am. Bd. Pathology. Mem. Coll. Am. Pathologists (chmn. com. edn. resources 1977-78), Am. Soc. Clin. Pathologists, Assn. Pathology Charimen, Am. Assn. Pathology, Internat. Acad. Pathology, Assn. Am. Med. Colls., Am. Assn. Blood Banks, Ohio Soc. Pathologists (gov. 1979—), AAAS, Ohio Hist. Soc., Columbus Art League, Sigma Xi. Lutheran. Club: Masons. Contbr. articles to profl. jours.; mem. editorial bd. Am. Jour. Clin. Pathology, 1965-76. Home: 1256 Clubview Blvd N Worthington OH 43085 Office: 333 W 10th Ave Columbus OH 43210

SENKIER, ROBERT JOSEPH, univ. dean; b. Poughkeepsie, N.Y., May 31, 1916; s. Michael J. and Mary Gilberta (Perrin) S.; A.B., Columbia U., 1939, M.A., 1940, Ed.D., 1961; m. Mary Theresa Kelly, Mar. 21, 1941; children—Pamela Jeanne Senkier Scott, Deborah Ann. Faculty, Columbia U., 1948-61, asst. dean Sch. Bus., 1958-61; faculty Seton Hall U., South Orange, N.J., 1962-74, dean Sch. Bus. Adminstrn., 1962-74; prof. mgmt., dean Grad. Sch. Bus., Fordham U., N.Y.C., 1975—; mgmt. cons. State Farm Ins. Cos., 1962—. Mem. alumni bd. dirs. Columbia Coll.; mem. John Jay Assos. Served to lt. comdr. USNR, 1940-45. Mem. Am. Econ. Assn., Acad. Mgmt., Acad. Internat. Bus., Columbia Alumni Assn., Phi Delta Kappa, Alpha Kappa Psi, Alpha Sigma Phi, Beta Gamma Sigma. Republican. Roman Catholic. Club: Princeton (N.Y.C.). Author: Revising a Business Curriculum—The Columbia Experience, 1961; contbr. articles to profl. jours. Home: 6 Amherst Ct Glen Rock NJ 07452 Office: Fordham U at Lincoln Center New York City NY 10023

SENKUS, MURRAY, tobacco co. exec.; b. Saskatoon, Sask., Can., Aug. 31, 1914; s. Nicholas and Anne (Waligurski) S.; came to U.S., 1936, naturalized, 1943; student Nutana Collegiate Inst., Sask., 1928-32; B.S. in Chemistry, U. Sask., 1934, M.S., 1936; Ph.D., U. Chgo., 1938; m. Emily Kulcheski, Dec. 31, 1938; children—Neal J., William M., Joanne K., David P. Chemist, Comml. Solvents Corp., Terre Haute, Ind., 1938-46, group leader, 1946-50; dir. research and devel. Daubert Chem. Co., Chgo., 1950-51; dir. chem. research R.J. Reynolds Tobacco Co., Winston-Salem, N.C., 1951-60, asst. dir. research, 1960-64, dir. research, 1964-76, dir. sci. affairs, 1976-79; ret., 1979; instr. chemistry North Park Coll., Chgo., 1936-38. Mem. N.C. Bd. Sci. and Tech., 1972—; mem. sci. commn. CORESTA. Served to sgt. maj. Canadian Officers Tng. Corps, 1934-36. Mem. AAAS, Am. Chem. Soc., N.Y. Acad. Scis. Clubs: Kiwanis, Forsyth Country. Contbr. articles to sci. jours. Patentee in field. Home: 2516 Country Club Rd Winston-Salem NC 27104

SENN, HERBERT CHARLES, scenic designer; b. Ilion, N.Y., Oct. 9, 1924; s. Robert Charles and Elizabeth Amelia (Dietsch) S.; A.B., Atlantic Union Coll., 1948; postgrad. Columbia U. Sch. Dramatic Arts, 1953-56; m. Helen Barbara Pond. Scenic designer over 300 plays, operas, ballets; designer numerous Broadway plays and musicals including What Makes Sammy Run, 1965; prin. designer with Helen Pond, Opera Co. Boston, 1969—; prin. designer Cape Playhouse, Dennis, Mass., 1956—. Served with U.S. Army, 1950-52. Mem. United Scenic Artists of Am. Home: 316 W 51st St New York NY 10019

SENNETT, WILLIAM CLIFFORD, lawyer; b. Erie, Pa., June 1, 1930; s. B. Walker and Rosanne (Cooney) S.; B.A., Holy Cross Coll., 1952; LL.B., Georgetown U., 1955; m. Pauline Wuenschel, Aug. 7, 1954; children—William, Timothy, Patrick, Mark, Kathleen, Carolyn. Admitted to Pa. bar, also U.S. Supreme Ct.; law clk. U.S. Ct. Appeals Judge Danaher, 1955-56; asso. firm Shreve, Sennett, Coughlin & McCarthy, Erie, 1956-65; solicitor Erie County Controller, 1961-63; partner firm Knox, Pearson & McLaughlin, Erie, 1965-66; adminstr. to lt. gov. Pa., 1966-67; atty. gen. Pa., 1967-70; partner law firm Knox, Graham, McLaughlin, Gornall & Sennett, Erie, 1970—. Trustee Mercyhurst Coll.; bd. corporators St. Vincent Hosp., Hamot Hosp. Named Erie County Jr. C. of C. Man of Year, 1961. Mem. Am., Pa., Erie County bar assns., Am. Judicature Soc., Automotive Assn. Erie (sec.-treas. 1971), Phi Delta Phi. Home: 6336 Red Pine Ln Erie PA 16506 Office: 120 W 10th St Erie PA 16501

SENSEMAN, RONALD SYLVESTER, architect; b. Collingswood, N.J., Oct. 19, 1912; s. Raphael and Louise (Tanner) S.; student Columbia Union Coll., 1931-34, Cath. U. Am., 1934-36; m. Lois Hatt, Aug. 18, 1935; children—Marilyn Louise (Mrs. John Whitson Rogers), Peggy June (Mrs. James Orvil Hutchinson). Pvt. practice architecture, Met. Washington area, 1935—; dir. Park Motels Inc., Manor Care, Inc.; pres. Reef Properties Inc., St. Croix, V.I.; lectr. Columbia Union Coll., Seventh Day Adventist Theol. Sem. Republican candidate Md. State Legislature, 1958. Mem. univ. councillors Loma Linda U.; trustee Atlantic Union Coll. Fellow A.I.A.; mem. Guild Religious Architecture, Washington Bd. Trade, Washington Bldg. Congress, Prince George's County C. of C., Cath. U. Alumni Assn. (Archtl. Achievement award 1967). Rotarian. Home: 901 McCeny Ave Silver Spring MD 20901 Office: 7676 New Hampshire Ave Langley Park MD 20783

SENSENBRENNER, FRANK JAMES, JR., congressman; b. Chgo., June 14, 1943; s. Frank James and Margaret Anita (Luedke) S.; A.B. in Polit. Sci., Stanford U., 1965; J.D., U. Wis., 1968: m. Cheryl Lynn Warren, Mar. 26, 1977. Admitted to Wis. bar, 1968, U.S. Supreme Ct. bar, 1972; mem. Wis. Assembly, 1969-75; mem. firm McKay and Martin, Cedarburg. Wis., 1970-75; mem. Wis. State Senate, 1975-79, asst. minority leader, 1977-79; mem. 96th Congress from 9th Wis. Dist. Mem. Am. Philatelic Soc. Republican. Episcopalian. Clubs: Shorewood Men's, Capitol Hill. Office: 315 Cannon House Office Bldg Washington DC 20515

SENTELL, JAMES OSCAR, court ofcl.; b. Luverne, Ala., July 3, 1909; s. James Oscar and Ida Stakley (Fonville) S.; A.B., U. Ala., 1930, LL.B., 1932; m. Jane Elizabeth Jones, June 6, 1937; children—Jane (Mrs. George Preiss III), James C., Edgar. Admitted to Ala. bar, 1932; practiced in Luverne, 1932-43, 46-51, Montgomery, 1953-62; price atty. OPA, Montgomery, 1943-46; counsel Office of Price Stblzn., 1951-53; first asst. U.S. Atty., Middle Dist. Ala., Montgomery, 1962-67; dep. clk. Supreme Ct. Ala., 1967, 68, clk., 1968—, clk. Ct. Civil Appeals, 1969-75. Recipient Alger Sidney Sullivan award U. Ala., 1932. Mem. Nat. Conf. Appellate Ct. Clks. (pres. 1973-74), Jasons, Phi Delta Phi, Phi Gamma Delta, Omicron Delta Kappa. Methodist. Mason. Editor: Alabama Lawyer, 1967—. Home: 3067 Ashley Ave Montgomery AL 36109 Office: Judicial Dept Bldg Montgomery AL 36104

SENTER, L. T., fed. judge; b. Fulton, Miss., July 30, 1933; s. L. T. and Eva Lee (Jetton) S.; B.S., U. So. Miss., 1956; LL.B., U. Miss., 1959; married. Admitted to Miss. bar, 1959; county pros. atty., 1960-64; U.S. commr., 1966-68; judge Miss. Circuit Ct., Circuit 1, 1968-78, U.S. Dist. Ct. for No. Dist. Miss., 1980—. Mem. Miss. State Bar, Am. Bar Assn. Democrat. Office: PO Box 727 Oxford MS 38655*

SENTER, ROGER CAMPBELL, hotel co. exec.; b. Manchester, N.H., Apr. 21, 1932; s. Kenneth Lee and Beatrice (Campbell) S.; B.A., Boston U., 1954, LL.B., 1956. Mem. grad. student tng. program Westinghouse Co., Pitts., 1956-59; asst. mgr. recruiting Semi-Condr. div. Raytheon Co., Boston, 1959-61; founder McGovern, Senter & Assos., Boston, 1961, v.p., 1961-65; dir. recruiting ITT World Hdqrs., N.Y.C., 1965-70; sr. v.p., dir. personnel Sheraton Corp., Boston, 1970—. Bd. dirs. Mass. Mental Health Assn. Mem. Am. Hotel and Motel Assn., Hotel Sales Mgmt. Assn. (pres.), Nat. Assn. for Corp. and Profl. Recruiters (pres.). Club: Corinthian Yacht (Marblehead, Mass.). Home: Roundy's Hill Marblehead MA 01945 Office: 60 State St Boston MA 02210

SENTER, WILLIAM JOSEPH, pub. co. exec.; b. N.Y.C., Dec. 4, 1921; s. Joseph and Sarah (Greenglass) S.; B.B.A., Coll. City N.Y., 1947; m. Irene Phoebe Marcus, Aug. 3, 1952; children—Adam Douglas, Caren Amy. Chmn. bd., mng. editor Deadline Data, Inc., N.Y.C., 1962-66; pres. Unipub, Inc. (merged with Xerox Corp. 1971), N.Y.C., 1966-72; v.p. planning and devel. Xerox Pub. Group, Greenwich, Conn., 1973-74; v.p. info. pub. Xerox Pub. Group and pres. R.R. Bowker Co., N.Y.C., 1974-75; pres. Xerox Pub. Group, Greenwich, Conn., 1976—; v.p. Xerox Corp., Stamford, Conn., 1978—. Served with U.S. Army, 1942-46. Mem. Assn. Am. Pubs. (dir. 1978—). Office: One Pickwick Plaza Greenwich CT 06830

SENTER, WILLIAM OSCAR, ret. air force officer; b. Stamford, Tex., June 15, 1910; s. William Oscar and Mary Ellen (Futrell) S.; student Hardin-Simmons U., 1929; B.S., U.S. Mil. Acad., 1933; postgrad. Mass. Inst. Tech., 1938, Air War Coll., 1948-49; Aero. Engr., U. Okla., 1957; m. Ruth Jane Tinsley, Apr. 10, 1937 (dec. Apr. 1967); children—Suellen Senter Bollé, Ruth Jane Senter Wood; m. 2d, Carolyn C. Fallon, Jan. 2, 1973. Commd. 2d lt. Coast Arty. Corps, U.S. Army, 1933, attached to air corps and apptd. student officer, 1934, advanced through grades to lt. gen. USAF, 1963; comdr. Oklahoma City Air Material Area, 1954-57; dir. Procurement and Prodn. Hdqrs., Air Material Command, Wright-Patterson AFB, 1957-59; asst. dep. chief staff material Hdqrs. USAF, 1959-63; dir. petroleum logistics policy Dept. Def., 1963-66, ret., 1966; exec. v.p. Natural Gas Supply Com., 1966-74. Mem. nominating com. Aviation Hall of Fame. Decorated D.S.M., Legion of Merit with oak leaf cluster. Mem. Air Force Assn., Am. Srs. Golf Assn., Fla. Srs. Golf Assn., So. Srs. Golf, Assn. Grads. U.S. Mil. Acad., Air Force Hist. Found., Mil. Order Carabao, Order Daedalians. Baptist. Clubs: Burning Tree, Tequesta Country, Army-Navy. Home: 72 River Dr Tequesta FL 33458

SERAPHINE, DANNY PETER, drummer; b. Chgo., Aug. 28, 1948; s. John Valentine and Mary (Colangelo) S.; grad. high sch.; m. Rosemarie Stevenson, June 3, 1967; children—Christine, Danielle. Mem. musical group Chicago, 1967—; owner night club B. Ginnings, Schaumberg, Ill., 1974—; owner clothing store Peabody's, Chgo., 1974—. Co-composer: Lowdown, 1972; Devil's Sweet, 1974; Aire, 1974. Address: Wald-Nanas Assos 6356 Santa Monica Blvd Beverly Hills CA 90210*

SERAYDARIAN, MARIA W(ARGON), biochemist; b. Warsaw, Poland, Jan. 30, 1924; d. Mieczyslaw and Bronislawa (Diettman) Wargon; came to U.S., 1949, naturalized, 1958; B.A., Am. U., Beirut, Lebanon, 1948, M.S., 1949; Ph.D., Tufts U., 1952; m. Kirkor H. Seraydarian, Aug. 24, 1950; children—Ann, Paul. Asso. research biochemist, nuclear medicine and zoology dept. UCLA, 1960-68, asso. prof. Sch. of Nursing, 1972-74, prof., 1974—; asso. research biochemist dept. biol. sci. U. So. Calif., 1968-72; cons. NIH, Nat. Heart and Lung Inst., 1970—. Mem. AAAS, Am. Physiol. Soc., Cardiac Muscle Soc., Internat. Soc. Heart Research. Contbr. articles to profl. jours. Home: 2256 Parnell Ave Los Angeles CA 90064 Office: U Calif Sch of Nursing Los Angeles CA 90024

SERBAN, ANDREI GEORGE, theatre dir.; b. Bucarest, Romania, June 21, 1943; s. George and Elpis (Lichiardopol) S.; came to U.S., 1969; student Theatre Inst. Bucarest, 1963-68. Asst. to Peter Brook Internat. Theatre Inst., Paris, 1970-71; dir. La Mama Exptl. Theatre, N.Y.C., 1970-77; asso. dir. Yale Repertory Theatre, 1977—; guest prof. drama Yale U., 1977, Pitts. Carnegie Tech., 1974, Sarah Lawrence U., 1974, Paris Conservatory, 1975. Recipient Obie award for distinguished direction of Greek tragedy, 1975, Drama Desk award for best prodn. Medea, Outer Critic Circle award for Cherry Orchard on Broadway, 1977, European Festival awards, 1972, 73, 75; Guggenheim fellow, 1976-77; Ford Found. fellow, 1969-70. Contbr. articles to profl. jours. Home and Office: 74 E 4th St New York NY 10003. *The path of the theatre is to be in tune with the movements of life. Theatre, as love does, can give us the fresh feeling of being in touch with the miraculous and the immediate.*

SERBER, ROBERT, educator; b. Phila., Mar. 14, 1909; s. David and Rose (Frankel) S.; B.S., Lehigh U., 1930, D.Sc., 1972; Ph.D., U. Wis., 1934; m. Charlotte Leof, June 15, 1933 (dec. May 1967); m. 2d, Fiona St. Clair, Dec. 4, 1979. NRC fellow U. Cal., 1934-36, research asso., 1936-38, prof. radiation lab., 1945- 51; asst. prof. U. Ill., 1938-40, asso. prof., 1940-45; war work Metall. Lab., Chgo., 1942-43, Los Alamos (N.Mex.) Lab., 1943-45; prof. physics Columbia, 1951—, chmn. dept. physics, 1975-77, prof. emeritus, 1977—. Cons., Brookhaven Nat. Lab.; mem. Solvay Conf., Brussels, Belgium, 1948, Atomic Bomb Group, Marianas, 1945; dir. phys. measurements Atomic Bomb Mission to Japan, Sept.-Oct. 1945; mem. sci. policy adv. coms. Brookhaven Nat. Lab., Argonne Nat. Lab., Stanford Linear Accelerator Center; adv. com. Fermi Nat. Accelerator Lab., 1967—, Los Alamos Meson Facility, 1979—. Trustee Asso. Univs., Inc., 1974—. Recipient Oppenheimer prize, 1972. Guggenheim fellow. Fellow Am. Phys. Soc. (v.p. 1970, pres. 1971), Am. Acad. Arts and Scis.; mem. Nat. Acad. Scis., Explorers Club, Sigma Xi. Contbr. to profl. jours. Home: Box 260 Cruz Bay St John VI 00830

SERENBETZ, WARREN LEWIS, leasing co. exec.; b. N.Y.C., Mar. 27, 1924; s. Lewis E. and Estelle (Weygand) S.; B.S., Columbia, 1944, M.S., 1949; m. Thelma Randby, Apr. 10, 1948; children—Warren Lewis, Paul Halvor, Stuart Weygand, Clay Raymond. Cons., Emerson Engrs., N.Y.C., 1949-51; with Oliver Corp., 1951-53; with REA Express, 1953-68, sr. v.p., 1966-68; v.p., dir. REA Leasing Corp., 1961-68; chmn. exec. com., chief exec. officer Interpool, Ltd., 1968—. Bd. dirs. Containerization Inst.; pres. Inst. Internat. Container Lessors. Served to lt. (j.g.) USNR, World War II. Mem. Am. Nat. Standards Inst., Am. Mgmt. Assn. (pres.'s council), U.S. C. of C. (com. on trends and perspectives). Presbyn. Clubs: University (Larchmont); Union League (N.Y.C.); Orienta Beach and Yacht. Home: Hunter Hill West St Harrison NY 10528 Office: 630 3d Ave New York NY 10017

SERENI, MARIO, baritone; b. Perugia, Italy, Mar. 25, 1928; student Acad. Chigiana, Siena, Italy, Acad. S. Cecilia, Rome; m. Elsa Sereni; 4 children. Opera debut as Wolfram in Tannhauser, Teatro Massimo, Palermo, Italy, 1956; Met. Opera debut as Gerald in Andrea Chenier, 1957; sang with maj. opera cos. in Europe, North and South Am.; resident mem. Met. Opera, Wiener Staatsoper, La Scala; appearances with symphony orchs.; recitalist; tchr. voice. Recipient Arena d'Oro, Verona, Italy, Verdi award, Parma, Italy. Office: care Met Opera Lincoln Center New York NY 10023*

SERENYI, PETER, art historian; b. Budapest, Hungary, Jan. 13, 1931; s. Nicholas and Emma (Josika) S.; came to U.S., 1950, naturalized, 1954; A.B. cum laude, Dartmouth Coll., 1957; M.A., Yale U., 1958; Ph.D., Washington U., St. Louis, 1968; m. Agnes Kertesz, Aug. 28, 1969; children—Peter, Denis. Part-time instr. art and archaeology Washington U., 1959-61; instr. fine arts Amherst Coll., 1961-64; vis. lectr. Smith Coll., 1962-63, U. Pa., 1964-66, Boston U., 1966-68; mem. faculty Northeastern U., Boston, 1968—, asso. prof. art history, 1973-80, prof., 1980—. Dir., Mass. Com. Preservation Archtl. Records. Served with AUS, 1953-55. Nat. Endowment Humanities grantee, summer 1970; Am. Philos. Soc. grantee, 1970; Graham Found. Advanced Studies Fine Arts grantee, 1974-75; Fulbright scholar, 1974-75. Mem. Soc. Archtl. Historians (pres. New Eng. chpt. 1978—), Victorian Soc. Am., Soc. Preservation New Eng. Antiquities, City Conservation League. Democrat. Roman Catholic. Editor, contbr.: Le Corbusier in Perspective, 1975; contbr. articles to profl. jours. Address: 79 Greenough St Brookline MA 02146

SERFASS, EARL JAMES, cons.; b. Allentown, Pa., Dec. 22, 1912; s. James M. and Ida Alice (Shafer) S.; B.S. in Chemistry, Lehigh U., 1933, M.S., 1935, Ph.D., 1938; m. Mabel Dowling, Sept. 5, 1935; children—Nancy Alice, Robert Earl, Richard Eric. Instr. analytical chemistry Lehigh U., Bethlehem, Pa., 1938-40, asst. prof., 1940-42, asso. prof., 1942-45, prof. 1946-59, curriculum dir. chemistry, 1950-52, head chemistry dept., 1952-59; pres. Serfass Corp.; v.p., research dir. Milton Roy Co., 1959-66, sr. v.p. 1966-68, pres., 1968-76, chmn. bd., chief exec. officer, 1974-78; pres. Sercon Corp., cons., 1978—. Project dir. Am. Electroplaters Soc.; cons. various indsl. firms; Fellow Instrument Soc. Am.; mem. Am. Chem. Soc., Am. Inst. Physics, Phi Beta Kappa, Sigma Xi, Tau Beta Pi. Contbr. numerous articles to profl. jours. Home: 102 Harbor View Ln Largo FL 33540

SERGEL, CHRISTOPHER ROGER, publisher; b. Iowa City, May 7, 1918; s. Roger Louis and Ruth (Fuller) S.; A.A., U. Chgo., 1939; m. Carol Johnston, Mar. 21, 1967; 1 dau., Kathryn; children by previous marriage—Ruth, Christopher Triton, Ingrid, Ann. With Dramatic Pub. Co., Chgo., 1941—, editor, 1945—, v.p., 1952-70, pres., 1970—; capt. schooner on expdn. to South Pacific, 1940; playwright, 1938—. Served to lt. comdr. USMCR, World War II; ETO, PTO. Mem. Dramatists Guild, Drama Desk, Beta Theta Pi. Clubs: Adventurers, Explorers', Cliff Dwellers. Author: The Ragtime Dance, 1975; dramatic versions of Lost Horizon, 1942, Winesburg, Ohio, 1958, To Kill a Mockingbird, 1970, Black Elk Speaks, 1975, others. Contbr. articles to mags. Home: 123 Sharp Hill Rd Wilton CT 06897 Office: 163 Main St Westport CT 06880

SERGIEVSKY, OREST, ballet dancer, tchr., choreographer; b. Kiev, Russia, Aug. 21, 1911; s. Boris and Ella S.; pvt. study ballet including Bronislava Nijinskaya, 1920, 40, Olga Preobrajenskaya, Paris, France, 1927-47, Michael Fokine, 1932-42, others; grad. drama dept. Columbia. Performed with Art of Musical Russia, 1935, Salmagi Opera, 1937, Fokine ballets, 1936-38, Met. Opera Co., 1938, 39, Ballet Theatre, 1939-41, Original Ballet Russe, 1941, 45-48; solo concerts, 1936-50; tchr. ballet arts own sch. Theatre Studio of Dance and Carnegie Hall Internat. Ballet Sch., 1950-71; dir., choreographer Dance Varieties; now free-lance tchr., choreographer. Served with USAAF, World War II. Author: (autobiography) Shadows-Memories, 1977. Address: 200 W 54th St New York NY 10019*

SERISAWA, SUEO, artist; b. Yokohama, Japan, Apr. 10, 1910; s. Yoichi Gaho and Masu (Aoki) S.; student Otis Art Inst., Los Angeles, 1939, Chgo. Art Inst., 1943; m. Marsha Monroe Davis, Nov. 29, 1977; 1 dau. by previous marriage, Margaret Marcotte. Exhbns. include: Carnegie Inst., Pitts., 1952, Tokyo Internat., 1952, San Paulo Biennale, Brazil, 1955, Whitney Mus. Am. Art, N.Y.C., 1960, Pacific Heritage, U.S. State Dept., Berlin, 1965; instr. painting Kann Inst. Art, West Hollywood, Calif., 1948-50, Scripps Coll., 1949-50, U. So. Calif., 1975-79, Idyllwild, Calif., 1974—; represented in permanent collections: Met. Mus. N.Y., Joslyn Mus., Omaha, Los Angeles County Mus. Art, Santa Barbara Mus. Art, Smithsonian Inst., San Diego Fine Arts Gallery. Mem. Artists for Econ. Action, Nat. Water Color Soc. (past pres.), Japanese-Am. Citizens League, Mingei Internat. La Jolla (Calif.). Home: 3033 Warren Ln Costa Mesa CA 92626 Office: 55315 S Circle Idyllwild CA 92349. *Painting brings to me an understandable scale which I can relate to nature. My particular interest is trying to extract the symbol from nature and to create an atmosphere in which I can break the laws of natural forms by intuitive improvisation. Through this I hope to let my hand guide me to true art awareness as cosmic awareness.*

SERKIN, PETER, pianist; b. N.Y.C., July 24, 1947; s. Rudolf and Irene (Busch) S.; student Curtis Inst. Music, 1958-64; m. Wendy Spinner, Oct. 5, 1968. Debut in N.Y.C., 1959; appearances including with Phila., Cleve., N.Y.C., London (Eng.), Zurick (Switzerland), Paris (France), Casals Festival orchs.; recitals in N.Y.C., London, Japan, maj. European and Am. cities; benefit performances for pacifism, aid to victims of war; rec. artist for RCA Victor. Office: care Frank Salomon Assos 201 W 54th St Suite 4C New York NY 10019*

SERKIN, RUDOLF, pianist; b. Eger, Bohemia, Mar. 28, 1903; s. Mordko Serkin and Augusta (Schargl) S.; thought a child prodigy at 4, studied piano with Richard Robert, and composition with J. Marx and Arnold Schoenberg; Mus.D., Curtis Inst. Music, Williams Coll., Temple U., U. Vt., Oberlin (Ohio) Coll., U. Rochester, Harvard U., 1973, Marlboro Coll.; m. Irene Busch; children—Ursula, Elisabeth, John, Peter, Judith, Marguerite. European concert debut as guest artist Vienna Symphony Orch., 1915; began concert career in Europe, 1920, in solo, concerto and chamber music recitals, appearing with Adolf Busch in series of sonatas for violin and piano, with Busch Chamber Players in the Bach suites and Brandenburg concertos; debut in America, Coolidge Festival, Washington, 1933; launched concert career in U.S. with N.Y. Philharmonic under Toscannini, 1936; played a series of Mozart and Beethoven, with Nat. Orchestral Assn., 1937; with Adolf Busch played complete series of Beethoven piano and violin sonatas, N.Y.C., 1938; has made ann. concert tours in U.S. since 1934; apptd. piano dept. Curtis Inst. Music, Phila.; artistic dir., pres. Marlboro Music Sch. and Festival, Vt.; dir. Curtis Inst. Music, 1968-76. Recipient Presdl. Medal Freedom, 1963; named grand officiale del Ordina. Fellow Am. Acad. Arts and Scis.; former mem. Nat. Council on Arts, Carnegie Commn. Report; hon. mem. Academia Nationale di Santa Cecilia, Rome, Verein Beethoven Haus, Bonn, Philharmonic Symphony Soc. N.Y., Riemenschneider Bach Inst. Home: RFD 3 Brattleboro VT 05301

SERLIS, HARRY GEORGE, inst. dir.; b. Kansas City, Feb. 22, 1912; s. Harry and Hattie (Weissenbach) S.; student U. Ill., 1928-29; m. Kathryn Isreal, Dec. 14, 1935; children—Charles Harry, Barry Edward; m. 2d, Roberta Maleville, 1962. Advt., investment banking, Midwest 1932-34; asst. gen. sales mgr. Schenley Distillers, Inc., 1936-41; gen. mgr. Schenley Import Corp., 1942; dir. sales, advt. CVA Co., 1943-51, chmn. bd., 1954-59, pres., chmn., 1955-58; pres., dir. Schenley Distillers, Inc., 1951-55; v.p., dir. Schenley Industries, Inc., 1952-59; with Harry G. Serlis & Assos., mgmt. cons.-pub. relations, San Francisco, 1961-69; pres. Wine Inst., San Francisco, 1969-75; sr. v.p. Jeré Helfat Assos., Inc., San Francisco, 1975—; dir. Robert Mondavi Winery, Oakville, Calif. Mem. Calif. Agrl. Fgn. Trade Adv.

Com. Decorated officier de l'Ordre National du Merit de France, Medaille d'Honneur du Comité Nationale des Vins de France; recipient gold insignia Club Oenologique. Mem. Pub. Relations Soc. Am., Am. Assn. Mgmt. Cons. Home: 570 Via Corta Palm Springs CA 92262 also 1250 Jones St San Francisco CA 94109

SERNETT, RICHARD PATRICK, pub. co. exec., lawyer; b. Mason City, Iowa, Sept. 8, 1938; s. Edward Frank and Loretta M. (Cavanaugh) S.; B.B.A., U. Iowa, 1960, J.D., 1963; m. Janet Ellen Ward, Apr. 20, 1963; children—Susan Ellen, Thomas Ward, Stephen Edward, Katherine Anne. Admitted to Ill. bar, 1965; with Scott, Foresman & Co., Glenview, Ill., 1963—, house counsel, asst. sec., 1967-70, sec., legal officer, 1970—; mem. adv. panel on internat. copyright U.S. State Dept., 1972-75. Mem. Am. (chmn. copyright div. sect. patent, trademark and copyright law 1972-73), Ill. (chmn. copyright law com. 1978-79), Chgo., bar assns., Am. Patent Law Assn. (chmn. copyright matters com. 1972-73), Patent Law Assn. Chgo. (chmn. copyright com. 1972-73, 77-78, bd. mgrs. 1979—), Copyright Soc. U.S.A. (trustee 1972-75, 77-80), Am. Judicature Soc., Am. Soc. Corporate Secs., Assn. Am. Pubs. (chmn. copyright com. 1972-73, vice chmn. 1973-75), Phi Delta Phi, Phi Kappa Theta. Home: 2071 Glendale Ave Northbrook IL 60062 Office: 1900 E Lake Ave Glenview IL 60025

SEROTA, HERMAN MICHAEL, psychiatrist, psychoanalyst, educator; b. Chgo., May 1, 1914; s. Hermon and Hannah (Pouhl) S.; B.S., U. Chgo., 1934, M.D., 1938, Ph.D., 1939; certified (Rockefeller fellow), Inst. for Psychoanalysis, Chgo., 1948; m. Hermia Sunshine, 1957. Intern Michael Reese Hosp., Chgo., 1938-39; resident U. Chgo. Hosps., 1939-42; practice medicine, specializing in psychiatry and psychoanalysis, Chgo., 1942—; asst. to asso. prof. psychiatry Northwestern U. Med. Sch., 1950-56, distinguished lectr., 1973-74; professorial lectr. U. Chgo., 1956-74, sr. attending psychiatrist Psychiat. and Psychosomatic Inst., 1966-74; dir. liaison psychiatry, 1950-56; mem. staff, tng., supervising analyst Inst. for Psychoanalysis, Chgo., 1956-74; tng. and supervising psychoanalyst San Diego Psychoanalytic Inst., LaJolla, Calif., 1974—; clin. prof. psychiatry U. Calif. at San Diego, 1974—; attending psychiatrist Univ. Hosp., San Diego. Life mem. Art Inst. Chgo.; asso. life mem. Field Mus. Natural History. Served to capt. M.C., AUS, 1942-46. Diplomate Am. Bd. Psychiatry and Neurology. Fellow Am. Psychiat. Assn. (life), A.A.A.S. (life; chmn. com. on liaison); mem. Am. Psychoanalytic Assn. (councillor-at-large 1971-75, 76-80), Chgo. Psychoanalytic Soc. (pres. 1965-66), Am. EEG Assn. (charter), Phi Beta Kappa, Sigma Xi, Alpha Omega Alpha. Office: 1020 Prospect Pl LaJolla CA 92037. *I have always been mindful of the state of human bonds which can be simply formulated as "I plus you equals We" or I U — UI a (affect in all personal interchange, the equation of the human bond.*

SERPA, THOMAS ROSE, drug co. exec.; b. Providence, Mar. 28, 1917; s. Anthony and Philomena (Rose) S.; A.B., Brown U., 1938; M.A., Fletcher Sch. Law and Diplomacy, 1940; m. Jean Campbell Worthington, Jan. 12, 1946; children—Carol Ann (Mrs. David M. Corcoran), Melanie. With fgn. div. Sterling Drug, Inc., N.Y.C., 1940—, worked in all areas of Brazil, 1942-65, v.p., gen. mgr. orgn., 1955-65, adminstrv. v.p. charge fgn. operations including Latin Am., Africa, So. Europe and Far East, N.Y.C., 1965-72, corp. v.p., 1972—, dir., 1974—; pres., chief exec. officer Sterling Products Internat., Inc., Winthrop Products, Inc., Sydney Ross Co., Dorothy Gray, Inc., Valmont, Inc., 1973. Mem. Phi Beta Kappa. Home: 350 S Ocean Blvd Boca Raton FL 33432 Office: 6th Floor 90 Park Ave New York NY 10016

SERRA-BADUE, DANIEL FRANCISCO, artist, educator; b. Santiago de Cuba, Sept. 8, 1914; s. Daniel Serra and Eloisa Badue; came to U.S., 1962; Licenciate in Law, U. Barcelona, 1936; LL.D., U. Havana, 1938, Dr. in Social, Polit. and Econ. Scis., 1949; M.F.A., Nat. Sch. Fine Arts, Havana, 1943; m. Aida Betancourt, Mar. 8, 1944; 1 dau., Aida Victoria. Prof., Sch. Fine Arts, Santiago de Cuba, 1945-60, Nat. Sch. Fine Arts, Havana, 1960-62; lectr. Columbia U., N.Y.C., 1962-63; instr. Bklyn. Mus. Art Sch., N.Y.C., 1962—; prof. St. Peter's Coll., Jersey City, 1967—; asst. dir. culture Ministry Edn., Havana, 1959-60; exhibited 30 one-man shows and over 100 group shows. Guggenheim Found. fellow, 1938, 39; Cintas Found. fellow, 1963-64; recipient Pa. Acad. prize, 1941, Bienal Hispano Americana prize, Havana, 1954. Mem. AAUP, Coll. Art Assn. Am., Soc. Archtl. Historians. Home: 15 W 72d St New York City NY 10023 Office: 2641 Kennedy Blvd Jersey City NJ 07306

SERRALLES, FELIX J., bank exec.; b. Ponce, P.R., Feb. 3, 1911; s. Juan E. and Rosa Maria (Sanchez) S.; B.S. in Elec. Engring., N.Y. U., 1931; m. Frances Nevares, Nov. 11, 1933; children—Felix J., Juan Oscar, Frances M., Michael J. With Ponce Elec. Co., 1931-33; with Empresas Serralles, Inc., Ponce, 1933—, now chief exec. officer, chmn.; chmn. Banco de Ponce, 1939—. Past pres., Amateur Softball Assn. P.R.; hon. pres. Sports Hall of Fame of P.R. Recipient Achievement award N.Y. U. Banking and Industry, 1957. Mem. Sociedad de Ingenierios de P.R., Bankers Club P.R., Aircraft Owners and Pilots Assn. Roman Catholic. Rotary (past pres.). Clubs: Deportivo de Ponce, Nautico de Ponce, Ponce Country, Nat. de San Juan. Home: E-36 Urb El Monte Ponce PR 00731 Office: Mercedita PR 00715

SERRIN, JAMES BURTON, educator; b. Chgo., Nov. 1, 1926; s. James B. and Helen Elizabeth (Wingate) S.; student Northwestern U., 1944-46; B.A., Western Mich. U., 1947; M.A., Ind. U., Ph.D., 1951; D.Sc., U. Sussex, 1972; m. Barbara West, Sept. 6, 1952; children—Martha Helen, Elizabeth Ruth, Janet Louise. With Mass. Inst. Tech., 1952-54; faculty U. Minn., Mpls., 1955—, prof. math., 1959—, head Sch. Math., 1964-65, Regents prof., 1968—. Vis. prof. U. Chgo., 1964, 75, Johns Hopkins, 1966, Sussex U., 1967-68, 72, 76, U. Naples, 1979. Mem. Met. Airport Sound Abatement Council, Mpls., 1969—. Recipient Disting. Alumni award Ind. U., 1979. Mem. Am. Math. Soc. (G.D. Birkhoff prize 1973). Math. Assn. Am., Soc. for Natural Philosophy (pres. 1969-70), A.A.A.S. Author: Mathematical Principles of Classical Fluid Mechanics, 1957. Co-editor: Archive for Rational Mechanics and Analysis. Home: 4422 Dupont Ave S Minneapolis MN 55409

SERRIS, NICHOLAS HARRY, banker; b. Glens Falls, N.Y., Sept. 27, 1924; B.S. in Bus. Adminstrn., Boston U., 1955; m. Mary Jane Verlangieri, May 21, 1967; children—Paul, Suzanne. With Coopers and Lybrand, N.Y.C., 1955-67, audit mgr., 1964-67; treas., financial v.p. Gen. Devel. Corp., Miami, Fla., 1967-73, sr. v.p. finance, 1973—; sr. v.p. Flagship Banks, Inc., 1974—; v.p., comptroller S.E. Banking Corp., 1975—. Trustee Bapt. Hosp. of Miami. Served with USNR, 1943-45. Mem. Am. Inst. C.P.A.'s, N.Y. State Soc. C.P.A.'s. Club: Riviera Country (Coral Gables, Fla.). Home 8390 SW 108th St Miami FL 33156 Office: 100 S Biscayne Blvd Miami FL 33131

SERVICE, ELMAN ROGERS, educator; b. Tecumseh, Mich., May 18, 1915; s. Joseph Duaine and Ethel (Rogers) S.; A.B., U. Mich., 1941; postgrad. U. Chgo., 1942; Ph.D., Columbia, 1950; m. Helen Stevenson, Dec. 2, 1942. Faculty, Columbia, 1949-53, U. Mich., 1953-69, prof. anthropology, 1960-69; faculty U. Calif. at Santa Barbara, 1969—. Anthrop. field research in Paraguay, 1948-49, Mexico, 1957-58, also Am. S.W. Served with AUS, 1942-46. Fellow Am. Anthrop. Assn.; mem. Am. Ethnol. Soc. (sec.-treas. 1949-52), Phi Beta Kappa. Author: Tobati: Paraguayan Town, 1954; A Profile of Primitive Culture, 1958; (with M.D. Sahlins) Evolution and Culture, 1960; Primitive Social Organization, 1962; Profiles in Ethnology, 1963; The Hunters, 1966; Cultural Evolutionism, 1971; Origins of the State and Civilization, 1975. Home: 459 El Cielito Rd Santa Barbara CA 93105

SERVICE, JAMES EDWARD, naval officer; b. Grosse Point, Mich., Jan. 20, 1931; s. Bruce Edward and Constance Irene (Mills) S.; B.A. in Polit. Sci., U.S. Naval Postgrad. Sch., 1965; student in def. studies U.S. Army War Coll., 1972-73; M.A. in Mass. Communications, Shippensburg State Coll., 1973; m. Natalie Gene Harpst, Apr. 15, 1955; children—Mark Earl, Bruce Edward, David Bryan. Commd. ensign U.S. Navy, 1952, advanced through grades to rear adm., 1978; comdg. officer Heavy Reconnaisance Squadron 62, Naval Air Sta., Jacksonville, Fla., 1969, Heavy Attach Squadron 123, Naval Air Sta., Whidbey Island, Wash., 1969-70, U.S.S. Sacramento, Bremerton, Wash., 1973-75, U.S.S. Independence, Norfolk, Va., 1975-77; exec. officer U.S.S. Independence, 1971-72; dir. aviation manpower and tng. Office of Chief of Naval Ops., Washington, 1978—. Decorated Legion of Merit with gold star, Bronze Star, Air with 6 gold stars,. Navy Commendation medal. Mem. Nat. Rifle Assn. Republican. Home: 2351 S Rolfe St Arlington VA 22202 Office: Dir Aviation Manpower and Tng (OP-59) Office Chief of Naval Ops Navy Dept Washington DC 20350

SERVIES, JAMES ALBERT, librarian; b. Lafayette, Ind., Sept. 2, 1925; s. Byron Beatty and Mildred Margaret (Boonstra) S.; Ph.B., U. Chgo. 1946, M.A., 1949; m. Ruth Janet Oostmeyer, Sept. 27, 1945 (div. 1971); children—Janet Lynn, Jeanne Ann, James Albert, John Edward; m. 2d, Lana Warren Stanley. Asst. to circulation librarian U. Miami, Coral Gables, Fla., 1949-53; reference and circulation librarian Coll. William and Mary, 1953-57, librarian, 1957-66; dir. libraries U. West Fla., Pensacola, 1966—. Served with AUS, 1945-46. Mem. Southeastern, Fla. library assns., Fla. Hist. Soc., Phi Gamma Delta. Democrat. Methodist. Editor: The Three Charters of the Virginia Company of London (with seven related documents), 1606-1621, 1957; co-editor: The Poems of Charles Hansford, 1961. Compiler: A Bibiography of John Marshall, 1956; (with E.G. Swem, J.M. Jennings) A Selected Bibliography of Virginia, 1607-1699, 1957; A Bibliography of West Florida, 1974. Home: 1305 Lansing Dr Pensacola FL 32504 Office: John C Pace Library U W Fla Pensacola FL 32504

SESKER, MONTE NEIL, editor; b. Des Moines, May 1, 1940; s. Neil H. and Marjory Q. (Hanks) S.; B.S., Iowa State U., 1963; m. Carolyn J. Gill, Mar. 10, 1961; children—Terry, Rick, Christine. News editor Democrat and Reporter, Emmetsburg, Iowa, 1963-64; field editor Wallaces Farmer, Farm Progress Publs., Des Moines, 1964-70, mng. editor, 1970-74, editor, 1974—. Recipient Meritorious Agrl. Service award Am. Soybean Assn., 1973. Mem. Am. Agrl. Editors Assn., Sigma Delta Chi. Methodist. Home: Rural Route 1 Cambridge IA 50046 Office: 1912 Grand Ave Des Moines IA 50305

SESLOWSKY, HARVEY MICHAEL, broadcasting exec.; b. N.Y.C., Apr. 25, 1942; s. Alan and Geraldine (Dworkin) S.; B.A., Queens Coll., 1964; certificate Sch. Radio Techniques, 1960; m. Helaine Lewander, June 14, 1964; children—Edward, Wendy, Cheryl, Alan. Account exec. ABC-TV Network, 1964-66; dir. program purchasing TV Stations, Inc., N.Y.C., 1966-70; v.p. Film Service Corp., N.Y.C., 1970—; pres. Broadcast Info. Bur., Inc., 1971—, also dir.; dir. Herb Altman Communications Research, Inc., Syntheprintics Corp. Vice pres. Transquility Alumni. Mem. Nat. Assn. TV Program Execs., Oyster Bay Jewish Center, Queens Coll. Alumni Assn. Author articles, composer. Office: 30 E 42d St New York City NY 10017

SESONSKE, ALEXANDER, nuclear, chem. engr.; b. Gloversville, N.Y., June 20, 1921; s. Abraham and Esther (Kreitzer) S.; B.Chem. Engring., Rensselaer Poly. Inst., 1942; M.S., U. Rochester, 1947; Ph.D., U. Del., 1950; m. Marjorie Ann Mach, Apr. 17, 1952; children—Michael Jan, Jana Louise. Engr., Chem. Constrn. Corp., N.Y.C., 1942; chem. engr. Manhattan Project, 1943-45, Columbia-So. Chem. Corp., 1945-46; staff Los Alamos Sci. Lab., 1950-54, 60-61, cons., 1961-63; faculty Purdue U., Lafayette, Ind., 1954, prof. nuclear and chem. engring., 1959—, asst. chmn. dept. nuclear engring., 1966-73. Cons. Oak Ridge Nat. Lab., 1963-67, Electric Power Research Inst., 1974; mem. rev. com. Argonne (Ill.) Nat. Lab., 1965-67, 75—. Fellow Am. Nuclear Soc.; mem. Am. Inst. Chem. Engrs., Am. Soc. Engring. Edn., Sigma Xi, Omega Chi Epsilon. Author: (with Samuel Glasstone) Nuclear Reactor Engineering, 1963, 2d edit., 1967; Nuclear Power Plant Design Analysis, 1973; (with Samuel Glasstone) Nuclear Power Reactor Engineering, 1979. Mem. editorial bd. Advances in Nuclear Sci. and Tech., 1972—. Contbr. numerous articles to profl. jours. Research on liquid metal heat transfer and nuclear reactor engring. Home: 608 Elm Dr West Lafayette IN 47906 Office: Nuclear Engring Purdue U Lafayette IN 47907

SESSA, FRANK BOWMAN, educator, librarian; b. Pitts., June 11, 1911; s. Thomas G. and Margaret Isabelle (Bowman) S.; A.B., U. Pitts., 1933, A.M., 1934, Ph.D., 1950; B.L.S., Carnegie Inst. Tech., 1942; m. Anne Marshall Johnston, Dec. 19, 1942; children—Anne Marshall, Jane Thomas, Gale Francesca. Research fellow Western Pa. Hist. Survey, 1935-36; librarian Hist. Soc. Western Pa., 1936-40; circulation librarian U. Pitts., 1941-42, prof. Grad. Sch. Library and Info. Scis., 1966—, acting dean, 1971-74, chmn. dept. library sci., 1973-76; instr. history U. Miami, 1947-50, asst. prof., 1951; dir. libraries City Miami, 1951-66. Served as lt. comdr. USNR, 1943-46; capt. Res. ret. Mem. A.A.U.P., A.L.A. (treas. 1972-76), Pa. Library Assn., Assn. Am. Library Schs., Hist. Soc. Western Pa., Beta Phi Mu (exec. sec.). Rotarian. Contbr. articles to profl. jours. Home: 346 Midway Rd Mt Lebanon PA 15216 Office: 135 N Bellefield Ave Pittsburgh PA 15260

SESSIONS, CICERO COLUMBUS, lawyer; b. Empire, C.Z., Oct. 5, 1908; s. Varner Vaughn and Laura Caroline (Browning) S.; student La. State U., 1926-29; LL.B., Tulane U., 1932, J.D., 1968; m. Phyllis Dilworth, Apr. 12, 1941; 1 dau., Mary Susan. Admitted to La. bar, 1932; individual practice law, New Orleans, 1932-40; gen. counsel La. Dept. Revenue, asst. atty. gen. State of La., 1940-42; asst. city atty., New Orleans, 1946; mem. firm Montgomery, Barnett, Brown, Sessions & Read, New Orleans, 1946-58; sr. mem. firm Sessions, Fishman, Rosenson, Snellings & Boisfontaine, New Orleans, 1958—. Served to 1st lt., inf., AUS, to lt. col., JAG, U.S. Army, 1942-46; ret. Fellow Am. Coll. Trial Lawyers (state chmn. 1963, com. to preserve oral argument in appellate cts. 1976—, chmn. 1977-78, mem. com. to preserve oral argument in trial cts. 1978—), Internat. Soc. Barristers; mem. Am. (spl. com. to cooperate with Internat. Commn. of Jurists 1957-64), La. (chmn. sect. internat. comparative and mil. law 1949-51, chmn. ins. sect. 1958-59, ho. of dels. 1957-60), New Orleans (chmn. com. on jud. reform 1952-54, chmn. com. on dist. ct. rules 1963-64, 66-67, exec. v.p. 1965) bar assns., Assn. Bar City N.Y., Am. Judicature Soc., Am. Soc. Internat. Law, Judge Advs. Assn., Fedn. Ins. Counsel, Internat. Assn. Ins. Counsel (chmn. marine ins. com. 1957-58), Maritime Law Assn. U.S., La., New Orleans assns. def. counsel, New Orleans Assn. Commerce (chmn. aviation com. 1950-52), U.S. Fifth Circuit Ct. of Appeals Jud. Conf. (hon. life), Supreme Ct. Hist. Soc. (founding), Sigma Alpha Epsilon (founder mem.), Pi Sigma Alpha, Tau Kappa Alpha. Democrat. Presbyterian. Clubs: Masons; Petroleum of New Orleans; City (Baton Rouge); Carnival. Co-author: Statement of the Rule of Law in the United States, 1960. Home: 1609 Frankfort St New Orleans LA 70122 Office: 21st Floor 1010 Common St New Orleans LA 70112

SESSIONS, CLIFF, govt. ofcl.; b. Bolton, Miss., Sept. 26, 1931; s. Valentine Hunter and Daisy (Farr) S.; B.S., U. So. Miss., 1955; m. Shirley Edwards, Dec. 31, 1952; children—Carol, Steven. Announcer, news reporter, program mgr. radio sta. WFOR, Hattiesburg, Miss., 1952-57; staff reporter, then mgr. Jackson (Miss.) bur. U.P.I., 1957-64, staff reporter Washington bur., 1964-66; with Dept. Justice, 1966-69, dir. pub. information, spl. asst. to atty. gen., 1967-69; mng. editor Nat. Jour., Washington, 1969-70, editor, pub., 1970-71; dep. exec. dir. Am. Bankers Assn., Washington, 1971-72, exec. dir., 1972-78; dep. asst. sec. HEW, Washington, 1978—. Served with AUS, 1951-52. Mem. Pub. Relations Soc. Am., Sigma Delta Chi. Home: 7702 Granada Dr Bethesda MD 20034 Office: Dept HEW Washington DC 20201

SESSIONS, PAUL STANLEY, patent lawyer; b. Ft. Wayne, Ind., May 5, 1899; s. Frank Lord and Jane Carson (Crighton) S.; B.S., Worcester (Mass.) Poly. Inst., 1921; LL.B., Cleve. Law Sch., 1929. Mech. engr. Frank L. Sessions, cons. engr., Cleve., 1921-29; admitted to Ohio bar, 1929, since practiced in Cleve.; of counsel firm Bosworth, Sessions & McCoy, 1974-78; of counsel firm Pearne, Gordon, Sessions, McCoy & Granger, 1979—. Trustee Cleve. Zool. Soc.; mem. president's adv. council Worcester Poly. Inst. Registered profl. engr., Ohio. Served with U.S. Army, 1918; to comdr. USNR, 1942-46. Mem. Am., Cleve. bar assns., Am., Cleve. (v.p. 1941) patent law assns., Newcomen Soc., Phi Gamma Delta, Delta Theta Phi. Republican. Clubs: Cleve. Yachting; Clifton. Home: 12700 Lake Ave Lakewood OH 44107 Office: 1200 Leader Bank Bldg Cleveland OH 44114

SESSIONS, ROBERT EVANS, mgmt. counsel; b. Huntsville, Ala., June 1, 1909; s. Robert Ernest and Yula (Stricklen) S.; A.B., U. Ala., 1930; LL.B., Yale, 1933; m. Janice de la Croix, Dec. 26, 1931; 1 son, Robert Evans. Admitted to Tenn. bar; atty. A.A.A., 1933-34; atty. TVA, 1934-38, asst. to chmn., 1938-40, asst. gen. mgr., 1943-45; dep. dir. OPA, 1940-43; partner Alderson & Sessions, mgmt. cons., Phila., 1945-58; pres. Edward Dalton Co. div., exec. v.p., dir., mem. exec. com. Mead Johnson & Co., 1958-62, sr. exec. v.p., vice chmn. exec. com. of bd., 1962-64; pres. Robert E. Sessions, mgmt. counsel, 1964—; pres. Krain & Canton, Inc., 1965-68; chmn. bd. Esterbook Pen Co., 1967-68. Mem. Mayor's Pub. Bldg. Commn.; dir. Old Phila. Corp., inter-agy. com. for met. study. Decorated knight officer Order Merit (Italy). Mem. C. of C. Greater Phila. (pres.), Am. Mktg. Assn. (Nat. award for contbn. field of theory in marketing, chmn. nat. awards program), Delaware Valley Council (exec. com.), Am. Mgmt. Assn., Soc. for Advancement Mgmt., Assn. Cons. Mgmt. Engrs., Franklin Inst., Newcomen Soc. Democrat. Clubs: Merion Cricket, Midday (Phila.); Yale (N.Y.C.). Home: 500 Wayne Dr Apt 318 King of Prussia PA 19406

SESSIONS, ROGER HUNTINGTON, composer; b. Bklyn., Dec. 28, 1896; s. Archibald Lowery and Ruth Gregson (Huntington) S.; A.B., Harvard U., 1915, Mus.D., 1964; Mus.B., Yale U., 1917; Mus.D., Wesleyan U., 1958, Rutgers U., 1962, New Eng. Conservatory, 1966, Amherst Coll., 1969, Williams Coll., 1971, Princeton U., 1972, Cleve. Inst. Music, 1975, Boston U., 1977; LL.D., Brandeis U., 1965; A.F.D., U. Pa., 1966; D.F.A., U. Calif. at Berkeley, 1967, Northwestern U., 1971; D.A., Rider Coll., 1978; m. Barbara Foster, 1920; m. 2d, Elizabeth Franck, Nov. 26, 1936; children—John Porter, Elizabeth Phelps. Instr. music Smith Coll., 1919-21; tchr. theory Cleve. Inst. Music, 1921-25; resided in Florence, Rome, Berlin, 1925-33; instr. Boston U. Coll. Music, 1933-35; lectr. N.J. Coll. for Women, 1935-37; instr. Princeton U., 1935-37, asst. prof., 1937-40, asso. prof., 1940-45; prof. music U. Calif. at Berkeley, 1945; Fulbright scholar Academia Luigi Cherubini, Florence, Italy, 1951-52; William Shubael Conant prof. music Princeton, 1953-65; faculty Juilliard Sch. Music, N.Y.C., 1965—; Ernest Bloch prof. music U. Calif., Berkeley, 1966-67; Charles Eliot Norton prof. Harvard U., 1968-69. John Simon Guggenheim fellow, 1926-28; Walter Damrosch fellow Am. Acad. in Rome, 1928-31. Mem. Am. Acad. Arts and Scis., Internat. Soc. Contemporary Music (hon.), Am. Acad. Arts and Letters, League of Composers, Internat. Soc. for Contemporary Music (co-chmn. U.S. sect.), Broadcast Music, Nat. Inst. Arts and Letters. Composer: Symphony No. 1, 1927; Sonata for Piano 1930; Suite from The Black Maskers, 1923; Three Chorales for Organ, 1926; Concerto for Violin, 1935; String Quartet (Coolidge Festival 1937), 1936; Chorale for Organ, 1938; Duo for Violin and Piano, 1942; Turn O Libertad (mixed chorus and piano, 4 hands), 1944; Sonata No. 2 for piano, 1946; Symphony No. 2, 1946; String Quartet No. 2, 1950-51; (opera) The Trial of Lucullus, 1947; Sonata for Violin, unaccompanied, 1953; Idyll of Theocritus, for soprano and orch., 1954; Mass in celebration of the 50th Anniversary of Kent School, 1955; Concerto for Piano and Orchestra, 1956; Symphony No. 3, 1957, No. 4, 1958; String Quintet, 1958; Divertimento for Orchestra, 1959-60; (opera) Montezuma, 1959-63; Psalm 140 for soprano and orch., 1963; Symphony Number 5, 1964; Sonata No. 3, 1965; Symphony No. 6, 1966; Six Pieces for Violoncello Solo, 1966, Symphony No. 7, 1967, Symphony No. 8, 1968; cantata When Lilacs Last in the Dooryard Bloom'd, soloists, chorus and orch., 1967-70; Rhapsody for Orch., 1970; Double Concerto for Violin, Violincello and Orch., 1970-71; Concertino for Chamber Orch., 1972; 3 Choruses on Bibl. Text with Small Orch., 1972; Five Pieces for Piano, 1974; Symphony No. 9, 1978. Recipient Creative arts award Brandeis U., 1958; elected Ausserordentliches Mitglied, Akademie der Kunste, Berlin, 1960; Gold medal Nat. Inst. Arts and Letters, 1961; Academico Corr., Academia Nacional de Bellas Artes, Argentina, 1965; medal Edward MacDowell Assn., 1968; charter mem. Berkeley Fellows, 1968. Author: The Musical Experience of Composer, Performer and Listener, 1950; Harmonic Practice, 1950; Questions About Music, 1970; Roger Sessions on Music, 1979. Address: 63 Stanworth Ln Princeton NJ 08540

SESSIONS, WILLIAM CRIGHTON, lawyer; b. Columbus, Ohio, Sept. 22, 1904; s. Frank Lord and Jane (Crighton) S.; B.S., Mass. Inst. Tech., 1926; J.D., Western Res. U., 1930; m. Marian Eloise Hill, June 16, 1931; children—Elizabeth (Mrs. Thomas V.A. Kelsey), Margaret (Mrs. Frank K. Penirian). Admitted to Ohio bar, 1930, since practiced in Cleve.; mem. firm Bosworth, Sessions & McCoy, 1941-79, Pearne, Gordon, Sessions, McCoy and Granger, 1979—. Mem. corp. devel. com., alumni council, ednl. council Mass. Inst. Tech.; mem. fiscal adv. com. Cleve. YWCA. Trustee Cleve. Health Mus. Mem. Internat. Patent and Trademark Assn., Am. Judicature Soc., Am., Cleve. (pres. 1963-64) patent law assns., Am., Cleve. bar assns., SAR, Newcomen Soc., Cleve. Engring. Soc., Bluecoats, Phi Gamma Delta. Republican. Clubs: Union, Clifton, Westwood Country, Rowfant, Rockwell Springs Trout. Home: 15710 West Shore Ct Lakewood OH 44107 Office: 1200 Leader Bldg Cleveland OH 44114

SESSLER, ANDREW M., theoretical physicist; b. N.Y.C., Dec. 11, 1928; s. David and Mary (Baron) S.; B.A., Harvard U., 1949; M.S., Columbia U., 1951, Ph.D., 1953; m. Gladys Lerner, Sept. 23, 1951;

children—Daniel Ira, Jonathan Lawrence, Ruth, Lorna Pool. Asst. in physics Columbia U., 1949-52; NSF predoctoral fellow, 1952-53; NSF postdoctoral fellow Cornell U., 1953-54; asst. prof. Ohio State U., 1954-60, asso. prof., 1960-61; on leave to Midwestern Univs. Research Assn., 1956, to Lawrence Radiation Lab., 1959-60; vis. staff Niels Bohr Inst., Copenhagen, summer 1961; sr. staff physicist Lawrence Berkeley Lab. (Calif.), 1961—, dir., 1973—; chmn. sci. policy bd. Stanford Synchrotron Radiation Lab., 1976-78, chmn. advanced fuels adv. com. CRRI, 1978—; U.S. adviser U.S.-India Coop. Program Improvement Sci. Edn. in India, Chandigarh, summer 1966; visitor European Orgn. Nuclear Research, 1966-67; mem. high energy physics adv. panel AEC, 1969-72; corr. Comments on Modern Physics, part A, 1969-72; editorial bd. Nuclear Instruments and Methods, 1969—. Recipient E.O. Lawrence award AEC, 1970. Fellow Am. Phys. Soc.; mem. AAAS, Sigma Xi. Contbr. articles to sci. jours., conf. procs. Home: 3071 Buena Vista Way Berkeley CA 94708

SESSOMS, STUART MCGUIRE, physician, educator; b. Autryville, N.C., July 16, 1921; s. Edwin Tate and Lillian Olive (Howard) S.; B.S., U. N.C., 1943; M.D., Med. Coll. Va., 1946; postgrad. Johns Hopkins U.; m. Thelma Ernestine Call, June 21, 1944; children—Stuart McGuire, Cristi Kay. Intern, U.S. Marine Hosp., Balt., 1946-47, resident internal medicine, 1947-50, asst. chief med. service, charge med. outpatient dept., 1950-52; asst. resident medicine Meml. Center Cancer and Allied Diseases, N.Y.C., 1952-53; with NIH, Bethesda, Md., 1953-68, mem. clin. medicine, surgery Nat. Cancer Inst., 1953-54, acting chief gen. medicine, 1954, asst. dir., 1958, asso. dir. collaborative research, 1961-62, chief cancer chemotherapy Nat. Service Center, 1958-62, asst. dir. clin. center NIH, 1955-57, dep. dir., 1962-68; asst. dir., clin. instr. medicine George Washington U., 1953-54; asso. dean, prof. medicine Duke Sch. Medicine, Durham 1968-75, dir. Duke U. Hosp., 1968-75, prof. health adminstrn., 1973-75; sr. v.p. Blue Cross and Blue Shield of N.C., 1976—. Active PTA. Recipient Distinguished Service award U.S. Jr. C. of C., 1957. Diplomate Am. Bd. Internal Medicine. Mem. AMA, Assn. Mil. Surgeons U.S., Am. Hosp. Assn., Am., N.C. hosp. assns., Am. Pub. Health Assn., N.Y. Acad. Sci., Phi Delta Chi, Rho Chi, Alpha Kappa Kappa. Presbyterian. Contbr. articles to profl. jours. Home: 3432 Dover Rd Durham NC 27707 Office: Blue Cross and Blue Shield PO Box 2291 Durham NC 22702

SESTANOVICH, STEPHEN N., found. exec.; b. Yugoslavia, Dec. 6, 1912; (parents Am. citizens); s. Roy and Florence (Lipanovich) S.; A.B., St. Mary's (Calif.) Coll., 1935; postgrad. U. Calif. at Berkeley, 1935-37; m. Molly Brown, July 9, 1949; children—Stephen R., Mary E., Robert Benjamin. Reporter, editor for newspapers, mags., also cons., mng. dir. pub. relations firm, San Francisco, 1937-40; dir. Nat. Herald Pub. Corp., 1937-39; adviser U.S. Mil. Govt. Austria, Korea, 1946-49; joined U.S. Fgn. Service, 1949; consul pub. affairs, Palermo and Naples, Italy, 1949-54; pub. affairs counselor embassy, Bangkok, Thailand, 1955-56; chief tng. officer overseas employees, also Far East personnel dir. USIA, 1957-60; consul, Singapore, 1960-64; counselor public affairs embassy, Helsinki, Finland, 1964-65; reg. dir. USIS, consul U.S. embassy Caracus, Venezuela, 1966-68; pub. affairs counselor Dept. State, 1968-70; pres. With These Hands Found., Moraga, Calif., 1970—. Information, internat. communications cons. NATO-South, 1951-54; U.S. rep. informational cultural and labor commn. SEATO, 1955-56, U.S. rep. U.S. Ednl. Found., Thailand, 1955-56, Finland, 1964-66. Mem. bd. edn. Am. Sch. System, Singapore, 1962-64. Candidate for Congress, 7th dist. Cal., 1972. Served with AUS, 1942-46. Mem. Am. Acad. Polit. and Social Sci. Democrat. Unitarian. Clubs: Commonwealth of Calif., Press (San Francisco). Contbr. articles to profl. jours. Writer, lectr. U.S. polit., ednl. and hist. topics. Office: 15 Idlewood Ct Moraga CA 94556

SETCHKAREV, VSEVOLOD, educator; b. Kharkov, Russia, Apr. 8, 1914; s. Michael and Maria (Zschentzsch) S.; Dr. phil., U. Berlin (Germany), 1938; Dr. phil. habil., U. Bonn (Germany), 1948; A.M. (hon.), Harvard, 1957. Came to U.S., 1957. Dozent, prof. Slavic philology U. Bonn, 1947-53; prof. Slavic philology U. Hamburg (Germany), 1953-57; prof. Slavic langs., lit. Harvard, 1957-64, Curt Hugo Reisinger prof. Slavic langs., lit., 1964—. Home: 72 Scott Rd Belmont MA 02178 Office: Dept Slavic Langs and Lit Harvard U Cambridge MA 02138

SETE, BOLA (DJALMA DE ANDRADE), guitarist; b. Rio de Janeiro, Brazil, July 16, 1923; s. Acacio and Hilda (Santos) de Andrade; M.Mus., Rio de Janeiro Conservatory of Music, 1945; m. Glada Anne Hurd, Feb. 17, 1971. Formed own mus. group, 1950, toured S.Am., 1950-53, Europe, 1953-58, played in P.R., 1959; with Dizzy Gillespie band, 1962; formed new group, 1966; solo acoustical guitar concerts, 1971—; recs. Takoma Records. Named New Guitarist of Year, Down Beat mag., 1965; recipient European Film Festival award for best original music in a documentary film, 1967; Cindy award 1968. Address: 66 Buckelew St Marin City CA 94965

SETH, OLIVER, judge; b. Albuquerque, May 30, 1915; s. Julien Orem and Bernice (Grefe) S.; A.B., Stanford U., 1937; LL.B., Yale U., 1940; m. Jean MacGillivray, Sept. 25, 1946; children—Sandra Bernice, Laurel Jean. Admitted to N.Mex. bar, 1940; practice law, Santa Fe, 1940, 46-62; judge U.S. Ct. Appeals for 10th Circuit, 1962—, chief judge, 1976—; dir. Santa Fe Nat. Bank, 1949-62; chmn. legal com. N.Mex. Oil and Gas Assn., 1956-59, mem. regulatory practices com., 1960-62; counsel N.Mex. Cattlegrowers Assn., 1950-62, N.Mex. Bankers Assn., 1952-62; govt. appeal agent SSS, 1948-52. mem. bd. regents Mus. of N.Mex., 1956-60. Bd. dirs. Boys Club, Santa Fe, 1948-49; New Mex. Land Resources Assn., 1956-60, Ghost Ranch Mus., 1962—; mng. bd. Sch. Am. Research, 1950—. Served from pvt. to maj. AUS, 1940-45; ETO. Decorated Croix de Guerre (France.). Mem. Santa Fe C. of C. (dir.), N.Mex., Santa Fe County bar assns., Phi Beta Kappa. Presbyterian. Office: US Ct Appeals PO Drawer 1 Santa Fe NM 87501*

SETHNA, PATARASP RUSTOMJI, educator; b. Bombay, India, May 26, 1923; s. R.E. and Naja (Engineer) S.; B. Engring., U. Bombay, 1946; Ph.D., U. Mich., 1953; m. Shiley S. Smith, Sept. 4, 1954; children—James, Michael, Susan, John. Came to U.S., 1947, naturalized, 1965. Sr. engr. Bendix Corp., 1953-56; faculty U. Minn., Mpls., 1956—, prof. mechanics, 1963—, head dept., 1966—. Vis. prof. applied math. Brown Univ., 1965-66; sr. vis. scholar U. Calif. at Berkeley, 1970; vis. prof. U. Warwick (Eng.), 1972. Recipient Gold medal in applied mechanics Bombay U., 1946. Mem. ASME, Am. Inst. Aeros. and Astronautics, Soc. Natural Philosophy, AAUP, Soc. Indsl. and Applied Math. Home: 2147 W Hoyt St St Paul MN 55108 Office: Dept Aero and Engring Mechanics U Minn Minneapolis MN 55414

SETHNESS, CHARLES OLIN, investment banker; b. Evanston, Ill., Feb. 24, 1941; s. Charles Olin and Alison Louise (Burge) S.; A.B., Princeton, 1963; M.B.A. (Baker scholar), Harvard, 1966; 1 son, Peter Worcester; m. 2d, Geraldine Greene, June 25, 1977; stepchildren—John, Carla, Sarah Houseman. Sr. credit analyst Am. Nat. Bank & Trust Co., Chgo., 1963-64; research asst. Harvard Bus. Sch., 1966-67; asso. Morgan Stanley & Co., N.Y.C., 1967-71, v.p., 1972, mng. dir., 1975—; mgr. Morgan & Cie Internat. S.A., Paris, France, 1971-73; U.S. exec. dir. Internat. Bank for Reconstrn. and Devel., spl. asst. to sec. treasury, Washington, 1973-75. Trustee, treas. Latin Am. Scholarship Program of Am. Univs., Cambridge, Mass. Club: Rocky Point (Old Greenwich, Conn.). Home: 131 Shore Rd Old Greenwich CT 06870 Office: 1251 Ave of Americas New York NY 10020

SETLOW, JANE KELLOCK, biophysicist; b. N.Y.C., Dec. 17, 1919; d. Harold A. and Alberta (Thompson) Kellock; B.A., Swarthmore Coll., 1940; Ph.D. in Biophysics, Yale U., 1959; m. Richard Setlow, June 6, 1941; children—Peter, Michael, Katherine, Charles. With dept. radiology Yale U., 1959-60; with biology div. Oak Ridge Nat. Lab., 1960-74; biophysicist Brookhaven Nat. Lab., Upton, N.Y., 1974—; mem. recombinant DNA molecule program adv. com. NIH, chmn., 1978-80. Predoctoral fellow USPHS, 1957-59, postdoctoral fellow, 1960-62. Mem. Biophys. Soc. (pres. 1977-78), Am. Soc. Microbiology. Democrat. Author articles, mem. editorial bd. jours. Home: 57 Valentine Rd Shoreham NY 11786 Office: Biology Dept Brookhaven Nat Lab Upton NY 11973

SETLOW, RICHARD BURTON, biophysicist; b. N.Y.C., Jan. 19, 1921; s. Charles Meyer and Elsie (Hurwitz) S.; A.B., Swarthmore Coll., 1941; Ph.D., Yale U., 1947; m. Jane Kellock, June 6, 1942; children—Peter, Michael, Katherine, Charles. Asso. prof. Yale U., 1956-61; biophysicist Oak Ridge Nat. Lab., 1961-74, sci. dir. biophysics and cell physiology, 1969-74; dir. U. Tenn.-Oak Ridge Grad. Sch. Biomed. Scis., 1972-74; sr. biophysicist Brookhaven Nat. Lab., Upton, N.Y., 1974—, chmn. biology dept., 1979—; prof. biomed. scis. U. Tenn., 1967-74; adj. prof. biochemistry State U. N.Y., Stony Brook, 1975—. Mem. Nat. Acad. Scis., Am. Acad. Arts and Scis., Biophys. Soc. (pres. 1969-70), Comité Internat. de Photobiologie (pres. 1972-76), Radiation Research Soc., Am. Soc. Photobiology, Phi Beta Kappa. Author: (with E.C. Pollard) Molecular Biophysics, 1962; editor: (with P.C. Hanawalt) Molecular Mechanisms for Repair of DNA, 1975. Home: 57 Valentine Rd Shoreham NY 11786 Office: Biology Dept Brookhaven Nat Lab Upton NY 11973

SETO, YEB JO, elec. engr., educator; b. China, July 31, 1930; s. Jo Ting and Shee (Chang) S.; came to U.S., 1951, naturalized, 1962; B.S., U. Idaho, 1957; M.S., U. Wash., 1960; Ph.D., U. Tex., 1964; m. Jane Mei-Chun Wong, Feb. 14, 1958; children—Samuel K., Susanna L. Research engr. Boeing Airplane Co., Renton, Wash., 1957-60; instr. U. Houston, 1960-61, asst. prof., 1964-66; instr. U. Tex., Austin, 1961-63; prof. elec. engring. Tulane U., New Orleans, 1966—, dir. electrosci. and biophysics research group, 1969—; pres., dir. Applied Research Corp., New Orleans, 1967-71, Sealong, Inc., New Orleans, 1971—. Served with U.S. Army, 1953-55. NASA-Am. Soc. Engring. Edn. fellow, 1964, 65. Mem. IEEE, Profl. Group on Antenna Propagation (sect. chmn. 1967—), Sigma Xi, Tau Beta Pi, Eta Kappa Nu. Contbr. sci. articles to profl. jours. Home: 4824 Purdue Dr Metairie LA 70003 Office: Tulane U New Orleans LA 70118

SETON, ANYA, author; b. N.Y.C.; d. Ernest Thompson and Grace (Gallatin) Seton; ed. pvt. tutors in Eng., France, Spence Sch., N.Y.C. Author: My Theodosia, 1941; Dragonwyck, 1944; The Turquoise, 1946; The Hearth and Eagle, 1948; Foxfire, 1950; Katherine, 1954; The Mistletoe and Sword (juvenile), 1955; The Winthrop Woman, 1958; Washington Irving (juvenile), 1960; Devil Water, 1962; Avalon, 1965; Green Darkness, 1973; Smouldering Fires (juvenile), 1975; (all translated into many langs.); also short stories mags. Recipient Medal of Honor, Soc. Colonial Wars, 1958. Mem. League Am. Penwomen, Pen and Brush Club (hon.), P.E.N. Home: Old Greenwich CT 06870

SETON, CHARLES B., lawyer; b. Bridgeport, Conn., Oct. 1, 1910; s. Charles Hillison and Stella (Rosen) Shapiro; B.A., Yale U., 1931, LL.B., 1934; m. Suzanne Alexia Maimin, Mar. 7, 1948; children—Pam Elinor Seton Lorenzo, Charles B. Admitted to N.Y. bar, 1934; practiced in N.Y.C., 1934—; asso. firm Rosenman, Goldmark, Colin & Kaye, and predecessors, 1935-51; partner Rosen & Seton, 1955-58, 74-79, Rosen, Seton & Sarbin, 1958-74; sec. Ziff-Davis Pub. Co., 1974-77, gen. counsel, 1958-79; sec. Ziff Corp., 1976-78; guest lectr. Advanced Copyright Seminar, N.Y. U. Law Sch., 1953-77, Yale U. Law Sch., 1954, Practising Law Inst., 1955-73. Vice pres., founding dir. Music for Westchester, Inc., 1962-75, Arthur Judson Found., Inc., 1959—. Served to lt. comdr. USNR, 1942-45. Mem. Fed. Bar Council (chmn. bd. trustees 1952-77), Internat. Law Assn., Inter-Am., Am., N.Y.C., Westchester bar assns., Consular Law Soc., Copyright Soc. U.S. (founding trustee 1953-77). Clubs: Copyright Luncheon Circle (co-chmn. 1952—), Yale. Participating author: The Business and Law of Music, 1965; Internat. Music Industry Conference, 1969; contbr. articles to profl. jours. Home: 16 Ervilla Dr Larchmont NY 10538 Office: 1889 Palmer Ave Larchmont NY 10538

SETTERBERG, CARL, artist; b. Las Animas, Colo., Aug. 16, 1897; s. Herman and Emma (Davidson) S.; student Chgo. Acad. Fine Arts, 1917, Chgo. Art Inst., 1920-23, Grand Central Sch. Art, N.Y.C., 1939. Paintings exhibited N.A.D., Am. Watercolor Soc., Audubon Artists, Allied Artists Am., Hudson Valley Artists, Knickerbocker Artists, Salmagundi Club, Nat. Arts Club, Swedish-Am. Club Chgo., Soc. Illustrators, Soc. Painters in Casein, Laguna Beach (Cal.) Art Assn., Birmingham (Ala.) Mus., Tweed Gallery, Duluth, Minn., Norton Gallery, West Palm Beach, Fla., Columbus (Ga.) Mus., Royal Watercolor Soc., London, also numerous travelling shows in U.S.; works represented in permanent exhbns. including Air Force Acad., Colorado Springs, Columbus (Ga.) Mus., McChord AFB, Washington, DeBeers Collections, N.Y. Met. Mus., N.Y.C., also pvt. collections. Recipient Adolph and Clara Obrig-prize N.A.D., 1956, Ranger purchase prize, 1958; 1958; citation world-wide operational art program USAF, 1956; medal Am. Artist mag., 1961; prize and medal Swedish-Am. Art Exbhn., 1959; Emily G. Clindinst prize Salmagundi Club, 1951; Sterling Silver Medal award Nat. Arts Club, 1972. Served as capt. AUS, 1942-43, 58. Mem. Am. Watercolor Soc. (Lena Newcastle Meml. award 1958, William Church Osborne award 1969, U.S.A. Watercolor award 1967), Nat. Acad. Design, Hudson Valley Art Assn. (Caroline Arcier prize 1953, Jane Peterson award 1970), Audubon Artists, Allied Artists Am. (1st prize 1966, Annonymous award 1970), Soc. Illustrators (life), N.A.D., Soc. Painters in Casein, Knickerbocker Artists. *

SETTERFIELD, GEORGE AMBROSE, biologist, educator; b. Halifax, N.S., Can., Aug. 29, 1929; s. Ambrose Charles and Ethyl Violet (Tarbuck) S.; B.A. with honors, U. B.C., 1951; Ph.D. in Botany, U. Wis., 1954; m. Diana Evelyn, May 19, 1951; children—Thomas, David, Jennifer, Wayne, Christopher. Instr. biology U. B.C., Vancouver, 1954-56; asst. research officer NRC, Ottawa, Ont., Can., 1956-58, asso. research officer, 1958-62; asso. prof. Carleton U., Ottawa, 1962-64, prof., 1964—, chmn. dept. biology, 1963-68; vis. scientist Laval U., Quebec, 1968-69, NRC, Saskatoon, Sask., Can., 1977-78. NRC sr. research fellow, 1968, research grantee, 1962—. Fellow Royal Soc. Can.; mem. Can. Soc. Cell Biology, Can. Soc. Plant Physiology, Genetics Soc. Can., Soc. Devel. Biology. Contbr. articles on structure, function of cells to sci. jours. Home: Rural Route 3 North Gower ON K0A 2T0 Canada Office: Carleton U Dept Biology Ottawa ON K1S 5B6 Canada

SETTLE, MARY LEE, author; b. Charleston, W.Va., July 29, 1918; d. Joseph Edward and Rachel (Tompkins) S.; student Sweet Briar Coll., 1936-38; m. William Littleton Tazewell, Sept. 2, 1978; 1 son, Christopher Weathersbee. Asso. prof. Bard Coll., Annandale-on-Hudson, N.Y., 1965-76; vis. lectr. U. Va., 1978, U. Iowa, 1976. Served with Womens Aux., RAF, 1942-43. Recipient Merrill Found. award, 1974, Nat. Book award, 1978. John Simon Guggenheim fellow, 1958, 60. Democrat. Author: The Love Eaters, 1954; The Kiss of Kin, 1955; O Beulah Land, 1956; Know Nothing, 1960; Fight Night on a Sweet Saturday, 1964; All The Brave Promises, 1966; The Clam Shell, 1971; Prisons, 1973; Blood Tie, 1977. Office: c/o Roberta Pryor Internat Creative Mgmt 40 W 57th St New York NY 10019

SETTLEMYER, CLAUDE HAROLD, ret. textile exec.; b. Lancaster, S.C., Oct. 9, 1912; s. Arthur Frank, and Cornelia Ethel (Dabney) S.; student Wingate Jr. Coll., 1928-31; A.B., Duke, 1934; m. Helen M. Grady, June 27, 1942; children—William Boyd, Anita Lynn, Susan Elizabeth. With Cannon Mills Co., Kannapolis, N.C., 1934-37; with Cannon Mills, Inc., N.Y.C., 1937—, v.p., 1956-59, exec. v.p., 1961-73, sr. v.p., 1973-78, ret., 1978. Served from lt. (j.g.) to lt. comdr. USNR, 1942-45. Mem. Phi Delta Theta. Clubs: Sea Pines Golf; Canoe Brook Country (Summit, N.J.); Water Gap (Pa.) Country. Home: 32 Plantation Dr Sea Pines Hilton Head Island SC 29928

SETTON, KENNETH M., educator, historian; b. New Bedford, Mass., June 17, 1914; s. Ezra and Louise (Crossley) S.; A.B., Boston U., 1936, Litt.D. (hon.), 1957; postgrad. U. Chgo., 1936, Harvard, 1939-40; A.M., Columbia, 1938, Ph.D., 1941; Dr. Phil. h.c., U. Kiel (Germany), 1979; m. Josephine W. Swift, Sept. 11, 1941 (dec. Aug. 1967); 1 son, George Whitney Fletcher; m. 2d, Margaret T. Henry, Jan. 4, 1969. Instr. classics, history Boston U., 1940-43; asso. prof. European history U. Man. (Can.), 1943-45, prof., head dept. history, 1945-50; Henry C. Lea asso. prof. medieval history, curator Lea Library U. Pa., Phila., 1950-53, Lea prof. history, 1953-54, Lea prof. history, dir. libraries, 1955-65, Univ. prof. history, 1962-65; prof. history Columbia, 1954-55; William F. Vilas research prof. history, dir. Inst. for Research in Humanities, U. Wis., 1965-68; prof. history Inst. for Advanced Study, Princeton, N.J., 1968—. Vis. lectr. medieval history Bryn Mawr (Pa.) Coll., 1952-53; research fellow Gennadius Library, Am. Sch. Classical Studies, Athens, Greece, 1960-61; mem. exec. and mng. coms. Am. Sch. Classical Studies, Athens. Guggenheim Meml. fellow to Greece, Italy, 1949, 50. Decorated Gold Cross Order George I (Greece); recipient Premi Catalonia, Barcelona, 1976; Prix Gustave Schlumberger, Paris, 1976. Fellow Mediaeval Acad. Am. (pres. 1971-72), Soc. Macedonian Studies (hon.), Am. Acad. Arts and Scis.; mem. Am. Philos. Soc. (John Frederick Lewis prize 1957, v.p. 1966-69), Am. Hist. Assn., Inst. Catalan Studies (corr.), Phi Beta Kappa. Episcopalian. Author: Christian Attitude Towards the Emperor in the Fourth Century, 1941; Catalan Domination of Athens, 1311-1388, 1948, rev. edit., 1975; (with Henry R. Winkler) Great Problems in European Civilization, 1954, 2d edit., 1966; Europe and the Levant in the Middle Ages and the Renaissance, 1974; Athens in the Middle Ages, 1975; Los Catalanes en Grecia, 1975; The Papacy and the Levant, 1204-1571, vol. I, 1976, vol. II, 1978. Contbr. articles to jours. Editor-in-chief History of the Crusades, 5 vols. Office: Institute for Advanced Study Princeton NJ 08540

SETZER, GENE WILLIS, found. exec.; b. Wichita, Kans., Oct. 9, 1918; s. Charles William and Eda (Hutchinson) S.; B.A., Wichita State U., 1941; M.A., U. Wash., 1947; postgrad. Columbia, 1949; m. Kathleen Elizabeth Hitchner, June 27, 1943; children—Janet E., Charles H., Dell W. Fellow, asso. polit. sci. U. Wash., 1941-42, 46-47; instr. govt., deptl. rep. Columbia Sch. Gen. Studies, 1949-53; asso. Rockefeller Bros. Fund, 1953-79, v.p., 1969-73; cons. Rockefeller Family Fund, 1972—. Bd. dirs. Nat. Audubon Soc., 1959-74, chmn. exec. com., 1963-64, chmn. bd., 1964-74, v.p., 1974—; treas. Am. Conservation Assn., 1963-64, exec. v.p., 1964-78, v.p., 1978—, trustee, 1972—; exec. v.p. Jackson Hole Preserve, 1964-78, v.p., 1978—, trustee, 1967—; trustee Regional Plan Assn., 1975—. Asst. treas. Sleepy Hollow (N.Y.) Restorations, 1960—, sec., 1964—; mem. Planning Bd. Nyack, N.Y., 1960-65, 71-74; chmn. Zoning Bd. Appeals, 1974—; mem. Hosp. Corp., 1962—; vice chmn. Nyack Urban Renewal Agy., 1963-65. Served with USNR, 1942-45. Decorated Bronze Star medal. Baptist. Home: 76 6th Ave Nyack NY 10960 Office: 30 Rockefeller Plaza New York NY 10020 also 950 3d Ave New York NY 10022

SETZLER, WILLIAM EDWARD, chem. co. exec.; b. Bklyn., Dec. 20, 1926; s. William Edward and Gertrude A. (Seyer) S.; B.Chem. Engring., Cooper Union, 1950; m. Dorothy C. Kress, Dec. 2, 1950; children—William John, Heather A. Vice pres. ops. Argus Chem. Corp., N.Y.C., 1950-66; v.p. engring., then group v.p. Witco Chem. Corp., N.Y.C., 1966-75, exec. v.p., dir., 1975—. Served with USAAF, 1945-46. Mem. Am. Inst. Chem. Engrs. Author, patentee in field. Home: 3921 Lincoln St Seaford NY 11783 Office: 277 Park Ave New York City NY 10017

SEUSS, DR. see Geisel, Theodor Seuss

SEVAREID, ARNOLD ERIC, broadcaster, author; b. Velva, N.D., Nov. 26, 1912; s. Alfred and Clare (Hougen) S.; A.B., U. Minn., 1935; student Alliance Francaise, Paris, 1937; m. Lois Finger, May 18, 1935 (div. 1962); children—Michael and Peter (twins); m. Belen Marshall, 1963 (div. 1974); 1 dau., Cristina. Copy boy Mpls. jour., 1931, later reporter; reporter Mpls. Star, 1936-37; reporter, city editor, Paris edit. N.Y. Herald-Tribune. 1938-39; night editor United Press, Paris, 1939; became European corr. Columbia Broadcasting System, Aug. 1939; with French Army and Air Force in France and Belgium; broadcast French capitulation from Tours and Bordeaux; has also broadcast news from Asia, Africa, Eng., Holland, Belgium, Luxembourg, Mexico, Brazil; nat. corr. CBS, to 1977, cons., 1977—. Recipient George Foster Peabody award, 1949, 64, 68. Mem. Radio-TV Corrs. Assn. (past pres.), Sigma Delta Chi. Clubs: Metropolitan, Garrick, Overseas Writers. Author: Canoeing with the Cree (children's book), 1935; Not So Wild a Dream, 1946, repub., 1976; In One Ear, 1952; Small Sounds in the Night, 1956; This Is Eric Sevareid, 1964. Editor: Candidates, 1960. Contbr. articles to mags. Address: 2020 M St NW Washington DC 20036

SEVCENKO, IHOR, educator; b. Radosc, Poland, Feb. 10, 1922; s. Ivan and Maria (Cherniatynska) S.; Dr.Phil., Charles U., Prague, Czechoslovakia, 1945; Doct. en Phil. et Lettres, U. Louvain (Belgium), 1949; m. Margaret M. Bentley, July 16, 1953 (div. 1966); m. 2d, Nancy Patterson, June 18, 1966; children—Catherine, Elisabeth. Came to U.S., 1949, naturalized, 1957. Fellow in Byzantinology, Dumbarton Oaks, 1949-50, dir. studies, 1966, prof. Byzantine history and lit., 1965—; lectr. Byzantine and ancient history U. Calif. at Berkeley, 1950-51; fellow Byzantinology and Slavic lit., research program USSR, 1951-52; instr., then asst. prof. Slavic langs. and lit. U. Mich., 1953-57; faculty Columbia, 1957-72, prof., 1962-65, adj. prof., 1965-72; vis. prof. U. Munich, 1969, Harvard, 1973-74, prof., 1974—; vis. fellow All Souls Coll., Oxford U., 1979-80. Vis. mem. Princeton Inst. for Advanced Study, 1956. Guggenheim fellow, 1963. Treas., acting treas., bd. dirs. Am. Research

Inst. in Turkey, 1964-66, 67, 75—; asso. dir. Harvard Ukrainian Research Inst., 1973—, acting dir., 1977; chmn. Nat. Com. Byzantine Studies, 1966-77. Fellow Mediaeval Acad. Am.; mem. Am. Philos. Soc., Am., Ukrainian acads. arts and scis., Am. Hist. Assn., Société des Bollandistes Belgium (adj. mem.), Accademia di Palermo (fgn. mem.), Internat. Assn. Byzantine Studies (v.p. 1976—), Austrian Acad. Sci. (corr.). Clubs: Cosmos (Washington); Harvard (N.Y.C.). Author: Etudes sur la polémique entre Théodore Métochite et Nicéphore Choumnos, 1962; co-author: Der Serbische Psalter, 1978. Contbr. articles to profl. jours. Home: 6 Follen St Cambridge MA 02138 Office: 319 Boylston Hall Harvard Univ Cambridge MA 02138

SEVCIK, JOHN GEORGE, business exec.; b. Chgo., May 15, 1909; s. Joseph and Rose (Kostal) S.; J.D., DePaul U., 1939, LL.D., 1958; B.S.C., Central YMCA Coll., 1945; M.B.A., U. Chgo., 1947; M.P.L., John Marshall Law Sch., 1950, LL.M., 1954; LL.D., St. Mary's Coll., Ill. Benedictine Coll., 1960; m. Rose Vanek, Mar. 27, 1934; children—Joanne, John Wayne. Asso., Burton Dixie Co., 1925—, dir., 1942—, pres., 1949-72, vice chmn. bd., 1972—; admitted to Ill. bar, 1940, since practiced law; chmn. bd. Financial Marketing Services Inc., 1971—; gen. mgr. McCormick Pl., Chgo., 1971—; dir. Central Nat. Bank Chgo., Brunswick Corp., Bus. Capitol Corp. Mem. bd. govs. Chgo. Furniture Mart; dir. Nat. Cotton Batting Inst.; mem. editorial bd. Bedding mag. Commr., Pub. Bldgs. Commn. Chgo.; chmn. adv. bd. Chgo. Youth Commn.; mem. adv. com. Chief Justice Municipal Ct. Chgo.; active work Boy Scouts; gen. finance chmn. Chgo. Cerebral Palsy Assn., 1956; mem. exec. bd. Nat. Conf. Christians and Jews; mem. Bd. Edn. Berwyn, Ill. Vice chmn. bd. trustees St. Procopius Coll.; mem., chmn. lay bd. trustees, mem. legal bd. trustees DePaul U.; mem. lay bd. trustees Rosary Coll., chmn. bd., 1966-70; asso. mem. lay bd. St. Xavier Coll., mem. adv. council Sch. of Bus.; citizens bd. U. Chgo.; adv. bd. St. Mary's Coll.; bd. dirs. MacNeal Meml. Hosp.; vice chmn. bd. Ill. Coll. Podiatric Medicine, 1968—; trustee John Marshall Law Sch. Chgo. Mem. Am. Judicature Soc., Am., Ill. bar assns., Nat. Assn. Bedding Mfrs. (pres. 1959-60), Ill. Mfrs. Assn., Furniture Club Am., AAUP, Internat. Assn. Auditorium Mgrs., DePaul U., John Marshall (pres. 1968-71) alumni assns. Phi Alpha Delta, Beta Gamma Sigma. Clubs: Executives, Economic, Union League. Address: McCormick Place Chicago IL 60616

SEVEL, BERNARD JEROME, lawyer; b. Balt., May 1, 1924; s. Edward A. and Reba (Stein) S. B.Engring., Johns Hopkins, 1949; LL.B., Mt. Vernon Sch. Law, Balt., 1957; J.D., U. Balt., 1970; m. Deane L. Siskind, Mar. 29, 1959; children—Adam J., Jonathan B. Aircraft engine design engr. Curtis Wright Co., Lodi, N.J., 1952-54; head specification dept. contracts div. Martin Co., Middle River, Md., 1954-61; admitted to Md. bar, 1958; practiced in Balt., 1961—; part-time tchr. sci., bus. law, math. Eastern Coll., Balt., 1958-64; atty. N.W. Balt. Corp., 1968—, Internat. Longshoremen's Assn. Served to 1st lt. inf. AUS, World War II; with C.E., Korea. Decorated Bronze Star, Combat Inf. badge. Mem. Am., Md., Balt. bar assns., Maritime Law Assn., Am., Md. trial lawyers assns. Jewish (chmn. legal com. congregation, also trustee). Club: Chestnut Ridge Country (dir., legal officer). Co-author material on workmen's compensation Md. Inst. Continuing Profl. Edn. of Lawyers. Home: 3305 Janellen Dr Baltimore MD 21208 Office: Suite 1410 Arlington Fed Bldg Baltimore MD 21201

SEVERA, GORDON, utility exec.; b. Clarkson, Nebr., Feb. 15, 1930; s. Rudolph G. and Olga (Indra) S.; B.S. in Bus. Adminstrn. cum laude, U. Nebr., Omaha, 1951; m. Dorothy Jacqueline Smith, Feb. 23, 1952; children—Susan, Dan, Siri Lyn and Sara Jane (twins). With No. Natural Gas Co., Omaha, 1951—, pres. Nat. Gas Group, 1977—; pres., chmn. bd. No. Border Pipeline Co. Trustee U. Nebr., Omaha, 1974—, pres., 1977. Mem. Am. (dir.), So., Midwest gas assns., Inst. Gas Tech. (dir.), Gas Research Inst. (dir.). Home: 9133 Shirley St Omaha NE 68124 Office: 2223 Dodge St Omaha NE 68102

SEVERINGHAUS, JOHN WALTER, ret. architect; b. Seymour, Ind., Dec. 20, 1905; s. Charles Edwin and Ida (Mock) S.; A.B., Ohio Wesleyan U., 1928; B.Arch., Ohio State U., 1931, L.H.D., 1970; m. Helen Merrill Clark, July 24, 1943; children—John Merrill, Nancy Clark. Archtl. designer Adams & Prentice, 1934-37; project mgr. Skidmore, Owings & Merrill, N.Y.C., 1937-42, asso. partner, 1946, gen. partner, 1949-75, former partner in charge Chase Manhattan Bank, Hdqrs., N.Y.C., now ret.; projects include Ford Central Staff Office Bldg., Deaborn, Mich., First City Nat. Bank Bldg., Houston, U.S. Air Bases, Morocco, N.Y.C. Conv. and Exbn. Center, Texaco Offices, Harrison, N.Y. Mem. Scarsdale (N.Y.) Bd. Edn., 1964-70; bd. dirs. N.Y. Bldg. Congress, 1962-64; mem. adv. bd. China Inst. Am., N.Y.C., 1975—; trustee YWCA, White Plains, N.Y. Served to maj. USAAF, 1942-46. Fellow AIA; mem. Am. Bible Soc. (vice chmn. exec. com.), Phi Beta Kappa Assos., Phi Beta Kappa, Tau Beta Pi, Tau Sigma Delta, Alpha Sigma Phi. Methodist. Clubs: Univ. (pres. 1975-78) (N.Y.C.); Scarsdale (N.Y.) Golf. Home: 38 Lockwood Rd Scarsdale NY 10583 Office: 400 Park Ave New York City NY 10022

SEVERINO, ALEXANDRINO EUSEBIO, educator; b. Olhao, Portugal, July 17, 1931; s. Eusebio Joaquim and Maria Alexandrina (Rato) S.; came to U.S., 1946, naturalized, 1946; B.A., U. R.I., 1958; Ph.D., U. Sao Paulo (Brazil), 1966; m. Dorothea Regel Bresslau, Jan. 7, 1961; children—Alexander, Cornelia, Roger, Katherine. Prof., Faculdade de Marilia (Brazil), 1960-66; asso. prof. U. Tex., Austin, 1966-69; prof. Spanish and Portuguese, chmn. dept. Spanish and Portuguese, Vanderbilt U., Nashville, 1969—. Served with U.S. Army, 1952-54. Mem. Modern Lang. Assn., Am. Assn. Tchrs. Spanish and Portuguese. Author: Fernando Pessoa na Africa do Sul, vol. 1, 1969, vol. 2, 1970; editor: (with Enrique Pupo-Walker) Studies in Short Fiction: Contemporary Latin America, 1971. Home: 6708 Rodney Ct Nashville TN 32705 Office: PO Box 1640 St B Vanderbilt U Nashville TN 37235

SEVERINO, DOMINICK ALEXANDER, educator; b. Boston, Sept. 14, 1914; s. Nicholas and Amalia (Giordano) S.; B.S., Mass. Sch. Art, 1937; Ed.M., Boston U., 1939; Ed.D. (Carnegie fellow A.I.A.), Harvard, 1943; m. Fehrn E. Dirkman, Aug. 20, 1940; children—Douglas Alexander, Donald Arthur. Art instr. R.I. Coll. Edn., 1939-43; asst. dean R.I. Sch. Design, Providence, 1947-48; chmn. art dept. Bradford Durfee Tech. Inst., 1948-52; prof. art U. Wis., 1952-55; dir. Ohio State U. Sch. Fine and Applied Arts, Columbus, 1955-57, asso. dean for acad. affairs Coll. Edn., 1957-75, prof. higher edn., 1975—, campus coordinator India Edn. Project, 1957-69; cons. continuing med. edn. Vis. summer prof. Harvard, 1942, U. Minn., 1948. Mem. Nat. Com. Art Edn.; mem. Franklin County Com. on Drug Edn., Columbus; mem. commn. on role professions in soc. Acad. for Contemporary Problems, Columbus. Served with USNR, 1943-46; PTO. Mem. Coll. Art Assn. Am., Nat. Art Edn. Assn., Am. Fedn. Art, Am. Assn. Sch. Adminstrs., N.E.A., Phi Delta Kappa. Presbyn. Contbr. articles on esthetic, environmental issues to profl. jours. Home: 6215 Olentangy River Rd Worthington OH 43085 Office: Coll Edn State U Columbus OH 43210

SEVERINSEN, CARL H. (DOC), condr., musician; b. Arlington, Oreg., July 7, 1927; children—Nancy, Judy, Cindy, Robin, Allen. Mem. Ted Fio Rito Band, 1945, Charlie Barnet Band, 1947-49; then with Tommy Dorsey, Benny Goodman, Norro Morales, Vaughn Monroe; soloist network band Steven Allen Show NBC-TV, 1954-55; mem. NBC Orch. Tonight Show, 1962—. music dir., 1967—; past host of NBC-TV show The Midnight Special; recs. RCA Records, including album Brass Roots, 1971. Address: care NBC Press Dept 30 Rockefeller Plaza New York NY 10020*

SEVERO, RICHARD, reporter; b. Newburgh, N.Y., Nov. 22, 1932; s. Thomas and Mary Theresa (Farina) S.; B.A., Colgate U., 1954; postgrad. N.Y. U. Inst. Fine Arts, 1955-56, Columbia U. Sch. Architecture and Urban Planning, 1964-65; m. Emöke Edith de Papp, Apr. 7, 1961. News asst. CBS, N.Y.C., 1954-55; reporter Poughkeepsie (N.Y.) New Yorker, 1956-57, A.P., Newark, 1957-61, N.Y. Herald Tribune, 1961-63; writer TV news CBS, N.Y.C., 1963-66; reporter Washington Post, 1966-68; investigative reporter N.Y. Times, N.Y.C., 1968-71, fgn. corr., Mex., C. Am. and Caribbean, 1971-73, investigative and environ. reporter, 1973—; asso. Seminar on the City, Columbia U., 1966-69; Poynter fellow-in-residence Vassar Coll., 1974 75. CBS News fellow, 1964-65. Recipient Front Page award Washington-Balt. Newspaper Guild, 1967; Journalistic award H.A.V.E.N., 1969; Schaeffer Gold Typewriter award N.Y. Newspaper Reporters Assn., 1969; Page One award Newspaper Guild of N.Y., 1970; hon. mention Mike Berger award Columbia U., 1970; George Polk Meml. award L.I. U. Sch. Journalism, 1975; Hudson River Fisherman's Assn. award, 1976; Mike Berger award Columbia U., 1976; James Wright Brown award Deadline Club, Sigma Delta Chi, N.Y.C., 1976; Feature award N.Y. Press Club, 1977; Page One award Newspaper Guild N.Y., 1977; Media award Am. Cancer Soc., 1977; hon. mention Heywood Broun Meml. award Am. Newspaper Guild, 1977; Penney-Mo. Newspaper award U. Mo. Sch. Journalism, 1978. Contbr. articles to mags. Office: New York Times 229 W 43d St New York NY 10036

SEVIK, MAURICE, researcher; b. Istanbul, Turkey, Mar. 19, 1923; s. Benjamin and Esther (Barzilai) S.; D.I.C., Imperial Coll. Sci. and Tech., London, 1946; Ph.D., Pa. State U., 1963; m. Jacqueline Delannoy, June 2, 1953; children—Michele, Martine. Came to U.S., 1959, naturalized, 1965. With Bristol Aircraft Corp. (U.K.), 1946-51; sr. structures engr. Avro Aircraft, Ltd. (Can.), 1952-59; prof. aerospace engring., dir. Garfield Thomas Water Tunnel, Pa. State U., University Park, 1959-72, also mem. Senate; asso. tech. dir. for ship acoustics Naval Ship Research and Devel. Center, Bethesda, Md., 1972—. Vis. prof. Cambridge (Eng.) U., 1970; cons. USAF Office Sci. Research, 1965—. Fellow Churchill Coll., Cambridge U., 1970. Registered profl. engr., Ont. Fellow Acoustical Soc. Am.; mem. ASME, Sigma Xi. Contbr. articles to profl. jours. Home: 7817 Horseshoe Ln Potomac MD 20854 Office: Naval Ship Research and Devel Center Bethesda MD 20034

SEVILLA, STANLEY, lawyer; b. Cin., Apr. 3, 1920; s. Isadore and Dienna (Levy) S.; B.A. in Econs. with high honors, U. Cin., 1942; J.D., Harvard, 1948; m. Lois A. Howell, July 25, 1948; children—Stanley, Susan, Donald, Carol, Elizabeth. Admitted to Calif. bar, 1949, since practiced in Los Angeles; asso. firm Williamson, Hoge & Curry, 1948-50; mem. firm Axelrod, Sevilla and Ross, 1950-75, Stanley Sevilla, P.C., 1975—. Served with USAAF, 1942-46. Mem. Los Angeles County Bar Assn., Phi Beta Kappa, Tau Kappa Alpha. Home: 16606 Merivale Ln Pacific Palisades CA 90272 Office: 10203 Santa Monica Blvd Los Angeles CA 90067

SEVY, ROGER WARREN, educator; b. Richfield, Utah, Nov. 6, 1923; s. Carl Spencer and Maude (Malmquist) S.; student Utah State U., 1941-43, Harvard, 1943-45; M.S., U. Vt., 1948; Ph.D., U. Ill., 1951, M.D., 1954; m. Barbara Florence Snetsinger, Aug. 16, 1948; children—Pamela Jane, Jonathan Carl. Asst. physiology U. Ill., 1948-51, instr., 1951-54; asst. prof. pharmacology Temple U., 1954-56, prof., 1956—, chmn. dept., 1957-73, dean Sch. Medicine, 1973-79. Adj. prof. biomed. engring. Drexel U.; v.p. sci. and edn. Univ. Creations, Inc. Served with AUS, 1943-45. Mem. Am. Soc. Pharmacology and Exptl. Therapeutics, Am. Physiol. Soc., Endocrine Soc., Mensa, AAAS, Sigma Xi. Alpha Omega Alpha. Research on hypertension and cardiovascular pharmacology. Home: 242 Mather Rd Jenkintown PA 19046 Office: 3420 N Broad St Philadelphia PA 19140

SEWARD, DORIS MARIE, univ. adminstr.; b. Bloomington, Ind., Mar. 26, 1917; d. Fred Allen and Dorothy Florence (Hopper) Seward; A.B., Ind. U., 1938; M.A., Syracuse U., 1943; Ph.D., 1953. Mem. staff Office Dean Women, Syracuse U., 1943-45; co-dir. Student Christian Movement N.Y.State, 1945-47; asso. dir. student activities U. Minn., 1947-49; asst. dean women Purdue U., 1952-57, acting dean women, asso. prof., 1955-56; lectr. Housemother's Tng. Sch., Purdue U. and U. Ky., 1949-62; dean women, prof. edn. U. Ky., 1957-67, dean of student affairs planning, 1967-70; exec. asst. to pres. Pa. State U., 1970—, prof. Coll. Human Devel., 1970—; mem. Am. delegation World Confedn. Orgns. Teaching Profession, Stockholm, 1962, Rio de Janeiro, 1963, Paris, 1964, Addis Ababa, 1965, Seoul, 1966; made comparative ednl. survey in Russia, 1967, 69, China, 1974. Recipient Distinguished Alumni Service award Ind. U., 1976. Mem. Nat. Assn. Women Deans and Counselors (chmn. univ. sect. 1958-60, treas. 1960-62), NEA, AAUW (corp. del. Pa. State U.), Am. Personnel and Guidance Assn., Am., So. coll. personnel assns., Phi Beta Kappa, Mortar Board, Kappa Kappa Gamma, Pi Lambda Theta, Psi Chi, Alpha Lambda Delta. Mem. Christian Ch. Home: 341 E Foster Ave State College PA 16801

SEWARD, GEORGE CHESTER, lawyer; b. Omaha, Aug. 4, 1910; s. George Francis and Ada Leona (Rugh) S.; B.A., U. Va., 1933, LL.B., 1936; m. Carroll Frances McKay, Dec. 12, 1936; children—Gordon Day, Patricia McKay (Mrs. Dryden G. Liddle), James Pickett, Deborah Carroll. Admitted to Va. bar, 1935, also N.Y., Ky., D.C., U.S. Supreme Ct. bars; with Shearman & Sterling, N.Y.C., 1936-53, Seward & Kissel, N.Y.C., 1953—. Trustee Benson Iron Ore Trust, Edwin Gould Found. for Children. Fellow Am. Bar Found. (chmn. model corp. acts com. 1956-65); mem. Internat. (founder, chmn. bus. law sect. 1969-74, now hon. life pres.), Am. (chmn. sect. corp. banking bus. law 1958-59, chmn. sect. com. corp. laws 1952-58, chmn. sect. banking com. 1960-61, mem. ho. of dels. 1959-60, 63-74) bar assns., Am. Law Inst. (mem. joint com. with Am. Bar Assn. on continuing legal edn. 1965-74), Cum Laude Soc., Raven Soc., Order of Coif, Phi Beta Kappa Assos. (pres. 1969-75), Phi Beta Kappa, Theta Chi, Delta Sigma Rho. Clubs: Downtown Assn., Knickerbocker, N.Y. Yacht (N.Y.C.); University (Chgo.); Metropolitan (Washington); Commerce (Atlanta); Scarsdale (N.Y.) Golf; Shelter Island Yacht (N.Y.). Author: Basic Corporate Practice; co-author: Model Business Corporation Act Annotated. Home: 48 Greenacres Ave Scarsdale NY 10583 also Ram Head Shelter Island NY 11964 Office: 63 Wall St New York NY 10005

SEWARD, HAROLD ALOYSIUS, safety engr., author; b. N.Y.C., July 29, 1905; s. Thomas Joseph and Anna (Gould) S.; B.A., Lehigh U., 1930; postgrad. Columbia U., 1938, Yale U., 1955, N.Y. U., 1956, 60; m. Kathryn Constance Spiegel, June 12, 1930 (dec. Jan. 6, 1976); children—Thomas Joseph, Anna Kathryn Seward Lambert; m. 2d, Jean Commerford Ward, June 14, 1976 (dec. Jan. 1979). Sales engr. Fed. Armored Cable Co., N.Y.C., 1930-36; sales mgr. R. A. Stewart & Co., N.Y.C., 1936-40; individual cons. in safety engring., N.Y.C. 1940-50; safety coordinator Bethlehem Steel Co. (Pa.), 1950-53; mgr., sec.-treas. Lehigh Valley Safety Council. Bethlehem, 1953-74; dir. research Internat. Safety Inst., Bethlehem, 1960-69, pres., 1969-74; owner, editor Ace Pub. Co., Caldwell, N.J.; editor, pub. bi-monthly newsletter Safety News Coordinator; coordinator Ann. Lehigh Valley Safety Conf., 1953-74; lectr. on safety Lehigh U., Bethlehem, 1954—, Rutgers U. Extension Service, 1955—, Pa. State U., University Park, 1954—; condr. seminars in creative writing, pub. speaking, sales psychology, 1940—; adviser to ins. co. groups on safety, 1940—; mem. adv. council Pres.'s Com. for Traffic Safety, 1956-61. Chmn. bd. McGarvey Found., 1953-58. Recipient Gold medal for superiority in math. and sci. Rensselaer Poly. Inst., 1925; Williams prize for pub. speaking Lehigh U., 1927; Holman trophy for athletic work with boys, 1941; Eastman medal for Boy Scout work, 1943; $500 award for manuscript Pa. Freedom League, 1953; Richardson Smith award for traffic safety, 1960. Mem. Assn. Safety Council Execs. (pres. 1956-61), Nat. Safety Council, Vets. of Safety, Am. Soc. Safety Engrs. (dir.), Pa. Fedn. Safety Councils (pres. 1973-74), Pa. Indsl. Safety Conf., Pa. Rural Safety Council, Lehigh U. Alumni Club (pres. 1951-53). Club: Lehigh Valley Pub. Relations (pres. 1972-73). Contbr. articles on safety to newspapers, tech. mags. Home: 612 Shady Retreat Rd Doylestown PA 18901 Office: PO Box 942 Buckingham PA 18912

SEWARD, HARRY PAUL, ins. co. exec.; b. Hardin, Mo., Aug. 30, 1917; s. Harry Paul and Sophia Park (Born) S.; B.S. in Bus. and Pub. Adminstrn., U. Mo., 1939; m. Frances Ann Robnett, Sept. 27, 1941; children—Anne Cordell Seward Crosby, Harry Paul, III. With Ralston-Purina Co., St. Louis, summer 1936, Mchts. Exchange, St. Louis, summer 1937, Frat. Mgmt., Inc., Lincoln, Nebr., 1939-40; chmn., chief exec. officer Bankers Life Ins. Co. of Nebr., Lincoln, 1940—; chmn. bd. Gateway Shopping Center, Inc.; dir., mem. exec. com. Island Gem Enterprises, Ltd., St. Maarten, Netherland Antilles. Past pres. United Way, 1964, Bryan Meml. Hosp., 1966-69, Lincoln Found., 1972-74. Served to maj., F.A., AUS, 1941-46. Decorated Bronze Star. C.L.U. Fellow Life Mgmt. Inst.; mem. Life Office Mgmt. Assn. (past chmn.), Am. Council Life Ins., Am. Coll. Life Underwriters, Pres.'s Profl. Assn., Life Ins. Mktg. Research Assn., Nebr. Assn. Commerce and Industry (pres. 1973), Lincoln C. of C. (pres. 1971). Republican. Presbyterian. Clubs: Masons (Shriner, Jester), Country of Lincoln, Lincoln University, Nebraska. Home: 3435 S 30th St Lincoln NE 68502 Office: PO Box 81889 Lincoln NE 68501

SEWARD, RALPH THEODORE, lawyer, labor arbitrator; b. N.Y.C., Mar. 16, 1907; s. John Perry and Edith (Hibbard) S.; A.B., Cornell U., 1927; M.A., N.Y. U., 1931; LL.B., Columbia U., 1935; m. Norma North, Mar. 5, 1939 (div.); children—Timothy North, Paul North; m. 2d, Clayton Cranwell, Dec. 26, 1954. Admitted to N.Y. bar, 1936; asso. Simpson, Thacher & Bartlett, 1935-36; atty. NLRB, 1936-37; exec. sec. N.Y. State Labor Relations Bd., 1937-39, gen. counsel, 1939; chmn. Bd. Immigration Appeals, U.S. Dept. Justice, 1939-41; exec. sec. Nat. Def. Mediation Bd., 1941-42; asso. pub. mem. W.L.B., 1942; impartial chmn. Met. N.Y. Milk Industry, 1942-44; impartial umpire UAW and Gen. Motors Corp., 1944-47; chmn. bd. conciliation and arbitration U.S. Steel Corp. and United Steelworkers Am., CIO, 1947-49; impartial umpire Internat. Harvester Co. and United Farm Equipment and Metal Workers Council, 1949-51; impartial umpire Bethlehem Steel Corp. and United Steelworkers Am., 1952-71, impartial chmn., 1972—; mem. Presdl. Bd. on Labor Disputes in Aerospace Industry, 1962; chmn. Arbitration Bd. 282, Nat. Mediation Bd., 1963-65; mem. aerospace spl. panel Cost of Living Council, 1973-74; mem. arbitration services adv. com. Fed. Mediation and Conciliation Service, 1974—; chmn. permanent arbitration tribunal Govt. of Bermuda, 1975—; mem. fgn. service grievance bd. Dept. State, 1976—. Mem. Nat. Acad. Arbitrators (pres. 1947-49), Indsl. Relations Research Assn. (exec. bd. 1968—), Am. Arbitration Assn. (mediation adv. com. 1974—). Author: (with L. M. Hacker, B.M. Selekman, W.J. Dickson and T.V. Smith) The New Industrial Relations, 1948. Home: 3103 P St NW Washington DC 20007 Office: 1054 31st St NW Washington DC 20007

SEWARD, RICHARD BEVIN, lawyer; b. Bartlesville, Okla., May 27, 1932; s. Fredrick W. and Kittie Lea (Hudson) S.; B.S., Okla. State U., 1954; postgrad. Tulsa U., 1959-62; J.D., So. Methodist U., 1971; m. Loydell E. Nash, Aug. 1, 1954; children—Ann M., Elizabeth, Amy M. Personnel mgr. Unit Rig and Equipment Co., Tulsa, 1958-62, Gifford-Hill Cos., Dallas, 1962-66; labor cons., Dallas, 1966-68; admitted to Tex. bar, 1968; partner firm Stanfield, Crooks & Seward, Dallas, 1974-78, Seward, Heitman, 1978—. Served with AUS, 1955-57. Mem. Order of Coif. Home: 738 Newberry Richardson TX 75080 Office: 510 Katy Bldg 701 Commerce Dallas TX 75202

SEWARD, WILLIAM WARD, JR., educator, author; b. Surry, Va., Feb. 2, 1913; s. William Ward and Elizabeth (Gwaltney) S.; A.B., U. Richmond, 1934, M.A., 1935; grad. fellow Duke U., 1938-39, 40-41; m. Virginia Leigh Widgeon, Dec. 27, 1941; children—Virginia R., Leigh W. English tchr. pub. schs., 1935-38; instr. U. Richmond, 1939-40, summer 1944; head English dept. Greenbrier Mil. Sch., 1941-42; prof., head English dept. Tift Coll., 1942-45; faculty Old Dominion U., Norfolk, Va., 1945, 47—, prof., 1957—, head dept. English, 1947-61. Lectr., U. Va. extension div., 1952-54. Recipient Charles T. Norman medal for best grad. in English, U. Richmond, 1934. Mem. Am. Assn. U. Profs., Modern Lang. Assn., Nat. Council Tchrs. English, Poetry Soc. Va. (pres. 1952-55), Poetry Soc. Am., Mystery Writers Am., Internat. Mark Twain Soc. (hon.), Phi Beta Kappa, Kappa Alpha, Pi Delta Epsilon. Methodist. Clubs: Norfolk Yacht and Country; Princess Anne Country (Virginia Beach). Author: The Quarrels of Alexander Pope, 1935. Editor: The Longer Thou Livest the More Fool Thou Art (W. Wager), 1939; Literature and War, 1943; Skirts of The Dead Night, 1950; Foreword to Descent of the White Bird (Barbara Whitney), 1955; Contrasts in Modern Writers, 1963; My Friend Ernest Hemingway, 1969. Editorial bd. Lyric Virginia Today, 1956. Contbr. articles to profl. jours. Home: 1421 Daniel Ave Lochhaven Norfolk VA 23505

SEWELL, BEN GARDNER, lawyer; b. Palestine, Tex., Mar. 23, 1911; s. Roy C. and Carrie (Gardner) S.; B.A., Rice U., 1933; LL.B., U. Tex., 1936; m. Elizabeth Hall, Nov. 14, 1947. Admitted to Tex. bar, 1936; partner firm Sewell & Riggs, Houston; dir. Capital Nat. Bank, Houston; dir., mem. exec. com. Southland Financial Corp., Dallas; dir. Richmond Tank Car Co. Served to lt. comdr. USNR, 1942-46. Fellow Am. Coll. Trial Lawyers; mem. Am. Law Inst., Phi Beta Kappa, Order of Coif, Phi Delta Phi. Home: 81 Saddlebrook Houston TX 77024 Office: Capital Nat Bank Bldg Houston TX 77002

SEWELL, DANIEL KEITH, metal co. exec.; b. Harrisburg, Ill., Jan. 3, 1922; s. Daniel Lee and Clara Anna (Cox) S.; B.M.E., N.D. State U., 1949; postgrad. U. Minn., 1951-53; m. Doris Clara Wrobbel, May 7, 1942; children—Deborah, Denise. Mgmt. engr. Am. Air Filter Co., Moline, Ill., 1951-58; prodn. design supr. Brunswick Corp., Muskegon, Mich., 1958-60; mgr. research engring. div. Louis Allis Co., Milw., 1960-62; asst. to pres. McQuay, Inc., Mpls., 1962-66, v.p. mfg., 1966-70, v.p. corp. planning and devel., 1970-71, exec. v.p. Perfex div. McQuay-Perfex, Inc., Milw., 1972-73, pres., 1973—, exec. v.p. parent co., 1976-77, pres. parent co., 1977—, also dir. Mem. corp., regent Milw. Sch. Engring. Served in AUS, 1943-46. Decorated Bronze star. Mem. Am. Soc. Heating, Air Conditioning and Refrigeration Engrs. Republican. Mem. Evang. Free Ch. Am. Clubs:

Mpls.; Univ. (Milw.). Home: 2840 Gale Rd Wayzata MN 55391 Office: 5401 Gamble Dr St Louis Park MN 55440

SEWELL, DUANE CAMPBELL, govt. ofcl.; b. Oakland, Calif., Aug. 15, 1918; s. Earl Ferris and Hazel Merle (Campbell) S.; B.A., Coll. Pacific, 1940; postgrad. U. Calif., 1941; m. Ruth Elizabeth Lombardi, July 25, 1943; 1 son, Barre Duane. Physicist, Lawrence Berkeley (Calif.) Lab., 1941-52, dir. sci. ops., 1952-59, physicist Lawrence Livermore Lab., Livermore, Calif., 1952-78, asso. dir. support, 1959-73, dep. dir., 1973-78; asst. sec. of Energy for def. programs, Dept. Energy, Washington, 1978—. Mem. Am. Phys. Soc. Office: 1000 Independence Ave Washington DC 20585

SEWELL, JACK VINCENT, museum curator; b. Dearborn, Mo., June 11, 1923; s. Arthur Bryan and Annie Laurie (Shortridge) S.; student St. Joseph (Mo.) Jr. Coll., 1941-43, Coll. City N.Y., 1943-44; M.F.A., U. Chgo., 1950; postgrad. Harvard, 1951-53. Staff, Oriental dept. Art Inst. Chgo., 1950—, asso. curator Oriental art, 1956-58, curator, 1958—. Vice pres., dir. Japan Am. Soc. Chgo. Served with AUS, 1943-46. Decorated Bronze Star medal. Mem. Disciples of Christ Ch. Clubs: Arts, Cliff Dwellers (Chgo.). Home: 1350 Lake Shore Dr Chicago IL 60610 Office: Art Inst Chicago Chicago IL 60603

SEWELL, JAMES LESLIE, engring. co. exec.; b. Coleman, Tex., Nov. 23, 1903; s. James McCord and Pearle (Davis) S.; B.M.E., Tex. A. and M. Coll., 1927; m. Charlotte Barnard, Aug. 27, 1929; children—George Barnard, Frederic Dana, James McCord, John Charles. Refinery supt. Taylor Refining Co., 1933-35, gen. supt., 1939-47, v.p., 1947-52; refinery supt. Coastal Refineries, Inc., 1935-39; v.p., mem. exec. com., dir. Petroleum Heat & Power Co., 1946-50; pres., dir. Taylor Oil & Gas Co., 1952-55, Delhi-Taylor Oil Corp., Dallas, 1955-68, Standard Lumber Co., 1968—; dir., mem. exec. com. dirs. Aztec Oil & Gas Co., 1969-76; dir. Delhi Internat. Oil Corp., Citizens Nat. Bank Dallas. Mem. Tex. Mid-Continent Oil and Gas Assn. (pres. 1963-65), Mid-Continent Oil and Gas Assn. (dir., pres. 1967-69), Am. Petroleum Inst. (dir.), ASME, Soc. Automotive Engrs., Tau Beta Pi. Presbyterian. Clubs: Dallas Petroleum, Dallas Country. Home: 4218 High Star Ln Dallas TX 75252 Office: Fidelity Union Life Bldg Dallas TX 75201

SEWELL, JOHN, mayor; b. Toronto, Dec. 8, 1940; s. William and Helen (Sanderson) S.; B.A., U. Toronto, 1961; LL.B., U. Toronto, 1964; 1 son, Nicholas. Called to bar, 1967; community organizer, Toronto, 1966-69; mem. Toronto City Council, 1969-78, mayor City of Toronto, 1978—. Author: Up Against City Hall, 1972; contbr. articles to mags., newspapers. Office: City Hall Toronto ON M5H 2N2 Canada

SEWELL, WILLIAM HAMILTON, sociologist; b. Perrington, Mich., Nov. 27, 1909; s. Will H. and Lulu (Collar) S.; A.B., Mich. State U., 1933, A.M., 1934, D.Sc. (hon.), 1973; Ph.D., U. Minn., 1939; m. Elizabeth Shogren, June 13, 1936; children—Mary, William, Robert. Instr., U. Minn., 1934-37; asst. prof. sociology Okla. State U., 1937-38, asso. prof., 1938-40, prof., 1940-44; prof. sociology, rural sociology U. Wis., 1946-64, Vilas research prof. sociology, 1964—, chmn. dept., 1951-53, chmn. social sci. research com., 1952-55, social sci. div., 1950-53, chmn. dept. sociology, 1958-63, univ. chancellor, 1967-68. Vis. scholar Russell Sage Found., 1968-69; Walker-Ames vis. prof. U. Washington, 1954; vis. prof. U. Tex., 1941, U. P.R., 1949, Garrett Inst., 1950, Columbia, 1952; Ford Found. vis. prof. Delhi, Bombay, Poona univs., 1956-57; cons. human resources Sec. War, Research and Devel. Bd., Dept. Def., 1946-54; cons. Nat. Inst. Mental Health, USPHS, 1957—, chmn. behavioral scis. study sect.; chmn. behavioral scis. tng. com. NIH, 1962-67, mem. metal health research adv. com., 1968-70; exec. com. behavorial sci. div. NRC, 1966-70; chmn. Nat. Commn. on Research, 1978—. Trustee Chatham Coll., Am. Coll. Testing Program Reseach Inst., Nat. Opinion Research Center; bd. dirs. Social Sci. Research Council. Served as lt. USNR, 1944-46. Recipient Outstanding Achievement award U. Minn., 1972, Distinguished Research award Am. Ednl. Research Assn., 1975. Fellow Center for Advanced Study in Behavioral Scis., 1959-60. Fellow A.A.A.S. (chmn. sect. K 1975-76), Am. Sociol. Assn. (chmn. social psychology sect. 1960-61, v.p. 1961-62, pres. 1970-71), Am. Acad. Arts and Scis.; mem. Rural (pres. 1955), Southwestern (pres. 1941), Midwestern (pres. 1954) sociol. socs., Nat. Acad. Scis., Am. Statis. Assn., Sociol. Research Assn. (pres. 1954), Soc. Research in Child Devel., Am. Philos. Soc. Clubs: Blackhawk Country, University. Author: Construction and Standardization of a Scale for the Measurement of Farm Family Socioeconomic Status, 1941; (with others) Scandinavian Students on An American Campus, 1961; Attitudes and Facilitation in Status Attainment, 1972; Education, Occupation and Earnings: Achievement in the Early Career, 1975. Co-editor; Uses of Sociology, 1967; Schooling and Achievement in American Society, 1976; asso. editor Am. Sociol. Rev., 1954-57, Sociometry, 1955-58; Human Resources, 1967—. Contbr. articles, monographs on sociology to profl. jours. Home: 1005 Merrill Springs Rd Madison WI 53705

SEWELL, WINIFRED, pharm. librarian; b. Newport, Wash., Aug. 12, 1917; d. Harold Arthur and Grace (Vickerman) Sewell; B.A., State Coll. Wash., Pullman, 1938; B.S. in Library Sci., Columbia, 1940; D.Sc. (hon.), Phila. Coll. Pharmacy and Sci., 1979. Asst., Columbia Library, 1938-42; asst. librarian Wellcome Research Labs., Tuckahoe, N.Y., 1942-43, librarian, 1943-46; librarian, Squibb Inst. Med. Research, 1946-61; subject heading specialist Nat. Library of Medicine, 1961-62, dep. chief bibliog. services div., 1962-65, head drug literature program, 1965-70; cons., 1970—; adj. asst. prof. U. Md. Sch. Pharmacy, 1970—; adj. lectr. U. Md. Coll. Library and Info. Services, 1969—; cons. Nat. Health Planning Info. Center, 1975—; editor Unlisted Drugs, 1949-59, 62-64; instr. pharmaceutical literature and librarianship Columbia, summer 1959. Mem. com. on modern methods for handling chem. info. Nat. Acad. Sci.-NRC. Mem. Am. Soc. for Info. Sci. (chmn. spl. interest group/classification research 1974-75), Med. Library Assn. (chmn. Rittenhouse award com. 1975-76, chmn. recert. com. 1979-80, chmn. public health and health adminstrn. sect. 1979-80), Spl. Libraries Assn. (chmn. pharm. sect., sci.-tech. div. 1952-53, pres. 1960-61, publs. award sci. and tech. div. 1966), ALA, Drug Information Assn. (v.p. 1966-67, pres. 1970-71), Am. Assn. Colls. Pharmacy (chmn. libraries/ednl. resources sect. 1979-80, del. council on sects. adv. bd. 1980—). Author: Guide to Drug Information (Ida and George Eliot award Med. Library Assn. 1977), 1976; (with Merle Harrison) Using MeSH for Effective Searching: a Programmed Guide, 1976; Readings in Medical Librarianship, 1973. Editor: Health Affairs Series, Gale Info. Guides, 1971—; editorial bd. Bull. Med. Library Assn., Drug Info. Jour. Home and office: 6513 76th Pl Cabin John MD 20731

SEXTON, IRWIN, librarian; b. Lafayette, Ind., Nov. 7, 1921; s. Orville C. and Mary Della (Hayth) S.; B.S. in Trade and Indsl. Edn., Purdue U., 1949; M.S. in L.S., Western Res. U., 1952; m. Kathryn Segee, Nov. 24, 1950; 1 son, David. Dir. St. Joseph (Mo.) Pub. Library, 1955-57, Oklahoma City Libraries, 1958-60, San Antonio Pub. Library 1961—. Pres., St. Joseph Mental Health Assn., 1957. Served with USAAF, 1942-46. Mem. Am., Tex. library assns. Rotarian. Club: San Antonio Torch. Author: Industrial Techniques for the School Shop, 1955. Office: 203 S St Mary's St San Antonio TX 78205

SEXTON, RICHARD, diversified mfg. co. exec.; b. Madison, Wis., May 9, 1929; s. Joseph Cantwell and Eleanor Carr (Kenny) S.; student Amherst Coll., 1947-49; B.S., U. Wis., 1951; LL.B., Yale U., 1958; m. Joan Fleming, Feb. 23, 1957; children—Mary, Joseph, Lucy, Michael, Ann, Katherine. Admitted to N.Y. bar, 1959; asso. firm Sullivan & Cromwell, N.Y.C., 1958-64; with SCM Corp., N.Y.C., 1964—, asst. counsel, 1964-67, gen. counsel Smith-Corona Marchant div., 1967-72, v.p., gen. counsel parent co., 1972—, sec., 1977—. Served to lt. (j.g.) USNR, 1951-55. Mem. Assn. Bar City N.Y. Club: Yale. Home: 532 3d St Brooklyn NY 11215 Office: SCM Corp 299 Park Ave New York City NY 10017

SEXTON, THOMAS MACKIN, food co. exec.; b. Chgo., June 2, 1919; s. Franklin C. and Alice (Philbin) S.; B.S., Holy Cross Coll., 1941; m. Alice Nancy McHugh, May 9, 1946; children—Thomas Mackin, Edward Franklin, Alice, Peter Dolan. With John Sexton & Co., Chgo., 1942—, gen. br. mgr., N.Y.C., 1958-59, pres., Chgo., 1959-76; v.p. Beatrice Foods Co., Chgo., 1976—, also dir.; dir. Sargent-Welch Sci. Co., Skokie, Ill., Smurfit Industries, Inc., Chgo. Mem. Econ. Club Chgo. Clubs: North Shore Country (Glenview, Ill.); Big Sand Lake (Phelps, Wis.). Home: 825 Mount Pleasant St Winnetka IL 60093 Office: 222 S Riverside Plaza Chicago IL 60606

SEXTON, WILLIAM COTTRELL, newspaper editor; b. Balt., Sept. 22, 1928; s. Hardigg and Grace Dean (Cottrell) S.; student U. N.C., 1946-47; m. Bonnie Stone, Dec. 18, 1976; 1 son, Paul Norman. With UPI, 1948-62, mgr. N.Y. bur., 1959-62; asso. dir. Am. Press Inst., Columbia U., 1963-66; mng. editor Louisville Courier-Jour., 1966-67; mng. editor, then editor World Book Sci. Service, 1967-70; editor Publishers-Hall Syndicate, N.Y.C., 1970-71; with Newsday, Inc., Melville, N.Y., 1971—, asst. to editor, 1972-73, asso. editor, 1973—; dir. Ford Found. seminar for African newspaper execs., 1965; vice chmn. N.Y. State Fair Trial Free Press Conf., 1977—. Served with AUS, 1951-52. Mem. Am. Soc. Newspaper Editors, Council Fgn. Relations. Home: 103 Pidgeon Hill Rd Huntington NY 11746 Office: Melville NY 11747

SEYBOLT, GEORGE CROSSAN, food processing co. exec.; b. N.Y.C., Apr. 18, 1914; s. George Lionel and Blanche (Crossan) A.; D.C.S., Suffolk U., 1961; m. Hortense E. Kelly, Sept. 2, 1947; children—Reva Blanche, Edwina Porter, George Crossan, Calvert Horace. With Orvis Bros. & Co., stockbrokers, N.Y.C., 1933-35; with Am. Can. Co., N.Y.C., 1935-50, asst. regional sales mgr., Balt., 1946-47, New Eng. sales mgr., Boston, 1947-50; with William Underwood Co. Voluntary Assn., 1950—, v.p., 1954-56, exec. v.p., 1956-57, pres., trustee, 1957-78, chmn. bd., 1975—, chief exec. officer, 1978—; pres. William Underwood Co. (Maine), 1957—; dir. William Underwood Co. (Can.) Ltd., Dorion-Vaudreuil, Que., 1957—, treas., 1957-61, pres., 1962-70, chmn. bd., 1968—; pres., dir. Richardson & Robbins Co., 1959-61, Burnham & Morrill Co., Portland, Maine, 1965-66, Village Inn Gourmet Foods, Inc., Watertown, 1974; pres. Diablitos Venezolanos, C.A., Caracas, Venezuela, 1960-72, dir., 1960—, chmn. bd., 1972—; pres., dir. Diablites Mexicanos S.A., Mexico City, 1974—; treas., dir. Sell's Splty., Inc., N.Y.C., 1960-63; dir. Ac'cent Internat. de Mexico, Mexico City, 1971—, pres., 1973—; dir. C. Shippam Ltd., Chichester, Eng., Cinta Azul, S.A., San Jose, Costa Rica, Bjelland & Co. A/S, Stavanger, Norway; adv. dir. New Eng. Mchts. Nat. Bank and New Eng. Mchts. Co., Inc., Boston, 1967-71, dir., 1971—. Dir. Asso. Industries Mass., 1963-74, mem. exec. com., 1965-67, hon. dir., 1974—; chmn. Maine Sardine Industry Research Com., 1953-59. Mem. Dedham Hist. Commn., 1963—, Dedham Town Meeting, 1956-74; 1st v.p., dir. Dedham Community Assn., 1954-70; mem. adv. com. Positive Program Boston, N.A.A.C.P., 1969-73; chmn. Boston Devel. and Indsl. Commn., 1968—, Econ. Devel. and Indsl. Corp. Boston, 1972—; mem. Nat. Mus. Services Bd., Washington, chmn., 1977—; mem. Bus. Com. for Arts, N.Y.C., 1970—, bd. dirs., 1974-78; mem. gen. council Ford Hall Forum, Boston, 1971-77. Trustee Suffolk U., Boston, 1962-72, chmn. bd., 1966-71, life trustee, 1972—; trustee Mus. Fine Arts, Boston, 1966-77, pres., 1968-73, pres. emeritus, 1973—; trustee Valley Forge Mil. Acad., 1966-73; bd. dirs. Mass. Taxpayers Found., 1967-72, Internat. Center New Eng., 1968-72; overseer Old Sturbridge Village, 1977. Mem. nat. adv. council Episcopal Ch. Found., N.Y.C., 1970-74; mem. corp. Mus. Sci. Boston, 1965-77, Wentworth Inst., Boston, 1969-77, Faulkner Hosp., Boston, 1957-77. Served from ensign to lt. USNR, 1942-45. Decorated Order Brit. Empire. Mem. Nat. Canners Assn. (adminstrv. council 1958-72, finance com. 1962-74, internat. trade com. 1964-68, dir. 1953-56, 59-62, 67-70, 73-77), Pan Am. Soc. New Eng. (bd. govs. 1966-69), Greater Boston C. of C. (dir. 1965-68, pres. 1968-69, chmn. 1969-70, hon. v.p. 1970—, chmn. nominating com. 1970), Nat. Council on Arts, Am. Assn. Museums (chmn. trustees com. 1973-77, legis. com. 1973-77). Episcopalian (vestryman 1958-60, 67-70, mem. Diocesan Council 1964-68, chmn. communications com. 1965-68, com. to select bishop 1969). Clubs: Tennis and Racquet, Brook (N.Y.C.); Country (Brookline, Mass.); St. James (London). Home: 1 Town Landing Ln Dedham MA 02026 Office: Wm Underwood Co One Red Devil Ln Westwood MA 02090

SEYDELL, MILDRED, writer, lectr., traveler; b. Atlanta; d. Vasser and Elizabeth Cobb (Rutherford) Woolley; student Washington Sem., Atlanta, Lucy Cobb Inst., Athens Ga., and Sorbonne, Paris; m. Paul Bernard Seydel (now dec.); children—Paul Vasser, John Rutherford; m. 2d, Max Seydel (dec.). Columnist, Charleston (W.Va.) Gazette, 1921; Hearst Crime Commn. rep. in Europe, 1926, collecting data for series of articles, interviews; traveled in Belgium, Ireland, 1927, Balkan States, Hungary, Turkey, Greece, 1929, Sweden, Germany, France, 1931; contributed to Talks with Celebrities; spl. study liquor regulation in Sweden. Travelled through Africa from Capetown to Cairo, Palestine, 1934; spl. study histroy diamonds and gold in S. Africa, native customs of Belgian Congo, investigation of activity of Jews in Palestine; adventure in friendship to South Sea Islands, New Zealand, Austrialia, 1937; Internat. News Service rep. in Germany, Czechoslovakia, 1938, Finland, 1939; corr. U.S. papers; adventures in Europe, 1955, Eng., Wales, 1956; pres. Mildred Seydell Pub. Co. Belgian dir. World Poetry Day; mem. adv. com. Fellowship in Prayer; hon. mem. Ladies Meml. Assn. Atlanta. Hon. mem. bd. A.G. Rhodes Home. Decorated chevalier Order of Leopold (Belgium); recipient Book of Golden Deeds plaque Nat. Exchange Club, 1979. Mem. Tape Talk Internat. (pres.), Nat. League Am. Pen Women, Beta Sigma Phi (hon.). Clubs: Peony Garden (hon.); Writer, Am. Women's (Brussels). Author: Secret Fathers, 1930; Then I Saw North Carolina, 1937; Chins Up, 1939; Come Along to Belgium, 1969. Editor: Poetry Profile of Belgium, 1960. Mem. adv. staff Sunshine Mag.; pub. Essays Wise and Otherwise. Address: 9530 Scott Rd Route 2 Roswell GA 30076. *When asked what does it take to be a successful journalist, I answer: "Calmness against injustice, humor for hardships, memory keen enough to recall observed details, ability to inspire confidence sufficient to make people talk."*

SEYFERTH, DIETMAR, educator, chemist; b. Chemnitz, Germany, Jan. 11, 1929; s. Herbert C. and Elisabeth (Schuchardt) S.; came to U.S., 1933; B.A. summa cum laude, U. Buffalo, 1951, M.A., 1953; Ph.D., Harvard, 1955; Dr. honoris causa, U. Aix-Marseille, 1979; m. Helena A. McCoy, Aug. 25, 1956; children—Eric Steven, Karl Dietmar, Elisabeth Mary. Fulbright scholar Tech. Hochschule, Munich, Germany, 1954-55; postdoctoral fellow Harvard, 1956-57; faculty Mass. Inst. Tech., 1957—, prof. chemistry, 1965—. Cons. to industry, 1957—. Recipient Distinguished Alumnus award U. Buffalo, 1964. Guggenheim fellow, 1968. Fellow AAAS; mem. Am. Chem. Soc. (Frederic Stanley Kipping award in organosilicon chemistry 1972), Chem. Soc. London, Gesellschaft Deutscher Chemiker, German Acad. Scientists Leopoldina, Phi Beta Kappa, Sigma Xi. Author: Annual Surveys of Organometallic Chemistry, 3 vols., 1965, 66, 67. Regional editor Jour. Organometallic Chemistry, 1963—; coordinating editor revs. and survey sects.; Contbr. research papers to profl. lit. Office: 77 Massachusetts Ave Cambridge MA 02139

SEYMOUR, ALLYN HENRY, radioecologist, fishery biologist; b. Seattle, Aug. 1, 1913; s. Alphonso Sherwood and Velma Jane (Smith) S.; B.S. in Fisheries, U. Wash., 1937, Ph.D., 1956; m. Barbara Jane Noonan, June 28, 1940; children—Allyn Henry, Denny Richard, Gary Noonan. Fishery biologist Internat. Fisheries Commn., 1937-39, 42-47, Wash. State Dept. Fisheries, 1940-42, Internat./Pacific Salmon Fisheries Commn., 1937-39; research scientist, asst. dir. applied fisheries lab. U. Wash., 1947-56, asso. dir. lab. radiation biology, 1958-66, dir. lab radiation ecology, 1967-78, prof. radioecology, fishery biology Coll. Fisheries, 1963-79; marine biologist div. biology and medicine AEC, Washington, 1956-58; cons. aquatic radioecology; dep. chmn. AEC Chariot Bioenviron. Program, 1959-64; mem. Nat. Acad. Scis.-NRC panel on Radioactivity in Marine Environ, 1966-72; mem. panels Nat. Acad. Scis.-NRC. Fellow AAAS; mem. Am. Fisheries Soc., Am. Inst. Fishery Research Biologists, Pacific Fishery Biologists (pres. 1947), Health Physics Soc., Sigma Xi (chpt. pres. 1979-80), Phi Sigma. Congregationalist. Author numerous reports on aquatic radioecology and fishery biology. Home: 5855 Oberlin Ave NE Seattle WA 98105 Office: Coll Fisheries U Wash Seattle WA 98195

SEYMOUR, ANNE, actress; b. N.Y.C., Sept. 11, 1909; d. William Stanley and May Davenport (Seymour) Eckert; student Am. Lab. Theatre Sch., N.Y.C., 1927-28. Profl. debut with the Jitney Players, 1928; appeared in numerous plays, Broadway theatres, East Coast theatres, 1928—, including: A School for Scandal, 1931, The Wind and the Rain, 1936, The Romantic Young Lady, 1942, Sunrise at Campobello, 1958, Medea, 1965; film debut as Lucy Stark in All the King's Men, 1949; film appearances include: Whistle at Eaton Falls, 1951, Man on Fire, 1957, Desire Under the Elms, 1958, Handle with Care, 1958, Pollyanna, 1959, Home from the Hill, 1960, All the Fine Young Cannibals, 1960, Where Love Has Gone, 1964, Stage to Thunder Rock, 1964; How to Succeed in Business Without Really Trying, 1966, Blendfold, 1966, Mirage, 1967, Stay Away, Joe, 1968, Gemini Affair, 1974, Hearts of the West, 1975; radio performances include: Grand Hotel, 1933, title role The Story of Mary Marlin, 1934-40, 41-44, A Woman of America, 1943, The Magnificent Montague, 1950, narrator My Secret Story, 1951, Ford Mystery Theater, Theatre Guild of the Air, Philip Morris Playhouse, Inner Sanctum, Somerset Maugham Playhouse, Studio One, Armstrong Theatre of Today, CBS Mystery Theatre, Heartbeat House, Fireside Playhouse, and numerous others; television appearances include: Studio One, Robert Montgomery Presents, Kraft Television Theatre, U.S. Steel Hour, Lux Television Playhouse, Alcoa Presents, Schlitz Playhouse of the Stars, Gunsmoke, Hawaiian Eye, Perry Mason; co-starred on Empire series and Tim Conway Show; appeared in numerous others television films and series including: Emergency, One Day at a Time, The Last Survivors, A Tree Grows in Brooklyn, Police Story, Police Woman, Another World, General Hosp., Portrait of Grandpa Doc, The Miracle Worker, Second Star to the Right. Mem. AFTRA (nat. bd. dirs., v.p., sec. 1927-52, v.p. Chgo. chpt. 1937, dir. 1937-40, dir. N.Y.C. chpt. 1940-52), Am. Theatre Wing (bd. 1959-62), Plays for Living (bd. dirs. 1959-73), Plays for Living of So. Calif., Veterans Hosp. Radio and Television Guild (1st v.p, 1961), Actors Fund Am. (bd. dirs. West Coast), Episcopal Actors' Guild, Theatre Authority (bd. dirs. West Coast 1977—), Screen Actors Guild (nat. bd. dirs. 1973—), Am. Nat. Theatre Acad. (dir. 1974-77).

SEYMOUR, ANNE, actress; b. N.Y.C., Sept. 11, 1909; d. William Stanley and May Davenport (Seymour) Eckert; student Am. Lab. Theatre Sch., 1927-28. Appeared in motion pictures All the King's Men, 1949, Man on Fire, 1957, Home from the Hill, 1959, All the Fine Young Cannibals, 1960, The Subterraneans, 1960, Sunrise at Campobello, 1960, Mirage, 1965, Blindford, 1966, Fitzwilly, 1967, Gemini Affair, 1974, (TV film) Dawn: Portrait of a Teenage Runaway, 1976; co-starred in television series Empire, 1962; appeared on TV shows Studio One, Robert Montgomery Presents, Armstrong Circle Theatre, Climax!, Gunsmoke, Ben Casey, Naked City, My Three Sons, Perry Mason, numerous others; Bd. dirs. Plays for Living of So. Calif. Mem. Actors Fund of Am.-West (dir. 1972—), Screen Actors Guild, Motion Picture and Television Fund, Episcopal Actors Guild. Democrat. Office: care Bret Adams Ltd 8282 Sunset Blvd Los Angeles CA 90046

SEYMOUR, ARTHUR HALLOCK, newspaperman; b. Des Moines, Oct. 22, 1928; s. Forrest Wilson and Pearl Bernice (Yeager) S.; B.A., Harvard, 1952; m. Ann Adele Knutson, Aug. 19, 1977; children—Forrest Wilson, Macy Yeager, Andrew Hallock. Reporter, A.P., Cheyenne, Wyo., 1952-53, Denver, 1953-55; mem. staff Mpls. Star, 1955—, bus. news editor, 1965-70, asst. news editor, 1970-72, news editor, 1972-78, asst. mng. editor, 1978—. Served with USMCR, 1946-49. Home: 7328 Landau Dr Bloomington MN 55438 Office: 425 Portland Ave Minneapolis MN 55488

SEYMOUR, ERNEST RICHARD, naval officer; b. Syracuse, N.Y., Oct. 6, 1931; s. Willard Renwick and Virginia (Smith) S.; B.S., U.S. Naval Acad., 1953; B.S., U.S. Naval Postgrad. Sch., 1961; Aero. E., Calif. Inst. Tech., 1962; m. Virginia Ann Metzler, Feb. 6, 1954; children—Ernest Richard, Deborah L., Stephen E. Commd. ensign, 1953; naval aviator, 1955—; asst. program mgr. for logistics A-7 aircraft Naval Air Systems Command, Washington, 1968, later project mgr., then dep. comdr. plans and program tour as mem. staff chief naval ops., exec. asst. to vice chief naval ops., asst. dep. chief naval ops. (air warfare), now vice chief naval material. Decorated Silver Star, Legion of Merit (3), D.F.C., Bronze Star, Air medal (23). Episcopalian. Home: 10204 Glencoe Dr Vienna VA 22180 Office: Chief Naval Material (MAT-09) Washington DC 20360

SEYMOUR, JAMES OWENS, lawyer; b. Columbus, Ohio, Aug. 23, 1904; s. Augustus T. and Evelyn (Owens) S.; A.B., Princeton, 1926; LL.B., Harvard, 1929; m. Jane H. Farrar, Mar. 30, 1940; 1 dau., Antoinette F. Admitted to Ohio bar, 1929, since practiced in Columbus; mem. firm Vorys, Sater, Seymour & Pease, 1936—; dir. Credit Life Ins. Co., Springfield. Mem. Am., Ohio, Columbus bar assns. Home: 26 Sessions Dr Columbus OH 43209 Office: 52 E Gay St Columbus OH 43215

SEYMOUR, JANE, actress; b. Hillingdon, Middlesex, Eng., Feb. 15, 1951; d. John Benjamin and Mieke Frankenberg; came to U.S., 1976; student Arts Ednl. Sch., London. Appeared in films: Oh What A Lovely War, 1968, The Only Way, 1968, Young Winston, 1969, Live and Let Die, 1971, Sinbad and the Eye of the Tiger, 1973, Somewhere in Time, 1979, Oh Heavenly Dog, 1979; TV spls., Frankenstein, The

True Story, 1972, Captains and The Kings (Emmy nomination), 1976, 7th Avenue, 1976, The Awakening Land, 1977, The Four Feathers, 1977, Battlestar Galactica, Dallas Cowboy Cheerleaders, 1979, Our Mutual Friend, PBS, Eng., 1975. Named Hon. Citizen of Ill., Gov. Thompson, 1977. Mem. Screen Actors Guild, AFTRA, Actors Equity, Brit. Equity. Office: care William Morris Agy 151 El Camino Beverly Hills CA 90212

SEYMOUR, LYLE EUGENE, coll. pres.; b. Milaca, Minn., Sept. 26, 1922; s. Edward and Elizabeth (Rodenberg) S.; student Wayne State Coll., 1940-42; B.S., Ia. State U., 1947, M.S., 1954; Ph.D., U. S.D., 1961; m. Virginia Ruth Melahn, Oct. 12, 1945; children—Linda, Pamela (Mrs. Galen Johnson), Ronald. With Comml. Solvents Corp., Terre Haute, Ind., 1947-50; tchr. sci. Wayne (Nebr.) City Schs., 1951; instr. chemistry Wayne State Coll., 1953-60, chmn. div. sci. and math., 1961-67, dean faculties, 1967-73, interim pres., 1973-74, pres., 1974—. Pres., Seymour's, Inc. Pres. bd. dirs. Wayne Hosp., 1972—; trustee Wayne Hosp. Found., Wayne State Found. Served to capt. USAAF, 1943-45. Decorated Air medal, D.F.C.; named Outstanding Tchr. Sci., 1962, 67. Mem. Sigma Xi. Republican. Lutheran. Home: 1100 Sunset Dr Wayne NE 68787

SEYMOUR, LYNN, dancer, choreographer; b. Wainwright, Alta., Can., Aug. 3, 1939; d. Edward Victor and Marjorie Isabelle (McIvor) Springbett; student Royal Ballet Sch., London, 1954-57; children—Adrian, Jerszy, Demian. Ballerina with Royal Ballet, London, 1956-66, 70-78; guest appearances with Stuttgart (Germany) Ballet Can. Nat. Ballet, Ballet de Marseilles, Deutsche Oper—Berlin, Hamburgische Staatsoper, Dutch Nat. Ballet Co., Am. Ballet Theater, London Contemporary Dance Theatre; guest artist Alvin Ailey Co., 1970-71; dir. ballet Bavarian State Opera, Munich, W.Ger., 1978—; choreographer: Two's Night Ride, Breakthrough, Gladly Badly Sadly Madly, Rashomon, A Court of Love, Intimate Letters, Boreas, Mac and Polly, Tatooed Lady, Leda and the Swan. Decorated comdr. Order Brit. Empire. Office: Bayerisches Staatsoper Munchen Federal Republic of Germany

SEYMOUR, RICHARD KELLOGG, educator; b. Hinsdale, Ill., June 21, 1930; s. William and Katharine (Fifield) S.; B.A., U. Mich., 1951, M.A., 1952; certificate U. Tübingen (Germany), 1953; Ph.D., U. Pa., 1956, postgrad. linguistics. 1957; m. Nancy Ann Nutt, June 23, 1951; children—Michael Bradley, William David. Asst. instr. U. Pa., 1952-55; instr. Princeton, 1954-58, linguist NDEA Summer Inst., 1963; asst. prof. Duke, 1958-63, asso. prof., 1963-67, endowment fellow, 1966; prof., chmn. dept. European langs. and lit. U. Hawaii, Honolulu, 1967-75, prof., 1977—; chmn. German dept. Pa. State U., University Park, 1975-77; vis. prof. Cologne (Germany) U., 1974. Princeton Research Council grantee, 1958; Am. Council Learned Socs. grantee, 1957. Mem. Linguistic Soc. Am., Internat. Linguistic Assn., Am. Dialect Soc., Am. Assn. Tchrs. German, Modern Lang. Assn., S. Atlantic Modern Lang. Assn. (exec. sec. 1962-67), Delta Phi Alpha (nat. sec.-treas. 1968—). Conglist. (bd. deacons, sec. 1970-71). Author: A Bibliography of Word Formation in the Germanic Languages, 1968. Asst. editor Unterrichtspraxis, 1969—. Contbr. articles to profl. jours. Office: Dept European Langs and Lit U Hawaii 470 Moore Hall Honolulu HI 96822

SEYMOUR, ROBERT EDWARD, utilities exec.; b. Meadville, Pa., May 6, 1916; s. Clinton Windsor and Nellie Grace (Byham) S.; student Meadville Comml. Coll., 1935, U. Pitts., 1948-52; m. Hazel Clare Dixon, Nov. 30, 1940; children—Robert Dixon, Donald Edward, John Windsor, Richard Allen. Pres., Peoples Natural Gas Co., Pitts., 1963-68; exec. v.p. Consol. Natural Gas Co., Pitts., 1968-70, pres., 1970-74, chmn. bd., 1974-79, chmn. exec. com., 1979—; dir. Pitts. Nat. Bank, Pitts. Nat. Corp., Rockwell Internat. Corp., Wheeling-Pitts. Steel Corp., Pitts. Brewing Co. Bd. dirs. Allegheny County chpt., mem. nat. bd. govs. ARC; bd. dirs. Pitts. Conv. and Visitors Bur., Inc., Montefiore Hosp., Gas Devel. Corp., Pitts. Ballet Theatre; trustee Carnegie-Mellon U.; bd. dirs. United Way of Allegheny County, chmn. fund drive, 1979; mem. Nat. Petroleum Council; vice chmn. Nat. Alliance of Bus., mem. exec. com. Allegheny Conf. on Community Devel. Served to capt. AUS, 1942-46. Decorated Bronze Star medal. Mem. Am. Gas Assn. (past chmn., dir.), Interstate Natural Gas Assn. Am. dir.), Inst. Gas Tech. (trustee, exec. com.). Presbyterian (elder). Clubs: Duquesne (dir.), Univ. (Pitts.); Longue Vue (dir.) (Verona, Pa.); Bay Point Yacht and Country (Panama City, Fla.). Home: 811 Rockwood Ave Pittsburgh PA 15234 Office: Four Gateway Center Pittsburgh PA 15222

SEYMOUR, THADDEUS, coll. pres.; b. N.Y.C., June 29, 1928; s. Whitney North and Lola Virginia (Vickers) S.; A.B., U. Calif., 1950; M.A., U. N.C., 1951, Ph.D., 1955; D.H.L., Wilkes Coll., 1968; LL.D., Butler U., 1971, Ind. State U., 1976; m. Polly Gnagy, Nov. 20, 1948; children—Elizabeth Halsey, Thaddeus, Samuel Whitney, Mary Duffie, Abigail Comfort. Teaching fellow U. N.C., 1951-52, teaching asst., 1952-54; faculty Dartmouth Coll., 1954-69, prof. English, dean coll., 1959-69; pres. Wabash Coll., Crawfordsville, Ind., 1969-78, Rollins Coll., Winter Park, Fla., 1978—. Mem. Bd. Environ. Quality Control, Ind. Bicentennial Commn.; del. N.H. Republican Conv., 1958, 64, vice chmn. N.H. Rep. Com., 1967-68; trustee Park-Tudor Sch., 1970-78; bd. dirs. Citizens Scholarship Found.; pres. Ind. Conf. Higher Edn., 1977; v.p. Asso. Colls. Ind., 1978. Mem. Nat. Rowing Found. (dir.), Internat. Brotherhood Magicians. Clubs: Rotary, University, Century Assn. (N.Y.C.). Home: 482 Lakewood Dr Winter Park FL 32789

SEYMOUR, WHITNEY NORTH, lawyer; b. Chgo., Jan. 4, 1901; s. Charles Walton and Margaret (Rugg) S.; A.B., U. Wis., 1920, LL.D., 1962; LL.B., Columbia, 1923, LL.D., 1960; LL.D., Dartmouth, 1960, Duke, U. Akron, U. Man., 1961, Trinity U., 1964; D.C.L., N.Y. U., 1971; m. Lola V. Vickers, June 17, 1922 (dec. Nov. 1975); children—Whitney North, Thaddeus. Admitted to N.Y. bar, 1924; asso. Simpson, Thacher & Bartlett, N.Y.C., 1923-29, partner, 1929-31, 33—; instr. N.Y. U. Law Sch., 1925-31; asst. solicitor gen. U.S., 1931-1933. Lectr., Yale Law sch. 1935-45. Mem. N.Y. Temporary Commn. on Cts., 1953-58; mem. Atty. Gen.'s Com. on Anti-trust Laws; spl. asst. atty. gen. N.Y., waterfront controversy, 1954; past mem. N.Y.C. Mayor's Com. on Judiciary; pres. Legal Aid Soc., N.Y.C., 1945-50. Trustee emeritus Practicing Law Inst.; trustee N.Y. Landmarks Conservancy, Law Center Found.; hon. chmn. bd. Freedom House; distbn. com. N.Y. Community Trust; past chmn. bd. trustees Carnegie Endowment, 1957-70; chmn. Council on Library Resources, William Nelson Cromwell Found., Council on Legal Edn. for Profl. Responsibility; pres. Joint Conf. Legal Edn. Decorated Knight Order St. John of Jerusalem; recipient Distinguished Service award U. Wis., 1974; Episcopal Layman award Bard Coll., 1976; President's medal Municipal Art Soc., 1976; N.Y.C. Mayor's citation for support of arts, 1977. Fellow Am. Bar Found. (pres. 1960-64), Am. Coll. Trial Lawyers (pres. 1963-64), Bar Assn. City N.Y. (pres. 1950-52), N.Y. County, Am. (Gold medal 1971, pres. 1960-61), Fed. (hon.), Minn. (hon.), Wis. (hon.), N.H. (hon.), Tenn. (hon.), Miss. (hon.). Ga. (hon.), Hawaii (hon.), Canadian (hon.), N.Y. State bar assns., Law Soc. Eng. (hon.), Am. Arbitration Assn. (pres. 1953-55, chmn. bd. 1955-57), Inst. Jud. Adminstrn. (pres. 1968-69), Lincoln's Inn (hon. bencher), Order Coif, Phi Gamma Delta. Republican. Episcopalian (sr. warden). Clubs: Century, Players, Downtown, Merchants, Church (pres. 1966-68), Salmagundi, Recess (N.Y.C.); National Lawyers, Metropolitan (Washington); Pilgrims; St. Nicholas Soc. (historian). Home: 40 Fifth Ave New York NY 10011 Office: 1 Battery Park Plaza New York NY 10004

SEYMOUR, WHITNEY NORTH, JR., lawyer; b. Huntington, W.Va., July 7, 1923; s. Whitney North and Lola (Vickers) S.; A.B. magna cum laude, Princeton, 1947; LL.B., Yale, 1950; LL.D. (hon.), N.Y. Law Sch., 1972; m. Catryna Ten Eyck, Nov. 16, 1951; children—Tryntje, Gabriel. Admitted to N.Y. bar, 1950; asso. firm Simpson Thacher & Bartlett, N.Y.C., 1950-53, 56-59, partner, 1961-70, 73—; asst. U.S. atty., 1953-56; chief counsel N.Y. State Commn. Govtl. Operations, N.Y.C., 1959-60; chief counsel Spl. Unit N.Y. State Commn. Investigation, 1960-61; mem. N.Y. Senate, 1966-68; U.S. atty. So. Dist. N.Y., 1970-73. Chmn. legal adv. com. Pres.'s Council on Environmental Quality, 1970-73; v.p. Art Commn., N.Y.C., 1975-77; pres. Municipal Art Soc., 1965, Park Assn. N.Y., 1962-64. Past bd. dirs. N.Y. Pub. Library, recipient Thelma K. Moore award, 1977; bd. dirs. Natural Resources Def. Council, recipient Environ. award, 1972; bd. dirs. Council for Pub. Interest Law, South St. Seaport Mus., Com. for Modern Cts., Urban Libraries Council; past bd. dirs. N.Y. Bot. Garden, Citizens Housing and Planning Council, Citizens for Clean Air, Boys Brotherhood Republic, Edward MacDowell Assn.; organizer, sec. Nat. Citizens Emergency Com. to Save Our Pub. Libraries, 1976—. Served from pvt. to capt. AUS, 1943-46. Fellow Am. Bar Found.; mem. N.Y. State Bar Assn. (pres. 1974-75, ho. of dels.), Am. Bar Assn. (chmn. centennial com. 1972-75), Am. Coll. Trial Lawyers, Am. Judicature Soc. (dir. 1973-76), Fed. Bar Council (Emory Buchner award 1977), Assn. Bar City N.Y. (exec. com. 1960-64, chmn. com. on criminal justice 1976—), N.Y. County Lawyers Assn. (dir. 1968-71), N.Y. Bar Found. (v.p., dir.), Authors Guild. Republican. Episcopalian. Clubs: India House, Century, Players (N.Y.C.). Author: The Young Die Quietly: The Narcotics Problem in America, 1972; Why Justice Fails, 1973; United States Attorney, 1975; For the People: Fighting for Public Libraries, 1979. Editor: Small Urban Spaces, 1969; contbr. articles to N.Y. Times Mag., Redbook, legal periodicals, others. Home: 290 W 4th St New York NY 10014 Office: One Battery Park Plaza New York NY 10004

SEZNEC, ALAIN, French scholar, educator; b. Paris, Mar. 20, 1930; s. Jean Joseph and Genevieve (Dunan) S.; came to U.S., 1941; Licence es lettres, U. Paris, 1951, Diplome d'Etudes Superieures, 1953; m. Janet E. Grade, June 15, 1950; children—Anne, Peter J., Catherine G., Dominique M., Michael A. Instr. French, Harvard U., Cambridge, Mass., 1953-55, 57-58; asst. prof. Cornell U., Ithaca, N.Y., 1958-63, asso. prof., 1963-69, prof., 1969—, asso. dean Coll. Arts and Scis., 1969-73, vice provost for humanities and performing arts, 1970-73, chmn. dept. Romance studies, 1976—, dean Coll. Arts and Scis., 1978—. Served with French Army, 1955-57. French Nat. fellow, 1965; recipient Clark award Cornell U., 1968. Mem. Modern Lang. Assn., Am. Assn. Tchrs. French. Editor: Princesse de Cleves (de Lafayette), 1961; author: Diderot and Pope's Essay on Man, 1975. Home: 131 Kline Rd Ithaca NY 14850 Office: 282 GS Cornell Univ Ithaca NY 14850

SFREDDO, ROBERT LOUIS, constrn. co. exec.; b. Stafford Springs, Conn., Aug. 13, 1934; s. Louis and Florence Augusta (Da Dalt) S.; B.A., Chapman Coll., 1964; M.B.A., George Washington U., 1968; m. Collette Maureen Conway, Dec. 28, 1957; children—Robert Scott, Elena Marie, Anthony Mark. Served with U.S. Navy, 1954-56; served as officer U.S. Marine Corps, 1956-77 advanced through grades to lt. col., 1977; comdg. officer Marine Fighter Attack Squadron 212; served at Hdqrs. Marine Corps, Washington, also service in Hawaii, Calif.; with Presley Cos., Newport Beach, Calif., 1977—, v.p., sec., treas., 1979—. Home: 11852 Gladstone St Santa Ana CA 92905 Office: Presley Cos 4600 Campus Dr Newport Beach CA 92660

SGARRO, LOUIS, bass; b. N.Y.C.; s. Anthony Fidele and Theodora (Morelli) S.; student Coll. City N.Y., 1937-39, Am. Theatre Wing., 1946-50; m. Charlene Harvey, Apr. 27, 1946; children—Anton, Christopher. Basso with Teatro alla Scala, Milan, 1951-53, Chgo. Lyric Theatre, 1954—, Phila. La Scala, 1954—, Met. Opera Assn., N.Y.C., 1954-75 (including inaugural performance at new Met. Opera House, Lincoln Center, Sept. 1966), Conn. Opera Soc., Hartford, 1955—, Boston Opera Group, 1960—, Pitts. Opera, 1968, 72, San Diego Symphony, 1968; sang Mefisto in Faust in Split, Yugoslavia Festival, July 1959; rec. artist Met. Opera Record Club, Record Corp. Am. Served with AUS, 1942-46. Winner Met. Auditions of the Air, 1954; recipient Grande Prix de Disque de L'Academie Charles Gros, 1956; Mattheus L. Sullivan Found. scholar, 1959. Home: 36 Buttonwood Dr Old Bridge NJ 08857

SHAARA, MICHAEL JOSEPH, JR., author; b. Jersey City, June 23, 1929; s. Michael Joseph and Florence Alleene (Maxwell) S.; B.S., Rutgers U., 1951; postgrad. Columbia U., 1952, U. Vt., 1953-54; m. Helen Elizabeth Krumwiede, Sept. 16, 1950; children—Jeffrey, Lila. Asso. prof. English, Fla. State U., Tallahassee, 1961-73; writer, producer, performer courses ednl. TV, 1961-65. Served with AUS, 1946-47. Recipient award for excellence in med. journalism A.M.A., 1966; Coyle Moore award for classroom excellence, 1967; Pulitzer Prize for fiction, 1975. Mem. AAUP, Internat. Platform Assn., Gold Key Honor Soc., Theta Chi, Omicron Delta Kappa. Author: The Broken Place, 1968; The Killer Angels, 1974. Contbr. short stories, articles to Am., fgn. mags. Home and office: 3019 Thomasville Rd Tallahassee FL 32312

SHABAIK, ALY HOSSNI, educator; b. Cairo, Egypt, Mar. 1, 1937; s. Abd Elkader and Aziza S.; came to U.S., 1961, naturalized, 1971; M.S., Renesselaer Poly. Inst., 1962; Ph.D., U. Calif., Berkeley, 1966; m. Virginia F. Secor, Dec. 23, 1967; children—Nadia, Safi. Asst. research engr. U. Calif., Berkeley, 1966-68; asst. prof. engring. UCLA, 1968-72, asso. prof., 1972-77, prof., 1977—; cons. to industry. Ford Motor Co. fellow, 1973-74. Mem. ASME, Soc. Mfg. Engrs. (sr.), Am. Soc. Metals, Am. Soc. Engring. Edn. (Disting. Teaching award 1971). Republican. Moslem. Contbr. articles in field to profl. jours. Home: 4133 Sunnyslope Ave Sherman Oaks CA 91423 Office: 6531 Boetler Hall Engring U Calif Los Angeles CA 90024

SHABAT, OSCAR E., coll. chancellor; b. 1913; M.A. in Sociology with honors, U. Chgo.; m. Ethel Kuzin; 1 son, Michael. With Chgo. pub. sch. system, 1937-66, dir. div. human relations, 1960-62, dean Wright Jr. Coll., 1962-65, exec. dean jr. coll. div. 1965-66, chancellor City Colls. Chgo., 1966—. Co-chmn. edn. sub-com. Chgo. Com. on Urban Opportunity; mem. Com. on Cooperation Higher Edn.; mem. exec. com. Nat. League for Experimentation in Community Jr. Coll. Bd. dirs. Welfare Council Chgo.; pres. Chgo. Met. Higher Edn. Council, 1977—. Author: Society and Man, Introduction to the Social Sciences. Mem. adv. bd. editors Am. School and Univ. Address: City Colls Chicago 180 N Michigan Ave Chicago IL 60601*

SHACKELFORD, BARTON WARREN, utility exec.; b. San Francisco, Oct. 12, 1920; s. Frank Harris and Amelia Louise (Schilling) S.; B.S. in Civil Engring., U. Calif., Berkeley, 1941; m. Charlaine Mae Livingston, July 24, 1949; children—Frank, Joan, Linda, Ann. Jr. engr. Todd-Calif. Shipbldg. Corp., 1941-44; with Pacific Gas & Electric Co., 1946—, sr. v.p., then exec. v.p., San Francisco, 1976-79, pres., chief operating officer, 1979—, also dir. Address: 77 Beale St San Francisco CA 94106

SHACKELFORD, DONALD BRUCE, financial exec., mgmt. cons.; b. Pitts., June 10, 1932; s. William Allen and Ruth Elizabeth (Mosher) S.; B.A., Denison U., 1954; M.B.A. with high distinction, Harvard U., 1959; m. Thekla Alice Reese, Apr. 10, 1956; children—Lee Elizabeth, Amy Rhys, Alison Grace. Asso., McKinsey & Co., Chgo., 1959-64; dir. McLagan & Co., Chgo., 1965—; chmn. First Nat. Bank, Cambridge, Ohio, 1972-78, Charter Franklin Inc., Columbus, Ohio, 1976—, State Savs. Co., Columbus, Ohio, 1972—; dir. Jeffrey Co., Limited Stores Inc., Progressive Corp. Trustee Denison U., Granville, Ohio, Mary Holmes Coll., West Point, Miss. Served to 1st lt. USAF, 1954-57. Mem. Mid-Ohio League Savs. Assn. (pres. 1976), Presbyn. Clubs: Union League (Chgo.); University (N.Y.C.); Columbus, Columbus Athletic; Rocky Fork Hunt and Country (Gahanna, Ohio). Address: 20 E Broad St Columbus OH 43215

SHAD, JOHN SIGSBEE REES, investment banker; b. Brigham City, Utah, June 27, 1923; s. John Sigsbee and Lillian (Rees) S.; B.S. cum laude, U. So. Cal., 1947; M.B.A., Harvard, 1949, LL.B., N.Y. U., 1959; m. Patricia Pratt, July 27, 1952; children—Leslie Anne, Rees Edward. Security analyst, account exec., investment banker, 1949-62; with E.F. Hutton Group Inc. and E.F. Hutton & Co., Inc., 1963—, vice chmn. bd., chmn. fin., investment, acquisition, underwriting coms., dir., mem. exec. com., also dir.; mem. fin. adv. panel Nat. R.R. Passenger Corp. (AMTRACK), 1970-75; dir. A-T-O, Inc., Scudder Duo-West, Inc., Sheller-Globe Corp., Katy Industries, Inc., Kaufman & Broad, Inc., Triangle-Pacific Corp., Scudder Duo-Vest Exchange Fund, Electro Audio Dynamics, Pratt-Shad Found., also others; faculty, N.Y. U. Grad. Sch. Bus. Adminstrn., 1961; speaker, writer corp. fin., mergers. Mem. N.Y. Stock Exchange. Served to lt. (j.g.) USNR, 1943-46. Recipient Investment Banker of Year award E. F. Hutton Group, 1972. Mem. Investment Assn. N.Y., Navy League, Beta Gamma Sigma, Phi Kappa Phi, Alpha Kappa Psi. Clubs: University, Wall Street, Harvard Business School, Bond, Economic, India House (N.Y.C.); Stockbridge Country. Author: Financial Realties of Mergers; Stock Reacquisition Programs; Why and How More European Companies Are Acquiring U.S. Companies; Critical Considerations in Going Public. Home: 535 Park Ave New York NY 10021 Office: 1 Battery Park Plaza New York NY 10004

SHADBOLT, DOUGLAS, educator; b. Victoria, B.C., Can., Apr. 18, 1925; s. Edmund and Alice Mary Maude (Healy) S.; B.Arch., U. Oreg., 1957; D.Eng. (hon.), N.S. Tech. Coll., 1969; m. Sidney Osborne Craig, June 29, 1960; stepchildren—James Osborne Craig, Catherine Shand Craig. Archtl. asst., Montreal, Ottawa, Vancouver, Victoria, Seattle and Boston, 1942-58; lectr. U. Oreg., 1955-57; asst. prof. McGill U., 1958-60, asso. prof., 1960-61; prof., dir. Sch. Architecture, N.S. Tech. Coll., 1961-68; prof., dir. Sch. Architecture, Carleton U., Ottawa, Ont., 1968-77, dir. Archtl. Research Group, 1977—; pvt. practice cons. architect, 1961—. Fellow Royal Archtl. Inst. Can.; mem. Ont. Assn. Architects. Office: Sch Architecture Carleton U Ottawa ON K1S 5B6 Canada

SHADDUCK, LOUISE, assn. exec.; b. nr. Coeur d'Alene, Idaho; d. Lester Carson and Mary Jeannette (Furgason) Shadduck; grad. high sch.; J.D. (hon.), U. Idaho, 1969. Reporter, women's editor, columnist Coeur d'Alene Press, 1936-47; Idaho corr. Spokesman-Rev., Spokane, Wash., 1942-47; asst. to lt. gov. Idaho, 1947-48, adminstrv. asst. to gov., 1949-50; exec. sec. to U.S. senator from Idaho, 1950-56; exec. sec. Idaho Dept. Commerce and Devel., Boise, 1958-68; adminstrv. asst. to Idaho congressman, Washington, 1969-74; exec. dir. Idaho Forest Industry Council, Coeur d'Alene, 1974—; exec. dir. North Idaho Forestry Assn., So. Idaho Forestry Assn.; mem. Am. Forest Inst./Forest Industry Council; mem. Idaho Hwy Users Conf., Idaho Pub. Lands Resource Council, Intermountain Logging Conf. Idaho liaison ofcl. U.S. Travel Service, 1964-69; mem. adv. council Yellowstone Nat. Park, 1958-68; mem. Rocky Mountain Govs.' Com. on Sci. and Tech., Assn. State Planning and Devel. Agys., Tri-State Council for Yellowstone Nat. Park; nat. adv. com. to U.S. commr. gen. Expo 67, Montreal; dir. No. State Bank; rep. Idaho forest products industry on U.S. Senate Fgn. Relations Com. Trade Del. to China, 1979. Idaho chmn. drive Am. Heart Assn., 1975-78; bd. dirs. Western Council for Travel Research, Idaho Heritage, 1977—; mem. Idaho Med. Bd. Profl. Discipline, 1977—; mem. adv. com. North Idaho Coll., 1975-78; mem. Idaho Gov.'s Com. on Rail Transp., Idaho Wildlife Tomorrow Com.; mem. Idaho Internat. Women's Year Commn.; del. Idaho and Nat. Internat. Women's Year Conf., 1977. Recipient Monongahela Forestry Leadership award, 1976; Silver Anvil award Pub. Relations Soc. Am., 1976. Hon. life mem. Idaho Press Assn., Quill and Scroll; mem. Western Forestry and Conservation Assn., Nat. Forest Products Assn., Idaho Assn. Commerce and Industry, Idaho Ad Club, Bus. and Profl. Women's Club, Altrusa, Nat. Assn. Travel Orgns. (Idaho v.p. 1960-68), Idaho (pres.), Nat. (Western regional dir., 1st v.p. nat. orgn. 1969-71) press woman, Nat. Fedn. Press Women (pres. 1971-73), Am. Newspaper Women, Women in Communications, Am. Indsl. Devel. Council. Club: U. Idaho Regents (chmn. 1974-75). Home: Mica Bay Marine Mail Route Coeur d'Alene ID 83814 Office: PO Box 657 Coeur d'Alene ID 83814

SHADDY, RAYMOND WILLIAM, univ. ofcl.; b. Omaha, Aug. 13, 1923; s. Gabriel A. and Mary (Zaroor) S.; D.D.S., Creighton U., 1953; m. Marjorie Rieth, June 20, 1949; children—Carol, Mary Beth, Martha, Robert, Scott, James, John, Marguerite. Pvt. practice dentistry, Omaha, 1956—; faculty Creighton U. Sch. Dentistry, Omaha, 1956—, asso. prof., chmn. dept. operative dentistry, 1956-61, dean, 1962-71, asso. v.p. for health sci. planning, 1971-77, dir. Creighton Inst. Internat. Programs, 1977—. Fellow Am. Coll. Dentists; mem. Internat. Coll. Dentists, Am. Acad. Gold Foil Operators, Am. Dental Assn., Woodbury Study Club, Delta Sigma Delta, Omicron Kappa Upsilon, Alpha Sigma Nu. Home: 5107 Cass St Omaha NE 68132

SHADEK, EDWARD THOMAS, broadcasting exec.; b. Teaneck, N.J., Aug. 2, 1929; s. Arthur Joseph and Wilhelmina Elizabeth (Uhlenbusch) S.; B.E., Yale U., 1951; M.B.A., U. Pa., 1953; m. Beverly Ann Bower, Apr. 3, 1954; children—Suzanne, Edward Thomas, Leigh. Dist. mgr. Air Products & Chems., Inc., Allentown, Pa., 1959-64; indsl. cons., Madison, Conn., 1964-68; gen. mgr. Internat. Controls Corp., Fairfield, N.J., 1968-70; pres. Southwestern Broadcasters Inc., San Diego, 1970—, Radio Alamo, Inc., 1977—. Served with AUS, 1955-56. Club: Madison Beach (Conn.). Home: 1975 Calle Madrigal San Diego CA 92037 Office: 5252 Balboa Ave San Diego CA 92117

SHAEFER, RICHARD FRANCIS, ret. air force officer; b. Lansing, Mich., Dec. 30, 1919; s. Francis Marion and Margaret Grace (Tubbs) S.; B.S., U. N.M., 1940; B.S., U.S. Mil. Acad., 1943; postgrad. U.K. Joint Services Staff Coll., 1953, U.S. Nat. War Coll., Ft. McNair, 1962, George Washington U., 1963; m. Caroline Longstreet Cavett, July 3, 1946; children—Richard Longstreet, Louisa Cavett. Commd. 2d lt. USAAF, 1943, advanced through grades to lt. gen. USAF, 1974; assigned Europe, 1944-45; instr. U.S. Mil. Acad., 1946-49; duty with Hdqrs. USAF, with operation units in Europe, with RAND Corp., with Joint Chiefs of Staff and with U.S. delegation to NATO, 1949-63;

dir. of plans NATO mil. com., 1963-65; vice comdr. U.S. 3d Air Force, Eng., 1965-67; chief of staff USAF Europe, 1967-68; asst. chief of staff for plans U.S. Mil. Command Vietnam, 1968-70; dep. dir. for plans and policy, joint staff Joint Chiefs of Staff, Washington, 1970-71; asst. chief staff for operations SHAPE, 1971-74; dep. chmn. mil. com. NATO, 1974-75; ret., 1975. Deacon, Presbyterian Ch. Decorated D.S.M. with oak leaf cluster, Legion of Merit with oak leaf cluster, D.F.C., Bronze Star, Air medal with 9 oak leaf clusters, Purple Heart; French Croix de Guerre with silver star; Korean Chung-Mu; Vietnam Nat. Order and Distinguished Service Order; Thailand Royal Order of White Elephant. Mem. Sigma Tau. Home: 6424 Crosswoods Dr Falls Church VA 22044. *In this era of increasing emphasis on social services, we must never forget that the greatest service a nation can provide its people is security and freedom. I have been blessed with a series of unique opportunities to serve this cause for our nation and the free world.*

SHAEFFER, CHARLES WAYNE, investment counselor; b. Bridgeton, Pa., Dec. 12, 1910; s. Bartram Augustus and Carolyn I. (Morton) S.; B.A., Pa. State U., 1933; M.B.A., Harvard, 1935; LL.D., Loyola Coll., 1974; m. Ruth S. Smyser, Oct. 2, 1937; children—Charles Wayne, Ann B. (Mrs. Clark F. MacKenzie), Julia P. Investment counselor Mackubin Legg & Co., Balt., 1935-37; with T. Rowe Price Assos., Inc. (formerly T. Rowe Price & Assos., Inc.), Balt., 1938—, chmn. bd., 1966-76, pres., 1963-74, cons., 1976—; pres. T. Rowe Price Growth Stock Fund, Inc., 1968-74, chmn. bd., 1974-76; chmn. bd. Rowe Price New Income Fund, 1973—; dir. Rowe Price New Horizons Fund, Inc., 1966—, Rowe Price New Era Fund, Inc., Rowe Price Prime Res. Fund; trustee Monumental Properties Trust; lectr. investment mgmt. Balt. Coll. Commerce, 1938-70, Johns Hopkins, 1960-72. Trustee Pa. State U., Franklin Sq. Hosp.; bd. mgrs. Bryn Mawr Sch., U. Balt.; Bd. dirs. Md. chpt. Nature Conservancy. Recipient Distinguished Alumni award Pa. State U. Coll. Bus. Adminstrn., 1971-72. Mem. Investment Counsel Assn. Am. (pres. 1970-73, gov. 1965—), No-Load Mut. Fund Assn. (pres. 1972-75), Investment Co. Inst. (gov. 1968—, chmn. 1975-76), Alpha Sigma Phi, Pi Gamma Mu, Delta Sigma Pi. Episcopalian. Clubs: Maryland, L'Hirodelle, Merchants, Center, Elkridge (Balt.); Green Spring Valley Hunt (Garrison, Md.); Laurel Fish and Game Assn., Lafayette (York, Pa.); Seaview Country (Absecon, N.J.); Farmington Country (Charlottesville, Va.), Home: 913 1/2 Poplar Hill Rd Baltimore MD 21210 Office: 100 E Pratt St Baltimore MD 21202

SHAFER, B. LYLE, bus. equipment co. exec.; b. Gettysburg, Ohio, Jan. 14, 1924; s. Raymond and Olive Augusta (Skinner) S.; A.B., Harvard U., 1948, postgrad. Sch. Bus. Adminstrn., 1955; J.D., Ohio State U., 1951; m. Helen Straker, June 6, 1953; children—Amy Louise, Thomas Lyle, Elizabeth Ann. Admitted to Ohio bar, 1952; mem. legal dept. NCR Corp., Dayton, Ohio, 1952-65, v.p. personnel resources, 1965—; dir. Home Savs. and Loan Assn., Dayton, Danis Industries Corp., Dayton. Councilman, Kettering, Ohio, 1959-62, mem. park bd., 1959; trustee Aviation Hall of Fame, 1971-75; bd. dirs. Miami Valley Conservation Dist., 1979—; mem. bd. visitors U. Dayton Law Sch. Served with USAAF, 1942-45. Mem. Am., Ohio, Dayton bar assns. Home: 4444 Southern Blvd Kettering OH 45429 Office: NCR World Hdqrs Patterson Blvd Dayton OH 45479

SHAFER, ELDON EUGENE, diversified industry exec.; b. Dayton, Ohio, Apr. 11, 1933; s. George Eldon and Lucinda May (Fertick) S.; B.S., Miami U., Oxford, Ohio, 1957; m. Ruthlynne Marshall, Apr. 26, 1958 (div. 1972); children—Susan, Betsy, Jodi; m. 2d, Betty Jo Lester Sheehy, Nov. 13, 1978; stepchildren—John, Peter and Barbary Sheehy. With Assos. Investment Co., South Bend, Ind., 1957-60; accountant Studebaker Corp., South Bend, 1960-62, adminstr. of leases, contracts and real estate, 1962-68; asst. treas. Studebaker-Worthington, Inc., N.Y.C., 1968-73, treas., asst. sec., 1973—. Served with U.S. Army, 1954-56; ETO. Mem. Delta Upsilon. Home: 150 Parsonage Hill Rd Short Hills NJ 07078 Office: One Dag Hammarskjold Plaza New York NY 10017

SHAFER, EVERETT EARL, office equipment co. exec.; b. Oelwein, Iowa, Apr. 19, 1925; s. Paul Emerson and Maude Blanche (Lovell) S.; B.S., Iowa State U., 1948; J.D., U. Iowa, 1951; M.B.A., U. Chgo., 1960; m. Kathryn Elaine Rose, Sept. 4, 1949. Admitted to Iowa bar, 1951, Ill. bar, 1952; mem. legal staff Motorola, Inc., Chgo., 1951-54, fin. adminstr. Motorola Fin. Corp., Chgo., 1954-60, asst. treas., credit mgr. Motorola Consumer Products, Inc., Chgo., 1960-68; asso. prof. bus. adminstrn. Buena Vista Coll., Storm Lake, Iowa, 1968-72, chmn. faculty senate, 1970-71; treas. Admiral Corp., Chgo., 1972-74; asst. treas. Addressograph Multigraph Corp., Cleve., 1975-76; pres., treas. Addressograph Multigraph Finance Corp., 1976—. Served with USAAF, 1943-45. Decorated D.F.C., Air medal; recipient Outstanding Tchr. award Buena Vista Coll., 1972. Methodist. Home: 36W934 Middlecreek Ln St Charles IL 60174 Office: 244 E West Ct Palatine IL 60067

SHAFER, GUY CARLTON, corp. exec.; b. Morgantown, W. Va., Dec. 9, 1918; s. Guy Carlton and Kathryn (Morris) S.; B.S. in Mech. Engring., W. Va. U., 1946; m. Anne Thompson, May 26, 1951; children—Joan Morris, Lisa Knight, Marc Thompson. Engr. Gen. Electric Co., Lynn, Mass., 1946-53, gen. mgr., 1953-59; gen. mgr. New Eng. Aircraft Products Co., Farmington, Conn., 1959-62; v.p. planning Chandler Evans, Inc., aircraft accessories, West Hartford, Conn., 1962, exec. v.p., 1962-63, pres., 1963-69; group v.p. Colt Industries, Inc., 1969—. Active A.R.C. Served from 2nd lt. to maj., AUS, 1941-46. Mem. Am. Soc. Me. E., Am. Helicopter Soc., Soc. Automotive Engrs., Am. Ordnance Assn., Am. Inst. Aeros. and Astronautics, Newcomen Soc., Conn. C. of C. Clubs: Hartford, Hartford Golf. Home: 71 Westerly Terr Hartford CT 06105 Office: Charter Oak Blvd West Hartford CT 06101

SHAFER, JOSEPH ERNEST, economist; b. Bluffton, Ind., Apr. 25, 1903; s. Otis Ernest and Ida March (Taylor) S.; A.B., DePauw U., 1925; M.A., U. Wis., 1929, Ph.D., 1932; m. Emily Cornell Marine, June 10, 1926; children—Sue Elizabeth (Mrs. Harlow G. Farmer, Jr.), Thayer Cornell. Spl. study labor problems, working incognito as factory laborer, 1925-26; asst. instr. econs. U. Wis., 1929-32; asso. prof. econs., head dept., coll. mines br. U. Tex., 1932-35; asso. prof. econs. Bowling Green State U., 1935-46; economist dist. office OPA, 1943-44, restaurant price br., Washington, 1944-46; prof. econs. U. N.H., 1946-60, chmn. dept., 1946-49; prof. econs., bus. adminstrn. Alaska Meth. U., 1960-70, dir. summer sessions, 1961-65, dean Coll. Bus. Adminstrn. and Econs., 1965-70. Vis. research prof. econs. N.Y. U. Grad. Sch. Bus. Adminstrn., summer 1956; research new interpretation mercantilism, Eng., 1953-54. Trustee Alaska Mut. Savs. Bank, 1963-73. Research grantee Alfred P. Sloan Found., 1953, W. Alton Jones Found., 1959. Mem. AAUP, Am., Western econs. assns., Pi Gamma Mu. Methodist. Mason, Rotarian. Author: Explanation of the Business Cycle, 1928; The Trend of Non-Monetary Consumption of Gold, 1932; Analysis of the Business System, 1956; Alaska's Economy in Case of a National Economic Pause, 1968; Chrematistics-Economics, 1969; Why I Alone Among Economists Understand the Basic Trouble We Suffer, 1978. Home: 12 Davis Ave Durham NH 03824 also 4944 Cass St Apt 509 San Diego CA 92109

SHAFER, RAYMOND PHILIP, lawyer, business exec.; b. New Castle, Pa., Mar. 5, 1917; s. David Philip and Mina Belle (Miller) S.; A.B. cum laude, Allegheny Coll., 1938, LL.D., 1963; LL.B., Yale, 1941; numerous hon. degrees; m. Jane Harris Davies, July 5, 1941; children—Diane Elizabeth, Raymond Philip, Jane Ellen. Admitted to N.Y., Pa. bars; asso. firm Winthrop, Stimson, Putnam & Roberts, N.Y.C.; practice law, Meadville, Pa., 1945-63; counsel Shafer, Dornhaffer, Swick and Bailey; dist. atty. Crawford County, 1948-56; mem. Pa. Senate from 50th Dist., 1959-63; lt. gov. Pa., 1963-67; gov. Commonwealth Pa., 1967-71; vis. prof. U. Pa., 1973—; counselor to v.p. of U.S., 1975-77; partner Coopers & Lybrand, 1977—; chmn. Cultural Resources, Inc. Chmn., Nat. Commn. on Marijuana and Drug Abuse; active charitable, community drives. Chmn. bd. trustees Allegheny Coll.; trustee Cleve. Clinic Found., Freedoms Found. Served with USNR, 1942-45; PTO. Recipient Gold Medal award Soc. Family of Man, 1972, numerous humanitarian and civic awards. Mem. Am., Pa., Crawford County (pres. 1961-63) bar assns., Phi Beta Kappa, Phi Kappa Psi. Republican. Mason (33 deg.). Home: 485 Chestnut St Meadville PA 16335 Office: Coopers & Lybrand 1800 M St NW Washington DC 20036. *One makes a living by what one gets. One makes a life by what one gives.*

SHAFER, STEPHEN JOHN, editor; b. N.Y.C., June 2, 1932; s. Chester W. and Esther E. (Orton) S.; B.A., Northwestern U., 1954; postgrad. in anthropology U. Mich., 1954-55; m. Patricia Wiley, July 12, 1960; children—Eric, Edward, Barton. Mem. staff Domestic Engring. and De Jour. Mags., Chgo., 1960—, editor-in-chief, 1970—. Served with USAF, 1955-57. Home: 110 N York Rd Elmhurst IL 60126 Office: 110 N York Rd Elmhurst IL 60126

SHAFER, STEWART ADAIR, ret. judge; b. Montrose, Colo., Aug. 24, 1911; s. Sylvester and Mattie (Kelly) S.; student U. Colo., 1929-31, U. Denver, 1931-33; LL.B., Westminster Law Sch., Denver, 1936; m. Helen Sickman, Apr. 14, 1937; children—Stewart Adair, Lawrence Harrah, Jean Ellen, Robert Kelly. Admitted to Colo. bar, 1936, since practiced in Denver; judge Probate Ct. City and County Denver, 1974-77, ret., 1977. Atty. ordnance dept. U.S. Army, 1942-44, chief legal div. small arms ammunition br., 1945. Chmn., Denver County Ct. Jud. Commn., 1967; mem. Denver Pub. Defenders Commn., 1967. Mem. Am., Colo. (bd. govs. 1964-67), Denver (pres. 1966-67) bar assns., Sigma Phi Epsilon. Mason (33 deg., past grand master Colo.). Club: Denver Athletic. Home: 795 S Alton Way Denver CO 80231

SHAFER, W. O., lawyer; b. nr. Sweetwater, Tex., July 6, 1917; s. William Oscar and Nancy (Brimberry) S.; student Ranger Jr. Coll., 1934-36; J.D., Cumberland U., 1937; m. Margaret Frances Crutsinger, Nov. 12, 1937. Admitted to Tex. bar, 1939, since practiced in Odessa; justice peace, 1941-44; county atty. Ector County, 1945-50; dist. atty. 70th Jud. Dist. Tex., 1951-52; pvt. practice, 1953—; pres. Shafer, Gilliland, Davis, McCollum & Ashley, Inc.; chmn. bd. First Savs. & Loan Assn., Odessa; dir. First Nat. Bank. Chmn. Nat. Conf. Bar President's, 1970-71; Tex. commr. Nat. Conf. on Uniform State Laws, 1967-70. Named Odessa's Outstanding Citizen, Am. Bus. Clubs, 1967; recipient Leadership award W. Tex. C. of C., 1967. Fellow Am., Tex. bar founds., Internat. Acad. Trial Lawyers (dir. 1969-72), Am. Coll. Trial Lawyers; mem. Fedn. Ins. Counsel, Am. (past Tex. ho. dels.), Tex. (dir. 1960-63, chmn. bd. 1962-63, v.p. 1964-65, pres. 1966-67), Ector County bar assns., Tex. Assn. Def. Counsel (pres. 1968-69), Odessa C. of C. (past dir., Distinguished Service award). Democrat. Mem. Ch. of Christ. Mason (Shriner). Home: 2500 Bainbridge Odessa TX 79763 Office: 1st Nat Bank Bldg PO Box 1552 Odessa TX 79760

SHAFER, WILLIAM GENE, educator, pathologist; b. Toledo, Nov. 15, 1923; s. Earl Arthur and Alice May (Misener) S.; B.S., U. Toledo, 1947; D.D.S., Ohio State U., 1947; M.S., U. Rochester, 1949; m. Ruth Eleanor Hertweck, Aug. 12, 1943. Eastman fellow dentistry U. Rochester, 1947-48, USPHS post doctorate research, research fellow, 1948-50; instr. oral pathology Ind. U. Sch. Dentistry, Indpls. 1950-53, asst. prof., 1953-56, asso. prof., chmn. dept. oral pathology, 1956-59, prof., chmn. dept., 1959—, Distinguished prof., 1971—. Cons. oral pathology VA, 1952—, Surgeon Gen., USAF, 1960—. Diplomate Am. Bd. Oral Pathology (past sec. treas.). Fellow Am. Acad. Oral Pathology (past pres.); mem. A.A.A.S., Internat. Assn. Dental Research, Am. Dental Assn., N.Y. Acad. Scis., Internat. Acad. Pathology, Sigma Xi. Author: (with M.K. Hine, B.M. Levy) Texbook of Oral Pathology, 1958. Contbr. articles to profl. jours. Home: 3306 Kenilworth Dr Indianapolis IN 46208

SHAFFER, CHARLES ELWOOD, wholesale co. exec.; b. Xenia, Ohio, June 6, 1913; s. Charles E. and Mary (Liddle) S.; B.S., Miami U., Oxford, Ohio, 1936; m. Mary Ruth Biasi, Aug. 28, 1943; children—Nancy (Mrs. Walter Hughs), Linda (Mrs. Mark Cheadle), Charles S. Exec. v.p. Eavey Co., wholesale food, Xenia, 1938-60; div. mgr. Super Valu Stores, Xenia, 1960-69; pres. Super Food Services, Inc., Dayton, Ohio, 1969—; dir. Peoples Savs. & Loan, Xenia; v.p., dir. Emsko, Inc.; pres., dir. Tevico, Xenia. Mem. Xenia Sch. Bd., 1961-69, pres., 1968. Served with AUS, 1942-46. Decorated Legion of Merit. Club: Greene Country. Home: 870 Meadow Lane Xenia OH 45385 Office: 3185 Elbee Rd Dayton OH 45439*

SHAFFER, CHARLES NORMAN, lawyer; b. N.Y.C., June 8, 1932; s. Charles Norman and Lucy (White) S.; A.B., Fordham U., 1954, LL.B., 1957; m. Diana Dolan, Aug. 20, 1955; children—Monica, Leslie, Charles Norman III, Camille. Admitted to N.Y. bar, 1958, U.S. Tax Ct. bar, 1966, U.S. Supreme Ct. bar, 1967, Md. bar, 1967; asst. U.S. atty. so. dist. N.Y., 1959-61; atty. Dept. Justice, 1960-66; spl. asst. to atty. gen., 1964-66; practice law, Rockville, Md., 1966—, now mem. firm Shaffer and Davis, Rockville. Mem. staff Pres.'s Commn. Assassination of Pres. Kennedy, 1963-64. Mem. Montgomery County (Md.) Crime Commn., 1968-70. Mem. Montgomery County (chmn. com. continuing legal edn. 1970; mem. exec. com. 1971-72, Md. bar assns. Home: 7 Hartman Ct Potomac MD 20854 Office: 10 S Adams St Rockville MD 20850

SHAFFER, GUY HENRY BASKERVILLE, naval officer; b. Jersey City, May 1, 1928; s. Carl Harry and Dorothy (Baskerville) S.; student Rensselaer Poly. Inst., 1946-47; B.S., U. S. Naval Acad., 1951; postgrad. Navy Nuclear Power Sch., 1956; m. Marie Meigs, June 2, 1951; children—Douglas Meigs, Craig Baskerville, Cayley Edmonds. Commd. ensign U.S. Navy, 1951, advanced through grades to rear adm., 1976; served on U.S.S. Helena, 1951-52, U.S.S. Sea Cat, Key West, Fla., 1953-56; mem. commissioning crew U.S.S. Skate, 1957-59, including patrols under Arctic ice to North Pole; engring. officer U.S.S. Scorpion, Groton, Conn., 1959-61; dir. fleet ballistic missile nuclear propulsion maintenance tng. div. Submarine Sch., New London, Conn., 1961-62; exec. officer Gold crew U.S.S. Theodore Roosevelt, 1962-64; comdg. officer Greenling Pre-commissioning Unit, Quincy, Mass., 1965-67, comdg. officer Greenling, 1967-69; ops. officer Staff of Comr. Submarine Devel. Group 2, 1969-70, chief staff officer, 1970-71; comdr. Submarine Devel. Group 2, 1972-74; assigned to Staff of Dept. Chief Naval Ops., Washington, 1971-72; dep. dir. Strategic Systems Project Office, Dept. Navy, Washington, 1974-76; dep. comdr. for planning, programming and resources mgmt. Naval Electronic Systems Command, Washington, 1976-77, project mgr. Command Control and Communications Project, Arlington, Va., 1977—; participant communications workshops. Decorated Legion of Merit with 2 gold stars, Meritorious Service medal with gold star, Navy Unit Commendation with 2 gold stars. Mem. U.S. Naval Inst., Armed Forces Communications and Electronics Assn., U.S. Yacht Racing Union, U.S. Navy Sailing Assn. Club: Off Soundings. Author classified manuals and papers on submarine tactics and operational performance. Office: Nat Center #1 Command Control and Communications Project NAVELECSYSCOM Navy Dept Washington DC 20360

SHAFFER, JAMES GRANT, med. educator; b. Washington, Kans., Jan. 17, 1913; s. Bowen Ross and Myrtle Katherine (Worley) S.; B.S., Manchester Coll., 1935, D.Sc., 1973; D.Sc., Johns Hopkins U., 1940; m. Esther Elizabeth Willard, Sept. 3, 1939; children—Carol (Mrs. Wesley Stieg), Susan (Mrs. John Willard), Janet (Mrs. Gregory Harsha), Nancy (Mrs. James Lanier). Tchr., Jackson Twp. High Sch., Flint, Ind., 1935-36, Jefferson Twp. High Sch., Ossian, Ind., 1936-37; student instr. immunology and filterable viruses Johns Hopkins U., Balt., 1937-40, instr., 1940-42; med. research biologist Am. Cyanamid Co., Stamford, Conn., 1942-43; asst. prof. preventive medicine Vanderbilt U., Nashville, 1946-48, vis. prof. bacteriology, 1947-48; asso. prof. bacteriology and virology U. Louisville, 1948-52; dir. labs. Louisville Children's Hosp., 1948-50, microbiologist, 1950-52; prof., chmn. dept. microbiology and pub. health Chgo. Med. Sch., 1952-60, asso. dean, prof. microbiology, 1967-74; dir. microbiology and hosp. epidemiology Luth. Gen. Hosp., Park Ridge, Ill., 1960-67; cons. hosp. epidemiology 1967-74; dir. edn1. and profl. programs Mt. Sinai Hosp. Med. Center of Chgo., 1974—; prof. microbiology Rush U., Chgo., 1975—, dir. undergrad. med. edn., 1975—; professorial lectr. microbiology U. Chgo., 1965-68; cons. VA Hosp., Hines, Ill., 1972—; coordinator devel. of projected urban-oriented med. sch. Mt. Sinai Hosp. Med. Center and Roosevelt U., 1974—. Pres. PTA Lincoln Sch., Elmhurst, Ill., 1956-57. Mem. sch. bd. dist. 46 Elmhurst Elementary Sch., 1958-67. Served to maj. AUS, 1943-46. Recipient Outstanding Alumni award Manchester Coll., 1965, award of merit Chgo Tech. Socs. Council, 1969. Diplomate Am. Bd. Microbiology. Fellow Am. Pub. Health Assn. (chmn. lab. sect. 1970-71, governing council 1971-76, mem. action bd.), Am. Inst. Chemists, Am. Acad. Microbiology, Inst. Medicine Chgo.; mem. Am. Soc. Microbiology, AAAS, Am. Soc. Tropical Medicine and Hygiene, Soc. Ill. Bacteriologists, Ill. Pub. Health Assn., Assn. Tchrs. Preventive Medicine, Royal Soc. Health, Assn. Am. Med. Colls. (chmn. com. fin. problems of med. students 1971-73), Alumni Assn. Manchester Coll. (pres. 1962-63), Sigma Xi, Alpha Omega Alpha, Delta Omega. Author: Amebiasis: A Biomedical Problem, 1965. Contbr. to publs. in field. Home: 605 Swain Ave Elmhurst IL 60126 Office: 15th St and California Ave Chicago IL 60608. *There is no greater success than to have the fruits of one's research being applied and expanded and the students one has helped to learn and grow, succeeding in their chosen profession. To see the family one has raised gaining in maturity, raising families and accomplishing their goals in professions or in domestic pursuits, is certainly the final fulfillment.*

SHAFFER, JAMES TRAVIS, gas co. exec.; b. Athens, La., Dec. 22, 1930; s. George Henry and Dorothy Velma (Bridges) S.; B.S., La. Tech. U., 1951; postgrad. La. State U.; m. Jean Ruffin, Feb. 5, 1955; children—Cynthia, Cheryl, James. With Ark.-La. Gas Co., Shreveport, 1954—, asst. sec., asst. treas., 1969-74, sec., asst. treas., 1974—. Past bd. dirs. Shreveport Assn. Blind, Shreveport YMCA, Shreveport Y's Men Club, Shreveport Jr. C. of C.; mem. adminstrv. bd. Neel Methodist Ch., Shreveport. Served with USAF, 1952-54. Mem. Am. Soc. Corporate Secs., Omicron Delta Kappa. Club: Riverside Swim and Tennis (past dir.). Home: 504 Huron St Shreveport LA 71106 Office: 525 Milam St Shreveport LA 71151

SHAFFER, JEROME ARTHUR, educator; b. Bklyn., Apr. 2, 1929; s. Joseph and Beatrice (Leibowitz) S.; B.A., Cornell U., 1950; Ph.D. (Woodrow Wilson fellow), Princeton U., 1952; m. Olivia Anne Connery, Sept. 3, 1960; children—Diana, David. Prof. philosophy Swarthmore (Pa.) Coll., 1955-67; prof. philosophy U. Conn., Storrs, 1965—, head dept., 1976—; exec. sec. Council Philos. Studies, 1965-72. Served with AUS, 1953-55. Fulbright fellow, 1952-53; fellow Center for Advanced Study Behavioral Scis., 1963-64; Nat. Endowment for Humanities sr. fellow, 1973-74. Mem. Am. Philos. Assn., Phi Beta Kappa, Phi Kappa Phi. Author: The Philosophy of Mind, 1968; Violence, 1970; Reality, Knowledge and Value, 1971; contbr. articles to profl. jours. Home: 312 Hanks Hill Rd Storrs CT 06268 Office: U Conn Storrs CT 06268

SHAFFER, JOHN HIXON, transp. co. exec.; b. Everett, Pa., Feb. 25, 1919; s. Samuel C. and Julia Ann (Hixon) S.; student U.S. Mil. Acad., 1943; B.S., Air Force Inst. Tech., 1945; M.S., Columbia, 1946; m. Joan Van Vleck, Jan. 20, 1943; children—Susan, Jacqueline, John Hixon. Commd. 2d lt. USAF, 1943, advanced through grades to lt. col., 1952, pilot, 1942-45, sr. pilot, 1949-54, resigned, 1954; gen. prodn. mgr., asst. plant mgr. Mercury div. Ford Co., 1955-57; with TRW, Inc., Cleve., 1957-68, v.p. customer requirements, 1960-68; adminstr. FAA, Washington, 1969-73; pres. Pioneer Van Line; dir. Beech Aircraft, TRE Corp. Mem. Econ. Commn. for Europe, 1966. Decorated Air medal with 9 oak leaf clusters. Recipient DOT Exceptional Service award, 1973, FAA Distinguished Service award, 1972; Wright Bros. Meml. trophy, 1972; Aero Club Achievement award, 1971 NAC Man of Yr. in aviation, 1971. Clubs: Burning Tree (Bethesda, Md.); Nat. Aviation (Washington); Columbia Country (Chevy Chase, Md.); Bay Hills Country (Orlando, Fla.); Wings (N.Y.C.); Royal and Ancient Golf (St. Andrews, Scotland). Home: 10001 Logan Dr Potomac MD 20854 Office: 2801 52d Ave Bldg A Hyattsville MD 20781

SHAFFER, MARY L., librarian; b. St. Clarisville, Ohio, Oct. 9, 1923; d. George and Alice (Demitrakis) Litis; B.S., W.Va. U., 1945; M.S., Pa. State U., 1948; M.S., Catholic U. Am., 1958; m. Wayne Crider Shaffer, Feb. 9, 1947; children—George David, Phillip Lloyd. Librarian, Arlington (Va.) County Schs., 1957-61; librarian Post Library, Ft. Belvoir, Va., 1962-64; hdqrs. librarian Def. Supply Agy., Washington, 1964-71; dir. Army Library, Pentagon, 1971—. Mem. ALA, Spl. Libraries Assn. Home: 135 Ft Williams Pkwy Alexandria VA 22304 Office: 1A530 Pentagon Washington DC 20310

SHAFFER, PAUL E., banker; b. Rockford, Ohio, Aug. 3, 1926; s. Randall J. and Zelah V. (Alspaugh) S.; grad. U. Wis. Sch. Banking, 1954; certificate Am. Inst. Banking; m. Dorothy L. Schumm, June 26, 1951; children—Paula Kay, Patti Lee. With Rockford Nat. Bank, 1945-48; asst. nat. bank examiner Treasury Dept., 1948-52; with Fort Wayne Nat. Bank (Ind.), 1952—, exec. v.p., 1965-68, pres., 1968—, chmn., 1970—, also dir.; dir. Old First Nat. Bank, Bluffton, Ind., Lyall Electric, Inc., Lincoln-Life Improved Housing, Inc.; trustee Magnavox Govt. and Electronics Co. Pres., Downtown Fort Wayne Assn., 1965, Credit Bur. Fort Wayne, 1962, Jr. Achievement Fort Wayne, 1967-69; treas. Fort Wayne Better Bus. Bur., 1968, Ind.-Purdue Devel. Fund; mem. regional adv. com. Comptroller Currency, 1968-70; commr. Ft. Wayne Conv. and Tourism Authority. Past bd. dirs. Fort Wayne Conv. Bur., Fort Wayne Philharmonic Orch., Parkview Meml. Hosp.; bd. dirs. Caylor-Nickel Hosp., Ft. Wayne campus Ind. U., Ind.-Purdue Found., Taxpayers Research Assn.; past bd. dirs. United Community Services, chmn. drive, 1970-71; past bd. dirs. Fort Wayne YMCA, v.p., 1964-67; bd. adviser

Ind. U.-Purdue U., Ft. Wayne; mem. fin. advisory bd. Luth. Social Services, Ft. Wayne; bd. govs. Asso. Colls. Ind.; chmn. vol. com. U.S. Savs. Bonds, Allen County, Ind.; numerous other civic activities. Served with USAAF, 1945. Mem. Am. Inst. Banking (past pres. Fort Wayne chpt.), Am. (governing council 1978-79), Ind. (past pres., dir.) bankers assns., Fort Wayne (past v.p., dir.), Ind. (state dir.) chambers commerce. Mason (Shriner). Clubs: Executives (past pres.), Fort Wayne Country, Summit, Quest, Fort Wayne Press, Mad Anthonys, Pine Valley Country. Home: 1804 Old Lantern Trail Fort Wayne IN 46825 Office: 110 W Berry St Fort Wayne IN 46802

SHAFFER, ROBERT HOWARD, educator; b. Delphi, Ind., Sept. 13, 1915; s. John William and Bessie Marie (Hall) S.; A.B., DePauw U., 1936, LL.D., 1976; M.A., Columbia, 1939; Ph.D., N.Y. U., 1945; m. Marjorie Jane Fitch, Sept. 22, 1940; children—James Burgess, Bruce William (dec.). Asst. to nat. dir. personnel Boy Scouts Am., 1936-41; asst. to dean, instr. bus. Ind. U., 1941-43, asst. dean jr. div., 1945-46, asst. prof. bus. adminstrn., 1945-54, also asst. dean students, 1946-54, asso. dean, asso. prof., 1954-55, dean students, 1955-69, prof. bus. adminstrn., 1956—, prof. edn., 1960, chmn. dept. higher edn., 1973—, acting dean jr. div., 1965. Vis. prof. edn. N.Y. U., 1951, Pa State U., 1954, Mich. State U., 1960; cons. adminstrn. student personnel services Nat. Coll. Edn. and Chulalongkorn U., Bangkok, Thailand, 1959, 61, Kabul (Afghanistan) U., 1967, 70; dir. Workingmen's Fed. Savs. & Loan Assn. Mem. at large Nat. council Boy Scouts Am., 1946—, exec. bd. local council, 1947—, pres., 1947-49; mem. adv. bd. YMCA, 1946-49, 50-53, 54-57; chmn. Bloomington Human Relations Commn., 1960-66; mem. exec. com. Gov.'s Youth Commn., 1950-56; adviser Nat. Student Assn., 1958-67; chmn. Council Student Personnel Assns. Higher Edn., 1965-66. Bd. overseers St. Meinrad Coll., 1969-78. Served to 1st lt. Transp. Corps, AUS, 1943-45; PTO. Recipient Silver Beaver award Boy Scouts Am., 1955; Distinguished Alumnus award DePauw U., 1961. Mem. Am. Personnel and Guidance Assn. (pres. 1951-53), Nat. Vocational Guidance Assn., Am. Coll. Personnel Assn. (sec. 1949-52), A.A.U.P., Nat. Assn. Student Personnel Adminstrs. (v.p. 1956-57, 65-66, Distinguished Service award 1969, Scott H. Goodnight award 1973), Phi Delta Kappa, Beta Gamma Sigma, Sigma Chi. Kiwanian. Author: Effect of an English Deficiency Upon a Student's Adjustment in College, 1948; Professional Opportunities in National Youth Serving Organizations, 1949; (with Daniel A. Ferber) The Residential College Concept: Campus Organizational Patterns for Quality with Quantity, 1965; (with William D. Martinson) Student Personnel Services in Higher Education, 1966: (with Leo R. Dowling) Foreign Students and their American Student Friends, 1966; (with others) College Student Personnel Work in the Years Ahead, 1966. Editor: Current Legal Developments Affecting Education, 1976; (with Edward H. Hammond) The Legal Foundations of Student Personnel Services in Higher Education, 1978. Editor: NASPA Jour., 1969-72; asso. editor Personnel and Guidance Jour., 1952-53; mem. editorial bd. Occupations Mag., 1949-52, Jour. Coll. Student Personnel, 1974-77. Contbr. articles to profl. jours. Home: 2420 E Maxwell Ln Bloomington IN 47401

SHAFFER, ROBERT NESBIT, ophthalmologist; b. Cochranton, Pa., Jan. 18, 1912; s. William Walter and Ethel Margaret (Nesbit) S.; B.A., Pomona Coll., 1934; M.D., Stanford U., 1939; m. Virginia Jane Miller, Aug. 12, 1939; children—John, Stuart, William. Intern, Stanford U. Hosp., San Francisco, 1938-39; resident in ophthalmology, 1939-41; practice medicine specializing in ophthalmology, glaucoma cons., San Francisco, 1941—; mem. staff U. Calif. Hosp., St. Mary's Hosp., San Francisco; dir. glaucoma clinic, clin. prof. ophthalmology U. Calif. Sch. Medicine, San Francisco, 1950—. Served to lt. M.C., U.S. Army, 1941. Recipient Pan-Am. medal for prevention of blindness, 1979. Diplomate Am. Bd. Ophthalmology (asst. sec.-treas. 1974-79, sec.-treas. 1980). Mem. Internat. Claucoma Club of the Internat. Congress, Oxford Ophthal. Congress, Can. Ophthal. Soc., Am. Acad. Ophthalmology, Am. Ophthal. Soc., AMA. Republican. Presbyterian. Clubs: Rotary, Mason. Contbr. articles, author textbooks on glaucoma. Office: 490 Post St San Francisco CA 94102

SHAFFER, RUSSELL K., advt. co. exec.; b. N.Y.C., Apr. 12, 1933; s. Russell Paul and Alice (Cole) S.; A.B., Brown U., 1954; M.B.A., Harvard, 1958; m. Leslie Van Nostrand, July 28, 1956; children—Cole Van Nostrand, Wendel L., Daniel W., Russell W. Account exec. McCann-Erickson, N.Y.C., 1958-62; account supr. Grey Advt., N.Y.C., 1962-66; exec. v.p. Richard K. Manoff, Inc., N.Y.C., 1966-71, pres., 1971-77, also dir.; pres. David H. Mann, Inc., 1977—. Served to lt. USNR, 1954-56. Home: 2 Richards Ave South Norwalk CT 06854 Office: 845 3d Ave New York NY 10022

SHAFFER, THOMAS LINDSAY, lawyer, educator; b. Billings, Mont., Apr. 4, 1934; s. Cecil Burdette and Margaret Jeanne (Parker) S.; B.A., U. Albuquerque, 1958; J.D., U. Notre Dame, 1961; m. Nancy Jane Lehr, Mar. 19, 1954; children—Thomas, Francis, Joseph, Daniel, Brian, Mary, Andrew, Edward. Admitted to Ind. bar, 1961; asso. firm Barnes, Hickam, Pantzer, & Boyd, Indpls., 1961-63; prof. law U. Notre Dame, 1963—, asso. dean, 1969-71, dean, 1971-75; vis. prof. UCLA, 1970-71, U. Va., 1975-76; Frances Lewis scholar Washington and Lee U., 1979; dir. Ft. Howard Paper Co. Mem. Ind. Constl. Revision Commn., 1969-70, Ind. Trust Code Study Commn., 1968-71; reporter Ind. Jud. Conf., 1963, 67; mem. adv. com. on rules U.S. Ct. Appeals, 1977-79; hearing officer Ind. Civil Rights Commn., 1975. Served with USAF, 1953-57. Recipient Emil Brown Found. Preventive Law prize, 1966; Presdl. citation U. Notre Dame, 1975. Mem. Am. Bar Assn., Bar Assn. 7th Fed. Circuit, Ind. State Bar Assn., St. Joseph County Bar Assn., Christian Legal Soc., Soc. Values in Higher Edn., AAUP. Roman Catholic. Author: Death, Property, and Lawyers, 1970; The Planning and Drafting of Wills and Trusts, 1972, 79; Legal Interviewing and Counseling, 1976; co-author: Lawyers, Law Students, and People, 1977; co-editor: The Mentally Retarded Citizen and the Law, 1976; contbr. articles in field to legal jours. Home: 18801 Burke St South Bend IN 46637 Office: The Law Sch U Notre Dame Notre Dame IN 46556

SHAFFER, WAYNE EUGENE, lawyer; b. Wauseon, Ohio, June 25, 1922; s. Chalmer L. and Leva L. (Rashley) S.; A.B., Ohio No. U., 1947, LL.B., 1949; m. Georgia G. Frey, June 4, 1949; 1 dau., Julie W. (dec.). Admitted to Ohio bar, 1949, since practiced in Bryan; partner firm Newcomer, Shaffer, Geesey & Hutton, 1949—. Mem. Ohio Bd. Edn., 1956—, v.p., 1960-61, pres., 1962-63; pres. Ohio Community Sch. Assn., 1954; chmn. Ohio Bar Com. on Legal Edn., 1971. Bd. govs. Ohio Bd. Real Estate. Chmn. Williams County U.S.O. Trustee Williams County Retarded Childrens Assn., Ohio No. U., 1971—, Bryan Area Found., 1975—. Served to lt. (j.g.) USNR, World War II. Named hon. state farmer Future Farmers Am., 1962; recipient Distinguished Alumni award Ohio No. U., 1972. Mem. Am., Ohio, Northwestern Ohio, Williams County bar assns., Bryan C. of C. (scholarship chmn.), Nat. Assn. State Bds. Edn. (v.p. 1967-68, pres. 1968-69), Nat. Com. on Assessing Progress Edn., Am. Legion, Delta Sigma Phi, Sigma Delta Kappa. Methodist (ofcl. bd.). Elk, Moose, Lion; mem. Order Police. Home: 604 Circle Dr Bryan OH 43506 Office: 117 W Maple St Bryan OH 43506

SHAFFNER, JOHN ELVIN, Can. govt. ofcl.; b. Lawrencetown, N.S., Can., Mar. 3, 1911; s. John Elvin and Naomi Winifred (Durling) S.; student Acadia U., Wolfville, N.S.; grad. Bentley Sch. Acctg. and Fin., Boston; m. Nell Margaret Potter, Sept. 4, 1936; children—Lynne, Susan. With Crowell, Balcom & Co., chartered accountants, Halifax, 1932-34; pres. family bus., 1934-40; sec.-treas. M.W. Graves & Co., Seven-Up Maritime Ltd., also Asso. Co., Halifax, 1941-49; pres. Seven-Up Maritime, Ltd., 1949-60, M.W. Graves & Co. Ltd., 1949-68, Acadia Foods Ltd., 1954-61, Can. Foods Ltd., 1950-68; past dir., v.p. Evangeline Investments Ltd.; past dir. Rothmans Pall Mall Can. Ltd., Can. Breweries Ltd., Avon Valley Greenhouses Ltd.; past adv. bd. Can. Permanent Mortgage Corp., Can. Permanent Trust Corp.; head Can. Trade Del. to U.K. and Western Europe, 1962; agt. gen. N.S. in U.K. and Europe, 1973-76; lt. gov. Province of N.S., 1978—. Bd. govs. Acadia U., 1962-78, vice chmn. bd., 1969-73. Clubs: Halifax, Ken-Wo Golf and Country, Halifax Bd. Trade, Royal N.S. Yacht Squadron. Home: Rural Route 1 Port Williams NS B0P 1T0 Canada Office: 1451 Barrington St Halifax NS B3J 1Z2 Canada

SHAFTER, ALBERT JENE, JR., educator; b. Carbondale, Ill., Sept. 15, 1924; s. Albert Jacob and Iva (House) S.; B.A., So. Ill. U., 1948, M.A., 1949; Ph.D., Iowa State U., 1953; m. Lynette R. Peek, Feb. 15, 1946; children—Albert James, Michael Brian, Belinda Jo. Instr. econs. and sociology Iowa State U., Ames, 1949-51; dir. social service Woodward (Iowa) State Hosp., 1951-56; mental health eductor Ill. Dept. Pub. Welfare, Springfield, 1956-57; asso. prof. sociology and guidance, asst. dir. Rehab. Inst., So. Ill. U., Carbondale, 1957-61, adj. prof., 1964—; supt. Enid (Okla.) State Sch., 1961-64; project co-ordinator Ill. Adv. Council Mental Retardation, 1964-65; supt. A.L. Bowen Developmental Center, Harrisburg, Ill., 1964—; asst. zone dir. mental retardation Carbondale Mental Health Zone, 1964-68; councilor Accreditation Council for Facilities for Mentally Retarded, 1971-74, 76-77. Served with AUS, 1943-46; ETO. Fellow Am. Assn. Mental Deficiency (past chmn. S. Central region, councilor at large 1965-69, v.p. adminstrn. 1969-71); mem. Am. Legion, So. Ill. U. Alumni Assn. (pres. 1974-75), Alpha Kappa Delta. Methodist. Clubs: Masons, Elks. Cons. editor Am. Jour. Mental Deficiency, 1959-69; column editor Mental Retardation. Home: Rural Route 2 Shaw St Apt 5 Harrisburg IL 62946

SHAFTO, ROBERT AUSTIN, ins. co. exec.; b. Council Bluffs, Iowa, Sept. 15, 1935; s. Glen Granville and Blanche (Radigan) S.; B.S. in Actuarial Sci., Drake U., Des Moines, 1959; m. Jeanette DeFino, Dec. 17, 1954; children—Robert, Dennis, Teri, Shari, Michael. Mgr. computer services Guarantee Mut. Life Ins. Co., Omaha, 1959-65; v.p. Beta div. Electronic Data Systems, Dallas, 1965-71; sr. v.p. policyholder and computer services New Eng. Mut. Life Ins. Co., Boston, 1972—; mem. Life Ins. Systems Planning Exec. Com. Mem. Life Office Mgmt. Assn. (systems research com.). Roman Catholic. Home: 15 Richardson St Medway MA 02053 Office: 501 Boylston St Boston MA 02117

SHAGAN, STEVE, screenwriter, novelist, film producer; b. N.Y.C., Oct. 25, 1927; s. Barnet Harry and Rachel (Rosenzweig) S.; grad. high sch.; m. Elizabeth Leslie Florance, Nov. 18, 1956; 1 son, Robert William. Film technician Consol. Film, Inc., N.Y.C., 1952-56, RCA, Cape Canaveral, Fla., 1956-59; asst. to publicity dir. Paramount Pictures, Hollywood, Calif., 1962-63; producer TV series Tarzan, 1966; producer, writer movies for TV, Universal and CBS, Hollywood, Calif., 1968-70; writer-producer TV shows: River of Mystery, Spanish Portrait, Sole Survivor, A Step Out of Line, numerous others; writer original screenplay Save the Tiger, Paramount Studios, 1972 (Writers Guild award, Acad. award nominee 1973), also producer film; writer screenplay City of Angels (produced as movie Hustle), 1975; writer novels Save the Tiger, City of Angels, The Formula, 1979; writer screenplay Voyage of the Damned (Acad. award Nomination), 1976; writer, producer film The Formula, MGM, 1980; writer TV teleplay House on Garibaldi Street, 1979. Served with USCG, 1944-46. Mem. Writers Guild Am. Office: care Norman Garey Rosenfeld Myer & Sussman 9601 Wilshire Blvd Beverly Hills CA 90210

SHAGASS, CHARLES, psychiatrist; b. Montreal, Que., Can., May 19, 1920; s. Morris and Pauline (Segal) S.; came to U.S., 1958, naturalized, 1965; B.A., McGill U., Montreal, 1940, M.D., C.M., 1949; M.S., U. Rochester, 1941; m. Clara Wallerstein, Nov. 1, 1942; children—Carla Louise, Kathryn Sharna, Thomas Alan. Intern, Royal Victoria Hosp., Montreal, 1949-50, resident, 1950-53; lectr. McGill U., 1952-56, asst. prof. psychiatry, 1956-58; asso. prof. U. Iowa, 1958-60, prof., 1960-66; prof. Temple U., 1966—; asst. psychiatrist Royal Victoria Hosp., 1952-58; psychiat. physician Eastern Pa. Psychiat. Inst., 1966—; cons. NIMH, Social Security Adminstrs. Served with RCAF, 1941-45. USPHS grantee, 1958—; certified in psychiatry, Que. Fellow Royal Coll. Physicians (Can.), Am. Psychiat. Assn.; mem. Am. Psychopathol. Assn. (pres. 1974-75, Samuel Hamilton award 1975), Soc. Biol. Psychiatry (pres. 1974-75, Gold medal award 1977), Am. Coll. Neuropsychopharmacology, Am. EEG Soc., Collegium Internationale Neuro-Psychopharmacologicum, Psychiat. Research Soc., Philadelphia County Med. Soc., Group for Advancement Psychiatry, Eastern Assn. Electroencephalographers, Sigma Xi, Alpha Omega Alpha. Democrat. Jewish. Author: Evoked Brain Potentials in Psychiatry, 1972; editor books, including: The Role of Drugs in Community Psychiatry. Modern Problems of Pharmacopsychiatry, Vol. 6, 1971; (with others) Psychopathology and Brain Dysfunction, 1977; research, numerous publs. on brain function in mental illness, 1941—. Home: 1301 Spruce Ln Wyncote PA 19095 Office: Eastern Pa Psychiat Inst Henry Ave and Abbottsford Rd Philadelphia PA 19129

SHAHAN, EWING POPE, educator; b. St. Louis, Jan. 25, 1914; s. William Ewing and Harriet (Bowen) S.; A.B., Cornell U., 1934; M.B.A., Harvard U., 1936; Ph.D., Columbia U., 1948; m. Anne Stobie, Aug. 24, 1940; children—William Ewing, Margaret Anne, John Stobie. Investment analyst Brown Bros. Harriman & Co., N.Y.C., 1936-38; part-time instr. Am. Inst. Banking, N.Y.C., 1938-40; instr. econs., philosophy U. Miami, Coral Gables, Fla., 1940-42; economist, sr. economist, regional office War Manpower Commn., Atlanta, 1942-44, chief, div. reports and analysis, state office, Montgomery, Ala., 1944-45; asst. prof. bus. adminstrn. Vanderbilt U., Nashville, 1945-51, asso. prof. econs., 1951-54, prof. econs., 1954-79, prof. econs. and bus. adminstrn. emeritus, 1979—, dean coll. arts and scis., 1951-60, dir. Inst. Communism and Constl. Democracy, 1962-66, Summer Inst. for Coll. Tchrs. Econs., 1970-71, lectr. religion, 1971-79; cons. IBRD, 1956-60; coll., univ. lectr. on communism, 1963-66. Recipient Excellence in Undergrad. Teaching award Vanderbilt U., 1966. Mem. Am., So. econ. assns., Am. Acad. Religion. Presbyterian. Author: Whitehead's Theory of Experience, 1950; co-editor, contbr. to TV series The Nature of Communism, 1964. Home: 1117 Sparta Rd Nashville TN 37205

SHAHEEN, JOHN MICHAEL, oil co. exec.; b. Lee County, Ill., Oct. 24, 1915; s. Michael and Sadie (Saied) S.; student U. Ill., 1934-36, U. Chgo., 1937-38; m. Barbara Tracy, Apr. 21, 1951; children—Tracy, Michael, Bradford. Pres., Shaheen Natural Resources Co., Inc., N.Y.C., Macmillan Ring-Free Oil Co., Inc., N.Y.C., 1968—, Golden Eagle Refining Co., Inc., N.Y.C., 1956-60; mem. U.S. Adv. Commn. on Info., 1971-77; mem. Nat. Petroleum Council, 1970-77; spl. U.S. ambassador to Colombia, 1974. Vestryman St. Bartholomew's Episcopal Ch., N.Y.C. Served as capt., OSS, USNR, 1941-45. Decorated Silver Star, Legion of Merit; recipient Outstanding Leadership in Energy Resources Devel. award ASME, 1974. Republican. Clubs: Union League, Met. Office: 90 Park Ave New York City NY 10016

SHAHEEN, MICHAEL EDMUND, JR., lawyer, govt. ofcl.; b. Boston, Aug. 5, 1940; s. Michael Edmund and Dorothy Wallace (Cameron) S.; B.A., Yale U., 1962; LL.B., Vanderbilt U., 1965; m. Polly Adair Dammann, Sept. 11, 1976; 1 son, Michael Edmund. Dir. ann. capital support fund, instr. physics, Memphis Univ. Sch., 1965-66; admitted to Tenn. bar, 1968; law clk. Judge Robert M. McRae, Jr., Memphis, 1966-68; individual practice law, Tenn., Miss., 1968-73; dep. chief voting and public accomodations sect. Dept. Justice, Washington, 1973-74, dep. chief fed. programs sect., civil rights div., 1974-75, counsel to Atty. Gen. for Intelligence, 1975, spl. adv. to Atty. Gen., counsel, dir. Office Profl. Responsibility, 1975—; mayor, Como, Miss., 1970-73; pres. Como Resources, Inc., 1971-72; mcpl. judge, Como, 1970-73; chmn. Como Indsl. Devel. Commn., 1970-73. Mem. Phi Delta Phi, Zeta Psi. Office: Dept Justice 10th and Constitution Aves NW Washington DC 20530

SHAHEEN, MICHAEL GEORGE, archbishop; b. Canton, Ohio, Apr. 27, 1924; s. George and Mary (Corey) S.; B.A., Kent State U., 1953. Ordained priest Syrian Orthodox Ch., 1951; elevated to archimandrite, 1954; consecrated archbishop, 1961; archbishop Toledo (Ohio) Antiochian Orthodox Archdiocese in N.Am., 1975—; apptd. aux. United Antiochian Christian Orthodox Archdiocese N.Am. Pres., Archdiocese Bd. Trustees. Served with Mil. Police, AUS, 1945-46. Decorated Golden Cross of St. Mark, Holy Cross of Mt. Sinai, medal Syrian Arab Republic. Mem. Holy Synod Antioch, Nat. Council Chs. in U.S.A. Author: Pontifical Orthodox Litury, 1961. Publisher Toledo Archdiocesan Messenger, 1962—. Address: 2656 Pemberton Dr Toledo OH 43606

SHAHEEN, WILLIAM HENRY, lawyer, govt. ofcl.; b. Dover, N.H., Dec. 30, 1943; s. William Nicholas and Josephine (Skeip) S.; B.A., U. N.H., 1965; J.D. with honors, U. Miss., 1973; m. Cynthia Jeanne Bowers, Oct. 15, 1969; children—Stefany Amber, Stacy Paige. Admitted to Miss. bar, 1973, N.H. bar, 1973; city atty. City of Somersworth (N.Y.), 1974-77; asso. to ret. judge Ovilia J. Gregoire, Dover (N.H.) Dist. Ct., 1973-76; partner firm Keefe, Dunnington & Shaheen, Dover, 1976-77; U.S. atty. Dist. N.H., Concord, 1977—. State chmn. Carter campaign N.H. Presdl. Primary and Gen. Election, 1975-76. Served to capt. U.S. Army, 1965-69. Mem. Am., N.H. bar assns. Democrat. Roman Catholic. Home: Dover Rd Durham NH 03824 Office: 55 Pleasant St Concord NH 03301

SHAHIDI, NASROLLAH THOMAS, pediatrician; b. Meshed, Iran, Dec. 11, 1926; s. Taber and Robab (Habib) S.; came to U.S., 1956, naturalized, 1970; B.S., U. Montplier (France), 1947; M.D., mention tres honorable, Sorbonne, 1954; m. Mary Alice Vandervoort, Sept. 29, 1962; children—John, Caroline, Mark. Resident in pediatrics Hospital des Enfants Malades, Paris, 1954-56; asst. resident in pediatrics Balt. City Hosp., 1956-57; research fellow in pediatrics Harvard U., 1957-60, instr. pediatrics, 1960-63; asst. physician Children's Hosp. Med. Center, Boston, 1960-63; vis. prof. pediatrics Kinderspital, Zurich, Switzerland, also vis. investigator Swiss Nat. Found., 1964-66; asso. prof. pediatrics U. Wis. Center for Health Scis., also hematologist Children's Hosp., Madison, 1966-70; prof. pediatrics, dir. pediatric hematology U. Wis. Center Health Scis., Madison, 1970—; pediatric rep. Wis. Clin. Cancer Center, 1973; cons. Madison Gen., St. Mary's hosps., 1966—; guest lectr.; vis prof. various profl. groups and univs. Recipient numerous pvt. and govt grants; diplomate Am. Bd. Pediatrics. Mem. Am., Midwest pediatric socs., Am. Soc. Hematology, Am. Soc. Pediatric Research, Central Soc. Clin. Research, Chilean Hematology Soc., (hon.), Dominican Republic Pediatric Soc. (hon.), Royal Soc. (affiliate). Contbr. articles to med. jours.; reviewer for Jour. Biol. Chemistry, Jour. Clin. Investigation, Jour. Lab. and Clin. Medicine, New Eng. Jour. Medicine; recognized for treatment of aplastic anemia. Home: 509 Ozark Trail Madison WI 53705

SHAHOVSKOY, JOHN, clergyman; b. Moscow, Russia, Aug. 23, 1902; s. Prince Alexis and Anna (Knina) S.; ed. Imperial Lyceum St. Petersburg, 1917, U. Louvain (Belgium), 1922-25; hon. degree St. Vladimir's Theol. Sem., 1976. Came to U.S., 1946, naturalized, 1951. Joined order in Mt. Athos, ordained monk priest Russian Orthodox Ch., 1926; priest in Yugoslavia, 1927-31; rector St. Vladimir Ch., Berlin, Germany, 1932-45; bishop of Bklyn., Russian Orthodox Greek Cath. Ch. of Am., 1947-50; dean St. Vladimir's Sem., N.Y.C., 1947-50; bishop San Francisco, 1950-61, archbishop San Francisco and Western U.S., 1961. Writer, announcer religious scripts Voice of Am., 1947—; mem. central com. World Council Chs., 1954-68. Author: The Philosophy of Pastorship, 1935; Life, 1935; Tolstoy and the Church, 1939; The Mystery of the Church, 1954; The Age of the Faith, 1954; The Leaves of the Tree, 1962; The Book of the Evidences, 1965; Selected Verses, Strannik, 1974; Moscow Dialogue of Immortality, 1972; The History of Russian Intelligentsia, 1975; Biography of My Youth, 1977; others. Contbr. numerous articles to religious publs. Home: 2040 Anza St San Francisco CA 94118 Office: Holy Trinity Cathedral Green and Van Ness San Francisco CA 94123 also 59 E 2d St New York City NY 10003

SHAIFER, NORMAN, communications exec.; b. Bklyn., Oct. 28, 1931; s. Abe and Rose (Cohen) S.; student Coll. City N.Y., 1949-52; m. Frankie Levine, Dec. 31, 1968. Founder, pres. Custom Communications Systems, Inc., S. Hackensack, N.J., 1962—, publisher Priest Forum mag., 1968—; chmn. bd. Inst. for Human Devel., 1977—; mem. bd. Mgmt. Decision Lab. Grad. Sch. Bus. Adminstrn. N.Y. U.; cons. to pub. and printing industry orgns.; cons. on communications and organizational and fund-raising to various churches. Served in U.S. Army, 1952-54. Mem. Printing Industries Met. N.Y. (v.p. Lithographers Industries Met. N.Y.), Printing Industries of Am., GraphicArts Tech. Found., Soc. Photog. Scientists and Engrs., Guild for Religious Architecture. Author: John Paul II, a Son of Poland. Patentee graphic arts color reprodn. control device, 1972. Home: 28 Pierrepont St Brooklyn NY 11201 Office: Custom Bldg South Hackensack NJ 07606

SHAIN, IRVING, univ. adminstr.; b. Seattle, Jan. 2, 1926; s. Samuel and Selma (Blockoff) S.; B.S. in Chemistry, U. Wash., 1949, Ph.D., 1952; m. Mildred Ruth Udell, Aug. 31, 1947; children—Kathryn Ann, Steven Terry, John Robert, Paul Stuart. Faculty chemistry U. Wis., Madison, 1952-75, prof., 1961-75, chmn. dept., 1967-70, vice chancellor, 1970-75; provost, v.p. academic affairs, prof. chemistry U. Wash., Seattle, 1975-77; chancellor, prof. chemistry U. Wis. at Madison, 1977—. Served with U.S. Army, 1943-46. Mem. Am. Chem. Soc., Electrochem. Soc., Internat. Soc. Electrochemistry, AAAS. Home: 130 N Prospect Ave Madison WI 53705

SHAINMAN, IRWIN, educator, musician; b. N.Y.C., June 27, 1921; s. Samuel and Gussie (Pollack) S.; B.A., Pomona Coll., 1943; M.A., Columbia, 1948; Premier Prix, Conservatoire Nat. de Musique de Paris (France), 1950; m. Bernice Cohen, Aug. 29, 1948; children—Joan, Jack. Prof. music, curator Paul Whiteman collection

Williams Coll., Williamstown, Mass., 1948—; chmn. music dept., 1971-77, dean faculty, 1972-73, coordinator performing arts, 1973-76. Tchr. extension U. Mass., 1952-55, Mass. State Coll., North Adams, 1957, also Bennington Coll. Composer's Conf. and Chamber Music Center; condr. Berkshire Symphony, 1950-65, also Williams Coll. band, brass ensemble and woodwind ensemble; 1st trumpet Albany (N.Y.) Symphony Orch., 1960-65, Vt. Symphony Orch., 1954-58. Cons. advanced placement program Coll. Entrance Exam. Bd., 1969—. Mem. edn. com. Saratoga Performing Arts Center, 1967-68; pres. Williamstown Theatre Found., 1972-77. Served with AUS, 1942-45. Decorated Purple Heart, Combat Inf. badge. N.Y. Philharmonic scholar, 1934-35. Recipient Danforth Found. Tchrs. award, 1957-58. Mem. Am. Musicological Soc., Coll. Music Assn. Contbr. articles to profl. jours. Home: Baxter Rd Williamstown MA 01267

SHAKESPEARE, FRANK, broadcasting co. exec.; b. N.Y.C., Apr. 9, 1925; s. Francis Joseph and Frances (Hughes) S.; B.S., Holy Cross Coll., 1945; D.Eng. (hon.), Colo. Sch. Mines, 1975; D.C.S. (hon.), Pace U., 1979; m. Deborah Anne Spaeth, Oct. 9, 1954; children—Mark, Andrea, Fredricka. Formerly pres. CBS-TV Services, sr. v.p. CBS-TV Network, exec. v.p. CBS-TV Stas.; dir. USIA, 1969-73; exec. v.p. Westinghouse Electric Corp., 1973-75; pres. RKO Gen. Inc., N.Y.C., 1975—, also dir.; dir. Frontier Airlines, Inc. Served to lt. (j.g.) USNR, 1945-46. Club: Union League. Home: Cliff Rd Greenwich CT 06830 Office: 1440 Broadway New York City NY 10018

SHAKESPEARE, WALTER SAMUEL, hosp. accreditation commn. adminstr.; b. Harrisburg, Pa., Aug. 17, 1925; s. Walter Leon and Daisy (Alleman) S.; student U. Pa., 1954; B.S. in Econs. and Bus. Adminstrn., Lebanon Valley Coll., 1968; m. Mildred Nicholson, June 28, 1947; 1 son, W. Jeffrey. Mem. staff Harrisburg Hosp., 1947-70, asst. adminstr., 1960-62, adminstr., 1962-70; field rep. Joint Commn. on Accreditation Hosps., 1970, asst. dir. accreditation program, Chgo., 1970-72, asso. dir., 1972—. Served with AUS, 1943-45. Decorated Breast Order of Yun-Hui (China). Fellow Am. Coll. Hosp. Adminstrs.; mem. Am. Hosp. Assn., Am. Assn. Hosp. Accountants (v.p Harrisburg 1958, mem. bd. 1961), Hosp. Assn. Pa. Home: 2626 N Lakeview Ave Chicago IL 60614 Office: Joint Commn on Accreditation Hosps 875 N Michigan Ave Chicago IL 60611

SHAKLEE, FORREST CLELL, SR., nutritional researcher; b. Carlisle, Iowa, Nov. 27, 1894; s. Robert Lenz and Martha Jane (Overton) S.; student D.C. Palmer Coll., 1915; Ph.C., West Coast Chiropractic Coll., Oakland, Calif., 1931; D.D., Calif. Coll., 1933; D.D., Coll. Divine Metaphysics, Indpls., 1933; A.B., Am. Humanist Sch., 1949; Ph.D. in Psychology, Commonwealth U., Los Angeles, 1957; Ruth Alice Chapin, Dec. 15, 1915 (dec. 1941); children—Forrest Clell, Raleigh L.; m. 2d, Dorothy Eleanor Potter, Aug. 8, 1957. Pvt. practice as chiropractor, Rockwell City, Iowa, 1915-23, Mason City, Iowa, 1924-30, Oakland, 1931-43; ordained to ministry Ch. of Christ, 1929; pastor, Portland, Iowa, 1928-29; founder Shaklee Corp., Emeryville, Calif., 1956, pres., chmn. bd., 1956-72, chmn. bd., 1972—; cons. human relations, Oakland, 1941-57. Recipient Outstanding Achievement award Standard Chiropractic Coll., San Jose, 1937, Spl. Recognition award Calif. Sec. State, 1968, Humanitarian award Nat. Health Fedn. Am., 1973, Ambassador of Good Will award Mayor of Chattanooga, 1977, numerous others. Mem. Hayward C. of C. (dir. 1965-66), Order Ky. Cols., Oakland Mus. Assn., Calif. Hist. Soc., Thoughtsmanship (founder, pres. 1947). Clubs: Masons; Shriners. Author: Thoughtsmanship Life's Questions and Answers, 1951; Thoughtsmanship for Well Being, 1951; Thoughtsmanship for the Salesman, 1951; Thoughtsmanship in Love and Marriage, 1951; Thoughtsmanship for the Bride, 1951; Shaklee Reference Treasure to Better Health Through Better Nutrition, 1960; Reflections on a Philosophy, 1973; When Nature Speaks: the Life of Forrest C. Shaklee, Sr. Home: 5286 Dunnigan Ct Castro Valley CA 94546 Office: Shaklee Corp 1900 Powell St Emeryville CA 94608

SHAKLEE, WILLIAM EUGENE, ret. poultry geneticist; b. Watonga, Okla., May 2, 1920; s. Vere Stalker and Nina Lillian (Pierce) S.; B.S., Okla. State U., 1942; M.S., Iowa State U., 1948; Ph.D., U. Md., 1953; m. Rose Marie Miller, Feb. 24, 1946; children—Ronald Vere, Janelle Marie Shaklee Waggoner, Lynda Rose Shaklee Henderson, Cynthia Jeanne. Research asst. Ill. Agr. Expt. Sta., Urbana, 1948-50; poultry geneticist Agrl. Research Center, Beltsville, Md., 1950-55, state expt. stas. div. Agrl. Research Service, Washington, 1955-62, Coop. State Expt. Sta. Service, Washington, 1962-63, Coop. State Research Service, Washington, 1963-76; vis. fellow Cornell U., 1963-64. Served with AUS, 1942-46; col. Res., ret. Recipient Nat. Honor award Orgn. Profl. Employees, Dept. Agr., 1973; certificate merit Coop. State Research Service, 1969; Meritorious Service medal U.S. Army, 1975. Fellow AAAS; mem. Poultry Sci. Assn. (rep. to AAAS 1961-77, editor-in-chief 1977—), Am. Genetic Assn. (mem. council 1976—), Civil Affairs Assn., Am. Poultry Hist. Soc., Res. Officers Assn., Ret. Officers Assn., Air Force Assn., Nat. Assn. Ret. Fed. Employees (chpt. v.p. 1977—), Orgn. Profl. Employees Dept. Agr. (profl. v.p. 1968-69, pres. 1969-71, mem. council 1975-76, 78—), Am. Assn. Ret. Persons (chpt. pres. 1977—), Am. Soc. Animal Sci., World Poultry Sci. Assn. (asso. editor 1973—, historian, archivist U.S. br. 1976—), Garfield County Geneal. Soc. (pres. 1977—), Garfield County Hist. Soc., Sons and Daus. Cherokee Strip Pioneers, Sigma Xi, Phi Kappa Phi. Republican. Methodist. Club: Enid Lions (editor 1978-79). Contbr. articles to profl. jours. Home: 2407 Indian Dr Enid OK 73701. *Any successes may be ascribed to a unique combination of genetic traits and to a favorable environment. A work ethic was instilled early by my parents and has been fostered through the years by a devoted and understanding wife.*

SHAKNO, ROBERT JULIAN, hosp. adminstr.; b. Amsterdam, Holland, Aug. 15, 1937; s. Rudy C. and Gertrude (Loeb) S.; came to U.S., 1939, naturalized, 1944; B.B.A. (scholar 1955), So. Methodist U., 1959; M.H.A., Washington U., St. Louis, 1961; m. Elka Linda Baum, June 10, 1962; children—Steven Lee, Deborah Sue. Adminstrv. asst. Mt. Sinai Hosp., Chgo., 1961-63; asso. adminstr. Tex. Inst. Rehab. and Research, Houston, 1963-65; asst. adminstr. Michael Reese Hosp., Chgo., 1965-70, v.p., hosp. dir., 1970-73; asso. exec. dir. Cook County Hosp., Chgo., 1973-75; exec. dir. Hackensack (N.J.) Hosp., 1975—; past clin. instr. Washington U., U. Chgo., Northwestern U. Pres., Bergen-Passaic County Hosp. Adminstrs. Council. Bd. dirs. Temple Beth Or. Served to 1st lt. USAR, 1960-66. Named Young Adminstr. of Year, Washington U., 1968. Fellow Am. Coll. Hosp. Adminstrs.; mem. Am., N.J. (chmn. com. on govt. relations) hosp. assns., Washington U. Alumni Assn. (past pres.), Sigma Alpha Mu (past pres.). Home: 11 Nowak Ct Woodcliff Lake NJ 07675 Office: 22 Hospital Pl Hackensack NJ 07601

SHALALA, DONNA EDNA, govt. ofcl.; b. Cleve., Feb. 14, 1942; d. James Abraham and Edna (Smith) Shalala; A.B., Western Coll., 1962; M.S.Sc., Syracuse U., 1968, Ph.D., 1970. Vol., Peace Corps, Iran, 1962-64; asst. to dir. met. studies program Syracuse U., 1965-69, instr. asst. to dean Maxwell Grad. Sch., 1969-70; asst. prof. polit. sci. Bernard M. Baruch Coll., U. City N.Y., 1970-72; asso. prof. politics and edn. Tchrs. Coll. Columbia U., 1972-77; asst. sec. for policy devel. and research HUD, Washington, 1977—; asst. to chmn. com. on local govt. N.Y. State Constl. Conv., 1967. Vice chmn. New Democratic Coalition of N.Y. State, 1970-72; trustee Western Coll.; bd. dirs. N.Y. Citizen's Union. Ohio Newspaper Women's scholar, 1958; Western Coll. Trustees scholar, 1958-62; Carnegie fellow 1966-68; Nat. Acad. Edn. Spencer fellow, 1972-73; Guggenheim fellow, 1975—. Mem. Am., N.Y. polit. sci. assns. Author: Neighborhood Governance, 1971; The city and the Constitution, 1972; The Property Tax and the Voters, 1973; The Decentralization Approach, 1974. Office: Dept of HUD 451 Seventh St SW Washington DC 20410

SHALLECK, MILTON, lawyer, ret. judge; b. N.Y.C., June 8, 1905; s. Morris and Dora (Sussman) S.; A.B., U. Pa., 1927; LL.B., Fordham U., 1930, LL.D.; m. Rosalyn Baron, June 24, 1934; children—Alan Bennett, Peter Blair. Admitted to N.Y. bar, 1931, also fed. cts., U.S. Supreme Ct.; pvt. practice, N.Y.C., 1932-33; sec. to Justice Samuel I. Rosenman, N.Y. Supreme Ct., 1934-43; head atty. Office Lend Lease Adminstrn., Washington, 1943; spl. counsel Fgn. Econ. Adminstrn., 1943-45; pvt. practice with Oscar Cox, N.Y.C. and Washington, 1945-46, with Samuel I. Rosenman, 1946-48; partner Shalleck & Krakower, 1948-53; pvt. practice, 1953-62; counsel to Gainsburg, Gottlieb, Levitan & Cole, 1976—; judge Criminal Ct. of City of N.Y., 1962-76, acting civil and supreme ct. judge. U.S. commr. on South Pacific Commn., 1948-53; spl. dep. supt. of ins. State of N.Y., 1955-59. Sec. Franklin D. Roosevelt Meml. Found., Inc., 1947-48. Mem. Am., Fed. N.Y. State bar assns., Bar Assn. City N.Y., Tau Delta Phi. Mason, Elk. Author: The Evolution of a Court, 1949; articles legal jours. Home: 88 The Intervale Roslyn Estates NY 11576 Office: 122 E 42d St New York NY 10017

SHALLENBERGER, GARVIN FLETCHER, lawyer; b. Beloit, Wis., Jan. 7, 1921; s. Garvin Dennis and Grace (Hubbell) S.; B.A., U. Mont., 1942; J.D., U. Calif., Berkeley, 1949; m. Mary Louise Hillman, May 5, 1945; children—Diane, Dennis. Admitted to Calif. bar, 1949, U.S. Supreme Ct. bar, 1960; mem. firm Crider, Tilson & Ruppe, Los Angeles, 1952-60; partner firm Rutan & Tucker, Santa Ana, Calif., 1960—. Mem. Am. Bar Assn., Calif. State Bar (bd. govs. 1976-78, pres. 1978), Orange County Bar Assn. (dir. 1968-72, pres. 1972, Franklin West award 1979), Am. Bd. Trial Advocates (founder, 1st sec.), Am. Coll. Trial Lawyers. Office: 401 Civic Center Dr W Santa Ana CA 92702. *Life, in my case, has been neither especially hard or especially easy. My upbringing certainly emphasized diligent application to studies and work. With this ingrained characteristic, success orientation seemed naturally to follow. But success, even such limited success as I have had, leaves bruises too, though not as ugly as those left by failure.*

SHALLENBERGER, ROBERT URSON, life ins. co. exec.; b. Chgo., Mar. 7, 1917; s. John Franklin and Olga Marguerite (Urson) S.; B.A., U. Chgo., 1937; M.B.A., Harvard, 1939; m. Barbara Leary, June 30, 1943; children—Robert, Peter, Elizabeth. Gen. agt. N.E. states World Ins. Co., 1946-50, Ind., 1951-53; dir. accident and sickness sales Mut. Life Ins. Co. N.Y., 1954-56, supt. agys, 1957-59, regional v.p., 1960-62, 2d v.p. sales, 1962-63, v.p. for merchandising, 1963-65, v.p. for pub. relations, 1965-69, v.p. for group ins., 1969-71, sr. v.p., 1972-76, exec. v.p., 1976-78, pres., 1978—. Served from pvt. to capt. Med. Adminstrv. Corps, AUS, 1941-45. Clubs: Metropolitan, Harvard (N.Y.C.); Innis Arden, Rocky Point Sailing. Home: 40 Lockwood Ave Old Greenwich CT 06870 Office: 1740 Broadway New York City NY 10019

SHALOWITZ, ERWIN EMMANUEL, civil engr.; b. Washington, Feb. 13, 1924; s. Aaron Louis and Pearl (Myer) S.; student U. Pa., U. Notre Dame, 1944-45; B.C.E., George Washington U., 1947, postgrad., 1948-49; grad. soil mechanics Cath. U., 1951; M.A. in Pub. Adminstrn. (fellow U.S. Civil Service Commn.), Am. U., 1954; m. Elaine Mildred Langerman, June 29, 1952; children—Ann Janet, Aliza Beth, Jonathan Avram. Engr., Klemitt Engring. Co., N.Y.C., 1947; with cons. firm Whitman, Requardt & Assos., Balt., 1947-48; chief structural research engr., head def. research sect., project officer and tech. adviser for atomic tests Bur. Yards and Docks, Dept. Navy, Washington, 1948-59; supervisory gen. engr. spl. asst. for protective constrn. programs, project mgr. for bldg. systems, chief research br., chief mgmt. information, chief contracting procedures Pub. Bldgs. Service, Gen. Services Adminstrn., Washington, 1959—. Chmn. fed. exec. tng. program U.S. Civil Service Commn., 1950; fallout shelter analyst Dept. Def.; mem. Nat. Evaluation Bd. Architect-Engr. Selections; mem. standing com. on procurement policy Nat. Acad. Sci. Bldg. Research Adv. Bd.; coordinator pub. bldgs. design and constrn. Small Bus. Program and Minority Enterprise and Minority Subcontracting Programs. Served to engring. officer USNR, 1944-46. Recipient Gen. Services Adminstrn. Commendable Service award, 1968; Outstanding Performance recognition, 1976, 77, 79, cash award, 1977, 79. Registered profl. engr., Washington. Fellow ASCE, Am. Biog. Inst.; mem. Soc. Advancement Mgmt., Soc. Am. Mil. Engrs., Sigma Tau, Pi Sigma Alpha. Jewish. Contbr. articles profl. jours. Home: 5603 Huntington Pkwy Bethesda MD 20014 Office: 19th and F Sts NW Washington DC 20405. *PRINCIPLES: Look beyond the material for lasting values and meaning, optimize managerial effectiveness by creating an objective and challenging climate in an organization, delve into the underlying causes of problem areas for meaningful solutions, and persevere in spite of obstacles. IDEAS: Cultural pluralism; the intrinsic potential of each individual; and love, appreciation, and support of one's family as indispensable for real accomplishment. GOALS: To attain the highest level of professional accomplishment within my capabilities and to continue to have a rich, happy, and fulfilling family life. STANDARDS OF CONDUCT: To be fair, consistent, and straightforward; and to avoid over-reacting.*

SHAMBUREK, ROLAND HOWARD, physician; b. Adell, Wis., June 7, 1928; s. William and Catherine (Illig) S.; B.S., U. Wis., 1950, M.D., 1953; M.P.H., Harvard U., 1960; m. Gladys Irene Gibbons, June 21, 1952; children—Steven J., Robert D., Daniel J. Intern, St. Joseph's Hosp., Marshfield, Wis., 1953-54; commd. 1st lt. M.C., U.S. Army, advanced through grades to col., 1968; resident in preventive medicine USAF Sch. Aerospace Medicine, Brooks AFB, 1960-63; service in Europe and Vietnam; comdr. U.S. Army Med. Personnel Support Agy., 1975-77; ret., 1977; exec. v.p. Aerospace Med. Assn., 1977-79. Decorated Legion of Merit with oak leaf cluster, Commendation medal, Meritorious Service medal; diplomate Am. Bd. Preventive Medicine. Mem. Assn. Mil. Surgeons (John Shaw Billings award 1968), Am. Coll. Preventive Medicine (v.p. 1968-69), Aerospace Med. Assn. (v.p. 1968-79), AMA (del. 1978), Soc. Med. Cons. Armed Forces, Soc. U.S. Army Flight Surgeons, Soc. NASA Flight Surgeons. Author papers in field. Address: 3700 Moss Dr Annandale VA 22003

SHAMOS, MORRIS HERBERT, educator; b. Cleve., Sept. 1, 1917; s. Max and Lillian (Wasser) S.; A.B., N.Y. U., 1941, M.S., 1943, Ph.D., 1948; postgrad. Mass. Inst. Tech., 1941-42; m. Marion Jean Cahn, Nov. 26, 1942; 1 son, Michael Ian. Faculty, N.Y. U., 1942—, prof. physics, 1959—, chmn. dept. Washington Sq. Coll., 1957-70; sr. v.p. research and devel. Technicon Corp., 1970-75, chief sci. officer, 1975—, also dir. Cons. pvt. industry; spl. research atomic and nuclear physics; cons. Armament Center, USAF, 1955-57, Tung-Sol Electric, Inc., 1949-65, Office Pub. Information, UN, 1958, NBC, 1957-67, AEC, 1957-70, N.Y. Eye and Ear Infirmary, 1961-64, 79—, L.I. Jewish Hosp., 1962—, N.Y.C. Health Dept., 1961-70, Technicon Instruments Corp., 1964-70, U.S. Office Edn., 1964-72. Dir. tng. N.Y.C. Office Civil Def., 1950-54; subscribing mem. N.Y. Philharmonic Soc.; mem. adv. council Pace U., 1971—. Trustee Hackley Sch., Westchester Arts Council. Fellow N.Y. Acad. Scis. (past chmn. phys. scis., bd. govs. 1977—, rec. sec. 1978-80, v.p. 1980—), AAAS; mem. Nat. Assn. Ednl. Broadcasters, Am. Phys. Soc., IEEE, AAUP, AFTRA, Am. Chem. Soc., Nat. Sci. Tchrs. Assn. Am. (pres. 1967), Assn. Physics Tchrs. Britain, Phi Beta Kappa, Sigma Xi, Pi Mu Epsilon, Sigma Pi Sigma. Club: Cosmos. Author: Great Experiments in Physics, 1959. Co-editor: Recent Advances in Science, 1956; Industrial and Safety Problems of Nuclear Technology, 1950; cons. editor Addison-Wesley Pub. Co., 1965-69. Adv. bd. Jour. Coll. Sci. Teaching, 1971-75, 76—, Clin. Lab. Guide, Am. Chem. Soc., 1972-76. Home: 3515 Henry Hudson Pkwy New York NY 10463

SHANAHAN, EDWARD P., utility exec.; b. N.Y.C., 1918; B.S., Fordham U., 1939; M.S., Columbia; married. Mgr. accounting staff Price Waterhouse & Co., N.Y.C., 1940-58; v.p., comptroller Fla. Gas. Co., Winter Park, 1958-60, sr. v.p., treas., asst. sec., 1960—; sr. v.p., treas. dir. Fla. Liquid Gas Co., Fla. Gas Exploration Co., Fla. Gas Transmission Co., Fla. Hydro Carbons Co., Fla. Computer Systems Co.; treas., dir. Fla. Gas Utilities Co.; dir. Comml. Bank at Winter Park, Combanks Corp. C.P.A., N.Y. Home: 3000 Westchester Ave Orlando FL 32803 Office: PO Box 44 Winter Park FL 32789

SHANAHAN, EILEEN, journalist; b. Washington, Feb. 29, 1924; d. Thomas Francis and Vena (Karpeles) Shanahan; A.B., George Washington U., 1944; m. John V. Waits, Jr., Sept. 16, 1944; children—Mary Beth, Kathleen. Copy aide Washington Post, summers 1942-43; dictationist Washington Bur., UP, 1944-45, reporter, 1945-47; reporter for Walter Cronkite, Washington Radio News Bur., 1949-50; reporter for columnist Robert S. Allen, 1951; reporter, editor Washington Office, Research Inst. Am., 1951-56; reporter Washington bur., Jour. Commerce, 1956-61, N.Y. Times, 1962-77; spl. asst. to asst. to sec. Dept. Treasury, Washington, 1961-62; asst. sec. for pub. affairs HEW, Washington, 1977-79; asst. mng. editor Washington Star, 1979—; faculty mem. Summer Program for Minority Journalists, U. Calif., Berkeley, 1976—; mem. advisory council Woodrow Wilson Sch. Govt., Princeton U., 1973-76; mem. adv. com. Nieman Found., 1975—; mem. exec. com. Reporters' Com. for Freedom of Press, 1972-76. Bd. govs. Fund for Investigative Journalism, 1973-76. Recipient Bus. Journalism award U. Mo. Sch. Journalism, 1966; named Newspaperwoman of Yr., N.Y. Women in Communications, 1972. Club: Washington Press. Home: 3608 Van Ness St NW Washington DC 20008 Office: 225 Virginia Ave SE Washington DC 20061

SHANAHAN, ELWILL MATTSON, state ofcl.; b. Salina, Kans., Sept. 22, 1912; d. August G. and Adine (Peterson) Mattson; grad. Swedish Covenant Hosp., Chgo., 1934; m. Paul R. Shanahan, Oct. 13, 1951 (dec. Apr. 1966); m. 2d, W. Keith Weltmer, July 11, 1976. Sec. of state State of Kans., Topeka, 1966-78; ret., 1978. Republican. Home: 1320 W 27th St Topeka KS 66611

SHANAHAN, ROBERT BART, banker; b. Buffalo, Jan. 8, 1928; s. Bart J. and Florence (Dietrich) S.; B.S., U. Pa., 1951; m. Janet I. Mulholland, Feb. 6, 1953; children—Maureen, Timothy, Karin, Molly, Colleen, Mark, Ellen. Sales rep. Assos. Discount Corp., Buffalo, 1951-55; sales rep. Universal Time Plan, Inc., Buffalo, 1955-63, exec. v.p., 1963-65, pres. 1965-67; v.p., sr. v.p. Liberty Nat. Bank & Trust Co., Buffalo, 1967-72, exec. v.p., 1972—, also dir.; chmn. bd. Eastern States Bankcard Assn., N.Y.C., 1972-73, now dir.; dir., mem. exec. com. Interbank Card Assn. N.Y., 1973-77. Served with AUS, 1945-46. Mem. Buffalo C. of C., Am. Bankers Assn. (mem. communications council 1975-79, chmn. adv. council 2d Fed. Res. dist. 1973-76, mem. exec. com. installment lending div. 1973—, chmn. 1978-79, bd. dirs. 1978, bd. govs. 1978, mem. edn., research and devel. council 1979—), N.Y. State (mem. exec. com. consumer div.). Clubs: U. of Pa. Western N.Y. (life dir., past pres. Buffalo); Buffalo; Cherry Hill (Ridgeway, Ont., Can.). Contbg. author: The Modern Banking Handbook, 1977. Mem. adv. bd. Bankers Mag., 1975—. Home: 42 Dorset Dr Kenmore NY 14223 Office: 424 Main St Buffalo NY 14202

SHANAMAN, RICHARD LOWELL, drug chain exec.; b. Tacoma, Apr. 30, 1935; s. Fred Charles and Marjorie Blanch (Jefferies) S.; A.B., Dartmouth Coll., 1958; postgrad. Stanford U., 1967-69; m. Nancy Jean Cottrell, Nov. 8, 1975; children—Christa Ann, Kurt Arik. Asst. cashier City Bank, N.Y.C., 1958-62; v.p. Bank of Calif. N.A., San Francisco, 1963-69, F.S. Smithers & Co., Inc., San Francisco, 1969-72; pres. Pacific Intermountain Capital, Sun Valley, Idaho, 1972-74; sr. v.p., treas. Skaggs Cos., Inc., Salt Lake City, 1974-79, exec. v.p., treas., 1979—. Served with Army NG, 1959. Office: PO Box 30658 Salt Lake City UT 84125

SHANAS, ETHEL, educator; b. Chgo., Sept. 6, 1914; d. Alex and Rebecca (Rich) S.; A.B., U. Chgo., 1935, M.A., 1937, Ph.D., 1949; m. Lester J. Perlman, May 17, 1940; 1 son, Michael S. Sr. research analyst City of Chgo., 1952-53; instr. human devel., research asso. U. Chgo., 1947-52, sr. study dir. Nat. Opinion Research Center, 1956-61, asso. prof. sociology, 1961-65; lectr. sociology U. Ill., Chgo. Circle campus, 1954-56, prof., 1965—, prof. Med. Center, 1973—; Kesten Meml. lectr. U. So. Calif., 1975. Vice chmn. UN Expert Com. on Aging, 1974; mem. U.S. Nat. Com. on Vital and Health Statistics, 1976-79; bd. govs. Chgo. Heart Assn., 1972—; mem. City of Chgo. Adv. Council on Aging, 1972-78; bd. dirs. Schwab Rehab. Hosp., 1972—. Fellow Am. Sociol. Assn., Gerontol. Soc. (pres. 1974, Kleemeier award 1977); mem. Ill. Sociol. Assn. (pres. 1971), Midwest Sociol. Soc., Nat. Council on Family Relations (Burgess award 1978), Groves Conf., Internat. Center of Social Gerontology (France). Author: (with others) The Health of Older People, 1962; Old People in Three Industrial Societies, 1968. Editor: (with G.F. Streib) Social Structure and the Family, 1965; (with R.H. Binstock) Handbook of Aging and the Social Sciences, 1976; (with M.B. Sussman) Family, Bureaucracy and the Elderly, 1977. Home: 222 Main St Evanston IL 60202 Office: U Ill at Chgo Box 4348 Chicago IL 60680

SHANDS, HARLEY CECIL, psychiatrist; b. Jackson, Miss., Sept. 10, 1916; s. Harley Roseborough and Bessie Webb (Nugent) S.; B.S., Tulane U., 1936, M.D., 1939; M.S. in Medicine, U. Minn., 1945; m. Janet Hoffman, Mar. 25, 1943; children—Kathy, Betsy, Paul. Fellow medicine Mayo Clinic, 1941-45; research fellow psychiatry Mass. Gen. Hosp., Boston, 1945-48; asso. prof. psychiatry U. N.C. Med. Sch., 1953-61; prof. State U. N.Y. Med. Sch., Bklyn., 1961-66; dir. dept. psychiatry Roosevelt Hosp., N.Y.C., 1966—; clin. prof. psychiatry Columbia Coll. Phys. and Surg., 1966—; impartial specialist Workmen's Compensation Bd. N.Y. State. Commonwealth Fund fellow, London, 1958-59. Fellow Am. Psychiat. Assn.; mem. Group Advancement Psychiatry, Semiotic Soc. Am. Club: Cosmos (Washington). Author: Thinking & Psychotherapy, 1960; Semiotic Approaches to Psychiatry, 1970; The War with Words, 1971; Language and Psychiatry, 1973; Speech as Instruction, 1977. Home: Box 353 Glenford NY 12433 Office: 428 W 59th St New York NY 10019

SHANDS, WILLIAM RIDLEY, JR., lawyer; b. Richmond, Va., Nov. 23, 1929; s. William Ridley and Josephine (Winston) S.; B.A., Hampden-Sydney Coll., 1952; LL.B., U. Va., Charlottesville, 1958; m. Lynneth Williams, May 31, 1958; children—William Tyler, Laura Sawyer. Admitted to Va. bar, 1958; atty., asso. firm Christian, Barton, Epps, Brent & Chappell, Richmond, 1958-61; counsel The Life Ins. Co. of Va., Richmond, 1961-66, asst. gen. counsel, 1966-68, asso. gen. counsel, 1968-71, gen. counsel, 1971-73, v.p., gen. counsel, 1973-78, sr. v.p., gen. counsel, 1978—. Chmn. Eastern Appeal Bd., Selective Service System, 1969; pres., chmn. bd. dirs. Trinity Episcopal High Sch., 1971-72; bd. dirs. Richmond Area Heart Assn., 1965-71; bd. dirs. Southampton Cotillion, 1970-72; vestryman St. Michael's Epis. Ch., 1965-68, sr. warden, 1968. Served with AUS, 1952-55; Philippines. Mem. Am., Va., Richmond bar assns., Assn. Life Ins. Counsel, Am. Life Ins. Assn. (state v.p. 1973-75), Health Ins. Assn. Am., Va. Assn. Life Underwriters. Club: Commonwealth. Home: 3811 Darby Dr Midlothian VA 23113 Office: PO Box 27601 Richmond VA 23261

SHANE, BOB, singer; b. Hilo, Hawaii, Feb. 1, 1934; s. Arthur C. and Margaret (Schauffelburger) Schoen; B.S., Menlo Sch. and Coll., 1956; m. Louise Glancy Brandon, Mar. 15, 1959; children—Jody Glancy, Susan Hull, Inman Brandon, Robin Castle, Jason McCall. Singer with Kingston Trio, 1957—; plays colls., univs., night clubs in U.S., tours Far East, Europe, Australia; owner-leader Kingston Trio; owner Shane Inc., investment co., Honolulu. Recipient Gold record for Tom Dooley; 8 gold albums, 2 Grammys, Nat. Acad. Rec. Arts and Scis.; trio named Best Group of Year, Billboard, Cashbox, Best Show Attraction of Year, Ballroom Operators. Mem. Screen Actors Guild, Nat. Acad. Rec. Arts and Scis. (life), A.F.T.R.A., Am. Fedn. Musicians, Hawaii Mission Soc., Nat. Skeet Shooting Assn. (life). Republican. Presbyn. Address: 24 Milton Ave Alpharetta GA 30201

SHANE, CHARLES DONALD, astronomer; b. Auburn, Calif., Sept. 6, 1895; s. Charles Nelson and Annette (Futhey) S.; A.B., U. Calif., 1915, Lick Obs. fellow, 1916-17, 19-20, Ph.D., 1920, LL.D., 1965; m. Ethel L. Haskett, Dec. 24, 1917 (dec. Jan. 1919); 1 son, Charles Nelson; m. 2d, Mary Lea Heger, Dec. 29, 1920; 1 son, William Whitney. Instr. nav. U.S. Shipping Bd. 1917-19; instr. math., astronomy U. Calif., 1920-24, asst. prof. astronomy, 1924-29, asso. prof., 1929-35, prof., 1935-45, chmn. astronomy dept., Berkeley, 1941-42, asst. dir. Radiation Lab., Manhattan Project, 1942-44, asst. dir. in charge personnel Los Alamos Lab., 1944-45, dir. Lick Obs., 1945-58, astronomer, 1958-63. Pres., Assn. Univs. for Research in Astronomy, 1958-62; chmn. U.S. nat. com. for astronomy Internat. Astron. Union, 1966-68. Mem. Astron. Soc. Pacific (pres. 1940), Am. Philos. Soc., Nat. Acad. Scis., Royal Astron. Soc. (asso.), Sigma Xi, Phi Beta Kappa. Republican. Club: Faculty (Berkeley). Contbr. papers to profl. lit. Address: PO Box 582 Santa Cruz CA 95061

SHANE, HAROLD GRAY, educator; b. Milw., Aug. 11, 1914; s. Bert L. and Grace (Gray) S.; B.E., Milw. State Tchrs. Coll., 1935; M.A., Ohio State U., 1939, Ph.D., 1943; m. Ruth Williams, Sept. 1, 1938 (dec.); children—Michael Stewart, Susan Hatker, Patricia Mills, Ann Gray; m. 2d, Catherine McKenzie, July 6, 1974. Tchr., Cin. Pub. Schs., 1935-37; prin. Ottawa Hills Elementary Sch., Toledo, 1937-41; supr. elementary edn. State of Ohio, 1941-43; asst. prof. edn. Ohio State U., 1943-46; supt. schs., Winnetka, Ill., 1946-49; prof. edn. Northwestern U., 1949-59; dean Sch. Edn., Ind. U., Bloomington, 1959-65, Univ. prof. edn., 1965—; cons. U.S. Office Edn., Dept. Def., Danforth Found., numerous corps. Served as officer USNR, 1944-46. Recipient Outstanding Ednl. Journalist award Ed Press, 1974. Mem. NEA, Assn. Childhood Edn., Assn. Supervision and Curriculum Devel. (pres. 1973-74, exec. council 1972-75), Nat. Assn. Nursery Edn., Am. Assn. Sch. Adminstrs., Nat. Soc. Study Edn. (dir. 1968-78), Phi Delta Kappa, Kappa Delta Pi. Author over 100 books including: The Solar System, 1938; Magic of Electricity, 1939; Power Boat Book, 1947; The New Baby, 1948; (with E.T. McSwain) Evaluation and the Elementary Curriculum, 1951, rev. edit., 1958; The American Elementary School, 1953; (with W. A. Yauch) Creative School Adminstration, 1954; The Twins, 1955; Research Helps in Teaching the Language Arts, 1956; Beginning Language Instruction, 1960; (with others) Improving Language Arts Instruction, 1962; Linguistics and the Classroom Teacher, 1967; (with others) Guiding Human Development, 1971; The Educational Significance of the Future, 1973; (with others) The Elementary School in the U.S., 1973; (with Alvin Toffler et al.) Learning for Tomorrow, 1974; The Future of Education, 1975; The Future As an Academic Discipline, 1975; (with others) Issues in Secondary Education, 1976; Curriculum Change: Toward the 21st Century, 1977; (with others) Alternative Educational Systems, 1979. Contbr. numerous articles to popular and profl. jours. Home: 1416 Sare Rd Bloomington IN 47401. *G.B. Shaw explained my efforts when he said: "Those who have the chill of poverty in their bones are never fully warm again."*

SHANE, LEONARD, savs. and loan exec.; b. Chgo., May 28, 1922; s. Jacob and Selma (Shayne) S.; student U. Chgo., 1939-41, Ill. Inst. Tech., 1941-42; m. Marjorie Cynthia Konecky, Jan. 14, 1941; children—Judith Shane Shenkman, Marsha Kay Shane Palmer, William Alan, Shelley Rose, Shane Asidon. Writer-editor UPI, 1942-44; cons. indsl. areas, 1944-46; writer-rancher, Tucson, 1946-48; writer-producer ABC, Los Angeles, 1948-49; owner cons. agency, Los Angeles, 1949-64; chmn. bd., dir., mng. officer Mercury Savs. and Loan Assn., Huntington Beach, Calif., 1964—; pres., dir. Shellrose Corp.; pres., dir. Hermes Fin. Corp. Chmn. United Jewish Welfare Fund of Orange County, 1972-73; pres. Western region, mem. internat. bd. govs. Am. Assos. Ben Gurion U., Israel; pres. Los Angeles Recreation and Park Commn., 1960-63, Jewish Fedn. Council of Orange County, 1973-74; trustee Ocean View Sch. Dist., 1970-72, City of Hope, 1968—. Mem. Calif. Savs. and Loan League (dir. 1969-73), Phi Sigma Delta. Clubs: Big Canyon Country, Masons, Shriners. Office: 7812 Edinger Ave Huntington Beach CA 92647. *My life has represented a most worthwhile combination of family, business and civic relationships. While business has always been a source of satisfaction, pride and enjoyment, the real values have manifested themselves in having my close family members as friends which makes this bond stronger and warmer. At the same time, I have been blessed with the opportunity to devote over one third of my productive hours to civic and community activities in areas of deep concern and interest, which has provided an enrichment which can be grasped only by those who have shared this type of experience on an ongoing basis.*

SHANE, RITA, opera singer; b. N.Y.C.: d. Julius J. and Rebekah (Milner) Shane; B.A., Barnard Coll., 1958; postgrad. Santa Fe Opera Apprentice Program, 1962-63, Hunter Coll. Opera Assn., 1962-64; pvt. study with Beverly Peck Johnson, 1961—; m. Daniel F. Tritter, June 22, 1958; 1 son, Michael Shane. Performer with numerous opera cos., including profl. debut Chattanooga Opera, 1964, N.Y.C. Opera, Chgo. Lyric Opera, San Diego Opera, Santa Fe Opera, Teatro alla Scala, Milan, Italy, 1970—, Bavarian State Opera, 1970—, Netherlands Nat. Opera, 1970—, Geneva Opera, 1971—, Vienna State Opera, 1973—, Phila., 1978—, New Orleans, 1975—, Met. Opera, 1973—, Balt. Opera, 1974—, Opera du Rhin, Strasbourg, 1974—, Scottish Opera, 1975—, Teatro Regio, Turin, 1976—, Opera Metropolitana, Caracus, 1978, others; participant Mozart Festival, Lincoln Center, N.Y.C., Munich Festival, Aspen Festival, Handel Soc., Vienna Festival, Salzburg Festival, Perugia Festival, Festival Canada, Glyndebourne Festival; performed with orchs. including Clarion, Berkshire, Albany, Santa Cecilia, Rome, Austrian Radio, Louisville, Cin., Cleve., Phila., Naples, Denver, Milw., Israel Philharmonic; rec. artist RCA, Columbia, Louisville labels. Recipient Martha Baird Rockefeller award, William Matheus Sullivan award. Mem. A.G.M.A. Office: care Herbert H Breslin Inc 119 W 57th St New York NY 10019

SHANE, SHELDON RICHARD, mag. pub.; b. Bklyn., July 22, 1929; s. Herman W. and Rose G. (Ritter) S.; B.A., Columbia U., 1950; m. Saundra C. Kaplan, Oct. 10, 1954; children—Scott Elliot, Cathy Lynn. Mem. staff Travel mag., Floral Park, N.Y., 1950—, exec. v.p., 1972-77, pub., 1977—; with Allsport Pub. Co., Floral Park, 1955—, pub., 1970—. Mem. Marine Resources Council, 1974-75; pres. 5-Town United Way, 1975-76; chmn. Environ. Mgmt. Council Nassau County, 1973—; trustee, dep. mayor, Hewlett Neck, N.Y., 1969-76, mayor, 1976—; adv. bd. Franklin Gen. Hosp., Valley Stream, N.Y., 1974—, trustee, 1979—; sr. v.p. Nassau County Village Officers Assn., 1979—. Served with M.C., AUS, 1950-51. Mem. Mag. Pubs. Assn. Republican. Clubs: Friars (N.Y.C.); Woodmere Bay Yacht (commodore 1975); Inwood Country.

SHANET, HOWARD STEPHEN, condr., educator; b. N.Y.C., Nov. 9, 1918; s. Eugene Joseph and Jennie (Diesenhouse) S.; A.B. with honors in Music (Pulitzer scholar), Columbia U., 1939, A.M. in Musicology (William Mitchell Honor fellow), 1941; m. Bernice Grafstein, Oct. 10, 1963; 1 son, Laurence Paul. Instr., Hunter Coll., 1941-42, 46-53; asst. condr. N.Y. City Symphony Orch., 1947-48, to Serge Koussevitzky on internat. tour, 1949-50; condr. Berkshire Music Center, Tanglewood, Mass., 1949-52, Huntington (W.Va.) Symphony Orch., 1951-53, Music-in-the-Making, N.Y.C., 1958-61, String Revival. N.Y.C., 1975—; asst. prof. music Columbia U., 1953-59, asso. prof., 1959-69, prof., 1969—, chmn. dept. music, 1972-78, dir. music performance, 1978—, condr. univ. orch., 1953—; mem. nat. screening com. for conducting Fulbright Awards, 1967-72, 76-77; judge various music competitions, 1966—; mem. advisory bd. Sta. WNCN, 1976—; author, participant TV series Learn to Read Music, 1962, 63; condr., guest condr. orchs., U.S. and abroad, including premieres of many Am. and European works. Served with U.S. Army, 1942-46; Iwo Jima. Decorated Bronze Service Star; recipient Presdl. citation Nat. Fedn. Music Clubs, 1977; certificate of distinguished service Inst. Internat. Edn., 1977; MacDowell Colony fellow, 1953, 63; Huntington Hartford Found. fellow, 1954; Martha Baird Rockefeller grantee, 1962-63. Mem. Coll. Music Soc. (nat. council), Am. Musicol. Soc., Sonneck Soc., Fed. Music Soc. (council advisers 1977—), Sibelius Soc. (adv. com.). Author: Learn to Read Music, 1956 (also Brit., Norwegian, Italian edits.); Philharmonic, A History of New York's Orchestra, 1975; editor: Early Histories of the New York Philharmonic, 1979; contbr. articles to Mus. Quar., Saturday Rev., N.Y.C. Symphony and N.Y. Philharmonic program notes; mus. compositions include: Allegro Giocoso for String Quartet (or String Orch.), Variations on a Bizarre Theme for orch.; also works for mil. band, piano, chamber ensembles. Home: 1235 Park Ave New York City NY 10028 Office: 703 Dodge Hall Columbia U New York City NY 10027

SHANGE, NTOZAKE, poet, playwright; b. Trenton, N.J., Oct. 18, 1948; d. Paul T. and Eloise Williams; B.A. in Am. Studies cum laude, Barnard Coll., 1970; M.A. in Am. Studies (NDEA fellow), U. So. Calif., 1973. Plays: for colored girls who have considered suicide/when the rainbow is enuf, 1976; negress, 1977; a photograph: lovers in motion, 1977; where the mississippi meets the amazon, 1977; from okra to greens: a different love story, 1978; boogie woogie landscapes, 1978; magic spell #7, 1979; author books: for colored girls..., 1975; sassafrass: a novella, 1976; nappy edges, 1978; 8 pieces & 'a photograph', 1979; contbr. poetry, essays and short stories to numerous mags. and anthologies, including: Black Scholar, Yardbird, Indigine, Ms., Third World Women, Sojourner, Bopp, Essence, Heresies, The Little Mag., Chgo. Rev., Am. Rag, Womansports; performing mem. Sounds in Motion Dance Co.; performed in various jazz/poetry collaborations; mem. faculty Sonoma State U., 1973-75, Mills Coll., 1975, CCNY, 1975, Douglass Coll., 1978; lectr. in field. Recipient award Outer Critics Circle, 1977; OBIE award, 1977; Audelco award, 1977; Frank Silvera Writer's Workshop award, 1978. Mem. Actors Equity, Nat. Acad. TV Arts and Scis., Acad. Am. Poets, Dramatist's Guild, PEN Am Center, 112 Workshop, Poets and Writer's, Inc., N.Y. Feminist Art Guild, Woman's Inst for Freedom of Press. Office: Zaki Pony Inc Suite 503 1270 Broadway New York NY 10001

SHANK, CLARE BROWN WILLIAMS, former asst. chmn. Republican Nat. Com.; b. Syracuse, N.Y., Sept. 19, 1909; d. Curtiss Crofoot and Clara Irene (Shoudy) Brown; B.Oral English, Syracuse U., 1931; m. Frank E. Williams, Feb. 18, 1940 (dec. Feb. 1957); m. 2d, Seth Carl Shank, Dec. 28, 1963 (dec. Jan. 1977). Tchr., 1931-33; merchandising exec., 1933-42; Pinellas County mem. Rep. State Com., 1954-58; life mem. Pinellas County Rep. Exec. Com.; exec. com. Fla. Rep. Com., 1954-64; mem. exec. com. Rep. Nat. Com., 1956-64, asst. chmn. and dir. women's activities, 1958-64; alt., mem. exec. arrangements com. Rep. Nat. Conv., 1960; alt., program and arrangement coms. Rep. Nat. Conv., 1964; pres. St. Petersburg Women's Rep. Club, 1955-57. Mem. Def. Adv. Com. on Women in Services, 1959-65; trustee St. Petersburg Housing Authority, 1976—. Recipient George Arents medal Syracuse U., 1959; citation for patriotic civilian service 5th U.S. Army and Dept. Def. Mem. AAUW, Gen. Fedn. Women's Clubs, DAR, Colonial Dames 17th Century, Fla. Fedn. Women's Clubs (dist. pres. 1976-78), Zeta Phi Eta, Pi Beta Phi (nat. officer 1945-48). Methodist. Clubs: Woman's (pres. 1974-76), Bath, Yacht (St. Petersburg). Home: 1120 North Shore Dr NE Apt 901 Saint Petersburg FL 33701

SHANK, HOWARD CORTLAND, advt. exec.; b. Tulsa, Oct. 20, 1921; s. Lloyd C. and Jessie Lena (Rice) S.; student Lake Forest Coll., 1942; m. Hollis McLaughlin, Apr. 5, 1966; children—Kathleen, Susan. Exec. v.p. Leo Burnett Co., Chgo., 1949-73, chmn. bd. U.S.A., 1973-78; pres., chief operating officer Leo Burnett Co., Inc., 1978—. Bd. dirs. Shedd Aquarium, Mus. Contemporary Art, Off-the-Street Club, Lake Forest Coll. Mem. Kappa Sigma. Clubs: Racquet, Arts, Saddle and Cycle, Mid America (Chgo.); Owentsia Country (Lake Forest, Ill.). Office: Leo Burnett Co Inc Prudential Plaza Chicago IL 60601*

SHANK, ROBERT ELY, physician; b. Louisville, Sept. 2, 1914; s. Oliver Orlando and Isabel Thompson (Ely) S.; A.B., Westminster Coll., 1935; M.D., Washington U., 1939; m. Eleanor Caswell, July 29, 1942; children—Jane, Robert Oliver, Bruce. Intern, house physician Barnes Hosp., 1939-41; asst. resident physician, asst. in research Hosp. Rockefeller Inst. Med. Research, 1941-46; research asso. div. nutrition and physiology Pub. Health Research Inst. City N.Y., 1946-48; prof. preventive medicine Washington U. Sch. Medicine, 1948-55, Danforth prof. preventive medicine, 1955—. Cutter lectr. preventive medicine Harvard, 1964. Mem. food and nutrition bd. NRC, 1949-69; spl. cons. nutrition USPHS, 1949-53; chmn. adv. bd. health and hosps. St. Louis County, 1949-54; med. adv. bd. St. Louis Vis. Nurses Assn., 1950—; mem. com. food and nutrition nat. adv. bd. health services A.R.C., 1950-53; mem. adv. com. metabolism Office Surgeon Gen., 1956-60, mem. adv. com. on nutrition, 1964-72; mem. Am. Bd. Nutrition, 1955-64, sec., treas. 1958-64; mem. Nat. Bd. Med. Examiners, 1957-58; co-dir. nutrition survey NIH, Peru, 1959, N.E. Brazil, 1963, mem. sci. adv. bd. Nat. Vitamin Found., 1958-61; mem. nutrition study sect. NIH, 1964-68, chmn. sect., 1966-68; mem. gastroenterology and nutrition tng. com., 1968-69, mem. nat. adv. child health and human devel. council, 1969-73; mem. clin. application and prevention adv. com. Nat. Heart, Lung and Blood Inst., 1976-80. Served as lt. comdr. M.C., USNR, 1942-46. Recipient Alumni Achievement award Westminster Coll., 1970. Diplomate Am. Bd. Nutrition. Fellow Am. Pub. Health Assn. (governing council 1955-56); mem. N.Y. Acad. Scis., Harvey Soc., Am. Soc. Biol. Chemists, Soc. Exptl. Biology and Medicine (council 1952-54), Central Soc. Clin. Research, Am. Soc. Clin. Investigation, Assn. Tchrs. Preventive Medicine (v.p. 1955-57, pres. 1957-58), A.M.A. (council on foods and nutrition 1960-69, chmn. 1963-66), Gerontological Soc., Assn. Am. Physicians, Am. Soc. Clin. Nutrition (council 1963-65, pres. 1967-68), Am. Dietetic Assn. (hon.), Am. Soc. for Study Liver Diseases (council 1963-66, pres. 1966), Am. Heart Assn. (chmn. nutrition com. 1973-76), Am. Inst. Nutrition, Sigma Xi, Alpha Omega Alpha. Author: sects. in med. textbooks; sci. paper relating to nutritional, metabolic disorders. Asso. editor: Nutrition Revs., 1948-58; editorial adv. bd. Nutrition Today, 1966-76. Home: 1325 Wilton Ln Kirkwood MO 63122 Office: 4566 Scott Ave St Louis MO 63110

SHANK, RUSSELL, librarian, univ. adminstr.; b. Spokane, Wash., Sept. 2, 1925; s. Harry and Sadie S.; B.S., U. Wash., 1946, B.A., 1949; M.B.A., U. Wis., 1952; Dr.L.S., Columbia, 1966; m. Doris Louise Hempfer, Nov. 9, 1951 (div.); children—Susan Marie, Peter Michael, Judith Louise. Reference librarian U. Wash., Seattle, 1949; asst. engrng. librarian U. Wis., Madison, 1949-52; chief personnel Milw. Pub. Library, 1952; engrng.-phys. scis. librarian Columbia U., N.Y.C., 1953-59, sr. lectr., 1964-66, asso. prof., 1966-67; asst. univ. librarian U. Calif. at Berkeley, 1959-64; dir. sci. library project N.Y. Met. Reference and Research Agy., 1966-68; dir. libraries Smithsonian Instn., Washington, 1967-77; univ. librarian, prof. U. Calif., Los Angeles, 1977—; cons. Indonesian Inst. Sci., 1970; bd. cons. Pahlavi Nat. Library, Iran, 1975-76; pres. U.S. Book Exchange, 1975; trustee OCLC, Inc., 1978—; mem. library del. People's Republic of China, 1979. Served with USNR, 1943-46. Recipient Distinguished Alumnus award U. Wash. Sch. Librarianship, 1968; fellow Council on Library Resources, 1973-74. Mem. ALA (pres. 1978-79, council 1961-65, 74—, exec. bd. 1975—, pres. info. sci. and automation div. 1968-69), Assn. Coll. and Research Libraries (pres. 1972-73), Assn. Research Libraries (dir. 1974-77), Spl. Libraries Assn., Am. Soc. Info. Sci., AAAS. Office: Univ Research Library U Calif Los Angeles CA 90024. *Intellectual freedom is the paramount human right. It is the American's premier heritage. Without it the pretension of democracy is a sham. Should the principles of our society fade or perish, the survival of this freedom alone would justify the nation's experience. The freedom to think, to read, and to speak will be our enduring monument. Their diffusion throughout the world must be our unending crusade.*

SHANK, STEPHEN GEORGE, lawyer, toy mfg. co. exec.; b. Tulsa, Dec. 6, 1943; s. Louis Warren and Lillian Margaret S.; B.A., U. Iowa, 1965; M.A. (Woodrow Wilson fellow), Fletchers Sch., Tufts U., 1966; J.D., Harvard U., 1972; m. Judith Frances Thompson, July 17, 1966; children—Susan, Mary. Admitted to Minn. bar, 1972; mem. firm Dorsey, Marquart, Windhorst, West & Halladay, Mpls., 1972-74, 78-79, Dorsey, Windhorst, Hannaford, Whitney & Halladay, Mpls., 1978-79; gen. counsel Tonka Corp., Hopkins, Minn., 1974-78, sec., 1974-79, pres., chief exec. officer, 1979—, also dir.; asst. prof. law William Mitchell Coll. Law, 1974-77. Bd. dirs. Loring-Nicollet-Bethlehem Center, Mpls., 1977. Served with U.S. Army, 1966-69. Decorated D.S.M. Mem. Am., Minn. State bar assns. Asso. editor Harvard Law Rev., 1971-72. Home: 5345 Oliver Ave S Minneapolis MN 55419 Office: 4144 Shoreline Blvd Spring Park MN 55384

SHANK, WILLIAM O., lawyer; b. Hamilton, Ohio, Jan. 11, 1924; s. Horace Cooper and Bonnie (Winn) S.; B.A., Miami U., Oxford, O., 1947; J.D., Yale, 1950; m. Shirleen Allison, June 25, 1949; children—Allison Kay, Kristin Elizabeth. Admitted to Ohio, Ill. bars, also U.S. Supreme Ct. bar; practice in Hamilton, Ohio, 1950-55, Chgo., 1955—; mem. firm Shank, Briede & Spoerl, 1950-55; asso. Lord, Bissell & Brook, 1955-58; atty. Chemetron Corp., 1958-60, sr. atty., 1960-61, gen. atty., asst. sec., 1961-71, sec., gen. counsel, 1971-78; v.p., gen. counsel, sec. Walgreen Co., Deerfield, Ill., 1978—. Mem. bus. adv. council Miami U., Oxford, 1975—; bd. dirs. Council for Community Services Met. Chgo., 1973-77; trustee Library Internat. Relations, 1971-78. Served to 1st lt. USAAF, World War II; ETO. Mem. Am., Ill., Chgo. bar assns., Am. Soc. Corp. Secs., Yale Law Sch. Assn. (past pres. Ill., exec. com. New Haven), Legal Club (pres.), Law Club, Northwestern U. Corp. Counsel Inst. (chmn. planning com. 1973), Sigma Chi, Omicron Delta Kappa, Phi Delta Phi. Clubs: Yale (N.Y.C.); University, Economic (Chgo.). Home: 755 S Shore Dr Crystal Lake IL 60014 Office: 200 Wilmot Rd Deerfield IL 60015

SHANKER, ALBERT, labor union ofcl.; b. N.Y.C., Sept. 14, 1928; s. Morris and Mamie S.; B.A., U. Ill., 1949; postgrad. Columbia U.; m. Edith Gerber, 1960; children—Adam, Jennie, Michael. Tchr. elementary schs., jr. high sch. math. pub. schs., N.Y.C., 1952-59; pres. United Fedn. Tchrs., N.Y.C., 1964—, Am. Fedn. Tchrs., Washington, 1974—; v.p. AFL-CIO, 1973—; exec. v.p. N.Y. State United Tchrs., 1972-78; v.p. N.Y. State AFL-CIO, 1973—; v.p. N.Y.C. Central Labor Council; sec. Jewish Labor Com., 1965—; asso. Univ. Seminar on Labor, Columbia; hon. vice chmn. Am. Trade Union Council for Histadrut; mem. exec. com. Workers Def. League. Mem. labor com. Boy Scouts Am., 1969. Bd. dirs. A. Philip Randolph Inst., 1965—, N.Y.C. Council Econ. Edn., 1969—, United Fund Greater N.Y., 1964—, Internat. Rescue Com., 1973—; mem. adv. council dept. sociology Princeton; mem. internat. adv. council Population Inst., 1976—; trustee Center for Urban Edn. Contbr. articles to profl. and popular publs. Office: 11 Dupont Circle Washington DC 20036 also 260 Park Ave S New York NY 10010

SHANKER, MORRIS GERALD, lawyer, educator; b. Cleve., Aug. 23, 1926; s. Hyman and Anna (Kaplan) S.; B.S. in Elec. Engring., Purdue U., 1948; M.B.A., J.D., U. Mich., 1952; m. Bernice Jacobs, Dec. 16, 1956; children—Chari, Jaymie Ann. Admitted to Ohio bar, 1952; asso. firm Grossman, Schlesinger & Carter, Cleve., 1952-61; prof. law Case Western Res. U., Cleve., 1961—, acting dean Law Sch., 1972—. Vis. prof. law. U. Mich., 1964, U. Cal. at Berkeley, 1966, Wayne State U., 1969, U. London, 1971; cons., asst. reporter adv. com. on bankruptcy rules U.S. Supreme Ct., 1965-68, mem. com., 1969-77; mem. Nat. Bankruptcy Conf., 1966—; comml. and labor arbitrator; spl. master r.r. reorgn. procedures; lectr. comml. and bankruptcy law throughout country, 1961—. Served with USNR, 1944-46. Mem. Am., Ohio, Cleve. bar assns., Am. Law Inst., Order of Coif, Tau Beta Pi, Eta Kappa Nu. Contbr. articles to profl. jours. Home: 15712 Chadbourne Rd Shaker Heights OH 44120 Office: Case Western Res U Cleveland OH 44106

SHANKLAND, ROBERT SHERWOOD, physicist; b. Willoughby, Ohio, Jan. 11, 1908; s. Frank North and Margaret Jane (Wedlock) S.; B.S., Case Inst. Tech., 1929, M.S., 1933, Ph.D., U. Chgo., 1935; m. Hilda C. Kinnison, June 20, 1931 (dec. 1970); children—Ruth (Mrs. William Fielder), Dorothy (Mrs. John Eisenhour), Ava (Mrs. Thomas Prebys), Lois (Mrs. Ronald McIntyre), Sherwood John; m. 2d, Eleanor Newlin Griffiths, 1971. Physicist, Nat. Bur. Standards, Washington, 1929-30; faculty physics dept. Case Inst. Tech., 1930— (on leave at U. Chgo. 1934-36), Ambrose Swasey prof. physics, 1941—, head physics dept., 1939-58 (on leave to Columbia 1942-45). Physicist, Naval Ordnance Lab., Washington, 1941; dir. Unnderwater Sound Reference, Labs. OSRD, N.Y.C., 1942-46; physics cons. Standard Oil Co. (Ohio), 1947—; physicist Radiation Lab., U. Calif., summers 1946, 49, AEC Materials Testing Reactor, Ida., summers 1955-58, 61-69; cons. Philips Petroleum Co., 1957—; cons. in archtl. acoustics. Chmn. hydrophone adv. com. USN, 1942-46. Mem. council of participating instns. Argonne Nat. Lab., 1946—, mem. exec. council, 1951-54. Pres. bd. trustees Andrews Sch. for Girls, Willoughby, Ohio; bd. dirs. Asso. Midwest Univs., 1958—, past v.p., pres., 1960-61. Recipient Presdl. certificate of Merit, 1948. Fellow Am. Phys. Soc. (pres. Ohio sect. 1947-48), Acoustical Soc. Am. (exec. council 1944-47), A.A.A.S.; mem. Am. Inst. Physics (chmn. com. on student orgn. 1958—, mem. governing bd. 1966-69), Am. Standards Assn. (chmn. underwater sound com. 1946-49), Optical Soc. Am., Franklin Inst., Clev. Physics Soc. (pres. 1948-49), Am. Assn. Physics Tchrs. (exec. council 1963-66), Sigma Xi, Sigma Pi Sigma, Tau Beta Pi, Theta Tau, Sigma Alpha Epsilon. Author: Atomic and Nuclear Physics, 1955, 60. Editor: Sonar Calibration Methods, 1946; Sonar Calibrations, 1946; Collected Papers of Arthur H. Compton, 1973. Asso. editor: Review of Scientific Instruments, 1949-52, Am. Jour. Physics. Contbr. articles to sci. publs. Home: 15800 Hazel Rd East Cleveland OH 44112 Office: 10900 Euclid Ave Cleveland OH 44106

SHANKLIN, J. GORDON, lawyer, former govt. ofcl.; b. Elkton, Ky., Dec. 10, 1909; s. William S. and Eva J. (Jones) S.; B.A., Vanderbilt U., 1932, LL.B., 1934; m. Emily Shacklett, July 15, 1933; children—Elizabeth Eve, William Samuel. Admitted to Tenn. bar, 1934, Tex. bar, 1975; with FBI, Washington, 1943-75, spl. agt. in charge, Mobile, Ala., 1952-55, Pitts. office, 1955-56, insp. hdqrs., Washington, 1956-58, spl. agt. in charge El Paso. (Tex.) office, 1958-59, Honolulu office, 1959-63, Dallas, 1963-75; partner firm Johnson, Guthrie, Nash & Shanklin, Dallas, 1975-78, Johnson, Shanklin, Billings, Kelton & Porter, Dallas, 1978—; instr. various police acads. Recipient numerous profl. awards and citations from civil and police orgns. Baptist. Home: 6023 Del Norte Dallas TX 75225

SHANKLIN, RICHARD VAIR, III, mech. engr.; b. Bklyn., Feb. 12, 1937; s. Richard Vair and Sue Hall (Morfit) S.; B.S.M.E., Duke U., 1959; M.S., U. Tenn., 1965, Ph.D., 1971; m. Sept. 6, 1958; children—Carolyn Dennett, Anne Landon Scott. Engring. asst. Phillips Petroleum Co. (Tex.), 1959-60; asso. engr. Boeing Co., Seattle, 1960-62; design engr. Aro Inc., Arnold Air Force Sta., Tenn., 1962-64; chief engr. J.B. Dicks & Assos., Inc., Tullahoma, Tenn., 1967-70; asso. prof. mech. engring. technology Nashville State Tech. Inst., 1971-72; asst. prof. U. Tenn., Tullahoma, 1972-73; sr. scientist Systems Research Labs., Dayton, Ohio, 1973-75; asst. dir. MHD div. ERDA, Washington, 1975-77; sr. staff engr. Energy Systems Group, TRW Inc., Morgantown, W.Va., 1977-78; dir. MHD div. Dept. Energy, Washington, 1978-79; mgr. combustion programs Energy Systems Group, TRW, Inc., Redondo Beach, Calif., 1979—. Recipient Spl. Achievement awards ERDA, 1976, 77. Mem. ASME (George Westinghouse silver medal 1976), Sigma Xi. Episcopalian. Author papers and reports in field. Home: 29600 Island View Dr Rancho Palos Verdes CA 90274 Office: TRW Inc Redondo Beach CA 90278

SHANKMAN, FLORENCE VOGEL, educator; b. Norwalk, Conn., July 16, 1912; d. Morris and Betty (Jacobson) Vogel; student Danbury State Coll., 1930; B.S., Tchrs. Coll., Columbia U., 1934, M.A., 1936; M.A., N.Y. U., 1955, Ed.D., 1959; m. Louis Shankman, Aug. 29, 1937 (dec. 1952) children—Martin, Robert S., Susan E. Pub. sch. tchr., Norwalk, Conn., 1930-37, 53-59; tchr. fgn. born and high sch. equivalency courses, Norwalk, 1939-47, New Rochelle, N.Y., 1950-51, Wilton, Conn., 1952-53; instr. N.Y. U. Sch. Edn., also N.Y. U. Reading Inst., 1955-59; supr. instrn. N.Y. U. Reading Inst., N.Y.C., 1959-62; asso. prof. edn. U. So. Calif., summer 1962; asst. prof. edn. U. Bridgeport (Conn.), 1962-65; asso. prof. edn. Keene (N.H.) State Coll., 1965-67; asso. prof. Temple U. Coll. Edn., Phila., 1967-72, prof. curriculum and instrn., 1972-79, prof. emerita, 1979—; guest prof. State U. Colo., Greeley, 1967; vis. prof. Coll. of Holy Names, Oakland, Calif., summer 1969; publs. cons. Silver Burdett (Gen. Learning Corp.), 1979; reading cons., author, 1955—. Mem. Acad. Reading Experts to assist N.Y.C. Bd. Edn., 1961-67; mem. N.H. Ednl. Policies Commn., 1966-68; del. World Congress of Reading, Sydney, Australia, 1970, Buenos Aires, Argentina, 1972. First aid instr. ARC; active Conn. Mental Health Assn., Tb and Health Assn., Crippled Children's Assn. drives; mem. women's com. Norwalk Symphony Orch.; exec. bd. Danbury State Coll. Mem. Nat. Soc. for Study Edn., NEA, Conn. Edn. Assn., AAUP, AAUW, Am. Psychol. Assn., Elementary Prins. Assn., Assn. Supervision and Curriculum Devel., Nat. Council Tchrs. English, Internat. Reading Assn., New Edn. Fellowship, Am. Assn. Sch. Adminstrs., Assn. Childhood Edn. Internat. (life), Nat. Council Jewish Women (pres. 1938), Am. Ednl. Research Assn., Assn. Student Teaching, Nat. Council Social Studies (exec. bd. dirs. New Edn. fellowship N.Y. chpt.), Coll. Reading Assn., Piaget Soc., Pa. Edn. Assn., N.Y. U. Faculty Club and Alumni Assn., Internat. Platform Assn.. U. Bridgeport, Newcomers Faculty Club (sec., treas., 1963—), Kappa Delta Pi (life), Pi Lambda Theta (mem. nat. publs. bd., pres. Phila. area chpt. 1978—), Phi Delta Kappa (rec. sec. Temple br. 1977—). Clubs: Women's Press (N.Y.C.); Temple U. Faculty Women's (sec., treas. 1973-74, pres. 1976-79). Author: (with Robert Kranyik) How to Teach Study Skills, 1963; Successful Practices in Remedial Reading, 1963; How to Teach Reference and Research Skills, 1964; Readings About Reading Instruction, 1968; Research Studies in Reading, Vol. I, II, 1969; Readings in the Language Arts, 3 vols., 1969; Reading Success for Young Children, 1970; Reading for Inner City Children, 1970; Methods of Teaching Reading, 1970; Specialized Methods of Teaching Reading, 1970; Teaching Reading and Language to Inner City Children, 1971; Teaching Techniques With Phonics, Linguistics and Games, 1971; Games and Activities to Reinforce Reading Skills, 2d edit., 1973; Crossword Puzzles for Phonics, 1972, 74; film We Discover the Encyclopedia, 1971; also revs. Contbr. to profl. mags. Home: 32 West Ave South Norwalk CT 06854 also Columbia Ave Philadelphia PA 19122

SHANKS, ANN ZANE, filmmaker, photographer, writer; b. N.Y.C.; d. Louis and Sadye (Rosenthal) Kushner; ed. Carnegie Mellon U., Columbia U.; m. Ira Zane (dec.); children—Jennifer, Anthony; m. 2d, Robert Horton Shanks, Sept. 25, 1959; 1 son, John. Filmmaker, photographer, writer for numerous mags., newspapers including Life, Time, Esquire, Fortune. N.Y. Times, Redbook, Cosmopolitan; producer Women on the Move, NBC-TV; script editor CBS; asso. producer World Video, Inc.; producer, dir. Central Park (movie short, U.S. engry Edinburgh Film Festival; Cine Golden Eagle, Cambodia Film Festival award), 1969; producer, dir. Denmark... A Loving Embrace (Cine Golden Eagle 1973), Tivoli (movie short, San Francisco Film Festival award, Am. Film Festival award), 1972-79, TV series American Life Style (one silver and four gold medal awards Internat. TV and Film Festival N.Y., two Golden Eagle awards); producer, dir., writer short Mousie Baby; dir. TV movie The Walls Came Tumbling Down; exhibited photographs Mus. Modern Art, Mus. City N.Y., Met. Mus. Art, Jewish Mus., Caravan Gallery, Parents Mag.; tchr., moderator spl. symposiums Mus. Modern Art, Ednl. Alliance, N.Y.C. Recipient 4 awards, internat. competitions. Mem. Am. Soc. Mag. Photographers (bd. govs.), Overseas Press Club Am. (chmn. 1970 photog. awards). Author: The Name's the Game (photographs and text), 1961; New Jewish Ency. (photographs), 1966; Adolescent Development (photographs), 1967; Old Is What You Get (photographs and text), 1976; writer, photographer: (juvenile) Garbage and Stuff. Home: 904 N Bedford Dr Beverly Hills CA 90210

SHANKS, EUGENE BAYLIS, mathematician, educator; b. Sumrall, Miss., Nov. 17, 1913; s. James William and Minnie Elnora (Baylis) S.; B.A., Millsaps Coll., 1938; M.A., Vanderbilt U., 1940; Ph.D., U. Ill., 1947; m. Mary Olivia Harris, June 13, 1940; children—Judith Olivia (Mrs. Ira Claude Denton, Jr.), Eugene Baylis Jr. Faculty math. Vanderbilt U., 1940-41, 47—, prof., 1954—, chmn. dept., 1956-69, dir. summer sessions, 1956, 57. Dir. summer insts. for high sch. tchrs. sci. and math. NSF and Vanderbilt U., 1959, 60; civilian instr. Air Force Preflight Nav. Sch., Maxwell Field, 1942; cons. to computation div. George C. Marshall Space Flight Center, Huntsville, Ala., NASA, 1962-69. Mem. holding bd. Am. Bapt. Theol. Sem. Served from 2d lt. to capt. USAAF, 1942-46. Recipient Wisdom award, 1970. Fellow Tenn. Acad. Sci. (chmn. math. sect.); mem. A.A.A.S., Am. Math. Soc., Math. Assn. Am. (chmn. Southeastern sect. 1961-62, cons. 1962—, lectr. 1962-63), Tenn. Math. Tchrs. Assn. (pres. 1955, past chmn. finance com.), Alumni Assn. Millsaps Coll. (dir.), Sigma Xi, Pi Mu Epsilon. Baptist (trustee, deacon). Kiwanian. Author numerous monographs on original solutions of differential equations by evaluations of functions through Runge-Kutta type procedures, including first developed formulas of orders seven, eight, nine and ten. Home: 4007 Harding Pl Nashville TN 37215

SHANKS, HERSHEL, lawyer, editor; b. Sharon, Pa., Mar. 8, 1930; s. Martin and Mildred (Freedman) S.; B.A., Haverford (Pa.) Coll., 1952; M.A., Columbia, 1953; LL.B., Harvard, 1956; m. Judith Alexander Weil, Feb. 20, 1966; children—Elizabeth Jean, Julia Emily. Admitted to D.C. bar, 1956; trial atty. Dept. Justice, 1956-59; pvt. practice, Washington, 1959—; partner firm Glassie Pewett, Beebe & Shanks, since 1964—; editor Bibl. Archaeology Rev., Washington, 1975—. Pres. Bibl. Archaeology Soc., 1974—. Mem. exec. com. United Jewish Appeal, 1972—; nat. council Joint Distbn. Com., 1975—. Mem. Am., Fed., D.C. bar assns., Am. Schs. Oriental Research, Phi Beta Kappa. Club: Nat. Lawyers (Washington). Author: The Art and Craft of Judging, 1968; The City of David, 1973; Judaism in Stone, 1979; also articles. Home: 5208 38th St NW Washington DC 20015 Office: 1737 H St NW Washington DC 20006. *I try to take time to identify what is important in my life, to focus on that and ignore the rest when it conflicts. It takes conscious effort not to dissipate energy on activities and attitudes that don't matter in the big picture of my priorities. Free to concentrate on what I value most, I try to accomplish something each day in a regular, habitual way.*

SHANLEY, BERNARD MICHAEL, lawyer; b. Newark, 1903; s. Bernard Michael and Regina (Ryan) S.; student Columbia U., 1925, Fordham U. Law Sch., 1928; m. Maureen Virginia Smith, Aug. 1, 1936; children—Maureen S. Kirk, Seton, Kevin, Brigid, Brendan. Admitted to N.J. bar, 1929, D.C. bar, 1969; in practice under name Shanley & Fisher, Newark, 1952; on leave of absence from firm to act as dep. chief staff and spl. counsel to Pres. U.S., 1953-55, sec. to Pres., 1955-57. Former chmn. N.J. Republican Fin. Com.; exec. com. Rep. Nat. Com.; mem. Rep. Nat. com. for N.J., vice chmn. N.E. area, 1968—; mem. Gen. Eisenhower's personal staff, 1952 campaign; chmn. adv. bd. St. Benedict's Prep. Sch., Newark; trustee Victoria Found., Am. Inst. Mental Studies, N.J. Research Found. for Mental Hygiene, Allocca Found.; mem. Found. for Ednl. Alternatives; mem. exec. com. Archbishop's Com. of Laity, Newark. Served with AUS, 1942-45. Designated knight St. Gregory the Great (Pope John Paul II); recipient War Dept. citation. Fellow Am. Bar Found.; mem. Am., N.J., Essex County, Somerset County bar assns., N.J. Golf Assn. (trustee). Roman Catholic. Clubs: Two Hundred Somerset County; Two Hundred, Essex County (Newark); Metropolitan, Capitol Hill (Washington); Nat. Golf Links Am. (Southampton); Roxiticus Golf (pres.) (Mendham, N.J.). Home: Bernardsville NJ 07924 Office: 550 Broad St Newark NJ 07102

SHANLEY, PAUL JOSEPH, publisher; b. Scranton, Pa., Dec. 24, 1925; s. Gerald Edward and Marcella Marie (Coyne) S.; B.S., U. Scranton, 1947; m. Isobel Culley, Mar. 28, 1953; children—Mimi, Kate, Eliza, Jane. Sales exec. Nat. Advt. Service, N.Y.C., 1953-62; pres. Fine Arts Media, N.Y.C., 1962-74; pub. Art in Am., N.Y.C., 1974—. Served with USAAF, 1943-44. Home: 141 Greenway S Forest Hills Gardens NY 11375 Office: 850 3d Ave New York City NY 10022

SHANNAHAN, JOHN HENRY KELLY, energy cons., assn. exec.; b. Sparrows Point, Md., Nov. 1, 1913; s. John Henry Kelly and Beulah Williams (Day) S.; A.B., Princeton, 1934; postgrad. U. Mich., 1954, sr. exec. program, Mass. Inst. Tech., 1959; m. Mary Reynolds Kline, Apr. 22, 1939; children—John H.K., James R., Jennifer K. (Mrs. Bernard R. Koerner, Jr.). Comml. mgr. Ind.-Mich. Electric Co., 1955-59; asst. v.p. Am. Electric Power Service Corp., 1959-61; asst. to pres. Kans. Power & Light Co., 1961-63; v.p., exec. dir. Electric Heating Assn., 1962-72; pres. Electric Energy Assn., 1972-75; sr. v.p. Edison Electric Inst., N.Y.C., 1975—; cons. energy matters, 1975—; dir. Energy Utilization Systems Inc., EUS Inc. Served to maj. F.A., AUS, 1942-45; ETO. Decorated Bronze Star with oak leaf cluster; recipient Trend Maker award Elec. Info. Publs. Inc., 1967. Mem. Am. Mktg. Assn. Presbyn. (elder). Clubs: Princeton (N.Y.C.); Leland Yacht. Home: Route 1 Box 36 Lake Leelanau MI 49653

SHANNON, DAVID ALLEN, univ. ofcl., historian; b. Terre Haute, Ind., Nov. 30, 1920; s. John Raymond and Esther (Allen) S.; B.S., Ind. State Coll., 1941; M.S., U. Wis., 1946, Ph.D., 1951; m. Jane Short, Aug. 31, 1940; children—Molly Shannon Osborne, Sarah Shannon Olson. Instr. history Carnegie Inst. Tech., 1948-51; asst. prof., then asso. prof. Columbia Tchrs. Coll., 1951-57; faculty U. Wis., 1957-65, prof. history, 1960-65; prof., chmn. dept. history U. Md., 1965-68, Rutgers U., 1968-69; prof. history, dean faculty arts and scis. U. Va., Charlottesville, 1969-71, v.p., provost, 1971—, Commonwealth prof. history, 1975—; tchr. U. Calif. at Berkeley, 1957, U. Stockholm, 1959, U. Lund (Sweden), 1960, U. Aix-Marseille (France), 1962-63; Thomas Jefferson vis. fellow Downing Coll., U. Cambridge (Eng.), fall 1976. Served with USAAF, 1943-45. Mem. Orgn. Am. Historians (past exec. com.), Am., So. hist. assns. Author: The Socialist Party of America: A History, 1955; The Decline of American Communism, 1959; Twentieth Century America, 1963; Between the Wars, 1965, 2d edit., 1979; co-author: A History of Teachers College Columbia University, 1954; editor: The Great Depression, 1960; Beatrice Webb's American Diary, 1898, 1963; Progressivism and Postwar Reaction, 1966. Home: Pavilion V West Lawn U Va Charlottesville VA 22903

SHANNON, DONALD HAWKINS, newspaperman; b. Auburn, Wash., Feb. 1, 1923; s. Ernest Victor and Fern (McConville) S.; B.A., Stanford, 1943, postgrad. Law Sch., 1946-47; m. Sally van Deurs, June 13, 1952; children—John McConville, Susanna Shepard. Reporter, Brazil Herald, Rio de Janeiro, 1947-48, U.P.I., London, Eng., 1949-51, Western Reporters, Washington, 1951-53; mem. staff Los Angeles Times, 1954—, bur. chief, Paris, France, 1962-65, Africa, 1965-66, Tokyo, Japan, 1966-71, UN, N.Y.C., 1971-75, Washington bur., 1975—. Served with AUS, 1944-46; PTO. Mem. Phi Gamma Delta. Clubs: Federal City, City Tavern (Washington); Overseas Press (N.Y.C.); Foreign Correspondents (Tokyo). Address: care Los Angeles Times Washington Bur 1700 Pennsylvania Ave NW Washington DC 20006

SHANNON, EDFRED L., JR., corp. exec.; b. 1926; B.S., U. Calif., Berkeley, 1951; married. Petroleum engr. Union Oil Co. of Calif., 1951-53; with Santa Fe Internat. Corp., 1953—, v.p. Orange, Calif., 1960-63, pres., chief exec. officer, 1963—, also dir. Office: Santa Fe Internat Corp 505 S Main St PO Box 1401 Orange CA 92668*

SHANNON, EDGAR FINLEY, JR., educator; b. Lexington, Va., June 4, 1918; s. Edgar Finley and Eleanor (Duncan) S.; A.B., Washington and Lee U., 1939, Litt.D., 1959; A.M., Duke U., 1941, Harvard U., 1947; Rhodes scholar Merton Coll., Oxford, 1947-50, D.Phil., Oxford U., 1949; LL.D., Southwestern at Memphis, 1960, Duke U., 1964, Hampden-Sydney Coll., 1971; H.H.D., Wake Forest Coll., 1964; D.H.L., Thomas Jefferson U., Phila., 1967; Litt.D., Centre Coll., 1968, Coll. William and Mary, 1973; L.H.D., Bridgewater Coll., 1970; m. Eleanor H. Bosworth, Feb. 11, 1956; children—Eleanor, Elizabeth, Lois, Susan, Virginia. Asso. prof. naval. sci. and tactics Harvard U., 1946, instr. English, 1950-52, asst. prof. English, 1952-56; asso. prof. English, U. Va., Charlottesville, 1956-59, prof. English, 1959-74, pres., 1959-74, Commonwealth prof. English, 1974—; mem. state and dist. selection coms. Rhodes scholars; pres. Council So. Univs., 1962-64, 71-72; pres. State Univs. Assn., 1963-64; exec. com. Nat. Assn. State Univs. and Land-Grant Colls., 1964-67, chmn. exec. com., 1966-67, pres., 1965-66; mem. So. Regional Edn. Bd., 1963-71; bd. govs. Nat. Commn. for Accrediting, 1961-67; mem. U.S. Nat. Commn. for UNESCO, 1966-67; mem. Pres.'s Commn. on CIA Activities within U.S., 1975. Bd. visitors U.S. Naval Acad., 1962-64, USAF Acad., 1965-67; bd. cons.'s Nat. War Coll., 1968-71; bd. dirs. Am. Council on Edn., 1967-70, vice chmn., 1971-72; trustee Washington and Lee U., 1973—, Thomas Jefferson Meml. Found., 1973—, Darlington Sch., 1966-76, Mariners Mus., 1966-75, Colonial Williamsburg Found., 1975—; chmn. Va. Found. Humanities and Pub. Policy, 1973-79; v.p. Oceanic Edn. Found., 1968—; bd. adminstrs. Va. Inst. Marine Sci., 1963-71; hon. v.p. Tennyson Soc., 1960—; mem. council White Burkett Miller Center for Pub. Affairs, 1975—. Guggenheim fellow, 1953-54; Fulbright research fellow, Eng., 1953-54. Served from midshipman to lt. comdr. USNR, 1941-46; capt. Res. ret. Decorated Bronze Star, Meritorious Service medal; Distinguished Eagle Scout, 1973; recipient Distinguished Service award Va. State C. of C., 1969; Medallion of Honor, Virginians of Md., 1964; Thomas Jefferson award U. Va., 1965; Algernon Sydney Sullivan award Washington and Lee U., 1939, U. Va., 1975; Jackson Davis award Va. chpt. AAUP, 1977. Mem. Assn. Va. Colls. (pres. 1969-70), Raven Soc., Signet Soc., Jefferson Soc., Modern Lang. Assn. Am., Soc. Cin., Phi Beta Kappa (senator 1967—, vis. scholar 1976-77, v.p. 1976-79, pres. 1979—), Omicron Delta Kappa, Phi Eta Sigma, Beta Theta Pi. Presbyterian. Clubs: Authors' (London); Century Assn.; Univ. (N.Y.C.). Author: Tennyson and the Reviewers, 1952; contbr. articles to various jours. Home: 1925 Blue Ridge Rd Charlottesville VA 22903

SHANNON, GAIL, univ. ofcl.; b. Wellsville, Kans., Apr. 25, 1917; s. Frank R. and Florence (Nolker) S.; B.S. in Edn., Kans. State Tchrs. Coll., 1939; M.A., Ohio State U., 1949, Ph.D., 1951; m. Helen Lorraine Edwards, May 28, 1939; children—Michael William, Mark Edward. Music instr. pub. schs., Kan., 1939-48; instr. edn. Coll. Edn. Ohio State U., 1949-51; faculty U. Okla., Norman, 1951-60, prof. edn., 1959-60, asst. dean Coll. Edn., 1958-60; dean acad. affairs Eastern N.Mex. U., Portales, 1960-67, v.p. acad. affairs, 1967-75, acting pres., 1975; exec. v.p. West Tex. State U., Canyon, 1977—. Served with USNR, 1942-45. Mem. Nat., Tex. edn. assns., Phi Delta Kappa, Kappa Delta Pi, Phi Kappa Phi, Phi Mu Alpha. Republican. Methodist. Club: Kiwanis. Home: 13 Eagle Pass Canyon TX 79015

SHANNON, IRIS REED, ednl. adminstr.; b. Chgo.; d. Ira Paul and Iola Sophia (Williams) S.; B.S. in Nursing, Fisk U.-Meharry Med. Coll., 1948; M.A., U. Chgo., 1954; m. Robert Alwood Shannon, Aug. 21, 1953. Staff nurse Chgo. Bd. Health, 1948-50; instr. pub. health nursing Meharry Med. Coll., Nashville, 1951-56; tchr.-nurse, health coordinator child devel. Head Start, Chgo. Bd. Edn., 1957-66; dir. community nursing Mile Sq. Neighborhood Health Center, Presbyn.-St. Luke's Hosp., Chgo., 1966-69; co-dir. nurse asso. programs Rush Presbyn.-St. Luke's Hosp., 1971-76; chairperson community nursing Rush U., Chgo., 1972-77; asst. prof. pub. health nursing U. Ill., 1971-74; asso. prof. community nursing Rush U., 1974—; adj. faculty Sch. Public Health, U. N.C., 1977—; mem. profl. adv. bd. Vis. Nurse Assn. Chgo., 1973-75; cons. Video Nursing, Inc.; mem. profl. adv. com. Mile Sq. Home Health Unit, Chgo., 1975—; mem. Nat. Adv. Council on Nurse Tng., HEW, 1978—. Recipient award of merit Ill. Public Health Assn., 1979. Rockefeller fellow, 1953-54. Fellow Am. Pub. Health Assn. (chmn. pub. health nursing sect. 1977-79); mem. Am. Nurses Assn., Am. Sch. Health Assn., Inst. Medicine of Nat. Acad. Scis., Delta Sigma Theta.

SHANNON, JAMES A., med. investigator, educator; b. Hollis, N.Y., Aug. 9, 1904; s. James A. and Anna (Margison) S.; A.B., Holy Cross Coll., Mass., 1925; M.D., N.Y. U., 1929, Ph.D., 1935; numerous hon. degrees from U.S., fgn. instns.; m. Alice Waterhouse, June 24, 1933; children—Alice, James Anthony. Intern, Bellevue Hosp., N.Y.C., 1929-31; asst. dept. physiology N.Y. U. Coll. Medicine, 1931-32, instr., 1932-35, asst. prof., 1935-40, asst. prof. dept. medicine, 1941, asso. prof., 1941-46; dir. research service N.Y. U. med. div. Goldwater Meml. Hosp., 1941-46; dir. Squibb & Sons, Squibb Inst. Med. Research, 1946-49; asso. dir. in charge research Nat. Heart Inst., 1949-52; asso. dir. NIH, 1952-55, dir., 1955-68; scholar-in-residence Nat. Library Medicine, 1975—; prof. biomed. scis., spl. adviser to pres. Rockefeller U., N.Y.C., 1970-75, adj. prof., 1975—; scholar in human biology Eleanor Roosevelt Inst. for Cancer Research, 1977—. Cons. tropical diseases to sec. war, 1943-46; spl. cons. surgeon gen. USPHS, 1946-49, asst. surg. gen., 1952-68; mem. Bd. for Coordination Malarial Studies, chmn. clin. panel, 1943-46; mem. subcom. on shock NRC, 1952-56, NRC exec. com., mem.-at-large, 1954-55, USPHS rep., 1955-63, chmn. panel on malaria Div. Med. Scis., 1951-56; mem. U.S. nat. com. Internat. Union Physiol. Scis., 1955-62; mem. expert adv. panel on malaria, WHO, 1956-66, founding mem. adv. com. on med. research, 1959-63; founding mem. adv. com. on med. research Pan Am. Health Orgn., 1962-66; cons. med. affairs AID, 1963-68; cons. Pres.'s Sci. Adv. Com., 1959-65; HEW rep. and vice-chmn. standing com. Fed. Council Sci. and Tech., 1960-68; mem. selection com. Rockefeller Pub. Service awards Princeton U., 1969-73; mem. N.Y.C. Bd. Health, 1970-71. Recipient Presdl. medal for Merit, 1948; Mendel medal Villanova U., 1961; Rockefeller Pub. Service award, 1964; Distinguished Service medal HEW, 1964; Presdl. Distinguished Fed. Civilian Service award, 1966;

3d Ann. award Hadasash Myrtle Wreath, 1968; Rosenberger medal U. Chgo., 1968; John Phillips Meml. award A.C.P., 1969; Nat. Medal Sci., 1974; award for distinguished contbns. Soc. Research Adminstrs., 1975. Fellow Am. Pub. Health Assn.; mem. Am. Soc. Pharmacology and Exptl. Therapeutics, Am. Physiol. Soc., Am. Soc. Clin. Investigation, Am. Acad. Arts and Scis., Am. Philos. Soc., Royal Soc. Physicians London, Soc. Exptl. Biology and Medicine, Harvey Soc., Assn. Am. Physicians, AAAS, Nat. Acad. Scis. (Pub. Service award 1964, mem. bd. on medicine 1967-70, academic council 1970-73, exec. com. 1970-73), Inst. on Medicine (founding mem. 1970), Nat. Acad. Pub. Adminstrn., Sigma Xi, Alpha Omega Alpha. Club: Cosmos. Contbr. articles to profl. jours. Home: 8302 SW Homewood St Portland OR 97225 Office: Rockefeller U New York NY 10021

SHANNON, JAMES MICHAEL, congressman; b. Methuen, Mass., Apr. 4, 1952; s. Martin J. and Mary J (Sullivan) S.; B.A., Johns Hopkins U., 1973; J.D., George Washington U., 1975; m. Silvia de Araujo Castro, Dec. 2, 1973. Admitted to Mass. bar, 1975, D.C. bar, 1976; practice law, Lawrence, Mass., 1976-78; mem. 96th Congress from 5th Mass. Dist. Democrat. Roman Catholic. Home: 142 E Haverhill St Lawrence MA 01841 Office: 226 Cannon House Office Bldg Washington DC 20515

SHANNON, JAMES PATRICK, lawyer, found. exec.; b. South St. Paul, Minn., Feb. 16, 1921; s. Patrick Joseph and Mary Alice (McAuliffe) S.; B.A. in Classics, Coll. St. Thomas, St. Paul, 1941; M.A. in English, U. Minn., 1951; Ph.D., Yale U., 1955; J.D., U. N.Mex., 1973; LL.D., U. Notre Dame, 1964, Macalester Coll., 1964, Lora Coll., 1964, DePaul U., 1965, St. Mary's Coll., 1965, Carleton Coll., 1965, Creighton U., 1966, Northland Coll., Ashland, Wis., 1979; Litt.D., Seton Hall, 1965, Coe Coll., Cedar Rapids, Iowa, 1966, U. Minn., 1966; J.U.D., Lawrence U., 1969; m. Ruth Church Wilkinson, Aug. 2, 1969. Ordained priest Roman Catholic Ch., 1946; asst. prof. history Coll. St. Thomas, 1954-56, pres., 1956-66; aux. bishop Archdiocese of St. Paul, 1965-68; pastor St. Helena Parish, Mpls., 1966-68; tutor Greek St. John's Coll., Santa Fe, 1969-70, v.p., 1969-70; mem. firm Sutin, Thayer & Browne, Albuquerque, Santa Fe, 1973-74; exec. dir. Mpls. Found., 1974-78; columnist, writer, found. cons., 1978—; dir. Toro Co., Inc., Foxley & Co., Denver. Bd. dirs. Bush Found., Citizens' League, Mpls., Council on Founds., Washington, Edward W. Hazen Found., New Haven, Conn., James J. Hill Library, St. Paul, dir. Walker Art Center, Mpls.; chmn. Minn. Council on Founds.; mem. Minn. State Bd. for Continuing Legal Edn.; chmn. Rhodes Scholarship Selection Com. for Upper Midwest Selection Com. Mem. D.C. Bar Assn., N. Mex. Bar, Assn., Minn. Bar Assn. Democrat. Author: Catholic Colonization on the Western Frontier, 1957. Address: PO Box 112 Wayzata MN 55391

SHANNON, LYLE WILLIAM, educator, sociologist; b. Storm Lake, Iowa, Sept. 19, 1920; s. Bert Book and Amy Irene (Sivits) S.; B.A., Cornell Coll., Mt. Vernon, Iowa, 1942; M.A., U. Wash., 1947, Ph.D., 1951; m. Magdaline W. Eckes, Feb. 27, 1943; children—Mary Louise, Robert William, John Thomas, Susan Michelle. Faculty, U. Wis., 1952-62, asso. prof., 1958-62; prof. sociology U. Iowa, 1962—, chmn. dept. sociology and anthropology, 1962-70. Vis. prof. Wayne State U., 1956-57, Portland State U., summer 1956, U. Colo., summers 1960, 61; dir. Iowa Urban Community Research Center, 1970—. Served with USNR, 1942-46. Mem. Am. Sociol. Assn., Midwest, Pacific sociol. socs., AAAS, Population Assn. Am., Soc. Applied Anthropology, Phi Beta Kappa. Author: Underdeveloped Areas, 1957; Minority Migrants in the Urban Community, 1973. Contbr. numerous articles to profl jours. Home: River Heights Iowa City IA 52240

SHANNON, MARGARET RUTLEDGE, newspaper reporter; b. New Albany, Miss., July 4, 1917; d. James Biggs and Fannie (Rutledge) Shannon; B.J., U. Mo., 1939. With Neshoba Democrat, Philadelphia, Miss., 1939-40, Suffolk (Va.) News-Herald, 1941, Tupelo (Miss.) Jour., 1942-43, Atlanta Jour., 1944-66, Washington corr., 1962-66; mem. staff Atlanta Jour.-Констn. mag., 1967—. Recipient Headliners, Sigma Delta Chi, Edn. Writers Assn. awards, 1951. Reid fellow, 1952. Presbyterian. Home: 570 Lakeshore Dr Duluth GA 30136 Office: 72 Marietta St NW Atlanta GA 30302

SHANNON, MELVIN LEROY, ins. co. exec.; b. Fort Morgan, Colo., June 15, 1925; s. Oren and Lodoska (McElhiney) S.; student U. Colo., 1948-53; m. Mary Ellen Palm, Nov. 15, 1946; children—John Edward, Ronald David, Randall James, Russell Dean, Jerold Paul. Asst. casualty actuary Nat. Farmers Union Property & Casualty Co., Denver, 1955-62; with Occidental Fire & Casualty Co. N.C., Denver, 1962—, v.p., treas., 1969-73, pres., 1973—; pres., dir. Wilshire Ins. Co., 1977—, Allied Mgmt. Co., 1979—. Served with USAAF, 1943-46. Mem. Ins. Accounting and Statis. Assn. (past sec.-treas., v.p. Rocky Mountain chpt.), Nat. Assn. Ind. Insurers (bd. govs. 1975—). Home: 9050 E Big Canon Pl Englewood CO 80111 Office: 5670 S Syracuse Circle Englewood CO 80111

SHANNON, MICHAEL EDWARD, steel co. exec.; b. Evanston, Ill., Nov. 21, 1936; s. Edward Francis and Mildred Veronica (Oliver) S.; B.A., U. Notre Dame (Ind.), 1958; M.B.A., Stanford U., 1960; m. A. Laura McGrath, July 4, 1964; children—Claire Oliver Mary, Kathryn Ann Elizabeth. With Continental Oil Co., Houston, 1960-62; with Gulf Oil Corp., 1962-75, asst. treas., 1965-66, treas. Gulf Oil Co.—U.S., Houston, 1970-72, Gulf Oil Co.—Eastern Hemisphere, London, 1972-75; treas. Republic Steel Corp., Cleve., 1975—, v.p., 1978—. Trustee Cancer Center, Inc., Cleve., 1976—, Beech Brook, Cleve., 1977—, Cleve. Inst. Music, 1978—, Laurel Sch., 1978—; mem. gen. bd. ARC, 1979—. Mem. Cleve. Treasurers Club (dir.), Cleve. Council World Affairs, Fin. Execs. Inst., Am. Iron and Steel Inst., Stanford Bus. Sch. Assn., Stanford Bus. Sch. Assn. Roman Catholic. Clubs: Cleve. Athletic, The Country; Univ. (N.Y.C.); Notre Dame Alumni Assn. Office: PO Box 6778 Cleveland OH 44101

SHANNON, THOMAS ALFRED, assn. exec.; b. Milw., Jan. 2, 1932; s. John Elwood and Eleanor Ann (Mitchell) S.; B.S., U. Wis, 1954; J.D., U. Minn., 1961; m. Barbara Ann Weidner, June 26, 1954; children—Thomas Alfred, Paul J., Suzanne L., Terrence D. Admitted to Minn. bar, 1961, Calif. bar, 1963, U.S. Supreme Ct. bar, 1965, D.C. bar, 1977; practiced law, Mpls., 1961-62; schs. atty. San Diego City Schs., 1962-73; dept. supt., gen. counsel, 1973-77; exec. dir. Nat. Sch. Bds. Assn., Washington, 1977—; adj. prof. law and edn. U. San Diego; mem. Edn. Commn. of States; prof. Nat. Acad. Sch. Execs., 1971—; legal counsel Am. Assn. Sch. Adminstrs., 1973-77. Chmn. San Diego County Juvenile Justice Commn. 1973-74; mem. Nat. council Boy Scouts Am., 1979—. Served with USN, 1954-59. Life cert. as sch. adminstr., Calif. Mem. Am. Bar Assn. (chmn. com. public edn. 1978—), Nat. Orgn. on Legal Problems of Edn. (pres. 1973), Nat. Sch. Bds. Assn. (chmn. council sch. attys. 1967-69). Exec. pub. The American School Board Jour., 1977—, Exec. Educator, 1977—. Home: 3811 N 26th St Arlington VA 22207 Office: 1055 Thomas Jefferson St Washington DC 20007

SHANNON, THOMAS FRANCIS, lawyer; b. Lowell, Mass., June 11, 1927; s. Philip F. and Catherine M. (Duffy) S.; A.B., Bowdoin Coll.; LL.B., U. Va.; m. Helen Joyce Gonyea, Sept. 2, 1950. Legis. asst. to Senator Styles Bridges of N.H., 1955-57; chief minority counsel U.S. Senate Com. on Appropriations, 1958; partner firm Collier, Shannon, Rill, Edwards & Scott, Washington, 1959—. Served with USNR, 1945-46. Mem. Am. Bar Assn. Clubs: Metropolitan, Congressional, University (Washington); Duquesne (Pitts). Home: 3006 P St NW Washington DC 20007 Office: 1055 Thomas Jefferson St NW Washington DC 20007

SHANNON, WILLIAM VINCENT, ambassador, former newspaperman; b. Worcester, Mass., Aug. 24, 1927; s. Patrick Joseph and Nora Agnes (McNamara) S.; A.B. magna cum laude, Clark U., 1947, D.Litt., 1964; M.A., Harvard U., 1948; D.Litt., New Rochelle Coll., 1971; L.H.D., Boston U., 1976; LL.D., Sacred Heart U., Bridgeport, 1978; m. Elizabeth McNelly, Aug. 5, 1961; children—Liam Anthony, Christopher Andrew, David Patrick. Free-lance writer, Washington, 1949-51; Washington corr., columnist N.Y. Post, 1951-64; editorial bd. N.Y. Times, 1964-77; ambassador to Ireland, 1977—. Bd. dirs., sec. Am. Irish Found.; trustee Clark U. Recipient Page One award for nat. coverage N.Y. Newspaper Guild, 1951, Edward J. Meeman award for conservation writings Scripps-Howard Found., 1968, 76; Gold medal Am. Irish Hist. Soc., 1979. Fellow in residence Center Study Democratic Instns., Santa Barbara, Calif., 1961-62; Alicia Patterson Fund fellow, London. 1969-70. Mem. Phi Beta Kappa. Roman Catholic. Clubs: Cosmos (Washington); Century (N.Y.C.). Author: (with R.S. Allen) The Truman Merry-Go-Round, 1950; The American Irish, 1964; The Heir Apparent, 1967; They Could Not Trust The King, 1974. Contbr. articles to mags. Office: Embassy of US 42 Elgin Rd Dublin 4 Ireland

SHANOR, LELAND, botanist, educator; b. Butler, Pa., July 21, 1914; s. Paul Leland and Marion (McCandless) S.; A.B., Maryville Coll., 1935; M.A., U. N.C., 1937; Ph.D., 1939; D.Sc. (hon.), Ill. Wesleyan U., 1961; m. Mary Williams Ward, June 20, 1940; children—Charles Algernon, Paul Leland II. Asst. biology Maryville Coll., 1933-35; grad. asst., teaching fellow botany U. N.C., 1935-39, fellow Highlands Lab., summer 1937, dir. Highlands Mus. Natural History, summer 1939; instr. botany Clemson Coll., 1939-40; instr. botany U. Ill., 1940-43, asst. prof., 1946-48, asso. prof., 1948-51, prof., 1951-56, curator mycol. collections, 1948-56; prof. botany Fla. State U. 1956-63, head dept. biol. sci., 1956-62, dean div. advanced studies Fla. Inst. for Continuing Univ. Studies, 1962-65; prof. U. Fla., Gainesville, 1965—, chmn. dept. botany, 1965-73. Sect. head div. sci. personnel and edn. NSF, 1964, dir. div. undergraduate edn. in sci., 1965; pathologist Dept. Agr., 1943-44; research mycologist OSRD, George Washington U., 1944-45; research asso. Johnson Found. U. Pa., Panama C.Z. Lab., 1946; mem. adv. com. C.Z. Biol. Area, 1954—; mem. sci. adv. com. Ill. Wesleyan U., 1956—, Inter-Inst. Commn. on Nuclear Research, 1957-63, sec., 1957-58, chmn., 1958-59; cons. div. sci. personnel and edn. NSF, 1960-63; mem. sci. adv. com. Fairchild Tropical Garden, 1966—, trustee, 1971—; treas. 2d Internat. Mycol. Congress, 1977; adv. com. Southeastern Plant Environment Labs., 1968-73. Bd. govs. Center for Research in Coll. Instrn. Sci. and Math., 1967-70, sec., 1968, chmn., 1970; trustee Highlands Biol. Sta., 1956—, pres. bd., 1958-63. Recipient Alumni citation Maryville Coll., 1965; Merit citation Highlands Biol. Sta., 1964. Guggenheim fellow, 1951-52. Fellow A.A.A.S., mem. Bot. Soc. Am. (chmn. south-eastern sect. 1966), Mycol. Soc. Am. (sec.-treas. 1951-53, editor newsletters 1950-53, pres. 1954, councilor 1955-57), Ill. Acad. Sci. (sec. 1949-51, councilor 1951-53, pres. 1955), Assn. Southeastern Biologists (treas. 1962-65, v.p. 1970-71, pres. 1972-73), Nature Conservancy, Sigma Xi, Phi Sigma, Gamma Sigma Delta. Rotarian. Editorial bd. Ill. Biol. Monographs, 1948-56, chmn., 1953-56; editorial bd. MYCOLOGIA, 1961-70. Contbr. articles to profl. pubs. Home: 2816 NW 21st Ave Gainesville FL 32605

SHANSBY, JOHN GARY, consumer products co. exec.; b. Seattle, Aug. 25, 1937; s. John Jay and Jule E. (Boyer) S.; B.A., U. Wash., 1959; m. Joyce Ann Dunsmore, June 21, 1959; children—Sheri Lee, Kimberly Ann, Jay Thomas. Dist. sales mgr. Colgate-Palmolive Co., N.Y.C., 1959-67; subs. pres. Am. Home Products Corp., N.Y.C., 1968-71; v.p. Clorox Co., Oakland, Calif., 1972-73; v.p. Booz, Allen & Hamilton, San Francisco, 1974-75; pres., chief exec. officer, dir. Shaklee Corp., Emeryville, Calif., 1975—. Bd. dirs. Bay Area Council; mem. San Francisco Internat. Film Festival Bd., San Francisco Host Com.; trustee Springfield Coll., Art Inst.; mem. bd. U. Calif. at Berkeley Bus. Sch. Founded J. Gary Shansby chair Mktg. Strategy, U. Calif., Berkeley. Mem. Calif. Roundtable, Am. Mgmt. Assn., Newcomen Soc., San Francisco C. of C. (dir.), Sigma Nu. Republican. Clubs: Commonwealth, Villa Traverna, Olympic (San Francisco); Silverado (Calif.) Country; Pennask Lake Fishing (B.C.).

SHANTZER, LOUIS, apparel co. exec.; b. Bklyn., Sept. 30, 1930; s. Herman and Irene (Turk) S.; B.B.A., Coll. City N.Y., 1953; m. Judith Glauber, Dec. 5, 1954; children—Sara, Hope. Audit mgr. firm Eisner & Lubin, C.P.A.'s, N.Y.C., 1953-65; controller Russ Togs, Inc., N.Y.C., 1965—, sec., 1972—. C.P.A., N.Y. Mem. N.Y. Soc. C.P.A.'s. Home: 12 Mohawk Ave Rockaway NJ 07866 Office: 1411 Broadway New York City NY 10018

SHAO, OTIS HUNG-I, commn. exec.; b. Shanghai, China, July 18, 1923; s. Ming Sun and Hannah (Chen) S.; came to U.S., 1949, naturalized, 1956; B.A., St. John's U., 1946; M.A., U. Colo., 1950; Ph.D., Brown U., 1957; m. Marie Sheng, Apr. 2, 1955. From instr. to prof. polit. sci. Moravian Coll., Bethlehem, Pa., 1954-62; asso. prof., then prof. polit. sci. Fla. Presbyn. Coll., St. Petersburg, 1962-68; prof. internat. politics, dean Grad. Sch., U. Pacific, 1968-74, dir. Pub. Affairs Inst., 1969-74; provost Callison Coll., 1974-76; dean faculty, v.p. Occidental Coll., 1976-78; asso. exec. dir. sr. commn. Western Assn. Schs. and Colls., 1978—. Mem. grad. students relations com. Council Grad. Schs. U.S., 1970-73; mem. exec. council undergrad. assessment program Ednl. Testing Service, 1978—. Chmn. bd. dirs. Fgn. Policy Assn. Lehigh Valley, 1961-62; bd. dirs. World Affairs Council San Joaquin County, 1969—; trustee Inst. Med. Scis., Pacific Med. Center, San Francisco, 1968-72, optical scis. group of Profl. and Pub. Service Found., San Francisco, 1969-72. Resident fellow Harkness House, Brown U., 1953-54; Danforth Asso., 1958—; recipient Distinguished Service award Fgn. Policy Assn. Lehigh Valley, 1962. Mem. AAUP (pres. Fla. Presbyn. Coll. chpt. 1965-66), Am. Assn. Higher Edn., Rho Psi, Tau Kappa Epsilon. Democrat. Presbyn. Contbr. articles to profl. jours. Home: 2959 Hedge Ct Oakland CA 94602

SHAPERE, DUDLEY, educator; b. Harlingen, Tex., May 27, 1928; s. Dudley and Corinne (Pupkin) S.; B.A., Harvard U., 1949, M.A., 1955, Ph.D., 1957; m. Hannah Hardgrave; 1 dau., Hannah Elizabeth; children by previous marriage—Alfred Dudley, Catherine Lucretia. Instr. philosophy Ohio State U., 1957-60; asst. prof. U. Chgo., 1960-65, asso. prof., 1965-67, prof., 1967-72, mem. com. on evolutionary biology, 1969-72, chmn. undergrad. program in history and philosophy of sci., 1966-72, chmn. com. on conceptual founds. sci., 1970-72; prof. U. Ill., Urbana, 1972-75 chmn. program in history and philosophy of sci., 1972-75; prof. U. Md., College Park, 1975—, mem. com. on history and philosophy of sci., 1975—; vis. prof. Rockefeller U., 1965-66, Harvard U., 1968; mem. Inst. Advanced Study, Princeton, N.J., 1978-79; spl. cons. (program dir.) program in history and philosophy of sci. NSF, 1966-75; Sigma Xi nat. bicentennial lectr., 1974-77. Served with AUS, 1950-52. Recipient Quantrell award for excellence in undergrad. teaching U. Chgo., 1968. Fellow AAAS (sect. sec. 1972); mem. Philosophy Sci. Assn., History Sci. Soc., Am. Philos. Assn., Am. Psychol. Assn. Author: Philosophical Problems of Natural Science, 1965; Galileo: A Philosophical Study, 1974; editorial bd. Philosophy of Sci., Jour. for History and Philosophy Sci.; rev. bd. Philosophy Research Archives; contbr. articles to profl. jours. Home: 11200 Buckwood Ln Rockville MD 20852 Office: U Md College Park MD

SHAPERO, MARTIN MURRAY, lawyer; b. Detroit, Feb. 10, 1924; s. Aubrey and Serla (Stone) S.; B.A., U. Mich., 1945, postgrad. Law Sch., 1945-48; LL.B., Pacific Coast U., 1949; m. Ray Levin, Dec. 17, 1950; children—Steven, Bella, Miriam. Admitted to Calif. bar, 1950, since practiced in Los Angeles; mem. firm Corinbilt, Shapero & Seltzer, 1968—. Mem. Mayor's Commn. on Govt. Efficiency, City of Los Angeles. Mem. Am., Hollywood bar assns., State Bar Calif., Am. Legal History Soc., Delta Sigma Rho. Democrat. Jewish religion. Home: 5817 Nagle Ave Van Nuys CA 91401 Office: 3700 Wilshire Blvd Los Angeles CA 90010

SHAPEY, RALPH, composer, condr., educator; b. Phila., Mar. 12, 1921; s. Max and Lillian (Paul) S.; student violin with Emanuel Zetin, composition with Stefan Wolpe; m. Vera Shapiro, Oct. 28, 1957; 1 son, Max Klement. Asst. condr. Phila. Nat. Youth Adminstrn. Symphony Orch., 1938-42; guest condr. Phila. Symphony Orch. at Robin Hood Dell (winner Phila. Finds Contest), 1942; condr. 1st performance saxophone quartet by Wolpe, McMillan Theatre, N.Y.C., 1950, repeat performance Times Hall, N.Y.C., 1950; condr. clarinet concerto N.Y. Philharmonic Chamber Soc., 1955, Internat. Soc. Contemporary Music, N.Y.C., 1961, 62, Phila., 1961-63, Fromm Found. Concert, N.Y.C., 1962; guest condr. London Symphony Orch. for BBC; mus. dir. orch. and chorus U. Pa., 1963-64, vis. prof., 1973; mus. dir. Contemporary Chamber Players, U. Chgo., 1964—, prof. music, 1964—. Chmn. admissions com. MacDowell Colony. Served with AUS, 1942-45. Recipient Frank H. Beebe award for Europe, 1953; MacDowell Colony fellow, 1956-58; Clarinet Concerto selected to rep. U.S. at Strasbourg Festival, 1958; grantee Italian govt., 1959-60; recipient Creative Arts award Brandeis U., 1962, Edgar Stern Family Fund award, 1962, William and Noma Copley Fund award, 1962; Naumberg Rec. award, 1966; awarded Dimitri-Mitropoulos commn. for symphony orch., 1960; numerous others; Mem. Internat. Soc. Contemporary Music (dir.), ASCAP, Am. Composers Alliance, Am. Music Center. Composer numerous works, 1946—. latest being Challenge-The Family of Man, for symphony orchestra, 1955, Mutations, for piano, 1956, Duo for Viola and Piano, 1957, Ontogeny for symphony orchestra, 1958, Form for piano, 1959, Rituals for symphony orchestra, 1959, Dimensions for soprano and 23 instruments, 1960, Incantations for soprano and 10 instruments, 1961, Convocation for chamber group, 1962, Birthday Piece for piano, 1962, Brass Quintet, 1963, String Quartet VI, 1963, VII, Sonance for carillon, 1964, Configurations for Flute and Piano; Praise, oratorio, Variations for piano, O Jerusalem, for soprano and flute, Songs of Eros, for soprano, orch. and tape, others. Recs. include: Evocation for Violin with Piano and Percussion, Incantations for Soprano and 10 Instruments, Seven for Piano 4 Hands, Rituals for Symphony Orch., String Quartet No. 6, Songs of Ecstacy for Soprano, Piano and Percussion; Music for a 20th Century Violinist; Praise: Oratorio for Bass-Baritone, Double Chorus and Chamber Group, The Covenant for soprano and 16 players, 21 Variations for Piano, 31 Variations for Piano, Song of Songs I, Three for Six, others. Address: 5835 S University Ave Chicago IL 60637

SHAPIRO, ALBERT, paper co. exec., physician; b. Somerville, Mass., Oct. 12, 1913; s. Joseph and Ida (Chenzer) S.; B.S., U. Md., 1934, M.D., 1937; m. Sylvia Feldman, May 7, 1947; children—Eileen, Jane. Intern, Sinai Hosp., 1937-38; resident in dermatology N.Y. U. Skin and Cancer Hosp., 1938-40; pres. Md. Baking Co., Balt., 1947-60; v.p., treas. Md. Cup Corp., Owings Mills, Md., 1961-77, sr. v.p., treas., 1977—; prof. clin. dermatology U. Md. Med. Sch., 1974—. Bd. dirs. Balt. Symphony, 1969—, Balt. Hebrew Congregation, 1967-70; trustee Park Sch., Balt., 1965-68; pres. Balt. chpt. Hebrew U., Jerusalem, 1970—, Associated Jewish Charities Balt., 1976—. Served to lt. col. M.C., AUS, 1941-46. Fellow Am. Acad. Dermatology; mem. AMA, Phi Delta Epsilon. Democrat. Home: One Slade Ave Baltimore MD 21208 Office: 3635 Old Court Rd Baltimore MD 21208

SHAPIRO, ALVIN PHILIP, physician, educator; b. Nashville, Dec. 28, 1920; s. Samuel and Mollie (Levine) S.; A.B., Cornell U., 1941; M.D., L.I. Coll. Medicine, Bklyn., 1944; m. Ruth Thomson, 1951; children—Debra, David. Intern L.I. Coll. Hosp., Bklyn., 1944-45; asst. resident internal medicine Goldwater Meml. Hosp., N.Y.C., 1945-46; asst. resident psychiatry L.I. Coll. Hosp. and Kings County Hosp., 1947-48; practice acad. medicine specializing in internal medicine, Cin., 1948-51, Dallas, 1951-56, Pitts., 1956—; research fellow Cin. Gen. Hosp., 1948-49, med. teaching fellow Commonwealth Fund Psychosomatic Program, 1949-51, attending physician, 1949-51; attending physician Parkland, VA hosps., Dallas, 1951-56; attending physician Presbyn.-Univ. Hosp., Pitts., 1957-61, sr. staff, 1962—; attending physician VA Hosp., Pitts., 1960-66, cons., 1967—; co-dir. hypertension-renal clinic Falk Clinic U. Pitts., 1956-65, dir. hypertension clinic, 1965—; instr. dept. internal medicine U. Cin. Coll. Medicine, 1949-51; asst. prof. Southwestern Med. Sch., U. Tex., 1951-56; asst. prof. depts. clin. sci. and medicine U. Pitts. Sch. Medicine, 1956-60, asso. prof. dept. medicine, 1960-67, prof., 1967—, dir. psychosomatic program dept. medicine, 1960-71, acting chief renal sect., 1962-65, chief clin. pharmacology-hypertension sect., 1960-71, asso. dean acad. affairs, 1971-75, vice-chmn. dept. medicine, 1975-79, acting chmn. dept. medicine, 1977-79. Cons. AMA Council on Drugs, 1959, Med. Letter of Drugs and Therapy, 1960; Fulbright vis. prof. U. Utrecht, The Netherlands, 1968; chmn. spl. projects study com. Nat. Heart Inst., 1970, chmn. adv. com. nat. hypertension study, 1972—. Served as capt. M.C., AUS, 1946-47. Diplomate Am. Bd. Internal Medicine. Fellow A.C.P.; mem. Am. Fedn. Clin. Research, Am. Psychosomatic Soc. (sec.-treas. 1969-73, pres. 1975), AAAS, AMA, Am. Heart Assn. (med. adv. bd. council high blood pressure, council on circulation), Pa., Allegheny County med. socs., Am. Assn. Med. Colls., N.Y. Acad. Scis., Am. Diabetes Assn., Am. Soc. Clin. Investigation, Soc. for Exptl. Biology and Medicine, Am. Soc. Nephrology, Am. Soc. for Pharmacology and Exptl. Therapeutics, Central Soc. Clin. Research, Internat. Soc. Hypertension, Alpha Omega Alpha. Author: (with S.O. Waife) Clinical Evaluation of New Drugs, 1959; Hypertension-Current Management, 1963, 77; Hypertension in Renal Disease, 1969; Pharmacologic Mechanisms in Control of Hypertension, 1971. Asso. editor: Psychosomatic Medicine, 1963—. Contbr. articles to profl. jours. Office: Univ Pitts Sch Medicine Pittsburgh PA 15261

SHAPIRO, ARTHUR KYLE, psychiatrist, educator; b. N.Y.C., Jan. 11, 1923; s. Morris M. and Fay M. (Feldman) S.; B.Social Sci. summa cum laude, Coll. City N.Y., 1951; M.D., U. Chgo., 1955; m. Elaine Schaffer, Jan. 20, 1949; children—Peter, Moira, Kaethe. Broadcast engr. Sta. WNEW, N.Y.C., 1942-43, 1947-49; intern Wayne County Gen. Hosp., Eloise, Mich., 1955-56; psychiat. resident Mass. Mental Health Center, Boston Psychopathic Hosp., teaching fellow Harvard Med. Sch., 1956-58; psychiat. resident Bronx Municipal Hosp. Center, Albert Einstein Coll. Medicine, 1958-59; psychiat. research, clin. asst. vis. neuropsychiatrist N.Y. U. Med. Center and Bellevue Hosp., 1959-60; pvt. practice, N.Y.C., 1959—; sr. psychiatrist, research teaching fellow, head VA Contract Clinic, also hosp. formulary com. Montefiore Hosp., N.Y.C., 1960-66; asso. clin. prof. N.Y. Hosp-Cornell Med. Center; asso. attending Payne Whitney Psychiat. Clinic, N.Y.C., 1967-72, prof. clin. psychiatry, also prof. clin. psychiatry in pharmacology Grad. Sch. Med. Scis., Cornell U.; attending N.Y. Hosp., dir. spl. studies lab. Payne Whitney Clinic, formulary com., research adv. com. hosp., 1972-77; research supr., cons. lectr. Westchester Mental Health Bd., 1966-67; research scientist, epidemiology of mental disorders Psychiat. Inst., N.Y. State Dept. Mental Hygiene, 1976-79; postdoctoral fellow in psychiat. epidemiology Dept. Pub. Health., Psychiatry and Sociology, Columbia U., 1977-78; prof. clin. psychiatry, dir. Tourette and Tic Lab. and Clinic, Mount Sinai Sch. Medicine, also attending psychiatrist Mt. Sinai Hosp., N.Y.C., 1977—. Served to ensign U.S. Maritime Service, 1943-47. Diplomate Nat. Bd. Med. Examiners, Am. Bd. Psychiatry and Neurology. Fellow Am. Psychiat. Assn.; mem. Am. Psychopath. Assn., Soc. Research in Psychotherapy, AAAS, Tourette Syndrome Assn. (med. adv. bd.), N.Y. Soc. for Clin. Psychiatry, Psychiat. Soc. Westchester County, Westchester County Med. Soc., Am. Med. Writers Assn., AMA, N.Y. County Med. Soc., Phi Beta Kappa. Contbr. articles to profl. jours. Office: 35 E 85th St New York City NY 10028 also 17 Colvin Rd Scarsdale NY 10583

SHAPIRO, ASCHER HERMAN, mech. engr., educator; b. Bklyn., May 20, 1916; s. Bernard and Jennie (Kaplan) S.; student Coll. City N.Y., 1932-35; S.B., Mass. Inst. Tech., 1938, Sc.D., 1946; D.Sc. (honoris causa), Salford U. (Eng.), 1978; m. Sylvia Charm, Dec. 24, 1939 (div. 1959); children—Peter Mark, Martha Ann, Bernett Mary; m. 2d, Regina Julia Lee, June 4, 1961 (div. 1972). Asst. mech. engring. Mass. Inst. Tech., 1938-40, faculty, 1940—, prof. mech. engring., 1952—, prof. charge fluid mechanics div., mech. engring. dept., 1954-65, Ford prof. engring., 1962-75, chmn. faculty, 1964-65, head dept. mech. engring., 1965-74, inst. prof., 1975—; vis. prof. applied thermodynamics U. Cambridge (Eng.), 1955-56; Akroyd Stuart Meml. lectr. Nottingham (Eng.) U., 1956; editor Acad. Press, Inc., 1962-65; cons. United Aircraft Corp., M.W. Kellogg Co., Arthur D. Little, Inc., Hardie-Tynes Mfg. Co., Carbon & Carbide Chems. Corp., Oak Ridge, Rohm & Haas Co., Ultrasonic Corp., Jackson & Moreland, Engrs., Stone & Webster, Bendix Aviation, Oak Ridge Nat. Lab., Acushnet Processing Co., Kennecott Copper Co., Welch Sci., Sargent-Welch, others; served on sub-coms. on turbines, internal flow, compressors and turbines NACA; mem. Lexington Project to study and report on nuclear powered flight to AEC, summer 1948; dir. Project Dynamo to study and report to AEC on technol. and econs. nuclear power for civilian use, 1953; dir. Lamp Wick study Office Naval Research, 1955; mem. tech. adv. panel aeronautics Dept. Def.; cons. ops. evaluation group Navy Dept.; sci. adv. bd. USAF, 1964-66; mem. Nat. Com. for Fluid Mechanics Films, 1962—, chmn., 1962-65, 71—; chmn. com. on ednl. films Commn. on Engring. Edn., 1962-65. Mem. Town Meeting Arlington (Mass.); chmn. 1st Mass. chpt. Atlantic Union Com., 1951-52, mem. council 1954—; dir. lab. for devel. power plants for use in torpedoes Navy Dept., 1943-45; mem. ad hoc med. devices com. FDA, HEW, 1970-72; mem. com. Nat. Council for Research and Devel., Israel, 1971—; mem. com. sci. and pub. policy Nat. Acad. Scis., 1970-74; bd. govs. Technion, Israel Inst. Tech., 1968—. Recipient Naval Ordnance Devel. award, 1945; joint certificate outstanding contbn. War and Navy depts., 1947; Richards Meml. award ASME, 1960, Worcester Reed Warner medal, 1965; Townsend Harris medal Coll. City N.Y., 1978. Fellow Am. Inst. Aeros. and Astronautics, Am. Acad. Arts and Scis. (councillor 1967-71), ASME; mem. Am. Sci. Films Assn., Nat. Acad. Scis. (com. on sci. and pub. policy 1973-77), Nat. Acad. Engring., Biomed. Engring. Soc. (charter mem. 1968), Am. Soc. Engring. Edn. (Lamme award 1977), AAAS, Sigma Xi, Tau Beta Pi, Pi Tau Sigma. Club: Mass. Inst. Tech. Faculty (Cambridge). Author: The Dynamics and Thermodynamics of Compressible Fluid Flow, vol. 1, 1953, vol. 2, 1954; Shape and Flow, 1961; also ednl. films and articles, tech. jours. Patentee fluid metering equipment, combustion chambers, propulsion apparatus and gas turbine aux., magnetic disc, magnetic disc storage device, vacuum pump, low-density wind tunnel. Editorial board Jour. Applied Mechanics, 1955-56; editorial com. Ann. Rev. Fluid Mechanics, 1967-71. Office: Mass Inst Tech 77 Massachusetts Ave Cambridge MA 02139

SHAPIRO, BURTON LEONARD, educator; b. N.Y.C., Mar. 29, 1934; s. Nat Lazarus and Fay Rebecca (Gartenhouse) S.; student Tufts U., 1951-54; D.D.S., N.Y. U., 1958; M.S., U. Minn., 1962, Ph.D., 1966; m. Eileen Roman, Aug. 11, 1958; children—Norah Leah, Anne Rachael, Carla Faye. Faculty, U. Minn. Sch. Dentistry, Mpls., 1962—, asso. prof. div. oral pathology, 1966-70, prof., chmn. div. oral biology, 1970—, dir. grad. studies, mem. grad. faculty genetics, 1966—, univ. senator, 1968—, also mem. med. staff Health Scis. Center, exec. com. Grad. Sch., chmn. Health Scis. Policy Rev. Council; hon. research fellow Galton Lab. dept. human genetics Univ. Coll., London, 1974. Served to lt. USNR, 1958-60. Am. Cancer Soc. postdoctoral fellow, 1960-62, advanced fellow, 1965-68. Fellow Am. Acad. Oral Pathology; mem. Internat. Assn. Dental Research (councilor 1969—), Am. Soc. Human Genetics, Craniofacial Biology Soc. (pres. 1972), A.A.A.S., Sigma Xi, Omicron Kappa Upsilon. Mem. adv. editorial bd. Jour. Dental Research, 1971—. Contbr. articles to profl. jours. Home: 76 Exeter Pl St Paul MN 55104 Office: Sch Dentistry U Minn Minneapolis MN 55455

SHAPIRO, DAVID, artist; b. N.Y.C., Aug. 28, 1916; s. Jacob and Ida (Katz) S.; student Ednl. Alliance Art Sch., 1933-35, Am. Artists Sch., 1936-39; m. Cecile Peyser, June 18, 1944; children—Deborah Jane, Anna Roberta. Instr., Smith Coll., 1946-47, Bklyn. Coll., summer, 1947; asst. prof. art U. B.C., 1947-49; mem. faculty dept. art Hofstra U., 1961—, prof. fine art New Coll., 1972—; one-man shows; Milch Gallery, N.Y.C., 1958, 61, 63, Galleria Dell' Orso, Milan, Italy, 1971, Tweed Art Mus., Duluth, Minn., 1978; represented in permanent collections: Bklyn. Mus., Met. Mus., Library of Congress, Smithsonian Instn. Fulbright grantee, 1951-52, 52-53; MacDowell fellow, 1976; Tamarind fellow, 1976; Nat. Endowment Arts, grantee, 1978. Mem. AAUP (pres. Hofstra U. chpt. 1969-71), Soc. Am. Graphic Artists (pres. 1968-70), Coll. Art Assn., Victorian Soc. Author: Social Realism: Art as a Weapon, 1973; Abstract Expressionism: An American Phenomenon, 1980. Home: RFD 77 Cavendish VT 05142 Office: New Coll Hofstra Univ Hempstead NY 11550. *My work and my family are the main interests in my life. Both make it very worthwhile.*

SHAPIRO, DAVID ISRAEL, lawyer; b. Bklyn., June 17, 1928; s. Louis Raymond and Rae (Remin) S.; student U. Wis., 1944-45, Bklyn. Coll., 1946; LL.B., Bklyn. Law Sch., 1949; m. Carol Ann Berger, Nov. 28, 1952; children—Claudia, Anthony, James, Miles. Admitted to N.Y. State bar, 1949, U.S. Supreme Ct. bar, 1955, D.C. bar, 1958; partner firm Dickstein, Shapiro & Morin and predecessor firms, Washington, 1953—, sr. partner, 1973—. Served with USNR, 1944-46. Mem. Am. Bar Assn., A.C.L.U. Democrat. Home: 3508 Prospect St NW Washington DC 20006 Office: 2101 L St NW Washington DC 20037

SHAPIRO, DAVID JOEL, poet, educator; b. Newark, Jan. 2, 1947; s. Irving and Fraida (Chagy) S.; B.A. magna cum laude, Columbia, 1968, Ph.D., 1973; B.A. with first honors (Kellett fellow), Clare Coll. Cambridge (Eng.) U., 1970, M.A., 1974; m. Jean Lindsay Stamm, Aug. 30, 1970. Asst. prof. Columbia, 1973—. Lectr. Acad. Am. Poets, 1964—; specialist Lincoln Center, N.Y.C., 1971, N.Y. State Council on Arts, N.J. Council on Arts. Recipient Avant-Garde Poetry award Gotham Book Mart, 1962; recipient Book of the Month Club award, Creative Artists award, 1974; Morton Dauwen Zabel award AAAL, 1977; Nat. Endowment Humanities grantee, 1979. Mem. P.E.N. Author: January: A Book of Poems, 1965; Poems From Deal, 1969; A Man Holding An Acoustic Panel, 1971; The Page-Turner, 1973; Lateness, 1977; John Ashbury, 1979; contbg. author: Poems of Our Moments, Possibilities of Poetry, Young American Writers, Under 30, other anthologies. Editor: Anthology of New York Poets; editorial asso. Art News, 1971; art critic Art in Am., Domus, Craft Horizons, New Yorker; contbr. numerous poems to lit. jours., popular mags.; contbr. lit. criticism to Poetry (Chgo.), Washington Post, Saturday Rev., Contemporary Poets. Home: 560 Riverside Dr New York NY 10027

SHAPIRO, DAVID LOUIS, lawyer, educator; b. N.Y.C. Oct. 12, 1932; s. Louis and Sara (Grabelsky) S.; grad. Horace Mann Sch., 1950; A.B., magna cum laude, Harvard, 1954, LL.B. summa cum laude, 1957; m. Jane Wilkins Bennett, June 19, 1954; 1 dau., Lynn Mayson. Admitted to D.C. bar, 1957, Mass. bar, 1964; asso. atty. firm Covington & Burling, Washington, 1957-62; law clk. Supreme Ct. Justice John M. Harlan, 1962-63; faculty Harvard Law Sch., 1963—, prof. law, 1966—, asso. dean, 1971-76. Mem. labor arbitration panel Am. Arbitration Assn., 1966—. Mem. Am. Bar Assn. (reporter adv. com. fair trial and free press 1965-68), Am. Law Inst. (asst. reporter study of div. of jurisdiction 1963-65, reporter Restatement of Judgments 2d 1970-74). Author: (with others) The Federal Courts and the Federal System, 1973. Editor: The Evolution of a Judicial Philosophy: Selected Opinions of Justice John M. Harlan, 1969. Contbr. articles to profl. jours. Home: 17 Wendell St Cambridge MA 02138

SHAPIRO, E. DONALD, ednl. adminstr.; b. York, Pa., Nov. 1, 1931; s. Samuel Milton and Sarah (Lavetan) S.; A.B. summa cum laude, Dickinson Coll., 1953, LL.D., 1975; student Sorbonne, Paris, 1952; J.D., Harvard U., 1956; LL.D., N.Y. Law Sch., 1973; m. Merle Judith Mandell, Aug. 12, 1956; children—Felicia, Rachel, Carol, Richard. Publicity dir. Cape Cod (Mass.) Melody Tent, 1954-55; drama critic Sta. WSBA-TV, York, 1955; admitted to Pa., D.C. bars, 1957, Mich. bar, 1967; with firm Freedman, Landy & Lorry, Phila., 1956-57; instr. Boston U. Law Sch., 1957-59; prof. law Detroit Coll. Law, 1959-60; dir. Inst. Continuing Legal Edn., U. Mich. Law Sch.-Wayne State U. Law Sch., also mem. faculty U. Mich. Law Sch., 1960-68; asso. dean state-wide edn. for continuing legal edn. U. Mich., 1965-68; lectr. U. Mich. Sch. Social Work, 1961-66, prof. social welfare law, 1966-68; adj. prof. law N.Y. U. Sch. Law, 1968-74, adj. prof. legal medicine Sch. Medicine, 1974-78; dean, prof. N.Y. Law Sch., from 1973, also trustee; adj. prof. social work Fordham U. Sch. Social Work, 1968-73; corr. mem. Anglo-Am. Studies Inst., U. Padua, 1969—, vis. prof., 1970; dir. Practising Law Inst., 1968-71; gen. partner Andresen & Co., 1972-73, spl. ltd. partner, 1973; chmn. bd. Struthers Sci. and Internat., Inc., 1971-72; pres. ABC Industries, 1971-72, dir., 1972—; mem. N.Y. Law Jour., 1972—, pres., 1971-72, vice chmn. bd. editors, 1972-77; dir. Loral Corp., United Mchts. and Mfrs., Inc., U.S. Banknote Corp., Continental Connector Corp., Group Health Inc., Fisher & Bro., Inc., Rand Info. Services, Inc., ABC Industries; adv. bd. Kenneth D. Laub & Co., Inc.; cons. continuing legal edn. com. Nat. Jr. Bar Conf., 1960-62; cons. joint com on continuing legal edn. Am. Law Inst. and Am. Bar Assn., 1962-64; chmn. com. on continuing legal edn. Assn. Am. Law Schs., 1966-68; dir. tng. Juvenile Ct. Hearing Officer Tng. Project, 1963-65; project dir. Tng. Ct. Officers, 1964-65; chmn. adv. com. (SAT Prep. Course, Adelphi U.; cons. Practising Law Inst., 1960-67, Jud. Conf. Mich, 1962-67, Am. Trial Lawyers Assn., 1965-67; adv. com. Fed. Jud. Center, 1968-70, co-chmn. jud. edn. subcom., 1968- 70; project dir. Tng. Inst. series on Supreme Ct. juvenile law decision in Gault case, 1967-68; cons. Criminal Law Tng. Films Project, 1966-67; funded by grants from Justice Dept., Office Law Enforcement Assistance; mem. nat. planning com. 2d World Meeting on Med. Law, Washington, 1970; dir. tng. U.S. AID-Central Bank Brazil Capital Markets Program, 1969-70; mem. com. to study and propose standards for admission to practice in fed. cts. U.S. Jud. Conf., 1976—; 1976—; dir. Com. Modern Cts., 1974—; adv. com. Fed. Jud. Center, Washington, co-chmn. jud. edn. subcom., 1968-70; faculty Fed. Appellate Judges Seminar, Phoenix, 1976; mem. Temporary N.Y. State Commn. Living Costs and the Economy, 1974-75, N.J. Commn. Against Alcoholism, Crime and Drug Abuse, 1974-75. Trustee, Nat. Center Automated Info. Retrieval, N.Y.C., 1969-73, trustee emeritus, 1976—; trustee Scoula d'Italia, N.Y.C., 1977—; trustee Milton Helpern Library Legal Medicine, N.Y.C., 1970—, chmn. and pres., 1977—; trustee Practising Law Inst. Found., 1969-72, exec. v.p., 1970-71, v.p., 1972—; mem. adv. bd. Milton Helpern Internat. Center for Forensic Scis., 1975—; trustee nat. adv. council Center Adminstrn. Justice, Wayne State U. Law Sch., Detroit, 1972—, Dickinson Coll., 1969—; bd. dirs. Am. Friends of Communidad Israelita de Madrid Sch., Inc., 1976—; chmn. task force on financing N.J. Bd. Edn., 1978-79; trustee, nat. bd. dirs. Odyssey House, N.Y.C., 1971-74; bd. dirs. Brotherhood in Action, N.Y.C., 1973—, exec. com., 1973—; adv. bd. N.Y. State Assn. Retarded Children, 1975—. Recipient U.S. Nat. Extemporaneous Speaking award, 1952; Nat. Achievement award Phi Epsilon Pi, 1967. Fellow Am. Coll. Legal Medicine Chgo. (hon.), Inst. Jud. Adminstrn., N.Y.C.; mem. Supreme Ct. Hist. Soc. (com. law student mems.), Fed. Bar Council, NAACP (life), State Bar Mich., Am. Acad. Forensic Sci., Am. Law Inst., Practising Law Inst. (trustee 1968-72), N.Y. County Lawyers Assn. (chmn. spl. com. penal reform 1978—), Bar Assn. City N.Y., Am. Bar Assn. (chmn. com. programs and insts. of criminal justice sect., chmn. nat. conv. 1977-78; chmn. spl. task force of legal edn. sect. 1978—, chmn. inspection teams on law sch. accreditation 1976, 77; chmn. nat. inst. for sect. on individual rights and responsibilities 1976—, mem. com. alcoholism and drug reform 1976—, chmn. insp. team Hamline U. Sch. Law 1976), AAUP, Harvard Law Assn. Mich., Scribes (chmn. legal writing nat. inst. com. 1977—), Phi Beta Kappa, Omicron Delta Kappa, Tau Kappa Alpha, Phi Epsilon Pi (Nat. Undergrad. of Year award 1953, Nat. Achievement award 1967). Jewish. Clubs: Lawyers (bd. govs. 1971—); Harvard. Author: (with Curran) Law, Medicine and Forensic Science, 1970, supplement, 1974; editor: Michigan Basic Practice Series, 1960; co-editor: Mich. Basic Practice Handbooks, 8 vols., 1962-67; Mich. Splty. Handbook Series, 25 vols., 1962-67; Mich. Course Handbooks, 30 vols., 1961-67; Personal Injury Library, 6 vols., 1965-67; various other legal publs.; editorial bd. Human Rights, 1978—, Am. Jour. Law and Medicine; internat. bd. editors Internat. Jour. Medicine and Law, 1978—; contbr. articles to legal and med. jours. Home: 1 Princeton Terr Short Hills NJ 07078 Office: 57 Worth St New York City NY 10013

SHAPIRO, ELI, bus. cons., educator, economist; b. Bklyn., June 13, 1916; s. Samuel and Pauline (Kushel) S.; A.B., Bklyn. Coll., 1936; A.M., Columbia U., 1937, Ph.D., 1939; m. Beatrice Ferbend, Jan. 18, 1946; children—F. Stewart, Laura J. Instr., Bklyn. Coll., 1936-41; research asso. Nat. Bur. Econ. Research, 1938-39, cons., 1939-42, research staff, 1955-62; asst. prof. fin. U. Chgo., 1946-47, asso. prof., 1948-52, prof., 1952; prof. fin. Mass. Inst. Tech., 1952-61, asso. dean Sch. Indsl. Mgmt., 1954-58, Alfred P. Sloan prof. mgmt., 1976—; prof. fin. Harvard Bus. Sch., 1962-70, Sylvan C. Coleman prof. fin. mgmt., 1968-70; chmn. fin. com., dir. Travelers Ins. Cos., Hartford, Conn., 1971-77, vice chmn. bd., dir., 1976-78; chmn. bd. Mass. Co., 1971-72; dir. Dexter Corp., Travelers Corp., Norlin Corp.; chmn. bd. Fed. Home Loan Bank Boston; econ. analyst div. monetary research U.S. Dept. Treasury, 1941-42; economist research div. OPA, 1941-42; staff cons. Com. Econ. Devel., 1950-51, mem. research adv. com., 1961-64, 69—, project dir., 1966-69; cons. to sec. treasury; mem. enforcement commn. WSB, 1952-53; cons. Inst. Def. Analyses; dep. dir. Research Com. on Money and Credit, 1959-61. Trustee, Mt. Holyoke Coll., Am. Coll., Bryn Mawr, Pa. Served from ensign to lt. USNR, 1942-46. Recipient Econ. Dept. award Bklyn. Coll. 1936, Honors Day award for distinguished alumni, 1949. Fellow Am. Acad. Arts and Scis.; mem. Nat. Bur. Econ. Research (dir., vice chmn.), Am. Econ. Assn., Council Fgn. Relations, Am. Fin. Assn. Author: (with others) Personal Finance Industry and Its Credit Standards, 1939; (with Steiner) Money and Banking, 1941; Development of Wisconsin Credit Union Movement, 1947; (with Steiner) Money and Banking, 1953; (with others) Money and Banking, 1958; (with D. Meiselman) Measurement of Corporate Sources and Uses of Funds, 1964; (with others) Money and Banking, 1969; (with Wolf) The Role of Private Placement in Corporate Finance, 1972. Editor: (with W.L. White) Capital for Productivity and Growth, 1977. Home: 180 Beacon St Boston MA 02116 Office: Mass Inst Tech Sloan Sch Mgmt 50 Memorial Dr Cambridge MA 02139

SHAPIRO, FRED DAVID, lawyer; b. Cleve., Nov. 10, 1926; s. Isadore R. and Lottie (Turetsky) S.; B.A. cum laude, Ohio State U., 1949; LL.B., Harvard, 1954; m. Helen Solomon, Sept. 5, 1948; children—Gary N., Ira R., Diane S. Admitted to Ohio bar, 1954; since practiced in Cleve., sr. partner firm Shapiro, Turoff & Gisser, 1976—. Served with USNR, 1945-46. Mem. Ohio, Greater Cleve., Cuyahoga County bar assns., Phi Beta Kappa. Jewish. Home: 19610 Lomond Blvd Shaker Heights OH 44122 Office: 1200 Standard Bldg Cleveland OH 44113

SHAPIRO, GEORGE M., lawyer; b. N.Y.C., Dec. 7, 1919; s. Samuel N. and Sarah (Milstein) S.; B.S., L.I. U., 1939; LL.B. (Kent scholar), Columbia U., 1942; m. Rita V. Lubin, Mar. 29, 1942; children—Karen Shapiro Spector, Sanford. Admitted to N.Y. bar, 1942; mem. staff gov. N.Y., 1945-51, counsel to gov., 1951-54; partner firm Proskauer, Rose, Goetz & Mendelsohn, N.Y.C., 1955—; pres. Edmond de Rothschild Found., 1964—; dir. Bank of Calif.; counsel, majority leader N.Y. Senate, 1955-59; counsel N.Y. Constl. Revision Commn., 1960-61. Chmn. council State U. Coll. Medicine, N.Y., 1955-71; mem. Gov.'s Com. Reapportionment, 1964, Mayor's Com. Jud. Selection, 1966-69; chmn. Park Ave. Synagogue, 1973—; active Council on Fgn. Relations, 1972—. Served with USAAF, 1943-45. Clubs: Harmonie, Metropolis. Home: 1160 Park Ave New York City NY 10028 Office: 300 Park Ave New York City NY 10022

SHAPIRO, GOODWIN, fgn. service officer; b. N.Y.C., Dec. 25, 1920; s. Bernard and Sarah (Klegnan) S.; student Pace Inst., 1938-40; B.A., George Washington U., 1954; m. Laura Leib, May 25, 1947; children—Richard Conrad, Lorie Margaret. Clk. stenographer Bur. Census, Washington, 1940-42; conf. reporter OPA, 1946-47; conf. reporter State Dept., 1947-54, staff asst., 1954-56, fgn. affairs officer, 1956-57, exec. officer Am. consulate, Nuevo Laredo, 1957-61, chief Protection-Welfare Office, Am. embassy, Mexico, 1962-64, chief consular sect. Am. embassy, Seoul, Korea, 1964-67, vis. officer Am. embassy, Madrid, Spain, 1967-70, chief consular sect., 1970-71, dept. dep. dir. Spl. Consular Services, Washington, 1971-73, Am. consul, prin. officer Am. Consulate, Ciudad Juarez, Chihuahua, Mexico, 1973-77, consul gen., 1975-77, consul gen., counselor for consular affairs Am. embassy, Buenos Aires, Argentina, 1977—. Served with USNR, 1942-46. Recipient Meritorious Honor award State Dept., 1969. Mem. El Paso C. of C. (internat. relations com. 1973-77), Delta Phi Epsilon. Rotarian. Home: 3102 Libertador Buenos Aires Argentina Office: Am Embassy 4300 Colombia Buenos Aires Argentina

SHAPIRO, HAROLD BENJAMIN, indsl. exec.; b. Marshfield, Wis., Aug. 25, 1937; s. Louis H. and Dorothy (Cohen) S.; B.S., B.A., Washington U., St. Louis, 1961, M.S., 1962; m. Yanait Perez, June 11, 1961; children—Sheryl Lynn, Laura Alise. Staff accountant Tiger, Fireside & Co., St. Louis, 1962-65, Moll, Blum, Rones Co., St. Louis, 1965-68; v.p., controller Diversified Industries, Inc., St. Louis, 1968—; faculty U. Mo.-St. Louis, 1966-68. C.P.A., Mo. Mem. Am. Inst. C.P.A.'s, Mo. Soc. C.P.A.'s, Nat. Assn. Accountants. Home: 12631 Conway Club Ct Creve Coeur MO 63141 Office: 1034 S Brentwood Blvd St Louis MO 63117

SHAPIRO, HAROLD TAFLER, economist, univ. pres.; b. Montreal, Que., Can., June 8, 1935; s. Maxwell and Mary (Tafler) S.; B.Comm., McGill U., Montreal, 1956; M.A. in Econs., Ph.D. in Econs. (Harold Helm fellow, Harold Dodd sr. fellow), Princeton U., 1964; m. Vivian Bernice Rapoport, May 19, 1957; children—Anne, Marilyn, Janet, Karen. Asst. prof. econs. U. Mich., 1964-67, asso. prof., 1967-70, prof., 1970-76, chmn. dept. econs., 1974-77, prof. econs. and public policy, 1977—, v.p. acad. affairs, 1977-79, pres., 1979—; research adv. Bank Can., 1965-72; cons., forecasting U.S. Treasury, 1965-68. Mem. divisional bd. St. Joseph Mercy Hosp., Ann Arbor, Mich., 1979. Recipient Lt. Gov.'s medal in commerce McGill U., 1956. Fellow Mich. Soc. Fellows (sr.); mem. Am. Statis. Assn. (council). Office: 2068 Adminstrn Bldg U Mich Ann Arbor MI 48109

SHAPIRO, HARRY, musician; b. Boston, Jan. 2, 1914; s. Max and Sarah (Nelson) S.; student Julliard Grad. Sch. Music, 1936-37; m. Frances G. Sidd, May 24, 1942; children—Emily (Mrs. Lewis H. Koplil), Laura. French horn player Boston Symphony Orch., 1937—; mem. faculty Boston U., 1962—, New Eng. Conservatory, 1962—; orch. mgr. Opera Co. Boston, 1960—, Boston Ballet Co., 1962—, Nat. Ednl. TV Opera, 1969—; travel mgr. Boston Symphony Orch., 1968—. Bd. dirs. Boston Symphony Orch. Pension Instn.; trustee Boston Ballet Co. Served with USAAF, 1944-46. Office: care Boston Symphony Orch Symphony Hall Boston MA 02115*

SHAPIRO, HARRY LIONEL, anthropologist; b. Boston, Mar. 19, 1902; s. Jacob and Rose (Clemens) S.; A.B., Harvard, 1923, A.M., 1925, Ph.D., 1926; m. Janice Sandler, June 26, 1938 (dec. Apr. 1962); children—Thomas, Harriet, James. Tutor, Harvard, 1925-26; asst. curator Am. Mus. Natural History, 1926-31, asso. curator, 1931-42, chmn. dept. anthropology, curator, 1942-70, chmn. emeritus, 1970—; research prof. Hawaii, 1930-35; prof. Columbia, 1939-74; prof. anthropology U. Pitts., 1970; asso. Bishop Mus., Honolulu. Chmn. div. anthropology, psychology NRC, 1953-54. Bd. dirs. Louise Wise Services; mem. bd. Field Found., 1966-71. Recipient Theodore Roosevelt Distinguished Service medal, 1964, award N.Y. Acad. Scis., 1977. Fellow Nat. Acad. Scis., Am. Acad. Arts and Scis., Die Anthropologische Gesellschaft in Wien (hon.); mem. Am. Ethnol. Soc. (pres. 1942-43), Am. Assn. Phys. Anthropologists (sec. 1935-39, v.p. 1941-42), Am. Anthrop. Assn. (pres. 1948), AAAS, Am. Eugenics Soc. (pres. 1956-63), Social Sci. Research Council. Author: Heritage of the Bounty, 1936; Migration and Environment, 1939;

Aspects of Culture, 1956; The Jewish People, 1960; Peking Man, 1975. Editor: Man, Culture and Society, 1956. Contbr. articles to sci. jours. Home: 26 E 91st St New York City NY 10028 Office: Am Mus Natural History New York City NY 10001

SHAPIRO, HARVEY, poet; b. Chgo., Jan. 27, 1924; s. Jacob J. and Dorothy (Cohen) S.; B.A., Yale U., 1947; M.A., Columbia U., 1948; m. Edna Lewis Kaufman, July 23, 1953; children—Saul, Dan. Instr. English, Cornell U., 1949-50, 51-52; creative writing fellow Bard Coll., 1950-51; mem. editorial staff Commentary, New Yorker, 1955-57; editorial staff N.Y. Times mag., N.Y.C., 1957, asst. editor, 1964-75, editor N.Y. Times Book Rev., 1975—; author: The Eye, 1953; The Book and Other Poems, 1955; Mountain, Fire, Thornbush, 1961; Battle Report, 1966; This World, 1971; Lauds, 1975, Nightsounds, 1978. Served with USAAF, World War II. Decorated D.F.C., Air medal with 3 oak leaf clusters. Rockefeller Found. grantee in poetry, 1967. Club: Elizabethan (New Haven). Home: 264 Hicks St Brooklyn NY 11201 Office: NY Times 229 W 43d St New York City NY 10036

SHAPIRO, HENRY, paper co. exec.; b. Cheslea, Mass., Mar. 18, 1915; s. Isaac and Fannie (Glicman) B.S., Northwestern U., 1937; m. Soretta Baim, July 25, 1937; children—Earl W., James A. Pres., Md. Cup Corp., Owings Mills. Home: 1540 Lake Shore Dr Chicago IL 60610 Office: 7575 S Kostner Ave Chicago IL 60652

SHAPIRO, HENRY, journalist, lectr.; b. Vaslui, Romania, Apr. 19, 1906; s. Simon and Buca (David) S.; C. brought to U.S., 1920, naturalized, 1928; A.B., Coll. City N.Y., 1929; student Columbia U. Summer Sch., 1928; Geneva Sch. Internat. Studies, 1932; J.D., Harvard, 1932; m. Ludmilla Nikitina, June 11, 1937; 1 dau., Irina. Admitted to N.Y. bar, 1932; practiced in N.Y.C., 1932-33; fgn. corr. N.Y. Herald-Tribune, London Morning Post, Reuters of London, United Press Internat., Atlantic Monthly, ABC, 1933-73; mgr. Moscow bur. United Press Internat., 1939-73; Kemper Knapp Univ. prof. U. Wis., 1973-75, adj. prof. and hon. fellow in journalism and mass communication, 1975—; U.S. war corr. Persian Gulf Command, 1944-46; cons. Russian Research Center, Harvard, 1955, Johnson Found., Racine, Wis., 1976—; vis. lectr. U. Calif. at Berkeley, 1962-63; guest prof. U. of Tel Aviv, 1964. Recipient Nat. Headliners award fgn. reporting, 1944, 64, Nieman fellow journalism Harvard, 1955, Distinguished Achievements award U. So. Calif., 1961, Ford Found. travel and research grant, 1962-63, award for distinguished service in journalism Sigma Delta Chi, 1965. Mem. Internat. Platform Assn., Ango-Am. Press Assn. Moscow (pres. 1942-43), Alumni Assn. Harvard Law Sch., Alumni Assn. City U. N.Y., Dobro Slovo Honor Soc., Phi Kappa Phi, Sigma Delta Chi. Club: Overseas Press of America. Author: L'U.R.S.S. Apres Staline (pub. in Paris), 1954. Home: 4902 Waukesha St Madison WI 53705 Office: 5146 Vilas Hall U Wis Madison WI 53706

SHAPIRO, IRVING MEYER, biochemist; b. London, Oct. 28, 1937; s. Syd and Betty (Silver) S.; came to U.S., 1969, naturalized, 1977; B.Dental Surgery, U. London, 1961, Ph.D., 1968; M.Sc., U. Liverpool (Eng.), 1964; m. Joan Poliner, July 4, 1965; 1 dau., Susan. Research fellow Royal Dental Hosp., London, 1966-69; mem. faculty U. Pa. Sch. Dental Medicine, Phila., 1969—, prof., chmn. dept. biochemistry, 1976—. Nuffield fellow, 1964-65. Mem. Internat. Assn. Dental Research (Basic Sci. award 1974), AAAS, Am. Soc. Biol. Chemists, Am. Chem. Soc. Contbr. articles to profl. jours. Home: 555 Haverford Rd Wynnewood PA 19096 Office: Dept Biochemistry Dental Med Sch U Pa Philadelphia PA 19104

SHAPIRO, IRVING SAUL, corp. exec.; b. Mpls., July 15, 1916; s. Sam I. and Freda (Lane) S.; B.S., U. Minn., 1939, LL.B., 1941; m. Charlotte Farsht, Mar. 1, 1942; children—Stuart Lane, Elizabeth Irene. Admitted to Minn. bar, 1941, Del. bar, 1958; atty. criminal div. Dept. Justice, 1943-51; with E.I. du Pont de Nemours & Co., Inc., 1951—, v.p., 1970-73, vice chmn. bd., 1973, chmn., chief exec. officer, 1974—; also dir., chmn. exec. com., chmn. pub. affairs com.; dir. Bank of Del., Citicorp., Citibank, IBM, Continental Am. Ins. Co. Mem. Adv. Council on Japan-U.S. Econ. Relations, U.S.-USSR Trade and Econ. Council, Bus. Council, Bus. Roundtable. Bd. dirs. Greater Wilmington Devel. Council; trustee Conf. Bd., U. Del., Ford Found., U. Pa. Recipient Chem. Industry medal Soc. Chem. Industry, London, 1979. Office: 9000 du Pont Bldg Wilmington DE 19898

SHAPIRO, IRWIN IRA, physicist, educator; b. N.Y.C., Oct. 10, 1929; s. Samuel and Esther (Feinberg) S.; A.B., Cornell U., 1950; A.M., Harvard U., 1951, Ph.D., 1955; m. Marian Helen Kaplun, Dec. 20, 1959; children—Steven, Nancy. Mem. staff Lincoln Lab. Mass. Inst. Tech., Lexington, 1954-70; Sherman Fairchild Distinguished scholar Calif. Inst. Tech., 1974; Morris Loeb lectr. physics Harvard, 1975; prof. geophysics and physics Mass. Inst. Tech., 1967—; cons. NSF. Recipient Albert A. Michelson medal Franklin Inst., 1975. Fellow Am. Geophys. Union, Am. Phys. Soc.; mem. Am. Acad. Arts and Scis., Nat. Acad. Scis. (Benjamin Apthorp Gould prize 1979), Am. Astron. Soc., Internat. Astron. Union, Phi Beta Kappa, Sigma Xi, Phi Kappa Phi. Contbr. articles to profl. jours. Home: 17 Lantern Ln Lexington MA 02173 Office: 77 Massachusetts Ave Cambridge MA 02139

SHAPIRO, JEROME HERBERT, radiologist, educator; b. Cleve., Aug. 5, 1924; s. Louis and Rose (Hamburgher) S.; student Western Res. U., 1942-44; M.D., Yale, 1948; m. Amy Elizabeth Alderman, June 16, 1948; children—Nancy Lee, Mathew Paul, Wendy Jane, Deborah Gail. Intern, Mt. Sinai Hosp., Cleve., 1948-49; resident radiology Montefiore Hosp., N.Y.C., 1949-52; fellow X-ray diagnosis Meml. Center, N.Y.C., 1952; attending radiologist Montefiore Hosp., 1952-63; asso. clin. prof. radiology N.Y. U., 1960-63; prof. radiology, chmn. dept. Boston U. Sch. Medicine, 1963—; dir. radiology Boston City, Univ. hosps., 1963—. Lectr. radiology Harvard, Tufts med. schs., 1963—. Fellow Am. Coll. Radiology (chancellor 1973-79); mem. AMA, Radiol. Soc. N.Am., Am., New Eng. (pres. 1974-75) Roentgen ray socs., Assn. U. Radiologists, Am. Soc. Neuroradiology, Mass. Radiol. Soc. (pres. 1970-71). Jewish religion (pres. temple 1968-72). Sr. author Cardiac Calcifications, 1963. Contbr. numerous articles to profl. jours. Home: 30 Wachusett Rd Wellesley Hills MA 02181 Office: 818 Harrison Ave Boston MA 02118

SHAPIRO, JOEL ELIAS, artist; b. N.Y.C., Sept. 27, 1941; s. Joseph and Anna (Lewis) S.; B.A., N.Y. U., 1964, M.A., 1969; One man-shows include: Paula Cooper Gallery, N.Y.C., 1970, 72, 74, 76, Inst. of Art and Urban Resources, N.Y.C., 1973, Mus. of Contemporary Art, Chgo., 1976, Albright-Knox Art Gallery, Buffalo, 1977; numerous group shows including Paula Cooper Gallery, N.Y.C., 1969, 72, Emily Lowe Gallery, Hofstra U., Hempstead, L.I., 1970, Whitney Mus. of Modern Art, N.Y.C., 1970, 73, 77, Soc. for Contemporary Art, Chgo., 1971, 75, Fogg Art Mus., Harvard U., Cambridge, Mass., 1973, N.Y. Cultural Center, 1974, Indpls. Mus. of Art, 1974, Art Inst. Chgo., 1974, Inst. of Contemporary Art, U. Pa., Phila., 1975, Fine Arts Gallery, U. Mass., Amherst, 1976, The Renaissance Soc., U. Chgo., 1976, Venice (Italy) Biennale, 1976, Am. Pavilion, Venice, Italy, 1976, Art Gallery of New South Wales, Australia, 1976; represented in permanent collections: Mus. Modern Art, N.Y.C., Whitney Mus. Art, N.Y.C., Walker Art Center, Mpls., Met. Mus. Art, N.Y.C., Albright Knox Art Gallery, Buffalo; represented by Paula Cooper Gallery, N.Y.C. Home: 284 Lafayette St New York NY 10012 Office: care Paula Cooper Gallery 155 Wooster St New York NY 10012

SHAPIRO, KARL JAY, poet; b. Balt., Nov. 10, 1913; s. Joseph and Sarah (Omanski) S.; student Johns Hopkins U., 1937-39; m. Evalyn Katz, Mar. 25, 1945 (div. Jan. 1967); children—Katharine, John J., Elizabeth; m. Teri Kovach, July 31, 1967. Cons. poetry Library of Congress, 1946-47; asso. prof. writing Johns Hopkins U., 1947-50; editor Poetry: A Magazine of Verse, 1950-56; prof. English, U. Nebr., Lincoln, 1956-66, U. Ill. Circle Campus, Chgo., 1966-68; prof. English, U. Calif. at Davis, 1968—. Served with AUS, 1941-45. Recipient Jeanette S. Davis prize, 1942; Levinson prize, 1943; Contemporary Poetry prize, 1943; Pulitzer prize (poetry), 1945; Shelly Meml. prize, 1945; Bollingen prize for poetry, 1969; Am. Acad. Arts and Letters grantee, 1944; fellow Kenyon Sch. Letters, 1956, 57; Guggenheim fellow, 1945-46, 53-54; fellow in Am. Letters, Library of Congress. Mem. Nat. Inst. Arts and Letters, Am. Acad. Arts and Scis. Author: Poems, 1935; Person, Place and Thing, 1942; The Place of Love, 1942; V-Letter and Other Poems, 1944; Essay on Rime, 1945; Trial of a Poet, 1947; Bibliography of Modern Prosody, 1948; Poems, 1942-53, 1953; Beyond Criticism, 1953; Poems of a Jew, 1958; In Defense of Ignorance, 1960; Prose Keys to Modern Poetry, 1962; (with James E. Miller, Jr. and Bernice Slote), 1960 Start with the Sun, The Bourgeois Poet, 1964; (with Robert Beum) A Prosody Handbook, 1964; Selected Poems, 1968; To Abolish Children, 1968; White-Haired Lover, 1968; (novel) Edsel, 1971; The Poetry Wreck (Selected Essays 1950-70), 1975; (poems) Adult Bookstore, 1976; (film) Karl Shapiro's America, 1976; Collected Poems 1940-1978, 1978. Office: Sproul Hall U Calif at Davis Davis CA 95616

SHAPIRO, LAWRENCE, advt. agy. exec.; b. N.Y.C., Feb. 25, 1937; s. Harold D. and Ciril S. (Seman) S.; B.S. in Commerce and Fin., Bucknell U., 1959; m. Dale Gottesman, Jan. 23, 1965. With Young & Rubicam Inc., N.Y.C., 1964—, mgmt. supr., 1977-78, sr. v.p., group dir. account mgmt., 1978—. Served to lt. USAR, 1960. Office: 285 Madison Ave New York NY 10003

SHAPIRO, LEON NATHAN, psychiatrist; b. Boston, Oct. 8, 1926; s. Jacob and Ruth (Yankelovich) S.; student Harvard, 1942-44; M.D., Boston U., 1948; m. Rose Kurhan, Oct. 16, 1948; children—Jean (Mrs. Joel Perwin), Carol, Robert, James. Intern Newton-Wellesley Hosp., 1948-49; resident psychiatry Menninger Clinic, Topeka, 1949-51; mem. Boston Psychoanalytic Inst., 1960; mem. faculty Boston U., 1953-57, Harvard, 1957-62; prof. psychiatry Tufts U. Sch. Medicine, 1969-75, also mem. faculty Boston Psychoanalytic Inst., 1968-75; prof. psychiatry Cornell Med. Sch., 1975-77; clin. prof. Harvard Med. Sch., 1978—. Served as lt. USNR, 1951-52. Mem. Am. Psychoanalytic Assn., Am. Psychiat. Assn. Home: 66 Norfolk Rd Chestnut Hill MA 02167 Office: Mass Mental Health Center 74 Fenwood Rd Boston MA

SHAPIRO, LEONARD, pipe mfg. co. exec.; b. Los Angeles, Aug. 8, 1928; s. Fred and Bertha (Grossman) S.; student pub. schs., Los Angeles; m. Annette Familian, Apr. 4, 1948; children—David Alan, Joel Jay, Ilyse Ellen. Sales trainee Gt. Am. Sales Co., 1949-50; salesman Pacific Cast Iron Pipe & Fitting Co., S. Gate, Calif., 1950-51, sales and asst. mgr., 1951-58, v.p., asst. mgr., 1953-55, pres., 1955-58; pres. Familian Pipe & Supply Co., 1959-70, pres. Familian Corp., Los Angeles, 1970-72, chmn. bd., 1972—; dir. NWS Constrn. Co., Relco Mfg. Co., Paragon Precision Products Co. Pres., 500 Club for City of Hope, 1952-54, founder, dir. Founders Club, 1970—; bd. dirs. Jewish Fedn. Council, 1974-75, U. Judaism, 1976—. Mem. Supply Assn. (past dir.), Pacific S.W. Distbrs. Assn. (past dir.). Clubs: Hillcrest Country; Palm Springs Tennis. Office: 12353 Wilshire Blvd Los Angeles CA 90025

SHAPIRO, LOUIS, judge; b. N.Y.C., Feb. 7, 1905; s. Max David and Beatrice (Altman) S.; student U. Conn. Coll. Law, 1930-34; m. Betty Reyna Older, May 3, 1936; children—Susan Jane, Andrew. Admitted to Conn. bar, 1934; practiced in Unionville, Conn., 1934-53; judge Borough Ct., Unionville, 1943-45; judge Conn. Superior Ct., Hartford, 1953-70, chief judge, 1966-70; asso. justice Conn. Supreme Ct., Hartford, 1970-75; state referee, 1975—. Mem. Conn. Ho. of Reps., 1941-51, majority leader, 1951, chmn. legis. council, 1951-53; mem. Conn. Statute Review Com., 1945-48. Chmn. Conn. Bd. Edn., Services for Blind; chmn. Council on Probate Jud. Conduct; mem. Commn. on Ofcl. Legal Publs. Mem. Am., Conn., Hartford County bar assns. Republican. Jewish religion. Mason. Home: 67 Tunxis Village Farmington CT 06032 Office: Chambers Supreme Court Bldg Hartford CT 06106

SHAPIRO, MARVIN LINCOLN, broadcasting co. exec.; b. Erie, Pa., Feb. 12, 1923; s. Hyman and Flora (Burstein) S.; B.S., Syracuse (N.Y.) U., 1948; m. B. Gertrude Berkman, Oct. 25, 1946; children—Susan Jo, Barbara Ann, Jonathan David. Account exec. sta. WSYR, Syracuse, 1948-50; account exec., then nat. sales mgr. sta. WCAU-TV, Phila., 1950-58; account exec. spot sales CBS-TV, Chgo., 1955-56, N.Y.C., 1958-60; with TV Advt. Reps., Inc., N.Y.C., 1961-66, pres., then vice chmn., 1968-77, chmn., 1978, dir., 1968-78; pres., then vice chmn., dir. Radio Advt. Reps., Inc., N.Y.C., 1966-77; exec. v.p., chief operating officer, pres. sta. group Westinghouse Broadcasting Co., Inc., N.Y.C., 1969-77, sr. v.p., 1978—, also dir.; chmn. bd. Micro-Relay, Inc., 1974—; chmn. bd., pres. CATV Enterprises, Inc., 1970—; dir. Group W Prodns., Inc., W-F Prodns., Inc.; mem. communications adv. council St. John's U., Jamaica, N.Y.; bd. dirs. TV Bur. Advt., 1974—, chmn., 1977-79; bd. dirs. Radio Advt. Bur., 1970-77. Committeeman, United Fund Greater N.Y., 1974; boxing judge Pa. Athletic Commn., 1952-55. Served with USAAF, 1942-45. Decorated Air medal with 9 oak leaf clusters; recipient Communications Alumni award Syracuse U., 1960. Mem. Internat. Radio and TV Soc., Alpha Epsilon Rho (hon.). Clubs: Pinnacle (N.Y.C.); Long Ridge (Stamford). Office: 90 Park Ave New York NY 10016

SHAPIRO, MARVIN LINCOLN, broadcasting exec.; b. Erie, Pa., Feb. 12, 1923; s. Hyman and Flora (Burstein) S.; B.S., Syracuse U., 1948; m. B. Gertrude Berkman, Oct. 25, 1946; children—Susan Jo, Barbara Ann, Jonathan David. Account exec. radio sta. WSYR, Syracuse, 1948-50; account exec. sta. WCAU-TV, Phila., 1950-55, nat. sales mgr., 1956-58; account exec. CBS TV spot sales, Chgo., 1955-56, N.Y.C., 1958-60; with TV Advt. Reps., Inc., N.Y.C., 1961-66, exec. v.p., 1965-66, pres., 1968-69, dir., vice chmn., 1969-77, chmn., 1978; pres. Radio Advt. Reps., Inc., N.Y.C., 1966-68, dir., vice chmn., 1969-77; exec. v.p., chief operating officer, pres. sta. group Westinghouse Broadcasting Co., Inc., N.Y.C., 1969-77, sr. v.p., 1978—, also dir.; dir. Group W Prodns., Inc., W-F Prodns., Inc.; chmn. bd. Micro-Relay, Inc., 1974—; chmn. bd., pres. CATV Enterprises, Inc., 1970—. Mem. communications adv. council St. John's U.; committeeman United Fund Greater N.Y., 1974; boxing judge Pa. Athletic Commn., 1952-55. Bd. dirs. TV Bur. Advt., 1974—, chmn., 1977-79; bd. dirs. Radio Advt. Bur., 1970-77. With USAAF, 1942-45. Decorated Air medal with 9 oak leaf clusters. Recipient Communications Alumni award Syracuse U., 1960. Mem. Internat. Radio and TV Soc., Alpha Epsilon Rho (hon.). Clubs: Pinnacle (N.Y.C.); Long Ridge (Stamford). Home: 26 Foxwood Rd Stamford CT 06903 Office: 90 Park Ave New York NY 10016

SHAPIRO, MAURICE MANDEL, physicist; b. Jerusalem, Nov. 13, 1915; s. Asher and Miriam R. (Grunbaum) S.; came to U.S., 1921, naturalized by Act of Congress; B.S., U. Chgo., 1936, M.S., 1940, Ph.D., 1942; m. Inez Weinfield, Feb. 8, 1942 (dec. Oct. 1964); children—Joel Nevin, Elana Shapiro Ashley, Raquel Tamar Shapiro Kislinger; m. 2d, Marion C. Gordon, Aug. 20, 1968 (div. May 6, 1976); stepchildren—Lisa Jane, Joshua, James Lincoln. Instr. physics and math. Chgo. City Colls., 1937-41; chmn. dept. phys. and biol. scis. Austin Coll., 1938-41; instr. math. Gary Coll., 1942; physicist Dept. Navy, 1942-44; lectr. physics and math. George Washington U., 1943-44; group leader, mem. coordinating council of lab. Los Alamos Sci. Lab., U. Calif., 1944-46; sr. physicist, lectr. Oak Ridge Nat. Lab., Union Carbon and Carbide Corp., 1946-49; cons. div. nuclear energy for propulsion aircraft Fairchild Engine & Aircraft Corp., 1948-49; head cosmic ray br. nucleonics div. U.S. Naval Research Lab., Washington, 1949-65, supt. nucleonics div., 1953-65, chief scientist Lab. for Cosmic Ray Physics, 1965—, apptd. to chair of cosmic ray physics, 1966; lectr. U. Md., 1949-50, 52—, asso. prof., 1950-51; cons. Argonne Nat. Lab., 1949; cons. panel on cosmic rays U.S. nat. com. IGY; lectr. physics and engring. Nuclear Products-Erco div. ACF Industries, Inc., 1956-58; lectr. E. Fermi Internat. Sch. Physics, Varenna, Italy, 1962; vis. prof. Weizmann Inst. Sci., Rehovoth, Israel, 1962-63, Inst. Math. Scis., Madras, India, 1971, Inst. Astronomy and Geophysics, Nat. U. Mex., 1976; vis. prof. physics and astronomy Northwestern U., Evanston, Ill., 1978; cons. space research in astronomy Space Sci. Bd., Nat. Acad. Scis., 1965; cons. Office Space Scis., NASA, 1965-66, prin. investigator Gemini S-9 Cosmic Ray Expts., NASA, 1964-69, Skylab, 1967-76, Long Duration Exposure Facility, 1977—; mem. Groupe de Travail de Biologie Spatiale, Council of Europe, 1970—; mem. steering com. DUMAND Consortium, 1976—; lectr. Summer Space Inst., Deutsche Physikalische Gesellschaft, 1972; dir. Internat. Sch. Cosmic-Ray Astrophysics, Ettore Majorana Centre Sci. Culture, 1977—, also sr. corr., 1977—; chmn. U.S. IGY com. on interdisciplinary research, mem. nuclear emulsion panel space sci. bd. Nat. Acad. Scis., 1959—; chief U.S. rep., steering com. Internat. Coop. Emulsion Flights for Cosmic Ray Research; cons. CREI Atomics, 1959—; vis. com. Bartol Research Found., Franklin Inst., 1967-74; mem. U.S. organizing com. 13th Internat. Conf. on Cosmic Rays; mem. sci. adv. com. Internat. Confs. on Nuclear Photography and Solid State Detectors, 1966—; mem. Com. of Honor for Einstein Centennial, Acad. Naz. Lincei, 1977—; Recipient Distinguished Civilian Service award Dept. Navy, 1967; Guggenheim fellow, 1962-63; medal of Honor, Société d'Encouragement au Progrès, 1978; Publs. award Naval Research Lab., 1970, 74, 76. Fellow Am. Phys. Soc. (chmn. organizing com. div. cosmic physics, chmn. 1971-72, com. on publs. 1977—), AAAS, Washington Acad. Scis. (past com. chmn.); mem. Am. Inst. Physics, Research Soc. Am., Am. Astron. Soc. (exec. com. div. high-energy astrophysics 1978—), Philos. Soc. Washington (past pres.), Am. Technion Soc. (Washington bd.), Assn. Los Alamos Scientists (past chmn.), Assn. Oak Ridge Engrs. and Scientists (past chmn.), Fedn. Am. Scientists (past mem. exec. com., nat. council), Internat. Astron. Union (exec. com. commn. on high-energy astrophysics), Phi Beta Kappa, Sigma Xi. Editorial bd. Astrophysics and Space Sci., 1968-75; asso. editor Phys. Rev. Letters, 1977—; contbr. to Ency. Physics, Am. Inst. Physics Handbook. Research in cosmic radiation: composition, origin, propagation, and nuclear transformations; high-energy astrophysics; particles and fields; nuclear physics; neutron physics and fission reactors, neutrino astronomy. Office: Lab Cosmic Physics US Naval Research Lab Code 7020 Washington DC 20375

SHAPIRO, MICHAEL, super market chain exec.; b. N.Y.C., Mar. 3, 1942; s. Jack and Celia (Schwartzbaum) S.; B.S., CCNY, 1962; m. Sara Louise Ress, Mar. 22, 1964; children—Jeffrey, Lisa, Kenneth. Acct., Sidney Kaminsky & Co., N.Y.C., 1964-68; supr. Hurdman Cranston, Penney & Co., C.P.A.'s, N.Y.C., 1968-71; with Mayfair Super Markets Inc., Elizabeth, N.J., 1971—, v.p. fin. and adminstrn., 1978—. C.P.A., N.Y. Mem. Am. Inst. C.P.A.'s, Food Mktg. Inst., N.Y. State Soc. C.P.A.'s, N.J. Food Council. Office: 681 Newark Ave Elizabeth NJ 07208

SHAPIRO, MILTON, mfg. co. exec.; b. Chgo., Feb. 26, 1926; s. Morris and Florence (Naiman) S.; student U. Wis., 1943-44, DePaul U., 1946-49, Loyola U., Chgo., 1950; M.B.A., U. Chgo., 1959; m. Phyllis Urow, Dec. 22, 1957; children—Fern, Sharon, David. With Maremont Corp., Chgo., 1950—, asst. treas., 1963-65, treas., 1965-69, v.p., treas., 1969—; pres., dir. Maremont Acceptance Corp., 1967—. Bd. dirs. Better Govt. Assn. Served with AUS, 1944-46. Home: 9416 Lawndale Ave Evanston IL 60203 Office: 200 E Randolph Dr Chicago IL 60601

SHAPIRO, MOSES, electronics mfg. co. exec.; b. N.Y.C., Nov. 30, 1910; s. Samuel and Rachel (Gochberg) S.; student Fordam U., 1929; LL.B., St. Lawrence U., 1932; m. Barbara Ann Hewson, Dec. 27, 1970; children—Robert B., Susan J., William B. Admitted to N.Y. bar, 1933; indsl. relations cons., 1934-52; impartial chmn., labor arbitrator for numerous nat. industries, 1936-45; exec. v.p. Gen. Instrument Corp., N.Y.C., 1955-60, pres., 1960-68, vice chmn., 1968-69, chmn., chief exec. officer, 1969-76, chmn. exec. com., 1977—; mgmt. cons., 1976—; lectr. Practising Law Inst., CCNY. Bd. dirs., treas. Theatre Devel. Fund; mem. Pres.'s Task Force Tech. Transfer, Nat. Planning Assn. CAMRAND Com., N.Y. Mayor's Contingency Task Force. Decorated commendatore dell' Ordine della Stella della Solidarieta Italiana (Italy), Govt. of the Republic of China. Mem. Electronics Industries Assn. (dir.). Jewish. Club: Harmonie. Contbr. articles on indsl. relations to profl. jours. Office: 52 S Howells Point Rd Bellport NY 11713

SHAPIRO, MYRON FREDERICK (MIKE), broadcasting co. exec.; b. Mpls., Dec. 16, 1918; s. Leo Miriam (Levin) S.; student Duluth Jr. Coll., 1937-38, U. Minn., 1939; m. Conway Helen King, Oct. 24, 1942; 1 dau., Lynne Carole Shapiro Covert. Mgr. Sta KTXL, San Angelo, Tex., Sta. KECK, Odessa, Tex.; sales rep. Sta. WFAA-TV, Dallas, 1952-53, mgr., 1958-60, gen. mgr., 1960-74; comml. mgr. Sta. KDUB, Lubbock, Tex., 1953-54; account exec. Avery Knodel Inc., Chgo., 1954-55; v.p., mng. dir. Griffin Telecasting Properties, Tulsa and Little Rock, 1956-58; pres. Belo Broadcasting Corp., Dallas, 1974—, dir., 1974—; dir. A.H. Belo Corp., Dallas, 1968—. Chmn. bd. Dallas chpt. Am. Cancer Soc., 1977-78; mem. advisory bd. Lon Morris Coll., Jacksonville, Tex., 1971—; bd. dirs. Dallas chpt. ARC, 1977-78, co-vice chmn., 1978-79, chmn., 1979-80; bd. dirs. Dallas March of Dimes, 1970-74, Tex. Soc. for Prevention of Blindness, 1976-79, Dallas Better Bus. Bur., 1961—, Dallas Jr. Achievement, 1972-74, Family Guidance Center, 1967-69; mem. advisory council U. Tex. Sch. Communications Found., 1969-79; mem. local broadcasters advisory com. Abe Lincoln awards So. Bapt. Radio-TV Commn., 1976-78, chmn., 1977-78. Served with USAAF, 1941-45. Recipient 1st Abe Lincoln Broadcasters merit award So. Bapt. Radio-TV Commn., 1970, Award for service to broadcasting students N. Tex. State U. Radio and TV Club, 1971. Mem. Salesmanship Club Dallas (bd. dirs. 1972-73, v.p. 1976-77), Nat. Assn. Broadcasters (mem. TV bd. dirs. 1963-66, 75-79, chmn. 1965-66, mem. TV code bd. 1968-71), ABC-TV Affiliates Assn. (bd. dirs. 1961-64, chmn. 1963), Assn. Broadcast Execs. Tex. (past pres., award 1962), Dallas Ad Club (bd. dirs. 1968-69), Dallas Ad League (bd. dirs. 1968-69), CBS Radio Affiliates (bd. dirs. 1975-78). Originator Let Me Speak to the Manager (name changed to Inside

Television 1974), 1961—. Home: 13825 Hughes Ln Dallas TX 75240 Office: Communications Center Dallas TX 75202

SHAPIRO, NILS ALLEN, mag. editor and pub.; b. Bayonne, N.J., May 18, 1933; s. Sol and Minnie (Weber) S.; B.B.A., City Coll. N.Y., 1954; m. Roberta Datz, Apr. 10, 1954 (div.); children—Brett Andree, Hillary Lynn. Dir. advt., promotion and pub. relations Grosset & Dunlap, Inc., N.Y.C., 1955-68; dir. mktg. and spl. projects Clairol, Inc., N.Y.C., 1968-69; asso. pub. Penthouse mag., N.Y.C., 1969-72; mktg. dir. Environ. Advt. of Am., Inc., N.Y.C., 1972-75; asso. pub. Gallery mag., N.Y.C., 1975-76, editor, pub., 1976-79; editor, pub. New Dawn mag., 1976-77; exec. v.p., dir. Montcalm Pub. Corp., N.Y.C., 1976—. Recipient nat. award Direct Mail Advt. Assn. Am., 1956. Home: 405 E 56th St New York NY 10022 Office: 800 2d Ave New York NY 10017

SHAPIRO, NORMA SONDRA LEVY, fed. judge; b. Phila., July 27, 1928; d. Bert and Jane (Kotkin) Levy; B.A. in Polit. Theory with honors, U. Mich., 1948; J.D. magna cum laude, U. Pa., 1951; m. Bernard Shapiro, Aug. 21, 1949; children—Finley, Neil, Aaron. Admitted to Pa. bar, 1952, U.S. Supreme Ct. bar, 1978; law clk. to judge Pa. Supreme Ct., 1951-52; instr. U. Pa. Law Sch., 1951-52, 55-56; asso. firm Dechert Price & Rhoads, Phila., 1956-58, 67-73, partner, 1973-78; judge U.S. Dist. Ct. for Eastern Pa., 1978—; asso. trustee U. Pa. Law Sch., 1978—; trustee Women's Law Project, 1978—; mem. lawyer's adv. panel Pa. Gov.'s Commn. on Status of Women, 1974; legal adv. Regional Council Child Psychiatry. Pres., Lower Merion County (Pa.) Bd. Sch. Dirs., 1968-77, 77, v.p., 1976; v.p. Jewish Community Relations Council of Greater Phila., 1975-77; chmn. legal affairs com., 1978; pres. Belmont Hills Home and Sch. Assn., Lower Merion Twp.; legis. chmn. Lower Merion Sch. Dist. Intersch. Council; mem. Task Force on Mental Health of Children and Youth of Pa.; treas., chmn. edn. com. Human Relations Council Lower Merion; v.p., parliamentarian, Nes Ami Penn Valley Congregation, Lower Merion Twp. Named Woman of Yr., Oxford Circle Jewish Community Center, 1979, Woman of Distinction, Golden Slipper Club, 1979; Gowen fellow, 1954-55. Mem. Am. Law Inst., Am. Bar Found., Am. Bar Assn. (vice chmn. com. on law and mental health sect. family law), Pa. Bar Assn. (ho. of dels. 1979—), Phila. Bar Assn. (chmn. com. women's rights 1972, 74-75, chmn. bd. govs. 1977—, chmn. public relations com. 1978), Fed. Bar Assn., Nat. Assn. Women Lawyers, Phila. Trial Lawyers Assn., Am. Judicature Soc., Phila. Fellowship Commn., Order of Coif (chpt. pres. 1973-75), Tau Epsilon Rho. Guest editor Shingle, 1972. Home: 417 Hidden River Rd Narberth PA 19072 Office: US Courthouse Room 10614 601 Market St Philadelphia PA 19106

SHAPIRO, NORMAN RICHARD, educator; b. Boston, Nov. 1, 1930; s. Harry Alexander and Eva (Goldberg) S.; B.A., Harvard, 1951, M.A., 1952, Ph.D., 1958; diplôme de Langue et Lettres Françaises (Fulbright fellow), Université D'Aix-Marseille, 1956; M.A. (hon.), Wesleyan U., 1972. Instr. French, Amherst (Mass.) Coll., 1958-60; asst. prof., asso. prof., prof. Romance langs. and lits. Wesleyan U., Middletown, Conn., 1960—. Mem. African Studies Assn., Am. Assn. Tchrs. French, Universala Esperanto-Asocio, Esperanto League N.Am., Judezmo Soc., Delta Kappa Epsilon. Jewish. Club: Signet Soc. (Harvard). Editor: Echos, 1965; Palabres, 1973. Translator, editor: Négritude, 1971. Translator: Four Farces by Georges Feydeau, 1970; Comedy of Eros, 1971; Kamouraska (by Anne Hébert), 1973; Virginie, or The Dawning of the World (by Joseph Majault), 1974; The Camp of the Saints (by Jean Raspail), 1975. Composer; Three Songs, 1961. Contbr. articles, transls. and revs. to profl. jours. Home: 214 High St Middletown CT 06457

SHAPIRO, PHILIP, financial exec.; b. Boston, Feb. 1, 1931; s. Jacob and Lillian (Cooper) S.; B.S., Boston U., 1951; m. Marilyn Freeman, Aug. 16, 1953; children—Rhonda Anne, Wendy Joyce, Alan Frank. With Irving Chernoff, C.P.A., Boston, 1954-57; audit supr. Touche, Ross & Co., C.P.A.'s, Boston, 1957-64, audit mgr., 1967-71; asst. treas. Garland Corp., Brockton, Mass., 1964-67, fin. v.p., treas., 1974-75; corporate controller Chelsea Industries, Inc., Brighton, Mass., 1971-74; controller Suburban Shoe Stores, Cambridge, Mass., 1976—. Mem. Town Meeting, Brookline, Mass., 1971-73; treas., mem. exec. bd. Jewish Def. League of Boston, 1970—, chmn., 1973—. Served with AUS, 1952-54. C.P.A., Mass. Mem. Am. Inst. C.P.A.'s, Mass. Soc. C.P.A.'s. Jewish (pres. congregation 1967-68). Contbr. to Ency. of Audit Techniques, 1965. Home: 27 Osborne Rd Brookline MA 02146 Office: Suburban Shoe Stores 1935 Revere Beach Pkwy Everett MA 02149

SHAPIRO, RICHARD GERALD, dept. store exec.; b. N.Y.C. Apr. 24, 1924; s. David and Sophie (Hayflich) S.; B.A., U. Mich., 1946; M.B.A., Harvard, 1948; m. Lila Eig, July 27, 1951; children—Judith, Amy, Donald. With Lord & Taylor, N.Y.C., 1948-64, v.p., 1959-63, sr. v.p., 1963-64, also mem. adv. bd.; pres. Wm. Filene's Sons Co., Boston, 1965-68, chief exec. officer, chmn. bd. 1968-73; pres. Gimbel Bros. Corp., N.Y.C., 1973-76; v.p. W.R. Grace & Co., pres. sporting goods div., 1977-79, pres. splty. store div., 1979—; dir. Asso. Merchandising Corp. Retail chmn. greater N.Y. Fund, 1963; chmn. merc. div. Mass. Bay United Fund, 1967. Mem. corp. Simmons Coll., Boston Mus. Fine Arts (permanent); bd. dirs. Mass. Mchts.; bd. dirs Family Counseling and Guidance Centers, 1969-72, v.p., 1970; trustee Brandeis U. Served with AUS, 1942-46. Mem. Harvard Bus. Sch. Assn. (gov.). Home: 7002 Blvd East Guttenberg NJ 07093

SHAPIRO, ROBERT FRANK, investment banking co. exec.; b. St. Louis, Dec. 19, 1934; s. Eugene J. and Clara (Katz) S.; grad. St. Louis Country Day Sch., 1952; B.A., Yale U., 1956; m. Anna Marie Susman, Dec. 21, 1960; children—Albert Andrew, Robert Jr., Jeanne. Asso. firm Lehman Bros., N.Y.C., 1956-67, partner, 1967-73, dir., sr. mng. dir., 1970-73; dir., exec. v.p. Wertheim & Co., Inc., N.Y.C., 1974-75, partner, 1974, pres., dir., 1975—; dir. Zayre Corp. Trustee Blythedale Children's Hosp. Mem. Bond Club N.Y., Securities Industry Assn. (gov.). Clubs: Bd. Room, Century Country. Home: 730 Park Ave New York City NY 10021 Office: 200 Park Ave New York City NY 10017

SHAPIRO, RONALD MAURICE, lawyer; b. Phila., Mar. 29, 1943; s. Mark and Lilian Constance (Dratch) S.; A.B., Haverford Coll., 1964; J.D. cum laude, Harvard, 1967; m. Lynn Huberman, Mar. 22, 1964; children—Mark A., Julie K., Laura R., David B. Law clk. U.S. dist. judge, 1967-68; admitted to Md. bar, 1967; asso. Frank, Bernstein, Conaway & Goldman, Balt., 1968-70, partner, 1970-72; pres. Shapiro, Vettori & Olander, 1972—; pres., dir. Personal Mgmt. Assos., Inc., 1977—. Lectr. in law U. Md., 1968—, faculty council Sch. Law, 1969-71; lectr., dir. Modern Bar Rev. Course, 1968—; lectr. evening div. Johns Hopkins, 1971, U. Balt. Sch. Law, 1971—; mem. Md. Blue Sky Adv. Commn., 1974-79; chmn. Md. Franchise Adv. Task Force, 1977—; panelist Square-Off, WJZ-TV, 1977—. Securities commr. State of Md., 19772-74. Pres., Md. Conf. Social Concern, 1975-76; pres. Balt. chpt. Am. Jewish Com., 1976-78. Bd. dirs. Balt. Legal Scholarship Fund; treas. Balt. Jewish Community Relations Council, 1976-78, pres., 1978-80; bd. dirs. Asso. Jewish Charities and Welfare Fund; Md. chmn. Harvard Law Sch. Fund, 1975-77; chmn. devel. com. Johns Hopkins Children's Center, 1978—; trustee Gilman Sch., Balt., 1977—. Recipient Pub. Affairs research grantee Ford Found., 1963. Mem. Am., Md. bar assns., Bar Assn. Balt. City. Club: Center, Serjeants Inn Law (Balt.). Co-author: Securities Regulation Forms, 1975, Maryland Corporate Forms—Practice, 1976. Contbr. articles to profl. jours. and newspapers. Home: 2404 W Rogers Ave Baltimore MD 21209 Office: 2000 Charles Center S 36 S Charles St Baltimore MD 21201

SHAPIRO, SAM, biostatistician; b. N.Y.C., Feb. 12, 1914; s. Meyer and Tillie (Sugarman) S.; B.S., Bklyn. Coll., 1933; postgrad. Columbia U., 1934-35; m. Selma Deitch, Apr. 26, 1938; children—Ellen Shapiro Fried, Robert. Chief natality analysis br. Nat. Office Vital Statistics, USPHS, 1947-54; sr. study dir. Nat. Opinion Research Center, Chgo., 1954-55; asso. dir. research and statistics Health Ins. Plan of Greater N.Y., N.Y.C., 1955-59, v.p., dir. research and statistics, 1959-73; dir. Health Services Research and Devel. Center Johns Hopkins Med. Instns., 1973—, prof. dept. health services adminstrn. Sch. Hygiene and Pub. Health Johns Hopkins U., 1973—; lectr. Columbia U. Sch. Pub. Health and Adminstrv. Medicine, 1962; adj. prof. dept. community medicine Mt. Sinai Sch. Medicine, N.Y.C., 1972; cons. Nat. Cancer Inst., WHO, Nat. Center Health Statistics, Health Care Fin. Adminstrn., Robert Wood Johnson Found., Nat. Center Health Services Research. Served with U.S. Navy, 1944-46. Fellow Am. Pub. Health Assn. (Domestic award 1977), Am. Statis. Assn., Am. Heart Assn.; mem. Inst. Medicine, Nat. Acad. Scis., Population Assn. Am., Am. Epidemiologic Soc., Internat. Soc. Cardiology, Internat. Epidemiol. Assn. Editorial bd. Am. Jour. Public Health. Home: 5903 Charlesmead Rd Baltimore MD 21212 Office: 624 N Broadway Baltimore MD 21205

SHAPIRO, SAMUEL BERNARD, cons.; b. Chgo., Nov. 15, 1909; s. Bernard and Ida (Schwartz) S.; B.S., U. Chgo., 1935; m. Mary Heller, Dec. 24, 1933; children—Judith Shapiro DeGraff, Richard B. Asst. to mgr. Greater Chgo. Safety Council, 1928-33; exec. sec. Authorized Ford Dealers Assn., 1933-38; mgr. Chgo. Automobile Trade Assn. and Chgo. Auto Shows, 1938-43; chief research and planning, automobile rationing br. OPA, 1943; exec. dir. Linen Supply Assn. Am., 1946-75; pres. Samuel B. Shapiro Cons. Inc., 1975—; v.p. Seminars, Speakers, Travel, Inc., Washington, 1976—. Sr. v.p., treas., dir. Am. Soc. Assn. Execs., 1958-62, pres., 1962-63, chmn. bd. trustees CAE-ASAE, 1972; pres. Assn. Execs. Forum Chgo., 1956-57; chmn. exec. operating council Insts. Orgn. Mgmt., Mich. State U., 1957; mem. exec. adv. council Fla. Atlantic U., 1974—. Served with AUS, 1943-45. Recipient Key award CAE-ASAE, 1960. Mem. Internat. Soc. Gen. Semantics (charter mem., v.p. 1969—, ACLU, Am. Vets. Com., Phi Beta Kappa. Co-author: Association Management (textbook), 1958; Forward Planning; author: The Whys of Association Executive Success (and Failure), 1977; Before and After Retirement, 1978; adv. bd. Adult Edn. mag., 1956-58; contbr. articles to profl. jours.; lectr. in field. Home: 5945 N Bay Rd Miami Beach FL 33140 Office: 311 Lincoln Rd Miami Beach FL 33140

SHAPIRO, SAMUEL HARVEY, lawyer, former gov. Ill.; b. Apr. 25, 1907; s. Joseph and Tillie (Bloom) S.; student St. Viator Coll.; J.D., U. Ill., 1929; m. Gertrude Adelman, May 21, 1939. Admitted to Ill. bar, 1929; with Shapiro & Lauridsen, Kankakee, 1929—; partner firm Friedman and Koven, Chgo., 1969—; city atty., Kankakee, 1933-35; state's atty., Kankakee County, 1936-40; mem. 65th-71st Ill. gen assemblies, chmn. pub. aid, health, welfare and safety com., 1959; lt. gov. Ill., 1960-68, gov., 1968-69; dir. Aetna State Bank, Chgo. Pres., Nat. Conf. Lt. Govs., 1960-62. Chmn., Ill. Mental Health Commn.; past mem. Council on Improvement Econ. and Social Status Older People, Intergovtl. and Narcotics commns.; mem. nat. civil rights com. Anti-Defamation League. Past sec., treas. Young Democratic Club Ill. Served with USNR, World War II. Named Man of Year Jewish Police Soc. Chgo., Jewish Nat. Fund, 1968. Mem. Am., Ill., Chgo., Kankakee County bar assns., Kankakee C. of C., Musician's Union (past pres.), Kankakee Fedn. Labor (past pres.), Am. Legion, Amvets, Alpha Epsilon Pi (past nat. pres.). Moose, Kiwanian, Elk; mem. B'nai B'rith. Clubs: Country (Kan Ka Kee); Covenant of Ill. (Chgo.). Home: 1300 Cobb Blvd Kankakee IL 60901 Office: 208 S LaSalle St Chicago IL 60604 also City Nat Bank Bldg Kankakee IL 60901

SHAPIRO, SEYMOUR, botanist; b. N.Y.C., Feb. 16, 1924; s. Abraham and Lillian (Moskowitz) S.; B.A., U. Mich., 1947, Ph.D., 1952; m. Harriett Sher, June 16, 1947; 1 son, Carl David. Asso. botanist Brookhaven Nat. Lab., 1952-61; asso. prof. biology U. Oreg., 1961-64; prof., head botany dept. U. Mass., Amherst, 1964-75, dean faculty natural sci. and math., prof. botany, 1975—; cons. NSF, 1962-69. Recipient Metawampe award, 1969, Outstanding Service medal, 1973 both from U. Mass. Mem. AAAS, Am. Soc. Plant Physiologists, Bot. Soc. Am., Am. Soc. Devel. Biology, Fedn. Am. Scientists. Home: 135 Lincoln Ave Amherst MA 01002 Office: South Coll U Mass Amherst MA 01003

SHAPIRO, SIDNEY, physicist, educator; b. Boston, Dec. 4, 1931; s. Samuel and Sadie (Aberblatt) S.; A.B., Harvard, 1953, A.M., 1955, Ph.D., 1959; m. Janice Ann Yeutter, May 14, 1960; children—Sara Ruth, Johanna Sue. Physicist, also group leader Arthur D. Little, Inc., 1959-64; mem. tech. staff Bell Telephone Labs., Inc., 1964-67; asso. prof. elec. engring. U. Rochester (N.Y.), 1967-73, prof., 1973—, asso. dean Coll. Engring. and Applied Sci., 1974-79; vis. prof. Physics Lab I, Tech. U. Denmark, 1972-73. Fellow Am. Phys. Soc.; mem. I.E.E.E. (sr.). Democrat. Jewish religion. Contbr. articles to profl. publs. Pioneer exptl. confirmation AC Josephson effect in superconducting tunneling. Home: 220 Parkwood Ave Rochester NY 14620 Office: Dept Elec Engring U Rochester Rochester NY 14627

SHAPIRO, SUMNER, naval officer; b. Nashua, N.H., Jan. 13, 1926; s. Maurice David and Hannah (Goodman) S.; B.S., U.S. Naval Acad., 1949; M.S., George Washington U., 1966; postgrad. Naval War Coll., 1966, U.S. Army Inst. Advanced Soviet and Eastern European Studies, 1961; m. Eleanor S. Hymen, June 14, 1949; children—Martha, Steven, Susan. Commd. ensign U.S. Navy, 1949, advanced through grades to rear adm.; asst. naval attache Am. embassy, Moscow, 1963-65; dep. asst. chief of staff U.S. Naval Forces Europe, London, 1967-69; comdg. officer Naval Intelligence Processing System Support Activity, Washington, 1969-72; asst. chief staff Atlantic Command, Atlantic Fleet, Norfolk, Va., 1972-76; dep. dir. naval intelligence, 1976-77; comdr. Naval Intelligence Command, Washington, 1977-78, dir. Naval Intelligence, 1978—. Decorated Legion of Merit and others. Mem. U.S. Naval Inst., U.S. Naval Acad. Alumni Assn. Jewish. Office: Office Naval Intelligence Dept Navy Washington DC 20350*

SHAPIRO, WILLIAM RICHARD, neurologist; b. Pitts., May 1, 1936; s. Carl S. and Jean R. (Fisch) S.; B.S., UCLA, 1958; M.D., U. Calif., San Francisco, 1961; m. Aug. 23, 1959; children—Matthew E., Rachel E. Intern, Kings County Hosp., Seattle, 1961-62; resident in medicine U. Wash. Hosps., Seattle, 1962-63; resident in neurology N.Y. Hosp.-Cornell U. Med. Coll., 1963-66, instr. in neurology, 1965-66; asst. registrar Nat. Hosp., London, 1965; staff asso. Nat. Cancer Inst., Bethesda, Md., 1966-69; asst. prof. neurology Cornell U. Med. Coll., N.Y.C., 1969-73, asso. prof., 1973-76, prof., 1976—; attending neurologist Meml. Sloan-Kettering Cancer Center and head lab. neuro-oncology Sloan-Kettering Inst. Cancer Research, 1976—. Served with USPHS, 1966-69. Recipient Research Career Devel. award NIH, 1971-76. Mem. Am. Assn. Cancer Research, Am. Acad. Neurology, AAAS, Am. Neurol. Assn., Am. Soc. Clin. Oncology, Harvey Soc., N.Y. Acad. Scis., Pan African Assn. Neurol. Scis. Contbr. numerous articles to med. jours.; research in biology and therapy of brain tumors, neuro-oncology, sleep. Office: 1275 York Ave New York NY 10021

SHAPLEIGH, WARREN MCKINNEY, food mfg. co. exec.; b. St. Louis, Oct. 27, 1920; s. Alexander Wessel and Lois (McKinney) S.; B.A. in Econs., Yale, 1942; m. Jane Howard Smith, Sept. 10, 1945; children—Jane Howard, Christine. Vice pres. Shapleigh Hardware Co., St. Louis, 1946-56, Sterling Aluminum Products, St. Louis, 1959-61; pres. Hipolite Co., St. Louis, 1956-59; mgr. diversification planning Ralston Purina Co., St. Louis, 1961-63, v.p. consumer products div., 1963-68, exec. v.p., 1968-70, pres. consumer products group, 1970-72, pres. co., 1972-78, vice chmn., 1978—, also dir.; dir. Tidewater Marine Service, New Orleans, Midland Container Co., Brown Group, Inc., St. Louis, First Nat. Bank, St. Louis Union Trust, Mo. Pacific Corp., Mo. Pacific R.R. Co., J.P. Morgan & Co., Morgan Guaranty Trust Co. Trustee Jefferson Nat. Expansion Meml. Assn., St. Louis Symphony Soc., Mo. Bot. Garden, Washington U., St. Louis, Govtl. Research Inst., Brookings Instn. Served to lt. USNR, 1942-46. Clubs: St. Louis County (pres., gov. 1959-61), Noonday (St. Louis). Home: 1310 Mason Rd St Louis MO 63131 Office: Checkerboard Sq St Louis MO 63188

SHAPLEN, ROBERT MODELL, journalist, author; b. Phila., Mar. 22, 1917; s. Joseph and Sonia (Modell) S.; B.A., U. Wis., 1937; M.S. in Journalism, Columbia, 1938; postgrad. (Nieman fellow), Harvard, 1947-48; m. Martha Lucas, Apr. 10, 1953 (div. 1962); 1 son, Peter Lucas; m. 2d, June Herman, Mar. 31, 1962; children—Kate, Jason. Reporter, N.Y. Herald Tribune, 1937-43; S.W. Pacific War corr. Newsweek mag., 1943-45, Far East bur. chief, Shanghai, 1945-47; writer Fortune mag., 1948-50; mem. fgn. staff Collier's mag., also fgn. corr. 15 newspapers 1950-52; staff writer New Yorker mag., 1952-62, Far East corr., Hong Kong, 1962—. Club: Harvard (N.Y.C). Author: A Corner of the World, 1949; Free Love and Heavenly Sinners, 1954; A Forest of Tigers, 1956; Kreuger: Genius and Swindler, 1960; Toward the Wellbeing of Mankind: 50 Years of the Rockefeller Foundation, 1962; The Lost Revolution, 1965; Time out of Hand: Revolution and Reaction in the Southeast Asia, rev., 1970; The Road from War, rev., 1971; (introduction) The Face of Asia, 1972; A Turning Wheel, 1979; also numerous articles, TV documentaries. Home: Princeton NJ 08540 Office: New Yorker 25 W 43d St New York NY 10036

SHAPLEY, ALAN HORACE, geophysicist; b. Pasadena, Calif., Mar. 23, 1919; s. Harlow and Martha (Betz) S.; A.B., Harvard; 1940; m. Kathryn Maloney, Mar. 10, 1956; 1 dau., Carol Louise Shapley. In charge solar-ionospheric research, dept. terrestrial magnetism Carnegie Instn. Washington, 1942-46; with central radio propagation lab. Nat. Bur. Standards, Washington, 1947-54, Boulder, Colo., 1954-65, chief CRPL Radio Warning Service, 1947-59, chief sun-earth relationships sect., 1956-59, asst. chief radio propagation physics div., 1959-60, chief Office CRPL liaison and program devel., 1960-65; sr. geophysicist Environmental Sci. Services Adminstrn., 1965-67, dir. office of programs, research labs., 1967-70, asso. dir. for geophysics nat. oceanic and atmospheric adminstrn. Environ. Data Services, 1970-74, dir. Nat. Geophys. and Solar Terrestrial Data Center, 1972—; research asso. Harvard Obs., 1955-63. Vice chmn. U.S. nat. com. Internat. Geophys. Year, Nat. Acad. Scis., 1953-64, mem. space sci. bd. 1958-61, cons., 1963—, com. polar research, 1958-70, spl. com. Internat. Geophys. Year, Internat. Council Sci. Unions, 1955-59, internat. rapporteur for world days and communications, mem. com. geophysics, 1958-67, mem. spl. com. internat. quiet sun years, 1962-67, mem. spl. com. on solar terrestrial physics, 1967—; mem. Com. on Solar Terrestrial Physics, 1971—; mem. solar-terrestrial commn. Pan Am. Inst. Geography and History. Mem. adv. com. U. Alaska Geophys. Inst. Fellow A.A.A.S.; mem. Fedn. Am. Scientists (exec. officer Washington 1948-53), Washington Acad. Scis., Am. Astron. Soc., Am. Geophys. Union (chmn. geophys. monograph bd. 1959-70), Internat. Sci. Radio Union (nat. com., chmn. worldwide ionospheric soundings com. 1955-61), Internat. World Days Service (chmn.). Office: Nat Oceanic and Atmospheric Adminstrn Environ Data Services Boulder CO 80302*

SHAPLEY, LLOYD STOWELL, mathematician; b. Cambridge, Mass., June 2, 1923; s. Harlow and Martha (Betz) S.; A.B., Harvard U., 1948; Ph.D. (Grad. Coll. Procter fellow), Princeton U., 1954; m. Marian Ludolph, Aug. 19, 1955; children—Peter, Christopher. Mathematician, Rand Corp., Santa Monica, Calif., 1948-50; 54—, instr. Princeton U., 1952-54; sr. research fellow Calif. Inst. Tech., 1955-56; fellow Inst. Advanced Studies, Hebrew U., Jerusalem, 1979-80; mem. adv. bd. Rand Grad. Inst. for Policy Studies, 1970—. Served with AC, U.S. Army, 1943-45. Decorated Bronze Star. Fellow Econometric Soc., Am. Acad. Arts and Scis.; mem. Nat. Acad. Scis., Am. Math. Soc., Math. Programming Soc. Author: (with S. Karlin) Geometry of Moment Spaces, 1953; (with R. Aumann) Values of Non-Atomic Games, 1974; editor: (with others) Advances in Game Theory, 1964; editorial bd. Internat. Jour. Game Theory, 1970—, Math. Programming, 1971—, Jour. Math. Econs., 1973—, Math. Ops. Research, 1975—; research in game theory, econs., polit. sci. Office: Rand Corp 1700 Main St Santa Monica CA 90406*

SHAPLIN, JUDSON TIFFANY, educator; b. East Stroudsburg, Pa., Mar. 16, 1918; s. Alfred C. and Helen (Tiffany) S.; student Girard Coll., Phila., 1927-36; B.S. summa cum laude, Harvard, 1942, M.A., 1951, Ph.D., 1954; m. Philippa Dunham, Feb. 19, 1944 (div. May 1968); children—Alfred Dows, John Dunham, Helen; m. 2d, Marjorie Lowry, June 18, 1968. With Universal Credit Co., Reading, Pa., 1936-38; jr. airport mgr. Pan Am. Airways, Australia, 1942, airport mgr., 1942, airport mgr. Hawaii, Canton Island, San Francisco, N.Y.C., 1943-46; asst. dean Harvard, 1946-49, asst. dean Grad. Sch. Edn., 1949-52, dir. freshman scholarships, 1952-54, asso. dean, asst. prof. edn., lectr. edn., 1954-63, dir. M.A. in teaching program, 1954-61, dir. Harvard-Newton Summer Program, 1955-60, dir. sch., univ. program for research and devel., 1958-61; dir. Washington U. Grad. Inst. Edn., St. Louis, 1963-69, prof. edn., 1963-77, prof. emeritus, 1978—. Ford Found. cons. tchr. tng., Caribbean, Nigeria, Chile, 1959-72; mem. com. research and devel. Coll. Entrance Exam. Bd., 1960-64; chmn. interim bd. dirs. Central Midwestern Regional Ednl. Lab., 1966; coordinator Western Nigerian Comprehensive High Sch., 1962-63. Mem. Cambridge (Mass.) Sch. Com., 1954-59. Mem. Am. Psychol. Assn., Phi Beta Kappa, Phi Delta Kappa. Author, co-editor: Team Teaching, 1964. Editor: Founds. of Edn. Series, 1963-69. Contbr. articles to profl. jours. Home: Rural Route 1 Box 59 Defiance MO 63341

SHAPO, MARSHALL SCHAMBELAN, lawyer, educator; b. Phila., Oct. 1, 1936; s. Mitchell and Norma (Schambelan) S.; A.B. summa cum laude, U. Miami, 1958, J.D. magna cum laude, 1964; A.M., Harvard U., 1961; S.J.D., 1974; m. Helene Shirley Seidner, June 21, 1959; children—Benjamin, Nathaniel. Copy editor, writer Miami (Fla.) News, 1958-59; instr. history U. Miami, 1960-61; admitted to Fla. bar, 1964, Va. bar, 1977; asst. prof. law U. Tex., 1965-67, asso. prof., 1967-69, prof., 1969-70; prof. law U. Va., 1970-78, Joseph M. Hartfield prof., 1976-78; Frederic P. Vose prof. Northwestern U. Sch. Law, Chgo., 1978—; vis. prof. Juristisches Seminar U. Gottingen (W. Ger.), 1976; mem. panel on food safety

Inst. Medicine, Nat. Acad. Scis., 1978-79; vis. fellow Centre for Sociol. Studies, Wolfson Coll., Oxford, vis. fellow of Coll., 1975; mem. Center for Advanced Studies, U. Va., 1976-77. Nat. Endowment Humanities sr. fellow, 1974-75. Mem. Am. Law Inst. Author: A Nation of Guinea Pigs, 1979; The Duty to Act: Tort Law, Power and Public Policy, 1978; Tort and Compensation Law, 1976; (with Page Keeton) Products and the Consumer: Deceptive Practices, 1972, Products and the Consumer: Defective and Dangerous Products, 1970. Mem. editor bd. Jour. Consumer Policy. Author: A Representational Theory of Consumer Protection: Doctrine, Function and Legal Liability for Product Disappointment, 1974; contbr. articles to legal jours. Home: 1910 Orrington Ave Evanston IL 60201 Office: Northwestern U Sch Law 357 E Chicago Ave Chicago IL 60611

SHAPP, MARTHA GLAUBER, editor, educator; b. N.Y.C., Jan. 16, 1910; d. Charles and Anna (Mendelson) Segall; A.B., Barnard Coll., 1929; M.A., Columbia Tchrs. Coll., 1940; m. Stanley E. Glauber, June 17, 1939 (dec. Dec. 1946); 1 son, William Donald; m. 2d, Charles Shapp, Dec. 23, 1953; 1 stepson, Mark. Ednl. research, nat. council YMCA, 1930-33; elementary sch. tchr., N.Y.C. Pub. Schs., 1933-49; curriculum research N.Y.C. Bd. Edn., Bur. Curriculum Research, 1949-52, N.Y. State Dept. Edn. Bur. Curriculum Devel., 1952-53; curriculum coordinator elementary schs., N.Y.C., 1953-60; editor-in-chief New Book of Knowledge, 1960—; dir. Young Peoples Publs., Grolier, Inc., 1970—. Mem. Assn. Supervision and Curriculum Devel., N.E.A., N.Y. State Assn. Supervision and Curriculum Devel., Assn. Childhood Edn. Internat., Nat. Com. Geog. Edn., Nat. Com. Social Studies, Nat. Council Adminstrv. Women in Edn. Author: (children's books) 42 books in Let's Find Out series. Office: Grolier Inc 575 Lexington Ave New York City NY 10022

SHAPP, MILTON J., gov. of Pa.; b. Cleve., June 25, 1912; s. Aaron Shapiro and Eva (Smelsey) S.; B.S. in Elec. Engring., Case Inst. Tech., 1933; m. Muriel Matzkin, May 19, 1947; children—Dolores (Mrs. Gary Graham), Richard, Joanne. Pres., chmn. bd. Jerrold Corp., Phila., 1947-66; pres. Shapp Corp., 1967—; gov. of Pa., 1971-79. Cons., Peace Corps, 1961-63, U.S. Dept. Commerce, 1961-63; vice chmn. Nat. Pub. Adv. Com. on Area Redevel., 1961-64. Del. Democratic Nat. Conv., 1968, 72, 76. organizer, chmn. Pa. Dem. Study Com., 1963-71. Recipient numerous awards including Humanitarian award Pa. State Baptist Conv., 1966, Reuben J. Miller Youth award B'nai B'rith, 1964, William Penn Lodge Youth award, 1964, Ann. award for good citizenship Pa. AFL-CIO, 1963; Alumni award Case Inst. Tech., 1963, Humanitarian award Nat. Bus. League, Phila., 1962. Home: 626 S Bowman Ave Merion PA 19066

SHAPPIRIO, DAVID GORDON, biologist; b. Washington, June 18, 1930; s. Sol and Rebecca (Porton) S.; B.S. with distinction, U. Mich., 1951; A.M., Harvard U., 1953, Ph.D., 1955; m. Elvera May Bamber, July 8, 1953; children—Susan, Mark. NSF postdoctoral fellow Cambridge (Eng.) U., 1955-56; research fellow Am. Cancer Soc.-NRC, U. Louvain (Belgium), 1956-57; mem. faculty U. Mich., Ann Arbor, 1957—, prof. zool. and biol. scis., 1967—, asso. chmn. div., 1976-79, acting chmn. div., 1978-79, coordinator NSF undergrad. sci. edn. program, 1962-67; cons. in field. Lalor Found. fellow, 1953-55; Danforth Found. asso., 1969—; recipient Disting. Teaching award U. Mich., 1967; Bausch & Lomb Sci. award, 1974; research grantee, cons. NIH, NSF. Fellow AAAS; mem. Am. Inst. Biol. Scis. (vis. lectr. 1966-68), Am. Soc. Cell Biology, Biochem. Soc., Entomol. Soc. Am., Royal Entomol. Soc., Lepidopterists Soc.. Soc. Exptl. Biology, Soc. Gen. Physiologists, Phi Beta Kappa. Author, editor, research on biochemistry and physiology growth, devel., dormancy. Address: Div Biol Scis Univ Mich Ann Arbor MI 48109

SHAPSHAK, RENE, sculptor; b. Paris, France, Apr. 18; s. Leo and Perle (Metz) S.; student Ecole Des Beaux Arts, Paris, 1923-26, Brussels, 1927, London, Internat. Am. Inst., Washington; Ph.D., St. Andrews Coll., Eng., 1956; m. Eugenie Palca, Dec. 13, 1938; children—Leon, Maurice, Paul. Exhibited in shows at UN Hdqrs., N.Y.C., 1955, Palais De Beaux Arts, Paris, 1955, Art Assn. New Orleans, 1955, 56, Expn. Internationale, Paris, 1955, Whitney Mus., N.Y.C., 1956, New Rochelle Pub. Library, 1957, Ind. Designers Expn., Detroit, 1958, Internat. Art Exhbn., N.Y.C., 1958, Bronx Courthouse, 1964, Art Show, Mt. Vernon, 1965, Art Show, Newark, 1965, Philathea Mus. Modern Art, London, Ont., Can., 1969, Musee de l'Art Moderne, Paris, 1970; represented in permanent collections at Buckingham Palace, London, Royal Collection, Denmark, South Africa House, London, City of Bulawayo, S.Rhodesia, USCG, Washington and Cal., Towmotor Corp., Pitts. Corning Corp., Westinghouse Electric Co., Kenmetal Corp., Alcoa, Jefferson Chem. Co., Collection of Prince and Princess Henri Paleologue, Cannes, France, also numerous pvt. collections, numerous portraits; bicentennial bronze sculpture of Pres. Truman for Truman Hosp. and Research Center, Kansas City, Mo.; dir. Spring Arts Festival for Edn. and Cultural Trust Fund of Elec. Industry, Flushing, N.Y., 1968—; curator Philathea Mus. Modern Art, London, 1970—; art dir. Yeru-Pax, N.Y.C., 1970—. Dep. Am. provost Gen. Eloy Alfaro Found. Panama, S.Am. Decorated medal Chevalier Order St. Dennis of Zonte (Greece), comdr. Order Konstantinien Nemagnique De St. Etienne, Knight Malta and St. John of Jerusalem; recipient Alfaro medal, 1960; Golden Jubille award Bronx Borough, N.Y., 1964; palmes academique Internat.-Am. Inst. Art lectr. Pinakotheki, Athens, 1951, Donnell Library, N.Y.C., 1959-65, Central Library, N.Y.C., 1959-61, City Art League, N.Y.C., 1960-65. Fellow Royal Soc. Arts (London); mem. Internat. Fine Arts Council, Am. Internat. Acad., Washington (hon. life). Sculpture subjects include Harry S. Truman, Arthur Miller, Yehudi Menuhin, Claudio Arrau, Cardinal Spellman. Home: Hotel Chelsea 222 W 23d St New York City NY 10011 Studio: 163 W 23d St New York City NY 10011

SHARAFF, IRENE, costume designer; b. Boston; student N.Y. Sch. Fine and Applied Arts, Art Students League N.Y., La Grande Chaumiere, Paris. Asst. to Aline Berstein, Civic Repertory Theatre, N.Y.C., 3 yrs., designer scenery and costumes Eva Le Gallienne's Alice Wonderland; designer costumes Broadway musical, Thousands Cheer; designer for musicals, other plays, including Boys from Syracuse, On Your Toes, Lady in the Dark, Star and Garter, Billion Dollar Baby, A Tree Grows in Brooklyn, The King and I, Me and Juliet, West Side Story, Candide, Flower Drum Song, Do Re Mi, The Girl Who Came to Supper, Sweet Charity, Hallelujah Baby; also the designer for ballets of Union Pacifc, Jeudes Cartes, Age of Anxiety, Fanfare, The Concert; designer for motion pictures (ballet) An American in Paris, Brigadoon, Call Me Madam, Guys and Dolls, The King and I, Porgy and Bess, Can Can, West Side Story, Taming of the Shrew, Funny Girl, The Sandpiper, Hello Dolly, Justine, The Great White Hope, The Other Side of Midnight, Ford TV Show (with Mary Martin and Ethel Merman). Recipient Oscar for American in Paris, The King and I (also Antoinette Perry award, Donaldson award), West Side Story, 1962, Cleopatra, 1964, Who's Afraid of Virginia Woolf, 1967. Address: care Gloria Safier 667 Madison Ave New York NY 10021*

SHARBAUGH, HARRY ROBERT, petroleum co. exec.; b. Pitts., Oct. 22, 1928; s. Oliver Michael and Sarah Marie (Wingenroth) S.; B.S. in Chem. Engring., Carnegie Inst. Tech., 1948; postgrad. U. Del., 1949-52; M.S. in Indsl. Mgmt., Mass. Inst. Tech., 1961; D.Sc., Ursinus Coll., 1970; m. Ivy L. Gallacher, Apr. 7, 1951; children—Robert W., Jeanne M., Stephen E. With Sun Co., Phila., 1946—, supt. lube oil and wax mfg., 1966, asst. to v.p. mfg., 1967-69, asst. to pres., chief operating officer of merged Sun-Sunray DX Orgn., 1969, pres., dir. 1970—, chief exec. officer, 1974-79, chmn., 1975-79; dir. Girard Co., Girard Bank, Phila. Mem. bd. com. on devel. Mass. Inst. Tech.; mem. exec. bd. Valley Forge council Boy Scouts Am. Trustee Carnegie Mellon U. Served with Chem. Corps, AUS, 1954-56. Mem. Am. Petroleum Inst. (dir.), Tau Beta Pi. Republican. Episcopalian. Club: Union League (Phila.). Home: 706 Larchwood Ln Villanova PA 19085 Office: One Aldwyn Center Villanova PA 19085

SHARFMAN, ROBERT JAY, lawyer; b. Chgo., Mar. 23, 1936; s. Nathan Stanley and Lillian Ann (Abrams) S.; B.S. in Commerce, Law, U. Ill., 1957; J.D., De Paul U., 1959; m. Barbara Ann Baskes, June 10, 1957; children—Glenn, Howard, Lauren. Admitted to Ill. bar, 1960; trust adminstr. Continental Ill. Nat. Bank & Trust Co. of Chgo., 1960-61; practice law, Chgo., 1961-63; asst. atty. gen. Ill., Chgo., 1963-65; gen. counsel to Ill. Savings, Loan Commr., Chgo., 1965-69; partner firm Gomberg & Sharfman, Ltd., Chgo., 1969—. Tchr. Inst. Financial Edn., Chgo., 1969—; lectr. Exec. Devel. Center, U. Ill., 1972—; contbg. author Inst. Continuing Legal Edn., Springfield, Ill., 1968—. Mem. Am. (pres. com. savs., loan law 1967—), Chgo., Ill. State bar assns. Clubs: Glen Flora Country (Waukeegan, Ill.); Pinehurst (N.C.) Country. Contbg. author handbooks: Creditor Rights, 1969, 72, 74, 77, Mortgages and Foreclosures, 1973; Administrative Law and Practice, 1976. Author 1969 Ill. revision state savings and loan act. Home: 1555 Sunnyside St Highland Park IL 60035 Office: 209 S La Salle St Chicago IL 60604

SHARIF, OMAR (BORN MICHAEL SHALHOUB), actor; b. Alexandria, Egypt, Apr. 10, 1932; s. Joseph and Claire (Saada) Shalhoub; attended Victoria Coll., Cairo; m. Faten Hamama, Feb. 5, 1955; 1 son, Tarek. Appeared in numerous Egyptian, French and Am. films, including: Lawrence of Arabia (Golden Globe award for best supporting actor), 1962, Behold a Pale Horse, 1964, The Fall of the Roman Empire, 1964, Genghis Khan, 1965, The Yellow Rolls Royce, 1965, Doctor Zhivago (Golden Globe award best actor), 1966, Night of the Generals, 1967, More Than a Miracle, 1967, Funny Girl, 1968, Mayerling, 1969, Che!, 1969, MacKenna's Gold, 1969, The Horsemen, 1970, The Last Valley, 1971, The Burglars, 1972, The Tamarind Seed, 1974, The Mysterious Island of Captain Nemo, 1974, Juggernaut, 1974, Funny Lady, 1975, Crime and Passion, 1975. Recipient Golden Globe award for best newcomer/male, 1963. Author: The Eternal Male, 1977; author syndicated columns on bridge. Office: care William Morris Agy (UK) Ltd 147 Wardour St London W1 England*

SHARITS, PAUL JEFFREY, film artist; b. Denver, Feb. 7, 1943; s. Paul Edward and Florence May (Romeo) S.; B.F.A. in Painting, U. Denver, 1964; M.F.A. in Visual Design, Ind. U., 1966; m. Frances Trujillo, July 28, 1962 (div. 1971); 1 son, Christopher. Instr. art Md. Inst. Art, Balt., 1967-70; asst. prof. Antioch Coll., Yellow Springs, Ohio, 1970-73; asso. prof. media State U. N.Y., Buffalo, 1973—; one-man exhbns. include Bykert Gallery, N.Y.C., 1972, 74; Galerie Ricke, Cologne, Ger., 1974, 77; Albright-Knox Art Gallery, Buffalo, 1976; Gallery A, Amsterdam, Netherlands, 1977; Galerie Waalkens, Finsterwolde, Netherlands, 1977; Droll/Kolbert Gallery, N.Y.C., 1977, Art Gallery Ont., Toronto, 1978; retropective of films Centre Georges Pompidou, Paris, 1977, Anthology Film Archives, N.Y.C., 1978; rep. catalogues, also magazines. Grantee Am. Film Inst., 1968, Ford Found., 1970, 71, Nat. Endowment Arts, 1974, Creative Artists Pub. Service, N.Y. State, 1975, 78, N.Y. State Council Arts-Nat. Endowment Arts, 1976. Home: 537 Lafayette Ave Buffalo NY 14222 Office: Center Media Study State Univ NY Buffalo NY 14214

SHARMAN, WILLIAM, basketball exec.; b. Abilene, Tex., May 25, 1926; student U. So. Calif. Basketball player Washington Capitols, 1950-51, Boston Celtics, 1951-61; coach Los Angeles/Utah Stars, 1968-71; coach Los Angeles Lakers, 1971-76, gen. mgr., 1976—. Named to Nat. Basketball Assn. All Star First Team, 1956-59, 2d Team, 1953, 55, 60; named Coach of Year, Nat. Basketball Assn., 1972; named to Naismith Basketball Hall of Fame, 1975. Author: Sharman on Basketball Shooting, 1965. Office: PO Box 10 Inglewood CA 90306

SHARP, AARON JOHN, botanist, educator; b. Plain City, Ohio, July 29, 1904; s. Prentice Daniel and Maude Katharine (Herriott) S.; A.B., Ohio Wesleyan U., 1923-27, D.Sc., 1952; M.S., U. Okla., 1927-29; Ph.D., Ohio State U., 1936-38; m. Cora Evelyn Bunch, July 25, 1929; children—Rosa Elizabeth, Maude Katharine, Mary Martha, Fred Prentice, Jennie Lou. Botanist technician Nat. Park Service, Great Smoky Mountains Nat. Park, summer, 1934, ranger-naturalist, summers, 1939-41; acting editor The Bryologist, 1943- 44, asso. editor, 1938-42, 1945-53; asso. editor Castanea, 1947-66; instr. summer sch. W.Va. U., 1939-41; instr. U. Tenn., 1929-37, asst. prof., 1937-40, asso. prof., 1940-46, prof., 1946-65, Distinguished Service prof., 1965-74, prof. emeritus, 1974—, curator herbarium, 1949-68, asso. curator, 1968—, head botany dept., 1951-61; mem. staff Hattori Bot. Lab., 1956—; vis. prof. Stanford U., 1951, U. Mich. Biol. Sta., 1954-57, 59-64, U. Minn. Biol. Sta., 1971, U. Mont. Biol. Sta., 1972, Nat. U. Taiwan, 1965, Instituto Universitario Pedagógico Experimental, Maracay, Venezuela, 1976; Cecil Billington lectr. Cranbrook Inst. Sci., 1947; vis. lectr. Am. Inst. Biol. Scis., 1967-70; trustee Highlands (N.C.) Biol. Labs., 1934-38, 1948-64, bd. mgrs., 1946-52; sec. of sect. Inter-Am. Conf. on Conservation of Renewable Natural Resources, Denver, 1948; mem. nat. adv. bd. Ministry of Ecology, 1975—. Bd. dirs. Gt. Smoky Mountains Nat. Hist. Assn., 1979—. Guggenheim Found. fellow, 1944-46. Fellow AAAS (v.p. 1963); mem. New Eng. Bot. Club, Internat. Soc. Phytomorphologists, Internat. Assn. Plant Taxonomy, So. Appalachian Bot. Club (pres. 1946-47), Sullivant Moss Soc. (pres. 1935), Am. Fern Soc., Bot. Soc. Am. (editorial com. 1948-53, treas. 1957-62, v.p. 1963, pres. 1965, Merit award 1972), Soc. for Study Evolution, Soc. Botanica de Mexico, Soc. Mexicana de Historia Natural, Tenn. Acad. Sci. (exec. com. 1943-44, v.p. 1952, pres. 1953), Am. Soc. Plant Taxonomists (pres. 1961), Assn. Southeastern Biologists (v.p. 1956, Meritorious Tchr. award 1972), Ecol. Soc. Am. (v.p. 1958-59), Torrey Bot. Club, Nature Conservancy (gov. 1955-61), Am. Soc. Naturalists, AAUP, Bot. Soc. Brit. Isles, Internat. Soc. Tropical Ecology, Internat. Phycolog. Soc., Nat. Assn. Biology Tchrs., Palynolog. Soc. India, Phycolog. Soc. Am., Systematics Assn., Am. Assn. Stratigraphic Palynol., Phi Beta Kappa, Phi Kappa Phi, Sigma Xi, Phi Sigma, Phi Epsilon Phi, Sigma Delta Pi. Club: Explorers. Contbr. articles to sci. jours., Ency. Brit.; asso. editor Hattori Bot. Jour., Nichinan, Japan, 1961—. Home: 1201 Tobler Rd Knoxville TN 37919 Office: U Tenn Knoxville TN 37916. *The Universe is so constructed that for every error committed someone must pay a penalty now or in the future.*

SHARP, ALLEN, judge; b. Washington, Feb. 11, 1932; s. Robert Lee and Frances Louise (Williams) S.; student Ind. State U., 1950-53; A.B., George Washington U., 1954; J.D., Ind. U., 1957; postgrad. Butler U., 1970-73; m. Beverly J. Hawley, May 16, 1964; children—Crystal Catholyn, Scarlet Frances. Admitted to Ind. bar, 1957, practiced in Williamsport, 1957-68; judge Ct. of Appeals Ind., 1969-73; U.S. dist. judge No. Dist. Ind., Hammond, 1973—. Bd. advisers Milligan (Tenn.) Coll. Served as maj., J.A.G., USAF, 1957. Mem. Ind. Judges Assn., Blue Key, Phi Delta Kappa, Pi Gamma Mu, Tau Kappa Alpha. Republican. Mem. Christian Ch. Mason. Office: US Dist Court 204 S Main St South Bend IN 46601*

SHARP, BERT LAVON, educator; b. Philadelphia, Miss., Nov. 4, 1926; s. Bert L. and Louie (MacBeth) S.; B.S., Miss. Coll., Clinton, 1949; M.Ed., U. Fla., Gainesville, 1953, D.Ed., 1960; m. Mary Warren, Dec. 24, 1948; children—Kenneth, Richard. Tchr., guidance dir., Miss. and Fla., 1945-55; dir. ednl. research Pinellas County, Fla., 1955-56; dir. secondary curriculum and ednl. services, 1958-61; asso. prof., chmn. counselor edn. Auburn (Ala.) U., 1961-63; mem. faculty U. Fla., 1956-58, 63—, prof. edn., 1968—, dean Coll. Edn., 1968-78; cons. in field. Mem. Am. Assn. Colls. Tchr. Edn. (dir. 1973-76, exec. com. 1974-76, 78-81, pres. 1979), Assn. Colls. Schs. Edn. in State Univs. and Land-Grant Colls (pres. 1976), Am. Personnel and Guidance Assn., Am. Assn. Counselor Edn. and Supervision, Fla. Council Deans, Am. Sch. Counselor Assn., Assn. Deans Edn. Land Grant Coll. and State Univs., Fla. Council Tchrs. Edn., Am. Assn. Sch. Adminstrs., Gov. Fla. Council Tchr. Edn. Centers, Phi Kappa Phi, Phi Delta Kappa, Alpha Kappa Delta. Contbr. articles to profl. jours. Home: 2801 SW 81st St Gainesville FL 32601 Office: Coll Edn U Fla Gainesville FL 32611

SHARP, CHARLES FREDERICK, corp. exec.; b. Maywood, Ill., Apr. 3, 1914; s. Frederick and Lois (Gaines) S.; B.S., U. Fla., 1935; m. Banks Carter Wood, June 10, 1939; children—Charles Frederick, Harry Carter. Salesman, B.A. Railton Co., Chgo., 1935-38, Swift & Co., Miami, Fla., 1937-38; dist. sales mgr. Nat. Airlines, 1938-42, gen. sales mgr., 1948-52, asst. v.p. sales, 1952-53, v.p. sales Miami, 1953-62; v.p. Frozen Valley Products, Miami, 1946-48; pres. Woodlawn Park Cemetery Co., 1962—, Nat. Monument Co., Electra Constrn. Co.; dir. Flagship 1st Nat. Bank, Miami, Saturn Airways. Served from 1st lt. to maj. F.A., AUS, 1942-46. Decorated Bronze Star (U.S.); Croix de Guerre (France). Mem. Am. (pres.), So. (pres.), Fla. (pres.) cemetery assns., Miami C. of C., Beta Theta Pi. Presbyn. (trustee). Kiwanian. Clubs: Miami Sales Executives (dir.), SKAL Internat. (pres.), Traffic. Home: 1866 Tigertail Ave Miami FL 33133 Office: 3260 Tamiami Trail Miami FL 33135

SHARP, DANIEL ASHER, corp. exec.; b. San Francisco, Mar. 29, 1932; s. Joseph C. and Miriam (Asher) S.; B.A., U. Calif. at Berkeley, 1954; J.D., Harvard, 1959; m. Jacqueline Borda, Feb. 24, 1967 (div. Feb. 1975); 1 son, Benjamin Daniel. Admitted to Calif. bar, 1959; dep. atty. gen. State of Calif., San Francisco, 1959-61; with U.S. Peace Corps, 1961-68; asst. dir. div. internat. programs U.S. Peace Corps, Washington, 1961-62, asso. dir. in Cuzco, Peru, 1962-64; acting dir. Peace Corps, La Paz, Bolivia, 1964; creator, dir. Staff Tng. Center Peace Corps, Washington, 1965-68, dir. div. edn. resources, 1966; dir. edn. and Latin Am. programs, asst. dir. Adlai Stevenson Inst., U. Chgo., 1968-70, dir. tng. Internat. Tel. & Tel. Co., Latin Am., 1970-72, mgr. mgmt. devel., N.Y.C., 1973; with Xerox Corp., 1973—, dir. human resources devel. Xerox Latinam. group, 1973-75, chmn. overhead value analysis task force, 1975-76, dir. ops. support, 1976, dir. Inter-Am. affairs, 1977-79, dir. internat. affairs Xerox Corp. Hdqrs., 1979—; cons. U.S. Dept. State, fgn. govts., corps., founds. Mem. U.S. delegation to UN Econ. and Social Council, Geneva, Switzerland, 1961; U.S. rep. Internat. Conf. on Vol. Programs, The Hague, Netherlands, 1961. Trustee Chgo. Council on Fgn. Relations, 1969, Latin Am. Scholarship Program of Am. Univs., 1971-74; trustee African Student Aid Fund, vice chmn. bd., 1973-77; chmn. adv. bd. Council of Ams.; bd. dirs. Fund for Multinat. Mgmt. Edn., Accion, Partners of Ams. Served with U.S. Army, 1954-55; capt. Res. Recipient Medalla de Oro y Diploma de Honor del Consejo Provincial del Cuzco, 1963. Mem. State Bar Calif., San Francisco Bar Assn., Council on Fgn. Relations. Club: Harvard. Editor: United States Foreign Policy and Peru, 1972; los Estados Unidos y La Revolucion Peruaña, 1972. Home: 94 Campbell Dr Stamford CT 06903 Office: Xerox Corp Long Ridge Rd Stamford CT 06904

SHARP, DAVID EARL, savs. and loan assn. exec.; b. Knoxville, Tenn., Mar. 10, 1938; s. John L. and Evelyn (Petree) S.; B.S., U. Tenn., 1959; postgrad. U. Ga. Savs. and Loan Exec. Devel. Sch., 1967, U. Ind. Grad. Sch. Savs. and Loan, 1969; grad. diploma Inst. Fin. Edn., 1975; m. Virginia Heiskell, Dec. 27, 1959; children—Jeffrey David, John C., Jennifer Lynne. Mgmt. trainee Quaker Oats Co., Memphis, 1960-62; with Home Fed. Savs. and Loan Assn., Knoxville, 1962—, exec. v.p., 1973-77, pres., 1977—. Chancellor's asso. U. Tenn.; bd. dirs. Neighborhood Housing Services, Inc., Knoxville. Baptist. Clubs: Kiwanis (dir. local club), City (dir.), Beaver Brook Country (dir.), Le Conte. Home: 3924 Arline Dr Knoxville TN 37918 Office: 515 Market St Knoxville TN 37902

SHARP, ELIOT HALL, publisher; b. Madison, Wis., Aug. 14, 1903; s. Frank Chapman and Bertha (Pitman) S.; B.A., U. Wis., 1925; m. Dorothy John, Apr. 27, 1927; children—Timothy John, Michael. Reporter, Japan Advertiser, 1925-26; tchr. Yamagata High Sch., 1926; publicity dept. Union Carbide & Carbon Co., 1926-27; analyst Howe, Snow & Bertles, 1927-28, Stranahan, Harris & Co., 1928-29; advt. mgr. Founders Gen. Corp. and Distbrs. Group, Inc., 1929-36; founder, pub. emeritus Investment Dealers' Digest, N.Y.C., 1935—; co-founder Investor mag., 1950; founder, pub., editor emeritus Eliot Sharp's Daily Corporate News Letter, 1945, Eliot Sharp's Daily Tax Exempt News Letter, 1950; dir. IDD Inc. Originator, dir. Invest in Am. Week, 1953—. Served as maj. AUS, World War II. Mem. N.Y. Soc. Security Analysts, Nat. Security Traders Assn., Financial Analysts Fedn., Soc. Am. Bus. Writers, Alpha Delta Phi, Sigma Delta Chi. Clubs: National Press (Washington); Overseas Press (N.Y.C.); Hudson Highland Ice Boat (Greenwood Lake, N.J.). Contbr. articles to mags., newspapers. Home and office: 2 Montague Terr Brooklyn NY 11201. *Belief in the soundness of the private enterprise system plus conviction that salutary labor relations result from a wisely conceived employee profit sharing program produced a successful business. Widely dispersed personal interests led to stimulating cultural experiences.*

SHARP, GEORGE STEVENSON, surgeon; b. Cadiz, Ohio, Apr. 15, 1901; s. George Cunningham and Agnes (Stevenson) S.; M.D., Harvard U., 1927; m. Pauline Casebeer, Nov. 15, 1927 (div. 1952); children—George S., Paula Sharp; m. 2d, Cecilia Retinger. Intern, Montreal Gen. Hosp. 1927-28; resident in surgery N.Y. Hosp., 1928-29; Rockefeller fellow Meml. Hosp., N.Y.C., 1929-32; asso. prof. surgery U. So. Calif. Med. Sch., Los Angeles, 1945-50, prof. oral pathology Sch. Dentistry, 1950-70; founder, dir. Pasadena (Calif.) Found. for Cancer Research, 1952—; vis. prof. U. Mexico, 1940—, U. Guadalahara, 1940—; dir. Pasadena Tumor Inst.; hon. prof. surgery Sch. Medicine, Athens, Greece, 1962. Diplomate Am. Bd. Radiology. Mem. A.C.S., Ewing Soc. (pres. 1942-45), Head and Neck Surgeons (co-founder). Clubs: Valley Hunt; Overland; Flintridge Riding (pres. 1965-67). Author: Oral Cancer and Tumors of Jaws; contbr. articles to med. jours. Home: 931 Emerald Bay Laguna Beach CA 92651 Office: 99 N El Molino Ave Pasadena CA 91101

SHARP, JERE WORTH, army officer; b. Monticello, Ga., Mar. 10, 1929; s. Joseph Worth and Mary Scott (Brightwell) S.; B.S., U.S. Mil. Acad., 1950; M.S., Purdue U., 1956; m. Louise Bragdon Bucher, Aug. 17, 1950; children—Linda, David, Mary, Nancy, Joy, Joseph. Commd. 2d lt. U.S. Army, 1950, advanced through grades to maj. gen., 1978; asst. prof. mechanics U.S. Mil. Acad., 1956-60; product mgr. goer vehicles, dir. procurement, 1970-73; chief ops. div. Office Asst. Sec. Army, Washington, 1973-74; comdt. Ordnance Sch., 1974-77; dir. procurement and production Hdqrs. U.S. Army Devel. and Readiness Command, Alexandria, Va., 1977—. Decorated Bronze Star, Purple Heart, Legion of Merit. Mem. Assn. U.S. Army, Am. Def. Preparedness Assn., Tau Beta Pi. Episcopalian. Home: 22B Lee Ave Fort Myer VA 22211 Office: 5001 Eisenhower Ave Alexandria VA 22333. *Success in organizations, and therefore for individuals, is the result of collective efforts toward a common goal. The most important thing a manager can do is to create an atmosphere in which things can happen and where people can work to their maximum capacity.*

SHARP, MITCHELL WILLIAM, Canadian govt. ofcl.; b. Winnipeg, Man., Can., May 11, 1911; s. Thomas and Elizabeth (Little) S.; B.A., U. Man., 1934, LL.D., 1965; postgrad. London Sch. Econs., 1937-38; hon. Dr. Social Sci., U. Ottawa, 1970; LL.D. (hon.), U. Western Ont., 1977; m. Daisy Boyd, Apr. 23, 1938 (dec.); 1 son, Noel; m. 2d, Jeanette Dugal, Apr. 14, 1976. Statistician, Sanford Evans Statis. Service, 1926-36; economist James Richardson & Sons, Ltd., 1936-42; officer Canadian Dept. Fin., Ottawa, 1942-51, dir. econ. policy div., 1947-51; asso. dep. minister Canadian Dept. Trade and Commerce, 1951-57, dep. minister, 1957-58, minister, 1963-65; v.p. Brazillian Traction, Toronto, Can., 1958-62; minister fin. Can., 1965-68; sec. state external affairs, 1968-74, pres. Privy Council, house leader, 1974-76, resigned, 1978; commr. No. Pipeline Agy., 1978— Address PO Box 1605 Sta B Ottawa ON KIP 5A0 Canada

SHARP, MORELL EDWARD, judge; b. Portland, Oreg., Sept. 12, 1920; s. Eugene Edward and Hazel E. (Eaton) S.; student U. Oreg., 1939-41; LL.B., J.D., Northwestern U., 1948; m. Betty Marie Parker, Apr. 3, 1948; children—Laurie, John. Admitted to Ill. bar, 1948, Wash. bar, 1951; asst. gen. atty. Milw. R.R., Chgo., Seattle, 1948-52; partner Williams, Kinnear & Sharp, Seattle, 1952-56; mem. firm Graham, Dunn, Johnston & Rosenquist, Seattle, 1957-67; judge Superior Ct., King County, Wash., 1967-70; justice Wash. Supreme Ct., 1970-71; judge U.S. Dist. Ct. Western Dist. Wash., Seattle, 1971—. Dir. Nat. Center for State Cts., 1970-71; Mayor, councilman Beaux Arts Village, Wash., 1952-56; councilman Municipality Met. Seattle, 1956-57. Served to capt. AUS, 1943-46. Fellow Am. Bar Assn.; mem. Wash., Ill. bar assns., Jud. Conf. U.S. Episcopalian. Clubs: Wash. Athletic (Seattle), Harbor, Overlake (Medina, Wash.). Bd. editors Am. Bar Assn. Jour., 1974—. Home: 9021 NE 10th Bellevue WA 98004 Office: 410 US Courthouse Seattle WA 98104

SHARP, MORRIS LOUIS, psychiatrist; b. St. Louis, Aug. 2, 1908; s. Henry and Rebecca (Boxerman) S.; M.D., Tufts U., 1932; m. Ida Reiser, Aug. 12, 1945; 1 dau., Harriet R. Rotating intern St. Mary's Hosp., East St. Louis, Ill, 1932-33; resident contagious diseases Belleville (N.J.) Hosp., 1933; mem. staff Foxboro (Mass.) State Hosp., 1934-52, asst. supt., dir. psychiatry, 1946-52; asst. to commr. Mass. Dept. Mental Health, 1952-53; supt. Westboro (Mass.) State Hosp., 1953-72, also hosp. area program dir.; pvt. practice psychiatry East Falmouth, Mass., 1972—. Served to maj. M.C., AUS, 1942-46; MTO. Recipient Cutting Gold award for medicine and religion, 1972. Diplomate Am. Bd. Psychiatry and Neurology. Life fellow Am. Psychiat. Assn.; mem. New Eng. Soc. Psychiatry (life), A.M.A., Mass., Barnstable County, med. socs. Contbr. articles to profl. jours. Address: 106 Striper Ln East Falmouth MA 02536

SHARP, PAUL FREDERICK, univ. adminstr.; b. Kirksville, Mo., Jan. 19, 1918; s. Frederick J. and L. Blanche (Phares) S.; A.B., Phillips U., 1939; Ph.D., U. Minn., 1947; LL.D., Tex. Christian U., 1961, Austin Coll.; L.H.D., Buena Vista Coll., 1967, U. Nev.; Litt.D., Limestone Coll.; m. Rosella Ann Anderson, June 19, 1939; children—William, Kathryn, Paul Trevor. Instr., U. Minn., 1942, 46-47, vis. lectr., 1948; asso. prof. Am. history Iowa State U., 1947-54; prof. Am. history, chmn. Am. Instns. program U. Wis., 1954-57, vis. lectr., 1953; vis. lectr. San Francisco State Coll., 1950, U. Oreg., 1955; Fulbright lectr. Am. Instns., univs. Melbourne, Sydney, 1952; pres. Hiram Coll., 1957-64; chancellor U. N.C., Chapel Hill, 1964-66; pres. Drake U., Des Moines, 1966-71; pres. U. Okla., 1971-78, pres. emeritus and Regents prof., 1978—; dir. Equitable of Iowa, Sterndent Corp., vis. lectr. Harvard Bus. Sch., 1970-72. Bd. dirs., priorities com., commn. on instnl. affairs Assn. Am. Colls., Washington. Served from ensign to lt. USNR, 1943-46. Minn. Hist. Soc. grantee, 1947, 48; Social Sci. Research Council grantee, 1949, 51; Ford Faculty fellow, 1954; Guggenheim fellow, 1957; recipient Iowa State U. Alumni Fund award, 1952; award of merit Am. Assn. State and Local History, 1955; Silver Spur award Western Writers Am., 1955; Fulbright award to Australia, 1952; Outstanding Achievement award U. Minn., 1975, Phillips U., U. Okla. Mem. Phi Beta Kappa, Phi Kappa Phi, Phi Delta Kappa, Pi Gamma Mu, Phi Alpha Theta. Mem. Disciples of Christ Ch. Author: Agrarian Revolt in Western Canada, 1948; Old Orchard Farm, Story of an Iowa Boyhood, 1952; Whoop-Up Country, Canadian American West, 1955; cons. author: Heritage of Midwest, 1958. Editor: Documents of Freedom, 1957. Contbr. articles to profl. jours. Home: 701 Mockingbird Ln Norman OK 73071

SHARP, PHILIP R., congressman; b. Balt., July 15, 1942; s. Riley and Florence Sharp; B.S. cum laude, Sch. Fgn. Service, Georgetown U., 1964; Ph.D. in Govt., 1974; postgrad. Exeter Coll., Oxford (Eng.) U., summer 1966; m. Marilyn Kay Augburn, 1972; 1 son, Jeremy Beck. Legis. aide to Senator Vance Hartke of Ind., 1964-69; asst. to asso. prof. polit. sci. Ball State U., Muncie, Ind., 1969-74; mem. 94th-96th Congresses from 10th Ind. Dist., mem. Com. Interstate and Fgn. Commerce, Com. Interior and Insular Affairs. Democrat. Methodist. Office: 1421 Longworth House Office Bldg Washington DC 20515

SHARP, ROBERT PHILLIP, geologist, educator; b. Oxnard, Calif., June 24, 1911; s. Julian Heber and Alice (Darling) S.; B.S., Calif. Inst. Tech., 1934, M.S., 1935; M.A., Harvard U., 1936, Ph.D., 1938; m. Jean Prescott Todd, Sept. 7, 1938; adopted children—Kristin S. Lytle, Bruce Todd. Faculty, U. Ill., 1938-42, U. Minn., 1945-47; faculty Calif. Inst. Tech., Pasadena, 1947—, chmn. div. geol. scis., 1952-67, prof. emeritus geology, 1979—. Served as capt. USAAF, 1942-45. Recipient Exceptional Sci. Achievement medal NASA; Eagle Scout award Boy Scouts Am., 1978. Fellow Geol. Soc. Am. (Kirk Bryan award, Penrose medal 1977), Am. Geophys. Union, Am. Acad. Arts and Scis.; mem. Glaciological Soc. (hon.), Nat. Acad. Sci. Contbr. articles to profl. jours. Home: 1901 Gibraltar Rd Santa Barbara CA 93105 Office: Calif Inst Tech Pasadena CA 91125

SHARP, ROBERT WEIMER, lawyer; b. Cleve., Feb. 12, 1917; s. Isaac Walter and Ruth (Weimer) S.; A.B., Oberlin Coll., 1939; LL.B., Harvard U., 1942; m. Norine Wines, Nov. 13, 1948; children—Kathleen L. (Mrs. Larry J. Samuel), Pamela J. (Mrs. David N. Adamson), Janet E., Andrea L., Gail N. Admitted to Ohio bar, 1944, since practiced in Cleve; partner firm Gallagher, Sharp, Fulton, Norman & Mollison and predecessors, 1958—; dir. Bulkley Bldg. Co., 1964-70, pres., 1966-70; dir. Nat. Terminals Corp., Hillside Dairy Co. Trustee St. Luke's Hosp. Assn., Christian Residence Found.; sec. Ohio East Area United Meth. Found., 1967-74, pres., 1974—; adv. trustee Ohio div. Am. Cancer Soc. Served with USNR, 1942-46. Mem. Am., Ohio, Cleve. bar assns. Republican. Methodist. Home: 3090 Fairmount Blvd Cleveland OH 44118 Office: Bulkley Bldg Cleveland OH 44115

SHARP, SUSIE MARSHALL, ret. state chief justice; b. Rocky Mount, N.C., July 7, 1907; d. James Merritt and Annie (Blackwell) Sharp; LL.B., U. N.C., 1929, LL.D. (hon.), 1970; LL.D., Woman's Coll. U. N.C., 1950, Queen's Coll., 1962, Elon Coll., 1963, Wake Forest U., 1965, Catawba Coll., 1970, Duke, 1974, U. N.C. at Wilmington, 1977; L.H.D., Pfeiffer Coll., 1960. Admitted to N.C. bar, 1928; gen. practice firm Sharp & Sharp, Reidsville, N.C., 1929-49; city atty. Reidsville, 1939-49; spl. judge Superior Ct. of N.C., 1949-62; asso. justice Supreme Ct. N.C., 1962-75, chief justice, 1975-79. Mem. Am. Law Inst., Order of Coif, Phi Beta Kappa, Order Valkyries, Delta Kappa Gamma. Democrat. Methodist. Clubs: Altrusa, Soroptimist. Home: 629 Lindsey St Reidsville NC 27320 also 521 Wade Ave Apt 26 Raleigh NC 27605

SHARP, ULYSSES S. GRANT, ret. naval officer; b. Mont., Apr. 2, 1906; s. Ulysses S. Grant and Cora (Krauss) S.; B.S., U.S. Naval Acad., 1927; grad. U.S. Naval Postgrad. Sch., 1936, Naval War Coll., 1950; D.Sc. (hon.), Mont. State U., 1971; m. Patricia O'Connor, Aug. 2, 1930; children—Patricia Sharp Milham, Grant Alexander. Commd. ensign USN, 1927, advanced through grades to adm., 1963; comdr. destroyers U.S.S. Hogan, 1942-43, U.S.S. Boyd, 1943-44; staff of comdr. Cruiser-Destroyer Force, Pacific Fleet, 1945-48; comdr. Sonar Sch., San Diego, 1948-50, Destroyer Squadron 3, 1950; staff of comdr. 2d Fleet, 1951, chief staff to comdr., 1952-53; comdr. cruiser U.S.S. Macon, 1953-54; dep. chief staff to comdr. in chief U.S. Pacific Fleet, 1954-55; comdr. Cruiser Div. 3, 1956-57; dir. strategic plans div. Navy Dept., 1957-59; comdr. Cruiser-Destroyer Force, U.S. Pacific Fleet, 1959-60, First Fleet, 1960; dep. chief naval ops. for plans and policy Navy Dept., 1960-63; comdr. in chief U.S. Pacific Fleet, 1963-64, Pacific, 1964-68; U.S. mil. adviser SEATO, 1964-68; ret., 1968. Bd. overseers U. Calif. at San Diego. Decorated Silver Star (2), Bronze Star (2), D.S.M. (2 Navy, 1 Army); Order of White Elephant (Thailand); Order of Rising Sun (Japan); Order of Cloud and Banner (China); other fgn. decorations. Mem. U.S. Naval Inst., U.S. Naval Acad. Alumni Assn., Naval History Found., Navy League, U.S. Naval Commandery. Author: Strategic Direction of the Armed Forces, 1977; Strategy for Defeat: Vietnam in Retrospect, 1978. Clubs: Rotary (hon.) (San Diego); LaJolla (Calif.) Country. Home: 876 San Antonio Pl San Diego CA 92106

SHARP, WARREN DONALD, ins. holding co. exec.; b. Jackson, Mich., Nov. 4, 1939; s. Warren Donald and Maxine M. Sharp; B.B.A., U. Mich., 1962, M.B.A., 1963; m. Patricia Sharp, Dec. 4, 1971; children—Michael Kevin, Connie Janine. Sr. investment analyst Conn. Gen. Life Ins. Co., Hartford, Conn., 1963-70, asst. sec., 1970-73, sec., 1973-76; treas. Conn. Gen. Ins. Corp. and subsidiaries, Hartford, 1976—; dir. CG Equity Ventures, CG Trust Co., Congen Properties, Inc., Realconn, Inc., Aetna Ins. Co. of M.W. Trustee, mem. exec. com. Noah Webster Found., West Hartford, Conn., Hist. Soc. of West Hartford. Served with USMC, 1957-58. Mem. Hartford Soc. Fin. Analysts, Fin. Analysts Fedn. Republican. Congregationlist. Home: 254 Griswold Dr West Hartford CT 06119 Office: Conn Gen Ins Corp Hartford CT 06152

SHARP, WILLIAM, soft drink co. exec.; b. Chgo., Aug. 1, 1929; s. William Sharp and Essie Mae (Kendall) S.; student Wilson Jr. Coll., 1948-50, Roosevelt U., 1950-52; m. Doris Ellen Wooten, May 16, 1952; children—William Gregory, Dianne, Michael. Owner, mgr. Card Gifters and Sharp Advt. Agy., Chgo., 1957-65; copywriter Tatham-Laird and Kudner Advt. Agy., 1965-67; copy supr. Leo Burnett Advt. Agy., 1967-68; group creative supr. J. Walter Thompson Advt., 1968-69; dir. communications OEO, Washington, 1969-72; v.p., advt. mgr. Coca Cola USA, Atlanta, 1972—. Served with U.S. Army, 1952. Mem. Assn. Nat. Advertisers (bd. dirs.), Am. Advt. Fedn. (past chmn., bd. dirs., mem. govt. relations com.). Home: 2940 Arrowood Dr East Point GA 30344 Office: 310 North Ave Atlanta GA 30301

SHARP, WILLIAM HARRY, univ. adminstr.; b. Moorestown, N.J., Apr. 20, 1930; s. Alvin L. and Anna L. (Stiles) S.; B.A., Denison U., 1952; M.A., Ohio U., 1954; Ph.D., Ohio State U., 1959; m. Margaret Brown Wiltshire, Aug. 16, 1952; children—William Timothy, Margaret Joyce, Brian Wiltshire, Julie Anna. Dir. counseling and testing U. Wyo., Laramie, 1965-70, mem. faculty dept. psychology, 1959-73, asst. prof., 1959-61, asso. prof., 1961-68, prof. 1968-73, dean of students, 1970-73; vice chancellor, dean of students U. Houston, 1973—; cons. Wyo. Div. Vocat. Rehab., 1965-68, S.E. Wyo. Mental Health Center, Cheyenne, 1967-69, St. Joseph's Home for Children, Torrington, Wyo., 1969-70; vocat. cons. Bur. Hearings and Appeals, Social Security Adminstr., HEW, 1965-73; mem. legis. subcom. Gov.'s Commn. on Mental Health Planning, 1965-66. Certified psychologist, Tex. Mem. Am. Psychol. Assn., Am. Coll. Personnel Assn., So. Coll. Personnel Assn., Tex. Assn. Coll. and Univ. Student Personnel Adminstrs., Omicron Delta Kappa, Psi Chi, Lambda Chi Alpha. Presbyterian. Home: 13018 Taylorcrest St Houston TX 77079 Office: Dean of Students U Houston Houston TX 77004

SHARP, WILLOUGHBY, artist; b. N.Y.C., Jan. 23, 1936; s. William Willoughby and Murielle (MacMahon) S.; B.A., Brown U., 1961; M.A., Columbia U., 1970; postgrad. U. Paris, 1957-58, U. Lausanne, 1958-59. Founder, pres. Kineticism Press, N.Y.C., 1968—; co-founder, pub. Avalanche mag., N.Y.C.; v.p. Center for New Art Activities, N.Y.C., 1970—; founder, exec. dir. Franklin St. Arts Center, N.Y.C., 1973—; founder, dir. Worldpool, N.Y.C., 1976—, Toronto, 1978—; pres. Sharpcom, N.Y.C., 1979—; telecommunications cons. Grantee Rockefeller Found., 1971, Nat. Endowment Arts, 1972, 76-80, N.Y. State Council Arts, 1973-80.

SHARPE, DAVID IRVIN, banker; b. Windber, Pa., June 27, 1928; s. Thomas Penman and Audrey Sharpe; student Columbus Coll., Washington, 1948-49; grad. Stonier Grad. Sch. Banking, 1966; m. Eleanor Jean Rudinac, Dec. 27, 1952; children—Peter, Timothy, Kevin. With U.S. Nat. Bank, Johnstown, Pa., 1952-63, Bank of Hanover (Pa.), 1963-69; with York Bank & Trust Co. (Pa.), 1969—, sr. v.p., sr. trust officer, 1977—. Treas. York Found., 1976-79; v.p. York Symphony Assn., 1978—. Served with U.S. Army, 1950-52. Republican. Methodist. Club: Lafayette (York). Address: York Bank & Trust Co Market and Beaver Sts York PA 17401

SHARPE, DORES ROBINSON, ch. ofcl.; b. Pembroke, N.B., Can., Jan. 23, 1886; s. Charles Frederick and Frances (Robinson) S; A.B., U. N.B., 1908, A.M., 1910, LL.D., 1943; B.D. (scholar, fellow), Rochester Theol. Sem., 1911; postgrad. U. Chgo., 1911-12; D.D., Hillsdale (Mich.) Coll., 1930; LL.D., Ark. Bapt. Coll., 1931; L.H.D., Wilberforce U., 1951; m. Harriet Maude Holdsworth, Sept. 8, 1914 (dec. 1917); children—Margaret Louise, Roger Holdsworth and Harriett Frances (twins); m. 2d, Ruth Leila Mitchell, Feb. 25, 1920 (dec. 1972). Ordained to Bapt. ministry, 1908; pastor in Edmonton and Calgary, Alta., also Moose Jaw, Sask., gen. sec. Sunday Sch. Assn. Sask. 1917-19; dir. Forward Movement for Protestant chs. in Sask., 1919; gen. supt. Bapt. chs. in Sask., 1917-25; exec. sec. Cleve. Bapt. Assn., 1925-53, exec. sec. emeritus, 1953—. Rauschenbusch lectr. Colgate-Rochester Sem., 1946; cons. Grad. Theol. Union, Berkeley, Calif. Former mem. Council of Finance and Promotion and Council of World Evangelization, No. Bapt. Conv.; past chmn. Com. on City Missions, Com. on Ch. and City of Ch. Fedn., Com. on Pub. Edn. and Service; mem. speakers bur. Community Chest; founder, dir. Cleve. Sunday Evening Hour; founder ann. Theol. Conf. Roger Williams Fellowship and Div. Sch. U. Chgo., also Dores Robinson Sharpe lectureship. Past mem. Calif. Democratic State Central Com.; Dem. candidate Assembly, 47th dist., Calif.; mem. exec. com. Los Angeles County Dem. Central Com.; foreman Grand Jury Cuyahoga, Cleve., which uncovered corruption in mental hosps. (recipient Albert Lasker award). Former dir. Bapt. Home No. Ohio., Northwestern Bapt. Hosp. Assns.; trustee Grad. Theol. Union; trustee emeritus Colgate-Rochester Div. Sch.; past trustee Rio Grande Coll.; past vice chmn. Cleve. Community Relations Commn.; hon. pres. Consumers League of Ohio; founder, past pres. Ohio Mental Hygiene Assn.; exec. com. Community Relations Bd., N.A.A.C.P.; former chmn. State Hosps. Betterment Com; founder, pres. Ch. Civic League; chmn. Interaward, Nat. Com. Mental Hygiene, 1946; v.p. Rauschenbusch Fellowship; past chmn. com. Internat. Justice and Peace, Pasadena Council Chs. Mem. Pi Gamma Mu. Mason. Club: Professional, Alpine (Can.). Author: (book) Rise and Place of American City, 1959, Call to Christian Action: The Triumph of Religious Liberty, Of One Blood, The Golden Fountain; also other pageants, Biography of Walter Rauschenbush. Lectr., writer, dir. instnl. finance, organizer. Home: 3725 Hampton Rd Pasadena CA 91107

SHARPE, HENRY DEXTER, JR., mfg. co. exec.; b. Providence, May 5, 1923; s. Henry Dexter and Mary Elizabeth (Evans) S.; grad. Brown U., Providence, 1945; m. Peggy Plumer Boyd, Aug. 1, 1953; children—Henry Dexter, Douglas, Sarah. With Brown & Sharpe Mfg. Co., Providence, 1946—, v.p., 1950-51, pres., 1951-76, chmn., chief exec. officer, 1976—; dir. Providence Jour. Co. Pres. R.I. Pub. Expenditure Council; trustee Brown U. Served from ensign to lt. (j.g.) USNR, 1943-46. Mem. Am. Soc. Tool Engrs., Council for Technol. Advancement, Nat. Machine Tool Builders Assn., ASME, Machinery and Allied Products Inst. Office: PO Box 456 North Kingstown RI 02852

SHARPE, JAMES RALPH, engring. constrn. co. exec.; b. Columbus, Ohio, Apr. 15, 1929; s. Leslie Purkis and Marion Francis (Hall) S.; B.S.C.E., Ohio State U., 1951; m. Sally Truit Knorr, Apr. 8, 1961; 1 son, James Douglas. Constrn. engr. Panhandle Eastern Pipeline Co., Kansas City, Mo., 1954-56, project engr., 1956-57; with Dravo Corp., Pitts., 1957—, v.p., gen. mgr. engring. constrn. div., 1970-74, group v.p., 1974-76, sr. v.p., 1976—; pres. Dravo Engrs. and Constructors, Pitts., 1980—. Served to lt. (j.g.) USN, 1951-54. Mem. Am. Iron and Steel Inst., Am. Mining Congress. Clubs: Duquesne, Laurel Valley Golf (Pitts.); Garden of the Gods (Colorado Springs, Colo.). Home: 817 White Oak Circle Pittsburgh PA 15228 Office: Dravo Engrs and Constructors One Oliver Plaza Pittsburgh PA 15222

SHARPE, JOHN CHARLES, physician; b. Long Beach, Calif., Feb. 1, 1907; s. James Wright and Jeanette (Greusel) S.; B.Sc., M.D., U. Nebr., 1932, m. Jane Francis Mullin, Jan. 19, 1952; children—Mary Hilary, Carla Catherine; children by previous marriage—Timothy, Mary Ellen (Mrs. Roland Peck), Sidney. Intern, Johns Hopkins Hosp., 1933-34, asst. resident medicine, 1934-35; practice medicine, Omaha, 1935-39, Sun Valley, Idaho, 1939-41, Los Angeles, 1942-73, Beverly Hills, Calif., 1970-72; instr. medicine U. Nebr., 1935-39; faculty U. Calif. at Los Angeles Med. Sch., 1950-73, clin. prof. medicine, 1955-73; chief staff St. Johns Hosp., Santa Monica, Calif., 1948-49, chief div. medicine, 1963-66, chief electrocardiography, 1972-78. Named papal knight Sovereign Mil. Order Malta, 1964. Diplomate Am. Bd. Internal Medicine. Fellow Am. Coll. Cardiology, A.C.P.; mem. Los Angeles Acad. Medicine, Los Angeles County Med. Assn. Contbr. articles to profl. jours. Editor: Management of Medical Emergencies, 2d edit., 1969. Home: Ocean Towers 201 Ocean Ave Santa Monica CA 90402

SHARPE, KEITH YOUNT, transp. co. exec.; b. Hiddenite, N.C., July 11, 1930; s. Ruel Yount and Eileen Lois (Lackey) S.; A.B., Duke U., 1952; J.D., Wake Forest Law Sch., 1957; m. Margaret Joyce Land, Aug. 27, 1955; children—Jonathan, Matthew, Leonora, Felicia. Admitted to N.C. bar, 1957; practiced law, Winston-Salem, N.C., 1957-62; asst. solicitor Mcpl. Ct. of Winston-Salem, 1958-60; with Pilot Freight Carriers Inc., Winston-Salem, 1962—, sr. v.p., 1967-76, exec. v.p., 1976—, also dir.; v.p., dir. Comml. Automotive Co., 1967-76, Tenn. Warehouse Corp., 1967—; bd. govs. So. Motor Carriers State Conf., 1977—. Served as cpl., inf. U.S. Army, 1952-54. Mem. N.C. Bar Assn., Am. Bar Assn., Assn. ICC Practitioners, Phi Alpha Delta, Theta Chi. Democrat. Episcopalian. Club: Torch. Home: 844 Glen Echo Trail Winston-Salem NC 27106 Office: Pilot Freight Carriers N Cherry St and Polo Rd Winston-Salem NC 27105

SHARPE, MYRON EMANUEL, publisher, editor, writer; b. Chester, Pa., Sept. 10, 1928; s. Abraham Maxwell and Emma (Friedman) S.; B.A., Swarthmore Coll., 1950; M.A., U. Mich., 1951, postgrad., 1951-54; m. Jacqueline Steiner, Dec. 20, 1959; children—Susanna, Matthew. Pres., Modern Factors Corp., Phila., 1957; founder, chmn. bd., pres. M.E. Sharpe, Inc., Pub., White Plains, N.Y., 1958—, writer, editor, 1955—; econ. cons., 1956—. Founder, exec. dir. Com. to Save the Life of Henry Spetter, 1974; co-founder, coordinator Initiative Com. for Nat. Econ. Planning, 1974-76. Mem. Am. Econ. Assn., Nat. Assn. Bus. Economists, Am. Assn. for Advancement Slavic Studies, Assn. for Asian Studies. Author: John Kenneth Galbraith and the Lower Economics, 1973. Editor: The Liberman Discussion: A New Phase in Soviet Economic Thought, 1966; Reform of Soviet Economic Management, 1966; co-editor, The Challenge of Economics, 1977; editor jours. Problems of Economics, 1958-60, The Soviet Rev., 1960-67; editor, pub. Challenge: The Mag. of Economic Affairs, 1973—; co-founder, pub. Social Policy, 1970-72. Home: 121 Ferris Hill Rd New Canaan CT 06840 Office: 901 N Broadway White Plains NY 10603

SHARPE, ROBERT FRANCIS, equipment mfg. co. exec.; b. Buffalo, Mar. 29, 1921; s. Bertram Francis and Agnes (Coppinger) S.; B.S. in Chem. Engring., Rensselaer Poly. Inst., 1942; m. Audrey Rembe, July 10, 1943; 1 son, Robert Francis. With Duriron Co., 1946—, mgr. pump sales, Dayton, 1955-58, dir. research, devel., 1958-63, v.p. plastics ops., 1963-65, exec. v.p., 1967-68, pres., chief operating officer, 1968-69, pres., 1969-76, chief exec. officer, 1969-79, chmn. bd., 1976—, also dir.; dir. Winters Bank, Price Bros. Co., Reynolds & Reynolds Co. (all Dayton). Served with USAAF, 1943-46. Mem. Am. Inst. Chem. Engrs., Hydraulic Inst. Club: Rotary. Home: 25 Turret Snell Ln Hilton Head SC 29938 Office: 425 N Findlay St Dayton OH 45404

SHARPE, RUEL YOUNT, trucking co. exec.; b. Alexander County, N.C., Mar. 28, 1905; s. Addison Clay and Ada Francis (Mitchell) S.; grad. Piedmont Aviation Sch., 1938; m. Eileen Lackey, Sept. 10, 1928; children—Shirley Sharpe Duncan, Keith Y., Lynn Sharpe Hill. Founder, pres. Pilot Freight Carriers, Inc., Winston-Salem, N.C., 1941-76, chmn. bd., 1976—, also dir.; pres., treas. Comml. Automotive Corp., 1950-76; pres., treas., dir. Terminal Warehouse Corp., Winston-Salem, 1950—; pres. Irregular Route Common Carrier Conf., 1952; trustee Am. Trucking Assn. Found. Mem. Sm. Trucking Assn. (state v.p. 1953, 55-76, v.p.-at-large 1979), N.C. Motor Carriers Assn. (dir. 1949—, pres. 1962), Winston-Salem Traffic

Club. Democrat. Methodist. Club: Forsyth Country. Home: 981 Arbor Rd Winston-Salem NC 27104 Office: 4103 N Cherry St Winston-Salem NC 27102

SHARPE, WILLIAM FORSYTH, fin. economist; b. Cambridge, Mass., June 16, 1934; s. Russell Thornley and Evelyn Forsyth (Jillson) S.; A.B., UCLA, 1955, M.A., 1956, Ph.D., 1961; m. Roberta Ruth Branton, July 2, 1954; children—Deborah Ann, Jonathan Forsyth. Economist, RAND Corp., 1957-61; asst. prof. econs. U. Wash., 1961-63, asso. prof., 1963-67, prof., 1967-68; prof. U. Calif., Irvine, 1968-70; Timken prof. fin. Stanford U., 1970—; trustee Coll. Retirement Equities Fund. Served with U.S. Army, 1956-57. Recipient Graham and Dodd award Fin. Analysts' Fedn., 1972, 73. Mem. Am. Fin. Assn. (v.p. 1979, pres. 1980), Western Fin. Assn., Am. Econ. Assn., Phi Beta Kappa. Author: The Economics of Computers, 1969; Portfolio Theory and Capital Markets, 1970; Investments, 1978. Office: Grad Sch Bus Stanford U Stanford CA 94305

SHARPE, WILLIAM NORMAN, JR., engr.; b. Chatham County, N.C., Apr. 15, 1938; s. William Norman and Margaret Horne (Womble) S.; B.S., N.C. State U., 1960, M.S., 1961; Ph.D., Johns Hopkins U., 1966; m. Margaret Ellen Strowd, Aug. 21, 1959; children—William N., J. Ashley. Instr. mech. engring. dept. Johns Hopkins U., Balt., 1965-66; asst. prof. to prof. Mich. State U., East Lansing, 1966-78; prof., chmn. mech. engring. dept. La. State U., Baton Rouge, 1978—. Mem. Am. Soc. Engring. Edn., Soc. Exptl. Stress Analysis, Mich. Soc. Profl. Engrs., ASME, Am. Acad. Mechanics, ASTM, Sigma Xi. Methodist. Contbr. articles to profl. jours. Office: Mech Engring Dept La State Univ Baton Rouge LA 70803

SHARPLES, WYNNE, physician; b. Merion, Pa., Oct. 15, 1923; d. Philip T. and Edith (Walz) Sharples; B.S., Radcliffe Coll., 1944; M.D., Columbia U., 1951; m. George de Mohrenschildt, Apr. 7, 1951 (div. May 1956); children—Sergei (dec.), Nadejda (dec.); m. 2d, Robert Denton, May 18, 1956 (div. July 1967); children—Ashley, Stuart, David; m. 3d, Robert I. Ballinger, Jr., Oct. 1967. Founder, Mucoviscidosis Found., 1954; founder Nat. Cystic Fibrosis Research Found., 1955, pres., 1955-60; founder, pres. Cystic Fibrosis Research Inst. Pa., 1960-67; staff physician Temple U. Hosp., 1967-70, asst. dir. emergency dept., 1969-70; staff Sacred Heart Hosp., Norristown, Pa., 1971. Mem. Pa. Adv. Health Bd., 1963-71. Hon. life trustee Temple U. Mem. Coll. Physicians Phila., AMA, Phila. County Med. Soc., Nat. Soc. Colonial Dames, Colonial Dames Am. Republican. Home: 1200 S Ocean Blvd Palm Beach FL 33480

SHARPLESS, RICHARD KENNEDY, lawyer; b. Springdale, Pa., Mar. 30, 1911; s. Charles Thomas and Luella Lincoln (Kennedy) S.; A.B., Boston U., 1932; LL.B., Harvard, 1935; m. Eleanor Ridgeway Crowther, Mar. 4, 1946; m. 2d, Nancy Jean Sleight, July 23, 1948; children—Kendall Deborah, Richard Kennedy, Lincoln Kennedy. Admitted to Pa. bar, 1936, Cal. bar, 1947, Hawaii bar, 1949; with firm Dalzell, McFall & Pringle, Pitts., 1936-42; mem. legal sect. trust dept. Bank of Am., Los Angeles, 1946-48; atty. Office Dist. Engr., Honolulu, 1948-49; with Office Atty. Gen., T.H., 1949-55, atty. gen., 1956-57; mem. Lewis, Saunders & Sharpless, and predecessor firm, 1957-68; mng. dir. City and County of Honolulu, 1968-72, 75-78, corp. counsel, 1973-75, 78—. Mem. Planning Commn. City and County of Honolulu, 1966-68, chmn., 1968. Served to capt. C.E., AUS, 1942-46. Mem. Bar Assn. Hawaii (pres. 1960-61), State Bar Cal., Harvard Law Sch. Assn., S.A.R. (pres. Hawaii 1961). Episcopalian (lay reader). Clubs: Outrigger Canoe, Uluniu Swimming. Home: 2003 Kalia Rd Apt 12-F Honolulu HI 96815 Office: City Hall Honolulu HI 96802

SHARPLEY, JOHN MILES, chem. co. exec.; b. Norfolk, Va., Jan. 28, 1918; s. John Edward and Annie Carter (Miles) S.; B.A., Hampden-Sydney Coll., 1941; M.S., U. Richmond, 1950; postgrad. USAF Command, Staff and War Coll., 1950-51; Ph.D., U. London, 1951; m. Mary Elwang Shannon, 1976. Asst. dir. Froehling & Robertson, Inc., Richmond, Va., 1945-49; chief microbiologist Buckman Labs., Inc., Memphis, 1952-62; pres. Sharpley Labs., Inc., Fredericksburg, Va., 1962—; prof. Va. Commonwealth U., Richmond, 1967-77. Past pres. Gallery Modern Art, Fredericksburg. Served to lt. col. USAAF, 1941-45. Decorated Silver Star, Purple Heart; named Distinguished Vis. Scientist, Am. Inst. Biol. Scis., 1970. Fellow AAAS, Am. Inst. Chemists; mem. Soc. Indsl. Microbiology, Am. Chem. Soc., Am. Soc. Microbiology, Soc. Gen. Microbiology (Gt. Britain). Author: Applied Petroleum Microbiology, 1962; Elementary Hydrocarbon Microbiology, 1967; International Biodegradation Symposium, 1976. Contbr. articles to profl. jours. Home: 2401 Plank Rd Fredericksburg VA 22401 Office: Sharpley Labs Inc Box 846 Fredericksburg VA 22401

SHARRAH, MARION LESTER, oil co. exec.; b. Hamilton, Mo., Oct. 23, 1922; s. Thomas Lester and Eunice Catherine (Bear) S.; B.A. in Chemistry, U. Colo., 1943, M.A., 1946, Ph.D. in Organic Chemistry, 1948; m. Mary Emma Norris, Aug. 16, 1957; children—John T., Karl L., Cynthia K. With Continental Oil Co., 1948—, mgr., then gen. mgr. research and engring., 1958-66, v.p., gen. mgr. research and engring., 1966-74, sr. v.p. research and engring., Stamford, Conn., 1974—; sr. dir. Conoco Coal Devel. Co., Conoco Methanation Co. Bd. dirs. Indsl. Research Inst. Served to lt. (j.g.) USNR, 1944-46. Mem. Am. Chem. Soc., Phi Beta Kappa, Sigma Xi, Phi Delta Chi. Methodist. Clubs: Darien (Conn.) Country. Home: 229 Lost District Dr New Canaan CT 06840 Office: Continental Oil Co High Rd Rd Stamford CT 06904

SHARRATT, RICHARD FITZGERALD, aluminum co. exec.; b. Mexico City, July 13, 1925; s. Cyprian Handel and Phyllis (Waterland) S.; B.Commerce, McGill U., 1948; certificate Centre d'Etudes Industrielles, Geneva, 1955; grad. Advanced Mgmt. Program, Harvard U., 1964. Sec., Alcan Aluminum Co. S. Africa, 1957-60; treas. Indian Aluminum Co. Ltd., 1960-64; chief fin. officer Alcan Aluminum Corp., 1965-75; v.p., chief fin. officer Aluminum Co. Can. Ltd., 1975—, also dir. Served with Canadian Navy, 1943-45. Chartered accountant, Que. Home: 1550 Dr Penfield Ave #1901 Montreal PQ H3G 1C6 Canada Office: Place Ville Marie Montreal PQ Canada

SHARROW, LEONARD, musician, educator; b. N.Y.C., Aug. 4, 1915; s. Saul and Sonia (Berson) S.; student Juilliard Sch. Music, 1932-35; m. Emily M. Kass, Oct. 22, 1942; 1 son, Neil Jason. Prin. bassoonist Nat. Symphony Orch., Washington, 1935-37; bassoonist NBC Symphony, N.Y.C., 1937-41, prin. bassoonist, 1947-51; prin. bassoonist Detroit Symphony, 1946-47, Chgo. Symphony Orch., 1951-64; faculty Juilliard Sch. Music, 1949-51; faculty, performer, Gunnison (Colo.) Music Camp, Western State Coll., 1962-63; pvt. teaching, 1946—; tchr. bassoon Ind. U. Sch. Music, part-time 1963-64, prof. music (bassoon), 1964-77; asso. prof. Indiana U. of Pa., 1979-80; faculty performer New Coll. Summer Music Festival, 1976, 77, 79; mem. Am. Woodwind Quintet, 1964-77; prin. bassoonist Pitts. Symphony Orch., 1977—; faculty, performer Aspen Music Festival, 1967-77, Waterloo Music Festival, 1979—; performances chamber music groups, Washington, N.Y.C., Chgo. others; participant Pablo Casals Festival, Prades, France, 1953; soloist NBC Symphony, Chgo. Symphony Orch. TV concerts; recorded Mozart Bassoon Concerto in B flat Major, with Arturo Toscanini and NBC Symphony, Vivaldi Concerti for Bassoon with Max Goberman and N.Y. Symphonietta, Leonard Sharrow Plays Bassoon Solos; assisting artist A Baroque Trumpet Recital; Concerto for Bassoon and Orch. by Ray Luke and Concerto da Camera for Bassoon and Orch. by Dan Welcher; orchestral recs. with Arturo Toscanini, Fritz Reiner and the Chgo. Symphony, Rafael Kubelik. Served with AUS, 1941-45. Mem. AAUP, Pi Kappa Lambda. Editor: U. Bertoni, 12 Studies for Bassoon; J.B. de Boismortier, Concerto in D Major for Bassoon; A. Corelli, Sonata in B Minor for Bassoon; H. Eccles, Sonata in G Minor; G.F. Händel, Concerto for Bassoon; F.H. Hoffman, Exercises and Studies for Bassoon; J.N. Hummel, Grand Concerto for Bassoon in F Major; B. Marcello, Sonata in E Minor for Bassoon, Sonata in C Major for Bassoon, Sonata in G Major for Bassoon, Sonata in A Minor for Bassoon; L. Milde, Tarantella; A. Orefici, 20 Melodic Studies for Bassoon; E. Ozi, 42 Caprices for Bassoon; P. Rode, 15 Caprices for Bassoon; A. Vivaldi, Concerto in A Minor for Bassoon, Concerto in E Minor for Bassoon, Concerto in F Major for Bassoon, Sonata No. 1 in B Flat Major, Sonata No. 2 in F Major, Sonata No. 4 in B Flat Major, Sonata No. 6 in B Flat Major; C.M. von Weber, Concerto in F Major for Bassoon. Office: care Pitts Symphony Soc 600 Penn Ave Pittsburgh PA 15222

SHARROW, MARILYN JANE, library adminstr.; b. Oakland, Calif.; d. Charles L. and H. Evelyn S.; B.S. in Design, U. Mich., 1967, M.A.L.S., 1969; m. Lawrence J. Davis. Librarian, Detroit Public Library, 1968-70; head fine arts dept. Syracuse U. Libraries, 1970-73; dir. library Roseville (Mich.) Public Library, 1973-75; asst. dir. libraries U. Wash., 1975-77, asso. dir. libraries, 1978-79; dir. libraries U. Man. (Can.), Winnipeg, 1979—. Recipient Josenhans Pre-profl. award Detroit Public Library, 1968. Mem. ALA, Can. Library Assn., Man. Library Assn. Office: Dafoe Library U Man Winnipeg MB R3T 2N2 Canada

SHARRY, JOHN JOSEPH, dentist; b. Somerville, Mass., Feb. 11, 1925; s. Thomas Martin and Mary Redmond (Murphy) S.; B.S., Tufts U., 1945, D.M.D., 1949; m. Rachel Thompson, Jan. 30, 1952; children—Paul Michael, Ann Margaret, Thomas Martin. Resident in oral surgery U. Ala. Dental Sch., 1949-51, asst. prof., then asso. prof., 1953-59, prof. dentistry, chmn. dept., 1960-68, dir. Office Learning Resources, 1968-71; dean Dental Sch., Med. U. S.C., 1971-75, U. Tex. Dental Sch., San Antonio, 1978—; Kellogg fellow, Brazil, 1963; vis. prof. U. Ill. Dental Sch., 1965; mem. biomed. library rev. com. NIH, 1971-74, mem. spl. programs adv. com., 1976—; cons. in field. Trustee Charleston (S.C.) Symphony Assn., 1973-78, Birmingham (Ala.) Symphony Assn., 1966-70. Kellogg fellow, 1951-53; NIH fellow, 1959-60. Mem. Acad. Denture Prosthetics, Am. Prosthodontics Soc. (exec. council 1971-74), Am. Coll. Prosthodontics (pres. 1975-76), Brit. Soc. Study Prosthetic Dentistry, Am. Equilibration Soc., Internat. Assn. Dental Research, Fedn. Prosthodontic Orgns. (chmn. edn. com. 1977—), Southeastern Acad. Prosthodontics (hon.), Am. Acad. History Dentistry, AAAS, Am. Assn. Dental Textbook Authors, Prosthodontics Research Group, ADA, Tex. Dental Assn., San Antonio Dist. Dental Soc., Sigma Xi, Omicron Kappa Upsilon. Club: Rotary. Author: Complete Denture Prosthodontics, 3d edit., 1974; also articles; editor books, jours. in field. Home: 3507 Elm Hollow San Antonio TX 78230 Office: 7703 Floyd Curl San Antonio TX 78284

SHARTLE, CARROLL LEONARD, psychologist; b. Ruthven, Iowa, June 26, 1903; s. Harry E. and Flora (Leonard) S.; student Iowa State Coll., 1922-25; A.B., Iowa State Tchrs. Coll., 1927; A.M., Columbia U., 1932; Ph.D., Ohio State U., 1933; m. Doris Phelan Brown, Sept. 2, 1931; children—Alexander Brown, Leonard Harry. Asst. psychologist, mem. edn. staff Milw. Electric Ry. & Light Co., 1927-31; faculty Marquette U., 1931, Ohio State U., 1931-33, Mich. State Coll., 1933-35; chief worker analysis sect. U.S. Employment Service, 1935-39, chief occupational analysis sect. Social Security Bd., 1939-42, chief, div. occupational analysis and manning tables War Manpower Commn., 1942-44, exec. dir. Personnel Research Bd., 1944-56, chmn., 1956-61; vis. prof., lectr. occupational analysis methods George Washington U., Washington, 1941-44; prof. psychology Ohio State U., Columbus, 1944-68, prof. emeritus psychology and administrv. sci., 1968—, asso. dean, dir. research div. Coll. Commerce and Adminstrn., 1964-68; now cons. manpower, social sci. research; cons. HEW, 1971-73; dir. research Human Resources Research Inst., Air. U., 1952-53; chief psychology and social scis. div. Office Dir. Def. Research and Engring., Office Sec. Def., 1961-64; dir. Ohio State leadership studies, 1946-52; cons. to asst. sec. def., 1954-59; mem. com. on classification of mil. personnel NRC, 1940-45; mem. Pres.'s Com. on Deferments, 1943-44; mem. labor market research com. Social Sci. Research Council, 1946-56, dir., 1954-60; treas. Am. Psychol. Found., 1947-57; mem. human resources com. Research and Devel. Bd., Nat. Mil. Establishment, 1947-52; mem. Am. Bd. Examiners in Profl. Psychology, 1947-51; mem. med. adv. com. Social Security Adminstrn., 1955-60; U.S. mem. NATO Adv. Group on Human Factors, 1961-64, Manpower Research Conf., Yugoslavia, 1973. Recipient Centennial Achievement award Ohio State U., 1970. Fellow Am. Psychol. Assn. (past treas., past pres. bus. and indsl. div.), AAAS; mem. Nat. Vocat. Guidance Assn., Ohio Psychol. Assn. (past chmn. Ohio bd. examiners), Internat. Assn. Applied Psychology, Phi Beta Kappa, Sigma Xi, Alpha Psi Delta, Tau Kappa Epsilon. Club: Cosmos (Washington). Author: (with W.H. Stead et al) Occupational Counseling Techniques, 1940; Occupational Information, 1946, rev., 1959; Executive Performance and Leadership, 1956; research articles on related subjects. Address: 218 Leland Ave Columbus OH 43214

SHARWELL, WILLIAM GAY, communications co. exec.; b. Newark, July 26, 1920; s. William G. and Lillian (Kenny) S.; B.S., Seton Hall U., 1941; M.B.A., N.Y. U., 1950; M.B.A., Harvard U., 1952, D.C.S., 1960; m. Jacqueline Larocque, Oct. 22, 1960; children—William L., Paul L. Vice pres. personnel N.Y. Tel. Co., N.Y.C., 1965-67, v.p., comptroller, 1967-68, v.p. ops., 1968-71, exec. v.p. ops., 1971-76; v.p. AT&T, N.Y.C., 1976—; dir. Bank N.Y. County Trust Region, White Plains, USLIFE Corp., N.Y.C., U.S. Life Ins. Co. in City N.Y., Bell Tel. Co. Pa., Phila.; trustee Bklyn. Savs. Bank. Trustee, vice chmn. bd. Pace U., N.Y.C., 1973—; trustee Westchester Community Coll., Valhalla, N.Y., 1971—, vice chmn. bd., 1974—; trustee Nat. Conf. Christians and Jews, 1964—; bd. dirs. NOW Legal Def. and Edn. Fund, 1978. Clubs: Harvard, City Midday. Contbg. author: Credit Management Handbook, 1958, Chief Executive's Handbook, 1976; editorial bd. Ency. Profl. Mgmt., 1978. Home: 171 Devon Rd Bronxville NY 10708 Office: 195 Broadway New York NY 10007

SHASTID, JON BARTON, wine co. exec.; b. Hannibal, Mo., Nov. 21, 1914; s. Jon Shepherd and Mary (Barton) S.; m. Natalie Kiliani, Dec. 16, 1944; children—Lucinda, Jon G.H., Victoria A., Thomas Bartwyn. Pub. accountant Dodge City, Kans., 1938-42; v.p. finance Johnson Bronze Co., New Castle, Pa., 1946-54; exec. v.p., treas. E. & J. Gallo Winery, Modesto, Calif., 1954—; admitted to Calif. bar, 1959; pres. Gallo Wine Co. of La. at New Orleans, 1960—. City councilman Modesto, 1961-69. Served to capt. USAAF, 1942-46. C.P.A., Calif., Kans. Mem. State Bar of Calif., Am. Bar Assn., Calif. Soc. C.P.A.'s. Home: Modesto CA 95350 Office: PO Box 1130 Modesto CA 95353

SHATIN, HARRY, educator, physician; b. N.Y.C., July 7, 1910; s. Samuel and Hannah (Papish) Shatinsky; B.S., Coll. City N.Y., 1930; M.D., Strasbourg U., France, 1936; postgrad. N.Y. U., 1949-50; m. Vera Brusilowsky, Oct. 30, 1943; 1 dau., Beth. Intern, Unity Hosp., N.Y.C., 1937-38; pvt. practice medicine, 1938-41; staff physician VA Hosp., Bronx, N.Y., 1946-51, chief sect. dermatology, 1951-74, sr. cons. dermatology, 1974—; prof. clin. medicine Mt. Sinai Sch. Medicine, City U. N.Y., 1969-74, prof. dermatology, chmn. dept., 1974—; dir. dermatology Mt. Sinai Hosp., N.Y.C., 1974—. Served from lt. to maj. AUS, 1942-46. Fellow Am. Acad. Dermatology, A.C.P. (asso.); mem. N.Y. Acad. Medicine, A.M.A., Soc. Investigative Dermatology, Manhattan Dermatol. Soc. (pres. 1967-68), Dermatol. Soc. Greater N.Y., Internat. Soc. Tropical Dermatology. Home: 3720 Independence Ave New York City NY 10463 Office: Mt Sinai Sch Medicine 100th St and Fifth Ave New City NY 10029

SHATKIN, AARON JEFFREY, biochemist; b. Providence, July 18, 1934; s. Morris and Doris S.; A.B., Bowdoin Coll., 1956, D.Sc. (hon.), 1979; Ph.D., Rockefeller Inst., 1961; m. Joan A. Lynch, Nov. 30, 1957; 1 son, Gregory Martin. Sr. asst. scientist NIH, Bethesda, Md., 1961-63, research chemist, 1963-68; vis. scientist Salk Inst., La Jolla, Callif., 1968-69; asso. mem. dept. cell biology Roche Inst. Molecular Biology, Nutley, N.J., 1968-73, full mem., 1973-77, head molecular virology lab., 1977—; adj. prof. cell biology Rockefeller U. Served with USPHS, 1961-63. Recipient U.S. Steel Found. prize in molecular biology, 1977; Rockefeller fellow, 1956-61. Mem. Am. Soc. Microbiology, Am. Soc. Biol. Chemists, AAAS, N.Y. Acad. Scis., Harvey Soc. Mem. editorial bd. Jour. Viology, 1969—, Archives of Bio-chemistry & Biophysics, 1972—, Virology, 1973-76, Comprehensive Virology, 1974—, Jour. Biol. Chemistry, 1977—. Home: 4 Tanglewood Rd North Caldwell NJ 07006 Office: Roche Inst Molecular Biology Nutley NJ 07110

SHATNER, WILLIAM, actor; b. Montreal, Canada, Mar. 22, 1931; s. Joseph and Anne Shatner; B.A., McGill U., 1952; m. Gloria Rand, Aug. 12, 1956 (div. Mar. 1969); m. 2d, Marcy Lafferty, Oct. 20, 1973; 3 daus. Stage debut 1952; appeared Montreal Playhouse, summers 1952, 53; played juvenile roles Canadian Repertory Theatre, Ottawa, 1952-53, 53-54; appeared Stratford Shakespeare Festival, Ont., 1954-56; Broadway appearances include Tamburlaine the Great, 1956: The World of Suzie Wong; 1958; A Shot in the Dark, 1961; films include The Brothers Karamazov, 1958: The Explosive Generation, 1961; Judgement at Nuremburg, 1961; The Intruder, 1962; The Outrage, 1964; Dead of Night, 1974; The Devil's Rain, 1975; Star Trek, 1979; also TV movies and appearances on Omnibus, Studio One, U.S. Steel Hour, Alfred Hitchcock Presents, Naked City, Alcoa Premiere, Twilight Zone, Bob Hope Chrysler Theatre, Name of the Game, Mission: Impossible, Testimony of Two Men, the Tenth Level, The Andersonville Trial; star of TV show Star Trek, 1966-69, animated Series, 1973-75; Barbary Coast, 1975-76, The Bastard, 1978, Disaster on the Coastliner, 1979. Recipient Tyrone Guthrie award, 1956; Theatre World award, 1958. Mem. Actors Equity Assn., A.F.T.R.A., Screen Actors Guild, The Bastard, 1978. A.C.T.A. Address: care Wm Morris Agy 151 El Camino Beverly Hills CA 90212

SHATTO, GLORIA MCDERMITH, coll. pres., economist; b. Houston, Oct. 11, 1931; d. Ken E. and Gertrude (Osborne) McDermith; B.A. with honors in Econs., Rice U., 1954, Ph.D. (fellow), 1966; m. Robert J. Shatto, Mar. 19, 1953; children—David Paul, Donald Patrick. Market research Humble Oil & Refining Co., Houston, 1954-55; tchr. pub. sch., C.Z., 1955-56; tchr. Houston Independent Sch. Dist., 1956-60; asst. prof. econs., U. Houston, 1965-69, asso. prof., 1969-72; prof. econs., asso. dean Coll. Indsl. Mgmt., Ga. Inst. Tech., Atlanta, 1973-77; George R. Brown prof. bus. Trinity U., San Antonio, 1977-79; pres. Berry Coll., Berry Acad., Mount Berry, Ga., 1979—; small bus. adv. com. U.S. Treasury, 1977—. Mem. Tex. Gov.'s Commn. on Status of Women, 1970-72; trustee Ga. Tech. Research Inst., 1975-77, Berry Coll., Ga., 1975—; mem. Ga. Gov.'s Commn. on Status of Women, 1975. OAS fellow, summer 1968. Mem. Royal, Am., So., Southwestern (pres. 1976-77) econ. assns., Am. Fin. Assn. (nominating com. 1976), Southwestern Social Scis. Assn., Fin. Execs. Inst. (chmn. Atlanta edn. com. 1976-77), AAUW (area rep. 1967-68, Tex. chmn. legis. program 1970-71, mem. internat. fellowships and awards com. 1970-76, chmn. 1974-76), Phi Beta Kappa, Phi Kappa Phi, Omicron Delta Epsilon. Contbr. articles to profl. jours. Editor: Employment of the Middle-Aged, 1972. Address: Berry Coll Mount Berry GA 30149

SHATTUCK, CHARLES HARLEN, educator; b. Belvidere, Ill., Nov. 23, 1910; s. Deazro Harlen and Katherine Margaret (Hines) S.; A.B., U. Ill., 1932, M.A., 1934, Ph.D., 1938; m. Susan Elizabeth Deuel, Nov. 24, 1936; children—Kate Shattuck Green, Judith Shattuck Sarason. Asst. in English, U. Ill., Urbana, 1934-38, instr., 1938-43, asst. prof., 1943-48, asso. prof., 1948-58, prof., 1958—, dir. U. Theatre, 1943-63, mem. Center for Advanced Study, 1961-62, 66; Henry Noble MacCracken Chair of English, dir. exptl. theatre Vassar Coll., Poughkeepsie, N.Y., 1948-49. Recipient George Freedley award for best book on theatre, 1969, 76; Folger Shakespeare Library fellow, 1959, 61, 74, 78; Guggenheim fellow, 1961-62, 68-69. Mem. Soc. Theatre Research, Am. Soc. Theatre Research (dir. 1968—), Shakespeare Assn. Am. (pres. 1979). Author: Bulwer and Macready, 1958; William Charles Macready's King John, 1962; Mr. Macready Produces As You Like It, 1963; The Shakespeare Promptbooks, 1965; The Hamlet of Edwin Booth, 1969; John Philip Kemble Promptbooks, 1975; Shakespeare on the American Stage, 1976. Editor: Accent, 1940-60, Folger Facsimile Promptbook Series, 1971—; Home: 103 N Busey St Urbana IL 61801

SHATTUCK, ROGER WHITNEY, author, educator; b. N.Y.C., Aug. 20, 1923; s. Howard Francis and Elizabeth (Colt) S.; grad. St. Paul's Sch., Concord, N.H., 1941; B.A., Yale, 1947; m. Nora Ewing White, Aug. 20, 1949; children—Tari Elizabeth, Marc Ewing, Patricia Colt, Eileen Shepard. Information officer UNESCO, Paris, France, 1947-48; asst. editor Harcourt, Brace & Co., 1949-50; mem. Soc. Fellows, Harvard, 1950-53, instr. French, 1953-56; faculty U. Tex., Austin, 1956-71, prof. English, French, 1968-71, chmn. dept. French and Italian, 1968-71; Commonwealth prof. French, U. Va., Charlottesville, 1974—. Adv. bd. Nat. Translation Center, 1964-69, chmn., 1966-69; provediteur gen. Coll. de Pataphysique, Paris, 1961—. Served to capt. USAAF, 1942-45. Decorated Ordre Palmes Academiques (France). Guggenheim fellow, 1958-59; Fulbright research fellow, 1958-59; Am. Council Learned Socs. research fellow, 1969-70. Author: (poems) Half Tame, 1964; Proust's Binoculars, 1963; Banquet Years, 1958; Marcel Proust (Nat. Book award 1975), 1974; The Forbidden Experiment, 1980. Editor or co-editor: Selected Writings of Guillaume Apollinaire, 1950; The Craft and Context of Translation, 1961; Selected works of Alfred Jarry, 1965; Occasions by Paul Valéry, 1970. Mem. editorial bd. PMLA, 1977-78. Office: Dept French Cabell Hall U Va Charlottesville VA 22903

SHATZ, STEPHEN SIDNEY, mathematician; b. Bklyn., Apr. 27, 1937; s. Nathan and Agusta S.; A.B., Harvard U., 1957, A.M., 1958, Ph.D., 1962; A.M. (hon.), U. Pa., 1971; children—Geoffrey, Adria. Instr., Stanford U., 1962-63, acting asst. prof., 1963-64; asst. prof. U. Pa., Phila., 1964-67, asso. prof., 1967-69, prof. math., 1969—; vis.

prof. U. Pisa, 1966-67. Mem. Am. Math. Soc. (editor trans. 1975-78, mem. council 1975—). Author: Profinite Groups, Arithmetic and Geometry, 1972; contbr. articles to profl. jours. Office: Dept Math U Pa Philadelphia PA 19104

SHATZKIN, LEONARD, pub. cons.; b. Warsaw, Poland, July 16, 1919; s. Isaac and Helen (Feiman) S.; came to U.S., 1920, naturalized, 1922; student City Coll. N.Y., 1935-38; B.S., Carnegie Inst. Tech., 1941; m. Eleanor Oshry, Aug. 4, 1940; children—Michael, Karen, Nancy. Production mgr. House Beautiful Mag., N.Y.C., 1941-43; research scientist Manhattan Project, N.Y.C., 1943-45; production mgr. Viking Press, N.Y.C., 1945-50; asst. to dir. mfg. Doubleday & Co., N.Y.C., 1950-55, dir. research, 1955-60; v.p. Crowell-Collier Macmillan Co., N.Y.C., 1960-63; dir. mfg. McGraw-Hill Book Co., N.Y.C., 1963-68, v.p., 1968-70; pres. Planned Production, N.Y.C., 1970-78, Two Continents Pub. Group, Ltd., N.Y.C., 1972—; prin. Shatzkin & Co., Cons., Croton-on-Hudson, N.Y., 1979—; instr. div. gen. studies N.Y. U., 1948-53; dir. Yates Industries, 1965-72; instr. Pratt Inst., 1971-72; cons. George Banta Co., Avon Industries, Macmillan Co., N.Y. Bot. Garden, Pahlavi Nat. Library, Teheran, Iran. Mem. Am. Inst. Graphic Arts (treas. 1952-59), Trade Book Clinic, Publishers Round Table, Tamiment Inst. Mem. Democratic Socialist Organizing Com. Editor and translator: The Stars Bear Witness, 1947; contbr. articles in field to Publishers Weekly, others; patentee field of book binding. Home: 132 Old Post Rd N Croton-on-Hudson NY 10520 Office: 310 E 44th St New York NY 10017

SHAUB, HAROLD ARTHUR, food processing co. exec.; b. Lancaster, Pa., Nov. 28, 1915; s. Arthur and Clara (Cramer) S.; B.S., Drexel Inst. Tech., 1939; m. Eileen B. Bair, Aug. 6, 1939; children—John A., Carole Sue (Mrs. Clifford Hoffman), Lynn E. (Mrs. Bill Benton). Indsl. engr. Talon, Inc., 1941-42; with Campbell Soup Co., Camden, N.J., Chgo., 1942-57, sr. v.p., 1968-69, exec. v.p., 1969-72, pres., 1972—, also dir.; v.p., gen. mgr. Campbell Soup Co. Ltd., Toronto, Can., 1957-58, pres., 1961-66, also dir.; pres. Pepperidge Farm, Inc., 1966-68; dir. Scott Paper Co., N.J. Bell Telephone Co., Exxon Corp., R.H. Macy & Co., Inc.; mem. internat. adv. council Canadian Imperial Bank of Commerce, Toronto. Chmn. bd. trustees Drexel U., Nutrition Found. Mem. N.A.M. (dir.), Grocery Mfrs. Am. (dir.). Home: 1250 Country Club Rd Gladwyne PA 19035 Office: Campbell Pl Camden NJ 08101

SHAUGHNESSY, DANIEL ROBERT, JR., restaurant and motel co. exec.; b. Boston, Mar. 8, 1927; s. Daniel Robert and Hester (DeVoy) S.; B.S., Boston Coll., 1951; postgrad. Harvard Bus. Sch., 1966; m. Norma Hayward, Oct. 1, 1948; children—Daniel Robert III, Dale, Keith, Bryan. Various mgmt. positions to gen. mgr. Southwestern states Montgomery Ward & Co., Chgo., 1952-67; v.p., treas. Hecht Co., Washington, 1967-69; exec. v.p. Howard Johnson Co., Boston, 1969-74; pres. Motel 6, Inc., Santa Barbara, Calif., 1975—. Served with USNR, 1944-46. Office: 51 Hitchcock Way Santa Barbara CA 93105*

SHAUGHNESSY, DONALD JOSEPH, consumer goods mfg. co. exec.; b. Chgo., Mar. 11, 1932; s. Emmett Michael and Margaret Mary (Shaughnessy) S.; B.S.C., Loyola U., Chgo., 1953; M.B.A., U. Chgo., 1966; m. Mary Ann Wall, Feb. 11, 1956; children—Mary Rita, Donald Joseph, Molly, Joseph, Margaret. With Armour & Co., since 1955—, pres., 1978—; group v.p. Greyhound Corp., 1977—. Served with AUS, 1953-55. Roman Cath. Clubs: Tavern (Chgo.); Desert Forest Golf (Carefree). Home: Box 843 Carefree AZ 85331 Office: Armour & C 111 W Clarendon St Phoenix AZ 85077

SHAULIS, NELSON JACOB, viticulturist, educator; b. Somerset, Pa., Sept. 10, 1913; s. Guy Stanley and Minnie (Stufft) S.; B.S., Pa. State Coll., 1935, M.S., 1937; Ph.D., Cornell U., 1941; m. Lillian Hedwig Huep, Aug. 16, 1941; children—Catherine Shaulis Osterhout, Margaret Shaulis Harty. Instr. pomology Pa. State Coll., 1938-44; asst. soil conservationist Soil Conservation Service, Arendtsville, Pa., 1938-44; asst. prof. pomology N.Y. State Agrl. Expt. Sta., Cornell U., Geneva, 1944-47, asso. prof., 1947-48, prof., 1948-67, prof. viticulture, 1967-78, prof. emeritus, 1978—. Mem. bd. edn. Geneva City Sch. Dist., 1964-67, v.p., 1966-67. Fulbright sr. research scholar, Australia, 1967-68. Fellow Am. Soc. Hort. Sci.; mem. Am. Soc. Enologists (hon. life mem.), Am. Soc. Agronomy, Soil Sci. Soc. Am., Crop Sci. Soc. Am., Sigma Xi, Phi Kappa Phi. Republican. Lutheran. Club: Torch. Contbr. chpts. to books, articles to profl. jours. Home: 505 W North St Geneva NY 14456 Office: Dept Pomology and Viticulture NY State Agr Expt Sta Geneva NY 14456

SHAULL, RICHARD, theologian, educator; b. Felton, Pa., Nov. 24, 1919; s. Millard and Anna (Brenneman) S.; B.A., Elizabethtown Coll., 1938, D.D., 1958; B.Th., Princeton Theol. Sem., 1941, Th.M., 1946, Th.D., 1959; m. Mildred Miller, May 17, 1941; children—Madelyn, Wendy. Ordained to ministry Presbyn. Ch., 1941; pastor in Wink, Tex., 1941-42; missionary in Colombia, 1942-50, U. Brazil, 1952-62; prof. ch. history Campinas (Brazil) Presbyn. Sem., 1952-60; v.p. Mackenzie Inst., Sao Paulo, Brazil, 1960-62; prof. ecumenics Princeton Theol. Sem., 1962—; cons. internat. programs, 1960—; chmn. N.Am. Congress Latin Am., 1966—, World Student Christian Fedn., 1968-73. Author: Encounter with Revolution, 1955; (with Carl Oglesby) Containment and Change, 1967; (with Gustavo Gutierrez) Liberation and Change, 1977; also 3 books in Portuguese. Home: 156 Maplewood St Philadelphia PA 19144

SHAVELSON, MELVILLE, writer-dir.; b. N.Y.C., Apr. 1, 1917; s. Joseph and Hilda (Shalson) S., A.B., Cornell U., 1937; m. Lucille T. Myers, Nov. 2, 1938; children—Richard, Carol-Lynne. Writer, Bob Hope Pepsodent Show, NBC radio, 1938-43; author screenplays including The Princess and the Pirate, 1944, Wonder Man, 1944, Room for One More, 1951, I'll See You in My Dreams, 1952; writer-dir. The Seven Little Foys, 1954, Beau James, 1956, Houseboat, 1957, The Five Pennies, 1958, It Started in Naples, 1959, On the Double, 1960, Yours, Mine and Ours, 1968, The War Between Men and Women, 1972; The Legend of Valentino, 1975; writer-dir.-producer The Pigeon That Took Rome, 1962, A New Kind of Love, 1963, Cast A Giant Shadow, 1966, Mixed Company, 1974, The Great Houdinis, 1976, Ike, 1979; creator Danny Thomas Show, ABC-TV, 1953, My World—And Welcome To It, NBC-TV, 1969; author Broadway musical Jimmy, 1969. Recipient Award of Merit, United Jewish Appeal, 1966; Screen Writers' Guild award, 1959; Christopher award, 1959; Sylvania TV award, 1953; Acad. Award Nominations (screenplay), 1955, 58; Screen Writers Ann. award nominations (screenplay), 1952 (2), 58, 59, 62, 68, 72, 75; Screen Writers award (best written Am. musical), 1959. Mem. Dirs.' Guild Am., Writers' Guild Am. (exec. bd. 1960-75, 78, pres. screen writers br. 1967, pres. found. 1975-79), Acad. Motion Picture Arts and Scis., Writer Guild Am. West (pres. 1969-70, 79—), Sigma Delta Chi. Author: How to Make a Jewish Movie, 1970; Lualda, 1975; The Great Houdinis, 1976; The Eleventh Commandment, 1977; Ike, 1979. Home: 11947 Sunshine Terr Studio City CA 91604

SHAVER, GEORGE JACOB, JR., broadcasting exec.; b. Chgo., Jan. 30, 1929; s. George J. and Elizabeth (Siddall) S.; B.A., Princeton U., 1951; m. Dorothy H. Breska, Aug. 21, 1954 (dec. Mar. 1974); children—Patricia, Pamela, Linda, George Jacob. Account exec. McCann-Erickson, Inc., N.Y.C., 1953-56; account exec. Dancer-Fitzgerald-Sample, Inc., N.Y.C., 1956-63, account supr., 1963-70, creative group head, 1970-73, v.p., 1963-69, creative dir., 1973-77, sr. v.p., 1969-77; v.p. advt. and creative services NBC-TV, N.Y.C., 1977—. Served with CIC, AUS, 1951-53. Clubs: Princeton (N.Y.C.); Lloyd Harbor Yacht, Yacht (Huntington). Home: 8 Woodhollow Ln Huntington NY 11743 Office: 30 Rockefeller Plaza New York City NY 10020

SHAVER, JESSE MILTON, mfg. co. exec.; b. Nashville, Nov. 16, 1919; s. Jesse M. and Daisy (Rule) S.; B.S. in Engring., Purdue U., 1942; M.B.A., U. Chgo., 1955; m. Louise L. Lyman, June 9, 1956; children—Jesse Milton III, John Warren. Mgmt. cons. Booz, Allen & Hamilton, 1952-58; div. mgr. Wells-Gardner Electronics Corp., 1958-62; exec. v.p. Am. Air Filter Co., Inc., Louisville, 1962-67, pres., chief operating officer, 1967, chmn. bd., chief exec. officer, 1968—; exec. v.p. Allis-Chalmers Corp., 1978—, also dir.; dir. Louisville Trust Bank, Inc., Reliance Universal, Inc., United Ky. Inc., South Central Bell Telephone Co., Commonwealth Life Ins. Co. Bd. dirs. Air Conditioning and Refrigeration Inst., pres., 1972. Served to maj. F.A., AUS, 1942-47; ETO, PTO. Decorated Bronze Star medal. Mem. IEEE, NAM (dir.), Am. Soc. Heating, Refrigerating and Air-Conditioning Engrs., Sigma Chi, Beta Gamma Sigma. Clubs: Economic, University (Chgo.); Louisville Country, Pendennis, Boat (Louisville); Metropolitan (N.Y.C.). Episcopalian. Home: 3105 Boxhill Ln Louisville KY 40222 Office: 215 Central Ave Louisville KY 40277

SHAVER, ROBERT HAROLD, educator; b. North Henderson, Ill., Sept. 8, 1922; s. Archibald Harold and Melvina (Edgar) S.; student Monmouth (Ill.) Coll., 1940-42; B.S., U. Ill., 1947, M.S., 1949, Ph.D., 1951; m. Beryl Margaret Burt, May 25, 1945; children—Joanne Lee, Mark Harold, Jill Margaret, Bruce Robert. Asst. prof. to prof. geology, chmn. dept. U. Miss., 1951-56; asso. prof., prof. geology Ind. U., Bloomington, 1956—, asst. chmn. dept., 1967-72, acting chmn., 1970. Paleontologist, head geology sect. Ind. Geol. Survey, 1956—; geologist Miss. Geol. Survey, Oxford, summer 1951, Shell Oil Co., Jackson, Miss., summer 1952; lectr. U. Ill., summer 1953; pres. Found. Advancement of Paleontology and Sedimentology, 1977—. Served to lst. lt. USAAF, 1942-45. Decorated D.F.C. Fellow Geol. Soc. Am.; mem. Am. Assn. Petroleum Geologists, Paleontol. Soc., Soc. Econ. Paleontologists and Mineralogists (v.p. Gt. Lakes sect. 1972-73, pres. sect. 1973-74, chmn. publs. com. 1971-75, nat. pres. 1976-77), Ind. Acad. Sci., Michigan Basin Geol. Soc. Editor: Jour Paleontology, 1964-69. Contbr. articles to profl., state jours. Home: 2012 Viva Dr Bloomington IN 47401

SHAW, ALLEN BENNETT, broadcasting exec.; b. New Orleans, Sept. 24, 1943; s. Allen Bennett and Olive Francis (Burson) S.; B.S. in Speech, Northwestern U., 1966; m. Jane G. Roberts, Aug. 28, 1965; children—Thomas Allen, David Andrew, Allison Lee. Asst. program dir. Sta. WCFL, Chgo., 1966-68; v.p. ABC Owned FM Radio Stas., N.Y.C., 1968-76, pres., 1976—. Office: 1330 Ave of the Americas New York NY 10019

SHAW, ARNOLD, author, composer; b. N.Y.C., June 28, 1909; s. David and Sarah (Coller) S.; M.A., Columbia, 1931; m. Ghita Milgrom; children—Mindy Sura, Elizabeth Hilda. Pianist on radio, 1926; orch. leader, 1932; exec. editor Musette Pubs., N.Y.C., 1941; dir. pub. relations, advt. Big Three Music Corp., 1944; editor Swank mag., 1945; dir. pub. relations, advt. Leeds Music Corp., 1946; v.p., gen. profl. mgr. Duchess Music Co., 1949, Hill & Range Songs, 1953, Edward B. Marks Music Corp., 1955-66. Lectr., Juilliard Sch. Music, 1945, New Sch., 1957; Fairleigh Dickinson U., 1964-65, U. Nev., Reno, U. Okla., 1971, U. Nev., Las Vegas, 1977-80; TV producer-narrator-writer-composer Curtain Time-Gt. Musicals series, host Window on the Arts series, 1972-73. Mem. Authors Guild, Am. Musicological Soc., ASCAP (Deems Taylor award 1968, 79), Am. Guild Authors and Composers, Nat. Acad. Rec. Arts and Scis., Nat. Soc. Lit. and The Arts, Songwriters Hall of Fame, Nat., Nev. (Nev. Composer of Yr. award 1973), Las Vegas (pres. 1975-77) music tchrs. assns. Author: Lingo of Tin Pan Alley, 1950; The Money Song, 1953; Belafonte, 1960; Sinatra: 20th Century Romantic, 1968; The Rock Revolution: What's Happening in Today's Music, 1969; The World of Soul, 1970; The Street That Never Slept: N.Y.'s Fabled 52d St., 1971; The Rockin' '50s, 1974; 52d St.: The Street of Jazz, 1977; Honkers and Shouters: The Golden Years of Rhythm & Blues, 1978; Music Scene, New Book of Knowledge Annuals, 1970-80. Editor: Mathematical Basis of the Arts by Joseph Schillinger, 1948; co-editor Schillinger System of Musical Composition, 1946. Composer: Sing a Song of Americans, 1941; A Man Called Peter and Other Songs, 1956; Mobiles for Piano, 1966; Stabiles for Piano, 1968; Plabiles for Piano, 1971; One Finger Piano, Kiss Me Another, Night Lights; A Whirl of Waltzes for Piano, 1974; The Mod Moppet: 7 Nursery Rip-Offs for Piano, 1975; They Had a Dream: An American Musical Odyssey, 1975-76; The Bubble-Gum Waltzes, 1977; An American Sonata, 1978; Snapshots of Three Friends, 1980. Address: 2288 Gabriel Dr Las Vegas NV 89109

SHAW, ARNOLD FRANKLIN, lawyer; b. Chgo., Apr. 24, 1910; s. Louis H. and Odyce (Kaufman) S.; student U. Ill., 1927-29, U. Chgo., 1929-30; B.S.L., Northwestern U., 1931, postgrad. Law Sch., 1931-33; m. Dolores Stewart, Apr. 25, 1941; children—Lois Holly, Janet Ann. Admitted to Ill. bar, 1933, D.C. bar, 1952; practiced law, Chgo., 1933-39; mfg. exec. Chgo. 1939-42, 46-48; exec. asst. to dir. Office Alien Property, Dept. Justice, 1949-50; spl. asst. to dir. OPS, Washington, 1951-52; dir. Mchts. Credit, Inc., Am. Research and Mfg. Corp. Served as lt. USNR, 1943-46; PTO. Mem. Am., Fed., D.C., Chgo. bar assns, Am. Legion, Amvets. Home: 4550 Brandywine St NW Washington DC 20016 Office: 503 D St NW Washington DC 20001

SHAW, ARTIE, musician; b. N.Y.C., May 23, 1910; s. Harry and Sarah (Strauss) S.; extension work in lit. Columbia; Mus.D. (hon.), U. Nebr., 1938; m. Margaret Allen; m. 2d, Lana Turner; m. 3d, Elizabeth Kern; 1 son, Steven Kern; m. 4th, Ava Gardner (div. Oct. 1946); m. 5th, Kathleen Winsor, Oct. 28, 1946; m. 6th, Doris Dowling, June 16, 1952 (div. 1956); 1 son, Jonathan Dowling; m. 7th, Evelyn Keyes, 1957. Orch. leader, 1936—, appeared in motion pictures Dancing Co-ed and Second Chorus; former owner firm Shooters Service and Dewey, gun mfs.; pres. Artixo Prodns., Ltd., film distbn. co.; lectr. colls. and univs.; also engaged in film, theatrical prodn.; producer Broadway mus. The Great Gatsby; ann. lectr. U. Calif., Santa Barbara. Former mem. exec. council, bd. Hollywood Ind. Citizens Com. Arts, Scis. and Professions. Served with USNR, 1942-44. Recipient Downbeat award best Am. swing band; Esquire Mag. Poll award as favorite band of armed services; Hall of Fame award for rec. Begin the Beguine, Nat. Acad. Rec. Arts and Scis., 1977. Composer: Summit Ridge Drive, Concerto for Clarinet, A Clarinet Method, numerous orchestral works. Author: The Trouble with Cinderella; I Love You, I Hate You, Drop Dead!; Three Variations on a Theme. Address: 2127 W Palos Ct Newbury Park CA 91320

SHAW, BERNARD, journalist; b. Chgo.; grad. U. Ill., Chgo.; married; 2 children. Reporter, Group W, Westinghouse Broadcasting Co., 1966-71, corr., 1968; reporter Washington bur. CBS News, 1971-74, corr., 1974-77; chief Miami (Fla.) bur. ABC News, 1977—; spl. corr. children's spls.: What's an Election About, What the Oil Crisis is About. Served with USMC. Office: care ABC News Latin Am Bur 2801 Ponce de Leon Blvd Suite 820 Coral Gables FL 33134*

SHAW, CHENG-MEI, neuropathologist; b. Taiwan, Oct. 24, 1926; s. Ching-Keng and Shok (Kang) S.; came to U.S., 1954, naturalized, 1969; M.D., Nat. Taiwan U., 1950; m. Shiu-Thi Koo, Nov. 2, 1951; children—Wen-Yee, Andrey, Robert, Kathryn. Intern, Taiwan U. Hosp., Taipei, 1950-52, resident, 1952-54; resident Lahey Clinic, Boston, 1954-55, Baylor U. Affiliated Hosps., Houston, 1955-58; fellow Coll. Medicine, Baylor U., Houston, 1958-60; practice medicine specializing in neuropathology, Seattle, 1960—; mem. staffs Univ. Hosp., VA Hosp., Harborview Med. Center, Children's Orthopedic Hosp.; cons. Swedish Hosp., Virginia Mason Hosp., USPHS Hosp.; asst. prof. dept. pathology U. Wash. Med. Sch., Seattle, 1964-68, asso. prof., 1968-74, prof., 1974—. Pres. bd. trustees Talent Edn., Seattle, 1972-73. Nat. Multiple Sclerosis Soc. fellow, 1960-63. Mem. Am. Assn. Neuropathologists, Am. Assn. Pathologists, Internat. Acad. Pathology. Contbr. articles to profl. jours. Home: 6541 29th St NE Seattle WA 98115

SHAW, DENIS MARTIN, educator, univ. dean; b. St. Annes, Eng., Aug. 20, 1923; s. Norman Wade and Alice Jane Sylvia (Shackleton) S.; B.Sc., Emmanuel Coll., Cambridge, Eng., 1943, M.Sc., 1948; Ph.D., U. Chgo., 1951; m. Pauline Mitchell, Apr. 6, 1946 (div. 1975); children—Geoffrey, Gillian, Peter; m. 2d, Susan L. Evans, Apr. 9, 1976. Came to Can., 1948. Lectr., McMaster U., Hamilton, Ont., Can., 1949-51, asst. prof., 1951-55, asso. prof., 1955-60, prof. geology, 1960—, chmn. dept., 1953-59, 62-66, dean grad. studies, 1979—; asso. prof. ENSGA, U. Nancy (France), 1959-60. Invited prof. Inst. de Minéralogie, U. Genève, 1966-67. Served with RAF, 1943-46. Fellow Royal Soc. Can.; mem. Geol. Assn. Can., Geochem. Soc., Mineral. Assn. Can. (pres. 1964), Am. Geophys. Union, A.A.A.S. Exec. editor Geochimica et Cosmochimica Acta, 1970—; asso. editor Handbook of Geochemistry, 1966—. Author: Masson Et Cie, 1964. Address: Dept Geology McMaster U Hamilton ON Canada

SHAW, DONALD HARDY, utility exec.; b. Oelwein, Iowa, June 1, 1922; s. John Hardy and Minnie (Brown) S.; B.S., Harvard, 1942; J.D., U. Iowa, 1948; m. Elizabeth Jean Orr, Aug. 16, 1946; children—Elizabeth Ann, Andrew Hardy, Anthony Orr. Admitted to Ill. bar, 1949, Ia. bar, 1948; with firm Sidley & Austin, Chgo., 1948-55; with Ia.-Ill. Gas & Electric Co., Davenport, Iowa, 1956—, treas., 1960-72, v.p. finance, 1973—, also dir.; dir. First Nat. Bank of Davenport. Mem. Iowa State Bd. Regents, 1969—, Iowa State Mental Hygiene Com., 1969—. Trustee St. Luke's Hosp., Davenport. Served to capt. USAAF, 1942-45. Recipient Philo Sherman Bennett award, 1942. Mem. Iowa Bar Assn., Order of Coif, Delta Theta Phi. Democrat. Conglist. Clubs: Davenport, Davenport Country, Outing. Home: 29 Hillcrest Ave Davenport IA 52803 Office: 206 E 2d St Davenport IA 52801

SHAW, E. CLAY, JR., mayor Fort Lauderdale (Fla.); b. Miami, Fla., Apr. 19, 1939; s. E. Clay and Rita (Walker) S.; B.S., Stetson U., 1961, J.D., 1966; M.B.A., U. Ala., 1963; m. Emilie Costar, Aug. 22, 1960; children—Emilie, Jennifer, E. Clay, John C. Admitted to Fla. bar, 1967; asst. city atty. City of Ft. Lauderdale, 1968, chief city pros., 1968-69, asso. municipal judge, 1969-71, city commr., 1971-73, vice mayor, 1973-74, mayor, 1975—. U.S. spl. ambassador to Papua, New Guinea Independence; pres. U.S. Conf. Republican Mayors; mem. adv. bd. U.S. Conf. Mayors. Chmn. municipal div. Ft. Lauderdale United Fund Campaign, 1971; active Young Rep. Club Broward County, Ft. Lauderdale Rep. Exec. Com.; mem. exec. com. Rep. Nat. Com.; bd. dirs. Ft. Lauderdale U., Broward County Traffic Assn. Home: 609 Coral Way Fort Lauderdale FL 33301 Office: Office of Mayor City Hall 100 N Andrews Ave Fort Lauderdale FL 33301

SHAW, EDGAR ALBERT GEORGE, research assn. exec.; b. Middlesex, Eng., July 10, 1921; s. Albert and Lily (Hill) S.; student U. London, 1938-40, Imperial Coll., London, 1946-50; B.Sc., asso. Royal Coll. Sci., 1948; Ph.D., Imperial Coll., 1950; m. Millicent Selina Chandler, Oct. 6, 1945; children—Jennifer, Kenneth. Tech. officer U.K. Ministry Aircraft Prodn., London, 1940-44, Brit. Air Commn., Washington, 1944-46; asst. NRC, Can., Ottawa, Ont., 1950-53, asso., 1953-60, sr. research officer, 1960-74, prin. research officer, 1974—, head acoustics sect., 1974—. Lectr., U. Ottawa, 1958—. Mem. com. hearing, bioacoustics and biomechanics U.S. Nat. Acad. Scis., 1965—; mem. Internat. Commn. on Acoustics, Internat. Union Pure and Applied Physics, 1972-78, chmn., 1975-78. Fellow Acoustical Soc. Am. (councilman 1960-63 v.p. 1968-70, pres. 1973-74), Royal Soc. Can.; mem. Inst. Physics (Eng.), Canadian Assn. Physicists. Presbyn. Contbr. articles to profl. jours. Patentee in field. Home: 1391 Wesmar Dr Ottawa ON KIH 7T4 Canada Office: Div Physics NRC Ottawa ON K1A OS1 Canada

SHAW, EDWARD ANDREW, editor; b. Lawton, Okla., Nov. 12, 1928; s. Roy B. and Eileen A. (Ryan) S.; B.A., U. Okla., 1954, M.A., 1955; m. Betty Jean Langford, Aug. 23, 1953; children—Mark Patrick, Ellen Joyce. Sci. editor, prodn. mgr. U. Calif. Press, Berkeley, 1956-59, 1961-63; mng. editor W.H. Freeman & Co., San Francisco, 1959-61, Am. Dental Assn., Chgo., 1963-66; dir. U. Okla. Press, Norman, 1966—. Served with AUS, 1950-52. Home: 815 S Ponca Norman OK 73071 Office: 1005 Asp Ave Norman OK 73019

SHAW, EDWARD PEASE, educator; b. Lowell, Mass., Dec. 18, 1911; s. Paul Hervey and Ruth (Pease) S.; A.B. magna cum laude, Harvard, 1933, A.M., 1934, Ph.D., 1937; m. Eleanor Lazelle Snell, Dec. 26, 1936; children—Dana Paul, Susan Barbara. Instr. French, U. Ill., 1938-42; asso. prof. Romance langs. Miami U., Oxford, Ohio, 1946-47; prof. French, State U. N.Y., Albany, 1947-73, prof. emeritus, 1973—, chmn. dept. Romance langs., 1959-61, 63-64, chmn. div. humanities, 1965-68. Served to maj. USAAF, 1942-45; ETO. Decorated Bronze Star; chevalier Order Acad. Palms France, 1962, officier, 1973. French Govt. traveling scholar, 1935; Harvard Sheldon traveling fellow, France, 1937-38. Mem. Am. Assn. U. Profs., Modern Lang. Assn., Am. Assn. Tchrs. French, N.Y. State Tchrs. Assn., Société d'Etude du 18e Siècle. Author: History of IX Air Force Service Command, 1946; Jacques Cazotte (1719-1792), 1942; (with C.W. Colman) Maurois, La Machine a Lire les Pensées, 1944; The Case of the Abbé de Moncrif, 1953; (with D.L. Demorest) French Civilization Through Fiction, 1956; Francois-Augustin Paradis de Moncrif (1687-1770), 1958; (with J.J. Fotos) Dix Contes, 1961; Problems and Policies of Malesherbes as Directeur de la Librairie in France (1750-1763), 1966; (with A. Rogers) Selected Literary References in the Manuscript Journal (1750-1769) of Joseph d'Hémery, 1973. Contbr. articles to profl. jours. Home: 9 Countryfield Circle Kennebunk ME 04043

SHAW, GAYLORD DEWAYNE, journalist; b. El Reno, Okla., July 22, 1942; s. Charley Smolt and Ruth Edith (Maloney) S.; student Cameron Coll., Lawton, Okla., 1960-62, U. Okla., Norman, 1962-64; m. Judith Kay Howard, Aug. 27, 1960; children—Randall, Kristine. Police reporter Lawton Constn.-Press, 1960-62; statehouse corr. AP, Oklahoma City, 1962-66, Washington bur. editor, 1966-67, investigative reporter spl. assignment team, 1967-69, editor spl. assignment team, 1969-71, White House corr., 1971-75; Washington bur. staff writer Los Angeles Times, 1975-78, Denver bur. chief,

1978—. Recipient Worth Bingham award for disting. reporting, 1968, Merriman Smith award for presdl. coverage White House Corrs. Assn., 1974, Sigma Delta Chi award for Washington corr., 1978, Pulitzer prize for nat. reporting, 1978. Office: 1415 Larimer Sq Suite 300 Denver CO 80202

SHAW, GEORGE ROBERT, assn. exec., editor; b. Circleville, Ohio, Apr. 22, 1930; s. Floyd and Bessie Mae (Cutright) S.; attended Lincoln Inst., U. Ga.; B.S./B.A., U. Md., 1954; m. Norma Jean Barthelmas, July 30, 1949; children—Bruce Robert, Brooks Cameron, Kara Elizabeth. Asst. to plant supt. Ralston Purina Co., Circleville, 1949-55; staff advisor Dept. of Army, Columbus, Ohio, 1955-57; mgr. dist. sales Nationwide Mut. Ins. Co., Columbus, 1957-64; pres. Bus. Builders Inc., Dayton, Ohio, 1964-68; dir. field ops. and pub. relations Nat. Mgmt. Assn., Dayton, 1968-79, v.p. mktg., 1979—, also editor-in-chief Manage mag. Pres. Nat. Found., 1957-59. Served with AUS, 1951-54. Named Master Motivator of Year, 1967; hon. State Senator La., 1973. Mem. Assn. U.S. Army, Public Relations Soc., Sales Execs. Am. Mason. Author: What's In It For Me?, 1967. Home: 4327 Wales Dr Dayton OH 45405 Office: 2210 Arbor Blvd Dayton OH 45439

SHAW, (FRANCIS) HAROLD, concert assn. exec.; b. Hebron, N.Y., June 11, 1923; student Ithaca Coll., 1942, Columbia, 1944, N.Y. U. Extension, 1948. Pres., owner Shaw Concerts, Inc., N.Y.C., also Shaw Attractions, Inc.; asso. Hurok Concerts Inc., concert mgr. Vladimir Horowitz, Nathan Milstein, Janet Baker, Julian Bream, others, featuring numerous concert and stage stars, also internat. touring programs including Chgo. Symphony, Phila. Orch. performing arts dir. Seattle World's Fair, 1961-62; exec. dir. Pres. Johnson's Shakespeare Ann. Com., 1964; exec. staff dir. performing arts com. Cultural Commn., N.Y.C., 1966; nat. chmn. Performing Arts Energy Comm., 1974; chmn. bd. trustees Am. Shakespeare Theatre, Stratford, Conn., 1974—. Served with USAAF, 1942-43. Mem. Internat. Performing Arts Adminstrs. (dir.), Am. Symphony Orch. League, Coll. and Univ. Mgrs. Assn., Auditorium and Arena Mgrs. Assn., Actors Equity Assn. (sr.), Am. Summer Stock Mgrs. Assn. (co-founder), Phi Mu Alpha. Office: Shaw Concerts Inc 1995 Broadway New York NY 10023

SHAW, HARRY ALEXANDER, III, mfg. co. exec.; b. Tacoma, Sept. 27, 1937; s. Harry Alexander and Gladys (Reynolds) S.; A.B., Dartmouth Coll., 1959; grad. Advanced Mgmt. Program, Harvard U., 1979; m. Phoebe Jo Crouch, Nov. 27, 1966; children—Harry Alexander IV, Austin R., Christine N. Various sales positions U.S. Steel Corp., 1962-69; div. mktg. v.p. Huffy Corp., 1969-74, corp. mktg. v.p., 1974-75, Calif. div. pres., 1975-77, group v.p., Dayton, Ohio, 1977-78, pres., 1979—; dir. Citizens Fed. Savs. & Loan Assn., Dayton, 1979—. Asso. bd. dirs. Dayton Art Inst., 1977—. Served with USNR, 1959-62. Mem. Bicycle Mfrs. Assn., Young Presidents Orgn. Club: Rotary. Home: 1135 Ridgeway Rd Dayton OH 45419 Office: Huffy Corp PO Box 1204 Dayton OH 45401

SHAW, HARRY LEE, JR., editor, writer; b. Fountain Inn, S.C., Feb. 19, 1905; s. Harry L. and Jane B. (Wilson) S.; A.B., Davidson Coll., 1926, Litt.D., 1969; M.A., U. S.C., 1927; postgrad. N.Y. U., 1928-31; m. Marie Louise Ragsdale, Aug. 12, 1931 (div.); children—Harry Lee III, Edward S., Stephen Willard; m. 2d, Joy Thomas, Oct. 30, 1953; children—Jill, Thomas. Fellow, English asst. U. S.C., 1926-27, instr., 1927-28; instr. English, N.Y. U., 1928-39, asst. prof., 1939-42, dir. Workshops in Composition, 1937-42; asso. editor, dir. editorial research Look Mag., 1942-43, mng. editor, 1943-44, editorial dir., 1944-47; editor in charge humanities Harper & Bros., N.Y., 1947-52; exec. v.p., mng. editor Tupper & Love, Inc., 1952-53; sr. editor E.P. Dutton & Co., N.Y.C., 1953-57, v.p., 1955-57; editor-in- chief gen. book div. Henry Holt & Co., 1957-59, mgr. gen. book div., 1958-59; free lance writer, 1959-61; cons. editor Barnes & Noble, 1961-63, dir. publs., 1963-64; editor W.W. Norton & Co., 1965—. Dir. Fed. Writers Project, N.Y.C., 1938; lectr. English, Columbia, 1948-52; guest dir. non-fiction workshop U. Colo. Western Writers' Conf., summer 1941, 42, dir. conf., 1947, 48; lectr. Writer's Conf. U. Ind., 1949, U. Utah, 1950. Mem. Phi Beta Kappa, Omicron Delta Kappa, Sigma Upsilon, Pi Kappa Phi. Republican. Episcopalian. Author: Writing and Rewriting, 1937, 55, 73; A Complete Course in English, 1940, 55, 59, 67, 73, 79; Spell It Right, 1961; Errors in English, 1962; Punctuate It Right, 1963; (with Marquis E. Shattuck) Harper's Handbook of English 1942; (with Douglas Bement) Reading the Short Story, 1942; (with Ruth Davis) Americans One and All, 1947; (with others) Dominant Types in British and American Literature, 1949; (with George Wykoff) The Harper Handbook of College Composition, 1952, 5th edit., 1980; (with Virginia Shaffer) The McGraw Hill Handbook of English, 1952, 4th edit. (sole authorship), 1978; The Shorter Handbook of College Composition, 1965; Say It Right, 1972; Dictionary of Literary Terms, 1972; Twenty Steps to Better Writing, 1975; Dictionary of Problem Words and Expressions, 1975; 30 Ways to Improve your Grades, 1976; Concise Dictionary of Literary Terms, 1976; Better Jobs Through Better Speech, 1979. Contbr. articles to nat. mags. Home: Old Mill Rd Fairfield CT 06430 Office: 500 Fifth Ave New York NY

SHAW, HENRY KING, former librarian, educator; b. Akron, Ohio, Nov. 22, 1904; s. Roy Arthur and Carrie Luella (King) S.; B.A., Phillips U., 1932; M.A. in Edn., U. Akron, 1942; D.D., Butler U., 1957; m. Edrie Ethel Stanton, June 8, 1929 (dec. Nov. 1966); 1 son, Roy Stanton; m. 2d, Ethel M. Cawthorne, Oct. 29, 1971. Ordained to ministry Ch. of Christ, 1932; pastor Riverside Ch. of Christ, Akron, 1929-30, 1st Christian Ch., Ada, Ohio, 1932-35, Medina, Ohio, 1935-42, Washington Ave. Christian Ch., Elyria, Ohio, 1943-57; faculty Butler U., 1957-58; librarian Christian Theol. Sem., Indpls., 1958-72, dir. publs., 1959-72, prof. Disciples lit., 1965-72, emeritus, 1972—. Mem. ALA, Am. Theol. Library Assn., Disciples of Christ (trustee emeritus), Am. Cath. hist. socs., AAUP, Am. Soc. Ch. History, Theta Phi. Author: Saga of a Village Church, 1937; The Amateur Philosopher, 1940; Buckeye Disciples, 1952; Hoosier Disciples, 1966; mng. editor Encounter, 1959-72. Home: 663 Hollis Ave El Jobean FL 33927

SHAW, HENRY OVERSTREET, transp. exec.; b. Adel, Ga., Oct. 21, 1893; s. Archibald Hiram and Elizabeth (Overstreet) S.; intensive course U.S. Naval Acad., 1918; m. Vivian Izona Riggs, June 19, 1920 (dec. May 1967); 1 dau., Sylvia Byron (Mrs. David Nicholas Blount); m. 2d, Mary H. Garnder, Apr. 28, 1971. With Ga. Lumber & Supply Co. and Shaws, Inc., Miami, Fla., 1914-29, v.p., treas., 1923-29; with Shaw Bros. Oil Co. and predecessor cos., Miami, 1916-61, chmn. bd. dirs. and exec. officer, 1950-61; land developer 1916—; partner Shaw Bros. Docks, Shaw Bros. Shipping Co. 1943—; pres. Shaw Gold Coast Co., 1955—, Shaw Marine Co.; owner Shaw Fgn. Trade Warehouse; pres. Fla. Fgn. Trade Zone, Inc., 1969—; dir. Fla. Nat. Bank & Trust Co. of Miami, Nat. Bank at Opa Locka. Bd. dirs. Hist. Assn. So. Fla. Mem. civilian aide com. of comdg. gen. Army Air Forces, 1942; chmn. Dade County chpt. A.R.C. war fund drive, 1942, dir. county chpt., 1942-43, vice chmn., 1943. Pres., So. Atlantic and Fla. Ports Conf. 1945-47; chmn. Miami Rate and Traffic Bd., 1927-33, Port and Harbor Bd., 1937-38, 1939; mem. Am. and Fla. petroleum industries coms. 1931—; mem. Fla. Gov.'s Spl. Com. on Freight Rates, 1940-45; mem. citizens bd. U. Miami 1946—, pres. 1950. Served to ensign Supply Corps, USNRF, 1918-19. Mem. Miami C. of C. (pres. 1944-46), Greater Miami Traffic Assn., Internat. Platform Assn., Newcomen Soc. Mason (K.T., Shriner), Elk, Rotarian (pres. 1934-35 Miami). Home: 700 Coral Way Apt 9 Coral Gables FL 33134 also Pinebrook 3A Highlands NC 28741 Office: 501 NE 1st Ave Miami FL 33132

SHAW, HERBERT WELLER, JR., advt. agy. exec.; b. Governors Island, N.Y., Feb. 8, 1935; s. Herbert Weller and Mary Edna (Smith) S.; B.A., Haverford (Pa.) Coll., 1956; m. Moira Elizabeth Buxton, Aug. 4, 1974; children—Suzanne, Christopher. Copywriter, Internat. Nickel Co., Inc., N.Y.C., 1958-59, Kenyon & Eckhardt, 1959-61; asso. creative dir. Marsteller, Inc., 1961-65; v.p., creative dir. Muller, Jordan & Herrick, 1965-66; pres. Shaw Elliott, Inc., N.Y.C., 1966-78. Treas., bd. dirs. Center for Living Force, Phoenicia, N.Y.; bd. dirs. theatre in a Trunk; mem. corp. U.S. com. UNICEF. Served with AUS, 1958-59. Home: Center for Living Force Phoenicia NY Office: 45 E 78th St New York City NY 10016. *My life began when I began to trust—in myself, in others, in the universe. In my frozen, untrusting state, my life was empty as I desperately tried every way almost every way almost every to be filled from the outside. I learned early how to take and justified it because I felt there was not enough for me. I became competitive and considered it a good quality. I convinced myself that my emptiness was a small price for power. But in recent years, in many big and little ways, I have learned the obvious—that the receiving, the filling, is in the giving. It is always my choice, then, to fill myself or remained starved. More and more, I am finding the joy in choosing to be full.*

SHAW, IRWIN, author; b. N.Y.C., Feb. 27, 1913; s. William and Rose (Tompkins) S.; A.B., Bklyn Coll., 1934; 1 son, Adam. Drama critic New Republic, 1947-48. Author: (plays) Bury the Dead, 1936; Siege, 1937; The Gentle People, 1939; Quiet City, 1939; Retreat to Pleasure, 1941; Sons and Soldiers, 1943; The Assassin, 1945; (books, collections of short stories) Sailor Off the Bremen, 1940; Welcome to the City, 1942; Act of Faith, 1946; (with Peter Viertel) The Survivors, 1948; The Young Lions (novel), 1948; The Troubled Air (novel), 1950; (with Robert Capa) The Face of Israel, 1950; Mixed Company (short stories), 1950; Lucy Crown (novel), 1956; Tip on a Dead Jockey (short stories), 1957; Selected Short Stories, 1959; Two Weeks in Another Town (novel), 1959; Children From Their Games (play), 1963; In The Company of Dolphins (travel), 1964; Voices of a Summer Day (novel), 1965; Love on a Dark Street (stories), 1965; Rich Man, Poor Man (novel), 1970; God Was Here But He Left Early (short stories), 1973; Evening in Byzantium (novel), 1973; Nightwork (novel), 1975; (essays) Paris! Paris!, 1977; Beggarman, Thief (novel), 1977; (short stories) Five Decades, 1978; The Top of The Hill, 1979. Contbr. to mags. Recipient O. Henry Meml. award 1944, 2d prize, 1945. Served with AUS, 1942-45. Home: Klosters Switzerland

SHAW, JAMES HOWARD, religious adminstr., clergyman; b. N.S., Can., Dec. 1, 1910; s. Daniel Jess and Emma (Huntley) S.; student U. N.B., Can., 1930-31; divinity diploma N.E. Sch. Theology, 1933; Th.B., Gordon Coll. Theology and Missions, 1933-34, student Div. Sch., 1942; student Evang. Sem., 1948-49; D.D., Aurora Coll., 1968; m. Ella von Helmolt, July 12, 1933; children—Beverly Louise (Mrs. Kelton Dexter Johnson), David Howard, Kenneth Reid. Ordained to ministry Advent Christian Ch., 1934; pastor Advent Christian Ch., Newport Center, Vt., 1934-36, Schenectady, 1936-40, Providence, 1940-47, College Ch., Aurora, Ill., 1947-56, Worcester, Mass., 1956-58, LaGrange, Ill., 1975-75; exec. sec. Advent Christian Gen. Conf. Am., 1958-75. Elective officer Advent Christian denomination, 1943-60; adv. council Am. Bible Soc., 1959—. Bd. dirs. Aurora Coll., 1975—. Mem. Am. Advent Mission Soc. (rec. sec., dir. 1957-58), R.I. (chmn. dept. evangelism), Greater Worcester councils chs., Aurora (pres.), Greater Worcester (pres.) ministerial assns. Rotarian. Home: 1525 Plainfield Rd LaGrange IL 60525. *A faith encounter with the living Christ and a commitment to Him, at the age of sixteen, gave direction and a unifying purpose to my life. This relationship with Him has motivated me and shaped my basic outlook and decisions as life has broadened and matured. A perspective definition of "education" which I heard at the age of eighteen has also influenced me helpfully in developing self-discipline and the constructive use of time: "Education is training the mind and the will so that one is able to do what he ought to do, when it ought to be done, whether he feels like doing it or not."*

SHAW, JAMES RAYMOND, physician, educator; b. Yale, Mich., Mar. 29, 1908; s. James W. and Nellie (Imeson) S.; A.B., Mich. State Normal Coll., 1936; M.D., U. Mich., 1936; D.Sc., Eastern Mich. U., 1961; m. Sylvia H. Gross, June 17, 1935; children—James W., Sandra Lee. Intern, USPHS Hosp., New Orleans, 1936-37; spl. fellow internal medicine Mayo Clinic, 1940-41; chief dept. medicine USPHS Hosp., San Francisco, 1941-44, med. officer charge out patient clinic, Los Angeles and San Pedro, Calif., 1944-49; med. officer charge USPHS Hosp., Detroit, 1949-52; chief hosp. div. USPHS, 1952-53; chief health br. Bur. Indian Affairs, Dept. Interior, 1953-55; chief div. Indian health USPHS, 1955-62; asst. surgeon gen., 1958-62; prof. microbiology, asso. coordinator research, dir. U. Ariz. Peace Corp. Tng. Program, 1962-68, prof. community medicine, 1968—; dep. coordinator Ariz. Regional Med. Programs, 1968-70. Served as sr. surgeon, dist. med. officer 11th Naval Dist., USCGR, 1943-46. Recipient commendations USCG, surgeon gen. USPHS. Fellow A.C.P.; mem. Am. Hosp. Assn., Am. Pub. Health Assn., Assn. Mil. Surgeons (Gorgas medal 1961), Am. Assn. Pub. Health Physicians, Commd. Officer Assn., Ret. Officers Assn., Alpha Omega Alpha. Contbr. numerous articles to profl. jours. Home: 6832 E Tiuani Dr Tucson AZ 85715

SHAW, JOHN HARRISON, physicist; b. Sheffield, Eng., Jan. 25, 1925; s. Herbert Ronald William and Ada (Harrison) S.; B.A., Cambridge (Eng.) U., 1946, M.A., 1949, Ph.D., 1952; m. Elizabeth Wroe, Sept. 10, 1949; children—Jennifer, Peter, Michael, Stephen. Came to U.S., 1949. Faculty, Ohio State U., Columbus, 1949—, prof. physics, 1964—. Fellow Optical Soc. Am., Am. Meteorol. Soc., Royal Meteorol. Soc. Contbr. articles profl. jours. Home: 4940 Sharon Ave Columbus OH 43214

SHAW, JOHN SHERMAN, JR., holding co. exec.; b. New Orleans, Oct. 8, 1915; s. John Sherman and Lucile C. (Crumbliss) S.; B.A., Vanderbilt U., 1937; M.B.A., Harvard, 1939; m. Mary Cornelia Holland, 1953; children—John Sherman III, Thomas Taylor. Engaged in comml. banking, N.Y.C., 1939-52; gen. partner Ingalls & Snyder, investments, N.Y.C., 1952-60; with So. Natural Gas Co., 1961—, chmn. bd., chief exec. officer, 1965-76; chmn. bd., pres., chief exec. officer So. Natural Resources, Inc., Birmingham, Ala., 1973—; chmn. bd., chief exec. officer Offshore Co., Houston, 1965-76; dir. Airco, Inc., Montvale, N.J., 1970-78, Ala. Bancorp., 1st Nat. Bank of Birmingham, Ala., Protective Life Ins. Co., Birmingham. Trustee Gulf Univs. Research Consortium, Houston, So. Research Inst., Birmingham. Served lt. comdr. USNR, World War II; ETO. Mem. Nat. Petroleum Council, Am. Gas Assn. Am. Petroleum Inst., Interstate Natural Gas Assn. Am. (dir., past chmn.). Clubs: Blind Brook, Links, Harvard (N.Y.C.); Ramada (Houston); Mountain Brook, Birmingham Country, Shoal Creek Country, Downtown, Relay House (Birmingham). Home: 3424 Westbury Rd Mountain Brook AL 35223 Office: So Natural Resources Inc PO Box 2563 Birmingham AL 35202

SHAW, JOSEPH THOMAS, educator; b. Ashland City, Tenn., May 13, 1919; s. George Washington and Ruby Mae (Pace) S.; A.B., U. Tenn., 1940, A.M., 1941; A.M., Harvard, 1947, Ph.D., 1950; m. Betty Lee Ray, Oct. 30, 1942; children—David Matthew, Joseph Thomas, James William. Asst. prof. Slavic langs. Ind. U., 1949-55, asso. prof., 1955-61; prof. Slavic langs. U. Wis., 1961—, chmn. dept. Slavic langs., 1962-68, 77—, chmn. div. humanities, 1964-65, 72-73, asso. dean Grad. Sch., 1965-68. Served to capt. USNR, 1942-46, 51-53. Mem. Am. Assn. Tchrs. Slavic and East European Langs. (mem. exec. council, pres. 1973-74). Author: The Letters of Alexander Pushkin, 1963; Pushkin's Rhymes: A Dictionary, 1974; Baratynskii: A Dictionary of the Rhymes and a Concordance to the Poetry, 1975; Batiushkov: A Dictionary of the Rhymes and a Concordance to the Poetry, 1975. Editor: The Slavic and East European Jour., 1957-70. Contbr. articles to profl. jours. Home: 4505 Mineral Point Rd Madison WI 53705

SHAW, JOSEPH THOMPSON, JR., advt. agy. exec.; b. N.Y.C., Mar. 26, 1926; s. Joseph Thompson and Hana (Muskova) S.; student Williams, 1943-44; B.A., Yale, 1947; m. Helen R. Jepson, Mar. 29, 1947; children—Richard S., Peter G., Christopher J., David T. With ABC, N.Y.C., 1947-53, TV cameraman, 1947-50, asst. TV program dir., 1950-53; with Dancer-Fitzgerald-Sample, Inc., N.Y.C., 1953—, sr. v.p., 1970—. Active publicity Boy Scouts, Community Fund, Town Club, Youth Recreation (all Scarsdale). Bd. dirs. Scarsdale Civic Orgn. Served to lt. (j.g.) USNR, 1945-46: PTO. Conglist. Home: 52 Tunstall Rd Scarsdale NY 10583 Office: 405 Lexington Ave New York NY 10017

SHAW, KENNETH ALAN, univ. pres.; b. Granite City, Ill., Jan. 31, 1939; s. Kenneth W. and Clara H. (Lange) S.; B.S., Ill. State U., Normal, 1961; Ed.M., U. Ill., Urbana, 1963; Ph.D., Purdue U., 1966; m. Mary Ann Byrne, Aug. 18, 1962; children—Kenneth William, Susan Lynn, Sara Ann. Tchr. history, counselor Rich Twp. High Sch., Park Forest, Ill., 1961-63; residence hall dir., instr. edn. Ill. State U., 1963-64; counselor Office Dean of Men, Purdue U., 1964-65, Office Student Loans, 1965-66; asst. to pres., lectr. sociology Ill. State U., 1966-69; acting dean coll., asso. prof sociology Towson State Coll., Balt., 1969-70, dean coll., asso. prof. sociology, 1970-71, v.p., dean coll., 1971-77; pres. So. Ill. U., Edwardsville, 1977-79; chancellor So. Ill. U. System, 1979—. Chmn., McLean County United Community Services Fund Drive, 1967, bd. dirs., 1967-69; M.C. for United Community Services Fund Drive, 1968-69, chmn. ednl. div., 1969-70; mem. Bloomington-Normal Town Meeting Com., 1967; mem. YMCA Midland Com., 1967-69; mem. Town Gown Com., Normal 1968; chmn. edn. com. Balt. chpt. NCCJ; mem. Baltimore County Task Force on Edn., 1975-77; governing bd. Ill. Council Econ. Edn., 1977—, St. Louis Symphony Soc., 1977—, St. Louis Regional Commerce and Growth Assn., 1978—. Mem. Am. Sociol. Assn., Am. Higher Edn. Assn., NEA, Phi Delta Kappa, Pi Gamma Mu. Home: 219 S Charles St Edwardsville IL 62025 Office: Office of Pres So Ill U Edwardsville IL 62026

SHAW, LEE CHARLES, lawyer; b. Red Wing, Minn., Feb. 17, 1913; s. Marvil T. and Bernice (Quinland) S.; student U. Mich. 1931-34; B.A., U. Chgo., 1936, J.D., 1938; m. Lorraine Schroeder, July 1, 1939; children—Lynda Lee (Mrs. Smith), Robert, Candace Jean (Mrs. Peterson), Lee Charles. Admitted to Ill. bar, 1938; asso. Pope & Ballard, Chgo., 1938-44, partner, 1944-45; partner Seyfarth, Shaw, Fairweather & Geraldson, 1945—. Dir. Interlake Inc., Walker Forge, Inc., Oakbrook Consol., Inc. Mem. arbitration services adv. com. Fed. Mediation and Conciliation Service. Adv. bd. Salvation Army. Mem. Am., Ill., Chgo. (bd. mgrs. 1956-57) bar assns., Indsl. Relations Research Assn. (past chpt. pres.), Phi Delta Phi. Contbr. articles to labor, econ. publs. Home: 2440 N Lakeview Ave Chicago IL 60614 Office: 55 E Monroe St Chicago IL 60603

SHAW, LEROY ROBERT, educator, author; b. Medicine Hat, Alta., Can., Jan. 15, 1923; s. Roy Albert and Ruby Ida (Johnson) S.; came to U.S., 1923, naturalized, 1947; A.B., U. Calif. at Berkeley, 1946, M.A., 1948, Ph.D., 1954; postgrad. U. Zurich, 1949-50, U. Vienna, 1950; m. Ida Rosmarie Mannaberg, June 29, 1959; children—Dion Desmond, Melissa Amanda. Instr. German, humanities Reed Coll., 1951-53; from instr. to asso. prof. German, U. Tex. at Austin, 1953-65; prof. German, U. Wis.-Milw., 1965-68; prof. German, U. Ill. at Chgo. Circle, 1968—, head dept., 1979—; vis. Fulbright prof. German, Trinity Coll., Dublin, Ireland, 1966-67; participant Brecht Symposium, Milw., 1970, Internat. Conf. Modern German Lit., Ludwigsburg, Germany, 1975. Grantee Am. Philos. Soc., 1958; Alexander von Humboldt fellow, 1962-64; Nat. Endowment for Humanities fellow, 1979-80. Mem. Am. Assn. Tchrs. German (exec. com. 1955-58), Modern Lang. Assn., Midwest Modern Lang. Assn., A.A.U.P., Brecht Soc. Author: Witness of Deceit: Gerhart Hauptmann as Critic of Society, 1958; The Playwright and Historical Change: Dramatic Strategies in Brecht, Hauptmann, Kaiser, Wedekind, 1970; Focus on German for Beginners, 1965; (with others) Focus on German for Intermediates, 1965; (with others) In einer deutschen Stadt, 1960; (with others) Review and Progress in German, 1959. Editor: (with introduction) The German Theatre Today, 1963. Home: 1137 N Euclid Ave Oak Park IL 60302 Office: Univ Hall Univ Ill Chicago Circle Chicago IL 60680

SHAW, LESLIE NELSON, savs. and loan assn. exec.; b. Columbus, Ohio, Aug. 2, 1922; s. Leslie Mervin and Kate (Hamilton) S.; B.Sc., Ohio State U., 1949; grad. extension student bus. U. Calif. at Los Angeles, 1953; m. Margaret Ann White, Dec. 18, 1947; children—Valerie, Leslie Nelson, Rebecca Ann. Vice pres. Family Savs. & Loan Assn. Los Angeles, 1951-63; postmaster Los Angeles, 1963-69; v.p., dir. community devel. Gt. Western Financial Corp., Beverly Hills, Calif., 1969—, pres. affiliate First City Savs. & Loan Assn.; dir. Lockheed Aircraft Corp. Mem. Los Angeles Area council Boy Scouts Am., Spl. Service for Groups; exec. bd. Braille Inst. Am. Bd. dirs. Community TV So. Calif. Served with inf. AUS, 1942-46. Mem. Soc. Real Estate Appraisers, Nat. PTA, NAACP. Episcopalian. Rotarian. Home: 1650 S Victoria Ave Los Angeles CA 90019 Office: 8484 Wilshire Blvd Beverly Hills CA 90211

SHAW, LUTHER GARDNER, educator, coll. adminstr.; b. Hurffville, N.J., June 9, 1920; s. Theodore and Blanche (Gardner) S.; B.S., Glassboro (N.J.), State Coll., 1941; M.S., U. Pa., 1948, Ed.D, 1954; m. Elizabeth M. Woods, July 14, 1975; children—Luther Gardner, John Duncan, Patricia Jean. Tchr., prin. N.J. pub. schs., 1941-42, 45-47; instr. Illman Sch., U. Pa., 1947-49; asst. prof. edn. Mt. Union (Ohio) Coll., 1949-53; prof. edn. Glassboro State Coll., 1953-62, dean adminstrn., 1962-66; pres. Atlantic Community Coll., Mays Landing, N.J., 1966-70, Garrett Community Coll., McHenry, Md., 1970-75; chmn. dept. edn. Cabrini Coll., Radnor, Pa., 1976-78; exec. v.p. Keuka Coll., Keuka Park, N.Y., 1978—; vis. summer prof. U. N.Mex., 1956, 58, Emory U., 1961, 62. Bd. dirs. Miss America Pageant. Served with USAAF, 1942-45. Mem. Assn. Higher Edn., N.E.A., Assn. N.J. State Coll. Faculties (pres. 1961-62), Am. Assn Sch. Adminstrs., Phi Delta Kappa, Author: (with Briggs, Gumaer) Handbook- -Readings in Grades 7-12, 1964. Home: The Lucina Keuka Coll Keuka Park NY 14478 Office: Keuka Coll Keuka Park NY 14478

SHAW, MANFORD AVIS, coll. chancellor; b. Tremonton, Utah, Nov. 14, 1906; s. N. Edward and LoVisa (Brent) S.; Ph.B., Yale, 1929; J.D., U. Utah, 1942; LL.D., Westminster Coll., Salt Lake City, 1957; m. Janet Walker, Feb. 4, 1932 (dec. 1950); children—Ann (Mrs. Ian McFarlane), Brent (Mrs. Eugene Foster); m. 2d, June Winward, May 6, 1953; children—Michael M., Karen (Mrs. G.M. Cordray), Cynthia (Mrs. R. Pitts), Debra (Mrs. F. Benzinger), Avis. Salesman, Dictaphone Corp., N.Y.C., 1929-32; v.p. E.B. Wicks Co., realtors, Salt Lake City, 1932-42; admitted to Utah bar, 1942; pres. Shaw Inc., realtor, Salt Lake City, 1946-67, Nat. Mortgage Co., Salt Lake City, 1963-65; pres. Westminster Coll., 1968-76, chancellor, 1976—; trustee, 1936-68, chmn. trustees, 1965-68. Pres., Salt Lake City Bd. Realtors, 1939, Utah Realty Assn., 1940, Utah Sales Exec. Assn., 1941. Served to maj. AUS, 1942-46. Methodist. Clubs: University, Cottonwood Country (Salt Lake City). Home: 2528 Wilshire Circle Salt Lake City UT 84109

SHAW, MARGERY WAYNE SCHLAMP, physician, lawyer; b. Evansville, Ind., Feb. 15, 1923; d. Arthur George and Louise (Meyer) Schlamp; student Hanover Coll., 1940-41; A.B. magna cum laude, U. Ala., 1945; M.A., Columbia U., 1946; postgrad. Cornell U., 1947-48; M.D. cum laude, U. Mich., 1957; J.D., U. Houston, 1973; D.Sc. (hon.), U. Evansville, 1977; m. Charles Raymond Shaw, May 31, 1942 (div. Nov. 1972); 1 dau., Barbara Rae. Intern, St. Joseph Mercy Hosp., Ann Arbor, Mich., 1957-58; practice medicine specializing in human genetics, Ann Arbor, 1958-67, Houston, 1967—; instr. dept. human genetics Med. Sch. U. Mich., 1958-61, asst. prof., 1961-66, asso. prof., 1966-67; asso. prof. dept. biology Grad. Sch. Biomed. Scis., U. Tex., Houston, 1967-69, prof., 1969—, dir. Med. Genetics Center, 1971—, acting dean Grad. Sch. Biomed. Scis., 1976-78; mem. genetics study sect. NIH, Bethesda, Md., 1966-70, mem. genetics tng. com., 1970-74, adv. com. to dir., 1979—; chromosome studies astronauts NASA, 1970-71; mem. med. adv. bd. Nat. Genetics Found., 1972—; research adv. bd. Planned Parenthood, Houston, 1972—; vis. scholar Yale Law Sch., 1974. First aid instr. ARC, 1962-67; unit chmn. United Fund, 1966. Recipient Billings Silver medal AMA, 1966; Achievement award AAUW, 1970-71; Am. Jurisprudence award, 1973; Mem. Am. Soc. Human Genetics (past sec., dir.), Genetics Soc. Am. (sec. 1971-73, pres. 1977-78, wilhelmene Key award 1977), Tissue Culture Assn. (trustee 1970-72), Environ. Mutagen Soc. (council), Am. Soc. Cell Biology, Phi Beta Kappa, Alpha Omega Alpha. Asso. editor: Am. Jour. Human Genetics, 1962-68; editorial bd. Am. Jour. Med. Genetics, 1977—, Am. Jour. Law and Medicine, 1977—; contbr. articles to profl. jours. Home: 7469 Brompton Blvd Houston TX 77025 Office: Med Genetics Center PO Box 20334 Houston TX 77025

SHAW, MICHAEL, educator; b. Barbados, W.I., Feb. 11, 1924; s. Anthony and Myra (Perkins) S.; B. Sc., McGill U., 1946, M. Sc., 1947, Ph.D., 1949, D.Sc., 1975; m. Jean Norah Berkinshaw, Oct. 16, 1948; children—Christopher A., Rosemary E., Nicholas R., Andrew L. Asso. prof. biology U. Sask., 1950-54, prof., 1954-67, prof., head dept. biology, 1961-67; dean faculty agrl. scis. U. B.C., 1967-75, v.p. acad. devel., 1975—. Mem. Sci. Council Can., Natural Scis. and Engring. Research Council Can. Recipient Queen's Silver Jubilee medal, 1977. Fellow Royal Soc. Can. (Flavelle medal 1976), Am. Phytopathol. Soc.; mem. Canadian Soc. Plant Physiologists (Gold medal 1971), Am. Soc. Plant Physiologists. Contbr. articles to profl. jours. Home: 1792 Western Pkwy Vancouver BC V6T 1V3 Canada Office: Office Vice Pres U British Columbia Vancouver BC V6T 1W5 Canada

SHAW, MICHAEL ALLAN, dept. store exec.; b. Evanston, Ill., July 14, 1940; s. Frank C. and Mabel I. (Peacock) S.; B.A., Colo. State U., 1962; J.D., U. Denver, 1965; M.B.A., DePaul U., 1969; postgrad. Columbia, 1970; m. Genevieve Schrodt, Aug. 16, 1964; children—M. Ian, Trevor N. Admitted to Ill. bar, 1965; practiced in Chgo., 1965—; asst. counsel, staff asst. to v.p. traffic Jewel Cos., Inc., Melrose Park, Ill., 1965-71; corporate sec., asst. treas., house counsel Wieboldt Stores, Inc., Chgo., 1972—. Mem. Village Planning Commn., Itasca, Ill., 1973-77. Home: 6 S 230 Cohasset Rd Naperville IL 60540 Office: 1 N State St Chicago IL 60602

SHAW, MILTON CLAYTON, educator; b. Phila., May 27, 1915; s. Milton Fredic and Nellie Edith (Clayton) S.; B.S. in Mech. Engring., Drexel Inst. Tech., 1938; M.Eng. Sci., U. Cin., 1940, Sc.D., 1942; Dr. h.c., U. Louvain (Belgium), 1970; m. Mary Jane Greeninger, Sept. 6, 1939; children—Barbara Jane, Milton Stanley. Research engr. Cin. Milling Machine Co., 1938-42; chief materials br. NACA, 1942-46; with Mass. Inst. Tech., 1946-61, prof. mech. engring., 1953-61, head materials processing div., 1952-61; prof., head dept. mech. engring. Carnegie Inst. Tech., Pitts., 1961-75, univ. prof., 1974-77; prof. engring. Ariz. State U., Tempe, 1978—. Cons. indsl. cos.; lectr. in Europe, 1952; pres. Shaw Smith & Assos., Inc., Mass., 1951-61; Lucas prof. Birmingham (Eng.) U., 1961; Springer prof. U. Calif. at Berkeley, 1972; Distinguished guest prof. Ariz. State U., 1977; mem. Nat. Materials Adv. Bd., 1971-74; bd. dirs. Engring. Found., 1976, v.p. conf. com., 1976-78. Recipient gold medal Am. Soc. Tool Engrs., 1958; Guggenheim fellow, 1956; Fulbright lectr., Aachen T.H., Germany, 1957; OECD fellow to Europe, 1964—; Fellow Am. Acad. Arts and Scis., ASME (Hersey award 1967, Thurston lectr. 1971, meeting theme organizer 1977, hon.); titular mem. Internat. Soc. Prodn. Engring. Research (pres. 1960-61, hon. mem. 1975); mem. Am. Soc. Metals (Wilson award 1971), Am. Soc. Lubrication Engrs. (Nat. award 1964, hon. life), Am. Soc. for Engring. Edn. (G. Westinghouse award 1956), Soc. Mfg. Engrs. (hon.; P. McKenna award 1975, Am. Machinery award 1973, Edn. award 1980), Nat. Acad. Engring., Polish Acad. Sci. Home: 3203 S College St Tempe AZ 85282 also Route 1 Central City PA 15926

SHAW, MILTON HERBERT, conglomerate exec.; b. Phila., June 16, 1918; s. Milton Herbert and Ethel (Shane) S.; B.S., U. Pa., 1949; m. Rita P. Revins, Nov. 24, 1971. Accountant, Franklin Sugar Refinery, Phila., 1945-52; with Kaiser Metal Products, Inc., Bristol, Pa., 1952-61, mgr. ins. and taxes, 1955-61; with Kidde Consumer Durables Corp., Bala Cynwyd, Pa., 1961—, asst. v.p., 1968—, dir. corp. services and risk mgmt., 1977—. Served with USNR, World War II. Mem. U.S. Power Squadron, Nat. Wildlife Fedn., Nat. Rifle Assn., Sigma Kappa Phi. Home: PO Box 51 Warrington PA 18976 Office: Kidde Consumer Durables Corp 2 Bala Cynwyd Plaza Bala Cynwyd PA 19004

SHAW, OSCAR MOORE, lawyer; b. Portsmouth, Ohio, Nov. 17, 1904; s. Edward Harrison and Fan Caldwell (Newman) S.; B.S., Harvard, 1926, LL.B., 1929; m. Margaret Curtis Pickering, Nov. 2, 1929; children— Margaret S. Dean, Edward McMichael. Admitted to Mass. bar, 1929; with firm Ropes & Gray, Boston, 1929—, mem. firm, 1937-76, of counsel, 1977—; past dir. Kendall Co., Colonial Fund, Am. Thread Co., Naumkeag Steam Cotton Co., Felters Co. Past bd. dirs. Student Ednl. Loan Fund. Fellow Am. Bar Found. (life); mem. Am. Law Inst. (life), Am., Boston bar assns., Phi Beta Kappa. Republican. Episcopalian. Clubs: Union (Boston); Country (Brookline, Mass.); Harvard (N.Y.C.). Home: 388 Beacon St Boston MA 02116 Office: 225 Franklin St Boston MA 02110

SHAW, PAUL DALE, biochemist; b. Morton, Ill., Aug. 12, 1931; s. Jesse Roy and Garnet Margaret (Sharp) S.; B.S., Bradley U., Peoria, Ill., 1953; Ph.D., U. Ill., 1957; m. Doris Jeanne Smith, June 11, 1955; children—Brian Paul, Alison Lorainne. Research fellow Harvard U., 1958-60; mem. faculty dept. plant pathology U. Ill., Urbana, 1960—, prof. biochemistry, 1973—. Served to 1st lt. USAF, 1956-57. U. Ill. fellow, 1955-56; postdoctoral fellow USPHS, 1959-60, research grantee, 1963-72, 77—. Mem. Am. Chem. Soc., Am. Soc. Biol. Chemists. Editor: Antibiotics, Vol. I, Mechanism of Action, 1967, Vol. II, Biosynthesis, 1967. Home: 20 Briarcliff Mahomet IL 61853 Office: S-524 Turner Hall Univ Ill Urbana IL 61801

SHAW, RAYMOND KENNETH, assn. exec.; b. Kansas City, Mo., Oct. 12, 1916; s. Hugh Ralph and Anna Elizabeth (Stevens) S.; grad high sch.; m. Katherine Geraldine Little, May 15, 1937; children—Judith Ann (Mrs. Gerald McConoughey), Barbara (Mrs. Thomas Ostrowski), William, Richard. With Internat. Harvester, East Moline, Ill., 1938-39, Rock Island (Ill.) Arsenal, 1939-45; insp. J.I. Case Co., 1947-62; co-organizer Internat. Assn. Tool Craftsmen, Rock Island, 1953, pres., 1959—. Mem. Nat. Fedn. Ind. Unions (exec. v.p. 1963-69), Am. Craftsmen Assn. (pres. 1973—). Moose, Elk. Address: 3243 37th Ave Rock Island IL 61201

SHAW, REID LONSDALE, broadcasting co. exec.; b. Norwalk, Conn., June 12, 1930; s. Donald Scholefield and Mary Reeves (West) S.; B.A., Trinity Coll., 1952; m. Marilyn Ann McCarthy, Apr. 11, 1953; children—Michael, Gayle, Stephen, Andrew. With Gen. Electric Co., Schenectady, 1952-59, 60-65; mgmt. cons. McKinsey & Co., Inc., N.Y.C., 1959-60; v.p., gen. mgr. Gen. Electric Broadcasting and Gen. Electric Cablevision Corp., Schenectady, 1965-71, pres., 1971-79; pres. Broadcasting Services div. John Blair & Co., N.Y.C., 1979—. Republican. Roman Catholic. Clubs: Mohawk Golf. Home: 50 Holly Ln Darien CT 06820 Office: 717 Fifth Ave New York NY 10022

SHAW, RICHARD, artist; b. Hollywood, Calif., Sept. 12, 1941; s. Richard Blake and Catherine (Dexter) S.; student Orance Coast Coll., Costa Mesa, Calif., 1961-63; B.F.A., San Francisco Art Inst., 1965; postgrad. U. Calif., Davis, 1967-68; m. Martha Helen Hall, Apr. 24, 1965; children—Alice, Virgil. Instr. ceramics San Francisco Art Inst., 1966—, U. Calif., Berkeley, 1970, U. Wis., 1971; exhibited in one-man shows San Francisco Art Inst., 1967, Dilexi Gallery, San Francisco, 1968, Quay Gallery, San Francisco, 1970, 71, 73, 75, 79, E.G. Gallery, Kansas City, Mo., 1974, Michael Berger Gallery, Pitts., 1979; exhibited in group shows Mus. Contemporary Crafts, N.Y.C., 1965, 66, 70, 71, Boston Soc. Arts and Crafts, 1966, Mus. West of Am. Craftsman's Council, San Francisco, 1966, Scripps Coll., Claremont, Calif., 1967, U. Sask., 1968, Smithsonian Instn., 1969, 76, San Francisco Art Inst., 1969, 71, Oakland Mus., 1970, Bklyn. Mus., 1970, Whitney Mus. Am. Art, N.Y.C., 1970, 74, 76, USIA, 1972, Nat. Mus. Modern Art, Tokyo and Kyoto, 1971-72, U. Miami, Coral Gables, Fla., 1972, Evanston (Ill.) Art Center, 1972, 74, Victoria and Albert Mus., London, 1972, Calif. State U., Hayward, 1972, Stanford U. Art Gallery, 1972, San Francisco Mus. Art, 1972, 74, David Stuart Gallery, Los Angeles, 1972, Emerson Mus. Art, Syracuse, N.Y., 1972, Sch. Arts and Crafts Soc., Portland, Oreg., 1973, 74, Kohler Art Center, Sheboygan, Wis., 1973, Balt. Mus. Art, 1973, Krannert Art Mus., Champaign, Ill., 1974, Phila. Coll. Art, 1974, Fendrick Gallery, Washington, 1975, Carborundum Mus., Niagara Falls, N.Y., 1975, U. Tex., Arlington, 1976, Campbell Mus., 1976, Contemporary Crafts Mus., 1976, Art Gallery U. Calif., Santa Barbara, 1976, Hopkins Art Center, Dartmouth, 1976-77, San Francisco Mus. Modern Art, 1976, Nat. Gallery Art, Washington, 1976, U. Calif., Fullerton, 1976, Laguna Beach (Calif.) Mus. Art, 1977, DeYoung Downtown Center, San Francisco, 1977, U. N.C., Chapel Hill, 1977, Grossmont Coll. Art Gallery, 1977, No. Ill. Art Gallery, DeKalb, Ill., 1977; rep. permanent collections at Oakland Mus., San Francisco Mus. Art, Nat. Mus. Art, Tokyo, Levi-Strauss Co., San Francisco, Utah Mus. Fine Arts, Salt Lake City, Stedelijk Mus., Gemeentemusea, Amsterdam. Chmn. artists com. San Francisco Art Inst. Recipient Nat. Endowment Arts grants, 1970, 74. Mem. Internat. Soc. Ceramists, Geneva, Switzerland. Home: 231 Frustuck St Fairfax CA 94930

SHAW, ROBERT, music condr.; b. Red Bluff, Calif., Apr. 30, 1916; s. Shirley Richard and Nelle Mae (Lawson) S.; A.B., Pomona Coll., 1938, Mus.D. (hon.), 1953; Mus.D., Coll. Wooster, 1951, Mich. State U., 1960, Cleve. Inst. Music, 1966, Emory U., 1967, Fla. State U., 1968; D.F.A., St. Lawrence U., 1955, U. Alaska, 1966; L.H.D., Kenyon Coll., 1963, Western Res. U., 1966, Westminster Choir Coll., Princeton, N.J., 1975, U. Akron, 1976, Morehouse U., 1977, Oglethorpe U., 1977; m. Maxine Farley, Oct. 15, 1939 (div. 1973); children—Johanna, Peter Thain, John Thaddeus; m. 2d, Caroline Sauls Hitz, Dec. 19, 1973; 1 son, Thomas Lawson. Dir. Fred Waring Glee Clubs, 1938-45; choral dir. Aquacades, 1942-43, Carmen Jones, 1943, Seven Lively Arts, 1944, My Darlin Aida, 1953; guest condr. CBS Symphony series, 1944-45, ABC Symphony series, 1945, NBC Symphony, 1946, N.Y.C. Symphony, 1946, Boston Symphony Orch., 1958, N.Y. Philharmonic, 1958, 70, Nat. Symphony Orch., 1959, 77, Chgo. Symphony Orch., 1960; dir. choral music Berkshire Music Center, 1946-49; dir. choral activities Juilliard Sch. Music, 1946-49; condr. San Diego Summer Symphony, 1953-58; asso. condr. Cleve. Symphony Orch., 1956-67; condr. Atlanta Symphony Orch., 1967—, Alaska Festival of Music, 1956-73. Guest condr. Cin. May Festival, 1967-75, Cleve. Orch. Blossom Music Festival, 1967-73, 2d Ann. Univ. Choral Festival, 1969, Aspen Festival Music, 1969, 72, Dallas Symphony Orch., 1969, Minn. Orch., 1970, 77, 78, Houston Symphony, 1970, 75, 3d Internat. Choral Festival, 1972, Brevard Music Festival, 1972-74, 77-78, Westminster Coll. Choir Summer Festival, 1972—, Ind. U. Summer Workshop, 1973—, Pitts. Symphony, Ambler Festival, 1973—, Ives Festival, New Haven, 1974, Mostly Mozart Festival, N.Y.C., 1974—, Cin. Symphony, 1974-75, Kansas City Philharmonic, 1974, Hamilton (Ont., Can.) Philharmonic, 1974, San Antonio Symphony, 1974, Buffalo Symphony, 1975, U. So. Calif.-Los Angeles Summer Workshop, 1976—, Los Angeles Philharmonic, 1976, 77, Memphis Symphony, 1976, Saratoga Festival, Phila. Orch., 1977; founder, dir. Robert Shaw Chorale ann. tours U.S., 1948-66, Middle East, Europe, 1956, USSR, 1962, S.Am., 1964; Collegiate Chorale, N.Y.C., 1941-60; festival music dir. 2d Internat. Choral Festival Composers and Condrs. Recipient award Outstanding Am.-born Condr. of Year, Nat. Assn. Am. Composers and Condrs., 1943; Alice M. Kitson award Columbia, 1955; Ga. Gov.'s award arts, 1973; Distinguished Service award Ga. Coll., 1973, Morehouse Coll., Atlanta, 1973, State U. N.Y. at Potsdam, 1975, Atlanta Boys' Clubs, 1975; ASCAP award, 1976; Harvard Glee Club medal, 1977; Nat. Fedn. Music Clubs award, 1975; 5 Grammy awards; 1 Gold Record. Guggenheim fellow, 1944. Home: 3707 Randall Mill Rd NW Atlanta GA 30327

SHAW, ROBERT FLETCHER, cons. civil engr.; b. Montreal, Que., Can., Feb. 16, 1910; s. John Fletcher and Edna Mary Baker (Anglin) S.; B.C.E., McGill U., Montreal, 1933; Sc.D. (hon.), McMaster U., 1967; D.Eng. (hon.), N.S. Tech. Coll., 1967; m. Johann Alexandra MacInnes, Dec. 24, 1935; 1 son, Robert Fletcher (dec.). With Found. Co. Can. Ltd., Montreal, 1933-63, pres., 1962-63, dir., 1968-71; shipyard mgr. Found. Maritime Ltd., Pictou, N.S., 1943-45; on loan to Govt. Can. as v.p., chief engr. Def. Constrn. (1951) Ltd., 1951-52; on loan as mem. working party mil. airfields NATO, 1952; dep. commr. gen., also dir. Expo '67, Montreal, 1963-68; v.p. adminstrn. McGill U., 1968-71; chmn. bd., dir. Found. Can. Engring. Corp., 1968-71; dep. minister environment Govt. Can., 1971-75; pres., dir. Monenco Pipeline Cons. Ltd., 1975-78; adv. N.S. Dept. Indsl. Devel., 1978—. Bd. govs. McGill U., 1964-68; bd. govs. U. N.B., 1973—, chmn., 1978—; bd. govs. Montreal Gen. Hosp., 1963—; pres. Canadian Assn. Mentally Retarded, 1963-65; bd. dirs. Montreal Internat. Music Competition, 1967—. Decorated companion Order Can., 1968; recipient Can. Centennial medal, 1967; citation Engring. News Record, 1967; Queen's Jubilee medal, 1977; registered profl. engr., Ont., Que. Fellow Engring. Inst. Can. (pres. 1975-76; Julian C. Smith award 1968); mem. Order Engrs. Que. (pres. 1953), Can. Council Profl. Engrs. (v.p. 1954, gold medal 1979), Grads. Soc. McGill U. (pres. 1964-65; Gold medal 1967), Assn. Profl. Engrs. Ont. (Gold medal 1968), Canadian Soc. Civil Engrs. Clubs: Royal Montreal Golf; Royal Ottawa Golf. Home: Apt C29 3980 Cote des Neiges Rd Montreal PQ H3H 1W2 Canada Office: PO Box 6088 Sta A Montreal PQ H5A 1E3 Canada. *Exploding population is creating a heavy demand on the world's resources. If species man is to survive and improve, he must innovate, mass produce, provide the additional energy required, and learn the value of interdependence. So far we are losing ground. The human reaction to these problems seems to be confrontation, conflict, fragmentation and increased social and economic nationalism. It is my hope that I may make a contribution to increasing productivity, better management and more interdependent action.*

SHAW, ROBERT NELSON, retail chain store exec.; b. Sault Ste. Marie, Mich., Jan. 23, 1912; s. Fred F. and Orpha L. (Lymburner) S.; A.B., U. Mich., 1934, M.B.A., 1935; m. Georgina L. Karlson June 23, 1937; 1 son, Frederick A. With Merc. Stores Co., Wilmington, Del., 1935-78, v.p. Glass Block Store, Duluth, Minn., 1947-48, pres., gen. mgr. McAlpin Co. store, Cin., 1948-64, also exec. v.p., dir. parent co., 1962-64, pres. parent co., 1964-72, chmn. bd., chief exec. officer, 1972-75, now dir., cons.; dir. Kroger Co., Cin. Bd. dirs. Cin. Retail Mchts., 1948-64, pres., 1956; pres. Cin. Credit Bur., 1958, chmn. bd., 1959-64; bd. dirs. Cin. Unlimited, Cin. Property Owners. Served to lt. USNR, 1944-46. Mem. Cin. C. of C., Navy League, Internat. Platform Assn., Newcomen Soc., Theta Xi. Mason (Shriner). Clubs: N.Y. Athletic, Union League; Kenwood Country; Old Pueblo, Skyline Country (Tucson); Le Mirador Country (Mt. Pelerin, Switzerland). Home: 4762 E Cherry Hills Dr Skyline Country Club Estates Tucson AZ 85718 Office: Merc Stores Co Inc 128 W 31st St New York City NY 10001

SHAW, RODRICK LUCIAN, judge; b. Milo, Iowa, Nov. 28, 1923; s. Reginald Arthur and Beulah (Green) S.; B.A. with high honors, Tex. Tech U., 1947; J.D., So. Meth. U., 1949; m. Bobbye Ruth Bockman, Aug. 21, 1949; children—Robin Rodrick, Luke Larkin. Admitted to Tex. bar, 1949; practiced in Amarillo, Tex, 1949-50, Lubbock, Tex., 1950-64; judge Lubbock County (Tex.), 1964—. Pres. bd. dirs. Wesley Found., 1954-57, Guadalupe Neighborhood Center, 1966-67; mem. U.S. Hwy. 87 Assn., 1965—; mem. campaign cabinet Lubbock United Fund, 1973-74; mem. Lubbock County Hist. Survey Com., 1966—; mem. Lubbock Community Planning Council, 1969-71; mem. adv. com. Tex. Urban Devel. Commn., 1970-71. Bd. dirs. YMCA, 1964-68, Lubbock Lake Site Inc., 1973—. Served with USNR, 1943-45. Mem. Lubbock County Bar Assn., West Tex. County Judges and Commrs. Assn. (pres. 1971), South Plains Assn. Govts. (pres. 1967-69). Mason (Shriner). Methodist (Sunday sch. tchr. 1954—, mem. ofcl. bd. 1971-74, charge lay leader 1968-69). Home: 2309 53d St Lubbock TX 79412 Office: 101 Courthouse Lubbock TX 79401

SHAW, RUSSELL BURNHAM, assn. exec., author; b. Washington, May 19, 1935; s. Charles Burnham and Mary (Russell) S.; B.A., Georgetown U., 1956, M.A., 1960; m. Carmen Hilda Carbon, July 19, 1958; children—Mary Hilda, Emily Anne, Janet, Charles, Elizabeth. Staff writer, Cath. Standard, Washington, 1956-57; reporter Nat. Cath. News Service, 1957-66; dir. publs., pub. info. Nat. Cath. Ednl. Assn., 1966-69; dir. Nat. Cath. Office for Info., 1969-73; asso. sec. for communication U.S. Cath. Conf., 1973-74; sec. for pub. affairs Nat. Conf. Cath. Bishops and U.S. Cath. Conf., 1975—; author sydicated newspaper column Arts of Leisure, 1965-67, monthly mag. columns Washington Report, 1966—, Washington Dispatch, 1967—, semi-monthly mag. column About Schs., 1967-69. Mem. Pub. Relations Soc. Am., Religious Pub. Relations Council. Roman Catholic. Club: National Press (Washington). Author: The Dark Disciple, 1961; Abortion and Public Policy, 1966; Abortion on Trial, 1968; Church and State, 1979; co-author: S.O.S. for Catholic Schools, 1970; Beyond the New Morality, 1974. Asso. editor New Patterns in Catholic Education, 1968; co-editor Catholic Education Today and Tomorrow, 1968; co-editor, contbr. Trends and Issues in Catholic Education, 1968. Contbr. articles to profl. jours. Home: 2928 44th Pl NW Washington DC 20016 Office: 1312 Massachusetts Ave NW Washington DC 20005

SHAW, SPENCER, gastroenterologist; b. N.Y.C., Apr. 28, 1946; s. Leo and Marjorie Alice (Goldstein) S.; A.B. with high distinction, U. Rochester, 1966, M.D. with honors, 1970; m. Joanne Bellafiore, June 28, 1971; children—Jonathan, Jennifer. Intern in medicine Mt. Sinai Hosp., 1970-71, resident in medicine, 1971-73, fellow in gastroenterology, 1973-75; staff physician Bronx VA Hosp., 1975—; asst. in medicine Mt. Sinai Sch. Medicine, 1974-75, instr., 1975-76, asso. in medicine, 1976-78, asst. prof. medicine, 1978—. Diplomate Am. Bd. Internal Medicine, Am. Bd. Gastroenterology. Mem. Research Soc. on Alcoholism, Am. Fedn. Clin. Research, Am. Assn. for Study Liver Disease, Alpha Omega Alpha. Home: 1245 Park Ave New York NY Office: Alcohol Research and Treatment Center Bronx VA Hosp 130 W Kingsbridge Rd New York NY 10468

SHAW, STANFORD JAY, educator; b. St. Paul, May 5, 1930; s. Albert G. and Belle (Jaffey) S.; B.A., Stanford, 1951; M.A., Princeton, 1955, Ph.D., 1958; M.A. (hon.), Harvard, 1966; m. Ezel Kural, June 6, 1967; 1 dau., Wendy Miriam Kural. Research fellow Center Middle Eastern Studies, Harvard, 1958-60, asst. prof. Turkish, 1960-65, asso. prof. Turkish history, 1965-68; prof. Turkish, Nr. Eastern history U. Calif. at Los Angeles, 1968—. Mem. exec. bd. Am. Research Inst. Turkey, 1964-68, 75—. Ford Found. fellow, 1955-58; Guggenheim fellow, 1966-67; fellow Am. Research Inst. Turkey, 1968, Royal Inst. Internat. Affairs, London, 1965, Nat. Endowment for Humanities, 1972-73. Mem. Middle East Studies Assn., Middle East Inst., Royal Asiatic Soc., Am. Hist. Assn., Internat. Soc. Oriental Studies, Turkish Hist. Soc. Author: The Financial and Administrative Organization and Development of Ottoman Egypt, 1517-1798, 1962; Ottoman Egypt in the Age of the French Revolution, 1966; The Budget of Ottoman Egypt, 1969; Between Old and New: The Ottoman Empire under Sultan Selim III, 1971; History of the Ottoman Empire and Modern Turkey, vol. 1 Empire of the Gazis: The Rise and Decline of Ottoman Empire 1280-1808, vol. 2 (with Ezel Kural Shaw) Reform, Revolution and Republic: The Rise of Modern Turkey 1808-1975, 1976-77. also articles. Editor in chief: Internat. Jour. Middle East Studies, 1968—. Office: History Dept U Calif Los Angeles CA 90024

SHAW, STANLEY MINER, bionucleonics scientist; b. Parkston, S.D., July 4, 1935; s. George Henry and Jensina (Thompson) S.; B.S., S.D. State U., 1957, M.S., 1959; Ph.D., Purdue U., 1962; m. Excellda J. Watke, Aug. 13, 1961; children—Kimberly Kay, Renee Denise, Elena Aimee. Instr., S.D. State U., 1960-62; asst. prof. bionucleonics Purdue U., West Lafayette, Ind., 1962-66, asso. prof., 1966-71, prof., 1971—. Recipient Lederle Pharmacy faculty awards, 1962, 65,

Parenteral Drug Assn. research award, 1970. Mem. Health Physics Soc., Am. Pharm. Assn., Acad. Pharmacy Practice (chmn. sect. nuclear pharmacy 1979—), Sigma Xi, Phi Lambda Upsilon, Rho Chi. Mem. Christian Ch. Contbr. sci. articles to profl. jours. Home: 610 Perry Ln West Lafayette IN 47906 Office: Sch Pharmacy Purdue U West Lafayette IN 47907

SHAW, STEVEN JOHN, educator; b. Hamilton, N.Y., Nov. 16, 1918; s. Constantine J. and Agnes (Tilicki) S.; B.S., N.Y. State U., 1941; M.S. in Retailing, N.Y. U., 1946, Ph.D., 1955; m. Aracelis Goberna, June 8, 1952. Instr. marketing U. Miami (Fla.), 1948-52; asst. prof. marketing Tulane U., 1954-55, U. Fla., 1955-57; asso. prof., prof. marketing U. S.C., Columbia, 1957—, dir. marketing, 1968—. Cons. Hoffman LaRoche, Nutley, N.J.; exec. sec. S.C.-Southwestern Colombia chpt. Partners of Ams., 1977—. Recipient N.Y. U. Founders Day award, 1956, Steven J. Shaw award for most scholarly article in Jour. Bus. Research. Mem. So. Marketing Assn. (pres. 1964), Beta Gamma Sigma (pres. 1965). Author: Salesmanship: Modern Viewpoints on Personal Communication, 1960; Marketing in Business Management, 1963; Cases in Marketing Management Strategy, 1971. Home: 4832 Forest Ridge Ln Columbia SC 29206 Office: Bull St Columbia SC 29208

SHAW, THELMA SKAGGS, social welfare vol.; b. Romont, W. Va., July 20, 1901; d. Edward Wallace and Lydia Goodridge (Spinks) Skaggs; A.B., W.Va. U., 1922; LL.D., W.Va. Wesleyan Coll.; m. Victor Shaw, July 24, 1928 (dec. 1928). Tchr. pub. schs., W.Va., Fla., Del., 1922-27; vol., speaker community affairs, 1932—; v.p. Assn. Jr. Leagues Am., 1938-40; mem. Nat. Conf. Social Welfare, 1938—, pres., 1960-61; v.p., sec. Family Service Assn. Am., 1958-60, mem. bd., 1949-62; sec. Nat. Social Welfare Assembly, 1958-60; mem. bd. Nat. Travellers Aid Assn., 1958-74, Internat. Social Service, 1958-64; mem. adv. Com. Nursing Project, So. Regional Edn. Bd.; chmn. vis. com. Sch. Nursing W.Va. U.; mem. Gov.'s Commn. for Nursing; mem. W.Va. Statewide Health Coordinating Council; awards com. W. Va. Welfare Conf., W.Va. League Nursing; chmn. citizens adv. com. Fairmont State Coll. Recipient Red Feather award United Community Funds and Councils Am., 1954; also awards Family Service Assn. Am., W.Va. Welfare Conf., others. Mem. A.A.U.W., Bus. and Profl. Womens Club, W.Va. League Women Voters, Jr. League (past pres.), Alpha Xi Delta, Beta Sigma Phi (hon.). Soroptimist. Home: 425 Morgantown Ave Fairmont WV 26554. *I am grateful for health, friends, freedom, the awareness of change and a degree of ability to adapt to it, the opportunity to participate in life around me and for the faith that keeps me going.*

SHAW, WALTER BURNS, constrn. co. exec.; b. N.Y.C., June 6, 1920; s. Walter Kelsey and Alma (Burns) S.; B.C.E., Cornell U., 1941; m. Beatrice Jean Scholl, Mar. 10, 1945; 1 son, Peter Lawrie. With Turner Constrn. Co., N.Y.C., 1940—, dir., 1961—, exec. v.p., 1968-71, pres., 1971-77, pres., chief exec. officer, 1977-78, chmn. bd., pres., 1978—; trustee Bowery Savs. Bank; dir. J. Ray McDermott & Co. Inc. Bd. dirs. Regional Plan Assn., N.Y.C.; trustee Lenox Hill Hosp. Served to lt. USNR, 1942-45. Mem. ASCE, Soc. Am. Mil. Engrs. Presbyn. Home: 799 Park Ave New York City NY 10021 Office: 150 E 42d St New York City NY 10017

SHAW, WILLIAM FREDERICK, statistician; b. Bklyn., Feb. 24, 1920; s. Charles Peter and Josephine Veronica (Seusing) S.; B.B.A., U. Miami, 1949; M.A., George Washington U., 1953; postgrad. studies in econometrics, math. and computer scis. U.S. Dept. Agr. Grad. Sch., 1964-74; Ph.D. (fellow), Walden U., 1977; m. Josephine Cannington Kerbey, Jan. 18, 1947; children—William Frederick, Teresa Anne. Research asst. U. Miami, 1948-49; with Research and Statistics div. FHA, Washington, 1950-73, chief statistician, 1969-73; chief statistician, dir. Advanced Statis. Analysis and Computer Applications Staff, HUD, 1974—; pres. Kerbey-Shaw Assos. Served with F.A., AUS, 1943-45. Decorated Bronze Star medal for heroism; recipient Superior Performance award HUD, 1977. Mem. Am. Statis. Assn., Am. Risk and Ins. Assn., Western Finance Assn., Am. Real Estate and Urban Econ. Assn., So. Econ. Assn., Va. Assn. Economists, Am. Econ. Assn., Am. Finance Assn., Assn. Computing Machinery, Am. Ednl. Research Assn., N.Y. Acad. Scis., Alpha Kappa Psi. Roman Catholic. Home: 6527 Byrnes Dr McLean VA 22101 Office: 7th and D Sts SW Washington DC 20411

SHAW, WILLIAM HENRY, educator; b. Durham, N.C., Aug. 6, 1902; s. Calvin High and Ora Mozelle (Bevers) S.; B.A., Duke, 1928, M.Ed., 1933; Ed.D., Auburn U., 1963; m. Mary Louise Carlton, June 1, 1929; children—William Henry, Carlton Reed. Tchr. Durham County (N.C.) schs., 1924-26, prin., 1926-30; prin. Needham Broughton High Sch., Raleigh, N.C., 1930-38; supt. Sumter (S.C.) City Schs., 1938-45; supt. edn. Muscogee County Sch. Dist., Columbus, Ga., 1945-73; prof. ednl. adminstrn. Columbus (Ga.) Coll., 1973—. Trustee Nat. Inf. Museum of Ft. Benning, 1970-75; bd. dirs. Museum Arts and Crafts, Columbus, 1950-75, Columbus YMCA, 1974—. Mem. Ga. Edn. Assn. (pres. 1955-56, Columbus Execs. (pres. 1947), Columbus C. of C. (life mem., dir. 1970-73), Am. Assn. Sch. Adminstrs. (life), N.E.A. (life). Phi Beta Kappa, Kappa Delta Pi, Phi Delta Kappa. Methodist. Rotarian (dist. gov. 1944-45). Home: 2870 Cromwell Dr Columbus GA 31906. *My life has been devoted to the service of mankind.... I have had many opportunities to leave the education field and go into business where I may have made considerable money, but the urge to serve outweighed all other attractions. I do not regret that I continued always where I thought I could be of most help to others.*

SHAW, WILLIAM VAUGHAN, architect; b. Los Angeles, Apr. 12, 1924; s. Norman Tooker and Elizabeth Allison (Kennedy) S.; student U. Calif. at Los Angeles, 1941-44; B.A. in Architecture, U. Calif. at Berkeley, 1950; m. Mary Morse, Sept. 14, 1967; stepchildren—Susan (Mrs. Kenneth Schley), Charles D. Osborne, Mary Lithgow Osborne, Ellen Osborne. Practice architecture, Carmel, Calif., 1951-55; partner Walter Burde, Burde Shaw & Assos., Carmel, 1955-69; founder, prin. Will Shaw & Assos., Monterey, Calif., 1969—. Pres. Calif. 7th Agr. Dist., 1964-65; founder, pres. Monterey County Citizens Planning Assn., 1960-65; chmn. design adv. com. Monterey County, 1960-65; exec. dir. Found. Environmental Design, 1963—; chmn. exec. com. Monterey Found., 1965-67, pres., 1972-73; bd. dirs. Pebble Beach Corp., 1976—; pres., founding mem. Big Sur Found., 1977—. Served to lt. USNR, 1944-47; PTO. Fellow Am. Acad. in Rome, 1968. Recipient Calif. Gov.'s award in environmental design for Shell Ser. Sta., Carmel, 1964, Urban Renewal Design Award Progressive Architecture mag., 1973. Mem. A.I.A. (pres. Monterey chpt. 1964, Honor award for Merchant Built houses 1968). Clubs: Old Capital, Pacific Biol. Lab. (Monterey). Home: 225A Cannery Row Monterey CA 93940 Office: 12 Prescot Ave Monterey CA 93940

SHAW, WILLIAM WHITFIELD, banker; b. Rocky Mount, N.C., July 30, 1903; s. Augustus Moore and Frances (Philips) S.; student U. of South, 1925, D.C.L., 1975; m. Burt Arrington Perry, Oct. 29, 1930. With Peoples Bank & Trust Co., Rocky Mount, 1931—, pres., 1954-67, chmn. bd., 1968-73; v.p., dir. Daniel's, Inc.; past v.p., dir. Carbisco Flour & Feed Co.; v.p., chmn. exec. com., dir. Rocky Mount Mills. Past chmn. Rocky Mount Zoning Commn., Rocky Mount Bus. Devel. Authority; past pres. Rocky Mount C. of C. Bd. dirs. Rocky Mount YMCA, Edenton Hist. Commn.; trustee, chmn. finance com. N.C. Wesleyan Coll.; trustee Thomas H. Battle Found.; pres. Park View Hosp., 1967-73, Braswell Meml. Library, 1951-53. Served with AUS, 1942. Recipient Disting. Citizenship award Rocky Mount C. of C., 1974. Mem. Am., N.C. (chmn. legis. com.) bankers assns., Phi Gamma Delta. Democrat. Episcopalian (past sr. warden). Rotarian (past pres. Rocky Mount). Club: Benvenue Country (Rocky Mount). Home: 513 Shady Circle Dr Rocky Mount NC 27801 Office: Peoples Bank & Trust Co Rocky Mount NC 27801

SHAW, WOODY HERMAN, jazz trumpeter, composer; b. Laurinburg, N.C., Dec. 24, 1944; s. Woody and Rosalie (Pegues) S.; m. Maxine Gregg; 1 son, Woody Louis Armstrong. Lead trumpet player Woody Shaw Quintet & Concert Ensemble; albums include: The Moontrane, 1976; Rosewood, 1978; Woody III, 1979. Nat. Endowment Arts grantee, 1977. Named #1 Trumpeter and #1 Album of year Downbeat Readers Poll, 1978; nominated for Grammy award (2), 1979. Office: 38 W 53d St New York NY 10019

SHAWAKER, WAYNE EDWARD, lawyer; b. Toledo, Oct. 7, 1903; s. Edward G. and Louisa C. (Schmidt) S.; A.B., U. Mich., 1925, J.D., 1927; m. Jeanne Eckhardt, June 23, 1928; children—Suzanne S. (Mrs. Allen D. Gutchess, Jr.), Stephen B. Admitted to Ohio bar, 1927, since practiced in Toledo. Chmn. Greater Toledo chpt. A.R.C., 1961-64; nat. chmn. Alumni Fund U. Mich., 1963; pres. Toledo Bd. Edn. 3 times. Bd. dirs. United Appeal, Flower Hosp., Lake Park Hosp. Recipient Distinguished Alumnus award U. Mich., 1959; Honor award Toledo Bar Assn., 1977. Clubs: Toledo, U. Mich. Alumni, Crestview (bd. dirs.), Inverness Country (Toledo); Lawyers (Ann Arbor, Mich.). Home: 3211 Kenwood Blvd Toledo OH 43606 also Eagle Point Rd Clark's Lake MI Office: Security Bldg Toledo OH 43604

SHAYNE, ALAN, TV prodn. co. exec.; b. Boston; s. Ralph and Bertha Shayne; student public schs., Mass. Actor, 1943-60; casting dir. David Merrick Prodns., 1961-62; producer Talent Assos., 1964-72; producer, creator Snoop Sisters TV series, 1973, House Without a Christmas Tree and various spls., 1972; v.p. spl. affairs Warner Bros. Inc., 1974, pres. TV programming, 1976—; v.p. talent CBS, 1975-76. Recipient Christopher award for House Without a Christmas Tree, 1973. Office: Warner Bros Inc 4000 Warner Blvd Burbank CA 91522

SHAYNE, NEIL T., lawyer; b. N.Y.C., May 2, 1932; s. Seymour S. and Mildred May (Isear) S.; student N.Y. U., 1949-51; LL.B., Bklyn. Law Sch., 1954; m. Marilyn Sorkin, Mar. 17, 1955; children—Mark, David, Jeffrey. Admitted to N.Y. bar, 1954, since practiced in Mineola; adj. asso. prof. bus. Adelphi U., 1972-75; dir. paralegal program L.I. U.; mem. faculty, program chmn. N.Y. State Trial Lawyers Acad., 1972—; asso. adj. prof. Hofstra U., 1977; faculty Am. Mgmt. Assn., N.Y. Law Jour. Pres., chmn. bd. Northeastern Title and Guarantee Co., 1968-71. Chmn. devel. adv. bd. Hofstra U. Law Sch., 1972-75; referee municipal ct. Kings County, N.Y., 1960-62, referee civil ct., 1965-69; adv. council Practicing Law Inst., 1973—. Democratic candidate for dist. ct. judge, 1963; treas. Nassau County Dem. Com., 1973. Trustee St. Joseph Hosp., Far Rockaway, N.Y., 1968-71; pres. Hewlett Park Civic Assn., 1961, Hofstra Law Sch. Assn., 1969—. Recipient award merit W.Va. Trial Lawyers Assn., 1971; guest of honor Hofstra Law Sch. reception, 1969, Mem. Nassau County Bar Assn. (legal edn. com.), Assn. Legal Assts. (certifying bd.). Author, editor jours. and procs. in field. Home: 171 S Middle Neck Rd Great Neck NY 11023 Office: 1501 Franklin Ave Mineola NY 11501

SHEA, DION WARREN JOSEPH, assn. exec., physicist; b. New London, Conn., June 10, 1937; s. Frank Steven and Violette Marie (Dion) S.; A.B., Sc.B. in Physics, Brown U., 1959; M.A. in Physics, Boston U., 1962; Ph.D., U. Colo., 1968; m. Mary Elizabeth Gingras, Sept. 10, 1960; children—Dion Warren Joseph, Nancy Wallace. Mem. tech. staff RCA, 1959-62; asst. prof. physics Creighton U., 1967-68; NRC/Environ. Sci. Services Adminstrn. fellow, research asso. Environ. Sci. Services Adminstrn., Boulder, Colo., 1968-70; dir. Soc. Physics Students, Am. Inst. Physics, 1970—, dir. edn. div., 1972-76. Active Boy Scouts Am. Fellow A.A.A.S.; mem. Am. Phys. Soc., Am. Assn. Physics Tchrs., Sigma Xi, Sigma Pi Sigma, Sigma Chi. Club: Appalachian Mountain. Author sci. articles. Home: 29 Spencer Ln Stony Brook NY 11790 Office: Am Inst Physics 335 E 45th St New York NY 10017

SHEA, DONALD JAMES, cosmetic co. exec.; b. Bronx, N.Y., Nov. 24, 1933; s. Andrew B. and Constance M. (Green) S.; A.B., Georgetown U., 1955; postgrad. Law Sch., Columbia U., 1955-56; m. Sarah O'Donnell, Feb. 9, 1957; children—Donald, Mary Ann, William, Robert, Joanna. With Boyle-Midway div. Am. Home Products Corp., N.Y.C., 1956-61, asst. to pres, 1959-60, product mgr., 1960-61; with Clairol, Inc., N.Y.C., 1961-66, 68—, dir. advt., 1968-71, v.p. advt., 1971-73, sr. v.p., haircolor, cosmetics and toiletries div., 1973, exec. v.p., corp., 1974-76, pres., 1977—; v.p. Bristol-Myers Co., 1977—; dir. sales and mktg. Clairol Ltd., London, 1966-68. Clubs: Creek (Locust Valley, N.Y.); Racquet and Tennis (N.Y.C.); Mill Reef (Antiqua, B.W.I.). Home: Brookville Rd Brookville NY 11545 Office: 345 Park Ave New York NY 10022

SHEA, DONALD RICHARD, educator; b. Mpls., July 15, 1926; s. John James and Marjorie (Jennings) S.; B.A., U. Minn., 1947, M.A., 1949, Ph.D., 1953; m. Mary Patricia Donovan, June 4, 1948; children—Barbara, John, Marjorie, Kathleen. Prof. polit. sci. U. Wis., Milw., 1949—, chmn. dept. polit. sci., 1958-62, dir. Inst. for World Affairs Edn., 1960-63, spl. asst. to chancellor, 1962-64, adminstr. Peace Corps Tng. Center, 1963—, dean Internat. Studies and Programs, 1964-70, dir. Center for Latin America, 1976—; dir. Inst. World Affairs, Summer Fgn. Student Seminar, 1962, 63, 71, 72; cons. Ford Found., 1967-68. Bd. dirs. World Affairs Council Milw., Inst. World Affairs, Milw. Internat. Student's Center. Served with USNR, 1944-46. Recipient Kiekhofer Meml. Teaching award, 1975. Mem. Am. Soc. for Internat. Law, Am. Polit. Sci. Assn., Midwest Latin Am. Assn. Author: The Calvo Clause: A Problem of Inter-American and International Law and Diplomacy, 1955. Editor: Business and Legal Aspects of Latin American Trade and Investment, 1976; sr. editor: Reference Manual on Doing Business in Latin America, 1979; contbr. to Ency. Americana. Home: 3346 N Summit Ave Milwaukee WI 53211

SHEA, EDWARD EMMET, chem. co. exec.; b. Detroit, May 29, 1932; s. Edward Francis and Margaret Katherine (Downey) S.; A.B., U. Detroit, 1954; LL.B., U. Mich., 1957; m. Ann Marie Conley, Aug. 28, 1957; children—Michael, Maura, Ellen. Admitted to Mich. bar 1957, N.Y. bar 1961; asso. firms Simpson Thacher & Bartlett, N.Y.C., 1960-63, Dykema, Wheat, Spencer, Goodnow & Trigg, Detroit, 1963-69, Cadwalader, Wickersham & Taft, N.Y.C., 1969-71; v.p., dir. Reichhold Chems., Inc., White Plains, N.Y., 1971—, chmn. bd., 1972—; officer, dir. Bluebeard's Castle, Inc., V.I., Reichhold Quimica de Mexico, S.A., Reichhold Chem. del Caribe, Inc., Reichhold Energy Corp., Henry Reichhold Found., 1972—; adj. prof. comml. law U. Detroit, 1965-69. Served as officer USAF, 1957-60. Mem. Phi Alpha Delta. Roman Catholic. Contbr. articles profl. jours. Office: Reichhold Chemicals Inc RCI Bldg White Plains NY 10602

SHEA, FRANCIS MICHAEL, lawyer; b. Manchester, N.H., June 16, 1905; s. Michael Francis and Margaret (Muldoon) S.; A.B., Dartmouth, 1925; LL.B., Harvard, 1928; m. Hilda Droshnicop, July 22, 1936; 1 son, Richard. Admitted to N.Y. bar, 1930, D.C. bar, 1946; on research project for Bernard Flexner, N.Y., 1928-29; asso. Slee, O'Brian, Hellings and Ulsh, Buffalo, 1929-33; chief of opinion sect., legal div., A.A.A., 1933-35; specialist, legal div. SEC, Feb.-July 1935; gen. counsel P.R. Reconstrn. Adminstrn., 1935-36; dean and prof. law U. Buffalo Law Sch., 1936-41 (on leave of absence, July 1939-Feb. 1941); asst. atty. gen. of U.S., 1939-Oct. 1945; asso. counsel for the prosecution of major Axis war criminals, 1945; mem. firm Shea & Gardner. Chmn. Atty. Gen.'s Com. on Bankruptcy Adminstrn., 1941-45, Jud. Conf. Com. Laws Pertaining Mental Disorders; dir. Joint Conf. Legal Edn., N.Y. State (exec. com. 1936-40). Mem. Am., New York State, D.C. bar assns., Assn. Bar City N.Y., D.C. Bar, Maritime Law Assn. Am. Law Inst. (life). Democrat. Roman Catholic. Clubs: Metropolitan, Univ., Cosmos, F Street (Washington). Contbr. to law jours. Home: 505 S Lee St Alexandria VA 22314 Office: 1800 Massachusetts Ave NW Washington DC 20036

SHEA, FRANCIS RAYMOND, clergyman; b. Knoxville, Tenn., Dec. 4, 1913; s. John Fenton and Harriet (Holford) S.; A.B., St. Mary's Sem., Balt., 1935; B.S.T., N.Am. Coll.- Gregorian U., Rome, Italy, 1939; M.A., Peabody Coll., Nashville, 1942; D.D., 1969. Ordained priest Roman Catholic Ch., 1939; tchr. Christian Bros. Coll. and Siena Coll., Memphis, 1940-45; prin. Father Ryan High Sch., Nashville, 1945-46; pastor Immaculate Conception Ch., Knoxville, 1956-69; named bishop Evansville, Ind., 1969, consecrated, 1970. Mem. planning bd. United Fund Agys., Knoxville, 1968-69. Bd. dirs. Buffalo Trace council Boy Scouts Am., Evansville, Child and Family Services, Knoxville. Office: 219 NW 3d St Evansville IN 47708*

SHEA, GEORGE BEVERLY, singer; b. Winchester, Ont., Can., Feb. 1, 1909; s. Adam Joseph and Maude (Whitney) S.; student Houghton Coll., 1928-29, D.F.A., 1956; D.Sacred Music, Trinity Coll., 1969; m. Erma Letta Scharfe, June 16, 1934; children—Ronald G., Elaine L. Came to U.S., 1928, naturalized, 1941. With Mut. Life N.Y., N.Y.C., 1929-38; announcer-singer radio sta. WMBI, Chgo., 1938-44; soloist ABC network Club Time, 1944-52; soloist Billy Graham crusades, U.S. and fgn. countries, 1947—, appearances include weekly NBC, ABC radio program The Hour of Decision, 3 a year TV series in U.S., Can., Australia; soloist weekly TV series, Can.; recorded 48 albums of hymns-spirituals RCA Victor, 1950-74, 4 albums Word Records, 1975—. Trustee Trinity Coll., Deerfield, Ill. Recipient Grammy award Nat. Acad. Rec. Arts and Scis., 1966; named to Gospel Music Hall of Fame, Nashville, 1978. Mem. AFTRA. Methodist. Composer song (words by R.H. Miller) I'd Rather Have Jesus, 1939, others; also compiler sacred song collections, GBS Favorites, 1957; The Crusade Soloist, 1963; (autobiography) The Sings My Soul, 1968; Songs That Lift The Heart, 1972. Office: Billy Graham Evangelistic Assn 1300 Harmon Pl Minneapolis MN 55403

SHEA, GEORGE WILLIAM, educator; b. Paterson, N.J., Oct. 7, 1934; s. George A. and Helen (Brueckmann) S.; B.A., Fordham Coll., 1956; M.A., Columbia, 1960, Ph.D., 1966; m. Shirley Ashton, Mar. 17, 1956; children—Sarah Kathleen, Susan Elizabeth, George Michael. Instr. classics Bklyn. Coll., 1966-67; asst. prof. Fordham U., 1967-70, asst. dean Fordham Coll., 1968-70, dean, asso. prof. Coll. at Lincoln Center, 1970—. Vice chmn. bd. dirs. Nat. Self-Govt. Com. Served to 1st lt. inf., AUS, 1956-57. Mem. Am. Philol. Assn., Am. Conf. Acad. Deans, N.Y. Classical Club. Home: 12 Zabriskie St Haledon NJ 07508 Office: 113 W 60th St New York NY 10023

SHEA, JACK, TV/film dir.-producer, writer; b. N.Y.C., Aug. 1, 1928; s. John F. and Mary (Maguire) S.; B.A., Fordham U., 1950; m. Patricia Carmody, Jan. 2, 1954; children—Shawn, Liz Ann, William, Michael, John Francis III. Stage mgr. NBC-TV, N.Y.C., 1950-52, asso. dir., Los Angeles, 1954-56, staff dir., 1956-59, contract producer/dir., 1959-61; freelance producer/dir., 1961—; prodns. include Bob Hope spls. 1956-68, Jerry Lewis spls., 1957-59, Glen Campbell Goodtime Hour, 1969-72, also Sanford and Son, Wonderful World of Disney, Hawaii Five-O, The Jeffersons, The Waltons, The Ropers, We'll Get By, Calucci's Department, others; films include Dayton's Devils, 1968, The Monitors, 1969. Served to 1st lt. USAF, 1952-54. Mem. Dirs. Guild Am. (4th v.p. 1967-71, sec. 1971-75, nat. bd. 1975—), Radio and TV Dirs. Guild (pres. Hollywood local 1958-60), Acad. TV Arts and Scis. (treas. 1977—), Caucus for Producers, Writers and Dirs. Office: SILKN Prodns care Freedman Kinzelberg & Broder 911 Gateway W Los Angeles CA 90067

SHEA, JAMES J., JR., toy, game and ednl. aids co. exec.; b. Springfield, Mass., Nov. 15, 1925; s. James J. and Henrietta (Delaney) S.; B.S. in Econs., Wharton Sch. Fin., U. Pa., 1949; m. Marisa Wealleans, Aug. 29, 1972; children by previous marriage—Thomas E., Carol A., James J., III, Barbara E. Shea Hatten, Christine H. With Milton Bradley Co., Springfield, 1949—, dir., 1957—, exec. v.p., 1963-67, pres., 1967—, chief exec. officer, 1969—, chmn. bd., 1972—; mem. Capital Funds Com.; dir., mem. exec. com. Valley Bank and Trust. Bd. dirs. Springfield Orch. Assn., Springfield Central Bus. Dist.; chmn. U.S. Savs. Bond Dr., Springfield; alumni trustee U. Pa.; trustee Wilbraham-Monson Acad., Wilbraham, Mass., New Eng. Colls. Fund; a founder Bus. Fund for Arts, Springfield. Served with USAF, 1943-45. Named Outstanding Young Man, C. of C. of Greater Springfield, 1959,; recipient Outstanding Citizens' award Jewish War Vets., 1968, William Pynchon award Advt. Club Springfield, 1976. Mem. Newcomen Soc. N. Am., Mass. Bus. Roundtable, Toy Mfrs. Am., Inc. (dir.), Lambda Chi Alpha. Clubs: Club Internat., Chgo. Athletic Assn. (Chgo.); Met., 200 Fifth Ave. (N.Y.C.); Les Ambassaduers, White Elephant Ltd., Annabels (London); Pa. U. Alumni. Office: 1500 Main St Springfield MA 01101

SHEA, JAMES J., JR., toy, game and ednl. aids co. exec.; b. Springfield, Mass., Nov. 15, 1925; s. James J. and Henrietta (Delaney) S.; B.S. in Econs., Wharton Sch., U. Pa.; m. Marilyn L. Hunderun, June 29, 1948; children—Thomas E., Carol A., James J. III, Barbara E., Christine H. With Milton Bradley Co., Springfield. 1955—, pres., 1967—, chief exec. officer, 1968—, chmn. bd., 1977—; vice chmn. bd. Playskool, Inc., pres., 1973—; chmn. Cap. Funds Com. mng. dir. MB Internat. N.V.; dir. Valley Bank & Trust Co.; adv. bd. Liberty Mut. Ins. Co.; trustee Springfield Five Center Savs. Bank. Active Joint Civic Agys., Future Springfield, Hampden Council; pres. United Fund Springfield; Bd. asso. trustees Regis Coll.; trustee Wilbraham Acad., Western New Eng. Coll. mem. pres.'s council Boston Coll.; lay adv. bd. St. Joseph Coll. Served with USAAF. Named Greater Springfield Outstanding Young Man, 1959; Outstanding Citizen, Greater Springfield Jewish War Vets., 1968. Mem. Toy Mfrs. Assn. Am. (dir.). Office: Milton Bradley Corp 1500 Main St Springfield MA 01115*

SHEA, JEREMIAH PATRICK, banker; b. Phila., Apr. 11, 1926; s. Jeremiah Francis and Bridget Margaret (McTiernan) S.; B.A., Yale U., 1946; M.A., Cath. U. Am., 1950; m. Mary Ann Robinson, Oct. 2, 1948; children—Mary, Jeremiah, Kathleen, Michael, John, Timothy, Daniel. Trainee, Fed. Res. Bank Phila., 1948-50; with Bank of Del., Wilmington, 1950—, pres., to 1980, chief exec. officer, chmn. bd., 1980—; instr. Am. Inst. Banking, 1955-69; mem. faculty Stonier Sch. Rutgers U., 1971-75. Vice pres. United Way; bd. dirs. St. Mark's High Sch. Served with USN, 1943-47. Certified comml. lender. Mem.

Robert Morris Assos., Am. Bankers Assn., Nat. Alliance Businessmen (chmn. local chpt.). Clubs: Wilmington Country, Yale of Del. Home: 2223 Old Orchard Rd Wilmington DE 19810 Office: 300 Delaware Ave Wilmington DE 19801

SHEA, JOHN JOSEPH, surgeon; b. Memphis, Sept. 4, 1924; s. John Joseph and Catherine (Flanagan) S.; B.S., Notre Dame, 1945; M.D., Harvard, 1947; grad. student U. Vienna (Austria), 1954; Ph.D. (hon.), Christian Bros. Coll., 1979; m. Gwyne Cooke Rainer, Mar. 12, 1949 (div. Sept. 1956); children—John Joseph III, Gwyn Rainer; m. 2d, Lynda Lee Mead, Dec. 26, 1964; children—Paul Flanagan, Susanna Mead, Peter Ryan. Intern Bellevue Hosp., N.Y.C., 1947-48; resident Mass. Eye and Ear Hosp., 1949-50; founder, 1952, since pres. Shea Clinic; founder Memphis Eye and Ear Hosp., 1967; clin. prof., dept otolaryngology and maxillofacial surgery U. Tenn.; cons. to surgeon gen. USN; cons. Kennedy VA Hosp., Memphis; spl. research removal stapes and replacement with artificial prothesis over vein graft for otosclerosis deafness. Served with USNR, 1943-45, to lt. (s.g.), M.C. 1950-52; now lt. comdr. Res. Decorated Order So. Cross (Brazil), 1962; recipient honors award Tenn. Speech and Hearing Assn., 1974. Diplomate Am. Bd. Otolaryngology. Mem. AMA, Pan Am., So., Tenn. med. assns., Am. Acad. Ophthalmology and Otolaryngology (1st Gold medal 1960), Acoustical Soc. Am., Am. Auditory Soc., Neuro-Otol. and Equilibiometric Soc., Am. Hearing Assn., Am. Assn. Mental Deficiency, Am. Triological Soc., Royal Soc. Medicine, French, Danish and Buenos Aires socs. otolaryngology, Australian Soc. Medicine (hon.), Memphis and Shelby County Med. Soc., Assn. Am. Physicians and Surgeons, Miss.-La. Soc. Ophthalmology and Otolaryngology (pres. 1978-79), Otosclerosis Study Club, Am. Council Otolaryngology, Pan Am. Assn. Oto-Rhino-Laryngology and Broncho-Esophagology, Australian, South African socs. otolaryngology, Am. Otol. Soc. Club: Centurian. Office: 1060 Madison Ave PO Box 4049 Memphis TN 38104

SHEA, JOHN MARTIN, JR., exec.; b. Santa Barbara, Calif., Nov. 14, 1922; s. John Martin and Karmel Kathryn (Knox) S.; B.A., U. Wash., 1944; m. Marion Abie; children—Michael Knox, Patrick Campbell, Katherine Martin. Vice pres., gen. mgr. Yaras & Co., Far East, Manila, P.I., Hong Kong, Tokyo, Japan, 1946-52; pres. Shea Oil Co., Pasadena, Calif., 1953-57; v.p., dir. Am. Petrofina, Inc.; sr. v.p. mktg., refining, transp., crude oil, dir. Am. Petrofina Co. of Tex., 1957-64; pres. Colonial Oil Products Co., Des Moines, Osmond Oil Co., Waco, Tex., 1958-64; chmn. bd. Freeman, Gossage & Shea, advt. and cons., San Francisco, 1964-65; chmn. bd., chief exec. officer Beacon Bay Enterprises Inc., Newport Beach, Calif., 1964—, Shea, S.A., Buenos Aires, Argentina, 1968—; dir. Commercebank, Newport Beach. Pres. bd. trustees Newport Harbor Art Mus., Newport Beach, Calif.; trustee Palm Springs Desert Mus. Served to lt. (j.g.) USNR, World War II. Office: Beacon Bay Bldg 260 Newport Center Dr Newport Beach CA 92660

SHEA, JOSEPH FRANCIS, mech. engr.; b. N.Y.C., Sept. 5, 1926; s. Joseph Anthony and Mary Veronica (Tully) S.; B.S. in Math., U. Mich., 1949, M.S. in Engring. Mechanics, 1950, Ph.D., 1955; m. Carol Dowd Manion; children from earlier marriage—Mary Linda Helt, Nancy Catherine, Patricia Ann Kelly, Elizabeth Carol Williams, Amy Virginia. Instr. engring. mechanics U. Mich., 1948-50, 53-55; research mathematician Bell Telephone Labs., 1950-53, mil. devel. engr., 1955-59; dir. advanced system research and devel., also mgr. Titan inertial guidance program AC Spark Plug div. Gen. Motors Corp., 1959-61; space program dir. Space Tech. Labs., 1961-62; dep. dir. systems, manned space flight NASA, 1962-63, mgr. Apollo spacecraft program office, Manned Spacecraft Center, 1963-67; v.p., dep. dir. engring. Polaroid Corp., Cambridge, Mass., 1967-68; v.p., gen. mgr. equipment div. Raytheon Co., Waltham, Mass., 1968—, sr. v.p., group exec., Lexington, Mass., 1975—. Served to ensign USNR, 1944-47. Recipient Arthur S. Flemming award U.S. Jr. C. of C., 1965. Fellow Am. Astronautical Soc., Am. Inst. Aeros. and Astronautics; mem. ASME, IEEE, Nat. Acad. Engring., Nat. Space Club. Home: 15 Dogwood Rd Weston MA 02193 Office: 141 Spring St Lexington MA 02173

SHEA, ROBERT MCCONNELL, lawyer; b. North Adams, Mass., May 28, 1924; s. Edward Michael and Margaret Frances (McConnell) S.; A.B. cum laude, Harvard U., 1948, LL.B., 1951; grad. sr. exec. program Mass. Inst. Tech., 1962. Admitted to Mass. bar, 1951; with John Hancock Mut. Life Ins. Co., Boston, 1951—, counsel, 1966-70, v.p., counsel, 1970—; Bd. trustees Laboure Jr. Coll., Boston, 1976—. Served with U.S. Army, 1943-46. Decorated Bronze Star medal. Mem. Am., Boston bar assns., Assn. Life Ins. Co., Am. Life Ins. Assn., Health Ins. Assn. Am. Republican. Catholic. Club: Harvard. Home: 146 Independence Dr Chestnut Hill MA 02167 Office: John Hancock Pl Post Office Box 111 Boston MA 02117

SHEA, STEPHEN MICHAEL, physician, educator; b. Galway, Ireland, Apr. 25, 1926; s. Stephen and Margaret Mary (Cooke) S.; came to U.S., 1956, naturalized, 1966; B.Sc. in Anatomy and Pathology, Univ. Coll., Galway Nat. U. Ireland, 1948; M.B., B.Ch. in Medicine, 1950, M.Sc. in Pathology, 1951, M.D., 1959. Intern, St. Vincent's Hosp., Dublin, Ireland, 1950-51; Dr. Keenan traveling scholar, dept. physiology Univ. Coll., London, 1951-53; asst. lectr. pharmacology Univ. Coll., Dublin, 1953-56; resident in pathology Mallory Inst. Pathology, Boston City Hosp., 1956-59, chief resident, 1958-59; asst. prof. pathology U. Toronto (Ont., Can.), 1959-61; instr. Harvard Med. Sch., 1961-63, instr. math. biology, 1963-65, asso. in pathology, 1965-67, asst. prof. pathology, 1967-70, asso. prof., 1970-73; asso. pathologist Mass. Gen. Hosp. and Shriners Burns Inst., both Boston, 1972-73; prof. pathology Coll. Medicine and Dentistry N.J.-Rutgers Med. Sch., 1973—. Diplomate Am. Bd. Pathology. Fellow Royal Coll. Pathologists (U.K.), Royal Coll. Physicians (Can.); mem. Am. Assn. Pathologists, Internat. Acad. Pathology, Am. Soc. Cell Biology, Biophys. Soc., Soc. Math. Biology, Microcirculatory Soc. Roman Catholic. Clubs: Harvard Travellers, Harvard of Boston. Contbr. articles to profl. publs. Home: 1050 George St Apt 12L New Brunswick NJ 08901 Office: Rutgers Med Sch Piscataway NJ 08854

SHEA, WILLIAM A., lawyer; b. N.Y.C., June 21, 1907; J.D., Georgetown U., 1931, L.H.D., 1971; L.H.D., St. Johns U., 1973, St. Francis Coll., 1974. Admitted to D.C. and N.Y. bars, 1932; now partner firm Shea & Gould, N.Y.C.; counsel liquidation bur. N.Y. State Banking Dept., 1934-36; asst. gen. counsel to supt. ins. N.Y. State, 1936-41; mem. N.Y. State Ins. Bd., 1956—; trustee, sec., gen. counsel Met. Savs. Bank; dir., gen. counsel Interboro Mut. Indemnity Ins. Co., N.Y.C.; dir. Asso. Madison Cos., Topps Chewing Gum Inc., N.Y.C., Diamond Internat. Corp., N.Y.C., Teleprompter Corp., N.Y.C. Office: 330 Madison Ave New York NY 10017

SHEAFFER, LOUIS, writer; b. Louisville, Oct. 18, 1912; s. Abraham and Ida (Jacobson) Slung; student U. N.C., 1930-31. Reporter Bklyn. Eagle, 1934-42, 46-47, movie critic, 1947-49, drama critic, 1949-55. Recipient Theater Library Assn.'s George Freedley award for O'Neill, Son and Playwright, 1969, Pulitzer prize biography for O'Neill, Son and Artist, 1974; Guggenheim fellow 1959, 62, 69; grantee Am. Council Learned Socs., 1960, 62, Nat. Endowment for Humanities, 1971-72. Author: O'Neill, Son and Playwright, 1968; O'Neill, Son and Artist, 1973. Home: 5 Montague Terr Brooklyn Heights NY 11201 Office: Little Brown & Co 34 Beacon St Boston MA 02106. *I believe that, in the long run, life is worthwhile and satisfying only when you work hard at something you really want to do and for which you have some ability.*

SHEAHAN, JOHN BERNARD, economist, educator; b. Toledo, Sept. 11, 1923: s. Bernard William and Florence (Sheahan) S.; B.A., Stanford, 1948; Ph.D., Harvard, 1954; m. Denise Eugénie Morlino, Nov. 29, 1946; children—Yvette Marie, Bernard Eugene. Econ. analyst Office Spl. Rep. in Europe, ECA, Paris, France, 1951-54; mem. faculty Williams Coll., 1954—, prof. econs., 1966—; mem. devel. adv. service Colombia adv. group Harvard, 1963-65; nat. research prof. Brookings Instn., 1959-60; vis. prof. El Colegio de Mexico, Mexico City, 1970-71; Fulbright research scholar Institut de recherche économique et de planification, Université de Grenoble (France), 1974-75. Mem. Presdl. Price Adv. Com., 1979—. Mem. Am. Econ. Assn., Latin Am. Studies Assn., Phi Beta Kappa. Author: Promotion and Control of Industry in Postwar France, 1963; The Wage-Price Guideposts, 1967; An Introduction to the French Economy, 1969. Home: Syndicate Rd Williamstown MA 01267

SHEALY, CLYDE NORMAN, physician; b. Columbia, S.C., Dec. 4, 1932; s. Clyde Lemuel and Palma Leona (Padget) S.; B.S. in Medicine, Duke U., 1956, M.D., 1956; Ph.D., Humanistic Psychology Inst., San Francisco, 1977; m. Mary-Charlotte Bayles, June 13, 1959; children—Brock Allison, Craig Norman, Laurel Elizabeth. Intern Duke U. Hosp., Durham, N.C., 1956-57; resident in neurosurgery Mass. Gen. Hosp., Boston, 1958-63; sr. instr., then asst. prof. neurosurgery Western Res. U. Med. Sch., 1963-66; chief neurosurgery Gundersen Clinic, LaCrosse, Wis., 1966-71; asso. clin. prof. neurosurgery U. Minn. Med. Sch., 1970-75; asst. clin. prof. U. Wis. Med. Sch., 1967-74; dir. Pain and Health Rehab. Center, S.C., LaCrosse, 1971—; bd. dirs. East West Acad. Healing Arts. Served with USNR, 1956-63. Fellow A.C.S., Am. Coll. Preventive Medicine; mem. AMA, Wis., LaCrosse County med. socs., Harvey Cushing Soc., Am. Holistic Med. Assn. (pres. 1978-80), Am. Assn. Study Headache, Wis. Heart Assn., Wis. Regional Med. Program Stroke Adv. Bd., Congress Neurol. Surgeons, Internat. Assn. Study Pain, Phi Beta Kappa, Alpha Omega Alpha. Author: Occult Medicine Can Save Your Life, 1975; The Pain Game, 1976; 90 Days to Self Health, 1977; also articles. Address: Route 2 Welsh Coulee La Crosse WI 54601

SHEAR, HAROLD EDSON, naval officer; b. N.Y.C., Dec. 6, 1918; s. Harold Edson Shear and Margaret Jane (Dillon) Shear Payne; stepson Kenneth H. Payne; B.S., U.S. Naval Acad., 1941; grad. Armed Forces Staff Coll., 1954, Nat. War Coll., 1965; m. Elizabeth Perry, Apr. 16, 1942; children—Kathleen Dillon, Kenneth Edward. Commd. ensign U.S. Navy, 1941, advanced through grades to adm., 1974; on destroyer and submarine assignments, World War II; comdg. officer U.S.S. Becuna, 1952-54, U.S.S. Patrick Henry, 1959-62, U.S.S. Sacramento, 1965-66; chief U.S. Naval Mission to Brazil, 1967-69; dir. submarine warfare Navy Dept., Washington, 1969-71, anti-submarine warfare, 1971-74; comdr. in chief U.S. Naval Forces in Europe, 1974-75; vice chief Naval Ops., Washington, 1975-77; comdr. in chief Allied Forces in So. Europe, 1977—. Decorated D.S.M. with gold star, Silver Star medal, Navy Commendation medal with gold star (U.S.) Order of Naval Merit (Brazil). Mem. U.S. Naval Inst., Mystic Marine Hist. Assn., Shelter Island Hist. Assn., Holly Soc. Am. Presbyterian. Club: N.Y. Yacht. Home: Shelter Island NY 11964 Office: Comdr in Chief Allied Forces So Europe FPO NY 09524

SHEARD, WILLIAM JAMES, credit agy. exec.; b. Woodmont, Conn., Dec. 6, 1925; s. William James and Martha Bernadina (Anderson) S.; B.C.S., Strayer Coll., Washington, 1948; m. Christlee Estep, July 26, 1947; 1 dau., Karen Leslie. With The Hecht Co., Washington, 1946-53, supr. machine accounting, 1948-51, div. mgr. control div., 1951-53; with Central Charge Service, Inc., Washington, 1953—, v.p. finance, 1963, dir., 1964—, exec. v.p., 1969—. Mem. Met. Washington Bd. Trade. Served with USAAF, 1943-45. Mem. Nat. Capitol Group of Controllers, Internat. Consumer Credit Assn., Washington Soc. Investment Analysts. Roman Catholic. Club: Falls Church Toastmasters (past pres.). Home: 2216 Toronto St Falls Church VA 22043 Office: 1215 E St NW Washington DC 20004

SHEARER, JESSE LOWEN, mech. engr., educator; b. Marengo, Ill., Apr. 25, 1921; s. Frank L. and Sarah A. (Ebert) S.; B.S., Ill. Inst. Tech., 1944; S.M., Mass. Inst. Tech., 1950, M.E., 1952, Sc.D., 1954; m. Jean Edith Mortensen, Sept. 10, 1944; children—Richard Michael, Ann Elizabeth, Douglas Ralph. Engr.-in-tng. Sundstrand Machine Tool Co., Rockford, Ill., 1939-44; mem. faculty and staff Mass. Inst. Tech., 1949-63, asso. prof. mech. engring., 1957-63, head control systems div., 1957-63; Rockwell Mfg. Co. prof. engring. Pa. State U., 1963-74, prof. mech. engring., 1974—; Gäst Forskare and lect. Svenska Textilforskningsinstitute, Chalmers Tekniska Högskolan Göteborg, Sweden, 1956-57; dir. spl. summer course fluid power control U. Calif. at Los Angeles, 1961; spl. lectr. fluid power control Svenska Teknologföreningen, Stockholm, Sweden, summer 1963; vis. prof. Tokyo Inst. Tech., 1969; guest scientist Royal Inst. Tech., Stockholm, summer 1970; chmn. Pa. Gov.'s Solid Waste Mgmt. Adv. Com., 1976-77; guest researcher Rheinischen-Westfälischen Technischen Hochschule, 1977; cons. in field to industry, govt. Served as officer USNR, 1944-46. Named Eminent Scholar and Tchr., Pa. State U., 1964; recipient Donald P. Eckman award Instrument Soc. Am., 1965; Ann. Achievement award Nat. Fluid Power Assn., 1972. Fellow ASME (Richards Meml. award 1966, exec. com. Boston 1961-63, exec. com. automatic control div. 1965-70, chmn. 1969, tech. editor jour. 1975—); mem. N.Y. Acad. Scis., Am. Soc. Engring. Edn., Instrument Soc. Am., Am. Inst. Aeros. and Astronautics, Am. Automatic Control Council (chmn. components com. 1961-63), Internat. Fedn. Automatic Control (chmn. tech. com. on components 1966-69), Sigma Xi, Tau Beta Pi, Pi Tau Sigma, Triangle. Elk. Author: (with Murphy, Richardson) Introduction to System Dynamics, 1967. Editor: (with Blackburn and Reethof) Fluid Power Control, 1960; cons. editor Addison-Wesley Pub. Co., 1961-69. Home: 136 Redwood Ln College Township PA 16801 Office: Mech Engring Bldg University Park PA 16802

SHEARER, JOHN CLYDE, educator; b. Phila., June 24, 1928; s. John Dwight and Edna Mildred (Moser) S.; student Cornell, 1945-46, 48-52; B.S., N.Y. State Sch. Indsl. and Labor Relations, 1952; postgrad. U. Manchester (Eng.), 1952-53; A.M., Princeton, 1958, Ph.D., 1960; m. Mary Ann Shafer, Apr. 30, 1955; children—John Peter, Rachel Alicia. Adminstrv. asst. indsl. relations Union Carbide Metals Co., Marietta, Ohio, 1952-56; research asst. indsl. relations Princeton, 1957-60; asst. prof. econs. Grad. Sch. Indsl. Adminstrn. Carnegie Inst. Tech., Pitts., 1960-65; asso. prof. econs. Pa. State U., State College, 1965-67; prof. econs., dir. Manpower Research and Tng. Center Okla. State U., Stillwater, 1967—. Labor arbitrator, 1965—; prof., economist Latin Am. Inst. Econ. and Social Planning, UN Econ Commn. for Latin Am., Santiago, Chile, 1962-63; cons. OAS, UN, Ford Found., Inter-Am. Devel. Bank, Council Internat. Progress in Mgmt., ILO, A.M.A., others; mem. arbitration panels Fed. Mediation and Conciliation Service, Pub. Employment Disputes Settlement Panel. Mem. for edn. Southwestern Regional Manpower Adv. Com. to Secs. Labor and HEW. Served with USMC, 1946-48. Fulbright fellow, Eng., 1952-53; Owen D. Young fellow, 1956-57, 57-58; Ford Found. fellow, 1958-59. Mem. Am. Econ. Assn., So. Econ. Assn., Okla. Civil Liberties Union, Indsl. Relations Research Assn., Soc. Internat. Devel., Nat. Acad. Arbitrators, Am. Arbitration Assn. (labor arbitration panels). Author: High-Level Manpower in Overseas Subsidiaries: Experience in Brazil and Mexico, 1960; La Importación y La Exportación de Los Recursos Humanos, 1964; (with Jacob Kaufman, Grant Farr) The Development and Utilization of Human Resources, 1967; Industrial Relations of American Corporations Abroad, 1967; (with Rafael Isaza) Employment and Unemployment in Colombia, 1969; Manpower Environments Confronting American Firms in Western Europe, 1970; Intra and International Movements of High-Level Human Resources, 1971; High-Level Human Resources in Economic Development, 1973; Arbitration and Changing Life Styles, 1974; Fact and Fiction Concerning Multinational Labor Relations, 1977; contbr. articles to profl. jours. Home: 2020 Crescent Dr Stillwater OK 74074

SHEARER, OTIS CLAUDE, III, lawyer; b. Beaver, Okla., Sept. 2, 1940; s. Otis Claude, Jr., and Rheba Eloise (Pate) S.; B.A., U. Tex., 1962, J.D., 1967; student Law Sch., Washburn U., 1963-65; m. Bonita Claudine Kliewer, Nov. 29, 1968; children—Claudia Ann, Cathy Jo. Admitted to Tex. bar, 1967; asso. Lemon, Close & Atkinson, 1967-70; partner Lemon, Close, Atkinson, Shearer & McCutcheon, Booker and Perryton, Tex., 1971—; city atty., Booker, 1968—; county atty. Lipscomb County, Tex., 1969-75. Served with USAF, 1962-65. Cert. in civil trial law Tex. Bd. Legal Specialization. Mem. N.E. Panhandle Bar Assn. (pres. 1973), Phi Kappa Tau, Delta Theta Phi. Methodist. Club: Booker Booster (pres. 1971). Home and office: Box 188 Booker TX 79005

SHEARER, RICHARD EUGENE, coll. pres.; b. Connellsville, Pa., Dec. 30, 1919; s. H.D. and Florence (Prinkey) S.; A.B., Eastern Bapt. Coll. and Sem., Phila., 1943, D.D., 1953; B.D., New Brunswick Theol. Sem., 1945; M.A., Columbia, 1948, Ed.D., 1959; LL.D., Denison U., 1958; H.H.D., Bishop Coll., 1977; m. Ruth Mansberger, June 16, 1944; children—Patricia (Mrs. Richard Wilson), Suzanne (Mrs. Terry Jones), Richard J. Ordained to ministry Bapt. Ch., 1943; minister, Atlantic Highlands, N.J., 1943-45, New Brunswick, N.J., 1945-5O; pres. Alderson-Broaddus Coll., Philippi, W.Va., 1951—; lectr. Mex. Pastor's Conf., summer 1955; pres. W.Va. Found. Ind. Colls.; mem. Commn. on Instnl. Funding, Am. Bapt. Chs., U.S.A.; coordinator Central Europe Coll. Program; pres. Am. Bapt. Assn. Sch. and Coll. Adminstrs., 1977. Mem. W.Va. Ednl. Found., W.Va. State Scholarship Commn. Bd. regents W.Va. Assn. Pvt. Colls. Trustee Broaddus Hosp. Named Phi Delta Kappa Profl. Educator of Year, 1964. Mem. Am. Assn. Sch. Adminstrs., W.Va. Assn. Coll. and Univ. Presidents (sec. mem. exec. com. 1963—), Assn. Am. Colls. (commn. coll. and soc.). Kiwanian. (past pres. Philippi). Address: Alderson-Broaddus Coll Philippi WV 26416. *The joint impact of good religion and good education has been the dominant theme of my life and work. I feel that education is a powerful force which can be directed in either constructive or destructive directions-good religion can assure that the power in education is constructive.*

SHEARER, RONALD ALEXANDER, economist; b. Trail, B.C., Can., June 15, 1932; s. James Boyd and Mary Ann (Smith) S.; B.A., U. B.C., 1954; M.A., Ohio State U., 1955, Ph.D., 1959; m. Renate Elisabeth Selig, Dec. 20, 1956; children—Carl, Bruce. Asst. prof. econs. U. Mich., 1958-62; economist Royal Commn. Banking and Finance, Toronto, 1962-63; mem. faculty U. B.C., Vancouver, 1963—, prof. econs., 1970—, head dept., 1972-76. Mem. Am., Canadian econs. assns., Royal Econ. Soc. Co-author: The Economics of the Canadian Financial System, 1972; Money and Banking, 1975. Editor: Trade Liberalization and a Regional Economy, 1971. Office: Dept Economics Univ BC Vancouver BC V6T 5 Canada

SHEARER, THADDEUS ERRINGTON, artist, cartoonist; b. Jamaica, W.I., Nov. 1, 1919; s. Samuel and Sophie Ruby (Parnell) S.; student Art Students League, Pratt Inst.; m. Phyllis Wildman, Dec. 23, 1945; children—John, Kathleen Shearer Maynard. Free lance cartoonist; illustrator Caravel Motion Picture Co.; art dir. Batten, Burton, Durstine & Osborn; syndicated cartoonist King Features Syndicate, N.Y.C., daily comic strip Quincy, mem. syndicated panel Next Door; artist Billy Joe Jive Super Pvt. Eye, childrens book series Dell Pub. Co., also presented on ednl. television program Sesame Street; art cons. Westchester County Pub. Schs. Served with inf., AUS, 1942-45. Decorated Bronze Star; recipient Gombart's award, Art Dirs. awards, Achievement award Nat. Assn. Minority Bankers; Art Students League scholar. Mem. Nat. Cartoonists Soc., Comics Council, Cartoonists Museum, Found. of Westchester Clubmen. Address: Route 1 Box 21 Tatumuck Rd Pound Ridge NY 10576

SHEARIN, JESS STEWART, JR., food ser. co. fin. exec.; b. Unionville, Tenn., May 18, 1934; s. Jess Stewart and Nettie Vaughn (Read) S.; B.S., Middle Tenn. State U., 1970; m. Sara Elizabeth Pewitt, Oct. 10, 1954 (div. 1975); 1 dau., Sandra Joyce. Jr. acct. Ernst & Ernst, Nashville, 1960-61; staff acct. Associates Capital, Nashville, 1961-68; asst. controller Ky. Fried Chicken Corp., Louisville, 1968-71; controller Shoney's Inc., Nashville, 1971-74, sec.-treas., 1974—. Mem. steering com. Howard Baker for Pres., 1979-80. Served with USAF, 1954-58. C.P.A., Tenn. Mem. Tenn. Soc. C.P.A.'s, Am. Inst. C.P.A.'s, Nat. Accts. Soc. (cert.). Republican. Baptist. Club: Rotary. Home: 2962 Brantley Dr Nashville TN 37013 Office: 1727 Elm Hill Pike Nashville TN 37202

SHEARING, GEORGE ALBERT, pianist, composer; b. London, Eng., Aug. 13, 1920; s. James Philip and Ellen Amelia (Brightman) S.; student Linden Lodge Sch. for Blind, London; m. Beatrice Bayes, May 1, 1941; 1 dau., Wendy Ann. Came to U.S., 1947, naturalized, 1956. Vice pres. Shearing Music Corp. Composer Lullaby of Birdland, numerous other popular songs; recs. English Decca and Parlophone, Am. Savoy, London, MGM Capital, Sheba Records. Bd. dirs. Guide Dogs for Blind, San Rafael, Hadley Sch. for Blind, Winnetka, Ill. Voted top English pianist, 1941-47; winner all Am. jazz polls, also many pvt. awards; recipient Golden Plate award Am. Acad. of Achievement, 1968. Mem. Broadcast Music Inc. Club: Bohemian (San Francisco). Office: ABC 9595 Wilshire Blvd Beverly Hills CA 90212*

SHEAROUSE, HENRY GRADY, JR., librarian; b. Sardis, Ga., May 2, 1924; s. Henry Grady and Byrdice (Askew) S.; B.S., Ga. Tchrs. Coll., Statesboro, 1945; A.B., Emory U., 1947; M.S., U. Ill., 1949. Tchr., Swainsboro (Ga.) Pub. Schs., 1945-46; reference asst. Savannah (Ga.) Pub. Library, 1946-48; research asst. in testing U. Ill., 1948-49; head reference dept. Atlanta Pub. Library, 1949-53; dir./spl. asst. to dir. Ga. Pub. Library Service, 1953-55; dir. Regional Library Service Center N.Y. State Library, Watertown, 1955-56; asso. supr. library extension div., 1957-63; asst. librarian, dir. pub. services Denver Pub. Library, 1963-69, librarian, 1969—. Cons. Colo. State Library, 1959, Lower Merion Twp., Pa., 1960, Delaware County Commrs., Pa., 1963; bldg. cons. Longmont (Colo.) Pub. Library, 1970, Westchester Library System, Mt. Vernon, N.Y., 1966; mem. Internat. Assn. Met. City Libraries, 1969—; mem. Colo. Council for Library Devel., 1971-74, chmn., 1972-74; mem. exec. bd. Adult Edn. Council Met. Denver, 1969—, v.p., 1972-73, pres., 1974-76; mem. bd. Bibliog. Center for Research, Rocky Mountain Region, 1969-75. Bd. dirs. Greater Denver Council for Arts and Humanities, 1970-73, treas., 1970-72. Mem. Am., Colo., Mountain Plains library assns. Home:

1285 Glencoe St Denver CO 80220 Office: 1357 Broadway Denver CO 80203

SHEASBY, EDWARD GORDON, pipeline co. exec.; b. Redcliff, Alta., Can., Mar. 5, 1925; s. Henry Gordon and Mary Jane (Webb) S.; LL.B., U. B.C., 1952; m. Dorothea F. M. Bussman, Aug. 28, 1954; children—Patricia Jane, Henry Gordon, Charlotte Maria, Bruce R. Admitted to B.C. bar, 1953, Ont. bar, 1969; asso. firm Campbell, Brazier & Co., Vancouver, B.C., 1953-55; sr. solicitor, asst. sec. Trans Mountain Oil Pipe Line Co., Vancouver, 1955-66; asst. gen. counsel Inter-Provincial Pipe Line, Ltd., Toronto, Ont., 1966-72, gen. counsel, 1972—, asst. sec., 1967-73, sec., 1973-77, v.p., 1977—; sec. Lakehead Pipe Line Co., Superior, Wis., 1973—; dir. IXL Industries & Assos. Cos., Medicine Hat., Alta. Served with Canadian Navy, 1942-47. Mem. Law Socs. B.C. and Ont. Clubs: Masons, Univ. (Toronto). Home: 3708 Beechhollow Crescent Mississauga ON C4Y 3T2 Canada Office: PO Box 48 1 First Canadian Pl Toronto ON M5X 1A9 Canada

SHEATS, PAUL HENRY, educator; b. Tiffin, Ohio, Dec. 5, 1907; s. Edward Hamlin and Katherine Ann (Koch) S.; A.B., Heidelberg Coll., Tiffin, 1929; A.M., Columbia, 1930; Ph.D., Yale, 1936; LL.D., U. Akron, 1966; m. Dorothea Burns, 1929; 1 son, Paul Douglas; m. Helen Johnson Taylor, Nov. 21, 1942 (dec. June 1967); children—Peter Warren, Michael Clarron; stepchildren—Vern Taylor, Marion; m. June Maseeger Dow, June 16, 1967. Instr. govt. N.Y. State Coll. for Tchrs., Albany, 1930-34; instr. dept. edn. Yale, 1934-36; dir. Fed. Forum Project, Chattanooga, 1936-37; adminstrn. asst. Fed. Forum Demonstration, U.S. Office Edn., 1937-39; asst. prof. edn. U. Wis., 1939-42; head adult edn. sect. OWI, 1942-43; dir. New Tools for Learning, N.Y.C., 1943-44; ednl. dir. Town Hall, Inc., N.Y.C., 1944-46; asso. dir. Univ. Extension, U. Calif., 1946-57, dir., 1957-58, univ. dean, 1958-67; asso. prof. edn. U. Calif., Los Angeles, 1946-49, prof. edn., 1949-75, prof. emeritus, 1975—; vis. prof. edn. U. Judaism, 1976, 77; Kellogg resident fellow Oxford U. Extra-Mural Delegacy, spring 1967; cons. Ford Found. Fund Adult Edn., 1951; sr. cons. So. Regional Edn. Bd., 1970-73; adv. com. on adult edn. Calif. Dept. Edn., 1968-70. Mem. UNESCO Nat. Commn., 1950-56, vice chmn. exec. com., 1954-56, U.S. del. UNESCO conf adult edn., Elsinore, Denmark, 1949, Montreal, 1960, U.S. del. 7th Gen. Conf., Paris, 1952; mem. Pres.'s Panel on Vocational Edn., 1961-62; chmn. AID Evaluation Panel for World Edn., 1973. Bd. dirs. Nat. Tng. Labs., 1961-64; chmn. bd. dirs. Internat. Coll., 1970-72; adv. bd. trustees City U. Los Angeles, 1979—. Recipient Delbert Clark award, 1970; Los Angeles Human Relations Commn. cert. of merit, 1979. Fellow Nat. Univ. Extension Assn. (dir. 1958-64, pres. 1962-63, Julius M. Nolte award 1975); mem. N.E.A. (pres. dept. adult edn. 1942-44), Am. Ednl. Research Assn., Adult Edn. Assn. U.S. (pres. 1953-54), Assn. State Univs. and Land Grant Colls. (exec. com. 1963-66), UCLA Emerti Assn. (pres. 1977-78), Guild of Tutors. Club: Faculty. Author: (with R.W. Frederick) Citizenship Education Through the Social Studies, 1936; (with J.W. Studebaker, C.S. Williams) Forums for Young People, 1937; Education and the Quest For a Middle Way, 1938; Forums on the Air, 1939; (with R. Spence, C. Jayne) Adult Education, 1953; (with James Farmer, J. David Deshler) Developing Community Service and Continuing Education Programs in California Higher Education Institutions, 1972; Developing Community Services in the Seventies: New Roles for Higher Education, 1975. Editor: Adult Education Bull., 1940-42; editorial bd. Lifelong Learning, The Adult Years, 1977—. Contbr. to Foundations of Education (Kneller), 1963, 67, 70; Handbook of Adult Education in the U.S. 1960, 1970; Materials and Methods in Adult Education, 1972, 76. Home: 11490 Laurelcrest Dr Studio City CA 91604 Office: Grad Sch Edn U Calif at Los Angeles Los Angeles CA 90024. *As a practitioner for many years in the field of adult continuing education, I have lived to see lifelong education accepted as a necessity by countries with many different political systems and cultural heritages. I have become more and more convinced that, in a free society intent upon remaining free, lifelong learning must be embraced as the major instrument through which the processes of self-government can be maintained.*

SHEATSLEY, PAUL BAKER, survey research dir.; b. N.Y.C., Aug. 3O, 1916; s. Paul Weidner and Nina Genevieve (Baker) S.; A.B., Princeton, 1936; m. Priscilla Ward Jones, May 25, 1940 (div. 1947); children—Pamela, Jo Ann (Mrs. Norman Cope); m. 2d, Natalie Bennett, May 31, 1947; 1 dau., Victoria. Editor, Boonton (N.J.) Tribune, 1937-39; pub. relations dir. Newark Internat. Baseball Club, 1939; dir. field staff Audience Research Inst., 1940-42; Eastern rep. Nat. Opinion Research Center, U. Chgo., 1942-63, dir. survey research service, 1963—, acting dir., 1970-71. Dir. field work wartime morale studies for OWI, 1942-44, studies Am. attitudes toward fgn. policy issues for State Dept., 1945-57; dir. nat. ambulatory med. care survey Nat. Center for Health Statistics, 1973—. Bd. dirs. Roper Center for Pub. Opinion Research. Mem. Am., (pres. 1967-68), World assns. for pub. opinion research, Soc. Psychol. Study Social Issues, Am. Sociol. Assn., Am. Pub. Health Assn. Editorial staff Record Research, 1961—; co-editor Blues Research, 1959-74; asso. editor Am. Social Rev., 1967-68. Contbr. to Ency. Americana, articles to profl. jours. Home: 1700 E 56 St Chicago IL 60637 Office: 6030 S Ellis Ave Chicago IL 60637 also 817 Broadway New York NY 10003

SHEBESKI, LEONARD HYLARY, univ. adminstr., geneticist; b. Aubigny, Man., Can., Aug. 5, 1914; s. Michael and Amelia S.; B.S.A., U. Man., Winnipeg, 1941, M.Sc., 1946; D.Sc. (hon.), Agrl. U., Warsaw, Poland, 1972; D.Sc. (hon.), Queen's U., Kingston, Ont., Can., 1974; LL.D. (hon.), U. Sask. (Can.), 1976; m. Laura, May 26, 1945; children—Janice, Elaine, Peggy, Kathy. Asst. prof. field husbandry U. Sask., Saskatoon, 1947, asso. prof., 1948-53; prof. plant sci., head dept. plant sci. U. Man., 1953-65, dean Faculty Agr., 1965—; chmn. Man. Research Council. Exec. v.p. Red Cross Soc., Winnipeg; mem. health services subcom. United Way of Greater Winnipeg. Served with RCAF, 1941-45. Decorated Mention-in-dispatches, officer Order Can.; recipient Alumni Jubilee award U. Man., 1966, Centennial medal Can., 1967. Fellow Agrl. Inst. Can., Royal Soc. Can.; mem. Can. Agrl. Research Council, Genetics Soc. Can. (hon. life), Can. Soc. Agronomy, AAAS, Assn. Sci., Engring. and Tech. Community Can., Internat. Inst. Tropical Agr. (Nigeria) (trustee), Can. Seed Growers' Assn. (hon. life), Lenin All-Union Acad. Agrl. Sci. (USSR) (fgn.). Contbr. numerous articles to profl. publs. Home: PO Box 97 Sanford MB R0G 2J0 Canada Office: Faculty Agr U Man Winnipeg MB R3T 2N2 Canada

SHECKELS, G. DALE, educator; b. Seattle, Jan. 11, 1917; s. Glenn and Lenore (Kohler) S.; B.S. in Elec. Engring., U. Wash., 1938, M.S., Mass. Inst. Tech., 1940; Ph.D., Iowa State U., 1955; m. Dorothy Jensen, Apr. 5, 1945; children—Thomas Glenn, William James. Engr., U.S. Bur. Fisheries, 1938-39, Standard Oil Co. Calif., 1939, Puget Sound Power & Light Co., 1940-41; instr. elec. engring. U. Wash., 1941-42; staff mem. Radiation Lab., Mass. Inst. Tech., 1942-45; from asst. prof. to prof. elec. engring. Mont. State U., 1945-59; prof. elec. engring. U. Mass., 1959—, chmn. dept., 1959-72; summer engr. Gen. Electric Co., 1957, Martin Co., Denver, 1959, autonetics div. N.Am. Aviation Co., 1960; cons. Holyoke Water Power Co., 1964-69. Chmn., Amherst Town Fin. Com., 1967-70; mem. Mass. Bd. Registration Profl. Engrs. and Land Surveyors, 1976—. Mem. I.E.E.E. (sr. mem., chmn. Springfield sect. 1966-67), Am. Soc. Engring. Edn., Eta Kappa Nu, Sigma Xi, Tau Beta Pi. Baptist. Mason. Rotarian. Contbr. articles to profl. jours. Patentee motor control system. Home: 93 Cherry Ln Amherst MA 01002

SHEDD, MARK REDANS, govt. ofcl.; b. Quincy, Mass., June 1, 1926; s. Guy Vaughn and Sarah Kathryn (Redans) S.; A.B., U. Maine, 1950, M.Ed., 1954, LL.D. (hon.), 1969; Ed.D., Harvard U., 1960; hon. degrees: LL.D., Coll. Wooster, 1970, Bates Coll., 1971, Litt.D., Drexel U., 1970; m. Shirley Greene, Oct. 18, 1968; children—Lynne Shedd Simonds, Mark Daniel, Dale Shedd Whitesell, Nancy Shedd Scott, Kim, Andrew Christopher. Ednl. adminstr. public schs., Bangor, Caribou and Auburn, Maine, 1950-60; rural dist. supt. Conn. Dept. Edn., 1960-62; supt. schs., Englewood, N.J., 1962-67, Phila., 1967-71; vis. prof. edn. Harvard U. Grad. Sch. Edn., Cambridge, Mass., 1972-74; commr. edn. State of Conn., Hartford, 1974—. Trustee, Hazen Found., U. Conn.; mem. exec. com. Conn. Public TV Corp.; mem. Conn. State Tchrs. Retirement Bd., Conn. State Library Bd. Served with USN, 1944-46. Recipient A. Philip Randolph award Negro Trade Union Leadership Council, Phila., 1968; Man of Year award Ednl. Equality League Phila., 1971; Disting. Service award Phila. Urban Coalition, 1972. Mem. Council Chief State Sch. Officers, Am. Assn. Sch. Adminstrs., Nat. Urban Coalition, NAACP, Harvard Grad. Sch. Edn. Alumni Council, Phi Delta Kappa. Democrat. Contbr. articles to profl. jours. Office: State Dept Edn Box 2219 Hartford CT 06115

SHEED, WILFRID JOHN JOSEPH, author; b. London, Eng., Dec. 27, 1930; s. Francis Joseph and Maisie (Ward) S.; came to U.S. 1947; B.A., Lincoln Coll., Oxford U., 1954, M.A., 1957; m. Miriam Ungerer; children—Elizabeth, Francis, Marion. Movie reviewer Jubilee mag., 1959-61, asso. editor, 1959-66; drama critic, former book editor Commonweal mag., N.Y.C.; movie critic Esquire magazine, 1967-69; vis. prof. Princeton, 1970-71; judge, mem. editorial bd. Book of Month Club, 1972—. Guggenheim fellow, 1971-72. Mem. P.E.N. Club. Roman Catholic. Author: A Middle Class Education, 1961; The Hack, 1963; Square's Progress, 1965; Office Politics, 1966; The Blacking Factory, 1968; Max Jamison, 1970; The Morning After, 1971; People Will Always Be Kind, 1973; Three Mobs: Labor, Church, and Mafia, 1974; Transatlantic Blues, 1978; The Good Word, 1979; editor: G. K. Chesterton's Essays and Poems, 1957. Contbr. articles to popular mags. Address: Sag Harbor NY 11963

SHEEHAN, DANIEL EUGENE, bishop; b. Emerson, Nebr., May 14, 1917; s. Daniel F. and Mary Helen (Crahan) S.; student Creighton U., 1934-36, LL.D. (hon.), 1964; student Kenrick Sem., St. Louis, 1936-42; J.C.D., Cath. U. Am., 1949. Ordained priest Roman Cath. Ch., 1942; asst. pastor, Omaha, 1942-46; chancellor Archdiocese Omaha, 1949—, aux. bishop Omaha, 1964-69; archbishop of Omaha, 1969—. Pres. Canan Law Soc. Am., 1953; del. 3d session Ecumenical Council, Rome, Italy, 1964; chaplain Omaha club Serra Internat., 1950—. Office: 100 N 62d St Omaha NE 68132*

SHEEHAN, DENNIS WILLIAM, lawyer; b. Springfield, Mass., Jan. 2, 1934; s. Timothy A. and H. Marjorie (Kelsey) S.; B.S., U. Md., 1957; J.D. Georgetown U., 1960; LL.M., 1962; m. Elizabeth M. Hellyer, July 27, 1957; children—Dennis William, Catherine Elizabeth, John Edward. Admitted to D.C., Md. bars, 1960, Mo. bar, 1976, Ohio bar, 1977; legal asst. to chmn. NLRB, Washington, 1960-61; trial atty. U.S. SEC, Washington, 1962-63; corporate atty. Martin Marietta, Balt., N.Y.C., 1963, 64; v.p., gen. counsel, sec. Bunker Ramo Corp., Oak Brook, Ill., 1964-73; exec. v.p., gen. counsel, dir. Diversified Industries, Inc., St. Louis, 1973-75; v.p., gen. counsel, dir. N-ReN Corp., Cin., 1975-77; v.p., gen. counsel, sec. Bliss & Laughlin Industries, Oak Brook, Ill., 1977—; dir. Am. Taping Tools of Can. Ltd., Ont., Jensen Tools & Alloys Inc., Phoenix, Compagnie Fischbein S.A., Brussels, BLK Steel Inc., Chgo. Served with AUS, 1954-56. Mem. Am., Fed., Cin. bar assns., Licensing Execs. Soc., Am. Soc. Corp. Secs., Phi Delta Phi, Pi Sigma Alpha, Delta Sigma Phi. Republican. Clubs: St. Louis; Economic (Chgo.); Bankers (Cin.); Metropolitan, Nat. Lawyers (Washington). Home: 450 Lexington Dr Lake Forest IL 60045 Office: 122 W 22d St Oak Brook IL 60521

SHEEHAN, DONALD THOMAS, govt. ofcl., univ. adminstr.; b. Winsted, Conn., Jan. 2, 1911; s. James J. and Louise (Coffey) S.; grad. Gilbert Sch., Winsted, 1931; B.S. in Edn., Syracuse U., 1935; student Sch. Pub. Affairs, Am. U., 1936; m. Betty Young, June 25, 1941; 1 son, Michael Terrence. Dir. health edn. D.C. Tb. Assn., 1937-39; dir. Washington office NCCJ, 1939-41; cons. on Williamstown (Mass.) Inst. Human Relations, Williams Coll., 1939-41; dir. bur. information Nat. Cath. Welfare Conf., dir. pub. relations Nat. Cath. Community Service, also Washington pub. relations liaison U.S.O., 1941- 42; spl. cons. to U.S. Commr. Edn., 1946; staff mem. John Price Jones Co., Inc., pub. relations cons., 1946-51; cons. civil def. edn. program, asst. adminstr. charge vol. manpower FCDA, 1951-54, cons. vol. manpower, 1954—; dir. pub. relations U. Pa., 1954-76, sec. corp., 1975-76, sec., v.p. emeritus, 1976—; spl. lectr. pub. relations, Drexel U., 1957-72; non. dir. Brakeley, John Price Jones Inc., N.Y.C.; cons. Nat. Bd. Med. Examiners, 1964—, Coll. Physicians Phila., 1973—, Citizens' Action Com. to Fight Inflation, 1974-75, Council for N.E. Econ. Action, 1978—, Wistar Inst. Anatomy and Biology, 1979; counselor Public Agenda Found., 1978—. Trustee United Phila., adv. com. Nat. Trust for Historic Preservation. Served from 1st lt. to lt. col. USAAF, 1942-46. Decorated Bronze Star medal. Fellow Coll. Physicians Phila. (hon. assoc.); mem. Pub. Relations Soc. Am., Am. Coll. Pub. Relations Assn., Am. Acad. Polit. and Social Sci., Pi Gamma Mu. Roman Catholic. Club: Nat. Press. Home: 332 W Springfield Ave Chestnut Hill Philadelphia PA 19118

SHEEHAN, EDWARD JAMES, tech. cons., former govt. ofcl.; b. Johnstown, Pa., Dec. 31, 1935; s. Louis A. and Ethel F. (Schaefer) S.; B.S. in Physics, St. Francis Coll., 1959; M.S. (Sloan fellow), Mass. Inst. Tech., 1972; m. Florence Ann Hartnett, June 17, 1958; children—Edward, James, John, William, Mary. Project engr. Electronics Command, Dept. Army, 1959-61, project team leader electro-optic equipment for tanks, 1961-63, project team leader electro-optic equipment for infantry, 1963-65, tech. area dir. electro-optic night vision equipment, 1965-73, asso. lab. dir. for devel. engring., 1973-76, lab. dir. Night Vision Lab., Fort Belvoir, Va., 1976-79; founder, pres. Sheehan Assos. Inc., Alexandria, Va., 1979—. Recipient numerous awards including Meritorious Civilian Service award Dept. Army. Home: 8502 Crestview Dr Fairfax VA 22031 Office: 611 Cameron St Alexandria VA 22314

SHEEHAN, HELEN LEE, lawyer; b. Washington, Oct. 6, 1927; d. Parklin and Lai Ping (Chew) Lee; student George Washington U., 1945-49, Catholic U. Law Sch., 1965; m. Mark Thomas Sheehan, Jr., Oct. 6, 1971. Admitted to D.C. bar, 1967, since practiced in Washington; adminstrv. asst. to U.S. congressman, 1966; partner firm Feldman Krieger Sheehan Goldman & Tish, and predecessor, 1974—. Mem. Am. Bar Assn., D.C. Bar Assn., Women's Bar Assn. D.C. Home: 6003 Lux Ln Rockville MD 20852 Office: 2019 Q St NW Washington DC 20009

SHEEHAN, JOHN C(LARK), chemist, educator; b. Battle Creek, Mich., Sept. 23, 1915; s. Leo Clark and Florence B. (Green) S.; B.S., Battle Creek Coll., 1937; M.S., U. Mich., 1938, Ph.D. in Organic Chemistry, 1941; D.Sc., U. Notre Dame, 1963; m. Marion M. Jennings, June 2, 1941; children—John Clark, David E., Elizabeth Sheehan Watkins. Research asso. Nat. Def. Research Com. project U. Mich., 1941; sr. research chemist Merck & Co., Inc., Rahway, N.J., 1941-46; asst. prof. chemistry Mass. Inst. Tech., 1946-49, asso. prof., 1949-52, prof. organic chemistry, 1952—, Camille Dreyfus prof. chemistry, 1969—. Reilly lectr. Notre Dame U., 1953, Swiss-Am. Found. lectr., Zurich, Basel, and Bern, 1958, McGregory lectr. Colgate U., 1958; Bachmann Meml. lectr. U. Mich., 1959; A.H. Robins Meml. lectr., Richmond, Va., 1975; chmn. Symposium Future B-Lactam Antibiotics, Internat. Meeting Heterocyclic Soc., 1975; speaker Stevens Inst. Tech., Hoboken, N.J., 1975. Sci. laison officer Am. Embassy Office Naval Research, London, Eng., 1953-54. Cons. Pres.'s Sci. Adv. Com., 1961-65; chmn. Pres.'s Sci. Adv. Com. Chemistry and Biology; mem. Pres.'s Sci. Adv. Com. Ltd. War Panel, 1961-65; former chmn. adv. com. on chem. methods radiol. protection Walter Reed Army Med. Center; nat. counselor Gordon Research Confs., Nat. Research Resources NIH. Chmn. bd. Sheehan Inst. for Research, Inc., SISA, Inc., Sharps Assos., Cambridge, Mass. Recipient Am. Chem. Soc. award in pure chemistry, 1951, award for creative work in organic chemistry, 1959; John Scott award City of Phila., 1964; Synthetic Organic Chem. Mfrs. Assn. medal, 1969; Outstanding Achievement award U. Mich., 1971. Fellow Am., N.Y. acads. arts and scis., Chem. Soc. Royal Inst. Chemists (London); mem. Am. Chem. Soc. (chmn. organic div. 1959-60, past dir., past chmn. grants and fellowships com., chmn. internat. activities com., nat. bd. dirs.) Nat. Acad. Scis., Sigma Xi, Alpha Chi Sigma, Phi Kappa Phi, Phi Lambda Upsilon. Editor-in-chief Organic Synthesis, 1958; past asso. editor Organic Reactions. Editorial bd. Jour. Organic Chemistry, Antimicrobial Agents and Chemotherapy. Research in chemistry of peniciliin, peptides, alkaloids, steroids, the synthesis of high explosives. Home: 10 Moon Hill Rd Lexington MA 02173 also 166 Harbor Dr Key Biscayne FL 33149 Office: Mass Inst Tech Cambridge MA 02139

SHEEHAN, JOHN EUGENE, bus. exec.; b. Johnstown, Pa., Dec. 11, 1929; s. Louis Anthony and Frances Ethel (Schaefer) S.; B.S. in Engring., U.S. Naval Acad., 1952; M.B.A. with distinction (George F. Baker scholar), Harvard U., 1960; m. Jean McEvers, Sept. 8, 1956; children—Kathleen Anne, John Kevin, Caroline Kelly. Commd. ensign U.S. Navy, 1952, advanced through grades to lt.; resigned, 1958; with McKinsey & Co., Inc., cons., N.Y.C., 1960-63; with Martin Marietta Corp., 1963-66, v.p. adminstrn., cement and lime div.; pres., chief exec. officer Corhart Refractories Co., Inc. subs. Corning Glass Works, Louisville, 1966-72; bd. govs. FRS, Washington, 1972-75; pres., chief operating officer White Motor Corp., 1975—; chmn., chief exec. Reading Industries, Inc.; chmn. Bristol Corp., Mored, Inc.; pres. Excelsior Brass Works, Inc. Office: Reading Industries Inc 2200 Bernville Rd Reading PA 19601

SHEEHAN, JOHN FRANCIS, cytopathologist, educator; b. Portsmouth, N.H., July 28, 1906; s. John Thomas and Ellen Agnes (Lynes) S.; B.S., U. N.H., 1928, M.S., 1930; Ph.D., State U. Iowa, 1945; postgrad. McGill U., 1949; m. Grace Anne O'Neil, Aug. 3, 1935; 1 son, John Thomas. Grad. asst. U. N.H., 1928-30; instr. biology Creighton U., 1930-38, asst. prof., 1938-44, asso. prof., 1944-49, prof. biology, 1949-67, prof. pathology Sch. Medicine, 1967—, prof. obstetrics and gynecology, 1975—; attending staff Creighton Meml., St. Joseph hosps. Omaha. Fellow Am. Soc. for Colposcopy and Cervical Pathology; mem. Am. Soc. Cytology, Internat. Coll. Surgeons, Am. Inst. Biol. Scis., Am. Soc. Zoologists, Omaha-Douglas County Med. Soc. (asso.), A.A.A.S., Am. Micros. Soc., A.A.U.P., Am. Assn. Anatomists, Am. Assn. Clin. Pathologists, Nebr. Heart Assn., Sigma Xi, Phi Sigma, Phi Kappa Theta, Phi Rho Sigma. Home: 1916 S 61st Ave Omaha NE 68106

SHEEHAN, JOHN JOSEPH, lawyer; b. Manchester, N.H., April 28, 1899; s. Daniel C. and Mary (Sullivan) S.; student Georgetown U.; m. Ellinor Nielsen, Jan. 8, 1943; children—Karen Ann Chicaderis, Susan Mary Pearsall, Mary Ellinor Sheehan. Admitted to N.H. bar, 1923, since practiced in Manchester; pres. Sheehan, Phinney, Bass & Green Assos. and predecessor firms, 1946—; U.S. atty. Dist. N.H., 1949-53. Mem. N.H. Ho. of Reps., 1925-28, N.H. Senate, 1931-32; county atty. Hillsborough County, 1933-37; del. N.H. Constl. Conv., 1930, 38, 41, 48, 56-59, 64, pres. pro tem; del. Democratic Nat. Conv., 1936, 40, 48, 60; mem. spl. adv. com. on rules Dem. Nat. Conv. 1956. Local chmn. SSS, 1940-42. Chmn. bd. trustees Carpenter Meml. City Library, Manchester; trustee Shaker Village, Inc. Served from capt. to maj. USAAF, 1942-45, with 8th and 9th Air Forces overseas. Mem. Am., N.H. (pres. 1966-67), Manchester (pres. 1940-41) bar assns., Am. Legion, VFW, Am. Judicature Soc., Nat. Assn. of R.R. Trial Counsel, N.E. Def. Counsel Assn., N.H., Manchester hist. socs., Nat. Trust for Historic Preservation, Nat. Hist. Soc. Clubs: Manchester Country, K.C. Home: 525 Concord St Manchester NH 03104 Office: 1000 Elm St Manchester NH 03101

SHEEHAN, JOHN WIGHT, oil co. exec.; b. Ann Arbor, Mich., Mar. 27, 1917; s. John Raleigh and Halcyon Ruth (Wheelock) S.; B.S., Tex. Tech. U., 1938, M.S., 1940; Ph.D. in Chem. Engring., U. Tex., 1948; m. Nelta Mayberry, Sept. 13, 1941; children—John Wight, Karen, Peggy. With Shell Oil Co., 1947-77, v.p., 1970-77; exec. v.p., chief ops. officer Commonwealth Oil Refining Co., Inc., San Antonio, 1977-78; cons. engr., Kerrville, Tex., 1978—; adv. council Engring. Found., U. Tex. Bd. dirs. Tex. Tech. Found. Named Distinguished Engr., Tex. Tech. U., 1975; Distinguished Grad., Coll. Engring. U. Tex., 1978; registered profl. engr., Tex. Mem. Am. Petroleum Inst., Nat. Petroleum Refiners Assn., Sigma Xi, Tau Beta Pi, Phi Lambda Upsilon. Congregationalist. Club: Houston. Home and office: Star Route Box 574-345 Kerrville TX 78028

SHEEHAN, JOSEPH GREEN, clin. psychologist, educator; b. Battle Creek, Mich., May 27, 1918; s. Leo Clark and Florence Belle (Green) S.; B.S. in Chemistry, Western Mich. U., Kalamazoo, 1941, M.A. Speech Pathology, in 1946; Ph.D. in Psychology, U. Mich., 1950; m. Vivian Mowat, Dec. 22, 1945; children—Marian Louise, Kathleen Florence, Joseph John; m. 2d, Margaret McMillan, June 4, 1966. Research chemist Gen. Foods Co., 1941-45; speech therapist U.S. Army Hosp., Ft. Custer, Mich., 1945-46; USPHS fellow, VA intern U. Mich., 1947-48; mem. faculty UCLA, 1949—, prof. psychology, 1963—; cons. clin. psychology VA, 1950—, Mental Hygiene Dept. Calif., 1966—; Commr. psychology exam. com. Calif. Bd. Med. Examiners. Fellow Am. Psychol. Assn., Am. Speech and Hearing Assn. Democrat. Author: Stuttering: Research and Therapy, 1970; co-author: Stuttering: A Second Symposium, 1975. Asso. editor Jour. Speech and Hearing Disorders; pubs. bd. Jour. Communication Disorders. Home: 371 20th St Santa Monica CA 90402 Office: Psychology Dept Univ Calif Los Angeles CA 90024

SHEEHAN, LOUIS JAMES, diversified co. exec.; b. Mt. Carmel, Pa., Dec. 4, 1934; s. Louis Andrew and Anna Veronica (Scully) S.; B.S., St. Vincent Coll., Latrobe, Pa., 1959; m. Joan Lois Fiebig, Sept. 1, 1959; children—Louis, Maryellen. Sr. accountant Price Waterhouse & Co., Pitts., Washington, 1959-64; mgr. Laventhol, Krekstein, Horwath & Horwath, Harrisburg, Pa., 1964-65; auditing mgr. Harsco Corp., Camp Hill, Pa., 1965-71, asst. treas., 1971-72, treas., 1972—. Served with USN, 1952-55. C.P.A., Pa. Home: 3832

Carriage House Dr Camp Hill PA 17011 Office: 350 Poplar Church Rd Camp Hill PA 17011

SHEEHAN, NEIL, journalist; b. Holyoke, Mass., Oct. 27, 1936; s. Cornelius Joseph and Mary (O'Shea) S.; A.B. cum laude, Harvard, 1958; Litt.D., Columbia Coll., Chgo., 1972; m. Susan Margulies, Mar. 30, 1965; children—Maria Gregory, Catherine Fair. Vietnam Bur. chief U.P.I., Saigon, 1962-64; reporter N.Y. Times, N.Y.C., Djakarta, Saigon, Washington, 1964—; obtained Pentagon Papers, 1971. Served with AUS, 1959-62. Recipient Louis M. Lyons award for conscience and integrity in journalism, 1964, Silver medal Poor Richard Club, Phila., 1964, certificate of appreciation for best article on Asia, Overseas Press Club Am., 1967, 1st Ann. Drew Pearson prize for excellence in investigative reporting, 1971, Columbia Journalism award, 1972, Sidney Hillman Found. award, 1972, Page One award Newspaper Guild N.Y., 1972, Distinguished Service award and Bronze medallion Sigma Delta Chi, 1972, citation of excellence Overseas Press Club, 1972. Guggenheim fellow, 1973-74; Adlai Stevenson fellow, 1973-75; Lehrman Inst. fellow, 1975-76; Rockefeller Found. fellow in humanities, 1976—. Author: The Arnheiter Affair, 1972. Contbr. to The Pentagon Papers, 1971; also articles, book revs. to popular mags. Home: 4505 Klingle St NW Washington DC 20016

SHEEHAN, WALTER FRANCIS, educator; b. Holyoke, Mass., Oct. 10, 1910; s. John Joseph and Margaret (Courtney) S.; ed. Deerfield (Mass.) Acad., 1927-29; A.B., Williams Coll., 1933; A.M., Amherst Coll., 1944; L.H.D. (hon.), Williams Coll., 1949; LL.D., U. Portland, 1964; m. Lillian Fontaine, June 28, 1941; chilldren—Peter John, Kevin Edward, Monica Mary. Mem. faculty English dept. Deerfield Acad., 1933-46, founder and editor Deerfield Alumni Jour., 1944-46; dean freshmen, athletic dir. Williams Coll., 1946-48; headmaster Canterbury Sch., New Milford, Conn., 1948-73, chmn. bd. trustees, 1973-77. Trustee New Milford Hosp. Decorated knight Holy Sepulchre. Mem. Headmasters Assn., Gargoyle Soc. (Williams Coll.), Alpha Delta Phi. Democrat. Roman Catholic. Home: 31 Marwick Manor New Milford CT 06776

SHEEHY, EUGENE PAUL, librarian; b. Elbow Lake, Minn., Oct. 10, 1922; s. Thomas Joseph and Roxy Odessa (Vincent) S.; B.A., St. John's U., Collegeville, Minn., 1950; M.A. in English, U. Minn., 1951, B.S. in L.S., 1952. Reference librarian Georgetown U., 1952-53; reference asst. Columbia U., 1953-65, head reference dept., 1965—. Served with USMC, 1942-46. Mem. ALA. Republican. Roman Catholic. Author: Joseph Conrad at Mid-Century, 1957; The Achievement of Marianne Moore, 1958; Yvor Winters, 1959; Frank Norris, 1959; Sherwood Anderson, 1960; Index to the Little Review, 1961; Index to Little Magazines, 1953-63, 5 vols., 1957-64; Guide to Reference Books, supplements 1-3 to 8th edit., 1968-72; Guide to Reference Books, 9th edit., 1976, Supplement, 1979. Home: 185 West End Ave New York NY 10023 Office: Columbia Univ Libraries 535 W 114th St New York NY 10027

SHEEHY, GAIL HENION, author; b. Mamaroneck, N.Y., Nov. 27, 1937; d. Harold Merritt and Lillian Rainey (Paquin) Henion; B.S., U. Vt., 1958; fellow Journalism Sch., Columbia U., 1970; m. Albert F. Sheehy, Aug. 20, 1960 (div. 1967); 1 dau., Maura. Traveling home economist J.C. Penney & Co., 1958-60; fashion editor Rochester Democrat & Chronicle, 1961-63; feature writer N.Y. Herald Tribune, N.Y.C., 1963-66; contbg. editor New York mag., 1968-77; sometimes contbr. to N.Y. Times mag., Esquire mag., McCall's, Ms., Cosmopolitan, Rolling Stone, others; books include: (novel) Lovesounds, 1970, Panthermania: The Clash of Black Against Black in One American City, 1971, Speed is of the Essence, 1971, Hustling: Prostitution in Our Wide-Open Society, 1973, Passages: Predictable Crises of Adult Life, 1976. Recipient Front Page award Newswomen's Club N.Y., 1964, 73; Nat. Mag. award Columbia U., 1973; Penney-Mo. Journalism award U. Mo., 1975. Mem. PEN, NOW, Authors Guild, Women's Ink. Office: William Morrow 105 Madison Ave New York NY 10016

SHEEHY, HOWARD SHERMAN, JR., clergyman; b. Denver, Mar. 19, 1934; s. Howard Sherman and Mildred Louise (Fishburn) S.; A.A., Graceland Coll., 1953; B.S., Central Mo. State Coll., 1955; M.S., U. Kans., 1960, postgrad., 1976—; m. Thelma Florine Cline, Sept. 4, 1954; children—John Robert, Lisa Florine, Michael Howard. Youth dir. Reorganized Ch. Jesus Christ Latter-day Saints, Independence, Mo., 1960-64; pastor, Des Moines, 1964-68; church supr., Haiti, 1968-70, Canada, 1970-74, Australia, 1970-75, N.Z., 1970-75, India, 1970-78, Japan, Korea, Republic of China, Philippines, 1976-78; mem. Council of Twelve Apostles, 1968-78, mem. 1st presidency, 1978—. Mem. nat. Protestant com. on scouting Boy Scouts Am., 1964-66, dir. internat. scouting program for church. Served to lt. USNR, 1955-59. Mem. Pi Omega Pi, Phi Delta Kappa. Republican. Home: 3403 S Crane St Independence MO 64055 Office: The Auditorium Independence MO 64051

SHEELINE, PAUL CUSHING, hotel exec.; b. Boston, June 6, 1921; s. Paul Daniel and Mary Cushing (Child) S.; B.S., Harvard, 1943, J.D., 1948; m. Harriet White Moffat, May 23, 1948 (dec. 1962); children—Christopher White, William Emerson, Mary Child, Leonora Moffat; m. 2d, Sandra Dudley Wahl, July 24, 1965; 1 dau., Abby Tucker. Admitted to N.Y. bar, 1948; asso. Sullivan & Cromwell, N.Y.C., 1948-54; with Lambert & Co., N.Y.C., 1954-65, gen. partner, 1958-65; chief financial officer Intercontinental Hotels Corp., N.Y.C., 1966-71, pres., 1971-74, chmn. bd., chief exec. officer, 1971—; dir. Nat. Bank N.Am., Pan Am. World Airways. Vice chmn. Community Service Soc. of N.Y., 1962-63; dir. Am. Assn. for UN, 1951-58; former mem. Harvard Overseers Com. to visit Center for Internat. Affairs and Dept. Romance Langs.; trustee East Woods Sch., Oyster Bay Cove, N.Y., 1959-68, Camargo Found.; bd. dirs. Bus. Council for Internat. Understanding. Served to capt. USAAF, 1942-46. Decorated Silver Star medal, French Legion of Honor, Croix de Guerre with palm, Moroccan Ouissam Alaouite. Mem. Council Fgn. Relations, Phi Beta Kappa. Clubs: Cold Spring Harbor Beach; Anglers (N.Y.); Harvard (N.Y.C. and L.I.). Home: Camel Hollow Rd Lloyd Harbor NY 11743 Office: 200 Park Ave New York NY 10017

SHEEN, MARTIN (RAMON ESTEVEZ), actor; b. Dayton, Ohio, Aug. 3, 1940; s. Francisco and Mary Ann (Phelan) Estevez; grad. high sch.; m. Janet; Dec. 23, 1961; children—Emilio, Ramon, Carlos, Renee. Made N.Y. stage debut as mem. Living Theatre in The Connection, 1959, Broadway debut in Never Live Over a Pretzel Factory, 1964; other stage appearances include: The Subject Was Roses, 1964-66, The Wicked Crooks, 1967, Hamlet, 1967, Romeo and Juliet, 1968, Hello and Goodbye, 1969, The Happiness Cage, 1970, Death of a Salesman, 1975; writer, dir. Down the Morning Line; film appearances include: The Incident, 1967, The Subject Was Roses, 1968, Catch-22, 1970, No Drums, No Bugles, 1971, Rage, 1972, Badlands, 1973, Cassandra Crossing, 1976, The Little Girl Who Lived Down the Lane, 1977, Apocalypse Now, 1979; regular TV series As the World Turns; TV movies include: Then Came Bronson, 1969, Mongo's Back in Town, 1971, Welcome Home, Johnny Bristol, 1972, That Certain Summer, 1972, Pursuit, 1972, Catholics, 1973, The Execution of Private Slovik, 1974, The California Kid, 1974, The Story of Pretty Boy Floyd, 1974, Sweet Hostage, 1975, The Last Survivors, 1975; TV drama Taxi!!, 1978; other TV appearances include: East Side, West Side, The Defenders, U.S. Steel Hour, Catholic Hour, Medical Center, FBI, Hollywood TV Theatre, Cannon, Mannix; TV spl. The Missiles of October, 1974. Office: care Paul Kohner Inc 9169 Sunset Blvd Los Angeles CA 90069*

SHEEN, ROBERT TILTON, mfg. co. exec.; b. Phila., Dec. 10, 1909; s. Milton Roy and Emma Elizabeth (Tilton) S.; B.S. in Chem. Engrinng., Lehigh U., 1931, Chem Engr., 1936; m. Dorothy Martha Dillenbeck, June 25, 1932; children—James D., Roberta Alace (Mrs. R. Donald Peterson); m. 2d. Mary Regina Orban, Aug 17, 1951; 1 dau., Regina Elizabeth; m. 3d, Frieda Marie Van Riter, July 19, 1972. Chem. engr. Swann Chem. Co., Anniston, Ala., 1931-32; tech. dir., then dir. cons. div. W.H. & L.D. Betz Co., 1932-43; co-founder Milton Roy Co., Phila and St. Petersburg, Fla., 1946, pres., chmn. bd., 1947-68, chmn. bd., chief exec. officer, 1968-72, chmn. bd., 1972-74, dir., chmn. exec. com., 1975—; dir. First Nat. Bank of St. Petersburg, Blue Cross of Fla. Pres., Jr. Achievement of St. Petersburg, 1965-66; chmn. Bayfront Med. Center, Inc., St. Petersburg, 1968-72; pres. Pinellas County Health Care Found., St. Petersburg, 1971-74 Bd. dirs. United Fund S. Pinellas, Fla., 1962; trustee Eckerd Coll., St. Petersburg, 1959—, chmn. bd., 1974-77; hon. trustee Sci. Center Pinellas County; mem. council advisers Fla. State U., Tallahassee, 1975—; former dir., chmn. health care com. Fla. Council of 100, 1969-77, chmn. human affairs com., 1978—. Recipient Diamond Jubilee award U.S. CSC, 1958; Outstanding Citizen award, 1967; West Coast Fla. Engr. of Year award, 1968; Silver Medallion Brotherhood award NCCJ, 1977. Registered profl. engr., Pa., N.J., Ohio, Ill. Fellow Instrument Soc. Am. (pres. 1955-56); hon. mem. Am. Mgmt. Assn. (dir. 1962-67, 70-73, mem. exec. com. 1965-67, 70-73, life mem.); mem. Am. Chem. Soc., Nat. Soc. Profl. Engrs., Am. Inst. Chem. Engrs., Aircraft Owners and Pilots Assn., Suncoasters Inc. (named Mr. Sun 1969, pres. 1974-75), Newcomen Soc. N.Am. Contbr. articles to profl. jours. Patentee chem. pumps, chem. feed systems. Home: 2432 Pelham Rd N Saint Petersburg FL 33710 Office: PO Box 12169 Saint Petersburg FL 33733

SHEETS, DONALD GUY, chemist, educator; b. Mt. Vernon, N.Y., Nov. 20, 1922; s. Guy W. and May (Wood) S.; A.B., Central Coll., Fayette, Mo., 1944; M.S., U. Mich., 1947, Ph.D., 1950; m. Emily Louise Mesley, Aug. 5, 1950. Instr., Central Coll., Fayette, 1944; research chemist Monsanto Chem. Co., St. Louis, 1944-45; asst. prof. Miss. State U., 1949-50; prof. chemistry St. Louis Coll. Pharmacy, 1950-62; prof. chemistry U.S. Naval Acad., Annapolis, Md., 1962—. Research fellow U. Mich., 1945-49. Mem. Am. Chem. Soc., Sigma Xi, Phi Lambda Upsilon, Alpha Chi Sigma. Contbr. articles to profl. jours. Home: 172 Williams Dr Annapolis MD 21401

SHEETS, GEORGE HENKLE, paper co. exec.; b. Washington Court House, Ohio, Apr. 22, 1915; s. George Lane and Lulu Belle (Henkle) S.; B.Chem. Engring., Ohio State U., 1937; M.S., Inst. Paper Chemistry, 1939, Ph.D., 1941; grad. Advanced Mgmt. Program, Harvard, 1956; m. Margaret Janet Muenchow, May 31, 1941; children—Cynthia (Mrs. Harold Webster), Karen (Mrs. Craig Campbell). With Mead Corp., 1941—, sr. v.p., 1964-68, exec. v.p., 1968—, also dir.; chmn. bd., dir. Northwood Pulp & Timber Ltd.; pres., dir. Escanaba Paper Co.; v.p., dir. Meadisc Inc., Brunswick Chem. Co., Mead Itab Inc.; chmn. bd., dir. Brunswick Pulp & Paper Co.; v.p., dir. Forest Kraft Co., Mead Timber Co., Brunswick Overseas, Inc.; dir. Mead Pulp Sales, Inc., B.C. Forest Products Ltd., Mead Packaging Internat., Inc., Mead Tech. Labs., B.C. Chems., Ltd.; mem. mgmt. com. Brunswick Pulp Land Co. Mem. TAPPI (pres. 1968-70), Am. Paper Inst. (exec. bd. pulp producers div.). Home: 60 Harmon Terr Dayton OH 45419 Office: Mead World Hdqrs Courthouse Plaza NE Dayton OH 45463

SHEETS, HERMAN ERNEST, educator; b. Dresden, Germany, Dec. 24, 1908; s. Arthur Chitz and Gertrude (Stern) S.: M.E., U. Dresden, 1934; Dr. Tech. Scis. in Applied Mechanics, U. Prague (Czechoslovakia), 1936; m. Norma Sams, Oct. 17, 1942; children—Lawrence S., Michael R., Arne H., Diana E., Elizabeth J., Norma K. Chief engr. Chamberlin Research Corp., East Moline, Ill., 1939-42; mgr. research St. Paul Engring. & Mfg. Co., 1942- 44: project engr. Elliott Co., Jeannette, Pa., 1944-46; engring. mgr. Goodyear Aircraft Corp., Akron, Ohio, 1946-53; with Electric Boat div. Gen. Dynamics Corp., 1953-69, v.p. engring, and research; prof. dept. ocean engring. U. R.I., 1969—, dept. chmn., 1971—. Recipient citation, sec. war. Fellow Am. Inst. Aeros. and Astronautics (asso.), ASME; mem. N.Y. Acad. Scis., Nat. Acad. Engring., Soc. Naval Architects and Marine Engrs., Am. Soc. Naval Engrs., AAAS, Marine Tech. Soc., Pi Tau Sigma. Author numerous articles in field. Home: 87 Neptune Dr Mumford Cove Groton CT 06340 Office: Lippitt Hall U RI Kingston RI 02881

SHEETZ, RICHARD LATRELLE, assn. exec.; b. Macon, Mo., Aug. 10, 1906; s. Robert Karl and Lena M. (Fetter) S.; A.B., Westminster Coll., 1928; m. Aagot Velline, Aug. 12, 1939; children—Robert K., Susan S. Laitsch, Timothy R., Ferne D. Holmes, Harold S., Geraldine M. Beck. Asst. sales mgr. Lowe and Campbell Athletic Goods Co., Kansas City, Mo., 1928-33; officer mgr., campaign asst. Kansas City Charities Fund, 1933-36; exec. dir., N.D. Community Chest, Fargo, 1936-39; exec. dir. Tex. Community Chest and Planning Council, Austin, 1939-43; exec. dir. Va. United Communities Fund, Norfolk, 1943-71; exec. dir. The Norfolk Found.-Community Trust, 1971—; pres. S.E. region Community Chests and Councils of Am., 1948-49; pres. Va. Fedn., 1949-59, bd. dirs., 1953-59. Named Mr. Citizen of his generation Norfolk Union Labor Council, 1971; recipient citation for outstanding service City of Norfolk, 1970, Golden Legion award Westminster Coll., 1978. Mem. Nat. Conf. Social Welfare, Beta Theta Pi. Club: Virginia. Author: Savannah, Georgia, A Study of Community Organization, 1950. Home: 2545 Murray Ave Norfolk VA 23518 Office: Suite 406 201 Granby Mall Bldg Norfolk VA 23510

SHEETZ, RICHARD SMEDLEY, mfg. co. exec.; b. Phila., June 18, 1924; s. John Wesley and Marian (Smedley) S.; grad. Episcopal Acad., Phila., 1942; student Pa. State Coll., 1943-44; B.S. in Elec. Engring., Bucknell U., 1946; M.B.A., Harvard, 1955; m. Ebba Jean Sterner, Jan. 2, 1954; children—Marian Christine, Rebecca Jane, Laura Jean, Sarah Elizabeth, Constance Smedley. With Westinghouse Electric Corp., 1946-61, gen. mgr. E. Springfield plant, 1959-61; exec. v.p. Ohio Crankshaft Co., Cleve., 1961-67; chmn. bd. Park Ohio-Industries, Inc., Cleve., 1967—; dir. S-P Mfg. Co., Cedar Point Inc., Cleve.-Cliffs Iron Co. Past chmn. bd. N.E. Ohio affiliate Am. Heart Assn. Served with USNR, 1943-46. Clubs: Union (Cleve.); Shaker Heights Country. Home: 22040 McCauley Rd Shaker Heights OH 44122 Office: 600 Tower E 20600 Chagrin Blvd Cleveland OH 44122

SHEFCHIK, THOMAS JOSEPH, JR., architect; b. Paris, France, Oct. 30, 1920 (parents Am. citizens); s. Thomas Joseph and Margaret Paddock (Rice) S.; student Pomona Coll., 1939-41; B.Arch., U. Minn., 1948; m. Dorothy Louella Carlson, June 17, 1946; children—Mark Thomas, Richard Sperling, Lisa Dorothy. Mem. firm Thomas J. Shefchik & Assos., Inc., Duluth, Minn., 1948-63, pres., 1963—. Adv. bd. Salvation Army, 1963—; exec. bd. Lake Superior council Boy Scouts Am., 1970-71. Served with USAAF, 1942-45. Decorated Air medal. Mem. A.I.A. (pres. Northeast Minn. chpt. 1972), Minn. Soc. Architects (dir. 1972—), Duluth C. of C. (treas. 1967, dir. 1964-67). Conglist. (trustee 1959-65, 71-72). Rotarian (dir. 1968-70, pres. 1970-71). Archtl. works include maj. additions and remodeling St. Luke's Hosp., Duluth, 1963-71; Duluth Area Inst. Tech., 1968; bldgs. Bemidji State Coll. and Itasca State Jr. Coll., 1971; Ramsey Manor Apts. (for elderly), Duluth, 1971; Tri-Tower Apts (for elderly), Duluth, 1973; City Hall, Ashland, Wis., 1977. Home: 2730 Greysolon Rd Duluth MN 55812 Office: 207 S 28th Ave E Duluth MN 55812

SHEFELMAN, HAROLD S., lawyer; b. N.Y.C., Apr. 15, 1898; s. Joseph and Henrietta (Lovett) S.; Ph.B., Brown U., 1920; LL.B., Yale, 1925; LL.D., Seattle Pacific Coll., Brown U.; m. Madolene Whitehead, Aug 12, 1924 (dec. June 1955); children—Thomas Whitehead, June Henderson Shefelman Hensley; m. 2d, Sylvia Rogers, 1958 (div.); m. 3d, Nona Proctor Church, 1977. Admitted to Wash. bar, 1926, since practiced in Seattle; mem. Roberts, Shefelman, Lawrence, Gay & Moch; lectr. Sch. Law, U. Wash., 1930-57. Mem. Seattle City Planning Commn., 1948-71, chmn., 1950-52; mem. interim com. nation-wide conf. on met. area problems, Lansing, Mich., 1957; chmn. Wash. Child Welfare Adv. Com., 1949-51; mem. Wash. State Bd. Edn., 1951-57; chmn. Wash. delegation White House Conf. on Edn., 1955; chmn. com. State Govt. Orgn., 1951-55; exec. com. Seattle Health and Welfare Council, 1950-52; chmn. State Citizens' Com. (survey state's pub. welfare problems), 1949-50; chmn. Seattle Civic Center Commn., 1956-72; pres. Seattle Municipal League, 1956-58; mem. adv. council Bonneville Power Authority, 1940-45. Mem. council Nat. Municipal League, 1955—, Gov.'s Constl. Revision Commn., 1968-69; chmn. Wash. State Tax Adv. Council, 1957-59; bd. regents U. Wash., 1957-75, past pres.; trustee emeritus Brown U.; trustee Pacific Sci. Center Found., also pres., chmn.; hon. life mem. exec. com., past v.p. Yale Law Sch. Assn.; trustee Century 21 Expn. Recipient citation of honor Wash. State chpt. AIA, 1955, Distinguished Citizen award Nat. Municipal League, 1961; Outstanding Citizen award Seattle Municipal League, 1961; Others award Salvation Army, 1963; Bishop's cross Diocese Olympia, 1956; Outstanding Alumnus award Brown U., 1970; Recognition award U. Wash., 1977; comdr. Order of Hosp. of St. John of Jerusalem; named Hon. Tex. Citizen, 1966. Served with U.S. Army, World War I. Fellow Am. Bar Found.; mem. Am. (ho. of dels. 1938-40, 54-56, past council on legal edn., council municipal law sect. 1948-61, chmn. sect. 1952-54), Wash., Seattle (pres. 1937-38) bar assns., Am. Law Inst. (life mem.), Am. Judicature Soc. (past dir.), Am. Soc. Planning Ofcls. (dir. 1957-62, pres. 1959-61), Municipal Forum (N.Y.C.), Acad. Polit. Sci., Order of Coif, Phi Beta Kappa Assos., Phi Beta Kappa. Episcopalian (chancellor Diocese of Olympia). Mason (Shriner). Clubs: College, Washington Athletic (Seattle), Oval, U. Wash. Office: IBM Bldg Seattle WA 98101

SHEFFEL, IRVING EUGENE, psychiat. instn. exec.; b. Chgo., July 5, 1916; s. Joseph and Jennie (Leibson) S.; A.B., U. Chgo., 1939; M.P.A., Harvard U., 1946; m. Beth Silver, Aug. 2, 1942; 1 dau., Anita (dec.). Insp., wage and hour div. Dept. Labor, Chgo., 1940-41; mgmt. and budget analyst VA, Washington, 1946-48; budget analyst U.S. Bur. of Budget, Washington, 1948-49; controller, treas. Menninger Found., Topeka, 1949-73, v.p., 1973—; instr. Menninger Sch. Psychiatry; dir. Volume Shoe Co. Bd. dirs. Washburn U. Art Center, 1969—, pres., 1971-73. Served to maj. U.S. Army, 1942-45. Fellow Assn. Mental Health Adminstrs. (charter); mem. Am. Soc. Public Adminstrn. (charter). Jewish. Home: 323 Greenwood Topeka KS 66606 Office: PO Box 829 Topeka KS 66601

SHEFFER, HAROLD VERMONT, community coll. pres.; b. Nicklesville, Pa., Feb. 25, 1921; s. George Peter and Theressa Marie Sheffer; B.A., Allegheny Coll., Meadeville, Pa., 1950; M.Div. cum laude, Drew U., Madison, N.J., 1954; postgrad. Columbia U. Tchrs. Coll.; m. Joycelyn Shirley Fitzke, Mar. 30, 1976; children—Eric, Lynda, Suzanne, Robert, Johanna, David. Ordained to minister Methodist Ch., 1950; cleric United Methodist Ch., Pa. and N.Y., 1947-55; cleric and canon to ordinary Episcopal Diocese Calif., 1956-60; asst. nat. field dir. Nat. Multiple Sclerosis Soc., 1960-63, 63-67; self-employed, 1967-72, successively instr., dean instrn., pres. Glen Oaks Community Coll., 1967-72; pres. Jackson (Mich.) Community Coll., 1972—; dir. Midwest Bank, Jackson. Bd. dirs., past pres. Ella Sharp Museum, Jackson. Served with USNR, 1944-45. Ezra Squier Tipple fellow, 1954-55. Mem. Am. Assn. Community and Jr. Colls., N. Central Assn., Mich. Community Coll. Assn. (past pres.), Jackson C. of C. (dir.). Republican. Roman Catholic. Clubs: Rotary, Elks. Home: 1135 Wickwire Rd Jackson MI 49201 Office: 2111 Emmons Rd Jackson MI 49201

SHEFFET, JOSEPH, cons. structural engr.; b. St. Louis, June 20, 1910; s. Joseph and Sadie Zelda (Siegel) S.; B.S. in Civil Engring., Calif. Inst. Tech., 1932, M.S. in Civil Engring., 1933; m. June Phyllis Miller, Apr. 5, 1942; children—Mary Jane, Laura Anne. With Donald B. Parkinson, architect, Los Angeles, 1935-46, chief structural engr., 1938-46; pvt. practice, 1946—; pres. Joseph Sheffet, Inc., Los Angeles, 1959—. Fellow Am. Cons. Engrs. Council (dir. 1967-68); mem. structural engrs. assns. Calif. (pres. 1959), So. Calif. (pres. 1958), Cons. Engrs. Assn. Calif. (pres. 1966), Sigma Xi, Tau Beta Pi, Pi Kappa Delta. Republican. Club: Indian Wells Country. Home: 75484 Montecito Dr Indian Wells CA 92260 Office: 7024 Melrose Ave Los Angeles CA 90038. *Lead a useful life. Be considerate of others. Carry your full share of burdens and responsibilities. Give your colleagues, your family, your profession, your school, your neighbors-something extra of yourself. You will be judged by your actions so be sure that they truly reflect you. Get along with others by being thoughtful of their views. Don't over value yourself.*

SHEFFEY, FRED CLIFTON, JR., army officer; b. McKeesport, Pa., Aug. 27, 1928; s. Fred Culmore and Julia Belle (Richardson) S.; B.S., Central State Coll., Wilberforce, O., 1950; M.B.A., Ohio State U., 1962; postgrad. Command and Gen. Staff Coll., 1965, Nat. War Coll., 1969; M.S. in Internat. Affairs, George Washington U., 1969; m. Jane Hughes, Dec. 27, 1952; children—Alan C., Steven C., Patricia C. Commd. 2d lt. U.S. Army, 1950, advanced through grades to maj. gen., 1976; mem. staff U.S. Army Communications Zone, Europe, 1962-64; div. supply officer 4th Inf. Div., Ft. Lewis, Wash., 1965, exec. officer 4th Div. Supply and Transport Bn., 1965-66; comdr. 266th QM Bn., Ft. Lewis, Vietnam, 1966; chief base operations br. Office Dep. Chief of Staff for Logistics, Dept. Army, 1967-68, dir. financial resources, 1972-73, dir. operation and maintenance resources, 1973-74, dep. dir. supply and maintenance, 1974-75; dir. materiel mgmt. U.S. Army Materiel Devel. and Readiness Command, Alexandria, Va., 1975-77; comdg. gen. U.S. Army Quartermaster Center, also comdt. U.S. Army Quartermaster Sch., Fort Lee, Va., 1977—; chief of plans br., J4, Pacific Command Hdqrs., Hawaii, 1969-71; comdr. 54th Gen. Support Group, Republic of South Vietnam, 1971-72. Decorated Legion of Merit with 2 oak leaf clusters, Bronze Star medal, Meritorious Service medal, Army Commendation medal with oak leaf cluster, Purple Heart, Combat Inf. badge. Home: 1 Normandy Rd Fort Lee VA 23801 Office: Comdg Gen US Quartermaster Center Fort Lee VA 23801

SHEFFIELD, GILBERT (LEROY), utility co. exec.; b. Oakland, Calif., Sept. 24, 1929; B.S. in Bus. Adminstrn., U. Calif., 1951; m. Barbara R. Sheffield; children—Gail Mark, Todd, Sally. Dept. mgr. J.C. Penney Co., Oakland, 1951; with Pacific Tel. & Tel. Co., San Francisco, 1953—, v.p. Bay, 1978, exec. v.p.-residence, 1978—; dir. Calif. Dept. Human Resources Devel., 1969-71. Trustee, Westmont

Coll.; bd. dirs. Bridgemont High Sch., San Francisco. Mem. U. Calif. at Berkeley Alumni Assn. Clubs: Olympic, Orindawoods, Las Cruces, Commonwealth (San Francisco). Office: 140 New Montgomery St San Francisco CA 94105

SHEFFIELD, HORACE LINDSEY, union ofcl.; b. Vienna, Ga., Feb. 22, 1916; s. Horace Lindsey and Georgie (Brown) S.; student Detroit Inst., 1937-41; student Wayne State U., 1941-42, 48, LL.D., 1972; student U. Calif. at Los Angeles, 1952; widower; children—Corliss Sheffield Williams, Kathryn, Lavonne Sheffield Hudson, Horace Lindsey III. Joined United Auto Workers, Detroit, 1940, internat. rep., 1942-67, adminstrv. asst. to internat. v.p., 1967-74, adminstrv. asst. to pres., 1975—; with Ford Motor Co., 1934—. Moderator weekly half hour program Sta. WCHB, Detroit, 1961-72; columnist Mich. Chronicle weekly. Bd. dirs. United Found., Legal Aid and Defender Assn., Am. Health Planning Assn., Nat. Health Council, Merrill-Palmer Inst.; sec. Nat. Coalition Black Trade Unionists; exec. dir. Trade Union Leadership Council; pres. Friends of Belle Isle, Detroit Coalition Black Trade Unionists. Recipient Ira W. Jayne Meml. medal Detroit NAACP, 1962, Liberty Bell award Mich. State Bar, 1964. Mem. NAACP (life), Kappa Alpha Psi. Lutheran. Home: 2101 Bryanston Crescent Detroit MI 48221 Office: 8000 E Jefferson St Detroit MI 48214

SHEFFIELD, ROY DEXTER, mathematician, educator; b. Dorsey, Miss., Sept. 5, 1922; s. G.W. and Esther (Martin) S.; B.A., U. Miss., 1948, M.A., 1949; Ph.D., U. Tenny, 1956; m. Sereda Franks, Nov. 27, 1946. Mem. faculty U. Miss., 1949-63, prof. math., 1957-63; prof. math., head dept. Miss. State U., 1963-71; chmn. dept. math. U. Miss., 1971-77, prof. math., 1977—. Served with AUS, 1942-46. Mem. Am. Math. Soc., Math. Assn. Am., Sigma Xi, Phi Kappa Phi. Baptist. Mason. Office: Dept Math Hume Hall Univ Miss University MS 38677

SHEFFIELD, WILLIAM JOHNSON, educator, ednl. adminstr.; b. Nashua, N.H., May 9, 1919; s. Edward Newton and Grace Capron (Johnson) S.; B.S. in Pharmacy, U. N.C., 1942, M.S., 1949, Ph.D., 1954; m. Nadine Jean Watson, June 3, 1955; children—Lisa Jean, Erin Kathleen, William Johnson. Asst. prof. Coll. Pharmacy, U. Tex., Austin, 1952-60, asso. prof., 1960-68, prof., 1968—, asst. dean, 1956-58, 68-73, acting dean, 1964, 71-73, asso. dean, 1973—. Pres. Pearce Jr. High PTA, Austin, 1973-74, Lyndon Baines Johnson High Sch. PTA, Austin, 1977-78. Served with USAAF, 1943-45. Recipient Teaching Excellence award U. Tex., 1958, 60, 62, 77, 79; Merit award for outstanding contbn. to pharm. edn. Longhorn Pharm. Assn., 1972. Fellow AAAS; mem. Tex. Pharm. Assn. (v.p. 1969-70, Pharmacist of Year 1979), Am. Pharm. Assn., Acad. Pharm. Scis., Sigma Xi, Phi Delta Chi (nat. pres. 1965-69), Rho Chi, Phi Kappa Phi. Contbr. articles to Jour. Am. Pharm. Assn., Drug Standards, Jour. Pharm. Scis. Home: 2204 Langford Cove Austin TX 78723 Office: Coll Pharmacy U Tex Austin TX 78712. *I have always tried to recognize and accept peoples' limitations but, whenever possible, help them to exceed those limitations.*

SHEFLER, STEPHEN ALAN, govt. ofcl.; b. Phoenix, Apr. 5, 1943; s. H. George and Selma (Reichenstein) S.; B.A. with distinction, Stanford U., 1965, LL.B., 1968. Admitted to Ariz. bar, 1968, Calif., 1969; atty. Navajo Legal Service, Window Rock, Ariz., 1968; mem. firm Heller, Ehrman, White and McHulliffe, San Francisco, 1969-70; mem. staff Senator Alan Cranston and U.S. Senate Banking Com., Washington, 1970-74; asst. U.S. atty., San Francsico, 1974-77; dep. asst. sec. Transp. for policy and internat. affairs, Dept. Transp., Washington, 1977—. Home: 425 S Fairfax Alexandria VA 22314 Office: Dept Transp 7th and D Sts SW Washington DC

SHEHAN, LAWRENCE JOSEPH, Cardinal; b. Balt., Mar. 18, 1898; s. Thomas Patrick and Anastasia (Schofield) S.; student St. Charles Coll., Balt., 1911-17; A.B., St. Mary Sem., Balt., 1919, A.M., 1920; S.T.D., N.Am. Coll., Rome, Italy, 1923. Ordained priest Roman Cath. Ch., 1922; asst. St. Patrick Ch., Washington, 1923-41, pastor, 1941-45; pastor Saints Philip and James Ch., Balt., 1945; named titular bishop Lydda, aux. bishop Balt. and Washington, 1945, aux. bishop Balt., 1948, 1st bishop Bridgeport, Conn., 1953, coadjutor archbishop Balt., 1961, archbishop, 1961-74; elevated to cardinal, 1965. Consultor, Post-Conciliar Commn. for Revision Code of Canon Law; pres. Permanent Commn. for Internat. Eucharistic Congresses, 1969-73; Papal legate 40th Internat. Eucharistic Congress, Melbourne, Australia, 1973. Home: 408 N Charles St Baltimore MD 21201 Office: 320 Cathedral St Baltimore MD 21201

SHEIB, SIMON, lawyer; b. Jan. 23, 1916; s. Benjamin and Fannie (Fine) S.; B.A., N.Y. U.; LL.B., Harvard; m. Stella Newman, Sept. 29, 1945; children—David, Fredda, Jonathan, James. Admitted to N.Y. State bar; practiced in N.Y.C.; pres., chief exec. officer, chmn. bd. Avnet, Inc., N.Y.C.; dir. Rexham Corp., Golden Crest Records, Inc. Home: 28 Pryer Ln Larchmont NY 10538 Office: 767 Fifth Ave New York City NY 10022

SHEINBERG, GEORGE CHARLES, stock brokerage co. exec.; b. N.Y.C., Feb. 9, 1935; s. Frank R. and Edith (Kupchick) S.; A.B., Harvard, 1956; M.B.A., N.Y. U., 1959, LL.B., 1965; m. Jacqueline Baliba, Mar. 30, 1958; children—Evan, Kenneth. With Bulova Watch Co., 1958—, treas., 1968—, v.p., 1972-76, exec. v.p., 1976-78, also dir.; sr. exec. v.p., dir. Shearson Hayden Stone, Inc. (Shearson Loeb Rhoades, Inc.), N.Y.C., 1978—; dir. Franks Broadcasting Co. Trustee Lexington Sch. for Deaf, R. Sturble Found. Served with USNR, 1956-58. Home: 11 Fifth Ave New York NY 10003 Office: 14 Wall St New York NY 10005

SHEINBERG, ISRAEL, computer co. exec.; b. Ft. Worth, Apr. 15, 1932; s. Samuel I. and Pauline C. (Fram) S.; B.S. in Physics, U. Tex., 1953; student U. Calif. at Los Angeles, 1957-58, Arlington (Tex.) State Coll., 1960, Southwestern Med. Sch., 1961; m. Betty S. Topletz, Aug. 19, 1962; children—Amy, Karen, David, Paula. Electronic engr. Hughes Aircraft Co., 1956-60, Nat. Data Processing Corp., 1961; exec. v.p., chief operating officer Recognition Equipment Inc., 1961—, now group v.p., also dir., also pres., dir. subs. Recognition Products Inc. Served with AUS, 1954-56. Mem. Optical Soc. Am., Am. Mgmt. Assn. Jewish (bd. dirs. synagogue). Contbr. articles to profl. jours. Speaker on optical character recognition, data processing. Home: 5706 Watson Circle Dallas TX 75225 Office: PO Box 22307 Dallas TX 75222

SHEINFELD, DAVID, composer; b. St. Louis, Sept. 20, 1910; s. Joseph and Feige (Sandler) S.; scholar of Ototrino Respighi, Santa Cecilia Acad., Rome, 1930-32; m. Dorothy Jaffe, Apr. 12, 1942; children—Daniel, Paul. Compositions performed by symphony orchs. in San Francisco, Chgo., Pitts., Phila., Phila. Chamber Symphony; chamber music performed numerous cities in U.S., Can.; pvt. tchr. composition; violinist San Francisco Symphony Orch., 1945-72. Mem. adv. panel San Francisco Chamber Music Soc. Mem. Broadcast Music, Inc. Composer orchestral and chamber music works; commd. to compose work for San Francisco Symphony Assn. orch.'s 60th anniversary, 1971. Recipient Norman Fromm award for chamber music composition, 1979. Home: 1458 24th Ave San Francisco CA 94122

SHEINFELD, MYRON, lawyer; b. Chelsea, Mass., Mar. 18, 1930; s. Robert and Sadye (Rosenberg) S.; B.A., Tulane U., 1951; J.D., U. Mich., 1954; m. Phyllis Jane Wolf, June 18, 1951; children—Michael Allen, Scott Patrick. Admitted to Tex. bar, 1956; researcher Legis. Research Inst. U. Mich., 1954; asst. U.S. atty. So. Dist. Tex., Houston, 1958-60, law clk. to U.S. Dist. Judge, 1960-61; partner firms Strickland, Gordon & Sheinfeld, Houston, 1961-68, Sheinfeld & Maley, Houston, 1968-70, Sheinfeld, Maley & Kay, Houston, 1970—; lectr. in field; dir. 1st City Bank, Bellaire; adj. asso. prof. Bates Coll. Law U. Houston, 1966-79; vis., also lectr. adj. prof., in law U. Tex. Law Sch., Austin, 1970, 76—; gen. counsel Foley Bros. Store Found., Houston, 1968-75; regional chmn. nat. com. fund raising U. Mich. Law Sch., 1971-73. Recipient S. Walter Stern award Tulane U., 1950. Mem. Tex., Am. bar assns., Nat. Bankruptcy Conf., Phi Beta Kappa, Pi Sigma Alpha. Clubs: Houston, Houston Athletic, Houstonian. Contbg. author: Texas Lawyers Practice Guide, 1967. Contbr. articles to profl. jours. Home: 6119 Ella Lee Ln Houston TX 77057 Office: 2130 Two Shell Plaza Houston TX 77002

SHEINGOLD, LEONARD SUMNER, cons.; b. Boston, Jan. 14, 1921; s. Julius J. and Minnie (Soloff) S.; student Northeastern U., 1938-40; B.S. in Elec. Engring., Syracuse U., 1947, M.S., 1949; M.A. in Applied Physics, Harvard, 1950, Ph.D., 1953; m. Shirley Kolodny, June 16, 1946; children—Beth Helene, Barry Jay, Terry Faye. Instr. elec. engring. Syracuse U., 1947-49; engring. specialist Sylvania Electronic Systems Co., Waltham, Mass., 1952-56, dir. applied research lab., 1956-61, v.p. advanced tech. 1962-68; cons., 1968—; chief scientist USAF, 1961-62; pres. Corporate-Tech. Planning, Inc., 1969-72; pres. Leonard S. Sheingold and Assos., Inc., 1973—. Mem. weapons systems evaluation group of Inst. Def. Analysis, 1956, cons., 1956—; cons. Project Mich., U. Mich., 1958; mem. USAF Sci. Adv. Bd., 1958-70, adv. group electronic warfare Office Dir. Def. Research and Engring., 1959—; cons. Pres.'s Sci. Adv. Com., 1964-70; mem. Def. Sci. Bd., 1965-70. Pres., New Eng. Villages, Inc., 1967—. Served with AUS, 1942-45. Recipient Exceptional Civilian Service award USAF. Fellow I.E.E.E.; mem. Am. Phys. Soc., Assn. U.S. Army, Am. Inst. Aeros. and Astronautics, A.A.A.S., Sigma Xi, Sigma Pi Sigma. Address: 156 Highland Ave Newtonville MA 02160

SHEINWOLD, ALFRED, columnist. Author syndicated column Sheinwold on Bridge; bridge editor Los Angeles Times. Chmn. bd. govs. Am. Contract Bridge League. Author: Five Weeks to Winning Bridge; Pocket Books of Bridge Puzzles. Home and office: 2625 Angelo Dr Los Angeles CA 90024

SHELANSKI, MICHAEL L., cell biologist; b. Phila., Oct. 5, 1941; s. Herman Alder and Bessie S.; student Oberlin Coll., 1959-61; M.D. (Life Ins. Med. Research Fund fellow), U. Chgo., 1966, Ph.D., 1967; m. Vivien Brodkin, June 9, 1963; children—Howard, Samuel, Noah. Intern in pathology Albert Einstein Coll. Medicine, N.Y.C., 1967-68, fellow in neuropathology, 1968-70, asst. prof. pathology, 1969-74; staff scientist NIH, Bethesda, Md., 1971-73; vis. scientist Inst. Pasteur, Paris, 1973-74; asso. prof. neuropathology Harvard U., Cambridge, Mass., 1974-78; sr. research asso., asst. neuropathologist Children's Hosp. Med. Center, Boston, 1974-78; prof., chmn. dept. pharmacology N.Y. U. Med. Center, N.Y.C., 1979—; mem. Neurology A study sect. NIH, 1974-78. Served as sr. asst. surgeon USPHS, 1971-73. Guggenheim fellow, 1973-74. Mem. Am. Soc. Cell Biology, Am. Assn. Neuropathologists, Assn. Med. Coll. Pharmacologists, Am. Soc. Neurochemistry. Research on fibrous proteins of brain, aging of human brain, devel. neurobiology. Office: Dept Pharmacology NY U Med Center 550 1st Ave New York NY 10016

SHELBY, RICHARD CRAIG, congressman; b. Birmingham, Ala., May 6, 1934; s. O.H. and Alice L. (Skinner) S.; A.B., U. Ala., 1957, LL.B., 1963; m. Annette Nevin, June 11, 1960; children—Richard Craig, Claude Nevin. Admitted to Ala. bar, 1961, D.C. bar, 1979; law clk. Supreme Ct. of Ala., 1961-62; practice law, Tuscaloosa, Ala., 1963-79; prosecutor City of Tuscaloosa, 1964-70; spl. asst. atty. gen. State of Ala., 1969-70; U.S. magistrate No. Dist. of Ala., 1966-70; mem. Ala. State Senate, 1970-76; mem. 96th Congress from 11th Ala. dist. Active Boy Scouts Am.; dir. Tuscaloosa County Mental Health Assn., 1969-70; bd. govs. Nat. Legis. Conf., 1975-78. Mem. Am. Bar Assn., Ala. Bar Assn., Tuscaloosa County Bar Assn., D.C. Bar Assn. Democrat. Presbyterian. Club: Exchange. Home: 66 High Forest Tuscaloosa AL 35406 Office: 1408 Longworth Bldg Washington DC 20515

SHELDON, DAVID FREDERICK, headmaster; b. N.Y.C., Feb. 2, 1929; s. Seward Ross and Zue Mac (Bronaugh) S.; A.B., Amherst Coll., 1951; M.B.A., Harvard, 1953, M.A.T. 1958; m. Judith West, June 18, 1954; children—Frederick William, Charles Seward, James Nias. Trainee, then account exec. McCann-Erickson Inc., advt., 1953-57; tchr. history and English, Middlesex Sch., Concord, Mass., 1957-59, dir. admissions, 1961-64, headmaster, 1964—. Pres., Sch. Scholarship Service, 1963-65. Trustee Charles River Sch., Dover, Mass., 1965-68, Carroll Sch., Lincoln, Mass., 1972—, Interalp, Princeton, N.J., 1973—; mem. corp. Emerson Hosp., Concord, Mass., 1970—; mem. overseers vis. com. Harvard, 1966—; exec. com. Ind. Schs. Found. Mass., 1966-68. Mem. Headmasters Assn. Episcopalian (vestryman). Address: Middlesex Sch Concord MA 01742

SHELDON, ELEANOR HARRIET BERNERT, sociologist; b. Hartford, Conn., Mar. 19, 1920; d. M.G. and Fannie (Myers) Bernert; A.A., Colby Jr. Coll., 1940; A.B., U. N.C., 1942; Ph.D., U. Chgo., 1949; m. James Sheldon, Mar. 19, 1950 (div. 1960); children—James, John Anthony. Asst. demographer Office Population Research, Washington, 1942-43; social scientist U.S. Dept Agr., Washington, 1943-45; asso. dir. Chgo. Community Inventory, U. Chgo., 1947-50; social scientist Social Sci. Research Council, N.Y.C., 1950-51, research grantee, 1953-55, pres., 1972-79; research asso. Bur. Applied Social Research, Columbia, 1950-51; social scientist UN, N.Y.C., 1951-52; lectr. sociology Columbia, 1951-52, vis. prof., 1969-71; research asso., lectr. sociology U. Calif., Los Angeles, 1955-61, asso. research sociologist, lectr. Sch. Nursing, 1957-61; sociologist, exec. asso. Russell Sage Found., N.Y.C., 1961-72; vis. prof. U. Calif. at Santa Barbara, 1971; dir. Rand Corp., Santa Monica, Equitable Life Assurance Soc., Citicorp, Citibank, Mobil Corp. Bd. dirs. Colby-Sawyer Coll., UN Research Inst. for Social Devel., 1973-79; trustee Rockefeller Found., 1978—. William Rainey Harper fellow U. Chgo., 1945-47. Fellow Am. Acad. Arts and Scis., Am. Sociol. Assn., Am. Statis. Assn.; mem. U. Chgo. Alumni Assn. (Profl. Achievement award), Sociol. Research Assn. (pres. 1971-72), Council on Fgn. Relations, AAAS, Am. Assn. Pub. Opinion Research, Eastern Sociol. Soc., Internat. Sociol. Assn., Internat. Union Sci. Study of Population, Population Assn. Am. (2d v.p. 1970-71), Inst. of Medicine (chmn. program com. 1976-77). Club: Cosmopolitan. Author: (with L. Wirth) Chicago Community Fact Book, 1949; America's Children, 1958; (with R.A. Glazier) Pupils and Schools in N.Y.C., 1965. Editor: (with W.E. Moore) Indicators of Social Change; Concepts and Measurements, 1968. Editor Family Economic Behavior, 1973. Contbr. articles to profl. jours. Home: 630 Park Ave New York NY 10021

SHELDON, ERIC, physicist, educator; b. Pilsen, Bohemia, Oct. 24, 1930; s. Robert Bernard and Martha (Martin) S.; B.Sc., London (Eng.) U., 1951, B.Sc. in Physics, with honors, 1952, Ph.D., 1955, D.Sc., 1971; m. Sheila Harper, July 8, 1959; 1 son, Adrian. Lectr., research asso. Acton Tech. Coll., London, 1952-55; asso. physicist IBM Research Lab., Switzerland, 1957-59; research asso. E.T.H., Zurich, Switzerland, 1959-62, lectr., 1962-64, prof., 1964-69; prof. physics and applied physics Lowell (Mass.) Technol. Inst. and U. Lowell, 1970—; vis. prof., NSF sr. fgn. sci. fellow U. Va., 1968-69; vis. prof. U. Tex., 1969-70. Mem. Convocation London U., 1951—. Chartered chemist. Fellow Inst. Physics, Royal Inst. Chemistry, Chem. Soc. London, Am. Phys. Soc., AAAS, Royal Astron. Soc.; mem. Zurich Physics Soc. (life), Royal Instn. Gt. Britain, Mensa. Anglican/Episcopalian (lay reader). Author: (with R. Szostak and P. Marmier) Kernphysik I, 1960, Kernphysik II, 1961; (with P. Marmier) Physics of Nuclei and Particles, Vol. I, 1969, Vol. II, 1970; editor: Proc. Internat. Conf. on Interactions of Neutrons with Nuclei, 1976; contbr. articles to profl. jours. Home: 38 Cathy Rd Chelmsford MA 01824 Office: Dept Physics U Lowell North Campus Lowell MA 01854. *The benefits of happiness in my work and throughout my life, of health, contentment, fulfillment and zest for living, impose an obligation to repay this good fortune in some measure through direct service to the world around me. And still the wonder remains: Life has given me so much more than I ever could contribute—inspiration from family, friends and scholars, the grace of beauty and the miracle of laughter.*

SHELDON, GEORGIANA HORTENSE, govt. ofcl.; b. Lawrenceville, Pa., Dec. 2, 1923; d. William Franklin and Georgiana (Root) Sheldon; B.A., Keuka Coll., 1945; M.S., Cornell U., 1949; m. James R. Sharp, May 18, 1979. Dir. admissions Stetson U. Coll. Law, 1954-56; exec. asst. Republican Nat. Com., 1956-61; exec. sec. Hon. Rogers Morton (rep., Md.), 1962-69; dep. dir. Def. Civil Preparedness Agy., Washington, 1969-75; dir. Office Fgn. Disaster Assistance, dep. dir. internat. disaster assistance AID, 1975-76; vice chmn. CSC, 1976-77; mem. Fed. Power Commn., 1977—; mem. Fed. Energy Regulatory Commn., 1977—. Recipient Alumni award for profl. advancement Keuka Coll., 1966. Republican. Presbyn. Home: 1200 N Nash St Arlington VA 22209 Office: 825 N Capitol St NE Washington DC 20426

SHELDON, GILBERT IGNATIUS, clergyman; b. Cleve., Sept. 20, 1926; s. Ignatius Peter and Stephanie Josephine (Olszewski) S.; student John Carroll U.; M.Div., St. Theol. Sem., 1970; D.Min., St. Mary Sem. and Ohio Consortium of Sems., 1974. Ordained priest Roman Catholic Ch., 1953; asso. pastor Cleve. Diocese 1953-64, diocesan dir. propagation of faith, 1964-74; pastor, Episcopal vicar, Lorain County, Ohio, 1974-76, aux. bishop, Cleve., 1976—, vicar for Summit County, 1979—; bd. dirs. Soc. Propagation of Faith, 1968-74; instr. theology St. John Coll. Served with USAAF, 1944-45. Mem. Nat. Conf. Cath. Bishops, Bishops Com. for Latin Am., Bishops Com. for Missions. Club: K.C. Office: 40 E Center St Akron OH 44308

SHELDON, JOHN WILLIAM, merchandising exec.; b. Chgo., June 12, 1911; s. James Milton and Edna Leona (Stevens) S.; B.A., Dartmouth, 1932; student Northwestern U. Inst. Mgmt., 1955; m. Marjorie Mercer, June 22, 1940; children—Edward Mercer, Barbara Stevens. With Chas. A. Stevens & Co., Chgo., 1932—, v.p., 1942-57, pres., 1957—, chief exec., 1963—, chmn. bd., 1974-79, also dir.; dir. Nat. Blvd. Bank of Chgo. Chgo. Mem. bd., chmn. State St. Council. Served to lt. USNR, 1943-46. Mem. Chgo Assn. Commerce and Industry (bd., v.p.), Nat. (dir.), Ill. (past vice chmn.) retail mchts. assns., Psi Upsilon. Clubs: University, Economic, Commonwealth, Commercial (Chgo.); Old Elm Golf; Exmoor Country. Home: 575 Groveland Ave Highland Park IL 60035 Office: 25 N State St Chicago IL 60602

SHELDON, RICHARD JAY, meat packing co. exec.; b. N.Y.C., Oct. 26, 1935; s. Mack Nathan and Lucille S.; B.S., U. Ala., 1958; m. Dorothy Litvak, June 15, 1958; children—Martin Neal, Leslie Ann. With Litvak Meat Co., Denver, 1959—, plant supt., 1964-72, exec. v.p., 1972—. Served with Q.M.C., U.S. Army, 1958. Mem. Colo. Meat Dealers Assn. (pres. 1977-78). Jewish. Office: 5900 York St Denver CO 80216

SHELDON, SIDNEY, author; b. Chgo., Feb. 11, 1917; s. Otto and Natalie (Marcus) S.; ed. Northwestern U.; m. Mary Jorja Curtright, Mar. 28, 1951. Started as reader Universal and 20th Century Fox Studios; author novels: The Naked Face, 1970, The Other Side of Midnight, 1975, A Stranger in the Mirror, 1976, Bloodlines, 1977; creator, writer, producer The Patty Duke Show, I Dream of Jeannie, Nancy; author plays including: Jackpot, Dream with Music, Alice in Arms, Redhead, Roman Candle, The Judge; writer screenplays including: The Bachelor and the Bobby-Soxer, Easter Parade, Annie Get Your Gun, Rich, Young and Pretty, Dream Wife (also dir.), Anything Goes, Never Too Young, The Buster Keaton Story (also dir.), Billy Rose's Jumbo. Served with USAAF, World War II. Recipient Acad. award for screenplay The Bachelor and the Bobby-Soxer, 1947; Tony award for Redhead, 1959; Writers Guild Am. Screen awards for Easter Parade, 1948, Annie Get Your Gun, 1950. *

SHELDON, THOMAS DONALD, coll. pres.; b. Canastota, N.Y., July 15, 1920; s. Harry Ellsworth and Sadie Joyce (McNulty) S.; B.S., Syracuse U., 1942, M.S., 1949, Ed.D., 1958; grad. USAF Air War Coll., 1972; m. Helen Elizabeth Kyser, Aug. 29, 1942; children—Thomas, Paul, Edward, Patricia, Curtis, Roberta, Kevin. Tchr. sci., coach Split Rock (N.Y.) High Sch., 1942-43; tchr. sci., coach, vice prin. Minoa (N.Y.) High Sch., 1946-54, prin., 1954-59; prin., asso. supt. Hempstead (N.Y.) High Sch., 1959-63; supt. schs. Hempstead Public Schs., 1963-68; supt. Balt. City Schs., 1968-71; dep. commr. N.Y. State Edn. Dept., Albany, 1971-77; pres. Utica Coll. of Syracuse U., 1977—; bd. dirs. Commn. on Ind. Colls. and Univs.; nat. trustee Aerospace Edn. Found., Center for Study of Presidency; speaker in field. Mem. Utica (N.Y.) Pvt. Industry Council; mem. Utica-Rome Research and Tech. Com.; bd. dirs. Utica United Appeal, Upper Mohawk Valley council Boy Scouts Am. Served with U.S. Army, 1943-46; USAF, 1961-62; Berlin; to brig. gen. Air N.G., 1955-76. First recipient Outstanding Grad. award Syracuse U. Sch. Edn., 1977; recipient Outstanding Md. Educator award Md. State Council PTA's, 1969; Disting. Am. Educator award Freedoms Found., 1966; Outstanding Citizen award Minoa Community, 1959, Hempstead Community, 1968, Balt. Community, 1971, N.Y.C. Community, 1978; Conspicuous Service medal N.Y. State Gov., 1976; named to Balt. Afro-Am. Honor Roll, 1970. Mem. Am. Assn. Sch. Adminstrs., N.Y. State Council Chief Sch. Dist. Adminstrs., N.Y. State PTA (hon. life), Md. PTA (hon. life), Air Force Assn., Militia Assn. N.Y., Phi Delta Kappa. Clubs: Lions (hon. life) (Balt.); Rotary, Torch, U.S. Naval Acad. Officers and Faculty, Univ. of Albany, Ft. Schuyler of Utica, Am. Legion. Author: The Relationships of Teacher Background and Preparation to Student Success in Regents Examinations, 1959; The Crisis in Urban Education, 1968; International Education Through International Teacher Exchange, 1970; co-author and editor various N.Y. State Regents publs., 1971-76. Office: Office of the Pres Utica Coll of Syracuse U Burrstone Rd Utica NY 13502

SHELESNYAK, MOSES CHAIM, biodynamicist, physiologist; b. Chgo., June 6, 1909; s. Jonas and Fay (Leavitt) S.; B.A., U. Wis., 1930; Ph.D. (U. fellow), Columbia, 1933; postgrad. Alliance Francaise, summer 1929, N.Y. Sch. Social Work, 1935-36; m. Roslyn Benjamin, Jan. 28, 1942; children—Betty Jane (Mrs. Franz Sondheimer), Henry Lawrence. Instr. physiology, pharmacology Chgo. Med. Sch., 1935-36; lectr. human growth New Coll., Tchrs. Coll., Columbia, 1936-37; research asso. Mt. Sinai Hosp., N.Y.C., 1936-40; research asso. Friedsam fellow Beth Israel Hosp., N.Y.C., 1940-42; acting head biophysics br. U.S. Office Naval Research, Washington, 1946-47, head human ecology br., 1946-49; lectr. ecology Johns Hopkins, 1949-50; dir. Arctic Inst. N.Am., Balt.-Washington, 1949-50; sr. scientist Weizmann Inst. Sci., Rehovoth, Israel, 1950-58, asso. prof., 1958-59, prof., 1959, head dept. biodynamics, 1960-68; asso. dir. Interdisciplinary Communications Program, Office Asst. Sec. Sci., Smithsonian Instn.-N.Y. Acad. Scis., 1967-68, exec. sec. Council Communication, 1968-72, dir. Interdisciplinary Communications Program, Smithsonian Instn., 1968-77, research asso., 1977—; dir. Internat. Program Population Analysis, 1972-77; pres., chmn. bd. Interdisciplinary Communication Assos., 1969—; vis. lectr. geography McGill U., 1948; vis. prof. Coll. de France, 1960; mem. bd. human ecology arid zones UNESCO, 1954-72; research com. Internat. Planned Parenthood Fedn., 1959-72; selection and adv. com. Internat. Tng. Program Physiology Reprodn., Worcester, Mass., 1959-70; neuroendocrinology panel Interdisciplinary Brain Research Orgn., 1961—; expert adv. panel biology human reprodn. WHO, 1965-70; cons. Am. Physiol. Soc., 1977—. Served to lt. comdr. USNR, 1942-46. Gen. Edn. Bd. fellow, 1936-38, Sir Simon Marks fellow Birmingham (Eng.) U., 1957-58, U. Research fellow Birmingham U., 1957-59. Fellow A.A.A.S., Arctic Inst. N.Am., Eugenics Soc.; mem. Aerospace Med. Assn., A.A.U.P., Israel, Am. chem. socs., Am. Inst. Biol. Sci., Am. Physiol. Soc. (dir. task force commemorative com., exec. editor The Physiology Tchr. 1977—, exec. editor hist. sect. The Physiologist 1979—), Am. Polar Soc., Am. Soc. Study Sterility, Animal Behavior Soc., Arctic Circle, Biochem. Soc. Israel, Brit. Glaciological Soc., Ecol. Soc. Am., Endocrine Soc. Am., Endocrine Soc. Israel, European Soc. Drug Toxicity, History Sci. Soc., Inst. Aero. Scis., Soc. Exptl. Biology and Medicine, Israel Fertility Soc., Israel Soc. Exptl. Biology and Medicine, Israel Soc. Undersea Exploration, N.Y. Acad. Scis., Internat. Soc. Research in Reprodn. (founding), Soc. Internat. Devel., Soc. Research Child Devel., Soc. Gen. Systems Research, Am. Acad. Polit. and Social Sci., Acad. Polit. Scis., Population Assn. Am., World Future Soc., Acad. Medicine Washington, Sigma Xi; fgn. mem. La Sociedad Chilena d'Obstetricia y Ginecologia, Societa Italiana per il progresso della zootecnica, Societe Royale Belge de Gynecologie et d'Obstetrique. Clubs: Cosmos (Washington); Explorers (N.Y.C.). Editor: Ovum Implantation, 1969; Growth of Population, 1969; editorial bd. Jour. Reprodn. and Fertility; Contraception; contbr. articles to profl. jours. Home: River House Cherryfield Rd Drayden MD 20630 Office: 9650 Rockville Pike Bethesda MD 20014

SHELINE, GLENN ELMER, radiation oncologist, educator; b. Flint, Mich., Mar. 31, 1918; s. Charles Earl and Onale (Newman) S.; B.S., U. Calif. at Berkeley, 1939, Ph.D. in physiology, 1943; M.D., U. Calif. at San Francisco, 1948; m. Patricia Brinton, June 14, 1948; 1 dau., Moira Lynn. Investigations plutonium chemistry Manhattan Dist. Engrs., 1942-45; NRC fellow, 1949-51; with dept. radiology U. Calif. Med. Sch., San Francisco, 1955—, prof., 1964—; program dir. for radiation therapy Nat. Cancer Inst. (on leave), 1975, adv. com. div. cancer control and rehab., 1977—. Mem. San Francisco Med. Soc., AMA, Calif. Med. Assn., Am. Thyroid Assn., Am. Radium Soc., Radiol. Soc. N.Am., Am. Roentgen Ray Soc., Am. Soc. Therapeutic Radiologists. Asso. editor Internat. Jour. Radiation Oncology Biology and Physics; mem. editorial bd. Radiology; contbr. articles to profl. jours. Home: 50 Mounds Rd San Mateo CA 94402 Office: Dept Radiology U Calif Med Center San Francisco CA 94143

SHELINE, RAYMOND K., nuclear chemist; b. Port Clinton, Ohio, Mar. 31, 1922; s. Raymond Kaiser and Rozena (Huard) S.; B.S. summa cum laude, Bethany Coll., 1943; Ph.D., U. Calif. at Berkeley, 1949; m. Yvonne Faith Engwall, June 9, 1951; children—Yvette Ingrid, Raymond Kenneth, Jonathan Lee, Hans Eric, Rebecca Ruth, Martin Engwall, Christian Thomas. Research asst. Manhattan Project War Research, Columbia, 1943-45; jr. sci. U. Calif. at Los Alamos Lab., 1945-46, cons. 1961; instr. Inst. Nuclear Studies and chemistry dept. U. Chgo., 1949-51; asso. prof. chemistry Fla. State U., 1951-55, prof., 1955-58, prof. chemistry and physics, 1958—, chmn. nuclear sci. program, 1959-70; research prof. Niels Bohr Inst., Copenhagen, 1964, Nordita prof., 1972. Fulbright lectr., Denmark, Holland, Germany, Norway, Sweden, 1955-58; Egyptian nat. lectr. Ein Shams U., Cairo, Egypt, 1956; cons. chem. div. Oak Ridge Nat. Lab., 1959-64; Nordita prof. U. Lund (Sweden); mem. Woodrow Wilson Fellowship Com., 1958-61; mem. com. on postdoctoral fellowships in chemistry Nat. Acad. Scis., 1958-63; mem. Gov.'s Com. on Quality Edn., 1961-63; cons. phys. facilities program NSF, 1963-66; cons. Los Alamos Sci. Lab., 1961—; co-chmn. Gordon Research Conf. on Nuclear Chemistry, 1967; lectr. Nuclear Physics Summer Sch., Mikolaki, Poland, 1974; Gillon lectr. Nat. U. Zaire, Kinshasa, 1976; vis. research prof. Inst. für Kernphysik, Kernforschungsanlage, Julich, W. Ger., 1976. Served with AUS, 1943-46. Fulbright fellow, Copenhagen, 1955-56, 57-58, Guggenheim fellow, 1955-56, 57-58, 64-65; appointee Ford Found. Research Project, Internat. Coop. Atomic Energy, 1957-58; recipient Niels Bohr award for coop. in devel. nuclear chemistry lab. Inst. Theoretical Physics, Copenhagen, 1958; alumni outstanding achievement award Bethany Coll., 1965, Nat. fellow, 1966; Distinguished Prof. of Year, Fla. State U., 1966; Alexander von Humboldt Sr. Scientist award, 1976. Fellow Am. Phys. Soc.; mem. Am. Chem. Soc., Danish Royal Acad. Scis. (fgn.), Sigma Xi. Contbr. articles numerous sci. jours., profl. publs. Home: 3268 Longleaf Rd Tallahassee FL 32304

SHELL, ARTHUR (ART), football player; b. Charleston, S.C., Nov. 26, 1946; B.S., Md. State-Eastern Shore Coll., 1968. Offensive tackle Oakland Raiders, 1968—; played in Pro Bowl, 1973-79. Office: care Oakland Raiders 7811 Oakport St Oakland CA 94621*

SHELL, BILLY JOE, univ. pres.; b. Ecorse, Mich., Sept. 2, 1925; s. Millard Wootson and Flossie Mae (Evans) S.; B.S., Mich. State U., 1947, M.S., 1949, Ph.D., 1955; m. Edythe Lorraine Roach, Dec. 25, 1948; children—Deborah (Mrs. William Wilkinson), Brian Jeffrey. Faculty U. Ariz., 1949-53, Mich. State U., 1955; v.p., chief engr. San Xavier Rock & Sand Co., Tucson, 1956-66; asso. dean engring. Miss. State U., 1966-70, acting v.p. for research, 1969-70; dean engring. Calif. State Poly. U., Pomona, 1970-73, acting v.p. acad. affairs, 1971-72; pres. Northrop U., Inglewood, Calif., 1973—, also trustee. Vice chmn. Ariz. Bd. Tech. Registration, 1965-66; chmn. Calif. Council for Pvt. Postsecondary Ednl. Instns. Mem. Environ. Quality Control Com., Los Angeles County, 1971. Chmn. bd. dirs. Tucson Boys Chorus, 1965-66. Served with USMCR, 1943-45. Recipient Engr. of Year award So. chpt. Ariz. Soc. Profl. Engrs., 1965, Outstanding Service award, 1966, Educator of Year award Region VII, Soc. Mfg. Engrs., 1973; Skill, Integrity and Responsibility award Asso. Gen. Contractors Calif., 1975. Registered profl. engr., Ariz., Miss., Tex. Fellow Inst. for Advancement Engring.; mem. Nat., Calif. (Outstanding Service award 1973, Edn. Achievement award 1975) socs. profl. engrs., ASCE, Nat. Council Engring. Examiners, Am. Water Works Assn., Water Pollution Control Fedn., Am. Soc. Engring. Edn., Am. Assn. Univ. Presidents, Sigma Xi, Chi Epsilon, Sigma Pi Alpha, Tau Beta Pi. Mason, Rotarian. Home: 1182 Steele Dr Brea CA 92621 Office: 1155 W Arbor Vitae Inglewood CA 90306

SHELL, CLAUDE IRVING, JR., educator; b. Pine Bluff, Ark., Oct. 15, 1922; s. Claude Irving and Ela (Hartsell) S.; B.A., Maryville Coll., 1947; M.S., U. Tenn., 1949; Ph.D., So. Ill. U., 1966; m. Mary Frances Robinson, July 27, 1952; children—Barbara Jane, Mary Louise, James Claude, William Joseph. Partner, Shell-Ross Co., 1951-54; asst. prof. bus. adminstrn. Tenn. Tech. U., 1948-51, asso. prof., 1954-57; product planner Ford Motor Co., 1957-60; asst. dir. Small Bus. Inst., So. Ill. U., 1960-65; asst. dir. placement services, 1965-66, chmn. dept. mgmt., 1966-67; prof., head dept. mgmt. Eastern Mich. U., Ypsilanti, 1967—, acting dean Coll. Bus., 1978-79; cons. Ill. Div. Vocational Rehab., 1964—. Bd. dirs. Bus. Opportunities for Blind, 1965-69; mem. bd., exec. com. Visually Handicapped Mgrs. Ill., 1972—, chmn., 1974—. Served to lt. F.A., AUS, 1943-46; ETO. Mem. Acad. Mgmt., Internat. Council Small Bus., Beta Gamma Sigma, Phi Kappa Phi, Alpha Kappa Psi, Pi Sigma Epsilon, Sigma Iota Epsilon. Presbyn. (elder). Contbr. articles to profl. jours. Home: 1910 Collegewood Dr Ypsilanti MI 48197

SHELL, OWEN G., banker; b. Greenville, S.C., June 19, 1936; s. Owen G. and Katherine W. (Walker) S.; B.S., U. S.C., 1960; postgrad. Stonier Grad. Sch. Banking, Rutgers U., 1971, Advanced Mgmt. Program. Harvard Bus. Sch., 1977; children—Katherine Sloan, Mary Carroll, Robert Owen. Tech. supt. Deering-Milliken, Inc., 1962-63; v.p. Citizens & So. Nat. Bank of S.C., Columbia, 1968-71, sr. v.p., 1971-74, exec. v.p., 1974-79; pres. First Am. Nat. Bank, Nashville, 1979—; vice-chmn. bd. First Amteen Corp., Nashville, 1979—; dir. Engineered Custom Plastics Corp., Sloan Constrn. Co., Inc. Chmn., Redevel. Authority City of Greenville (S.C.), 1972-74, Richland County Library Bd., 1978-79; bd. dirs. Am. Cancer Soc. Served to capt. USAF, 1960-64. Mem. S.C. Bankers Assn. (exec. com. 1973-74). Greenville C. of C. (past v.p., dir.), Downtown Greenville Assn. (past pres.), S.C. C. of C. (dir.), Kappa Alpha, Omicron Delta Kappa. Presbyterian. Clubs: Rotary. Home: 4633 Pine Grove Ct Columbia SC 29206 Office: PO Box 727 Columbia SC 29222

SHELLEY, BRIAN HOLINGER, pub. co. exec.; b. Manchester, Eng., 1917; s. William Edmund and Blanche (Holinger) S.; grad. high sch.; m. Pauline Mary Vidler, Feb. 16, 1946; children—Pamela Joy (Mrs. Peter Williamson), Martin William, Leslie Anne. With Morris Gregory & Co., chartered accountants, Manchester, 1935-39, 46-47; audit supr. McDonald Currie & Co., Toronto, 1947-50; internal auditor Brazilian Traction Light & Power Co., Ltd., Sao Paolo, Brazil, 1950-56; v.p. fin., sec. Southam Inc., Toronto, Ont., Can., 1957—. Served with RAF, 1939-45. Chartered accountant. Fellow Inst. Chartered Accountants of Eng. and Wales; mem. Inst. Newspaper Controllers and Finance Officers (dir.). Clubs: Royal Canadian Yacht; Royal Canadian Mil. Inst. Home: 33 Valentine Dr Don Mills ON Canada Office: 321 Bloor St E Ste 801 Toronto ON M4W 1H3 Canada

SHELLEY, CAROLE AUGUSTA, actress; b. London, Aug. 16, 1939; came to U.S., 1964; d. Curtis and Deborah (Bloomstein) S.; studied ballet at Arts Ednl. Sch., 1943-56, Prep. acad. R.A.D.A., 1956-57; studied voice with Iris Warren; m. Albert G. Woods, July 26, 1967. Child actress, beginning at age 3; later appeared in revues, films, West End comedies, including New Cranks and Mary Mary at the Globe Theatre; appeared as Gwendolyn Pigeon in stage, film and TV versions of The Odd Couple; Broadway appearances include: The Astrakhan Coat, Loot, Sweet Potato, Little Murders, Hay Fever, The Norman Conquests (Los Angeles Drama Critics Circle award 1975); appeared as Rosalind in As You Like It, King Lear and She Stoops to Conquer at Stratford, Ont., Can., 1972, and their European and Russian tours; appeared as Mrs. Margery Pinchwife in The Country Wife at Am. Shakespeare Festival, Stratford, Conn., 1973, as Nora in A Doll's House, Goodman Theatre, Chgo.; appeared in Man and Superman and as Epifania in The Millionairess, Shaw Festival, 1977; appeared in The Play's The Thing and The Devil's Disciple, Bklyn. Acad. Music, 1978; other stage appearances include The Royal Family (Los Angeles Drama Critics Circle award 1977), The Elephant Man (Outer Critics Circle award for 1978-79 season, Tony award for best actress 1978-79 season); appeared in film The Boston Strangler; created voice characters in Walt Disney films The Aristocats and Robin Hood; trustee Am. Shakespeare Theatre. Jewish. Office: care Lionel Larner 850 7th Ave New York NY 10019

SHELLEY, JAMES LAMAR, lawyer; b. Joseph City, Ariz., Dec. 8, 1915; s. Thomas Heber and Eva (Tanner) S.; B.A., Ariz. State Coll., 1936; J.D., U. Ariz., 1949; m. Virginia Rand, Nov. 21, 1942; children—Carol (Mrs. Danny Parker Boyle), Marlene (Mrs. J. Robert Tolman), Jana (Mrs. Gunn B. McKay), Mary (Mrs. Mark Hutchings), Gerald LaMar, James Rand. Admitted to Ariz. bar, 1948, since practiced in Mesa; asst. city atty., 1948-50, city atty., 1950—; mem. firm Johnson Shelley & Roberts and predecessor firms, 1951—; gen. counsel League Ariz. Cities and Towns, 1963—. Mem. exec. bd. Theodore Roosevelt council Boy Scouts Am., 1962—, Mesa Dist. chmn., 1967-68; v.p. Mesa United Fund, 1967-69, pres., 1970; pres. bd. mgmt. Mesa br. YMCA; pres. Mesa Christmas Basket Assn., Mesa Fine Arts Assn., 1978—. Served to lt. USNR, 1942-45. Named Mesa Man of Year, 1965. Mem. Ariz. Acad., Nat. Inst. Municipal Law Officers (trustee). Republican. Mem. Ch. of Jesus Christ of Latter-day Saints (regional rep. of The Twelve). Clubs: Exchange (past pres.), Southside Dinner (past pres. Mesa). Home: 550 N Emerson St Mesa AZ 85201 Office: 48 N Macdonald St Mesa AZ 85201

SHELLEY, JOHN RICHARD, architect; b. Warroad, Minn., Jan. 14, 1923; s. John S. and Clara (Pryor) S.; archtl.-engring. degree Wash. State U., 1947; m. Gladys Elaine Cox, June 21, 1947 (dec. May 1977); children—Leslye, Rodney, Jeffrey. Prin., J. Richard Shelley & Assos., Long Beach, Calif., 1956; architect, owner, developer hotels, apts., office bldgs. in Midwest, Calif., Hawaii; sr. adviser tourism and resort devel. and cons. to World Bank, Indonesia, 1974—; cons. urban redevel. projects. Dir. Long Beach Heart Assn., 1961-62, Long Beach Family Service Agy., 1957-60, Long Beach Muscular Dystrophy, 1955-56, Long Beach Civic League, 1961-62. Served with USAAF, World War II. Recipient 4 archtl. design awards, 1st prize for community fallout shelter design Dept. Def., 1964. Mem. AIA, Calif. Jr. C. of C. (life, dir. 1954-56), Sigma Nu. Republican. Clubs: University (pres., dir. 1954-66), International City, Long Beach Yacht (Long Beach). Home: 197 Rivo Alto Canal Long Beach CA 90803

SHELLEY, WALTER BROWN, physician, educator; b. St. Paul, Feb. 6, 1917; s. Patrick K. and Alfaretta (Brown) S.; B.S., U. Minn., 1940, Ph.D., 1941, M.D., 1943; M.A. honoris causa, U. Pa., 1971; M.D. honoris causa, U. Uppsala (Sweden), 1977; children—Peter B., Anne E. Kiselewich. Instr. physiology U. Pa., Phila., 1946-47, asst. instr. dermatology and syphilology, 1947-49, asst. prof. dermatology, 1950-53, asso. prof., 1953-57, prof., 1957—, chmn. dept., 1965—; instr. dermatology Dartmouth, 1949-50. Regional cons. dermatology VA, 1955-59; mem. com. on cutaneous system NRC, 1955-59, Commn. Cutaneous Diseases, Armed Forces Epidemiological Bd. 1958-61, dep. dir., 1959-61; cons. dermatology Surgeon Gen. USAF, 1958-61, U.S. Army, 1958-61; mem. NRC, 1961-64. Served as capt. M.C., AUS, 1944-46. Recipient Spl. award Soc. Cosmetic Chemists, 1955; Hellerstrom medal, 1971; Am. Med. Writers Assn. Best Med. Book award, 1973. Diplomate Am. Bd. Dermatology (pres. 1968-69, dir. 1960-69). Fellow A.C.P. (master), Assn. Am. Physicians, St. John's Dermatol. Soc. London (hon.); mem. AMA (chmn. residency rev. com. for dermatology 1963-67, chmn. sect. dermatology 1969-71), Assn. Profs. Dermatology (pres. 1972-73), Pacific (hon.), Am. (dir., pres. 1975-76) dermatol. assns., Soc. Investigative Dermatology (pres. 1961-62), Am., Phila. physiol. socs., Brit. (hon.), Phil. (pres. 1960-61) dermatol. socs., Am. (pres. 1971-72), Pa. (pres. 1972-73) acads. dermatology, Am. Soc. for Dermatologic Surgery; corr. mem. Nederlandse Vereniging Van Dermatologen, Israeli Dermatol. Assn., Finnish Soc. Dermatology, Swedish Dermatol. Soc., French Dermatologic Soc.; fgn. hon. mem. Danish Dermatol. Assn., Dermatol. Soc. S.Africa. Author: (with Crissey) Classics in Clinical Dermatology, 1953; (with Pillsbury, Kligman) Dermatology 1956; Cutaneous Medicine, 1961; (with Hurley) The Human Apocrine Sweat Gland in Health and Disease, 1960; (with Botelho and Brooks) The Endocrine Glands, 1969; Consultations in Dermatology with Walter B. Shelley, 1972, Consultations II, 1974. Mem. editorial bd. Jour. Investigative Dermatology, 1961-64, Archives of Dermatology, 1961-62, Skin and Allergy News, 1970—, Excerpta Medica Dermatologica, 1960—, Cutis, 1972—; asso. editor Jour. Cutaneous Pathology, 1972—; editorial cons. Medcom., 1972—. Home: 505 County Line Rd Radnor PA 19087 Office: 3600 Spruce St Philadelphia PA 19104

SHELLHASE, LESLIE JOHN, educator; b. Hardy, Nebr., Jan. 12, 1924; s. John Clayton and Sanna Belle (Muth) S.; A.B., Midland Coll., 1947; M.S.W., U. Nebr., 1950; D.Social Work, Catholic U. Am., 1961; m. Fern Eleanor Kleckner, June 8, 1948; children—Jeremy Clayton, Joel Kleckner. Parole supr. Child Welfare, Omaha, 1948-49; psychiat. social work intern Letterman Gen. Hosp. San Francisco, 1950-51; commd. 2d lt. U.S. Army, 1949, advanced through grades to lt. col., 1966; chief social worker 6th Inf. Div., Ft. Ord, Calif., 1952-55; chief med. social worker Walter Reed Gen. Hosp., Washington, 1955-57; research investigator Walter Reed Inst. Research, Washington, 1957-63; head social work faculty Med. Field Service Sch., Ft. Sam Houston, Tex., 1963-66; chief sociologist U.S. Army, Washington, 1966-68; prof. Sch. Social Work, U. Ala., University, 1968—; cons. Family Service Assn. Am., 1969—. Bd. dirs. Crisis Intervention Center; bd. dirs., chmn. Soc. for Crippled Children and Adults; chmn. bd. social ministry So. Dist. Lutheran Ch. Decorated Legion of Merit, Bronze Star, Purple Heart, recipient letters of commendation from Pres., 1968, Surgeon Gen., 1961. Fellow Am. Sociol. Assn.; mem. Nat. Assn. Social Workers (dir. 1963-66), Council Social Work Edn., Nat. Conf. Social Welfare, Acad. Certified Social Workers, ACLU, Am. Vets Com., Ret. Officers Assn., So. Sociol. Soc. Democrat. Author: The Group Life of the Schizophrenic Patient, 1961; Bibliography of Army Social Work, 1962; contbr. articles on social and behavioral sci. to nat. and internat. profl. jours., books. Home: 148 Woodland Hills Tuscaloosa AL 35405 Office: Box 1935 University AL 35486

SHELLHORN, RUTH PATRICIA, landscape architect; b. Los Angeles, Sept. 21, 1909; d. Arthur Lemon and Lodema (Gould) S.; student dept. landscape architecture Oreg. State Coll., 1927-30; L.A., Cornell U. Coll. Architecture, 1933; m. Harry Alexander Kueser, Nov. 21, 1940. Pvt. practice landscape architecture, various cities, Calif., 1933—; exec. cons. landscape architect Bullocks Stores, Calif., 1945-78, Fashion Sqs. Shopping Centers, Calif., 1958—, Marlborough Sch., Los Angeles, 1968—, El Camino Coll., Torrance, Calif., 1970-78, Harvard Sch., North Hollywood, Calif., 1974—; cons. landscape architect, site planner Disneyland, Anaheim, Calif., 1955, U. Calif., Riverside, Campus, 1956-64, numerous others, also numerous gardens and estates; landscape architect Torrance (Calif.) City Goals Com., 1969-70; cons. landscape architect City of Rolling Hills (Calif.) Community Assn., 1972—. Named Woman of Year, Los Angeles Times, 1955, S. Pasadena-San Marino (Calif.) Bus. Profl. Women, 1955; recipient numerous nat., state, local awards for excellence. Fellow Am. Soc. Landscape Architects (past pres. So. Calif. chpt.), Phi Kappa Phi, Kappa Kappa Gamma (Alumni Achievement award 1960). Contbr. articles to garden and profl. publs. Home and office: 362 Camino De Las Colinas Redondo Beach CA 90277. *Integrity, honesty, dependability, sincerity, dedication, and a willingness to give more than is expected in service, are the basic principles which have guided my career. Never losing sight of the importance of the individual, I have tried to create total environments of harmony and beauty to which each individual can relate in a very personal and pleasureable way, and for a little while, can find a calm oasis in a busy and demanding world.*

SHELLOW, JAMES MYERS, lawyer; b. Milw., Oct. 31, 1926; s. Henry Gershon and Sadie (Myers) S.; B.A., U. Chgo., 1949; LL.B., Marquette U., 1961; m. Gilda Bloom, Sept. 3, 1950; children—Jill, Robin. Univ. research fellow U. Chgo., 1950; engr. Servo, Capehart, Farnsworth affiliate ITT, 1950; sr. systems engr. Chance Vought Aircraft Corp., Grand Prairie, Tex., 1951; ops. analyst Inst. for Air Weapons Research, Chgo., 1952; dir. long range planning Calif. Research and Devel. affiliate Standard Oil Calif., Livermore, 1953; admitted to Wis. bar, 1961; mem. firm Shellow & Shellow, Milw., 1961—. Research asso. Mental Health Research Center, U. Mich., 1966-67; lectr. Beloit (Wis.) Coll., 1968; lectr. trial advocacy U. Wis. Law Sch., 1971, lectr. advanced criminal procedure, 1972-74; asst. clin. prof., div. human behavior Med. Coll. Wis., 1971-74; lectr. Nat. Legal Aid and Defender Assn., 1968-74, Practicing Law Inst., 1972. Mem. Gov.'s Task Force on Computerization of Criminal Justice System, mem. Com. on Criminal Rules of Wis. Jud. Council, 1966; mem. adv. council on Handbook for Wis. Criminal Def. Attys., Inst. for Continuing Legal Edn., 1972; bd. dirs. Freedom Through Equality, 1969-73, Milw. Legal Services, 1973-74. Fellow Nat. Coll. Criminal Def. Lawyers (v.p. 1972-73, pres. 1975.), mem. Am. Judicature Soc., Am. (past rep. to Nat. Conf. Lawyers and C.P.S.'s, lectr. nat. inst. 1972), Wis. (mem. exec. com. criminal law sect. 1967, past chmn.), Milw. (mem. profl. responsibility com. 1971-74, ethics com. 1967-70, fair trial-free press com. 1968, cts. com. 1973-74), 7th Fed. Circuit (chmn. com. on criminal law and prodecure) bar assns., ACLU (chpt. exec. bd. 1966-74), Nat. Assn. Criminal Def. Lawyers (dir. 1967-70), Am. Law Inst. Home: 3212 N Lake Dr Milwaukee WI 53211 Office: 222 E Mason St Milwaukee WI 53202

SHELOKOV, ALEXIS, physician; b. Harbin, China, Oct. 18, 1919; s. Ivan T. and Maria M. (Zolotov) S.; came to U.S., 1938, naturalized, 1944; A.B., Stanford, 1943, M.D., 1948; m. Paula Helbig, June 10, 1947; 1 son, Alexis Paul. Physiologist climatic research lab. War Dept., 1943-44; research asst. Stanford, 1946-47; house officer Mass. Meml. Hosps., Boston, 1947-50; instr. medicine Boston U. Sch. Medicine, 1948-50; asst. in pediatrics Harvard Med. Sch., 1949-50; clin. instr. medicine Georgetown U., 1953-57; cons. D.C. Gen. Hosp., 1955-57, Gorgas, Coco Solo hosps., C.Z., 1958-61; dir. Middle Am. Research Unit, C.Z. 1957-61; mem. sci. adv. bd. Gorgas Meml. Inst., Panama, 1959-72, 76—; chief lab. tropical virology Nat. Inst. Allergy and Infectious Diseases, NIH, 1959-63; chief lab. virology and rickettsiology Div. Biologics Standards, NIH, 1963-68; officer (med. dir.) USPHS, 1950-68; prof., chmn. dept. microbiology U. Tex. Health Sci. Center, San Antonio, 1968—; mem. U.S. del. on virus diseases to USSR, 1961, chmn. U.S. del. on hemorrhagic fevers to USSR, 1965,

69; exec. council Am. Com. for Arthropod-borne Viruses, 1960-67; panel for arthropod-borne virus reagents. Nat. Inst. Allergy and Infectious Diseases, 1962-66, cons. geog. medicine br., 1972-76; mem. sci. adv. bd. WHO Serum Bank, Yale, 1964-68; cons. Pan Am. Health Orgn., 1958-63, 71, WHO, 1966; mem. commn. on viral infections Armed Forces Epidemiological Bd., 1967-68; mem. virology study sect. div. research grants NIH, 1968-70; mem. viral disease panel U.S.-Japan Coop. Med. Sci. Program, 1971-76; mem. Am. Tropical Medicine del. to China; adv. bd. virology CRC Press, 1975—. Trustee Am. Type Culture Collection, 1969-72; bd. sci. counselors Nat. Inst. Dental Research, NIH, 1971-75. Decorated Order Rodolfo Robles (Guatemala). Diplomate Am. Bd. Microbiology, Am. Bd. Preventive Medicine. Mem. Am. Assn. Immunologists, Soc. Exptl. Biology and Medicine, Am. Soc. Tropical Medicine and Hygiene, Am. Epidemiologic Soc., A.M.A., Infectious Disease Soc. Am., Soc. Epidemiological Research, Am. Soc. Microbiology, Council Biology Editors, Assn. Med. Sch. Microbiology Chairmen. Mem. editorial bd. Am. Jour. Tropical Medicine and Hygiene, 1973—, Jour. Clin. Microbiology, 1976—, Archives of Virology, 1979—. Home: 4134 High Sierra Dr San Antonio TX 78228 Office: U Tex Health Sci Center San Antonio TX 78284

SHELTON, DAVID HOWARD, univ. dean; b. Winona, Miss., Nov. 30, 1928; s. Tuttle M. and Kate (Moss) S.; B.A., Millsaps Coll., 1951; M.A., Ohio State U., 1952, Ph.D., 1958; m. Margaret Murff, Feb. 4, 1951; children—David Keith, Sarah Katherine, Susan Esther. Instr., Ohio State U., 1958; asst. prof. U. Del., 1958-63, asso. prof., 1963-65; prof. U. N.C. at Greensboro, 1965—, head dept. econs., bus. adminstrn., 1967-70, dean Sch. Bus. and Econs., 1970—. Cons. Joint Council on Econ. Edn., 1969-72, N.C. Dept. Pub. Instrn., 1970-73. Trustee N.C. Council on Econ. Edn., 1971—, chmn., 1971-75, pres., 1975—. Served with USNR, 1946-48. M.D. Lincoln fellow, 1956-57, H.L. and Grace Doherty fellow, 1957. Mem. Beta Gamma Sigma, Omicron Delta Kappa, Kappa Sigma. Episcopalian. Home: 3609 Dogwood Dr Greensboro NC 27403

SHELTON, GEORGE CALVIN, univ. dean; b. Stephenville, Tex., Apr. 26, 1923; s. William Dewey and Georgia (Tucker) S.; D.V.M., Tex. A. and M. U., 1948; M.S., Auburn U., 1952; Ph.D., U. Minn., 1965; m. Quata Joy Shelton, Feb. 5, 1949; children—Kay Ellen, Darrell Glen. Pvt. practice vet. medicine, California, Mo., 1948-49; mem. faculty U. Mo. at Columbia, 1949-51, 52-73, prof. vet. microbiology, 1959—, chmn. dept., 1965-69, asso. dean acad. affairs, 1967-73; research asst. Auburn U., 1952; dean Tex. A. and M. U. Coll. Vet. Medicine, Bryan, 1973—. Cons. in field. Vice pres. Residential Housing Assn., 1968-70, bd. dirs., 1967—. Served with USAAF, 1942-45. Decorated Air medal with 3 oak leaf clusters, Purple Heart; Faculty sci. fellow NSF, 1961-62. Mem. Am. Vet. Med. Assn., Am. Soc. Parasitological Research Workers, Am. Assn. Vet. Parasitologists (pres. 1966-67), Sigma Xi, Gamma Sigma Delta. Baptist. Kiwanian (pres. Columbia 1970-71). Contbr. articles to profl. jours. Home: 3708 Sunnybrook Ln Bryan TX 77801

SHELTON, JAMES TRUESDALL, physician, hosp. adminstr.; b. Los Angeles, Aug. 30, 1922; s. William Cortez and Ruth (Zimmerman) S.; A.B., Pomona Coll., 1944; M.D., U. So. Calif., 1946; m. Betty Ellen Faith, Dec. 26, 1945; children—Susan, Jane, Robert, Betsy, Jeffrey, John. Intern Santa Fe Coast Lines Hosp., Los Angeles, 1946-47; resident psychiatry Langley Porter Neuropsychiat. Inst., San Francisco, 1951-52; resident psychiatry Mendocino State Hosp., Talmage, Calif., sr. physician and surgeon, 1950; dir. pre-admission and diagnostic service Sonoma State Hosp., Eldridge, Calif., 1952-53; asst. supt. med. service Porterville State Hosp., 1953-54, supt., med. dir., 1954—; clin. instr. psychiatry U. Calif. Sch. Medicine, 1953-72; mem. Nebr. Mental Retardation Panel, 1975-78; adv. bd. mental health Tulare County, 1963-68; dir. Porterville Assn. Retarded Children's Workshop, 1958-68; bd. trustees Porterville Elementary Sch. Dist., 1965-77; chmn. 1969-75. Served to capt. M.C., AUS, 1947-49. Recipient Golden Rule award Calif. Council Retarded Children, 1961. Diplomate Am. Bd. Psychiatry and Neurology. Fellow Am. Psychiat. Assn. (mem. com. on mental retardation 1964-71), Am. Assn. Mental Deficiency (chmn. Region III 1970-71); mem. Am. Assn. Psychiat. Adminstrs. (councillor 1976-78), Central Calif. Psychiat. Soc. (past pres.), Am. Contract Bridge League, P.T.A. (hon. life). Clubs: Rotary (Porterville); Commonwealth of Calif. Contbr. articles to profl. publs. Address: Porterville State Hospital PO Box 2000 Porterville CA 93257

SHELTON, KARL MASON, banker; b. Lincolnton, N.C., June 8, 1933; s. Karl and Annie (Grace) S.; grad. Am. Inst. Banking, 1960, Carolinas Sch. Banking, 1963, Stonier Grad. Sch. Banking, 1967; m. Deloris Hundley, May 8, 1954; children—Melanie Dwain, Leslie Elaine, Kevin Karl. Vice pres. N.C. Nat. Bank, Charlotte, 1954-71; sr. v.p., treas. Seattle-First Nat. Bank, 1971-79; pres. Citizens Fidelity Corp., Louisville, 1979—, also dir.; dir. Citizens Fidelity Bank and Trust Co., Louisville. Served with AUS, 1952-54. Mem. Am. Bankers Assn., Am. Inst. Banking, Dealer Bank Assn. Methodist. Contbg. editor Bankers Handbook, 1978. Office: Box 33000 Louisville KY 40232

SHELTON, LARRY BRANDON, apparel co. exec.; b. Paducah, Ky., Aug. 4, 1934; s. Brandon and Annabelle (Jones) S.; B.S. in Commerce, Bowling Green Coll. Commerce, 1956; m. Lura Jane Peyton, Aug. 26, 1955; children—Tracey Jean, Ted Peyton. With Genesco Inc., Nashville, 1956—, sr. internal auditor, 1961, spl. finance asst. exec. dept., 1961-62, v.p. Eastern control office, 1962-69, v.p. Central control, 1969, sec., 1973-75, vice chmn. bd., 1975-77, exec. v.p., 1977—. C.P.A., Tenn. Mem. Am. Inst. C.P.A.'s, Tenn. Soc. C.P.A.'s. Methodist. Home: 1809 Laurel Ridge Dr Nashville TN 37215 Office: 111 7th Ave N Nashville TN 37202*

SHELTON, LEWIS SAMUEL, mus. adminstr.; b. Jacksonville, Fla., Nov. 19, 1933; s. Lewis Samuel and Mattie (Wansley) S.; B.S., U. Ga., 1955, M.A., 1963, Ed.D. (NSF fellow), 1965; m. Patricia Clarke Rae, Aug. 20, 1955; children—Barbara, Catherine, Jeffrey. Prof. dept. biology DeKalb Coll. and Oglethorpe U., Atlanta, 1964-66; dir. Fernbank Sci. Center, Atlanta, 1966—; pres. Druid Hills Civic Assn., 1975-77; bd. dirs., pres. Druid Hills Civitan Club, 1976-77; bd. dirs. Planned Parenthood, Inc., 1973—; mem. cabinet Met. Ga. Heart Assn., 1975-76. Mem. Nat. Sci. Tchrs. Assn., Am. Mgmt. Assn. Home: 1133 E Clairmont Rd Decatur GA 30030 Office: 156 Heaton Park Dr NE Atlanta GA 30307

SHELTON, MERCEL JOSEPH, civil engr.; b. South Haven, Mich., Apr. 4, 1906; s. Walter C. and Anna (Cordier) S.; B.S., Purdue U., 1930; m. Maxine Leiter, Oct. 20, 1928 (dec.); children—Roselyn Anne, Max Leiter (dec.), m. 2d, Margaret Perry, Sept. 2, 1979. Engr., Ind. & Mich. Elec. Co., South Bend, Ind., 1928-33; cons. engr., San Diego, 1936-42; operations officer WPA, San Diego County. 1937-38; engr. La Mesa Lemon Grove and Spring Valley Irrigation Dist., La Mesa, Calif., 1946-56, chief engr., gen. mgr., 1948-56; dir. San Diego County Water Authority, 1948-56, 65-77, San Diego Regional Water Pollution Control Bd., 1950-53; dir. Calif. Water Pollution Control Bd. 1953-58; dep. dir. Calif. Dept. Water Resources, 1956-58; chief engr. Koebig & Koebig, Inc., engrs.-architects, San Diego, 1959-71, v.p., 1963-71; propr. M.J. Shelton, cons. engr., San Diego, 1971—; asso. Tudor Engring. Co., San Diego, 1972-73. Pres., Grossmont Community Concert Assn., 1969-70, 78; dir., mem. adv. council East County Performing Arts Center, 1976—. Served as 2d lt. C.E. Civilian Conservation Corps, 1933-36; 2d lt. to capt. U.S. Army, 1942-46. Registered civil engr., Calif., Ariz., Nev. Mem. ASCE (sec. San Diego sect. 1947, pres. 1948, nat. dir. 1952-55, nat. v.p. 1963-65), Am. Water Works Assn. (chmn. Calif. sect. 1956-57), Engrs. Council Profl. Devel. (council 1959-65), Soil Conservation Soc. Am. (pres. Calif. chpt. 1964), Cons. Engrs. Council U.S. (v.p. 1970-71), Cons. Engrs. Council Calif. (pres. 1969). Presbyterian. Clubs: Engineers (sec. 1938), Masons. Contbr. articles to engring. mags. Address: 8701 Mesa Rd Sp 114 Santee CA 92071

SHELTON, RAYMOND ORRIS, supt. schs.; b. Powersville, Mo., Nov. 25, 1928; s. Alpha Basil and Mildred Faye (Noel) S.; A.B., B.S. in Edn., Mo. State U., 1948; M.A. in City Sch. Adminstrn., Mo. State U., 1956; Ph.D., State U. Iowa, 1965; m. Laura Jane Johnson, Nov. 11, 1951 (dec. Sept. 1972); children—Raymond Mark, Gina Marie; m. 2d, Eileen Grace Marsh, Jan. 25, 1974; stepchildren—Jody (Mrs. Don Yarboro), Larry Russell Marsh, Russell Jason Marsh. Tchr. high sch., Iowa, 1948-56; supt. Bonaparte (Iowa) Sch., 1956-58, Hartwick, Ladora and Victor Sch., Victor, Iowa, 1958-60; adminstrv. asst. intern, asst. bus. Omaha Public Schs., 1960-62; asst. supt. schs. for bus. Omaha pub. schs., 1962-67; supt. schs. Hillsborough County, Tampa, Fla., 1967—. Mem. Fla. Vocat. Adv. Council, 1969—, pres., 1976-77; bd. dirs., exec. com. Fla. West Coast Ednl. TV, 1967—; mem. Fla. Council on Econ. Edn., 1976—. Bd. dirs. YMCA Tampa, Tampa chpt. Nat. Football Found. and Hall of Fame; exec. com., bd. dirs. United Fund Greater Tampa; exec. com. Gulf Ridge council Boy Scouts Am.; trustee Univ. Community Hosp., Tampa. Served with USAF, 1951-53. Recipient Top Mgmt. award Tampa Sales and Mktg. Execs., 1969; named hon. Future Farmer Am., 1968. Mem. Am. Assn. Sch. Adminstrs., N.E.A. (life), Fla. Assn. Dist. Sch. Supts. (pres. 1975), Fla. (life), Nebr. (life) P.T.A.'s, Greater Tampa C. of C., Fellowship Christian Athletes, Phi Delta Kappa. Mason, Kiwanian. Clubs: North Dale Golf and Country, University (Tampa). Home: 3026 Samara Dr Tampa FL 33618 Office: PO Box 3408 Tampa FL 33601

SHELTON, REID LEROY, actor; b. Salem, Oreg., Oct. 7, 1924; s. Roy Van and Jennie (White) S.; Mus.B., Willamette U., 1948; Mus.M., U. Mich., 1951. Appeared in Broadway shows: Wish You Were Here, 1953, Saint of Bleeker Street, 1954-55, My Fair Lady, 1956-57 (toured from 1957-60 including Cultural Exchange to USSR), Oh What a Lovely War, 1964, Carousel (Lincoln Center), 1965, Canterbury Tales, 1968-69, Rothschilds, 1971-72, 1600 Pennsylvania Avenue, 1976, Annie, 1977; off-Broadway shows include: Phedre, 1966 (also tour to Festival of Arts, Am. embassy London), Man With a Load of Mischief, 1966, Beggar's Opera, 1972, Contractor, 1973, TV-Contractor, 1974, Adams Chronicles, 1975, Equal Justice under Law, 1976; guest artist: U. R.I. in Inherit the Wind, 1967, Purdue U. in Uncle Vanya, Incident at Vichy, Homecoming, Bus Stop, 1968; mem. Inst. Advanced Studies in Theater Arts, 1962-65. Served with cav. AUS, 1943-46; PTO. Named Best Actor in a musical for Man With a Load of Mischief, Jersey Jour., 1966; nominated for Drama Desk award for Man With a Load of Mischief, 1966, Annie, 1977, Best Actor in a musical for Annie, Antoinette Perry award, 1977. Mem. Actors Equity Assn., Screen Actors Guild, AFTRA. Democrat. Club: Players. Office: c/o Actors Equity Assn 1500 Broadway New York NY 10036

SHELTON, ROBERT DUANE, educator; b. Dublin, Tex., Sept. 14, 1938; s. Duane McAfee and Bertie Ella (Honea) S.; B.S. in Elec. Engring., Tex. Tech U., 1960; S.M. (Kaiser Aluminum fellow, NSF fellow), M.I.T., 1962; Ph.D., U. Houston, 1967; m. Ruth Klein, Nov. 28, 1963; aerospace technologist NASA Johnson Space Center, Houston, 1963-64; asst. prof. U. Houston, 1964-68; asso. prof. Tex. Tech U., Lubbock, 1968-70; prof. elec. engring. and computer sci. U. Louisville, 1970—, chmn. dept. applied math. and computer sci., 1974-77. NASA-NSF grantee, 1967-73. Mem. IEEE, Instn. Elec. Engrs. (London), Assn. Computing Machinery, Am. Soc. Engring. Edn. Home: Rural Route 2 Box 434A New Albany IN 47150 Office: Elec Engring Dept U Louisville Louisville KY 40208

SHELTON, SALLY ANGELA, ambassador; b. San Antonio, Aug. 29, 1944; d. Harlan Bryan and Edith Angela (Pratka) S.; B.A. with honors, U. Mo., 1966; M.A. (univ. fellow; NDEA fellow), Johns Hopkins Sch. Advanced Internat. Studies, Bologna, Italy and Washington, 1968; postgrad. (Fulbright scholar) Institut de Sciences Politiques, Paris, 1968-69; postgrad. Georgetown U., 1968. Ministry of Fgn. Affairs fellow, Italy, 1966-67; research asso. Brookings Instn., Washington, 1969—; prof. U.S. fgn. policy Mexico City/Iberoam. U. and Nat. Autonomous U. Mexico; legis. asst. for fgn. policy to Senator Lloyd Bentsen, U.S. Senate, 1971-77; dep. asst. sec. for inter-Am. affairs Dept. State, 1977-78; now ambassador to Barbados, Grenada, Dominica, St. Lucia, St. Vincent and spl. rep. to Antigua, St. Kitts-Nevis-Anquilla, Montserrat and Brit. W.I.; adv. U.S. del. UN Gen. Assembly; mem. Dept. State Women's Action Orgn. Named Outstanding Young Woman Am., 1979. Mem. Council Fgn. Relations, NOW, Nat. Women's Polit. Caucus, Fulbright Alumni Assn., Phi Beta Kappa. Office: US Embassy Bridgetown Barbados

SHELTON, STEPHANI, news corr.; b. Boston, Aug. 17, 1938; d. Phil and Babette (Belloff) Saltman: B.S., Boston U., 1960; m. Frank Herold, Nov. 9, 1969. Prodn. asst. NBC-TV, N.Y.C., 1960-63; actress, N.Y.C. and Boston, 1963-65; reporter WCOP, Boston, 1965-66; reporter, anchor Manhattan Cable TV, N.Y.C., 1966-69; free lance radio documentary writer Westinghouse Group W Broadcasting, N.Y.C., 1969-73; reporter, news broadcaster WPAT, Paterson, N.J., 1972-73; writer, reporter, corr. CBS News, N.Y.C., 1973—. Recipient Peabody award, 1972. Mem. Am. Women in Radio and Television (award for news radio feature What's Happening 1978), Aftra, Screen Actors Guild. Office: CBS News 524 W 57th St New York NY 10019. *Guiding principles; a questioning mind, a refusal to take no for an answer, and a child-like belief that if you work hard enough toward a goal...you'll realize it (all that's called a New England upbringing!).*

SHELTON, TRAVIS DUANE, lawyer; b. Tahoka, Tex., Jan. 30, 1921; s. Santford Lane and Lena Mae (Ansley) S.; student Tex. Tech. U., 1940-42; LL.B., U. Tex., 1949; m. Mary Lou Metcalf, Apr. 14, 1946; children—Shelly, Christy, Steve. Admitted to Tex. bar; dist. atty. 72d Jud. Dist., Lubbock, Tex., 1951-57; practice law, Lubbock, 1957—; v.p. Tex. State Bar, 1975-76, pres., 1977-78. Mem. Tex. State Democratic Exec. Com., 1964-68. Served with USCG, 1942-46. Fellow Tex. Bar Found., Am. Bar Found.; mem. Am. Coll. Trial Lawyers, Lubbock County Bar Assn. (past pres.), Nat. Conf. Bar Pres. Presbyterian. Club: Lions. Home: 3810 27th St Lubbock TX 79410 Office: 1507 13th St Lubbock TX 79401*

SHELTON, TURNER BLAIR, ambassador; b. Louisa County, Va., Dec. 3, 1915; s. David Rice and Lillie Blanche (Gibson) S.; student U. Va., 1932-34, 36-40, U. Richmond, 1935-36; m. Lesly Starr, Sept. 23, 1951. With Loew's, Inc., Washington, 1941-42; asst. to dir. Treasury Dept., Washington, 1942-46; asst. to exec. producer Monogram Studios, Hollywood, Calif., 1946-47; producer Eagle Lions Studios, Hollywood, 1948-49; asso. producer motion picture T-Men Exec. Warner Bros. Studios, 1949-51; cons. State Dept., 1951-54, dep. asst. dir. U.S.I.A., 1954-55, asst. dir., 1955-61; spl. asst. Soviet and Eastern European Exchanges Staff, Bur. European Affairs, 1961; counselor of legation, Budapest, Hungary, 1962-64, spl. asst. to asst. sec. state, Washington, 1964-66; consul gen., Nassau, The Bahamas, 1966-70; U.S. ambassador to Nicaragua, 1970-75; Dept. State adviser to Pres., Naval War Coll., Newport, R.I., 1976—; del. meeting on post-war financing, Paris, France, 1945; negotiator for State Dept. portion of sci., tech., ednl. and cultural exchange agreement with U.S. and USSR, 1958, mem. U.S. del. which negotiated new agreement with USSR, 1959, which negotiated cultural agreement with Rumania, 1960. Recipient Distinguished Service award U.S.I.A., 1956; Unit award for valor Dept. State, 1973. Mem. Motion Picture Acad. Arts and Scis. Mason. Clubs: International (Washington); Lyford Cay (Nassau, Bahamas); Nejapa Country (Managua, Nicaragua). Home: 1121 Tower Rd Beverly Hills CA 90210 Office: Dept State Washington DC 20515

SHEMIN, DAVID, biochemist, educator; b. N.Y.C., Mar. 18, 1911; s. Louis and Mary (Bush) S.; B.S., Coll. City N.Y., 1932; A.M., Columbia, 1933, Ph.D., 1938; m. Mildred B. Sumpter (dec. 1962); children—Louise P., Elizabeth; m. 2d, Charlotte Norton, Mar. 1963. Asst. prof. biochemistry Columbia, 1945-49, asso. prof., 1949-53, prof., 1953-68; chmn. dept. biochemistry and molecular biology Northwestern U., Evanston, Ill., 1968—, prof. biochemistry, 1968—. Recipient Pasteur medal, Stevens award. Guggenheim fellow; Commonwealth fellow; Fogarty Internat. scholar, 1979—. Mem. Nat. Acad. Sci., Am. Acad. Arts and Scis. Contbr. articles to sci. publs. Home: 902 Lincoln St Evanston IL 60201 Office: Dept Biochemistry and Molecular Biology Northwestern U Evanston IL 60201

SHEN, BENJAMIN SHIH-PING, scientist, univ. ofcl.; b. Hangzhou, China, Sept. 14, 1931; s. Nai-cheng and Chen-chiu (Sun) S.; naturalized U.S. citizen; A.B. summa cum laude, Assumption Coll. (Mass.), 1954, Sc.D. (hon.), 1972; A.M. in Physics, Clark U., 1956; D.Sc.d'Etat in Physics, U. Paris (France), 1964; M.A. (hon.), U. Pa., 1971; m. Lucia Simpson, July 31, 1971; children—William Li, Juliet Ming. Tchr., Assumption Prep. Sch., Worcester, Mass., 1954-56; asst. prof. physics State U. N.Y. at Albany, 1956-59; asso. prof. space sci., dept. aeros. and astronautics Engring. Sch., N.Y. U., 1964-66; asso. prof. U. Pa., Phila., 1966-68, prof., 1968-72, Reese W. Flower prof. astronomy and astrophysics, 1972—, asso. provost, 1979—, chmn. council grad. deans, 1979—, chmn. dept. astronomy and astrophysics, 1973-79, dir. Flower and Cook Obs., 1973-79, mem. Energy Center, 1976—, founding chmn. roundtable on sci., law and pub. policy, 1976—; cons. Space Sci. Lab., Gen. Electric Co., 1961-68, Am. Inst. Physics, 1965, 72-75, cosmic physics div. Am. Phys. Soc., 1972-75; cons. Office of Tech. Assessment, U.S. Congress, 1977-78; sci. and tech. adviser U.S. Senate Budget Com., 1976-77; guest staff mem. Brookhaven Nat. Lab., 1963-64, 65-70; gen. chmn. Internat. Symposium on High-Energy Nuclear Reactions in Astrophysics, 1967; founding chmn. Com. on Public Understanding of Sci., N.Y. Acad. Scis., 1972-75; gen. chmn. Internat. Conf. on Spallation Nuclear Reactions and Their Applications in Astrophysics and Radiotherapy, 1975. Bd. dirs. Pa. Ballet, 1974-79; bd. govs. N.Y. Acad. Scis., 1976-78; mem. Hayden Planetarium com. of bd. trustees Am. Mus. Natural History, N.Y.C., 1978—; mem. sci. adv. bd. Children's TV Workshop, N.Y.C., 1977, 79—; mem. adv. com. Mt. John Obs., N.Z., 1978—. Recipient Frederick Gardner Cottrell grant Research Corp., 1957-59; Dupont scholar Wesleyan U., 1956; Vermeil medal for sci. Société d'Encouragement au Progrès, 1978. Fellow Am. Phys. Soc. (mem. congl. sci. fellow selection com. 1980), AAAS (com. on sci. engring. and pub. policy 1978—, internat. subcom. 1978—, chmn. subcom. on fed. research and devel. budget and policy 1978—), Royal Astron. Soc. (U.K.), Joint Assn. for Geophysics (U.K.); mem. Am. Astron. Soc., Internat. Astron. Union, Am. Soc. Internat. Law, Sigma Xi. Author: Contribution à l'Etude du Passage des Protons dans des Milieux Condensés, 1964; editor, co-author: High-Energy Nuclear Reactions in Astrophysics, 1967; co-editor, co-author: Spallation Nuclear Reactions and Their Applications, 1976; asso. editor Biosci. Communications, 1974-77; mem. editorial bd. Earth and Extraterrestrial Scis., 1974-78, asso. editor, 1978-79; asso. editor Comments on Astrophysics, 1979—; editor Astronomical Series of U. Pa., 1973-79; contbr. articles profl. jours. Office: David Rittenhouse Lab E-1 U Pa Philadelphia PA 19104

SHEN, CHIA THENG, shipping co. exec.; b. Chekiang, China, Dec. 15, 1913; s. Foo Sheng and Feng Hsu (Hsai) S.; came to U.S., 1952, naturalized, 1964; B.E.E., Chiao Tung U., 1937; Litt.D. (hon.), St. John's U., 1973; m. Woo Ju Chu, Apr. 21, 1940; children—Maria May Shen Jackson, Wilma Way Shen George, David Chuen-Tsing, Freda Foh. With Central Elec. Mfg. Works, China, 1937-44, factory mgr., 1942-44; dep. coordinating dept. Nat. Resources Commn., Govt. of China, 1945-47; pres. China Trading and Indsl. Devel. Corp., Shanghai, 1947-49; mng. dir. China Trading & Indsl. Devel. Co. Ltd., Hong Kong, 1949-53; with TransAtlantic Financing Corp., 1954-62, pres., 1958-62; pres. Pan-Atlantic Devel. Corp., N.Y.C., 1955-70; with Marine Transport Lines Inc., N.Y.C., 1958-70, sr. v.p., 1964-70; with Am. Steamship Co., Buffalo, 1967—, chmn. bd., chief exec. officer, 1971—. Trustee, pres. Inst. Advanced Studies World Religions, N.Y.C., 1970—; trustee China Inst. in Am., N.Y.C., 1963—, vice chmn., 1970-79, chmn., 1979—, mem. exec. com., 1963—; trustee C.T. Loo Ednl. Fund, N.Y.C., 1971—; trustee, v.p. Buddhist Assn. U.S., N.Y.C., 1964—. Mem. Chinese Inst. Engring. Home: 131 Tekening Dr Tenafly NJ 07670 Office: 2150 Center Ave Fort Lee NJ 07024. *To benefit all human beings and to work toward freeing them from fear is my goal. The collective wisdom of all world religions furnishes us the direction and means to achieve that goal. To introduce such wisdom into the daily life of mankind in general and America in particular, is therefore what I devote my energy to. To the extent that I succeed in this endeavor, I consider my life successful.*

SHEN, SHAN-FU, mech. and aerospace engr.; b. Shanghai, China, Aug. 31, 1921; s. Tsu Wei and Sien Wha (New) S.; came to U.S., 1945, naturalized, 1962; B.S., Nat. Central U. China, 1941; Sc.D., Mass. Inst. Tech., 1949; m. Ming-Ming Tung, Dec. 16, 1950; children—Hsueh-Yung, Hsueh-Lang. Research asst. Bur. Aero. Research Chinese Air Force, 1941-45; research asso. math. Mass. Inst. Tech., 1948-50; mem. faculty U. Md., 1950-61, asso. prof. aero. engring., 1952-57, prof., 1957-61; prof. mech. and aerospace engring. Cornell U., 1961—, John Edson Sweet prof. engring., 1978—; vis. asso. prof. U. Va., summer 1954; professeur associe U. Paris, 1964-65, 69-70; vis. prof. Technische Universität, Vienna, 1977; cons. instns., govt. agys. Recipient Achievement award Washington Acad. Sci., 1959; Guggenheim fellow, 1957-58. Mem. Internat. Acad. Astronautics (corr.), Academia Sinica. Contbr. articles to profl. jours. Home: 119 N Sunset Dr Ithaca NY 14850 Office: Upson Hall Cornell U Ithaca NY 14850

SHENAR, (ALBERT) PAUL, actor, stage and film dir.; b. Milw., Feb. 12, 1936; s. Eugene Joseph and Mary Rosella (Puhek) S.; B.S., U. Wis., Milw., 1962. Actor numerous plays in repertory A.C.T., off-Broadway, N.Y.C., also San Diego Shakespeare Festival, Long Wharf Theatre, 1979; TV appearance Execution of Pvt. Slovac, 1974, The Night That Panicked America, 1975, Cyrano de Bergerac, 1974, Suddenly Love, 1978, Ziegfeld: The Man and His Women; tchr. A.C.T. Conservatory, 1965-74, Conservatory Theatre, San Francisco, 1965—. Served with USAF, 1954-57. Office: care Richard M Rosenthal PC 12301 Wilshire Blvd Suite 610 Los Angeles CA 90025

SHENAUT, JOHN FREDERICK, symphony condr.; b. Galesburg Ill., Nov. 9, 1916; s. Charles Willard and Emelia Louise (Haggenjos) S.; student Knox Coll. Conservatory Music, 1922-35; B.Mus., Am. Conservatory Music, 1938; M.Mus., U. Mich., 1940; studied at Paris Conservatory, Mozarteum, Salzburg, Austria, Berlin Acad. Music; m. Frances Bustillo, June 12, 1971. Condr. Natchitoches-Northwestern Symphony, 1944-48; music dir., condr. Shreveport (La.) Symphony Orch., 1948—; guest condr. Rheinische Philharmonic, Germany, Bodensee Symphony; Switzerland tour Pro Musica Chamber Orch., Swiss Radio Beromunster, Choeur et Orchestre Philharmonique, Paris, Craiova and Ploiesti Symphonies, Rumania. Office: Shreveport Symphony Orchestra PO Box 4057 Shreveport LA 71104*

SHENEFIELD, JOHN HALE, govt. ofcl.; b. Toledo, Jan. 23, 1939; s. Hale Thurel and Norma (Bird) S.; A.B., Harvard U., 1960, LL.B., 1965; m. Anna Larson, Sept. 6, 1962; children—Stephen Hale, Christopher Newcomb. Admitted to Va. bar, 1966, D.C. bar, 1966; mem. firm Hunton & Williams, Richmond, Va., 1965-77; dep. asst. atty. gen. antitrust div. Dept. Justice, Washington, 1977, asst. atty. gen., 1977-79, asso. atty. gen., 1979—; asso. prof. law U. Richmond, 1975; chmn. Nat. Commn. for Rev. Antitrust Law and Procedures, 1978-79. Sec., Va. Democratic Com., 1970-72, treas., 1976-77; chmn. Richmond Dem. Party, 1975-77. Served as 2d lt. U.S. Army, 1961-62; to capt. Res., 1965. Mem. Am. Bar Assn. Contbr. articles on antitrust law to profl. jours. Home: 4501 Arlington Blvd Arlington VA 22203 Office: Office Asso Atty Gen Dept Justice Washington DC 20530

SHENK, JOHN CHRISTIAN, JR., savs. and loan co. exec.; b. Evanston, Ill., May 7. 1926; s. John Christian and Anabel (Kroell) S.; A.B., Wash. U., 1950; J.D., State U. Iowa, 1955; m. Mary Elizabeth Strobel, July 18, 1950; children—John Christian III, Mary Elizabeth II. Admitted to Iowa bar, 1955; practice in Davenport, 1955-61; v.p., gen. counsel First Trust and Savs. Bank, Davenport, 1961-62; gen. counsel First Fed. Savs. and Loan Assn., Davenport, 1962-74, exec. v.p., 1965-74, pres., 1974-78, chmn., 1978—, also dir. Bd. dirs. United Community Services Scott County, Iowa, 1967—, pres., 1970; bd. dirs. Jr. Achievement Scott County, 1963-65, pres., 1964, chmn. bd., 1965. Served with U.S. Army, World War II, Korea. Mem. Am., Iowa, Scott County bar assns., U.S. Savs. and Loan League, Davenport C. of C. (bd. dirs. 1964-67), Delta Theta Phi. Unitarian. Mason. Club: Davenport. Home: 1730 Harmony Ct Bettendorf IA 52722 Office: 131 W 3d St Davenport IA 52801

SHENK, WILLIS WEIDMAN, newspaper exec.; b. Manheim, Pa., Nov. 2, 1915; s. John Horst and Amanda (Weidman) S.; m. Elsie Sherer, Aug. 31, 1940; 1 son, J. David. Acct., Raymond D. Shearer, Lancaster, Pa., 1937-39; sr. acct. Lancaster Newspapers, Inc., 1940-50, sec.-controller, 1950-61, v.p., sec., 1961-76, pres., 1977—; dir. Commonwealth Nat. Bank, Lancaster. Pres., United Way of Lancaster County, 1961; pres., bd. trustees Lancaster Country Day Sch., 1971-72; trustee Franklin and Marshall Coll., Lancaster, 1977—; sec. Pequea Twp. Planning Commn., 1965-77. Mem. Nat. Assn. Accts., Pa. Inst. C.P.A.'s. Lutheran. Clubs: Hamilton, Masons. Office: 8 W King St Lancaster PA 17604

SHENKIR, WILLIAM GARY, ednl. adminstr.; b. Three Rivers, Tex., June 27, 1938; s. William and Lydia (Jancik) S.; B.B.A., Tex. A & M U., 1960; postgrad. (Rockefeller Bros. Theol. fellow), Drew U. Sem., 1960-61; M.B.A., U. Tex., 1962, Ph.D., 1964; m. Missy Smith, Jan 1, 1973. Asst. prof. McIntire Sch. Commerce, U. Va., Charlottesville, 1967-69, asso. prof., 1969-72, prof., 1972-73, dean, 1977—; project dir. Fin. Acctg. Standards Bd., Stamford, Conn., 1973-76; vis. prof. N.Y. U. Grad. Sch. Bus., N.Y.C., 1976-77. Served to lt. USAF, 1964-67. Mem. Am. Acctg. Assn., Am. Inst. C.P.A.'s, Va. Soc. C.P.A.'s, Beta Gamma Sigma, Phi Kappa Phi. Presbyterian. Clubs: Boar's Head Sports, Raven Soc. Editor: Carman Blough: His Professional Career and Accounting Thought, 1978; contbr. articles to profl. jours. Home: 420 Rookwood Dr Ednam Forest Charlottesville VA 22903

SHENNAN, JAMES GRIERSON, business exec.; b. Hazleton, Pa., June 11, 1910; s. Maurice Grierson and Anne (Burt) S.; student Blair Acad., 1925-28; A.B., Princeton, 1932; m. Elizabeth Rich, Sept. 23, 1939 (dec. 1969); children—James Grierson, Melissa Shennan Reily, Elizabeth Shennan Loring, Jerome R.; m. 2d, Elizabeth Wood Haywood, July 2, 1975. With Elgin Nat. Watch Co., 1932-60, successively time study engr., foreman, factory supt., 1938, 2d v.p., 1942, v.p., 1946, exec. v.p. 1947, pres., dir., 1948-60. chmn. Weldstar Co., Aurora, Ill., 1962—; dir. Dukane Corp., St. Charles, Ill. Presbyn. Home: 34W791 Army Trail Rd Wayne IL 60184 Office: 1750 Mitchell Rd Aurora IL 60504

SHENSTONE, ALLEN GOODRICH, educator; b. Toronto, Ont., Can., July 27, 1893; came to U.S., 1910; s. Joseph Newton and Eliza (Hara) S.; B.S., Princeton, 1914, A.M., 1920, Ph.D., 1922; B.A., Cambridge U., 1921, M.A., 1935; D.Sc. (hon.), York U., Toronto, 1972; m. Mildred Madeline Chadwick, July 28, 1923 (dec. Apr. 1967); 1 son, Michael; m. 2d, Tiffin H. Harper, Aug. 22, 1969; children—Katherine Mead, Daisy Fitch. Instr. Toronto U., 1922-25; prof. physics Princeton U., 1925—, Class 1909 prof., 1945-62, chmn. dept. physics, 1949-60. Mem. NRC-Can. on War Work, 1940-45. Served with Royal Engrs., 1915-19. Awarded Mil. Cross, 1918; Officer Order Brit. Empire, 1943. Fellow Royal Soc. of London; mem. AAAS, Am. Phys. Soc., Am. Assn. Physics Tchrs., Optical Soc. Am. (Meggers prize 1971). Baptist. Clubs: Princeton of N.Y.; Nassau (Princeton); Athenaeum (London). Contbr. numerous papers on atomic spectroscopy to sci. jours. Home: 111 Mercer St Princeton NJ 08540

SHENTON, JAMES PATRICK, educator; b. Passaic, N.J., Mar. 17, 1925; s. Walter Gardiner and Lillian (Spitzel) S.; A.B. Columbia, 1949, M.A., 1950, Ph.D., 1954. Mem. faculty Columbia, 1951—, prof. Am. history, 1967—, departmental rep. history dept., 1963-69; lecturer ednl. television sta. WNDT, 1963-64. Served with AUS, 1943-46. Mem. Am. Hist. Assn., AAUP, Am. Cath. Hist. Assn. (bd. dirs. 1962-65). Author: Robert John Walker, a Politician from Jackson to Lincoln, 1960; Reconstruction, the South After the War, 1963; An Historian's History of the United States, 1966; Melting Pot, 1971. Home: 80 Passaic Ave Passaic NJ 07055 Office: 324 Fayerweather Hall Columbia University New York City NY 10027

SHEPACK, LAWRENCE FREDERICK, accountant; b. St. Louis, Feb. 12, 1917; s. Frederick A. and Bertha (Thiessen) S.; B.S. Washington U., St. Louis, 1938; M. Marie B. Saitta, May 11, 1940; children—Joan (Mrs. Maher), James, Edward, David. Partner Price Waterhouse & Co., C.P.A.'s, St. Louis, 1938-59, New Orleans, 1959-62, Newark, 1962-74, Morristown, N.J., 1974—. Served with USNR, 1945-46. Mem. Am. Inst. C.P.A's Nat. Assn. Accountants, Mo. Soc. C.P.A.'s (past pres.) St. Louis; Club: Baltusrol Golf (Springfield, N.J.). Home: 15 Pembroke Road Summit NJ 07901 Office: 65 Madison Av Morristown NJ 07960

SHEPARD, ADRIAN BRUCE, clergyman; b. Wilmington, N.C., Mar. 5, 1937; s. Walter McCrae and Ethel Bertelle (Blake) S.; B.S. in Psychology Aurora Coll., 1963, B.Theology, 1963; B.D., Evang. Theol. Sem., 1965; m. Joyce Arlene Hathaway, Nov. 7, 1964; children—Kevin, Kirby, Kristoffer, Kenneth. Ordained to ministry Advent Christian Ch., 1965; pastor Advent Christian Ch., Waycross, Ga., 1965-68, Walterboro, S.C., 1968-75; exec. v.p. Advent Christian Gen. Conf. Am., Charlotte, N.C., 1975—; bd. dirs. Advent Christian Home, Aurora Coll., Berkshire Coll. Served with USNR, 1956-63. Democrat. Office: PO Box 23152 Charlotte NC 28212

SHEPARD, ALAN BARTLETT, JR., astronaut, constrn. co. exec.; b. East Derry, N.H., Nov. 18, 1923; s. Alan Bartlett and Renza (Emerson) S.; student Admiral Farragut Acad. 1940; B.S., U.S. Naval Acad., 1944; grad. Naval War Coll., 1958; M.S. (hon.), Dartmouth Coll.; D.Sc. (hon.), Miami U.; m. Louise Brewer, Mar. 3, 1945; children—Juliana, Laura. Commd. ensign U.S. Navy, 1944, advanced through grades to rear adm., 1971; designated naval aviator, 1947; assigned destroyer U.S.S. Cogswell, Navy Test Pilot Sch., Pacific, World War II, Fighter Squadron 42, 1947-49, aircraft carriers in Mediterranean, 1947-49; with U.S. Navy Test Pilot Sch., 1950-53, 55-57; took part in high altitude tests, expts. in test and devel. in-flight refueling system, carrier suitability trials of F2H3 Banshee, also trials angled carrier deck ops. officer Fighter Squadron 193, Moffett Field, Calif. and in carrier U.S.S. Oriskany, Western Pacific, 1953-55; test pilot for F3H Demon, 1956, F8U Crusader, 1956, F4D Skyray, 1955, F11F Tigercat, 1956; project test pilot F5D Skylancer, 1956; instr. Naval Test Pilot Sch., 1957; aircraft readiness officer staff Comdr.-in-Chief, Atlantic Fleet, 1958-59; joined Project Mercury man in space program NASA, 1959; first Am. in space May 5, 1961; chief of astronaut office, 1965-74; selected to command Apollo 14 Lunar Landing Mission, 1971, became 5th man to walk on moon, hit 1st lunar golf shot; ret., 1974; partner, chmn. Marathon Constrn. Co., Houston, 1974--; pres., partner Windward Distbg. Co., 1976—; apptd. by Pres. as del. to 26th Gen. Assembly UN, 1971. Decorated Congl. Medal of Honor (space), D.S.M., D.F.C. Presdl. unit citation, NASA Distinguished Service medal; recipient Langley medal Smithsonian Instn., 1964. Mem. Soc. Exptl. Test Pilots, Order Daedlians, Soc. Colonial Wars. Clubs: Lions, Kiwanis, Rotary.

SHEPARD, ALLAN GUY, state justice; b. Gardner, Mass., Dec. 18, 1922; s. Guy H. and May (Kendall) S.; student Boston U., 1942-43; B.S. U. Washington, 1948, J.D., 1951; m. Donna K. Soderlund, 1972; children—Lynn Kendall, Paul Vernon, Ann Kendall. Admitted to Idaho bar 1951; asst. atty. gen. Idaho, 1951-57; chief counsel Idaho Dept. Hwys., 1952-57; pvt. practice, Boise, 1957-63; mem. Idaho Ho. of Reps. from Ada County, 1958-63; atty. gen. Idaho, 1963-69; justice Idaho Supreme Ct. 1969—, chief justice, 1974—. Mem. Western States Hwy. Policy Com., 1959-63. Mem. youth and govt. com. YMCA Idaho, 1953—, chmn. 1969. Adv. bd. Booth Meml. Hosp., Boise. Mem. Am., Idaho, 3d Dist. bar assns., Western (chmn. 1965-66), Nat. (pres. 1968) assns. attys. gen., Delta Theta Phi. Republican. Episcopalian. Home: 4023 Del Monte St Boise ID 83704 Office: Supreme Ct Bldg Boise ID 83707

SHEPARD, CHARLES CARTER, physician; b. Ord, Nebr., Dec. 18, 1914; s. Charles Carter and Margaret Catherine (Ferguson) S.; student Stanford U., 1932-35; B.S., Northwestern U., 1936, M.S., 1938, M.D., 1941; m. Regina Elizabeth Schmidt, Nov. 22, 1939. Commd. med. officer, USPHS, 1941; research in rickettial disease and biophys. technique NIH, Bethesda, Md., 1942-48, 49-51; guest mem. Biochemistry Inst. Uppsala U. (Sweden), 1948-49; research in biophys. technique Rocky Mountain Lab., 1951-53; with Center for Disease Control, Atlanta, 1953—, now chief leprosy and rickettsia br.; chmn. U.S. Leprosy Panel, U.S.-Japan Coop. Med. Sci. Program; cons. WHO, others; adj. asso. prof. Emory U., U. N.C. Recipient World Leprosy Day award, 1970, others. Fellow AAAS; mem. Am. Assn. Immunologists, Am. Acad. Microbiology, Am. Soc. Microbiology, Internat. Leprosy Soc., Soc. Exptl. Biol. Medicine. Contbr. articles in field of leprosy and rickettsial diseases to profl. jours. Home: 1001 Castle Falls Dr Atlanta GA 30329 Office: Center for Disease Control Atlanta GA 30333

SHEPARD, CLARENCE DAY, oil co. exec.; b. Winnipeg, Man., Can. July 31, 1914; s. Clarence Day and May (Merrill) S.; student McGill U., 1931-33; LL.B., U. Man., 1937; m. Caroline Faith Spring, Apr. 23, 1938; children—Clarence Day, Caroline (Mrs. Hugh Nangle), Merrill, Sarah. Called to Man. bar, 1938, created Queen's counsel, 1951; internal solicitor Grain Ins. & Guarantee Co., Winnipeg, 1937-39; Western supr. Phoenix Ins. of Hartford Group, Winnipeg, 1939-40; partner firm Thompson, Shepard, Dilts, Jones & Hall, Winnipeg, 1945-57; lectr. Man. Law Sch., 1946-53; chief commnr. Bd. Transport Commrs. Can., 1957-58; acting chmn. Air Transport Bd., Ottawa, 1958; v.p., gen. counsel, dir. Gulf Oil Can. Ltd., Toronto 1959-64, chmn. bd., 1964—, chief exec. officer, 1976—, also dir.; dir. Toronto Dominion Bank. Mem. Ont. Alcoholism and Drug Addiction Research Found., Toronto. Trustee Hosp. for Sick Children, Toronto. Served to capt. Can. Army, World War II. Fellow Ins. Inst. Am.; mem. law socs. Man. (bencher 1952-57), Ont., Bd. Trade Met. Toronto, Law Soc. Upper Can. Mem. Anglican Ch. Clubs: Manitoba (Winnipeg); Rideau, Country (Ottawa); York, Donalda, Toronto. Home: 202 Sandringham Dr Downsview ON M3H IE3 Canada Office PO Box 460 Sta A Toronto ON M5W IE3 Canada

SHEPARD, EARL EMANUEL, orthodontist; b. Marine, Ill., Sept. 3, 1908; s. Earl W. and Elma (Sutter) S.; D.D.S., cum laude, Washington U., St. Louis, 1931; m. Wilma Schwartz, Dec. 26, 1931. Gen. practice dentistry, Edwardsville, Ill., 1931-38; orthodontic practice, St. Louis, 1938—; mem. staff Barnes Hosp., 1954—, St. Luke's Hosp., 1979—; mem. faculty Sch. Dentistry, Washington U., 1931—, prof. orthodontics, chmn. dept., 1953-75, prof. emeritus, lectr., 1975—; pres. Denver Summer Meeting for Advancement Orthodontic Practice and Research, 1970, President's award, 1976. Alumni rep. bd. dirs. Washington U., 1956-59; bd. dirs. Boys Town Mo., 1961—, Playgoers, St. Louis, 1966-72. Served to lt. col., Dental Corps, AUS, World War II ETO. Decorated Bronze Star, Army Commendation medal; recipient Alumni Faculty award Washington U., 1964; Distinguished Alumnus award Washington U. Sch. Dentistry, 1968; Albert H. Ketcham award, 1979. Diplomate Am. Bd. Orthodontics (dir. 1970-77, sec.-treas. 1971-77, exec. dir. 1977—; Albert H. Ketcham Meml. award 1979). Fellow Am., Internat. colls. dentists; mem. Am. Assn. Orthodontists (sec. treas. 1957-62 pres. 1964), Midwestern Soc. Orthodontists (sec-treas. 1947-51, pres. 1953), Am., Mo. (council 1958-61, 1st v.p. 1965), dental assns., St. Louis Dental Soc. (council 1950-54), Omicron Kappa Upsilon, Delta Sigma Delta (grand master Upsilon chpt. 1931, Grad. chpt. 1952). Club: University (life). Author: Technique and Treatment with Twin Wire Appliance, 1961; History of Marine, Ill.; (with J.D. McCoy) Applied Orthodontics, 1956; also articles; asst. editor Am. Jour. Orthodontics, 1953—; editor: Pictures That Hang on Memories Wall. Home: 900 S Hanley Rd Saint Louis MO 63105 Office: 225 S Meramec Ave Saint Louis MO 63105

SHEPARD, ELAINE ELIZABETH, writer; b. Olney, Ill.; d. Thomas J. and Bernice E. (Shadle) S.; m. Terry D. Hunt, Apr. 16, 1938; m. 2d, George F. Hartman, Oct. 1, 1943 (div. June 1958). Film and theater actress, Hollywood, N.Y.C., Europe, 1939-50; cover girl John Robert Powers, 1939-43; under contract to RKO and Metro-Goldwyn-Mayer, 1940-45; covered nat. polit. convs. for Stas. WTTG-TV and WINS, Chgo., 1952, Chgo., 1956, polit. reporter for NANA and WINS, Chgo. and Los Angeles, 1960; reporter Congo rebellion for N.Am. Newspaper Alliance and N.Y. Mirror, 1960-61; corr. covering Pres. Eisenhower's Middle East, Far East and S. Am. tour, 1959-60; Vietnam corr. MBS, 1965-66; guest commentator for Voice of Am.; contbr. feature articles to various mags., including McCall's, Pageant, Better Homes and Gardens, Parade, N.Y. News Sunday Mag., 1953—; columnist, contbg. editor Twin Circle mag. Nat. Cath. Press, 1969-74; granted interviews with Khrushchev, Castro, Tito, Chou En-lai, Nasser, Shah of Iran, King Hussein, King Faisel, Duvalier, Lumumba, Chiang-Kai-Shek, Nehru, Menzies, John F. Kennedy, Richard M. Nixon, others; mem. White House Press Corps accompanying Pres. Nixon to Austria, Iran, Poland, Moscow, 1972. Recipient 2 citations for participating in armed helicopter assaults with 145th Aviation Bn., Vietnam. Mem. Screen Actors Guild, AFTRA, Actors Equity. Club: Overseas Press (N.Y.C.). Author: Forgive Us Our Press Passes, 1962; The Doom Pussy, 1967. Home: 12 E 62nd St New York City NY 10021

SHEPARD, JEAN, vocalist, rec. artist; b. Pauls Valley, Okla., Nov. 21, 1933; attended high sch., Visalia, Calif.; m. Hawkshaw Hawkins (dec. 1963); m. Bennie Birchfield; children—Don Robin Hawkins, Harold F. Hawkins II, Corey Birchfield. Originally sang and played bass with Melody Ranch Girls; regular on Red Foley Show, Sta. KWTO; later appeared on Jubilee, U.S.A., ABC-TV, WSM Grand Ole Opry, Nashville; signed with Capitol Records, 1953; albums include: Slippin' Away, This is Jean Shepard, I'm a Believer, For the Good Times, Lighthearted and Blue, Lonesome Love, Jean Shepard and Ferlin Husky, Mercy Ain't Love Good, Poor Sweet Baby, The Good Shepard, The Best of Jean Shepard, Heartaches and Tears, Got You on My Mind, First of the Famous. Named Top Female Singer, Cash Box, 1959. Office: care Bill Goodwin Agy 1303 N Gallatin Rd Madison TN 37115*

SHEPARD, MERRILL, lawyer; b. Winnipeg, Man., Can., Mar. 30, 1905; s. Clarence Day and May (Merrill) S., came to U.S., 1928, naturalized, 1934; B.A., Yale U., 1925; LL.B., U. Man., 1928; M.A., Columbia U., 1943; m. Brenda Forbes, June 17, 1947. Admitted to Man. bar, 1929, Minn. bar, 1930, Ill. bar, 1936; commerce atty. G.N. Ry., 1929-33; asso. firm Best, Flanagan & Rogers, Mpls., 1933-36; partner law firm Pope, Ballard, Shepard & Fowle, and predecessor, Chgo., 1936—. Life trustee, past pres. Chgo. Symphony Orch.; past pres. Welfare Council Met. Chgo., United Charities Chgo. Served to lt. comdr. USNR., World War II. Mem. Assn. ICC Practitioners (charter), Am. Bar Assn. (charter sect. labor relations law), Phi Beta Kappa, Zeta Psi. Clubs: Law, Legal, Chicago, Commercial (Chgo.). Home: Rock Ridge Route 9-W Box 134 Alpine NJ 07620 Office: 69 W Washington St Chicago IL 60602

SHEPARD, PAUL HOWE, educator, author; b. Kansas City, Mo., July 12, 1925; s. Paul Howe and Clara (Grigsby) S.; A.B., U. Mo., 1949; M.S., Yale, 1952, Ph.D., 1954; m. Melba Wheatcroft, 1950 (div.); children—Kenton, Margaret, Jane; m. 2d, June Smith, Mar. 21, 1965. From instr. to asso. prof. biology and dir. Green Oaks, Knox Coll., 1954-64; lectr. biology Smith Coll., 1965-70; vis. prof. environ. perception Dartmouth Coll., 1971-73; Avery prof. natural philosophy and human ecology Pitzer Coll. and Claremont Grad. Sch., 1973—; faculty Internat. Coll. Served with AUS, 1943-46. Fulbright research scholar, Wellington, N.Z., 1961; Guggenheim fellow, 1969; USPHS grantee, 1962; Rockefeller Found. fellow, 1977. Author: Man in the Landscape: A Historic View of the Esthetics of Nature, 1967; The Subversive Science: Essays Toward an Ecology of Man, 1969; Environmental: Essays on the Planet as a Home, 1971; The Tender Carnivore and the Sacred Game, 1973; Thinking Animals, 1977. Home: 5241 Palmer Canyon Rd Claremont CA 91711

SHEPARD, ROBERT ANDREWS, educator; b. Gaziantep, Turkey, Oct. 22, 1923 (parents Am. citizens); s. Lorrin Andrews and Virginia (Moffat) S.; grad. Deerfield (Mass.) Acad., 1941; B.S., Yale U., 1944, Ph.D., 1950; m. Eugenia Melzar, June 18, 1949; children—Virginia, Andrew Moffat, Marjorie, Alan Melzar (dec.). Instr. chemistry Yale, 1946-50; mem. faculty Northeastern U., Boston, 1950—, prof. chemistry, 1958-68, 76—, chmn. dept., 1958-68, dean Coll. Liberal Arts, 1968-76, acting dir. Marine Sci. Inst., Nahant, Mass., 1979—. Served with U.S. Army, 1944-46. Mem. Am. Chem. Soc. (chmn. Northeastern sect. 1966), AAAS, Sigma Xi. Mem. United Ch. Co-author: General Chemistry, 1965. Home: RFD 4 Georgetown MA 01833 also Willow Rd Boxford MA Office: Northeastern U Marine Sci Inst Nahant MA 01908. *Two main principles guide my conduct: first, I know that God loves me and therefore fear is foolish; second, I assume that others are honest and kind unless they prove to be otherwise. Accordingly I risk often; and the results, though occasionally painful, are usually rewarding.*

SHEPARD, ROBERT EARL, assn. adminstr.; b. Riverside, Ill., Mar. 2, 1917; s. Earl Herbert and DeMarguerite (Ashbrook) Sieweke; student Central YMCA Coll., Chgo., 1936-40; m. Miriam Bates, Apr. 24, 1943; children—William Robert, James Alan. Factory accountant Westinghouse Electric Corp., Little Rock, 1948-51; with Central Transformer Inc., Pine Bluff, Ark., 1951-71; bus. adminstr. Ark. Enterprises for the Blind, Little Rock, 1972—, also pres. bd. dirs. Served with AUS, 1941-45. Decorated Combat Infantry badge, Bronze Star. Mem. C. of C. Lion (dep. dist. gov. 1968-69, dist. gov. 1973-74). Presbyn. Home: 3005 Ridge Pass Rd Little Rock AR 72207 Office: 2811 Fair Park Blvd Little Rock AR 72204

SHEPARD, ROGER NEWLAND, psychologist, educator; b. Palo Alto, Calif., Jan. 30, 1929; s. Orson Cutler and Grace (Newland) S.; B.A., Stanford U., 1951; Ph.D., Yale U., 1955; A.M. (hon.), Harvard U., 1966; m. Barbaranne Bradley, Aug. 18, 1952; children—Newland Chenoweth, Todd David, Shenna Esther. Research asso. Naval Research Lab., 1955-56; research fellow Harvard, 1956-58; mem. tech. staff Bell Telephone Labs., 1958-66, dept. head, 1963-66; prof. psychology Harvard U., 1966-68, dir. psychol. labs., 1967-68; prof. psychology Stanford U., 1968—. Guggenheim fellow Center for Advanced Study in Behavioral Scis., 1971-72. Fellow AAAS, Am. Psychol. Assn. (Distinguished Sci. Contbn. award 1976); mem. Nat. Acad. Scis., Psychometric Soc. (pres. 1973-74), Psychonomic Soc., Soc. Exptl. Psychologists. Office: Stanford U Stanford CA 94305

SHEPARD, SAM, author; b. Ft. Sheridan, Ill., Nov. 5, 1942; s. Samuel Shepard and Jane Elaine (Schook) Rogers; student Mt. San Antonio Jr. Coll., Walnut, Calif., 1961-62; m. O-Lan Johnson Dark, Nov. 9, 1969; 1 son, Jesse Mojo. Grantee Guggenheim Found., Rockefeller Found.; fellow Yale, U. Minn.; recipient Obie award distinguished playwriting for The Tooth of Crime, 1973; Nat. Inst. Arts and Letters award, 1974. Author: Five Plays, Operation Sidewinder, The Unseen Hand, Mad Dog Blues, The Tooth of Crime, La Turista, Action, Killer's Hand, Angel City, Curse of the Starving Class (Obie award 1977), Seduced, Buried Child (Pulitzer prize 1979, Obie award 1979), Suicide in Bb, Cowboys #2, Geography for a Horse Dreamer; (screenplays) Zabriski Point, Me and My Brother. Office: care Toby Cole 234 W 44th St New York NY 10036*

SHEPARD, TAZEWELL TAYLOR, petroleum co. exec., former navy officer; b. Mobile, Ala., Jan. 22, 1921; s. Tazewell Taylor and Martha (Webb) S.; B.S., U.S. Naval Acad., 1942; B.S. in Elec. Engring., U.S. Naval Postgrad. Sch., 1951; M.S. in Applied Physics, U. Calif. at Los Angeles, 1952; m. Julia Ann Sparkman; 1 son, Tazewell Taylor III. Commd. ensign USN, 1942, advanced through grades to rear adm., 1968; naval aide to Pres., 1961-64; comdg. officer U.S.S. Aucilla, 1964-65, U.S.S. Princeton, 1966-67; dep. dir. operations Joint Chiefs Staff, 1968; dir. East Asia and Pacific region Office Asst. Sec. Def. for Internat. Security Affairs, 1968-70; comdr. Anti-Submarine Warfare Group 2, 1970-72, Joint Strategic Integrated Planning System, 1972-73; ret., 1973; exec. v.p. Occidental Internat. subsidiary Occidental Petroleum Corp., Washington, 1973—; dir. Fed. Home Loan Bank of Atlanta. Decorated Navy Cross, Legion of Merit, Navy Commendation medal. Mem. Delta Kappa Epsilon. Episcopalian. Author: John F. Kennedy, Man of the Sea, 1965. Office: 1747 Pennsylvania Ave NW Washington DC 20006

SHEPARD, THOMAS HILL, physician; b. Milw., May 22, 1923; s. Francis Parker and Elizabeth Rhodes (Buchner) S.; A.B., Amherst Coll., 1945; M.D., U. Rochester, 1948; m. Alice B. Kelly, June 24, 1946; children—Donna Elizabeth, Ann. Intern, Strong Meml. Hosp., Rochester, N.Y., 1948-49, resident, 1950-52; resident Albany (N.Y.) Med. Center, 1949-50; pediatrician U. Wash., Seattle, 1955-61, teratologist, 1961—, prof. pediatrics, head central lab. for human embryology, 1961—; cons. NIH, FDA, EPA, 1971—; vis. prof. pediatrics U. Geneva, 1972. Served with U.S. Army, 1946-48, USAF, 1952-54. Mem. Teratology Soc. (pres. 1968), Western Soc. Pediatric Research (pres. 1970). Author: A Catalog of Teratogenic Agents, 1973, 3d edit., 1980; contbr. articles to profl. jours. Home: 3015 98th St NE Bellevue WA 98004 Office: U of Wash Sch Medicine Dept Pediatrics Seattle WA 98195

SHEPARD, THOMAS ROCKWELL, JR., publishing cons.; b. N.Y.C., Aug. 22, 1918; s. Thomas Rockwell and Marie (Dickinson) S.; B.A., Amherst Coll., 1940; m. Nancy Kruidenier, Sept. 20, 1941; children-Sue (Mrs. R. Gerald Mould), Molly (Mrs. Karl K. Lunkenheimer), Amy K., Thomas Rockwell III. With Look Mag., N.Y.C., 1946-72, advt. sales mgr., 1961-64, advt. dir., 1964-67, pub., 1967-72; cons. Cowles Communications, Inc. Pres., Inst. Outdoor Advt., 1974-76. Pres. Greenwich Community Chest, 1964-65; chmn. Robert A. Taft Inst. Govt. Bd. dirs. Advt. Council. Served to lt. comdr. USNR, 1941-45. Recipient George Washington honor medal for pub. address Freedoms Found., 1970, 73. Republican. Club: Round Hill (Greenwich). Co-author: The Disaster Lobby, 1973. Contbr. articles to various publs. Home: 44 Lismore Ln Greenwich CT 06830

SHEPARD, THOMAS ZACHARY, rec. co. exec.; b. Orange, N.J., June 26, 1936; s. Seymour Deber and Dorothy (Kahn) S.; B.A. in Music, Oberlin Coll., 1958; postgrad. Yale, 1959; m. Irene Clark, Dec. 4, 1960; 1 dau., Elizabeth. Asso. producer Columbia Records, N.Y.C., 1960-63, producer classical and Broadway cast albums and film soundtracks, 1963-71, dir. Masterworks div., 1971-74; v.p. Red Seal div. RCA Records, N.Y.C., 1974—. Arranger, pianist, condr.; composer several shows; composer score for film Such Good Friends, 1971. Recipient numerous Grammy awards, 1963-78; Gold Record for Sesame St. Cast Album, 1971. Mem. Nat. Acad. Rec. Arts and Scis. (trustee, gov.), Am. Fedn. Musicians, Broadcast Music Inc., Am. Guild Authors and Composers. Contbr. articles to profl. jours. Composer: (opera) The Last of the Just, 1977. Office: 1133 6th Ave New York NY 10036

SHEPARD, TRENT ALLEN, ins. co. exec.; b. Normal, Ill., May 20, 1920; s. Lawrence Freeman and Mildred (Oster)S.; B.S. in Econs., U. Ill., 1942, LL.B., 1945; m. Myra Jane Rodgers, Dec. 5,1948; children—Trent Allen, Karen Jane, Gregory Mark, Tracy Morgan. Pres., trustee Union Automobile Indemnity Assn., Bloomington Ill., 1952—, Prairie State Farmers Ins. Assn., Bloomington, 1952—; pres., treas., dir. Union Ins. Exchange, Bloomington, 1952—; pres., chmn. bd. Am. Union Life Ins. Co., Bloomington, 1961—, Am. Diversified Investors Fund, Inc., Bloomington, 1964—; pres., dir. Am. Investors Mgmt. Corp., Bloomington, 1964—; pres., treas., dir. Farmers Deposit Co., Bloomington, Mid-Am. Financial Corp. Admitted to Ill. bar, 1946—. Bd. dirs. Bloomington YMCA, Bloomington United Fund, Bloomington chpt. Am. Cancer Soc., Brokaw Hosp., Normal. Served with inf. AUS, 1942-44. C.L.U. Mem. Ill. Bar Assn., Chartered Property and Casualty Underwriters. Mem. Christian Ch. (bd. dirs.). Office: Union Ins Group 303 E Washington St Bloomington IL 61701*

SHEPARDSON, WALLACE LLOYD, advt. agy. exec.; b. Springfield, Mass., Nov. 5, 1919; s. Lloyd M. and Florence (Wallace) S.; student Rochester Bus. Inst., 1940-41, Dickinson Coll., 1943; grad. Advanced Mgmt. Program Harvard, 1955; m. Janet Marion Rice, Oct. 14, 1939; children—Laurinda Lee, Christina Lloyd. Dept. mgr. Photoreflex Studios, Inc., 1939-43; sales promotion mgr. Hood Rubber Co. div. B.F. Goodrich Co., 1945-47; account exec. James T. Chirurg Co., Boston, 1947-50, v.p., 1950-55, pres., 1955-60, dir. 1950—; pres., dir. Chirurg & Cairms, Inc., 1960-68, chmn. bd., 1968-76; vice chmn. LKP Internat. Ltd., 1976—. Served as lt. USAAF 1943-45. Mem. Am. Assn. Advt. Agys. (dir., chmn. N.E. council), Nat. Indsl. Advertisers Assn., World Bus. Council, Harvard Bus. Sch. Assn., Chief Execs. Forum (dir.), Radio and TV Broadcasters Club, Advt. Club Boston. Clubs: Algonquin (Boston); Cape Cod Tuna; Longwood Cricket; Badminton and Tennis; Truro Fish and Game; Rolling Hills Tennis; Weston (Mass.) Golf. Office: Gen Motors Bldg 767 Fifth Ave New York City NY 10022

SHEPHARD, ALFRED HENRY, psychologist, educator; b. Vancouver, B.C., Can., Mar. 4, 1917; s. William and Elsie (Bates) S.; B.A., U. B.C., 1939; M.A., U. Iowa, 1948, Ph.D., 1950; m. Jean Mary Nicholson, Aug. 20, 1957; children—Suzanne, Jeannette. Mem. faculty U. Toronto, 1950-62; prof. psychology U. Man., Winnipeg, 1962—. Mem. Am., Canadian psychol. assns. Contbr. articles to profl. jours. Home: 265 Harvard Ave Winnipeg MB R3M OK1 Canada

SHEPHARD, RONALD WILLIAM, educator; b. Portland, Oreg., Nov. 22, 1912; s. Robert E. and Jessie W. (Hunter) S.; A.B. in Math. and Econs., U. Calif. at Berkeley, 1935, Ph.D. in Math. and Statistics, 1940; m. Hilda May Maloy, Dec. 26, 1940; children—Jessie M., William H. Statis., cons. Bell Aircraft Corp., 1943-46; sr. economist RAND Corp., 1950-52; mgr. systems analysis dept. Sandia Corp., 1952-56; prof. engring. sci. U. Calif. at Berkeley, 1957—, chmn. ops. research center, 1966-72, also chmn. indsl. engring. and ops. research dept., 1970-76, past chmn. indsl. engring. dept.; cons. ops. research OECD, Paris, France, 1959-60; dir. Market Research Corp. Am., 1961-66; cons. to industry, 1950—; internat. authority on math. econ. theory of prodn. and tech. Served as lt. (j.g.) USNR, World War II. Recipient Humboldt prize Alexander von Humboldt Found., Bonn, 1976. Fellow Econometric Soc.; mem. Ops. Research Soc. Am. (past pres. Western sect.), Inst. Mgmt. Sci. (past chmn. No. Calif. sect.), Phi Beta Kappa, Sigma Xi. Author: Theory of Cost and Production Functions, 1970; Indirect Production Functions, 1974; Dynamic Theory of Production Correspondences, 1978. Home: 1089 Keeler Ave Berkeley CA 94708

SHEPHERD, ALAN J., constrn. mgmt. cons. exec.; b. Bklyn., Jan. 15, 1942; s. Morris Elijah and Jean (Birnbaum) Shapiro; B.S. in Mech. Engring., Mich. State U., M.S. in Indsl. Engring., Wayne State U., 1966; m. Barbara M. Moss, Sept. 8, 1963; children—Robin Elyse, Kevin Peter. Mgmt. trainee Chrysler Corp., Detroit, 1964-65, product engr., 1965-66; exec. v.p. Bruce Erts & Assos., Southfield, Mich., mgmt. cons., 1966-70; pres. Creative Mgmt. Group, Inc., Southfield, 1970-76, chmn. bd., 1976; pvt. cons., 1976—; dir. planning and coordination Mgmt. Support Assos., Tel Aviv, Israel, 1979—; instr. Lawrence Inst. Tech., 1971, 73. Mem. Am. Inst. Indsl. Engrs., Project Mgmt. Inst. Home: 31416 Stonewood Ct Farmington Hills MI 48018 Office: Mgmt Support Assos Tel Aviv APO New York NY 09672

SHEPHERD, CYBILL, actress, singer; b. Memphis, Feb. 18, 1950; d. William Jennings and Patty Shobe (Micci) S.; student Hunter Coll., 1969, Coll. of New Rochelle, 1970, Washington Sq. Coll., N.Y. U., 1971, U. So. Calif., 1972, N.Y. U., 1973; m. David Ford, Nov. 19, 1978. Appeared in Motion pictures The Last Picture Show, 1971, The Heartbreak Kid, 1973, Daisy Miller, 1974, At Long Last Love, 1975, Taxi Driver, 1976, Special Delivery, 1976, Silver Bears, 1977, A Guide for the Married Woman, 1978, The Lady Vanishes, 1978; record albums include Cybill Does It To Cole Porter, 1974, Cybill and Stan Getz, 1977, Vanilla with Phineas Newborn, Jr., 1978. Office: care Harry Ufland Agy Inc 190 N Canon Dr Beverly Hills CA 90210

SHEPHERD, DENNIS GRANVILLE, educator; b. Ilford, Essex, Eng., Oct. 6, 1912; s. George Granville and Lillian (Stubbins) S.; came to U.S., 1948, naturalized, 1951; B.S.E. in Math, B.S.E. in Physics, U. Mich., 1934; m. Gertrude May Pitman, Sept. 1, 1939; children—Julian Granville, Joanna Ruth, Barbara Lynn. Engr., Crittall Mfg. Co., Braintree, Eng., 1935-39, Power Jets. Ltd., Lutterworth, Eng., 1940-46; chief exptl. engr. A.V. Roe Can., Ltd., Toronto, 1946-48; mem. faculty Cornell U., 1948—, prof. mech. engring., 1952—, dir. Sch. Mech. Engring., 1965-72. Cons. in field. Mem. ASME, Inst. Mech. Engrs., Combustion Inst., Sigma Xi. Author: Introduction to the Gas Turbine, 2d edit., 1960; Principles of Turbomachinery, 1956; Elements of Fluid Mechanics, 1965; Aerospace Propulsion, 1972. Home: 518 Highland Rd Ithaca NY 14850

SHEPHERD, GEORGE WILLIAM, JR., educator, writer; b. Shanghai, China, Oct. 26 1926; s. George William and Clara (Sargent) S.; B.A., U. Mich, 1949; Ph.D., London U., 1951; m. Shirley Brower, June 19, 1948; children—Mary Claire, Holland, Sharon, Harold. Came to U.S., 1936, naturalized, 1944. Econ. adviser Fedn. Uganda African Farmers, Kampala, Uganda, 1951-53, assisted formation Uganda Nat. Congress, 1952; asst. minister First Congl. Ch., Flushing, N.Y., 1954-56; lectr. govt. and world politics Bklyn. Coll., 1956; asst. prof. polit. sci., dir. fgn. service program St. Olaf Coll., 1959-61; asso. prof., spl. lectr. African politics U. Minn., 1961; asst. prof. internat. relations dept. U. Denver, 1961-64, asso. prof., 1964-68, prof. internat. relations, 1968—, dir. Center on Internat. Race Relations, 1969-74. Vis. lectr. U. Khartoum, Sudan, 1964-65; vis. scholar UN, 1973. Rockefeller Found. fellow, 1962; Internat. African Inst. fellow, 1973. Recipient Anisfield-Wolf award for contbn. field race relations, 1955. Fellow African Studies Assn.; mem. Am. Acad. Polit. and Social Sci., Am. Polit. Sci. Assn. Mem. United Ch. Christ (council for social action bd.). Author: They Wait in Darkness, 1955; Politics of African Nationalism, 1962; Nonaligned Black Africa, 1970; Race Among Nations, 1970; Anti-Apartheid: Transnational Conflict and Western Policy, 1977. Past editor, founder Africa Today; editor Racial Influences on U.S. Foreign Policy, 1971. Address: U Denver Denver CO 80210

SHEPHERD, HERMAN ROBERT, chem. mfg. co. exec.; b. Bklyn., May 20, 1921; B.S., Cornell U., 1943; L.H.D., Villanova U., 1973; m. Carol Ruth Shapiro, 1943; children—John, Marjorie (Mrs. Simmitt John Loeper, Jr.), Beth, Benjamin. Vice pres. research Conn. Chem. Research Corp., 1946-55; founder ATI, Inc. (Aerosol Techniques, Inc.), Milford, Conn., 1955, since pres., now also chmn. Bd. dirs. Park City Hosp.; past chmn. bd. dirs. Silvermine Coll. Art; trustee Aldrich Mus. Contemporary Art; past chmn. bd. trustees U. Bridgeport; bd. govs. Yeshiva U. Grad. Sch. Served with A.C., AUS. Fellow Aspen Inst. Humanistic Studies; mem. Soc. Cosmetic Chemists, Chem. Spltys. Mfgrs. Assn. (past chmn. aerosol div.), Chemist Club, World Bus. Council, Met. Presidents Assn. Editor: Aerosols: Science Technology. Contbr. chapters to books. Home: New Canaan CT 06840 Office: 5 Taft St Totowa NJ 07511

SHEPHERD, JOHN CALVIN, lawyer; b. Memphis, June 27, 1925; s. Calvin and Beatrice (Newton) S.; student Ill. Coll., 1946-48; J.D., St. Louis U., 1951; LL.D. (hon.), Ill. Coll., 1979; m. Bernice Hines, Sept. 4, 1948; children—J. Michael, William N. Admitted Mo. bar, 1951, Ill. bar, 1962; practiced in St. Louis, 1951—; partner firm Shepherd, Sandberg & Phoenix; lectr. U. Mich. Advocacy Inst., 1962-78. Bd. dirs. St. Louis Municipal Opera, 1973—, Barnes Hosp., 1978—; trustee Ill. Coll., 1979—; bd. overseers Hoover Inst. War, Revolution and Peace, 1979—. Served with USMCR, 1943-46. Recipient Lon O. Hocker award Mo. Bar Found., 1957; Alumni Merit award St. Louis U., 1970; named Distinguished Alumnus, Ill. Coll., 1965. Fellow Am. Coll. Trial Lawyers, Internat. Acad. Trial Lawyers; mem. Am. (state del. 1968-73, assembly del. 1974-79, chmn. ho. of dels. 1978—), Mo. (chmn. medico-legal com.), Ill. (chmn. admiralty sect. 1973-74) bar assns., Maritime Law Assn. St. Louis Bar (past pres. 1963-64) Clubs: Noonday, Missouri Athletic, St. Louis, Bellerive Country (St. Louis). Home: 20 Bellerive Country Club Grounds Saint Louis MO 63141 Office: One Mercantile Center Saint Louis MO 63101

SHEPHERD, JOHN HERBERT, labor union ofcl.; b. Kearney, Nebr., Sept. 21, 1918; s. Arthur LaVerne and Fannie (Hoselton) S.; grad. high sch.; m. Marjorie Elnora Line, June 12, 1939; children—Ronald J., Jacqueline K. Bassin. Switchman, U.P. R.R. Co., 1940, 53-55, chmn. gen. grievance com., 1955-60; v.p. Brotherhood of R.R. Trainmen, Denver and Los Angeles, 1960-68, dir., 1964-68; gen. sec., treas., dir. United Transp. Union, Cleve., 1969—; adminstrv. officer, dir., gen. sec., treas. United Transp. Union Ins. Assn., 1971—. Bd. dirs. United Community Chest, Omaha, 1955. Served with USMCR, 1944-46. Decorated Purple Heart. Mem. Fraternal Investment Assn., Nat. Fraternal Congress Am. Democrat. Mem. Christian Ch. Mason (32 deg., Shriner), Elk. Home: 17600 Detroit St Apt 1214 Lakewood OH 44107 Office: 14600 Detroit Ave Cleveland OH 44107

SHEPHERD, JOHN J., exec.; b. Lancashire, Eng., Feb. 20, 1929; B.A. with honors, London U., 1954; M.A. in Polit. Sci., McMaster U., Hamilton, Ont., Can., 1958; m. Leigh Hamilton Findlay, May 10, 1956; children—William Paul, Andrew Duncan, Adam John, Kristin Hamilton, Victoria Mary, Matthew Thomas. Exec. officer Air Ministry U.K.; contracts mgr. Computing Devices Can.; chmn., pres. Leigh Instruments Ltd.; vice chmn. Sci. Council Can., Ottawa, Ont.; pres. Can. Inst. Econ. Policy; dir. Lumonics Ltd., Nordco Ltd. Trustee Forum for Young Canadians. Mem. Can. Inst. Strategic Studies. Roman Catholic. Club: Rideau (Ottawa). Office: 100 Metcalfe St Ottawa ON K1P 5M1 Canada*

SHEPHERD, MARK, JR., electronics co. exec.; b. Dallas, Jan. 18, 1923; s. Mark and Louisa Florence (Daniell) S.; B.S. in Elec. Engring., So. Meth. U., 1942; M.S. in Elec. Engring., U. Ill., at Urbana, 1947; m. Mary Alice Murchland, Dec. 21, 1945; children—Debra Aline (Mrs. Rowland K. Robinson), MaryKay Theresa, Marc Blaine. With Gen. Elec. Co., 1942-43, Farnsworth Television and Radio Corp., 1947-48; with Tex. Instruments Inc., Dallas, 1948—, v.p., gen. mgr. semicondr.-components div., 1955-61, exec. v.p., chief operating officer, 1961-66, dir., 1963—, pres., chief operating officer, 1967-69, pres., chief exec. officer, 1969-76, chmn. bd., chief exec. officer, 1976—; dir. Republic Nat. Bank Dallas, Republic of Tex. Corp., U.S. Steel; mem. internat. council Morgan Guaranty Trust Co. Mem. Adv. Council on Japan-U.S. Econ. Relations; bd. dirs. Found. for Sci. and Engring. So. Meth. U.; mem. Center for Strategic and Internat. Studies, Internat. Council on Future of Bus.; bd. govs., trustee So. Meth. U.; trustee Com. for Econ. Devel., Am. Enterprise Inst. Pub. Policy Research; co-chmn. bd. trustees Conf. Bd.; mem. adv. council Am. Ditchley Found.; mem. Bus. Council, Dallas Citizens Council, European Community-U.S. Businessmen's Council, Trilateral Commn.; mem. nat. bd. Com. on the Present Danger. Served to lt. (j.g.) USNR, 1943-46. Registered profl. engr., Tex. Fellow IEEE; mem. Soc. Exploration Geophysicists, Newcomen Soc., Council on Fgn. Relations, Internat. C. of C. (trustee U.S. council), Nat. Acad. Engring., Sigma Xi, Eta Kappa Nu. Home: 5006 Middlegate Rd Dallas TX 75229 Office: Texas Instruments Inc PO Box 225474 MS 236 Dallas TX 75265

SHEPHERD, MASSEY HAMILTON, JR., clergyman; b. Wilmington, N.C., Mar. 14, 1913; s. Massey Hamilton and Alice Louise Gladstone (Melville) S.; A.B., U. S.C., 1932, A.M., 1933; Ph.D., U. Chgo., 1937; B.D. (hon.), Berkeley Div. Sch., 1941, S.T.D. (hon.), 1951; D.D. (hon.), Anglican Theol. Coll., 1957; Litt.D. (hon.), U. South, 1961; m. Gabriella Taylor Conner, Jan. 3, 1950; 1 dau., Nancy Lloyd. Instr. div. U. Chgo., 1937-40; ordained to ministry Episcopal Ch., 1941; instr. Episcopal Theol. Sch., Cambridge, Mass., 1940-42, asst. prof., 1942-46; prof. ch. history, 1946-54; minister in charge Ch. of Our Saviour, Allerton, Mass., 1940-41; asso. rector St. John's Ch., Roxbury, Mass., 1945-54; dir. Grad. Sch. Theology, U. South, Sewanee, Tenn., 1952-70; prof. liturgies Ch. Div. Sch. of Pacific, Berkeley, Calif., 1954—, vice dean, 1972-75; Anglican observer II Vatican Council, 1964; mem. liturgy commn. Roman Catholic Ch., 1966-70. Mem. World Council Chs. (commn. on ways of worship 1947-64), Am. Soc. Ch. History (pres., 1949), Soc. Bibl. Lit. and Exegesis, Mediaeval Acad. Am., Ch. Hist. Soc. (pres. 1961-74), Henry Bradshaw Soc., Alcuin Club, Phi Beta Kappa, Blue Key. Episcopalian (mem. liturgical com. 1946-76). Author: The Living Liturgy, 1946; The Oxford American Prayer Book Commentary, 1950; At All Times and In All Places, 1947; The Worship of the Church, 1952; The Liturgy and the Christian Faith, 1957; The Paschal Liturgy and the Apocalypse, 1960; The Reform of Liturgical Worship, 1961; Liturgy and Education, 1965; A Liturgical Psalter for the Christian year, 1976; The Psalms in Christian Worship, 1976; A Companion of Prayer for Daily Living, 1978; editor: Munera Studiosa (with S.E. Johnson), 1946; The Liturgical Renewal of the Church, 1960; The Eucharist and Liturgical Renewal, 1960; Worship in Scripture and Tradition, 1963. Home: 624 Euclid Ave Berkeley CA 94708 Office: 2451 Ridge Rd Berkeley CA 94709

SHEPHERD, RICHARD ALLAN, motion picture exec.; b. Kansas City, Mo., June 4, 1927; s. William Bertram and Harriette (Hirschfield) S.; B.A., Stanford U., 1948. Theatrical agt. MCA Artists, Ltd., 1948-55; head talent Columbia Picture Corp., 1956-57; motion picture producer, partner Jurow Shepherd Prodns., 1958-62; v.p. Creative Mgmt. Assos., Inc., Los Angeles, 1962-68, exec. v.p. motion pictures and dramatic TV divs., 1968-72; exec. v.p. prodn. Warner Bros. Pictures, Inc., Burbank, Calif., 1972-74; pres. Richard Shepherd Co., Burbank, 1974-76; sr. v.p. world wide prodn. MGM, Inc., Culver City, Calif., 1976—; films produced include: The Hanging Tree, 1959, Fugitive Kind, 1960, Breakfast at Tiffanys, 1961, Robin and Marian, 1976, Alex and the Gypsy, 1976. Served with USNR, 1944-46, U.S. Army, 1950-51. Office: MGM Inc 10202 W Washington Blvd Culver City CA 90230

SHEPHERD, ROBERT ASHLAND, lawyer; b. Huntsville, Tex., July 7, 1894; s. James L. and Julia (Josey) S.; grad. Sam Houston State Tchrs. Coll., 1914; LL.B., U. Tex. at Austin, 1917; m. Opal Powell, July 8, 1922; children—Robert Ashland, William Leftwich. Admitted to Tex. bar, 1921; with James L. Shepherd, Cisco, Tex., 1921; with Vinson, Elkins, Weems & Searls, Houston, 1921, partner, 1929—, mng. partner, 1951-59, then partner Vinson, Elkins, Searls, Connally & Smith (name change); ret., 1971. Vice pres., dir. Duval Corp., 1947-70; sr. chmn. bd., dir. Heights State Bank, Houston. Trustee, Lon Morris Coll., Tex. Med. Center, Meth. Hosp., Houston, Tex. Meth. Found. Served as 2d lt. F.A. and aviation, U.S. Army, World War I. Mem. Am., Houston bar assns., State Bar Tex., S.A.R., Sons Republic of Tex. Democrat. Methodist (trustee). Mason (Shriner, K.T.). Home: 2136 Inwood Dr Houston TX 77019

SHEPHERD, WILLIAM GERALD, ednl. adminstr.; b. Fort William, Ont., Can., Aug. 28, 1911; s. William Charles and Catherine Alice (Noble) S.; came to U.S., 1914, naturalized, 1922; B.S., U. Minn., 1933, Ph.D., 1937; m. Frances Elizabeth Bruce, Aug. 26, 1936; children—William Bruce, Anne Elizabeth, Sarah Louise. Teaching fellow U. Minn., 1933-37; mem. tech. staff Bell Tel. Labs, N.Y., 1937-47; engr., 1937-47; prof. elec. engring. U. Minn., 1947-79, prof. emeritus, 1979—, asso. dean. Inst. Tech., 1954-56, head dept. elec. engring., 1956-63, v.p. acad. adminstrn., 1963-73, dir. space sci. center, 1974-79. Civilian OSRD; space tech. adv. com. NASA; engring. div. adv. com. NSF, 1964—. Bd. dirs. Walker Art Inst., 1964-70, 71-77, Minn. Orch. Assn., 1963-74; bd. govs. Mpls. YMCA. Recipient citation Bur. Ships 1947; medal of honor Nat. Electronics Conf., 1965; Minn. Engr. of Year, 1966. Fellow I.E.E.E. (v.p. 1964-65, pres. 1965-66); mem. Am. Phys. Soc., Am. Soc. Engring. Edn., A.A.U.P., Internat. Sci. Radio Union (pres. commn. VII 1957), Nat. Assn. State Univs. and Land Grant Colls. (chmn. academic council 1965-66), Nat. Acad. Engring., Sigma Xi, Tau Beta Pi, Eta Kappa Nu. Contbr. articles to sci. jours. Home: 2197 Folwell St St Paul MN 55108 Office: University of Minn Minneapolis MN 55455

SHEPLEY, ETHAN ALLEN HITCHCOCK, JR., banker; b. St. Louis, Mar. 5, 1923; s. Ethan Allen Hitchcock and Sophie (Baker) S.; B.A., Yale, 1945; J.D., Washington U., St. Louis, 1949; m. Margaret B. Meyer, June 18, 1970; children by previous marriage—Michael Ethan, Lela Lockwood, Virginia Cochran. Admitted to Mo. bar, 1949; with firm Shepley, Kroeger, Fisse & Shepley, St. Louis, 1949-53; with Boatman's Nat. Bank, St. Louis, 1953—, vice chmn., 1977—, also dir.; pres. Boatman's Bancshares, Inc., 1969—, also dir.; dir. Credit Systems Inc., Boatmen's Bank West County, Boatmen's Bank O'Fallon. Bd. dirs., mem. exec. com. United Way Greater St. Louis; bd. dirs. Downtown St. Louis, Municipal Theatre Assn. St. Louis, Webster Coll.; bd. dirs. Barnard Free Skin and Cancer Hosp., St. Louis; pres. Reproductive Biology Research Found. Served with USAAF, 1943-45. Decorated Air medal with four oak leaf clusters, D.F.C. Recipient Distinguished Service award Boy Scouts Am. Mem. Mo. Bar Assn., Am. Inst. Banking, Scroll and Key, Fence Club, Phi Delta Phi. Republican. Episcopalian. Home: 8 Arbor Rd Saint Louis MO 63132 Office: 100 N Broadway Saint Louis MO 63102

SHEPLEY, HUGH, architect; b. Boston, Mar. 17, 1928; s. Henry Richardson and Anna Lowell (Gardiner) S.; B.A., Harvard, 1951; postgrad. Boston Archtl. Center, 1953-58, Mass. Inst. Tech., 1958-59; m. Mary Waters Niles, Dec. 27, 1950; children—Hamilton Niles, Philip Foster. Mem. archtl. firm Shepley, Bulfinch, Richardson & Abbott, Boston, 1955-63, partner, 1963—. Bd. dirs. Greater Boston Red Cross, 1967-73, mem. exec. com., 1968-69; bd. dirs. Community

Music Center Boston, 1968-72, Boston Center for Blind Children, 1979—; trustee New Eng. Conservatory Music, 1978—. Fellow AIA; mem. Mass. Assn. Architects (pres. 1972), Boston Soc. Architects (pres. 1974), Boston Archtl. Center (pres. 1969-71). Republican. Episcopalian. Clubs: Tavern (Boston); Century Assn. (N.Y.C.). Home: 18 Forster Rd Manchester MA 01944 Office: One Court St Boston MA 02108

SHEPLEY, JAMES ROBINSON, journalist; b. Harrisburg, Pa., Aug. 16, 1917; s. Charles Laurence and Jean (Robinson) S.; student Dickinson Coll., 1935-37, Litt.D., 1959; D.Sc., Clarkson Coll. Tech., 1966; m. Jean Stevens, Mar. 27, 1937; children—Steven, Jean Lucile, James, Lynn Hammond; m. 2d, Yvonne Hudson; 1 dau., Genoa Laurence. Corr., Pitts. Press, 1937; Pa. legis. corr. U.P.I., 1937-40, Washington corr., 1940-42, Time mag., 1942, fgn. policy corr., 1946-48; war corr. Time and Life mags., CBI, S.W. Pacific Theatre, ETO, 1942-44, chief Washington corr., 1948-57, chief corr. for co.'s U.S. and Canadian new service, 1957-60; asst. pub. Life, 1960-63; pub. Fortune, 1964-67, pub. Time mag., 1967-69, pres. Time, Inc., 1969—. U.S. staff officer at Potsdam Conf., 1945; collaborator Gen. Marshall's ofcl. report World War II, 1945. Served as capt. Gen. Staff Corps. attached Chief of Staff Gen. G.C. Marshall, 1945-46; attache to spl. presdl. envoy to China, 1946; capt. U.S. Army Res., 1946-50; maj. USAF Res. Awarded War Dept. Letter of Commendation. Clubs: Manhasset Bay Yacht; Chicago; Army and Navy; N.Y. Yacht; Nat. Press; Conquistadores del Cielo; Storm Trysail, Cruising of America. Co-author: The Hydrogen Bomb. Office: Time & Life Bldg Rockefeller Center New York NY 10020

SHEPP, BRYAN EUGENE, psychologist; b. Cumberland, Md., Sept. 13, 1932; s. Bryan Evert and Dorothy Lorene (Stell) S.; B.S., U. Md., 1954, M.S., 1956, Ph.D., 1960; M.S. (hon.), Brown U., 1966; m. June Lee Langeluttig, Jan. 31, 1953; children—Karen Suzanne, David Bryan. Research prof. U. Conn., 1961-63; asst. prof. psychology George Peabody Coll., 1963-64; asst. prof. Brown U., 1964-66, asso. prof., 1966-69, prof., 1969—; cons. in field; vis. scientist Oxford (Eng.) U., 1970. Served with USN, 1955-59. Decorated letter of commendation Sec. of Navy; USPHS postdoctoral fellow, 1959-61; Nat. Inst. Child Health and Human Devel. grantee, 1965—. Fellow Am. Psychol. Assn.; mem. Psychonomic Soc., Soc. Research in Child Devel., AAAS, AAUP. Club: Univ. Contbr. numerous articles to profl. publs.; ad hoc editor for several psychol. jours. Office: 89 Waterman St Providence RI 02912

SHEPPARD, ALBERT PARKER, JR., electronics engr., educator; b. Griffin, Ga., June 6, 1936; s. Albert Parker and Cornelia (Cooper) S.; B.S., Oglethorpe U., 1958; M.S., Emory U., 1959; Ph.D., Duke U., 1965; m. Eleanor C. Davis, Feb. 8, 1978; children—Albert Parker III, Frank Phillip. Sr. engr. Orlando (Fla.) research div. Martin Marietta Co., 1960-63; physicist U.S. Army Research Office, Durham, N.C., 1963-65; prin. research engr., head spl. techniques br., electronics div. Ga. Inst. Tech., 1965-71, chem. scis. and materials div., 1971-72, asso. dean coll. engring., 1972-74, prof. elec. engring., 1972—, asso. v.p. for research, 1974—; mem. eve. faculty Dekalb Coll., Clarkston, Ga., 1967-71; partner Microwave and Electronics Cons., Atlanta. Recipient Distinguished Alumni award Oglethorpe U., 1974. Woodrow Wilson fellow, 1959. Mem. IEEE (sr.), Internat. Solar Energy Soc., Internat. Microwave Power Inst., Am. Soc. for Engring. Edn., Engring. Research Council (dir. 1976-79, chmn. com. research adminstrn. 1975-79, com. univ./industry research 1979—), Sigma Xi, Sigma Pi Sigma. Club: Ansley Golf (Atlanta). Contbr. articles to profl. jours. Home: 3591 Norwich Dr Tucker GA 30084

SHEPPARD, CHARLES STEWART, univ. dean; b. Caerphilly, Wales, Nov. 25, 1915; s. Henry Arthur and Mary F. (Edwards) S.; came to U.S., 1939, naturalized, 1941; B.A. with honors, U. Wales, 1939; M.B.A., N.Y. U., 1940; Ph.D., Columbia, 1950; m. Maria Elena Moreno, Dec. 22, 1968; children—Linda Peterson, David Jones, Glennys, Bettina Williams. Prof. econs., asso. dean N.Y. U., 1946-55; prof., dean Grad. Sch. Bus. and Pub. Adminstrn., Cornell U., 1955-61; prof. bus. adminstrn. U. Va., Charlottesville, 1961-72, Tipton R. Snavely prof., dean Darden Grad. Sch. Bus. Adminstrn., 1972—. Dir. Hazleton Labs., Inc. Research dir. Econometric Inst., N.Y.C., 1945-46; exec. dir. Inst. Chartered Financial Analysts, also Financial Analysts Research Found., Charlottesville, 1961-72, now trustee; exec. dir. Financial Analysts Fedn., N.Y.C., 1968-70. Served to 1st lt. AUS, 1940-45. Mem. Raven Soc., Beta Gamma Sigma, Omicron Delta Epsilon. Presbyn. Clubs: Farmington Country, Greencroft, Rotary, Colonnade (Charlottesville). Contbr. articles to profl. jours. Home: Pavilion IV East Lawn U Virginia Charlottesville VA 22903

SHEPPARD, CLAUDE-ARMAND, lawyer; b. Ghent, Belgium, May 26, 1935; B.A., McGill U., 1955; B.C.L., 1958; m. Claudine Proutat; children—Jean-Pierre, Michel, Marie-Claude, Stephane, Annabelle. Admitted to Que. bar, 1959; partner firm Robinson, Cutler, Sheppard, Borenstein, Shapiro, Langlois & Flam, Montreal, 1965—; legal commentator for French and English radio and television networks in Can.; lectr. various instns.; counsel various royal commns.; counsel to com. Canadian Ho. of Commons; legal supr. Que. Commn. of Inquiry Lang. Rights. Past pres. Canadian Civil Liberties Union; former mem. Canadian Adv. Council on Status of Women. Mem. Canadian Bar Assn. Author: The Law of Languages in Canada, 1965; The Organization and Regulation of the Health and Social Welfare Professions in Quebec, 1970; Language Rights in Quebec, 1973; also numerous papers. Office: 800 Place Victoria Suite 612 Montreal PQ H4Z 1H6 Canada

SHEPPARD, JOHN GAVIN, steel co. exec.; b. Ottawa, Ont., Can., July 2, 1916; s. Frank Eugene and Lillie (MacFarlane) S.; grad. high sch.; m. Mary Suzanne Wood, May 19, 1945; children—Gavin Wood, John Scott, Carol Jane, Blair Hesson. With Dominion Foundries & Steel, Ltd., Hamilton, Ont., 1935—, v.p., sec., comptroller, 1961-64, exec. v.p.-financial, sec., 1964-68, exec. v.p.-financial, 1968—; chmn., dir. Prudential Steel Ltd.; dir. Dominion Foundries & Steel, Ltd., Nat. Steel Car Corp., Ltd., Arnaud Ry. Co., Ltd., Wabush Lake Ry. Co., Ltd., Nat. Trust Co., Ltd., Beachvilime Ltd., Internat. Portable Pipe Mills Ltd. Past pres. Jr. C. of C., Hamilton and Can. Chmn. Hamilton United Appeal, 1955-56; past pres. Hamilton YMCA; past pres. Art Gallery of Hamilton; past v.p. Nat. Councils of YMCA's. Chmn. bd. Royal Bot. Gardens of Hamilton. Mem. Am. Iron and Steel Inst., Financial Execs. Inst., Financial Execs. Inst. Can., Hamilton C. of C., Can.-U.S. Com. C. of C. Clubs: Hamilton, Hamilton Golf and Country, Tamahaac (Hamilton); Toronto (Ont.). Home: 399 Queen St S Hamilton ON L8P 3T8 Canada Office: PO Box 460 Hamilton ON L8N 3J5 Canada

SHEPPARD, POSY (MRS. JOHN WADE SHEPPARD), social worker; b. New Haven, Aug. 23, 1916; d. John Day and Rose Marie (Herrick) Jackson; student Vassar Coll., 1938; m. John W. Sheppard, May 16, 1936; children—Sandra S. (Mrs. Allan Gray Rodgers), Gail G. (Mrs. J. Truman Bidwell, Jr.), Lynn S. (Mrs. William Muir Manger), John W. Vol. field cons. Conn. A.R.C., 1955-60; vice chmn. bd. govs. Am. Nat. Red Cross, 1962-66; rep. League Red Cross Socs. to UN, 1957—; rep. Am. Nat. Red Cross to com. internat. social welfare Nat. Social Welfare Assembly, 1957-61; chmn. Non-Govtl. Orgn. Com. for UNICEF, 1963-64, 71-73; chmn. Non-Govtl. Orgn. Com. exec. com. for Office Pub. Information, UN, 1964-66; pres. conf. non-govtl. orgns. in consultative status with UN Econ. and Social Council, 1966-69. Mem. Nat. Council Women (mem.-at-large bd.), Nat. Inst. Social Scis. (vice chmn.), Am. Soc. Polit. and Social Sci., Soc. Internat. Devel., Nat. Soc. Colonial Dames, Descs. Signers of Declaration Independence, Jr. League Greenwich. Clubs: Cosmopolitan, Field of Greenwich, Round Hill. Home: 535 Lake Ave Greenwich CT 06830

SHEPPARD, ROBERT BLAIR, ins. co. exec.; b. San Francisco, Sept. 11, 1922; s. Robert Boone and Joy Winifred (Sivers) S.; A.B., U. Calif. at Berkeley, 1943; m. June Wayne Phillips, Dec. 13, 1944; children—Stephen Robert, James Mark. Sales mgr. Calif. State Auto Asso., Walnut Creek, 1946-53; with Allstate Ins. Co., Northbrook, Ill., 1953—, exec. v.p., 1971—, pres., 1972—. Dir. Council Better Bus. Burs. Bd. dirs. Advt. Council, Inc., Chgo. Urban League, Coll. of Ins. Served to capt. USMCR, 1942-46. Named Sales and Mktg. Exec. of Year, Sales and Mktg. Execs. Assn. Chgo., 1974. Clubs: Skokie Country (Glencoe, Ill.); Bay Hill (Orlando, Fla.); Carmel Valley Golf (Carmel, (Calif.). Office: Allstate Plaza Northbrook IL 60062

SHEPPARD, THOMAS RICHARD, lawyer; b. Pasadena, Calif., Aug. 8, 1934; s. James Carroll and Ruth Mary (Pashgian) S.; A.B., Stanford U., 1956; LL.B., Harvard U., 1961; m. Arlene Clubb, June 23, 1956; children—Eileen Diana, Pamela Lynn, Thomas Richard. Admitted to Calif. bar, 1962; asso. firm Sheppard, Mullin, Richter & Hampton, Los Angeles, 1961-66, partner, 1966—; dir. numerous small corps.; pres. Legal Aid Found. Los Angeles, 1973. Trustee Harold Lloyd Found., Los Angeles, 1971—, Della Martin Found., Los Angeles, 1979—. Served to lt. (j.g.), USN 1956-58. Mem. Am. Bar Assn., State Bar Assn. Calif., Los Angeles County Bar Assn., Am. Law Inst., Beta Theta Pi. Club: Calif. (Los Angeles). Home: 1680 Oak Grove Ave San Marino CA 91108 Office: 333 S Hope St Suite 4800 Los Angeles CA 90071

SHEPPARD, WILLIAM JACOB, educator; b. Ft. Scott, Kans., Feb. 28, 1917; s. James Gifford and Lucile (Dillard) S.: student Fort Scott Jr. Coll., 1934-35, Washburn Coll., 1937-38, U. Kansas City, 1939-42; A.B., George Washington U., 1950; M.A.P.A., U. Calif. at Berkeley, 1968; m. Ruth Flora, children—Lucy Ann, James Cecil. Adminstrv. asst. Fed. Crop Ins. Corp., 1939-42; adminstrv. officer WPB, 1942-43; spl. asst. to dir. U.S. Bur. Budget, 1946-48; dir., orgn. and mgt. ECA, Paris, France, 1948-49; spl. asst. to Sec. State, 1949-50; dep. dir., exec. sec. Dept. State, Washington, 1950-51; exec. asst. to dir. internat. security affairs Dept. State, Feb.-Nov. 1951; exec. asst., dir. for Mut. Security, 1951-54, asst. to dep. dir. for mgmt., 1954-56; dir. Fgn. Ops. Thailand, 1956-57; spl. asst., exec. asst. to asst. sec. state for adminstrn., 1957-58; dep. ops. coordinator Dept. State, 1959-60; regional dir. Far East, ICA, 1960-62; dir. adminstrn. Asia Found., 1962-66. dir. pub. affairs, 1966-68; acting asst. dean Grad. Sch. Pub. Affairs, U. Calif. at Berkeley, 1968-70; lectr. Calif. State U., Hayward, 1968—, coordinator grad. program in pub. adminstrn., 1971—, acting chmn. dept. pub. adminstrn., 1971-73, dir. Center for Pub. Service Edn. and Research, 1974—. Served as C.W.O., USAF, 1943-46; capt. USAF Res. Recipient William A. Jump Meml. award, 1953. Mem. Am. Soc. for Pub. Adminstrn., Calif. Assn. Pub. Adminstrn. Educators (pres. 1977—). Am. Fgn. Service Assn., Phi Delta Theta. Presbyterian. Home: 2707 Oakes Dr Hayward CA 94542 Office: Calif State U 25800 Hillary St Hayward CA 94542

SHEPPERD, JOHN BEN, life ins. and petroleum co. exec.; b. Gladewater, Tex., Oct. 19, 1915; s. Alfred Fulton and Berthal (Phillips) S.; LL.B., U. Tex., 1941; LL.D. (hon.), North Tex. State Coll., 1951, Chapman Christian Coll., Los Angeles, 1953, Southwestern U., 1955; m. Maimie Strieber, Oct. 6, 1938; children—Alfred Lewis, John Ben, Marianne and Suzanne (twins). Admitted to Tex. bar, 1941; sec. state State of Tex., 1950-52, atty. gen., 1952-56; officer El Paso Products Co., Trebol Oil Co., Odessa Natural Gasoline Co., West Tex. Gathering Cos. (all Odessa); chmn. bd. Republic Nat. Life Ins. Co., Dallas; dir. Am. Bank, Odessa, Nat. Western Life Ins. Co., Austin, Tex. Former mem., chmn. Tex. Indsl. Commn., Tex. Civil War Centennial Commn., Tex. Hist. Commn., Tex. Commn. Arts and Humanities; mem. Tex. State Library and Archives Commn.; trustee St. Edward's U., Austin. pres. Tex. Jaycees 1941, U.S. Jaycees, 1947; Mem. Nat. Assn. Attys. Gen. (pres. 1956). Democrat. Mem. Christian Ch., Author: The President's Guide to Club and Organizations Management and Meetings. Home: 3107 Windsor Dr Odessa TX 79762 Office: Republic Nat Life Ins Co 3988 N Central Expy Dallas TX 75204

SHEPPERSON, WILBUR STANLEY, educator; b. Arbela, Mo., May 23, 1919; s. Clinton Artis and Ruby (Dietrich) S.; B.S., N.E. Mo. State Coll., 1941; M.A., U. Denver, 1947; Ph.D., Western Res. U., 1951; postgrad. Johns Hopkins, 1941-42, U. London, 1948-49; m. Margaret Loraine Dietze, Feb. 17, 1945; children—Stanley Carlyle, Tara Loraine. Personnel cons. Glen L. Martin Aircraft Co., Balt., 1941-42; interviewer USES, Denver, 1947-48; instr. Western State Coll., 1947-48; instr., asst. prof., asso. prof. U. Nev., Reno, 1951-63, prof., 1963—, chmn. dept. history, 1966-74, 79—, dir. U. Nev. Press, 1965-66; Fulbright prof. U. Liverpool, Eng., 1967-68; historian research div. U.S. Dept. State, Washington, 1952; vis. lectr. U. Wales, 1954-55; apl. agt. U.S. Bur. Census, Reno, 1963-66; cons. U.S. Dept. Interior, 1958-60. Chmn. Nev. Humanities Com., 1973—. Served with USAAF, 1942-46. Fellow Hon. Soc. Cymmrodorion; mem. Nat. Hon. History Soc. (nat. councillor 1958-62). Author: British Emigration to North America, 1957; Samuel Roberts, A Welsh Colonizer in Tennessee, 1961; Emigration and Disenchantment, 1965; Retreat to Nevada: A Socialist Colony During World War I, 1966; Restless Strangers: Nevada's Immigrants, 1970; Questions from the Past, 1973; Hardscrabble: A Narrative of the California Hill Country, 1975. News editor Historian, 1951-53; editor Nev. Studies in History and Polit. Sci., 1960—; mng. editor Nev. Hist. Soc. Quar., 1970-73, Halcyon: Jour. of Humanities, 1978—; contbr. numerous articles to profl. jours. Home: 2490 Pioneer Dr Reno NV 89502

SHEPS, CECIL GEORGE, physician; b. Winnipeg, Man., Can., July 24, 1913; s. George and Polly (Lirenman) S.; M.D., U. Man., 1936; M.P.H., Yale, 1947; D.Sc. (hon.), Chgo. Med. Sch., 1970; m. Mindel Cherniack, May 29, 1937 (dec. Jan. 1973); 1 son, Samuel B.; m. 2d, Ann Shepherd. Came to U.S., 1946, naturalized, 1956. Intern St. Joseph's Hosp. Gen. Hosp., Winnipeg; resident Corbett Gen. Hosp., Stourbridge, Eng., Queen Mary's Hosp. for East End, London, Eng., Camp Shilo Mil. Hosp., Can., Ft. Osborne Mil. Hosp., Can., gen. dir. Beth Israel hosp., Boston, also clin. prof. preventive medicine Harvard Med. Sch., 1953-60; prof. med. and hosp. adminstrn. Grad. Sch. Pub. Health, U. Pitts., 1960-65; gen. dir. Beth Israel Med. Center, N.Y.C., also prof. community medicine Mt. Sinai Sch. Medicine, 1965-68; prof. social medicine U. N.C., 1969—, dir. Health Services Research Center, 1969-71, vice chancellor health scis., 1971-76; cons. in field, 1947—. Chmn. health services research study sect. NIH, 1958-62; cons. med. affairs Welfare Adminstrn., HEW, 1964-67; mem. spl. commn. social scis. NSF, 1968-69; chmn. Milbank Meml. Fund. Commn. on Higher Edn. for Pub. Health, 1972-75. Served as capt. Royal Can. Army Med. Corps., 1943-46. Mem. Nat. Council Aging (v.p., bd. mem.), Am. Nurses Found. (bd. mem. sec.-treas.), Inst. Medicine, Nat. Acad. Scis. Author: Needed Research in Health and Medical Care-A Biosocial Approach, 1954; Community Organization-Action and Inaction, 1956: Medical Schools and Hospitals, 1965. Home: Route 7 Arboretum Dr Chapel Hill NC 27514

SHER, ALLAN LOUIS, brokerage co. exec.; b. Superior, Wis., Oct. 19, 1931; s. Robert Edward and Pearl (Wolpert) S.; B.A., Princeton U., 1953; grad. Advanced Mgmt. Program, Harvard U., 1975; m. Judy Biegel, June 17, 1962; children—Allison, Victoria, Robert. With Merrill Lynch, Pierce, Fenner & Smith Inc., N.Y.C., 1956—, exec. v.p. services, 1976-79, exec. v.p. fin./adminstrn., 1979—, also dir.; dir. Depository Trust Co.; ofcl. Am. Stock Exchange. Trustee, Congregation Emanu-El, Scarsdale, N.Y. Served with U.S. Army, 1954-56. Democrat. Club: Century Country. Home: 51 Paddington Rd Scarsdale NY 10583 Office: 165 Broadway New York NY 10080

SHER, DAVID, lawyer; b. Omaha, Jan. 27, 1908; s. Philip and Rebecca (Saxe) S.; B.S., Harvard, 1928, LL.B., 1931; m. Phyllis Tulin, Nov. 3O, 1934; 1 son, Michael. Admitted to N.Y. Bar, 1932; asst. to gen. counsel Gen. Motors Corp., 1931-46; partner firm Stroock & Stroock & Lavan, N.Y.C., 1946—; dir. Tosco Corp. Pres., Jewish Family Service N.Y., chmn. Nat. Community Relations Adv. Council; chmn. publ. com. Commentary mag.; chmn. bd. Community Council Greater N.Y.; asso. chmn. bd. N.Y. Fedn. Jewish Philanthropies; chmn. exec. com. Internat. Rescue Com. Mem. Am. Council on Germany, Am. Soc. for Technion (v.p.). Clubs: Harmonie, Lotos, Century Country (N.Y.C.). Home: 1120 Park Ave New York NY 10028 Office: 61 Broadway New York NY 10006

SHER, STANLEY OWEN, lawyer; b. Milw., June 3, 1935; s. Abo S. and Mary Rose Sher; B.S., U. Wis., 1956; LL.B., Harvard U., 1959; m. Linda Rosenberg, Aug. 11, 1963; children—Jeremy Jay, Helen Sue. Admitted to D.C. bar, 1960, since practiced in Washington; v.p. firm Billig, Sher & Jones, 1973—. Served as officer AUS, 1959-60. Mem. D.C., Wis. bar assns., Maritime Adminstrn. Bar Assn. (v.p.), Phi Beta Kappa. Home: 6120 33d St NW Washington DC 20015 Office: 2033 K St NW Washington DC 20006

SHERA, JESSE HAUK, librarian, educator; b. Oxford, Ohio, Dec. 8, 1903; s. Charles H. and Jessie (Hauk) S.; A.B., Miami U., Oxford, 1925; M.A., Yale, 1927; Ph.D., U. Chgo., 1944; LL.D., Ball State U., 1976; m. Helen M. Bickham, 1928; children—Mary Helen, Edgar Brookins. Asst. cataloger Miami U. Library, 1927-28, bibliographer Scripps Found. for Research in Population Problems, 1928-40; chief census library project Library of Congress, 1940-41; asst. chief, central information div. O.S.S., 1941-44; asst. dir. U. Chgo. Library, 1944-47; asst. prof. Grad. Library Sch., U. Chgo., 1947-51, asso. prof., 1951-52; dean sch. library sci. Western Res. U., Cleve., 1952-70, prof., dean emeritus, 1972—; Brazilian lectr. Inst. Bibliography and Documentation, 1957; vis. prof. Grad. Sch. Library Sci., U. Tex., Austin, 1970-71, U. Ariz., summer 1973, U. Ky., summer 1974, U. Minn., spring 1977; lectr. seminar on library edn. Liverpool (Eng.) Poly., 1974, U. P.R., 1979. Mem. Pres.'s Com. Employment of the Handicapped, 1969—, Pres.'s Com. Library Research and Edn. U.S. del. UNESCO Internat. Conf., Paris. 1950; U.S. del. Internat. Conf. on Bibliog. Classification, Dorking, Eng., 1957; bd. educators United Educators, Inc. Dir. Center Documentation and Communication Research, Western Res. U., 1960-71. Trustee Council Nat. Library Assns. Recipient Beta Phi Mu award, 1965; Melvil Dewey award A.L.A., 1968, Lippincott award, 1973; Distinguished Service award Drexel U., 1971; award of merit Am. Soc. for Info. Sci., 1973; Scarecrow Press award A.L.A., 1974; Hilbert T. Ficken award Baldwin-Wallace Coll., 1976; Alumni award U. Chgo., 1977, Gold Medal, Kaula Found. (India); elected to Ohio Library Hall Fame, 1973. Mem. Spl. Libraries Assn., AAAS, Assn. Am. Library Schs. (pres. 1964-65), English-Speaking Union, ALA (hon. life mem., chmn. com. on bibliography 1950-52; council 1964-68), Ohio (pres. 1963-64, Librarian of Year 1969), Chgo. library assns., Bibliog. Soc. Am., Miss. Valley Hist. Assn., Phi Beta Kappa, Beta Phi Mu (pres. 1970-71), Phi Alpha Theta. Clubs: Cliff Dwellers; Caxton, Rowfant. Author: Foundations of the Public Library, 1949; Bibliographic Organization (with Margaret E. Egan), 1951; Historians, Books, and Libraries, 1953; The Classified Catalog (with M.E. Egan), 1956; Libraries and the Organization of Knowledge, 1965; Documentation and the Organization of Knowledge, 1966; The Compleat Librarian, 1970; Sociological Foundations of Librarianship, 1971; Foundations of Education for Librarianship, 1972; Knowing Books and Men, 1973; Introduction to Library Science, 1976. Editor: American Documentation, 1953-60; Western Res. U. Press, 1954-59; Documentation in Action, 1956; Information Systems in Documentation, 1957: Information Resources: A Challenge to American Science and Industry, 1958; Toward a Theory of Librarianship (Conrad H. Rawski), 1973. Editorial bd. Jour. Library History; asso. editor Library Quar., 1947-52, adv. editor, 1952-55; adv. editor Jour. Cataloging and Classification, 1947-57; editor-in-chief Wiley-Interscience texts in Documentation and Library Science, 1958—; editorial bd. Library Sci. (India); bd. editors United Educators, 1961-74. Home: 2368 Overlook Rd Cleveland Heights OH 44106 Office: Baker Bldg Case Western Res Univ Cleveland OH 44106

SHERAN, ROBERT JOSEPH, judge; b. Waseca, Minn., Jan. 2, 1916; s. Michael J. and Eleanor A. (Bowe) S.; B.A., Coll. St. Thomas, St. Paul, 1936; LL.B., U. Minn., 1939; m. Jean M. Brown, Feb. 3, 1940; children—Michael, Thomas, Kathleen, John, Daniel. Admitted to Minn. bar, 1939; practice in Glencoe, 1939-42, Mankato, 1945-63; spl. agt. FBI, 1942-45; asso. justice Supreme Ct. Minn., 1963-70, chief justice, 1973—; mem. firm Lindquist & Vennum, Mpls., 1970-73. Mem. Minn. Bd. Law Examiners, 1956- 62, 70-73; mem. Minn. Bd. Tax Appeals, 1961-63; chmn. Gov.'s Commn. on Crime Prevention and Control, 1970-73. Mem. Minn. Ho. of Reps. from Blue Earth County, 1946-50. Trustee Coll. St. Thomas, 1964-73. Fellow Am. Coll. Trial Lawyers, Internat. Acad. Trial Lawyers, Am. Bar Found.; mem. Am. Law Inst., Am. Judicature Soc., Inst. Jud. Adminstrn., Conf. Chief Justices U.S. (chmn.-elect 1979-80), U. Minn. Alumni Assn. (pres. 1979-80). Home: 1077 Sibley Meml Hwy Saint Paul MN 55118 Office: 230 State Capitol Saint Paul MN 55155

SHERARD, JOHN HOLMES, IV, hosp. exec.; b. Memphis, Aug. 23, 1937; s. John Holmes and Mary Allison (Arnold) S.; student Tex. A. and M. U., 1956-57; B.S. in Agronomy, Miss. State U., 1959; m. Margaret Nicholas, Dec. 24, 1976; 1 son, Holmes V. Pres., chief exec. officer John H. Sherard Inc., Sherard, Miss., 1961—; chmn. bd. mgrs., chmn. exec. com. Methodist Hosp., Memphis, also chmn. fund-raising campaign; trustee, dir. Coahoma Bank; dir. Grenada Bank. Bd. dirs. Lee Acad., N. Delta Compress, Farm Bur.; trustee Clarksdale Library. Served to capt. U.S. Army, 1959-61. Recipient Nat. Trustee of Yr. award United Meth. Ch., 1977. Mem. Cotton Council, Southeastern Pecan Assn., Delta Council, Miss. Pecan Growers Assn., Miss. Forestry Assn., Miss. Cattlemen Assn. Clubs: Rotary, Univ., Ward Lake Hunting, Clarksdale Country. Home and office: Sherard MS 38669

SHERA (SHAPIRO), MARK, actor; b. Bayonne, N.J., July 10, 1949; s. Nathan and Bette Shapiro; B.F.A. in Acting, Boston U., 1971. Appeared as Jesus in Godspell, Boston, nat. touring co., Off-Broadway; appeared in television series SWAT, 1975-76; appears in television series Barnaby Jones in role of J.R. Jones, 1976—. Office: CBS Television Network 7800 Beverly Blvd Los Angeles CA 90036

SHERBELL, RHODA, sculptor; b. Bklyn.; d. Alexander and Syd (Steinberg) S.; student Art Students League, 1950-53, Bklyn. Mus. Art Sch., 1959-61; also pvt. study art, Italy, France, Eng., 1956; m. Mervin Honig, Apr. 28, 1956; 1 dau., Susan. Exhibited one-woman shows: Country Art Gallery, Locust Valley, N.Y., Bklyn. Mus. Art Sch., Adelphia Coll., A.C.A. Galleries, N.Y.C., 1967, Capricorn Galleries, Rehn Gallery, Washington, 1968, Gallery Modern Art, N.Y.C., 1969; one-woman retrospective at N.Y. Cultural Center, 1970, Nat. Art Mus. of Sport, 1977; two-woman shows at Bklyn. Mus., Country Art Gallery, Rehn Gallery, Port Washington Library; exhibited group shows: Downtown Gallery, N.Y.C., Maynard Walker Gallery, N.Y.C., F.A.R. Gallery, N.Y.C., Provincetown Art Assn., Detroit Inst. Art, Pa. Acad. Fine Arts, Bklyn. and L.I. Artists Show, Old Westbury Gardens Small Sculpture Show, Audubon Artists, NAD, Allied Artists, Heckscher Mus., Nat. Art Mus. Sports, others; represented permanent collections: Stony Brook (N.Y.) Mus., Colby Coll. Mus., Oklahoma City Mus., Montclair (N.J.) Mus., Colby Coll. Mus., Smithsonian Instn., Baseball Hall of Fame, Nassau Community Coll., Hofstra U. Emily Lowe Gallery, also pvt. collections; TV shows ABC, 1968; ednl. TV spl. Rhoda Sherbell-Woman in Bronze, 1977; important works include Walking Ballerina, Adolescent Girl, The Sunday Hat, Standing Woman, Seated Ballerina; portraits Casey Stengel, Yogi Berra, Marguerite and William Zorach, The Gypsie Troupe, Aaron Copland. Cons., council mem. Emily Lowe Gallery, Hofstra U., Hempstead, N.Y., 1978; council mem. Nassau County Mus., 1978; asso. trustee Nat. Art Mus. of Sports, Inc.; cons., community liaison WNET Channel 13; trustee Women's Boxing Fedn., 1978. Recipient Am. Acad. Arts, Letters and Nat. Inst. Arts and Letters grant, 1960; Louis Comfort Tiffany Found. grant, 1962; Alfred G. B. Steel Meml. award Pa. Acad. Fine Arts, 1963-64; Helen F. Barnett prize NAD, 1965; Jersey City Mus. prize for sculpture, 1961; 1st prize sculpture Locust Valley Art Show, 1966, 67; Ann. Sculpture prize Jersey City Mus.; Bank for Savs. 1st prize in sculpture, 1950; Ford Found. purchase award, 1964; MacDowell Colony fellow, 1976; 2 Top Sculpture awards Mainstreams 77; Cert. of Merit, Salmagundi Club, 1978. Mem. Nat. Assn. Women Artists (Jeffery Childs Willis Meml. prize 1978), Allied Artists Soc., Audubon Artists (Greta Kempton Walker prize 1965), Woman's Caucus for Art, Coll. Art Assn., Am. Inst. Conservation Historic and Artistic Works, N.Y. Soc. Women Artists, Artists Equity Assn. N.Y., Nat. Sculpture Soc., Internat. Platform Assn., Profl. Artists Guild L.I., Painters and Sculptors Soc. N.J. (Bertrum R. Hulmes Meml. award), Catharine Lorillard Wolfe Club (hon. mention 1968). Appeared several TV shows; guest various radio programs. Contbr. articles to newspapers, popular mags. and art jours. Home: 64 Jane Ct Westbury NY 11590

SHERBO, ARTHUR, educator; b. Haverhill, Mass., May 27, 1918; s. Pasquale and Angela (Torchia) S.; student U. N.H., 1937-38; B.A., Bowdoin Coll., 1947; M.A., Columbia U., 1948, Ph.D. (Univ. fellow), 1950; m. Irene Frankel, June 20, 1947; children—Angela, Laura, Barbara. Instr. to asst. prof. English, U. Ill., Urbana, 1950-56; asst. prof. Mich. State U., East Lansing, 1956-57, asso. prof., 1957-62, prof., 1962—; vis. scholar Corpus Christi Coll., Cambridge (Eng.) U., 1973. Served with AUS, 1943-46. Guggenheim fellow, 1956. Mem. Modern Lang. Assn. Am., Modern Humanities Research Assn., A.A.U.P., Phi Beta Kappa. Author: Samuel Johnson Editor of Shakespeare, 1956; English Sentimental Drama, 1957; Christopher Smart, Scholar of the University, 1967; Studies in the Eighteenth-Century English Novel, 1969; English Poetic Diction From Chaucer to Wordsworth, 1975. Editor: New Essays by Arthur Murphy, 1963; Johnson on Shakespeare, 2 vols., 1968; Hesther Piozzi: Anecdotes of Samuel Johnson with William Shaw, Memoirs of Dr. Johnson, 1974; Christoper Smart's Verse Translation of the Odes of Horace, 1979. Home: 243 Kensington Rd East Lansing MI 48823

SHERBOURNE, ARCHIBALD NORBERT, educator; b. Bombay, India, July 8, 1929; s. Manekji and Sarah Agnes (Sherbourne) Bulsara; B.Sc., U. London, 1953, D.Sc., 1970; B.S., Lehigh U., 1955, M.S., 1957; M.A., Cambridge, 1959, Ph.D., 1960; m. Jean Ducan Nicol, Aug. 15, 1959; children—Mary, Sarah, Jeffrey, Nicolas, Jonathan, Simon. Mem. faculty U. Waterloo (Ont., Can.), 1961—, prof. civil engring., 1963—, dean Faculty Engring., 1966-74. Dir. Frew & Sherbourne Consultants Ltd. Vis. prof. U. W.I., Trinidad, 1969-70, Nat. C.E. Lab., Lisbon, Portugal, 1970, Ecole Polytechnique Federale, Lausanne, Switzerland, 1975-77; spl. cons. technol. edn. for developing countries Canadian Internat. Devel. Agy. Registered profl. engr., Ont. OECD fellow, Switzerland, 1964. Recipient Engring. medal Assn. Profl. Engrs. Province Ont., 1975. Fellow Instn. Structural Engrs. London, Royal Soc. Arts, mem. Internat. Assn. Bridge and Structural Engring. Contbr. articles to profl. jours. Home: Tigh-Na-Bruadar 46 Glasgow St N Conestogo ON N0B 1N0 Canada Office: Faculty Engring U Waterloo Waterloo ON Canada

SHERBURNE, DONALD WYNNE, philosopher, educator; b. Proctor, Vt., Apr. 21, 1929; s. Hermon Kirk and Alma May (Bixby) S.; A.B., Middlebury Coll., 1951; B.A., Balliol Coll., Oxford U., 1953; M.A., Yale U., 1958, Ph.D., 1960; m. Elizabeth Statesir Darling, July 30, 1955; children—Kevin Darling, Nancy Elizabeth, Lynne Darling. Instr. philosophy Yale, 1959-60; asst. prof. Vanderbilt U., Nashville, 1960-64, asso. prof., 1964-68, prof. philosophy, 1968—, chmn. dept., 1973—. Troop leader Cub Scouts, 1965-67. Served with U.S. Army, 1954-56. Dutton fellow, Oxford U., 1951-53; sr. fellow Nat. Endowment for Humanities, 1977—. Mem. Metaphys. Soc. Am. (governing council 1969-73), So. Soc. Philosophy and Psychology (governing council 1971-74, treas. 1974-77, pres. elect 1977, pres. 1978, Jr. award for Excellence 1962), Am. Philos. Assn., Am. Soc. Aesthetics, AAUP (pres. Vanderbilt chpt. 1966-67), Phi Beta Kappa (chpt. pres. 1975-77). Author: A Whiteheadian Aesthetic, 1961; A Key to Whitehead's Process and Reality, 1966; co-editor: Corrected Edition of Whitehead's Process and Reality, 1978. Home: 227 Leonard Ave Nashville TN 37205

SHERBURNE, JAMES WILSON, educator; b. Toledo, Apr. 8, 1905; s. John C. and Martha (Headley) S.; A.B., Greenville Coll., 1927; M.A., U. Mich., 1928; Ph.D., Ohio State U., 1938; m. Mildred Lasswell, Dec. 29, 1928; children—Harry R., James W. Prof. ednl. psychology Wessington Springs Coll., 1928-29; supt. schs., Lane, S.D., 1929-34; instr. psychology Ohio State U., 1934-38; asst. prof. psychology Oreg. State Coll., 1938-40, asso. prof., 1940-42, prof., 1942-56, head dept. psychology, 1951-56; vis. prof. Syracuse U., summer 1937, U. Idaho, summers 1940-41, U. Alta., summer 1953; dean gen. extension div. Oreg. System Higher Edn., 1956-62, vice chancellor of state system, 1962—. Served as maj. AUS, 1942-46. Mem. Portland C. of C., Phi Delta Kappa, Kappa Delta Pi. Clubs: University, City (Portland); Rotary. Author: Industrial Psychology, 1948; Scientific Study of Mental Activities of Normal Individuals, 1948. Home: 1030 Cleveland St Corvallis OR 97330 Office: Agr Hall U Campus Corvallis OR 97331

SHERE, DENNIS, editor; b. Cleve., Nov. 29, 1940; s. William and Susan (Luskay) S.; B.S. in Journalism, Ohio U., 1963, M.S. in Journalism 1964; m. Maureen Jones, Sept. 4, 1965; children—Rebecca Lynn, David Matthew, Stephen Andrew. Staff writer Dayton (Ohio) Daily News, 1966-69; asst. prof. Sch. Journalism Bowling Green (Ohio) State U., 1969-70; fin. editor Detroit News, 1970-72, city editor, 1973-75; editor Dayton Jour. Herald, 1975—. Served with AUS, 1964-66. Mem. Sigma Alpha Epsilon, Omicron Delta Kappa. Home: 66 E Dixon Ave Dayton OH 45419 Office: 4th and Ludlow Sts Dayton OH 45401

SHERE, LOUIS, economist; b. Oxbow, Sask., Can., Apr. 8, 1900; s. Elkon and Hattie (Gotleib) S.; B.A., U. Man., Winnipeg, Can., 1921, M.A., 1922; Ph.D., Columbia U., 1932; m. Della Michael Ebert, June 7, 1940; 1 dau., Anne Elizabeth. Lectr. econs. U. Toronto, 1928-29; economist Wall St. banking, investment trust and brokerage firms, N.Y.C., 1929-31; research staff N.Y. State Commn. for revision N.Y. tax laws, 1931-32; research staff Columbia, 1932-33; economist U.S. Treasury Dept., 1934-48, asso. dir. tax research, June 1946, acting dir., Oct. 1946, dir., Jan.-Sept. 1948; prof. econs. and dir. tax research, Ind. U., 1948-70, emeritus prof. econs., 1970—; cons. on govt. finances; staff Council Econ. Advisers, 1953-54, 1955-56; UN cons. Pakistan Tax Commn., 1958; Pan Am., Union cons. to Colombia, 1960, El Salvador, 1962. Fulbright Sr. Research scholar, U.K., 1960-61; cons. AID, 1962. Mem. Am. Econ. Assn. Author books relating to field, latest: Report of the Haitian Fiscal System, 1944; A Tax Program for the Philippines, 1950; Taxation of International Airlines, 1950; A Tax Program for Puerto Rico, 1951; Sugar Taxation in the Caribbean and Central American Countries, PAU and UN, 1952; A Tax Program for Columbia, 1960; A Tax Program for El Salvador, 1962; contbr. to econ. publs. Home: 800 S Rose Ave Bloomington IN 47401. *To be constructive we must find the way to happiness in daily life as we work and play and we must find the way to make all our associates more hopeful, enthusiastic and optimistic. Pessimism is the great personal and social evil to be avoided as the greatest sin. There are a multitude of ways, to build perspective and a cheerful approach. History and poetry helped me as did the beauty I found in the various arts. The aimless in life are the unhappy ones. It is best to be flexible and follow circumstances from goal to goal as changing opportunities unfold.... The doors to happiness are open to all who will cultivate a constructive attitude and look for ways to serve others as well as self.*

SHERER, LEWIS MICHAEL, JR., hotel exec.; b. Dayton, Ohio, Apr. 11, 1929; s. Lewis Michael and Gertrude Beatrice (Uhl) S.; B.A. in Econs., Cath. U., 1951; m. Stella Marie Davis, Sept. 5, 1953; children—William M., Robert L., Karen L., Lauranne E. With Sheraton-Park Hotel, Washington, 1954-61; Washington hotel rep. for group/sales William P. Wolfe, Inc., 1961-63; with Mariott Hotels, 1963—, gen. mgr. Marriott Hotel, Saddle Brook, N.J., 1969-71, Marriott Hotel, Newton, Mass., 1971-74, Marriott Hotel, New Orleans, 1974—; v.p. Greater New Orleans Tourist and Conv. Commn., New Orleans Exhibit Hall Authority, 1978—. Served with U.S. Army, 1952-54. Mem. La. Hotel-Motel Assn. (pres. 1979-80), Hotel-Motel Assn. Greater New Orleans (v.p.). Office: Marriott Hotel Canal and Chartres St New Orleans LA 70140

SHERER, THOMAS E., bearing co. exec.; b. Indpls., May 24, 1928; s. Carl J. and Frances M. (Byrne) S.; B.S. in Acctg., U. Notre Dame, 1950; grad. Advanced Mgmt. Program, Harvard U., 1975; m. Marcia J. Porter, Sept. 8, 1956; children—Thomas E., Marcia J., Marc P., Sara E. With new departure div. Gen. Motors Corp., Bristol, Conn., 1952-56; with Fafnir Bearing Co. (became div. Textron Corp. 1968), 1956—, v.p. ops., New Britain, Conn., 1972-74, exec. v.p., 1974-75, pres. Fafnir Bearing div., 1975—; dir. First Conn. Bancorp. Bd. dirs. New Britain Gen. Hosp.; trustee Conn. Public Expenditure Council. Served with U.S. Army, 1950-52. Mem. Anti Friction Bearing Mfrs. Assn. (chmn.), Mfrs. Assn. Hartford County (Conn.) (chmn.). Roman Catholic. Clubs: Shuttle Meadow Country; Rotary (New Britain). Office: 37 Booth St New Britain CT 06050

SHERF, ARDEN FREDERICK, educator; b. Brooklyn Center, Minn., Aug. 7, 1916; s. Fred Elmer and Alice (Stubbs) S.; B.S., U. Minn., 1939; Ph.D., U. Nebr., 1948; m. Jean Marian Voigt, Jan. 25, 1942; children—Carol (Mrs. Herbert Flower, Jr.), David, Stephen, Andrea (Mrs. Dale Smith). Research asst. plant pathologist U. Minn., 1937-39; research asst. plant pathologist, then asst. plant pathologist U. Nebr., 1939-49; asso. prof. Iowa State U., 1949-54; mem. faculty Cornell U., 1954—, asso. prof. plant pathology, 1954-59, prof., 1959—, dept. extension leader, 1965—; lectr. U. Calif. at Davis, 1961; cons. to Brit. minister agr., 1968, New South Wales Dept. Agr., Australia, 1975. Served with USNR, 1942-46. Fellow AAAS; mem. Am. Phytopath. Soc., Res. Officers Assn. (pres. Ithaca-Cornell U. chpt. 1962-63, 68-70, 76-77), Sigma Xi, Gamma Sigma Delta. Methodist. Co-author: Vegetable Diseases and Their Control, 1960. Contbr. articles to profl. jours. Home: 10 Bean Hill Ln Ithaca NY 14850

SHERIDAN, EDWARD PHILIP, educator; b. Merced, Calif., July 9, 1916; s. Edward Philip and Ruth (Knox) S.; A.B., Stanford, 1939, M.A., 1941; Ph.D., Yale, 1949; m. Harriet Susan Waltzer, June 30, 1950; children—Alison Ellen Cowdery, Ruth Emily Knox. Instr., Calif. Inst. Tech., 1945-46, Yale, 1948-52; mem. faculty Carleton Coll., 1952—, prof. English, 1966—, chmn. dept., 1967-70. Pres., Midwest Athletic Conf., 1974-75. Served with AUS, 1942-45. Mem. Modern Lang. Assn., Milton Soc., Caribbean Conservation Corp. Episcopalian. Home: 501 E 2d St Northfield MN 55057

SHERIDAN, HARRIET WALTZER, educator; b. N.Y.C., July 21, 1925; d. Ben and Mildred (Wolff) Waltzer; A.B. (Helen Gray Cone fellow 1945-46), Hunter Coll., 1944; M.A. (Trustee fellow 1944-45, Marjorie Hope Nicholson fellow 1945-46), Smith Coll., 1945; Ph.D. (Univ. fellow 1946-47), Yale, 1950; m. E.P.Sheridan June 30, 1950; children—Alison, Ruth. Instr. English, Hunter Coll., 1947-49; asst. to asso. prof. English and edn. Carleton Coll., Northfield, Minn., 1953-67, prof., 1967—, Andrew W. Mellon prof. humanities, 1974—, dean, 1976—, acting pres., Jan.-Aug., 1977, chmn. faculty, 1971-73, chmn. English dept., 1973-75; dir. Northwest Bancorp. Field reader curriculum improvement program U.S. Office Edn., 1963—; tchr. NDEA Inst. in English, summer 1965, dir., summer 1966; coordinator McKnight Edn. Found. English awards; mem. Gov. Minn. adv. council Minn. Right to Read Program; Sloan Commn. on Higher Edn. and Govt.; mem. fellowships adv. council Danforth Found., 1974—; mem. nat. bd. consultants Nat. Endowment for Humanities; mem. bd. Minn. Humanities Commn., 1977—, mem. exec. com., 1978—; mem. corp. bd. Bishop Whipple Schs., 1977—; trustee Breck Sch., 1977—. Louis W. and Maud Hill Family Found. Research grantee, 1962—. Mem. Nat. (Minn. chmn. achievement awards program 1962-65), Minn. (mem. liaison com. to Minn. Bd. Edn. 1969-72, chmn. editorial bd. 1973-75) councils tchrs. English, Internat. Reading Assn., AAUP, AAUW, Modern Lang. Assn., Orton Soc.; Assn. Minn. Dept. English Chairmen (chmn. 1973-77); Assn. Depts. English (exec. com., chmn. com. on pub. literacy), Phi Beta Kappa (pres. Carleton chpt. 1968-69). Author: Structure and Style: An Analytical Approach to Prose Writing, 1966. Editor: Minn. English Jour. Home: 501 E 2d St Northfield MN 55057

SHERIDAN, JAMES, corp. exec.; b. Jersey City, June 21, 1919; s. James and Raphaela (Capicciotti) S.; student N.Y. U., 1945-47; m. Jean M. Rice, Jan. 10, 1943 (dec. Aug. 1977); children—Keith A., Brian D., Margaret C.; m. 2d, Sharon H. Green, Dec. 16, 1977. Salesman Monroe Calculating Machine Co. Inc. (merged with Litton Industries 1958), Orange, N.J., 1947-53, pres., 1970-74; sr. v.p., group exec. Bus. Machines & Retail Systems Group, Litton Industries, Orange, 1974; pres., chief exec. officer Victor Comptometer Corp. (merged into Walter Kidde & Co., Inc. 1977), Chgo., 1974-77, pres., chief exec. officer Victor United, Inc. subs. Walter Kidde & Co., Inc., Chgo., 1977—. Served with USN, 1942-45. Mem. Am. Mgmt. Assn. Clubs: Executives, Economic (Chgo.); Sunset Ridge Country. Home: 1555 N Astor St Chicago IL 60610 Office: 3900 N Rockwell St Chicago IL 60618

SHERIDAN, JAMES EDWARD, educator; b. Wilmington, Del., July 15, 1922; s. Phillip Lambert and Ida Alverna (Green) S.; B.S., U. Ill., 1949, M.A., 1950; Ph.D., U. Calif. at Berkeley, 1961; m. Sonia Landy, Sept. 27, 1947; 1 son, Jamy. Lectr. Chinese history Stanford, 1960; mem. faculty Northwestern U., 1961—, prof. history, 1968—, chmn. dept., 1969-74. Served to ensign USN, 1941-46. Fulbright fellow, France, 1950-51; Ford Found. fellow, 1958-60; grantee Am. Council Learned Socs.-Social Sci. Research Council, 1966-67, 71-72. Mem. Am. Hist. Assn., Assn. Asian Studies (China council 1970-71). Author: Chinese Warlord: The Career of Feng Yu-hsiang, 1966; China: A Culture Area in Perspective, 1970; China in Disintegration: The Republican Era in Chinese History, 1912-1949, 1975. Home: 718 Noyes St Evanston IL 60201 Office: Dept History Northwestern Univ Evanston IL 60201

SHERIDAN, JAMES MICHAEL, automotive parts co. exec.; b. Muskegon, Mich., Oct. 9, 1940; s. Edward James and Nell (Fairchild) S.; student Lawrence U., 1958-60; B.B.A., U. Mich., 1962, J.D., 1965; m. Nancy Ann Nolen, Aug. 1, 1964; children—Christine, Charles, William. Admitted to Ill. bar, 1965, Mich. bar, 1972; asso. firm Price, Cushman, Keck & Mahn, Chgo., 1965-71; mem. firm Landman, Hathaway Latimer Clink and Robb, Muskegon, 1971-76; sec., gen. counsel Sealed Power Corp., Muskegon, 1976—; dir. Mich. Spring Co., Sandmold Systems, Inc. Mem. Am. Bar Assn., Mich. State Bar Assn., Muskegon County Bar Assn., Muskegon Area C. of C. (dir., mem. exec. com.), Order of Coif. Republican. Home: 335 Mid Oak Dr North Muskegon MI 49445 Office: 100 Terrace Plaza Muskegon MI 49443

SHERIDAN, JOHN EDWARD, mfg. co. exec.; b. Pitts., Feb. 21, 1935; s. John Raymond and Violet Mildred (Steinberger) S.; B.A., Dartmouth, 1956; M.B.A., Harvard, 1962; m. Mary Ann Hemry, Dec. 27, 1971; 1 dau., Mary Katharine. Fin. analyst W. R. Grace Co., N.Y.C., 1962-64; treas. Corporate Equities, N.Y.C., 1964-67; dir. acquisition and venture investments Westinghouse Electric Co., Pitts., 1967-71; v.p. corporate finance F. S. Smithers Co., investment bankers, N.Y.C., 1971-73; v.p. fin., treas., chief fin. officer Fairchild Industries, Germantown, Md., 1973-75; v.p. fin., chief fin. officer AMF Inc., 1975—, also chmn. pension com.; chmn. AMF Ins. Ltd.; vis. lectr. bus. schs. Founder, v.p. coordinating council Allegheny Conf., profl. assistance to minority businessmen, Pitts., 1969-71. Trustee Fairchild Industries Found., 1973-75. Served to lt. comdr. (naval aviator) AC, USNR, 1956-60. Mem. U.S. Naval Inst., Am. Mgmt. Assn. (com. on govt. liaison), Fin. Execs. Inst., Smithsonian Assos., Republican. Episcopalian. Clubs: Harvard, India House, Wings (N.Y.C.); Pequot Yacht (Southport, Conn.); Fairfield Hunt; Harvard-Yale-Princeton (Pitts.). Home: 421 Sasco Hill Rd Fairfield CT 06430 Office: AMF Inc 777 Westchester Ave White Plains NY 10604

SHERIDAN, MARTIN, editor, publisher; b. Providence, Aug. 1, 1914; s. S.H. and Edna (Sherman) S.; student Coll. William and Mary, 1932-33, R.I. State Coll., 1933-34; m. Margaret A. Cooke, June 10, 1944; children—Margaret Ann, Jean Randall. Free-lance writer, photographer, 1936-39; staff Boston Am., Providence News, Financial Observer, N.Y.C., 1939-42; war corr. Boston Globe, 1943-46; account exec. Carl Byoir & Assos., 1948-51; dir. pub. relations Admiral Corp., 1951-57, v.p., 1961-71; dir. communications NARDA, Chgo., 1971-77; editor, pub. NEDA Jour., 1977—; dir. information and publs. New Eng. Council Econ. Devel., 1957-59. Mem. Am. Polar Soc., Soc. Midland Authors, Sigma Delta Chi. Clubs: Adventurers (Chgo.); Overseas Press (N.Y.C.). Author: Comics and Their Creators, 1942, 71, 77; Overdue and Presumed Lost, 1947. Contbr. articles to mags. Home: 2545 Greeley Ave Evanston IL 60201 Office: Suite 214 1480 Renaissance Dr Park Ridge IL 60068

SHERIDAN, PATRICK MICHAEL, ins. co. exec.; b. Grosse Pointe, Mich., Apr. 13, 1940; s. Paul Phillip and Frances Mary (Rohan) S.; B.B.A., U. Notre Dame, 1962; M.B.A., U. Detroit, 1975; m. Jane Louise Hansinger, May 30, 1962; children—Mary, Patrick, Kelly, Kevin, James. Acct., Peat, Marwick, Mitchell & Co., Detroit, 1962-72, audit mgr., 1969-72; exec. v.p. fin. Alexander Hamilton Life Ins. Co., Farmington, Mich., 1973-76; sr. v.p. ops. Sun Life Ins. Co. Am., Balt., 1976-78, exec. v.p., 1978-79; pres. Sun Ins. Services, Inc., 1979—. Republican candidate for U.S. Congress, 1972. Served to capt. AUS, 1963-65. Recipient various Jaycee awards. Mem. Am. Inst. C.P.A.'s, Mich. Assn. C.P.A.'s, Ga. Assn. C.P.A.'s, U.S. (treas. 1973-74), Mich. (pres. 1971-72), Detroit (pres. 1968-69) jaycees, Mensa. Club: Notre Dame (Atlanta). Home: 175 Spalding Mill Dr Atlanta GA 30338 Office: 260 Peachtree St NW Atlanta GA 30303. *Most of my life I set goals, achieved them, and immediately felt the compulsion to set more goals.*

SHERIDAN, STAN ROGER, army officer; b. Hollywood, Calif., Mar. 27, 1928; s. Stanley Jerome and Peggy (Lenz) S.; B.S., U.S. Mil. Acad., 1951; M.S. in Mech. Engring., U. So. Calif., 1958; attended Armor Officer Base Course, Ft. Knox, Armo Officer Career Course, Ft. Knox, Army Command and Gen. Staff Coll., Indsl. Coll. Armed Forces; m. Ruth Ann Perrill, Feb. 18, 1954; children—Stan Roger, Jeffrey David. Commd. 2d lt. U.S. Army, 1951, advanced through grades to maj. gen., 1979; analyst Strategic Studies, Joint Chiefs of Staff, 1970-71; project mgr. M60 Series Tank family, Warren, Mich., 1971-74; comdr. Support Command, 2d Armored Div., Ft. Hood, Tex., 1975; program mgr. for fighting vehicle systems, Warren, Mich., 1975-78; dir. battlefield systems integration Materiel Devel. and Readiness Command, 1978-79, dir. devel. and engring., Alexandria, Va., 1979—. Decorated Silver Star, Legion of Merit with 2 oak leaf clusters, D.F.C., Bronze Star with V, Air medal with 11 oak leaf clusters, Army Commendation medal with oak leaf cluster, Purple Heart (U.S.); Service medal, Commendation medal, Cross of Gallantry with palm, gold and silver stars (Vietnam); recipient Frank Pace award Sec. Army, 1968. Mem. Assn. U.S. Army, U.S. Army Armor Assn., Am. Def. Preparedness Assn. Episcopalian. Contbr. numerous articles to profl. jours. Office: HQ US Army DARCOM Attention: DRCDE 5001 Eisenhower Ave Alexandria VA 22333

SHERIDAN, WILLIAM COCKBURN RUSSELL, bishop; b. N.Y.C., Mar. 25, 1917; s. John Russell Fortescue and Gertrude Magdalene (Hurley) S.; student U. Va.; B.A., Carroll Coll., 1939; S.T.M., Nashotah House Sem., 1968, D.D., 1966; m. Rudith Treder, Nov. 13, 1943; children—Elizabeth Sheridan Beeler, Margaret Sheridan Wilson, Mary Sheridan Janda, Peter, Stephen. Ordained priest Episcopal Ch., 1943, bishop, 1972; asst. priest St. Pauls Ch., Chgo., 1943-44; rector Gethsemane Ch., Marion, Ind., 1944-47, St. Thomas Ch., 1947-72; Episc. chaplain Culver (Ind.) Mil. Acad., 1953-58, 70-72; bishop Diocese of No. Ind., South Bend, 1972—. Clerical dep. to Gen. Conv., Nat. Synod, 1952-70. Pres. bd. trustees Howe (Ind.) Mil. Sch.; v.p. bd. trustees Nashotah House Sem. Mem. Alumni Assn. Nashotah House Sem. (pres. 1953-55). Author: Journey to Priesthood, 1950; For High School Boys Only, 1955; Between

Catholics, 1968. Home: 2502 S Twyckenham Dr South Bend IN 46614 Office: 117 N Lafayette Blvd South Bend IN 46601

SHERIF, CAROLYN WOOD, psychologist; b. Loogootee, Ind., June 26, 1922; d. Lawrence Anselm and Bonny (Williams) Wood; B.S., Purdue U., 1943; M.A., State U. Iowa, 1944; Ph.D. in Psychology, U. Tex., 1961; m. Muzafer Sherif, Dec. 29, 1945; children—Sue, Joan, Ann. Asst. to research dir. Audience Research, Inc., Princeton, N.J., 1944-45; asst. Princeton, 1945-47; research, free-lance writer, Norman, Okla., 1949-58; research asso. Inst. Group Relations, U. Okla., Norman, 1959-65, asso. prof. sociology, 1963-65; cons. asst. prof. U. Okla. Med. Sch., 1963-65; vis. lectr. Pa. State U., 1962, asso. prof. psychology, 1965-66, asso. prof., 1966-69, prof., 1970—; vis. prof. psychology and sociology, Cornell U., 1969-70; disting. vis. prof. Smith Coll., 1979; cons. NSF. Fellow Am. Psychol. Assn. (policy and planning bd. 1979—, pres. div. 35, 1979-80); mem. Am. Sociol. Assn., AAUW, AAAS, Mortar Bd., Sigma Xi, Theta Alpha Phi, Alpha Lambda Delta, Pi Beta Phi. Author: (with M. Sherif) Groups in Harmony and Tension, 1953, An Outline of Social Psychology, 1956, Problems of Youth; Transition to Adulthood in a Changing World, 1965, Attitude, Ego-Involvement and Change, 1967, Interdisciplinary Relationships in the Social Sciences, 1969, Social Psychology, 1969; (with M. Sherif, O.J. Harvey, B.J. White, W.R. Hood) Intergroup Conflict and Cooperation, 1961; (with M. Sherif and R. Nebergall) Attitude and Attitude Change, 1965; Instructor's Manual for Social Psychology, 1969; Orientation in Social Psychology, 1976; contbr. numerous articles to profl. jours. Home: 507 Shannon Ln State College PA 16801 Office: 515 Moore St Pa State U University Park PA 16802. *Enlarging the human circle within which individuals treat one another equitably has been the goal guiding my work conduct. The woman's movement provided fresh air, preventing institutional oversight of my work and promoting my renewed endeavor in activities I love.*

SHERIFF, HILLA, physician; b. Easley, S.C., May 29, 1903; d. John Washington and Mary Lenora (Smith) Sheriff; student Coll. of Charleston (S.C.): 1920-22; M.D., Med. U. of S.C., Charleston, 1926; M.P.H., Harvard, 1937; m. George Henry Zerbst, M.D., July 10, 1940. Interne Hosp. of Woman's Med. Coll., Phila., 1926-27, Children's Hosp., Washington, 1928-29, Willard Parker Contagious Disease Hosp., N.Y.C ., 1929; practice of pediatrics, Spartanburg, S.C., 1929-33; dir. Spartanburg County Health Dept., 1933-40; med. staff Spartanburg Gen. Hosp., med. dir. Am. Women's Hosp. Units in Spartanburg and Greenville Counties, S.C., 1931-36; med. dir. research study in Spartanburg County, S.C. for Milbank Meml. Fund, N.Y.C., 1935-39; asst. dir. of div. maternal and child health in Dept. Health and Environmental Control, State of S.C., Columbia, 1940-41, dir., 1941—, chief bur. community health services, asst. state health officer, 1968-73, dep. commr. personal health services, past dir. crippled children's services; clin. prof. pediatrics Med. U. S.C., 1972—. Mem. S.C. State Youth Conservation Com., chmn. health and med. care sub com.; rep. from S.C. to White House Conf., 1940, 50, 60; mem. State Adv. Com. on Adult Edn., 1947. Mem. S.C. Council for Handicapped Children, Gov.'s Interagy. Council on Mental Retardation Planning; chmn. S.C. State Nutrition Com.; bd. dirs. Winthrop Coll. Found., Rock Hill, S.C. Recipient meritorious award S.C. Mental Health Assn., 1972, spl. pioneer award; Outstanding State Employee award S.C. State Employees Assn., 1974; award S.C. Hosp. Assn., 1975; named to Order of Palmetto, Gov. of S.C. Diplomate Am. Bd. Preventive Medicine. Fellow Am. Pub. Health Assn. (council mem. maternal and child health sect., Ross award 1969), Am. Acad. Pediatrics (chpt. pres. 1972), Assn. State Maternal and Child Health and Crippled Children's Dirs. (pres. 1960-62), Am. Assn. Pub. Health Physicians, Columbia Med. Soc. (v.p. 1962), Am. Med. Women's Assn. (2d v.p. 1946), Am. So., S.C. med. assns., S.C. Pub. Health Assn., (pres. 1947), Pan Am. Med. Women's Alliance, S.C. Obstet.. and Gynecol. Soc. (hon. mem.), S.C. Pediatric Soc. (sec.-treas. 1941-46, pres. 1972-73), S.C. Mental and Social Hygiene Soc. (pres. 1948-49), S.C. Thoracic Soc., S.C. Conf. Social Work, Delta Kappa Gamma, Alpha Epsilon Iota. Episcopalian. Clubs: S.C. Federation of Women's, Business and Professional Women's (charter mem. Spartanburg club), Survey (Columbia, S.C.); Harvard of S.C. (sec.-treas. 1977-79). Home: 807 Hampton Hill Dr Columbia SC 29209

SHERIFF, SEYMOUR, lawyer; b. Rye, N.Y., Aug. 22, 1917; s. Michael and Anna (Rosenfeld) S.; B.S.S., Coll. City N.Y., 1935; J.D., Yale, 1938; m. Selene Gloria Wolf, Oct. 15, 1950; children—Steven, Susan, Ellen, Carol. Admitted to D.C. bar, 1938, since practiced in Washington; sr. partner firm Gardner, Morrison, Sheriff & Beddow, 1958—. Served with AUS, 1942-45. Decorated Legion of Merit. Mem. Phi Beta Kappa. Home: 6910 Blaisdell Rd Bethesda MD 20034 Office: Suite 1126 Woodward Bldg Washington DC 20005

SHERK, ROBERT KENNETH, educator; b. Buffalo, Dec. 12, 1920; s. Lloyd William and Magdalena (Gurtner) S.; B.A., U. Buffalo, 1947; Ph.D., Johns Hopkins, 1950; m. Beatrice Schifano, Feb. 17, 1947; 1 son, Kenneth. Instr. U. Maine, 1950-53, asst. prof., 1953-56, asso. prof., 1956-58, prof. classics and German, 1958-62; prof. classics State U. N.Y. at Buffalo, 1962—. Served to 1st lt. USAF, 1942-45. Decorated Air Medal with oak leaf cluster. Mem. Am. Philos. Assn., Archaeol. Inst. Am. Author: Legate of Galatia, 1951; Roman Documents from Greek East, 1969; Municipal Decrees of Roman West, 1970; also articles. Home: 5165 Mapleton Rd Lockport NY 14094 Office: Dept Classics Clemens Hall State Univ NY at Buffalo Buffalo NY 14260

SHERLOCK, JOHN MICHAEL, bishop; b. Regina, Sask., Can., Jan. 20, 1926; s. Joseph and Catherine S.; student St. Augustine's Sem., Toronto, Ont., Can., 1950; student canon law Catholic U. Am., 1950-52. Ordained priest Roman Cath. Ch., 1950, bishop, 1974; asst. pastor St. Eugene's, Hamilton, Ont., 1952-59, St. Augustine's Dundas, Ont., 1959-63, Cathedral Christ the King, Hamilton, also Guelph and Maryhill, Ont., 1950-52; pastor St. Charles Ch., Hamilton, 1963-74; aux. bishop London (Ont.), 1974-78, bishop, 1979—; chaplain Univ. Newman Club, McMaster U., Hamilton, 1963-66; mem. Wentworth County Roman Cath. Separate Sch. Bd., 1964-74, chmn., 1972-73. Address: 1070 Waterloo St London ON N6A 3Y2 Canada

SHERLOCK, PAUL, physician; b. N.Y.C., Oct. 7, 1928; s. Joseph and Estelle (Salzman) S.; B.S., Queens Coll., 1950; M.D., Cornell U., 1954; m. Marcia Regina Rohr, Mar. 29, 1952; children—Diane, Susan, Nancy. Intern, Bellevue Hosp., N.Y.C., 1954-55; resident Bellevue Hosp.-Meml. Sloan-Kettering Cancer Center, 1957-60; trainee Nat. Cancer Inst., 1959-60; postdoctoral research fellow Am. Cancer Soc., 1960-62; head gastrointestinal physiology sect. Sloan Kettering Inst. for Cancer Research, N.Y.C., 1963-70, asso., 1963-78, mem., 1978—; chief gastroenterology service Meml. Sloan-Kettering Cancer Center, 1970-78, asso. chmn. dept. medicine, 1976-77, acting chmn., 1977-78, chmn., 1978—; cons. med. staff North Shore U. Hosp., 1978—; vis. physician Rockefeller U. Hosp., 1978—; practice medicine specializing in gastroenterology and internal medicine, N.Y.C., 1962—; attending physician N.Y. Hosp.; prof. medicine Cornell U. Med. Coll., N.Y.C., 1975—; med. dir. Moore McCormack Lines, Inc., N.Y.C., 1967—. Trustee Lenox Sch., N.Y.C., Alumni Assn. Queens Coll., Flushing, N.Y. Served to lt. comdr. USNR, 1955-57. Recipient Gold medal VII Internat. Congress Gastroenterology, 1968; diplomate Am. Bd. Internal Medicine. Fellow A.C.P., Am. Coll. Gastroenterology, N.Y. Acad. Gastroenterology, N.Y. Acad. Scis.; mem. Am. Soc. Internal Medicine, AMA, Am. Fedn. Clin. Research, Soc. Surg. Oncology (exec. council 1976-79), Am. Soc. Gastrointestinal Endoscopy (mem. governing bd. 1974—, pres. 1978—), Am. Soc. Clin. Oncology, Am. Gastroent. Assn. (chmn. council on cancer 1975-78), N.Y. Gastroent. Assn. (pres. 1973-74), Harvey Soc., Am. Cancer Soc., (nat. task force on colon and rectal cancer), N.Y. Cancer Soc., Nat. Found. Ileitis and Colitis, Am. Assn. Study Liver Diseases. Asso. editor Am. Jour. Digestive Diseases, 1973-77, mem. editorial bd., 1977—; editorial staff Gastroenterology, 1973-76; contbr. articles to profl. jours. Home: 345 E 68th St New York NY 10021 Office: 425 E 67th St New York NY 10021

SHERMAN, ALICE E., retail chain exec.; b. Ill., Apr. 16, 1927; d. Elmer L. and Edna B. (Mathews) S.; student Bradley U., 1944-45; B.A. in Bus. Adminstrn., Northwestern U., 1948. Mem. internal audit staff Fed. Res. Bank, Chgo., 1948-50; partner Vineyard, Sherman & Brown, acctg. firm, Winter Haven, Fla., 1950-68; v.p., treas. Scotty's, Inc., Winter Haven, 1968—. Treas. Ridge chpt. ARC. C.P.A., Ill. Mem. Am. Inst. C.P.A.'s, Fla. Soc. C.P.A.'s. Republican. Presbyterian. Club: Pilot (pres.) (Winter Haven). Office: PO Box 939 Winter Haven FL 33880

SHERMAN, BENJAMIN MAX, lawyer; b. Rolfe, Iowa, Jan. 28, 1909; s. Fred and LuVerna (Ferguson) S.; B.S., U. Ill., 1931; LL.B., U. Calif. at Berkeley, 1934; m. Helen Hood, July 2, 1940; children—Benjamin Karl, Carroll Sue, Frederick Hood, Robert David, Kathleen Louise; m. Janet Ray, 1976. Admitted to Calif. bar, 1934, N.Mex. bar, 1936; practiced in Calif. and N.Mex., 1934-36; engaged in exporting bus., 1936-39; practice in Deming, N.Mex., 1940—; mem. firm Sherman & Sherman, 1940—; city atty., Deming, 1946-47. Pres. Southwest Loan & Investment Corp.; atty., dir. and chmn. bd. Home Fed. Savs. & Loan Assn.; atty., dir. chmn. bd. Deming Nat. Bank, 1962—; sec. Columbis Telephone Co., 1963—; partner Southwest Underwriters, Ins. Agy. Mem. Interstate Streams Commn., 1969-74, N.Mex. Jud. Council, 1969-74. Sec., Mimbres Meml. Hosp., 1954-60. Served to capt. USAAF, 1942-45. Mem. N.Mex. Bar Assn. (bar commr. 1949-59, pres. 1959-60), N.Mex. Bar Found. (dir.), 6th Jud. Bar (pres. 1948—), Luna County Bar Assn. (pres. 1948-77). Club: Rotary (pres. 1963). Home: 704 S Zinc St Deming NM 88030 Office: 210 S Silver Ave Deming NM 88030

SHERMAN, CHARLES DANIEL, JR., surgeon; b. Avon Park, Fla., Oct. 5, 1920; s. Charles Daniel and Mary Alice (Oliver) S.; B.S., U. Fla., 1942; M.D., Johns Hopkins U., 1945; m. Jean Riebling, Aug. 13, 1943; children—Rachel, Charles Daniel, Edward. Intern, Duke U. Hosp., Durham, N.C., 1945-46; resident U. Rochester Med. Center, 1948-52, instr., 1952-56, asst. prof., 1956-64, clin. asso. prof. surgery, 1964-70, clin. prof., 1970—; fellow Meml. Center for Cancer, 1951; practice medicine specializing in cancer surgery, Rochester, 1953—; mem. staff Strong Meml., Highland Hosps. Vice-pres. Redd Labs., Clearwater, Fla., 1961-70; advisor N.Y. State Bur. Cancer Control, 1964—; sec.-treas. Monroe County Health Council, 1967—; mem. Monroe County Bd. Health, 1966—; advisor to WHO, 1971; mem. advisory com. Nat. Cancer Insts.; dir. Internat. Union Against Cancer Project to Survey Cancer Edn. in Latin Am., 1976, Asia, 1977. Served to lt. USMC, 1946-48. Fulbright fellow, Mendoza, Argentina, 1963; diplomate Am. Bd. Surgery. Mem. AMA, Am. Radium Soc., Soc. Head and Neck Surgeons, A.C.S., Royal Soc. Medicine, Am. Assn. Cancer Edn. (pres. 1975-76), Am. Fedn. Clin. Oncologic Socs. (bd. govs. 1974—), N.Y. Acad. Sci., N.Y. State Cancer Programs Assn. (pres. 1970-71), Monroe County Med. Soc. (pres. 1965), Monroe County Cancer and Leukemia Assn. (pres. 1962-66), U.S. Squash Rackets Assn. (dir. 1963-65), James Ewing Soc., Phi Beta Kappa, Alpha Phi Omega. Author: Clinical Concepts in Cancer Management, 1976; co-author: Clinical Oncology, 1974; editor: (with others) Programmed Instruction in Medical Education; Newsletter in Cancer, 1968—; chmn. editorial bd. Clinical Oncology (monograph), Internat. Union against Cancer, 1978; contbr. articles to profl. jours. Home: 127 Southern Parkway Rochester NY 14618

SHERMAN, CHARLES EDWIN, broadcast exec.; b. Phila., Mar. 20, 1934; s. Abe and Rae (Ginsberg) S.; B.S., Temple U., Phila., 1960, M.A., 1962; Ph.D., Wayne State U., Detroit, 1967; m. Elaine Landsburg, Sept. 11, 1960; children—Jean, Eric, David. Announcer, program producer Radio Sta. WHAT, Phila., 1957-62; mem. prodn. staff WFIL-TV, Phila., 1961; grad. asst. Temple U., 1960-62; TV producer-dir., prodn. supr. Wayne State U., 1962-64, instr. dept. speech, 1964-66, asst. to dir. div. mass communication, 1966-67; asst. prof. dept. speech U. Wis., 1967-70, asso. chmn., asso. prof. dept. communication arts, 1970-73, acting chmn., asso. prof., 1974, prof., asso. chmn. dept. communication arts, 1974-75; cons. Forward Communications, Inc., Wausaw, Wis., 1974—; prof., chmn. dept. telecommunications Ind. U., Bloomington, 1975—; pres., gen. mgr. WTRF-TV/FM, Wheeling, W.Va., 1979—; chmn. Task Force on Citizens Rights and Access, Wis. Commn. on Cable TV, 1973. Served with U.S. Army, 1955-57. Recipient Communications award Temple U., 1960, Sigma Delta Chi award Temple U., 1960, Distinguished Service award in broadcasting Wayne State U., 1966. Mem. Speech Communication Assn., Broadcast Edn. Assn. (chmn. Internat. Seminar 1974, chmn. Internat. Interest Group 1974), Nat. Assn. Ednl. Broadcasters, Alpha Epsilon Rho, Sigma Delta Chi. Democrat. Jewish. Contbr. articles on broadcasting to profl. jours. Home: 1307 Valley Forge Rd Bloomington IN 47401 Office: Radio-TV Center Room 101 Ind U Bloomington IN 47401

SHERMAN, EDWARD DAVID, physician; b. Sydney, N.S., Can., Mar. 15, 1908; s. Frederick and Sara (Epstein) S.; M.D., C.M., McGill U., 1932; m. 1938; 1 son, Neil; m. 2d, Anne Helen Doner, Feb. 22, 1955. Intern Womans Gen. Hosp., Montreal, 1931-33; resident Mt. Sinai Hosp., N.Y.C., 1933-35; practice internal medicine, Sydney, N.S., 1935-46, N.Y.C. 1947- 55, Montreal, 1956—; became asso. physician-in-chief Maimonides Hosp. and Home for Aged, Montreal, 1956, now hon. attending staff; dir. research Rehab. Inst. Montreal, 1962—; became asso. physician med. staff, also geriatric clinic Jewish Gen. Hosp. Montreal, 1956, now hon. attending staff; med. dir. Sheltered Workshop of Jewish Vocational Service, Montreal, 1959—, v.p. Inst. Gerontology, U. Montreal, 1962-65, lectr. geriatrics Sch. Rehab., 1958—, mem. med. research com. and superior studies Faculty Medicine, 1973—. Cons., sr. citizens' program Quebec div. Canadian Red Cross Soc. Exec. com. Canadian Conf. on Aging, 1963-66; Canadian rep. White House Conf. on Aging, Washington, 1971. Bd. dirs. med. com. Herzl Dispensary, 1958—, Baron de Hirsch Inst., 1958-65. Served with Royal Canadian Army Med. Corps, 1943-44. Recipient Malford W. Thewlis award Am. Geriatrics Soc., 1965, Rabbi Harry J. Stern award Temple Emanu-El, Canadian Silver Jubilee medal, 1977. Fellow Royal Coll. Physicians Can., A.C.P., Internat. Coll. Angiology, Am. Geriatrics Soc. (dir. 1961-71, past pres., past chmn. bd.), Royal Soc. Medicine, Am. Coll. Preventive Medicine, Royal Soc. Arts; mem. Que. Med. Assn. (chmn com. aging 1963-77, dir.), Canadian Assn. Phys. Medicine and Rehab., Internat. Soc. Internal Medicine, Internat. Assn. Gerontology (council 1963-66, mem. history com. 1975), Gerontol. Soc., N.Y. Acad. Scis., Canadian Med. Assn. (chmn. com. on aging 1963-67, mem. gen. council), Am. Psychosomatic Soc., Canadian Geriatric Research Soc. (med. adv. bd.), Canadian Assn. Gerontology, St. James Lit. Soc., St. John Ambulance Assn. (hon. life), Sigma Xi, Pi Lambda Phi. Jewish. Mason. Contbr. articles in field. Abstract editor N.S. Med. Bull., 1942-46. Address: 4330 Hampton Ave Montreal PQ H4A 2L2 Canada

SHERMAN, FRANK H., corp. exec.; b. Bellevue, Pa., 1916; ed. Queen's U., 1939. Pres., chief exec. officer Dominion Foundries and Steel, Ltd.; dir. Arnaud Ry. Co., Bank of N.S., Canron Ltd., Crown Life Ins. Co., Dominion Foundries and Steel Ltd., Great Lakes Waterways Devel. Assn., Knoll Lake Minerals Ltd., Nat. Steel Car Corp. Ltd., Wabush Lake Ry. Co. Ltd., Can. Devel. Corp., Canadian Pacific Ltd. Bd. govs. Art Gallery Hamilton, McMaster U., Hamilton Philharmonic Orch. Mem. Canadian Mfrs. Assn. (mem. nat. exec. council), Am. Iron and Steel Inst. (dir.). Clubs: Jockey of Can.; Ontario Jockey (trustee). Home: 9 Turner Ave Hamilton ON L8P 3K4 Canada Office: 1330 Burlington St E Hamilton ON Canada

SHERMAN, FREDERICK GEORGE, educator; b. McGregor, Mich., Apr. 16, 1915; s. William James and Mary Helen (McCullough) S.; B.S., U. Tulsa, 1938; Ph.D., Northwestern U., 1942; m. Barbara Corrine Tenney, Aug. 7, 1942; children—Susan, Martha, Sarah. Univ. fellow Sch. Medicine, Washington U., St. Louis, 1946; from instr. to prof. biology Brown U., 1946-60; prof. zoology Syracuse U., 1960—, chmn. dept., 1960-68; with Brookhaven Nat. Lab., Upton, N.Y., 1955-56; mem. sci. adv. council Masonic Med. Research Lab., Utica, N.Y., 1970-78. Served to capt. USAAF, 1942-46. Fellow Picker Found., 1951-52; spl. research fellow USPHS, 1967-68. Fellow A.A.A.S.; mem. Am. Physiol. Soc., Soc. Gen. Physiologists (sec. 1957-59, councilor 1963- 65), Soc. Study Growth and Devel., Am. Chem. Soc., Gerontol. Soc., Phi Beta Kappa, Sigma Xi. Home: 106 DeWitt Rd Syracuse NY 13214

SHERMAN, JEROME KALMAN, anatomist, cryobiologist; b. Bklyn., Aug. 14, 1925; s. Murray and Beatrice (Freilich) S.; A.B., Brown U., 1947; M.S., Western Res. U., 1949; Ph.D., State U. Iowa, 1954; m. Hildegard Schroeder, Dec. 26, 1952; children—Karen Sherman Vesole, Marc, Keith. Research asso. U. Iowa, 1952-54, Am. Found. Biol. Research, Madison, Wis., 1954-58; mem. faculty U. Ark. for Med. Scis. Med. Coll., Little Rock, 1958—, prof. anatomy, 1967—; spl. prof. chair of cryobiology Chung Hsin U., Taiwan, 1973-74; cons. human male fertility, human semen cryobanking. Active local Boy Scouts Am., also Explorer Scouts; bd. dirs. Temple B'nai Israel, Little Rock; mem. adv. bd. Day Care Center, Little Rock. Served with USN, 1943-46. Recipient Lederle Med. Faculty award, 1961-64; Fulbright sr. research award, Germany, 1965-66; Taiwan Nat. Sci. Council grantee, 1973-74. Club: Lions. Author articles in field. Home: 3012 N Grant St Little Rock AR 72207 Office: U Ark for Med Scis Dept Anatomy 4301 W Markham St Little Rock AR 72205. *The key to a happy and productive life, one which mutually benefits all, is—consideration. Whatever one's profession or station in life living with consideration of others, in the long run will result in a legacy to mankind which exceeds professional accomplishment.*

SHERMAN, JOHN CLINTON, educator; b. Toronto, Ont., Can., May 3, 1916; s. Harold C. and Grace (Ubbes) S.; B.A., U. Mich., 1937; M.A., Clark U., 1942; Ph.D., U. Wash., 1947; m. Helen Jean Loyd, Mar. 15, 1941; children—Constance Jean (Mrs. Roger Newell), John Harold (dec.), Mary Helen (Mrs. Stephen Wood), Barbara Lillian. Mem faculty U. Wash., Seattle, 1942—, prof. geography, 1963—, chmn. dept., 1963-73. Mem. sub-com. on geography adv. to U.S. Geol. Survey space programs for earth observation Nat. Acad. Sci.-NRC, 1965—; mem. Wash. State Bd. on Geog. Names. Mem. Assn. Am. Geographers, Assn. Pacific Coast Geographers, Internat. Cartographic Assn. (mem. U.S. com.). Research and publs. on maps for the blind, maps and graphics for partially seeing children. Author: Atlas of a Single ERTS Image, 1975. Adv. co-editor Oxford Regional Economics Atlas of U.S. and Can., 1967, visual and tactile map of met. Washington, tactile atlas of The Mall, Washington. Home: 7424 55th Ave NE Seattle WA 98115

SHERMAN, JOHN FOORD, assn. ofcl.; b. Oneonta, N.Y., Sept. 4, 1919; s. Henry C. and Ruth (Foord) S.; B.S., Albany Coll. Pharmacy of Union U., 1949, D.Sc., 1970; Ph.D., Yale U., 1953; m. Betsy Deane Murray, Feb. 8, 1944; children—Betsy Deane, Mary Ann. With NIH, 1953-74, asso. dir. extramural programs Nat. Inst. Neurol. Diseases and Blindness, 1961-62, asso. dir. extramural programs Nat. Inst. Arthritis and Metabolic Disease, 1962-63, asso. dir. for extramural programs Office Dir., NIH, 1964-68, dep. dir. NIH, 1968-74; v.p. Assn. Am. Med. Colls., Washington, 1974—; asst. surgeon gen. USPHS, 1964-68; spl. research chemotherapy and neuropharmacology; mem. Nat. Multiple Sclerosis Med. Adv. Bd.; mem. panel on data and studies NRC, 1976—. Served with U.S. Army, 1941-46. Decorated Bronze Star; recipient Meritorious Service award USPHS, 1965, Distinguished Service award HEW, 1971, Sec.'s Spl. Citation award, 1973, award Nat. Civil Service League, 1973; Distinguished Alumnus award Union U.-Pharmacy Coll. Council, 1974. Mem. AAAS, Nat. Soc. for Med. Research (v.p.), Inst. Medicine, Nat. Acad. Scis., Sigma Xi. Congregationalist. Club: Cosmos. Office: AAMC One Dupont Circle NW Suite 200 Washington DC 20036

SHERMAN, JONATHAN GOODHUE, clergyman; b. St. Louis, June 13, 1907; s. Stephen Fish and Marion Louise (Goodhue) S., Jr.; student Kent Sch., Conn., 1921-25; A.B., Yale U., 1929; S.T.B., Gen. Theol. Sem. 1936, S.T.D., 1949, D.C.L., Nashotah House Sem., 1971; m. Frances Le Baron Casady, Jan. 1, 1938; children—Thomas Oakley, Sallie Goodhue, Marilyn Nancy, Jonathan Goodhue. Fellow and tutor Gen. Theol. Sem., 1933-35; ordained priest Episcopal Ch., 1934; priest in charge St. Thomas's Ch., Farmingdale, N.Y., 1935-38; rector St. Thomas Ch., Bellerose, N.Y., 1939-49; suffragan bishop, L.I., 1949—, bishop, 1966-77; instr. Holy Scripture, George Mercer Jr. Meml. Sch. Theology, 1956—; Protestant chaplain Creedmoor State Hosp., 1940-49; sec. Trustees of Estate Belonging to Diocese of L.I., 1945-48; mem. nat. council Episcopal Service for Youth, 1945-56, pres., 1952-56; pres. Ch. Mission of Help of Diocese of L.I., 1944-51; pres. Episc. Ch. Bldg. Fund, 1955—; chmn. Joint Comm. Ch. Architecture and Allied Arts, 1956-65; mem. Standing Liturgical Commn., 1965-71; pres. 2d Province, 1970-73; mem. Dept. Christian Edn., 1937-44, dir., 1956-60; visitor Poor Clares of Reparation, 1966; mem. Anglican-Orthodox Consultation, 1968-77; vice chmn. Ho. of Bishops, 1974-76; dean Diocesan Leaders' Conf., 1938, 45, 46; chmn. Commn. on Relations with Eastern Chs., 1972-77. Mem. exec. council C.W. Post Coll., 1964-70. Trustee Ho. of Redeemer, 1949—, Gen. Theol. Sem., 1961-76, Walter H.D. Killough Estate, 1966—. Mem. Anglican Soc. (pres. 1953-62), Nat. Assn. Episcopal Schs. (gov.), Phi Beta Kappa. Clubs: Union League (N.Y.C.); Kiwanis; University of L.I. Author: The Christian Faith, 1935; The Spirit of Knowledge, 1961; Editor: Tidings, 1943-45. Home and Office: 36 Cathedral Ave Garden City NY 11530

SHERMAN, LAWRENCE M., lawyer, retail stores exec.; b. N.Y.C., May 23, 1940; s. Philip and Goldie (Brown) S.; B.A., N.Y. U., 1962, LL.B., 1965; m. Barbara Zuckerman, June 10, 1962; children—Roger, Jacqueline. Admitted to N.Y. bar, 1965, Calif. bar, 1977; asso. firm Proskauer Rose Goetz & Mendelsohn, N.Y.C., 1965-71, Nickerson Kramer Lowenstein Nessen Kamin & Soll, N.Y.C., 1971-74, Fried

Frank Harris Shriver & Jacobson, N.Y.C., 1974-76; exec. v.p. legal and adminstrn. Fed-Mart Corp., San Diego, 1976—. Office: Fed-Mart Corp 3851 Rosecrans St San Diego CA 92110

SHERMAN, MALCOLM LEE, retail co. exec.; b. Boston, Aug. 3, 1931; s. Samuel Richard and Celia (Marcus) S.; B.A., Cornell U., 1953; m. Barbara Cantor, Jan. 28, 1959; 1 dau., Robin. Men's shoe buyer Morton Shoe Co., Boston, 1957-60; exec. v.p., gen. mdse. mgr. Ideal Shoe Co., Phila., 1960-68; with Zayre Corp., Framingham, Mass., 1968—, sr. v.p., gen. mdse. mgr., 1973-76, exec. v.p., 1976—; pres. Two/Ten Nat. Found., Boston, 1970—. Bd. dirs. Horizons for Youth, Sharon, Mass., 1978—, Jewish Vocat. Service, Horizons for Youth. Served with U.S. Army, 1953-56. Fellow Brandeis U., Waltham, Mass., 1971—. Mem. Nat. Mass Retailing Inst. (dir.), AIM (pres.'s council 1968—), Vol. Footwear Retailers Assn. (dir.), Am. Footwear Inst. (trustee), Confrerie de la Chaine des Rotisseurs (chevalier 1968—). Home: 10 Albion Rd Wellesley MA 02181 Office: 235 Old Connecticut Path Framingham MA 01701

SHERMAN, MERRITT, banker; b. Holly, Colo., Oct. 25, 1903; s. Dr. Edward Merritt and Mary (Sherman) S.; student U. Calif. at Los Angeles, 1922-23; A.B., Stanford U., 1926; mem. Adminstr. Staff Coll., Henley, Eng., 1958; m. Beatrice Dorothy Cross, Mar. 1, 1927; children—Stephen Merritt, Stanley, Stuart, Sandra Sherman Decker. Research asst. Fed. Res. Bank of San Francisco, 1926-29, mgr. div. analysis and research, 1930-41, asst. cashier, 1941-46, asst. sec. bd. govs. Fed. Res. System, Washington, 1946-58, sec. bd., 1958-68, asst. to the bd., 1968-69, cons., 1969—, also asst. sec. fed. open market com., 1951-69. Conglist. Club: Bretton Woods (Germantown, Md.). Home: 13610 Deakins Ln Germantown MD 20767 Office: Federal Reserve Bldg Washington DC 20551

SHERMAN, PATRICK, journalist; b. Newport, Eng., Mar. 16, 1928; s. Daniel James and Kathleen (Crowley) S.; student grammar sch., Eng.; m. Kathleen Maureen Haggerty, Sept. 29, 1951; children—Michael, Susan, Janet, Wendy. With Yorkshire Conservative Newspaper Co., Leeds, 1949-52; with Vancouver (B.C.) Province, 1952—, editor, 1965—, pub., 1972—; dir. Pacific Press Ltd.; mem. exec. com. Can. Press. Founding dir. Mountain Rescue Group B.C., 1956; leader mountaineering expdns. in N.Am. and Peru. Bd. dirs. Outward Bound Trust of B.C. Clubs: Alpine of Canada (Banff, Alta.); University (Vancouver); American Alpine (N.Y.C.). Author: Cloud Walkers, 1964; Bennett, 1965. Home: 556 Newdale Rd West Vancouver BC Canada Office: 2250 Granville St Vancouver BC Canada

SHERMAN, RICHARD FREEMAN, lawyer, restaurant chain exec.; b. Boston, Dec. 6, 1943; s. Harry H. and Sarah A. (Freeman) S.; B.A., Pa. State U., 1965; J.D., U. Tex., 1970; m. Yvonne J. Hinton, Dec. 16, 1972; children—Merida L., Nicholas H. Admitted to Tex. bar, 1970; atty. Foster Capital Corp., El Paso, Tex., 1970; staff atty. Hardee's Food Systems, Inc., Rocky Mount, N.C., 1971-72, corp. counsel, 1972-74, dir. legal services, asst. sec., 1974-75, sec., 1975—, v.p.-legal, 1975-77, sr. v.p.-legal, 1977-79, sr. v.p. adminstrn., 1979—, mem. sr. mgmt. com., 1977—, also sec. all subs.'s. Mem. N.C. Mental Health Council. Mem. Am., Tex. bar assns., Internat. Franchise Assn. (legal and legis. com.), Food and Lodging Inst. (dir.), Nat. Restaurant Assn. Democrat. Jewish. Clubs: Northgreen Country, Masons. Home: 104 Candle Ct Rocky Mount NC 27801 Office: 1233 N Church St Rocky Mount NC 27801

SHERMAN, RICHARD MORTON, composer, lyricist; b. N.Y.C., June 12, 1928; s. Al and Rosa (Dancis) S.; student U. So. Calif., 1945; B.A., Bard Coll., 1949; m. Ursula Gluck, July 6, 1957; children—Linda Sue, Gregory Vincent, Victoria Lynn. Composer popular songs including Tall Paul, Pineapple Princess, You're Sixteen, 1950-60; with Walt Disney Prodns., Burbank, Calif., 1960—, film song scores include: The Parent Trap, 1961, The Sword in the Stone, 1962, Summer Magic, 1963, Mary Poppins, 1964, That Darn Cat, 1965, Winnie The Pooh, 1965, Follow Me Boys, 1966, Happiest Millionaire, 1967, Jungle Book, 1967, Family Band, 1968, Chitty, Chitty Bang Bang, 1969, Aristocats, 1970, Bedknobs and Broomsticks, 1971, Snoopy Come Home, 1972, Charlotte's Web, 1973; Song Scores and Screenplays: Tom Sawyer, 1973, Huckleberry Finn, 1974; composer songs Walt Disney's Wonderful World of Color, TV, 1961—, also for Disneyland attractions. Served with AUS, 1953-55. Recipient Acad. award for best score for Mary Poppins, 1964, Best Song, Chim Chim Cheree, 1964; Grammy award for best film score, 1965; Christopher medal, 1965. Mem. Acad. Motion Picture Arts and Scis., Broadcast Music, Inc., Nat. Acad. Recording Arts and Scis., Composers and Lyricists Guild, Wrtiers Guild Am. Office: 280 S Beverly Dr Beverly Hills CA 90212*

SHERMAN, ROBERT ARTHUR, corp. exec., lawyer; b. Providence, Apr. 19, 1940; s. Robert Hiram and Olivia Mae (Latham) S.; A.B. cum laude, Harvard, 1962, LL.B. cum laude, 1965; m. Edith Ordway Clifford, June 11, 1964; children—Daniel Ordway, Charles Latham. Admitted to N.Y. bar, 1966; since practiced in N.Y.C., asso. law firm Dewey, Ballantine, Bushby, Palmer & Wood, N.Y.C., 1965-70; gen. counsel Wallace-Murray Corp., N.Y.C., 1971-73, sec., 1973-79, v.p., 1979—. Mem. Assn. Bar City N.Y., Am., N.Y. State bar assns. Club: University (N.Y.C.). Home: 1035 Park Ave New York NY 10028 Office: 299 Park Ave New York NY 10017

SHERMAN, ROBERT BERNARD, songwriter, writer; b. N.Y.C., Dec. 19, 1925; s. Al and Rosa (Dancis) S.; student U. Calif. at Los Angeles, 1943; B.A., Bard Coll., 1949; m. Joyce Ruth Sasner, Sept. 27, 1953; children—Laurie Shane, Jeffrey Craig, Andrea Tracy, Robert Jason. Popular songwriter, 1950-60, including Tall Paul, Pineapple Princess, You're Sixteen; songwriter Walt Disney Prodns., Beverly Hills, Calif., 1960-68, including for films The Parent Trap, 1961, Summer Magic, 1963, Mary Poppins, 1964, That Darn Cat, 1965, Winnie The Pooh, 1965, Jungle Book, 1967; writer screenplays Tom Sawyer, Huckleberry Finn, The Slipper and The Rose, The Magic of Lassie; composer, lyricist United Artists, Beverly Hills, 1969—, songs and scores for film Chitty, Chitty, Bang, Bang, 1969, The Aristocats, 1970, Bedknobs and Broomsticks, 1971, Charlotte's Web, 1973, Tom Sawyer, 1973; composer for film Snoopy, Come Home; Broadway show Over Here!, 1974; composer, writer for film Huckleberry Film, 1974; composer for Walt Disney's Wonderful World of Color, TV, 1961—; co-producer NBC-TV spl. Goldilocks, 1970; writer screenplay, songscore The Slipper and the Rose, 1976, The Magic of Lassie, 1978. Served with inf. AUS, 1943-45. Decorated Purple Heart, Combat Infantry badge; recipient Acad. award best score for Mary Poppins, 1964, for Best Song, Chim Chim Cheree, 1965; Christopher award for Mary Poppins, 1964, Tom Sawyer, 1974; 9 acad. award nominations including Chitty Chitty Bang Bang, 1968, Bedknobs and Broomsticks, 1972, Tom Sawyer, 1974, The Slipper and the Rose, 1977, Magic of Lassie, 1978; four golden record albums, 1965, 68, 69, 74; 1st prize Moscow Film Festival for Tom Sawyer, 1973. Mem. Acad. Motion Picture Arts and Scis. (exec. com., music br.), N.A.R.A.S., Composers and Lyricists Guild, Writers Guild Am., Dramatists Guild, Authors League. Pub. song score of Mary Poppins, most translated in the world. Office: 280 S Beverly Dr Beverly Hills CA 90212

SHERMAN, ROGER JAMES, engring. cons. co. exec.; b. N.Y.C., Feb. 17, 1913; s. Charles T. and Frances A. (O'Sullivan) S.; B.S. in Mech. Engring., N.Y. U. Coll. Engring., 1939, postgrad., 1940-41; postgrad. in nuclear engring. Columbia U., 1953; m. Rosalind Brooks, Sept. 4, 1937; children—Susan Jane, Roger Brooks. With Ebasco Services Inc., N.Y.C., 1939—, mgr. bus. devel. and fgn. ops., until 1963, v.p. in charge engring., bus. devel. and fgn. ops, 1963-69, sr. v.p. in charge engring., constrn., nuclear projects and purchasing activities, 1969, pres., chief exec. officer, 1969—, chmn. bd., 1978—, also dir. parent co. and subsidiaries. Served from lt. (j.g.) to lt. comdr., U.S. Navy, 1943-46. Recipient Achievement award N.Y. U., 1971, Distinguished Engr. in Pvt. Practice award N.Y. State Soc. Profl. Engrs. Fellow ASME; mem. Am. Nuclear Soc., Nat. Soc. Profl. Engrs., Am. Nuclear Energy Council (dir.), Atomic Indsl. Forum (chmn., dir.). Clubs: Capital City, Union League, White Beeches Golf and Country, Whitehall Luncheon; George Town. Home: 30 Colgate St Closter NJ 07624 Office: 2 Rector St New York NY 10006

SHERMAN, SAMUEL S., JR., lawyer; b. Wilmette, Ill., Jan. 22, 1909; student U. Colo.; A.B., U. Mich., 1931; LL.B. cum laude, U. Denver, 1935. Admitted to Colo. bar, 1935; mem. firm Dawson, Nagel, Sherman & Howard, Denver. Mem. Am., Colo., Denver bar assns., Phi Delta Phi. Office: 2900 First of Denver Plaza Denver CO 80202

SHERMAN, SAUL LAWRENCE, lawyer, govt. ofcl.; b. N.Y.C., Sept. 5, 1926; s. Louis and Hannah Jean (Auerbach) S.; grad. Fieldston Sch., 1943; S.B. magna cum laude, Harvard, 1946, J.D. cum laude, 1949; m. Carol Esberg, Nov. 12, 1964 (dec. 1972); children—Kate M., William Benjamin; m. 2d, Judith Shonkoff, June 5, 1977. Admitted to N.Y. bar, 1949, also U.S. courts; with U.S. Fgn. Service in Frankfurt, Germany, 1949-51, London, Eng., 1951-52; with firm Lord, Day & Lord, N.Y.C., 1952-62; partner Rivkin Sherman & Levy and predecessor firms, N.Y.C., 1962—; exec. sec. U.S. affiliate Internat. Commn. Jurists, 1962-66; U.S. mem. bd. Validation German Dollar Bonds, 1962—; adv. on multilateral trade negotiations U.S. Dept. Commerce, 1978—; adv. working party on customs valuation Internat. C. of C., Paris, 1979—; lectr. internat. trade to profl. and bus. groups. Served with USNR, 1944-45. Mem. Am. Bar Assn., Am. Soc. Internat. Law, Am. Fgn. Law Assn., Assn. Bar City N.Y., Assn. Customs Bar (dir. 1972—), Am. Importers Assn. (dir. 1974—), Phi Beta Kappa. Contbr. articles to profl. jours. Home: 4920 Arlington Ave Bronx NY 10471 Office: 750 3d Ave New York NY 10017

SHERMAN, SAUL S., mfg. co. exec.; b. 1917; B.A., U. Chgo., 1939; married. Pres., treas. Emerman Machy Corp., 1937-66; mem. Chgo. Bears, profl. football team, 1939-40; pres. Am. Eagle Corp., 1962-65; with Allied Products Corp., Chgo., 1963—, chmn. exec. com., pres. (merger Am. Eagle Corp. and Allied Products Corp.), 1965-73, also chmn. bd., 1973—, also chmn. subsidiaries Continental/Moss-Gordin Inc., Aurora Corp. of Ill. Pres. Davis & Thompson Co., United Crane & Shovel Corp., also dir. Office: Allied Products Corp 10 S Riverside Plaza Chicago IL 60606*

SHERMAN, STUART CAPEN, librarian; b. Amherst, Mass., Oct. 30, 1916; s. Clarence Edgar and Inez (Copeland) S.; A.B., Brown U., 1939, Litt.D., 1964; B.L.S., Columbia U., 1940; m. Mary Elliott Thompson, June 7, 1941; children—Nancy Elliott (Mrs. John M. Walker, Jr.), Robert Thompson. Summer substitute N.Y. Pub. Library, 1940; br. librarian Enoch Pratt Free Library, Balt., 1940-43; br. supr. Providence Pub. Library, 1943-44, asst. librarian, 1945-53, asso. librarian, 1954-56, librarian, 1957-68; asso. prof. bibliography Brown U., 1968-78, prof., 1978—, John Hay librarian, 1968-76, library bibliographer, 1976—, acting Univ. librarian, 1978—; extension lectr. R.I. Coll. Edn., U. R.I., 1957-62; exec. sec. Friends of Library of Brown U., 1976—. trustee Citizens Savs. Bank, also chmn. bldg. com., mem. investment com. Mem. joint com. ALA-NEA, N.E.A., 1962-65, chmn., 1964; R.I. chmn. Nat. Library Week, 1958; research adv. com. Council Community Services, 1954-60; mem. corp. Narragansett council Boy Scouts Am.; charter mem. R.I. Heritage Week Com. of R.I. Devel. Council, 1956- 67; adv. council U.S. Civil War Centennial Commn., 1958-65; adv. bd. R.I. Civil War Centennial Commn., 1960-65; vice chmn. City of Providence Historic Dist. Commn., 1960-68; chmn. adv. com. sch. libraries State Bd. Edn., 1959-63; chmn. human relations task force, mem. Providence Master Plan Adv. Com., 1958-60; mem. vis. com. and publ. com. Mystic Seaport. Asso. John Carter Brown Library; v.p., dir. R.I. Philharmonic Orch., 1958-60; bd. dirs. Com. for New Eng. Bibliography; trustee R.I. Sch. Design, 1957-68, Impact, R.I., Inc., 1963-67, Research & Design Inst., Inc., Union Chapel, Oak Bluffs; mem. bd. mgmt. Annmary Brown Meml.; mem. adv. com. Brown U. Study Library Coop.; mem. Am. civilization exec. com. Brown U.; mem. corp. Providence Tb League, 1952-60, Providence Boys Club, 1956, Providence Pub. Library. Mem. ALA (life), R.I. (pres. 1947-49), New Eng. (v.p. 1947-49), Mass. library assns., Bibliog. Soc. Am., R.I. Hist. Soc. (library com. 1957-62, planning com. 1960-62; chmn. publs. com. Nathanael Greene papers, trustee, pres.), Am. Antiquarian Soc., Manuscript Soc., Old Dartmouth (New Bedford), Dukes County (Mass.) hist. socs., East Chop Assn. (pres. 1959-61), Citizens TV Council R.I. (gov. 1958-60), Marine Hist. Assn. (Mystic), Asso. Alumni Brown U. (past dir.; sec. class 1939), Friends Library Brown U., R.I. Marine Soc. (incorporator, v.p.), Greater Providence C. of C., Downtown Bus. Coordinating Council, Melville Soc., Friends of Peabody Mus., Vineyard Conservation Soc. (dir.), Soc. Colonial Wars, Am. Printing History Assn., Phi Beta Kappa, Theta Delta Chi. Conglist. (deacon). Clubs: Rotary (dir. 1958-59), Art, Review (Providence); Club of Odd Volumes (Boston); Brown of R.I. (past dir., past sec.); Grolier (N.Y.); Book of California. Author: The Voice of the Whaleman, 1965; The First Ninety Years of the Providence Public Library, 1968; The Providence Public Library: A Century of Service, 1878-1978; co-author of The Melville Bibliography; mem. editorial bd. Brown Alumni Monthly, 1960—; editor Books at Brown, 1976—; contbr. articles, book reviews to profl. publs. Home: 654 Angell St Providence RI 02906 Office: Brown U Providence RI 02912

SHERMAN, STUART HOLMES, JR., air force officer; b. Lenoir, N.C., Mar. 20, 1932; s. Stuart Holmes and Grace (Turner) S.; B.S. in Engring., U.S. Naval Acad., 1953; M.S., U. Mich., 1960; grad. Armed Forces Staff Coll., 1966, Nat. War Coll., 1972; m. Stella Theresa Hedrick, June 20, 1953; children—Deborah Theresa, Stuart Holmes, III, Clyde Reitzel. Commd. 2d lt. USAF, 1953, advanced through grades to maj. gen., 1978; exec. asst. to undersec. air force, 1969-71; comdr. 1st Strategic Aerospace Div., Vandenberg AFB, Calif., 1975-77; dir. manpower and orgn. Hdqrs. USAF, Washington, 1977—. Decorated Air Force Disting. Service medal, Legion of Merit, Meritorious Service medal, Air Force Commendation medal with oak leaf cluster, Army Commendation medal. Mem. Air Force Assn. Home: 86 Westover Ave Bolling AFB DC 20336 Office: Hdqrs USAF Washington DC 20330

SHERMAN, THOMAS MONROE, steel co. exec.; b. Independence, Mo., Sept. 1, 1916; s. Amos Monroe and Pearl Gertrude (King) S.; student William Jewell Coll., 1936-37, Mo. U., 1935, 37-38; m. Vera Marie Anderson, Sept. 27, 1941. Sales rep. Inter-Collegiate Press, 1945-46; sales mgr. Anderson-Egner Motor Co., Independence, Mo., 1946-47; dist. account mgr. Armco Steel Corp., Kansas City, Mo., 1947—; pres. bd. publs. Herald House Pub. Co., Independence, Mo., 1975—. Mem. highest judicial council, mem. presidency Santa Fe stake Reorganized Ch. of Jesus Christ of Latter-day Saints; mem. Richard-Gebaur AFB Community Council, 1975-77. Served with AUS, 1943-44. Mem. William Jewell Coll. Alumni Assn. Republican. Clubs: Kansas City Royal Stadium. Home: 11964 E 44th St Kansas City MO 63144 Office: 7000 Roberts Kansas City MO 64125. *The years have taught me the infinite value of human life. The great worth of persons outweighs the apparent decadence of our society, and has challenged me to help each individual I touch to achieve the highest potential of their giftedness.*

SHERMAN, VERNON WESLEY, elec. engr.; b. Oscoda, Mich., Apr. 7, 1907; s. Henry C. and Mabel F. (Nolan) S.; A.B., Coll. City of Detroit, 1931; B.S. in Mech. Engring., Wayne U., 1937, M.S. in Elec. Engring., 1941; B.S. in Edn., Central Mich. U., 1964; m. June Roach, Sept. 2, 1930; children—Nola Marie, Vernon Clayton; m. 2d, Helen L. McNair, July 28, 1948; 1 son, Vernon Wesley. Asst. to supt. Gen. Elec. Co. Detroit, 1925-33; project engr. Chrysler Corp., Detroit, 1933-42; mgr. indsl. electronics div. Fed. Telephone & Radio Corp., Newark, 1942-45; pres., chief engr. Sherman Indsl. Electronics Co., Belleville, N.J., 1945-58; gen. mgr. Sherman Indsl. Electronics div., Engring. Design, Inc., State College, Pa., 1958-59; prop. Lake City Marine (Mich.), 1959-64; tchr. math. and sci. dept. Manton (Mich.) High Sch., 1964-72. Chmn. bd. Civilian Def. Communications, Belleville, 1953-57. Recipient War Dept. Atomic Bomb certificate, 1945, Distinguished Alumnus award Coll. Engring. Wayne State U., 1958; Order of Engr., 1974. Registered profl. engr., Mich., N.J. Mem. Am. Soc. for Metals, Quarter Century Wireless Assn. (life mem.), Mich. Soc. Profl. Engrs. (edn. com. 1969-71, pres. No. chpt. 1974-75), IEEE (sr. mem.; bd. editors, 1943-54, mem. indsl. electronics com. 1946-48), Am. Assn. Physics Tchrs., Nat. Council Tchrs. Math. (life mem.), Epsilon Sigma. Presbyn. Club: Kiwanis. Lectr. and contbr. numerous tech. papers including: Thin Case Hardening with Radio Frequency Energy, 1943; Electronic Heating of Food, 1944; Dehydration of Food, 1944; Electronic Heating of Preforms, 1944; Case Hardening by Megacycle Induction Heat, 1944; New Induction Heater, 1950; contbr. New Voices in American Poetry, 1977, 78; holder of 23 patents granted or applied for in field of high frequency induction and dielec. heating. Home: Apple Acres Rural Route 2 Manton MI 49663. *I'm grateful for the standards I learned at home in a family of nine, including two parents who worked very hard and quarrelled and stayed married. I think I learned then that the tight times and bad spots in life were nothing as compared to its remembered joys and satisfactions. Overall my life has been wonderful. I've been a bit surprised about earlier convictions: First, my dearest memories all turn out to be strictly subjective; and secondly, the objective parts of my life which show up in Who's Who now seem to me as largely due to the audacity of youth (well, age 30). I now view audacity as an essential of creativity. I ventured all in the High Frequency Heating field. Education and experience were basic requirements, but engineering audacity was the very key.*

SHERMAN, WILLIAM COURTNEY, fgn. service officer; b. Edmonton, Ky., Sept. 27, 1923; s. George Frederick and Katherine Courtney (Kinnaird) S.; A.B., U. Louisville, 1946; student U. Colo., 1946, Okla. A. and M. Coll., 1945-46; student Nat. War Coll., 1967-68; m. Mary Jane Hazelip, Apr. 28, 1945; children—Katherine Courtney, John Justin, Roger Woodson. With Mil. Govt. in Korea, 1946-48, ECA mission to Korea, 1948-50; joined U.S. Fgn. Service, 1951; vice consul, Yokohama, Japan, 1952-54; 3d sec. embassy, Tokyo, Japan, 1954-56; assigned State Dept., 1956-60; 1st sec. embassy, Rome, Italy, 1960-65; spl. asst. to dep. under sec. state for adminstrn., 1966-67; consul general Kobe-Osaka, Japan, 1968-70; counselor for polit. affairs Am. embassy, Tokyo, 1970-73, minister-counselor, dep. chief mission, 1977—; dir. for Japanese affairs State Dept., Washington, 1973-77. Served to lt. (j.g.) USNR, 1943-46, 50-51. Mem. Omicron Delta Kappa. Home: 11422 Orchard Ln Reston VA 22090 Office: Dept of State Washington DC 20520

SHERMAN, WILLIAM SAMUEL, journalist; b. N.Y.C., Dec. 9, 1946; s. Murray George and Beatrice Hannah (Nathanson) S.; B.A., Bard Coll., 1968; M.Jour., Boston U., 1969. Reporter, N.Y. Daily News, 1969—; corr. ABC TV News, 1978—; adj. prof. journalism Hunter Coll. Recipient George Polk Meml. award for outstanding community service N.Y. Newspaper Guild, 1973, Page One award for lifestyle features, 1973, Page One award for crusading journalism, 1974, Page One award, 1976; Outstanding Journalism award Soc. Silurians, 1972, award for investigative reporting, 1975; Deadline Club award Sigma Delta Chi, 1974, 78; Women's Press Club award, 1974; Pulitzer prize, 1974; 1st place and hon. mention for best newspaper stories of yr. AP, 1978. Club: New York Press Byline (Gold Typewriter award 1974). Home: 115 Central Park W New York NY 10023 Office: 220 E 42d St New York NY 10017

SHERMOEN, RICHARD EUGENE, educator; b. Fargo, N.D., Nov. 26, 1930; s. Clarence and Margaret Delia (Spotts) S.; B.S., N.D. State U., 1953, M.S., 1958; M.A., U. Ill., 1961; postgrad. U. N.M., 1961-62; Ed.D., Okla. State U., 1965; m. Nancy Lee Hanks, June 17, 1956; children—Richard Clarence, James Willard, Margaret Marie. Tchr. math. and sci., Harvey, N.D., 1953-55; life ins. salesman, 1955; tchr. math. and sci., Hart, Mich., 1956; instr. math. N.D. State U., 1956-60, asst. prof. math., 1964-67; chmn. math. dept. Washburn U., Topeka, 1967—. Served with USNR, 1948-49. NSF Summer Inst., Iowa State U., NSF Acad. Year Inst., U. Ill., 1960-61. Sci. Faculty fellow Okla. State U., 1962-63. Mem. Math. Assn. Am. (past chmn. Kans. sect., gov. 1976—), Nat. Council Tchrs. Math., Phi Kappa Phi, Pi Mu Epilson, Kappa Mu Epsilon. Home: 1405 McAlister Ave Topeka KS 66604

SHERNOFF, WILLIAM M., lawyer; Prin. firm William M. Shernoff, P.C., Claremont, Calif., br. office in San Diego. Named Trial Lawyer of Year, Los Angeles Trial Lawyers Assn., 1975. Mem. Calif. Trial Lawyers Assn. (gov., past chpt. pres.), Assn. Trial Lawyers Am., Los Angeles County Bar Assn. Contbr. articles to profl. jours. Office: 666 S Indian Hill Claremont CA 91711

SHERO, FRED ALEXANDER, profl. hockey coach; b. Winnipeg, Man., Can., Oct. 23, 1925. Profl. hockey player, 1943-57; defenseman N.Y. Rangers Nat. Hockey League team, then coach N.Y. Rangers farm clubs, 1957-58; coach Am. Hockey League team, Buffalo, 1968-70, Omaha Central Hockey League team, 1970-71, Phila. Flyers Nat. Hockey League team, 1971-78; gen. mgr., coach N.Y. Rangers Nat. Hockey League Team, 1978—. Address: care NY Rangers 4 Pennsylvania Plaza New York NY 10001

SHEROCKMAN, ANDREW ANTOLCIK, former steel co. exec.; b. Raccoon, Pa., July 19, 1913; s. Andrew and Anna (Antolcik) S.; B.A., Dubuque (Iowa) U., 1935; postgrad. Columbia, 1944; M.A., Pitts. U., 1945, Ph.D., 1955; postgrad. Harvard, 1949; m. Anna Yesko, Oct. 31, 1943. Tchr. high sch., Burgettstown, Pa., 1935-42; prof. chemistry U. Evansville (Ind.), 1946-55; dir. naval reactor tng. Bettis Atomic Power div. Westinghouse Co., Pitts., 1955-59; dir. tech. info. services Nat. Steel Corp., Weirton, W.Va., from 1959. Cons. in sci. edn. to colls., univs.; dir. sems. in sci. edn. Pres. Robinson Township (Pa.) Civic League, 1972. Trustee Allegheny Acad., Pitts Tech. Inst. Served to maj. inf. AUS, 1942-46. Fellow A.A.A.S.; mem. Am. Chem. Soc., Spl. Libraries Assn., Nat. Sci. Tchrs. Assn., Soc. Tech. Communications,

Presbyn. Beneficial Union, Am. Legion, Alpha Chi Sigma, Phi Delta Kappa, Phi Alpha Theta, Pi Kappa Delta. Republican. Presbyn. (elder). Kiwanian. Author: Manual for General Chemistry, 1948; Caleb Mills, Pioneer Educator in Indiana, 1955. Contbr. sci. articles to profl. jours. Home: RD 5 McMichael Rd Box 596-B Pittsburgh PA 15205

SHERR, RUBBY, physicist; b. Long Branch, N.J., Sept. 14, 1913; s. Max and Anna (Jacobson) S.; B.A., N.Y. U., 1934; Ph.D., Princeton, 1938; m. Rita P. Ornitz, Sept. 11, 1936; children—Elizabeth, Frances. Instr., Harvard, 1938-42; staff Radiation Lab., Mass. Inst. Tech., 1942-44, Manhattan Project, Los Alamos, 1944-46; asst. prof. Princeton, 1946-49. asso. prof., 1949-58, prof., 1958—; exptl. research nuclear physics. Sr. research fellow NSF, 1958-59. Mem. Am. Phys. Soc., Sigma Xi. Home: 73 McCosh Circle Princeton NJ 08540

SHERRER, CHARLES DAVID, coll. pres., clergyman; b. Marion, Ohio, Sept. 21, 1935; s. Harold D. and Catherine E. (Fye) S.; A.B., U. Notre Dame, 1958, M.A., 1965; S.T.L., Gregorian U., 1962; Ph.D., U. N.C., 1969. Ordained priest Roman Cath. Ch., 1961; instr. English U. Portland, 1963-64, asst. prof., 1969-74, chmn. dept., 1970-74; pres. King's Coll., Wilkes Barre, Pa., 1974—; dir. studies Holy Cross Fathers, Ind. Province, 1979—. Bd. dirs., v.p. Wyoming Valley United Way; bd. dirs. Greater Wilkes-Barre C. of C. and Indsl. Fund, Osterhout Library; mem. exec. com. Econ. Devel. Council Northeastern Pa. Mem. Commn. Ind. Colls. and Univs., AAUP, MLA, Shakespeare Soc., Wyoming Valley Hist. and Geol. Soc. Club: Westmoreland. Office: 133 N River St Wilkes-Barre PA 18711

SHERRER, JAMES WYLIE, SR., mfg. co. exec.; b. Enterprise, Ala., Jan. 24, 1935; s. Fred Alfred and Gladys (Godwin) S.; B.S. in Textile Engring., Auburn U., 1956; m. Shirley Spurlin, Dec. 19, 1954; children—James, Michael. With Crompton Co., Griffin, Ga., 195—59; sales, devel. and mktg. mgr. Formex div. Huyck Corp., 1959-70, v.p., gen. mgr. Felt div., 1970-73, exec. v.p. Huyck Corp., Wake Forest, N.C., 1973—. Mem. Paper Industry Mgmt. Assn., TAPPI. Republican. Baptist. Office: Huyck Corp Drawer 1 US 1 N Wake Forest NC 27587

SHERRER, WAYMAN GRAY, lawyer; b. Birmingham, Ala., Nov. 15, 1927; s. Claude Wayman and Rosalee (Garner) S.; A.B., Samford U., 1952; LL.B., U. Ala., 1956; m. Betty Rodgers, Aug. 13, 1960; children-Elizabeth Ann, William Jefferson. Spl. agt. FBI, 1956-62; admitted to Ala. bar, 1956, also Supreme Ct. U.S., U.S. Dist. Ct. No. Dist. Ala., U.S. Ct. of Appeals 5th Circuit; practiced in Oneonta, Ala., 1962-69, 77—; U.S. atty. No. Dist. Ala., 1969-77; county solicitor Blount County, 1965-69. Atty. Blount County Republican Party, 1962-69, mem., 1964-69; mem. Ala. Rep. Exec. Com. 7th Congl. Dist., 1965-66, 68-69; Rep. candidate for Congress for 7th Congl. Dist., 1966; del. Rep. Nat. Conv., 1968. Served with USMCR, 1946-48. Mem. Former FBI Agts. (past chmn. Ala. chpt.), Am. Fed. (past chmn. Birmingham chpt.), Ala., Blount County (past chmn.) bar assns., Oneonta C. of C., Sigma Nu, Alpha Kappa Psi, Pi Gamma Mu, Omicron Delta Kappa. Methodist. Rotarian. Home: 107 Redbud Rd Oneonta AL 35121 Office: 231 2d Ave E Oneonta AL 35121

SHERRICK, RONALD PAUL, meat processing co. exec.; b. Phila., Sept. 3, 1933; s. John Joseph and Edith Louise (Sternberger) S.; student U. Pa., 1958, Temple U., 1965-72; m. Marilyn Joyce Woehr, Sept. 7, 1953; children—Michael Paul, Donna Lynn. Budget analyst Alan Wood Steel Co., Conshohocken, Pa., 1959-62; chief accountant Lummis & Co. div. U.S. Tobacco Co., Phila., 1962-66; supr. gen. acctg. Nat. Sugar Refining Co., Phila., 1966-71; chief accountant Acme Hardesty Co. Inc. div. Jacob Stern & Sons, Inc., Phila., 1971-73; treas. Blue Bird Food Products Co. subs. Bluebird, Inc., Phila., 1973—. Served with USAF, 1950-54. Office: 3501 S 3d St Philadelphia PA 19148

SHERRIFFS, ALEX CARLTON, educator; b. San Jose, Calif., Dec. 14, 1917; s. Alexander and Ruth (Turner) S.; A.B., Stanford, 1939, M.A., 1941, Ph.D., 1946; LL.D., Pepperdine U., 1974; m. Mary Rock Edwards, May 10, 1948; children—Anna, Nancy, John, Alex; m. 2d, Dawn Hart Wisner, Apr. 1, 1966. Mem. faculty U. Calif. at Berkeley, 1944-73, prof. psychology, 1960-73, research asso. Inst. Human Devel., 1944-60, vice chancellor student affairs, 1958-65; edn. adviser to Gov. of Calif., 1968-73; vice chancellor acad. affairs Calif. State U. and Colls. System, Los Angeles, 1973—; lectr. in field. Pres. Berkeley Mental Health Assn., 1951-52, Alameda County Mental Health Assn., 1952-53. Mem. Am. Psychol. Assn., AAAS, Sigma Xi. Contbr. to profl. publs. Research on higher edn., social stereotypes of roles of sex groups and effects. Home: 1620 Via Machado Palos Verdes Estates CA 90274 Office: 400 Golden Shore Long Beach CA 90802

SHERRILL, HUGH VIRGIL, investment banker; b. Long Beach, Calif., 1920; ed. Yale. Pres., Bache Halsey Stuart Shields Inc., 1977—; dir. Alberto-Culver Co. Trustee Meml. Hosp., N.Y.C., Boys' Club N.Y.C. Address: 100 Gold St New York NY 10038

SHERRILL, WILLIAM W., bus. exec.; b. Houston, Aug. 23, 1926; s. Harry C. and Iva (Haywood) S.; B.B.A. with honors, U. Houston, 1950; M.B.A. with distinction in Finance, Harvard U., 1952; m. Marilyn Sue Poer, June 18, 1948 (div.); children—Cynthia Lea, Sandra Lynn, Suzanne Elise; m. 2d, Sharon J. Blansfield, Oct. 28, 1972. Adminstr., City Houston, 1954, then exec. asst. to mayor, chief adminstrv. officer, city treas.; pres. Homestead Bank, Houston, 1963-66; exec. v.p. Jamaica Corp., Houston, 1963-66; dir. Fed. Deposit Ins. Corp., 1966-67; bd. govs. Fed. Res. System, 1967-71; former pres., former dir. Assos. Corp. N. Am., South Bend, Ind.; dir. Gulf & Western Industries, Inc., N.Y.C. Mem. U.S. nat. com. UNESCO, 1967-69. Active local Boy Scouts Am., YMCA. Served with USMC, World War II. Decorated Purple Heart; recipient outstanding Alumnus award U. Houston, 1955. Mem. U. Houston Alumni Assn. (past treas., dir.). Home: 2139 Tangley St Houston TX 77005 Office: 777 1700 West Loop South Suite 1200 Houston TX 77027

SHERRIS, JOHN CHARLES, microbiologist; b. Colchester, Eng., Mar. 8, 1921; s. Cyril and Dorothy S.; came to U.S., 1959, naturalized, 1969; MRCS, LRCP, M.B., B.S., U. London, 1948, M.D., 1950; M.D. (hon.), Karolinska Inst., Stockholm, Sweden, 1975; m. Elizabeth, July, 1944; children—Peter, Jacqueline. House surgeon and physician King Edward VII Hosp., Windsor, Eng., 1944-45; trainee, asst. pathologist central lab. Sector V. Ministry Health, 1945-48; sr. registrar in pathology Aylesbury and Dist. Lab., Stoke, Mandeville, Eng., 1948-50, Radcliffe Infirmary, Oxford (Eng.) U., 1950-52; lectr. in bacteriology U. Manchester (Eng.), 1953-56, sr. lectr., 1956-59; dir. clin. microbiology labs. U. Wash. Hosp., 1959-70; asso. prof. microbiology U. Wash., 1959-63, prof., 1963—, chmn. dept. microbiology and immunology, 1970—; bd. dirs. Nat. Found. Infectious Diseases. Diplomate Am. Bd. Pathology, Am. Bd. Med. Microbiology. Fellow Royal Coll. Pathologists, Am. Acad. Microbiology (gov. 1974-78, v.p. 1976-78); mem. Am. Soc. Microbiology (Becton-Dickinson award 1978), Soc. Gen. Microbiology, Can. Soc. Microbiologists, Assn. Clin. Pathologists, Acad. Clin. Lab. Physicians, Scientists, Am. Bd. Med. Microbiology (chmn. 1971-73). Editor: Cumitech Series, Am. Soc. Microbiology, 1974—. Research in antibiotic susceptibility and resistance of bacteria, automation in microbiology. Home: 10021 Lake Shore Blvd NE Seattle WA 98125 Office: Dept Microbiology and Immunology SC-42 U Wash Seattle WA 98195

SHERROD, ROBERT LEE, writer; b. Thomas County, Ga., Feb. 8, 1909; s. Joseph Arnold and Victoria Ellen (Evers) S.; A.B., U. Ga., 1929; m. Elizabeth Hudson, Oct. 8, 1936 (dec. Dec. 1958); children—John Hudson, Robert Lee; m. 2d, Margaret Carson Ruff, May 5, 1961 (div. 1972); m. 3d, Mary Gay Labrot Leonhardt, Aug. 26, 1972 (dec. July 1978). Reporter Atlanta Constn., Palm Beach (Fla.) Daily News, and others, 1929-35; with Time and Life mags. as Wash. corr., asso. editor, war and Far East corr., 1935-52; Far East corr. Sat. Eve. Post, 1952-55, mng. editor, 1955-62; editor, 1962, editor-at-large, 1963-64; v.p., editorial coordinator Curtis Pub. Co., 1965-66; writing on fgn. affairs and history, 1966—; contract writer Life Mag., N.Y.C., 1966-68. Mem. history adv. com. USMC, 1973-76, U. Ga. Pres.'s Adv. Council, 1975-78. Trustee Corrs. Fund, 1963—. Commended by USN Dept., Battle of Attu, May 1943, Battle of Tarawa, Nov. 1943; recipient Headliners Club award for war reporting, 1944; Banjamin Franklin award U. Ill., 1954; Overseas Press Club certificate, 1955. Episcopalian. Clubs: Federal City, Nat. Press (Washington); Overseas Press, Century (N.Y.C.). Author: Tarawa, the Story of a Battle, 1944, 3d edit., 1973; On to Westward, 1945; History of Marine Corps Aviation in World War II, 1952; also text for Life's Picture History of World War II, 1950 and Kobunsha's Picture History of the Pacific War (in Japanese), 1952; (with others) Apollo Expeditions to the Moon, 1975. Home and office: 4000 Cathedral Ave NW Washington DC 20016

SHERRY, ARTHUR HARNETT, educator; b. Berkeley, Calif., Mar. 10, 1908; s. Arthur V. and Cecilia D. (Harnett) S.; A.B., St. Mary's (Calif.) Coll., 1929; J.D., U. Cal. at Berkeley, 1932; m. Mary Ellen Leary, July 25, 1949; children—Suzanne, Judith, Virginia. Admitted to Calif. bar, 1932, also U.S. Supreme Ct.; asst. dist. atty. Alameda County, Calif., 1935-50; chief asst. atty. gen. Calif., 1951-53; Walter Perry Johnston prof. law, prof. criminology emeritus U. Calif. at Berkeley, 1953—; prof. law Hastings Coll. Law, San Francisco. Project dir. survey adminstrn. criminal justice Am. bar Found., 1954-58; dir. revision project Calif. Penal Code, 1964-69; chmn. adv. com. criminal statistics atty. gen. Calif., 1954-62. Bd. dirs. Hanna Center for Boys, Sonoma, Calif., 1964-69; pres. St. Mary's Coll. Alumni Assn., 1963-65. Served to lt. col. USAAF, 1942-45. Decorated Bronze Star; recipient Signum Fidei award St. Mary's Coll., 1968, citation Boalt Hall Alumni Assn., 1976. Mem. Am. Law Inst., Am. Justice Inst. (dir., mem. exec. com. 1969-77), Am. Bar Assn. Catholic. Club: Bohemian (San Francisco). Home: 319 El Cerrito Ave Piedmont CA 94611 Office: Hastings Coll Law Univ California San Francisco CA 94102

SHERRY, JOSEPH A., architect; b. N.Y.C., May 2, 1936; s. Anthony and Carrie (Gultz) S.; A.A.S., Pratt Inst., 1962, B.S., 1967; m. Patricia A. Manti, Aug. 22, 1959; 1 dau., Michelle P. Archtl. draftsman, N.Y. area, 1955-61; asst dir. Urban Renewal Rehab. N.Y.C., 1961-66, dir. Urban Renewal Planning, 1968; dir. architecture and planning N.Y.C. Housing & Devel. Adminstrn., 1969-72; staff architect Office S.I. Devel., 1972-75; project mgr. Housing and Devel. Adminstrn., N.Y.C., 1975-76, chief Bklyn. devel., 1976—; archtl. cons., S.I., N.Y., 1969—; instr. Inst. Design & Constrn. Pres. Bay Terrace Civic Assn., 1969—. Mem. A.I.A. (dir. S.I. chpt. 1965-74), C. of C., Reserve Officers Assn., Naval Reserve Assn., N.Y. Assn. Architects. Home and office: 112 Kelvin Ave Staten Island NY 10306

SHERRY, PETER JOSEPH, automobile mfg. co. exec.; b. Mahanoy City, Pa., Apr. 20, 1924; s. Richard Terrence and Petronella (Schumacher) S.; B.S., Bowling Greene (Ohio) State U., 1948; m. Natalie Dolores Alonzi, Dec. 1, 1951; children—Richard, Peter, Mary Martha, Christopher, Joanne. With Ford Motor Co., Dearborn, Mich., since 1948, dir. compensation planning office, 1968-70, v.p. indsl. relations Ford of Europe, 1970-72, exec. dir. personnel and orgn. staff, Dearborn, 1972-73, v.p. personnel and orgn., 1973—. Active Overseas Schs. Adv. Council, Jr. Achievement. Mem. Orgn. Resources Counselors, Joint Council Econ. Edn., Bus. Edn. Alliance. Club: Birmingham Athletic. Office: Ford Motor Co American Rd Dearborn MI 48121

SHERRY, RICHARD, newspaper syndicate exec.; b. Chgo., Sept. 23, 1929; s. Edward and Pearl (Andelson) S.; B.F.A., Va. Commonwealth U., 1951; m. Ruth Elisabeth Thierfeldt, Jan. 20, 1956. Circulation promotion Hearst Newspapers, 1957-59; spl. events mgr. N.Y. World-Telegram & Sun, 1959-62; promotion editor Miami (Fla.) Herald. 1962-65; with Field Newspaper Syndicate, Irvine, Calif., and predecessor. Chgo., 1965—, exec. v.p., 1972-75, pres., 1975—, chief exec. officer, 1977—, also dir.; pres., dir. Hall House, book pubs., 1975—. Mem. PEN, Sigma Delta Chi.

SHERRY, SOL, physician, educator; b. N.Y.C., Dec. 8, 1916; s. Hyman and Ada (Greenman) S.; A.B., N.Y. U., 1935, M.D., 1939; m. Dorothy Sitzman, Aug. 7, 1946; children—Judith Anne, Richard Leslie. Successively fellow, intern, resident 3d med. div. Bellevue Hosp., N.Y.C., 1939-42, 46; asst. prof. medicine N.Y.U. Coll. Medicine, 1946-51; dir. May Inst. Med. Research, Cin., 1951-54; dir. medicine Jewish Hosp., St. Louis, 1954-58; prof. medicine Washington U. Sch. Medicine, St. Louis, 1958-68, co-chmn. dept., 1964-68; chmn. dept. Temple U. Sch. Medicine, 1968—, dir. Thrombosis Research Center, 1970—. Cons. emeritus surgeon gen. army; past chmn. com. thrombolytic agts. USPHS; past chmn. com. on thrombosis USPHS, council on thrombosis Am. Heart Assn.; past mem. com. blood, past chmn. task force on thrombosis NRC; mem. Internat. Commn. on Hemostasis and Thrombosis; past chmn. and pres. Internat. Socs. on Thrombosis and Hemostasis; past mem. sci. adv. com. St. Louis Heart Assn., also St. Louis Multiple Sclerosis Soc. Mem. bd. Hillel, 1961-67; pres. S.E. Pa. chpt. Am. Heart Assn., 1978-79. Served as flight surgeon USAAF, 1942-46; ETO. Recipient medal for typhus control Lower Bavaria, U.S. Army Typhus Commn., 1946; Research Career award USPHS, 1962; Distinghished Achievement award Modern Medicine, 1963, A.C.P., 1968, Am. Coll. Cardiology, 1971. Mem. AMA (past mem. and chmn. council drugs, chmn. sect. exptl. medicine and therapeutics), Assn. Am. Physicians, Assn. Profs. Medicine (council 1973-75, pres. 1976), Am. Soc. Clin. Investigation, Central Soc. Clin. Research (council 1962-64), Am. Physiol. Soc., Soc. Exptl. Biology and Medicine, A.C.P. (master), Phi Beta Kappa, Sigma Xi (pres. Washington U. chpt. 1962-63), Alpha Omega Alpha. Contbr. articles to profl. jours. Home: 408 Sprague Rd Narberth PA 19072

SHERRY, WILLIAM JAMES, oil producer; b. Salamanca, N.Y., Aug. 13, 1899; s. William and Bridget (Dunn) S.; student U. Notre Dame, 1917-19; B.S., Mass. Inst. Tech., 1921; m. Margaret Harrington, Oct. 2, 1928; children—Patricia, Margaret (Mrs. Andrew McNearney), Mary (Mrs. Lucius F. Cassidy), William James, Anne (Mrs. Rodger P. Erker), Jane (Mrs. Robert E.D. Harper), Teresa, Richard J. Petroleum geologist Shaffer Oil & Refining Co., 1921-23; oil producer, 1923—; pres. dir., Sherry Petroleum Corp., Tulsa 1931—, Rock Creek Oil Co., 1953-59. Mem. Tulsa Utility Bd., 1950-53; pres. Eastern Okla. Arthritis and Rheumatism Found., 1949-53, Tulsa Cath. Community Center, 1951-70, St. John's Hosp., Tulsa, 1969-72; v.p. Nat. Council Alcoholism, 1966. Trustee Mass. Inst. Tech., 1954-59, St. Gregory's Coll.; gov. U. Notre Dame Found., Okla. State U. Found. Served with U.S. Army, 1918. Created Papal Knight, 1943, Knight Grand Cross, 1951. Chancellor of Equestrian Order of Holy Sepulchre, Western Lietenantcy, 1950. Mem. Am. Assn. Petroleum Geologists. Am. Inst. Mining and Metall. Engrs., Am. Petroleum Inst., Ind. Petroleum Assn., Tulsa Geol. Soc., U. Notre Dame Alumni Assn. (dir. 1951-53, v.p. 1953), Mass. Inst. Tech. Alumni Assn. (v.p. 1966), Am. Legion. Republican. Roman Catholic. K.C. Clubs: Serra (hon.), Tulsa, Petroleum, University. Home: Townhouse 147 Center Plaza Tulsa OK 74119 Office: 320 S Boston Ave Tulsa OK 74103

SHERTZER, BRUCE ELDON, educator; b. Bloomfield, Ind., Jan. 11, 1928; s. Edwin Franklin and Lois Belle Shertzer; B.S., Ind. U., 1952, M.S., 1953, Ed.D., 1958; m. Carol Mae Rice, Nov. 24, 1948; children—Sarah Ann, Mark Eldon. Tchr., counselor Martinsville (Ind.) High Sch., 1952-56; dir. div. guidance Ind. Dept. Pub. Instrn., 1956-58; asso. dir. project guidance of superior students, North Central Assn. Coll. and Secondary Sch. 1958-60; mem. faculty Purdue U., 1960—, now prof., chmn. counseling and personnel services; vis. prof. ednl. psychology U. Hawaii, 1967; Fulbright sr. lectr., Reading, Eng., 1967-68; chmn. Nat. Adv. Council for Career Edn., 1976. Served with AUS, 1946-47. Mem. Am. Personnel and Guidance Assn. (pres. 1973-74). Author: Career Exploration and Planning 1973, 2d edit., 1976; Fundamentals of Counseling, 2d edit., 1974; Fundamentals of Guidance, 3d edit., 1976; also articles. Home: 1620 Western Dr West Lafayette IN 47906 Office: Edn Bldg Purdue Univ Lafayette IN 47907

SHERTZER, GEORGE EDWIN, lawyer; b. Hershey, Pa., June 9, 1928; s. Lester E. and Edna S. (Weaver) S.; B.A., Yale U., 1950; LL.B., Columbia U., 1953; m. Margaret Delano, Oct. 6, 1957; children—John D., Anne E. Admitted to N.Y. bar, 1957; with firm Winthrop, Stimson, Putnam & Roberts, N.Y.C., 1955-59; asst. counsel GTE Service Corp., 1959-66, gen. atty., 1966-72, v.p., 1969-72; sr. v.p., gen. counsel Gen. Telephone & Electronics Corp., Stamford, Conn., 1972—, v.p., 1969-76, sr. v.p., 1976—. Fellow Am. Bar Found.; mem. Am., N.Y. State bar assns. Home: 111 Maywood Rd Darien CT 06820 Office: 1 Stamford Forum Stamford CT 06904

SHERVHEIM, LLOYD OLIVER, ins. co. exec.; b. Kensington, Minn., June 22, 1928; s. Lewis and Ruth Amanda (Thronson) S.; student Gustavus Adolphus Coll., 1948-50, U. Minn., 1950-52; B.S., William Mitchell Coll. Law, 1958, LL.B., 1958; m. Ruth Elaine Rhodes, Oct. 29, 1950; children—Daniel, Anne, Heidi, Garold, Robette, Shanna, Bryce. Admitted to Minn. bar, 1959; sr., asst. to corp. sec. Investors Diversified Services, Inc., 1952-59; legal counsel Investors Syndicate Life Ins. Co., Mpls., 1959-66; gen. counsel Western Life Ins. Co., St. Paul, 1966-72; corporate sec. St. Paul Cos., Inc., 1969—, chief legal officer, 1972-78, v.p. legal affairs, 1978—; corporate sec. St. Paul Fire and Marine Ins. Co., 1969—; dir. St. Paul Ins. Co. (Tex.), St. Paul Surplus Lines Ins. Co., St. Paul Mercury Ins. Co., St. Paul Guardian Ins. Co., St. Paul Ins. Co. (Ill.). Charter patron Minn. Theatre Co. Mem. Lake Elmo City Council, 1970-78; past chmn. protection open space task force Met. Open Space Adv. Bd. Served with U.S. Army, 1946-48. Mem. Am., Minn. (chmn. ins. com. 1964-65), Fed. (pres. Minn. chpt.), Ramsey County (ethics com. 1978—) bar assns., Assn. Life Ins. Counsel, Am. Soc. Corporate Secs., Am. Life Conv. (v.p. Minn. chpt. 1969-71), Am. Judicature Soc., Corp. Counsel Assn. Minn. (dir., pres.). Lutheran (chmn. bd. trustees). Club: Minnesota (St. Paul). Home: 3065 Klondike Ave N Lake Elmo MN 55042 Office: 385 Washington St Saint Paul MN 55102

SHERWIN, CHALMERS WILLIAM, physicist; b. Two Harbors, Minn., Nov. 27, 1916; s. Louis Blanchard and Georgia (Polhemus) Sherwin B.S.; Wheaton (Ill.) Coll., 1937; Ph.D., U. Chgo., 1940; m. Irene Ackerman, Sept. 18, 1937; children—Margaret, Priscilla, Catherine, Louise, Louis, Julia, Susan. Research asst. U. Chgo., 1940-41; mem. staff Radiation Lab., Mass. Inst. Tech., 1941-45; asso. Columbia, 1946; from asst. prof. physics to prof. U. Ill., 1946-60; chief scientist USAF, 1954-55; asso. dir. Coordinated Scis. Lab, U. Ill., 1959-60; v.p., gen. mgr. labs. div. Aerospace Corp., El Segundo, Calif., 1960-63, trustee, 1960; dep. dir. def. research and engring. for research and tech. Dept. Def., Washington, 1963-66; dep. asst. sec. of commerce for sci. and tech. Dept. Commerce, Washington, 1966-68; dir. tech. evaluation and asst. dir. lab. Gulf Gen. Atomic Corp., San Diego, 1968-69; v.p., gen. mgr. spl. products Gen. Atomic Co., San Diego, 1970-79; v.p. Cerprobe Corp., Tempe, Ariz., 1979—. Mem. sci. adv. bd. USAF, 1956-63; bd. dirs. WEMA, 1973-76. Recipient Presdl. Certificate of Merit, 1947; Sci. award Air Force Assn., 1956. Fellow Am. Phys. Soc.; mem. Sigma Xi. Author: Introduction to Quantum Mechanics, 1959; Basic Concepts pf Physics, 1961. Home: 2117 Willowspring Pl Encinitas CA 92024 Office: Cerprobe Corp 2121 Priest Dr Tempe AZ 85282

SHERWIN, JAMES TERRY, lawyer; b. N.Y.C., Oct. 25, 1933; s. Oscar and Stella (Zins) S.; B.A., Columbia, 1953, LL.B. (Stone scholar), 1956; m. Judith Johnson, June 21, 1955; children—Miranda, Alison Dale, Galen Leigh. Admitted to N.Y. bar, 1956, U.S. Supreme Ct. bar, 1963; atty. with firm Kaye, Scholer, Fierman, Hays & Handler, N.Y.C., 1957-60; with GAF Corp., N.Y.C., 1960—, asso. counsel, gen. mgr. European ops., 1969-71, group v.p. photography, 1971-74, exec. v.p. fin. and adminstrn., 1974-78, exec. v.p. legal and investment services 1978—, also dir. Bd. dirs., v.p. Internat. Rescue Com.; bd. dirs. New Music for Young Ensembles. Served to lt. comdr. USCGR, 1956-57. Mem. Am. Bar Assn., Assn. Bar City N.Y., Am. Chess Found. (pres., dir.), Belgian-Am. C. of C. (dir.), Marshall (N.Y.) Chess Club (pres. 1967-69, gov.), Phi Beta Kappa. Club: Economic (N.Y.C.). U.S. intercollegiate chess champion, 1951-53, N.Y. State champion, 1951, U.S. speed champion, 1956-57, 59-60; internat. master. Home: 271 Central Park West New York NY 10024 Office: 140 W 51st St New York NY 10020

SHERWIN, JUDITH JOHNSON, poet, playwright, author; b. N.Y.C., Oct. 3, 1936; d. Edgar and Eleanor (Kraus) Johnson; student Radcliffe Coll., 1954-55; B.A. cum laude, Barnard Coll., 1958; postgrad. (Woodrow Wilson fellow) Columbia, 1958-59; m. James T. Sherwin, June 21, 1955; children—Miranda, Alison Dale, Galen Leigh. Contbr. poetry and fiction to numerous publs.; readings, lectr. workshops univs., cultural instns., radio and TV; cons. N.Y. State Council on Arts, 1976, Poets and Writers, Inc., 1976-77. Recipient Acad. Am. Poets prize, 1958, Amy Loveman prize, 1958, Van Rensselaer prize, 1957, Yale Series Younger Poets prize, 1968, Playboy fiction prize, 1977. Poetry Soc. Am. fellow, 1964; Yaddo fellow, 1964; Rose fellow in fiction Aspen Writers Workshop, 1967. Mem. Poetry Soc. Am. (exec. bd. 1973-75, pres. 1975-78, chmn. exec. com. 1979-80), P.E.N., Authors Guild, Phi Beta Kappa. Author: Uranium Poems, 1968; (short stories) The Life of Riot, 1970; (poems) Impossible Buildings, 1973; The Town Scold, 1977, How The Dead Count, 1978, Transparencies, 1978, Dead's Good Company, 1978. Home: care Charlotte Sheedy Lit Agts 145 W 86th St New York NY 10024

SHERWOOD, AARON WILEY, educator; b. St. Louis, Jan. 13, 1915; s. Charles Vliet and Amelia Pauline (Kappler) S.; M.E., Rensselaer Poly. Inst., 1935; M.S., U. Md., 1943; m. Helene M. Gysin, 1944; children—Susan Helene, Mark Wiley. Exptl. engr. Wallace &

Tiernan Co., Inc., 1936-38; devel. engr. Asso. Engring., 1938-39; layout engr. Glenn L. Martin Co., 1939-40; instr. U. Md., 1940-44, aero. project engr. David Taylor Model Basin, 1944-46, prof. aerodynamics, 1946—, acting head dept. aero. engring., 1950-58, head dept. aerospace engring., 1958-67, prof. dept. aerospace engring., 1967-77; in charge wind tunnel lab. Glenn L. Martin Inst. Tech., 1946-55; owner, engring. cons. Aerolab. Fellow ASME (chmn. Washington sect. 1954-55); mem. Am. Inst. Aeros and Astronautics (sect. chmn.), Am. Soc. Engring. Edn., Sigma Xi, Tau Beta Pi, Phi Kappa Phi, Phi Kappa Tau. Author: Aerodynamics, 1946. Home: 3411 Chatham Rd Hyattsville MD 20783 Office: Aerolab 9580 Washington Blvd Laurel MD 20810. *Instead of carefully planned progress toward long-term fixed goals, I advocate frequent modifications of both goals and access routes according to current circumstances. One should follow his interests, tempered only by the needs of his associates and by firm ethical standards — a sort of intelligent muddling along.*

SHERWOOD, ARTHUR MURRAY, lawyer; b. Portland, Oreg., Dec. 4, 1913; s. Arthur Murray and Evelyn (Wilson) S.; grad. Milton Acad., 1932; B.S., Harvard U., 1936; J.D., Columbia, 1939; m. Marjorie F. Catron, Dec. 27, 1947; children—Philip T., Thomas C., Evelyn W. Admitted to N.Y. bar, 1940, N.J. bar, 1972; asso. atty. firm Shearman & Sterling, N.Y.C., 1939-41, 46-54; counsel law dept. Mobil Oil Corp., N.Y.C., 1954-55, asst. sec., 1955, sec., 1956-72; asso. atty. Smith, Stratton, Wise & Heher, Princeton, N.J., 1972—. Bd. visitors Columbia U. Sch. Law, 1963-77, Woodrow Wilson vis. fellow, 1974-75. Served from pvt. to lt. col. U.S. Army, 1941-46; asst. chief staff G-1, 2d Inf. Div., 1944-45. Decorated Legion of Merit, Bronze Star; Croix de Guerre with palm (France); Mil. Cross (Czechoslovakia). Clubs: Fly (Cambridge, Mass.); Nassau (Princeton, N.J.). Home: 19 Cleveland Ln Princeton NJ 08540 Office: 1 Palmer Sq Princeton NJ 08540

SHERWOOD, BERNATH PARDEE, JR., banker; b. Grand Haven, Mich., Oct. 7, 1907; s. Bernath Pardee and Gertrude (Miller) S.; A.B., U. Mich., 1929; m. Elizabeth Krause, Oct. 13, 1934 (dec. Apr. 1976); children—Bernath Pardee III, Peter Krause; m. 2d, Helene N. Dodd, Feb. 18, 1977. With Security First Bank & Trust Co., and predecessor, Grand Haven, 1929—, cashier, 1936-47, pres., 1947-72, chmn. bd., 1972—. treas., dir. Mich. Plastic Products, Inc., 1946-72, Grand Haven; dir. Fed. Res. Bank, Chgo., Detroit br., 1966-71; chmn. bd. Pacesetter Fin. Corp., 1973-76, dir., 1972-77; dir. JSJ Corp., Grand Haven. Pres. Tri Cities Indsl. Fund, Grand Haven, 1961- 66; campaign chmn. Tri Cities Community Fund, 1949. Trustee Mich. Heart Assn., 1961-67, Citizens Research Council Mich., 1962—. Mem. Mich. Bankers Assn. (pres. 1952-53). Presbyn. (elder, trustee). Rotarian (pres. Grand Haven 1944-45). Clubs: Spring Lake (Mich.) Country; Peninsular, University (Grand Rapids, Mich.). Home: 18003 Fruitport Rd Spring Lake MI 49456 Office: Security First Bank & Trust Co Grand Haven MI 49417. *Always seek the truth. Give quality service or build a quality product and you will always have business if there is any. Whether the customer is large or small make them feel important and treat them alike.*

SHERWOOD, BETTE WILSON, artist, lectr.; b. Sheffield, Ala., Nov. 1, 1920; d. Hardison S. and Jennis M. (Gaut) Wilson; grad. Miss. Synodical Jr. Coll., M.S., 1940; student Corcoran Sch. of Art, 1939-40, Art Inst. Chgo., 1940-43; m. Sidney James Sherwood, June 2, 1945; children—Bette Anne, Sidney James III. Jr. engr. TVA, Sheffield, Ala., 1941; photographer, reporter Reynolds Aluminum Co., Listerhill, Ala., 1942-45; one man shows at Miss. Synodical Coll., 1937, Heath & Brown Gallery, Houston, 1968, Lynn Kottler Galleries, N.Y.C., also Houston Oaks Hotel; exhibited in group shows at Nat. League Am. Pen Women, Art League Houston, Briar Club, Houston, Unitarian Fellowship Hall, numerous others; represented in permanent collections at River Oaks Bank & Trust, Kirby at San Filepe, numerous others; lectr. art and poetry Sam Houston Book Store, 1972, Galleria, Houston, 1972, Jr. League Houston, 1973, Lakeside Country Club, 1974, numerous others; judge numerous art shows, 1967—. Fine arts dir. Found. for Children, Houston Med. Center, 1971—. Recipient numerous awards including 2d and 3d pl. Nat. League Show, Houston, 1968, Best in Show, 1969, 2d and 3d pl., 1975; citation city of Houston and Bicentennial Commn. Mem. Nat. League of Am. Pen Women (founder meml. br. 1970, state bi-centennial chmn. 1974—, Best of Show in Portraiture award 1970). Mem. Am. Security Council (nat. adv. bd.), Visual Arts and Galleries Assn., Internat. Soc. Artists, Mus. Fine Arts, Houston Ballet Soc., Nat. Hist. Soc. Republican. Mem. Berachah Ch. Address: 9215 Bronco Houston TX 77055

SHERWOOD, DONALD, investment exec.; b. Colville, Wash., Sept. 29, 1901; s. Edward and Anna (Cameron) S.; B.S., Whitman Coll., 1922, LL.D., 1962: m. Virginia Kelly, Dec. 7, 1929; children—Gene Sherwood, Claire (dec.). With stock, traffic depts., also dist. auditor Standard Oil Co. of Calif., 1922-29; ins. and investment salesman, 1929-32; pres., dir. Sherwood & Roberts, Inc. (became unit Equitable Savs. & Loan, Portland, Oreg. 1971), Walla Walla, Wash., 1932-69, chmn. finance com., dir., 1969—; treas. Walla Walla Union-Bull., Inc., 1932-45, v.p., dir., 1945-71, pres., 1951-71, pub., 1962-71, pub. emeritus, 1971—; v.p., dir., Walla Walla Canning Co., 1945-51, pres. 1951-61; dir. Rogers-Walla Walla Inc., 1961—; dir., v.p. Church Grape Juice Co., Kennewick, 1932-48, pres., 1948-53, pres. successor firm Pioneer Investment Co., 1953—; pres. Gen. Credit Co., Columbia Center Corp.; chmn. Am. Sign & Indicator Corp., Spokane, Wash.; dir. emeritus Pacific Power & Light Co. Mem. finance com., pres. emeritus bd. trustees Whitman Coll.; pres. Walla Walla Found., Inc. Served with USN, 1943-45, comdr. Res. ret. Mem. C. of C. (pres. 1937), Phi Delta Theta. Republican. Conglist. Mason (32, Shriner), Rotarian. Clubs: Rainier, Balboa, Country, Wash. Athletic. Home: 1107 Alvarado Terr Walla Walla WA 99362 Office: 106 Second Ave Walla Walla WA 99362

SHERWOOD, FOSTER HALL, educator; b. Golden, Colo., Apr. 6, 1916; s. George Eulas Foster and Mabel (Hall) S.; A.B., U. Calif. at Los Angeles, 1938, Ph.D 1941; LL.D., Colgate U. 1963; m. June Elizabeth Hallberg, July 10, 1940 (div. 1961); children—Foster Hallberg, John. m. 2d, Georgia Gage, 1962; 1 child, Gage D. Research fellow Brookings Instn., 1941-42; adminstrv. officer U.S. Govt., 1942-43; instr. polit. sci. U. Calif. at Los Angeles 1943-45, asst. prof., 1945-50, asso. prof. polit. sci., 1950-56, prof., 1956—, chmn. dept. polit. sci., 1959-60, vice chmn. acad. senate, 1958-60, vice chancellor acad. affairs, 1960-63, vice chancellor, 1963-70, acad. cons. to pres., 1976—; sr. research fellow Fulbright Commn. Oxford (Eng.) U., 1949-50; vis. prof. Northwestern U., summer 1953; research fellow Rockefeller Found., Lincoln Inn, London, 1956-57. Commr. Western Interstate Commn. High Edn., 1959-68. Trustee Mt. St. Mary's Coll., Los Angeles, 1969—. Mem. Am. Assn. Internat. Law, Soc. Internat. and Comparative Law, Phi Beta Kappa. Author: (with C.G. Haines) The Supreme Court in American Government and Politics, 1835-1864, 1957. Contbr. articles to profl. jours. Home: Cul de Sac Sint Maarten Netherlands West Indies Office: U Calif Los Angeles CA 90024

SHERWOOD, LOUIS MAIER, endocrinologist; b. N.Y.C., Mar. 1, 1937; s. Arthur Joseph and Blanche (Burger) S.; A.B., Johns Hopkins U., 1957; M.D., Columbia U., 1961; m. Judith Brimberg, Mar. 27, 1966; children—Jennifer, Beth, Arieh David. Intern, Presbyn. Hosp., N.Y.C., 1961-62, asst. resident in medicine, 1962-63; clin. asso., research fellow Nat. Heart Inst., NIH, Bethesda, Md., 1963-66; NIH trainee endocrinology and metabolism Coll. Physicians and Surgeons, Columbia U., N.Y.C., 1966-68; asso. medicine Beth Israel Hosp. and Harvard Med. Sch., Boston, 1968-69; chief endocrinology Beth Israel Hosp., 1968-72; asst. prof. medicine Harvard U., 1969-71, asso. prof., 1971-72; physician in chief, chmn. dept. medicine Michael Reese Hosp. and Med. Center, Chgo., 1972—; prof. medicine div. biol. scis. and Pritzker Sch. Medicine, U. Chgo., 1972—; bd. dirs. Physicians and Surgeons Corp., Michael Reese Med. Center, 1973—, Barren Found., 1974—; Josiah Macy Jr. Found. fellow and vis. scientist Weizmann Inst., Israel, 1978-79. Trustee Michael Reese Med. Center, 1974-77. Served as surgeon USPHS, 1963-66. Diplomate Am. Bd. Internal Medicine (asso. mem. bd. on subcom. endocrinology and metabolism 1977—). Fellow A.C.P.; mem. AAAS, Am. Fedn. Clin. Research, Am. Inst. Chemists, Am. Soc. Biol. Chemists, Am. Soc. Clin. Investigation, Assn. Am. Physicians, Endocrine Soc., N.Y. Acad. Sci., Mass. Med. Soc., Central Soc. Clin. Research, Assn. Program Dirs. Internal Medicine (mem. council 1979—), Chgo. Soc. Internal Medicine, Phi Beta Kappa, Alpha Omega Alpha. Recipient Joseph Mather Smith prize for outstanding alumni research Coll. Physicians and Surgeons, Columbia U., 1972; Sr. Class Teaching award U. Chgo., 1976, 77. Editor: Beth Israel seminars New Eng. Jour. Medicine, 1968-71; editorial bd. Endocrinology, 1969-73; asso. editor Metabolism, 1970—, Gen. Medicine B Study Sect., NIH, 1975-79; editorial bd. Yr. in Endocrinology, 1976—, Calcified Tissue Internat., 1978—, Internal Medicine Alert, 1979—. Contbr. numerous articles on endocrinology, protein hormones, calcium metabolism and ectopic proteins to jours. Office: Michael Reese Hospital and Medical Center 29th St and Ellis Ave Chicago IL 60616. *To be a successful administrator, you must have the willingness to surround yourself with outstanding individuals (even smarter than yourself), to give them your support and to watch them grow. By supporting and enjoying the growth of those around you, you grow yourself and also have some free time to pursue your own intellectual interests.*

SHERWOOD, RICHARD EDWIN, lawyer; b. Los Angeles, July 24, 1928; s. Benjamin Berkley and Jennie (Goldeen) S.; B.A., Yale U., 1949; LL.B., Harvard U., 1952, Sheldon traveling fellow, 1953-54; m. Dorothy Lipsey Romonek, July 25, 1953; children—Elizabeth Deirdre, Benjamin Berkley II. Admitted to Calif. bar, 1953; law clk. to Justice Felix Frankfurter, U.S. Supreme Ct., 1954-55; with firm O'Melveny & Myers, Los Angeles, 1955—, partner, 1964—. Mem. Calif. Little Hoover Commn., 1961-67, White House Task Force Antitrust Policy, 1967-68. Pres. bd. trustees Los Angeles County Mus. Art, 1974-78, chmn., 1978—; chmn. Planned Parenthood/World Population Los Angeles, 1971-75; chmn. Los Angeles chpt. Am. Jewish Com., 1972-75, nat. v.p., 1977—; mem. vis. com. Harvard Law Sch., 1969-75, Harvard Art Museums, 1975—; pres. Partnership for The Arts in Calif. Inc., 1975-79; trustee Asia Soc., 1978—. Served to 2d lt. USAF, 1952-53. Mem. Los Angeles County Bar Assn. (chmn. human rights sect. 1970-71). Home: 803 N Elm Dr Beverly Hills CA 90210 Office: 611 W 6th St Los Angeles CA 90017

SHERWOOD, ROBERT SPENCER, machine tool mfg. co. exec.; b. Manhattan, Kans., Apr. 12, 1915; s. Ross M. and Ida L. (Spencer) S.; B.S., Tex. A. and M. Coll., 1936; M.S., Iowa State U., 1939; m. Marian Susan Dougan, June 4, 1941; children—Ross, Jane, Scott. Asst. dir. corp. research Worthington Corp., Harrison, N.J., 1951-55, mgr. engring., steam turbine div., 1955-61, gen. mgr. advanced products div., 1962-63; sr. v.p. Gleason Works, Rochester, N.Y., 1963—, dir., 1971—; dir. Alliance Tool Corp. Mem. City Planning Commn. Rochester, 1975—; chmn. exec. com. Center for Govtl. Research, 1975—; trustee Alfred U. Served with C.E., U.S. Army, 1941-46. Fellow ASME; mem. Am. Mgmt. Assn., NAM, Sigma Alpha Epsilon, Tau Beta Pi, Pi Tau Sigma. Republican. Club: Genesee Valley. Editor machine design sect. McGraw Hill Ency. of Sci. and Tech., 1960-63. Home: 1881 Highland Ave Rochester NY 14618 Office: Gleason Works 1000 University Ave Rochester NY 14692

SHERWOOD, SIDNEY, former UN adviser; b. Balt., May 10, 1901; s. Sidney and Mary A. (Beattie) S.; grad. Storm King Sch., Cornwall-on-Hudson, N.Y. 1919; A.B., Princeton U., 1923; m. Olita Schlichten, May 28, 1927. With Bankers Trust Co., N.Y.C. and Phelps Dodge Corp., Bisbee, Ariz., 1923-32, Farm Credit Adminstrn., U.S. Treasury Dept. 1933-35; supr. alcohol tax unit, also co-ordinator Treasury enforcement agys., New Eng., 1933-40; asst. sec. adv. commn. Council of Nat. Def., asst. liaison officer Office for Emergency Mgmt., Exec. Office of Pres., dir. Nat. Policy Com., exec. officer Div. of Industry Operations, WPB, Combined Prodn. and Resources Bd. and cons. on fgn. programs Office of War Moblzn., White House, spl. asst. to adminstr. Fgn. Econ. Adminstrn., 1940-45; sec. Export-Import Bank of Washington and chief of econ. survey missions to Afghanistan, Saudi Arabia and Israel 1945-59; econ. attache Am. embassy, New Delhi, India, representing Export-Import Bank, and loan adviser to U.S. AID Mission in India, 1959-64; Am. investment adviser Indian Investment Centre, and U.S. adviser The Central Bank of India, Ltd., cons. to Govt. of Ceylon, cons. to UNIDO, 1964-69; sr. financial adviser UN Devel. Program, 1969-72. Bd. govs. Middle East Inst.; Mem. Washington Inst. Fgn. Affairs, Am. Soc. for Internat. Devel., Asia Soc. Club: Cosmos (Washington) Address: 3320 Runnymede Pl NW Washington DC 20015

SHERWOOD, THORNE, architect; b. Montclair, N.J., Dec. 3, 1910, s. William Carman and Lida Crawford (Ramsey) S; A.B., Williams Coll., 1932; M. Arch., Columbia, 1936, Perkins Boring travelling fellow study in Europe, 1937-39; m. Nancy Davol Chapman, June 23, 1934; children—Thorne, Nancy Frost (Mrs. C.M. O'Hearn, Jr.), Michael. Founding partner Sherwood Mills & Smith, Stamford, Conn., N.Y.C., New Canaan, Conn., 1946-69; works include Ramapo Regional High Sch. (awards AIA, Am. Assn. Sch. Architects), Franklin Lakes, N.J., Rehab. Center of S.E. Conn., Stamford, Dorr Oliver exec. hdqrs. (Boston Fine Arts Festival medal 1957), Olmsted Hall, Vassar Coll., Mut. Ins. Co. (1st honor award AIA 1960), also pub. and private schs., coll. and univ. bldgs., residential, indsl., comml. and religious architecture U.S. and abroad; now engaged in individual archtl. practice. Former park commr., Stamford; mem. planning bd., chmn. joint com. parks and recreational facilities, Stamford; mem. pub. adv. panel on archtl. services, region 1-Boston, Gen. Services Adminstrn., 1967-69. Bd. dirs. Stamford Mus. and Nature Center. Served as lt. USNR, 1942-45. Fellow A.I.A.; mem. Nat. Inst. Archtl. Edn. (past bd. trustees), Archtl. League N.Y., Municipal Art. Soc., Conn. Soc. Architects, Columbia U. Fedn. Alumni Assos. (past dir.), Stamford Good Govt. Assn. (past dir.), Soc. Colonial Wars, Alumni Assn. Columbia Sch. Architecture (pres. 1957-59), N.A.D. (asso.), Alpha Delta Phi. Episcopalian. Clubs: Century Assn. (N.Y.C.). Address: West Morris Rd Morris CT 06763 winter PO Box 52 Gov Harbour Round House Eleuthera Bahamas

SHESTACK, ALAN, museum ofcl.; b. N.Y.C., June 23, 1938; s. David and Sylvia P. (Saffran) S.; B.A., Wesleyan U., 1961, D.F.A. (hon.), 1978; M.A. (Woodrow Wilson fellow), Harvard U., 1963; m. Nancy Jane Davidson, Sept. 24, 1967. Mus. curator graphic art Nat. Gallery Art, Washington, 1965-67; asso. curator prints and drawings Yale Art Gallery, New Haven, 1967-68, curator prints and drawings, 1968-71, dir., 1971—; adj. prof. history of art Yale U., 1971—; mem. adv. com. Art Mus., Princeton, 1972-76; mus. panel Nat. Endowment for the Arts, 1974-77; mem. com. prints and illustrated books Mus. Modern Art, N.Y.C., 1972—. David E. Finley fellow, 1963-65. Mem. Print Council Am. (dir., v.p. 1970-71), Coll. Art Assn. (dir. 1972-76), Am. Assn. Museums, Assn. Art Mus. Dirs., Alpha Delta Phi, Phi Beta Kappa. Author: Fifteenth Century Engravings of Northern Europe, 1967; The Engravings of Martin Schongauer, 1968; Master LCZ and Master WB; 1971; Exhibitions Organized and Catalogued: Master E.S., 1967; The Danube School. 1969. Contbr. articles to profl. jours. Home: 191 Bishop St New Haven CT 06511 Office: Box 2006 Yale Station New Haven CT 06520

SHESTACK, JEROME JOSEPH, lawyer; b. Atlantic City, Feb. 11, 1925; s. Isidore and Olga (Shankman) S.; A.B., U. Pa., 1944; LL.B., Harvard, 1949; m. Marciarose Schleifer, Jan. 28, 1951; children—Jonathan Michael, Jennifer. Teaching fellow Northwestern Law Sch., Evanston, Ill., 1949-50; asst. prof. law, faculty editor La. State Law Sch., Baton Rouge, 1950-52; dep. city solicitor, City of Phila., 1952, 1st dep. solicitor, 1953-55; adj. prof. law U. Pa. Law Sch., Phila., 1953, Rutgers U. Law Sch., Camden, N.J., 1953-60; partner law firm Schnader, Harrison, Segal and Lewis, Phila., 1956—. Mem. Southeast Pa. Transit Authority, 1965-72; mem. nat. adv. com. on legal services OEO, 1965-72; bd. dirs., mem. exec. com. Lawyers Com. for Civil Rights Under Law, Washington, 1963—; U.S. rep. UN Human Rights Commn. Mem. fin. com. Democratic Nat. Com., 1975—; bd. govs. Hebrew U., Jerusalem, Israel, 1967—; bd. dirs. Am. sect. Internat. Commn. Jurists, N.Y.C., 1973—; bd. overseers Gratz Coll., Phila., 1965—. Served to lt. (j.g.) USNR, 1943-46; PTO. Mem. Fedn. Jewish Agys. (dir. 1962—), Jewish Theol. Soc. Am. (bd. overseers 1968—), Jewish Publ. Soc. (pres. 1973-75, trustee 1955—), Nat. Legal Aid and Defender Assn. (dir., mem. exec. com. 1970—), Internat. League Human Rights (pres. 1971—), Phila. (chmn. com. local govt. 1968-69), Am. (chmn. sect. on individual rights and responsibilities 1970-71, mem. ho. of dels. 1971-73, 77—, chmn. commn. mentally disabled 1973-76, chmn. standing com. on legal aid 1978—) bar assns., Am. Law Inst., Order of Coif. Jewish. Clubs: Harvard, Varsity (Phila.). Home: 2201 The Parkway Philadelphia PA 19130 Office: Packard Bldg 15th and Chestnut Sts Philadelphia PA 19102

SHESTACK, MELVIN BERNARD, editor, found. exec., author; b. Bklyn., Aug. 18, 1931; s. David and Sylvia Pearl (Saffran) S.; A.B., U. So. Calif., 1953; postgrad. U. Rochester, N.Y. U., New Sch. Social Research; m. Jessica Gifford, Feb. 13, 1965; 1 dau., Victoria J.; 1 dau. by previous marriage, Lisa F. Staff producer CBS-TV News, 1967-69; asso. editor Sat. Eve. Post, 1969-70; asso. producer sta. WOR-TV, 1970; exec. editor True mag., N.Y.C., 1971-75, editor-in-chief, 1975; editor In The Know mag., N.Y.C., 1975—; exec. dir. Ponca Inst. Am. Studies, 1976; exec. editor Antelope Classics, Empire Edits., 1977—; producer, writer documentary The Forgotten American, 1967. Served with AUS, 1953-55. Recipient Brown-Nickerson award for best religious radio program, 1967. Mem. Pi Lambda Phi. Author: The Country Music Encyclopedia, 1974; co-author: (filmscript) The Soul, 1978; (mystery) The Soho Murders; Secrets of Success, 1980; also articles. Home: 4 Great Jones St New York NY 10012 Office: Gallery Press 800 2d Ave New York NY 10012

SHETH, JAGDISH NANCHAND, educator; b. Rangoon, Burma, Sept. 3, 1938; came to U.S., 1961, naturalized, 1975; s. Nanchand Jivraj and Diwaliben (Nanchand) S.; B.Com. with honors, U. Madras, 1960; M.B.A., U. Pitts., 1962; Ph.D., 1966; m. Madhuri Ratilal Shah, Dec. 22, 1962; children—Reshma J., Raju J. Research asso., asst. prof. Grad. Sch. Bus., Columbia U., 1963-65; asst. prof. M.I.T., 1965-66; asst. prof. Columbia U., 1966-69; vis. prof. Indian Inst. Mgmt., Calcutta, 1968; vis. lectr. Internat. Mktg. Inst., Harvard U., 1969; asso. prof. bus. adminstrn. U. Ill., Urbana, 1969-71, acting head dept., 1970-72, prof. and research prof., 1971-73, I.B.A. Disting. prof. and research prof., 1973-79, Walter H. Stellner Disting. prof. and research prof., 1979—; Albert Frey vis. prof. mktg. U. Pitts., 1974; condr. seminars for industry and govt.; cons. to industry. Recipient gold medal for 1st standing pub. exams., India, 1960; Mgmt. Program for Execs. fellow, S & H Green Stamps fellow, 1963-64. Fellow Am. Psychol. Assn.; mem. Am. Mktg. Assn., Am. Statis. Assn., Am. Assn. Decision Scis., Assn. Consumer Research, Acad. Internat. Bus., Acad. Mktg. Sci. Author: (with John A. Howard) The Theory of Buyer Behavior, 1969; (with S.P. Sethi) Multinational Business Operations: Advanced Readings, 4 vols., 1973; (with A. Woodside and P. Bennett) Consumer and Industrial Buying Behavior, 1977; editor: Models of Buyer Behavior, 1974; (with Peter L. Wright) Marketing Analysis for Societal Problems, 1974; Multivariable Methods for Market and Survey Research, 1977; series editor Research in Marketing, 1978—; contbr. articles profl. jours. Home: 414 Brookens Dr Urbana IL 61801

SHETTERLY, ROBERT BROWNE, food and household products mfg. co. exec.; b. Corning, N.Y., May 28, 1915; s. Fred F. and Izora A. (Burns) S.; B.A., U. Rochester, 1936; m. Phyllis E. Galloway, June 20, 1942; children—John A., Robert Browne, Thomas H. With Procter & Gamble Co., Cin., 1936-68, in advt. dept., 1936-55, advt. mgr. Food Products div., 1955-60, asso. mgr. div., 1960-61, mgr., 1961-65, v.p., gen. mgr. Clorox Co. div., Oakland, Calif., 1965-68, pres., 1968—; pres., dir. Clorox Co., 1968-78, chmn., 1979—; dir. Crocker Nat. Bank. Mem. New Oakland Com.; vice chmn. San Francisco Bay Area Council. Served to capt. USAAF, 1942-46. Mem. Grocery Mfrs. Am. (dir.), Psi Upsilon. Republican. Episcopalian. Clubs: Claremont (Calif.) Country; Pacific Union, Stock Exchange (San Francisco); Sankaty Head Golf (Nantucket, Mass.). Home: 26 Via Hermosa Orinda CA 94563 Office: 1221 Broadway Oakland CA 94612

SHETTLES, LANDRUM BREWER, obstetrician-gynecologist; b. Pontotoc, Miss., Nov. 21, 1909; s. Basil Manly and Sue (Mounce) S.; B.A., Miss. Coll., 1933, D.Sc. (hon.), 1966; M.S., (fellow 1933-34), U. N.M., 1934; Ph.D., Johns Hopkins, 1937, M.D., 1943; m. Priscilla Elinor Schmidt, Dec. 18, 1948; children—Susan Flora, Frances Louise, Lana Brewer, Landrum Brewer, David Ernest, Harold Manly and Alice Annmarie (twins). Instr. biology Miss. Coll., 1932-33, biologist U.S. Bur. Fisheries, 1934; instr. biology Johns Hopkins, 1934-37, research fellow, 1937-38; research fellow Nat. Com. Maternal Health, N.Y.C., 1938-43; intern Johns Hopkins Hosp., 1943-44; resident Columbia-Presbyn. Med. Center, N.Y.C., 1947-51, attending obstetrician-gynecologist, 1951-73; attending obstetrician-gynecologist Doctors, Polyclinic and Flower-Fifth Av hosps., N.Y.C., 1974-75, chief obstetrician-gynecologist Gifford Meml. Hosp., Randolph, Vt., 1975—. Markle Found. scholar Columbia Coll. Phys. and Surg., 1951-56; asso. prof. clin. obstetrics-gynecology Coll. Phys. and Surg. Columbia, 1951-73; individual practice, N.Y.C., 1951-75; dir. research N.Y. Fertility Research Found., 1974-75; Anglo-Am. lectr. Royal Coll. Obstetricians and Gynecologists, London, Eng., 1959. Research cons. Office Naval Research, Am. embassy, London, 1951-52. Served to maj., M.C., AUS, 1944-46. Recipient Ortho medal and award Am. Soc. Study Fertility, Sterility and Allied Subjects, 1960. Diplomate Am. Bd. Obstetrics and Gynecology, N. Am. sect. obstetrics and gynecology Pan Am. Med. Assn. Fellow Am. Coll. Obstetricians and Gynecologists, A.C.S., A.A.A.S., World Med. Assn., Royal Soc. of Health (London), Royal Soc. Medicine (London); mem. Am. Soc. Zoologists, Am. Physiol. Soc., Soc. Exptl. Biology and Medicine, Vt.

Med. Sco., Soc. U. Gynecologists, Harvey Soc., Am., N.Y. State, N.Y. County med. assns., Phi Beta Kappa, Sigma Xi, Omicron Delta Kappa, Gamma Alpha. Author: Ovum Humanum, 1960; Your Baby's Sex: Now You Can Choose, 1970; From Conception to Birth, 1971; Choose Your Baby's Sex, 1976; also numerous articles. Spl. research fisheries biology, physiology, human reprodn., fertility and sterility, hemorrhagic disease in newborn infants, sperm biology; discovered, identified male and female producing sperms. Home: 9 Highland Ave Randolph VT 05060 Office: Gifford Meml Hosp 44 S Main St Randolph VT 05060

SHEVENELL, RAYMOND HENRY, coll. dean; b. Rollinsford, N.H., Apr. 20, 1908; s. Henry Israel and Helena (Theoret) S.; came to Can., 1935; B.L., U. Montreal, 1927; B.A., U. Ottawa (Can.), 1929, Ph.L., 1931, M.A., 1946, Ph.D., 1949; D.Ed, Sherbrooke U. (Can.), 1967; D.Sc.Ps., Moncton U., 1976. Joined Order of Mary Immaculate, 1932, ordained priest Roman Catholic Ch., 1934; tchr. high sch. Ottawa, Ont., 1935-38; founder, dir. Inst. Psychology, Ottawa, 1941, Guidance Center, Ottawa, 1942-53, Child Guidance Clinic, Ottawa, 1953—; mem. faculty U. Ottawa, 1938—, prof. psychology, 1955—, dean Faculty Psychology and Edn., 1965-73. Diplomate Am. Bd. Examiners in Profl. Psychology; registered psychologist, Ont. Fellow Canadian Psychol. Assn. (dir. 1950-54); mem. Am. Psychol. Assn., A.A.A.S., Am. Cath. Psychol. Assn., Am. Edn. Research Assn., Nat. Vocational Guidance Assn., Psychologists in Advancement of Psychotherapy. Author: Research and Theses, 1951. Home: 305 Nelson Ave Ottawa ON K1N 7S5 Canada

SHEVIN, ROBERT LEWIS, lawyer; b. Miami, Fla., Jan. 19, 1934; s. Aaron and Pauline (Bott) S.; B.A., U. Fla., 1955; J.D. magna cum laude, U. Miami, 1957; m. Myrna Bressack, Jan. 27, 1957; children—Laura Dawn, Hilary Beth, Harry Alan. Admitted to Fla. bar, 1957; partner firm Shevin, Goodman & Holtzman, 1957-67; partner firm Shevin & Shevin, Fla., 1967-70; mem. Fla. House of Reps., 1963-65; mem. Fla. State Senate, 1965-70; atty. gen. State of Fla., 1970-79; partner firm Sparber, Shevin, Rosen, Shapo & Heilbronner, Miami, 1979—; city atty. City of Miami Beach (Fla.), 1979—; chmn. Fla. Legislature's Select Com. to Investigate Organized Crime and Law Enforcement; chmn. Intermin Com. on Crime and Law Enforcement; chmn. Legislature's Interim Study Com. on Urban Affairs, chmn. Legislature's Interim Study Com. on Urban Affairs, chmn. subcom. on jurisprudence; chmn. Help Stop Crime Program subcom. Gov.'s Council on Criminal Justice. Chmn., Dade County Housing Fin. Authority, 1979—. Recipient Allen Morris award, 1969; named One of 10 Most Valuable Members of Fla. Legislature, Capital Press Corps, 1965; recipient Furtherance of Justice award Fla. Pros. Attys. Assn.; Conservationist of Year awards Fla. Wildlife Fedn., 1973, Audubon Soc., 1974; Furtherance of Justice award Fla. Pros. Attys. Assn., 1974; Peace award State of Israel, 1977. Mem. Am. Bar Assn., Fla. Bar, Jud. Council Fla., Nat. Assn. Attys. Gen. (chmn. So. region). Democrat. Jewish (trustee). Club: Sertoma. Home: 4745 SW 80th St Miami FL 33143 Office: 30th Floor 1st Fed Bldg One SE 3d Ave Miami FL 33131

SHEWALTER, CHARLES ELLIS, banker; b. Butler, Pa., Jan. 31, 1930; s. Charles Ellis and Helen (Green) S.; B.S., U. Notre Dame, 1951; postgrad. Northwestern U., 1955- 56; m. Mary Bickel, June 20, 1953; children—Anne, Catherine, James, Ellen, Mary, John, William, Thomas. Audit mgr. Arthur Andersen & Co., Chgo., 1955-65; controller Commerce Trust Co., Kansas City, Mo., 1965—, sr. v.p., 1966—; v.p., treas. Commerce Bankshares, Inc.; v.p., comptroller First Banc Group Ohio; v.p. City Nat. Bank & Trust Co., Columbus, O. Treas., Park Forst (Ill.) Community Chest, 1961-62. Republican precinct capt. Rich Twp., Ill., 1964-65. Trustee Park Forest Pub. Library, 1959-65, pres. bd., 1963-65. Served with USNR, 1952-55. Mem. Civil War Round Table, Mo., Ohio socs. C.P.A.'s, Am. Inst. C.P.A.'s, Financial Execs. Inst. Roman Catholic. Home: 4080 Fairfax Dr Upper Arlington OH 43220 Office: 100 E Broad St Columbus OH 43215

SHEWMAKE, CHARLES BURREL, constrn. co. exec.; b. Clarke County, Ala., May 10, 1916; s. Thomas J. and Martha C. S.; student pub. schs., Ala.; children—Sherrel Jane, Charles Burrel. With Algernon Blair, Inc., Montgomery, Ala., 1936—, exec. v.p., 1952-60, pres., owner, 1960—; dir. Union Bank & Trust Co., Montgomery, Tide Constrn. Co., Algernon Blair Indsl. Contractors, Inc. Pres. bd. Met. Montgomery YMCA. Clubs: Montgomery Country, Shriners. Address: 1 Blair Pl Montgomery AL 36116

SHEWMAKER, RUSSELL NEWTON, govt. ofcl.; b. Washington, Mar. 15, 1915; s. Ulysses S. and Adelle (Weddington) S.; J.D., George Washington U., 1941, A.B., 1942; m. Ruth Lenore Horn, Aug. 3, 1940; children—John Russell, Wayne Allan, Dale Pryor, Diane Ruth, Roger Brett. With Bur. Customs, Treasury Dept., 1935- 51; admitted to D.C. bar, 1940, since practiced in Washington; atty. U.S. Tariff Commn., 1951-56, asst. gen. counsel, 1956-63, gen. counsel, 1964—. Drafted Tariff Classsification Act, 1962; organized, drafted Tariff Schedules of U.S., 1963; liaison officer, cons. House Ways and Means Com. and Senate Finance Com. on tariff and trade matters, 1964-76; U.S. rep. to EEC on tariff nomenclature, Brussels, 1963, Geneva, 1964; del. Customs Cooperation Council, Brussels, 1964-65; mem. U.S. delegation GATT, Geneva, 1967. Cubmaster, committeeman Nat. Capital area council Boy Scouts Am., 1950-57; legislative chmn. D.C. Congress Parents and Tchrs., 1955-58. Recipient letters of commendation Pres. Kennedy, 1962. Mem. Fed., D.C. bar assns., Phi Eta Sigma, Phi Delta Phi. Home: 5857 Nebraska Ave NW Washington DC 20015 Office: US Internat Trade Commn 8th and E Sts Washington DC 20436. *A public law officer can serve no master other than the public trust. To that end, I have given freely of my time and energies—that I might, through experience, gain knowledge of my chosen profession, and what is fair and just among an honorable people; that I might, to the best of my ability and in good conscience, advise and counsel others with respect thereto, forthrightly, and without equivocation or compromise of my obligations as a public servant.*

SHEWMON, PAUL GRIFFITH, metall. engr., educator; b. Rochelle, Ill., Apr. 18, 1930; s. Joe Allen and Mildred Elizabeth (Griffith) S.; B.S. in Metall. Engring., U. Ill., 1952, M.S., Carnegie Mellon U., 1954, Ph.D., 1955; m. Dorothy E. Bond, Aug. 30, 1952; children—David A., Joan E. (dec.), Andrew B. Staff, Westinghouse Research Lab., Pitts., 1955-58; prof. metall. engring. Carnegie Mellon U., Pitts., 1958-67; asso. dir. metal div., Exptl. Breeder Reactor II Project, Argonne Nat. Lab., 1969-70, dir. material sci. div., 1971-73, dir. div. materials research NSF, 1973-75; prof., head dept. Ohio State U., 1976—; mem. adv. com. on reactor safeguards U.S. Nuclear Regulatory Commn., 1977—. Dow fellow, 1952-55, NSF sci. faculty fellow, 1963-64. Mem. Nat. Acad. Engring., Am. Soc. Metals, Am. Nuclear Soc., Am. Inst. Metall. Engring. (asso. editor trans., R. Raymond award 1959, Noble award 1959). Author: Diffusion in Metals, 1963; Phase Transformations, 1969. Home: 2477 Lytham Rd Columbus OH 43220 Office: 116 W 19th Ave Columbus OH 43210

SHICK, GEORGE BARTON, JR., naval officer; b. Trenton, N.J., Aug. 12; s. George Barton and Euphemia Duffis (Anderson) S.; B.S., U.S. Naval Acad., 1950; M.A. in Internat. Relations, George Washington U., 1970; m. Bernice Marie Milligan, June 3, 1950; children—George Barton, III, Beverly Ann, Mary Ann. Commd. ensign U.S. Navy, 1950, advanced through grades to rear adm., 1976; service in India, Japan and Eng.; communications officer Office Chief Naval Ops., 1970-71; comdg. officer U.S.S. Worden, 1971-73; mem. communications staff to comdr.-in-chief U.S. Naval Forces Europe, 1973-76; comdr. Naval Telecommunications Command, Washington, 1976—. Decorated Legion of Merit, Bronze Star, Meritorious Service medal. Mem. Armed Forces Communications Electronics Assn., U.S. Naval Acad. Alumni Assn., U.S. Naval Acad. Athletic Assn., U.S. Naval Inst. Episcopalian. Home: 3230 Sleepy Hollow Rd Falls Church VA 22042 Office: 4401 Massachusetts Ave Washington DC 23090

SHIDELER, EMERSON WAYNE, educator; b. Chgo., May 7, 1913; s. Noah M. and Hazel (Crull) S.; A.B., U. Pitts., 1937; B.D., Chgo. Theol. Sem., 1940; Ph.D., U. Chgo., 1948; student U. Manchester (Eng.), 1957-58; m. Mary Katharine McDermott, June 8, 1940. Ordained to ministry Ch. of Brethren, 1939, transferred to United Ch. Christ, 1945; 1940; pastor in Ch. of Brethren, 1940-45, Congl.-Christian Ch., 1945-46; asst. prof. philosophy Hamline U., 1947-48, Carleton Coll., 1948-50; mem. faculty Iowa State U., 1950—, prof. philosophy, 1963-71, chmn. dept., 1969-71, prof. emeritus, 1971—. Fulbright travel award, Taiwan, 1964; Iowa State U. Faculty Improvement leave, Japan, 1968-69. Mem. Am. Theol. Soc. (pres. Midwest div. 1963-64), Am. Acad. Religion, Am. Philos. Assn., AAUP, Phi Kappa Phi. Author: Believing and Knowing, 1966; also articles, revs. Home: Boulder Heights Boulder CO 80302

SHIDELER, JAMES HENRY, historian, educator; b. Oxford, Ohio, Dec. 10, 1914; s. William Henry and Katherine (Hoffman) S.; A.B., Miami U., Oxford, 1936; M.A., U. Calif. at Berkeley, 1938, Ph.D., 1945; m. Idella Pindell, June 24, 1941; children—Sarah, William, Katherine. Mem. faculty, U. Calif. at Davis, 1945—, prof. history, 1960—, chmn. dept., 1967-68, dir. Agrl. History Center, 1964—; vis. prof. U. Wis. at Madison, 1959-60; editor Agrl. History Jour., 1964—; cons. U.S. Dept. of Agriculture. Mem. Agrl. History Soc. (pres. 1972-73), Orgn. Am. Historians, Am. Hist. Assn., AAUP. Author: Farm Crisis, 1919-1923, 1957; also articles. Home: 210 E 8th St Davis CA 95616

SHIDEMAN, FREDERICK EARL, pharmacologist, educator; b. Albion, Mich., Oct. 16, 1915; s. George Washington and Mary Anne (Klein) S.; B.A., Albion Coll., 1936; Ph.D. (Wis. Alumni Research Found. research asst.), U. Wis., 1941, postdoctoral fellow, 1941-42; M.D., U. Mich., 1946; LL.D. (hon.), Yonsei U., 1978; m. Margaret Elizabeth Reiner, Aug. 12, 1939; children—Frederick C., Jeffrey R., Ethel M., Elizabeth M. Instr. U. Mich., 1943-47, asst. prof. pharmacology, 1947-49, asso. prof., 1949-52; prof. pharmacology and toxicology U. Wis., 1952-62, chmn. dept., 1954-62; prof. and head dept. pharmacology U. Minn., 1962—. Chmn. adv. com. abuse of depressant and stimulant drugs FDA, HEW, 1966-68; chmn. sci. adv. com. on drugs Bur. Narcotics and Dangerous Drugs, U.S. Dept. Justice, 1968-72; chmn. pharmacology and exptl. therapeutics study sect. NIH, 1960-65, mem. pharmacology and toxicolgy tng. com.; mem. com. Narcotic Addiction and Drug Abuse, NIMH, 1971-75; chmn. Pharmacology com. Nat. Bd. Med. Examiners, 1967-72; chmn. drug research bd. Nat. Acad. Scis.-NRC, 1972-76; mem. adv. com. on personnel for research Am. Cancer Soc., 1974—, chmn., 1976-78; vice pres., trustee U.S. Pharmacopeial Conv., 1975—; vice chmn. Nat. Council on Drugs, 1976-78, chmn., 1978—. Recipient travel award Am. Physiol. Soc. to XVIII Internat. Physiol. Congress, Copenhagen, Denmark, 1950. Fellow Royal Soc. Medicine; mem. Am. Soc. Pharmacology and Exptl. Therapeutics (pres. 1963-64), Soc. Exptl. Biology and Medicine, AAAS, Wis. Med. Soc. (hon.), Japanese, Peruvian (hon.) pharmacology socs., Korean Med. Assn. (hon.). Editor: Take As Directed; cons. editor: Am. Scientist. Contbr. articles to profl. jours. Home: 4503 Moorland Ave Minneapolis MN 55424

SHIELD, RICHARD THORPE, educator; b. Newcastle, Eng., July 9, 1929; s. Thomas and Hilda (Thorpe) S.; B.Sc., King's Coll., Durham (Eng.) U., 1949; Ph.D., 1952; m. Lois Ann Schmitt, Sept. 12, 1958; children—Thomas William, Margaret Ann. Research asso. Brown U., 1951-53, asst. prof. 1955-57, asso. prof., 1957-60, prof. applied math., 1960-65; sr. research fellow Ft. Halstead, Kent, Eng., 1953-55; prof. applied mechanics Calif. Inst. Tech., 1965-70; prof., head dept. theoretical and applied mechanics U. Ill., Urbana, 1970—; Alcoa vis. prof. U. Pitts., 1970-71. Guggenheim Meml. fellow, 1961-62. Fellow Am. Acad. Mechanics (sec. 1973-77, pres. 1977-78); mem. AAAS, ASME, Am. Soc. Engring. Edn., Soc. Engring. Sci., Assn. Chairmen Depts. Mechanics (v.p. 1976, pres. 1978—), Soc. Indsl. and Applied Math., Sigma Xi, Pi Tau Sigma. Co-editor Jour. Applied Math. and Physics, 1965—; editorial bd. SIAM Jour. Applied Math., 1968—, Jour. Elasticity, 1970—. Office: 216 Talbot Lab U Ill Urbana IL 61801

SHIELD, WILBUR LEE, JR., lawyer; b. Mathews Court House, Va., Feb. 1, 1913; s. Wilbur Lee and Daisy (Martin) S.; student Ohio State U., 1931-35; LL.B., Franklin U., 1937; J.D., Capital U., 1966; m. Virginia Ann Orr, June 20, 1936; children—Cynthia Ann (Mrs. Harold Bohmer), Ralph Philip. Admitted to Ohio bar, 1938, D.C. bar, 1975; practiced, Sidney, 1938-41; asst. atty. gen. Ohio, 1941-47; supt. ins. Ohio, 1947- 49; counsel Am. Life Conv., Chgo., 1949-52, asso. gen. counsel, 1952-58; v.p. Union Central Life Ins. Co., Cin., 1959-60; exec. v.p., gen. counsel Am. Life Conv., 1960-63, pres., 1963-72; pres., Am. Life Ins. Assn., 1973-75; of counsel Scribner, Hall, Thornburg & Thompson, Washington, 1975, Crabbe, Brown, Jones, Potts & Schmidt, Columbus, Ohio, 1976—. Trustee Griffith Found. Ins. Edn.; chmn., treas., mem. bd. govs. Internat. Ins. Hall Fame. Served with AUS, 1944-46. Mem. Assn. Life Ins. Counsel, Am., D.C., Ohio bar assns., Presbyterian. Republican. Clubs: Brookside Country (Columbus); Pass e Internat. Home: 1330 Carriage Rd Powell OH 43065

SHIELDS, ALEXANDER, fashion designer; b. San Francisco, Oct. 21, 1921; s. Henry Howard and Grace Champagne (Ste. Marie) S.; student Calif. Inst. Tech., 1936-38, Georgetown U. Sch. Fgn. Service, 1938-40; m. Aina Constant, Aug. 29, 1946; 1 dau., Zia Alexandra. Founder, pres. Alexander Shields, Inc., N.Y.C., 1948—. Mem. Ethics Com., Centre Island, Oyster Bay, N.Y.C.; mem. 1st panel Sheriff's Jury N.Y.C. Served to comdr. USNR, 1942-46. Recipient Coty Menswear award. Mem. SAR, Soc. War of 1812. Republican. Roman Catholic. Clubs: Met., 7th Regiment Tennis, Tennisport, Internat. Lawn Tennis. Office: 484 Park Ave New York NY 10022

SHIELDS, ALLEN LOWELL, mathematician, educator; b. N.Y.C., May 7, 1927; s. Thomas Arthur and Esther Julia (Lowell) S.; B.S., Coll. City N.Y., 1949; Ph.D., Mass. Inst. Tech., 1952; m. Joan Porter, Dec. 22, 1956 (separated); children—Katherine, Thomas, Jean. Instr. math. Tulane U., New Orleans, 1952-54, asst. prof., 1954-56; asst. prof. math. U. Mich., Ann Arbor, 1956-60, asso. prof., 1960-64, prof., 1964—. Served with inf. AUS, 1945-47. Mem. Am. Math. Soc., Math. Assn. Am. Office: Math Dept Univ Mich Ann Arbor MI 48109

SHIELDS, CHARLES DANIEL, physician; b. Buffalo, Feb. 18, 1910; s. Daniel L. and Elizabeth F. (McMahon) S.; student Canisius Coll., 1928-30; M.D., Georgetown U., 1934; M.P.H., Harvard, 1937. Rotating intern Sisters of Charity Hosps., Buffalo, 1934-35; commd. 1st lt., M.C., U.S. Army, 1935, served from capt. to col., 1941-54; asst. resident phys. medicine, rehab. Walter Reed Army Hosp., Washington, 1947-48, resident, 1948-49, sr. resident, 1949-50; chief phys. medicine service Brooke Army Hosp., Ft. Sam Houston, San Antonio, 1950-53; dir. dept. phys. medicine, rehab. Med. Field Service Sch., 1950-53; chief cons. phys. medicine Office Surg. Gen. U.S. Army, 1953-54; prof., chmn. dept. phys. medicine, and rehab. Georgetown U., 1954-66, asso. dean, 1956-58, exec. dir. Georgetown U. Hosp., 1961-66; prof., chmn. dept. phys. medicine Coll. Medicine, U. Vt., Burlington, 1966-69; cons. phys. medicine, rehab. VA Hosp., Washington, 1954—; cons. Trenton (N.J.) area VA, 1955—, nat. cons., mem. spl. med. adv. group VA, 1956-61; cons. Walter Reed Army Hosp., 1956-64; nat. med. adv. bd. Am. Rehab. Found., 1957-68. Recipient Presdl. Citation for aid physically handicapped, 1956. Diplomate Nat. Bd. Med. Examiners, Am. Bd. Phys. Medicine and Rehab. Mem. So. Med. Assn., Assn. Mil. Surgeons, Am. Congress Rehab. Medicine, Am. Acad. Phys. Medicine and Rehab., Am. Public Health Assn., Alpha Omega Alpha. Clubs: Cosmos, Army and Navy. (Washington). Contbr. articles to profl. jours. Address: 1500 Oak Ave Evanston IL 60201

SHIELDS, CLIFFORD DALE, petroleum co. exec.; b. Unionport, Ohio, Aug. 9, 1921; s. Walter E. and Mae (Johnston) S.; B.A., Mt. Union Coll., 1943; postgrad. Northwestern U., 1946-47; m. Betty E. Hatton, Aug. 22, 1945; children—Richard K., Kermit E., Diane E. With Standard Oil Co. (Ohio), Cleve., 1947—, mgr. controllers staff, 1962-63, asst. controller, 1963-77; controller Vistron Corp., Cleve., 1967-77, dir. ednl. relations and corporate contbns., 1977—. Mem. adv. council Kent (Ohio) State U., Toledo (Ohio) State U. Trustee Mt. Union Coll. Served with AUS, 1943-45. Mem. Am. Mgmt. Assn., Cleve. Growth Assn., Financial Execs. Inst., Planning Execs. Inst. (pres., (dir.). Presbyn. Home: 4939 Anderson Rd Cleveland OH 44124 Office: Midland Bldg Cleveland OH 44115

SHIELDS, CURRIN VANCE, educator; b. LaPorte, Ind., Feb. 18, 1918; s. Clarence Vance and Harriet (Swanson) S.; A.B., U. Nebr., 1941; Ph.M., U. Wis., 1943; Ph.D., Yale U., 1950; m. Phyllis Rae Greene, June 10, 1941 (div.); children—Currin Burk, Craig Vance, Malinda Rae, Colin Kent; m. 2d, Marjorie Miller Rowe, May 28, 1960. With advt. art dept. Chgo. Tribune, 1937-38; research asst. Legislative Council, Nebr., 1939-41; research asst. dept. polit. sci. U. Wis., 1941-43, asst. to dir. Civil Affairs Tng. Sch., 1943-44; asst. in instrn., Cowles fellow dept. polit. sci. Yale, 1946-47, instr., 1948-50; asst., asso. prof. dept. polit. sci. U. Calif. at Los Angeles, 1950-60; prof. govt., U. Ariz., 1960—, head govt. dept., 1960-69; dir. Inst. Govt. Research, 1963-72, dir. community services, 1972—; vis. lectr. Boston U., summer 1947, U. N.H., 1948, U. Wis., 1955; mem. adv. council Electric Power Research Inst., Palo Alto, Calif.; asso. Consumer Affairs Assos., Washington, Virginia Knauer & Assos., consumer consultants, Washington. Dir. Group Health of Ariz., 1975-78, Nat. Consumer Symposium, Inc., 1977—. Radio program, What's the Issue?, sta. KFWB, Hollywood, 1953-55; cons. legislative edn. program United Steelworkers Am., 1953-61; co-chmn. corp. seminar Fund for Republic, 1959-60; cons. Nat. Endowment for Humanities, 1969-75; pres. Ariz. Consumers Council, 1969—; bd. mem. Consumer Fedn. Am., 1969-74, mem. exec. com., 1970-74, resolutions chmn., 1971-74, v.p., 1973-74; chmn. Nat. Conf. Consumer Orgns., 1974-77; mem. consumer adv. com. Fed. Energy Adminstrn., 1973-75, mem. constrn. adv. com., 1974-76; mem. Nat. Advt. Rev. Bd., 1975—; mem. President's Consumer Adv. Council; dir. Nat. Consumer Affairs Internship Program, 1976—. Vice chmn. 22d Congl. Dist., Democratic Council Calif., 1953, 54, chmn., 1955; co.-chmn. polit. action com. Calif. Dem. Council, 1955-57; candidate for gov., Ariz., 1968; chmn. 1970 Platform Com. Dem. Party Ariz. Mem. exec. bd. Arizona Acad. Served as 2d lt. U.S. Army, 1944-46. Mem. Am. (chmn., com. on relations with regional assos.), Western (exec. bd., pres. 1971-72) polit. sci. assns., Am. Soc. Pubilc Adminstrn., AAUP, UN Assn. Tucson (pres. 1964-67), Western Govs. Research Assn., Tucson Council Fgn. Relations, Am. Council on Consumer Interests, Am. Soc. Assn. Execs., Phi Beta Kappa, Pi Sigma Alpha (nat. council 1968—). Episcopalian. Club: University Faculty (U. Ariz.) (pres.). Author: Democracy and Catholicism in America, 1958. Bd. editors Western Polit. Quar. Contbr. numerous articles to profl. publs. Home: 6480 Camino de Michael Tucson AZ 85718

SHIELDS, JAMES GETTY, JR., financial cons., banker, lawyer; b. Des Moines, Mar. 25, 1918; s. James Getty and Bertha O. (McClure) S.; B.S., U. Calif. at Berkeley, 1938, J.D., 1941; m. Valerie Moore, Aug. 9, 1947; children—Victoria G., Cinthia S., James K. Admitted to Calif. bar, 1941; exec. v.p., dir. Indsl. Indemnity Co., San Francisco, 1946-64; chmn. bd. Calif. Canadian Bank, 1964-72; pres. Gt. State Fin. Services, 1972; exec. v.p., Crocker Nat. Corp., 1972-75; dir. Commonwealth Am. Guaranty Ins. Co., McNeil Money Market Fund. Bd. dirs. Franklin Hosp., San Francisco, Brentano Found., U. Calif. Hosp. Aux. Served from ensign to comdr. USNR, 1941-46. Decorated Bronze Star, 17 campaign stars. Mem. Am., San Francisco bar assns., State Bar of Calif., Canadian Am. Assn. (dir.), Beta Theta Pi, Phi Delta Phi. Clubs: Stock Exchange, Pacific Union, Bohemian (San Francisco); California (Los Angeles). Home: 120 Santa Paula Ave San Francisco CA 94127 Office: 235 Montgomery St San Francisco CA 94104

SHIELDS, JOHN HAROLD, automotive co. exec.; b. Shawnee Twp., Ohio, Aug. 29, 1902; s. Charles H. and Edith E. (DeLong) S.; student LaSalle Extension U., 1924-27; m. Alvena Theresia Steveley, Apr. 18, 1923; children—Dwayne A., Thomas E., John Harold, Patricia S. (Mrs. Galligan). Cost accountant Lima Locomotive Works, 1923-25; with Superior Coach Corp. (merged with Sheller-Globe Corp.), Lima, Ohio, 1925—, exec. v.p., 1941-47, pres., 1947-65, chmn., 1965-70, hon. chmn., 1970—; dir. Nat. Bank Lima. Dir. St. Rita's Hosp. Bldg. Fund and Meml. Hosp., 1944-46; co-chmn. Community Chest, 1951-55; campaign dir. First United Fund Drive, 1955-56; co-chmn. Urban Renewal Lima, 1961. Bd. dirs. Meml. Hosp., Bradfield Community Center; trustee Lima Pub. Library, YMCA, Automotive Safety Found.; trustee, pres. bd. dirs., chmn. devel. fund com., gen. chmn. fund-raising com. Bethesda Meml. Hosp., Boynton Beach, Fla.; mem. adv. bd. St. Rita's Hosp. Recipient Boss of Year award Jr. C. of C., 1949, 50, 51, Human Relations award Frontiers Club, 1964, award of merit Ambulance Assn., 1965. Mem. N.A.M., Lima Assn. Commerce, Lima Mfrs. Assn. Presbyn. Clubs: Elks, Shawnee Country (Lima); Pine Tree Country, Little, Delray Beach, Country (Delray Beach, Fla.). Home: 86 Macfarlane Dr Apt 6B Delray Beach FL 33444 Office: Superior Coach Corp 1200 E Kibby St Lima OH 45802

SHIELDS, L(ORAN) DONALD, univ. pres.; b. San Diego, Sept. 18, 1936; s. Clifford L. and Malta Shields; B.A., U. Calif. at Riverside, 1959; postgrad. (grad. asst. teaching fellow) U. Ill., 1959, U. So. Calif., 1959; postgrad. (grad. asst. teaching fellow) U. Calif. at Los Angeles, 1959, Ph.D. (duPont teaching fellow), 1964; m. Patricia Ann Baldwin, Sept. 1, 1957; children—Ronald, Steven, Cynthia, Laurie. Asst. prof. chemistry Calif. State U., Fullerton, 1963-66, asso. prof., 1966-67, prof., 1967—, v.p. for adminstrn., 1967-70, acting pres., 1970-71, pres., 1971—; vis. prof. chemistry U. Calif. at Los Angeles, summers, 1964-67. Cons. NSF, 1970—; mem. Nat. Sci. Bd., 1974—, mem. programs, budget and sci. edn. adv. coms., 1974—; Mem. Orange County Econ. Devel. Council, 1972—; trustee Nat. Commn. Coop. Edn., 1977—, World Affairs Council Orange County. Recipient Calif. State Legislature Distinguished Teaching award, 1965; named one of

Five Outstanding Young Men, Calif. Jr. C. of C., 1971; du Pont fellow, 1961-62. Mem. AAAS, Am. Chem. Soc., Am. Coll. Pub. Relations Assn., Am. Inst. Chemists, Orange County C. of C., Town Hall Calif., Sigma Xi, Phi Lambda Upsilon. Author: Analytical Methods of Organic and Biochemistry, 1968, 76; Modern Methods of Chemical Analysis, 1968, 2d edit., 1976. Contbr. articles to profl. jours. Office: Calif State U Fullerton CA 92634

SHIELDS, RICHARD TYNER, investor; b. Kansas City, Mo., Feb. 22, 1908; s. Edwin Willis and Martha (Deardorff) S.; grad. St. George's Sch., 1925; Ph.B., Yale, 1929; M.B.A., Harvard, 1931; m. Jean Koehler, Mar. 5, 1949 (div. 1954); m. 2d, Elizabeth Bayne de Vegh, May 21, 1964. With Bankers Trust Co., N.Y.C., 1937-63, asst. trust officer, 1939-44, asst. v.p. 1944-50, v.p., investment research, 1950-63; with WPB, 1942-43, Office Lend Lease, 1943-44; v.p., dir., mem. exec. com. One William St. Fund, Inc., 1963-65, dir., mem. exec. com., 1965-71; dir. Partners Fund, Inc., 1975—. Adviser Gen. Electric Pension Fund, 1955-63. Mem. Yale Devel. Bd., 1967—. Trustee, mem. finance com. Boys Club of N.Y., 1964—. Club: The River of N.Y., University (N.Y.C.); Pauma Valley Country (Calif.). Home: 812 Fifth Ave New York NY 10021 Office: 30 Rockefeller Plaza New York NY 10020

SHIELDS, ROBERT CAMPBELL, petroleum co. exec.; b. Kosse, Tex., Sept. 15, 1923; s. Barton Warren and Rena (Small) S.; B.S., U. Tex., 1949; m. Edith Sue Alexander, June 13, 1947; children—Rana Colleen, Renee Caryn. With Texaco, Inc., 1949—, asst. gen. mgr. producing dept., N.Y.C., 1970, gen. mgr., 1970-71, v.p. producing dept. Latin Am., 1971-77, v.p. Eastern Hemisphere, 1977—. Served to 1st lt. USAAF, 1942-45; ETO; prisoner of war. Decorated Air medal. Mem. Am. Inst. Mining, Metall. and Petroleum Engrs., Tau Beta Pi. Home: 58 Llewylln New Canaan CT 06840 Office: 2000 Westchester Ave White Plains NY 10650

SHIELDS, ROBERT EMMET, lawyer; b. Ridley Park, Pa., May 18, 1942; s. Joseph Leonard and Kathryn J. (Walsh) S.; A.B., Coll. Holy Cross, 1964; LL.B. cum laude, N.Y. U., 1967; m. Mary Katherine Reid, July 22, 1967; children—Christopher D., David R., Kevin M., Kathleen. Admitted to Pa. bar, 1968; mem. faculty U. Calif. Boalt Hall Sch. Law, 1967-68; asso. firm Drinker Biddle & Reath, Phila., 1968-74, partner, 1974—. Mem. Am. Law Inst., Am. Bar Assn., Pa. Bar Assn., Phila. Bar Assn. Club: Union League (Phila.). Author: (with Eliot B. Thomas) Federal Securities Act Handbook, 4th edit., 1977. Home: 206 Atlee Rd Wayne PA 19087 Office: 1100 Philadelphia Nat Bank Bldg Philadelphia PA 19107

SHIELDS, THOMAS WILLIAM, surgeon, educator; b. Ambridge, Pa., Aug. 17, 1922; s. John Jr. and Elizabeth (Flanagan) S.; B.A., Kenyon Coll., Gambier, O., 1943, D.Sc. (hon.), 1978; M.D., Temple U., 1947; m. Dorothea Ann Thomas, June 12, 1948; children—Thomas William, John Leland, Carol Ann. Resident surgery Northwestern U. Med. Sch., Chgo., 1949-55, prof. surgery, 1968—; practice medicine specializing in surgery, Chgo., 1956—; chief of surgery VA Lakeside Hosp., Chgo., 1968—. Dir. Shields Rubber Co., Loman Shields Rubber Co. Served with U.S. Army, 1951-53. Mem. A.C.S., Am. Assn. for Thoracic Surgery, Soc. Throacic Surgery, Central, Western surg. assns., Société Internationale de Chirurgie, Phi Beta Kappa, Sigma Xi, Alpha Omega Alpha. Editor: General Thoracic Surgery, 1972; Bronchial Carcinoma, 1974; asso. editor Surgery, Gynecology and Obstetrics. Contbr. articles to profl. jours. Home: 1721 Jenks Ave Evanston IL 60201 Office: 333 E Huron St Chicago IL 60611

SHIELS, EUGENE F., oil co. exec.; b. Dallas, 1920; grad. Tex. A. and M. U., 1941; married. With Ideco div. Dresser Industries, Inc., 1946-66; sr. v.p. operations Zapata Corp. (fomerly Zapata Norness, Inc.), Houston, 1966-69, exec. v.p., 1969—, also dir.; chmn., pres., dir. Zapata Tech. Services Corp.; chmn. Carrier Ins. Co., Ltd. Club: Petroleum (1st v.p., dir.) (Houston). Home: 11219 Tynewood Dr Houston TX 77024 Office: Zapata Tower PO Box 4240 Houston TX 77001

SHIELY, ALBERT RAYMOND, JR., ret. air force officer; b. St. Paul, July 14, 1920; s. Albert Raymond and Helene (Paulet) S.; B.S., U.S. Mil. Acad., 1943; M.S., U. Ill., 1947; grad. Indsl. Coll. Armed Forces, 1962; m. Edith C. Morrison, Sept. 9, 1944; children—Diane M., Albert Raymond III, Barbara J. Served with Minn. N.G., 1938-40; commd. 2d lt. USAAF, 1943, advanced through grades to maj. gen. USAF, 1970; exchange officer with RAF, 1949-51; research and devel. engr., program dir. for devel. Air Def. Systems and Air Traffic Control Systems, 1951-65; vice comdr. electronic systems div. Air Force Systems Command, 1965-67; comdr. European communications area Air Force Communications Service, 1967-69, became vice comdr., Richards-Gebaur AFB, Mo., 1969; comdr. electronics systems div., L.G. Hanscom Field, Bedford, Mass., 1971-74; selectman Town of Barrington (N.H.), 1978—. Commr., Little League, Syosset, N.Y., 1955-57; commr. Rhineland Dist. Boy Scouts Am., 1967-69, mem. Okaw Valley council, 1969—. Decorated D.S.M., Legion of Merit with 3 oak leaf clusters, Air medal, Air Force Commendation medal. Mem. Air Force Assn., Ret. Officers Assn., Sigma Nu. Roman Catholic. Club: Kiwanis. Address: Woodhaven Dr Barrington NH 03825

SHIENTAG, FLORENCE PERLOW, lawyer; b. N.Y.C.; d. David and Ester (Germane) Perlow; B.S., N.Y.U., 1940, then LL.B., J.D.; m. Bernard L. Shientag, June 8, 1938. Admitted to N.Y. bar, 1933; law aide Thomas E. Dewey, 1937; law sec. Mayor La Guardia, 1939-42; justice Domestic Relations Ct., 1941-42; mem. Tchrs. Retirement Bd., N.Y.C., 1942-46; asst. U.S. atty. So. dist. N.Y., 1943-53; lectr. on internat. divorce. Mem. Nat. Commn. on Wiretapping and Electronic Surveillance, 1973—. Candidate N.Y. State senate, 1954. Bd. dirs. U.N. Devel. Corp., 1972—; bd. dirs., asso. treas. YM and YWHA. Hon. commr. commerce N.Y.C. Mem. Fed. (exec. com.), Internat., Am., N.Y. Womens (pres.), N.Y. State, N.Y.C. (chmn. law and art sect. bar assns., N.Y. County Lawyers Assn. (dir.), Nat. Assn. Women Lawyers (sec.). Club: City (N.Y.C.). Contbr. articles to profl. jours. Home: 737 Park Ave New York NY 10021 Office: 1 E 57th St New York NY 10022. *Success is a product of self respect, even self appreciation, allowing associates to be as they are, not as you prefer them to be, and hard work at what you do well.*

SHIFFLER, NEIL FREDERICK, educator; b. Altoona, Pa., Aug. 15, 1922; s. Edgar Harold and Amelia Elizabeth (Herr) S.; B.S., U. Pa., 1948; M.B.A., U. Mich., 1950; Ph.D., U. Pitts., 1960; m. Ruth Gertrude Garman, Feb. 23, 1946; children—Neil Frederick II, Alan Lee, Dale Stewart, Sandra Kay, Douglas H. From instr. to prof. bus. adminstrn. Bucknell U., 1950—, also chmn. dept. mgmt.; lectr. U. Pitts., 1955-56; mgmt. cons.; mem. panel Am. Arbitration Assn. Active Little League Baseball, Cub Scouts; chmn. Twp. Planning Commn. Served with USAAF, 1943-45. Mem. Am. Mktg. Assn., Acad. Mgmt. Methodist. Mason. Co-author: Principles of Marketing, 1960; also numerous articles in field. Home: Stein Ln Lewisburg PA 17837

SHIFFMAN, BERNARD, mathematician; b. N.Y.C., June 23, 1942; s. Max and Bella (Manel) S.; B.S., M.I.T., 1964; Ph.D. (NSF fellow), U. Calif., Berkeley, 1968; m. Doris Judith Yaffe, July 11, 1965; children—Jonathan, Daniel. C.L.E. Moore instr. M.I.T., 1968-70; asst. prof. math. Yale U., 1970-73; asso. prof. Johns Hopkins U., 1973-77, prof., 1977—; mem. Inst. Advanced Study, Princeton, N.J., fall 1975; series lectr. U. Kaiser-slautern (W. Ger.), 1977, Inst. Math., Academia Sinica, Peking, China, 1978, U. Paris VI, 1979. Hon. Woodrow Wilson fellow, 1964; Alfred P. Sloan research fellow, 1973-75; recipient Woodrow Wilson Faculty Devel. award, 1979. Mem. Am. Math. Soc. Research, publs. in complex analysis. Office: Dept Math Johns Hopkins U Baltimore MD 21218

SHIFLEY, RALPH LOUIS, ret. naval officer, corp. exec.; b. Mounds, Ill., Oct. 26, 1910; s. Marion Monroe and Elizabeth Alice (Hawkins) S.; student U. Ill., 1928; B.S., U.S. Naval Acad., 1933; m. Frances Ellen Norman, Sept. 8, 1936; 1 dau., Susan Elizabeth. Commd. ensign U.S. Navy, 1933, advanced through grades to vice adm., 1967; designated naval aviator, 1937; various assignments in ships, 1933-40; comdg. officer Bombing Squadron 8, 1943-44; comdr. Air Group 8, 1944; supt. tng. Naval Air Sta., Jacksonville, Fla., 1945-47; assigned U.S.S. Randolph, 1947, U.S.S. Leyte, 1948-49; operations officer to comdr. Air Force, Atlantic Fleet, 1949-51; grad. Naval War Coll., 1952; mem. staff chief naval operations in aviation plans div., 1952-54; staff comdr. 6th fleet, 1954-56; comdg. officer, Badoeng Strait, 1956-57; sr. aide to chief naval operations, 1957-58; comdg. officer U.S.S. Franklin D. Roosevelt, 1958-59; asst. dir., then dir. aviations plans div., staff chief naval operations, 1959-62; comdr. Carrier Div. 7, 1962-63; vice chief naval material, 1963-67; dep. chief naval operations (logistics), 1967-71; ret., 1971; exec. v.p., treas. Stanwick Corp., Arlington, Va., 1971-78, pres., treas., 1978—; pres. Stanwick Internat., Inc., Arlington, 1971-78. Decorated Navy Cross, Legion of Merit, D.F.C. with 3 gold stars, D.S.M., Air medal with 2 gold stars. Clubs: Army and Navy (Washington); New York Yacht; Army-Navy Country (Arlington, Va.); Pinehurst (N.C.) Country. Home: 4738 Tilden St NW Washington DC 20016 Office: Stanwick Corp PO Box 9184 Rosslyn Sta Arlington VA 22209

SHIH, CHIA SHUN, educator, cons. engr.; b. Kiangsi, China, Sept. 7, 1938; s. I Ming and Chih-Yung (Chang) S.; came to U.S., 1963, naturalized, 1973; B.S., Taiwan Cheng Kung U., 1960; M.S., U. Tex., Austin, 1966, Ph.D., 1967; m. Hester F. Chiao, Aug. 6, 1966; children—R. Liren, Rainee L. Engr., Taiwan Water Supply Commn., Taipei, 1961-63; supr. research dept. Roy F. Weston, Inc., West Chester, Pa., 1967-70; asso. prof. indsl. engring. dept. Tex. A. and M. U., College Station, 1970-73; prof., dir. environ. studies div. U. Tex., San Antonio, 1973-75, prof. environ. and energy systems, 1976—; cons. Fed. Energy Adminstrn., Washington, 1975-77, Dept. Energy, 1977-78, Southwest Research Inst., 1978—; partner Marco Polo Assos., Corpus Christi, 1971-78; v.p. S&W Enterprise, Inc., N.Y.C., 1976—; pres. H. Garden, Inc., Tex., 1977—, Resources Info. Assos. Inc. Served as engring. officer Chinese Army, 1960-61. Registered profl. engr., Tex. Mem. Am. Inst. Inst. Engrs., ASCE (state chmn.), Ops. Research Soc. Am., AAAS, Tex. Assn. Profl. Engrs., Sigma Xi, Phi Kappa Phi, Alpha Pi Mu, Chi Epsilon. Contbr. chpts. to books on environ pollution. Research in environ. quality, water resources systems analysis, and energy resources mgmt. Home: 7010 Evening Sun Dr San Antonio TX 78238 Office: Environ Div U Tex FM 1604 San Antonio TX 78285. *My oriental culture has taught me to always respect and follow the advice of those who are older, more knowledgeable and more experienced. Now I find that it is not only a proper approach but also a profitable way.*

SHIH, HSIO-YEN, mus. ofcl.; b. Wuchang, Hubei, China, July 27, 1933; s. Shih Chao-ying and Wu Fang-jing; naturalized Can. citizen, 1966; B.A., Wellesley Coll., 1955; M.A., U. Chgo., 1958; Ph.D., Bryn Mawr Coll., 1961. Teaching asst. dept. history of art Bryn Mawr (Pa.) Coll., 1959-60; asst. curator Far Eastern dept. Royal Ont. (Can.) Mus., 1961-63, curator, 1968-76; asst. prof. dept. East Asian studies U. Toronto (Ont.), 1961-63, asso. prof., coordinator for Chinese studies, 1964-68, prof., 1971-77; dir. Nat. Gallery of Can., Ottawa, 1977—; vis. prof. Trinity Coll., Hartford, Conn., 1962, York U., Toronto, 1970, U. Calif., Berkeley, 1971; vis. prof., chmn. bd. studies in fine arts Inst. Chinese Studies, Chinese U., Hong Kong, 1973-74. Mem. Coll. Art Assn. Am., Canadian Soc. for Archaeology Abroad. Home: 215 MacKay St Ottawa ON K1M 2B6 Canada Office: Lorne Bldg Room 715 Ottawa ON K1A 0M8 Canada

SHIH, J. CHUNG-WEN, educator; b. Nanking, China; d. Cho-kiang and Chia-pu (Fang) S.; came to U.S., 1948, naturalized, 1960; B.A., St. John's U., Shanghai, 1945; M.A., Duke U., 1949, Ph.D., 1955. Asst. prof. English, Kings Coll. N.Y., 1955-56; asst. prof. U. Bridgeport (Conn.), 1956-60; postdoctoral fellow East Asian Studies, Harvard, 1960-61; asst. prof. Chinese, Stanford, 1961-64; asso. prof. Chinese, Pomona Coll., 1965-66; asso. prof. George Washington U., 1966-71, prof., chmn. dept. East Asian langs. and lit., 1971—. Bd. dirs. Sino-Am. Cultural Soc., Washington, 1971—. AAUW fellow, 1964-65; Social Sci. Research Council fellow, 1976-77. Mem. Assn. Asian Studies, Am. Council Fgn. Lang. Tchrs., Chinese Lang. Tchrs. Assn. (chmn. exec. bd.), Zonta, Delta Kappa Gamma. Author: Injustice to Tou O, 1972; the Golden Age of Chinese Drama: Yuan Tsa-chu, 1976. Home: Apt 602-S 2500 Virginia Ave NW Washington DC 20037 Office: Dept East Asian Langs and Lit George Washington U Washington DC 20052

SHIKLER, AARON, artist; b. Bklyn., Mar. 18, 1922; s. Frank and Annie (Blai) S.; B.F.A., B.S. in Edn., M.F.A., Tyler Sch. Fine Arts, Temple U., 1948; student Barnes Found., Merion, Pa., 1941-43, Hans Hoffmann Sch., N.Y.C., 1949-51; m. Barbara Lurie, Oct. 4, 1947; children—Cathy M., Clifford M. One man shows Davis Galleries, N.Y.C., 1953, 54, 56, 58, 60, 62, 64, 67, 71, Bklyn. Museum, 1971, Palace of Legion of Honor, San Francisco, 1971, Long Gallery, Houston, 1972, 76, Davis & Long Co., 1975, 79; represented in permanent collections Montclair (N.J.) Mus., Hofstra Mus. Art, L.I., Met. Mus. Art, Mint Mus. Art, Charlotte, N.C., Parrish Mus. Art, Southampton, L.I., N.A.D., Bklyn. Mus., Hirshorn Mus., Washington, Nat. Art Gallery, Wellington, N.Z., Nat. Gallery, Singapore, New Britain Mus. Am. Art, Sun Rise Mus., Charleston, W.Va., Sheldon Meml. Art Gallery, Lincoln, Nebr.; executed portraits Pres. and Mrs. John F. Kennedy for White House, Robert Lehman Pavilion at Met. Mus. Art, Henry F. duPont for Winterthur (Del.) Mus., Robert F. Kennedy for Dept. Justice, Washington, Sec. Carla Hills for HUD, Mrs. Lyndon B. Johnson for Johnson Library, Austin, Tex., Senator Mike Mansfield for U.S. Senate, Washington. Recipient Tiffany award, 1958, Ranger award, 1959; Proctor prize N.A.D., 1959, 60, Thomas B. Clarke prize, 1961, Benjamin Altman prize, 1976. Served with inf. AUS, 1943-46. Dept. State grantee, S.E. Asia and South Pacific, 1976. Mem. N.A.D. Club: Century Assn. Address: 44 W 77th St New York NY 10024

SHILENSKY, MORRIS, lawyer; b. Oserany, Poland, Nov. 20, 1910; s. Louis and Esther (Kachonofsky) S.; came to U.S., 1912, naturalized, 1925; student Columbia, 1929; LL.B., St. Lawrence U., 1932; m. Celia Binder, Nov. 6, 1932; children—Sylvia E. (Mrs. Gerald Freed), Michael. Admitted to N.Y. bar, 1933; with firm Hays, St. John, Abramson & Heilbron, 1928—, partner, 1938—; sec., dir. Henry I. Siegel Co., Inc.; dir. Questor Corp., Alfred Dunhill of London Inc. Pres. bd. dirs. Billy Rose Found.; bd. dirs., chmn. fin. com. Am. Friends Israel Museum; bd. dirs., v.p. Samuel Schulman Inst. Mem. N.Y. County Lawyers Assn. Club: Bankers (N.Y.C.). Home: 63-42 Haring St Rego Park NY 11374 Office: 120 Broadway New York City NY 10005

SHILLING, KENNETH, lawyer; b. Kingston, Okla., Mar. 25, 1920; s. Marvin French and Grace (Corder) S.; student Okla. State U., 1937-40; J.D., U. Okla., 1943; grad. Nat. Coll. State Judiciary, Reno, Nev., 1971; m. Elizabeth Thomas, Apr. 23, 1943; children—Linda Jean (Mrs. Wayne L. Rhodes Jr.), Cynthia Ann (Mrs. William E. Black), Thomas K. Admitted to Okla. bar, 1943; partner law firm Shilling & Shilling, Ardmore, Okla., 1946-54, 75—; legal asst. to Supreme Ct. of Okla., Oklahoma City, 1954-59; dist. judge 20th Jud. Dist., Ardmore, 1959-75. Pres. Chickasaw dist. Boy Scouts Am., 1960-61. Served with AUS, 1943-46, 51-52. Mem. Am., Carter County (pres. 1949-50), Okla. bar assns., Jud. Conf. Okla., Acacia, Am. Legion, V.F.W. Democrat. Methodist. Home: 505 Regent St Ardmore OK 73401 Office: PO Box 217 Ardmore OK 73401

SHILLING, ROY BRYANT, JR., coll. pres.; b. Enville, Okla., Apr. 7, 1931; s. Roy Bryant and Lila M. (Prestage) S.; B.A., McMurry Coll., 1951; B.D., So. Meth. U., 1957; M.S., Ind. U., 1966, Ph.D., 1967; m. Margaret Riddle, Oct. 16, 1952; children—Roy Bryant III, Nancy Gale. Presdl. asst. McMurry Coll., Abilene, Tex., 1959-61; asst. to pres. Tenn. Wesleyan Coll., 1961-64; asst. in devel. Ball State U., 1964-65; research asso. Ind. U., 1965-67; dir. planning and research Baldwin Wallace Coll., 1967-68; exec. v.p. Southwestern U., 1968-69; pres. Hendrix Coll., 1969—; dir. Comml. Nat. Bank, Little Rock, 1973—. Mem. Ark. Arts and Humanities Council, 1970-78, chmn., 1974-75; state gen. chmn. Ark. Childrens' Hosp. Fund Dr., 1978-79; mem. United Meth. Ch. Bd. Higher Edn. and Ministry, 1972-80. Served with U.S. Army, 1952-54. Mem. Young Pres.'s., Orgn., North Central Assn. Colls. and Schs. (cons./examiner 1970—, exec. bd. 1976—), Nat. Assn. Schs. and Colls. of United Meth. Ch. (pres. 1976-77), Nat. Council Ind. Colls. and Univs. (dir. 1972-76), Alpha Chi, Phi Delta Kappa. Clubs: Conway (Ark.) Country, Masons, Rotary (hon.); Univ. (hon.) (N.Y.C.). Author: (with Philip C. Chamberlain) Private Liberal Arts Colleges and Their Changing Purposes, 1967. Office: Hendrix Coll Conway AR 72032

SHILLITO, BARRY J., industrialist; b. Dayton, Ohio, Jan. 1, 1921; s. Lucian W. and Mary Ellen (O'Connor) S.; B.S. in Bus. Adminstrn., B.S. in Econs., U. Dayton, 1949; postgrad. U. Cal. at Los Angeles, 1958; m. Eileen Elizabeth Cottman, Dec. 2, 1942; children—Barry L., Elaine (Mrs. Tanavage), Daniel G., James K., Colleen A. Gen. mgr. Harris-Lincoln Supply Co., Dayton, 1945-49; sect. chief procurement div. USAF, Wright Patterson AFB, 1949-54; dir. material Hughes Aircraft Co., 1954-58, dir. sales, 1958-59; exec. v.p. Houston Fearless Co., Los Angeles, 1959-60, pres., 1960-62; pres. Logistics Mgmt. Inst., Washington, 1962-68; asst. sec. navy for installations and logistics, 1968-69; asst. sec. def. for installations and logistics, 1969-73; pres. Teledyne Ryan Aeronautical, San Diego, 1973-76; v.p. Teledyne Inc., 1976—; mem. council of NATO Armaments Dirs., 1969-73. Served to 1st lt., pilot, USAF, 1942-45; prisoner of war, 1944-45. Decorated Purple Heart; recipient Navy Distinguished Pub. Service award, 1968; distinguished pub. service medal, Sec. Defence, 1972; medal of cloud and banner, Republic of China, 1973; Nat. order of Vietnam, Republic of Vietnam, 1973. Fellow Soc. Logistics Engrs.; mem. Armed Forces Mgmt. Assn., Young Pres. Orgn. 1959-71, alumni assns. U. Dayton, UCLA (Disting. Alumnus award 1978), Nat. Contract Mgmt. Assn. (adv. bd.), Am. Legion. K.C. Clubs: Burning Tree (Washington); Moraine Country (Dayton). Office: Teledyne Inc 1501 Wilson Blvd Suite 900 Arlington VA 22209

SHILS, EDWARD B., educator; b. Phila., May 29, 1915; s. Benjamin and Dinah (Berkowitz) S.; B.S. in Econs., U. Pa., 1936, M.A. in Polit. Sci., 1937, Ph.D., 1940; LL.D., Phila. Coll. Textiles and Sci., 1975; m. Shirley Seigle, July 31, 1942; children—Ronnie Lois, Nancy Ellen, Edward Barry. Research asso. Pa. Economy League, 1938-42; cons. job classification and wage adminstrn. Phila. City Council, 1942-43; chief coordination and planning VA, Phila., 1947-48; cons. tchr. salary schedules Phila. Bd. Pub. Edn., 1948-50; dir. pub. edn. survey Greater Phila. Movement, 1950-51; sr. dept. head WSB, Phila., 1951; methods cons. Budget Office Gov. Pa., 1951-55; cons. Phila. County Med. Soc., 1955-56; chmn. social sci. dept. Community Coll. of Temple U., grad. lectr. pub. adminstrn. Grad. Sch. Bus. and Pub. Adminstrn., 1948-56; faculty Wharton Sch. U. Pa., Phila., 1956—, prof. mgmt., chmn. mgmt dept., 1968-76, George W. Taylor prof. entrepreneurial studies, 1979—, dir. Wharton Entrepeneurial Center, 1973—. Personnel cons. Phila. Bd. Pubs. Edn., 1946-75, Phila. Psychiat. Center, 1971-76, Am. Bd. Internal Medicine, 1973—, Girard Coll., 1974, Dental Mfrs. Am., 1952—; cons. Royal Coll. Physicians and Surgeons Canada, 1977—; v.p. Fedn. Jewish Agys. for Phila., 1976—; pres. Jewish Publs. Soc. Am., 1978. Served as officer Signal Corps, U.S. Army, 1943-46. Life trustee, hon. chmn. trustee com. on edn. Phila. Coll. Textiles and Sci.; chmn. bd., hon. pres. Pathway Sch., Jeffersonville, Pa., 1970—. Author: Financial Administration Public School Systems, 1940; Automation and Industrial Relations, 1963; co-author: Teachers, Administrators and Collective Bargaining, 1968; Industrial Peacemaker: George W. Taylor's Contributions to Collective Bargaining, 1979. Home: 335 S Woodbine Ave Narberth PA 19072 Office: Wharton Sch U Pa Philadelphia PA 19174

SHIM, ROGER VERNON FRANCIS, ballet dancer; b. Port of Spain, Trinidad, Jan. 29, 1949; s. Vernon Cecil and Roma Raphaella (Chang) S.; came to Can., 1967, naturalized, 1977; B.Sc. in Physics, Lake Head U., Thunder Bay, Ont., Can., 1970; grad. (company scholar) profl. program Royal Winnipeg (Man., Can.) Ballet, 1972; student Les Grands Ballets Canadiens, Montreal, Que., 1969, Banff (Alta.) Sch. Fine Arts, Vera Volkova, 1971; student (Can. Council grantee) Maggie Black, N.Y.C., 1975, Zolotova, 1977, York U. (Can. Council grantee), 1979. Debut in corps de ballet Royal Winnipeg Ballet, 1972, with corps de ballet, 1972-75, soloist, 1975-77, prin. dancer, 1977-79; prin. dancer Ballet Geneva Opera (Switzerland), 1980—; guest tchr. Caribbean Sch. Dance, Trinidad, Royal Winnipeg Ballet Apprentice Program. Mem. Canadian Actors' Equity Assn., Assn. Canadian TV and Radio Artists,

SHIMAMOTO, GEORGE GENTOKU, architect, archtl. engr.; b. Wakayama, Japan, Nov. 15, 1904; s. Gennosuke and Oiwa Shimamoto; B.Sc., Sch. Architecture Poly. Coll. Engring., 1927; postgrad. extension program Waseda U., Tokyo, Japan, 1928-31; m. Masayo Mine, Aug. 4, 1934; children—Teruko (Mrs. Herbert Neuwalder), Lily Ayako (Mrs. Wilfred Tashima). Cons., archtl. advisor Buddhist Mission Am., 1928-39; cons. Golden Gate Internat. Expn., San Francisco, 1939-41; resident project engr. Relocation Center, Topaz, Utah, 1942-44; asso. firm Kelly & Gruzen, Architect-Engrs. (name later changed to Gruzen & Partners 1964), N.J. and N.Y.C., 1945-50, sr. asso., 1951-63, sr. partner, gen. mgr., 1964-73; archtl., archtl. engring. cons., N.Y.C., 1974—; cons. Toda-Am. Inc., N.Y.C., Archtl. Inst. Japan; mem. N.Y.C. Housing Task Force. Chmn. bd. Buddhist Ch., N.Y.C.; bd. dirs. Japanese Am. Help for Aging, Inc., N.Y.C. Decorated Order of Rising Sun (Japan); recipient citation San Francisco C. of C., N.Y.C. Housing Task Force, HHFA. Fellow Archtl. Inst. Japan (citation of services), ASCE (emeritus); mem. A.I.A. (emeritus), Nat. Soc. Profl. Engrs. (emeritus), Am. Soc. Mil. Engrs., Japan Soc. (life, patron), ASTM, Japanese Am. Citizens League (San Francisco), Japanese Am. Assn. N.Y. (v.p. 1974-75, 77-78, chmn. fin. commn. 1975-76, pres. 1979—). Buddhist.

Clubs: Nippon (house com.) (N.Y.C.); N.Y. Japanese Lions (charter). Designer: Horizon House (Design award FHA); Chatham Towers, N.Y.C. (Design award Bard Commn.); Japan House, N.Y.C. (Design award N.Y. State Architects Assn.); traveled extensively for housing studies in Europe and Far East; established scholarship trust at Archtl. Inst. Japan, 1978. Home: 2150 Center Ave Fort Lee NJ 07024 Office: Gruzen & Partners 1700 Broadway Suite 2100 New York NY 10019. *Retain that spotless purity like a white lotus flower blossoming in the midst of mire.*

SHIMKIN, DEMITRI BORIS, anthropo-geographer, educator; b. Omsk, Siberia, July 4, 1916; s. Boris Michael and Lydia (Serebrova) S.; came to U.S., 1923, derivative citizen; A.B., U. Calif. at Berkeley, 1936, Ph.D., 1939; m. Edith Manning, Aug. 19, 1943; children—Alexander, Eleanor. Johnson scholar, univ. and research fellow U. Calif., Berkeley, 1937-41; instr. Nat. War Coll., 1946-47, Inst. for Advanced Study, Princeton, 1947-48; research asso. Russian Research Center, Harvard, 1948-53; social sci. analyst, then sr. research specialist U.S. Bur. Census, Washington, 1953-60; prof. anthropology, geography and pub. health U. Ill., Urbana, 1960—; field work in Wyo., 1937-39, 66, 75, Alaska, 1949, Ill., 1963—, Miss., 1966-72, 78, Ala., 1976; vis. prof. anthropology Harvard, 1964-65, summer 1970. Mem. NRC, 1964-67; mem. U.S. nat. com. Internat. Biol. Program, 1965-69; mem. task force environ. health HEW, 1968-69, task force on civil engring. ASCE, 1975-78. Col. AUS (ret.). Decorated Legion of Merit. Fellow Center Advanced Study Behavioral Scis., 1970-71. Fellow AAAS, Am. Anthrop. Assn.; mem. Assn. Am. Geographers, Phi Beta Kappa, Sigma Xi. Author: Minerals: A Key to Soviet Power, 1953; (with others) Trends in Economic Growth, 1955; (with others) Man's Health and Environment, 1970, The Water's Edge, 1972, The Extended Family in Black Societies, 1978, Anthropology for the Future, 1978. Home: 106 W Pennsylvania Ave Urbana IL 61801

SHIMKIN, LEON, book publisher; b. Bklyn., Apr. 7, 1907; s. Max and Fannie (Nickelsberg) S.; B.C.S., N.Y. U., 1926; m. Rebecca Rabinowitz, Aug. 17, 1930; children—Emily, Michael. Began career as an accountant; later bus. mgr., treas., and dir. various book pub. enterprises; became pres. and dir. Simon & Schuster, Inc., N.Y.C., 1924, now chmn. bd.; co-founder Pocket Books, Inc., 1939. Trustee Com. Econ. Devel., N.Y. U., N.Y.C., Westchester Jewish Community Services. Clubs: Rockefeller Center City Athletic; Rock Rimmon Country (Pound Ridge, N.Y.); Beach Point (Mamaroneck, N.Y.). Home: 8 East Dr Larchmont NY 10538 Office: 1230 Ave of Americas New York NY 10020

SHIMKIN, MICHAEL BORIS, physician, educator; b. Tomsk, Siberia, Oct. 7, 1912; s. Boris Michael and Lydia (Serebrova) S.; came to U.S., 1923, naturalized, 1928; A.B., U. Calif. at Berkeley, 1933; M.D., U. Calif. at San Francisco, 1937; m. Mary Louisa North, July 2, 1938; children—Peter Michael, Ann Mary, Philip North. Resident medicine U. Tex., 1937-38; research fellow Harvard, 1938-39; officer USPHS, 1939-63, med. dir., 1950; with Nat. Cancer Inst., NIH, 1939-44, 46-63, chief biometry and epidemiology br., 1954-60, asso. dir. field studies, 1960-63; asst. chief Office Internat. Health, USPHS, 1945-46; clin. prof. oncology, chief lab. exptl. oncology U. Calif. Sch. Medicine, San Francisco, 1947-54; prof. medicine Temple U. Sch. Medicine, 1963-69, asst. v.p. research Health Scis. Center, 1966-69; chief cancer biology Fels Research, 1963-69; prof. community medicine and oncology U. Calif. at San Diego, 1969—, asso. dean for health manpower, 1970-72. Coordinator regional med. program San Diego & Imperial Co., 1969-73. Advisor U.S. delegation WHO constn. conv., 1945-46, OSRD, 1943-44; med. officer UNRRA, 1944-45; pub. health ofcr. G-5, 3rd Army, 1944-45; adviser Am. Cancer Soc. Diplomate Am. Bd. Internal Med., Am. Bd. Preventive Med. Fellow A.C.P., Am. Coll. Preventive Medicine; mem. Am. Assn. Cancer Research (pres. 1973), Soc. Exptl. Biology and Medicine, Phi Beta Kappa, Sigma Xi. Author: Science and Cancer, 1964; Contrary to Nature, 1977. Sci. editor Jour. Nat. Cancer Inst., 1955-60. Editor: Cancer Research, 1964-69. Home: 7246 Rue de Roark LaJolla CA 92037 Office: U Calif at San Diego Sch Medicine LaJolla CA 92093

SHIMURA, GORO, mathematician, educator; b. Hamamatsu, Japan, Feb. 23, 1930; s. Kurao and Yone (Nishigaki) S.; B.S., U. Tokyo, 1952, S.D., 1958; m. Chikako Ishiguro, Aug. 16, 1959. Came to U.S., 1962. Asst. prof. U. Tokyo, 1957; mem. Inst. Advanced Study, Princeton, 1958-59; prof. Osaka (Japan) U., 1961; vis. prof. Princeton, 1962-64, prof. math., 1964—. Mem. Math. Soc. Japan, Am. Math. Soc. Home: 25 Evergreen Circle Princeton NJ 08540

SHINALL, VERN, bass-baritone; b. St. Louis, June 22, 1936; attended Ind. U.; studied with Frank St. Leger, Charles Kullman, Tibor Kozma, Frank Randolfi; m. Marylin Ballard; 3 children. Opera debut as Scarpia in Tosca, Kansas City Lyric Opera, 1964; Met. Opera debut as Rangoni in Boris Godunov; appearances with maj. U.S. cos. including: N.Y.C. Opera, Opera Co. Boston, Cin. Opera, Houston Grand Opera, Milw. Florentine Opera, New Orleans Opera, Phila. Grand Opera; resident mem. Met. Opera; recitalist; appearances with symphony orchs. Office: care Joseph A Scuro Internat Artist's Mgmt 111 W 57th St New York NY 10019*

SHINBROT, MARVIN, mathematician, educator, author; b. Bklyn., May 30, 1928; s. Meyer and Sylvia (Pokross) S.; A.B., Syracuse U., 1948, M.A., 1949; Ph.D., Stanford, 1961; m. Sue Louise Cline; children—Mia, Adam, Troy. Aero. research scientist NACA, 1949-57; research scientist Lockheed Aircraft Co., 1957-59; cons. Atlantic Research Corp., Palo Alto Med. Research Found., 1959-61; instr. U. Chgo., 1961-62; asst. prof. U. Calif., Berkeley, 1962-65; asso. prof. Northwestern U., 1965-68, prof., 1968-72; vis. prof. U. B.C., Vancouver, 1970-72; vis. prof. U. Victoria, 1972-73, prof., 1973-79; research asso. U. Montreal (Que., Can.), 1979—. Mem. grants selection com. NRC of Can., 1975-77; mem. organizing com. Can. Congress Applied Mechanics, 1976. Fellow Royal Soc. Can.; mem. Can. Math. Soc. (council 1975—, chmn. research com. 1977-79), Am. Math. Soc., Math. Assn. Am., Soc. for Indsl. and Applied Math. (spl. lectr.), N.Y. Acad. Scis. Author: Lectures on Fluid Mechanics. Contbr. articles on fluid mechanics, statis. mechanics, differential equations, operator theory to profl. jours. Office: CRMA U Montreal Montreal PQ Canada

SHINDELL, SIDNEY, educator; b. New Haven, May 31, 1923; s. Benjamin Abraham and Freda (Mann) S.; B.S., Yale U., 1944; M.D., State U. N.Y., 1946; postgrad. Emory U., 1948-49; LL.B., Geo. Washington U., 1951; m. Gloria Emhoff, June 17, 1945; children—Barbara, Roger, Lawrence, Judith. With USPHS, 1947-52; med. dir. Conn. Commn. on Chronically Ill and Aged, 1952-57; med. dir. Am. Joint Distbn. Com., 1957-59; asst. prof. preventive medicine U. Pitts., 1960-65; dir. Hosp. Utilization project Western Pa., 1965-66; prof., chmn. dept. preventive medicine Med. Coll. Wis., Milw., 1966—; exec. dir. Health Service Data of Wis., 1967-73. Mem. Sch. Bd. Fox Point-Bayside (Wis.), Sch. Dist., 1970-71; vice-chmn. Citizens' Adv. Com. Met. Problems, 1971-72. Bd. dirs. Med. Care Evaluation S.E. Wis., 1973-76. Served with AUS, 1943-46. Diplomate Am. Bd. Preventive Medicine. Fellow Am. Coll. Preventive Medicine, Am. Coll. Legal Medicine, Am. Pub. Health Assn.; mem. Am. Occupational Medicine Assn., Am. Assn. Health Data Systems (sec. 1972-73), Assn. Tchrs. Preventive Medicine (dir. 1973-74, pres. 1976-77). Mason. Author: Statistics, Science and Sense, 1964; A Method of Hospital Utilization Review, 1966; The Law In Medical Practice, 1966; A Course Book on Health Care Delivery, 1976. Home: 929 N Astor Milwaukee WI 53202 Office: PO Box 26509 Milwaukee WI 53226

SHINE, HENRY JOSEPH, educator; b. London, Jan. 4, 1923; s. Nathan and Esther (Lewkovich) S.; B.Sc., London U., 1944, Ph.D., 1947; m. Sellie Schneider, June 14, 1953; children—Stephanie, Trevor Paul. Research chemist Shell Oil Co., Eng., 1944; research chemist U.S. Rubber Co., Passaic, N.J., 1951-54; asst. prof. chemistry Tex. Tech. U., Lubbock, 1954-57, asso. prof., 1957-60, prof., 1960—, Paul Whitfield Horn prof., 1968—, chmn. dept., 1969-75. Mem. Am. Chem. Soc. (exec. com. div. organic chemistry 1973-75, alt. councillor 1975-78, councillor 1978—), Chem. Soc. London, AAAS, Sigma Xi (pres. chpt. 1976-77), Phi Kappa Phi. Author: Aromatic Rearrangements, 1967. Contbr. articles to profl. jours. Home: 4705 17th St Lubbock TX 79416 Office: Dept Chemistry Tex Tech U Lubbock TX 79409

SHINE, NEAL JAMES, newspaper editor; b. Grosse Pointe Farms, Mich., Sept. 14, 1930; s. Patrick Joseph and Mary Ellen (Conlon) S.; A.B. in Journalism, U. Detroit, 1952; m. Phyllis Theresa Knowles, Jan. 24, 1953; children—Judith Ann, James Conlon, Susan Brigid, Thomas Patrick, Margaret Mary, Daniel Edward. Mem. staff Detroit Free Press, 1950—, asst. city editor, 1963-65, city editor, 1965-71, mng. editor, 1971—. Trustee, vice chmn. bd. trustees Youth for Understanding, 1973-75, chmn., 1975-78; mem. U. Mich. Bd. for Student Publs. Served with U.S. Army, 1953-55. Mem. Am. Soc. Newspaper Editors, Mich. Press Assn., A.P. Mng. Editors. Club: Detroit Press (charter; bd. govs. 1966—, sec. 1967—, v.p. 1969-71, pres. 1971-73). Home: 1169 Bedford Rd Grosse Pointe Park MI 48230 Office: 321 W Lafayette St Detroit MI 48231

SHINEMAN, EDWARD WILLIAM, JR., drug co. exec.; b. Canajoharie, N.Y., Apr. 9, 1915; s. Edward W. and Bertelle H. (Shubert) S.; A.B., Cornell U., 1937; m. H. Doris Thompson, Apr. 15, 1939; children—Edward T., Alan B. With apparatus dept., accounting div. Gen. Electric Co., 1938-46, line auditor, 1942-46; with Beech-Nut, Inc., and predecessor cos., 1946-68, asst. treas., 1948-63, controller, 1959-63, treas., 1963-68; asst. sec.-treas. Squibb Corp., 1968—; dir. Central Nat. Bank, Canajoharie. Trustee, v.p., treas. Arkell Hall Found. Mem. Financial Execs. Inst., Nat. Assn. Accountants. Republican. Home: 420 E 51st St New York NY 10022 Office: Squibb Corp 40 W 57th St New York NY 10019

SHINER, VERNON JACK, JR., chemist, educator; b. Laredo, Tex., Aug. 11, 1925; s. Vernon Jack and Mildred (Meerscheidt) S.; B.S., Tex. Western Coll., 1947; Ph.D., Cornell U., 1950; m. Reva Percival, Dec. 26, 1946; children—Lora, David, Diane. Fulbright fellow Univ. Coll., London, Eng., 1950-51; DuPont fellow Harvard, 1951-52; mem. dept. chemistry Ind. U., 1952—, from instr. to asso. prof., 1952-60, prof., 1960—, chmn. dept., 1962-67, dean Coll. Arts and Scis., 1973-78. Served with USNR, 1944-46. Alfred P. Sloan research fellow, 1957-61; NSF sr. postdoctoral fellow, 1958-59, 65-66. Mem. Am. Chem. Soc., Chem. Soc. London, Sigma Xi, Alpha Chi Sigma. Episcopalian. Contbr. articles to profl. publs. Home: Maple Grove Rd Bloomington IN 47401

SHINKLE, ROBERT THOMAS, banker; b. Cin., Oct. 12, 1916; s. Clyde and Carolyn (Nixon) S.; B.S., Yale, 1938, LL.B., 1941; m. Margery Joan Kneip, June 13, 1944; children—John, Joan, James. Admitted to N.Y. bar, 1941, Calif. bar, 1948, D.C. bar, 1972; with firm Blake & Voorhees, N.Y.C., 1941-42, Blake, Voorhees & Stewart, N.Y.C., 1946-47; counsel Bank of Am. Nat. Trust & Savs. Assn., San Francisco, 1948-60, v.p., trust officer, 1960-62, v.p., sr. trust officer, 1962-65, sr. v.p., 1965-68; v.p. finance World Airways, Inc., 1968-69; exec. v.p. World Am. Investors Corp.; v.p., asso. counsel Crocker Nat. Bank, 1969-74; counsel Visa U.S.A. Inc., 1974—. dir.. First Western Bank & Trust Co., 1968-69. Mem. Las Lomitas Sch. Bd., 1959-68, pres. 1961. Served to lt. USCGR, 1942-45. Mem. San Francisco Bar Assn., Asso. Trust Cos. No. Calif. Clubs: Press, Army and Navy (Washington); St. Francis Yacht, Stock Exchange (San Francisco); Berkeley Tennis. Home: 77 Clarewood Ln Oakland CA 94618 Office: PO Box 8999 San Francisco CA 94128

SHINN, ALLEN MAYHEW, ret. naval officer, business exec.; b. Niles, Calif., June 6, 1908; s. Joseph Clark and Florence Maria (Mayhew) S.; B.S., U.S. Naval Acad., 1932; grad. Nat. War Coll., 1953; m. Sevilla Hayden Shuey, June 20, 1936; children—Allen Mayhew, James Washburn, Jonathan Hayden. Commd. officer USN, 1932, advanced through grades to vice adm.; served in battleships, 1932-36; naval aviator, 1937; served in various fleet aircraft squadrons, comdr. 3, also comdr. attack carrier air group, 1944-45; served on various staffs; comdr. 2 carriers USS Saipan, 1956, USS Forrestal, 1959; comdt. midshipmen U.S. Naval Acad., Annapolis, Md., 1956-58; comdr. Anti-Submarine Warfare Carrier Task Group, 1960-61; comdr. Attack Carrier Task Force, 1963-64; chief Bur. Naval Weapons, Washington, 1964-66; comdr. Naval Air Force Pacific Fleet, 1966-70; ret. 1970; chmn. bd. Harvard Industries, Inc., 1970-71, All-Am. Industries, 1973-78; pres. Internat. Controls Corp., 1973-78, dir., 1973-79; dir. Loral Corp., 1973—, Pennzoil Co., 1970—. Bd. dirs. Navy Mut. Aid Assn., 1962-66; bd. editorial control U.S. Naval Inst., 1964-66; bd. mgrs. Navy Relief Soc., 1962-64; pres. Naval Acad. Athletic Assn., 1956-58; pres. North Water St. Corp., Edgartown, Mass., 1948-50. Trustee Longfellow Sch. Boys, Bethesda, Md., 1950-53. Mem. Soc. Mayflower Descendants. Delta Tau Delta. Republican. Unitarian. Clubs: Cosmos, Outrigger Canoe, N.Y. Yacht, Edgartown Yacht, Tantallon Country. Home: 12345 Hatton Point Rd Oxon Hill MD 20022 also Edgartown MA 02539 also Montserrat West Indies

SHINN, GEORGE LATIMER, investment banker; b. Newark, Ohio, Mar. 12, 1923; s. Leon Powell and Bertha Florence (Latimer) S.; A.B., Amherst Coll., 1948; LL.D., Denison U., 1975; m. Clara LeBaron Sampson, May 21, 1949; children—Deborah, Amy, Martha, Sarah, Andrew. Trainee Merrill Lynch, Pierce, Fenner & Beane (now Merrill Lynch, Pierce, Fenner & Smith Inc.), 1948-49, account exec., Boston, 1949-57, office mgr., Boston, 1957-60, v.p., office mgr., Phila., 1960-64, various sales and adminstrv. positions, N.Y.C., 1964-69, exec. v.p., 1969, vice chmn., 1970-73, pres., 1973—; pres. Goodbody & Co., Inc., 1970—; pres. Merrill Lynch & Co., Inc., 1974-75; chmn. bd. 1st Boston Corp., 1975—; dir. N.Y. Times Co.; trustee Greenwich Savs. Bank, N.Y.C.; mem. adv. com. Instl. Investor Study SEC, 1961-71; gov. Am. Stock Exchange, 1970-74; dir. N.Y. Stock Exchange, 1977—. Gen. chmn. United Hosp. Fund, N.Y.C., 1973-74; trustee Kent Pl. Sch., Summit, N.J., 1966-73, Carnegie Found. for Advancement Teaching, 1976—, Pingrey Sch., 1977-79; chmn. bd. trustees Amherst Coll., 1973—; adv. council Grad. Sch. Bus. U. Chgo., 1969—; bd. dirs. Research Corp., 1975—, Wildcat Service Corp., 1973—; trustee Morris Mus. Arts and Scis., Morristown, 1973-78, N.J. Shakespeare Festival, Madison. Served to capt. USMCR, 1943-46. Home: Spring Valley Rd Morristown NJ 07960 Office: 20 Exchange Pl New York NY 10005

SHINN, RICHARD RANDOLPH, life ins. co. exec.; b. Lakewood, N.J., Jan. 7, 1918; s. Clayton Randolph and Carrie (McGravey) S.; B.S., Rider Coll., 1938; m. Mary Helen Shea, Nov. 8, 1941; children—Kathleen, Patricia, John. With Met. Life Ins. Co., 1939—, 2d v.p., 1959-63, v.p., 1963-64, sr. v.p., 1964-66, exec. v.p., 1966-68, sr. exec. v.p., 1968- 69, pres., dir., 1969—, chief exec. officer, 1973—. C.L.U., 1949. Clubs: The Blind Brook (Port Chester, N.Y.); The Stanwich (Old Greenwich, Conn.); Riverside Yacht; Links (N.Y.C.) Home: 31 Lindsay Dr Greenwich CT 06830 Office: 1 Madison Ave New York NY 10010

SHINOZUKA, MASANOBU, civil engr.; b. Tokyo, Dec. 23, 1930; s. Akira and Kiyo S.; came to U.S., 1957, naturalized, 1971; B.S., Kyoto (Japan) U., 1953, M.S., 1955; Ph.D., Columbia U., 1960; m. Fujiko Sakamoto, Oct. 25, 1954; children—Rei, Naomi, Megumi. Research asst. civil engring. Columbia U., N.Y.C., 1958-61, asst. prof., 1961-65, asso. prof., 1965-69, prof., 1969—, Renwick prof., 1977—; vis. scholar N.C. State U., Raleigh, 1967-68; pres. Modern Analysis Inc., Ridgewood, N.J., 1972—; cons. in field. NSF grantee, 1968—. Mem. Nat. Acad. Engring., ASCE (Walter L. Huber prize 1972; State-of-the-Art of Civil Engring. award 1973, Alfred M. Freudenthal medal 1978), ASME, Am. Inst. Aeros. and Astronautics, ASTM, Japan Soc. Civil Engrs., Sigma Xi. Editor: Reliability Approach in Structural Engineering, 1975. Home: 825 Norgate Dr Ridgewood NJ 07450 Office: 610 Mudd Columbia U New York NY 10027

SHIP, IRWIN, dental educator; b. N.Y.C., July 11, 1932; s. Max and Lillian (Gootnick) S.; student Columbia U., 1949-52; D.M.D., Harvard U., 1956; M.S. in Epidemiology and Preventive Medicine, U. Pa., 1965; m. Gabriella Wolfsohn, June 24, 1956; children—Jonathan Avram, Sara Ann, Jordan Robert. Intern in oral surgery and oral medicine Mass. Gen. Hosp., Boston, 1956-57; prin. investigator clin. br. NIH, Bethesda, Md., 1957-60, clin. asso., cons. oral medicine, 1962-73; asst. chief dental research Phila. Gen. Hosp., 1960-62, research com., 1962-73, chief dental research, 1962-73, sr. attending dentist, 1973-74; attending dentist Children's Hosp., Phila., 1962—; asst. prof. oral medicine U. Pa. Sch. Dental Medicine, Phila., 1960-63, asso. prof., 1963-66, prof., 1966—, dir. hosp. edn., 1963-73, chmn. dept. oral medicine, 1973-78, prof. dept. otorhinolaryngology, 1974—, dir. Clin. Research Center, 1978—; mem. staff Hosp. U. Pa., Presbyn. U. Hosp.; vis. prof. oral medicine Hebrew U., Jerusalem, 1968, 69-70, 72, dir. affiliated program, 1975—; vis. prof., Japan, 1976; dir. Robert Wood Johnson Found. Rural Dental Health Program, U. Pa., 1975—. Chmn. adult edn. Temple Beth Hillel, 1964-69, bd. dirs., 1965-70, mem. exec. com., 1966-70, fin. sec., 1966-69; mem. Public Com. for Humanities in Pa., 1977—, vice chmn., 1979, 80; vice chmn. dental div. Am. Friends of Hebrew U., 1978—. Served with USPHS, 1957-60. Recipient Grace Milliken award Harvard U., 1956; Myrle Wreath award Phila. chpt. Hadassah, 1973; spl. citation Am. Friends Hebrew U., 1978. Mem. ADA, Am. Public Health Assn., Am. Acad. Oral Medicine (Samuel) Charles Miller award 1978), Am. Soc. Hosp. Dentists, Am. Bd. Oral Medicine (bd. examiners), Am. Soc. Dentistry for Handicapped, Internat. Assn. Dental Research (sec.-treas. 1963-66, pres. Phila. sect. 1965-67, counsellor 1967-68), Coll. Physicians Phila. Cons. to editorial bds.; reviewer for med. and dental jours.; contbr. chpts. to books, articles to profl. publs. Home: 340 Haverford Rd Wynnewood PA 19096 Office: U Pa Sch Dental Medicine Philadelphia PA 19104

SHIPLER, DAVID KARR, journalist; b. Orange, N.J., Dec. 3, 1942; s. Guy Emery Jr. and Eleanor (Karr) S.; A.B., Dartmouth, 1964; m. Deborah S. Isaacs, Sept. 17, 1966; children—Jonathan Robert, Laura Karr, Michael Edmund. News clk. N.Y. Times, 1966-67, news summary writer, 1968, reporter met. staff, 1968-73, fgn. corr. Saigon bur., 1973-75, fgn. corr. Moscow Bur., 1975—, bur. chief, 1977-79, chief Jerusalem bur., 1979—. Served with USNR, 1964-66. Recipient award for distinguished reporting Soc. Silurians, 1971; award for distinguished pub. affairs reporting Am. Polit. Scis. Assn., 1971; Page One award for best local reporting N.Y. Newspaper Guild, 1973, Page One award (with others) for most crusading newspaper, 1973; award N.Y. chpt. Sigma Delta Chi, 1973. Mem. N.Y. Newspaper Guild. Contbr. articles to nat. mags. Home: 21 Hovevei Zion Jerusalem Israel Office: care New York Times 229 W 43d St New York NY 10036. *I have been governed professionally by the conviction that an open society needs open examination of itself to survive. Defining problems, inspecting blemishes, probing wounds, and exposing injustice are the required pastimes of a free people. Nothing intelligent can come from ignorance. If information does not guarantee wisdom, it is at least a prerequisite, for the only wise course is through knowledge. To write about current affairs, then, is to play a small role in a great endeavor. It is to measure one's own performance continually against the highest standards of honesty, fairness, thoroughness, intelligence, to search every day for a bit of truth, then share it. These are the ingredients of happiness, for such a job involves a life of constant learning, perpetual self-education. It keeps a man whole.*

SHIPLEY, JAMES ROSS, educator, designer; b. Marion, Ohio, Dec. 26, 1910; s. Jay R. and Anna M. (Bolley) S.; diploma Cleve. Inst. Art, 1935; B.S., Western Res. U., 1936; grad. student, U. So. Calif., summer 1940; A.M., U. Ill., 1949; m. Dorothy J. Elliott, May 29, 1941; children—Ann, Robert E. and David E. Engaged as artist J.H. Maish Advt. Agy.; 1929-31; designer styling sect. Gen. Motors Corp., 1936-38; salesman Proctor and Gamble Co., 1938-39; instr. art, charge curriculum indsl. design U. Ill., Urbana, 1939-41, asso., 1941-45, asst. prof., 1945-48, asso. prof., 1949, prof., 1949-78, prof. emeritus, 1978—, head dept. art and design, 1956-77; prof., acting head dept. art Pa. State U., University Park, 1978—; art dir. VioBin Corp., 1944-54; design cons., 1944—; acad. dir. advanced studies for designers. Inst. Contemporary Art, 1958; exhibited paintings Cleve. Mus. Art, Detroit Inst. Arts. Mem. visual arts com. Festival of Americas, Chgo., 1959; mem. Exploratory com. visual arts Am. Council Learned Societies, 1949; mem. Ill. Bd. Higher Edn. com. Z on grad. and profl. edn. in humanities and arts, 1969-70; mem. visual arts panel Ill. Arts Council, 1971-76; cons. Ind. Commn. for Higher Edn., 1976. Fellow Nat. Assn. Schs. Art (v.p., 1960-61, pres., 1961-63; major writer standards, procedures and manuals for accrediting profl. programs in art); mem. Am. Soc. Indsl. Designers (ednl. sec. 1959-61), AAUP, College Art Assn., Indsl. Design Edn. Assn. (pres. 1959-61), Indsl. Designers Inst. (chmn. edn. com.; vice chmn. Midwest chpt. 1949), Citizens Ednl. Council, Midwest Coll. Art Conf. (pres. 1961- 62). Home: 27 Greencroft Dr Champaign IL 61820 Office: Dept of Art and Design U of Ill Champaign IL 61820. *The American system of education, often criticized for low standards, has the virtue, beyond any other system known to me, of being very forgiving and for attempting to give each of its citizens the chance to make the most of his talents. Along with many others I was a late starter; yet our system was forgiving, gave me time, gave me a second chance so to speak. I often thank God I was born an American, for I doubt I would have done very well under most other systems. I hope American education never loses this quality of magnanimity.*

SHIPLEY, JOSEPH T., editor, writer, radio commentator; b. Bklyn., Aug 19, 1893; s. Jay R. and Jennie (Fragner) S.; A.B., Coll. City N.Y., 1912; A.M., Columbia U., 1914, Ph.D., 1931; m. Helen Bleet; children—Margaret (Mrs. Fiedler), Paul D.; m. 2d, Ann Ziporkes; children—J. Burke, H. Thorne. Instr. in English, Stuyvesant

High Sch., 1914-57; lecturer on poetry, Bd. of Edn., 1916-20; instr. in lit. criticism Coll. City of N.Y., 1928-38, Bklyn. Coll., 1932-38; with Yeshiva Coll., 1928-44, sec. of faculty, successively asst. prof., asso. prof. English; drama critic New Leader, 1922-62, radio station WEVD, 1940—; Am. corr. Assn. pour le Rencontre des Cultures, 1965—; Vocabulary cons. Sci. Research Assos.; instr. Playwrights Seminar Dramatic Workshop, dean, 1952-54; mng. dir. Theatre of UN; fgn. editor Contemporary Verse, 1919-26; apptd. to make survey and scenarios for motion picture survey of N.Y. C. Sch. System, 1939; founder and exec. sec. Inst. Pub. Arts in Edn., 1939-41; asst. editor Jour. History of Ideas, 1940-44; asso. editor Jour. Aesthetics; editor American Bookman; Dictionary of World Lit., 1943; Ency. of Lit., 1946; editorial asso. Philos. Library. Chmn. Nat. Com. on Edn. in Public Arts; Am. rep. Theatre des Nations Festival, Paris. Am. director Far East Research Inst.; mem. cultural adv. bd. American Coll. in Paris; hon. trustee Hwa Kiu U. (Macao), Canton U. (Hong Kong). Recipient Townsend Harris medal for distinguished contbns. in field, 1975. Mem. Assn. Internationale de la Critique Dramatique (U.S. v.p.), English Assn., N.Y. Drama Critics' Circle (pres. 1952-54, sec.), London Drama Critics' Circle, Phi Beta Kappa. Author translations from the French, also original works, latest of these being, Trends in Literature, 1948; Guide to Great Plays, 1952; Dictionary of Forgotten Words, 1953; Dictionary of World Literary Terms, 1955, rev. 1968, 72; Playing with Words, 1960; Word Play, 1972. Author: Mentally Disturbed Teacher, 1961; Word Games for Play and Power, 1962; Five plays by Ibsen, 1965; Vocabulab, 1968; Anthology: Modern French Poetry, 1975; In Praise of English, 1977. Contbr. to Ency. Brit., also articles, poems and critical essays to mags. in U.S., Eng., France, India, Pakistan. Editor: Study-Master Guides to Drama. Office: 29 W 46th St New York NY 10036 also 13 Gledhow Gardens London SW5 OAY England

SHIPLEY, L(INWOOD) PARKS, private banker; b. Cockeysville, Md., 1905; s. Walter Vincent and Edith (Parks) S; grad. U. Md., 1927; m. Emily Herzog, 1930; children—Linwood Parks, Frederick H., Walter V., Emily Jane. With Brown Brothers Harriman & Co., N.Y.C., 1933—, mgr., 1946—, partner, 1953—. Dir. The Shipleys of Md. Decorated Order of Sitara-l-quaid-i-Azam, (Pakistan). Fellow Royal Soc. Arts; mem. Swedish C. of C. U.S.A. (dir.), Pakistan-Am. C. of C., Norwegian Am. C. of C. (dir.). Presbyn. Clubs: Baltusrol Golf (Short Hills, N.J.); India House, Union League (N.Y.). Home: 81 Oak Ridge Ave Summit NJ 07901 Office: 59 Wall St New York City NY 10005

SHIPLEY, SAMUEL LYNN, advt. and pub. relations exec.; b. Marlborough, Mass., Nov. 14, 1929; s. Clifford Lynn and Esther (Jacobs) S.; student Charles Morris Price Sch. Advt. and Journalism, U. N.H., 1948-50; m. Sue Finucan, Sept. 5, 1955; children—Jeffrey Lynn, Beth Ann, Amy. Exec. dir. Democratic Party N.H., 1953-56; sales promotion and pub. relations mgr. Nat. Advt. Splty. Firm, Phila., 1958-62; pres. Shipley Assos., Inc., Wilmington, Del., 1962—, Internat. Toy Shows, Inc., 1977—; pub. relations dir. Democratic Party Del., 1964-68; dir. Del. Devel. Dept., Dover, 1965-69; Mem. Com. of 39, Inc., 1964—; chmn. exec. com. Del. Bicentennial Commn., 1973; del. Bicentennial Council of Thirteen Original States, 1976—; nominee for U.S. Congress, 1976. Served with U.S. Army, 1951-53. Recipient Freedoms Found. Honor medal, 1966, Outstanding Grad. award Charles Morris Price Sch., 1974. Mem. Am. Advt. Fedn., Wilmington Advt. Club. Mason, Rotarian. Club: Masonic of Del. (Wilmington). Home: Curtis Mill Rd RD 3 Newark DE 19711 Office: Powder Mill Sq Greenville DE 19807. *One is almost always successful if he is blessed with good health, normal intelligence, a truly giving spirit, positive mind, good imagination, some self-discipline, hard work, and persistence. In America these ingredients spell success and happiness.*

SHIPLEY, VERGIL ALAN, educator; b. Amber, Okla., June 25, 1922; s. Guy and Ida Jean (Grant) S.; B.A., U. Okla., 1947, M.A., 1948; postgrad. U. Tex., 1947; Ph.D., London (Eng.) Sch. Econs., 1950; m. Zannie May Manning, May 3, 1947; children—Douglass Manning, John Grant. Asso. prof. polit. sci. Wichita State U., 1950-56; asst. prof. govt. U. Miami, Coral Gables, Fla., 1957-61, asso. prof., 1962-68, prof. politics and pub. affairs, 1968—, chmn. dept., 1970-77, acting dean Sch. Bus. Adminstrn., 1968-69. Polit. election analyst WTVJ-CBS, 1962—; cons. to study commn. on local govt., 1971-72. Served to capt. AUS, 1942-46; ETO. Mem. Am. Polit. Sci. Assn., Am. Soc. Pub. Adminstrn., Phi Beta Kappa, Phi Eta Sigma, Pi Sigma Alpha, Beta Gamma Sigma (pres. U. Miami chpt. 1969), Delta Sigma Pi (faculty adviser 1968-76). Democrat. Home: 1127 Alberca St Coral Gables FL 33134 Office: Dept Politics and Pub Affairs U Miami Coral Gables FL 33124

SHIPLEY, WALTER VINCENT, banker; b. Newark, Nov. 2, 1935; s. L. Parks and Emily (Herzog) S.; student Williams Coll., 1954-56; B.S., N.Y. U., 1960; m. Judith Ann Lyman, Sept. 14, 1957; children—Barbara, Allison, Pamela, Dorothy, John. With Chem. Bank, 1956—, head London br. Internat. Div., 1973-74, head ops. Europe and Can., 1974-75, dep. dir. internat. div., 1975, exec. v.p. charge internat. div., N.Y.C., 1975—; dir. Bayer Fgn. Investments Ltd., Banco General de Negocios, S.A., Buenos Aires, Argentina; bd. dirs. Nat. Fgn. Trade Council. Bd. dirs. Goodwill Industries Greater N.Y.; trustee Central Presbyterian Ch., Summit, N.J. Mem. Council Fgn. Relations, Overseas Devel. Council, English-Speaking Union, Pilgrims of U.S., Japan Soc. Clubs: Links; Baltusrol Golf (Springfield, N.J.); Beacon Hill. Home: 21 Prospect Hill Ave Summit NJ 07901 Office: 20 Pine St New York NY 10015*

SHIPMAN, CHARLES WILLIAM, engr.; b. Phillipsburgh, N.J., Aug. 29, 1924; s. George Funk and Elizabeth (Johnston) S.; S.B., Mass. Inst. Tech., 1948, S.M., 1949, Sc.D., 1952; m. Louise Jean Hendrickson, Aug. 31, 1946; children—Nancy Ruth, Jane Louise, Robert Walter George. Instr. chem. engring. Mass. Inst. Tech., 1949-50, research asso., 1955-58; asst. prof. U. Del., 1952-55; mem. faculty Worcester (Mass.) Poly. Inst., 1958-74, prof. chem. engring., 1964-74, dean grad. studies, 1971-74; engr. Cabot Corp., Billerica, Mass., 1974—; cons., 1953-74. Served with USMCR, 1944-46. Mem. Combustion Inst. (co-recipient Silver Combustion medal 1964), Am. Chem. Soc., Am. Inst. Chem. Engrs., Sigma Xi, Alpha Chi Sigma, Chi Phi. Contbr. articles to profl. jours. Home: 14-C 105 Spitbrook Rd Nashua NH 03060 Office: Cabot Corp Billerica MA 01821

SHIPMAN, FURNEY GEORGE, coll. pres.; b. Clarkton, N.C., June 11, 1917; s. Daniel Lency and Lemie Ann (Melvin) S.; A.B., Livingstone Coll., 1939; M.A., Boston Coll., 1952; Ed.D., George Peabody Coll. Tchrs., Nashville, 1961; m. Louise McKoy, Dec. 22, 1948; 1 son, Sheldon René. Tchr. high sch., Clarkton, 1940-51; prin. Branch High Sch., Lumberton, N.C., 1951-52, Southside High Sch., Rowland, 1952-57, Dillard High Sch., Goldsboro, N.C., 1957-59; mem. faculty Fisk U., 1959-61; prof., chmn. dept. edn. N.C. Central U., 1961-69; pres. Livingstone Coll., 1969—; cons. in field; dir. First Union Nat. Bank, Salisbury, N.C. Bd. dirs. CORD, 1968-69. Served with USNR, 1944-46. Mem. A.A.U.P., Am. Assn. Sch. Adminstrs., Am. Assn. Higher Edn., NEA (life), Salisbury C. of C., Educators N.C., Common Cause, Phi Delta Kappa, Kappa Delta Pi. Mem. A.M.E. Zion Ch. Mason, Optimist. Author publns. in field. Office: 702 W Monroe St Salisbury NC 28144*

SHIPMAN, PETER HERBERT, stock broker; b. London, Ont., Can., Aug. 25, 1934; s. Gerald Totten and Cora Fern (Foster) S.; came to U.S., 1940, naturalized, 1954; A.B., Dartmouth, 1956; postgrad. Gen. Motors Inst., 1957; m. Joan Chessman, June 16, 1962; children—Julie, James, Jerrold. With Gen. Motors Corp., Detroit, 1956-57, Merrill, Lynch, Pierce, Fenner & Smith, San Francisco, 1960-65, N.Y.C., 1965-69; sr. v.p., dir. William D. Witter, Inc., N.Y.C., 1969-76; exec. dir. SEC, Washington, 1976-77; sr. v.p. Kuhn Loeb & Co. Inc., 1977—, also dir.; exec. v.p. Blyth Eastman Dillon & Co., Inc., 1978—, also dir.; pres. Am. Banker-Bond Buyer Inc., N.Y.C., 1978—, also dir. Served to capt. USMCR, 1957-60. Mem. Psi Upsilon. Presbyn. Clubs: Appawamis Country, Shenorock Shore (Rye, N.Y.). Bd. Room (N.Y.C.). Home: Windcrest Rd Rye NY 10580 Office: One Chase Manhattan Plaza New York NY 10005

SHIPMAN, ROBERT JACK, ins. co. exec.; b. Mullens, W.Va., Dec. 15, 1933; s. Jack K. and Gladys G. (Goode) S.; A.B. in History, W.Va. U., 1955, LL.B., 1958; m. Marilyn O'Dell, July 9, 1959; children—Andrew. Jeff. Admitted to W.Va. bar, 1960; claims supr. USF&G Co., Charleston, W.Va., 1961-66; ins. commr. State of W.Va., 1966-69, asst. atty. gen., 1969-71; v.p., gen. counsel Foremost Ins. Co., Grand Rapids, Mich., 1971—. Served with AUS, 1958-60. Mem. Am., W.Va. bar assns. Democrat. Presbyterian. Home: 1718 Pembroke St SE Kentwoods MI 49508 Office: 5800 Foremost Dr SE Grand Rapids MI 49501

SHIPPEE, NATHAN MATHEWSON, banker; b. Providence, May 1, 1919; s. Harold R. and Beatrice M. (Wright) S.; B.S., U. R.I., 1941; m. Patricia R. Morel, Dec. 20, 1967; children—Elizabeth, Robert, Richard, Arthur. Cashier, Chase Manhattan Bank, Shanghai, 1946-49; asst. to pres. H & B Machinery Co., Pawtucket, R.I., 1949-53; founder, chmn., pres., treas. Inpak Systems, Inc., N.Y.C., 1959; founder The Prudential Group, Inc., N.Y.C., 1959. Trustee Mus. of the Am. Indian. Served to maj. AUS, World War II. Decorated Bronze Star; Chevalier du Merite Maritime (France). Home: Sandpiper Point Rd Old Lyme CT 06371 Office: 90 Broad St New York NY 10004. *Once an individual has found out how to make a living, he then turns to a higher question—how to make a life.*

SHIPPEN, ZOE, portrait artist; b. Boston, Nov. 12, 1902; d. Eugene Rodman and Elizabeth Herrick (Blount) S.; student Mary C. Wheeler Sch., Providence, Boston Museum Sch., Art Students League, N.Y., Ecole des Beaux Arts Americaine, Fontaine Bleau, France; m. Laurent Kimball Varnum, Feb. 28, 1959. Began painting portraits professionally, 1925; has specialized in portraits of children, 1930—; exhbns. include Palm Beach, Miami Beach, Washington, N.Y., East Hampton, N.Y., Newport, R.I. El Lyceum y Lawn Tennis Club, Havana, Cuba, 1947; one-man show Newton Galleries, N.Y., 1946; portraits include children of internationally famous people residents of both the U.S. and fgn. countries. Author: Cooking with a Light Touch, 1966; Four for Lunch...Dinner for Eight, 1975. Address: 220 Fairview Rd Palm Beach FL 33480

SHIPPEY, DAVID B., bus. exec.; b. San Francisco, Dec. 30, 1927; s. Gertrude H. Shippey; B.S., U. Calif., Berkeley, 1950; m. Roberta E. Long, June 23, 1951; children—Matthew, Ann, Elizabeth. Corp. exec. DiGiorgio Corp., San Francisco, 1959-71; v.p., treas. Saga Corp., Menlo Park, Calif., 1971—; dir. Gentran, Inc., BBK Internat. Fund, Inc., Ross Valley Homes, Inc. Pres. bd. dirs. Miramonte Mut. Health Services, Inc. Served with USNR, 1945-46. C.P.A., Calif. Mem. Am. Inst. C.P.A.'s, Fin. Execs. Inst., Calif. Soc. C.P.A.'s. Home: 557 Cresta Vista Ln Portola Valley CA 94025 Office: 1 Saga Ln Menlo Park CA 94025

SHIRA, ROBERT BRUCE, dentist, univ. adminstr.; b. Butler, Pa., Dec. 2, 1910; s. Thomas Plummer and Erla (Brown) S.; student Bartlesville (Okla.) Jr. Coll., 1927-28; D.D.S., U. Mo., Kansas City, 1932; D.Sc., Georgetown U., 1976; m. Anne Eileen Anderson, Mar. 27, 1933; children—Sharon Lu, Mary Ann, Linda Kay. Pvt. practice dentistry, Pawhuska, Okla., 1932-38; commd. 1st lt., Dental Corps, U.S. Army, 1938, advanced through grades to maj. gen., 1967; chief oral surgery Walter Reed Gen. Hosp., 1954-64; dental surgeon U.S. Army Europe, 1964-66; dir. dental activities Walter Reed Army Med. Center, 1966-67; asst. surgeon gen., chief Army Dental Corps, 1967-71; ret., 1971; dean Sch. Dental Medicine, Tufts U., Boston, 1972-78, sr. v.p., acting provost, Medford, Mass., 1979—, prof. oral surgery, 1971—; vis. prof. U. of Pacific, 1954-71, U. Pa., 1956-71; professorial lectr. Georgetown U., 1955-71. Decorated D.S.M., Legion of Merit with 2 oak leaf clusters, Army Commendation medal; recipient Sword of Hope award Am. Cancer Soc., 1959; named Man of Year, U. Mo., Kansas City, 1960. Diplomate Am. Bd. Oral and Maxillofacial Surgery (pres. 1974-75). Mem. ADA (pres. 1975-76, cons. Council on Therapeutics, Disting. Service award), Am. Assn. Oral and Maxillofacial Surgery (pres. 1965-66), Am. Acad. Oral Pathology. Democrat. Presbyterian. Contbr. chpts.: Textbook of Oral Surgery, 1973; Management of Office Emergencies, 1979; Improving Dental Practice through Preventive Measures, 1965; contbr. articles to profl. jours. Home: 17 Phinney Rd Lexington MA 02173 Office: Office of Provost Tufts U Medford MA 02155

SHIRCLIFFE, HAROLD ARNOLD, lawyer; b. Chgo., Jan. 5, 1906; s. Arnold and Louisa M. (Mace) S.; student U. Ill., 1923-26; LL.B., DePaul U., 1930; m. M. Virginia Allen, Aug. 5, 1930. Admitted to Ill. bar, 1930, Cal. bar, 1957; asst. to trust atty. Chgo. Title & Trust Co., 1930-32, trust adminstr., 1932-42, asst. trust officer, 1942-48, tax counsel, 1949-56; trust officer United Calif. Bank, Los Angeles, 1956-57, v.p., 1957—, trust counsel, 1957-68, v.p., sr. trust officer, 1968-73; counsel, Bolton & Hemer, 1972-73, Volney Morin, Inc., Hollywood, Calif., 1973—; dir. Santa Maria Valley Ry., 1970-72; sec. E.R. Moore Cap & Gown Co., 1944-46. Lectr., Ill. State Bankers Trust Devel. Sch. at Northwestern U., 1950-55. Mem. adv. council Comdt. Chgo. Harbor, 1953-54. Fellow N.Y. Hist. Soc. Mem. Calif., Los Angeles County bar assns., Chgo. Power Squadron (post comdr., exec. com. 1952-56), Beverly Hills Navy League Council, Los Angeles C. of C. Republican. Presbyn. Contbr. articles to profl. jours. Home: 11951 Mayfield Ave Los Angeles CA 90049 Office: 1341 Cahuenga Blvd Hollywood CA 90028

SHIRE, DAVID LEE, composer; b. Buffalo, July 3, 1937; s. Irving Daniel and Esther Miriam (Sheinberg) S.; B.A., Yale U., 1959; m. Talia Rose Coppola, Mar. 29, 1970; 1 son, Matthew Orlando. Film scores include: The Conversation, 1974, The Taking of Pelham 1-2-3, 1974, Farewell, My Lovely, 1975, The Hindenburg, 1975, All the President's Men, 1977, Saturday Night Fever (adaptation and additional music), 1977, Old Boyfriends, 1979, Norma Rae, 1979; TV scores include: Tell Me Where It Hurts, 1974, Raid on Entebbe, 1977, The Defection of Simas Kudirka, 1978; Theatre scores include: The Sap of Life, 1961, Graham Crackers, 1962, The Unkown Solider and His Wife, 1967, How Do You Do, I Love You, 1968, Love Match, 1970, Starting Here, Starting Now, 1977; composer: Sonata for Cocktail Piano, 1965; recorded songs include: Autumn, 1959, Starting Here, Starting Now, 1965, What About Today?, 1969, Manhattan Skyline, 1977, The Promise, 1978, It Goes Like It Goes, 1979, With You I'm Born Again, 1979; albums include: Saturday Night Fever, 1977 (Grammy award 1978), Starting Here, Starting Now, 1977. Served with Army N.G., 1960-66. Mem. Composers and Lyricists Guild Am., Am. Fedn. Musicians, Broadcast Music Inc., Acad. Motion Picture Arts and Scis., Nat. Acad. Rec. Arts and Scis., Nat. Acad. TV Arts and Scis. Jewish. Office: care Plant Cohen & Co 9777 Wilshire Blvd Beverly Hills CA 90212

SHIRE, DONALD THOMAS, corp. exec.; b. Boston, Jan. 13, 1930; s. Thomas J. and Nellie M. S.; B.S. in Bus. Adminstrn., Boston U., 1951, LL.B., 1953; m. Anne Court Bither, Nov 21, 1953; children—Jennifer Anne, Andrew Carter, Daniel Orchard. Atty., Air Products and Chems., Inc., 1957-64, sec., atty., 1964-75, sec., asst. gen. counsel, 1975—, v.p. energy and materials, 1978—. Dir. Indsl. Devel. Corp. Lehigh County; trustee Muhlenberg Coll.; bd. dirs. Family and Children's Service. Served to lt. USNR, 1954-57. Mem. Am., Boston bar assns., Am. Soc. Corp. Secs., Pa. Soc. Mem. P.E. Ch. (mem. com. episcopate Diocese Bethlehem). Home: 1133 N Main St Allentown PA 18104 Office: Air Products and Chemicals Inc Trexlertown PA 18087

SHIRE, TALIA ROSE, actress; b. Jamaica, N.Y., Apr. 25, 1946; d. Carmine and Italia (Pennino) Coppola; m. David Lee Shire, Mar. 29, 1970 (div.); 1 son, Matthew Orlando. Films include: Godfather, 1972 Godfather II (Oscar nominee for Best Supporting Actress), 1974, Rocky (Oscar nominee for Best Actress, N.Y. Film Critics award for Best Actress), 1977, Old Boyfriends, 1979, Rocky II, 1979, Windows, 1980; TV appearances include Rich Man, Poor Man, 1976, Kill Me If You Can, 1977. Office: care Creative Artists Agy Inc 1888 Century Park E Suite 1400 Los Angeles CA 90067*

SHIRER, WILLIAM LAWRENCE, journalist, author; b. Chgo., Feb. 23, 1904; s. Seward Smith and Bessie Josephine (Tanner) S.; A.B., Coe Coll., 1925, Litt. D. (hon.); m. Theresa Stiberitz, 1931 (div. 1970); children—Eileen Inga, Linda Elizabeth. Journalist, Paris edit. Chicago Tribune, 1925-26; fgn. corr., Tribune, 1926-33, Universal News Service, 1935-37; became Continental rep. CBS, 1937; war corr., 1939-45, commentator, 1945-47; commentator on Mutual network, 1947-49. Mem. Authors Guild (pres.), P.E.N., Council on Fgn. Relations, Fgn. Policy Assn., Legion of Honor, Phi Beta Kappa. Club: Centry (N.Y.C.). Author: Berlin Diary, 1941; End of a Berlin Diary, 1947; The Traitor, 1950; Midcentury Journey, 1952; Stranger Come Home, 1954; The Challenge of Scandinavia, 1955; The Consul's Wife, 1956; The Rise and Fall of the Third Reich (Nat. Book award 1961), 1960; The Rise and Fall of Adolf Hitler, 1961; The Sinking of the Bismarck, 1962; The Collapse of the Third Republic, 1969; 20th Century Journey, 1976; Gandhi-A Memoir, 1979. Contbr. to Atlantic Monthly, Harper's, others. Address: Box 487 34 Sunset Ave Lenox MA 01240

SHIRES, GEORGE THOMAS, II, physician, educator; b. Waco, Tex., Nov. 22, 1925; s. George Thomas and Donna Mae (Smith) S.; M.D. (Life Ins. Med. Research fellow), U. Tex. at Dallas, 1947; m. Robbie Jo Martin, Nov. 27, 1948; children—Donna (Mrs. James G. Blain), George Thomas III, Jo Ellen. Intern Mass. Meml. Hosp., Boston, 1948-49; resident Parkland Meml. Hosp., Dallas, 1950-52; mem. faculty U. Tex. Southwestern Med. Sch. at Dallas, 1952-74, asso. prof. surgery, acting chmn. dept., 1960-61, prof., chmn. dept., 1961-74 surgeon in chief surg. services Parkland Meml. Hosp., 1960-74; prof., chmn. dept. surgery U. Wash. Sch. Medicine, Seattle, 1974-75; chief of service Harborview Med. Center, Seattle, Univ. Hosp., Seattle, 1974-75; chmn. dept. surgery N.Y. Hosp.-Cornell Med. Center, 1975—; cons. Childrens Orthopedic Hosp., Seattle, 1974-75; cons. to Surgeon Gen., Nat. Inst. Gen. Med. Sci., 1965—, to Surgeon Gen. Army, 1965—; mem. com. metabolism and trauma Nat. Acad. Sci./NRC, 1964-71, com. trauma, 1964-71; mem. research program evaluation com., reviewer clin. investigation applications career devel. program VA, 1972—; mem. gen. med. research program progress com. NIH, 1970-74, mem. Surgery A study sect., 1970-74, chmn., 1976—; cons. editorial bd. Jour. Trauma, 1968—, Tex. Medicine. Served to lt. M.C., USNR, 1949-50, 53-55. Diplomate Am. Bd. Surgery (dir. 1968-74, chmn. 1972-74). Mem. Dallas Soc. Gen. Surgeons (pres.-elect, pres. 1972-74), Am. Assn. Surgery Trauma, A.C.S. (bd. regents 1971—, chmn. bd. regents 1978—), A.M.A., Am. Surg. Assn. (sec. 1969-74), Digestive Disease Found. (founding mem.), Halsted Soc., Internat. Soc. Burn Injuries, Internat. Surg. Soc., Pan-Am. Med. Assn. (surgery council, 1971—), Pan Pacific Surg. Assn., Soc. Clin. Surgery, Soc. Surgery Alimentary Tract, Soc. Surg. Chairmen (pres. 1972-74), Soc. Univ. Surgeons (chmn. publs. com. 1965-68), So. Surg. Assn., Surg. Biology Club (sec. 1968-70), Western Surg. Assn., Allen O. Whipple Surg. Soc., James IV Assn. Surgeons, Alpha Omega Alpha, Alpha Pi Alpha, Phi Beta Pi. Editorial bd. Year Book Med. Publs., 1970—, Annals of Surgery, 1972—, Surgical Techniques Illustrated: An International Comparative Text, 1974-75, Am. Jour. Surgery, 1968—, Contemporary Surgery, 1973—. Home: 450 E 63d St New York NY 10021 Office: 525 E 68th St New York NY 10021

SHIRK, CHARLES ALBERT, engring. and bldg. co. exec.; b. Gary, Ind., May 15, 1920; s. Joel B. and Mary A. (Pearson) S.; B.S. in Civil Engring., U. Notre Dame, 1942; m. Norma Fisher, Oct. 26, 1944; children—Peter J., Wendy C., Jill K. Structural engr. Curtiss-Wright Corp., Buffalo, 1942-46, Hazelet & Erdal, Chgo., 1946-48; with Austin Co., Cleve., 1948—, supr. engring., Chgo., 1948-57, asst. dist. engr., 1957-60, mgr. research and devel. div., Cleve., 1961-62, dist. engr., Chgo., 1962-65, asst. dist. mgr., 1965-70, v.p., process div. mgr., 1970-72, asst. gen. mgr., Cleve., 1972-73, pres., gen. mgr., chief exec. officer, 1973—, dir., 1971—, dep. chmn., 1979—. Mem. gen. bd. Greater Cleve. chpt. ARC; trustee Euclid Gen. Hosp. Assn., Cleve. Health Edn. Mus.; bd. dirs. Greater Cleve. Growth Assn., Bluecoats, Inc., The 50 Club. Registered profl. engr., 49 states, D.C. Fellow ASCE; mem. Nat. Soc. Profl. Engrs., Am. Welding Soc., Am. Concrete Inst., Cleve. Engring. Soc., Newcomen Soc. N.Am. Roman Catholic. Club: Union (Cleve.). Home: 31681 Meadowlark Way Pepper Pike OH 44124 Office: 3650 Mayfield Rd Cleveland OH 44121

SHIRLEY, DAVID ALLEN, chemist, educator; b. Knoxville, Tenn., Sept. 15, 1918; s. John Fletcher and Tennie Marie (Beets) S.; B.S. in Chemistry, U. Tenn., 1939, M.S., 1940; Ph.D., Ia. State U., 1943, postdoctoral research fellow, 1943-44; m. Ruth Charlotte Wright, Aug. 30, 1941; children—Carolyn R., Allen C., Robert E., Elizabeth M. Research chemist E.I. duPont de Nemours & Co., Inc., 1944-47; asst., then asso. prof. Tulane U., 1947-53; mem. faculty U. Tenn., 1953—, prof. chemistry, 1955—, head dept., 1962—. Mem. Am. Chem. Soc. (chmn. E. Tenn. sect. 1959), Chem. Soc. (London, Eng.), AAUP, Tenn. Acad. Sci., Phi Beta Kappa (pres. U. Tenn. chpt. 1976-77), Sigma Xi (pres. U. Tenn. chpt. 1960), Phi Kappa Phi. Author: Preparation of Organic Intermediates, 1951; Organic Chemistry, 1964. Asso. editor: (Gilman) Organic Chemistry-An Advanced Treatise, vols. III and IV, 1953; (Adams) Organic Reactions, Vol. VIII, 1954. Contbr. articles to profl. jours. Home: 1116 Montview Dr Knoxville TN 37914

SHIRLEY, GEORGE IRVING, tenor; b. Indpls., Apr. 18, 1934; s. Irving Ewing and Daisy (Bell) S.; B.S. in Edn., Wayne State U., 1955, grad. student, 1955-56; H.D.H., Wilberforce U., 1967; m. Gladys Lee Ishop, June 24, 1956; children—Olwyn, Lyle. Operatic debut in Die Fledermaus, Turnau Opera Players, Woodstock, N.Y., 1959; other appearances include Teatro Nouvo, Milan and Teatro Della Pergola, Florence, Italy, 1960, New Eng. Opera Theatre, 1961, Spring Opera

San Francisco, 1961, Festival of Two Worlds, Spoleto, Italy, 1961, Sante Fe Opera, 1961, N.Y.C. Opera, 1961, Met. Opera Co., 1961, Opera Soc. Washington, 1962, Teatro Colon, Buenos Aires, Argentina, 1964, La Scala, Milan, Italy, 1965, Glyndebourne Festival, Sussex, Eng., 1966, Scottish Opera, 1967, Royal Opera, Covent Garden, London, Eng., 1967, San Francisco Opera, 1977, Chgo. Lyric Opera, 1977. Rec. sec. Am. Guild Mus. Artists, 1963-73. Winner Met. Opera Audition, 1961, Am. Opera Audition, 1960; recipient Nat. Arts Club award, 1960; winner Il Concorso di Musica e Danza, Italy, 1960. Mem. Alpha Phi Alpha, Phi Mu Alpha. Address: care Ann Summers Internat Via Mario dei Fiori 42 00187 Rome Italy also Box 95 Sta A Willowdale Toronto ON M2N 5S7 Canada

SHIRLEY, HARDY LOMAX, forester, educator; b. Orleans, Ind., Nov. 20, 1900; s. Charles Hicks and Maud (Hardy) S.; A.B., Ind. U., 1922; Ph.D., Yale, 1928; Doctor honoris causa, U. Helsinki, 1958; D.Sc., Syracuse U., 1966; m. Mary Hayward Connard, Apr. 22, 1930; children—Frank Connard, Jon Hardy, Emily Knapp, (Mrs. Castner). Instr., later asst. prof. math. U. Nev., 1922-25; asst. biochemistry Boyce Thompson Inst., Yonkers, N.Y., 1927-29; silviculturist Lake States Forest Expt. Sta., St. Paul, 1929-39; dir. Allegheny Forest Expt. Sta., Phila., 1939-41, Northeastern Forest Expt. Sta., 1942-45; asst. dean State U. N.Y., Coll. Forestry at Syracuse U., 1945-51, dean, 1952-67; cons. forestry edn. FAO, UN, 1966—, AID, 1967; study dir. Pres.'s Adv. Panel on Timber and Environment, 1972-73; pres. Shirley Forests, Inc., Elizabethtown, N.Y., 1978—. Fellow Oberlaender Trust, to study tree seed testing and seed certification, 1935; mem. sixth Bot. Congress, Amsterdam 1935; on spl. mission to Caribbean region, 1937; recommendation of this mission carried out by establishment of Tropical Forest Expt. Sta. in P.R., 1939. Mem. 3d World Forestry Congress, Helsinki, Finland, 1949, 4th congress at Dehra Dun, India, 1954, del. 5th congress, Seattle, 1960, 6th congress, Madrid, Spain, 1966; del. Internat. Union Forest Research Orgns. Congress, Oxford, 1957, Vienna, 1961, Munich, Germany, 1967, Gainesville, Fla., 1971. Fellow A.A.A.S. (council 1950-52), Soc. Am. Foresters (council 1944-45); mem. Bot. Soc. Am., Am. Forestry Assn., Nat. Research Council (div. biology and agr. 1944-47), Ecol. Soc. Am., Societas Forestalia Fenniae, Forest Hist. Soc., Empire State Forest Products Assn. (hon. mem.), Phi Beta Kappa, Sigma Xi, Gamma Alpha. Club: Torch (Syracuse). Author: Forestry and its Career Opportunities, 1952, 2d edit., 1964, 3d edit., 1973; (with Paul Graves) Forest Ownership for Pleasure and Profit, 1967; also profl. articles and bulls. Editor-in-chief Jour. of Forestry, 1946-49. Home: 14 Centennial Dr Syracuse NY 13207 also Elizabethtown NY 12932

SHIRLEY, LEMUEL BARNETT, bishop; b. Colon, Panama, July 23, 1916; s. Michael Barnett and Leanna Pricilla (Perry) S.; student La Boca Normal Tng. Sch., 1935-38; B.D., Bishop Payne Div. Sch., 1941; postgrad. Union Theol. Sem., N.Y.C., 1953, St. Augustine's Coll., Canterbury, 1958; D.D. (hon.), Va. Theol. Sem., 1973; m. Olga Gwendolyn Hinds, Apr. 17, 1969; 1 dau., Mariela Cecilia. Ordained deacon Episc. Ch., 1941, priest, 1942, bishop, 1972; bishop Episc. Ch., Balboa, C.Z., 1972—; pres. 9th Province, Episc. Ch. Chmn. Ecumenical Com., 1973; mem. Latin Am. Scholarship Com., 1965; pres. bd. Bella Vista Childrens Home, Child Day Care Center; pres. Colegio Episcopal, Instituto San Cristobal, Christ Ch. Acad.; bd. dirs. Balboa YMCA, United Way. Home: 334 Gorgas Rd Ancon CZ 00101 Office: Box R Balboa CZ 00101

SHIRLEY, ROGER JOHN, utilities exec.; b. Bathurst, N.B., Can., Aug. 7, 1921; s. Edgar Russell and Lydia (LeMarquand) S.; student Dalhousie U., Halifax, N.S., 1939-41; B.A., U. Western Ont., 1948; m. Janet Armour Ince, Feb. 14, 1953; children—Anne Lydia, David John, Peter Strachan. Cons. Woods, Gordon & Co., Toronto, 1948-57, partner, 1957-71, adminstrv. partner Vancouver office, 1957-64, Montreal office, 1964-69, regional partner Eastern Can., 1969-71; exec. v.p., dir. Canadian Internat. Power Co. Ltd., Montreal, 1972-73; pres., dir. Bowater Can. Ltd., 1974—; chmn. Perkins Papers Ltd., Buchmin Industries Inc.; pres. Vinland Holdings Ltd.; dir. Bowater Inc., Bowater Nfld. Ltd., Bowater Mersey Paper Co. Ltd., Bowater Power Co. Ltd., MPG Investment Corp. Bd. dirs., treas. Centraide, Montreal; chmn. Red Feather Found.; trustee Rachael Ship Found. Served to lt. comdr. RNCVR, 1941-45. Anglican. Clubs: St. James (Montreal); Rideau (Ottawa); University (Toronto). Home: 89 Sunnyside Ave Montreal PQ H3Y 1C7 Canada Office: 800 Dorchester Blvd W Montreal PQ Canada

SHIRPSER, CLARA, former mem. Democratic Nat. Com.; b. San Francisco, Aug. 25, 1901; d. Leo and Alexandra (Shragge) Garfinkle; student U. Calif., 1919-21; m. Adolph Shirpser, Nov. 10, 1940; 1 dau., Barbara (Mrs. Robert De Liban); m. 2d, Nat Levy, 1976. Owner, mgr. retail bus., Berkeley, Calif., 1925-45. Mem. Alameda County, Calif. State Dem. central coms., 1950-56, Dem. Nat. Com., 1952-56; vice chmn. nat. and Calif. Kefauver primary campaign for pres., 1956; co-chmn. nat. exec. com. Stevenson-Kefauver presdl. campaign gen. election, 1956; del. to Dem. nat. conv., 1952, 56, 60; Dem. nominee for Assembly, Calif. Legislature, 1950; Calif. campaign com. Brown for gov., 1958; mem. Kennedy Nat. Inaugural Com., 1961; chmn. Alameda County Women for Johnson and Humphrey, 1964; mem. No. Calif. Com. Cranston for U.S. Senator Campaign. Former mem. Berkeley Soc. Welfare Com.; Grey lady ARC, Navy Oak Knoll Hosp., Blood Bank, 1946-49; chmn. women's div. Herrick Meml. Hosp., Berkeley, 1956-74, hon. trustee 1968—; mem. franchise, taxation, charter amendment coms. Berkeley City Council, 1948-50; mem. Menninger Found.; past mem. nat. bd. Atlantic Union; chmn. Bldg. Fund, East Bay Rehab. Center, Women's Div., 1958; mem. Gov.'s Adv. Com. to Calif. Consumers Council, 1959-67; pres. Arch Herrick Hosp. Guild, 1957-74; past bd. dirs. Calif. Heritage Council, Planned Parenthood San Francisco and Alameda Counties; chmn. viewpoints com. Center for Learning in Retirement, U. Calif. Extension Div., 1975-76; pres. League Women Voters Berkeley, 1948-49, Town Meeting chmn. 1949-50; mem. nat. bd. Women's Crusade for a Common Sense Economy. Mem. U. Calif. Alliance, World Affairs Council, UN Assn. U.S. (dir.). Author: Clara Shirpser-One Woman's Role in Politics (2 vol. transcript oral history project Bancroft Library), U. Calif., Berkeley, 1975. Home: 1201 California St San Francisco CA 94109

SHISTER, JOSEPH, educator, labor arbitrator; b. Montreal, Can., Nov. 27, 1917; s. Eli Harry and Pearl (Millman) S.; B.S., U. Montreal, 1939; M.A., Harvard, 1941, Ph.D., 1943; m. Edna Louise Tuck, Dec. 28, 1941; children—Neil Barry, Jayne Ellen, Gail Marilyn, Diane Marjorie. Came to U.S., 1939, naturalized, 1943. Instr. econs. Cornell U., 1942-43; research asso. study trade-unionism Rockefeller Found., 1944-45; asst. prof. econs. Syracuse U., 1945-46; asst. prof., dir. research, labor and mgmt. center Yale U., 1946-49; mem. faculty State U. N.Y. at Buffalo, 1949—, prof., 1950—, chmn. dept. indsl. relations, 1950-78; vis. prof. Tufts U., Wesleyan U., Montreal U., 1949-55; moderator U. Buffalo Round Table of the Air, WBEN, WBEN-TV, WBEN-FM, 1952-72; labor arbitrator, 1944—. Cons. economist Nat. War Labor Bd., 1944; pub. mem. constrn. commn. Nat. Wage Stblzn. Bd., 1951-52; referee System Boards of Adjustment, 1959—; chmn. Presdl. Emergency Dispute Bd., 1961, 62, 64; spl. adviser labor legislation Gov. Conn., 1948-50; mem. social stratification com. Social Sci. Research Council, 1952-53; mem. N.Y. State Bd. Mediation, 1966-68; spl. cons. N.Y. State Med. Bd., 1968—; also spl. Mayor's Office Settlement Emergency Labor Disputes, 1959—; spl. cons. Buffalo Full Employment Com., 1958-60; chmn. Erie County Grievance Bd., 1963-70; mem. N.Y. State Minimum Wage Bd. in Amusement and Recreation Industry, 1957-59; mem. White House Conf. on Nat. Econ. Issues, 1962, White House Conf. on Indsl. World Ahead, 1972; mem. labor dispute panels various bds. and commns. Served as pvt. AUS, 1943-44. Mem. Nat. Acad. Arbitrators, Am. Arbitration Assn., Fed. Mediation and Conciliation Service, Am. Econ. Assn., Indsl. Relations Research Assn. (mem. exec. bd. 1959-62); panels various bds. and commns.), Beta Kappa, Beta Gamma Sigma. Author: Economics of the Labor Market, rev. edit., 1956; Readings in Labor Economics and Industrial Relations, rev. edit., 1956. Co-author: Job Horizons, 1948; Conflict and Stability in Labor Relations, 1952; contbg. author: A Decade of Industrial Relations Research, 1958, Unions, Management and the Public, 1967; Problems de Planification, 1964; Economic Issues and Policies, 1965; Negotiation and Administration of Collective Bargaining Agreements, 1966; The Business World, 1967; Rights and Obligations of Parties Under Collective Agreements, 1967. Co-editor: Insight Into Labor Issues, 1948; Public Policy and Collective Bargaining, 1962. Contbr. articles to profl. jours. Home: 310 Brantwood Rd Snyder NY 14226 Office: Dept Indsl Relations State U NY Buffalo NY 14214

SHIVE, THOMAS M., controls co. exec.; b. Clinton, Iowa, Apr. 7, 1924; s. Philip W. and Helen (Gradert) S.; B.S., Iowa State U., 1948; m. Joanne La Doux, May 29, 1949; children—Katherine, Mark T. With Fisher Governor Co., 1948—, pres., 1969—; pres., chmn. Fisher Controls Co., 1969—; dir. Comml. State Bank, Marshalltown, Iowa. Bd. govs. Iowa State U. Found. Served to capt. USAAF, 1942-45. Decorated Air medal, Purple Heart. Mem. Instrument Soc. Am., Sci. Apparatus Mfrs. Assn. (dir.), Iowa Mfrs. Assn. (dir. 1979), Marshalltown C. of C. (pres. 1965-66). Rotarian. Home: 1911 Knollwood Dr Marshalltown IA 50158 Office: 201 S Center St Marshalltown IA 50158

SHIVE, WILLIAM, educator; b. Commerce, Tex., Dec. 20, 1916; s. William Claud and Myrtle Blanch (Bradford) S.; B.A., E. Tex. State Coll., 1937; M.A., U. Tex., 1939, Ph.D., 1941; m. Gwyn White, Sept. 4, 1941; children—Kathleen, Karen. From instr. to research asst. Univ. Research Inst., U. Tex., 1939- 41; research chemist, cons. Pitts. Coke & Chem. Co., 1941-45; research asst. Nat. Def. Research Council, U. Ill., 1941, instr. organic chemistry at univ., 1942; instr., then asst. prof. Tulane U., 1942-45; research asso. Clayton Found. Biochem. Inst., U. Tex., 1945—, prof. chemistry at univ., 1950—, chmn. dept., 1961-70; cons. Eli Lilly & Co., 1947-55. Mem. nutrition study sect. NIH, 1969-73, chmn., 1972-73; chmn. interdisciplinary cluster on nutrition President's Biomed. Research Panel, 1975-76. Recipient award biol. chemistry Am. Chem. Soc.-Eli Lilly & Co., 1950; Five Outstanding Young Texans award Tex. Jr. C. of C., 1951; Distinguished Alumnus award E. Tex. State U., 1973. Mem. Am. Chem. Soc. (chmn. central Tex. 1951-52), Am. Soc. Biol. Chemists, Am. Inst. Nutrition, Sigma Xi, Phi Lambda Upsilon, Phi Kappa Phi, Alpha Chi Sigma. Mem. Church of Christ. Asso. editor Chem. Rev., 1953-55; editorial adv. bd. Jour. Medicinal and Pharm. Chemistry, 1959-61. Home: 843 E 38th St Austin TX 78705

SHIVELY, DONALD HOWARD, educator; b. Kyoto, Japan, May 11, 1921 (parents Am. citizens); s. Benjamin Franklin and Grace (Ressler) S.; A.B. summa cum laude, Harvard, 1946, A.M., 1947, Ph.D., 1951; m. Emily Mary King, Sept. 1, 1942 (div. Aug. 1957); 1 son, Bruce King; m. 2d, Ilse Dorothea Raacke, Sept. 11, 1957 (div. June 1979); children—Kent Raacke, Evan Raacke. Jr. fellow Soc. Fellows, Harvard, 1947-50; asst. prof., then asso. prof. Oriental langs. U. Calif. at Berkeley, 1950-62; prof., exec. head dept. Asian langs. Stanford, 1962-64; prof. Japanese history and lit. Harvard U., 1964-77, dir. Lang. and Area Center for East Asian Studies, 1964-77, exec. dir. Japan Inst., 1975—, chmn. dept. East Asian langs. and civilizations, 1977—; Lowell lectr. Boston Pub. Library, 1949; dir. Far Eastern Assn., 1952-54; chmn. Center for Japanese Studies U. Calif., 1958-60. Mem. U.S. Nat. Commn. for UNESCO, 1959-60; mem. Com. for U.S.-Japan Cultural and Ednl. Interchange, 1966-69, co-chmn., 1969-71. Served from 2d lt. to maj., USMCR, 1942-46. Decorated Bronze Star. Mem. Assn. Asian Studies, Am. Oriental Soc. (dir. 1969—), Am. Hist. Assn. Author: The Love Suicide At Amijima: A Study of a Japanese Domestic Tragedy by Chikamatsu Monzaemon, 1953; co-author Studies in Kabuki: Its Acting, Music, and Historical Context, 1978. Editor: (with Albert M. Craig) Personality in Japanese History, 1970; Tradition and Modernization in Japanese Culture, 1971. Mng. editor. Jour. Asian Studies, 1955-59; editor Harvard Jour. Asiatic Studies, 1975—. Contbr. articles to profl. jours. Office: 2 Divinity Ave Cambridge MA 02138

SHIVELY, JOHN ADRIAN, pathologist, univ. ofcl.; b. Rossville, Ind., Oct. 29, 1922; s. Henry Adam and Lucy (Gascho) S.; B.A., Ind. U., 1944, M.D., 1946; m. Lois Lorene Faris, Aug. 26, 1945; children—David A., Ann M., Theodore J., Janet S. Intern Phila. Gen. Hosp., 1946-47; resident internal medicine Clinic Hosp., Bluffton, Ind., 1949-50; resident pathology South Bend Med. Found., 1950-52; asst. prof. clin. pathology Ind. U. Sch. Medicine, 1954-57; asso. prof. pathology U. Ky. Med. Sch., 1962-63; prof. pathology, chief clin. pathology U. Tex. M.D. Anderson Hosp., 1963-68; prof. pathology U. Mo. Med. Sch., 1968-71; prof. pathology, chmn. dept. U. Tenn. Coll. Medicine, 1971-76, vice chancellor for acad. affairs Center for Health Scis., 1976—; pathologist-in-chief City of Memphis Hosps., 1971-76. Served with AUS, 1947-49. Mem. Am. Soc. Clin. Pathologists, Coll. Am. Pathologists, A.C.P., Am. Soc. Hematology, Am. Assn. Blood Banks (pres. 1967-68), Phi Beta Kappa, Sigma Xi, Alpha Omega Alpha. Research on platelet physiology. Home: 2205 Kirby Pkwy Memphis TN 38138

SHIVELY, WILLIAM JEROME, wax co. exec.; b. Columbus, Ohio, Jan. 3, 1929; s. Robert C. and Audrey P. (Gutchess) S.; B.A., Colgate U., 1950; M.B.A., Harvard U., 1952; m. Eleanor Jackson, Dec. 26, 1953; children—William Kent, Meredith Maye, Orrin Jerome, Lucie Burnell. With S.C. Johnson & Son, Inc., Racine, Wis., 1953—, v.p., 1968-73, exec. v.p.-European ops., 1973-76, exec. v.p. Johnson Wax Assos. & Worldwide Innochem Ops., 1976—; dir. Heritage Bank Mt. Pleasant; dir. Johnson Wax Cos. in Britain, Iran, Ireland, Nigeria and Norway. Bd. dirs. Jr. Achievement Racine; trustee Ocean Trust Found., San Francisco, Ripon Coll. Served to 2d lt. USAF, 1952-53. Mem. Racine Symphony Orch. Assn. Clubs: Colagate U. Pres.'s., Racine Country, Racine Squash, Somerset. Office: 1525 Howe St Racine WI 53403

SHIVELY, WILLIAM PHILLIPS, polit. scientist; b. Altoona, Pa., Mar. 31, 1942; s. Arthur Willard and Ruth Phillips S.; B.A., Franklin and Marshall Coll., 1963; Ph.D., U. N.C., 1968; m. Barbara Louise Shank, Aug. 29, 1964; children—Helen, David. Mem. faculty U. Oreg., Eugene, 1967-68, Yale U., 1968-71; mem. faculty U. Minn., Mpls., 1971—, prof. polit. sci., 1979—. Author: Craft of Political Research, 1974, rev. edit., 1979; editor Am. Jour. Polit. Sci., 1977-79; contbr. articles on elections and voting to profl. jours. Home: 1572 Northrop St Saint Paul MN 55108 Office: Dept Polit Sci U Minn Minneapolis MN 55455

SHIVERS, ALLAN, former gov. Tex., investment exec.; b. Lufkin, Tex., Oct. 5, 1907; s. Robert A. and Easter (Creasy) S., B.A., U. Tex., 1931, LL.B., 1933; m. Marialice Shary, Oct. 5, 1937; children—John, Allan, Marialice Sue, Brian McGee. Mem. Tex. Senate from 4th dist., 1935-46; lt. gov. of Tex., 1947-49; gov. of Tex., 1949-57; chmn. bd. Western Pipe Line, Inc., 1957-63, Austin Nat. Bank (Tex.); farmer, lawyer and other bus. interests; dir. Tex. Gulf Inc., Celanese Corp. Am., N.Y., Tex. Good Roads Assn., Austin, Global Marine, Inc., Los Angeles, Citizens State Bank of Woodville, Houston 1st Savs. Assn., Houston First Financial Group; adv. dir. Chem. Bank and Trust Co., Houston, People's Nat. Bank of Spring Branch. Past chmn. adv. bd. dirs. Export-Import Bank U.S. chmn. bd. regents U. Tex. system. Mem. C. of C. U.S. (past pres.). Democrat. Baptist. Clubs: Masons (33 deg.), Shriners. Office: Austin Nat Bank Bldg Austin TX 78701

SHIVLER, JAMES FLETCHER, JR., civil engr., engring. co. exec.; b. Clearwater, Fla., Feb. 17, 1918; s. James Fletcher and Estelle (Adams) S.; B.C.E., U. Fla., 1938, M.S., 1940; m. Katherine Lucille Howlett, Feb. 2, 1946; children—James Fletcher, Susan (Mrs. William J. Schilling). Mem. engring. faculty U. Fla., 1940-41; with Reynolds, Smith & Hills, Architects-Engrs.-Planners, Inc. (formerly Reynolds, Smith & Hills, architects and engrs.), Jacksonville, Fla., 1941—, partner, 1950—, pres., 1970—; partner Lewis-Eaton Partnership, Architects-Engrs. & Planners, Jackson, Miss., 1969—; dir. Environ. Sci. & Engring. Inc., Gainesville, Fla. Mem. Fla. Bd. Engr. Examiners, 1964-70, v.p., 1964-65, pres. 1965-70. Served to lt. j.g. USNR, 1943-46. Recipient Outstanding Service award Fla. Engring. Soc., 1971, Distinguished Alumnus award U. Fla., 1972, citation for service to constrn. industry Engring. News Record, 1973. Registered profl. engr., Fla., Ga., N.C. Fellow ASCE (pres. Fla. sect. 1952), Am. Cons. Engrs. Council, Fla. Engring. Soc. (pres. 1960-61); mem. Nat. Soc. Profl. Engrs. (pres. 1972-73), Fla. (dir.-at-large 1971—), Jacksonville Area chambers commerce, Tau Beta Pi. Presbyn. Clubs: Jacksonville Exchange, University, River, Deerwood, Florida Yacht, Jacksonville Power Squadron. Home: 8191 Hollyridge Rd Jacksonville FL 32216 Office: PO Box 4850 Jacksonville FL 32201

SHIYA, GEORGE GILBERT, lawyer; b. Fremont, Ohio, Feb. 15, 1898; s. Kalil and Elizabeth (Thomas) S.; diploma Ecole de la Sagesse, Beirut, Lebanon, 1913; A.B., Columbia, 1922; M.A., 1923, LL.B., 1923; m. Margaret Flannery, Aug. 7, 1930. Admitted to N.Y. bar, 1923; since practiced in N.Y.C.; asso. Loucks, Griffin, Connet & Cullen, 1923-25, Blandy, Mooney & Shipman, 1925-28; partner Bibb, Shiya & Cullen, 1928-33; individual practice, 1933—; counsel Republic Lebanon, N.Y.C., 1943—; legal adviser, exec. dir. U.S. Lebanese C. of C., 1961—. Pres., Class of 1922, Columbia Coll., 1974—, chmn. fund, 1970—. Served with USNR, 1918-19. Recipient Diplome D'Honneur de la Republique Lebanaise, 1940. Mem. Consular Law Soc., Acad. Polit. Sci., Am. Polit. Sci. Assn., Assn. Bar City N.Y., Soc. Older Grads. Columbia, Ohio Soc. N.Y., Delta Chi. Clubs: University, Lawyers, Columbia University, World Trade Center (N.Y.C.); Ridgewood (N.J.) Country. Contbr. articles to profl. jours. Home: 116 Woodland Ave Ridgewood NJ 07450 Office: 5 World Trade Center New York NY 10048

SHKLAR, GERALD, oral pathologist, periodontist, educator; b. Montreal, Que., Can., Dec. 2, 1924; s. Louis and Ann (Schleifstein) S.; came to U.S., 1950, naturalized, 1955; B.S., McGill U., 1947, D.D.S., 1949; M.S., Tufts U., 1952; M.A. (hon.), Harvard U., 1971; m. Judith Nisse, June 16, 1948; children—David, Michael, Ruth. Asst. prof. oral pathology Tufts U. Sch. Dental Medicine, Boston, Mass., 1953-59, asso. prof., 1960-61, prof., 1961-71, research prof. periodontology, 1961-71; Charles A. Brackett prof. oral pathology, head dept. oral medicine and oral pathology Harvard Sch. Dental Medicine, Boston, 1971—; cons. oral pathology Children's Hosp. Med. Center, Peter Bent Brigham Hosp., Mass. Gen. Hosp. Fellow Am. Acad. Dental Sci., AAAS, Am. Acad. Oral Pathology, Am. Coll. Dentists, Internat. Coll. Dentists; mem. ADA, Internat. Assn. Dental Research, Am. Acad. Periodontology, Am. Cancer Soc., Am. Assn. Cancer Edn., Am. Acad. Oral Medicine, Sigma Xi, Omicron Kappa Upsilon. Author books, articles on oral diseases, exptl. pathology, exptl. oral cancer. Home: 33 Clinton Rd Brookline MA 02146 Office: 188 Longwood Ave Boston MA 02115

SHKOLNICK, RODNEY, educator, lawyer; b. Davenport, Iowa, Dec. 3, 1931; s. Jake Sam and Jeanette Rose (Rohrbach) S.; B.A., U. Iowa, 1953, J.D., 1955; m. Lois Ann Greenblatt, Aug. 22, 1954; children—Jeffrey Mark, Stuart Craig. Admitted to Iowa bar, 1955, Nebr. bar, 1961; mem. faculty Sch. Law, Creighton U., Omaha, 1961—, asso. dean, 1972-77, dean, 1977—; partner firm McGrath, North, Nelson, Shkolnick & Dwyer, 1965-71. Served with U.S. Army, 1955-57. Mem. Am. Bar Assn., Iowa Bar Assn., Nebr. Bar Assn. Jewish. Club: Rotary. Office: Creighton Univ Sch Law Omaha NE 68178

SHLAUDEMAN, HARRY WALTER, ambassador; b. Los Angeles, May 17, 1926; s. Karl Whitman and Florence (Pixley) S.; B.A., Stanford, 1952; m. Carol Jean Dickey, Aug. 7, 1948; children—Karl Frederick, Katherine Estelle, Harry Richard. Joined U.S. Fgn. Service, 1955; vice consul, Barranquilla, Colombia, 1955-56; polit. officer, Bogota, Colombia, 1956-58; assigned lang. tng. Washington, 1958-59; consul, Sofia, Bulgaria, 1960-62; chief polit. sect., Santo Domingo, Dominican Republic, 1962-64; officer charge Dominican Affairs, State Dept., 1964-65; asst. dir. Office Caribbean affairs, 1965-66; Sr. Seminar Fgn. Policy, State Dept., 1966-67; spl. asst. to sec. state, 1967-69; dir. INR/RAR, 1969; dep. chief of mission, counselor of embassy, Santiago, Chile, 1969-73; dep. asst. sec. state for Inter-Am. affairs, Washington, 1973-75; ambassador to Venezuela, 1975-76; asst. sec. state for Inter-Am. affairs, 1976-77; ambassador to Peru, Lima, 1977—. Served with USMCR, 1944-46. Recipient Distinguished Honor award Dept. State, 1966. Mem. Phi Gamma Dalta. Club: Bethesda (Md.) Country. Office: Am Embassy Lima Corner Avenidas Inca Garcilasode la Vega and Espana PO Box 1995 Lima Peru

SHMOYS, JERRY, educator; b. Warsaw, Poland, Oct. 6, 1923; s. Abram and Ella (Kac) S.; came to U.S., 1941; B.Eng., Cooper Union Sch. Engring., 1945; Ph.D. in Physics, N.Y.U., 1952; m. Eva Halpern, Aug. 9, 1953; children—Susan, David. Engr., Sperry Gyroscope Co., Garden City, N.Y., 1945-46; research asst. and asso. N.Y.U., 1946-55; prof. electrophysics Poly. Inst. N.Y., 1955—. Nat. Acad. Sci.-NRC sr. research asso., 1967-68. Mem. I.E.E.E. (sr.), Am. Phys. Soc., Am. Geophys. Union, Tau Beta Pi. Contbr. articles to profl. jours. Home: 18 Crandon St Melville NY 11747 Office: Route 110 Farmingdale NY 11735

SHNAYERSON, ROBERT BEAHAN, editor; b. N.Y.C., Dec. 8, 1925; s. Charles and Madalene (Griffin) Beahan; A.B., Dartmouth, 1950; m. Lydia Conde Todd, Dec. 23, 1950 (dec. Sept. 1973); children—Michael, Kate. Reporter, N.Y. Daily News, 1946; reporter Life mag., N.Y.C., 1950-54; corr. Time-Life News Service, 1954-56; contbg. editor Time mag., 1957-59, edn. editor, 1959-64, law editor, 1964-67, sr. editor, 1967-71; editor-in-chief Harper's Mag., N.Y.C., 1971-76; editor, pub. Quest/80 mag., N.Y.C., 1976—. Served with USNR, 1943-46. Home: 118 Riverside Dr New York NY 10024 Office: 1133 Ave of Americas New York NY 10036

SHNEIDEROV, ANATOL JAMES, cosmophysicist; b. Ekaterinburg, Russia, July 29, 1894; s. James G. and Alexandra (Petukhov) S.; came to U.S., 1941, naturalized, 1950; C.E., Petrograd Mil. Engring. Sch., 1917, Mag. Mil. Eng., 1918; B.E.E., George Washington U., 1944; M.A., Tchrs. Coll. Columbia, 1948; postgrad. Johns Hopkins, 1945-46, Cath. U. Am., 1944-45, 55-58; m. Siren O. Martirosiantz, Sept. 30, 1930 (dec. Dec. 1958); 1 dau., Svetozara Anatol'evna (Mrs. Maxim D. Persidsky). Owner, Izida Assns., Harbin-Shanghai, China, 1924-41; mng. dir. Shneider Process Co., Ltd., Hong-Kong, Shanghai, Washington, 1941-45; chmn., pres. Polycultural Instn. Am., Washington, 1945—, prof. Russian lang. and culture, 1950—. Geophysicist, U.S. Geol. Survey, 1958-62; fellow European Center for Research on Gravitation, Rome, Italy, 1961, del. to U.S., 1962, prof., 1964; engr., geophysicist arctic bibliography project Arctic Inst. N.Am., Washington, 1962-74; world lectr., 1964-65. Mem. Am. Geophys. Union, Am. Phys. Soc., Philos Soc. Washington, U.S. Naval Inst., AAAS, Am. Def. Preparedness Assn., Arctic Inst. N.Am., Washington Acad. Scis., Am. Inst. Aeros. and Astronautics. Orthodox. Author: The Dreams I Dreamt and the Life I Lived, 1927; The Little Blue Book of Shanghai, 1932. Editor: Dynamics and Mobilism of an Expanding Earth. Research, publs. on radional field theory; pioneer earth's expansion theory; author expulsion planetery theory. Home: 1673 Columbia Rd NW Washington DC 20009

SHNEIDMAN, EDWIN S., educator, thanatologist, suicidologist; b. York, Pa., May 13, 1918; s. Louis and Manya (Zukin) S.; A.B., U. Calif. at Los Angeles, 1938, M.A., 1940; M.S., U. So. Calif., 1947, Ph.D., 1948; m. Jeanne E. Keplinger, Oct. 1, 1944; children—David William, Jonathan Aaron, Paul Samuel, Robert James. Clin. psychologist VA Center, Los Angeles, 1947-50, chief research, 1950-53, co-dir. Central Research Unit for Study Unpredicted Deaths, 1953-58; co.-dir. Suicide Prevention Center, Los Angeles, 1958-66; prof. psychiatry U. So. Calif. Sch. Medicine, 1963-66; chief Center Studies Suicide Prevention, NIMH, Bethesda, Md., 1966-69; lectr. psychiatry Johns Hopkins Sch. Medicine, 1967-69; clin. prof. psychiatry George Washington U. Sch. Medicine, 1967-69; vis. prof. Harvard, 1969; fellow Center Advanced Study in Behavioral Scis., Stanford, 1969-70; prof. med. psychology U. Calif., Los Angeles, 1970-75, prof. thanatology, 1975—, dir. lab. for study life-threatening behavior, 1970—. Served to capt. USAAF, 1942-45. Recipient Harold M. Hildreth award Psychologists in Pub. Service, 1966; Louis I. Dublin award Am. Assn. Suicidology, 1969. Diplomate Am. Bd. Examiners Profl. Psychology (past v.p.). Mem. Am. Assn. Suicidology (founder, past pres.), Am. Psychol. Assn. (past div. pres.), Soc. Projective Techniques (past pres.). Author: Deaths of Man, 1973; Voices of Death, 1980. Editor: Thematic Test Analysis, 1951; (with N.L. Farberow) Clues to Suicide, 1957, The Cry for Help, 1961; Essays in Self-Destruction, 1967; (with M. Ortega) Aspects of Depression, 1969; On the Nature of Suicide, 1969; (with N.L. Farberow, L.E. Litman) Psychology of Suicide, 1970; Death and the College Student, 1972; Death: Current Perspectives, 1976; Suicidology: Contemporary Developments, 1976. Home: 11431 Kingsland St Los Angeles CA 90066 Office: U Calif at Los Angeles 740 Westwood Plaza Los Angeles CA 90024

SHNEOUR, ELIE ALEXIS, neurochemist; b. Neuilly-sur-Seine, France, Dec. 11, 1925; s. Zalman and Salomea (Landau) S.; brought to U.S., 1941, naturalized, 1945; B.A., Columbia U., 1947; M.A., U. Calif. at Berkeley, 1955; Ph.D., U. Calif. at Los Angeles, 1958; D.Sc. (hon.), Bard Coll., 1969; m. Joan Haight Brewster, Jan. 22, 1955; children—Mark Zalman, Alan Brewster. Tchg., research fellowship U. Calif. at Berkeley, 1953-55; Nat. Cancer Inst. research fellow, 1956-57; research, tchg. fellowship U. Calif. at Los Angeles, 1958; Am. Heart Assn. research fellow N.Y. U., 1958-59, U. Calif. at Berkeley, 1958-62; research asso. genetics Stanford, 1962-65; prof. biology and neurosciences U. Utah, 1965-69; research neurochemist City of Hope Nat. Med. Center, Duarte, Calif., 1969-71; dir. research Calbiochem., 1971-75; pres. Biosystems Assos. Ltd., 1975—; mem. exec. com. Nat. Acad. Sci. Study Group on Biology and the Exploration of Mars, 1964; chmn. Western Regional council Research in Basic Bioscis. for Manned Orbiting Missions, Am. Inst. Biol. Scis., NASA, 1966-69; mem. adv. council Cousteau Soc., 1977—. Recipient William Lockwood prize, 1947. Mem. Am. Chem. Soc., N.Y. Acad. Scis., I.E.E.E., A.A.A.S., Am. Inst. Biol. Scis., Am. Soc. Biol. Chemists (chmn. sci. advisers program 1973-75; mem. com. on pub. policy 1974-76), Am. Soc. Neurochemistry (council 1971-73), Soc. Neurosci., Internat. Soc. Neurochemistry, Sigma Xi, Phi Sigma. Author: Extraterrestrial Life, 1965; (with S. Moffat) Life Beyond the Earth, 1966; The Malnourished Mind, 1974. Contbr. numerous articles to sci. and lay jours. Home: 8492 Cliffridge Ave La Jolla CA 92037 Office: PO Box 1414 La Jolla CA 92038. *My working philosophy can best be defined by this statement: A CHALLENGE OVERCOME IS AN ACT OF CREATION.*

SHOBER, EDWARD WHARTON, JR., hosp. mgmt. co. exec.; b. Bryn Mawr, Pa., Nov. 16, 1927; s. Edward Wharton and Catherine Earle (Mather) S.; student Ga. Mil. Acad., 1942-44, Princeton U., 1946-50; D.Sc., Wilkes Coll., 1975; m. Ellen Frances Smith, May 30, 1959; children—Jorie Von S., Edward Wharton III, Paula Mather. With Butler Co., Chgo., 1952-57; pres. Atec Corp., Phila., 1957-69, Joshua B. Powers, Inc., N.Y.C., 1969-71; pres., chief exec. officer Hahnemann Med. Coll. and Hosp. of Phila., 1971-77, emeritus, 1977—; co-founder, chief exec. officer Gen. Arabian Med. and Allied Services Ltd., Riyadh, Saudi Arabia, 1978—; chmn. Hahnemann-Jefferson-Temple-Med. Coll. Pa. Comprehensive Cancer Center; dir. Old Phila. Devel. Corp. Mem. adv. panel Nat. Health Ins. Congl. Subcom. Health Ways and Means; hon. consul of Nicaragua, 1964; mem. adv. panel Temple U. Sch. Bus. Bd. dirs. Rush Meml. Hosp., 1965-67, Bryn Mawr Hosp., 1967-71, University City Sci. Center, 1971—; trustee New Sch., Newport, R.I., 1969-74; bd. govs. Newport Casino, 1965-75; co-founder, co-chmn. Cuban Aid Relief, 1960-61. Recipient Presdl. E, 1963. Mem. English Speaking Union (trustee). Served to 1st lt. U.S. Army, 1950-52. Office: PO Box 3412 Riyadh Saudi Arabia

SHOBERT, ERLE IRWIN, II, mfg. co. exec.; b. DuBois, Pa., Nov. 19, 1913; s. Erle Irwin and Edna Mae (Gray) S.; A.B. summa cum laude, Susquehanna U., 1935, D.Sc. (hon.), 1957; student Georg August U., Goettingen, Germany, 1935-36; M.A. in Physics, Princeton, 1939; m. Marjorie E. Sullivan, Apr. 6, 1939; children—Judith Ann (Mrs. Edward Marsden), Margaret (Mrs. William G. Hayes). With Stackpole Carbon Co., St. Mary's, Pa., 1934-79, v.p. tech., 1971-79; chmn. bd. dirs. Chemcut Corp., State College, Pa., 1978—. Mem. materials adv. panel Pa. Dept. Commerce, 1972, indsl. and adv. com. Pa. State U., 1968-71; adv. com. Am. Carbon Conf., 1967-73; bd. dirs. Engrs. Joint Council, 1969-72; exec. standards council Am. Nat. Standards Inst., 1973, bd. dirs., 1974—. Pres. Elk County Soc. Crippled Children and Adults; pres. St. Mary's Youth Council. Pres., bd. dirs. Susquehanna U., 1978—. Recipient Outstanding Alumni award Susquehanna U., 1969; Ragnar Holm Sci. Achievement award, 1974. Fellow ASTM (bd. dirs. 1966-74, pres. 1971-72), IEEE, AAAS; mem. Sigma Xi. Republican. Presbyterian. Clubs: Masons, Kiwanis (pres. St. Mary's 1963), St Mary's Country. Author 3 books, tech. papers. Patentee carbon products, electronic materials and applications. Home: Box 343 St Mary's PA 15857

SHOCH, DAVID EUGENE, physician, educator; b. Warsaw, Poland, June 10, 1918; s. Henry and Hannah (Dembina) S.; B.S., Coll. City N.Y., 1938; M.S., Northwestern U., 1939, Ph.D., 1943, M.D., 1946; m. Gertrude Amelia Weinstock, June 10, 1945; children—James, John. Intern Cook County Hosp., Chgo., 1945-46, resident ophthalmology, 1948-52; practice medicine, specializing in ophthalmology, Chgo., 1952—; asst. prof. ophthalmology dept. Northwestern U., Chgo., 1952-66, prof. head ophthalmology dept., 1966—; head ophthalmology dept. Northwestern Meml. Hosp., Childrens Meml. Hosp., VA Research Hosp. Trustee Assn. U. Profs. (pres. 1973). Opthalmology; bd. dirs., sec. Heed Ophthalmic Found. Served to capt., M.C., AUS, 1946-48. Diplomate Am. Bd. Ophthalmology (dir., vice chmn. 1978, chmn. 1979). Fellow A.C.S.; mem. A.M.A., AAAS, Am. Acad. Ophthalmology (sec. for instrn. 1972-78), Assn. Research in Vision and Ophthalmology, Inst. Medicine Chgo., Chgo. (past pres.), Am., Pan-Am., French ophthalmol. socs., Sigma Xi. Editorial cons. in ophthalmology Postgrad. Med.; abstract editor Am. Jour. Ophthalmology. Home: 1070 Hohlfelder Rd Glencoe IL 60022 Office: 303 E Chicago Ave Chicago IL 60611

SHOCK, NATHAN WETHERILL, gerontologist; b. Lafayette, Ind., Dec. 25, 1906; B.S., Purdue U., 1926, M.S., 1927, D.Sc. (hon.), 1954; Ph.D., U. Chgo., 1930; m. Margaret B. Truman, Sept. 9, 1928; children—Joseph B., John H. Research asso. dept. pediatrics, instr. physiology U. Chgo., 1930-32; research asso. Inst. Child Welfare, asst. prof. physiology U. Calif. at Berkeley, 1933-41; chief gerontology research center Nat. Inst. on Aging NIH, USPHS and Balt. City Hosps., 1941-76, sci. dir., 1975-76, scientist emeritus, 1977—; vis. physiologist Balt. City Hosps., 1941—. Mem. Md. Commn. on Aging, 1967-75; mem. North Am. com. First Pan-Am. Gerontol. Congress, Mexico City, 1956, Am. com. 4th Internat. Congress on Gerontology, Merano, Italy, 1957. Recipient Ciba travel award 2d Internat. Gerontol. Congress, London, 1954, award Gerontol. Research Found., St. Louis, 1956; Modern Medicine achievement award, 1960, Willard O. Thompson award Am. Geriatrics Soc., 1965; 1st Ann. Research award Gerontol. Soc., 1965; Superior Service award HEW, 1965, Distinguished Service award, 1976; Distinguished Service award Am. Heart Assn., 1965; Chancellor's medal Syracuse U., 1977. Fellow N.Y. Acad. Scis., Am. Psychol. Assn. (pres. maturity and old age div. 1952-53, chmn. research com. 1958-64), Am. Heart Assn. (council circulation), Am. Physiol. Soc., Gerontol. Soc. (sec. 1951-58, pres. 1960, chmn. publs. com. 1969-75); mem. Internat. Assn. Gerontol. Socs. (governing bd.; pres. 1969-71), Soc. Exptl. Biology and Medicine (chmn. Md. sect. 1956), Am. Inst. Biol. Scis. (chmn. com. basic biol. research on aging 1955), Am. Geriatric Soc., Soc. Research Child Devel., Psychometric Soc., A.A.A.S. (v.p. sect. N-med. sci. 1959); hon. mem. Socidad Argentina de Gerontologia y Geriatrai, Brit. Soc. Research on Aging. Author: Trends in Gerontology, rev. edit., 1957; A Classified Bibliography of Gerontology and Geriatrics, rev. edit., 1963. Editor Biol. Aspects of Aging, 1962; Perspectives in Experimental Gerontology, 1966. Editor-in-chief Jour. Gerontology, 1963-69; editor gerontology section Biol. Abstracts, 1953; editor Conf. on Problems of Aging, Josiah Macy Found., 1950-54. Home: 6505 Maplewood Rd Baltimore MD 21212 Office: Gerontology Research Center Balt City Hosps Baltimore MD 21224

SHOCKLEY, LOREN COLSON, dept. store exec.; b. Milan, Ind., Jan. 1, 1907; s. Jesse and Melissa Jane (Colson) S.; A.B., DePauw U., 1928; m. Eva Mae Hoffman, July 6, 1935. With McCrory Stores Corp. (now McCrory Stores div. Rapid Am. Corp.), 1928—, mdse. buyer, N.Y.C., 1933-43, 46-48, head sales devel. and advt. dept., 1948-59, v.p. corp., 1952-59, sr. v.p. in charge of buying, 1959-65, asst. to pres., 1965—. Co-chmn. for variety store industries Nat. Father's Day Council, 1949—. Served to lt. col. AUS, 1943-46. Decorated Legion of Merit. Mem. Pa. Retailers Assn. (v.p.). Republican. Methodist. Clubs: Columbia University (N.Y.C.); Roslyn (L.I.) Rifle; Revolver (Carle Place, L.I.). Home: 34-14 81st St Jackson Heights NY 11372 Office: 245 Fifth Ave New York City NY 10016

SHOCKLEY, THOMAS DEWEY, educator; b. Haynesville, La., Nov. 2, 1923; s. Thomas Dewey and Inez (Hudson) S.; B.S. in Elec. Engring., La. State U., 1950, M.S. in Elec. Engring., 1952; Ph.D., Ga. Inst. Tech., 1963; m. Willie Belle Austin, Feb. 13, 1947; children—Dianne, Cecilia. Instr. La. State U., 1950-53; aerophysics engr. Gen. Dynamics, 1953-56; research engr., asst. prof. Ga. Inst. Tech., 1956-63; asso. prof. U. Ala., 1963-64; prof. U. Okla., 1964-67; prof., chmn. dept. elec. engring. Memphis State U., 1967—; pres. SSC, Inc., Germantown, Tenn., 1978—; system cons. ITT, Md. Co., State Farm Fire & Casualty Co., Ripley Industries, Aetna Ins. Cos., CNA Ins. Co. Served with AUS, 1942-46, 1950. Mem. I.E.E.E. (treas. Memphis sect. 1970-71, sec. 1971-72, vice chmn. 1972-73, chmn. 1973-74), N.Y. Acad. Sci., Sigma Xi (chpt. pres. 1969-71), Phi Kappa Phi (chpt. pres. 1973-74). Home: 1526 Poplar Estates Pkwy Germantown TN 38038 Office: Memphis State U Memphis TN 38111

SHOEMAKE, SHOCKLEY TALIAFERRO, lawyer; b. Bennington, Okla., Nov. 5, 1922; s. Ceph and Ora Belle (Shockley) S.; B.A., U. Okla., 1946, LL.B., 1947; student City U., Paris, France, 1945; m. Hazel Ann Hunt, Oct. 5, 1955; children—Bransford, John, Shelley, Sheila. Admitted to Okla. bar; partner firm Shoemake & Briggs, Pawhuska, Okla., 1947—; pres. Osage Diamond Coring & Drilling Co., Pawhuska, 1962—, Patriot Oil and Gas Co. Mem. Okla. Legislature, 1950-60; state-co-chmn. Constn. Reorgan. Com., 1970; chmn. Pawhuska Democratic Com., 1966-70; mem. City Planning Commn., 1967-70. Served with AUS, 1943-45, 1950-52. Mem. Okla., Fed., U.S. Supreme Court, Osage County bar assns. Mason. K.P.; mem. Order Eastern Star. Home: 501 E 6th St Pawhuska OK 74056 Office: Triangle Bldg Pawhuska OK 74056

SHOEMAKER, ALVIN VARNER, investment banker; b. Somerset, Pa., Oct. 4, 1938; s. Alvin Moore and Sarah Rosemary (Varner) S.; B.S. in Econs., U. Pa., 1960; J.D., U. Mich., 1963; m. Sally Prevost, June 30, 1962; children—Peter, John, Christopher, Julie. Admitted to Pa. bar, D.C. bar; atty. Office Controller of Currency, Dept. Treasury, Washington, 1963-65; atty. Investment Bankers Assn., Washington, 1965-69; sr. v.p., dir., mem. mgmt. com. First Boston Corp., 1969-78; pres., chief exec. officer Blyth Eastman Dillon & Co., Inc., N.Y.C., 1978—. Clubs: Links; Canoe Brook Country; Seaview Country; University (Washington). Office: Blyth Eastman Dillon & Co Inc 1221 Ave of the Americas New York NY 10020

SHOEMAKER, DAVID POWELL, chemist, educator; b. Kooskia, Idaho, May 12, 1920; s. Roy Hopkins and Sarah (Anderson) S.; B.A., Reed Coll., 1942; Ph.D., Calif. Inst. Tech., 1947; m. Clara Brink, Aug. 5, 1955; 1 son, Robert Brink. Research asst. Calif. Inst. Tech., 1943-45, NRC fellow, 1945-47, sr. research fellow, 1948-51; fellow John Simon Guggenheim Meml. Found. Inst. Theoretical Physics, Copenhagen, Denmark, 1947-48; asst. prof. chemistry Mass. Inst. Tech., Cambridge, 1951-56, asso. prof., 1956-60, prof., 1960-70; prof., chmn. dept. chemistry Oreg. State U., Corvallis, 1970—; vis. scientist Lab. Cristallographie, CNRS, Grenoble, France, 1967, 78-79; vis. lectr. Kemisk Institut, Aarhus, Denmark, June 1979; cons. Exxon Co. U.S.A., Baton Rouge, 1957—; sec.-treas. U.S.A. Nat. Com. for Crystallography, 1962-64, chmn., 1967-69. Mem. Am. Chem. Soc., Am. Phys. Soc., Am. Crystallographic Assn. (pres. 1970), Am. Acad. Arts and Scis., AAAS, Internat. Union Chrystallography (mem. exec. com., 1972-78), Phi Beta Kappa, Sigma Xi, Phi Lambda Upsilon, Phi Kappa Phi. Author: (with Carl W. Garland, Jeffrey I. Steinfeld) Experiments in Physical Chemistry, 1962, 67, 74. Am. co-editor: Acta Crystallographica, 1964-69. Home: 3453 NW Hayes Ave Corvallis OR 97330 Office: Dept Chemistry Oreg State U Corvallis OR 97331

SHOEMAKER, DON(ALD CLEAVENGER), editor; b. Montreal, Que., Can., Dec. 6, 1912 (parents Am. citizens); s. Richard Samuel and Alberta (Stone) S.; A.B., U. of N.C., 1934; Litt.D., Hollywood Coll.; m. Lyal Reynolds, Oct. 30, 1937 (dec. July 1968); children—Elizabeth Shoemaker Powell; m. 2d, Suzanne Statler, Aug. 2, 1969; 1 dau., Charlotte. Telegraph editor, Greensboro (N.C.) Record, 1934-37, Asheville (N.C.) Times, 1937-41; asso. editor, Asheville Citizen, 1941-47, editor, 1947-55; exec. dir. So. Edn. Reporting Service, 1955-58; editor, editorial page The Miami Herald, 1958-62, editor, 1962-78, sr. editor, 1978—; columnist Knight-Ridder Newspapers, 1978—. Sec. Fla. World's Fair Authority; mem. Orange Bowl Com., dir., Fla. Bicentennial Commn.; past vice chmn. Fla. Council of 100; chmn. N.C. Conf. Editorial Writers, 1951-52; pres. Buncombe County Community Chest, 1951; chmn., Miami com. on fgn. relations; chmn. Dade Coordinating Council, 1974-75; chmn., Fla. region NCCJ, also nat. trustee; dir., Mental Health Clinic; mem. Fla. Organized Crime Control Council; trustee, U. Miami, Mus. of Sci.; trustee United Way Dade County, pres., 1976, chmn. bd., 1977; dir., chief U.S. del. United Way Internat., Hong Kong, 1977; mem. Fla. Edn. Council, Fla. Task Force on Student Assessment; bd. dirs. Met. Art Mus. Recipient Silver medallion award, NCCJ, 1970, medal of merit, The Asheville Sch., Diamond Jubilee award Nat. Jewish Hosp., 1974; Disting. Eagle Scout award, 1978. Mem. Inter-Am. Press Assn., Asociacion de Amigos del Pais (Guatemala), Internat. Press Inst., Am. Soc. Newspaper Editors, Order of Golden Fleece (U. N.C.), Newcomen Soc., Pi Kappa Alpha, Sigma Delta Chi. Episcopalian. Clubs: Bath, Miami, Standard (Miami); Palm Bay, Jockey, Racquet. Editor: Henry George: Citizen of the World (by Anna George de Mille), 1950; Middle East Journey; The Case of the Lively Ghost, 1957; With All Deliberate Speed, 1957; Spanish Diary, 1974. Contbr. to mags. and encys. Home: 617 Sabal Palm Rd Bay Point Miami FL 33137 Office: The Miami Herald 1 Herald Plaza Miami FL

SHOEMAKER, EUGENE MERLE, geologist, educator; b. Los Angeles, Apr. 28, 1928; s. George Estel and Muriel May (Scott) S.; B.S., Calif. Inst. Tech., 1947, M.S., 1948; M.A., Princeton U., 1954, Ph.D., 1960; Sc.D., Ariz. State Coll., 1965, Temple U., 1967; m. Carolyn Jean Spellmann, Aug. 18, 1951; children—Christine Carol, Patrick Gene, Linda Susan. Exploration uranium deposits and investigation salt structures Colo. and Utah, U.S. Geol. Survey, 1948-50, regional investigations geochemistry, vulcanology and structure Colorado Plateau, 1951-56, research structure and mechanics of meteorite impact and nuclear explosion craters, 1957-60, with E.C.T. Chao, discovered coesite, Meteor Crater, Ariz., 1960, investigation structure and history of moon, 1960-73, established lunar geol. time scale, methods of geol. mapping of moon, 1960, application TV systems to investigation extra-terrestrial geology, 1961—, geology and paleomagnetism Colo. Plateau, 1969—, systematic search for planet-crossing asteroids, 1973—; organized br. of astrogeology U.S. Geol. Survey, 1961; co-investigator TV expt. Project Ranger, 1961-65; chief scientist, center of astrogeology U.S. Geol. Survey, 1966-68, research geologist, 1976—; prin. investigator geol. field investigations in Apollo lunar landing, 1965-70, also television expt. Project Surveyor, 1963-68; prof. geology, 1969—, Calif. Inst. Tech., chmn. div. geol. and planetary scis., 1969-72. Recipient (with E.C.T. Chao), Wetherill medal Franklin Inst., 1965; Arthur S. Flemming award, 1966; NASA medal for exceptional sci. achievement, 1967; honor award for meritorious service U.S. Dept. Interior, 1973. Mem. Geol. Soc. Am., Mineral Soc. Am., Soc. Econ. Geologists, Geochem. Soc., Am. Assn. Petroleum Geologists, Am. Geophys. Union, Seismol. Soc. Am., Astron. Soc. Pafific, Internat. Astron. Union. Home: PO Box 984 Flagstaff AZ 86002 Office: US Geol Survey 2255 N Gemini Dr Flagstaff AZ 86001

SHOEMAKER, FRANK CRAWFORD, physicist, educator; b. Ogden, Utah, Mar. 26, 1922; s. Roy Hopkins and Sarah Parker (Anderson) S.; A.B., Whitman Coll., 1943, D.Sc. (hon.), 1978; Ph.D., U. Wis., 1949; m. Ruth Elizabeth Nelson, July 11, 1944; children—Barbara Elaine, Mary Frances. Staff mem. Radiation Lab., Mass. Inst. Tech., 1943-45; instr. physics U. Wis., 1949-50; mem. faculty Princeton, 1950—, prof. physics, 1962—; asso. dir. Princeton-Pa. Accelerator, 1962-66; vis. scientist Rutherford High Energy Lab., 1965-66; main accelerator sect. head Nat. Accelerator Lab., 1968-69. Fellow Am. Phys. Soc.; mem. Am. Assn. Physics Tchrs., Phi Beta Kappa, Sigma Xi, Tau Kappa Epsilon. Co-author proposal for 3 billion electron volt Princeton-Pa. Accelerator, 1955. Home: 361 Walnut Ln Princeton NJ 08540

SHOEMAKER, GRADUS LAWRENCE, chemist, educator; b. Zeeland, Mich., Jan. 18, 1921; s. Corey and Hattie (Lubbers) S.; A.B., Hope Coll., 1944; M.S., U. Ill., 1947, Ph.D., 1949; m. Florence Etta Wright, June 5, 1952; children—Robert Neil, Betty Lynn. Mem. faculty U. Louisville, 1949—, prof. chemistry, 1965—, chmn. dept., 1963-64, 65-67, chmn. div. natural sci., 1967—. Served as ensign USNR, 1944-45. Mem. Am. Chem. Soc. (councillor 1968—), AAUP, Ky. Acad. Sci., Blue Key, Sigma Xi, Alpha Epsilon Delta, Phi Kappa Phi, Phi Lambda Upsilon, Presbyn. Home: 2815 Meadow Dr Louisville KY 40220

SHOEMAKER, LOUISE PROEHL, educator, univ. dean; b. Clinton, Iowa, July 7, 1925; d. Otto Ludwig and Caroline Wilemina (Reinhard) Proehl; B.A., U. Ill., 1945; M.S.W., U. Pa., Phila., 1947, D.S.W., 1965; L.H.D., Upsala Coll., 1975; m. Bryce Wayne Shoemaker, July 19, 1947; children—Paul, Caroline, Lisa. Program dir. Elliot Park Neighborhood House, Mpls., 1947-49; dir. Home for Emotionally Disturbed Children Luth. Social Services of Minn., St. Paul, 1949-51, cons., 1954-57; lectr. U. Edinburgh (Scotland), 1952; lectr., supr. Nachbarschaftshaus, Bremen, West Germany, 1951-53; supr. Manhattanville Community Center, N.Y.C., 1957-58; chief div. tng. Balt. Dept. Social Services, 1959-63; cons. U.S. Children's Bur., Md. Dept. Pub. Welfare, Cumberland, Md., 1963-65; asst. prof. social work U. Pa., 1965-68, asso. prof., 1968-71, prof., 1971—, dean Sch. Social Work, 1971—. Prof. U. N.C., Chapel Hill, summer 1956, U. Minn., Mpls., summer 1958, summers 1965, 66, Rutgers U., New Brunswick, N.J., summer 1966; vis. prof. W.Va. U., 1968, U. Hamburg (Germany), 1969; cons. VA, Lyons, N.J., 1969-72. Commr., Phila. Commn. on Children and Youth; bd. dirs. Mary Drexel Home for Aged, Phila., 1965-70, Presbyn.-U. Hosp., 1973-79, Luth. Retirement Homes; bd. dirs. YWCA, Phila., 1968—, chairperson com. personnel, tng., 1968-75. U. Pa. Research grantee, 1968, 69; West German Travel grantee, 1968. Mem. A.A.U.P. (pres. chpt. 1970-71), Nat. Assn. Social Workers (chairperson Council Group Services, 1975—), Pa. Council Deans and Dirs. Social Work Schs. (pres. 1976-79), Council Social Work Edn., Nat. Conf. Social Welfare (dir. 1979—), Conf. Deans Grad. Schs. Social Work, Phi Beta Kappa. Democrat. Lutheran (exec. bd. synod 1969-75). Author: Parent and Family Life Education for Low-Income Families, 1965. Pioneer in use of groups in giving service in pub. welfare. Home: 2265 Bryn Mawr Ave Philadelphia PA 19131 Office: 3701 Locust Walk Philadelphia PA 19174

SHOEMAKER, ROBERT JOHN, physician; b. Erie, Pa., Feb. 7, 1919; s. Robert Harrison and Loraine (Underhill) S.; B.S., U. Pitts., 1941, M.D., 1944; student Pitts. Psychoanalytic Inst., 1961-67; m. Mary Louise Altenbaugh, Sept. 4, 1943 (dec. 1965); children—Suzanne (Mrs. Carl VonEnde), Robert H., Bonnie L., John H.; m. 2d, Gloria Lee Maruca, Dec. 15, 1973. Staff psychiatrist Western Psychiat. Inst., Pitts., 1950; pvt. practice, Pitts., 1950; instr. psychiatry U. Pitts. Sch. Medicine, 1950-55, clin. asso. prof., 1964-66; asso. psychiatrist Stauton Clinic, Pitts., 1955; supt. Woodville State Hosp., Carnegie, Pa., 1966-72; faculty mem. Pitts. Psychoanalytic Inst. Chmn. task force religion and mental health Pa. Comprehensive Mental Health Planning, 1964; chmn. subsect. medicine, regional com. region I, 1964-65. Served with AUS, 1946-48. Mem. A.M.A. Pa., Allegheny County med. socs., Am. Psychiat. Assn., Mental Health Soc. Allegheny County, Pa. State Psychiat. Soc. (pres. 1972-73, chmn. planning com.), Pitts. Neuropsychiat. Soc. (pres. 1964-65), Pitts. Psychoanalytic Soc., Am. Psychoanalytic Assn. Contbr. articles to profl. jours. Office: 121 University Pl Pittsburgh PA 15213

SHOEMAKER, ROBERT MORIN, army officer; b. Almont, Mich., Feb. 18, 1924; s. Uriah Beebe and Pomala (Morin) S.; B.S., U.S. Mil. Acad., 1946; grad. U.S. Army Command and Gen. Staff Coll., 1959, Army War Coll., 1967; m. Mary Alice Rickard, July 17, 1948. Commd. 2d lt. U.S. Army, 1946, advanced through grades to gen., 1978; pilot comdr., bn. staff officer, co. comdr. 18th Inf., Germany, 1947-50; co. comdr., regtl. S2 and S3, 23d Inf., Korea, 1953-54; action officer inf. br. DA, 1954-56; student, faculty officer U.S. Army Aviation Sch., Ft. Rucker, Ala., 1959-62; project officer Army Concept Team in Vietnam, 1962-63; bn. comdr., asst. chief of staff, G-3, 11th Air Assault Div., Ft. Benning, Ga., 1963-65; bn. comdr., squadron comdr., exec. officer 1st Cav. Div., Vietnam, 1965-66; chief plans and programs Army Aviation DA, 1967-69; chief of staff, asst. div. comdr. 1st Cav., Vietnam, 1969-70; dep. comdr., chief of staff III Corps and Ft. Hood, Tex., 1970; dep. comdr. MASSTER, Ft. Hood, 1971-72, comdr. 1st Cav., 1973-75; comdr. III Corps and Ft. Hood, 1975-76; dep. comdr. FORSCOM, Ft. McPherson, Ga., 1977-78, comdr., 1978—. Decorated D.S.M., Silver Star medal with oak leaf cluster, Legion of Merit, D.F.C., Bronze Star medal, Air medal with 48 oak leaf clusters, Army Commendation medal with oak leaf cluster, French Croix de Guerre, Republic of Vietnam Gallantry Cross with palm, RVN Honor medal 1st class. Home: 10 Wheeler Dr Fort McPherson GA 30330

SHOEMAKER, VAUGHN, cartoonist, painter, lectr.; b. Chgo., Aug. 11, 1902; s. William Henry and Estella Jane (Vaughn) S.; ed. grammar sch. and Bowen High Sch., Art Inst. Chgo., Chgo. Acad. Fine Arts; Litt.D. (hon.), Wheaton Coll., Wheaton, Ill., 1945; m. Evelyn Marian Arnold, July 3, 1926; 1 son, Vaughn Richard, Jr. With art dept. Chgo. Daily News, 1922, chief cartoonist, 1925-52; editorial cartoonist N.Y. Herald Tribune, 1956-61, 70; became chief cartoonist Chgo. Am. and Chgo. Today, 1961-71, now ret.; syndicated Des Moines Register and Tribune, Nat. Newspaper syndicate, Chgo. Tribune, N.Y. News, 1930-71; instr. Chgo. Acad. Fine Arts, 1927-42. Awarded Pulitzer prize in cartooning, 1938, 47; Nat. Headliner's Award, Atlantic City, 1943; Nat. Safety Council Grand Award, 1946, 49, outstanding achievement award, 1952, 53, 58; Sigma Delta Chi awards, 1945, 50; Freedom Found. Gold Medals Valley Forge 1949 through 1969; Christopher Gold Medal award, 1957; Lincoln Nat. Life Found. awards, 1955, 66, 68. Mem. Christian Bus. Men's Com., The Gideons; treas. Eastern European Mission, Pasadena; mem. Nat. Cartoonist Soc. N.Y., Assn. Am. Editorial Cartoonists, Soc. Western Artists San Francisco, Sigma Delta Chi. Clubs: Palette and Chisel Acad. Fine Art (hon.), Ill. Athletic, Jackson Park Yacht (dir. 1948), Great Lakes Cruising (commodore 1949), Chgo. Press, Chgo. Headline (Chgo.); San Francisco Press, Union League, Marine's Memorial (San Francisco); National Press (Washington, D.C.). Author: 1938 A.D.; 1939 A.D.; 1940 A.D.; '41 and '42 A.D.; '43 and '44 A.D.; '45 and '46 A.D.; The Best of Shoemaker Cartoons, 1966 (books of cartoons). Permanent Editorial Cartoon Collection, Huntington Library, San Marino, Cal., Syracuse (N.Y.) U., U. Mo., Wheaton (Ill.) Coll., one-man water color exhbn. Obrien Galleries, Chgo., 1935, 36, Marshall Field Galleries, 1938; one-man oil exhbn. Masters Gallery, Carmel, Calif., 1973; first telecasting of cartoons in Chgo. Station W9XAP, 1930; television shows, Over Shoemakers' Shoulder, WBKB, NBC, ABC, 1949-50. Home: Drawer V Carmel CA 93921

SHOEMAKER, WILLIE (WILLIAM LEE), jockey; b. Fabens, Tex., Aug. 19, 1931; s. Bebe S.; m. Virginia McLaughlin, 1950 (div. 1960); m. 2d, Bessie May Masterson, Nov. 29, 1961 (div.); m. 3d, Cynthia Barnes, March 7, 1978. Jockey, 1949—; winner Ky. Derby, 1955, 59, 65, Belmont Stakes, 1957, 59, 62, 67, Preakness Stakes, 1963, 67; 1st jockey to have 7,000 wins; winner more than 700 Stakes races. Office: care Ryder Stilwell Inc 5900 Wilshire Blvd Suite 1100 Los Angeles CA 90036

SHOEN, LEONARD SAMUEL, bus. exec.; b. McGrath, Minn., Feb. 29, 1916; s. Samuel J. and Sophia B. (Appert) S.; B.S., Oreg. State U., 1941; postgrad. U. Oreg. Med. Sch., 1941-44; LL.B., Northwestern U., 1955; m. Anna Mary Carty, 1944 (dec. 1957); m. 2d, Suzanne Gilbaugh, 1958 (div. 1977); m. 3d, Suzanne Whitmore, Jan. 7, 1978 (div. 1978); children—Samuel, Michael, Edward, Mark, Mary, Paul, James, Sophia, Cecelia, Theresa, Katrina, Scott. Founder of U-Haul Rental System, 1945; pres. Arcoa, Inc., 1951, chmn. bd., 1968; founder Amerco Systems, Phoenix, 1969, chmn. bd., 1969—. Mem. Pres.'s Council Coll. of Holy Cross, Worcester Mass.; mem. emeritus Bd. of Regents Brophy Coll. Prep. Sch., Phoenix; mem. Marylhurst Edn. Center Adv. Council (Ore.); mem. parents com. Harvard U. Grad. Sch. Bus. Adminstrn. Served with USNR, 1944-45. Mem. Oreg. Bar Assn., Am. Bar Assn., Law Soc. Ariz. State U. Democrat. Roman Catholic. Club: K.C. Office: Suite 22A Regency Towers 3111 Bel Air Dr Las Vegas NV 89109

SHOESMITH, THOMAS PAUL, fgn. service officer; b. Palmerton, Pa., Jan. 25, 1922; s. Thomas and Emma Irene (Mitch) S.; B.A. in Edn., U. Pa., 1943; M.A. in Internat. Affairs, Harvard U., 1951; m. Martha Flagler Houser, Apr. 28, 1945; children—Thomas M., Jo Ann. Various positions Dept. State, 1951-55, commd. fgn. service officer, 1955; assigned Hong Kong, Korea and Japan, 1956-66; dir. office Republic of China affairs, 1966-71; mem. sr. seminar Dept. State, 1971-72; dep. chief of mission Am. embassy, Tokyo, 1972-77; consul gen. U.S. Consulate, Hong Kong, 1977—. Served to 1st lt. U.S. Army, 1943-48. Mem. Am. Fgn. Service Assn. Democrat. Episcopalian. Home: 411 E Bryant St Stroudsburg PA 18360 Office: Am Consulate Gen Hong Kong Box 30 FPO San Francisco CA 96659*

SHOKEIR, MOHAMED HASSAN KAMEL, pediatrician, educator; b. Mansoura, Egypt, July 2, 1938; s. Hassan Sayed and Lolis Nora (Kira) S.; came to Can., 1969, naturalized, 1974; M.D., Cairo U., 1960, D.Ch., 1963, D.Ch. in Orthopedics, 1964; M.D., U. Mich., 1965, Ph.D., 1969; m. Donna Jean Nugent, Feb. 27, 1968; children—Omar Hassan Karim, Vanessa May. Intern, Cairo U. Hosps., 1960-61, resident, 1961-64; Fulbright research scholar, dept. human genetics U. Mich., 1964-69; asst. prof. pediatrics U. Sask., Saskatoon, 1969-71, asso. prof., 1971-73, prof., 1977—, dir. div. med. genetics, 1975—, head dept. pediatrics, 1979—; head sect. clin. genetics U. Man., Winnipeg, 1973-75; mem. staffs Univ. Hosp., Saskatoon City Hosp., St. Paul's Hosp.; cons. Winnipeg Health Scis. Centre, St. Vital Hosp. Chmn. Scouts Movement, Saskatoon. Queen Elizabeth II scientist, 1969-75; Med. Research Council grantee, 1970—; Canadian Coll. Med. Geneticists Found. fellow, 1975—. Fellow Can. Coll. Med. Geneticists, Can. Soc. Clin. Investigation (councillor), Can. Med. Assn.; mem. Am. Pediatric Soc., Soc. Pediatric Research, N.Y. Acad. Scis., Am. Geriatrics Soc., Am. Fedn. Clin. Research, Mid-Western Soc. Pediatric Research, Western Pediatric Soc., Am. Soc. Human Genetics, Genetics Soc. Am., Genetics Soc. Can., Am. Genetic Assn., Can. Soc. Immunology, Am. Pub. Health Assn. Contbr. articles to profl publs. Home: 108 Riel Crescent Saskatoon SK S7J 2W6 Canada Office: Ellis Hall Univ Hosp Saskatoon SK S7N 0X0 Canada. *Never tried to imagine what the future will bring, found the present and its implications enough to occupy me. The overriding passions in my life have been the love of man and the pity for his suffering. I have come to accept the futility of eliminating bias, even prejudice—mine or others'; my hope now is to recognize it and shield one's actions from it. What the world needs is more tolerance. Always found praise a bit embarrassing, confusing and altogether inhibiting—the most lavish for the least deserved accomplishment. Always thought the world is, at best, approximate.*

SHOLANDER, MARLOW CANON, mathematician, educator; b. Topeka, Mar. 13, 1915; s. Canon Calmer and Florence (Johnson) S.; B.A. (Summerfield scholar), U. Kans., 1936, M.A., 1940; Ph.D., Brown U., 1949; m. Patricia Cordelia Green, Aug. 10, 1940; children—Mark, Diane, Susan. Clk., A.T. & S.F. Ry., 1936-38; asst. U. Kans., 1938-40; asst. Brown U., 1940-46; instr., asst. prof., asso. prof. Washington U., St. Louis, 1946-54; asso. prof., prof. Carnegie Inst. Tech., 1954-60; prof. Western Res. U., Case Western Res. U., Cleve., 1960—. Mem. Am. Math. Soc., Math. Assn. Am., AAUP, Phi Beta Kappa, Sigma Xi. Home: 2921 Warrington Rd Shaker Heights OH 44120 Office: Case Western Res U Cleveland OH 44106

SHON, FREDERICK JOHN, nuclear engr.; b. Pleasantville, N.Y., July 24, 1926; s. Frederick and Lucy (Stelz) S.; B.S., Columbia, 1946; postgrad. Ohio State U., U. Cal. at Berkeley; m. Dorothy Theresa Patterson, June 8, 1946; 1 son, Robert Frederick. With Publicker Alcohol Co., Phila., 1946-47, Thermoid Co., Trenton, N.J., 1947-48, Mound Lab., Miamisburg, Ohio, 1948-51; radiation chemist Atomics Internat., Canoga Park, Calif., 1951-52; cons., 1962-63; physicist, reactor ops. supr. Lawrence Radiation Lab., Livermore, Cal., 1952-61; chief examining br., div. licensing and regulations U.S. AEC, Washington, 1961-62, chief reactor safety br., div. operational safety, 1963-67, asst. dir. for nuclear facilities, 1967-72; mem. atomic safety and licensing bd. panel U.S. Nuclear Regulatory Commn., 1972—; cons. nuclear firms including Danish AEC, Risoe, Denmark, 1959; also lectr. nuclear engring. U. Calif. at Berkeley 1955-63. Mem. Am. Nuclear Soc., Health Physics Soc., Tau Beta Pi. Research, publs. on nuclear reactor fuels, reactor ops., safety procedures. Home: 4212 Flower Valley Dr Rockville MD 20853 Office: US Nuclear Regulatory Commn Washington DC 20555

SHONIKER, FINTAN RAYMOND, librarian, clergyman; b. Rochester, N.Y., Nov. 13, 1914; s. Benjamin P. and Mary F. (McConville) S.; A.B., St. Vincent Coll., 1938, M.A., 1940; student St. Vincent Sem., 1936-42; B.S. in L.S., Rosary Coll., 1943; LL.D., Gannon Coll., 1970. Joined Benedictine Order, 1936; ordained priest Roman Catholic Ch., 1942; librarian St. Vincent Prep. Sch., 1936-39, instr., 1940-45; asst. librarian St. Vincent Coll., Latrobe, Pa., 1939-44, librarian, 1944-68, 1972—, dir. libraries, 1949-68, 1972—, dir. pub. relations, 1947-54, alumni sec., 1950-54, faculty 1939—, pres., 1968-71, bd. dirs., 1969—, sec., 1976—, coordinator St. Vincent Coll.-Seton Hill Coll. Coop. Program, 1971—; mem. Am. commn., Survey of U. Montreal; mem. Middle States evaluation teams. Mem. Am., Cath. (exec. council 1959-61), Pa. library assns., Am. Benedictine Acad. (chmn. library sect. 1948), Assn. Coll. and Research Libraries (pres. Tri-State chpt. 1962-63), Pitts. Bibliophiles, Nat. Fedn. Cath. Coll. Students (nat. chaplain 1952-54, 56-58). Contbr. articles to profl. jours. Address: St Vincent Coll Latrobe PA 15650

SHONNARD, LUDLOW, JR., gas utility exec.; b. Kansas City, Mo., Dec. 23, 1912; s. Ludlow and Erna (Rambach) S.; B.S., U. So. Calif., 1934; m. Christy Fox, Sept. 26, 1936 (dec. Nov. 1975); children—Ludlow III, Christy Susan; m. 2d, Nedeane Fallas, Jan. 15, 1977. With So. Counties Gas Co. of Calif., Los Angeles, 1934-70, mgr. personnel and claims, 1942-53, v.p., dir., 1953-70; v.p. Pacific Lighting Service Co., 1970-72; v.p., So. Calif. Gas Co., 1972-78, Dual Fuel Systems, Inc., 1970-78; ret., 1978; dir. The Morris Plan Co. Calif., CrediThrift Fin., Inc. Trustee, Webb Sch. of Calif., 1978—; personnel commr. Pasadena United Sch. Dist., 1979—. Mem. Am., Pacific Coast gas assns. Club: Valley Hunt (dir. 1976—) (Pasadena, Calif.). Home and office: 1151 Arden Rd Pasadena CA 91106

SHOOK, KAREL FRANCIS ANTONY, balletmaster, choreographer, author; b. Renton, Wash., Aug. 29, 1920; s. Walter Burnell and Ida Maria Teresa (Tack) S.; student Cornish Sch. Allied Arts, Seattle, Sch. Am. Ballet. Dancer, Ballet Russe de Monte Carlo, 1940-47, 49-52, N.Y.C. Ballet, 1949; tchr. Katherine Dunham Sch., 1952-54, Studio Dance Arts, 1954-57, June Taylor Sch., 1957-59, Het Nationale Ballet, Amsterdam, Holland, 1959-68; co-dir. Dance Theatre Harlem, N.Y.C., 1968—; artistic adviser Maris Battaglia's Am. Acad. Ballet, Tonawanda, N.Y.; choreographer: Souvenir, 1954, Jazz-Nocturne, 1959, Alceste, 1966, Le Corsaire, 1972, Don Quixote, 1974; author: Beyond The Mist, 1968; Elements of Classic Ballet Technique, 1978. Recipient Human Resources award N.Y.C. Housing Authority, 1976. Mem. Am. Guild Mus. Artists. Roman Catholic. Home: 60 E 9th St New York NY 10003 Office: 466 W 152d St New York NY 10031

SHOOMAN, MARTIN LAWRENCE, elec. engr., computer scientist, educator; b. Trenton, Feb. 24, 1934; s. Lou and Ada (Pearl) S.; B.S., M.I.T., 1956, M.S., 1956; D.Elec. Engring., Poly. Inst. Bklyn., 1961; m. Sylvia Rose Bashoff, Dec. 23, 1962; children—Andrew Michael, Alice Helen. Test engr. Gen. Electric Co., 1953-55; teaching fellow Mass. Inst. Tech., 1955-56, vis. asso. prof. elec. engring., 1971; research engr. Sperry Gyroscope Co., 1956-58; asso. prof. elec. engring. Poly. Inst. Bklyn., 1958-72; prof. elec. engring and computer sci. Poly. Inst. N.Y., 1973—. Spl. lectr. IBM, Arma Corp., Ford Instruments Co., Grumman Aerospace, others; cons. to govt. agys. and industry, including Bell Labs., NASA. Tech. chmn. Internat. IEEE Computer Soc. Symposium Software Reliability, 1973, 76, 79, gen. chmn., 1975, chmn. com. software engring., 1975; prin. investigator Poly. Inst. N.Y. research Contracts with NASA, Office Naval Research, Air Force, Dept. Transp., others; mem. adv. coms. NASA, Nat. Acad. Scis. Fellow IEEE (spl. lectr., mem. adminstrv. com. reliability group, Best Tech. Paper on Reliability award 1967, 71, 77, Ann. Reliability award 1977, Best Paper on Software award 1977); mem. Sigma Xi, Tau Beta Pi, Eta Kappa Nu. Author: Probabilistic Reliability, 1968; also chpts. in 6 textbooks; numerous research papers and reports on reliability, safety, computers, software, and control systems. Home: 12 Broadfield Pl Glen Cove NY 11542 Office: 333 Jay St Brooklyn NY 11201

SHOQUIST, JOSEPH WILLIAM, newspaper editor; b. Lone Tree, Iowa, Nov. 30, 1925; s. Walter E. and Bertha (McCurdy) S.; B.A., U. Iowa, 1948, M.A., 1951; m. Dorothy Lee Ormond, June 30, 1951; children—Paul Steven, Sally. With Milw. Jour., 1955—, news editor, 1964-67, mng. editor, 1967—; dir., Newspapers Inc., 1973—. Mem. Internat. Press Inst., A.P. Mng. Editors Assn. (pres. 1978-79), Sigma Delta Chi. Club: Milw. Press. Unitarian. Home: 1105 E Wabash Ave Waukesha WI 53186 Office: 333 W State St Milwaukee WI 53201

SHOR, EDGAR LEROY, educator; b. Pitts., May 17, 1916; s. Samuel and Eva (Richman) S.; B.A., U. Pitts., 1938; M.A., U. Chgo., 1948; Ph.D., 1954; m. Marian L. Gaynor, Oct. 31, 1948; children—Terry D., Laurel Ann. Instr., then asst. prof. Ind. U., 1954-60; asst. prof. U. Chgo., 1960-63; mem. faculty Colgate U., 1963—, prof. polit. sci., 1966—, chmn. dept., 1964—. Field asst. Social Security Bd., 1939-41; dir. research Inst. Pub. Adminstrn., Thammasat U. Bangkok, Thailand, 1956-58. Served to capt. AUS, 1941-46. Mem. Am. Polit. Sci. Assn., Am. Soc. Pub. Adminstrn. Contbr. articles to profl. jours. Home: 14 University Ave Hamilton NY 13346

SHOR, GEORGE G., JR., geophysicist, educator; b. N.Y.C., June 8, 1923; s. George Gershon and Dorothy (Williston) S.; B.S., Calif. Inst. Tech., 1944, M.S., 1948, Ph.D., 1954; m. Elizabeth Louise Noble, June 11, 1950; children—Alexander Noble, Carolyn Elizabeth, Donald Williston. Joined Seismic Explorations, Inc., Houston, 1948, party chief, 1949-50; asst. research geophysicist to research geophysicist Scripps Inst. Oceanography, La Jolla, Calif., 1953-69, prof. marine geophysics, 1969—, asso. dir., 1968—, mgr. Sea Grant program, 1969-73. Mem. NAS-NRC panel on Mohole site selection, 1959; com. on underwater telecommunications, 1968; USN Marine Geophys. Survey Liaison Council, 1965-67, adv. bd., 1968; vice chmn. Univ.-Nat. Oceanographic Lab. System, 1974-76; mem. or sci. leader oceanographic expdns. to various parts of Pacific and Indian oceans, 1953—. Served to lt. (j.g.) USNR, 1943-46; now comdr. Res. Fellow Geol. Soc. Am., Am. Geophys. Union; mem. Seismol. Soc. Am., Soc. Exploration Geophysicists, Sigma Xi. Research in geol. structure of sea floor, seismic methods, marine technology. Home: 2655 Ellentown Rd La Jolla CA 92037

SHOR, SAMUEL WENDELL WILLISTON, naval engr.; b. N.Y.C., June 25, 1920; s. George Gershon and Dorothy (Williston) S.; student Harvard, 1937-39; B.S., U.S. Naval Acad., 1942; Naval Engr., Mass. Inst. Tech., 1949; M.S. in Math., N.Y.U., 1963; m. Joan Bopp, June 21, 1958; children—Peter Williston, Molly Hathaway. Commd. ensign U.S. Navy, 1942, advanced through grades to capt., 1962; served in cruisers Chicago, St. Louis, and Quincy, Pacific and Atlantic, 1942-46; assigned San Francisco Naval Shipyard, 1949-52; AEC rep. for nuclear matters in U.S.S. Nautilus and U.S.S. Seawolf, also for testing Shippingport (Pa.) Atomic Power Sta., 1953-58; design supt., prodn. engring. officer N.Y. Naval Shipyard, 1958-63; dir. sonar systems office Naval Ship Systems Command 1963-67, exec. dir. plans, 1967-69, dep. comdr. for engring., 1969-71; project mgr. electronic warfare, 1971-72; Naval Electronic Systems Commd., 1973; with Bechtel Power Corp., San Francisco, 1973—. Mem. Soc. Naval Architects and Marine Engrs., Soc. Naval Engrs., Am. Math. Soc., Am. Phys. Soc., Sigma Xi. Unitarian. Author tech. papers. Home: 318 Montford Ave Mill Valley CA 94941 Office: 50 Beale St San Francisco CA 94119

SHORB, EUGENE MURRAY, utility exec.; b. Cleve., Mar. 6, 1920; s. Charles F. and Beth M. Shorb; B.S. in Mech. Engring., Purdue U., 1949; m. Harriet Elizabeth Colman, July 14, 1951; children—Janet E., William M., Thomas C. With No. Ind. Public Service Co., 1949—, v.p. gas ops. and fuel procurement, then sr. v.p., Hammond, 1974-79, 1st v.p., 1979—. Served with USNR, 1942-45. Mem. Am. Gas Assn., Ind. Electric Assn., Ind. Gas Assn. (dir.). Methodist. Home: 1401 Fran-Lin Pkwy Munster IN 46321 Office: 5265 Hohman Ave Hammond IN 46325

SHORE, DINAH (FRANCES ROSE SHORE), singer, TV talk-show hostess; b. Winchester, Tenn., Mar. 1, 1921; d. S.A. and Anna (Stein) Shore; B.A., Vanderbilt U., 1939; m. George Montgomery, Dec. 5, 1943 (div. 1962); children—Melissa Ann, John David; m. 2d, Maurice F. Smith, May 26, 1963 (div. 1964). Became singer WNEW, N.Y., 1938; joined NBC as sustaining singer 1938; started contract RCA-Victor, 1940; star Chamber Music Soc. of Lower Basin St. program, 1940; joined Eddie Cantor radio program, 1941; star own radio program for Gen. Foods, 1943; entertained Allied Troops ETO, 1944; radio program Proctor & Gamble; star TV show for Chevrolet, 1951-61; star show Dinah's Place, NBC-TV, 1970-74, Dinah!, CBS-TV, 1974-79, Dinah! and Friends, 1979—. Awarded New Star of Radio Motion Picture Daily Poll and World Telegram-Scripts Howard Poll, 1940; Best Popular Female Vocalist Motion Picture Daily Fame's Annual Radio Poll, 1941-61; Michael Award, Best Female Vocalist, Radio and T-V, 1950, 51, 52; Billboard Award, Favorite Female Vocalist on Records, 1947; Billboard Award, favorite popular female singer in radio, 1949; Gallup poll, America's best known and favorite female vocalist, 1950, 51; Emmy award, Acad. TV Arts and Sciences, 1954, 55, 56, 57, 58, 59, 72, 73; Peabody Award for 1958; Sylvania Award for 1958. Author: Someone's in the Kitchen with Dinah, 1971. Address: care Henry Jaffe Enterprises 5800 Sunset Blvd Los Angeles CA 90028*

SHORE, FERDINAND JOHN, physicist, educator; b. Bklyn., Sept. 23, 1919; s. Ferdinand John and Magdalene (Schwarz) S.; B.S., Queens Coll., 1941; M.A., Conn. Wesleyan U., 1943; Ph.D., U. Ill., 1952; m. Paulina Barbara Pucko, May 25, 1946; children—Gregory, David, Carolyn, Pamela, Jonathan. Lab. asst. War Research NDRC Project Conn. Wesleyan U., 1941-45; research asst. U. Ill., 1946-51; asso. physicist Brookhaven Nat. Lab., 1952-60; with Queens Coll., Flushing, N.Y., 1960—, prof. physics, 1964—; cons. physics dept. Brookhaven Nat. Lab., 1961-72, cons. dept. applied sci., 1976—; mem. Nat. Council on Radiation Protection and Measurements, 1962-71. Mem. Nat. Council on Radiation Protection and Measurements (consociate mem.), Sigma Xi. Home: 77 Southern Blvd East Patchogue NY 11772 Office: Dept Physics Queens Coll Flushing NY 11367

SHORE, JAMES H(ENRY), psychiatrist; b. Winston-Salem, N.C., Apr. 6, 1940; s. James Henry and Ellen Elizabeth (Hayes) S.; M.D., Duke U., 1965; m. Christine Lowenbach, Aug. 24, 1963; children—Ellen Ottilie, James Henry. Intern, U. Utah Med. Center, 1965-66; resident in psychiatry U. Wash., 1969; chief mental health office Portland (Oreg.) Area Indian Health Service, 1969-73; asso. prof. psychiatry, dir. community psychiatry tng. program U. Oreg. Health Scis. Center, 1973-75, prof., chmn. dept. psychiatry, 1975—; mem. exptl. and spl. edn. com. NIMH-Internal Rev. Group; cons. in field; mem. mental health adv. bd. Oreg. Commn. on Crime and Delinquency; mem. community bds. for child treatment center, suicide prevention service and community coll. paraprofl. tng. Served with USPHS, 1969-73. Decorated USPHS Commendation medal; various grants. Diplomate Am. Bd. Psychiatry and Neurology. Mem. Am. Psychiat. Assn., Oreg. Psychiat. Assn., North Pacific Soc. for Neurology and Psychiatry, AMA, Mental Health Assn. Contbr. numerous articles to profl. publs. Home: 2608 SW Buena Vista Pl

Portland OR 97201 Office: 3181 SW Sam Jackson Park Rd Portland OR 97201

SHORE, MILES FREDERICK, psychiatrist, educator; b. Chgo., May 26, 1929; s. Miles Victor and Margaret Elizabeth S.; B.A., U. Chgo., 1948; B.A., Harvard U., 1950, M.D., 1954; m. Eleanor M. Gossard, July 4, 1953; children—Miles Paul, Rebecca Margaret, Susanna Gladys. Intern, U. Ill. Research and Edn. Hosp., Chgo., 1954-55; resident in psychiatry Mass. Mental Health Center, Beth Israel Hosp., Boston, 1956-61; asst. prof. psychiatry Tufts U. Sch. Medicine, Medford, Mass., 1964-68, asso. prof., 1968-71, prof., 1971-75, prof. community health, 1972-75, founder, dir. Tufts Community Mental Health Center, 1968-74, asso. dean community affairs, 1972-75; mem. faculty Boston Psychoanalytic Inst., 1973—; Bullard prof. psychiatry, head dept. psychiatry Mass. Mental Health Center, Harvard Med. Sch., Boston, 1975—; cons. in field. Bd. dirs. Federated Dorchester Neighborhood Houses, Boston, 1975-78. Served to capt. U.S. Army, 1956-58. Community Mental Health Center grantee, 1964-75. Fellow Am. Psychiat. Assn. (mem. Joint Commn. on Public Affairs); mem. Group for Advancement of Psychiatry (chmn. public edn. com. 1972-76, mktg. bd. 1975—, dir. 1977—), Boston Psychoanalytic Soc. and Inst. (chmn. bd. trustees 1970-73), Mass. Psychiat. Soc. (pres. 1970-71), Am. Hist. Assn., Roxbury Clin. Record Club. Club: Aesculapian. Contbr. articles to Archives of Gen. Psychiatry, Brit. Jour. Med. Psychology, Jour. Interdisciplinary History. Office: 74 Fenwood Rd Boston MA 02115

SHORE, NATHAN ALLEN, dentist; b. N.Y.C., Feb. 2, 1914; s. Moritz and Jeanette (Bricianer) Shapiro; D.D.S., Marquette U., 1938; m. Miriam Felder, Feb. 4, 1943; 1 dau., Elizabeth Ann. Practice dentistry specializing in temporomandibular joint dysfunction, N.Y.C.; lectr. N.Y. U., Loma Linda U.; lectr. in field to profl. socs., seminars. Served with Dental Corps U.S. Army, 1943-46. Recipient Presidential Citation award Belgian Govt. Fellow Am. Coll. Dentists, Internat. Coll. Dentists; mem. Soc. Oral Physiology, Occlusion (founder 1954, pres. 1955-59, Steven W. Brown Gold medal 1968), Am. Equilibration Soc., Royal Soc. Medicine, Periodontal Soc. Rome (hon.). Author: Temporomandibular Joint Dysfunction and Occlusion Equilibration, 2d edit., 1976; (with Miriam Felder Shore) How to Test and Hire for the Professional Office, 1967; producer two sound color films on occlusal equilibration, temporomandibular joint dysfunction; contbr. numerous articles to med. and dental jours. Home: 77 W 55th St New York NY 10019

SHORE, SIDNEY, educator; b. Phila., Sept. 13, 1921; s. Maurice William and Freda (Sillman) S.; B.S. in Civil Engring., U. Pa., 1943; M.S. in Civil Engring., Columbia, 1949; Ph.D., Harvard, 1960; m. Mildred Cohen, Dec. 21, 1946; children—Neal Adam, Monica Gail, Fred Eric. Research and test engr. Bur. Aeros., U.S. Navy, 1943-45; asst. prof. Princeton, 1946-52; mem. faculty U. Pa., 1952—, prof. civil and urban engring., 1960—, chmn., dept. civil and urban engring., 1973-78; dir. ops. analysis standby unit USAF, 1963-66; teaching fellow Harvard, 1950-51; vis. lectr. Swarthmore Coll., 1961; vis. prof. Royal Inst. Tech., Stockholm, Sweden, 1962-63; partner Structural Mechanics Assos. Served with USNR, 1945-46. Fulbright scholar, Sweden, 1962-63. Registered profl. engr., Pa. Fellow ASCE; mem. Am. Soc. Engring. Edn., Internat. Assn. Bridge and Structural Engring., Am. Acad. Mechanics, Soc. Exptl. Stress Analysis, Sigma Xi, Tau Beta Pi. Contbr. articles to profl. jours. Home: 1433 Sandy Circle Narberth PA 19072 Office: U Pa Philadelphia PA 19104

SHORE, THOMAS SPENCER, JR., lawyer; b. Akron, Ohio, Jan. 1, 1939; s. T. Spencer and Harriet G. (Delicate) S.; B.A., Brown U., 1961; J.D., Northwestern U., 1964; m. Margaret F. Kudzma, Aug. 12, 1961; children—Thomas Spencer III, John Christopher, Daniel Andrew, Mary Margaret. Admitted to Ohio bar, 1964; asso. firm Taft, Stettinius and Hollister, Cin., 1964-69; asso. firm Rendigs, Fry, Kiely & Dennis, Cin., 1969-71, partner, 1972—; adj. asst. prof. Chase Law Sch., U. No. Ky. Bd. dirs., treas. United Cerebral Palsy of Cin., 1978—; trustee Family Service of Cin. Area; past pres. Vis. Nurse Assn. of Cin., hon. trustee. Mem. Cin. Bar Assn., Ohio State Bar Assn., Am. Bar Assn. Clubs: Cin. Country, Queen City. Home: 3441 Observatory Pl Cincinnati OH 45208 Office: 900 Central Trust Tower Cincinnati OH 45202

SHORES, JANIE LEDLOW, state justice; b. Georgiana. Ala., Apr. 30, 1932; d. John Wesley and Willie (Scott) Ledlow; J.D., U. Ala., Tuscaloosa, 1959; m. James L. Shores, Jr., May 12, 1962; 1 dau., Laura Scott. Admitted to Ala. bar, 1959; pvt. practice, Selma, 1959; mem. legal dept. Liberty Nat. Life Ins. Co., Birmingham, Ala., 1962-66; asso. prof. law Cumberland Sch. Law, Samford U., Birmingham, 1)66-74; asso. justice Supreme Ct. Ala., 1974—; legal adviser Ala. Constn. Revision Commn., 1973; mem. Nat. Adv. Council State Ct. Planning, 1976—. Mem. Am. Bar Assn., Am. Judicature Soc., Farrah Order Jurisprudence. Democrat. Episcopalian. Contbr. articles to legal jours. Office: Judicial Bldg Montgomery AL 36104*

SHORES, LOUIS, ret. univ. dean, author, editor; b. Buffalo, Sept. 14, 1904; s. Paul and Ernestine (Lutenberg) S.; A.B., U. Toledo, 1926; M.S., Coll. City N.Y., 1927; B.L.S., Columbia U., 1928; student U. Chgo., 1930-31; Ph.D., George Peabody Coll., 1934; D.H.L. (hon.), Dallas Bapt. Coll., 1970; m. Geraldine Urist, Nov. 19, 1931. Asst., Toledo Pub. Library, 1918-22, U. Toledo Library, 1924-26; reference asst. N.Y. Pub. Library, 1926-28; librarian, prof. library sci. Fisk U., 1928-33; librarian George Peabody Coll., Nashville, 1933-35, dir. Library Sch., 1933-46; asso. editor Collier's Ency., 1946-60, editor in chief, 1960—; dean Library Sch., Fla. State U., 1946-67, prof. and dean emeritus, 1967—; Fulbright research fellow U.K., 1951-52; spl. lectr. library sci. McGill U. 1930, U. Dayton, 1931, Colo. State Coll. Edn., 1936; vis. prof. U. So. Ill., 1968, U. Colo., 1969; vis. lectr. Dalhousie U., 1970; dir. Tex-Tec, 1967-68. Served from 1st lt. to maj. USAAF, 1942-46; maj. Res., 1946-53. Decorated Legion of Merit. Recipient Beta Phi Mu award, 1967; Mudge citation, 1967; cited as founder library-coll. movement Library-Coll. Assos., 1971; named charter mem. Pres.'s Club, Fla. State U., 1977. Mem. Assn. Coll. and Reference Librarians (dir.), ALA, NEA, Southeastern Library Assn. (pres. 1950-52), Phi Kappa Phi, Phi Delta Kappa, Kappa Delta Pi, Pi Gamma Mu. Author: Origins of the American College Library, 1638-1800, 1935; Bibliographies and Summaries in Education, 1936; Basic Reference Books, 1937, 2d edit., 1939; Highways in the Sky, 1947; Challenges to Librarianship, 1953; Basic Reference Sources, 1954; Instructional Materials, 1960; Mark Hopkins' Log and Other Essays, 1965: The Library-College, 1966; Around the Library World in 76 Days, 1967; Tex-Tec. 1968; Library-College USA, 1970; Looking Forward to 1999, 1972; Library Education, 1972; Audiovisual Librarianship, 1973; Reference as the Promotion of Free Inquiry, 1974; Quiet World, 1975; The Generic Book, 1977; Speculation: Concerns with Ultimates, 1977; Encyclopedia: A Commonplace Book, 1977; also articles in various library jours., also The Ednl. Forum, Sch. and Soc., N.Y. Herald-Tribune Books, Saturday Rev.; contbg. author: Best Methods of Study, 1938, Compton's Picture Ency.; editor Current Reference Books, Wilson Bull.; Current Reference Aids, Coll. and Research Libraries; Ann. Reference Check List Library Jour., 1954-58; Jour. Library History, 1965-68; contbg., adv. editor Learning Today. Home: 2013 W Randolph Circle Tallahassee FL 32303

SHORT, BYRON ELLIOTT, educator; b. Putnam, Tex., Dec. 29, 1901; s. Samuel W. and Florence Gertrude (Sublett) S.; B.S., U. Tex., 1926, M.S., 1930; M.M.E., Cornell U., 1936, Ph.D., 1939; m. Mary Jo Fitzgerald, June 1, 1937; children—Mary Aileen (Mrs. James L. Gauntt), Byron Elliott, Jr. Cadet engr. Tex Co., summers 1926-27, mech. engr., summers 1928-30, instr. U. Tex., 1926-29, asst. prof., 1929-36, charge heat-power, fluid mechanics lab. 1930-65, mech. engr., summers 1932-36, 40, asso. prof., 1936-39, prof. mech. engring., 1939-73, prof. emeritus, 1973—, chmn. dept., 1945-47, 51-53, acting dean Coll. Engring., 1948-49; teaching fellow Cornell, 1935-36; cons. Oak Ridge Nat. Lab., research participant, 1956, 57. Fellow ASME (chmn. Tex. sect. 1938-39, mem. heat transfer and power test code com.); life mem. Am. Soc. Heating, Refrigerating and Air Conditioning Engrs. (asso. editor Databook 1953, 55), Am. Soc. Engring. Edn., Sigma Xi, Tau Beta Pi, Phi Kappa Phi, Pi Tau Sigma. Mason (33 deg., K.T., Shriner). Author: Flow, Measurement and Plumping of Fluids, 1934; Engineering Thermodynamics (with H.L. Kent, B.F. Treat), 1953; Pressure Enthalpy Charts (with H.L. Kent and H.A. Walls), 1970. Editor: Design Volume, Am. Soc. Refrigerating Engrs. Databook, 10th edit. Contbr. articles to engring. jours. Home: 502 E 32d St Austin TX 78705

SHORT, DAVID GAINES, food co. exec.; b. Abilene, Tex., Apr. 29, 1939; s. D. Gaines and Christine (Boyd) S.; B.A., Tex. Tech. U., 1961; J.D., U. Tex., 1964; m. Ingrid Moody, June 6, 1964; children—Michael, Christopher, Melissa. Admitted to Tex. bar, 1964; with Tex. Securities Bd., 1964-68, SEC, 1968; counsel Eppler, Guerin & Turner, Inc., investment bankers, Dallas, 1968-74; sec. Campbell Taggart. Inc., Dallas, 1975—. Mem. Am. Soc. Corporate Secs., State Bar Tex. Home: 9501 Milltrail Dallas TX 75238 Office: 6211 Lemmon Ave PO Box 222640 Dallas TX 75222

SHORT, HEDLEY VICARS ROYCRAFT, bishop; b. Toronto, Ont., Can., Jan. 24, 1914; s. Hedley Vicars and Martha Hallam (Parke) S.; B.A., U. Toronto, 1941; L.Th., Trinity Coll., Toronto, 1943, B.D., 1945, D.D., 1964; m. Elizabeth Frances Louise Shirley, Apr. 14, 1953; children—Martha, Elizabeth, Janet, Margaret, Desmond. Ordained deacon Anglican Ch. of Ca., 1943, priest, 1944, consecrated bishop, 1970; asst. curate ch., Toronto, 1943-46; jr. chaplain St. Michael's Cathedral, Coventry, Eng., 1946-47; lectr., sr. tutor, dean of residence Trinity Coll., Toronto, 1947-51; rector, Cochrane, Ont., 1951-56, St. Catharines Ch., Ont., 1956-63; canon Diocese of Niagara, 1963-70; dean, rector St. Alban's Cathedral, Prince Albert, Sask., Can., 1963-70; archdeacon of Prince Albert, 1966-70; bishop of Sask., 1970—; pres. council Coll. Emmanuel, St. Chad; chancellor U. Emmanuel Coll., Saskatoon. Chmn. high sch. bd., Cochrane, 1953-56, Prince Albert, 1970; chmn. bd. dirs. Prince Albert Community Coll., 1974-77. Home: Bishopsthorpe 427 21st St W Prince Albert SK Canada Office: PO Box 1088 Prince Albert SK Canada

SHORT, JAMES FRANKLIN, JR., educator; b. Sangamon County, Ill., June 22, 1924; s. James Franklin and Ruth L. (Walbaum) S.; student Shurtleff Coll., Alton, Ill., 1942-43; B.A., Denison U., 1947, hon. degree, 1975; M.A., U. Chgo., 1949, Ph.D., 1951; m. Kelma E. Hegberg, Dec. 27, 1947; children—Susan Elizabeth, James Michael. Instr., Ill. Inst. Tech., 1950, Ind. U., S. Bend extension, 1950-51; mem. faculty Wash. State U., Pullman, 1951—, prof. sociology, 1963—. dir. Sociol. Research Lab., 1962-65, dean Grad. Sch., 1964-68, dir. Social Research Center, 1970—; vis. asso. research prof. (NIMH grantee) U. Chgo., 1959-62; vis. prof. law and sociology Stanford, 1975; vis. scholar Inst. of Criminology, Cambridge U., 1976; co.-dir. research Nat. Commn. on Causes and Prevention of Violence, 1968-69; fellow Center for Advanced Study in the Behavioral Scis., Stanford, 1969-70. Cons. NIMH, 1961—, mem. behavioral scis. fellowship rev. panel, 1963-66, mem. behavior sci. review panel, tng. grant br., 1967-71, chmn., 1970-71; mem. assembly behavioral and social scis. NRC, 1973-75; Am. Sociol. Assn. rep. to Nat. Acad. Scis., 1970-72; cons. NSF, 1970—, mem. social adv. com., 1971-72, research adv. com., 1973; cons. Ford Found., 1962-64. Served to 2d lt. USMCR, 1943-46; PTO. Faculty Research fellow Social Sci. Research Council, 1953-56; Guggenheim fellow, 1976. Mem. Am. (chmn. research com. 1963, mem. council 1967-70, 76—, com. on exec. office and budget, 1971, 76—, chmn., 1977—, mem. publs. com. 1972-74, 76—, sec. 1977—), Pacific (pres. 1966—) sociol. assns., Soc. Study Problems (exec. com. 1965-66), Western Assn. Grad. Schools (exec. com. 1965-67). Author: (with A.F. Henry) Suicide and Homicide, 1954; (with F.L. Strodtbeck) Group Process and Gang Delinquency, 1965, 2d edit., 1974; also articles chpts. in books. Editor: Gang Delinquency and Delinquent Subcultures, 1968; Modern Criminals, 1970, 2d edit., 1973; The Social Fabric of Metropolis, 1971; (with Marvin Wolfgang) Collective Violence, 1972; editor, contbr. Delinquency, Crime and Society, 1976; asso. editor Am. Sociol. Rev., 1960-63, 70-71, editor, 1972-74; asso. editor Social Problems, 1958-61, 67-69, Am. Jour. Sociology, 1964-72; adv. editor Jour. Life Threatening Behavior, 1971-75, Jour. Research in Crime and Delinquency, 1969—, Am. Sociologist, 1967-68; adv. editor Jour. Criminal Law and Criminology, 1976—; contbr. to encys., yearbooks. Home: 425 Dexter St SE Pullman WA 99163

SHORT, RAY EVERETT, clergyman, educator; b. Coffeyville, Kans., Jan. 5, 1919; s. Franklin Marion and Jennie (Messersmith) S.; A.B., Willamette U., 1944; postgrad. U. Chgo., 1946; B.D., Duke, 1948, Ph.D., 1961; postgrad. U. Ida., 1950-51; m. Jeannette Louise Stephens, June 12, 1954; children—Glenn Alan, Linda Louise, Kenneth Ray, Timothy Wesley, Karen Amy; 1 stepdau., Mary Jennings. Ordained to ministry Methodist Ch., 1946; dir. Westminster Found., Duke, 1944-46; asst. prof. religion, dir. chapel programs Fla. So. Coll., Lakeland, 1947-48; exec. dir. Fla. br. United World Federalists, 1948-50, dir. Intermountain Region, 1953-54; dir. Wesley Found., U. Idaho, 1950-51; exec. dir. Student YMCA-YWCA, U. Denver, 1951-53; pastor Fairmont Meth. Ch., Lockport, Ill., 1954-56; grad. asst. sociology Duke, 1956-57; asso. prof. religion, head div. religion and philosophy, chaplain Tenn. Wesleyan Coll., 1957-60; asso. prof. sociology and religion, head dept. sociology U. Dubuque (Iowa), 1960-65, acting chmn. div. social sci., 1962-65; asso. prof. sociology, head dept. sociology and anthropology U. Wis.-Platteville, 1965-70, prof. sociology, 1966—, prof. sociology and anthropology U. Wis. Copenhagen Study Center, Copenhagen, Spring 1974; vis. prof. sociology Adams State Coll., Alamosa, Colo., 1963; chmn. Peace and World Order div. North Iowa Meth. Conf., 1963-69. Rep. U.S. Jr. C. of C. in testimony before U.S. Senate Com. on Fgn. Relations, 1950; Midwest Region rep. on Nat. Council World Federalists U.S.A., 1964-73, pres. Midwest Region, 1967-69, chmn. Nat. Council, 1971-72, nat. v.p., 1975—; mem. spl. Wis. Conf. called with Pres.'s Commn. for Observance 25th Anniversary of UN, 1970; vice chmn. Wis. gov. commn. on UN, 1970—; mem. Wis. legislative council, 1972-76; mem. Wis. Methodist Bd. on Church and Society, 1973—, chmn. World Peace div., mem. exec. com., 1975—; founder, Wis. chmn. ecumenical program Exert Religious Influence on Nat. Leaders, 1973-74; Democratic Party candidate for Wis. 3d Dist. Congl. seat, 1970, 72, del. Dist. and State Convs., 1969—, mem. state platform com., 1975—. Bd. dirs. Dubuque Salvation Army, 1961-65; mem. nat. bd. Am. Freedom Assn.; nat. vice chmn. UN Reform Electoral Campaign Com., 1975-78; dir., founder Wis. Ann. High Sch. World Peace Study Program, 1975—. Recipient NSF grant Anthropology Inst., Fairmont State Coll., W.Va., 1962. Fellow Am. Sociol. Assn.; mem. Midwest Sociol. Soc., Nat. Council on Family Relations, Fedn. Am. Scientists, AAUP, Assn. Wis. State U. Faculties. Author: Sex, Love or Infatuation: How Can I Really Know?, 1978; contbr. articles to profl. jours. Home: 365 W Dewey St Platteville WI 53818 Office: Dept Sociology U Wis-Platteville Platteville WI 53818

SHORT, ROBERT ALLEN, educator; b. Dayton, Wash., Nov. 7, 1927; s. Dallas Allen and Conchita Kathleen (Miller) S.; B.S., Oreg. State U., 1949, B.A., 1952; M.S., Stevens Inst. Tech., 1956; Ph.D., Stanford, 1961; m. Barbara Ellen Lemert, June 18, 1949; children—Kathleen (Mrs. Steven Westfall), Rebecca (Mrs. Thomas Cator), Kevin, Jennifer, Amy, Brian, Emily. Mem. tech. staff Bell Labs, Whippany, N.J., 1952-56; sr. research engr. Stanford Research Inst., 1956-66; lectr. Santa Clara (Calif.) U., 1966; prof. elec. engring. Oreg. State U., Corvallis, 1966—, chmn. dept. computer sci., 1972—. Served with 82d Airborne Div., AUS, 1946-48. Mem. I.E.E.E., I.E.E.E. Computer Soc. (bd. govs. 1970-72, 76—, publs. com. 1970—, editor 1970-75), Assn. Computing Machinery, A.A.A.S., Am. Soc. Engring. Edn., Am. Soc. Cybernetics, Sigma Xi, Phi Kappa Phi, Tau Beta Pi, Sigma Tau, Eta Kappa Nu, Pi Mu Epsilon. Home: 1815 Hawthorne Pl Corvallis OR 97330

SHORT, ROBERT EARL, motor freight co. exec., hotel exec.; b. Mpls., July 20, 1917; s. Robert Lester and Frances (Niccum) S.; A.B., Coll. St. Thomas, 1940; postgrad. U. Minn. Law Sch., 1940-41, Harvard U., 1941-42, Fordham U. Law Sch., 1945-46; LL.B., Georgetown U., 1948; m. Marion McCann, Sept., 1947; children—Robert, Brian, Marianne, Kevin, Elizabeth, Carolyn, Colleen. Asst. U.S. Dist. Atty., 1948-50; pres. Mueller Transp. Co., from 1950 (name changed to Admiral Merchants Motor Freight), now chief exec. officer; pres., owner Leamington Hotel, Leamington Motor Inn, Francis Drake Hotel, Dyckman Hotel, Mpls. Trustee Coll. St. Thomas, St. Paul; mem. bd. trustees St. Mary's Hosp., Mpls; mem. law sch. adv. council Notre Dame U.; candidate U.S. Senate, 1978; treas. Nat. Democratic Com., 1968; nat. treas. Humphrey-Muskie campaign, 1968; past mem. Council Twin Cities Area. Served to comdr. USN, 1941-47. Mem. Minn. Motor Transport Assn., Ill.-Minn. Motor Carriers Conf. (past pres.), Am. Trucking Assn., Am. Bar Assn., Minn. Bar Assn., Hennepin County Bar Assn. Roman Catholic. Clubs: Interlachen Country (Edina, Minn.), Mpls. Athletic, Minn. Office: Leamington Hotel 1014 3d Ave S Minneapolis MN 55404

SHORT, ROBERT HENRY, utility co. exec.; b. Klamath Falls, Oreg., Oct. 15, 1924; s. Judge Haywood and Henrietta Luella (Lyon) S.; B.S. in Journalism, U. Oreg., 1950; m. Ruby Madalyn Rice, Aug. 1, 1946; children—Robert L., Victoria (Mrs. Gregory Baum), Casey. City editor Klamath Falls Herald and News, 1950-52; dir. pub. relations Water and Elec. Bd., Eugene, Oreg., 1952-55; mgr. pub. info. Portland Gen. Electric Co. (Oreg.), 1955-57, asst. to chmn., 1957-62, v.p., 1962-71, sr. v.p., 1971-73, exec. v.p., 1973-77, pres., 1977—, also dir.; dir. First Nat. Bank of Oreg. Bd. dirs. Oreg. Ind. Colls. Found., Oreg. United Way; trustee Oreg. Grad. Center. Served with USNR, 1942-45. Mem. Edison Elec. Inst. (com. on cost of money and taxes). Clubs: Congl. Country, Astoria (Oreg.) Country, Portland Golf, Arlington. Home: 1210 SW 61st St Portland OR 97221 Office: 121 SW Salmon St Portland OR 97204

SHORT, ROBERT WALTRIP (BOBBY), entertainer, author; b. Danville, Ill., Sept. 15, 1924; s. Rodman Jacob and Myrtle (Render) S.; grad. high sch. Singing pianist as child and after high sch.; appeared in night clubs in U.S. and abroad; concerts in maj. cities; recordings, TV appearances, Broadway prodns., 1956—; appeared at White House for Duke and Duchess of Windsor at request of Pres. Nixon, 1970. Mem. N.A.A.C.P. (life). Author: Black and White Baby, 1971; also articles. Address: care Betty Lee Hunt Assos 1501 Broadway New York City NY 10036

SHORT, WALTER JOSEPH, airline exec.; b. Blairsville, Pa., Jan. 10, 1918; s. Charles J. and Margaret E. (Caulfield) S.; B.S. cum laude, U. Notre Dame, 1939; m. Martha J. Hammill, June 13, 1942; children—Charles W., Robert A., Debra Ann. Accounting supr. Capital Airlines, Washington, 1941-46; treas. Luke Harris Industries, Inc., Willow Run, Mich., 1946-47; office mgr. Giant Food Co., Washington, 1948-49; chief accountant All Am. Airways, Inc. (now Allegheny), Washington, 1949; asst. treas. Allegheny Airlines, Washington, 1949-53, treas., 1953-59, v.p., treas., 1955-59, v.p. finance, 1959-61, sr. v.p. finance, adminstr., 1961-69, exec. v.p. finance, 1969—; dir. Aero. Radio & ARINC Research, Annapolis, Md. First v.p. Airline Finance and Accounting Conf., 1955, pres., 1956, 2d v.p., 1968. Mem. Air Transp. Assn. (chmn. council 1974), Financial Execs. Inst. (past nat. dir., chpt. pres., dir., area v.p.), John Carroll Soc. Washington. K.C. Club: Notre Dame (Washington). Home: 4741 Rock Spring Rd Arlington VA 22207 Office: Allegheny Airlines Hangar 12 Washington Nat Airport Washington DC 20001

SHORT, WINTHROP ALLEN, footwear co. exec.; b. Newark, Nov. 14, 1919; s. Walter Edwin and Mary (Hosley) S.; A.B., Princeton, 1941; LL.B., Yale, 1944; LL.M., N.Y.U., 1949; m. Janet Gerdes, Sept. 12, 1944; children—Winthrop A., John G., Andrew B., David H. Admitted to N.Y. bar, 1944, Mass. bar, 1956; practice in N.Y.C., 1945-55; with Knapp King-Size Corp. (formerly Knapp Bros. Shoe Mfg. Corp.), Brockton, Mass., 1955—, treas., 1959-62, pres., 1962—; dir. Ludlow Corp., Needham, Mass., Shawmut First County Bank, Brockton, Markem Corp., Keene, N.H., Liberty Mut. Ins. Co., Boston. Trustee, Brockton Hosp., Princeton U., Hurricane Island Outward Bound Sch., Rockland, Maine. Mem. Am. Footwear Industries Assn. (dir.), Asso. Industries Mass. (dir.). Home: 146 Nichols Rd Cohasset MA 02025 Office: 1 Knapp Centre Brockton MA 02401

SHORTER, FRANK C., sportscaster, lawyer, marathon runner; b. 1947; B.A., Yale U., 1969; J.D., U. Fla.; m. Louise Shorter. Winner, Gold medal in marathon, 1972 Olympics, Silver medal 1976 Olympics; sportscaster NBC Sports, 1978—; owner Frank Shorter Running Gear, Boulder, Colo., 1977—. Recipient Sullivan award (nation's top amateur athlete), 1972. Office: care Frank Shorter Running Gear 3675 Frontier Ave Boulder CO 80301*

SHORTER, WAYNE, musician; b. Newark, Aug. 25, 1933; B.A., N.Y. U., 1956. Played saxophone with Art Blakey, 1959-63, Miles Davis, 1964-70, Weather Report, 1970—. Served with U.S. Army, 1956-58. Winner numerous Down Beat mag. awards. 1970-77. Office: care Cavallo-Ruffalo Mgmt 9885 Charleville Blvd Beverly Hills CA 90212*

SHORTHILL, RICHARD WARREN, physicist; b. Aberdeen, Wash., Dec. 28, 1928; s. William Warren and Elizabeth Ann (Boyle) S.; student Westminster Coll. Salt Lake City, 1947-48; B.A. in Physics, U. Utah, 1954, Ph.D., 1959; m. Ruth Louise Wood, Sept. 10, 1948 (dec.); children—David Warren, Ann Louise; m. 2d, Ellen Eggleston, June 19, 1968. TV cameraman sta. KSL-TV, 1949-50, TV audio engr., 1952-55; lab. instr. physics, then research asst. physics and teaching fellow U. Utah, 1955-59; research physicist, space physics, aero-space div. Boeing Co., 1960-62; research physicist, lunar physics, Boeing Sci. Research Lab., 1962-74; adj. prof. geology and geophysics U. Utah, 1973—, dir. geospace scis. lab. U. Utah Research Inst., 1974—; vis. scientist, Lunar Sci. Inst., 1972. Cons. Lunar Sci.

Inst., NASA, Office Space Scis., 1976—; prin. investigator phys. properties Viking 75 Mission to Mars, 1970—; mem. Working Group Extra-Terrestrial Resources. Served with Utah N.G., 1947-50, AUS, 1950-52. Recipient Pub. Service award NASA, 1977, Group Achievement award, 1977. Mem. Optical Soc. Am., Am. Astron. Soc., Am. Inst. Physics, Royal Astron. Soc. Can., Astron. Soc. Pacific, AAAS, Soc. Photoptical Instrument Engrs., Am. Geophys. Union, Sigma Xi, Sigma Pi Sigma. Mem. Disciples of Christ Ch. (chmn. bd., chmn. bd. elders). Mason. Mem. editorial bd. Modern Geology, 1972—, The Moon and Planets, 1974—. Discovered anomolous cooling lunar ray craters; research on thermal, photometric properties of lunar surface, phys. properties surface of Mars and satellites of solar system, properties atmosphere of Jupiter, optical fibers, geophysics; research on new guidance systems. Home: 4562 Fortuna Way Salt Lake City UT 84117

SHORTWAY, RICHARD ANTHONY, publishing co. exec.; b. Fairlawn, N.J., Feb. 17, 1924; s. Anthony and Blanche (Wiley) S.; student Western Res. U., 1942-43; m. Dorothy McDonald, Oct. 6, 1945 (div. Apr. 1963); children—Catherine Carina, Mary Lida; m. 2d, Sue Ann Taylor, Aug. 6, 1963 (div. Dec. 1969); m. 3d, Gretchen Swartzwelder, Nov. 27, 1971 (div. Apr. 1977); 1 son, Richard Anthony; m. 4th, Kay R. Larson, May 1977. Advt. rep. Womens Wear Daily, N.Y.C., 1946-50; advt. rep. Glamour mag., 1950-54, Eastern mgr., 1954-59, advt. mgr., 1959-63; advt. mgr. Vogue mag., 1963-64, advt. dir., 1964—, pub., 1970—. Served to 1st lt. USAAF, 1944-45. Decorated D.F.C., Air medal with oak leaf clusters. Clubs: Westchester Country, Coveleigh (Rye, N.Y.). Home: 6 Philips Ln Rye NY 10580 Office: 350 Madison Ave New York NY 10017

SHORY, NASEEB LEIN, dentist, state ofcl.; b. Birmingham, Ala., Sept. 27, 1925; s. Lein George and Fomeyi (Buhana) S.; B.S., U. Ala., 1948; D.D.S., Loyola U., Chgo., 1952; M.P.H., U. Mich., 1962; m. Mary Jo Howard Sept. 8, 1951; children—Lawrence G., Richard L., Carl B., Celeste Marie. Pvt. practice dentistry, Montgomery, Ala., 1952-60; dir. Bur. Dental Health, Ala. Dept. Pub. Health, 1961-68, 73—; asso. clin. prof. Med. Coll. Ala., 1966-68; asso. prof., head dept. community and preventive dentistry La. State U. Sch. Dentistry, 1968-70; prof., chmn. dept. community dentistry Loyola U. of New Orleans, 1968-70; lectr. Tulane U. Sch. Pub. Health and Tropical Medicine, 1968-70; prof., dir. div. health services Sch. Dental Medicine, So. Ill. U., Edwardsville, 1970-72, asst. to dean, 1972-73, chmn. dept. health ecology, 1970-73; mem. Ala. Bd. Dental Scholarships, 1965-68, 73—; dir. Ala. Smile Keeper Program, 1976—; mem. Ala. State Health Advisory Commn., 1977—. Pres., Profl. Men's Credit Assn. Montgomery, 1960-61; mem. Montgomery Community Council, 1960-61, Youth Adv. Council, Montgomery Police Dept., 1960-61. Bd. dirs. Catholic Charities, 1959, 65, 66, New Orleans Area Health Planning Council, 1968-70; mem. Montgomery Cath. High Sch. Sch. Bd., 1975—. Served with AUS, 1943-45; ETO. Decorated Purple Heart; recipient Most Excellent Fellow award Ala. Dental Assn., 1968. Diplomate Am. Bd. Dental Pub. Health. Mem. ADA (chmn. nat. task force on prohibition confection sales in schs. 1978-79), Ill., La. (chmn. council on dental health 1969-70), Ala. dental assns., Am. Assn. Pub. Health Dentists, Assn. State and Territorial Dental Dirs. (pres.-elect 1978-80). Contbr. articles to profl. jours. Home: 410 Bellehurst Dr Montgomery AL 36109 Office: 4E VFW Bldg 304 Dexter Ave Montgomery AL 36104

SHOSID, JOSEPH LEWIS, govt. ofcl.; b. Ft. Worth, Aug. 27, 1927; s. Samuel and Lilly Minna (Schneider) S.; B.A., Tex. Christian U., 1950; children—Sharon Suzann, Steven Stanford. Former exec. profl. baseball with Los Angeles (Bklyn.) Dodgers farm orgn.; bus. mgr. Ft. Worth Baseball Club, 1950-54; with various newspapers, radio & television stations as sportscasting and advt. exec.; pres. Advt. Unlimited, Inc., Ft. Worth, 1954-76; spl. asst. to U.S. Ho. of Reps. Majority Leader Jim Wright 12th Dist. Tex., 1955—. Chmn., Ft. Worth Airpower Council, 1972-74; mem. adv. council Pres.'s Nat. Com. for Employer Support of Guard and Res., 1971—; spl. asst. to Vice Pres. Hubert H. Humphrey, 1966-69; supr. ofcls. Metro 7 Conf. Served with AUS, World War II; brig. gen. USAF Res. Recipient Exceptional Service award USAF, 1975. Mem. Air Force Assn. (past nat. pres. and chmn. bd., Nat. Man of Year 1963, Medal of Merit 1962, Exceptional Service Plaque 1971, life mem., nat. bd. dirs.), S.W. Basketball Ofcls. Assn. (past pres.), Congl. Staff Club, Aerospace Edn. Found. (Dolittle fellow), Ft. Worth C. of C., Res. Officers Assn., Am. Basketball Assn., Fed. Internat. Basketball Assn., Naismith Basketball Hall of Fame, Ft. Worth Press Club. Mason (32 deg., Shriner). Mem. Christian Ch. Club: Ridglea Country. Home: 1612 Ems Rd W Fort Worth TX 76116 Office: PO Box 824 Fort Worth TX 76101

SHOTTS, BRYAN MEEKS, air force officer; b. Laurel, Miss., Oct. 29, 1922; s. Bryan N. and Bernice Ester (Meeks) S.; student U. Omaha, 1959-61, Indsl. Coll. Armed Forces, 1965, Air Command and Staff Sch., 1953; m. Betty Jean Bissell, Dec. 22, 1942; children—Sheila, Jacqueline, Beverly, Sheryl. Commd. 2d lt. U.S. Air Force, 1942, advanced through grades to lt. gen., 1975; chief of staff March AFB, Calif., 1970; comdr. Turkey/U.S. Logistics Group, Ankara, 1971-73; comdr. Keesler Tech. Tng. Center, Miss., 1973; comdr. 15th Air Force, March AFB, Calif., 1975—. Decorated D.S.M., D.F.C., Legion of Merit with oak leaf cluster, Bronze Star, Air medal with 4 oak leaf clusters, Purple Heart, others. Episcopalian. Clubs: Rotary, Masons, Shriners, Knights Templar. Office: 527 Front Beach Ocean Springs MS 39564

SHOTZBERGER, MARTIN LUTHER, coll. pres.; b. Balt., Jan. 10, 1923; s. John Irvin and Alice (McKenna) S.; B.S., U. Richmond, 1948, M.S., 1949, LL.D., 1974; Ph.D., Ohio State U., 1960; m. Edith Lavinia Cosby, July 5, 1942; children—Martin Edward, Jo Ann, Gary Robert, Beverly Paige. Asst. prof. Lynchburg (Va.) Coll., 1949-51; grad. asst. Ohio State U., 1951; dir. evening div. U. Richmond (Va.), 1953-57, dean Univ. Coll., 1962-68; prof. econs., dir. Mgmt. Center, Kalamazoo Coll., 1957-62; pres. Catawba Coll., Salisbury, N.C., 1968—; lectr. Bur. Indsl. Relations, U. Mich.; lectr. Sch. Bank Adminstrn., U. Wis., Madison, 1972—; pres. Piedmont Univ. Center, 1973-75; mem. exec. com. N.C. Assn. Ind. Colls. and Univs., 1976, v.p., 1978-80; mem. exec. com. Ind. Coll. Fund of N.C., vice chmn., 1977-80; Salisbury dir. Security Bank & Trust Co. Pres. Nat. Council for Small Bus. Mgmt. Devel., 1960-61. Bd. dirs. N.C. Heart Assn.; pres. N.C. Found. Ch. Related Colls., 1970-71; chmn. United Church of Christ Council of Higher Edn., 1973-74. Served with AUS, 1942-45. Decorated Silver Star, Purple Heart; recipient Distinguished Alumnus award U. Richmond, 1976. Mem. N.C. Council Econ. Edn. (dir.), Kappa Alpha, Omicron Delta Kappa, Tau Kappa Alpha, Alpha Kappa Psi, Beta Gamma Sigma. Democrat. Mem. United Ch. of Christ. Contbr. articles to profl. jours. Home: 104 N Park Dr Salisbury NC 28144

SHOULBERG, HARRY, artist; b. Phila., Oct. 25, 1903; s. Max and Tessie (Derfer) S.; student Coll. City N.Y., 1931-35; m. Sylvia Hendler, June 1, 1931; 1 son, Ted. Painter, serigrapher, 1931—; represented in numerous permanent collections including Met. Mus., Carnegie Inst., San Francisco Mus., Smithsonian Instn., U.S. Army, Denver Pub. Schs., Brooks Meml. Art Gallery, U. Wis., N.Y.U., Denver Mus., Balt. Mus., Tel Aviv Mus., Ain Harod Mus., U. Oreg., Norfolk Mus. Arts and Scis., Butler Inst. Am. Art, Albrecht Gallery, St. Lawrence U., N.J. State Coll., Wichita State U., State U N.Y. at Binghampton; one-man exhbn. Salpeter Gallery, 1951, Hudson Guild, 1955, Carnegie Inst. Art, 1958, Harbor Gallery, 1968, others; work rep. Prize Prints of 20th Century, 1949. Dir. Studio Art Gallery, N.Y.C. Recipient 1st prize Am. Color Print Soc.; 1st prize Guild Hall, Easthampton, N.Y., 1955; 1st prize, Bronx, N.Y.; purchase prize Nat. Serigraph Soc.; Jane Phillips prize, 1956; Emily Lowe award, 1956; Jane Peterson prize Soc. N.J. Artists, 1956; Albert Kapp award Silvermine Artists, 1957; Grumbacker award N.J. Soc. Painters and Sculptors, 1963; Peterson medal of honor Audubon Artists, 1965; Talen's award N.J. Mus., 1966: M.J. Kaplan Meml. award Am. Soc. Contemporary Artists, 1967, Grumbacher prize, 1976; prize Jersey City Mus., 1973. Mem. Nat. Serigraph Soc., Nat. Soc. of Painters in Casein, N.J. Soc. Painters and Sculptors (Pearl award 1979), Bklyn. Soc. Artists, Artists Equity Assn., Audubon Artists, Artists League Am., League Present Day Artists, Artist Circle. Address: 112-114 W 14th St New York NY 10011

SHOULDICE, KENNETH JAMES, coll. pres.; b. Milw., June 13, 1924; s. Herbert and Marie (Decker) S.; B.S., Marquette U., 1949; M.S., Northwestern U., 1955; Ph.D., State U. Iowa, 1960; m. Marie Bergemann, Jan. 24, 1943; children—Gail (Mrs. Marshall Puckett), Susan, Bradley, William, Jeffrey. Sales rep. Bauer & Black, Inc., Chgo., 1949-52; dist. rep. Davis & Geck div. Am. Cyanamid, Danbury, Conn., 1952-55; adminstrv. resident Milw. County (Wis.) Hosp., 1955-56, adminstrv. asst., 1956-57, asst. adminstr., 1957-58; teaching asst. U. Iowa, Iowa City, 1958-59, instr., 1959-60, asst. prof., 1960; adminstr. War Meml. Hosp., Sault Ste. Marie, Mich., 1960-65; v.p. Mich. Tech. U., Houghton, 1965-66; pres. Lake Superior State Coll., Sault Ste. Marie, 1965—. Mem. adv. bd. Catholic Social Services Upper Mich., Gov.'s Health Facilities Adv. Council, 1969, Pere Marquette Tercentenary Commn.; chmn. Tri-Centennial Com. Sault Ste. Marie, 1968, Mich. United Fund Combined Health Services, Indsl. Study com. City of Sault Ste Marie, 1966. Bd. dirs. United Cerebral Palsy Mich., Mich. Kenny Found., Mich. United Fund, Inc., Mich. Arthritis Assn.; mem. health care cost com. Mich. Hosp. Assn.; budget rev. com. Mich. Blue Cross-Blue Shield; bd. dirs. Chippewa County Red Cross; trustee War Meml. Hosp.; mem. exec. com. Operation Action-Upper Peninsula of Mich. Served with U.S. Army, 1943-45. Decorated Purple Heart, Bronze star. Named Man of Year, Elks Club, Sault Ste Marie, 1964; recipient Gov.'s award, Mich., 1967. Fellow Am. Coll. Hosp. Adminstrs.; mem. Am., Mich. (trustee, grad. med. edn. com., govt. regulations com.) hosp. assns., Am. Council Edn., Am. Assn. State Colls. and Univs. (com. continuing and profl. devel.), Mich. Acad. Arts, Sci. and Letters, Mich. Council State Coll. Pres., Internat. Assn. Univ. Pres.'s. Club: Rotary (v.p. Sault Ste. Marie chpt.). Home: 803 N Campus Ct Sault Sainte Marie MI 49783

SHOUP, CARL SUMNER, economist; b. San Jose, Calif., Oct. 26, 1902; s. Paul and Rose (Wilson) S.; A.B., Stanford U., 1924; Ph.D., Columbia U., 1930; Ph.D. (hon.), U. Strasbourg, 1967; m. Ruth Snedden, Sept. 27, 1924; children—Dale, Paul Snedden, Donald Sumner. Mem. faculty Columbia U., 1928-71, dir. Internat. Econ. Integration Program and Capital Tax Project, 1962-64. Editor Bull. Nat. Tax Assn., 1931-35; staff mem. N.Y. State Spl. Tax Commns., 1930-35; tax study U.S. Dept. Treasury, June-Sept. 1934, Aug.-Sept. 1937, asst. to sec. Treasury, Dec. 1937-Aug. 1938, research cons., 1938-46, 62-68; interregional adviser, tax reform planning UN, 1972-74; sr. Killam fellow Dalhousie U., 1974-75; staff Council of Econ. Advisers, 1946-49; dir. Twentieth Century Fund Survey of Taxation in U.S., 1935-37; dir. Fiscal Survey of Venezuela, 1958; dir. Shoup Tax Mission to Japan, 1949-50; dir. Tax Mission to Liberia, 1969; co-dir. N.Y.C. finance study, 1950-52; pres. Internat. Inst. Pub. Finance, 1950-53; cons. Carnegie Center for Transnat. Studies, 1976, Harvard Inst. for Internat. Devel., 1978-79; Disting. fellow Am. Econ. Assn.; mem. Nat. Tax Assn. (pres. 1949-50, hon. mem.), Decorated Order Sacred Treasure (Japan). Author: The Sales Tax in France, 1930; (with E.R.A. Seligman) A Report on the Revenue System of Cuba, 1932: (with Robert M. Haig and others) The Sales Tax in the American States, 1934; Facing the Tax Problem (with others), 1937; The Fiscal System of Cuba (with Roswell Magill), 1939; Federal Finances in the Coming Decade, 1941; Taxing to Prevent Inflation (with others), 1943; Principles of National Income Analysis, 1947; (with others) Report on Japanese Taxation, 1949, The Fiscal System of Venezuela, 1959; Ricardo on Taxation, 1960; The Tax System of Brazil, 1965; Federal Estate and Gift Taxes, 1966; Public Finance, 1969 (transl. into Japanese 1974, Spanish 1979); The Tax System of Liberia (with others), 1970. Editor: Fiscal Harmonization in Common Markets, 1966. Address: Sandwich NH 03270

SHOUP, HAROLD ARTHUR, advt. exec.; b. Pontiac, Mich., Mar. 30, 1930; s. Claude Frank and Jessie Margaret (Forney) S.; B.A., Mich. State U., 1952; m. Mary Ann Brinegar, May 31, 1958; children—Christopher Allen, Leslie Ann, Lisa Margaret. With Babcock & Wilcox Co., N.Y.C., 1957-58, Barberton, Ohio, 1958-59; asso. account exec. Carr Liggett Advt., Cleve., 1959-60, account exec., 1960-65, account supr., 1965-66, asst. to pres., 1965-67, v.p. creative services, 1967-71, sr. v.p. and dir. client services, 1971-76, pres., 1976—, chmn. bd., chief exec. officer, 1978—; bd. dirs. Nat. Advt. Agy. Network, 1971, 72, 73, bd. chmn., 1974. Served to 1st lt. USAF, 1952-56. Mem. Indsl. Mktg. Assn., Internat. Advt. Assn. Republican. Presbyterian. Clubs: Union of Cleve.; Lakewood Country, Cleve. Playhouse. Office: 815 Superior Ave Cleveland OH 44114

SHOUP, ROBERT JOHN, lawyer; b. Xenia, Ohio, Jan 30, 1911; s. Marcus and Mary (Mahanna) S.; B.S. in Econs., U. Pa., 1933; LL.B., U. Cin., 1936; m. Madeleine Marchand Cole, Sept. 4, 1937; children—Suzanne (Mrs. William M. Wehner), Carol (Sister M. Madelaine), Robert G., Bruce D., Charles C. Partner firm Baker, Hostetler and Patterson, Cleve., now ret. Fellow Am., Ohio bar assn. founds. Home: 34102 Chagrin Blvd Chagrin Falls OH 44022 Office: Union Commerce Bldg Cleveland OH 44115. *Motivated to the extent of doing more than is required or expected.*

SHOUPP, WILLIAM EARL, cons.; b. Troy, Ohio, Oct. 5, 1908; s. William Albert and Lydia (Slack) S.; A.B., Miami U., 1931, D.Sc., 1957; A.M., U. Ill., 1933, Ph.D., 1937; D.Sc., Ind. Inst. Tech., 1972; m. Kathryn Elizabeth Torbeck, June 13, 1933; 1 son, William Joseph. Research fellow, 1938-42; mgr. electronics, nuclear research Westinghouse Electric Corp., 1942-43, dir. research Bettis atomic power div., 1948-53, tech. dir. atomic power dept., 1953-61, tech. dir. astronuclear labs., 1961-62, v.p. corp. research, 1962-73, cons., 1973—. Mem. divisional com. engring. NSF, 1964-67; com. biotech. and human factors research NASA, 1962-64, mem. space and electric propulsion com., chmn. subcom. on power conditioning; mem. adv. bd. for oceanography and ocean engring. Fla. Inst. Tech., 1973-74; mem. task force on tech. aspects, tech. adv. commn. on conservation energy FPC, 1973-74; mem. commn. natural resources NRC, 1973-74; mem., chmn. gen. tech. adv. com. ERDA, 1975-77; chmn. fossil energy adv. com. Dept. of Energy, 1977—; mem. sci. adv. com. USCG, 1969-74; mem. commerce tech. adv. bd. U.S. Dept. Commerce, 1971-73; mem. vis. com. nuclear engring. dept. Mass. Inst. Tech., 1972-73, mem. vis. com., ocean engring. dept., 1973-77; adv. bd. Navy Oceanographers, 1974—. Named man of year in sci. Pitts. Jr. C. of C., 1949; awarded Order of Merit, Westinghouse, 1953; Alumni award U. Ill. Fellow IEEE (Frederik Philips award 1978), Am. Phys. Soc., Am. Nuclear Soc. (dir., pres. 1964, chmn. honors and awards com. 1973-75), ASME (chmn. nuclear engring. div. 1958); mem. Nat. Acad. Engring. (mem. integrated utility systems bd. 1972-74, chmn. marine bd. 1970-74, v.p. 1974-78), Am. Soc. Engring. Edn., Indsl. Research Inst. (medal 1973), U.S.A. Standards Inst. (chmn. nuclear standards bd. 1967), Marine Tech. Soc. (pres. 1972-74), Nat. Security Indsl. Assn. (research and devel. adv. com. 1962-73), Phi Beta Kappa, Sigma Xi. Author numerous tech. reports. Patentee. Home and office: 343 Maple Ave Pittsburgh PA 15218

SHOWALTER, ENGLISH, ret. banker, lawyer; b. Snowville, Va., Oct. 15, 1897; s. Chester David Michael and Lou Ella (English) S.; B.A., Lynchburg Coll., 1916; J.D., U. Va., 1919; m. Jean Lee Staples, June 25, 1934; children—English, David Watts, Jean (Mrs. John Olaf Strom-Olsen). Atty. Colonial-Am. Nat. Bank, Roanoke, Va., 1947-72, chmn. exec. com., 1947-71, chmn. bd., 1971-73; individual practice law, Roanoke, 1921-78; ret., 1978. Mem. Roanoke (pres. 1941), Va., Am. bar assns. Episcopalian. Home: 2700 Longview Ave SW Roanoke VA 24014

SHOWER, ROBERT WESLEY, corp. exec.; b. Harvey, Ill., Sept. 5, 1937; s. Glenn Wesley and Chrissie Irene (Ford) S.; B.S., U. Tulsa, 1960; P.M.D., Harvard Business Sch., 1972; m. Sandra Marie Stough, June 27, 1959; children—David Wesley, Lynece Marie. Sr. auditor Arthur Andersen & Co., Tulsa, 1960-64; with The Williams Cos., Tulsa, 1964—, asst. v.p., 1968-69, v.p. adminstrn., 1969-71, v.p., treas., 1971, v.p. fin. 1971-73, sr. v.p. fin., 1973-77, exec. v.p. fin. and adminstrn., 1977—. Mem. Am. Inst. C.P.A.'s, Okla. Soc. C.P.A.'s, Fin. Execs. Inst., U. Tulsa Alumni Assn. (dir.), Mid-Continent Harvard Bus. Sch. Assn. (dir.), Harvard Bus. Sch. Assn. (exec. council), Lambda Chi Alpha, Delta Sigma Pi. Clubs: Tulsa, Southern Hills Country, U. Tulsa Hurricane (Tulsa); Grandfather Golf and Country (N.C.). Home: 6625 S 75th E Ave Tulsa OK 74133 Office: 1 Williams Center Tulsa OK 74103

SHOWERS, DONALD MCCOLLISTER, govt. ofcl., ret. naval officer; b. Iowa City, Aug. 25, 1919; s. Charles Nathan and Hedwig Marie (Potratz) S.; student U.S. Naval Res. Midshipman Sch., Northwestern U., Chgo., 1941; B.A., State U. Iowa, 1944; postgrad. U.S. Naval War Coll., Newport, R.I., 1960-61; m. Sarah Vivian Gilliland, June 12, 1948; children—Donna Lynn, Donald McCollister, David Vance. Newspaper reporter, desk editor Daily Iowan, Iowa City, 1939-41; commd. ensign USN, 1941, advanced through grades to rear adm., 1965; staff comdr.-in-chief U.S. Naval Forces Eastern Atlantic and Mediterranean, London, Eng. and Naples, Italy, 1950-52; staff U.S. Naval Sch. (naval intelligence), Washington, 1953-55; asst. chief of staff intelligence, staff comdr. 1st Fleet, San Diego, 1955-57; chief naval operations Office Naval Intelligence, Washington, 1957-60, chief operational intelligence br., chief naval operations, 1961-62; asst. chief of staff intelligence, staff comdr.-in-chief Pacific Fleet, Pearl Harbor, Hawaii, 1962-66; asst. chief of staff plans and programs Def. Intelligence Agy., Washington, 1966-69, chief of staff, 1970; now ret., engaged in civilian U.S. Govt. service. Decorated Legion of Merit, Bronze Star Navy Commendation medal, D.S.M. Mem. Sigma Delta Chi, Alpha Tau Omega. Lutheran. Home: 3829 N 26th St Arlington VA 22207 Office: Intelligence Community Staff Washington DC 20505

SHOWERS, RALPH MORRIS, educator; b. Plainfield, N.J., Aug. 7, 1918; s. Ralph W. and Angelina (Jackson) S.; B.S., U. Pa., 1939, M.S., 1941, Ph.D., 1950; m. Beatrice Anne Cicko, July 11, 1944; children—Virginia Ann, Janet Lynne, Carolin Joan. Lab. asst. Farnsworth Radio & Television, 1939-40; test engr. Gen. Electric Co., Phila., Schenectady, 1940-41; lab. asst. U. Pa., Phila., 1941-43, instr. elec. engring., 1942-43, research engr., lab. supr., 1943-45, asst. prof. elec. engring., 1945-53, prof., 1959—; v.p. Internat. Spl. Com. on Radio Interference, 1973-79, chmn., 1979—; v.p. U.S. nat. com. Internat. Electrotech. Commn., 1975—; chmn. Am. Nat. Standards Com. C63, 1968—; cons. Dept. Navy; cons. interference reduction panel research and devel. bd. Dept. Def., 1945; mem. spl. mission OSRD, Washington, 1945; Fellow IEEE; life mem. Group on EMC; mem. Ops. Research Soc. Am., Am. Soc. Engring. Edn., AAUP, Sigma Xi. Contbr. articles to profl. jours. Home: 223 Oxford Rd Havertown PA 19083 Office: Moore Sch Elec Engring U Pa Philadelphia PA 19104

SHRADER, ERWIN FAIRFAX, physicist; b. Pitts., Nov. 1, 1916; s. James Edmund and Ava (Ross) S.; A.B., Swarthmore Coll., 1937; Ph.D., Yale, 1940; m. Nancy Jane Siverd, Aug. 1, 1942; children—Stephen P., Ellen R., Ann E., Nancy Jane, Erwin Fairfax. Prof. physics Case Western Res. U. Cleve., 1940-69; dir. devel., crystal and electronic products, Harshaw Chem. Co., 1970—; with div. war research Columbia, 1943-45; with U.S. Army C.E., Oak Ridge, 1945; with Clinton Lab., Oak Ridge, 1945-46; acting chief phys. and math. br., div. research AEC, 1955-57. Mem. Ohio Atomic Energy Adv. Com., 1958-71. Fellow Am. Phys. Soc.; mem. Phi Beta Kappa, Sigma Xi. Home: 2042 Brunswick Rd East Cleveland OH 44112 Office: 6801 Cochran Rd Solon OH 44139

SHREEVE, CHARLES ALFRED, JR., mech. engr., educator; b. Balt., Mar. 29, 1915; s. Charles Alfred and Ida Brice (Lockerman) S.; B.Engring., Johns Hopkins, 1935; M.S., U. Md., 1943; student Cath. U. Am., 1959-62; m. Elsie M. Starks, June 20, 1940; children—Charles Alfred III, Harry Stark, Mark Whisler. Lab. asst. U.S. Indsl. Alcohol Co., 1935-37; mem. design dept. Babcock & Wilcox Co., 1937-38; instr. Pratt Inst., 1938-41; engr. Naval Ordnance Lab., 1945; mem. faculty U. Md., 1941-45, 45—, prof. mech. engring., 1955—. head dept., 1959-70; dir. Bowles Engring. Corp.; cons. to industry, 1940—. Registered profl. engr., Md., D.C. Mem. ASME, Am. Soc. Engring. Edn., AAUP, AAAS, Tau Beta Pi, Pi Tau Sigma, Omicron Delta Kappa, Phi Kappa Phi. Home: 4612 Drexel Rd College Park MD 20740

SHREEVE, JEAN'NE MARIE, chemist, ednl. adminstr.; b. Deer Lodge, Mont., July 2, 1933; d. Charles William and Maryfrances (Briggeman) S.; B.A., U. Mont., 1953; M.S., U. Minn., 1955; Ph.D., U. Wash., 1961; NSF postdoctoral fellow U. Cambridge (Eng.), 1967-68. Asst. prof. chemistry U. Idaho, Moscow, 1961-65, asso. prof., 1965-67, prof., 1967-73, acting chmn. dept. chemistry, 1969-70, 1973, head dept., and prof., 1973—; Lucy W. Pickett lectr. Mt. Holyoke Coll., 1976; mem. Nat. Com. Standards in Higher Edn., 1965-67, 69-73. Recipient Distinguished Alumni award U. Mont., 1970; named Hon. Alumnus U. Idaho, 1972; recipient Outstanding Achievement award U. Minn., 1975; award for creative work in fluorine chemistry, 1978; Sr. U.S. Scientist award Alexander von Humboldt Found., 1978. U.S. hon. Ramsay fellow, 1967-68; Alfred P. Sloan fellow, 1970-72. Mem. Am. Chem. Soc. (Garvan medal), AAUW (officer Moscow br. 1962-69), Phi Beta Kappa, Sigma Xi, Phi Kappa Phi. Editorial bd. J. Fluorine Chemistry, 1970—, Accounts Chem. Research, 1973-75, Inorganic Synthesis, 1976—; contbr. articles to chem. jours. Office: Dept Chemistry Univ Idaho Moscow ID 83843

SHREVE, RONALD LEE, educator; b. Los Angeles, Oct. 18, 1930; s. Austin L. and Dorothy (Powell) S.; B.S., Calif. Inst. Tech., 1952, Ph.D., 1959; m. Jean Malcolm, Apr. 14, 1962; 1 dau., Elizabeth. NSF fellow Calif. Inst. Tech., 1954-57, instr., 1957-58; NSF postdoctoral fellow Swiss Fed. Inst. Tech., 1958-59; instr. to prof. geology and geophysics U. Calif. at Los Angeles, 1958—; hon. research fellow

Harvard, 1965-66; vis. asso. prof. U. Minn., 1968; vis. prof. geology and Crosby lectr., Mass. Inst. Tech., also hon. research asso., Harvard, 1971-72; Sherman Fairchild disting. scholar Calif. Inst. Tech., 1978-79. Recipient Kirk Bryan award Geol. Soc. Am., 1969. Fellow Geol. Soc. Am; mem. Am. Geophys. Union, Internat. Glaciol. Soc., AAAS, Sierra Club. Research on theoretical geomorphology, glaciology, glacial geology, geophysics. Office: Dept Earth and Space Sciences Univ California Los Angeles CA 90024

SHRIER, ADAM LOUIS, energy co. exec.; b. Warsaw, Poland, Mar. 26, 1938; s. Henry Leon and Mathilda June (Czamanska) S.; came to U.S., 1943, naturalized, 1949; B.S., Columbia U., 1959; M.S. (Whitney fellow), M.I.T., 1960; D.Engr. and Applied Sci. (NSF fellow), Yale U., 1965; postdoctoral visitor U. Cambridge (Eng.), 1965-66; J.D., Fordham U., 1976; m. Diane Kesler, June 10, 1961; children—Jonathan, Lydia, Catherine, David. With Esso Research & Engring. Co., Florham Park and Linden, N.J., 1963-65, 66-72, head. environ. scis. research area, 1969-72; coordinator pollution abatement activities, tanker dept. Exxon Internat. Co., N.Y.C., 1972-74; project mgr., energy systems Exxon Enterprises Inc., N.Y.C., 1974-75, mgr. solar energy projects, 1975-77, gen. mgr. solar heating div., 1977-78, pres. solar thermal systems div., 1979—; dir. Solar Power Corp., North Billerica, Mass., Daystar Corp., Burlington, Mass.; adj. lectr. chem. engring. Columbia U., N.Y.C., 1967-69. Mem. Am. Inst. Chem. Engrs., Am. Chem. Soc., AAAS, N.Y. Acad. Scis., Am. Bar Assn. Contbr. articles to profl. jours.; patentee in field. Home: 543 Park St Upper Montclair NJ 07043 Office: Solar Thermal Systems PO Box 592 Florham Park NY 07932

SHRIVER, DONALD WOODS, JR., educator, ednl. adminstr.; b. Norfolk, Va., Dec. 20, 1927; s. Donald Woods and Gladys (Roberts) S.; B.A., Davidson Coll., 1951; B.D., Union Theol. Sem., 1955; S.T.M., Yale U., 1957; Ph.D. (Rockefeller Doctoral fellow), Harvard U., 1963; LL.D. (hon.), Central Coll., 1970; D.D. (hon.), Wagner Coll., 1978; m. Peggy Ann Leu, Aug. 9, 1953; children—Gregory Bruce, Margaret Ann, Timothy Donald. Ordained to ministry Presbyterian Ch., 1955; pastor Linwood Presbyn. Ch., Gastonia, N.C., 1956-59; u. minister, prof. religion N.C. State U., Raleigh, 1963-72, dir. u. program on sci. and soc., 1968-72; prof. ethics and soc. Emory U., Atlanta, 1972-75; pres. faculty, William E. Dodge prof. applied Christianity Union Theol. Sem., N.Y.C., 1975—; lectr. Duke U., Va. State U., Ga. State U., numerous colls., univs. in Canada, Kenya, India, Japan, Korea. Dir. Urban Policy Study N.C. State U., 1971-73; precinct chmn. Democratic Party, Raleigh, N.C., del. to nat. conv., 1968; mem. Mayor's Com. on Human Relations, Raleigh, 1967-71; chmn. Urban Policy Seminar, Center for Theology and Public Policy, 1978-80. Served with Signal Corps, U.S. Army, 1946-47. Kent fellow in religion, 1959. Mem. Am. Soc. Christian Ethics (pres. 1979-80), Soc. for Values in Higher Edn., Soc. for Health and Human Values, Soc. for Sci. Study of Religion, AAAS, Am. Sociol. Assn., Am. Soc. Engring. Edn. (chmn. liberal arts div. 1972-73), United Christian Youth Movement of Nat. Council of Chs. (nat. chmn. 1951-53). Author: How Do You Do and Why: An Introduction of Christian Ethics for Young People, 1966; Rich Man Poor Man: Christian Ethics for Modern Man Series, 1972; (with Dean D. Knudsen and John R. Earle) Spindles and Spires: A Restudy of Religion and Social Change in Gastonia, 1976; (with Karl A. Ostrom) Is There Hope for the City?, 1977. Editor: The Unsilent South, 1965; Medicine and Religion: Strategies of Care, 1979. Home: 606 W 122d St New York NY 10027 Office: 3041 Broadway St New York NY 10027

SHRIVER, EUNICE MARY KENNEDY (MRS. ROBERT SARGENT SHRIVER, JR.), civic worker; b. Brookline, Mass.; B.S. in Sociology, Stanford U., 1943; student Manhattanville Coll. of Sacred Heart, L.H. D., 1963; Litt.D., U. Santa Clara, 1962; L.H.D., D'Youville Coll., 1962; LL.D., Regis Coll., 1963; L.H.D., Newton Coll., 1973, Brescia Coll., 1974; m. Robert Sargent Shriver, Jr., May 23, 1953; children—Robert Sargent III, Maria Owings, Timothy Perry, Mark Kennedy, Anthony Paul Kennedy. With spl. war problems div. State Dept. Washington, 1943-45; sec. Nat. Conf. on Prevention and Control juvenile Delinquency, Dept. of Justice, Washington, 1947-48; social worker Fed. Penitentiary for Women, Alderson, W.Va., 1950; exec. v.p. Joseph P. Kennedy, Jr. Found., 1950—; social worker House of Good Shepherd, Chgo., also Juvenile Ct., Chgo., 1951-54; regional chmn. women's div. Community Fund-Red Cross Joint Appeal, Chgo., 1958; mem. Chgo. Commn. on Youth Welfare, 1959-62; cons. to Pres. John F. Kennedy's Panel on Mental Retardation, 1961. Active worker in congl. and presdl. campaigns of John F. Kennedy, 1948-60; co-chmn. women's com. Democratic Nat. Conv., Chgo., 1956. Decorated Legion of Honor; recipient Lasker award, Humanitarian award A.A.M.D., 1973, Nat. Vol. Service award, 1973, Phila. Civic Ballet award, 1973, Prix de la Couronne Française, 1974, others. Address: care Joseph P Kennedy Jr Found 1701 K St NW Washington DC 20006

SHRIVER, GARNER EDWARD, govt. ofcl., former congressman; b. Towanda, Kans., July 6, 1912; s. Edward Arthur and Olive (Glass) S.; A.B., U. Wichita, 1934; J.D., Washburn U., 1940; D. Pub. Service, Friends U., Wichita, 1970; m. Martha Jane Currier, June 4, 1941; children—Kay Kwon, David Garner, Linda Ann Breeding. Instr. English and speech South Haven (Kans.) High Sch., 1936-37; admitted to Kan. bar, 1940; mem. firm Bryant, Cundiff, Shriver & Shanahan, Wichita, 1940—; atty. Wichita Bd. Edn., 1951-60; mem. Kan. Legis. Council, 1955-60; mem. 87th-94th Congresses, 4th Kans. Dist. minority counsel Senate Vet. Affairs Com., 1975—. Mem. Kansas Interstate Coop. Commn., 1953-55. Mem. Kans. Ho. of Reps. from Sedgwick County, 1947-51, Kans. Senate, 27th Dist., 1953-61. Bd. dirs. Sedgwick County Assn. for Mental Health, Legion of Honor DeMolay, Naval Res. Served to lt. USNR, World War II. Mem. Am., Kans., Wichita bar assns., V.F.W., Am. Legion, Nat. Sojourners. Republican. Methodist. Mason (33 deg., Shriner), Moose, Kiwanian. Home: 6349 Crosswoods Dr Falls Church VA 22044 Office: Senate Office Bldg Washington DC 20515

SHRIVER, HARRY CLAIR, judge; b. Gettysburg, Pa., Oct. 2, 1904; s. Edward Simpson and Minnie B. (Snyder) S.; student Shippensburg State U., 1924, Dickinson Coll., 1925-26, Gettysburg Coll., 1926-27; J.D., George Washington U., 1930, LL.M., 1931, A.B., 1932; m. Florence Basehoar, Oct. 10, 1944; children—Anne Basehoar Bielot, Harry Clair, Florence Louise Armstrong. Tchr., Adams County, Pa., 1924-25; staff Library of Congress, 1928; admitted to D.C. bar, 1931, U.S. Supreme Ct., 1935, Ct. Claims, 1945; practice of law, Washington, 1932-37, 47; staff Law Library of Congress, 1935, spl. agt., 1936; del. D.C. Bar Assn., 2d Congress Internat. and Comparative Law, 1937; atty. FTC, 1942, War Shipping Adminstrn., 1944, Maritime Commn., 1946, Maritime Adminstrn., 1950; asst. gen counsel, gen. counsel St. Lawrence Seaway Devel. Corp., 1958-62; hearing examiner FPC, 1963-72, adminstrv. law judge, 1972—; dir., pub. The Fox Hills Press, Potomac, Md., 1970—. Mem. Am., Fed. bar assns., Am. Soc. Internat. Law, Pa. Hist. Junto (pres. 1968-72), Phi Beta Gamma, Theta Chi. Republican. Lutheran. Clubs: Rotary; Old Georgetown (co-founder, dir.) (Washington). Author: Justice Oliver Wendell Holmes: His Book Notices and Uncollected Letters and Papers, 1936; How to Find the Law of Administrative Agencies, 1940; Judicial Opinions of Oliver Wendell Holmes, 1940; History of the Shriver Family, 1962; What Gusto, 1970; The Government Lawyer, 1975; What Justice Holmes Wrote; And What Has Been Written About Him, 1978; contbr. articles to law jours., periodicals. Home: 8409 Fox Run Potomac MD 20854

SHRIVER, PHILLIP RAYMOND, univ. pres.; b. Cleve., Aug. 16, 1922; s. Raymond Scott and Corinne Ruth (Smith) S; B.A., Yale, 1943; M.A. Harvard, 1946; Ph.D., Columbia, 1954; Litt.D., U. Cin., 1966; LL.D., Heidelberg Coll., 1966; LL.D., Eastern Mich., 1972, Ohio State U., 1973; D.H., McKendree Coll., 1973; D.P.S., Albion Coll., 1974; L.H.D., Central State U., 1976; m. Martha Damaris Nye, Apr. 15, 1944; children—Carolyn (Mrs. Richard Helwig), Susan (Mrs. Lester La Vine), Melinda (Mrs. David Williams), Darcy, Raymond Scott II. Mem. faculty Kent (Ohio) State U., 1947-65, prof. Am. history, 1960-65, dean Coll. Arts and Scis., 1963-65; pres. Miami U., Oxford, Ohio, 1965—. Dir. Cin. br. Fed. Res. Bank of Cleve., 1968-75, chmn. bd., 1975; dir. Ohio Nat. Life Ins. Co.; pres. Ohio Coll. Assn., 1974-75; chmn. council presidents Mid-Am. Conf., 1971-77; chmn. council pres.'s Nat. Assn. State Univs. and Land-Grants Colls., 1975-76, mem. exec. council, 1976-78. Bd. dirs. Cin. Center Sci. and Industry, 1965-70; trustee Ohio Coll. Library Center, 1968-74; chmn. bd. Univ. Regional Broadcasting, 1975-76, 78-79. Served to lt. (j.g.) USNR, 1943-46; PTO. Recipient Most Distinguished Faculty Mem. award Kent State U., 1961; Distinguished Acad. Service award AAUP, 1965; Gov.'s award, 1969; A.K. Morris award, 1974. Mem. Orgn. Am. Historians, Ohio Acad. History, Ohio Hist. Soc., Am. Studies Assn., Phi Beta Kappa, Omicron Delta Kappa, Phi Alpha Theta, Alpha Kappa Psi, Kappa Delta Pi, Phi Eta Sigma, Phi Kappa Phi, Kappa Kappa Psi, Beta Gamma Sigma, Sigma Delta Pi, Alpha Phi Omega, Delta Upsilon. Presbyn. Author: The Years of Youth, 1960; George A. Bowman: The Biography of an Educator, 1963; (with D.J. Breen) Ohio's Military Prisons of the Civil War, 1964. Home: 310 E High St Oxford OH 45056

SHRIVER, ROBERT SARGENT, JR., lawyer; b. Westminster, Md., Nov. 9, 1915; s. Robert Sargent and Hilda (Shriver) S.; student Canterbury Sch.; B.A. cum laude, Yale, 1938, LL.B., 1941; LL.D., St. Procopius Coll., 1959, Notre Dame U., DePaul U., Seton Hall Coll., 1961, St. Louis U., Kansas State U., Brandeis U., 1962, St. Michael's Coll. (Vt.), Fordham U., Boston Coll., Yale U., Duquesne U., N.Y.U., Wesleyan U.; D.C.L., U. Liberia, 1963; H.H.D., Salem Coll., 1963, Bowling Green State U.; L.H.D., Springfield (Mass.) Coll., 1963, U. Scranton, Providence Coll.; Dr. Polit. Sci., Chulalongkorn U., Bangkok, Thailand; m. Eunice Mary Kennedy, May 23, 1953; children—Robert Sargent III, Maria, Timothy, Mark Kennedy, Anthony Paul Kennedy. Admitted to N.Y. State bar, 1941, Ill. bar, 1959, U.S. Supreme Ct. bar, 1969, D.C. bar, 1971; with Winthrop, Stimson, Putnam & Roberts, 1940-41; asst. editor Newsweek, 1945-46; asso. Joseph P. Kennedy Enterprises, 1947-48; asst. gen. mgr. Merchandise Mart, Chgo., 1948-61; dir. Peace Corps., Washington, 1961-66; dir. Office Econ. Opportunity, 1964-68; U.S. ambassador to France, 1968-70; spl. asst. to the Pres., 1965-68; sr. partner law firm Fried, Frank, Harris, Shriver & Jacobson, N.Y.C., Washington, London, Eng., 1971—. Pres. Chgo. Bd. Edn., 1955-60; mem.-at-large Nat. Council Boy Scouts Am.; pres. Cath. Interracial Council Chgo., 1955-60; chmn. Internat. Orgn. Patrons of Israel Museum, 1972-75. Democratic candidate for v.p., 1972; ran for Dem. presdl. election, 1976. Served as lt. comdr. USNR, 1940-45. Recipient Yale U. medal, 1957; Chgo. medal of Merit, 1957; James J. Hoey award Cath. Interracial Council of N.Y., 1958; named Lay Churchman of the Year by Religious Heritage Am., 1963; Golden Heart Presdl. award Phillippines, 1964; Laetare medal, U. Notre Dame, 1968. Mem. Yale U. Law Sch. Assn. (exec. com.), Navy League (life), Chgo. Council Fgn. Relations (dir.), Delta Kappa Epsilon. Roman Catholic. Clubs: Serra, Economic, Racquet, Executives (Chgo.); Onwentsia (Lake Forest, Ill.); Yale (N.Y.C.); University (Washington); Chevy Chase (Md.). Author: Point of the Lance, 1964. Extensive world travel to visit Peace Corps projects, 1961-66. Office: 120 Broadway New York NY 10005 also 600 New Hampshire Ave NW Washington DC 20037*

SHROCK, ROBERT RAKES, geologist; b. Waupecong, Ind., Aug. 27, 1904; s. Andrew and Stella (Glassburn) S.; A.B., Ind. U., 1925, A.M., 1926, Ph.D., 1928, D.Sc. (hon.), 1971; m. Theodora Antoinette Weidman, Feb. 2, 1933; children—Wendolyn Theodora, Robert Ellsworth. Asst. in geology U. Wis., 1928-29, instr. 1929-31, asst. prof., 1931-37; asst. prof. geology Mass. Inst. Tech., 1937-43, asso. prof., 1943-49, exec. officer dept. geology, 1946-49, acting chmn., 1949-50, chmn., 1950-65, prof. of geology, 1949-70, emeritus prof. geology, 1970—; vis. lectr. geology Harvard, 1948-49, asso. in invertebrate paleontology, 1950-70; cons. various mining and petroleum cos. and engring. groups, 1925—; sr. indsl. specialist WPB, 1943; cons. Research and Devel. Bd., 1946-52. Mem. corp., hon. trustee, hon. mem. Woods Hole Oceanographic Instn. Fellow Geol. Soc. Am., Paleontol. Soc. (patron 1977), AAAS (chmn. sci. 1957, v.p.); mem. Am. Acad. Arts and Scis., Soc. Econ. Paleontologists and Mineralogists (pres. 1956-57, Twenhofel medal 1976), Am. Assn. Petroleum Geologists, Nat. Assn. Geology Tchrs. (pres. 1959), Phi Beta Kappa, Sigma Xi, Sigma Gamma Epsilon. Mason. Author:(with W.H. Twenhofel) Invertebrate Paleontology, 1935; (with H.W. Shimer) Index Fossils of North America, 1944; Sequence in Layered Rocks, 1948; (with W.H. Twenhofel) Principles of Invertebrate Paleontology, 1953; The Geologists Crosby of Boston, 1972; Geology at MIT 1865-1965, 1977. Contbr. articles to sci. jours. Home: 18 Loring Rd Lexington MA 02173

SHRODES, CAROLINE, educator; b. Madison, Minn.; d. George H. and Clara (Blasing) Shrodes; Ph.B., U. Chgo., 1928, M.A., 1934; Ph.D., U. Calif., 1949. Instr. U. Wis., 1937-39, Stockton (Calif.) Coll., 1939-46; prof. San Francisco State U., 1946—, chmn. English dept., 1964-73, also mem. core faculty Union Grad. Sch. Mem. Am. Psychol. Assn., Nat. Council Tchrs. English, Assn. Depts. English (pres. 1969-70), Modern Language Assn. Author: Patterns for Living (with Campbell, Van Gundy), 1940; Psychology Through Literature (with Husband, Van Gundy), 1943; English at Work (with Grant, Van Gundy), 1943; Approaches to Prose (with Van Gundy), 1959; (with Josephson, Wilson) Reading for Rhetoric, 1962, 67, 75, 79: (with Van Gundy, Dorius) Reading for Understanding, 1968; (with Finestone, Shugrue) The Conscious Reader, 1974, 78; editor: Harper and Row series, Studies in Language and Literature, 1973-75; Calif. Council for the Humanities in Pub. Policy, 1977-78. Home: 89 Cloud View Rd Sausalito CA 94965

SHRONTZ, FRANK ANDERSON, bus. exec.; b. Boise, Idaho, Dec. 14, 1931; s. Thurlyn Howard and Florence Elizabeth (Anderson) S.; LL.B., U. Idaho, 1954; postgrad. George Washington U., summer 1953; M.B.A., Harvard, 1958; postgrad. Stanford, 1969-70; m. Harriet Ann Houghton, June 12, 1954; children—Craig Howard, Richard Whitaker, David Anderson. Admitted to Fed. bar, 1954; asst. contracts coordinator Boeing Co., Seattle, 1958-65, asst. dir. contract adminstrn., 1965-67, asst. to v.p. comml. airplane group, 1967-69, asst. dir. new airplane program, 1969-70, dir. comml. sales operations, 1970-73; asst. sec. Dept. Air Force, Washington, 1973-76, Dept. Def., 1976-77, v.p. planning and contracts Boeing Co., Seattle, 1977-78; v.p., gen. mgr. 707/727/737 div. Boeing Comml. Airplane Co., Seattle, 1978—. Chmn. bd. Lake Hills Assn., Bellevue, Wash., 1968. Served to 1st lt. AUS, 1954-56. Mem. Blue Key, Phi Eta Sigma, Phi Alpha Delta, Beta Theta Pi. Club: Mercer Island Beach. Home: 8434 W Mercer Way Mercer Island WA 98040

SHROPSHIRE, DONALD GRAY, hosp. adminstr.; b. Winston-Salem, N.C., Aug. 6, 1927; s. John Lee and Bess L. (Shouse) S.; B.S., U. N.C., 1950; Erickson fellow hosp. adminstrn., U. Chgo., 1958-59; m. Mary Ruth Bodenheimer, Aug. 19, 1950; children—Melanie Gray, John Devin. Personnel asst. Nat. Biscuit Co., Atlanta, 1950-52, asst. personnel mgr., Chgo., 1952-54; adminstr. Eastern State Hosp., Lexington, Ky., 1954-62; asso. dir. U. Md. Hosp., Balt., 1962-67; adminstr. Tucson Med. Center, 1967—. Pres. Tucson Hosps. Med. Edn. Program, 1970-71, sec., 1971—; pres. So. Ariz. Hosp. Council, 1968-69; bd. dirs. Ariz. Blue Cross, 1967-76, chmn. provider standards com., 1972-76; bd. dirs., exec. com. Health Planning Council Tucson, 1969-74; chmn. profl. div. United Way Tucson, 1969-70; chmn. dietary services com. Md. Hosp. Council, 1966-67; bd. dirs. Ky. Hosp. Assn., 1961-62, chmn. council profl. practice, 1960-61; past pres. Blue Grass Hosp. Council; trustee Assn. Western Hosps., 1974—, pres., 1979-80; bd. govs. Pima Community Coll., 1970-76, sec., 1973-74, chmn., 1975-76; mem. Tucson Airport Authority, 1976—; v.p. Tucson Econ. Devel. Corp., 1977—; bd. dirs. Vol. Hosps. Am., 1977—, treas., 1979—. Named Ky. col. Mem. Am. (trustee 1975-78, ho. dels. 1972-78, chmn. council profl. services 1973-74, regional adv. bd. 1969-78, chmn. joint com. with Nat. Assn. Social Workers 1963-64), Ariz. (bd. dirs. 1967-72, pres. 1970-71) hosp. assns., Assn. Am. Med. Colls. (mem. assembly 1974-77), Tucson C. of C. (bd. dirs. 1968-69), United Comml. Travelers, Nat. League Nursing, Ariz. Acad., Tucson Community Council. Baptist (ch. moderator, chmn. finance com., deacon, ch. sch. supt., trustee). Rotarian. Home: 5301 E Grant Rd Tucson AZ 85712 Office: Box 42195 Tucson AZ 85733. *It seems important to put something back into life-for all we take from it.*

SHROPSHIRE, THOMAS BAILEY, brewing co. exec.; b. Little Rock, Oct. 15, 1925; s. Bruce and Irene S.; B.S., Lincoln U., 1950; m. Jacqulyn Calloway, June 14, 1961; children—Terilyn, Tom. Coll. supr. Philip Morris, Inc., 1952-59, sales mgr. West Africa Philip Morris Internat., 1959-67, chmn., mng. dir. Philip Morris Nigeria, 1968-72; v.p. Miller Brewing Co., Milw., 1972-78, sr. v.p., treas., dir., 1978—; dir. Key Banks, Inc., Albany, N.Y. Bd. dirs. Miller High Life Found., United Way Greater Milw., U. Wis. Hosps., YMCA Met. Milw., Urban League; mem. adv. council W. Paul Stillman Sch. Bus., Seton Hall U. Served with USNR, 1944-46. Recipient B'nai B'rith Humanitarian award, 1979; Ebony Achievement award, 1979; NAACP Bus. award, 1979. Mem. Am. Mktg. Assn., Internat. Advt. Assn., Nat. Assn. Market Developers. Clubs: Milw. Athletic, Ozaukee Country. Office: 3939 W Highland Blvd Milwaukee WI 53208

SHROPSHIRE, WALTER, JR., biophysicist; b. Washington, Sept. 4, 1932; s. Walter and Mary Virginia (Anderson) S.; B.S. in Physics, George Washington U., 1954, M.S. in Botany, 1956, Ph.D. in Plant Physiology, 1958; postdoctoral fellow biophysics, Calif. Inst. Tech., 1957-59; m. Audrey Marie McConkey, June 28, 1958; children—Janet Marie, Susan Lynn, Edward Allen. Physicist, Smithsonian Instn., 1959-63; asst. dir. Smithsonian Radiation Biology Lab., 1963—; Gast prof. U. Freiburg (Germany), 1968-69; professorial lectr. botany George Washington U., 1960—. Recipient Smithsonian Outstanding Performance award, 1967, Smithsonian Research award, 1968; NSF grantee, 1960-66. Charter mem. Biophys. Soc.; fellow AAAS, Internat. Solar Energy Soc. (dir.), Am. Soc. Plant Physiologists. United Methodist Ch. (ordained pastor). Editor: Phytochrome, 1972. Contbr. articles to profl. jours. Home: 4816 Flower Valley Dr Rockville MD 20853 Office: 12441 Parklawn Dr Rockville MD 20852

SHROYER, FREDERICK BENJAMIN, educator, author; b. Decatur, Ind., Oct. 28, 1916; s. Benjamin Franklin and Huldah (Mutschler) S.; student U. Mich., 1935-37; B.A., U. So. Calif., 1948, M.A., 1949, Ph.D., 1955; m. Patricia Grace Connor, Jan. 13, 1949; 1 dau., Madeline Gwynn. Mem. faculty Calif. State U. at Los Angeles, 1950-76, prof. English and Am. lit., 1959-75, emeritus, chmn. dept. lang. arts, 1951-53; vis. prof. U. So. Calif. 1958; vis. lect. U. So. Calif., 1961, Redlands U., 1965, Eastern Ky. U., 1966; Bingham prof. humanities U. Louisville, 1969-70; founder, dir. Pacific Coast Writers Conf., 1953-55, novelist-in-residence, 1965, 66, 67; founder, dir. Idyllwild Writers Conf., 1956-57; literary editor, columnist Los Angeles Herald-Examiner, 1962-77; lit. cons., moderator, lectr. many TV programs. Served to capt. USAAF, 1942-46. Named Alumnus of Distinction, U. So. Calif., 1961; resident fellow Huntington Hartford Found., 1958, 65; recipient Sylvania award, 1959, Christopher award, 1965; outstanding prof. award, Calif. State U. at Los Angeles, 1967; Cine Gold Eagle award, 1970; named Ky. col. Mem. Nat. Acad. TV Arts and Scis., Blue Key, Epsilon Phi, Phi Delta Kappa, Phi Kappa Phi. Clubs: Greater Los Angeles Press; Hollywood Authors (dir. 1966—, exec. v.p. 1967-77); Kent County Cricket (Canterbury, Eng.); Athenaeum (London); So. Calif. Cricket (Los Angeles); British United Services. Author: (novels) Wall Against the Night, 1957; It Happened in Wayland, 1963; There None Embrace, 1966; author, editor (with H. Richardson) Muse of Fire, 1971. Editor: (with Paul A. Jorgensen) A College Treasury, 2d edit., 1967, The Informal Essay, 1961, The Art of Prose, 1965; (with Dorothy Parker) Short Story; A Thematic Anthology, 1965: (with Louis Gardemal) Types of Drama, 1969. Home: 362 Coral View Monterey Park CA 91754

SHRYOCK, EDWIN HAROLD, anatomist, educator; b. Seattle, Apr. 14, 1906; s. Alfred Quimby and Stella Louisa (Tefft) S.; B.S., Pacific Union Coll., 1930; M.D., Loma Linda U., 1934; A.M., U. So. Calif., 1939; m. Daisy May Bagwell, Apr. 30, 1929; children—Patricia Helen, Edwin Forrest. Instr. dept. micro-anatomy Loma Linda U., 1934-39, asst. prof., 1939-45, asso. prof. anatomy, 1945-57, prof., 1957-75, prof. emeritus, 1975—, past chmn. dept. anatomy, dean Preclinic div. Med. Sch., 1945-50, asso. dean, 1950-51, dean Sch. Medicine, 1951-54. Diplomate Nat. Bd. Med. Examiners, 1935. Mem. Am. Assn. Anatomists, Sigma Xi. Republican. Mem. Seventh-day Adventist Ch. Author: Happiness for Husbands and Wives, 1949; Happiness and Health, 1950; On Becoming a Man, 1951; On Becoming a Woman, 1951; Highways to Health, 1953; Living, 1958; Mind If I Smoke?, 1959; On Being Sweethearts, 1966; On Being Married Soon, 1968; Your Amazing Body, 1971; What To Do in an Emergency, 1978; Modern Medical Guide, 1979; co-author You and Your Health, 3 vols., 1970, author rev. edit., 3 vols., 1978; also articles on developmental anatomy in sci. publs.; mental hygiene in nat. publs. Home: PO Box 638 Loma Linda CA 92354

SHRYOCK, GERALD DUANE, educator; b. Sharon, Okla., Jan. 24, 1933; s. Elton Leroy and Cecil Irene (Taylor) S.; B.S., Northwestern State Coll., 1956; M.S., Okla. State U., 1959; Ph.D., U. Pacific, 1966; m. Carmen Jean Lawson, June 6, 1959; children—Lori Denise, Dennis Duane, Darin Wayne, Daryl Neal. Instr. Murray State Coll., 1958-59, 61-62; instr. Imperial Ethiopian Coll., Dire Dawa, 1959-61; asst. prof. Black Hills State Coll., Spearfish, S.D., 1963-65, asso. prof., 1966-68, prof., chmn. div. sci. and math., 1968—. NSF grantee, 1962-63, 64. Mem. Am. Chem. Soc., Phi Kappa Phi, Phi Lambda Upsilon. Contbr. articles to profl. jours. Home: 908 Spartan Dr Spearfish SD 57783

SHRYOCK, RUSSELL WEBSTER, business exec.; b. Mansfield, Ohio, Apr. 22, 1917; s. Hoyt S. and Lottie (Kurtz) S.; B.S., Ohio State U., 1943; m. Margaret E. Backus, Aug. 2, 1941; children—Randa Kay, Ronald Allen, Richard Scott. Vice pres., gen. mgr. Davidson Motors,

Inc., Cleve., 1949-57; v.p., gen. mgr. United Leasing Service, Inc., Cleve., 1951-58; exec. v.p. Lee Fleet Systems, Cleve., 1958-60; v.p. U.S. Leasing Corp., San Francisco, 1960-66; v.p. Marine Midland Banks, Inc., Buffalo, 1966-68; sr. v.p. Marine Midland Bank-Western, Buffalo, 1968-76; pres., chief exec. officer Marine Midland Leasing Corp., 1970-76; pres., chief exec., chmn. bd. Xyovest, Inc., XyoQuip Inc., XyoMed, Inc., Cin., 1976—; instr. Ohio State U., 1942. Mem. Downtown Council C. of C. Served to capt. F.A., U.S. Army, 1943-46; ETO. Mem. Cin. C. of C., Beta Alpha Psi. Clubs: Exchange (past pres.) (Cleve.); Cincinnati. Contbr. articles to profl. jours. Home: 762 Woodfield Rd Cincinnati OH 45231 Office: 130 Tri-County Pkwy Cincinnati OH 45240

SHUART, JAMES M., univ. pres.; b. College Point, N.Y., May 9, 1931; s. John and Barbara (Schmidt) S.; B.A., Hofstra U., 1953, M.A., 1962; Ph.D., N.Y. U., 1966; m. Marjorie Strunk, Apr. 5, 1953; children—James Raymond, William Arthur. Group rep. Home Life Ins. Co., N.Y.C. and Buffalo, 1955-57; rep., group ins. N.Y. Life Ins. Co., N.Y.C., 1957-59; asst. dir. admissions Hofstra U., Hempstead, N.Y., 1959-70, asst. dean faculty, asst. pres., exec. dean student services, asso. dean liberal arts scis., v.p. adminstrv. services, 1975-76, pres., 1976—, trustee, 1973-75; trustee Molloy Coll., 1973-77; adv. bd. Adelphi U. Sch. Social Work, 1973—; dep. county exec. County of Nassau (N.Y.), 1973-75, commr. social services, 1971-73. Trustee Uniondale (N.Y.) Pub. Library, 1967-68, L.I. (N.Y.) Health Hosp. Planning Council, 1971-75; pres., dir. Health Welfare Council Nassau County (N.Y.), 1971—; chmn. Nassau (N.Y.) Bd. Social Services, 1971-73; mem. Nassau Youth Bd., 1971-73, Nassau Mental Health Bd., 1971-73; trustee Nassau-Suffolk Comprehensive Health Planning Council, 1974-75. Recipient Founders Day award N.Y. U., 1967; Outstanding Alumnus award Hofstra U., 1973, George M. Estabrook Disting. Service award Alumni Assn., 1974; Leadership in Govt. award C.W. Post. Coll., L.I. U., 1978; Hempstead Man of Yr. award, 1978; L.I. Personnel and Guidance Assn. award, 1976. Home: 25 Cathedral Ave Garden City NY 11530 Office: Hofstra Univ Hempstead NY 11550

SHUBERT, GUSTAVE HARRY, research exec.; b. Buffalo, Jan. 18, 1929; s. Gustave Henri and Ada Shubert (Smith) S.; B.A., Yale U., 1948; M.A., N.Y. U., 1951; m. Rhea Brickman, Mar. 29, 1952; children—Wendy J., David L. Staff mem. Lincoln Lab., M.I.T., 1955-57; adminstr. systems engring. Hycon Eastern, Inc., Paris, 1957-59; with Rand Corp., Santa Monica, Calif., 1959—, v.p. domestic programs, 1968-75, sr. v.p. domestic programs, 1975-78, sr. v.p., 1978—, dir. Inst. Civil Justice, 1979—, trustee, 1973—; trustee N.Y.C. Rand Inst., 1972—, pres., 1972-73; trustee Housing Allowance Offices of Brown County and South Bend, Ind., 1973—; mem. adv. council Sch. Engring., Stanford U.; mem. policy adv. com. Clin. Scholars Program, UCLA; mem. Nat. Acad. Scis. Com. on Evaluation of Poverty Research. Served with USAF, 1951-55. Decorated Air medal with 2 oak leaf clusters, Commendation medal. Mem. Inst. Strategic Studies (London). Clubs: Commonwealth (San Francisco); Yale (N.Y.C.). Home: 13838 Sunset Blvd Pacific Palisades CA 90272 Office: Rand Corp 1700 Main St Santa Monica CA 90406

SHUBERT, JOSEPH FRANCIS, librarian; b. Buffalo, Sept. 17, 1928; s. Joseph Francis and Lena M. (Kohn) S.; B.S., State U. Tchrs. Coll., Geneseo, N.Y., 1951; M.A., U. Denver, 1957; m. Dorothy Jean Whearty, Feb. 5, 1955; children—Julia Ellen, Alan Joseph. Reference and extension librarian Nev. State Library, Carson City, 1951-57, library cons. 1957-59, state librarian, 1959-61; asst. dir. internat. relations office ALA, 1962-66; state librarian Ohio, 1966-77; state librarian, asst. commr. libraries N.Y. State Edn. Dept., 1977—: mem. adv. council to U.S. Pub. Printer, 1974-77; adv. com. White House Conf. Library and Info. Services, 1977-79; trustee Ohio Coll. Library Center, 1976-78. Mem. ALA, Nev. (pres.), North Collins (N.Y.), Meml. library assns., Ohio Library Assn., Am. Soc. Pub. Adminstrn., Chief Officers State Library Agencies (chmn. 1977-78), Nev. Congress Parents and Tchrs., Kappa Delta Pi. Roman Catholic. Author: Public Library Service to Englewood, Colorado, 1957; A Community Librarian's Training Program, 1973. Contbr. to numerous periodicals. Home: 494 Madison Ave Albany NY 12208 Office: NY State Library State Edn Dept Cultural Edn Center Albany NY 12230

SHUBIK, PHILIPPE, physician, educator; b. London, Apr. 28, 1921; s. Joseph L.M. and Sara (Soloweiczyk) S.; came to U.S., 1949, naturalized, 1957; B.M.B.Ch., Oxford (Eng.) U., 1943, D.Phil., 1949, D.M., 1971; m. Valerie Helen Reid, July 22, 1964; children—Anna, Peter, Katherine. Intern, London (Eng.) Hosp., 1943; demonstrator pathology, mem. cancer research unit Sir William Dunn Sch. Pathology, U. Oxford, 1947-49; instr. pathology, biologist exptl. cancer project Northwestern U. Med. Sch., Evanston, Ill., 1949-50; cancer coordinator, asst. prof. surgery Chgo. Med. Sch., 1950-53, asso. prof. surgery, dir. div. oncology, 1953-68, prof. oncology, 1953-68, dir. Inst. Med. Research, 1966-68; prof., dir. Eppley Inst. Research Cancer, U. Nebr. Coll. Medicine, Omaha, 1968—; mem. subcom. carcinogenesis prevention Nat. Cancer Adv. Bd., 1970—, chmn. subcom. environ. carcinogens, 1974-75; mem. U.S.A. nat. com. Internat. Union Against Cancer, 1971—; mem. adv. com. environ. carcinogenesis Internat. Agy. Research Cancer WHO; mem. com. environ. carcinogenesis Am. Assn. Cancer Research, 1971—; pres. Toxicology Forum, 1976—. Served to maj. M.C., Brit. Army, 1944-47. Nat. Cancer Inst. grantee, 1950—. Fellow N.Y. Acad. Scis.; mem. Sigma Xi. Editorial bd. Cancer Research, 1956-70, Internat. Jour. Cancer, 1964-66, Am. Jour. Pathology, 1967-72, Jour. Toxicology Environ. Health, 1975—, Preventive Medicine, 1975—; co-mng. editor Cancer Letters, 1975—; contbr. articles to med. jours. Home: 3321 S 101st St Omaha NE 68124 Office: Eppley Inst Cancer Research Univ Nebraska Coll Medicine 42nd and Dewey Ave Omaha NE 68105

SHUCART, WILLIAM ARTHUR, neurosurgeon; b. St. Louis, Oct. 23, 1935; s. Frank M. and Beatrice S.; A.B., Washington U., 1957; M.D., U. Mo., 1961; m. Laura Huber, Dec. 16, 1971. Intern, U. Utah Hosp., Salt Lake City, 1961-62; resident in surgery Columbia-Presbyterian Hosp., N.Y.C., 1967-71; mem. faculty dept. neurosurgery Tufts Med. Sch., Boston, 1971-76, asso. prof., 1976; neurosurgeon Tufts-New Eng. Med. Center, 1972-76; prof., chmn. dept. neurosurgery SUNY, Downstate Med. Center, Bklyn., 1976—. Served with U.S. Army, 1964-67. Diplomate Am. Bd. Neurol. Surgery. Mem. A.C.S., Am. Assn. Neurol. Surgeons, Soc. Neurol. Surgeons. Home: 16 Broadmoor Rd Scarsdale NY 10583 Office: 450 Clarkson Ave Brooklyn NY 11203

SHUCHTER, CLAUDE F., banker; m. Adele Greeley; children—Alan F., Barbara. Chmn., chief exec. officer, dir. Mfrs. & Traders Trust Co., Buffalo; pres., chief exec. officer, dir. 1st Empire State Corp.; v.p., dir. M. & T. Capital Corp.; dir. M & T Bank Internat. N.V., Pollack Printing Co., Upson Co., 1st Nat. Bank of Highland. Address: 1 M & T Plaza Buffalo NY 14240

SHUCK, EMERSON CLAYTON, educator; b. Findlay, Ohio, Apr. 15, 1916; s. Clayton B. and Mary Ethel (Biddle) S.; B.S., Otterbein Coll., Westerville, Ohio, 1938, Litt.D., 1963; M.A., Ohio State U., 1939; Ph.D., U. Wis., 1943; m. Sarah LeGrand Beidleman, May 24, 1936; children—William C., Sarah (Mrs. David Demchak), Mary (Mrs. David Bertram), Jane Stewart (Mrs. Roger Vermillion). Grad. asst. English, Ohio State U., 1939-40, U. Wis., 1941-43; asst. prof. English, Bowling Green State U., 1943-46, asso. prof., 1946-48, prof., 1948-63, dir. Grad. Sch., 1946-50, dean Grad. Sch., 1950-55, chmn. dept. English, 1952-55, dean Coll. Liberal Arts, 1955-63; v.p. acad. affairs Ohio Wesleyan U., Delaware, 1963-67; pres. Eastern Wash. State Coll., Cheney, 1967-76, prof. English, 1968—; pres. Am. Assn. State Colls. and Univs., 1975-76; mem. Commn. on Colls., N.W. Assn. Schs. and Colls., 1978—. Mem. Omicron Delta Kappa, Sigma Zeta, Sigma Alpha Epsilon. Presbyn. Contbr. articles to profl. jours. Home: 716 Clover Ct Cheney WA 99004. *I have tried to use as guides to my own behavior the relatively simple principles that love and trust in others is always better than hate and suspicion, that concentration is as important as brilliance, that I am responsible for matters with which I have been involved, that openness and honesty are productive and rewarding, and that it is important to have something larger than one's self to believe in and work for. I accept the evidence that human life is frequently whimsical, unfair to individual needs and desires, and probably basically tragic; but I am not willing to allow that perception to dominate my own acts.*

SHUFF, LILY, artist, wood engraver; b. N.Y.C.; B.A., M.A., Hunter Coll.; student Art Students League, Bklyn., Acad. Fine Arts, N.Y. Sch. Social Research, Columbia U.; m. Martin Shir, May 12, 1950; children—Lewitt, Lawrence. One-woman shows include: Argent Gallery, N.Y.C., 1947, 56, Van Dieman Lilenfeld Gallery, N.Y.C., 1948, 52, Giraudeau Gallery, Paris, 1951, Utica (N.Y.) Library Gallery, Cortland (N.Y.) Gallery, Mercersburg (Pa.) Acad., Thiel Coll., Greenville, Pa., Freemont (Mich.) Found., St. Vincent's Coll., Latrobe, Pa., 1960, State Coll., Conn., Purdue U., Inc., McPherson Coll., Kans., Regar Mus., Ala., Fairleigh Dickinson Coll., 1961, East Side Gallery, Erie (Pa.) Pub. Mus., Pack Meml. Mus., Asheville, N.C., State U. N.Y., U. N.D., Wesleyan U., S.D., Oreg. Coll., East Side Gallery, N.Y., 1962, 64, 66, others; exhibited in group shows: NAD, Whitney, Riverside, Bklyn., Jersey City museums, Nat. Print Show Library of Congress, Portland Mus. Arts, Nat. Sarasota Smithsonian Instn., also in France, Belgium, Holland, Switzerland, Can., Greece, Japan, Latin Am., India, S.AM., Mex., Scotland, Eng., Israel; represented in permanent collections: Bat Yam Mus., Israel, Met. Mus., N.Y.C., Pakistan Consulate, James Fenimore Cooper High Sch., Robert Mueller, Paris, Mme. Germaine Richier, Paris, Yale U., Ga. Mus. Art, Am. Fedn. Art, Library of Congress, Monsieur Rene de Solier, Paris, Bezalel Nat. Mus., Jerusalem, Norfolk Mus., Neville Mus., Purdue U., Regar Mus., Dakota Wesleyan U., State U. N.Y., Baylor U., Mayville State Coll., St. Vincent Coll., Central Okla. Mus., Phila. Mus. Art, Baruch Coll., N.Y.C., Butler Mus. Am. Art, City Coll. N.Y., McPherson Coll., U. N.D., Rosenberg Library, Galveston, Tex., Erie (Pa.) Mus., many pvt. collections. Recipient prize oil Bklyn. Soc. Artists, 1953, 56; N.J. Painters and Sculptors Soc., 1956, 68, 69, 70, oil, 1960; wood block print Conn. Acad. Fine Art, 1956, 1st prize oil, Caravan Gallery, 1957, print Nat. Assn. Women Artists, 1959, Caseim, 1958; Casein prize, Argent Gallery, 1958, Riverside Mus. Print, 1959, Nat. Soc. Painters in Casein, 1963, 65; Bklyn. Soc. Artists prize oil, 1960; gold medal of honor Jersey City Mus., 1962; prize Nat. Soc. Casein Painters, 1966-67-70-73, 75, 76, 77; prize in oil Knickerbocker Artists, 1966; prize in oil Am. Soc. Contemporary Artists, 1966, 67, 68, 70; Nat. Assn. Women Artists prize, 1969, 70, 71, 75, 78; Silver medal for creative oil Audubon Artists, 1979; others. Mem. Bklyn. Soc. Artists (dir., oil jury), N.Y. Soc. Woman Artists (dir., treas.), Nat. Assn. Woman Artists (dir., chmn. membership jury, oil jury, mem. adv. bd.), Nat. Soc. Casein Painters (sec.), Nat. Casein Soc. (oil jury), Artists Equity, Mus. Modern Art, Silvermine Guild Artists, Soc. Wash. Printmakers, Conn. Acad. Fine Arts, N.J. Painters and Sculptors Soc. (jury selection), Audubon Artists Assn., Hunterdon County Art Center, Am. Soc. Contemporary Artists, Am. Color Print Soc., Physicians Wives League Greater N.Y. Club: Woman Pays. Contbr. to Art Collector's Almanac, Prize Winning Art Smithsonian Instn., Archives Am. Art, Today's Art, Allied Arts, Talk of N.Y., Artists U.S.A., others. Address: 155 W 68th St Apt 212 New York NY 10023. *I belong to an idealistic school that acclaims romanticism but accepts realities for study and style. Therefore, throughout my life I have held an optimistic view of mankind and of man's intellect.*

SHUFORD, HARRY ALEXANDER, banker, lawyer; b. Tyler, Tex., Feb. 26, 1915; s. Harry Dawson and Alla Mae (Duke) S.; B.S. in Commerce, So. Methodist U., 1936, LL.B., 1939; m. Virginia Waters, Oct. 14, 1939 (dec. Aug. 1975); children—Harry Lindsley, David William; m. Claire Tucker Blakeney, Sept. 23, 1976. Admitted to Tex. bar, 1939; research and evidence asst. with atty. gen. Tex., 1939-41; briefing atty. Supreme Ct. Tex., 1941-42; with firm Malone, Lipscomb, White & Seay, Dallas, 1941-42, Malone, Lipscomb, Seay & Shuford, Dallas, 1946-47; asst. atty. Dr. Pepper Co., Dallas, 1947-48; counsel Fed. Res. Bank Dallas, 1948-52, v.p., gen. counsel, 1952-59, 1st v.p., 1959-62; pres. Fed. Res. Bank of St. Louis, 1962-66; chmn. trust com. 1st Nat. Bank in Dallas, 1966-72, chmn. bd., 1972-77, chmn. exec. com., 1978—. Bd. dirs. Cotton Bowl Athletic Assn., Salvation Army; trustee Meth. Hosp. of Dallas. Served to lt. (s.g.) USNR, 1942-45. Named Alumnus of Year, So. Meth. U. Sch. Law, 1960; Distinguished Alumnus award So. Meth. U., 1963; Mem. Am., Tex., Dallas bar assns., Salesmanship Club Dallas. Methodist. Home: 3604 Beverly Dr Dallas TX 75205 Office: PO Box 83300 Dallas TX 75283

SHUGART, HOWARD ALAN, physicist, educator; b. Orange, Calif., Sept. 21, 1931; s. Howard Ancil and Bertha Elizabeth (Henderson) S.; B.S., Calif. Inst. Tech., 1953; M.A., U. Calif. at Berkeley, 1955, Ph.D., 1957; m. Elizabeth L. Hanson, Feb. 6, 1971. Teaching asst. physics U. Calif. at Berkeley, 1953-56, asso., 1957, lectr., 1957-58, acting asst. prof., 1958-59, asst. prof., 1959-63, asso. prof., 1963-67, prof., 1967—, atomic beam group leader Lawrence Berkeley Lab., 1965—. Cons. Convair div. Gen. Dynamics Corp., 1960-61; mem. com. nuclear constants NRC, 1960-63. Fellow Am. Phys. Soc. (acting sec. Pacific Coast, 1961-64, exec. com. div. electron and atomic physics 1972-74), Nat. Speleological Soc. (gov. 1954-56); mem. Sigma Xi. Office: Dept Physics U Calif Berkeley CA 94720

SHUKER, GREGORY BROWN, pub. and production co. exec.; b. Charleston, W.Va., Oct. 3, 1932; s. George and Florence (Brown) S.; B.S. in Journalism, Northwestern U., 1954; m. Nancy Swift Frederick, June 9, 1956; children—John Frederick, Allison Gregory, Frances Swift. Corr. Life mag., 1959-60; producer Drew Assos., 1961-66; producer Pub. Broadcast Lab., 1967-68; dir. programming CBS-EVR, 1969; program dir. Time-Life Video, 1970; exec. prod., v.p. Eden House Pub. Inc., N.Y.C., 1971—; exec. producer Playback Assos., Inc., 1972—. Vice pres., dir. The Loft Film and Theatre Center, Bronxville, N.Y. Served to lt. (j.g.) USNR, 1955-58. Mem. Deru, Sigma Delta Chi, Alpha Tau Omega, Kappa Tau Alpha. Club: Bronxville Field. Producer documentary films TV: Crisis: Behind a Presidential Committment, 1963; The Chair (Grand Prix Cannes), 1963; Faces of November (1st prize Venice), 1964; Free at Last (1st prize Venice), 1968; exec. producer What Do We Do Now? - The Need for Direction, 1976. Home: 17 Sunset Ave Bronxville NY 10708 Office: 30 Rockefeller Plaza New York City NY 10020. *I think often of Joseph Conrad's sentence, "Art is long and life is short and success is very far off. . . ." It seems to me that those of us in this volume who may have achieved a "success," albeit modest, could dwell on this humbling reminder, whatever our endeavor (our "art") may be, and achieve that most elusive entity—perspective.*

SHULA, DON FRANCIS, profl. football coach; b. Grand River, Ohio, Jan. 4, 1930; s. Dan and Mary (Miller) S.; B.S., John Carroll U., Cleve., 1951, H.H.D., 1972; M.A., Western Res. U., 1953; Sc.D., Biscayne Coll., 1974; m. Dorothy Bartish, July 19, 1958; children—David, Donna, Sharon, Anne, Michael. Profl. football player, Cleve. Browns, 1951-52, Balt. Colts, 1953-56, Washington Redskins, 1957; asst. coach U. Va., 1958, U. Ky., 1959, Detroit Lions, 1960-62; head coach Baltimore Colts, 1963-69; head coach, v.p. Miami (Fla.) Dolphins, 1970—. Fla. crusade chmn. Nat. Cancer Soc., 1975; co-chmn. Jerry Lewis March Against Dystrophy, 1975; nat. bd. dirs. Jesuit Program for Living and Learning, 1976; mem. nat. sports com. Multiple Sclerosis Soc., Muscular Dystrophy Assn.; bd. dirs. Heart Assn. Greater Miami; hon. chmn. Belen Jesuit Intercultural Fund Campaign to Build Sch. Served with Ohio N.G., 1952. Recipient Coach of Yr. awards, 1964, 70, 71, 72; coached five superbowl teams, winner, 1972, 73; overall coaching percentage, .737; named Balt. Colts Silver Anniversary Coach, 1977; recipient Brotherhood award Fla. region NCCJ, 1977, Light of Flames Leadership award Barry Coll., 1977. Roman Catholic. Author: The Winning Edge, 1972. Home: 16220 W Prestwick Pl Miami Lakes FL 33014 Office: 330 Biscayne Blvd Bldg Miami FL 33132. *Success is never final; defeat is never fatal.*

SHULER, JACK HAYWARD, utility co. exec., lawyer; b. Detroit, Dec. 7, 1917; s. Herbert and Ethel (Hayward) S.; B.S.E., U. Mich., 1940, J.D., 1942; m. Elizabeth Graham, Oct. 9, 1942; children—John G., Elizabeth Stuart, Janet H. Admitted to Mich. bar, 1942; atty. Mich. Bell Telephone Co., Detroit, 1946-49, 50—, v.p., gen. counsel, 1972-77, v.p., gen. counsel, sec., 1977—; atty. AT&T, N.Y.C., 1949-50. Bd. dirs. Mich. State C. of C., 1973-78, Citizen Research Council, Detroit, 1973—, Blue Cross Blue Shield of Mich., 1977—. Served to lt. USN, 1942-45. Mem. Am. Bar Assn., Mich. Bar Assn., Detroit Bar Assn., Am. Judicature Soc. Home: 3140 Wellington Ct Orchard Lake MI 48033 Office: 444 Michigan Ave Room 1700 Detroit MI 48226

SHULER, KURT EGON, chemist, educator; b. Nuremberg, Germany, July 10, 1922; s. Louis and Donie (Wald) Schulherr; came to U.S., 1937, naturalized, 1944; B.S., Ga. Inst. Tech., 1942; Ph.D., Cath. U. Am., 1949; postdoctoral fellow Johns Hopkins U., 1949-51; m. Beatrice Gwyn London, Nov. 11, 1944; Sr. staff mem., asst. group supr., chem. physics group Applied Physics Lab., Johns Hopkins, 1951-55; supervisory phys. chemist Nat. Bur. Standards, 1955-58, cons. to dir., 1958-61, asst. dir., sr. research fellow, 1963-68; mem. research staff, sci. adviser to v.p. research Gen. Motors Corp., 1958; spl. asst. to dir. research Inst. Def. Analyses, 1961-63; vis. prof. chemistry, U. Calif. at San Diego, 1966-67; prof. chemistry U. Calif., San Diego, 1968—, chmn. dept., 1968-70; cons. to govt. and industry, 1956—. Mem. Solvay Conf., 1962, 78; mem. adv. panel, chemistry div. NSF, 1973-75. Served with U.S. Army, 1944-46. Recipient Distinguished Service award Nat. Bur. Standards, 1959, Gold medal award Dept. Commerce, 1968. Solvay Found. fellow, 1975. Fellow Am. Inst. Chemists, Am. Phys. Soc., Washington Acad. Sci.; mem. Am. Chem. Soc., Washington Philos. Soc., AAAS. Club: Cosmos (Washington). Author, editor tech. books. Asso. editor Jour. Math. Physics, 1963-66; bd. editors Jour. Statis. Physics, 1968—; adv. bd. Chem. Engring. News, 1967-70. Contbr. articles to profl. jours. Home: Box 1504 Rancho Santa Fe CA 92067 Office: Dept Chemistry U Calif at San Diego La Jolla CA 92093

SHULEVITZ, URI, author, illustrator; b. Warsaw, Poland, Feb. 27, 1935; s. Abraham and Szandla (Hermanstat) S.; student Tel-Aviv Inst., 1953-55; Tchrs. Cert. Tchrs. Coll. Israel, 1956; student Bklyn. Museum Art Sch., 1959-61. Came to U.S., 1959, naturalized, 1965. Author, illustrator: The Moon In My Room, 1963; One Monday Morning, 1967; Rain Rain Rivers, 1969; Oh What a Noise, 1971; Soldier and Tsar in the Forest, 1972; Dawn, 1974, The Treasure, 1978; illustrator: The Fool of the World and the Flying Ship (Caldecott medal 1969), 1968, The Twelve Dancing Princesses, 1966; The Touchstone, 1976; Hannkah Morey, 1978; The Lost Kingdom of Karnica, 1979; instr. Sch. Visual Arts N.Y., 1967-68, Pratt Inst., 1970-71; illustrator, writer children's books The New Sch., 1970—. Served with Israeli Army, 1956-59. Mem Authors Guild. Office: care Farrar Straus & Giroux Inc 19 Union Sq W New York NY 10003

SHULL, CLIFFORD G., physicist, educator; b. Pitts., Sept. 23, 1915; s. David H. and Daisy I. (Bistline) H.; B.S., Carnegie Inst. Tech., 1937; Ph.D., N.Y.U., 1941; m. Martha-Nuel Summer, June 19, 1941; children—John C., Robert D., William F. Research physicist Texas Co., 1941-46; chief physicist Oak Ridge Nat. Lab., 1946-55; prof. physics Mass. Inst. Tech., 1955—. Chmn. vis. com. Brookhaven Nat. Lab., 1961-62; chmn. vis. com. Nat. Bur. Standard reactor, 1972-73; chmn. vis. com. solid state div. Oak Ridge Nat. Lab., 1974-75; chmn. policy com. Nat. Small-Angle-Scattering Center, 1978-79. Recipient award of merit Alumni Assn. of Carnegie-Mellon U., 1968; Humboldt Sr. U.S. Scientist award, 1979. Fellow Am. Phys. Soc. (Buckley prize 1956; chmn. solid state physics div. 1962-63), A.A.A.S., Am. Acad. Arts and Scis., N.Y. Acad. Scis., Nat. Acad. Scis. (vice chmn. panel on neutron sci. 1977); mem. Am. Crystallographic Assn., Research Soc. Am., Sigma Xi, Tau Beta Pi, Phi Kappa Phi. Contbr. articles to sci. jours. Home: 4 Wingate Rd Lexington MA 02173 Office: Dept Physics Mass Inst Tech Cambridge MA 02139

SHULL, FRANKLIN BUCKLEY, physicist, educator; b. Ann Arbor, Mich., Apr. 23, 1918; s. Aaron Franklin and Margaret (Buckley) S.; A.B., U. Mich., 1939, A.M., 1940, Ph.D., 1948; m. Barbara Bair, Aug. 26, 1947; children—Margaret E., Catherine A., Sarah F., Dorothy E. Asso. physicist U.S. Naval Ordnance Lab., 1941-46; asst. prof. Washington U., St. Louis, 1948-53, asso. prof., 1953-63, prof., 1963—. Mem. Sigma Xi. Research on nuclear physics, beta decay, nuclear polarization, scattering and nuclear reactions. Home: 40 Picardy Ln St Louis MO 63124

SHULL, FREMONT ADAM, JR., bus. mgmt. scientist, educator; b. Findlay, Ohio, Apr. 28, 1924; s. Fremont A. and Gladys Pearl (Walcutt) S.; Ph.D., Mich. State U., 1958; children—Scott Alden, Marcy Lee. Instr., Drake U., 1949-51; instr. mgmt. Mich. State U., 1951-56; asst. prof. mgmt. Ind. U., Bloomington, 1956-63; prof., chmn. dept. So. Ill. U., Carbondale, 1963-67; vis. prof. orgn. theory U. Wis., Madison, 1967-68, U. Ky., 1968-69; research prof. mgmt. and soc. U. Ga., Athens, 1969—; cons. Del. Correctional System, Warner Robins Air Logistic Command, Anaconda Aluminum Co., Ala. Welfare System. Fellow Acad. Mgmt.; mem. Beta Gamma Sigma (Distinguished Scholar), Alpha Kappa Psi. (Distinguished Prof.). Author: (with Delbecq and Cummings) Organizational Decision-Making, 1970. Home: 175 Kings Ct Watkinsville GA 30677 Office: U Ga Athens GA 30602

SHULL, HARRISON, chemist, educator; b. Princeton, N.J., Aug. 17, 1923; s. George Harrison and Mary (Nicholl) S.; A.B., Princeton U., 1943; Ph.D., U. Calif. at Berkeley, 1948; m. Jeanne Louise Johnson, 1948 (div. 1962); children—James Robert, Kathy, George Harrison, Holly; m. 2d, Wil Joyce Bentley Long, 1962; children—Warren Michael Long, Jeffery Mark Long, Stanley Martin, Sarah Ellen. Asso. chemist U.S. Naval Research Lab., 1943-45; asst. prof. Iowa State U., 1949-54; asso. prof., mem. faculty Ind. U., 1955-79, research prof., 1961-79, dean Grad. Sch., 1965-72, vice chancellor for research and devel., 1972-76, dir. Research Computing Center, 1959-63, acting chmn. chemistry dept., 1965-66, acting dean arts and scis., 1969-70, acting dean faculties, 1974; mem. faculty, provost, v.p. acad. affairs Rensselaer Poly. Inst., 1979—; asst. dir. research, quantum chemistry group Uppsala (Sweden) U., 1958-59; vis. prof. Washington U., St. Louis, 1960, U. Colo., 1963. Founder, supr. Quantum Chemistry Program Exchange, 1962—; chmn. subcom. molecular structure and spectroscopy NRC, 1958-63; chmn. Fulbright selection com. chemistry, 1963-67, mem. adv. com. Office Sci. Personnel, 1957-60; chmn. First Gordon Research Conf. Theoretical Chemistry, 1962; mem. com. survey chemistry Nat. Acad. Sci., 1964-65; mem. adv. panel chemistry NSF, 1964-67, mem. adv. panel Office Computer Activities, 1967-70, cons. chem. information program, 1965-71, mem. adv. com. for research, 1974-76; mem. vis. com. chemistry Brookhaven Nat. Lab., 1967-70; mem. adv. com. Chem. Abstracts Service, 1971-74. Trustee Argonne U. Assn., 1970-75, Asso. Univs., Inc., 1973-76. Served as ensign USNR, 1945. NRC postdoctoral fellow phys. scis. U. Chgo., 1948-49; Guggenheim fellow U. Uppsala, 1954-55, NSF sr. postdoctoral fellow, 1968-69; Sloan research fellow, 1956-58. Fellow Am. Acad. Arts and Scis. (v.p. 1976—, chmn. Midwest Center 1976-79), Am. Phys. Soc.; mem. Nat. Acad. Scis. (com. on sci. and public policy, 1969-72; council, exec. com., 1971-74, chmn. U.S.-USSR sci. policy subgroup for fundamental research 1973—, naval studies bd. 1974-79, chmn. Commn. on Human Resources 1977-80, nominating com. 1978), Am. Chem. Soc., AAAS, AAUP, Assn. Computing Machinery, Royal Swedish Acad. Scis. (fgn. mem.), Royal Acad. Arts and Scis. Uppsala (corr. mem.), Phi Beta Kappa, Sigma Xi, Phi Lambda Upsilon. Club: Cosmos (Washington). Asso. editor Jour. Chem. Physics, 1952-54; editorial adv. bd. Spectrochimica Acta, 1957-63, Internat. Jour. Quantum Chemistry, 1967—, Proc. Nat. Acad. Scis., 1976—; cons. editor Allyn and Bacon. Contbr. articles to profl. jours. Home: 352 Hoosick St Troy NY 12180

SHULL, LEO, publisher, editor; b. Milw., Feb. 8, 1913; s. David John and Anna (Blumencranz) S; B.S., U. Pa., 1936; M.A., Temple U., 1938; m. Claire Kiar, Aug. 9, 1948; 1 dau., Lee. Pub., Actors Cues, Show Business, Summers Theatres, Models Guide, Casting Guide, Prodn. Directory, Angels, 1,000 Filmmakers, Who's Where, others, 1941—; N.Y. editor Writer's Digest, 1942—; vice cultural commr. City of N.Y., 1960; founder, 1st sec. N.Y. Drama Desk, Pubs. Assn., Inc.; producer plays on Broadway, off Broadway, films and weekly TV Leo Shull Show. Author: Playwriting for Broadway, 1946; How to Break Into Show Business, 1964; New York Show Business Celebrities, 1966; Playwriting for the Broadway Stage, 1967. Producer: Apollo (stage show), 1957. Home: 420 E 72d St New York NY 10021 Office: 136 W 44th St New York NY 10036

SHULL, LEON, orgn. exec.; b. Phila., Nov. 8, 1913; s. Samuel and Yetta Shull; m. Anne Wollod, Dec. 29, 1938; children—Jane Ellen, Susan Deborah. Owner, Logan Furniture Co., 1936-41; dir. Jewish Labor Com., Phila., 1946-50; mem. staff Ams. for Democratic Action, Phila., 1951-63, nat. dir., Washington, 1964—; dir. several polit. campaign coms. Pa., 1951-63. Served with AUS, 1942-46. Home: 6417 Western Ave NW Washington DC 20015 Office: 1411 K St NW Washington DC 20005

SHULL, WILLARD CHARLES, III, retailing financial exec.; b. St. Paul, Dec. 6, 1940; s. Willard Charles II and Rosanna (Robbins) S.; B.A., Yale U., 1963; M.B.A., Harvard U., 1965; m. Laurie Jane Syverton, Dec. 17, 1977; children by previous marriage—Martha Williams, Willard Charles IV. Budget dir. Archer Daniels Midland Co., Mpls., 1965-69; v.p., treas. Northland Equity Corp., Mpls., 1969-71; successively mgr. fin. services, asst. treas., treas., v.p. fin., sr. v.p. fin. Dayton Hudson Corp.. Mpls., 1971—. Trustee Minn. Outward Bound Sch., 1971-77; bd. dirs. Met. Econ. Devel. Assn., 1972-76, chmn., 1977. Mem. Fin. Execs. Inst. Clubs: Minneapolis, Woodhill Country, Yale (N.Y.C.). Office: 777 Nicollet Mall Minneapolis MN 55402

SHULLAW, JAMES HAROLD, fgn. service officer; b. Peoria, Ill., Dec. 5, 1916; s. George F. and Ella T. (Pauli) S.; A.R., Knox Coll., 1938; M.A., Cath. U., 1940; grad. study U. Minn., 1939-41; m. Jean Sullivan, May 11, 1942; children—Richard Kurt, Mari Kevin. Appointed to position of fgn. service officer, vice consul career, sec. Diplomatic Service, 1941; vice consul, Windsor, Canada, 1941-42; 3d sec., vice consul, Cairo, Egypt, 1942, Jidda, Saudi Arabia, 1942-44; 3d sec., Pretoria, Union S. Africa, 1944, 2d sec., 1947-48; acting asst. chief div. Brit. Commonwealth Affairs, Dept. State, 1948, consul, 1949-56; assigned Canadian Nat. Def. Coll., Kingston, Ontario, 1956; 1st sec. The Hague, Netherlands, July 1952-57; 1st sec., London, 1957-62; dir. Office Brit. Commonwealth and No. European Affairs, Dept. State, Washington; dep. chief of mission, Helsinki, Finland, 1968-70. Mem. Phi Beta Kappa, Roman Catholic. Home: Wyoming IL Office: 34 Margaretta Terr London SW3 England

SHULMAN, ARNOLD, judge; b. Phila., Apr. 12, 1914; s. Edward Nathaniel and Anna (Leshner) S.; student Emory U., 1931; J.D., U. Ga., 1936; m. Mary Frances Johnson, Nov. 26, 1943; children—Diane Shulman Lifshey, Warren Scott, Amy Lynn Shulman Haney. Admitted to Ga. bar, 1937; mem. firm Shulman, Shulman, Bauer & Deitch, and predecessors, Atlanta, to 1977; judge Ga. Ct. Appeals, 1977—; prof. Atlanta Law Sch., 1964—. Chmn. DeKalb County (Ga.) Sch. Salary Commn., 1960-62, DeKalb County Sch. Study Commn., 1962-64; mem. Fulton County-Atlanta Ct. Study Commn., 1961-62. Served to capt. U.S. Army, 1941-46. Mem. Am., Atlanta bar assns., Ga. State Bar. Club: Lawyers (Atlanta). Author: (with Wiley H. Davis) Georgia Practice and Procedure, 1948, 3d edit., 1968, 4th edit. (with Warren S. Shulman), 1975; contbr. articles to legal jours. Home: 1420 Stephens Dr NE Atlanta GA 30329 Office: State Judicial Bldg Atlanta GA 30334

SHULMAN, ARTHUR, publisher; b. N.Y.C., Mar. 4, 1927; s. Jack and Sarah (Hochman) S.; B.A., Syracuse U., 1950; m. Joan Plaut, Jan. 31, 1958; children—James, Karen. Regional mgr. TV Guide mag., 1953-60, asst. to publisher, 1960-63, dir. pub. relations, 1963-70; publisher Seventeen mag., N.Y.C., 1973—. Served with AUS, 1945-46. Mem. Nat. Acad. TV Arts and Scis., Internat. Radio and TV Soc. Author: (with Roger Yoaman) How Sweet It Was, 1966, The Television Years, 1973. Clubs: Overseas Press (N.Y.C.); Poor Richard (Phila.). Home: 1919 County Line Rd Villanova PA 19085 Office: Radnor PA 19088

SHULMAN, HERMAN L., educator; b. N.Y.C., Feb. 24, 1922; s. Samuel and Sophie (Kaufman) S.; B.Ch.E., Coll. City N.Y., 1942; M.S., U. Pa., 1948, Ph.D., 1950; m. Florence Israel, Dec. 24, 1942; children—Nancy Lynn (Mrs. Paul Weigel), Richard Alan. Devel. engr. Gen. Motors Corp., Trenton, N.J., 1942-43; research chem. engr. Barrett div. Allied Chem. & Dye Corp., Phila., 1943-46; devel. chem. engr. Publicker Industries, Inc., Eddington, Pa., 1946-47; DuPont fellow in chem. engring. U. Pa., 1947-48; asst. prof. chem. engring. Clarkson Coll. Tech., Potsdam, N.Y., 1948-51, asso. prof., 1951-54, asso. dir. div. research, 1954-58, prof. chem. engring., 1954—, chmn. dept. chem. engring., 1958-64, dir. div. research, 1958-73, dean Grad. Sch., 1964-73, v.p., 1966-77, dean Sch. Engring., 1968—, provost, 1977—. Chmn. St. Lawrence County Planning Bd., 1970-74; commr., St. Lawrence-East Ontario Commn. Fellow Am. Inst. Chem. Engrs.; mem. Am. Chem. Soc. (past sec.-treas., chmn., counselor No. N.Y. sect.), Am. Soc. Engring. Edn., St. Lawrence County C. of C. (1st v.p., pres., dir.), Sigma Xi, Tau Beta Pi, Omega Chi Epsilon. Rotarian. Club: Potsdam Town and Country. Contbr. articles to profl. jours. Home: 32 Hillcrest Dr Potsdam NY 13676

SHULMAN, IRVING, novelist, educator; b. Bklyn., May 21, 1913; s. Max and Sarah (Ress) S.; A.B. magna cum laude, Ohio U., 1937; A.M., Columbia, 1938; Ph.D., U.C.L.A., 1972; m. Julia Grager, July 9, 1938; children—Joan, Leslie. Personnel technician, statistician, admistrv. officer, information specialist various govt. agys., 1941-47; faculty dept. English, George Washington U., 1943-47; teaching asst. U. Calif., Los Angeles, 1962-64; asst. prof. English dept. Calif. State Coll., Los Angeles, 1964-65; author, collaborator various screen plays. Mem. Modern Lang. Assn., English Grad. Assn., AAUP, Writers Guild Am., Acad. Motion Picture Arts and Scis., Am. Film Inst., Ohio U. Alumni Assn. (Certificate of Merit, 1958), Columbia Univ. Alumni Assn., Zeta Beta Tau. Phi Epsilon Pi. Author: The Amboy Dukes (motion picture City Across the River), 1947; Cry Tough (also motion picture), 1949; The Big Brokers, 1951; The Square Trap (motion picture The Ring), 1953; Children of the Dark (motion picture Rebel Without a Cause) 1956; Good Deeds Must be Punished, 1956; Calibre, 1957; The Velvet Knife, 1959; The Short End of the Stick, 1959; The Roots of Fury, 1961; Harlow, 1964; Valentino, 1967; Jackie: The Exploitation of a First Lady, 1970; The Devil's Knee, 1973; Saturn's Child, 1976. Office: care William E Stein CPA 9454 Wilshire Blvd Suite 801 Beverly Hills CA 90212

SHULMAN, KENNETH, neurosurgeon; b. Worcester, Mass., Sept. 6, 1928; s. Hyman Abraham and Sophie (Levine) S.; A.B. with highest honors, Clark U., 1950; M.D. with honors, Washington U., 1954; m. Jean Carol Lewit, June 25, 1955; children—Michael Eben, Daniel Richard. Intern, Yale-New Haven Hosp., 1954-55; resident in neurosurgery Neurol. Inst., Columbia-Presbyn. Med. Center, N.Y.C., 1957-61; asst. prof. neurosurgery N.Y. U. Med Sch., 1961-64; asst. prof. neurosurgery U. Pa. Med. Sch., 1964-65, asso. prof., 1965-67; prof. neurosurgery Albert Einstein Coll. Medicine, N.Y.C., 1967—, chmn. dept., 1972—; dir. neurosurgery Montefiore Hosp. Med. Center. Served with USNR, 1955-57. Mem. Am. Assn. Neurol. Surgeons (past pres. pediatric sect.), A.C.S., Soc. Neurol. Surgeons. Contbr. articles to profl. jours. Home: 43 Cambridge Rd Scarsdale NY 10583 Office: 1300 Morris Pkwy Bronx NY 10461

SHULMAN, MARCY LEE, dentist; b. Union City, N.J., Sept. 5, 1911; s. Jacob and Eva (Barnett) S.; grad. Juilliard Sch. Music, 1929; student N.Y. U., 1929-30; D.D.S., U. Md., 1935; postgrad. Columbia and N.Y. U. Dental Schs., 1947-55; m. Rosemary Stanger, May 31, 1936; 1 dau., Susan Deborah. Practice dentistry, Hackensack, N.J., 1936—; asst. clin. prof. Seton Hall Coll. Dentistry, 1960-66, spl. lectr. postgrad. dept., 1962-66; vis. lectr. Fairleigh Dickinson Dental Sch., 1974; mem. med.-dental staff Bergen Pines County Hosp.; essayist, lectr. Trinidad-Tobago Dental Soc.; dental clinician N.J., Ind., N.Y., Hawaii, Calif., N.Y. 1st Dist., Phila. Greater, Am. Dental Assn., Chgo. Midwinter, Irish Dental Soc., World Dental Congress F.D. (London); cons. Aetna Casualty Co., Firemen's Fund Ins. Cos., Liberty Mut. Ins. Co. Mem. Bergen Community Coll. Art Council, 1974—. Chmn. bd. govs. Bergen County Players Community Theatre. Served from 1st lt. to maj. AUS, 1943-46. Diplomate Am. Bd. Hypnosis in Dentistry. Fellow Internat. Coll. Dentists; mem. Am. Dental Assn., Bergen County Dental Soc. Mason (32 deg.). Contbr. articles to profl. jours., chpt. to Lawyers Med. Ency. Home: 26 Winthrop Rd Hillsdale NJ 07642 Office: 241 Main St Hackensack NJ 07601. *Being a member of the healing arts is a privilege. Working with and for people is a joy. Being recognized for these things is an honor to be cherished.*

SHULMAN, MARSHALL DARROW, educator; b. Jersey City, Apr. 8, 1916; s. Harry Max and Bessie (Waldman) S.; A.B., U. Mich., 1937; student Harvard, 1939-40; M.A. Columbia, 1948, Ph.D., 1959, certificate Russian Inst., 1948; m. Elizabeth Van Anda Thomson, 1948 (dec. Nov. 1956); children—Elizabeth, Michael; m. 2d, Colette Schwarzenbach, 1960. Newspaper reporter Detroit News, 1937-38; writer Nat. Safety Council, 1938-39; v.p. Council for Democracy, 1940-42; information officer U.S. Mission to UN, 1949-50; spl. asst. to sec. state, 1950-53; Rockefeller Pub. Service award, 1953-54; asso. dir. Russian Research Center, Harvard, 1954-62, lectr. dept. govt., 1956-60, research asso., 1962-67; prof. internat. politics Fletcher Sch. Law and Diplomacy, 1961-67; prof. govt. Columbia U., 1967-74, dir. Russian Inst., 1967-74, 76-77, Adlai E. Stevenson prof. internat. relations, 1973-77; ambassador, spl. advisor on Soviet affairs to sec. state, 1977—; scholar in residence Aspen Inst. Humanistic Studies, summer 1973. Adv. com. East-West trade U.S. Dept. Commerce, 1975—. Mem. council Internat. Inst. for Strategic Studies (London); Carnegie vis. research scholar, 1963-64; Whitney Shepardson fellow Council Fgn. Relations, 1974-75. Served from pvt. to capt. USAAF, 1942-46, glider pilot, psychol. warfare officer. Decorated Bronze Star. Fellow Am. Acad. Arts and Scis.; mem. Internat. Polit. Sci. Assn., Council Fgn. Relations (dir.) (N.Y.), Am. Polit. Sci. Assn. Club: Harvard (N.Y.C.). Author: Stalin's Foreign Policy Reappraised, 1963; Beyond the Cold War, 1966. Home: 3032 N St NW Washington DC 20007 Office: 420 W 118th St New York NY 10027

SHULMAN, MARTIN, air freight co. exec.; b. Phila., Feb. 14, 1924; s. Benjamin and Anna (Litvin) S.; B.S., Temple U., 1948; postgrad. student U. Pa., 1948-49; student Cambridge (Eng.) U., 1945; m. Lucille Russell, Sept. 11, 1952; children—Linda, Marcia, Robert, Debra, Nancy, Benjamin. Chief exec. officer Shulman Air Freight, Inc., Phila., 1950—, sec.-treas., 1950-64, pres., 1964—; pres., chief exec. officer Shulman Transp. Enterprises Inc., Cherry Hill, N.J., 1969-78, pres., chmn. bd. dirs., 1972-78; pres. Sky Cab, Inc., East Brunswick, N.J., 1979—. Served with AUS, 1943-46. Mem. U.S. C. of C. (transp. com. 1972-74). Jewish. Clubs: Wings (N.Y.C.); Union League (Phila.). Home: 5 E Riding Dr Cherry Hill NJ 08003 Office: 16 Edgeboro Rd East Brunswick NJ 08816

SHULMAN, MAX, author; b. St. Paul, Mar. 14, 1919; s. Abraham and Bessie (Karchmer) S.; A.B., U. Minn., 1942; m. Carol Rees, Dec. 21, 1941 (dec. 1963); children—Daniel, Max, Peter, Martha; m. 2d, Mary G. Bryant, 1964. Freelance writer, 1942—. Served with USAAF, 1942-44. Mem. Authors Guild, Dramatists Guild. Author: Barefoot Boy with Cheek, 1943 (musical comedy version produced by George Abbott, 1947); The Feather Merchants, 1944: The Zebra Derby, 1946; Sleep Till Noon, 1949; Rally Round the Flag, Boys, 1957; also movies: A Steak for Connie, Confidentially Connie (with Herman Wouk), Affairs of Dobie Gillis, Half a Hero; The Tender Trap (play), 1954; I Was a Teen Age Dwarf, 1959; Anyone Got a Match?, 1964; (musical comedy) How Now Dow Jones, 1967; Potatoes Are Cheaper, 1971; also short stories in Sat. Eve. Post, Good Housekeeping, Esquire, Mademoiselle, others; author TV series Dobie Gillis. Office: care Dell Pub Co 1 Dag Hammarskjold Plaza 245 E 47th St New York NY 10017*

SHULMAN, MAX L., lawyer; b. N.Y.C., Oct. 18, 1908; s. Jacob and Dora (Silverman) S.; grad. Boys' High Sch., 1925; LL.B., Nat. U. Washington, 1930; m. Sylvia Weinstein, June 25, 1939; children—Lloyd J., Gail P. Admitted to Washington bar, 1930, N.Y. bar, 1942; pvt. practice law, Washington, 1930-39; with J.W. Mays, Inc., Bklyn., 1939—, v.p., dir., 1946-53, pres., dir., 1953—, chmn. bd., chief exec. officer, 1978—. Served as maj. U.S. Army, 1941-45. Paul Harris fellow. Decorated Army Commendation Ribbon with oak leaf clusters. Clubs: Harmonie, Rotary. Office: 510 Fulton St Brooklyn NY 11201

SHULMAN, ROBERT GERSON, biophysicist; b. N.Y.C., Mar. 3, 1924; s. Joshua S. and Freda (Lipshay) S.; A.B., Columbia, 1943, M.A., 1947, Ph.D., 1949; m. Saralee Deutsch, Aug., 1952; children—Joel, Mark, James. Research asso. Columbia U. Radiation Lab., N.Y.C., 1949; AEC fellow in chemistry Calif. Inst. Tech., Pasadena, 1949-50; head semicondr. research sect. Hughes Aircraft Co., Culver City, Calif., 1950-53; mem. tech. staff Bell Labs., Murray Hill, N.J., 1953-66, head biophysics research dept., 1966-79; prof. molecular biophysics and biochemistry Yale U., 1979—; Rask Oersted lectr. U. Copenhagen, 1959; Guggenheim fellow in lab. molecular biology MRC Cambridge (Eng.) U., 1961-62; vis. prof. Ecole Normale Superieur, Paris, 1962; Appleton lectr. Brown U., 1965; vis. prof. physics U. Tokyo, 1965; Reilly lectr. U. Notre Dame, Ind., 1969; vis. prof. biophysics Princeton U., 1971-72; Regents lectr. UCLA, 1978. Mem. Nat. Acad. Scis. Researcher spectroscopic techniques applied to physics, chemistry, biology. Home: Dryden Rd Bernardsville NJ 07924 Office: JW Gibbs Research Lab Yale U New Haven CT

SHULMAN, STEPHEN NEAL, lawyer; b. New Haven, Apr. 6, 1933; s. Harry and Rea (Karrel) S.; B.A., Harvard, 1954; LL.B. cum laude (editor-in-chief Law Jour. 1957-58), Yale, 1958; m. Sandra Paula Still, Aug. 14, 1954; children—Harry, Dean, John. Indsl. relations Bendix Aviation Corp., 1954-55; admitted to Conn. bar, 1958, also U.S. cts.; law clk. to Justice Harlan, U.S. Supreme Ct., 1958-59; vis. asst. pro. U. Mich. Law Sch., 1959; asso. firm Covington & Burling, Washington, 1959-60; asst. U.S. atty., Washington, 1960-61; exec. asst. to sec. labor, 1961-62, dept asst. sec. of def., 1962-65; gen. counsel U.S. Air Force, 1965-66; chmn. Equal Employment Opportunity Commn., 1966-67; mem. firm Kane, Shulman & Schiei, Washington, 1967-70; mem. firm Cadwalader, Wickersham & Taft, N.Y.C., also Washington, 1971—; vis. prof. mgmt. U. Okla., 1965-66. Mem. Order of Coif, Cum Laude Soc., Phi Alpha Delta, Book and Gavel. Home: 3732 N Oakland St Arlington VA 22207 Office: 1333 New Hampshire Ave NW Washington DC 20036

SHULMAN, STEVEN, environ. control co. exec.; b. N.Y.C., Apr. 6, 1941; s. Jack and Esther (Lester) S.; M.E., Stevens Inst. Tech., 1962, M.S., 1963; m. Pamela Levy, Dec. 10, 1967; children—Jason Zachary, Eliza Philippa, Alexander Nathaniel. Cons., Am. Appraisal Co., N.Y.C., 1963-67; asso., corporate finance dept. Burnham & Co., N.Y.C., 1967-69; sr. v.p. Wheelabrator-Frye, Inc., N.Y.C., 1969—; chmn. Wheelabrator Internat., Inc., 1974—; officer, dir. several Wheelabrator subs. and joint venture cos. Served with U.S. Army, 1963-69. Mem. Chi Psi. Clubs: MAPI, Princeton (N.Y.C.). Home: 29 Old Locke Rd North Hampton NH 03862 Office: Liberty Ln Hampton NH 03842

SHULTS, ROBERT LUTHER, JR., lawyer; b. Pine Bluff, Ark., Oct. 25, 1925; s. Robert Luther and Gay (Moseley) S.; B.S., in Elec. Engring. cum laude, La. State U., 1950; LL.B. cum laude, Harvard U., 1953; m. Barbara Jo Taylor, Aug. 19, 1950; children—Steven Taylor, Elizabeth Gay. Admitted to Ark. bar, 1953, since practiced in Little Rock; partner firm Wright, Lindsey, Jennings, Lester & Shults, 1956-65, Lester and Shults, 1965—. Chmn. Little Rock Great Decisions Program, 1961, Little Rock Com. Fgn. Relations, 1954—. Bd. dirs. Little Rock, Central YMCA, Ark. chpt. Arthritis Found.; chmn. bd. Winthrop Rockefeller Found., Econ. Opportunity Agy. Pulaski County; trustee U. Ark., 1970—, chmn. bd. trustees, 1976—; trustee Ark. Blue Cross-Blue Shield, Inc., Ark. Arts Center, 1978—. Served to 1st lt. AUS, 1943-46; ETO. Mem. Am., Ark. (chmn. legal edn. council 1963-66, chmn. exec. com. 1968-69) bar assns., Am. Judicature Soc., Am. Inst. for Public Service (bd. of selectors), Sigma Chi, Tau Beta Pi, Omicron Delta Kappa. Democrat. Methodist. Clubs: Little Rock Country, Capital. Editor: Harvard Law Rev., 1952-53. Home: 11 Glenridge Rd Little Rock AR 72207 Office: Worthen Bank Bldg Little Rock AR 72201

SHULTZ, GEORGE PRATT, constrn. co. exec., educator; b. N.Y.C., Dec. 13, 1920; s. Birl E. and Margaret Lennox (Pratt) S.; B.A., Princeton U., 1942; Ph.D. in Indsl. Econs., Mass. Inst. Tech., 1949; m. Helena M. O'Brien, Feb. 16, 1946; children—Margaret Ann, Kathleen Pratt Shultz Jorgensen, Peter Milton, Barbara Lennox, Alexander George. Mem. faculty Mass. Inst. Tech., 1946-57, asso. prof. indsl. relations, 1955-57, prof. indsl. relations Grad. Sch. Bus., U. Chgo., 1957-68, dean sch., 1962-68; fellow Center for Advanced Studies in Behavioral Scis., 1968-69; U.S. sec. labor, 1969-70, dir. Office Mgmt. and Budget, 1970-72; U.S. sec. treasury, also asst. to Pres., 1972-74; exec. v.p., Bechtel Corp., San Francisco, 1974-75, pres., 1975—, also dir.; prof. mgmt. and pub. policy Stanford U., 1974—; dir. J.P. Morgan & Co., Inc., Morgan Guaranty Trust Co., Sears Roebuck & Co. Bd. dirs. Alfred P. Sloan Found. Served to capt. USMCR, 1942-45. Mem. Am. Econ. Assn., Indsl. Relations Research Assn. (pres. 1968), Nat. Acad. Arbitrators. Author: (with T.A. Whisler) Management Organization and the Computer, 1960; (with Arnold R. Weber) Strategies for the Displaced Worker, 1966; (with A. Rees) Workers and Wages in the Urban Labor Market, 1970; (with Kenneth W. Dam) Economic Policy Beyond the Headlines, 1978; also articles, chpts. in books, reports. Home: 776 Dolores St Stanford CA 94305 Office: Bechtel Corp 50 Beale St San Francisco CA 94105

SHULTZ, RICHARD CARL, mus. dir.; b. York, Pa., Nov. 9, 1927; s. Pius Milton and Hattie Bell (Smith) S.; B.A., Pa. State U., 1950; m. Diane Gail McKnight, Jan. 9, 1973. Field sec. Pi Kappa Alpha Frat., Memphis, 1950-52; staff asst. Pa. Bankers Assn., Harrisburg, 1952-53; treas. P.M. Shultz & Sons, Inc., York County, Pa., 1953-63; mgr. York Symphony Assn., 1963-73; exec. dir. Hist. Soc. York County, 1968-73, Rochester (N.Y.) Mus. and Sci. Center, 1973—; mem. Atty. Gen.'s Mus. Adv. Com.; bd. govs. N.E. Museums Conf. Dir. GVGHA Group Health Plan; commr. York Twp., Pa., 1968-73. Served with AUS, 1946-47. Mem. N.Y. State Assn. Museums (treas.), Am. Assn. State and Local History, Am. Assn. Museums, Rochester Com. Fgn. Relations, Pi Kappa Alpha. Republican. Club: Univ. (Rochester). Editorial bd. Bicentennial U.S.A., 1971-72. Home: 286 Park Ave Rochester NY 14607 Office: 657 East Ave Rochester NY 14603

SHUMACKER, HARRIS B, JR., surgeon, educator; b. Laurel, Miss., May 20, 1908; s. Harris B. and Corinne (Teller) S.; B.S., U. Chattanooga, 1927; A.M., Vanderbilt U., 1928; M.D., Johns Hopkins, 1932; m. Myrtle E. Landau, Dec. 1, 1933; children—Peter D., James N. Asst. in surgery Johns Hopkins U., 1932-35, instr., 1938-41, asst. prof., 1941-46; asst. in surgery Yale, 1936-37, instr., 1937-38, asso. prof., 1946-48; prof. surgery Ind. U., 1948—, chmn. dept., 1948-68, Disting. prof., 1970-78, Disting. prof. emeritus, 1978—; hon. mem. surg. faculties in Peoples Republic of China, 1979—; dir. sect. cardiovascular-thoracic surgery St. Vincent Hosp., 1973-78, sr. surg. cons., 1978—. Served from capt. to lt. col. M.C., U.S. Army, 1942-46; cons. surgeon gen. 1949-60. Recipient Roswell Park award, 1968, Medal of Honor, Evansville U., 1970, Distinguished Alumnus award, U. Chattanooga, Curtis medal, 1970, Spl. Alumnus award Johns Hopkins U., 1973. Chmn. subcom. on cardiovascular diseases NRC, 1954-55. Mem. Am. Assn. Surgery of Trauma, Am. (1st v.p. 1961, sec.

1964-68), So., Central, Pan-Pacific (council of bd. trustees 1961-64, v.p. 1964-75, 78—, pres. 1975-78) surg. assns., A.M.A. (chmn. sect. gen. surgery), Internat. Surg. Soc., Soc. Clin. Surgery (pres. 1961-63), Internat. Cardiovascology Soc. (pres. N.Am. br. 1956-58, v.p. 1958), A.C.S. (chmn. forum com. 1955-60, chmn. nat. television com. 1964-68, Disting. Service award 1968), Soc. U. Surgeons (pres. 1951), Soc. for Vascular Surgery (pres. 1958-59), Am. Thoracic Surg. Assn., Internat. Surg. Group (v.p. 1974-75, pres. 1975-76), Società Italiana di Chirurgia (hon.), Phi Beta Kappa, Sigma Xi, Alpha Omega Alpha. Home: 7481 Holliday Dr E Indianapolis IN 46260 Office: 8402 Harcourt Rd Indianapolis IN 46260

SHUMAKER, THOMAS PAINE, chem. co. exec.; b. Phila., Oct. 4, 1918; s. Harry Adam and Mary Margaret (Walsh) S.; B.S., U. Ala., 1942; m. Mildred Julia Smith, Mar. 15, 1946; children—Karl Thomas, Laurie Ellen Sumaker Berry, Lewis Adam. With Reichhold Chemis, Inc., 1946—, lab. tech., pilot plant operator, product devel., asst. plant supt., tech. service dir., div. sales mgr., v.p. sales So. div., 1946-64, v.p., gen. mgr., 1964-71, regional mgr., 1971-75, sr. v.p., 1972-75, exec. v.p., 1975—, also dir. Chmn., Friedman-Tuscaloosa County Library Bd., 1967—; co-chmn. Council Environ. Quality, 1969—. Bd. dirs. Warrio-Tombigbee River Devel. Assn. Served with USAAF, 1942-46. Mem. Am. Chem. Soc., Area C. of C. Baptist (deacon 1967—). Author: The Roman Campaign in Judea A.D. 66-A.D. 70, 1966; Soldier Under, 1968; From Calvary to Computers, 1969; Essays on Christian Subjects-Easy Charlie Sugar One, 1974. Patentee in field. Home: 46 Cherokee Hills Tuscaloosa AL 35401 Office: PO Box 1610 Tuscaloosa AL 35401

SHUMAN, CHARLES ROSS, physician, educator; b. Harrisburg, Pa., Sept. 18, 1918; s. Charles Ross and Esther (Gramme) S.; B.A., Gettysburg Coll., 1940, D.Sc., 1973; M.D., Temple U., 1943, M.S. in Internal Medicine, 1949; m. Mary H. DeSheilds Moss, May 27, 1944; children—Charles Ross III, Sandra J. Intern Temple U. Hosp., Phila., 1943-44, resident, 1944-49; practice medicine, specializing in internal medicine, Phila., 1950—; chief dept. metabolism Temple U. Hosp., 1952—; prof. medicine Temple U. Sch. Medicine, 1966—; Eastern Pa. coordinator Am. Diabetes Assn., 1965—. Served to maj. M.C., AUS, 1946-48. Diplomate Am. Bd. Internal Medicine. Mem. A.C.P., Phila. Coll. Physicians, A.M.A., Am., Delaware Valley diabetes assns., Am. Fedn. Clin. Research, Pa., Phila. County med. socs., Union League Phila., Sigma Xi, Alpha Omega Alpha. Author chpts. in textbooks. Contbr. articles to profl. jours. Home: 1111 Delene Rd Jenkintown PA 19046 Office: 3401 N Broad St Philadelphia PA 19140

SHUMAN, FREDERICK GALE, meteorologist; b. South Bend, Ind., July 13, 1919; s. Fred William and Catherine (Grimm) S.; B.S., Ball State U., 1941; M.S., Mass. Inst. Tech., 1948, Sc.D., 1951; m. Elena Fragomeni, June 15, 1946; children—Frederick Gale, Marianne, Deborah Joan. Chief computation br. Nat. Meteorol. Center, U.S. Weather Bur., Washington, 1955-58, chief devel. br., 1958-64, dir. center, 1964—; mem. meteorology group Inst. Advanced Study, Princeton, N.J., 1952-54; vis. prof. N.Y.U., 1961. Served to maj. USAAF, 1941-45, Recipient Meritorious Service award U.S. Dept. Commerce, 1957, gold medal award, 1967; Alumni Distinguished Service award Ball State U., 1965. Mem. Am., Royal meteorol. socs., Am. Geophys. Union, AAAS. Home: 212 Inverness Ln Oxon Hill MD 20022 Office: Nat Meteorol Center Nat Weather Service Washington DC 20233

SHUMAN, NICHOLAS ROMAN, newspaper editor; b. Chgo., June 30, 1921; s. Roman William and Pauline (Stasevich) S.; B.A., U. Ill., 1943; m. Marilyn Elaine Johnson, Feb. 23, 1952; children—Kristin Mary, Elizabeth Carol, Mark Nicholas. With Chgo. Jour. Commerce, 1938-46; staff Herald-American, Chgo., 1946-51, asst. photo editor, 1947-51; staff Chgo. Daily News, 1951-78, financial editor, 1961-65, asst. mng. editor, 1965-69, nat. and fgn. editor, 1969-77, chief editorial writer, 1977-78; editorial writer Chgo. Sun-Times, 1978—; sr. editor World Book Ency., 1965-66; profl. instr. Medill Sch. Journalism, Northwestern U., 1954-61; freelance mag. writer, 1951—; TV commentator, 1958-61. Founding pres. Arlington Heights (Ill.) Human Relations Com., 1965. Served to 1st lt. AUS, 1943-46; ETO. Mem. Alpha Kappa Lambda, Sigma Delta Chi. Home: 1001 W Clarendon Rd Arlington Heights IL 60004 Office: Chgo Sun-Times 401 N Wabash Ave Chicago IL 60611

SHUMAN, R(OBERT) BAIRD, author, educator; b. Paterson, N.J., June 20, 1929; s. George William and Elizabeth (Evans) S.; A.B. (Trustees scholar), Lehigh U., 1951; M.Ed., Temple U., 1953; Ph.D. (Univ. scholar), U. Pa., 1961; cert. in philology, U. Vienna (Austria), 1954. Tchr., Phila. Pub. Schs., 1953-55; asst. instr. humanities U. Pa., 1955-57; instr. Drexel U., Phila., 1957-59; asst. prof. English, San Jose (Calif.) State U., 1959-62; asst. prof. Duke U., 1962-63, asso. prof., 1963-66, prof. edn., 1966-77; prof. English, dir. English edn. U. Ill., Urbana-Champaign, 1977—, dir. freshman rhetoric, 1979—; vis. prof. Moore Inst. Art, 1958, Phila. Conservatory Music, 1958-59, Lynchburg Coll., 1965, King Faisal U., Saudi Arabia, 1978, Bread Loaf Sch. English, 1980. Mem. Nat. Council Tchrs. English (evaluator ERIC Clearing House), Internat. Council Edn. of Tchrs., N.C. English Tchrs. Assn., Ill. English Tchrs. Assn., Conf. English Edn. (exec. com.), Internat. Reading Assn., MLA, Internat. Assn. Univ. Profs. English, Nat. Soc. Arts and Humanities, Nat. Soc. Study Edn., Am. Fedn. Tchrs., ACLU. Democrat. Author: Clifford Odets, 1962; Robert E. Sherwood, 1964; William Inge, 1965; Strategies in Teaching Reading: Secondary, 1978; (with Robert J. Krajewski) The Beginning Teacher: A Guide to Problem Solving, 1979; Elements of Early Reading Instruction, 1979; editor: Nine Black Poets, 1968; An Eye for an Eye, 1969; A Galaxy of Black Writing, 1970; Creative Approaches to the Teaching of English: Secondary, 1974; Questions English Teachers Ask, 1977; Educational Drama for Today's Schools, 1978; Education in the 80's—English, 1980; exec. editor The Clearing House, 1976—; cons. editor Poet Lore, 1977—, Cygnus, 1978—, Jour Aesthetic Edn., 1978—; contbg. editor Reading Horizons, 1975—; editor monthly column Speaking Out, The Clearing house; editor quar. column Profl. Concerns, Reading Horizons. Home: Box 1687 Champaign IL 61820. *I try to be the sort of person on whom no experience is lost, no demonstration of trust and confidence misplaced.*

SHUMAN, SAMUEL IRVING, educator, lawyer; b. Fall River, Mass., Aug. 7, 1925; s. Max and Fannie S.; A.B., U. Pa., 1947, M.A., 1948, Ph.D., 1951, J.D., U. Mich., 1954; S.J.D., Harvard U., 1959; m. Maria Barbetsea, Mar. 22, 1964; children—Maxim Erric, Michael A. Admitted to Mich. bar, 1954; research asst. Legis. Research Center, U. Mich., Ann Arbor, 1953-54, vis. prof. law, 1961; vis. prof. U. Rome, 1963-64; asst. prof. law Wayne State U., Detroit, 1954-55, asso. prof., 1955-56, prof., 1957—, prof. dept. psychiatry Wayne State U. Med. Sch.; lectr. Internat. Faculty Comparative Law, Luxembourg, 1964; prof. forensic psychiatry, spl. counsel Lafayette Clinic, Mich. Dept. Mental Health; gen. counsel Mich. Psychiat. Assn., Epilepsy Center Mich. Recipient Wayne State U. Bd. Govs. Faculty Recognition award, 1978; Probus Club award Disting. Acad. Achievement in Humanities, 1963; Fulbright fellow, Italy, 1961; Rockefeller Found. grantee, 1959, 61; Fulbright travel grantee, Germany, 1961; Wayne State U. research grantee, 1960-64; Internat. Research & Exchanges Bd. grantee, 1973. Mem. Am. Law Inst., Am. Soc. Polit. and Legal Philosophy, Internat. Assn. Philosophy of Law and Social Philosophy, Mich Bar Assn., Mich. Soc. Mental Health (dir.). Author: Legal Positivism: Its Scope and Limitations, 1963; (with N.D. West) Introduction to American Law: Cases and Materials, 1971; Psychosurgery and the Medical Control of Violence: Autonomy and Deviance, 1977; editorial bd. Am. Jour. Jurisprudence, 1969—; Am. editor Jour. Internat. Assn. Philosophy of Law and Social Philosophy, 1962—. Office: 3111 Kettering Houston TX 77027

SHUMAN, STANLEY SAXE, investment banker; b. Cambridge, Mass., June 22, 1935; s. Saul Aaron and Sarah Lillian (Saxe) S.; grad. Phillips Andover Acad., 1952; B.A., Harvard U., 1956, J.D., 1959, M.B.A., 1961; m. Ruth Helen Lande, Nov. 19, 1967; children—David Lande, Michael Adam. Admitted to Mass. bar, 1959; with Allen & Co., Inc., N.Y.C., 1961—, now exec. v.p., dir., mem. exec. com.; dir. Internat. Foodservice Corp., Horizon Corp., Genesis Project, News Group Publs. Inc., New York Mag., News Am. Pub. Inc. Mem. N.Y. Gov.'s Task Force on Unemployment; mem. Emergency Fin. Control Bd. N.Y.C. Bd. dirs. Wiltwyck Sch., pres., 1970-78; trustee, exec. com. Dalton Sch.; bd. dirs., mem. exec. com., v.p. Jewish Guild for Blind; chmn. bd. dirs. Nat. Econ. Devel. Law Project. Mem. Am. Bar Assn. (mem. comml. arbitration com.). Mason. Clubs: Harvard (Boston and N.Y.C.); City Athletic; East Hampton Tennis; Quaker Ridge Golf. Home: 17 E 73d St New York NY 10021 Office: 711 Fifth Ave New York NY 10022

SHUMATE, JOSEPH DAVENPORT, judge; b. Pauls Valley, Okla., Aug. 23, 1914; s. Carl Alonzo and Margaret Freer (Matthews) S.; B.A., U. Okla., 1936, LL.B., 1938, J.D., 1970; m. Anna Lee Moore, May 4, 1941; children—Joanna (Mrs. C.D. Klingensmith), Joseph Kent. Admitted to Okla. bar, 1938; practice law, 1938-40, 46-55; dist. judge 21st Jud. Dist. Okla., Pauls Valley, 1955-75; presiding judge South Central Jud. Adminstrv. Dist., State of Okla., 1975—, Okla. Ct. Bank Rev., 1973-75. Vice pres. council Boy Scouts Am., 1969-72. Served with AUS, 1940-46. Mem. Am., Okla., Garvin County bar assns., Okla. Jud. Conf. (past pres.), Pauls Valley C. of C. (past dir.), Am. Legion (past post comdr.). Elk, K.P., Rotarian (past pres.). Home: 1721 S Walnut St Pauls Valley OK 73075 Office: Box 419 Pauls Valley OK 73075

SHUMATE, STUART, railroad ofcl.; b. Calverton, Va., Aug. 22, 1915; s. Sidney and Stuart (Strother) S.; B.S. in Civil Engring., Va. Poly. Inst., 1936; m. Mary Kossuth, May 6, 1943; children—Susan, John. With Richmond, Fredericksburg & Potomac R.R. Co., Richmond, 1946—, pres., 1961—, also dir.; pres., dir. Richmond Land Corp., 1961—, S. Washington Land Corp., 1961—; dir. First & Mchts. Corp., First & Mchts. Nat. Bank, A.H. Robins Co., Colonial Stores; chmn. bd. mgrs. Potomac Yard, Alexandria, Va.; bd. mgrs. Washington Terminal. Bd. visitors Va. Commonwealth U.; bd. assos. U. Richmond; bd. govs. United Givers Fund Richmond. Served to col. U.S. Army, World War II; col. Res. Mem. Greater Richmond C. of C. (chmn.). Clubs: Commonwealth, Country of Va. (Richmond). Home: 4690 Arrowhead Rd Richmond VA 23235 Office: Richmond Fredericksburg & Potomac R R Co 2134 W Laburnum Ave Richmond VA 23230*

SHUMWAY, FORREST NELSON, corp. exec., lawyer; b. Skowhegan, Maine, Mar. 21, 1927; s. Sherman Nelson and Agnes Brooks (Mosher) S.; student Deerfield (Mass.) Acad., 1943-45; A.B., Stanford U., 1950, LL.B., 1952; LL.D. (hon.), U. So. Calif., 1974, Pepperdine U., 1978; m. Patricia Ann Kelly, Aug. 12, 1950; children—Sandra Brooks, Garrett Patrick. Admitted to Calif. bar, 1952; staff Office County Counsel, Los Angeles, 1953-57; sec. Signal Oil & Gas Co., Los Angeles, 1959-61, gen. counsel, 1961-64, group v.p. operations, 1963-64, pres., 1964-68; pres., chief exec. officer The Signal Cos., 1968—, also dir.; dir. Mack Trucks, Inc., Transamerica Corp., W.R. Grace & Co., UOP, Inc., Garrett Corp., Golden West Baseball Co., Golden West Broadcasters, United Calif. Bank, Natomas Co. Trustee U. So. Calif., Deerfield (Mass.) Acad. Served to 1st lt. USMCR, 1945-46, 49-55. Mem. Am., Los Angeles County bar assns., State Bar Calif., Phi Delta Theta. Clubs: Cypress Point (Pebble Beach, Calif.); Los Angeles Country, California (Los Angeles); Newport Harbor Yacht (Newport Beach, Calif.); Tuna (Avalon, Calif.); Bohemian (San Francisco), Masons, Shriners. Office: 9665 Wilshire Blvd Beverly Hills CA 90212

SHUMWAY, FRANK RITTER, corp. exec.; b. Rochester, N.Y., Mar. 27, 1906; s. Robert Crittenden and Adelina (Ritter) S.; grad. Hotchkiss Sch., Lakeville, Conn., 1924; A.B., Princeton, 1928; M.A., Univ. Coll., Oxford U., Eng., 1931; m. Hettie Beaman Lakin, Sept. 8, 1930; children—Mary Ellen (Mrs. Preston A. Gaylord, Jr.), Frank Ritter, Charles Lakin. With Sybron Corp. (formerly Ritter Co., later Ritter Pfaudler Corp.), Rochester, 1934—, sec., 1936-53, treas., 1940-53, v.p., 1939-53, pres., 1953-65, chmn., 1965-71, hon. chmn., 1971-76, hon. dir., 1976—; dir. Lehman Corp., N.Y.C.; adv. bd. Security Trust Co. Adv. bd. United Community Chest; past pres., now mem. adv. bd. Rochester YMCA; mem. adv. com. Center for Strategic and Internat. Studies, Georgetown U.; trustee Rochester Center for Governmental and Community Research, Inc., Rochester Boys Club, Rochester Area Found., Project Hope, Nat. Fund for Med. Edn., Am. Fund for Dental Health; exec. com. bd. trustees Rochester Inst. Tech.; pres. Family Service of Rochester, 1943-46. Mem. NAM (dir. 1952-53, 60-61), U.S. (pres. 1970-71), Empire State (pres. 1950-53, 64-66, chmn. bd. 1966-68, dir.), Rochester (trustee, past pres.) chambers commerce, U.S. Power Squadrons (chief comdr. 1948-49, mem. governing bd.), U.S. Figure Skating Assn. (pres. 1961-63, hon. mem. exec. com.), Am. Dental Trade Assn. (pres. 1968-70). Republican. Presbyn. Clubs: Country of Rochester (pres. 1946), Rochester Yacht (commodore 1951-53), Genesee Valley (Rochester); Great Lakes Cruising (commodore 1972-73, dir.); Skating (N.Y.C., Phila., Genesee) (pres.). Home: 375 Ambassador Dr Rochester NY 14610 Office: 1100 Midtown Tower Rochester NY 14604

SHUMWAY, NORMAN EDWARD, surgeon, educator; b. Kalamazoo, 1923; M.D., Vanderbilt U., 1949; Ph.D. in Surgery, U. Minn., 1956. Intern, U. Minn. Hosps., 1949-50, med. fellow surgery, 1950-51, 53-54, Nat. Heart Inst. research fellow, 1954-56, Nat. Heart Inst. spl. trainee, 1956-57; mem. surg. staff Stanford U. Hosps., 1958—, asst. prof. surg., 1959-61, asso. prof., 1961-65, prof., 1965—, head div. cardiovascular surgery, 1964-74, prof., chmn. dept. cardiovascular surgery Sch. Medicine, 1974—. Served to capt. M.C., USAF, 1951-53. Diplomate Am. Bd. Surgery, Am. Bd. Thoracic Surgery. Mem. A.M.A., Soc. Univ. Surgeons, Am. Assn. for Thoracic Surgery, Am. Surg. Assn., A.C.S., Soc. Thoracic Surgery, Am. Coll. Cardiology, Transplantation Soc., Samson Thoracic Surg. Soc., Soc. for Vascular Surgery, Alpha Omega Alpha. Office: Dept Cardiovascular Surgery Stanford U Medical Center Stanford CA 94305

SHUMWAY, RODEN GRANT, savs. and loan assn. exec.; b. Kanab, Utah, Nov. 6, 1921; s. Merlin Grant and Ruth (Glazier) S.; grad. in mortgage banking, Northwestern U., 1961; B.S., Ind. U., 1977; m. Naomi Maxfield, Mar. 8, 1945; children—Sharene, Jana Lee, Roger. Asst. v.p. Walker Bank & Trust Co., Salt Lake City, 1946-61; exec. v.p. Pioneer Savs. & Loan Assn., Salt Lake City, 1961-73; dir., 1961—; pres., chief exec. officer, dir. State Savs. & Loan Assn. Salt Lake City, 1973—; pres., dir. Gt. States Service Corp., Salt Lake City, 1973—; pres. Davis Indsl. Bur., Farmington, Utah, 1968-69; instr. Am. Inst. Banking. Del. Utah Republican Conv., 1972-76; commnr. power Bountiful, Utah, 1966-76; mem. city council, Bountiful, 1970-74. Served with USAAF, 1943-46. Recipient Alumni Merit citation Utah State U., 1977. Mem. Utah Mortgage Bankers Assn. (pres. 1969), Utah Home Builders Assn., Utah Savs. and Loan League, S. Davis C. of C. (past pres.). Mormon. Clubs: University, Sertoma (pres. Bountiful 1967). Home: 767 North 800 East Bountiful UT 84010 Office: 125 S Main St Salt Lake City UT 84111

SHUPE, JOHN WALLACE, univ. adminstr.; b. Liberal, Kans., Mar. 30, 1924; s. Eldon E. and Nelle (Brentlinger) S.; B.S., Kans. State U., Manhattan, 1948; M.S., U. Calif. at Berkeley, 1951; Ph.D., Purdue U., 1958; m. Elizabeth Mendenhall, Dec. 28, 1944; children—John Wallace, George, Christine, Steve. Instr., Kans. State U., 1948-49; lectr. U. Calif. at Berkeley, 1949-51; asst. prof. mechanics Kans. State U., 1951-53, asso. prof., 1954-56, asso. dean engring. and architecture, 1959-65; structural engr. Convair Aircraft Co., San Diego, 1953-54; research engr. Purdue U., 1956-58; dean engring. U. Hawaii, 1965-79, energy research coordinator, 1980—; sci. advisor to asst. sec. for energy tech. U.S. Dept. Energy, 1977-78. Mem. water quality adv. bd. City and Country of Honolulu, State of Hawaii Environ. Council, chmn. State Com. Alt. Energy Sources for Hawaii. Served as navigator USAAF, 1943-46; ETO. Recipient Distinguished Engring. Alumnus award Purdue U., 1967. Danforth Tchr. Study grantee, 1956; NSF faculty fellow, 1957. Registered profl. engr., Kan. Mem. Am. Soc. Testing Materials (Templin award 1960), Am. Soc. Engring. Edn., Am. Soc. C.E., Nat. Soc. Profl. Engrs., Hawaii Engring. Soc., Sigma Xi, Pi Tau Sigma, Sigma Tau, Chi Epsilon, Phi Kappa Phi. Author articles, sect. in books. Home: 1629 Wilder Ave Honolulu HI 96822 Office: U Hawaii 2540 Dole St Honolulu HI 96822

SHUPERT, GEORGE THOMAS, broadcasting exec.; b. Alpena, Mich., July 24, 1904; s. Harry L. and Grace (Bostwick) S.; A.B. in Lit., U. Mich., 1926; m. Evlyn LaLonde, Feb. 21, 1928; children—George Thomas, Sally Jean (Mrs. James Shepard), Joanne (Mrs. David Johnsen). Engaged in investment banking, Detroit, 1926-38 founder George T. Shupert & Co., 1936, gen. partner, 1936-38; dir. sales comml. film div. Paramount Pictures Corp., 1940-42, TV dept. 1942-51; v.p., dir. comml. TV operations Paramount TV Prodns., Inc., 1946-51; v.p. Peerless TV Prodns., Inc., 1951-52; v.p., gen. mgr. United Artists TV Corp., 1952-53; v.p. film syndication ABC, 1953-54; pres. ABC Films, Inc., 1954-59; v.p. charge TV, MGM, Inc., 1959-61; v.p. 20th Century Fox TV Corp., 1961-64; pres. Sunrise Broadcasting Corp., Ft. Lauderdale, 1964-77; dir. Am. Video Corp., Pompano Beach, Fla. Mem. Am. TV Soc. (past pres., dir., spl. award 1941-42), Radio and TV Execs. Soc. (past pres., hon. life mem.), Television Pioneers Soc., Acad. TV Arts and Scis., Pompano Beach C. of C. (pres. 1968-69), Broward County Council 100 (vice-chmn.), U. Mich. Alumni Assn. Home: 333 Sunset Dr Fort Lauderdale FL 33301

SHUR, RUDY, publisher; b. Munich, W. Ger., Feb. 22, 1946; came to U.S., 1947, naturalized, 1963; s. Isak and Sonia (Levine) S.; B.A., C.W. Post Coll., N.Y.C., 1968; m. Erica Rajman, Feb. 1, 1969; children—Shoshana, Justinian. Rep., Charles E. Merrill Publishing Co., 1968; asso. editor William C. Brown Pub. Co., Dubuque, Iowa, 1972, Kendall/Hunt Pub. Co., Dubuque, 1972; pres., mng. editor Avery Pub. Group, Inc., Wayne, N.J., 1976—; pub. cons. Doctorate Assn. Office: 89 Baldwin Terr Wayne NJ 11040

SHUR, WALTER, ins. co. exec.; b. N.Y.C., Feb. 1, 1929; B.S., U. Tex., 1949, M.A., 1951; grad. Advanced Mgmt. Program, Harvard U., 1975; m. Ruth Schram, Aug. 28, 1949; children—Robert, Richard, James. With N.Y. Life Ins. Co., N.Y.C., 1952—, asst. actuary, 1956-59, asso. actuary, 1959-62, actuary, 1962-64, group actuary, 1964-65, 2d v.p., group actuary, 1965-69, v.p. in charge group ins., 1969-71, sr. v.p. in charge individual ins. ops., 1971-74, exec. v.p., 1974—. Fellow Soc. Actuaries; mem. Acad. Actuaries. Office: 51 Madison Ave New York City NY 10010

SHURCLIFF, SIDNEY NICHOLS, landscape architect; b. Boston, Mar. 24, 1906; s. Arthur Asahel and Margaret Homer (Nichols) S.; A.B. magna cum laude, Harvard U., 1927, student Sch. Landscape Architecture, 1927-28, 29-30; m. Katharine Noyes Balch, June 28, 1935; 1 foster son, James C. Heigham. Assisted Restoration of Williamsburg, Va., 1928-40; landscape architect, town planner, 1930—; partner Shurcliff and Merrill; prepared town plans for Dedham, Falmouth, Sherborn, Randolph, Marion, Mattapoisett, Needham, Mass.; adviser Boston Park Dept., Met. Dist. Commn. of Mass., 1930—, also colls., univs., instns.; prepared recreation plan for Taiwan, 1971. Mem. adv. com. Trustees of Reservations (Mass.), 1963—; mem., sec. Commonwealth of Mass. Art Commn., 1954-77. Served as lt. comdr. USNR, 1942-45. Fellow Am. Soc. Landscape Architects (v.p. 1952-54); mem. Am. Inst. Planners, Internat. Fedn. Landscape Architects (pres. 1958-62), N.A.D. (asso.), Gore Place Soc. (gov.). Clubs; St. Botolph, Harvard Travellers, Veteran Motor Car of Am. (Boston); Country (Brookline, Mass.). Author: Jungle Islands, 1929; Upon Road Argilla, 1958; The Day it Rained Fish, 1977; Roughing It in Roughwood, 1979; contbr. to mags. Home: 167 Argilla Rd Ipswich MA 01938 Office: 2 Central Sq Cambridge MA 02139

SHURCLIFF, WILLIAM ASAHEL, physicist, assn. exec.; b. Boston, Mar. 27, 1909; s. Arthur Asahel and Margaret (Nichols) S.; A.B. cum laude, Harvard U., 1930, Ph.D., 1934; m. Joan Hopkinson, Jan. 18, 1941; children—Arthur A. 2d, Charles H. Head spectrophotometric lab. Am. Cynamid Co., 1935-42; sr. tech. aide Office Sci. Research and Devel., 1942-45; sci. advisor N.Y. Dept. Commerce, 1945-46; head Office of Tech. Historian of 1st Atomic Bomb Tests, Bikini, 1946-47; program analyst A.E.C., 1947-48; sr. scientist, project leader Polaroid Corp., 1948-59; sr. research asso. Cambridge Electron Accelerator of Harvard, 1960-74; dir. Citizens League Against Sonic Boom, 1967—; hon. research asso. physics dept. Harvard U., 1974—; cons. on solar heating of houses, 1974—. Mem. A.A.A.S., Am. Optical Soc. Author: Operation Crossroads: The Official Pictorial Record, 1946; Bombs at Bikini, 1947; Polarized Light: Production and Use, 1962; (with S.S. Ballard) Polarized Light, 1964; SST and Sonic Boom Handbook, 1970; Solar Heating of Buildings, A Brief Survey, 13th edit., 1977. Contbr. articles profl. jours., encys. Holder U.S. and Canadian patents. Home: 19 Appleton St Cambridge MA 02138

SHURICK, EDWARD PALMES, TV exec., rancher; b. Duluth, Minn., Dec. 15, 1912; s. Edward P. and Vera (Wheaton) S.; student U. Minn., 1932-33; B.A. in Econs., U. Mo., 1946; m. F(lossie) Dolores Pipes, Aug. 1, 1933; children—Patricia Annette (Mrs. Robert Dube), Sandra Sue Hackley, Linda Jean (Mrs. James McBride), Edward P. III. Gen. sales mgr. Intermountain Network, Salt Lake City, 1937-41; advt. mgr. sta. KMBC, Kansas City, Mo., 1941-47; research mgr. Free & Peters, N.Y.C., 1947-49; v.p. CBS TV, N.Y.C., 1949-57; exec. v.p. Blair TV, N.Y.C., 1957-62; chmn., treas. H-R TV, N.Y.C., 1962-76; dir. Broadcast Data Base, N.Y.C.; v.p., owner Sta. KXXX-AM-FM, Colby, Kans., 1963—; v.p. treas., H-R Rep. Cos., 1970-73; pres. Nutmeg of Va., Charlottesville, 1959—, S & S Ranch Corp., Aspen, Colo., 1965—, mem. bd. Chgo. Internat. Live Stock Expn., 1972-76. Pres. Shurick Research Found., Bridgewater, 1959-72; v.p. Internat. Radio and TV Found., N.Y.C., 1964-73. Recipient Alumnus award U.

Mo. at Kansas City, 1968; ordre du merit for contbns. to agr. Govt. France, 1970; Ordre du Charolais Francais, 1971. Mem. Internat. Radio and TV Soc. N.Y. (pres. 1967-69), Am. Internat. Charolais Assn. (pres. 1968-69), Colonial Charolais Breeders (dir. 1967-71), World Fedn. Charolais (pres. 1973-74), Broadcast Pioneers, Am. Nat. Cattlemen's Assn. (tax com. 1968-76). Episcopalian (lay reader). Mason (32 deg., Shriner). Clubs: Union League (N.Y.C.); Farmington (Charlottesville); Windemere (Eleuthera, The Bahamas). Author: First Quarter-Century of American Broadcasting, 1946. Home: Hickory Ridge Earlysville VA 22936 also Pompano Beach FL 33062 Office: 750 3d Ave New York NY 10017. *The opportunity to succeed as a self-made person still exists in the United States today. This may seem hackneyed and out-of-date, but it isn't. Honesty, dedication, long hours of hard work with an average amount of luck will build a fortune from a few cents to a million or so dollars. I say this because this happened to me.*

SHURMAN, MICHAEL MENDELSOHN, educator, physicist; b. St. Louis, Aug. 4, 1921; s. Michael and Dorothy (Mendelsohn) S.; B.A., U. Wis., 1943, M.S., 1946, Ph.D., 1951. Mem. staff Los Alamos Sci. Lab., 1952-55; mem. faculty U. Wis.-Milw., 1955—, prof. physics, 1961—. Served with U.S. Army, 1943-44. Mem. Am. Assn. Physics Tchrs., Sigma Xi. Home: 2582 N Stowell Ave Milwaukee WI 53211 Office: Dept Physics U Wisconsin PO 413 Milwaukee WI 53201

SHURRAGER, PHIL SHERIDAN, psychologist; b. Erie, Pa., Dec. 26, 1907; s. Frederick and Margaret (Lautersbach) S.; B.S., Muskingum Coll., 1930; A.M., Ohio U., 1932; research fellow, U. of Ill., 1936-38, Ph.D., 1939; m. Harriett Cantrall, Dec. 11, 1937; 1 dau., Margaret Lynn. Dept. zoology and physiology, Ohio Univ., 1931-35; research fellow, Clark U., 1935-36; research fellow, 1938-39, and Nat. Research Council fellow U. of Rochester and Rochester Sch. of Medicine, 1939-40; vis. asst. prof. psychology, Univ. of Pa., 1940-41, St. Lawrence U., 1941-42; dep. asst. dir. and design engr., Brit. Ministry of Supply, U.S., 1942-44; indsl. cons. and psychologist Stevenson, Jordon and Harrison, Inc. engrs., 1944-46; prof. of psychology and chmn., dept. of psychology and edn., Ill. Inst. Tech., Chicago, 1946-73, prof. emeritus, 1973—; psychologist neurophysiol. labs. Northwest Inst. Med. Research, 1973—. Cons. to business and industry, 1946—. Mem. curriculum council Chgo. Bd. Edn. Diplomate indsl. psychology Am. Bd. of Profl. Psychology, Fellow Am. Acad. Neurology; mem. Am., Ill., Midwest psychol. assns., Soc. Exptl. Biology and Medicine, N.Y. Acad. of Scis. (life mem.), A.A.A.S., Soc. Advancement Engring. Edn., Am. Assn. Univ. Profs., Sigma Xi (pres. Ill. Inst. Tech. chapter 1958-59), Pi Gamma Mu. Mason. Club: Chicago Psychology, Chicago Literary. Contbr. articles in fields of biology and exptl. psychology to professional journals and co-author of an occupational aptitude test series. Originator of spinal conditioning and learning at a motor neurone synapse; co-discoverer biochem., phys. changes paralleling light and dark adaptation in vitreous humor of mammalian eyes. Home: 1127 Lucerne Ave Cape Coral FL 33904

SHURTLEFF, DAVID BERTRAND, physician; b. Fall River, Mass., July 1, 1930; s. Bertrand Leslie and Hope (Seal) S.; student Harvard U., 1948-51; M.D., Tufts U., 1955; m. Cynthia Helen Fuguet, June 18, 1952; children—Michael David, Hillary Anne, Matthew David. Intern, resident pediatrics Mass. Gen. Hosp., Boston, 1955-57; chief resident, asso. in pediatrics Children's Orthopedic Hosp. and U. Wash. Med. Sch., Seattle, 1957-58, mem. staff, 1960—; chief pediatric sect. U.S. Army Sta. Hosp., Ft. Hood, Tex., 1958-59; mem. staff Harborview Med. Center, Seattle, 1960—; sr. cons. Madigan Army Hosp., Tacoma, 1961—; cons. Rainier Sch., Buckley, Wash., 1961-69; dir. Congenital Defects Clinic, U. Hosp., Seattle, 1961-69, dir. Pediatric Outpatient Clinic, 1962-68, dep. chief pediatric services, 1968-69, chief, 1970-74; vis. prof., cons. for spina bifida, dept. child health Welsh Nat. Sch. Medicine, Cardiff, Wales, 1969-70; vis. scientist Nat. Insts. Neurol. Diseases and Stroke, Bethesda, Md., 1970; cons. Nat. Inst. Child Health and Human Devel., 1974, Nat. Acad. Scis., 1975; instr. dept. pediatrics U. Wash. Med. Sch., 1960-62, asst. prof., 1962-65, asso. prof., 1965-71, prof., 1971—, head div. congenital defects, 1963-69, 70—, coordinator integrated pediatric residency com., 1960-63, chmn., 1964-68, chmn. grant com. Child Devel. and Mental Retardation Center CORE, 1973, chmn. ad hoc ambulatory search and program com., 1974—; mem. Nat. Residency Rev. Bd. for Pediatrics, 1974—, chmn., 1978—. Served to capt., M.C., U.S. Army, 1958-60. Recipient Golden Acorn award for health teaching Wash. PTA, 1968, Western Soc. Pediatrics Research award, 1969. Diplomate Nat. Bd. Med. Examiners, Am. Bd. Pediatrics. Mem. AMA, Wash. Med. Soc. (chmn. edn. for all laws com.), Ambulatory Pediatric Assn., Am. Acad. Pediatrics (council on grad. edn. 1978—), Am. Pub. Health Assn., North Pacific, Puget Sound (program chmn. 1972, pres. 1973) pediatric socs., Wash. Soc. Pediatrics (trustee 1970-73, chmn. com. handicapped children 1965-68, edn. for all laws com. 1973-75), Western Soc. for Pediatric Research. Republican. Methodist. Contbr. articles to med. jours. Home: 9119 NE 24th St Bellevue WA 98004 Office: Childrens' Orthopedic Hosp and Med Center 4800 Sand Point Way Seattle WA 98105

SHURTLIFF, MARVIN KARL, lawyer, govt. ofcl.; b. Idaho Falls, Idaho, Nov. 6, 1939; s. Noah Leon and Melba Dorothy (Hunting) S.; B.A., Idaho State Coll., 1962; J.D., U. Idaho, 1968; m. Peggy J. Griffin, Nov. 23, 1963; 1 dau., Jennifer Karyl. Tchr. pub. schs., Jefferson County, Idaho, 1964-65; admitted to Idaho bar, 1968; atty. Dept. Justice, Washington, 1968-74; commr. Idaho Pub. Utilities Commn., 1974-75, pres., 1975-76; spl. asst., legal counsel Gov. of Idaho, Boise, 1977; U.S. atty. for Dist. of Idaho, Boise, 1977—; mem. Idaho Ho. of Reps., 1962-64. Mem. Am., Idaho bar assns. Democrat. Home: Box 441 Boise ID 83701 Office: 550 W Fort St Boise ID 83724

SHUSTER, ALVIN, journalist; b. Washington, Jan. 25, 1930; s. Fred and Dora (Levy) S.; A.B., George Washington U., 1951; m. Miriam Schwartz, June 22, 1952; children—Fred, Jessica, Beth. Reporter Washington bur. N.Y. Times, 1952-61, asst. news editor, 1961-66, reporter London Bur., 1967-70, bur. chief, Saigon, 1970-71, London, 1972-75, Rome, 1975-77; chief editorial writer, dep. editor editorial pages Los Angeles Times, 1977—. Nieman fellow Harvard, 1966-67. Club: Reform (London). Editor: Washington, The New York Times Guide to the Nation's Capital, 1967. Office: Editorial Page Los Angeles Times Times Mirror Sq Los Angeles CA 90053

SHUSTER, BUD, congressman; b. Glassport, Pa., Jan. 23, 1932; B.S., U. Pitts., 1954; M.B.A., Duquesne U., 1960; Ph.D., Am. U., 1967; m. Patricia Rommell, 1955; children—Peg, Bill, Deb, Bob, Gia. Former bus. exec.; mem. 93d-96th Congresses from 9th Dist. Pa.; mem. budget com., chmn. House Republican Policy com., ranking minority mem. surface transp. subcom., mem. Edn. and Labor Com. Pres. 93d congress Republican Freshman Class; chmn. Nat. Transp. Policy Study Commn. Mem. Chowder and Marching Soc., Phi Beta Kappa. Office 2455 Rayburn House Office Bldg Washington DC 20515

SHUSTER, WILLIAM WEYMANN, educator; b. Norristown, Pa., Dec. 10, 1917; s. William Christian and Jessie (Brewster) S.; B.Chem. Enging., Rensselaer Poly. Inst., 1939, M.Chem. Engring., 1948, D.Chem. Engring., 1952; m. Nancy Duffie, June 12, 1948; children—Barbara (Mrs. Benjamin Huntington), Dale, William, Robert, Edward, Charles. Process engr. E.I. duPont de Nemours & Co., Inc., 1939-46; mem. faculty Rensselaer Poly. Inst., 1946—, prof. chem. engring., 1956-64, prof. environmental engring., chmn. dept., 1964-75, dir. environment program, 1975—; cons. to industry, 1950—. Active local Boy Scouts Am. Mem. Christian edn. com. Albany Presbytery, 1962—. Fellow Am. Inst. Chem. Engrs. (chmn. Upper N.Y. sect. 1967-68); mem. Sigma Xi, Phi Lambda Upsilon. Presbyn. (elder). Home: Ave A Melrose NY 12121 Office: Rensselaer Poly Inst Troy NY 12181

SHUTAN, ROBERT HARRY, lawyer; b. Chgo., May 12, 1918; s. Arthur J. and May (Flower) S.; B.S., U. Calif. at Los Angeles, 1939, LL.B., 1942; children—Peter, Anne. Admitted to Calif. bar, 1943; mem. firm Shutan & Trost, Los Angeles, 1971—; lectr., panelist Calif. Continuing Edn. of Bar Programs. Served to lt. USNR, 1942-46. Mem. Am., Calif. (chmn. com. on debtor/creditor relations and bankruptcy 1978-79), Los Angeles County, Beverly Hills (dir. public counsel) bar assns. Democrat. Office: 1880 Century Park E Los Angeles CA 90067

SHUTIAK, JAMES, oil co. exec.; b. Saskatoon, Sask., Can., July 1, 1932; s. Nicholas and Anna (Zabaczinski) S.: M.B.A., Simon Fraser U., 1977; m. M.L. Suzanne, June 21, 1961; children—David A., Peter J., Laura E., Teresa S. Partner, Winspear, Higgins, Stevenson & Co., C.A., 1951-61; comptroller, treas. Wainwright Producers & Refiners, Calgary, Alta., Can., 1961-63; sec., treas. Peace River Oil Pipeline Co., Ltd., Calgary, 1963-69; asst. to treas., asst. treas. Columbia Cellulose Co., Ltd., Vancouver, 1969-71; mgmt. cons. J. Shutiak, C.A., Vancouver, 1971-73; asst. gen. mgr., dep. chmn. Man. Devel. Corp., Winnipeg, 1973-75; treas. Alta. Gas Trunk Line Co., Ltd., Calgary, 1975-77; v.p., treas. Algas Mineral Enterprises, Ltd., Calgary, 1977-79; v.p. fin. CDC Oil & Gas Ltd., Calgary, 1979—. Bd. govs. Strathcona-Tweedsmuir Sch., Okotoks, Alta. C.A., 1958. Mem. Canadian Inst. Chartered Accountants, Fin. Execs. Inst., Simon Fraser U. Alumni Assn., Calgary Petroleum Club: Home: PO Box 333 Midnapore AB T0L 1J0 Canada Office: PO Box 1051 Calgary AB T2P 2K7 Canada

SHUTLER, KENNETH EUGENE, mfg. co. exec.; b. Wichita, Kans., Mar. 27, 1938; s. Walter Kenneth and Charlene Belle (Swearingen) S.; A.B., U. Pa., 1960; LL.B., Yale, 1963; m. Jean E. Rohner, June 24, 1967; children—Samantha Elizabeth, Whitney Anne. Admitted to Pa. bar, 1965, Calif. bar, 1971; practiced in Phila., 1965-68; asso. firm Stradley, Ronon, Stevens & Young, Phila.; v.p. Shareholders Mgmt. Co., Los Angeles, 1968-72; v.p., gen. counsel Republic Corp., Los Angeles, 1972-78; sr. v.p., gen. counsel Nat. Med. Enterprises, Inc., Los Angeles, 1978—; dir. Rollcut, Inc. Bd. dirs. Constl. Rights Found. Served to capt. U.S. Army, 1963-65. Mem. Am., Pa., Calif., Los Angeles County bar assns., Yale (schs. com.), U. Pa. (pres. So. Calif. 1971-72) alumni assns. Clubs: Venice (Calif.) Squash; Bel-Air Bay. Home: 16801 Severo Pl Encino CA 91316 Office: 1900 Ave of Stars Suite 2700 Los Angeles CA 90067

SHUTLER, RICHARD, JR., anthropologist, archaeologist; b. Longmont, Colo., Dec. 8, 1921; s. Richard D. and Tessa Flo (Burnett) S.; A.A., Salinas Jr. Coll., 1942; B.A., U. Calif., Berkeley, 1949, M.A., 1950; Ph.D., U. Ariz., 1961; m. Jamie Sue Evrard, Mar. 26, 1978; children—Kathryn Allice, John Hall, Richard Burnett. With Nevada State Mus., Carson City, 1959-65; mem. faculty U. Hawaii, 1965-66, San Diego State Coll., 1967-68, U. Victoria, B.C., Can., 1968-72; mem. faculty dept. anthropology U. Iowa, Iowa City, 1972—, prof., chmn. dept., 1972—; hon. asso. in anthropology Bernice P. Bishop Mus., 1963—; hon. curator of archaeology Nat. Mus. of Philippines, 1976—. Served with AUS, 1942-44, USAAF, 1944-46. NSF grantee, 1962, 63, 76. Fellow Am. Anthrop. Assn., AAAS; mem. Soc. Am. Archaeology, Indo-Pacific Prehistory Assn. Author: Pleistocene Studies in Southern Nevada, 1967; Oceanic Prehistory, 1975. Office: Dept Anthropology U Iowa Iowa City IA 52240

SHUTT, STEPHEN JOHN, profl. hockey player; b. Toronto, Ont., Can., July 1, 1952; s. John Frederick and May Ivy (Murray) S.; m. Ninon Malinosky, June 14, 1975; 1 son, Jason John. With Montreal (Que., Can.) Canadiens, Nat. Hockey League, 1972—. Played on team which won 3 Stanley Cups; mem. First All-Star Team for making most goals (60) for a left winger Nat. Hockey League. Office: 2313 Saint Catherine St W Montreal PQ H3H 1N2 Canada*

SHUTTLEWORTH, HARRY BENSON, r.r. ofcl.; b. Montclair, N.J., Dec. 27, 1923; s. Sydney and Margaret May (Smith) S.; B.S., Lehigh U., 1947; m. Barbara Anne Turner, Sept. 16, 1950; children--John, Richard, Anne. With treas. dept. Standard Oil Co. (N.J.), N.Y.C., 1947-54; mgr. corporate investment Gen. Electric Co., N.Y.C., 1955-60; mgr. banking relations and fund procurement Gen. Electric Credit Corp., N.Y.C., 1961-67, treas., 1968-69; treas. Union Pacific Corp., N.Y.C., 1969—; treas. U.P. R.R. Served to ensign USNR, 1943-45. Mem. Chi Psi. Clubs: Wee Burn Country (Darien, Conn.); Marco Polo (N.Y.C.). Home: 106 Inwood Rd Darien CT 06820 Office: 345 Park Ave New York City NY 10022

SHUTTLEWORTH, HERBERT LEWIS, II, bus. exec.; b. Amsterdam, N.Y., Nov. 2, 1913; s. Arthur Wellesley and Manie (Manning) S.; A.B., Dartmouth, 1935; grad. Mass. Inst. Tech., 1937; m. Jean Dutcher, Aug. 11, 1937; 1 dau., Molly Jean. With Mohawk Carpet Mills, Inc., 1937—, dir., 1940—, v.p., 1940-48, exec. v.p., 1948-52, pres., 1952-55; pres. Mohasco Corp., 1955-74, chmn. bd., 1974—; dir. Bankers Trust Co. Albany N.A. Pres., dir. Community Chest, Amsterdam, 1948-50; chmn. adv. bd. St. Mary's Hosp.; trustee Amsterdam City Hosp., 1939-48, Manlius (N.Y.) Sch. 1947-57, Am. Carpet Inst. (chmn. bd. 1958-59). Mem. bd. overseers Amos Tuck Sch. Bus. Adminstrn., Dartmouth Coll.; trustee Albany Med. Coll. Served as maj. Q.M.C., U.S. Army, 1942-45. Mason. Home: Golf Course Rd Amsterdam NY 12010 Office: Lyon St Amsterdam NY 12010

SHUTZ, BYRON CHRISTOPHER, realtor; b. Kansas City, Mo., Feb. 16, 1928; s. Byron Theodore and Maxine (Christopher) S.; A.B. in Econs., U. Kans., 1949; m. Marilyn Ann Tweedie, Mar. 30, 1957; children—Eleanor, Byron Christopher, Collin, Allison, Lindley. Partner Herbert V. Jones & Co., Kansas City, Mo., 1953-72; pres. Herbert V. Jones Mortgage Corp., Kansas City, 1967-72; pres. The Byron Shutz Co., Kansas City, 1973—; dir. Bus. Men's Assurance Co. Am., 1st Am. Financial Corp., Faultless Starch-Bon Ami Co. Chmn. bd. trustees U. Kansas City, 1979—; trustee Pembroke-Country Day Sch., 1974-77; bd. dirs. Kansas City Crime Commn. Served to 1st lt. USAF, 1951-53. Mem. Mortgage Bankers Assn. Am. (bd. govs. 1966-74), Am. Inst. Real Estate Appraisers. Clubs: Kansas City Country, Kansas City, University, Mercury, Vanguard. Home: 1001 W 58th Terr Kansas City MO 64113 Office: 800 W 47th St Kansas City MO 64112

SHUTZ, BYRON THEODORE, realtor, mortgage banker; b. New Philadelphia, Ohio, June 26, 1899; s. George E. and Millie (Auman) S.; student U. Kans., 1917-18; m. Maxine Christopher, Dec. 27, 1924; children—Byron Christopher, Laura Ann Shutz Cray, Susanne Shutz Curry. Joined Herbert V. Jones & Co., 1919, jr. partner, 1924, co. became inc., 1934, exec. v.p., 1939-44, pres., 1944-72; chmn. Bryon Shutz Co., 1973—; pres. Companion Investments, Inc.; v.p. Andrew, Drumm Inst.; adv. dir. Rothschild & Sons, Inc., 1st Nat. Bank of Kansas City (Mo.); dir., vice chmn. Farm & Home Savs. Assn., Downtown, Inc., Kansas City Power & Light Co.; dir., mem. adv. trust investment com. 1st Nat. Bank of Kansas City Dir. Real Estate Bd., Kansas City, 1927-30, pres., 1934-35; apptd. by Gov. F.C. Donnell as 1 of 3 original Mo. real estate commrs., 1941-45; chmn. War Fund Campaign of Kansas City-Jackson County chpt., A.R.C., 1944, mem. chpt. bd. dirs., 1945-46, chpt. chmn., 1945, 46, chmn. nat. nominating com., 1948, mem. Midwestern area adv. council, hon. mem. chpt. bd. dirs. Bd. govs. Am. Royal Live Stock and Horse Show; bd. dirs. Starlight Theatre Assn.; soc. fellows Nelson Gallery Found.; trustee Jacob L. Loose and Ella C. Loose Charity Funds, U. Kans. Endowment Assn.; hon. dir. Rockhurst Coll. Mem. Mo. Real Estate Assn. (organizer 1936, past pres.), Mortgage Bankers Assn. Am. (pres. 1939-40, life mem. bd. govs., mem. past pres. adv. council; trustee Research and Ednl. Trust Fund), Kansas City C. of C. (past dir.), U.S. C. of C., Friends of Art, Am. Soc. Real Estate Counselors, Midwest Research Inst. (dir., trustee, adv.), Phi Kappa Psi. Mem. Christian Ch. Mason (Jester). Clubs: Kansas City, Kansas City Country, University, River, Mercury (Kansas City, Mo.); Flat Rock (Mack's Inn, Idaho); Ocean Reef (Key Largo, Fla.). Home: 1000 W 66th St Kansas City MO 64113 Office: 800 W 47th St Kansas City MO 64112

SHUVAL, ANDREW JACKSON, lawyer; b. Meknes, Morocco, Apr. 6, 1933; s. Peter and Helene (Tatistcheff) Schouvaloff; came to U.S., 1936, naturalized, 1948; grad. Phillips Exeter Acad., 1950; student Harvard U., 1950-52; B.A., Tex. A. and M. U., 1960; law edn., U. Tex., 1963; m. Elizabeth Louise Walterscheid, May 25, 1968; children—Sonia, Elena, Peter Kevin, Nina and Lisa (twins). Admitted to Tex. bar, 1965; pvt. practice law, Hereford, 1965—; county atty. Deaf Smith County, Tex., 1970-71, dist. atty., 1971-78; exec. dir. Tex. Prosecutors Coordinating Council, Austin, 1978—. Div. chmn. Nat. Young Dems., 1964-66; pres. Tex. Young Dems., 1963-65. Served with USAF, 1952-56. Certified criminal law specialist. Mem. Tex. Bar Assn., Tex. County and Dist. Attys. Assn., Am. Judicature Soc., Nat. Dist. Atty. Assn. Roman Catholic. K.C. Home: 8203 Loyola St Austin TX 78723 Office: 1414 Colorado Tex Law Center Austin TX 78711

SHWAYDER, DAVID SAMUEL, educator; b. Denver, Oct. 21, 1926; s. Sol and Ida (Weitz) S.; student Northwestern U., 1944, Coll. St. Thomas, 1944-45; A.B., U. Calif. at Berkeley, 1948, B.A., Oxford U., 1950, M.A., 1954, D.Phil., 1954. Mem. faculty U. Ill., Urbana, 1954-58, 68—, prof. philosophy, 1968—, chmn. dept., 1969-70; mem. faculty U. Calif. at Berkeley, 1958-68, prof., 1967-68, chmn. dept., 1966-68. Mem. Am. Studies Seminar, Kyoto, Japan, 1968. Served with USNR, 1944-46. Guggenheim fellow, 1967; Fulbright Research fellow, New Zealand, 1961. Mem. Am. Philos. Assn. Author: Modes of Referring and the Problems of Universals, 1961; Stratification of Behavior, 1965. Home: 1802 S Race St Urbana IL 61801

SHWAYDER, KING DAVID, luggage and furniture mfg. co. exec.; b. Denver, Aug. 21, 1910; s. Jesse and Nellie (Weitz) S.; student U. Pa., 1928-30, also U. Colo.; m. Rose Friedland, Dec. 30, 1934; children—Keith Roger, Jessie Lou (Mrs. Theodore Harsham). Credit mgr. Samsonite Corp. (formerly Shwayder Bros., Inc.), mfrs. folding furniture, Ecorse, Mich., 1930-34, asst. gen. mgr., Detroit, 1934-46, v.p., gen. mgr., 1946-60, exec. v.p., 1960-61, pres., 1961—, also chief exec. officer; dir. Pub. Service Co. Colo., Centennial Turf Club, Denelcor, Inc., Discount Fabrics, United Bank of Denver. Regional co-chmn. NCCJ, Denver; mem. exec. bd. Denver, mem. nat. council Boy Scouts Am.; trustee U. Denver. Mem. Colo. Assn. Commerce and Industry. Jewish. Clubs: Green Gables Country, Rotary, The Town, Denver Athletic. Home: 1201 Williams St Denver CO 80218 Office: 4155 E Jewell Ave Denver CO 80222

SHY, JOHN WILLARD, educator; b. Dayton, Ohio, Mar. 23, 1931; s. Willard Alden and Margaret (Brush) S.; B.S., U.S. Mil. Acad., 1952; M.A., U. Vt., 1957; Ph.D., Princeton, 1961. Instr. history Princeton, 1959-62, asst. prof., 1962-66, asso. prof., 1966-68; prof. history U. Mich., 1968—. Fulbright prof. U. London, 1975-76. Served with U.S. Army, 1952-55. Guggenheim fellow, 1969-70. Recipient Dunning prize, 1966. Mem. Am. Hist. Assn., Orgn. Am. Historians, Am. Antiquarian Soc. Author: Guerrillas in the 1960's, 1962; Toward Lexington, 1965; A People Numerous and Armed, 1976. Office: History Dept U Mich Ann Arbor MI 48109

SHYER, HERBERT PAUL, ins. co. exec.; b. Los Angeles, Apr. 29, 1930; s. Nathaniel and Cele (Caine) S.; A.B., U. Calif., Los Angeles, 1950, M.A., 1952; postgrad. Grad. Sch. Arts and Scis., Harvard U., 1951-53; LL.B., Harvard U., 1956; postgrad. (Fulbright Scholar), Oxford U., 1956-57. Teaching fellow dept. govt. Harvard U., 1952-56; admitted to N.Y. bar, 1957; asso. firm Cleary, Gottlieb, Steen & Hamilton, N.Y.C., 1957-67; with Equitable Life Assurance Soc. of U.S., N.Y.C., 1967—, sr. v.p., gen. counsel, 1975—. Mem. Am., N.Y. State bar assns., Assn. Bar City N.Y., N.Y. County Lawyers Assn., Assn. Life Ins. Counsel (pres.), Phi Beta Kappa Assos. Home: 24 W 55th St New York NY 10019 Office: 1285 Ave of Americas New York NY 10019

SHYTLE, JOHN DAVID, health adminstr.; b. Shelby, N.C., Mar. 30, 1918; s. Johnson D. and Oster (Whisnant) S.; B.S. in Bus. Adminstrn., Am. U., 1954; M.A. in Pub. Adminstrn., George Washington U., 1966; M.S. in Mgmt., Frostburg (Md.) U., 1972; m. Lois Tate Shell, May 2, 1941; children—Linda Shell, John David. Cost accountant Dover Mill Corp., Shelby, 1936-41; budget examiner VA, 1946-48; sr. cost analyst U.S. Steel Co., 1948-49; with VA, 1949-74, controller, Washington, 1962-72, dir. McGuire VA Hosp., Richmond, Va., 1972-74; asst. v.p. for health affairs/adminstrn. Duke U. Med. Center, Durham, N.C., 1974—. Served to capt. USAAF, 1941-46. Decorated D.F.C. (4), Air medal (2); Chinese Nat. Govt. medal; recipient Exceptional Service award VA. Mem. Fed. Govt. Accountants Assn., Assn. Am. Med. Colls., Am. Soc. Pub. Adminstrn., Shelby Jr. C. of C. (charter), Am. Legion, D.A.V., V.F.W. Democrat. Mem. Christian Ch. (chmn. ofcl. bd. 1963-64, also other coms.). Methodist. Mason. Address: 2756 McDowell Rd Durham NC 27705

SIAS, DAVID KENNETH, JR., banker; b. Orange, N.J., Nov. 14, 1937; s. D. Kenneth and Mabel Louise (Lewi) S.; B.S., Yale U., 1959; M.B.A., N.Y. U., 1965; m. Patricia Lee Milback, Jan. 2, 1967; children—Christopher, Robin. Gen. mgr. Deutsche Unionbank GmbH, Frankfurt, W.Ger., 1970-74; sr. v.p. in charge Europe div. Bankers Trust Co., N.Y.C., 1974-77, sr. v.p. in charge adminstrn, ops. and personnel, internat. dept., 1977-79, exec. v.p. in charge internat. dept., N.Y.C., 1979—. Served with U.S. Army, 1959-63. Home: 17 Point O'Woods Rd Darien CT 06820 Office: 280 Park Ave New York NY 10017

SIATOS, THOMAS JOHN, magazine pub.; b. Los Angeles, Sept. 13, 1923; s. John and Kaleope (Kontos) S.; B.S. in Bus. Adminstrn., U. Calif. at Los Angeles, 1949; m. Farrel Dale Solberg, Aug. 17, 1957; 1 dau., Dena Ann. Engaged in banking and life ins. bus., 1950-53; free-lance writer firearms and hunting, 1953—; mng. editor Western Outdoor Pub. Co., Los Angeles, 1954-58; editor Guns and Ammo mag. pub. Petersen Pub. Co., Los Angeles, 1958-64, editorial dir. Petersen Publishing Co., 1964-65; pub. Guns & Ammo mag., 1965-73, exec. pub., 1973—; exec. pub. Hunting Mag., also Outdoor Specialty

Books, 1973—, corporate v.p., 1975—. Served with USMCR, 1942-45; PTO. Mem. Am. Ordnance Assn., Nat. Rifle Assn., Am. Mus. Natural History, Aircraft Owners and Pilots Assn., Theta Delta Chi. Mason. Home: Los Angeles CA Office: 8490 Sunset Blvd Los Angeles CA 90069

SIBAL, ABNER WOODRUFF, lawyer; b. Ridgewood, N.Y., Apr. 11, 1921; s. Charles L. and Elizabeth (Buckett) S.; A.B., Wesleyan U., 1943; LL.B., St. John's Law Sch., 1949; m. Mary Ellen Igou, 1944; children—Susan Wells, John Woodruff. Admitted to Conn. bar, 1949, D.C. bar, 1965; partner Sibal, Hefferan & Rimer, Norwalk, Conn., 1952-70, Gadsby & Hannah, Washington, 1970-74; gen. counsel Equal Employment Opportunity Commn., 1975-79; resident partner firm Whitman and Ransom, Washington, 1979—; pros. atty., Norwalk City Ct.; corp. counsel City of Norwalk; mem. 87th-88th congresses, 4th Dist. Conn. Past chmn. Norwalk-Wilton chpt. A.R.C.; chmn. Conn. Commn. Corp. Law, 1959. Mem. Conn. Senate, 1956-60, minority leader, 1959-60. Served to 1st lt. AUS, World War II. Mem. Am. Legion, V.F.W., Psi Upsilon. Republican. Congregationalist. Club: Masons. Home: 4101 Cathedral Ave NW Washington DC 20016 Office: 1333 New Hampshire Ave NW Washington DC 20036

SIBIGTROTH, JOSEPH CLARENCE, ins. co. exec.; b. Mendota, Ill., Nov. 29, 1915; s. Joseph and Alma (Leifheit) S.; B.A., U. Ill., 1939, M.S., 1940; m. Marjorie Ward, June 12, 1941; children—Alan, Joan. With Met. Life Ins. Co., N.Y.C., 1940-52; adminstrv. asst. N.Y. Life Ins. Co., N.Y.C., 1952-54, exec. asst., 1954-56, asst. v.p., 1956-57, actuary, 1957-59, 2d v.p., actuary, 1959-66, v.p., actuary, 1966-71, sr. v.p., chief actuary, 1971—. Served to lt. USNR, 1942-45. Fellow Soc. Actuaries; mem. Am. Acad. Actuaries, Canadian Inst. Actuaries. Lutheran. Home: 90 South Rd Port Washington NY 11050 Office: 51 Madison Ave New York City NY 10010

SIBLEY, ALDEN KINGSLAND, orgn. exec., ret. army officer; b. Tuscaloosa, Ala., Jan. 3, 1911; s. Frederick Hubbard and Annabelle (Pearson) S.; student U. Nev., 1928-29; B.S., U.S. Mil. Acad., 1933; B.A. (Rhodes scholar), Magdalen Coll., Oxford U., Eng., 1936, B.Sc., 1936, M.A., 1943; student Engr. Sch., Ft. Belvoir, Va., 1937-38; grad. Nat. War Coll., 1957; doctoral study nuclear physics George Washington U., 1955—; D.Sc., Coll. Advanced Sci., Canaan, N.H., 1962; m. Evira Trowbridge, Nov. 15, 1945; 1 son, Frederick Drake. Commd. 2d lt. C.E. U.S. Army, 1933, advanced through grades to maj. gen., 1961; condr. sci. expdn. around world, 1935; bn. commdr. 1st Bn., 5th Engr. Regt., Ft. Belvoir, Va., 1936; mil. aide to pres., White House, 1937-38; exec. officer constrn. Conchas Dam, N.Mex., 1938; chief, inspection constrn. John Martin Dam, Colo., 1939; exec. officer St. Lawrence Seaway and Power Project, 1940-41; dist. engr. African Engr. Dist., Cairo, Egypt, 1942; asst. chief staff G-4 (logistics), Middle-East Theater Ops., Cairo, 1942; comdg. officer Eritrea and Tripoli Base commands, N. Africa, 1943; chief Army component Joint Brit.-U.S. Operations and Planning Group, Middle East, 1943; dep. chief staff Middle East Theater Operations, 1943; exec. officer, asst. chief staff G-4 (logistics), SHAEF, London, 1943-44; chief SHAEF Mission to France, 1944-45; dep. asst. chief staff G-4, War Dept. Gen. Staff, 1945; mem. joint logistics com. Joint Chiefs Staff, 1946; chief theaters br. Gen. Staff Army, 1946-48; chief ops. planning group Office Chief Staff Army, 1949; mil. sec. Army Policy Council, Office Sec. Army, also spl. asst. under sec. army for politico-mil. affairs, 1950-52; chief, logistic plans br. SHAPE, Paris, 1952-55; dir. ednl. devel., faculty Nat. War Coll., 1955-57; chief staff U.S. del. for negotiations Fed. Republic of Germany, Bonn, 1956, Philippine Base Negotiations, Manila, 1956; div. engr. U.S. Army Engr. Div., New Eng., 1957-60; dep. chief Mil. Assistance Adv. Group, Saigon, Vietnam 1960-61; dep. chief engrs., Washington, 1961-62; comdg. gen. U.S. Army Mobility Command, Center Line, Mich., 1962-64; dep. chief staff logistics, acting chief of staff U.S. Army Europe, Heidelberg, Germany, 1964-66; comdg. gen. XI U.S. Army Corps, St. Louis, 1966-67; dep. comdg. gen. 5th U.S. Army, Chgo., 1967-68; exec. asst. to chmn. bd. Champion Internat. Corp., N.Y.C., 1968-74, Econ. Devel. Council, N.Y.C., 1974-78. Mem. Rhodes Scholarship selection com., Europe, 1954, Mass., 1958, Mich., 1963, Mo., 1966; dir. World Affairs Council, Boston; dir. Boston Regional Conf. on NATO Affairs; trustee Nat. U., Winter Park, Fla., Canaan (N.H.) Coll. Decorated D.S.M., Legion of Merit, Bronze Star, Army Commendation ribbon with oak leaf cluster (U.S.); Medal of Honor 1st class (Vietnam); Order Brit. Empire; comdr. Legion of Honor, Croix de Guerre with palm (France); grand marshall knight comdr. Order St. John of Jerusalem; knight Malta; recipient Diamond Jubilee Anniversary medal ASME, 1956, Disting. Leadership Cause Freedom award Detroit-Windsor Internat. Freedom Festival, 1962, Author's award Automotive Industries, 1963-64. Mem. Am. Def. Preparedness Assn., AAAS, Armed Forces Mgmt. Assn., Assn. U.S. Army (pres. N.Y. chpt.), Am. Soc. French Legion of Honor (exec. v.p., dir., chmn. exec. com.), Pilgrims U.S., S.A.R., Nat. Aviation Hall of Fame, Oxford Soc., Soc. Am. Mil. Engrs. (founding pres. Saigon chpt., nat. dir., pres. Boston chpt.), West Point Alumni Assn. N.E. (pres.), Registered Profl. Engrs. Mass., ASCE, ASME, Newcomen Soc., Soc. Am. Rhodes Scholars, Nat. Inst. Social Scis., Société des Indépendents of Paris, Tir Aux Pigeons of Paris, Anysetiers du Roy, Chevalliers du Tastevin (grand officier), Seigneur de Franc-Pineau, St. Georges Soc. (dir.), Sigma Xi, Tau Beta Pi. Clubs: Army-Navy Country, Army-Navy, Chevy Chase (Washington); River (N.Y.); Detroit; Marco Palo; St. Louis; Jockey (Paris) Contbr. articles to profl. publs. Exhibited original oil paintings Grand Palais, Societe des Independents, 1954. Home: 969 Park Ave New York NY 10028

SIBLEY, CHARLES GALD, biologist, educator; b. Fresno, Calif., Aug. 7, 1917; s. Charles Corydon and Ida (Gald) S.; A.B., U. Calif. at Berkeley, 1940, Ph.D., 1948; M.A. (hon.), Yale U., 1965; m. Frances Louise Kelly, Feb. 7, 1942; children—Barbara Susanne, Dorothy Ellen, Carol Nadine. Biologist, USPHS, 1941-42; instr. zoology U. Kans., 1948-49; asst. prof. San Jose (Calif.) State Coll., 1949-53; asso. prof. ornithology Cornell U., 1953-59, prof. zoology, 1959-65; prof. biology Yale, 1965—, William Robertson Coe prof. ornithology, 1967—, dir. div. vertebrate zoology, curator birds Peabody Mus., 1965—, dir. mus., 1970-76; cons. systematic biology, 1963-65. Mem. adv. com. biol. medicine NSF, 1968—; exec. com. biol. agr. NRC, 1966-70. Served to lt. USNR, 1943-45. Guggenheim fellow, 1959-60. Fellow AAAS; mem. Am. Inst. Biol. Scis., Soc. Study Evolution, Am. Soc. Zoology, Am. Soc. Naturalists, Soc. Systematic Biology, Am. Ornithol. Union, Royal Australian Ornithol. Union, Deutsche Ornithol. Gesellschaft, Internat. Ornithol. Congress (sec.-gen. 1962). Contbr. profl. jours. Home: Old Quarry Rd Guilford CT 06437 Office: Peabody Museum Yale U New Haven CT 06520

SIBLEY, HARPER, JR., pvt. investor; b. Rochester, N.Y., May 2, 1927; s. Harper and Georgiana (Farr) S.; grad. Groton Sch., 1945; A.B., Princeton, 1949; m. Beatrice Blair, Feb. 19, 1949 (div. Sept. 1970); children—Elizabeth, Harper III, Montgomery Blair, John Durbin; m. 2d, Stuart Franken, Dec. 14, 1970. Pres. Sibley Corp., mortgage bankers, 1955-69, Dietrich-Sibley Agy., Inc., 1959-69; chmn. bd. Ocean Reef Club, North Key Largo, Fla., Jockey Club, Miami, Fla.; owner, operator Sibleyville Farms, Honeoye Falls, N.Y., Taryall Ranch, Jefferson, Colo.; dir. Western Union Corp., Central Trust Co., Rochester, N.Y., Median Mortgage Investors, 1st Nat. Bank Miami (Fla.). Pub. safety commr., Rochester, 1965-66. Trustee U. Miami, chmn. Med. Sch.; trustee United Fund Dade County, Jackson Meml. Hosp. Clubs: Metropolitan (Washington); Country Genesee Valley (Rochester); Princeton (N.Y.); Miami (Fla.). Home: 10640 SW 53d Ave Miami FL 33156 Office: Ocean Reef Club Key Largo FL 33037

SIBLEY, JAMES MALCOLM, lawyer; b. Atlanta, Ga., Aug. 5, 1919; s. John Adams and Nettie Whitaker (Cone) S.; A.B., Princeton U., 1941; student Woodrow Wilson Sch. Law, 1942, Harvard Law Sch., 1946; m. Karen Norris, Apr. 6, 1942; children—Karen Mariea, James Malcolm, Jack Norris, Elsa Alexandria Victoria, Quintus Whitaker. Admitted to Ga. bar, 1942; asso. firm King & Spalding, Atlanta, 1942-47, partner, 1947—, chmn. mgmt. com., 1976—; dir. Trust Co. of Ga., also chmn. exec. com.; dir. Trust Co. Bank, Trust Co. of Ga. Assos., John H. Harland Co., Life Ins. Co. of Ga., Rock-Tenn Co. Trustee, Emily and Ernest Woodruff Fund, Joseph B. Whitehead Found., Lettie Pate Evans Found., Emory U., Berry Schs., A. G. Rhodes Home, Inc., Trebor Found.; trustee David, Helen and Marian Woodward Fund, also vice-chmn.; chmn. trustees Jess Parker Williams Hosp. Served with USAAF, 1942-45. Mem. Am., Ga., Atlanta bar assns., Atlanta Lawyers Club, Am. Coll. Probate Counsel, Am. Bar Found., Am. Law Inst. Episcopalian. Clubs: Piedmont Driving, Commerce, Capital City. Home: 63 Peachtree St NE Atlanta GA 30309 Office: 2500 Trust Co Tower Atlanta GA 30303

SIBLEY, JOHN ADAMS, lawyer; b. Milledgeville, Ga., Jan. 4, 1888; s. James Longstreet and Mattie (Erwin) S.; prep. course Ga. Mil. Coll., Milledgeville, Ga.; LL.B., U. Ga., 1911; LL.D., Oglethorpe U., 1950, Mercer U., 1952, Emory U., 1962; m. Nettie Whitaker Cone, Nov. 25, 1914 (dec. Mar. 1934); children—John A. (dec.), James Malcolm, Jeannette Sibley Yow, Martha Sibley George; m. 2d, Barbara Sanford Thayer, Mar. 29, 1937; children—Barbara Thayer, Horace Holden, John Adams, III, Stephen Thayer. Admitted to Ga. bar, 1911, began practice under title of Sibley & Sibley, Milledgeville; mem. firm King & Spalding, Atlanta, Spalding, Sibley & Troutman, 1918-46; judge County Ct., Baldwin County, Ga., 1914-18; chmn. bd. Trust Co. Ga., 1946-63, adv. dir., chmn. adv. council, dir.; dir. Trust Co. of Ga. Assos., Coca-Cola Co., Coca-Cola Export Corp. Hon. chmn. bd. trustees Henrietta Egleston Hosp. for Children; chmn. Gen. Assembly Com. on Schs. (Sibley Commn.), 1960-61, Higher Ednl. Facilities Commn. for Ga., 1963-66. Mem. Am. (v.p. 1922), Ga., Atlanta bar assns. Democrat. Presbyn. Rotarian. Clubs: Capital City, Piedmont Driving, The Ten (Atlanta). Home: 165 W Wesley Rd NW Atlanta GA 30305 Office: Trust Co of Ga Atlanta GA 30302

SIBLEY, JOHN MEARES, JR., banker; b. New Orleans, May 10, 1923; s. John Meares and Esther Regina (Wagner) S.; student Tulane U., 1941, La. State U. Sch. Banking of South, 1966-68; m. Louise Theresa Buysse, June 14, 1956; 1 son, John David. With Central Bank & Trust Co., Miami, 1953-54; asst. v.p. Am. Bank & Trust Co., South Bend, Ind., 1954-61, Mut. Nat. Bank Chgo., 1961-62; sr. v.p. Nat. Am. Bank, New Orleans, 1963-74; pres. First Progressive Bank, Metairie, La., 1974—, vice chmn. bd., 1978—. Served with USNR, 1943-46. Clubs: Chateau Golf and Country, various carnival orgns. Home: 2520 Judith St Metairie LA 70003 Office: 1501 Veterans Blvd Metairie LA 70005

SIBLEY, WILLIAM ARTHUR, educator; b. Ft. Worth, Nov. 22, 1932; s. William Franklin and Sada (Rasor) S.; B.S., U. Okla., 1956, M.S., 1958, Ph.D., 1960; m. Joyce Elaine Gregory, Dec. 21, 1957; children—William Timothy, Lauren Shawn, Stephen Marshall. Teaching and research asst. U. Okla., 1956-60; postdoctoral research in defect solid state Kernforschungsanlage Julich and Tech. U. Aachen, Germany, 1960-61; research solid state div. Oak Ridge Nat. Lab., 1961-70; prof., head physics Okla. State U., Stillwater, 1970-76, dir. Sch. Phys. and Earth Scis., 1976-78, asst. v.p. research, 1978—; mem. solid state sci. com. Nat. Acad. Sci., 1977—. Served to lt. AUS, 1951-53; maj. Res., 1953-60. Fellow Am. Phys. Soc.; mem. Sigma Xi, Sigma Pi Sigma, Pi Mu Epsilon. Baptist. Contbr. articles to profl. jours. Home: 3119 W 27th St Stillwater OK 74074

SIBLEY, WILLIAM AUSTIN, neurologist, educator; b. Miami, Okla., Jan. 25, 1925; s. William Austin and Erna Johanna (Quickert) S.; B.S., Yale U., 1945, M.D., 1948; m. Joanne Shaw, Sept. 4, 1954; children—John, Mary Jane, Peter, Andrew. Intern Univ. Hosp., Cleve., 1948-50; asst. resident neurologist Neurol. Inst. Presbyn. Hosp., N.Y.C., 1953-55, chief resident neurologist, 1955-56; asst. prof. neurology Western Res. U., Cleve., 1956-63, asso. prof., 1963-67; prof., head dept. neurology U. Ariz. Coll. Medicine, Tucson, 1967—. Chmn. adv. com. on etiology, diagnosis and therapy Nat. Multiple Sclerosis Soc., 1970-74, 76-78. Served to capt. M.C. USAF, 1951-53. Recipient LaFayette B. Mendel prize in physiol. chemistry Yale, 1945. Mem. Am. Neurol. Assn. (v.p. 1979-80), Am. Acad. Neurology, Central Soc. for Neurol. Research (pres. 1968). Home: 2150 E Hampton St Tucson AZ 85719 Office: 1501 N Campbell Ave Tucson AZ 85724

SIBLEY, WILLIS ELBRIDGE, educator; b. Nashville, Feb. 22, 1930; s. Elbridge and Elizabeth Reynolds (LaBarre) S.; B.A., Reed Coll., 1951; M.A., U. Chgo., 1953, Ph.D., 1958; m. Barbara Jean Grant, June 9, 1956; children—Sheila Katherine, Anthony Grant, Michael David. Instr. sociology and anthropology Miami (Ohio) U., 1956-58; asst. prof. anthropology U. Utah, 1958-60; asst. prof. anthropology Wash. State U., 1960-64, asso. prof., 1964-69, prof. anthropology, 1969-71, acting chmn. dept., fall 1969-70, asst. to dean Coll. Arts and Scis., spring 1969-70; prof. anthropology Cleve. State U., 1971—, chmn. dept., 1971-77; sr. program analyst EPA, Washington, 1977-78; Govtl. fellow Am. Council on Edn., 1977-78; research asst. Philippine Studies Program, U. Chgo., 1955-56, research asso., summer 1959; asst. prof. anthropology Fordham U., summer 1957, U. Alta., Edmonton, Can., summer 1963; Rockefeller Found. vis. prof. anthropology U. Philippines, Quezon City, 1968-69; lectr. Am. Anthropol. Assn. Vis. Lectr. Program, 1962-63, 66-68, 70-71, 72-74, 76-77. Fulbright grantee, 1954-55, 64; NIMH grantee, 1959-61; NSF grantee, 1964-71; Nat. Acad. Scis.-NRC travel grantee, 1966; Office Edn., HEW research grantee, 1967. Fellow Am. Anthropol. Assn., AAAS, Soc. Applied Anthropology (sec. 1977-80); mem. Assn. Asian Studies, Am. Ethnol. Soc., Anthropol. Soc. Washington, Central States Anthropol. Soc. (exec. bd.), AAUP (treas. Wash. State U. chpt. 1962-63, v.p. 1963-64, pres. 1965-66), ACLU (pres. Pullman chpt. 1963, 66), Wash. Assn. Profl. Anthropologists, Sigma Xi. Club: Edgewater Yacht (Cleve.) (trustee 1979—). Asso. editor Research Studies, 1963-66. Home: 2615 Lee Rd Cleveland Heights OH 44118 Office: Dept Anthropology Cleve State U Cleveland OH 44115

SICA, ALBERT JOSEPH, state ofcl.; b. N.Y.C., Oct. 9, 1915; s. Enrico and Antionetta (D'Ambrosio) S.; B.S. in Pharmacy cum laude, Fordham U., 1937, M.S., 1941, Ph.D., in Biochemistry, 1948; m. Lee Belloise, July 1, 1944; children—Albert Joseph, Robert, Michael, William, Gregory, John. Pharm. cons. Centaur Co., also Burroughs Wellcome & Co., 1940-42; faculty Coll. Pharmacy, Fordham U., 1942-70, chmn. dept., 1952-56, prof., 1954-70, asso. dean, 1954-56, dean, 1956-70; mem. N.Y. State Bd. Pharmacy, 1961—, pres., 1966-67, sec., 1970—. Mem. Am. Pharm. Assn., N.Y. State Pharm. Soc., Sigma Xi, Rho Chi, Phi Lambda Upsilon. Home: 83 Greenock Rd Delmar NY 12054

SICA, NICHOLAS ALPHONSE, banker; b. N.Y.C., Dec. 6, 1920; s. Nicholas and Rose (Vesta) S.; Asso. Bus. Adminstrn., Pace Coll., 1955; m. Carmela E. Yaiulla, Apr. 5, 1947; children—Dennis R., Roseann R., Barbara C., Richard B., Glen S. With European-Am. Banking Corp. and predecessor firms, N.Y.C., 1941—, sr. v.p., sr. loan officer, 1968-72, exec. v.p., dir. European-Am. Bank & Trust Co. and European-Am. Bancorp, 1972-78, pres., dir., 1978—; pres., dir. European Am. Fin. (Bermuda) Ltd., European Am. Banking Corp.; dir. Euram Realty Corp., Euramcor Realty Corp., Disk-Pack Leasing Corp.; pres. Euramlease, Inc., 1976—. Served with AUS, 1942-45; ETO. Decorated Silver Star medal. Roman Catholic. Clubs: Wall Street (N.Y.C.); Westchester Country (Rye, N.Y.); K.C. Home: Appleby Dr Bedford Village NY 10506 Office: 10 Hanover Sq New York NY 10015

SICHERMAN, MARVIN ALLEN, lawyer; b. Cleve., Dec. 27, 1934; s. Harry and Malvina (Friedman) S.; B.A., Case Western Res. U., 1957, LL.B., 1960, J.D., 1968; m. Sue Kovacs, Aug. 18, 1957; children—Heidi Joyce, Steven Eric. Admitted to Ohio bar, 1960, since practiced in Cleve.; mng. partner Dettelbach & Sicherman, 1971—. Mem. Beachwood (Ohio) Civic League, 1972—, Beachwood Bd. Edn., 1978—; bd. dirs. Beachwood Arts Council, 1977—. Mem. Am., Ohio (lectr. truth in lending 1969, lectr. bankruptcy 1972), Cuyahoga Country, Cleve. (lectr. practice and procedure clinic 1965—, chmn. bankruptcy ct. com. 1971-73) bar assns., Comml. Law League Am., Jewish Chautauqua Soc., Tau Epsilon Rho, Zeta Beta Tau. Jewish (trustee Temple brotherhood 1968-76). Editorial bd. Case-Western Res. Law Rev., 1958-60. Contbr. articles to legal jours. Home: 24500 Albert Ln Beachwood OH 44122 Office: Ohio Savs Plaza Cleveland OH 44114

SICILIANO, ROCCO CARMINE, financial corp. exec.; b. Salt Lake City, Mar. 4, 1922; s. Joseph Vincent and Mary (Arnone) S.; B.A. with honors, U. Utah, 1944; LL.B., Georgetown U., 1948; m. Marion Stiebel, Nov. 8, 1947; children—Loretta, A. Vincent, Fred R., John, Maria. Admitted to D.C. bar, 1949; legal asst. to bd. mem. NLRB, Washington, 1948-50; asst. sec.-treas. Procon Inc., Des Plaines, Ill., 1950-53; asst. sec. labor charge employment and manpower Dept. Labor, Washington, 1953-57; spl. asst. to Eisenhower for personnel mgmt., 1957-59; partner Wilkinson, Cragun & Barker, 1959-69; pres. Pacific Maritime Assn., San Francisco, 1965-69; under sec. of commerce, Washington, 1969-71; chmn. bd., chief exec. officer Ticor, Los Angeles; dir. Pacific Lighting Corp., So. Pacific Co.; mem. Fed. Pay Bd., 1971-73. Mem. nat. adv. council U. Utah; mem. adv. council Stanford Bus. Sch.; mem. vis. com. Grad. Sch. Mgmt., U. Calif. at Los Angeles; pres. Los Angeles Philharmonic Assn.; mem. Calif. Roundtable; trustee Com. for Econ. Devel. Served with AUS, 1943-46; 1st lt., 10th Mountain Div., Italy; personnel officer G-1, Hdqrs., U.S. Forces, Austria. Decorated Combat Infantryman Badge, Bronze Star, Army Commendation Ribbon (U.S.); Order Merit Italian Republic. Mem. Am. Bar Assn., Calif. (dir.), Los Angeles Area (dir.) chambers commerce. Clubs: Met. (Washington); Family (San Francisco); Los Angeles. Home: 612 N Rodeo Dr Beverly Hills CA 90210 Office: 6300 Wilshire Blvd Los Angeles CA 90048

SICK, WILSON WILLIAM, JR., mfg. co. exec.; b. Wayland, N.Y., Dec. 23, 1933; s. Wilson William and Aldene Bauter (Snell) S.; B.S. in Elec. Engring., Carnegie Mellon U., 1955, M.S. in Indsl. Adminstrn., 1957; m. Mary Louise McClure, Sept. 8, 1956; children—Wilson, Robert, Deborah. With Ford Motor Co., 1957-73, gen. mgr. indsl. engine and turbine div., 1972-73; sr. v.p. Allen Group, Inc., Mellville, N.Y., 1973-75; exec. v.p. Bell & Howell Co., Chgo., 1976-78; group v.p., chief fin. and adminstrv. officer Am. Motors Corp., Southfield, Mich., 1978—; dir. Student Loan Mktg. Assn. Bd. dirs. Ypsilanti (Mich.) Community Chest, 1966-67, Plymouth (Mich.) Symphony Soc., 1969-72; treas. Plymouth Twp. Sch. Bd., 1971-72. Andrew Mellon fellow, 1955-57. Mem. Fin. Execs. Inst. Clubs: Economic (Chgo. and Detroit). Home: 1582 Apple Ln Bloomfield Hills MI 48013 Office: 27777 Franklin Rd Southfield MI 48034

SICKMILLER, EDWARD PAUL, found. exec.; b. Port Clinton, Ohio, Apr. 18, 1934; s. Edward Gale and Evelyn Eleanor (Clucky) S.; student Ohio U., 1953; B.A. in History, Bowling Green (Ohio) U., 1957; m. Joan M. Duncan, Dec. 1, 1962; children—Anya Elaine, Darcy Ann. Purchasing agt. W.K. Kellogg Found., Battle Creek, Mich., 1960-63, adminstrv. asst., 1963-66, asst. sec., 1967-70, asst. treas., 1970, sec., 1970-78. Served with U.S. Army, 1957-59. Mem. Adminstrv. Mgmt. Soc., Battle Creek C. of C. Roman Catholic. Home: 498 Morningside Dr Battle Creek MI 49015

SIDAMON-ERISTOFF, ANNE PHIPPS, museum ofcl.; b. N.Y.C., Sept. 12, 1932; d. Howard and Harriet Dyer (Price) Phipps; B.A., Bryn Mawr Coll., 1954; m. Constantine Sidamon-Eristoff, June 29, 1957; children—Simon, Elizabeth, Andrew. Vice pres. Am. Mus. Natural History, N.Y.C., 1974—. Bd. dirs., sec. Conservation Found.; bd. dirs. Greenacre Found., Highland Falls (N.Y.) Pub. Library. Home: 120 East End Ave New York NY 10028 Office: 79th and Central Park W New York NY 10024

SIDAMON-ERISTOFF, CONSTANTINE, lawyer; b. N.Y.C., June 28, 1930; s. Simon C. and Anne Huntington (Tracy) Sidamon-E.; B.S.E. in Geol. Engring., Princeton U., 1952; LL.B., Columbia U., 1957; m. Anne Phipps, June 29, 1957; children—Simon, Elizabeth, Andrew. Clk, then asso. firm Kelley Drye Newhall Maginnes & Warren, N.Y.C., 1957-64; individual practice law, N.Y.C., 1964-65, 74-77; exec. asst. for Congressman John V. Lindsay, 1964-65; city coordinator Lindsay Mayoral Campaign, N.Y.C., 1965; asst. to mayor City of N.Y., 1966, commr. hwys., 1967-68, transp. adminstrn., 1968-73; partner firm Sidamon-Eristoff, Morrision, Warren, Ecker & Schwartz, N.Y.C., 1978—; mem. N.Y. State Met. Transp. Authority Bd., 1974—; trustee United Mut. Savs. Bank, N.Y.C., 1979—, Phipps Houses, N.Y.C., 1979—; mem. policy bd. N.Y. State Legis. Inst.; mem. bd. overseers Grad. Sch. Mgmt. and Urban Professions, New Sch. Social Research; mem. adv. bd. N.Y.C. Project for Public Spaces, Met. Assn. Urban Designers and Environ. Planners. Trustee, Allaverdy Found., N.Y.C., 1962—, Am. Farm Sch., Thessalonki, Greece, 1963-79, Carnegie Hall, N.Y.C., 1966—, Millbrook (N.Y.) Sch., 1971—, Orange County (N.Y.) Citizens Found., 1974—; bd. dirs. Caramoor Center for Music and Arts, Katonah, N.Y., 1961—, Yorkville Republican Club, 1962—; v.p., bd. dirs. Tolstoy Found., Inc., N.Y.C., 1975—, chmn., 1979; bd. dirs., mem. exec. com. Mid-Hudson Pattern for Progress, Poughkeepsie, N.Y., 1975—; chmn., bd. dirs. Council on Mcpl. Performance, N.Y.C., 1979—. Served to 1st lt. arty. AUS, 1952-54; Korea. Decorated Bronze Star; recipient Honor award Kings County chpt. N.Y. State Soc. Profl. Engrs., 1969, Greater N.Y. council Girl Scouts U.S.A., 1973. Mem. Assn. Bar City N.Y., N.Y. County Lawyers Assn., Am. Bar Assn., N.Y. State Bar Assn., Orange County Bar Assn., AIME, Kent Moot Ct., Phi Delta Phi, Delta Psi. Republican. Eastern Orthodox. Clubs: Century Assn., Knickerbocker, St. Anthony's, Racquet and Tennis (N.Y.C.). Office: 551 Fifth Ave Suite 800 New York NY 10017

SIDBURY, JAMES BUREN, physician; b. Wilmington, N.C., Jan. 13, 1922; s. James Buren and Willie Wellington (Daniel) S.; B.S., Yale U., 1944; M.D., Columbia U., 1947; m. Alice Lucas Rayle, Aug. 29, 1953; children—Anne, Mary, Patricia, James, Robert. Intern, then asst. resident in internal medicine Roosevelt Hosp., N.Y.C., 1947-49;

intern Johns Hopkins Hosp., 1949-50; asst. resident in pediatrics Univ. Hosp., Cleve., 1950-51; with Communicable Disease Center, USPHS, Atlanta, 1951-53; practice medicine specializing in pediatrics, Wilmington, 1953-54; research fellow Johns Hopkins Hosp., 1955-57; asst. prof. Johns Hopkins U. Med. Sch., 1957-61; asso. prof. pediatrics Duke U. Med. Center, 1961-65, prof., 1965—, dir. clin. research unit, 1961-75; on leave as sci. dir. intramural research program Nat. Inst. Child Health and Human Devel., Bethesda, Md., 1975—; cons. Lennox Baker Hosp., Durham; lectr. Johns Hopkins Hosp.; cons. developmental evaluation services for children Montgomery County schs., 1976—. Served with USNR, 1943-45. Recipient Bicentennial medallion in pediatrics Columbia U. Coll. Physicians and Surg., 1967. Mem. Am. Acad. Pediatrics, Am., So. socs. pediatric research, AAAS, Am. Soc. Human Genetics, Am. Pediatric Soc. Contbr. profl. jours. Home: 5200 W Cedar Ln Bethesda MD 20014 Office: NIH NICHD 31/2A-50 Bethesda MD 20014

SIDDIQUI, WASIM AHMAD, microbiologist; b. India, May 10, 1934; s. Abdul Ahad and Waslunnisa Siddiqui; Ph.D., U. Calif., Berkeley, 1961; m. Saltanat Siddiqui, Jan. 24, 1965; children—Jamal, Omar. Research asso. Rockefeller U., N.Y.C., 19 1962-65; instr. Stanford U. Sch. Medicine, 1965-69; asso. prof. U. Hawaii Sch. Medicine, Honolulu, 1969-72, prof., 1972—; cons. Children's Hosp. Honolulu. First v.p. Spl. Edn. Center of Oahu, Honolulu, 1973—. Mem. Am. Soc. Protozoologists, Am. Soc. Parasitologists, Am. Soc. Tropical Medicine and Hygiene. Author book. Contbr. articles to profl. jours. Home: 512 Halemaumau St Honolulu HI 96821 Office: 3675 Kilauea Ave Honolulu HI 96816

SIDEBOTTOM, JOHN HERBERT, electronic co. exec.; b. Montclair, N.J., Sept. 7, 1917; s. Herbert Graf and Ann Nottingham (Stites) S.; B.S. in Mech. Engring., U. Va., 1940; m. Dorothy Gray Winlock, Sept. 19, 1942; children—Richard Winlock, William Jeffrey, David Gray. Engr., Pratt & Whitney div. United Aircraft Corp., 1940-43; asst. tech. dir. Aircraft Industries Assn., 1943-53; v.p. Flight Refueling, Inc., 1953-57; dir. sales Wright aero. div. Curtiss-Wright Corp., 1957-58; exec. v.p. Indsl. Acoustics Corp., 1958-59; v.p. def. electronics products RCA, 1959-70; v.p. Raytheon Co., Lexington, Mass., 1970—. Mem. bd. U. Va. Engring. Found. Asso. fellow Am. Inst. Aeros. and Astronautics (treas.); mem. Nat. Aero. Assn., Armed Forces Communications and Electronics Assn., Assn. U.S. Army. Clubs: Wings (N.Y.C.); Cosmos, Nat. Aviation (Washington); Gibson Island; Congressional Country; New Bedford Yacht. Home: 8321 Persimmon Tree Bethesda MD 20034 Office: Raythen Co 400 Army Navy Dr Arlington VA 22202

SIDELL, WILLIAM, union ofcl.; b. Chgo., May 30, 1915; s. Samuel and Fannie (Freeman) S.; grad. high sch.; m. Frankie Scruggs, Aug. 14, 1936; children—Barton, Gary and Suzann (Mrs. Jerome Cook) (twins). With United Brotherhood of Carpenters and Joiners Am., 1939—, bus. mgr. local 721, Los Angeles, 1948-57, exec. sec., Los Angeles, 1957-63, mem. gen. exec. bd., 1963—, 2d gen. v.p., 1964-69, 1st gen. v.p., 1969-72, gen. pres., 1972—; mem. exec. council AFL-CIO, 1972—, mem. bldg. and constrn. trades dept. exec. council, 1972—; v.p. Calif. Labor Fedn., AFL-CIO, 1958-64; mem. exec. bd. Calif. State and Los Angeles County Bldg. and Constrn. Trades Council, 1957-63; sec. So. Calif. Conf. Carpenters, 1957-63. Mem. Calif. Gov.'s Adv. Commn. on Housing Problems, 1957-63, Mayor's Labor-Mgmt. Com., Los Angeles, 1957-63; mem. Pres.'s Labor-Mgmt. Constrn. Com., 1975—, constrn. adv. com. Fed. Energy Adminstrn., 1975—, labor policy adv. com. trade negotiations, 1975—. Trustee Carpenters Health and Welfare Trust So. Calif., Carpenters Pension Trust So. Calif., Carpenters Joint Apprenticeship Com. Fund So. Calif., Carpenters Vacation Savs. Plan So. Calif. Home: 2301 Glenallan Ave Apt 115 Silver Spring MD 20906 Office: 101 Constitution Ave NW Washington DC 20001

SIDEY, HUGH SWANSON, correspondent; b. Greenfield, Iowa, Sept. 3, 1927; s. Kenneth H. and Alice Margaret (Swanson) S.; B.S., Iowa State U., 1950; m. Alice Anne Trowbridge, Dec. 5, 1953; children—Cynthia Anne, Sandra, Bettina, Edwin. Reporter, Adair County (Iowa) Free Press, 1950, The Nonpareil, Council Bluffs, Iowa, 1950-51, Omaha World-Herald, 1951-55, Life mag., 1955-58; corr. Time mag., 1958—, columnist The Presidency, 1966—, chief Washington Bur., 1969-78, Washington contbg. editor, 1978—. Served with AUS, 1945-46. Author: John F. Kennedy, President, 1963; A Very Personal Presidency, Lyndon Johnson in the White House, 1966; These United States, 1975; Portrait of a President, 1975; co-author: 1,000 Ideas for Better News Pictures, 1956. Contbr. The Kennedy Circle. Office: 888 16th St NW Washington DC 20006

SIDIMUS, JOYSANNE, ballet dancer and tchr.; b. N.Y.C., June 21, 1938; d. Jerome Hillel and Bessie (Brodsky) S.; student Barnard Coll., 1955-57, Sch. Am. Ballet, 1946-58; studied with Robert Joffrey, also Am. Ballet Theatre Sch.; m. John Hugh Selleck, June 8, 1975; 1 dau., Anya Janine. Dancer corps de ballet N.Y. City Ballet, 1958-63; soloist London's Festival Ballet, London, Eng., 1963; prin. dancer Nat. Ballet Can., Toronto, Ont., 1963-68; prin. dancer Pa. Ballet Co., Phila., 1968-70; staged George Balanchine's ballet Serenade, 1969, 75; tchr. Nat. Ballet Sch., Toronto, summer 1966; tchr. Pa. Ballet Sch., Phila., 1969-70, Mary Anthony Dance Studio, N.Y.C., 1970-71; tchr. ballet Nat. Music Camp, Interlochen, Mich., summer 1969, Dance Theatre Harlem, N.Y.C., 1972, Briansky Saratoga Ballet Centre, Saratoga Springs, N.Y., summers 1972-76; ballet mistress Grand Theatre de Geneva, Geneva, Switzerland, 1971; staged George Balanchine's ballet La Source, 1971; ballet mistress Ballet Repertory Co., N.Y.C., 1973-76; ballet faculty N.C. Sch. Arts, Winston-Salem, 1976—; mem. exec. com. Actor's Equity, Toronto, 1966-68. Mem. Am. Guild Mus. Artists. Jewish. Home: 4720 Hawkedale Dr Winston-Salem NC 27106 Office: care NC Sch of Arts 200 Waughtown St Winston-Salem NC 27101

SIDJAKOV, NICOLAS, designer, illustrator; b. Riga, Latvia, Dec. 16, 1924; s. Nicolas and Lydie (Somac) S.; grad. French Lyceum, Riga, 1940; student l'Ecole des Beaux Arts (Paris), 1946-48; m. Diane M. Sullivan, Oct. 3, 1975; children by previous marriage—Nicolas, Gregory. Freelance designer French movie industry, 1950-55; freelance designer, San Francisco, 1956—; designed, illustrated The Friendly Beasts (Am. Inst. Graphic Arts award for one of 50 best children's books; N.Y. Times award as one of 10 best illustrated children's books of 1958); designed, illustrated Baboushka and the Three Kings (Am. Inst. Graphic Arts, N.Y. Times awards, 1960; Caldecott medal 1961); The Emperor and the Drummer Boy (New York Times award 1962). Recipient awards, certificates of merit San Francisco, Los Angeles, Chgo., Detroit, N.Y. art dirs. clubs exhibits, N.Y. Soc. Illustrators, N.Y. ann., Chgo. ann.; Am. Inst. Graphic Arts award for one of 50 best ads of yr. Mem. San Francisco Soc. Communicating Arts. Home: 114 San Carlos Ave Sausalito CA 94965

SIDMAN, RICHARD LEON, neuroscientist; b. Boston, Sept. 19, 1928; s. Manuel and Annabelle (Seltzer) S.; A.B., Harvard U., 1949, M.D. (Jeffries Wyman scholar), 1953; m. Ljiljana Lekic, Aug. 11, 1974; children—David, Peter. Intern in medicine Boston City Hosp., 1953-54; asst. resident in neurology Mass. Gen. Hosp., Boston, 1955-56; staff scientist NIH, Bethesda, Md., 1956-58; instr. to prof. neuropathology Harvard U. Med. Sch., 1959—, Bullard prof., 1969—; chief dept. neurosci. Children's Hosp. Med. Center, Boston, 1972—; 1st Richard Stearns Meml. lectr. Albert Einstein Coll. Medicine, 1958; Bailey Meml. lectr. U. Sask. (Can.), 1978; Waisman Meml. lectr. U. Wis.; mem. sci. adv. com. Nat. Paraplegia Found., Retinitis Pigmentosa Found.; bd. sci. overseers Jackson Lab., Bar Harbor, Maine. Served with USPHS, 1956-58. Recipient Soma Weiss student research prizes Harvard U. Med. Sch., 1951-53, Boylston Soc. Essay prize, 1953; Harvard U. Mosley Travelling fellow, 1954-55; Neuroscis. Research Program fellow, 1971-79. Fellow Am. Acad. Arts and Scis., Nat. Acad. Sci.; mem. Am. Acad. Neurology, AAAS, Am. Assn. Anatomists, Am. Assn. Neuropathologists, Am. Soc. Cell Biology, Histochem. Soc., Soc. Developmental Biology, Soc. Neurosci., Tissue Culture Assn. Author: (with M. Sidman) Neuroanatomy - A Programmed Text, vol. 1, 1965; (with others) Catalog of the Neurological Mutants of the Mouse, 1965; (with R.D. Adams) Introduction to Neuropathology, 1968; (with others) Atlas of the Mouse Brain and Spinal Cord, 1971; contbr. numerous articles, book chpts., revs. on neuroembryology, pathology, and genetics to profl. jours. Office: Dept Neurosci Children's Hosp Med Center 300 Longwood Ave Boston MA 02115

SIDNEY, GEORGE, motion picture dir.; b. Long Island City, N.Y., Oct. 4, 1916; s. Louis K. and Hazael (Mooney) S.; ed. pub. and pvt. schs.; m. Jane Robinson, Mar. 22, 1978. Messenger boy Metro-Goldwyn-Mayer Pictures, Hollywood, Calif., 1933-34, prodn. dept. workman, 1934, sound technician, 1934-35, film editor, 1935, asst. dir., 1935-36, test dir., 1936, short subjects dir., 1936-41, dir., 1941. Productions include Free and Easy, 1941; Pacific Rendezvous, 1942; Pilot No. 5, 1942; Thousands Cheer, 1943; Bathing Beauty, 1944; Anchors Aweigh, 1945; The Harvey Girls, 1945; Holiday in Mexico, 1946; Cass Timberlane, 1947; The Three Muskeeters, 1948; The Red Danube, 1949; Key to the City, 1949, Annie Get Your Gun, 1949, Show Boat, 1950, Scaramouche, 1951, Young Bess, 1952, Kiss Me Kate, 1953, Jupiters Darling, 1954, The Eddie Duchin Story, 1955, Jeanne Eagels, 1957, Pal Joey, 1957, Who Was That Lady, 1960; Pepe, 1960; Bye Bye Birdie, 1963, A Ticklish Affair, 1963, Viva Las Vegas, 1963, Half a Sixpence, 1968, The Swinger, 1966 Who Has Seen the Wind? Mem. exec. bd., past pres. Dirs. Guild Am. Received Acad. award for short subjects, Quicker'n A Wink, 1940, Of Pups and Puzzles, 1941. Recipient citation USAF, 1951. Mem. Motion Picture Assn. Am. (mem. prodn. code review bd.), Screen Producers Guild.*

SIDNEY, SYLVIA (KOSSOW, SOPHIA), actress; b. N.Y.C., Aug. 8, 1910; d. Victor and Rebecca (Saperstein) Kossow; attended N.Y.C. pub. schs.; attended Theater Guild Sch., 1925; m. Bennett Alfred Cerf, 1935 (div.); m. 2nd Luther Adler, 1938 (div.); 1 son, Jacob L.; m. 3rd Carlton Alsop, 1945 (div.). Made stage debut starring in Prunella at the Garrick theater, 1926; subsequent stage appearances include: The Challenge of Youth, Washington, 1926, The Squall, N.Y.C., 1927, Crime, 1927, Mirrors, 1928, The Breaks, 1928, The Gods of the Lightning, 1928, Nice Women, N.Y.C., 1929, Cross-Roads, 1929, Many a Slip, 1930, Bad Girl, 1930, To Quito and Back, N.Y.C., 1937, Pygmalion, 1938, The Gentle People, N.Y.C., 1939, Accent on Youth, 1941, Angel Street, 1942, 64, Pygmalion, 1943, Joan of Lorraine, 1947, Kind Lady, 1948, The Two Mrs. Carrolls, 1949, Pygmalion, 1949, O Mistress Mine, 1949, Goodbye My Fancy, 1950, Anne of the Thousand Days, 1950, Innocents, Black Chiffon, 1951, The Gypsies Wore High Hats, 1952, The Fourposter, 1952, A Very Special Baby, 1956, Auntie Mame, 1958, Enter Laughing, 1963, Silver Cord, 1964, Kind Lady, 1964, Come Blow Your Horn, 1968-69, Vieux Carré, Sabrina Fair; appearances in Nat. Repertory Theatre plays includes: Mad Woman of Chaillot-NRT, The Rivals, 1965-66, The Little Foxes, 1966, The Importance of Being Earnest, 1966, She Stoops to Conquer, 1968; appeared on Broadway in Bad Girl, The Gentle People, Nice Women, Crossroads; film career began in 1930; movie appearances include: An American Tragedy, Street Scene, Dead End, You Only Live Once, Sabotage, Accent on Youth, Mary Burns, Fugitive, Fury, Dead End, Through Different Eyes, City Streets, Confessions of a Co-ed, Ladies of the Big House, The Miracle Man, Merrily We Go to Hell, Madam Butterfly, Pick Up, Jennie Gerhardt, You and Me, The Wagons Roll at Night, Blood on the Sun, Love From a Stranger, Mr. Ace, Searching Wind, Trail of the Lonesome Pine, Les Miserables, Violent Saturday, Behind the High Wall, Summer Wishes, Winter Dreams (Acad. award nominee for best supporting actress), Demon, I Never Promised You A Rose Garden, You Only Live Once, Accent on Youth, 30 Day Princess, Behold My Wife, Sabotage, 1/3 of a Nation, Damien: Omen 2; TV appearances include: Schlitz Playhouse of Stars, Tales of Tomorrow, Lux Video Theatre, Broadway TV Theatre, Ford Theatre, Philco Playhouse, Kraft Theatre, Climax, Star Stage, Playwrights '56, 20th Century-Fox Hour, Playhouse 90, G. E. Theatre, June Allyson Show, Naked City, Route 66, Defenders, Eleventh Hour, Yom Kippur Special, Nurses, My Three Sons; TV movies: Do Not Fold, Spindle, or Mutilate, Siege, Catch My Boy on Sunday. Author: Sylvia Sidney's Needlepoint Book, 1968; The Sylvia Sidney Question and Answer Book on Needlepoint, 1975. Office: care John Springer 667 Madison Ave New York NY 10021

SIDRANSKY, HERSCHEL, pathologist; b. Pensacola, Fla., Oct. 17, 1925; s. Ely and Touba (Bear) S.; B.S., Tulane U., 1948, M.D., 1953, M.S., 1958; m. Evelyn Lipsitz, Aug. 18, 1952; children—Ellen, David Ira. Intern, Charity Hosp. La., New Orleans, 1953-54, vis. asst. pathologist, 1954-58; practice medicine, specializing in pathology, Washington, 1977—; pathologist Nat. Cancer Inst., NIH, Bethesda, Md., 1958-61; instr. pathology Tulane U., 1954-58; prof. pathology U. Pitts., 1961-72; prof., chmn. dept. pathology U. South Fla., Tampa, 1972-77; prof., chmn. dept. pathology George Washington U., 1977—; cons. VA Hosp. and Children's Hosp., Washington. Served with AUS, 1944-46. Life Ins. Med. Research fellow, 1956-57; USPHS fellow, 1957-58, 67-68; NIH research grantee, 1961—. Diplomate Am. Bd. Pathology. Mem. Am. Assn. Pathologists, Soc. Exptl. Biology and Medicine, Am. Assn. Cancer Research, Am. Inst. Nutrition, Am. Soc. Clin. Nutrition, Internat. Acad. Pathologists, Med. Mycology Soc. of Americas, Reticuloendothelial Soc., N.Y. Acad. Scis., AAAS, Washington Acad. Medicine, Washington Soc. Pathologists, Sigma Xi. Jewish. Mem. editorial bd. Jour. Nutrition, 1973-77, Cancer Research, 1974-77, Human Pathology, 1979—, Am. Jour. Clin. Nutrition, 1979—; contbr. articles to med. jours. Home: 5144 Macomb St NW Washington DC 20016 Office: 2300 Eye St NW Washington DC 20037

SIEBEN, HARRY ALBERT, JR., lawyer, state legislator; b. Hastings, Minn., Nov. 24, 1943; s. Harry A. and Mary S. (Luger) S.; B.A., Winona State Coll., 1965; J.D., U. Minn., 1968; m. Wanda Kay Alphin, Aug. 21, 1971; children—Jeffrey Scott, Thomas Allan. Admitted to Minn. bar, 1968; since practiced in Mpls.; mem. firm Grose, Von Holtum, Sieben & Schmidt, Ltd. Mem. Minn. Ho. of Reps., 1971—. Served with AUS, 1968. Democrat. Home: 90 Valley Ln Hastings MN 55033 Office: 371 State Office Bldg St Paul MN 55155

SIEBEN, HORST OTTO, mfg. co. exec.; b. Neustadt, Germany, Oct. 25, 1938; s. Jakob and Rita (Ohlenschlaeger) S.; came to U.S., 1959, naturalized, 1962; M.B.A., Johannes Gutenberg U., Mainz, Germany, 1962; m. Billiee J. Bemis, Oct. 29, 1958; children—Jeffrey Scott, Jody Sue. Financial mgmt. trainee Gen. Electric Co., Sowersworth, N.H., 1962-66; mgr. financial reporting Pa. R.R. Co., Phila., 1966-68; with Nashua Corp. (N.H.), 1968—, internat. comptroller, 1973—. Home: East Rd Greenfield NH 03047 Office: 44 Franklin St Nashua NH 03060

SIEBENTHALER, HAROLD JACOB, lawyer; b. Cin., Oct. 23, 1892; s. Louis F. and Mollie (Mohlenhoff) S.; J.D., Salmon P. Chase Coll. Law, Cin., 1914, LL.D.; m. Florence Burkhardt, Mar. 20, 1920; 1 dau., Phyllis A. (Mrs. William H. Hopple, Jr.). Admitted to Ohio bar, 1914, since practiced in Cin.; counsel firm Frost & Jacobs, 1915—; dir. Witt Co., Charles V. Maescher & Co., Inc., W.A. Natorp Co., Inc., F.F. Co. Former pres., trustee Salmon P. Chase Coll. Law. Mem. Am., Ohio, Cin. bar assns. Clubs: Cincinnati Country, Queen City, Cincinnati, Cin. Rotary, Masons (33 deg.), Shriners. Home: 3666 Willowlea Ct Cincinnati OH 45208 Office: Central Trust Center Cincinnati OH 45202

SIEBER, HARRY CHARLES, educator; b. Oklahoma City, Oct. 4, 1941; s. Richard Teller and Marilyn Mae S.; student San Bernardino Valley Coll., 1959-60; B.A., Baylor U., 1963; Ph.D., Duke U., 1967; m. Claudia Winn, 1963; 1 dau., Diane Elizabeth. Asst. prof. Romance langs. Johns Hopkins U., Balt., 1967-73, asso. prof., 1973-76, prof., 1976—. Woodrow Wilson fellow (hon.), 1963; NDEA fellow, 1963-66; Woodrow Wilson fellow, 1966-67; Guggenheim Found. fellow, 1979. Mem. MLA, Am. Assn. Tchrs. Spanish and Portuguese, Asociación Internacional de Hispanistas. Author: The Picaresque, 1977; Language and Society in La vida de Lazarillo de Tormes, 1978; co-editor Modern Lang. Notes, 1967—. Office: Johns Hopkins Univ Baltimore MD 21218

SIEBER, ROY, educator; b. Shawano, Wis., Apr. 28, 1923; s. Roy L. and Margaret (Collard) S.; B.A., New Sch. Social Research, 1949; M.A., State U. Iowa, 1951, Ph.D., 1957; m. Sophia Yeran, June 10, 1950; children—Mark, Thyne, Ellen, Matthew. Instr., then asst. prof. art history State U. Iowa 1950-62; mem. faculty Ind. U., 1962—, prof. art history, 1964—, Rudy prof. fine arts, 1974—, chmn. fine arts dept., 1967-70; vis. prof. U. Ghana (W. Africa), 1964, 67; vis. research prof. U. Ife (Nigeria), 1971; Benedict distinguished vis. prof. Carleton Coll., 1976-77; curator primitive art Ind. U. Art Mus., 1962—. Mem. primitive art adv. com. Met. Mus.; mem. joint com. Africa, Am. Council Learned Socs.-Social Sci. Research Council, 1962-71; mem. fgn. area fellowship program Africa Screening Com., 1959-63. Cons. Mus. African Art, Washington. Fgn. Area Fellowship Program postdoctoral grantee, 1957-58; African-Am. Univs. grantee, 1964; Ind. U. Internat. Studies grantee, 1964, 67; sr. fellowship Nat. Endowment for Humanities, 1970-71. Mem. Royal Anthrop. Inst., African Studies Assn. (chmn. arts and humanities com. 1963), Coll. Art Assn., AAUP. Author monograph, articles, exhbns., books on African art. Home: 114 Glenwood Ave E Bloomington IN 47401

SIEBERS, JACK ALAN, ins. co. exec.; b. East Grand Rapids, Mich., Nov. 12, 1941; s. Herman and Grace (Sluiter) S.; A.B., Hope Coll., 1963; J.D., U. Mich., 1966; M.B.A., Western Mich. U., 1974; m. Mary B. Sagendorf, Feb. 15, 1963; children—Jennifer Beth, Jonathan Jack. Admitted to Mich. bar, 1966; asso. firm Varnum, Riddering, Wierengo & Christenson, Grand Rapids, 1966-69; corporate atty. Foremost Ins. Co., Grand Rapids, 1969—, v.p., sec., 1975—; v.p., sec. parent co. Foremost Corp. Am., 1975—. Bd. dirs. Jellema House, Grand Rapids, 1974-77; sec., trustee Fifth Reformed Ch., Grand Rapids, 1975-77. Mem. Mich., Grand Rapids bar assns., Lowell Area Arts Council. Clubs: Rotary (Lowell, Mich.); Charlevoix Athletic; Macatawa Bay Yacht. Home: 706 Riverside Dr Lowell MI 49331 Office: 5800 Foremost Dr SE PO Box 2450 Grand Rapids MI 49501

SIEBERT, CALVIN D., economist, educator; b. Hillsboro, Kans., Feb. 11, 1934; s. Ira and Margaret (Everett) S.; B.A., U. Kans., 1958, M.A., 1960; Ph.D. in Econs., U. Calif., Berkeley, 1966; m. Valerie Dawn Nanninga, Feb. 18, 1960; children—Douglas Erik, Derek Christopher. Asst. prof. econs. U. Iowa, 1965-68, asso. prof., 1968-75, prof., 1975—, chmn. dept., 1969-71, 75-79; Rockefeller Found. vis. asso. prof. U. Philippines, 1971-72. Served with U.S. Army, 1954-56. Ford Found. grantee, 1964-65. Mem. Am. Econ. Assn., AAUP, Phi Beta Kappa. Contbr. articles to profl. jours. Home: 341 N 7th Ave Iowa City IA 52240 Office: 663 Phillips Hall Dept Econs Univ of Iowa Iowa City IA 52242

SIEBERT, MURIEL, state ofcl.; b. Cleve.; d. Irwin J. and Margaret Eunice (Roseman) Siebert; student Western Res. U., 1949-52; D.C.S. (hon.), St. John's U., St. Bonaventure U. Security analyst Bache & Co., 1954-57; analyst Utilities & Industries Mgmt. Corp., 1958, Shields & Co., 1959-60; partner Stearns & Co., 1961, Finkle & Co., 1962-65, Brimberg & Co., N.Y.C., 1965-67; chmn., pres. Muriel Siebert & Co., Inc., 1969-77; trustee Manhattan Savs. Bank, 1975-77; supt. banks dept. banking State of N.Y., 1977—; dir. Urban Devel. Corp., N.Y.C., 1977—, Job Devel. Authority, N.Y.C., 1977—, State of N.Y. Mortgage Agy., 1977—; first woman mem. N.Y. Stock Exchange; asso. in mgmt. Simmons Coll.; guest lectr. numerous colls. Mem. women's adv. com. Econ. Devel. Adminstrn., N.Y.C.; trustee Manhattan Coll.; v.p., mem. exec. com. Greater N.Y. Area council Boy Scouts Am.; mem. N.Y. State Econ. Devel. Bd., N.Y. Council of Economy. Clubs: Wings (dir., chmn. finance com.) Sales Executives (dir., v.p.) (N.Y.C.). Home: 435 E 52d St New York NY 10022 Office: Two World Trade Center New York NY 10047

SIEBERT, WILLIAM MCCONWAY, educator; b. Pitts., Nov. 19, 1925; s. Charles Theodore, Jr. and Isabel (McConway) S.; S.B., Mass. Inst. Tech., 1943, Sc.D., 1952; m. Anne Decker, Sept. 10, 1949; children—Charles R. (dec.), Thomas McC., Peter W., Terry A., Theodore D. Jr. engr. Westinghouse Research Labs., 1946- 47; group leader Lincoln Lab., Mass. Inst. Tech., 1953-55, mem. faculty, 1952—, prof. elec. engring., 1963—; cons. to govt. and industry, 1952—. Served with USNR, 1943-46. Fellow I.E.E.E.; mem. Acoustical Soc. Am., Sigma Xi, Tau Beta Pi, Eta Kappa Nu. Research in applications of communication theory to radar and biol. systems. Home: 40 Martha's Point Rd Concord MA 01742 Office: 77 Massachusetts Ave Cambridge MA 02139

SIEBRING, BARTELD RICHARD, educator; b. George, Iowa, Sept. 24, 1924; s. Richard and Katie (Snuttjer) S.; B.A., Macalester Coll., 1947; B.S., U. Minn., 1948, M.S., 1949; Ph.D., Syracuse U., 1953. Instr. Worthington (Minn.) Jr. Coll., 1948-50; asst. prof. Wis. State Coll. at Milw., 1953-56; asso. prof. U. Wis.-Milw., 1956-62, prof. chemistry, 1962—. Served with USNR, 1944-46. Mem. Am. Chem. Soc., History Sci. Soc., Nat. Assn. Research in Tchg., Math. Assn. Am., Phi Kappa Phi. Author: Chemistry, 1967; Chemistry: A Comprehensive Laboratory Course, 1970; (with Mary Ellen Schaff) Chemistry: A Basic Approach, 1972, Japanese edit., 1974. Contbr. articles to profl. jours. Home: 12808 N Colony Dr Mequon WI 53092

SIECKMAN, WALTER, indsl. mfg. and engring. co. exec.; b. Duesseldorf, Ger., July 6, 1931; came to U.S., 1958; s. Heinrich and Erni (Neschen) S.; M.S. in Metallurgy, Tech. Hochschule Aachen, 1958; m. Edith Erdelyi, July 28, 1956; children—Michael, Martin. Metallurgist, Crucible Steel Co., 1958-59; project engr., dir. vacuum process dept. Lectromelt Corp., 1959-65, pres., 1967-69; exec. v.p. Heraeus-Engelhard Co., 1965-67; sr. v.p. Pa. Engring. Corp., 1967-69, exec. v.p., chief operating officer, 1969—; also dir.; dir. Birdsboro Corp. Mem. Am. Iron and Steel Inst., Am. Iron and Steel Engrs., AIME. Clubs: Duquesne, Univ. (Pitts.); St. Clair Country (Upper St.

Clair, Pa.). Home: 2387 Morrow Rd Pittsburgh PA 15241 Office: PO Box 4055 32d St at AVRR Pittsburgh PA 15201. *My father used to say, "Whatever you have in your head, nobody can take away." I believe one of man's greatest assets is his natural curiosity. Once you lose the drive to learn, to understand, to explore, you are dead mentally and physically.*

SIECKMANN, EVERETT FREDERICK, physicist; b. Tobias, Nebr., Dec. 31, 1928; s. Frederick W. and Ruth E. (Shafer) S.; B.A., Doane Coll., 1950; M.S., Fla. State U., 1952; Ph.D., Cornell U., 1960; m. Lois L. Rippe, Aug. 28, 1951; children—Sharlene K., Christine E. Asst. prof. physics U. Ky., 1957-62; prof. U. Idaho, Moscow, 1962—; vis. prof. physics U. Calif., Berkeley, 1976-77; cons. USAF Holloman AFB, N.Mex., 1962-63. Mem. Am. Phys. Soc., Am. Assn. Physics Tchrs. Club: Elks. Home: 509 S Polk St Moscow ID 83843

SIEFERT, RUSSELL EUGENE, investment banker; b. Belleville, Ill., May 18, 1907; s. Julius H. and Anna B. S.; B.A., Northwestern U., 1931; m. Dorothy Stowell, May 2, 1936; children—Peter, Jane. Trader, First Boston Corp., N.Y.C., 1931-38; exec. v.p. Stern Bros. & Co., Kansas City, Mo., 1938—, also dir. Episcopalian. Clubs: Univ. (Kansas City); Mission Hills Country (Shawnee Mission, Kans.). Home: 2402 W 70 Terr Shawnee Mission KS 66208 Office: 9 W 10th St Kansas City MO 64199

SIEGAL, ALLAN MARSHALL, newspaper editor; b. N.Y.C., May 1, 1940; s. Irving and Sylvia Norma (Wrubel) S.; grad. N.Y. U., 1962; m. Gretchen M-P. Leefmans, May 31, 1977. With New York Times, 1960—, editor Pentagon Papers, 1971, asst. fgn. editor, 1971-76, asst. to exec. editor in charge newsroom automation, 1976-77, news editor, 1977—; tchr. journalism N.Y. U., 1966, Columbia U., 1967-69. Office: 229 W 43d St New York NY 10036

SIEGAL, JACOB J., mgmt. and fin. cons.; b. Phila., Apr. 4, 1929; s. Louis and Henrietta (Greenberg) S.; B.S., Temple U., 1951, LL.B., 1954; postgrad. U. Chgo., 1973; m. Dolores Berg, June 8, 1952; children—Marla, Karen, Leslie. Admitted to Pa. bar, 1955, Ill. bar, 1973; with City of Phila., 1954-61, chief counselor, 1959-61, dep. city solicitor, 1958-61; pvt. practice law, partner firm Meltzer & Schiffrin, Phila., 1961-72; v.p., gen. counsel, dir. Bluebird Inc., Phila., 1972-74, exec. v.p., 1974-78, pres., 1978-79, chmn., chief exec. officer, 1979—. Mem. Am. Bar Assn., Am. Soc. Corp. Secs., Am. Meat Inst. (dir., conv. speaker 1978). Home: 600 Fairview Rd Narberth PA 19072 Office: 301 City Line Bala Cynwyd PA 19004

SIEGAN, BERNARD HERBERT, lawyer; b. Chgo., July 28, 1924; s. David and Jeannette (Seitz) S.; student Herzl. Jr. Coll., Chgo., 1943, 46, Roosevelt Coll., Chgo., 1946-47; J.D., U. Chgo., 1949; m. Sharon Goldberg, June 15, 1952. Admitted to Ill. bar, 1950, practiced in Chgo.; partner firm Siegan & Karlin, 1952-73. Pres., sec. various small corps. and gen. partner in partnerships engaged in real estate ownership and devel., 1955-70; weekly columnist Freedom newspaper chain, other papers, 1973—; cons. law and econs. program U. Chgo. Law Sch., 1970-73; adj. prof. law U. San Diego Law Sch., 1973-74, prof., 1974-75, distinguished prof., 1975—; cons. windfalls and wipeouts project HUD, 1973-74. Served with AUS, 1943-46. Research fellow law and econs. U. Chgo. Law Sch., 1968-69; Urban Land Inst. research fellow, 1976—; recipient Leander J. Monks Meml. Fund award Inst. Humane Studies, 1972. Mem. Am., Chgo. bar assns., Am. Judicature Soc. Author: Land Use Without Zoning, 1972; Other People's Property, 1976; also numerous articles on zoning and land use regulation. Editor: Planning without Prices, 1977; The Interaction of Economics and the Law, 1977; Regulation, Economics and the Law, 1977; Government, Regulation and the Economy, 1980. Home: 6005 Camino de la Costa LaJolla CA 92037

SIEGEL, ALAN MICHAEL, communications and design cons.; b. N.Y.C., Aug. 26, 1938; s. Eugene and Ruth S.; B.S., Cornell U., 1960; m. Gloria Fern Mendel, Nov. 6, 1965; 1 dau., Stacey Ruth. Account exec., sec. new products devel. group Batten, Barton, Durstine and Osborn, N.Y.C., 1964-67; account exec. Ruder & Finn Inc., N.Y.C., 1967-68; account exec. Sandgren & Murtha Inc., N.Y.C., 1968-69; pres. Siegel & Gale Inc., N.Y.C., 1969—; adj. asso. prof. Fordham U. Sch. Law; adj. asso. prof., co-dir. Communications Design Center, Carnegie-Mellon U.; mem. exec. com. document design project Nat. Inst. Edn. Mem. Soc. Consumer Affairs Profls. in Bus., Internat. Assn. Bus. Communicators, Am. Bus. Communication Assn., Indsl. Communications Council, N.Y.C. C. of C. Club: N.Y. Athletic. Author: Simplified Consumer Credit Forms; contbr. to Drafting Documents in Plain English, 1979; contbr. articles to profl. jours. Office: Siegel & Gale Inc 445 Park Ave New York NY 10022

SIEGEL, ALBERTA ENGVALL (MRS. SIDNEY SIEGEL), educator; b. Pasadena, Calif., Feb. 24, 1931; d. Albert and Portia (Powers) Engvall; B.A., Stanford, 1951, M.A., 1954, Ph.D., 1955; m. Sidney Siegel, July 31, 1954 (dec. 1961). Faculty, Pa. State U., 1955-63; faculty Stanford, 1963—, prof. psychology in psychiatry, 1969—, asso. dean undergrad. studies, 1971. Fellow Center Advanced Study Behavioral Scis., 1961-63; mem. research scientist devel. com. NIMH, 1965-69, mem. panel research consultants to dir., research task force, 1973; mem. sci. adv. com. on TV and social behavior U.S. Surgeon Gen., 1969-71; mem. growth and devel. research and tng. com. Nat. Inst. Child Health and Human Devel., 1972-76; mem. adv. com. on ethical and human value implications of sci. and tech. NSF, 1973-76; dir. Gt. Western Fin. Corp.; mem. developmental problems research rev. com. NIMH, 1977—. Bd. dirs. Population Edn., 1974—; bd. visitors Learning Research and Devel. Center, U. Pitts., 1975—. Fellow Am. Psychol. Assn. (pres. div. developmental psychology 1973-74); mem. Soc. Research Child Devel. (governing council), A.A.A.S., Phi Beta Kappa, Sigma Xi. Democrat. Club: Stanford Faculty (pres., 1973-74). Editor: Child Development, 1964-68. Contbr. articles to profl. jours. Home: 1850 Willow Rd Palo Alto CA 94304 Office: Dept Psychiatry and Behavioral Scis Stanford U Sch Medicine Stanford CA 94305

SIEGEL, ARTHUR, corp. exec.; b. N.Y.C., July 4, 1908; s. Louis and Helena (Kaufman) S.; B.S., N.Y. U., 1930; m. Mirian Bierman, Sept. 3, 1939; children—Barbara Joan Siegel Frankfort, Louise Susan Siegel Riordan. Vice pres. Congress Financial Corp., N.Y.C., 1963-68; v.p., dir. Commonwealth United Corp., Chgo., 1969—; pres., dir. Williams Electronics Inc., Chgo., 1969—; sr. v.p., dir. Seeburg Corp., Chgo., 1968—; sr. v.p., dir. Inland Credit Corp., N.Y.C., 1953-63; v.p., dir. Indsl. Equipment Credit Corp., N.Y., 1948-53. Home: 437 Golden Isles Dr Hallandale FL 33009 Office: 1500 N Dayton Chicago IL 60622

SIEGEL, BENJAMIN M., educator; b. Superior, Wis., Mar. 26, 1916; s. Aaron and Pauline (Josephs) S.; B.S., Mass. Inst. Tech., 1938, Ph.D., 1940; m. Rachel Josefowitz, June 15, 1944; children—Charles E., H. Barry, Ruth V. Vis. fellow Calif. Inst. Tech., 1940-41; research asso. Mass. Inst. Tech., 1941-42, 44-46, 48-49, Harvard, 1942-44; asso. Weizman Inst. Sci., 1946-48; asso. prof. engring. physics Cornell U., Ithaca, N.Y., 1949-59, prof. applied and engring. physics, 1959—; vis. prof. exptl. physics Hebrew U., Jerusalem, Israel, 1962-63; vis. fellow Salk Inst. Biol. Studies, La Jolla, Calif., 1971. Mem. Nat. Council Joint Dist. Com. Mem. Am. Assn. Jewish Edn., Am. Friends Hebrew U., Am. Jewish Congress. Am. Jewish League for Israel, Electron Microscopy Soc. Am. (pres. 1973, past dir.), Am. Phys. Soc., Optical Soc. Am., Am. Vacuum Soc., Biophys. Soc., A.A.A.S., Fedn. Am. Scientists, Sigma Xi, Sigma Alpha Mu. Jewish (trustee temple). Author: Modern Developments in Electron Microscopy, 1964. Editor: Physical Aspects of Electron Microscopy and Microbeam Analysis, 1975. Research in high resolution electron microscopy, image processing, submicron fabrication with electron and ion beams. Home: 203 Forest Dr Ithaca NY 14850 Office: Clark Hall Cornell U Ithaca NY 14853

SIEGEL, BERNARD JOSEPH, educator; b. Superior, Wis., Oct. 26, 1917; s. Elias and Evelyn (Aronsohn) S.; A.B., Harvard U., 1939; M.A., U. Chgo., 1941, Ph.D., 1943; m. Charlotte Brest, May 21, 1942; children—Eve Linda, Paul Jeffrey. Research asso. Yale, 1942-44; instr. Bklyn. Coll., 1944-46; asst. prof. anthropology U. Wyo., 1946-47; asst. prof. Stanford, 1947-49; asso. prof., 1949-55, prof., 1955—, head dept. anthropology, 1961-64, dir. Center for Latin Am. Studies, 1972-75. field work, Taos Pueblo, N.Mex., 1947, Brazil, 1950-51, 66-67, Mountain View, Calif., 1951, 52, Portugal, 1954-55, Italy, 1972-73; Picturis Pueblo, 1957-60. Research fellow Coordinator Inter-Am. Affairs, 1942-44; Social Sci. Research Council faculty research fellow, 1953-56. Mem. Anthrop. Assn., Am. Anthrop. Assn., Am. Sociological Soc., Latin Am. Studies Assn. AAAS, Phi Beta Kappa, Sigma Xi. Author: Slavery During the Third Dynasty of Ur, 1947; Acculturation Critical Abstracts, 1955; Ann. Review of Anthropology; also sci. papers and critical rev.; co-author: Divisiveness and Social Conflict, 1966; To See Ourselves: Anthropology and Modern Issues, 1973. Home: 853 Mayfield Ave Stanford CA 94305 Office: Stanford U Stanford CA 94305

SIEGEL, DAVID DONALD, lawyer; b. Bklyn., Oct. 18, 1931; s. Harry Wilbur and Ida Claire (Scharaga) S.; B.A., Bklyn. Coll., 1953; J.D., St. John's U., 1958; LL.M., N.Y. U., 1964; m. Rosemarie Ann Duffy, Dec. 21, 1969; children—Sheela Nell, Rachel Ann. Admitted to N.Y. bar, 1958; law sec. to chief judge N.Y. Ct. Appeals, 1958-59; practiced law, N.Y.C., 1960-62; asst. prof. law St. John's U., 1962-65, asso. prof., 1965-67, prof., 1967-72, vis. prof., 1972—; prof. Albany Law Sch., 1972—; vis. prof. N.Y. U., 1967-70, SUNY, Buffalo, 1971-72, Cornell U., 1978; adv., cons. on procedure Am. Arbitration Assn.; chmn. adv. com. on civil practice N.Y. State Jud. Conf. Served with U.S. Army, 1953-55. Mem. Am. Law Inst., Am. Bar Assn., N.Y. State Bar Assn., Assn. Bar City N.Y. Democrat. Jewish. Author: New York Practice, 1978; author Practising Law Inst. monographs on conflict of laws, fed. jurisdiction and practice; ann. commentaries N.Y. civil practice McKinney's Consol. Laws N.Y.; editor N.Y. State Law Digest, 1977—; draftsman N.Y. Appellate Div. Handbook, 1978. Office: Albany Law Sch 80 New Scotland Ave Albany NY 12208

SIEGEL, DON, film dir.; b. Chgo., Oct. 26, 1912; ed. Jesus Coll. Cambridge (Eng.) U.; m. Doe Avedon. Films include Hitler Lives, 1945, Star in the Night, 1945, The Verdict, 1946, Night unto Night, 1948, The Big Steel, 1949, Duel at Silver Creek, 1952, No Time for Flowers, 1952, Count the Hours, 1953, China Venture, 1954, Riot in Cell Block Eleven, 1954, Private Hell, 36, 1954, An Annapolis Story, 1955, Invasion of the Body Snatchers, 1956, Crime in the Streets, 1956, Baby-Face Nelson, 1957, Spanish Affair, 1958, The Line-up, 1958, The Gun Runners, 1958, Hound-Dog Man, 1959, Edge of Eternity, 1959, Flaming Star, 1960, Hell is for Heroes, 1962, The Killers, 1964, The Hanged Man, 1965, Madigan, 1967, Coogan's Bluff, 1968, Two Mules for Sister Sara, 1969, The Beguiled, 1970, Dirty Harry, 1971, Charley Varrick, 1973, Black Windmill, 1974, The Shootist, 1976, Telefon, 1977, Escape From Alcatraz, 1979; dir., actor Play Misty for Me, 1971; actor Invasion of the Body Snatchers, 1978 (remake); appeared with Royal Acad. Dramatic Arts, London, Contemporary Theatre Group, Hollywood, Calif. Recipient Acad. awards (2) for shorts, 1945. Address: care Leonard Hirshon William Morris Agency 151 El Camino Dr Beverly Hills CA 90212*

SIEGEL, HERBERT BERNARD, co. exec.; b. N.Y.C., Mar. 10, 1934; s. Jacob and Clara Dora (Goldgeier) S.; B.S., N.Y. U., 1959, postgrad. in bus., 1960-63; postgrad. in bus. Harvard U., 1975; m. Joan Miriam Goodkin, Nov. 6, 1955; children—Jeffrey Roy, Lori Robin, Amy Hope, Jonathan Stuart. With William Iselin & Co., Inc., N.Y.C., 1957-67; asst. v.p., treas. Bates Mfg. Co., Inc., N.Y.C., 1968; pres. Emie Industries, Inc., N.Y.C., 1968-72; pres., chief exec. officer, fed. trustee Interstate Stores, Inc., N.Y.C., 1973-78; pres. Nat. Silver Co., N.Y.C., 1978—, F.B. Rogers Silver Co., N.Y.C., 1978—; trustee, chmn. mortgage rev. com. Dime Savs. Bank of Williamsburg, N.Y.C.; thesis examiner Grad. Sch. Banking, Rutgers U., 1963-64; lectr. Grad. Sch. Mgmt. and Orgn., Yale U. Bd. dirs. United Cerebral Palsy, Nassau, N.Y. Served with AUS, 1955-57. Mem. N.Y. U. Club, Prime Raters Financial Club (pres.). Home: 515 E Bay Dr Long Beach NY 11561 Office: 241 Fifth Ave New York NY 10011

SIEGEL, HERBERT JAY, mfg. co. exec.; b. Phila., May 7, 1928; s. Jacob and Fritzi (Stern) S.; B.A., Lehigh U., 1950; m. Ann F. Levy, June 29, 1950; children—John C., William D. Sec., dir. Official Films, Inc., N.Y.C., 1950-55; v.p., dir. Bev-Rich Products, Inc., Phila., 1955-56; v.p., dir. Westley Industries, Inc., Cleve., 1955-58, Phila. Ice Hockey Club, Inc., 1955-60; chmn. bd. Fort Pitt Industries, Inc., Pitts., 1956-58, Seeburg Corp., 1958-60, Centlivre Brewing Corp., Ft. Wayne, Ind., 1950—, Baldwin-Montrose Chem. Co.; pres. Gen. Artists Corp., 1963-65; chmn. bd., pres. Chris-Craft Industries, Inc., 1967—; dir. Baldwin Rubber Co., Pontiac, Mich., Mono-Sol Corp., Gary, Inc., Piper Aircraft Corp., 1967-77. Bd. dirs. Phoenix House, 1978—. Club: Friars. Home: 190 E 72d St New York NY 10022 Office: 600 Madison Ave New York NY 10022

SIEGEL, IRENE, artist, educator; b. Chgo., Jan. 26, 1936; d. Ignatius R. and Anna Yarovich; B.S., Northwestern U., 1953; M.S. (Moholy-Nagy scholar), Inst. Design, Ill. Inst. Tech., 1956; m. Artaur Siegel, 1955 (dec.); children—Julie, Adam, Ezra. Mem. faculty dept. art and design U. Ill., Chgo., 1970—, research fellow, 1973, asso. prof., 1975—; one-woman shows of drawings and paintings: LoGiudice Gallery, Chgo., 1968, Capper Gallery, San Francisco, 1969, LoGuidice Gallery, 1971. One Ill. Center, Chgo., 1975, Northwestern U., Evanston, 1977, Young Hoffman Gallery, Chgo., 1978; group shows include: Mus. Fine Arts, Houston, 1959, Art Inst. Chgo., 1959, 65, 66, 71, 73, 74, 76, 77, Mus. Modern Art, N.Y.C., 1959, 69, Gray Gallery, Chgo., 1968, Los Angeles County Mus., 1968, Madison (Wis.) Art Center, 1970, Boston Mus. Fine Arts, 1970, U. So. Ill., Carbondale, 1971, Mus. Contemporary Art, Chgo., 1972, Relativerend Realisme, Eindheven, Holland, 1972, Palais des Beaux Arts, Brussels, 1972, N.Y. Cultural Center, 1972, LoGiudice Gallery, N.Y.C., 1972, Bklyn. Mus., 1973, Calif. Palace Legion of Honor, San Francisco, 1973, U. Chgo., 1973, 74, U. N.D., Vermillion, 1973, Lake Forest (Ill.) Coll., 1974, Utah State U., Logan, 1974, 77, U. Wis., Madison, 1975, U. Mo., St. Louis, 1975, U. Ga. Gallery, Atlanta, 1975, Graphics Gallery, San Francisco, 1975, N.Y. U., Potsdam, 1976, 77, Hyde Park Art Center, Chgo., 1976, St. Thomas U., Houston, 1976, Women's Bldg., Los Angeles, 1977, Basle (Switzerland) Art Fair, 1977, Cologne (Germany) Art Fair, 1977, U. Houston, 1977, Indpls. Mus. Art, 1978, Nat. Collection of Fine Arts, Washington, 1979, Evanston (Ill.) Art Center, 1979; represented in permanent collections: Art Inst. Chgo., Mus. Modern Art, N.Y.C., Los Angeles County Mus., U. Wis., Madison, World Bank, Washington, Ill. Bell Telephone Co., Chgo., FMC Corp., Chgo., Nat. Collection Fine Arts, Washington, Indpls. Mus. Art, also pvt. collections. Recipient numerous prize awards Art Inst. Chgo.; Tamarind fellow; U. Ill. Research grantee, 1973. Author: 70 Instructions on How to Make Certain Drawings, 1979. Office: Dept Art U Ill Chgo Circle Chicago IL 60680

SIEGEL, JEFFREY, pianist; b. Chgo., Nov. 18, 1942; s. Harold and Ruth (Berman) S.; D.Mus. Art, Juilliard Sch. Music, 1970; D.Letters (hon.), Nat. Coll. Edn., 1975; m. Laura Mizel, May 20, 1973. Concert pianist, including appearances in London, Berlin, Amsterdam, Zurich, Switzerland, Brussels; guest soloist with maj. Am. orchs., including N.Y. Philharmonic, Chgo. Symphony Orch., Boston Symphony Orch., Phila. Orch.; concert pianist Keyboard Conversations, informal concerts at univs. Recipient Silver medal award Queen Elisabeth Competition, Brussels, 1968. Home: 613 Kincaid St Highland Park IL 60035 Office: care Columbia Artists 165 W 57th St New York City NY 10019

SIEGEL, LAURENCE, educator; b. N.Y.C., Feb. 11, 1928; s. Jacob Maurice and Carolyn (Blum) S.; A.B., N.Y.U., 1946, M.A., 1948; Ph.D., U. Tenn., 1950; m. Betty S. Smith, Oct. 2, 1971; 1 son, Brent G. Asst. prof. Wash. State U., 1950-53; research asso. Ohio State U., 1954-55; asso. prof. Miami U., Oxford, Ohio, 1956-61, prof., 1961-65, dir. instructional research service, 1960-66; prof., chmn. dept. psychology La. State U., 1966—; indsl. and ednl. cons. Served with AUS, 1955-56. Fellow Am. Psychol. Assn.; mem. Southeastern (pres. 1976-78), Southwestern, La. psychol. assns., Sigma Xi. Author: Industrial Psychology, 1962, 69, 74; Instruction—Some Contemporary Viewpoints, 1967. Home: 4608 Whitehaven St Baton Rouge LA 70808

SIEGEL, LEO HAROLD, physician; b. Newark, July 25, 1919; s. Aaron and Rose (Bass) S.; student U. Md., 1937-40; M.D., George Washington U., 1943; m. Gloria G. Shayman, Mar. 7, 1943; children—Barbara, Richard, Elise. Intern St. Barnabas Hosp., Newark, 1943, resident pathology, 1946-47; practice internal medicine specializing in gastroenterology, Newark, 1947-71, West Orange, N.J., 1971—; attending gastroenterologist Presbyn. Hosp., Newark, 1956—, St. Barnabas Med. Center, Livingston, N.J., 1962—; dir. dept. medicine Presbyn. Hosp., 1963-72; cons. W. Hudson Hosp., Kearny, N.J., 1958—; asso. clin. prof. medicine N.J. Coll. Medicine, 1969-79, clin. prof. medicine, 1979—; vice chmn. Adv. Council Grad. Med. Edn. N.J., 1978—. Trustee Suburban YMHA of Essex County, 1962-65. Served with AUS, 1944-46. Decorated Bronze Star. Fellow A.C.P., Am. Coll. Gastroenterology, Am. Fedn. Clin. Research, N.J. Gastroenterol. Soc. (pres. 1963-64), Acad. Medicine N.J. (trustee 1964—, v.p. 1970-72, pres. 1972-73); mem. Am. Soc. Gastrointestinal Endoscopy, Am. Gastroenterol. Assn., N.J. Soc. Internal Medicine (trustee 1965—). Contbr. articles to profl. jours. Home: 21 Sheffield Terr West Orange NJ 07052 Office: 100 Northfield Ave West Orange NJ 07052

SIEGEL, MARC MONROE, TV and film producer, writer and dir.; b. N.Y.C., Dec. 8, 1916; s. Isaac and Annie N. (Natelson) S.; B.A., Washington Sq. Coll., 1936; M.A., N.Y. U. Sch. Edn., 1938; m. Anne Dorothy Fishman, Sept. 8, 1940; 1 son, Peter Kieve. Sec. campaign affairs bur. Fedn. Jewish Philanthropies, N.Y.C., 1940-41; public relations writer United Jewish Appeal, N.Y.C., 1941-42; nat. public relations dir. Russian Relief, Inc., 1942-43, 45-46; asst. nat. public relations dir. Joint Distbn. Com., 1946-48; free-lance mag. writer, especially for New Yorker mag., 1948-50; writer Eternal Light radio series NBC, N.Y.C., 1950-60; writer-dir-producer Directions, ABC-TV, N.Y.C., 1961-78; exec. producer Jewish civilization project WNET, N.Y.C., 1978—; cons. in field; author feature screenplays A Child is Crying, 1961, The Young Adventurers, 1963; author ABC News Bicentennial spls. Rendezvous With Freedom, 1973, The Right to Believe, 1975, The Will to Be Free, 1976; author ABC News feature The Panama Canal, 1977 (Writers Guild award). Served with USAAF, 1943-45. Recipient numerous awards, including: Edinburgh Film Festival award, 1948, Venice Film Festival award, 1962, Cannes Film Festival award, 1964, Eternal Light award Jewish Theol. Sem. Am., 1969, Peabody award 1979, Gabriel award Nat. Assn. Catholic Broadcasters, 1979, also several awards Freedoms Found. Mem. Nat. Acad. TV Arts and Scis., Writers Guild Am., East (council 1972-73, 78-79, awards 1959, 73, 78), Dirs. Guild Am. Democrat. Home: 75 Central Park W New York NY 10023 Office: WNET 356 W 58th St New York NY 10010

SIEGEL, MAX, psychologist; b. N.Y.C., July 22, 1918; s. Harry and Fanny (Goodman) S.; B.A., CCNY, 1939, M.S., 1940; Ph.D., N.Y. U., 1951; postgrad. William Alanson White Inst., 1951-56; m. Frieda Friedman, Nov. 23, 1941; children—Ozzie, Shelley. Psychologist, VA, N.Y.C., 1946-47, N.Y.C. Domestic Relations Ct. Psychiat. Clinic, 1947-48; asst. prof. psychology Bklyn. Coll., 1955-61, asso. prof., 1961-68, prof., 1968-79, prof. emeritus, 1979—, chief psychologist, 1948-55, dean of students, 1965-68; adj. prof. Fla. Atlantic U.; mem. profl. adv. com. Queens County (N.Y.) Mental Health Soc. Served to capt. U.S. Army, 1942-46. Diplomate Am. Bd. Profl. Psychology. Fellow Am. Psychol. Assn. (dir. 1976-79, pres. div. clin. psychology 1976-77, pres. div. psychotherapy, 1972-73), Am. Group Psychotherapy Assn.; mem. N.Y. State Psychol. Assn. (pres. 1961-62), Eastern Group Psychotherapy Soc. (pres. 1965-66). Democrat. Jewish. Club: Boca West (Boca Raton, Fla.). Editor: The Counseling of College Students, 1968; Remedial Reading With Children, 1955. Home: 1575 Bridgewood Dr Boca Raton FL 33434 Office: 600 S Dixie Hwy Boca Raton FL 33432

SIEGEL, MILTON P., ret. internat. ofcl., assn. exec., mgmt. cons., educator; b. Des Moines, July 23, 1911; s. Barney and Sylvy (Levinson) S.; ed. Drake U., Des Moines; m. Rosalie Rosenberg, May 25, 1934; children—Betsy Lee, Larry (dec.), Sally (dec.). Dir. finance, statistics Iowa Emergency Relief Adminstrn., also treas. Ia. Rural Rehab. Adminstrn., 1933-35; regional finance and bus. mgr. Farm Security Adminstrn., U.S. Dept. Agr., 1935-41, chief fiscal officer, 1942-44; asst. treas., dir. Office for Far East, UNRRA, 1944-45; asst. dir. fiscal br. prodn. and marketing adminstrn. U.S. Dept. Agr., 1945-47; asst. dir.-gen. WHO, 1947-71; prof. internat. health Sch. Pub. Health, U. Tex. Health Scis. Center, Houston, 1971-75; health mgmt. cons. Imperial Govt. of Iran, Nat. Health Ins. Orgn., 1975-76; sr. cons. to adminstr. UN Devel. Program, 1976-77; chmn. bd. trustees Mgmt. Planning Systems Internat., Inc., 1977—; pres., chief exec. officer Fedn. World Health Founds.; mem. permanent scale contbns. commn. League Red Cross Socs., 1967—; sr. mgmt. scientist Children's Nutrition Research Center, Baylor Coll. Medicine, Houston, 1979—; cons. U. N.C., Chapel Hill, 1970, Carolina Population Center, 1970; vis. prof. U. Mich., 1967; chmn. bd. trustees World Health Found. U.S.A., 1976—. Recipient Sam Beber award, 1960. Mem. Am. Acad. Polit. and Social Sci., Am. Public Health Assn., Acad. Polit. Sci., AAAS. Home: 2833 Sackett Houston TX 77098

SIEGEL, MORRIS J., herb tea mfg. co. exec.; b. Salida, Colo., Nov. 21, 1949; s. Joe E. and Betty S.; student Western State Coll., Gunnison, Colo., U. Colo., Boulder; m. Peggy Lester, Oct. 16, 1970; children—Gabriel, Sarah, Megan. Originator, co-founder Celestial Seasonings Herb Tea Co., Boulder, Colo., now pres. Pres. Boulder Arts & Humanities, Democrat. Tour leader on study tour of Soviet

Union. Author numerous articles, patentee teas. Office: 1780 55th St Boulder CO 80301

SIEGEL, NATHANIEL HAROLD, univ. ofcl.; b. Bklyn., May 17, 1929; s. Victor and Yetta (Kogel) S.; A.B., Bklyn. Coll., 1950; A.M., N.Y.U., 1952, Ph.D., 1956; m. Annabelle Replansky, Mar. 3, 1958; children—Anthony, Jennifer. Asst. prof. sociology Columbia, 1956-59; sociologist Hillside Hosp., Queens, N.Y., 1958-63; asso. dir. behavioral research N.Y.C. Dept. Health, 1963-64; chief social sci. tng. sect. NIMH, 1964-67, cons., 1970—; prof. sociology Queens Coll., 1967-79, chmn. dept., 1967-70, v.p., dean faculty, 1970-74, provost, 1974-77, acting pres., 1977-78; v.p. acad. affairs SUNY, Purchase, 1979—. Served with M.C., AUS, 1950-51. Home: 8 Birchfield Rd Larchmont NY 10538 Office: SUNY at Purchase Purchase NY 10577

SIEGEL, PETER VINCENT, physician, govt. ofcl.; b. Syracuse, Mo., Oct. 22, 1916; s. Carl Christian and Mary (DeHaven) S.; A.B., U. Mo., 1939, B.S., 1942; M.D., N.Y.U., 1943; m. Mary Elizabeth Cunningham, Sept. 14, 1940; children—Peter Vincent, Mary Elizabeth, Audrey Evelyn. Intern U.S. Navy Hosp., Seattle, 1943; pvt. practice, Smithton, Mo., 1947-61; with FAA, 1961—, fed. air surgeon, 1965-75, chief occupational health service Navy Regional Med. Center, Jacksonville, Fla., 1975—. Served to lt. U.S. Navy, 1943-47, 50-51; capt. Res. Recipient Howard K. Edwards award Aerospace Med. Assn.; meritorious service awards FAA, Dept. Transp.; Sec. Transp.'s award, 1973; Air Line Med. Dirs. award, 1975. Diplomate in aerospace medicine Am. Bd. Preventive Medicine. Fellow Am. Coll. Preventive Medicine, Aerospace Med. Assn. (v.p. 1966); asso. fellow Am. Inst. Aeros. and Astronautics; founders mem. Flying Physicians Assn.; mem. Am., Mo. med.. assns., D.C. Med. Soc. Home: 4965 Ortega Blvd Jacksonville FL 32210 Office: Navy Regional Med Center Jacksonville FL 32212

SIEGEL, ROBERT TED, physicist; b. Springfield, Mass., June 10, 1928; s. Charles V.D. and Ida B. S.; B.S., Carnegie-Mellon U. 1948, M.S., 1950, D.S., 1952; m. Rebecca Weisberg, June 13, 1951; children—Carol D., Naomi L., Joan E., Jonathan D., Richard M. Research asso. Carnegie Mellon U., 1952-57, asst. prof. physics, 1957-60, asso. prof., 1960-63; prof. Coll. William and Mary, 1963—, dean grad. studies, 1965-67, dir. space radiation effects lab., 1967-79. Mem. Am. Phys. Soc., AAAS, AAUP. Jewish. Office: Physics Dept Coll William and Mary Williamsburg VA 23185

SIEGEL, SAMUEL, metals co. exec.; b. Elizabeth, N.J., Oct. 30, 1930; s. Morris and Anna (Fader) S.; B.B.A., City U. N.Y., 1952; m. Raenea Kershenbaum, Mar. 29, 1953; children—Daryl Lynn, Annie Roslyn. Cost accountant Seaporcel Metals, Inc., Long Island City, N.Y., 1955-56; asst. to controller Deltown Foods, Inc., Yonkers, N.Y., 1956-57; sr. accountant Touche Ross & Co., N.Y.C., 1957-61; v.p. fin., treas., sec., dir. Nucor Corp., Charlotte, N.C., 1961—. C.P.A., N.Y., Ariz. Mem. Am. Soc. Corp. Secs., Fin. Execs. Inst., Am. Inst. C.P.A.'s. Home: 3318 Tinkerbell Ln Charlotte NC 28210 Office: 4425 Randolph Rd Charlotte NC 28211

SIEGEL, SAMUEL, educator; b. Lake Mills, Wis., Feb. 15, 1917; s. Harry and Rose (Perlman) S.; B.S. with honors in Chemistry, U. Calif. at Berkeley, 1938; M.A., U. Calif. at Los Angeles, 1940, Ph.D., 1942; m. Betty Howard, Mar. 7, 1948; children—Jonathan Howard, Robert Varner. Research asso. Northwestern U., 1942-43; with div. 9, NDRC, Harvard, 1943-45; asst. prof. chemistry Ill. Inst. Tech., 1946-51; faculty U. Ark., Fayetteville, 1951—, prof. chemistry, 1957—, chmn. dept., 1957-63. Vis. prof. Queen's U., Belfast, No. Ireland, 1963-64, Research Inst. for Catalysis Hokkaido, Sapporo, Japan, 1977; cons. Universal Oil Products Co., 1957-63. Recipient Am. Chem. Soc.-Petroleum Research Fund Internat. Faculty award in petroleum field, 1963-64. Fellow AAAS; mem. Am. Chem. Soc., Chem. Soc. (London), AAUP, Sigma Xi, Phi Lambda Upsilon. Home: 16 N Sang Ave Fayetteville AR 72701

SIEGEL, SEYMOUR, clergyman, educator; b. Chgo., Sept. 12, 1927; s. David and Jeanette (Morris) S.; B.A., U. Chgo., 1947; M.H.L., Jewish Theol. Sem., 1951, D.H.L., 1958. Rabbi, 1951; registrar, postgrad. dept. Jewish Theol. Sem. Am., 1951-59, asso. prof. theology, 1959-67, sem. prof. theology, Young Men's Philanthropic League prof. ethics and rabbinic thought, 1967—, Ralph Simon prof. ethics and theology, 1976—, asst. dean Herbert H. Lehman Inst. Ethics, 1962—; vis. prof. Seminario Rabinico, Buenos Aires, Argentina, 1962-64; adj. prof. Jewish studies Coll. City N.Y., 1971-73; lectr. ethics Union Theol. Sem.; sr. research fellow Kennedy Inst. for Bioethics, 1976-77. Bd. dirs. Jewish Mus. Fellow Inst. Religious and Social Studies, Soc. for Religion in Higher Edn., Conf. on Sci., Philosophy and Religion. Mem. B'nai B'rith. Author: Conservative Judasim and Jewish Law, 1976; The Jewish Dietary Laws; Contemporary Issues in Jewish Ethics; mem. editorial bd. Jewish Publ. Soc.; editorial adv. bd. Kennedy Inst. for Study Human Reprodn. and Bioethics; div. editor Ency. Judaica; bd. editors Ency. Bio-Med. Ethics. Home: 380 Riverside St New York NY 10025. *I have tried all my life to guide myself by the values inherent in the Jewish tradition. These values are a sense of the holy; responsibility to God and to fellowman; the development of the rational faculties; a reverence for tradition; and a healthy good humor about the failings and foibles of human beings.*

SIEGEL, SHELDON C., physician; b. Mpls., Jan. 30, 1922; s. Carl Siegel; A.A., Va. Jr. Coll., 1940; B.A., B.S., U. Minn., 1942, M.D., 1945; m. Priscilla Rikess, Mar. 3, 1946; children—Linda, Nancy. Intern, U. Minn. Hosp., 1946, resident in pediatrics, 1947-48; fellow in pediatric allergy, Rochester, N.Y., 1949-50; practice medicine specializing in pediatric allergy and pediatrics, St. Paul, 1950-52, San Antonio, 1952-54, Los Angeles, 1954—; clin. instr. pediatrics U. Rochester, 1949-50, U. Minn., 1950-51; asst. prof. pediatrics U. Tex., 1952-54; asst. clin. prof. U. Calif. at Los Angeles Med. Sch., 1955, clin. asso. prof., 1957-62, clin. prof., 1963—, co-chief pediatric allergy clinic, 1957—; mem. staff Harbor Gen. Hosp., Torrance, Calif., Daniel Freeman Hosp., Inglewood, Calif., Centinela Valley Community Hosp., Inglewood, Hawthorne (Calif.) Community Hosp. Fellow Am. Acad. Allergy (pres. 1974), Am. Coll. Allergists, Am. Acad. Pediatrics; mem. AMA, Allergy Found. Am. (pres. 1976), Calif., Los Angeles County med. assns., Los Angeles Pediatric Soc., Calif., Los Angeles socs. allergy, Western Pediatric Research Soc., Am. Bd. Med. Specialists, Sigma Xi. Editorial bd. Jour. Allergy, 1973-75; contbr. articles to med. jours. Office: 8540 S Sepulveda Blvd Los Angeles CA 90045

SIEGEL, SID, composer, lyricist; b. Chgo., Jan. 20, 1927; s. Michael and Rose (Wolfson) S.; B.Mus. in Composition, Roosevelt Coll., Chgo., 1950; m. Carrie Patricia Zeigler, May 18, 1952; children—David, Jodi, Mark. Composer-lyricist for local TV shows, nightclub performers and popular songs, also commls. for radio and TV, nightclub shows; composer-lyricist, arranger, condr. for radio and TV commls., films, slide presentations, industry shows. Served with USNR, 1945-46. Recipient numerous awards for music for commls. and films including Cindy Indsl. Film Producers Am. and Capa Chgo. Audio-Visual Producers Assn. Mem. ASCAP, Am. Fedn. Musicians. Address: 640 Wicklow Rd Deerfield IL 60015

SIEGEL, STUART SAMUEL, publishing co. exec.; b. Davenport, Iowa, Apr. 16, 1926; s. Benjamin M. and Edna (Abrahamson) S.; B.A., U. Iowa, 1947; m. Louise Slotsky, Aug. 3, 1947; children—Barbara, Steven, Laurie. With McGraw-Hill Co., N.Y.C., 1947—, pub. Modern Plastics mag., 1962—, founder Modern Plastics Internat. mag., Lausanne, Switzerland, 1970—; v.p.-pub. McGraw Hill Publs. Co., N.Y.C. Served with USMC, 1943-44. Mem. Soc. Plastics Industries, Soc. Plastics Engrs., Plastics Pioneers. Home: 206 Goodhill Rd Weston CT 06880 Office: 1221 Ave of Americas New York City NY 10020

SIEGEL, THOMAS LOUIS, lawyer; b. N.Y.C., Oct. 7, 1939; s. Jack M. and Helen S. (Simpson) S.; B.A., Rutgers U., 1961; J.D., Cornell U., 1964; m. Ruth L. Rosenthal, June 23, 1963; children—Peter, Karen. Admitted to N.Y. State bar, 1964, D.C. bar, 1967; atty. advisor Office of Gen. Counsel, FHA, Washington, 1968; asso. mem. firm Arent, Fox, Kintner, Plotkin & Kahn, Washington, 1968-70; gen. counsel Group Health Assn., Inc., 1970-74; partner firm Diuguid, Siegel & Kennelly, Washington, 1974—; legal cons. div. organizational devel. HEW, 1974—. Pres. bd. trustees St. Luke's House, Bethesda, Md. Served with USAF, 1965-67. Mem. Am., N.Y. State bar assns., Bar Assn. D.C., Am. Soc. Hosp. Attys., Nat. Health Lawyers Assn., Rutgers, Cornell U. alumni assns. Club: Georgetown Prep Golf. Home: 5218 Rayland Dr Bethesda MD 20014 Office: Suite 1112 1000 Connecticut Ave NW Washington DC 20036

SIEGEL, WILLIAM M., food service co. exec.; b. 1931; B.S., Mich. State U., 1951, M.S. in Food Tech., 1952; M.S. in Bus., Northwestern U., 1954; married. With Interstate Host & Host Internat., 1960-62; with Brass Rail, N.Y.C., 1962-64; with N.Y. Restaurants, 1964-65; with Playboy Internat., 1965-68; with Dunkin' Donuts, Quincy, Mass., 1968; with Continental Travel Co., 1968-69; pres. ARASERV Inc., 1969-71; became v.p. ARA Services Inc., 1971, sr. v.p., 1973-77, exec. v.p., 1977—; pres. ARA Food Services Inc. Served to capt. AUS, 1952-54. Office: Independence Sq West 6th and Walnut Sts Philadelphia PA 19106

SIEGELMAN, DON EUGENE, state ofcl.; b. 1946; B.A., U. Ala.; J.D., Georgetown U., 1972; postgrad. Oxford (Eng.) U., 1972-73. Admitted to Ala. bar, 1972; exec. dir. Ala. Democratic Exec. Com., 1973-78; sec. and coordinator Ala. Election Law Commn., 1974-77; sec. of state State of Ala., Montgomery, 1979—. Office: Office of Sec of State State Capitol Montgomery AL 36130

SIEGERT, ARNOLD JOHN FREDERICK, research physicist, educator; b. Dresden, Germany, Jan. 1, 1911; s. Frederick Ludwig and Lea (Rosenberg) S.; student Inst. Tech., Dresden, Germany, 1928-30, U. Vienna (Austria), 1929, U. Innsbruck, 1930; Ph.D., U. Leipzig, 1934; m. Anna Beatrice Brown, Feb. 12, 1944; 1 son, Allan. Came to U.S. 1936, naturalized, 1942. Lorentz Funds fellow, Leiden, Holland, 1934-36; grad. asst. Stanford (Calif.) U., 1936-39; physicist The Texas Co., Houston, 1939-42, Nat. Geophys. Co., Dallas, May-Sept. 1942, Stanolind Oil & Gas Co., Tulsa Sept.-Dec. 1942, Radiation Lab., Mass. Inst. Tech., 1942-45; asso. prof. physics Syracuse U., 1946-47; prof. physics Northwestern U., 1947—; research in theoretical physics. Guggenheim fellow, 1953-54; mem. Inst. Advanced Study, Princeton, 1953-54; NSF sr. postdoctoral fellow at Instituut voor Theoretische Fysica, U. Amsterdam (Netherlands), 1962-63, at physics dept. Weizmann Inst. Sci., Rehovoth, Israel, 1963-64, guest prof. U. Utrecht (Netherlands), 1971-72; vis. prof. Technion (Israel Inst. Tech.), Haifa, 1978. Fellow Am. Phys. Soc.; mem. Sigma Xi. Co-author: Radiation Laboratory Technical Series; author and co-author numerous sci. articles on physics in sci. jours., revs., etc. Bd. editors Phys. Rev., 1951, Jour. Math. Physics, 1961-63, 74-76; Jour. Statis. Physics, 1970-75. Holder several patents in geophys. exploration and invention of gravity integrator. Home: 2347 Lake Ave Wilmette IL 60091 Office: Physics Dept Northwestern U Evanston IL 60201

SIEGFRIED, ROBERT EDWIN, engring. and constrn. co. exec.; b. Allentown, Pa., Jan. 16, 1922; s. Harold Edwin and Bessie (Davies) S.; B.S. in Chem. Engring., Lehigh U., 1943; S.M., Mass. Inst. Tech., 1947; postgrad. Center for Mgmt. Devel., Northeastern U., 1960; m. Blanche Worth, Aug. 17, 1945; children—Martha Siegfried Fritz, Jay Worth. Process engring. supr. Stone & Webster Engring. Co., London, 1951-52; process engr. E.B. Badger & Sons Co., Boston, 1947-51; process engring. supr. Badger Co., Cambridge, Mass., 1952-54, project mgr., 1954-56, project and engring. coordinator, 1956-59, asst. engring. mgr., 1959-60, engring. mgr., 1960-65, dir., 1963—, v.p., engring. mgr., 1965-68, pres., 1968—, chief exec. officer, 1971—, chmn. bd., 1977—; dir. State St. Bank & Trust Co., State St. Boston Corp. Mem. corp., v.p., trustee Boston Mus. Sci.; mem. corp. Northeastern U.; trustee New Eng. Gas and Electric Assn. Served with AUS, 1943-46. Registered profl. engr., Mass., Ky., La. Mem. Am. Inst. Chem. Engrs., Fla. Engring. Soc., Nat. Soc. Profl. Engrs., Sigma Xi, Tau Beta Pi. Patentee desalination of sea water. Office: One Broadway Cambridge MA 02142

SIEGLER, HOWARD MATTHEW, physician, surgeon; b. N.Y.C., May 26, 1932; s. Samuel Lewis and Shirley Kendall (Matthews) S.; B.S. in Biochemistry, Hofstra U., 1951; postgrad. Yale U., 1952; M.B., Ch.B., St. Andrews U., 1958; M.D., N.Y. Med. Coll., 1965; m. Toinette Andrau, Dec. 1, 1953; children—Samuel Lewis, Karel Lynn, Jacqueline Andrau, Todd Bradford. Intern, N.Y. U. Med. Center, N.Y.C., 1965, New Rochelle (N.Y.) Hosp., 1966-67; asst. to dean U. Tex., Southwestern Med. Sch., Dallas, 1967-68; sr. fellow dept. phys. medicine Baylor Coll., Houston, 1968-69; resident family practice program Meml. Bapt. Hosp., Houston, 1971; gen. practice medicine, Houston, 1971, 72—; clin. fellow in obstetrics and gynecology St. Lukes Episcopal Hosp., Houston, 1971-72, mem. staff, 1972—; mem. staff St. Joseph's Hosp., Center Pavilion Hosp., St. Anthony's Med. Center, Tex. Childrens Hosp., St. Lukes Episcopal Hosp. (all Houston). Co-chmn. Muscular Dystrophy Soc., 1964-65; cons. div. disability determination Tex. Rehab. Commn., 1973; sr. dir. Pacer Devel. Corp., 10 Main Baytown Ltd. Active Assn. To Help Retarded Children, 1965-76; chmn. sr. div. Protestant Charities N.Y., 1964-65; asso. trustee Kinkaid Sch., Houston, 1972-77. Served to maj. U.S. Army; maj. Tex. Army N.G., USAR. Col., aide-de-camp Gov. of La., Gov. of Miss., Gov. of Tenn., lt. col., aide-de-camp Gov. of Ala. Honored by Internat. Soc. Cardiology, 1978. Fellow Royal Soc. Health, Royal Soc. Medicine (London); mem. Am. Fertility Soc., Am. Geriatric Soc., AAAS, N.Y. Acad. Scis. (life), Am. Diabetes Assn., Am. Social Health Assn., Am. Soc. Bariatrics, Christian, So. med. assns., Am. Med. Soc. Alcoholism, Am. Assn. Gynec. Laparoscopists, Am. Soc. Contemporary Medicine and Surgery, Tex. Acad. Family Physicians, Denton A. Cooley Cardiovascular Surg. Soc., Harris County Acad. Medicine, Harris County Med. Soc., Internat. Acad. Preventive Medicine, Tex. Assn. Disability Examiners, Internat. Platform Assn., Phi Chi. Episcopalian. Home: 1 Longfellow Ln Houston TX 77005 Office: Suite 1020 Hermann Profl Bldg 6410 Fannin St Houston TX 77030. *I recognize that a bridge must be created between human effort and human frailty, and that bridge is man's compassion to man.*

SIEGMAN, HENRY, clergyman; b. Germany, Dec. 12, 1930; s. Mendel and Sara (Scharf) S.; came to U.S., 1942, naturalized, 1948; rabbi, Torah Vodaath Sem., N.Y.C., 1951; B.A., New Sch. Social Research, 1961; postgrad. New Sch. Social Research, 1961-64; m. Selma Goldberger, Nov. 8, 1953; children—Bonnie, Debra, Alan. Nat. dir. community activities div. Union Orthodox Jewish Congregations Am., 1953-59; exec. sec. Am. Assn. Middle East Studies, 1959-64; dir. internat. affairs Nat. Community Relations Adv. Council, N.Y.C., 1964-65; exec. v.p. Synagogue Council Am., N.Y.C., 1965—; exec. dir. Am. Jewish Congress, N.Y.C., 1978—; guest lectr. U. Ill., Columbia, Williams Coll. An organizer White House Conf. Civil Rights, 1967; nat. vice chmn. Religion in Am. Life, 1966—; exec. com. Interreligious Com. on Peace, 1966—; chmn. Interreligious Com. Gen. Secs. (Nat. Council Chs.-U.S. Cath. Conf.-Synagogue Council Am.), 1973. Bd. dirs. Nat. Com. Against Discrimination in Housing, 1966—; steering com., exec. com. Nat. Urban Coalition. Served to 1st lt., chaplain, AUS, 1952-54. Decorated Bronze Star; designated Distinguished Am. by Pres. U.S., 1970. Mem. Am. Assn. U. Profs., Rabbinical Council Am., Nat. Conf. Jewish Communal Service, Assn. Jewish Community Relations Workers. Editor: Middle East Studies, 1959-64. Contbr. articles in field. Home: 287 Redmont Rd West Hempstead NY 11552 Office: 15 E 84th St New York NY 10028

SIEGMEISTER, ELIE, composer; b. N.Y.C., Jan. 15, 1909; s. William and Bessie (Gitler) S.; B.A., Columbia U., 1927; diploma Ecole Normale de Musique, Paris, 1931; fellow Juilliard Grad. Sch. Music, 1935-38; m. Hannah Mersel, Jan. 15, 1930; children—Willa, Miriam, Nancy. Student of Music since age of 8; first composition performed at Columbia Coll. at age of 17; lived and studied in Paris, 1927-31; composer orchestral and stage works on native Am. themes, performing and publicizing native Am. music, 1931—; pres. Pioneer Edits., 1967-68; prof. music Hofstra U., composer-in-residence, 1966-76; condr. Hofstra Symphony Orch., 1953-65, Pro Arte Symphony Orch., 1965-66. Works have been performed by Toscanini, Stokowski, Mitropoulos, Maazel; commd. by N.Y. Philharmonic, NBC, Phila., Cleve. and other symphony orchs., also in Germany, France, Italy, Norway, Israel, USSR, Mexico, Eng., Australia; organized Am. Ballad Singers, 1939, dir. in numerous concerts including Town Hall, 1939, 40, 41, 45, 46; made nation-wide tours, 1942-44; vis. lectr. U. Minn., 1948. Expert cons. to War Dept., 1945. Mem. Kennedy Center Black Music Competition 1977-79. Recipient 38th ann. Acad.-Inst. award Am. Acad. and Inst. Arts and Letters, 1978. Mem. ASCAP (bd. dirs.), Am. Music Center, Council Creative Artists, Libraries and Museums (chmn. 1971—). Composer numerous musical works in various forms; latest include: (for orch.) Symphony No. 1, 1947, From My Window, 1949; Symphony No. 2, 1950; Divertimento, 1954; Clarinet Concerto, 1956; Symphony No. 3, 1957; Theater Set, 1959; Flute Concerto, 1960; Dick Whittington and His Cat, 1966; Five Fantasies of the Theater, 1967; The Face of War, 1968; Symphony No. 4, 1970; Symphony No. 5, 1971; Piano Concerto, 1974; Shadows and Light, 1975; Fables from the Dark Wood, 1976; Double Concerto for violin, piano and orch., 1976; Violin Concerto, 1978; (for Symphonic band) Five American Folk Songs, 1948; Deep Sea Chanty, 1948; Hootenanny, 1950, Front Porch Saturday Night, 1977, Celebration, 1978; (for chorus) The New Colossus, 1949; In Our Time, 1965; I Have A Dream, 1967; A Cycle of Cities, 1974; operas include: Darling Corie, 1952, The Plough and the Stars, 1969; Miranda and the Dark Young Man, 1955; The Mermaid in Lock No. 7, 1958; Night of the Moonspell, 1976; (chamber music) String Quartet No. 2, 1960; String Quartet No. 3 (on Hebrew Themes), 1973; Piano Sonata No. 2, 1964; Piano Sonata No. 3, 1979; Sextet for Brass and Percussion, 1965; Violin Sonata No. 2, 1965; Violin Sonata No. 3, 1970; Violin Sonata No. 4, 1971; Violin Sonata No. 5, 1972; Songs of Experience for voice, viola and piano, 1977: others. Author or co-author several books relating to music; latest publ. Invitation to Music, 1959; Harmony and Melody, 2 vols., 1965-66; The New Music Lover's Handbook, 1973. Contbr. to Ency. Americana, N.Y. Times, Opera News, Mus. America. Address: 56 Fairview Ave Great Neck NY 11023. *Dedication to one's deepest feelings, to the substance of life rather than conformity to passing fashions or manners; belief in human dignity and the beauty of man's vision despite dark forces of greed, ambition, and cruelty of some powerful men toward others; devotion to art and imagination as basic forces in man's life; and the use of intelligence as a means of combatting surrounding evil. Life is to be struggled for, lived, and enjoyed, in love of one's fellows. (And the hopelessness of mere words to express these beliefs!)*

SIEKEVITZ, PHILIP, educator; b. Phila., Feb. 25, 1918; s. Joseph and Tillie (Kaplan) S.; B.S. in Biology, Phila. Coll. Pharmacy and Scis., 1942, Ph.D. (hon.), 1972; Ph.D. in Biochemistry, U. Calif. at Berkeley, 1949; Ph.D. (hon.), U. Stockholm (Sweden), 1974; m. Rebecca Burstein, Aug. 7, 1949; children—Ruth, Miriam. USPHS fellow Mass. Gen. Hosp., 1949-51; fellow oncology McArdle Lab., U. Wis., 1951-54; mem. faculty Rockefeller U., 1954—, now prof. cell biology. Mem. molecular biology panel NSF, 1964-67; panel Internat. Cell Research Orgn., 1963—. Bd. dirs., treas., chmn. Scientists Com. Pub. Information N.Y., 1962—; bd. dirs. N.Y. Univs. Com., 1965—; council Am. Fedn. Scientists, 1967—. Served with USAAF, 1942-45. Mem. Am. Soc. Biol. Chemists, Am. Soc. Cell Biology (pres. 1966-67), A.A.A.S., Am. Inst. Biol. Scientists, N.Y. Acad. Scis. (governing bd. 1973—, pres. 1976), Nat. Acad. Scis., Sigma Xi. Author: (with A. Loewy) Cell Structure and Function, 2d edit., 1969. Editor: Jour. Cell Biology, 1962-65, Jour. Cellular Physiology, 1970—, Biosci., Jour. Exptl. Zoology, 1969-73, Biochim. Biophysica Acta. mem. editorial bd. Jour. Cell Sci. Home: 290 West End Ave New York NY 10023

SIEKMAN, WILLIAM AUGUST, paper co. exec.; b. Independence, Kans., Nov. 18, 1916; s. Albert Charles and Elsie (Hein) S.; B.S. in Mktg., Okla. A. and M. U., 1939; m. Martha Hill Boyd, Oct. 12, 1946; children—Charles, Frances. With War Manpower Commn., 1942-46; with Appleton Coated Paper Co. (Wis.), 1947—, chmn. bd., 1962-70; chmn. Sequence Corp., Appleton; vice chmn. Appleton Papers div. NCR, 1970—; pres. Alcan, Ltd., Pioneer Investments Co. (both Appleton); dir. First Nat. Bank, Appleton. Trustee Western Mich. U. Home: 940 E College Ave Appleton WI 54911 Office: 825 E Wisconsin Ave Appleton WI 54911

SIELING, DALE HAROLD, ret. lab. dir.; b. McCracken, Kans., June 7, 1909; s. Wilhelm Theodor Johan and Mabel May (Rixon) S.; student Ft. Hays (Kans.) State Coll., 1926-28; B.S., Kans. State U., 1931, M.S., 1932; Ph.D., Iowa State U., 1936; m. Naomi Nell Larson, Sept. 2, 1933; children—Sonja Nan Sieling Blackmur, Hal Dale. Foreman, Civilian Conservation Corps, 1932-34; grad. asst. Iowa State Coll., 1934-35; instr. chemistry, 1935-37; instr. agrl. chemistry Purdue U., 1937-38, asst. prof. soil chemistry, 1938-40; prof. soil chemistry U. Mass., 1940-47, head dept. agronomy, 1947-50, dean Coll. Agr., also dir. Agrl. Expt. Sta., 1950-59, dir. extension service, 1958-59; sci. dir. U.S. Army Natick Labs., Natick, Mass., 1959-79. Served as maj. San. Corps, AUS 1942-46. Mem. Am. Soc. Agronomy, Soil Sci. Soc. Am., Sigma Xi, Kappa Sigma, Phi Lambda Upsilon, Phi Kappa Phi, Gamma Sigma Delta. Alpha Zeta. Conglist. Home: 43 Hartford St Natick MA 01760

SIEMER, DEANNE C., govt. ofcl.; b. Buffalo, Dec. 25, 1940; d. Edward D. and Dorothy J. (Helsdon) Siemer; B.A. magna cum laude, George Washington U., 1962; LL.B. cum laude, Harvard U., 1968. Economist, Office Mgmt. and Budget, Washington, 1964-65; admitted to N.Y. State bar, 1968, D.C. bar, 1968, Md. bar, 1970, U.S. Supreme Ct. bar, 1972, U.S. Ct. Appeals for 2d circuit, 1975, 4th circuit, 1976, D.C. circuit, 1969, Trust Ty. Pacific Islands bar, 1976; asso., then partner firm Wilmer, Cutler & Pickering, Washington, 1968-77; gen. counsel Dept. Def., 1977—; mem. faculty Nat. Inst. Trial Advocacy, 1975-77, Law Sch., State U. N.Y., Buffalo, 1974-76; exec. com. Washington Lawyers Com. Civil Rights Under Law, 1970-76. Bd. overseers vis. com. Law Sch., Harvard U., 1970-76. Mem. Am., D.C. bar assns. Co-author: Briefing Papers for the Delegates to the Northern Marianas Constitutional Convention, 2 vols., 1976; also articles. Address: 3E980 The Pentagon Washington DC 20301

SIEMER, JOHN WILLIAM, diversified industry exec.; b. Ross, Calif., Dec. 28, 1925; s. Albert Henry and Mabel Meta (Jones) S.; A.B. in Econs., Stanford U., 1947; m. Elizabeth Jane Sampson, Feb. 6, 1954; children—Alan Ewing, Lesley Jane, Geoffrey David. Purser, Am. Pres. Lines, San Francisco, 1947-51, freight sales rep., Chgo., 1951-53; asst.-in-tng.-agr. Hawaiian Sugar Planters' Assn., Honolulu, 1954-55; field supt. Waimea Sugar Mill Co., Ltd., Kauai, Hawaii, 1955-59; v.p. Siemer & Hand, Ltd., San Francisco, 1959-61; indsl. relations dir. Kekaha Sugar Co., Kauai, 1961-62; mng. dir. Cia Agricola E Industrial Del Norte S.A., Montevideo, Uruguay, 1962-66; pres., mgr. Pioneer Mill Co., Lahaina, Hawaii, 1966-74; v.p. Amfac Inc., Honolulu, 1975-77, exec. v.p., 1977—; dir. Grace Bros., Ltd., Calif. & Hawaiian Sugar Co., Bay & River Nav. Co.; bd. dirs. U.S. C. of C. Food and Agr. Com., Hawaii Employers' Council. Pres. Maui County council Boy Scouts Am., 1971-74, bd. dirs. Aloha council, 1975—; trustee Lahaina Restoration Found. Served with USNR, World War II. Recipient Bill Hall award Hugh A. Wichert & Assos., 1974, also Master of Bus. Enterprise. Mem. Hawaiian Sugar Planters' Assn. (dir.), Hawaiian Sugar Technologists, Sugar Club, C. of C. of Hawaii, Stanford Alumni Assn. Republican. Episcopalian. Club: Rotary (Honolulu). Home: 4340 Pahoa Ave PH-C Honolulu HI 96816 Office: PO Box 3230 Honolulu HI 96801

SIENA, JAMES VINCENT, govt. ofcl.; b. Cleve., Sept. 25, 1932; s. Vincent James and Virginia Catherine (Johnson) S.; student Miami U., 1951-52; B.A., Western Res. U., 1955; LL.B., Stanford U., 1961; m. June Elizabeth Harvey, 1954 (dec. 1974); children—Katherine June, James Harvey, Margaret Johnson; m. 2d, Lynn Bonde, Dec. 31, 1978. Admitted to D.C. bar, 1962, Calif. bar, 1976; asso. firm Covington & Burling, Washington, 1961-67; dep. undersec. Army for internat. affairs, Washington, 1967-69; legal adv. to pres. Stanford U., 1970-77; dep. asst. sec. Def. for European and NATO affairs Dept. Def., Washington, 1977—; cons. OEO, 1964-65. Bd. dirs. ACLU, Washington, 1963-67, Sierra Club Legal Def. Fund, 1972-77. Served with USMCR, 1955-58. Mem. Calif. Bar Assn., D.C. Bar Assn. Democrat. Home: 65 Observatory Circle Washington DC 20008 Office: The Pentagon Washington DC 20301

SIENKO, MICHELL J., chemist, educator; b. Bloomfield, N.J., May 15, 1923; s. Felix and Teofila (Kislova) S.; A.B., Cornell U., 1943; Ph.D., U. Calif. at Berkeley, 1946; m. Carol Tanghe, Aug. 25, 1946; 1 dau., Tanya. Research asso. Stanford, 1946-47; instr. chemistry Cornell U., Ithaca, N.Y., 1947-50, asst. prof., 1950-53, asso. prof., 1953-58, prof., 1958—. Fulbright lectr. U. Toulouse, France, 1956-57; vis. prof. Am. Coll. in Paris, France, 1963-64; guest prof. U. Vienna, Austria, 1974-75; vis. fellow Cambridge U., 1978-79. Recipient Sporn award Coll. Engring, Cornell U., 1963. Guggenheim fellow, Grenoble, France, 1970-71. Mem. Am. Chem. Soc., Am. Phys. Soc., Phi Beta Kappa, Sigma Xi, Phi Kappa Phi. Author: (with Robert A. Plane), Chemistry, 5th edit., 1976, Experimental Chemistry, 5th edit., 1976, Physical Inorganic Chemistry, 1963; Stoichiometry and Structure, 1964; Equilibrium, 1964; Principles and Properties, 2d edit., 1974; Chemistry Problems, 2d edit., 1972; Chemistry Principles and Applications, 1979; editor (with Gerard Lepoutre) Solutions Metal-Ammoniac, 1964; (with Joseph Lagowski) Metal-Ammonia Colloque Weyl II, 1970; Jour. Solid State Chemistry. Home: 493 Ellis Hollow Creek Rd Ithaca NY 14850 Office: Cornell U Dept Chemistry Ithaca NY 14853. *I have always believed that man could do anything he set his mind to provided he was willing to work hard enough. However, no goal is worth pursuing if it means that human qualities are destroyed. Respect for one's fellowman comes first.*

SIEPI, CESARE, opera singer; b. Milan, Italy, Feb. 10, 1923. Operatic debut, Rigoletto, Schio, at age of 18; debut in Il Nabucco, LaScala Opera, Switzerland, 1945, in Don Carlo, Met. Opera, N.Y.C., 1950; soloist Carnegie Hall, N.Y.C., 1951; sang in Mozart and Verdi requiems Edinburgh Festival, Albert Hall, London; leading bass at Salzburg Festival, LaScala, Milan; appeared in play Bravo Giovanni, 1962; appeared Vienna Staatsoper; made many opera recordings for London Records. Winner Nat. Singing Competition, Florence, 1941; recipient Italy's Orfeo award, 1956. Home: 1200 NE 87th St Miami FL 33138

SIERAKOWSKI, ROBERT LEON, aero. engr.; b. Vernon, Conn., Apr. 11, 1937; s. Stanley F. and Amelia C. (Misiaszek) S.; B.S. in Engring., Brown U., 1958; M.S., Yale U., 1960, Ph.D., 1964; m. Nina A. Shopa, May 3, 1975; children—Steven R., Sandra M. Engr., United Techs Corp., East Hartford, Conn., 1958-60, research engr., 1963-67; research asst. Yale U., New Haven, 1960-63; adj. asst. prof. engring. mechanics Rensselaer Poly. Inst. Hartford Grad. Center, 1965-67; vis. asst. prof. engring. mechanics U. Fla., 1967-68, asso. prof., 1968-72, prof., 1972—. Mem. Vernon Bd. Edn., 1965-67; mem. Vernon City Commn., 1967; mem. Gainesville (Fla.) Citizens Adv. Council for Elementary Schs., 1973-75. NRC sr. research fellow, 1972-73, Fellow AIAA (asso.); mem. ASME, Soc. Exptl. Stress Analysis, Soc. Engring. Sci. (editor procs. 1978), Soc. Materials Process Engrs., Yale Engring. Assn., Sigma Xi, Sigma Tau, Tau Beta Pi, Phi Kappa Phi. Roman Catholic. Club: K.C. Contbr. numerous articles and revs. to profl. publs. Home: 1502 NW 52d Terr Gainesville FL 32605 Office: U Fla Dept Engring Gainesville FL 32601

SIESEL, ALFRED J., advt. exec.; b. N.Y.C., May 22, 1929; s. Harold J. and Frieda (Wolff) S.; B.A., Union Coll., Schenectady, 1949; m. Dorothy Renner, Dec. 17, 1950; children—David Lawrence, Anne Hillary. With Harold J. Siesel Co. Inc., N.Y.C., 1949—, pres., 1955-67, chmn. bd., 1967—. Pres. League Advt. Agencies, 1960, bd. dirs., 1961-66. Bd. dirs. Friends of Grace Ch. Sch., 1966—. Home: 40 E 83d St New York City NY 10028 Office: 845 3d Ave New York City NY 10022*

SIESS, CHARLES PRESTON, JR., mfg. co. exec.; b. Lake Charles, La., Jan. 28, 1927; s. Charles Preston and Burem (Henderson) S.; B.S. in Chem. Engring., La. State U., 1948; m. Jean Dorris Muchard, Sept. 27, 1979; children—Charles P., Stephen Kurt; 1 stepson, Thomas L. Muchard. Field engr. tretolite div. Petrolite Corp., Monroe, La., 1948-52, Anoco, Venezuela, 1953-57, asst. sales mgr., Webster Groves, Mo., 1957-59, sales mgr. Petreco div., 1959-60, v.p., gen. mgr., 1961-64, v.p., gen. mgr. tretolite div., 1964-68; exec. v.p. Apco Oil Corp., Houston, 1969-72, pres., chief exec. officer, 1972-75; pres. Marathon Mfg. Co., Houston, 1976—, dir.; dir. Camco, Inc. Bd. dirs. La. State U. Found. Served with USNR, 1944-46. Mem. Am. Petroleum Inst. (past dir.), Am. Inst. Mining and Metall. Engrs. Clubs: Lakeside Country, Petroleum (Houston); Balboa (Mazatlan, Mexico). Home: 242 Gessner Houston TX 77024 Office: 600 Jefferson Houston TX 77002

SIESS, CHESTER PAUL, educator; b. Alexandria, La., July 28, 1916; s. Leo C. and Adele (Liebreich) S.; B.S., La. State U., 1936; M.S., U. Ill., 1939, Ph.D., 1948; m. Helen Kranson, Oct. 5, 1941; 1 dau., Judith Ann. Party chief La. Hwy. Commn., 1936-37; research asst. U. Ill., 1937-39; soil engr. Chgo. Subway Project, 1939-41; engr., draftsman N.Y.C. R.R. Co., 1941; mem. faculty U. Ill., 1941—, prof. civil engring., 1955-78, emeritus, head dept. civil engring., 1973-78. Mem. adv. com. on reactor safeguards Nuclear Regulatory Commn., 1968—, chmn., 1972. Recipient award Concrete Reinforcing Steel Inst., 1956. Mem. ASCE (hon. mem.; Research prize 1956, Howard medal 1968, Reese award 1970), Nat. Acad. Engring., Am. Concrete Inst. (pres. 1974—, Wason medal 1949, Turner medal 1964, hon. mem.), Reinforced Concrete Research Council (chmn., Boase award 1974), Internat. Assn. Bridge and Structural Engring., Sigma Xi, Tau Beta Pi, Phi Kappa Phi, Omicron Delta Kappa, Gamma Alpha, Chi Epsilon. Research reinforced and prestressed concrete structures and hwy. bridges. Home: 805 Hamilton Dr Champaign IL 61820 Office: Civil Engring Bldg Urbana IL 61801

SIEVER, RAYMOND, educator; b. Chgo., Sept. 14, 1923; s. Leo and Lillie (Katz) S.; B.S., U. Chgo., 1943, M.S., 1947, Ph.D., 1950; M.A. (hon.), Harvard, 1960; m. Doris Fisher, Mar. 31, 1945; children—Larry Joseph, Michael David. With Ill. Geol. Survey, 1943-44, 47-56, geologist, 1953-56; research asso., NSF sr. postdoctoral fellow Harvard, 1956-57, mem. faculty, 1957—, prof. geology, 1965—, chmn. dept. geol. scis., 1968-71, 76—; research asso. geology Woods Hole (Mass.) Oceanographic Instn., 1957—; cons. to industry, 1957—. Served with USAAF, 1944-46. Recipient Best Paper award Soc. Econ. Paleontologists and Mineralogists, 1957; Pres.'s award Am. Assn. Petroleum Geologists, 1952. Fellow Am. Acad. Arts and Scis., AAAS, Geol. Soc. Am.; mem. Geochem. Soc. (pres. organic geochemistry group 1965), Am. Geophys. Union. Author: (with others) Geology of Sandstones, 1965; Sand and Sandstone, 1972; Earth, 2d edit., 1978; Planet Earth, 1974; also numerous articles, papers. Home: 38 Avon St Cambridge MA 02138 Office: Hoffman Lab Harvard Univ Cambridge MA 02138

SIEVERING, NELSON FREDERICK, JR., energy cons.; b. Newark, Dec. 8, 1924; s. Nelson Frederick and Clarice Elizabeth (Taylor) S.; B.Engring., Yale, 1945; M.S., Columbia, 1948; student N.Y.U. Grad. Sch. Bus. Adminstrn., 1948-51; m. Dorothy Rothberg, Dec. 9, 1945; children—Nelson Frederick III, Scott Moore, Keith Donald, Jeffrey Taylor. Research chemist White Lab., Newark, 1946-47; with AEC, 1948-65, dep. for Euratom affairs U.S. Mission to European Communities, Brussels, Belgium, also AEC European sci. rep., 1959-61, asso. dir. advanced systems, div. reactor devel. and tech., Washington, 1961-65; sr. asso. internat. sci., technol. affairs, Dept. State, 1965-69, dir. Office Gen. Sci. Affairs, 1969-72, dep. dir. Bur. Internat. Sci. and Technol. Affairs, 1972-75; asst. adminstr. for internat. affairs ERDA, 1975-77; dep. asst. sec. for internat. programs Dept. Energy, 1977-78; prin. cons. Internat. Energy Assos., Ltd., Washington, 1978—; mem. U.S. del. 3d UN Internat. Conf. Peaceful Uses Atomic Energy, 1964. Active local Boys Scouts Am., PTA. Served to lt. (j.g.) USNR, 1943-46. Registered profl. engr., D.C. Mem. AAAS, Am. Nuclear Soc., Yale Engring. Assn., Phi Gamma Delta. Home: 6402 Orchid Dr Bethesda MD 20034 Office: Internat Energy Assos Ltd 2600 Virginia Ave Washington DC

SIEVERS, ALBERT JOHN, III, educator; b. Oakland, Calif., June 28, 1933; s. Albert John and Martha (McDowell) S.; B.A., U. Calif. at Berkeley, 1958, Ph.D., 1962; m. Betsy Floy Ross, Feb. 6, 1959; children—Karla Jean, John Charles, Martha Caroline, Sylvia Jane. Machinist Varian Assos., Palo Alto, Calif., 1951-58; research asso. Cornell U., 1962-64; asst. prof. physics, 1964-67, asso. prof., 1967-71, prof., 1971—; cons. Lockheed Research Lab., 1966, Los Alamos Sci. Lab., 1967-69, ARPA Materials Research Council, 1969—; lectr. NATO Summer Sch., Italy, 1966, Holland, 1968. NSF sr. postdoctoral fellow, 1970-71; Erskine fellow U. Canterbury (N.Z.), 1976. Mem. Am. Phys. Soc., AAAS, Am. Optical Soc., Phi Beta Kappa, Sigma Xi. Club: Sierra. Research far infrared spectroscopy of solids and liquids, solar energy research, 1960—. Home: 115 Winston Dr Ithaca NY 14850

SIEVERS, ALLEN MORRIS, economist, educator; b. Boston, Oct. 15, 1918; s. Maurice J. and Esther (Bloom) S.; A.B., U. Chgo., 1939; M.A., Columbia, 1941, Ph.D., 1948; m. Anita Ress, Aug. 29, 1954; 1 son, Marc Jonathan. Asst. prof. U. N.C. at Greensboro, 1945-48; asso. prof. Tufts U., 1948-49, U. Mass. at Amherst, 1949-51; prof. U. Fla. at Gainesville, 1954-68; prof. econs. U. Utah, Salt Lake City, 1968—, chmn. dept., 1968-71; chief econ. analysis sect. Bur. Fgn. Commerce, Dept. Commerce, 1952-53; mem. U.S. del. to 17th, 18th sessions UN ECOSOC, 1952-53; cons. Korea, 1953, Indonesia, 1962-64, chief of party, 1964, Thailand, 1972. Served to capt. USAAF, 1942-45. Mem. Am. Econ. Assn. Author: Has Market Capitalism Collapsed? A Critique of Karl Polanyi's New Economics, 1948; General Economics, 1952; (with others) An Economic Programme for Korean Reconstruction, 1954; Revolution, Evolution, and The Economic Order, 1962; The Mystical World of Indonesia: Culture and Economic Development in Conflict, 1975. Home: 701 I St Salt Lake City UT 84103

SIEVERS, ROBERT H., film processing co. exec.; b. San Francisco, Nov. 2, 1941: s. Howard H. and Minnie A. (Sommers) S.; B.A. in Finance, Calif. State U., San Francisco, 1968; m. Judith Falk; children—Kirk Robert, Allison Jill, Paige Julie, Tracy Michele, Jeremy David. Audit mgr. Hurdman and Cranstoun, San Francisco, 1968-76; treas. Falstaff Brewing Corp., San Francisco, 1976-77, also dir.; v.p. fin. Capital Film Labs., Washington, 1977—. C.P.A., Calif. Mem. Am. Inst. C.P.A.'s, Calif. Soc. C.P.A.'s. Home: 3905 Parsons Rd Chevy Chase MD 20015 Office: 470 E St SW Washington DC 20024

SIEVERT, JAMES LEE, mfg. co. exec.; b. Manitowoc, Wis., Sept. 7, 1934; s. Lyman R. and Verona F. (Peronto) S.; B.S., Marquette U., 1956; m. Anita J. Henneke, May 4, 1957; children—Suzanne, Shari. Asst. controller J.I. Case Co., 1963-65; treas. Dietz Electric Co., Milw., 1965-68; v.p. V.I.P. Corp., Milw., 1968-70, also dir.; fin. v.p., treas. Medalist Industries, Inc., Milw., 1970—; dir. Blue Shield of Wis. Served with U.S. Army, 1957, 61-62. Mem. Wis. Soc. C.P.A.'s (Achievement award 1978, v.p. 1973-75, dir. 1969-75), Fin. Execs. Inst. (dir. and sec. Milw. chpt.). Roman Catholic. Clubs: Milw. Athletic, North Shore Country. Home: 8121 Aberdeen Ct Wauwatosa WI 53213 Office: 735 N 5th St Milwaukee WI 53203

SIEVERTS, FRANK ARNE, govt. ofcl.; b. Frankfurt am/Main, Germany, June 19, 1933; s. Helmut J. and Cecilie M. (Behrendt) S.; came to U.S., 1938, naturalized, 1945; B.A., Swarthmore Coll., 1955; B.Phil. (Rhodes scholar), Balliol Coll., Oxford U., 1957, postgrad. Nuffield Coll., 1957-59; m. Jane Baldwin Woodbridge, Dec. 31, 1957; children—Elisabeth, Michael. News corr. Time mag., 1959-60; legis. asst. U.S. Senator, 1960-62; spl. asst. Dept. State, 1962, spl. asst. to under sec. state, dep. staff dir. Sr. Inter-Deptl. Group, 1966, spl. asst. to ambassador at large, Washington, 1967-68, also adviser on prisoner of war matters to U.S. delegation to Vietnam peace talks; spl. asst. to dep. sec. of state for prisoner of war matters, 1969-75, dep. coordinator for human rights and humanitarian affairs, 1975—, dep. asst. sec. for refugee and migration affairs, 1978—, mem. advance team for release Am. prisoners of war, Hanoi, 1973. Mem. U.S. delegation to 20th Internat. Conf. Red Cross, Vienna, 1965, 21st Conf., Istanbul, 1969, 22d Conf., Tehran, 1973; chmn. 23d Conf., Bucharest, 1977; mem. U.S. del. Diplomatic Conf. on Humanitarian Law in Armed Conflicts, Geneva, 1974-77, to exec. com. of UN High Commn. for Refugees, 1978. Mem. Am. Assn. Rhodes Scholars (dir. 1974—, v.p. 1978—). Editorial bd. The Am. Oxonian. Home: 4216 Mathewson Dr NW Washington DC 20011 Office: Dept State Washington DC 20520

SIFFERT, ROBERT SPENCER, orthopaedic surgeon; b. N.Y.C., June 16, 1918; s. Oscar and Sadye (Rusoff) S.; A.B. with honors in Biology, N.Y. U., 1939, M.D., 1943; m. Miriam Sand, June 29, 1941; children—Joan, John. Intern, Kings County Hosp., Bklyn., 1943; resident orthopaedic surgery Mt. Sinai Hosp., N.Y.C., 1946-49, fellow pathology, 1949-52, mem. staff, 1949—, dir. orthopaedic surgery, orthopaedic surgeon in chief, 1960—; sr. orthopaedic cons. N.Y.C. Dept. Health, 1952—; pvt. practice, N.Y.C., 1949—; attending orthopaedic surgeon Blythedale Childrens Hosp., Valhalla, N.Y., 1960—; dir. orthopaedic surgery City Hosp. at Elmhurst; prof., chmn. dept. orthopaedics Mt. Sinai Sch. Medicine. Med. adv. bd. CARE-MEDICO, 1972—; adv. bd. Orthopaedics Overseas; bd. dirs., profl. adv. com. Easter Seal Soc. for Crippled Children and Adults, 1st v.p., 1977-79. Served to capt. USAAF, 1944-46; CBI. Recipient annual award medicine N.Y. Pub. Health Assn., 1958, N.Y. Philanthropic League, 1959. Diplomate Am. Bd. Orthopaedic Surgery, Nat. Bd. Med. Examiners. Fellow Am. Pub. Health Assn., A.C.S.; mem. Am. Orthopaedic Assn., Am. Acad. Orthopaedic Surgery (chmn. com. care handicapped child), Assn. Bone and Joint Surgeons, Internat. Soc. Orthopaedic Surgery and Traumatology, Orthopaedic Research Soc., N.Y. Acad. Medicine (fellow orthopaedic sect. 1952, sec. 1962-63, chmn. 1963-64), N.Y. State Med. Soc. (chmn. orthopaedic sect. 1967-68), Phi Beta Kappa, Alpha Omega Alpha. Club: Century Assn. (N.Y.C.). Contbr. articles to profl. jours. Home: 45 E 85th St New York NY 10028 Office: 955 Fifth Ave New York NY 10022

SIFTON, CHARLES PROCTOR, judge; b. N.Y.C., Mar. 18, 1935; s. Paul F. and Claire G. Sifton; A.B., Harvard U., 1957; LL.B., Columbia U., 1961; m. Elisabeth Niebuhr, July 7, 1962; children—Samuel, Tobias, John. Admitted to N.Y. bar, 1961; asso. firm Cadwalader, Wickersham & Taft, 1961-62, 64-66; staff atty. U.S. Senate Fgn. Relations Com., 1962-63; asst. U.S. atty., N.Y.C., 1966-69; partner firm Leboeuf, Lamb, Leiby and MacRae, N.Y.C., 1969-77; U.S. Dist. judge, Eastern Dist. of N.Y., Bklyn., 1977—. Mem. Bar Assn. City of N.Y. Club: Century Assn. Office: 226 Cadman Plaza E Brooklyn NY 11201

SIFTON, DAVID WHITTIER, mag. editor; b. N.Y.C., Sept. 12, 1940; s. David William and Dorothy (Whittier) S.; B.A., Trinity Coll., Hartford, Conn., 1962; M.A., Stanford U., 1967. Editor, Inside Edn., N.Y. State Edn. Dept., 1968-70; adminstrv. editor Med. Econs., Oradell, N.J., 1970-72; editor Drug Topics, Oradell, 1972-75; editor-in-chief Current Prescribing, Oradell, 1975-78, RN mag., Oradell, 1978—. Served to 1st lt. USAF, 1963-66. Decorated Air Force Commendation medal; grantee Ford Found., 1967. Mem. Am. Bus. Press (chmn. editorial com. 1975-76). Republican. Episcopalian.

SIFTON, MICHAEL CLIFFORD, broadcasting pub. exec.; b. Toronto, Ont., Can., Jan. 21, 1931; s. Clifford and Doris Margaret (Greene) S.; student U. Western Ont., 1950- 54; m. Heather Ann McLean, Sept. 8, 1956; children—Clifford McLean, Michael Gregory, Derek Andrew. Pres., Armadale Co. Ltd., Armadale Enterprises Ltd., Regina Leader-Post Ltd., Armadale Pubs. Ltd. (Saskatoon Star-Phoenix), Armadale Communications Ltd. (CKCK Radio, Regina, Radio CKRC, Winnipeg), Toronto Airways Ltd., Radio CKOC, Hamilton; dir. H.A. McLean Chevrolet-Oldsmobile Ltd., Phoenix Leasing Ltd., Eastern Ont. Broadcasting (CFJR). Named hon. col. 411th Air Res. Squadron, 1975. Clubs: Toronto, Toronto and North York Hunt, Toronto Polo (pres.); Saskatoon; Canadian; Empire; Assiniboia. Office: care Armadale Co Ltd Buttonville Airport Markham ON L3P 3J9 Canada

SIGAL, CLANCY, writer; b. Chgo., Sept. 6, 1926; s. Leo and Jenny (Persily) S.; B.A. in English Lit., U. Calif. at Los Angeles, 1950. Mem. staff UAW-CIO, Detroit, 1946-47; story analyst Columbia Pictures Corp., Los Angeles, 1952-54; agt. Jaffe Agy., Los Angeles, 1954-56; author, critic, editor, journalist, Britain, 1957—. Served with inf. AUS, 1944-46. Author: Weekend in Dinlock, 1961; Going Away, 1962; Zone of the Interior, 1976. Home: care Elaine Greene Ltd 31 Newington Green London N16 England

SIGBAND, NORMAN BRUCE, ednl. adminstr., educator; b. Chgo., June 27, 1920; s. Max and Bessie S.; B.A., U. Chgo., 1940, M.A., 1941, Ph.D., 1954; m. Joan C. Lyons, Aug. 3, 1944; children—Robin, Shelley, Betsy. Asst. prof. bus. communication De Paul U., 1946-50, asso. prof., 1950-54, prof., 1954-65; prof. mgmt. communication U. So. Calif., 1965—, chmn. dept. mktg., 1970-72, asso. dean Sch. Bus., 1976—; cons. to industry; speaker, condr. workshops, seminars in field. Served to capt. AUS, 1942-46; ETO. Decorated Bronze Star; recipient Excellence in Teaching award U. So. Calif., 1975, Dean's award, 1972, outstanding Educator award, 1973. Fellow Am. Bus. Communication Assn. (pres. 1964-65); mem. Internat. Communication Assn. Democrat. Jewish. Author books, including: Practical English for Everyday Use, 1954; Effective Report Writing for Business, Industry and Government, 1960; Communication for Management, 1970; Communicacion Para Directivos, 1972; Management Communication for Decision Making, 1972; Communication for Management and Business, 1976; Communication for Results in Business, 1980; contbr. numerous articles to profl. jours., mags. Home: 3109 Dona Susana Dr Studio City CA 91604 Office: U So Calif Grad Sch Bus University Park Los Angeles CA 90007

SIGEL, BERNARD, medical educator; b. Wilno, Poland, May 14, 1930; s. Zundel and Hinda (Lubetska) S.; came to U.S., 1937, naturalized, 1945; student So. Meth. U., 1947-49; M.D., U. Tex., 1953; m. Lois Savitch, Dec. 1, 1956; children—Paul, Carin, Gwynne, Ellen, Adam. Intern Grad. Hosp. U. Pa., Phila., 1953-54, resident, 1954-58; resident VA Hosp., Coral Gables, Fla., 1958-59, surg. staff, 1959-60; instr. gen. surgery U. Miami Sch. Medicine, 1959-60; practice medicine specializing in gen. surgery, Phila., 1960—; mem. staff Med. Coll. Pa. Hosp.; asso. in surgery Med. Coll. Pa., Phila., 1960-62, asst. prof., 1962-64, asso. prof., 1964-69, prof., 1969-74, dean, 1969-74, acting pres., 1971-74; prof. surgery Abraham Lincoln Sch. U. Ill. Coll. Medicine, Chgo., 1974—, dean, 1974-78. Fellow A.C.S.; mem. Soc. U. Surgeons, AMA, Am. Soc. Exptl. Pathology, Am. Gastroenterological Assn., Soc. Surgery Alimentary Tract. Home: 936 Fisher Ln Winnetka IL 60093 Office: 1853 W Polk St Chicago IL 60012

SIGEL, M(OLA) MICHAEL, microbiologist; b. Nieswiez, Poland, June 24, 1920; s. Zundel and Hinda (Lubecka) S.; came to U.S., 1937, naturalized, 1941; B.A., U. Tex., 1941; Ph.D., Ohio State U., 1944; m. Mary Elizabeth Wynne, Dec. 22, 1941; children—Suzanne Lea Sigel Barth, Vicki Adelaide Breina Sigel Sroka, Rachel Delelaw Sarah Sigel Blancher, Valerie Harriet Louise, David Edward Burl. Asso. in virology U. Pa., 1946-50, asst. prof. virology, 1950-53; head virus diagnostic lab. Children's Hosp., Phila., 1946-53; chief reference diagnosis and research unit Center for Disease Control, USPHS, Montgomery, Ala., 1953-55; spl. cons. WHO, Europe, 1956; asso. prof. U. Miami (Fla.), 1955-58, prof. microbiology Sch. Medicine, 1958-78, prof. oncology, 1975-78; prof., chmn. microbiology and immunology U. S.C. Sch. Medicine, Columbia, 1978—; research asso. Lerner Marine Lab., Bimini, Bahamas, 1963—; hon. prof. U. W.I., 1960—. Served to col. AUS. Fellow AAAS, N.Y. Acad. Scis.; mem. Am. Soc. Microbiology (pres. So. Fla. br. 1969-70), Soc. Exptl. Biology Medicine, Soc. Pediatric Research, Am. Assn. Immunologists, Soc. Gen. Microbiology, Reticuloendothelial Soc. (counselor, chmn. nat. meeting 1975, pres. 1978-79), Am. Soc. Cell Biology, Am. Assn. Cancer Research, Tissue Culture Assn. (program chmn. 1969-70, counselor-at-large 1974-78), Phi Beta Kappa, Sigma Xi (pres. U. Miami chpt. 1976-77). Author: (with A. R. Beasley) Viruses, Cells and Hosts, 1962; editor: Lymphogranuloma Venereum, 1962; Differentiation and Defense Mechanisms in Lower Organisms in Vitro, 1968; (with R. A. Good) Tolerance, Autoimmunity and Aging, 1972; asso. editor Cancer Research, 1969-72; contbr. articles to profl. jours. Home: 1174 Quail Run Columbia SC 29206 Office: Dept Microbiology and Immunology Sch Medicine U SC Columbia SC 29208

SIGEL, STANLEY JORDAN, economist; b. Boston, Feb. 10, 1920; s. Max and Ida (Klebanov) S.; B.A., Harvard, 1940, M.A. (Social Sci. Council demblzn. fellow 1946-47, Littauer fellow 1946-47), 1947, Ph.D., 1953; student U. Calif. at Berkeley, 1940-41; m. Madeleine Bartfeld, Mar. 9, 1947; children—Karen P., Joan B. Chief flow of funds and savs. sect., div. research and statistics, bd. govs. Fed. Res. System, 1947-61, asst. to dir., 1964-65, asso. adviser, 1965-68, adviser, 1969-75, asst. to bd., 1975—; dir. statistics and nat. accounts OECD, 1962-64; adj. prof. Am. U., Washington, 1964-67. U.S. rep. internat. tech. meetings, 1959-64. Served to lt. (s.g.) USNR, 1942-46. Mem. Am. Econ. Assn., Conf. Research Income and Wealth, Internat. Assn. Research Income and Wealth, Phi Beta Kappa. Author articles, research bulls. Home: 6530 E Halbert Rd Bethesda MD 20034 Office: Bd Govs Fed Reserve System Washington DC 20551

SIGERSON, DAVID KINLEY, lawyer; b. Yonkers, N.Y., July 1, 1924; s. Wilfred H. and Bertha (Gauble) S.; A.B. cum laude, Harvard, 1947; J.D. cum laude, Yale, 1950; m. Marjorie Lorraine Parke, Apr. 9, 1943; children—Diane Parke (Mrs. John Dando), David Kinley. Admitted to N.Y. bar, 1950, Fla. bar, 1962; practice in Daytona Beach, 1962-76; partner firm Cobb, Cole, Sigerson, McCoy, Bell & Bond, 1964-76; individual practice law, Ormond Beach, Fla., 1976—; pres., dir. N.D.G., Inc., S&W, Inc. Legal officer Daytona Beach Power Squadron, 1965-75. Pres. Levittown (N.Y.) Civic Council, 1952-54. Trustee Daytona Beach Mus. Arts and Scis., 1964—, pres., 1967-69, 73-75, 1st v.p., 1972. Served with USAAF, 1942-45. Mem. Am., N.Y. State, Volusia County bar assns., Fla. Bar., Volusia County Anthrop. Soc., Daytona Beach Community Coll. Photog. Soc., Ormond Beach C. of C. Presbyn. (sec. 1967-69, deacon 1966-69). Clubs: University (bd. dirs.) Quarter Back (Daytona Beach); Halifax Kiwanis; Halifax; Oceanside Country. Home: 410 John Anderson Dr Ormond Beach FL 32074 Office: 142 E Granada Blvd Ormond Beach FL 32074

SIGETY, CHARLES EDWARD, lawyer, health care exec.; b. N.Y.C., Oct. 10, 1922; s. Charles and Anna (Toth) S.; B.S., Columbia, 1944; M.B.A. (Baker scholar), Harvard, 1947; LL.B., Yale, 1951; m. Katharine K. Snell, July 17, 1948; children—Charles, Katharine, Robert, Cornelius, Elizabeth. With Bankers Trust Co., 1939-42; instr. adminstrv. engring. Pratt Inst., 1948; instr. econs. Yale, 1948-50; vis. lectr. accounting Sch. Gen. Studies, Columbia, 1948-50, 52; admitted to N.Y. State bar, 1952, D.C. bar, 1958; rapporteur com. fed. taxation for U.S. council, Internat. C. of C., 1952-53; asst. to com. fed. taxation Am. Inst. Accountants, 1950-53; vis. lectr. law Yale, 1952; law practice, N.Y.C., 1952-67; pres., dir. Video Vittles, Inc., N.Y.C., 1953-67; dep. commr. FHA, 1955-57; of counsel Javits and Javits, 1959-60; 1st asst. atty. gen., N.Y., 1958-59; dir., mem. exec. com. Gothem Bank, N.Y.C., 1961-63; dir. N.Y. State Housing Finance Agy., 1962-63; pres., exec. adminstr. Florence Nightingale Nursing Home, N.Y.C., 1965—; professorial lectr. Sch. Architecture, Pratt Inst., N.Y.C., 1962-66; mem. Sigety Assos., cons. in housing mortgage financing and urban renewal, 1957-67. Housing cons. Govt. Peru, S.Am., 1956. Bd. dirs., sec., v.p. Nat. Council Health Care Services, 1969—; bd. dirs. Am.-Hungarian Found., 1974-76. Served to lt. (j.g.) USNR, 1943-47. Mem. N.Y. County Lawyers Assn., Am. Bar Assn., Guild N.Y. Nursing Homes (pres. 1969-72), Am. Hosp. Assn., Harvard Bus. Sch. Assn. (exec. council 1966-69, area chmn. 1967-69), Alpha Kappa Psi, Phi Delta Phi. Presbyn. Clubs: Yale, Harvard Bus. Sch. (pres. 1964-65, chmn. 1965-66, dir. 1964—), Harvard (N.Y.C.); Metropolitan (Washington). Office: 175 E 96th St New York NY 10028

SIGGELKOW, RICHARD ALBERT, univ. adminstr.; b. Madison, Wis., Feb. 10, 1918; s. Herbert Scott and Florence Edna (Perkins) S.; B.S., U. Wis., 1941, M.S., 1948, Ph.D., 1953; m. Lois Vandall, Dec. 27, 1946; children—Richard Todd, James Alan. Asst. dir. to asso. dir. tchr. placement bur. U. Wis., 1949-56, asst. prof. edn., asst. dean, 1956-58; dean, students, asso. prof. edn. State U. N.Y. at Buffalo, 1958-67, v.p. student affairs, prof. edn., 1967—. Mem. Nat. Assn. Student Personnel Adminstrs., Am. Coll. Personnel Assn., N.Y. State Assn. Deans and Guidance Personnel, Am. Assn. Higher Edn., Phi Delta Kappa, Sigma Delta Chi. Editor of NASPA, 1964-69. Home: 304 Brantwood Rd Buffalo NY 14226

SIGLER, ANDREW CLARK, forest products co. exec.; b. Bklyn., Sept. 25, 1931; s. Andrew J. and Eleanor (Nicholas) S.; A.B., Dartmouth, 1953; M.B.A., Amos Tuck Sch., 1956; m. Margaret Romefelt, June 16, 1956; children—Andrew Clark, Patricia, Elizabeth. With Champion Papers Co., Hamilton, Ohio, 1957—; pres. Champion Papers div. Champion Internat. Corp., 1972, exec. v.p., dir. parent co., 1972-74, pres., chief exec. officer, Stamford, Conn., 1974-79, chmn. bd., chief exec. officer, 1979—; dir. A.M.F. Corp., Cabot Corp., Chem. Bank, Thomson Newspapers. Served from 2d lt. to 1st lt. USMCR, 1953-55. Office: 1 Landmark Sq Stamford CT 06921

SIGLER, JAY ADRIAN, polit. scientist, educator; b. Paterson, N.J., June 21, 1933; s. Benjamin and Lucille (Pakula) S.; B.A. with honors, Rutgers U., 1954, J.D. (Law Alumni scholar), 1957, M.A. (fellow), 1960, Ph.D., 1962; m. Margaret Davis, Sept. 5, 1961; children—Niall, Ian. Asst. prof. polit. sci. Kent (Ohio) State U., 1961-63, U. Vt., Burlington, 1963-64; instr. dept. polit. sci. Rutgers U., Camden, N.J., 1960-61, asso. prof., 1965-70, prof., 1970-73, Disting. prof. polit. sci., chmn. dept., 1973—, asso. dean, 1970-71. Mcpl. chmn. Democratic Party, Haddonfield, N.J., 1968-70; mem. Camden County Dem. Com., 1968-71. Served with U.S. Army, 1957-58. Rutgers Research fellow, 1973-74; Eagleton fellow, 1978-79; Am. Polit. Sci. Assn. Project 87 fellow, 1979; Nat. Endowment for Humanities summer fellow, 1979. Mem. AAUP, Law and Soc. Assn., Policy Studies Orgn., Nat. Assn. Schs. Public Affairs and Adminstrn., Am. Polit. Sci. Assn. Club: Rutgers Faculty. Author: Double Jeopardy, 1969; Courts and Public Policy, 1970; El Pensamento Conservador en los Estados Unidos, 1971; Contemporary American Government, 1972; American Rights Policies, 1975; The Legal Sources of Public Policy, 1977; contbr. articles to profl. jours. Home: 4631 Pine St Philadelphia PA 19143 Office: 311 N 5th St Camden NJ 08102. *The contemplation of the limits of a life, of the mixture of luck and planning for more luck, is a source of balance and calm. Discovering that a few persons mean more than any things is the hard and painful part.*

SIGLER, LEROY WALTER, banker, lawyer; b. Racine, Wis., Aug. 3, 1926; s. LeRoy I. and Ruth Ann (Wacynski) S.; B.B.A., U. Wis., 1952, J.D., 1952; m. Sylvia L. Schmidt, Sept. 20, 1969; children—Suzanne Sigler Storer, Cynthia Sigler Idezak, Lee Scott, Robb Nash, Paul Grant. Admitted to Wis. bar, 1952, Ohio bar, 1967; corp. counsel, asst. sec. J.W. Butler Paper Co., 1952-66, Butler Paper Co., 1952-66; asst. mgr. law dept. Nekoosa Edwards Paper Co., 1952-66; asst. sec., gen. counsel Seilon, Inc., 1966-68, v.p., sec., gen. counsel, 1968-70, pres., gen. counsel, dir., 1970-79; pres., gen. counsel, dir. Bancorp. Leasing, 1973-79, Thomson Internat. Co., Thomson Veracruz S.A., Thomson-Poole, Inc., Inmobilaria Elda S.A., 1971-79, Air-Way Sanitizor, Inc., 1972-79; various positions including pres., vice chmn., dir., sec., gen. counsel Nev. Nat. Bank, 1969-79; v.p., sec. gen., counsel, dir. Nev. Nat. Bancorp., 1969-79; sec., gen. counsel Lamb Enterprises, Inc., Lamb Communications, Inc., 1970-79; chmn. Greenwood's Bancorp., Inc., 1976—; chmn., pres. Nekoosa Port Edwards Bancorp., Inc., 1979—. Chmn. fund drive South Wood County United Fund; co-chmn. 5 Community Planning Commn.; pres. Port Edwards Water Utility, Tri City Airways, Village of Port Edwards; chmn. South Wood County Airport Commn. Served with AUS, 1945-47. Mem. Wisconsin Rapids C. of C. (dir., Spl. Citizen award 1964), Tri-City Bar Assn. (pres.), 7th Circuit Bar Assn. (v.p.), Toastmasters Club (v.p.), Phi Delta Phi. Elk (exalted ruler, trustee). Home and Office: 2908 River Rd Maumee OH 43537. *Play all games possible. Play by the rules. Play devotedly, sincerely and graciously.*

SIGLER, WILLIAM FRANKLIN, cons.; b. LeRoy, Ill., Feb. 17, 1909; s. John A. and Bettie (Homan) S.; B.S., Iowa State U., 1940, M.S., 1941, Ph.D., 1947; postdoctoral studies U. Calif. at Los Angeles, 1963; m. Margaret Eleanor Brotherton, July 3, 1936; children—Elinor Jo, John William. Conservationist, Soil Conservation Service, Ill., 1935-37; cons. Central Engring. Co., Davenport, Iowa, 1940-41; research asso. Iowa State U., 1941-42; 1945-47; asst. prof. wildlife sci. Utah State U., 1947-50, prof., head dept., 1950-74; pres. W.F. Sigler & Assos., Inc., 1974—; cons. Cons. U.S. surgeon gen., 1963-67, FAO, Argentina, 1968. Mem. Utah Water Pollution Control Bd., 1957-65, chmn., 1963-65. Served as lt. (j.g.) USNR, World War II. Named wildlife conservationist of year Nat. Wildlife Fedn., 1970, Outstanding Educator of Year, 1971. Fellow Internat. Acad. Fishery Scientists, AAAS; mem. Ecol. Soc. Am., Wildlife Soc., Am. Fisheries Soc., AAUP, Outdoor Writers Am., Sigma Xi. Author: Theory and Method of Fish Life History Investigations, 1952; Wildlife Law Enforcement, 1956, 3d edit., 1980; Fishes of Utah, 1963; also numerous articles. Home: 980 E 2d S Logan UT 84321

SIGMOND, ROBERT M., med. economist; b. Seattle, June 18, 1920; s. Harry and Alice (Gottfield) S.; B.A., Pa. State Coll., 1941, M.A., 1942; m. Barbara, June 29, 1941; children—Alison (Mrs. Elden J. Gatwood), Laurence. Research asso. Gov.'s Commn. on Hosp. Facilities, Standards and Orgn., Phila., 1945-46, Hosp. Council Phila., 1946-50; asst. to v.p., Albert Einstein Med. Center, Phila., 1950-55, exec. v.p. for planning, 1968-70, exec. v.p., 1971-75, recipient trustee medal, 1975; dir. fiscal studies Nat. Commn. Financing. of Hosp. Care, Chgo., 1952-54; exec. dir. Hosp. Council Western Pa., Pitts., 1955-64, Hosp. Planning Assn. Allegheny County, Pitts., 1964-68; adj. prof. health adminstrn. Sch. Bus. Adminstrn., Temple U., 1968—; cons. Blue Cross Assn. and Blue Cross of Greater Phila., 1976-77; spl. adviser on hosp. affairs Blue Cross and Blue Shield Assns., Chgo., 1977—; cons. Nat. Center Health Services Research; mem. adv. panel on cost effectiveness Congl. Office of Tech. Assessment; past cons. com. community health care council on med. services AMA, Social Security Adminstrn., Pa. Gov.'s Hosp. Study Commn., USPHS, OEO, Pitts. Found., U. Mich. Study of Hosp. and Med. Econs., hosp. utilization project Calif. Dept. Health; expert Office Asst. Sec. for Health, HEW. Chmn. nat. adv. com. Johnson Found. Community Hosp. Med. Staff Group Practice Program; trustee Dorothy Rider Pool Health Care Trust, Allentown, Pa.; mem. North Phila. Sub-Area Council of Health Systems Agency of Southeastern Pa.; past. chmn. health facilities rev. and study com. Regional Comprehensive Health Planning Council, Phila. Edwin L. Crosby fellow Nuffield Provincial Hosps. Trust, London, 1976. Fellow Am. Pub. Health Assn. (mem. editorial bd. jour.); mem. Am. Hosp. Assn. (mem. adv. panels on data base devel. and research policy), Am. Statis. Assn., Am. Coll. Hosp. Adminstrs. (Dean Conley award 1969), Pa. Pub. Health Assn., Am. Assn. Hosp. Planning, Am. Health Planning Assn., Nat. League Nursing, Internat. Hosp. Fedn., Hosp. Assn. Pa. Author: Methods of Making Experimental Inferences 2d edit., 1945; (with Thomas Kinser) The Hospital-Blue Cross Plan Relationship, 1976; numerous monographs for profl. jours. Home: 1801 John F Kennedy Blvd Philadelphia PA 19103

SIGMUND, PAUL EUGENE, educator; b. Phila., Jan. 14, 1929; s. Paul Eugene and Marie (Ramsey) S.; A.B., Georgetown U., 1950; Fulbright scholar U. Durham, Eng., 1950-51; M.A., Harvard, 1954, Ph.D., 1959; postgrad. U. Paris (France), U. Heidelberg, U. Cologne (Germany) 1955-56; m. Barbara Rowena Boggs, Jan. 25, 1964; children—Paul Eugene, David, Stephen. Teaching fellow Harvard, 1953-55, 58-59, instr., 1959-63; asso. prof. politics Princeton, 1963-70, prof. politics, 1970—. Cons. AID, 1961, UNESCO, 1963-65, Peace Corps, 1966, U.S. Dept. State Div. Exchange of Persons, 1968. Cons. Platform com. Democratic Party, 1968. Adv. bd. Georgetown U. Coll. Arts and Sci., 1962-64, Stuart Country Day Sch., Princeton, N.J., 1969-72; bd. dirs. Georgetown U., 1970—. Served to 1st lt., USAF, 1956-57. Mem. Am. Polit. Sci. Assn., Am. Soc. Polit. and Legal Philosophy, Latin Am. Studies Assn., Phi Beta Kappa. Author: Nicholas of Cusa and Medieval Political Thought, 1963; (with Reinhold Niebuhr) The Democratic Experience, 1969; Natural Law in Political Thought, 1971; The Overthrow of Allende and the Politics of Chile, 1977. Editor: The Ideologies of the Developing Nation, 1963, 67, 72; Models of Political Change in Latin America, 1970. Home: 8 Evelyn Pl Princeton NJ 08540

SIGNORET, SIMONE (SIMONE-HENRIETTE-CHARLOTTE KAMINKER), actress; b. Wiesbaden, Germany, Mar. 25, 1921; d. Andre and Georgette (Signoret) Kaminker; ed. Solange Sicard Sch., Paris; m. Marc Allegret, 1947 (div.); 1 dau., Catherine; m. 2d, Yves Montand, June 15, 1950. Tutor, English and Latin, Paris; typist for newspaper Le Nouveau Temps; appeared in motion picture Des Demons d l'Aube, 1946, other roles in Dédée d'Anvers, La Ronde, 1950, Thérèse Raquin, 1953, La mort en ce jardin, Diabolique, 1955, Les Sorcières de Salem (with husband in play version Paris stage, 1954), 1958, Room at the Top, 1958, also appeared as Roberte in Naked Autumn, 1963, Adua e le Compagne, Term of Trial, 1963, Ship of Fools, 1965, The Sleeping Car Murders, 1966, The Deadly Affair, 1967, Games, 1967, The Seagull, 1968, The Confession, 1971, Madame Rosa, 1978; TV acting debut in Don't You Remember, Gen. Electric Theater, 1960. Recipient Prix Suzanne Bianchetti for performance in Macadam, 1946, Prix Féminin du Cinéma, 1952, Grand Prix d'Intérpretation féminine de l'Académie du Cinema, 1953; Brit. Film Acad. award for performance as queen of Apaches in Casque d'Or, 1951; Best Actress award Brit. Film Acad. and Cannes Film Festival, 1959; prize as best fgn. actress German Film Critics, 1959; Acad. Award for best actress of 1959. Author: Nostalgia Isn't What It Used to Be, 1978. *

SIGNORI, EDRO ITALO, psychologist, educator; b. Calgary, Alta., Can., July 29, 1915; s. Giovanni Battista and Angela Teresa (Chicchiani) S.; B.A., U. Alta., 1937; M.A., U. Toronto, 1938-41, Ph.D., 1947; m. Dolores Alba Scarpelli, Apr. 24, 1942; children—Dolores Anne and Donna Lea (twins). With NRC Can., 1940-41; instr. U. Toronto, 1946-48; asst. prof. Queens U., 1948-49; asso. prof. U. B.C., Vancouver, 1949-59, prof., 1959—, acting head dept. psychology, 1961-65, 69-72; individual practice psychology, 1949—. Cons. to industry, 1949—; dir. research B.C. Commn. on Edn., 1958-61; coordinator and spl. cons. B.C. Govt. Community Care Services Soc., 1974-75. Served to lt. RCAF, 1942-46. Mem. B.C. Acad. Scis. (pres. 1957), Canadian (dir. 1954-57), Am., B.C. (pres. 1952-53) psychol. assns., Can. Assn. Gerontology. Co-author: Interpretive Psychology, 1957. Contbr. numerous articles to profl. jours. Home: 4621 W 6th Ave Vancouver BC V6R 1V6 Canada

SIGOLOFF, SANFORD CHARLES, retail conglomerate co. exec.; b. St. Louis, Sept. 8, 1930; s. Emmanuel and Gertrude (Breliant) S.; B.A., U. Calif., Los Angeles, 1950; m. Betty Ellen Greene, Sept. 14, 1952; children—Stephen, John David, Laurie. Cons. AEC, 1950-54, 57-58; gen. mgr. Edgerton, Germeshausen & Grier, Santa Barbara, Calif., 1958-63; v.p. Xerox Corp., 1963-69; pres. CSI Corp., Los Angeles, 1969-70; sr. v.p. Republic Corp., Los Angeles, 1970-71, pres., 1971-72; mgmt. cons., Los Angeles, 1972-74; pres., chmn. bd., chief exec. officer Daylin, Inc., Los Angeles, 1974-79; vice chmn., chief operating officer Kaufman & Broad, Inc., Los Angeles, 1979—. Bd. govs. Cedars-Sinai Hosp. Served in USAF, 1954-57. Recipient Tom May award Nat. Jewish Hosp. and Research Center, 1972. Mem. AAAS, Am. Chem. Soc., Am. Inst. Aeronautics and Astronautics, Am. Nuclear Soc., IEEE, Radiation Research Soc. Contbr. articles on radiation dosimetry to profl. jours. Home: 220 N Cliffwood Ave Los Angeles CA 90049 Office: 10801 National Blvd Los Angeles CA 90064

SIGWORTH, OLIVER FREDERIC, educator; b. Glendale, Ariz., July 31, 1921; s. Jay and Bjorg (Fredericksson) S.; student Phoenix Jr. Coll., 1940-42, U. So. Calif., 1942-43; B.A., U. Calif., Berkeley, 1947, M.A., 1948, Ph.D., 1951; m. Alice V. Gibbs, Dec. 17, 1953 (dec. 1958); 1 son, George F.; m. 2d, Heather Brooks, Apr. 28, 1963; 1 stepdau., Rosalind. Instr. English, U. Nev., Reno, 1951-52; instr. English and humanities San Francisco State Coll., 1952-53; mem. faculty U. Ariz., Tucson, 1953—, prof. English, 1967—, dir. grad. studies in English, 1968-77, chmn. univ. faculty, 1979—. Fund for Advancement Edn. fellow, 1955-56. Mem. Am., Western (treas. 1975-77, 1st v.p. 1978—, socs. eighteenth century studies, Modern Lang. Assn. Am., Philol. Assn. Pacific Coast, Rocky Mountain Modern Lan. Assn., Rocky Mountain Coll. English Assn. (v.p. 1974-76). Author: Four Styles of a Decade, 1960; Nature's Sternest Painter, 1965; William Collins, 1965; editor: Criticism and Aesthetics, 1660-1800, 1971; contbr. articles to profl. jours. Home: 4241 N Camino Pintoresco Tucson AZ 85705

SIH, CHARLES JOHN, educator; b. Shanghai, China, Sept. 11, 1933; s. Paul Kwang-Tsien and Teresa (Dong) S.; A.B. in Biology, Caroll Coll., 1953; M.S. in Bacteriology, Mont. State Coll., 1955; Ph.D. in Bacteriology, U. Wis., 1958; m. Catherine Elizabeth Hsu, July 11, 1959; children—Shirley, Gilbert, Ronald. Sr. research microbial biochemist Squibb Inst. for Med. Research, New Brunswick, N.J., 1958-60; mem. faculty U. Wis.-Madison, 1960—, Frederick B. Power prof. pharm. biochemistry, 1966—; sci. adviser Miles Labs., Elkart, Ind., 1972; cons. Schering Corp., 1975. First recipient Ernest Volwiler award, 1977. Mem. Am. Chem. Soc., Soc. Am. Biol. Chemists, Acad. Pharm. Scis., Soc. Am. Microbiologists. Home: 6322 Landfall Dr Madison WI 53705

SIH, JULIUS WEI WU, engr.; b. Shanghai, China, July 2, 1922; s. C.C. and Y.F. (Dai) S.; B.S., Nat. Chekiang U., 1944; M.S. in Engring., U. Mich., 1948; doctoral candidate N.Y. U., 1952; m. Susan D. Wang, Aug. 30, 1950; children—Jeanette, Daniel. Came to U.S., 1947, naturalized, 1956. Lectr., Chiao-Yang Coll.; dir., exec. com. Min-Ku-Jin-Pao, newspaper; dir. Tao-Sih-Pao, newspaper, Shanghai, China, 1944-48; cons. engr. major projects for cons. engring. firms in N.Y.C. and Chgo., 1948-59; chief structural engr. Chgo. Fed. Center Architects, 1959-65; pres. J.W. Sih & Assos., Inc., architects and engrs., Chgo., 1965—; projects include Lake County Govt. Complex, Casual Commons, Community Hosp., numerous Ill. State regional office bldgs., indsl. facilities Inland Steel Co., Ill. State Mental Retardation Facility, New Loop Coll. for City Colls. Chgo., Orr High Sch., Lawndale High Sch., Chgo., 6th Dist. Circuit Ct. Bldg., Ill. Chmn., Citizens Com. on Sr. Coll. Fellow ASCE; mem. Am. Concrete Inst., Internat. Soc. Soil Mechanics and Found. Engring., Internat. Assn. Bridge and Structural Engrs., Nat. Assn. Profl. Engrs., Am. Inst. Steel Constrn., Ill. Soc. Profl. Engrs., Chgo. Chamber Commerce and Industry. Clubs: Union League, Chicago Athletic, Executives (Chgo.). Contbr. to profl. jours. Home: 608 Earlston Rd Kenilworth IL 60043 Office: 35 E Wacker Dr Chicago IL 60601

SIHLER, WILLIAM WOODING, educator; b. Seattle, Nov. 17, 1937; s. William and Helen Alice (Wooding) S.; A.B. summa cum laude in Govt. (Sheldon traveling fellow), Harvard U., 1959, M.B.A. with high distinction, 1962, D.B.A., 1965; m. Mary Elizabeth Unwin, Aug. 21, 1963; children—Edward Wooding, Jennifer Mary. Instr., asst. prof. Harvard U. Bus. Sch., 1964-67; asso. prof. Darden Grad. Bus. Sch., U. Va., Charlottesville, 1967-72, prof., 1972-76, A.J. Morris prof., 1976—, dir. D.B.A. Program, 1971-73, asso. dean acad. affairs, 1972-77, exec. dir. Center for Internat. Banking Studies, 1977—; dir. Southeastern Cons. Group, Ltd., Cenco, Inc., Ohio-Sealy Mattress Mfg. Co. Class sec. Harvard M.B.A. Class, 1962; mem. vis. com. Sch. Mgmt., Case Western Res. U., 1976—. Recipient DeL. K. Jay prize; C.J. Bonaparte scholar. Mem. Fin. Mgmt. Assn., Am. Fin. Assn., Am. Econ. Assn., Phi Beta Kappa, Beta Gamma Sigma. Clubs: University (N.Y.C.); Harvard (Boston); Colonnade (U. Va.). Contbr. articles to mgmt. publs. and anthologies of readings. Home: 202 Sturbridge Rd Charlottesville VA 22901 Office: PO Box 6550 Charlottesville VA 22906

SIIPOLA, ELSA MARGAREETA (MRS. HAROLD E. ISRAEL), educator; b. Fitchburg, Mass., Mar. 15, 1908; d. George William and Lydia (Tikka) Siipola; B.A., Smith Coll., 1929, M.A. (Marjorie Hope Nicholson fellow), 1931; Ph.D. (Mary E. Ives fellow), Yale, 1939; m. Harold E. Israel, July 24, 1939 (dec. Oct. 1961). Faculty Smith Coll., 1929—, asst., instr., asst. prof., asso. prof., 1929-54, prof. psychology, 1954-69, Harold E. Israel prof. psychology, 1969—, chmn. dept., 1956—, sci. research dept. psychology, 1933—; vis. prof. psychology U. Calif., 1962-63. Chmn. Mass. Adv. Com. on Service to Youth, 1965—. Mem. Am. Psychol. Assn., Phi Beta Kappa, Sigma Xi. Contbr. numerous articles in field. Home: 42 West St Northampton MA 01060

SIKER, EPHRAIM S., physician; b. Port Chester, N.Y., Mar. 24, 1926; s. Samuel S. and Adele (Weiser) S.; student Duke, 1943-45; M.D., N.Y.U., 1949; m. Eileen Mary Bohnel, Aug. 5, 1951;

children—Kathleen Ellen, Jeffrey Stephen, David Allan, Paul William, Richard Francis. Intern Grasslands Hosp., Valhalla, N.Y., 1949-50, resident in anesthesia, 1950; resident dept. anesthesiology Mercy Hosp., Pitts., 1952-53, asso. dir. dept. 1955-62, chmn., 1962—; practice medicine, specializing in anesthesiology, Pitts., 1954—; sr. staff St. Clair Meml. Hosp., Pitts., 1954—; dir. anesthesia services Central Med. Pavilion, Pitts., 1973—; cons. staff St. Margaret Meml. Hosp., 1962—; pres. Pitts. Anesthesia Assos., Ltd., 1967—; clin. prof. dept. anesthesiology U. Pitts. Sch. Medicine, 1968—; mem. exec. com. Am. Bd. Med. Spltys., 1978—. Exchange cons. Welsh Nat. Sch. Medicine, Cardiff, 1955-56; mem. Pa. Gov.'s Commn. on Profl. Liability Ins., 1968-70; mem. adv. panel U.S. Pharmacopeia, 1970-76; mem. Am. acupuncture anesthesia study group of Nat. Acad. Scis. to Peoples Republic China, 1974; mem. adv. com. on splty. and geog. distbn. of physicians Inst. Medicine, Nat. Acad. Scis., 1974-76. Served to lt. M.C., USNR, 1950-52. USPHS postdoctoral research fellow, 1954; hon. fellow faculty anaesthetists Royal Coll. Surgeons (Eng.), 1974. Diplomate Am. Bd. Anesthesiology (dir. 1971—, sec.-treas. 1974—), Nat. Bd. Med. Examiners. Mem. Am. Soc. Anesthesiologists (pres. 1973—, dir.), A.M.A. (alternate del. 1962), Pa., Allegheny County med. socs., Pa. Soc. Anesthesiologists (pres. 1965), Royal Soc. Medicine (Eng.), Pitts. Acad. Medicine, Am. Coll. Anesthesiologists (gov. 1969-71), World Fedn. Socs. Anesthesiologists (vice chmn. exec. com. 1976—). Author: (with F.F. Foldes) Narcotics and Narcotic Antagonists, 1964; sect. on narcotic Ency. Brittanica; numerous other publs. in med. lit. Developed Siker Laryngoscope, 1956. Home: 185 Crestvue Manor Dr Pittsburgh PA 15228 Office: 1400 Locust St Pittsburgh PA 15219. *If you have to tell someone who you are, then you probably aren't. People are measured by more than their deeds, and such estimations are frequently made on the basis of their inter-personal relationships. While achievement and effort usually bear a linear relationship to each other, the impact that the achiever has on society depends upon the impact he makes on individuals.*

SIKES, CHARLES RENFORD, retail food chain exec.; b. Talco, Tex., Dec. 3, 1917; s. J.E. and Maude (Herring) S.; grad. pub. high sch.; m. Sarah Frances McClelland, Sept. 10, 1939; children—Charlotte (Mrs. John Caffey), Charles Randall, Tamera Jo. Owner, pres. Affiliated Food Stores, Dallas, 1939—; dir. Paris Bank of Tex. Served with USAAF, 1943-46. Mem. Tex. Retail Grocers Assn. (dir.). Baptist. Mason (Shriner). Club: Paris Golf and Country. Home: 3230 Hubbard St Paris TX 75460 Office: 15 W Provine St Paris TX 75460. *Behind every successful man there is another after his job.*

SIKES, G. GRIFFIN, lawyer; b. Booth, Ala., May 4, 1922; s. Joseph Cleveland and Belle (deRamus) S.; LL.B., U. Ala., 1947, J.D., 1964; m. Norma Loraine Evers, Sept. 7, 1947; children—Griffin, Margaret, Nancy, Anne, Steven, Clayton. Admitted to Ala. bar, 1947; asso. firm Edward F. Reid, Andalusia, Ala., 1951-54; partner firm Smith & Sikes, Andalusia, 1954-58, Powell & Sikes, Andalusia, 1966-79, Tipler, Fuller & Sikes, Andalusia, 1979—; individual practice law, Andalusia, 1958-65; mem. Ala. Bar Com., 1958-67; lectr. on history. Mem. Andalusia City Council, 1959-66. Served with USAAC, 1940-42. Mem. Ala. Def. Lawyers Assn. (v.p. 1977-78), Andalusia C. of C. (pres. 1958). Methodist. Club: Kiwanis (pres. local club 1951). Editor: Gridiron Internat., 1956-79. Office: Tipler Fuller & Sikes 218 S 3-Notch St PO Box 1397 Andalusia AL 36420

SIKES, ROBERT L.F., former Congressman; b. Isabella, Worth County, Ga., June 3, 1906; s. Benjamin Franklin and Clara Ophelia (Ford) S.; B.S., U. Ga., 1927; M.S., U. Fla., 1929; LL.D., Stetson U., 1969, U. West Fla., 1970; L.H.D., St. Leo Coll., 1969; hon. doctorate U. Inca Garcilaso de la Vega, Peru, 1970, Hangyang U., Seoul, Korea, 1975; H.H.D. (hon.), Gulf Coast Sem., Fla., 1979; m. Inez Tyner; children—Bobbye Serrene (Mrs. Edward F. Wicke), Robert Keyes. Agrl., indsl. research, 1928-32; published Okaloosa News-Jour., Crestview, Fla., and other newspapers, 1933-40. Mem. Fla. Legislature, 1936-40; chmn. Okaloosa County Democratic Com., 1934; mem. 77th-87th Congresses, 3d Fla. Dist., 88th-95th Congresses, 1st Fla. Dist., mem. appropriations com.; dir. 1st Bank Crestview (Fla.). Chmn. Fla. delegation Dem. Nat. Conv., 1956, 60, mem., 1972; del. Dem. Mid-Term Conf., 1974. Pres. Fla. Press Assn., 1937; bd. visitors Civil Air Patrol, USAF Acad., 1971-74, U.S. Naval Acad., 1975—; v.p., dir. Water Resources Congress (formerly Nat. Rivers and Harbors Congress), 1959-71, 1st v.p., 1970-71, exec. com., 1971; del. Pan Am. Roads Conf., Venezuela, 1954, Inter-parliamentary Conf. Poland, 1959, 6th World Forestry Congress, Madrid, Spain, 1966, 7th Congress, Buenos Aires, 1972; Congressional adv. U.S. dels. SALT II, Geneva, UN Gen. Assembly Spl. Session on Disarmament, Conf. Com. on Disarmament, Geneva; adv. com. Am. Enterprise Inst.; mem. Americana com. Nat. Archives. Served with AUS, World War II; ETO; maj. gen. Res. ret. Decorated Legion of Merit; Guatamalan Order Merit, 1961; Peruvian Order of Merit, 1970; recipient Governor's Conservation award, 1960; Fla. award Young Dem. Clubs, 1961; George Washington Meml. award Nat. Rivers and Harbors Congress, 1966; Distinguished Service award Water Resources Congress, 1972; Fla. Pub. Service award U.P.I., 1968; Nat. Leadership award Gun Dealer's Assn., 1959; Distinguished Service awards Am., Fla. forestry assns., 1972; named Hon. State Farmer, Fla. Assn. Future Farmers Am., 1967; Distinguished Service award Fla. Dept. Agr., 1973; faculty chair in govt. named in his honor at Okaloosa-Walton Jr. Coll.; recipient Gen. Louis E. Brereton award Fla. Air Force Assn., 1972; Man of Year award Nat. Fedn. Ind. Businesses, 1972; Certificate of Appreciation Nat. Small Bus. Assn. and Nat. Com. for Small Bus. Tax Reform, 1972; Distinguished Service award Nat. Assn. State Foresters, 1972; Fla. West Port Authority Leadership award, 1972; Distinguished Alumnus award U. Fla., 1972; J. Sterling Morton award, Arbor Day Found., 1973; distinguished service awards Fla. V.F.W., 1974, Fla. Bankers Assn., 1975; Patriot's award N.Y. State Res. Officers Assn., 1974; Man of Year awards Forest Farmers Assn., 1974, H.H. Arnold chpt. Air Force Assn., 1974; spl. commendation Fla. C. of C., 1974; award for distinguished service to U.S., Assn. U.S. Army, 1974; distinguished service citation Civil Affairs Assn., 1974; resolution of commendation Adj. Gens. Assn., 1974; Square and Compasses award for distinguished service Grand Lodge Masons of Fla., 1975; Silver Distinguished Achievement award Am. Heart Assn., 1975; Certificate of Appreciation, U.S. Army Ranger Assn., 1976; City of Milton (Fla.), 1978; named Bicentennial Patriot, Fla. Bicentennial Commn., 1976; Gold Good Citizen medal SAR, 1978; numerous other honors and awards. Mem. Naval Aviation Mus. Assn. (trustee), Fla. Hist. Soc., Mil. Order World Wars, Am. Legion (Distinguished Service award 1962), V.F.W., Nat. Assn. Suprs. (hon.), 40 and 8, Res. Officers Assn. (Distinguished Service awards 1958, 66, named to Minute Man Hall of Fame 1964, recipient Man of Year award 1967, Distinguished Service award Coast Guard Affairs Com. 1970), Ret. Officers Assn. (hon.), Nat. Rifle Assn. (life, dir. 1965-67), Nat. Assn. Master Mechanics and Foremen (hon. mem. Pensacola chpt.), Am. Fedn. Govt. Employees, United Fedn. Postal Clks., Fleet Res. Assn. (hon. life), Navy League (hon. life), Sons Confederate Vets., Am. Soc. Arms Collectors (hon.), SAR (gold good citizenship medal nat. congress 1978), Blue Key (U. Ga. award 1972), Phi Kappa Phi, Sigma Delta Chi, Alpha Zeta, Phi Sigma, Alpha Gamma Rho. Democrat. Methodist. Mason (33 deg., Shriner, K.T.), K.P., Elk, Moose; hon. mem. Order Ahepa (Leadership award 1969). Toastmasters (Communications and Leadership award 1969). Clubs: Kiwanis (lt. gov. 1940); Lions (hon.), Civitan (hon.), Rotary (hon.). Home: Crestview FL 32536 Office: Robert LF Sikes Public Library Crestview FL 32536

SIKKING, ARTHUR LELAND, JR., marketing cons., former publishing co. exec.; b. Decatur, Ill., Jan. 19, 1921; s. Arthur Leland and Myn Sue (Paxton) S.; student S.E. Mo. State Tchrs. Coll., 1944, Tulane U., 1945; B.S. in Bus. Adminstrn., U. Calif. at Los Angeles, 1947; postgrad. U. Humanities, 1949; m. Angela Seraph; children—James Seraph, Athena Daphne, Arthur Leland III. Br. mgr. Ency. Americana, Los Angeles, 1947-53; dist. mgr. Ency. Britannica, Inc., 1954-55. div. mgr., Atlanta, 1955-59, v.p., Scarsdale, N.Y., 1960-61, Chgo., 1961-62, nat. sales mgr., sr. v.p., sales, 1962-65, exec. v.p., 1965-71; pres. Personal Jet Inc., Chgo. Served to lt. (j.g.) USNR, 1941-45. Mem. Delta Tau Delta. Home: 1809B Wildberry Dr Glenview IL 60025

SIKOROVSKY, EUGENE FRANK, elec. equipment mfg. co. exec.; b. Jackson, Mich., Nov. 27, 1927; s. Frank Joseph and Betty Dorothy (Malik) S.; B.S. in Elec. Engring., U. Mich., 1948; LL.B., Harvard U., 1951; m. Patricia O'Byrne, July 11, 1953; children—Paul, Charles, Catherine, Elizabeth, Emily. Admitted to N.Y. bar, 1952, Va. bar, 1970, Ill. bar, 1978; asso. predecessor firms Cahill, Gordon & Reindel, 1954-63, partner, 1964-68; v.p., gen. counsel, dir. Reynolds Metals Co., Richmond, Va., 1969-76; gen. counsel Gould Inc., Rolling Meadows, Ill., 1977-79, v.p., 1977—. Served to lt. USNR, 1951-54. Mem. Am. Bar Assn., Va. Bar Assn., Assn. Bar City N.Y., Tau Beta Pi, Eta Kappa Nu, Phi Eta Sigma, Phi Delta Theta. Episcopalian. Home: 31 E Pembroke St Lake Forest IL 60045 Office: 10 Gould Center Rolling Meadows IL 60008

SIKULA, ANDREW FRANK, educator; b. Akron, Ohio, Oct. 7, 1944; s. John and Anna Marie (Shimko) S.; B.A. cum laude, Hiram Coll., 1966; M.B.A., Mich. State U., 1967, Ph.D., 1970; m. Celeste Marie Casey, June 12, 1971; children—Andrew Casey, Ana Celeste. Instr., Mich. State U., 1966-70; asst. prof. mgmt. U. Ill. Chgo. Circle, 1970-73, asso. prof., 1973-76; asso. dean, dir. grad. programs, prof. mgmt. Murray (Ky.) State U., 1976-78; dean, prof. mgmt. Coll. Bus. and Adminstrn., Chgo. State U., 1978—; Chief exec. officer, chmn. bd. Human Resource Mgmt. Inc., Oak Brook, Ill., 1974-76. Recipient Aaron H. Kelker award for top student athlete Hiram Coll., 1966, Allyn A. Young prize Hiram Coll., 1966. Mem. Acad. Mgmt. (v.p., chmn. programs 1975—, pres. Midwest div. 1977-78), Nat. Acad. Mgmt. (asso. chmn. placement com. 1973-74), Am. Mgmt. Assn. (Disting. Service cert. 1975), Am. Soc. Tng. and Devel., Soc. Advancement Mgmt., Ill. One-A-Year Pub. Club. Author: Conflict Via Values and Value Systems, 1971; Values, Motivation and Management, 1972; Management and Administration, 1973; Essays in Management and Administration, 1973, Fundamentals of Modern Personnel Management, 1974; Personnel Administration and Human Resources Management, 1976; Proc. 19th Conf. Midwest Sect. Acad. Mgmt., 1976; Personnel Management: A Short Course for Professionals, 1977; contbr. articles to profl. jours. Home: Elliott and Evergreen Olympia Fields IL 60461 Office: Chgo State U Chicago IL 60628

SILAGI, SELMA (MRS. ROBERT SILAGI), biomed. researcher; b. Montreal, Que., Can., Sept. 5, 1916; d. Israel Jacob and Anna (Dorinson) Epstein; brought to U.S., 1916, naturalized, 1928; B.A. magna cum laude, Hunter Coll., 1936; M.A., Columbia U., 1938, Ph.D., 1961; m. Robert Silagi, Nov. 26, 1936; children—Daniel, Laura. Tchr. biology N.Y.C. secondary schs., 1938-43, 46-50, 52-56; lectr. Queens Coll., 1956-59; research asso. Rockefeller U., 1962-65; asst. prof. Cornell U. Med. Coll., N.Y.C., 1965-70, asso. prof. genetics, obstetrics and gynecology dept., 1970-74, prof., 1974—. Mem. spl. program cancer adv. com. Nat. Cancer Inst., NIH, 1973-75. Pres. Queensview Summer Playschool, Inc., 1950-52. Research grantee USPHS, 1967—, Damon Runyon Meml. Fund grantee, 1970-77, faculty research award Am. Cancer Soc., 1970-75; elected to Hunter Coll. Hall of Fame; USPHS fellow, 1959-62. Mem. Am. Soc. Cell Biology, Genetics Soc. Am., Tissue Culture Assn., Harvey Soc., AAAS, Phi Beta Kappa, Sigma Xi. Contbr. articles to profl. jours. Home: 21-36 33d Rd Long Island City NY 11106 Office: 1300 York Ave New York NY 10021

SILAS, CECIL JESSE, petroleum co. exec.; b. Miami, Fla., Apr. 15, 1932; s. David Edward and Hilda Videll (Carver) S.; B.S. in Chem. Engring., Ga. Inst. Tech., Atlanta, 1954; m. Theodosea Hejda, Nov. 27, 1965; children—Karla, Peter, Michael, James. With Phillips Petroleum Co., 1953—, mng. dir. NRG Europe/Africa, London, 1974-77, v.p. natural resources group gas and gas liquids, Bartlesville, Okla., 1977-78, sr. v.p. group, 1978—. Adv. bd. Ga. Inst. Tech. Served to 1st lt. Chem. Corps, AUS, 1954-56. Decorated comdr. Order St. Olav (Norway). Mem. Am. Mgmt. Assn., Natural Gas Men Okla. Club: Bartlesville Rotary. Office: 18 Phillips Bldg Bartlesville OK 74004

SILAS (KOSKINAS), bishop; b. Corfu, Greece, Dec. 27, 1919; came to U.S., 1946; grad. U. Athens Theol. Sch., 1943; M.S.T., Boston U., 1957. Ordained deacon Greek Orthodox Ch. 1941, ordained priest, 1943; pastor Greek Orthodox Ch., Albuquerque, 1946, parishes in New London Conn., Boston, Pitts.; dean of St. Nicholas Cathedral, Pitts.; elevated to bishop, 1960; bishop of 8th archdiocesan dist., New Orleans, 1960-65; bishop of 1st archdiocesan dist., N.Y.C., 1965—; bishop new diocese of N.J., 1979—; mem. spl. del. to Rumania, 1970; v.p. of Religion in Am. Life, 1972—; v.p. Archdiocesan Council of Greek Orthodox Archdiocese, 1972—; chmn. Office of Fgn. Missions, Greek Orthodox Ch. Mem. bd. Appeal of Conscience Found. Recipient Gold Medallion award NCCJ. Contbr. numerous articles on Greek Orthodox faith to religious publs. Address: 10 E 79th St New York City NY 10021

SILBAUGH, PRESTON NORWOOD, savs. and loan assn. exec., lawyer; b. Stockton, Cal., Jan. 15, 1918; s. Herbert A. and Della Mae (Masten) S.; A.B. in Philosophy, U. Wash., 1940; J.D., Stanford U., 1953; m. Maria Sarah Arriola; children—Judith Ann (Mrs. Harvey Freed), Gloria (Mrs. Alan Lethers), Ximena Carey (Mrs. Arturo Braun), Carol Lee (Mrs. Michael Morgan). With Lockheed Aircraft Corp., 1941-44, Pan Am. World Airways, 1944, Office Civilian Personnel, War Dept., 1944-45; engaged in ins. and real estate in Calif., 1945-54; admitted to Calif. bar; mem. faculty Stanford Law Sch., 1954-59, asso. prof. law, 1956-59, asso. dean, 1956-59; chief dep. savs. and loan commnr. for Calif., 1959-61; bus. and commerce adminstr., dir. investment, savs. and loan commr., mem. gov.'s cabinet, Calif., 1961-63; dir. Chile-Calif. Aid Program, Sacramento and Santiago, 1963-65; chmn. bd. Beverly Hills Fed. Savs. & Loan Assn. (Calif.), 1965—; chmn. bd. Southland Co., Beverly Hills, Service Corp. of Beverly Hills; dir. Cie. Europeenne de Reassurance Internationale, Belgium, Cie. Europeenne de Reassurance Internationale (U.K.) Ltd., Beverly-Hawaiian, Inc.; chmn. bd., pres. Simon Bolivar Fund, Beverly Hills; of counsel firm Miller, Boyko & Bell, San Diego. Mem. pres.'s real estate adv. com. U. Calif., 1966—; mem. Beverly Hills Pub. Bldg. Adv. Com., 1970—. Served with USMCR, 1942-43. Mem. Am., San Diego County, Beverly Hills bar assns., Soc. Internat. Devel., U.S., Nat., Calif. savs. and loan leagues, State Bar Calif., U. Wash., Stanford alumni assns.; Calif. Aggie Alumni Assn., Los Angeles World Affairs Council, Order of Coif, Phi Alpha Delta. Clubs: Commonwealth, Town Hall (Los Angeles); Beverly Hills Men's. Author: The Economics of Personal Insurance, 1958; also articles. Home: 344 N Palm Dr Beverly Hills CA 90210 Office: 9401 Wilshire Blvd Beverly Hills CA 90212 also Security Pacific Plaza 1200 3d Ave Suite 1324 San Diego CA 92101

SILBER, GORDON RUTLEDGE, educator; b. N.Y.C., Nov. 6, 1909; s. Arthur Moore and Edith May (Anderson) S.; A.B., Princeton, 1931, Ph.D., 1935; student U. Grenoble, 1932, U. Chgo., 1933, U. Florence, 1935; m. Barbara Coney, June 30, 1936 (div.); children—Anderson, Cristina; m. 2d, Beatrice Shepherd Blane, Feb. 18, 1961. Instr. Latin, Princeton 1931-32, instr. French research asst. Roman d'Alixandre project, 1935-36; instr. French and Italian, Union Coll., Schenectady, 1936-42, asst. prof., 1942-46, asso. prof., 1946-47, prof., 1947-60, chmn. modern lang. dept., 1946-59, chmn. div. humanities, 1952-55; prof. romance langs. State U. N.Y. at Buffalo, 1960—, chmn. dept. modern langs. and lit., 1960-68, chmn. dept. French, 1968; dir. European office Inst. Internat. Edn., Paris, 1951-52; prof.-in-charge Sweet Briar Coll. Jr. Year in France, 1963-64, mem. adv. com., 1962—. Research analyst U.S. War Dept., 1943-46; chmn. nat. screening com. Fulbright program, France, 1961; cons. fgn. lang. instrn. Schenectady Pub. Schs., 1953-60; mem. Council on Jr. Year Abroad, 1952-60; chmn. com. II Northeast Conf. Fgn. Lang. Teaching, 1958-59; cons. Lang. Teaching by TV, Mass. Council on Pub. Schs., 1958-65; mem. exec. com. Nat. Fedn. Modern Lang. Tchrs. Assns., 1965-77, sec.-treas., 1968-77, sec. emeritus, 1978—; bd. dirs. Buffalo Philharm. Orch., 1978—. Decorated officier d'Academie, 1956, officier des Palmes Academiques, 1969 (France). Mem. N.Y. State Fedn. Fgn. Lang. Tchrs. (sec.-treas. 1948-51), Am. Assn. Tchrs. French (exec. council, 1953-57), Am. Assn. Tchrs. Italian (v.p. 1941-44), AAUP, Modern Lang. Assn., Am. Council on Teaching Fgn. Langs., Dante Soc., Phi Beta Kappa. Democrat. Unitarian. Author: The Influence of Dante and Petrarch on Certain of Boccaccio's Lyrics, 1940. Editor Italian lit. sect. Collier's Ency. Research in 18th Century French lit., especially lit. of Freemasonry. Home: 124 Brookedge Dr Williamsville NY 14221

SILBERMAN, CHARLES ELIOT, mag. editor, author; b. Des Moines, Jan. 31, 1925; s. Seppy I. and Cel (Levy) S.; A.B., Columbia, 1946, postgrad. in econs., 1946-49; L.H.D. (hon.), Kenyon Coll., 1972; m. Arlene Propper, Sept. 12, 1948; children—David, Richard, Jeffrey, Steven. Tutor econs. Coll. City N.Y., 1946-48; instr. econs. Columbia, 1948-53, lectr. econs., 1955-66; asso. editor Fortune mag., 1953-60, mem. bd. editors, 1961-71; dir. Study Law and Justice, 1972-79; dir. The Study of Jewish Life, 1979—. Mem. joint commn. on juvenile justice standards Am. Bar Assn.; dir. Carnegie Corp. Study Edn. Educators, 1966-69. Bd. dirs. Synagogue Council Am., Inst. Jewish Policy Planning and Research, United Synagogue Am.; mem. exec. com. bd. visitors Columbia U. Law Sch. Served to lt. (j.g.) USNR, 1943-46. Field Found. fellow, 1971-72. Fellow Nat. Assn. Bus. Economists. Co-author: Markets of the Sixties, 1960. Author: Crisis in Black and White, 1964; The Myths of Automation, 1966; Crisis in the Classroom, 1970; The Open Classroom Reader, 1973; Criminal Violence, Criminal Justice, 1978. Contbr. to various publs. Home and office: 535 E 86th St New York NY 10028

SILBERMAN, H. LEE, pub. relations exec.; b. Newark, Apr. 26, 1919; s. Louis and Anna (Horel) S.; B.A., U. Wis., 1940; m. Ruth Irene Rapp, June 5, 1948; children—Richard Lyle, Gregory Alan, Todd Walter. Radio continuity writer Radio Star WTAQ, Green Bay, Wis., 1940-41; reporter Bayonne (N.J.) Times, 1941-42; sales exec. War Assets Adminstrn., Chgo., 1946-47; copy editor Acme Newspictures, Chgo., 1947; reporter, editorial writer Witchita (Kans.) Eagle, 1948-55; reporter Wall St. Jour., N.Y.C., 1955-57, banking editor, 1957-68; 1st v.p., dir. corporate relations Shearson-Hamill & Co., N.Y.C., 1968-74; N.Y. corr. Economist of London, 1966-72; contbg. editor Finance mag., 1970-74, editor in chief 1974-76; v.p., dir. Fin. Services Group, Carl Byoir & Assos., Inc., N.Y.C., 1976-78, sr. v.p., 1978—. Served to capt. C.E., AUS, 1942-46. Recipient Loeb Mag. award U. Conn., 1965; Loeb Achievement award for distinguished writing on fin. Gerald M. Loeb Found., 1968. Mem. N.Y. Fin. Writers Assn., Deadline Club N.Y., Sigma Delta Chi, Phi Kappa Phi, Zeta Beta Tau, Phi Sigma Delta. Republican. Contbr. articles to profl. jours. Home: 80 Miller Rd Morristown NJ 07960 Office: 380 Madison Ave New York NY 10017

SILBERMAN, JAMES HENRY, editor, publisher; b. Boston, Mar. 21, 1927; s. Henry R. and Dorothy (Conrad) S.; A.B., Harvard, 1950; children—Michael, Ellen. Asst. to pub. Writer, Inc., 1950-51; asst. to advt. mgr. Little, Brown & Co., 1951-53; publicity dir. Dial Press, Inc., 1953-55, editor, 1954-55, exec. editor, 1955-59, v.p., editor-in-chief, 1959-63; editor The Dial, 1959-62; sr. editor Random House, Inc., N.Y.C., 1963-65, exec. editor, 1965-66, exec. editor, v.p., 1966-68, v.p., editor-in-chief, 1968-76, also pub., 1975-76; pres., editor-in-chief Summit Books div. Simon & Schuster, Inc., 1976—. Served as pfc. AUS, World War II. Mem. Freedom To Read Com., Assn. Am. Pubs., PEN Club: Harvard (N.Y.C.). Home: 315 E 70th St New York NY 10021 Office: 1230 Ave of the Americas New York NY 10020

SILBERMAN, LAURENCE HIRSCH, lawyer, banker; b. York, Pa., Oct. 12, 1935; s. William and Anna (Hirsch) S.; A.B., Dartmouth, 1957; LL.B., Harvard, 1961; m. Rosalie G. Gaull, Jan. 5, 1957; children—Robert Steven, Katherine De Boer, Anne Gaull. Admitted to Hawaii bar, 1961, D.C. bar, 1973; asso. firm Moore, Torkildson & Rice (name changed to Quinn & Moore 1963), Honolulu, 1961-64; partner firm Moore, Silberman & Schulze, Honolulu, 1964-67; atty. appellate div. gen. counsel's office NLRB, Washington, 1967-68; solicitor of labor U.S. Dept. Labor, Washington, 1969-70, under sec. labor, 1970-73; partner Steptoe & Johnson, Washington, 1973-74; dep. atty. gen. of U.S., 1974-75; ambassador to Yugoslavia, 1975-77; President's spl. envoy on ILO affairs, 1977; sr. fellow Am. Enterprise Inst., 1977-78, vis. fellow, 1978—; partner firm Morrison & Foerster, Washington, 1978-79; exec. v.p. legal and govt. affairs Crocker Nat. Bank, San Francisco, 1979—; lectr. labor law and legislation U. Hawaii, 1962-63. Bd. dirs. Com. on Present Danger, 1978—; vice chmn. adv. council on gen. govt. Republican Nat. Com., 1977—. Served with AUS, 1957-58. Mem. Am. Bar Assn. (labor law com. 1965—, corp. and banking com. 1973), Bar Assn. Hawaii (ethics com. 1965-67), Bar Assn. D.C., Council on Fgn. Relations. Home: 6 Kittery Ct Bethesda MD 20034 Office: Crocker Nat Bank One Montgomery St San Francisco CA 94104

SILBERMAN, LOU HACKETT, educator, rabbi; b. San Francisco, June 23, 1914; s. Lou Harry and Myrtle (Mueller) S.; student U. Calif. at Los Angeles, 1931-33; A.B., U. Calif. at Berkeley, 1934, postgrad., 1935; B.H.L., Hebrew Union Coll., Cin., 1939, M.H.L., 1941, D.H.L., 1943; postgrad. U. Basel, 1959; m. Helen Sue Epstein, June 14, 1942 (dec. 1979); children—Syrl Augusta, Deborah (Mrs. Alan Cohn). Rabbi, 1941; instr. medieval Bibl. exegesis Hebrew Union Coll., 1941-43; asst. rabbi Temple Emanuel, Dallas, 1943-45; rabbi Temple Israel, Omaha, 1945-52; asso. prof. Jewish lit. and thought Vanderbilt U., 1952-55, Hillel prof. Jewish lit. and thought, 1955—, dir. grad. studies Bibl. field, 1960-65, 67-69, acting chmn. grad. dept. religion, 1960-61, chmn. dept. religious studies, 1970-77; vis. prof. Oriental Inst., U. Vienna, 1965-66; vis. prof. Carleton Coll., 1972, Emory U., 1973; Rosenstiel fellow Notre Dame U., 1972; Touhy lectr. interreligious studies John Carroll U., 1973; vis. prof. U. Chgo.

Divinity Sch., 1978; vis. scholar Postgrad. Center Hebrew Studies Oxford, 1978. Chmn. community relations com. Nashville Jewish Community Council, 1956-61; vice chmn. Nat. Jewish Community Relations Adv. Council, 1964-70. Mem. Soc. Bibl. Lit. and Exegesis (pres. So. sect. 1959-60), Am. Acad. Religion, Central Conf. Am. Rabbis, Am. Soc. Study Religion, Assn. for Jewish Studies, Am. Theol. Soc., Studiorum Novi Testamenti Societas. Mem. B'nai B'rith. Clubs: Freolac, University, Shamus (Nashville). Editorial adviser Ency. Internat.; contbr. Ency. Brit., Ency. Judaica. author studies dealing with Dead Sea Scrolls, rabbinic lit., contemporary theology. Home: 600 Hillwood Dr Nashville TN 37205

SILBERMAN, PETER HENRY, journalist; b. Berlin, May 28, 1930; s. George and Frida Silberman; B.A. in English, Queen's Coll., N.Y.C., 1952; M.A. in Journalism, U. Mo., 1956. Mem. staff Kansas City (Mo.) Star, 1956-60; mem. staff Washington Post, 1960—, nat. editor, 1971-74, asst. mng. editor bus. and fin., 1974—; vis. lectr. George Washington U., 1979. Served with AUS, 1952-54. Mem. Am. Assn. Bus. and Econ. Writers. Clubs: Nat. Press, Washington Press, Fed. City (Washington). Office: 1150 15th St NW Washington DC 20071

SILBERMAN, RICHARD THEODORE, state ofcl., former pvt. investor and banker, Democratic nat. committeeman; b. Los Angeles, Apr. 22, 1929; s. Isadore A. and Sophie (Mechanic) S.; student Ohio U., 1948; B.S., San Diego State Coll., 1950; m. Roberta F. Rosenfeld, July 1, 1951; children—Craig, Karen, Jeffrey. Asso. prof. physics San Diego State Coll., 1949-50; partner Video Service, San Diego, 1950-57; v.p. Brown Corp., San Diego, 1951-52; v.p., dir. Cohu Electronics Co., 1952-59, pres. Kin Tel div., 1952-59; v.p. Video Antenna Systems, Inc., San Diego, 1953-57; v.p., sec., dir. Electronics Investment Corp., San Diego, 1954-65; exec. v.p., treas., dir. Electronics Capital Corp., San Diego, 1959-65, Electronics Internat. Capital Ltd., Hamilton, Bermuda, 1960-65; pres. Electronics Corp. Advisers, Inc., San Diego, 1960-65, Electronics Internat. Mgmt. Ltd., Hamilton, 1960-65; v.p., dir. Electronics Investment Mgmt. Corp., San Diego, 1960-65; v.p., sec. Republic Tech. Fund, Inc. (formerly Electronics Investment Corp.), San Diego, 1965; gen. partner Foodmaker Co., San Diego, 1965—; vice chmn., treas., dir. Foodmaker, Inc., San Diego, 1965-70; pres. Checkerboard Properties (subsidiary Ralston Purina Co.), 1968-70; vice chmn. bd. So. Calif. First Nat. Corp., 1969-75; pres. So. Calif. First Nat. Bank/Corp., 1974-75, Centre City Devel. Corp., 1976-77; dir., mem. exec. comm. So. Calif. First Nat. Bank; mem. Democratic Nat. Com. from Calif., 1976—; mem. Fed. Jud. Commn., 1977-78. bd. govs. San Diego Stadium, 1965-72, chmn., 1969; chmn. San Diego Transit Corp., 1972, dir., 1972-77; chmn. Calif. Fed. Selection Commn., 1978—; sec. Bus. and Transp. Agy. State of Calif., 1977-78, dir. fin., 1978—; mem. Gov. Brown's cabinet. Mem. pub. adv. council Peer Rev. Commn., Calif. Med. Assn., 1973-75. Recipient Outstanding Alumni award San Diego State Coll., 1959. Mem. Western (bd. dirs. 1958-59), West Coast (chmn. San Diego 1963), electronics mfrs. assns., IEEE (sec. San Diego 1953), Sigma Phi Sigma. Address: PO Box 3745 San Diego CA 92103

SILBERT, EARL J., lawyer; b. Boston, Mar. 8, 1936; s. Coleman and Lillian (Rosenburg) S.; A.B., Harvard U., 1957, LL.B., 1960; m. Patricia Ann Allott, Oct. 18, 1969; children—Sarah Elizabeth, Leslie Kathryn. Admitted to Mass. bar, 1960, D.C. bar, 1963; atty. tax div. Dept. Justice, Washington, 1960-64, Office Criminal Justice, 1969-70; asst. U.S. atty. for D.C., 1964-69, exec. asst. U.S. atty., 1970-72, prin. asst. U.S. atty., 1972-73, U.S. atty. for D.C., 1974-79; partner firm Schwalb, Donnenfeld, Bray & Silbert, Washington, 1979—. Bd. dirs. Metro Athletic Cultural and Ednl. Assn., Washington, 1961-64; participant YWCA Tutorial Project, Washington, 1965-70; bd. dirs. Eastern br. Boys' Club Greater Washington, 1974—. Mem. Am. Bar Assn., D.C. Bar Assn., Am. Coll. Trial Lawyers. Home: 6617 31st St NW Washington DC 20015 Office: 1333 New Hampshire Ave NW Washington DC 20036

SILBERT, JULES, retail dept. store exec.; b. Winston-Salem, N.C., Dec. 21, 1927; s. Benjamin and Rebecca Silverstein; B.Elec. Engring., N.C. State U., Raleigh, 1949; m. Nancy Loeb, Nov. 1, 1959; children—Thomas Jon, Wendy Lynn. Market research specialist Gen. Electric Co., Pittsfield, Mass., 1949-60; gen. mgr. mail order div. Lane Bryant, Inc., Indpls. and N.Y.C., 1960-76, pres. retail div., 1975—, corp. exec. v.p., N.Y.C., 1975—, also dir. Served with U.S. Army, 1953-55. Mem. Nat. Retail Mchts. Assn. Home: 120 E 81st St New York NY 10028 Office: 11 W 42d St New York NY 10036

SILBERT, THEODORE H., banker; b. Boston, July 5, 1904; m. Silvia Friedlander, 1939; LL.B. (hon.), Bard Coll., Western State U., Anaheim, Calif.; 1 son, Arthur Frederick. With Standard Financial Corp., 1934—, pres., 1945—, also dir.; pres., dir. various subsidiaries; pres., chief exec. officer, dir. Standard Prudential Corp., until 1968, chmn., chief exec. officer, dir., 1968—; chmn., dir. Yuba Industries, Inc., Sterling Nat. Bank & Trust Co. N.Y. Past pres. and former chmn. Assn. Comml. Finance Cos.; former trustee Bronx-Lebanon Hosp. Center; trustee, chmn. Jewish Assn. for Services for Aged; hon. vice chmn. Anti-Defamation League Nat. Commn., nat. chmn. Anti-Defamation League Appeal, nat. treas.; mem. exec. com., bd. dirs. N.Y.C. div., also life mem. Am. Cancer Soc.; bd. dirs., hon. treas., mem. campaign cabinet United Jewish Appeal Greater N.Y.; asso. trustee mem. pres.'s council Bard Coll., Annandale-on-Hudson, N.Y.; trustee Brandeis U.; trustee Fedn. Jewish Philanthropies N.Y.; founder Albert Einstein Coll. Medicine, past pres. Soc. Founders; bd. dirs., mem. exec. com. Jewish Theol. Sem. Am.; bd. dirs. Fashion Inst. Tech. Mem. Newcomen Soc., Fgn. Policy Assn. (asso.), Def. Orientation Conf. Assn. Clubs: Standard (Chgo.); Board Room, Harmonie, Friars (N.Y.C.); Old Oaks Country (past pres.) (Purchase, N.Y.); Hillcrest Country (Los Angeles). Contbr. articles to bus. publs. Home: 936 Fifth Ave New York NY 10021 Office: 540 Madison Ave New York NY 10022

SILBEY, JOEL HENRY, educator; b. Bklyn., Aug. 16, 1933; s. Sidney Richard and Estelle Harriet (Mintzer) S.; B.A., Bklyn. Coll., 1955; M.A., U. Iowa, 1956, Ph.D., 1963; m. Rosemary Johnson, Aug. 13, 1959; children—Victoria Elizabeth, David Sidney Johnson. Asst. prof. San Francisco State Coll., 1960-64, U. Md., 1965-66; asst. prof. Am. history Cornell U., 1966-67, asso. prof., 1967-68, prof., 1968—; vis. asst. prof. history U. Pitts., 1964-65; editorial cons. numerous pubs. Social Sci. Research Council fellow, 1958-60, 69-70; Am. Philos. Soc. fellow, 1969-70; NSF fellow, 1970-74. Mem. Am. Hist. Assn. (program com. 1977), Orgn. Am. Historians, So. Hist. Assn., Social Sci. History Assn. (co-chmn. membership com., mem. exec. com.). Author: The Shrine of Party, 1967; The Transformation of American Politics, 1967; A Respectable Minority: The Democratic Party in the Civil War Era, 1977. Editor: (with others) Voters, Parties and Elections, 1972, American Political Behavior, 1974, The History of American Electoral Behavior, 1978. Home: 105 Judd Falls Rd Ithaca NY 14850 Office: Cornell U 453 McGraw Hall Ithaca NY 14853

SILCOX, DAVID P., city ofcl.; b. Moose Jaw, Sask., Can., Jan. 28, 1937; s. Albert Phillips and Marjorie Emilia S.; B.A., M.A., U. Toronto (Ont., Can.). Sr. arts officer Can. Council, 1965-60; asso. dean. Faculty Fine Arts, York U., Toronto, 1970-73, asso. prof. fine arts., 1970-77; dir. cultural affairs Met. Toronto, 1974—; cons. to fed. and provincial govts. on cultural policies; bd. govs. Massey Hall, 1974—; bd. dirs. Can. Conf. of Arts, 1977—; mem. acquisitions com. Art Gallery Ont., 1970—; vice chmn. Can. Film Devel. Corp., 1970-77. Recipient Sr. award Can. Council, 1979. Fellow Royal Soc. Arts (Gt. Britain); mem. Assn. Cultural Execs. (dir. 1976—). Author: (with others) Tom Thomson: The Silence and the Storm, 1977; contbr. numerous articles on cultural policy and visual arts to profl. jours. Office: Metro Toronto New City Hall/West Tower Toronto ON M5H 2N1 Canada

SILEN, WILLIAM, physician, educator; b. San Francisco, Sept. 13, 1927; s. Dave and Rose (Miller) S.; B.A. in Med. Sci., U. Calif. at Berkeley, 1946; M.D., U. Calif. at San Francisco, 1949; m. Ruth Heppner, July 13, 1947; children—Stephen, Deborah, Mark. Intern U. Calif. Hosp., San Francisco, 1949-50, asst. resident gen. surgery, 1950, 52-56, chief resident gen. surgery, 1956-57; asst. chief surgery Denver VA Hosp., 1957-59, chief surgery, 1959-60; asst. chief surgery San Francisco Gen. Hosp., 1960-61, chief surgery, 1961-66; surgeon-in-chief Beth Israel Hosp., Boston, 1966—; instr. surgery, then asst. prof. surgery U. Colo. Sch. Medicine, 1957-60; asst. prof. surgery, then asso. prof. surgery U. Calif. Sch. Medicine, 1960-66; Johnson & Johnson prof. surgery Harvard Med. Sch., 1966—. Served with M.C., USAF, 1950-52. Recipient numerous outstanding tchr. awards. Mem. Soc. Univ. Surgeons, A.C.S., H.C. Naffziger Surg. Soc., Cal., San Francisco med. socs., A.M.A., Am. Fedn. Clin. Research, Soc. Exptl. Biology and Medicine, San Francisco Surg. Soc., Am. Gastroenterol. Assn., Soc. Surgery Alimentary Tract, Assn. Am. Med. Colls., Pacific Coast, Am., New Eng. surg. assns., Mass. Med. Soc., Boston Surg. Soc., Phi Beta Kappa, Alpha Omega Alpha. Address: 710 Wellesley St Weston MA 02193

SILER, EUGENE EDWARD, JR., judge; b. Williamsburg, Ky., Oct. 19, 1936; s. Eugene Edward and Lowell (Jones) S.; B.A. cum laude, Vanderbilt U., 1958; LL.B., U. Va., 1962; LL.M., Georgetown U., 1964; m. Christy Dyanne Minnich, Oct. 18, 1969; children—Eugene Edward, Adam Troy. Admitted to Ky. bar, 1963; individual practice law, Williamsburg, 1964-65; atty. Whitley County, Ky., 1965-70; U.S. atty. Eastern Dist. Ky., Lexington, 1970-75, judge U.S. Dist. Ct., Eastern and Western Dists., 1975—. Campaign co-chmn. Congressman Tim L. Carter, 1966; 5th Congl. Dist. campaign co-chmn. U.S. Senator J.S. Cooper, 1966; trustee Cumberland Coll., Williamsburg, 1965-73. Served with USNR, 1958-60. E. Barrett Prettyman fellow, 1963-64; recipient medal Freedom's Found., 1968. Mem. Fed., Ky., D.C. bar assns., Va. State Bar. Republican. Baptist. Club: Optimists (pres. Williamsburg 1969). Home: 818 Walnut St Williamsburg KY 40769 Office: Fed Bldg London KY 40741

SILER, WALTER ORLANDO, JR., bus. exec.; b. Atascadero, Calif., May 21, 1920; s. Walter Orlando and Hylda Ruth Martyn (Jackson) S.; B.S., U. So. Calif., 1941; m. Violet Mae Smith, 1942; children—Robert Eugene, Barbara Ellen, Susan Jane; m. 2d, Dona Jean Delanoy, 1962; children—Donald Walter, David Brian; m. 3d, Carolyn Louise Townsend, 1978. Partner, Arthur Andersen & Co., C.P.A.'s, Phoenix, 1958-61; pres., treas., dir. Bargain City, U.S.A., Inc., Phila., 1962; treas., dir. Getty Oil Co., Los Angeles, 1963-67, v.p., 1966-67, asst. controller, 1968-70; controller Fluor Corp., Los Angeles, 1970-72; gen. mgr. Saudi Arabian ops. Whittaker Corp., 1972-73; bus. mgr. Northrop Aircraft Div., Taif, Saudi Arabia, 1973-74; v.p. fin. Fluor Arabia Ltd., Dhahran, Saudi Arabia, 1974-77; mgr. accounting The Ralph M. Parsons Co., Pasadena, Calif., 1977-78; v.p., treas. Parsons Constructors Inc., Pasadena, 1978—; treas., dir. Mission Corp., 1963-68; treas. Mission Devel. Co., 1963-67; dir. Skelly Oil Co., 1963-68. Served to maj. USAAF, 1941-46. C.P.A., Calif. Mem. Fin. Execs. Inst., Am. Inst. C.P.A.'s. Address: 703 N Stoneman Ave Alhambra CA 91801

SILETS, HARVEY MARVIN, lawyer; b. Chgo., Aug. 25, 1931; s. Joseph Lazarus and Sylvia (Dubner) S.; B.S. cum laude, DePaul U., 1952; J.D. (Frederick Leckie scholar), U. Mich., 1955; m. Elaine Lucy Gordon, June 25, 1961; children—Hayden Leigh, Jonathan Lazarus, Alexandra Rose. Admitted to Ill. bar, 1955, N.Y. bar, 1956; asso. firm Paul, Weiss, Rifkind, Wharton & Garrison, N.Y.C., 1955-56; asst. U.S. atty. No. Dist. Ill., 1958-60, chief tax atty., Chgo., 1960-62; partner firm Harris, Burman & Silets, Chgo., 1962-79, firm Silets & Martin, Ltd., Chgo., 1979—; asst. advance tng. program IRS, U. Mich., 1952-53; law lectr. John Marshall Law Sch., 1962-66; gen. counsel Nat. Treasury Employees Union, 1968—; mem. Chgo. Crime Commn., 1975—; mem. adv. com. tax litigation U.S. Dept. Justice, 1979—. Trustee, Latin Sch., Chgo., Rodfei Zedek; bd. assos. DePaul U. Served with AUS, 1956-58. Fellow Am. Coll. Trial Lawyers; mem. Bar Assn. 7th Fed. Circuit Ct. (chmn. com. criminal law and procedure 1972—), Am. (com. fed. taxation 1960—, criminal justice 1963—, chmn. com. prosecution and def. criminal tax cases 1979—, subcom. on civil and criminal tax penalties 1965—, subcom. on grand jury 1978—, ad hoc com. sensitive payments audit techniques 1978—), Fed. (dir. 1971—, v.p. 7th fed. circuit 1978— dir. 1971—, chmn. judiciary com. 1971—, chmn. fed. rules com. 1972—, sec. 1975, v.p. 1976, pres. 1977-78), Chgo. (com. devel. law 1966-72, 78—, com. fed. taxation 1968—, com. evaluation candidates 1978—) bar assns., Decalogue Soc. Lawyers, Nat. Assn. Criminal Def. Lawyers. Clubs: Standard (Chgo.); Biltmore Country. Home: Chicago IL also Wandering Tree Barrington IL Office: Suite 400 10 S LaSalle St Chicago IL 60604

SILHA, OTTO ADELBERT, newspaper pub. exec.; b. Chgo., Jan. 15, 1919; s. Emil Albert and Alice Lucille (Lindstrom) S.; B.A. magna cum laude, U. Minn., 1940; m. Helen Elizabeth Fitch, Sept. 4, 1942; children—Stephen Fitch, David William (dec.), Alice Barbara, Mark Albert. Copyreader, Mpls. Star, 1940-41; promotion dir. Mpls. Star and Tribune, 1947-51, promotion and personnel dir., 1951-54, bus. mgr., 1954-65, gen. mgr., 1965-68, v.p., 1956-68, exec. v.p., pub., 1968-73, pres., 1973— chmn. bd., 1979—, dir., 1954—; dir. Newspaper Advt. Bur., 1970-73, vice-chmn., 1974-76, chmn., 1976-78; dir. Harper & Row, Pubs., Inc., Northwestern Nat. Bank, AP. Mem. Gov. Minn.'s Adv. Com. Dept. Bus. Devel., 1955-63, chmn., 1957-59. Pres. Mpls. Aquatennial Assn., 1956; v.p., dir. North Star Research Inst., 1963-75; chmn. steering com. Minn. Exptl. City Project, 1966—. Bd. regents U. Minn., 1961-69; bd. dirs. Tyrone Guthrie Theatre Found., 1960-62, Minn. Theatre Co. Found., 1962-72; trustee Mpls. Soc. Fine Arts, 1966-74, Midwest Research Inst., 1975—, U. Minn. Found., 1974—; bd. dirs. Greater Mpls. Met. Housing Corp., 1971—; bd. dirs. Upper Midwest Council, 1971—, pres., 1975-77. Served from pvt. to maj. USAAF, 1942-46. Named one of 100 outstanding young men, Mpls., 1953, Boss of Year, Mpls. Jaycees, 1971; recipient Silver medal award Am. Advt. Fedn., 1972; Outstanding Achievement award U. Minn., 1974, Minn. award for disting. service in journalism, 1978. Mem. Internat. Newspaper Promotion Assn. (pres. 1953-54), Am. Newspaper Pubs. Assn. (dir. Research Inst. 1960-70, pres. 1967-69), Mpls. C. of C. (dir. 1960-69, v.p. 1963-69), U. Minn. Alumni Assn. (dir. 1959-63), Phi Beta Kappa, Delta Tau Delta (regional v.p. 1947-52), Sigma Delta Chi. Clubs: Minneapolis, Minikahda, 5:55 (pres. 1956-57) (Mpls.); Minneapolis Athletic; Minnesota (St. Paul). Office: 425 Portland Ave Minneapolis MN 55488

SILIPIGNI, ALFREDO, opera dir.; b. Atlantic City, Apr. 9, 1931; s. Alfredo and Elizabeth (Calhoun) S.; student Westminster Choir Coll., Princeton, N.J., 1948, Juilliard Sch. Music, 1953; pupil of conductor Alberto Erede, 1953; L.H.D. (hon.), Kean Coll., 1978; m. Gloria Rose DiBenedetto, Apr. 11, 1953; children—Marisa, Elisabetta Luisa, Alfredo Roberto. Artistic dir., condr. N.J. State Opera, 1965—; condr. NBC Symphony, Boston, Bklyn. and Conn. operas, Newark Symphony; guest condr. in Caracas, Venezuela, San Remo, Italy, Sirmione, Italy, Milano, Italy, Paris, France, Santo Domingo, Dominican Republic. Tampa Opera, Providence, Ont., Manitoba and Alta., Can.; prin. condr. Mexican Nat. Opera; debut as condr. Vienna State Opera, 1976, Gran Liceo di Barcelona, 1976, London, 1977; established statewide auditioning program for young artists, N.J. State Opera Young Artists Program, 1969; frequent judge vocal competitions; guest lectr. Glassboro (N.J.) State Coll.; instituted operalogues, Paper Mill Playhouse, Millburn, N.J., 1968; organist, choir master Chelsea Presbyn. Ch., Atlantic City, 1946, Calvary Bapt. Ch., N.Y.C., 1958; founder, conductor Lauter Opera Theatre of Air, Newark, 1951, Suburban Concerts N.J., 1955; conducted, recorded world revival of Leoncavallo's Zaza, 1970; rec. artist for Cetra. Recipient Centennial medallion St. Peters Coll., 1972; named hon. citizen Trenton, 1972; recipient Distinguished Service to Culture award City San Remo, 1972, Columbian Found. award, Boys Town of Italy award. Club: Essex (Newark). Office: NJ State Opera 1020 Broad St Newark NJ 07102

SILK, GEORGE, photographer; b. Levin, New Zealand, Nov. 17, 1916; s. Arthur and Constance (Naylor) S.; ed. New Zealand schs.; m. Margery G. Schieber, Nov. 28, 1947; children—Stuart, Georgiana B., Shelley G. With photographic store in New Zealand, 1935-39; ofcl. photographer Australian Inf. Forces in Middle East, 1940-42, New Guinea, 1942-43; photographer Life mag., 1943-73, corr. in ETO, 1944-45, PTO, 1945, China, 1946, N.Y.C., 1947-73; free lance photographer, 1973—. Recipient gold medal Art Dirs. Club, 1961; Photographer of Year award Ency. Brit., 1960; Am. Soc. Mag. Photographers Meml. award, 1962; Photographer of Year awards Nat. Press Photographers Assn., U. Mo., World Book, 1960, 62, 63, 64; Brehm Meml. award Rochester Inst. Tech., 1966. Pictures in color sect. 1959 annual Ency. Brit.; photographs in photography in Fine Arts exhibit, 1962, 63. Home: Owenoke Park Westport CT 06880

SILK, LEONARD SOLOMON, economist, columnist, editor; b. Phila., May 15, 1918; s. Harry Lewis and Ida (Ender) S.; A.B., U. Wis., 1940; Ph.D., Duke, 1947, LL.D. (hon.), 1978; D.H.L. (hon.), Southeastern Mass. U., 1976; LL.D., Montclair State Coll., 1979; m. Bernice Harriet Scher, June 20, 1948; children—Mark Reuel, Andrew David, Adam Jonathan. Instr. econs. Duke, 1941-42, U. Maine, 1947-48; asst. prof. econs. Simmons Coll., 1948-50; economist HHFA, 1951; asst. econ. commr. U.S. mission to NATO, 1952-54; econs. editor Business Week mag., 1954-69, sr. editor, 1959-69, editor editorial page, chmn. editorial bd., 1967-69; Ford Found. distinguished vis. research prof. Carnegie Inst. Tech., 1965-66; vis. prof. Salzburg Seminar in Am. Studies, 1968; sr. fellow Brookings Instn., also adj. prof. Am. U., 1969—; columnist, mem. editorial bd. N.Y. Times, 1970—. Mem. research adv. bd. Com. Econ. Devel.; mem. steering group Task Force on War Against Poverty, 1964; cons. Pres.'s Adv. Com. on Labor-Mgmt. Policy, 1962; mem. Carnegie Endowment Seminar on Space; mem. Pres.'s Commn. on Budget Concepts, 1967; chmn. Task Force on Employment and Income Maintenance, 1968-69; pres. N.Y. State Council on Econ. Edn., 1973-75. Mem. bd. advisers U. Mass., trustee Montclair Adult Sch.; bd. overseers Tuck Sch. Bus. Adminstrn., Dartmouth Coll.; bd. visitors U. City N.Y. Grad. Sch.; vis. com. social scis. U. Chgo. Served with USAAF, 1942-45. F. Lincoln Cromwell fellow in Sweden, Am. Scandinavian Found., 1946; Fulbright research scholar in Norway, 1951; recipient Loeb award distinguished bus. and financial journalism, 1961, 66, 67, 69, 71, 72; G.L. Loeb Meml. award UCLA, 1978; Overseas Press Club citation for fgn. reporting, 1966, Bache award for best bus. reporting, 1972; U. Mo. certificate of outstanding merit, 1967; Poynter fellow in journalism Yale, 1974-75. Fellow Nat. Assn. Bus. Economists; mem. Nat. Assembly Social Policy and Devel. (pres.), Am. Econ. Assn., Council Fgn. Relations, Phi Beta Kappa, Beta Gamma Sigma, Phi Kappa Phi, Artus. Jewish religion. Author: Sweden Plans for Better Housing, 1948; Forecasting Business Trends, 1956; The Education of Businessmen, 1960; The Research Revolution, 1960; Veblen, 1966; Economic Commentary, 1967; (with P. Saunders) The World of Economics, 1969; Readings in Economics, 1969; Contemporary Economics: Principles and Issues, 1970, 75; Readings in Contemporary Economics, 1970; (with M.L. Curley) A Primer on Business Forecasting, 1970; Nixonomics, 1972, 74; Capitalism, The Moving Target, 1973. Editor: (with Mark Silk) The Evolution of Capitalism, 1973; (with Mark Sick) The Economists, 1976; (with David Vogel) Ethics and Profits, 1976; Economics in Plain English, 1978; (with Rawleigh Warner) Ideals in Collision: The Relationship between Business and the News Media, 1979; contbr. The Best From Yank, 1945; Outer Space, Prospects for Man and Society, 1962; Space and Society, 1964; America as an Ordinary Country, 1976. Home: 115 S Fullerton Ave Montclair NJ 07042 Office: 229 W 43d St New York NY 10036

SILL, STERLING WELLING, ch. ofcl.; b. Layton, Utah, Mar. 31, 1903; s. Joseph A. and Marietta (Welling) S.; student Utah State U., 1921-22, U. Utah, 1926-27, LL.D., 1953; m. Doris Mary Thornley, Sept. 4, 1929; children—John Michael, David S., Carolyn (Mrs. Perry Fitzgerald). Tchr., Layton, 1927-29; agt. N.Y. Life Ins. Co., 1928-32, mgr. Intermountain br. office, 1933-39, insp. agys., field v.p., 1940-54, hon. insp. agys., 1954-68, ret., 1968; asst. to Quorum of 12 Apostles, Ch. of Jesus Christ of Latter-day Saints, Salt Lake City, 1954-76, First Qurom of Seventy, 1976—. Mem. Layton City Council, 1928-32. Bd. regents U. Utah, 1940-51, chmn., 1947-51. Recipient Carnegie Hero medal, 1959. C.L.U. Mem. Am. Coll. Life Underwriters. Author numerous books on religious, social themes. Speaker radio program Sunday Evening on Temple Sq., Sta. KSL, Salt Lake City, 1960-77. Office: 50 East North Temple St Salt Lake City UT 84111. *The greatest waste there is in the world is not the devastation that goes with war, it is not the cost of crime, the erosion of our soil, or the depletion of our raw materials. The greatest waste there is in the world is that human beings, you and I, live so far below the level of our possibilities. Compared with what we might be, we are just partly alive.**

SILL, WEBSTER HARRISON, JR., educator; b. Wheeling, W.Va., Dec. 4, 1916; s. Webster Harrison and Grace Elaine (Clark) S.; B.S., W.Va. Wesleyan Coll., 1939; postgrad. Pa. State U., 1942; M.A., Boston U., 1947; Ph.D., U. Wis., 1951; m. Charlyn Alice Adams, July 25, 1943; children—Webster Harrison III, Susan C. (Mrs. Craig Calamaio), Warren T. Research asso. U. Wis., Madison, 1951-52; asst. prof. botany and plant pathology Kans. State U., 1952-56, asso. prof., 1956-63, prof., 1963-69; chmn. dept. biology, prof. U. S.D., Vermillion, 1969—, dir. Black Hills Natural Scis. Field Sta., 1970-73, dir. Center for Environ. Studies, 1972—; food and agrl. officer FAO, UN, 1962-63; dir. research Andhra Pradesh Agrl. U., Hyderabad, India, AID, 1966-68; pres. Environ. Cons., Inc., 1971—; cons. H.J. Heinz Co., Gen. Foods Corp., Frontier Chem. Co., Eli Lilly Co. Co-chmn. Kans. Centennial Com., 1961; active Boy Scouts Am., 1952—; bd. dirs. Sioux council, 1968—; chmn. United Campus Christian Fellowship; hon. life PTA; P.T.A.; pres. Westminster

Found., 1964. Served to 1st lt. USMCR, 1941-46. Wis. Alumni Research fellow, 1948-51; Lisle fellow, 1937; Danforth fellow, 1957; NSF sr. postdoctoral fellow Marine Lab., Duke, 1972; Food Inst., East-West Center sr. fellow, Honolulu, 1974-75; Ace govtl. fellow, 1976-77. Mem. Am. Phytopath. Soc., Bot. Soc. Am., AAAS, Am. Inst. Biol. Scis., N.Y. Acad. Scis., Sigma Xi, Phi Sigma, Gamma Sigma Delta, Gamma Alpha, Pi Sigma Alpha. Republican. Methodist (lay minister 1939-68; named Kans. Layman of Year 1957). Kiwanian, Rotarian. Co-author: Sourcebook of Laboratory Exercises in Plant Pathology; author: The Plant Protection Discipline; also numerous articles on research. Home: 515 N Prentis St Vermillion SD 57069. *Genius resides in individuals; never in institutions or governments. The only good governments are those which allow genius the freedom to flower and give individuals the chance to be creative.*

SILLCOX, LEWIS KETCHAM, educator; b. Germantown, Pa., Apr. 30, 1886; s. George Washington and Georgiana (Parker) S.; student Trinity Sch., N.Y. and L'Ecole Polytechnique, Brussels, 1903; D.Sc., Clarkson Coll., 1932; D.Eng., Cumberland U., 1941, Purdue U., 1951; LL.D., Syracuse U., 1948, Queen's U., 1955; D.H.L., Norwich U., 1963; m. Edna May Harris, Sept. 14, 1918 (dec. Feb. 1961); children—Elsie Winifred (Mrs. Donald G. Bridge), Esther Harris (Mrs. Stanley L. Whittemore), Enid Burnham (Mrs. Fred E. Brown), Edith May (Mrs. Conrad F. Reiman), Robert Lewis. Machinist apprentice N.Y.C. & H.R. R.R., High Bridge, N.Y., 1903-07; foundry apprentice McSherry Mfg. Co., Middletown, Ohio, 1907-09; shop. engr. Canadian Car & Foundry Co., Montreal, Que., Can., 1909-12; mech. engr. Canadian No. Ry., Toronto, Ont., 1912-16; mech. engr. I.C. R.R., 1916-18; gen. supt. motive power C.,M. & St.P. Ry., Chgo., 1918-27; asst. to pres., exec. v.p., vice chmn. bd. N.Y. Air Brake Co., N.Y.C., 1927-59; dir. Office of Transp., Exec. Dept. State of N.Y., Albany, 1959-60; prof., lectr. engring. Purdue U., 1946—; lectr. transp. various colls., univs. Chmn. mech. engring. adv. com. Princeton, 1938- 58; vis. com. dept. mech. engring. Mass. Inst. Tech., 1955-57; trustee, gen. chmn. vis. coms. Norwich U.; hon. curator Baker Library, Harvard, 1935—; mem. Alfred Noble Joint Prize Com., 1943-78. Ret. trustee Hosp. Rev. and Planning Council Central N.Y., Inc.; mem. adv. bd. Salvation Army. Recipient gold medals ASME, Inst. Mech. Engrs., George Washington Honor medal, 1954, Freedoms Found. award, 1955; first recipient Transp. Research Forum award, 1977. Fellow Inst. Mech. Engrs., IEEE, AAAS; hon. mem. ASME (past pres.), A.R.E.A., Engring. Inst. Can.; mem. ASCE (life, past pres.), Am. Inst. Mining and Metall. Engrs. (life), other nat., state, local profl. engring. socs., Sigma Xi, Pi Tau Sigma, Tau Beta Pi. Episcopalian. Mason (32 deg., K.T., Shriner). Clubs: Harvard (Boston); University (N.Y.C., Chgo.); Black River Valley (Watertown, N.Y.); Seigniory (Can.). Author: Mastering Momentum, 1941. Contbr. to tech. publs. Home: 241 Clinton St Apt 4 Watertown NY 13601. *You cannot manage anything you cannot measure.*

SILLESKY, JOHN DARRISON, actuary; b. Lockport, N.Y., Mar. 8, 1915; s. John Roscoe and Miriam Laura (Darrison) S.; A.B. cum laude Syracuse U., 1937, M.A., 1938; postgrad. Sch. Inst. Adminstrn., 1956; postgrad. advanced mgmt. program Harvard U., 1961; m. Mary Dixon Pike, Oct. 12, 1940; children—Anne Sillesky Morgan, Carolin Sillesky Davis, John Dixon. Various actuarial positions Travelers Ins. Co., Hartford, Conn., 1938-45; with John Hancock Mut. Life Ins. Co., Boston, 1945-79, v.p., 1978-79; ret., 1979. Bd. dirs. Needham (Mass.) YMCA, 1973—, corp. sec., 1975-77, pres., 1977—; bd. dirs. Greater Boston YMCA, 1979—; mem. Com. on Racial Imbalance in Needham Schs., 1966-67, Needham Fin. Commn.; mem. west metro council Health Planning Council for Greater Boston, Inc. Fellow Soc. Actuaries; mem. Am. Acad. Actuaries, Internat. Actuarial Assn., Boston Actuaries Club. Episcopalian. Home: 41 Perry Dr Needham MA 02192

SILLETTO, CHARLES DAVID, ins. co. exec.; b. Des Moines, Mar. 22, 1931; s. Charles Vyatt and Ada (Nelson) S.; B.A. in Actuarial Math., U. Iowa, 1952; m. Ann Kathleen Larson, June 28, 1953; children—David L., John C., Mary A. With Lincoln Nat. Life Ins. Co., Ft. Wayne, Ind., 1954-67, 71—, v.p., 1967, 71-73, sr. v.p., 1973-78, exec. v.p., 1978—, also dir.; pres. Lincoln Nat. Life Ins. Co. of N.Y., 1967-71; dir. Dominion Life Assurance Co. (Can.), LNC Life Ins. Co., Insurers Fund, Lincoln Nat. Sales Corp., Security-Conn. Life Ins. Co. Bd. dirs. Ft. Wayne Fine Arts Found, 1975—, Ft. Wayne Museum Art, 1979. Served with USAF, 1952-54. Fellow Soc. Actuaries; mem. Am. Acad. Actuaries, Phi Beta Kappa. Presbyterian. Club: Quest (Ft. Wayne). Home: 3526 N Washington Rd Fort Wayne IN 46804 Office: 1300 S Clinton St Fort Wayne IN 46801

SILLIN, LELAN FLOR, JR., utility exec.; b. Tampa, Fla., Apr. 19, 1918; s. Lelan Flor and Ruth (Berry) S.; A.B. with distinction, U. Mich., 1940, LL.B., 1942; m. Joan Outhwaite, Sept. 26, 1942; children—Lelan Flor, John Outhwaite, Andrew Borden, William Berry. Admitted to N.Y. bar, 1946; with firm Gould & Wilkie, N.Y.C., 1945-51; with Central Hudson Gas & Electric Corp., Poughkeepsie, N.Y., 1951-68, v.p., asst. gen. mgr., 1955-60, pres., 1960-68, chief exec. officer, 1964-67, also dir.; chmn. N.E. Utilities, Hartford, Conn., 1968-78, chief exec., 1969—, chmn. bd., 1970—, also trustee; chmn., chief exec. officer NE Utilities Service Co., Hartford, 1968—; chmn. Conn. Yankee Atomic Power Co., 1971—, NE Nuclear Energy Co.; dir. Charter N.Y. Corp., Irving Trust Co., Hartford Steam Boiler Inspection & Ins. Co.; adv. dir. Arthur D. Little, Inc. Chmn. Fed. Power Commn. Nat. Power Survey Exec. Adv. Com., 1965-72; past mem. Pres.'s Adv. Com. on Environ. Quality; dir. Atomic Indsl. Forum, Edison Electric Inst. Mem. steering com. Nat. Urban Coalition. Life trustee, past pres. Vassar Bros. Hosp., Poughkeepsie; formerly trustee New Eng. Natural Resources Center; adv. trustee Edwin Gould Found for Children; trustee Wesleyan U. Served to maj. USMCR, 1942-45. Mem. Am. Bar Assn., N.Y. State Bar Assn., Edison Electric Inst., U.S.C. of C., Conf. Bd., Conn. Bus. and Industry Assn. (past dir.), Am. Judicature Soc., Conf. Bd. Clubs: Century Assn., Economic, University (N.Y.C.); Hartford. Home: RD 2 Route 156 Lyme CT 06371 Office: Northeast Utilities PO Box 270 Hartford CT 06101

SILLIPHANT, STIRLING DALE, motion picture writer, producer; b. Detroit, Jan. 16, 1918; s. Leigh Lemuel and Ethel May (Noaker) S.; B.A. magna cum laude, U. So. Calif., 1938; m. Tiana Du Long, July 4, 1974; children—Stirling, Dayle, Loren (dec.). Publicity dir. 20th Century-Fox, N.Y.C., 1946-53; screenwriter, independent producer various studios in Hollywood, 1953—. Recipient Image award for prodn. of Shaft, N.A.A.C.P., 1972; named Box Office Writer of Year, Nat. Assn. Theater Owners, 1974. Mem. Phi Beta Kappa. Club: Calif. Yacht. Author: (motion pictures) In The Heat of the Night (Motion Picture Arts and Scis. Acad. award for best screenplay, Golden Globe award Fgn. Press Assn.), 1968, Charly (Golden Globe award Fgn. Press Assn.), 1969; (television series) Naked City, 1960, Route 66, 1960; others.

SILLOWAY, CHARLES THOMPSON, health industry cons.; b. Duluth, Minn., Apr. 7, 1913; s. George Elbridge and Margaret (Thompson) S.; grad. William Penn Charter Sch.; A.B. cum laude, Princeton U., 1934; m. Greta Burgess, Oct. 23, 1947; 1 son, Robert Lathrop. Clk., Guaranty Trust Co., N.Y.C., 1934-36; investment research Eastman Dillon & Co., 1936-39; v.p., dir. Warner-Hudnut (formerly Maltine Co., then Chilcott Labs., now Warner-Lambert Co.), 1952-55; pres. Warner-Chilcott Labs. div. 1954-55; pres., dir. Chemway Corp. and subsidiaries, Wayne, N.J., 1955-62; exec. v.p. CIBA Pharm. Co., Summit, N.J., 1962-64, pres., 1964-69; pres. Silloway & Co., Inc., 1969—; chmn. Primary Med. Communications, Inc., 1971-75; dir. Buildex, Inc. Clubs: University (N.Y.C.); Nassua (Princeton, N.J.). Home: van Beuren Rd Morristown NJ 07960

SILLS, ARTHUR JACK, lawyer; b. Bklyn., Oct. 19, 1917; s. Herman Silverman and Ida (Rosenzweig) S.; B.A., Rutgers U., 1938; LL.B. (Kirkpatrick scholar 1938), Harvard, 1941; LL.D., Rutgers U., 1966, Newark State Coll.; m. Mina Minzer, May 7, 1947; 1 dau., Hedy Erna. Admitted to N.J. bar, 1941; pub. rate counsel N.J., 1958-61; atty. gen. N.J., 1962-70; sr. partner Sills, Beck, Cummis, Radin & Tischman, 1971—. Counselor-lectr. counselors course Rutgers U., 1953-55. Dir. WHYY-TV, Channel 12, City Title Ins. Co., Channel Cos., Packaging Products and Design Corp., Devel. Corp. Am.; mem. Nat. Council Responsible Firearms Policy, Inc.; trustee WNDT-TV, Channel 13; trustee N.J. Easter Seal Soc., Rabbinical Coll. Am.; bd. dirs. J.F.K. Community Hosp., Edison, N.J.; pres. Hillell Bldg. Corp., Rutgers U.; adv. bd. Fed. Bar Assn. Recipient Louis Brownlow Meml. prize for article in State Govts. publ., 1967, Pope Paul VI Humanitarian award, 1968. Mem. Internat. Platform Assn., Am. Bar Assn., N.J., Middlesex County bars, Am. Judicature Soc., Nat. Assn. Attys. Gen. (pres. 1969-70), Phi Beta Kappa. Democrat. Jewish. Co-author: The Imbroglio of Constitutional Revision; contbr. to profl. publs. Home: 204 Dellwood Rd Metuchen NJ 08840 Office: 33 Washington St Newark NJ 07102

SILLS, BEVERLY (MRS. PETER B. GREENOUGH), coloratura soprano; b. Bklyn., 1929; grad. pub. schs.; student voice Estelle Leibling, piano Paolo Gallico, stagecraft Desire Defrere; hon. doctorates Harvard U., N.Y. U., New Eng. Conservatory, Temple U.; m. Peter B. Greenough, 1956; stepchildren—Lindley, Nancy, Diana; children—Meredith, Peter B. Radio debut as Bubbles Silverman on Uncle Bob's Rainbow House, 1932; appeared on Major Bowes Capitol Family Hour, 1934-41, on Our Gal Sunday; toured with Shubert Tours, Charles Wagner Opera Co., 1950, 51; debut with N.Y.C. Opera Co., as Rosalinda in Die Fiedermaus, 1955; debut San Francisco Opera, 1953, La Scala, Milan, 1969, Royal Opera, Covent Garden, London, 1971, Met. Opera, N.Y.C., 1975; recital debut, Paris, 1971; appeared throughout U.S., Europe, S. Am., including Vienna State Opera, Teatro Fenice, Venice, Teatro Colon, Buenos Aires, N.Y. State Theatre, 1966, Boston Symphony, Tanglewood Festival, 1968, 69, Robin Hood Dell, Phila., 1969; star roles in Handel's Julius Caesar, Manon, La Traviata, Tales of Hoffman, Lucia di Lammermoor, Roberto Devereux, Anna Bolena, Maria Stuarda, Siege of Corinth, Thaïs; gen. dir. N.Y.C. Opera, 1979—. Address: care Mgmt Ludwig Lustig 111 W 57th St New York NY 10019

SILLS, DAVID LAWRENCE, sociologist; b. N.Y.C., Aug. 24, 1920; s. R. Malcolm and Charlotte Noyes (Babcock) S.; B.A., Dartmouth Coll., 1942; M.A., Yale U., 1948; Ph.D., Columbia U., 1956; m. Yole Laura Granata, Feb. 18, 1948; 1 son, Gregory Lawrence. Research analyst pub. opinion and sociol. research div. Allied Occupation of Japan, 1947-50; research asso. Bur. Applied Social Research Columbia U., 1952-61, acting dir., 1961-62, dir. research, 1962; expert UN Tech. Assistance Orgn., Bombay, India, 1960-61; editor Crowell Collier and Macmillan, N.Y.C., 1962-67; asso. dir. demographic div. Population Council, N.Y.C., 1968-70, dir., 1970-72; exec. asso. Social Sci. Research Council, N.Y.C., 1973—; fellow Center for Advanced Study in Behavioral Scis., Stanford, Calif., 1967-68; vis. scholar Russell Sage Found., 1973. Served with U.S. Army, 1942-46. Mem. AAAS (chmn. sect. on social and econ. sci. 1979-80), Am. Sociol. Assn., Scientists Inst. Pub. Info., Sociol. Research Assn. Democrat. Episcopalian. Editor: International Encyclopedia of the Social Sciences, 17 vols., 1968. Home: 95 Circle Dr Hastings-on-Hudson NY 10706 Office: 605 3d Ave New York NY 10016

SILLS, STANLEY S., publishing co. exec.; b. N.Y.C., Nov. 3, 1925; s. Morris N. and Shirley (Bahn) S.; B.S., State U. N.Y., 1950; M.A., Columbia, 1951; m. Shirley Dieter, Nov. 20, 1951; children—Michael N., David C. From salesman to mktg. mgr. Sci. Research Assos., Chgo., 1955-65; v.p. Am. Book Co., N.Y.C., 1965-68; product line mgr. Internat. Tel. & Tel., N.Y.C., 1968-71; pres. Howard W. Sams & Co., subsidiary ITT, Indpls., 1971—, also dir.; pres. Filmways Pub. Group, 1980—; gen. mgr. ITT Pub. Co. Served to 2d lt. USAAF, 1943-46; ETO. Decorated Presdl. citation, five battle stars. Office: 51 Madison Ave New York NY 10010

SILLS, THEODORE ROOSEVELT, pub. relations counsel; b. Chgo., Aug. 31, 1904; s. Harry B. and Jeanne (Forman) S.; grad. Northwestern U., 1928; m. Annie Laurie McPherson, Dec. 23, 1934. With Chgo. Eve. Am., 1925-28; partner Seaberg-Sills, 1933-36; pres. Theodore R. Sills, Inc., Chgo., 1936—; dir. Studio City Bank (Calif.). Pres., Los Angeles Psychiat. Service, 1973-75. Mem. Spain-U.S. C. of C., Pub. Relations Soc. Am. (nat. dir. 1949-55, pres. Chgo. chpt. 1950), Nat. Assn. Pub. Relations Counsel (nat. v.p. 1945-46), N.W. Golf League (pres. 1953), Sigma Delta Chi. Episcopalian. Clubs: Winged Foot Golf (Mamaroneck, N.Y.); Barrington Hills Country; Lincoln Park Gun, Northwestern U., Headline (Chgo.); Nat. Press (Washington); Riviera Golf (Pacific Palisades, Calif.). Co-author: Public Relations, Principles and Procedures, 1946. Home: 1501 Umeo Rd Pacific Palisades CA 90272 Office: 3600 Wilshire Blvd Los Angeles CA 90010

SILLS, THOMAS ALBERT, artist; b. Castalin, N.C., Aug. 20, 1914; s. Baldie and Cynthey S.; m. Jeanne Reynal, 1952; 2 children. One-man shows include: Betty Parsons Gallery, N.Y.C., 1955, 57, 59, 61, Paul Kantor Gallery, Los Angeles, 1962, Bodley Gallery, N.Y.C., 1964, 67, 70, 72, Fine Arts Gallery Creighton U., Omaha, 1967, Cushing Gallery, Newport, R.I., 1970; group shows include: Mus. Modern Art, N.Y.C., 1969, Univ. Art Mus., U. Tex., Austin, 1971, Mus. Fine Arts, Boston, 1967, Mpls. Inst. Art, 1967, PVI Gallery, N.Y.C., 1960; represented in permanent collections: Met. Mus. Art, N.Y.C., Whitney Mus. Am. Art, N.Y.C., Mus. Modern Art, N.Y.C., Syracuse U. Mus., Phoenix Art Mus., Los Angeles County Mus., Rockefeller U., Fisk U., San Francisco Mus. Art, Bklyn. Mus. Address: 240 W 11th St New York NY 10014

SILSBY, WILLIAM SANDS, lawyer, justice; b. Aurora, Maine, May 15, 1902; s. Herbert Trafton and Margaret (Schoppee) S.; student Maine Central Inst., 1921, Suffolk Law Sch., 1937; m. Myrle Coombs, July 26, 1924; children—Herbert Trafton II, William Sands, Beverly (Mrs. Preston A. McLean). Operator various lumbering, road constrn. projects, Maine, 1921-31; admitted to Maine bar, 1936, U.S. Supreme Ct. bar; mem. firm Clarke & Silsby, 1938-47; mem. firm Silsby & Silsby, 1947—; now of counsel mem. Maine Ho. Reps., 1947-53, speaker, 1951-52; mem. Senate, 1953-58; justice Superior Ct., Maine, 1961-72; of counsel Silsby & Silsby, 1972—; promoter Northeastern Packing Co., 1941; pres. Union River Electric Coop., Union River Telephone Co. Appeal agt. SSS, Ellsworth, 1941-72; mem. Maine Gov.'s Exec. Council, 1959-60; adv. com. Maine Publicity Bur., 1959. Trustee Higgins Classical Inst., 1959-74. Mem. Am., Maine (pres. 1958-59) bar assns., Am. Judicature Soc. Conglist. Mason (Shriner), Rotarian. Home: 4 Union St Ellsworth ME 04605 Office: Silsby Bldg Ellsworth ME 04605

SILVA, FELIPE, tobacco co. exec.; b. Cienfuegos, Cuba, Feb. 27, 1919; s. Felipe and Hortensia (Cardenas) S.; student U. Mich., 1936-38; D. Law, U. Havana, 1942, Public Acct., 1943; came to U.S., 1960, naturalized, 1968; m. Dolores Alvarez, Feb. 3, 1945; children—Ana, Felipe Rafael, Maria Dolores, Lourdes. Pres., Tabacalera Cubana, S.A., 1949-60; spl. sales rep. ACC div. Am. Tobacco Co., St. Petersburg, Fla., 1960-62, mgr. P.R. br., San Juan, 1963-67; export mgr. Am. Tobacco Co. div. Am. Brands, Inc., N.Y.C., 1968-78, pres. Am. Cigar div., 1978—. Mem. U. Mich. Alumni Assn. Roman Catholic. Club: Rotary. Home: 244 Virginia Ct Paramus NJ 07652 Office: Am Cigar Div Am Brands Inc 245 Park Ave New York NY 10017

SILVA, RUTH CARIDAD, polit. scientist; b. Lincoln, Nebr.; d. Ignatius Dominic and Beatrice (Davis) S.; A.B., U. Mich., 1943, M.A., 1943, Ph.D., 1948. Instr., Wheaton Coll., Norton, Mass., 1946-48; mem. faculty Pa. State U. at Univ. Park, 1948—, prof. polit. sci., 1959—; Fulbright prof. polit. sci., Cairo U., 1952-53; vis. prof. Hunter Coll., N.Y.C., 1948, Johns Hopkins U., 1965; spl. cons. U.S. Dept. Justice, 1957, N.Y. State Constn. Commn., 1959-60, Pa. State Constn. Commn., 1967-68; mem. Pres.'s Commn. Post Secondary Edn., 1972-73. Mem. Am. Polit. Sci. Assn. (past sec., chmn. com. status of women in profession 1972-73, v.p. 1972-73), Acad. Polit. Sci., AAUP (chmn. com. relation of govt. to higher edn. 1964-68), Nat. Municipal League, Phi Kappa Phi, Chi Omega. Republican. Roman Catholic. Clubs: University, U. Mich. President's (Ann Arbor); Pa. State U. Faculty. Author: Presidential Succession, 1951; Legislative Apportionment in New York, 1960; Rum, Religion and Votes: 1928 Re-examined, 1962; co-author: American Government, Democracy and Liberty in Balance, 1976; contbr. articles in field to profl. jours. Home: 1000 Plaza Dr State College PA 16801 Office: Burrowes Bldg University Park PA 16802

SILVEIRA, AUGUSTINE, JR., educator; b. Mattapoisett, Mass., July 17, 1934; s. Augustine and Mildred (Lewis) S.; B.S., Southeastern Mass. U., 1957, Sc.D. (hon.), 1975; Ph.D., U. Mass., 1962; m. Beverly Ann Washburn, Aug. 20, 1960; children—Linda Ann, Karen Louise. Research chemist Acushnet Process Co. (Mass.), 1957-58; instr. U. Mass., 1960-62; asst. prof. Rutgers U., 1962-63; asso. prof. State U. N.Y. at Oswego, 1963-64, prof., 1964-67, prof., chmn. dept. chemistry, 1967—, distinguished teaching prof., 1976—. Am. Council on Edn. fellow U. Calif. At Irvine, 1969-70, vis. prof., 1976-77; vis. prof. Calif. State U., Long Beach, 1976-77; cons. to edn. and industry; guest lectr.; evaluator State U. N.Y. Grad. Programs, 1968—, Patent Policy Bd., 1971; mem. commn. higher edn. Middle States Assn., 1971—. Mem. alumni adv. council U. Mass., 1971-75. Research grantee. Fellow Am. Inst. Chemists; mem. Am. Chem. Soc. (dist. rep.), AAUP (v.p. 1965-66), Sigma Xi (pres. 1972-73, 78-79), Delta Kappa Phi, Alpha Kappa Phi. Contbr. articles to profl. jours. Home: 2021 Benson Ave Minetto NY 13115 Office: Chemistry Dept State Univ New York Oswego NY 13126

SILVER, CHARLES HAL, ret. dept. store exec.; b. Anderson, Ind., July 18. 1924; s. Charles B. and Dorothy Geneve (Carroll) S.; B.S., Butler U.. Indpls., 1948; m. Betty Van Arendonk, Sept. 6, 1947; children—Stephen H., Craig B., Annette M. With L.S. Ayres & Co., Indpls., 1949-69, v.p., gen. mgr., 1965-69; with Meier & Frank Co., Portland, Oreg., 1969-74, pres., 1973-74; pres., chief exec. officer Kaufmann's, Pitts., 1975-79. Served with U.S. Army, 1943-45. Republican. Presbyn. Clubs: Duquesne, Pitts. Field. Home: 1440 Thatch Palm Dr Boca Raton FL 33432

SILVER, CHARLES MORTON, communications co. exec.; b. New Haven, Sept. 22, 1929; s. Sam and Rose (Fischman) S.; B.S., U Conn., 1954; m. Rose Charek, Mar. 27, 1960; children—Ronni Ellen, Suzanne Paula, Steven Mitchell. With Arthur Andersen & Co., N.Y.C., 1954-61; with Internat. Tel. & Tel., N.Y.C., 1961—, now v.p., asso. treas., dir. fgn. treasury ops. Served with U.S. Army, 1947-48, 50-51. Mem. Am. Inst. C.P.A.'s, N.Y. State Soc. C.P.A.'s. Club: Roxbury Swim and Tennis. Home: Akbar Rd Stamford CT 06902 Office: 320 Park Ave New York NY 10022

SILVER, DAVID MAYER, coll. dean; b. West Pittston, Pa., July 16, 1915; s. Morris Jacob and Flora (Mayer) S.; A.B. magna cum laude, Butler U., 1937; A.M. (history scholar 1938), U. Ill., 1938, Ph.D. (fellow history 1938-40), 1940; m. Anita Rose Cohen, May 10, 1942; children—Gregory, Terence. Mem. faculty Butler U., 1940—, prof. history, 1954—, dean Coll. Liberal Arts and Scis., 1963—. Cons.-evaluator North Central Assn., 1974—. Pres. Indpls. Bd. Pub. Safety, 1956-63; mem. youth study com. Ohio Valley Council of Hebrew Congregations, 1963-65. Research dir. Ind. Democratic Central Com., 1944; Dem. nominee Ind. Legislature, 1944; Dem. candidate for Indpls. City Council, 1955. Bd. dirs. Indpls. Jewish Social Services, 1953-56. Butler U. Faculty fellow, 1950-51; recipient J.I. Holcomb award Butler U., 1955. Mem. Am. Hist. Assn., Orgn. Am. Historians, Ind. Hist. Soc., AAUP, Ind. Conf. Acad. Deans (chmn. 1972), Phi Beta Kappa, Phi Kappa Phi, Phi Eta Sigma, Sigma Alpha Mu. Jewish religion (bd. dirs., pres. congregation). Mem. B'nai B'rith. Author: Lincoln's Supreme Court, 1956; also articles. Home: 8230 N Illinois St Indianapolis IN 46260

SILVER, DONALD, educator, surgeon; b. N.Y.C., Oct. 19, 1929; s. Herman and Cecilia (Meyer) S.; A.B., Duke U., 1950, B.S. in Medicine, M.D., 1955; m. Helen Elizabeth Harnden, Aug. 9, 1959; children—Elizabeth Tyler, Donald Meyer, Stephanie Davies, William Paige. Intern, Duke Med. Center, 1955-56, asst. resident, 1958-63, resident, 1963-64; mem. faculty Duke Med. Sch., 1964-75, prof. surgery, 1972-75; cons. Watts Hosp., Durham, 1965-75; cons. VA Hosp., Durham, 1970-75, chief surgery, 1968-70; prof. surgery, chmn. dept. U. Mo. VA Med. Center, Columbia, 1975—; cons. Harry S. Truman Hosp., Columbia, 1975—; mem. bd. sci. advisers Cancer Research Center, Columbia, 1975—; mem. surg. study sect. A, NIH. Served with USAF, 1956-58. James IV Surg. traveler, 1977. Diplomate Am. Bd. Surgery, Am. Bd. Thoracic Surgery. Fellow A.C.S., Deryl Hart Soc.; mem. Am., Mo. med. assns., Boone County Med. Soc., AAAS, Internat. Cardiovascular Soc., Soc. Univ. Surgeons, Am. Heart Assn. (Mo. affiliate research com.), Soc. Surgery Alimentary Tract, Assn. Acad. Surgery, So. Thoracic Surg. Assn., Internat. Soc. Surgery, Soc. Vascular Surgery, Am. Assn. Thoracic Surgery, Am., Central, Western surg. assns., Phi Beta Kappa, Alpha Omega Alpha. Contbr. articles to med. jours., chpts. to books. Home: 1050 W Covered Bridge Rd RD 4 Columbia MO 65201 Office: Dept Surgery M580 Univ Mo Med Center Columbia MO 65201

SILVER, GERALD, univ. adminstr.; b. N.Y.C., Feb. 19, 1939; s. Harry and Freida (Cohen) S.; B.A., Queens Coll., 1961; M.B.A., Columbia U., 1963, Ed.D., 1973. Fin. analyst Hotel Corp. Am., Washington, 1963-64; prof., chmn. dept. mgmt. and computer sci. Fairleigh Dickinson U., Rutherford, N.J., 1966-73, acting dean Coll. Bus. Adminstrn., 1974-76; dean Coll. Bus. Adminstrn., Ohio U., Athens, 1976—. Trustee Ohio Council on Econ. Edn., 1976—. Served with U.S. Army, 1963. Recipient Outstanding Service award Bergen County C. of C., 1975. Mem. Am. Assn. Higher Edn., Am. Assn. Univ. Adminstrs., Acad. Mgmt., Am. Mgmt. Assn., Nat. Assn. Mgmt. Educators. Clubs: Rotary, Athens Country, Lancaster Indoor Tennis, Tuckahoe Racquet. Home: 9-201 Monticello Dr Athens OH 45701 Office: Coll of Bus Adminstrn Ohio U Athens OH 45701

SILVER, HAROLD FARNES, inventor and mfg. exec.; b. Salt Lake City, Mar. 15, 1901; s. Joseph A. and Elizabeth (Farnes) S.; student Columbia, 1921-22, U. Utah, 1924-27; m. Madelyn C. Stewart, Feb. 20, 1929 (dec. Sept. 1961); children—Elizabeth (Mrs. Robert M. Clawson, Jr.), Barnard S., Judith A. (Mrs. W. Peter Poulsen, Jr.); m. 2d, Ruth Stanlie Smith, Sept. 16, 1964. Pres., Silver Corp., Denver, 1940—; hon. dir. Ideal Basic Industries, Inc., Mountain States Tel. & Tel. Co. Industry mem. regional WLB, 1942-45; industry adv. regional War Manpower Commn., 1942-45; mem. regional bd. govs. Smaller War Plants Corp., 1942-45; pres. Mountain States Employers Council, Inc., 1947-48, now hon. dir. Campaign chmn. Denver Community Chest, 1949-50, pres., 1951 (hon. mem. award 1957); pres. Denver area council Boy Scouts Am., 1960-62 (recipient Silver Beaver 1956). Hon. trustee U. Denver; bd. dirs. Med. Care and Research Found. Recipient award of merit for Bus. Achievement U. Colo. Sch. Bus., 1944, award Am. Soc. Sugar Beet Technologists, 1960; Sertoma Service to Mankind award, 1961, Civis Princeps award, Regis Coll., 1961, Brotherhood Citation award NCCJ, 1965, Jesse Knight Indsl. Citizenship award Brigham Young U., 1965; Humanitarian award Cenikor Found., 1974; Pub. Service award Colo. Assn. Commerce and Industry, 1974; named Outstanding Businessman of Colo. C. of C., 1951. Mem. N.A.M. (past dir.), Mfrs. Assn. Colo. (pres. 1939-40), Denver C. of C. (dir. 1941-44), Newcomen Soc. N.Am.; hon. mem. Tau Beta Pi, Beta Gamma Sigma, Omicron Delta Kappa. Mem. Ch. of Jesus Christ of Latterday Saints. Clubs: Denver, Denver Country, Denver Athletic, Mile High (Denver). Inventor sugar beet piler, continuous diffusion process for the sugar industry, continuous coal mining machine, non-flammable dry cleaning process. Home: 315 Clermont St Denver CO 80220 Office: First Nat Bank Bldg Denver CO 80293

SILVER, HENRY K., pediatrician, educator; b. Phila., Apr. 22, 1918; s. Samuel and Dora (Kreitzer) S.; B.A., U. Calif., Berkeley, 1938, M.D., 1942; m. Harriet Ashkenas, June 15, 1941; children—Stephen, Andrew. Intern, U. Calif. Hosp., San Francisco, 1941-42; resident Children's Hosp., Phila., 1942-43; instr., then asst. prof. pediatrics, U. Calif. Med. Sch., San Francisco, 1946-52; asso. prof. Yale Med. Sch., 1952-57; prof. pediatrics U. Colo. Med. Sch.. Denver, 1957—, asso. dean admissions, 1977—; clin. prof. nursing U. Colo. Sch. Nursing, 1976—. Rosenberg Found. fellow, 1945-47; recipient George Armstrong award Ambulatory Pediatric Assn., 1972; Martha May Eliot award Am. Pub. Health Assn., 1974; Eleanor Roosevelt Humanitarian award Denver chpt. Hadassah, 1973; diplomate Am. Bd. Pediatrics. Mem. Inst. Medicine of Nat. Acad. Sci., Am. Acad. Pediatrics, Western Soc. Pediatric Research (Ross award in edn. 1962), Soc. Pediatric Research, Am. Pediatric Soc., Colo., Denver med. socs., Sigma Xi, Alpha Omega Alpha. Co-author: Healthy Babies-Happy Parents, 1958; Current Pediatric Diagnosis and Treatment, 5th edit., 1978; Handbook of Pediatrics, 12th edit., 1977. Developer of first nurse practitioner program and child health associate program in U.S.; first to describe Silver's Syndrome, 1953, Deprivation Dwarfism, 1967. Home: 135 S Ivy St Denver CO 80224 Office: 4200 E 9th Ave Denver CO 80262

SILVER, HORACE WARD MARTIN TAVARES, composer, pianist; b. Norwalk, Conn., Sept. 2, 1928; s. John and Gertrude (Edmonds) S.; ed. pub. schs., Norwalk. Pres., Ecaroh Music, Inc., N.Y.C., 1955—; leader Horace Silver Quintet, 1955—. Recipient Budweiser Mus. Excellence award, 1958; Silver Record award Blue Note Records, 1959; Citizen Call Entertainment award, 1960. Mem. A.S.C.A.P., Am. Fedn. Musicians. Composer: Senor Blues, 1956, Doodlin', 1956, The Preacher, 1956, Nica's Dream, 1956, Home Cookin', 1956 Enchantment, 1956, Cookin' at the Continental, 1957, Moon Rays, 1957, Soulville, 1957, Sister Sadie, 1959, Come on Home, 1959, Peace, 1959, Finger Poppin, 1959, Blowin' the Blues Away, 1959, Strollin', 1960, Filthy McNasty, 1961, The Tokyo Blues, 1962, Silver's Serenade, 1963, Song For My Father, 1965, Que Pasa, 1965, Lonely Woman, 1956, others. Office: care Jack Whittemore 80 Park Ave New York NY 10016*

SILVER, HOWARD, lawyer; b. Detroit, May 1, 1925; s. Frank and Ethel (Horwitz) S.; B.A., Wayne State U., 1947, LL.B., 1950; m. Hermine Lipman, Dec. 27, 1958; children—Greta A., Abby E. Admitted to Mich. bar, 1951; sr. partner firm Maile, Leach & Silver, 1951-67, Sugar, Schwartz, Silver, Schwartz & Tyler, 1967-73, Sommers, Schwartz, Silver & Schwartz, Southfield, Mich., 1978—; trustee Nat. Inst. Trial Advocacy, 1972—; speaker Detroit Acad. Surgery Trauma. Mem. Assn. Trial Lawyers Am. (pres. Detroit chpt. 1964, Mich. chpt. 1965, 6th circuit bd. govs. 1966-67; chmn. Nat. Coll. Advocacy com. 1973; mem. continuing legal edn. com. 1975—, med. malpractice com. 1975—), Am., Mich. (negligence sect, counsel 1972-74), Detroit Southfield (v.p. 1978-79) bar assns., Nat. Inst. Trial Advocacy, Nat. Coll. Advocacy. Contbr. articles to legal jours. Home: 32546 Scottsdale St Franklin MI 48025 Office: 26555 Evergreen St Southfield MI 48076

SILVER, JAMES WESLEY, educator; b. Rochester, N.Y., June 28, 1907; s. Henry Dayton and Elizabeth (Squier) S.; A.B., U. N.C., 1927; A.M., Peabody Coll., 1929; Ph.D., Vanderbilt, 1935; hon. doctoral degree Morehouse Coll., 1967, U. So. Fla., 1976; m. Margaret McLean Thompson, Dec. 31, 1935; children—James William, Virginia, Margaret. Asso. prof. history Southwestern Coll., Winfield, Kans., 1935-36; asst. prof. history U. Miss., 1936-42, asso. prof., 1942-46, prof., 1946-65, chmn. dept., 1946-57; became prof. history U. Notre Dame, South Bend, Ind., 1965; now emeritus prof. history U. South Fla., Tampa; Fulbright scholar U. Aberdeen, Scotland, 1949-50, Ford Found. scholar Harvard, 1951-52; summer lectr. Emory U., Harvard, others. Mem. State Hist. Commn. Miss. 1948-57. Mem. South Bend Human Relations Commn. Bd. dirs. Forest History Found. Served with A.R.C. in Pacific area, 1945. Recipient Anisfield-Wolfe Race Relations award, 1965. Mem. Am. Acad. Arts and Scis., Am., So. (mem. exec. council, pres.) hist. assns., Orgn. Am. Historians, Miss. Hist. Soc., Phi Beta Kappa, Omicron Delta Kappa, Tau Kappa Alpha, Pi Gamma Mu, Phi Kappa Phi. Rotarian. Author: Edmund Pendleton Gaines: Frontier General, 1949; Confederate Morale and Church Propaganda, 1957; A Life for the Confederacy, 1959; Mississippi in the Confederacy, 1961; Mississippi: The Closed Society (Sidney Hillman Found. award for 1964), 1964; The Confederate Soldier, 1973. Mem. bd. editors: Jour. Miss. History, 1947-48, Jour. So. History, 1952-56, Mississippi Valley Hist. Rev., 1963—. Contbr. articles to various hist. jours., Dictionary Am. History. Home: 4929 SW 10th Ave Cape Coral FL 33904

SILVER, JOE, actor; b. Chgo., Sept. 28, 1922; s. Morris and Sonia (Genis) S.; student U. Wis., 1940-42; m. Evelyn Colton, Jan. 8, 1950; children—Christopher Michael, Jennifer. Appeared in numerous motion pictures, 1950—, including Rhinoceros, 1973, Apprenticeship of Duddy Kravitz, 1974; Broadway shows include Lenny (Tony award nominee), 1972, Promises, Promises (N.J. Drama Critics award nominee), 1973; appeared in numerous TV programs. Served with Signal Corps, AUS, 1944-47, Mem. Screen Actors Guild (dir. 1967—), AFTRA, Actors Equity Assn.

SILVER, JULIUS, lawyer; b. Phila., Dec. 17, 1900; s. Louis and Esther (Miller) S.; B.A., N.Y. U., 1922, D.C.L. (hon.); J.D., Columbia U., 1924; D.Sc. in Tech. (hon.), Israel Inst. Tech.; D.H.L. (hon.), Jewish Theol. Sem. Am.; m. Roslyn Schiff, July 3, 1929; 1 dau., Enid (Mrs. Winslow). Admitted to N.Y. bar, 1925, since practiced in N.Y.C.; sr. partner firm Silver, Saperstein, Barnett & Solomon, 1944—. Dir. Polaroid Corp., Cambridge, Mass., v.p., chmn. exec. com., 1937—. Asso. counsel com. on banking and currency U.S. Senate, 1932-34. Donor Julius Silver Residence Center, N.Y. U., 1963; founder Julius Silver Inst. Biomed. Engring., Technion U., Israel, 1968. Trustee N.Y. U., mem. exec. and finance coms., 1963-75, emeritus, 1975—. trustee Middlesex Coll. (now Brandeis U.), 1946; trustee Jewish Theol. Sem., pres. Library Corp. 1965—. Recipient Achievement award N.Y.U. Alumni Assn., 1961; Silver Towers named in his honor, N.Y.U., 1974. Mem. Bar Assn. N.Y.C., N.Y. County Lawyers Assn., Gallatin Soc. (v.p. 1964-68), Phi Beta Kappa, Phi Epsilon Pi (Achievement award 1963), Zeta Beta Tau. Clubs: Old Oaks Country (Purchase, N.Y.); Harmonie, N.Y. U. (N.Y.C.). Home: Byram Shore Rd Greenwich CT 06830 Office: 60 E 42d St New York City NY 10017

SILVER, LEON THEODORE, educator; b. Monticello, N.Y., Apr. 9, 1925; s. Jacob and Bessie (Kramer) S.; B.S., U. Colo., 1945; M.S., U. N.Mex., 1948; Ph.D., Calif. Inst. Tech., 1955; m. Geraldine Sinars, 1974; children by previous marriage—Stuart Lynds, Victoria Alleyne. With U.S. Geol. Survey, Pasadena, Calif., 1947—, geologist, 1970-76; mem. faculty dept. geology Calif. Inst. Tech., Pasadena, 1948—, asso. prof., 1962-65, prof., 1965—. Mem. adv. com. Lunar Sci. Inst., Houston, 1972—; mem. bd. mineral resources NRC, 1975—, vice chmn. Served to lt. (j.g.) USN, 1943-46. Guggenheim fellow, 1964; recipient exceptional sci. achievement medal NASA, 1971. Fellow Geol. Soc. Am. (councillor 1974-76, v.p. 1978, pres. 1979), Mineralogical Soc. Am.; mem. Nat. Acad. Scis., Am. Geophys. Union, Geochem. Soc., Meteoritical Soc., Soc. Economic Geologists, AAAS, AAUP, Sigma Xi. Office: 1201 California Blvd Pasadena CA 91125

SILVER, MARC STAMM, chemist; b. Phila., Jan. 5, 1934; s. Robert and Mae (Stamm) S.; A.B., Harvard Coll., 1955; Ph.D. (NSF fellow), Calif. Inst. Tech., 1959; M.A. (hon.), Amherst Coll., 1969; m. Carol Joan Dinnes, Aug. 13, 1961; children—David Abraham, Daniel Clark, Benjamin Richard. Instr., asst. prof., asso. prof. Amherst (Mass.) Coll., 1958-69, prof. chemistry, 1969—, dept. chmn., 1975-77; vis. prof. Yale U., 1977-78. NSF fellow, 1961-62, 66-67; research grantee NSF, 1974-80, NIH, 1964-74, Research Corp., 1959-63, Petroleum Research Fund, 1959-63. Mem. Am. Chem. Soc., AAAS, Am. Soc. Biol. Chemists, Phi Beta Kappa, Sigma Xi. Contbr. articles to chem. jours. Home: 317 S Pleasant St Amherst MA 01002 Office: Dept Chemistry Amherst Coll Amherst MA 01002

SILVER, MELVIN J., lawyer; b. St. Paul, Nov. 12, 1904; s. Alexander and Edith (Silberstein) S.; student U. Minn., 1923-26; LL.B., St. Paul Coll. Law, 1927; m. Eleanor Kaufman, Jan. 12, 1930; 1 dau., Sandra (Mrs. Robert Alch). Tchr. violin Mpls. Sch. Music, 1924-27; admitted to Minn. bar, 1927; spl. counsel for atty. gen. Minn., 1944; sr. mem. Silver and Ryan; v.p., gen. counsel U.S. Arlington Corp.; pres., dir., gen. counsel Minn. Capital Corp.; gen. counsel, dir. C.G. Rein Investment Co., Twin City Textile Mills Inc.; gen. counsel Ralph R. Kriesel Enterprises, ATR Electronics, Inc.; chmn. bd., gen. counsel Sacred Design Assos. Inc., Smithcraft, Inc., Schmidt Printing, Inc. Mem. Bd. Edn. St. Paul, 1950-52; mem. initial gifts com. St. Paul Community Chest; chmn. spl. gifts com. St. Vincent de Paul Soc. Chmn. U. Minn. scholarships Dr. William Ginsburg and Edward Hoffman awards; chmn. Alex Dim scholarship award com.; chmn. Albert and Annie Schapira Found. for Scholarships. Mem. exec. com. Minn. Jewish Council; v.p. St. Paul Jewish Council; dir. Jewish Vocat. Service; chmn. State of Israel Bond Com. Recipient B'nai B'rith award for outstanding service to St. Paul, 1951. Received Scroll of Honor for service by City Bd. Edn., 1952. Mem. Am., Minn. (plaque for distinguished services to community for 50 yrs 1977), Ramsey County bar assns., Alpha Tau Mu (past chief justice). Jewish. Mason (32 deg., Shriner); mem. B'nai B'rith (past pres. Minn. lodge, award of Honor Scroll by Supreme Lodge 1958). Clubs: Hillcrest Country, Standard, St. Paul Athletic; Lost Spur Country. Home: 2029 Upper St Dennis Rd Saint Paul MN 55116 Office: Minnesota Bldg Saint Paul MN 55101

SILVER, RALPH DAVID, distilling co. exec.; b. Chgo., Apr. 19, 1924; s. Morris J. and Amelia (Abrams) S.; B.S., U. Chgo., 1943; postgrad. Northwestern U., 1946-48; J.D., DePaul U., 1952; m. Lois Reich, Feb. 4, 1951; children—Jay, Cappy. Staff accountant David Himmelblau & Co., C.P.A.'s, 1946-48; internal revenue agt. U.S. Dept. Treasury, 1948-51; admitted to Ill. bar, 1952; practice in Chgo., 1952-55; atty. Lawrence J. West, 1952-55; chief fin. exec. Barton Brands, Ltd., Chgo., 1955—, also dir. bd. dirs., pres. Silver Found. Served to lt. (j.g.) USNR, 1943-46. Mem. Am., Chgo. bar assns., Am. Inst. C.P.A.'s. Clubs: Green Acres Country; University (Chgo.). Home: 1124 Old Elm Ln Glencoe IL 60022 Office: 55 E Monroe St Chicago IL 60603

SILVER, SAMUEL MANUEL, clergyman; b. Wilmington, Del., June 7, 1912; s. Adolph David and Adela (Hacker) S.; B.A., U. Del., 1933; M.H.L., Hebrew Union Coll., 1940, D.D., 1965; m. Elaine Shapiro, Feb. 9, 1953; children—Leon David, Joshua J., Barry M., Noah, Daniel. Ordained rabbi, 1940; dir. Hillel Found., U. Md., 1940-42; asst. rabbi in Cleve., 1946-52; rabbi Temple Sinai, Stamford, Conn., 1959-77, Jewish Community Center of Lee County, Cape Coral, Fla., 1977-79, Reform Hebrew Congregation of Delray (Fla.), 1979—. Sec., Temple of Understanding, Greenwich, Conn., 1969; v.p. Stamford-Darien Council of Chs. and Synagogues; exec. bd. Fellowship in Prayer, 1970—. Served as chaplain AUS, 1942-46. Mem. Central Conf. Am. Rabbis (nat. exec. bd. 1954-56), Jewish War Vets, Am. (chaplain 1966-70), Assn. Jewish Chaplains U.S. (pres. 1959-62), Stamford-Darien Ministers League (pres. 1961-62), Alpha Epsilon Pi. Author: (with Rabbi M.M. Applebaum) Sermonettes for Young People, 1964; How To Enjoy This Moment, 1967; Explaining Judaism to Jews and Christians, 1971; When You Speak English You Often Speak Hebrew, 1973; Mixed Marriage Between Jew and Christian, 1977; Speak to the Children of Israel, 1977. Editor: Am. Judaism, 1952-59; The Quotable American Rabbis, 1967. Columnist, Nat. Jewish Post, 1955—, Seven Arts Feature Syndicate, 1962—. Home and Office: Rainberry Lake 2015 NW 9th St Delray Beach FL 33440. *The greatest of all miracles is that we need not be tomorrow what we are today but that we can improve if we make use of the potential implanted within us by God.*

SILVER, STUART MARTIN, museum ofcl., designer; b. N.Y.C., May 4, 1938; s. Hyman and Miriam (Bornstein) S.; B.F.A., Pratt Inst., 1960; postgrad. Yale, 1960; m. Elizabeth Ann Munson, May 13, 1962; children—Lauren Davi, Jessica Leah, Leslie Eve. Jr. designer Met. Mus. Art, N.Y.C., 1962-65, asso. design mgr., 1965-67, mgr., 1967-71, adminstr. for design, 1971-76, design dir., 1976—; pres. Exhbn. Planning, Inc., 1969; v.p. design communications Knoll Internat., 1979—; cons. Govts. of Iran, Japan, N.Y. State Council on Arts, Yale Gallery Art, N.Y.C. Parks Dept., Mellon Center Brit. Studies, Yale, pvt. industry; instr. design Pratt Inst.; dir. Bicentennial Exhbn., Scarsdale, N.Y., 1975—. Arbitrator, Am. Arbitration Assn., 1975, 76; trustee, sec. bd. Museums Collaborative, N.Y. Served with AUS, 1956-58. Mem. Soc. Publ. Designers (Silver award 1974, 77, Gold award 1977, certificates of excellence 1972-75), Am. Inst. Graphic Arts (certificates of excellence 1972-77), Art Dirs. Club N.Y. (certificates of excellence 1969, 75, 77), Type Dirs. Club (certificates of excellence 1973, 77), Illuminating Engring. Soc. (Lumen award 1971, 78), Am. Assn. Museums. Club: Town (Scarsdale). Contbr. articles to Mus. Quar., Connoisseur. Home: 11 Gorham Ct Scarsdale NY 10583 Office: Fifth Ave and 82d St New York NY 10028. *My parents, who are immigrants, instilled in their children an abiding and deep respect for accomplishment, for the maximal use of ones talents, intellect, or particular gifts. I have no doubt that that guiding principle, plus a healthy measure of work and luck, is responsible for whatever success I have achieved thus far.*

SILVERBERG, LORENCE A., retail exec.; b. Sioux City, Iowa, June 19, 1914; s. Abraham and Blanche (Magasiner) S.; A.A., U. Minn., 1934; m. Lillian Baker, June 14, 1936; children—Barry J., Cheri Lou (Mrs. Robin Fern), Keith C. Mgr. store Silverberg Bros., Sioux City, Ia., 1934-42; wholesale clothing distbr., 1943-46; mfrs. rep. William Schwartz & Co., Phila., 1946-50; pres. Coombs Mfg. Co., Mpls., 1950-62; chmn. Asso. Apparel Industries, N.Y.C., 1962-64; dir. restaurants concessions McCrory-McLellan-Green Stores, York, Pa., 1964-66, pres., 1966-68; exec. v.p. S. Klein Dept. Stores, N.Y.C., 1968-72; chmn. bd. Leeds Travelwear, N.Y.C., 1972; chief operating officer, pres., chmn. bd. dirs. Kenton Corp., N.Y.C., 1972-74; pres. McCrory Stores, York, Pa., chmn. bd., chief exec. officer, 1977—; exec. v.p. McCrory Corp., N.Y.C., 1974-77, pres., chief exec. officer, 1977—, also dir.; exec. v.p. Rapid Am. Corp. Served with AUS, 1942-43. Mem. Sigma Alpha Mu. Home: 800 Fifth Ave New York NY 10021 Office: care McCrory Corp 888 7th Ave New York NY 10019

SILVERBERG, ROBERT, author; b. N.Y.C.; s. Michael and Helen (Baim) S.; B.A., Columbia, 1956; m. Barbara Brown, Aug. 26, 1956. Author: (novels) Thorns, 1967; The Masks of Time, 1968; Hawksbill Station, 1968; Nightwings, 1969; To Live Again, 1969; Tower of Glass, 1970; The World Inside, 1971; Son of Man, 1971; A Time of Changes, 1971; Dying Inside, 1972; The Book of Skulls, 1972; Born With the Dead, 1974; Shadrach in the Furnace, 1976; Lord Valentine's Castle, 1980; (non-fiction) Lost Cities and Vanished Civilizations, 1962; The Great Wall of China, 1965; The Old Ones: Indians of the American Southwest, 1965; Scientists and Scoundrels: A Book of Hoaxes, 1965; The Auk, the Dodo and the Oryx, 1966; The Morning of Mankind: Prehistoric Man in Europe, 1967; Mound Builders of Ancient America: The Archaeology of a Myth, 1968; If I Forget Thee, O Jerusalem: American Jews and the State of Israel, 1970; The Pueblo Revolt, 1970; The Realm of Prester John, 1971. Recipient Hugo award World Sci. Fiction Conv., 1956, 69, Nebula award Sci. Fiction Writers of Am., 1970, 72, 75. Mem. Sci. Fiction Writers of Am. (pres. 1967-68). Address: Box 13160 Station E Oakland CA 94661

SILVERBERG, STEVEN, hotel exec.; b. USSR, Aug. 5, 1944; s. Morris and Goldie S.; ed. Bebail Inst., Israel, 1964; m. Dvora Silverberg, Jan. 17, 1967; 1 dau., Shelly. Owner, operator 5 hotels, N.Y.C.; pres., chief exec. Am. Land Co., N.Y.C.; mem. adv. com. to ways and means com. N.Y. State Assembly. Mem. Associated Hotels and Motels (dir.), Nat. Realty Club. Jewish. Office: 304 E 42d St New York NY 10017

SILVERBLATT, ARTHUR, lawyer; b. Wilkes-Barre, Pa., July 27, 1910; s. Jacob and Henrietta (Menkle) S.; A.B. cum laude, Harvard U., 1930, LL.B., 1933, m. Elizabeth Friend, Apr. 27, 1946; children—Anne, Arthur. Admitted to Pa. bar, 1933, since practiced in Wilkes-Barre; partner firm Silverblatt & Townend, 1950—; 1st asst. dist. atty., Luzerne County, Pa., 1956-60; dir. Diamond Mfg. Co., Percy A. Brown & Co., Northeastern Bank Pa., Pa. Millers Mut. Ins. Co. Chmn. Luzerne County Mental Health Bd., 1966-69; pres. Wilkes-Barre Law and Library Assn., 1970—. Bd. dirs. Family Service Assn., Children's Service Center; chmn. Luzerne County Bicentennial Commn., 1976; pres. Osterhout Free Library, 1977—. Served with U.S. Army, 1942-46. Recipient certificate of Recognition, NCCJ, 1964. Fellow Am. Bar Found.; mem. Am., Pa. (bd. govs.) bar assns., Internat. Assn. Ins. Counsel. Club: Masons. Home: 192 James St Kingston PA 18704 Office: United Penn Bank Bldg Wilkes-Barre PA 18701

SILVERLIGHT, IRWIN JOSEPH, judge; b. Newark, Nov. 10, 1924; s. Benjamin and Rose (Breitkopf) S.; student Newark Coll. Engring., 1945-46, John Marshall Coll., 1946-47, John Marshall Coll. Law Sch., 1947-49; m. Lois S. Cohen, Oct. 30, 1949; children—Than, Scott, Brad. Admitted to N.J. bar, 1950, U.S. Supreme Ct. bar, 1956, V.I. bar, 1971; asso. firm Foreman & Foreman, Elizabeth, N.J., 1950-52; trial counsel Weiner & Weiner, Roselle, N.J., 1952-54; individual practice law, Westfield, 1954-62; partner firm Silverlight & Berenson, Westfield, 1962-64; partner firm Sachar, Sachar & Bernstein, Plainfield, 1964-69; asst. atty. gen. V.I., 1970-71; partner firm Nichols & Silverlight, St. Croix, V.I., 1971-76; judge Territorial Ct. V.I., St. Croix, 1977—; instr. zoning, planning and municipal law Rutgers U. Extension Div., 1967-69. Pres., Progressive Republican Party, St. Croix, 1972—; trustee Good Hope Sch., St. Croix. Served with USAAF, 1942-45. Decorated Air medal with 4 oak leaf clusters. Mem. V.I. (bd. govs. 1975, chmn. legis. and law reform 1974-76), N.J., Essex County, Plainfield, Union County bar assns., Assn. Trial Lawyers Am., Am. Judges Assn., Am. Judicature Soc., St. Croix C. of C. Jewish. Contbr. to Legal Aspects of Zoning and Planning, 1968, Opinions of the Attorney General, Virgin Islands, 1970-71. Home: PO Box 2726 Christiansted Saint Croix VI 00820 Office: PO Box 929 Christiansted Saint Croix VI 00820

SILVERMAN, AL, book club editor; b. Lynn, Mass., Apr. 12, 1926; s. Henry and Minnie (Damsky) S.; B.S., Boston U., 1949; m. Rosa Magaro, Sept. 9, 1951; children—Thomas, Brian, Matthew. Asso. editor Sport mag., 1951-52; sports editor True mag., 1952-54; asst. editor Argosy mag., 1954-55; free-lance mag. writer, contbr. Sat. Eve. Post, Coronet, Pageant, This Week, Am. Weekly, Am. Heritage, Sat. Review, others, 1955-60; editor-in-chief Saga mag., Impact mag., Sport Library, Sport Mag., 1960-72; exec. v.p., editorial dir. Book-of-the-Month Club, 1972—. Mem. Authors Guild. Author: Warren Spahn, 1961; Best from Sport, 1961; (with Phil Rizzuto) The Miracle New York Yankees, 1962; The World of Sport, 1962; Mickey Mantle, Master Yankee, 1963; World Series Heroes, 1964; (with Paul Hornung) Football and the Single Man, 1965; The Specialist in Pro Football, 1966; Sports Titans of the 20th Century, 1968; (with Frank Robinson) My Life is Baseball, 1968; More Sport Titans of the 20th Century, 1969; Joe DiMaggio, The Golden Year, 1969; I Am Third (with Gale Sayers), 1970; Foster and Laurie, 1974. Home: 311 Rosedale Ave White Plains NY 10605 Office: 485 Lexington Ave New York NY 10017

SILVERMAN, ALBERT A., mfg. exec.; b. Copenhagen, Denmark, Oct. 14, 1908; s. Louis and Anna (Mendelsohn) S.; came to U.S., 1909, naturalized, 1921; student Northwestern U., 1929-34; A.A., Central YMCA Coll., Chgo., 1936; J.D., Loyola U., Chgo., 1940; m. Gertrude Adelman, 1929 (div. 1934); 1 dau., Violet (Mrs. Robert Blumenthal); m. 2d, Florence Cohen, Aug. 5, 1939 (dec. 1966); m. 3d, Mrs. Francie Seifert, Oct. 1, 1975. With Central Republic Bank & Trust Co., Chgo., 1926-32; sec.-treas. Central-Ill. Co., 1932-42; sec. Republic Drill & Tool Co., 1942-44; asst. to treas. Hansen Glove Corp., Milw., 1944-45; v.p. Vilter Mfg. Corp., Milw., 1945-49, pres.,

1949—, chmn. bd., 1970—, also dir., chief legal counsel; admitted to Ill. bar, 1940, Wis. bar, 1959, U.S. Supreme Ct. bar, 1960. Bd. dirs., pres. Vilter Found., Inc.; mem. council Engring. Sch., Marquette U., 1974—; adv. council Sch. Bus. Adminstrn., U. Wis.-Milw. Named Man of Year, Milw. chpt. Unico Nat., 1967; recipient Francis J. Rooney-St. Thomas More award Loyola U. Law Sch., Chgo., 1974; Community Relations award Milw. police chief, 1974. Mem. Am., Wis., Chgo., Milw. bar assns., Am. Soc. Heating, Refrigerating and Air Conditioning Engrs., Master Brewers Assn. Am., Milw. Assn. Commerce, Zool. Soc. Milw. County, Loyola U. Alumni Assn. Jewish. Mason (32 deg., Shriner). Clubs: Tripoli Country, Milw. Athletic, Milw. Press (Knight of Bohemia award 1979), Wisconsin. Office: 2217 S 1st St Milwaukee WI 53207

SILVERMAN, ALBERT JACK, educator, psychiatrist; b. Montreal, Que., Can., Jan. 27, 1925; s. Norman and Molly (Cohen) S.; B.Sc., McGill U., 1947, M.D., C.M., 1949; grad. Washington Psychoanalytic Inst., 1964; m. Halina Weinthal, June 22, 1947; children—Barry Evan, Marcy Lynn. Came to U.S., 1950, naturalized, 1955. Intern, Jewish Gen. Hosp., Montreal, 1949-50; resident psychiatry Colo. U. Med. Center, 1950-53, instr., 1953; from asso. to asso. prof. psychiatry Duke Med. Center, 1953-63; prof. psychiatry, chmn. dept. Rutgers U. Med. Sch., 1964-70; prof., chmn. dept. psychiatry U. Mich. Med. Sch., Ann Arbor, 1970—; cons. to area hosps. Mem. biol. scis. tng. rev. com. NIMH, 1964-69, chmn., 1968-69, mem. research scientist devel. award com., 1970-75, chmn., 1973-75; mem. merit rev. bd. in behavioral scis. VA, 1975-78, chmn., 1976-78. Bd. mgrs. N.J. Neuropsychiat. Inst., 1965-69; trustee N.J. Fund Research and Devel. Nervous and Mental Diseases, 1965-67; bd. dirs. N.J. Mental Health Assn., 1964-69; mem. behavioral sci. com. Nat. Bd. Med. Examiners, 1978—. Served as capt. M.C., USAF, 1955-57. Diplomate Am. Bd. Psychiatry and Neurology. Fellow Am. Coll. Psychiatry (charter), Am. Psychiat. Assn. (chmn. council on med. edn. 1970-75), Am. Acad. Psychoanalysis, Am. Coll. Neuropsychopharmacology; mem. Am. Psychosomatic Soc. (council 1964-68, 70-74, pres. 1976-77), N.J. Psychoanalytic Soc. (trustee 1968-70), Assn. Research Nervous and Mental Diseases, N.J. Neuropsychiat. Assn. (council 1966-69), Group Advancement Psychiatry (chmn. com. psychopathology 1968-74), Soc. Psychophys. Research, Soc. Biol. Psychiatry, Mich. Psychiat. Soc. (council 1975-77). Cons. editor Psychophysiology, 1970-74, Psychosomatic Medicine, 1972—. Contbr. articles in field. Home: 19 Regent Dr Ann Arbor MI 48104

SILVERMAN, ALVIN MICHAELS, pub. relations cons.; b. Louisville, Jan. 16, 1912; s. Alvin and May (Michaels) S.; student Adelbert Coll., Western Res. U., 1930-32; m. Phyllis Israel, Nov. 22, 1936; children—Susy, Lora (Mrs. A. Gene Samburg), Jane (Mrs. Carl Culos). With Cleve. Plain Dealer, 1930-65, beginning as sportswriter, successively schs. editor, city hall reporter, state house corr., Columbus, editorial columnist, day city editor, 1930-57, chief Washington bur., 1957-65; pres. Pearl-Silverman Agy., pub. relations consultants, Washington, 1965—; dir. Tiffin Amusement Co., Ellet Co., Bklyn. Devel. Corp. Mem. White House Corrs. Assn., Ohio Legis. Corrs. Assn., Sigma Delta Chi, Zeta Beta Tau. Clubs: Nat. Press; Press of Ohio; Cleveland Press; Woodmont Country (Rockville, Md.); Gridiron, Federal City, LaSalle (Washington). Author: The American Newspaper, 1965. Home: 4100 Cathedral Ave NW Washington DC 20016 Office: 1125 17th St NW Washington DC 20036

SILVERMAN, BENEDICT ARTHUR, mortgage banker; b. N.Y.C., June 4, 1929; s. Bernard and Frances (Schleffer) S.; B.S., U. Fla., 1952, LL.B., 1952; m. Gerry Lou Rose, Nov. 24, 1954; children—Jill, Jonathan. Admitted Fla. bar, 1952; atty. legal firms in Miami, 1952-62; pres. Coin Meter Co., Miami, 1962-64; with Mortgage Corp. Am., N. Miami, 1965—, chmn. bd., 1976—. Home: 53 E 66th St New York NY 10021 Office: 770 Lexington Ave New York NY 10021

SILVERMAN, BURTON PHILIP, artist; b. Bklyn., June 11, 1928; s. Morris Daniel and Anne (Firstenberg) S.; B.A., Columbia U., 1949; m. Claire Guss, June 12, 1969; children—Robert Arthur, Karen Lila. Freelance illustrator Life, Fortune, Esquire, Time, Newsweek, Sports Illus., New York, The New Yorker mags., 1959—; one-man exhbns. include Davis Gallery, N.Y.C., 1956, 58, 62, Kenmore Galleries, Phila., 1963, 67, 70, FAR Gallery, N.Y.C., 1965, 70, 75, 77, Genesis Gallery, N.Y.C., 1979, Gallery 52, South Orange, N.J., 1967, 70, 77, Harbor Gallery, L.I., 1971, 74, U. Utah, 1967; group exhbns. include Butler Inst. Am. Art, Youngstown, Ohio, 1954-71, 74, 76, 79, NAD, N.Y.C., 1958-79, Pa. Acad. Fine Art, 1949, New Britain (Conn.) Mus. Am. Art, 1964, Wadsworth Atheneum, Hartford, Conn., 1961, Am. Acad. Arts and Letters, 1967, 74, 76, 79, N.Y. Hist. Soc., 1976, Pa. State Mus. Art, 1976, Portsmouth (W.Va.) Mus. Art, 1976, 78; instr. Sch. Visual Arts, N.Y.C., 1964-67. Served with AUS, 1951-53. Recipient numerous awards and prizes including: S.J. Wallace Truman prize, 1961, Benjamin Altman figure prize, 1969, gold medal Am. Watercolor Soc., 1979. Mem. NAD (prize 1965-66, 67). Co-author: Abel, 1968; A Portfolio of Drawings, 1968; author: Painting People, Watson-Guptill, 1977; contbr. articles and drawings to profl. jours. Address: 324 W 71st St New York NY 10023. *My painting is devoted to a direct observation of the world with an eye for anomalies, contrasts and contradictions. In art I am wary of things too facile, or appealing. Tempermentally I am drawn towards struggle and to the humor that sometimes attends it. Art is my life and my life is in my art.*

SILVERMAN, FRED, hosp. exec.; b. N.Y.C., lMay 31, 1935; s. Joseph and Bella (Brenman) S.; B.B.A. in Indsl. Engring., CCNY, 1958; postgrad. N.Y. U. Sch. Bus. Adminstrn., 1962-68; m. Lois Leichtman, Dec. 3, 1972; children—Mark, Gail, Karyn, Jeffrey. Mgr. central supply dept. Montefiore Hosp., Bronx, N.Y., 1958-62, asst. adminstr. for method and procedures, 1962-63, asst. adminstr., 1963-68, dep. dir., 1972-77; adminstr. Hosp. of Albert Einstein Coll. Medicine, 1969-72; pres. Bronx-Lebanon Hosp. Center, 1977—; asst. prof. hosp. adminstrn. CCNY, 1970—; asso. clin. prof. N.Y. U. Sch. Public Adminstrn.; lectr. Lehman Coll. Nursing Practice; dir. FOJP Service Corp., malpractice ins. co., 1977—; mem. Ins. Profl. Adv. Com.; mem. health com. Task Force on N.Y. Crisis, 1978—. Served with M.C., U.S. Army, 1958. Mem. Am. Coll. Hosp. Adminstrs., Am. Hosp. Assn., Am. Public Health Assn., Greater N.Y. Hosp. Assn. (dir.), Hosp. Assn. N.Y. State, Public Health Assn. N.Y.C., Bronx C. of C. Home: 28 Clubway Hartsdale NY 10530 Office: 1276 Fulton Ave Bronx NY 10456. *To reach a place at the top, one must have determination, direction, and self-discipline. Additionally, one must have the tenacity of a street fighter, the cunning of a politician, while understanding humility. You must carefully select those who grow with you. But more than anything else, frankness and honesty will open the doors to the executive suite. Also, remember your friends who helped you along the way.*

SILVERMAN, FRED, broadcasting exec.; b. N.Y.C., Sept. 1937; grad. Syracuse U.; M. in TV and Theatre Arts, Ohio State U.; m. Cathy Kihn; children—Melissa Anne, William Lawrence. With WGN-TV, Chgo.; exec. position WPIX-TV, N.Y.C.; dir. daytime programs CBS-TV, N.Y.C., v.p.-programs, 1970-75; pres. ABC Entertainment, 1975-78; pres. NBC, 1978—. Office: NBC-TV 30 Rockefeller Plaza New York NY 10020

SILVERMAN, HENRY JACOB, educator; b. New Haven, Feb. 22, 1934; s. Morris Samuel and Ethel (Ullman) S.; B.A. (Univ. scholar), Yale U., 1955, M.A., 1956 (Ford Found. fellow); postgrad. Stanford U., 1959-60; Ph.D., U. Pa., 1963; m. Ann Beryl Snyder, Apr. 12, 1957; children—Edwin Stodel, Emily Davies. Fgn. service officer Dept. States, 1961-63; bibliographer Am. history Library of Congress, Washington, 1963-64; asst. prof. Am. thought and lang. Mich. State U., East Lansing, 1964-68, asso. prof., 1968-71, prof., 1971—, chmn. dept. Am. thought and lang., 1977—. Danforth Found. Asso., 1969-73; Nat. Endowment for Humanities/U. Iowa grantee, 1979. Mem. Am. Hist. Assn., Am. Studies Assn., Orgn. Am. Historians, Coll. English Assn., AAUP (mem. exec. bd. Mich. State U. chpt. 1975-77), ACLU (mem. exec. bd. Lansing 1975-78). Author: American Radical Thought, 1970. Home: 1158 Snyder Rd East Lansing MI 48823 Office: Dept Am Thought and Lang Mich State U East Lansing MI 48823

SILVERMAN, HERBERT R., business exec.; b. N.Y.C., June 10, 1912; s. Jacob and Minnie (Stein) S.; B.S., N.Y.U., 1932; J.D., St. Lawrence U., 1935; m. Roslyn Moskowitz, Dec. 17, 1933 (dec. Dec. 1965); children—Karen (Mrs. Daniel K. Mayers), Henry; m. 2d, Nadia Gray, Oct. 17, 1967. Admitted to N.Y. bar, 1935; organizer, pres. Centaur Credit Corp., 1933-44, merged with James Talcott, Inc. of N.Y., v.p. James Talcott, Inc., 1944-46, exec. v.p., 1956-58, dir., 1956-75, pres., 1958-64, chmn. bd., chief exec. officer, 1961-73; chmn., chief exec. officer Talcott Nat. Corp., 1968-73, also chmn. exec. com., dir., 1968-75; chmn. fin. com. Helmsley-Spear, Inc., 1974—; pres. Nat. Comml. Finance Conf., 1948-52, chmn., 1952-58; dir., mem. exec. com. Penn Dixie Industries, Inc.; dir. Am. Savs. & Loan Assn., Baer-Am. Banking Corp., Partners Fund, Inc., Energy Fund, Inc., Nat. Spinning Co., Nat. Silver Industries, Inc.; chmn. credit policy com., dir. Baer Am. Banking Corp.; adj. prof. fin. N.Y. U. Coll. Bus. and Pub. Adminstrn., 1973—. Vice chmn. bd. N.Y. U., trustee N.Y. U. Med. Center. Named Man of Year banking and finance Phi Alpha Kappa; recipient Golden Medallion for humanitarian services B'nai B'rith; Albert Gallatin award N.Y. U., 1978. Mem. Am., N.Y. bar assns., N.Y. Univ. Alumni Fedn. (pres. 1958-60), Phi Alpha Kappa, Iota Theta. Clubs: Harmonie (N.Y.C.); Navesink Country (Middletown, N.J.); N.Y. Univ. (past pres.). Home: 375 Cooper Rd Red Bank NJ 07701 Office: 60 E 42d St New York NY 10017

SILVERMAN, HIRSCH LAZAAR, univ. adminstr.; b. N.Y.C., June 19, 1915; s. Herman Bear and Ida (Mackta) S.; B.Sc., Coll. City N.Y., 1936, M.Sc., 1938; M.A., N.Y.U., 1947; Ph.D., Yeshiva U., 1951; M.A., Seton Hall U., 1956; D.Sc. (hon.), Lane Coll., 1962; LL.D., Fla. Meml. Coll., 1965; L.H.D., Ohio Coll. Podiatric Medicine, 1972; m. Mildred Friedlander, Mar. 1, 1942; children—Hyla Susan. Morton Maier, Stuart Edward. Asst. prof. philosophy and psychology, chmn. dept. Philosophy Mohawk Coll., 1946-48; ednl. and vocational cons., psychol. lab. Stevens Inst. Tech., 1948-49; asst. prof. psychology Rutgers U., 1949-53; asst. to supt. schs., dir. psychol. services Nutley (N.J.) Bd. Edn., 1953-59; chmn. dept. ednl. and sch. psychology Yeshiva U. Grad. Sch., 1959-61, prof. psychology grad. div., 1959-65; prof. ednl. adminstrn., chmn. dept. Seton Hall U., 1965—; research clin. psychologist Columbus Hosp., Newark, 1963-72; psychol. cons. N.J. Rehab. Hosp., East Orange, N.J.; vis. prof. psychology Lane Coll., 1961—, Fla. Meml. Coll., 1961—; research clin. psychologist N.Y. Med. Coll., 1961-65; clin. psychologist, med. staff St. Vincent's Hosp., Montclair, N.J. Chmn. N.J. Bd. Marriage Counsel Examiners, 1968-74; mem. N.J. Mental Health Council, 1966-69; mem. N.J. Bd. Psychol. Examiners, 1975—, chmn., 1979—; mem. nat. adv. com. White House Conf. on Families. Bd. dirs. Family Service Bur., Newark, 1961—. Served with U.S. Army, 1942-46. Decorated Army Commendation medal; grand cross St. John of Jerusalem; Maltese cross Order St. John Denmark. Diplomate in sch. psychology and clin. psychology Am. Bd. Profl. Psychology, Am. Assn. Clin. Counselors (asso. editor); v.p. Am. Bd. Forensic Psychology, 1978—. Fellow Coll. Preceptors Eng., Philos. Soc. Eng. (hon. v.p.), Royal Soc. Health, Royal Soc. Arts, Gerontological Soc., A.A.A.S., Assn. Advancement Psychotherapy, Am. Assn. Social Psychiatry, Am. Orthopsychiat. Assn., Assn. Advancement Psychotherapy, Am. Psychol. Assn., Am. Med. Writers Assn., Am. Pub. Health Assn., Am. Assn. Psychiat. Services for Children, Royal Soc. Medicine, World Acad. Art and Sci.; mem. N.J. Assn. Marriage and Family Counselors (pres. 1967-70), Acad. Psychology in Marital Therapy (pres. 1964-67), Essex County Psychol. Assn. (exec. com., sec., editor), Internat. Council Psychologists (treas. 1971-73), Phi Beta Kappa, Sigma Xi, Psi Chi, Phi Sigma Tau, Kappa Delta Pi, Phi Delta Kappa. Author 15 books, numerous articles in field. Home: 123 Gregory Ave West Orange NJ 07052 Office: McQuaid Hall Seton Hall Univ South Orange NJ 07079. *One's standard ultimately is to be measured not in gold, but in growth; not in position, but in personal inner power; not in capital, but in character.*

SILVERMAN, JACOB, chemist; b. N.Y.C., May 11, 1923; s. Meyer and Esther (Fried) S.; B.Sc., Wayne U., 1943, Ph.D., 1949; m. Shirley Seldin, Mar. 25, 1951; children—Sharon, David. Lectr. chemistry, research asso. U. So. Calif., 1949-51; radiol. chemist U.S. Naval Radiol. Def. Lab., 1951-53; research chemist Aerojet Gen. Corp., 1953-54; sr. research engr. Rocketdyne, 1954-56, supr. theoretical chem. research, 1956-58, group leader propellant chem. research, 1958-59, chief chem. research, 1960-67, mgr. chem. and material scis., 1967-70, mgr. sci. and tech. programs, 1971-73, dir. sci. and tech., 1973-75, dir. energy systems, 1975-78; dir. fossil energy systems Energy Systems group Rockwell Internat., Canoga Park, Calif., 1978—. Served with USAAF, 1944-45. Mem. Am. Chem. Soc., A.A.A.S., Sigma Xi, Phi Lambda Upsilon. Office: Energy Systems Group Rockwell Internat 8900 De Soto Ave Canoga Park CA 91304

SILVERMAN, JOSEPH, educator, scientist; b. N.Y.C., Nov. 5, 1922; s. Jakob and Mary (Chechick) S.; B.A., Bklyn. Coll., 1944; A.M., Columbia, 1948, Ph.D., 1951; m. Joan Aline Jacks, Jan. 14, 1951; children—Joshua Henry, David Avrom. Head research dept. Walter Kidde, nuclear labs., Garden City, N.Y., 1952-54; v.p., tech. dir. RAI Research Corp., L.I. City, N.Y., 1954-59; asso. prof. chemistry State U. N.Y., Stony Brook, 1959-60; prof. dept. chem. engring. U. Md., College Park, 1960—, dir. Inst. Phys. Sci. and Tech., 1976—. Cons. Danish AEC, Indsl. Research Inst., Japan, Boris Kidric Inst., Yugoslavia, Internat. Atomic Energy Agy., Vienna; distinguished vis. prof. Tokyo U., 1974. Served with AUS, 1944-46. Research fellow Brookhaven Nat. Lab., 1949-51; Guggenheim fellow, 1966-67. Mem. Am. Chem. Soc., Am. Phys. Soc., Am. Nuclear Soc. (Radiation Industry award 1975), Am. Inst. Chemists, Sigma Xi. Club: Cosmos. Editor Internat. Jour. Applied Radiation and Isotopes, 1973—, Internat. Jour. Radiation Engring., 1970-73. Home: 320 Sisson St Silver Spring MD 20902 Office: Inst Phys Sci and Tech U Md College Park MD 20742

SILVERMAN, LAWRENCE F., educator; b. N.Y.C., Mar. 31, 1922; s. Aaron and Rachel (Mazur) S.; B.A., U. Mo., 1949; M.A., Harvard, 1953, Ph.D., 1967; m. Libby Rubin, Aug. 6, 1946; children—Matthew, Rachel. Mem. faculty U. Tenn., Knoxville, 1954-70, asst. dean Coll. Liberal Arts, 64-67, asso. dean, 1967-68, vice chancellor acad. affairs, 1968-70; v.p., provost U. Colo., Boulder, 1970-74, v.p., chancellor, Colorado Springs, 1974-77, prof. history and pub. adminstrn., Boulder, 1977—; disting. vis. prof. USAF Acad., 1979-80. Served with USAAF, World War II. Am. Council Edn. fellow acad. adminstrn.; Ford Found. fellow fgn. area studies. Mem. Phi Beta Kappa. Contbr. to books on communism and Soviet society. Office: Dept History Boulder CO 80309

SILVERMAN, LEON, lawyer; b. N.Y.C., June 9, 1921; B.A., Bklyn. Coll., 1942; LL.B., Yale U., 1948; postgrad. London Sch. Econs., 1948-49. Admitted to N.Y. bar, 1949; asso. firm Riegelman, Strasser, Schwartz & Spiegelberg, N.Y.C., 1949-53; asst. U.S. atty. So. Dist. N.Y., 1953-55, asst. dep. atty. gen. Dept. Justice, Washington, 1958-59; partner firm Fried, Frank, Harris, Shriver & Jacobson, N.Y.C., 1960—; counsel N.Y. Gov.'s Com. to Rev. N.Y. Laws and Procedure in the Area of Human Rights, 1967-68, Com. to Rev. Legis. and Jud. Salaries, 1972-73; mem. adv. com. on criminal rules to com. on rules of practice and procedure Jud. Conf. U.S.; mem. joint com. to monitor N.Y. drug laws; pres. N.Y. Legal Aid Soc., 1970-72, dir., 1966—. Mem. Am. Coll. Trial Lawyers (regent 1979—), Am. Law Inst., Am. Judicature Soc., Practising Law Inst. (trustee), Assn. Bar City N.Y. (exec. com.), N.Y. State, Fed., Am. bar assns., Fed. Bar Council. Home: 16 Oak Dr Great Neck NY 11021 Office: Fried Frank Harris Shriver & Jacobson 120 Broadway St New York NY 10005

SILVERMAN, MATTHEW, lawyer; b. N.Y.C., Feb. 1, 1908; A.B., Amherst Coll., 1928; M.A., Harvard, 1929, LL.B., 1932. Admitted to N.Y. State bar, 1933, D.C. bar, 1969; gen. counsel Emergency Relief Bur. N.Y., 1935-38; asst. corp. counsel N.Y.C., 1938-41; mem. firm Robinson, Silverman, Pearce, Aronsohn, Sand & Berman, N.Y.C. Mem. Assn. Bar City N.Y., N.Y. County Lawyers Assn., Nat. Lawyers Guild, Phi Beta Kappa. Office: 230 Park Ave New York City NY 10017

SILVERMAN, PAUL HYMAN, zoologist, univ. and research adminstr.; b. Mpls., Oct. 8, 1924; s. Adolph and Libbie (Idlekope) S.; student U. Minn., 1942-43, 46-47; B.S., Roosevelt U., 1949; M.S. in Biology, Northwestern U., 1951; Ph.D. in Parasitology, U. Liverpool (Eng.), 1955, D.Sc., 1968; m. Nancy Josephs, May 20, 1945; children—Daniel Joseph, Claire. Research fellow Malaria Research Sta., Hebrew U., Israel, 1951-53, debt. entomology and parasitology Sch. Tropical Medicine U. Liverpool, 1953-56; sr. sci. officer dept. parasitology Moredun Inst., Edinburgh, Scotland, 1956-59; head dept. immunoparasitology Allen & Hanbury, Ltd., Ware, Eng., 1960-62; prof. zoology and veterinary pathology and hygiene U. Ill., Urbana, 1963-72, chmn. dept. zoology, 1964-65, head dept. zoology, 1965-68, sr. staff mem. Center for Zoonoses Research, 1964; prof. biology, head div. natural scis. Temple Buell Coll., Denver, 1964-72; prof. biology, chmn. dept. biology, acting v.p. research, v.p. research and grad. affairs, asso. provost for research and acad. services U. N.Mex., 1972-77; provost for research and grad. studies SUNY, Central Adminstrn., Albany, 1977-79; pres. Research Found., SUNY, Albany, 1979—; cons., examiner Middle States Assn. Schs. and Colls., Commn. Colls. and Univs., North Central Assn. Colls. and Secondary Schs., 1964—, chmn. Commn. on Instns. Higher Edn., 1974-76; adj. prof. U. Colo., Boulder, 1970-72; Fulbright prof. zoology Australian Nat. U., Canberra, 1969; adjoint prof. biology U. Colo., Boulder, 1970-72; examiner for Western Assn. Schs. and Colls., Accrediting Commn. for Sr. Colls. and Univs., Calif., 1972—; mem. bd. (Nat.) Council on Postsecondary Accreditation, Washington, 1975-77; faculty apointee Sandia Corp., Dept. Energy, Albuquerque, 1974—; project dir. research in malaria immunology and vaccination AID, 1965-76; project dir. research in Helminth immunity USPHS, NIH, 1964-72; sr. cons. to Ministry Edn. and Culture, Brasilia, Brazil, 1975—; adv. on malaria immunology WHO, Geneva, 1967; bd. dirs. Inhalation Toxicology Research Inst., Lovelace Biomed. and Environ. Research Inst., Albuquerque, 1967—; mem. N.Y. State Gov.'s High Tech. Opportunities Task Force; chmn. research and rev. com. N.Y. State Sci. and Tech. Found.; bd. advs. Lovelace-Bataan Med. Center, Albuquerque, 1974-77. Bd. dirs. Historic Albany Found. Fellow Royal Soc. Tropical Medicine, Hygiene; mem. Am. Soc. Parasitologists, Soc. Exptl. Biology, Inst. Biology, Am. Soc. Immunologists, Brit. Soc. Parasitology (council), Brit. Soc. Immunologists, Soc. Gen. Microbiology, Soc. Protozoologists, Am. Soc. Zoologists, Am. Inst. Biol. Scis., AAAS, N.Y. Acad. Scis., N.Y. Soc. Tropical Medicine, Sigma Xi, Phi Kappa Phi. Club: B'nai B'rith. Contbr. articles to profl. jours. Patentee process for prodn. parasitic helminth vaccine. Office: State U NY State Univ Plaza Albany NY 12246

SILVERMAN, ROBERT, concert pianist; b. Montreal, Que., Can., May 25, 1938; s. Abraham and Fanny (Segal) S.: B.Mus., McGill U., Montreal, 1964: M.Mus., Eastman Sch. Music, Rochester, N.Y., 1965, artist diploma, 1968, D.Mus.Arts, 1970; m. Ellen Ruth Nivert, June 12, 1966. Mem. faculty U. Calif., Santa Barbara, 1969-70, U. Wis., Milw., 1970-73, U. B.C., Vancouver, 1973—; performances with maj. N.Am. and European orchs.; solo recitals in USSR, S. Am., N.Am., Australia, Asia; rec. artist Orion Records; host, writer documentaries CBC radio. Winner grand prize Concours Jeunesses Musicales, Quebec, 1967; winner Grand Prix du Disques Liszt for piano solo, Budapest, 1977. Mem. Coll. Music Soc., Can. Assn. Univ. Schs. Music, Am. Liszt Soc., Iota Kappa Lambda. Office: Music Dept Univ BC Vancouver BC V6T 1W5 Canada

SILVERMAN, ROBERT EUGENE, educator, psychologist; b. Providence, Mar. 1, 1924; s. Samuel and Natalie (Jess) S.; A.B., Brown U., 1948; Ph.D., Ind. U., 1952; m. Margaret Takacs, Dec. 23, 1949; children—Jill Anne, Pamela Kaye. Mem. faculty N.Y. U., 1952—, prof. psychology Coll. Arts and Sci., 1961—, chmn. dept., 1961-69; cons. Bolt, Beranek and Newman, Cambridge, Mass., 1964-71, VA, 1956-63. Dir. programmed instrn. World ORT Union, Geneva, Switzerland, 1962—. Served with AUS, 1943-46. Mem. Am. Psychol. Assn., AAAS, Psychomonic Soc., Sigma Xi. Author: Psychology, 1971. Contbr. articles profl. jours. Home: 4 Avalon Rd Great Neck NY 11021 Office: New York Univ New York City NY 10003

SILVERMAN, SAMUEL JOSHUA, judge; Ct.; b. Odessa, Russia, Sept. 25, 1908; s. Benjamin and Ida (Kagarlitzky) S.; came to U.S., 1913; student N.Y.U., 1925; A.B., Columbia U., 1928, LL.B., 1930; m. Claire Gfroerer, Aug. 21, 1941. Admitted to N.Y. bar; with firm Gilman & Unger, 1930-32, firm Engelhard, Pollak, Pitcher, Stern & Clarke, 1932-35; asst. corp. counsel, N.Y.C., 1938-40; partner firm Paul, Weiss, Rifkind, Wharton & Garrison, N.Y.C., 1946-62; asso. justice N.Y. Supreme Ct., 1963-66, 71-75, appellate div., 1976—; surrogate N.Y. County, 1967-70; lectr. Nat. Coll. State Trial Judges, Boulder, Colo., 1966. Bd. dirs. Univ. Settlement, N.Y.C., 1960-74, Louis and Pauline Cowan Found. Fellow Am. Coll. Trial Lawyers; mem. Assn. Bar City N.Y., Am. Law Inst., N.Y. County Lawyers Assn. Democrat. Home: 210 E 68th St New York City NY 10021 Office: 27 Madison Ave New York City NY 10010

SILVERMAN, SOL RICHARD, educator; b. N.Y.C., Oct. 2, 1911; s. David and Sarah (Sheiken) S.; A.B., Cornell, 1933; M.S., Washington U., 1938, Ph.D., 1942; D.Litt., Gallaudet Coll., 1961; L.H.D., Hebrew Union Coll., 1962; LL.D., Emerson Coll., 1966; m. Sara Ella Hill, Sept. 3, 1938; 1 dau., Rebecca Ann (Mrs. Richard John Howard). Rockefeller fellow Central Inst. for the Deaf, St. Louis, 1933-35, instr., 1935-41, adminstrv. exec., 1941-47, dir., 1947-72, dir. emeritus, 1972—; asso. prof. edn. Washington U., 1946-49, prof. audiology, 1949—, prof. otolaryngology Med. Sch., 1946—; guest lectr. numerous univs.; lectr. profl. socs., assns., orgns. Dir. project on hearing and deafness Central Inst. for Deaf through OSRD, 1943-46; expert cons. problems of deafness to Sec. War, 1944-48; cons. audiology USAF, 1951; Social Planning Council Bd., St. Louis, 1957-60; adv. council on Handicapped Children, So. Regional Edn. Bd., 1956-59; adv. council on Speech and Hearing, HEW, 1957-60. Pres. Council on Edn. Deaf, 1960-63; mem. Nat. Adv. Council Vocat. Rehab., 1962-66; co-chmn. Internat. Congress on Edn. of Deaf, 1963; chmn. Nat. Adv. Com. on Edn. of Deaf, 1966-70; mem. communicative disorder research tng. com. Nat. Inst. Neurol. Diseases and Blindness, 1967—. Recipient certificate of appreciation War Dept., 1946; voted honors Am. Speech and Hearing Assn., 1954; Distinguished Alumni citation Wash. U., 1955, Edgar Allen Fay award Conf. Execs. Am. Schs. for Deaf, 1965; Humanities award St. Louis Globe-Democrat, 1969; Health Care Leadership award St. Louis Hosp. Assn., 1973; Ben Breslow Auditory Sci. award Hope for Hearing Research Found., U. Cal. Los Angeles, 1974. Fellow Am. Coll. Dentists (hon.), Am. Speech and Hearing Soc. (pres. 1952-53), Am. Acad. Ophthalmology and Otolaryngology (hon.); mem. Acoustical Soc. Am., Alexander Graham Bell Assn. for Deaf (pres. 1957), Am. Otological Soc. (asso.), Cleve. (hon.). Kansas City (hon.) otolaryng. socs., St. Louis Ear, Nose and Throat Soc., AAAS, St. Louis Ear, Nose and Throat Soc. (hon.), La Federacion Argentina de Sociedades de Otorrinolaringologia de Rie de Janeiro (hon.), Sociedad Chilena de Oto-Rino-Laringologia (hon.), Sigma Xi, Sigma Alpha Mu. Jewish. Club: Cosmos (Washington). Contbr. profl. jours. Home: 7574 Cornell Ave Saint Louis MO 63130 Office: 818 S Euclid Ave Saint Louis MO 63110

SILVERMAN, SYD, newspaper pub.; N.Y.C., Jan. 23, 1932; s. Sidne L. and Marie (Saxon) S.; A.B., Princeton, 1954; m. Jan McNally, June 26, 1954; children—Marie, Michael, Mark, Matthew. With Variety, Inc., N.Y.C., 1956—, exec. editor, 1973—, also pub.; pres. Daily Variety, Ltd., 1956—. Served to 1st lt. AUS, 1954-56. Office: 154 W 46th St New York NY 10036*

SILVERMAN, THEODORE N., ins. co. exec.; b. Chgo., May 11, 1927; s. Albert and Lillian (Rosenberg) S.; student DePaul U., Chgo., 1946, U. Chgo., 1957-58; m. Helen Eileen Siegel, Mar. 6, 1949; children—Lori Michelle, Carol Lynn. Partner, South End Cleaners and Dyers, Inc., Chgo., 1946-62; chief exec. officer Vienna Fisher Cleaners, Inc., Chgo., 1962-73; dep. dir. for internat. trade Ill. Dept. Bus. and Econ. Devel., 1973-74, acting dir. dept., 1974-75, dep. dir., 1975-77; v.p. Spic and Span, Inc., 1977-78, Nat. Detergents, Inc., 1979—; agt. Equitable Life Assurance Soc., 1980. Pres. Young Cleaners Guild Chgo., 1951; sec.-treas. Ill. Drycleaners Assn., 1957-58; pres. Chgo. Drycleaners Assn., 1959-63; mem. All Ill. Action Com., Ill. Indsl. Devel. Authority, President's Regional Export Adv. Com., Ill. Devel. Council. Industry chmn. Chgo. chpt. U.S.O., 1951, United Jewish Appeal, 1953; mem. Ill. Bicentennial Commn., 1974; commr. Gt. Lakes Commn., 1975—, exec. com., 1975—. Bd. dirs. Ind. Voters Ill., 1968-73, vice chmn. polit. action com., 1969-72. Bd. dirs. Sao-Paulo-Ill. Partners of the Americas, 1974—. Served with USAAF, 1945-46. Recipient Man of Year award Chgo. Drycleaners Assn., 1963; Edwin Astrin award Ind. Voters Ill., 1972. Democrat. Jewish (pres. congregation sch. bd. 1964-70). Club: Internat. Trade (Chgo.). Home: 4250 N Marine Dr Chicago IL 60613 Office: 505 N Michigan Ave Chicago IL 60610

SILVERMAN, WILLIAM JOSEPH, hosp. adminstr.; b. Mpls., Sept. 4, 1916; s. Maurice and Dora (Berkuvitz) S.; B.A., U. Minn., 1939, M.S. in Psychometrics, 1942; m. Lynne Helen Houts, 1950; children—Sandra Lynne, Pamela Ann, James Laurence, Deborah Marie. Psychometrist, Minn. Civil Service, 1939-42; cons. pub. adminstrn. Pub. Adminstrn. Service, Chgo., 1946-50; adminstr. Guam Meml. Hosp., Island of Guam, 1950-52; asso. dir. Michael Reese Hosp., Chgo., 1952-59, exec. dir., 1960-70; dir. health services and facilities div. Comprehensive Health Planning, Inc., 1970-72; asst. dir. Chgo. Hosp. Council, 1970-72; dir. Cook County Hosp., Chgo., 1972—. Mem. Southside Planning Bd., Chgo., 1960-70; chmn. emergency med. services Commn. Met. Chgo., 1974-76. Bd. dirs., mem. exec. com. Chicago Community Fund, 1962-68; bd dirs. Video Nursing, Inc., 1968-74, Hosp. Service Corp. (Blue Cross), 1970-71; Mid South Side Health Planning Orgn., 1970-71; vice chmn. bd. dirs. Ill. Regional Med. Program, 1969-70. Served from pvt. to capt. U.S. Army, 1942-46. Fellow Am. Coll. Hosp. Adminstrs.; mem. Am., Ill. hosp. assns., Chgo. Hosp. Council (pres. 1964). Home: 25 Braeburn Dr Park Forest IL 60466 Office: 1825 W Harrison St Chicago IL 60612

SILVERS, EARL REED, JR., food chain exec.; b. Rahway, N.J., Oct. 3, 1917; s. Earl Reed and Edith (Terrill) S.; grad. Deerfield (Mass.) Acad., 1935; B.A., Rutgers U., 1939; m. Janet Gray, Mar. 17, 1951; children—Earl Reed III, Robert Gray, Margaret Ann, Peter Colfax Terrill. With Grand Union Co., 1941—, v.p. charge devel., 1957-66, v.p. in charge corporate planning, 1966-67, adminstrv. v.p., 1968-78, v.p., sec., 1978—, also dir.; chmn. bd. dir. Eastern Shopping Centers, Inc., 1967-72; dir. First Nat. Bank N.J. Bd. dirs. Super Market Inst., 1957-60. Trustee Rutgers U., 1970-76. Mem. Phi Beta Kappa, Cum Laude Soc., Delta Phi. Home: 101 Del Rio Blvd Boca Raton FL 33432 Office: 100 Broadway Elmwood Park NJ 07407

SILVERS, PHIL, actor; b. Bklyn., May 11, 1912; m. Jo Carroll Dennison, Mar. 2, 1945 (div.); m. 2d, Evelyn Patrick, Oct. 21, 1956 (div.); five daus. First appeared on stage in a vaudeville act in Gus Edwards' School Days Revue, 1925-28; later toured in vaudeville with Morris and Campbell; toured with Minsky Burlesque troupe, 1934-39; on legitimate stage in Yokel Boy (musical), 1939; made film debut in Hit Parade, 1940; appeared in numerous pictures the latest being You'll Never Get Rich, 1955, 40 Pounds of Trouble, 1963, It's a Mad, Mad, Mad World, 1963, A Guide for the Married Man, 1967, Buona Sera, Mrs. Campbell, 1969, The Boatniks, 1970, The Strongest Man in the World, 1975, WonTonTon, the Dog Who Saved Hollywood, 1976, The Chicken Chronicles, 1977, The Cheap Detective, 1978; in USO performances in Mediterranean area, World War II; leading role in Broadway prodn. High Button Shoes, 1947- 50; leading role Top Banana, 1951-52, on tour, 1953, and in film of same name, 1954; with CBS-TV, after 1955; in role of Sgt. Bilko in the Phil Silvers TV Show (first named You'll Never Get Rich), 1955-59; leading role in Broadway prodn. Do-Re-Mi, 1960, A Funny Thing Happened On The Way to The Forum, 1972; has appeared as entertainer in night clubs and as guest on radio shows; appeared in TV movie The Night They Took Miss Beautiful, 1977. Recipient triple citation (best comedian, best comedy series, best actor in continuing performance) Acad. TV Arts and Scis., 1955, Emmy award for best comedy series show, 1957, Tony awards, 1951, 72. Mem. Screen Actors Guild, A.F.T.R.A., Am. Guild Variety Artists. Clubs: Friars; California Country. Author: (with Robert Saffron) The Laugh Is On Me: The Phil Silvers Story, 1973. Address: care Internat Creative Mgmt 8899 Beverly Blvd Los Angeles CA 90048*

SILVERS, WILLYS KENT, geneticist; b. N.Y.C., Jan. 12, 1929; s. Lewis Julian and Miriam Elizabeth (Rosenzweig) S.; B.A., Johns Hopkins U., 1950; Ph.D., U. Chgo., 1954; m. Abigail M. Adams, Sept. 29, 1956; children—Deborah Elizabeth, Willys Kent. Asso. staff scientist Jackson Lab., Bar Harbor, Maine, 1956-57; asso. mem. Wistar Inst., Phila., 1957-65; mem. faculty U. Pa. Med. Sch., 1965—, prof. human genetics, 1967—; mem. allergy and immunology study sect. NIH, 1962-66, mem. primate research centers adv. bd., 1968-71; mem. com. cancer immunobiology Nat. Cancer Inst., 1974-78. Recipient Research Career Devel. award NIH, 1964-71. Author: The Immunobiology of Transplantation, 1971; The Coat Colors of Mice: A Model for Mammalian Gene Action and Interaction, 1979. Editorial bd. Transplantation, 1963-71, Jour. Exptl. Zoology, 1965-70, Jour. Immunology, 1973-77, Jour. Reticuloendothelial Soc., 1974-77. Contbr. profl. jours. Home: 210 Mill Creek Rd Ardmore PA 19003 Office: Dept Human Genetics Sch Medicine Univ Pa Philadelphia PA 19174

SILVERSTEIN, ADOLPH TRAUB, mfg. co. exec.; b. Chgo., Jan. 30, 1927; s. Merrill E. and Irene (Traub) S.; B.B.A., U. Mich., 1949; m. Gloria Cataline Gray; children—Susan Gray, Karen. With Fruehauf Corp., 1955—, controller, 1965—. Served with AUS, 1944-46. C.P.A., Mich. Mem. Am. Inst. C.P.A.'s, Mich. Assn. C.P.A.'s. Home: 31655 Bellvine Ct Birmingham MI 48010 Office: 10900 Harper St Detroit MI 48213

SILVERSTEIN, JOSEPH HARRY, violinist; b. Detroit, Mar. 21, 1932; s. Bernard and Ida (Katz) S.; student Curtis Inst. Music, 1945-50; m. Adrienne Shufro, Apr. 27; children—Bernice, Deborah, Marc. Violinist, Houston Symphony Orch., Phila. Orch., concert-master Denver Symphony Orch., Boston Symphony Orch.; formerly chmn. string dept. New Eng. Conservatory Music, also chmn. faculty Berkshire Music Sch.; mem. faculty Boston U. Sch. Music, Yale U. Sch. Music; music dir. Boston Symphony Chamber Players, Boston U. Symphony Orch.; interim music dir. Toledo Symphony Orch. Recipient Silver medal Queen Elisabeth of Belgium Internat. contest, 1959, Naumberg Found. award, 1960; named one of ten outstanding young men. Boston C. of C., 1962. Fellow Am. Acad. Arts and Scis. Office: care Maxim Gershunoff Inc Delmonico's 502 Park Ave at 59th St New York NY 10022*

SILVERSTEIN, LEONARD LEWIS, lawyer; b. Scranton, Pa., Jan. 21, 1922; s. Robert Philip and Blanche (Raker) S.; A.B., Yale, 1943; LL.B., Harvard, 1948; m. Elaine Wise, June 24, 1951; children—Thomas, Susan. Admitted to Pa. bar, 1949, D.C. bar, 1953; practiced in Scranton, 1949-51, Washington, 1954—; atty. Office Chief Counsel, IRS, Washington, 1951-52; mem. legal adv. staff Dept. Treasury, Washington, 1952-54; mem. firm Silverstein and Mullens, Washington, 1959—; adj. prof. Law Sch., Georgetown U., Washington, 1960-61; spl. tax counsel SBA, Washington, 1958-59; lectr. law N.Y. U., N.Y.C., 1954-60. Chmn. exec. com. Nat. Symphony Orch., Washington, 1974—; exec. dir. Commn. on Pvt. Philanthropy and Pub. Needs, Washington, 1973-77, mem. task force Council on Environ. Quality, Washington, 1970-71. Mem. adv. group House Ways and Means Com., 85th Congress; mem. task force on taxes Pres.-elect Nixon, 1968-69. Trustee Corcoran Gallery of Art, Washington, 1974—; chmn. exec. com. Nat. Symphony Assn.; mem. U.S. Adv. Commn. on Public Diplomacy. Served to lt. (j.g.) USNR, 1943-46. Mem. Am. Bar Assn., Am. Law Inst. Chief editor Tax Mgmt. Inc. 1959—. Home: 5402 Goldsboro Rd Bethesda MD 20034 Office: 1776 K St NW Washington DC 20006

SILVERSTEIN, SAMUEL CHARLES, physician; b. N.Y.C., Feb. 11, 1937; s. Paul Robert and Jeanette (Kamen) S.; A.B., Dartmouth Coll., 1958; M.D., Albert Einstein Coll. Medicine, 1963; m. JoAnn Kleinman, Apr. 2, 1967; children—David Paul, Jennifer Kate. Intern in medicine U. Colo. Med. Center, 1963-64; postdoctoral fellow dept. cell biology Rockefeller U., 1964-67, asst. prof. cellular physiology and immunology, 1968-71, asso. prof., physician, 1972—; asst. resident in medicine Mass. Gen. Hosp., Boston, 1967-68; established investigator Am. Heart Assn., 1972-77; mem. sci. adv. com. Damon Runyon-Walter Winchell Cancer Fund, 1975-79; mem. study sect. Nat. Inst. Allergy and Infectious Diseases, 1977-78; vice chmn. Gordon Conf. Lysosomes, 1980; chmn. Dahlem Conf. on Transport Macromolecules, Berlin, 1978. Recipient John Oliver LaGorce medal Nat. Geog. Soc., 1967; Helen Hay Whitney fellow, 1964-67. Mem. Am. Soc. Cell Biology, Am. Soc. Clin. Investigation, Am. Soc. Microbiology, Am. Assn. Immunologists, Infectious Diseases Soc. Am., AAAS, Am. Alpine Club (dir. 1963-64, 69-74), Appalachian Mountain Club, Sierra Club. Research, numerous publs. on virology, cell biology, immunology; contbr. articles on mountaineering to mags.; editor: Transport of Macromolecules in Cellular Systems, 1979; editorial bd. Jour. Cell Biology, 1979—. Home: 325 E 79th St New York NY 10021 Office: Rockefeller U 1230 York Ave New York NY 10021

SILVERSTEIN, SHELBY (SHEL), author, cartoonist, composer, folksinger; b. Chgo., 1932. Former corr. Stars and Stripes, Pacific area; now cartoonist, writer Playboy Mag., Chgo. Author: Lafcodio, the Lion Who Shot Back; Uncle Shelby's ABZ Book; Giraffe and a Half; Giving Tree; Now Here's My Plan, 1976; Uncle Shelby's Zoo: Don't Bump the Glump; Where the Sidewalk Ends, 1974; The Missing Piece, 1976; (drawings) Different Dances, 1979; composer: Boa Constrictor; A Boy Named Sue; One's On The Way; Comin' After Jinny. Address: care Grapefruit Prodns 106 Montague St Brooklyn NY 11201*

SILVERSTEIN, STEPHEN HOWARD, publishing co. exec.; b. Lowell, Mass., July 5, 1948; s. Jerry L. and Gertrude S.; B.B.A. in Econs., U. Mass., 1970; M.B.A., U. Chgo., 1972; m. Linda Gerhardt, Aug. 16, 1970; children—David, Daniel. Asso., J. Lloyd Johnson Assos., Northbrook, 1972-75; v.p. fin. Car-X Service Systems, Ill., 1975-77; v.p., treas. Playboy Enterprises, Inc., Chgo., 1977—. Served to lt. USAF, 1972. Mem. Am. Mgmt. Assn., Soc. Internat. Treas.'s, Beta Gamma Sigma. Office: 919 N Michigan Ave Chicago IL 60611

SILVERSTONE, DAVID, advt. agy. exec.; b. N.Y.C., Sept. 21, 1932; s. Max and Rose (Orliansky) S.; grad. Queens Coll., 1954; postgrad. Columbia U., Baruch Sch., UCLA; m. Caroline A. Hill, June 14, 1963; children—Eva Hilary, Joshua David. Sr. research analyst McCann-Erickson Inc., N.Y.C., 1956-63, mgr. media research, 1963-68, mktg. devel. supr., 1972-74, mgr. mktg. planning and research, 1974-75, dir. planning services, 1975-77, dir. research, 1977-78, sr. v.p., dir. mktg. planning, 1978—; v.p., dir. mktg. Dataplan, Inc., 1968; founder Media Info. Services, 1969, dir., 1969-72; mem. Advt. Agy. Research Dirs. Council, 1977—; guest lectr., speaker in field. Bd. dirs. United Way of Larchmont, 1974-77. Mem. Am. Assn. Advt. Agys. (chmn. spl. com. info. mgmt. 1969-73, vice chmn. EDP com. 1970, initiated, organized AAAA Advt. Agy. Computer System Catalog 1972). Author papers and articles for U.S. and fgn. trade and profl. publs.; editor: (with D.E. Sexton, Jr.) Understanding the Computer, Marketing Managers Handbook, 1973. Developer system for defining TV mktg. areas, 1968, quantitative research methodology for measuring consumer need states, 1975, participant development industry's 1st computer model for media planning optimization and simulation of consumer media exposure, 1964. Home: 22 Glenn Rd Larchmont NY 10538

SILVERSTONE, HARRIS JULIAN, chemist, educator; b. N.Y.C., Sept. 18, 1939; s. Sidney M. and Estelle C. (Cohen) S.; A.B., Harvard, 1960; Ph.D. (NSF grad. fellow), Calif. Inst. Tech., 1964; postgrad. (NSF postdoctoral fellow) Yale, 1964; m. Ruth C. Federman, June 19, 1960; children—Robert A., Aron L., Nancy M., Murray D. Asst. prof. chemistry Johns Hopkins U., Balt., 1965-68, asso. prof., 1968-71, Alfred P. Sloan Found. research fellow, 1969-73, prof., 1971—. Mem. Am. Chem. Soc., Am. Phys. Soc., AAAS, Phi Beta Kappa. Researcher quantum chemistry. Office: Dept Chemistry Johns Hopkins Univ Baltimore MD 21218

SILVESTRO, CLEMENT MARIO, museum dir., historian; b. New Haven, Sept. 7, 1924; s. Joseph and Rose (Griego) S.; B.S., Central Conn. State Coll., 1949; M.S., U. Wis., 1951; Ph.D., 1959; m. Betty C. Mack, June 26, 1950; 1 dau., Elizabeth Jane. Asst. to dir. Wis. Hist. Soc., 1956-57; dir. Am. Assn. State and Local History, 1957-64, editor History News, 1957-64; asso. dir. Chgo. Hist. Soc., 1964-65, dir., 1965-74, sec., 1970-74; dir. Mus. of Our Nat. Heritage, Lexington, Mass., 1974—. Mem. exec. com. Am. Assn. Museums, 1965-71, v.p., 1966-71; mem. Chgo. Archtl. and Landmark Com., 1968-74, Ill. Historic Sites Adv. Council, 1970-74; mem. U.S. ICOM, Nat. Com., 1970-74; chmn. Pres.'s Adv. Council on Historic Preservation, 1974-77; mem. adv. bd. Eleutherian Mills-Hagley Found., 1973-76; U.S. rep. to UNESCO Internat. Adv. Com. to Safeguard City of Venice, 1975. Trustee U.S. Capitol Hist. Soc. Served with USAAF, 1943-45. Decorated Air medal with oak leaf clusters. Mem. Am. Hist. Assn., Am. Assn. Museums, Orgn. Am. Historians (chmn. historic sites com. 1973-78), Am. Assn. State and Local History, Ill., Chgo. hist. socs., Colonial Soc. Mass., Nat. Trust for Historic Preservation. Club: Masons. Home: 98 Pepperell Rd Groton MA 01450 also Box 42 Hancock Point ME 04610 Office: 33 Marrett Rd Lexington MA 02173

SILVOSO, JOSEPH ANTON, educator; b. Benld, Ill., Sept. 15, 1917; s. Biagio and Camilla (Audo) S.; B.Ed., Ill. State U., 1941; A.M., U. Mo., 1947, Ph.D., 1951; m. Wilda Lucille Miller, Nov. 16, 1942; children—Joseph A., Gerald R. Instr., U. Mo., 1947-48, 50-51; asst. U. Ill., 1948-49; staff accountant Touche Ross & Co. and predecessor, C.P.A.'s, 1951-55, ednl. dir., 1956; mem. faculty U. Mo., 1955-56, 57—, prof. accountancy, 1958—, Peat Marwick Mitchell prof. profl. acctg., 1978—, chmn. dept. accountancy, 1964-75, dir. Sch. Accountancy, 1975—; cons. in field, 1956—. Chmn. Joint Adv. Council Accounting, 1962-64. Served with USAAF, 1942-45. C.P.A., Mo., Kans. Mem. Am. Accounting Assn. (chmn. membership com. Mo. 1956-58, nat. chmn. accounting careers com. 1961-63, sec. treas. 1971-73), Am. Inst. C.P.A.'s (contbg. editor jour. 1958-61, editorial bd. 1970-72), Mo. Soc. C.P.A.'s (chmn. accounting careers com. 1966-67, dir., sec. ednl. found. 1968-70), Central States Conf. C.P.A.'s (treas. 1975, sec. 1976, v.p. 1977, pres. 1978), Fedn. Schs. Accountancy (dir. 1977-78), Nat. Assn. Accountants, Inst. Internal Auditors, Fin. Exec. Inst., Midwest Econs. Assn., Delta Sigma Pi, Beta Gamma Sigma, Alpha Pi Zeta. Beta Alpha Psi (named Nat. Acad. Accountant of Year 1977). Methodist. Author: Auditing, 1965; Illustrative Auditing, 1965; Audit Case, 1966. Home: 818 Greenwood Ct Columbia MO 65201

SIM, JOHN CAMERON, educator; b. Grand Forks, N.D., Feb. 7, 1911; s. John Cameron and Katherine Gertrude (Mason) S.; B.A., U. N.D., 1932; M.A., U. Minn., 1940; m. Mary L. Hanson, Sept. 10, 1946; children—Erin Terese, John Cameron III. Mng. editor E. Grand Forks (Minn.) Record, 1931-39; tchr. journalism U. N.D., 1934-40, U. Ala., 1940-41; univ. editor U. N.H., 1941-42; editor, co-publisher East Grand Forks Record, 1946-56; mem. faculty U. Minn., 1956—, prof. journalism, 1967—, asst. dir. Sch. Journalism and Mass Communication, 1970—. Editor, Asso. Coll. Press Bus. Rev., 1960-66, conf. mgr., 1960-66; pres. Red River Valley Editorial Assn., 1949-50; dir. Minn. High Sch. Press Assn., 1964—; nat. conf. mgr. Nat. Sch. Press Assn., 1959-61; cons. on scholastic press, also mass media teaching UNESCO, 1975. Sec. E. Grand Forks C. of C., 1935-39; pres. East Grand Forks Rotary Club, 1954-55. Served with AUS, 1942-46. Towley award Journalism Edn. Assn., 1978; U. Minn. Grad. Sch. grantee, 1970. Mem. AAUP, Minn. Press Assn. (hon.), Phi Beta Kappa, Sigma Delta Chi, Kappa Tau Alpha. Clubs: Minn. Press, Campus (Mpls.). Author: The Grass Roots Press: America's Weekly Newspapers-Ames, Iowa, 1969. Home: 2901 29th Ave S Minneapolis MN 55406

SIMARD, ARTHUR, aluminium co. exec.; b. Sorel, Que., Can., Aug. 29, 1915; s. Joseph and Rose Blanche (Pontbriand) S.; ed. McGill U., Montreal, U. Montreal; m. Madeleine Ouellette, June 5, 1945; children—Pierre, Paul. Called to Que. Bar, 1940, queen's counsel, 1962; with Reynolds Aluminium Co. Can., St. Joseph de Sorel, Que., now vice chmn. bd.; vice chmn. bd. Quebecair; chmn. bd. Trust Gen. du Can.; pres. Cie de Charlevoix Ltee., Cie Simclaire Ltee., Corp. Equitable Canadienne, Les Immeubles Cramis Inc., Car-Lex Ltd., Sherbrooks Trust; v.p. Simcor Inc., Voyage Richelieu Inc.; dir. Immeubles Themis Ltee. Mem. Inst. Recherches Cliniques Montreal (dir.), Atlantic Salmon Assn. (dir.). Clubs: St. Denis (Montreal); Mt. Bruno Country and Golf. Home: 47 De La Rive Ste-Anne de Sorel PQ J3P 1K1 Canada Office: 101 Montcalm St St Joseph de Sorel PQ J3R 1Bp Canada

SIMARD, RENE, physician; b. Quebec, Que., Can., Mar. 12, 1912; s. Louis Eugene and Florida (Malouin) S.; B.A., Que. Sem., 1932; M.D., Laval U., 1937; postgrad. Paris U., 1938-39; m. Albina Petitclerc, Aug. 7, 1937; children—Genevieve (Mrs. Rene Paquet), Jacqueline (Mrs. Roland Truchon). Asso. dept. obstetrics and gynecology Laval U., 1942, prof., 1946—, head dept., 1957-71; chief staff Hosp. de la Misericorde, 1945-72; cons. in field. Fellow Royal Coll. Surgeons Can.; mem. Soc. Obstetricians and Gynecologists Can. (pres. 1955-56). Home: 2590 Plaza Sillery Quebec PQ G1T 1X2 Canada Office: 246 St Jean Quebec 4 PQ Canada

SIMCHES, SEYMOUR OLIVER, educator; b. Boston, Sept. 22, 1919; s. Meyer and Rebecca (Nadell) S.; A.B., Boston U., 1941; M.A., Harvard, 1942, Ph.D., 1950; m. Marcia Harriet Goldberg, Sept. 13, 1953; children—Judith Ellen, Jonathan David. Teaching fellow Romance langs. Harvard, 1947-50, instr., 1950-53; asst. prof. Amherst Coll., 1953-54; mem. faculty Tufts U., 1954—, chmn. dept. Romance langs., 1958-70, John Wade prof. modern langs., 1962—, dir. Tufts Coll. Within, 1971-74, dir. Center for European Studies, 1978—. Mem. Mass. Adv. Com. Fgn. Langs., 1961—; cons. U.S. Office Edn., 1964; dir. Fgn. Lang. Insts., NDEA, 1960-62, 65; mem. bd. examiners advanced placement Coll. Entrance Exam. Bd., 1968—; mem. Mass. Adv. Bd. Non-Traditional Edn. Served with USAAF, 1942-46. Decorated Medaille Aero., officier Palmes Academiques (France). Mem. New Eng. Modern Lang. Assn. (chmn. Eastern Mass. 1955-56), Am. Assn. Tchrs. French (pres. Boston 1958-60), NE Conf. Fgn. Lang. Tchrs. (vice chmn. 1964-65), Modern Lang. Assn., AAUP, Renaissance Soc. Am., Phi Beta Kappa, Phi Sigma Iota (hon.). Sheldon traveling fellow Harvard, 1949. Author: (with H.H. Golden) Modern French Literature and Language: A Bibliography of Homage Studies, 1956; Modern Iberian Literature and Language: A Bibliography of Homage Studies, 1958; Modern Italian Literature and Language: A Bibliography of Homage Studies, 1958; Le Romantisme et le Gout Esthetique du XVIII ième Siècie, 1964; The Theatre of Jacinto Grau. Home: 5 Burbank Rd Medford MA 02155

SIMCOX, EDWIN JESSE, state ofcl.; b. LaPorte, Ind., Jan. 12, 1945; s. J. Willard and Rachel (Gibbs) S.; B.S., Ind. U., 1967, J.D., 1971; m. Sandra Sue Stephenson, Aug. 30, 1970; 1 son, Edwin J. Admitted to Ind. bar, 1971; sec. Ind. State Hwy. Commn., 1969-71;

sec. Public Service Commn. of Ind., 1971; chief dep. Office of Reporter of Supreme Cts. and Judicial Ct. of Appeals, State of Ind., 1973-78; sec. of state of Ind., Indpls., 1978—; sec. Ind. State Repubican Central Com., 1972-77. Chmn. adminstrv. bd. White Harvest United Meth. Ch., 1975-76. Mem. Am. Bar Assn., Ind. Bar Assn., Indpls. Bar Assn. Clubs: Masons, Shriners. Office: 201 State House Indianapolis IN 46204

SIME, DONALD RAE, univ. adminstr.; b. Los Angeles, July 20, 1926; s. Chester I. and Gaynal (Ramage) S.; B.A., Pepperdine Coll., 1949, M.A., 1951; B.D., Princeton, 1954; Ph.D., U. Chgo., 1962; m. Patricia Evelyn Hawes, Sept. 4, 1949; children—Julia, Paul, Jill. Prof. religion Harding Coll. and Harding Grad. Sch., 1954-66; prof. dept. religion and psychology Pepperdine Coll., 1966-68, chmn. dept. bus. adminstrn., 1968-69, dean Sch. Bus. and Mgmt., 1969, v.p., 1973-78, v.p. corp. relations, 1978—; cons. orgnl. devel., affirmative action programs Webco, Page Group, Conceptual Consultants. Served with USNR, 1944-46. Mem. Am. Mgmt. Assn., Soc. Advancement Mgmt., Am. Assn. Collegiate Schs. Bus., Am. Acad. Polit. and Social Scis., Am. Acad. Mgmt., Calif. Aviation Council. Contbr. articles to religious publs. Home: 6779 Las Olas Way Malibu CA 90265

SIMECHECK, DON MAC, engring. co. exec.; b. Kansas City, Mo., Oct. 24, 1923; s. Stanley John and Virginia (McCall) S.; B.S. in Chem. Engring., Okla. U., 1947; m. Marjorie Maines, Feb. 18, 1945; children—Craig, Susan. Engr., Dow Chem. Co., Freeport, Tex., 1947-53; with Fish Engring. & Constrn., Inc., Houston, 1953—, v.p., then exec. v.p., 1961-68, pres., 1968—, dir. Fish Investment Corp. Served with F.A. AUS, 1943-46. Decorated Commendation medal. Episcopalian. Clubs: River Oaks Country, University (Houston). Home: 741 W Creekside Dr Houston TX 77024 Office: 5051 Westheimer St Houston TX 77027

SIMEONE, FIORINDO ANTHONY, surgeon, educator; b. St. Ambrose, Italy, Jan. 20, 1908; s. Antonio and Antonia (Rivera) S.; A.B., Brown U., 1929, Sc.M., 1930, Sc.D. (hon.), 1954; M.D., Harvard, 1934; perpetual student St. Bartholomew's Hosp. Med. Sch., London; m. Martha Toothill, Aug. 16, 1941 (dec.); children—Timothy A., Maria Antonia, Francesca Angelica, Martha Christina, Walter John; m. Margaret Jacoy, June 15, 1972. Came to U.S., 1914, naturalized, 1930. Intern, Mass. Gen. Hosp., 1934-36, surg. resident, 1938-40; G.U. surg. resident Peter Bent Brigham Hosp., 1940-41; NRC fellow Harvard, 1936-38, asst. prof. surgery Med. Sch., 1946-50; prof. surgery Western Res. U., also dir. surgery Cleve. Met. Gen. 1950-67; prof. med. sci. Brown U., 1967—; surgeon-in-chief Miriam Hosp., Providence, R.I., 1967—; spl. asst. for cancer control to gov. State of R.I.; cons. to Surgeon Gen., U.S. Army, 1946—; mem. bd. cons. Mass. Gen. Hosp., Boston. Served from capt. to col. M.C., AUS, 1942-46; ETO. MTO. Decorated Comdr. Nat. Order of Cedars (Republic of Lebanon), Legion of Merit; recipient Verrazzano Day award, 1973; Disting. Service award Hosp. Assn. R.I., 1978; named to R.I. Hall of Fame, 1973. Diplomate Am. Bd. Surgery, Am. Bd. Thoracic Surgery. Fellow A.C.S., AAAS, N.Y. Acad. Sci., Internat. Coll. Surgeons (hon.); mem. AMA, Am. Surg. Assn., Soc. U. Surgeons, Central Surg. Soc., Cleve. Surg. Soc. (pres.), Cleve. Area Heart Soc. (pres.), Soc. Exptl. Biology and Medicine (pres. chpt.), U.S. Med. Cons. World War II, Phi Beta Kappa, Sigma Xi (pres.), Alpha Omega Alpha. Author: The Autonomic Nervous System (with J. C. White and R. H. Smithwick), 1952; (with J. B. Kinmonth and C. G. Rob) Vascular Surgery, 1962. Contbr. articles to profl. jours. Address: Div Biol and Med Scis Brown U Providence RI 02912

SIMEONE, JOSEPH JOHN, justice Supreme Ct. Mo.; b. Quincy, Ill., Oct. 8, 1921; J.D., Washington U., St. Louis, 1946; B.S., St. Louis U., 1953; LL.M., U. Mich., 1956, S.J.D., 1962. Admitted to Mo. bar, 1946, Ill. bar, 1946; asst. prof. law St. Louis U., 1947-50, asso. prof., 1950-57, prof., 1957-71; judge Mo. Ct. Appeals, St. Louis Dist., 1972; now justice Mo. Supreme Ct. Mem. Mo. Bar (Smithson award 1976), Bar Assn. Met. St. Louis. Office: Supreme Ct Mo Supreme Ct Bldg Jefferson City MO 65101*

SIMES, DIMITRI KONSTANTIN, fgn. policy analyst; b. Moscow, Oct. 17, 1947; came to U.S., 1973; s. Konstantin M. and Dina (Kaminsky) Simis; M.A. in History, Moscow State U., 1969; grad. Inst. World Economy and Internat. Relations, Moscow, 1972; m. Natasha Timofeyev, Feb. 11, 1967. Research asso. Inst. World Economy and Internat. Relations, 1967-72; sr. fellow Center Strategic and Internat. Studies, Georgetown U., 1973-76, dir. Soviet studies, 1976—, mng. editor Soviet Report, 1979—; adv. bd. Negotiation Inst.; sec. adv. bd. Union Councils Soviet Jews. Mem. Am. Assn. Advancement Slavic Studies. Author: Detente and Conflict: Soviet Foreign Policy 1972-1977, 1977, Soviet Successiion: Leadership in Transition, 1979; also articles. Home: 4430 Vacation Ln Arlington VA 22207 Office: 1800 K St NW Washington DC 20006

SIMES, FRANK JAMES, educator; b. Brockport, N.Y., Jan. 18, 1916; s. James A. and Janet (Hummel) S.; A.B., U. Mich., 1938; M.A., State U. N.Y., Albany, 1948; D.Ed., Pa. State U., 1951; m. Mary Alice Stever, Apr. 16, 1949; 1 dau., Amy Caroline. Prodn. expediter Trico Products Corp., 1939- 41; tchr., guidance counselor Honeoye Falls High Sch., 1947-49; dir. residence counseling Pa. State U., 1950-51, asst. dean of men, 1951-52, dean of men, asso. prof. counselor edn., 1952-67; v.p., acad. dean Hampden-Sydney (Va.) Coll., 1967-75, prof. psychology, 1975—. Served as capt. C.A.C., U.S. Army, 1941-46. Lic. profl. counselor, Va. Mem. Am. Personnel and Guidance Assn., Assn. for Counselor Edn. and Supervision, Pa. Soc., Phi Delta Kappa, Psi Chi, Phi Kappa Sigma, Omicron Delta Kappa. Mason. Home: Box 25 Hampden-Sydney VA 23943

SIMIC, CHARLES, author, educator; b. Beograd, Yugoslavia, May 9, 1938; s. George and Helen (Matijevich) S.; came to U.S., 1954, naturalized, 1971; B.A., N.Y. U., 1967; m. Helen Dubin, Oct. 1964; children—Anna, Philip. Editorial asst. Aperture, Quar. of Photography, N.Y.C., 1966-69; prof. English, Calif. State U., Hayward, 1970-73, U. N.H., Durham, 1973—. Served with U.S. Army, 1961-63. Recipient PEN Internat. award for translation, 1970, Edgar Allan Poe award, 1975, Nat. Inst. Arts and Letters and AAAL award, 1976. Guggenheim fellow, 1972-73, Nat. Endowment for Arts fellow, 1974-75. Author: (poems) What the Grass Says, 1967, Somewhere Among us a Stone is Taking Notes, 1969, Dismantling the Silence, 1971, White, 1972, Return to a Place Lit by a Glass of Milk, 1974, Biography and a Lament, 1976, Charon's Cosmology, 1977. Translator, editor (with C.W. Truesdale) Fire Gardens, 1970; (with Mark Strand) Another Republic, 1976; translator, The Little Box, 1970, Four Modern Yugoslav Poets, 1970. Contbr. poems to mags. and anthologies. Home: Box 192 Strafford NH 03884 Office: Dept English U NH Durham NH 03824

SIMINOVITCH, DAVID, agronomist; b. Montreal, Que., Can. May 29, 1916; s. Nathan and Golda (Wachtman) S.; B.Sc. (Maj. Hiram Mills Gold medal biology 1936), McGill U., Montreal, 1936, M.Sc., 1937, Ph.D. (Nat. Research Council Can. bursary and studentship 1937-38), 1939; Ph.D., U. Minn., 1946; m. Helen Elizabeth Daubney, Sept. 4, 1945; children—David Jonathan, Sara Jane, Michael Jeremy. Research asst. McGill U., 1937-38; research asso. Macdonald Coll., Montreal, 1943-45; Frasch Found. research asso., lectr. U. Minn., 1945-50; research scientist Chemistry and Biology Research Inst., Can. Dept. Agr., Ottawa, 1950—, head winter hardiness sect., 1968—. Mem. Royal Soc. Can. (travelling fellow 1940-41), Can. Soc. Plant Physiologists (Gold medal 1972), Soc. Cryobiology (editorial bd.), Am. Soc. Plant Physicologists (editorial bd.). Contbr. articles to profl. publs. Home: 1118 Agincourt Rd Ottawa ON Canada Office: Chemistry and Biology Research Inst Dept Agr KW Neatby Bldg Ottawa ON K1A 0C6 Canada

SIMIS, THEODORE LUCKEY, telephone co. exec.; b. N.Y.C., June 17, 1924; s. Theodore E. and Helen (Luckey) S.; B.S., N.Y. U., 1950, M.B.A., 1952; m. Laura Cushman Ingraham, Sept. 8, 1946; children—Nancy, Theodore S., Karen, June. With Am. Tel. & Tel. Co., 1941—, asst. v.p., 1970—; v.p. N.Y. Telephone Co., also v.p., dir. Empire City Subway Co., 1965-67; v.p. N.J. Bell Telephone Co., 1969-70; adj. asso. prof. N.Y. U. Grad. Coll. Engring., 1956-59. Bd. dirs. Luth. Sem., Phila., 1964; trustee Upsala Coll., N.J. Served with U.S. Army, 1942-45. Mem. U.S. C. of C., Inst. Mgmt. Sci. Republican. Lutheran. Home: Mile Dr Chester NJ 07930 Office: American Tel & Tel Co 195 Broadway New York City NY 10007

SIMKIN, PETER ANTHONY, physician, educator; b. Morgantown, W.Va., Nov. 22, 1935; s. William Edward and Ruth Helen (Commons) S.; B.A., Swarthmore Coll., 1957; M.D., U. Pa., 1961; m. Penelope Hart Payson, Aug. 9, 1958; children—Andrew, Caroline, Mary, Elizabeth. Intern, N.C. Meml. Hosp., Chapel Hill, 1961-62, resident, 1962-63; resident Univ. Hosps. Cleve., 1965-66; fellow in medicine U. Wash., Seattle, 1966-69, asst. prof., 1968-74, asso. prof., 1974—. Bd. dirs. Western Wash. chpt. Arthritis Found., chmn. med. and sci. com., 1974-78. Served with U.S. Army, 1963-65. Mem. Am. Rheumatism Assn., Western Soc. Clin. Research, Am. Fedn. Clin. Investigation. Quaker. Contbr. articles to profl. jours. Home: 1100 23d Ave E Seattle WA 98112 Office: Dept Medicine RG-20 U Wash Seattle WA 98195

SIMKINS, LEON JACK, paper co. exec.; b. Phila., Dec. 15, 1927; s. Samuel and Dorothy (Sherman) S.; B.S., Wharton Sch. of U. Pa., 1948; div.; children—S. Alberto, David, Michael, Ronald S.; m. 2d, Kathryn Ann Sears; 1 dau., Michelle Ann. With Nat. Paper Box Mfg. Co., Inc., Phila., 1956—, Simkins Paper Box Mfg. Co., Inc., Phila., 1956—, Miami Paper Board Mills, Inc. (Fla.), 1956—, Benner Box Inc., Miami, 1956—; pres., chmn. bd. Simkins Industries, Inc., 1963—; vice chmn. bd. Capital Banks. Mem. Beta Gamma Sigma, Phi Epsilon Pi. Home: 5740 N Bay Rd Miami Beach FL 33140 Office: 259 East St New Haven CT 06508

SIMMEL, MARIANNE LENORE, psychologist, designer; b. Jena, Germany; d. Hans E. and Else R. (Rapp) Simmel; A.B., Smith Coll., 1943; A.M., Harvard, 1945, Ph.D., 1949. Intern psychology Worchester (Mass.) State Hosp., 1943; research asst. Neurol. Lab., Boston Dispensary, Tufts Coll. Med. Sch., Boston, 1943-45; instr. psychology Cambridge (Mass.) Jr. Coll., 1945-46; vol. asst. neurol. unit Childrens Hosp., Harvard Med. Sch., 1945-46; instr. psychology Hofstra Coll., 1946-48; vis. lectr. dept. psychology Wellesley Coll., 1948-49; from instr. to clin. asso. prof. psychology dept. psychiatry Coll. Medicine, U. Ill., 1950-58; psychophysiologist, head psychol. lab. Ill. State Psychopathic Inst., Chgo., 1952-58, asst. dir., 1952-55; vis. lectr. med. psychology Duke Med. Sch., 1958-59; spl. research fellow USPHS, NIMH, 1959-61, 69-70; asst. psychologist in neurosurgery Mass. Gen. Hosp., 1959-61, 63—; research asso. dept. psychology Brandeis U., 1959-61, from asso. prof. to prof. 1963—; research asso. in neurology Mt. Sinai Hosp., N.Y.C., 1961—. Recipient Research award Am. Rehab. Counseling Assn., 1964. Diplomat Am. Bd. Examiners Profl. Psychology. Fellow Am. Psychol. Assn.; mem. Eastern Psychol. Assn., Psychonomic Soc., AAUP, Am. Soc. Aesthetics, Phi Beta Kappa, Sigma Xi. Contbr. articles to profl. jours. Editor: The Reach of Mind: Essays in Memory of Kurt Goldstein, 1968. Home: Box 562 North Eastham MA 02651. *Methodology is the last refuge of a sterile mind.*

SIMMERMON, JAMES EVERETT, credit bur. exec.; b. Arnold, Pa., Mar. 23, 1926; s. Joseph C. and Melba J. (McGeary) S.; B.S. in Bus. Adminstrn., Ashland (Ohio) Coll., 1949; m. Lois Bowden, Apr. 19, 1952; children—James, Thomas, John, Lisa, William. Pres., Credit Bur. Services Inc., New Kensington (Pa.), 1955—, Simmermon Telephone Answering Service, 1955—; v.p. Credit Bur. Sales Promotion Group, 1964—; v.p. MBW Holding Corp., Manchester, N.H., 1978—; dir. Asso. Credit Burs. Inc., Houston, 1965-73, chmn. bd., 1972-73; dir. Consumer Credit Counseling Service of Western Pa., 1976. Trustee Citizens Gen. Hosp., New Kensington. Served with USNR, 1944-46. Mem. New Kensington Area C. of C. (pres. 1961, dir. 1973—). Rotarian (pres. New Kensington 1957). Club: Oakmont (Pa.) Country. Home: 239 Elmtree Rd New Kensington PA 15068 Office: PO Box 560 New Kensington PA 15068

SIMMONDS, GEOFFREY ROY, mfg. co. exec.; b. Southampton, Eng., Jan. 15, 1929; s. Oliver E. and Gladys (Hewitt) S.; grad. Harrow Sch., 1947; student Magdelene Coll., Cambridge (Eng.) U., 1948; m. Doreen Treseder-Griffin, Mar. 7, 1951; children—Levinia, David, Geoffrey Craig. Came to U.S., 1949, naturalized, 1954. Successively sales mgr., v.p., gen. mgr. Pinnacle Products Corp., N.Y.C., 1951-58; pres., chief exec. officer Simmonds Precision Products, Inc., Tarrytown, N.Y., 1958-74, chmn. bd., chief exec. officer, 1974—; dir. Hayden Pub. Co. Pres., bd. dirs. Simmonds Found. Clubs: Racquet and Tennis, N.Y. Yacht (N.Y.C.); Round Hill (Greenwich, Conn.); Royal Thames Yacht (London). Home: Edge Tide Smith Rd Greenwich CT 06830 Office: 150 White Plains Rd Tarrytown NY 10591

SIMMONDS, JAMES HENRY, lawyer; b. Lynchburg, Va., Apr. 19, 1905; s. Sidney J. and Elsie (Febrey) S.; student George Washington U., 1923-25; B.S., U. Va., 1927, LL.B., 1930; LL.M., Columbia, 1931; m. Elisabeth Welch (div.); children—James G., John S.; m. 2d, Jeane F. Deeley, Feb. 6, 1954; children—Sidney G., Susan Jeane. Admitted to Va. bar, 1930, N.Y. bar, 1932; asso. Root, Clark, Bockner & Ballantine, N.Y.C., 1931-33; asst. commonwealth atty., Arlington, Va., 1933-40; partner firm Simmonds, Culler, Damm & Coleburn, 1940—; dir. 1st Am. Bank of Va., Fellow Am. Bar Found.; mem. Va. State Bar (pres. 1958-59), Am. Coll. Trial Lawyers, Am. Judicature Soc., Arlington Bar Assn. (pres. 1948), Phi Beta Kappa, Order of Coif, Phi Delta Phi. Clubs: Farmington Country, Washington Golf and Country. Home: 3615 N 27th St Arlington VA 22207 Office: 1500 N Courthouse Rd Arlington VA 22201

SIMMONS, ADELE SMITH, coll. adminstr.; b. Amherst, Mass., June 21, 1941; d. Hermon Dunlap and Ellen (Thorne) Smith; B.A. with honors, Radcliffe Coll., 1963; D.Phil., Oxford U., 1969; m. John Leroy Simmons, Sept. 18, 1966; children—Ian, Erica. Dir., African Youth Leadership program Operation Crossroads, N.Y., Africa, 1963-64; asst. prof. history Jackson Coll., Medford, Mass., 1969-72, asst. dean, 1969-70, dean, 1970-72; dean student affairs Princeton U., 1972-77; pres. Hempshire Coll., Amherst, Mass., 1977—; dir. Marsh and McLennan Cos., Sci. Research Assos. Trustee, Carnegie Found. for Advancement of Teaching, 1978—, Southeastern Mass. U., 1971-72; bd. overseers Harvard U., 1972-78; mem. Pres.'s Commn. on World Hunger, 1978—. Home: 15 Middle St Amherst MA 01002 Office: Cole Science Center Hampshire Coll Amherst MA 01002

SIMMONS, CHARLES, journalist; b. N.Y.C., Aug. 17, 1924; s. Charles and Mary (Landrigan) S.; A.B., Columbia, 1948; m. Helen Elizabeth Fitzgerald, Feb. 8, 1947 (div.); children—Deirdre, Maud; m. Nancy Nicholas, Sept. 17, 1977. Picture editor Unicorn Press, N.Y.C., 1948-51; mem. staff N.Y. Times, 1951—, asst. book rev. editor, 1963—. Served with AUS, 1943-46. Mem. P.E.N. Author: Powdered Eggs (William Faulkner award notable 1st novel), 1964; An Old-Fashioned Darling, 1971; Wrinkles, 1978; also stories, articles, lit. criticism. Editor: (with Nona Balakian) The Creative Present: Notes on Contemporary American Fiction, 1963. Home: 221 W 82d St New York NY 10024 Office: 229 W 43d St New York NY 10036

SIMMONS, CHARLES EDWARD PHILLIP, univ. adminstr.; b. Boston, Mar. 11, 1932; s. Charles Lenard and Isabella Constance (Young) S.; B.A., Seattle U., 1960; M.A., Drake U., 1960; Ph.D., Wash. State U., 1966; m. JoAnn C. Apthorp, June 6, 1959; children—Andrea, Damon, Alexia. Asst. prof. history U. Idaho, 1965-67; chmn. dept. history Bradley U., Peoria, Ill., 1967-70; acting dean arts and humanities Moorhead (Minn.) State Coll., 1970-73, dean Social and Behavioral Scis., 1970-73; academic v.p. U. Evansville (Ind.), 1973-77; pres. Lake Erie Coll., Painsville, Ohio, 1977—; cons. N.S. Dept. Pub. Welfare, 1968; vis. fellow Dalhousie U., Halifax, N.S., 1965-66; faculty fellow Hamline U., summer 1969. Trustee, Wilmington (Del.) Coll., 1977—. Served with AUS, 1948-52. Mem. Am. Council Edn., Phi Kappa Alpha, Phi Alpha Theta, Phi Delta Kappa. Clubs: Kiwanis; Union (Cleve.); Hunt. Contbr. articles to profl. jours. Office: Lake Erie Coll Painesville OH 44077

SIMMONS, CHARLES FERDINAND, educator; b. Andalusia, Ala., May 17, 1910; s. William Ferdinand and Lela (Morgan) S.; student Southwestern U., Memphis, 1928-30; B.S., Auburn U., 1932. M.S., 1934; Ph.D., Ohio State U., 1937; m. Edith Gosnell, Feb. 17, 1940; 1 dau., Margaret Hannah. Extension agronomist Coll. Agr., U. Ark., 1937-44; asso. agronomist Agrl. Expt. Sta., La. State U., 1944-46; head dept. agronomy and soils Auburn U., 1946-50, asso. dean Sch. Agr., 1951—, asso. dir. Agrl. Expt. Sta., 1951-55, asst. dir. sta., 1955—. Mem. Am. Inst. Biol. Scis., Am. Soc. Agronomy, Soil Sci. Soc. Am. Presbyterian (elder). Home: 357 S Gay St Auburn AL 36830

SIMMONS, DANIEL H., educator, physician; b. N.Y.C., June 22, 1919; s. Simon and Mollie (Zerof) S.; B.A., U. Calif. at Los Angeles, 1941; M.D., U. So. Calif., 1948; Ph.D., U. Minn., 1953; m. Ethelyn Sternberger, Mar. 3, 1942; children—Anthony Carl, Michael Scott. Sect. chief gen. medicine, chief respiration labs. VA Center, Los Angeles, 1953-61; dir. research, asso. dir. div. medicine Mt. Sinai Hosp., Los Angeles, 1961-64; dir. Med. Research Inst., Cedars-Sinai Med. Center, Los Angeles, 1964-66; mem. faculty U. Calif. at Los Angeles Med. Sch., 1953—, prof. medicine and physiology, 1966—; cons. VA Hosp., Cedars-Sinai Med. Center, Los Angeles. Served to 2d lt. USAAF, 1942-44. Diplomate Am. Bd. Internal Medicine. Fellow A.C.P., Am. Coll. Chest Physicians; mem. Am. Physiol. Soc. Western Assn. Physicians, Am. Fedn. Clin. Research, Med. Research Assn. Calif. (pres. 1972-74), Phi Beta Kappa, Sigma Xi. Contbr. articles to profl. jours. Home: 11901 Saltair Terr Los Angeles CA 90049

SIMMONS, DARRELL AUBREY, sportswriter; b. Jacksonville, Fla., Oct. 12, 1934; s. Chester Charles and Doris Muriel (Peacock) S.; student Jacksonville Jr. Coll., 1953-54, Jacksonville U., 1957-58; B.A. in English, U. Fla., 1961; m. Marise J. Charter, Apr. 13, 1963 (div.); 1 son, Chet Simmons; stepchildren—Sherri Weitnauer, Cliff Bussard. Reporter, AP, Jacksonville, Fla., 1953-58; corr. Jacksonville Jour., Miami News, Pensacola Jour., 1958-62; staff writer Jacksonville Jour., 1962-67; staff writer Atlanta Jour., 1967—, columnist, 1979—. Mem. Profl. Basketball Writers Assn. Democrat. Lutheran. Home: 2320 Melante Atlanta GA 30324 Office: 72 Marietta St Atlanta GA 30302

SIMMONS, DAVID ARTHUR, engr., quality control cons.; b. Flint, Mich., July 25, 1935; s. Thomas Arthur and Dorothy Pearl (Borton) S.; A.S. in Electronic Engring., Northeastern U., 1964, B.S., 1966; Sc.D., Ind. No. U., 1973; m. Patricia Elaine Evans, Feb. 2, 1957; children—John David, Laura Maureen, Richard Keith, William Andrew. Electronic technician A.C. Spark Plug, Milw., 1954-57; supr. quality control engring. Raytheon Co., Waltham, Mass., 1958-61, L.F.E. Inc., Boston, 1961-63; quality control engr. systems div. Sylvania Co., Bedford, Mass., 1963-65, quality assurance mgr., 1965-67; founder, operator Quality Control Assos., Reading, Mass., 1967-72; engring. supr. Polaroid Corp., Cambridge, Mass., 1968-70; dir. quality control and reliability Bendix, Sturbridge, Mass., 1970-71; dir. engring. and maintenance St. Vincent Hosp., Worcester, Mass., 1972; chief biomed. engring. VA, Washington, 1972-76; chief biomed. engring. I.H.S., Tucson, 1976-79, dir. biomed. engring. Fairfax Hosp., Falls Church, Va., 1979—; mem. faculty Northeastern U., 1967-74. Mem. Commn. Product Quality, 1967—; quality control dir. Center Profl. Advancement, Hopatcong, N.J., 1967-68. Served with U.S. Army, 1954-57. Registered profl. engr.; certified clin. engr. Fellow AAAS; mem. Am. Soc. Quality Control (sr., dir.; testimonial award 1971), Emergency Care Research Inst., Am. Nat. Standards Inst., Assn. Advancement Med. Instrumentation. K.C. Club: Commonwealth Swim (dir.) (Fairfax, Va.). Author: Commercial Quality Control, 1966; Reliability Engineering, 1967; Precision Electrical Measurements, 1968; Practical Quality Control, 1970; Medical and Hospital Control Systems, 1975. Contbr. articles to profl. jours. Patentee in field. Home: 5406 Earps Corner Pl Fairfax VA 22032 Office: Fairfax Hosp Falls Church VA 22032

SIMMONS, EDWARD DWYER, ednl. adminstr.; b. North Dighton, Mass., Aug. 29, 1924; s. Percy Briggs and Anna Cecilia (O'Connell) S.; student St. Charles Coll., 1942-44; A.B., St. Mary's U., 1945, S.T.B., 1947; M.A., U. Notre Dame, 1949, Ph.D., 1952; m. Marguerite Mary Scheibelhut, Aug. 12, 1950; children—Kathleen, Marguerite, Edward, Patricia, Thomas, Mary, Susan, Timothy, Martha, Carol, Michael, Jeanne. Instr., U. Notre Dame, 1950-52; mem. faculty Marquette U., Milw., 1952—, prof., 1965—, chmn. dept. philosophy, 1966-68, acting dean Grad. Sch., 1967-68, asso. v.p. for acad. affairs, 1968-74, v.p. for acad. affairs, 1974—. Chmn. bd. dirs. Trinity Meml. Hosp., Cudahy, Wis.; bd. overseers St. Francis Sem., Milw., 1977—; bd. dirs. St. Mary's Acad., Milw., 1976—. Mem. Am. Philos. Assn., Jacques Maritain Assn., Metaphys. Soc. Am., Am., Am. Cath. (exec. council 1960-63) philos. assns., Nat. Cath. Ednl. Assn (exec. com. coll. and univ. dept. 1969-72), Am. Assn. Higher Edn., AAUP (v.p. Marquette U. chpt. 1965-66). Author: The Scientific Art of Logic, 1961; Editor: Essays on Knowledge and Methodology, 1965. Contbr. chpts. to books, articles, papers to profl. lit. Home: 411 Hawthorne Ave S Milwaukee WI 53172

SIMMONS, EDWIN HOWARD, marine corps officer, historian; b. Paulsboro, N.J., Aug. 25, 1921; s. Edwin Lonsdale and Nettie Emma (Vankirk) S.; B.A., Lehigh U., 1942; M.A., Ohio State U., 1955; postgrad. Amphibious Warfare Sch., 1949-50, Nat. War Coll., 1966-67; m. Frances Bliss, Apr. 25, 1962; children—Edwin Howard, Clarke Vankirk, Bliss, Courtney. Commd. 2d lt. USMC, 1942, advanced through grades to brig. gen., 1967; asst. prof. NROTC, Ohio State U., 1952-55; with Hdqrs. Marine Corps, 1955- 59; naval attache Dominican Republic, 1959-60; with Hdqrs. Marine Corps and Joint Staff, 1962-65; with 3d Marine Div., 1965-66, 1st Marine Div., Vietnam, 1970-71; dep. fiscal dir. Marine Corps, 1967-70; dir. Marine

Corps history and museums USMC Hdqrs., Arlington, Va., 1971—. Trustee, Am. Mil. Inst. Decorated D.S.M., Silver Star, Legion of Merit with two gold stars, Bronze Star with gold star, Meritorious Service medal, Navy Commendation medal, Purple Heart, knight Nat. Order of Vietnam, Vietnamese Cross of Gallantry with 2 palms and silver star; recipient Centennial Distinguished Grad. medallion Ohio State U., 1970. Fellow Co. Mil. Historians; mem. Am. Soc. Mil. Comptrollers (nat. v.p. 1967-69, pres. 1969-70), Nat. War Coll. Alumni Assn. (v.p. 1969-70, 74-75), Phi Beta Kappa, Omicron Delta Kappa, Phi Sigma Kappa. Author: The United States Marines, 1974. Mng. editor Marine Corps Gazette, 1946-49; sr. editor Publs. Group, Marine Corps Schs., 1960-61. Contbr. to numerous books, encys., mags., jours. and annuals. Home: 9020 Charles Augustus Dr Alexandria VA 22308 Office: Hdqrs USMC Washington DC 20380

SIMMONS, FORREST WIEMANN, lawyer, investment co. exec.; b. Brooking, S.D., Mar. 9, 1924; s. Forrest E. and Violet E. (Wiemann) S.; B.A., Oreg. State U., 1950; J.D., U. Mich., 1952; m. Betty Jean Manoles, Aug. 25, 1950; children—Forrest Bradford, Mark, Gregory, Douglas. Admitted to Oreg. bar, 1952; sr. partner Souther, Spaulding, Kinsey, Williamson & Schwabe, Portland, Oreg., 1952—; chmn. bd., chief exec. officer First Farwest Corp., Portland, 1965—; dir. Webster Industries, Tiffin, Ohio, Trans Pacific Leasing Services, Ltd., Vancouver, B.C.; pres. Pacific Ins. Investment Co., Portland. Served with U.S. Army, 1942-46. Decorated Bronze Star. Mem. Am., Oreg., Multnomah bar assns. Republican. Methodist. Clubs: Arlington, Waverley Country, Multnomah Athletic. Home: 11700 SW Military Ln Portland OR 97219 Office: 400 SW 6th Ave Portland OR 97208

SIMMONS, FRANCIS BLAIR, otolaryngologist; b. Los Angeles, Nov. 15, 1930; s. Francis J. and Kathryn B. Simmons; A.B. cum laude, Transylvania Coll., Lexington, Ky., 1952; M.D., U. Louisville, 1956; children—Kathryn, Holly, Kevin, Iris. Research asso. psychoacoustic labs. Harvard U., 1955; rotating intern Madigan Army Hosp., Tacoma, 1956-57; research asso. neurophysiology and audio physiology Walter Reed Inst. Research, 1958-59; resident in otolaryngology Stanford U. Hosp., 1959-62, research asso. Stanford U. Med. Sch., 1959-61, mem. faculty, 1961—, prof. otolaryngology, head dept., 1971—; mem. study sect. sensory communication Nat. Inst. Neurol. Communicative Disorders and Stroke, 1969-71; bd. dirs. Calif. Oral Deaf Edn., 1967-71; mem. grants rev. study sect. HEW-Vocat. Rehab. Adminstrn., 1969-72; cons. San Mateo County (Calif.) Schs., 1972—. Diplomate Am. Bd. Otolaryngology. Mem. Am. Assn. Ophthalmology Otolaryngology (research award 1963, Physicians Recognition award 1973), Am. Physiol. Soc., Santa Clara County Med. Soc., Acoustical Soc. Am., Nat. Assn. Hearing and Speech Agencies, Soc. Univ. Otolaryngologists, Otoneurology Study Group, Am. Audiology Soc., Am. Laryngological, Rhinological Otol. Soc., Am. Otol. Soc. Asso. editor Annals Otology Rhinology and Laryngology, 1969—; editor home study sect. hearing aids Am. Acad. Ophthalmology Otolaryngology. Home: 628 Westridge St Portola Valley CA 94025 Office: Stanford Univ Med Center Stanford CA 94305

SIMMONS, GRANT G., JR., bedding and home furnishings mfg. co. exec.; b. Jan. 3, 1920; s. Grant G. and Nancy O. Simmons; A.B., Yale, 1942; postgrad. Harvard; children—Allison, Leslie Frances, Grant G. III; m. 2d, Elizabeth Richardson Darlington, Aug. 31, 1965; stepchildren—Henry Darlington III, Elizabeth A. Darlington, Victoria W. Darlington. With Simmons Co., 1945—, v.p., dir., 1952-57, pres., chief exec. officer, 1957-68, chmn. bd., chief exec. officer after 1968, now hon. chmn.; dir. IBM World Trade Corp., ACF Industries, Inc., 1st Nat. Bank of Atlanta, 1st Nat. Holding Corp. Bd. dirs. Internat. Exec. Service Corps; adv. dir. Boys Clubs of Am.; mem. pres.'s council Brandeis U.; mem. assos. council Amos Tuck Sch., Dartmouth; hon. trustee Trudeau Inst., Com. for Econ. Devel. Served with USNR, 1942-45. Mem. Nat. Assn. Bedding Mfrs., Am. Def. Preparedness Assn., Am. Soc. Corporate Execs., Nat. Audubon Soc. (dir., life mem.), Am. Ornithol. Union (life), Wilson Ornithol. Soc. (life), N.Y. State Conservation Council, Friends Art Mus. (Princeton), Am. Philatelic Soc., Met. Mus. Art, Am. Library in Paris, Irish Georgian Soc., Point Reyes Bird Obs. Episcopalian. Clubs: Brook, University, Pilgrims of U.S.; Plantation (Hilton Head, S.C.), Piedmont Driving; Atlanta Commerce. Office: Simmons Co PO Box 49000 Atlanta GA 30340*

SIMMONS, HAROLD A., retail trade co. exec.; b. Los Angeles, Aug. 4, 1931; s. Arthur Harold and Kathyrne Marie (Craig) S.; student Boise Jr. Coll., 1950, Wash. State U., 1950-51; B.S. in Bus., U. Idaho, 1959; m. Jane Perry, Sept. 28, 1952; children—Janene, Chad M. With Lincoln G. Kelly & Co., C.P.A.'s, 1959-62; audit mgr. Coopers & Lybrand, C.P.A.'s, Salt Lake City, 1962-74; treas., asst. sec. Grand Central, Inc., Salt Lake City, 1975—; dir. Investment Income, Inc. Served with USAF, 1952-56. C.P.A., Utah. Mem. Am. Inst. C.P.A.'s, Utah Assn. C.P.A.'s. Republican. Presbyterian. Clubs: Hidden Valley Country, Masons, Elks. Home: 2537 Wilshire Circle Salt Lake City UT 84109 Office: 2233 S 3d East Salt Lake City UT 84115

SIMMONS, HOWARD ENSIGN, JR., research adminstr., chemist; b. Norfolk, Va., June 17, 1929; s. Howard Ensign and Marie Magdalene (Weidenhammer) S.; B.S. in Chemistry, Mass. Inst. Tech., 1951, Ph.D. in Organic Chemistry, 1954; m. Elizabeth Anne Warren, Sept. 1, 1951; children—Howard Ensign III, John W. Mem. research staff E.I. duPont de Nemours & Co., central research and devel. dept., Wilmington, Del., 1954-59, research supr., 1959-70, asso. dir., 1970-74, dir. research, 1974-79, dir., 1979—; adj. prof. chemistry U. Del., 1974—; Sloan vis. prof. Harvard, 1968; Kharasch vis. prof. U. Chgo., 1978. Trustee Gordon Research Confs., 1974—. Fellow N.Y. Acad. Scis.; mem. Am. Acad. Arts and Scis., Nat. Acad. Scis., Soc. Chem. Industry, Am. Chem. Soc., Indsl. Research Inst., AAAS, Delta Kappa Epsilon. Author: (with A.G. Anastassiou) Theoretical Aspects of the Cyclobutadiene Problem in Cyclobutadiene, 1967. Editorial bd. Jour. Organic Chemistry, 1969-74, Synthesis, 1969—, Chem. Revs., 1972-74. Home: 104 Delview Rd Wilmington DE 19810 Office: Central Research and Development Dept DuPont Experimental Station Wilmington DE 19898

SIMMONS, JEAN, actress; b. London, Eng., Jan. 31, 1929; d. Charles and Winifred Ada (Loveland) Simmons; ed. Orange Hill Sch., Burnt Oak, London; m. Stewart Granger, Dec. 20, 1950 (div. June 1960); 1 dau., Tracy; m. 2d, Richard Brooks, Nov. 1, 1960; 1 dau. Motion picture actress, appearing in English and Am. films, including Great Expectations, Black Narcissus, Hamlet, The Actress, Guys and Dolls, Young Bess, Adam and Evelyn, Big Country, 1958; Home Before Dark, 1958; Spartacus, Elmer Gantry, 1959; The Grass Is Greener, 1960; All the Way Home, 1963; Rough Night in Jericho; Divorce American Style; The Happy Ending; also theatre appearance A Little Night Music, Phila. and on tour, 1974; appeared in TV mini-series The Dain Curse, 1978. Office: Care Morgan Maree 6363 Wilshire Blvd Los Angeles CA 90048*

SIMMONS, JEAN ELIZABETH MARGARET (MRS. GLEN R. SIMMONS), educator; b. Cleve., Jan. 20, 1914; d. Frank Charles and Sarah Anne (Johnston) Saurwein; B.A., Western Reserve U., 1933; Ph.D. (Stieglitz fellow 1935-37), U. Chgo., 1938; m. Glen R. Simmons, Nov. 14, 1935; children—Sally Anne, (Frank) Charles, James Fraser. Faculty, Barat Coll., Lake Forest, Ill., 1938-58, prof., chmn. dept. chemistry, 1948-58; faculty Upsala Coll., East Orange, N.J., 1959—, prof., 1963—, chmn. dept. chemistry, 1965-71, 74, 76—, chmn. sci. curriculum study, Luth. Ch. Am. grantee, 1965-68, chmn. div. natural scis. and maths., 1965-69, asst. to pres., 1968-73, cons. to pres., 1978—. Coordinator basic scis. Evang. Hosp. Sch. Nursing, Chgo., 1943-46; lectr. sci. topics; participant various White House Confs. Troop leader Girl Scouts U.S.A., Wheaton, Ill., 1952-58, neighborhood chmn., 1956-57, dist. chmn. DuPage County, 1958; chmn. U. Chgo. Alumni Fund Dr., Wheaton, 1957, 58, Princeton, N.J., 1964, 65; mem. nursing advisory com. East Orange (N.J.) Gen. Hosp., 1963-73; pres. Virginia Gildersleeve Ednl. Fund. Recipient Lindback Found. award for disting. teaching, 1964. Fellow Am. Inst. Chemists, AAAS (council 1969-71); vis. fellow Princeton U., 1977; mem. Am. Chem. Soc., AAUW (br. treas. 1960-62, chmn. sci. topic, 1963—, state v.p. program 1964, nat. sci. topic implementation chmn. 1965, 66, state dir. 1967-68, 71-72, state pres. 1968-70), Fedn. Orgns. Profl. Women (nat. pres. 1974-75), Internat. Fedn. Univ. Women (alt. del. for U.S. at conf. 1968, 77, del. conf. 1974, ofcl. observer UN Conf. Vienna 1979), AAUP (charter, past chpt. pres.), Phi Beta Kappa (pres. North Jersey alumni assn. 1973-74), Sigma Xi, Sigma Delta Epsilon (nat. pres. 1970-71, dir. 1972—). Episcopalian. Contbr. articles to publs. in field. Home: 40 Balsam Ln Princeton NJ 08540 Office: Upsala Coll East Orange NJ 07019

SIMMONS, JOHN EDWARDS, publisher; b. Osceola, Iowa, May 30, 1918; s. Paul Murray and Gladys (Edwards) S.; B.A., U. Iowa, 1947; m. Eleanor Pownall, Apr. 1, 1947; children—Frederick Pownall, Mary Murray. Bus. mgr. U. Pa. Press, 1950-54; asst. mgr. Cornell U. Press, 1954-60; sr. editor U. Chgo. Press, 1960-61; dir. publs. U. Iowa, Iowa City, 1961-77, dir. U. Iowa Press, 1977—. Served with U.S. Army, 1941-45. Home: 329 River St Iowa City IA 52240 Office: U Iowa Press Iowa City IA 52242

SIMMONS, JOHN KAUL, educator; b. Beloit, Kans., July 12, 1938; s. Fred Cole and Bernice Eva (Kaul) S.; B.S., Kans. State U., 1960; M.B.A., U. Denver, 1961; Ph.D., Ohio State U., 1967; m. Gail Ruth Parrish, Aug. 22, 1959; children—Kauleen Kaye, Laura Elizabeth. Teaching fellow U. Denver, 1960-61; instr. Ohio State U., Columbus, 1961-63; accountant Peat, Marwick, Mitchell & Co., Columbus, 1963-64; asst. prof. U. Minn., Mpls., 1965-69, asso. prof., 1969-73, prof., 1973-74; prof., chmn. dept. accounting U. Fla., Gainesville, 1974-77, dir. Sch. Accounting, 1977—. Cons. NASA Manned Spacecraft Center 1968; mem. written profl. exam. com. Fla. Bd. Accountancy, 1975-77. Bd. dirs. Fla. Athletic Assn., 1975-77. Co-recipient award for outstanding contbn. to accounting lit. Am. Inst. C.P.A.'s, 1969. C.P.A., Kans. Mem. Am. Accounting Assn. (mem. editorial research adv. com. 1974-75, sec./treas. 1977-79), Am. Inst. C.P.A.'s, Fla. Inst. C.P.A.'s, Fedn. Schs. Accounting (sec./treas. 78, pres.-elect 1979, pres. 1980), Nat. Assn. State Bds. Accountancy (C.P.A. exam. rev. bd. 1979—), Beta Alpha Psi, Beta Gamma Sigma, Alpha Kappa Psi, Sigma Chi. Contbr. articles to profl. jours. Home: 1615 NW 19th Circle Gainesville FL 32605 Office: 202 Matherly Hall U Fla Gainesville FL 32611

SIMMONS, JOHN WILLIAM, mfg. co. exec.; b. Toledo, Aug. 12, 1919; s. Francis W. and Stella (Arnsman) S.; B.A., Williams Coll., 1941; grad. Advanced Mgmt. Program, Harvard, 1958; m. Paula Marie Johnston, Oct. 10, 1944; children—Lorraine (Mrs. John Tuohy), Carol, Paula (Mrs. Mark Butler), John William Jr. With Scott Paper Co., 1945-46; with Becton, Dickinson & Co., Rutherford, N.J., 1946-72, exec. v.p., chief ops. officer, dir., chmn. exec. com., mem. finance com., 1961-72; with Morton-Norwich Products, Inc., Chicago, 1972—, pres., chief exec. officer, dir., chmn. exec. com., mem. fin. com., chmn. bd., 1976—; chmn. bd., dir. Eaton Labs. P.R., Inc., Canadian Salt Co. Ltd.; vice chmn., dir. Rohm Pharma GmbH; dir. Noroma Produtos Quimicos Ltd. (Brazil), Williams (Hounslow) Ltd. (Eng.), Burlington Industries, Morton Bahamas Ltd.; adv. dir. Arkwright-Boston Ins. Co. Mem. Brazil-U.S. Bus. Council; governing mem. Orchestral Assn.; mem. citizens bd. U. Chgo.; trustee Am. Health Found., Rush-Presbyn.-St. Luke's Med. Center; bd. dirs. Lyric Opera of Chgo. Served to lt. USCGR, 1941-45. Named master knight Sovereign Mil. Order of Malta, 1962. Mem. Pharm. Mfrs. Assn. (dir.). Clubs: Arcola (N.J.) Country; Casino, Glen View, Mid-America, Chicago, Metropolitan, Commercial, The Plaza, Saddle and Cycle, Economic, Tower (Chgo.); Devon Yacht (East Hampton, N.Y.); Maidstone (L.I., N.Y.); Union League, Williams (N.Y.C.); Lyford Cay (Nassau, Bahamas). Home: 1500 Lake Shore Dr Chicago IL 60610 Office: 110 N Wacker Dr Chicago IL 60606

SIMMONS, JOSEPH JACOB, III, oil co. exec.; b. Muskogee, Okla., Mar. 26, 1925; s. Jacob, Jr. and Eva (Flowers) S.; student U. Detroit, 1942-44, 46-47; B.S. in Geol. Engring., St. Louis U., 1949; m. Bernice Elizabeth Miller, Jan. 30, 1947; children—Jacob, Mary Agnes, Bernice, Jacolyn, Eva Frances. Vice pres., sec. bd. dirs. Simmons Royalty Co., Muskogee, 1949-61; asst. dir. Office Oil and Gas, Dept. Interior, Washington, 1961-68, dep. adminstr. oil imports, 1968-69, adminstr., 1969-70; v.p. Hess Oil & Chem. div. Amerada Hess Corp., Woodbridge, N.J., 1970-73, v.p. govt. relations, asst. to chmn. Amerada Hess Corp., N.Y.C., 1973—; mem. fuel oil mktg. adv. com. Dept. Energy, 1978—; mem. President's Commn. on Exec. Exchange, 1978—. Youth dir. NAACP, 1950-55; candidate Okla. Ho. of Reps., 1956; candidate City Council, 1956. Trustee Madonna Coll., Livonia, Mich., 1969-76. Served with USAAF, 1944-46. Recipient Alumni Merit award St. Louis U., 1968, Spl. Act of Service award Dept. Interior, 1963, Outstanding Performance award, 1968, Distinguished Service award, 1970. Registered profl. engr., Okla. Mem. Am. Assn. Petroleum Geologists, Soc. Petroleum Engrs., Am. Inst. Mining, Metall. and Petroleum Engrs., Petroleum Exploration Soc. of N.Y. Home: 1549 Ashbrook Dr Scotch Plains NJ 07076 Office: Amerada Hess Corp 1185 Ave of Americas New York NY 10036

SIMMONS, LAWRENCE WHITLEY, chocolate mfg. co. exec.; b. Gettysburg, Pa., June 17, 1925; s. Millard Bingham and Wilma Lacey (Lawrance) S.; B.E.E., Cornell U., 1946; M.B.A., Harvard, 1950; m. Mary Glenn Pennell, Oct. 6, 1951; children—Lawrance Whitley, Mary Glenn, Barbara Pennell. Engr., Gen. Electric Co., 1947-48; with Hershey Foods Corp., 1950—, asst. comptroller, 1957-59, comptroller, 1959-78, treas., 1971-76, asst. v.p., 1976—. Served to lt. (j.g.) USNR, 1943-46. Mem. Fin. Execs. Inst., Nat. Assn. Accountants, S.A.R. Republican. Presbyn. Mason. Rotarian. Home: 129 Para Ave Hershey PA 17033 Office: 19 E Chocolate Ave Hershey PA 17033

SIMMONS, MABEL CLARKE, journalist; b. Tuscumbia, Mo., Sept. 5, 1899; d. Charles H. and Mattie (Clark) Clarke; B.J., U. Mo., 1923; m. George Evans Simmons, June 25, 1921; children—George Clarke. Kirksey. Reporter, Nashville Tennessean, 1922-24; free lance writer, 1925-52; lit. editor New Orleans Times Picayune, 1954—, also travel editor. Home: 2439 Nashville Ave New Orleans LA 70115 Office: 3800 Howard Ave New Orleans LA 70140

SIMMONS, MARVIN GENE, educator; b. Dallas, May 15, 1929; s. Burt H. and Mable (Marshall) S.; B.S., Tex. Agrl. and Mech. Coll., 1949; M.S., So. Methodist U., 1958; Ph.D., Harvard, 1962; div.; children—Jon Eric, Debra Lynn, Sandra Kay, Pamela Jean. Petroleum engr. Humble Oil Co., 1949-51; propr. gravel business, 1953-58; asst. prof. So. Meth. U., 1962-65; prof. geophysics Mass. Inst. Tech., 1965—. Cons. NASA, 1965-72, chief scientist Manned Spacecraft Center, Houston, 1969-71; sec. Internat. Heat Flow Com., 1967-71; chmn. com. drilling for sci. purposes Nat. Acad. Scis., 1965; Mem. geophysics panel NSF. Served with USAF, 1951-53. NSF postdoctoral fellow, 1961-62. Fellow Geol. Soc. Am., Am. Geophys. Union; mem. AAAS, Boston Geol. Soc. (pres. 1967-68), Mineral. Soc. Am., Soc. Exploration Geophysicists, Sigma Xi, Tau Beta Pi. Research phys. properties materials, lunar exploration, marine geophysics, temperature of earth, regional geophysics. Home: 9 Edgehill Rd Winchester MA 01890 Office: 77 Massachusetts Ave Cambridge MA 02139

SIMMONS, MATTY, pub. co. exec., theatrical and film producer, author, editor; b. Bklyn., Oct. 3, 1926; s. Irving and Kate (Sharp) S.; student Coll. City N.Y.; m. Lee Easton, Feb. 28, 1952; children—Michael, Julie, Andrew. Newspaper reporter, 1944-45; pub. relations cons., 1947-58; exec. v.p. Diners' Club, 1950-67, also dir.; exec. editor Signature, Diners' Club mag. 1950-66; exec. editor Bravo mag., also pres. Bravo, Inc., 1965-66; chmn. bd. San Francisco Warriors, mems. Nat. Basketball Assn., 1963; engaged in racing and breeding harness horses, 1960-70; pres. Wayfarer's Club, 1966; editor, pub., chmn. 21st Century Communications Inc., chmn., chief exec. officer subsidiary Nat. Lampoon, 1970—, Heavy Metal mag., 1977—; producer mus. comedies Nat. Lampoon Lemmings, 1972-74, Nat. Lampoon Show, 1974-76, That's Not Funny, That's Sick, 1977—; producer Nat. Lampoon's Animal House, 1978. Author: On the House, 1955; The Best Of, 1962; The Card Castle (novel), 1970. Editor: The Diners' Club Drink Book, 1960—, Weight Watchers mag., 1968-75. Office: 21st Century Communications Inc 635 Madison Ave New York NY 10019

SIMMONS, NORMAN STANLEY, biophysicist, educator; b. N.Y.C., May 28, 1915; B.S., City U. N.Y., 1935; D.M.D., Harvard, 1939; Ph.D., U. Rochester, 1950. Carnegie fellow dental research U. Rochester, 1939-41, fellow dental research, 1947-50, sr. fellow, 1948-50; instr. Periodontology Columbia Dental Sch., 1941-43; mem. faculty U. Calif. at Los Angeles Med. Sch., 1950—, research biochemist, 1959—, prof., 1963—. Fellow in chemistry Harvard, 1955; NIH career research award, 1963—. Mem. Internat. Assn. Dental Research, Biophys. Soc., Am. Soc. Biol. Chemists, Internat. Assn. Pure and Applied Biophysics, Sigma Xi, Omicron Kappa Upsilon. Contbr. articles to profl. jours. Address: Center Health Sci Univ Calif Los Angeles CA 90024

SIMMONS, OZZIE GORDON, sociologist, educator; b. Winnipeg, Man., Can., Oct. 9, 1919 (parents Am. citizens); s. Max and Rose (Goldstone) S.; B.S., Northwestern U., 1941; M.A., Harvard U., 1948, Ph.D., 1952; m. Charlotte Sonenklar, Dec. 9, 1942; children—Gregor, Lauren, Paula. Dir. in Peru for Inst. Social Anthropology, Smithsonian Instn., also vis. prof. U. San Marcos, Lima, Peru, 1949-52; cons. anthropologist Inst. Inter-Am. Affairs, Santiago, Chile, 1953; asso. prof. anthropology Harvard U. Sch. Pub. Health, 1953- 61; prof. sociology, also dir. Inst. Behavioral Sci., U. Colo., Boulder, 1961-68; sr. faculty research asso. Brandeis U., 1961-65; program officer internat. div. Ford Found., 1968—; lectr. behavioral sci. Johns Hopkins U., Balt., 1968-71; cons. NIH, also mem. health services research study sect., 1961-65; cons. VA, Ford Found.; chmn. research study sect. alcoholism and alcohol-related problems Nat. Center Prevention and Control of Alcoholism, NIMH, 1967-68. Served with USAAF, 1942- 46. Co-recipient Hofheimer prize Am. Psychiat. Assn., 1963; Sigmund Livingston fellow, Arnold traveling fellow Harvard. Fellow Am. Sociol. Assn. (past mem. exec. council sect. med. sociology), Am. Anthrop. Assn., AAAS, Soc. Applied Anthropology, Population Assn. Am., Internat. Union Sci. Study Population; mem. Phi Beta Kappa. Author: Social Status and Public Health, 1958; After Hospitalization: The Mental Patient and his Family, 1960; (with Howard E. Freeman) The Mental Patient Comes Home, 1963; Work and Mental Illness: Eight Case Studies, 1965; Mexican Americans and Anglo Americans in South Texas, 1974; also numerous research articles in behavioral and health scis. Asso. editor Am. Sociol. Review, 1959-62, Jour. Health and Human Behavior, 1959-66, Social Sci. and Medicine, 1966-76, Jour. Health and Social Behavior, 1967-71. Address: 320 E 43d St New York NY 10017

SIMMONS, PAUL ALLEN, judge; b. Monongahela, Pa., Aug. 31, 1921; s. Perry C. and Lilly D. (Allen) S.; B.A., U. Pitts., 1942; J.D., Harvard U., 1949; m. Gwendolyn O. Gladden, Sept. 2, 1950; children—Paul A., Gwendolyn Dale, Anne Marie. Mem. faculty dept. law S.C. State Coll. Law, 1949-52; prof. law N.C. Central U., 1952-56; pvt. practice law, Monongahela, 1956-73; judge Ct. of Common Pleas, Washington County, Pa., 1973-78; judge U.S. Dist. Ct., Western Dist. Pa., Pitts., 1978—. Mem. Pa. Human Relations Commn., 1963-68; mem. Pa. Minor Jud. Edn. Bd., 1970—; mem. Washington County Redevel. Authority, 1970-73. Mem. Pa. Bar Assn., N.C. Bar Assn., Am. Bar Assn., Washington County Bar Assn., Pa. Bar Assn., Am. Judicature Soc., NAACP. Democrat. Mem. African Meth. Episcopal Ch. Clubs: Masons, Elks. Office: US Post Office and Court House Grant St Pittsburgh PA 15219

SIMMONS, PETER, educator, univ. adminstr.; b. N.Y.C., July 19, 1931; s. Michael L. and Mary A. S.; A.B., U. Calif., Berkeley, 1953, LL.B., 1956; postgrad. (Alvord fellow) U. Wis., 1956-58; postgrad. SUNY, Buffalo, 1963-67, Ohio State U., 1967-75, Case Western Res. U., 1974-75, U. Ill., 1972; m. Ruth J. Tanfield, Jan. 28, 1951; children—Sam, Lizzard. Prof. law and urban planning Rutgers U. Coll. Law, Newark, 1975—, dean, 1975—. Mem. Ohio State Housing Commn., 1972-74; commr. Ohio State Reclamation Rev. Bd., 1974-75. Mem. Am. Inst. Planners, Am. Soc. Planning Ofcls., Urban Land Inst., Am. Law Inst., AAUP (nat. council 1973-75). Contbr. articles to profl. jours. Home: 422 Wyoming Ave Millburn NJ 07041 Office: 15 Washington St Newark NJ 07102

SIMMONS, RALPH OLIVER, physicist, educator; b. Kensington, Kans., Feb. 19, 1928; s. Fred Charles and Nellie (Douglass) S.; B.A., U. Kans., 1950; B.A. (Rhodes scholar), Oxford U., 1953; Ph.D., U. Ill., 1957; m. Janet Lee Lull, Aug. 31, 1952; children—Katherine Ann, Bradley Alan, Jill Christine, Joy Diane. Research asso. U. Ill., Urbana, 1957-59, faculty physics, 1959—, asso. prof., 1961-65, prof. physics, 1965—, head physics dept., 1970—; mem. governing bd. Internat. Symposia on Thermal Expansion, 1970—; cons. Argonne Nat. Lab., 1978—. Chmn. Office of Phys. Scis., NRC, 1978—, mem. Assembly of Math. and Phys. Scis., 1978—, mem. Geophysics Research Bd., 1978—; trustee Argonne Univs. Assn., 1979—. Sr. postdoctoral fellow NSF, 1965. Fellow Am. Phys. Soc. (vice chmn., chmn. div. solid state physics 1975-77); mem. AAAS, Am. Assn. Physics Tchrs., Phi Beta Kappa, Sigma Xi, Pi Mu Epsilon. Mem. internat. adv. bd. Jour. Physics C (Solid State Physics), 1971-76; mem. editorial bd. Physical Review B, 1978—. Research on atomic defects in solids, quantum solids, molecular crystals, crystal dynamics, radiation damage. Home: 1005 Foothill Dr Champaign IL 61820

SIMMONS, RICHARD D., pub. co. exec.; b. 1934; A.B., Harvard, 1955; LL.B., Columbia, 1958; married. Admitted to N.Y. bar; asso. firm Satterlee, Warfield & Stephens, 1958-62; gen. counsel Giannini Sci. Corp., 1962-64; v.p., gen. counsel Southeastern Pub. Service Corp., 1964-69; counsel Dun & Bradstreet Inc., N.Y.C., 1969-70, v.p., gen. counsel, 1970-72; pres. Moody's Investors Service, 1973-76, Dun & Bradstreet, Inc., 1975-76; exec. v.p. Dun & Bradstreet Cos., Inc., N.Y.C., 1976-78, dir., vice chmn. bd., 1979—; trustee Am. Savs. Bank. Office: 299 Park Ave New York NY 10017

SIMMONS, RICHARD MORGAN, JR., furniture mfg. co. exec.; b. Martinsville, Va., Sept. 28, 1926; s. Richard Morgan and Margaret (Sydnor) S.; student Va. Mil. Inst., 1944; B.A., U. Va., 1948; m. Louise Henry Acker, Oct. 9, 1948; children—Catherine, Lee, Morgan, Elizabeth, Louise. With Am. Furniture Co., Inc., Martinsville, Va., 1948—, pres., chief exec. officer, 1961-74, chmn. bd., pres., 1974—; dir. Dibrell Bros., Piedmont Trust Bank, Renfro Co., Tultex Corp., Warren Trucking Co. Served with U.S. Mcht. Marine, 1945. Mem. So. Furniture Mfrs. Assn., Furniture Factories Mktg. Assn. Episcopalian. Home: 214 Oakdale St Martinsville VA 24112 Office: PO Box 5071 Martinsville VA 24112

SIMMONS, RICHARD SHERIDAN, lawyer; b. N.Y.C., Sept. 28, 1928; s. William and Mary E. (Sheridan) S.; B.A. summa cum laude, Princeton U., 1951; LL.B., Yale U., 1954; m. Margaret Patricia Casey, June 30, 1955; 1 son, William. Admitted to N.Y. bar, 1956; mem. firm Cravath, Swaine and Moore, N.Y.C., 1956—, partner firm, 1963—. Dep. supt. Banks of State of N.Y., 1959-60. Served with U.S. Army, 1954-56. Mem. Internat., Am., (chmn. banking com. 1970-75), N.Y. State bar assns., Assn. Bar City of N.Y., Council on Fgn. Relations, Soc. Colonial Wars, St. Nicholas Soc., SAR. Mem. Dutch Reformed Ch. Clubs: Wall St., Univ., North Hempstead Country. Editor Yale Law Jour., 1954. Home: 27 Stonytown Rd Plandome Manor LI NY 11030 Office: One Chase Manhattan Plaza New York City NY 10005

SIMMONS, ROY WILLIAM, banker; b. Portland, Oreg., Jan. 24, 1916; s. Henry Clay and Ida (Mudd) S.; student U. Utah, 1934-37; m. Elizabeth Ellison, Oct. 28, 1938; children—Julia (Mrs. W. Mack Watkins), Matthew R., Laurence E., Elizabeth Jane, Harris H., David E. Asst. cashier First Nat. Bank Layton (Utah), 1944-49; Utah bank commr., 1949-51; exec. v.p. Bank of Utah, Ogden, 1951-53; pres. Lockhart Co., Salt Lake City, 1953-64; pres., dir. Zion's First Nat. Bank, Salt Lake City, 1964—, Zion's Utah Bancorp., 1965—; chmn. bd. Zion's Savs. & Loan Assn., 1961-69, Lockhart Co., 1964—; dir. Salt Lake City br. Fed. Res. Bank San Francisco, 1971-77; dir. Kennecott Copper Corp., Beneficial Life Ins. Co., Hotel Utah, Utah Portland Cement Co., Mountain Fuel Supply Co., Denver & Rio Grande R.R., Rio Grande Industries, Ellison Ranching Co. Chmn. Utah Bus. Devel. Corp., 1969—. Mem. Utah State Bd. Regents, 1969—. Mem. Salt Lake City C. of C. (treas. 1964-65), Sigma Pi. Republican. Mem. Ch. of Jesus Christ of Latter Day Saints. Home: Crestwood Rd Kaysville UT 84037 Office: Zion's First Nat Bank 1 Main St Salt Lake City UT 84110

SIMMONS, SAMUEL LEE, cosmetic co. exec.; b. St. Louis, Dec. 27, 1929; s. David Mayo and Mayme Pearle (Looney) S.; B.A. with honors, Principia Coll., 1951; J.D. cum laude, Harvard U., 1957; m. Joan Miller, Oct. 8, 1959; children—Lesley, Samuel Lee. Admitted to N.Y. bar, 1958; atty. Standard Oil Co. N.J., N.Y.C., 1957-59, firm Arthur, Dry & Dole, N.Y.C., 1959-63; with ITT, 1963-75, staff counsel, gen. counsel ITT Credit Corp., 1963-67, v.p. parent co., gen. counsel European hdqrs., Brussels, Belgium, 1967-75; v.p., gen. counsel Revlon Inc., N.Y.C., 1975-76, sr. v.p., gen. counsel, dir., 1976—, corp. sec., 1979—. Served with U.S. Army, 1952-54. Mem. Bar Assn. City N.Y., Am. Bar Assn. Home: 800 Park Ave New York NY 10021 Office: 767 Fifth Ave New York NY 10022

SIMMONS, SHERWIN PALMER, lawyer; b. Bowling Green, Ky., Jan. 19, 1931; s. Carl Smith and Helen (Creasy) S.; A.B., Columbia U., 1952, LL.B., 1954, J.D., 1969; m. Mary Anne Rodriguez Leal, Dec. 25, 1974; children—Leslie Palmer (dec.), Sherwin P.; 1 stepson, Stephen Leal. Admitted to Tenn. bar, 1954, Fla. bar, 1957; atty.-advisor U.S. Tax Ct., Washington, 1954-56; asso. law firm Fowler, White, Collins, Gillen, Humkey & Trenam, Tampa, Fla., 1956-60, partner, 1960-70; partner law firm Trenam, Simmons, Kemker, Scharf, Barkin, Frye & O'Neill and predecessor firms, Tampa, 1970-77; mem. firm Trenam, Simmons, Kemker, Scharf, Barken, Frye & O'Neill, P.A., 1977—; adj. prof. law Stetson Univ. Coll. Law, 1956-73; dir. Reeves Southeastern Corp., Scotty's Inc., Shop & Go, Inc., Nat. Trust Bank of Fla.; mem. adv. group Commr. Internal Revenue, 1978-79; mem. U.S. Tax Ct. Nominating Commn., 1978-79. Pres., Hillsborough County Soc. Crippled Children and Adults, 1960-61; treas., chmn. com. on bus. and fin. Hillsborough County Pub. Edn. Study Commn., 1965-66; mem. adv. bd. Salvation Army, 1959-62, 64-66, sec. 1960-61. Trustee Shimberg Found., Inc., So. Fed. Tax Inst., Inc. Mem. Internat., Fed., Tampa and Hillsborough County (treas. 1963-65), Fla. (mem. exec. council 1958—), Am. (mem. commn. on law and economy 1976-78; chmn. sect. taxation 1975-76) bar assns., Am. Trial Lawyers Assn. Author: Federal Taxation of Life Insurance, 1966. Home: 58 Bahama Circle Tampa FL 33606 Office: PO Box 1102 Tampa FL 33601

SIMMONS, T.F. DENYS, fin. exec.; b. Watford, Eng., July 25, 1921; s. Thomas H. and Violet (Prentice) S.; student Malvern Coll., Eng., 1935-39; B.A. in Econs., Trinity Hall, Cambridge, Eng., 1948; m. Bona De Seta, Sept. 19, 1946; children—Francesca, Maria, Giovanna, Thomas. With Alcan, Can., Eng., India, Switzerland, 1952—, fin. dir. Alcan Aluminium (U.K.) Ltd., also Alcan Booth Industries Ltd., London, 1969-73, treas. Alcan Aluminium Ltd., Montreal, Que., Can., 1973—. Served as capt. Brit. Army, 1940-45. Clubs: Mt. Bruno (Que.), Saint James's (Montreal). Address: Alcan Aluminium Ltd PO Box 6090 Montreal PQ H3C 3H2 Canada

SIMMONS, THOMAS JEFFERSON, editor; b. Dallas, Aug. 13, 1914; s. John Middleton and Ada May (Lindop) S.; student Jefferson Sch. Law, 1932-33; m. Jean Adelaide Webb, Nov. 11, 1939; 1 dau., Susan Adelaide (Mrs. Eric Weir). Reporter Dallas Jour., 1931-34; reporter, editor Dallas Morning News, 1934-68, mng. editor, 1968-75, v.p., exec. editor, 1975—; journalism instr. So. Meth. U., 1947-62. Chmn., Tex. Election Bur. Served with AUS, 1944-46. Mem. Am. Soc. Newspaper Editors, Tex. Asso. Press Mng. Editors Assn. (past pres.). Sigma Delta Chi. Christian Scientist. Clubs: Kiwanian (past pres.), Press of Dallas (past pres.), Northwood, Dallas Knife and Fork (past pres.). Home: 3601 Shenandoah St Dallas TX 75205 Office: care AH Belo Corp Communications Center Dallas TX 75265

SIMMONS, WILLIAM PINCKNEY, banker, mfg. co. exec.; b. Bainbridge, Ga., Dec. 25, 1915; s. John Middleton and Virginia (Ramsay) S.; A.B., Duke, 1937; m. Betty Sweet Smith, Nov. 24, 1937; children—William Pinckney, Betty Sweet (Mrs. William Francis Ladson), Charles Smith. Chmn. bd., pres. First Nat. Bank & Trust Co.; chmn. So. Crate & Veneer Co., Macon, Ga., 1950—; v.p. Elberta Crate & Box Co., Bainbridge, Ga.; dir. Trust Co. of Ga., Atlanta, Trust Co. Bank Atlanta, The Bibb Co., Macon, Trust Co. of Ga. Assos., Atlanta, Ga. So. & Fla. R.R. Co. Treas., Bibb County Bd. Edn., 1942-67; past pres. Central Ga. council Boy Scouts Am., Macon Council on World Affairs; mem. Gov.'s Commn. for Efficiency and Improvement in Govt., 1962-66; chmn. Ga. Adv. Com. on Edn., 1970-72. v.p. Forward Macon. Trustee Emory U., Wesleyan Coll., Macon, Com. for Econ. Devel., N.Y., Walter F. George Found., Mercer U., Macon, Forward Macon, Macon. Recipient Silver Beaver award Boy Scouts Am.; Algernon Sydney Sullivan award. Mem. U.S. (past dir.), Greater Macon (past pres.) chambers commerce, Sigma Nu, Omicron Delta Kappa, Alpha Kappa Psi, Tau Kappa Alpha. Methodist. Rotarian (dist. gov. 1953-54), Elk, Moose. Clubs: Idle Hour Golf and Country (past pres.) (Macon); Piedmont Driving, Commerce (Atlanta). Home: 2694 Stanislaus Circle Macon GA 31204 Office: First Nat Bank & Trust Co Macon GA 31208 also Southern Crate & Veneer Co Macon GA 31208

SIMMS, ARTHUR BENJAMIN, mgmt. cons., financier; b. Atlanta, Sept. 20, 1921; s. Arthur B. and Eva (Hurt) S.; grad. Darlington Sch., 1938; student Ga. Inst. Tech., 1939-40; B.S., U. Pa., 1942; M.B.A., Harvard, 1947; m. Jane Laurice Griffin, Nov. 7, 1953; children—Arthur Benjamin IV, Jane Griffin, Anne Woodruff. Bus. cons. Elec. Bond & Share Co., N.Y.C., 1947-50; pres. A. B. Simms & Assos., mgmt. cons., Atlanta, 1950—; prof. bus. adminstrn. Ga. State U., 1951-52; pres., chmn. bd. Peachtree House, Inc., 1957-65, S. & L. Corp., 1959-62, 1st Atlanta Investment Corp., 1960-65, Consol. Equities Corp., Atlanta, 1965—; dir. 1st Gen. Ins. Co., Atlanta. Trustee Pop Warner Little Scholars, Inc. Served from ensign to lt. USNR, 1942-46; ETO. Mem. Am. Mktg. Assn., Atlanta Apt. Assn. (dir. 1964-65), Nat. (gov. 1963), So. Regional (pres. 1963) assns. small bus. investment cos., Am. Mgmt. Assn., Atlanta C. of C., A.I.M. (mem. pres.'s council), Newcomen Soc. N.Am. (Ga. com.), Sigma Alpha Epsilon (past dir.), Presbyn. (deacon, elder). Kiwanian. Clubs: Breakfast, Harvard Bus. Sch. (past dir.), Piedmont Driving, Capital City (Atlanta); Harvard (N.Y.C.). Home: 195 Valley Rd NW Atlanta GA 30305 Office: 1280 W Peachtree St NW Atlanta GA 30309

SIMMS, LEROY ALANSON, newspaper exec.; b. Emelle, Ala., Sept. 17, 1905; s. John Thomas and Minnie Epes (Thomas) S.; student U. Ill., 1924-25; m. Virginia Hammill, June 30, 1926 (dec.); 1 dau., Lucie Grey (Mrs. Lucie S. Grubbs, dec.); m. 2d, Martha Alice Holliman, May 17, 1969. Reporter, Birmingham (Ala.) News, 1924-26, Tampa (Fla.) Morning Tribune, 1926-27; city editor Birmingham Post, 1927-28, mng. editor, 1929-31; asst. editor Newspaper Enterprise Assn., Cleve., 1931-32; day editor Asso. Press, Birmingham bur., 1933-38, Ala. corr., 1938-58; mng. editor Birmingham News, 1959-61; editor Huntsville (Ala.) Times, 1961—, v.p., dir., 1963—, pub., 1964—. Dir., Huntsville Indsl. Expansion Com., 1966—, v.p., 1966-70, pres., 1970-71. Mem. Am., So. newspaper pubs. assns., Ala. Press Assn. (dir. 1964-66), Ala. A.P. Assn. (pres. 1965-66), Am. Soc. Newspaper Editors, Sigma Delta Chi (chmn. Ala. 1960), Theta Chi. Rotarian. Clubs: Huntsville Country; Valley Hills Country. Author: Road to War: Alabama Leaves the Union, 1960. Home: 1 Cruse Alley SE Huntsville AL 35801 Office: Huntsville Times Memorial Pkwy Huntsville AL 35807

SIMMS, RICHARD LEE, JR., business exec.; b. Atlanta, Nov. 8, 1919; s. Richard Lee and Lois (Beckham) S.; student Ga. Inst. Tech., 1938-41; m. Anne Marie Roney, Oct. 12, 1945; children—Louise LaValle, Deborah Lee, Richard Lee III, Anne Marie. Account exec. Robert E. Martin Co., Atlanta, 1947-48; sales, advt. mgr. Communications Co., Inc., Miami, Fla., 1949-51; account exec. Grizzard Advt., Atlanta, 1951-54; account supr. D'Arcy Advt., Atlanta, 1955-65; exec. v.p., dir. Tucker Wayne & Co., Atlanta, 1965-73, vice chmn., 1973-78; ret., 1978; co-owner, operator S&S Christmas Tree Farm. Chmn. Atlanta Vol. Advt. Com., 1975-76. Served to lt. (s.g.) USNR, 1941-45. Decorated D.F.C. with gold star, Air medal with two gold stars, Purple Heart; lic. real estate agt. Mem. Atlanta Advt. Club (pres.), Alpha Delta Sigma. Clubs: Piedmont Driving (Atlanta); Rotary, Washington-Wilkes Country. Home: Route 1 Danburg GA 30632

SIMMS, ROBERT D., justice Supreme Ct. Okla.; b. Tulsa, Feb. 6, 1926; s. Matthew Scott and Bessie L. (Moore) S.; student Milligan Coll., Phillips U.; LL.B., U. Tulsa; m. Patricia C., Feb. 16, 1950; 1 son, Robert D. Admitted to Okla. bar, 1950; practiced law, Sand Springs, Okla., from 1950; asst. county atty. Tulsa County, 1953-54, chief prosecutor County Atty.'s Office, 1955-58, county atty., 1958-62; judge Okla. Dist. Ct., Dist. 14, 1962-71, Okla. Ct. Criminal Appeals, 1971-72; justice Okla. Supreme Ct., 1972—; mem. Okla. Crime Commn. Mem. Gov.'s Spl. Com. on Drug Abuse, 1970; sponsor and coach Pee-Wee Baseball. Served with USN, 1943-46. Mem. Tulsa County Bar Assn., Okla. Bar Assn. (chmn. dist. atty. sect. 1959). Office: Supreme Ct Okla 202 State Capitol Bldg Oklahoma City OK 73105*

SIMOENS, ALVIN COSMAN, investment co. exec.; b. Nucla, Colo., June 28, 1934; s. Constantine and Vessie Vera (Wilson) S.; B.S. in Elec. Engring., U. Colo., 1959, B.S. in Fin. magna cum laude, 1976, J.D., 1979; m. Earlene Joyce Herman, Feb. 14, 1956; 1 son, Alvin Cosman. Field rep. Philco Corp., Army Air Def. Sch., Ft. Bliss, Tex., 1959-61, New Boston Satellite Tracking Sta., New Boston, N.H., 1961-64; propr. Securities Tng. Inst., Denver, 1964-67; v.p., sec. Westam. Securities, Inc., Denver, 1967—. Served with AUS, 1956-58. Mem. Beta Gamma Sigma. Lion (dir. 1970). Editor The Westamerican and the Best of Westamerica, 1967, 68. Home: 7802 E Hampden Circle Denver CO 80237 Office: Westam Securities 1288 S Lincoln St Denver CO 80210. *Nothing is impossible; there are always ways to lead to everything; and if we had sufficient will we should always have sufficient means.*

SIMOKAITIS, FRANK JOSEPH, air force officer; b. St. Louis, Dec. 12, 1922; s. Frank and Constance (Ladish) S.; student Washington U., St. Louis, 1945-47; LL.B., St. Louis U., 1950, J.D., 1970; m. Mary Jane Feeny; children—Frank, Peggy, Mary. Commd. 2d lt. USAAF, 1943, advanced through grades to maj. gen. USAF, 1973; admitted to Supreme Ct. bar, U.S., 1950, Mo. bar, 1950, also other fed. cts.; plans and operations officer Hdqrs. Pacific Air Force, 1960-63; staff officer Hdqrs. USAF, Washington, 1963-69, exec. asst. to sec. air force, 1969-73; comdt. Air Force Inst. Tech., 1973-78; dir. Dept. Def. affairs Hdqrs. NASA, Washington, 1978—. Bd. dirs. Dayton chpt. ARC. Decorated D.S.M., Legion of Merit, Air medal with 4 oak leaf clusters, Air Force Commendation medal. Mem. Phi Alpha Delta. Clubs: Wright-Patterson AFB Officers'; Moraine Country, One Hundred, Dayton Racquet (Dayton). Home: 4689 S 34th St Arlington VA 22206 Office: Hdqrs NASA Washington DC 20546

SIMON, ABBEY, pianist; b. N.Y.C., Jan. 8, 1922; s. Solomon and Vera (Seldin) S.; grad. Curtis Inst. Music, 1941; m. Dina Levinson, July 28, 1942; 1 son, Jonathan Dean. Concert tours include Australia, Europe, S. Am., Soviet Union, New Zealand, N.Am.; rec. artist Philips, Epic, RCA, HMV, Vox; mem. faculty music Ind., U., Juilliard Sch. Music; Cullen Distinguished prof. U. Houston. Recipient Walter Naumburg Found. award, Nat. Orchestral Assn. award, Fedn. Music Clubs award, Elizabeth Sprague Coolidge medal. Jewish. Club: Lotos (N.Y.C.). Office: care of Shaw Concerts Inc 1995 Broadway New York NY 10023*

SIMON, ALBERT, physicist, educator; b. N.Y.C., Dec. 27, 1924; s. Emanuel D. and Sarah (Leitner) S.; B.S., Coll. City N.Y., 1947; Ph.D., U. Rochester, 1950; m. Harriet E. Rubinstein, Aug. 17, 1947 (dec. June 1970); children—Richard, Janet, David; m. 2d, Rita Shiffman, June 11, 1972. Physicist, Oak Ridge Nat. Lab., 1950-54, asso. dir. neutron physics div., 1954-61; head plasma physics div. Gen. Atomic Co., San Diego, 1961-66; prof. dept. mech. and aerospace scis. U. Rochester (N.Y.), 1966—, prof. physics, 1968—, chmn. dept. mech. and aerospace scis., 1977—; mem. Inst. for Advanced Study, Princeton, 1974-75; sr. vis. fellow U.K. Sci. Research Council, Oxford U., 1975. John Simon Guggenheim fellow, 1964-65. Fellow Am. Phys. Soc. (chmn. plasma physics exec. com. 1963-64); mem. Sigma Xi. Author: An Introduction to Thermonuclear Research, 1959; contbr. to Ency. Americana, 1964, 74. Editor: Advances in Plasma Physics, 1967—. Home: 263 Ashley Dr Rochester NY 14620

SIMON, ALEX JOSEPH, educator, cons., arbitrator; b. Maurice, La., May 22, 1918; s. Leonard Joseph and Elda (Trahan) S.; grad. Lamar Jr. Coll., Beaumont, Tex., 1947; B.B.A., U. Tex., 1950, M.B.A., 1956, Ph.D., 1962; m. Mary E. Benefiel, Dec. 19, 1942; children—Laura Beatrice Kulp, Carolyn Jane Johnson. Labor relations rep. to Ford Motor Co. assembly plant, Kansas City, Mo., 1951-52; personnel mgr. A. Brandt Co., Ft. Worth, 1952; tng. mgr. Day & Zimmermann, Inc., Texarkana, Tex., 1953-54; labor relations mgr. Jonco Aircraft Corp., 1954-55; lectr., dept. mgmt. Coll. Bus. Adminstrn., U. Tex., 1955-57; asst. prof. bus. mgmt. U. Okla., 1957-61; asso. prof. mgmt. Coll. Commerce, U. Southwestern La., 1961-62; asst. prof. mgmt. U. So. Calif., 1962-65; asso. prof. mgmt., asst. dean Sch. Bus., U. Colo., Denver, 1965-68; prof. bus., dir. Bur. Bus. Research, dean Coll. Bus., Idaho State U., Pocatello, 1968-70; prof. bus. adminstrn. U. Miss., 1970-73; prof. bus. adminstrn. Middle Tenn. State U., Murfreesboro, 1974-78, prof. emeritus, 1978—; vis. prof. indsl. relations Auburn (Ala.) U., 1978-79; pres., Indsl. Relations Cons., Inc., 1970—; prin. Simon & Assos., 1979—; labor arbitrator, cons. Served with U.S. Army, 1941-45. Decorated Purple Heart with 2 clusters, Bronze Star, Combat Inf. badge. Mem. D.A.V. (comdr. Austin (Tex.) chpt. 1949-50, Tex. chpt. 1950-51, nat. vice comdr. 1952-53), Am. Legion, Soc. Advancement Mgmt., Am. Arbitration Assn., Am. Soc. Personnel Adminstrn., So. Mgmt. Assn., V.F.W., Ex-students Assn. U. Tex., Acad. Mgmt., Delta Sigma Pi, Beta Alpha Psi, Sigma Iota Epsilon. Democrat. Mason. Contbr. articles. Home: 4001 Chevy Chase Ln Port Arthur TX 77640 Office: PO Box 1116 Port Neches TX 77651. *The greatest reward in life is witnessing the emergence of the youth in today's society; to help them to "become." Man (in the neuter sense) is America's greatest resource. My drive in life has been to help make each of my students a better person; if I have succeeded than I have "emerged."*

SIMON, ARTHUR BERNARD, educator; b. N.Y.C., Jan. 17, 1927; s. Joseph and Bess (Abrams) S.; B.S., St. Louis U., 1949; M.S., U. Miami, 1954; Ph.D., Tulane U., 1957; m. Dolores J. Svehla, July 7, 1951; children—Irene Shelly, Richard William. Instr. Yale, 1957-59; asst. prof. math. Northwestern U., 1959-63, asso. prof., 1963-68, prof., 1968-72; prof. Calif. State U., Hayward, 1972—. Served with AUS, 1944-46. NSF fellow, 1963-64, 70-71. Mem. Am. Math. Soc. Author: Calculus Book, 1970. Contbr. articles to profl. jours. Office: Calif State U Hayward CA 94542

SIMON, CARLY, singer, composer; b. June 25; d. Richard Simon; studied with Pete Seeger; m. James Taylor, 1972; children—Sarah Maria, Benjamin Simon. Singer, composer, rec. artist, 1971—. Recipient Grammy award as best new artist, 1971. Albums include Carly Simon, 1971, Anticipation, 1972, No Secrets, 1973, Hotcakes 1974, Playing Possum, 1975, The Best of Carly Simon, 1975, Another Passenger, 1976, Boys in the Trees, 1978, Spy, 1979; single record Nobody Does It Better, 1977. Address: Arlyne Rothberg Inc 145 Central Park W New York NY 10023

SIMON, CAROLINE KLEIN, lawyer, judge; b. N.Y.C.; d. David and Julia (Feist) Klein; LL.B., N.Y. U.; L.H.D. (hon.), Hebrew Union Coll. Religion, 1966; m. Leopold King Simon (dec. 1952); m. 2d, Irving W. Halpern, July 1, 1953 (dec. Dec. 1966); children—Lee Simon, Cathy Silver. Past mem. N.Y. State Commn. Against Discrimination; publicist and journalist; expert in field crime prevention and problems of women's and children's courts; former commr. N.Y. State Youth Commn.; former dir. group activities 2d Def. Area, Office Civil Def.; past mem. Workmen's Compensation Bd. N.Y. State; mem. Com. on Discrimination in Employment, State War Council; legal adviser U.S. delegation 14th session UN Human Rights Commn.; sec. of state N.Y., 1959-63; judge N.Y. State Ct. Claims, 1963-71; counsel firm Surrey, Karasik, Morse & Seham, 1970-77; individual practice, 1977—; chmn. subcom. on jury 1st and 2d depts. Appellate Div. N.Y. State Supreme Ct.; mem. med. malpractice mediation 2d Jud. Dept.; legal adviser U.S. delegation UN Human Rights Commn., 1958; mem. N.Y. State Youth Commn., 1956-59, N.Y. State Commn. on Discrimination, 1945-55. Mem. Joint Legis. Com. on Ct. Reorgn.; chmn. lawyers com. Community Service Soc.; Republican candidate for pres. N.Y.C. Council, 1957. Trustee and asst. treas. Freedom House, v.p. Willkie Meml. Bldg.; bd. dirs., mem. exec. com. Com. for Modern Cts.; U.S.O. of N.Y. Recipient Woman of Year award Women's Expn., 1957, presdl. citation N.Y. U., 1962. Mem. N.Y. County Lawyers Assn. (profl. ethics com., forum and practical edn. com.), Assn. Bar City N.Y. (com. on profl. responsibity), Internat., Am. (spl. com. on no-fault automobile ins. legislation, past mem. spl. com. on crime prevention and control adv. com.), N.Y. State (com. cts. and the community, com. on centennial) bar assns., Nat. Council on Crime and Delinquency (past chmn. bd.), Nat. Jewish Welfare Bd., Am. Jewish Com. (life mem. exec. bd., adminstrv. com.), Jewish Bd. Guardians and Family Service Assn. (hon. trustee, exec. com., chmn. com. pub. interest and social responsibility), Nat. Conf. Christians and Jews, World Habeas Corpus (exec. com.), Am. Arbitration Assn. (mem. panel, mem. arbitrator roster), Delta Kappa Gamma (hon.). Home: 200 E 66th St New York NY 10021 Office: 500 Fifth Ave New York NY 10036

SIMON, CHARLES JACOB, investment banker; b. N.Y.C., Nov. 19, 1911; s. Joseph and Nettye (Levy) S.; student Coll. William and Mary, Williamsburg, Va., 1929-30, N.Y. U. Grad. Sch. Bus., eves. 1945-65; widower; 1 dau., Patricia. With Salomon Bros., N.Y.C., 1930—, partner, 1946-76, limited partner, 1977—, mem. adminstrv. com., 1958-76. Trustee Animal Med. Center, Museum Am. Indian, New Sch. for Social Research; treas. Whitney Mus. Am. Art; bd. dirs. YM-YWHA; mem. investment adv. com. N.Y. State Tchrs. Retirement System. Mem. N.Y. State Bankers Assn. (chmn. investment seminars, mem. council adminstrn. 1950-60), Money Marketeers (pres. 1965), Phi Alpha Kappa. Jewish. Clubs: Beach Point, City Athletic, Ocean Reef. Home: 190 E 72d St New York NY 10021 Office: 1 New York Plaza New York NY 10004

SIMON, DAVID, lawyer; b. Bklyn., Apr. 20, 1924; s. Solomon and Lena (Fisher) S.; B.A., Cornell U., 1944; LL.B. magna cum laude, Harvard, 1950; m. Deborah Sheen, June 29, 1969; children—Michael, S. Andrew. Russian editor USIS, Dept. State, 1947, 51; law clk. Judge Augustus N. Hand, 1950-51; admitted to N.Y. State bar, 1952; asso. Barrett Smith Schapiro Simon & Armstrong, and predecessor firms, N.Y.C., 1952-57, partner, 1958—; vis. lectr. law Yale Law Sch., 1972-73; lectr. Practising Law Inst., Am. Mgmt. Assn. Served to 1st lt. AUS, 1943-46. Recipient Sears prize Harvard Law Sch., 1948, 49. Mem. Am., N.Y. State (chmn. com. on internat. taxation 1966-68) bar assns., Assn. Bar City N.Y., Phi Beta Kappa, Phi Kappa Phi. Jewish religion. Staff editor Amerika mag., 1947, 51. Note editor Harvard Law Rev., 1949-50. Co-translator: The Wandering Beggar, 1942; The Wise Men of Helm, 1945. Home: 1120 Park Ave New York NY 10028 Office: 26 Broadway New York NY 10004

SIMON, DOLPH B(ERTRAM) H(IRST), lawyer, jewelry co. exec.; b. Dallas, Mar. 20, 1933; s. Bertram H. and Leta P. Simon; B.B.A., U. Tex., 1954, J.D., 1958; m. Nancy Carlson, Dec. 2, 1972; children—Debbie, Dolph, Terri, Beau, Lindsey, Carey. Admitted to Tex. bar, 1957; atty. SEC, Washington, 1962-64; asso. firm Turner, Atwood, Meer & Francis, Dallas, 1964-67; partner firm Meer, Chandler, Simon & Bates, Dallas, 1967-70, Tobolowsky & Schlinger, Dallas, 1970-78; sr. v.p., gen. counsel Zale Corp., Dallas, 1978—. Served with USAF, 1955-57. Mem. Am. Bar Assn., State Bar Tex., Dallas Bar Assn. Jewish. Office: 3000 Diamond Park Dr Dallas TX 75247

SIMON, DOROTHY MARTIN, chemist, bus. exec.; b. Harwood, Mo., Sept. 18, 1919; d. Robert William and Laudell (Flynn) Martin; A.B., S.W. Mo. State U., 1940; Ph.D., U. Ill., 1945; postdoctoral work Cambridge (Eng.) U., 1953-54; Sc.D. (hon.), Worcester Poly. Inst., 1971; D.Eng. (hon.), Lehigh U., 1978; m. Sidney L. Simon, Dec. 6, 1946 (dec. Nov. 26, 1975). Grad. teaching asst. U. Ill., 1941-45; research chemist rayon div. E. I. Du Pont de Nemours & Co., Inc., Buffalo, 1945-47; chemist Oak Ridge Nat. Lab., 1947; asso. chemist Argonne (Ill.) Nat. Lab., 1948-49; aero. research scientist, group leader NACA, Cleve., 1949-53, asst. br. chief chemistry, 1954-55; group leader combustion fundamentals Magnolia Petroleum Co. subs. Mobil Corp., Dallas, 1955-56; prin. scientist, tech. asst. to pres. research and advanced devel. div. Avco Corp., Greenwich, Conn., 1956-62, dir. corp. research def. and indsl. products group, 1962-64, group v.p. Avco Corp., 1964-68, corp. v.p. research, 1968—; Marie Curie lectr. State U. Pa., 1962; dir. Conn. Nat. Bank, Crown Zellerbach Corp.; mem. Pres.'s Com. on Nat. Medal Sci., 1979-81; mem. space systems and tech. adv. com. NASA; mem. NSF panel sci. and tech., 1973—; mem. adv. vis. com. Nat. Bur. Standards, 1979—; vis. com. aeros. and astronautics M.I.T., 1980—. Trustee, Worcester Poly. Inst.; mem. vis. com. sponsored research Mass. Inst. Tech., 1972-78; mem. overseers' com. for applied research Harvard U. Recipient Rockefeller Pub. Service award, 1953, Outstanding Alumnus award S.W. Mo. State U., 1957, Outstanding Profl. Woman award Bus., Profl. Women's Club N.Y., 1966. Fellow Am. Inst. Chemists; mem. Am. Chem. Soc., Internat. Combustion Inst., AIAA (chmn. sect. 1977-79, nat. dir. 1979—), Soc. Woman Engrs. (Achievement award 1966), Sigma Xi. Contbr. articles to profl. jours. and collected symposia books. Home: 69 Londonderry Dr Greenwich CT 06830 Office: 1275 King St Greenwich CT 06830

SIMON, ECKEHARD (PETER), educator; b. Schneidemühl, Germany, Jan. 5, 1939; s. Herbert and Doris (Keiler) S.; came to U.S., 1955, naturalized, 1960; A.B., Columbia U., 1960; A.M., Harvard U., 1961, Ph.D., 1964; m. Eileen Higginbottom, Dec. 19, 1959; children—Anders, Conrad, Matthew, Frederick. Instr., German Harvard, Cambridge, Mass., 1964-65, asst. prof., 1965-69, asso. prof., 1969-71, prof., 1971—, head tutor and lang. coordinator, 1965-76, chmn. dept. German, 1976—. Woodrow Wilson fellow, 1960-61; Nat. Endowment for the Humanities Younger Scholar fellow, 1968-69, research fellow, 1977-78; Guggenheim fellow, 1968-69. Mem. Am. Assn. Tchrs. German, Medieval Acad. Am., Modern Lang. Assn. Am. Author: Neidhart von Reuental: Geschichte der Forschung und Bibliographie, 1968; Neidhart von Reuental, 1975. Contbr. articles to profl. jours. Home: 120 Highland Ave Arlington MA 02174 Office: Boylston Hall Harvard University Cambridge MA 02138

SIMON, ERIC JACOB, neurochemist; b. Wiesbaden, Germany, June 2, 1924; s. Joseph and Paula (Meyer) S.; came to U.S., 1938, naturalized, 1945; B.S., Case-Western Res. U., 1944; M.S., U. Chgo., 1947, Ph.D., 1951; m. Irene M. Ronis, Aug. 9, 1947; children—Martin A., Faye Ruth, Lawrence D. Postdoctoral trainee in biochemistry Columbia U. Coll. Physicians and Surgeons, 1951-53; lectr. in chemistry Coll. City N.Y., 1952-59; research asso. Cornell U. Med. Coll., 1953-59; asst. prof. medicine N.Y. U. Med. Center, 1959-64, asso. prof. exptl. medicine, 1964-72, prof. exptl. medicine, 1972-80, prof. psychiatry and pharmacology, 1980—; mem. initial rev. com. Nat. Inst. Drug Abuse, 1976-80, chmn., 1979-80; Sterling-Winthrop lectr. Albany Med. Coll., 1977. Trustee, Teaneck (N.J.) Bd. Edn., 1975-79. Served with U.S. Army, 1944-46. Recipient Research Pace Setter award Nat. Inst. Drug Abuse, 1977; Health Research Council N.Y.C. career scientist, 1959-75. Fellow AAAS, N.Y. Acad. Scis.; mem. Am. Soc. Biol. Chemists, Am. Soc. Neurochemistry, Am. Soc. Pharmacology, Internat. Soc. Neurochemistry, Am. Chem. Soc., Sigma Xi. Club: B'nai B'rith. Research, publs. on opiate receptors, endorphins, biochemistry of analgesic action, vitamin E metabolism, acyl-coenzyme A synthesis. Home: 375 Edgewood Ave Teaneck NJ 07666 Office: 550 1st Ave New York NY 10016

SIMON, ERNEST ROBERT, physician, govt. ofcl.; b. Karlsruhe, Germany, June 24, 1929; s. Frederick David and Hedwig (Michel) S.; came to U.S., 1938, naturalized, 1944; student U. Calif. Berkeley, 1947-50; M.D. cum laude, Harvard, 1954; m. Eve Renee Maier, June 28, 1953; children—Carol, Lori, Renee. Intern Boston City Hosp., II and IV Med. Services (Harvard), 1954-55; resident Stanford U. Hosps., 1955-56; clin. asso. NIH, 1956-58; Helen Hay Whitney research fellow in biochemistry, Bethesda, Md., 1958-59; hematology research fellow U. Wash. Sch. Medicine, Seattle, 1959-61, asst. prof. medicine, 1961-63; mem. faculty U. N.Mex. Sch. Medicine, Albuquerque, 1963-74, prof. medicine, 1969-74; dir. div. blood diseases and resources Nat. Heart and Lung Inst., NIH, Bethesda, Md., 1973-76; dep. dir. div. blood and blood products Bur. Biologics FDA, Bethesda, 1976—; prof. medicine George Washington U. Sch. Medicine, Washington, 1973—; U.S.A. coordinator U.S.A.-USSR Health Exchange in Blood Transfusion, 1973—. Mem. hematology study sect. NIH, 1966-70, cons. Nat. Blood Resources Program, also rep. for implementation nat. blood policy, 1973—; State Dept. observer to Council Europe com. of specialists on blood transfusion and immunohematology, 1975—. Served as sr. asst. surgeon USPHS, 1956-58, med. dir., 1973—. Named Outstanding Faculty Mem., U. N.Mex. Sch. Medicine, 1970. Fellow A.C.P.: Mem. Am. Soc. Clin. Investigation, Western Soc. Clin. Research (councilor), Am. Soc. Hematology, Phi Beta Kappa, Alpha Omega Alpha. Author: Red Cell Manual, 3d edit., 1966. Mem. editorial bd. Transfusion, 1967—, Am. Jour. Physiology, 1968-70, Jour. of Applied Physiology, 1968-70. Contbr. articles to profl. jours. Home: 7015 Oak Forest Ln Bethesda MD 20034

SIMON, GEORGE THOMAS, author, jazz critic, producer; b. N.Y.C., May 9, 1912; s. Leo L. and Anna (Mayer) S.; grad. Fieldston Sch., N.Y.C., 1930; A.B., Harvard, 1934; m. Beverly Alt, Nov. 6, 1947; children—Julie A., Thomas G. With Metronome mag., 1935-55, Introducing pioneer dance band revs. and serving as editor, 1939-55; writer, asst. to producer Jackie Gleason America's Greatest Bands series, other TV shows, 1955-56; program dir. Jazztone Soc., 1956-57; pres. Bouree Prodns., Inc., ind. rec. producers and cons., 1958-60, Bouree Enterprises, Ltd., 1958-60; exec. dir. Nat. Acad. Rec. Arts and Scis., 1961-72, cons., 1972—. Mem. bd. advisers Newport Jazz Festival, TV series; writer asso. producer Timex All Star Jazz TV shows, Sammy Kaye, 1958-59; The Swinging Years, The Singing Swinging Years (NBC-TV), 1960; idea man Play Your Hunch, 1962; asso. producer, talent coordinator The Best on Record, TV spls., 1963-67; music cons. ABC-TV music spls., 1966-68, Time-Life Records, 1970-72, 78-79, Timex All-Star Swing Festival, 1972. Served with AUS, World War II; mem. Glenn Miller Band, later rec. chief V Discs. Recipient Grammy award for best album notes, 1978. Mem. ASCAP, Writers Guild. Author: Don Watson Starts His Band, 1940; (also photographer) The Bandleader, 1950; (songs) Mother Goose for the Swing Set, 1958; The Feeling of Jazz, 1961; The Big Bands, 1967 (1st prize A.S.C.A.P.-Deems Taylor award 1968), rev., enlarged edit., 1971, 74; The Sinatra Report, 1965; Simon Says: The Sights and Sounds of The Swing Era, 1971; Glenn Miller and his Orchestra, 1974; The Big Bands Songbook, 1975; editor revision The World of Jazz, 1975; producer jazz recs. for RCA Victor, Warner Bros., Golden Records, Grand Award, Fantasy, Everest, Capitol, Columbia, 20th Century-Fox, and others. Regular commentator on jazz N.Y. Herald Tribune, 1961-64; contbr. articles on jazz to N.Y. Times, Cosmopolitan, Esquire, Downbeat, Mademoiselle. Home: 34 Overbrook Dr Stamford CT 06906 Office: 21 W 58th St New York NY 10019

SIMON, HERBERT ALEXANDER, social scientist; b. Milw., June 15, 1916; s. Arthur and Edna (Merkel) S.; A.B., U. Chgo., 1936, Ph.D., 1943, LL.D., 1964; D.Sc., Case Inst. Tech., 1963, Yale U., 1963; Fil. Dr., Lund U., Sweden, 1968; LL.D., McGill U., 1970, U. Mich., 1978, U. Pitts., 1979; Dr. Econ. Sci., Erasmus U. Rotterdam (Netherlands), 1973; m. Dorothea Pye, Dec. 25, 1937; children—Katherine (Mrs. David L. Frank), Peter Arthur, Barbara. Research asst. U. Chgo., 1936-38; staff mem., Internat. City Mgrs.' Assn., also asst. editor Pub. Mgmt. and Municipal Year Book, 1938-39; dir. adminstrv. measurement studies Bur. Pub. Adminstrn., U. Calif., 1939-42; asst. prof. polit. sci. Ill. Inst. Tech., 1942-45, asso. prof., 1945-47, prof., 1947-49; also chmn. dept. polit. and social sci., 1946-49; prof. adminstrn. and psychology Carnegie-Mellon U., Pitts., 1949-65, Richard King Mellon univ. prof. computer scis. and psychology, 1965—, head dept. indsl. mgmt. 1949-60, asso. dean Grad. Sch. Indsl. Adminstrn., 1957-73, trustee, 1972—; cons. to Internat. City Mgrs. Assn., 1942-49, U.S. Bur. Budget, 1946-49, U.S. Census Bur., 1947, Cowles Found. for Research in Econs., 1947-60; cons. and acting dir. Mgmt. Engring. br. Econ. Cooperation Adminstrn., 1948; Ford Distinguished lectr. N.Y. U., 1959; Vanuxem lectr. Princeton, 1961; William James lectr. Harvard, 1963, Sigma Xi lectr., 1964, 76-78; Harris lectr. Northwestern U., 1967; Karl Taylor Compton lectr. Mass. Inst. Tech., 1968; Wolfgang Koehler lectr. Dartmouth, 1975; Katz-Newcomb lectr. U. Mich., 1976; Carl Hovland lectr. Yale, 1976; Ueno lectr., Tokyo, 1977; chmn. bd. dirs. Social Sci. Research Council, 1961-65; chmn. div. behavioral scis. NRC, 1968-70; mem. President's Sci. Adv. Com., 1968-71; cons. bus. and govtl. orgns. Chmn. Pa. Gov.'s Milk Inquiry Com., 1964-65. Recipient adminstrs. award Am. Coll. Hosp. Adminstrs., 1957; Frederick Mosher award Am. Soc. Pub. Adminstrn., 1974; Alfred Nobel Meml. prize in econ. scis., 1978. Distinguished fellow Am. Econ. Assn. (Ely lectr. 1977); fellow Econometric Soc., AAAS, Am. Acad. Arts and Scis., Am. Psychol. Assn. (Disting. Sci. Contbn. award 1969), Am. Sociol. Soc.; mem. Inst. Mgmt. Scis. (v.p. 1954), Am. Polit. Sci. Assn., Assn. for Computing Machinery (A.M. Turing award 1975), Nat. Acad. Scis. (mem. com. sci. and pub. policy 1967-69, chmn. com. air quality control 1974; chmn. com. behavioral scis. NSF 1975-76, mem. council 1978—), Soc. Exptl. Psychologists, Am. Philos. Soc., Royal Soc. Letters (Lund) (fgn. mem.), Orgnl. Sci. Soc. (Japan) (hon.), Phi Beta Kappa, Sigma Xi. Democrat. Unitarian. Clubs: Cosmos (Washington); University (Pitts.). Author or co-author books relating to field, including: Administrative Behavior, 1947, 3d edit., 1976; Public Administration, 1950; Models of Man, 1956; Organizations, 1958; New Science of Management Decision, 1960, rev. edit., 1977; The Shape of Automation, 1965; The Sciences of the Artificial, 1968; Human Problem Solving, 1972; Skew Distributions and Business Firm Sizes, 1976; Models of Discovery, 1977; Models of Thought, 1979. Home: 5818 Northumberland St Pittsburgh PA 15217

SIMON, JACK AARON, state ofcl.; b. Champaign, Ill., June 17, 1919; s. Abraham and Lenore (Levy) S.; B.A., U. Ill., 1941, M.S., 1946; postgrad. Northwestern U., 1947-49. Tech. and research asst. Ill. State Geol. Survey, Urbana, 1937-42, asst. to asso. geologist, 1945-53, geologist, head, coal sect., 1953-67, prin. geologist, 1967-74, asst. chief, 1973-74, chief, 1974—; occasional cons.; asso. prof. dept. metallurgy and mining engring. U. Ill., 1967-74, prof., 1974-77, adj. prof. dept. geology, 1979—. Served with F.A., AUS, 1942-43, USAAF, 1943-45. Decorated Air medal with 4 oak leaf clusters. Fellow AAAS, Geol. Soc. Am. (chmn. coal geology div. 1962-63, Gilbert H. Cady award 1975, mem. council 1979—); mem. Am. Assn. Petroleum Geologists, Am. Inst. Mining, Metall. and Petroleum Engrs. (chmn. Midwest coal sect. 1966), Am. Inst. Profl. Geologists (v.p. 1973), Am. Mining Congress, Ill. Mining Inst. (hon. life; exec. sec.-treas. 1963-68), Ill. Soc. Coal Preparation Engrs. and Chemists, Ill. Geol. Soc., Ill. Acad. Sci., Soc. Econ. Geologists, Soc. Econ. Paleontologists and Mineralogists, Sigma Xi. Mem. B'nai B'rith. Club: Exchange (Urbana, pres. 1969). Home: 502 W Oregon Urbana IL 61801 Office: Ill State Geol Survey 121 Natural Resources Bldg Urbana IL 61801

SIMON, JOANNA, singer; b. N.Y.C., Oct. 20, 1940; d. Richard Leo and Andrea S.; B.A., Sarah Lawrence Coll., m. Gerald R. Walker, Dec. 4, 1976. Appeared with maj. opera cos. in U.S. and Europe, including cos. of Washington, Seattle, Balt., Phila.; mem. N.Y.C. Opera; appeared with Salzburg (Austria) Festival, and Teatro Colon, Buenos Aires, Argentina; regular appearances as guest soloist with maj. U.S. orchs., including N.Y. Philharmonic, Chgo. Symphony, Boston Symphony, Phila. Orch. Office: care Herbert H Breslin Inc 119 W 57th St New York NY 10019

SIMON, JOEL NORMAN, lawyer; b. Chgo., Aug. 18, 1936; s. Daniel Merrill and Sylvia (Riskind) S.; B.S. in Acctg. with high honors, U. Ill., 1957; J.D., U. Mich., 1960; m. Joan Susan Berman, June 21, 1959; children—Marcia Jill, Roger Neil, Jeremy Scott. Admitted to D.C. bar, 1960; atty. tax civ. Dept. Justice, 1960-62; asso. firm Arent, Fox, Kintner, Plotkin & Kahn, Washington, 1962-69, partner, 1969—; lectr. Catholic U. Am. Law Sch., 1962-63; lectr. continuing legal edn. programs in estate planning Am. Law Inst.-Am. Bar Assn. Bd. dirs. Nat. Child Day Care Assn., 1964—. Mem. Am. Bar Assn., Fed. Bar Assn. Club: Nat. Lawyers (Washington). Home: 6404 Danville Ct Rockville MD 20852 Office: 1815 H St NW Washington DC 20006

SIMON, JOHN BERN, lawyer; b. Cleve., Aug. 8, 1942; s. Seymour Frank and Roslyn (Schultz) S.; B.S., U. Wis.-Madison, 1964; J.D., DePaul U., 1967; m. Lynda Lou Cohn, Aug. 11, 1966; children—Lindsey Helaine, Douglas Banning. Admitted to Ill. bar, 1967; asst. U.S. atty. U.S. Justice Dept., Chgo., 1967-70, dep. chief civil div., 1970-71, chief civil div., 1971-74; spl. counsel to dir. Ill. Dept. Pub. Aid, Chgo., 1974-75; legal cons. to Commn. on Rev. of Nat. Policy Toward Gambling, Chgo., 1975-76; partner firm Friedman and Koven, 1975—; spl. cons. to adminstr. Drug Enforcement Adminstrn. Dept. Justice, 1976-77; counsel to Gov.'s Revenue Study Commn. on Legalized Gambling, 1977-78; spl. counsel Ill. Racing Bd., 1979—; lectr. tng. seminars and confs.; instr. U.S. Atty. Gen.'s Advocacy Inst., Washington, 1974; lectr. Nat. Conf. Organized Crime, Washington, 1975; faculty Cornell Inst. Organized Crime, Ithaca, N.Y., 1976; judge Miner Moot Ct. competition Northwestern U., 1971-73; mem. law council DePaul U., 1974—, chmn., 1975-79, instr. Coll. Law, 1977—. Mem. exec. com. govt. agys. Jewish United Fund, 1973-75, chmn., 1975, mem. gen. gifts com. lawyers div., 1976—; bd. dirs. Community Film Workshop of Chgo., 1977—; bd. dirs. Friends of Glencoe Parks, 1977-78, sec., 1978—; mem. nominating com. Glencoe Sch. Bd., 1978—; pres. Glencoe Hist. Soc., 1979—. Recipient Bancroft-Whitney Am. Jurisprudence award, 1965, 66. Mem. Am., Ill., Chgo. bar assns., Ill. Police Assn., U.S. Treasury Agts. Assn., Alpha Epsilon Pi. Clubs: Chgo. Justice Lodge, B'nai B'rith (dir. 1975-77), Standard (Chgo.). Contbr. articles to profl. jours. Office: 208 S LaSalle St 900 Chicago IL 60604

SIMON, JOHN GERALD, legal educator; b. N.Y.C., Sept. 1928; s. Robert Alfred and Madeleine (Marshall) S.; grad. Ethical Culture Schs., 1946; A.B., Harvard U., 1950; LL.B., Yale U., 1953; m. Claire Aloise Bising, June 14, 1958; 1 son, John Kirby. Admitted to N.Y. bar, 1953; asst. to gen. counsel Office Sec. Army, 1956-58; with firm Paul, Weiss, Rifkind, Wharton & Garrison, N.Y.C., 1958-62; mem. faculty Yale Law Sch., 1962—, prof. law, 1967-76, Augustus Lines prof. law, 1976—, dir. program on non-profit orgns. Yale U., 1977—. Pres. Taconic Found., 1967—. Trustee, sec. Potomac Inst., 1961—; mem. grad. bd. Harvard Crimson, 1950—; chmn. bd. dirs. Coop. Assistance Fund, 1970-76, vice chmn., 77—. Served to 1st lt. U.S. Army, 1953-56. Recipient Certificate of Achievement, Dept. Army, 1956. Mem. Phi Beta Kappa. Clubs: Century, Harvard (N.Y.C.). Author: (with Powers and Gunnemann) The Ethical Investor, 1972. Office: Yale Law Sch Yale Univ New Haven CT 06520

SIMON, JOHN IVAN, film and drama critic; b. Subotica, Yugoslavia, May 12, 1925; s. Joseph and Margaret (Reves) Simmon; came to U.S., 1941; A.B., Harvard U., 1946, A.M., 1948, Ph.D., 1959. Teaching fellow Harvard U., 1950-53; instr. U. Wash., 1953-54, Mass. Inst. Tech., 1954-55; asst. prof. Bard Coll., 1957-59; asso. editor Mid-Century Book Soc., 1959-61; drama critic The Hudson Rev., 1960—, Theater Arts mag., 1962; drama and film critic The New Leader, 1962-73, 75-77, cultural critic, 1974—; drama critic WNET-TV, 1963, Commonweal, 1967-68; drama critic New York mag., 1968-75, 77—, film critic, 1975-77; film critic Esquire, 1973-75, lang. critic, 1977—; film critic Nat. Rev., 1977—; guest prof. U. Pitts., lectr. in field. Served with USAF, 1944-45. Recipient George Polk Meml. award in film criticism, 1968; George Jean Nathan award for dramatic criticism, 1969-70; Lit. award Am. Acad. Arts and Letters, 1976; Fulbright fellow U. Paris, 1949-50. Mem. P.E.N., N.Y. Drama Critics Circle, N.Y. Film Critics Circle. Author: Acid Test, 1963; Private Screenings, 1967; Movies into Film, 1971; Ingmar Bergman Directs, 1972; Uneasy Stages, 1976; Singularities, 1976; editor Film 67/68, 1968; (with Richard Schickel) Fourteen for Now, 1969. Office: New York Mag 755 2d Ave New York NY 10017*

SIMON, JOHN JACOB, pub. co. exec.; b. N.Y.C., Oct. 30, 1934; s. Abraham I. and Jeannette (Feldman) S.; B.A., Bard Coll., 1956. Editor, Basic Books, N.Y.C., 1960, Alfred A. Knopf, N.Y.C., 1961-62, World Pub. Co., N.Y.C., 1962-64, Premier Books, Fawcett Publs., N.Y.C., 1964-65; sr. editor Random House, N.Y.C., 1965-74, exec. editor Vintage and Modern Library Books, Random House, 1966-71, exec. editor internat., 1971-74; founder, dir. Ramp Co., pubs., 1974—; sr. editor McGraw-Hill Book Co., 1974-76; exec. editor Quadrangle, N.Y. Times Book Co., 1976-79; editorial dir. Schocken Books, Inc., N.Y.C., 1979—. Bd. dirs. Pacifica Found., 1964-66; mem. adv. bd. L.M. Rabinowitz Found. Inc. Office: care Schocken Books Inc 200 Madison Ave New York NY 10016

SIMON, JOHN KENNETH, educator; b. N.Y.C., Dec. 23, 1935; s. Jack Horace, and Marian (Frank) S.; B.A. in French and English, Yale, 1956. Ph.D. in Comparative Lit., 1963; student U. Paris (France), 1954-55, 56-57; m. Jacqueline Chalaire, Sept. 6, 1957; children—Julie, Marc. Asst. instr. French, Yale, 1957-59, instr., 1959-61, 62-63; asst. prof. French and English, U. Ill., Urbana, 1963-66, asso. prof., 1966-69; prof. French State U. N.Y., Buffalo, 1969—, chmn. dept. French, 1969-75. French govt. grantee, 1956-57, 67; Am. Philos. Soc. grantee, 1964. Home: 217 High Park Blvd Eggertsville NY 14226

SIMON, JOSEPH PATRICK, food services exec.; b. Phila., Nov. 9, 1932; s. Joseph Patrick and Elizabeth Gertrude (McLaughlin) S.; B.S., Cornell U., 1955; m. Vera Cornelia Steiner, Sept. 15, 1956; children—Joseph Walter, Walter Joseph, Leslie Vera, Ernest William. With Slater Systems, 1955-59; with ARA Services, Inc., Phila., 1959-72, regional v.p., 1964-66, area v.p., 1966-68, group v.p. and sr. v.p., 1968-70, pres. community and school food service div., 1970-71, gen. mgr. internat. ops., 1971-72; v.p., gen. mgr. airline services div. Dobbs Houses Inc., Memphis, 1972-73; group v.p. Service Systems Corp., Buffalo, 1973—, also nat. dir. Dist. chmn. Detroit United Fund, 1966-67, Nat. Alliance of Businessmen, 1969. Mem. adv. bd. McComb Jr. Coll. Served as 1st lt., U.S. Army, 1955-56. Mem. Assn. Food Service Mgmt. (dir.), Cornell Hotel Soc. Mich. (pres.), Zeta Psi. Episcopalian. Club: Memphis Athletic; Detroit Athletic; Park Country (Buffalo). Home: 382 Dan Troy Dr Williamsville NY 14221 Office: PO Box 352] Buffalo NY 14240

SIMON, JULIAN LINCOLN, educator; b. Newark, Feb. 12, 1932; s. Philip Mordechai and Mae (Goodstein) S.; B.A., Harvard U., 1953; M.B.A., U. Chgo., 1960, Ph.D., 1961; m. Rita Mintz James, June 25, 1961; children—David Meyer, Judith Debs, Daniel Hillel. Advt. copywriter William Douglas McAdams, Inc., N.Y.C., 1956; sales promotion Ziff-Davis Pub. Co., N.Y.C., 1957-61; owner Julian Simon Assos., Newark, 1961-63; prof. econs., mktg. and advt. U. Ill., Urbana, 1963—; first Lipson prof. internat. mktg. Hebrew U., Jerusalem, 1970-71. Served to lt. (j.g.) USN, 1953-56. Mem. Am. Econ. Assn., Am. Mktg. Assn., Population Assn. Am. Jewish religion. Author: How to Start and Operate a Mail-Order Business, 1965, 2d edit., 1976; Basic Research Methods in Social Science, 1969, 2d edit., 1978; (with Herman H. Fussler) Patterns of Use of Books in Large Research Libraries, 1969; Issues in the Economics of Advertising, 1970; The Management of Advertising, 1971; The Effects of Income on Fertility, 1974; Applied Managerial Economics, 1975; The Economics of Population Growth, 1977. Home: 1105 S Busey Ave Urbana IL 61801

SIMON, LEE WILL, astronomer; b. Evanston, Ill., Feb. 18, 1940; s. Clarence Turkle and Dorothy Elizabeth (Will) S.; B.A., Northwestern U., 1962, M.S., 1964, Ph.D. in Astronomy, 1972; m. Mary Jo Welsh, Feb. 19, 1966; children—John, Dan, Steve. Staff astronomer, program supr. Adler Planetarium, Chgo., 1969-77; dir. Morrison Planetarium, Calif. Acad. Scis., San Francisco, 1977—. Mem. AAAS, Am. Astron. Soc., Royal Astron Soc., Internat. Planetarium Soc., Sigma Xi. Presbyterian. Home: 245 San Marin Dr Novato CA 94947 Office: Morrison Planetarium Calif Acad Scis Golden Gate Park San Francisco CA 94118

SIMON, LEONARD SAMUEL, banker; b. N.Y.C., Oct. 28, 1936; s. Nathaniel and Lena (Pasternack) S.; B.S., M.I.T., 1958; M.S., Columbia U., 1959, Ph.D., 1963; m. Marion Appel, Sept. 1, 1957; children—Andrew, Jonathan. Mem. faculty Grad. Sch. Mgmt., U. Rochester, 1962-79, prof., 1974-79; v.p. Community Savs. Bank, Rochester, N.Y., 1969-74, sr. v.p., 1974-77, exec. v.p., 1977—; chmn. Telephone Computing Service Corp., 1974-79. Chmn., Rochester-Monroe County chpt. ARC, 1979—; vice chmn. Rochester Area Ednl. TV Assn., 1979—; mem. Women's Career Center Adv. Council, 1978—; mem. Urban Policy Conf., Brookings Instn.,

1972-73. Ford Found. grantee, 1964. Mem. Inst. Mgmt. Scis., Am. Mktg. Assn., Savs. Bank Assn. N.Y. State, Nat. Assn. Mut. Savs. Banks, Beta Gamma Sigma. Club: Ski Valley. Editor-in-chief, founding editor Interfaces, 1970-76. Author books in field. Office: 235 Main St E Rochester NY 14618

SIMON, LOTHAR, pub. co. exec.; b. Wuppertal, Germany, Sept. 17, 1938; s. Fritz and Erna (Backhaus) S.; came to U.S., 1961, naturalized, 1973; m. Jeannine Rechtman, Oct. 30, 1964; 1 son, Charles. Mgr. book dept. Franz Bader Book Shop and Globe Book Shop, Washington, 1961-66; sales mgr. Humanities Press Inc., N.Y.C., 1966-73; pres. Longman Inc., N.Y.C., 1973—. Mem. Am. Med. Pubs. Assn., Assn. Am. Pubs. Democrat. Home: 230 Nelson Rd Scarsdale NY 10583 Office: Longman Inc 19 W 44th St New York NY 10036

SIMON, MAX MICHAEL, surgeon; b. Poughkeepsie, N.Y.; s. Isaac and Goldie (Katz) S.; B.S., Union Coll., 1921; M.D., Cornell U., 1925; m. Zerline Lehman, Nov. 18, 1928 (dec. 1962); children—Georgene (Mrs. Irving Dreishpoon), Babette (Mrs. Seymour Stall), Fredrica (Mrs. Jack Goodman). Mem. house staff Hosp. for Joint Diseases, N.Y.C., 1925-26; house surgeon Lebanon Hosp., N.Y.C., 1926-28; jr. surgeon St. Francis Hosp., Poughkeepsie, 1928-32, sr. surgeon, 1932-38, chief of staff, 1938-39, sr. attending surgeon, 1939—, mem. med. bd.; cons. surgeon Highland Hosp., Matteawan State Hosp., Harlem Valley-State Hosp., Wingdale, N.Y., 1957—. Served with F.A., U.S. Army, 1917-18; commd. 1st lt. Med. O.R.C., 1925. Diplomate Internat. Bd. Surgery, 1952. Fellow A.C.S. (internat. bd. govs. 1958—), Internat. Coll. Surgeons (pres. Hudson Valley Guild 1941—, vice regent 1954, essayist, panelist on goiter surgery various congresses, pres. N.Y. surg. sect. 1956, mem. credentials and adv. bd., gov.), Am. Jewish Physicians Com. (nat. dir.), Roman Coll. Surgeons (hon.), Madrid Coll. Surgeons (hon.), Miss. Valley Med. Soc. (hon.); mem. AMA, N.Y. State, Dutchess County med. socs., Am. Legion, Kappa Nu, Phi Delta Epsilon. Jewish religion. Mason, Elk. Author sects. in books: Simon Triangle for Localization of Recurrent Laryngeal Nerve in Thyroid Surgery, Pitfalls To Be Avoided in Cholecystectomy. Contbr. to surg. jours. Home: Fox Run Farm Pleasant Valley NY 12569

SIMON, MORDECAI, religious assn. adminstr., clergyman; b. St. Louis, July 19, 1925; s. Abraham M. and Rose (Solomon) S.; B.A., St. Louis U., 1947; M.A., Washington U., St. Louis, 1952; M.H.L., Rabbi, Jewish Theol. Sem. Am., N.Y.C., 1952, D.D. (hon.), 1977; m. Maxine R. Abrams, July 4, 1954; children—Ora, Eve, Avrom. Ordained rabbi, 1952; asst. rabbi in Mpls., 1952-56; rabbi in Waterloo, Iowa, 1956-63; exec. dir. Chgo. Bd. Rabbis, 1963—; nat. chaplain Jewish War Vets., 1977-78; host weekly TV program What's Nu?, Sta. WGN-TV, 1973—; mem. exec. bd. Chgo. Conf. Religion and Race, 1963—, Community Council Jewish Orgns., Tri-Faith Employment Project, Jewish Student Service, pub. affairs com. Jewish United Fund. Mem. exec. council Chgo. Com. Urban Opportunity, 1964—; mem. nat. council Joint Distbn. Com. Bd. dirs. Citizens Greater Chgo., Chgo. Bd. Jewish Edn., Chgo. USO, Greater Chgo. Jewish Welfare Bd., Armed Forces Council. Served with AUS, 1943-46. Recipient citation Jewish War Vets., 1967, Boy Scouts Am., 1966, 74, Chgo. chpt. Am. Jewish Congress, 1973, Chgo. Conf. Jewish Women's Orgns., 1973, Chgo. Bd. Rabbis, 1973. Mem. Rabbinical Assembly. Home: 621 County Line Rd Highland Park IL 60035 Office: 72 E 11th St Chicago IL 60605

SIMON, NEIL, playwright, TV writer; b. N.Y.C., July 4, 1927; s. Irving and Mamie S.; student N.Y. U., 1946; m. Joan Bain, Sept. 30, 1953 (dec.); 2 daus.; m. 2d, Marsha Mason, 1973. Author materials for Tamiment (Pa.) revues, 1952-53; author sketches (with brother Danny) for Catch a Star, 1955, New Faces of '56; author (with brother) Come Blow Your Horn, 1961; book for musicals Little Me, 1962, Sweet Charity, 1966, Promises, Promises, 1968; plays include: Barefoot in the Park, 1963, The Odd Couple, 1965, The Star-Spangled Girl, 1966, Plaza Suite, 1968, The Last of the Red Hot Lovers, 1969, The Gingerbread Lady, 1970, The Prisoner of Second Avenue, 1971, The Sunshine Boys, 1972, The Good Doctor, 1973, God's Favorite, 1974, California Suite, 1976, Chapter Two, 1977, They're Playing Our Song, 1979; screenplays adapted from own plays: Barefoot in the Park, 1967, The Odd Couple, 1968, Plaza Suite, 1971, Last of the Red Hot Lovers, 1972, The Prisoner of Second Avenue, 1975, The Sunshine Boys, 1975, The Goodbye Girl, 1977, California Suite, 1978, Chapter Two, 1979; screenplays include After the Fox, 1966, The Out-of-Towners, 1970, The Heartbreak Kid, 1972, Murder by Death, 1976, The Goodbye Girl, 1977, The Cheap Detective, 1978; wrote for TV shows: The Phil Silver Arrow Show, 1958, The Tallulah Bankhead Show, 1951, The Sid Caesar Show, 1956-57, Phil Silvers Show, 1958-59, Garry Moore Show, 1959-60, also NBC spls. Served to cpl. USAAF, 1945-46. Recipient Emmy award nominations for Sid Caesar Show, 1956-57, Phil Silvers Show, 1958-59; Tony award nominations for Little Me, 1963, Barefoot in the Park, 1963; Sam S. Shubert award, 1968; Antoinette Perry awards, 1965, 75; Writers Guild screen awards, 1968, 70, 75. Mem. Dramatists Guild. Address: care Eugene O'Neill Theatre 230 W 49th St New York NY 10019*

SIMON, NORTON WINFRED, industrialist; b. Portland, Oreg., Feb. 5, 1907; s. Myer and Lillian (Glickman) S.; student U. Calif., Berkeley, 1923; m. Jennifer Jones, May 30, 1971; children by previous marriage—Donald Ellis, Robert Ellis (dec.). Founder, former chief exec. officer, now cons. Norton Simon, Inc., N.Y.C.; founder, chief exec. officer 5 corp. and 1 family found., Los Angeles; former dir., chmn. fin. com. Burlington No., Inc. Mem. Courtauld Inst., London; former mem. Carnegie Commn. on Future of Higher Edn., Nat. Programming Council; mem. Nat. Com. on U.S.-China Relations, Founding Friends of Can.; lifetime chmn. bd. dirs. The Founders, Los Angeles Music Center; affiliated Calif. Sch. Profl. Psychology; bd. dirs., trustee Norton Simon Mus., Pasadena, Calif.; trustee Inst. Advanced Study, Princeton, N.J.; formerly bd. dirs. Reed Coll., Inst. Internat. Edn., Los Angeles County Mus. Art; former regent U. Calif.; mem. advisory bd. Columbia U.-McGraw Hill Lectures; fellow Pierpont Morgan Library, N.Y.C.; chmn. State Transp. Commn. Address: PO Box 367 Malibu CA 90265

SIMON, PAUL, musician, composer; b. Newark; s. Louis and Belle S.; B.A., Queens Coll.; postgrad. Bklyn. Law Sch.; m. Peggy Harper; 1 son, Harper. With mus. group Simon and (Art) Garfunkel, 1964-71; soloist, 1972—; songs recorded with Garfunkel include: The Sounds of Silence, Dangling Conversation, Homeward Bound, I Am a Rock, At the Zoo, Mrs. Robinson (Grammy award), The Boxer, Bridge Over Troubled Water (Grammy award); albums with Garfunkel: Wednesday Morning 3 A.M., 1964; Sounds of Silence, 1966; Parsley, Sage, Rosemary and Thyme, 1966; The Graduate (soundtrack) (Grammy award), 1968; Bookends, 1968; Bridge over Troubled Waters, 1970; record albums as soloist: There Goes Rhymin' Simon, 1973; Live Rhymin', 1975; Still Crazy After All These Years (Grammy award), 1975. Address: 36 E 61st St New York NY 10021

SIMON, PAUL, congressman, educator, author; b. Eugene, Oreg., Nov. 29, 1928; s. Martin Paul and Ruth (Troemel) S.; student U. Oreg., 1945-46; student Dana Coll., Blair, Nebr., 1946-48, LL.D., 1965; D.Litt., McKendree Coll. (Ill.), 1965; D.C.L., Greenville (Ill.) Coll., 1968; LL.D., Concordia (Nebr.) Coll., 1968, Lincoln (Ill.) Coll., 1969, Loyola U., Chgo., 1969, Valparaiso U., 1976; m. Jeanne Hurley, Apr. 21, 1960; children—Sheila, Martin. Pub., Troy (Ill.) Tribune, 1948-66; mem. Ill. Ho. of Reps., 1955-63, Ill. Senate, 1963-69; lt. gov. Ill., 1969-73; fellow John F. Kennedy Inst. Politics Harvard, 1973; prof. pub. affairs Sangamon State U., Springfield, Ill., 1973; mem. 94th-96th Congresses from 24th Dist. Ill. Bd. dirs. Dana Coll., McKendree Coll. Served with CIC, AUS, 1951-53. Recipient Am. Polit. Sci. Assn. award, 1957; named Best Legislator 7 times. Mem. Luth. Human Relations Assn., Am. Legion. V.F.W., N.A.A.C.P., Urban League. Lutheran. Author: Lovejoy: Martyr to Freedom, 1964; Lincoln's Preparation for Greatness, 1966; A Hungry World, 1966; (with Jeanne Hurley Simon) Protestant-Catholic Marriages Can Succeed, 1967; You Want to Change the World? So Change It, 1971; co-author: The Politics of World Hunger, 1973. Contbr. articles to periodicals, including Sat. Rev., Harper's. Office: 227 Cannon House Office Bldg Washington DC 20515

SIMON, RALPH, clergyman; b. Newark, Oct. 19, 1906; s. Isaac and Yetta (Biddleman) S.; B.A., Coll. City N.Y., 1927; M. in Hebrew Lit., Jewish Theol. Sem., 1931; M.A., Columbia, 1943; postgrad. Oriental Inst. U. Chgo., 1944-47; D.D., Jewish Theol Sem., 1964; D.H.L., Spertus Coll. Judaica, 1972; m. Kelsey Hoffer, June 30, 1931; children—Matthew, Tamar (Mrs. Tamar Hoffs), Jonathan Carmi. Rabbi, 1931; rabbi Congregation Rodef Sholom, Johnstown, Pa., 1931-36, Jewish Center, Jackson Heights, N.Y., 1937-43, Congregation Rodfei Zedek, Chgo., 1943—; dir. Jewish Fedn. Met. Chgo., 1949-61; founder Camp Ramah, Conover, Wis., 1947. Pres. Chgo. Bd. Rabbis, 1952-54, Chgo. Council Rabbinical Assembly, 1943-45, Council Hyde Park and Kenwood Churches and Synagogues, 1956; mem. Ill. Bd. Mental Health Commrs., 1957-67; mem. Chgo. Commn. on Human Resources, 1958-71; gen. chmn. Combined Jewish Appeal Met. Chgo., 1967; gen. chmn. Bonds for Israel Campaign Greater Chgo., 1965-66; v.p. Rabbinical Assembly Am., 1966-67, pres., 1968-69; v.p. Bur. for Careers in Jewish Service, 1969-70; bd. dirs. World Council Synagogues, 1974—. Jewish Theol. Sem. created professorship, Ralph Simon chair in Jewish Ethics and Mysticism, 1959. Clubs: Standard, Idlewild Country (Chgo.). Home: 5000 East End Ave Chicago IL 60615 Office: 5200 Hyde Park Blvd Chicago IL 60615

SIMON, RICHARD HEGE, lawyer; b. Englewood, Colo., Jan. 15, 1911; s. John and Anna (Hege) S.; A.B., U. Denver, 1934, J.D., 1936; m. Barbara Bayliss, July 11, 1936; children—Cynthia Claire (Mrs. Robert E. Raynor), Susan C. Admitted to Colo. bar, 1938; undersheriff, Araphaoe County, Colo., 1933-40; dist. atty. 1st Jud. Dist., Colo., 1941-49; practiced in Englewood, 1941—; mem. firm Simon & Lee, 1942-46, Simon, Lee, Shivers, 1946-49, Simon, Kelley, Hoyt & Malone, 1967-69, Simon, Eason, Hoyt & Malone, 1969-76; dir. First Nat. Bank of Englewood, Key Savs. & Loan Assn., Englewood. Bd. dirs. Arapahoe County Fair Assn., Araphoe County Mental Health Center, Arapahoe County Mile High United Fund; trustee Denver Met. United Way, Iliff Sch. Theology. Fellow Am. Bar Found.; mem. Colo. Bar Assn. (pres. 1970), Englewood C. of C. Mason (33 deg., Shriner), Elk, Odd Fellow. Clubs: Columbine Country (Littleton); Denver Athletic. Home: 2 Viking Dr Englewood CO 80110 Office: 333 W Hampden Ave Englewood CO 80110

SIMON, RITA JAMES (MRS. JULIAN SIMON), educator; b. Bklyn., Nov. 26, 1931; d. Abraham and Irene (Waldman) Mintz; B.A., U. Wis., 1952; Ph.D., U. Chgo., 1957; m. Julian Simon, June 25, 1961; children—David Meyer, Judith Debs, Daniel Hillel. Research asso. Law Sch., U. Chgo., 1957-61, asst. prof. sociology dept., 1959-61; research asso. Columbia, 1961-63; prof. sociology U. Ill. at Urbana, 1963—, head dept. sociology, 1968—, research prof. communications, 1963—. Guggenheim fellow, 1966-67; Ford Found. fellow, 1970-71. Mem. Am. Sociol. Assn., Soc. Study Social Problems. Jewish. Author: The American Jury: The Plea of Insanity, 1966; (with Jeffrey O'Connell) Payment For Pain and Suffering, 1972; Public Opinion in America, 1930-1970, 1974; Women and Crime, 1975; Continuity and Change: A Study of Two Ethnic Communities in Israel, 1978; editor: As We Saw the Thirties, 1967; The Sociology of Law, 1968; The Jury System: A Critical Assessment, 1975; (with Howard Altstein) Transracial Adoption, 1977; Am. Sociol. Rev., 1977—; (with Fred Adler) Women in Crime and the Criminal Justice System, 1978. Home: 1105 S Busey St Urbana IL 61801

SIMON, SEYMOUR F., judge; b. Chgo., Aug. 10, 1915; s. Ben and Gertrude (Rusky) S.; B.S., Northwestern U., 1935, J.D., 1938; m. Roslyn Schultz Biel, May 26, 1954; children—John B., Nancy Harris, Anthony Biel. Admitted to Ill. bar, 1938; spl. atty. Dept. Justice, 1938-42; practice law, Chgo., 1946-74; judge Ill. Appellate Ct., Chgo., 1974—, presiding justice 1st Dist., 3d Div., 1977—. Mem. Bd. Commrs. Cook County, 1961-66, pres., 1962-66; pres. Cook County Forest Preserve Dist., 1962-66; mem. Pub. Bldg. Commn., City Chgo., 1962-67. Alderman, 40th ward, Chgo., 1955-61, 67-74, Democratic ward committeeman, Chgo., 1960-74. Bd. dirs. Schwab Rehab. Hosp., 1961-71, Swedish Covenant Hosp., 1969-75. Served with USNR, 1942-45. Decorated Legion of Merit; recipient citation for distinguished service North Park Coll., Chgo., 1967, 9th Ann. Pub. Service award Tau Epsilon Rho, 1963. Mem. Ill., Chgo. bar assns., Chgo. Hist. Soc., Izaak Walton League, Chgo. Hort. Soc., Phi Beta Kappa, Order of Coif. Clubs: Standard, Variety (Chgo.). Home: 1555 N Astor St Chicago IL 60610 Office: Richard J Daley Center Chicago IL 60602

SIMON, SHELDON, electronics co. exec.; b. N.Y.C., May 30, 1918; s. Henry and Hannah (Cyge) S.; B.B.A., Coll. City N.Y., 1939; B.Indsl. Engring., N.Y. U., 1950; m. Eleanor F. Block, Apr. 5, 1951. Gen. mgr. Sossner Tap & Tool Corp., Lynbrook, N.Y., 1940-50; mgr. indsl. engring. Loral Electronics Corp., Bronx, N.Y., 1950-55; v.p., exec. asst. to pres. Loral Corp., 1955-63, exec. asst. to pres., 1963-68, v.p., sec., Scarsdale, N.Y., 1968-72, v.p. adminstrn., N.Y.C., 1972-77; v.p. indsl. engring. Loral Electronic Systems, Yonkers, N.Y., 1977—. Served with USAAF, 1941-43. Mem. Am. Inst. Indsl. Engrs., Am. Soc. Interior Designers, Alpha Pi Mu. Home: Woodlands Rd Harrison NY 10528 Office: Loral Electronic Systems 999 Central Park Ave Yonkers NY 10704

SIMON, SIDNEY, sculptor; b. Pitts., May 21, 1917; s. James and Minnie (Lipman) S.; student Barnes Found., 1938-40; B.F.A. (Cresson fellow, Edwin Austin Abbey fellow), Pa. Acad. Fine Arts and U. Pa., 1941; postgrad. Grand Chaumiere, Paris, 1948-49; m. Joan E. Lewisohn, May 26, 1945 (div. Aug. 1964); children—Mark, Teru Simon Bratton, Rachel, Nora, Juno; m. 2d, Renee Lane Adriance, June 16, 1968; children—John Nicholas, James Anthony. One man shows include: Branford Coll. of Yale, 1967, Sarah Lawrence Coll., Manhattanville, N.Y., 1972, Graham Gallery, N.Y.C., 1974, Sculpture Center, 1978, Long Point Gallery, 1978, numerous others; group shows include: State U. N.Y., Binghamton, 1973, many others; represented in permanent collections Prospect Park, Bklyn., Downstate Med. Center, N.Y.C., Williams Coll. Mus., Smith Coll. Mus., Colby Coll. Mus., Met. Mus., N.Y.C., others; instr. New Sch. for Social Research, 1963—, Art Students League, 1973—, Castle Hill, Truro, Mass., 1973-79, Skowhegan (Maine) Sch. Painting and Sculpture, 1975-76; artist-in-residence Am. Acad. Rome, 1968-69; mem. N.Y.C. Art Commn., 1975-78. Bd. dirs. Skowhegan Sch. Painting and Sculpture, 1946—. Served to capt. C.E., U.S. Army, 1941-45. Decorated Bronze Star; recipient Acad. Arts and Letters award, 1976; Silver medal Nat. Arts Club, 1978. Mem. NAD, Artists Equity, Archtl. League, Sculptors Guild (v.p. 1974—). Club: Century Assn. Home and studio: 95 Bedford St New York NY 10014

SIMON, STANLEY, mgmt. and financial cons.; b. N.Y.C., July 7, 1917; s. Louis and Cecile (Kashowitz) S.; student Amherst Coll., 1932-33; A.B., Harvard, 1936; m. Marcelle Kramer, Sept. 17, 1939; 1 son, Frederick K. Staff Bristol & Willett, investment securities, 1936-40; asst. mdse. mgr. A. Harris & Co., 1940-43; with Bulova Watch Co., Flushing, N.Y., 1943-58, v.p., 1950-58, dir., 1955—; sr. partner Stanley Simon and Assos., 1958—; dir. Williamhouse-Regency, Inc., Swedlow, Inc., Gerber Sci. Instrument Co., Wetterau Inc., Vornado, Inc., Nat. Shoes, Inc., Shire Nat. Corp. Home: 44 E 67th St New York NY 10021 Office: 70 Pine St New York NY 10005

SIMON, STANLEY CORNELIUS, lawyer; b. Memphis, May 6, 1926; s. Stanley and Gladys E. (Eilbott) S.; B.S. cum laude, N.Y. U., 1954; LL.B., U. Tenn., 1948; children—Mark Philip, John Matthew; m. Carol Buehrens, 1977. Admitted to Tenn. bar, 1947, Tex. bar, 1957; tax accountant Lybrand, Ross Bros. & Montgomery, N.Y.C., 1953-56, tax mgr., Dallas, 1956-61; tax atty. firm Atwell, Grayson & Atwell, Dallas, 1961-69, firm Grayson & Simon, Dallas, 1969-73, Simon & Twombly, Dallas, 1973—; lectr. So. Meth. U., 1969-75. Served with AUS, 1950-52. Mem. Am. Bar Assn., State Bar Tex., Internat. Fiscal Assn., Profit Sharing Council Am. (legal and legis. com. 1973—), Dallas Bar Assn. (chmn. taxation sect. 1969, com. continuing legal edn. 1969, com. legal edn. 1972), Phi Eta Sigma, Phi Kappa Phi. Home: 8916 Capri Dr Dallas TX 75238 Office: 2 Turtle Creek Village Suite 202 Dallas TX 75219

SIMON, TODD, newspaper editor; b. Cleve., Mar. 1, 1913; s. Samuel and Rose (Frankel) S.; A.B., Case Western Res. U., 1937; M.A., Ohio State U., 1938; postgrad. (Sage scholar) Cornell U., 1938-41; m. Doris Harriet Babin, June 11, 1938; children—Julie (Mrs. Ted Cohen), Jeffrey, Amy (Mrs. Philip Skerry), Alice. With The Plain Dealer, Cleve., 1942—, successively reporter, day city editor, editorial writer, columnist, asso. editor. Mem. Cuyahoga County Community Mental Health and Retardation bd., 1968-78, chmn., 1968-69; bd. overseers Case Western Res. U., 1971-72. Developed Key-Vote voter profile analysis. Home: 19801 Van Aken Blvd Shaker Heights OH 44122 Office: 1801 Superior Ave Cleveland OH 44114

SIMON, WERNER, psychiatrist, educator; b. Bremen, Germany, June 5, 1914 (came to U.S. 1937, naturalized 1941); s. Louis and Elise (Halle) S.; student U. Frankfurt (Germany), 1932-36; M.D., U. Berne (Switzerland), 1937; m. Elizabeth Strawn, Apr. 24, 1939. Intern, Lutheran Hosp., Omaha, 1937-38, resident psychiatry, 1938-39; resident physician Cherokee State Hosp., Cherokee, Iowa, 1939-41; psychiatrist Vets. Hosps., Palo Alto, Calif., American Lake, Wash., 1941-44, VA Hosp., St. Cloud, Minn., 1946-48; chief psychiatry VA Hosp., Mpls., 1948-71, now cons.; prof. psychiatry U. Minn. Med. Sch., Mpls., 1956-71, clin. prof. psychiatry and medicine, 1971—; cons. Hastings (Minn.) State Hosp., 1960-73; cons. Hennepin County Gen. Hosp., 1971—, VA Hosp., Mpls., 1971—. Served to capt., M.C., AUS, 1944-46. Fellow Am. Psychiat. Assn. (life), A.C.P.; mem. Minn. Psychiat. Soc. (pres. 1967-69), Minn. Soc. Neurol. Scis. Club: Evergreen (Mpls.). Author: (with Dr. R.D. Wirt) Differential Treatment and Prognosis in Schizophenia, 1959. Contbr. articles on schizophrenia, suicide, drug addiction, music therapy to publs. Home: 8915 River Ridge Rd Minneapolis MN 55420 Office: VA Hosp Minneapolis MN 55417

SIMON, WILLIAM, biomathematician; b. Pitts., May 27, 1929; B.S. in Physics, Carnegie Inst. Tech., 1950; M.A. in Applied Physics, Harvard U., 1952, Ph.D., 1958; m. Maxine Check, June 27, 1965; children—Robert, Steven, Alan. Staff physicist Comstock & Wescott, Inc., cons. engrs., Cambridge, Mass., 1951-53; head instruments sect. Spencer Kennedy Lab., Boston, 1953-57; sr. systems engr. Nat. Radio Co., Malden, Mass., 1957-59; chief physicist Image Instruments, Inc., Newton Lower Falls, Mass., 1959-60; mem. staff M.I.T. Lincoln Lab. and Center for Computer Tech. in Biomed. Scis., 1961-64; research asso. dept. physiology, dir. biomed. tech. cons. group Harvard U. Med. Sch., 1964-68; asso. prof., head div. biomath. U. Rochester Sch. Medicine and Dentistry, 1968-77, prof., head div. biomath., 1977—; vis. asso. prof. dept. elec. engring. M.I.T., 1974-75. Author: Mathematical Techniques for Physiology and Medicine, 1972; Mathematical Techniques for Biology and Medicine, 1977; contbr. articles to profl. jours. Office: U Rochester Box 316 Rochester NY 14642

SIMON, WILLIAM EDWARD, financial cons., past sec. treasury; b. Paterson, N.J., Nov. 27, 1927; B.A., Lafayette Coll., 1952, LL.D. (hon.), 1973; LL.D. (hon.), Pepperdine U., 1975; D.C.L., Jacksonville U., 1976; Doctor Philosophiae honoris causa, Tel Aviv (Israel) U., 1976; hon. scriptual degree Israel Torah Research Inst., Jerusalem; m. Carol Girard, 1950; 7 children. With Union Securities Co., N.Y.C., 1952-57, asst. v.p., 1955-57; v.p. Weeden & Co., N.Y.C., 1957-64; sr. partner Salomon Bros., N.Y.C., 1964-72; dep. sec. Dept. Treasury, Washington, 1973-74, sec. treasury, 1974-77; adminstr. Fed. Energy Office, Washington, 1973-74; sr. cons. Blyth Eastman Paine Webber, Inc.; cons. chmn. adv. council Brazilinvest; dir. Citibank/Citicorp, INA Corp., Xerox Corp., Dart Industries Haliburton Company, Power Corp. of Canada. Past chmn. Oil Policy Com., Econ. Policy Bd., East-West Fgn. Trade Bd., Nat. Adv. Council on Internat. Monetary and Fin. Policies, Council on Internat. Econ. Policy, Joint U.S.-Saudi Arabian Commn. on Econ. Cooperation, U.S.-Israel Joint Com. on Investment and Trade, Fed. Financing Bank, U.S. sect. Joint U.S.-USSR Commercial Commn., U.S.-Japan Joint Econ Com., Council on Wage and Price Stability, Emergency Loan Guarantee Bd.; past vice chmn. Nat. Commn. on Supplies and Shortages; past hon. chmn. U.S.-USSR Trade and Econ. Council, Inc.; past U.S. gov. IMF, Inter-Am. Devel. Bank, Asian Devel. Bank, IBRD; past mem. Energy Resources Council, Domestic Council, Devel. Loan Com., Adv. Com. on Export Policy, Nat. Council on Organized Crime, Nat. Commn. on Productivity and Work Quality, Trade Policy Com., Group of Ten, OECD Ministerial Council, Adv. Com. on Reform of Internat. Monetary System, Agrl. Policy Com., Task Force on Questionable Corporate Payments Abroad, Joint Com. on Reduction of Fed. Expenditures, Cabinet Com. on Internat. Narcotics Control, Cabinet Com. to Combat Terrorism. Chmn. Library of Commerce Trust Fund Bd.; pres. John M. Olin Found.; treas. U.S. Olympic Com. Director John D. and Catherine T. MacArthur Found.; co-chmn. bd. Inst. for Ednl. Affairs; bd. overseers Hoover Instn. on War, Revolution and Peace; bd. dirs. Heritage Found., Damon Runyon-Walter Winchell Cancer Fund; trustee Lafayette Coll., Hudson Inst.; trustee, former chmn. fin. com. Wolf Trap Center for Performing Arts. Served as lt. AUS, 1946-48. Decorated Order of the Nile (Egypt); recipient Man of Year award ASME; Dean's citation Am. U.; Trustees Distinguished Service award Fairleigh Dickinson U.; Am. Eagle award Invest in Am. Council; Govt. Service award Pub. Relations Soc. Am.; Pres.'s Cup award Nat. Def. Transp. Assn.; Gold Medal award Nat. Inst. Social Scis.; Exec. Govt. award OIC Govt. Relations Service; Distinguished Pub. Service award The Tax Found.; Bicentenneal award U.S. Citizen's Congress; named Outstanding Citizen of Year, Advt. Club N.J. Mem. Council Fgn. Relations, Pilgrims U.S., Mt. Pelerin Soc., Friendly Sons of St. Patrick. Order of Malta. Roman Catholic. Clubs:

Chevy Chase, Links, Brook, Madison Square Garden River (N.Y.C.); Maidstone (East Hampton, N.Y.); Burning Tree, Federal City (Washington); Balboa Bay; Morris County Golf, Mendan Valley Gun (N.J.); Balboa Bay (Calif.). Author: A Time for Truth, 1978. Office: Blyth Eastman Paine Webber Inc 1221 Ave of the Americas New York NY 10020

SIMON, WILLIAM GEORGE, lawyer; b. Douglas, Ariz., Apr. 17, 1913; s. George Elias and Mary (Shamas) S.; A.B., St. Mary's Coll., 1937; J.D., U. Calif. at Berkeley, 1940; m. Alice Van Hecke, Feb. 22, 1941; children—Gregory, Stephanie (Mrs. William Branon), Douglas, Suzette. Admitted to Calif. bar, 1940; insp. FBI, Washington and N.Y.C., 1952, spl. agt. in charge maj. cities, 1954-64; practice law, Los Angeles, 1964—; partner law firm Simon & Sheridan, Los Angeles, 1964--; pres., dir. Fidelity TV, Inc., Los Angeles, 1967—. Del., 9th Circuit Jud. Conf., 1966, mem. com. on rules criminal procedure, 1967-76. Bd. dirs., exec. v.p. Damon Runyon-Walter Winchell Cancer Fund, N.Y.C.; regent Mt. St. Mary's Coll., Los Angeles, 1967—; bd. dirs., v.p. J. Edgar Hoover Found., Washington, 1964—; trustee Alumni Found., U. Calif. at Berkeley, 1972—; adv. bd. Am. Arbitration Assn., 1967, St. Vincent's Hosp., Los Angeles, 1971—. Mem. Los Angeles County (chmn. law office mgmt. sect. 1971-72), Cal., Am. bar assns., Boalt Hall Alumni Assn. (dir. 1973—), Phi Delta Phi. Home: 2035 Lombardy Rd San Marino CA 91108 Office: 2404 Wilshire Blvd Suite 400 Los Angeles CA 90057. *I feel that perhaps life's most important asset is peace of mind—both the acquisition of peace of mind for one's own self, and giving assistance to others to enable them to achieve peace of mind. I believe that truth, perseverance, hard work, and progress through merit are guidelines which have been most helpful to me.*

SIMON, WILLIAM JOHN, dental educator; b. Mpls., June 12, 1911; s. Jay Alois and Grace Julia (Funk) S.; A.B., U. Minn., 1935, D.D.S., 1936, M.S.D., 1940; m. Lela Belle Tarter, Feb. 26, 1933; children—Elizabeth Grace, Jay Daniel. Dental intern U. Minn., Mpls., 1936-37, instr., 1937-39, asst. prof., 1939-41, asso. prof., 1941-43, prof., chmn. div. oral diagnosis, 1945-48, prof., chmn. div. operative dentistry, 1948-53; dean, prof. operative dentistry Coll. Dentistry, State U. Iowa, 1953-61; practice dentistry, Mpls., part time, 1936-43; dental dir. mem. nat. adv. council dental research USPHS, 1959-62, dir. clin. devel., 1962-70; prof. dentistry U. Louisville Sch. Dentistry, 1970--; chmn. advisory com. health careers program Dakota County Vocat. Center, 1976—. Trustee Rosemount United Methodist Ch. Served as 1st lt. Dental Corps, U.S. Army, 1943-45. Diplomate Am. Bd. Oral Medicine. Fellow Am. Coll. Dentistry, Internat. Coll. Dentists; mem. Am. Dental Assn., Internat. Assn. Dental Research, Minn. Acad. Sci., Am. Acad. Oral Roentgenology, AAAS, Minn. Dental Found., Dakota County Hist. Soc. (dir. 1978—), Nat. Sojourners, Heroes of 76 (past comdr.), Sigma Xi, Omicron Kappa Upsilon, Alpha Sigma Epsilon, Psi Omega. Methodist. Mason, Rotarian. Author: Clinical Dental Assisting, 1973. Co-author: Clinical Operative Dentistry, 1948; Review of Dentistry, 1949. Contbr. articles to profl. jours. Home: 2261 W 130th St Rosemount MN 55068

SIMONDS, CHARLES FREDERICK, artist, architect; b. N.Y.C., Nov. 14, 1945; s. Robert and Anita I. (Bell) S.; B.A., U. Calif., Berkeley, 1967; M.F.A., Rutgers U., 1969. One man exhbns. include: Mus. Modern Art, N.Y.C., 1976, Albright Knox Art Gallery, Buffalo, 1977, Nat. Galerie Berlin, 1978, Walraf-Richartz Mus., Koln, 1978; group exhbns. include: 8th and 9th Biennales, Paris, 1973, 75, Whitney Mus., N.Y.C., 1975, 77, Venice Biennale, 1976, 78, documenta 6, Kassel, 1977; represented in permanent collections: Mus. Modern Art, N.Y.C., Walker Art Center, Mpls., Allen Meml. Art Mus., Oberlin, Ohio, Centre Georges Pompidou, Paris, Mus. Ludwig, Cologne, Germany. Bd. dirs. Lower East Side Coalition for Human Housing, 1973-76. Nat. Endowment Arts grantee, 1973. Author: Three Peoples, 1975; Floating Cities and Other Architectures, 1978. Home: 138 Prince St New York NY 10012

SIMONDS, JOHN ORMSBEE, landscape architect; b. Jamestown, N.D., Mar. 11, 1913; s. Guy Wallace and Marguerite Lois (Ormsbee) S.; B.S., Mich. State U., 1935, also hon. D.Sc.; M.Landscape Architecture (scholar 1936-37, Eugene Dodd medal), Harvard, 1939; m. Marjorie C. Todd, May 1, 1943; children—Taye Anne, John Todd, Polly Jean, Leslie Brook. Landscape architect Mich. Dept. Parks, 1935-36; partner Simonds and Simonds, Pitts., 1939-70, Collins, Simonds and Simonds, Washington, 1952-70; partner The Environ. Planning and Design Partnership, Pitts., also Miami Lakes, 1970—; lectr., vis. critic urban and regional planning Carnegie-Mellon U., 1955-67; vis. critic Grad. Sch. Planning, also Sch. Architecture, Yale, 1961-62. Cons. Chgo. Central Area Com., 1962, Allegheny County Dept. Regional Parks, 1961-74, Allegheny County Housing Authority, 1960; U.S. cons. community planning Inter-Am. Housing and Planning Center, Bogota, Colombia, 1960-61; mem. jury Am. Acad. Rome, 1963, 65, 66, 69; mem. Nat. Adv. Com. on Hwy. Beautification; chmn. panel on parks and open space White House Conf. on Natural Beauty; mem. Interprofl. Commn. on Environ. Design, Joint Com. on Nat. Capital; mem. urban hwy. adv. bd. U.S. Bur. Pub. Rds., 1965-68; mem. landscape architecture adv. panel U.S. C.E., 1968-71, Pres.'s Task Force on Resources and Environment, 1968-70; mem. design adv. panel Operation Breakthrough, HUD, 1970-71; mem. Mid-Atlantic regional adv. bd. Nat. Park Service, 1976— Asso. trustee U. Pa., 1962-66, mem. bd. fine arts, 1962-66; chmn. joint com. planning Carnegie-Mellon U. and U. Pitts., 1959-60; overseer's vis. com. Harvard Grad. Sch. Design, 1962-68, exec. council alumni assn., 1960-63; adv. com. Sch. Design, N.C. State U., 1965-67; mem. Fla. Gov.'s Task Force on Natural Resources, 1979—. Bd. dirs. Hubbard Ednl. Trust, 1974—; bd. govs. Pitts. Plan for Arts. Recipient citation Top Men of Year, Engring. News-Record, 1973; Charles L. Hutchinson medal Chgo. Hort. Soc. Fellow Am. Soc. Landscape Architects (mem. exec. com. 1959-67, pres. 1963-65, pres. Found. 1966-68, recipient medal 1973), Royal Soc. Arts (Gt. Britain); mem. N.A.D. (asso.), Urban Land Inst., Nat. Assn. Housing Ofcls., Archtl. League N.Y., Royal Town Planning Inst. (hon. corr.); hon. asso. Pa. chpt. A.I.A. Presbyn. (ruling elder). Clubs: Harvard, Yale, Princeton (Pitts.). Author: Landscape Architecture, the Shaping of Man's Natural Environment, 1961; Earthscape, a Manual of Environmental Planning, 1978. Editor: The Freeway in the City; Virginia's Common Wealth, 1965. Home: 17 Penhurst Rd Pittsburgh PA 15202 Office: 100 Ross St Pittsburgh PA 15219. *Perhaps the most important lesson in life is to learn to address oneself with intensity to each person, object and event. One may be with friends without awareness of either friend or friendship, live with family as an almost stranger, partake of food and drink without savor, pass burgeoning tree, splashing stream, or splendid view without appreciation . . . unless one learns to address all powers of perception-first consciously, and then by habit, to the subject at hand. Only thus may each experience be made rich and rewarding, and life, the sum of experience, be lived to the full.*

SIMONDS, PHILIP DOUGLAS, landscape architect; b. Jamestown, N.D., May 9, 1916; s. Guy Wallace and Marguerite Lois (Ormsbee) S.; B.A., Wooster (Ohio) Coll., 1938; postgrad. Harvard Grad. Sch. Design, 1938-39; m. Alison Stewart, Jan. 29, 1946; children—James Stewart, Kirk Douglas. Landscape architect, 1939—; co-founder, partner Simonds & Simonds (now The Environ. Planning and Design Partnership), Pitts. and Miami Lakes, Fla., 1940—; lectr. Carnegie-Mellon U., 1963-73, Mich. State U., 1971-73, Pa. State U., 1968. Mem. Gov.'s Adv. Com. to Pa. State Bd. Edn., 1962-72. Served to USAF, 1943-46. Fellow Am. Soc. Landscape Architects (v.p. 1973-74, chmn. com. on code profl. ethics 1973-77); mem. Soc. Am. Mil. Engrs., Am. Soc. Planning Ofcls., Urban Land Inst., Pitts. Archtl. Club (life). Republican. Presbyterian. Club: Harvard-Yale-Princeton (Pitts.). Contbr. articles to archtl. jours. Home: Brightwood Trail Pittsburgh PA 15237 Office: 100 Ross St Pittsburgh PA 15219

SIMONE, JOSEPH VINCENT, physician; b. Chgo., Sept. 19, 1935; s. Peter and Josephine (Casablanca) S.; student Loyola U., Chgo., 1953-56, M.D., 1960; m. Patricia Ann Sheahan, May 28, 1960; children—Patricia Marie, Julie Ann, Margaret Mary. Intern, Presbyn.-St. Luke's Hosp., Chgo., 1960-61, resident in medicine, 1961-63; resident in pediatrics U. Ill. Research and Edn. Hosp., Chgo., 1965-66, fellow in pediatric hematology-oncology, 1963-66; mem. staff St. Jude Childrens' Research Hosp., Memphis, 1967-77, 78—, asso. dir. clin. research, 1978—; prof. pediatrics Stanford U., physician in chief Children's Hosp. at Stanford, Palo Alto, Calif., 1977-78; clin. prof. pediatrics U. Tenn., 1978. Diplomate Am. Bd. Pediatrics, Am. Bd. Internal Medicine. Mem. Am. Soc. Clin. Oncology (dir.), Am. Assn. for Cancer Research, Am. Soc. Hematology, Soc. for Pediatric Research, Am. Pediatric Soc. Roman Catholic. Editor: Clinics in Hematology, 1978. Contbr. articles on therapeutic research in childhood cancer to profl. jours. Home: 506 Princeton Cove Memphis TN 38117 Office: St Jude Children's Research Hosp 332 N Lauderdale Ave Memphis TN 38101

SIMONE, NINA, singer, pianist, composer; b. Tryon, N.C., Feb. 21, 1933; d. John Divan and Kate (Irvin) Waymon; student piano and theory with Carl Freidberg, Juilliard Sch. Music, 1954; student Vladimir Sokoloff, Curtis Inst. Music, 1950-53; m. Andrew B. Stroud, Dec. 4, 1961; 1 dau., Lisa Celeste. Accompanist for vocal student Arlene Smith Studio, Phila., also tchr. pvt. lessons, 1954; appearances in night clubs, in concert, on radio and television, 1954—; rec. for RCA Victor Records; albums include: It Is Finished, Here Come the Sun, Gifted and Black. Recipient numerous awards for fund raising efforts; named Woman of Year Jazz at Home Club, Phila., 1966; recipient YMCA life award for fund raising. Mem. A.S.C.A.P., A.F.T.R.A, Am. Fedn. Musicians. Composer; Mississippi Goddam, 1963; Four Women, 1964; (with Langston Hughes) Backlash Blues, 1966. Home: Mount Vernon NY 10553 Office: care Asso Booking Corp 445 Park Ave New York NY 10022*

SIMONELLI, CHARLES FRANCIS, business exec.; b. Bklyn., May 28, 1925; s. Charles and Catherine (Simonelli) S.; m. Rose Mary Strafaci, Oct. 26, 1961; children—Angela C., Donna C. With Universal Pictures Co. Inc., 1945-62, asst. to pres., 1959-62; v.p. Technicolor Inc., 1963-66, exec. v.p., 1966-68, past dir., mem. finance com.; dir., chmn. exec. com. Thompson Starrett, 1954-56, chmn. bd., 1956-57; dir., mem. exec. com. Superior Tool and Die Co., 1956-57, Bethelem Machine and Foundry, 1956-57; chmn. mgmt. com. Bib Corp., 1956-57; exec. v.p., dir. Nat. Industries, Inc., Louisville, 1968-70, pres., 1970-72, also dir. numerous subsidiaries; sr. v.p., also dir., REA Holding Corp., 1972-74; exec. v.p., chief adminstrv. officer, dir. Nat. Bulk Carriers, Inc., Princess Properties Internat. Ltd., Am. Hawaiian Steamship Co., 1974-77; mng. dir., chief exec. officer Numinter BV, 1977-79; vice-chmn., chief operating officer, dir. Movie Lab., Inc., N.Y.C., 1979—; dir. Walter Reade Orgn., Pillar Corp. Del., Democratic Nat. Conv., 1952. Club: N.Y. Athletic (N.Y.C.). Home: 291 Chestnut Hill Rd Stamford CT 06903 Office: 19 rue de Berri 75008 Paris France. *A conviction that every individual has the right to see the view from his own window, without fear of prejudice or recrimination. That the individual who wears his crown on his heart, not his head, leaves a lasting mark upon those he touches in his business, civic, and family life.*

SIMONET, JOHN THOMAS, banker; b. Stillwater, Minn., Aug. 11, 1926; s. Joseph S. and Helen (Martin) S.; B.B.A., U. Minn., 1948, LL.B., 1951; m. Helen Kennedy, Sept. 8, 1951; children—William T., Joseph K., Mary, Michelle, Ann. With First Nat. Bank, St. Paul, 1951-72, cashier, 1958-60, v.p., 1960-71; exec. v.p. First Trust Co., St. Paul, 1972-74, pres., chief adminstrv. officer, 1974—; dir. Donovan Cos., Inc. Asst. treas. Port Authority St. Paul, 1966-71. Mem. lay adv. bd. exec. com. St. Joseph's Hosp., St. Paul, 1965-70, trustee, 1971—, chmn. bd. trustees, 1976-79; pres. adv. bd. Catholic Social Service St. Paul, 1968-70; chmn. Archbishop's Appeal Com., 1970; exec. bd. dirs. St. Paul Council Arts and Scis., 1967-69; trustee St. Paul Sem., 1969—; bd. dirs. United Way, St. Paul, 1976—. Served with USNR, 1953-55. Club: St. Paul Athletic (treas. 1966-68). Home: 782 S Syndicate Saint Paul MN 55116 Office: 332 Minnesota St Saint Paul MN 55101

SIMONI, JOHN PETER, educator, art critic; b. Denver, Apr. 12, 1911; s. Achille and Amabile Maria (Callierotti) S.; student Gymnasium of Trent, Italy 1924-29, Nat. U. Mex., 1938, Kansas City Art Inst., 1938-41; B.A., Colo. State Coll. Edn., 1948, M.A., 1949; student U. Colo., 1949; Ph.D., Ohio State U., 1952, Mass. Inst. Tech., 1958; cert. Command and Gen. Staff Coll., 1971; cert. in museology, conservation and restoration art objects Internat. U. Art, Florence, Italy, 1979; m. Vera Huffman, Apr. 8, 1939; children—John Stephen, Alan Gregory, Brian Randall. Tchr., supr. adult edn. Works Progress Adminstrn., Denver, 1935-37; dir. arts and crafts Denver YWCA, 1936-37, Student Christian Movement Conf. YM-YWCA, Estes Park, Colo., 1937-41, Cheley (Colo.) Camps, summers 1940-42, 61-65, head dept.; head dept. art Baker U., 1937-55, dir. Elsie Allen Art Gallery, 1953-55; prof. Wichita State U., 1955-78, chmn. dept. art, 1957-64; former art critic and columnist Wichita Eagle; now corr. Estes Park (Colo.) Trail Gazette, El Dorado (Kans.) Times; muralist, paintings and sculpture; color cons. Western Lithograph Co., Wichita, Hertzler Research Found., Halstead, Kans. Mem. Nat. Council Arts and Govt., Mus. Modern Art; pres. Southwest Coll. Art Conf., 1963-64. Mem. Coutts Art Scholarship com. Butler County Community Coll. and Washburn U.; trustee Halstead (Kans.) Fine Arts Assn., Warren Hall Coutts III Meml. Art Gallery, El Dorado, Kans. Civil affairs officer Allied Control Commn. and Allied Mil. Govt., Italy, 1944-47; dir. reorgn. Italian, Slovene, Croat Schs., Ter. of Venezia Giulia; consular corr. of Italy in Kans., Italian Consulate, St. Louis, 1961-78. Served from pvt. to capt., AUS, 1942-47; lt. col. Res. (ret.). Decorated knight Order of Crown, knight officer Order of Merit (Republic of Italy); Bronze Star (U.S.); recipient Trentino art prize, 1928, Carter art prize, 1931. Fellow Internat. Inst. Arts and Letters; mem. Internat. Soc. Edn. Through Art, Kans. Art Edn. Assn. (v.p., editor 1942), Coll. Art Assn., Am. Soc. Aesthetics and Art Criticism, AAUP, Kans. Art Fedn. (trustee), VFW, Am. Legion (mem. past comdrs. club), Kappa Pi. Lutheran (Sunday sch. supt. 1958-62). Author: Report on Education in Venezia Giulia, 1947; Formal Organization in Painting, 1949; Writings on Art Criticism in Nineteenth Century America, 1951; Art Critics and Criticism in Nineteenth Century America, 1952; The Structure of Form in Painting and Design, 1973; contbr. articles, book revs. learned jours. Home: PO Box 1154 Estes Park CO 80517. *An unsophisticated and sincere view of life, never holding nationality, racial, political, or religious prejudices; belief in fine craftsmanship; seeing life as a configurational experience, whole and complete, in its diversities of purpose and action, have brought human understanding for successful achievement and related identification.*

SIMONPIETRI, ANDRE C., ret. fgn. service officer; b. Richmond, Va., July 23, 1911; s. Auguste and Alma Cecilia (Dominici) S.; A.B., 1931, M.A., 1932, Ph.D., 1935, Universita Urbana, Rome, Italy; S.T.B., Universita Gregoriana, Rome, 1934; m. Grace Marie Boland, May 24, 1941; children—Andre C., Grace Alma (Mrs. Christian W. Brix, Jr.), D. Augustine III, Pierre Antoine, Raymond, Paul Philippe. Instr. U. Md., 1936-37; pub. agt., 1937-38; exec. asst. div. internat. confs. Dept. State, 1938- 42; lectr. Washington Coll. of Fgn. Service, 1939-41; sec. Commn. on Cartography, Pan-Am. Inst. of Geography and History, Mexico City, 1942- 44, Washington, 1944-51, sec. exec. com., 1944-51, sec. gen., Mexico City, 1951-56; spl. adviser on cartography Dept. State, 1945-51; liaison officer Joint Chiefs of Staff, 1947-51; asso. dir. Office Internat. Relations, Nat. Acad. Scis.-Nat. Research Council, Washington, 1956-62; apptd. sci. officer Fgn. Service Res., 1962; sci. attache Am. Embassy, Rio de Janeiro, Brazil, 1962-67; assigned Am. embassy, Buenos Aires, Argentina, 1967-71, counselor for sci. affairs, 1970-71; counselor for sci. and technol. affairs Am. Embassy, Mexico City, 1971-75; cons. Dept. State, 1975—; liaison officer Internat. Union Geodesy and Geophysics-Pan-Am. Inst. Geography and History, 1957-63; chmn. U.S. Regional Sci. Office for Latin Am., 1962-67. Chmn. delegation to numerous internat. confs.; mem. bd. U.S.-Brazil Ednl. (Fulbright) Commn., 1964-67, U.S.-Argentina, 1970-71; mem. Inter-Am. Com. on Sci. and Tech. OAS, 1974-78. Mem. or hon. mem. numerous U.S. and fgn. profl. assns. Clubs: Cosmos (Washington); Clube de Golfe de Brasilia, San Andres (Buenos Aires); Gavea Golf (Rio de Janeiro); Club de Golf Mexico; Culpeper (Va.) Country. Editor, author, linguist, internat. sci. affairs authority. Home: Box 94 Route 1 Rixeyville VA 22737

SIMONS, ALBERT, JR., lawyer; b. Charleston, S.C., Nov. 20, 1918; s. Albert and Harriet Porcher (Stoney) S.; A.B., Princeton, 1940; LL.B., Yale, 1947; m. Caroline Pinckney Mitchell, June 18, 1948; children—Albert III, Julian Mitchell, Cotesworth Pinckney, Caroline Pinckney. Admitted to S.C. bar, 1947, also U.S. Fed. Dist. Ct. Eastern and Western Dists. S.C., U.S. Circuit Ct. of Appeals 4th Circuit, U.S. Supreme Ct.; practiced in Charleston, 1948—; asso. Sinkler & Gibbs, 1948; partner Sinkler Gibbs & Simons, and predecessor firms, 1949—. Mem. City Council, Charleston, 1954-59; mem. Charleston County Bd. of Assessment Control, 1965—; dir. S.C. Municipal Council. Bd. dirs. Legal Aid Soc., Family Agy., Charleston Library Soc., Served from pvt. to maj. AUS, 1941-46. Decorated Bronze Star medal. Fellow Am. Coll. Probate Counsel; mem. Am., S.C., Charleston County bar assns., St. Cecilia Soc., S.C. Soc., Soc. of Cin., Soc. Colonial Wars, St. Georges Soc., Carolina Art Assn. (former dir.), S.C. Hist. Soc. (dir.), Charleston Library Soc. (trustee), Hibernian Soc., Princeton Alumni Assn. of S.C. (past pres.), Alpha Tau Omega, Phi Delta Phi. Episcopalian. Mason, Rotarian. Clubs: Carolina Yacht, Charleston (Charleston). Home: 8 S Battery St Charleston SC 29401 Office: 160 E Bay St Charleston SC 29402

SIMONS, CHARLES EARL, JR., U.S. judge; b. Johnston, S.C., Aug. 17, 1916; s. Charles Earl and Frances (Rhoden) S.; A.B., U. S.C., 1937, LL.B. cum laude, 1939; m. Jean Knapp, Oct. 18, 1941; children—Charles Earl III, Paul Knapp, Richard Brewster, Jean Brewster. Admitted to S.C. bar, 1939; mem. firm Lybrand, Simons and Rich, Aiken, S.C., 1939-64, U.S. dist. judge Dist. S.C., 1964—. Mem. S.C. Constl. Revision Com., 1948; mem. Bd. Discipline and Grievance S.C. Bar, 1958-61. Fourth Circuit dist. judge rep. Jud. Conf. of U.S., 1973-79, mem. ethics adv. panel, mem. subcom. on fed. jurisdiction of com. on ct. adminstrn. Mem. S.C. House Reps. 1942, 1947-48, 1961-64, mem. ways and means com., 1947-48, 61-64. Served with USNR, World War II. Recipient Algernon Sidney Sullivan award, 1937, 64. Mem. S.C. (mem. exec. com.), Am. bar assns., Am. Law Inst., Am. Judicature Soc., Am. Legion, V.F.W., U. S.C. Alumni Assn. (past pres.), Baptist (past mem. bd. deacons, past chmn. finance com.). Rotarian (hon.). Club: Aiken Business Men's. Home: PO Box 2185 910 Valley Green Dr SW Aiken SC 29801 Office: US Courthouse Aiken SC 29801

SIMONS, CHARLES J., airline co. exec.; b. 1918; B.S., Fordham U., 1938; married. With Lehigh Coal & Nav. Co., 1938-40; with Eastern Air Lines, Inc., Miami, 1940—, vice chmn., exec. v.p., 1976—, also dir., pres. dir., chief exec. officer Dorado Beach Devel. Inc., Dorado Beach Estates Inc., 1971—; dir. S.E. 1st Nat. Bank of Miami, Bank of Commerce, Wometco Enterprises, Inc., Exec. Sports, Inc., Twin Fair, Inc., Aero Spacelines, Inc. Mem. Harvard Bus. Sch. Assos. (exec. council). Home: 631 Arvida Pkwy Coral Gables FL 33156 Office: Internat Airport Miami FL 33148

SIMONS, DOLPH COLLINS, editor; b. Lawrence, Kans., Nov. 24, 1904; s. W.C. and Gertrude (Reineke) S.; A.B., U. Kans., 1925; m. Marie Nelson, Feb. 16, 1929; children—Dolph Collins, John Nelson. Reporter, A.P., Chgo., 1924; office mgr. Lawrence (Kans.) Daily Jour.-World 1925, editor, 1950-79, pub., 1944-63; pres. World Co., 1951-69, chmn. bd., 1969—. Dir. Fed. Res. Bd., Kansas City, 1962-70, dep. chmn., 1963-66, chmn., 1967-70. Mem. Pulitzer Awards Jury, 1962-63. Del. Republican Nat. Conv., 1944, 1960; v.p. Eisenhower Found., 1951—. Trustee, past pres. U. Kan. Endowment Assn.; v.p., past chmn. trustees, Kan. 4-H Found.; bd. trustees Midwest Research Inst., Kansas City. past pres. William Allen White Found. Civilian observer round-the-world Navy Flight, 1949. Recipient Distinguished Service citation U. Kans., 1956, Ellsworth award, 1975, Pub. Service award Baker U., 1976; Distinguished Service in Journalism award U. Minn., 1966. Mem. Lawrence C. of C. (past pres., dir.), U. Kans. Alumni Assn. (dir., past pres.), Kans. Press Assn. (past dir. and pres.), Am. Soc. Newspaper Editors, (dir. A.P. 1951-60, v.p. 1950-51, 1959-60), Kans. (dir.), Lawrence (past pres.) hist. socs., Phi Kappa Psi, Sigma Delta Chi. Republican. Baptist. Mason (Shriner), Rotarian. Clubs: Lawrence (Kans.) Country; Kansas City, River, Kansas City Country, Mercury (Kansas City, Mo.); Kansas Day Republican (past pres.); Garden of Gods (Colorado Springs, Colo.). Author: Germany and Austria, May-June 1947; A Globe-Circler's Diary, 1949. Home: 444 Country Club Terr Lawrence KS 66044 Office: 6th and New Hampshire Sts Lawrence KS 66044

SIMONS, DOLPH COLLINS, JR., newspaper pub.; b. Lawrence, Kans., Mar. 11, 1930; s. Dolph Collins and Marie (Nelson) S.; A.B., U. Kans., 1951, LL.D. (hon.), Colby Coll., 1972; m. Pamela Counseller, Feb. 7, 1952; children—Pamela, Linda, Dolph Collins, Dan. Reporter, Lawrence Jour.-World, 1953, asso. pub., 1957, pub., 1962—, editor, 1978—, pres., 1969—; reporter The Times, London, 1956; reporter Johannesburg (S. Africa) Star, 1958; pres. World Co.; dir. Commerce Trust Co., Kansas City, Mo. Mem. adv. com. Nieman Found., Harvard; trustee, past pres. William Allen White Found.; trustee, mem. exec. com. Midwest Research Inst., Menninger Found.; mem. governing bd. Children's Mercy Hosp., Kansas City, Mo.; trustee U. Kans. Endowment Assn. Served to capt. USMCR, 1951-53. Recipient Elijah Parish Lovejoy award, 1972; Fred Ellsworth award for significant service to U. Kans., 1976. Mem. Newspaper Advt. Bur. (dir.), Am. Soc. Newspaper Editors, Inland Daily (past dir.), Kans. (past pres., dir.) press assns., AP (past dir.), Am. Newspaper Pubs. Assn. (dir., nat. sec.), Lawrence C. of C. (past pres., dir.), U. Kans. Alumni Assn. (past dir.), Sigma Delta Chi, Phi Delta Theta.

Republican. Episcopalian. Clubs: Masons, Rotary; Lawrence Country; Kansas City Country; Kansas City River. Home: 2425 Vermont St Lawrence KS 66044 Office: 609 New Hampshire St Lawrence KS 66044

SIMONS, ELWYN LAVERNE, paleontologist, educator; b. Lawrence, Kans., July 14, 1930; s. Verne Franklin and Verna (Cuddeback) S., A.B. in Biology, Rice U., 1953; M.A., Princeton U., 1955, Ph.D. in Paleobiology, 1956; D.Phil. (Marshall scholar), Oxford (Eng.) U., 1959; M.A. (hon.), Yale U., 1965; m. 2d, Friderun Annursel Ankel, Dec. 2, 1972; children—Cornelia V.M., Verne F.H.; 1 son by previous marriage—David D.B. Lectr. geology Princeton, 1958-59; asst. prof. zoology U. Pa., 1959-61; vis. asso. prof. geology, curator vertebrate paleontology Yale, 1960-61, mem. faculty, 1961-77, prof. geology, curator charge div. vertebrate paleontology Peabody Mus., 1965-77; prof. anthropology and anatomy Duke U., Durham, N.C., 1977—, dir. Duke Primate Center; research asso. Am. Mus. Natural History; dir. Paleontol. Expdns. Egypt, 1961-68, 77-79, No. India, 1968-69; research expdns. for fossil mammals, Wyo., 1960-75, Iran, 1970, Spain, 1971; Barbour-Schramm Meml. lectr. U. Nebr., 1974; David French lectr. Claremont Colls., 1974; traveling lectr. Bur. Fgn. Affairs, Govt. of France, 1976. Recipient Annadale Meml. medal Asiatic Soc. Bengal, 1973; Sr. U.S. Scientist award Alexander von Humboldt Found. (Fed. Republic Germany), 1975. Richard C. Hunt Meml. fellow Wenner-Gren Found., 1965. Mem. Soc. Vertebrate Paleontology, Am. Soc. Naturalists, Inst. Human Paleontology, AAAS, Assn. Phys. Anthropology, Geol. Soc. Am., Soc. Study Human Biology, Soc. Study Evolution, Am. Soc. Zoologists, Internat. Assn. Human Biologists, Sigma Xi. Author: Primate Evolution: An Introduction To Man's Place In Nature, 1972. Co-editor Macmillan Series in Physical Anthropology; A Simons Family History in England and America, 1975. Contbr. numerous articles to profl. publs. Research on early mammals and early primate evolution spl. interest in higher primate and human evolution with recovery of earliest known apes in Oligocene of Africa, 1961-68, 77-78, Gigantopithecus in India, 1968, Dryopithecus, 1969, also studies earliest hominid, Ramapithecus, 1961—. Office: Dept Anthropology Duke U Durham NC 27708

SIMONS, GORDON DONALD, JR., statistician; b. Kansas City, Mo., Dec. 26, 1938; s. Gordon Donald and Delora (Kellogg) S.; B.A. in Math., U. Minn., 1960, M.A. in Math., 1964, Ph.D. in Stats., 1966; m. Karen Janell Lee, Aug. 31, 1962; children—Delora Ann, Sylvia Kay, Melinda Lee. Research asso. dept. stats. Stanford U., 1966-68; asst. prof. stats. U. N.C., Chapel Hill, 1968-71, asso. prof., 1971-75, prof., 1975—, chmn. dept. stats., 1976—; bd. dirs. Carolina Study Center. Air Force Office Sci. Research grantee, 1968, 72-75; NSF grantee, 1969-71, 75—. Mem. Inst. Math. Stats., Am. Statis. Assn. (asso. editor jour. 1971-76), Am. Sci. Affiliation. Presbyterian. Home: 2937 Welcome Dr Durham NC 27705 Office: 315 Phillips Hall U NC Chapel Hill NC 27514

SIMONS, HOWARD, newspaper editor; b. Albany, N.Y., June 3, 1929; s. Reuben and Mae (Chesler) S.; B.A., Union Coll., Schenectady, 1951, Litt.D., 1973; M.S. in Journalism, Columbia, 1952; m. Florence Katz, Nov. 11, 1956; children—Anna, Isabel, Julie, Rebecca. Writer, editor Sci. Service, Washington, 1954-59; free-lance writer, 1959-61; Am. corr., New Scientist, London, Eng., 1964-67; with Washington Post, 1961—, mng. editor, 1971—. M. Lyle Spencer vis. prof. Syracuse U., 1975; Intellectual Interchange scholar, Japan, 1975. Served with AUS, 1952-54. Recipient AAAS/Westinghouse Electric Corp. Sci. writing award, 1962, 64, Raymond Clapper Journalism award, 1966. Nieman fellow Harvard, 1958-59. Mem. Overseas Writers, Council Fgn. Relations. Club: Federal City (Washington). Author: (with Joseph A. Califano, Jr.) The Media and the Law, 1976; Simons' List Book, 1977; Business and Media, 1979; Home: 906 N Overlook Dr Alexandria VA 22305 Office: 1150 15th St NW Washington DC 20005

SIMONS, LAWRENCE B., govt. ofcl.; b. S.I., N.Y., Oct. 19, 1924; LL.B., Columbia U., 1949; married. Asso. law firm Spring & Eastman, N.Y.C., 1949-53; v.p., gen. mgr. Hemisphere Corp., P.R., 1953-54; gen. mgr. Monitor Industries, P.R., 1954-55; v.p., gen. mgr. Caribe Knitting Mills, Inc., P.R., 1955-57; engaged in real estate and constrn. bus., S.I., 1957-67; pres. LBS Constrn. Co., S.I., 1967-77; asst. sec. for housing and fed. housing commr. HUD, Washington, 1977—; dir. Nat. Housing Conf., 1976. Bd. dirs. N.Y. State Urban Devel. Corp., N.Y.C. Public Devel. Corp.; commr. Greater N.Y. council Boy Scouts Am. Named Man of Year, N.Y.C. Builders Assn., 1972. Mem. S.I. C. of C. (v.p.), Nat. Assn. Home Builders (exec. com. 1968-76), N.Y. State Builders Assn. (pres. 1965). Office: HUD 451 7th St SW Washington DC 20410

SIMONS, LEONARD NORMAN RASHALL, advt. exec.; b. Youngstown, Ohio, July 24, 1904; s. William Rashall and Minna (Williams) S.; LL.D., Wayne State U., 1957; D.H.L., Hebrew Union Coll.-Jewish Inst. Religion, 1964; m. Harriette Lieberman, Jan. 21, 1930; children—Mary Lou (Mrs. Morton Zieve), Susan (Mrs. Monte Nagler). Partner, Simons-Michelson Co., investments, Troy, Mich., 1929—; ret. founding dir. City Nat. Bank of Detroit; former vis. lectr. N.Y. U.; v.p. Simons Michelson Zieve, Inc., advt. agy., Troy, 1977—. Past pres. Wayne State U. Press; pres. emeritus Detroit Hist. Commn.; past chmn. bd. Mich. Cancer Found.; past chmn. United Negro Coll. Fund Mich. Bd. dirs., former v.p. Jewish Welfare Fedn. Detroit; bd. dirs. Am. Jewish Com., Jewish Nat. Fund, Det. Service Group, Nat. Found. Infantile Paralysis S.E. Mich. (former chmn.), Sinai Hosp. (former v.p.), Jewish Home for Aged (past chmn. bd.), NCCJ (brotherhood chmn. 1952), Detroit Round Table Caths., Jews and Protestants. Fellow Brandeis U. Decorated chevalier dans l'Ordre Nationale du Merite (France); recipient Prime Minister's medal State of Israel; LNS Forest given in Israel Jewish Nat. Fund; recipient various other citations. Jewish (past pres. temple). Mem. Jewish Hist. Soc. Mich. (dir.), Am. Jewish Hist. Soc. (dir.), Detroit Hist. Soc. (dir.), The Hundred Club Detroit (dir.), Jewish War Vets. (hon.), Phi Beta Kappa, Zeta Beta Tau. Mason. Clubs: Franklin Hills Country (past pres.), Standard, Adcraft. Home: 16300 W 9 Mile Rd Apt 1002 Southfield MI 48075 Office: Simons-Michelson Co 3250 W Big Beaver Rd Troy MI 48084

SIMONS, LEWIS MARTIN, journalist; b. Paterson, N.J., Jan. 9, 1939; s. Abram and Goldie (Fleisher) S.; student Rutgers U., 1956-58; B.S., N.Y. U., 1962; M.S., Columbia, 1964; m. Carol Seiderman, Feb. 7, 1965; children—Justine, Rebecca, Adam. Corr. assigned Saigon, Malaysia-Singapore for AP, N.Y.C., 1964-70; corr. S. Asia, Washington Post, India, 1971-75, S.E. Asia, 1975-77, Washington, 1977—. Served with USMCR, 1962-63. Edward R. Murrow fellow Council Fgn. Relations, N.Y.C., 1970-71. Office: Washington Post 1150 15th St NW Washington DC 20071

SIMONS, SAMUEL STONEY, health cons.; b. Charleston, S.C., May 10, 1920; s. Albert and Harriet Porcher (Stoney) S.; A.B., Princeton, 1942, postgrad., 1946; m. Virginia Laurie Cooke, Sept. 9, 1944; children—Samuel Stoney, Richard C., Ellen Daniel, Anne Dixon, Elizabeth Gaillard. Successively market research analyst, asst. to exec. v.p., head new products dept., asst. mgr. research and devel. Smith Kline & French Labs., Phila., 1946-66; v.p. Western Savs. Bank, Phila., 1966-70, exec. v.p., 1970-77; prin. Third Age Inc., life care and long term care consultants, 1978—. Vice pres. Children's Aid Soc., Children's Services, Inc.; chmn. bd. Chestnut Hill Hosp., 1974-78, Oncological Hosp.; chmn. bd. Springside Sch., 1961-66, Council Voluntary Child Care Agys., Phila., 1968-73, Health and Welfare Council Phila., 1955-61. Bd. dirs. Tri-County Health and Welfare Council. Served with USNR, 1942-46. Decorated Purple Heart. Republican. Episcopalian (vestryman). Home: 540 E Evergreen Ave Philadelphia PA 19118 Office: 511 Welsh St Chester PA 19013

SIMONS, SAVILLA MILLIS, former social work adminstr.; b. Chgo.; d. Harry Alvin and Alice (Schoff) Millis; Ph.B., M.A., U. Chgo.; m. V. Dodge Simons, Jr. Legis. sec. Ill. LWV, 1931-32; exec. dir. Douglas Smith Fund, Chgo., 1932-40; pres. Lower North Community Council, Chgo., 1936-39; specialist spl. studies unit Children's Bur., U.S. Dept. Labor, 1940-43; chief assistance analysis sect., bur. pub. assistance Social Security Bd., 1943-46; asst. dir. office internat. relations Fed. Security Agy., 1946-51; asst. chief, acting chief, health, manpower and edn. div. Tech. Coop. Adminstrn., Dept. State, 1951-52, dir. manpower and community services staff, 1952-53; gen. sec. YWCA of U.S., 1953-58; gen. dir. Nat. Travelers Aid Assn., 1958-67; adviser to U.S. rep. on UN Econ. and Social Council, 6th, 8th, 9th sessions, 1947-49; chmn. U.S. del. UN Conf. of Host Govts. for Social Welfare Fellowship Program in Western Hemisphere, 1949; chmn. com. residence laws Nat. Social Welfare Assembly, 1958-63; dir. Am. Immigration Conf., 1958-67; dir. Social Legis. Service; cons. gen. bd. Nat. Council Chs. of Christ in U.S., 1953-58; bd. dirs. United Community Def. Services, 1954-57; bd. govs. USO, 1954-65; mem. U.S. com. Internat. Conf. Social Work, 1954-65, U.S. rep. preconf. working group, Italy, 1960; chmn. group work sect. Nat. Conf. Social Work, 1954-55; mem. council of dels. dir. Council Social Work Edn., 1954-57; chmn. Conf. Nat. Agy. Execs., Nat. Social Welfare Assembly, 1959-60; exec. com. Nat. Conf. on Social Welfare, 1959-62; mem. adv. com. on young workers U.S. Dept. Labor, 1959-61, travel adv. com. U.S. Travel Service, 1963-64; dir. Community Devel. Found., Save Children Fedn., 1958-73. Recipient Pub. Service citation U. Chgo. Alumni Assn., 1955. Mem. Am. Assn. Social Workers (chmn. Chgo. chpt. 1938-40, nat sec. 1939-40, chmn. nat. com. on internat. welfare 1946-48), Nat. Assn. Social Workers, LWV, AAUW, Phi Beta Kappa. Contbr. articles to profl. jours. Home: 1508 Canyonwood Ct No 1 Walnut Creek CA 94595. *I have undertaken a job, whether governmental or private, local or national, only if I believed it was worth doing because it would make some contribution to the public good.*

SIMONS, THOMAS CUNNINGHAM, holding co. exec.; b. Pasadena, Calif., Nov. 12, 1928; s. Seward Churchyard and Evelyn (Cunningham) S.; grad. Thacher Sch., Ojai, Calif., 1946; A.B., Harvard, 1950; m. Joan Gardiner, Sept. 16, 1950; children—Thomas Seward, Martha Gardiner, Sarah Carver, John Caldwell. With Conn. Gen. Life Ins. Co., 1953-78, mgr. Los Angeles, 1960-63, v.p. agy. dept., 1936-69, v.p., 1969-71, sr. v.p., 1971-76, exec. v.p., 1976-78; chmn., pres., chief exec. officer, dir. Capital Holding Corp., Louisville, 1978—; dir. Citizens Fidelity Corp., Citizens Fidelity Bank and Trust Co. (all Louisville). Past pres. Urban League Greater Hartford (Conn.); bd. dirs. Louisville Fund for Arts, Louisville Metro United Way, Ky. Rural Devel. and Housing Found.; bd. overseers U. Louisville; v.p. Louisville/Jefferson County Downtown Devel. Corp. Served to lt. (j.g.) USNR, 1950-53. C.L.U. Mem. Louisville C. of C. (dir.). Clubs: Louisville Country, Jefferson, Pendennis. Home: 3606 Glenview Ave Glenview KY 40025 Office: PO Box 32830 Louisville KY 40232

SIMONSON, HUGH MELVIN, ret. adj. gen. Wis.; b. Pittsville, Wis., Apr. 2, 1917; s. Carl Sigrid and Leah Leonore (Lewis) S.; children—Mark W., Lynne M., Acct., Consol. Papers, Wisconsin Rapids, Wis., 1937-40; with Wisconsin Rapids Police Dept., 1940-53; with Wis. Nat. Guard, 1947-79, chief auditor, 1953-59, dep. adj. gen., 1969-77, adj. gen. dept. mil. affairs State of Wis., 1977-79. Served with AUS, 1942-46. Recipient Meritorious Service award Nat. Guard Assn. U.S., 1975; decorated Legion of Merit. Mem. Nat. Guard Assn. U.S. (mem. exec. council). Lutheran. Clubs: Masons, Shriners. Home: 1621 Tarragon Dr Madison WI 53716

SIMONSON, ROY WALTER, soil scientist; b. Agate, N.D., Sept. 7, 1908; s. Otto and Johanna (Carlson) S.; B.S., N.D. Agrl. Coll., 1934; Ph.D., U. Wis., 1938; m. Susan Miller, Nov. 14, 1942; children—Walter, Bruce. Asst. prof. soils Iowa State Coll., Ames, 1938-43; in charge classification and nomenclature soils Southeastern U.S., Dept. of Agr., 1944-47, devel. soil classification program islands of Western Pacific, 1947-48, head soil sci. Pacific area, 1948, asst. chief div. soil survey Agrl. Research Adminstrn., 1949-52, dir. soil classification and correlation Soil Conservation Service, 1953-73; cons. Ministry Agr., Brazil, 1954, FAO, UN, Rome, Italy, 1959, Ministry Agr., Venezuela, 1974, Dept. Agrl. Tech. Services, South Africa, 1978. Fellow AAAS, Am. Soc. Agronomy, Soil Sci. Soc. Am. (hon.); mem. Brit. Soc. Soil Sci., Internat. Soc. Soil Sci. Author: (with Riecken, Smith) Understanding Iowa Soils, 1951. Editor: Non-agricultural Applications of Soil Surveys, 1974. Cons. editor Soil Science, 1950—; asso. editor Soil Science America Proc., 1957-60; cons. editor Geoderma, 1967-71, editor in chief, 1971—. Contbr. articles to sci. jours. Home: 4613 Beechwood Rd College Park MD 20740 Office: PO Box 427 College Park MD 20740

SIMONT, MARC, artist; b. Paris, France, Nov. 23, 1915 (came to U.S. 1927, naturalized 1936); s. José and Dolores (Basté) S.; student Academie Julian, Academie Ranson, André Lhote Sch. (all Paris), 1932-35, N.A.D., N.Y.C., 1936; m. Sara Dalton, Apr. 7, 1945; 1 son, Marc D. Asst. to Ezra Winter on Jefferson Wing mural, Library of Congress, 1940; author, illustrator children's books, 1939—. Tiffany Found. fellow, 1937; recipient Caldecott award, 1957. Mem. Am. Vets. Com. Author, illustrator: Opera Soufflé, 1950; Polly's Oats, 1951; The Lovely Summer, 1952; (with Red Smith) How to Get to First Base, 1952; Mimi, 1955; The Plumber Out of the Sea, 1955; The Contest at Paca, 1959; How Come Elephants?, 1965; Afternoon in Spain, 1965; A Childs' Eye View of the World, 1972. Translator: The Lieutenant Colonel and the Gypsy, 1971. Home: RFD 96 Town St West Cornwall CT 06796

SIMONTON, WESLEY CLARK, librarian; b. Cin., June 22, 1921; s. Walter Clark and Lily Bell (Whitney) S.; A.B., U. Cin., 1941; B.S.L.S., Columbia U., 1946, M.S.L.S., 1948; Ph.D., U. Ill., 1960; m. Susan Humphrey, July 28, 1973; children—Ann Elizabeth Simonton Rockwell, Katherine Byrne Simonton. Sr. cataloger Columbia U. Libraries, 1947-48; chief catalog librarian U. Minn., 1949-56; asst. prof. U. Minn. Library Sch., 1956-60, asso. prof., 1960-65, prof., 1965—, dir., 1974—. Served with USNR, 1943-46. Mem. AAUP, ALA, Am. Soc. Info. Sci., Assn. Am. Library Schs., Minn. Library Assn., Phi Beta Kappa. Editor: Information Retrieval Today, 1963; Information Retrieval with Special Reference to the Biomedical Sciences, 1966. Home: 1779 Dupont Ave S Minneapolis MN 55403 Office: U Minn 117 Pleasant St SE Minneapolis MN 55455

SIMOONS, FREDERICK JOHN, educator; b. Phila., Nov. 2, 1922; s. Frederick John and Stephanie (Ryckeboer) S.; B.A. in Sociology, Rutgers U., 1949; postgrad. U. Wis., spring, 1949; postgrad. Harvard, 1949-50; M.A., U. Calif. at Berkeley, 1952, Ph.D. in Geography, 1956; m. Elizabeth Stadler, Apr. 16, 1949. Instr., Ohio State U., 1956-57; from asst. prof. to prof. geography U. Wis., 1957-66; prof. geography La. State U., 1966-67, U. Tex., Austin, 1967-69; prof. U. Calif. at Davis, 1969—, chmn. dept. geography, 1973-77. Served with AUS, 1944-46. Guggenheim fellow, 1963-64. Mem. Phi Beta Kappa. Author: Northwest Ethiopia: Peoples and Economy, 1960; Eat Not This Flesh: Food Avoidances in the Old World, 1961; A Ceremonial Ox of India, 1968; contbr. articles to profl. jours. Office: Dept Geography U Calif Davis CA 95616

SIMPICH, WILLIAM MORRIS, pub. affairs cons.; b. Washington, Sept. 24, 1924; s. Frederick and Margaret (Edwards) S.; student George Washington U., 1942-43; B.S., U.S. Naval Acad., 1946; m. Margaret Pearson Hunter, Sept. 9, 1950; children—William Morris, Margaret Edwards, John Hunter, Joseph Pearson. Asso. Ivy Lee & T.J. Ross (name later changed to T.J. Ross & Assos., Inc.), N.Y.C., 1949-51, 54-63, v.p., 1964, sec., treas., 1965—, sr. v.p., 1977—, also dir. Served with U.S. Navy, 1946-49, 51-53. Mem. Nat. Investor Relations Inst. Episcopalian. Clubs: Union League (N.Y.C.); Riverside (Conn.) Yacht; Army-Navy Country (Arlington, Va.). Home: 19 Old Club House Rd Old Greenwich CT 06870 Office: T J Ross & Assos Inc 405 Lexington Ave New York NY 10017

SIMPKIN, LAWRENCE JAMES, utilities exec.; b. Sault Ste Marie, Mich., Jan. 1, 1933; s. Fred Bernard and Helen Clara (Goetz) S.; B.S. in Elec. Engring., Mich. Technol. Inst., 1954; M.S., Wayne State U., 1965; m. Agnes Diane L'Huillier, Sept. 3, 1960; children—Lawrence J., Lynn Marie, Dawn Catherine. Engr., Detroit Edison Co., 1957-67, supr. engring. instrumentation, 1967-69, dir. elec. div., 1969-72, dir. engring. research, 1972-75, dir. tech. systems planning, 1975-76, gen. dir. div. services, 1976—; lectr. Lawrence Inst. Tech., 1965-72; adj. prof. U. Mich., 1974 Served to capt. USAF, 1954-57. Registered profl. engr., Mich. Mem. IEEE, Engring. Soc. Detroit, Sigma Xi. Contbr. articles to profl. jours. Home: 6206 Fairwood Rd Dearborn Heights MI 48127 Office: 2000 2d Ave Detroit MI 48226

SIMPKINS, GILBERT ARNOTT, fin. co. exec.; b. Kew Gardens, N.Y., Mar. 17, 1928; s. Gilbert Charles and Ruby (Wilson) S.; B.S., Syracuse U., 1950; LL.B., Cornell U., 1953; grad. Advanced Mgmt. Program, Harvard U., 1973; m. Joy Y. Grady, Sept. 19, 1953; children—Gilbert Charles II, Gracia Parks, Mary Louise, Sarah Elizabeth. With Coopers & Lybrand, N.Y.C., 1953-59; tax mgr. Abex Corp., N.Y.C., 1959-61; comptroller Abex of Can., Montreal, Que., 1961-65; v.p. fin. Norlin Corp., N.Y.C., 1967-79, sr. v.p., 1979—, also dir. Served with U.S. Army, 1945-47. Mem. Am. Bar Assn., Am. Inst. C.P.A.'s, Fin. Execs. Inst. Home: Rural Route 2 Box 100 Poundridge NY 10576 Office: Westchester Dr E White Plains NY 10601

SIMPKINS, JOE, bus. exec.; b. St. Louis, Sept. 15, 1905; s. Leo and Ella (Fredkin) S.; m. Mildred Underwood, Dec. 21, 1933; 1 dau., Linda (Mrs. Farrel Kahn). Pres. Joe Simpkins Ford Agy., St. Louis, 1947-56; pres. Joe Simpkins Oil Devels., St. Louis, 1964—; pres., chmn. bd. Tiffany Industries, St. Louis, 1968—. Vice pres., charter mem. Herbert Hoover's Boys Club. Bd. dirs. Jewish Hosp., Jewish Fedn., City of Hope, Dismas House, Our Lady of Grace Child Center, Internat. Variety Clubs; trustee Israel Bond Com. Recipient Eleanor Roosevelt Humanitarian award, 1970; St. Louis Humanities award, 1972. Home: 2220 S Warson Rd Saint Louis MO 63124 Office: 100 Progress Pkwy Maryland Heights MO 63043. *No human has any control over his birth. All my life I have tried to put myself in the place of less fortunate persons and keep reminding myself that I could have been born in their place instead of my own, especially when I see the unfortunates in Africa and other similar surroundings.*

SIMPKINS, JOHN EDWARD, coll. dean; b. Detroit, Oct. 18, 1932; s. Samuel Isaac and Evelyn (Simmons) S.; B.A., Wayne State U., 1955, M.A., 1961; M.A. (Univ. fellow 1968, Martin Luther King fellow and Woodrow Wilson fellow 1968-69), Harvard, 1969, Ed.D. (Martin Luther King fellow and Woodrow Wilson fellow 1969-70), 1971; m. Alice Mann, Dec. 22, 1957; children—Edward, Ann Marie, Evelyn. Vice pres. Detroit Fedn. Tchrs., 1962-68; asst. dean Harvard, 1969-71; chief negotiator Phila. Pub. Schs., 1971-72, Balt. Pub. Schs., 1973-74; dean Coll. Edn., Wayne State U., 1974—. Labor cons.; arbitrator. Am. Arbitration Assn., Mich. Employment Relations Cons. Bd. dirs. Merrill-Palmer Inst., Detroit, 1975—. Served with AUS, 1956-58. Recipient Human Rights award for contbns. to labor Commn. on Community Relations, City of Detroit, 1968, Spirit of Detroit award Detroit Common Council, 1974. Mem. Mich. Assn. Study Afro-Am. Life and History (exec. dir. 1972), Mid Am. Assn. Edn. Opportunity, Phi Delta Kappa, Kappa Alpha Psi. Author: (with Frank Ross) Success and Language, 1962; Problems, Issues and Techniques in the Resolution of School Disputes, 1970. Home: 4255 W Outer Dr Detroit MI 48221

SIMPSON, ADELE, costume designer; b. N.Y.C., Dec. 8, 1908; d. Jacob and Ella (Bloch) Smithline; grad. Pratt Inst., Bklyn.; m. Wesley William Simpson, Oct. 8, 1930; children—Jeffrey R., Joan Ellen. Pres., dir. Adele Simpson, Inc. Work displayed in Met. Costume Inst., Bklyn. Mus., Dallas Library. Recipient Neiman-Marcus Fashion award, 1946, Coty Fashion award, 1947, First Nat. Cotton Council award, 1953. Mem. Fashion Group, Inc., N.Y.C. Office: 530 7th Ave New York NY 10018

SIMPSON, ALAN, former coll. pres.; b. Gateshead, Eng., July 23, 1912 (came to U.S., 1946, naturalized, 1954); s. George Hardwick and Isabella (Graham) S.; B.A. with 1st class honors in History (scholar), Worcester Coll., Oxford U., 1933, M.A. (Harmsworth scholar), Merton Coll., 1935, D.Phil., 1940; Commonwealth fellow Harvard, 1935-37; LL.D., Colgate U., Knox Coll.; L.H.D., Nat. Coll. Edn., R.I. Coll., U. Rochester; m. Mary McEldowney, Aug. 8, 1938; children—Barbara (Mrs. Frank T. Flynn III), Carol (Mrs. J.A. Stern), Rupert. Sr. lectr. modern Brit. history U. St. Andrews, Scotland, 1938-46; asst. prof. history U. Chgo., 1946-54, asso. prof., 1954-59, Thomas E. Donnelley prof. history, dean of coll., 1959-64; pres., prof. Vassar Coll., Poughkeepsie, N.Y., 1964-77. Sec. Midwest Conf. Brit. Historians, 1954-61; mem. council Inst. Early American History and Culture, Williamsburg, Va., 1957-60; mem. N.Y. Gov.'s Hudson River Valley Commn., 1966-73; trustee Colonial Williamsburg (Va.), Salve Regina Coll., Newport, Va. Served to maj., arty. Brit. Army, 1940-45. Mem. Am. Council Edn. (dir.), Assn. Am. Colls., Am. Hist. Assn., Am. Antiquarian Soc., Conf. on Brit. Studies. Episcopalian. Clubs: Tavern (Chgo.); Century Assn. (N.Y.). Author: Puritanism in Old and New England (Book prize Inst. Early Am. History and Culture), 1955; The Wealth of the Gentry, 1540-1660; East Anglian Studies, 1961; (with wife) Mark Twain's Great Niece: The Story of Jean Webster, 1979; co-editor: The People Shall Judge: Readings in the Formation of American Policy, 1949; (with Mary Simpson) Diary of King Philip's War (1675-76) by Colonel Benjamin Church, 1975; I Too Am Here: Selections from the Letters of Jane Welsh Carlyle, 1977. Home: Yellow Gate Farm Little Compton RI 02837

SIMPSON, ALAN KOOI, U.S. senator; b. Denver, Sept. 2, 1931; s. Milward Lee and Lorna (Kooi) S.; B.S., U. Wyo., 1954, J.D., 1958; m. Ann Schroll, June 21, 1954; children—William Lloyd, Colin Mackenzie, Susan Lorna. Admitted to Wyo. bar, 1958, U.S. Supreme Ct. bar, 1964; asst. atty. gen. State of Wyo., 1959; partner firm Simpson, Kepler, Simpson & Cozzens, and predecessor, Cody, Wyo., 1959-78; mem. Wyo. Ho. of Reps., 1964-77, majority whip, 1973-75, majority floor leader, 1975-77, speaker pro tem, 1977; mem. U.S. Senate from Wyo., 1978—; city atty. City of Cody, 1959-69; legis. participant Eagleton Inst. Politics, Rutgers U., 1971; former vice chmn. Wyo. Gov.'s Com. on Inter-govtl. Cooperation; former dir. First Wyo. Bank, Cody. Formerly v.p., pres., trustee N.W. Community Coll., Powell, Wyo., 1968-76; trustee Buffalo Bill Hist. Center, Cody; bd. dirs. Western Arts Found., Cody; trustee Gottsche Found. Rehab. Center, Thermopolis, Wyo.; vestryman Christ Ch. of Cody, 1960-64; del. Nat. Triennial Episcopal Ch. Conv., 1973, 76. Mem. Wyo. Bar Assn., Park County Bar Assn., Fifth Jud. Dist. Bar Assn., Am. Bar Assn., Assn. Trial Lawyers Am., U. Wyo. Alumni Assn. (pres. 1962, 63), VFW (life). Clubs: Eagles, Elks, Masons, Shriners; Rotary (pres. local club 1972-73) (Cody). Home: 1112 Brentfield Dr McLean VA 22101 Office: 6203 Dirksen Office Bldg Washington DC 20510

SIMPSON, CARY HATCHER, broadcasting sta. exec.; b. Huntingdon, Pa., Jan. 25, 1927; s. Frederick Miller and Lois (Hatcher) S.; B.S., Juniata Coll., 1949; m. Betty Louise Finnegan, Aug. 16, 1958; children—Barbara Ellen, John Frederick. Program dir. Sta. WHUN, Huntingdon, Pa., 1947-49, Sta. KCOW, Alliance, Nebr., 1949, Sta. WMRN, Marion, Ohio, 1949-50; founder, pres. Allegheny Mountain Network, 1950—; coordinator Internat. Broadcasters Idea Bank, 1975-76; Pa. chmn. FCC Emergency Broadcast System, 1965—. Bd. dirs. Pa. div. Am. Cancer Soc., 1964—; v.p. Tyrone (Pa.) Parking Authority, 1959—; mem. Tyrone Downtown Revitalization Commn., 1977—. Named Boss of Yr., Tyrone Jaycees, 1964, recipient Disting. Service award, 1971. Served with USNR, 1945-46. Mem. Pa. Assn. Broadcasters (pres. 1964-65), Pa. Asso. Press Broadcasters (pres. 1973-74), Radio Advt. Bur. (sec., bd. dirs.). Presbyterian (elder 1963—, Sunday sch. supt. 1966-77). Clubs: Masons, Shriners, Elks. Home: 601 5th St Tyrone PA 16686 Office: Box 247 Tyrone PA 16686. *It's so much more fun to be a medium-sized toad in a relatively small pond, but to have known and to have worked with some of the super-achievers of the bigger-sized ponds. I have found that people are very much alike-whether it's one of the top executives of a large national organization, or the men who helped to count the collection at Sunday Sch.*

SIMPSON, CHARLES HAMMOND, indsl. gas co. exec.; b. Oolahga, Okla., Mar. 28, 1929; s. Charles Hammond and Lelah (Taylor) S.; B.S. in Bus. Adminstrn., U. Tulsa, 1953, B.A., 1953; B.S. in Metallurgy, Purdue u., 1961; m. Shirley M. Barbour, Mar. 24, 1952; children—Cynthia, Cathryn, Christine, Caren. With Union Carbide Corp., Tex., Okla., Ind., 1951-63, asst. gen. mgr. N.Y.C., 1963; v.p. Liberty Nat. Bank, Oklahoma City, 1963-65; gen. mgr. Kerr-McGee Corp., Oklahoma City, 1965-67; pres. Airco Indsl. Gases, Murray Hill, N.J., 1967-73; pres., dir. C.S. Industries, Inc., 1973; chmn. bd. Carbonic Engring. Corp., 1973—, also dir. Gen. chmn. 1980 U.S. Open Golf Championship. Mem. Am. Iron and Steel Inst., Iron and Steel Engrs., Metall. Engring. Soc., Compressed Gas Assn. (dir.), Alpha Tau Omega. Republican. Presbyn. Mason. Author: Chemicals from the Atmosphere, 1969. Home: 95 Tanglewood Dr Summit NJ 07901 Office: 11764 Harrells Ferry Rd Suites E and F Baton Rouge LA 70816

SIMPSON, CHARLES REAGAN, U.S. judge; b. Danville, Ill., June 16, 1921; s. Frank and Mamie (Moreland) S.; B.A. with highest honors, U. Ill., 1944, J.D. with high honors, 1945; LL.M., Harvard, 1950; m. Ruth V. Thomason, June 5, 1948. Admitted to Ill. bar, 1945; practiced in Champaign, Ill., 1946-49; atty. OPS, 1951-52; with legislation and regulations div. Office Chief Counsel, IRS, 1952-65, dir. office, 1964-65; judge U.S. Tax Ct., 1965—. Teaching fellow Harvard Law Sch., 1950-51. Chmn. Champaign County chpt. Nat. Found. Infantile Paralysis, 1947-49. Mem. Ill. Gen. Assembly from 24th Dist., 1947-50. Recipient Justice Tom C. Clark award Fed. Bar Assn., 1964. Mem. Am. Bar Assn., Am. Law Inst., Am. Judicature Soc., Phi Beta Kappa, Order of Coif, Phi Kappa Phi. Home: 2500 Virginia Ave NW Washington DC 20037 Office: US Tax Court 400 2d St NW Washington DC 20217

SIMPSON, DAVID WILLIAM, artist; b. Pasadena, Calif., Jan. 20, 1928; s. Frederick and Mary Adeline (White) S.; B.F.A., Calif. Sch. Fine Arts, 1956; M.A., San Francisco State Coll., 1958; m. Dolores D. Debus, July 30, 1954; 1 stepson, Gregory C. Vose; 1 dau., Lisa C. Instr. art Am. River Jr. Coll., Sacramento, 1958-60, Contra Costa Jr. Coll., San Pablo, Calif., 1960-65; prof. art U. Calif., Berkeley, 1967—; exhibited in one-man shows including: Robert Elkton Gallery, N.Y.C., 1961, 63, 64, David Stuart Galleries, Los Angeles, 1966, 68, San Francisco Mus. Art, 1967, Henri Gallery, Washington, 1968, Oakland Museum, 1978; exhibited in group shows including: Mus. Modern Art, N.Y.C., 1963, Carnegie Internat., Pitts., 1961-62, 66-67, Los Angeles Mus. Art, 1964, U. Ill., 1969, Expo '70, Osaka, Japan, 1970, Josly Art Mus., Omaha, 1970, John Berggruen Gallery, San Francisco, 1979; represented in permanent collections including: Phila. Mus. Art, Nat. Collection Fine Arts, Washington, Seattle Art Mus., La Jolla (Calif.) Mus. Art, Mus. Modern Art, N.Y.C., San Francisco Mus. Art, Oakland (Calif.) Mus. Home: 565 Vistamont St Berkeley CA 94708 Office: Art Dept U Calif Berkeley CA 94720

SIMPSON, DONALD BRUCE, librarian; b. Ithaca, N.Y., Dec. 13, 1942; s. Francis Alfred and Drusilla Lucille (Dickson) S.; B.A., Alfred (N.Y.) U., 1964; M.S. in L.S., Syracuse (N.Y.) U., 1970; m. Lupe M. Rodriguez; 1 son, Michael John. Asst. librarian Keuka (N.Y.) Coll., 1970-71; head catalog center State Library Ohio, Columbus, 1971-75; exec. dir. Bibliog. Center Research, Rocky Mountain Region, Inc., Denver, 1975—; cons. in field; mem. adv. bd. Satellite Library Network Project, 1976-77, Telefacsimile Library Network, 1978—; mem. users council Ohio Coll. Library Center, 1978—. Served with USAF, 1965-69. Decorated Air Force Commendation medal. Mem. ALA, Assn. State Library Agencies (pres. 1977-78), Am. Soc. Info. Sci., Spl. Libraries Assn., Am. Soc. Pub. Adminstrn., Beta Phi Mu. Author reports, articles in field. Home: 2603 S Balsam St Lakewood CO 80227 Office: 245 Columbine St Suite 212 Denver CO 80206. *If history and the profession of librarianship deem my accomplishments as successful, it is because I have undertaken every task and assignment as important in its own right. Each activity has been pursued with honor since the events and how they were met will live beyond me.*

SIMPSON, DONALD JAMES, lawyer; b. Des Moines, Sept. 28, 1907; s. John Clarence and Ora E. (Barlow) S.; B.S., Northwestern U., 1929, E.E., 1930; LL.B., George Washington U., 1935; m. Genevieve Wheeler, July 6, 1931; children—John Douglas, Marcia Lynne. Elec. engr. Gen. Electric Co., 1930, with patent dept., 1931-36; admitted to D.C. bar, 1934, Ill. bar, 1939; practiced in Chgo., 1936—; asso. firm Hill, Gross, Simpson, VanSanten, Steadman, Chiara and Simpson, 1936-43, partner, 1943—. Mem. Chgo. Patent Law Assn. (past mem. bd. mgrs.), Am., Ill., Chgo. bar assns., Chgo. Mountaineering Club, Evanston Hist. Soc. (former trustee), Tau Beta Pi, Sigma Xi. Republican. Congregationalist. Clubs: Union League, Chicago Yacht, Adventurers, Metropolitan, Westmoreland Country; American Alpine; Alpine of Canada; Swiss Alpine; Chgo. Mountaineering (past pres.). Home: 2733 Lincoln St Evanston IL 60201 Office: 70th Floor Sears Tower Chicago IL 60606

SIMPSON, DOUGLAS GORDON, assn. exec.; b. Glasgow, Scotland, May 3, 1910; s. Fred Gordon and Minnie (Addie) S.; chartered accountant, Glasgow U., 1932; m. Annette Kidd, Nov. 28, 1936; children—Gordon Douglas, Aline Anderson (Mrs. William D. Cousens). With McFarlane Hutton & Patrick, chartered accountants, Glasgow, 1927-32, Brown & Co. Ltd., Colombo, Ceylon, 1934-47; sec. DeHavilland Propellers Ltd., 1947-52; dir. DeHavilland Aircraft Can. Ltd., 1952-54; controller Trans-Can. Pipe Lines Ltd., 1954-70, mgr. adminstrn. N.W. project study group, 1971-72; dir. Willson Assos. Ltd., Calgary, 1973; exec. v.p. Fin. Execs. Inst. Willowdale, Ont., 1973—. Active blood donor service Canadian Red Cross Soc. Bd. dirs. Mid-Can. Devel. Found. Served to lt. comdr. Royal Naval Vol. Res., 1939-45. Mem. Fin. Execs. Inst. (pres. Toronto 1963-64, chmn. Canadian com. 1966-67). Clubs: Granite (Toronto); Glencoe (Calgary). Home: 4000 Yonge St Apt 733 Toronto ON M4N 2N9 Canada Office: 207 141 Adelaide St W Toronto ON M5H 3L5 Canada

SIMPSON, ERNEST CLIFFORD, govt. engr.; b. Huntington, W.Va., Sept. 4, 1917; s. E. Wellington and Mabel G. (Wilson) S.; B.S. in Mech. Engring. with distinction, U. Ky., 1939; M.S. in Mech. Engring., Ohio State U., 1948; m. Vivian Busse, Nov. 27, 1940; children—James Clifford, Thomas Lee. Field engr. Trane Co., LaCrosse, Wis., 1939-40; design engr. Mawen Motor Corp., Lexington, Ky., 1940-42; project engr. USAF Propulsion Lab., 1945-50; dir. turbine engine div. USAF Aero Propulsion Lab., Wright-Patterson AFB, Ohio, 1952—. Served from lt. to capt., AUS, 1942-45; from capt. to maj., USAF, 1950-52. Registered profl. engr., Ohio. Fellow Am. Inst. Aeros. and Astronautics (Goddard award 1968); mem. Research Soc. Am., Tau Beta Pi. Episcopalian. Office: USAF Aero Propulsion Lab Wright-Patterson AFB OH 45433. *Be true to your profession or you are less than whole.*

SIMPSON, FRED BRYAN, lawyer; b. Birmingham, Ala., Sept. 4, 1935; s. Joseph Woodly and Nellie Demayze (Ware) S.; LL.B., Vanderbilt U., 1964; m. Peggy Ann Holloway, Aug. 20, 1961; children—Bryan, Cynthia, Derek. Admitted to Ala. bar, 1965, U.S. Supreme Ct. bar; atty. U.S.Army Redstone Arsenal, Huntsville, Ala., 1964-65; with firm Morring, Giles, Watson & Willisson, Huntsville, 1965-69; dist. atty. 23d Jud. Circuit Ala., Huntsville, 1969—. Vice pres. Huntsville Christmas Charities. Alternate del. Dem. Nat. Conv., 1972. Served with USAF, 1953-57. Mem. Fed., Am., Ala., Madison County bar assns., Nat., Ala. (pres.) dist. attys. assns., Am. Judicature Soc. Baptist (trustee). Elk; mem. Fraternal Order of Police (trustee). Home: 724 Mira Vista Dr SE Huntsville AL 35802 Office: Madison County Courthouse Huntsville AL 35801

SIMPSON, FREDERICK JAMES, research adminstr.; b. Regina, Sask., Can., June 8, 1922; s. Ralph James and Lillian Mary (Anderson) S.; B.Sc., U. Alta. (Can.), 1944, M.Sc. in Agr., 1946; Ph.D. in Bacteriology, U. Wis., 1952; m. Margaret Christine Simpson, May 28, 1947; children—Christine Louise, Steven James, Leslie Coleen, Ralph Edwin, David Glen. With Nat. Research Council Can., 1946—, asst. dir. Atlantic Regional Lab., Halifax, N.S., 1970-73, dir. Atlantic Regional Lab., 1973—; vis. scientist U. Ill., Urbana, 1955-56, vis. prof., 1964; mem. exec. council Atlantic Provinces Interuniv. Com. on Scis., 1976-79. Decorated Queen's Silver Anniversary medal. Mem. Can. Soc. Microbiologists (sec.-treas. 1969-70, v.p., 1971-72, pres. 1972-73), Am. Soc. Microbiology, Am. Soc. Biol. Chemists, Nova Scotian Inst. Sci. (v.p. 1975-76, pres. 1977-78), Internat. Phycological Soc., Sigma Xi. Mem. United Ch. of Canada. Contbr. numerous articles to profl. jours. Home: 54 Tangmere Crescent Halifax NS B3M 1K Canada Office: Atlantic Regional Lab 1411 Oxford St Halifax NS B3H 3Z1 Canada

SIMPSON, GEDDES WILSON, entomologist; b. Scranton, Pa., Aug. 15, 1908; s. Frank Morton and Mary Elizabeth (Wilson) S.; A.B., Bucknell U., 1929; M.A., Cornell U., 1931; Ph.D., 1935; m. Blanche May Thomas, Oct. 21, 1933; children—Mary Elizabeth, Frank Thomas, Blanche Amy, Geddes Wilson. Research asst. N.Y. State Coll. Agr., 1930-31; asst. entomologist Maine Agrl. Expt. Sta., 1931-44, asso. entomologist, 1944-52, entomologist, 1952-54, entomologist, chmn. dept. Agrl. Expt. Sta. and Coll. Life Scis. and Agr., Orono, 1954-74, prof. entomology emeritus, 1974—; asst. to dir. Maine Agrl. Expt. Sta., 1976—. Fellow AAAS; mem. Canadian, Am. entomol. socs., Pa. Acad. Sci., Potato Assn. Am., Acadian Entomol. Soc., Phi Beta Kappa, Phi Kappa Phi (Disting. mem.), Delta Upsilon. Mason (32 deg.). Editor-in-chief: Am. Potato Jour., 1974—. Contbr. articles to sci. publs. Home: 15 Cedar St Orono ME 04473

SIMPSON, GEORGE GAYLORD, educator, vertebrate paleontologist; b. Chgo., June 16, 1902; s. Joseph Alexander and Helen Julia (Kinney) S.; student U. Colo., 1918-19, 20-22; Ph.B., Yale U., 1923, Ph.D., 1926, Sc.D., 1946; Sc.D., Princeton, 1947, U. Durham, 1951, Oxford U., 1951, U. N.Mex., 1954, U. Chgo., 1959, Cambridge (Eng.), 1965, York U., 1966, Kenyon Coll., 1968, U. Colo., 1968; LL.D., U. Glasgow, 1951; Dr. h.c., U. Paris (France), 1965; D. Honoris Causa, Universidad de La Plata (Argentina), 1977; m. Lydia Pedroja, Feb. 2, 1923 (div. Apr. 1938); children—Helen Frances, Patricia (dec.), Joan, Elizabeth; m. 2d, Anne Roe, May 27, 1938. Marsh fellow Peabody Mus. (Yale), research on Mesozoic mammals, 1924-26; field asst. Am. Mus. Natural History, N.Y.C., 1924, asst. curator of vertebrate paleontolgy, 1927, asso. curator, 1928-42, curator of fossil mammals, 1942-59, chmn. dept. geology and paleontology, 1944-58; prof. vertebrate paleontology Columbia, 1945-59; Agassiz prof. vertebrate paleontology Mus. Comparative Zoology, Harvard, 1959-70; prof. geoscis. U. Ariz; Tucson, 1967—; pres., trustee Simroe Found., 1968—. NRC and Internat. Edn. Bd. fellow in work on early fossil mammals, chiefly in Brit. Mus., London, also other instns. Eng., France and Germany, 1926-27; expdns. to collect fossil animals include-Northern Tex., Mont., N.Mex., Fla. and S.E. states, Argentina, Venezuela, Brazil. Served from capt. to maj. U.S. Army, 1942-44. Recipient Cross medal Yale Grad. Assn., 1969, Lewis prize Am. Philos. Soc., 1942, Thompson medal Nat. Acad. Scis., 1943, Elliot medal, 1944, 65, Gaudry medal Geol. Soc. France, 1947; Hayden medal, 1951, Penrose medal Geol. Soc. Am., 1952, André H. Dumont medal Geol. Soc. Belgium, 1953, Darwin-Wallace medal Linnean Soc., 1958, Darwin Plakette, Deutsche Akad. Naturforscher Leopoldina, 1959, Gold medal Linnean Soc., 1962, Darwin medal Royal Soc., 1962, Nat. Medal Sci., 1966, distinguished achievement medal Am. Mus., 1969; Paleontol. Soc. medal, 1973; Internat. award Nat. Mus. Natural History, 1976, Fellow Am. Acad. Arts and Scis., Nat. Acad. Scis., Am. Philos. Soc., Geol. Soc. Am., Paleontol. Soc., AAAS; mem. Soc. Vertebrate Paleontology (sec.-treas. 1940-41, pres. 1942), Soc. Study Evolution (pres. 1946), Am. Soc. Mammalogists, Soc. Systematic Zoology (pres. 1962), Am. Soc. Zoologists (pres. 1964), Academia Nazionale dei Lincei (Italy), Academia Nae dei XL (Italy), Academia de Ciencias (Argentina) (fgn. mem.), Sociedad Argentina de Estudios Geog. Gaea (hon. corr.), Zool. Soc. London (fgn. mem.), Royal Soc. (fgn. mem.), Linnean Soc. London (fgn. mem.), Academia de Ciencias (Venezuela, Brazil, Argentina), Asociacion Paleontologica Argentina (hon. mem.), Deutsche Gesellschaft für Saugetierkunde (hon.), Senkenbergische Naturforschende Gesellschaft, Phi Beta Kappa, Sigma Xi. Author books relating to field, 1928—, latest publ.; The Meaning of Evolution, rev. edit., 1967; Horses, 1951; Life of the Past, 1953; The Major Features of Evolution, 1953; Evolution and Geography, 1953; Life, 1957; Quantitative Zoology, 1960; Principles of Animal Taxonomy, 1961; This View of Life: The World of an Evolutionist, 1964; The Geography of Evolution, 1965; Biology and Man, 1969; Penguins, 1976; Concession to The Improbable, an Unconventional Autobiography, 1978. Contbr. articles to profl. publs. Home: 5151 E Holmes St Tucson AZ 85711

SIMPSON, GORDON, lawyer; b. Gilmer, Tex., Oct. 30, 1894 s. Robert Walton and Adeline (Fuller) S.; student Baylor U., 1911-13; A.B., U. Tex., 1915, J.D., 1919; m. Grace Jones, Sept. 20, 1921; children—Mary Margaret (Mrs. Harry Edward Carloss, Jr.), Barbara (Mrs. John Charles Cooper). Admitted to Tex. bar, 1919, U.S. Supreme Ct., 1942; practiced law, Tyler, Tex., 1920-42; mem. Tex. Ho. Reps. 1923-27; judge 7th dist. Tex., 1930; asso. justice Tex. Supreme Ct., 1945-49; practiced law, Dallas, 1949—; pres. Gen. Am. Oil Co. Texas, 1955-60; asso. firm Thompson & Knight, and predecessor, 1960—. Mem. Tex. Civil Jud. Council, 1946-56, pres. 1955-56. Chmn. commn. for investigation war crime cases Dept. Army, Dachau, Germany, 1948. Served to lt. U.S. Army, 1917-19; lt. col. JAG. dept. AUS, 1942-44; col. Res. ret. Decorated Bronze Star. Fellow Am. Bar Found.; mem. Internat., Am., Smith County, Dallas bar assns., Judge Adv. Assn. (pres. 1955-56), Am. Law Inst. (life), Tex. Presbyn. Found. (chmn. 1953-57, 60-62, 63-66), State Bar Tex. (pres. 1941-42), Ind. Petroleum Assn. Am. (pres. 1958-59, life mem.), Am. Petroleum Inst., Delta Chi. Democrat. Presbyterian. Mason, Elk. Clubs: Town and Gown, Petroleum, Dallas Country. Home: 4409 Belclaire Dallas TX 75205

SIMPSON, HARRELL ABNER, lawyer, former judge; b. Evening Shade, Ark., Feb. 19, 1913; s. James Monroe and Laura Frances (Harrell) S.; grad. Ark. Tech., Russellville, 1933; LL.B., U. Ark., 1938; grad. Nat. Coll. State Trial Judges, 1968; m. Norma Jeanne Belford, Oct. 24, 1941; children—Harrell Abner, Anne Belford. Admitted to Ark. bar, 1938, U.S. Supreme Ct. bar, 1952; dep. pros. atty. Randolph County, Ark., 1939-44; dep. 16th Jud. Circuit, 1944, Pocahontas, Ark., pros. atty., 1945-48, judge, 1954-79; ret., 1979; mem. firm Simpson, Simpson and Riffel, Pocahontas, 1979—; tchr. rural schs. Lawrence County, Ark., 1933-35; mem. Ark. Criminal Code Revision Commn., chmn. com. for revision Ark. Criminal Code; mem. Ark. Jud. Council, pres., 1972-73; mem. State-Fed. Jud. Council; mem. com. on model jury instrn. under crminial code Ark. Supreme Ct. Chmn. March of Dimes; commr. Little League Baseball; cub master Cub Scouts Am. Nat. Coll. State Trial Judges fellow. Mem. Am. Judges Assn., Am. Judicature Soc., Am., Ark., Randolph-Lawrence, Eighth Chancery bar assns., Pocahontas C. of C. (past sec.), Pi Kappa Alpha. Methodist (bd. stewards). Mason; mem. Order Eastern Star. Home: 511 Pine St Pocahontas AR 72455 Office: Pocahontas AR 72455

SIMPSON, JAMES RICHARDSON, electric utility exec.; b. Lewisburg, Pa., May 7, 1910; s. Frank M. and Mary (Wilson) S.; B.S., Bucknell U., 1931; M.B.A., N.Y. U., 1933; m. Helen Hoffner, Aug. 8, 1936; 1 dau., Ann Elizabeth (Mrs. Moeder). With Guaranty Trust Co., N.Y.C., 1933-35, Mfrs. Trust Co., N.Y.C., 1935-37; asst. cashier, investment officer First Nat. Bank, Glens Falls, N.Y., 1936-46; asst. treas., sec. investment com. Cornell U., 1946-59; asst. treas. Kennecott Copper Corp., 1959-60, treas., 1960-61; v.p. First Nat. City Bank N.Y., 1961-66; asso. Goldman Sachs & Co., 1966-71; pres. Citizens Electric Co., Lewisburg. Pa., 1971-79, chmn. bd., 1980—. Trustee Bucknell U. Club: Scarsdale (N.Y.) Golf. Home: Valley View RD 2 Lewisburg PA 17837

SIMPSON, JAMES SHORES, sportscaster; b. Washington, Dec. 20, 1927; s. Elmer Orem and Elizabeth Louise (Shores) S.; student George Washington U., 1945-46; m. Sara Catherine Kanaga, Aug. 12, 1950; children—Bret, Kim, Sherry, Susanne, Barbara. Sportscaster NBC-TV, Washington, 1955, NBC, N.Y.C., 1964—. Served with USNR, 1951-53. Mem. Sigma Alpha Epsilon. Republican. Lutheran. Clubs: Touchdown, Nat. Press (Washington). Office: NBC 4001 Nebraska Ave NW Washington DC 20016*

SIMPSON, JOANNE MALKUS, meteorologist; b. Boston, Mar. 23, 1923; d. Russell and Virginia (Vaughan) Gerould; B.S., U. Chgo., 1943, M.S., 1945, Ph.D., 1949; m. Robert H. Simpson, Jan. 6, 1965; children by previous marriage—David Starr Malkus, Steven Willem Malkus, Karen Elizabeth Malkus. Instr. physics and meteorology Ill. Inst. Tech., 1946-49, asst. prof., 1949-51; meteorologist Woods Hole Oceanographic Instn., 1951-61; prof. meteorology UCLA, 1961-65; dir. exptl. meteorology lab. NOAA, Dept. Commerce, Washington, 1965-74; prof. environ. scis. U. Va., Charlottesville, 1974-76, W.W. Corcoran prof. environ. scis., 1976—. Mem. Fla. Gov.'s Environ. Coordinating Council, 1971-74. Recipient Disting. Authorship award NOAA, 1969, Silver medal, 1967, Gold medal, 1972 both from Dept. Commerce; Community Headliner award Women in Communications, 1973; Profl. Achievement award U. Chgo. Alumni Assn., 1975; named Woman of Year, Los Angeles Times, 1963; Guggenheim fellow, 1954-55. Fellow Am. Meteorol. Soc. (Meisinger award 1962; council 1975-77, 79—, exec. com. 1977, 79—); mem. Weather Modification Assn. (Vincent J. Schaefer award 1979), Royal Meteorol. Soc., Nat. Weather Assn., Phi Beta Kappa, Sigma Xi. Author: (with Herbert Riehl) Cloud Structure and Distributions Over the Tropical Pacific Ocean; asso. editor Revs. Geophysics and Space Physics, 1964-72, 75-77; contbr. articles to profl. jours. Home: PO Drawer 5508 Charlottesville VA 22905 Office: Dept Environ Scis U Va Charlottesville VA 22903

SIMPSON, JOHN ALEXANDER, physicist; b. Portland, Oreg., Nov. 3, 1916; s. John A. and Janet (Brand) S.; A.B., Reed Coll., 1940; M.S., N.Y. U., 1942, Ph.D., 1943; m. Elizabeth Alice Hilts, Nov. 30, 1946 (div. Sept. 1977); children—Mary Ann, John Alexander. Research asso. OSRD, 1941-42; sci. group leader Manhattan Project, 1943-46, instr. U. Chgo., 1945-47, asst. prof., 1947-49, asso. prof., 1949-54, prof. physics, dept. physics and Fermi Inst. Nuclear Studies, 1954- 68, Edward L. Ryerson Distinguished Service prof. physics, 1968-74, Arthur H. Compton Distinguished Service prof. physics, 1974—, also dir. Enrico Fermi Inst., 1973-78. Mem. Internat. Com. IGY; chmn. bd. Ednl. Found. Nuclear Sci.; mem. tech. panel cosmic rays NRC; mem. Internat. Commn. Cosmic Radiation, 1962—; mem. astronomy missions bd. NASA, 1968; vis. asso. physics Calif. Inst. Tech.; vis. scholar U. Calif., Berkeley. Founder Lab. Astrophysics and Space Research in Enrico Fermi Inst. Nuclear Studies, 1964; bd. overseers, vis. com. astronomy Harvard; mem. Pres.'s Sci. Adv. Group on Sci. Problems, 1975-76; trustee Adler Planetarium, 1977—. Recipient medal for exceptional sci. achievement NASA. Fellow Center Policy Study, U. Chgo.; Guggenheim fellow, 1972. Fellow Am. Acad. Arts and Scis., Am. Geophys. Union, Am. Phys. Soc. (chmn. cosmic physics div. 1970-71; mem. Nat. Acad. Sci. (mem. space sci. bd.), Internat. Union Pure and Applied Physics (pres. cosmic ray commn. 1963-67), Atomic Scientists Chgo. (chmn. 1945-46, bd. bull. 1945—), Am. Astron. Soc., Internat. Acad. Astronautics, Phi Beta Kappa, Sigma Xi. Research in nuclear radiation and instrumentation, also origin of cosmic radiation, solar physics, high energy astrophys. problems, and acceleration of charged particles in space; expts. in earth satellites and deep space probes, also probes to Mercury, Venus, Mars, Jupiter and Saturn; inventor teaching reading devices, nuclear radiation instruments. Office: Fermi Inst 5630 Ellis Ave Chicago IL 60637

SIMPSON, JOHN AROL, govt. exec.; b. Toronto, Ont., Can., Mar. 30, 1923; came to U.S., 1926, naturalized, 1938; s. Henry George and Verna Lavinia (Green) S.; B.S., Lehigh U., 1946, M.S., 1948, Ph.D., 1951; m. Arlene Badel, Feb. 11, 1948; 1 son, George Badel. Research physicist Nat. Bur. Standards, Washington, 1948-60, supervisory physicist, 1960-68, exec. dir. Center for Mech. Engring. and Process Tech., 1968—. Served with U.S. Army, 1943-46. Recipient Gold medal Dept. Commerce, 1976. Fellow Am. Phys. Soc.; mem. Sigma Xi. Contbr. articles on electron optics to profl. jours. Home: 312 Riley St Falls Church VA 22046 Office: Nat Bur Standards Washington DC 20234

SIMPSON, JOHN DUNCAN, transp. exec.; b. Chgo., Mar. 7, 1937; s. Duncan Ross and Josephine (Gleeson) S.; B.S., U.S. Mil. Acad., 1959; M.S., Princeton U., 1962, M.P.A., 1969; m. Elli Hatcher, Feb. 1, 1964; children—Heather, Sean. Commd. 2d lt. U.S. Army, 1959, advanced to lt. col., 1972; spl. asst. to U.S. comdr., Berlin, 1964-66; asst. prof. econs. and public policy U.S. Mil. Acad., 1968-71; exec. asst. Office Emergency Preparedness, spl. asst. to chmn. Pres.'s Oil Policy Com., 1971-72; ret., 1972; dep. commr. Environ. Protection Commn., N.Y.C., 1972-73; exec. dir., gen. mgr. Regional Transp. Dist., Denver, 1973-79; pres. Value Capture Opportunities, Inc., Denver, 1976-79; exec. dir. Met. Transp. Authority, N.Y.C., 1979—. Served with USMC, 1954-55. Decorated Bronze Star (3), Air Medal, Meritorious Service medal. Mem. Am. Public Transit Assn. (v.p., dir. 1974—), Transp. Research Bd., West Point Soc. Roman Catholic. Club: Army-Navy (Washington). Contbr. articles to profl. jours. Office: 347 Madison Ave New York NY 10017

SIMPSON, JOHN MCLAREN, steel co. exec.; b. Chgo., July 27, 1908; s. James and Jessie (McLaren) S.; student U. Chgo., 1933; m. 2d, Nancy Townsend Heyser, Dec. 29, 1951; children—Susan Simpson; (by previous marriage)—Michael, Patricia. Pvt. sec., 1933-34; with A.M. Castle & Co., steel distbrs., Chgo., 1934—, asst. to pres., 1936-37, v.p., 1937-43, pres., 1944-61, chmn., 1961-77, chmn. exec. com., 1977—. Trustee, Rush-Presbyn.-St. Luke's Med. Center, Chgo., Field Mus. Natural History. Republican. Clubs: Chicago, Shore Acres, Onwentsia, Tavern, Racquet (Chgo.). Home: 1161 Lake Rd Lake Forest IL 60045 Office: 3400 N Wolf Rd Franklin Park IL 60131

SIMPSON, JOHN WISTAR, energy cons., former mfg. co. exec.; b. Glenn Springs, S.C., Sept. 25, 1914; s. Richard Caspar and Mary (Berkeley) S.; student Wofford Coll., 1932-33, D.Sc., 1972; B.S., U.S. Naval Acad., 1937; M.S., U. Pitts., 1941; D.Sc. (hon.), Seton Hill Coll., 1970; m. Esther Slattery, Jan. 17, 1948; children—John Wistar, Carter B., Patricia A., Barbara J. With Westinghouse Electric Corp., 1937-77, mgr. Navy and Marine switchboard engring., switchgear div., on leave as mgr. nuclear engring. Daniels pile group, Oak Ridge Nat. Lab., successively asst. engring. mgr. tech. dir. mgr. (Shippingport) project Bettis Atomic Power div., 1949-58, v.p. Westinghouse Electric Corp., gen. mgr. Bettis atomic power lab., 1958-59, v.p., gen. mgr. atomic power divs., 1959-62, v.p. engring. and research 1962-63, v.p. electric utility group, 1963-69, pres. power systems, corp. exec. v.p., dir., 1969-74, dir.-officer, chmn. energy com., 1974-77; now pvt. energy cons.; dir. Off Shore Power Systems. Mem. Naval Tech. Mission to Japan, 1945; del. 1st Internat. Conf. on Peaceful Uses Atomic Energy, Geneva, Switzerland, 1955, 2d Internat. Conf., 1958; chmn. Atomic Industrial Forum; mem. sci. adv. bd. Notre Dame. Trustee, Seton Hill Coll., Point Park Coll., Wofford Coll. Recipient Gold medal for advancement of research Am. Soc. Metals. Fellow IEEE (Edison medal 1971), ASME (hon. mem.; George Westinghouse gold medal, 1975), Am. Nuclear Soc. (pres.); mem. Newcomen Soc., Am. Ordnance Assn., Soc. Naval Architects and Marine Engrs., Nat. Acad. Engring., Franklin Inst. (Newcomen Gold medal), Navy League. Clubs: St. Clair Country, Duquesne (Pitts.); Rolling Rock, Laurel Valley Golf (Ligonier, Pa.); Farmington Country (Charlottesville, Va.); Plantation (Hilton Head S.C.); New York Yacht; Amelia Island. Home and Office: 36 E Beach Wagon Dr Hilton Head SC 29928. *The guiding principles of my career have been to work in an area I considered to be of major importance, to have the most competent people working for me, to know enough technically that I could properly evaluate performance and, as far as possible, always make my position clear to all.*

SIMPSON, LEWIS PEARSON, educator; b. Jacksboro, Tex., July 18, 1916; s. John Pearson and Grace (Sidebottom) S.; B.A., U. Tex., 1938, M.A., 1939, Ph.D., 1948; m. Mary Elizabeth Ellis, July 14, 1941; 1 son, Lewis David. Instr. U. Tex., 1941-42, 44-48; civilian instr. Navy Flight Sch., 1942-44; mem. faculty La. State U., Baton Rouge, 1948—, prof. English, 1960—, William A. Read prof., 1971—. Cons. sr. fellowship program in Am. lit. Nat. Endowment for Humanities, 1970-74; Lamar lectr. So. lit. Mercer U., 1973; mem. Christian Gauss award com. Phi Beta Kappa, 1975-77, chmn., 1977. Guggenheim fellow, 1954-55; Named Distinguished Research Master, recipient Univ. medal La. State U., 1977. Nat. Endowment for Humanities fellow, 1977-78. Mem. AAUP, Modern Lang. Assn. (Hubbell award com. Am. lit. sect. 1976—, exec. com. Early Am. lit. div. 1977—), Am. Studies Assn., Soc. Study So. Lit. (exec. council 1968-70, 74-75, v.p. 1975-76, pres. 1977-78), Orgn. Am. Historians, So. Hist. Assn., South Central Modern Lang. Assn., Thoreau Soc. Author: The Federalist Literary Mind, 1962; The Man of Letters in New England and the South, 1973; The Dispossessed Garden: Pastoral and History in Southern Literature, 1975; also articles. Co-editor: So. Rev., 1964—; editor Library of Southern Civilization, 1970—; (with introduction) Profile of Robert Frost, 1971; The Poetry of Community: Essays on the Southern Sensibility of History and Literature, 1972; The Possibilities of Order: Cleanth Brooks and his Work, 1976; adv. editor Studies in Am. Humor; Southern Studies; editorial bd. Am. Lit., 1969-72. Home: 965 Aberdeen Ave Baton Rouge LA 70808

SIMPSON, LOUIS ASTON MARANTZ, educator, author; b. Jamaica, B.W.I., Mar. 27, 1923; s. Aston and Rosalind (Marantz) S.; higher schs. certificate Munro Coll., Jamaica, 1939; B.S., Columbia U., 1948, A.M., 1950, Ph.D., 1959; D.H.L., Eastern Mich. U., 1977; m. Jeanne Claire Rogers, 1949 (div. 1954); 1 son, Louis Matthew; m. 2d, Dorothy Mildred Roochvarg, June 19, 1955; children—Anne Borovoi, Anthony Rolf. Editor, Bobbs-Merrill Pub. Co., N.Y.C., 1950-55; instr. Columbia U., 1955-59, prof. English, U. Calif., Berkeley, 1959-67, State U. N.Y., Stony Brook, 1967—. Served with AUS, 1943-45. Decorated Purple Heart with oak leaf cluster, Bronze Star; recipient Prix de Rome, 1957, Millay award, 1960, Distinguished Alumnus award Columbia U., 1960, Pulitzer prize for poetry, 1964, medal for excellence Columbia U., 1965; Hudson Rev. fellow, 1957; Guggenheim fellow, 1962, 70; Am. Council Learned Socs. grantee, 1963. Fellow Am. Acad. in Rome. Author: (poems) The Arrivistes, 1949; Good News of Death, 1955; A Dream of Governors, 1959; At the End of the Open Road, 1963; Selected Poems, 1965; Adventures of the Letter I, 1971; Searching for the Ox, 1976; (books) Riverside Drive, 1962; James Hogg, A Critical Study, 1962; North of Jamaica, 1972; Three on the Tower: The Lives and Works of Ezra Pound, T.S. Eliot and William Carlos Williams, 1975; A Revolution in Taste: Studies of Dylan Thomas, Allen Ginsburg, Sylvia Plath and Robert Lowell, 1978; editor: An Introduction to Poetry, 1967; The New Poets of England and America, 1957. Address: PO Box 91 Port Jefferson NY 11777

SIMPSON, LYLE LEE, lawyer; b. Des Moines, Oct. 15, 1937; s. R. Clair and Martha B. (Accola) S.; B.A., Drake U., 1960, J.D., LL.B., 1963; m. Marci Tesdell; children—Sondra Sue, Donald Scott. Asst. to dean students Drake U., 1960-62; admitted to Iowa bar, 1963; prin. Lyle L. Simpson, atty., Des Moines, 1963-64; mem. firm Beving & Swanson, Des Moines, 1964-68, Peddicord, Simpson & Sutphin, Des Moines, 1968—; sec.-treas. K & S Devel., Inc., 1977—; sec. 1st Iowa Properties, Inc., 1978—; dir. Americare Growth Fund. Instr. mil. leadership Iowa Mil. Acad., 1965-68. Treas., Mental Health Coordinating Commn., 1975-77; mem. exec. bd. Polk County Republican Central Com., 1964-68; bd. counselors Drake U. Law Sch., 1969-72; chmn. bd. trustees Broadlawns Med. Center; bd. dirs. Polk County Health Services Corp., 1976-78, Polk County Mental Health Center, 1977—. Served to capt. AUS, 1955-68; comdr. USN Res. Recipient Class of 1915 award Drake U., 1960; Oren E. Scott award, 1960. Mem. Am. Humanist Assn. (humanist counselor 1974—, gen. counsel 1975—, dir. 1976—), Naval Res. Lawyers Assn., Res. Officers Assn., JAG Officers Assn., Am. Acad. Trial Lawyers, Am. (coms. recent devels. real estate, condominiums, mil. lawyers and probate 1970—), Iowa (coms. ethics, mill. affairs 1968—), Polk County (coms. ethics and grievance 1963-69) bar assns., Drake U. Alumni Assn. (dir. 1963-70), Delta Theta Phi, Omicron Delta Kappa, Psi Chi, Tau Kappa Epsilon, Phi Eta Sigma. Clubs: Masons (officer), Shriners; Des Moines Golf and Country, Embassy, Morning (pres. 1964). Home: 3901 SW 28th Pl Des Moines IA 50321 Office: 300 Fleming Bldg Des Moines IA 50309. *To me only two aspects of life have relevance: (1) Your life becomes "meaningful" as you share in happiness, and (2) Your own life becomes "significant" to the extent the world is a better place because of your efforts. The fully actualized person keeps both in appropriate balance.*

SIMPSON, O.J. (ORENTHAL JAMES), profl. football player, actor; b. San Francisco, July 9, 1947; s. Jimmie and Eunice (Durton) S.; student U. So. Calif.; grad. City Coll. San Francisco; m. Marguerite Whitley, June 24, 1967; children—Arnelle, Jason. Halfback, Buffalo Bills, 1969-78, San Francisco 49'ers, 1978-79; sports commentator ABC; motion picture appearances include: The Towering Inferno, 1974, The Cassandra Crossing, 1977, Killer Force, 1976, A Killing Affair (TV), 1977 Goldie and the Boxer (TV), 1979. Recipient Heisman trophy N.Y. Downtown Athletic Club, 1968; voted Coll. Player of Decade, ABC Sports, 1970; mem. world record 440 yd. relay team (38.6 secs.), 1967; record holder for most yards rushing gained in a season, most yards rushing gained in a game; named to Am. Football League All-Star Team, 1970, ProBowl Team, 1972, 73, 74, 75, 76; named Nat. Football League Player of Decade, Pro Football Monthly, 1979. Address: care OJ Simpson Enterprises 11661 San Vicente Blvd Suite 600 Brentwood CA 90049

SIMPSON, RICHARD CLAUDE, indsl. distbn. exec.; b. Los Angeles, Apr. 23, 1918; s. Claude Vernon and Evelyn (Bowers) S.; A.B., Stanford, 1940; M.B.A., Harvard, 1942; div.; children—Barbara (Mrs. Edwin A. Meserve, Jr.), Diane (Mrs. James Cunningham), Carol; m. 2d, Mary Alice Clark, Mar. 1971; stepchildren—Karin, Susan (Mrs. John Janneck), Michael and James Burnap, Anne Marie and Bruce Cordingly. Mdse. mgr. Rexall Drug & Chem. Co., Los Angeles, 1946-56; dir. marketing devel. Ducommun, Inc., Los Angeles, 1956-58, v.p., 1958-66, dir., 1960—, gen. mgr., 1964-66, exec. v.p., 1966-73, pres., 1973-77, vice chmn., 1977—; dir. 1st Am. Financial Corp., Mattel Inc., Calif. Fed. Savs. & Loan Assn. Bd. dirs. Los Angeles YMCA, 1964—, Los Angeles C. of C. Served to lt. USNR, 1942-46. Mem. Los Angeles C. of C. (dir.), Phi Beta Kappa, Zeta Psi. Clubs: California; Los Angeles Country; Tuna (Avalon, Calif.); Newport Harbor Yacht (Newport, Calif.). Home: 1072 N Beverly Dr Beverly Hills CA 90210 Office: 612 S Flower St Los Angeles CA 90017

SIMPSON, RICHARD HOWARD, pub. co. exec.; b. Mpls., Dec. 19, 1909; s. Laurens Luther and Pearl C. (Howard) S.; student Bradley Polytech. Inst., 1927-28, 29-30, U. Pa., 1928-29; B.S., U. Ill., 1931, postgrad., 1931-32; m. Katherine Eva Law, Nov. 24, 1936; children—Thomas Lauren, Kathy Lynn Simpson Simpson. With Chas. A. Bennett Co. Inc., Peoria, Ill., 1934—, bd. dirs. 1939—, v.p., 1947-52, pres., 1952-75, chmn. bd., 1975—. Mem. exec. com. W.D. Boyce council Boy Scouts Am., 1966; former trustee Lakeview Center for Arts and Sci., 1970-71; del., v.p. Lakeview Council Arts and Sci., 1979-80. Paul Harris fellow. Mem. Am. Vocat. Assn., Am. Council on Indsl. Arts Tchrs. Edn., Am. Indsl. Arts Assn., Ill. Indsl. Edn. Club (hon.), Peoria Assn. Commerce, Nat. Art Edn. Assn., Nat. Small Bus. Assn. (pres. 1977, chmn. bd. 1977-79), Peoria Philatelic Soc., Trans Miss. Philatelic Soc., Soc. Philatelic Ams., Am. Philatelic Soc., Alpha Pi, Pi Beta Alpha. Club: Rotary (Peoria). Home: 516 W Richwoods Blvd Peoria IL 61604 Office: 809 W Detweiller Dr Peoria IL 61615

SIMPSON, ROBERT EDWARD, economist; b. Chgo., July 7, 1917; s. James Albert and Mabel Grace (Farrell) S.; A.B., Amherst Coll., 1938; student Nat. Inst. Pub. Affairs, 1939; M.A., George Washington U., 1964; m. Anna Margareta Nelson, May 22, 1954; children—Karen Anne, Heather Margot, John Frederick. Student U.S. Central Statis. Bd., 1938-39; economist U.S. Nat. Resources Com., 1939-40; personnel work Office Sec. of War, 1941; economist civilian supply div. WPB, 1941-42; econ., adminstrv. work Nat. Housing Adminstrn., 1946-47; asst. dir. European div., later dept. asst. dir. for econ. affairs Office Internat. Trade, U.S. Dept. Commerce, 1947-53; dir. Office Econ. Affairs, Bur. Fgn. Commerce, 1953-61, dir. Office Regional Econs., Bur. Internat. Commerce, 1961-70, dir. Office Internat. Comml. Relations, 1970-73; counsellor for econ. and comml. affairs Am. embassy, Canberra, Australia, 1973-77; dir. Office Country Affairs, U.S. Dept. Commerce, Washington, 1978—; assigned Nat. War Coll., Washington, 1961-62. Mem. U.S. dels. to various internat. confs., 1948-73; bd. examiners for U.S. Fgn. Service. Served with USNR, 1942-46; PTO and in U.S.S. Europa; comdr. Res. Decorated Bronze Star. Mem. Am. Econ. Assn., Phi Beta Kappa, Delta Tau Delta, Kappa Theta. Home: 10317 Riverwood Dr Potomac MD 20854 Address: US Dept Commerce Washington DC 20230

SIMPSON, ROBERT LEATHAM, clergyman, ch. ofcl.; b. Salt Lake City, Aug. 8, 1915; s. Heber C. and Lillie Clarissa (Leatham) S.; A.A., Santa Monica City Coll., 1937; student U. So. Calif., 1942, Yale, 1944; m. Jelaire Kathryn Chandler, June 24, 1942; children—Steven Chandler, Jelaire Christine, Kathryn Marie, Robert Michael. Missionary, Ch. of Jesus Christ of Latter-day Saints to New Zealand, 1937-40; pres. New Zealand Mission, 1958-61, 1st counselor Presiding Bishopric, Salt Lake City, 1961-72, asst. to Council of Twelve Apostles, 1972-76, 1st Quorum of the Seventy, 1976—, mng. dir. Social Services dept., Salt Lake City, 1972-74, ch. area supr., South Pacific, 1975-78; former dir. Zion Securities Corp., ZCMI Dept. Stores, Heber J. Grant Ins. Co., Beneficial Life Ins. Co., Deseret Gymnasium. Former mem. Utah Bd. Alcoholism and Drugs; former mem. adv. bd. Great Salt Lake council and nat. speakers bur. Boy Scouts Am.; former mem. adv. com. Utah Tech. Coll. Served to capt. USAAF, 1943-46. Home: 3563 Cove Point Dr Salt Lake City UT 84109 Office: 50 E North Temple Salt Lake City UT 84150. *As a very young man, a Church call sent me to the South Pacific for three years to work closely with the Polynesians (Maoris of New Zealand). These loving, warm folks lived simple lives. They taught me that the most important thing in life is people and that caring about others brings the greatest fulfillment. My priorities changed dramatically as these wonderful new friends taught me to simplify my life style, to accept all people, to be forgiving, and indeed to follow the teachings of the Master. I had been sent 8,000 miles to teach, and I was taught.*

SIMPSON, ROBERT WHITESIDE, beverage co. exec.; b. Chgo., May 17, 1909; s. Robert Whiteside and Mary (Wright) S.; B.S., Northwestern U., 1931; m. Jacqueline Jean Fleming, May 4, 1964; children—Carl, Grant, Nancy, Robert Whiteside. With Ill. Bell Telephone Co., 1931-34; route mgr. Jewel Tea Co., 1934-38; with 7-Up Co., 1938—, franchise dir., then asst. sec., St. Louis, 1948-65, v.p., sec., St. Louis, 1965—. Chmn. trustees Seven-Up Co. Charitable Trust. Served with AUS, 1943-45. Mem. Am. Soc. Corporate Secs. (v.p. 1974, pres. St. Louis regional group 1975). Republican. Presbyn. Mason (Shriner). Home: 708 Claymont Dr Ballwin MO 63011 Office: 121 S Meramec St St Louis MO 63105

SIMPSON, ROY BERTRAM, indsl.-consumer products co. exec.; b. N.Y.C., Sept. 12, 1923; s. David and Elsie S.; student Acad. Aeros., 1941-43, Yale U. Aviation Engring. Cadet Program, 1943-44; m. Edith Joy Immerman, May 5, 1945; children—Roy Bertram, Mary Elizabeth. Vice pres. Fabrex Corp., 1953-58; pres. Crown Fabrics Co., 1958-63, Bangor-Punta Textile Ops., 1963-68; chmn. exec. com. Duplan Corp., 1968-79; chmn. Everfast, Inc., 1970—; v.p. Am. Can Co., Greenwich, Conn., 1974-78, sr. v.p., sector exec. consumer products, 1978—; dir. Hayden Pub. Co., Bradford Nat. Served with USAAF, 1943-46; PTO. Mem. Am. Arbitration Assn. Club: Stanwich (Greenwich). Office: Am Can Co American Ln Greenwich CT 06830

SIMPSON, SEYMOUR DAVID, food chain exec.; b. N.Y.C., Dec. 31, 1923; s. Philip and Mae (Levy) S.; B.B.A., Coll. City N.Y., 1942; m. Diane Rosengarten, May 19, 1946; children—Tina Carol, Adrienne Lee, Ronald Allen. With Garden Markets, Inc., N.Y.C., 1946-62; exec. v.p. Shopwell Inc. (formerly Daitch Crystal Dairies, Inc.), N.Y.C., 1962—, chief adminstrv. officer, 1971—, also dir. Food Industry chmn. United Jewish Appeal N.Y., 1964- 66. Served to 1st lt. USAAF, 1943-46; PTO. Mem. Nat. Assn. Food Chains (dir. 1966-69, 70-76), N.Y. State Food Mchts. Assn. (dir. 1971—). Mason. Club: Elmwood Country (treas., bd. govs. 1963-69) (White Plains, N.Y.). Home: Cayuga Trail Harrison NY 10528 Office: 400 Walnut Ave New York City NY 10454

SIMPSON, VINSON RALEIGH, JR., electric mfg. co. exec.; b. Chgo., Aug. 9, 1928; s. Vinson Raleigh and Elsie (Passeger) S.; S.B. in Chem. Engring., Mass. Inst. Tech., 1950; M.B.A., Ind. U., 1955; m. Elizabeth Caroline Matte, Sept. 9, 1950; children—Kathleen Simpson Jackson, Nancy Jane, James Morgan. With Trane Co., LaCrosse, Wis., 1950-75, mgr. mktg. services, 1957-64, mgr. dealer devel., 1964-66, mng. dir. Trane Ltd., Edinburgh, Scotland, 1966, v.p. internat., LaCrosse, 1967, exec. v.p., 1968-70, exec. v.p., gen. mgr. comml. air conditioning div., 1970-73, pres., 1973-75; pres. Simpson and Co., La Crosse, 1975-76; pres., chief operating officer Marathon Electric Mfg. Corp., Wausau, Wis., 1976—; dir. RTE Corp. Regional chmn. Edn. Council, Mass. Inst. Tech.; mem. Pres.'s Club, Viterbo Coll.; mem. pastor-parish relations com. 1st United Meth. Ch., Wausau; mem. adv. bd. Wausau Area Performing Arts Found.; mem. adv. bd., also mem. steering com. Marathon Center, U. Wis.; bd. dirs. Woodson YMCA, Central Wausau Corp.; trustee Northland Coll.; mem. ann. support com. Wausau Hosp. Found. Served to 1st lt. USAF, 1951-53. Mem. ASHRAE, Kappa Kappa Sigma, Alpha Tau Omega, Beta Gamma Sigma (dirs. table). Clubs: Masons, Shriners, Jesters; Wausau (trustee), Wausau Country; U. Chgo. Address: 1010 Highland Park Blvd Wausau WI 54401

SIMPSON, (BESSIE) WALLIS WARFIELD. see Windsor, Duchess of (Bessie Wallis Warfield Simpson)

SIMPSON, WILBUR HERMAN, musician; b. Montpelier, Ohio, Dec. 6, 1917; s. Glenn Olen and Hannah Katherine (Kohl) S.; B.Music Edn., Northwestern U., 1940, Mus.M., 1946; m. Margaret Jane Kleinhuizen, June 25, 1944; children—Michael H., Jeffrey A., Joan M. Dir. instrumental music Forest Park (Ill.) pub. schs., 1940-42; bassoonist Chgo. Symphony Orch., 1946—; instr. bassoon Northwestern U., 1948-72, prof., 1972—; instr. De Paul U., 1947-74, Chgo. Conservatory Coll., 1958—; mem. Chgo. Symphony Woodwind Quintet, 1946-72. Served with USNR, 1942-45. Mem. Phi Mu Alpha, Pi Kappa Lambda. Home: 2333 Meadow Dr N Wilmette IL 60091 Office: care Chicago Symphony Orch 220 S Michigan Ave Chicago IL 60604

SIMPSON, WILLIAM KELLY, educator, mus. curator, Egyptologist; b. N.Y.C., Jan. 3, 1928; s. Kenneth Farrand and Helen L.K. (Porter) S.; student Phillips Acad., Andover, Mass.; B.A., Yale, 1947, M.A., 1948, Ph.D., 1954; m. Marilyn E. Milton, June 19, 1953; children—Laura Knickerbacker (Mrs. Grover O'Neill 3d), Abby Rockefeller. Asst., Egyptian Art, Met. Mus. Art, 1948-54; research fellow Center MIddle East Studies, Harvard, 1957-58; mem. faculty Yale, New Haven, Conn., 1958—, prof. Egyptology, 1965—, chmn. dept. Near Eastern langs., 1966-69, dir. editor of papers Penn-Yale Archaeol. Expdn. to Egypt, 1960—; curator Egyptian and ancient Near Eastern art Mus. Fine Arts, Boston, 1970—; partner Kin and Co., 1967-69, Venrock, 1970—. Mem. adv. council fgn. currency program Smithsonian Instn., 1966-69. Trustee, Am. Sch. Classical Studies, Athens, Am. U. in Cairo, Mus. Primitive Art; mem. internat. council Mus. Modern Art, N.Y.C.; pres. Wrexham Found., 1965-67. Fulbright fellow, Egypt, 1955-57; Guggenheim fellow, 1965. Mem. Am. Oriental Soc., Archaeol. Inst. Am., Egypt Exploration Soc., Soc. francaise d'egyptologie, German Archaeol. Inst., Foundation egyptologique Reine Elisabeth. Clubs: Century, Met. Opera, University, Union (N.Y.C.); Union Boat (Boston); Bedford (N.Y.) Golf and Tennis. Author: Papyrus Reisner I-Records of a Building Project, 1963; Hekanefer and the Dynastic Material from Toshka, 1963; Papyrus Reisner II-Accounts of the Dockyard Workshop, 1965; Papyrus Reisner III: Records of a Building Project in the Early Twelfth Dynasty, 1969; The Terrace of the Great God at Abydos, 1974; The Mastabas of Qar and Idu, 1976; The Offering Chapel of Sekhem-ankh-ptah, 1976; (with others) The Ancient Near East, A History, 1971, The Literature of Ancient Egypt, 1972, The Mastaba of Queen Mersyankh III, 1974. Home: RD 1 Box 327 Katonah NY 10536

SIMPSON, WILLIAM TRACY, educator; b. Berkeley, Calif., Dec. 7, 1920; s. Tracy Whittelsey and Cornelia (Ewing) S.; A.B., U. Calif. at Berkeley, 1943, Ph.D., 1948; m. Ann Bruck; children—Elizabeth, Jane; m. 2d, Carmen Tschudi, Sept. 10, 1961; children—Carlos, Marjorie, John. Teaching asst. U. Calif. at Berkeley, 1946-48, vis. lectr., 1960; from instr. to prof. U. Wash., 1948-64; vis. prof. U. Oreg., 1963, prof. chemistry, 1964-77, chmn. dept., 1972-75; vis. prof. Fla. State U., 1961, Catholic U., Santiago, Chile, 1970. Asso. Neuroscis. research program, 1963; chmn. Gordon Conf. Theoretical Chemistry, 1967. Served with AUS, 1943-46. Decorated Bronze Star; recipient Calif. Sect. award Am. Chem. Soc., 1959. Fulbright Lectureship in Chemistry, Lima, Peru, 1970. Mem. Phi Beta Kappa, Sigma Xi, Psi Upsilon. Democrat. Episcopalian. Author monograph, research papers. Asso. editor Jour. Chem. Physics, 1966-69; mem. editorial bd. Chem. Reviews, 1971. Home: 500 Fair Oaks Eugene OR 97401

SIMPSON, ZELMA ALENE, family history researcher; b. Bristow, Okla., Nov. 2, 1923; d. Robert E. and Zelma (Wolfe) Tidrow; B.S. in Edn., Central State U., Edmond, Okla., 1948, postgrad., 1961—; m. Eugene Lester Simpson, Dec. 26, 1945 (dec. 1967); 1 son, Lantz Eugene. Sch. tchr., Oklahoma County, Okla., 1948-65; library dir. Okla. Hist. Soc., Oklahoma City, 1965-79; tchr. Oscar Rose Junior Coll., Midwest City, Okla., 1972-73. Lectr. history and geneaology. Sec.-treas. Broncho Basketball Booster Club, Central State U., 1967—. Recipient Certificate of Recognition, D.A.R., 1975, Award of Honor, Oklahoma City Bicentennial Commn., 1975; named Distinguished Former Student, Central State U., 1977. Mem. Hist. Soc. Mo., Okla. Geneal. Soc. (life, past acquisition's chmn., past 1st v.p., pres. 1972-73), DAR (lineage research chmn. Samuel King chpt., regent 1978—), Okla. Hist. Soc., Sapulpa Hist. Soc., Indian Ter. Pioneer Geneal. and Hist. Soc. (pres. 1976—), Central State U. Alumni Assn. (life), Pontotoc Hist. and Geneal. Soc., Southwest Okla. Geneal. Soc., Washington County, Eastern Okla. hist. socs., Delta Kappa Gamma. Home and Office: 33 E 9th St Edmond OK 73034

SIMRALL, HARRY CHARLES FLEMING, coll. dean, engr.; b. Memphis, Oct. 16, 1912; s. William Crutcher and Wilhelmina (Reagin) S.; B.S. in Elec. Engring., Miss. State U., 1934, B.S. in Mech. Engring., 1935; M.S. in Elec. Engring., U. Ill., 1939; postgrad. U. Pitts., 1944-45; m. Mary Virginia Miller, Dec. 18, 1936. Instr. elec. engring. Miss. State U., 1934-35, instr. drawing, 1935-37, instr. elec. engring., 1937-39, asst. prof. elec. engring., 1939-43, asso. prof., 1943-44; central station engr., industry engring. dept. Westinghouse Electric Corp., 1944-45, supr. engring. tng., student tng. dept., 1945; asso. prof. elec. engring. Miss. State U., 1945-47, prof. and head elec. engring. dept., 1947-57, dean Sch. Engring., dir. Engring. and Indsl. Research Sta., dir. Engring. Extension Service, prof. elec. engring., 1957-63, dean Coll. Engring., 1963-78, dean and prof. emeritus, 1978—; mem. Miss. Bd. Registration for Profl. Engrs. and Land Surveyors, 1960-78; v.p., dir. So. Zone Nat. Council Engring. Examiners, 1972-74. Named Engr. of Year, Miss. Engring. Soc., 1963; Alumnus of Year, Miss. State U. Alumni Assn., 1963; Disting. Service cert. Nat. Council Engring. Examiners, 1971; Disting. Alumnus award U. Ill. Elec. Engring. Alumni Assn., 1978. Registered profl. engr., Ala., La., Tenn., Miss. Fellow IEEE (life mem.); mem. Illuminating Engring. Soc., Am. Soc. Agrl. Engrs., Am. Soc. E.E., Nat. (pres. 1970-71), Miss. socs. profl. engrs., Omicron Delta Kappa, Eta Kappa Nu, Sigma Xi, Tau Beta Pi, Alpha Tau Omega, Phi Kappa Phi, Pi Tau Sigma. Democrat. Presbyn. Club: Rotary (Starkville, Miss.). Home: 107 White Dr W Starkville MS 39759

SIMS, BENNETT JONES, clergyman; b. Greenfield, Mass., Aug. 9, 1920; s. Lewis Raymond and Sarah Cosette (Jones) S.; A.B., Baker U., 1943; postgrad., Princeton Theol. Sem., 1946-47; B.D., Va. Theol. Sem., 1949, D.D., 1966; D.D., U. of South, 1972; Merrill fellow Harvard, 1964-65; postgrad. Cath. U., 1969-71; m. Beatrice May Wimberly, Sept. 25, 1943; children—Laura (Mrs. John P. Boucher), Grayson, David. Ordained to ministry Protestant Episcopal Ch. as deacon, 1949, priest, 1950; rector Ch. of Redeemer, Balt., 1951-64; dir. continuing edn. Va. Theol. Sem., 1966-72; bishop, Atlanta, 1972—; priest-in-charge St. Alban's Ch., Tokyo, 1962; spl. lectr. Diocesan Confs., U.S., overseas, 1969. Trustee U. of South. Served with USNR, 1943-46. Named Young Man of Year, Balt. C. of C., 1953, Distinguished Alumnus of Year, Baker U., 1972. Home: 22 Springlake Pl NW Atlanta GA 30318 Office: 2744 Peachtree Rd NW Atlanta GA 30305

SIMS, EDWARD HOWELL, editor, publisher; b. Orangeburg, S.C., May 29, 1923; s. Hugo Sheridan and Jesse Lucile (Howell) S.; A.B., Wofford Coll., 1943; postgrad. Emory U., 1946-47; m. Frances Dell Hartt, Jan. 5, 1946; m. 2d, Martha Lurene Bass, July 18, 1960; children—Edward H., Robert; m. 3d, Bente Thorlund Christensen, Oct. 4, 1969; children—Edward Christian, Frederik. Mng. editor Orangeburg Times and Democrat, 1946, editor, 1952—; Washington corr., founder Washington bur. for number S.C. dailies, 1947; columnist, Looking South From Washington, 1948—; Washington Bur. chief Editor's Copy syndicate, 1950-52, editor-pub., 1952—; radio news analyst The News of The Week In Washington, 1951—; dir. Sims Pub. Co., Orangeburg. White House corr. covering President's confs., 1948—; mem. Senate and House press galleries, 1947—. Am. consul, Munich, Germany, 1963-65; cons. Exec. Office of White House, 1966-67. Served from cadet to first lt., USAAF, World War II; ETO. Recipient Young Man of the Year award, S.C. Jr. C. of C., 1959. Mem. White House Corrs. Assn., Am. Legion, V.F.W. Methodist. Clubs: Rotary, Nat. Press; Metropolitan (Washington); R.A.F. (London). Author: American Aces 1958; Greatest Fighter Missions, 1962; The Fighter Pilots, 1967; Fighter Tactics 1914-70, 1972. Contbr. articles to publs. Home: 408 Partridge Circle Sarasota FL 33577 also Box 813-E Route 6 Asheville NC 28803 Office: Box 532 Orangeburg SC 29115

SIMS, EVERETT MARTIN, publishing co. exec.; b. Morristown, N.J., June 27, 1920; s. Walter Leonard and Amy Ethel (Coleman) S.; B.A., Drew U., Madison, N.J., 1941; M.A., Harvard U., 1947. Dir. project planning div. Prentice-Hall, Inc., Englewood Cliffs, N.J., 1950-60, asst. v.p., 1956-60; with Harcourt Brace Jovanovich, Inc., N.Y.C., 1960—, v.p., dir. coll. dept., 1970—; pres. Media Systems Corp., 1974-77, chmn., 1977—. Served with USAAF, 1942-45, USAF, 1950-51; ETO. Decorated Air medal; Croix de Guerre (France). Home: 68 W 87th St New York NY 10024 Office: 757 3d Ave New York NY 10017

SIMS, HOWARD FRANCIS, archtl. co. exec.; b. Detroit, July 25, 1933; s. Joseph James and Ann Lee (Glover) S.; B.Arch., U. Mich., 1961; M.Arch., U. Mich., 1966; m. Judity Pamela Perry, Sept. 13, 1958; children—Frances Ann, Gregory Michael, Laurence Howard, Wesley Joseph. Pvt. practice architecture, Ann Arbor, Mich., 1964-69; pres. Howard Sims & Assos., Detroit, 1969-76; pres. Sims-Varner & Assos., Inc., Detroit, 1976—; chmn. Mich. State Constrn. Code Commn., 1972-76; dir. Detroit chpt. The Fed. Reserve Bank of Chgo. Chmn. emeritus Inner-City Bus. Improvement Forum, 1969-78; trustee New Detroit, Inc., 1972-75; vice chmn., trustee Merrill-Palmer Inst., Detroit, 1975—; dir. Detroit Econ. Growth Corp., 1978—. Served with U.S. Navy, 1951-55. Recipient Cert. of Excellence Detroit Minority Bus. Opportunity Com., 1972; Trailblazer award Assn. Bus., Engring. and Sci. Students and Profls., 1977. Fellow AIA; mem. Engring. Soc. Detroit, Council on Urban Econ. Devel., Council of Ednl. Facilities Planners, Sigma Pi Phi, Kappa Alpha Psi. Office: 1900 Fisher Bldg Detroit MI 48202

SIMS, IVOR DONALD, ret. steel co. exec.; b. Coquimbo, Chile, Mar. 14, 1912; s. George and Florence Kate (Johns) S.; B.S., Lehigh U., 1933, LL.D., 1970; LL.D., U. Liberia, 1967; m. Christine Buchman, June 19, 1937; 1 dau., Christine. With Bethlehem Steel Corp. (Pa.), 1933-73, successively jr. buyer, buyer, asst. purchasing agt., purchasing agt., 1933-57, asst. v.p., 1957-63, v.p. adminstrn., 1963-66, exec. v.p., 1966-73, also dir., 1957-73. Trustee Lehigh U., Hollins Coll. Decorated knight comdr. Liberian Humane Order African Redemption (Liberia); comdr. Star Equatorial Africa (Gabon); recipient L in Life award Lehigh Club N.Y., 1970. Mem. Am. Iron and Steel Inst., C. of C., NAM (dir. 1969-73), Pa. Soc., Newcomen Soc. N.Am. Episcopalian. Clubs: Saucon Valley Country (Bethlehem); Univ. (N.Y.C.); Mid Ocean (Bermuda); Sky Top (Pa.). Home: 1723 Cloverleaf St Bethlehem PA 18017

SIMS, JAMES REDDING, educator; b. Macon, Ga., July 2, 1918; s. Thomas Banks and Ella (Jones) S.; B.S., Rice Inst., 1941; M.S., U. Ill., 1950, Ph.D., 1956; m. Marjorie Brittain, Dec. 28, 1946; children—Susan, Deborah, Thomas Bradford, Jr. engr. Am. Republics Corp., 1941-42; instr. civil engring. Rice U., Houston, 1942-44, 46-47, asst. prof., 1947-52, asso. prof., 1952-58, prof., chmn. dept. civil engring., 1958-63, prof. civil engring., 1963—, Herman and George R. Brown prof. civil engring., 1974—, campus bus. mgr., 1963-74, v.p. univ., 1969-72, adviser to men, 1958-61; cons. Lockwood and Andrews, Humble Oil & Refining Co., chief of staff USAF. Served from ensign to lt. (j.g.), USNR, 1944-46. Fellow ASCE (past sec.-treas., pres. Tex. sect., past chmn. awards com., nat. dir. 1965-68, v.p. 1970-71); mem. Am. Congress Surveying and Mapping, ASTM, Nat. Soc. Profl. Engrs., Tex. Soc. Profl. Engrs. (dir. San Jacinto chpt. 1957-59, v.p. 1959-61, pres. 1961-62), Internat. Assn. Bridge and Structural Engring., Houston Philos. Soc., Sigma Xi, Tau Beta Pi, Chi Epsilon, Sigma Tau, Phi Kappa Phi. Clubs: Seabrook Sailing, Rice Univ. Faculty. Patentee in field. Home: 2532 Bluebonnet Houston TX 77030

SIMS, JOE, lawyer; b. Phoenix, Sept. 29, 1944; s. Joe and Pauline Jane (Saunders) S.; B.S., Ariz. State U., 1967, J.D., 1970; m. Robin Ann Reed, Jan. 30, 1965; 1 dau., Shannon Dane. Admitted to Ariz. bar, 1970, U.S. Supreme Ct. bar, 1975, D.C., 1978; trial atty. antitrust div. Dept. Justice, Washington, 1970-73, spl. asst. to Asst. Atty. Gen., 1973-74, dep. asst. Atty. Gen. for policy planning and legislation, 1975-77, dep. asst. Atty. Gen. for regulatory matters and fgn. commerce, 1977-78; mem. firm Jones, Day, Reavis & Pogue, Washington, 1978-79, partner firm, 1979—; resident fellow Am. Enterprise Inst. for Public Policy Research, Washington, 1978-79, vis. fellow, 1979—. Mem. Am. Bar Assn., D.C. Bar Assn., Ariz. State Bar Assn., Fed. Bar Assn. Home: 2792 Hyson Ln Falls Church VA 22043 Office: 1735 Eye St NW Washington DC 20006

SIMS, JOHN HALEY (ZOOT), jazz saxophonist; b. Inglewood, Calif., Oct. 29, 1925; s. Peter and Kate (Haley) S.; grad. high sch.; m. Louise Choo, Nov. 17, 1970. Saxophonist, Benny Goodman, Woody Herman, Bobby Sherwood orchs., 1941-50, Stan Kenton, Benny Goodman, Gerry Mulligan, 1950-59; formed Zoot Sims-Al Cohn Quintet, 1959; toured Europe, U.S. with Norman Granz, Jazz At The Philharmonic, 1966-67, Monterey Jazz Festival, 1971, Newport Jazz Festival, 1972-77, 79, Montreux Festival, 1975, 77, 1st White House Jazz Concert, 1978, Smithsonian Instn., 1978. Mem. N.Y. Jazz Repertory Co. Served with USAAF, 1944-46. Recipient Grammy award, 1977. Mem. ASCAP (Popular award 1976, 77, 78, 79), Defenders of Wildlife Soc. Democrat. Composer: Red Door, 1949; Dark Cloud, 1956; Nirvana, 1974; Blues for Nat Cole, 1975; Bloos for Louise, 1976. Numerous jazz recs. Address: 16 Sunset View Dr West Nyack NY 10994

SIMS, JOHN LEROY, physician, educator; b. Houston, Sept. 21, 1912; s. Frank Jacob and Jennie Elizabeth (Ramsay) S.; A.B., Rice U., 1933; M.D., U. Tex., 1937; m. Anne M. Schurch, May 30, 1942; children—John Ernest, Elizabeth Ann, Thomas LeRoy. Intern, Wis. Gen. Hosp., U. Wis.-Madison, 1937-38, resident, 1939-42; practice medicine specializing in internal medicine, Madison, 1946—; instr. medicine U. Wis., 1946-47, prof., 1959—, mem. faculty senate, 1975—; former cons. medicine, to surgeon 5th U.S. Army, U.S. VA. Served to maj. AUS, 1942-46; col. Res. (ret.). Fellow A.C.P. (gov. for Wis. 1963-69); mem. AMA, AAAS, Wis. Soc. Internal Medicine (pres. 1957), Wis. Med. Assn., Central Soc. Clin. Research, Central Clin. Research Club, Phi Beta Kappa, Sigma Xi, Alpha Omega Alpha, Alpha Kappa Kappa. Presbyn. (elder). Home: 942 S Midvale Blvd Madison WI 53711 Office: University Hosp Madison WI 53706

SIMS, JOHN ROGERS, JR., lawyer; b. Red Star, W.Va., Apr. 10, 1924; s. John Rogers and Myrtle (Hutchison) S.; B.S. in Commerce, U. Va., 1950, LL.B., 1952; m. Geraldine L. Bucklew, Oct. 8, 1966; children—John Rogers III, Joyce Rebecca. Asso. firm Dow, Lohnes & Albertson, Washington, 1953-57; gen. counsel D.C. Transit System, Inc., Washington, 1957-65; individual practice law, Washington, 1965-68; partner firm Wrape and Hernly, Arlington, Va., 1968-71, Goff, Sims, Cloud, Stroud, Shepherd & Walker, P.C. and predecessor firm, Washington, 1972—. Chmn. bd. dirs. John Sims Assos., Inc.; chmn. bd. dirs., gen. counsel A Presdl. Classroom for Young Ams., Inc.; dir. Super Service Bus. Co. Vice chmn. Falls Church (Va.) Planning Commn., 1958-64. Pres., Falls Church Republican party, 1961-62. Bd. dirs., v.p., gen. counsel Commonwealth Doctors Hosp., Fairfax, Va., 1967-74. Served with Armed Forces, 1943-45. Mem. Am., W.Va., D.C. bar assns., State Bar Va., Motor Carrier Lawyers Assn., Assn. ICC Practitioners (nat. pres. 1971-72), Delta Theta Phi, Phi Gamma Delta. Presbyn. Rotarian, Mason (Shriner). Clubs: Washington Golf and Country, Nat. Lawyers; Farmington Country (Charlottesville, Va.). Home: 815 Nethercliffe Hall Rd Great Falls VA 22066 Office Suite 915 425 13th St NW Washington DC 20004

SIMS, JOHN WILLIAM, lawyer; b. Vicksburg, Miss., Mar. 25, 1917; s. John Ernest and Helen Ross (Moore) S. B.A., Tulane U., 1937, LL.B., 1939; m. Marie Elise Hebert, Sept. 28, 1940; 1 dau., Helen Moore. Admitted to La. bar, 1939, since practiced in New Orleans; mem. firm Phelps, Dunbar, Marks, Claverie & Sims; mem. permanent adv. bd. and planning com. Tulane U. Admiralty Law Inst., 1966—. Mem. Met. Area Com. New Orleans; trustee Gulf South Research Inst., 1965—, Children's Hosp., 1975-78; bd. dirs. Council for Better La., Bur. Govt. Research; bd. dirs., v.p. New Orleans Opera Assn., 1974—; mem. men's adv. bd. Christian Woman's Exchange. Served to lt. USCGR, 1942-45. Fellow Am. Coll. Trial Lawyers; mem. Am., La. (past sec.-treas.), New Orleans bar assns., Def. Research Inst., Average Adjusters Assn. U.S., Maritime Law Assn. U.S. (2d v.p. 1976-78, 1st v.p. 1978—, com. Supreme Ct. admiralty rules 1963-69, com. limitation of liability 1963-75, com. Comite Maritime Internat. 1965—, com. uniformity admiralty law 1975—, com. liquified natural gas transp. 1978—; del. Comite Maritime Internat. conv. N.Y.C., 1965, Rio de Janeiro, 1977, adv. cons. Hamburg 1974, titular mem. Comite Maritime Internat. 1979—), SAR, Soc. Colonial Wars, Phi Beta Kappa, Omicron Delta Kappa, Phi Delta Theta, Phi Delta Phi. Clubs: Boston, Louisiana. Asso. editor Am. Maritime Cases, 1974—; contbr. articles to profl. jours. Home: 21 Audubon Blvd New Orelans LA 70118 Office: Hibernia Bldg New Orleans LA 70112

SIMS, JOSEPH SHERRER, banker; b. Jackson, Miss., Apr. 3, 1927; s. Matthew David and Laura (Parker) S.; student Hampden-Sydney Coll., 1944-45; A.B., Princeton, 1947; LL.B., Vanderbilt U., 1951; m. Vivian Jane Walker, June 4, 1949; children—Joseph Walker, Sherrie Jane. With First Nat. Bank Memphis, 1954—, sr. v.p., trust officer, 1968-72, exec. v.p., 1972—; adminstrv. v.p. First Tenn. Nat. Corp., 1974-76, vice chmn., 1976—; admitted to Tenn. bar, 1951. Served with USNR, 1944-46, 52-54. Mem. Tenn., Memphis and Shelby County bar assns., Am., Tenn. (pres. trust div. 1969) bankers assns., Estate Planning Council Memphis (pres. 1969), Princeton Alumni Assn. Memphis (pres. 1969), Phi Alpha Delta. Methodist. Home: 1311 Hayne Rd Memphis TN 38117 Office: 165 Madison Ave Memphis TN 38103

SIMS, KENT OTWAY, bank exec.; b. Chickasha, Okla., Nov. 2, 1940; s. Jesse Otway and Mable Vela (Bear) S.; B.A., U. Colo., Boulder, 1963, Ph.D., 1966; m. Jeanette McCollum, June 9, 1962; children—Marketa, Adam. Economist, Urban Renewal Authority, Denver, 1965-66, AID. Washington and Pakistan, 1966-69; with Fed. Res. Bank San Francisco, 1969—, v.p. charge research, 1972-74, sr. v.p. research, 1974-75, sr. v.p. charge dist. depts., 1975—. Mem. World Affairs Council No. Calif., Am. Econs. Assn., Marin Conservation League, Am. Mus. Natural History, Commonwealth Club Calif. Office: 400 Sansome St San Francisco CA 94120

SIMS, MELVIN EARL, farmer, agrl. coop. exec.; b. Liberty, Ill., July 31, 1920; s. Earl R. and Golden (Dean) S.; B.S. in Agr., U. Ill., 1941; m. Carol Marie Humphrey, Sept. 4, 1943; children—Randall Lee, Judith Kay (Mrs. Michael C. Walsten). Farm owner and operator, 1946—; pres. FS Services, Inc., 1959—, Central Nitrogen, Inc., 1962-71, Ill. Grain Corp., 1969—; shareholder rep. CF Industries, Long Grove, Ill., 1959—; dir. Farm Credit Banks St. Louis, 1958-65, Found. Am. Agr., 1965—, Farm Found., Chgo., 1970—; chmn. bd. Coop. Fertilizers Internat., Chgo., 1970—; dir. Agrl. Coop. Devel. Internat., 1965—, chmn. bd., 1975-79; bd. govs. Agr. Hall of Fame, 1965—; trustee Am. Inst. Coop., 1968-73, Farm Film Found., 1969—. Trustee Blessing Hosp., Quincy, Ill., 1967-70, Fed. Farm Credit Bd., 1972-78; mem. Adv. Council U.S.-Japan Econ. Relations, 1973—. Served to capt. AUS, 1941-46. Decorated Bronze Star; named Outstanding Young Farmer in Ill., 1955; recipient Disting. Service award Nat. Future Farmers Am., 1968, Hon. Am. Farmer degree Nat. Future Farmers Am., 1973; award of merit Agr. Alumni Assn., U. Ill., 1964. Mem. Alumni Assn. Coll. Agr. U. Ill. (dir. 1959-66, pres. 1961), Nat. Coop. Refinery Assn. (dir. 1963—), Nat. Council Farmer Coops. (dir. 1961-73, pres. 1969-71), C. of C. of U.S. (agr. com. 1975), Farm House, Alpha Zeta, Gamma Sigma Delta. Methodist. Mason. Office: 1701 Towanda Ave Bloomington IL 61701

SIMS, NAOMI RUTH, wig co. exec., former model; b. Oxford, Miss., Mar. 30, 1949; d. John and Elizabeth (Parham) S.; student Fashion Inst. Tech., also N.Y. U., 1966-67; m. Michael Alistair Findlay, Aug. 4, 1973; 1 son, John Phillip Sims. Fashion model Ford Modeling Agy., N.Y.C., 1967-73; founder, owner, chief exec. officer Naomi Sims Collection, N.Y.C., 1973—; introduced Naomi fragrance, owner Naomi Sims Inc., 1979—. Freelance writer, 1970—; lectr., participant panels for schs., Univs., social groups. Vol. tchr. remedial reading pub. schs., N.Y.C., 1973-75. Bd. dirs. Northside Center For Child Devel. Named Model of Year, Internat. Famous Mannequinns Assn., 1969, 70; recipient N.Y.C. Bd. Edn. award, 1970; Woman of Achievement medal Ladies Home Jour., 1970, Am. Cancer Soc., 1972; Top Hat award New Pitts. Courier, 1974. Mem. NAACP (hon. life). Roman Catholic. Author: All About Health and Beauty for the Black Woman, 1976; How To Be A Top Model, 1979; columnist Right On mag; contbr. articles on fashion and beauty to popular mags. Co-developer synthetic hair fiber for wigmaking, 1972-73. Office: Naomi Sims Collection 48 E 21st St New York NY 10010. *To be born both female and Black is to be denied those advantages usually required for high accomplishment yet I constantly rejoice in my womanhood and in my color. I do not trust in luck but in my ability to judge the worth of people and projects. Once I have chosen a particular goal I pursue it with single-minded vigor. I try to select goals that are emotionally challenging.*

SIMS, PAUL KIBLER, govt. geologist; b. Newton, Ill., Sept. 8, 1918; s. Dorris Lee and Vere (Kibler) S.; A.B., U. Ill., 1940, M.S., 1942; Ph.D., Princeton, 1950; m. Dolores Carsell Thomas, Sept. 15, 1940; children—Thomas Courtney, Charlotte Ann. Spl. asst. geologist Ill. Geol. Survey, 1942-43; geologist U.S. Geol. Survey, 1943-61; prof. geology, dir. Minn. Geol. survey U. Minn., 1961-73; research geologist U.S. Geol. Survey, 1973—; pres. Econ. Geology Pub. Co., 1979—. Bd. dirs. North Star Research and Devel. Inst., Mpls., 1966-73. Adviser Minn. Outdoor Recreation Resources Commn., 1963-67. Served with USNR, 1943-46. Fellow Geol. Soc. Am.; mem. Soc. Econ. Geologists (councilor 1965-68, pres. 1975), Internat. Assn. on Genesis of Ore Deposits, Internat. Union Geol. Sci. (U.S. subcom. Precambrian stratigraphy, sec. 1976—). Co-editor Geology of Minnesota, 1972. Research geology metalliferous ore deposits Colo., Minn., Wis., N.J., Ariz., Wash., also early evolution earth's crust in N.Am. Home: 1315 Overhill Rd Golden CO 80401

SIMS, PHILIP STUART, indsl. distbg. co. exec.; b. Cleve., Nov. 21, 1927; s. Edward Paul and Hortense Jean (Feldman) S.; B.B.A. cum laude, Cleve. Coll., Western Res. U., 1956; m. Barbara Ann Less, Jan. 31, 1951; children—Wendy Lou, Debra Sue. With Am. Steel & Wire Co., U.S. Steel Corp., 1947-56, fin. analyst, 1951-56; with Premier Indsl. Corp., Cleve., 1956—, v.p., treas., 1968-74, sr. v.p., treas., 1975—, also officer, dir. all subsidiaries and trustee pension trust and charitable found. Served with AUS, 1945-47. Mem. Planning Execs. Inst., Am. Statis. Assn., Beta Alpha Psi. Home: 2460 Saybrook Rd University Heights OH 44118 Office: 4415 Euclid Ave Cleveland OH 44118

SIMS, RICHARD LEE, hosp. adminstr.; b. Columbus, Ohio, Jan. 6, 1929; s. Dorwin Delos and Christine Anna (Hanstein) S.; B.S., Ohio State U., 1951; m. Marilyn Lou Atkinson, June 2, 1951; children—John Christopher, Steven Paul. Adminstr., Doctors Hosp., Columbus; preceptor faculty Ohio State U. Coll. Health Care Adminstrn.; chmn. adminstrs. council Mid Ohio Health Planning Fedn.; adminstr. Sattelite Hosp.-Doctors Hosp. West, Columbus; chmn. Hosp. Shared Service Inc. Past pres. Franklin County Crippled Childrens Soc.; pres. Franklin County chpt. ARC, 1978—; chmn. 1st Community Village Bd. Served with Med. Service, AUS, 1953-56; to maj. Ohio N.G., 1956-74. Recipient Distinguished Service award Columbus Jr. C. of C., 1960-63. Mem. Am. Coll. Hosp. Adminstrs., Am. Coll. Osteo. Hosp. Adminstrs., Ohio Trade Assn. Execs. (past pres.), Ohio Hosp. Assn. (past chmn. bd.), Ohio Osteo. Hosp. Assn. (pres.), Am. Legion (past post comdr.), Sigma Chi. Clubs: University, Rotary (pres. 1978-79) (Columbus). Home: 2431 Southway Dr Columbus OH 43221 Office: 1087 Dennison Ave Columbus OH 43201

SIMS, ROBERT BARRY, lawyer; b. N.Y.C., Aug. 20, 1942; s. Irving Zach and Laura (Levine) S.; A.B., Franklin and Marshall Coll., 1964; J.D., George Washington U., 1967; M.B.A., N.Y. U., 1969; m. Roberta Jane Donner, Nov. 17, 1973. Admitted to N.Y. bar, 1968, Conn. bar, 1979, D.C. bar, 1969, U.S. Supreme Ct. bar, 1979; asso. firm Cahil, Gordon & Reindel, N.Y.C., 1967-69, Whitman & Ransom, N.Y.C., 1969-72; asst. counsel Gen. Signal Corp., N.Y.C., also Stamford, Conn., 1972-76; v.p., sec., gen. counsel Raybestos-Manhattan, Inc., Trumbull, Conn., 1972—. Mem. Am. Bar Assn., N.Y. State Bar Assn., Assn. Bar City N.Y., D.C. Bar Assn., Westchester-Fairfield Corp. Counsel Assn. Home: 40 Timber Ln Fairfield CT 06430 Office: 100 Oakview Dr Trumbull CT 06611

SIMS, WILSON, lawyer; b. Nashville, Dec. 24, 1924; s. Cecil and Grace (Wilson) S.; B.A., U. N.C., 1946; J.D., Vanderbilt U., 1948; m. Linda Bell, Aug. 12, 1948; children—Linda Rickman, Suzanne, Wilson. Admitted to Tenn. bar, 1948; since practiced in Nashville; partner firm Bass, Berry & Sims, 1948—; gen. counsel, dir. Synercon Corp., 1968-76, Martha White Foods, Baird Ward Printing Co., Tenn., 1950-76. Chmn. Commn. for Human Devel., 1970. Mem.

Tenn. Gen. Assembly, 1959; bd. dirs. Nashville YMCA, 1955-65, United Cerebral Palsy; trustee Meharry Med. Coll., Webb Sch., Bell Buckle, Tenn.; adv. bd. Jr. League. Served to 1st lt. USMCR, 1942-45, 50-52. Mem. Am., Tenn. (ho. dels. chmn. 1973-75), Nashville (past pres., dir.) bar assns., Am. Judicature Soc., Am. Acad. Polit. Sci., Vanderbilt Law Alumni (pres. 1974-75), Nashville C. of C. (bd. govs. 1965-70). Mem. Christian Ch. (elder). Clubs: Belle Meade Country (dir. 1969-72), Cumberland (Nashville); Bay Point Yacht and Country (Panama City, Fla.). Home: 405 Westview Ave Nashville TN 37205 Office: 27th Floor 1st Am Center Nashville TN 37238

SINAI, ARTHUR, govt. ofcl.; b. Bklyn., Sept. 23, 1939; s. Hyman and Miriam (Savitsky) S.; B.A., Bklyn. Coll., 1960; J.D., Georgetown U., 1970; m. Carol Goldstein, Nov. 28, 1965; 1 son, Jeffrey Sinai. With IRS, 1960-68, criminal investigator, 1961-68; chief investigator Dept. Commerce, Washington, 1968-70, U.S. Senate Labor Subcom., 1970-71; field dir. GSA, 1971-72; 1st asst. welfare insp. gen., State of N.Y., 1972-73; asst. supt. Ill. Bur. Investigation, 1973-74; dep. dir. Office of Spl. Investigation, State of Ill., 1974-75; dir. Office of Spl. Investigation, Ill. Dept. Law Enforcement, 1975-76, asst. dir., 1976-77; cons. U.S. Dept. Labor, 1977; dep. asst. sec. enforcement Dept. Treasury, Washington, 1977—. Mem. Internat. Assn. Chiefs Police, Am. Judicature Soc., Am. Soc. Public Adminstrn. Democrat. Jewish. Office: Treasury Dept Washington DC 20220. *Do not try to attain a goal which entails the selling of your soul. Be true to thyself.*

SINAI, ISAAC ROBERT, educator, author; b. Lithuania, Oct. 10, 1924; (came to U.S. 1962, naturalized 1969); s. Boris and Ella (Zotnick) S.; ed. in South Africa; Ph.D., Union Grad. Sch., 1975; m. Anne Witten, Aug. 18, 1946; 1 son, Joshua B. Freelance journalist, Johannesburg, London and Paris, 1946-51; editor Work Jour., Israel Fedn. Labour, 1952-55, officer internat. relations dept., 1957-60; rep. Israel Labour Party on Secretariat Asian Socialist Conf., Rangoon, Burma, 1955-57; information officer Israel Fgn. Office, 1962; instr. New Sch. for Social Research, N.Y.C., 1962—, N.Y.U., 1964-73; asso. prof. polit. sci. L.I.U., 1966-73; asso. prof. State U. N.Y. at Potsdam, 1973—; cons. Fgn. Policy Research Inst., U. Pa., 1963; guest lectr. Princeton, U. Wis., Columbia Research Inst. Communist Affairs. Rockefeller Found. fellow, 1965-66. Fellow Middle East Studies Assn. N.Am.; mem. Authors League Am., Authors Guild, AAUP, Acad. Polit. Sci., Am. Polit. Sci. Assn., Am. Hist. Assn., Am. Sociol. Assn. Author: The Challenge of Modernization, 1964; In Search of the Modern World, 1967; The Emergence of the State of Israel, 1945-1948, 1972; The Decadence of the Modern World, 1978; editor: Modernization and the Middle East, 1970. Home: 21 Grant St Potsdam NY 13676

SINANOGLU, OKTAY, educator, chemist; b. Feb. 25, 1935; s. Nüzhet Hasim and Rüveyde (Karacabey) S.; grad. Ankara (Turkey) Coll., 1953; B.S. in Chem. Engring. with highest honors, U. Calif. at Berkeley, 1956, Ph.D. in Phys. Chemistry (Univ. fellow 1958-59), 1959; M.S. in Chem. Engring. (Whitney fellow 1956-57), Mass. Inst. Tech., 1957; m. Paula Armbruster, Dec. 21, 1963; children—K. Levni, Elif-Lâle, Murat Haslm. Postdoctoral chemist AEC, Radiation Lab., Berkeley, 1959-60; mem. faculty Yale, New Haven, Conn., 1962—, prof. chemistry, 1963—, fellow Trumbull Coll., 1961—; spl. research intermolecular forces, atomic structure, solvent effects, quantum theory organic and bio-molecules, other spl. research; A. and R. Sloan vis. lectr. Harvard, spring 1962; vis. prof. Orta Dogu Tekn. U., Ankara, summer 1962, now cons. Prof., dir. NATO Internat. Summer Sch. of Quantum Chemistry, Istanbul, 1964, NATO Internat. Advance Study Inst. on New Directions in Atomic Physics, Izmir, Turkey, 1969; hon. chmn. ODTU, Ankara, 1968; cons. prof. Bogazici U., Istanbul, Turkey, 1973. Recipient Turkish sci. award, 1966, Alexander von Humboldt sr. scientist award West Germany, 1973, sr. scientist award Japanese Soc. for Promotion Sci., 1975. Fellow Am. Acad. Arts and Scis.; mem. Am. Chem. Soc., Am. Phys. Soc., Am. Inst. Chem. Engrs. (award Western sect. 1955), Inst. Am. Chemists (award 1955-56), Phi Beta Kappa, Sigma Tau, Tau Beta Pi. Author: (with K.B. Wiberg) Sigma Molecular Orbital Theory; (with K.A. Brueckner) Three Approaches to Electron Correlation in Atoms. Editor, co-author: Modern Quantum Chemistry Istanbul Lectures, 3 vols., 1966; (with E.U. Condon) New Directions In Atomic Physics, 2 vols., 1970. Gen. editor (with E.U. Condon) Yale Series in the Sciences, 1969—. Contbr. articles to profl. jours., chpts. in books.

SINATRA, FRANK (FRANCIS ALBERT SINATRA), singer, actor; b. Hoboken, N.J., Dec. 12, 1915; s. Anthony and Natalie (Garaventi) S.; student Demarest High Sch., Hoboken, also Drake Inst.; m. Nancy Barbato, Feb. 4, 1939 (div.); children—Nancy, Frank Wayne, Christine; m. 2d, Ava Gardner (div.); m. 3d, Mia Farrow, 1966 (div.); m. 4th, Barbara Marx, 1976. Sang with sch. band and helped form sch. glee club; worked after sch. on news truck of Jersey Observer, copy boy on graduation with sports div. covering coll. sports events; won first prize on Maj. Bowes Amateur Hour, touring with co. for 3 months; sustaining programs on 4 radio stas. and in Rustic Cabin, N.J.; toured with Harry James Band, then Tommy Dorsey's; solo night club and concert appearances; starred on radio program Lucky Strike Hit Parade; appeared in motion pictures Las Vegas Nights, Ship Ahoy, Miracle of the Bells, Kissing Bandit, Take Me Out to the Ball Game, Higher and Higher, Step Lively, Anchors Aweigh, It Happened in Brooklyn, From Here to Eternity (Acad. award as best supporting actor 1953), Guys and Dolls, Not as a Stranger, The Tender Trap, The Man With the Golden Arm, Johnny Concho, 1956, The Pride and the Passion, 1957, Pal Joey, 1957, Some Came Running, 1959, Never So Few, 1960, Can-Can, 1960, Oceans 11, 1960, Pepe, 1960, The Devil at 4 O'Clock, 1961, The Manchurian Candidate, 1962, Come Blow Your Horn, 1963, None But the Brave, 1964, Assault on a Queen, 1965, Von Ryan's Express, 1966, Tony Rome, 1966, Lady in Cement, 1967, The Detective, 1968, Dirty Dingus McGee, 1970; TV movie Contract on Cherry Street, 1977; hit songs include Night and Day, 1943, Nancy, 1945, Young at Heart, 1954, Love and Marriage, 1955, The Tender Trap, 1955, How Little We Know, 1956, Chicago, 1957, All the Way, 1957, High Hopes, 1959, It Was a Very Good Year, 1965, Strangers in the Night, 1966, My Way, 1969; (with Nancy Sinatra) Somethin Stupid, 1969; writer lyrics for This Love of Mine. Recipient Sylvania TV award, 1959; Peabody and Emmy awards, 1965; Jean Hersholt award Acad. Motion Picture Arts and Scis., 1971; Golden Apple award as Male Star of Year, Hollywood Women's Press Club, 1977. Recs. Columbia, Capitol. Club: Friars (abbot). Address: Sinatra Enterprises 1041 N Formosa Ave Hollywood CA 90046*

SINATRA, NANCY SANDRA, rec. artist, actress; b. Jersey City, N.J., June 8, 1940; d. Frank Albert and Nancy (Barbato) Sinatra; student U. So. Calif., m. Hugh Lambert, Dec. 12, 1970; children—Angela Jennifer, Amanda Katherine. Rec. artist Warner Bros.; nightclub performer Las Vegas; performed USO tours, Viet Nam, 1967; actress films. Chmn. Young Adult group United Cerebral Palsy Fund; active Thalians, Sugar Ray Youth Found., Cedars-Sinai Womens' Guild. Recipient Gold records for These Boots Are Made for Walkin', Sugartown, Something Stupid, Boots. Democrat. Office: care Boots Enterprises Inc 9145 Sunset Blvd Los Angeles CA 90069

SINCLAIR, ALAN MURRAY, univ. exec.; b. St. John, N.B., Can., Feb. 27, 1929; s. Rankine Murray and Greta Maud (Parlee) S.; LL.B., Dalhousie U., 1956; LL.M. in Comparative Law, So. Methodist U., 1957; LL.M., U. Mich., 1960, S.J.D., 1965; m. Mary Verne MacDougall, June 5, 1954; children—Caroline Jane, Marilyn Anne. Called to N.S. bar, 1957, N.B. bar, 1961, created Queen's Counsel, 1978; asst. prof. law So. Meth. U., 1957-61; asso. prof. U. N.B. (Can.), Fredericton, 1961-65, prof., 1965-74, dean, 1974-78; pres. Acadia U., Wolfville, N.S., Can., 1978—. NATO fellow, 1969. Mem. Barrister's Soc. N.B., Can. Bar Assn. Author: Introduction to the Law of Real Property, 1969. Office: Acadia U Wolfville NS 30P 1X0 Canada

SINCLAIR, ALFORD CHARLES, banker; b. Rowland, N.C., Feb. 1, 1930; s. Alexander Charles and Rena Helen (Parker) S.; B.S., Wake Forest Coll., 1952; M.Ed., U. N.C., 1955; m. Sylvia Marie Ferrell, Sept. 9, 1967; 1 son, Alexander Charles, II. From trainee to v.p. N.C. Nat. Bank, Winston-Salem, 1956-68; sr. v.p. Union Bank and Trust Co., Montgomery, Ala., 1968-73; pres. Nashville City Bank & Trust Co., 1973-76; pres., chief exec. officer Atlantic Nat. Bank, Jacksonville, Fla., 1976—; lectr. in field. Trustee U. N.Fla. Found.; bd. dirs. Jacksonville Symphony Orch.; mem. exec. com. Jacksonville Area United Way, Jacksonville Area chpt. ARC. Served with AUS, 1952-54. Decorated Purple Heart, Combat Inf. badge. Mem. Am., Fla. bankers assns., Robert Morris Assos. (gov. council policy div., regent loan mgmt. seminar), Jacksonville Area C. of C. (exec. com.). Republican. Episcopalian. Clubs: Timuquana Country, River, Sawgrass Beach. Fla. Yacht. Home: 4651 Arapahoe Ave Jacksonville FL 32210 Office: 200 W Forsyth St Jacksonville FL 32202

SINCLAIR, BRUCE, historian, educator; b. Artesia, N.Mex., Apr. 30, 1929; s. Bert Thomas and Helen Evelyn (Cleveland) S.; B.A., U. Calif., Berkeley, 1956; M.A., U. Del., 1959; Ph.D., Case Inst. Tech., 1966; m. Christine E. Roen, June 17, 1956 (div. Jan. 1968); children—Alan Douglas, Margaret Elizabeth; m. 2d, Mary P. Winsor, Feb. 15, 1975. Dir. Merrimack Valley Textile Museum, North Andover, Mass., 1959-64; mem. faculty Kans. State U., 1966-69; mem. faculty U. Toronto, 1969—, prof. history, dir. Inst. History and Philosophy of Sci. and Tech., 1975—. Served with USAF, 1950-54. Eleutherian Mills-Hagley fellow, 1957-59; grantee NSF, Am. Philos. Soc., Can. Council. Mem. Soc. History Tech. (Dexter prize 1975), Orgn. Am. Historians, Canadian Soc. History and Philosophy Sci., Canadian Hist. Assn. Author: Early Research at the Franklin Institute, 1966; Philadelphia's Philosopher Mechanics, 1974; Let Us Be Honest and Modest: Technology and Society in Canadian History, 1974. Address: 550 Spadina Crescent Toronto ON M5S 2J9 Canada

SINCLAIR, GEORGE, telecommunications co. exec.; b. Hamilton, Ont., Can., Nov. 5, 1912; s. Charles Thomson and Elizabeth Gilchrist (MacKenzie) S.; B.Sc., U. Alta., 1933, M.Sc., 1935; Ph.D., 1946, D.Sc. (hon.), 1973; m. Helen Marie Carscadden, Sept. 8, 1951; children—Andrea Joan, Valerie June, Dorothy Elizabeth. Dir. antenna lab. Ohio State U., Columbus, 1942-47; mem. dept. elec. engring. U. Toronto, 1947-78, prof., 1974-78; chmn. bd. Sinclair Radio Labs., Ltd., Concord, Ont., 1951—. Guggenheim fellow, 1958. Fellow Royal Soc. Can., IEEE (Gen. A.G.L. McNaughton award 1975); mem. Can. Soc. Elec. Engrs., Assn. Profl. Engrs. Ont. Presbyterian. Club: Kiwanis. Office: 122 Rayette Rd Concord ON L4K 1B6 Canada

SINCLAIR, IAN DAVID, railroad co. ofcl.; b. Winnipeg, Man., Can., Dec. 27, 1913; s. John David and Lillian (Matheson) S.; B.A. in Econs., Wesley Coll., U. Man., 1937, LL.D., 1967; LL.B., Man. Law Sch., 1941; m. Ruth Beatrice Drennan, July 17, 1942; children—Ian R., Susan L., Christine R., Donald L. Barrister, Guy, Chappell & Co., Winnipeg, 1937-41; called to Man. bar, 1941, apptd. Queen's counsel, 1961; lectr. torts U. Man., 1942-43; with Canadian Pacific Ltd., 1942—, asst. solicitor, 1942, solicitor, Montreal, Que., Can., 1946, asst. to gen. counsel, 1951, gen. solicitor, 1953, v.p., gen. counsel, 1960, v.p. law, 1960-61, v.p., 1961-66, mem. exec. com., dir., 1961—, pres., 1966-72, chief exec. officer, 1969—, chmn. bd., 1972—; chmn., dir. Can. Pacific Air Lines, Ltd.; pres., dir. Midland Simcoe Elevator Co., Ltd.; chmn., chief exec. officer, dir. Can. Pacific Investments, Ltd.; v.p., dir. Pan Canadian Petroleum Ltd., Cominco Ltd.; dir. subsidiaries Canadian Pacific Securities Ltd., Canadian Pacific Steamships Ltd., Canadian Pacific (Bermuda) Ltd., Pacific Logging Co. Ltd., Marathon Realty Co. Ltd., Soo Line RR Co., Great Lakes Paper Co. Ltd.; dir., v.p. Royal Bank Can.; dir. Canadian Marconi Co., Sun Life Assurance Co. Can. Ltd., MacMillan Bloedel Ltd., Canadian Investment Fund, Union Carbide Corp., Union Carbide Can. Ltd., Canadian Fund Inc., Seagram Co. Ltd.; mem. internat. adv. com. Chase Manhattan Corp. Mem. The Conf. Bd. N.Y., Canadian C. of C., La Chambre de Commerce (Montreal), Montreal Bd. Trade. Clubs: Canadian Railway, Canadian, Mount Royal (Montreal); Rideau (Ottawa, Ont.). Office: Canadian Pacific Limited Windsor Sta Montreal PQ H3C 3E4 Canada

SINCLAIR, JOHN TAYLOR, JR., oil co. exec.; b. Paterson, N.J., Mar. 14, 1918; s. John Taylor and Anne (Bolte) S.; A.B., Wesleyan U., Middletown, Conn., 1939; M.S. in Phys. Sci., U. So. Calif., 1943; m. Ethel Mae Edwards, Sept. 18, 1941; children—John Taylor III, Lawrence Glenn. Trainee, Tide Water Asso. Oil. Co., Los Angeles, 1939-41, asst. dist. petroleum engr., 1941-45; div. engr., geologist Pantepec Oil Co., Eastern Venezuela, 1945-48, field supt., 1948-49, chief engr., geologist, 1949-51, asst. sec.-treas., 1951-53, dir., 1951—; chief engr., geologist Pancoastal Oil Corp., Caracas, Venezuela, 1949-51, sec. treas., 1951-53, dir., 1949-53; pres., dir. United Canso Oil & Gas Ltd., and predecessors, Calgary, Alta., Can., also Houston, 1954-69; dir. Coastal Caribbean Oils, 1968; operations coordinator Catawba Corp., Houston, 1958-65; dir. Coastel Caribbean Oils & Minerals Ltd., Pancoastal Petroleum Co. Registered profl. engr., Calif. Mem. Am. Inst. Mining, Metall. and Petroleum Engrs., Am. Petroleum Inst., Am. Assn. Petroleum Geologists, AAAS, Phi Beta Kappa, Sigma Xi, Phi Kappa Phi, Chi Psi. Presbyn. Clubs: Houston; Calgary Petroleum. Home: 201 Vanderpool 57 Houston TX 77024

SINCLAIR, JOSEPH SAMUELS, broadcasting co. exec., retail mcht.; b. Narragansett, R.I., June 14, 1922; s. James and Bertha (Samuels) S.; student Williams Coll., 1940-41; B.S., U.S. Naval Acad., 1945; D.B.A. (hon.), Johnson and Wales Coll., 1976; m. Betty Virginia Hintz, Feb. 16, 1946 (dec. 1968); children—Sherry Murr, Lani Patricia, Jodie Carol; m. 2d, Rosalyn K. Dwares, Oct. 24, 1969; children—Sara Ellen Sinclair, Steven Dwares. Asst. to program mgr. sta. WJAR-TV, Providence, 1949-57, sta. mgr., 1957-60, gen. mgr., 1960—; pres. WNYS-TV Inc., Syracuse, N.Y.; chmn. Cherry and Webb; dir. Outlet Co., 1955-58, exec. com., 1958-60, v.p., 1960, pres., 1960-68, chmn. bd., 1968—; dir. Indsl. Nat. Bank, Indsl. Bancorp., Exec. Jet Aviation, Columbus, Ohio. Mem. Mayor's Adv. Council, R.I., Kent County, Miriam hosps.; mem. Pres.'s Council Providence Coll.; trustee R.I. Council Econ. Edn., U. R.I. Found., Public Expenditure Council, Trinity Square Theater. Served to lt. (s.g.) USN, 1945-47, USNR, 1950-52. Decorated Italian Star Solidarity; recipient R.I. Advt. Silver medal, 1968. Mem. Navy League R.I., Naval War Coll. Found., Nat. (dir.), R.I. (v.p.) assns. broadcasters, TV Pioneers, Internat. Radio and TV Soc., World Bus. Council, R.I. Commodores (adm.). Clubs: N.Y. Athletic; Sports Car Am.; East Greenwich Yacht (East Greenwich, R.I.); Cat Cay, University (Providence); Nat. Broadcasters; Atlantic Tuna; R.I. 100 (pres.); Pt. Judith Country, Dunes, Squantum. Home: 30 Alton Rd Providence RI 02906 Office: 176 Weybosset St Providence RI 02903

SINCLAIR, KEITH VAL, educator; b. Auckland, N.Z., Nov. 8, 1926; s. Valentine Leslie and Dorothy Coral (Keith) S.; B.A., U. New Zealand, 1948, M.A., 1949; Licence ès Lettres, U. Paris, 1951, Docteur, 1954; D.Phil., St. Catherine's Coll., Oxford U., 1960; Lit. D., Victoria U., Wellington, New Zealand, 1973. Came to U.S., 1972. Instr. English, Lycée Montaigne, Paris, 1950-52; part time instr. French, Oxford U., 1952-55; lectr., then sr. lectr. French, Australian Nat. U., 1955-62; asso. prof. French, U. Cal. at Davis, 1963-64; sr. lectr., then asso. prof. French Sydney (Australia) U., 1964-71; vis. prof. French and Italian, Northwestern U., 1971; prof. French, U. Conn., 1972—. Exec. sec. Australian Humanities Research Council, 1964-69; mem. N.S.W. State Edn. Syllabus Com., 1965-72; mem. Australian UNESCO Com. for Libraries, 1967-72. Decorated officier Ordre National du Merite, officier de l'Ordre des Palmes Académiques, chevalier de l'Ordre de la Couronne (France); cavaliere ufficiale nell'Ordine al Merito (Italy). French Govt. postgrad. scholar, 1949-50; Brit. Inst. in Paris scholar, 1950-51; Australian Research Grants Com. award, 1965-66; French Govt. personnalité invitée, 1971. Exec. dir. Unisyd Credit Union, 1968-72. Fellow Australian Acad. Humanities (found. fellow, exec. sec. 1969-71, 72-73, exec. treas. 1971-72), Soc. Antiquaries (London), Royal Geog. Soc.; mem. Mediaeval Acad. Am., Modern Lang. Assn., Anglo-Norman Text Soc., Australian Univs. Lang. and Lit. Assn., Australian and New Zealand Assn. for Medieval and Renaissance Studies. Author: The Melbourne Livy, 1961; Anglo-Norman: the last twenty years, 1966; Catalogue of Exhibition of Medieval MSS at Fisher Library, 1967; Treasures of the Ballarat Art Gallery: the Crouch MSS, 1968; Descriptive Catalogue of Medieval MSS in Australia, 1969; Tristan de Nanteuil: chanson de geste inédite, 1971; Prières en encien français, 1978; French Devotional Texts of the Middle Ages, 1979; also articles in profl. jours. Home: Slade Rd Warrenville CT 06278 Office: Dept Romance Langs U Conn Storrs CT 06268

SINCLAIR, LISTER SHEDDEN, broadcasting exec.; b. Bombay, India, Jan. 9, 1921; s. William Shedden and Lillie Agnes (Smith) S.; B.A., U. B.C. (Can.), Vancouver, 1942, LL.D. (hon.), 1970; M.A., U. Toronto (Ont., Can.), 1945; D.Litt., Mt. Allison U., 1968; Litt.D. (hon.), Meml. U., Nfld., Can., 1969; LL.D. (hon.), 1970; m. Margaret Alice, Dec. 24, 1942; m. 2d, Margaret, June 2, 1965; children—Peter Elliot, William Andrew Alexander. Lectr. in math. U. B.C., 1942, U. Toronto, 1950; exec. producer CBC-TV, Toronto, 1967-72, exec. v.p., 1972-74, v.p. programs, 1974—. Decorated Silver Jubilee medal; recipient numerous awards for broadcasting, including Columbus award (12), Japanese Sci. Film award, Hugo award, John Drainie award. Mem. Assn. Can. Radio, TV Film Artists (hon. life). Author numerous radio, TV, film and theater scripts; author books: A Play on Words; The Blood is Strong; Socrates; The Art of Norval Morrisseau; contbr. numerous articles to profl. jours. Office: CBC 790 Bay St Toronto ON M5G 1N8 Canada

SINCLAIR, ROLF MALCOLM, physicist, govt. ofcl.; b. N.Y.C., Aug. 15, 1929; s. Nathan and Elizabeth (Stout) S.; B.S., Calif. Inst. Tech., 1949; M.A. (Reade scholar), Rice U., 1951, Ph.D. (Inst. fellow), 1954; m. Margaret Lee Andrews, June 13, 1959 (div. 1978); children—Elizabeth Ann, Andrew Caisley. Physicist, Westinghouse Research Labs., 1953-56; vis. scientist U. Hamburg (Germany), 1956-57, U. Paris (France), 1957-58, U.K. Atomic Energy Authority, Culham Lab., Eng., 1965-66; research physicist Princeton, 1958-69; program dir. NSF, Washington, 1969—. Cons. to industry, 1960-69. Fellow Am. Phys. Soc. (panel pub. affairs), AAAS (sec. physics sect. 1972—, mem. council 1972-73), Sigma Xi. Research and publs. on physics, tech. and instrumentation. Patentee in field. Home: 1838 Belmont Rd NW Washington DC 20009 Office: NSF Washington DC 20550

SINCLAIR, WARREN KEITH, physicist; b. Dunedin, N.Z., Mar. 9, 1924; s. Ernest W. and Jessie E. (Craig) S.; came to U.S., 1954, naturalized, 1959; B.Sc., U. Otago (N.Z.), 1944, M.Sc., 1945; Ph.D., U. London, 1950; m. Elizabeth J. Edwards, Mar. 19, 1948; children—Bruce W., Roslyn E., Allen. Radiol. physicist U. Otago, 1945-47; radiol. physicist U. London Royal Marsden Hosp., 1947-54; chmn. dept. physics, prof. U. Tex. M.D. Anderson Hosp., 1954-60; sr. biophysicist Argonne (Ill.) Nat. Lab., 1960—, div. dir., 1970-74, asso. lab. dir., 1974—; prof. radiation biology U. Chgo., 1964—; mem. Internat. Commn. on Radiation Units and Measurements, 1969—, Internat. Commn. on Radiol. Protection, 1977—; dir. Nat. Council on Radiation Protection and Measurements, 1967—, pres., 1977—; sec. gen. 5th Internat. Congress Radiation Research, 1974. Served with N.Z. Army, 1942-43. Nat. N.Z. scholar, 1942-45. Fellow Inst. Physics; mem. Am. Assn. Physicists in Medicine (pres. 1961-62), Radiation Research Soc. (council 1964-67, pres. 1978-79), Brit. Inst. Radiology (council 1953-54), Internat. Assn. Radiation Research (council 1966-70, 76—), Radiol. Soc. N.Am., Biophys. Soc., Soc. Nuclear Medicine. Club: Innominates (U. Chgo.). Contbr. numerous articles to profl. jours., also chpts. to books. Home: 1419 87th St Downers Grove IL 60515 Office: 9700 S Cass Ave Argonne IL 60439

SINDEN, HARRY, profl. hockey team exec.; m. Eleanor Sinden; children—Nancy, Carol, Dawn, Julie. Player Hull-Ottawa Eastern Pro League hockey team; player-coach Kingston team, from 1961; coach numerous teams Central League until 1967; coach Boston Bruins Nat. Hockey League team, 1967-70, mng. dir., 1972—; v.p. Storer Broadcasting Co.; TV hockey commentator, 1970-72. Coach Team Can., 1973. Coach Stanley Cup team, 1970. Address: care Boston Bruins Boston Gardens 150 Causeway St Boston MA 02114*

SINEATH, TIMOTHY WAYNE, librarian, univ. adminstr.; b. Jacksonville, Fla., May 21, 1940; s. Holcombe Asbury and Christine Marcel (Cook) S.; B.A., Fla. State U., 1962, M.S., 1963; Ph.D. (Higher Edn. Act fellow), U. Ill., 1970; m. Patricia Ann Greenwood, June 8, 1962; children—Philip Greenwood, Paul Byron. Reference librarian U. Ga., 1963-64, catalog librarian, 1964-66; acad. coordinator continuing edn. in library sci. U. Ill., 1966-68; asst. prof. library sci. Simmons Coll., 1970-74, coordinator doctoral program, 1974-77; prof., dean Coll. Library Sci., U. Ky., 1977—; cons. to libraries, schs., chs., industry; mem. Lexington (Ky.) Public Library Bd., 1978—. Mem. Am. Soc. Info. Sci., ALA, Assn. Am. Library Schs., Episcopalian. Author profl. reports; contbr. articles on library and info. sci., gen. info. mgmt., organizational and small group behavior to profl. jours. Home: 3418 Bay Leaf Dr Lexington KY 40502 Office: 459 Patterson Office Tower U Ky Lexington KY 40506

SINEL, NORMAN MARK, lawyer; b. New Haven, Dec. 8, 1941; s. Nathan and Mona S.; B.A., Yale U., 1963; LL.B., Stanford U., 1966; m. Ellen Winnick, June 16, 1963; children—Joshua, Natasha. Admitted to Calif. bar, 1967, D.C. bar, 1968; law clk. to judge Dist. Ct. No. Dist. Calif., 1966-67; asso. firm Wilmer, Cutter & Pickering, Washington, 1967-71; gen. counsel Public Broadcasting Service, Washington, 1971-73, v.p., gen. counsel, 1973-76, sr. v.p. for corp. mgmt., gen. counsel, 1976-79; of counsel firm Arnold & Porter, Washington, 1979—. Mem. Calif. Bar Assn., D.C. Bar Assn. Home: 3710 Harrison St NW Washington DC 20015 Office: 1229 19 St NW Washington DC 20036

SINEX, FRANCIS MAROTT, educator, biochemist; b. Indpls., Jan. 11, 1923; s. Francis Herr and Helen Myrtilla (Marott) S.; A.B., DePauw U., 1944; M.A., Ind. U., 1946; Ph.D., Harvard, 1950; m.

Virginia Hofer, 1948 (dec.); 1 dau., Katherine; m. 2d, Joan S. Martin, May 19, 1951; children—Ellen Jane, Margaret Ann. Exec. officer biochemistry div., med. dept. Brookhaven Nat. Lab., Upton, N.Y., 1952-57; chmn. dept. biochemistry Boston U. Sch. Medicine, 1957-77, co-dir. Gerontology Center, 1974-77, head bio-med. gerontology sect., 1977—. Fellow Gerontol. Soc. (pres. 1969-70); mem. Soc. Biol. Chemists. Home: C 705 77 Pond Ave Brookline MA 02146 Office: 80 E Concord St Boston MA 02118

SINEY, MARION CELESTIA, historian, educator; b. Muskegon, Mich., Aug. 11, 1913; d. Andrew Joseph and Vina Lillian (Carpenter) S.; A.B., U. Mich., 1933, M.A., 1934, Ph.D., 1938. Mem. residence halls staff, teaching fellow U. Mich., 1939-41; mem. faculty dept. history Case Western Res. U., Cleve., 1941—, prof., 1965—, Hiram C. Haydn prof., 1977—. Social Sci. Research Council fellow, 1935-36; Rackham fellow, 1936-38; Social Sci. Research Council grantee, 1957-58; Am. Council Learned Socs. and Am. Philos. Soc. grantee, 1966-67; Alfred Lloyd postdoctoral fellow, 1938-39. Fellow Royal Hist. Soc. (London); mem. Am. Hist. Assn., AAUP, Phi Beta Kappa. Author: The Allied Blockade of Germany, 1914-1916, 1973; contbr. articles to profl. jours. Home: 2676 Mayfield Rd Cleveland Heights OH 44106 Office: Dept History Case Western Res Univ Cleveland OH 44106

SINFELT, JOHN HENRY, chemist; b. Munson, Pa., Feb. 18, 1931; s. Henry Gustave and June Lillian (McDonald) S.; B.S., Pa. State U., 1951; Ph.D., U. Ill., 1954; m. Muriel Jean Vadersen, July 14, 1956; 1 son, Klaus Herbert. Research engr. Exxon Research Engring. Co., Linden, N.J., 1954-57, sr. research engr., 1957-62, research asso., 1962-68, sr. research asso., 1968-72, sci. advisor, 1972-79, sr. sci. advisor, 1979—; vis. prof. chem. engring. U. Minn., 1969; Lacey lectr. Calif. Inst. Tech., 1973; Reilly lectr. U. Notre Dame, 1974. Recipient Dickson prize Carnegie-Mellon U., 1977; Internat. prize for new materials Am. Phys. Soc., 1978. Mem. Am. Inst. Chem. Engrs. (Alpha Chi Sigma award 1971, Profl. Progress award 1975), Am. Chem. Soc. (Petroleum Chemistry award 1976), Catalysis Soc. (Emmett award 1973), Nat. Acad. Scis., Nat. Acad. Engring. Methodist. Contbr. articles in field to sci. jours.; inventor polymetallic cluster catalysts used commercially in petroleum reforming. Office: Exxon Research Engineering Co PO Box 45 Linden NJ 07036

SINGER, ALLEN MORRIS, lawyer; b. Mpls., Dec. 30, 1923; s. William and Ida (Simonstein) S.; J.D., U. Chgo., 1948; LL.M., Harvard U., 1958. Admitted to Ill. bar, 1948, Calif. bar, 1949; practiced law, 1949-55, 59—; v.p., sec., gen. counsel Am. Bldg. Maintenance Industries, San Francisco, 1969—; asso. prof. law U. Oreg., 1955-59; lectr. law Stanford, 1960-62. Mem. U. Chgo. Nat. Alumni Cabinet, 1978-80. Served as 2d lt., USAAF, 1943-45. Mem. Am., San Francisco bar assns., State Bar Calif. Contbr. articles to profl. jours. Home: 1070 Green St San Francisco CA 94133 Office: 44 Montgomery St San Francisco CA 94104

SINGER, ARMAND EDWARDS, educator; b. Detroit, Nov. 30, 1914; s. Elvin Satori and Fredericka Elizabeth (Edwards) S.; A.B., Amherst Coll., 1935; M.A., Duke, 1939, Ph.D., 1944; diplôme, Université de Paris, 1939; postgrad. Ind. U., summer 1964; m. Mary Rebecca White, Aug. 8, 1940; 1 dau., Fredericka Ann Schmidt. Teaching fellow in sci. Amherst Coll., 1935-36, instr. French and Spanish, part-time Duke, 1938-40; teaching fellow Romance langs. W. Va. U., Morgantown, 1940-41, instr., 1941-47, asst. prof., 1947-55, asso. prof., 1955-60, prof., 1960—, chmn. humanities, 1963-72, chmn. dept. integrated studies, 1963, acting chmn. dept. religion and program for humanities, 1973. Bd. dirs. Community Concert, Morgantown, 1959-60. Mem. Modern Lang. Assn. (internat. bibliography com. 1956-59, nat. del. 1975-78), So. Atlantic Modern Lang. Assn. (exec. com. 1971-74), Am. Assn. Tchrs. French, Am. Assn. Tchrs. Spanish and Portuguese, AAUP, Am. Philatelic Soc., Am. Philatelic Congress, Phi Beta Kappa. Republican. Author: A Bibliography of the Don Juan Theme: Versions and Criticism, 1954; The Don Juan Theme, Versions and Criticism: A Bibliography, 1965; (with J.F. Stasny) Anthology of Readings: Humanities I, 1966; Anthology of Readings: Humanities II, 1967; Paul Bourget, 1976. Editor: W. Va. U. Philol. Papers, 1948-50, 52-54, editor-in-chief, 54—. Home: 248 Grandview Ave Morgantown WV 26505. *In an age of deteriorating standards, I want to be counted among those educators who stood against the tide. We ask too little of others, we ask too little of ourselves; others ask too little of us. When we constantly encounter shoddy construction, shoddy merchandise, shoddy performances, shoddy ethics, we may be tempted to forswear our standards. But through our hands pass tomorrow's leaders. As teachers we must help stop this corrosion undermining our national pride. If we fail, let us never forget that it could well destroy us all.*

SINGER, ARTHUR LOUIS, JR., found. exec.; b. Scranton, Pa., Feb. 14, 1929; s. Arthur Louis and Isabel Agnes (Corcoran) S.; A.B., Williams Coll., 1950; M.B.A., U. Mich., 1952; m. Joan Cristal, July 26, 1952; children—Arthur Louis, Philip Edward, Charles Martin. Asst. dean Mass. Inst. Tech., 1955-63; exec. asso. Carnegie Corp., N.Y.C., 1963-66; pres. Edn. Devel. Center, Newton, Mass., 1966-68; v.p. Alfred P. Sloan Found., N.Y.C., 1968—; cons. Yale U., 1968, City U. N.Y., 1968, Hunter Coll., 1970. Chmn., N.Y.C. Mayor's Adv. Com. on Appointments to Bd. Higher Edn., 1968-72; trustee Tougaloo Coll., Inst. for Services to Edn.; mem. vis. com. Mass. Inst. Tech. Center for Internat. Studies, City U. N.Y. Grad. Sch. and Univ. Center; mem. publs. com. The Pub. Interest. Served to lt. (j.g.) USNR, 1952-55. Club: Yale (N.Y.C.). Home: 23 Owenoke Park Westport CT 06880 Office: 630 Fifth Ave New York NY 10020

SINGER, ESTHER FORMAN (MRS. SIDNEY SINGER), artist; b. N.Y.C.; d. Maurice and Sarah (Shaller) Forman; R.N., N.Y. U., 1957; postgrad. Fairleigh Dickinson U., 1960-63, New Sch. Social Research, 1965-71; m. Sidney Singer, Oct. 29, 1950; children—Keith Arlen, Maurene Forman. One-man shows: Papermill Playhouse Galleries, 1965, Bambergers Dept. Store, 1965, Gallery 9-Chatham, 1967, Seton Hall U., 1969, Centenary Coll., Hackettstown, N.J., 1970, Bloomfield Coll., 1970, County Coll. of Morris, 1971, Mus. Modern Art, Paris, 1973, Gallery 52, 1973, N.J. State Mus., 1973, 76, one-man tour Old Bergen Art Guild, 1973-75, Hait Gallery Retrospective, 1976, Brandeis U., 1977; exhibited numerous group shows throughout U.S., including: Morris Mus., Morristown, N.J., 1978, NABISCO World Hdqrs., East Hanover, N.J.; represented in permanent collections at Finch Mus. Contemporary Art, N.Y.C., Newark Mus., Hudson River Mus., Yonkers, N.Y., N.J. State Mus., Trenton, Seton Hall U. Mus. Collection, N.Y. Hosp.-Cornell Collection, Whitney Mus., Morris (N.J.) Mus., others; art critic Am. Artist mag., Worrall Publs.; tchr. elementary sch. art class Recreation Center S. Orange (N.J.); guest lectr. B'nai B'rith; guest panelist TV, 1967-68, radio, 1968-69; guest speaker TV program Focus on Art, 1976-77; judge local and regional art shows. Served as 1st lt. Army Nurse Corps, 1944-46. Recipient Painting prize Paris Mus. Modern Art, 1973. Mem. Artists Equity N.J., Artists Equity N.Y., Old Bergen Art Guild, Painters and Sculptors Soc. N.J., Am. Vets. Soc. Artists, Miniature Art Soc. N.J. . *It's not what I do, but how I do it which has had enormous impact in every phase of my artistic growth and development. "How" to me has always meant complete dedication with absolute follow-through in all things—large and small.*

SINGER, HENRY A., orgn. exec.; b. Mt. Vernon, N.Y., Apr. 13, 1919; s. A.D. and Evelyn (Zierler) S.; B.S., Columbia U., 1942; M.A., N. Y. U., 1947, Ph.D. (grad. fellow 1947-48), 1950, 2d Ph.D., 1973; m. Rosina Scimonelli, Jan. 7, 1944; children—Victoria, David Anthony. Instr., N.Y. U. Human Relations Center, 1948-50; asso. prof. State U. N.Y., Fredonia, 1950-51; adviser U.S. Mission to Philippines, 1951-54; cons. Conn. Edn. Assn., 1954-56; dir. edn. Hilton Hotel Corp., 1956-58; cons. Conn. Assn. Mental Health, 1958-59; dir. edn. Remington Rand div. Sperry Rand, 1959-62; exec. dir. Soc. Advancement Mgmt., 1963-66; higher edn. officer City U. N.Y., 1966-68; exec. dir. Human Resources Inst. Inc., Westport, Conn., 1969—; vis. prof. Cornell U., 1949—, U. Philippines, 1952-53, N.Y. U., 1960-62, City U. N.Y., 1962-63, Columbia, 1963-64, Western Conn. Coll., 1964-70; vis. prin. lectr. Hong Kong Poly., 1976-78. Vis. expert AID mission, Spain, 1962, Internat. Human Resources, Tehran, Iran, 1965; asso. dir. engring. mgmt. workshops Columbia, 1963-66. Bd. dirs. Conn. Assn. Mental Health, 1960-62. Recipient award Council Internat. Progress in Mgmt., 1963; Rockefeller fellow, 1948-49. Fellow Am. Soc. Applied Anthropology, Hong Kong Psych. Soc.; mem. Am. Psychol. Assn., AAAS. Clubs: Overseas Press, Hong Kong Fgn. Corrs., Columbia U. (N.Y.C.). Editor: Connecticut Teacher, 1954-56, Connecticut Mental Health News, 1958-59, Advanced Management, 1959-66. Contbr. articles to profl. jours. Home: Woodland Dr Westport CT 06880 Office: 310 Main St Westport CT 06880. *Perhaps life teaches us that relating successfully to others is the one sure road to survival in an increasingly crowded environment. One measurement of this successful human relationship is the degree to which one human being is able to inconvenience himself for another.*

SINGER, IRVING, philosopher; b. N.Y.C., Dec. 24, 1925; s. Isidore and Nettie (Stromer) S.; A.B. summa cum laude, Harvard U., 1948, M.A., 1949, Ph.D., 1952; m. Josephine Fisk, June 10, 1949; children—Anne, Margaret, Emily, Benjamin. Instr. philosophy Cornell U., 1953-56; asst. prof. U. Mich., 1956-59; vis. lectr. Johns Hopkins U., 1957-58; mem. faculty M.I.T., 1958—, prof. philosophy, 1969—. Served with AUS, 1944-46. Fellow Guggenheim Found., 1965, Rockefeller Found., 1970, Bollingen Found., 1966; grantee Am. Council Learned Socs., 1966; Fulbright fellow, 1955. Mem. Am. Philos. Assn., Am. Soc. Aesthetics. Author: Santayana's Aesthetics, 1957; The Nature of Love: Plato to Luther, 1966; The Goals of Human Sexuality, 1972; Mozart and Beethoven, 1977. Office: Room 20E210A MIT Cambridge MA 02139

SINGER, ISAAC BASHEVIS, writer; b. Radzymin, Poland, July 14, 1904; came to U.S. 1935, naturalized 1943; s. Pinchos Menachem and Bathsheba (Zylberman) S.; student Rabbinical Sem., Warsaw, Poland, 1920-27; Litt.D. (hon.), L.I. U., 1979; m. Alma Haimann, Feb. 14, 1940; 1 son, Israel. With Hebrew and Yiddish publs. in Poland, 1926-35, Jewish Daily Forward, N.Y.C., 1935—. Recipient Epstein Fiction award, 1963; Playboy award for best fiction/short story, 1967; Poses Creative Arts award, 1970; Nat. Book awards, 1970, 74; Nobel Prize for lit., 1978. Fellow Jewish Acad. Arts and Scis., Nat. Inst. Arts and Letters, Polish Inst. Arts and Scis. in Am.; mem. Am. Acad. Arts and Scis. Club: Pen (N.Y.C.). Author: Satan in Goray, 1935, The Family Moskat, 1950, Gimpel The Fool, 1957, The Magician of Lublin, 1960, The Spinoza of Market Street, 1961, The Slave, 1962, Short Friday, 1964, In My Father's Court, 1966, The Manor, 1967, The Seance, 1968, The Estate, 1969, A Friend of Kafka, 1970, Enemies, A Love Story, 1972, A Crown of Feathers, 1973, Passions, 1976, persons, and other stories, 1976, A Young Man in Search of Love, 1978, Shosha, 1978, Old Love, 1979; also books for children including A Day of Pleasure (Nat. Book award), 1970. Address: care Farrar Straus and Giroux Inc 19 Union Sq W New York NY 10003*

SINGER, ISADORE MANUAL, mathematician, educator; b. Detroit, May 4, 1924; s. Simon and Freda (Rose) S.; B.S., U. Mich., 1944, M.S., U. Chgo., 1948, Ph.D., 1950; m. Sheila Ruff, Sept. 24, 1961; children—Steven, Eliot, Natasha. C.L.E. Moore instr. Mass. Inst. Tech., 1950-52; asst. prof. U. Cal. at Los Angeles, 1952-54, Columbia, 1955; vis. mem. Inst. Advanced Study, Princeton, 1956; mem. faculty Mass. Inst. Tech., Cambridge, 1956—, prof. math., 1959—, Norbert Wiener prof. math., 1970—. Served with AUS, 1944-46. Sloan fellow, 1959-62; Guggenheim fellow, 1968-69; recipient Bôcher prize, 1969. Mem. Nat. Acad. Sci., Am. Acad. Arts and Scis., Am. Math. Soc., Math. Assn. Am., Phi Beta Kappa, Sigma Xi. Editor trans. Am. Math. Soc., 1960-66. Contbr. research articles to profl. jours. Office: Dept Math Mass Inst Tech Cambridge MA 02139

SINGER, JACQUES, (Kuba), condr.; b. Przemysl, Poland, May 9, 1917; s. Mark Eli and Rachela (Bach) S.; student Curtis Inst. Music, 1926; grad. Juilliard Grad. Sch. Music, 1931; Mus.D., Corpus Christi U., 1962; m. Leslie Wright, Jan. 28, 1946; children—Claude, Mark, Lori and Gregory (twins). Came to U.S., 1921, naturalized, 1931. Music dir., conductor Dallas Symphony, 1937-42, Vancouver (B.C., Can.) Symphony, 1947-51; music dir. N.Y. prodn. Shakespeare and Shaw Cleopatras with Lawrence Olivier and Vivian Leigh, 1952, Tel Aviv (Israel) Philharmonic, Haifa, 1953; condr. 1st symphony concert in Nazareth, 1953; music dir., Corpus Christi, 1954; guest condr. Mexico, Guatemala, also Indpls. symphonies, 1956, Peru, 1957, Portugal, 1958; mus. dir. Filharmonic de Buenos Aires, 1959, 60, Havana, 1959, Caracas, 1961, Florence, Italy, 1962, London Philharmonic, 1962, Portland Symphony Orch., 1962—; condr. Colombia Sinfonica, 1966, Filharmonica de Chile, Santiago, 1966, London Royal Philharmonic, 1970, Congress of Strings, U. So. Calif., 1970, Cin., 1970, N.Z. B.C. Symphony, N.Z. and Dublin, Ireland, 1971, Ind. U. Philharmonic, Orquesta Sinfonica Venezuela, Honolulu Symphony, 1972, Filharmonia de Wroclaw, de Krakow, de Gdansk (all Poland), Sacramento Symphony, Orquestra Filarmonica de Lisboa (Portugal), 1973, Warsaw Philharmonic, Poznan Philharmonic, Lodz Philharmonic, 1975, also Louisville Philharmonic, Naumburg Orch., N.Y.C., 1976-78; gen. music dir., comdr. Oreg. Symphony Orch., 1962-73; prof. No. Ill. U., 1977-80, condr. No. Ill. U. Philharmonic, Portugal Festival, Lisbon, 1978. Served with AUS, 1942-46. Recipient gold medal Buenos Aires Filharmonica, 1959. Mem. Nat. Assn. Am. Composers and Condrs. Home: 325 W 86th St New York NY 10024 Office: care Sol Hurok 730 Fifth Ave New York NY 10019. *Fleeting time is our only fortune and possession. If only we could spend it wisely.*

SINGER, KURT DEUTSCH, news commentator, author; b. Vienna, Austria, Aug. 10, 1911 (came to U.S., 1940, naturalized, 1951); s. Ignaz Deutsch and Irene (Singer) S.; student U. Zurich (Switzerland), 1930, Labor Coll., Stockholm, Sweden, 1936; Ph.D., Div. Coll. Metaphysics, Indpls., 1951; m. Hilda Tradelius, Dec. 23, 1932; children—Marian Alice Birgit, Kenneth Walt; m. 2d, Jane Sherrod, Jan. 1955. Author, editor underground weekly Mitteilungsblatter, Berlin, Germany, 1933; escaped to Sweden, 1934; founder Ossietzky Com. (successful in release Ossietzky from concentration camp); corr. Swedish mag. Folket i Bild, 1935-40; founder Niemoller Com.; pub. biography Goring in Eng. (confiscated in Sweden), 1940; co-founder pro-Allied newspaper Trots Allt, 1939; corr. Swedish newspapers in U.S., 1940; editor News Background, 1942; lectr. U. Minn., U. Kans., U. Wis., 1945-49; radio commentator WKAT, 1950; corr. N.Am. Newspaper Alliance, N.Y.C., 1953—; editorial dir. B.P. Singer Features Syndicate; dir. Oceanis Press Service, North Hollywood, Calif. Mem. UN Speakers Research Com., UN Children's Emergency Fund, Menninger Found. Mem. Nat. Geog. Soc., Smithsonian Assos., Internat. Platform Assn. (v.p.), United Sch. Assemblies (pres.). Author: The Coming War, 1934; Germany's Secret Service in Central America, 1943; Spies and Saboteurs in Argentina, 1943; Duel for the Northland, 1943; White Book of the Church of Norway, 1944; Spies and Traitors of World War II, 1945; Who are the Communists in America, 1948, 3000 Years of Espionage, 1951; World's Greatest Women Spies, 1952; Kippie the Cow (juvenile), 1952; Gentlemen Spies, 1953; The Man in the Trojan Horse, 1954; World's Best Spy Stories, 1954; Charles Laughton Story (adapted TV, motion pictures), 1954; Spy Stories and Asia, 1955; More Spy Stories, 1955; My Greatest Crime Story, 1956; My Most Famous Case, 1957; The Danny Kaye Saga; My Strangest Case, 1958; Spy Omnibus, 1959; Spies for Democracy, 1960; Crime Omnibus Spies Who Changed History, 1961; Hemmingway-Life and Death of a Giant, 1961; True Adventures in Crime; Dr. Albert Schweitzer, Medical Missionary, 1962; Kurt Lyndon Baines Johnson-Man of Reason, 1964; Ho-i-man (juvenile), 1965; Kurt Singer's Ghost Omnibus, 1965; Kurt Singer's Horror Omnibus, The World's Greatest Stories of the Occult, The Unearthly, 1965; Mata Hari-Goddess of Sin, 1965; Lyndon Johnson-From Kennedy to Vietnam, 1966; Weird Tales Anthology, 1966; I Can't Sleep at Night, 1966; Weird Tales of Supernatural, 1967; Tales of Terror, 1967; Famous Short Stories, 1967; Folktales of the South Pacific, 1967; Tales of The Uncanny, 1968; Gothic Reader, 1968; Bloch and Bradbury, 1969; Folktales of Mexico, 1969; Tales of the Unknown, 1970; Tales of the Macabre, 1971; Ghouls and Ghosts, 1972; Satanic Omnibus, 1973; Gothic Horror Omnibus, 1974; Dictionary of Household Hints and Help, 1974; They are Possessed, 1976; True Adventures into the Unknown, 1980; I Spied—And Survived, 1980. Editor UN Calendar, 1959-58. Contbr. articles to newspapers, popular mags., U.S., fgn. countries; all his books and papers in Boston U. Library-Spl. Collections. Address: 3164 Tyler Ave Anaheim CA 92801

SINGER, LEON, lawyer; b. Savannah, Ga., Dec. 31, 1899; s. Heiman and Bertha (Kapan) S.; B.S., U. Ga., 1921; J.D., Columbia U., 1923; m. Lee Lillian Gladstone, Dec. 31, 1928 (dec. May 1962); 1 son, Harlan Sanford; m. 2d, Leonora Rein, Jan. 25, 1963. Admitted to N.Y. State bar, 1924, U.S. District Ct. So. Dist. N.Y. bar, 1931, U.S. Supreme Ct. bar, 1956; practiced in N.Y.C., 1924—; asso. firm Paul Hellinger, 1924-26; asso. firm Schlesinger & Krinsky, 1926-42; partner firm Blumberg, Singer, Ross, Gottesman & Gordon, 1942—. Tchr. English to foreigners N.Y.C. Bd. Edn., 1925-26; active Boy Scouts Am.; sec. B'nai Jeshurun, 1954-68, trustee, 1957—, vice chmn. bd. trustees, 1963, chmn. bd. trustees, 1964—. Served with USN, 1918-19. Recipient Math. prize U. Ga., 1921. Mem. Cigar Mfrs. Assn. Am. (sec. 1961-74), Cigar Inst. Am. (sec.-treas. 1960-74), Cigar Assn. Am. (sec. 1974-76), Cigar Research Council (sec. 1971-74), Am. Arbitration Assn. (mem. panel arbitrators), Jewish War Vets. (judge adv. Kings County 1930-31), Am. Bar Assn. (chmn. alcohol, tobacco, firearms taxes com. 1964-65), Am. Jewish Com., Am. Jewish Congress, U. Ga. Alumni Assn., Columbia Law Sch. Alumni Assn., Alpha Mu Sigma (nat. vice prior 1968). Democrat. Club: Nat. Dem. Exhibited oil paintings, Atlantic City, N.J., 1967. Home: 300 E 54th St New York NY 10022 Office: 245 Park Ave New York NY 10017

SINGER, MARCUS GEORGE, educator, philosopher; b. N.Y.C., Jan. 4, 1926; s. David Emanuel and Esther (Kobre) S.; A.B., U. Ill., 1948; Ph.D. (Susan Linn Sage fellow), Cornell U., 1952; m. Blanche Ladenson, Aug. 10, 1947; children—Karen Beth, Debra Ann. Asst. in philosophy Cornell U., Ithaca, N.Y., 1948-49, instr. philosophy, 1951-52; instr. philosophy U. Wis.-Madison 1952-55, asst. prof., 1955-59, asso. prof., 1959-63, prof. philosophy, 1963—, chmn. dept. philosophy, 1963-68, chmn. philosophy dept. U. Wis. Center System, 1964-66; vis. fellow Birkbeck Coll., U. London, 1962-63; research asso. U. Calif. at Berkeley, 1969; vis. Cowling prof. philosophy Carleton Coll., Northfield, Minn., 1972; vis. prof. humanities U. Fla., Gainesville, 1975; vis. Francis M. Bernardin disting. prof. humanities U. Mo., Kansas City, 1979. Served with USAAF, 1944-45. Am. Philos. Assn. Western Div. fellow, 1956-57; Summer Research Tng. grant Social Sci. Research Council, 1958; Guggenheim fellow, 1962-63; Mem. Am. Philos. Assn., AAAS, AAUP, Aristotelian Soc., Mind Assn., Ams. for Democratic Action, Phi Beta Kappa, Phi Kappa Phi. Author: Generalization in Ethics, 2d edit., 1971. Editor: Morals and Values, 1977. Contbr. Essays in Moral Philosophy, 1958; Ency. of Philosophy, 1967; Skepticism and Moral Principles, 1973. Co-editor: Introductory Readings in Philosophy, 2d edit., 1974; Reason and the Common Good, 1963; Belief, Knowledge and Truth, 1970. Home: 5021 Regent St Madison WI 53705

SINGER, MARCUS JOSEPH, educator, biologist; b. Pitts., Aug. 28, 1914; s. Benjamin and Rachel (Gershenson) S.; B.S., U. Pitts., 1938; M.A., Harvard, 1940, Ph.D., 1942; m. Leah Horelick, June 8, 1938; children—Robert H., Jon Fredric. Mem. faculty Harvard Med. Sch., 1942-51, asst. prof. anatomy until 1951; vis. prof. anatomy L.I. Coll. Medicine, 1950; asso. prof., then prof. zoology and child devel. Cornell U., 1951-61; vis. fellow Dutch Brain Inst., Amsterdam; H.W. Payne prof. anatomy, dir. dept. Case Western Res. U. Sch. Medicine, Cleve., asso. dir. Devel. Biology Center, 1961-69, dir., 1969—; vis. prof. anatomy Hebrew U., Jerusalem, 1974; Zyskind hon. vis. prof. faculty health scis. Ben Gurion U. Negev, Beersheba, Israel, 1975-76; vis. prof. Gunma U., Japan, 1977; mem. cell biology study sect. NIH, 1971-74, neurology study sect., 1976—. Guggenheim fellow, Rome, 1967. Fellow Am. Acad. Arts and Scis., Ohio Acad. Sci., AAAS; mem. Am. Neurol. Assn. (asso.), Am. Assn. Anatomists, Soc. Zoologists, Internat. Brain Research Orgn., Assn. Research Nervous and Mental Diseases, Soc. Devel. and Growth, Biol. Stain Commn., Sigma Xi. Author: (with P. Yakovlev) Human Brain in Sagittal Section, 1954; Dog Brain in Section, 1962. Editor Jour. of Morphology, 1965-70, asso. editor, 1970-72. Asso. editor Jour. Exptl. Zoology, 1963-68, 70-71, editorial bd., 1970-74. Contbr. articles on nervous system, histochemistry regeneration, cytology to profl. publs. Home: 2905 Berkshire Rd Cleveland Heights OH 44118 Office: Sch of Medicine Case Western Res U Cleveland OH 44106

SINGER, MAXINE FRANK, biochemist; b. N.Y.C., Feb. 15, 1931; d. Hyman S. and Henrietta (Perlowitz) Frank; A.B., Swarthmore Coll., 1952, D.Sc. (hon.), 1978; Ph.D., Yale U., 1957; D.Sc., Wesleyan U., 1977; m. Daniel Morris Singer, June 15, 1952; children—Amy Elizabeth, Ellen Ruth, David Byrd, Stephanie Frank. USPHS postdoctoral fellow NIH, Bethesda, Md., 1956-58, research chemist (biochemistry), 1958-74, head sect. on nucleic acid enzymology Nat. Cancer Inst., 1974-79; chief Lab. of Biochemistry, Nat. Cancer Inst., 1979—. Bd. dirs. Found. for Advanced Edn. in Scis., 1972-78; trustee Wesleyan U., Middletown, Conn., 1972-75, Yale Corp., New Haven, 1975—. Recipient award for achievement in biol. scis. Washington Acad. Scis., 1969, award for research in biol. scis. Yale Sci. and Engring. Assn., 1974, Superior Service Honor award HEW, 1975, Dirs. award NIH, 1977. Fellow Am. Acad. Arts and Scis.; mem. AAAS, Am. Soc. Biol. Chemists, Am. Soc. Microbiologists, Am. Chem. Soc., Inst. Medicine (Nat. Acad. Scis.), Nat. Acad. Scis. Editor: Jour. Biol. Chemistry, 1968-74; Sci. mag., 1972—. Contbr. articles to scholarly jours. Home: 5410 39th St NW Washington DC 20015 Office: Bldg 37 4E-28 Bethesda MD 20205

SINGER, NORMAN, music group exec.; b. N.Y.C., Apr. 16, 1921; s. Julius and Rose (Wiener) S.; B.A., Cornell U., 1941, student law, 1940-42; M.A., Columbia U., 1948. With Juilliard Sch. Music, N.Y.C., 1948-57, Aspen (Colo.) Music Festival and Music Sch., 1955-62, Hunter Coll., 1962-68; exec. dir. City Center Music and Drama, N.Y.C., 1968-74; now exec. dir. Chamber Music Soc. Lincoln Center; music cons. govt. panels; v.p. Dance Notation Bur. Pres. Neighborhood Improvement Assn., 1966-68, 70-71. Chmn. bd. trustees Sch. Mus. Edn., N.Y.C., 1962—. Served with U.S. Army, 1942-45. Decorated officier Ordre des Arts et Lettres (France). Mem. Country Dance and Song Soc. Am. (pres. emeritus). Home: 55 Central Park W New York NY 10023 Office: Alice Tully Hall 1941 Broadway New York NY 10023

SINGER, ROBERT NORMAN, educator; b. Bklyn., Sept. 27, 1936; s. Abraham and Ann (Norman) S.; B.S., Bklyn. Coll., 1961; M.S., Pa. State U., 1962; Ph.D., Ohio State U., 1964; children—Richard, Bonni Jill. Instr. phys. edn. Ohio State U., Columbus, 1963-64, asst. prof., 1964-65; asst. prof. Ill. State U., Normal, 1965-67, dir. motor learning lab., 1965-69, asso. prof., 1968-69, asst. dean Coll. Applied Sci. and Tech., 1967-69; asso. prof., dir. motor learning lab. Mich. State U., East Lansing, 1969-70; prof. Fla. State U., Tallahassee, 1970—, dir. motor learning lab., 1970-72, dir. div. human performance, 1972-75, dir. Motor Behavior Center, 1975—; lectr. N. Am., Asia and Europe; cons. in field. Served with U.S. Army, 1955-58. Mem. Am. Ednl. Research Assn., AAHPER, N. Am. Soc. Sport Psychology and Phys. Activity, Am. Acad. Phys. Edn. Author: Motor Learning and Human Performance, 1968, rev. edit., 1975, 80; Coaching, Athletics, and Psychology, 1972; Physical Education, 1972; Teaching Physical Education, 1974, rev. edit., 1980; Laboratory and Field Experiments in Motor Learning, 1975; Myths and Truths in Sports Psychology, 1975; editor: Readings in Motor Learning, 1972; The Psychomotor Domain, 1972; Foundations of Physical Education, 1976; editor Completed Research in Health, Phys. Edn. and Recreation, 1968-74; mem. editorial bd. Research Quar., 1968—, Jour. Motor Behavior, 1968—, Jour. Sport Psychology, 1979—; reviewer numerous jours. contbr. articles in field to numerous anthologies and profl. jours. Home: Route 1 Box 3155 Havana FL 32333 Office: 106 Montgomery Gym Fla State U Tallahassee FL 32306. *I have always enjoyed my activities and have looked forward to new challenges and horizons. Intrinsic motivational values have guided my involvement in various endeavors, and the outcomes have been extremely rewarding.*

SINGER, RONALD, anatomist, educator; b. Cape Town, South Africa, Aug. 12, 1924; s. Solomon Charles and Sonia (Swirsky) S.; M.B., Ch.B., U. Capetown, 1947, D.Sc., 1962; m. Shirley Bernice Gersohn, Dec. 10, 1950; children—Hazel Lynn, Eric Gersohn, Sonia Esther, Charles Malcolm. Resident med. officer Kimberley Hosp., South Africa, 1947-48; govt. med. officer, supt. Gwelo Native Hosp., Rhodesia, 1948-49; faculty U. Capetown, 1949-62, asso. prof., 1960-62; vis. prof. anatomy U. Ill., 1959-60; prof. anatomy U. Chgo., 1962—, dept. chmn., prof. anatomy and anthropology, 1963—, Robert R. Bensley prof. biology and med. scis., 1973—. Recipient Americanism medal DAR, 1979. Rotary Found. fellow Carnegie Instn. Washington Embryology Labs., Johns Hopkins, 1951-52. Fellow Royal Soc. So. Africa, Royal Anthrop. Inst.; mem. Am. Assn. Anatomists, Am. Assn. Phys. Anthropologists, Anat. Soc. Gt. Britain and Ireland, Soc. Study Human Biology, A.A.A.S., Sigma Xi. Contbr. articles to profl. jours. Home: 5822 Blackstone Ave Chicago IL 60637

SINGER, S(IEGFRIED) FRED, geophysicist, educator; b. Vienna, Austria, Sept. 27, 1924; came to U.S., 1940, naturalized, 1944; s. Joseph B. and Anne (Kelman) S.; B.E.E., Ohio State U., 1943, D.Sc. (hon.), 1970; A.M., Princeton, 1944, Ph.D. in Physics, 1948. Instr. physics Princeton, 1943-44; physicist, applied physics lab. Johns Hopkins, 1946-50; sci. liaison officer Office Naval Research, Am. embassy, London, 1950-53; asso. prof. physics U. Md., College Park, 1953-59, prof., 1959-62; dir. Nat. Weather Satellite Center, Dept. Commerce, 1962-64; dean Sch. Environ. and Planetary Scis., U. Miami, 1964-67; dep. asst. sec. for water quality and research Dept. Interior, Washington, 1967-70; dep. asst. adminstr. EPA, Washington, 1970-71; prof. environmental scis. U. Va., Charlottesville, 1971—; vis. research prof. Jet Propulsion Lab., Calif. Inst. Tech., 1961-62; Fed. Exec. fellow Brookings Instn., 1971; vis. Sid Richardson prof. LBJ Sch., U. Tex., 1978; head sci. evaluation group, astronautics and space exploration com. Ho. of Reps., 1958; mem. research adv. bd. Center for Strategic and Internat. Studies, Georgetown U.; cons. U.S. Treasury, GAO, Office Tech. Assessment, U.S. Congress. Mem. bd. Nat. Com. on Am. Fgn. Policy. Served with USNR, 1944-46. Recipient Presdl. commendation, 1958, gold medal for exceptional service Dept. Commerce, 1965; named Outstanding Young Man U.S. Jr. C. of C., 1959. Fellow Am. Geophys. Union, Am. Phys. Soc.; mem. Internat. Acad. Astronautics, AAAS (com. council affairs 1970—), Pan Am. Med. Assn. (pres. sect. on environ. health scis. 1973—). Club: Cosmos (Washington). Author: Geophysical Research with Artificial Earth Satellites, 1956; Manned Laboratories in Space, 1970; Global Effects of Environmental Pollution, 1970; Is There an Optimum Level of Population?, 1971; The Changing Global Environment, 1975; Arid Zone Development: Potentialities and Problems, 1977; The Economic Effects of Demographic Changes, 1977; Energy, 1979. Contbr. articles on space, energy, environment and population problems to profl. publs. Home: Colonnade Club Charlottesville VA 22903

SINGER, S(EYMOUR) J(ONATHAN), biologist; b. N.Y.C., May 23, 1924; s. Hyman and Rose (Fink) S.; A.B., Columbia U., 1943, A.M., 1945; Ph.D., Poly. Inst. Bklyn., 1947; m. Ruth Elizabeth Aronson, May 31, 1947; children—Russell Jonson, Julianne Dale, Matthew Anson. USPHS postdoctoral fellow Calif. Inst. Tech., 1947-51; from asst. prof. to prof. chemistry Yale U., 1951-61; prof. biology U. Calif., San Diego, 1961—; Am. Cancer Soc. lifetime research prof., 1976—. Mem. Nat. Acad. Scis., Am. Acad. Arts and Scis., Am. Chem. Soc., Am. Soc. Biol. Chemists, Am. Assn. Immunologists, Am. Soc. Cell Biology. Office: Dept Biology B-022 Univ Calif San Diego La Jolla CA 92093*

SINGER, SAMUEL L(OEWENBERG), journalist; b. Phila., May 2, 1911; s. Benjamin and Hattie May (Loewenberg) S.; B.S. in Journalism, Temple U., 1934; m. Betty Janet Levi, June 12, 1939; children—Ruth Babette, Samuel Lawrence, Robert Bookhammer. Mem. staff Phila. Inquirer, 1934—, music editor, 1955—, pub. service editor, 1973—. Tchr. undergrad. journalism course Temple U., 1946—, tchr. music criticism, 1965-70; organist Congregation Temple Judea, 1933-41, Main Line Reform Temple, 1951-55, Beth Israel, Phila., 1956-65, Coatesville, Pa. 1967—, Zion Evang. Luth. Ch., 1956—, St. Matthew's Evang. Luth. Ch., 1972—; condr. radio program This Week's Music, 1961-72. Served with USNR, 1943-45. Mem. Am. Guild Organists (editor Phila. chpt. publ. Crescendo 1971-76), Am. Newspaper Guild, Phila. Press Assn., Mus. Fund Soc. Phila., Music Critics Assn., Phila. Mus. Art, Phila. Orch. Assn., Sigma Delta Chi (life). Author: Reviewing the Performing Arts, 1973. Home: 1431 Greywall Ln Philadelphia PA 19151 Office: Philadelphia Inquirer Philadelphia PA 19101. *Never do anything you can't tell your children.*

SINGER, SANFORD R., diversified energy co. exec.; b. 1930; B.A., M.A., U. Tenn.; Ph. D. in Econs., Ohio State U., 1960; married. With Fed. Res. Bank Dallas, 1960-63; with ENSERCH Corp. (formerly Lone Star Gas Co.), 1963—, sr. v.p., chief fin. officer, 1968—, dir. various corp. subs. Address: 301 S Harwood St Dallas TX 75201

SINGER, SARAH BETH, poet; b. N.Y.C., July 4, 1915; d. Samuel and Rose (Dunetz) White; B.A., N.Y. U., 1934; postgrad. New Sch. Social Research, 1961-63; m. Leon Eugene Singer, Nov. 23, 1938; children—Jack, Rachel. Tchr. creative writing Hillside Hosp., Queens, N.Y., 1964-75. Recipient Stephen Vincent Benet award Poet Lore, 1968, 71; Dellbrook award Shenandoah Valley Acad. Lit. and Dellbrook-Shenandoah Coll. Writers' Conf., 1978, 79. Mem. Nat. League Am. Penwomen (poetry chmn. L.I. br. 1957—, Marion Doyle Meml. award 1976, 1st prize nat. poetry contest 1976, Drama award 1977, Poetry award 1977, 1st prize for modern rhymed poetry 1978), Poetry Soc. Am. (v.p. 1974—, exec. dir. L.I. 1979—; James Joyce award 1972, A. Consuelo Ford award 1973, Gustav Davidson award 1974, 1st prize award 1975, Celia Wagner award 1976), Poets and Writers. Author: Magic Casements, 1957; After the Beginning, 1975. Poems rep. in anthologies, including: American Women Poets, 1976. Cons. editor Poet Lore. Address: 38 Stephan Marc Ln New Hyde Park NY 11040. *As a poet, I have sought never to compromise my standards as to what constitutes poetry, despite fads that come and go. My goal has been to achieve whatever perfection I can in my work, and to preserve enough humility to realize that the best is never good enough.*

SINGER, STEPHEN LEE, retail exec.; b. N.Y.C., Aug. 12, 1935; s. Sidney and Dorothy (Hirshberg) S.; B.A., Harvard U., 1957, M.B.A., 1959; student U. Birmingham, 1957; m. Linda Gross, June 12, 1958; children—Juliette Lee, Stuart Lyle, Lauren Jan. With Finlay Depts., N.Y.C., 1958—, pres., 1977—; dir., mem. exec. com. Seligman & Latz, Inc., N.Y.C., 1968—; dir. Equity Enterprises. Urban cons.; active Am. Mus. Natural History, Mus. Modern Art, Neuberger Mus., Harvard Coll., United Jewish Appeal, Am. Jewish Com. Club: Harvard of N.Y. Address: Finlay Div Seligman & Latz Inc 521 Fifth Ave New York NY 10017

SINGER, THOMAS ERIC, advt. agy. exec.; b. Vienna, Austria, Mar. 6, 1926; s. Henry and Berthe (dePokroi) S.; came to U.S. 1938, naturalized 1944; B.A., George Washington U., 1950; M.A., Harvard U., 1952; m. Ellen Colt, Dec. 20, 1952; children—Dominique, Mary F., Carlyle, Henry, Ellen. Fgn. affairs officer State Dept., 1952-55; export mgr. Polaroid Corp., Cambridge, Mass., 1955-58; with Gillette Co., 1958-79, exec. v.p., 1971-79; sr. v.p. Ingalls Assos., Boston, 1979—; dir. Nat. CSS, S.T. DuPont, Braun AG, Beirat Deutsche Bank, Frankfurt, W.Ger. Trustee Faulkner Hosp., Boston; corporator Babson Coll., Wellesley, Mass., Childrens Mus., Boston; mem. Mayor's Com. for Cultural Affairs. Served with U.S. Army, 1944-46. Named hon. consul of Peru in Boston, 1969. Mem. Phi Beta Kappa. Clubs: Algonquin (Boston); Harvard (N.Y.C.); Dedham Country and Polo; Essex Country (Manchester, Mass.). Home: 101 Chestnut St Boston MA 02108 Office: 857 Boylston St Boston MA 02116

SINGER-MAGDOFF, LAURA JOAN SILVER (MRS. SAMUEL MAGDOFF), psychotherapist; b. N.Y.C., Mar. 21, 1917; d. Max David and Minnie (Stabsky) Silver; student N.Y. U., 1936-38, U. Minn., 1938-39; B.S., M.A., Columbia U., 1946, Ed.D., 1961; m. Edward I. Plotkin, 1938 (dec. 1945); 1 dau., JoAnn Melanie; m. 2d, Arthur I. Singer, 1948 (div. 1962); m. 3d, Samuel Magdoff, Dec. 23, 1963. Nursery, elementary sch. tchr., dir., Bronxville, N.Y., 1943-45; tchr. Cherry Lawn Sch., Darien, Conn., 1943-44, Columbia Grammar Sch., 1951-53, N.Y. Children's Colony, 1953-54; psychotherapist, marital, family counselor Community Guidance Service, N.Y.C., 1958—; pvt. practice, 1958—; founder, pres. Save A Marriage, Inc.; adj. prof. Tchrs. Coll., Columbia, 1961—; mem. adv. bd. League for Parent Edn.; vis. faculty New Sch. for Social Research; faculty Nat. Acad. Profl. Psychologists; cons. parent edn. State Edn. Dept.; psychotherapist TV series Living Together. Mem. exec. bd. Sex Info. and Edn. Council of U.S., Community Sex Info.; adviser bd. trustees Nat. Accreditation Assn. for Psychoanalysis, Inc. Certified sex educator, therapist Am. Assn. Sex Educators, Counselors and Therapists. Fellow Am. Inst. for Psychotherapy and Psychoanalysis, Am. Assn. Marriage and Family Counselors (past pres.); mem. N.Y. Soc. Clin. Psychologists (past editor Newsletter, mem. exec. bd.), Am. Psychol. Assn., Assn. for Applied Psychoanalysis, Nat. Council Family Relations. Co-author: Sex Education on Film. Cons. editor Jour. Sex and Marital Therapy; adv. bd. Jour. Marriage and Family Counselors; editorial bd. Jour. Divorce. Address: 41 Central Park W New York NY 10023

SINGH, BALJIT, polit. scientist; b. Budaun, India, Oct. 1, 1929; s. Sardar Baboo and Kartar (Kaur) S.; came to U.S., 1957, naturalized, 1966; B.A., Agra U., 1951; M.A., Aligarh U. (India), 1953; postgrad. (Ford Found. fellow), U. Pa., 1957-58; Ph.D., U. Md., 1961; m. Barbara Leona Hassler, Aug. 11, 1962; children—Balkrishna, Balram. Lectr. polit. sci. U. Baroda (India), 1953-55; research fellow Indian Sch. Internat. Studies, New Delhi, 1955-57; research asst. Embassy of India, Washington, 1958; asst. prof. polit. sci. Mich. State U., East Lansing, 1961-62, 63-65, asso. prof., 1965-71, prof., 1971—, asst. dean Coll. Social Sci., 1967—, chmn. asst. deans group, 1977-78; asst. prof. polit. sci. Wayne State U., Detroit, 1962-63. Served to 2d lt. Indian Army, 1954-58. Asia Found. fellow, 1961. Mem. Internat. Studies Assn. (founding life mem.), Mich. Acad. Sci., Arts and Letters, Pi Sigma Alpha, Delta Phi Epsilon. Author: (with Ko-Wang Mei) The Theory and Practice of Modern Guerrilla Warfare, 1971; Indian Foreign Policy: An Analysis, 1975. Mem. editorial bd. Terrorism, 1977. Contbr. chpts. to books, articles to profl. jours. Home: 2400 Tulane Dr Lansing MI 48912 Office: College of Social Science Michigan State U 205 Berkley Hall East Lansing MI 48824. *Strive to attain your own potential without infringing upon the rights and privileges of others around you. After all is said and done, we have to come to terms with our inner selves, however briefly. Success and its operational outcome, happiness, ultimately depend upon how we organize our own inner "four walls."*

SINGHAL, RADHEY LAL, pharmacologist, educator; b. Gulaothi, India, July 12, 1940; s. Panna Lal and Nanoon; came to Can., 1965, naturalized, 1973; B.Sc., Lucknow (India) U., 1957, M.Sc., 1959, Ph.D., 1961; m. Nirmala Gupta, June 23, 1961; children—Ajay, Rajiv, Niraj. Research asso. Ind. U. Med. Sch., Indpls., 1962-64, instr., 1964-65, asst. prof., dept. pharmacology U. Ottawa (Ont., Can.), 1966-67, asso. prof., 1967-72, prof., 1972—, acting chmn. dept., 1974-76, chmn. dept., 1976—, dir. grad. tng. program, 1972—. Med. Research Council Can. scholar, 1967-72, grantee, 1966—; Health and Welfare Dept. Can. grantee, 1971-76; Ont. Mental Health Found. grantee, 1970—; Upjohn Co. grantee, 1970-72; Eli Lilly & Co. grantee, 1970-72; Lab. Supplies (Ottawa) Ltd. grantee, 1972-73. Fellow Royal Inst. Chemistry (Eng.); mem. Am. Soc. Pharmacology and Exptl. Therapeutics, Am. Soc. Biol. Chemists, Biochem. Soc. (Eng.), Endocrine Soc., Pharm. Soc. Can., Am. Soc. Cell Biology, Am. Fedn. Clin. Research, Internat. Soc. Biochem. Pharmacology, Ottawa Biochem. and Biol. Soc. (1st v.p. 1971-72). Co-editor: Advances in Sex Hormone Research, 1974, 75, 76, 80; Neuroendocrine Regulation of Altered Behaviour, 1980. Contbr. articles to profl. jours. Home: 49 Lillico Dr Ottawa ON K1V 9L7 Canada Office: 275 Nicholas St Ottawa ON K1N 9A9 Canada

SINGHER, MARTIAL, baritone, educator, stage dir; b. Oloron St.-Marie, France, Aug. 14, 1904; s. Joseph-Paul and Marie (Dubourg) S.; Ph.D., Normal Superior Sch., St. Cloud, Seine, France, 1927; Mus.D. (hon.), Met. Sch. Music, 1950; Dr. honoris causa, Chgo. Mus. Coll., 1954; m. Eta Busch, Jan. 10, 1940; children—Charles-Michael, Jean-Pierre, Philip. Leading baritone Paris Grand Opera, 1930-40, Teatro Colon, Buenos Aires, 1936-43, Met. Opera, N.Y.C., 1943-60; recitalist and concert singer throughout Europe, Am.; soloist N.Y. Philharmonic, Phila., Cleve., Nat., Mpls., Chgo., Balt., Boston, St. Louis symphony orchs.; leading baritone Chgo. Civic Opera Co. Rio de Janeiro Teatro, San Francisco Opera and others; dir. opera dept., vocal instr. Curtis Inst. Music, Phila., 1955-68; dir. voice and opera dept. Music Acad. West, Santa Barbara, Calif., 1962—; recorded with RCA Victor, Columbia, Decca, Vanguard, 1750 Arch Records. Decorated knight Legion of Honor (France). Roman Catholic. Home: 840 Deerpath Rd Santa Barbara CA 93108

SINGLAUB, JOHN KIRK, army officer; b. Independence, Calif., July 10, 1921; s. John A. and Ethel (Newby) S.; B.A., U. Calif. at Los Angeles, 1942; grad. Command and Gen. Staff Coll., 1954, Air War Coll., 1960; m. Mary Irene Osborne, Jan. 6, 1945; children—Elisabeth Janet (Mrs. Geir Finne), John Osborne, Mary Ann. Commd. 2d lt. inf., U.S. Army, 1943, advanced through grades to maj. gen., 1972; French Resistance leader, 1944, Chinese guerrilla leader, 1945; observer Chinese Civil War, Manchuria, 1946-48; comdr. inf. bn., Korean War, 1952-53; adviser, Vietnam, 1966-68; chief staff Project Masster, 1969-71; dep. asst. sec. def. (drug and alcohol abuse), 1971-73; comdg. gen. Army Readiness Region VIII, Denver, 1973-76; chief of staff UN Command-U.S. Forces in Korea, 1976-77; chief of staff Army Forces Command, Fort McPherson, Ga., 1977-78; ret., 1978. Decorated D.S.M. with oak leaf cluster, Silver Star, Legion of Merit with 2 oak leaf clusters, Soldiers medal, Bronze Star with oak leaf cluster, Air medal, Army Commendation medal, Purple Heart with oak leaf cluster. Mem. U.S. Parachute Assn., Am. Legion, VFW, Assn. U.S. Army, Am. Security Council, Mil. Order World Wars. Address: Tabernash CO 80478

SINGLETARY, CLARENCE EDWARD, judge; b. Pinopolis, S.C., Mar. 16, 1918; s. Joseph Matthew and Charlotte Elvira (Mims) S.; B.S., Coll. of Charleston, 1940; LL.B., U. Mich., 1948; m. Pollie Obear Lacour, Aug. 2, 1950; children—Nancy Judson, Judith Lacour, Clarence Edward. Admitted to S.C. bar, 1948; pvt. practice law, Charleston, 1948-61; judge 9th Jud. Circuit, Charleston, 1961—. Faculty adviser Nat. Coll. State Trial Judges, 1970; instr. The Citadel, 1948. Mem. S.C. Gen. Assembly, 1961. Trustee Charleston Pub. Schs., 1960. Served to lt. comdr. USCG, 1941-45. Episcopalian. Club: Carolina Yacht (Charleston). Home: 1603 Ventura Pl Mount Pleasant Charleston SC 29464 Office: Charleston County Courthouse Charleston SC 29401

SINGLETARY, OTIS ARNOLD, JR., univ. pres.; b. Gulfport, Miss., Oct. 31, 1921; s. Otis Arnold and May Charlotte (Walker) S.; B.A., Millsaps Coll., 1947; M.A., La State U., 1949, Ph.D., 1954; m. Gloria Walton, June 6, 1944; children—Bonnie, Scot, Kendall Ann. Mem. faculty U. Tex., Austin, 1954-61, prof. history, 1960-61, asso. dean arts and scis., 1956-59, asst. to pres., 1960-61; chancellor U. N.C. at Greensboro, 1961-66; v.p. Am. Council on Edn., Washington, 1966-68; on leave as dir. Job Corps, Office Econ. Opportunity, Washington, 1964-65; exec. vice chancellor acad. affairs U. Tex. System, 1968-69; pres. U. Ky., Lexington, 1969—. Dir., Fed. Res. Bank, Cleve., 1973-78, Anchor Hocking, Dana Corp., Howell Corp. Regional chmn. Woodrow Wilson Nat. Fellowship Found., 1959-61; chmn. N.C. Rhodes Scholarship Com., 1964-66, Ky. com., 1970, 71, 73, 74, 77; bd. dirs. Ednl. Change, Inc., 1968—, Inst. Services to Edn., 1969—; mem. So. Regional Edn. Bd., 1969—; chmn. dept. Army Hist. adv. com., 1972—. Bd. visitors Air U., Maxwell AFB, 1973-76. Served with USNR, 1943-46, 51-54. Recipient Scarborough Teaching Excellence award U. Tex., 1958, Students Assn. Teaching Excellence award 1958, 59. Carnegie Corp. grantee 1961. Mem. Am., So. hist. assns., Am. Mil. Inst. (Moncado Book Fund award 1954), Am. Assn. Higher Edn. (dir. 1969—), Phi Beta Kappa (senator 1977—), Phi Alpha Theta, Omicron Delta Kappa, Pi Kappa Alpha. Democrat. Methodist. Author: Negro Militia and the Reconstruction, 1957; The Mexican War, 1960; American Universities and Colleges, 1968. Office: U Ky Lexington KY 40506

SINGLETON, CHARLES SOUTHWARD, educator; b. McLoud, Okla., Apr. 21, 1909; s. Ellison Oliver and Lucy (Pennington) S.; A.B., U. Mo., 1931; Ph.D., U. Calif., 1936; M.A. (honoris causa), Harvard U., 1948; D.Litt. (hon.), U. Mo., U. Bologna (Italy). Western Md. Coll.; L.H.D., Middlebury Coll.; m. Eula Duke, June 27, 1935. Exchange fellow to Italy from Internat. House, Berkeley, Calif., 1934-36; instr. Italian, U. Calif., 1936; instr. French and Italian, U. Mo., 1936-37; successively asso. in Italian, asso. prof., prof. Italian lit., chmn. dept. Romance langs. Johns Hopkins U., Balt., 1937-48, prof. humanistic studies 1957—, dir. Humanities Center, 1966—; vis. lectr. Italian lit. Harvard, 1947, prof. Romance langs., 1948-57, chmn. dept., 1950-52; prof.-at-large Cornell U. Decorated Commendatore dell 'ordine al merito della Republica (Italy). Recipient Internat. prize Italian lit., Forte dei Marmi, Italy; Haskins medal Mediaeval Acad. Am., 1977. Guggenheim fellow, 1962. Mem. Am. Philos. Soc., Am. Assn. U. Profs., Modern Lang. Assn., Arcadia, Phi Beta Kappa. Author: Canti Carnascialeschi del Rinascimento (Scrittori d'Italia), 1936; Nuovi canti carnascialeschi del Rinascimento, 1940; An Essay on the Vita Nuova, 1949, reprinted, 1977; Dante Studies, 1954, reprinted, 1977; Il Decameron, 1955; Journey to Beatrice, 1958, reprinted, 1977; (with collaborators) Illuminated Mss. of the Divine Comedy, 1969; Dante's Divine Comedy (transl. with commentary), 1970-75, 6 vols. (finalist Nat. Book award). Editor: Art, Science and History in the Renaissance, 1967; Modern Language Notes: Toynbee Dante Dictionary, 1968; Interpretation, Theory and Practice, 1969. Contbr. to jours. Home: New Windsor MD 21776

SINGLETON, DONALD EDWARD, journalist; b. Morristown, N.J., Nov. 8, 1936; s. Edward Leslie and Charlotte (Angerbauer) S.; student Fairleigh Dickinson U., 1955-58; m. Maureen Ann McNiff, Aug. 8, 1959 (div. 1977); children—Nancy Ann, Mark Aram, Jill Susan. Reporter, Dover (N.J.) Advance, 1959-61, Morristown Daily Record, 1961-63, Newark Eve. News, 1963-64; feature reporter-writer N.Y. Daily News, 1964—. Organizer Com. to Save Church Sq. Park, Hoboken, N.J.; vice chmn. Hoboken Environment Com.; mem. due process com. ACLU. Mem. bd. edn. City of Hoboken, 1974-77. Recipient Pub. Service award N.Y. Council Civic Affairs, 1967; President's Distinguished Service award N.Y.C. Council, 1969; Newspaper award merit Women's Press Club N.Y.C., 1970, 79; citation VFW, 1970; Heywood Broun Meml. award Am. Newspaper Guild, 1970; Silver medal for pub. service journalism N.Y. chpt. Pub. Relations Soc. Am., 1970; certificate merit Am. Bar Assn., 1971; Page One award Newspaper Guild N.Y., 1970; Feature award Newspaper Reporters Assn. N.Y., 1972. Mem. Am. Newspaper Guild. Club: Press (N.Y.C.). Home: 628 Garden St Hoboken NJ 07030 Office: 220 E 42d St New York NY 10017. *In reporting, I try very hard to avoid gathering facts in such a way as to fulfill a preconception. I also attempt to force myself to review constantly my* *opinions about my subjects, and to keep my mind as open as possible. In writing, I try to ask myself the following questions regularly: "Is this what I really believe? Or am I simply writing this way because I believe that this is what some other person or group would like me to write?" Unless I can answer the first question in the affirmative, and the second in the negative, I am not satisfied with a particular story.*

SINGLETON, EDWARD MARION, ednl. adminstr.; b. Horry County, S.C., Oct. 9, 1922; s. Benjamin Franklin and Floride (Brakefield) S.; B.S., U. S.C., 1949, M.Ed., 1956, Ph.D., 1971; m. Elizabeth Jane Parker, Nov. 14, 1953; children—Francesca, Stephen, Kim. Principal, Conway (S.C.) High Sch., 1958-59, supt. schs., 1960-62; v.p., chancellor Coastal Carolina Coll. of the U. S.C., Conway, 1963—, also trustee. Past mem. Horry County Tech. Edn. Commn.; past chmn. Horry County TB Assn. Served with U.S. Army, 1944-46. Named Young Man of Year Conway Jaycees, 1958. Mem. Conway C. of C. (pres. 1968-69). Presbyterian. Clubs: Dunes Golf and Beach (Myrtle Beach, S.C.); Am. Legion (past comdr., Disting. Service award 1959). Author: A History of the Regional Campus System of the University of South Carolina, 1971; A History of Coastal Carolina College, 1964; A Study of the Private School Movement in South Carolina, 1967. Home: 1503 Oconee Rd Conway SC 29526 Office: Route 6 Box 275 Conway SC 29526

SINGLETON, FRED G., bus. exec.; b. Ft. Meade, Fla., Mar. 16, 1914; s. Gray and Lilian (Varn) S.; B.S., U. Fla., 1935, Ph.D., 1940; postgrad. (Inst. Internat. Edn. fellow), U. Paris, France, 1938-39; m. Mary Ellen Springer, Mar. 4, 1939 (dec. May 1974); 1 son, Donald Gray; m. Frances Temple Alvarez, Nov. 27, 1976. Instr. organic chemistry Kans. State Coll., Manhattan, 1940-41; asso. Mellon Inst., Pitts., 1941—, adv. fellow, 1955—, bd. advs., 1975—; with H.H. Robertson Co., Pitts., 1956—, v.p. chem. ops. and research, then sr. v.p., 1968—, also dir. Trustee, Robert Morris Coll., Pitts., 1964—. Mem. Am. Chem. Soc., AAAS, Soc. Plastics Engrs., Soc. Plastics Industry, Sigma Xi, Alpha Tau Omega. Clubs: Duquesne, St. Clair Country. Research in synthetic resins; pioneer in devel. reinforced plastics. Home: 1190 Lakemont Dr Pittsburgh PA 15243 Office: 2 Gateway Center Pittsburgh PA 15222

SINGLETON, GEORGE MONROE, food industry cons.; b. Wynnewood, Okla., Mar. 21, 1931; s. James William and Ruby Mae (Robison) S.; grad. Program Mgmt. Devel., Harvard U., 1967; m. Jacqueline R. Williams, Apr. 16, 1949; children—George Ronald, Debra Mae, Loretta Kay, Gregory Dean. Vice pres. Fleming Co., Topeka, 1957-69, Kimball Inc., Ft. Worth, 1969-70, Shop-Rite Foods, Grand Prairie, Tex., 1970-71; ind. cons., Ft. Worth, 1971-72; v.p. M. Loeb Ltd., Ottawa, Can., 1972-73; pres. S.M. Flickinger Co. Inc., Buffalo, 1973-77, Farm House Wholesale Corp., Milw., 1977-78; dir. Farm House Foods, Milw.; cons. to food industry, Buffalo, 1977—; pres. Better Bus. Bur., Lincoln, Nebr., 1966. Republican. Baptist. Club: Harvard Bus. Sch. (Buffalo). Home and office: 103 Shadow Wood Dr East Amherst NY 14051

SINGLETON, HENRY EARL, industrialist; b. Haslet, Tex., Nov. 27, 1916; s. John Bartholomew and Victoria (Flores) S.; S.B., S.M., Mass. Inst. Tech., 1940, Sc.D., 1950; m. Caroline A. Wood, Nov. 30, 1942; children—Christina, John, William, James, Diana. Vice pres. Litton Industries, Inc., Beverly Hills, Calif., 1954-60; chmn. bd., chief exec. officer Teledyne Inc., Los Angeles, 1960—. Home: 384 Delfern Dr Los Angeles CA 90024 Office: 1901 Ave of the Stars Los Angeles CA 90067

SINGLETON, JOHN PAUL, banker; b. Boston, Dec. 21, 1936; s. Fred Robert and Elizabeth (Csakany) S.; B.S. in Mgmt. (Univ. scholar, Marshall Fund scholar), Ariz. State U., 1960; postgrad. Calif. Poly. Coll., 1963, Calif. State Coll. at Los Angeles, 1966, U. So. Calif., 1968; m. Sharon Maurine de Young, Oct. 7, 1960; children—Michael, Janet, Robert. Head, adminstrv. systems and financial control sect. Aerojet Gen. Corp.-Calif., Azusa, 1960-63; mgmt. systems adminstr. Gen. Dynamics Co., Pomona, Calif., 1963-65; head financial planning and pricing systems sect. Hughes Aircraft Co., Fullerton, Calif., 1965-66; mgr. bus. systems Boeing Co., Cape Kennedy, Fla., 1966-67; mgr. info. systems planning and analysis McDonnell Douglas Corp., Huntington, Calif., 1967-69; chief operating office div. data processing Fed. Res. Bd., Washington, 1969-71; sr. v.p. banking service div. Security Nat. Bank, N.Y.C., 1971-73; v.p., mgr. systems and data processing div. Gt. Western Financial Corp., Beverly Hills, Calif., pres. subs. MISAC Corp. 1972—; dir., lectr. mng. data processing Advanced Mgmt. Research, Inc., N.Y.C., 1973—; sr. v.p. bank ops. and Data Processing div. Md. Nat. Bank, Balt., 1976—; mem. Mgmt. Information Systems Requirements Council, U.S. Senate, 1969—; nat. lectr. on mgmt. to state govts., industry, mgmt. devel. programs IBM. Mem. Am. Mgmt. Assn. (mgmt. systems and sci. council), Soc. Mgmt. Information Systems (charter), Blue Key, Phi Kappa Phi, Delta Sigma Pi. Baptist (supt. Sunday sch., deacon, tchr. adult Bible class). Home: 2101 Highland Ridge Dr Phoenix MD 21131 Office: Md Nat Bank 225 N Calvert St Baltimore MD 21203. *Press on. Nothing in the world can take the place of persistence. Talent will not: nothing is more common than unsuccessful men with talent. Genius will not: unrewarding genius is almost a proverb. Education alone will not: the world is full of educated derelects. Persistence and determination alone are omnipotent. Out of our beliefs are born deeds; out of our deeds we form habits; out of our habits grow our character; on our character we build our destination.*

SINGLETON, JOHN VIRGIL, JR., U.S. dist. judge; b. Kaufman, Tex., Mar. 20, 1918; s. John Virgil and Jennie (Shelton) S.; B.A., U. Tex. Law Sch., 1942; m. Jane Guilford Tully, Apr. 18, 1953. Admitted to Tex. bar, 1942; mem. firm Fulbright & Jaworski, 1953-57; partner Bates, Riggs & Singleton, 1953-57, Bell & Singleton, 1957-61, Barrow, Bland, Rehmet & Singleton, 1962-66; U.S. dist. judge So. Dist. Tex., 1966—, chief judge, 1979—; pres. Houston Jr. Bar Assn., 1952-53; co-chmn. 5th circuit dist. judges div. Jud. Conf., 1969, chmn., 1970, chmn. legis. com.; dir. Central Nat. Bank, Houston, 1964-66. Mem. Tex. Depository Bd., 1963-66. Co-chmn. Harris County Lyndon B. Johnson for Pres. Com., 1960-61; del.-at-large Democratic Nat. Conv., 1956, 60, 64; regional coordinator 7-state area Dem. Nat. Com., Lyndon B. Johnson-Hubert Humphrey Campaign for Pres., 1964; mem. exec. com., chmn. fin. com. Tex. Dem. Com., 1962-66; former bd. dirs. Houston Speech and Hearing Center; trustee Houston Legal Found.; mem. chancellor's council U. Tex. Served to lt. comdr. USNR, 1942-46. Mem. Am., Houston (v.p. 1956-57, editor Houston Lawyer 1954-55) bar assns., Tex. State Bar (chmn. grievance com. for Harris County 1963-66, dir. 1965-66), U. Tex. Ex-Students Assn. (life mem., pres. Houston 1961-62, mem. exec. com., chmn. scholarship com.), Cowboys (foreman, straw boss), Delta Tau Delta (pres. 1940-41), Phi Alpha Delta. Episcopalian. Rotarian. Club: Lakeside Country (past sec., dir.) (Houston). Home: 221 Sage Rd Houston TX 77056 Office: 515 Rusk St Houston TX 77002

SINGLETON, PHILIP ARTHUR, corp. exec.; b. Detroit, May 2, 1914; B.S. in Mech. Engring., U. Mich., 1935; cert. Harvard Bus. Sch., 1940; J.D., Yale U., 1941; m. Eleanor A. DeVilbiss, Aug. 16, 1941; children—Kimberley P., Janet D., John R.M., Tobias T. (dec.). With Monsanto Chem. Co. and asso. cos., 1940-55, successively at Merrimac div., Everett, Mass., asst. to pres., Washington, v.p. Nealco-Monsanto Co., Everett, asst. dir. fgn. dept., St. Louis, 1949-50, mng. dir. Monsanto Chems., Ltd., London, Eng., 1951-55, asst. to pres., sec. exec. com., St. Louis, 1956; dir., mem. exec. com. Forth Chems., Ltd., Scotland; dir. Monsanto Chems., India, Bombay, Monsanto Chem., Australia, Tororo Exploration Syndicate, Uganda, Monsanto Boussois S/A, Paris, Casco A/B, Stockholm, S.I.D.A.C. S/A, Brussels; exec. v.p. Prophy-lactic Brush Co., Florence, Mass., 1956, pres., dir., 1957-66; v.p. Vistron Corp., pres. Pro Brush and Prolon Dinnerware divs., 1967-68; with Warner-Lambert Pharm. Co., Morris Plains, N.J., 1956-63, sr. v.p., 1960-63, with responsibility for Md. Glass Corp., Balt., Gulfport Glass Corp. (Miss.), Nepera Chem. Co., Harriman, N.Y.; chmn. bd. Hoodfoam Industries, Inc., Marblehead, Mass., 1968-72; chmn. bd., dir. Mazzucchelli, Inc., N.Y.C., 1968-71; pres. Singleton Assos. Internat.; dir. Koehring Co., Milw., Keuffel & Esser Co., Morristown, N.J., Mass. Mut. Life Ins. Co. (exec. com.), Davis Bros. Inc., Denver, Hershey Foods Corp. (Pa.), Porter Paint Co., Louisville, Courier Corp., Lowell, Mass., Deerfield Plastics Co., South Deerfield, Mass., Barry Wright Corp., Watertown, Mass., Hardigg Industries Inc., South Deerfield, Mass., Howard Mfg. Co., Littleton, Colo., Werner & Pfleiderer Corp., Waldwick, N.J.; mem. Park St. Investment Trust, Boston. Mem. regional appeals bd. War Manpower Commn., 1943-45; employer mem. U.S. delegation ILO, Geneva, Switzerland, 1953-54. Admitted to Conn. bar, 1941, U.S. Supreme Ct., 1946. Mem. nat. adv. council Hampshire Coll., Amherst, Mass.; mem. corp. Northeastern U., Boston. Mem. NAM (dir. 1961-63), Am. Chem. Soc., Soc. Plastics Industry (dir.-at-large 1962-64, v.p. 1965-66, pres., dir. 1967-69), Pilgrims Soc., Soc. Chem. Industry London, U.S. C. of C. London (dir. 1953-56), Internat. C. of C. (overseas investment com., Paris, 1953-55), Am. Brush Mfrs. Assn. (dir., pres.), Asso. Industries Mass. (v.p. 1963-65, dir. 1966—), Beta Gamma Sigma (hon.), Phi Kappa Psi, Tau Beta Pi, Phi Eta Sigma. Republican. Presbyn. Clubs: Comml., Mchts., Union (Boston); Five Island Yacht (Maine); Colony (Springfield, Mass.); Ends of the Earth, Philippics, Royal Cruising, Royal Thames Yacht (London); Intrepids, Travellers Century (Calif.); Cruising of Am. Home: RD 1 On Fiddler's Green Amherst MA 01002 Office: 1072 S East St Amherst MA 01002

SINGLETON-WOOD, ALLAN JAMES, publisher; b. Newport, Monmouthsire, Eng., Feb. 13, 1933; s. Charles James and Violet Anne (Bond) S.-W.; came to Can., 1968; student London U., 1949-51; m. Joan Davis, June 23, 1956; children—Ceri, Glendon. TV and radio musical dir., 1953-57; TV producer, 1957-61; freelance producer for BBC, 1962-64; indsl. advt. mgr. Western Mail, Cardiff, Wales, 1964; advt. dir. Voice of Brit. Industry Mags., London, 1966; mktg. services exec. The Sun and The People, I.P.C. Newspapers, London, 1966-68; mktg. services mgr. Fin. Post, Toronto, Ont., Can., 1969-71, research mgr., 1971-76, nat. sales mgr., 1976-77, pub., 1978—; lectr. at various univs.; cons. Mem. Mag. Can. Conservative. Mem. Anglican Ch. Composer contemporary music including title theme of Swing High, BBC nat. network series, 1953-57. Home: 1254 Lakeview Dr Oakville ON Canada Office: 481 University Ave Toronto ON M5W 1A7 Canada

SINGLEY, MARK ELDRIDGE, educator; b. Delano, Pa., Jan. 25, 1921; s. Maurice and Clara (Rhodes) S.; B.S., Pa. State U., 1942; M.S., Rutgers U., 1949; m. Janet Twichell, Oct. 3, 1942; children—Donald Heath, Frances Marvin, Jeremy Mark, Paul Victor. Adminstrv. asst. UNRRA, 1946; prof. biol. and agrl. engring. Rutgers U., New Brunswick, N.J., 1947—, chmn. dept., 1961-71. Chmn. Hillsborough Twp., Somerset County (N.J.) Planning Bd., 1956-73. Served with USNR, 1942-46. Fellow Am. Soc. Agrl. Engrs. (chmn. N. Atlantic region 1966, dir. 1973-75), AAAS (mem. sect. com. O); mem. Am. Forage and Grassland Council (dir. 1966-69). Home: Belle Mead NJ 08502 Office: Rutgers U-Cook Coll PO Box 231 New Brunswick NJ 08903

SINK, CHARLES STANLEY, architect; b. Valparaiso, Ind., May 24, 1923; s. Stanley B. and Mabel (Van Buren) S.; student U. Pa., 1941-43; B.Arch., Harvard U., 1947, M.Arch., 1970; children by previous marriage—Carol, Jennifer, Mark. Apprentice architect Victor Hornbein Denver, 1950-52; asso. I. M. Pei & Partners, Denver, 1956-60; prin. Moore, Sink & Bush, Denver, 1960-62, Charles S. Sink, Architect, Denver, 1962-67, Charles S. Sink & Assos., Denver, 1967-79; pres. Sink/Combs & Assos., P.C., Denver, 1979—. Chmn., Denver Art Commn., 1968—. Served with AC, U.S. Army, 1943-45. Decorated D.F.C., Air medal with 4 oak leaf clusters; recipient local and regional design awards. Fellow AIA (pres. Colo. Central chpt. 1972, chmn. Western Mountain Region Conf. 1979. Democrat. Work pub. in various nat., fgn. publs., 1962—.

SINKFORD, JEANNE CRAIG, dentist, educator; b. Washington, Jan. 30, 1933; d. Richard E. and Geneva (Jefferson) Craig; B.S., Howard U., 1953, M.S., 1962, D.D.S., 1958, Ph.D., 1963; D.Sc. (hon.), Georgetown U., 1978; m. Stanley M. Sinkford, Dec. 8, 1951; children—Dianne Sylvia, Janet Lynn, Stanley M. III. Instr. prosthodontics Howard U. Sch. Dentistry, Washington 1958-60, mem. faculty dentistry, 1964—, asso. dean research coordinator, co-chmn. dept. restorative dentistry, 1968-75, dean Coll. Dentistry, 1975—; instr. research and crown and bridge Northwestern U. Sch. Dentistry, 1963-64; cons. prosthodontics and research VA Hosp., Washington, 1965—; cons. St. Elizabeth's Hosp.; mem. attending staff Freedman's Hosp., Washington, 1964—; adv. bd. D.C. Gen. Hosp., 1975—; mem. Nat. Adv. Dental Research Council, Nat. Bd. Dental Examiners; mem. ad hoc adv. panel Tuskegee Syphilis Study for HEW; sponsor D.C. Pub. Health Apprentice Program; mem. adv. council to dir. NIH. Contbr. Nat. Symphony Orch. Louise C. Ball fellow grad. tng., 1960-63. Fellow Internat., Am. colls. dentists; mem. Internat. Assn. Dental Research, Dist. Dental Soc., Am. Inst. Oral Biology, North Portal Civic League, ADA (chmn. appeal bd. council on dental edn. 1975-78), Inst. Grad. Dentists (trustee), Wash. Council Adminstrv. Women, Assn. Am. Women Dentists, Am. Assn. Dental Schs., Am. Pedodontic Soc., Inst. Medicine (council), Am. Soc. Dentistry for Children, N.Y. Acad. Scis., Sigma Xi, Phi Beta Kappa, Omicron Kappa Upsilon, Psi Chi, Beta Kappa Chi. Address: 1765 Verbena St NW Washington DC 20012

SINKS, LUCIUS FREDERICK, pediatrician; b. Newburyport, Mass., Mar. 14, 1931; s. Allen Thurman and Anne Chase (Batchelder) S.; B.S., Yale U., 1953; M.D., Jefferson Med. Coll., Phila., 1957; M.S., Ohio State U.; m. June 23, 1956; children—George W., Lillian Ferguson, Lucius Frederick. Chief dept. pediatrics Roswell Park Meml. Inst., Buffalo, 1967-76; prof. pediatrics State U. N.Y. Med. Sch., Buffalo, 1973-76, Georgetown U. Med. Center, 1976—; chmn. Childhood Solid Tumor Group; cons. Assn. Research Childhood Cancer. Served to capt. USAF. Recipient award USPHS, 1963-64; Nat. Cancer Inst. fellow, 1964-66, grantee, 1977. Mem. Am. Soc. Clin. Oncology, Am. Assn. Cancer Research, Soc. Pediatric Research, Am. Soc. Hematology. Clubs: Derby (pres. 1968-69, 74-75), Mantoloking Yacht; Bay Head Yacht; Cosmos (Washington). Author: Conflicts in Childhood Cancer, 1975. Asso. editor Med. and Pediatric Oncology. Home: 2728 36th Pl NW Washington DC 20007 Office: 3800 Reservoir Rd NW Washington DC 20007

SINN, MELVIN EARL, fgn. service officer; b. West Paterson, N.J., Mar. 3, 1924; s. William Frederick and Lillian (West) S.; A.B., Brown U., 1946; M.A., Fletcher Sch. Law and Diplomacy, 1949; m. Lois Adean Kinney, Sept. 14, 1944; children—Jeffrey Grant, Leslie Claire. Various econ., polit., and consular posts Dept. State, Washington and overseas, including Uruguay, Chile and Colombia, 1955—, now Am. consul gen., Barcelona, Spain. Served to lt. USN, 1943-46. Brown Club N.Y. scholar. Mem. Am. Fgn. Service Assn. Clubs: Royal Polo of Barcelona, Circulo del Gran Teatro del Liceo Barcelona. Co-author, Commercial Treaties and Agreements, 1951. Office: American Consulate General Via Layetana 33 Barcelona Spain

SINNESS, LESTER SNOWDON, chem. co. exec.; b. Minnewaukan, N.D., Apr. 7, 1909; s. Torger and Isabel (Sheldon) S.; B.A. in Chemistry, Carleton Coll., 1931; Ph.D. in Phys. Chemistry, U. Wis., 1935; m. Doris Fortain Downs, Jan. 10, 1942; 1 son, Warren Snowdon. With E.I. du Pont de Nemours & Co., 1935—, various positions in research, mfg., sales, gen. mgmt., 1935-63, v.p., mem. exec. com., 1963-72, also dir. Bd. dirs. People-to-People Health Found. (Project Hope); chmn. Del. Council on Econ. Edn. Home: Box 145 Mendenhall PA 19357 Office: 2016 DuPont Bldg Market St Wilmington DE 19898

SINNOTT, MAURICE JOSEPH, educator; b. Detroit, Jan. 19, 1916; s. Maurice and Margaret (Quigley) S.; B.Ch.E., U. Mich., 1938, M.Ch.E., 1941, Sc.D., 1946; m. Mary Louise DeClaire, Nov. 23, 1944; children—Mary K., William P., Margaret A., James M., Daniel J. Metallurgist, Great Lakes Steel Co., Detroit, 1938-40; research engr. U. Mich., 1940-43, instr., 1943-46, asst. prof., 1947-50, asso. prof., 1950-54, prof., 1955—, asso. dean engring., 1973—; on leave to Dept. Def., 1970-73, dir. Materials Sci. Office, Adv. Research Projects Agy., 1970-72, dep. dir., 1973. Recipient Distinguished Faculty Service award, 1969; Def. Meritorious Civilian Service medal, 1972. Mem. Am. Soc. for Metals (teaching award 1954), Am. Inst. M.E., Am. Soc. for Engring. Edn., ASTM, Sigma Xi, Tau Beta Pi. Author: Structure and Properties of Solids, 1952; Solid State for Engineers, 1958. Contbr. articles to sci. jours. Home: 2115 Woodside Rd Ann Arbor MI 48104

SINOR, DENIS, educator; b. Kolozsvar, Hungary, Apr. 17, 1916; s. Miklos and Marguerite (Weitzenfeld) S.; B.A., U. Budapest, 1938; M.A., Cambridge (Eng.) U., 1948; hon. doctorate U. Szeged (Hungary) 1971; m. Eugenia Trinajstic; children—Christophe (dec.), Sophie. Attache, Centre National de la Recherche Scientifique, Paris, 1939-48; univ. lectr. Altaic studies Cambridge U., 1948-62; prof. Uralic and Altaic studies and history Ind. U., Bloomington, 1962—, distinguished prof., 1975—, chmn. dept. Uralic and Altaic studies, 1963—, dir. Lang. and Area Center, 1963—, dir. Asian studies program, 1965-67, Asian studies Research Inst., 1967-79, dir. Research Inst. for Inner Asian Studies, 1979—. Sec. gen. Permanent Internat. Altaistic Conf., 1960—; research project dir. U.S. Office Edn., 1969-70; sec. Internat. Union Orientalists, 1954-64; vis. prof. Institut Nat. des Langues et Civilizations Orientales, Paris, spring 1974; scholar-in-residence Rockefeller Found. Study Center, Bellagio, 1975. Served with Forces Francaises de l'Intérieur, 1943-44, with French Army, 1944-45. Recipient Jubilee prize U. Budapest, 1938; Am. Philos. Soc. Research grantee, 1963; Am. Council Learned Soc. research grantee, 1962; Guggenheim fellow, 1968-69. Fellow Körösi Csoma Soc. (hon.); mem. Royal Asiatic Soc. (hon. sec. 1954-64), Am. Oriental Soc. (pres. Midwest br. 1968-70, nat. v.p. 1974-75, nat. pres. 1975-76), Assn. for Asian Studies, Am. Hist. Assn., Société Asiatique, Société de Linguistique, Tibet Soc. (pres. 1969-74), Deutsche Morgenlandische Gesellschaft, Suomalais-Ugrilaisen Seura (Finland) (hon. corr. mem.), Societas Uralo-Altaica (W. Ger.) (v.p. 1964—), Internat. Assn. for Hungarian Studies (v.p. 1977—), Hungarian Acad. Scis. (hon.). Clubs: Cosmos (Washington); Explorers (N.Y.C.); United Oxford and Cambridge (London). Author: Orientalism and History, 1954; History of Hungary, 1959; Introduction a l'étude de l'Eurasie Centrale, 1963; Aspects of Altaic Civilization, 1963; Inner Asia, 1968; Inner Asia and its Contacts with Medieval Europe, 1977; editor, contbr.: Modern Hungary, 1977; Studies in Finno-Ugric Linguistics, 1977; also numerous articles. Editor: Jour. Asian History; Cambridge History of Inner Asia. Home: 5581 E Lampkins Ridge Rd Bloomington IN 47401 Office: Dept Uralic and Altaic Studies 101 Goodbody Hall Indiana U Bloomington IN 47405

SINSABAUGH, ART (ARTHUR REEDER), photographer, educator; b. Irvington, N.J., Oct. 31, 1924; s. Grant Regynold and Helyn Edna (Reeder) S.; B.S., Inst. Design, Chgo., 1949, M.S., Ill. Inst. Tech., 1967; children—Elisabeth Helyn, Katherine Anne. Jr. photographer War Dept., 1942-43; instr. Inst. Design, Ill. Inst. Technology, Chgo., 1949-52, instr., head eve. div. photography, 1951-59; with U. Ill., Champaign-Urbana, 1959—, prof. art, 1969—, head dept. photography and cinematography program, 1959-77, head photography program, 1959—, founder, co-dir. Visual Research Lab., 1974-78; vis. artist U. Oreg., Eugene, 1964, U. N.H., Durham, 1968, Williams Coll., Williamstown, Mass., 1973, Chgo. Art Inst., 1968; photog. surveys City of Chgo. and City of Balt. Served with USAAC, 1943-46. Guggenheim fellow, 1969; asso. Center for Advanced Studies, U. Ill., 1972-73; grantee Ill. Arts Council, 1966, Graham Found., 1966, Nat. Endowment for Arts, 1976. Mem. Soc. for Photog. Edn. (founding mem.). Author: (with Anderson) 6 Mid-American Chants/11 Midwest Photography, 1964. Art Sinsabaugh Archive established at Ind. U. Art Mus., Bloomington, 1978. Home: Box 322 Champaign IL 61820 Office: 132 A&D Bldg U Illinois Champaign IL 61820

SINSHEIMER, RICHARD, lawyer; b. Bronxville, N.Y., Nov. 23, 1922; s. Bernard and Mathilde (Brady) S.; A.B., UCLA, 1942, M.A. in Polit. Sci., 1947, J.D., 1956; m. Ina Kaufman, Aug. 10, 1947; children—Jeffrey A., Peter J., Thomas A. Admitted to Calif. bar, 1956; individual practice law Los Angeles and Beverly Hills, Calif., 1956—. Pres. Am. Lung Assn., 1978-79, pres. elect, 1979-80. Served with USAAF, 1943-46. Mem. Am. Bar Assn., Los Angeles County Bar Assn., Beverly Hills Bar Assn. Office: 315 S Beverly Dr Suite 515 Beverly Hills CA 90212

SINSHEIMER, ROBERT LOUIS, educator; b. Washington, Feb. 5, 1920; s. Allen S. and Rose (Davidson) S.; S.B., Mass. Inst. Tech., 1941, M.S., 1942; Ph.D., 1948; m. Flora Joan Hirsch, Aug. 8, 1943 (div. 1972); children—Lois June (Mrs. Wickstrom), Kathy Jean, Roger Allen; m. 2d, Kathleen Mae Reynolds, Sept. 10, 1972. Staff mem. radiation lab. Mass. Inst. Tech., Cambridge, 1942-46; asso. prof. biophysics, physics dept. Iowa State Coll., Ames, 1949-55, prof., 1955-57; prof. biophysics Calif. Inst. Tech., Pasadena, 1957—, chmn. div. biology 1968-77; chancellor U. Calif., Santa Cruz, 1977—. Named Calif. Scientist of Year, 1968; recipient N.W. Beijerinck-Virologie medal Netherlands Acad. Sci., 1969. Fellow Am. Acad. Arts and Scis.; mem. Am. Soc. Biol. Chemists, Biophys. soc. (pres. 1970), AAAS, N.Y. Acad. Scis., Nat. Acad. Scis. (mem. council 1970-73, chmn. bd. editors Proc. 1972—), Inst. Medicine. Editor: Jour. Molecular Biology, 1959-67, Ann. Rev. Biochemistry, 1966-72. Home: University House U Calif at Santa Cruz Santa Cruz CA 95064

SINSHEIMER, WARREN JACK, lawyer, electronic equipment co. exec.; b. N.Y.C., May 22, 1927; s. Jerome William and Elizabeth (Berch) S.; student Ind. U., 1943-47; J.D. cum laude, N.Y. Law Sch., 1950; LL.M., N.Y.U., 1957; M.Phil., Columbia U., 1977; m. Florence Dubin, Mar. 30, 1950; children—Linda Ruth, Ralph David, Alan Jay, Michael Neal. Admitted to N.Y. bar, 1950; partner Sinsheimer, Sinsheimer & Dubin, N.Y.C., 1950-78, Satterlee & Stephens, N.Y.C.,

1978—; pres. Plessey, Inc., N.Y.C., 1956-70, chmn., chief exec. officer, 1970—; dir. overseas ops. and devel. Plessey Co., Ltd., Ilford, Essex, Eng., 1969-70, now dep. chief exec.; dir. Plessey Co., Ltd., Plessey, Inc., Eagle Star Ins. Co. Am. Chmn. Com. of 68, 1964-67. Mem Westchester County Republican Com., 1956-73; chmn. Nat. Scranton for Pres. Com., 1964; mem. N.Y. State Assembly, 1965-66. Bd. visitors Wassaic State Sch., 1962-64; dir. Westchester Jewish Community Services. Served with USNR, 1944-45; with USAF, 1950-52. Mem. Am. Bar Assn., Assn. Bar City N.Y., Torch and Scroll, Zeta Beta Tau. Jewish. Clubs: Beach Point (Mamaroneck, N.Y.), Harmonie (N.Y.C.). Home: 22 Murray Hill Rd Scarsdale NY 10583 Office: 277 Park Ave New York NY 10017

SINTON, WILLIAM MERZ, astronomer; b. Balt., Apr. 11, 1925; s. Robert Nelson and Alma (Summers) S.; A.B., Johns Hopkins, 1949, Ph.D., 1953; m. Marjorie Anne Korner, June 4, 1960; children—Robert William, David Theodore, Alan Nelson. Research asso. Johns Hopkins, 1953-54; research asso. Harvard, 1954-56; astrophysicst Smithsonian Instn., Washington, 1956-57; astronomer Lowell Obs., Flagstaff, Ariz., 1957-66; prof. U. Hawaii, 1966—. Served with AUS, 1943-46. Recipient Adolph Lomb medal Optical Soc. Am., 1954. Fellow Optical Soc. Am.; mem. Am. Astron. Soc., Astron. Soc. Pacific, Internat. Astron. Union, Phi Beta Kappa, Sigma Xi. Author: (with G.R. Miczaika) Tools of Astronomer, 1961. Home: 3137A Woodlawn Dr Honolulu HI 96822

SINTZ, EDWARD FRANCIS, librarian; b. New Trenton, Ind., Feb. 6, 1924; s. John and Edith E. (Rudicil) S.; B.A., U. Kans., 1950; M.A. in L.S., U. Denver, 1954; M.S. in Pub. Adminstrn., U. Mo., 1965; m. Donna Norris, Apr. 12, 1952; children—Ann Kristin, Lesley Elizabeth, Julie Melinda. With Kansas City (Mo.) Pub. Library, 1954-66, asst. dir., 1964-66; asso. librarian St. Louis Pub. Library, 1966-68; dir. pub. libraries, Miami, Fla., 1968—; instr. Washington U., St. Louis, 1966-67; library surveys for Mo. State Library, 1967-68. Served with USAAF, 1942-45. Mem. Am., Fla. (pres. 1975-76), Southeastern library assns. Kiwanian. Editor Mo. Library Assn. Quar., 1956-58. Home: 5730 SW 56th Terr Miami FL 33143 Office: 1 Biscayne Blvd Miami FL 33132

SINYKIN, GORDON, lawyer; b. Madison, Wis., June 18, 1910; s. Sam and Dora (Dansin) S.; A.B., U. Wis., 1931, LL.B., 1933; m. Dorothy b. Edelstein, May 2, 1941; children—Daniel, Philip and Susan (twins). Admitted to Wis. bar, 1933; practiced in Madison, 1933-35, 38-42, 45—; exec. counsel Gov. of Wis., 1935-38; spl. counsel, Wis., 1935-38; partner La Follette, Sinykin, Anderson & Munson and predecessors, 1945—; chmn. bd. The Progressive, Inc.; dir. United Bank and Trust of Madison, United Banks of Wis. Dir., adv. bd. Wis. div. Am. Automobile Assn., 1967—; lectr. U. Wis. Law Sch., 1950-52; spl. counsel State Wis. Ins. Dept., 1962-65; Madison Mayor's Commn. on Human Rights, 1958-63, mem. State Legislative Council Com. Ins. Law Revision, 1966-78, Wis. Jud. Commn., 1978—, U.S. Circuit Judge Nominating Commn., 1978-79. Bd. dirs. Methodist Hosp., 1969—, v.p., 1972-75, chmn. bd. 1975-78; bd. dirs. United Community Chest; bd. dirs., pres. Community Welfare Council, Madison, 1961-63; bd. dirs. Madison Legal Aid Soc., 1964-66. Served to maj. USAAF, 1942-45. Decorated Bronze Star. Fellow Am. Bar Found.; mem. Am. (del. 1975—), Wis. (gov. 1957-60, chmn. com. research planning 1965-67), Dane County (pres. 1956-57) bar assns., Order of Coif, Wis. Bar Found. (dir., pres. 1970-77), Am. Law Inst., Phi Beta Kappa, Phi Eta Sigma, Phi Kappa Phi. Co-author: Insurance Management Contracts. Editor-in-chief: Wis. Law Rev., 1932. Contbr. articles to profl. jours. Home: 721 Seneca Pl Madison WI 53711 Office: United Bank Tower 222 W Washington Ave Madison WI 53703

SINZER, JOSEPH FRANCIS, coll. adminstr.; b. Bklyn., Sept. 11, 1912; s. Francis B. and Josephine (O'Connor) S.; B.A., St. John's Coll., 1934; M.A., St. John's U., 1937, Ph.D., 1950; m. Mary Elizabeth Higgins, Aug. 28, 1948; children—Joseph Francis, John Paul, Mary Louise, Michael H. Faculty mem. St. John's U., 1937-42, 46-50; mem. faculty Pace U., N.Y.C., 1950—, chmn. dept. social scis., 1950-55, dean acad. affairs, 1955—, now Richard C. Pace prof., univ. historian. Mem. Bd. Edn. and Battalion Forum, Glen Ridge, N.J. Mem. Acad. Polit. Sci., Am. Cath. Hist. Assn., Am. Hist. Assn., Am. Studies Assn., AAUP, Assn. Higher Edn., Acad. Pub. Edn., Nat. Council Cath. Laity. Roman Catholic. Kiwanian (pres. local club). Club: Serra (pres.) (West Essex, N.J.). Editor: An Introduction to the Social Sciences, 1954. Home: 365 Ridgewood Ave Glen Ridge NJ 07028 Office: Pace U Plaza New York NY 10038

SION, MAURICE, educator; b. Skopje, Yugoslavia, Oct. 17, 1928; s. Max and Sarah (Alalouf) S.; B.A., N.Y. U., 1947, M.S., 1948; Ph.D., U. Calif. at Berkeley, 1951; m. Emilie Grace Chisholm, Sept. 15, 1957; children—Crispin, Sarah, Dirk, Robin (dec.). With Nat. Bur. Standards, Washington, 1951-52; instr. U. Calif. at Berkeley, 1952-53; mem. Inst. for Advanced Study, Princeton, 1955-57, 62; asst. prof. U. Calif. at Berkeley, 1957-60; faculty U. B.C., Vancouver, Can., 1960—, prof., 1964—; vis. prof. U. Calif. at Santa Barbara, 1965-66, U. Strasbourg (France), 1975-76; dir. Summer Research Inst. Canadian Math. Congress, 1967; guest speaker Internat. Congress Mathematicians, Nice, France, 1970; dir. Quadra Inst. Math. Served with AUS, 1953-55. Can. Council fellow, 1970-71. Mem. Am. Math. Soc., Canadian Math. Congress (v.p. 1971—.), Phi Beta Kappa, Sigma Xi. Author: Introduction to the Methods of Real Analysis, 1968; (with others) Basic Linear Algebra, 1971; A Theory of Semigroup Valued Measures, 1973. Asso. editor Canadian Jour. Math., 1969-70. Home: 6061 Chancellor Blvd Vancouver BC V6T 1E8 Canada Office: Math Dept U British Columbia Vancouver BC V6T 1W5 Canada

SIPES, DONALD, motion picture co. exec.; b. 1928; B.A., Ohio U., 1948; LL.B., Harvard U., 1951; married. Admitted to bar; asso. law firm, N.Y.C., 1953-57; atty., legal and bus. affairs NBC, 1957-61; agt. Frank Cooper Agy., 1961-63; v.p. bus. affairs and planning CBS, 1963-74; sr. exec. v.p. ICM, 1974-75; with MCA Inc., Universal City, Calif., 1975—, v.p. Universal TV Co., 1975-76, sr. v.p., 1976-77, corp. v.p. and exec. v.p. Universal TV, 1977-78, pres. Universal TV, 1978—. Served with U.S. Army, 1951-53. Office: Office of Pres Universal TV MCA Inc 100 Universal City Plaza Universal City CA 91608*

SIPPEL, JOHN PARKER, banker; b. Balt., Feb. 9, 1913; s. William F. and Marie (Parker) S.; A.B., Duke U., 1934; m. Ruth I. Jenkins, Nov. 10, 1934; children—John Parker, Marjorie R.M., William A.J. Nat. bank examiner, Balt., 1935-49; v.p. Nat. Met. Bank, Washington, 1950-58, Am. Security & Trust Co., Washington, 1958-60; with Citizens Nat. Bank, Laurel, Md., 1960—, pres., 1961-76, vice chmn., 1976—; dir. Balt. Gas & Electric Co., Balt. br. Fed. Res. Bank Richmond, 1964-69. Served to lt. USNR, 1942-45. Mem. Laurel C. of C. (past pres.), Fin. Pub. Relations Council Greater Washington (pres. 1965-66), Am. (v.p. for Md. 1969-70), Md. (pres. 1968-69) bankers assns. Presbyn. Clubs: Masons (Shriner), Rotary, Sherwood Forest, Annapolis Yacht. Home: 1111 Montgomery St Laurel MD 20810 Office; Citizens Nat Bank Laurel MD 20810

SIRAGUSA, ROSS DAVID, electronics appliance mfg. co. exec.; b. Buffalo, June 12, 1906; s. John A. and Maria (Barreca) S.; ed. parochial schs.; student Loyola U., Chgo.; m. Mary Irene O'Brien, Apr. 24, 1929 (dec. Apr. 1969); children—Ross David, John, Richard Donald, Mary Irene; m. 2d, Martha Ellen Peace Reibman, Aug. 28, 1973. Founder Admiral Corp. (merger with Rockwell Internat. Corp. 1974), Chgo., 1934, pres., 1934-63, chmn., 1963-74, ret.; founder RDS Enterprises, Rosemont, Ill., 1974—. chmn., dir. Gen. Aniline & Film, 1961-64. Mem. Pres. L.B. Johnson's bd. visitors USAF, 1970-71. Mem. bd. lay trustees, citizens bd. Loyola U., 1950-55. Decorated knight of Malta; knight Order Holy Sepulchre. Clubs: Conseil Internat. De La Chasse; Chicago, The Casino; Palm Bay, Jockey, Ocean Reef, Cat Cay, Lyford Cay. Home: 179 E Lake Shore Dr Chicago IL 60611 Office: 424 E Howard Ave Des Plaines IL 60018

SIREK, OTAKAR VICTOR, scientist, educator; b. Bratislava, Czechoslovakia, Dec. 1, 1921; s. Otakar and Alice (Wagner) S.; M.D., Slovak U., Bratislava, 1946; M.A., U. Toronto (Can.), 1951, Ph.D., 1954; m. Anna Janek, July 27, 1946; children—Ann, Jan, Peter, Terese. Came to Can., 1950. Research asso. Hosp. for Sick Children; 1955-57; mem. faculty U. Toronto, 1957—, prof. physiology, 1968—; vis. prof. U. Tel Aviv, 1978; cons. Hoechst Pharms. Can. Chmn. organizing com. Can. Workshops on Diabetes, 1971—; mem. council, faculty of medicine U. Toronto. Recipient Starr medal U. Toronto, 1958; Hoechst Centennial medal Frankfurt, Germany, 1966; C.H. Best prize Canadian Workshop on Diabetes, 1975. Wellcome fellow, 1962-63. Mem. Am. Diabetes Assn., Am. Physiol. Soc., Canadian Diabetes Assn., Canadian Assn. U. Tchrs., Internat. Diabetes Fedn., Canadian Physiol. Soc., Endocrine Soc., Canadian Soc. Endocrinology and Metabolism. Club: Faculty. Abstractor Jour. Diabetes 1964-70. Home: 93 Farnham Ave Toronto ON M4V 1H6 Canada

SIREK, WILLIAM MARTIN, ednl. adminstr.; b. Birchwood, Wis., Nov. 20, 1918; s. Jacob William and Rose Magdeline (Papousek) S.; B.S. in Edn., U. Wis., River Falls, 1941; M.S., U. Wis., Stout, 1954; m. June K. Holm, Nov. 12, 1942; children—Steven William, Mary Katherine, Judith Ann, James Martin. Tchr., prin. Roberts (Wis.) State Graded Sch., 1941-42; instr. math., sci. Wausau (Wis.) Tech. Inst., 1947-51, trades and industry coordinator, 1951-63; dir. Oshkosh (Wis.) Tech. Inst., 1963-67; dist. dir. Fox Valley Vocat., Tech. and Adult Edn. Dist., Appleton, Wis., 1967—; dir. Valley Western Bank, Appleton. Bd. dirs. St. Elizabeth Hosp.; mem. Outagamie County Manpower Council. Served with USNR, 1944-46. Mem. Wis. Vocat. Tech. and Adult Edn. Adminstrs. Assn. (past pres.), Am. Vocat. Assn., Wis. Assn. Vocat. and Adult Edn., Adult Edn. Assn., Nat. Assn. Public Sch. Adminstrs., Am. Tech. Edn. Assn., Nat. Assn. Public Continuing and Adult Edn., Nat. Council Community Relations. Roman Catholic. Clubs: Rotary, K.C. Office: 1825 N Bluemound Dr Appleton WI 54911

SIRI, WILLIAM EMIL, physicist, educator; b. Phila., Jan. 2, 1919; s. Emil Mark and Caroline (Schaedel) S.; student U. Chgo., 1937-43, U. Calif. at Berkeley, 1947-50; m. Margaret Jean Brandenburg, Dec. 3, 1949; children—Margaret Lynn, Ann Kathryn. Research engr. Baldwin-Lima-Hamilton Corp., 1943; physicist Radiation Lab., U. Calif. at Berkeley, 1943-45, physicist Donner Lab., Berkeley, 1945-74, mgr. energy analysis program Lawrence Berkeley Lab., 1974—; exec. v.p. Am. Mt. Everest Expdn., Inc. Pres., Save San Francisco Bay Assn., 1968—. Bd. dirs. Sierra Club Found. Co-recipient Hubbard medal Nat. Geog. Soc., 1963, Elisa Kent Kane medal Phila. Geog. Soc., 1963, Sol Feinstone Environmental award, 1977. Licensed profl. engr., Calif. Mem. Am. Phys. Soc., Biophys. Soc., Am. Assn. Physicists in Medicine, Sigma Xi. Democrat. Lutheran. Clubs: Sierra (dir. 1955-74, pres. 1964-66, William Colby award 1975); American Alpine (v.p.); Explorers (certificate of merit 1964). Author: Nuclear Radiations and Isotopic Tracers, 1949; papers on biophysics research, articles on conservation and mountaineering. Field leader U. Calif. Peruvian Expdns., 1950-52; leader Calif. Himalayan Expdn., 1954; field leader Internat. Physiol. Expdn. to Antarctica, 1957; dep. leader Am. Mt. Everest Expdn., 1963. Home: 1015 Leneve Pl El Cerrito CA 94530 Office: Lawrence Berkeley Lab U Calif Berkeley CA 94720

SIRICA, JOHN J., judge; b. 1904; LL.B., Georgetown U., 1926; hon. degrees Coll. New Rochelle (N.Y.), Brown U., New Eng. Sch. Law, Boston, Fairfield (Conn.) U., City U. N.Y., Duke U., Georgetown U.; m. Lucile M. Camalier, Feb. 26, 1952; children—John J. Jr., Patricia Anne, Eileen Marie. Former mem. firm Hogan & Hartson, Washington; judge U.S. Dist. Ct. for D.C., 1957—, chief Judge, 1971-74. Mem. Am. Bar Assn., Bar Assn. D.C. (hon.), Phi Alpha Delta. Clubs: Congressional Country, Nat. Lawyers, Lido Civic. Office: US Ct House Washington DC 20001

SIRIGNANO, WILLIAM ALFONSO, aerospace and mech. scientist; b. Bronx, N.Y., Apr. 14, 1938; s. Anthony P and Lucy (Caruso) S.; B.Aero.Engring., Rensselaer Poly. Inst., 1959; Ph.D., Princeton U., 1964; m. Molly Van Leeuwen, Oct. 29, 1966 (div. 1975); 1 dau., Monica Ann; m. 2d, Lynn Haisfield, Nov. 26, 1977; 1 dau., Jacqueline Hope. Mem. research staff Guggenheim Labs., aerospace, mech. scis. dept. Princeton U., 1964-67, asst. prof. aerospace and mech. scis., 1967-69, asso. prof., 1969-73, prof., 1973-79, dept. dir. grad. studies, 1974-78; George Tallman Ladd prof., head dept. mech. engring. Carnegie-Mellon U., 1979—; cons. industry and govt., 1966—; mem. emissions control panel Nat. Acad. Scis., 1971-73; chmn. tech. confs. United Aircraft research fellow, 1973-74. Mem. Combustion Inst. (vice chmn. Eastern sect.), Soc. Indsl. Applied Math., AIAA, ASME. Asso. editor Combustion Sci. and Tech., 1969-70; contbr. articles to profl. jours., also research monographs. Home: 5391 Northumberland St Pittsburgh PA 15217 Office: Carnegie-Mellon U Pittsburgh PA 15213

SIRNA, ANTHONY ALFRED, III, investment co. exec.; b. N.Y.C., May 22, 1924; s. Alfred Anthony and Frances Ruth (Lasky) S.; B.S. cum laude, Harvard U., 1944, postgrad., 1944-46; postgrad. Columbia U., 1946-47, N.Y. Inst. Finance, 1953; m. Allison Porter, Jan. 12, 1946 (dec. 1971); m. 2d, Therese Cooper, Feb. 25, 1972; children—Meredith Allison, Corinne Hart, Anthony Alfred IV, Rebecca Cooper, James Cooper. Pres. East 55th St. Corp., N.Y.C., 1946-50; writer, editor med. econs. Unicorn Press, N.Y.C., 1950-53; fin. adviser to chmn. bd. Am. Securities Corp., 1953—, dir., 1956—; dir. Western Union Internat. Inc., Mangood Corp., Union Stock Yards, Ametek, Inc. Lt. col. N.Y.C. Aux. Police; capt., trustee Riverview Manor Hose Co. 3, Hastings-on-Hudson, N.Y. Trustee N.Y. Coll. Music. Mem. N.Y. Soc. Security Analysts. Clubs: Harvard N.Y.C., Boston and Westchester County, N.Y.); Westchester Country (Rye, N.Y.); Riverview Manor Tennis (Hastings-on-Hudson, N.Y.); Westhampton (N.Y.) Yacht Squadron, Westhampton Country; American (London, Eng.). Author: (with Allison Sirna) The Wanderings of Edward Ely, 1945. Contbr. articles to profl. jours. Home: 784 Park Ave New York NY 10021 Office: 122 E 42d St New York NY 10017

SIROTKIN, PHILLIP LEONARD, ednl. adminstr.; b. Moline, Ill., Aug. 2, 1923; s. Alexander and Molly (Berghaus) S.; B.A. (McGregor Found. scholar), Wayne State U., 1945; M.A., U. Chgo., 1947, Ph.D. (Walgreen Found. scholar, Carnegie fellow), 1951; m. Cecille Sylvia Gussack, May 1, 1945; children—Steven Marc, Laurie Anne. Lectr., U. Chgo., 1949-50; instr. Wellesley Coll., 1950-52, asst. prof. polit. sci., 1953-57; asso. dir. Western Interstate Commn. Higher Edn., Boulder, Colo., 1957-60; exec. asst. to dir. Calif. Dept. Mental Hygiene, Sacramento, 1960-63; asst. dir. NIMH, 1964-66, asso. dir., 1967-71, cons., 1971-73; exec. v.p., acad. v.p. State U. N.Y. at Albany, 1971-76; exec. dir. Western Interstate Commn. Higher Edn., Boulder, Colo., 1976—; cons. Bur. Health Manpower Edn., NIH, 1972-74, Nat. Center Health Services Research, 1975—; spl. cons. AID, 1963-64; case writer Resources for the Future, 1954-55; mem. 1st U.S. mission on Mental Health to USSR, 1967. Bd. dirs. Council Social Work Edn., 1959-60. Served to 1st lt. AUS, 1943-46. Recipient Superior Service award HEW, 1967; Wellesley Coll. Faculty Research award, 1956. Mem. Am. Assn. Higher Edn., AAAS, Am. Pub. Health Assn., Am. Polit. Sci. Assn., Am. Soc. Pub. Adminstrn. Author: The Echo Park Dam Controversy and Upper Colorado River Development, 1959. Home: 299 Green Rock Dr Boulder CO 80302 Office: PO Drawer P Boulder CO 80302

SIROVICH, LAWRENCE, mathematician, educator; b. N.Y.C., Mar. 1, 1933; s. Herman and Lillian (Silverstein) S.; A.B. in Math., Johns Hopkins U., 1956, Ph.D. in Fluid Mechanics, 1960; m. Carole Ann Hochman, Oct. 16, 1960; children—Brenda Ellen, Matthew Ivan. Research scientist Courant Inst., N.Y. U., 1958-61; Fulbright scholar Universite Libre, Brussels, Belgium, 1961-62; asst. prof. applied math. Brown U., Providence, 1963-65, asso. prof., 1965-67, prof., 1967—; prof. Inst. Henri Poincare, U. Paris, 1968-69; adj. prof. Rockefeller U.; exchange prof. U. Paris, 1974. Guggenheim fellow, 1978. Mem. Am. Phys. Soc., Am. Math. Soc., Soc. Indsl. and Applied Math., AAUP, AAAS. Author: Techniques of Asymptotis Analysis, 1971. Editor: Applied Mathematical Sciences, 1974; Mathematics in Science, 1974; Quar. of Applied Math., 1978—; contbg. editor Le Bulletin des Sciences Mathematiques, Paris, 1976. Contbr. articles to math. jours. Home: 37 Riverside Dr New York NY 10023 Office:

SIROWITZ, LEONARD, advt. exec.; b. N.Y.C., June 25, 1932; s. Abraham and Sadie (Schoenwetter) S.; student Pratt Inst., 1950-53; m. Myrna Florman, Jan. 22, 1955; children—Laura, Michael. Advt. designer CBS-TV Network, N.Y.C., 1957; sr. v.p. Doyle, Dane, Bernbach, N.Y.C., 1959-70, creative mgmt. supr., 1959-70; prin. exec. v.p., co-dir. creative dept. Rosenfeld, Sirowitz & Lawson, N.Y.C., 1970—. Head Nat. Campaign for Eugene McCarthy, 1968; vol. ChildFind Project for Handicapped Children, 1976. Served with U.S. Army, 1953-55. Recipient over 100 awards and medals from profl. orgns. Mem. Am. Assn. Advt. Agys., Art Dirs. Club N.Y. Home: 44 W 77th St New York NY 10024 Office: 1370 Ave of Americas New York NY 10019

SIS, RAYMOND FRANCIS, veterinarian, educator; b. Munden, Kans., July 22, 1931; s. Frank J. and Edvie (Shimanek) S.; B.S., Kans. State U., 1953, D.V.M., 1957; M.S., Iowa State U., 1962, Ph.D., 1965; m. Janice L. Murphy, Aug. 31, 1953; children—Susan, Valerie, Mark, Michael, Amy. Clinician, Blue Cross Animal Hosp., Albuquerque, 1957; asst. prof. small animal surgery Iowa State U., Ames, 1964-65; asso. prof. anatomy Tex. A. and M. U., College Station, 1965-68, prof., head dept. vet. anatomy, 1968—. Served with USAF, 1957-61; mem. Res. Mem. Am., Tex. (dir.) vet. med. assns., Am. Animal Hosp. Assn., Am., Tex. (pres. 1973) assns. lab. animal sci., Am. (sec.-treas. 1973, pres. 1975), World assns. vet anatomists, Am. Assn. Vet. Clinicians, Brazos Valley Vet. Med. Assn. (pres. 1971), Nat. Soc. for Med. Research, Am. Assn. Vet. Med. Colls., Tex. Acad. Vet. Practice (v.p. 1973), Internat. Assn. for Aquatic Animal Medicine, Am. Soc. Lab. Animal Practitioners, Res. Officers Assn., Blue Key, Sigma Xi, Phi Zeta (exec. councilman 1969), Alpha Zeta, Phi Kappa Phi, Alpha Gamma Rho (adviser 1962-65, 77—, pres. 1953, pres. alumni assn. 1976—). K.C. (trustee 1969, pres. 1968). Home: 2519 Willow Bend Bryan TX 77801 Office: Tex A and M U College Station TX 77843

SISCO, JOSEPH JOHN, univ. pres., govt. ofcl.; b. Chgo., Oct. 31, 1919; student Morton Jr. Coll., 1937-39; A.B. magna cum laude, Knox Coll., 1941, L.H.D., 1970; M.A., U. Chgo., 1947, Ph.D., 1950; m. Jean Churchill Head, Mar. 26, 1946; children—Carol Bolton, Jane Murdock. Newspaper reporter, 1936-40; with City News Bur., Chgo., 1937; high sch. tchr., 1941; govt. service, 1950-51; staff Dept. State, 1951-76, successivley fgn. affairs officer, specialist internat. orgnl. affairs, officer-in charge Gen. Assembly, Security Council affairs, fgn. service officer, officer-in-charge UN polit. affairs, 1951-58, dep. dir. Office UN Polit. and Security Affairs, 1958-60, dir., 1960-63; dep. asst. sec. Bur. Internat. Orgn. Affairs, 1963-65, asst. sec. state internat. orgn. affairs, 1965-69, asst. sec. state Near East-South Asia, 1969-74, under sec. state for polit. affairs, 1974-76; pres. Am. U., Washington, 1976—. Mem. U.S. delegation UN Collective Measures Com., 1952, U.S. delegations to UN Gen. Assembly, 1952-68; U.S. del. spl. UN Gen. Assembly session of Middle East, 1967; exec. officer, 1954-57; polit. adviser U.S. delegation Internat. Atomic Energy Agy., 1959; lectr. Fgn. Service Inst. Served as 1st lt., inf., AUS, 1941-45. Recipient Top Ten Career Service award Civil Service League, 1966, Rockefeller pub. service award, 1971; Silver Helmet Peace award Am. Vets. Com., 1973. Mem. Am. Polit. Sci. Assn., Am. Soc. Internat. Law, Am. Fgn. Service Assn., Phi Beta Kappa, Tau Kappa Epsilon. Contbr. articles on internat. orgn., fgn. affairs to publs. Home: 3300 Nebraska Ave NW Washington DC 20016 Office: Am Univ Washington DC 20016

SISK, DANIEL ARTHUR, lawyer; b. Albuquerque, July 12, 1927; s. Arthur Henry and Myrl (Hope) S.; student U. N.Mex., 1946-48; B.A., Stanford, 1950, J.D., 1954; m. Katharine Banning, Nov. 27, 1954; children—John, Nancy, Thomas. Admitted to N.Mex. bar, 1955; asso. firm Simms & Modrall, 1954-59; partner firm Modrall, Sperling, Roehl, Harris & Sisk, Albuquerque, 1959-70, 71—; justice N.Mex. Supreme Ct., Santa Fe, 1970. Chmn. bd. First N.M. Bankshare Corp., Albuquerque, 1975—. Trustee Sandia Sch., Albuquerque, 1968-72, Albuquerque Acad., 1971-73, A.T. & S.F. Meml. Hosps., Topeka, 1966—. Served with USNR, 1945-46, PTO; to capt. USMCR, 1951-52; Korea. Mem. N.Mex., Albuquerque (dir. 1962-63), Am. bar assns., State Bar Calif. Presbyn. (elder). Home: 5917 Camino Placido NE Albuquerque NM 87109 Office: 800 Pub Service Bldg Albuquerque NM 87103

SISK, JOHN KELLY, communications co. exec.; b. Cookeville, Tenn., Mar. 3, 1913; s. Thurman Kelly and Martha Jane (Sewell) S.; B.S., U. Ala., 1934; LL.D. (hon.), Livingston (Ala.) Coll., 1975; m. Isbell Lane, Sept. 30, 1936; children—John Kelly, Lane Sisk Irick. With Greenville (S.C.) News-Piedmont Co., 1948—, chmn. bd., 1963—, publisher, 1966—; chmn. bd. Multimedia, Inc., Greenville, 1973—; dir. S.C. Nat. Corp., S.C. Nat. Bank, Liberty Life Ins. Co., Dan River Inc. Trustee Duke Endowment, Converse Coll.; adv. trustee Furman U.; chmn. trustees Greenville Gen. Hosp., 1959. Mem. Am. Newspaper Pubs. Assn., So. Newspaper Pubs. Assn. (pres. 1963, chmn. 1964), S.C. Press Assn. (pres. 1962), Greater Greenville C. of C. (pres. 1953). Methodist. Clubs: Nat. Press (Washington); Green Valley Country, Greenville Country, Poinsett, Cotillion, Biltmore Forest Country, Plantation. Home: 20 Southland Ave Greenville SC 29601 Office: PO Box 1688 305 S Main St Greenville SC 29602. *It has always been my feeling that no one can succeed in life alone, but with the help of competent people, can do well.*

SISK, PHILIP LAURENCE, lawyer; b. Lynn, Mass., Oct. 25, 1913; s. Joseph R. and Mary (Casey) S.; A.B., Coll. of Holy Cross, 1935; J.D., Boston Coll., 1938; m. Barbara Gardner, July 1, 1947; 1 son, Gardner P. Admitted to Mass. bar, 1938, individual practice law, Lynn, 1938—. Mem. Lynn Sch. Com., 1939-51, Mass. Defenders

Com., 1973—; trustee Mass. Continuing Legal Edn., Inc., 1974-78; mem. Mass. Bd. Bar Overseers. Served with AUS, 1943-46. Fellow Am. Coll. Trial Lawyers (mem. state com. 1969-70, state chmn. 1969-70), Am., Mass. (treas. 1978—, trustee) bar founds.; mem. Am. (ho. of dels., mem. standing com. on forums 1974—, chmn. 1978—), Mass. (exec. com. 1959-62, bd. dels. 1963—, pres. 1968-70), Lynn (pres. 1960-62), Essex (exec. bd. 1955—) bar assns., Def. Research Inst. (Mass. chmn. 1965-68), Mass. Assn. Def. Counsel (pres. 1966-67), Mass. Assn. Bank Counsel, Internat. Assn. Ins. Council (chmn. state com.), Am. Judicature Soc. (dir. 1976—), Assn. Ins. Counsel. Home: Flint St Marblehead Neck MA 01945 Office: 38 Exchange St Lynn MA 01901

SISKEL, EUGENE KAL (GENE), journalist; b. Chgo., Jan. 26, 1946; s. Nathan W. and Ida (Kalis) S.; B.A., Yale U., 1967; postgrad. Dept. Def. Info. Sch., 1968. Film critic Chgo. Tribune, 1969—; movie critic WBBM-TV, Chgo., 1974—; co-host Sneak Previews, PBS Network, 1978—. CORO Found. fellow, 1968. Mem. Acad. TV Arts and Scis., Sigma Delta Chi. Clubs: Yale, Culver; Arts (Chgo.). Office: care Chicago Tribune 435 N Michigan Ave Chicago IL 60611

SISLER, DAVID MICHAEL, investment broker; b. St. Louis, Oct. 16, 1931; s. George Harold and Kathleen (Holznagle) S.; B.Basic Engring. magna cum laude, Princeton U., 1953; postgrad. Washington U., St. Louis, 1956-59; m. Janet D. Beck, Oct. 6, 1956; 1 son, David G. Profl. baseball player, Boston, 1956-58, Detroit, 1959-60, Washington, 1961, Cin., 1962; with A.G. Edwards & Sons, Inc., St. Louis, 1960—, br. dir., sr. v.p., 1960-70. Served with U.S. Army, 1954-56. Office: Edwards & Sons Inc One N Jefferson Ave Saint Louis MO 63103

SISLER, GEORGE COOPER, psychiatrist, educator; b. Winnipeg, Man., Can., Dec. 28, 1923; s. William James and Agnes Ellen (Martin) S.; M.D., U. Man., 1946; m. Berenice Barbara Warne, Sept. 18, 1948. Intern Winnipeg Gen. Hosp., 1946-47, resident, 1947-49; resident U. Louisville Hosps., 1950-52; asso. psychiatry U. Louisville, 1952; staff psychiatrist Psychiat. Inst., Winnipeg, 1952-54; prof., head dept. U. Man. Med. Sch., Winnipeg, 1954-75, prof. psychiatry, 1975—; psychiatrist in chief Winnipeg Gen. Hosp., 1954-75; staff psychiatrist Health Scis. Centre, Winnipeg, 1975—. Served with M.C., Royal Canadian Army, 1944-46. Fellow Royal Coll. Physicians Canada, Am. Psychiat. Assn.; mem. Canadian Psychiat. Assn., Canadian Med. Assn. Office: Health Sciences Centre Winnipeg MB R3E 0W3 Canada

SISLER, HARRY HALL, chemist, educator; b. Ironton, Ohio, Mar. 13, 1917; s. Harry C. and Minta A. (Hall) S.; B.Sc., Ohio State U., 1936; M.Sc., U. Ill., 1938, Ph.D., 1939; Doctorate honoris causa, U. Poznan (Poland), 1977; m. Helen E. Shaver, June 29, 1940; children—Elizabeth A., David F., Raymond K., Susan C.; m. 2d, Hannelore L. Wass, Apr. 13, 1978. Instr. Chgo. City Colls., 1939-41; from instr. to asso. prof. U. Kans., Lawrence, 1941-46; from asst. prof. to prof. chemistry Ohio State U., Columbus, 1946-56; Arthur and Ruth Sloan vis. prof. chemistry Harvard, fall, 1962-63; prof., chmn. dept. chemistry U. Fla., Gainesville, 1956-68, Disting. Service prof. chemistry, 1979—, dean Coll. Arts and Scis., 1968-70, exec. v.p., 1970-73, dean grad. sch., 1973-79; indsl. cons. W.R. Grace & Co., Martin Marietta Aerospace, Naval Ordnance Lab., TVA; chemistry adv. panel, also vis. scientists panel NSF, 1959-62; cons. USAF Acad., Battelle Meml. Inst., chmn. interinstl. com. nuclear research, Fla., 1958-64; mem. Fla. Nuclear Devel. Commn. Teaching Sci. and Math., 1958; chemistry adv. panel Oak Ridge Nat. Lab., 1965-69. Decorated Royal Order North Star (Sweden). Named Outstanding Chemist in South, 1969, Outstanding Chemist in Southeast, Am. Chem. Soc., 1960, James Flack Norris award, 1979; recipient Outstanding Centennial Achievement award Ohio State U., 1970. Mem. Am. Chem. Soc. (nat. chmn. div. chem. edn. 1957-58, exec. com. 1957-60, bd. publ. Jour. Chem. Edn. 1956-58), Sigma Xi, Phi Delta Kappa, Phi Lambda Upsilon, Phi Kappa Phi, Alpha Chi Sigma. Baptist. Rotarian. Author: Electronic Structure, Properties, and the Periodic Law; Starlight-A Book of Poems, 1976; (with others) Gen. Chemistry—A Systematic Approach, 2d edit., 1959; Coll. Chemistry—A Systematic Approach, 4th edit., 1980; Essentials of Chemistry, 2d edit., 1959; A Systematic Laboratory Course in Chemistry, 1950; Essentials of Experimental Chemistry, 2d edit., 1959; Semimicro Qualitative Analysis, 1958, rev. edit., 1965; Comprehensive Inorganic Chemistry, Vol. V., 1956; Chemistry in Non-Aqueous Solvents, 1961; Starlight (poems), 1976; The Chloramination Reaction, 1977; cons. editor Dowden, Hutchinson & Ross, 1971-78; series editor Phys. and Inorganic Textbook Series, Reinhold Pub. Corp., 1958-70; contbr. articles to profl. jours. Patentee in field. Home: 6014 NW 54th Way Gainesville FL 32601

SISSON, EVERETT ARNOLD, diversified industry exec.; b. Chgo., Oct. 24, 1920; s. Emmett B. and Norma (Merbitz) S.; A.B., Valparaiso U., 1942; m. Roberta E. Blauman, Mar. 20, 1943; children—Nancy Lee Sisson Genz, Elizabeth Anne Sisson Levy. Sales mgr. Ferrotherm Corp., Cleve., 1946-51, Osborn Mfg. Co., Cleve., 1951-56; dir. sales Patterson Foundry & Machine Co., East Liverpool, Ohio, 1956-58; mgr. sonic energy products Bendix Corp., Davenport, Iowa, 1958-60; pres., chief exec. officer, dir. Lamb Industries, Inc., Toledo, 1960-65, Lehigh Valley Industries, Inc., N.Y.C., 1965-66; pres., chief exec. officer, dir. Am. Growth Industries, Inc., Chgo., 1966—, Workman Mfg. Co., Chgo., 1966-69, Am. Growth Devel. Corp., Chgo., 1968—, Oak Brook Club Co. (Ill.), 1969—; chmn. bd., chief exec. officer Hausske-Harlen Furniture Mfg. Co., Peru, Ind., 1976—; pres. Peru Properties, Inc., Oak Brook, 1976—; chmn. bd. Lutheran Mut. Life Ins. Co., Waverly, Iowa; dir. Libco Corp., Chgo., Tecco Mktg. Services, Inc., Chgo. Pres. council, Mayfield Heights, Ohio, 1952-57. Adviser to bd. trustees Valparaiso (Ind.) U., 1960-69; bd. regents Calif. Lutheran Coll., 1968—, fellow, 1969. Served Pres. capt. USAAF, 1943-46. Mem. Am. Mgmt. Assn., Cleve. Engring. Soc., President's Assn., Tau Kappa Epsilon. Club: Burr Ridge. Home: 1405 Burr Ridge Club Burr Ridge IL 60521 Office: 1550 Spring Oak Brook IL 60521

SISSON, GEORGE ALLEN, physician, educator; b. Mpls., May 11, 1920; s. Clark R. and Alberta (Chatfield) S.; A.B., Syracuse U., 1942, M.D., 1945; m. Mary Alice Reed, Mar. 25, 1944; children—Marjorie Ann (Mrs. Jack Swelsted), George Allen, Kathryn Alberta. Intern Syracuse (N.Y.) Med. Center, 1945-46, Bellevue Hosp.-N.Y. U. Postgrad. Sch., 1948-49; resident Manhattan Eye, Ear and Throat Hosp., N.Y.C., 1949-51, head and neck fellow, 1952-53; practice medicine specializing in head and neck surgery, Syracuse, 1953-67, Chgo., 1967—; prof., chmn. dept. otolaryngology and maxillofacial surgery Northwestern U. Med. Sch., 1967—; chmn. dept. otolaryngology and maxillofacial surgery Northwestern Meml. Hosp., 1967—; attending physician Cook County Hosp., Children's Meml. Hosp., VA Lakeside Hosp., Chgo. Chmn. rehab. com. head and neck surgery Ill. div. Am. Cancer Soc.; adv. com. Nat. Inst. Neurol. Diseases, 1975-78. Served to capt., M.C., AUS, 1946-48. Diplomate Am. Bd. Otolaryngology (examiner 1959—, bd. dirs. 1962—). Fellow A.C.S. (gov. 1965); mem. Am. Laryngeal, Rhinol. and Otolog. Soc., Am. Acad. Ophthalmology and Otolaryngology, Am. Soc. Head and Neck Surgery (pres. 1969-70), Assn. Acad. Depts. Otolaryngology (pres. 1978-79), Soc. U. Otolaryngologists (pres. 1971-72), Am. Acad. Facial Plastic and Reconstructive Surgery (v.p. 1972, pres. 1978-79), Soc. Head and Neck Surgeons, Am. Laryngol. Soc. Contbr. articles to profl. jours. Mem. editorial bd. Archives of Otolaryngology, Head and Neck Cancer Jour. Producer movies illustrating operative techniques for control of cancer. Home: Dunham Rd Wayne IL 60184 Office: 303 E Chicago Ave Chicago IL 60611

SISSON, JOSEPH ANDREW, pathologist, educator; b. San Diego, Oct. 24, 1930; s. Harvey Gladden and Myrtle Sophronia (Anderson) S.; A.B. cum laude, San Diego State Coll., 1955; M.D. cum laude, Washington U., 1960; m. Virginia Joan Ford, Dec. 29, 1959 (div. 1973); children—Edwin Andrew, Donna Virginia; m. Eugenia Legan, Dec. 25, 1977. Intern, Yale, 1960-61; resident pathology Albany Med. Coll., 1961-64, instr., 1964-68; prof. pathology Creighton U., 1969-79, chmn. dept., 1968-73; dir. labs. Creighton Meml. St. Joseph Hosp., 1968-72; prof. pathology Eastern Va. Med. Sch., 1979—; chief lab. service VA Med. Center, Hampton, Va., 1979—. Served with AUS, 1950-52. Decorated Bronze Star. Mem. AMA, Tidewater Assn. Pathologists, Am. Soc. Pathologists and Bacteriologists, Coll. Am. Pathologists. Author: The Bare Facts of General Pathology, 1971, 3d edit., 1979; The Bare Systemic Pathology, 1972, 2d edit., 1978; Handbook of Clinical Pathology, 1975. Contbr. articles to profl. jours. Home: Box 5474 VA Med Center Hampton VA 23667

SISTRUNK, JAMES DUDLEY, educator, clergyman, librarian; b. Jayess, Miss., Aug. 13, 1919; s. James Cannon and Amelia Frances (Smith) S.; student La. State U., 1945-46, Clarke Meml. Coll., 1951-52; B.A., Baylor U., 1954; B.D., Southwestern Bapt. Theol. Sem., 1957, M.Div., 1972; B.S. in L.S., North Tex. State U., 1959; postgrad. U. N.C., 1960; m. Helen Anna Wilson, Dec. 19, 1942; children—James Dudley, Richard Stanley. With Interstate Oil Pipe Line Co., Natchez, Miss., 1946-51; ordained to ministry Bapt. Ch., 1952; pastor Belfalls (Tex.) Bapt. Ch., 1952-54, Fairview Bapt. Ch., Valley Mills, Tex., 1955-57, Tolarsville (N.C.) Bapt. Ch., 1969—; circulation librarian Southwestern Bapt. Theol. Sem., 1957-59; adminstrv. librarian Southeastern Bapt. Theol. Sem., 1959-64; librarian, mem. faculty Campbell Coll., Buies Creek, N.C., 1964—, now prof. library sci. and dir. library services. Served with USAAF, 1940-45. Mem. ALA, Southeastern, N.C. library assns., Am. Theol. Library Assn. Lion (dir., membership chmn. pres.). Author: The History of Carie Rich Memorial Library from 1887 to 1966. Address: Box 415 Buies Creek NC 27506

SITES, WILLIAM MORRIS, ins. co. exec.; b. Nankin, Ohio, May 31, 1917; s. Harry Daniel and Florence Idel (Fluke) S.; m. Wilma Alice Blaney, June 28, 1947; children—Robert William, Jane Ann Sites Mackey. Acct., Lincoln Mut. Ind. Co., Mansfield, Ohio, 1936-40; underwriter Buckeye Union Casualty Co., Columbus, Ohio, 1941-47; with Shelby Mut. Ins. Co. (Ohio), 1947—, v.p., 1976—, sec., 1975—, also dir.; v.p., sec., dir. Shelby Life Ins. Co., IPBS, Inc.; dir. Shelby Fin. Corp.; chmn. bd. Shelby Printing, Inc. Trustee, mem. fin. com., mem. adminstrv. bd. First United Meth. Ch., Shelby. Served with U.S. Army, 1943-46. Mem. Chartered Property and Casualty Underwriters (past pres. Akron-Canton chpt.), Am. Ins. Assn., Conf. Casualty Ins. Cos. Republican. Club: Rotary. Home: 79 Parkwood Dr Shelby OH 44875 Office: 19 Mansfield Ave Shelby OH 44875

SITKIN, IRWIN JAY, ins. co. exec.; b. Middletown, Conn., Apr. 2, 1930; s. Leo and Anna (Gurland) S.; B.S., Cornell U., 1952; m. Helen Fiedel, Sept. 1, 1951; children—Marc Benton, Jill Marion. With Aetna Life & Casualty Co., Hartford, Conn., 1954—, IBM supervisory trainee. 1954-58, programmer, systems analyst, supr. central tabulating, 1958-60, asst. sec., 1960-65, sec., 1965-68, asst. v.p. data processing devel. dept. casualty div., 1968-69, asst. v.p. corporate data processing services, 1969-72, v.p. corporate data processing services, 1972-76, v.p. corporate data processing and adminstrv. services, 1976—; pres. SPAN subs. Aetna Life & Casualty Co., 1969—; corporator Liberty Bank for Savs., Middletown, Conn. Pres., No. Middlesex County YMCA, Middletown, 1971-72, trustee, 1972—; bd. dirs., chmn. audit com. Middlesex Meml. Hosp., Middletown; trustee Ward Tech. Coll. U. Hartford; chmn. ins. sect. Greater Hartford United Way, 1977. Served with USAF, 1952-54. Recipient YMCA Youth Services award, 1971-73. Mem. Data Processing Mgmt. Assn. (Individual Performance award 1965, past pres. and internat. dir., Computer Scis. Man-of-Yr. award 1978), Life Office Mgmt. Assn. (chmn. ops. and systems council, dir.), Nat. Computer Conf. Com., Am. Council Life Ins., Am. Ins. Assn. Republican. Jewish. Club: B'nai B'rith (Service award 1977, dir. Middletown lodge). Home: 180 Clover St Middletown CT 06457 Office: 151 Farmington Ave Hartford CT 06156

SITOMER, CURTIS JOHN, newspaper editor; b. N.Y.C., Nov. 17, 1932; s. Harry L. and Ethel Belle S.; B.A., Principia Coll., 1955; postgrad. Boston U., U. Calif., Santa Barbara; m. Mary Lou Allen, Aug. 31, 1957; children—Amy, Laura. Engaged in radio publicity and coll. public relations; newspaper reporter, editor; now with Christian Sci. Monitor, Boston. Recipient writing awards. Mem. Am. and Calif. bar assns., ACLU. Christian Scientist. Office: 1 Norway Sr Boston MA 02115

SITTERLEY, THEODORE SYNYER, JR., savs. and loan co. exec.; b. Bronxville, N.Y., Oct. 21, 1937; s. Theodore S. and Charlotte Ann (Meyer) S.; B.S., U. Ariz., 1959. With Home Fed. Savs. and Loan Assn., Tucson, 1960—, loan group mgr., 1971-73, exec. v.p., 1973-75, pres., 1975—. Mem. Tucson Airport Authority; bd. dirs. United Way, Ariz. Tng. Center for the Handicapped, Jr. Achievement; fin. chmn. Tucson Conquistadores, 1976-77. Mem. Ariz. Savs. and Loan League (pres. 1977-76), Beta Gamma Sigma, Alpha Kappa Psi, Phi Delta Theta. Clubs: El Dorado, Tucson Racquet, Tucson Nat. Golf, Old Peublo, Rotary. Home: 6562 Calle Cavalier Tucson AZ 85715 Office: 32 N Stone St Tucson AZ 85701

SITTLER, DARRYL GLEN, hockey player; b. Kitchener, Ont., Can., Sept. 18, 1950; m. Wendy; children—Ryan, Megan. Hockey player Toronto Maple Leafs, 1970—, capt., 1975. Office: 60 Carlton St Toronto ON M5B 1L1 Canada*

SITTON, CLAUDE FOX, newspaper editor; b. Emory, Ga., Dec. 4, 1925; s. Claude B. and Pauline (Fox) S.; A.B., Emory U., 1949; m. Eva McLaurin Whetstone, June 5, 1953; children—Lauren Lea, Clinton, Suzanna, McLaurin. Reporter, Internat. News Service, 1949-50; with U.P., 1950-55, writer-editor, N.Y.C., 1952-55; information officer USIA, 1955-57; mem. staff N.Y. Times, 1957-68, nat. news dir., 1964-68; editorial dir. The News and Observer Pub. Co., Raleigh, N.C., 1968—, dir., 1969, v.p., 1970—, editor News and Observer, 1970—. Served USNR, 1943-46. Mem. Am. Soc. Newspaper Editors (dir. 1977—), Sigma Delta Chi. Presbyn. Clubs: Watauga, Kiwanis. Home: 3104 Monticello Dr Raleigh NC 27612 Office: News and Observer 215 S McDowell St Raleigh NC 27602

SITTON, FRED MONROE, educator; b. Pyote, Tex., Mar. 27, 1924; s. Fitzhugh Lee and Aurie Hester (Hutchison) S.; B.A., Tex. Western Coll., 1943, M.A., 1951; M.F.A., U. Tex., 1954; L.D.A., U. N.C., 1959; Ph.D., Northwestern U., 1962; m. Kathryn Irene Means, July 19, 1947. Tchr. pub. schs., Pecos, Tex., 1947-52, Charlotte, N.C., 1954-58; instr. U. N.C., Chapel Hill, 1957-59; prof. speech and drama Valparaiso (Ind.) U., 1961—, chmn. dept. speech and drama, 1970—; producer, dir. Summer Stock Theatre, Pocono Pines, Pa., 1962-67; dir. Profl. Stock, Valparaiso, 1968-72; founder Children's Theatre, Valparaiso, 1963. Served with U.S. Maritime Service, 1943-46. U. N.C. grantee in theatre, 1958-59. Mem. Am. Theatre Assn., Children's Theatre Assn., Pi Kappa Alpha. Democrat. Address: Valparaiso Univ Valparaiso IN 46383

SIVE, DAVID, lawyer; b. Bklyn., Sept. 22, 1922; s. Abraham Leon and Rebecca (Schwartz) S.; A.B., Bklyn. Coll., 1943; LL.B., Columbia U., 1948; m. Mary Robinson, July 23, 1948; children—Rebecca, Helen, Alfred, Walter, Theodore. Admitted to N.Y. bar, 1948, also U.S. Supreme Ct.; partner firm Winer, Neuburger & Sive, and predecessors, N.Y.C., 1957—; adj. asso. prof. grad. div. N.Y. U. Law Sch., 1963—; lectr., vis. prof. Columbia, Colo., Utah, Wis., Wash. schs. law; counsel Rockland County Charter Commn., 1965-66; exec. dir. com. on natural resources 1967 N.Y. Constl. Conv.; mem. legal adv. com. to Presdl. Council on Environ. Quality; mem. Adminstrv. Conf. U.S., 1970-74; chmn. environ. planning lobby N.Y. State, 1971-74; mem. N.Y. State Energy Research and Devel. Authority, 1976—. Democratic candidate for congress, 1958, N.Y. State Supreme Ct., 1965. Bd. dirs., mem. exec. com. Friends of Earth; bd. dirs., sec. John Muir Inst.; trustee Natural Resources Def. Council, N.Y. Lawyers for Pub. Interest, Inc.; bd. dirs. Scientists Inst. for Public Info.; chmn. Environ. Law Inst. Served with AUS, World War II. Decorated Purple Heart and oak leaf cluster. Mem. Am., N.Y. State bar assns., Assn. Bar City N.Y. (mem. exec. com. 1972-76, chmn. com. environ. law 1968-72), Sierra Club (chmn. Atlantic chpt. 1968-69, nat. dir. 1968-69). Author: (with Reed Rowley) Rowley on Partnerships, 1959. Contbr. articles to law revs. Home: 89 Lark St Pearl River NY 10965 Office: 425 Park Ave New York NY 10022

SIX, ROBERT FORMAN, airline exec.; b. Stockton, Cal., June 25, 1907; s. Clarence Logan and Genevieve (Peters) S.; ed. pub. schs. of Stockton; D.Sc. (hon.), U. Colo.; m. Audrey Meadows, Aug. 1961. Instr. Stockton and Frisco, Stockton, Calif., 1929-33; dist. circulation mgr. San Francisco Chronicle, 1933-35; owner Mouton & Six, 1935-37; pres., dir. Continental Airlines, 1938—; chmn. bd., Continental Air Services, 1966—; dir. United Bank of Denver. Mem. nat. citizens bd. Eisenhower Med. Center; bd. nominations Nat. Aviation Hall of Fame; mem. Airlift Com. Nat. Def. Transp.; mem. Wright Bros. Hall of Fame Com.; Air Force Acad. Found., Nat. Football Found. and Hall of Fame; mem. bd. nominators Internat. Aerospace Hall of Fame; mem. Gen. McArthur Adv. Bd.; vice chmn. UN Day Com., 1973; trustee City of Hope Med. Center. Served as lt. col. USAAF, 1942-44; PTO. Decorated Army Commendation medal. Mem. Air Transport Assn. Am. (dir.), Wings Club of Am., Conquistadores del Cielo, Nat. Aviation Club, Sky Club, Rocky Mountain Food and Wine Soc., Chevaliers du Tastevin, Confrerie de la Chaine des Rotiesseurs, First Flight Soc., Nat. Aeros. Assn., Colo. Aviation History Soc., Los Angeles, Calif. chambers commerce, Am. Soc. Traffic and Transp., Newcomen Soc. Clubs: Burlingame (Cal.) Country; Brown Palace, Denver, Denver Country; Aero (Washington); Garden of Gods (Colorado Springs); Vallejo Gun, Mt. Kenya Safari; Am. Sportsman; Kansas City; Raffles; Racquet (Palm Springs). Home: 350 Trousdale Pl Beverly Hills CA 90210 Office: Continental Airlines Inc Los Angeles Internat Airport Los Angeles CA 90009

SIZEMORE, WILLIAM GENE, naval officer; b. Chauncey, Ill., Aug. 4, 1927; s. Boyd Monroe and Cliffa Milburn (Fielden) S.; B.A., U. Calif., Berkeley; postgrad. U.S. Naval Postgrad. Sch., Monterey, Calif.; m. Hellen Harriett Fish, Aug. 8, 1950; children—William G., Robert C. Commd. ensign U.S. Navy, 1949, advanced through grades to rear adm., 1977; comdg. officer Attack Squadron 93, 1965-66, Attack Carrier Air Wing One, 1969-70, Naval Air Sta., Jacksonville, Fla., 1972-74; head aviation plans br. Office Chief Naval Ops., 1974-75; head aviation officer distbn. control div. Bur. Naval Personnel, 1975-77; dep. dir. for ops. Nat. Mil. Command Center, Orgn. Joint Chiefs Staff, 1977-78; U.S. def. attache to USSR, Moscow, 1979—. Decorated Legion of Merit, D.F.C. with 3 gold stars, Def. Meritorious Service medal, Bronze Star, Air medal with 3 silver stars and 1 gold star, Navy Commendation medal with 2 gold stars, Republic of Vietnam Cross of Gallantry with Bronze Star, Korean Presdl. citation.

SIZER, IRWIN WHITING, univ. dean; b. Bridgewater, Mass., Apr. 4, 1910; s. Ralph Waldo Emerson and Annie Jenkins (Scott) S.; A.B., Brown U., 1931, Sc.D. (hon.), 1971; Ph.D., Rutgers U., 1935; m. Helen Whitcomb, June 23, 1935; 1 dau., Meredith Ann (Mrs. Twomey). Teaching fellow Rutgers U., 1931-35; dir. oyster pest control investgation for N.J., U.S. Bur. Fisheries, 1935; instr. Mass. Inst. Tech., Cambridge, 1935-39, asst. prof., 1939-42, asso. prof. physiology, 1942-56, prof. biochemistry, 1956—, exec. officer biology, 1954-55, acting head biol. dept., 1955-56, head biol. dept. 1956-67, dean Grad. Sch., 1967-75, cons. resource devel., 1975—. Pres. Whitaker Health Sci. Fund, Inc., 1974—; dir. Leader Fed. Savs. & Loan Assn., Lexington, Mass. Cons. in biochemistry to pharm. industry, Ford Found., Latin Am.; dir. Biol. Scis. Curriculum Study. Trustee, bd. govs. Rutgers U.; trustee Boston Biomed. Research Inst.; corp. mem. Lesley Coll.; trustee Mus. of Sci. Honored by Irwin Sizer award for acad. innovation, 1975—; named hon. mem. Mass. Inst. Tech. Class of 1924. Fellow Am. Acad. Arts and Sci., Am. Inst. Chemists; mem. Am. Physiol. Soc., Am. Soc. Zoologists, Am. Soc. Biol. Chemists, Am. Chem. Soc., Sigma Xi (pres. Mass. Inst. Tech. 1958-59), Phi Beta Kappa (hon. mem.), Delta Omega. Contbr. sci. papers, enzymology, biochemistry to profl. jours. Mem. adv. bd. Tech. Rev. Home: 52 Percy Rd Lexington MA 02173 Office: Room 4-234 Mass Inst Tech Cambridge MA 02139

SIZER, PHILLIP SPELMAN, oil field service co. exec.; b. Whittier, Calif., Apr. 11, 1926; s. Frank Milton and Helen Louise (Saylor) S.; B.M.E., So. Meth. U., 1948; m. Evelyn Sue Jones, Aug. 16, 1952; children—Phillip Spelman, Ves Warner. With Otis Engring. Corp., Dallas, 1948—, project engr., 1958-62, chief devel. engr., 1962-70, v.p. research and devel., 1970-73, v.p. engring. and research, 1973-76, sr. v.p., tech. dir., 1977—, dir., 1975—; dir. Sun Contracting. Registered profl. engr., Tex., Okla., Alta. Fellow ASME (Engr. of year N. Tex. sect. 1971, chmn. exec. com. petroleum div. 1974-75); mem. Assn. Well Head Equipment Mfrs. (pres. 1976), Offshore Tech. Conf. (exec. com. 1976-79), Soc. Petroleum Engrs., Nomads, Kappa Sigma, Kappa Mu Epsilon, Tau Beta Pi, Petroleum Engrs. Club Dallas. Patentee in field. Home: 14127 Tanglewood Dr Dallas TX 75234 Office: PO Box 34380 Dallas TX 75234

SIZER, THEODORE RYLAND, headmaster; b. New Haven, June 23, 1932; s. Theodore and Caroline Wheelwright (Foster) S.; B.A., Yale, 1953; M.A.T., Harvard, 1957, Ph.D., 1961; Ped.D. (hon.), Lawrence U., 1969; Litt. D. (hon.), Union Coll., 1972; m. Nancy Ellen Faust, July 2, 1955; children—Theodore II, Judith R., Harold F., Lydia E. Tchr., Roxbury Latin Sch., 1955-56, Melbourne (Australia) Grammar Sch., 1958; asst. prof., dir. masters teaching program Harvard, 1961-64, dean faculty edn., 1964-72; headmaster Phillips Acad., Andover, Mass., 1972—; vis. prof. Bristol (Eng.) U., 1971; dir. Baybank Merrimack Valley N.A. Bd. dirs. Commn. Ednl. Issues. Served with AUS, 1953-55. Guggenheim fellow, 1971. Author: Secondary Schools at the Turn of the Century, 1964; Places for Learning, Places for Joy: Speculations on American School Reform, 1972. Editor: Religion and Public Education, 1967; The Age of the

Academies, 1964; (with Nancy F. Sizer) Moral Education: Five Lectures, 1970. Home: 189 Main St Andover MA 01810

SJOBERG, SIGURD ARNOLD, govt. ofcl.; b. Mpls., Sept. 9, 1919; s. John and Anna (Erickson) S.; B.S., U. Minn., 1942; D.Sc., De Pauw U., 1972; m. Elizabeth Jane Ludwig, Sept. 22, 1944; children—Eric Sigurd, Stephen Lee, Robert John. Dir., gen. mgr. OAO Corp. NASA, 1942—, dep. dir. flight ops., Houston, 1963-69, dir. flight ops., 1969-72, dep. dir. Johnson Space Center, 1972-79. U.S. rep. to Internat. Fedn. Aero., 1968—. Recipient Superior Achievement of commendation, 1970, Disting. Ser. medal, 1971. Fellow Am. Astronautical Soc., Am. Inst. Aeros. and Astronautics; mem. Nat. Acad. Engring. Contbr. papers to tech lit. Home: 203 Pine Shadows Dr Seabrook TX 77586 Office: 1730 Rd1 Suite 204 NASA Houston TX 77058

SJOSTRAND, FRITIOF STIG, educator, biologist; b. Stockholm, Sweden, Nov. 5, 1912; s. Nils Johan and Dagmar (Hansen) S.; M.D., Karolinska Institutet, Stockholm, 1941, Ph.D., 1945; Ph.D. (hon.), U. Siena, 1974; m. Marta Bruhn-Fahraeus, Mar. 24, 1941 (dec. June 1954); 1 son, Rutger; m. 2d, Ebba Gyllenkrok, Mar. 28, 1955; 1 son, Johan; m. 3d, Birgitta Petterson, Jan. 23, 1969; 1 son, Peter. Asst. prof. anatomy Karolinska Institutet, Stockholm, 1945-48, asso. prof., 1949-59, prof. histology, 1960-61; research asso. Mass. Inst. Tech., 1947-48; vis. prof. U. Calif. at Los Angeles, 1959, prof. zoology, 1960—. Decorated North Star Orden (Sweden); recipient Jubilee award Swedish Med. Soc., 1959, Anders Retzius gold medal, 1967; Paul Ehrlich-Ludwig Darmstätter prize, 1971. Fellow Royal Micros. Soc. (hon.; London), Am. Acad. Arts and Scis.; mem. Japan Electron Microscopy Soc. (hon.), Scandinavian Electron Microscopy Soc. (hon.). Author: Über die Eigenfluoreszenz Tierischer Gewebe Mit Besonderer Berucksichtigung der Saugertierniere, 1944; Electron Microscopy of Cells and Tissues, Vol. I, 1967; also numerous articles. Devel. technique for high resolution electron microscopy of cells, fluorescence microspectrography; invented ultramicrotome.

SJOSTROM, GEORGE WILLIAM, newspaper exec.; b. Mpls., Oct. 19, 1924; s. George and Ester (Olson) S.; student U. Nebr., 1943, U. Minn., 1947; B.S. in Advt., U. So. Calif., 1954; m. Joan Kjarstad, June 4, 1949; children—Gregory Stevens, Geoffrey Charles. Advt. dept. Mpls. Star-Tribune, 1947-48; with Los Angeles Examiner, 1948-62, asst. advt. dir., 1959-62; with Los Angeles Herald-Examiner, 1962—, asst. bus. mgr., 1962-65, bus. mgr., 1965-67, gen. mgr., 1967—; v.p., treas. So. Calif. Contractors, Inc.; pres. Calgraphics, 1978—. Served with inf. AUS, 1943-46; ETO. Mem. Beta Gamma Sigma. Club: Jonathan (Los Angeles). Home: 815 Tierra Rejada Rd Simi CA 93065 Office: 1150 S Olive St Suite 2620 Los Angeles CA 90015

SKADDEN, DONALD HARVEY, educator; b. Danville, Ill., Jan. 26, 1925; s. Harvey Frank and Lois Mary (Strawbridge) S.; B.S., U. Ill., 1948, M.S., 1949, Ph.D., 1955; m. Barbara Ann Meade, June 16, 1946 (dec.); children—John D., David H. Grad. asst. U. Ill., Urbana, 1948-52, instr., 1952-55, asst. prof., 1955-58, asso. prof., 1958-61, prof. accountancy, 1961-73, asso. dean Coll. Commerce and Bus. Adminstrn., 1969-71; sr. accountant Haskins & Sells, 1957-58; vis. prof. Mich. State U., Okinawa Project, 1965; Arthur Young prof. accounting U. Mich., Ann Arbor, 1973—, chmn. acctg. faculty, 1976-79, asso. dean for acad. affairs, 1979—; dir. Paton Acctg. Center, 1976-79; dir. Illini Pub. Co. Alderman, City of Urbana, 1961-69, mayor, 1969. Served with AUS, 1943-46; ETO. Decorated Combat Inf. badge. C.P.A., Ill. Mem. Am. Inst. C.P.A.'s (chmn. tax publs. com. 1972-75), Ill. Soc. C.P.A.'s (dir. 1966-68, chair in accountancy 1968-73), Am. Accounting Assn. (v.p. 1975-76, pres. 1979-80), Am. Taxation Assn. (pres. 1977-78), Fin. Acctg. Standards Adv. Commn., Urbana Assn. Commerce and Industry (dir. 1970-73), Beta Gamma Sigma, Phi Kappa Phi, Beta Alpha Psi. Methodist. Club: Masons. Author: Federal Income Tax: Student Workbook, 1965. Editor The Illinois CPA, 1964-66; editorial bd. The Tax Adviser, 1969-74, The Accounting Review, 1973-75. Home: 1230 Naples Ct Ann Arbor MI 48103

SKAGGS, HARVEY TEAGUE, chem. co. exec.; b. Warren County, Ky., Jan. 25, 1921; s. Alva Lee and Elizabeth (Teague) S.; student Cornell U., 1945-46; B.S., Western Ky. State Coll., 1947; m. Bertha Emmalee Johnston, June 2, 1945; children—Harvey Teague, Brady Kenyon, Anna Christina; m. 2d, Carolyn Holt Stadey, 1979. With Amica Burnett Chem. Co., Jacksonville, Fla., 1947—, pres., 1954-60 (merged with F.H. Ross & Co. 1960); v.p., dir. F.H. Ross & Co., 1960— (merged with Ashland Oil Inc. 1968), v.p., gen. mgr. indsl. chems. and solvents div., Columbus, Ohio, 1968—; group v.p. Ashland Chems., 1976-79, sr. v.p., 1979—; pres. Amica Land, Inc., Jacksonville, Fla., 1961—. Co-trustee F.H. Ross & Co. Employees Profit Sharing Trust; trustee Syracuse U. Grad. Sch. Mgmt. and Marketing. Served to lt. AC, USNR, 1942-45. Decorated Air medal with 3 stars. Mem. Am. Chem. Soc., Am. Water Works Assn., Sales and Mktg. Execs.-Internat. (pres. 1964-65), Am. Mgmt. Assn., Alpha Delta Phi, Pi Sigma Epsilon. Republican. Universalist. Home: 4605 Sandringham Dr Columbus OH 43220 Office: PO Box 2219 Columbus OH 43216

SKAGGS, JAMES BONNER, computer systems co. exec.; b. Richland Springs, Tex., July 3, 1937; s. Marion Mallory and Elizabeth (Hampton) S.; B.S.M.E., U. Wash., 1959; m. Betty Carita Thomas, Aug. 3, 1962; children—Mark Douglas, David Michael, Catherine Diane. Engr., program control supr. Boeing Co., Seattle, 1959-64; dir. Apollo program control NASA, Washington, 1964-70; dir. mgmt. and ops. Gen. Dynamics, N.Y.C., 1970-71; v.p. System Devel. Corp., Santa Monica, Calif., 1971-77, exec. v.p., 1977—. Office: 2500 Colorado Ave Santa Monica CA 90406

SKALLER, LAURENCE DONALD, constrn. co. exec.; b. Bronx, N.Y., July 26, 1932; s. Joseph and Ethel (Braunstein) S.; B.S., Lehigh U., 1954; postgrad. Inst. Design and Constrn., 1959; m. Rona Joy Taub, Aug. 24, 1957; children—Jill Lisa, David Matthew, Julie Beth. With Central Foundry Div., Gen. Motors Corp., 1954-55; with Sovereign Constrn. Co., Ltd., Paramus, N.J., 1957—, pres., 1972-77, pres. T.G.I., East Coast Constrn. Corp., Paramus, 1977—, exec. v.p. Titan Group, Inc., 1979—. Bd. dirs. Jewish Community Center on the Palisades, 1969—, v.p., 1975—; bd. dirs. Temple Emanuel, 1974—; mem. exec. bd., head Explorer Post 656 Bergen council Boy Scouts Am., 1975-77. Served with inf. AUS, 1955-57. Mem. Lehigh U. Asa Packer Soc. Club: Edgewood Country (bd. govs. 1979—). Home: Lambs Ln Cresskill NJ 07626 Office: Titan Group Inc East 81 State Hwy 4 Paramus NJ 07652

SKALLERUP, WALTER THORWALD, JR., lawyer; b. Chgo., Feb. 17, 1921; s. Walter Thorwald and Ruth (White) S.; B.A., Swarthmore Coll., 1942; LL.B., Yale, 1947; m. Nancy McGhee Baxter, Dec. 16, 1950; children—Paula Skallerup Osborn, Walter Thorwald III, Andrew (dec.), Nancy. Admitted to D.C. bar, 1948, atty. AEC, 1947-52; partner firm Volpe, Boskey & Skallerup, Washington, 1953-61; dep. asst. sec. def. for security policy, 1962-67; partner firm Cox, Langford & Brown, Washington, 1968-71; pvt. practice law, 1973—. Spl. cons. to undersec. state, 1968-69; legal cons. Joint Congressional Com. on Atomic Energy, 1973-74; mem. panel U.S. AEC Atomic Safety and Licensing Bd., 1970-71. Treas. Citizens for Jackson campaign, 1971-72; treas., counsel Jackson for Pres. Com., 1974-76; bd. mgrs. Swarthmore (Pa.) Coll., 1977—. Served with USNR, 1943-45. Home: 1155 Crest Ln McLean VA 22101 Office: 1001 Connecticut Ave NW Washington DC 20036

SKALNIK, JOHN GORDON, elec. engr., educator; b. Medford, Okla., May 30, 1923; s. John Robert and Ella Catherine (Semrad) S.; B.S. in Elec. Engring., Okla. State U., 1944; M.E., Yale, 1947; Ph.D., 1955; m. Dianne Virginia Fleck, May 30, 1947; children—John Robert, David Gordon. Asst. prof. Yale, 1944-55, asso. prof., 1955-65; prof. elec. engring. U. Calif. at Santa Barbara, 1965—, chmn. elec. engring., 1968-70, dean Coll. Engring., 1970-76. Served with USNR, 1944. Mem. IEEE, Electrochem. Soc., Am. Soc. Engring. Edn., Sigma Xi. Author: Microwave Theory and Techniques, 1953; Microwave Principles, 1957; Theory and Applications of Active Devices, 1966. Home: 567 Ronda Dr Santa Barbara CA 93111

SKANTZE, LAWRENCE ALBERT, air force officer; b. Bronx, N.Y., June 24, 1928; s. Albert Julius and Nina (Washington) S.; B.S., U.S. Naval Acad., 1952; M.S., Air Force Inst. Tech., 1959; m. Patricia A. Bowers, Aug. 22, 1953; children—Lawrence Michael, Patricia Anne, Vanessa Maria. Served with U.S. Navy, 1946-52; commd. 2d lt. USAF, 1952, advanced through grades to lt. gen., 1979; bomber pilot, Korea, 1954; various assignments in engring., 1955-69; dir. personnel Air Force System Command, 1969-71; program mgr. Short Range Attack Missile Program, 1971-73, Airborne Waring and Control System, 1973-77; dep. chief staff for system devel. Hdqrs. Air Force Systems Command, Andrews AFB, Md., 1977-79; comdr. Aero. Systems Div., Wright-Patterson AFB, Ohio, 1979—; author, lectr. air force mgmt. techniques. Decorated D.S.M., Legion of Merit, Meritorious Service medal, Commendation medal. Mem. Air Force Assn. (Outstanding Program Mgr. award 1973; Theodore Von Karman award 1975), Am. Nuclear Soc. Roman Catholic. Home: 523 Johnson Dr Wright-Patterson AFB OH 45433 Office: Aero Systems Div Wright-Patterson AFB OH 45433

SKARDON, JAMES ALTICK, pub. relations cons.; b. Chgo., May 18, 1922; s. Kenneth Bruner and Mary (Altick) S.; B.A., Yale, 1944; M.S., Columbia, 1948; m. Miriam Steen, Jan. 7, 1950; children—Mary Hope, James Todd. Asst. editorial promotion mgr. King Features Syndicate, 1948-52; article editor Today's Woman mag., 1952-54; editor Cavalier mag., 1954; mng. editor Cosmopolitan mag., 1954-56; sr. editor Coronet Mag., 1956-59; articles editor Good Housekeeping Mag., 1959-60; exec. editor Coronet mag., N.Y.C., 1961; research dir. CBS, 1962-63, editorial dir., 1963-64; pres. James A. Skardon Asso., Inc., corporate pub. relations cons., N.Y.C., 1964—. Served as 1st lt. F.A., AUS, 1943-46. Contbr. articles to popular mags., U.S. and Can. Home: 106 Spectacle Ln Wilton CT 06897 Office: 295 Madison Ave New York NY 10017

SKEELS, JACK WILLIAM, economist, educator; b. Wausau, Wis., Nov. 3, 1929; s. Lawrence John and Gertrude (Preuss) S.; B.A., U. Wis., 1951, Ph.D., 1957; m. Joyce Vivian Goldy, Jan. 29, 1956 (div. Mar. 1977); children—Jack Allen, Jennifer Joy. Asst. prof. econs. Mich. State U., 1957-59; vis. asst. prof. U. Mich., summer 1959, fall 1961; asst. prof. Inst. Labor and Indsl. Relations, Wayne State U. and U. Mich.-Wayne State U., 1959-62; asso. prof. No. Ill. U., DeKalb, 1963-65, prof. econs., 1965—, chmn. dept., 1965-69, 77—, asso. dean Coll. Liberal Arts, 1969, asso. provost, 1975-76. Cons. UN, 1974—. Chmn. Gov. Mich. Task Force on Unemployment Compensation Panel, 1959. Served with USNR, 1951-53. Mem. Assn. Comparative Econs. (sec.-treas. 1964-71), Assn. Comparative Econ. Studies (exec. sec. 1971-73), Am. Econ. Assn., Midwest Econs. Assn. (v.p. 1975-76), AAUP, Indsl. Relations Research Assn., Phi Beta Kappa, Omicron Delta Epsilon. Contbr. articles to profl. jours. Home: 608 Russell Rd DeKalb IL 60115

SKEGGS, LEONARD TUCKER, JR., educator, biochemist; b. Fremont, O., June 9, 1918; s. Leonard Tucker and Frances (Wolfe) S.; A.B. in Chemistry, Youngstown Coll., 1940; M.S. in Biochemistry, Western Res. U., 1942, Ph.D. in Biochemistry, 1948; D.Sc. (hon.), Youngstown U., 1960; m. Jean Hossel, Dec. 13, 1941; children—Laura Skeggs Tradowsky, David, Josephine Skeggs Dick. Chief biochemistry sect., co-dir. hypertension research lab. VA Hosp., Cleve., 1947-70, dir. lab., 1970—; research fellow clin. biochemistry, dept. biochemistry Western Res. U., Cleve., 1948-49, instr. biochemistry, dept. biochemistry, 1950-51, sr. instr. biochemistry dept. pathology, 1951-52, asst. prof. biochemistry dept. pathology, 1952-59, asso. prof. biochemistry dept. pathology, 1959-69, prof. biochemistry dept. biochemistry, 1969—; dir. Whitehead Inst. for Med. Research, 1974—; med. investigator hypertension VA, 1976—. Pres., Lake County YMCA, 1978—; trustee Cleve. Mus. Natural History, 1975—. Served to lt. (j.g.) USNR, 1943-46; ETO, PTO. Recipient Arthur S. Fleming award U.S. Jr. C. of C., 1957, Van Slyke medal N.Y met. sect. Am. Assn. Clin. Chemists, 1963, Middleton award VA, 1968; Career Service award Greater Cleve. Growth Assn., 1968, Stouffer award Council High Blood Pressure of Am. Heart Assn., 1968, Bendetti-Pichler award, 1972, John Scott award, 1972; Cleve. award Internat. Soc. for Artificial Organs, 1978. Fellow N.Y. Acad. Scis., Am. Assn. Clin. Chemists (Ames award 1966); mem. Am. Heart Assn. (council high blood pressure, council basic sci.), Am. Soc. Biol. Chemists, Am. Chem. Soc. (award clin. instrumentation 1966), Am. Bd. Clin. Chemists, Sigma Xi. Club: Kirtland. Bd. editors Clin. Chemistry, 1967-71, Circulation Research, 1977—; contbr. numerous articles to publs. Patentee in field; research in hypertension, automatic chem. analysis, multiple automatic analysis. Home: 10212 Blair Ln Kirtland OH 44094

SKEHAN, JAMES WILLIAM, educator; b. Houlton, Maine, Apr. 25, 1923; s. James William and Mary Effie (Coffey) S.; A.B. in Philosophy, Boston Coll., 1946, A.M., 1947; Ph. Licentiate in Philosophy, Weston Coll., 1947, S.T.B., 1954, S.T.L., 1955; A.M. in Geology, Harvard, 1951, Ph.D., 1953. Joined Soc. of Jesus, 1940, ordained priest Roman Catholic Ch., 1954; asst. prof. geology Boston Coll., 1956-61, founder, chmn. dept. geology, 1958-68, asso. prof. geology dept. geology and grad. dept. geophysics, 1962-68, prof., 1968—, chmn. dept. geology and geophysics, 1968-70, asst. to dir. Weston Obs., 1956-68, asso. dir., 1968-72, dir. Environ. Center, 1970-72, acting dean Coll. Arts and Scis., 1972-73, dir. Weston Obs., 1974—, dir. Energy Research Center, 1974—; Prin. investigator, dir. Narragansett Basin Coal Exploration Project, 1976—; mem. Northeast Energy Congress. Chmn. bd. overseers St. Joseph Coll., North Windham, Mass., 1969-76. Fellow Geol. Soc. Am. (chmn. Northeast sect. 1970-71, chmn. engring. geology div. 1976), Geol. Soc. London; mem. Assn. Profl. Geol. Scientists, Boston Geol. Soc. (pres. 1958-59), Nat. Assn. Geology Tchrs. (pres. 1971-72, Neil Miner award for contbns. to interest in earth scis. 1976), AAAS, Assn. Geol. Study Deeper Zones of Earths Crust, Am. Geol. Inst. (sec.-treas. 1973), Assn. Engring. Geologists (chmn. New Eng. sect. 1974-75), Sigma Xi. Author: The Green Mountain Anitclinorium in the Vicinity of Wilmington and Woodford, Vermont, 1961; co-author: Investigating The Earth-Text and Teachers Guide, 2d edit., 1973; The Geology of Newton, 1973; Puddingstone, Drumlins and Ancient Volcanoes, A Geologic Field Guide along Historic Trails of Boston, 1975; The Planet we Live On-An Illustrated Encyclopedia of the Earth Sciences, 1976. Contbr. numerous articles to profl. jours. Editor: (with R.L. Carovillano) Science and the Future of Man, 1971; (with D.P. Murray) The Coal-Bearing Narragansett Basin of Massachusetts and Rhode Island Vol. 1: Geology, 1978. Research on metamorphic coal fields, related regional geology, plate tectonics models. Address: Weston Obs Boston Coll Concord Rd Weston MA 02193

SKEHAN, PATRICK WILLIAM, clergyman, educator; b. N.Y.C., Sept. 30, 1909; s. William F. and Johanna A. (Dwyer) S.; A.B., Fordham U., 1929; student theology St. Joseph's Sem., Dunwoodie, N.Y., 1929-33; S.T.D., Cath. U. Am., 1938; LL.D., Boston Coll., 1957, Manhattan Coll., 1962. Ordained priest Roman Catholic Ch., 1933, papal chamberlain, 1954, domestic prelate, 1958; instr. Cath. U. Am., Washington, 1938-43, asst. prof., 1943-46, asso. prof., 1946-51, prof. Semitic langs., 1951—, chmn. dept. Semitic and Egyptian langs. and lits., 1951-54, 56-65, 67-71; vis. prof. Johns Hopkins, 1947-58, Pontifical Bibl. Inst., Rome, Italy, 1969-70; ann. prof. Am. Sch. Oriental Research, Jerusalem, 1954-55, dir., 1955-56, asso. trustee, 1957-58, 60-64, cons. pontifical Bibl. com., 1965-71. Recipient Pro ecclesia et pontifice medal, 1970. Mem. Cath. Bibl. Assn. (pres. 1946-47, exec. bd. 1959-65, 73-75, treas. 1978—), Am. Oriental Soc., Phi Beta Kappa. Author: Studies in Israelite Poetry and Wisdom, 1971. Vice chmn. editorial bd. New American Bible, 1947-70; publ. editor Cath. Bibl. Quar., 1946-49, asso. editor, 1966-73, 76—. Contbr. articles to tech. lit. Research in Dead Sea Scrolls, 1954—. Address: Cath U Am Washington DC 20064

SKELDON, PHILIP CASS, zool. park adminstr.; b. Toledo, Apr. 12, 1922; s. Frank L. and Helen M. (Halpin) S.; student DeSales Coll., Toledo, 1940-42; D.Pub. Service, U. Toledo, 1976; m. Bernadine G. Wambold, Oct. 12, 1946; children—Thomas, Claudia, Martin, Constance, Barry, Stephen, Kim, Peter, Jeffery, Monica, Philip. Zoo keeper Toledo Zoo, 1950-51, bus. mgr., 1952, exec. dir., 1953—. Served with USMCR, 1942-46. Decorated Purple Heart. Mem. Am. Assn. Zool. Parks and Aquariums (pres. 1958-59), Internat. Union Dirs. of Zool. Gardens. Home: 2355 Townley St Toledo OH 43614 Office: 2700 Broadway Toledo OH 43609

SKELL, PHILIP S., chemist; b. N.Y.C., Dec. 30, 1918; s. Jacob M. and Mollie (Lipfriend) S.; B.S., Coll. City N.Y., 1938; M.S., Columbia U., 1940; Ph.D., Duke U., 1942; LL.D., Lewis Coll., Ill., 1966; m. Margaret E. Fosse, Dec. 25, 1948; children—Deborah J., Victoria A., Jeffrey M., Aviva M. Chemist, Dept. Agr., Peoria, Ill., 1942-43; mem. faculty U. Portland (Oreg.), 1947-52; mem. faculty Pa. State U., 1952—, prof. chemistry, since 1959, Evan Pugh prof. chemistry, 1974—; cons. in field; vis. prof. univs. and colls. Pres. Unitarian Fellowship, State College, Pa., 1960. Sr. fellow NSF, 1961, Guggenheim Found., 1961, Alexander von Humboldt Found., 1975. Fellow N.Y. Acads. Sci.; mem. Nat. Acad. Sci., Am. Chem. Soc., Chem. Soc. London. Contbr. articles to research jours. Home: 919 W Fairmount Ave State College PA 16801 Office: 152 Davey Lab Pa State U University Park PA 16802

SKELLY, THOMAS FRANCIS, mfg. co. exec.; b. Boston, Jan. 19, 1934; s. Michael Gerard and Katherine Agnes (Kelly) S.; B.S., Northeastern U., 1956; M.B.A., Babson Coll., 1966; m. Patricia A. Limerick, Sept. 6, 1958; children—Thomas Francis, John M., Peter G., Matthew M. Mgr., Peat, Marwick, Mitchell & Co., C.P.A.'s, Boston, 1957-67; with Gillette Co., Boston, 1967—, controller, 1973—, v.p., 1979—. Served to capt. AUS, 1957-59. Home: 54 Magnolia Dr Westwood MA 02090 Office: Prudential Tower Bldg Boston MA 02199

SKELTON, ALAN GORDON, librarian; b. Fayetteville, Ark., Aug. 3, 1912; s. James Lee and Josephine (Carter) S.; B.L.S., U. Okla., 1933, B.A. in Polit. Sci., 1934; m. Martha Hope Butcher, Jan. 26, 1940; children—Ann Hope Skelton Fentress, Gordon William. Librarian pub. sch., Alice, Tex., 1934-36, Robstown, Tex., 1936-38; librarian geol. library U. Okla., Norman, 1938-44; librarian, research asst. Mid-Continent Oil and Gas Assn., Tulsa, 1944-47; head Research Center Library, U.S. Army Engrs. Waterways Expt. Sta., Vicksburg, Miss., 1947-71, chmn. expt. sta. arboretum bd., 1978—, chief Tech. Info. Center, 1971—, fgn. intelligence officer, 1972—; rep. Fed. Lab. Consortium Tech. Transfer, 1978—. Chmn., Vicksburg Municipal Rose Garden, 1957—, Vicksburg City Beautification Commn., 1963-65; mem. exec. bd. Vicksburg-Warren Beautiful, Inc., 1969-70; mem. adv. com. for title programs Miss. Library Commn., 1969—, pres. State Library Adv. Council, 1978—; dep. exec. dir. Miss. Nat. Library Week, 1971, exec. dir., 1972, steering com., 1978; parliamentarian Gov.'s Conf. on Library and Info. Services, 1979. Recipient award of merit Vicksburg City Beautification Commn., 1965; Quality award Waterways Expt. Sta., 1971, Outstanding Service award, 1974, 75, 76, 77, 78. Mem. Miss. Library Assn. (pres. 1961, chmn. constn. and by-laws com. 1966, long range planning com., Miss. libraries 1972—, elections com. 1978, parliamentarian 1975, 76, 77, 78, 79, merit award 1972, outstanding achievement award 1978), Spl. Libraries Assn. (pres. La. chpt. 1959-60, editor La. chpt. Bull. 1958-59, mem. nat. adv. council 1959-60), Am. Soc. Info. Sci., Friends of Miss. Libraries, Miss. Ornithol. Soc., Am. Rose Soc., Washington County (Ark.), Carroll County (Ark.) hist. socs., N.W. Ark., Ark. geneal. socs., Mid-Continent Oil and Gas Assn. (sec. nomenclature com. 1944-47), Phi Beta Kappa, Phi Eta Sigma, Phi Delta Kappa. Democrat. Presbyterian. Contbr. articles to profl. jours. Home: 103 Stonewall Rd Vicksburg MS 39180 Office: P O Box 631 Vicksburg MS 39180

SKELTON, BYRON GEORGE, judge; b. Florence, Tex., Sept. 1, 1905; s. Clarence Edgar and Avis (Bowmer) S.; student Baylor U., 1923-24; A.B., U. Tex., 1927, M.A., 1928, LL.B., 1931; m. Ruth Alice Thomas, Nov. 28, 1931; children—Sue, Sandra. Admitted to Tex. bar, 1931, Circuit Ct. Appeals, 1937, U.S. Supreme Ct. bar, 1946, FCC, 1950, Tax Ct. U.S., 1952, U.S. Treasury Dept., 1952, ICC, 1953; practice of law, Temple, Tex., 1931-66; partner Saulsbury & Skelton, 1934-42, Saulsbury, Skelton, Everton, Bowmer & Courtney, 1944-55, Skelton, Bowmer & Courtney, 1955-66; judge U.S. Ct. Claims, Washington, 1966-77, sr. fed. judge, 1977—; county atty. Bell County, Tex., 1934-38; spl. asst. U.S. ambassador to Argentina, 1942-44; city atty., Temple, 1944-60. Dir. First Nat. Bank of Temple. Democratic nat. committeeman, 1956-64; del. Dem. Nat. Cov., 1948, 56, 60, 64, Tex. Dem. Conv., 1946, 48, 50, 52, 54, 56, 58, 60, 62, 64, vice chmn., 1948, 58; chmn. Dem. Adv. Council of Tex., 1955-57. Former pres. Temple YMCA; pres. Temple Indsl. Found., 1966. Appointed Ky. Col. and Adm. in Tex. Navy, 1959. Mem. State Bar Tex., Am., Bell-Lampasas and Mills Counties (past pres.) bar assns., Am. Law Inst., Am. Judicature Soc., Temple C. of C. (past pres., dir.), Ex-Students' Assn. U. Tex. (past pres., mem. exec. council), Phi Beta Kappa, Pi Sigma Alpha, Sigma Delta Pi, Delta Theta Phi (hon.). Democrat. Methodist. Mason (past worshipful master; Shriner), Kiwanian (past pres.). Home: Salado TX 76571 also 1101 Dakota Dr Temple TX 76501 Office: 305 WR Poage Fed Bldg Temple TX 76501

SKELTON, ISAAC NEWTON, IV, Congressman; b. Lexington, Mo., Dec. 20, 1931; s. Isaac Newton and Carolyn (Boone) S.; A.B., U. Mo., 1953, LL.B., 1956; m. Susan B. Anding, July 22, 1961; children—Ike, Jim, Page. Admitted to Mo. bar, 1956; practiced in Lexington; pros. atty. Lafayette County (Mo.), 1957-60; spl. asst. atty. gen. State of Mo., 1962-65; mem. Mo. Senate from 28th dist., 1971-77; mem. 95th-96th Congresses from 4th Mo. Dist. Chmn., Lafayette County Tom Eagleton for Senator campaign, 1968; active Cub Scouts. Mem. Phi Beta Kappa, Sigma Chi. Democrat. Mem.

Christian Ch. Clubs: Masons, Shriners, Elks. Home: 712 Highland St Lexington MO 64067

SKELTON, JOHN FREDERICK, JR., utility co. exec.; b. Frost, Tex., Oct. 4, 1914; s. John Frederick and Estelle (Van Hook) S.; corr. student LaSalle U.; student So. Meth. U., Tex. A. and M. U.; m. Doris Dye (McKamy) Oct. 19, 1940; children—John Frederick III, Joan M., Michael T., Stephen T. With Corsicana Cotton Mills (Tex.), 1933-35, Wolf Brand Products, Corsicana, 1936; with Tex. Power & Light Co., Dallas, 1937—, financial v.p., sec., 1964-72, pres., 1972-77, chmn. bd., 1977—, chief exec. officer, 1972-78. Past chmn. fund drives for A.R.C., Community Chest; past dist. chmn. Boy Scouts Am.; past bd. dirs. local A.R.C., Salvation Army. Served with USAAF, 1942-45. Decorated Air medal with oak leaf cluster. Mem. Edison Electric Inst. (dir.), Am. Radio Relay League (past bd. dirs.), Amateur Radio Club of Dallas. Methodist (ofcl. bd.). Clubs: City, Dallas Country. Contbr. articles to publs. Home: 3601 Euclid Ave Dallas TX 75205 Office: 1511 Bryan St Dallas TX 75222

SKELTON, (RICHARD) RED, comedian; b. Vincennes, Ind., July 18, 1913; s. Joseph and Ida Mae Skelton; grad. high sch., 1938; student coll. extension courses; hon. degrees, Vincennes U., Emerson Coll., U. Ind.; m. Edna Marie Stillwell, June 1932 (div. 1940); m. 2d, Georgia Maurine Davis, Mar. 1945 (dec.); children—Valentina Maris Alonso, Richard Freeman (dec.); m. 3d, Lothian Toland, Mar. 1973. Began acting career at age of 10 yrs.; successively with a tent show, a ministrel show, on a show boat, a clown in Hagenbeck & Wallace Circus, on burlesque circuit in Middle West, Walkathon contests (as master of ceremonies); appeared at Loew's Montreal Theatre in vaudeville (developed the doughnut drinking pantomime), 1936; made Broadway debut, June 1937; radio debut on Rudy Vallee program, Aug. 1937; first motion picture appearance in Having a Wonderful Time, 1938; has since appeared in Flight Command, The People vs Dr. Kildare, 1941, Whistling in the Dark, Whistling in Dixie, 1942, Whistling in Brooklyn, Lady Be Good, 1943, Maisie Gets Her Man, Panama Hattie, Ship Ahoy, I Dood It, 1943, DuBarry Was A Lady, Thousands Cheer, Bathing Beauty, 1944, The Show Off, Merton of the Movies, The Fuller Brush Man, A Southern Yankee, Neptune's Daughter, 1948, The Yellow Cab Man, 1949, Three Little Words, Watch the Birdie, Excuse My Dust, 1950, Texas Carnival, Lovely to Look At, 1951, The Clown, 1952, Public Pigeon Number One, 1957, Those Magnificent Men in Their Flying Machines, 1966; had first own radio program, 1937, Red Skelton's Scrapbook of Satire, 1942; The Red Skelton Show on TV, 1951-71; nightclub performer, also writer and composer for radio, TV, movies; entertained service men World War II and Korea as pvt. in F.A. Bd. dirs. Red Skelton Needy Children's Fund. Recipient AMVETS Silver Helmet Americanism award, 1969; Freedoms Found. award, 1970; Nat. Comdrs. award Am. Legion, 1970; winner three Emmy awards; Golden Globe award, 1978. Mem. ASCAP, Screen Actors Guild, AFTRA. Mason (33 deg.). Read his pledge before Joint Session of Congress. Office: care Van Bernard Prodns 37-715 Thompson Rd Rancho Mirage CA 92270*

SKELTON, ROBERT BEATTIE, educator; b. Auburn, Mich., Apr. 23, 1913; s. Glen Beattie and Irene (Richardson) S.; student Bay City (Mich.) Jr. Coll., 1934-35; A.B., Eastern Mich. U., 1937; M.A. (univ. scholar 1937-38), U. Mich., 1938, Ph.D. (Horace H. Rackham spl. fellow 1949-50, Am. Council Learned Socs. grantee Linguistics Inst. 1950), 1950; postgrad. (fellow) U. Brazil, 1942-43; postgrad. (Chilean Govt. fellow) U. Chile, 1943; postgrad. U. Salamanca, U. Paris, 1972, U. Perugia, 1975; m. Mary Carmack, June 2, 1940; children—Susan, Robert Thomas, Rebecca and Melissa (twins). Mem. faculty Auburn (Ala.) U., 1939-76, prof., 1954-76, research prof. comparative linguistics, 1967-76, head dept. fgn. langs., 1954-67; vis. scholar Linguistics Inst., 1967. Served from ensign to lt., USNR, 1943-46. Mem. Nat. Geog. Soc., Modern Lang. Assn., Am. Assn. Tchrs. French, Am. Assn. Tchrs. German, Am. Assn. Tchrs. Spanish and Portuguese, Linguistic Soc. Am., Inst. Internat. Edn. (asso.), Nat. Assn. Standard Med. Vocabulary, Am. Mus. Natural History (asso.), Acad. Tamil Culture (asso.). Contbr. articles, monographs to profl. jours. Home: 426 Scott St Auburn AL 36830

SKENDZIEL, FLOYD RAYMOND, union ofcl.; b. Superior, Wis., Jan. 14, 1922; s. Walter Anthony and Pearl (Matushak) S.; student Virginia (Minn.) Jr. Coll., U. Minn.; m. Elaine Francis Telega, Sept. 10, 1949; 1 dau., Mary-Jo. Motive power supr. Duluth, Winnipeg and Pacific R.R., Duluth, Minn.; successively field rep. Am. Railway Suprs. Assn., Chgo., v.p., bd. dirs., now treas., bd. dirs. Served with USAF. Decorated Bronze star. Clubs: Am. Legion, K.C., Friars. Home: 919 E Pratt Dr Palatine IL 60067 Office: 4250 W Montrose Ave Chicago IL 60641

SKERNICK, ABRAHAM, musician; b. N.Y.C., June 4, 1923. Asst. first violist St. Louis Symphony, 1946-48; first viola Balt. Symphony, 1948-49, Cleve. Orch., 1949-76; mem. faculty Peabody Conservatory, 1948-49, Cleve. Inst. Music, 1963-76, Blossom Music Sch., 1968-76; prof. music Ind. U., 1976—; first violist Aspen Music Festival, Casals Festival, Chautauqua Music Festival, Blossom Music Festival, Cleve. Orch. String Quartet, Berkshire Quartet. Mem. Pi Kappa Lambda. Home: 126 Hampton Ct Bloomington IN 47401 Office: Dept Music Ind U Bloomington IN 47401

SKERRITT, THOMAS ROY, actor; b. Detroit, Aug. 25, 1933; s. Roy Phileman and Helen Jane (Maybee) S.; B.A., UCLA, 1962; m. Susan Oran, Sept. 16, 1975; children—Andrew, Erin, Matthew, Collin. Starred in movies: MASH, 1970, Fuzz, 1971, Turning Point, 1978 (Nat. Bd. Rev. Best Supporting Actor 1978), Ice Castles, 1979, Alien, 1979; Silence of the North; appeared in Italian movies, 1972-76. Served with USAF, 1953-57. Office: care Mishkin Agy Inc 9255 Sunset Blvd Los Angeles CA 90069

SKIBELL, CARL ALBERT, lawyer; b. N.Y.C., Apr. 11, 1932; s. Sam and Lillian (Gallup) S.; B.B.A., U. Tex., 1953; J.D., So. Meth. U., 1958; m. Carol Klatsky, Dec. 29, 1957; children—Susan, Harris, Caren. Admitted to Tex. bar, 1957, since practiced in Dallas; partner firm Skibell & Blicker, 1960-65, firm Skibell, Russ & Adams, Dallas, 1965-75; individual practice law, 1975—; dir. Summit Sales Co. Municipal judge, Farmers Branch, Tex., 1963—. Bd. dirs., founder Goals Inc., 1960-63. Served as 1st lt. AUS, 1953-55; Korea. Mem. Phi Alpha Delta, Sigma Alpha Mu. Home: 13823 Tanglewood Dr Dallas TX 75234 Office: 2700 Mercantile Bank Bldg Dallas TX 75201

SKIBINE, GEORGE BORIS, artistic dir. ballet; b. Yasnaya, Polyana, Russia, Jan. 17, 1920; s. Boris Nicolayevitch and Vera (Hobe) S.; ed. Lycee Albert de Mun, Nogent, France, Paris (France) Opera Sch.; pvt. study ballet; m. Marjorie Tall Chief, Dec. 27, 1947; children—Alexandre, George T. Soloist Ballet de Monte Carlo, 1939; first dancer Ballet Theatre, 1940; mem. Grand Ballet du Marquis de Cuevas, 1947; tour U.S. with Ruth Page Co., 1956; ballet master Paris Opera, 1956-62, guest artist, choreographer, 1962-64; choreographer, artistic dir. Harkness Ballet, N.Y.C., 1964-69; artistic dir. Dallas Civic Ballet, 1969—; vis. prof. North Tex. State U., 1970—; free-lance choreographer, works performed Paris Opera, La Scala, Milan, Italy, Royal Ballet London (Eng.), Teatro Colon, Buenos Aires, Argentina, Teatro Municipal, Rio de Janeiro, Brazil. Adviser dance Tex. Commn. Arts and Humanities. Served with U.S. Army, 1942-46. Decorated Officier des Arts et Lettres (France), chevalier du Merit Culturel; Niham Iftikar (Tunisia); recipient Prix de la Critique Lyrique (France), 1956-58, Italia prize, 1962, Prix Diaguilef Inst. Paris, 1964. Home: 7260 Kenny Ln Dallas TX 75230 Office: 3601 Rawlins Dallas TX 75219

SKIBINE, MARJORIE LOUISE TALLCHIEF, ballerina; b. Denver; d. Alexander and Ruth (Porter) Tallchief; ballet tng. with Bronislava Nijinska, David Lichine. Became soloist Am. Ballet Theater while in teens; bacame ballerina Grand Ballet du Marquis de Cuevas at age 19; 1st American to become premiere danseuse etoile Paris Opera, 1st American to star at Bolshoi Theater, Moscow; now artistic dir. Dallas Civic Ballet Soc. Decorated chevalier du Nisham Iftikar for artistic achievement (Tunisia); recipient Outstanding Indian of Yr. award Council Am. Indians, 1977. Home: 7260 Kenny Ln Dallas TX 75230

SKIDMORE, HOWARD FRANKLYN, pub. relations exec.; b. Bklyn., Sept. 24, 1917; s. William F. and Mae (White) S.; student Coll. City N.Y., 1938-39; m. Zaza Irina O'Hara, Dec. 4, 1943; children—Joel Michael, Susan Irina. Editorial staff N.Y. Herald Tribune, 1937-42, 45-47; asst. to dir. pub. relations C. & O. Ry., N.Y.C., 1948, exec. asst. to v.p. passenger traffic, pub. relations, advt., Cleve., 1949-53, dir. pub. relations, 1954-59, dir. pub. relations and passenger traffic, 1959-63, v.p. C. & O. Ry., also B. & O. Ry., 1963-77, Western Md. Ry., 1973-77, Chessie System, Inc., 1974-77; pres. Howard Skidmore Co., Inc., Cleve., 1977—. Trustee Cleve. Music Sch. Settlement, 1958—. Served with USNR, 1942-45. Mem. Soc. Silurians, R.R. Pub. Relations Assn. (pres. 1958), Pub. Relations Soc. Am., Sigma Delta Chi. Clubs: Nat. Press (Washington); Press, Advertising, Canterbury Golf (Cleve.). Home: 3157 Belvoir Blvd Shaker Heights OH 44122 Office: Two Commerce Park Sq 23200 Chagrin Blvd Cleveland OH 44122

SKIDMORE, REX AUSTIN, educator; b. Salt Lake City, Dec. 31, 1914; s. Charles H. and Louise (Wangsgaard) S.; A.B., U. Utah, 1938, A.M., 1939; Ph.D., U. Pa., 1941; m. Knell Spencer Aug. 31, 1939; children—Lee Spencer, Larry Rex. Instr. sociology U. Pa., 1940-41, Utah State Agrl. Coll., Logan, 1941-42; spl. agt. FBI, Miami, Fla., San Francisco, San Antonio, 1943-45; dir. bur. student counsel U. Utah, 1947-57, asso. prof., 1947-50, prof., 1950—, dean Grad. Sch. Social Work, 1956-75. Chmn. Western Mental Health Council, Western Interstate Commn. Higher Edn., 1964-65; mem. Nat. Adv. Council Nat. Manpower and Tng. Recipient distinguished service awards Community Service Council, Nat. Assn. Social Work, 1975, Utah Conf. on Human Services, 1976. Mem. Council on Social Work Edn. (dir. 1968-71), Phi Kappa Phi, Pi Kappa Alpha, Pi Gamma Mu. Mem. Ch. of Jesus Christ Latter-Day Saints. Author: Mormon Recreation: Theory and Practice, 1941; Building Your Marriage, 1951, 3d edit., 1964; Marriage Consulting, 1956; Introduction to Social Work, 1964, rev. edit., 1976; Introduction to Mental Health, 1979; contbr. articles to sociol. jours. Home: 1444 S 20th E Salt Lake City UT 84108. *A significant idea for successful living is knowing that: Loving is the central ingredient in human relationships; and the essence of loving is giving, not getting.*

SKIDMORE, THOMAS ELLIOTT, educator; b. Troy, Ohio, July 22, 1932; s. Ernest Anton and Josephine (Hale) S.; B.A., Denison U., 1954, Litt.D., 1975; B.A. (Fulbright fellow), Oxford (Eng.) U., 1956; Ph.D., Harvard, 1961; m. Felicity Margaret Hall, Aug. 31, 1957; children—David, James, Robert. Instr. history Harvard, 1960-61, research fellow in Latin Am. studies, 1961-64, asst. prof. history, 1964-66; asst. prof. dept. history U. Wis., Madison, 1966-67, asso. prof., 1967-68, prof., 1968—; vis. prof. Oxford U., 1972; lectr. Fgn. Service Inst., State Dept. Social Sci. Research Council fellow, 1966-67; Woodrow Wilson Internat. Center for Scholars fellow, 1971-72; Guggenheim fellow, 1974-75; Fulbright Faculty Research Abroad grantee, 1979. Mem. Am. Hist. Assn., A.A.U.P., Latin Am. Studies Assn. (pres., past mem. exec. council), Council Fgn. Relations, Center for Inter-Am. Relations. Author: Politics in Brazil, 1967; Black Into White: Race and Nationality in Brazilian Thought, 1974; co-editor Luso-Brazilian Rev., 1977—. Home: 2025 Chadbourne Ave Madison WI 53705

SKIFF, ROBERT WOLTZ, fgn. service officer; b. Sebring, Fla., Oct. 31, 1923; s. Ernest Gage and Clara (Woltz) S.; student U. Fla., 1942-43, Georgetown U., 1946-50; m. Christian Agnes Kirkwood Carritt, Feb. 20, 1970; 1 son, Luke David Robert. With Dept. State, 1946-54; with U.S. Fgn. Service, 1954—; prin. officer to Fiji, until 1973; polit. officer, Bangkok, Thailand, 1973-74, polit.-mil affairs officer, 1974-76, permanent rep. to UN ESCAP, 1976—. Served with AUS, 1943-46. Decorated Bronze Star medal, Croix de Guerre with palm. Mem. Sigma Alpha Epsilon. Episcopalian. Club: Metropolitan (Washington). Home: 1114 SE 9th St Fort Lauderdale FL 33316 Office: Dept State Washington DC 20520

SKILES, ELWIN LLOYD, univ. chancellor; b. Scranton, Tex., June 15, 1912; s. Asa Irvin and Leoma (Parks) S.; student Hardin-Simmons U., 1930-32, H.H.D. (hon.), 1977; B.A., Baylor U., 1934, M.A., 1935; Th.M., So. Baptist Theol. Sem., 1938, Ph.D., 1941; m. Lavonia Ruth Kinder, Aug. 17, 1938; children—Elwin Lloyd, Ann Collier, Sarah Parks. Teaching fellow So. Bapt. Theol. Sem., 1938-41; ordained to ministry Bapt. Ch., 1932; pastor in Russellville, Ky., 1941-43, Richmond, Va., 1943-44, Georgetown, Ky., 1946-49, Pensacola, Fla., 1949- 53, Abilene, Tex., 1953-66; pres. Hardin-Simmons U., 1966-77, chancellor, 1977—; preaching missions, Hong Kong and Philippines, 1960. Mem. fgn. mission bd. So. Bapt. Conv., 1949; pres. Abilene Ministerial Alliance, 1956; exec. bd. Tex. Baptists, 1957-60; mem. program coordinating com. Bapt. Gen. Conv. Tex., 1961-66. Pres. bd. Central Bapt. Hosp., Lexington, Ky., 1948; trustee Bapt. Hosp., Pensacola, Fla., 1950-53, Hendrick Meml. Hosp., Abilene, 1953-66, Hardin-Simmons U., 1953-66; trustee Golden Gate Bapt. Theol. Sem., Mill Valley, Calif., 1950-66, chmn., 1963-66; bd. dirs. Abilene Mental Health Assn., 1964-67; exec. bd. Ind. Coll. Funds Am., 1970-75, Tex. Assn. Colls. and Univs., 1976—; bd. examiners Tex. Edn. Agy., 1976-78. chmn. Tex. Found. Voluntarily Supported Colls. and Univs., 1968-70. Served as chaplain USNR, 1944-46. Mem. So. Sem. Alumni Assn. (pres. 1962-63), Abilene C. of C. (bd. dirs. 1966-78). Democrat. Rotarian (pres. Russellville 1943, Pensacola 1953). Home: 916 Westwood Dr Abilene TX 79603

SKILLIN, EDWARD SIMEON, magazine publisher; b. N.Y.C., Jan. 23, 1904; s. Edward Simeon and Geraldine Madeleine (Fearons) S.; grad. Phillips Acad., Andover, Mass., 1921; A.B., Williams Coll., 1925; M.A., Columbia, 1933; L.H.D., St. Benedict's Coll., 1954, Fordham U., 1974; LL.D., St. Vincent's Coll., 1959, St. Francis Xavier U., 1966, Stonehill Coll., 1979; m. Jane Anne Edwards, Jan. 27, 1945; children—Edward John, Elizabeth Ann, Arthur Paul, Susan Geraldine, Mary Jane. With ednl. dept. Henry Holt & Co., N.Y.C., 1925-33; mem. staff Commonweal, N.Y.C., 1933-38, editor, 1938-67, publisher, 1967—. Recipient Centennial citation St. John's U., Collegeville, Minn., 1957. Mem. Cath. Commn. Intellectual and Cultural Affairs, Phi Beta Kappa, Phi Gamma Delta. Editor: The Commonweal Reader, 1949. Office: 232 Madison Ave New York NY 10016

SKILLING, HUGH HILDRETH, educator; b. San Diego, Sept. 2, 1905; s. William Thompson and Bird (Hildreth) S.; student San Diego State Coll., 1922-24; A.B., Stanford, 1926, E.E., 1927, Ph.D., 1931; S.M., Mass. Inst. Tech., 1930; mem. Kings Coll., Cambridge U., 1951; m. Hazel Dillon, June 21, 1932; 1 dau., Ann Katharine. Elec. engr. So. Calif. Edison Co., Los Angeles, 1927-29; instr. elec. engring. Stanford, 1929, 31-35, asst. prof., 1935-39, asso. prof., 1939-42, prof., 1942—, acting head dept., 1941-44, exec. head dept. elec. engring, 1944-64; acting dean Sch. Engring. 1944-46, asso. dean, 1952-54; Fulbright prof. elec. engring. Cambridge U., Eng., 1951-52, vis. prof., 1965; lectr. electric power transmission Mass. Inst. Tech., 1934; lectr., Madrid, 1952, U. Chile, Santiago, 1957; cons. elec. engring. edn. Dartmouth Coll., 1958, U. Hawaii, 1958, U. Alaska, 1964; cons. editor John Wiley & Sons, Inc., 1951-71; mem. rev. team U. Philippines, 1953. Supr. U.S. Army Signal Corps Radio Tng. Program, Stanford, 1942-43; ofcl. investigator Nat. Def. Research Com., 1942-44; expert cons. Army Service Forces, 1944. Sci. observer, atomic bomb tests, Bikini Atoll, 1946. Registered profl. elec. engr., Calif. Fellow IEEE (medal for edn. 1964), AAAS; mem. Phi Beta Kappa, Sigma Xi. Editor: Alternating Current Circuits (K.Y. Tang), 1940. Author: Transient Electric Currents, 1937: Fundamentals of Electric Waves, 1942, 2d edit., 1948; Prelude to Bikini, 1947; Exploring Electricity, 1948; Electric Transmission Lines, 1951; Electrical Engineering Circuits, 1957, 2d edit., 1965; A First Course in Electromechanics, 1960; Electromechanics, 1962; Do You Teach?, 1969; Electric Networks, 1974; Teaching: Guidance by Distinguished Teachers, 1977; works transl. Spanish, Russian, Polish, Vietnamese, Thai. Contbr. articles to tech. jours., also articles McGraw-Hill Ency. Sci. and Tech., 1968. Home: 672 Mirada Ave Stanford CA 94305

SKILLING, JOHN BOWER, structural and civil engr.; b. Los Angeles, Oct. 8, 1921; s. Harold C. and Helen M. (Bower) S.; B.S., U. Wash., 1947; m. Mary Jane Stender, May 1, 1943; children—William, Susan, Ann. Design engr. W.H. Witt Co., Seattle, 1947-54; partner Worthington, Skilling, Helle and Jackson, Seattle, 1959-67; partner Skilling, Helle, Christiansen, Robertson, Seattle, 1967—; mem. Bldg. Research Adv. Bd. Mem. Seattle Found.; mem. Seattle Municipal Art Commn., 1964-67. Fellow ASCE; mem. Nat. Acad. Engring., Am. Concrete Inst., Assn. Shell Structures, Internat. Assn. Bridge and Structural Engring., Soc. Am. Mil. Engrs., Structural Engrs. Assn. Wash., Am. Inst. Steel Constrn. (adv. com.). Home: 539 McGilvra Blvd E Seattle WA 98112 Office: 2200 The Financial Center Seattle WA 98161

SKILLMAN, HOPE, fabric converter, stylist, civic worker; b. Grand Rapids, Mich.; d. Frederic Cameron and Mary (Christie) Skillman; graduate Goucher Coll., 1961; m. Saul Schary, Dec. 15, 1934. Asso. editor Parnassus Mag., N.Y.C., 1932-33. The Fine Arts, 1933-34; asst. stylist Ameritex div. Cohn-Hall-Marx Co., 1934-35, stylist, 1935-39, dir., 1939-42; mgr. N.Y.C. office Tabin-Picker Co., 1942-43; pres. Hope Skillman Inc., N.Y.C., 1942, Skillmill, Inc., 1944—. Mem. Joint Manpower Commn., Washington. Bd. govs. Phila. Mus. Sch. bd. dirs. Council Nat. Voluntary Orgns., 1977—. Mem. Fashion Group Inc. (bd. govs., exec. com., pres. 1958-60), Textile Fabrics Assn., Nat. Council of Women (past v.p., fin. chmn., pres. 1970-72, 76—, hon. pres. 1972-74, pres. 1976—), Internat. Council Women (1st v.p. 1973—), Kappa Alpha Theta. Clubs: Goucher College, Inner Circle: Cosmopolitan (N.Y.C.). Address: 56 W 10th St New York City NY 10011 also New Milford CT 06776

SKILLMAN, JOHN FROSCH, JR., ednl. adminstr.; b. Princeton, N.J., May 16, 1934; s. John Frosch and Elsie (Wright) S.; student Gunnery Sch., 1949-52, Kings Sch., Worcester, Eng., 1952-53; A.B., Yale, 1957, M.A. in Teaching, 1959; m. Sally L. Cott, Aug. 4, 1956; children—Gregory John, Mark Randall, Lee Kirsten. Coach freshman squash and tennis, Yale, 1956-65; tchr. English, North Haven (Conn.) High Sch., 1958-62; tchr. English Hopkins Grammar Sch., New Haven, 1962-68, dir. admissions, 1965-68; now pres. Packer Collegiate Inst., Bklyn. Asst. to pres. Conn. Found. for Ind. Schs., 1965-68. Trustee Bklyn. Hosp., Ind. Ednl. Services. Mem. Bklyn. Heights Assn., English Speaking Union. Trustee Bklyn. Bur. Community Service. Mem. Guild Ind. Schs., Middle States Assn., Nat. Assn. Ind. Schs., N.Y. State Assn. Ind. Schs. (state treas.), St. Anthony Assn. Yale (trustee), St. Anthony Ednl. Assn. (trustee), Delta Psi. Republican. Episcopalian. Rotarian. Clubs: Bklyn., Heights Casino. Home: 1 Pierrepont St Brooklyn NY 11201 Office: 170 Joralemon St Brooklyn NY 11201

SKILLMAN, THOMAS GRANT, physician, educator; b. Cin., Jan. 7, 1925; s. Harold Grant and Faustina (Jobes) S.; B.S., Baldwin-Wallace Coll., 1946; M.D., U. Cin., 1949; m. Elizabeth Louise McClellan, Sept. 6, 1947; children—Linda, Barbara. Intern, Cin. Gen. Hosp., 1949-50, resident, 1952-54; instr. medicine U. Cin., 1952-57; asst. prof. medicine Ohio State U., Columbus, 1957-61, prof., 1963-67, Ralph Kurtz prof. endocrinology, 1974—; dir. endocrinology and metabolism Coll. Medicine, 1967-74, asso. prof. medicine Creighton U., Omaha, 1961-67; Bd. dirs. Central Ohio Diabetes Assn. Served with USNR, 1943-45; 1950-52; Korea. Recipient Golden Apple award Student Am. Med. Assn., 1966. Mem. Am. Diabetes Assn., Central Soc. Clin. Investigation, Am. Fedn. for Clin. Research, Alpha Omega Alpha. Club: Ohio State Golf (Columbus). Editor: Case Studies in Endocrinology, 1971. Contbr. numerous articles to med. jours. Home: 2367 Cambridge Blvd Columbus OH 43221 Office: Univ Hosp Columbus OH 43210

SKILLMAN, THOMAS J., JR., diaper service exec.; b. Newark, July 12, 1909; s. Thomas J. and Louise C. (Jenkinson) S.; B.S., Princeton, 1931; postgrad. U. Pa., 1932; m. Shirley B. Swift, Aug. 15, 1934; children—Thomas J. III, David M., Dean S., Sara. With Dy-Dee Wash, Phila., and successor firms (now called Blessing Corp.), N.Y.C., 1932—, v.p., 1946-68, pres., 1968-70, chmn. exec. com., 1970-77, mem. adv. com. to bd., 1977—; treas., dir. Dy-Dee Wash, Inc. (Collingswood, N.J.). Clubs: St. Davids (Pa.) Golf; Princeton (N.Y.C., Phila.); Pine Valley Golf (Clementon, N.J.). Home: 744 Clarendon Rd Narberth PA 19072 Office: 4136 Mitchel St Philadelphia PA 19128

SKINNER, BRIAN JOHN, educator, geologist; b. Wallaroo, South Australia, Dec. 15, 1928 (came to U.S. 1958, naturalized 1963); s. Joshua Henry and Joyce Barbara Lloyd (Prince) S.; B.Sc., U. Adelaide (Australia), 1950; A.M., Harvard, 1952, Ph.D., 1955; m. Helen Catherine Wild, Oct. 9, 1954; children—Adrienne Wild, Stephanie Wild, Thalassa Wild. Lectr., U. Adelaide, 1955-58, research geologist U.S. Geol. Survey, 1958-62, chief br. exptl. geochemistry and mineralogy, 1962-66; prof. geology and geophysics, chmn. dept. Yale, New Haven, Conn., 1966-73, Eugene Higgins prof., 1972—. Mem. exec. com. div. earth scis. NRC, 1966-69; chmn. com. mineral resources and the environment Nat. Acad. Scis.-NRC, 1973-75; mem. Lunar Sample Analysis Planning Team, 1968-70, Lunar Sci. Rev. Bd., 1971-72, U.S. Nat. Com. for Geochemistry, 1966-67, U.S. Nat. Com. for Geology, 1973-77; dir. Econ. Geology Pub. Co. Guggenheim fellow, 1970. Fellow Geol. Soc. Am. (councillor 1976-78); mem. Geochem. Soc. (pres. 1972-73). Author: Earth Resources, 1969, 77; Man and the Ocean, 1973; Physical Geology, 1974, 77; Rocks and Rock Minerals, 1979. Editor: Econ. Geology, 1969. Editorial bd. Am. Scientist, 1974—. Home: 70 High St New Haven CT 06511

SKINNER, BURRHUS FREDERIC, psychologist, educator; b. Susquehanna, Pa., Mar. 20, 1904; s. William Arthur and Grace (Burrhus) S.; A.B., Hamilton Coll., 1926, Sc.D., 1951; M.A., Harvard, 1930, Ph.D., 1931; Sc.D., N.C. State U., 1960, U. Chgo., 1967, U. Mo., 1968, Alfred U., 1969, U. Exeter (Eng.), 1969, Ind. U., 1970, McGill U., 1970, C.W. Post Center L.I. U., 1971, Dickinson Coll., 1972, Lowell Technol. Inst., 1974, Nasson Coll., 1976; Litt.D. (hon.), Ripon Coll., 1961, Tufts U., 1977; L.H.D., Rockford Coll., 1971, Framingham (Mass.) State Coll., 1972, U. Md.-Balt. County, 1973, New Coll., Hofstra U., 1974, Exptl. Coll. Inst. Behavioral Research, 1974, Johns Hopkins U., 1979; LL.D., Ohio Wesleyan U., 1971, Hobart and William Smith Coll., 1972, Western Mich. U., 1976; D.Soc.Sci., U. Louisville, 1977; D.Laws, Keio U., Tokyo, 1979; m. Yvonne Blue, Nov. 1, 1936; children—Julie (Mrs. Ernest Vargas), Deborah (Mrs. Barry Buzan). Research fellow NRC, Harvard, 1931-33, jr. fellow Harvard Soc. Fellows, 1933-36; instr. psychology U. Minn., Mpls., 1936-37, asst. prof., 1937-39, asso. prof., 1939-45; conducted war research sponsored by Gen. Mills, Inc., 1942-43; prof. psychology, chmn. dept. Ind. U., 1945-48; William James lectr. Harvard, 1947, prof. psychology, 1948-57, Edgar Pierce prof., 1958-74, prof. emeritus, 1974—. Recipient distinguished sci. contbn. award, 1958, Nat. medal Sci., 1968, Gold medal Am. Psychol. Assn., 1971, Joseph P. Kennedy, Jr. Found. award, 1971. Guggenheim fellow, 1944-45. Fellow Royal Soc. Arts; mem. Am. Psychol. Assn., A.A.A.S., Nat. Acad. Sci., Am. Acad. Arts and Scis., Swedish, Brit., Spanish psychol. socs., Am. Phil. Soc., Phi Beta Kappa, Sigma Xi. Author: Behavior of Organisms, 1938; Walden Two, 1948; Science and Human Behavior, 1953; Verbal Behavior, 1957; (with C.B. Ferster) Schedules of Reinforcement, 1957; Cumulative Record, 1959, rev. 1961, 72; (with J.G. Holland) The Analysis of Behavior, 1961; The Technology of Teaching, 1968; Contingencies of Reinforcement: A Theoretical Analysis, 1969; Beyond Freedom and Dignity, 1971; About Behaviorism, 1974; Particulars of My Life, 1976; Reflections on Behaviorism and Society, 1978; The Shaping of a Behaviorist, 1979. Home: 13 Old Dee Rd Cambridge MA 02138

SKINNER, CARLTON, mgmt. cons.; b. Palo Alto, Calif., Apr. 8, 1913; s. Macy M. and Marian W. (Junkins) S.; student Wesleyan U., Middletown, Conn., 1931; A.B., U. Calif. at Los Angeles, 1934; m. Jeanne Rowe, May 1, 1943 (div. 1970); children—Franz C., Andrea W., Barbara M.; m. 2d, Solange Petit, 1970. Staff, United Press, Washington, 1934-36, Wall St. Jour., 1936-38; asst. dir. info. wage and hour div. U.S. Dept. Labor, 1938-39; asst. dir. info. U.S. Maritime Commn., 1939-40, acting dir., 1940-41, chief sales and charter sect., 1945-46; dir. info. spl. asst. to sec. Dept. of Interior, 1946-49; gov. Ter. Guam, 1949-53; chmn. bd. dirs. Bank of Guam, 1949-51; exec. asst. to pres. Am. President Lines, San Francisco, 1953-58; fin. v.p., dir. Fairbanks Whitney Corp., N.Y.C., 1958-63; chmn. bd. Pratt & Whitney Co., 1962-63; propr. Skinner & Co., San Francisco, 1963—; chmn. bd. Air Micronesia, Inc., 1968—. U.S. commr. S. Pacific Commn., 1961-64, sr. U.S. commr., 1964-70; mem. Fed. Ter. Commn. to prepare econ. plan for Guam, 1964-66; hon. consul gen. Republic of Nauru for U.S., 1971—. Served with USCGR, 1941-45; comdg. officer U.S.S. Seacloud, 1944, U.S.S. Hoquiam, 1945; permanent appt. comdr. Res. Mem. Am. Legion, Democrat. Clubs: St. Francis Yacht (San Francisco); Explorers (N.Y.C.). Address: 110 Sutter St San Francisco CA 94104

SKINNER, DAVID BERNT, surgeon; b. Joliet, Ill., Apr. 28, 1935; s. James Madden and Bertha Elinor (Tapper) S.; B.A. with high honors, U. Rochester (N.Y.), 1958; M.D. cum laude, Yale U., 1959; m. May Elinor Tischer, Aug. 25, 1956; children—Linda Elinor, Kristin Anne, Carise Berntine, Margaret Leigh. Intern, then resident in surgery Mass. Gen. Hosp., Boston, 1959-65; sr. registrar thoracic surgery Frenchay Hosp., Bristol, Eng., 1963-64; teaching fellow Harvard U. Med. Sch., 1965; from asst. prof. surgery to prof. Johns Hopkins U. Med. Sch., also surgeon Johns Hopkins Hosp., 1968-72; Dallas B. Phemister prof. surgery, chmn. dept. U. Chgo. Hosps. and Clinics, 1972—; mem. President's Biomed. Research Panel, 1975-76; past cons. USPHS, Office Surgeon Gen. U.S. Navy. Elder, Fourth Presbyn. Ch., Chgo., 1976—. Served to maj. M.C., USAF, 1966-68. Grantee NIH, 1968—; John and Mary Markle scholar acad. medicine, 1969-74. Diplomate Am. Bd. Surgery (dir. 1974-80), Am. Bd. Thoracic Surgery. Fellow A.C.S.; mem. Am., Western, So. surg. assns., Soc. Univ. Surgeons (pres. 1978-79), Am. Soc. Artificial Internal Organs (pres. 1977), Soc. Surg. Chmn. (sec.-treas. 1977, pres. elect 1978-80), Am. Assn. Thoracic Surgery, Soc. Vascular Surgery, Soc. Thoracic Surgery, Soc. Surgery Alimentary Tract, Am. Coll. Chest Physicians, Central Surg. Soc., Assn. Acad. Surgery, Halsted Soc., Soc. Clin. Surgery, Phi Beta Kappa, Alpha Omega Alpha. Clubs: Quadrangle (Chgo.); Cosmos (Washington). Co-author: Gastroesophageal Reflux and Hiatal Hernia, 1972. Editor Jour. Surg. Research, 1972—, Current Topics in Surg. Research, 1969-71. Contbr. profl. jours., chpts. in books. Home: 5490 South Shore Dr Chicago IL 60615 Office: 950 E 59th St Chicago IL 60637

SKINNER, DAVID EDWARD, investment co. exec.; b. Seattle, July 31, 1920; s. Gilbert Whittemore and Winifred (Swalwell) S.; B.A., Dartmouth Coll., 1942; m. Dec. 29, 1942; children—David Edward, Pail Whittemore, Peter Gilbert. Pres., dir. Pacific Cruise Lines, 1946-49; with Alaska S.S. Co., 1950-70, pres., 1953-70; dir. Skinner Corp., Seattle, 1946—, pres., 1953—; dir. Alpac Corp., 1959—, chmn. bd., 1979—; chmn. bd., dir. N.C. Machinery Co., 1976—; dir. SAFECO Co., Boeing Co., Pacific N.W. Bell Telephone Co., BankCal Tri-State Corp., Bank Calif., N.A. Chmn., Econ. Devel. Council Puget Sound, 1976; trustee Wash. Internat. Trade Fair, 1961—; adv. bd. U. Wash. Grad. Sch. Bus. Adminstrn., 1966—; trustee, v.p. Corp. Council Arts, Seattle, 1975—; bd. dirs., exec. com. United Way King County, 1972-73, bd. dirs., 1978-81, campaign chmn., 1977; nat. bd. Smithsonian Assos., 1978—; pres. trustees Lakeside Sch., 1961-63; men's adv. bd. Children's Orthopedic Hosp., Seattle, 1961—. Served as officer USNR, 1942-45. Mem. Seattle C. of C. (dir. 1956-59, 63-66, trustee 1978-81). Clubs: Confrerie des Chevaliers du Tastevin (Los Angeles); Bohemian, Pacific Union (San Francisco); Rainier, Seattle Golf, Seattle, Yacht, Univ., Wash. Athletic (Seattle); Cruising of Am. Office: 711 Skinner Bldg Seattle WA 98101

SKINNER, DAVID HAVEN, mfg. co. exec.; b. Rockford, Ill., Sept. 21, 1927; s. Bertram Eugene and Alida Helen (Moss) S.; B.S. in Mech. Engring., Purdue U., 1949; M.B.A., U. Pa., 1951; m. Shelby June Peden, Feb. 16, 1979; children—Michael H., Janet E., Linda S. Project engr. Owens-Ill. Glass Co., Toledo, 1951-55; fin. mgr. Ford Motor Co., Detroit, 1955-68; corporate controller Western Gear Corp., Lynwood, Calif., 1968-71; asst. controller Signal Companies, Beverly Hills, Calif., 1971-74, treas., 1974-75, v.p., treas., 1975—. Served with AUS, 1946-48. Registered profl. engr., Ohio, cert. mgmt. accountant. Mem. Fin. Execs. Inst. Home: 2615 Angelo Dr Los Angeles CA 90024 Office: 9665 Wilshire Blvd Beverly Hills CA 90212

SKINNER, DOROTHY M., biologist, educator; b. Newton, Mass., May 22, 1930; d. Vincent George and Martha Jane (Borden) S.; B.S., Jackson Coll., 1952; Ph.D., Harvard, 1958; m. John S. Cook, July 24, 1965. Asst. dir. admissions Jackson Coll. for Women, Tufts U., 1952-54; asst. prof. N.Y. U. Sch. Medicine, 1962-66; research participant Oak Ridge Inst. Nuclear Studies, 1966-68; research staff mem. biology div. Oak Ridge Nat. Lab., 1967—, group leader growth and regeneration, 1969—; prof. biomed. scis. U. Tenn.-Oak Ridge Grad. Sch. Biomed. Scis., 1968—; mem. panel molecular biology NIH, USPHS, 1972-76. USPHS fellow, 1955-58, 58-61. Mem. Am. Soc. Cell Biology (exec. council 1972-73), Soc. Gen. Physiologists (treas. 1973-75), AAAS (com. on nominations 1977-78, mem. at large sect. biol. sci. 1978—), Am. Physiol. Soc., Am. Soc. Biol. Chemists, Am. Soc. Zoologists, Internat. Soc. Devel. Biology, Soc. Developmental Biology, Assn. for Women in Sci., NOW, Women's Equity Action League, Phi Beta Kappa. Asso. editor Growth; contbr. articles to profl. jours. Office: Oak Ridge Nat Lab Biology Div PO Box Y Oak Ridge TN 37830

SKINNER, FREDERICK JAMES, mfg. co. exec.; b. Gananoque, Ont., Can., May 21, 1924; s. Frederick Van Heusen and Eleanor Emery (Wright) S.; came to U.S., 1961, naturalized, 1969; B.Sc., Queen's U., Kingston, Ont., 1947; m. Elizabeth Anne Regan, Apr. 26, 1944; children—Ellen Anne, Mary Elizabeth Susanne. Pres., Houdaille Industries, Ltd., Oshawa, Can.; exec. v.p., dir. Houdaille Industries, Inc., Buffalo; now pres., chief exec. officer SKF Industries Inc., King of Prussia, Pa.; dir. Warner & Swasey Corp. Bd. mgrs. Franklin Inst., Phila.; bd. dirs. Pa. Ballet. Mem. Assn. Profl. Engrs. Ont. Clubs: Phila. Country, Union League (Phila.); Nat. (Toronto). Home: 155 Mill Creek Terr Gladwyne PA 19035 Office: SKF Industries Inc PO Box 239 King of Prussia PA 19406

SKINNER, G(EORGE) WILLIAM, anthropologist, educator; b. Oakland, Calif., Feb. 14, 1925; s. John James and Eunice (Engle) S.; student Deep Springs (Calif.) Coll., 1942-43; B.A. with distinction in Chinese Studies, Cornell U., Ithaca, N.Y., 1947, Ph.D. in Cultural Anthropology, 1954; m. Carol Bagger, Mar. 25, 1951; children—Geoffrey Crane, James Lauriston, Mark Williamson, Jeremy Burr. Field dir. Cornell U. S.E. Asia program, also Cornell Research Center, Bangkok, Thailand, 1951-55, research asso. in Indonesia, 1956-58, asso. prof., then prof. anthropology, Ithaca, N.Y., 1960-65; asst. prof. sociology Columbia, 1958-60; sr. specialist in residence East-West Center, Honolulu, 1965-66; prof. anthropology Stanford, 1966—; vis. prof. U. Pa., 1977, Duke U., spring, 1978; field research Szechwan, China, 1949-50, S.E. Asia, 1950-51, Thailand, 1951-53, 54-55, Java and Borneo, 1956-58; mem. joint com. contemporary China, Social Sci. Research Council-Am. Acad. Learned Socs., 1961-65, internat. com. Chinese studies, 1963-64; mem. subcom. research Chinese Soc. Social Sci. Research Council, 1961-70, chmn., 1963-70; dir. program on East Asian Local Systems, 1969-71; dir. Chinese Soc. Bibliography Project, 1964-73; asso. dir. Cornell China Program, 1961-63; dir. London-Cornell Project Social Research, 1962-65; mem. com. on scholarly communication with People's Republic of China, Nat. Acad. Scis., 1966-70; mem. adv. com. Center for Chinese Research Materials, Assn. Research Libraries, 1967-70. Served to ensign USNR, 1943-46. Fellow Center for Advanced Study in Behavioral Scis., 1969-70; Guggenheim fellow, 1969; NIMH spl. fellow, 1970. Fellow Am. Anthrop. Assn., Royal Anthrop. Inst., A.A.A.S., Am. Sociol. Assn.; mem. Assn. Asian Studies (bd. dirs. 1962-65, chmn. nominating com. 1967-68), Am. Acad. Polit. and Social Sci., Social Sci. History Assn., Am. Ethnol. Soc., Siam Soc., Soc. Ch'ing Studies, Soc. Applied Anthropology, Phi Beta Kappa, Sigma Xi. Author: Chinese Society in Thailand, 1957; Leadership and Power in the Chinese Community of Thailand, 1958; also articles, Editor: The Social Sciences and Thailand, 1956; Local, Ethnic and National Loyalties in Village Indonesia, 1959; Modern Chinese Society: An Analytical Bibliography, 3 vols., 1973; (with Mark Elvin) The Chinese City Between Two Worlds, 1974; (with A. Thomas Kirsch) Change and Persistence in Thai Society, 1975; The City in Late Imperial China, 1977; The Study of Chinese Society, 1979. Home: 80 Pearce Mitchell Pl Stanford CA 94305 Office: Dept Anthropology Stanford Univ Stanford CA 94305

SKINNER, GORDON SWEETLAND, educator, economist; b. New Britain, Conn., Nov. 9, 1924; s. Dwight and Dorothy (Sweetland) S.; B.S. cum laude, Boston U., 1948; M.S., U. Wis., 1949, Ph.D. in Econs., 1953; m. Virginia May Knodel, Aug. 20, 1955; children—Michael, Jo Ann, Jonathan. Instr. econs. Whitewater (Wis.) State Coll., 1950-51, U. Wis., 1952-53; mem. faculty U. Cin., 1953—, prof. econs., 1961—, head dept., 1963-74, chmn. univ. faculty, 1976-78. Mem. Cin. Full Employment Commn.; adv. com. Cin. Office Ohio Employment Service. Served to 1st lt. USAAF, 1943-46. Decorated D.F.C., Air medal with 3 oak leaf clusters. Mem. Am. Arbitration Assn. (labor arbitration panel), Am., Midwest econ. assns., Indsl. Relations Research Assn., AAUP, Ohio Assn. Economists and Polit. Scientists (pres. 1975-76), Cin. Civil War Round Table, Ohio Acad. Sci., Omicron Delta Epsilon, Alpha Kappa Psi, Beta Gamma Sigma, Phi Kappa Tau. Author: (with J.M. Kuhlman) The Economic System, rev. edit., 1964; (with E. Herman) Labor Law, 1973; (with D. Heisel) Costing Union Demands, 1977. Home: 547 Abilene Trail Cincinnati OH 45215

SKINNER, JOHN WILLIAM, educator, economist; b. Washington, Mar. 11, 1921; s. Clarence A. and Mabel C. (Ditchburn) S.; B.A., Wesleyan U., Middletown, Conn., 1942; M.A., George Washington U., 1947, Ph.D., 1954; m. Elizabeth Dalley, June 20, 1953; children—David, Susan. Teaching fellow George Washington U., 1947-50, mem. faculty, 1950-53, 55-65, prof. econs., 1963-65, chmn. dept., 1961-67; prof. and head dept. econs. U. Guelph (Ont., Can.), 1965-70, dean Coll. Social Sci., 1970—; asst. prof. Stetson U., 1953-55. Served with USAAF, 1942-45. Mem. Am. Econ. Assn., Omicron Delta Kappa, Pi Gamma Mu, Phi Sigma Kappa. Home: 8 Maplewood Dr Guelph ON Canada

SKINNER, KENNETH BARNES, life ins. co. exec.; b. Dallas, Aug. 12, 1919; s. Hugh Leon and Erma (Brower) S.; student Hardin-Simmons U., 1936-38; B.B.A., U. Tex., 1940; M.B.A., U. Pa., 1941; m. Elizabeth Bagwell, Jan. 9, 1942; children—Denny Elizabeth (Mrs. James A. Anderson), Sheryl (Mrs. James D. Schroeder). With Southwestern Life Ins. Co., 1941-42, N.Am. Aviation, Inc., 1943-44; with Southland Life Ins. Co., Dallas, 1944-67, v.p., agy. dir., 1952-65, v.p. mktg., 1965-67, also dir.; pres., dir. N.Am. Mgmt., 1971—; sr. v.p., dir. Midland Nat. Life Ins. Co., Sioux Falls, S.D., 1967—, Investors Life Ins. Co. Nebr., 1970—. Pres. Life Ins. Agy. Mgmt. Assn., 1961, bd. dirs., 1959-62. Mem. Am. Coll. Life Underwriters (ex officio trustee 1961-62), Am. Soc. C.L.U.'s (pres. Dallas 1949-50). Home: 4216 Thunderbird Trail Sioux Falls SD 57103 Office: One Midland Plaza Sioux Falls SD 57101

SKINNER, KNUTE RUMSEY, poet, educator; b. St. Louis, Apr. 25, 1929; s. George Rumsey and Lidi (Skjoldvig) S.; student Culver-Stockton Coll., 1947-49; B.A., U. No. Colo., 1951; M.A., Middlebury Coll., 1954; Ph.D., U. Iowa, 1958; m. Jeanne Pratt, 1953 (div. 1954); 1 son, Francis; m. 2d, Linda Kuhn, Mar. 30, 1961 (div. Sept. 1977); children—Dunstan, Morgan; m. 3d, Edna Kiel, Mar. 25, 1978. Instr. in English, U. Iowa, Iowa City, 1955-56, 57-58, 60-61; asst. prof. English, Okla. Coll. for Women, 1961-62; lectr. creative writing Western Wash. U., Bellingham, 1962-71, asso. prof. English, 1971-73, prof. English, 1973—. Nat. Endowment for the Arts fellow, 1975. Mem. Poetry Soc., Am. Com. Irish Studies. Author: Stranger with a Watch, 1965; A Close Sky Over Killaspuglonane, 1968, 75 In Dinosaur Country, 1969; The Sorcerers: A Laotian Tale, 1972. Contbr. poetry, short stories to anthologies, textbooks, periodicals. 412 N State St Bellingham WA 98255

SKINNER, LLOYD EDWARD, food co. exec.; b. Marinette, Wis., Aug. 22, 1914; s. Lloyd Merten and Emma Louise (Leroy) S.; B.A., Creighton U., 1936; m. Kathryn Garrett, May 31, 1941; children—James Garrett, Lloyd Edward, Kathryn Louise, Mary Elizabeth. With Skinner Macaroni Co. (now subs. Hershey Foods Corp.), Omaha, 1938—, sec., 1942-47, exec. v.p., 1947-50, pres., 1950-70, chmn. bd., 1971—; pres., sec., treas. Quaker Baking Co., Council Bluffs, Iowa, 1952-53. Bd. dirs. Nat. SBA, 1952—, v.p., 1961-62, pres., 1963-66, chmn. bd., 1967-68; bd. dirs. Miss. Valley Assn., 1953-69, Midwest Employers Council, 1957-63, Crop Quality Control Council, 1961—; chmn. 6th Dist. Water Resources Congress, 1970—; bd. dirs. Nat. Macaroni Mfrs. Assn., 1953—, pres., 1957-58; pres. Nebr. Small Bus. Assn., 1949-55; pres. Iowa-Nebr. River Devel. Assn., 1952-53; mem. nat. marketing adv. com. U.S. Dept. commerce, 1969—, exec. com., 1970; chmn. Macaroni Industry-Grain Food Products Sub-council, 1970. Chmn. Douglas County chpt. A.R.C. drive, 1949, Douglas County Am. Cancer Soc. drive, 1962, Omaha Archdiocesan Com. to Support Lay Missionaries drive, 1962; v.p., dir. United Community Services Omaha, 1957; pres. Douglas County Campfire Girls, 1952-53, Omaha Civic Opera Soc., 1959-63; trustee Nutritional Found., Mid-Am. council Boy Scouts Am., Nebr. Council Econ. Edn.; dir. Nebr. Clergy Econ. Edn., 1969—; exec. bd. Project Equality, Nebr., 1967-69, pres., 1968-69; exec. bd. Project Equality, Nebr.-Iowa, 1970-72; bd. dirs. Douglas County Cancer Soc., 1962—, Omaha Safety Council, 1948, Omaha Salvation Army, 1953—, Nebr. div. NCCJ, 1957—; bd. dirs. Nebr. chpt. Arthritis and Rheumatism Found., 1955—, pres., 1961-65; S. Omaha Youth Center, 1957-63, Cath. Interracial Council Omaha, 1963-64; mem. exec. com. Omaha Jr. Achievement, 1963—, pres., 1969-70; adv. bd. St. Catherines Hosp., Omaha, 1958-63, Creighton Prep. Sch., 1961-67, Omaha Urban League, 1953-63, Duchesne Coll., Omaha, 1960-67; Cath. co-chmn. NCCJ, 1961—; pres. Nebr. chpt. Arthritis and Rheumatism Found., 1961-64; trustee Nat. Arthritis Found., 1968—; mem. pres.'s council Creighton U.; mem. Nebr. Republican Finance Com., 1956; mem. adv. bd. Archbishop Bergen Mercy Hosp., 1963—, chmn., 1975-77; mem. Archbishop's Com. for Ednl. Devel., 1971; trustee mem. exec. com. Omaha Archdiocesan Ednl. Found., 1976—. Served to maj. AUS, 1942-46; ETO. Recipient Blessed Philippine Duchesne award, 1962, Omaha Musical Service award, 1959; Outstanding Service award Midwest Employers Council, 1964; Award Merit, Nebr. chapter Arthritis Foundation, 1964; Service Award Merit, Omaha Urban League, 1964; Distinguished Service award National Arthritis Found., 1966; Distinguished Service award Jr. C. of C., 1949; Outstanding Service award U.S. Durum Wheat Growers Assn., 1974; decorated Papal Knight of St. Gregory, 1964; recipient Mercian medal Coll. St. Mary, 1968; Nat. Council for Small Bus. Mgmt. Devel.'s award as Outstanding Small Businessman Central Region, 1969; Nat. Humanitarian award City of Hope Nat. Pilot Med. Center, 1972, Nat. Idealism award, 1979; Alumni Merit award Creighton U., 1975; Humanitarian award Nat. Jewish Hosp. and Research Center, 1978; Meritorious Service award Catholic Archdiocese of Omaha, 1979. Mem. Sr. Omaha C. of C. (dir. 1949), Nat. Small Bus. Assn. (dir. emeritus), Grocery Mfrs. Am. (dir. 1964-76), Am. Legion (post comdr. 1952), Serra Club, Alpha Sigma Nu (pres. Alumni chpt. 1967-68), Beta Gamma Sigma (hon.). K.C. Home: 843 S 96th St Omaha NE 68132 Office: 6848 F St Box 75 Downtown Station Omaha NE 68117

SKINNER, OLIVIA, journalist; b. Evanston, Ill., Oct. 2, 1919; d. Charles George and Myra (Wilson) Little; student Nat. Coll. Edn., 1941-42; m. Claiborne Adams Skinner, July 18, 1953; children—Charles Cole Claiborne, Claiborne Adams. Free lance travel writer, N.Y.C., S.Am., London, Eng., 1944-51; co-editor Guide to Europe, travel, entertainment feature writer Paris edition N.Y. Herald Tribune, Paris, France, 1949-50; pre-sch. tchr. McKnight Sch., Central Presbyn. Sch., St. Louis, 1958-60; feature writer St. Louis Post Dispatch, 1960-64, 1st woman city desk reporter, 1964-65, 1st women's editor, 1965-66, feature writer, 1966-75. Mem. Nursery Edn. Council Greater St. Louis, 1958-60, St. Louis Jr. League, 1956-59, St. Louis Children's Art Bazaar, 1955, 56, 57; bd. dirs. Santa Fe Vol. Info. Service, 1977. Recipient Nat. Fedn. Press Women Nat. award, 1965-66, 67, 69. Mem. Santa Fe LWV, Les Cheneaux Hist. Soc., Santa Fe Hist. Soc. Home: Romancoke Hessel MI 49745 also 153 W Zia Rd Santa Fe NM 87501

SKINNER, PATRICK JAMES, archbishop; b. St. John's, Nfld., Can., Mar. 9, 1904. Ordained priest Roman Catholic Ch., 1929; aux. to archbishop of St. John's, 1950; titular bishop of Zenobia, 1950-51; archbishop of St. John's, 1951—. Address: PO Box 37 Basilica Residence Bonaventure Ave Saint John's NF Canada*

SKINNER, ROBERT ALEXANDER, civil engr.; b. N.Y.C., Feb. 24, 1895; s. Andrew Jackson and Helen Sigismunda (Lee) S.; student Cornell U., 1914-17, U. So. Calif., intermittently, 1928-43, U. Calif., 1947; m. Gladys Marian Jones, July 11, 1927; children—Anne Lee Skinner Kelly, Roger Haines. In various indsl. engring. positions, Fundamental Corp., Bklyn., 1919; Gen. Electric Co., Harrison, N.J., 1919-20, Utah-Apex Mining Co., Bingham, 1920-21, Stone & Webster, Caribou, Calif., 1921, Standard Felt Co., Alhambra, Calif., 1921-23; with Los Angeles Bur. Engring., 1924-33; with Met. Water Dist., So. Calif., 1933-67, office engr., 1941-51, asst. chief engr., 1952-61, gen. mgr., 1962-67; cons. engr., Glendale, Calif., 1967-78, Balboa Island, Calif., 1978-80. Served to lt., j.g., USN, 1917-19. Recipient Golden Beaver award in engring. Beavers, 1972; Riverside County, Calif., reservoir named Lake Skinner by Met. Water Dist. So. Calif., 1971; registered profl. engr., Calif. Fellow Inst. Advancement Engring.; mem. ASCE (hon.; pres. Los Angeles sect. 1959), Am. Water Works Assn. (life), Los Angeles City and County Engrs. Assn. (hon.; pres. 1945), So. Calif. Water Conf., So. Calif. Water Utilities Assn. Republican. Clubs: Town Hall of Calif., Masons (life), Optimists, Los Angeles Breakfast, Am. Legion (Los Angeles). Co-author Metropolitan Water District of Southern California Water Pricing Policy Study, 1969. Address: 86A Calle Aragon Laguna Hills CA 92653

SKINNER, ROBERT GLENN, accountant; b. Cleve., Feb. 25, 1918; s. Glenn Greenwood and Lolo (Fiser) S.; A.B., Western Res. U., 1949; LL.B., Cleve.-Marshall Law Sch., 1951; m. Delores Marie Crouch, Jan. 26, 1943; children—Stephen Robert, Joanne Marie. With Gen. Motors Corp., 1950-51, Ernst & Ernst, C.P.A.'s, Cleve., 1952—, nat. partner charge tax services, chmn. nat. tax com., 1966-78; speaker in field, 1957-79; mem. White House Tax Adv. Com., 1977-78; adv. bd. N.Y. U. Inst. on Fed. Taxation, 1972-76; adv. group to commr. IRS, 1973-74. Pres. Cuyahoga County (Ohio) Bd. Edn., 1965, 68; trustee Ashland Theol. Sem. Found., 1978—, Helping Hand Halfway Home, Cleve., Good Samaritan Youth Center; trustee Cleve. City Mission, pres., 1973-75; bd. mgrs., fin. advisor New Wilmington Missionary Conf.; treas. No. Ohio Billy Graham Crusade, 1971-72; pres. City Mission Endowment Found., Cleve., 1975—, New Wilmington Missionary Conf. Endowment Found., Cleve., 1975—; chmn. sponsoring com. Here's Life, Cleve., 1976-77; co-chmn. Cleve. Center for Theol. Edn., 1978—. Served to capt. AUS, 1941-46. Mem. Am. Inst. C.P.A.'s (gen. chmn. taxation div. 1971-74), Phi Beta Kappa. Clubs: Union (Cleve.); Chagrin Valley Country (Moreland Hills, Ohio). Home: 34740 Sherwood Dr Solon OH 44139 Office: Union Commerce Bldg Cleveland OH 44115

SKINNER, STANLEY THAYER, utility co. exec., lawyer; b. Fort Smith, Ark., Aug. 18, 1937; s. John Willard and Irma Lee (Peters) S.; B.A. with honors, San Diego State U., 1960; M.A., U. Calif., Berkeley, 1961, J.D., 1964; m. Margaret Olsen, Aug. 16, 1957; children—Steven Kent, Ronald Kevin. Admitted to Supreme Ct. Calif. bar, 1965, U.S. Circuit Ct. Appeals for 9th Circuit bar, 1965, 10th Circuit bar, 1966; atty. Pacific Gas and Electric Co., San Francisco, 1964-73, sr. counsel, 1973, treas., 1974-76, v.p. fin., 1976, sr. v.p., 1977, exec. v.p., 1978—; dir. Pacific Gas Transmission Co., Nuclear Mut. Ltd., Natural Gas Corp. Calif., Calaska Energy Co., Eureka Energy Co. Founding dir., pres. Friends of the Moraga Library, Inc., 1972. Mem. Calif. State Bar Assn., Fin. Officers No. Calif., Pacific Coast Elec. Assn., Pacific Coast Gas Assn. Republican. Presbyterian. Clubs: Bankers, Commonwealth. Office: 77 Beale St San Francisco CA 94106

SKINNER, TRUMAN ARNOLD, lawyer; b. Greenwood, Ark., Aug. 13, 1936; s. James Truman and Bonnie Beatrice (Crow) S.; B.S., U. Fla., 1958, LL.B., 1964; m. Constance Leigh Berry, Aug. 16, 1963; children—Tracey Alaina, Carrie Aileen. Admitted to Fla. bar, 1965; dir. Am. Bankers Ins. Co. of Fla., 1972—, sec., counsel, 1975—; dir. UA Columbia Cablevision, Inc. Mem. Dade County Charter Rev. Bd., 1968-69. Served to lt. comdr. USCGR, 1958-75. Mem. Am., Fla., Dade County bar assns. Democrat. Baptist. Clubs: Miami, Bankers, Jockey. Home: 9304 SW 54th Ct Miami FL 33156 Office: 7900 Red Rd South Miami FL 33143

SKINNER, WALTER JAY, judge; b. Washington, Sept. 12, 1927; s. Frederick Snowden and Mary Waterman (Comstock) S.; A.B., Harvard, 1948; J.D., 1952; m. Sylvia Henderson, Aug. 12, 1950; 4 children. Admitted to Mass. bar, 1952, U.S. Dist. Ct. bar, 1954; asso. firm Gaston, Snow, Rice & Boyd, Boston, 1952-57; pvt. practice law, Scituate, Mass., 1957-63; asst. dist. atty. Plymouth County, 1957-63; town counsel, Scituate, 1957-63; asst. atty. gen., chief Criminal Div., Commonwealth of Mass., 1963-65; mem. firm Wardwell, Allen, McLaughlin & Skinner, Boston, 1965-74; U.S. dist. judge, Mass., 1974—. Bd. dirs. Douglas A. Thom Clinic, 1966-70. Mem. Am. Judicature Soc., Am. Bar Assn. Clubs: Longwood Cricket; City; Eight O'Clock (Newton, Mass.). Office: 1503 Post Office and Courthouse Boston MA 02109

SKINNER, WICKHAM, educator; b. Cin., Feb. 20, 1924; s. Charles Wickham and Ruth (Hargrave) S.; B.Engring., Yale, 1944; M.B.A., Harvard, 1948, D.B.A., 1961; m. Alice Sturges Blackmer, May 18, 1946; children—Polly Gay (Mrs. Dennis Duval), Charles Barry. Chem. engr. Manhattan project U. Calif. at Los Alamos, 1946-48; with Honeywell Corp., 1948-58, asst. sec., 1957-58; mem. faculty Harvard Grad. Sch. Bus. Adminstrn., 1958—, prof., 1967-74, James E. Robison prof. bus. adminstrn., 1974—, asso. dean, 1974-77, dir. div. internat. activities, 1967-70; tchr. Pakistan, France, Vietnam, Australia, Singapore, Turkey, Tunisia, Italy, Iran and Nicaragua; dir. Wilevco Corp., Dynamics Research Corp., Helix Tech. Corp., DBX Corp. Mem. spl. coms. Weston (Mass.) Sch. Com., 1962-64, 64-68; mem. planning com., Wayzata, Minn., 1955-56; pres. Eastern Acad. Mgmt., 1968-69. Candidate for mayor, Wayzata, 1955. Bd. dirs. Fla. Philharmonic Orch., 1956-58; class agt. Yale Alumni Fund, 1944-69; trustee, treas. Urbana (Ohio) U., 1960-70. Served with AUS, 1944-46. Fellow Acad. Mgmt.; mem. Am. Inst. Indsl. Engrs., Acad. Mgmt. Mem. Swedenborgian Ch. Author: American Industry in Developing Economics, 1968; Manufacturing in Corporate Strategy, 1977; also articles. Home: 368 Strawberry Hill Rd Concord MA 01742 Office: Harvard Business Sch Soldiers Field Rd Boston MA 02163

SKINSNES, OLAF KRISTIAN, pathologist; b. Sinyang, Honan, China, Apr. 20, 1917 (parents Am. citizens); s. Casper Christianson and Mathilde Fredrikke (Olson) S.; B.A., St. Olaf Coll., 1939; M.S., U. Chgo., 1946, M.D., 1947, Ph.D., 1947; m. Serene Elizabeth Anderson, Jan. 30, 1943; children—Fredrikke Marie Skinsnes Scollard, Anwei Viveca, Kasper Oscar, Virginia D. Murison. Intern, N.Y. Hosp.-Cornell Med. Center, N.Y.C., 1947-48; lectr. U. Hong Kong Med. Sch., 1950-53, sr. lectr., 1953-59; prof. pathology U. Chgo., 1959-67; pathologist Hay Ling Chau Leprosarium, 1950-59; prof. pathology Sch. Medicine, U. Hawaii, 1967—; practice medicine specializing in pathology, Honolulu, 1967—; mem. staff Leahi Hosp.; vis. prof. pathology Nihon U., Tokyo; vis. prof. microbiology Yonsei U., Seoul, Korea, 1978—; mem. spl. study sect. NIH, 1966-68, mem. bacteriology and mycol. study sect. 1969-72, mem. expert com. on leprosy WHO, 1972—. Bd. dirs. Am. Leprosy Missions, 1960-78, sr. med. cons., 1978—; mem. Hawaii Citizens Com. on Leprosy, 1969—. Recipient Disting. Alumnus award St. Olaf Coll., 1956; Disting. Service award U. Chgo. Sch. Medicine, 1977. China Med. Bd. traveling fellow, 1955-56; NIH grantee, 1961-75. Diplomate Am. Bd. Pathology. Mem. Am. Assn. Pathologists and Bacteriologists, Internat., Argentine, Japanese leprosy assns., AAAS, Reticuloendothelial Soc., Fed. Assn. Socs. Exptl. Biology, Royal Asiatic Soc. (London), N.Y. Acad. Sci., Am. Leprosy Missions. Lutheran. Editor: Internat. Jour. Leprosy, 1968-78; spl. work in immunology of granulomatous inflammations, especially leprosy; cultivation and identification of leprosy bacillics; debilitation of biol. def. mechanisms; oriental medicine, med. edn., history and culture. Home: 438 Portlock Rd Honolulu HI 96825 Office: 3675 Kilauea Ave Honolulu HI 96816. *All human "rights" are gifts from society or from "Heaven" as expressed through society, depending on one's view, and such "rights" could not persist without the response of responsibility. To meet these responsibilities each individual has a spectrum of talents, the development and direction of which are largely determined by the individual's perception of and response to opportunities or needs. In this response, made possible by "rights," lies development, service and the satisfaction derived from accruing interest and understanding of man, nature and spirituality.*

SKIPPER, JAMES EVERETT, librarian; b. Bartow, Fla., Dec. 10, 1920; s. Glenn Blount and Nina (Bigham) S.; A.B., U. N.C., 1943; B.S. in L.S., U. Mich., 1948. M.S. in L.S., 1949, Ph.D., 1960; postgrad. (Carnegie fellow advanced library adminstrn.), Rutgers U., 1958; m. Florene Wilkins, Aug. 9, 1947 (div.); children—Glenn Michael, Nancy Sue; m. 2d, Margaret L. Meigs, June 10, 1961; children—William Meigs, Ann Meigs. Asst. librarian Washington and Jefferson Coll., 1949-50; asst. acquisitions librarian, then acquisitions librarian Ohio State U., 1950-55; instr. library sci. U. Mich., 1954; asst. librarian tech. services Mich. State U., 1956-59; dir. libraries U. Conn., Storrs, 1959-63; exec. sec. Assn. Research Libraries, 1963-67; asso. librarian Princeton Library, 1967-68; chief U. Calif. at Berkeley Library, 1968-71; exec. v.p. Kraus-Thomson Orgn., 1971-74, dir. Research Libraries Group, 1974—. Served with AUS, 1943-45; ETO. Mem. Am., Mich. (pres. coll. sect. 1957-58), New Eng., Conn., Franklin County (Ohio) (pres. 1953-54) library assns., Mich. Acad. Arts, Letters and Sci., Conn. Acad. Arts and Scis., Phi Eta Sigma, Beta Phi Mu. Clubs: Cosmos, Yale. Contbr. articles to profl. jours. Home: 113B Florence Rd Branford CT 06405

SKIRVING, JOHN LIONEL, publishing co. exec.; b. London, Ont., Can., Aug. 28, 1907; s. Herbert Robertson and Constance (Elliott) S.; came to U.S., 1912, naturalized, 1939; student Columbia, 1930; m. Dorothy W. Stein, Oct. 18, 1930 (dec. May 1978); children—Susan C. (Mrs. Robert R. Hansel), Mary C. (Mrs. David Oyer); m. 2d, Helen E. Bonnoitt, Mar. 10, 1979. Salesman, then sales mgr. Banks-Baldwin Law Pub. Co., Cleve., 1930-37; with W.H. Anderson Co., Cin., 1937—, pres., 1964-73, chmn. bd., 1973—; dir., treas. Underwriters List Pub. Co., Cin. Served with USNR, 1942-45. Named Ky. col. Mem. Am. Forestry Assn., Izaak Walton League, Nat. Audubon Soc., Nat. Wildlife Fedn., Cumberland Falls Preservation Assn., DAV, Sierra Club, U.S. Naval Inst. Episcopalian. Club: Cincinnati. Home: 455 Old South Circle Murrells Inlet SC 29576 Office: 646 Main St Cincinnati OH 45201

SKLAR, GEORGE, writer; b. Meriden, Conn., June 1, 1908; s. Ezak and Bertha (Marshak) S.; B.A., Yale, 1929; postgrad. dept. drama, 1929-31; m. Miriam Blecher, Aug. 22, 1935; children—Judith, Daniel, Zachary. Author: (plays) Merry Go Round (with Albert Maltz), produced Avon Theatre, New York, 1932; Peace On Earth (with Albert Maltz), Theatre Union, 1933; Stevedore (with Paul Peters), produced Theatre Union, 1934; Parade (with Paul Peters), produced Theatre Guild, N.Y.C., 1935; Life and Death of An American, produced by Fed. Theatre Project, 1939; (novel) The Two Worlds of Johnny Truro, 1947; (play) Laura (with Vera Caspary), produced at Cort Theatre, N.Y.C., 1947; (novel) The Promising Young Men, 1951; (novel) The Housewarming, 1953; The Identity of Dr. Frazier, 1961; (play) And People All Around, 1966 (1966-67 selection Am. Playwrights Theatre); (play) Brown Pelican, 1972. John Golden fellow, 1939. Mem. Dramatists' Guild, Authors' Guild, Phi Beta Kappa. Address: 530 N Fuller Ave Los Angeles CA 90036. *I am essentially an idealist. I believe in man's aspirations and his potential for good. And though I am continually dismayed that he uses his creative genius to unlock the secrets of the universe to construct the bomb, that he still kills his fellows in needless wars, and that he despoils the planet on which he lives, I will not and cannot yield to cynicism. I have insisted - and shall continue to - that anything I write must in some measure contribute to man's hope and strivings for the betterment of life.*

SKLAR, RICHARD J. (RICK), broadcasting co. exec.; b. Bklyn., Nov. 21, 1929; s. William and Cecile F. (Fox) S.; B.S., N.Y. U., 1952; m. Sydelle Helfgott, July 8, 1954; children—Scott Richard, Holly. Announcer Sta. WPAC, 1953; copywriter, producer Sta. WINS, 1954-58, program dir., 1959-60; program dir. Sta. WMGM, N.Y.C., 1961; production dir. Sta. WABC, 1962, program dir., 1964-72; operations dir. sta. WABC, N.Y.C., 1973-74, v.p., dir. program devel. ABC AM Stations, 1974-76, v.p. programming ABC Radio, N.Y.C., 1977—; adj. prof. St. Johns U. Sighted advisor U.S. Assn. Blind Atheletes, 1977; mem. St. Johns Industry Adv. Council. Recipient Pres.'s medal St. John's U., 1978. Mem. Internat. Radio and Television Soc. (bd. govs.). Author childrens book: Tom Swift and His Giant Robot, 1954. 10023 Office: 1330 Ave of the Americas New York City NY 10019

SKLAR, RICHARD LAWRENCE, educator; b. N.Y.C., Mar. 22, 1930; s. Kalman and Sophie (Laub) S.; A.B., U. Utah, 1952; M.A., Princeton, 1957, Ph.D., 1961; m. Eva Molineux, July 14, 1962; children—Judith Anne, Katherine Elizabeth. Mem. faculty Princeton, Brandeis U., U. Ibadan (Nigeria), U. Zambia, State U. N.Y. at Stony Brook; now prof. polit. sci. U. Calif. at Los Angeles; mem. fgn. area fellowship program Africa Nat. Com., 1970-73; Simon vis. prof. U. Manchester (Eng.), 1975. Served with U.S. Army, 1952-54. Rockefeller Found. grantee, 1967. Mem. Am. Polit. Sci. Assn., African Studies Assn. (dir. 1976-78). Author: Nigerian Political Parties: Power in an Emergent African Nation, 1963; Corporate Power in an African State, 1975. Contbr. articles to profl. jours. Home: 1951 Holmby Ave Los Angeles CA 90025

SKLAR, ROBERT ANTHONY, educator, author; b. New Brunswick, N.J., Dec. 3, 1936; s. Leon George and Lilyn (Fuchs) S.; A.B. summa cum laude, Princeton, 1958; student U. Bonn (West Germany), 1959-60; Ph.D., Harvard, 1965; m. Kathryn Sue Kish, Nov. 27, 1958; children—Leonard, Susan. Rewrite man AP, Newark, 1958-59; staff reporter Los Angeles Times, 1959; asst. prof. program Am. culture U. Mich. at Ann Arbor, 1965-69, asso. prof. history, 1969-75, prof. history, 1975-76, mem. nat. humanities faculty, 1972-73; vis. prof. U. Auckland (New Zealand), 1970, U. Tokyo, 1971, Bard Coll., 1975-76; cultural historian, writer on movies, TV, Am. culture and soc. Guggenheim fellow, 1970-71; Rockefeller Found. Humanities fellow, 1976-77; prof. cinema, chmn. dept. cinema studies N.Y. U., 1977—. Mem. Am. Studies Assn. (v.p. 1971). Author: F. Scott Fitzgerald, The Last Laocoon, 1967; Movie-Made America: A Cultural History of the American Movies, 1975. Editor: The Plastic Age, 1917-1930, 1970—; contbg. editor Am. Film Mag. Contbr. essays, articles, revs. to publs. Address: 347 W Broadway New York City NY 10013

SKLARE, MARSHALL, sociologist; b. Chgo., Oct. 21, 1921; s. Irving and Bee (Lippman) S.; student Northwestern U., 1938-39, 40-43; diploma Coll. Jewish Studies, Chgo., 1943; M.A. in Sociology, U. Chgo., 1948; Ph.D., Columbia U., 1953; m. Rose Bernards, June 8, 1947; children—Daniel Avram, Judith Eve, Joshua Mayer. Lectr. dept. sociology and anthropology City Coll. N.Y., 1952-53; study dir. to dir. Div. Sci. Research, Am. Jewish Com., 1953-66; lectr. Wurzweiler Sch. Social Work, Yeshiva U., 1960-66, Stern Coll. for Women, 1963-64, prof. sociology Wurzweiler Sch. Social Work and Ferkauf Grad. Sch. Humanities and Social Sci., 1966-70; Fulbright lectr. Hebrew U. of Jerusalem, 1965-66; vis. lectr. Princeton Theol. Sem., 1968-69; vis. prof. Am. Jewish sociology Brandeis U., Waltham, Mass., 1969-70, prof. Am. Jewish studies and sociology, 1970-79, Klutznick Family prof. Am. Jewish studies and sociology, 1979—; vis. prof. sociology Clark U., 1970-72; sr. fellow Nat. Endowment for Humanities, 1972-73; chmn. award com. Fred Sherrow Meml. Prize; cons. Max Weinreich Center for Advanced Jewish Studies, YIVO Inst. for Jewish Research. Adviser univ. nominations com. Tel Aviv U.; mem. acad. adv. bd. Synagogue Council Am., Acad. for Jewish Studies Without Walls; mem. adv. bd. Tay-Sachs Found.; mem. acad. adv. council Nat. Found. for Jewish Culture. Mem. Assn. for Sociol. Study of Jewry (pres., chmn. com. on curriculum and resources), Am. Jewish Hist. Soc. (mem. acad. adv. council), Assn. for Jewish Studies (dir.), Am. Sociol. Assn. (program organizer). Author: Conservative Judaism: An American Religious Movement, 1955, rev. edit., 1972; (with M. Vosk) The Riverton Study: How Jews Look at Themselves and Their Neighbors, 1957; The Jews: Social Patterns of an American Group, 1958, 77; (with J. Greenblum) Jewish Identity on the Suburban Frontier: A Study of Group Survival in the Open Society, 1967, 2d edit., 1979; (with J. Greenblum and B.B. Ringer) Not Quite at Home: How an American Jewish Community Lives with Itself and its Neighbors, 1969; America's Jews, 1971; The Jew in American Society, 1974; The Jewish Community in America, 1974. Contbr. articles to profl. jours. Mem. editorial bd. Am. Jewish History. Office: Lown Bldg Brandeis U Waltham MA 02154

SKLENAR, HERBERT ANTHONY, indsl. products mfg. co. exec.; b. Omaha, June 7, 1931; s. Michael Joseph and Alice Madeline (Spicka) S.; M.B.A., Harvard, 1954; B.S. in Bus. Adminstrn. summa cum laude, U. Omaha, 1952; m. Eleanor L. Vincenz, Sept. 15, 1956; children—Susan Allison, Patricia Irene. Vice pres., comptroller Parkersburg-Aetna Corp., Parkersburg, W.Va., 1956-63; v.p., dir. Marmac Corp., Parkersburg, 1963-66; mgr. fin. control Boise Cascade Corp. (Idaho), 1966-67; exec. v.p. fin. and adminstrn., sec. Cudahy Co., Phoenix, 1967-72; exec. v.p., chief adminstrv. officer, dir. Vulcan Materials Co., Birmingham, Ala., 1972—; mem. task force on conceptual framework project, funds flows and liquidity Fin. Acctg. Standards Bd., 1979—. Served with U.S. Army, 1954-56. Recipient Alumni Achievement award U. Nebr. at Omaha, 1977; C.P.A., W.Va. Mem. Am. Inst. C.P.A.'s, Nat. Assn. Accountants, Fin. Execs. Inst., Phi Kappa Phi, Omicron Delta Kappa, Phi Eta Sigma, Delta Sigma Pi. Clubs: The Club, Racquet Place, Mountain Brook Racquet and Swim. Author: (with others) The Automatic Factory-A Critical Examination, 1955. Home: 3908 Knollwood Dr Birmingham AL 35243 Office: One Metroplex Dr Birmingham AL 35209

SKOK, RICHARD ARNOLD, educator; b. St. Paul, June 19, 1928; s. Clarence Francis and Madeline Eleanor (Arnold) S.; B.S., U. Minn., 1950, M.F., 1954, Ph.D., 1960; m. Helen Pauline Earnest, Nov. 17, 1951; children—Kenneth Earnest, Kathryn Paulette. Asst. prof. Sch. Forestry, U. Mont., 1958-59; asst. prof. Coll. Forestry, U. Minn., St. Paul, 1960-61, asso. prof., 1962-63, prof., 1965—, asst. dir., 1967-71, asso. dean, 1971-74, dean, 1974—. Chmn. McIntire-Stennis adv. bd. U.S. Dept. Agr., 1977, 78; mem. joint council on food and agrl. scis., 1979—. Trustee Wilderness Res. Fedn., 1977—. Served with AUS, 1950-52. Fellow Soc. Am. Foresters; mem. Forest Products Research Soc., Assn. State Coll. and Univ. Research Orgns. (v.p. 1979-80), Sigma Xi, Xi Sigma Pi. Home: 1873 Shryer Ave W Saint Paul MN 55113

SKOLNIK, BARNET DAVID, lawyer; b. N.Y.C., Feb. 8, 1941; s. Jack and Edythe (Savitz) S.; A.B. in Am. Govt. cum laude, Harvard U., 1962, LL.B., 1965; m. Joyce Elaine Hallock, July 14, 1973; children—Sarah, Deborah, Daniel, Joseph, Benjamin, Rebecca. Admitted to D.C. bar, 1966; atty. criminal div. U.S. Dept. Justice, Washington, 1966-68, asst. U.S. atty. for Dist. Md., Balt., 1968-78, chief public corruption unit U.S. Atty.'s Office, Balt., 1973-78; individual practice law, Washington, 1978—; tchr., lectr. on trial practice, white collar criminality, public corruption. Recipient Spl. Achievement award Dept. Justice, 1972, 74, Spl. Commendation for Outstanding Service, 1978; Younger Fed. Lawyer award Fed. Bar Assn., 1974; Atty. Gen.'s Disting. Service award, 1974; Legal award Assn. Fed. Investigators, 1977. Mem. D.C. Bar. Am. Bar Assn. Office: 1709 New York Ave NW Suite 205 Washington DC 20006

SKOLNIKOFF, EUGENE BERTRAM, educator; b. Phila., Aug. 29, 1928; s. Benjamin H. and Betty (Turoff) S.; B.S., Mass. Inst. Tech., 1949, M.S., 1950, Ph.D., 1965; B.A., Oxford (Eng.) U., 1952, M.A., 1952; m. Winifred S. Weinstein, Sept. 15, 1957; children—David, Matthew, Jessica. Research asst. in elec. engring. Uppsala U., Sweden, 1950; adminstrv. staff mem. Mass. Inst. Tech., 1952-55, prof. polit. sci., 1965—, chmn. polit. sci. dept., 1970-74, dir. Center for Internat. Studies, 1972—; vis. research prof. Carnegie Endowment for Internat. Peace, Geneva, 1969-70; systems analyst Inst. for Def. Analyses, Washington, 1957-58; mem. White House staff Office Spl. Asst. to Pres. for Sci. and Tech., Washington, 1958-63; adj. prof. Fletcher Sch. Law and Diplomacy, Tufts U., Medford, Mass., 1965-72; sr. cons. White House Office of Sci. and Tech. Policy, also vice chmn. adv. com. on sci., tech. and devel.; cons. White House Office Sci. and Tech., Dept. State AID, Orgn. Econ. Cooperation and Devel., Resources for the Future, Am. Soc. Internat. Law, Ford Found., Inst. Def. Analyses; chmn., pres. Sci. and Pub. Policy Studies Group, 1967-73; mem. Internat. Council Sci. Policy Studies, 1972—; Montague Burton vis. prof. U. Edinburgh. Trustee German Marshall Fund, UN Research Inst. for Social Devel.; bd. dirs. Overseas Devel. Council; mem. U.S. delegation UN Commn. for Social Devel., 1979. Served with U.S. Army Security Agy., 1955-57. Registered profl. engr., D.C. Rhodes scholar, 1950-52, Rockefeller Found. fellow, 1963-65; Fellow Am. Acad. Arts and Scis. (councillor 1973—), AAAS (sec. sect. K 1967-69, mem. com. on sci. and pub. policy 1972-74); mem. UN Assn., Council Fgn. Relations, Fedn. Am. Scientists (council 1971-75), Am. Polit. Sci. Assn., Internat. Studies Assn., Am. Assn. Rhodes Scholars, Soc. for Internat. Devel., Am. Acad. Arts and Scis., Soc. for Social Studies of Sci., Pugwash Com., Sigma Xi, Tau Beta Pi, Eta Kappa Nu. Author: Science, Technology and American Foreign Policy, 1967; International Imperatives of Technology, 1972. Co-editor: World Eco-Crisis, 1972. Contbr. articles to publs. Chmn. editorial bd. Pub. Sci; editorial bd. Sci. Studies, Tech. Rev., Internat. Orgn. Patentee hybrid circuits. Home: 3 Chandler St Lexington MA 02173 Office: Mass Inst Tech Cambridge MA 02139

SKOLOVSKY, ZADEL, concert pianist; b. Vancouver, B.C., Can. (brought to U.S. 1923, naturalized 1929); s. Max and Kate (Jones) S.; student Curtis Inst. Music, 1928-37; studied piano with Isabelle Vengerova, conducting with Fritz Reiner, violin with Edwin Bachmann; m. Alice Maffett Glass, July 29, 1947 (div. 1953). Debut at Town Hall, as winner of the Walter W. Naumburg award, 1939; appeared in recitals in Carnegie Hall, N.Y.C., and various states and Can., 1939—; soloist with N.Y. Philharmonic Symphony Orch. under condrs. Dimitri Mitropoulos, Charles Muench, Arthur Rodzinski, also Paul Paray; appeared as a soloist Lewishohn Stadium, N.Y. and Robin Hood Dell, Phila., under condrs. Vladimir Golschmann, Pierre Monteux, Alexander Smallens; soloist with NBC Orch., Nat. Orch. Assn., Phila. Orch., Nat. Orch. Washington, San Francisco Symphony, Israel Philharmonic, Residentie Orch. at The Hague, L'Orchestre Nat. de Belgique, B.B.C. Scottish Orch., orchs. of Luxembourg, Lisbon (Portugal), Hilversum Radio (Holland), Paris, London, Ravinia, Chgo., N.Y.C.; also appeared on TV; first performance Second Piano Concerto by Prokofieff with N.Y. Philharmonic Orch. under Charles Munch, 1948; world premier Concerto No. 4 of Darius Milhaud with Boston Symphony, 1950; first extensive European tour, 1953, appeared with Residency Orch. of the Hague, 2d tour, appeared as soloist with Israel Philharmonic Orch. at opening concert World Festival Music, 1954; appeared in Mexico, 1965; European tour, Eng., Holland, Scandinavia, Belgium, 1965-66, 67; recital Queen Elizabeth Hall, London, Eng., 1971, 73; reticals, B.C., 1975; prof. music Ind. U., 1976—; concert tour of S. Am., 1978; jurior N.Y. U. Internat. Tchaikovsky Piano Competition, 1978, 3d Latin Am. Teresa Carreno Piano Competition, Caracas, Venezuela, 1978. Records for Columbia Masterworks Records, Philips Records. Recipient prizes from Nat. Fedn. Music Clubs, Nat. Music League; The Robin Hood Dell Young Am. Artists award, 1943. Club: Lotos (N.Y.C.). Home: 240 E 79th St New York NY 10021 Office: 5 E 66th St New York NY 10021

SKOLSKY, SIDNEY, journalist, motion pictures producer; b. N.Y.C., May 2, 1905; s. Louis and Mildred (Arbeit) S.; student N.Y. U., 1925; m. Estelle Lorenz, Aug. 27, 1928; children—Nina, Steffi. Press agt., 1925-29; Broadway columnist, 1929-33; Hollywood columnist, 1933—; writer monthly column From A Stool at Schwabs, Photoplay mag.; producer Columbia film The Jolson Story, 1946, The Eddie Cantor Story, 1953; producer TV spl., 1961; writer TV documentary, 1962, Hollywood, The Golden Years, 1970. Author: Don't Get Me Wrong—I Love Hollywood, 1975. Office: Schwabs Drug Store Sunset Blvd Hollywood CA 90046

SKONING, WARREN GERALD, retail dept. store chain exec.; b. Elgin, Ill., Mar. 14, 1915; s. Walter and Edna (Hendricks) S.; grad. U. Chgo., 1937; m. Betty Jean Dunlap, Apr. 26, 1941; children—Gerald D. Mark S., Elissa S. With Sears, Roebuck and Co., Chgo., now v.p. facilities planning; dir. Homart Devel. Co.; trustee Am. Fletcher Mortgage Investors Northwestern Mut. Life Mortgage & Realty

Investors; officer, dir. Dearborn Park Corp. Trustee, Community Hosp., Geneva, Ill.; bd. dirs. Rehab. Inst. Chgo., Met. Housing Devel. Corp., Chgo., Nat. Realty Com. Served with USN; ETO. Home: 1101 Geneva Rd Saint Charles IL 60174 Office: Sears Tower Chicago IL 60684

SKOOG, CHARLES VERNON, JR., advt. exec.; b. N.Y.C., June 2, 1918; s. Charles Vernon and Clara (Peterson) S.; B.S. in Marketing, N.Y. U., 1942, student Grad. Sch. Bus., 1947. Advt. mgr. Frederick Loeser Dept. Store, 1947; with Hicks & Greist, N.Y.C., 1948—, chmn. bd., 1965—; dir. Gentry Corp., King Kullen Supermarkets. Served to maj. AUS, World War II. Decorated Bronze Star. Mem. Sales Execs. Club, Mktg. Execs. Club. Advt. Writers N.Y.C. Home: 2 Gramercy Park New York City NY 10003 Office: 522 Fifth Ave New York City NY 10036

SKOOG, FOLKE KARL, educator; b. Fjäräs, Sweden, July 15, 1908 (came to U.S. 1925, naturalized 1935); s. Karl Gustav and Sigrid (Person) S.; B.S., Calif. Inst. Tech., 1932, Ph.D., 1936; Ph.D. (hon.), U. Lund (Sweden), 1956; m. Birgit Anna Lisa Bergner, Jan. 31, 1947; 1 dau., Karin. Teaching asst., research fellow biology Calif. Inst. Tech., 1934-36; NRC fellow U. Calif., 1936-37, summer 1938; instr., tutor biology Harvard, 1937-41, research asso., 1941; asso., asso. prof. biology Johns Hopkins, 1941-44; chemist Q.M.C., also tech. rep., U.S. Army ETO, 1944-46; asso. prof. botany U. Wis.-Madison, 1947-49, prof., 1949—, now C. Leonard Huskins prof. botany. Vis. physiologist Pineapple Research Inst., U. Hawaii, 1938-39; asso. physiologist NIH, USPHS, 1943; vis. lectr. Washington U., 1946, Lantbrukshögskolan, Ultuna, Sweden, 1952; v.p. physiol. sect. Internat. Bot. Congress, Paris, 1954, Edinburgh, 1964, Leningrad, 1975. Recipient certificate of merit Bot. Soc. Am., 1956. Mem. Nat. Acad. Scis. U.S., Bot. Soc. Am. (chmn. physiol. sect. 1954-55), Am. Soc. Plant Physiologists (v.p. 1952-53, pres. 1957-58, Stephen Hales award 1954, Reid Barnes life membership award 1970), Scandinavian Soc. Plant Physiologists, Soc. Developmental Biology (pres. 1971), Am. Soc. Gen. Physiologists (v.p. 1956-57, pres. 1957-58), Internat. Plant Growth Substances Assn. (v.p. 1976-79, pres. 1979—), Am. Soc. Biol. Chemists, Am. Acad. Arts and Scis., Deutsche Akademie der Naturforscher Leopoldina, Swedish Royal Acad. Scis. (fgn.). Editor: Plant Growth Substances, 1951. Contbr. articles to profl. jours. Patentee in field. Track and field mem. Swedish Olympic Team, 1932. Home: 2134 Chamberlain Ave Madison WI 53705

SKOOG, RALPH EDWARD, lawyer; b. Topeka, Dec. 17, 1929; s. Ralph O. and Anna C. (Haley) S.; B.S., Kans. State U., 1952; J.D., Washburn U., 1959; m. Beth Henry, Nov. 19, 1953; children—Eric S., Peter R., Carl E., Curt A., Edward. Engr. and geologist Howard, Needles, Tammen & Bergendoff, Topeka, 1954-59; admitted to Kans. bar, 1959; partner firm Cook, Flatt & Skoog, Cons. Engrs., Topeka, 1960-63; partner law firm Dickinson, Crow & Skoog, 1962-71, Crow & Skoog, Attys., 1971-74, Skoog & Reed, Topeka, 1974—; treas. Steel Fixture Mfg. Co.; lectr. Washburn U., 1971—. Pres., Community Resources Council, 1970-71. Mem. Kans. Ho. of Reps., 1961-65, 67-69; mem. finance com. Rep. State Com., 1971-72; mem. Rep. State Com., 1973-74, chmn. 2d Congl. Dist., 1977-78; del. Rep. Nat. Conv., 1976. Bd. dirs. Topeka Inst. Urban Affairs, 1966-74. Served to 1st lt. AUS, 1952-54. Registered profl. engr., Kans. Mem. Geol. Soc. Am., ASCE, Nat. Soc. Profl. Engrs., Kans. State U. Alumni Assn. (internat. pres. 1967-69, bd. govs. 1970-74), Kans. Trial Lawyers Assn. (bd. govs., v.p. 1978—), Am., Kans. bar assns., Phi Alpha Delta, Sigma Tau, Sigma Alpha Epsilon, Phi Kappa Phi, Sigma Gamma Epsilon. Congregationalist. Home: 235 Greenwood Ave Topeka KS 66606 Office: 434 Topeka Ave Topeka KS 66603

SKOPIL, OTTO RICHARD, JR., judge; b. Portland, Oreg., June 3, 1919; s. Otto Richard and Freda Martha (Boetticher) S.; B.A. in Econs., Willamette U., 1941, LL.B., 1946; m. Janet Rae Lundy, July 27, 1956; children—Otto Richard III, Casey Robert, Shannon Ida, Molly Jo. Admitted to Oreg. bar, 1946, IRS, U.S. Treasury Dept., U.S. Dist. Ct. Oreg., U.S. Circuit Ct. of Appeals, 9th Circuit, U.S. Supreme Ct. bars; asso. firm Skopil & Skopil, 1946-51; partner Williams, Skopil, Miller, Beck & Wylie (and predecessor firms), Salem, Oreg., 1951-72; judge U.S. Dist. Ct., Portland, 1972-79, chief judge, 1976-79; circuit judge for 9th Circuit Ct. Appeals, Portland, 1979—. Hi-Y adviser Salem YMCA, 1951-52; appeal agt. Selective Service System, Marion County (Oreg.) Draft Bd., 1953-66; master of ceremonies 1st Gov.'s Prayer Breakfast for State Oreg., 1959; mem. citizens' adv. com. City of Salem, 1970-71; chmn. Gov.'s Com. on Staffing Mental Instns., 1969-70. Pres., bd. dirs. Marion County Tb and Health Assn.; bd. dirs. Willamette Valley Camp Fire Girls, Internat. Christian Leadership, Fed. Jud. Center; trustee Willamette U. Served to lt. USNR, 1942-46. Mem. Am., Oreg. (gov.), Marion County bar assns., Am., Judicature Soc., Oreg. Assn. Def. Counsel (dir.), Def. Research Inst., Assn. Ins. Attys. U.S. and Can. (Oreg. rep. 1970), Internat. Soc. Barristers, Prayer Breakfast Movement (fellowship council). Mem. Christian Ch. (deacon, trustee, elder). Clubs: Salem Exchange (pres.), Illahe Hills Country (pres., dir.). Office: Pioneer Courthouse Portland OR 97024

SKORNIA, HARRY JAY, educator, lectr., author, cons.; b. nr. Petoskey, Mich., Apr. 2, 1910; s. Charles and Josephine (Schluttenhofer) S.; A.B., Mich. State U., 1932; A.M., U. Mich., 1933, Ph.D., 1937; m. 2d, Lorene M. Kelly; children by former marriage—Mary Margaret, Lee Charles. Faculty, U. Mich., 1932-34, 36-38, Arkansas City Jr. Coll., 1934-36, DePauw U., 1938-40; program dir. NBC radio sta. WIRE, Indpls., 1940-42; asso. prof., chmn. dept., dir. radio Ind. Univ., Bloomington, 1942-53; weekly radio commentary, sta. WSUA, WTTS, Bloomington, 1946-48; vis. expert Office Mil. Govt., Germany, Austria, 1948-49; radio officer, radio attache Fgn. Service USIA, Dept. State, Vienna, 1951-53; exec. dir. Nat. Assn. Ednl. Broadcasters, 1953-59, pres., 1959-60; prof. TV-radio U. Ill., Urbana, 1960-69, U. Ill., Chicago Circle, 1969-75, prof. emeritus, 1975—; prof. mass communications U. South Fla., 1975—; cons. Italian Broadcast System, 1972, 73; lectr. in field. Sr. specialist East West Center, 1967; past mem. exec. com. Council Nat. Orgns.; former mem. Fullbright adv. screening com. radio and TV; former chmn. mass communication com. U.S. Nat. Commn. for UNESCO, 1958-60; cons. to bd. nat. missions Presbyn. Ch. Recipient Pioneer award Internat. Broadcasters Soc., 1968. Mem. Nat. Assn. for Better Broadcasting (dir.), Broadcast Edn. Assn., Nat. Assn. Ednl. Broadcasters. Author: Basic Manual for German Radio, 1949; (with Robert H. Lee, Fred Brewer) Creative Broadcasting, 1950; Television and Society, 1965; Television and the News, 1968; co-author: Problems and Controversies in Radio and Televison 1968. Contbr. tech. articles to profl. jours. Home: 224 S Pebble Beach Blvd Sun City Center FL 33570

SKORNICKA, JOEL L., mayor; b. Green Bay, Wis., Jan. 29, 1937; s. Lester A. and Jean U. (Hanson) S.; B.S. in Polit. Sci., U. Wis., Madison, 1959, M.S., 1964; m. Carol Nechrony, Feb. 2, 1962; children—Christopher, Jennifer. Mem. adminstrv. staff U. Wis., Madison, 1960-79, asst. to vice chancellor, then asst. vice chancellor, 1970-77, asst. chancellor, 1977-79; mayor of Madison, 1979—; mem. Wis. Correction Industries Adv. Bd., Dane County Public Affairs Council; adv. com. Dane County Regional Airport Commn. Bd. dirs. Madison Civic Music Assn., Wis. Arts Bd., Central Madison Council, Hist. Soc. Wis., Madison Art Assn.; pres. Greater Madison Found. Arts, 1974-77. Served to 2d lt. USAR, 1959-60. Home: 3830 Council Crest Madison WI 53711 Office: 210 Monona Ave Madison WI 53709

SKORSKI, ROMAN, educator; b. Jarczowce, Poland, July 9, 1911; s. Jan and Josephin (Jawnicz) S.; B.S., Mining and Metall. Acad., Poland, 1934, M.S., 1938, D.Sc., 1949; m. Genovefa Protasiewicz, Sept. 9, 1950; children—Maria, Margarette. Came to U.S., 1963, naturalized, 1968. Asso. prof., head physics, metall. div. Polytechnic Warsaw (Poland), 1950-54; head tech. physics div. Precision Mechanics Inst., Warsaw, 1954-63; vis. prof. U. Del., 1963, Busan Nat. U., Korea, 1975; prof. dept. metall. engring. U. Ala., 1963—. Served to flight lt. Polish br. Royal Air Force, 1943-46. Fellow A.A.A.S. (council 1968-73), Internat. Platform Assn., Mech. Engring. Soc. Warsaw (chmn. ednl. dept. 1949-54), Ala. Acad. Sci. (v.p. 1968-69), Sigma Xi. Author: Fundamentals of Metallurgy, 1953; The Elements: Their Atoms and Crystals, 1976. Contbr. articles sci. jours. Home: 7 B Northwood Lake Northport AL 35476 Office: Dept Metall Engring U Ala University AL 35486

SKOTHEIM, ROBERT ALLEN, coll. pres.; b. Seattle, Jan. 31, 1933; s. Sivert O. and Marjorie F. (Allen) S.; B.A., U. Wash., Seattle, 1955, M.A., 1958, Ph.D., 1962; LL.D., Hobart and William Smith Colls., Geneva, N.Y., 1975; m. Nadine Vail, June 14, 1953; children—Marjorie, Kris, Julia. Prof. history U. Wash., 1962-63; prof. history Wayne State U., Detroit, 1963-66; prof. UCLA, 1966-67; prof. U. Colo., Boulder, 1967-72; provost, dean faculty Hobart and William Smith Colls., 1972-75; pres. Whitman Coll., Walla Walla, Wash., 1975—. Guggenheim fellow, 1967-68. Mem. Phi Beta Kappa (hon.). Author: American Intellectual Histories and Historians, 1966; Totalitarianism and American Social Thought, 1971. Editor: The Historian and the Climate of Opinion, 1969; co-editor: American Social Thought: Sources and Interpretations, 2 vols., 1972. Home: 515 Boyer St Walla Walla WA 99362 Office: Whitman Coll Walla Walla WA 99362

SKOUFIS, PETER JOHN, govt. ofcl.; b. Bangor, Maine, May 7, 1919; s. John L. and Katina (Boretos) K.; A.B. in History and Govt., U. Maine, 1941; student George Washington U. Sch. Law, 1941-42; m. Helen Mahanic, Oct. 22, 1949. Boys supr. Indsl. Home Sch., Washington, 1941-42; registration officer div. vocational rehab. VA, Washington, 1946-47; joined U.S. Fgn. Service, 1947; assigned Am. embassies at Paris, Rome, Pretoria, 1947-55; asst. exec. dir. bur. security and consular affairs, Dept. State, 1955-58; 1st sec. Am. embassy, The Hague, 1958-61; fgn. service insp., 1961-63; exec. officer Office of Sec., 1964-66; counselor embassy adminstrv. affairs, London, Eng., 1966-71, Paris, France, 1971-75; dep. insp. gen. Dept. of State, 1975-77; asst. dir. gen. for adminstrn. and fin. FAO of UN, 1977—. Served to 1st lt. USAAF, World War II. Club: American (Rome). Home and Office: FAO Via delle Terme di Caracalla 00100 Rome Italy

SKOURAS, SPYROS SOLON, shipping co. exec.; b. St. Louis, Oct. 28, 1923; s. Spyros P. and Sarah K. (Briuglia) S.; B.A., Yale U., 1945; m. Barbara Jane Feldmann, May 29, 1951; children—Cassandra M., Spyros Solon, II, George A., Damaris B. Pres., Skouras Theatres Corp., 1952-60, chmn. bd., 1960-72; pres. Prudential Lines, Inc., N.Y.C., 1960—. Bd. dirs. USO Met. N.Y., 1971—, Catholic Interracial Council, 1972—, United Cerebral Palsy of N.Y., 1973—; mem. exec. com. Am. Museum Immigration, 1972—; trustee Alfred E. Smith Meml. Fund, 1974—. Served with U.S. Army, 1943-46. Decorated knight of Malta, 1958. Mem. Am. Steamship Owners Mut. Protection and Indemnity Assn. (dir.), Hellenic-Am. C. of C. (dir.), N.Y. C. of C., Am. Steamship Lines Assn. (vice chmn., exec. com.). Republican. Roman Catholic. Clubs: Met., Recess, Stanwich. Home: East Middle Patent Rd Greenwich CT 06830 Office: Prudential Lines Inc 1 World Trade Center New York City NY 10048

SKOVE, THOMAS MALCOLM, mfg. co. exec.; b. Cleve., June 27, 1925; s. Thomas Malcolm and Ethel C. (Rush) S.; B.S., Bucknell U., 1949; m. Helen Busing, June 12, 1948; children—Margaret, Thomas, Richard, Marcie, Douglas. Controller, treas. Cleve. Twist Drill Co., 1949-68; treas. Acme-Cleve. Corp., 1968—. Councilman, City of Aurora, Ohio, 1977—. Served with USN, 1943-46. Mem. Machinery and Allied Products Inst., Cleve. C. of C., Treas. Club Cleve. Republican. Club: Walden Country. Home: 624 W Acadia St Aurora OH 44202 Office: PO Box 5617 Cleveland OH 44101

SKRABLE, KENNETH WILLIAM, educator; b. Teaneck, N.J., Oct. 10, 1935; s. Robert and Gladys (Simms) S.; B.S., Moravian Coll., Bethlehem, Pa., 1958; M.S., Vanderbilt U., 1964; Ph.D., Rutgers U., 1969; m. Sidna Ann Jones, Sept. 7, 1957; children—Kenneth Paul, Stacy Ann. Health physics supr. Indsl. Reactor Labs., Plainsboro, N.J. 1959-63; radiation safety officer, lectr. radiation scis. Rutgers U., 1963-68; prof., head dept. radiol. scis. Lowell Tech. Inst., 1968-74; prof. radiol. scis. U. Lowell, 1974—. Diplomate Am. Bd. Health Physics. Mem. Am. Nuclear Soc., Health Physics Soc., Sigma Xi. Home: 6 Ruthellen Rd Chelmsford MA 08124 Office: 1 University Ave Lowell MA 01854

SKRAMSTAD, HAROLD KENNETH, JR., assn. exec.; b. Takoma Park, Md., June 3, 1941; s. Harold Kenneth and Sarah Catherine (Shroat) S.; A.B., George Washington U., 1963, Ph.D., 1971; m. Susan Edith Chappelear, Dec. 28, 1963; children—Robert Christopher, Elizabeth Ann. Instr. Am. lit. and Am. civilization George Washington U., 1966-67; project dir. community devel. Peace Corps, 1966-67; research fellow material culture Smithsonian Instn., 1967-68, acting dir. Office Am. Studies, 1968-69, asst. dir., 1969-71, spl. asst. to dir. Nat. Mus. History and Tech., 1971, chief spl. projects, 1971-72, chief of exhibits programs, 1972-74; dir. Chgo. Hist. Soc., 1974—; mem. Chgo. Commn. on Hist. and Archtl. Landmarks, 1975—, Joint Com. on Landmarks of Nat. Capital, 1972—. Bd. dirs. Kendall Coll. Mem. Am. Assn. Museums, Am. Assn. State and Local History, Am. Hist. Assn. Clubs: Arts, Tavern, Economic (Chgo.); Caxton. Home: 2436 Orrington Ave Evanston IL 60201 Office: Clark St at North Ave Chicago IL 60614

SKREBNESKI, VICTOR, photographer; b. Chgo., Dec. 17, 1929; s. Joseph and Anna (Casper) S.; student Art Inst. Chgo., 1945, Inst. Design, 1947. Propr. Skrebneski Studio, Chgo., 1956—. Bd. dirs. Chgo. Internat. Film Festival. Recipient award Art Directors Soc., 1958-75. Mem. Dirs. Guild Am., Soc. Photographers in Communications. Club: Arts (Chgo.). Author: Skrebneski, 1969; The Human Form, 1973; Skrebneski Portraits: A Matter of Record, 1978. Address: 1350 N LaSalle St Chicago IL 60610

SKRINDE, ROLF THORSTEN, environ. engr.; b. Stanwood, Wash., Sept. 1, 1928; s. Rolf Olson and Annie Evarna (Lindbak) S.; B.S. in Civil Engring., Wash. State U., 1946-50; M.S., Mass. Inst. Tech., 1952, San. Engr., 1955, Ph.D., 1958; m. Marjorie Eleanor Martin, Nov. 1, 1958; children—Kirsten, Karen, Rolf. Asst. prof., then asso. prof. civil engring. and san. engring. Wash. State U., 1958-61; asso. prof. environ. and san. engring. Washington U., St. Louis, 1961-63, chmn. dept. civil and environ. engring., 1963-65; prof., dir. research Asian Inst. Tech., Bangkok, Thailand, 1965-67; prof. civil engring. U. Mass.-Amherst, 1967-69; chmn. dept. civil engring. U. Iowa, 1969-71; v.p. Reynolds, Smith and Hills, Jacksonville, Fla., 1971-77; v.p. Tracey and Brunstrom Co., Seattle, 1977—; research asst. Mass. Inst. Tech., 1951-53, 55-58; with Ryckman, Edgerley, Tomlinson and Assos., St. Louis, 1961-71; san. engring. adviser Ministry Health Saudi Arabia, 1953-54, div. san. engring. Thailand Dept. Health, 1954-55; mem. study sect., engring. and urban health scis. Consumer Protection and Environ. Health Service, 1967-69; mem. environ. health rev. com. Bur. Health Professions Edn. and Manpower Tng., NIH, 1970-71; cons. NSF, 1972-75, ERDA, 1976-77, Dept. of Energy, 1977—. Served with USPHS, 1953-55. Registered profl. engr., Mass., Iowa, Fla., Ga., Mo., Wash. Mem. ASCE, Nat. Soc. Profl. Engrs., Am. Pub. Works Assn., Am. Water Works Assn., Water Pollution Control Fedn., Air Pollution Control Assn., Am. Pub. Health Assn., AAAS, Sigma Xi. Club: Masons. Contbr. numerous articles to profl. jours. Office: 1214 John St Seattle WA 98109

SKROMME, LAWRENCE HILMER, agrl. engr.; b. Roland, Iowa, Aug. 26, 1913; s. Austin and Ingeborg (Holmdal) S.; B.Sc., Iowa State Coll., 1937; m. Margaret E. Gleason, June 24, 1939; children—Cherlyn Sue, Inga Jean, Karen Ann. Design and devel. engr., tractor and implement tires Goodyear Tire & Rubber Co., Akron, Ohio, 1937-41; project engr., asst. to dir. engring., asst. chief engr. Harry Ferguson, Inc., Detroit, 1941-51; chief engr. New Holland div. Sperry Rand Corp. (formerly Sperry Corp.), New Holland, Pa., 1951-61, v.p. engring., 1961—. Mem. Pa. Gov.'s Com. Agr., 1965-67; research advisory com. U.S. Dept. Agr., 1964—; mem. div. engring. NRC. Vice pres. Farm & Home Found. Lancaster County. Bd. dirs., mem. awards com. Engrs. Joint Council; mem. adv. council Cornell U. Coll. Agr. Decorated chevalier Merit du Agricole (France); recipient Profl. Achievement citation Iowa State Coll., 1972. Registered profl. engr., Pa. Fellow Am. Soc. Agrl. Engrs. (pres. 1959-60, past v.p.; Gold medal 1974); mem. Internat. Commn. Agrl. Engrs. (dir., pres. tech. sect. III, v.p.), Nat. Soc. Profl. Engrs., Am. Soc. Engring. Edn., Soc. Automotive Engrs., Farm and Indsl. Equipment Inst. (engring. advisory com.), AAAS, N.Y. Acad. Scis., Nat. Acad. Engring., Alpha Zeta, Tau Beta Pi, Phi Kappa Phi. Methodist. Home: 2150 Landis Valley Rd Lancaster PA 17601 Office: Sperry New Holland Div Sperry Rand Corp New Holland PA 17557

SKROWACZEWSKI, STANISLAW, conductor, composer; b. Lwow, Poland, Oct. 3, 1923; s. Pawel and Zofia (Karszniewicz) S.; diploma faculty philosophy U. Lwow, 1945; diploma faculties composition and conducting Acad. Music Lwow, 1945, Conservatory at Krakow (Poland), 1946; L.H.D., Hamline U., 1963, Macalester Coll., 1972; m. Krystyna Jarosz, Sept. 6, 1956; children—Anna, Paul, Nicholas. Came to U.S., 1960. Composer, 1931—; first symphony and overture for orch. written at age 8, played by Lwow Philharmonic Orch., 1931; pianist, 1928—, violinist, 1934—, condr., 1939—; permanent condr., music dir. Wroclaw (Poland) Philharmonic, 1946-47, Katowice (Poland) Nat. Philharmonic, 1949-54, Krakow Philharmonic, 1955-56, Warsaw Nat. Philharmonic Orch., 1957-59, Minnesota Orch., 1960-79; guest condr. in Europe, S.A., U.S., 1947—. Recipient nat. prize for artistic activity Poland, 1953; First prize Santa Cecilia Internat. Concours for Condrs., Rome, 1956. Mem. Union Polish Composers, Internat. Soc. Modern Music, Nat. Assn. Am. Composers-Condrs., Am. Music Center. Composer: 4 symphonies; Prelude and Fugue for Orchestra (conducted first performance Paris), 1948; Overture 1947 (2d prize Szymanowski Concours, Warsaw 1947), 1947; Cantiques des Cantiques, 1951; String Quartet (2d Prize Internat. Concours Composers, Belgium 1953), 1953; Suite Symphonique (first prize, gold medal Composers Competition Moscow 1957), 1954; Music at Night, 1954; Ricercari Notturni, 1978 (3d prize Kennedy Center Friedheim Competition, Washington); also music for theatre, motion pictures, songs and piano sonatas, English horn concerto. Address: PO Box 700 Wayzata MN 55391

SKRYPYNK, MSTYSLAV STEPHAN, archbishop; b. Poltava, Ukraine, Apr. 10, 1898; s. Ivan and Mariamna (Petlura) S.; M. Polit. Sci., Sch. Polit. Sci., Warsaw, Poland, 1930; Ph.D. (hon.), Ukrainian Free U., 1951; m. Ivanna Witkovtsky, Jan. 8, 1921; children—Yaroslav, Tamara Yarovenko, Mariamna Suchoversky. Came to U.S., 1950. Acting bishop, Pereyaslav, Ukraine, 1942-44; sec. to Council of Bishops in Exile, Offenbach, Germany, 1945-46; bishop Ukrainian Orthodox Ch. Western Europe, 1946-47, archbishop Can., Winnipeg, Man., 1947-50; archbishop, pres. consistory U.S., South Bound Brook, N.J., 1950-71; met. archbishop in Diaspora, 1969—; met. archbishop Ch. U.S., 1971—. Dir. Coop. Union, Halychyna, 1923-26. Dep. mayor Riven, Volyn, Ukraine, 1930-31; mem. Polish (Seym) Parliament, sec. presidium, mem. fgn. affairs, budget commns., 1931-39; mem. Orthodox Council Volyn, 1932-39. Served to lt. Tsarist Army, 1916-17, Ukrainian Nat. Army, 1917-22. Address: PO Box 495 South Bound Brook NJ 08880

SKUBITZ, JOSEPH, congressman; b. Frontenac, Kans., May 6, 1906; s. Joseph and Mary (Youvan) S.; B.S., Kans. State Coll., 1929, M.S., 1934; student Washburn Law Sch., Topeka, 1938; LL.B., George Washington U., 1946; m. Mary Jess McClellan, Sept. 27, 1930. Mem. 88th-96th Congresses, 5th Dist. Kans. Recipient citation outstanding work in govt. Kans. State Coll., Pittsburg, 1961. Republican. Office: Rayburn House Office Bldg Washington DC 20515

SKULTETY, F(RANCIS) MILES, surgeon; b. Rochester, N.Y., June 6, 1922; s. Frank J. and Hazel (Kaitz) S.; B.S., U. Rochester, 1944, M.D., 1946; Ph.D. in Anatomy, State U. Iowa, 1958; m. Constance T. Schmitt, Dec. 26, 1945; children—Miles Christian, John Scott, William Kent. Intern, Worcester (Mass.) City Hosp., 1946-47; asst. resident in neurology Cushing VA Hosp., Farmingham, Mass., 1949-50; fellow in neurosurgery Lahey Clinic, Boston, 1950-51; sr. resident in neurosurgery Univ. Hosps., Iowa City, 1951-52; practice medicine specializing in neurosurgery, Iowa City, 1952-66, Omaha, 1966—; instr. State U. Iowa, Iowa City, 1952-53, asso. in surgery, 1953-54, asst. prof., 1954-56, asso. prof., 1958-63, prof. surgery div. neurosurgery, 1963-66; Shackleford prof. neurosurgery and neuroanatomy U. Nebr., Omaha, 1966—, mem. grad. faculty, 1967—, prof. anatomy, 1967—, asso. dean for clin. affairs, 1974—, chmn. dept. neurosurgery, 1975—, interim dean Coll. Medicine, 1978-79; mem. staffs U. Nebr. Hosp., Douglas County Hosp., Omaha, 1966—; asso. mem. staff Bishop Clarkson Meml. Hosp., 1967—; cons. Iowa City VA Hosp., 1952-66, Children's Meml. Hosp., Omaha, 1966—; cons. neurosurgery Omaha VA Hosp., 1966—, Lincoln (Nebr.) VA Hosp., 1968—; mem. task force for stroke Nebr.-S.D., Regional Med. Program, 1966; mem. spl. study sect. rev. coop. aneurysm study NIH, 1968. Pres. Hawkeye council Boy Scouts Am., 1964-66, chmn. regional tng. com., 1973—, mem. nat. tng. com., 1973-75. Served to capt. M.C., AUS, 1947-49. Recipient Silver Beaver award Boy Scouts Am., 1966, Silver Antelope award, 1975; diplomate Am. Bd. Neurol. Surgery. Fellow A.C.S., Royal Soc. Medicine; mem. Inst. Neurol. Diseases and Blindness (central registry com. study treatment intracranial aneurysms 1963-66, tng. com. B. 1966-70), Congress Neurol. Surgeons (sci. and edn. com. 1959-62, 64-65, program com. 1965-66, 70—, by-laws com. 1970—), AMA, Johnson County Med. Soc., Iowa State Med. Soc., Omaha-Douglas County Med. Soc., Nebr. State Med. Soc., Interurban Neurosurg. Soc., Iowa-M.W. Neurosurg. Soc. (pres. 1963),Assn. Research Nervous and Mental Diseases, Am. Assn. Neurol. Surgeons, Am. Assn. Anatomists, Soc. Exptl. Biology and Medicine, N.Y. Acad. Scis., Am. Neurol. Assn., Cajal Club,

Sigma Xi, Alpha Omega Alpha. Contbr. numerous articles to profl. jours. Home: 1503 S 83d St Omaha NE 68124 Office: Sch Medicine U Nebr 42d St and Dewey Ave Omaha NE 68105. *The guiding philosophical principle of my life has been that I am obligated to contribute to the community through my chosen profession and through volunteer services in the hope that the world will be a better place to live in by the time I die than it was when I was born.*

SKURDAHL, DALE MAYNARD, bank holding co. exec.; b. Warren, Minn., July 5, 1927; s. Norman Arthur and Helen Irma (Kays) S.; B.B.A., U. Minn., 1960, postgrad., 1960-63; m. Hilda G. Jones, June 1, 1948; children—Gail Constance, Dale Norman. Audit mgr. Ernst & Ernst, Mpls., 1961-74; sr. v.p., treas. Western Bancorp., Los Angeles, 1974—; instr. U. Minn., 1969-71. Served with USAAF, 1945-46, USN, 1948-56. C.P.A., Minn., Calif. Mem. Am. Inst. C.P.A.'s, Minn., Calif. socs. C.P.A.'s, Nat. Assn. Accountants. Republican. Methodist. Club: Jonathan (Los Angeles). Office: 707 Wilshire Blvd PO Box 54068 Los Angeles CA 90054

SKURLA, GEORGE MARTIN, aerospace co. exec.; b. Newark, July 2, 1921; B.S. in Aero. Engring., U. Mich., 1944; postgrad. Harvard U. Bus. Sch., 1973; m. Marie Brignoli; children—George Martin, Thomas, Martin, James. With Grumman Aerospace Corp., Bethpage, N.Y., 1944—, v.p., 1970-74, pres., chief operating officer, 1974—, chmn. bd., chief exec. officer, 1976—; dir. Grumman Corp., Grumman Ecosystems Corp., Grumman Allied Industries, Inc. Vice pres. United Way of Nassau-Suffolk counties, N.Y.; 1975—; trustee L.I. Forum for Tech., Poly. Inst. N.Y., Urban League of L.I., Hall of Sci. Mus., N.Y.C. Recipient Distinguished Citizen award Suffolk County council Boy Scouts Am., 1977; named Outstanding Man of Year in Aviation Mgmt., Roth Grad. Sch. Bus. Adminstrn., L.I. U., 1976. Fellow Am. Inst. Aeros. and Astronautics; mem. Soc. Logistics Engrs. (Founders medal 1977), Air Force Assn. (Man of Yr., H.H. Arnold chpt. 1975), Am. Def. Preparedness Assn., Assn. U.S. Army. Office: Grumman Aerospace Corp Bethpage NY 11714*

SKUTT, VESTOR JOSEPH, ins. exec.; b. Deadwood, S.D., Feb. 24, 1902; s. Roy N. and Catherine (Gorman) S.; ed. pub. and pvt. schs. in S.D.; LL.B., Creighton U., 1923, LL.D., 1971; LL.D., U. Nebr. at Omaha, 1958, U. Nebr. Coll. Medicine, 1964; m. Angela Anderson, June 8, 1926; children—Donald Joseph, Thomas James, Sally Jane (Mrs. John G. Desmond, Jr.). Admitted to Nebr. bar, 1923, practiced in Omaha, 1923-24; mem. legal dept. Mut. of Omaha Ins. Co., 1924-30, v.p., 1947-48, exec. v.p., 1948-49, pres., 1949-64, dir., 1947—, chmn. bd., chief exec. officer, 1953—; v.p. United Benefit Life Ins. Co., Omaha, 1936-49, chmn. bd., 1963—; pres., dir. Companion Life Ins. Co., N.Y.C., 1949-63, chmn. bd., 1963—; chmn. bd. Mut. of Omaha Fund Mgmt. Co., 1968—; dir. Omaha Nat. Bank, 1954-71, advisory council, 1971—; dir. Fairmont Foods Co., 1958-73, H.F. Ahmanson & Co., 1972-73. Former mem. civilian advisory com. to comdg. gen., Fifth Army. Gen. chmn. Omaha War Bond campaign, 1942; gen. chmn. United War and Community Chest campaign of Omaha, 1945, pres., 1948; mem. pres.'s com. on Employment of the Handicapped; mem. Nat. Civilian War Injury Policy Pool Com., 1942-45; mem. Bd. of World Rehabilitation Fund, Inc.; mem. Nat. Bus. Council Consumer Affairs. Founding pres. Nebr. Wildlife Fedn., 1970-72, chmn. bd., 1972-74; nat. brotherhood chmn. NCCJ, 1966, Cath. co-chmn., 1978—, vice chmn. nat. bd. trustees; nat. crusade chmn. Am. Cancer Soc., 1967; chmn. Jr. Achievement Omaha, 1974; nat. chmn. Explorer Scouts Bicentennial Exhbn., 1975-76; Nebr. chmn. United Negro Coll. Fund, 1975, nat. distinguished service award, 1975; dir., mem. exec. com., chmn. Region VII Nat. Alliance of Businessmen, nat. chmn., 1976-77; mem. Nat. 4-H Advisory Council; bd. regents Municipal U. Omaha, 1944-50; bd. dirs. Health Ins. Inst., 1972-75, Nat. Arthritis Found., 1972-74; trustee Am. Study Forum, Creighton U., 1968-76; mem. corp. Radio Free Europe Fund; trustee U. Nebr. Found., Creighton Hall, 1953-71, hon. trustee Joslyn Liberal Arts Soc.; mem.-at-large nat. council Boy Scouts Am.; chmn. communications com. North Central region Boy Scouts Am.; past trustee-at-large Nebr. Ind. Coll. Found.; bd. govs. Boys' Clubs Omaha; trustee Nat. Little League Found., 1976—; hon. chmn. Boys Republic ann. Della Robia wreath program, 1978. Recipient Harold R. Gordon Meml. award 1950; Air Force Exceptional Service medal, 1963; Golden Sword of Hope, Am. Cancer Soc., 1966; Can Do award Omaha C. of C., 1968; named Internat. Boss of Year, Nat. Secs. Assn., 1964, Nebraskan of Year, Nebr. Broadcasters Assn., 1964, Scouting Man of Year, 1971, Man of Year, Fedn. Ins. Counsel, 1971; recipient Nat. Salesman of Yr. award Nat. Sales and Mktg. Execs., 1972; Golden Plate award Am. Acad. Achievement, 1976; Silver Beaver award Mid-Am. council Boy Scouts Am., 1976. Mem. Am. Life Conv. (chmn. legal sect. 1947), Nebr., Tex., Okla. bar. assns., Health and Accident Underwriters Conf. (pres. 1948), Internat. Assn. Health Underwriters, Ins. Fedn. Nebr. (exec. council), Ins. Econs. Soc. Am., Health Ins. Assn. Am. (charter dir., pres. 1959), Fedn. Ins. Counsel, Creighton U. Alumni (nat. pres. 1935), Omaha Safety Council (chmn. bd. trustees), Newcomen Soc. N.Am., Delta Theta Phi, Ak Sar-Ben (Omaha, mem. bd. govs.). Clubs: Rotary; Omaha Country, Omaha; Chicago, Marco Polo. Home: 400 N 62d St Omaha NE 68132 Office: Mut of Omaha 33d and Dodge Sts Omaha NE 68131

SKYLSTAD, WILLIAM S., bishop; b. Omak, Wash., Mar. 2, 1934; s. Stephen Martin and Reneldes Elizzbeth (Danzl) S.; student Pontifical Coll., Josephinum, Worthington, Ohio; M.Ed., Gonzaga U. Ordained priest Roman Catholic Ch., 1960; asst. pastor, Pullman, Wash., 1960-62; tchr. Mater Cleri Sem., 1961-68, rector, 1968-74; pastor Assumption Parish, Spokane, 1974-76; chancellor Diocese of Spokane, 1976-77; ordained bishop, 1977; bishop of Yakima (Wash.), 1977—. Office: St Peter Retreat Center PO Box 87 Cowiche WA 98923*

SKYNNER, HENRY JOHN, librarian; b. Ft. William, Ont., Can., Nov. 10, 1930; s. Henry John and Susan Beatrice (Carter) S.; B.A., U. Man., Winnipeg, Can., 1951; L.Th., St. Johns Coll., Winnipeg, 1952; S.T.M., McGill U., Montreal, Que., 1956; B.L.S., U. Toronto (Ont., Can.), 1962. Ordained to ministry Anglican Ch., 1952; curate St. James Ch., Winnipeg, 1952-53, St. Johns Cathedral, Winnipeg, 1953-54, St. Matthias Ch., Montreal, 1954-56, St. John Evangelist Ch., Montreal, 1956-58; rector St. John Baptist Ch., Winnipeg, 1958-61; asst. prof. Near Eastern langs. St. Johns Coll., 1958-68, librarian, 1962-68; asso. dir. tech. services library U. Man., 1968—. Recipient Inkster medal, 1957; Birks div. fellow, 1956-57; H.W. Wilson scholar, 1961-62. Mem. Canadian Assn. Coll. and Univ. Libraries (past pres.), Can. Library Assn., Man. Library Assn. Home: 407-2945 Pembina Hwy Winnipeg MB R3T 3R1 Canada Office: Tech Services Elizabeth Dafoe Library U Manitoba Winnipeg MB R3T 2N2 Canada

SLAATTE, HOWARD ALEXANDER, clergyman, educator; b. Evanston, Ill., Oct. 18, 1919; s. Iver T. and Esther (Larsen) S.; A.A., Kendall Coll., 1940; B.A. cum laude, U. N.D., 1942; B.D. cum laude, Drew U., 1945, Ph.D., 1956; Drew fellow Mansfield Coll., Oxford (Eng.) U., 1949-50; m. Mildred Gegenheimer, June 20, 1951; children—Elaine Slaatte Tran, Mark, Paul. Ordained to ministry Methodist Ch., 1943; pastor Detroit Conf. United Meth. Ch., 1950-56; asso. prof. systematic theology Temple U., 1956-60; vis. prof. philosophy and religion McMurry Coll., 1960-65; prof., chmn. dept. philosophy Marshall U., Huntington, W.Va., 1965—, mem. grad. council, 1970-73, mem. research bd., 1974—, mem. acad. standards and policy com., 1975-77, research grantee, 1976, 77, mem. bd. Campus Christian Center, 1973-75; lectr. Traverse City (Mich.) State Hosp., 1966-71, other orgns.; baritone soloist. Mem. W.Va. Conf. United Meth. Ch., 1966—. NSF fellow, 1965; Benedum Found. research grantee, 1970; NSF research grantee, 1965, 71. Mem. W.Va. (pres. 1966-67), Am. philos. assns., AAUP, Am. Acad. Religion. Author: Time and Its End, 1962; Fire in the Brand, 1963; The Pertinence of the Paradox, 1968; The Paradox of Existentialist Theology, 1971; Modern Science and The Human Condition, 1974; The Arminian Arm of Theology, 1977; The Dogma of Immaculate Perception, 1979; contbr. numerous to theol. and philos. jours. Home: 407 Grand Blvd Huntington WV 25705

SLACK, DERALD ALLEN, plant pathologist, educator; b. Cedar City, Utah, Dec. 22, 1924; s. Fredrick and Marscella (Perry) S.; B.S., Utah State U., 1949, M.S., 1950; Ph.D., U. Wis., 1952; m. Betty Lue Stevens, Dec. 4, 1944; children—Steven Allen, Bonnie Lue Huens. Asst. prof. U. Ark., Fayetteville, 1952-54, asso. prof., 1954-59, prof., 1959-64, prof., head dept., 1964—. Bd. dirs., sec. Ark. Plant Bd., 1964—. Served with USAAF, 1943-45. Recipient Outstanding Instr. award U. Ark., 1956, Disting. Achievement award for research and teaching, 1961. Mem. Am. Phytopathol. Soc. (pres. So. div. 1970-71, sec. 1977—), Soc. Nematologists (charter mem.; editor Nematology Newsletter 1958-62), Ark. Hort. Soc., Ark. Pesticide Assn., Helminthological Soc., Washington, Ark. Acad. Sci., Sigma Xi (pres. Ark. chpt. 1961-63), Gamma Sigma Delta, Ark. Farm House Assn. (pres. 1961). Author: (with others) Plant Pathology Laboratory Manual, 3d edit., 1968; contbr. articles to sci. jours. Home: 1535 Hefley St Fayetteville AR 72701

SLACK, JOHN M., JR., Congressman; b. Charleston, W.Va., Mar. 18, 1915; s. John M. and Jennie (Gilchrist) S.; ed. Va. Mil. Acad.; m. Frances J. Reid; 1 son. Mem. 86th-87th Congresses from 6th Dist. W.Va., 88th to 96th Congresses from 3d Dist. W.Va. Mem. Kanawha County (W.Va.) Ct., 1948-52; assessor Kanawha County, 1952-58. Mem. SAR. Democrat. Presbyterian (treas., deacon). Clubs: Masons, Shriners, Exchange. Address: House Office Bldg Washington DC 20515

SLACK, LEWIS, orgn. adminstr.; b. Phila., Apr. 15, 1924; s. Lewis and Martha (Fitzgerald) S.; S.B., Harvard, 1944; Ph.D., Washington U., St. Louis, 1950; m. Sarah Hunt Wyman, Dec. 29, 1948; children—Elizabeth Wyman, Susan Towne, Christopher Morgan. Physicist, U.S. Naval Research Lab., 1950-54; asso. prof. physics George Washington U., Washington, 1954-57, prof. physics, 1957-62, acting head physics dept., 1957-60; asst. exec. sec. div. phys. scis. Nat. Acad. Scis., NRC, Washington, 1962-67, sec. com. nuclear sci. NRC, 1962-67, mem. commn. human resources, 1974-78; asso. dir. gen. activities Am. Inst. Physics, N.Y.C., 1967—; cons. Gen. Atomics div. Gen. Dynamics Corp., La Jolla, Calif., summers, 1959, 60; chmn. phys. scis. Am. exhibit Internat. Conf. Peaceful Uses Atomic Energy, Geneva, Switzerland, 1958; mem. Sci. Manpower Commn., 1968—, pres., 1974-75, treas., 1976; mem. U.S. nat. com. Internat. Union for Pure and Applied Physics, 1972-78, sec., 1974-78. Served with USNR, 1943-46. Fellow Washington Acad. Scis., AAAS (mem. council 1971-72, 76-78); mem. Am. Phys. Soc., Am. Assn. Physics Tchrs. Episcopalian. Mem. adv. com. Physics Today, 1963-67, chmn., 1967. Research beta ray and gamma ray spectroscopy. Home: 27 Meadowbank Rd Old Greenwich CT 06870 Office: 335 E 45th St New York NY 10017

SLADE, GERALD JACK, publishing co. exec.; b. Utica, N.Y., May 24, 1919; s. John H. and Sada (Jacobson) S.; B.A. summa cum laude, Colgate U., 1941; M.B.A., Harvard, 1943; m. Dorothy Casler, Oct. 24, 1942; children—John, Carolyn, David. Chmn. bd., pres., chief exec. officer Western Pub. Co., Racine, Wis.; dir. Mattel, Inc., Wells-Gardner Electronics Corp., 1st Nat. Bank of Racine, Joseph Schlitz Brewing Co. Past pres. Nat. Assn. Electronic Organ Mfrs. Mem. Phi Beta Kappa, Kappa Delta Rho. Home: 110 Raven Turn E Racine WI 53402 Office: 1220 Mound Ave Racine WI 53404

SLADE, HUTTON DAVISON, educator, microbiologist; b. London, Eng., Aug. 6, 1912 (came to U.S. 1913, naturalized 1920); s. Francis and Florence (Davison) S.; B.S., U. Md., 1935, M.S., 1936; Ph.D., Iowa State U., 1942; m. Eileen Fay Pryor, June 7, 1941; children—Richard Gary, Robert Bryan. Research biologist Wallerstein Co., N.Y.C., 1942-43; chief microbiology Rheumatic Fever Research Inst., Chgo., 1948-57; mem. faculty Northwestern U. Med. Sch., 1957—, prof. microbiology, 1959-78, prof. emeritus, 1978—; vis. prof. U. Colo. Dental Sch., 1978—; cons. Naval Med. Research Unit 4, Great Lakes, Ill., 1958—, Office Naval Research, 1967-70; mem. metabolic biology panel NSF, 1966-69; mem. grad. tng. grant. com. NIH, 1967-71, mem. oral biology and medicine study sect., 1976—; Found. Microbiology lectr., 1971-72; vis. lectr. Oreg. State U., 1972. Mem. sch. bd. 37, Cook County, Ill., 1954-58. Served to maj., Med. Corps, AUS, 1943-46, col. Res. ret. Established investigator Am. Heart Assn., 1956-61; recipient Research Career award NIH, 1962. Mem. AAAS, Am. Acad. Microbiology, Am. Soc. Microbiology, Soc. Gen. Microbiology, Ill. Soc. Microbiology (pres. 1962, Pasteur award 1976), Sigma Xi. Home: 1800 Twin Dr Estes Park CO 80517 Office: U Colo Med Center Denver CO 80262

SLADE, JARVIS JAMES, investment banker; b. Paris, France, Feb. 12, 1926; s. Henry L. and Elena (De Arostegui) S. (parents Am. citizens); B.A., Yale, 1947; M.B.A., Stanford, 1950; m. Alice Patterson, June 26, 1954 (div. Jan. 1976); children—Shelley Rodes, Georgiana James, Jarvis James; m. 2d, Mary Carlyle Lind, June 2, 1976. With N.Y. Trust Co., 1947-50; with F. Eberstadt & Co., N.Y.C., 1950-62, partner, 1958-62; founder N.Y. Securities Co. Inc., 1962, co-chmn., sr. v.p., 1962-75; pres. Computer Investors Group, Inc., N.Y.C., 1975-76; gen. partner Hampton Capital Co., N.Y.C., 1976—; dir. AIC Photo, Inc., Church & Dwight, Gaylords Nat. Corp.; chmn. Market Compilation and Research Bur. Trustee Big Bros. Orgn. Served with CIC, AUS, 1945-46. Clubs: Maidstone, River, Racquet and Tennis (N.Y.C.). Home: 446 E 52d St New York NY 10022 Office: 65 W 55th St New York NY 10019

SLADE, JOHN HANS, stockbroker; b. Frankfurt, Germany, May 30, 1908; s. Paul and Alice (Schmidt) Schlesinger; grad. Goethe Gymnasium, Frankfurt, 1920; m. Margit Steinharter, Sept. 25, 1943 (dec.); children—Barbara Slade Boelsterli, Nicole Slade Weinberg; m. 2d, Marianne Rosenbaum. Came to U.S., 1936, naturalized, 1943. With Bear Stearns & Co., N.Y.C., 1936—, founder internat. dept., 1946, partner, 1951—. Served with U.S. Army, 1942-45. Decorated Bronze Star. Clubs: Economic, Harmonie (N.Y.C.). Home: 700 Park Ave New York NY 10021 Office: 55 Water St New York NY 10041

SLADE, LLEWELLYN EUGENE, lawyer, engr.; b. Carroll, Iowa, May 1, 1911; s. Llewellyn and Mary (Veach) S.; B.S. in Elec. Engring., Iowa State U., 1938, M.S., 1942; J.D., Drake U., 1951; m. Jane England Dickinson, June 8, 1945; 1 dau., Yvonne (Mrs. Kim Tidd). With Iowa Power & Light Co., Des Moines, 1940-68, exec. v.p. ops., dir., 1964-68, cons. Nebr. Public Power Dist. nuclear project; pvt. practice as exec. counsellor, atty., profl. engr.; fed. ct. bankruptcy trustee; dir. Wright Tree Service Cos.; mem. panel arbitrators U.S. Fed. Mediation and Conciliation Service, Am. Arbitration Assn. Former chmn., trustee Des Moines Metro Transit Authority; bd. dirs. Iowa Luth. Hosp., West Des Moines Devel. Corp., Theta Chi Corp. Registered profl. engr., Iowa. Mem. Fed., Am., Iowa, Polk County bar assns., IEEE, Iowa Engring. Soc. (Anson Marston award for outstanding service 1957), Nat. Soc. Profl. Engrs., Engrs. Club Des Moines, Am. Judicature Soc., Atomic Indsl. Forum, Aircraft Owners and Pilots Assn., Greater Des Moines C. of C. Lutheran. Mason (32 deg., Shriner), Rotarian. Clubs: Des Moines, Embassy, Wakonda, Bohemian (Des Moines); Men's Garden of Am. Home: 5833 Pleasant Dr Des Moines IA 50312 Office: 400 Hubbell Bldg Des Moines IA 50309

SLADEK, RONALD JOHN, educator; b. Chgo., Sept. 19, 1926; s. James Joseph and Rose (Vachulka) S.; Ph.B., U. Chgo., 1947, S.B., 1949, S.M., 1950, Ph.D. (AEC fellow), 1954; m. Jeanne T. McFadden, Sept. 19, 1953; children—Linda, James, Frances, Stephen, Rosemarie, Edward. Research physicist Westinghouse Research Labs., Pitts., 1953-60, fellow scientist, 1960-61; asso. prof. physics Purdue U., Lafayette, Ind., 1961-66, prof., 1966—, acting head dept. physics, 1969-71, asso. dean sci., 1974—; vis. scientist Sci. Center, N.Am. Rockwell Corp., Thousand Oaks, Calif., summer 1967; sabbatical scientist Xerox Research Center, Palo Alto, Calif., 1976-77. Served with USNR, 1945-46. Fellow Am. Phys. Soc.; mem. AAUP, Sigma Xi. Contbr. articles to profl. jours. Home: 311 Lindberg Ave West Lafayette IN 47906 Office: Dept Physics Purdue U Lafayette IN 47907

SLADEN, WILLIAM JOSEPH LAMBART, physician, educator, ecologist; b. Newport, Eng., Dec. 19, 1920; s. Hugh A. Lambart and C. Motee (Booth-Tucker) S.; M.B., B.S., Middlesex Hosp., London (Eng.) U., 1946; M.D., London U., 1952; D.Phil. in Zoology, Oxford (Eng.) U., 1955; m. Brenda Kathleen Macpherson, May 31, 1955 (div. Aug. 1976); children—Catherine Adelie Lambart, Hugh St. George Lambart. Came to U.S., 1956, naturalized, 1963. Intern Princess Alice Hosp., Eastborne, Sussex, Eng., 1946; resident surgeon plastic surgery unit, Basingstoke with Sir Harold Gillies, 1946-47; med. officer, biologist, photographer Falkland Islands Dependencies Survey (now Brit. Antarctic Survey), 1947-55; Rockefeller Found. fellow Johns Hopkins Hosp. and Sch. Hygiene and Pub. Health, Balt., 1956-57, research asso. dept. pathobiology, 1957-58, asst. prof., 1958-61, asso. prof., 1961-68, prof. ecology and comparative behavior dept. pathobiology, 1969—. Mem. panel on biol. and med. scis. Com. on Polar Research, Nat. Acad. Scis., 1958-68, chmn., 1958-59; collaborator research and clin. work on Pribilof Islands, Arctic Health Research Center, Alaska Native Health Service, 1958-62; U.S. rep. biology working group Sci. Com. for Antarctic Research-Internat. Com. Sci. Union, 1964-69, also chmn. subcom. Antarctic bird banding; coordinator No. waterfowl project problem area V, U.S.-USSR Environ. Protection Agreement; travel, expdns. to Swedish Lapland, 1947, Antarctica and Falkland Islands, 1947-51, Central Iceland, 1953, Macedonia, 1955, Antarctica, 1958-59, 62, 64-66, 68-70, Alaska, 1960-62, summers 1967-78, Wrangel Island N.E. Siberia, summer 1975. Served with London Emergency Med. Service, 1943-45. Decorated mem. Order Brit. Empire, 1948; recipient Brit. Polar medal, 1953. Fellow Am. Ornithological Union, London Zool. Soc.; mem. Scott Polar Research Inst. (Eng.), Arctic Inst. N.Am., Internat. Waterfowl Research Bur. (exec. bd. 1970—, coordinator swan research group), Am. Inst. Biol. Scis., A.A.A.S., Wildlife Disease Assn., Wildlife Soc., Balt. Zool. Soc. (founding chmn. bd. trustees 1967-72), Antarctian Soc. (v.p., pres. 1971-73), Wildlife Soc., Nature Conservancy (v.p. Md. chpt. 1976—), Brit. Ornithol. Union, Wildfowl Trust, Chesapeake Bay Found. Contbr. articles on Arctic and Antarctic ecology, penguins and waterfowl to profl. jours., TV and documentary films. Spl. sci. interest in conservation of natural resources; polar animal ecology and ethology with spl. emphasis on sea birds and waterfowl and study of marked animals of known age; upper respiratory infections of man and animals; bot. ecology; sci. motion photography especially in study of animal behavior. Home: PO Box 1179 Pasadena MD 21122 Office: Dept Pathobiology Sch Hygiene and Pub Health Johns Hopkins U 615 N Wolfe St Baltimore MD 21205

SLAMECKA, VLADIMIR, info. scientist; b. Brno, Czechoslovakia, May 8, 1928 (came to U.S. 1956, naturalized 1961); s. Alois and Kristina (Vasicek) S.; B.Sc., Brno U., 1949; M.S., Columbia, 1958, D. Library Sci., 1962; postgrad. U. Sydney (Australia), 1951-53, U. Munich (Germany), 1954-56; m. Elba I. Seoane, Oct. 1962; children—John Vladimir, Alois William. Chem. engr. Brookvale Brewery, New South Wales, 1953-54; head librarian Columbia, 1958-62; mgr. spl. studies Documentation, Inc., Bethesda, Md., 1963; mgr. cancer chemotherapy Nat. Data Service, Documentation, Inc., 1964; dir. Sch. Info. and Computer Sci., Ga. Inst. Tech., Atlanta, 1964-78, prof., 1964—; vis. prof. Emory U., 1968, clin. prof. Sch. Medicine, 1979—; cons. NSF, UN, OAS, HEW, USAF, Washington, Computer Scis. Corp., Scott Paper Co., Coca-Cola Co., Aqua-Ion Co. Mem. AAAS, Assn. Computing Machinery, Am. Soc. Info. Sci., Sigma Xi. Author: Science in Czechoslovakia, 1963; Science in East Germany, 1963; The Coming Age of Information Technology, 1965; Studies in Technical Data Management, 1967; National Science Information Systems, 1972 (all monographs); also articles. Patentee in field. Home: 1661 Doncaster Dr NE Atlanta GA 30309

SLANETZ, LAWRENCE WILLIAM, microbiologist, educator; b. Islip, N.Y., Apr. 14, 1908; s. Charles and Rose (Volovka) S.; B.S., U. Conn., 1929; Ph.D., Yale, 1932; m. Helen C. Colby, Sept. 17, 1927; children—Lawrence William, Robert Colby, Caryl Jane. Asst. instr. Yale, 1931-32; instr. bacteriology U. N.H., Durham, 1932-38, asst. prof., 1938-41, asso. prof., 1941-48, prof. bacteriology, chmn. dept., 1948-62, prof. microbiology, chmn. dept., 1962-69, dean Sch. Health Studies, 1969-73, prof. microbiology, 1973-77, emeritus, 1977—; asst. bacteriologist N.H. Agrl. Expt. Sta., 1934-41, bacteriologist, 1941-62, microbiologist, 1962-69. Health officer Town of Durham, N.H., 1935—. Fellow Am. Pub. Health Assn.; mem. Am. Soc. Microbiology, Am. Acad. Microbiology, Royal Soc. Health, N.H. Acad. Sci., Sigma Xi, Gamma Alpha, Phi Sigma, Phi Kappa Phi. Home: 16 Bagdad Rd Durham NH 03824

SLAPPEY, STERLING GREENE, educator, former editor; b. Ft. Valley, Ga., June 18, 1917; s. Jenkins Sterling and Elma Louise (Greene) S.; student Ala. Poly. Inst. (now Auburn U.), 1937, 38, U. Ga., Atlanta, 1938-39; m. Margaret Byne Sellers, Jan. 13, 1945; children—Margaret, Charles. Reporter, Atlanta Georgian & Sunday Am., 1938-39, Atlanta Constn., 1940, 41, 45, 46, A.P., Atlanta, London, Moscow, 1947-59; specialist in racial affairs U.S. News & World Report, 1960-62; Central European bur. chief Los Angeles Times, based in Bonn, West Germany, 1963-66; sr. editor Nation's Bus., Washington, 1966-78; dir. Future of Bus. Program, Georgetown U. Center for Strategic and Internat. Studies, Washington, 1978—; columnist Washingtonian Mag., 1971-74; free lance writer various publs.; sec. Iberian Imports Inc., Alexandria, 1969—; pres. Alexandria Bath and Linen Co., 1978—. Served with AUS, 1941-45. Mem. Overseas Writers, White House, State Dept. corrs. assns., Friends Kennedy Center, Assn. for Preservation Va. Antiquities, Smithsonian Assos., Alexandria Assembly, Nat. Trust Historic Preservation, Am. Acad. Polit. Sci., Acad. Social and Polit. Sci., Phi Delta Theta. Clubs: Overseas Press; International (Washington). Author: (novel) Exodus of the Damned, 1968; Pioneers of American Business, 1973. Home:

121 Cameron Mews Alexandria VA 22314 Office: 1800 K St NW Washington DC 20006

SLATE, FLOYD OWEN, engring. educator; b. Carroll County, Ind., July 26, 1920; s. Ora George and Gladys Marie (Miller) S.; B.S., Purdue U., 1941, M.S., 1942, Ph.D., 1944; m. Margaret Mary Magley, Oct. 14, 1939; children—Sally Lee Slate Sanderson, Sandra Kay Slate Miller, Rex Owen. Chemist, Manhattan Project, N.Y.C., Oak Ridge and Decatur, Ill., 1944-46; asst. prof. civil engring. Purdue U., Lafayette, Ind., 1946-49; v.p., dir. Geotechnics & Resources Inc., White Plains, N.Y., 1959-63; prof. engring. materials Cornell U., Ithaca, N.Y., 1949—; internat. lectr., cons. concrete, low-cost housing. Recipient Excellence in Teaching award Cornell U., 1976, sr. fellow East-West Center, 1976, NSF research grantee, 1960-79. Fellow Am. Concrete Inst. (Wason Research medal 1957, 65, 74), Am. Inst. Chemists; mem. Am. Chem. Soc., ASCE, ASTM. Author books, research papers on concrete, low-cost housing, soil stabilization, 1944-79; research on internal structure of concrete vs. properties and chemistry applied to engring. problems. Home: 7 Redwood Ln Ithaca NY 14850 Office: Hollister Hall Cornell U Ithaca NY 14853. *Think positively and be optimistic. Be considerate of others, try to help others, and enjoy life.*

SLATE, JOE HUTSON, psychologist; b. Hertselle, Ala., Sept. 21, 1930; s. Murphy Edmund and Marie (Hutson) S.; B.S., Athens Coll., 1960; M.A., U. Ala., 1965, Ph.D., 1970; m. Rachel Holladay, July 1, 1950; children—Marc Allan, John David, James Daryl. Mem. faculty Athens (Ala.) State Coll., 1965—, prof. psychology, 1974—, chmn. behavioral scis., 1974—; pvt. practice psychology, Athens, 1970—. Named hon. prof. Montevallo U., 1973. Mem. Am., Ala. psychol. assns., Inst. Parapsychol. Research (founder, pres.), Council for Nat. Register Health Service Providers in Psychology, NEA, Ala. Edn. Assn., Delta Tau Delta, Phi Delta Kappa, Kappa Delta Pi. Home: Box 451 Hwy 31 N Hartselle AL 35640 Office: Dept Psychology Athens State Coll Athens AL 35611

SLATER, COURTENAY MURPHY, economist; b. Durham, N.C., July 23, 1933; d. Charles Springs and Kate Chestney (Graham) Murphy; B.A., Oberlin Coll., 1955; M.A., Am. U., 1965, Ph.D., 1968; m. Whitney S. Slater, Sept. 2, 1954; children—Charles S., W. Ruffin, Harold B. Staff economist Council Econ. Advisers, 1967-69, Joint Econ. Com., U.S. Congress, 1969-77; chief economist Dept. Commerce, Washington, 1977—. Mem. Am. Econ. Assn., So. Econ. Assn., Indsl. Relations Research Assn., Am. Statis. Assn., Phi Kappa Phi, Omicron Delta Epsilon. Office: Dept Commerce Washington DC 20230

SLATER, ELLIS DWINNELL, ret. beverage co. exec. b. Chgo., Mar. 22, 1895; s. John and Mary (Dwinnell) S.; A.B., U. Mich., 1917; m. Priscilla Allen, Oct. 8, 1921; children—Allen Dwinnell, Cynthia Linda (Mrs. Richard Stammers); m. 2d, Grace Taylor Harman, Sept. 8, 1973. Salesman, U.S. Indsl. Alcohol Co., Chgo., 1920-22, N.E. mgr., 1922-26 gen. sales mgr., 1926-33; v.p. Frankfort Distilleries, Inc., N.Y.C., 1933-43; pres. Frankfort Distillers Corp., 1943-55; cons. Joseph E. Seagram & Sons, Inc., 1955-60; dir. Emery Air Freight, 1955—, chmn. bd., 1958-62, chmn. exec. com., 1963-68, mem. exec. com.; cons. Riviana Foods, Inc. (formerly River Brand Rice Mills, Inc.), 1962-63, dir., 1962—, chmn. exec. com., 1963—. Hon. mem. Com. for Econ. Devel. Trustee emeritus Johns Hopkins Hosp.; trustee Am. Field Service, Eisenhower Coll., 1968-74. Served with AEF, 1917-19. Mem. Delta Kappa Epsilon. Presbyn. Clubs: Augusta (Ga.) Nat. Golf; Red Fox Country (Tryon, N.C.); Everglades (Palm Beach); Lost Tree (North Palm Beach, Fla.). Home: 11510 Turtle Beach Rd North Palm Beach FL 33408. *I have long advocated that one should plan his life into three parts - Number 1 - getting ready - Number 2 - doing - Number 3 - enjoying the fruits of the first two. Unless one's life is planned this way, Part Number 3 often lasting twenty-five years can be dull and unrewarding.*

SLATER, GEORGE RICHARD, banker; b. Indpls., Feb. 13, 1924; s. George Greenleaf and Chloe (Shoemaker) S.; B.S., Purdue U., 1946, M.S., 1957, Ph.D., 1963; m. Helen Irene Goodwill, July 1, 1945; children—George Greenleaf II, Kathleen Anne Slater Hamar, John Goodwill, Frederick Richard. Mgr. die casting plant Guide div. Gen. Motors Corp., Anderson, Ind., 1950-55; instr. Purdue U., 1955-57; chief economist Allis-Chalmers Corp., Milw., 1957-60; v.p. Citizens Nat. Bank, Decatur, Ill., 1960-64; sr. v.p., group exec. Met. Group, Harris Trust & Savs. Bank, Chgo., 1964-76; pres., chief exec. officer Marine Corp., Milw., 1976—. Mem. Greater Milw. Com.; treas., bd. dirs. Froedtert Meml. Hosp.; bd. dirs. United Performing Arts Fund; trustee Milw. Art Center, Marquette U.; mem. dean's advisory council Krannert Grad. Sch., Purdue U.; mem. pres.'s council Purdue U.; pres. bd. visitors U. Wis., Milw.; mem. adv. bd. Sch. Bus., U. Wis., Madison; mem. exec. bd. Milwaukee County council Boy Scouts Am. Served to 1st lt., F.A., AUS, 1943-46. Mem. Assn. Res. City Bankers. Episcopalian. Clubs: Milw. Country, Milwaukee; Town; Chicago, Economic (Chgo.). Office: 111 E Wisconsin Ave Milwaukee WI 53202. *Man has the obligation to his fellow man to strive for productivity, excellence and harmony.*

SLATER, JOHN GREENLEAF, banker; b. Milw., Mar. 25, 1935; s. Thomas McIndoe and Margaret Mary (McAnarney) S.; B.S. in Econs., Marquette U., 1958, M.A., 1960; m. Colleen Mary Conway, July 19, 1958; children—James C., John T., Ann E. With First Wis. Nat. Bank, Milw., 1960-69; with First Wis. Nat. Bank, Madison, 1969-79, exec. v.p., 1973-79, also dir.; sr. v.p. Fifth Third Bank, Cin., 1979—. Mem. Wis. Adv. Com. Equal Ednl. Opportunity, 1971-72, Madison Adv. Com. Drug Abuse, 1970-71; mem. long range planning com. Edgewood High Sch., Madison, 1972-75; bd. dirs. First Offenders Sch., 1975-79. Mem. Wis. Bus. Economists Assn. (pres. 1973), Nat. Assn. Bus. Economists, Phi Gamma Mu. Roman Catholic. Home: 10606 Orinda Dr Montgomery OH 45242 Office: 38 Fountain Sq Plaza Cincinnati OH 45202

SLATER, JOSEPH ELLIOTT, inst. exec.; b. Salt Lake City, Aug. 17, 1922; B.A. with honors, U. Calif. at Berkeley, 1943, postgrad., 1943; LL.D., U. Denver, 1976, Colo. Coll., 1976, U. N.H., 1977; m. Annelore Kremser, Dec. 20, 1947; children—Bonnie Karen Hurst, Sandra Marian Porat. Teaching asst., reader U. Calif. at Berkeley, 1942-43; dep. U.S. sec. Allied Control Council, Berlin, Germany, 1945-48; UN planning staff Dept. State, Washington, 1949; sec.-gen. Allied High Commn. for Germany, Bonn, 1949-52; exec. sec. U.S. Spl. Rep. in Europe, U.S. sec. to U.S. del. to NATO and OEEC, Paris, France, 1952-53; chief economist Creole Petroleum Corp. (Standard Oil Co. N.J.), Caracas, Venezuela, 1954-57; mem. and dir. internat. affairs program Ford Found., 1957-68, study dir. spl. com. to establish policies and programs, 1961-62; asst. mng. dir. Devel. Loan Fund, Washington, 1960-61; dep. asst. sec. state for edn. and cultural affairs, 1961-62; pres. Salk Inst., LaJolla, Calif., 1967-72, now trustee, spl. fellow; pres., trustee Aspen Inst. for Humanistic Studies, 1969—; pres. Anderson Found., N.Y.C., 1969-72; vis. prof. U. Colo., 1970—. Sec. Pres.'s Com. on Fgn. Assistance (Draper Com.), 1959; mem. devel. assistance panel Pres.'s Sci. Adv. Com., 1960-61; cons. Dept. State, 1961-68; mem. U.S. Inst. Human Rights. Founder, dir., mem. bd. Creole Found., 1956-57; mem. vis. com., dept. philosophy Mass. Inst. Tech., 1971—; trustee Asia Soc., Acad. for Ednl. Devel., Carnegie Hall, Internat. Fedn. Insts. Advanced Studies, Internat. Council Ednl. Devel., John J. McCloy Fund, The Villages, Topeka, Internat. Broadcast Inst., Aspen Center for Physics; bd. dirs. UN Assn. U.S.A., Am. Council on Germany, Eisenhower Exchange Fellowships, Tchrs. Ins. and Annuity Assn., Internat. Inst. Environ. Devel. Served to lt. USNR, 1943-46; mil. govt. planning officer, London, Paris, Berlin. Decorated Order of Merit (Fed. Republic Germany). Mem. Inst. Strategic Studies (London), Soc. Internat. Devel., Council Fgn. Relations, Center for Inter-Am. Relations, Phi Beta Kappa. Clubs: Century Assn., University (N.Y.C.); Cosmos (Washington). Home: 870 UN Plaza New York NY 10017 Office: Aspen Inst 717 Fifth Ave New York NY 10022 also Aspen Inst for Humanistic Studies 1000 N 3d St Aspen CO 81611

SLATER, JOSEPH LOCKE, educator; b. Elyria, Ohio, July 17, 1916; s. Joseph Hayden and Mabel Florence (Locke) S.; B.A., Colgate U., 1937; M.A., Columbia, 1939, Ph.D., 1956; m. Vivien Harvey, Aug. 19, 1939; children—Lydia, John. Instr. English, Lafayette Coll., 1938-41; instr., then asso. prof. Rutgers U., New Brunswick, N.J., 1947-61; Fulbright prof. Julius-Maximilians Universität Wûrzburg, Germany, 1957-58; prof. English, Colgate U., Hamilton, N.Y., 1961—, chmn. dept. English, 1961-66, 69-70, 76-77; vis. prof. Universitat Konstanz, Germany, 1971. Served to lt. (j.g.) USNR, 1944-46. Mem. Modern Lang. Assn., AAUP, Phi Beta Kappa. Editor: The Correspondence of Emerson and Carlyle, 1964; gen. editor Collected Works of Ralph Waldo Emerson. Contbr. articles to profl. jours. Home: Poolville NY 13432 Office: Colgate U Hamilton NY 13346

SLATER, MANNING, broadcasting exec.; b. Springfield, Mass., Aug. 29, 1917; s. Ely and Sarah Deenah (Hurwitz) Slotnick; B.A., Am. Internat. Coll., 1939; m. Anita Norman, July 1, 1977; children—Gary Edward, Richard Stuart. Pres., Community Markets, Springfield, Mass., 1939-46; v.p., treas. Bridgeport Broadcasting Co. (Conn.), 1947-58; pres., chmn. bd. Hercules Broadcasting Co.. Sacramento and Seattle, 1959—, also Slater Broadcasting Co.; pres. Slater Investment Co. Bd. govs. Mercy Hosp., Sacramento. Mem. Nat. Assn. Broadcasters, Radio Advt. Bur., Sacramento C. of C. Democrat. Jewish. Mem. B'nai B'rith. Clubs: University, Comstock Club Sacramento. Home: 7921 Wildridge Dr Fair Oaks CA 95628 Office: Suite 110 1337 Howe Ave Sacramento CA 95825

SLATER, OLIVER EUGENE, bishop; b. Sibley, La., Sept. 10, 1906; s. Oliver Thornwell and Mattie (Kennon) S.; A.B., So. Meth. U., 1930, LL.D., 1964; B.D., 1932; D.D. (hon.), McMurray Coll., 1951; L.H.D., Southwestern Coll., Winfield, Kans., 1961; LL.D., Baker U., 1962; m. Eva B. Richardson, Nov. 25, 1931; children—Susan (Mrs. H. Kipling Edenborough), Stewart Eugene. Ordained to ministry Meth. Ch., 1932; pastor in Rochelle, Tex., 1932-33, Menard, Tex., 1933-36, Ozona, Tex., 1936-42, San Antonio, 1942-44, Houston, 1944-50, Polk St. Ch., Amarillo, Tex., 1950-60; consecrated bishop, 1960; bishop Kans. area Meth. Ch., 1960-64, San Antonio-N.W. Tex. area, 1964-68, San Antonio area United Meth. Ch., 1968-76; bishop-in-residence Perkins Sch. Theology, So. Meth. U., 1976—. Mem. jurisdictional confs. Meth. Ch., 1948, 56, 60, gen. confs., 1956, 60, pres. gen. bd. edn. (now of United Meth. Ch.), 1964-72; mem. commn. on archives and history United Meth. Ch., 1968—, mem. interboard com. on enlistment for ch. occupations, 1968-72; v.p. Council Bishops, 1971-72, pres., 1972-73. Chmn. Commn. on Archives, 1972—. Trustee So. Meth. U., vice chmn. trustees, 1973-76; trustee Southwestern U.; mem. Bd. Global Ministries, 1972—. Recipient Distinguished Alumnus award So. Meth. U., 1975. Home: 7424-9 W Northwest Hwy Dallas TX 75255

SLATER, ROBERT JAMES, physician; b. Toronto, Ont., Can., May 7, 1923 (came to U.S. 1962); s. James Henry and Helen Isobel (Lockhart) S.; M.D., U. Toronto, 1946, B.Sc., 1948; m. Elizabeth Joan Hall, Aug. 12, 1950; children—Robert Matthew, Mary Elizabeth, John Barrie, Brian Andrew. Intern, Toronto Gen. Hosp., 1946-47; resident Hosp. Sick Children, Toronto, 1948-50; asst. physician Hosp. Rockefeller Inst. Med. Research, 1950-54; fellow pediatrics Cornell Med. Sch.-N.Y. Hosp., 1954-55; mem. Research Inst., Hosp. Sick Children, Toronto, 1955-61; asso. pediatrics faculty medicine U. Toronto, 1955-61; dean Coll. Medicine, U. Vt., Burlington, 1962-66; pres. Found. For Child Devel., N.Y.C., 1967-73; vis. prof. Yale, 1973-74; pres. Med. Coll. Pa., Phila., 1974-76; sr. research fellow Sch. Public Health, Harvard, 1976-79; dir. med. programs. Nat. Multiple Sclerosis Soc., N.Y.C., 1977—; med. adv. bd. Internat. Fedn. Multiple Sclerosis Socs., 1978—; mem. subcom. dental research NRC Can., 1960; chmn. med. adv. bd. Vt. Assn. Crippled, 1962-66; mem. Vt. Adv. Council Spl. Edn., 1962-66, com. student affairs Assn. Am. Med. Colls., 1962-66, mem. Nat. Rev. Com. Regional Med. Programs, 1967-70, chmn., 1969-70; bd. dirs. US Com. for UNICEF, 1969—, sec., 1972-78; bd. dirs. Pub. Health Research Inst., N.Y., 1973-76; mem. com. on future of women in engring. and scis. Nat. Acad. Scis., 1975—. Diplomate Am. Bd. Pediatrics. Fellow Royal Coll. Physicians and Surgeons Can.; mem. Soc. Pediatric Research (council 1958-60), Canadian Soc. Clin. Investigation (council 1958-59, pres. 1960), Harvey Soc., Am. Pediatric Soc., AMA, N.Y. Acad. Scis., N.Y. Acad. Medicine (trustee 1971-74), Am. Acad. Pediatrics, AAAS, Can. Pediatrics Soc. Office: Nat Multiple Sclerosis Soc 205 E 42d St New York City NY 10017

SLATER, ROBERT JOSEPH, steel co. exec.; b. Buffalo, May 13, 1937; s. John Joseph and Anna Mae (McMoil) S.; B.S., Canisius Coll., 1959; m. Patricia Ann Brennan, Oct. 8, 1960; children—Diane, Cynthia. Various positions N.Y. Central R.R., N.Y.C., 1959-67; supt. Ohio div. Penn Central R.R., Columbus, 1968, Toledo div., 1968, gen. supt. transp., Cleve., 1969, Phila., 1970; pres. C & W Ry., Pueblo, Colo., 1971; with CF & I Steel Corp., Pueblo, 1972—, v.p., 1972-76, pres., 1976—; dir. Republic Nat. Bank, Denver Metals Co., Albuquerque Metals Co. Bd. dirs. Easter Seal Fund Pueblo County, 1972—, Rocky Mountain council Boy Scouts Am., 1975—. Served with U.S. Army, 1960-62. Mem. Am. Iron and Steel Engrs., Am. Iron and Steel Inst. (mem. mfg. com. 1973-76, dir. 1976—), Colo. Mining Assn. (dir. 1977—), Pueblo C. of C., Mensa, Alpha Kappa Psi. Republican. Roman Catholic. Clubs: Rotary, Pueblo Country (bd. dirs. 1973-76); Garden of Gods (Colorado Springs). Home: 415 Starlite Dr Pueblo CO 81005 Office: PO Box 316 Pueblo CO 81002

SLATKIN, LEONARD, conductor; b. Sept. 1; s. Felix Slatkin and Eleanor Aller; began violin study, 1947, piano study with Victor Aller and Selma Cramer, 1955, composition study with Castelnuovo-Tedesco, 1958, viola study with Sol Schoenbach, 1959; conducting study with Felix Slatkin, Amerigo Marino and Ingolf Dahl; attended Ind. U., 1962, Los Angeles City Coll., 1963, Juilliard Sch. (Irving Berlin fellow in musical direction), beginning 1964; student of Jean Morel and Walter Susskind. Conducting debut as asst. condr. Youth Symphony of N.Y., Carnegie Hall, 1966; asst. condr. Juilliard Opera Theater and Dance Dept., 1967; asst. condr. St. Louis Symphony Orch., 1968-71, asso. condr., 1971-74, asso. prin. condr., 1979—; founder, music dir. and condr. St. Louis Symphony Youth Orch., beginning 1969; debut with Chgo. Symphony Orch., 1974, N.Y. Philharmonic, 1974, Phila. Orch., 1974; European debut with Royal Philharmonic Orch., 1974; debut with USSR orchs., 1976-77; prin. guest condr. Minn. Orch., beginning 1974, summer artistic dir., 1979-80; music dir. New Orleans Philharmonic Symphony Orch., 1977-78, musical adv., 1979-80; guest condr. orchs. throughout world; former vis. asst. prof. music Washington U., St. Louis; initiated Friday afternoon lecture series; hosted weekly radio program. Office: care Mariedi Anders Artist Mgmt 535 El Camino Del Mar San Francisco CA 94121 also St Louis Symphony Orch Powell Symphony Hall 718 N Grand Blvd Saint Louis MO 63103*

SLATOFF, WALTER JACOB, educator; b. N.Y.C., Mar. 1, 1922; s. Ellis and Jeannette (Armstrong) S.; B.A., Columbia, 1943; M.A., U. Mich., 1950, Ph.D., 1955; m. Jane Metzger, Sept. 10, 1946; children—Joan, Donald. Free lance writer, 1946-49; faculty Cornell U., Ithaca, N.Y., 1955—, asso. prof., 1961-66, prof. 1966—. Served with AUS, 1943-46. Recipient Clark award for disting. teaching, 1978. Mem. AAUP. Author: Quest For Failure: A Study of William Faulkner, 1960; With Respect to Readers: Dimensions of Literary Response, 1970. Editor: Epoch mag., 1955—. Home: 23 Renwick Heights Rd Ithaca NY 14850

SLATTERY, JAMES JOSEPH (JOE SLATTERY), actor; b. Memphis, Feb. 7, 1922; s. James Joseph and Katie May (Carlin) S.; A.B., Hendrix Coll., Conway, Ark., 1947; m. Mary Margaret Costello, May 23, 1944; children—James Joseph, John P., Ann, Mary, Nancy. Actor; pres. Am. Fedn. TV and Radio Artists, 1976-79; dir. First Trust & Savs. Bank, Glenview, Ill. Served with USAAF, 1942-46. Mem. Screen Actors Guild. Roman Catholic. Address: 820 Chatham Rd Glenview IL 60025

SLATTERY, KENNETH F., univ. ofcl., clergyman; b. Bklyn., June 12, 1921; s. James J. and Ethel (Kegelman) S.; student St. Joseph's Coll., Princeton, N.J., 1935-41, St. Vincent's Sem., Phila., 1941-43, Mary Immaculate Sem., Northampton, Pa., 1943-48; M.A., Cath U. Am., 1949, Ph.D., 1952; LL.D. (hon.), St. John's U., Jamaica, N.Y., 1969; H.H.D. (hon.), Cath. U. P.R., 1977. Ordained priest Roman Catholic Ch., 1948; tchr. Greek and German, St. Joseph's Coll., Princeton, 1948-49; tchr. philosophy Cath. U. Am., 1950-52; tchr. philosophy Niagara (N.Y.) U., 1952-54, dean studies Mary Immaculate Sem., Northampton, Pa., 1954-56; tchr. philosophy St. John's U., Jamaica, N.Y., 1956-61; dean Grad. Sch., Sch. Edn., Niagara U., 1961-65; superior of Vincentians, 1965-69, chmn. bd. trustees, pres., 1965-76; v.p. communications St. John's U., 1976-79, acad. v.p S.I. campus, 1979—. Bd. dirs. Manresa Ednl. Corp.; trustee Cardinal Newman Coll., St. Louis, 1979—. Recipient Interfaith award B'nai B'rith, 1970. Mem. Am. Cath. Philos. Assn. Address: St John's U Jamaica NY 11439

SLATTERY, SISTER MARGARET PATRICE, coll. pres.; b. St. Louis, June 19, 1926; d. Patrick Joseph and Margaret (Harris) S.; B.A., Incarnate Word Coll., 1952; M.A., Marquette U., 1955; Ph.D., Catholic U. Am., 1966. Mem. Order Congregation Sisters of Charity of Incarnate Word, Roman Catholic Ch., 1947—; instr. English, Incarnate Word Coll., San Antonio, 1952-54, asst. prof., 1955-61, asso. prof., 1966-72, prof., chmn. dept. English, 1966-69, asst. acad. dean, 1953-54, acad. dean, 1969-72, pres., 1972—. Hon. adv. Brit. univs. summer schs., 1968—. Bd. dirs. SW Research Inst., KLRN-TV, ARC. Mem. Nat. Council Tchrs. English, MLA, Assn. Tex. Colls. and Univs. (v.p., pres.-elect 1979-80). Home: 4301 Broadway San Antonio TX 78209

SLAUGHTER, ADOLPH JAMES, govt. ofcl., journalist; b. Chgo., Dec. 20, 1928; s. William H. and Ruth (Yates) S.; student U. Dubuque, 1947-48, U. Ill., 1955-57; m. Geraldine Claire Glover, Oct. 28, 1961; children—Adrienne Janna, Geraldine Anne. Reporter, feature writer Chgo. Defender, 1957-62; bur. chief, White House corr. Assos. Negro Press, 1962-64; asso. editor Negro Heritage Library, 1964-66; founder, 1964, since propr. Nat. News Services, Washington, 1964—; author column The Slaughter Pen, 1966—; information, press cons. Bur. Work Programs, Dept. Labor, 1966, and info. asst. to adminstr. Bur. Work-Tng. Programs, 1966-69; dir. office community relations and information D.C. Dept. Manpower, 1969—. Trustee Corcoran Gallery Art. Served with AUS, 1953-55. Mem. Alpha Phi Alpha. Clubs: Nat. Press, Capitol Press (Washington). Home: 4869 Colorado Ave NW Washington DC 20011 Office: Employment Security Bldg 500 C St NW Washington DC 20001

SLAUGHTER, EDWARD RATLIFF, JR., lawyer; b. Raleigh, N.C., Sept. 15, 1931; s. Edward Ratliff and Mary McBee (Hoke) S.; A.B., Princeton U., 1953; postgrad. (Rotary Found. fellow) U. Brussels, 1955-56; LL.B., U. Va., 1959; m. Anne Limbosch, July 25, 1957; children—Anne Marie, Hoke, Bryan. Admitted to Va. bar, 1959; asso. firm McGuire, Woods & Battle and predecessors, Charlottesville, Va., 1959-64, partner, 1964-79, head dept. litigation, 1964-79; spl. asst. to atty. gen. U.S. for litigation, 1979—; vis. lectr. trial advocacy U. Va., 1970-77. Chmn. Albemarle County (Va.) Democratic Com., 1969-73; pres. Charlottesville-Albemarle United Way, 1972. Served with USNR, 1953-55. Fellow Am. Bar Found., Am. Coll. Trial Lawyers; mem. Am. Bar Assn., Assn. Ins. Attys., Charlottesville-Albemarle Bar Assn. (pres. 1976-77), Internat. Soc. Barristers, Va. Assn. Def. Attys., Va. Bar Assn. (pres. 1978), Va. State Bar, Va. Trial Lawyers Assn. Clubs: Boar's Head Sports. Home: 111 Falcon Dr Charlottesville VA 22901 Office: Dept Justice Washington DC 20530

SLAUGHTER, FRANK G., author, physician; b. Washington, Feb. 25, 1908; s. Stephen Lucius and Sallie Nicholson (Gill) S.; A.B., Duke U., 1926; M.D., Johns Hopkins U., 1930; m. Jane Mundy, June 10, 1933; children—Frank G., Randolph M. Intern, asst. resident and resident surgeon Jefferson Hosp., Roanoke, Va., 1930-34; practice medicine specializing in surgery, Jacksonville, Fla., 1934-42, ret., 1946; lectr. W. Colston Leigh, Inc., N.Y.C., 1947-49. Served from maj. to lt. col., M.C., U.S. Army, 1942-46. Diplomate Am. Bd. Surgery. Fellow A.C.S. Presbyterian (elder). Author: That None Should Die, 1941; Spencer Brade, M.D., 1942; Air Surgeon, 1942; Battle Surgeon, 1944; A Touch of Glory, 1945; In a Dark Garden, 1946; The New Science of Surgery, 1946; The Golden Isle, 1947; Sangaree, 1948; Medicine for Moderns, 1948; Divine Mistress, 1949; The Stubborn Heart, 1950; Immortal Magyar, 1950; Fort Everglades, 1951; The Road to Bithynia, 1951; East Side General, 1952; The Galileans, 1953; Storm Haven, 1953; The Song of Ruth, Apalachee Gold, 1954; The Healer, Flight from Natchez, 1955, The Scarlet Cord, 1956; The Warrior, 1956; Sword and Scalpel, 1957; The Mapmaker, 1957; Daybreak, 1958; The Thorn of Arimathea, 1958; The Crown and the Cross, 1959; Lorena, 1959; The Land and the Promise, 1960; Pilgrims in Paradise, 1960; Epidemic, 1961; The Curse of Jezebel, 1961; David: Warrior and King, 1962; Tomorrow's Miracle, 1962; Devil's Harvest, 1963; Upon This Rock, 1963; A Savage Place, 1964; The Purple Quest, 1965; Constantine: The Miracle of the Flaming Cross, 1965; Surgeon, U.S.A., 1966; God's Warrior, 1967; Doctor's Wives, 1967; The Sins of Herod, 1968; Surgeon's Choice, 1969; Countdown, 1970; Code Five, 1971; Convention M.D., 1972; Women in White, 1974; Stonewall Brigade, 1975; Plague Ship, 1976; Devil's Gamble, 1977; The Passionate Rebel, 1979. Home: PO Box 14 Ortega Sta Jacksonville FL 32210

SLAUGHTER, HARRISON T., lawyer; b. Leesburg, Ohio. Aug. 6, 1910; s. Thomas Terry and Mary (Polk) S.; student Ohio U., 1928-32; LL.B., Nat. U., 1937; m. Ruth Nations, Dec. 20, 1938; children—Mary Teresa, Harrison T. With USDA, Washington, 1933-34; clk. FCC, Washington, 1934-38, atty., 1938-43; admitted to D.C. bar, 1937; practiced in Washington, 1943—; sr. partner firm

Pierson, Ball & Dowd, Washington, 1946—. Industry adviser U.S. del. 3d N.Am. Broadcasting Conf., Montreal, 1949, Washington, 1950, U.S.-Mexican Broadcasting Conf., Mexico City, 1954. Mem. Am. Bar Assn., Bar Assn. D.C., Fed. Communications Bar Assn., Lambda Chi Alpha. Methodist. Clubs: International, Congressional Country, Columbia Country, Counsellors (Washington). Home: 5206 Manning Pl Washington DC 20016 Office: Ring Bldg 18th and M Sts Washington DC 20036

SLAUGHTER, JOHN BROOKS, univ. adminstr.; b. Topeka, Mar. 16, 1934; s. Reuben Brooks and Dora (Reeves) S.; student Washburn U., 1951-53; B.S.E.E., Kans. State U., 1956; M.S. in Engring., UCLA, 1961; Ph.D. in Engring. Scis., U. Calif., San Diego, 1971; m. Ida Bernice Johnson, Aug. 31, 1956; children—John Brooks, Jacqueline Michelle. Electronics engr. Gen. Dynamics Convair, San Diego, 1956-60; with Naval Electronics Lab. Center, San Diego, 1960-75, div. head, 1965-71, dept. head, 1971-75; dir. applied physics lab. U. Wash., 1975-77; asst. dir. NSF, Washington, 1977-79; acad. v.p., provost Wash. State U., 1979—; dir., vice chmn. San Diego Transit Corp. Bd. dirs. San Diego Urban League, 1962-66, pres., 1964-66; chmn. Navy Equal Employment Opportunity Council, San Diego C. of C. Energy Task Force, Seattle Citizens Transit Adv. Com. Recipient Engring. Alumnus award UCLA, 1978; Naval Electronics Lab Center fellow, 1969-70; registered profl. engr., Wash. Fellow IEEE (Region 6 Com. Service award 1972), AAAS; mem. Sigma Tau, Eta Kappa Nu, Alpha Phi Alpha. Editor Jour. Computers and Elec. Engring., 1972—. Office: French Ad Bldg Washington State U Pullman WA 99163

SLAUGHTER, WILLIAM EDWARD, JR., ret. petroleum co. exec.; b. Chgo., Dec. 5, 1908; s. William Edward and Maggie (Ferguson) S.; student Northwestern U., 1927-28, Detroit Inst. Tech., 1931-33; m. Betty Helen Pesch, Dec. 27, 1961; children—Gloria, William Edward IV, Kent. Various sales, marketing positions in oil industry, 1929-32; co-founder, pres., dir. Aurora Gasoline Co., 1932-61; v.p., dir. Marathon Internat. Oil Co., 1961-65, v.p. gen. services Marathon Oil Co., 1965-70; ret. Mem. businessmen's adv. com. Wayne State U. Religious Center, 1960-70; chmn. Mich. Turnpike Authority, 1953-55. Bd. dirs. Boys Clubs of Met. Detroit, 1958-75, pres., 1970-71, vice chmn., 1971—, chmn., 1972-73, exec. com., 1974-75, trustee, 1975—; bd. dirs. Jr. Achievement Northwestern Ohio, Inc., 1965-70, Boys Clubs Broward County (Fla.), 1974—; trustee Detroit Osteo. Hosp. Corp., 1951-73; trustee, pres. Wm. E. Slaughter, Jr. Found., 1957—. Mem. Am. Petroleum Inst., NAM, Asso. Petroleum Industries of Mich. (chmn. 1956-61), Mich. C. of C. (charter mem., dir.), Hundred Club Detroit, Hundred Club Broward County, Hundred Club South Palm Beach County. Clubs: Detroit Athletic, Oakland Hills Country, Hunters Creek. Home: 32949 Bingham Ln Birmingham MI 48010 also 4545 N Ocean Blvd Boca Raton FL 33431

SLAVENSKA, MIA, ballerina, choreographer; b. Slavonski Brod, Jugoslavia, Feb. 20 1916; d. Milan and Hedda (Palme) Corak; student Royal Acad. Music, Zagreb, Jugoslavia, 7 yrs.; ballet student, Vienna, Paris; studied with Dubois, Egorova, Preobrajenska, Froman Celli; m. Kurt Neumann; 1 dau., Maria. Came to U.S., 1938, naturalized, 1947. Began ballet dancing Nat. Opera House, Zagreb, 1921, engaged Nat. Opera House, 1923; first recitals, Spalato, Jugoslavia, 1928; soloist, Zagreb, 1931, ballerina assoluta, 1933; concert tours, Europe, North Africa, 1936; motion picture La Mort du Cigne, 1937; prima ballerina Ballet Russe de Monte Carlo, concerts N.A., S.A., 1938-42; formed own ballet co., Hollywood, Calif., 1941; with concert co. toured U.S., S.A., Can., 1947-52; former dir. Ft. Worth Ballet; formed Slavenska-Franklin Ballet, 1952, prod. ballet Street Car Named Desire based on play by T. Williams, dancing part of Blanche, toured U.S., Japan, 1953; prima ballerina with Met. Opera Co., 1955-56; TV debut in Nat. Broadcasting Spectacular, 1956; now tchr. ballet technique UCLA, Calif. Inst. Arts, Valencia, pvt. studio, Santa Monica. Recipient 1st prize World Tournament of Dancing, Sports Olympiad, Berlin, 1936; Plac d'Honneur, France; Tanr Olympiad, Berlin; Elirey Polis. Composer ballets: Schoenberg's Transfigured Night; Chopin's Concerto in E Minor (Triology); Schubert's Schubertiana; Glazounoff Salome; Chopin's Suite Classic; Debussy's Pastells Tajtchevich; Balcan Plays; Cesar Frank, Symphonic Variations; Saint-Saëns Concerto in G Minor, Namaste.

SLAVIN, ARTHUR JOSEPH, educator; b. Bklyn., Feb. 15, 1933; s. David and Mildred (Eisner) S.; student N.Y. U., 1950-51; B.A. summa cum laude, La. State U., 1958; Ph.D. with honors (Woodrow Wilson fellow 1958-59), U. N.C., 1961; m. Inger-Johanne Espe, Nov. 30, 1968; children—Ruth, Aaron, Rebecca, Laura, Solveig. Asst. prof. dept. history Bucknell U., 1961-65; asso. prof. U. Calif. at Los Angeles, 1965-70, prof., 1971-74; dean arts and sci., prof. history U. Louisville, 1974-77, Justus Bier disting. prof. humanities, prof. history, 1977—; Clark Library lectr., 1977; Danforth asso., 1979—. Served with USAF, 1951-55. Folger Library Sr. fellow, 1970-71; Guggenheim fellow, 1967-68. Fellow Royal Hist. Soc. Great Britain; mem. Am. Hist. Assn. Author: Politics and Profit, 1966; Thomas Cromwell on Church and Commonwealth, 1968; Humanism and Reform, 1969; Tudor Men and institutions, 1972; The Precarious Balance, 1973; The Way of the West, 3 vols., 1973-75. Home: 502 Club Ln Louisville KY 40207 Office: Bingham Humanities 324 U Louisville Louisville KY 40208

SLAVIN, NEAL, photographer; b. Bklyn., Aug. 19, 1941; s. Harry and Ida (Pomerantz) S.; B.F.A., Cooper Union, 1963. Graphic designer Macmillan Pub. Co., 1965; instr. photographer Cooper Union, Sch. Visual Arts, Queens Coll., Manhattanville Coll.; one-man shows: Royal Ont. (Can.) Mus., Toronto, 1976, Light Gallery, N.Y.C., 1976, Center for Creative Photography, Tucson, 1976, Wadsworth Atheneum, Hartford, 1976; group shows include: Galerie Zabriskie, Paris, 1977, Chgo. Center for Contemporary Photography, 1978; represented in permanent collections: Met. Mus. Art, N.Y.C., Mus. Modern Art, N.Y.C., Mus. of Photography, Rochester, N.Y., Center for Creative Photography, Tucson, Exchange Nat. Bank, Chgo. Fulbright grantee, 1968; Nat. Endowment Arts grantee, 1972. Mem. Soc. Photog. Edn. Photog. books include: Portugal, 1971; When Two or More are Gathered Together, 1976. Address: 62 Greene St New York NY 10012. *Nothing in my life has been worth anything unless it has had risk.*

SLAVIN, RAYMOND GRANAM, allergist, immunologist; b. Cleve., June 29, 1930; s. Philip and Dinah (Baskind) S.; A.B., U. Mich., 1952; M.D., St. Louis U., 1956; M.S., Northwestern U., 1963; m. Alberta Cohrt, June 10, 1953; children—Philip, Stuart, David, Linda. Intern, U. Mich. Hosp., Ann Arbor, 1956-57; resident St. Louis U. Hosp., 1959-61; fellow in allergy and immunology Northwestern U. Med. Sch., 1961-64; asst. prof. internal medicine and microbiology St. Louis U., 1965-70, asso. prof., 1970-73, prof., 1973—, dir. div. allergy and immunology, 1965—; cons. U.S. Army M.C. Served with M.C., U.S. Army, 1957-59. NIH grantee, 1967-70; Nat. Inst. Safety and Health grantee, 1974—. Diplomate Am. Bd. Internal Medicine, Am. Bd. Allergy and Immunology (dir.). Fellow A.C.P., Am. Acad. Allergy (exec. bd.); mem. Am. Assn. Immunologists, Central Soc. Chem. Research, AAAS, Alpha Omega Alpha. Democrat. Jewish. Contbr. numerous articles to med. publs.; editorial bd. Jour. Allergy and Clin. Immunology, 1975—, Iice Practice Medicine, 1973—, Current Views in Allergy and Immunology, 1976—, Jour. Club of Allergy, 1978—. Home: 631 E Polo Dr Clayton MO 63105 Office: 1402 S Grand Blvd Saint Louis MO 63104

SLAVIN, SIMON, univ. dean; b. N.Y.C., Jan. 20, 1916; s. Isadore and Mary (Sushansky) S.; B.S. in Social Sci., Coll. City N.Y., 1937; M.A., Columbia, 1938, Ed.D., 1953; m. Jeannette Rose Littinsky, Jan. 16, 1938; children—Rayna (Mrs. Robert Epstein), Vicky Jane, Johanna. Regional supr. United Service Orgn. Jewish Welfare Bd., Chgo., 1945-46; exec. dir. YM-YWHA, Mt. Vernon, N.Y., 1946-53; exec. sec. div. recreation and group work and sect. on services to handicapped Welfare and Health Council of N.Y.C., 1953-54; exec. dir. Ednl. Alliance, N.Y.C., 1954-60; asso. prof. social work Columbia, 1960-63, prof., 1963-68, chmn. community orgn. area, 1960-66, chmn. advanced programs, 1966-67; Simon Sr. Research fellow U. Manchester (Eng.), 1967-68; dean Sch. Social Adminstrn., Temple U., 1968-78, prof., 1978—; chmn. regional adv. com. Region III Dept. Pub. Welfare, Phila., 1972-74; instr. Adelphi Coll., 1955-58, N.Y. U., 1956-57, Chgo. U., 1958-59; cons. N.Y.C. Commr. of Drug Addiction Services. Mem. personnel adv. com. Nat. Urban League, 1964-66. Editor: Adminstrn. in Social Work quar.; Social Administration: The Management of Social Services, 1978. Contbr. chpts. to Migration and Social Welfare, 1971, Evaluation of Social Intervention, 1972, A Design for Social Work Practice, 1974; also numerous articles to profl. jours. Home: 317 Crest Park Rd Philadelphia PA 19119

SLAVSKY, FRANK, architect; b. Denver, Aug. 17, 1919; s. Charles and Celia (Sokoloff) S.; B.A., U. Cal., 1943; div.; 1 dau., Stefanie O'Dell. Pres., sr. architect Frank Slavsky & Assos., Inc., Honolulu, 1951—; prin. works include Makua Alii Housing for Elderly, Queen Liliuokalani Children's Center. Mem. Hawaii State Adv. Commn. Hosps. and Med. Facilities, 1960-63; sec., dir. Hawaii Council for Housing Action, 1966-68. Served with C.E., USAAF, 1943-45. Recipient Honor award for design, Hawaii chpt. AIA, 1955, 60, 69, 70, 71, Merit award for design excellence HUD, 1968. Fellow AIA (sec. Hawaii chpt. 1961). Contbr. articles to profl. jours. Address: 700 Richards St Suite 2001 Honolulu HI 96813

SLAWECKI, TADEUSZ KAROL, educator; b. East Chicago, Ind., Nov. 4, 1919; s. Joseph A. and Josephine (Truszkiewicz) S.; B.S., U. Ill., 1943; M.S., U. Pa., 1948, Ph.D., 1952; m. Louise O. Elder, Mar. 25, 1945. Research asso. U. Pa., 1950-53; research engr. Frankford Arsenal, Phila., 1953-56, cons., 1957-58; cons. engr., mgr. Gen. Electric Co., Phila., 1956-68; dir. chem. engring. and chemistry div., chmn. chem. engring. dept. Ind. Inst. Tech., Ft. Wayne, 1968-71, Essex Internat. prof. in chem. engring., 1968-71; chmn. chem. engring. and materials sci. dept. Youngstown (Ohio) State U., 1971—; cons. Villanova U., 1956-57, Franklin Electric Co., 1968—; tech. adviser Gridcraft, Inc., 1969—. Served with AUS, 1944-46. Mem. Am. Inst. Chem. Engrs., Am. Chem. Soc., N.Y. Acad. Scis., Am. Soc. Engring. Edn., Sigma Xi. Unitarian. Home: 4446 Mellinger Rd Canfield OH 44406

SLAWSKY, ZAKA ISRAEL, physicist, educator; b. Bklyn., Apr. 2, 1910; s. Simon and Mollie (Brimberg) S.; B.S., Rensselaer Poly. Inst., 1933; M.S., Cal. Inst. Tech., 1935; Ph.D., U. Mich., 1938; m. Dorothy Altman, Jan. 19, 1945; children—Albert Altman, Richard Charles. Faculty, Bklyn. Coll., 1939-40, Union Coll., Schenectady, 1940-41; staff Naval Ordnance Lab., White Oak, Md., 1941—, chief physics research, 1960—; faculty U. Md., College Park, 1946—, prof. physics, 1964—. Pres., Joint Bd. in Sci. Edn., Washington Area, 1969-70; pres. bd. trustees Georgetown Day Sch., 1956-63. Recipient Meritorious Civilian Service award USN, 1952, 58, Distinguished Civilian Service medal, 1971. Fellow Am. Phys. Soc., Washington Acad. Sci.; mem. Fed. Prof. Assn. (pres. 1971), Washington Philos. Soc. Club: Cosmos (Washington). Contbr. articles to profl. jours. Research on tech. of antimine warfare, torpedo hydrodynamics, guided and ballistic missiles, antisubmarine warfare. Patentee in field. Home: 4701 Willard Ave Apt 318 Chevy Chase MD 20015 Office: Dept Physics U Md College Park MD 20742

SLAWSON, HUGH MACDONALD, oil co. exec.; b. Craftonville, Calif., Sept. 19, 1918; s. Frank MacDonald and Gladys (Bate) S.; A.A., Los Angeles Jr. Coll., 1937; B.S., U. Calif., Los Angeles, 1941; postgrad. Harvard Grad. Sch. Bus. Adminstrn., 1943; m. Margaret Pauline Straus, Aug. 3, 1940; children—Hugh Paul II, Michael Frank. Chief accountant Universal Pictures Co., Inc., Universal City, Calif., 1946-58; finance mgr. Tidewater Oil Co., Manila, Philippines, 1958-62; internat. finance mgr. Getty Oil Co., Los Angeles, 1963-65, 67-70, treas., 1970—; finance mgr., dir. Iranian Offshore Petroleum Co., Tehran, Iran, 1965-67; treas., asst. sec., dir. Getty (Iran), Ltd.; dir. Mitsubishi Oil Co. Ltd., Getty Oil Devel. Ltd., Minnehoma Corp., Tidewater Oil Co., Chembond Corp. Youth group leader YMCA, 1953-57. Served to capt. USAAF, 1942-46, USAF, 1951-53; ETO. Mem. Am. Petroleum Inst., Nat. Soc. Pub. Accountants, Mgmt. Assn. Philippines, Am. Mgmt. Assn., Petroleum Accountants Soc., Los Angeles World Affairs Council. Republican. Mem. Christian Ch. (deacon). Mason (32 deg.). Clubs: Braemer Country (Tarzana, Calif.); Manila Polo; Royal Tehran Sports. Home: 3010 Dona Susana Dr Studio City CA 91604 Office: 3810 Wilshire Blvd Los Angeles CA 90010

SLAY, ALTON DAVIS, air force officer; b. Crystal Springs, Miss., Nov. 11, 1924; s. Melvin F. and Zelma C. Slay, Flying Sch., Craig Field, Ala., 1944; B.S. in Math., George Washington U.; grad. Advanced Mgmt. Program, Harvard U.; grad. Can. Def. Coll.; Navy Parachutist Sch.; m. Jean Simmons, Feb. 19, 1944; 1 son, Alton Davis. Enlisted U.S. Army Air Corps, 1942, advanced through grades to gen., 1978; various operational, command and research and devel. assignments prior to promotion to gen.; since then served as asst. dep. chief of staff, plans and ops. U.S. Air Forces, Europe, 1967-68; comdr. Air Force Flight Test Center, Edwards AFB, Calif., 1968-70; dep. chief of staff ops. Air Force Systems Command, Andrews AFB, Md., 1970-71; dep. chief of staff ops. 7th Air Force, SE Asia, 1971-72; dir. ops. Mil. Assistance Command, Vietnam, 1972; comdr. Lowry Tech. Tng. Center, Denver, 1972-73; vice comdr. Air Tng. Command, San Antonio, 1973-74; dir. ops. requirements and devel. Hdqrs, USAF, Washington, 1974, dep. chief of staff research and devel., 1975-78; comdr. Air Force Systems Command, Andrews AFB, Md., 1978—; speaker on Air Force to various service orgns. Decorated D.S.M. with 2 oak leaf clusters, Legion of Merit with 4 oak leaf clusters, Soldier's medal, Air medal with 6 oak leaf clusters, Air Force Commendation medal with oak leaf cluster, Army Commendation medal (U.S.); Medal of Honor (Republic of Korea); Disting. Service Order, 1st class, Cross of Gallantry with palm (Republic of Vietnam); recipient Eugene M. Zuckert Mgmt. award U.S. Air Force, 1977, Jimmy Doolittle Fellow award Nat. Air Force Association, 1978, Theodore von Karman Trophy, 1979. Office: Hdqrs AFSC Andrews AFB MD 20334

SLAYBAUGH, DAVID JAMES, editor; b. East Cleveland, Ohio, Oct. 18, 1944; s. Andrew James and Charlotte Evelyn (Bancroft) S.; B.S.J., Ohio U., 1967; m. Nancy Elizabeth Quere, Mar. 23, 1968; children—Stephen David, Matthew James, Rachel Anne. Asst. editor Sch. Product News mag., Indsl. Pub. Co., Cleve., 1968, asso. editor, 1968-73, editor, 1973-76; editor Golf Bus. mag. Harvest Pub. Co., Cleve., 1976-79, Nursery Product News mag., 1979—, exec. editor Golf. Bus., Lawn Care Industry, Pest Control, Weeds Trees & Turf mags., The Land Reclamation Report, 1977—. Mem. Am. Soc. Bus. Press Editors (pres. chpt. 1976-77, nat. sec.-treas. 1977-78, nat. dir. 1978—). Home: 5165 Manchester Circle North Ridgeville OH 44039 Office: 9800 Detroit Ave Cleveland OH 44102

SLAYDEN, JAMES BRAGDON, dept. store exec.; b. Seattle, Sept. 28, 1924; s. Philip Lee and Ruth Alwin (Bragdon) S.; B.A., U. Wash., 1948; M.B.A., U. So. Calif., 1949; m. Barbara Marie McBride, May 7, 1955; children—Tracy Anne, James Bragdon. Buyer, Frederick & Nelson, dept. store, Seattle, 1949-59, div. mdse. mgr., 1959-65; gen. mgr. Bullocks, dept. store, Los Angeles, 1965-69; exec. v.p., gen. mdse. mgr. May D&F Co., dept. store, Denver, 1969-72; pres., chief exec. officer J.W. Robinson, dept. store, Los Angeles, 1972-78; exec. v.p. ops. Marshall Field & Co., Chgo., 1978—. Active United Crusade, United Way, Los Angeles, 1973-78, Chgo. Heart Assn., 1978-79. Served with U.S. Army, 1943-45. Mem. U. So. Calif. Assos., Phi Kappa Psi. Republican. Christian Scientist. Club: Bel Air Bay (Los Angeles). Home: 401 Burr Ridge Club Dr Burr Ridge IL 60521 Office: 111 N State St Chicago IL 60691

SLAYTON, DONALD KENT, astronaut; b. Sparta, Wis., Mar. 1, 1924; s. Charles Sherman and Victoria Adelia (Larson) S.; B.Aero. Engring., U. Minn., 1949; Sc.D. (hon.) Carthage Coll., 1960; D.Eng. (hon.), Mich. Tech. Inst.; m. Marjory Lunney, May 15, 1955; 1 son, Kent Sherman. Served to capt., pilot USAAF, 1942-46; engr. Boeing Aircraft Co., 1949-51; commd. capt. USAF, 1951, advanced to maj., 1959, resigned, 1963; fighter pilot, maintenance officer, Germany, 1952-55; fighter test pilot Edwards AFB, Cal., 1955-59; joined Project Mercury, manned space flight, NASA, 1959, chief astronaut, 1962-63, asst. dir. flight crew ops., 1963-66, dir. flight crew ops., 1966-74; mem. crew Apollo-Soyuz test project, 1974-75, pilot docking module, 1975; mgr. Space Shuttle Approach and Landing Test, 1975-77, mgr. Space Shuttle Orbital Flight Test, 1978—. Fellow Soc. Exptl. Test Pilots, AIAA (asso.), Am. Astronautical Soc.; mem. Order of Daedalians, Am. Fighter Aces, Houston C. of C. Home: PO Box 637 Friendswood TX 77546 Office: Johnson Space Center NASA Houston TX 77058

SLAYTON, MARIETTE ELIZABETH PAINE (MRS. RONALD ALFRED SLAYTON), artist, author; b. Danielson, Conn., May 31, 1908; d. James Monroe and Agnes Caroline (Halliday) P.; student Conn. Coll. Women, 1925-26, Grand Central Art Sch., 1928-29, Art Students League, 1928-29; studied painting with Robert Brackman, 1954-55, Frederick Taubes, 1957-58; studied decorative arts with William Crowell, 1930-45, Walter Wright, 1950-51; m. Ronald Alfred Slayton, Apr. 15, 1960; step-children—Thomas Kennedy, Peter Whitney, Gail (Mrs. Mark Le Grand). Freelance comml. artist, Danielson, 1935-60; tchr. Early Am. decoration, privately, 1945-60, Fletcher Farm Crafts Sch., 1954-69, Thousand Island Mus. Crafts Sch., 1966-67, U. Conn., Storrs, 1955-56, U. Conn. Extension, Willimantic, 1955-56; treas. Dog River Arts Sch., Montpelier, Vt., 1969-72; exhibited one-man shows Chaffee Gallery, Rutland, Vt., 1968, Wood Art Gallery, Montpelier, 1966. Sec. Montpelier Theatre Guild, 1971-73; bd. dirs. Bugbee Meml. Library, Danielson. Recipient Decorative Arts Book award Am. Life Found., 1972; certificate appreciation New Eng. Crafts Fair, 1967. Mem. Hist. Soc. Early Am. Decoration, Inc. (tech. research com.), League Women Voters (v.p. Montpelier chpt. 1966-68). Author: Early American Decorating Techniques, 1972. Home: RFD 2 Montpelier VT 05602

SLAYTON, WILLIAM LAREW, govt. ofcl.; b. Topeka, Dec. 2, 1916; s. Clarence Harvey and Mary (Larew) S.; student U. Omaha, 1937-39, A.B., U. Chgo., 1940, M.A., 1942; D.H.L. (hon.), Clarkson Coll. Tech., 1965; m. Mary Prichard, Aug. 30, 1941; children—Mary Elizabeth Slayton McKean, Barbara Slayton Shelton. Polit. sec. Alderman Paul H. Douglas, Chgo., 1940-42; planning analyst Milw. Planning Commn., 1944-45, 46-47; municipal reference librarian, Milw., 1947-48; asso. dir. Urban Redevel. Study, Chgo., 1948-50; field rep. div. slum clearance and urban redevel. HHFA, Washington, 1950; dir. redevel. Nat. Assn. Housing and Redevel. Ofcls., Washington, 1950-55; v.p. planning, redevel. Webb & Knapp, Inc., Washington, 1955-60; planning partner I.M. Pei & Partners, N.Y.C., 1956-61; commr. Urban Renewal Adminstrn., HHFA, HUD, Washington, 1961-66; dir. Urban Policy Center, Urban Am., Inc., Washington, 1966; exec. v.p. Urban Am., Inc., 1966-69, pres., 1969; exec. v.p. AIA, Washington, 1969-77, exec. v.p. AIA Found., 1970-77, mem. bd. AIA Corp., 1970-77, vice chmn. AIA Research Corp., 1973-77; chmn. urban devel. advisory com. HUD, 1967-68; mem. U.S. del. Econ. Commn. for Europe, 1970; dep. asst. sec. of state for fgn. bldgs., 1978—. Served with USNR, 1945-46. Recipient Gold medal Royal Instn. Chartered Surveyors, Great Britain, 1965. Mem. Potomac Inst. (dir.), AIA (hon.). Home: 3411 Ordway St NW Washington DC 20016 Office: Dept State 20520 C St Washington DC 20520

SLECHTA, ROBERT FRANK, biologist, educator; b. N.Y.C., June 4, 1928; s. Frank C. and Helen (Pospisil) S.; A.B., Clark U., 1949, M.A., 1951; postgrad. Columbia, 1951-52; Ph.D., Boston U., 1955; m. Betty S. Youngren, May 16, 1953; 1 son, Marc William. Research asst. Worcester Found., Shrewsbury, Mass., 1952-53; biologist U.S. Army Med. Nutrition Lab., Denver, 1953-55; instr., research asso. Tufts U., 1955-58; mem. faculty Boston U., 1958—, prof. biology, 1965—, asso. dean Grad. Sch., 1967-78. Mem. Boston Zool. Soc. (dir. 1967-78, trustee 1978-79), Am. Inst. Biol. Scis., AAAS, Microcirculation Soc., Am. Soc. Zoologists, Soc. Study Reprodn., Sigma Xi. Author: (with M. Hawthorne and E. Blaustein) Laboratory Manual for General Biology, 1965; also articles. Research on limb regeneration in urodeles, starvation in prisoners of war, human factors in aircraft seating, effects on progestational compounds on reprodn. (early work on contraceptive pill), quantitative studies of blood flow in living microscopic vessels in mammals and amphibians. Home: 101 Wilson Rd Bedford MA 01730 Office: 705 Commonwealth Ave Boston MA 02215

SLEDD, HERBERT DAVIS, lawyer; b. Paris, Ky., Mar. 19, 1925; s. Herbert Thomas and Soule (Davis) S.; student U. Ky., 1946-48; J.D., Chgo.-Kent Coll. Law, 1952; m. Carolyn Gay McCann, Apr. 30, 1947; children—Mary Miles, Herbert Davis, Sarah Gay. Admitted to Ky. bar, 1952, since practiced in Lexington; mem. firm Brown, Sledd & McCann, 1956—; asst. atty. Fayette County, Lexington, 1960-64. Vice chmn. dist. com. Blue Grass council Boy Scouts Am., 1956-58; mem. Ky. Statute Revision Commn., 1965-68. Bd. dirs. United Cerebral Palsy of Blue Grass; vice chmn. bd. govs. Lexington unit Shriners Hosps. for Crippled Children; trustee Lexington Theol. Sem. 1959—, chmn. bd., 1966-69. Served USMCR, 1943-45. Fellow Am. Coll. Trial Lawyers, Am. Bar Found.; mem. Am. Law Inst., Am. (ho. of dels., bd. govs., sec. 1975—), Ky. (past pres. Younger Lawyer's Conf., pres. 1965-66, named Outstanding Lawyer 1959, bd. govs. 1958-69), Fayette County (gov. 1955-61, pres. 1958) bar assns., Ky. Bar Found. (pres. 1964-70), Ky. Peace Officers council (chmn. 1967-68), Lexington C. of C. (pres. 1974), U. Ky. Alumni Assn., Am. Legion, Spindletop Hall. Mem. Disciples of Christ Central Christian Ch. (chmn. adminstrn. bd. 1959-60, chmn. congregation 1966-70, elder). Mason (33 deg., Shriner). Clubs: Lexington Optimist, Lexington Country, Pyramid, (Lexington). Home: 1617 Richmond Rd Lexington KY 40502 Office: 300 W Short St Lexington KY 40507

SLEDD, JAMES HINTON, educator; b. Atlanta, Dec. 5, 1914; s. Andrew and Annie Florence (Candler) S.; B.A., Emory U., 1936; B.A. with honors (Rhodes scholar), Oxford U., 1939; Ph.D., U. Tex., 1947; postdoctoral studies U. Mich., 1948, U. Chgo., 1951; m. Joan Webb, July 16, 1939; children—Andrew, Robert, James Jr., John, Ann. Instr. English, U. Chgo., 1945-46, asst. prof., 1948-55, asso. prof., 1955-56; asst. prof. Duke, 1946-48; asso. prof. U. Calif. at Berkeley, 1956-59; vis. prof. U. Ceylon, 1959-60; prof. Northwestern U., Evanston, Ill., 1960-64; prof. U. Tex., Austin, 1964—; vis. prof. U. Mich., summer 1956, U. London, 1963, U. Wash., summer 1963, Mont. State U., summer 1967, others. Guggenheim fellow, 1953-54; Ford Found. grantee, 1950-51; Rockefeller Found. grantee, 1952-53. Mem. Modern Lang. Assn., Linguistic Soc., Modern Humanities Research Assn., Nat. Council Tchrs. English, Am. Dialect Soc., Internat. Assn. Univ. Profs. English. Democrat. Methodist. Author, editor of books; contbr. articles to profl. jours. Home: 3704 Gilbert Austin TX 78703 Office: Dept English Univ Texas Austin TX 78712. *Such petty success as I've enjoyed has resulted from (1) great foresight in being born into an intelligent and respected family, (2) some cunning and more luck in evading detection when engaged in nefarious activity, (3) a quite censurable pleasure in using voice and typewriter as weapons in academic controversy.*

SLEDD, MARVIN BANKS, educator; b. Greensboro, Ala., Aug 24, 1912; s. Andrew and Annie Florence (Candler) S.; A.B., Emory U., 1935, M.S., 1936; M.S. in Elec. Engring., Mass. Inst. Tech., 1947, Ph.D., 1954; m. Mary Eloise McDonald, July 24, 1940; 1 son, Charles McDonald. Elec. engr. Gen. Electric Co., 1937-40; elec. engring. dept. Mass. Inst. Tech., 1941-43; staff math. dept. Emory U., Atlanta, 1946, 1948-50; staff Sch. Math., Ga. Inst. Tech., Atlanta, 1951—, former dir., now Regents' prof. math. Served from 2d lt. to 1st lt. USMCR, 1943-46. Mem. Soc. Indsl. and Applied Math., Phi Beta Kappa, Sigma Xi, Phi Kappa Phi. Home: 306 Kenilworth Circle Stone Mountain GA 30083 Office: Ga Inst Tech Atlanta GA 30332

SLEDGE, CLARENCE LINDEN, banker; b. Pearsall, Tex., Apr. 25 1929; s. Clarence Williamson and Lillian (Manford) S.; B.B.A., U. Tex., Austin, 1956; m. Ann Sledge; children—Susan Leigh, Scott Linden, John Tobin, Linda Claire. With Frost Nat. Bank, San Antonio, 1956—, v.p., 1962-65, mem. exec. com., 1963—, sr. v.p., 1965—; exec. v.p., mem. mgmt. com., trust com., sec. pres., dir. Frost Realty Co., 1969-71, pres., vice chmn. bd., 1973—, also dir.; pres., chief exec. officer Frost Nat. Bank; pres., dir. Cullen/Frost Bankers, Inc., Main Plaza Corp.; dir. Citizens Nat. Bank of San Antonio and Dallas. Pres. San Antonio Clearing House, 1973—. Vice pres., bd. dirs., mem. exec. com. Bexar County Muscular Dystrophy Assn.; bd. dirs. ARC, U. Tex. San Antonio Coll. Bus., St. Mary's U. Sch. Bus., NCCJ; trustee Trinity U., San Antonio, S.W. Research Inst.; mem. civic adv. com. South Tex. Regional Blood Bank; pres. Alamo council Boy Scouts; chmn. devel. bd. U. Tex., San Antonio. Served to capt. USAF, 1951-54. Mem. Greater San Antonio C. of C. (exec. com., pres. 1974-75), Am., Tex. bankers assns., Res. City Bankers Assn., Tex. Cavaliers, Phi Kappa Psi. Home: 4001 N New Braunfels Apt 1610 San Antonio TX 78209 Office: PO Box 1600 San Antonio TX 78296

SLEEPER, SHERWIN JAMES, businessman; b. Rockland, Maine, Jan. 22, 1928; s. George Dustin and Margaret Jenny (Aylward) S.; B.S. in Engring., Maine Maritime Acad., 1949, B.S., 1973; M.A., Central Mich. U., 1976; m. Eleanor Lorraine Patterson, Jan. 22, 1967; children—Christine, Kathleen, Theresa, Stanley, Brandt, Marrianne, Andrea, Pamela. Commd. ensign U.S. Navy, 1949, advanced through grades to capt., 1969; service in Korea and Vietnam; supt. U.S. Naval Obs., 1973-76; assigned Bur. Naval Personnel, Washington, 1976; comdg. officer Naval Alcohol Rehab. Center, Jacksonville, Fla., 1977-79, ret., 1979; adminstr. J.R.C. Enterprises and Palm Beach Inst., West Palm Beach, Fla., 1979—; adv. com. alcoholism Jacksonville Dist. Mental Health Bd., 1977—. Dist. commr. Boy Scouts Am., 1973—. Decorated Legion of Merit, Bronze Star with combat V, Meritorious Service medal, Navy Commendation medal with V and gold star, Meritorious Commendation ribbon with star; Vietnam Navy Distinguished Order 2d class, Vietnam Cross Gallantry. Mem. U.S. Power Squadrons (gov. 1972-76). Home: 1114 E Maple Ave Sterling VA 22170 Office: Palm Beach Inst 1014 N Olive Ave West Palm Beach FL 33401

SLEICHER, CHARLES ALBERT, chem. engr.; b. Albany, N.Y., Aug. 15, 1924; s. Charles Albert and Beatrice Eugena (Cole) S.; B.S., Brown U., 1946; M.S., M.I.T., 1949; Ph.D., U. Mich., 1955; m. Janis Jorgensen, Sept. 5, 1953; children—Jeffrey Mark, Gretchen Gail. Asst. dir. M.I.T. Sch. Chem. Engring. Practice, Bangor, Maine, 1949-51; research engr. Shell Devel. Co., Emeryville, Calif., 1955-59; asso. prof. chem. engring. U. Wash., Seattle, 1960—, dept. chmn., 1977—; cons. Westinghouse-Hanford Co. Served with USN, 1943-47. NSF postdoctoral fellow, 1959-60, SEED grantee, 1973-74; research grantee NSF, Chevron Research Corp., Am. Chem. Soc. Mem. Am. Inst. Chem. Engrs. (program, awards coms.), Am. Chem. Soc., AAAS, Am. Soc. Enologists, Sigma Xi. Chem. reactor design patentee. Contbr. articles on extraction, heat transfer, fluid mechanics to profl. jours. Home: 5002 Harold Pl NE Seattle WA 98105 Office: U Wash Dept Chem Engring BF 10 Seattle WA 98195

SLEMMONS, DAVID BURTON, geologist, geophysicist, educator; b. Alameda, Calif., Dec. 31, 1922; s. Claude Hayes and Gladys (Hinton) S.; B.S. in Econ. Geology, U. Calif. at Berkeley, 1947, Ph.D., 1953; m. Ruth Marillyn Evans, Sept. 7, 1946; children—David Robert, Mary Anne. Faculty, U. Nev., Reno, 1951—, prof. geology, 1963—, dir. Seismographic Stas., 1952-65, chmn. geology-geography dept., 1966-70; cons. geologist, geophysicist to various mining cos., utilities, geol. engring. firms, govt. agys., 1954—; mem. com. on safety of dams NRC. Recipient G. K. Gilbert award in seismic geology Carnegie Instn. Washington, 1962. Fellow Geol. Soc. Am.; mem. Earthquake Engring. Research Inst., Seismol. Soc. Am., Am. Inst. Mining, Metall. and Petroleum Engring., Am. Geophys. Union, Sigma Xi, Phi Kappa Phi. Author: Faults and Earthquake Magnitude. Contbr. articles to profl. jours. Home: 2995 Golden Valley Rd Reno NV 89506

SLEMON, GORDON RICHARD, educator; b. Bowmanville, Ont., Can., Aug. 15, 1924; s. Milton Everitt and Selena (Johns) S.; B.A.Sc., U. Toronto, 1946, M.A.Sc., 1948; D.I.C., Imperial Coll. Sci., London (Eng.) U., 1951, Ph.D., 1952, D.Sc., 1968; m. Margaret Jean Matheson, July 9, 1949; children—Sally, Stephen, Mark, Jane. Asst. prof. elec. engring. N.S. Tech. Coll., Can., 1953-55; asso. prof. U. Toronto, Ont., Can., 1955-63, prof., 1964—, chmn. dept. elec. engring., 1966-76, dean Faculty of Applied Sci. and Engring., 1979—; Colombo plan adviser, India, 1963-64; pres. Elec. Engring. Consociates, 1976-79. Recipient excellence in teaching award Western Electric, 1965. Fellow Inst. Elec. Engring., IEEE; mem. Am. Soc. for Engring. Edn., Canadian Elec. Assn., others. Author: Magnetoelectric Devices; (with J.M. Ham) Scientific Basis of Electrical Engineering; (with A. Straugher) Electric Machinery. Patentee in field. Contbr. articles to profl. jours. Home: 40 Chatfield Dr Don Mills ON Canada Office: Faculty Applied Sci and Engring Univ Toronto Toronto ON Canada

SLEPIAN, DAVID, mathematician, communications engr.; b. Pitts., June 30, 1923; s. Joseph and Rose Grace (Myerson) S.; student U. Mich., 1941-43; M.A., Harvard U., 1947, Ph.D., 1949; m. Janice Dorothea Berek, Apr. 18, 1950; children—Steven Louis, Don Joseph, Anne Maria. With Bell Labs., Murray Hill, N.J., 1950—, head math studies dept., 1970—; prof. elec. engring. U. Hawaii, Honolulu, 1970—; McKay prof. elec. engring. U. Calif., Berkeley, 1957-58; regents lectr., 1977. Served with U.S. Army, 1943-46. Fellow IEEE, Inst. Math. Statistics, AAAS; mem. Nat. Acad. Scis. Nat. Acad. Engring., Soc. Indsl. and Applied Math. Patentee in field. Contbr. articles to profl. jours. Home: 212 Summit Ave Summit NJ 07901 Office: Bell Labs 600 Mountain Ave Murray Hill NJ 07974

SLEPIAN, PAUL, mathematician, educator; b. Boston, Mar 26, 1923; s. Philip and Ida (Goldstein) S.; S.B., Mass. Inst. Tech., 1950; Ph.D., Brown U., 1956; m. Florence Weiner, Apr. 3, 1949; children—Laura, Jean. Mathematician Hughes Aircraft Co., 1956-60; asso. prof. math. U. Ariz., 1960-62; mem. faculty Rensselaer Poly. Inst., Troy, N.Y., 1962-69, prof. math., 1965-69; prof., chmn. dept. math. Bucknell U., Lewisburg, Pa., 1969-70; prof. math. Howard U., Washington, 1970—; summer vis. staff mem. Los Alamos Sci. Lab., 1976, 78, 79. Mem. Am. Math. Soc., Soc. Indsl. and Applied Math., Math. Assn. Am., IEEE. Home: 11235 Oak Leaf Dr Apt 1909 Silver Spring MD 20901

SLESINGER, REUBEN EMANUEL, educator; b. Windber, Pa., Feb. 12, 1916; s. Isaac and Sarah (Zimmerman) S.; B.S., U. Pitts., 1936, M.A., 1938, Ph.D., 1940; postgrad. Harvard, 1937-39, U. Wis., 1939-40; m. Natalie May Friedman, Dec. 17, 1950; children—Sarah, James (dec.), Diane. Mem. faculty U. Pitts., 1936—, prof. econs., 1955—; cons. to legal profession, govt. and industry. Served to col. AUS, World War II. Decorated Legion of Merit. Club: Press (Pitts.). Home: 6636 Wilkins Ave Pittsburgh PA 15217

SLESNICK, WILLIAM ELLIS, mathematician, educator; b. Oklahoma City, Feb. 24, 1925; s. Isaac Ralph and Adele (Miller) S.; B.S., U.S. Naval Acad., 1945; B.A., U. Okla., 1948; B.A. (Rhodes scholar), Oxford (Eng.) U., 1950, M.A., 1954; M.A., Harvard, 1952; A.M. (hon.), Dartmouth, 1972. Math. master St. Paul's Sch., Concord, N.H., 1952-62; vis. instr. Darmouth, 1958-59, mem. faculty, 1962—, prof. math., 1971—, asst. dir. ednl. uses Kiewit Computation Center, 1966-69; mem. N.H. Rhodes Scholar Selection Com.; mem. advanced placement exam. com. math. Coll. Entrance Exam. Bd., 1967-71; mem. Nat. Humanities Faculty, 1972—. Active Boy Scouts Am., 1937—, dist. chmn., 1974-76, council exec. bd., 1964—; mem. nat. com. Order of Arrow, 1965—, mem. internat. com., 1974—; mem. Nat. Jewish Com. Scouting, 1973—; attache Boy Scouts World Bur., 1955, 67; mem. corp. Mary Hitchcock Meml. Hosp., Hanover; trustee Lawrence L. Lee Mus., Hanover-Norwich Youth Fund, New Hampton (N.H.) Sch. Served to ensign U.S. Navy, 1942-47. Recipient Vigil Honor, 1948; Nat. Distinguished Service award Order of Arrow, 1967; Silver Beaver award Boy Scouts Am., 1967, Silver Antelope award, 1972; Wendall E. Badger award for contbn. to rowing Dartmouth Coll., 1978. Mem. Nat. Council Tchrs. Math., Math. Assn. Am., Assn. Tchrs. Math. in New Eng., Assn. Am. Rhodes Scholars, Phi Beta Kappa (chpt. pres. 1974-77), Phi Eta Sigma, Pi Mu Epsilon, Alpha Phi Omega. Co-author 12 math. textbooks including: (with R.H. Crowell) Calculus With Analytic Geometry, 1968. Home: 19 S Park St Hanover NH 03755

SLETTEBAK, ARNE, astronomer, educator; b. Danzig, Aug. 8 1925; s. Nicolai and Valerie (Janczak) S.; came to U.S. 1927, naturalized 1932; B.S. in Physics, U. Chgo., 1945, Ph.D. in Astronomy, 1949; m. Constance Pixler, Aug. 28, 1949; children—Marcia Diane, John Andrew. Mem. faculty Ohio State U., Columbus, 1949—, prof. astronomy, 1959—, dir. Perkins Obs., Delaware, Ohio, 1959-78, chmn. dept. astronomy, 1962-78, mem. steering com. Earth Sci. Curriculum Project, 1965-68. Mem. NRC Commn. on Astronomy adv. to Office Naval Research, 1963-65; mem. adv. panel for astronomy NSF, 1968-71. Fulbright research fellow Hamburg, Germany, 1955-56; Fulbright lectr., vis. prof. U. Vienna, 1974-75. Mem. Assn. Univs. for Research Astronomy (dir. 1961-79, chmn. sci. com. 1970-73), Am. Astron. Soc. (council 1964-67), Internat. Astron. Union (v.p. commn. 45 1976-79, pres. 1979—), Sigma Xi. Home: 601 Seabury Dr Worthington OH 43085 Office: Dept Astronomy Ohio State U Columbus OH 43210

SLEVIN, EDWARD DEAN, lawyer; b. Hanover, Pa., Feb. 19, 1937; s. Edward Joseph and Jane Ann (Dean) S.; B.A., Dickinson Coll., 1959; LL.B., U. Pa., 1962; m. Kay Marie Mummert, Aug. 27, 1960; children—Mark William, Courtney Ann, Edward Dean. Admitted to Pa. bar, 1963; asso. firm Montgomery, McCracken, Walker & Rhoads, Phila., 1962-69, partner, 1969—; fellow Salzburg Seminar in Am. Studies, 1972. Mem. Phila. Bar Assn., Pa. Bar Assn., Am. Bar Assn., Am. Law Inst. Democrat. Roman Catholic. Clubs: Merion Golf, Rittenhouse, Peale. Home: 2341 Pheasant Hill Ln Malvern PA 19355 Office: 20th Floor Three Parkway Philadelphia PA 19102

SLEZAK, JOHN, printing co. exec.; b. Stara Tura, Czechoslovakia, Apr. 18 1896 (came to U.S. 1916); s. Simon and Ann (Trokan) S.; B.S. in Mech. Engring., U. Wis., 1923; m. Dorothy Goodwill, Aug. 23, 1926; children—Nancy Jean, Doris Ann. Mech. engr. Western Electric Co., Chgo., 1923-30; pres. Turner Brass Works, Sycamore, Ill., 1930-53; chmn. bd. Kable Printing Co., Mt. Morris, Ill., 1947-72; pres., chmn. bd. Pheoll Mfg. Co., Chgo., 1948-53; asst. sec. of Army, 1953, under sec., 1953-55; dir. Hazeltine Corp., Clayton Mark Co., Roper Corp., Hazeltine Research, Inc., Western Pub. Co. Chmn. res. forces policy bd. Dept. Def., Washington, 1957—; dir. Inst. Am. Strategy, 1958—. Trustee Ill. Inst. Tech., 1949—, Found. for Econ. Edn., 1955-67, Am. Mus. Immigration, 1955-69. Served as col. AUS, 1943-46, chief Chgo. Ordnance Dist., 1944-46; cons. Army and Navy Munitions Bd., 1947. Decorated Legion of Merit with oak leaf cluster, Freedom medal. Mem. Am. Ordnance Assn. (dir.), Ill. Mfrs. Assn. (pres., chmn. bd. 1950-52), NAM (dir. 1952-53), Western Soc. Engrs., Ill. C. of C. (past dir.), Assn. U.S. Army (pres. 1955-57), Am. Legion. Moose. Clubs: Chicago, Commercial, Chicago Athletic (Chgo.). Home: 711 W State St Sycamore IL 60178

SLICHTER, CHARLES PENCE, physicist, educator; b. Ithaca, N.Y., Jan. 21, 1924; s. Sumner Huber and Ada (Pence) S.; A.B., Harvard, 1946, M.A., 1947, Ph.D., 1949; m. Gertrude Thayer Almy, Aug. 23, 1952 (div. Sept. 1977); children—Sumner Pence, William Aimy, Jacob Huber, Ann Thayer. Research asst. Underwater Explosives Research Lab., Woods Hole, Mass., 1943-46; mem. faculty U. Ill. at Urbana, 1949—, prof. physics, 1955—, prof. Center for Advanced Study, 1968—; Morris Loeb lectr. Harvard, 1961; dir. Polaroid Co.; mem. Pres.'s Sci. Adv. Com., 1964-69, Com. on Nat. Medal Sci., 1969-74, Nat. Sci. Bd., 1975—, Pres.'s Com. Sci. and Tech., 1976—. Mem. corp. Harvard U.; trustee, mem. corp. Woods Hole Oceanographic Instn. Recipient Langmuir award Am. Phys. Soc., 1969. Alfred P. Sloan fellow, 1955-61. Mem. Nat. Acad. Scis., Am. Acad. Arts and Scis., Am. Philos. Soc. Author: Principles of Magnetic Resonance, 1963, rev. edit., 1978. Contbr. articles to profl. jours. Home: 705 W Church Apt P Champaign IL 61820

SLICHTER, WILLIAM PENCE, chemist; b. Ithaca, N.Y., Mar. 31, 1922; s. Sumner Huber and Ada (Pence) S.; B.A., Harvard U., 1944, M.A., 1949, Ph.D., 1950; m. Ruth Kaple, June 17, 1950; children—Nancy, Carol, Catherine, Margaret. Mem. tech. staff Bell Telephone Labs., Murray Hill, N.J., 1950—, head chem. physics research dept., 1958-67, chem. dir., 1967-73, exec. dir. research-materials sci. and engring. div., 1973—; mem. adv. coms. Nat. Bur. Standards, NSF, NASA, Harvard U., Northwestern U., Dartmouth Coll., Rutgers U., SUNY, Albany. Served to lt. U.S. Army, 1943-46. Fellow Am. Phys. Soc. (award in high polymer physics 1970); mem., Nat. Acad. Engring., Am. Chem. Soc., Electrochem. Soc., AAAS, ASTM (dir.), Sigma Xi. Research on molecular motion and structure in high polymers, nuclear magnetic resonance spectrosocopy. Home: 55 Van Doren Ave Chatham NJ 07928 Office: Bell Telephone Labs Murray Hill NJ 07974

SLICK, GRACE WING, entertainer; b. Chgo., Oct. 30, 1939; d. Ivan W. and Virginia (Barnett) Wing; student Finch Coll., 1957-58, U. Miami (Fla.), 1958-59; m. Gerald Robert Slick, Aug. 26, 1961 (div. 1970); 1 dau., China; m. 2d, Skip Johnson, Nov. 29, 1976. Singer with Great Society, 1965-66, Jefferson Airplane, 1966-72, Jefferson Starship, 1974—. Address: 44 Montgomery St San Francisco CA 94118

SLICK, WILLIAM THOMAS, JR., oil co. exec.; b. Cleve., Sept. 17, 1923; s. William Thomas and Clare (Sheahan) S.; B.S. in Mech. Engring., Brown U., 1948; m. Patricia Gregg, May 25, 1946; children—Steven, Susan. With Exxon Co. U.S.A., Houston, 1948—, asst. mgr. corp. planning dept., 1969-72, mgr. pub. affairs, 1972-73, sr. v.p., 1973—; mem. adv. council U. Tex. Engring. Found., 1974. Trustee Brown U., 1976—; v.p., bd. dirs. Houston Assn. for Community TV, 1972—; adv. bd. Houston Salvation Army, 1977—. Served with USAF, 1943-46. Mem. Am. Petroleum Inst., Am. Inst. Mining and Metall. Engrs., U.S. C. of C. (council on trends and perspective), Tex. Assn. Taxpayers, Tex. Research League (dir. 1977—). Roman Catholic. Club: River Oaks Country, Petroleum Houston. Office: PO Box 2180 Houston TX 77001

SLIEPCEVICH, CEDOMIR M., educator; b. Anaconda, Mont., Oct. 4, 1920; s. Maksim and Jovanka (Lubibratich) S.; B.S., U. Mich., 1941, M.S., 1942, Ph.D., 1948; m. Cleo L. Whorton, Oct. 21, 1955. Asso. prof. dept. chem. and metall. engring. U. Mich., 1946-55; prof., chmn. Sch. Chem. Engring., also asso. dean Coll. Engring., U. Okla., 1955-62, research prof. engring., 1963—; pres. Univ. Engrs., Inc., 1965-78; dir. Autoclave Engrs., Inc.; also cons. chem. engr. Recipient Curtis W. McGraw Research award, 1958; Ipatieff award, 1959, George Westinghouse award, 1964; Sesquicentennial award U. Mich., 1967; Okla. Outstanding Scientist award, 1975; Disting. Service citation U. Okla., 1975; William H. Walker award, 1978; named Okla. Profl. Engr. of Yr., 1972, Nat. Profl. Engr. of Year, 1974; inducted into Okla. Hall Fame, 1974. Fellow Am. Inst. Chem. Engrs.; mem. Nat. Acad. Engrs. Author numerous tech. papers. Home: 2500 Butler Dr Norman OK 73069

SLIFE, HARRY G., broadcasting co. exec.; b. Hawarden, Iowa, Feb. 7, 1923; s. Earl V. and Bernice (Venard) S.; LL.B., State U. Iowa, 1948; m. Polly Young Prichard, May 12, 1945; children—James, Peggy, Polly, Sarah. Admitted to Iowa bar, 1948; practiced in Forest City, 1948-56; house counsel Rath Packing Co., Waterloo, Iowa, 1956-60, asst. sec., 1960-61, v.p., gen. counsel, 1961-63, v.p. fin., sec., 1963-66, exec. v.p., sec., 1966-67, pres., 1967-74; pres. Black Hawk Broadcasting Co., Waterloo, 1974—, also dir.; dir. Nat. Bank of Waterloo. County atty. Winnebago County, Iowa, 1954-56. Mem. Iowa Bd. Regents, 1973-74. Served with USMCR, 1943-46. Mem. Am., Iowa bar assns., Am. Mgmt. Assn., Iowa Taxpayers Assn. (dir. 1963-73), Iowa Mfrs. Assn. (dir. 1967-75), Am. Meat Inst. (dir. 1968-75). Republican. Methodist. Mason, Elk. Home: 2306 Rainbow Dr Cedar Falls IA 50613 Office: Black Hawk Broadcasting Co KWWL Bldg Waterloo IA 50704

SLIFER, LUTHER WALTER, JR., physicist; b. Guntur, India, Dec. 17, 1928; s. Luther Walter and Matilda Joanne (Anderson) S.; B.A., Gettysburg Coll., 1948; postgrad. Pa. State Coll., 1949, U. Md., 1951-54; m. Janice Miller Hill, June 11, 1949; children—Sheryl, John, Audrey, Leslee, Marshia, Mathew, Grant, Maureen. Instr. physics Pa. State Coll., 1948-50; physicist Nat. Bur. Standards, Washington, 1951-53; physicist, aero. research engr. Naval Ordnance Lab., White Oak, Md., 1953-61; aerospace technologist, physicist NASA Goddard Space Flight Center, Greenbelt, Md., 1961-78, staff engr., 1978—. Mem. AIAA. Republican. Lutheran. Patentee in field. Home: 7023 Dolphin Rd Lanham MD 20801 Office: NASA Greenbelt Rd Greenbelt MD 20771

SLIFKA, ALAN BRUCE, securities co. exec.; b. N.Y.C., Oct. 13, 1929; s. Joseph and Sylvia S.; m. Virginia Bayer, Oct. 31, 1976; children—Michael, Randolph, David. Now partner L. F. Rothschild, Unterberg, Towbin, N.Y.C. Office: 55 Water St New York NY 10041

SLIGER, BERNARD FRANCIS, univ. pres.; b. Chassell, Mich., Sept. 30, 1924; s. Paul and Hazel (McLauchlin) S.; A.B. in Econs. with high honors, Mich. State U., 1949, M.A., 1950, Ph.D., 1955; postgrad. U. Minn., 1961-62; m. Greta Taube, Sept. 1, 1945; children—Nan, Paul, Greta Lee, Sten. Mem. faculty La. State U., 1953-68, prof. econs., 1961, head dept., 1961-65, vice chancellor, dean acad. affairs, 1965-68; sec. adminstrn., chief budget officer State of La., 1968-69; sec.-treas. La. Office Bldg. Corp., 1969-72; exec. dir. La. Coordinating Council Higher Edn., 1969-72; exec. v.p. Fla. State U., Tallahassee, 1972-76, chief acad. officer, 1973-76, interim pres., 1976-77, pres., 1977—; prof. econs., 1973—; mem. Fla. Articulation Com., 1974—; cons. in field. Served with U.S. Army, 1943-46. Named Dr. Pratical Politics, La. Ho. of Reps., 1969. Mem. Am. Council Edn., So. Econ. Assn., AAUP (past chpt. pres.). Lutheran. Contbr. profl. publns. Home: 1030 W Tennessee St Tallahassee FL 32304 Office: 211 Westcott Fla State Univ Tallahassee FL 32306

SLINGLUFF, THOMAS ROWLAND, JR., pub. co. exec.; b. Balt., Aug. 10, 1919; s. Thomas Rowland and Gertrude Seckel (Jenkins) S.; B.A., Stanford, 1948; diplôme d'Études, Sorbonne U. Paris (France), 1949; m. Pamela Lloyd, Mar. 30, 1953; children—Michael St. Clair, Pamela Devereux, Deirdre Ann. Staff officer London (Eng.) Embassy U.S. Foreign Service, 1949-52, Paris (France) Embassy, 1952-53; dir. Pa. State U. Press, University Park, Pa., 1958-72; treas., gen. mgr. Am. U. Pubs. Group Ltd., London, 1965-72; chmn., chief exec. officer Univ. Park Press Inc., Balt., 1967—; owner Augean Stables, Balt. Trustee Walters Art Gallery, Balt., Md. Hist. Soc. Served with USAAC, 1942-45. Decorated D.F.C. with oak leaf cluster, Air medal. Mem. Soc. Colonial Wars, English-Speaking Union (bd. govs.), Pi Gamma Mu. Clubs: Md., Merchant's, Elkridge, Greenspring Hunt (Balt.); Hurlingham (London). Home: 6009 N Charles St Baltimore MD 21212 Office: Garrett Bldg Baltimore MD 21202

SLIPE, WALTER JAMES, city mgr.; b. N.Y.C., Mar. 13, 1933; s. Walter and Pauline Sally (Chrust) S.; B.A., Columbia U., 1954; M.City Planning, U. Calif., Berkeley, 1958. Dep. city mgr. community devel. Fresno (Calif.), 1966-69; asst. city mgr. community devel. Sacramento, 1969-76, city mgr., 1976—. Mem. Internat. City Mgmt.

Assn. Home: 1251 Noonan Dr Sacramento CA 95822 Office: City Hall Sacramento CA 95814

SLITOR, RICHARD EATON, financial cons., economist; b. St. Paul, July 1, 1911; s. Ray Francis and Nelle (Eaton) S.; student U. Wis., 1928-30; S.B. magna cum laude, Harvard U., 1932, Ph.D., 1940; M.A. (Carnegie Teaching fellow), Colgate U., 1934; m. Louise Bean, Dec. 24, 1937; children—Prudence Van Zandt (Mrs. William M. Crozier, Jr.), Deborah, Nicholas, Christopher W. Eaton. Instr., tutor econs. Harvard, 1934-41, Radcliffe Coll., 1940-41; asso. prof., chmn. dept. econs. and bus. adminstrn. Mt. Union Coll., 1941-42; economist div. tax research Treasury Dept., 1942-49, asst. dir. tax adv. staff Sec. of Treasury, 1949-51, taxation specialist, 1951-53, fiscal economist, tax analysis staff, U.S. Treasury, 1953-61, chief bus. taxation staff, asst. dir., office tax analysis, 1961-72; head Richard E. Slitor Assos., 1972—. Fed. exec. fellow Brookings Instn., 1963-64; vis. prof. econs. U. Mass., 1967-68; cons. Nat. Commn. on Urban Problems, 1967-68, Colombian Commission on Tax Reform, 1968, Com. for Econ. Devel., 1970-71, RAND Corp., 1972-74, Adv. Commn. Intergovtl. Relations, 1973-75, EPA, 1976-79, Council Environ. Quality, 1976-77, FRS, 77-78, others. Mem. Am. Econ. Assn., Internat. Inst. Pub. Fin., Royal Econ. Soc., Nat. Tax Assn., Phi Beta Kappa, Chi Phi. Episcopalian. Club: Harvard (Washington). Author articles and books on taxation. Address: 9000 Burning Tree Rd Bethesda MD 20034

SLIVE, SEYMOUR, museum ofcl., educator; b. Chgo., Sept. 15, 1920; s. Daniel and Sonia (Rapoport) S.; A.B., U. Chgo., 1943, Ph.D., 1952; M.A. (hon.), Harvard, 1958; M.A., Oxford (Eng.) U., 1972; m. Zoya Gregorevna Sandomirsky, June 29, 1946; children—Katherine, Alexander, Sarah. Instr. fine arts Oberlin (O.) Coll., 1950-51; chmn. art dept. Pomona (Cal.) Coll., 1952-54; mem. faculty Harvard, Cambridge, Mass., 1954—, prof. fine arts, 1961—, Gleason prof. fine arts, 1973—, chmn. dept. fine arts, 1968-71, dir. Fogg Art Mus., 1975—; exchange prof. Leningrad (USSR) U., 1961; Reyerson lectr. Yale, 1962; Slade prof. Oxford (Eng.) U., 1972-73. Trustee Solomon R. Guggenheim Found., 1978—. Served as lt. (j.g.) USNR, 1943-46; PTO. Decorated officer Order Orange Nassau (Netherlands), 1962; Fulbright fellow, Netherlands, 1951-52; Guggenheim fellow, 1956-57, 78-79; Fulbright research scholar Utrecht (Netherlands) U., 1959-60. Fellow Am. Acad. Arts and Scis.; hon. mem. Karel van Mander Soc.; mem. Coll. Art Assn. (dir. 1958-62, 65-69), Renaissance Soc., Dutch Soc. Scis. (fgn. mem.). Author: Rembrandt and His Critics; 1630-1730, 1953; The Rembrandt Bible, 1959; Catalogue of the Paintings of Frans Hals, 1962; (with Jakob Rosenberg and E.H. ter Kuile) Dutch Art and Architecture 1600-1800, 1966; Rembrandt's Drawings, 1965; Frans Hals, 3 vols., 1970-74. Office: Fogg Art Museum Harvard U Cambridge MA 02138

SLIVINSKY, CORNELL J., corp. exec.; b. Sewickley, Pa., Sept. 18, 1925; s. Joseph J. and Florence M. (Cornell) S.; B.S., Tulsa U., 1944; m. Ann M. Campolong, July 24, 1948; children—Kyra, Valerie. Structural engr. Kellett Aircraft Corp., Phila., 1947-49; project engr. Vertol div. Boeing Co., Phila., 1949-60; v.p., gen. mgr. Parsons Corp., Traverse City, Mich., 1960-68; dir. plans and programs Gates Learjet Corp., Wichita, Kans., 1968-71; v.p., gen. mgr. Vero Beach Facility, Piper Aircraft Corp., Lock Haven, Pa., 1971-74; pres. Gen. Aviation div. Rockwell Internat., Bethany, Okla., 1974—. Mem. adv. bd. Okla. U. Aerospace Sch. Served with USAAF, 1944-47. Patentee in field. Home: 3009 Raintree Rd Oklahoma City OK 73120 Office: 5001 N Rockwell Ave Bethany OK 73008

SLOAN, ALBERT RAYMOND, mfg. co. exec.; b. Los Angeles, Oct. 2, 1926; s. Albert C. and Grace (Brown) S.; B.S. in Mech. Engring., UCLA, 1949; grad. AMP, Harvard Sch. Bus., 1975; m. Janet M. Kelley, June 25, 1949; children—Nancy L., Carol A., Laurie E., Andrew C. With Continental Can Co., 1949—, v.p., asst. gen. mgr. metal div., N.Y.C., 1969-72, v.p., gen. mgr. mfg. ops. Chgo., 1972-73, v.p., gen. mgr. ops., 1974-75, pres. Continental Can Internat. Corp., Stamford, Conn., 1976—, also v.p. Continental Group, Inc., Stamford. Served with USNR, 1944-46. Mem. Delta Sigma Phi. Roman Catholic. Office: 72 Cummings Point Rd Stamford CT 06904

SLOAN, DAVID EDWARD, diversified industry exec.; b. Winnipeg, Can., Mar. 29, 1922; s. David and Annie (Gorvin) S.; B.Commerce, U. Man., 1942; m. Kathleen Lowry Craig, Dec. 26, 1947; children—Pamela Jane, John David, Kathleen Anne. With Monarch Life Assurance Co., Winnipeg, 1946-47; with Can. Pacific Ltd., 1947—, treas., 1969—; dir. Fire Ins. Co. Can.; mem. adv. com. Can. Pension Plan, Can. Govt., 1967-76, chmn., 1974-76. Served to lt. Royal Can. Army, 1942-45. Mem. Fin. Execs. Inst. Can. (past pres., dir. Montreal chpt.), Fedn. Fin. Analysts, Soc. Investment Analysts (U.K.), Soc. Internat. Treasurers (council advs. 1978), Assn. Am. R.R.'s, Can. C. of C., Nat. Assn. Bus. Economists. Mem. United Ch. of Canada. Clubs: Univ. (Toronto); Toronto Hunt (Scarborough, Ont.); Royal Montreal Golf (Ile Bizard, Que.). Home: 316 Rosemary Rd Toronto ON M5P 3E3 Canada Office: Canadian Pacific Ltd 20 King St W 7th Floor Toronto ON M5H 1C4 Canada

SLOAN, EDWARD WILLIAM, JR., former govt. ofcl., ret. mining and shipping co. exec.; b. Cleve., Aug. 20, 1907; s. Edward William and Laura (Biggar) S.; student Yale, 1925-26; Ph.B., Western Res. U., 1929; m. Josephine Rudolph, Dec. 20, 1930; children—Edward William III, James R. Personal trust adviser Union Trust Co., 1929-35; with Oglebay Norton Co., Cleve., 1935-70, v.p., treas., dir., 1949-56, exec. v.p., dir., 1956-59, pres., 1959-70, dir., 1970—; pres. Lake Erie Region Transp. Authority, Cleve., 1972-79. Mem. Cleve. Commn. Higher Edn., 1965-73; mem. Businessmen's Interacial Com. on Community Affairs, Cleve. Little Hoover Commn., 1965, Nat. Com. for Social Work Edn. Trustee United Appeal, campaign chmn., 1968, pres., 1969; trustee Ednl. Research Council Greater Cleve., 1961-75; trustee, former pres. bd. U. Sch., Cleve.; trustee, former chmn. Cleve. Devel. Found.; trustee Cleve. State U., 1964-70, Gates Mills Improvement Soc.; mem. exec. bd., chmn. finance com. Greater Cleve. council Boy Scouts Am.; bd. dirs. Greater Cleve. Growth Assn., 1966-71; bd. overseers Case Western Res. U., 1961-71; trustee, former chmn. Ednl. TV Assn. Met. Cleve., Cleve. Scholarship Programs, Cleve. Nat. Air Show, 1974-78; mem. adv. council Supplementary Ednl. Centers, Natural Sci. Mus., Health Fund Greater Cleve. Mem. Nat Coal Assn. (dir.), Am. Mining Congress, Am. Iron and Steel Inst. Presbyn. Clubs: Pepper Pike (dir.), Union, 50 of Cleve. (pres. 1970-71), Chagrin Valley Hunt. Home: Berkshire Rd Gates Mills OH 44040

SLOAN, FRANK KEENAN, lawyer; b. Johnson City, Tenn., Oct. 11, 1921; s. Z. Frank and Maria Pearl (Witten) S.; B.A., U. S.C., 1943, LL.B., J.D., 1948; m. Helen Rhett Yobs, Feb. 23, 1946 (dec. 1978); children—Richard O., Lewis W., Christine McC., Frank Keenan; m. Alice E. Hamburger, June 22, 1979. Admitted to S.C. bar, 1948; with firm Cooper & Gary, Columbia, S.C., 1948-62; dep. asst. sec. Dept. Def., Washington, 1962-65; S.E. regional dir. OEO, Atlanta, 1965-67; individual practice law, Columbia, 1967-77; dep. atty. gen. State of S.C., Columbia, 1977—; from instr. to asso. prof. law U. S.C., 1954-62. Exec. dir., sec. S.C. Dem. Party, 1960-62; county atty., county exec. Richland County, S.C., 1970-72. Served with USN, 1943-46, 51-52; capt. Res. (ret.). Mem. Am. Law Inst., Am. Bar Assn., S.C. Bar (chmn. com. on procedure 1958-62, 70-72), Richland County Bar Assn., S.C. Trial Lawyers Assn., S.C. Def. Attys. Assn., Am. Legion, VFW, Naval Res. Assn., Ret. Officers Assn. Democrat. Lutheran. Clubs: Rotary, Summit, Forest Lake (Columbia). Contbr. articles to legal jours. Home: 3320 Devereaux Rd Columbia SC 29205 Office: Wade Hampton State Office Bldg PO Box 11549 Columbia SC 29211

SLOAN, HERBERT ELIAS, physician and surgeon; b. Clarksburg, W.Va., Oct. 10, 1914; s. Herbert Elias and Luella (Dye) S.; A.B., Washington and Lee U., 1936; M.D., Johns Hopkins U., 1940; m. Doris Edwards, May 3, 1943; children—Herbert, Ann, Elizabeth, John, Robert. Resident in surgery Johns Hopkins Hosp., 1941-44, U. Mich. Hosp., 1947-49; instr. dept. surgery Johns Hopkins U., 1943-44; instr. thoracic surgery U. Mich., Ann Arbor, 1949-50, asst. prof., 1950-53, asso. prof., 1953-62, prof. surgery, head sect. thoracic surgery, 1970—; mem. staff VA Hosp., Ann Arbor, 1953—, cons., 1968—; mem. staff Wayne County Gen. Hosp., 1967—, cons., 1970—. Served to maj. M.C., U.S. Army, 1944-47. Recipient Bruce Douglas award in thoracic diseases, 1974; diplomate Am. Bd. Surgery, Am. Bd. Thoracic Surgery (pres. 1979-80). Mem. Am. Surg. Assn., A.C.S., Am. Heart Assn., Am. Assn. Thoracic Surgery (pres. 1979-80), Soc. Thoracic Surgery (pres. 1974-75), Central Surg. Assn., Soc. Univ. Surgeons, So. Thoracic Surgery Assn. (hon.), John Alexander Soc., Cardiovascular Surgeons Club, Detroit Heart Club, Am. Trudeau Soc., Mich. Heart Assn., Mich. Trudeau Soc., Am. Acad. Pediatrics, Soc. Vascular Surgery, Frederick A. Coller Surg. Soc., Research Club, Phi Beta Kappa, Alpha Omega Alpha, Sigma Xi. Club: Ann Arbor Figure Skating (pres. 1963-66). Author: (with Marvin M. Kirsh) Blunt Chest Trauma, General Principles of Management, 1977; contbr. chpts. to books, articles to profl. jours. Home: 471 Barton North Dr Ann Arbor MI 48105 Office: Sect Thoracic Surgery Univ Hosp Ann Arbor MI 48109

SLOAN, LEROY (MIKE) HENDRICK, advt. agy. exec.; b. Aurora, Ill., Nov. 13, 1929; s. LeRoy Hendrick and Anne J. (Harmon) S.; student Yale, 1947-49; B.A., Stanford, 1951; m. Jane A. Mumford, Nov. 25, 1961; children—Elizabeth, Kenneth, Scott, Peter. Copywriter Buchanan & Co., San Francisco, 1954-55; writer, v.p. Botsford, Constantine & Gardner, San Francisco, 1956-60; account exec. Ogilvy & Mather, San Francisco, 1960-61; account supr., v.p. Papert, Koening & Lois, N.Y.C., 1961-65; founder Mike Sloan, Inc., Miami, Fla., 1966, chmn., creative dir., 1966—. Served with U.S. Army, 1951-53. Named in Top 100 Advt. Creators, Ad Daily poll, 1972-76. Club: Royal Palm Tennis (Miami). Home: 10350 SW 56th Ave Miami FL 33156 Office: 2699 S Bayshore Dr Miami FL 33133

SLOAN, MACEO ARCHIBALD, ins. co. exec.; b. Newport, Ark., Aug. 10, 1913; s. Cleveland Eugene and Sammie (Patterson) S.; A.B., Prairie View State Coll., 1937; LL.D., Livingstone Coll., 1977; m. Charlotte Alicia Kennedy, Dec. 27, 1943; children—Sylvia M. (Mrs. Frederick Black), Maceo Kennedy. With N.C. Mut. Life Ins. Co., Durham, 1938—, v.p., asso. agy. dir., 1962-64, v.p. home office ops., 1964-69, sr. v.p., 1969-73, exec. v.p., 1973—; chmn., dir. Fed. Res. Bank of Richmond; dir. Duke Power Co. Former trustee Nat. Assembly for Social Policy and Devel.; bd. dirs. N.C. United Way, Durham United Fund; bd. govs. U. N.C.; past mem. nat. adv. council, former chmn. adv. bd. Salvation Army; past chmn. bd. N.C. Zool. Soc. Recipient Alumni Achievement award Prairie View State Coll., 1955. C.L.U. Mem. Nat. Ins. Assn. (past pres.), Alpha Phi Alpha, Sigma Pi Phi. Mason. Home: 2100 Otis St Durham NC 27707 Office: 411 W Chapel Hill St Durham NC 27701

SLOAN, RAYMOND PATON, ret. editor, publishing co. exec.; b. Bklyn., Dec. 12, 1893; s. Alfred Pritchard and Katharine (Mead) S.; student Bklyn. Prep. Inst., 1908-11; L.H.D., Colby Coll., 1946; LL.D., St. Lawrence U., 1954; D. Social Welfare, Women's Med. Coll. Pa., 1958; m. Mabel V. MacArthur, Nov. 20, 1916. Mem. editorial staff Automobile Topics, N.Y.C., 1920-33; editor The Modern Hospital, Chgo., 1933-53, pres., dir. The Modern Hosp. Pub. Co., Inc., 1953-58; v.p. Alfred P. Sloan Found., N.Y.C.; spl. lectr. Sch. Pub. Health, Columbia, 1945—. Bd. dirs. Thayer Hosp., Waterville, Me.; trustee Community Hosp. at Glen Cove, N.Y., Colby Coll., Waterville; bd. mgrs. Meml. Center for Cancer and Allied Diseases, N.Y.C.; chmn. N.Y. City Hosp. Vis. Com. Recipient la Grande Medaille d'Argent de la-ville de Paris, 1961. Hon. fellow Am. Coll. Hosp. Adminstrs.; mem. Am. Hosp. Assn. (hon.). Clubs: Creek (Locust Valley, N.Y.); Metropolitan, Sky (N.Y.C.). Author: Hospital Color and Decoration, 1944; This Hospital Business of Ours, 1952; On A Shoestring and A Prayer, 1964; Today's Hospital, 1966; Not for Ourselves Alone: The Story of Norfolk General Hospital, 1969. Contbr. articles on hosp. and health topics to profl. and nat. publs. Home: 19 E 72d St New York NY 10021 Office: 36 E 70th St New York NY 10021

SLOAN, ROBERT DYE, physician; b. Clarksburg, W.Va., Feb. 17, 1918; s. Herbert Elias and Luella Theresa (Dye) S.; A.B., Washington and Lee U., 1939; M.D., Johns Hopkins, 1943; m. Harriet Jean Stech, Mar. 2, 1946; children—Catherine Luella, Harriett Leedy. Intern in surgery Johns Hopkins Hosp., Balt., 1943-44, house officer dept. radiology, 1946-48; instr. dept. radiology Johns Hopkins U., 1948-49, asst. prof., 1949-54, asso. prof. dept. radiology, 1954-55; prof. dir. dept. radiology U. Miss. Med. Center, 1955. Served as 1st lt. M.C., AUS, 1944-45, capt. M.C., USAF, 1953-55. Diplomate Am. Bd. Radiology, 1950. Mem. AMA, Am. Coll. Radiology, Radiol. Soc. N.Am., Am. Roentgen Ray Soc., Assn. U. Radiologists, Alpha Omega Alpha, Phi Chi. Home: Route 3 Box 337A Jackson MS 39213 Office: University of Miss Medical Center Jackson MS 39216

SLOAN, ROBERT HOOD, mfg. co. exec.; b. Worcester, Mass., Nov. 20, 1926; s. Harold Hall and Ola May (Hood) S.; B.S. in Textile Engring., Lowell (Mass.) Tech. Inst., 1950; m. Valerie Mauss, July 1, 1951; children—Robert Hood, Rebecca J., Stephen R. With Albany Internat. Corp. (N.Y.), and predecessor, 1950—, pres., chief operating officer, 1976—, also dir.; dir. State Bank Albany. Trustee Coll. of St. Rose, Albany. Served with USN, 1944-46. Mem. Am. Mgmt. Assn., NAM, Asso. Industries N.Y. State, Albany Area C. of C. Clubs: Ft. Orange, Schuyler Meadows. Office: 1 Sage Rd Albany NY 12201

SLOAN, STEPHEN CHARLES, football coach; b. Austin, Tex., Aug. 19, 1944; s. Charles Lester and Virginia (Byrd) S.; B.A., U. Ala.; m. Brenda Fau, May 12, 1968; children—Stephen Charles, Jonathan Paul. Mem. Atlanta Falcons, 1966-67; head football coach Vanderbilt U., 1973-74, Tex. Technol. U., 1975-77, U. Miss., 1977—. Served with Air N.G., 1965-72. Methodist. Author: Calling Life's Signals, 1966; A Whole New Ball Game, 1975. Office: Athletic Dept U Miss University MS 38677

SLOAN, WILLIAM ALEXANDER, lawyer; b. Boston, Aug. 15, 1910; s. William and Margaret (Wallace) S.; A.B magna cum laude, Harvard, 1931, LL.B., 1934; m. Betty Clark, 1973; children by previous marriage—Diane M. (Mrs. William G. Pearson), Geoffrey W., Robert G. Admitted to Mass. bar, 1934, N.M. bar, 1938; law clk. Mass. Supreme Jud. Ct., 1934-37; pres. Rodey, Dickason, Sloan, Akin and Robb, P.A., Albuquerque, 1937—. Served to lt. comdr. USNR, 1942-46. Mem. State Bar N.Mex. (pres. 1958-59). Home: 2520 Elfego Rd NW Albuquerque NM 87107 Office: 20 First Plaza Suite 700 Albuquerque NM 87103

SLOANE, GEORGE HARVEY INGALLS, former mayor; b. N.Y.C., May 11, 1936; B.A., Yale U., 1958; M.D., Western Res. U., 1963; m. Kathleen McNally, June 7, 1969; children—Abigail, Patrick, Curtis. Intern, Cleve. Clinic, 1963-64; with USPHS in Appalachia, 1964-66; vol. physician, Vietnam, 1966; dir. Park DuValle Neighborhood Health Center, Louisville, 1967-72; mayor of Louisville, 1973-75; mem. Nutrition Survey Team to Malaysia, 1962, Pres.'s Advisory Com. on Nat. Health Ins., 1977—; mem. Pres.'s Strategy Council on Drug Abuse, 1977—; asst. clin. prof. comprehensive medicine U. Louisville Med. Sch., 1974—; bd. dirs. Nat. Urban Coalition, Preservation Action, Center Growth Activities, 20th Century Fund; mem. mayors advisory com. Nat. Council Urban Econ. Devel.; chmn. Ky. Health Security Action Council, 1971-72. Mem. Mid-Appalachian Environ. Service Bd., 1971-73; founder, chmn. Action Clean Air, 1968-70; bd. dirs. Louisville-Jefferson County Air Pollution Control Dist., 1969-73; mem. Ky. Democratic Central Com., 1976; del. Dem. Nat. Conv., 1976, mem. rules com., 1976. Recipient Outstanding Young Man award Ky. Jaycees, 1971, Louisville Jaycees, 1969; Floyd D. Rector Meml. award Citizens Met. Planning Council, Louisville, 1970; Outstanding Community Service award Zeta Phi Beta, 1971; named One of 200 Young Leaders in the Nation Time Mag., 1976. Mem. Ky. Pub. Health Assn. (pres. 1971). Episcopalian. Home: 1401 S 4th St Louisville KY 40208 Office: Box 34518 Louisville KY 40232

SLOANE, PATRICIA HERMINE, painter; b. N.Y.C., Nov. 21, 1934; d. David and Marian (Frauenthal) Sloane; student (scholar 1949) Dayton Art Inst., 1947-49; B.F.A. (scholar 1953, 54) R.I. Sch. Design, 1955; student (scholar) Ohio U. Grad. Coll., 1955-56, (scholar) NAD, 1956-58; M.A., Hunter Coll., 1968; Ph.D., N.Y. U., 1972; pvt. study with Hans Hoffman, Provincetown, summer 1954. One-woman shows: Camino Gallery, 1962, Brata Gallery, 1963, U. R.I., 1968, Grand Central Moderns Art Gallery, 1968, Fordham U., 1968, Amerika-Haus, Vienna, 1970; two-person shows: Camino Gallery, N.Y.C., 1962; exhibited in group shows: Corcoran Gallery, Providence Art Club, R.I. Artists' Ann., Beryl Lush Gallery, Provincetown, Dayton Art Inst., Ohio U., Camino Gallery, Terrain Gallery, Moris Gallery, NAD, Village Art Center, Brata Gallery, Osgood Gallery, Alan Stone Gallery, Silvermine Guild, others; represented in lending collection Mus. Modern Art; represented in pub. collections; Andrew Dickson White Mus., Cornell U., Notre Dame U., others; also pvt. collections; films shown: Runnymeade Film Festival, 1971, Film Forum, 1972, Fifth Ave. Cinema, 1972, Millenium Filmmakers Workshop, 1972, N.Y. Cultural Center, 1972, Mus. of 20th Century, Vienna, 1974, Mus. Johanneum, Gratz, Austria, 1974, Artists Space, 1974, Mus. Modern Art, Paris, 1974, Westbeth Feminists Playrites Collective, 1974, 75; free-lance or cons. book design layout, graphic and typog. design, 1960-66; tchr. Scarsdale Studio Workshop, 1965, N.Y. U., 1966, Mercer County Community Coll., 1966-68, U. R.I., summer 1967, Kingsborough Community Coll., 1968, New Sch. for Social Research, 1971-72; prof. City U. N.Y., 1969—. Lyra Brown Nickerson scholar, 1952; Scholastic Mags. scholar, 1957; N.Y. State Regents scholar, 1967-68, 69-70; Nat. Endowment Humanities grantee, 1973; Guggenheim fellow, 1974. Mem. Coll. Art Assn., Am. Soc. Aesthetics. Author: Colour: Basic Principles and New Directions, 1968; contbr. articles to profl. mags. and jours. Address: 53 Duffield St Brooklyn NY 11201. *I have tried to live in the assumption that God, being everywhere in the universe, is also in you and me.*

SLOANE, RICHARD, law librarian, lawyer; b. N.Y.C., May 22, 1916; s. Isaac and Leonie S.; B.S., CCNY, 1937; B.S. in Library Service, Columbia U., 1940; read law privately at Cravath, Swaine & Moore, N.Y.C., 1957-62. Reference librarian Queens Coll., 1940-42; librarian firm Cravath, Swaine & Moore, N.Y.C., 1948-62, atty. in charge library, 1962-71; Biddle law librarian, prof. law U. Pa., 1971—; admitted to N.Y. bar, 1962; adj. prof. Columbia U. Library Sch., 1971-78; cons. to law firms, corp. legal depts. on library planning, legal research and computer applications in law practice. Served with USAAF, 1942-46. Mem. Am. Bar Assn., Am. Assn. Law Libraries (Joseph Andrews award 1970), Am. Law Inst. Author: (with Marke) Coordinated Law Research, 1977; (with Wallace) Private Law Library: 1980's and Beyond, 1979; editor: Recommended Law Books, 1969. Home: 224 Delancey St Philadelphia PA 19106 Office: 3400 Chestnut St Philadelphia PA 19104

SLOANE, ROBERT BRUCE, psychiatrist; b. Harrogate, Eng., Mar. 28, 1923; s. Robert and Violet (Kitson) S.; M.B., B.S., London (Eng.) U., 1945, M.D., 1950; m. Vera Taylor, Apr. 25, 1946; children—Judith, Joanna, William, Polly, Robin, Eve. Intern Nat. Hosp. For Nervous Diseases, London, 1949; resident Guy's Hosp., London, 1950, Maudsley Hosp., London, 1950-52, 54-55, Mass. Gen. Hosp., 1953-54; lectr. McGill U., 1955-57; practiced medicine specializing in psychiatry, Kingston, Ont., 1957-64, Phila., 1964-72; prof., head dept. psychiatry Queens U., 1957-64; prof., chmn. dept. psychiatry Temple U. Health Sci. Center, 1964-72; prof., chmn. dept. psychiatry U. So. Calif. Sch. Medicine, Los Angeles, 1972—; vis. prof. Inst. Psychiatry U. London, 1978-79; vis. prof. dept. psychiatry U. Cambridge, 1978-79. Served with RAF, 1946-48. Fulbright scholar, 1953, Nuffield scientist, 1964. Fellow Royal Coll. Physicians (London), Royal Coll. Physicians and Surgeons Can. Office: Dept Psychiatry U So Calif Sch Medicine 1934 Hospital Pl Los Angeles CA 90033

SLOANE, ROBERT MALCOLM, hosp. adminstr.; b. Boston, Feb. 11, 1933; s. Alvin and Florence (Goldberg) S.; A.B., Brown U., 1954; M.S., Columbia U., 1958; m. Beverly LeBov, Sept. 27, 1959; 1 dau., Alison. Adminstrv. resident Mt. Auburn Hosp., Cambridge, Mass., 1957-58; med. adminstr. AT&T, N.Y.C., 1959-60; asst. dir. Yale New Haven Hosp., 1961-67; asso. adminstr. Monmouth Med. Center, Long Branch, N.J., 1967-69; adminstr. City of Hope Nat. Med. Center, Duarte, Calif., 1969—; mem. faculty Columbia U. Sch. Medicine, 1958-59, Yale U. Sch. Medicine, 1963-67, Quinnipiac Coll., 1963-67, Pasadena City Coll., 1972-73, Calif. Inst. Tech., 1973-76, U. So. Calif., 1976—; chmn. bd. Health Data Net, 1971-73. Bd. dirs. Health Systems Agy. Los Angeles County, 1977-78, Calif. Hosp. Polit. Action Com. Served to lt. (j.g.) USNR, 1954-56. Fellow Am. Coll. Hosp. Adminstrs.; mem. Am. Pub. Health Assn., Am. Hosp. Assn., Hosp. Council So. Calif. (dir.). Author: (with B. L. Sloane) A Guide to Health Facilities: Personnel and Management, 1971, 2d edit., 1977; editorial and adv. bd. Health Devices, 1972—; contbr. articles to hosp. jours. Home: 1301 N Santa Anita Ave Arcadia CA 91006 Office: 1500 E Duarte Rd Duarte CA 91010

SLOANE, THOMAS O., educator; b. West Frankfort, Ill., July 12, 1929; s. Thomas Orville and Blanche (Morris) S.; B.A., So. Ill. U., 1951, M.A., 1952; Ph.D., Northwestern U., 1960; m. Barbara Lee Lewis, Nov. 1, 1952; children—Elizabeth Alison, David Lewis, Emily. Instr. English, Washington and Lee U., 1958-60; asst. prof. speech U. Ill., 1960-65, asso. prof., 1965-70, asso. head dept., 1967-68, asst. dean liberal arts and scis., 1966-67; prof. rhetoric, chmn. rhetoric dept. U. Calif., Berkeley, 1970—; dir. Nat. Endowment Humanities Summer Seminar for Coll. Tchrs., 1979. Served to lt. USNR, 1952-55. Faculty research fellow, 1964; U. Ill. instructional devel. awardee, 1965; Henry H. Huntington Library research awardee, 1967; U. Calif. humanities research fellow, 1974. Mem. MLA, Renaissance Soc. Am. Editor: The Oral Study of Literature, 1966; The Passions of the Minde in Generall (Thomas Wright), 1971; (with Raymond B. Waddington) The Rhetoric of Renaissance Poetry, 1974; (with Joanna H. Maclay) Interpretation, 1972; contbr. articles to profl. jours. Home: 366 San Carlos Ave Piedmont CA 94611 Office: U Calif Berkeley CA 94720

SLOBODIN, ALEX, dept. store exec.; b. Clarion, Utah, 1914; ed. N.Y. U., 1937. Exec. v.p., treas., dir. J.W. Mays, Inc. (Mays Dept. Stores), Bklyn.; treas., dir. Loma Holding Corp., Sylflo, Inc., J.W. Enterprises, Inc., J. Weinstein Found., Inc., Gailoyd Enterprises Corp., C.W. Co., Inc., 512 Fulton St. Corp.; v.p., treas., dir. Pherbo Realty Corp. Mem. N.Y. Met. Retail Fin. Execs. Assn. (dir.). Home: 9 Willow Dr Englewood Cliffs NJ 07632 Office: 510 Fulton St Brooklyn NY 11201

SLOCOMBE, WALTER BECKER, lawyer, govt. ofcl.; b. Albuquerque, Sept. 23, 1941; B.A., Princeton U., 1963; postgrad. Balliol Coll., Oxford U., 1963-65; LL.B., Harvard U., 1968; children—Sarah Cody, Merrin Hayes. Admitted to D.C. bar, 1970; law clk. Justice Abe Fortas, U.S. Supreme Ct., 1968-69; mem. Nat. Security Council staff, 1969-70; research asso. Internat. Inst. Strategic Studies, London, 1970-71; mem. firm Caplin and Drysdale, Washington, 1971-76, partner, 1974-76; prin. dep. asst. sec. for internat. security affairs, dir. Def. Dept. SALT Task Force, Dept. Def., Washington, 1977-79, dep. under sec. for policy plans, 1979—. Rhodes scholar, 1963-65. Mem. Council Fgn. Relations, Internat. Inst. Strategic Studies, Am. Bar Assn., ACLU. Democrat. Office: Pentagon Washington DC 20301

SLOCUM, JOHN HOWARD, educator; b. Burlington, Vt., Aug. 8, 1919; s. Harold Wilson and Emma (Miller) S.; A.B., U. Chgo., 1941, A.M., 1946; Ph.D., N.Y. State Sch. Indsl. and Labor Relations, 1950; m. Margaret Wheeler, Aug. 15, 1941 (div.); children—Peter, Sally; m. 2d, Adele Trenchi, May 29, 1968. Instr. Rensselaer Poly. Inst., 1946-48; grad. asst., asst. prof. N.Y. State Sch. Indsl. and Labor Relations, 1948-50; nat. edn. dir. Amalgamated Clothing Workers Am., 1950-52; sec. bd. trustees State U. N.Y., 1952-55, sec. univ., asst. to chmn. bd., 1955-57, exec. dean four-year and profl. colls., 1957-58, v.p. for adminstrn., 1958-63; dir. State U. Indonesian Edn. Project, 1963-74; prof. polit. economy State U. N.Y. at Albany, 1966—, dir. internat. programs, 1966-70, research prof. Inst. Cypriot Studies, 1971, dir. polit. economy, 1972—. Exec. com. Assn. for Cultural Exchange, London, 1963—. Civilian tech. instr. USAAF, 1941-43, USN, 1943-45. Home: PO Box 56 Hollowville NY 12530 Office: 1400 Washington Ave Albany NY 12222

SLOMAN, MARVIN SHERK, lawyer; b. Ft. Worth, Apr. 17, 1925; s. Richard J. and Janette S. S.; A.B., U. Tex., 1948, LL.B. with honors, 1950; m. Margaret Jane Dinwiddie, Apr. 11, 1953; children—Lucy Carter, Richard Dinwiddie. Asso. firm Sullivan & Cromwell, N.Y.C., 1950-56; asso. firm Carrington, Coleman, Sloman & Blumenthal and predecessor firms, Dallas, 1956-60, partner, 1960—. Home: 6009 St Andrews Dr Dallas TX 75205 Office: 3000 1 Main Pl Dallas TX 75250

SLOMINSKI, LEO FRANK, machine mfg. co. exec.; b. Saginaw, Mich., June 20, 1909; s. Michel A. and Valentine (Brzeczkiewicz) S.; grad. high sch.; m. Eleonore Rita Konieczka, Nov. 29, 1941. With Gen. Motors Corp., Saginaw, 1927-45; with Allied Tool & Die Co., mfr. spl. and exptl. automotive precision machines, Saginaw, 1945—, pres., 1959—. Tchr. machine shop Saginaw High Sch., 1941. Mem. 7 man U.S. Trade Mission to USSR, 1971. Mem. Nat. Tool and Die and Precision Machining Assn. (pres. 1975—). Home: 1740 N Center Rd Saginaw MI 48603 Office: 3545 Janes Rd Saginaw MI 48605

SLONE, DENNIS, physician; b. Pretoria, S. Africa, Jan. 9, 1930; s. Simon and Jane (Gerber) S.; came to U.S., 1961, naturalized, 1967; M.B., B.Ch., U. Witwatersrand, Johannesburg, S.Africa, 1956; M.A. (fellow pediatric endocrinology), Harvard U., 1964; m. Annetta Roman Korsunski, Feb. 16, 1956; children—Gregory, Alan, Mark. Intern in medicine and surgery Johannesburg Gen. Hosp., 1956-57; resident in pediatrics Baragwanath Hosp., Johannesburg, 1957-58; asso. dir. clin. pharmacology unit Lemuel Shattuck Hosp., Boston, 1964-69; co-dir. Boston Collaborative Surveillance Program, Boston U. Med. Center, 1969-75, co-dir. drug epidemiology unit, 1975—; asst. prof. medicine Tufts U. Med. Center, Boston, 1968-71; asso. prof. Boston U. Med. Sch., 1971—. Mem. Am. Diabetes Assn., Am. Pub. Health Assn., Soc. Epidemiol. Research, Drug Info. Assn., Am. Acad. Pediatrics, Am. Soc. Clin. Pharmacology and Therapeutics, Lawson Wilkins Pediatric Endocrine Soc., Internat. Epidemiol. Assn. Jewish. Author books; contbr. articles to med. publs. Home: 22 Peacock Farm Rd Lexington MA 02173 Office: 10 Moulton St Cambridge MA 02138

SLONIMSKY, NICOLAS, condr., composer, writer; b. St. Petersburg, Russia, Apr. 27, 1894 (came to U.S. 1923, naturalized 1931); s. Leonid and Faina (Vengerova) S.; ed. Conservatory of Music, St. Petersburg; m. Dorothy Adlow, July 30, 1931; 1 dau., Electra. Concert tours as pianist, Europe, 1921-22, U.S., 1923—, S.Am., 1941-42; instr. Eastman Sch. Music, Rochester, N.Y., 1923-25, Boston Conservatory Music, 1925-45; condr. Pierian Sodality, Harvard, 1928-30, instr. Slavic langs. and lits., 1946-47; vis. prof. Colo. Coll., summer 1940, 47-49; lectr. music Simmons Coll., 1947-49, Peabody Conservatory, 1956-57, U. Calif. at Los Angeles, 1964-67; condr. Apollo Club Chorus, 1947-49; guest condr., Paris, Berlin, Budapest, Havana, San Francisco, Los Angeles, Hollywood and S.A. Wrote for ballet, orch., piano, voice. Author: Music since 1900, 4th edit., 1971; Music of Latin America, 4th edit., 1972; Lexicon of Musical Invective, 1953. Editor: Internat. Cyclo. of Music and Musicians, 4th-8th edits., 1946-58; Baker's Biog. Dictionary of Musicians, 5th edit., 1958, 6th edit., 1978; mem. Am. music editorial bd. Ency. Brit., 1958—. Contbr. ann. music surveys to Ency. Brit. Year Books, 1950-68. Home: 10847 3/4 Wilshire Blvd Los Angeles CA 90024

SLOSBERG, SAMUEL LOUIS, shoe mfg. co. exec.; b. Chelsea, Mass., Mar. 30, 1897; s. Jacob A. and Bessie (Abromovitz) S.; A.B. cum laude, Harvard, 1917; m. Helen Sagoff, May 30, 1922; children—Florence (Mrs. Sumner M. Gerstein), Edna (Mrs. Bela Kalman). With Stride Rite Boston, 1919—, chmn. bd., 1963—. Pres. Beth Israel Hosp., Boston, 1964—. Trustee Children's Hosp., Boston, Brandeis U. Served with U.S. Navy, World War I. Mem. Nat. Shoe Mfrs. Assn. (past pres.). Home: The Fairfield Prudential Center Apts Boston MA 02199 Office: 960 Harrison Ave Boston MA 02118

SLOSS, ROBERT LEE, lawyer; b. Louisville, Feb. 16, 1911; s. Stanley E. and Carrye (Kohn) S.; A.B., U. Mich., 1931, J.D., 1933; m. Carolyn Reese, Oct. 12, 1947; children—Robert R., Richard S., Martha L. Admitted to Ky. bar, 1933; atty. Fed. Emergency Adminstrn. Pub. Works, Washington, 1933-35; partner firm Willis & Sloss, Louisville, 1935-42, Wyatt, Grafton & Sloss, Louisville, 1946—; asst. atty. Jefferson County, Ky., 1937-42. Mem. Falls Region Health Council, 1969-72, pres., 1969-71; mem. Ky. Registry Election Fin., 1972-76, chmn., 1972-76; mem. Jefferson Area Devel. Dist., 1972-74. Bd. dirs. Louisville Legal Aid Soc., 1941-66, pres., 1955-56; overseer Ursuline Coll. 1961-68. Served from 2d lt. to maj., AUS, 1942-46. Mem. Am., Fed., Ky., Louisville (past pres.) bar assns., Newcomen Soc. N.Am., Soc. Profl. Journalists. Clubs: Pendennis, Jefferson, Standard Country (Louisville); Rotary. Home: 2549 Woodbourne Ave Louisville KY 40205 Office: Citizens Plaza Louisville KY 40202

SLOSSON, PRESTON WILLIAM, author; b. Laramie, Wyo., Sept. 2, 1892; s. Edwin Emery and May (Preston) S.; B.S., Columbia, 1912, M.A., 1913, Ph.D., 1916; LL.D., Hillsdale Coll., 1944; m. Lucy Denny Wright, 1927 (dec. 1974); children—Lucy Chase (Mrs. J. B. Stephenson), Mary Elizabeth (Mrs. G. Fearnehough); step children—Rev. Flora May (Mrs. W. Wuellner), Edith (Mrs. D. Tyson). Asst. in history Columbia U., 1913-17; mem. staff N.Y. Independent, 1917; with Dept. State, 1917-18; asst. librarian Am. Commn. to Negotiate Peace, 1918-19; lit. editor N.Y. Independent, 1920-21; instr. history U. Mich., 1921-23, asst. prof., 1923-27, asso. prof., 1927-37, prof., 1937-62, prof. emeritus, 1962—; distinguished prof. Kans. State U., 1960; Carnegie vis. prof. at Bristol, Manchester and Glasgow univs., 1932-33, at Bristol, Sheffield and Aberystwyth univs., 1938-39; radio broadcaster, 1941—; Haynes fellow Redlands (Calif.) U., 1954-55. Democratic candidate for House of Reps., 1948. Mem. Phi Beta Kappa. Congregationalist. Club: Research (University of Mich.). Author: Fated or Free, 1914; The Decline of the Chartist Movement, 1916; Twentieth Century Europe, 1927; The Problems of Austro-German Union, 1928; The Great Crusade and After, 1930; Europe since 1870, 1935; The Growth of European Civilization (with A.E.R.) Boak and H. R. Anderson), 1942; Why We Are at War, 1942; History of the English-Speaking Peoples (with R. B. Mowat), 1943; After the War: What?, 1943; From Washington to Roosevelt (with Lucy Slosson), 1950; Europe Since 1815, 1954; The History of Our World (with Boak, Anderson and Bartlett), 1959; A Teacher's Report Card, 1975; Pitt and Fox, 1978; Bright and Cobden, 1979. Home: RD 2 Knox PA 16232

SLOTKIN, EDWARD JAMES, corp. exec.; b. N.Y.C., Oct. 12, 1915; s. Samuel and Fanny (Rivkin) S.; A.B., Rutgers U., 1937; m. Shirley Eder, Mar. 29, 1944; children—Toni Eder, John S. With Hygrade Food Products Corp., Detroit, 1937-70, v.p., 1945-54, dir., 1945-70, exec. v.p., 1954-68, pres., 1968-70; pres. HR & I Inc., Detroit, 1970—. Trustee Rutgers U. Served as capt. AUS, 1942-45. Mem. N.Y. Merc. Exchange. Clubs: Hollywood (Deal, N.J.); Bankers (N.Y.C.); Franklin Hills (Mich.); Standard (Detroit). Home: 16500 North Park Dr Southfield MI 48075 Office: 13238 Harper St Detroit MI 48213

SLOTKIN, RICHARD SIDNEY, educator; b. Bklyn., Nov. 8, 1942; s. Herman and Roselyn B. (Seplowitz) S.; B.A., Bklyn. Coll., 1963; Ph.D., Brown U., 1967; M.A. (hon.), Wesleyan U., Middletown, Conn., 1976; m. Iris F. Shupack, June 23, 1963; 1 son, Joel Elliot. Mem. faculty Wesleyan U., 1966—, prof. English, 1976—, chmn. dept. Am. studies, 1976—. Fellow Center Humanities, Wesleyan U., 1969-70, 74-75, Nat. Endowment Humanities, 1973-74, Rockefeller Found., 1976-77. Mem. Am. Film Inst., Am. Studies Assn., Am. Hist. Assn., Orgn. Am. Historians, Modern Lang. Assn., Western History Assn., Popular Culture Assn. Jewish. Author: Regeneration Through Violence: The Mythology of the American Frontier, 1600-1860 (Albert Beveridge award Am. Hist. Assn.), 1973; (with J.K. Folsom) So Dreadfull a Judgement: Puritan Responses to King Philip's War, 1675-1677, 1978; also articles. Address: English Dept Wesleyan Univ Middletown CT 06457

SLOTNICK, HERBERT NORMAN, fast food co. exec.; b. Syracuse, N.Y., Oct. 20, 1925; s. Samuel Philip and Tillie (Steinberg) S.; B.A., Haverford Coll., 1944; m. Joan E. Pence, July 2, 1948; 1 son, David M. Vice pres. Slotnick Enterprises, Syracuse, 1950-60, pres., chmn. bd., 1960—; pres., chmn. bd. Carrols Devel. Corp., 1960—; dir. Mchts. Nat. Bank & Trust Co. Pres., bd. dirs. Central N.Y. Arthritis Found., 1969-70; bd. dirs. Syracuse Jewish Welfare Fedn., Salvation Army, 1972-74, United Way Central N.Y., 1974-76. Served with inf., AUS, 1944-45. Mem. Am. Mgmt. Assn., Nat. Assn. Theatre Owners, Nat. Restaurant Assn. Home: 410 Brookford Rd Syracuse NY 13224 Office: 968 James St PO Box 6969 Syracuse NY 13217

SLOUGH, MAJOR CARL, lawyer; b. Cin., Aug. 11, 1918; s. Carl Paul and Elizabeth Lucille (McAuley) S.; A.B., Columbia, 1938; J.D., Ind. U., 1941; m. Adele Bernero, July 27, 1950; children—Robert Bernero, James Anthony. Admitted to Ind. bar, 1941, also Kans. bar, U.S. Supreme Ct. bar; practiced with Kivett & Kivett, Indpls., 1941-46; asst. prof. law U. Kan., 1946-48, asso. prof. law, 1948-55, prof. law, 1955-61, dean, 1957-61; practiced law, Shawnee Mission, Kans., 1961—; mem. firm Wagner, Leek & Mullins. Mem. Kans. Commn. on Constl. Revision, 1957—. Mem. state com. U.S.O.; pres. Lawrence United Fund, Inc., 1957, Westwood Assn., 1951-58. Served with USNR, 1943-45. Mem. Cath. Lawyers Guild of Kans. (pres. 1956-58), Am., Kans. bar assns., Am. Law Inst., Am. Judicature Soc., Phi Kappa Psi, Phi Delta Phi, Order of Coif. Club: Kansas City (Mo.). Author: Kansas Civil Code, 1955, 60; Obscenity and Constitutional Freedom, 1964; Privacy, Freedom and Responsibility, 1969; Obscenity, Freedom and Responsibility, 1976. Contbr. articles to legal and med. publs. Home: 8811 Riggs Circle Shawnee Mission KS 66212 Office: 4101 W 54th Terr Shawnee Mission KS 66205

SLOVER, GEORGE, JR., lawyer; b. Bryn Mawr, Pa., Dec. 15, 1926; s. George and Emma (Neale) S.; A.B., U. Tenn., 1945; LL.B., Harvard, 1949; m. Jane Prescott Grayson, Oct. 3, 1953; children—George Prescott, John Grayson, Elizabeth Neale, Thomas Winward. Admitted to Tex. bar, 1950; asso. firm Johnson, Bromberg, Leeds & Riggs, Dallas, 1949—, partner, 1958—; sec. UNC Resources, Inc., Whitehall Corp., 1969—. Served with USNR, 1945-46. Mem. Am. Law Inst. Home: 3236 Southwestern Dallas TX 75225 Office: 4400 Republic Nat Bank Tower Dallas TX 75201

SLOVES, MARVIN, advt. exec.; b. N.Y.C., Apr. 22, 1933; s. John H. and Evelyn (Wishan) S.; A.B. cum laude, Brandeis U., 1955; postgrad. (Ford Found. scholar, NEA fellow) Oriental Inst. U. Chgo., 1955-61. Mem. staff research dept. Leo Burnett Co., Chgo., 1962; dir. research Earle Ludgin Co., Chgo., 1963-64; account exec. Ted Bates Co., N.Y.C., 1964; account supr., v.p., Papert, Koenig, Lois Co., Inc., N.Y.C., 1965-67; pres., chief exec. officer Scali, McCabe, Sloves, Inc., N.Y.C., 1967—. Bd. dirs. Burden Center for Aged, N.Y.C. Democrat. Jewish. Clubs: Lotos, Players. Home: PO Box 431 Windcroft Upper Black Eddy PA 18972

SLOVITER, HENRY ALLAN, medical educator; b. Phila., June 16, 1914; s. Samuel and Rose (Seltzer) S.; A.B., Temple U., 1935, A.M., 1936; Ph.D., U. Pa., 1942, M.D., 1949; m. Dolores Korman, Apr. 3, 1969. Chemist U.S. Naval Base, Phila., 1936-45; intern Hosp. U. Pa., 1949-50; research fellow U. Pa. Sch. Medicine, 1945-49, asst. prof., 1952-56, asso. prof., 1956-68, prof., 1968—; vis. scientist biochemistry dept., Tokyo U., Japan; U.S. project officer USPHS Fogarty Internat. Center program Inst. for Biology, Belgrade, Yugoslavia, 1971, 74. Am. Cancer Soc. fellow Nat. Inst. Med. Research, London, Eng., 1950-52; College de France endocrinology dept. research fellow, Paris, 1952; sr. internat. fellow USPHS Fogarty Internat. Center, St. Mary's Hosp. Med. Sch., London, 1978; recipient Glycerine Research award, 1954; exchange scholar Tokyo U., 1963, U.S.S.R., 1965, 71, India, 1967. Fellow A.A.A.S.; mem. Internat. Soc. Neurochemistry, Am. Soc. Biol. Chemists, Am. Physiol. Soc. Contbr. articles profl. jours. Home: 2215 Panama St Philadelphia PA 19103.

Criticize yourself as severely as you do other people, and try to be as generous to others as to yourself.

SLOWEY, JACK WILLIAM, astronomer; b. Milw., Mar. 19, 1932; s. Howard William and Viola (Lang) S.; B.S., U. Wis., 1955, M.S., 1956; student Harvard, 1961-62; m. Auralie P. Smith, July 28, 1952; children—Sean, Kevin, Niall, Kathleen. Physicist, Smithsonian Astrophys. Obs., Cambridge, Mass., 1956-59, astronomer, 1959—; lectr. gen. edn. Harvard, 1957-61; sci. cons. IBM, 1961-75, Boston Coll., 1975—; lectr. Boston U., 1968-69. Chmn. Standing Sch. Bldg. Com., Burlington, Mass., 1964-66. Bd. dirs. Lexington chpt. A.R.C., 1965-67, chmn., 1968-71. Mem. Am. Geophys. Union, Am. Astron. Soc. Computed orbit of first artificial satellite, 1957; sci. advisor satellite tracking program, 1959-60; research on earth's upper atmosphere. Home: 13 Paulson Dr Burlington MA 01803 Office: 60 Garden St Cambridge MA 02138

SLOWINSKI, EMIL JOHN, educator; b. Newark, Oct. 12, 1922; s. Emil John and Helen (Zaworski) S.; B.S., U. Mass., 1946; Ph.D., Mass. Inst. Tech., 1949; m. Emily Dayton, June 16, 1951; children—David A., Walter D., Nathan T., Amy H., Marya R. Instr., Swarthmore Coll., 1949-52; instr., asst. prof., asso. prof. U. Conn., 1952-64; prof. chemistry Macalester Coll., St. Paul, 1964—, chmn. dept., 1964-70; NSF sci. faculty fellow Oxford U., 1960-61; Nat. Acad. Scis. Exchange prof. U. Warsaw, 1968-69. Served with AUS, 1943-46; ETO. Mem. Am. Chem. Soc., AAUP. Author: (with W.L. Masterton) Chemical Principles, 1966, 4th edit., 1977, Chemical Principles with Qualitative Analysis, 1978; Chemical Principles in the Laboratory, 1969, 2d edit., 1973; Mathematical Preparation for General Chemistry, 1970; Elementary Mathematical Preparation for General Chemistry, 1974; Chemical Principles in the Laboratory with Qualitative Analysis, 1974; Qualitative Analysis and the Properties of Ions in Aqueous Solution, 1971. Office: Dept Chemistry Macalester Coll St Paul MN 55105

SLOWINSKI, WALTER ALOYSIUS, educator, lawyer; b. Newark, Oct. 28, 1920; s. Walter A. and Eugenia (Stawski) S.; B.S., St. Vincent Coll., 1941, LL.D. (hon.), 1975; J.D., Cath. U., 1948; m. Annette Carter Roberts, Jan. 31, 1953; children—Francis Hill, John Bowie, Mary Carroll, Walter Kent, Annette Carter, Elizabeth Snowden, Eugenia Calvert, Richard Lee. Admitted to D.C. bar, 1947, Ill. bar, 1957; resident partner Baker & McKenzie, Washington, 1957—; adj. prof. Georgetown U. Grad. Law Sch., 1956-70; gen. counsel Council of Americas, Assn. Am. Chambers Commerce Latin Am., Fund for Multinat. Mgmt. Edn., Internat. Mgmt. and Devel. Inst.; mem. adv. com. transnat. enterprises U.S. Dept. State, 1975—; lectr. U. Va. Law Sch., Dept. Commerce Seminars for Comml. Attaches, Dept. State Fgn. Service Inst., Am. Mgmt. Assn., Columbia U., George Washington U. Trustee Nat. Catholic Ednl. Assn., 1976—. Served with USNR, 1942-45, 50-53. Recipient Distinguished Service award Sch. Govt. and Bus. Adminstrn., George Washington U., 1974. Fellow Am. Bar Found.; mem. Washington Fgn. Law Soc. (pres. 1969-70), Am. Bar Assn. (sec. sect. taxation 1952-53, mem. com. fgn. tax problems 1957—, mem. council sect. internat. and comparative law 1968-70, vice chmn. com. treasury dept. sect. adminstrv. law 1970-74), Am. Law Inst., Am. Judicature Soc., Tax Inst. Am. (past gov.), Internat. Fiscal Assn., Bar Assn. D.C. dir. 1970-72, pres. research found. 1970-72). Club: Cosmos (pres. 1978-79) (Washington). Mem. editorial bd. The Tax Adviser, 1970-75. Home: 4400 Edmunds St NW Washington DC 20007 Office: 815 Connecticut Ave NW Washington DC 20006

SLOYAN, GERARD STEPHEN, educator, clergyman; b. N.Y.C., Dec. 13, 1919; s. Jerome James and Marie (Kelley) S.; A.B., Seton Hall U., 1940; S.T.L., Cath. U. Am., 1944, Ph.D., 1948. Ordained priest Roman Catholic Ch., 1944; asst. pastor in Trenton, Maple Shade, N.J., 1947-50; mem. faculty Cath. U. Am., Washington, 1950-67, chmn. dept. religion, 1957-67; prof. N.T. studies Temple U., Phila., 1967—, chmn. dept. religion, 1970-74. Recipient Pro Ecclesia et Pontifice medal, 1970. Mem. Am. Acad. Religion, Cath. Bibl. Assn., Soc. Bibl. Lit., Cath. Theol. Soc. Am., Coll. Theology Soc. (pres. 1964-66), AAUP, Liturg. Conf. (pres. 1962-64, v.p. 1970-71, 75—). Democrat. English editor N.T., The New American Bible, 1970. Author: Jesus on Trial: Development of the Passion Narratives, 1973; Commentary on the New Lectionary, 1975; Is Christ the End of the Law?, 1978. Office: Dept Religion Temple U Philadelphia PA 19122

SLOYAN, SISTER MARY STEPHANIE, educator; b. N.Y.C., Apr. 18, 1918; d. Jerome J. and Marie V. (Kelley) Sloyan; B.A., Georgian Court Coll., 1945; M.A., Cath. U. Am., 1949, Ph.D. in Math., 1952. Asst. prof. Georgian Court Coll., Lakewood, N.J., 1952-56, asso. prof., 1956-59, prof. math., 1959—, pres., 1968-74; vis. lectr. Grad. Sch. Arts and Scis., Cath. U. Am., summers 1960—. Mem. Am. Math. Soc., Math. Assn. Am., AAUW, Sigma Xi. Address: Georgian Court Coll Lakewood NJ 08701

SLUDIKOFF, STANLEY ROBERT, pub.; b. Bronx, N.Y., July 17, 1935; s. Harry and Lillie (Elberger) S.; B.Arch., Pratt Inst., 1957; grad. student U. So. Calif., 1960-62; m. Ann Paula Blumberg, June 30, 1972; children—Lisa Beth, Jaime Dawn. Project planner Robert E. Alexander, F.A.I.A. & Assos., Los Angeles, 1965-66, Daniel, Mann, Johnson & Mendenhall, City and Regional Planning Cons., Los Angeles, 1967-70; pres. SRS Enterprises, Inc.; pres., publisher Gambling Times, Am. Casino Promotions, Inc., also Two Worlds Mgmt., Inc., Los Angeles, 1971—; pres. Las Vegas TV Weekley, also Postal West, Las Vegas, 1975—; founder Stanley Roberts Sch. Winning Blackjack, 1976; instr. city and regional planning program U. So. Calif., 1960-63. Mem. Destination 90 Forum, Citizens Planning Group, San Fernando Valley, Calif., 1966-67. Served to lt. col. U.S. Army Res. Recipient commendation from mayor Los Angeles for work on model cities funding, 1968. Lic. architect, real estate broker. Mem. AIA, Am. Planning Assn., Am. Inst. City Planners, Res. Officers Assn. (life), Mensa (life). Author: (under pen name Stanley Roberts) Winning Blackjack, 1971; How to Win at Weekend Blackjack, 1973; Robert's Rules of Gambling, 1977—. Home: 11836 C Moorpark St Studio City CA 91064 Office: 839 N Highland Ave Hollywood CA 90038. *The challenge of being alive lies in the development of one's maximum potential. To do less is to fly in the face of the gifts of creation, to shorten the aspect of one's life and to deny the fullness of existence. The "weakness of the flesh" prevents anyone's full development from reaching fruition but the personal and societal loss lies in giving up too soon, before we have fully tested our limits.*

SLYKHUIS, JOHN TIMOTHY, plant pathologist; b. Carlyle, Sask., Can., May 7, 1920; s. William and Emma (Hodgson) S.; B.S.A., U. Sask., Saskatoon, 1942, M.S.C., 1943; Ph.D., U. Toronto (Ont., Can.), 1947; m. Ruth Enid Williams, July 6, 1946; children—Grace, Margaret, Dorothy, Timothy, Alan. Plant pathologist Can. Dept. Agr. Research Sta., Harrow, Ont., 1947-49, Lethbridge, Alta., 1952-57, Ottawa, Ont., 1957-76, Summerland, B.C., 1976—; asso. plant pathologist S.D. State Coll., Brooking, 1949-52; Fellow Am. Phytopathol. Soc., Royal Soc. Can.; mem. Can. Phytopathol. Soc., Internat. Soc. Plant Pathology, Agrl. Inst. Can. Unitarian. Research on virus diseases of cereal crops. Home: 13404 Bristow Rd Summerland BC V0H 1Z0 Canada Office: Research Sta Agr Can Summerland BC V0H 1Z0 Canada

SMAGORINSKY, JOSEPH, meteorologist; b. N.Y.C., Jan. 29, 1924; s. Nathan and Dinah (Azaroff) S.; B.S., N.Y. U., 1947, M.S., 1948, Ph.D., 1953; Sc.D. (hon.), U. Munich (Ger.), 1972; m. Margaret Knoepfel, May 29, 1948; children—Anne, Peter, Teresa, Julia, Frederick. Research asst., instr. meteorology N.Y. U., 1946-48; with U.S. Weather Bur., 1948-50, 53-65, chief gen. circulation research sect., 1955-63; meteorologist Inst. Advanced Study, Princeton, N.J., 1950-53; acting dir. Inst. Atmospheric Scis., Environ. Scis. Services Adminstrn., Washington, 1965-66; dir. Geophys. Fluid Dynamics Lab., Environ. Scis. Services Adminstrn.-Nat. Oceanic and Atmospheric Adminstrn., Washington and Princeton, 1964—; vice chmn. U.S. Com. Global Atmospheric Research Program, Nat. Acad. Sci., 1967-73, officer, 1974-77; chmn. joint organizing com. Global Atmospheric Research Program, Internat. Council Sci. Unions/World Meteorol. Orgn., 1976—, officer, 1967—; mem. climate research bd. Nat. Acad. Scis., 1978, chmn. com. on internat. climate programs, 1979; vis. lectr. with rank prof. Princeton U., 1968—. Served to 1st lt. USAAF, 1943-46. Decorated Air medal; recipient Gold medal Dept. Commerce, 1966; award for sci. research and achievement Environ. Sci. Services Adminstrn., 1970; Buys Ballot Gold medal Royal Netherlands Acad. Arts and Scis., 1973; prize and Gold medal World Meteorol. Orgn., 1974. Fellow Am. Meteorol. Soc. (councilor 1974-77, asso. editor jour. 1965-74; Meisinger award 1967, Wexler Meml. lectr. 1969, Carl-Gustaf Rossby Research Gold medal 1972); mem. Royal Meteorol. Soc. (Symons Meml. lectr. 1963). Contbr. to profl. publns. Home: 21 Duffield Pl Princeton NJ 08540 Office: Geophys Fluid Dynamics Lab Princeton Univ PO Box 308 Princeton NJ 08540

SMALE, JOHN GRAY, diversified industry exec.; b. Listowel, Ont., Can., Aug. 1, 1927; s. Peter John and Vera Gladys (Gray) S.; B.S., Miami U., Oxford, Ohio, 1949, LL.D., 1979; LL.D., Kenyon Coll., Gambier, Ohio, 1974; m. Phyllis Anne Weaver, Sept. 2, 1950; children—John Gray, Catherine Anne, Lisa Beth, Peter McKee. With Vick Chem. Co., 1949-50, Bio-Research, Inc., N.Y.C., 1950-52; pres., dir. Procter & Gamble Co., 1974—; dir. Eastman Kodak Co. Bd. dirs. Cin. Area chpt. ARC; chmn. bd. trustees Kenyon Coll.; nat. corp. campaign chmn. United Negro Coll. Fund, 1979, 80. Served with USNR, 1945-46. Clubs: Commercial, Commonwealth, Queen City, Cincinnati Country. Office: PO Box 599 Cincinnati OH 45201

SMALE, STEPHEN, educator; b. Flint, Mich., July 15, 1930; s. Lawrence A. and Helen (Morrow) S.; B.S., U. Mich., 1952, M.S., 1953, Ph.D., 1956; m. Clara Davis, Jan. 31, 1955; children—Nathan, Laura. Instr., U. Chgo., 1956-58; staff Inst. for Advanced Study, Princeton, 1958-60; asso. prof. U. Calif. at Berkeley, 1960-61, prof. math., 1964—; prof. Columbia, N.Y.C., 1961-64. Recipient Fields medal Internat. Union Math., 1966. Mem. Am. Math. Soc. (Veblen prize 1965, mem. council 1965—), Vietnam Day Com. (co-chmn. 1965), Nat. Acad. Sci. Research in immersion theory, Poincare conjecture, structural stability, math. econs. Home: 69 Highgate Rd Berkeley CA 94707

SMALES, FRED BENSON, corp. exec. b. Keokuk, Iowa, Oct. 7, 1914; s. Fred B. and Mary Alice (Warwick) S.; student pub. schs. Los Angeles; m. Constance Brennan, Dec. 11, 1965; children—Fred Benson III, Catherine; children by previous marriage—Patricia (Mrs. Murray Pilkington), Nancy (Mrs. Bruce Clark). With Champion Internat., Inc., 1933-68, successively San Francisco mgr., 1938-44, Los Angeles, Western div. mgr., 1944-55, v.p. Western sales div., Los Angeles, 1955-65, v.p. Pacific area, 1965-68, pres. Lewers & Cooke, Inc. div., Honolulu, 1966-68; chmn., pres., dir. Cyprus-Hawaiian Cement Corp.; dir. Pacific Resources Inc., Hawaiian Ind. Refinery, Portland Cement Assn., Pryor-Giggey Co. Bd. dirs. Oahu Devel. Conf. Vice chmn. bd. trustees Hawaii-Pacific Coll. Mem. C. of C. Hawaii (chmn.-elect), Mfrs. Assn. Hawaii (pres.). Clubs: Balboa Yacht (staff commodore, Newport Beach, Calif.); Sequoia Yacht (staff commodore, Redwood City, Calif.); So. Calif. Yachting Assn. (staff commodore), Transpacific Yacht (Honolulu chmn.); Waikiki Yacht (staff commodore), Pacific, Rotary, Oahu Country (Honolulu); Kaneohe (Hawaii) Yacht. Home: 46-422 Hulupala Pl Kaneohe HI 96744 Office: Suite 610 700 Bishop St Honolulu HI 96813

SMALL, BURRELL LESLIE, communications exec.; b. Kankakee, Ill., Apr. 2, 1918; s. Leslie Charles and Grace Olive (Burrell) S.; B.S. in Journalism, U. Ill., 1940; m. Reva Arlene Gray, Dec. 3, 1938; children—Susanne Gray, Leslie Howard, Stephen Burrell. With Kankakee Daily Jour., 1940-69, pres., co-pub., 1957-69; pres. Mid Am. Media, Kankakee, 1947—; pres. Mid Am. Audio-Video, Mid Am. Radio, Mid Am. Broadcasting, Imagery Corp.; dir. First Trust & Savs. Bank, First Bank of Meadowview. Fin. chmn. Asbury United Methodist Ch.; chmn. ARC. Mem. Kankakee C. of C. (pres.), U. Ill. Journalism Alumni (pres.). Republican. Office: 6 Dearborn Sq Kankakee IL 60901

SMALL, ERWIN, veterinarian; b. Boston, Nov. 28, 1924; cert. Vt. State Sch. Agr., 1943; B.S., U. Ill., 1955, D.V.M., 1957, M.S., 1965. Intern, Meml. Animal Hosp., Boston, 1957-58; with U. Ill. Coll. Vet. Medicine, Urbana, 1958—, prof. vet. clin. medicine, 1968—, asso. dean alumni and public affairs, chief of medicine, 1970—. Served with USMC, 1944-46, 50-51; PTO. Recipient Nat. Zeta award Auburn U., 1974, Nat. Gamma award, 1971; named Outstanding Tchr., Mordens Labs., 1967; Outstanding Educator, 1973. Mem. AVMA, Am. Animal Hosp. Assn., Am. Coll. Vet. Dermatology (pres.), Internat. Vet. Symposia (pres.), Am. Assn. Vet. Clinics (pres. elect), Am. Coll. Vet. Internal Medicine (pres.), Am. Acad. Vet. Dermatology, Ill. Vet. Med. Assn. (service award 1973), Ill. Vet. Med. Polit. Action Com. (past chmn.). Republican. Jewish. Club: Moose. Contbr. articles to profl. jours. Home: 58 E Daniel St Champaign IL 61820 Office: Vet Med Teaching Hosp Coll Vet Medicine U Ill Urbana IL 61801

SMALL, GEORGE MILTON, architect; b. Collinsville, Okla., Aug. 13, 1916; s. George Milton and Elsie (Sigmon) S.; B.Arch., B.S. in Archtl. Engring., U. Okla., 1939; postgrad. with Mies Van der Rohe, 1946-47; m. June Marie Volck, Feb. 20, 1942; children—George Milton III, June Marie. Design architect Perkings & Will, Chgo., 1947, W.H. Deitrick, Raleigh, N.C., 1948-49; founder, owner firm G. Milton Small & Assos., Raleigh, 1949—; mem. regional pub. adv. panel archtl. and engring. services GSA, 1976; important works include Student Center and Music Bldg. at N.C. State U., 1972; Med. Soc. N.C. Hdqrs. Bldg., 1971; Carter Football Stadium at N.C. State U., 1967, Raleigh Municipal Bldg., 1960. Vice chmn. Raleigh City Planning Commn., 1950-60, 75-76; mem. Raleigh Bd. Adjustment, 1960-71. Pres. Design Found., N.C. State U., 1966-67. Served to lt. (j.g.) USNR, 1943-45. Fellow AIA. Home: 310 Lake Boone Trail Raleigh NC 27608 Office: 105 Brooks Ave Raleigh NC 27607

SMALL, LAVERNE DOREYN, educator; b. Black Earth, Wis., Dec. 22, 1916; s. Harry William and Gladys Rebecca (Barber) S.; B.S., U. Minn., 1938, M.S., 1943, Ph.D., 1945; m. Nora Constance Romstad, Sept. 29, 1938; children—Lawrence D., James W. Registered pharmacist, Minn., 1938-42; sr. research chemist Sterling-Winthrop Research Inst., 1945-48; mem. faculty U. Nebr., 1948—, prof. pharm. chemistry, chmn. dept., 1954-72; spl. research medicinal chemistry. Mem. Am. Chem. Soc., Am., Nebr. pharm. assns., Lancaster County Pharm. Soc., Am. Assn. Colls. Pharmacy, Sigma Xi, Rho Chi, Phi Delta Chi. Methodist. Home: 1540 Sunburst Ln Lincoln NE 68506

SMALL, LAWRENCE FARNSWORTH, educator; b. Bangor, Maine, Dec. 30, 1925; s. Irving Wheelock and Geneva May (Turner) S.; B.D., Bangor Theol. Sem., 1948; B.A., U. Maine, 1948, M.A., 1951; Ph.D., Harvard, 1955; m. Elfie Joan Ames, Aug. 9, 1947; children—Kathleen Ann, Linda Jean, Lawrence Farnsworth, Daniel Irving. Ordained to ministry Congregational Ch., 1950; minister Paramus (N.J.) Congl. Ch., 1955-59; asso. prof. history Rocky Mountain Coll., Billings, Mont., 1959-61, prof., 1975—, dean of Coll., 1961-65, acting pres., 1965-66, pres., 1966-75. Chmn., Mont. commn. Higher Edn. Facilities Act, 1965-74. Pres., Yellowstone County Council Chs., 1968-70; treas. Mont. Conf., United Ch. of Christ, 1970-73; chmn. bd. dirs. Western Independent Colls. Found.; bd. dirs. Community Concert Assn., Yellowstone County Mental Health Assn., Billings Citizens for Community Devel., Billings United Fund; trustee Billings Deaconess Hosp. Mem. Phi Beta Kappa, Phi Kappa Phi. Club: Kiwanis (v.p. Billings). Home: 7320 Sumatra Pl Rural Route 4 Billings MT 59102 Office: 1511 Poly St Billings MT 59102

SMALL, MILTON MORRIS, state ofcl.; b. Notus, Idaho, Jan. 1, 1923; s. Linus E. and Gustine M. (Ohren) S.; B.A. with honors in History, U. Oreg., 1942; M.A. in History (Ford fellow), U. Wis., 1953; postgrad. (Coe fellow) Stanford U., 1960; m. Muriel L. Burtch, June 25, 1943; children—Barbara, Douglas, Mary. Tchr., Adrian (Oreg.) High Sch., 1946-47, Boise (Idaho) High Sch., 1947-59, counselor, 1959-61; supr. secondary edn. Boise Public Schs., 1961-67; dep. dir. Idaho Office Higher Edn., Boise, 1969-72; dir. spl. programs Idaho Bd. Edn., Boise, 1967-69, exec. dir., 1972—; lectr. evening programs U. Idaho, 1958-70, Coll. Idaho, 1960-71. Sec., Boise Com. Fgn. Relations, 1958-74. Served with U.S. Army, 1943-46. Mem. NEA, State Higher Edn. Exec. Officers, Phi Beta Kappa, Pi Delta Phi. Home: 822 Haines St Boise ID 83702 Office: 650 W State St Boise ID 83720

SMALL, PARKER ADAMS, JR., physician, educator; b. Cin., July 5, 1932; s. Parker Adams and Grace (McMichael) S.; student Tufts U., 1950-53; M.D., U. Cin. 1957; m. Natalie Settimelli, Aug. 26, 1956; children—Parker Adams, Peter McMichael, Carla Edmea. Med. intern Pa. Hosp., Phila., 1957-58; research asso. Nat. Heart Inst. NIH, Washington, 1958-60; research fellow St. Mary's Hosp., London, Eng., 1960-61; sr. surgeon NIMH, Washington, 1961-66; prof. immunology and med. microbiology U. Fla., 1966—, chmn. dept., 1966-75; vis. prof. U. Lausanne (Switzerland), 1972; vis. scholar Assn. Am. Med. Colls., Washington, 1973. Cons. in field. Sec.-treas. Oakmont, Md., 1964-65, mayor, 1965-66; chmn. Citizens for Pub. Schs. Gainesville, Fla., 1969-70. Served with USPHS, 1958-60, 61-66. NIH spl. fellow, 1960-61; research grantee, 1966—. Mem. Am. Assn. Immunologists, Phi Beta Kappa, Sigma Xi, Theta Delta Chi. Editor: The Secretory Immunologic System, 1971. Home: 3454 NW 12th Ave Gainesville FL 32605

SMALL, RAY, coll. dean; b. Winters, Tex., Aug. 2, 1915; s. George Norman and Etta (Thompson) S.; B.A., West Tex. State Coll., 1937; M.A., U. Tex., 1941, Ph.D., 1958; m. Dollee Georgia Meyer, Aug. 8, 1938; children—Marilynn Small Wilmeth, Andra Small Sherrill. Adminstr. and tchr. Tex. pub. schs., 1938-42; successively prof. English, dir. pub. relations, dean men Amarillo Coll., 1946-61; prof. English, U. Tex., El Paso, 1961—, asst. to pres., 1961-63, dean Sch. Arts and Scis., 1963-66, dean Coll. Liberal Arts, 1966-79. Served to comdr. USNR, 1943-46. Presbyterian (elder). Home: 4425 Buckingham St El Paso TX 79902

SMALL, ROBERT SCOTT, textile co. exec.; b. Charleston, S.C., July 18, 1915; s. Robert Scott and Louise (Johnson) S.; B.S., Coll. Charleston, 1936; LL.D., Clemson U., 1964, Furman U., 1968, Coll. Charleston, 1970; m. Sallie Tyler, June 17, 1938; children—Sallie Small Johnson, Robert Scott, Oscar Johnson, Charles Innes, Elizabeth Johnson. Mgr., S.C. Nat. Bank, Pickens, 1936-38, asst. mgr., Greenville, 1938-41, cashier, trust officer, 1941-47, now dir., Charleston; pres., treas. Ottaray Textiles, Inc., Anderson, S.C., Haynsworth Mills, Anderson, 1947-51; v.p., dir. Woodside Mills, Greenville, S.C., 1951-58, pres., 1958-66, chief exec. officer, treas., dir.; pres., chief exec. officer Dan River Mills, Inc., 1966-77, chmn., chief exec. officer, 1977—; dir. So. Bell Tel. & Tel., Liberty Corp., Greenville, Piedmont Natural Gas Co., Charlotte, N.C., Textile Hall Corp., Greenville, Dan River Mills, Inc. Campaign mgr. United Fund, 1957. Trustee, chmn. Greenville Gen. Hosp., 1960-66, Coll. Charleston, 1960-66; trustee J.E. Sirrine Found.; adv. com. Furman U.; fin. com. Episcopal Ch. Home for Children. Mem. Am. Textile Mfrs. Assn. (past pres.), S.C. Textile Mfrs. Assn. (pres. 1963). Clubs: Green Valley Country (pres. 1961), Cotillion (sr. com. 1960-62), Greenville Country, Poinsett (all Greenville); Carolina Yacht (Charleston). Home: E Parkins Mills Rd Greenville SC 29607 Office: PO Box 6126 107 Frederick St Greenville SC 29606

SMALL, ROLAND E., savs. and loan holding co. exec.; b. Glendale, Calif., Mar. 12, 1934; s. Willis V. and Ora E. (Morrison) S.; B.S., Stanford U., 1956; m. Judith E. Stanley, Nov. 7, 1971; children—David V., Doug D., Karen L., Sarah J., Katherine D. Asst. to pres. First Charter Fin. Corp., Beverly Hills, Calif., 1962-66; sr. v.p. Equitable Savs. & Loan Assn. and v.p. holding co., Los Angeles, 1966-70; exec. v.p. Columbia Savs. and Loan Assn., Denver, 1971-73; pres., mem. exec. com., dir. First S & L Shares, Inc. and Majestic Savs. and Loan Assn., Denver; chmn. bd. Majestic Investment Co. of Denver and Commerce Savs. and Loan Assn., Shawnee, Kans., 1974—. Served with USMC, 1956-60. Office: 2420 W 26th Ave Denver CO 80211

SMALL, S(AUL) MOUCHLY, psychiatrist; b. N.Y.C., Oct. 11, 1913; s. Joseph and Esther (Mouchly) S.; B.S. cum laude, Coll. City N.Y., 1933; M.D., Cornell U., 1937; m. Sophie Scholl, June 13, 1937; children—Susan Ellen, Laurie Jean, Jonathan, Cynthia A. Intern N.Y. Hosp., 1937-38, resident psychiatrist Payne Whitney Clinic, 1939-43, psychiatrist rehab. clinic, 1944-46; asst. resident psychiatry New Haven Hosp., asst. psychiatry Yale Med. Coll., 1938-39; asst. instr. psychiatry Cornell U. Med. Coll., 1940-43; asst. med. dir., psychiat. cons. Nat. Hosp., N.Y.C., 1943-47; psychiat. cons. VA, Buffalo, also chief psychiat. cons., mem. dean's com., 1952—; neuropsychiat. cons. Vassar Coll., 1943-47; asso. psychiatrist Mt. Sinai Hosp., 1946-51; cons. neuropsychiatry Surgeon Gen. U.S. Army, 1947-70; prof. psychiatry SUNY at Buffalo Sch. Medicine, 1951—, chmn. dept. psychiatry, 1951-78; dir. psychiatry Meyer Meml. Hosp., Buffalo, 1951-68, 74—, med. coordinator psychiatry, 1968-74; head psychiatry Buffalo Gen. Hosp., 1963—; univ. chief dept. psychiatry Buffalo Children's Hosp., 1968—; lectr. Columbia Med. Coll., 1948-51; dir. mental health services Erie County, N.Y., 1955-57; mem. Erie County Commn. Mental Health Bd., 1957—; psychiat. examiner USIA, 1959-62; psychiat. cons. Peace Corps., 1963—, U.S. Dept. Def., 1966—. Mem. N.Y. State Adv. Com. on Alcoholism. Bd. dirs. Muscular Dystrophy Assn. Am., chmn. nat. sci. adv. bd., 1975—. Qualified psychiatrist, certified examiner N.Y. State, 1942; certified mental hosp. adminstr.; com. on psychiatry Nat. Bd. Med. Examiners, chmn. Part III, 1975—. Diplomate Am. Bd. Psychiatry and Neurology (mem. exams. com. 1969—, dir. 1975—), Pan-Am. Med. Assn. Fellow Am. Psychiat. Assn. (life), N.Y. Acad. Medicine, A.M.A., Am. Coll. Psychiatrists, Am. Coll. Psychoanalysts, Am. Pub. Health Assn., Am. Assn. for Social Psychiatry (bd. councilors, v.p. 1978—); mem. Am. Psychoanalytic Assn., Nat. Council Alcoholism, A.A.A.S., Am. Psychosomatic Assn., Internat. Psychoanalytic Assn., Assn. Am. Med. Colls., Western N.Y. Psychoanalytic Soc. (pres.), N.Y. State Med. Soc., N.Y. Acad. Scis., Buffalo Acad. Medicine, N.Y. Psychoanalytic Soc., N.Y. State Pub. Health Assn., Western N.Y. Psychiat. Soc. (pres. 1959-60), Royal Soc. for Promotion Health (Eng.), N.Am. Assn. Alchoholism Programs, Phi Beta Kappa, Alpha Omega Alpha, Phi Delta Epsilon. Author: (with P.M. Lichtenstein) Handbook of Psychiatry, 1943; (with Hugh T. Carmichael and Peter F. Regan) Prospects and Proposals: Lifetime Learning for Psychiatrists, 1972. Contbr. articles, chpts. to profl. publs. Mem. internat. adv. bd. Jour. Behavioral Neuropsychiatry, 1969—; mem. editorial bd. Jour. Psychiat. Edn.; mem. adv. editorial bd. Internat. Jour. Social Psychiatry. Home: 75-G Oakbrook Dr Buffalo NY 14221

SMALL, STANTON HARRISON, mfg. co. exec.; b. San Francisco, Aug. 8, 1922; s. Cecil Stanton and Helena Clara (Newton) S.; B.A. in Econs. and Bus., U. Wash., 1949; m. Evaline Agnes Morton, Aug. 16, 1945; children—Katherine Claire, David Stanton. With Gen. Electric Co., 1949-70, mgr. fin. med. systems dept., 1964-70; v.p. fin., treas. Allen-Bradley Co., Milw., 1970—. Chmn. Benson (Wash.) unit Am. Cancer Soc., 1962-64. Trustee, chmn. planning com. St. Francis Hosp., Milw. Served with USAAF, 1942-45. Decorated D.F.C., Air medal. Mem. Fin. Execs. Inst. Home: 1360 Valley Ridge Rd Brookfield WI 53005 Office: 1201 S 2d St Milwaukee WI 53204

SMALL, SYDNEY LLEWELLYN, network radio exec.; b. Bklyn., Feb. 18, 1941; s. Vernon and Clara Belle (Cook) S.; B.B.A., Pace U., 1961. Bus. mgr. ABC, N.Y.C., 1963-69; bus. mgr. Time, Inc., N.Y.C., 1969-73; exec. v.p., co-founder Unity Broadcasting Network, Inc., Nat. Black Network, N.Y.C., 1973—, Unity Broadcasting Network-Penna., Inc., Phila., 1979—; dir. recruitment and tng. program World Inst. Black Communications, N.Y.C. Served with U.S. Army, 1961-63. Mem. Internat. TV and Radio Soc., Nat. Assn. Broadcasters, NAACP, N.Y. C. of C. (commerce-communications com. 1978—). Office: National Black Network 1350 Ave of Americas New York NY 10019

SMALL, WILLIAM ANDREW, educator; b. Cobleskill, N.Y., Oct. 16, 1914; s. James Arner and Lois (Patterson) S.; B.S., U.S. Naval Acad., 1936; A.B., U. Rochester, 1950, M.A., 1952, Ph.D., 1958; m. Bela Savkovich, Apr. 20, 1939; children—Lois (Mrs. Paul Gindling). James (dec.). Commd. ensign U.S. Navy, 1936, advanced through grades to lt. comdr., 1944; comdt. cadets, instr. DeVeaux Sch., Niagara Falls, N.Y., 1945-48; instr. U. Rochester, 1951-55. Alfred (N.Y.) U., 1955-56; asst. prof. math. Grinnell (Iowa) Coll., 1956-58, asso. prof., chmn. dept., 1958-60; prof. math. Tenn. Tech. U., 1960-62; prof. math. State Univ. Coll., Geneseo, N.Y., 1962—, chmn. dept. math., 1962-78. Fulbright-Hays lectr. math. Aleppo U., Syrian Arab Republic, 1964-65. Pres. Federated Orgn. Am.-Arab Relations, 1967—; Liberal Party candidate for N.Y. assemblyman, 1968. Mem. Am. Math. Soc., Math. Assn. Am., U.S. Naval Inst., AAUP, Phi Beta Kappa. Episcopalian. Contbr. profl. jours. Home: 28 Court St Geneseo NY 14454

SMALL, WILLIAM EDWIN, JR., recreation exec., editorial cons.; b. Jackson, Mich., Jan. 18, 1937; s. William Edwin and Lena Louisa (Hunt) S.; A.S., Jackson (Mich.) Community Coll., 1959; B.S. in Geology, Mich. State U., 1961, M.A. in Journalism, 1964; m. Ruth Ann Toombs, Mar. 28, 1959; children—Suzanne Marie, William Edwin III, Bryan Anthony. Copy editor Gillette Pub. Co., Lansing, Mich., 1961; reporter Sci. Service, Washington, 1961-62; writer sci. U. Chgo., 1963-64; sci. info. officer Pa. State U., State College, 1964-66; corr. McGraw-Hill, Washington, 1966-69; mem. staff com. pub. works U.S. Senate, 1969; founding editor Biomed. News, Falls Church, Va., 1969-71; pres. Editorial Cons., Washington, 1970—; dir. pub. info. Nat. Bur. Standards, Washington, 1972-76; owner recreation resort Small Country Va., Louisa, Va., 1975—; editor Am. Pharmacy, jour. Am. Pharm. Assn., Washington, 1979—; editorial cons., Washington, 1970—. Press sec. Pa. Acad. Scis., 1964-66; press officer Nat. Heart Fund, 1964-66; cons. HEW, EPA, 1970-72; mem. design and improvement task force U.S. Sec. Commerce, 1974-75. Chmn., leader Cub Scouts Am., 1973-75; active Little League Baseball, 1973-75. Served with Security Agy., AUS, 1955-59. Recipient Order of Arrow, Boy Scouts Am. Recipient Superior Accomplishment award U.S. Dept. Commerce, 1974. Fellow AAAS; mem. Nat. Assn. Sci. Writers, Sigma Delta Chi. Author: Third Pollution, 1971. Contbg. editor: Groliers Ency., 1959-61. Contbr. articles to profl. and lay publs. Home: Route 5 Box 201 Louisa VA 23093 Office: Small Country Va Louisa VA 23093 also Am Pharm Assn 2215 Constitution Ave NW Washington DC 20037

SMALL, WILLIAM JACK, broadcasting co. exec.; b. Chgo., Sept. 20, 1926; s. Louis and Libby (Mell) S.; M.A. in Social Scis., U. Chgo., 1951; m. Gish Rubin, Dec. 20, 1947; children—Tamar Helen Small Greif, Willa Susan. News dir. Sta. WLS, Chgo., 1951-56; news dir. Sta. WHAS-AM and TV, Louisville, 1956-62; dir. news and Washington bur. chief CBS, 1962-74; sr. v.p. CBS News, N.Y.C., 1974-78, v.p. CBS, Inc., Washington, 1978-79; pres. NBC News, N.Y.C., 1979—. Served with U.S. Army, 1944-45. Recipient Paul White award Radio TV News Dirs. Assn., 1974. Mem. Radio-TV News Dirs. Assn. (past pres.), Sigma Delta Chi (pres. 1974-75), Nat. Assn. Broadcasters (exec. bd.), Nat. Journalism Center (dir.). Author: To Kill a Messenger: Television and the Real World, 1970; Political Power and the Press, 1972. Office: 30 Rockefeller Plaza New York NY 10020

SMALL, WILLIAM NEWELL, naval officer; b. Little Rock, Feb. 22, 1927; s. John Clay and Ruth (Bass) S.; B.S., U.S. Naval Acad., 1948; postgrad. Naval War Coll., 1961; m. Janet Cubbison, June 17, 1950; children—James, Janet, Joan. Commd. ensign U.S. Navy, 1948, advanced through grades to vice adm., 1978; various assignments as aviator, 1949-64; comdr. Attack Squadrons 42 and 65, U.S.S. Necsho, U.S.S. Independence, 1964-73; comdr. Carrier Group 3, 1975-76; dir. Navy planning and programs div. Dept. Navy, Washington, 1976-79; comdr. U.S. 6th Fleet and comdr. Allied Striking Forces, So. Europe, 1979—. Decorated D.S.M., Legion of Merit with 2 oak leaf clusters, Air medal, Cross of Gallantry (Vietnam). Office: Comdr 6th Fleet FPO New York NY 09501

SMALLEY, HAROLD EUGENE, SR., educator; b. nr. Birmingham, Ala., Apr. 9, 1921; s. Harley Marvin and Nellie Estelle (Thompson) S.; student Howard Coll., 1940-41; B.S. in Indsl. Engring., U. Ala., 1946; M.S. in Indsl. Engring., Purdue U., 1947; postgrad. Columbia U., 1951-52; Ph.D., U. Pitts., 1957; postgrad. Case Inst. Tech., 1958; m. Elizabeth Louise Loehr, Feb. 11, 1944; children—Elizabeth Estelle, Janet Marie, Harold Eugene. Indsl. engr. Stockham Valves, Inc., 1941-43; asst. prof. U. Ala., 1947-50; asso. prof. U. Conn., 1950-54; asst. to vice chancellor U. Pitts., 1955-58; prof. Ga. Inst. Tech., Atlanta, 1958-68, Regents' prof. indsl. engring., 1968—, dir. Health Systems Research Center, 1969—, dir. Sch. Health Systems, 1977—; Regents' prof. Med. Coll. Ga., 1968—. Cons. to numerous mfg. firms, labor unions, govt. agys., hosps., health-care orgns., med. schs. Active Boys Scouts Am. Served with USNR, 1943-44. Recipient Editorial award Hosp. Mgmt., 1964, Distinguished Engring. Alumnus award Purdue U., 1976; also numerous research and tng. grants. Registered profl. engr., Ala., Conn., Pa., Ga. Fellow Am. Inst. Indsl. Engrs. (distinguished research award 1974, Frank and Lillian Gilbreth award 1979); mem. Hosp. Mgmt. Systems Soc. (founder), Am. Hosp.

Assn., Pi Kappa Alpha. Methodist. Author: Hospital Industrial Engineering (Book of Year award Am. Inst. Indsl. Engrs. 1968), 1966. Home: 4650 Huntley Dr NE Atlanta GA 30342

SMALLEY, ROY FREDERICK, III, profl. baseball player; s. Los Angeles, Oct. 25, 1952; s. Roy Frederick, Jr. and Norma Jolene (Mauch) S.; student Los Angeles City Coll., 1970-72, U. So. Calif., 1972-73; m. Christine Cecile Sherry, Jan. 14, 1978. Shortstop, Tex. Rangers Baseball Team, 1975-76, Minn. Twins Profl. Baseball Team, 1976—. Named to Am. League Allstar Team, 1979, also AP and UPI All Star Teams; mem. Allstar Exhbn. Team touring Japan, 1979. Office: 8001 Cedar Ave S Bloomington MN 55420. *My goal in life is to explore the utmost the physical, mental and artistic abilities imbued in me; to approximate as closely as possible the unlimited human potential in all aspects of existence.*

SMALLS, CHARLIE, composer, lyricist; b. N.Y.C., Oct. 25, 1943; s. Charles Henry and Rebecca Derotha (McNeil) S.; grad. Juilliard Sch. Music, N.Y.C., 1961; m. Marilyn Rose Simson, May 3, 1964; 1 son, Charles Michael. Mus. dir. Club Improvisation, N.Y.C., 1960, The Scene, N.Y.C., 1960, Harry Belafonte on tour in Paris and Stockholm, 1964, Hugh Masekela Group, 1966; composer theme film Faces, 1967-68; composer scores for film Drum, 1976; composer, lyricist stage prodn. The Wiz, 1974, film version, 1977. Served with USAF, 1961-63. Recipient Drama Desk award, 1974, 75, Show of Month award Tour-A-Trail Cultural Club, 1976; Grammy award Best Cast Show Album for The Wiz, 1976; Tony awards best mus. score (music and lyrics) for The Wiz, 1975. Mem. Broadcast Music Inc. Address: 924 West End Ave New York NY 10025. *Believe in myself; dealing with people and life straight down the middle. My word is my bond; don't make promises you can't keep. Laugh more. Please and thank you will get you over (from my Momma).*

SMALLWOOD, JAMES WRAY, publisher; b. Sutton, Ont., Can., Feb. 8, 1923; s. Alan Roy and Mabel Alma (Wray) S.; student pub. schs., Sutton; m. Joan Margaret Turner, Feb. 6, 1943; children—Dan Richard, Dianne Rose, David James. Sales mgr. Liberty mag., Can., 1946-47; br. mgr. Curtis Distbg. Co. Ltd., London, Ont., 1947-64; pres. Simon & Schuster Can. Ltd., Markham, Ont., 1964-76; v.p., gen. mgr. Paperjacks Ltd., Markham, 1976—; v.p. Rexwood Publns.; pres. World of Horse Ltd. Served with RCAF, 1942-45. Mem. Canadian Thoroughbred Horse Soc. (past pres.). Home: 36 Cousins Dr Aurora ON L4G 1B4 Canada Office: 330 Steelecase Rd Markham ON L3R 2M1 Canada

SMALTZ, DONALD CALVIN, lawyer; b. Harrisburg, Pa., Feb. 5, 1937; s. Monroe Calvin and Adaline Teresa (Chickini) S.; B.A., Pa. State U., 1958; J.D., Dickinson Sch. Law, 1961; children—Connie, Carrie Sue, Jennifer. Admitted to Pa. bar, 1961, Calif. bar, 1965; practiced in Los Angeles, 1964—; asst. U.S. atty. Central Dist. Calif., 1964-66, spl. asst. U.S. atty., 1967-68; partner Keatinge & Sterling, 1966-68; partner firm Grossman, Smaltz, Graven & Perry, 1968-74; individual practice law, 1974-77; mem. firm Smaltz & Neelley, P.C., 1977—; adj. prof. law Southwestern U., Los Angeles. Served to capt. JAGC, AUS, 1962-64. Clubs: Univ., Los Angeles Athletic (Los Angeles). Office: 530 W 6th St Los Angeles CA 90014

SMART, CHARLES RICH, surgeon; b. Ogden, Utah, Nov. 7, 1926; s. Junius Hatch and Avon (Rich) S.; B.S. with honors, U. Utah, 1945; M.D. with honors, Temple U., 1955; m. Dorotha Jean Cannon Sharp, Dec. 23, 1953; children—Thomas, Edward, Christopher, Angela, Cynthia, David. Intern, Los Angeles County Hosp., 1955-56; resident Hosp. of U. Pa., Phila., 1956-61; asst. prof. surgery in residence U. Calif., Los Angeles, 1963-66; asso. prof. surgery Coll. Medicine, U. Utah, 1966-69, cancer coordinator, 1967-69, clin. asso. prof. surgery, 1969-75, clin. prof. surgery, 1975—; mem. staff Latter-day Saints Hosp., chief of surgery, 1974—; chmn. SEER Group, Nat. Cancer Inst., 1976-78; dir. Rocky Mountain Coop. Tumor Registry, 1969—; mem. cancer commn. Am. Cancer Soc., also 1976—. bd. dirs. Fellow A.C.S.; mem. Utah Med. Assn., AMA, Pan - Pacific, Bay, Los Angeles Salt Lake surg. socs., Internat. Soc. Chemotherapists, Am. Assn. Cancer Edn., Am. Soc. Clin. Oncology, Soc. Head and Neck Surgeons, Am. Soc. Surg. Oncologists, Alpha Omega Alpha. Republican. Mormon. Contbr. research articles to med. jours. Home: 1262 Chandler Dr Salt Lake City UT 84103 Office: Latter-day Saints Hosp 325 8th Ave Salt Lake City UT 84143

SMART, CLIFTON MURRAY, JR., sch. ofcl., architect; b. Blytheville, Ark., Aug. 8, 1933; s. Clifton Murray and Elizabeth (Haley) S.; B.Arch., Tulane U., 1956; M.S. in City Planning, U. Ill., 1960; m. Carolyn Jo Jones, Aug. 22, 1959; children—Clifton Murray III, John David. Instr. dept. city planning U. Ill., 1960; asso. Uzzell S. Branson, Architect, Blytheville, 1960-66; faculty U. Ark. Sch. Architecture, Fayetteville, 1966—, prof., dean sch., 1975—; pvt. practice architecture, Fayetteville, 1967—; Fulbright-Hays lectr. U. Kabul, Afghanistan, 1972-73. Deacon, Fayetteville 1st Bapt. Ch., 1970—, mem. Ark. Bapt. Exec. Bd., 1978—. Served with Signal Corps, AUS, 1957-59. Mem. AIA (dir. Ark. chpt. 1977—), Soc. Archtl. Historians, Fayetteville C. of C. Democrat. Author: (with Charles Carnes) City Appearance and the Law, 1972. Home: 858 Woodlawn Fayetteville AR 72701 Office: Vol Walker Hall Room 218 Fayetteville AR 72701

SMART, FREDERICK KELLOGG, food co. exec.; b. Larchmont, N.Y., Jan. 22, 1925; s. Frederick Kellogg and Silvia Anna (Mueller) S.; B.S. in Bus. Adminstrn., Northwestern U., 1949; m. Colleen Wolfe, June 28, 1951; children—Deborah, Kimberly, Frederick, William. Group mgr. mktg. Post Cereals, Battle Creek, Mich., 1955-60; corp. dir. promotions Gen. Foods Co., White Plains, N.Y., 1963; exec. v.p. Galbraith, Hoffman & Rogers Advt. Agy., N.Y.C., 1964; pres. Smart Assos., mktg. cons., Upstage Productions Film Co., N.Y.C., 1965-72; exec. v.p. Nalley's Fine Foods, Tacoma, 1972—; partner Temvros Shipping Co., Piraeus, Greece, 1967—; dir. Myrhe Advt., Mont.; adv., cons. Dept. State, 1970. Adv., Jr. Achievement, 1959; v.p. Boy Scouts Am., 1958; chmn. Calhoun County (Mich.) Republican Party, 1960; active New Canaan (Conn.) Indian Guides, 1969. Served with USAAF, 1943-46. Recipient awards for devel. of TV by Constantine of Greece, 1966; Am.-Egypt Trade award Pres. Nasser, 1970; Commendation for promotion of understanding between Middle East and U.S.A., Saab Salam (Prime Minister), Lebanon, 1970. Mem. Assn. Nat. Advertisers, Western Assn. Food Chains, Sales and Mktg. Execs. Internat., Am.-Hellenic C. of C. Episcopalian. Clubs: Assn. Ex-Mems. Squadron A (N.Y.C.); Tacoma Golf and Country, Elks. Author 1st consumer-published motivation research in Middle East, 1970; co-editor Man's Funniest Friends, anthology dog cartoons, 1967; inventor paper table, 1965; developer reusable zipper bag packaging for textile industry, 1967. Home: 10 Forest Glen Ln SW Tacoma WA 98498 Office: Nalley's Fine Foods 3303 S 35th St Tacoma WA 98411

SMART, GEORGE NORMAN RUSSELL, educator; b. Montreal, Can., May 28, 1921; s. George L.P. and Elizabeth (Weeks) S.; B.Sc. in Chemistry, McGill U., 1942, Ph.D., 1945; post-doctoral research fellow U. Toronto, 1945-46, Ia. State U., 1946-47; m. Margaret Gwendolen Howe, July 6, 1946; children—Megan, David G.P., Derek H.B. Came to U.S., 1947. Sessional lectr. McGill U., 1944-45; asst. prof. Muhlenberg Coll., Allentown, Pa., 1947-50, asso. prof., 1950-56, prof., 1956—, head chemistry dept., 1961-78; industry cons. for organic chemistry and air and stream pollution control and abatement; exec. dir. Tuition Exchange. Trustee Kirkridge, Inc. Recipient Lindbach award for distinguished teaching, 1962. Mem. Am. Chem. Soc., AAUP, Sigma Xi. Presbyn. Home: 2219 Gordon St Allentown PA 18104

SMART, JACKSON WYMAN, JR., business exec.; b. Chgo., Aug. 27, 1930; s. Jackson Wyman and Dorothy (Byrnes) S.; B.B.A., U. Mich., 1952; M.B.A., Harvard, 1954; m. Suzanne Tobey, July 6, 1957; children—Jackson W. III, Alison Tobey. Asst. v.p. First Nat. Bank Chgo., 1956-64; exec. v.p. comml. banking Bank of Commonwealth, Detroit, 1964-69; pres., dir. MSP industries Corp. (subsidiary W.R. Grace & Co. 1972), 1969-71, pres., chief exec. officer, 1971-75; v.p. leisure/performance group, parent co., 1973-75; chmn., pres., treas., dir. The Delos Internat. Group, Inc. (now subs. Automatic Data Processing Inc.), Princeton, N.J., 1975-77; pres., chief exec. officer, dir. Central Nat. Bank, Chgo., 1977—, chmn., 1978—; chmn. fin. com., dir. Fed. Express Corp., Memphis, 1977—; dir. Thomas Industries, Inc., Louisville, Gulf Resources & Chem. Corp., Houston. Served to 1st lt. AUS, 1954-56. Mem. Young Pres. Orgn., Assn. Res. City Bankers, Psi Upsilon. Republican. Presbyterian. Clubs: Detroit; Orchard Lake (Mich.) Country; Birmingham (Mich.) Athletic; Economic, University (Chgo.), Hundred of Cook County, Mid-Day (Chgo.), Chicago, Indian Hill (Winnetka); Coral Beach and Tennis (Bermuda). Home: 1090 Westmoor Rd Winnetka IL 60093 Office: 120 S LaSalle St Chicago IL 60603

SMART, JACOB EDWARD, cons.; b. Ridgeland, S.C., May 31, 1909; s. William Edward and Alma (Nettles) S.; student Marion Mil. Inst., 1926-27; B.S., U.S. Mil. Acad., 1931; student Nat. War Coll., 1949-50; m. Elizabeth Gohmert, Feb. 20, 1932 (div. 1946); children—Joan Elizabeth, Jacklyn Cabell, William Edward, Rosemary. Commd. lt. USAF, 1931, advanced through grades to gen., 1963; served various posts U.S. and Europe, 1931-55; asst. vice chief of staff USAF, Washington, 1955-59; comdr. 12th Air Force, Waco, Texas, 1959-60; vice comdr. tactical air command Langley AFB, 1960-61; comdr. U.S. Forces in Japan, 1961-63, Pacific Air Forces, 1963-64; dep. comdr. in chief Hdqrs. U.S. European Command, 1964-66; ret., 1966; spl. asst. to adminstr. NASA, 1966-67, asst. adminstr. for policy, 1967-68; asst. adminstr. for Dept. Def. and inter-agy. affairs, 1968-73; v.p. Earth Satellite Corp., Washington, 1973-75; cons., 1975—. Decorated D.S.C., D.S.M. with 4 oak leaf clusters, Legion of Merit, D.F.C., Air medal with 3 oak leaf clusters, Purple Heart, Commendation Ribbon; hon. comdr. Order Brit. Empire; Order of Service Merit 1st class (Korea); Medal of Cloud and Banner with Grand Cordon (China); comdr. Legion of Honor (France); Order of Sacred Treasures (Japan). Mem. Assn. Grads. U.S. Mil. Acad., Air Force Assn. Home: PO Box Y Ridgeland SC 29936

SMART, JOHN KENNETH, newspaper publisher; b. Dallas, Oct. 6, 1932; s. John Paul and Faye (McDonald) S.; B.A., North Tex. State U., 1953; postgrad. journalism and govt. U. Tex. at Austin, 1953-54; m. Betty Kathryn Burns, Nov. 27, 1953; children—Deborah Kathryn, Scott Burns. Reporter, Carrollton (Tex.) Chronicle, 1951, Ft. Worth Star-Telegram, 1952; with Dallas Times Herald, 1954-75, mng. editor, 1971-75; publisher White Rocker News, 1975-78, Kilgore News Herald, 1979—; part-time lectr. journalism North Tex. State U., 1952-53. Mem. pub. relations adv. com. Baptist Gen. Conv. Tex., 1967-70. Bd. dirs. West Dallas Community Centers, 1963-65; bd. mgmt. Dallas Downtown YMCA, 1969-71; mem. adv. council Southwestern Bapt. Theol. Sem., 1976—; mem. journalism adv. council North Tex. State U., 1975—. Served with AUS, 1954-56. Mem. Nat., Tex. A.P. mng. editors assns., Res. Officers Assn., East Dallas C. of C. (dir. 1977-78). Baptist. Clubs: Roy H. Laird Country, Kilgore Rotary, Dallas Press (dir. 1968-69). Author: A Sacred Trust, 1970. Home: 3005 Joy Dr Kilgore TX 75662 Office: 610 E Main St Kilgore TX 75662

SMART, L(OUIS) EDWIN, JR., bus. exec.; b. Columbus, Ohio, Nov. 17, 1923; s. Louis Edwin and Esther (Guthery) S.; A.B. magna cum laude, Harvard U., 1947, J.D. magna cum laude, 1949; m. Virginia Alice Knouff, Mar. 1, 1944 (div. 1958); children—Cynthia Stephanie, Douglas Edwin; m. 2d, Jeanie Alberta Milone, Aug. 29, 1964; 1 son, Dana Gregory Milone. Admitted to N.Y. State bar, 1950; asso. firm Hughes, Hubbard & Ewing, N.Y.C., 1949-56; partner firm Hughes, Hubbard, & Reed, N.Y.C., 1957-64; pres. Bendix Internat., dir. Bendix Corp. and fgn. subsidiaries, 1964-67; sr. v.p. external affairs Trans World Airlines, Inc., 1967-71, sr. v.p. corp. affairs, 1971-75, vice chmn., 1976, chmn. bd., chief exec. officer, 1977-78, chmn. bd., 1979—, also dir., mem. exec. and fin. coms.; chmn. bd., pres., chief exec. officer Trans World Corp., 1978—; chmn. bd. Hilton Internat. Co., 1978—; chmn. exec. com., dir. Canteen Corp., 1973—, Spartan Food Systems, Inc., 1979—; dir. So. Natural Gas Co., So. Natural Resources, Inc., ACF Industries, Inc., Continental Corp. Trustee Com. Econ. Devel., 1977—, Conf. Bd., 1977—. Served to lt. USNR, 1943-46. Mem. Am. Bar Assn., N.Y. County Lawyers Assn., Am. Soc. Travel Agents, Phi Beta Kappa, Sigma Alpha Epsilon. Clubs: Economic, Presidents, Sky (N.Y.C.). Home: 535 E 86th St New York City NY 10028 also Coakley Bay St Croix VI 00820 Office: 605 3d Ave New York City NY 10016

SMART, STEPHEN BRUCE, JR., container mfg. exec.; b. N.Y.C., Feb. 7, 1923; s. Stephen Bruce and Beatrice (Cobb) S.; student Milton Acad.; A.B. cum laude, Harvard, 1945; M.S., Mass. Inst. Tech., 1947; m. Edith Minturn Merrill, Sept. 10, 1949; children—Edith Minturn (Mrs. E.M. Moore III), William Candler, Charlotte Merrill, Priscilla. Sales engr. Permutit Co., N.Y., 1947-51; various sales, gen. mgmt. positions Continental Group, Inc. (formerly Continental Can Co.), N.Y.C., 1953—, v.p. Central metal div., 1962-65, v.p. marketing and corporate planning, 1965-67, v.p., asst. gen. mgr. paper operations, 1967-69, group v.p. paper operations, 1969-71, exec. v.p. paper operations, 1971-73, vice chmn. bd., 1973-75, pres., 1975—; dir. Rexnord Inc., Chase Manhattan Corp., Chase Manhattan Bank, Life Ins. Co. Va., Lawyers Title Co. Vice-chmn. bd. trustees Smith Coll.; mem. adv. bd. Columbia U. Sch. Bus. Served to 1st lt. AUS, 1943-46, C.E., 1951-53. Mem. Council Fgn. Relations, Conf. Bd., Sigma Xi. Clubs: Country of Fairfield (Conn.); Pequot Yacht; Pinnacle, Blind Brook, River (N.Y.C.); N.Y. Yacht; Clove Valley Rod and Gun. Home: 4375 Congress St Fairfield CT 06430 Office: care Continental Group Inc 633 3d Ave New York NY 10017

SMART, WILLIAM BUCKWALTER, editor, gen. mgr.; b. Provo, Utah, June 27, 1922; s. Thomas Laurence and Nellie (Buckwalter) S.; student U. Wyo., 1943-44, U. Utah, 1949-51; B.A., Reed Coll., 1948; m. Donna Toland, July 15, 1945; children—William Toland, Melinda, Kristen, Thomas Toland, Alfred Lawrence. Reporter, Internat. News Service, Portland, Oreg., 1941-43; reporter The Oregonian, Portland, 1946-48; reporter The Deseret News-Salt Lake Telegram, Salt Lake City, 1948-52, chief editorial writer, editor, 1952-66, exec. editor, 1966-72, editor, gen. mgr., 1972—. Bd. dirs. Utah Symphony, Salt Lake Art Center, Sweetwater, Inc., Am. Council Alcohol Problems, Utah Council Econ. Edn., Utah Endowment for Humanities, Deseret Utah Art Found., Pioneer State Theatre Found. mem. Jud. Council Adv. Com., Downtown Council, South Temple Task Force Com.; mem. nat. adv. bd. Snowbird Summer Arts Inst., Courses by Newspaper. Served to 1st lt., inf. AUS, 1943-46; PTO. Mem. Am. Soc. Newspaper Editors (ethics com.), Am. Newspaper Pubs. Assn., Am. Enterprise Inst. (nat. adv. bd.), Downtown Council, Salt Lake Area C. of C., Phi Beta Kappa, Sigma Delta Chi, Kappa Tau Alpha. Mem. Ch. of Jesus Christ of Latter-day Saints. Clubs: Bonneville Knife and Fork, Timpanogos, Fort Douglas (Hidden Valley), Salt Lake Exchange (past pres., nat. v.p. Rocky Mountain region, nat. bd. dirs.), Aztec, Alta. Home: 55 Laurel St Salt Lake City UT 84103 Office: The Deseret News Box 1257 Salt Lake City UT 84110

SMARTT, CHARLES HINKLEY, librarian; b. McMinnville, Tenn., Aug. 11, 1906; s. Dan Thomas and Myrtle L. (Hinkley) S.; B.A., Bethell Coll., 1929; postgrad. Cumberland Presbyn. Theol. Sem., 1944; M.A., George Peabody Coll., 1960; m. Vista Beulah Perryman, Aug. 26, 1941; children—Judith Ann (Mrs. Larry Freeman Keen), Lela Frances. Ordained to ministry Presbyn. Ch., 1929; pastor Detroit, 1932-35, Overton, Tex., 1935-37, Greenville, Ky., 1937-40, Mt. Pleasant, Utica, Ky., 1944-45, 46-48, Morning Sun, Arlington, Tenn., 1945-46, Fairview, Marshall, Tex., 1948-53, Bowling Green, Ky., 1953-57, Arrington St., Nashville, 1957-58; asst. prof. Greek, Bethel Coll., McKenzie, Tenn., 1940-44; librarian Memphis Theol. Sem. (formerly Cumberland Presbyn. Theol. Sem.), 1958-72; asst. editor Cumberland Presbyn., 1972-77; prin. Snyder Elementary Sch., Owensboro, Ky., 1944-45. Mem. Bd. Fgn. Missions, Cumberland Presbytery, 1938-41, permanent com. on judiciary, 1954-63; trustee Cumberland Presbyn. Sem., 1956-57; asst. moderator 146th Gen. Assembly, Cumberland Presbyn. Ch. Mem. A.L.A., Am. Theol. Library Assn., Memphis Librarians Com., Beta Phi Mu. Democrat. Editor: Steering Wheel, 1951-52; reviser The Cumberland Presbyterian Digest, 1975. Home: 221 N Auburndale St Memphis TN 38112 Office: 168 E Pkwy S Memphis TN 38104

SMATHERS, BRUCE ARMISTEAD, lawyer; b. Miami, Fla., Oct. 3, 1943; s. George Armistead and Rosemary (Towney) S.; B.A. in Econs. with honors, Yale U., 1965; J.D., U. Fla., 1970. Admitted to Fla. bar, 1970; asst. state atty. 4th Jud. Circuit Ct. Fla., 1970-72; mem. Fla. Senate, 1972-74; sec. of state State of Fla., Tallahassee, 1974-79; practice law, 1979—. Active U. North Fla. Found. Served with USNR, 1965-67; Vietnam. Named Outstanding Fla. Jaycee, 1972, One of Outstanding Young Men of Fla., 1976. Mem. Jacksonville C. of C. Home: 5000 San Jose Blvd Jacksonville FL 32207 Office: 3103 Independent Sq Jacksonville FL 32202

SMATHERS, GEORGE A., lawyer, former senator; b. Atlantic City, Nov. 14, 1913; s. Frank and Lura (Jones) S.; A.B., U. Fla., 1937, LL.B., 1938; children—John Townley, Bruce A.; m. 2d, Carolyn Hyder, Jan. 1972. Began practice of law in partnership with Walter Dunigan, 1938; apptd. asst. U.S. dist. atty. in charge Miami office, 1940; firm of Smathers and Thompson, formed, 1939; asst. to atty. gen. for prosecution of war fraud cases, 1946-47; mem. 80th-81st Congresses (1947-51), 4th Fla. Dist.; U.S. senator from Fla., 1951-69; sr. partner Smathers & Thompson, Miami, Fla., 1969—, Smathers, Symington and Herlong, Washington, 1969—. U.S. del. Internat. Tariff Conf., Geneva, 1966, OAS, Buenos Aires, 1967. Served from 1st lt. to maj., USMC, 1942-45. Mem. Am., D.C., Fla., Dade County (v.p.) bar assns. Democrat. Methodist. Clubs: Kiwanis, Elks. Office: Alfred I du Pont Bldg Miami FL 33131 also 1700 17th St NW Washington DC 20006

SMATHERS, JAMES BURTON, engr., educator; b. Prairie du Chien, Wis., Aug. 26, 1935; s. James Levi and Irma Marie (Stindt) S.; B.Nuclear Enging., N.C. State Coll., 1957, M.S., 1959; Ph.D., U. Md., 1967; m. Sylvia Lee Rath, Apr. 20, 1957; children—Kristine Kay, Kathryn Ann, James Scott, Ernest Kent. Research engr. Atomics Internat., Canoga Park, Claif., 1959, Walter Reed Army Inst. Research Washington, 1961-67; prof. nuclear engring. Tex. A. and M. U., College Station, 1967—, prof., head bioengring., 1976—; cons. U.S. Army, also pvt. industry. Served with U.S. Army, 1959-61. Recipient Excellence in Teaching award Gen. Dynamics, 1971; Excellence in Research award Tex. A. and M. U. Former Students Assn., 1976; registered profl. engr., Tex. Mem. Am. Nuclear Soc., Health Physics Soc., Am. Assn. Physcists in Medicine, Am. Soc. Enging. Edn. (Outstanding Tchr. award in nuclear engring. div. 1972), Radiation Research Soc., Nat. Soc. Profl. Engrs., Tex. Soc. Profl. Engrs., Sigma Xi, Sigma Pi Sigma, Phi Kappa Phi. Home: 1402 Glade St College Station TX 77840

SMEAL, ELEANOR CUTRI, orgn. exec.; b. Ashtabula, Ohio, July 30, 1939; d. Peter Anthony and Josephine E. (Agresti) Cutri; B.A., Duke U., 1961; M.A., U. Fla., 1963; m. Charles R. Smeal, Apr. 27, 1963; children—Tod, Lori. Mem. bd. Upper St. Clair (Pa.) chpt. League Women Voters, 1968-72, sec.-treas. Allegheny County Council, 1971-72; mem. NOW, 1971—, convenor, 1st pres. S. Hills (Pa.) chpt., 1971-73, 1st pres., state coordinator Pa., 1972-75, nat. bd. dirs., 1973-75, chairwoman bd., 1975-77, pres., 1977—, mem. bd. Legal Def. and Edn. Fund, 1975—, chairwoman ERA Strike Force, 1977—; mem. 1st nominating com., founding conf. Nat. Women's Polit. Caucus, 1971; bd. dirs. Allegheny County Women's Polit. Caucus, 1971-72; co-founder, bd. dirs. S. Hills NOW Day Nursery Sch., 1972—; mem. Nat. Commn., Observance of Internat. Women's Year, 1977; mem. exec. com. Leadership Conf. on Civil Rights, 1979; mem. Nat. Adv. Com. on Women, 1978. Named One of 25 Most Influential Women in U.S., World Almanac, 1978. Home: 132 Sunridge Dr Pittsburgh PA 15234 Office: 425 13th St NW Suite 1048 Washington DC 20004

SMEAL, FRANK PAUL, investment banker; b. Sykesville, Pa., Aug. 7, 1918; s. Samuel and Mary Smeal; A.B., Pa. State U., 1942; M.B.A., Harvard, 1947; LL.B., N.Y. U., 1951; m. Mary Jean Popp, Aug. 15, 1942; children—Henry Frank, Mary Margaret. With Morgan Guaranty Trust Co., and predecessor, Guaranty Trust Co., N.Y.C., 1947—, asst. treas., 1952-57, asst. v.p., mgr. municipal bond dept., 1957-59, v.p., 1959-65, sr. v.p., 1965-68, exec. v.p., treas. govt. portfolio and bond div., 1968-77; partner Goldman, Sachs & Co., N.Y.C., 1977—; dir. Am. Reins. Co. Exec. com. Greater N.Y. councils Boy Scouts Am. Served to lt. USNR, 1942-45. Mem. Securities Industry Assn. (mem. govt. and fed. agys. securities com.). Clubs: Bond, Harvard (N.Y.C.). Home: 2 Orchard Ln Rumson NJ 07760 Office: Goldman Sachs & Co 55 Broad St New York NY 10004

SMEDA, RALPH, assn. exec.; b. Aduard, Groningen, Netherlands, May 12, 1933; s. Reit Jan and Jantje (Haalstra) S.; A.B., Calvin Coll., 1964; M.A., U. Rochester, 1969, Ed.D., 1972; m. Anne DeHaan, Feb. 18, 1961. Mgr. evaluation research and manpower program devel. Singer Edn. Systems, Rochester, N.Y., 1971-73; mgr. tng., evaluation and research Xerox Internat. Center for Tng. Mgmt. Devel., Leesburg, Va., 1974-75; exec. dir. Am. Bankers Assn., Washington, 1975—. NDEA scholar, 1968-69. Mem. Am. Personnel and Guidance Assn., Soc. for Nat. Program Instrn., Am. Soc. Assn. Execs., Am. Mgmt. Assn., Nat. Assn. for Higher Edn. Patentee game. Office: Am Bankers Assn 1120 Connecticut Ave NW Washington DC 20036. *Success lies within a person and is seldom found outside of the individual. Unless a person is determined to succeed, and totally and committedly so, the chances for success are slim. Determination and persistence are, in my view, the prime ingredients needed to become successful regardless of the undertaking.*

SMEDBERG, WILLIAM RENWICK, IV, naval officer; b. Coronado, Calif., Sept. 13, 1929; s. William Renwick and Claudia Stuart (Barden) S.; B.S., U.S. Naval Acad., 1951; M.S., George Washington U., 1971; m. Ann Evans Parker, June 28, 1957; children—Susan Stuart, William Renwick V. Commd. ensign U.S. Navy, 1951, advanced through grades to rear adm., 1975; comdr. U.S.S. Lawrence County, 1958-59, U.S.S. Bronstein, 1964-65, U.S.S. Berkeley, 1966-67, Destroyer Squadron Ten, 1974-75; asst. chief naval personnel, Washington, 1975-78; comdr. Cruiser Destroyer Group Twelve, 1978—. Decorated Legion of Merit (2), Meritorious Service medal, Navy Commendation medal, others. Mem. Naval. Inst., Naval Acad. Alumni Assn., C. of C. of Jacksonville, Republican. Episcopalian. Club: Meninak (Jacksonville). Home: 212 Moale Ave Mayport FL 32227 Office: COMCRUDESGRU Twelve FPO New York NY 09501

SMEDEGAARD, NORMAN H., lawyer; b. Denver, May 6, 1916; s. G.N. and Metha (Thompson) S.; B.S., U. Colo., 1938, LL.B., 1940, J.D., 1968; m. Rose Marie Hewlett, May 1, 1971; children by previous marriage—Brian, Eric. Admitted to Colo., Calif., U.S. Supreme Ct. bars; pvt. practice, Denver, 1940-42; supr. security clearances Denver ordinance plant E.I. duPont deNemours and Co., Inc., 1941-42; practice in Santa Ana, Calif., 1947—; now sr. partner law firm; gen. counsel Calif. for Western Mobile Home Assn., Christian Rousing, Inc.; dir. Reason Co., Inc.; past chmn. and adv. dir. Bank Am., Anaheim, 1972—. Chmn. Orange County Bar Disciplinary Com., 1964. Chmn. wills and gifts com. Children's Shrine Hosp., 1960—; Orange County chmn. wills and gifts Los Angeles Shrine Hosp. Bd. dirs. Masonic Temple Assn., 1950-58, pres., 1953-58; bd. dirs. Orange County Philharmonic Soc., 1979—. Served with AUS, 1942-45; capt. Res. Recipient Orange County Outstanding Citizen of Day award, 1960. Mem. Am., Colo., Orange County bar assns., State Bar Calif., Santa Ana (Ambassador award 1960), Anaheim (chmn. legislative com. 1972) chambers commerce, Jasmine Creek Home Owners Assn. Clubs: Masons, Shriners (pres. Orange County 1960, sec. 1977); Newport Beach (Calif.); Balboa Bay (gov., vice chmn. 1974) (Indian Wells). Home: 23 Jasmine Creek Dr Corona Del Mar CA 92625 Office: Meredith Financial Centre Tustin CA

SMELSER, NEIL JOSEPH, sociologist; b. Kahoka, Mo., July 22, 1930; s. Joseph Nelson and Susie Marie (Hess) S.; B.A., Harvard U., 1952, Ph.D., 1958; B.A., Magdalen Coll., Oxford (Eng.) U., 1954, M.A., 1959; grad. San Francisco Psychoanalytic Inst., 1971; m. Helen Thelma Margolis, June 10, 1954 (div. 1965); children—Eric Jonathan, Tina Rachel; m. 2d, Sharin Fateley, Dec. 20, 1967; children—Joseph Neil, Sarah Joanne. Mem. faculty U. Calif. at Berkeley, 1958—, prof. sociology, 1962—, asst. chancellor ednl. devel., 1966-68, asso. dir. Inst. Internat. Relations, 1969-73, Univ. prof. sociology, 1972, dir. edn. abroad program for U.K. and Ireland, 1977-79. Bd. dirs. Found. Fund for Research in Psychiatry, 1967-70; bd. dirs. Social Sci. Research Council, 1968-71, chmn., 1971-73. Editor Am. Sociol. Rev., 1962-65; advisory editor Am. Jour. Sociology, 1960-62; mem. com. econ. growth Social Sci. Research Council, 1961-65; chmn. sociology panel Behavioral and Social Scis. survey Nat. Acad. Scis. and Social Sci. Research Council, 1967-69. Rhodes scholar, 1952-54; jr. fellow Soc. Fellows, Harvard U., 1955-58. Mem. Am. (council 1962-65, 67-70, exec. com. 1963-65), Pacific sociol. assns. Author: (with T. Parsons) Economy and Society, 1956; Social Change in the Industrial Revolution, 1959; Theory of Collective Behavior, 1962; The Sociology of Economic Life, 1963, 2d edit., 1975; Essays in Sociological Explanation, 1968; Sociological Theory: A Contemporary View, 1971; Comparative Methods in the Social Sciences, 1976. Editor: (with W.T. Smelser) Personality and Social Systems, 1963, 2d edit., 1971; (with S.M. Lipset) Social Structure and Mobility in Economic Development, 1966; Sociology, 1967, 2d edit., 1973; (with James Davis) Sociology, a Survey Report, 1969; Karl Marx on Society and Social Change, 1973; (with Gabriel Almond) Public Higher Education in California, 1974; Comparative Methods in the Social Sciences, 1976; (with Robin Content) The Changing Academic Market, 1980. Home: 8 Mosswood Rd Berkeley CA 94704

SMELT, RONALD, aircraft co. exec.; b. Houghtonle-Spring, Durham, Eng., Dec. 4, 1913; s. Henry Wilson and Florence (Bradburn) S.; B.A., King's Coll., Cambridge (Eng.) U., 1935, M.A., 1939; Ph.D., Stanford, 1961; m. Marie Anita Collings, Nov. 2, 1940 (dec. May 1964); 1 son, David; m. 2d, Jean Stuart, Jan. 15, 1965. Came to U.S., 1948, naturalized, 1955. With Royal Aircraft Establishment, 1935-48, chief high speed flight, 1940-45, chief guided weapons dept., 1945-48; dep. chief aeroballistic research dept. USN Ordnance Lab., 1948-50; chief gas dynamics facility ARO, Inc., Tullahoma, Tenn., 1950-57; dir. research and devel. Lockheed Aircraft Corp., missile systems div., Sunnyvale, Calif., 1958-59, mgr. Discoverer Satellite system, 1959-60, chief scientist, 1960-62, v.p., gen. mgr. space programs div., 1962-63, v.p., chief scientist, 1963—. Mem. com. on space vehicle aerodynamics NASA, 1965-66, chmn. research adv. com. on space vehicles, 1966-73, chmn. research and tech. adv. council, 1973-77; chmn. tech. adv. bd. Dept. Transp., 1970-74. Fellow Cambridge Philos. Soc., Royal Aero. Soc. (London), Am. Astronautical Soc., Am. Inst. Aeros. and Astronautics (dir.-at-large 1966-68, pres. 1969, 70); mem. Nat. Acad. Engring., Internat. Acad. Astronautics (corr.). Home: Gamecock Canyon Ranch PO Box 782 Watsonville CA 95076 Office: PO Box 551 Burbank CA 91520

SMELTZER, NORMAN HAROLD, finance co. exec.; b. Bellefonte, Pa., Mar. 6, 1907; s. William C. and Sally (Garbrick) S.; B.S., Lehigh U., 1927; m. Ruth E. Shepherd, Oct. 10, 1931; 1 son, William S. Bus. tng. student Gen. Electric Co., Schenectady, 1927-33; accountant Gen. Electric Credit Corp., N.Y.C., 1933-35, asst. treas., 1935-43, treas., 1943-45, sec.-treas., 1945-56, v.p., 1956-60, v.p., gen. mgr. consumer financing dept., 1960-72; dir., exec. v.p. Homemakers Loan and Consumer Discount Corp., 1967-72; dir., chmn. bd. Gen. Electric Credit Corp. Ga., 1969-72; dir., chmn. bd., pres. Gen. Electric Credit Corp. P.R.; v.p. GECC Leasing Corp.; sec.-treas., dir. Boom Inc., 1974—, I-PLi, Inc., 1974— Precision Panel Products Inc., 1977—; dir. Manhattan Fire and Marine Ins. Co., 1970—, Universal Mobile Services Corp., 1972-73. Chmn., Fairfield County chpt. SCORE; bd. dirs. Stamford Girls' Club, 1976—, Wild Assos., 1976—, Vis. Nursing Assn.; mem. Scarsdale (N.Y.) Bd. Edn., 1958-65, pres., 1963; village trustee, Scarsdale, 1945-47. Mem. Am. Mgmt. Assn. (pres.'s council), Phi Beta Kappa. Presbyn. (elder). Clubs: Scarsdale (N.Y.) Golf, Silvermine Golf, Men's Garden of Fairfield County (dir., treas.). Home: 339 Indian Rock Rd New Canaan CT 06840

SMERLING, JULIAN MELVIN, investment co. exec.; b. N.Y.C., July 27, 1928; s. Louis and Eva (Singer) S.; B.B.A., Coll. City N.Y., 1949; m. Barbara Albert, Sept. 8, 1962; 1 dau., Fern Iris. With various C.P.A. firms, N.Y.C., 1949-57; v.p. Dreyfus Corp., N.Y.C., 1958-75, sr. v.p., 1975—; v.p., dir. Dreyfus Service Corp., other subsidiaries. Bd. dirs., sec. Dreyfus Med. Found., 1965-77. C.P.A., N.Y. Mem. Am. Inst. C.P.A.'s, N.Y. State Soc. C.P.A.'s. Home: 84 Lotus Oval South Valley Stream NY 11581 Office: 767 Fifth Ave New York City NY 10022

SMETHURST, ROBERT GUY, lawyer; b. Calgary, Alta., Can., May 28, 1929; s. Herbert Guy and Muriel (Wilson) S.; student U. B.C., 1946-47; LL.B., U. Man., 1952; children—Linda Anne, David Guy. Called to Man. bar, 1953, created Queen's counsel, 1968; practice in Winnipeg, 1954—; partner firm D'Arcy and Deacon (formerly D'Arcy, Irving, Haig & Smethurst), 1965—; commr. Uniform Law Conf., 1964—, pres., 1978—; counsel Man. Pub. Utility Bd., 1968-69. Mem. Man. Law Reform Com.; pres. Victorian Order Nurses Can., 1976—. Mem. Canadian (pres. Man. br. 1971-73), Man. (pres. 1969-70) bar assns., Phi Delta Theta. Mem. Progressive Conservative Party. Home: 308 Lamont Blvd Winnipeg MB R3P 0G1 Canada Office: 300 286 Smith St Winnipeg MB Canada

SMIDDY, JOSEPH CHARLES, coll. chancellor; b. Jellico, Tenn., June 20, 1920; s. Joseph F. and Sara Nan (Tye) S.; B.A., Lincoln Meml. U., 1948, L.H.D., 1970; M.A., Peabody Coll., 1952; LL.D., U. Richmond, 1975; m. Rosebud Stickley, Dec. 13, 1941; children—Joseph F., Elizabeth Lee. Tchr., Jonesville High Sch., 1948-51, prin., 1951-52; sec.-treas. Powell Valley Oil Co., Big Stone Gap, Va., 1952-53; prof. biology Clinch Valley Coll., U. Va., Wise, 1953-56, dean, 1956-57, dir., 1957-68, chancellor, 1968—. Dir., Wise County Nat. Bank. Bd. dirs. Wise Clinic. Served with AUS, 1942-45; PTO. Named Outstanding Citizen of Wise County, 1970. Mem. Baptist Gen. Assn. Va. (pres. 1974—), Phi Delta Kappa. Clubs: Masons, Shriners, Kiwanis. Folk music performer, collector and composer. Home: Ridgefield Acres Wise VA 24293 Office: Clinch Valley College Wise VA 24293

SMIDT, SEYMOUR, educator; b. Chgo., Nov. 2, 1928; s. Joseph and Harriet (Morrison) S.; A.B., U. Chgo., 1948, M.A., 1952, Ph.D., 1954; m. Rita Barbara Liss, Jan. 28, 1951; children—Tamar Rachelle, Stanley Adam. Asst. prof. econs. and fin. Cornell U. Grad. Sch. Bus. and Public Adminstrn., Ithaca, N.Y., 1956-59, asso. prof., 1959-65, prof., 1965-78, Nicholas H. Noyes prof., 1978—; asso. dir. Instl. Investor Study, SEC, 1969-70. Mayor, Village of Lansing (N.Y.), 1975—. Served with U.S. Army, 1954-56. Mem. Am. Econ. Assn., Am. Fin. Assn., Fin. Mgmt. Assn., Fin. Mgmt. Assn., AAUP. Author: (with Harold Bierman, Jr.) The Capital Budgeting Decision, 1960, 66, 71, 75; (with others) Management Decision-Making Under Uncertainty, 1969; contbr. articles to profl. jours. Home: 120 Oakcrest Rd Ithaca NY 14850 Office: Cornell U Malott Hall Ithaca NY 14853

SMIGHT, JOHN RONALD, film dir., producer; b. Mpls.; s. Harold Alexander and Beatrice Mary (Feeney) S.; B.A., U. Minn., 1949; m. Joyce Catherine Cunning, Aug. 18, 1950; children—Timothy John, Alexander Dow. Stage mgr. NBC, Los Angeles, 1950-53, asst. dir., 1953-54, dir., 1954-55; film dir., writer, producer films, TV shows including: Harper-Kaleidoscope, 1966, No Way to Treat A Lady, 1967, The Illustrated Man, 1969, The Travelling Executioner, 1971, Airport '75, 1971, Midway, 1975, Frankenstein, The True Story, 1974, Fast Break, 1978. Served to lt. USAF. Decorated Air medal with 4 oak leaf clusters. Mem. Dirs. Guild Am. Democrat. Office: 9200 Sunset Blvd Penthouse 25 Los Angeles CA 90069

SMILEY, CHARLES JACK, educator; b. Mt. Vernon, Wash., Dec. 2, 1924; s. Charley and Julia Carolina (Watson) S.; B.A. Western Wash. State Coll., 1951; M.A., U. Calif. at Berkeley, 1954, NSF fellow, 1954-55, Ph.D., 1960; postgrad. (fellow) Harvard, 1961-62; m. Marguerite Anna Clayton, Aug. 24, 1954; children—John Clayton, Sharifah. Asst. prof. geology Macalester Coll., St. Paul, 1956-61; asst. prof. U. Idaho, Moscow, 1962-65, asso. prof., 1965-67, prof., 1967—, asso. dean Coll. Mines, 1976—; vis. Fulbright prof. U. Malaya, Kuala Lumpur, 1968-69; investigator Artic Inst. N.Am., No. Alaska, 1956-67; NSF vis. scientist, Japan, 1973. Judge sci. fairs, 1956—. Served with USNR, 1943-47, 51-52. Mem. Am. Assn. Petroleum Geology, Paleontol. Soc., Internat. Paleontol. Union, Sigma Xi, Phi Kappa Phi, Phi Sigma. Author: The Ellensburg Flora of Washington, Tertiary, 1963; Later Mesozoic Flora of Maran Pahang, West Malaysia, 1970. Contbr. articles to profl. jours. Research in fossil plants. Home: Route 4 Box 381 Moscow ID 83843

SMILEY, DONALD BURDETTE, retailing exec., lawyer; b. Albany, Ill., Apr. 6, 1915; s. Ralph and Etta (Stafford) S.; B.A., Augustana Coll., 1936; J.D., Northwestern U., 1940; m. Dick Cutter, Apr. 10, 1942; children—Margot (Mrs. A.P. Humphrey), Sandra (Mrs. G.B. Weiksner, Jr.), Stafford, Daryl. Admitted to N.Y. bar, 1940, U.S. Supreme Ct. bar, 1945; asso. Breed, Abbott & Morgan, N.Y.C., 1940-42; with R.H. Macy & Co., Inc., N.Y.C., 1945—, became sec. and gen. atty., 1953, v.p., treas., dir., 1956-64, exec. v.p., treas., 1964-66, vice chmn., treas., 1966-68, chmn., treas., 1968-71, chmn. bd., chief exec. officer, 1971—; dir. Ralston Purina Co., RCA Corp., NBC, Met. Life Ins. Co., Fidelity Union Bancorp., U.S. Steel Corp., Charter N.Y. Corp., Irving Trust Co., Garden State Plaza, Macy's Banks, Texasgulf, Inc. Trustee Met. Mus. Art. Served as lt. USNR, World War II. Mem. Bar Assn. City N.Y., Fgn. Policy Assn. (dir.), N.Y. State Bar Assn., Am. Arbitration Assn., Nat. Retail Mcts. Assn. Order of Coif. Clubs: Union League, University (N.Y.C.); Round Hill, Indian Harbor Yacht (Greenwich, Conn.); Blind Brook (Port Chester, N.Y.). Home: 1 Putnam Hill Greenwich CT 06830 Office: 151 W 34th St New York NY 10001

SMILEY, FLOYD FRANKLIN, JR., foods co. exec.; b. Caribou, Maine, Apr. 27, 1924; s. Floyd Franklin and Geraldine (Hallett) S.; B.A., Bates Coll., 1948; postgrad. U. Maine, U. Rochester, 1950-55; m. Gloria Redman, June 12, 1945; children—Scott Thomas, Alison Smiley Rukeyser. Group mktg. mgr. R.T. French Co., Rochester, N.Y., 1957-64; v.p. Carnation Co., Los Angeles, 1964-70; group v.p. Borden Foods, Columbus, Ohio, 1970-74; pres., chief exec. officer Banquet Foods div. RCA, St. Louis, 1974—, also dir.; dir. Whitworth Mills, Western Fruit Packers, Frozen Food Action Communication Team. Served with USNR, 1941-45. Mem. Nat. Frozen Food Assn., Am. Frozen Food Inst. (dir.), Chefs de Cuisine Assn. St. Louis. Club: Westborough Country. Home: 720 Twin Fawns Dr Saint Louis MO 63131 Office: 100 N Broadway Saint Louis MO 63102

SMILEY, JOSEPH ROYALL, educator; b. Dallas, Mar. 17, 1910; s. S. Lehman and Mabel (Royall) S.; A.B., So. Meth. U., 1931, A.M., 1932, LL.D., 1964; Ph.D. Columbia, 1947; LL.D., U. Denver, 1966; m. Mary Fincher, May 25, 1935; children—Stephen, Mary. Instr. Ark. A. & M. Coll., Magnolia, 1934-35; instr., asst. prof., asso. prof. North Tex. State Coll., Denton, 1935-38, 40-43, 46-47; lectr. Columbia, 1938-40; asst. prof. U. Ill., 1947-49, asst. dean grad. coll., 1949-50, asso. dean, 1950-51, prof. French, 1951-58, head dept., 1952-54, dean coll. liberal arts and scis., 1954-58; pres. Tex. Western Coll., U. Tex., 1958-60; v.p., provost U. Tex., Austin, 1960-61, pres., 1961-63; pres. U. Colo., Boulder, 1963-69; pres. U. Tex., El Paso, 1969-73, pres. emeritus, H.Y. Benedict prof. modern langs., 1973—. Vis. prof. U. Colo., 1974. Mem. bd. advisers Mountain States Telephone; dir. El Paso Electric Co. Commr. Western Interstate Commn. on Higher Edn., 1963- 67, exec. com., 1965-67; chmn. U.S. Adv. Commn. on Internat. Ednl. and Cultural Affairs, 1966-69; mem. Govt. Adv. Com. Internat. Book Programs, 1966-68; chmn. Boulder Housing Authority, 1966-68; mem. adv. com. for instl. relations NSF, 1967-69. Mem. bd. Asso. Rocky Mountain Univs., 1963, sec.-treas., 1965-66, vice chmn., 1966-67. Fulbright research fellow, France, 1953-54; mem. President's Commn. on White House Fellows. Bd. dirs. East-West Center, Honolulu, 1966-69; bd. visitors Air U., 1968-71. Served as lt. USNR, 1943-46. Decorated chevalier Legion of Honor (France). Mem. Phi Kappa Phi, Kappa Alpha, Phi Beta Kappa. Episcopalian. Author: Diderot's Relations with Grimm, 1950. Bd. editors Tex. Western Press, 1973—. Contbr. articles to profl. jours. Address: 5713 Burning Tree El Paso TX 79912

SMILEY, MALCOLM FINLAY, educator; b. Monmouth, Ill., Dec. 15, 1912; s. Robert Rennsalear and Annie Laurie (Kerr) S.; B.S., U. Chgo., 1934, M.S., 1935, Ph.D., 1937; m. Dorothy Manning, Aug. 20, 1941. Mem. Inst. Advanced Study, 1937-38; instr. Lehigh U., 1938-40, asst. prof., 1940-42, asso. prof., 1946; vis. instr. U. Chgo., 1939, vis. asst. prof., 1941; instr. U.S. Naval Postgrad. Sch., 1942-46; asso. prof. Northwestern U., 1946-48; prof. State U. Iowa, 1948-60; prof. U. Calif., Riverside, 1960-67, chmn. dept. math., 1962-63; prof. state U. N.Y., Albany, 1967—, asso. dean div. scis. and math., 1972-73. Hon. research asso. in math. Harvard, 1975. Served from lt. (j.g.) to lt. comdr., USNR, 1942-46. Fellow Fund Advancement of Edn., 1954-55. Mem. Am. Math. Soc., Math. Assn. Am., Phi Beta Kappa, Sigma Xi. Home: 42 W Bayberry Rd Glenmount NY 12077 Office: Dept Math State U NY at Albany 1400 Washington Ave Albany NY 12222

SMILEY, PRIL, composer, ednl. adminstr.; b. Mohonk Lake, N.Y., Mar. 19, 1943; d. Daniel and Alice (Plumlee) S.; B.A. in Music, Bennington Coll., 1965. Resident composer Columbia-Princeton Electronic Music Center, N.Y.C., 1963—, instr., 1965—, asso. dir., 1974—; dir. Composers Recs. Inc., sec., 1977—; cons. in electronic music Lincoln Center Repertory Theatre, N.Y.C., 1968-74. Bd. dirs. Smiley Bros. Inc. of Mohonk Mountain House; trustee Smiley Bros. Trust. Nat. Endowment for Arts grantee, 1974; Guggenheim fellow, 1975—. Mem. Am. Composers Alliance. Quaker. Composer: Eclipse, electronic composition, 1968 (winner First Internat. Electronic Music Contest 1968); film score for Trip, 1974 (first finalist Currents First Internat. Contest for Electronic Music and Film 1974). Composer over 40 music scores for theatre prodns., films, dance and free-style skiing ballet. Home: 7 Pine Rd New Paltz NY 12561

SMILEY, ROBERT W., JR., fin. cons. co. exec.; b. Lansing, Mich., Nov. 17, 1943; s. Robert William and Rebecca Lee (Flint) S.; B.A. in Econs., Stanford, 1970; postgrad. Coll. Law U. San Fernando Valley, 1973-75; M.B.A., City U. Los Angeles, 1979. Sr. v.p. mktg. Actuarial Systems, Inc., San Jose, Calif., 1972-73; founder, chmn. Benefit Systems, Inc., Los Angeles, 1973—; lectr. in field; instr. Am. Coll. Life Underwriters; founder, pres., bd. dirs. Employee Stock Ownership Plan Council Am. Served with USN, 1961-64. Fellow Life Mgmt. Inst; mem. Am. Soc. C.L.U.'s, Western, S.W. (charter) pension confs., Am. Soc. Pension Actuaries (asso.). Home: 327 S Carmelina Ave Los Angeles CA 90049 Office: 11661 San Vicente Blvd Los Angeles CA 90049

SMILEY, ROBERT WILLIAM, indsl. engr.; b. Phila., Oct. 18, 1919; s. Albert James and Laura Emma (Hoiler) S.; certificate in Indsl. Engring., Gen. Motors Inst., 1942; student U. Rochester, 1948, mgmt. program for execs. U. Pitts. Grad. Sch. Bus., 1968, San Jose State Coll., 1969; B.S. in Bus. Adminstrn., Coll. Notre Dame, Belmont, Calif., 1972, M.B.A., 1974; m. Barbara Joan New, Oct. 18, 1977; children—Robert, James, Lauralee, Mary; stepchildren—Deborah, Sheila, Vicki, Judy, Sonja. With A.S. Hamilton, cons. engrs., Rochester, N.Y., 1946-48; commd. lt. USN, 1952, advanced through grades to comdr., 1960; engaged in tech. contract mgmt. Poseidon/Polaris and Terrier Missile Programs, 1952-64; officer in charge Polaris Missile Facility Pacific, Bremerton, Wash., 1964-66; resigned, 1966; mgr. product assurance Missile Systems div. Lockheed Missiles and Space Co., Sunnyvale, Calif., 1966-72, mgr. materiel, 1972-77; mgr. product assurance McDonnell Douglas Astronautics, 1977-78, dir. product assurance Aerojet Tactical Systems, Sacramento, 1978—; frequent guest lectr. at colls. on quality control and reliability; chmn. Polaris/Minuteman/Pershing Missile Nondestruct Test Com., 1958-64; quality control cons. Dragon Missile Program, U.S. Army, 1971. Served with USNR, 1942-46, 51-52; now capt. Res. Recipient letters of Commendation for work on Polaris/Poseidon Sec. of Navy, 1960, certificate of Honor, Soc. for Nondestructive Testing, 1966. Registered profl. engr., Calif. Fellow Am. Soc. Quality Control (chmn. San Francisco sect. 1969-70, exec. bd. 1966—, chmn. reliability div. 1971); mem. Am. Ordnance Assn., Navy League, AAAS, Am. Mgmt. Assn. Contbr. articles to sci. jours., chpt. to Reliability Handbook, 1966. Home: 9144 Green Ravine Ln Fair Oaks CA 95628 Office: PO Box 13400 Sacramento CA 95813. *A man can consider himself successful only if he leaves the world better than he found it partly through his efforts.*

SMILEY, SAUL CHARLES, architect, archtl. and engring. firm exec.; b. Mpls., Feb. 5, 1918; s. Paul and Sarah (Braman) S.; B.Arch., U. Minn., 1942; m. Maxine Goldie, Apr. 16, 1943; children—Leslie (Mrs. Robert Melamed), Linda Sue (Mrs. Dan Burke), Lisa Francis. Asso. archtl. firms, Minn., 1946-50; pres. S.C. Smiley & Assos., Mpls., 1950-72; pres. Smiley Glotter Assos., Mpls., 1972—. Mem. Metro 85 Com. for Devel. Core City, Mpls., 1972—; mem. Gov. Minn. Com. for Mental Health, 1970—; mem. Mayor Mpls. Commn. for Mpls. Work House, 1968-72. Served to lt. USNR, 1943-46; PTO. Recipient Meritorious Service award Mpls. Fedn. Jewish Service, 1965, First Nat. Instl. award in energy conservation Owens Corning Fiber-Glass Co., 1972, Hosp. award Modern Hosp. Mag., 1969, 71. Registered architect, Man. (Can.), Minn., Iowa, Wis., Tex., N.D., Mich., Pa., Ohio, Mo. Fellow AIA (pres. chpt. 1964-65, minute men program 1967); mem. Minn. Soc. Architects (dir., pres. 1966-73, regional dir. 1976—), Royal Archtl. Inst. Can., Am. Hosp. Assn., Am. Assn. Hosp. Planners, Mpls. C. of C. Jewish (Men's Club). Mem. B'nai B'rith. Clubs: Minneapolis, Oak Ridge Country. Designer: Harrison Elementary Sch., Mpls., 1960; Evans Reiley Clinic, Mpls., 1962; St. Cloud Coll. Learning Resource Center, 1969; VA Restorative Facility, St. Cloud, 1970; Mercy Hosp., Cedar Rapids, Minn., 1972; St. Louis Park (Minn.) Recreation Center, 1973; Hennepin County (Minn.) Med. Center, Mpls., 1975; Unity Hosp., Fridley, Minn., 1971, U. Minn. Basic Scis. Bldg., Duluth, 1975, Duluth Med. Sch., Watertown (Wis.) Med. Center, 1970. Home: 9700 Oak Ridge Trail Minnetonka MN 55343 Office: 1021 LaSalle St Minneapolis MN 55403

SMILEY, TERAH LEROY, educator; b. Oak Hill, Kans., Aug. 21, 1914; s. Terah Edward and Frances Angelina (Huls) S.; student U. Kans., 1934-36; M.A., U. Ariz., 1949; m. Marie Lemley, July 1935; 1 dau., Terrie Lucille Scheele; m. 2d, Winifred Whiting Lindsay, June 10, 1947; children—John, Maureen, Kathlyn; 1 stepdau., Margaret Ann Taylor. With U.S. Nat. Park Service, 1939-41, U.S. Immigration Service, 1941-42; research Lab. of Tree-Ring, U. Ariz., Tucson, 1946-60, dir., 1958-60, dir. geochronology labs., 1957-67, head dept. geochronology, 1967-70, prof. geosciences, 1970—. Gen. chmn. Internat. Conf. on Forest Tree Growth, Tucson, 1960; vice chmn. U.S. Com. on Internat. Assn. for Quaternary Research, Nat. Acad. Sci., 1961-66; gen. chmn. First Internat. Conf. on Palynology, Tucson, 1962; mem. U.S. Com. on Internat. Hydrological Decade, Nat. Acad. Sci., 1964-66; gen. chmn. Internat. Conf. on Arid Lands, Tucson, 1969. Served with USNR, 1942-45. Research fellow Clare Coll., Cambridge, U., 1970; vis. prof. Kvartärgeologiska Institutionen, Uppsala (Sweden) U., 1970-71; hon. v.p. 2d Internat. Conf. on Palynology, Utretch, 1966. Fellow Geol. Soc. Am., A.A.A.S., Am. Anthrop. Soc., Ariz. Acad. Sci.; mem. Am. Geophys. Union, Am. Assn. Stratigraphical Palynologists, Ecol. Soc. Am., Am. Meteorol. Soc., Soc. Am. Archeology, Tree-Ring Soc., N.Y. Acad. Scis., Ariz.

Geol. Soc. (past pres.), Ariz. Archeol. Soc. (past pres.), Sigma Xi. Editor: (with James H. Zumberge) Polar Deserts and Modern Man, 1974. Contbr. articles to profl. jours. Home: 2732 N Gill Ave Tucson AZ 85719

SMISEK, JOSEPH THOMAS, union ofcl.; b. New Prague, Minn., Dec. 21, 1918; s. Joseph Martin and Anna S.; student in voice McPhail Sch. Music, 1938-41, 62-64, in labor and econs. U. Minn., 1948-50; m. Nov. 20, 1943; children—Joseph, Thomas, Quentin, Karen. Owner, operator service sta., New Prague, 1939-67; with Internat. Multifoods Co., New Prague, 1939-67, stock control, 1946-50, prodn. coordinator, 1950-67; pres., bus. agt. Local 55, Am. Fedn. Grain Millers, New Prague, 1947-67, v.p. Am. Fedn. Grain Millers, Mpls., 1967-77, gen. sec.-treas., 1977—; mem. exec. bd. food and beverage dept. AFL-CIO; mem. joint adminstrv. pension bd. Am. Fedn. Grain Millers and Gen. Mills, Internat. Multifoods Co., Peavey Co., Pillsbury Co., Archer-Daniels-Midland Co., ConAgra Co.; sec., trustee Am. Fedn. Grain Millers Industry Wide Employees Pension Program. Coordinator communications CD, New Prague, 1952-62; mem. New Prague Mcpl. Planning Commn., 1952-62; mem. choir St. Paul Roman Catholic Cathedral. Served with Q.M.C., U.S. Army, 1942-46. Mem. Am. Radio Relay League (Public Service award 1956, 73, 75), Catholic Workmen, Twin City Schola Contorum. Democrat. Home: 16003 Birch Ln Minnetonka MN 55343 Office: 4949 Olson Memorial Hwy Minneapolis MN 55422

SMISZKO, STEPHAN E., airlines exec.; b. 1929; B.B.A., Pace Coll., 1964; postgrad. N.Y. U. Grad. Sch. Bus., 1964-67; m. With Eastern Air Lines, Inc., 1951—, dir. tax adminstrn., 1961-65, dir.-treas. adminstrn., 1965-67, asst. treas., 1967-68, treas., 1968—, v.p., 1970-75, v.p.-fin., 1975-77; v.p., treas. Western Union Corp., holding co., also Western Union Telegraph Co. subs., 1977—. Office: One Lake St Upper Saddle River NJ 07458

SMIT, JACOBUS WILHELMUS, educator; b. Utrecht, Netherlands, Aug. 25, 1930; s. Johan and Gijsbertha (Willemse) S.; B.A., Utrecht U., 1953, Ph.D., 1958; m. Pamela Spence Richards, June 2, 1969; children—Guy, Marijke; children by previous marriage—Valentijn, Michiel. Co-dir. Hist. Inst., Utrecht, 1960-65; Queen Wilhelmina prof. history, lang. and lit. of Low Countries, Columbia U., N.Y.C., 1965—; cons. State U. N.Y., Old Westbury, L.I., N.Y., 1970—. Am. Council Learned Socs. fellow, 1971-72. Mem. Nederlands Historisch Genootschap, Am. Hist. Assn., Société Paul-Louis Courier. Mem. Dutch Socialist party. Author: Fruin en de partijen tijdens de Republiek, 1958; contbg. author: Britain and the Netherlands, I, 1960; Britain and the Netherlands, III, 1968; Early Modern Revolution, 1970. Editor: Brandt's History of the Reformation in The Netherlands, 1979. Home: 90 Morningside Dr New York NY 10027

SMITH, A. ANTHES, banker; b. Fort Madison, Iowa, Nov. 17, 1920; s. Clarence W. and Marie (Anthes) S.; B.S. in Commerce, U. Iowa, 1942; M.B.A., Harvard, 1947; m. Bette Lee Rhea, Nov. 17, 1943; children—Stephanie M., A. Jeffrey. Vice pres. Anthes Force Oiler Co., Fort Madison, 1949-56, pres., 1956-60; v.p. domestic operations W.A. Sheaffer Pen Co., Fort Madison, 1961-63, exec. v.p., 1964-67; now pres. Fort Madison Bank & Trust Co. Chmn., Fort Madison Indsl. Devel. Com., 1948-55; city chmn. Iowa Coll. Found., 1963-78. Served to capt. AUS, 1942-46; PTO. Mem. Ft. Madison C. of C. (bd. dirs. 1948-57), Iowa Mfrs. Assn. (v.p. 1960-67), U. Iowa Alumni Assn. (dir. 1955-61), Phi Gamma Delta (pres. Mu Deuteron Alumni assn. 1950-60, mem. bd. chpt. advisers 1964—, archon, internat. councilor 1978—). Presbyn. (deacon, trustee, elder). Mason, Rotarian. Home: 926 Denmark Hill Dr Fort Madison IA 52627 Office: Fort Madison Bank & Trust Co Fort Madison IA 52627

SMITH, A. ROBERT, newspaper columnist, editor, author; b. York, Pa., Feb. 13, 1925; s. Arthur R. and Inez (Dunnick) S.; B.S., Juniata Coll., 1950; postgrad. George Washington U., 1950; m. Elizabeth McDowell Morgan, May 28, 1967; children—Dana C., Philip S. Morgan IV, Edward A. M. Morgan, Elizabeth A. Morgan. Reporter, Huntingdon (Pa.) Daily News, 1947, Evening Star, Washington, 1950, Bremerton (Wash.) Sun, 1950; Washington corr. Eugene (Oreg.) Register-Guard, 1951-78; Portland Oregonian, 1953-72; asso. editor Virginian-Pilot, Norfolk, Va., 1978—. Served with USNR, 1943-46; PTO. Mem. Nat. Press Club, Assn. for Research and Enlightenment. Author: The Tiger in the Senate, 1962; (with Eric Sevareid and Fred J. Maroon) Washington: Magnificent Capital, 1965; (with others) The Press in Washington, 1966; (with James V. Giles) An American Rape, 1975. Address: 933 Bobolink Dr Virginia Beach VA 23451

SMITH, ADA BEATRICE QUEEN VICTORIA LOUISA VIRGINIA (BRICKTOP), performing artist; b. Alderson, W.Va., Aug. 14, 1894; d. Thomas Milton and Harriet Elizabeth (Thompson) Smith; D.Arts, Columbia, 1975; m. Peter Du Conge, Dec. 29, 1929. Dancer, singer throughout U.S.A., 1910-24; singer, dancer in Paris Clubs, 1924-26; owner, mgr., singer/hostess Chez Bricktop, Paris, 1926-39, Mexico City, 1944-49, Bricktops, Rome, Italy, 1949-62. Recipient scroll Du Sable Mus. African Am. History, Chgo., 1975. Home: New York NY 10023*

SMITH, ADAM. see Goodman, George Jerome Waldo

SMITH, AGNES (MRS. RICHARD BRUCE PARRISH), author; b. Clarksburg, W.Va.; d. Lewis Oscar and Sarah (Boggess) Smith; grad. Acad. St. Joseph, Brentwood, L.I., N.Y.; B.S., Fairmont State Coll., W.Va.; m. Richard Bruce Parrish. Recipient Spring Book Festival award N.Y. Herald Tribune, 1959. Author: An Edge of the Forest, 1959, 74 (Aurianne award ALA 1961); The Bluegreen Tree, 1977; Speaking as a Writer, 1979. Home: Westwind Farm Route 1 Box 208 Farmington WV 26571

SMITH, ALBERT BARNES, JR., univ. pres.; b. Pitts., Apr. 21, 1915; s. Albert Barnes and Valeria (Fetterman) S.; B.B.A., Westminster Coll., 1937; M.Litt., U. Pitts., 1938; Pd.D., Westminster Coll., 1956; m. Lucile Nevin, June 22, 1940; children—Albert Barnes III, Sandra Lucile, Deborah Ann. With U. Pitts., 1938—, beginning as research asst. Sch. Retailing, successively sr. fellow research, asst. prof. retailing, asso. prof., asst. dir., 1938-53, prof. retailing, 1951-61, dean Grad. Sch. Retailing, 1953-61, dir. devel., 1959-62, prof. bus. adminstrn., 1961—, asso. dean grad. sch. bus., 1961-63, asst. to chancellor, 1962-63; pres. U. Pitts. at Greensburg, 1963—. Past bd. dirs. WQED. Served as lt. (j.g.), Supply Corps, USNR, 1944-46. Mem. Alpha Sigma Pi, Eta Mu Pi. Presbyn. (elder). Rotarian. Home: 970 Bridge Ave Greensburg PA 15601

SMITH, ALBERT CHARLES, biologist; b. Springfield, Mass., Apr. 5, 1906; s. Henry Joseph and Jeanette Rose (Machol) S.; A.B., Columbia, 1926, Ph.D., 1933; m. Nina Grönstrand, June 15, 1935; children—Katherine (Mrs. L.J. Campbell), Michael Alexis; m. 2d, Emma van Ginneken, Aug. 1, 1966. Asst. curator N.Y. Bot. Garden, 1928-31, asso. curator, 1931-40; curator herbarium Arnold Arboretum of Harvard U., 1940-48; curator div. phanerogams U.S. Nat. Mus., Smithsonian Instn., 1948-56; program dir. systematic biology NSF, 1956-58; dir. Mus. of Natural History, Smithsonian Instn., 1958-62, asst. sec., 1962-63; prof. botany, dir. research U. Hawaii, Honolulu, 1963-65, Gerrit Parmile Wilder prof. botany, 1965-70, prof. emeritus, 1970—; Ray Ethan Torrey prof. botany U. Mass., Amherst, 1970-76, prof. emeritus, 1976—; editorial cons. Pacific Tropical Bot. Garden, Hawaii, 1977—; bot. expdns., Colombia, Peru, Brazil, Brit. Guiana, Fiji, West Indies, 1926-69; del. Internat. Bot. Congresses, Amsterdam, 1935, Stockholm, 1950 (v.p. systematic sect.), Montreal, 1959, Internat. Zool. Congress, London, 1958. Bishop Museum fellow Yale U., 1933-34, Guggenheim fellow, 1946-47; Robert Allerton award for excellence in tropical botany, 1979. Fellow Am. Acad. Arts and Scis., Linnean Soc. London; mem. Bot. Soc. Am., Assn. Tropical Biology (pres. 1967-68), Internat. Assn. Plant Taxonomy (v.p. 1959-64), Nat. Acad. Scis., Fiji Soc. (hon.). Club: Washington Biologists' Field (pres. 1962-64). Author: Flora Vitiensis Nova: a New Flora of Fiji, Vol. I, 1979; also tech. articles. Editor: Brittonia, 1935-40, Jour. Arnold Arboretum, 1941-48, Sargentia, 1942-48, Allertonia, 1977—, editorial com. International Code Botanical Nomenclature, 1954-64. Office: Dept of Botany Univ of Hawaii Honolulu HI 96822

SMITH, ALBIN WILLIAM, corp. exec.; b. Paterson, N.J., Feb. 3, 1923; s. Albin M. and Aleaze F. S.; B.A., Kenyon Coll., 1950; B.S., U.S. Merchant Marine Acad., 1944; m. Joan V. Smith, Dec. 22, 1948; children—Jim, Mary, Susan. Vice-pres. Oils Inc., N.Y.C., 1951-53; salesman Shell Oil Co., N.Y.C., 1953-56; asst. mgr. internat. dept. Phillips Petroleum Co., N.Y.C., 1956-66; sr. v.p., dir. Shaheen Nat. Research Co., N.Y.C., 1966-76; sr. v.p. refining Coastal States Gas Corp., Houston, 1976—. Mem. adv. bd. U.S. Mcht. Marine Acad., 1970-73. Served to lt. comdr. USNR, 1944-46. Mem. Nat. Petroleum Refiner Assn. (dir.), Am. Mgmt. Assn. Republican. Clubs: Pine Forest Country Houston City (Houston); Met. (N.Y.C.). Home: 831 Thornvine Houston TX 77079 Office: 9 Greenway Pl Houston TX 77046

SMITH, ALEXANDER GOUDY, educator; b. Clarksburg, W.Va., Aug. 12, 1919; s. Edgell Ohr and Helen (Reitz) S.; B.S., Mass. Inst. Tech., 1943; Ph.D., Duke, 1949; m. Mary Elizabeth Ellsworth, Apr. 19, 1942; children—Alexander G. III, Sally Jean. Physicist, Mass. Inst. Tech., Radiation Lab., Cambridge, 1943-46; research asst. Duke U., Durham, 1946-48; asst. prof. to prof. physics U. Fla., Gainesville, 1948-61, asst. dean grad. sch., 1961-69, acting dean grad. sch., 1971-73, chmn. dept. astronomy, 1962-71, prof. physics and astronomy, 1956—; dir. U. Fla. Radio Obs.; cons. USN, USAF. Fellow Optical Soc. Am., Am. Phys. Soc., AAAS; mem. AAUP, Am. Astron. Soc. (editor Photo-Bull. 1975—), Astron. Soc. Pacific, Am. Geophys. Union, Internat. Astron. Union, Internat. Sci. Radio Union, Fla. Acad. Scis. (treas. 1957-62, pres. 1963-64, medal 1965), Assn. Univs. for Research in Astronomy (dir., cons.), Am. Assn. Physics Tchrs., Soc. Photog. Scientists and Engrs., Sigma Xi (nat. lectr. 1968, past pres. Fla. chpt.), Sigma Pi Sigma. Republican. Christian Scientist. Club: Athenaeum (past pres.). Author: (with others) Microwave Magnetrons, 1958; (with T.D. Carr) Radio Exploration of the Planetary System, 1964 (also Swedish, Spanish and Polish edits.); Radio Exploration of the Sun, 1966; also numerous articles in field. Home: 1417 NW 17th St Gainesville FL 32605

SMITH, ALEXANDER JOHN COURT, cons. actuary; b. Glasgow, Scotland, Apr. 13, 1934; s. John Court and Mary Walker (Anderson) S.; student Scottish schs.; m. Margaret Gillespie, Oct. 15, 1968. Actuarial trainee Scottish Mut. Ins. Co., Glasgow, 1957; asst. actuary Continental Life Ins. Co., Toronto, Can., 1958-61; from actuary to exec. v.p. William M. Mercer Ltd., Toronto, 1961-74; sr. v.p., dir. Marsh & McLennan Inc., N.Y.C., 1974-78; pres. William M. Mercer, Inc., N.Y.C., 1974—; trustee Employee Benefit Research Inst., 1979—. Fellow Faculty Actuaries Edinburgh, Can. Inst. Actuaries, Conf. Actuaries in Public Practice; asso. Soc. Actuaries; mem. Am. Acad. Actuaries, Internat. Congress Actuaries, Internat. Assn. Cons. Actuaries. Clubs: Racquet and Tennis (N.Y.C.); Royal Can. Yacht; Apawamis (Rye, N.Y.). Home: 630 Park Ave New York NY 10021 Office: 1211 Ave of Americas New York NY 10036

SMITH, ALEXANDER WYLY, JR., lawyer; b. Atlanta, June 9, 1923; s. Alexander Wyly and Laura (Payne) S.; grad. Marist Sch., 1941; student Holy Cross Coll., 1941-42; B.B.A., U. Ga., 1947, LL.B. cum laude, 1949; m. Betty Rawson Haverty, Aug. 31, 1946; children—Elizabeth Smith Cluderay, Clarence Haverty, Laura Smith Brown, James Haverty, Edward Kendrick, Anthony Marion, William Rawson. Admitted to Ga. bar, 1948; since practiced in Atlanta, partner firm Smith, Cohen, Ringel, Kohler & Martin, and predecessor, 1949—; gen. counsel Nat. Bank Ga.; dir. Haverty Furniture Cos., Inc., Audichron Co. Sec., dir. Our Lady of Perpetual Help Free Cancer Home; bd. dirs. fin. council Cath. Archdiocese Atlanta, S.W. Community Hosp., Marist Sch., Atlanta, John and Mary Franklin Found. Served with USAAF, 1943-46. Mem. Am., Ga., Atlanta bar assns., Internat. Assn. Ins. Counsel, Central Atlanta Progress (pres., dir. 1966), Phi Delta Phi, Chi Phi. Clubs: Piedmont Driving, Commerce, Peachtree Golf (Atlanta). Home: 158 W Wesley Rd NW Atlanta GA 30305 Office: First Nat Bank Tower Atlanta GA 30303

SMITH, ALEXIS, actress; b. Penticton, B.C., Can., June 8, 1921; ed. Los Angeles City Coll.; m. Craig Stevens, 1944. Actress numerous films, stage plays, 1941—; films include The Lady With Red Hair, 1940, Dive Bomber, 1941, The Smiling Ghost, 1941, Gentleman Jim, 1942, The Constant Nymph, 1942, The Doughgirls, 1944, Conflict, 1945, Rhapsody in Blue, 1945, San Antonio, 1945, Night and Day, 1946, Of Human Bondage, 1946, Stallion Road, 1947, The Woman in White, 1947, The Decision of Christopher Blake, 1948, Any Number Can Play, 1950, Undercover Girl, 1952, Split Second, 1953, The Sleeping Tiger, 1955, The Eternal Sea, 1956, The Young Philadelphians, 1959, Once is Not Enough, 1975, Casey's Shadow, 1977; stage appearances include Follies (Tony award 1972), 1971, 72, The Women, 1973, Summer Brave, 1975, Sunset, 1977, Platinum, 1978, The Best Little Whorehouse in Texas, 1979. Address: care International Creative Mgmt 8899 Beverly Blvd Los Angeles CA 90048*

SMITH, ALFRED GLAZE, JR., economist, educator; b. Urbana, Ill., Dec. 28, 1913; s. Alfred Glaze and Lucy Catharine (Prutsman) S.; A.B., Columbia, 1934, A.M., 1939, Ph.D., 1954; m. Katharine Cushing Brown, May 9, 1936; children—Alfred Glaze III, LeRoy Fairchild. With personal div. S.H. Kress & Co., 1936-38; instr. econs. U. S.C., 1938-42, asst. prof., 1942-47, asso. prof., 1947- 54, prof., 1954—, head dept. econs., 1958-70, acting asso. v.p. for instrn., 1974-76; discussant First Ann. Conf. Econ. Devel. South, 1960; Fulbright prof., Bologna, Italy, 1963-64. Owner, operator farm, Lexington County, S.C. Served as officer USNR, 1943-46; comdr. Res. Mem. Am., So. econ. assns., Econ. History Assn. Club: Torch. Author: Economic Readjustment of an Old Cotton State; South Carolina, 1820-1860, 1958. Home: 1816 Enoree Ave Columbia SC 29205

SMITH, ALFRED GOUD, educator; b. The Hague, Netherlands, Aug. 20, 1921; s. William G. and Joan (Wraslouski) S.; A.B. (Simon Mandlebaum scholar, Am. Council Learned Socs. fellow in Oriental Langs.), U. Mich., 1943; postgrad. Princeton U., Yale U., 1943; M.A., U. Wis., 1947, Ph.D., 1956; m. Britta Helen Bonazzi, May 30, 1946. Far East analyst OSS and Dept. State, Washington, 1944-46; asst., instr. philosophy and anthropology U. Wis., 1946-50; supr. linguistics, Pacific area specialist Trust Ter. Pacific Islands and Dept. Interior, Micronesia and Washington, 1950-53; asst. prof. anthropology Antioch Coll., Yellow Springs, Ohio, 1953-56; asst. prof., asso. prof. anthropology Emory U., Atlanta, 1956-62; asso. prof., prof. anthropology, community service and pub. affairs. U. Oreg., Eugene, 1962-73; dir. Center for Communication Research, U. Tex., Austin, 1973-78, prof. Sch. Communication, 1973—; cons. Ga. Dept. Pub. Health, 1956-60, Peace Corps, 1965-69, Job Corps, 1968-70; cons. on problems of communication and anthropology to state and fed. agys., industry, museums, instns. of higher learning; staff mem. AID Communication Seminars, 1966-73. Served to 1st lt. AUS, 1942-45. Fellow Am. Anthrop. Assn., AAAS; mem. Internat. Communication Assn. (pres. 1973-74, dir.), Linguistic Soc. Am. Clubs: Rotary, Town and Gown. Author: Communication and Culture, 1966; Cognitive Styles in Law Schools, 1979; editorial bd. Jour. Communication, Jour. Law and Human Behavior, Biosciences Communications, Human Communication Research, Communication Yearbook, Communication and Information Sciences. Contbr. articles to profl. jours. Home: 1401 Ethridge Ave Austin TX 78703 Office: Sch of Communication U Tex Austin TX 78712

SMITH, ALLAN FREDERICK, univ. ofcl.; b. Belgrade, Nebr., Dec. 19, 1911; s. Charles Henry and Alice (Kliese) S.; A.B. in Edn., Nebr. State Tchrs. Coll., 1933; LL.B. cum laude, U. Nebr., 1940; S.J.D., U. Mich., 1950; m. Alene Mullikin, June 9, 1939; children—Stephanie, Gregory Allan. Admitted to Nebr. bar, 1940, Mich. bar, 1951; chief counsel OPA, Washington, 1941-43, 46; vis. asso. prof. law Stanford, 1946-47; prof. law U. Mich., 1947—, dean Law Sch., 1960-65, v.p. for acad. affairs, 1965-74, interim pres., 1979—. Served with AUS, 1943-45. Fellow Am. Bar Found.; mem. Am., Mich. bar assns., Am. Judicature Soc., Order of Coif, Phi Kappa Phi, Phi Delta Phi. Clubs: University of Mich. Research, Lions (Ann Arbor). Author: Personal Life Insurance Trusts, 1950; Cases and Materials on Property, rev. edit., 1960; (with L.M. Simes) The Law of Future Interests, 1956; (with Browder, Julin and Cunningham) Basic Property Law, 1979. Home: 811 Berkshire St Ann Arbor MI 48104

SMITH, ALLEN ELMER, lawyer, educator, adminstr.; b. Kewanee, Ill., Sept. 25, 1932; s. Donald Elmer and Pauline Anne (Sullivan) S.; B.A., U. Tex., 1960, LL.B., 1961; m. Tot Porter, Dec. 21, 1953; children—Teresa M., Donovan P. Admitted to Tex. bar, 1961, Mo. bar, 1977; law clk. to U.S. Circuit Ct. Judge J.C. Hutcheson, Jr., Houston, 1961-62; asso. firm Orgain Bell & Tucker, Beaumont, Tex., 1962-64; prof. law U. Tex. Sch. Law, Austin, 1964-77; dean U. Mo. Sch. Law, Columbia, 1977—; partner firm Salmanson & Smith, Austin, 1970-77. Served with USN, USMC, 1950-57. Mem. Am. Bar Assn. Club: Rotary. Co-author: Cases and Materials on Torts, 1968, 77. Home: 104 W Brandon Rd Columbia MO 65201 Office: Sch of Law Univ Missouri Columbia MO 65211. *Such modest progress as I have been able to make in my life is attributable mostly to good luck, to being in the right place at the right time, to the kind help of others, and to refusal to take either life or myself too seriously. I have found moderation in all things except hard work and physical exercise satisfying and rewarding. An aggressive personality has helped in achieving goals, while a tendency toward compulsivity has been a substitute for self-discipline.*

SMITH, ANDREW CANNON, educator; b. Natchez, Miss., July 27, 1898; s. Andrew J. and Margaret (Cannon) S.; A.B., Gonzaga U., 1922; A.M., Cath. U., 1930; Ph.D., U. Chgo., 1934; D.H.L. (hon.), Spring Hill Coll., 1975; Entered Soc. of Jesus, 1916; ordained priest Roman Catholic Ch., Enghien, Belgium, 1927; instr. English, Spring Hill (Ala.) Coll., 1923-24, dean, 1934-52, pres., 1952-59; vice provincial of Jesuits, New Orleans, 1959-61; pres. Loyola U., New Orleans, 1961-66; prof. English lit. St. Charles Coll., Grand Coteau, La., 1967; prof. English lit. Spring Hill Coll., Mobile, Ala., 1967-74, prof. emeritus, 1975—; sec. coll., 1967—; asst. prof. Loyola U. South, 1931-32; regional dir. edn. Jesuit Ednl. Assn., 1940-52. Treas. Ind. Coll. Funds Am., 1964-66. Bd. govs. Spring Hill Coll. Mem. founding com. Mobile Town Meeting, Inc., 1948. Mem. Cath. Edn. Assn., Modern Lang. Assn. So. Assn. Colls. and Secondary Schs. (v.p. 1948). Clubs: Roundtable, Internat. House. Contbr. articles to ednl. jours. Address: Spring Hill Coll Mobile AL 36608

SMITH, ANDREW VAUGHN, telephone co. exec.; b. Roseburg, Oreg., July 17, 1924; s. Andrew Britt and Ella Mae (Vaughn) S.; B.S. in Elec. Engring., Oreg. State U., 1950; m. Dorothy LaVonne Crabtree, Apr. 25, 1954; children—Janet L., James A. With Pacific N.W. Bell Telephone Co., 1951—, asst. v.p. ops., Seattle, 1965, v.p., gen. mgr., Portland, Oreg., 1965-70, v.p. ops., Seattle, 1970-78, pres., Seattle, 1978—; dir. U.S. Bank/U.S. Bancorp, Portland, Blue Cross of Wash. and Alaska, Unigard Mutual and Unigard Ins. Cos.; trustee Wash. Mutual Savs. Bank. Trustee Oreg. State U. Found.; trustee U. Wash. Grad. Sch. of Bus. and Oreg. Grad. Center; asso. gen. chmn. United Way of King County, 1979-80; dir. Econ. Devel. Council of Puget Sound, 1978—; mem. Wash. State Council on Alcholism Labor/Mgmt. Task Force; trustee Wash. State Internat. Trade Fair; mem. Seattle Urban League. Served with USNR, 1943-46. Registered profl. engr., Oreg. Episcopalian. Clubs: Harbor, Washington Athletic, Seattle Yacht, Rainier, Seattle Golf, Arlington, Multnomah, Masons. Office: 1600 Bell Plaza Room 3101 Seattle WA 98191

SMITH, ANGIE FRANK, JR., lawyer; b. Detroit, Tex., Nov. 3, 1915; s. A. Frank and Bess Patience (Crutchfield) S.; B.A., Rice U., 1937; LL.B., U. Tex., 1940; LL.D., Southwestern U., 1976; m. Mary Hannah, June 15, 1939; children—Tweed Smith Kezziah, Karen Smith Rehm, A. Frank III, Alison Smith Campbell, Leslie Ann. Partner Vinson & Elkins and predecessor, 1950—, mng. partner, 1972—; dir. Cullen Center Bank & Trust, Cullen/Frost Bankers, Inc., Tex. Eastern Corp.; adv. bd. Internat. Oil and Gas Edn. Center, Internat. and Comparative Law Center; research fellow, trustee Southwestern Legal Found. Chmn. bd. trustees, mem. exec. com. Meth. Hosp., Houston, Southwestern U., Georgetown, Tex.; trustee Baylor Coll. Medicine, Cullen Found., Tex. Med. Center, Houston; bd. dirs. Houston Symphony Soc., Tex. Assn. Taxpayers, Tex. Research League; mem. exec. com. Houston Mus. Fine Arts. Served with USNR, 1942-45. Fellow Am., Tex. bar founds.; mem. Am. Judicature Soc., Houston C. of C. (past vice chmn. bd. dirs.), Tex. Philos. Soc., Sons Republic Tex., Knight San Jacinto, Am., Tex., Houston bar assns., Order of Coif, Phi Delta Phi, Phi Delta Theta. Methodist. Clubs: River Oaks Country; Broadmoor Golf, Garden of Gods (Colorado Springs). Home: 3420 Piping Rock Ln Houston TX 77027 Office: First City Nat Bank Bldg 21st Floor Houston TX 77002

SMITH, ANGUS FRANK, chem. mfg. co. exec.; b. Altrincham, Cheshire, Eng., Apr. 15, 1941; came to U.S., 1973; s. William and Gwen M. (Sutton) S.; M.B.A., Columbia U., 1967; m. Irina Maria Somerville, Aug. 8, 1964; children—Sophie Evelyn, Luisa Helen. Acct., Deloitte, Plender, Griffiths, London, 1959-63; auditor Deloitte, Plender, Haskins & Sells, N.Y.C., 1964-65; fin. mgr. Rohm & Haas Milan (Italy), 1967-72, Rohm & Haas France, (Paris), 1972-73, Rohm & Haas Co., Phila., 1973-78, treas., 1978—; occasional broadcaster on fgn. exchange. Bd. dirs. Central br. Phila. YMCA, St. Peter's Sch., Phila. Fellow Inst. Chartered Accts. of Eng. and Wales. Contbr. articles to profl. jours. Home: 321 S 6th St Philadelphia PA 19106 Office: Rohm & Haas Co Independence Mall W Philadelphia PA 19105

SMITH, ANNE MOLLEGEN, editor; b. Meridian, Miss., July 28, 1940; d. Albert Theodore and Ione (Rush) Mollegen; B.A. (Smith Coll. Club of Washington scholar), Smith Coll., 1961; m. David Fay Smith, Nov. 3, 1962; 1 dau., Amanda Wetherbee. Asst. editor Ladies' Home Jour., Phila., 1961-62; advt. copywriter Hutzler's Dept. Store, Balt., 1962-64; feature editor China Post, Taipei, Taiwan, 1965; staff writer house organ J. C. Penney Co., N.Y.C., 1966; asso. editor Redbook, N.Y.C., 1967-73, fiction editor, 1973-77; mng. editor Your Place mag. McCall Pub. Co., 1977-78; mng. editor Redbook, N.Y.C., 1978—; mem. faculty La Jolla (Calif.) Writers' Conf., 1974, 78, Pacific N.W. Writers' Conf., Seattle, 1975; parent cons. Redbook Toy Symposium, 1974; mem. selection com. for Specialized Journalism Nat. Mag. award Sch. Journalism, Columbia U., 1975-76; guest lectr. Womanschool, N.Y.C., 1977. Recipient 2d prize I Speak for Democracy contest, Alexandria, Va., 1955, Karig Writing prize, 1957. Mem. Am. Soc. Mag. Editors (Redbook received Nat. Mag. award for fiction 1975), Women's Media Group (pres. 1978), NOW. Club: Smith Coll. of N.Y. Home: 451 W 24th St New York NY 10011 Office: Redbook Mag 230 Park Ave New York NY 10017

SMITH, ANTHONY WAYNE, lawyer, assn. exec.; b. Pitts.; s. Anthony Woodward and Janey Mulhern (Coard) S.; B.A. with high honors, U. Pitts.; J.D., Yale, 1934; mem. bd. editors Yale Law Jour., 1931-34; m. Anya E. Freedel, June 20, 1930. Sec. to gov. Pa., 1932-33; admitted to N.Y. State bar, 1935, U.S. Supreme Ct. bar, 1940, D.C. bar, 1947; with firm Donovan, Leisure, Newton & Lumbard, N.Y.C., 1934-37; pvt. practice law, Washington, 1949—; asst. gen. counsel CIO, Washington, 1937-56, asst. dir. state and city indsl. union councils, 1941-55, exec. sec. housing com., 1937-39, 41-42, asst. sec. Latin Am. com., 1939-40, observer UN, 1954-56; atty. polit. edn. com. AFL-CIO, 1956-58. Pres., gen. counsel Nat. Parks and Conservation Assn., 1958—; comml. dairyman, Franklin County, Pa., 1954—. Exec. committeeman Emergency Com. on Natural Resources, 1952-53, Citizens Com. on Natural Resources, 1953-78, C & O Canal Assn., 1954-71; pres. South Central Pa. Citizens Assn., 1962—; gen. counsel Citizens Permanent Conf. Potomac River Basin, 1968—; chmn. Environ. Coalition for N.Am., 1969—; co-chmn. Everglades Coalition, 1969—; observer to UN Conf. on Human Environ., Stockholm, Sweden, 1972, UN Environ. Programme, Geneva, Switzerland, 1973; mem. adv. com. to sec. state on UN Conf. on Human Environment, 1972; mem. adv. com. to sec. state UN Conf. Law of Sea, 1972—, mem. U.S. Delegation, 1973—; mem. adv. com. to Council on Environmental Quality on U.S.-USSR Sci. Exchange, 1974. Served as 2d lt. AUS, 1926-30. Mem. Am. Farm Bur. Fedn., Pa., Franklin County farmers assns., Nat., Pa., Concord granges, Nat. Lawyers Club, D.C. Bar Assn., Assn. Bar City N.Y., Delta Tau Delta, Phi Mu Sigma, Delta Sigma Rho, Omicron Delta Kappa. Contbr. numerous articles to profl. jours. Home: 1330 New Hampshire Ave NW Washington DC 20036 also Cove Mountain Farm Box 141D Route 3 Mercersburg PA 17236 Office: 1701 18th St NW Washington DC 20009

SMITH, ARTHUR, composer, radio and TV producer; b. Clinton, S.C., Apr. 1, 1921; s. Clayton Seymour and Viola (Fields) S.; grad. high sch.; m. Dorothy Byars, Apr. 12, 1941; children—Arthur Reginald, Constance (Mrs. Wiley Brown), Robert Clayton. Rec. artist RCA Victor, 1936-38; band leader, composer radio sta. WSPA, Spartanburg, S.C., 1938-41, radio sta. WBT, Charlotte, N.C., 1941-43; band leader, composer, producer CBS Radio, WBT, WBTV, Charlotte, 1945-70; producer WSOC-TV Cox Broadcasting Co., Charlotte, 1970—, prin. The Arthur Smith Show, 1971-76; dir. Hardware Mut. Ins. Co., Am. Bank & Trust Co., Meat Centers; pres. Clay Music Corp., Charlotte, 1960-76; owner Arthur Smith Studios, Charlotte, 1961—; v.p. CMH Records, Los Angeles. Bd. dirs. Charlotte Sch. of Arts; trustee, dir. Gardner Webb Coll.; trustee Boys Homes N.C. Served with USNR, 1943-45. Named Bapt. Layman of Year Southeastern Sem., Louisville, 1969; recipient Religion Emphasis award Am. Legion, 1971, S.C. Tourism award State of S.C., 1979. Mem. Am. Fedn. Musicians (dir. local 342, pres. local 342, 1943-76), AFTRA, Salt Water Anglers Tournament Soc. (founder, chmn. bd.). Democrat. Mason (Shriner), Kiwanian. Clubs: Charlotte City, Red Fez. Composer numerous compositions, including: Guitar Boogie, 1946 (also rec. artist); Dueling Banjos, 1973 (BMI Song of Year 1973); composer (with Clay Smith) sound track of film Death Driver, 1975, Dark Sunday, 1976, musical score for Living Legend and Lady Grey-Superstar, 1979. Founder Arthur Smith King Mackerel Tournament, Myrtle Beach, S.C., 1976. Home: 7224 Sardis Rd Charlotte NC 28212 Office: Arthur Smith Studios 5457 Old Monroe Rd Charlotte NC 28211. *To me, success is not a destination - it's a journey. Integrity is not a business principle - it's a matter of right or wrong. Whatever I shall achieve in this world I owe to complete trust in, and commitment to God through Christ, a loving and understanding wife and family and loyal associates.*

SMITH, ARTHUR ALVIN, banker, economist; b. Monett, Mo., Mar. 1, 1905; s. Edward George and Carrie (Lyons) S.; B.S., Mo. State Coll., 1927; M.A., Peabody Coll., 1929; Ph.D., Vanderbilt U., 1933; m. Winifred Ann Campbell, Aug. 30, 1930; children—Natalie Judith Smith Moore, Kirby Campbell. Asso. prof. econs. DePauw U., 1934-38; prof. So. Meth. U., 1938-50; regional dir. Bur. Labor Statistics, 1942-47; sr. v.p., economist First Nat. Bank, Dallas, 1950-70; distinguished prof. econs. and fin. E. Tex. State U., 1970-76; econ. cons. Dallas Times Herald; dir. Dallas Fed. Savs. and Loan Assn., 1970—; mem. investment advisory com. Tex. Permanent Sch. Fund, 1962—. Pres. trustees Dallas Pub. Library, 1966-74; bd. dirs. Greater Planning Council, Dallas Health and Sci. Mus.; trustee Peabody Coll., Southwestern Coll., Winfield, Kans. Episcopalian. Rotarian. Home: 7328 Kenshire Ln Dallas TX 75230 Office: PO Box 6031 Dallas TX 75283

SMITH, ARTHUR HENRY, bus. cons.; b. Milw., Mar. 11, 1912; s. Charles Arthur and Margaret (Duckart) S.; B.A., U. Wis., 1936; grad. Advanced Mgmt. Program, Harvard, 1952; m. Isabelle Marie Skarolid, June 1, 1940; children—Gary Arthur, Virginia Isabelle, Judy Anne. Within Gen. Mills, Inc., 1936-60, dir. mgmt. analysis, 1956-60; v.p., dir. Midwest Tech. Devel. Corp., Mpls., 1960-63; pres., dir. Turbomatic, Inc., Mpls., 1962-63; dir. Dynasonics Corp., 1960-62, Electra Sci. Corp., 1961-63; controller Hunt Foods & Industries, Inc., dir. finance Hunt-Wesson foods div., 1963-65; mgmt. cons. Price Waterhouse & Co., 1965-66; v.p., controller Libby, McNeill & Libby, 1966-67; fin. v.p., treas. Internat. Industries, Inc., 1967-71, also dir.; pres. A. Smith & Assos., 1971—; exec. v.p. Solar Conversion Corp. Am., Van Nuys, Calif., 1975-76. Treas. Stuart Cameron McLeod Soc. C.P.A., Wis. Mem. Am. Inst. C.P.A.'s, Minn., Calif. socs. C.P.A.'s, Nat. Assn. Accountants (past pres. Mpls. chpt., past nat. dir. and v.p.), Harvard Bus. Sch. Assn. (past mem. nat. exec. council), Phi Beta Kappa. Contbr. articles in field to profl. jours. Home and office: 5243 Yarmouth Ave Unit #2 Encino CA 91316

SMITH, ARTHUR JAMES MARSHALL, author; b. Montreal, Que., Can., Nov. 8, 1902; s. Octavius Arthur and Alexandra Louise (Whiting) S.; came to U.S., 1930, naturalized, 1941; B.S., McGill U., 1925, M.A., 1926, Litt.D. (hon.), 1958; Ph.D., Edinburgh U., 1931; LL.D., Queen's U., Kingston, Ont., 1966, Dalhousie U., 1969; D.C.L. (hon.), Bishop's U., 1967; m. Jeannie Dougall Robins, Aug. 15, 1927; 1 son, Peter George Marshall. Instr. to prof. and poet in residence English dept. Mich. State U., East Lansing, 1936-72; vis. prof. U. Toronto, 1946-47, Queens U., summers 1952, 60, U. B.C., summer 1956, Sir George Williams U., Montreal, summers 1967, 69, Dalhousie U., 1966-67, State U. N.Y. at Stony Brook, 1969, McGill U., 1969-70; Claude Bissell chair Can.-Am. studies U. Toronto, 1976-77. Recipient Gov.-Gen.'s medal for poetry, 1943, medal Royal Soc. Can., 1966, Dominion of Can. Centennial medal, 1967, Can. Council medal, 1968; Guggenheim fellow, 1941-42, Rockefeller fellow, 1945-47. Author: The Book of Canadian Poetry, 1943; News of the Phoenix (poems), 1943; Seven Centuries of Verse, 1947, 57, 67; The Worldly Muse, 1951; A Sort of Ecstasy, 1954; (with M.L. Rosenthal) Exploring Poetry, 1955, 73; (with F.R. Scott) The Blasted Pine, 1957; The Oxford Book of Canadian Verse, 1960; Collected Poems, 1962; Modern Canadian Verse, 1967; Poems, New and Collected, 1967; Towards a View of Canadian Letters, 1973; The Canadian Experience, 1973; The Colonial Century, 1973; The Canadian Century, 1973; Essays on Poetry and Poets, 1977; The Classic Shade, Selected Poems, 1978. Contbr. articles to profl. jours. Home: 640 Bailey St East Lansing MI 48823

SMITH, ARTHUR JOHN STEWART, physicist, educator; b. Victoria, B.C., Can., June 28, 1938; s. James Stewart and Lillian May (Geernaert) S.; B.A., U. B.C., 1959, M.Sc., 1961; Ph.D., Princeton U., 1966; m. Norma Ruth Askeland, May 20, 1966; children—Peter James, Ian Alexander. Postdoctoral fellow Deutsches Electronen-Synchrotron, Hamburg, W. Germany, 1966-67; mem. faculty dept. physics Princeton U., 1967—, prof., 1978—, asso. chmn. dept., 1979—; vis. scientist Brookhaven Nat. Lab., 1967—, Fermilab, 1974—. Mem. Am. Phys. Soc. Contbr. articles to profl. jours. Home: 4 Ober Rd Princeton NJ 08540 Office: PO Box 708 Princeton NJ 08544

SMITH, AUSTIN, physician, investment co. exec.; b. Belleville, Ont., Can., Nov. 25, 1912; s. Wilfred and Keitha (Crouter) S.; came to U.S., 1939, naturalized, 1943; M.D., C.M., Queens U., Kingston, Ont., 1938, M.Sc. in Medicine, 1940, LL.D., 1954; D.Sc., New Eng. Coll Pharmacy, 1962, Phila. Coll. Pharmacy and Sci., 1963, Albany Med. Coll., 1964, Mass. Coll. Pharmacy, 1968; 1 son, Craig. Editor, mng. pub. Jour. of AMA, editor-in-chief AMA splty. jours., 1949-58; pres. Pharm. Mfrs. Assn., Washington, 1959-65; vice chmn. bd. Parke, Davis & Co., Detroit, 1966-67, chmn. bd., chief exec. officer, 1967-73, pres., 1968-70; vice chmn. bd. Warner-Lambert Co., 1971-73; founder, mng. dir. Invemed Assos., Inc., N.Y.C., 1974-76; founder, chmn. bd. MacKenzie Assos., 1976—. Bd. dirs. Bklyn. Coll. Pharmacy. Fellow Internat. Coll. Surgeons (hon.); mem. Am. Pharm Assn. (life mem.), Alpha Omega Alpha, Alpha Kappa Kappa, Sigma Delta Chi, Kappa Psi (hon.). Clubs: Chicago Press; Overseas Press, Pharm. Advt. N.Y. (hon.) (N.Y.C.). Author books and articles relating to field. Editor-in-chief: Med. Times, 1975-77. Home: PO Box 616 Lenox Hill Station New York NY 10021 Office: 12th Floor 711 Fifth Ave New York NY 10022

SMITH, BALLARD FLANDERS, JR., baseball club exec.; b. Indpls., June 20, 1946; s. Ballard Flanders and Mildred Smith; B.A. in Sociology, Carleton Coll., 1968; J.D., U. Minn., 1971; m. Linda Ardell Smith, Sept. 5, 1970; children—Allison, Amy, Amanda, Holly. Mem. firm Pepicelli & Pepicelli, Meadville, Pa., 1971-76; dist. atty., Crawford County, Pa., 1976; v.p., gen. mgr. San Diego Mariners Hockey Club, 1976-77; exec. v.p. San Diego Nat. League Baseball Club, Inc., San Diego Padres, 1977-79, pres., 1979—. Bd. dirs., Kroc Found., Santa Ynez Valley, Calif., San Diego County Boy Scouts Am., 1978—. Mem. Am. Bar Assn., Pa. Bar Assn., Am. Arbitration Assn., San Diego C. of C. (dir.). Episcopalian. Office: PO Box 2000 9449 Friars Rd San Diego CA 92120

SMITH, BARBARA BARNARD, educator; b. Ventura, Calif., June 10, 1920; d. Fred W. and Grace (Hobson) S.; B.A., Pomona Coll., 1942; Mus.M., U. Rochester, 1943, performer's certificate, 1944. Mem. faculty piano and theory Eastman Sch. Music, U. Rochester, 1943-49; mem. faculty U. Hawaii, Honolulu, 1949—, asso. prof. music, 1953-62, prof., 1962—, sr. fellow East-West Center, 1973; lectr., recitals in Hawaiian and Asian music, U.S., Europe and Asia, 1956—; field research in Asia, 1956, 60, 66, 71, Micronesia, 1963, 70. Mem. Internat. Soc. Music Edn., Internat., Am. Musicological socs., Soc. Ethnomusicology, Internat. Folk Music Council, Asia Soc., Coll. Music Soc., Music Educators Nat. Conf., Phi Beta Kappa, Mu Phi Epsilon. Author publs. on ethnomusicology. Home: 581 Kamoku St Honolulu HI 96826

SMITH, BARBARA HERRNSTEIN, educator; b. N.Y.C., Aug. 6, 1932; d. Benjamin and Ann (Weinstein) Brodo; student Coll. City N.Y., 1950-52; B.A. summa cum laude, Brandeis U., 1954, M.A., 1955, Ph.D., 1965; m. Richard J. Herrnstein, May 28, 1951 (div. Aug. 1961); 1 dau., Julia; m. 2d, Thomas H. Smith, Feb. 21, 1964 (div. Nov. 1974); 1 dau., Deirdre Maud. Instr. English, Sanz Sch. Langs., Washington, 1956-57; teaching and research asst. Brandeis U., 1959-61, instr. dept. English and Am. lit., 1961-62; faculty div. lit. and langs. Bennington (Vt.) Coll., 1962-74; vis. lectr. Annenberg Sch. Communications, U. Pa., 1973-74, prof. English and communications, 1974—, dir. Center for Study Art and Symbolic Behavior, 1979—. Judge William Riley Parker prize com. Modern Lang. Assn., 1970-71; mem. bd. judges Explicator Award, 1975—; mem. supervising com. English Inst., 1977—. Recipient Christian Gauss award, 1968, Explicator award, 1968, Huber Found. grants, 1965, 66, Ford Found. Humanities Faculty Devel. grant, 1968. Nat. Endowment for Humanities fellow, 1970; Guggenheim fellow, 1977-78; Princeton U. Council for Humanities fellow, 1980. Mem. MLA, Semiotics Soc. Am., Soc. for Critical Exchange. Author: Poetic Closure: A Study of How Poems End, 1968; On the Margins of Discourse: the Relation of Literature to Language, 1978. Editor: Discussions of Shakespeare's Sonnets, 1964; Shakespeare's Sonnets, 1969; mem. editorial bd. Critical Inquiry, PMLA; asso. editor Poetics Today. Address: 4632 Larchwood Ave Philadelphia PA 19143

SMITH, BARDWELL LEITH, educator; b. Springfield, Mass., July 28, 1925; s. Winthrop Hiram and Gertrude (Ingram) S.; grad. Phillips Andover Acad., Andover, Mass., 1943; B.A., Yale, 1950, B.D., 1953, M.A., 1957, Ph.D., 1964; postgrad. Harvard, 1964-65; postgrad. research U. London (Eng.), 1972-73; m. Charlotte McCorkindale, Aug. 19, 1961; children—Peter McKay, Susan McCorkindale, Laura Bardwell, Brooks Campbell, Samuel Bardwell. Asst. in instrn. Yale, 1958-60; asst. prof. religion Carleton Coll., Northfield, Minn., 1960-65, asso. prof., 1965-69, prof., 1969-72, dean coll., 1967-72, John W. Nason prof. Asian studies, 1972—. Chmn. com. on Yale Coll., Yale U. Council, 1969-73. Del. to Minn. conv. Democratic Farmer-Labor party, 1968. Served to cpl. USMCR, 1944-46; PTO. Nat. Def. Edn. Act research grantee, 1964-65; Am. Council Learned Socs. research grantee, 1972-73. Mem. Am. Acad. Religion (dir., chmn. Asian religions sect. 1968-72), Assn. Asian Studies, Internat. Assn. Buddhist Studies (exec. com.), Soc. Sci. Study Religion, Am. Soc. Christian Ethics, AAUP, Am. Oriental Soc., Royal Asiatic Soc., Soc. Values in Higher Edn., Canadian Assn. South Asian Studies (v.p. 1972-73), Phi Beta Kappa. Editor, contbr.: The Two Wheels of Dhamma: Essays on the Theravada Tradition in India and Ceylon, 1972; The Tenure Debate, 1973; Unsui: A Diary of Zen Monastic Life, 1973; Religion and Social Conflict in South Asia, 1976; Hinduism: New Essays in the History of Religions, 1976; Religion and Legitimation of Power in Sri Lanka, 1978; editor: Tradition and Change in Theravada Buddhism: Essays on Ceylon and Thailand in the 19th and 20th Centuries, 1973; Religion and the Legitimation of Power in South Asia, 1978; Religion and Legitimation of Power in Thailand, Laos and Burma, 1978; co-editor, contbr.: Essays on T'ang Society: The Interplay of Social, Political and Economic Forces, 1976; Warriors, Artists and Commoners: Japan in the Sixteenth Century, 1980. Contbr. articles to profl. jours. Home: 104 Maple St Northfield MN 55057

SMITH, BARNARD ELLIOT, educator; b. Mpls., May 6, 1926; s. Sheldon Strong and Jessie (Gould) S.; B.S. in Mech. Engring. with distinction, U. Minn., 1949, M.S., 1950; Ph.D., Stanford, 1961; M.A. (hon.), Dartmouth, 1971; m. Betty Lou Strohschein, Aug. 28, 1949; children—Carolyn Louise, Eileen Elizabeth. Asst. prof. mech. engring. U. N.D., 1950-51; mfg. specialist A.O. Smith Co., Milw., 1951-54; asst. prof. indsl. engring. Ore. State Coll., 1954-58, Stanford, 1958-61; asso. prof. mgmt. Sloan Sch. Mgmt., Mass. Inst. Tech., 1961-68; prof. mgmt. Indian Inst. Mgmt., Calcutta, 1965-68; prof. engring. Thayer Sch. Engring., Dartmouth, 1968-71; dean Stuart Sch. Mgmt. and Finance, Ill. Inst. Tech., 1971-75, prof. mgmt., 1975—; cons. in field. Dir. Wilkinson Computer Scis. Co. Served with USNR, 1944-46. Mem. Am. Soc. Quality Control (scholarship 1960), Am. Inst. Indsl. Engrs., Inst. Mgmt. Scis., Am. Acad. Mgmt., Am. Soc. Engring. Edn. (bd. dirs. engring. economy div. 1969-72), Sigma Xi, Pi Tau Sigma. Home: 5316 Howard Ave Western Springs IL 60558 Office: Stuart Sch Mgmt and Finance Ill Inst Tech Chicago IL 60616

SMITH, BARRY VINCENT, ins. co. exec.; b. Leeds, Eng., Jan. 15, 1932; s. Ernest and Mary (Hezelgrave) S.; came to U.S., 1959, naturalized, 1977; M.A., Balliol Coll., Oxford (Eng.) U., 1953; m. Jane Claire Rutherford, July 16, 1966; children—Philippa, Jessica, Julia, Jocelyn. Actuarial asst. Norwich Union Life Ins. Co. (Eng.), 1953-54, Yorkshire Life Ins. Co. (Eng.), 1954-56; sr. v.p. Equitable Life Assurance Soc. N.Y., N.Y.C., 1975—; chmn. bd. Informatics Inc. Chmn. United Fund, Westport, Conn. Served with RAF, 1956-59. Fellow Soc. Actuaries; mem. Inst. Actuaries (asso.), Acad. Actuaries. Home: 15 Richmond Hill Rd Weston CT 06883 Office: 1285 Ave of Americas New York City NY 10019

SMITH, BETTY FAYE, textile chemist; b. Magnolia, Ark., June 29, 1930; d. Carl Excel and Nannie (Nall) S.; B.S., U. Ark., 1951; M.S., U. Tenn., 1957; Ph.D., U. Minn., 1960, 65. Home agt. Ark. Agrl. Extension Service, 1951-56; mem. faculty Cornell U., 1965-70, asso. prof. textiles, 1965-70, chmn. dept., 1968-69; prof. textiles, chmn. dept. U. Md., 1970—. Fellow Textile Inst.; mem. Fiber Soc., Am. Chem. Soc., Am. Assn. Textile Chemists and Colorists, Soc. Dyers and Colourists, Am. Home Econs. Assn., Info. Council Fabric Flammability, AAUP, Sigma Xi, Omicron Nu, Phi Upsilon Omicron, Iota Sigma Pi. Democrat. Methodist. Author papers in field. Home: 9216 St Andrews Pl College Park MD 20740 Office: Dept Textiles and Consumer Econs Univ Md College Park MD 20742

SMITH, BETTYE JANE, univ. dean; b. Fairfield, Ala., Apr. 7, 1926; d. Jesse Doswell and Ethel (McCarthy) S.; R.N., Birmingham (Ala.) Baptist Hosp., 1947; B.S., George Peabody Coll., Nashville, 1954; M.A., Columbia U. Tchrs. Coll., 1958, Ed.D., 1971. Staff and sr. nurse Jefferson County Health Dept., Birmingham, 1948-50; student health nurse, clin. instr. Mobile Infirmary Sch. Nursing, 1950-53; sr. nurse, supr. Jefferson County Health Dept., 1954-59; asst. prof. U. Ky. Sch. Nursing, Lexington, 1959-60; instr. Tex. Woman's U. Sch. Nursing, Dallas, 1960-63; asst. prof., then asso. prof. Troy (Ala.) State U. Sch. Nursing, 1970-75; prof., dean Sch. Nursing, Miss. U. Women, Columbus, 1975-79; chmn. deans and dirs. council, bd. trustees Miss. Instns. Higher Learning. Adminstrv. Bd., 1977-79, fin. com. Wesley United Methodist Ch., Columbus, 1977-78. Isabel Hampton Robb scholar, 1964-65; Sigma Theta Tau grantee, 1968. Mem. Nat. League Nursing, Am. Nurses Assn., Am. Pub. Health Assn., Am. Acad. Polit. and Social Sci., Pi Lambda Theta. Address: 408 Springdale Dr Columbus MS 39701

SMITH, BRUCE HARRY, architect; b. Stanton, Mich., Nov. 20, 1923; s. Ralph Armstrong and Grace (Thurber) S.; B.A. in Physics and Math., Albion Coll., 1949; B.S. in Archtl. Engring., U. Colo., 1950; m. Doris H. Fishbeck, July 10, 1948; children—Kendall A., Clayton H., Brooke C. Draftsman firm W.C. Kruger Asso., Santa Fe, N.M., 1951; archtl. and structural designer firm Harold Ekman, Phoenix, 1952-53; asso. firm Harry M. Denyes, Birmingham, Mich., 1953-56; pres. firm Smith Plus Smith Assos. Architects, Inc., Royal Oak, Mich., 1956—. Mem. Royal Oak Citizens Council for Better Schs., pres., 1958-59. Served with AUS, 1943-46; PTO. Fellow AIA (nat. com. on architecture for edn. 1962-72, gold medal Detroit chpt. 1973); mem. Mich. Soc. Architects (pres. 1964-65), Council for Ednl. Facilities Planners, Mich. Assn. Professions. Presbyn. (elder). Home: 1288 Dorchester St Birmingham MI 48008 Office: 301 W 4th St Royal Oak MI 48067 also 733 St Antoine St Detroit MI 48226

SMITH, BRYAN FRANCIS, lawyer, corp. dir.; b. Jersey City, July 9, 1920; s. Bryan Smith and Grace M. (Hannon) S.; B.A., Harvard U., 1941; postgrad. M.I.T., 1942-43; J.D., Columbia U., 1947; LL.D. (hon.), U. Dallas, 1979; m. June E. Rafferty, June 24, 1950; children—Patricia, Bryan F., James, Peter, Michael, Paul, Mary. Admitted to N.Y. State bar, 1948; mem. firm Mitchell, Capron, Marsh, Angulo and Cooney, N.Y.C., 1947-51; with Tex. Instruments, Inc., Dallas, 1951—, treas., 1953-60, v.p. fin., sec., 1966-67, sr. v.p., sec., from 1967, dir., sec., 1972-75, gen. dir., 1975—; trustee U. Dallas, chancellor, 1976-78, chancellor emeritus, 1978—; bd. dirs. Engraph, Inc., French Am. Banking Corp., Mary Kay Cosmetics, Inc., Merrill Lynch & Co., Inc., Preston State Bank. Bd. dirs. Dallas chpt. NCCJ; mem. Cotton Bowl Council; trustee Dallas Symphony Assn., Dallas Symphony Pension Plan; bd. dirs. Cistercian Prep. Sch. for Boys; trustee Hockaday Sch.; mem. com. on univ. resources, nominating com. for bd. overseers Harvard U. Mem. Am. Bar Assn., Am. Soc. Corp. Secs. (past nat. v.p., dir.), Conf. Bd., Community Council Greater Dallas (chmn. countrywide health dept. com. 1975-76), Dallas C. of C. (past dir.), Tex. Research League (past dir.), Dallas Found. (past bd. govs.), Better Bus. Bur. Met. Dallas (dir.). Clubs: Dallas Petroleum, Northwood, 2001. Home: 12 Royal Way Dallas TX 75229 Office: PO Box 225474 Dallas TX 75265

SMITH, BULKELEY, JR., educator; b. Worcester, Mass., Mar. 11, 1921; s. Bulkeley and Elizabeth (Bright) S.; B.A., Yale, 1947, M.A., 1954, Ph.D., 1958; m. Helen Abigail Wade, June 28, 1947; 1 dau., Abigail Earle. Instr. English, Yale, 1947-48; self-employed, 1949-53; mem. faculty Mt. Holyoke Coll., 1957—, prof. sociology, 1971—, chmn. dept., 1969-74. Cons., No. Ednl. Service, Springfield, Mass., 1963-64; mem. grad. faculty U. Mass., 1970—. Dir., cons. Assn. Improvement Minorities, Holyoke, 1963—. Trustee Wilbraham and Monson (Mass.) Acad., 1968—. Served with Am. Field Service, 1942-43, 44-45, U.S. Merchant Marine, 1943. Henry A. Page fellow, 1955-57; Milbank Fund grantee, 1965. Fellow Am. Sociol. Assn.; mem. Eastern Sociol. Soc., Holyoke Human Relations Council (charter mem., dir. 1963—, also cons.), Inst. Race Relations (London), Traditional Small Craft Soc., Cat Boat Assn., Phi Beta Kappa. Author monographs; contbr. to profl. jours. Home: 6 Jewett Ln South Hadley MA 01075

SMITH, BUNNIE OTHANEL, educator; b. Clarksville, Fla., May 29, 1903; s. Isma Isaac and Lula (Cox) S.; B.S., U. Fla., 1925; M.A., Columbia, 1932, Ph.D., 1938; m. Tommie Naomi Harkey, Aug. 29, 1929; children—Norman Harkey, Hamilton Othanel. Asst. prin., Panama City, Fla., 1925-26; sci. tchr., Brooksville, Fla., 1926-27; high sch. prin., supervising prin., Tallahassee, 1927-30; asst. prof. U. Fla., 1930-37; mem. faculty U. Ill., 1937-70, prof. history and philosophy edn., 1945-70, chmn. dept. history and philosophy of edn., 1966-70, prof. emeritus, 1970—; prof. edn. U. South Fla., Tampa, 1970-75, prof. emeritus, 1975—; vis. prof. U. Fla., summer 1940, Columbia, summer 1945; mem. internat. group to prepare manuscript on curriculum devel. for UNESCO, 1955; adv. edn. editor Rand McNally and Co., 1953—; chmn. grad. records exam. in edn. Ednl. Testing Service, 1967-73; mem. Nat. Inst. Advanced Study Teaching Disadvantaged Youth, 1966-68; chmn. adv. council Asso. Orgns. Tchr. Edn., 1963; mem. Ill. Council Econ. Edn., 1968. Dir. Leadership Tng. Inst. U.S. Office Edn., 1970-75. Recipient Centennial award U. Fla., 1953, Distinguished Alumnus award, 1975; citation Nat. Tchr. Corps, 1977. Mem. Philosophy Edn. Soc. (pres. 1956-57, exec. com. 1957-58), Nat. Soc. Coll. Tchrs. Edn. (pres. 1949, exec. com. 1948), Am. Ednl. Research Assn. (v.p. 1967-69; mem. at large exec. bd. 1970-73), NEA (life), Nat. Soc. Study Edn., John Dewey Soc. (award 1975), Assn. Supervision and Curriculum Devel., AAAS, Phi Kappa Phi, Phi Delta Kappa, Kappa Delta Pi, Chi Phi. Democrat. Author: Logical Aspects of Education Measurement, 1938; (with others) The Improvement of Practical Intelligence, 1950; (with others) Fundamentals of Curriculum Development, 1950; (with others) Social Foundations of Education, 1956; (with Robert H. Ennis) Language and Concepts in Education, 1961; (with Milton Meux) A Study of the Logic of Teaching, 1962; (with others) Democracy and Excellence in Secondary Education, 1963; (with others) A Study of the Strategies of Teaching, 1967; (with Donald Orlosky) Socialization and Schooling, 1975, Curriculum Development: Concepts and Issues, 1978. Mem. editorial bd. Ency. Ednl. Research, 1960, 70, Jour. Tchr. Edn., 1959-62; editor Progressive Education, 1947-52, Research in Teacher Education: A Symposium, 1971; asst. editor Curriculum Jour., 1934-40. Home: 854 Island Way Clearwater FL 33515 Office: Coll Edn U South Fla Tampa FL 33620

SMITH, BURTON JOSEPH (B. J.), chem. coatings mfg. co. exec.; b. Portland, Oreg., Sept. 13, 1941; s. Burton Merle and Dorothy Madelaine (Esch) S.; B.B.A., U. Notre Dame, 1963; m. Ruth Ann Schnaus, June 6, 1963; children—Kathryn, Scott, Steven. Jr. acct. Price, Waterhouse & Co., San Francisco, 1963-64, sr. acct., 1964-65; v.p., treas. Reliance Panelyte, Kalamazoo, 1965-67; asst. treas. Reliance Universal Inc., Louisville, 1967-69, sec.-treas., 1969—, v.p. fin., 1975—; dir. Meidinger and Assos., Louisville. Mem. Fin. Execs. Inst. Republican. Roman Catholic. Club: Notre Dame of Ky. Home: 811 Rugby Pl Louisville KY 40222 Office: 1930 Bishop Ln Suite 1600 Louisville KY 40218

SMITH, BYRON CAPLEESE, ophthalmologist; b. Tonganoxie, Kans., Aug. 28, 1908; s. Fountain Michie and Annie Frances (Capleese) S.; B.S., U. Kans., 1929, M.D., 1931; m. Virginia Batton Stentz, Apr. 13, 1942 (div.); 1 dau., Constance Batton (Mrs. Stanley Williams); m. 2d, Margarite Elizabeth Fox, Oct. 15, 1948; children—Grady Livingston, Lindsay Byron. Resident physician Topeka State Hosp., 1931-33; resident surgeon Newington Hosp. Crippled Children, 1933-35; intern surgery, obstetrics and gynecology New Haven Hosp., 1935-37, asst. resident ophthalmology, 1937-38; resident ophthalmology N.Y. Eye and Ear Infirmary, 1938-40, asst. surgeon, 1941-46, sr. asst. surgeon, 1946-49, jr. surgeon, 1949-50, cons. ophthalmic plastic surgery, 1950—; asst. surgeon Manhattan Eye, Ear and Throat Hosp., 1946-49, attending surgeon, 1950, surgeon, 1957—, bd. dirs., 1951—, chmn. dept. ophthalmology, 1963—, dir. dept. ophthalmic plastic surgery, 1958—, now cons. ophthalmic plastic surgery; sr. surgeon cons. ophthalmology Park Med. Group, N.Y.C., cons. ophthalmology Monmouth (N.J.) Med. Center; asst. in surgery Yale U. Sch. Medicine, 1935-37, asst. ophthalmic plastic surgery Oxford U., Eng., 1945; clin. prof. ophthalmology N.Y. Med. Coll., 1973—; lectr. Scheie Eye Inst., Phila., 1978—; cons. ophthalmology Armed Forces U.S., 1947—; lectr. Am. Acad. Ophthalmology, 1949, Wendell Hughes lectr., 1971; ophthal. cons. Kingsbridge VA Hosp., 1949—, also Southampton Hosp.; civilian cons. ophthalmology Surg. Gen. U.S. Armed Forces, also Far East Command, 1950; asst. clin. prof. ophthalmology N.Y. U., 1951-55, asso. prof., 1955-62; ophthalmic plastic surgeon N.Y. U. Med. Center, 1955-63; E.J. Curran lectr. U. Kans., 1951; Albert B. Snell lectr. U. Rochester (N.Y.), 1955; Internat. Symposium lectr., Ethiopia, Greece, Italy, Uganda and Kenya; Alfred D. Ruedman lectr. Am. Soc. Ocularists, 1974; bd. advisers Am. Soc. Ophthalmic Plastic and Reconstructive Surgery, 1975—. Vice pres. bd. trustees The Searing Sch., N.Y.C., 1967—. Mem. med. adv. council Am. Acad. Ocularists, 1967—. Served to maj. AUS, 1942-46; chief ophthalmology Tilton Gen. Hosp., Fort Dix, N.J., 1942-43; chief ophthalmology and plastic surgery 1st Gen. Hosp., Eng., France and Germany, 1943-45; sr. cons. ophthalmology ETO, 1944-45. Decorated Conspicuous Service Cross N.Y., Bronze Star; numerous awards from U.S. and fgn. univs. and orgns., including Barraquen Meml. award, 1965; Egyptian Med. Syndicate award, 1968; New Orleans Acad. Ophthalmology award, 1968; Ocularists award, 1970; Herman Hosp. award U. Tex., 1970; Univ. Far East award, 1970; U. Republic of China award, 1971; Israel award, 1971; Becario award, 1972; Simposia Internazionale Di Chirurgia Oculare award, 1972. Diplomate Am. Bd. Ophthalmology. Mem. A.M.A., N.Y. County Med. Soc., N.Y. Acad. Medicine (sec. 1956-57, pres. 1961-62, 75), Am. Acad. Ophthalmology and Otolaryngology, N.Y. (sec. 1960, pres. 1973), Am. ophthalmol. socs., Soc. Med. Cons. World War II, Soc. Research Ophthalmology, Ophthalmol. Found., Tokyo Bay Med. Soc., Pan Am. Ophthalmol. Assn., Physicians Sci. Soc., Oxford (Eng.) Ophthalmol. Congress, Ophthalmol. Soc. No. Spain (hon.), Soc. Rehab. Facially Disfigured, Am. Polar Soc., Phi Beta Pi. Lion (hon.). Clubs: N.Y. Athletic, Gipsy Trail, Explorers, Strollers Soc. Author: (with Dr. R. Townley Palon, Dr. Herbert M. Katzin) Atlas of Eye Surgery, rev. edit., 1962; Plastic and Reconstructive Surgery of the Eye and Adnexa, 1962; (with Dr. John M. Converse) Plastic and Reconstructive Surgery of the Ocular Adexa, 1968; Oculoplastic Surgery, 1970. Contbr. numerous articles profl. jours. Home: Manhattan House 200 E 66th St New York NY 10021 Office: 32 E 64th St New York NY 10021. *Positive, consistent thinking aiming toward a goal in life. Honesty, diligence, generosity, and persistent motivation toward maximum achievement at all times.*

SMITH, BYRON CHARLES, corp. exec.; b. Glens Falls, N.Y., June 7, 1931; s. Charles A. and Alice I. (Prince) S.; B.S. in Econs., U. Pa., 1953; m. Lois Lindsay, Dec. 20, 1952; children—Carol, Deborah, Robert, Donna. With Borden, Inc., N.Y.C., 1953-70, controller Borden Chem. div., 1968-70; with Giffen Industries, Inc., Kerrville, Tex., 1970-77, sr. v.p. adminstrn. and fin., 1971-74, dir., 1972-77, treas., 1971-73, 77—, vice chmn. bd., exec. v.p., 1974-77; chmn., pres., chief exec. officer Bylo Corp., Dallas, 1977—; dir. Pounds Photog. Labs., Austin, Tex. Mem. Fin. Execs. Inst. Home: 4239 Nashwood Ln Dallas TX 75234 Office: 2254 Valdina St Dallas TX 75207

SMITH, BYRON OWEN, lawyer; b. Mitchell, S.D., July 28, 1916; s. Frank B. and Elizabeth (Klosterman) S.; A.B., Stanford, 1937, J.D., 1940; m. Jean Knox Harris, Dec. 20, 1938; children—Sheryl S. (Mrs. Kenneth P. King), Laird W., Ryland R., Ford R. Admitted to Calif. bar, 1940; asso. Stephens, Jones, Inch & LaFever, Los Angeles, 1940-41; partner Stephens, Jones, LaFever & Smith, Los Angeles, 1945-77, Adams, DuQue & Hazeltine, Los Angeles, 1977—. Served to comdr. USNR, 1942-45, 51. Fellow Am. Coll. Probate Counsel; mem. Calif. State Club Assn. (dir. 1970—, pres. 1974), So. Calif. Golf Assn. (dir. 1966-71), Phi Delta Phi, Alpha Delta Phi. Clubs: Annandale Golf (dir. 1963-66, pres. 1966); Eldorado Country (sec., dir. 1970-72); California. Home: 765 Canterbury Rd San Marino CA 91108 Office: 523 W 6th St Los Angeles CA 90014

SMITH, C(HARLES) CARNEY, trade assn. exec.; b. Kalamazoo, Nov. 17, 1912; s. Henry and Helen (Carney) S.; student Kalamazoo Coll., 1929-31; A.B., Western Mich. Coll., 1932-33; M.A., U. Mich., 1938; postgrad. Northwestern U., 1940; LL.D. (hon.), Alma (Mich.) Coll., 1972; m. Mildred Krohne, June 18, 1934; children—Patricia Marie (Mrs. M. Kent Barker), Clark K. With Kalamazoo City Welfare Dept., 1933-35; head dept. speech, dir. forensics No. High Sch., Flint, Mich., 1935-38; chmn. dept. speech Alma Coll., 1938-42; regional dir. Eastern Area ARC, Washington, 1942-46; mgmt. tng. program Mut. Benefit Life Ins. Co., Newark, 1946-48, gen. agt., Washington, 1948-63; exec. v.p. Nat. Assn. Life Underwriters, Washington, 1963-79, cons., 1979—; trustee Life Underwriters Tng. Council; chmn. Gen. Agts. and Mgrs. Conf., 1962-63. Bd. dirs. D.C. chpt. ARC. Recipient 1970 John Newton Russell Meml. award for outstanding contbns. to life ins. industry, 1970; Distinguished Alumnus award Western Mich. U., 1972; Golden Plate award Am. Acad. Achievement, 1975. Mem. U.S., D.C. chambers commerce, Tau Kappa Alpha, Republican. Conglist. Lion. Clubs: Capitol Hill, University (Washington); Congressional (Potomac, Md.). Contbr. profl. jours. Home: 809 Vassar Rd Alexandria VA 22314 Office: 1922 F St NW Washington DC 20006

SMITH, C. KENNETH, cons.; b. Brackenridge, Pa., Feb. 1, 1918; s. Clarence H. and Mary (Ferguson) S.; ed. U. Pitts., 1942; m. AnnaBell Amlin. Partner in charge Ernst & Whinney, C.P.A.'s, Columbus, Ohio, 1964-78; guest lectr. Ohio State U. Mem. exec. com. Nat. Football Found. and Hall Fame, Columbus Sports Arena Task Force; past pres. Greater Columbus Arts Council; mem. Forward Columbus Com. Bd. dirs. Devel. Com. Greater Columbus, Quality Edn. Com., Columbus Zool Park; trustee Columbus Symphony Orch., gen. chmn. symphony grand ball, 1975; trustee, vice chmn. Franklin U. Named One of 10 Top Men in Columbus, Columbus Citizen Jour., 1971; Columbus Dispatch Blue Chip Profile, 1977. Mem. Columbus Area (chmn. bd. 1968-70), Ohio (dir. 1974—, Man of Yr. award 1979) chambers commerce, Columbus Soc. Fin. Analysts, Am. Mgmt. Assn. (pres.'s council), Nat. Assn. Corp. Dirs., Am. Inst. C.P.A.'s, Am. Acctg. Assn., Columbus Assn. Performing Arts (pres., chmn. bd. 1970-72, chmn. profl. theatre com.), Columbus Gallery Fine Arts, Columbus Civic Ballet, Nat. Audubon Soc., Am. Forestry Assn., Nature Conservancy, Am. Acad. Arts and Scis., Ohio Hist. Soc. Conglist. Mason (32 deg., Shriner), Rotarian (dir. 1976—, pres. 1978-79). Clubs: Columbus (dir. 1968-74), Columbus Country, Torch (pres. 1979-80), Athletic (Columbus); Zanesfield Rod and Gun; Maennerchor; U. Pitts. Alumni Century; Faculty, Presidents (Ohio State U.), Torch (pres.), Press of Ohio, Ohio Commodore. Home and office: Fairoaks Farm Route 3 Westerville OH 43081

SMITH, CARL REGINALD (REGGIE), baseball player; b. Shreveport, La., Apr. 2, 1945; attended Compton Community Coll., Calif. With Boston Red Sox, Am. League, 1966-73; with St. Louis Cardinals, Nat. League, 1973-76; with Los Angeles Dodgers, Nat. League, 1976—. Played in All Star Game, 1969, 72, 74, 75, 77, 78. Address: care of Los Angeles Dodgers Dodger Stadium 1000 Elysian Park Ave Los Angeles CA 90012*

SMITH, CARLETON, art authority, found. exec.; b. Bement, Ill., Feb. 19, 1910; s. Roy Harte and Kathryn Cosette (Ravellon) S.; B.S., U. Ill., 1927; M.A., U. Md., 1928; student U. Chgo., 1928-30, also London Sch. Econs.; research in Brit. Mus., Bibliothèque Nationale, Preussische Staatsbibliothek, Hofbibliothek, Vienna and other European libraries; LL.D., Marietta Coll., 1952; A.F.D. (hon.), James Milliken U., 1956; m. Anne Josephe Boireau, Feb. 19, 1957; children—Christophe C., Colombe A., Raphael. Research staff Sch. Commerce and Bus. Adminstrn., U. Chgo., 1928; instr. econs. and fgn. trade DePaul U., 1928-30, asst. prof., 1930-34; music editor Esquire, 1934-42; critic and columnist Coronet, 1936-42; fin. adviser Rubber Devel. Corp., Reconstruction Fin. Corp. subs., 1942-43; asst. to pres. Celotex Corp., 1943-45; advisor pub. relations to various corps.; dir. Nat. Arts Found., 1947—, chmn. adv. com. 1954—; cons. public affairs Austrian Fgn. Ministry, 1962-68; chmn. adv. com. Internat. Communications Found., 1969-79; European corr. N.Y. Herald Tribune, summers 1932-37; visited composers Sibelius, Strauss, Shostakovich, Ravel, Elgar, Delius, deFalla, Vaughan Williams and others; collected and recorded folk songs in Finland, Lapland, Ukraine, Uzbekistan, Kajikistan, Iran, Iraq, Afghanistan, Senegal, Congo, Kenya, Tanzania, Zaire, Brazil, Chile and Peru; interview Hitler, Molotov, Trotsky, Mussolini, Shah of Iran and presidents and leading statesmen of African and S.Am. republics; broadcasted via NBC short-wave from many European and S.Am. capitals; radio commentator N.Y. Philharmonic-Symphony Stadium Concerts, 1938; guest speaker for Met. Opera, Phila. Orch., BBC; gave lecture recitals (with Josef Hofmann and others); remarks on music recorded and broadcast by RCA-Victor; lectured at Art Inst. Chgo., Berkshire Symphonic Festival. Curtis Inst. Music, Eastman Sch. Music, San Francisco Mus. Art, N.Y. Philharmonic-Symphony League, Chgo., Cleve., Cin., Mpls., St. Louis, and Kansas City symphonies; also at Columbia, Princeton, Stanford univs., univs. of Ill., Ind., Minn., Tex., Bryn Mawr Coll., principal town halls and forums of U.S.; vis. lectr. Cambridge (Eng.) U. Cons. to Nat. Found. Mem. advisory com. Schola Cantorum of N.Y.; co-founder Ballet Theatre Found.; organizer, sec. to jury Getty Wildlife Conservation prize, 1974, Internat. Architecture prize, 1978; chmn. Internat. Awards Found., 1979—; cons. to sec. Smithsonian Instn., Washington; cons. to pres. Ind. U.; founder, dir. M.U.S.I.C. (Music from Univs. and State of Ind. Colls.); cons. on philanthropy to J. Paul Getty, Jay Pritzker, H.M. King of Saudi Arabia, edn. ministers Orgn. Petroleum Exporting Countries, numerous Am. founds. Knight Order of the White Rose conferred by Pres. of Finland, 1950; Order of Merit conferred by Pres. of Austria, 1960. Mem. Am. Acad. Polit. and Social Sci., Am. Econ. Assn., Council on Fgn. Relations, Phi Beta Kappa. Clubs: Arts, Attic (Chgo.); St. James's, Savage (London); Racquet, Lotos (N.Y.). Author: Our World after Hitler; Science; The Adventure of Tomorrow; Notes on Composers (trans. into French, German, Spanish, Russian, Chinese and Arabic); The Search for Autograph Musical Manuscripts Lost During World War II. Contbr. to newspapers and mags. Home: Bement IL 61813 also Chalet le Stop CH1882 Gryon Switzerland Office: 30th Floor Two 1st Nat Plaza Chicago IL also Postfach 34722 Vaduz Liechtenstein. *"Sell ideas, never sell time" enables me to choose each day what seems to be the most important and rewarding use of myself. "Nothing human is alien" encourages me to understand the motivation and causes of the actions of every person whose path crosses mine.*

SMITH, CAROL CASTLEMEN, JR., naval officer; b. Montgomery, Ala., Sept. 7, 1930; d. Carol Castleman and Edith (Stollenwerck) S.; B.S., U.S. Naval Acad., 1952; M.S. in Physics, U.S. Naval Postgrad. Sch., 1963; m. Sara Jane Clyde, May 4, 1957; children—Paul, Casey, lMiddleton, Laura. Commd. ensign U.S. Navy, 1952, advanced through grades to rear adm., 1976; comdg. officer Reconaissance Attack Squadron 6, Albany, Ga., 1967-68; exec. officer U.S.S. Enterprise, 1970-72, 74-76; comdg. officer U.S.S. San Jose, 1972-73; comdr. Carrier Group 8, 1977-78; dir. carrier programs div. Navy Dept., Washington, 1978—. Decorated Legion of Merit, D.F.C. Office: OPNAV 989 Navy Dept Washington DC 20350

SMITH, CATHERINE AGNES, anatomist; b. St. Louis, Jan. 5, 1914; d. John Paul and Rosa (Bahr) S.; A.B., Washington U., St. Louis, 1935, M.S., 1948, Ph.D., 1951. Research asst. otolaryngology Washington U. Med. Sch., 1948-54, instr. anatomy, 1952-54, research asso., 1954-58, asst. research prof., 1958-61, asso. research prof., 1961-66, research prof., 1966-69; research asso. Central Inst. for Deaf, 1954-62; NIH postdoctoral fellow Karolinska Inst., Stockholm, Sweden, 1958-60; prof. otolaryngology U. Oreg. Med. Sch., Portland, 1969—; cons. HEW, 1962—, mem. study sect. communication sci. NIH, 1966-70, 73-75. NIH grantee, 1955—. Fellow Accoustical Soc. Am.; mem. Am. Assn. Anatomists, Am. Otol. Soc. (award of merit 1975), Soc. Cell Biology, Neurosci. Soc., Collegium Oto-Rhino-Laryngol. (Shambaugh prize 1977), Am. Acad. Ophthalmology and Otolaryngology. Contbr. articles to profl. jours. Home: 6170 SW Lombard St Apt 12 Beaverton OR 97005 Office: 3515 SW Veterans Hosp Rd Portland OR 97201

SMITH, CECE, restaurant co. exec.; b. Washington, Nov. 16, 1944; d. Linn Charles and Grace Inez (Walker) S.; B.B.A., U. Mich., 1966; M.L.A., So. Meth. U., 1974; m. John Ford Lacy, Apr. 22, 1978. Staff accountant Arthur Young & Co., C.P.A.'s, Boston, 1966-68; staff accountant, then asst. to controller Wyly Corp., Dallas, 1969-72; controller, treas. sub. Univ. Computing Co., Dallas, 1972-74; controller Steak and Ale Restaurants Am., Inc., Dallas, 1974-76, v.p. fin., 1976—. Vice pres., bd. dirs. Jr. Achievement Dallas. C.P.A., Tex. Mem. Am. Inst. C.P.A.'s, Fin. Execs. Inst., Tex. Soc. C.P.A.'s (v.p., dir. Dallas chpt.). Home: 3609 Normandy Ave Dallas TX 75205 Office: 12890 Hillcrest Rd Dallas TX 75230

SMITH, CECIL HOWARD, III, drama critic; b. Marlow, Okla., May 22, 1917; s. Cecil Howard and Elsie (Foster) S.; student Stanford, 1935-36, U. Calif. at Los Angeles, 1936-39; m. Cleo Marion Mandicos, July 14, 1961; children—Marcus Jared, Tina Marlene. Freelance writer for radio and motion pictures, 1938-42; mem. staff Los Angeles Times, 1947—, TV critic, entertainment editor, 1958-64, drama critic, 1964-69; nationally syndicated TV columnist, 1969—; appeared edl. television, 1964—; juror Monte Carlo TV Festival; participant theatre confs. Nat. Endowment for Arts, 1965—. Served to capt. USAAF, 1942-46; PTO. Decorated D.F.C. with 2 oak leaf clusters, Air medal with 7 oak leaf clusters. Mem. Writers Guild Am. W., Drama Critics Circle. Office: Los Angeles Times Times-Mirror Sq Los Angeles CA 90053

SMITH, CHARLES ALPHONSO, pub. relations exec.; b. Chapel Hill, N.C., Mar. 18, 1909; s. C. Alphonso and Susie McGee (Heck) S.; student U. Va., 1927-31; m. Priscilla Wright, Apr. 10, 1943 (div. Apr. 1952); children—Sandra, Joanna; m. 2d, Anne Vaughan, Dec. 21, 1956; 1 son, Jonathan Richardson. Advt. research N.Y.C., 1931-33; editor, pub. Albemarle News, Charlottesville, Va., 1933-35; copywriter Vick Chem. Co., 1935-37; info. specialist Bur. Agrl. Econs., Washington, 1938-41; staff Nat. Housing Agy. and Office of Housing Expediter, Washington, 1946-47; mng. editor All Hands mag., Navy Dept., Washington, 1947; Washington rep. Burlington Industries, 1947-52; pub. relations Electric Boat, submarines, Groton, Conn., 1953-54; publs. ed. Signal Corps, Dept. of Army, 1955; dir. publs. Mfg. Chemists Assn., Washington, 1956-57; spl. Asst. Mut. Security Adminstrn., Dept. State, Washington, 1958-62; spl. asst. Domestic and Internat. Bus., Dept. Commerce, 1962-70; dir. pub. relations Keswick Virginia Co., 1970-71; pres. Super Sr. Tennis, Inc. Served from lt. (j.g.) to comdr. USNR, World War II. Mem. Va. Folklore Soc. (v.p.). Democrat. Presbyn. Clubs: Nat. Press (Washington); Army-Navy Country (Arlington, Va.); Boar's Head Sports (Charlottesville). Asso. editor World Tennis. Contbr. naval articles to mags.; winner 31 nat. tennis championships over 55 yr. period; listed in Guinness Book World Records. Home: PO Box 5165 Charlottesville VA 22905

SMITH, CHARLES ANDERSON, grocery chain exec.; b. Loch Sheldrake, N.Y., Apr. 8, 1889; s. John H. and Mary (Farquhar) S.; student pub. schs., Hurleyville, N.Y.; m. Agnes Judson, Apr. 19, 1913; children—Charles Anderson, Barbara, Hamilton, Mary Lou. Salesman, W.H. Dunne Wholesale Grocery Co., Norwich, N.Y., 1973—; officer, dir. Victory Markets Inc., Norwich, 1973—, chmn. exec. com., 1977—, also dir.; dir. Great Am. Stores, 1st City Nat. Bank. Bd. dirs. YMCA, Norwich. Methodist. Clubs: Elks, Shriners, Masons. Home: Atlantic Towers Fort Lauderdale FL 33316 also Chenango Lake PO Box 307 Norwich NY 13815 Office: Victory Markets Inc 54 E Main St Norwich NY 13815

SMITH, CHARLES CURTIS, banker; b. Sedgwick, Colo., Aug. 24, 1917; s. George Albert and Titania (Curtis) S.; B.S., Colo. State U., 1939; M.B.A., Stanford U., 1948; m. Eloise Lorraine Conant, Sept. 21, 1941; children—Gregory Conant, Bradford Kingsley. Various sales and mgmt. positions with IBM Corp. to v.p. IBM World Trade Corp., 1948-67; exec. v.p. Bankers Trust Co., N.Y.C., 1967—. Chmn. adv. bd. CIMS program Nat. YMCA, also mem. nat. bd. dirs.; bd. dirs. Downtown Manhattan Assn. Served to lt. col. U.S. Army, 1941-46. Decorated Bronze Star. Mem. Am. Bankers Assn., Assn. Res. City Bankers. Methodist. Clubs: Econo. (N.Y.C.); Blind Brook; Tamarack Country (Greenwich, Conn.). Home: 5 Dogwood Dr Armonk NY 10504 Office: 280 Park Ave New York City NY 10017

SMITH, CHARLES EDWARD, univ. chancellor; b. White County, Tenn., May 19, 1939; s. Cecil Edward and Christine (Newsome) S.; B.S. in Journalism, U. Tenn., 1961; M.A. in English, George Peabody Coll., Nashville, 1966, Ph.D. in Higher Edn., 1976; m. Shawna Lea Hickerson, Dec. 15, 1962; children—Chip, Tandy. Editor, Sparta (Tenn.) Expositor, 1961-63; mng. editor Putnam County Herald-Cookville (Tenn.) Citizen, 1963-64; asst. news editor Nashville Tennessean, 1964-67; news bur. dir. U. Tenn., Knoxville, 1967-68, pub. relations dir., 1968-70, exec. asst. to chancellor, 1970-73; exec. asst. to pres. U. Tenn. System, Knoxville, 1973-75; chancellor U. Tenn., Nashville, also v.p. pub. service U. Tenn. System, 1975—; mem., 1st v.p. Ensworth Sch. Bd., Nashville, 1976—. Bd. dirs. Nashville Better Bus. Bur., 1976—; pres. Urban Obs., 1979. Recipient Single Best Editorial award Tenn. Press Assn., 1962. Mem. Council Advancement and Support Edn., Am. Assn. State Colls. and Univs. Democrat. Mem. Ch. of Christ. Club: Nashville Downtown Rotary. Contbr. articles to profl. jours. Home: Owl's Hill Beech Creek Rd Brentwood TN 37027 Office: U Tenn 10th and Charlotte Sts Nashville TN 37203

SMITH, CHARLES HADDON, Canadian govt. ofcl.; b. Darmouth, N.S., Can., Sept. 3, 1926; s. Albion Benson and Dora Pauline (McGill) S.; B.Sc. and Diploma in Engring., Dalhousie U. (Can.), 1946, M.Sc.

in Geology, 1948; M.S., Yale U., 1951, Ph.D. in Econ. Geology, 1952; m. May Gertrude Saint, Sept. 5, 1949; children—Charles Douglas, Richard David, Alan Michael, Timothy McGill. Instr., Dalhousie U., Halifax, N.S., 1946-48; geologist Cerro de Pasco Copper Corp., Morococha, Peru, 1949; geologist Geol. Survey of Can., Ottawa, Ont., 1952-64, chief petrological scis. div., 1964-67, chief crustal geology div., 1967-68; sci. adviser Sci. Council Can., Ottawa, 1968-70; dir. planning Dept. Energy Mines and Resources, Ottawa, 1970-71, asst. dep. minister sci. and tech., 1972-74, sr. asst. dep. minister, 1975—. Mem. adv. council, dept. geol. and geophys. scis. Princeton, 1967-76. Fellow Royal Soc. Can., Mineral Soc. Am., AAAS; mem. Soc. Econ. Geologists, Canadian Inst. Mining and Metallurgy, Geol. Assn. Can. Editorial bd. Am. Jour. Sci., 1966-69, Mineralium Deposita, 1968-72, Jour. of Petrology, 1967-70. Contbr. articles to profl. jours. Home: 2056 Thistle Crescent Ottawa ON Canada Office: 580 Booth St Ottawa ON Canada

SMITH, CHARLES HENRY, JR., indsl. exec.; b. Cleve., July 28, 1920; s. Charles H. and Florence (Reno) S.; B.S., Mass. Inst. Tech., 1942; m. Rhea Day, Sept. 18, 1943; children—Charles Henry, Deborah Rhea Smith Morris, Hudson Day. Pres., dir. Steel Improvement & Forge Co., Cleve., 1943-70, chmn., chief exec. officer, 1970— (name changed to Sifco Industries, Inc.), pres. Canadian Steel Improvement, Etobicoke, Ont., 1951-54; chmn. bd. Custom Tool & Mfg. Co., Mpls., Sifco Metachem., Inc., Cleve.; chmn. bd. Formmet Corp., Avon, Ohio, 1970—; chmn., consultative council Sifco do Brazil, Sao Paulo; adv. com. bd. dirs. New Eng. Mut. Life Ins. Co., 1973-77; dir. Bharat Forge Co. Ltd., Poona, India, Aikoh Sifco Co. Ltd., Tokyo, Industrias Kaiser Argentina, 1958-63; mem. Com. on Manpower Resources for Nat. Security, 1953-54; del. Internat. Labor Conf., Geneva, 1956, Buenos Aires, 1961; mem. adv. council U.S.-Japanese econ. relations U.S. State Dept., 1970—; dir., mem. com. experts study relationship between multinat. corps. and social policy ILO, mem. governing body, 1975-78, U.S. employer del., 1975, 76, 77; dir. U.S.-USSR Econ. and Trade Council, 1975; chmn. U.S. sect. Brazil-U.S. Bus. Council, 1976-77. Trustee Cleve. YMCA, chmn. bd. mgrs. Addison br., chmn. internat. adv. com. Center Internat. Mgmt. Studies; vice chmn. No. Ohio Rep. Fin. Com.; chmn. No. Ohio Rep. Small Bus. Com., 1956; chmn. Partners of Alliance for Ohio, 1969-72; trustee Defiance Coll., 1958-74, St. Alexis Hosp., 1960-70, Booth Meml. Hosp., 1964-74; trustee Ednl. Research Council Am., 1976—, chmn., 1978—; pres. bd. trustees Forging Industry Edn. and Research Found., 1961-65; adv. bd. Salvation Army. Named One of Ten Outstanding Young Men Am., 1955. Mem. Forging Industry Assn. (dir. 1954-55, pres. 1956-58), Young Pres.'s Orgn. (chmn. Cleve. chpt. 1956-57), U.S. C. of C. (dir. 1967—, v.p. 1970-73, treas. 1973-74, chmn. bd. 1974-75). Clubs: Union (Cleve.); Shaker Heights Country (dir.); Pine Lake Trout; Burning Tree (Bethesda, Md.); Va. Hot Springs Golf and Tennis. Home: 22500 McCauley Rd Shaker Heights OH 44120 also North Ridge Hot Springs VA Office: 970 E 64th St Cleveland OH 44103

SMITH, CHARLES ISAAC, geologist; b. Hearne, Tex., Feb. 9, 1931; s. Walter Lee and Nellie Lucille (Clearwater) S.; B.S., Baylor U., 1952; M.A., La. State U., 1955; Ph.D., U. Mich., 1966; m. Anita Low Howell, Aug. 22, 1961; children—Lanita Maylene, James Emmett, Timothy Stephen, Sheila Nell. Geologist, Shell Devel. Co., Houston, 1955-60, 62-65; prof. geology U. Mich., Ann Arbor, 1965-77, chmn. dept., 1970-77; prof. geology, chmn. dept. U. Tex., Arlington, 1977—. Mem. Geol. Soc. Am., Am. Assn. Petroleum Geologists, Soc. Econ. Paleontologists and Mineralogists, Nat. Assn. Geology Tchrs., Sigma Xi, Sigma Gamma Epsilon, Phi Kappa Phi. Club: Rotary. Author research papers. Home: 2404 Highgate Dr Arlington TX 76016 Office: Dept Geology Univ Tex Arlington TX 76019

SMITH, CHARLES LLEWELLYN, JR., investment adviser; b. St. Paul, May 27, 1928; s. Charles Llewellyn and Leone (Prigge) S.; B.A. in Econs., Harvard U., 1950, M.B.A., 1955; m. Lois Gates Baer, June 3, 1951; 1 son, Charles Llewellyn, III. Security analyst, then partner State St. Research & Mgmt. Co., Boston, 1955-71, mng. partner, 1971—; v.p., treas., dir. State St. Investment Corp., 1966—; v.p., treas., dir. Fed. St. Fund, 1969—; dir. Boston Insulated Wire & Cable Co.; trustee Home Savs. Bank, Boston; gov. Investment Co. Inst. Mem. exec. com., trustee New Eng. Deaconess Hosp., Boston, 1967—; mem. com. of bd. overseers to visit Harvard U. Library, 1977; treas. Harvard Coll. Class 1950; sec. Harvard Grad. Sch. Bus. Adminstrn. Class 1955; bd. dirs. Asso. Harvard Alumni; trustee Mus. Am. China Trade. Served with USAF, 1950. Decorated Bronze Star. Mem. Financial Analysts Fedn., Boston Econs. Club. Clubs: Cohasset Golf, Cohasset Yacht; Harvard, Somerset (Boston). Office: 225 Franklin St Boston MA 02110

SMITH, CHARLES OLIVER, engr.; b. Clinton, Mass., May 28, 1920; s. Oliver E. and Flora (Small) S.; B.M.E., Worcester Poly. Inst., 1941; S.M., Mass. Inst. Tech., 1947, Sc.D. in Metallurgy, 1951; m. Mary J. Boyle, Feb. 9, 1946; children—Mary J., Charles M., John P., Susan M., Peter G., Robert A., Katherine M. Instr. mech. engring. Worcester Poly. Inst., 1941-43; instr., then asst. prof. Mass. Inst. Tech., 1946-51; research engr. Alcoa Research Lab., 1951-55, New Oak Ridge Nat. Lab., 1955-65; prof. engring. U. Detroit, 1965-76, U. Nebr., 1976—; cons. materials and design, 1941—. Active local Boy Scouts Am. Served with USNR, 1943-46. Recipient St. George award Boy Scouts Am. Mem. Am. Inst. Mining, Metall. and Petroleum Engrs., Am. Soc. Metals, Am. Welding Soc., Am. Soc. Naval Engrs., ASME, Am. Soc. Engring. Edn., Research Soc. Am., Sigma Xi, Tau Beta Pi, Pi Tau Sigma, Phi Kappa Theta. Author: Nuclear Reactor Materials; Science of Engineering Materials, 2 edits.; Introduction to Reliability in Design; also articles in field. Home: 3105 N 97th St Omaha NE 68134

SMITH, CHARLES PHILIP, state ofcl.; b. Chgo., June 18, 1926; s. William Arthur and Lillian Christine (Christensen) S.; B.A., Milton Coll., 1950; m. Bernadette C. Carroll, Aug. 23, 1947; children—Charles Philip, II, Stephen, Megan, Haley. Field rep. Guardian Life Ins. Co., Coll. Life Ins. Co., 1958-67; prodn. supr. Olin Corp., Baraboo, Wis., 1967-71; treas. State of Wis., Madison, 1971—. Pres. Madison Rivers and Lakes Commn., 1965-71; vice chmn. Dane County (Wis.) Democrats., 1969-70; McGovern del. Nat. Dem. Conv., 1972; trustee Milton Coll.; bd. dirs. Big Bros. of Dane County, Madison Opportunity Center, Wis. Spl. Olympics. Served with USMC, 1944-45. Decorated Purple Heart. Mem. Nat. Assn. State Treasurers (regional v.p.). Roman Catholic. Home: 509 S Spooner St Madison WI 53711 Office: 111 W State Capitol Madison WI 53702

SMITH, CHARLES ROGER, coll. dean, veterinarian; b. Hartville, Ohio, Mar. 31, 1918; s. Charles Roger and Ethel Olive (Seeman) S.; student Ohio U., 1936-38, 40-41; D.V.M., Ohio State U., 1944, M.Sc., 1946, Ph.D., 1953; m. Genevieve Lorraine Taylor, Aug. 9, 1946; children—Ronald Roger, Debra Smith Beckstett, Eric William. Instr. veterinary medicine Ohio State U., 1944-53, asst. prof., 1953-55, asso. prof., chmn. dept. veterinary physiology and pharmacology, 1955-59, prof., 1957-69, research prof., chmn. dept. veterinary edn., 1969-71, acting dean Coll. Veterinary Medicine, 1972-73, dean, 1973—; research asso. dept. dairy sci. U. Minn., summer 1947; asst. research veterinarian Purdue U. Agrl. Expt. Sta., summers 1949, 50, 51; vis. scholar dept. physiology Coll. Medicine, U. Wash., summer 1960; cons. Morris Animal Found.; mem. nat. adv. com. Bur. Veterinary Medicine, FDA, 1968-74; mem. com. veterinary med. rev. NIH, 1970-73. Served with ASTP, 1943-44. Recipient Gamma award Omega Tau Sigma, 1964. Diplomate in cardiology Am. Coll. Veterinary Internal Medicine. Fellow Am. Coll. Vet. Pharmacology and Therapeutics; mem. Ohio, Am. (chmn. affiliate com. research 1976—, rev. and adv. com. 1975—, chmn. 1976—) heart assns., AVMA (council on research 1959-69, chmn. 1967—), Sigma Xi, Phi Zeta. Republican. Methodist. Club: Masons. Contbg. author: Duke's Physiology of Domestic Animals, 9th edit., 1977; reviewer Am. Jour. Veterinary Research, 1959-73; contbr. numerous articles to profl. jours. Home: 4873 Chevy Chase Ave Columbus OH 43220

SMITH, CHARLES SYDNEY, JR., educator; b. Lorain, Ohio, Apr. 29, 1916; s. Charles Sydney and Mabel (Isaacson) S.; B.S., Case Inst. Tech., 1937; Sc.D., Mass. Inst. Tech., 1940; m. Barbara Fellows, Dec. 28, 1940; children—David Kingsbury, Shirley Anne, Barbara Fellows. Instr., U. Pitts., 1940-42; faculty Case Inst. Tech., 1942-68, prof. physics, 1956-68; Univ. Distinguished prof., dir. Materials Research Center, U. N.C., 1968—. Cons. to industry. Fellow Am. Phys. Soc. Spl. research solid state physics. Home: 604 Caswell Rd Chapel Hill NC 27514

SMITH, CHARLES THOMAS, dentist, educator; b. San Diego, Mar. 22, 1914; s. Sydney Alexander and Lydia Ellen (Hoff) S.; A.B., Pacific Union Coll., 1935, D.D.S., Coll. Phys. and Surg., 1940; LL.H., Loma Linda U. Sch. of Dentistry, 1971; m. Ruth Anita Anderson, May 20, 1935 (dec. Jan. 1979); children—Charlyn Ruth, Charles Thomas; m. 2d, Mary Lou Sussman, July 21, 1979. Tchr., Glendale Union Acad., 1935-36; pvt. practice dentistry, San Diego, 1940-53; dean-elect Sch. Dentistry, Loma Linda U., 1959-60, dean, 1960-71; dean emeritus, 1971—; program coordinator div. Physicians and Health Profession Edn., NIH, 1971-73; prof. dept. community dentistry U. Tex. at San Antonio, 1973—, acting dean student affairs Dental Sch., 1975-76, asso. dean for acad. affairs, 1976-77, acting chmn. dept. community dentistry, 1977—. Cons. dental facilities review com. USPHS, 1964—; mem. grants and allocations com. Am. Found. for Dental Health, 1973—. Dir. Paradise Valley Sanitarium and Hosp., 1947-59; San Diego Union Acad., 1947-53; founder San Diego Children's Dental Health Center; exhibit chmn. Pacific Coast Dental Conf., 1957; pres. Am. Cancer Soc., 1950; trustee Loma Linda U., 1976—. Served as maj. AUS Dental Corps, 1953-55. Fellow Am. Coll. Dentists (vice chmn. So. Calif. chpt. 1967-68, chmn. 1968-69), Internat. Coll. Dentists; mem. So. Calif. Dental Assn. (chmn. council on dental edn. 1963-68), San Diego County Dental Soc. (pres. 1949), Am. Acad. Dental Practice Adminstrn., Western Dental Deans Assn. (chmn. 1960-67), Western Deans and Dental Examiners (v.p. 1969—, pres. 1970), Am. Assn. Dental Schs. (mem. exec. com., v.p. council deans, 1971), Nat. Assn. Seventh Day Adventists, Am. Acad. Periodontology, Delta Sigma Delta, Tau Kappa Omega, Omicron Kappa Upsilon. Home: 5515 King Richard San Antonio TX 78229

SMITH, CHARLES WALLACE, hockey coach; b. St. Paul, Jan. 5, 1930; s. Charles Wallace and Rose Ann (Schultheis) S.; B.S., St. Thomas Coll., 1951, M.A. in Guidance, 1968; m. Mary Rand McNally, June 16, 1951; children—Christine, Cynthia, Mike, Cheryl, Greg, Sheila, Tom, Mary Beth. With Concord Beverage Co., 1951-52; tchr., South St. Paul, Minn., 1953-68; hockey coach U. Notre Dame (Ind.), 1968—. Pres. Wakota Arena Inc., Kids Inc., South St. Paul. Recipient Distinguished Citizen award South St. Paul Jaycees; named Coach of Yr., Western Coll. Hockey Assn., 1973. Mem. Am. Fedn. Tchrs. K.C. Home: 2619 Summit Ridge South Bend IN 46628 Office: Athletic Dept U Notre Dame South Bend IN 46656

SMITH, CHARLES WHITLEY, distbn. systems design counsellor; b. Kansas City, Mo., Jan. 27, 1913; s. Walter Grey and Ada Rachel (Tucker) S.; B.S., U. Mo., 1933; m. Mary Kathryn Cotten, Nov. 5, 1938; children—Kathryn Hunnicutt, Sarah Tucker. Asst. to v.p. H. T. Poindexter & Sons Mdse. Co., 1933-34; sales promotion Hills Bros. Coffee, Inc., 1934-36; distbn. analyst Gen. Electric Co., 1936-44; mgmt. cons. McKinsey & Co., N.Y.C., 1944-56; sr. cons. McKinsey & Co., Inc., 1956-59; dir. distbn. planning and research Nat. Biscuit Co. (now Nabisco, Inc.), 1959-78; counsellor total distbn. systems design. Former chmn. distbn. statistics com. Fed. Statistics Users Conf.; mem. Council on Marketing Research. Mem. Am. Marketing Assn. (treas. 1952-55, v.p. 1955-56, pres. 1956-57), Am. Statis. Assn., Nat. Council Phys. Distbn. Mgmt. (chmn. finance com., chmn. research com.). Club: Sales Executives (mem., former chmn. research com.) (N.Y.). Author: Targeting Sales Effort, 1958; Making Your Sales Figures Talk, 1963. Home and office: 25 The Loch Roslyn Estates NY 11576

SMITH, CLYDE FUHRIMAN, educator, entomologist; b. Franklin County, Ida., Aug. 10, 1913; s. Isaac and Elizabeth (Fuhriman) S.; B.S., Utah Agricultural Coll., 1935, M.S., 1938; Ph.D., Ohio State U. 1939; m. Crystle Keller, June 9, 1936; children—Clara Beth, Carolynn, Clyde Leslie. Asst. in entomology Utah Agr. Expt. Sta., 1934-36; asst. extension entomol., Ohio, summers, 1938-39; asst. entomol. N.C. Agr. Expt. Sta., 1939-43, asso. entomol., 1942-47; asst. prof. entomology N.C. State Coll., 1941-45, asso. prof., 1945-47; research prof. entomol. N. C. State Coll. and N.C. Expt. Sta., 1947-50, head dept. entomology, 1950-64, research prof. entomology, 1964—. Chmn. N.C. Structural Pest Control Commn., 1955-67. Mem. N.C. Entomol. Soc. (pres. 1956-57, award for outstanding contribution to entomology 1972), AAAS, Entomol Soc. Am. (pres. Southeastern br. 1972-73), N.C. Acad. Sci., U.S. Power Squadron, Phi Kappa Phi, Sigma Xi, Gamma Sigma Delta. Mem. Ch. Jesus Christ of Latter-Day Saints. Author: The Aphidlinae of North America; The Pemphiginae (Homoptera Aphididae) of North America; Bibliography of the Aphididae of the World. Home: 2716 Rosedale St Raleigh NC 27607

SMITH, CULLEN, lawyer; b. Waco, Tex., May 31, 1925; s. Curtis Cullen and Elizabeth (Brient) S.; student Emory U., 1943-44, Duke U., 1944; B.B.A., Baylor U., 1948, J.D., 1950; m. Laura Risher Dossett, Mar. 6, 1948; children—Sallie Chesnutt Smith Wright, Alethea Risher, Elizabeth Brient. Admitted to Tex. bar, 1950; partner firm Smith, McIlheran & Smith, Weslaco, Tex., 1950-53, Naman, Howell, Smith, Lee & Muldrow, P.C., Waco, 1953—; dir. Westview Nat. Bank, Waco, Tex. Life Ins. Co.; lectr. law Baylor U. Sch. Law, 1964-72. Mem. standing com. Episcopal Diocese of Tex., 1960-63, 74-75; trustee Episc. Theol. Sem. of S.W., 1962-67. Served to 1st lt. USMCR, 1943-46. Named One of 5 Outstanding Young Texans, Tex. Jr. C. of C., 1957. Fellow Am., Tex. (chmn. bd. 1973-74) bar founds.; mem. Am. (chmn. standing com. econs. law practice 1965-69, chmn. spl. com. on law book pub. practices 1970-72, chmn. gen. practice sect. 1973-74, mem. ho. of dels. 1974—), Waco-McLennan County (pres. 1956-57), Mont. (hon.) bar assns., State Bar Tex. (pres. jr. bar 1957-58, chmn. profl. econs. com. 1959-61, chmn. spl. com. on revision Tex. Canons Ethics 1969-71, dir. 1971-74, pres. 1978-79), Baylor U. Law Alumni Assn. (pres. 1962-63), Order of Coif, Delta Sigma Phi, Phi Delta Phi. Clubs: Rotary; Ridgewood Country (pres. 1965), Hedonia (pres. 1957), City (pres. 1968) (Waco). Contbr. articles to legal publs. Home: 2701 Lake Air Dr Waco TX 76710 Office: Tex Center PO Box 1470 Waco TX 76703

SMITH, CURTIS GRIFFIN, educator, biologist; b. Milw., Nov. 14, 1923; s. Joseph Griffin and Clara (Shanbarker) S.; A.B., U. Chgo., 1947, Ph.D., 1954; m. Elaine Thompson, June 21, 1947; children—Eliot Randall, Katherine Anne, Alison Gay. Instr. biophysics U. Cal. at Los Angeles Med Sch., 1954-55; mem. faculty Mt. Holyoke Coll., 1955—, prof. biology, 1969—; vis. prof. biophysics U. E. Anglia, Norwich, Eng., 1969-70. Served with AUS, 1943-46. Grantee NSF, 1959-68. Mem. Am. Soc. Biol. Chemists, N.Y. Acad. Scis., Soc. Gen. Microbiology, Sigma Xi. Author: Introduction to Biophysics, 1971; also articles. Home: 32 Atwood Rd South Hadley MA 01075

SMITH, CYRIL JAMES, pipeline co. exec.; b. N.Y.C., Aug. 29, 1930; s. Franklin W. and Elizabeth (Cowley) S.; A.B., Brown U., 1952; LL.D., U. Va., 1955. Admitted to N.Y. bar, 1959; with firm Lord, Day & Lord, N.Y.C., 1955-65, Paris, France, 1965-66; resident atty. N.Y.C., Panhandle Eastern Pipe Line Co., 1966-67, corp. sec., Houston, 1967—, asst. to pres., 1974-77; corp. sec. Trunkline Gas Co., Century Refining Co., Youghiogheny & Ohio Coal Co., 1978—. Served with USNR, 1956-57. Home: 7534 del Monte Houston TX 77063 Office: 3000 Bissonnet Houston TX 77005

SMITH, CYRUS ROWLETT, business exec.; b. Minerva, Tex., Sept. 9, 1899; s. Roy Edgerton and Marion (Burck) S.; ed. U. Tex., 1920-24; m. Elizabeth L. Manget, Dec. 29, 1934 (div.); 1 son, Douglas Manget. Pub. accountant Peat, Marwick Mitchell & Co., Dallas, 1924-26; asst. treas. Tex.-La. Power Co., Ft. Worth, 1926-28; v.p. Tex. Air Transport, Inc., Ft. Worth, 1929-30; v.p. Am. Airways, Inc., Ft. Worth and St. Louis, 1930-33; v.p. Am. Airlines, Inc., Ft. Worth, 1934, pres., Chgo. and N.Y.C., 1934-42, chmn. bd., 1946-68, chmn., chief exec. officer, 1973-74; U.S. sec. commerce, 1968; partner Lazard Freres and Co., 1968-73. Served from col. to maj. gen. USAAF, 1942-45; dep. comdr. Air Transport Command, 1942-45. Decorated D.S.M., Legion of Merit, Air Medal (U.S.); comdr. Order Brit. Empire; recipient Disting. Ser. award Wings Club, 1978; named to Aviation Hall of Fame, 1974, Travel Hall of Fame, 1973, Bus. Hall of Fame, 1975. Democrat. Baptist. Club: Metropolitan (Washington). Address: 2358 Massachusetts Ave NW Washington DC 20008

SMITH, D. DAVID, c. of c. exec.; b. Bargersville, Ind., July 10, 1928; s. Donald Edgar and Velva Doris (Whitehead) S.; B.S., Ind. U., 1950; m. Rachel Irene Maddux, Sept. 4, 1950; children—David Gregory, Elizabeth Anne. Asst. mgr., retail div. mgr. San Leandro (Calif.) C. of C., 1956-60; exec. mgr. Woodland (Calif.) Dist. C. of C., 1960-65; exec. v.p. Greater Stockton (Calif.) C. of C., 1965—. Served with USAF, 1951-55. Mem. Calif. Assn. C. of C. Execs. (pres. 1970-71), Nat. Inst. for Orgn. Mgmt. (chmn. bd. regents). Home: 1421 W Alpine St Stockton CA 95204 Office: 1105 N El Dorado St Stockton CA 95202

SMITH, D. RICHARD, univ. adminstr.; b. Lafayette, Ind., Dec. 27, 1930; s. Guy M. and Hilda (Sattler) S.; B.S., Purdue U., 1953, M.S., 1957, Ph.D., 1960; m. Virginia Lehker, Aug. 24, 1957; children—Richard, Steven. Asst. prof. speech Albion Coll., 1960-62; asst. dir. Ft. Wayne campus Purdue U., 1962-65, dean, dir., 1965-70, prof. gen. studies, 1965—, v.p. Purdue U., Lafayette, Ind., 1970—, asst. to v.p., 1970-74, asst. to provost, 1974-76, asst. dir. internat. edn. and research, 1976-79, asso. dir., 1979—, asso. dir. internat. programs in agr., 1979—. Dir. Ft. Wayne Fine Arts Found., 1967-69, Ft. Wayne Y.M.C.A., 1969, Northeastern Ind. Mental Health Center, 1967-69, Adult Psychiat. Center, 1965-67. Vice presdl. alternate Ind. State U. Telecommunication Coordinating Council, 1970—; mem. community devel. com., greater Lafayette C. of C. Served with AUS, 1953-55; decorated Army Commendation medal. Purdue Research Found. Research fellow. Mem. Am. Assn. U. Profs., Isaac Walton League, Fort Wayne C. of C. (dir. 1967-70), Kappa Delta Pi, Phi Mu Alpha. Tenor soloist Operation Friendship European Tour, 1953; timpanist Jackson (Mich.) Symphony, 1961-62; timpanist Lafayette (Ind.) Symphony, 1970—. Clubs: Fort Wayne Quest, Fortnightly Sec. Home: 2851 Ashland Dr West Lafayette IN 47906 Office: 121 Agrl Adminstrn Purdue U Lafayette IN 47907

SMITH, DACOSTA, JR., lawyer; b. Weston, W.Va., Apr. 22, 1917; s. DaCosta and Mattie Jane (Callison) S.; A.B., W.Va. U., 1937, J.D., 1941; m. Florence Gray Koblegard, Apr. 12, 1947; children—Linda, Marcia, DaCosta III. Admitted to W.Va. bar, 1941, since practiced in Weston; dir. Midland Enterprises, Inc., 1956-62, Ohio River Co., 1956-61; trustee, dir. Eastern Gas & Fuel Assos., 1962-74; v.p., gen. counsel Eastern Associated Coal Corp., 1964-74. Served to lt. (s.g.) USNR, World War II. Mem. W. Va., W.Va. State, Lewis County bar assns., Weston C. of C. (dir.), Kappa Alpha, Phi Delta Phi. Episcopalian. Clubs: Weston Rotary, Deerfield Country. Home: 440 Center Ave Weston WV 26452 Office: 135 Main St Weston WV 26452

SMITH, DALE EDWIN, publisher; b. Taylorville, Ill., Nov. 8, 1930; s. Floyd R. and Mildred L. (Buffington) S.; B.S., U. Ill., 1960; m. Florence Harris, Aug. 28, 1958; children—Laurie, Greg. Advt. salesman Champaign (Ill.) News Gazette, 1954-60, Meredith Pub. Co., Chgo., 1960-62; advt. salesman Chgo. Farm Jour., 1963-64, Chgo. mgr., 1965-71, v.p., sales mgr., Phila., 1971-74, v.p. sales, mktg. mgr., Phila., 1974-75, v.p., pub., Phila., 1975-76, pres., pub., Phila., 1976—. Served with AUS, 1951-53. Mem. Mag. Pubs. Am. (dir.), Agrl. Pubs. Assn. (dir.), Nat. Agr. and Mktg. Assn. Office: 230 W Washington Sq Philadelphia PA 19105

SMITH, DAN THROOP, economist, educator, govt. ofcl.; b. Chgo., Nov. 20, 1907; s. Elbert Ellis and Olive (Cole) S.; A.B., Stanford U., 1928; student U. London, 1928-29; Ph.D., Harvard, 1934; D.Sc., Iowa Wesleyan Coll., 1962; m. Martha Louise Vaughan, June 15, 1935; children—Deborah Throop (Mrs. Charles M. Leighton), Louise Lord (Mrs. William G. Bowman), Dan Throop Smith. Mem. faculty Harvard, 1930—, prof. finance, 1945-69, prof. emeritus, 1969—; lectr. Stanford, 1968-73; sr. research fellow Hoover Instn., 1969—; dir. AAF Statis. Sch., spl. cons. to comdg. gen. U.S. Air Force, 1943-45; asst. to sec. Dept. Treasury, 1953-55, spl. asst. to sec., 1955-57, dep. to sec., 1957-59. Dir. Cambridge Research Inst., CML Group, Hon Industries. Mem. Pres.' Task Force on Bus. Taxation, 1969-70; mem. Commn. on Internat. Trade and Investment, 1970-71; chmn. tax adv. com. Council on Environ. Quality, 1970-73. Trustee Iowa Wesleyan Coll., 1962-76, life trustee, 1976—. Mem. Am. Econ. Assn., Am. Finance Assn., Tax Inst. Am. (pres. 1963), Nat. Tax Assn. (pres. 1967), Phi Beta Kappa. Republican. Unitarian. Clubs: Harvard (N.Y.C.); Cosmos (Washington). Author: Deficits and Depressions, 1936; Taxable and Business Income (with J. Keith Butters), 1949; Effects of Taxation on Corporate Financial Policy, 1952; Federal Tax Reform; The Issues and a Program, 1961; Tax Factors in Business Decisions, 1968. Contbr. articles to profl. jours. Home: 501 Portola Rd Box 8140 Portola Valley CA 94025 Office: Hoover Instn Stanford CA 94305

SMITH, DANIEL CLAYTON, lawyer; b. Spokane, Mar. 9, 1916; s. James Clayton and Helen (Carmody) S.; A.B., U. Chgo., 1937, J.D., 1940; m. Louise Hoyt, Sept. 14, 1940; children—Daniel, Ellen (Mrs. Michael E. Withey), Sheila, Lawrence, Monica, Rita (Mrs. Stephen Bauersmith), Clayton, Nora. Admitted to Ill. bar, 1940, Wash., State bar, 1953; tchr. U. Chgo. Law Sch., 1940-41; pvt. practice law, Chgo., 1941-50; with Weyerhaeuser Co., 1950-55, asst. gen. counsel, 1959-61, gen. counsel, 1961-69, v.p., 1969-75; v.p., gen. counsel FMC Corp., 1976—. Mem. vis. com. U. Chgo. Law Sch., U. Puget Sound

Law Sch. Mem. Am. Bar Assn., Assn. Gen. Counsel, Phi Beta Kappa, Order of Coif, Alpha Delta Phi. Clubs: Mid-Am., University, Saddle and Cycle (Chgo.). Home: Apt 26-E 990 N Lake Shore Dr Chicago IL 60611 Office: FMC Corp 200 E Randolph Dr 67th Floor Chicago IL 60601

SMITH, DANIEL JAMES, JR., civil engr.; b. Los Angeles, Sept. 27, 1914; s. Daniel James and Maria Magdalena (Santa Maria) S.; student Los Angeles City Coll., 1940-42, Oreg. State U., 1943-44; B.S. in Civil Engring., U. So. Calif., 1948; m. Madeleine Darthea Lehmann, Feb. 8, 1942; children—Kathleen Darthea, Gregory James. Engring. designer Clyde C. Deuel, cons. engr., Los Angeles, 1948-54; civil engr., project mgr. Koebig & Koebig, Inc., Los Angeles, 1954-67; civil engr. Met. Water Dist. So. Calif., Los Angeles, 1967-77, sr. engr. for spl. projects. Served in U.S. Army, 1942-46. Mem. ASCE (Thomas Fitch Rowland prize 1976), Earthquake Engring. Research Inst., Structural Engrs. Assn. So. Calif. Roman Catholic. Home: 919 University Ave Burbank CA 91504 Office: 1111 Sunset Blvd Los Angeles CA 90054

SMITH, DANIEL RICHARD, banker; b. Kalamazoo, Mar. 19, 1934; s. Claud Faust and Ruth M. (Lill) S.; B.A., Western Mich. U., 1955; m. Julia Ann Marquardt, June 18, 1955; children—Jeffrey, Cynthia, Melinda. With 1st Nat. Bank & Trust Co. Mich., Kalamazoo, 1955—, sr. v.p., trust officer, 1972-76, pres., 1976—. Pres. Kalamazoo Jaycees, 1962, Indian Prarie P.T.A., 1969; pres., dir. Kalamazoo Nature Center, 1968—. Bd. dirs. Kalamazoo Community Caucus, 1960—; bd. dirs., treas. Kalamazoo Sr. Citizens Fund, 1971—; mem. bd. control Tau Kappa Epsilon, 1965-70. Mem. Am. Bankers Assn., Kalamazoo C. of C. (dir. 1962). Episcopalian (vestryman 1965-70). Clubs: Kalamazoo Country, Park (Kalamazoo). Office: 108 E Michigan Ave Kalamazoo MI 49001*

SMITH, DARWIN EATNA, paper mfg. co. exec.; b. Garrett, Ind., Apr. 16, 1926; s. K. Bryant and Hazel (Sherman) S.; B.S. in Bus. with distinction, Ind. U., 1950; LL.B. cum laude, Harvard, 1955; m. Lois Claire Archbold, Aug. 19, 1950; children—Steven, Pamela, Valerie, Blair. Admitted Ill. bar, 1955, Wis. bar, 1958; asso. atty. firm Sidley, Austin, Burgess & Smith, Chgo., 1955-58; With Kimberly-Clark Corp., Neenah, Wis., 1958—, gen. atty., 1960—, v.p. 1962-67, v.p. finance and law, 1967-70, pres., 1970—, chmn., chief exec. officer, 1971—. Served with AUS, 1944-46. Mem. Am., Wis. bar assns., Am. Legion. Presbyn. Mason (32). Home: Rural Route 1 Box 211 Menasha WI 54952 Office: Kimberly-Clark Corp Neenah WI 54957

SMITH, DATUS CLIFFORD, JR., found. exec.; b. Jackson, Mich., May 3, 1907; s. Datus Clifford and Marion (Houston) S.; B.S., Princeton, 1929, M.A. (hon.), 1958; m. Dorothy Hunt, Aug. 29, 1931 (dec. 1973); children—Sandra, Karen. Grad. mgr. student employment Princeton U., 1929-30, asst. editor Princeton Alumni Weekly, 1930-31, editor, 1931-40; asst. mng. editor Public Opinion Quar., 1937-39; asst. editor Princeton U. Press, 1940-41, editor 1941-1953, dir. sec., 1942-53; asso. prof. Princeton U., 1943-47, prof., 1947-53, mem. adv. council dept. East Asian studies; pres. Franklin Book Programs, 1952-67, chmn., 1975-79; v.p. JDR 3d Fund, 1967-73; asso. John D. Rockefeller 3d, 1967-73; coordinator Japan philanthropy project Council on Founds., 1974-75; cons. Asia Soc., Nat. Endowment for Humanities, Hazen Found., Am. Council Learned Socs., Assn. Am. Pubs., UNESCO, Indo-U.S. Subcom. Edn. and Culture; past chmn. Found. Internat. Group; Bowker lectr. N.Y. Pub. Library, 1958; adv. council Center for Book, Library of Congress; past pres. Assn. Am. Univ. Presses; dir. Am. Book Pub. Council. Past chmn. editorial com. Pub. Opinion Quar.; vis. com. Harvard Press; Nat. Book Com.; trustee Center Applied Linguistics, Japan Center Internat. Exchange, Asia Soc., United Bd. Christian Higher Edn. in Asia, JDR 3d Fund, Haskins Labs., Nat. Council for Children and TV, Internat. Bd. on Books for Young People; trustee, pres. U.S. Com. for UNICEF; past mem. U.S. nat. commn. UNESCO. Decorated Order of Homayoun (Iran); recipient Distinguished Service award Assn. Am. Univ. Presses, 1975. Mem. Council Fgn. Relations. Clubs: Princeton, Rockefeller Center (N.Y.C.). Author: Land and People of Indonesia, 1961; Guide to Book Publishing, 1966; Economics of Book Publishing in Developing Countries, 1976. Contbr. to Atlantic Monthly, Saturday Review, Publishers Weekly, Fgn. Affairs, others. Home: 29 Wilson Rd Princeton NJ 08540 Office: Asia Soc 112 E 64th St New York NY 10021

SMITH, DAVID COLES, univ. adminstr.; b. LaPorte, Ind., June 10, 1932; s. Earl Lawrence and Winifred (Burton) S.; B.A., State Coll. Iowa, 1954, M.A., 1958; Ph.D., Northwestern U., 1966; m. Elizabeth Rule, Mar. 15, 1952; children—Pauline Louise, Earl Coles. Prin., Cresco (Iowa) Public Schs., 1954-60; dir. elem. edn. Decorah (Iowa) Community Sch. Dist., 1960-61; prin. Crow Island Sch., Winnetka, Ill., 1961-66; asso. prof. adminstrn. Mich. State U. Sch. Edn., 1966-70; div. coordinator U. Ark. Coll. Edn., 1972-76, dir. Ark.-in-Athens, 1973-76; dean U. Mont. Sch. Edn., 1976-78; dean U. Fla. Coll. Edn., 1978—. Bd. dirs. Profl. Archers Assn. Mem. Nat. Assn. Elem. Prins., Am. Assn. Advancement Internat. Edn. (dir.), Nat. Center Career Edn. (dir.), Profl. Archer's Assn., Phi Delta Kappa (pres. Upsilon campus chpt. 1964-66). lMethodist. Author monographs: A Cooperative Enterprise: Teachers and Teachers' Aides, 1969; Auditing Academic Programs—A Model, 1974. Home: 8612 SW First Pl Gainesville FL 32601 Office: Office of Den Coll Edn 140 Norman Hall U Fla Gainesville FL 32611

SMITH, DAVID EDMUND, geophysicist; b. Brentford, Eng., Nov. 3, 1934; s. Alfred Edmund and Violet (Hicks) S.; came to U.S., 1968; B.Sc. in Math., U. Durham (Eng.), 1958; M.Sc. in Math., U. London, 1962, Ph.D. in Satellite Geodesy, 1966; m. Veronica Mary Sparnon, July 1, 1961; children—Keri Elizabeth, Alistair David, Jeremy Edmund, Meredith Louise. Sci. officer Radio and Space Research Sta., Slough, Eng., 1958-68; sr. scientist Wolf Research and Devel. Corp., Riverdale, Md., 1968-69; staff scientist NASA Goddard Space Flight Center, Greenbelt, Md., 1969-71, head geodynamics br., 1971—; mem. Internat. Union Geodesy and Geophysics Commn. on Satellite Geodesy; mem. Internat. Assn. Geodesy Study Group on Fundamental Constants and Study Group on Reference Systems for Geodesy; mem. Internat. Astron. Union Working Group on Earth Rotation. Recipient Exceptional Sci. Achievement medal NASA, 1974, John C. Lindsay Meml. award Goddard Space Flight Center, 1978. Fellow Royal Astron. Soc.; mem. Am. Geophys. Union. Contbr. numerous articles to profl. publs. Home: 13920 Blair Stone Ln Wheaton MD 20906 Office: Code 921 Geodynamics Br Goddard Space Flight Center Greenbelt MD 20771

SMITH, DAVID ENGLISH, physician, educator; b. San Francisco, June 9, 1920; s. David English and Myrtle (Goodin) S.; A.B., Central Coll. Mo., 1941; M.D. cum laude, Washington U., St. Louis, 1944; m. Margaret Elizabeth Bronson, June 9, 1948; children—Ann English Smith Aberle, David Bronson, Mary Margaret. Intern, resident pathology Barnes Hosp., St. Louis, 1944-46; instr. pathology Washington U. Med. Sch., 1948-51, asst. prof., 1951-54, asst. head dept., 1953-54, asso. prof., 1954-55; prof. pathology U. Va. Sch. Medicine, 1955-73, chmn. dept., 1958-73, dir. div. Cancer Studies, 1972-73; prof. pathology Northwestern U. Sch. Medicine, 1974-75, U. Pa. Sch. Medicine, 1976—; asso. dir. Am. Bd. Med. Spltys., 1974-75; v.p., sec., dir. undergrad. evaluation Nat. Bd. Med. Examiners, 1975—; trustee Am. Bd. Pathology, 1966-73, v.p., 1973; mem. Nat. Bd. Med. Examiners, chmn. pathology test com., 1966-72, exec. com., 1970-74; mem. sci. bd. cons.'s Armed Forces Inst. Pathology, 1970-74. Pres. Va. div. Am. Cancer Soc., 1967-69. Served from 1st lt. to capt. M.C., AUS, 1946-48. Mem. Va. Soc. Pathology (pres. 1960), Am. Assn. Pathologists, Internat. Acad. Pathology (council 1956-59, pres. 1964-65), Am. Soc. Clin. Pathologists (co-dir. self assessment program 1970-75), AMA, Am. Acad. Neurology, AAAS, Sigma Xi, Alpha Omega Alpha, Phi Beta Pi, Alpha Epsilon Delta. Editor: Survey of Pathology in Medicine and Surgery, 1966-70. Contbr. articles to profl. publs. Home: 1320 Grenox Rd Wynnewood PA 19096 Office: 3930 Chestnut St Philadelphia PA 19104

SMITH, DAVID GILBERT, educator; b. Norman, Okla., Oct. 10, 1926; s. Gilbert H. and Virginia (Haizlip) S.; A.B., U. Okla., 1948, M.A., 1950; Ph.D, Johns Hopkins, 1953; student London (Eng.) Sch. Econs., 1955-56; m. Eleanor C. Gergen; children—Alison Claire, Joel Anthony. Instr. polit. sci. Swarthmore Coll., 1953-55; asst. prof. Stanford, 1956-57; mem. faculty Swarthmore Coll., 1957—, prof. polit. sci., 1967—, chmn. dept., 1970—; cons. HEW, Nat. Acad. Scis.-NRC, Ford Found. Chmn. Delaware County chpt. ACLU, 1965-70; mem. bd. Delaware County Health and Welfare Council, 1970—, chmn., 1971. Served with AUS, 1945-46; PTO. Mem. Am. Polit. Sci. Assn., Am. Soc. Polit. and Legal Philosphy, Phi Beta Kappa Author: (with J. Roland Pennock) Political Science; An Introduction, 1965; The Convention and the Constitution, 1965; also articles. Home: 3 Whittier Pl Swarthmore PA 19081

SMITH, DAVID HAMILTON, pediatrician, educator; b. Canton, Ohio, May 17, 1931; s. Cloyd D. and Mary W. S.; A.B., Ohio Wesleyan U., 1953; M.D., U. Rochester, 1958; children—Andrea, Jennifer, Rachel. Asso. prof. pediatrics Harvard Med. Sch., Boston, 1969-76; chief infectious diseases div. dept. medicine Children's Hosp. Med. Center, Boston, 1968-76; prof., chmn. dept. pediatrics U. Rochester Sch. Medicine and Dentistry, 1976—; vis. prof. U. Geneva, 1974-75; pediatrician-in-chief Strong Meml. Hosp., Rochester, 1976—. Served to capt. M.C., USAF, 1959-61. Recipient Disting. Scientist award Med. Soc. Czechkolovakia, 1972; E. Mead Johnson award, 1975; Milton Found. fellow, 1964-65; Guggenheim Found. fellow, 1974-75. Mem. AAAS, Am. Soc. Microbiology, Soc. Pediatric Research, New Eng. Pediatric Soc., Soc. Infectious Diseases, Am. Soc. Clin. Investigation, Am. Pediatric Soc., Alpha Omega Alpha. Contbr. articles to med. jours. Home: 334 Clover Hills Dr Rochester NY 14618 Office: 601 Elmwood Ave Rochester NY 14642*

SMITH, DAVID LEE, sports editor; b. Shelby, Ohio, Apr. 4, 1939; s. Ferris Francis and Rita Ann (Metzger) S.; student Pontifical Coll. Josephinum, Worthington, Ohio, 1953-56, Ohio State U., Mansfield, 1971; m. Betty Stewart Walker, Sept. 10, 1960; children—Stacie Lynn, Stefanie Linn, David Lee, II. Sports writer Mansfield News-Jour., 1960-61; sports editor Ashland (Ohio) Times-Gazette, 1961-63, Miami (Fla.) News, 1963-67, Ft. Lauderdale (Fla.) News, 1967-70, Boston Globe, 1970-78, Washington Star, 1978—; condr. seminars. Served with USMCR, 1957-60. Mem. AP Sports Editors Assn. (1st pres. 1974-75), Baseball Writers Assn., Football Writers Assn. Roman Catholic. Home: 11403 Drop Forge Ln Reston VA 22091 Office: Washington Star 225 Virginia Ave SE Washington DC 20061

SMITH, DAVID MARTYN, educator; b. Bryan, Tex., Mar. 10, 1921; s. John Blackmer and Doris (Clark) S.; B.S., U. R.I., 1941; postgrad. N.Y. U., 1942; M.F., Yale, 1946, Ph.D., 1950; m. Catherine Van Aken, June 16, 1951; children—Ellen, Nancy. Instr., Sch. Forestry and Environ. Studies, Yale, 1946-47, 48-51, asst. prof., 1951-57, asst. dean, 1953-58, asso. prof., 1957-63; prof., 1963—, Morris K. Jesup prof. silviculture, 1967; silviculture cons. Pres.'s Adv. Panel on Timber and Environment, 1972-73. Pres., dir. Connwood, Inc. Pres. Conn. Forest and Park Assn. Served to capt. USAAF, 1942-45. Fellow Soc. Am. Foresters; mem. Ecol. Soc. Am., Sigma Xi, Phi Kappa Phi. Republican. Mem. United Ch. of Christ. Author: Practice of Silviculture, 1962. Home: 55 Woodlawn St Hamden CT 06517 Office: 205 Prospect St New Haven CT 06511

SMITH, DAVID SHIVERICK, ambassador, lawyer; b. Omaha, Jan. 25, 1918; s. Floyd Monroe and Anna (Shiverick) S.; Degre Superieur, Sorbonne, Paris, 1938; B.A., Dartmouth Coll., 1939; J.D., Columbia U., 1942; m. June Noble, Dec. 8, 1945 (div. 1968); children—Noble, David Shiverick, Jeremy T., Bradford D. m. 2d, Mary Edson, Feb. 14, 1972. Admitted to N.Y. bar, 1942, Conn. bar, 1950, D.C. bar, 1954; asso. with Breed, Abbott & Morgan, N.Y.C., 1946-48; legal dept. ABC, N.Y.C., 1948-50; partner Chapman, Bryson, Walsh & O'Connell, N.Y.C., also Washington, 1950-54; spl. asst. Under Sec. State, Washington, 1954, asst. sec. Air Force, 1954-59; dir. internat. fellows program Columbia, 1959-75, coordinator internat. studies, 1960-75, asso. dean sch. internat. affairs, 1960-74, cons. AEC, 1959-60; partner firm Baker & McKenzie and predecessor firm, N.Y.C., Washington, until 1974; partner firm Martin, Whitfield, Smith & Bebchick, Washington, 1975-76, 77—; ambassador to Sweden, 1976-77; dir. United Services Life Ins. Corp., United Interests Corp. Mem. Council Fgn. Relations; dir. Fedn. Protestant Welfare Agys., Inc., Fgn. Policy Assn.; mem. adv. council Sch. Advanced Internat. Studies, Johns Hopkins U., 1962—; pres. Center for Inter-Am. Relations, N.Y.C, 1969-74. Bd. dirs. Boys' Clubs Am., N.Y.C.; chmn. bd. advisers Nat. Trust for Historic Preservation, 1963-70; dir., sec. Nat. Multiple Sclerosis Soc., 1965-70; mem. adv. Council Sch. Advanced Internat. Studies; alumni council Dartmouth; mem. adv. com. Nat. Cultural Center, Washington, 1959-62; chmn. bd. George Olmsted Found. Served as lt. USNR, 1942-54; col. USAFR, 1955-75. Decorated Purple Heart, Mem. Am. Soc. Internat. Law, Internat., Am. Fgn. law assns., Am., N.Y. State, Conn., Fed. (v.p. for N.Y., N.J., Conn.) bar assns., Pilgrims of U.S., France-Am. Soc., English-Speaking Union, Asia House, Washington Inst. Fgn. Affairs, Phi Beta Kappa. Clubs: Round Hill (Greenwich); Brook (N.Y.C.); Metropolitan (Washington); Bathing Corp. of Southampton, Meadow (Southampton, N.Y.). Adv. and contbg. editor Jour. Internat. Affairs, 1960-74; editor: The Next Asia, 1969; Prospects for Latin America, 1970; Concerns in World Affairs, 1973; From War to Peace, 1974. Home: 3046 R St NW Washington DC 20007 Office: 1701 Pennsylvania Ave NW Washington DC 20006

SMITH, DAVID THORNTON, lawyer, educator; b. Pawtucket, R.I., Dec. 11, 1935; s. Herbert Jeffers and Harriet Amelia (Thornton) S.; B.A., Yale U., 1957; J.D. cum laude, Boston U., 1960; m. Sandra June Gustavson, Dec. 20, 1958; children—David T., Douglas A., Daniel H. Admitted to Mass. bar, 1961, U.S. Supreme Ct. bar, 1964; instr. law Ind. U., Bloomington, 1960-62; asst. prof. law Duquesne U., Pitts., 1962-63; asst. prof. law Case Western Res. U., Cleve., 1963-65, asso. prof., 1965-68; asso. prof. law U. Fla., Gainesville, 1968-69, prof., 1969—; lectr. Fla. Bankers Assn., Fla. Trust Sch., 1973—. Mem. Am. Bar Assn., Mass. Bar Assn., Am. Law Inst., Am. Judicature Soc., AAUP (past pres. U. Fla. chpt.), Fla. Blue Key, Selden Soc., Omicron Delta Kappa, Phi Alpha Delta. Lutheran. Author: (with M. Sussman and J. Cates) The Family and Inheritance, 1970; Florida Probate Code Manual, 1975. Home: 6405 NW 18th Ave Gainesville FL 32605 Office: Coll of Law Univ of Fla Gainesville FL 32611

SMITH, DAVID WALDO EDWARD, physician, educator; b. Fargo, N.D., Apr. 3, 1934; s. Waldo Edward and Martha (Althaus) S.; B.A., Swarthmore Coll., 1956; M.D., Yale, 1960; m. Diane Leigh Walker, June 18, 1960. Intern, asst. resident, research fellow pathology Yale Med. Sch., 1960-62; research asso. lab. molecular biology Nat. Inst. Arthritis and Metabolic Diseases, 1962-64, investigator lab. exptl. pathology, 1964-67; asso. prof. pathology and microbiology Ind. U. Med. Sch., 1967-69; prof. pathology Northwestern U. Med. Sch., 1969—. Guest investigator Internat. Lab. Genetics and Biophysics, Naples, Italy, 1969; mem. ad hoc biochemistry study sect. NIH, 1974-75, mem. pathobiol. chemistry study sect., 1975-79. Served to sr. surgeon USPHS, 1958-67. Recipient Career Devel. award NIH, 1968-69. mem. Am. Assn. Pathologists, Am. Soc. Hematology, Am. Soc. Biol. Chemists, AAAS, Sigma Xi, Alpha Omega Alpha. Author research papers, chpts. in books. Editorial bd. Yale Jour. Biology and Medicine, 1957-60. Home: 843 Belden Ave Chicago IL 60614 Office: Dept Pathology Northwestern Univ Med Sch 303 E Chicago Ave Chicago IL 60611

SMITH, DAVID WAYNE, psychologist, univ. exec.; b. Ind., Apr. 16, 1927; s. Lowell Wayne and Ruth Elizabeth (Westphal) S.; B.S., Purdue U., 1949; M.S., Ind. U., 1953, Ph.D., 1955; m. Marcene B. Leever, Oct. 20, 1948; children—David Wayne, Laurreen Lea. Prof. rehab., dir. Rehab. Center, asso. dean, now asst. v.p. acad. affairs Ariz. Health Scis. Center, U. Ariz., Tucson, 1955—; pres. allied health professions sect. Nat. Arthritis Found., bd. dirs. S.W. chpt., nat. vice chmn. bd. dirs.; mem. NIH Nat. Arthritis Adv. Bd., 1977—, also chmn. subcom. community programs and rehab.; mem. staff Ariz. Legislature Health Welfare, 1972-73. Mem. Gov.'s Council Dept. Econ. Security, 1978—; pres., bd. dirs. Tucson Assn. for Blind. Recipient Gov.'s awards for leadership in rehab., 1966, 69, 72, 73; awards for sci. and vol. services Nat. Arthritis Found., 1973, 75. Mem. Am. Psychol. Assn. (div. 17 counseling psychology), Assn. Schs. Allied Health Professions, Nat. Rehab. Assn., Ariz. Psychol. Assn. Author: Employment Potential Profile; Worksamples; contbr. chpts. to books and articles to profl. jours. Home: 5341 E 4th St Tucson AZ 85711 Office: Ariz Health Scis Center U Ariz Tucson AZ 85724

SMITH, DEAN CARLTON, mgmt. cons.; b. Alliance, Nebr., Dec. 27, 1936; s. Harold Ernest and Alta Elliott (Morgan) S.; B.J., U. Nev., 1965; m. Gloria Ann Elquist, May 2, 1961; 1 dau., Rachael Jane. Classified advt. sales rep. Nev. State Jour., also Reno Evening Gazette, 1957-59; co-owner Sparks (Nev.) Tribune, 1959-61; govt.-polit.-edn.-ct. reporter Reno Evening Gazette, 1965-67, state capitol bur. chief, 1967, classified advt. mgr., 1967-73; advt. dir. Gazette-Jour., Reno, 1973-75, v.p., 1975-76; pres., pub. Sioux Falls (S.D.) Argus-Leader, 1977-78; pres. Dean C. Smith Enterprises, mktg. and mgmt. cons., Reno, 1979—. Pres. Young Democrats, 1960; mem. Washoe County Probation Com., Reno, 1975-77. Recipient disting. service citation U. Nev., Reno, 1977. Mem. Nat. Alliance Bus. Clubs: Elks. Home and Office: 2301 Rodney Dr Reno NV 89509

SMITH, DEAN EDWARDS, basketball coach; b. Emporia, Kans., Feb. 28, 1931; s. Alfred Dillon and Vesta Marie (Edwards) S.; B.S. in Math. and Phys. Edn., U. Kans., 1953; m. Linnea Weblemoe, May 21, 1976; children—Sharon, Sandy, Scott, Kristen. Asst. basketball coach U.S. Air Force Acad., 1955-58; asst. basketball coach U. N.C., 1958-61, head basketball coach, 1961—; mem. U.S. and Canadian Basketball Rules Com., 1967-73. U.S. basketball coach Olympics, Montreal, Que., Can., 1976; lectr. basketball clinics, U.S., Canary Islands, Israel, Greece, Eng., Yugoslavia, Switzerland, Germany, Italy. Served with USAF, 1954-58. Named Coach of Year, Atlantic Coast Conf., 1967, 1968, 1971, 1976, 1977, 79, Nat. Basketball Coach of Year, 1977, Nat. Coach of Yr., U.S. Basketball Writers, 1979. Mem. Nat. Assn. Basketball Coaches (Nat. Basketball Coach of Year, 1976, dir. 1972—), Fellowship Christian Athletes (dir. 1965-70). Baptist. Office: PO Box 2126 Chapel Hill NC 27514

SMITH, DENTON HENRY, mfg. co. exec.; b. Greene County, Mo., Jan. 19, 1910; s. Oren H. and Bessie E. (Goodin) S.; student Drury Coll., 1929-30; m. Kathryn E. Gilmore, Aug. 13, 1938; children—Judy Kay Smith Sipe, Allen J., Rebecca E. Smith Bowman (dec.). Eleanor Anne (O'Connell). Pres., Springfield Motor Sales (Mo.), distbr. Willys-Overland, 1944-51; pres., chmn. bd. Mono Mfg. Co., mfr., distbr. garden tillers, power mowers, brush cutters, Springfield, 1951—; dir. Ozark Air Lines, Inc., St. Louis, 1969-73, vice chmn. bd., 1973—; chmn. bd. Northpark Properties, Inc., Springfield; pres. Smith Investment Co., Springfield, Denton H. Smith Warehouse Corp., Springfield. Dir. Blue Springs Bank (Mo.), Commerce Bank of Willard (Mo.) Midland Bank, Lee's Summitt, Mo., First State Bank, Raytown, Mo., Jackson County State Bank, Kansas City, Mo. Trustee Drury Coll., 1971—; vice chmn. bd. Springfield City Utilities, 1975—; mem. Mo. Democratic Com.; del. Dem. Nat. Conv. Presbyterian. Club: Elks. Office: PO Box 2787 C S S Springfield MO 65803*

SMITH, DEWITT CLINTON, JR., army officer; b. Balt., Aug. 31, 1920; s. DeWitt Clinton and Mary Gladys (Benson) S.; B.A., U. Md., 1963; grad. numerous service schs.; LL.D. (hon.), Dickinson Sch. Law; m. Margaret Elizabeth Bond, Aug. 20, 1943; children—DeWitt Clinton, III, Dana Florence, Shelley Bond, Kevin Murray, Betsy Lynn, Barbara Helen. Commd. 2d lt. U.S. Army, 1943, advanced through grades to lt. gen. U.S. Army, 1977; service in ETO, Korea and Vietnam; dep. chief info. Hdqrs. U.S. Army, 1971-73; asst. dept. chief staff personnel, 1973-74; comdt. Army War Coll., 1974-77, 78—; dep. chief staff personnel Hdqrs. U.S. Army, 1977; trustee Civilian-Mil. Inst.; counselor Army Mut. Aid Assn.; mem. internat. advisory bd. Kennedy Inst. Ethics; Kermit Roosevelt lectr., 1977; fellow Inter-Univ. Seminar on Armed Forces and Soc. Decorated D.S.M., Silver Star, Legion of Merit with 3 oak leaf clusters, Bronze Star with oak leaf cluster, Purple Heart with 2 oak leaf clusters, Combat Inf. badge; Chung Mu with gold star (Korea); French Fourragere; named to Inf. Hall of Fame, 1970. Mem. Council Fgn. Relations, Internat. Inst. Strategic Studies, Newcomen Soc., English-Speaking Union, Ends of Earth, NAACP, Assn. U.S. Army, 4th Armored Div. Assn., Phi Delta Theta. Clubs: Army-Navy Country, M. Contbr. mil. jours. Home: Quarters 1 Carlisle Barracks PA 17013 Office: US Army War Coll Carlisle Barracks PA 17013

SMITH, DONALD CAMERON, physician, educator; b. Peterborough, Ont., Can., Feb. 2, 1922; s. James Cameron and Clarice (Leighton) S.; M.D., Queen's U., 1945; M.Sc. in Medicine, U. Toronto, 1948, D.P.H., 1949; m. Jean Ida Morningstar, Sept. 11, 1946; children—Douglas Frazer, Scot Earle, Donald Ian. Came to U.S., 1952, naturalized, 1960. Intern Victoria Hosp., London, Ont., 1945-46; fellow in physiology U. Toronto, 1947-48; asst. med. officer health East York-Leaside (Ont.) Health Unit, 1949-50; lectr. pub. health adminstrn. U. Toronto, 1949-50; med. officer health, dir. Kent County (Ont.) Health Unit, 1950-51; Commonwealth Fund fellow in pediatrics U. Mich. Hosp., 1952-55; asst. prof. maternal and child health, clin. instr. pediatrics U. Mich., Ann Arbor, 1956-57, asso. prof. maternal and child health, research asso. pediatrics, 1957-61, prof. maternal and child health Sch. Pub. Health, prof. pediatrics Med. Sch., 1961-79, chmn. dept. health devel., 1963-72; prof. psychiatry and behavioral scis. Northwestern U. Med. Sch., Chgo., 1979—; pres. Barton Hills Corp., 1970-72. Mem. adv. council on health protection and disease prevention Dept. Health, Edn. and Welfare, 1969-72, chmn. med. assistance adv. council, 1969-72; prin. advisor on health and med. affairs to gov. Mich., 1972-78; dir. Mich. Dept. Mental Health, 1974-78; chmn. health care policy bd. Mich. Dept. Corrections, 1976-79; v.p. for accreditation Joint Commn. on Accreditation Hosps., Chgo., 1979—; chief med. cons. Sisters of Mercy Health Corp., 1978-79; spl. cons. on maternal and child health and family planning programs South Korean Ministry Social Affairs, 1969; chmn., cross-national study of health care services HEW, 1971; vis. prof. maternal and child health Harvard, 1969-72. Chmn. Ann Arbor Youth Commn., 1962-64; med. dir. Mich. Crippled Children Commn., 1962-64. Bd. dirs. Nat. Soc. for Prevention Blindness, 1966-68, Mich. United Fund, 1964-67, Mich. League for Human Services, 1964-67. Served to Surgeon lt. Royal Canadian Navy, 1946-47. Diplomate Am. Bd. Preventive Medicine (ofcl. examiner 1966—), Am. Bd. Pediatrics. Fellow Am. Pub. Health Assn. (chmn. com. pub. med. care for children 1967-70, chmn. sect. maternal and child health 1968-70), Am. Acad. Pediatrics (chmn. com. on legis. 1966-73, mem. council pediatric practice 1966-73), Royal Coll. of Physician and Surgeons of Canada; mem. AMA, Assn. Ambulatory Pediatric Services, Internat. Epidemiol. Assn., Delta Omega (pres. 1967-68). Presbyn. Author: Contbr. to Manual on Standards of Child Health Care, 1971, Barnett's Pediatrics, 1971, Pediatric Clinics of North America; also articles in med. and pub. health jours. Home: 175 E Delaware Pl Chicago IL 60611 Office: 875 N Michigan Ave Chicago IL 60611

SMITH, DONALD EDWARD, educator; b. Pitts., Jan. 12, 1936; s. Edward Patrick and Margaret Mary (Hamill) S.; B.S., Allegheny Coll., 1958; M.A., Columbia, 1959, Ph.D., 1961; m. Rosemarie Eury, Aug. 31, 1957; children—Linda, William, Marianne, Michael, Thomas. Instr. chemistry Northwestern U., Evanston, Ill., 1961-63, asst. prof., 1963-66, asso. prof., 1966-71, prof., 1971—, chmn. dept., 1975—. Sci. adv. Chgo. Dist. Lab., FDA, 1966—. NSF grantee, 1962—; recipient Dept. Health, Edn. and Welfare citation for work with FDA, 1970. Mem. Am. Chem. Soc., Electrochem. Soc., Internat. Soc. Electrochem. AAAS, Am. Assn. U. Profs., Western Electroanalytical-Theoretical Soc., Phi Lambda Upsilon. Author: Electrochemical Methods of Process Analysis, 1972; also articles. Home: 2457 Pioneer Rd Evanston IL 60201

SMITH, DONALD H., community coll. pres.; b. Rochester, N.Y., Jan. 16, 1926; s. Harry P. and Ina A. Smith; B.S. in Econs., Purdue U., 1952; M.A., U. Rochester, 1961; Ed.D., Columbia U., 1969; m. Loraine Marie Hajjar, Aug. 15, 1959; 1 son, Kevin. With Am. Airlines, Rochester, 1946-47, Am. Overseas Airlines, Keflavik, Iceland, 1947-48, Eastman Kodak Co., Rochester, 1953-56, Arabian Am. Oil Co., Ras Tanura, Saudi Arabia, 1956-59; mem. faculty Coll. Edn., U. Rochester, 1959-62, Monroe Community Coll., Rochester, N.Y., 1962-64; dean instrn. Parkland Coll., Champaign, Ill., 1967-69; campus pres. Cuyahoga Community Coll., Cleve., 1970-74; pres. Brookdale Community Coll., Lincroft, N.J., 1974—; bd. dirs. League Innovation in Community Colls., Nat. Center Higher Edn. Mgmt. Systems. Bd. dirs. Monmouth/Ocean Devel. Council. Served with AUS, 1944-46. Kellogg fellow, 1965-66. Mem. Am. Assn. Community and Jr. Colls., Assn. Community Coll. Presidents N.J. (chmn. 1977-78). Home: 178 Ballantine Rd Middletown NJ 07748 Office: Brookdale Community Coll Newman Springs Rd Lincroft NJ 07738

SMITH, DONALD HOUSTON, lawyer; b. Peach Orchard, Ark., Mar. 18, 1930; s. Harmon and Mary (Cox) S.; B.A., Ark. State Coll., 1953; LL.B., U. Ark., 1959; m. Rose Mary Albano, Aug. 31, 1957; children—Donald Houston, Mary Ann, Brian Davis. Admitted to Ark. bar, 1959; practice in Blytheville, 1959, Pine Bluff, 1959—; partner firm Reinberger, Eilbott and Smith, 1964—. Chmn. Pine Bluff-Jefferson County Econ. Opportunity Com., 1964-65; pres. S.E. Ark. Econ. Devel. Dist., 1967—. Pres. Jefferson County Democrats, 1964-65; mem. exec. com. Ark. Dem. Central Com. Served to 1st lt. AUS, 1953-56. Mem. Am., Ark. (Outstanding Lawyer award 1965), Jefferson County (pres. 1971-72) bar assns., Am. Trial Lawyers Assn., Am. Judicature Soc., Ark. Assn. Devel. Orgn. (pres. 1974-75, dir. 1974—), Pine Bluff Jr. C. of C. (Civilian Distinguished Service award 1963), Pi Kappa Alpha, Blue Key. Baptist. Clubs: Rosswood Country (past pres., dir.), Eden Park Country (Pine Bluff). Home: 718 W Harding St Pine Bluff AR 71602 Office: 219 W 5th Ave Pine Bluff AR 71611

SMITH, DONALD KAYE, ins. co. exec.; b. Berea, Ohio, July 11, 1932; s. Harry Leonard and Goldie Estelle (Erwin) S.; B.A., U. Md., 1954; J.D., George Washington U., 1957; m. Sarah Elizabeth Glascock, Aug. 20, 1955; children—Blair Webster, Gregory Mason, Eric Vaughan. Admitted to D.C. bar, 1958, U.S. Supreme Ct. bar, 1968; practiced in Washington, 1958-63; with Govt. Employees Ins. Co., Washington, 1963—, gen. counsel, 1972—, v.p., 1972-77, sr. v.p., 1977—, dir., 1979—; gen. counsel Govt. Employees Life Ins. Co., 1972—; v.p., gen. counsel Criterion Ins. Co., 1974—. Pres., Old Farm Civic Assn., Rockville, Md., 1967; trustee Farmland Elementary Sch., Rockville, 1968-71; treas. Landon Sch. Fathers Club, 1979. Mem. Bar D.C., Am. Bar Assn., Fed. City Council, Washington Assembly, Phi Alpha Delta, Sigma Phi Epsilon. Methodist. Clubs: Terrapin, George Washington U., Chesapeake Country, Rotary (pres. North Bethesda, Md. 1977), Masons. Home: 7108 Wolftree Ln Rockville MD 20852 Office: 5260 Western Ave Washington DC 20076

SMITH, DONALD KLIESE, educator; b. Belgrade, Neb., Nov. 29, 1915; s. Charles Henry and Alice Maude (Kliese) S.; B.A., Neb. State Tchrs. Coll., Kearney, 1936; Ph.M., U. Wis., 1942, Ph.D., 1951; m. Kathleen Claire Rossiter, June 18, 1941 (dec. Jan. 1971); children—Christopher D., Kathleen Cynthia, Melinda Frances; m. 2d, Eileen Anne McAvoy, Aug. 14, 1971. Tchr., Holdrege (Neb.) High Sch., 1936-38; prin. Kimball (Neb.) High Sch., 1938-39; tchr. Wis. High Sch., Madison, 1939-42; instr. Coll. Edn., U. Wis., 1946-49; mem. faculty U. Minn., 1949-73, prof. speech, 1957-73, chmn. dept. speech and theatre arts, 1959-63, asst. v.p. acad. adminstrn., 1963-66, asso. v.p. acad. adminstrn., 1966-68, v.p. adminstrn., 1968-73; v.p. acad. affairs U. Wis. System, 1973-77, sr. v.p., 1977—; prof. communication arts U. Wis.-Madison, 1973—. Resident dir. AID, Higher Agricultural Edn., Indonesia, 1972-73. Cons. adminstrv. communication VA Hosp. Adminstrn. Insts., 1959-63; chmn. bd. trustees Upper Midwest Regional Ednl. Lab., 1966-68. Vice pres., mem. exec. com. Minn. Theatre Found. Served to capt., inf., AUS, 1943-46. Mem. Speech Assn. Am., Nat. Council English, Central States Speech Assn. (pres. 1960-61), Minn Assn. Tchrs. Speech (pres. 1954-56). Co-author: Discussion, 1956; The Teaching of Speech, 1952; Speaking and Listening, 1956. Author: Man Speaking, 1969. Asso. editor Quar. Jour. Speech, 1962-65. Contbr. chpts. to books, articles jours. Home: 62 Oak Creek Trail Madison WI 53717

SMITH, DONALD MCEWEN, govt. ofcl.; b. Lawrence, Mass., Apr. 19, 1911; s. Charles Porter and Jessie (McEwen) S.; B.A., Bates Coll., 1934; student Harvard, 1934; M.A., U. Chgo., 1935; m. Eda Osano, Sept. 13, 1932; 1 dau., Barbara (Mrs. Gene D'Andrea). Exec. sec. unemployment compensation div. N.H. Bur. Labor, 1937-38; with U.S. R.R. Retirement Bd., 1938—, dir. bur. retirement claims, 1961—. Mem. Internat. Assn. Personnel in Employment Security, Am. Fedn. Govt. Employees, Soc. for Personnel Adminstrn. Conglist. Co-author: Experience Rating in Unemployment Compensation, 1938. Home: Countryside Lake Mundelein IL 60060 Office: 844 N Rush St Chicago IL 60611

SMITH, DONALD NICKERSON, restaurant exec.; b. Kirkland Lake, Ont., Can., Sept. 12, 1940; s. Frederick and Hazel (Nickerson) S.; came to U.S., 1946, naturalized, 1956; B.A. in Mktg., U. Mont., 1961; m. Mary Ann Brogan, May 11, 1979; children by previous marriage—Jeffrey, Stacy, Darby. Ops. mgr. McDonald's Corp., Los Angeles, 1967-68, ops. dir. all West Coast stores, 1968-70, v.p. Mid-Atlantic region, Chgo., 1970-73, exec. v.p. for ops., 1973-77, sr. exec. v.p., chief ops. officer, 1977; pres., chief exec. officer Burger King Corp., Miami, Fla., 1977—; dir. Steak & Ale Corp. Mem. U. Miami Citizens Bd. Named Adman of Year, Advt. Age, 1979. Mem. Young Pres.'s Orgn. Office: 7360 N Kendall Dr Miami FL 33156

SMITH, DONN L., univ. dean; b. Denver, Nov. 1, 1915; s. Arthur M. and Elizabeth (Setzer) S.; A.B., U. Denver, 1939, M.S. (Upjohn scholar 1941), 1941; Ph.D., U. Colo., 1948, M.D., 1958; m. Ruth E. Perrin, Apr. 3, 1937; children—Eileen Smith Burg, Darlene Louise Smith Osterholt. Asst. prof. physiology U. Denver, 1948-50; asso. prof. physiology U. Colo. Sch. Medicine, 1950-60, asso. dean, 1960-63; prof. physiology, dean Sch. Medicine, U. Louisville, 1963-70; dir. Med. Center, dean Coll. Medicine, U. South Fla., Tampa, 1970-76, prof. comprehensive medicine and pharmacology, 1976—. Med. adv. Ky. SSS. Served with AUS, 1942-46. Mem. Am. (council on drugs 1965-72), Ky. med. assns., AAAS, Soc. Exptl. Biology and Medicine, Am. Soc. Pharmacology and Exptl. Therapeutics, Alpha Omega Alpha. Author: (with Philip Ellis) Handbook of Ocular Therapeutics and Pharmacology, 3d edit., 1969; also numerous articles. Home: 5212 E 127th St Tampa FL 33617

SMITH, DOUGLAS, newspaperman; b. Success, Ark., June 18, 1918; s. William Cortez and Dorcas (Douglas) S.; A.B., U. Ark., 1940; m. Margery Goding Neil, Dec. 28, 1948 (div.); 1 son, Douglas Wilfred. Asst. dir. pub. relations, U. Ark., 1940-41; editor Russellville (Ark.) Courier-Democrat, 1941-42; reporter New Orleans Times-Picayune, 1943-45; Washington corr. Scripps-Howard Newspapers of Ohio (Cleve. Press, Cin. Post, Columbus Citizen), 1945-52; editorial writer Scripps-Howard Newspaper Alliance, 1952-57; Washington corr. for Pitts. Press, 1957-78. Served as sgt. USAAF, 1942-43. Mem. Omicron Delta Kappa. Club: Nat. Press (Washington). Office Box 3015 Jonesboro AR 72401

SMITH, DOUGLAS ALBERTSON, food corp. exec.; b. East Orange, N.J., Mar. 25, 1934; s. Sidney W. and Evelyn (Albertson) S.; A.B., Brown U., 1956; postgrad. N.Y. U., 1962; m. Nevann Winslow, Apr. 26, 1957; children—Susan Leslie, Geoffrey Winslow, Ronald Sidney. Security analyst Marine Midland Corp., N.Y.C., 1959-62; with Gen. Foods Corp., White Plains, N.Y., 1962—, controller instl. food service div., 1968-69, controller Jello div., 1969-71, corp. asst. controller, 1971-72, corp. controller, 1972-73, corp. v.p., controller, 1973-77, v.p. fin., 1977, sr. v.p. fin., 1977—. Mem. exec. bd. Westchester-Putnam council Boy Scouts Am.; trustee South Salem Library Assn. Served to lt. USNR, 1956-59. Mem. Fin. Execs. Inst. Club: Economic of N.Y. Office: Gen Foods Corp 250 North St White Plains NY 10625

SMITH, DOUGLAS HILL, ins. co. exec.; b. Salt Lake City, May 11, 1921; s. Virgil Howarth and Winifred Pearl (Hill) S.; A.B., U. Utah, 1941; m. Barbara Jean Bradshaw, June 16, 1941; children—Sandra Jean, Lillian Kaye, Barton Douglas, Lowell Virgil, Blaine Kendall, Catherine Ann, Barbara Sherilynn. With Utah Home Fire Ins. Co., Salt Lake City, 1941—, exec. v.p., sec., 1950-58, pres., 1958—; pres. Beneficial Life Ins. Co., 1972—. Chmn. bd. govs. Latter-day Saints Hosp., Salt Lake City, 1971—. Mem. Pi Kappa Alpha, Tau Kappa Alpha. Mem. Ch. of Jesus Christ Latter-day Saints (bishop, 1946—, regional rep.). Office: 36 S State St Salt Lake City UT 84111*

SMITH, DOUGLAS LARUE, marketing exec.; b. Madison, Minn., July 25, 1917; s. Julius Waldo and Blanche (LaRue) S.; B.A., U. Minn., 1948; m. Jean Hefty, Feb. 8, 1941; children—Pamela Jean (Mrs. Robert Graham), and Gregory Douglas. Employed with U.S. Gypsum Company, Chicago, Ill., 1938-42; account exec. Melamed-Hobbs, Inc., advt., Mpls., 1946-49; product mgr. Swift & Co., Chgo., 1949-53; account exec. Batten, Barton, Durstine & Osborn, 1953-55; advt. mgr. Johnson's Wax Co., Racine, Wis., 1955-56, dir. advt. and mktg., 1956-64; sr. v.p. Lennen & Newell, Inc., N.Y.C., 1965-70, also dir., mem. exec. com.; sr. v.p. Planmetrics and On-Line Decisions, Inc., N.Y.C., 1970—. Chmn. bd. dirs. Assn. Nat. Advertisers, N.Y.C., 1965; bd. dirs. Advt. Fedn. Am., 1961—, Advt. Assn. West, 1962—. Mem. exec. com. Republican Party N.Y.C. Served to maj., inf., AUS, 1942-46; ETO. Decorated Bronze Star. Mem. Am. Assn. Advt. Agys. (gov. Eastern div.), Internat. Radio and Television Soc. (dir., treas.). Clubs: University (N.Y.C., Milw., Chgo.); Mid-Am. (Chgo.); Winged Foot Golf. Home: 249 E 48th St New York NY Office: 666 Fifth Ave New York City NY 10019. *Give-but never give up! For there is always a solution!*

SMITH, DOUGLAS RATHBONE, banker; b. Edmonton, Can., Aug. 13, 1915; s. W. Rathbone and Reba (Barrett) S.; came to U.S., 1925; naturalized, 1940; B.S.C. with honor, Southeastern U., 1942; grad. Rutgers U. Grad. Sch. Banking, 1951; m. Rice Barrett, Apr. 20, 1940; children—Anne Camden White, Rice Barrett II (Mrs. Robert Flanders), Elizabeth Hogarth (Mrs. Joseph P. Nye Jr.). With Nat. Savs. & Trust Co., Wash., 1931—, v.p., 1950-59, exec. v.p., 1959-60, pres., dir., 1960-66, chmn. bd., pres., 1966-76, chmn. bd., 1976-78, chief exec. officer, 1976-78; v.p. dir. Rosiclare Lead and Flourspar Mining Co. (Ill.), Pigmy Corp.; dir. Acacia Mutual Life Ins. Co., District-Realty Title Ins. Co., Eastern Broadcasting Corp., Home Casualty & Surety Co., Consumers Gas Utility Co., Union Trust Nat. Bank, Parkersburg; trustee Lyford Cay Investment Co. Mem. Greater Nat. Capital Com.; mem. Met. Washington Bd. Trade; bd. dirs. Washington Heart Assn., Washington Salvation Army, Travelers Aid Soc., Internat. Social Service of Am. Am., D.C. chpt. ARC, Care, Inc.; treas., dir. Anson Mills Found., Kiwanis Found., Anthony Francis Lucas Found. (all Washington); trustee National Florence Crittendon Mission; men's bd. Washington Florence Crittendon Home; dir. Travelers Aid Soc. Washington, 1950—, 1956; exec. bd., v.p. Washington council Boy Scouts Am.; asst. treas., Episcopal Home for Children, Washington; trustee, finance com. Group Hospitalization Inc., Washington; trustee, exec. com. Med. Service D.C.; dir. Interracial Council for Business Opportunity; trustee Fed. City Council; treas. Benning Park Terrace, Inc.; treas., dir. Boys' Club Greater Wash.; dir. Nat. Conf. Christians and Jews; trustee D.C. div. Nat. Jewish Hosp., Denver, treas. Gainesville Found.; trustee, chmn. finance com. Mt. Vernon Coll.; trustee George Washington U. Served with Signal Corps, World War II. Mem. Newcomen Soc., Soc. Va. (hon. v.p.), UN Assn. U.S.A. (dir.). Episcopalian (sr. warden). Clubs: Kiwanis (dir., treas.), University, 1925 F Street, Aviation, Fauquier (Warrenton); Metropolitan, Alfalfa, Chevy Chase; Friendly Sons of St. Patrick, Lyford Cay (dir.); George Washington University. Home: Ridgelea Warrenton VA 22186 Office: Nat Sav & Trust Co 15th St and New York Ave NW Washington DC 20005

SMITH, EARL E.T., financier; b. Newport, R.I.; s. Sydney J. and Fannie Bogert (Tailer) S.; student Taft Sch., 1922, Yale, 1926; m. Consuelo Vandebilt, Jan. 7, 1926; children—Iris (Mrs. Iris Christ), Virginia (Mrs. William Langdon Hutton); m. 2d, Florence Pritchett, July 12, 1948 (dec. 1965); 1 son, Earl E.T.; m. 3d, Lesly Stockard Hickox, 1968. Mem. N.Y. Stock Exchange, 1926—; partner Paige, Smith & Remick, investment brokers, 1930-39; mayor of Palm Beach, Fla., 1971-77; dir. Bank of Palm Beach & Trust Co., U.S. Sugar Corp., CF&I Steel Corp. Ambassador to Cuba, 1957-59. Mem. Rep. Nat. Finance Com., 1954-56, del. Rep. Nat. Conv., 1952, 56, 60, mem. platform com.; chmn. Fla. State Rep. Finance Com., 1954-56. Trustee John F. Kennedy Meml. Library. With div. OPM, later WPB, 1941-42. Served to lt. col. AUS, USAAF, World War II. Recipient Freedom award Order of Lafayette, 1963; George E. Sokolsky Meml. award Am. Jewish League Against Communism, 1963. Mason. Clubs: Brook (gov.), Racquet and Tennis, Deepdale Golf (N.Y.C.); Seminole Golf, Everglades (gov.) (Palm Beach); Nat. Golf Links of America. Author: The Fourth Floor, 1962. Home: 1021 N Ocean Blvd Palm Beach FL 33480

SMITH, EARL WILLIAM, supermarket chain chief exec.; b. Santa Ana, Calif., Apr. 25, 1921; s. Earl William and Clara Delight (Rounds) S.; student Santa Ana Jr. Coll., 1939-40; d. Virginia M. Richardi, May 7, 1966; children—Sheri Smith Partridge, Cathy Smith Russo, Pamela Smith Doheney. With Safeway Stores Inc., 1939-75, mgr. N.W. region, Bellevue, Wash., 1973-75; chmn. bd., chief exec. officer Allied Supermarkets Inc., Detroit, 1975—. Vice pres., bd. dirs. Los Angeles council Boy Scouts Am.. 1967-72, v.p. Seattle council, 1974, mem. Detroit council, 1975—; bd. dirs. Better Bus. Bur. Los Angeles County, 1968-72; mem. council Los Angeles Orthopaedic Hosp., 1970-73. Served with AUS, 1944-45. Named Citizen of Year, Stockton, Calif., 1955; recipient Silver Beaver award Boy Scouts Am., 1973. Mem. Food Employers Council So. Calif. (past dir.), Vernon (Calif.) C. of C. (past pres.). Clubs: Elks, Rotary; Pauma Valley Country, San Diego County; Seattle Golf, Wash. Athletic (Seattle). 8542 NE 13th St Bellevue WA 98004 also 2154 Barona Rd Palm Springs CA 92262 . *There is a tremendous opportunity to succeed in our country. This is the one place where rich or poor, college educated or self-trained has equal opportunity. Do unto others as you will wish others to do unto you. Believe in what you practice and portray. Be human, be fair, be demanding and you will succeed.*

SMITH, EDWARD BYRON, physician, educator; b. Petersburg, Ind., Apr. 24, 1912; s. Jacob Owen and Estella Merle (Richardson) S.; student Hanover Coll., 1930-31, D.Sc. (hon.), 1970; B.S., Ind. U., M.D., 1938; m. Edith Cash, Nov. 18, 1937; children—Michael Edward, Allen Richardson, Philip Allison. Intern Cleve. City Hosp., 1938-39; resident pathology Charity Hosp., Cleve., 1939-40; instr. pathology Washington U., 1940-42, asst. prof., 1949-51; asso. pathology Presbyn. Hosp., also U. Pa., 1946-48; cons. pathology Valley Forge Army Hosp., 1946-48; asso. prof. pathology Baylor Med. Coll., 1948-49; prof. pathology Ind. U. Sch. Medicine, 1951-62, chmn. dept., 1952-62; chief hematologic pathology br. Armed Forces Inst. Pathology, Washington, 1962-65; clin. prof. pathology George Washington U. Sch. Medicine, 1962-65; prof. pathology U. Mich., Ann Arbor, 1965-68; pathologist Patterson-Coleman Labs., Tampa, Fla., 1968—; clinical prof. pathology, U. South Fla., Tampa, 1972—; cons. Ind. U. Hosps., Indpls. Gen., Sunnyside, VA hosps.; cons. Surgeon Gen. U.S. Army, 1959-61. Mem. Adv. Bd. Med. Specialties, 1956-64; trustee Am. Bd. Pathology, 1955-67, sec., 1955-65, pres., 1965-66; mem. bd. sci. cons. Armed Forces Inst. Pathology, 1957-61; mem. Forensic Scis. Commn. Ind., 1959-62; dir. Marion County unit Am. Cancer Soc., com. profl. edn. Ind. div. Served from lt. to maj. AUS, 1942-46. Recipient Alumni Achievement award Hanover Coll., 1967. Mem. Internat. Acad. Pathology (council 1951-55, pres. 1956), Ind. Med. Assn. (chmn. commn. on conv. arrangements 1959), Ind. Soc. Pathologists, A.M.A., Am. Assn. Pathologists and Bacteriologists, Am. Soc. Hematology, Electron Microscopy Soc. Am., Am. Soc. Exptl. Biology, Am. Soc. Clin. Pathologists, Coll. Am. Pathologists, N.Y. Acad. Scis., Phi Gamma Delta, Nu Sigma Nu, Alpha Omega Alpha. Author: (with others) Principles of Human Pathology. Mem. editorial bd. Directory Med. Specialists, 1956-67, Survey Pathology in Medicine and Surgery, 1964-70. Home: Route 4 Box 38 Inverness FL 32650 Office: Citrus Meml Hosp 502 Highland Blvd Inverness FL 32650

SMITH, EDWARD BYRON, banker; b. Chgo., Mar. 22, 1909; s. Solomon A. and Fredrika (Shumway) S.; A.B., Yale, 1932; m. Louise de Marigny Dewey, May 23, 1934; children—Louise de Marigny Smith Bross, Marie Suzette de Marigny Smith Faux, Edward Byron. With No. Trust Co., 1932—, became dir., 1946—, pres., 1957, chmn. bd., 1963-78, chmn., 1978-79, chmn. exec. com., 1979—; dir. Ill. Tool Works, Inc. Trustee, treas. Field Mus., Art Inst. Chgo., Chgo. Zoöl. Soc. Served as lt. USNR, 1942-46. Clubs: Racquet, Chicago, Commercial (Chgo.); Onwentsia, Old Elm (Lake Forest); Metropolitan (Washington); Shoreacres (Lake Bluff, Ill.); River (N.Y.C.). Home: 1133 Lake Rd Lake Forest IL 60045 Office: 50 S LaSalle St Chicago IL 60675

SMITH, EDWARD KENNETH, consumer goods co. exec.; b. Peru, Ill., Apr. 29, 1915; s. Edward L. and Kathryn (Kehlenbach) S.; B.A., U. Chgo., 1937; m. Kathleen P. Barden, July 17, 1954; children—Martin, Margaret, Paul. Field auditor Gen. Mills Inc., Mpls., 1937-48, div. controller, Kankakee, Ill., 1948-60, div. controller, v.p., Mpls., 1960-69, corporate controller, v.p., 1969-78, sr. v.p., 1978—. Served to capt., CAC, AUS, 1942-45; ETO. Mem. Nat. Assn. Accountants, Financial Exec. Inst. Home: 6112 Ashcroft Ave S Edina MN 55424 Office: 9200 Wayzata Blvd Minneapolis MN 55440

SMITH, EDWARD SAMUEL, judge; b. Birmingham, Ala., Mar. 27, 1919; s. Joseph Daniel and Sarah Jane (Tatum) S.; student Ala. Poly. Inst., 1936-38; B.A., U. Va., 1941, J.D., 1947; m. Innes Adams Comer, May 5, 1942; children—Edward Samuel, Innes Smith Cameron Richards. Admitted to Va. bar, 1947, D.C. bar, 1948, Md. bar, 1953; asso., then partner firm Blair, Korner, Doyle & Appel, Washington, 1947-54; partner firm Blair, Korner, Doyle & Worth, 1954-61; chief trail sect., tax. div. Dept. Justice, 1961, asst. for civil trials, 1961-63; partner firm, head tax dept. Piper & Marbury, Balt., 1963-78, mng. partner, 1971-74; asso. judge U.S. Ct. Claims, Washington, 1978—. Bd. dirs. Roland Park Civic League, Inc., Balt., 1977-78; past pres., trustee St. Andrew's Soc. Washington. Served to lt. USNR, 1941-46. Mem. Am. Bar Assn. (chmn. com. on tax litigation 1977-78), Fed. Bar Assn., Md. State Bar Assn. (chmn. sect. on taxation 1971-72), Balt. City Bar Assn., D.C. Bar Assn. Va. State Bar, Lambda Chi Alpha. Democrat. Episcopalian. Clubs: Met., Nat. Lawyers (Washington); Chevy Chase (Md.); Mountain Brook (Birmingham). Home: 3708 Taylor St Chevy Chase MD 20015 Office: 717 Madison Pl NW Washington DC 20005. *The second most important rule of life is that we should never become disillusioned with the Golden Rule when others do not follow it.*

SMITH, EDWARD STEVENS, mfg. co. exec.; b. Hankow, China, May 18, 1919; s. Donald L. and Mildred Margaret (Stevens) S.; student Stanford, 1941, Harvard Bus. Sch., 1966; m. Joan Frances Furch, Apr. 3, 1943; children—Candace L. Mann, Robin L. (Mrs. Stanley Smith), Philip S. Internat. sales corr., account exec., group sales mgr. Frazar & Hansen, 1945-59; with Omark Industries, Inc., Portland, Oreg., 1959—, export mgr., gen. mgr. Omark Internat. Ltd., v.p., 1963-67, group v.p., 1967-70, exec. v.p., 1970-72, dir., 1972—, pres., chief exec. officer, 1973—; dir. First Nat. Bank of Oreg., Brooks-Scanlon, Inc., Bend, Oreg., Dillingham Corp., Honolulu. Trustee Lewis & Clark Coll., Portland. Served to maj. USAAF, 1941-45. Clubs: Multnomah Athletic, Waverley Country, Arlington (Portland). Home: 142 S Cornell Ct Lake Oswego OR 97034 Office: 2100 SE Milport Rd Portland OR 97222

SMITH, EDWIN BURROWS, educator; b. Washington, Mar. 11, 1919; s. William Silas and Mae (McMichael) S.; A.B., Swarthmore Coll., 1938; M.A., Brown U., 1939, Ph.D., 1950; postgrad. U. Paris, 1939-40; m. Dorothea Lyman, June 14, 1947; children—Michael Lyman, Margaret Fulton. Lectr. English, U. Paris, 1939-40; grad. asst. Brown U., 1940-41, instr., 1947-50; faculty Wayne State U., Detroit, 1950—, asso. prof., 1959-64, prof., 1964—, asst. to v.p. acad. adminstrn., 1958-64, chmn. dept. Romance and Germanic langs. and lits., 1964-71; asso. dean coll. liberal arts, 1971-72, asso. provost, acad. adminstr., 1971—. Chmn. world affairs council Met. Detroit, 1961; exec. vice chmn. Met. Detroit Gt. Decisions Program, 1959-63; chmn. Huntington Woods Human Rights Assn., 1963-64. Vice pres., trustee Bd. Edn. Sch. Dist. City Royal Oak, 1961-70. Served to capt. M.I., AUS, 1941-47. Decorated Bronze Star medal; French Croix de Guerre; Belgian Croix de Guerre, Order Leopold with palm, Palmes Academiques. Mem. Modern Lang. Assn., A.A.U.P., Council for Basic Edn., Archeol. Inst. Am. Clubs: Torch (Detroit). Author: Jean-Sylvain Bailly, Astronomer, Mystic, Revolutionary 1736-1793, 1954. Home: 26637 York Rd Huntington Woods MI 48070 Office: Asso Provost Academic Adminstrn Wayne State U Detroit MI 48202

SMITH, ELAINE DIANA, fgn. service officer; b. Glencoe, Ill., Sept. 15, 1924; d. John Raymond and Elsie (Gelbard) S.; B.A., Grinnell Coll., 1946; M.A., Sch. Advanced Internat. Studies, Johns Hopkins U., 1947; Ph.D., Am. U., 1959. Commd. fgn. service officer U.S. Dept. State, 1947; assigned to Brussels, 1947-50, Tehran, Iran, 1951-53, Wellington, N.Z., 1954-56, Dept. State, Washington, 1956-60, Ankara, Turkey, 1960-69, Istanbul, Turkey, 1969-72, Dept. Commerce Exchange, 1972-73; dep. examiner Fgn. Service Bd. Examiners, 1974-75; Turkish desk officer Dept. State, Washington, 1975-78; consul gen., Izmir, Turkey, 1978—. Recipient Alumni award Grinnell Coll., 1957. Mem. AAUW, U.S. Fgn. Service Assn., Phi Beta Kappa. Author: Turkey: Origins of the Kemalist Movement 1919-1923, 1959. Office: US Consulate Gen Izmir Turkey APO New York NY 09224

SMITH, ELDRED GEE, church leader; b. Lehi, Utah, Jan. 9, 1907; s. Hyrum Gibbs and Martha E. (Gee) S.; student U. Utah; m. Jeanne A. Ness, Aug. 17, 1932 (dec. June 1977); children—Miriam (Mrs. Edwin C. Skeen), Eldred Gary, Audrey Gay (Mrs. Arden A. Vance), Gordon Raynor, Sylvia Dawn (Mrs. Craig E. Isom); m. 2d, Hortense H. Child, May 18, 1978; stepchildren—Carol Jane Child Burdette, Thomas Robert Child. Employed with Bennett Glass & Paint Co., sales div., Salt Lake City, 6 years, Remington Arms Co., as mech. designs engr., 2 years, mech. design engr., prodn. equipment design, Tenn. Eastman Corp., Oak Ridge, 3 years; now presiding patriarch Ch. of Jesus Christ of Latter-day Saints. Home: 2942 Devonshire Circle Salt Lake City UT 84108 Office: 47 E South Temple St Salt Lake City UT 84111

SMITH, ELDRED REID, librarian; b. Payette, Idaho, June 30, 1931; s. Lawrence E. and Jennie (Reid) S.; B.A., U. Calif. at Berkeley, 1956, M.A., 1962; M.L.S., U. So. Calif., 1957; m. Judith Ausubel, June 25, 1953; children—Steven, Janet. Aquisition reference librarian Long Beach State Coll. Library, 1957-59; reference librarian San Francisco State Coll. Library, 1959-60; bibliographer U. Calif. at Berkeley Library, 1960-65, head search div. acquisition dept., 1966-69, head loan dept., 1969-70, asso. univ. librarian, 1970-72, acting univ. librarian, 1971-72; dir. libraries, also prof. State U. N.Y. at Buffalo, 1973-76; dir. libraries, prof. U. Minn., 1976—; lectr. Sch. Library Sci., U. Wash., 1972. Bd. dirs. Center for Research Libraries, 1975-77. Council on Library Resources fellowship, 1970. Mem. ALA, Assn. Research Libraries (dir. 1979—), Assn. Coll. and Research Libraries (pres. 1977-78, dir., 1976-79, com. on academic status 1969-74, pres. univ. libraries sect. 1974-75). Editor: Libraries and Librarianship; contbr. articles to library jours. Home: 576 Montcalm Pl Saint Paul MN 55116 Office: 477 Wilson Library U Minn Minneapolis MN 55455

SMITH, ELLIS WENDLE, diversified co. exec.; b. Bethany, Okla., May 23, 1923; s. Houston Travis and Ruby Ruth (Wilson) S.; student Okla. State U., 1941-42; S.B. cum laude in Econ., Harvard, 1947, M.B.A. with distinction, 1950; m. Doris Rae Hamer, July 5, 1958; 1 son—Richard Alan. With Kendall Co. and divs., 1946-65, v.p. finance, treas. Marmon Group, Chgo., 1965-67; v.p. finance, treas. Reliance Electric Co., Cleve., 1967-73; sr. v.p. Allegheny Ludlum Industries, 1973-75; sr. v.p. finance, dir. F.W. Woolworth Co., 1975—; dir. Arvin Industries, Kinney Shoe Co., Richman Bros. Co. Trustee, Deerfield, Ill., 1963-67, chmn. finance com., 1964-67; bd. dirs. Golden Age Center, Cleve., 1968-73, pres., 1973; bd. dirs. Pitts. Civic Light Opera, 1973-75. Mem. Nat. Harvard Bus. Sch. Fund Council, 1960-63. Served with USNR, 1943-46, 52-53. Decorated Commendation medal. Mem. Financial Execs. Inst. (pres. Cleve. chpt., nat. dir., nat. v.p., dir. N.Y.C. chpt. 1976), Nat. Elec. Mfrs. Assn. (fin. and acctg. council 1967-73), German-Am. C. of C. (dir.), Nat. Assn. Corp. Dirs., Harvard Bus. Sch. Assn. (trustee, pres. Cleve.). Clubs: World Trade Center, Harvard (N.Y.C.); Roxiticus Country, Boca Teeca (Boca Raton, Fla.); Quail Ridge (Boynton Beach, Fla.); Harvard Business School (sec., v.p., dir. 1959-63) (Chgo.). Home: Northgate Rd Oak Knoll Mendham NJ 07945 Office: Woolworth Bldg 233 Broadway New York NY 10007

SMITH, ELSDON COLES, lawyer; b. Virginia, Ill., Jan. 25, 1903; s. Dr. George Walter and Eva (Coles) S.; B.S., U. Ill., 1925; student U. Chgo., 1925; LL.B., Harvard, 1930; m. Clare Irvette Hutchins, Dec. 23, 1933; 1 dau., Laurel Gleda. Admitted to Ill. bar, 1930; faculty Chgo. Law Sch., 1933-35; asso. Follansbee, Shorey & Schupp, Chgo., 1933-48; mem. firm Blumberg & Smith, 1949-58; mem. firm Blumberg, Smith, Wolff, Pennish, 1958-62; asso. Koven, Salzman, Koenigsberg, Specks & Homer, 1965-76; lecturer onomatology. Mem. Am., Ill., Chgo. bar assns., Am. Name Soc. (pres. 1951-54, 70; bd. editors), English Place Name Soc., Internat. Com. Onomastic Scis. Presbyn. Mason. Author: Naming Your Baby, 1943; Story of Our Names, 1950; The Dictionary of American Family Names, 1956, new enlarged edit., 1972; Treasury of Name Lore, 1967; American Surnames, 1969; The Book of Smith, 1978. Compiler: Bibliography of Personal Names, 1950. Contbr. publs. Home: 8001 Lockwood Ave Skokie IL 60077

SMITH, ELTON ROBERT, assn. exec., farmer; b. Caledonia, Mich., Apr. 19, 1911; s. Robert D. and Mary (Beck) S.; grad. high sch.; student Mich. State U., 1931; m. Youlonda Raab, Jan. 26, 1938; children—Barbard (Mrs. Paul Schantz), Virginia (Mrs. Harry Shelton). Pres. Farm Bur. Services, 1961—, Mich. Farm Bur., 1964—, MACMA, 1964—, MASA, 1966—; bd. dirs. Am. Farm Bur. Fedn., 1964—, Farm Bur. Ins. Companies, Nat. Council Farmer Co-ops; mem. bd. Fed. Farm Credit; shareholder rep. Central Farmers Fertilizer Co., United Co-op, Inc.; pres. Caledonia Co-op., 1949-59. Trustee 4-H Found.; mem. exec. com. Am. Farm Bur., 1977. Recipient Disting. Service to Agr. award Mich. State U., 1963, Dairyman of Year award, 1963; 4-H Leadership award, 1969, hon. alumnus award Mich. State U., 1976. Mem. Alpha Zeta (hon.). United Methodist. Home: 5337 100th St Caledonia MI 49316 Office: 7373 W Saginaw Hwy Lansing MI 48904

SMITH, ELWYN ALLEN, assn. exec.; b. Wilmington, Del., Sept. 17, 1919; s. H. Framer and Mary (Closson) S.; student U. Omaha, 1936-38; B.A., Wheaton (Ill.) Coll., 1939; M.A., Harvard, 1941, Ph.D., 1942; B.D., Yale, 1943; Th.M., Princeton, 1944; m. Malvine Rose Maguire, Oct. 5, 1946; children—Paul, Rebecca, Scott. Dir., Westminster Found., Washington, 1943-45; asso. youth editor Bd. Christian Edn., Phila., 1945-49; dean, prof. ch. history Dubuque Theol. Sem., 1950-56; prof. ch. history Pitts. Theol. Sem., Pitts., 1957-66; prof. religion Temple U., Phila., 1966-70, v.p. student affairs, 1970-72; provost, v.p. acad. affairs Eckerd Coll., St. Petersburg, 1972-75; exec. dir. Continuing Edn. for Ch. Profls., 1976—; sr. pastor Garden Crest United Presbyn. Ch., St. Petersburg, 1977—. Author: The Presbyterian Ministry in American Culture, 1962; Church and State in Your Community, 1963; Religious Liberty in the U.S., 1972. Editor: Church State Relations in Ecumenical Perspective, 1966; Religion of the Republic, 1971; What the Religious Revolutionaries are Saying, 1971; Co-editor: Jour. of Ecumenical Studies, 1964—. Contbr. articles profl. jours. Home: 2500 Driftwood Dr SE St Petersburg FL 33705 Office: 2500 Driftwood Rd SE St Petersburg FL 33705

SMITH, EPHRAIM PHILIP, univ. adminstr., educator; b. Fall River, Mass., Sept. 19, 1942; s. Jacob Max and Bertha (Horvitz) S.; B.S., Providence Coll., 1964; M.S., U. Mass., 1965; Ph.D., U. Ill., 1968; m. Linda Sue Katz, Sept. 3, 1967; children—Benjamin, Rachel. Chmn. dept. accounting U. R.I., Kingston, 1968-73; dean Sch. Bus., Shippensburg (Pa.) State Coll., 1973-75; dean Coll. Bus. Adminstrn., Cleve. State U., 1975—. Mem. Am. Accounting Assn., Fin. Mgmt. Assn., Beta Gamma Sigma, Beta Alpha Psi. Contbr. articles to profl. jours. Home: 22325 Rye Rd Shaker Heights OH 44122 Office: Coll Bus Adminstrn Cleveland State U Cleveland OH 44115

SMITH, ERNEST ELWOOD, labor union exec.; b. Lawrence County, Tenn., Mar. 2, 1917; s. Reuben A. and Sallie Ann (Pollock) S.; student pub. schs., Toledo; m. Grace Margaret Bouya, Oct. 24, 1940; children—David, Daniel. Mem. Mechanics Ednl. Soc. Am., 1942—, shop steward, 1947-50, vice chmn. shop com., 1951-64, nat. rep., 1964-75, nat. sec.-treas., 1975—; mem. labor studies adv. com. Toledo U. Democrat. Office: Mechanics Ednl Soc Am 1421 First Nat Bldg Detroit MI 48226

SMITH, ESTUS, univ. ofcl.; b. Crystal Springs, Miss., Oct. 13, 1930; s. David D. and Margaret G. (Thompson) S.; B.S., Jackson State Coll., 1953; M.Music Edn., Ind. U., 1960; Ph.D., U. Iowa, 1970; m. Dorothy Triplett, Dec. 13, 1953; 1 son, Donald Gregory. Dir. bands Mickens High Sch., Dade City, Fla., 1953-58, Burglund High Sch., McComb, Miss., 1958-61, Brinkley High Sch., Jackson, Miss., 1961-62; dir. bands Jackson State U., 1968-72, dean Sch. Liberal Studies, 1973, v.p. for acad. affairs, 1973—; chmn. bd. State Mut. Fed. Savs. and Loan Assn. Mem. exec. bd. Miss. Com. for Humanities, exec. bd. All Saints Sch., Vicksburg, Miss.; pres. Opera/South Co.; trustee Dept. Archives and History, State of Miss.; mem. Commn. on Leadership Devel. in Higher Edn., Arts Center Space Allocation Com.; mem. exec. bd. Gov.'s Conf. Higher Edn.; mem. adv. com. Academic Adminstrn. Internship Program; active Boy Scouts Am., NAACP, YMCA. Named Outstanding Alumni and Scholar, 1970; Am. Council Edn. fellow, 1969. Mem. U. Iowa, Ind. U., Jackson State U. alumni assns., So. Conf. Deans of Faculties and Academic Pres.'s (past v.p.), Mus. Educators Nat. Conf., Nat. Assn. Humanities Edn., Miss. Assn., State TV Council on Higher Edn., Miss. Assn. Colls. and Univs., Phi Delta Kappa, Alpha Lambda Delta, Omega Psi Phi, Sigma Pi Phi. Episcopalian. Home: 1441 School Park Dr Jackson MS 39213

SMITH, EUGENE PRESTON, educator; b. Obetz, Ohio, Sept. 30, 1919; s. Silas Preston and Ruth (Cuckler) S.; B.S., Ohio State U., 1941, M.A., 1949, Ph.D., 1959; LL.D., Mt. Allison U., N.B., Can., 1973; m. Clara May Faris, Jan. 31, 1943; 1 son, Eugene Lynn. Tchr. math. and sci. Mifflin High Sch., 1941-42; tchr. math., gunnery and tactics Officer Candidate Prep. Sch., Ft. Sill, Okla., 1943-44; tchr. math. Bedford (Ohio) High Sch., 1946-47; chmn. math. dept. Univ. Sch., Ohio State U., 1947-58; supr. math. Wilmington (Del.) Pub. Schs., 1958-60; prof. math. edn. Wayne State U., Detroit, 1960—, chmn. dept. math. edn., 1960—; cons. to U.S. Office Edn., NSF, Ednl. Testing Service; mem. Conf. Bd. Math. Scis., 1972-75, trustee, 1977—, sec., 1978—. mem. div. math. scis. NRC, 1971-75. Recipient Centennial award medallion Ohio State U. Coll. Edn., 1970. Mem. Math. Assn. Am., Sch. Sci. and Math. Assn., Assn. Supervision and Curriculum Devel., NEA, Nat. (pres. 1972-74), Mich., Detroit, Ohio (pres. 1956-58) councils tchrs. math., AAUP, Alliance Assn. for Advancement Edn. (exec. com. 1972-75), Kappa Phi Kappa, Phi Delta Kappa. Presbyterian (elder). Club: Masons. Author: (with others) Discoveries in Modern Mathematics, Course One, 1972, Course Two, 1972; (with Joseph N. Hirsch) Computer Mathematics, 1966; (with Carlos Wilhite) Retriev-O-Math, 1968; contbr. articles to profl. jours., also chpts. to books. Home: 18031 Snow Rd Dearborn MI 48124 Office: Wayne State U Coll Edn Cass Ave Detroit MI 48202

SMITH, EWELL LEE, JR., lawyer; b. Denton, Tex., Jan. 29, 1923; s. Ewell Lee and Viola Beatrice (Price) S.; B.B.A., So. Methodist U., 1947, J.D., 1949; m. Mary Edith Taylor, June 17, 1950 (dec.); children—Lisa Ann, Douglas Marshall, Sally Jean, Mary Linda. Admitted to Tex. bar; practice in Dallas; sr. partner firm Smith, Smith, Dunlap & Canterbury, 1969—; lectr. in field. Appeal agt. Dallas SSS; mem. labor relations com. U.S. C. of C. Chmn. Dallas County Democratic Exec. Com., 1960-64, chmn. convs., 1958, 60. Mem. adv. bd. U. Tex., Arlington, also mem. devel. bd.; trustee Oallas Symphony Assn., Dallas Civic Opera. Served with AUS, 1942-45. Decorated D.S.C., Bronze Star (3), Purple Heart (4); Belgium Fourragère; recipient Alumni award outstanding profl. achievement U. Tex. at Arlington, 1967. Mem. Am., Tex., Dallas (past sec.-treas.) bar assns., Am. Mgmt. Assn. (chmn. seminars), N. Dallas C. of C., Dallas Personnel Assn., Tex. Assn. Lefthanded Golfers (past pres.). Presbyn. (deacon, ruling elder, trustee, stated clk.). Mason. Clubs: Brookhaven Country; Petroleum, Press (Headliner award) (Dallas). Author: Supervisor's Guide on Personnel Relations and Labor Laws; Labor Laws from Management Viewpoint. Home: 3860 Whitehall St Dallas TX 75229 Office: 4050 First Nat Bank Bldg Dallas TX 75202

SMITH, F(REDERICK) DOW(SWELL), physicist, coll. pres.; b. Winnipeg, Man., Can., Jan. 2, 1921; s. Edgar Nelson and Clara Branum (Dowswell) S.; B.A. with honors, Queen's U., 1947, M.A., 1948; Ph.D., U. Rochester, 1951; m. Margaret Lavinia Watson, July 2, 1949; children—Eric, Douglas, Linda, Murray. Came to U.S., 1948, naturalized, 1955. Research asst. Nat. Research Council of Can., 1947-48, Bausch & Lomb Optical Co., Rochester, N.Y., 1949-51; instr. dept. physics Boston U., 1951-52, asst. prof., 1952-54, asso. prof., 1955-58, chmn. dept. physics, 1953-58, dir. Boston U. Phys. Research Lab., 1955-58; dir. research Itek Corp., Boston, 1958-63, mgr. optics div., 1963—, v.p., 1967-74; interim pres. New Eng. Coll. Optometry, Boston, 1979—; v.p., treas. Internat. Commn. Optics, 1975—. Fellow Optical Soc. Am. (pres. 1974), A.A.A.S.; mem. Com. Sci. Soc. Presidents (sec.-treas. 1976), Sigma Xi. Home: 39 Gray Cliff Rd Newton Centre MA 02159 Office: 424 Beacon St Boston MA 02115

SMITH, FLOYD RODENBACK, utilities exec.; b. San Francisco, June 25, 1913; s. Floyd M. and Elizabeth (Rodenback) S.; student Long Beach (Calif.) Jr. Coll., 1931-33; B.S., N.Mex. State U., 1935; postgrad. Harvard U., 1962; m. Marion LaFrae Blythe, Oct. 5, 1935; children—Marion Katherine Smith Crain, Virginia Helene. With Gulf States Utilities Co., Beaumont, Tex., 1935-78, dir., 1965-78, v.p. Baton Rouge div., 1965-67, v.p. div. ops., 1967-69, exec. v.p., 1969, pres., 1970-73, prin. exec. officer, 1970-78, chmn. bd., prin. exec. officer, 1973-78; dir. First Security Nat. Corp., First Security Nat. Bank, Beaumont; pres. Southwest Atomic Energy Assos., 1971-77; mgmt. cons., 1978—. Bd. dirs., past chmn. Beaumont chpt. ARC; trustee United Appeals, pres., 1975; pres. Tex. Atomic Energy Research Found., 1976-78; bd. regents Devel. Council Lamar U. Named Distinguished Alumnus, Engrng. Sch., N.Mex. State U., 1977; registered profl. engr., Tex. Mem. Tex. Atomic Energy Research Found. (dir. 1970-78, pres. 1976-78), Tex. Research League (dir. 1970-78), Southeastern Elec. Exchange (pres. 1975-76, dir. 1970-78), Assn. Electric Cos. Tex. (chmn. 1978-79), Beaumont C. of C. (dir. 1970-76). Presbyterian (deacon). Clubs: Beaumont Country, Beaumont (past dir. 1974-76), Rayburn Country. Home: 5795 Longwood St Beaumont TX 77707 Office: 285 Liberty St Beaumont TX 77701

SMITH, FOSTER LEE, ret. air force officer, Sci. co. exec.; b. Okla., Sept. 6, 1922; s. John Richard and Nola Katherine (Shofner) S.; student Southeastern State Coll., Durant, Okla., 1939-41; B.S., U.S. Mil. Acad., 1944; M.P.A., Harvard U., 1962; postgrad. Nat. War Coll., 1965-66; m. Audrey Maxine Morris, Nov. 22, 1945; children—Paula Lee, Lynn Katherine, Todd Peyton. Commd. 2d lt. USAAF, 1944, advanced through grades to maj. gen. USAF, 1971; bomber pilot, World War II; aide to chmn. Joint Chiefs of Staff, 1950-51; fighter pilot, Korean War; comdr. first U.S. supersonic fighter squadron, 1954; dir. ops. and tng. 19th Air Force, 1955-57; plans officer Hdqrs. Air Force, 1957-61; chief war plans div. Hdqrs. USAF in Europe, 1962-65; vice comdr., comdr. combat crew tng. wing Davis Monthan AFB, Ariz., 1966-67; vice comdr. 3d Tactical Fighter Wing, Bien Hoa Air Base, Vietnam, 1967; dep. dir. 7th Air Force Tactical Air Control Center, Tan Son Nhut Air Base, 1967-68; mem. staff group, chmn. Joint Chiefs of Staff, 1968-69; dep. dir. ops. Nat. Mil. Command Center, 1970-71; chief Far East div. Office Joint Chiefs of Staff, 1970-71; dir. plans and policy Hdqrs. U.S. European Command, Stuttgart, Germany, 1971-74; asst. dep. chief staff plans and ops. Hdqrs. USAF, 1974-75, ret., 1975; asst. v.p. Sci. Applications, Inc., 1975—; pres. Topal Assos. Internat., 1975—. Vice pres. Trans-Atlantic council Boy Scouts Am., 1972—. Decorated D.S.M. with two oak leaf clusters, Silver Star, Legion of Merit, D.F.C. with three oak leaf clusters, Bronze Star with oak leaf cluster, Air medal with 10 oak leaf clusters, Air Force Commendation medal. Mem. Air Force Assn., Assn. Grads. U.S. Mil. Acad., Harvard Alumni Assn., Order of Daedalians. Address: 1331 Kingston Ave Alexandria VA 22302

SMITH, FRANK EARL, c. of c. exec.; b. Fremont Center, N.Y., Feb. 4, 1931; s. Earl A. and Hazel (Knack) S.; B.S., Syracuse U., 1952; m. Caroline R. Gillin, Aug. 14, 1954; children—Stephen F., David S., Daniel E. With Mellor Advt. Agy., Elmira, N.Y., 1954-55; asst. mgr. Assn. of Commerce, Elmira, 1955-56; asst. mgr. C. of C., Binghamton, N.Y. and mgr. Better Bus. Bur. Broome County, N.Y., 1956-60; exec. v.p. C. of C. Chemung County, Elmira, 1960-65; exec. v.p. Schenectady County (N.Y.) C. of C., 1965-69; exec. v.p. Greater Cin. C. of C., 1969-78; pres. Greater Detroit C. of C., 1978—. Served to 1st lt. USAF, 1952-54. Named Young Man of Yr., Jr. C. of C. Elmira, 1964. Mem. C. of C. Execs. Mich., Am. C. of C. Execs. (chmn.), N.Y. State C. of C. Execs. (past pres.), Ohio C. of C. Execs. (past pres.), C. of C. of U.S. (past chmn. nat. bd. regents Insts. for Orgn. Mgmt.). Presbyterian. Clubs: Detroit, Detroit Athletic, Renaissance, Lochmoor Golf. Home: 45 Renaud Rd Grosse Pointe Shores MI 48236 Office: 150 Michigan Ave Detroit MI 48226

SMITH, FRANK EDWARD, publisher, editor; b. Easton, Pa., Oct. 1, 1912; s. Frank Edward and Ella (Heavener) S.; B.S., State Coll., East Stroudsburg, Pa., 1934; M.A., N.Y. U., 1946; m. Lena June Popenciu, Sept. 16, 1950; 1 dau., Nancy Joan. Tchr., coach pub. schs., Easton, 1934-36, supervising prin., 1936-38; dir. employee activities Riegel Paper Co., Milford, N.J., 1938-43; nat. field rep. ARC, 1943-44; recreation dir. Gen. Electric Co., Erie, Pa., 1947-50; adminstrv. asst. C. J. La Roche Advt. Agy., N.Y.C., 1950-52; promotion mgr. McFadden Publs., N.Y.C., 1952-54; mgr. Buttenheim Pub. Co., Cleve., 1954-62; pub. School Product News, editor Changing Sch. Market Indsl. Pub. Co., Cleve., 1962-77; editorial cons., staff columnist Peter Li Inc., Dayton, Ohio, 1977-79; staff columnist The Woodsman, New Port Richey, Fla., 1979—; chmn. Frank E. Smith Inc., 1978-79. Bd. dirs. Beacon Woods (Fla.) Civic Assn., 1979. Served as warrant officer U.S. Mcht. Marines, 1945-46. Recipient Spl. award Nat. Sch. Supply and Equipment Assn., 1971, Black Hills Gang plaque, 1976, Spl. Pres.'s award, 1976; Alumni award East Stroudsburg State Coll., 1979; cert. of appreciation Assn. Sch. Bus. Ofcls., 1975-76. Mem. Nat. Sch. Supply Assn. (dir., exec. com. 1973-74, com. long range planning 1975-79), Nat. Audio Visual Assn. (cert. media specialist; faculty U. Ind. Inst. 1970-79, Spl. award 1973, 77, profl. devel. bd. 1974-80, public relations com. 1976-79, Inst. cert. 1970-75, vice chmn. continuing edn. com.), Edn. Industries (dir., sec.-treas. 1974—), Assn. Ednl. Communications and Tech. (exhibitors com. 1971—), Edn. Mgmt. Council (chmn. 1976), Phi Delta Kappa, Kappa Delta Pi. Club: Masons. Chief co-author: It Doesn't Pay to Work Too Hard. Monthly columnist Ednl. Dealer; contbr. articles to profl. jours. Home: 7702 Ironwood Circle New Port Richey FL 33553

SMITH, FRANK MACGREGOR, JR., broadcasting co. exec.; b. Indpls., May 28, 1927; s. Frank MacGregor and Freida (Boes) S.; grad. Deerfield Acad., 1945; B.A., N.Y.U., 1950; m. Abigail Goodmanson, Oct. 21, 1970; children—Frank MacGregor III, Braddock Monroe, Thaddeus Monroe. Adminstrv. asst. CBS films, CBS, Inc., 1951-52, copywriter TV Sales Dept., N.Y.C., 1952-53, adminstrv. asst., 1953-57, acct. exec., 1957-65, gen. sales exec., 1965-66, v.p. TV sales, 1966-78; pres. CBS Sports div., 1978—. Chmn. bd. Greenville Fire Dist. Commrs.; mem. N.Y.C. Council Hofstra U. Trustee Baldwin Sch. Served with AUS, 1945-47. Mem. Internat. Radio and Television Soc. (past gov.), Am. Marketing Assn., Acad. Television Arts and Scis., Sigma Phi Epsilon. Mem. Dutch Ref. Ch. (deacon). Clubs: Scarsdale Golf, Devon Yacht, Saw Mill River Kennel, Poodle Club of Am. Home: 1175 Park Ave New York NY 10028 Office: 51 W 52d St New York NY 10019

SMITH, FRED GEORGE, JR., medical educator; b. San Pedro, Calif., Jan. 1, 1928; s. Fred George and Agnes Proven (Melville) S.; B.S., U. Calif. at Los Angeles, 1951, M.D., 1955; m. Lurene Claire Roman, July 1, 1951; children—Randy, Richard, Cynthia. Intern U. Calif. at Los Angeles Hosp., 1955-56; resident U. Minn. Hosp., 1956-58; asst. prof. pediatrics, div. nephrology U. Cal. at Los Angeles, Med. Center, 1963-66, asso. prof., 1966-71, chief div. nephrology, 1966-73, prof. 1971-73; chmn. dept. pediatrics U. Iowa Med. Sch., 1973—. Served with USAF, 1958-60; USPHS spl. research fellow,

1968-69. Diplomate Am. Bd. Pediatrics. Fellow Am. Acad. Pediatrics; mem. Soc. Pediatric Research, Am. Pediatrics Soc., Western Soc. Clin. Investigation, Am. Soc. Nephrology, AAAS, Am. Soc. Pediatric Nephrology, Sigma Xi, Alpha Omega Alpha. Research: Fetal maturation and fetal renal function. Home: 329 MacBride Rd Iowa City IA 52240

SMITH, FREDERICK ADAIR, JR., army officer, educator; b. Trinity, Tex., Dec. 8, 1921; s. Frederick Adair and Alice Lorraine (Mansell) S.; student U. Tex., 1938-41; B.S., U.S. Mil. Acad., 1944; M.S., Johns Hopkins U., 1949; postgrad. Command and Staff Coll., 1954-55, Armed Forces Staff Coll., 1958-59, Indsl. Coll. Armed Forces, 1962-63; M.B.A., George Washington U., 1963; Ph.D., U. Ill., 1968; m. Katherine Bailey Egerton, Dec. 28, 1949; children—Katherine Lorraine, Carolyn Egerton. Commd. 2d lt. U.S. Army, 1944, advanced through grades to brig. gen., 1974; service in Europe, 1945-47, Korea, 1953-54; instr. Staff and Command Coll., 1955-58; instr. U.S. Mil. Acad., West Point, N.Y., 1949-52, prof. mechanics, 1965-74, head dept., 1969-74, dean acad. bd., 1974—. Trustee Assn. Grads. U.S. Mil. Acad. Decorated Bronze Star with 2 oak leaf clusters; recipient Engring. Alumni Honor award for distinguished service U. Ill. Coll. Engring., 1976. Mem. Am. Acad. Mechanics. Research in heavy box beams in structures. Home: 107 Washington Rd West Point NY 10996

SMITH, FREDERICK COE, mfg. co. exec.; b. Ridgewood, N.J., June 3, 1916; s. Frederick Coe and Mary (Steffee) S.; B.S., Cornell U., 1938; M.B.A., Harvard U., 1940; m. Ruth Pfeiffer, Oct. 5, 1940; children—Frederick Coe, Geoffrey, Roger, William, John. With Armstrong Cork Co., Lancaster, Pa., 1940-41; with Huffy Corp., Dayton, Ohio, 1946—, pres., chief exec. officer, 1961-72, chmn., chief exec. officer, 1972-76, chmn., 1976—, chmn. exec. com., 1979—; dir. Third Nat. Bank, Pitney Bowes Corp., Dayton Malleable, Inc. Trustee Sinclair Community Coll., Miami Valley Hosp., United Way Dayton Area; chmn. nat. bd. dirs. Planned Parenthood Fedn. Am., chmn. Dayton Found. Served to lt. col. USAAF, 1941-46. Decorated Legion of Merit. Home: 6320 Mad River Rd Dayton OH 45459 Office: PO Box 1204 Dayton OH 45401

SMITH, FREDERICK EDWARD, educator; b. Springfield, Mass., July 23, 1920; B.S., U. Mass., 1941; Ph.D. in Zoology, Yale, 1950; m. 1945; three children. Mem. faculty U. Mich., 1950-69, prof. natural resources, 1966-69; prof. resources and ecology Grad. Sch. Design, Harvard, 1969—. Mem nat. sci. bd. NSF, 1968-74; mem. climate research bd. Nat. Acad. Scis., 1977—; chmn. bd. Inst. Ecology, 1977—. Served with AUS, 1942-46. Mem. Ecol. Soc. Am. (pres. 1973-74). Address: Grad Sch Design Harvard Cambridge MA 02138

SMITH, FREDERICK GEORGE WALTON, marine biologist, oceanographer; b. Bristol, Eng., Jan. 28, 1909; s. Frederick George and Nelly Maud (Belton) S.; B.S., Royal Coll. Sci., London (Royal Scholar 1929-31), 1931, Ph.D., 1934; D.Sc. (hon.), Meml. U. Nfld., 1967, U. Miami (Fla.), 1974; m. Florence May Walker, Jan. 21, 1939; 1 dau., Alexandra. Commonwealth fellowship, 1934-36; biologist, sponge fishery investigation, Bahamas Govt., 1936-40; mem. faculty U. Miami, 1940—, prof. zoology, 1944-48, prof. marine biology, 1949—, dir. Inst. Marine Sci., 1942-69, dean Rosenstiel Sch. Marine and Atmospheric Sci., 1969-73, dean emeritus, disting. prof. oceanography, 1973—; editor Sea Frontiers, 1953—; dir. Planet Ocean Marine Sci. Expn., 1974; dir. Fla. Oyster Div., 1949-53; fisheries adviser Bahamas Govt., 1945—; tech. adviser to Gulf States Fisheries Commn. and Atlantic States Fisheries; chmn. Gulf and Caribbean Fisheries Inst.; chmn. exec. com. Joint Oceanographic Instns. Deep Earth Sampling, 1967-68, 72-73; chmn. Fla. Commn. for Marine Sci. and Tech., 1967-69. Recipient Achievement medal Fla. Acad. Sci., 1942, Gold medal, 1969; Naval Ordnance Devel. award for exceptional service U.S. Navy, 1945. Fellow Am. Geog. Soc., AAAS; mem. Am. Geophys. Union, Am. Soc. Limnology and Oceanography, Internat. Oceanographic Found. (founder, pres.), Am. Soc. Zoologists, Marine Biol. Assn. U.K., Fla. Acad. Sci., Fla. State Fisheries Com., Council Oceanographic Lab. Dirs. (chmn. 1967-68), Nat. Oceanography Assn. (dir. 1967-70), Miami (Fla.) Com. of 100. Clubs: Cosmos (Washington); Cat Cay (Bahamas) (past commodore); Biscayne Bay Yacht (past commodore); Cruising of Am. (rear commodore). Author: Atlantic Reef Corals, 1948, rev. edit., 1971; Spiny Lobster Industry of the Caribbean, 1949; Sea Turtles and the Turtle Industry (with R.M. Ingle), 1949; The Ocean River (with H. Chapin); The Sun, the Sea and Tomorrow (with H. Chapin), 1954; The Seas in Motion, 1973; Handbook of Marine Science, Vols. I, II, 1974; contbr. articles to sci. jours. Home: 720 Harbor Dr Key Biscayne FL 33149 Office: Planet Ocean Internat Oceanographic Found 3979 Rickenbacker Causeway Miami FL 33149. *A positive approach is not an infallible guarantee of success. But a negative approach leads only to certain failure.*

SMITH, FREDERICK GORDON, educator, geologist; b. Toronto, Ont., Can., Mar. 27, 1914; s. John Breigan and Christina Winifred (Marshall) S.; B.Sc., U. Man., 1937, M.Sc., 1939; Ph.D., U. Toronto, 1942; m. Mary Irene Closs, Sept. 19, 1942; children—F. Marshall, Susan Smith Wilkinson, Donald A., Bruce G., Christina Smith Eckersley, James O. Research metallurgist Internat. Nickel Co., 1942-43; phys. chemist Geophys. Lab., Washington, 1943-44; research engr. Research Enterprises, Ltd., Leaside, Ont., 1944-45; mem. faculty U. Toronto, 1945-79, prof. geology, 1965-79, prof. emeritus, 1979—; cons. in field. Fellowships, research grants NRC Can., 1939-42, 44—. Mem. Mineral Assn. Can., Geol. Assn. Can., Internat. Assn. Math. Geology, Am. Soc. Info. Sci., Geochem. Soc. Author: Historical Development of Inclusion Thermometry, 1953; Physical Geochemistry, 1963; Geological Data Processing, 1966; also articles. Home: 201 Mason Dr Whitby ON L1N 2B2 Canada Office: Dept Geology Univ Toronto Toronto ON M5S 1A1 Canada

SMITH, FREDERICK PLIMPTON, banker; b. Burlington, Vt., June 5, 1915; s. Levi Pease and Julia (Pease) S.; A.B., Princeton U., 1937; J.D., Harvard U., 1940; m. Marjorie Finlay Hewitt, Aug. 6, 1938; children—Susan Huntington Smith Strachan, Sybil Proctor Smith, Peter Plimpton, Frederick Hewitt, Charles Plimpton. Admitted to Vt. bar, 1940; asso. with Guy M. Page, atty., Burlington, 1940-42, 46-50; partner with David W. Yandell, Burlington, 1950-59; corporator Burlington Savs. Bank, 1942—, trustee, 1953—, v.p., gen. counsel, 1956-58, pres., 1959-74, chmn. bd., 1968—; dir., counsel Howard Nat. Bank & Trust Co., Burlington, 1948-66; dir. New Eng. Tel. & Tel. Co., chmn. audit com., 1977; dir., mem. exec. and fin. com. Nat. Life Ins. Co. Vt.; dir. Union Mut. Life Ins. Co. of Vt., Mt. Mansfield Co., Inc. Mem. Vt. Legislature, 1947-48, Vt. senate, 1973-74; chmn. Vt. Republican Com., 1948-49, fin. chmn., 1950-52; del., mem. credentials com. Rep. Nat. Conv., 1952; trustee U. Vt., 1947-53, Bennington Coll., 1967-74, Champlain Coll., Burlington, 1966-72. Served to lt. (s.g.) USNR, 1943-45. Mem. Am., Vt., Chittenden County (pres. 1957) bar assns., Nat. Assn. Mut. Savs. Banks (dir. 1960-69, chmn. fed. legis. com. 1963-65, v.p. 1965-66, pres. 1966-67). Congregationalist. Club: Princeton (N.Y.C.). Home: 195 S Willard St Burlington VT 05401 Office: 148 College St Burlington VT 05401

SMITH, FREDERICK ROBERT, JR., educator; b. Lynn, Mass., Sept. 19, 1929; s. Frederick Robert and Margaret Teresa (Donovan) S.; A.B., Duke U., 1951; M.Ed., Boston U., 1954; Ph.D., U. Mich., 1960; m. Mary Patricia Barry, Aug. 28, 1954; children—Brian Patrick, Barry Frederick, Brendan Edmund. Tchr. social studies public Jackson, Mich., 1954-58; instr. Eastern Mich. U., 1959, U. Mich., 1959-60; mem. faculty Sch. Edn., Ind. U., Bloomington, 1960—, prof., 1969—, chmn. social studies edn., 1964-73, chmn. secondary edn. dept., 1969-72, asso. dean adminstrn. and devel., 1975-78; vis. prof. U. Wis., summer 1967, U. Hawaii, summer 1972. USAF, 1951-53. Recipient Booklist award Phi Lambda Theta, 1965, 69. Mem. Ind. Council Social Studies (pres. 1968-69), Internat. Reading Assn., Nat. Council Social Studies (pres. 1968-69), Internat. Reading Assn., Nat. Council Social Studies (com. on sexism and social justice 1976—), Phi Delta Kappa, Kappa Sigma, Phi Kappa Phi. Roman Catholic. Co-author: New Strategies and Curriculum in Social Studies, 1969; Secondary Schools in a Changing Society, 1976; co-editor 2 books. Home: 2306 Edgehill Ct Bloomington IN 47401 Office: Sch of Education Rm 309 Indiana Univ Bloomington IN 47405

SMITH, FREDERICK RUTLEDGE, editor; b. Montgomery, Ala., Apr. 5, 1925; s. Frederick Rutledge and Mary Burton (Hale) S.; A.B., U. Ala., 1946, M.A., 1948. Asst. to mng. editor Charm mag. Street & Smith Pub. Co., 1948-49; asso. editor True mag., 1949-54; sr. editor Sports Illustrated mag., N.Y.C., 1954-69; editor-in-chief Am. Home mag., N.Y.C., 1969-73; editor and pub. Photo World Mag., N.Y.C., 1973-74; editor Photography Year, 1975 edit., Time-Life, N.Y.C., 1974-75; series editor Time-Life Books, 1975-76; v.p., editorial dir. East/West Network, pubs., N.Y.C., 1976-78, editor-in-chief, Los Angeles, 1978—. Served to 2d lt. USAAF, World War II. Organized, catalogued exhbn. at Mus. Modern Art, N.Y.C., summer 1965. Contbr. articles to nat. mags. Home: 511 Huntley Dr Los Angeles CA 90048 Office: 5900 Wilshire Blvd Los Angeles CA 90036

SMITH, G. E. KIDDER, architect, author; b. Birmingham, Ala., Oct. 1, 1913; s. F. Hopkinson and Annie (Kidder) S.; A.B., Princeton U., 1935, M.F.A., 1938; Ecole Americaine, Fontainbleau, France, 1935; m. Dorothea Fales Wilder, Aug. 22, 1942; children—G.E. Kidder, Hopkinson Kidder. Architect, Princeton Expdn. to Antioch, Syria, 1938; designer, site planner, camoufleur with Caribbean Architect-Engr. on Army bases in Caribbean, 1940-42; own archtl. practice, 1946—; lectr. numerous European archtl. socs., also many Am. univs. and museums; archtl. critic Yale U., 1948-49; vis. prof. M.I.T., 1955-56; mem. commn. on architecture Nat. Council Chs.; exhibits: Stockholm Builds, 1940, Brazil Builds, 1943, installed Power in the Pacific, USN, 1945 (all at Museum Modern Art, N.Y.C.); New Churches of Germany for Goethe House, N.Y.C., and Am. Fedn. Arts, 1957-58; Masterpieces of European Posters (donated), Va. State Mus., Richmond, 1958; Work of Alvar Aalto for Smithsonian Instn., 1965—; photographs in collection Mus. Modern Art. Served to lt. USNR, 1942-46. Registered architect, N.Y., Ala., N.C. Recipient Butler prize Princeton, 1938; fellow Am. Scandinavian Found., 1939-40; Guggenheim Found. fellow, 1946-47; President's fellow Brown U., 1949-50; research Fulbright fellow in Italy, 1950-51, India, 1965-66; Samuel H. Kress grant to India, 1967; Brunner scholar, 1959-60; Graham Found. for Advancement Arts-Nat. Council on Arts joint fellowship, 1967-69, Nat. Council Arts fellow, 1974-75, Ford Found. grant, 1970-71, 75-76; decorated Order So. Cross (Brazil); Premio ENIT gold medal (Italy); recipient gold medal (archtl. photography) A.I.A., 1964; E.M. Conover award, 1965. Fellow A.I.A., Internat. Inst. Arts and Letters (life; Switzerland); mem. Soc. Archtl. Historians, Assn. Collegiate Schs. of Architecture, Municipal Art Soc. N.Y.C., Coll. Art Assn. Episcopalian. Clubs: Century Assn., Princeton, Badminton (N.Y.C.); Cooperstown Country. Author: Brazil Builds, 1943; (with P.L. Goodwin) Switzerland Builds, 1950; Italy Builds, 1955; Sweden Builds, 1950, rev. edit., 1957; The New Architecture of Europe, 1961; The New Churches of Europe, 1963; A Pictorial History of Architecture in America, 1976; The Architecture of the United States, 1980; also contbr. articles to encys. Address: 163 E 81st St New York NY 10028

SMITH, G(ORDON) ROYSCE, JR., assn. exec.; b. Dothan, Ala., Mar. 7, 1924; s. Gordon Roysce and Mary Lucile (Brown) S.; student Ala. Poly. Inst., 1942-43, La. State U., 1947-49. Asst. buyer book dept. Davison's, Atlanta, 1949-57; book dept. mgr. Yale Coop., New Haven, 1957-71; ednl. project dir. Am. Booksellers Assn., N.Y.C., 1971-72, exec. dir., 1972—; pub. monthly mag. Am. Bookseller, 1977—; pub. Book Rev., 1978. Commentator The Book Smith, Sta. WELI, New Haven, 1966-71; producer/moderator The Opinionated Man, Sta. WNHC-TV, New Haven, 1966-71; Vanderhoff Meml. lectr. Sch. Library Sci., U. Iowa, 1973. Co-founder Booksellers Sch., 1965. Bd. dirs. North Branford (Conn.) Pub. Library, 1968-71, Starlight Festival Music, New Haven, 1964-71, Franklin Book Programs, 1977—; mem. exec. com. Festival of Arts, New Haven, 1959-69. Served with USNR, 1943-46. Recipient Outstanding Achievement award Ala. Library Assn., 1976. Mem. Am. Book Sellers Assn. (dir. 1968-71, 3d v.p. 1970-71), Kappa Sigma. Democrat. Methodist. Club: Dutch Treat. Co-editor: A Manual on Bookselling, 1974. Contbr. articles to profl. jours. Home: 640 Totoket Rd Northford CT 06472 Office: 122 E 42d St New York NY 10017. *Early on in my life I became convinced that the written word was the best way for one man to convey his thoughts to another, or for one generation to pass its collective wisdom (and follies) to succeeding generations. The book is the most permanent form for the preservation of the written word.*

SMITH, G(ODFREY) T(AYLOR), coll. adminstr.; b. Newton, Miss., Nov. 12, 1935; s. Taylor and Edna Young (Blanton) S.; B.A., Coll. Wooster, 1956; M.P.A. with distinction (Alfred P. Sloan fellow), Cornell U., 1960; LL.D. (hon.), Bethany Coll. 1979; m. Martha Joan Eaton, Sept. 1, 1956; children—Paul Brian, Sherry Lynn. Asso. dir. devel. Cornell U., 1960-62; dir. devel. Coll. Wooster, 1962-66, v.p., 1966-77; pres. Chapman Coll., 1977—; lectr. in field. Bd. dirs. Wayne County (Ohio) Indsl. Devel. Corp., 1966-72, World Affairs Council Orange County (Calif.), 1978—, Orange County chpt. NCCJ, 1979—, Goodwill Industries Orange County, 1979—, div. Higher Edn., Christian Ch. (Disciples of Christ), 1980—. Recipient William A. Galpin prize Coll. Wooster, 1956. Republican. Presbyterian. Clubs: Balboa Bay (Newport Beach, Calif.); Lincoln (Orange County); Univ. (Washington). Contbr. numerous articles on coll. mgmt. to profl. publs. Home: 9631 Fleet Rd Villa Park CA 92667 Office: Chapman Coll Orange CA 92666. *All that we are and have is a gift. Our imaginative response to that gift is gratitude that we express through what we do with what we have or can influence.*

SMITH, GARDNER WATKINS, physician; b. Boston, July 2, 1931; s. George Van Siclen and Olive (Watkins) S.; grad. Phillips Acad., 1949; M.D., Harvard, 1956; A.B., Princeton, 1969; m. Susan Elizabeth Whiteford, Sept. 6, 1958; children—Elizabeth Whiteford, Rebecca Tremain, George Van Siclen II. Intern Johns Hopkins Hosp., Balt., 1956-57, asst. resident, 1958-59, fellow, 1957-58, asst. in surgery, 1957-59, prof. surgery, 1970—, surgeon, 1970—, dep. dir. dept. surgery, 1978—; asst. resident U. Va., Charlottesville, 1959-61, resident, 1961-62, asst. in surgery, 1959-63, cardiovascular resident, 1962-63; instr., 1963-65, asst. prof., 1965-68, asso. prof., 1968-70, surgeon, 1963-70; prof. surgery U. Md., Balt., 1970—; chief surgery Balt. City Hosp., 1970-79, vis. surgeon, 1979—; cons. Greater Balt. Med. Center, 1970—; cons. Lock Raven VA Hosp., Balt., 1971—, Walter Reed Army Med. Center, 1976—. Diplomate Am. Bd. Surgery, Am. Bd. Thoracic Surgery. Mem. Soc. U. Surgeons, Am., So. surg. assns., A.C.S., Am. Gastroenterol. Assn., Assn. for Acad. Surgery, Balt. City Med. Soc., Halsted Soc., Med. and Chirurgical Faculty of Md., Soc. Surgery Alimentary Tract, Soc. Vascular Surgery, Internat. Cardiovascular Soc., So. Soc. Clin. Surgeons, Southeastern Surg Congress, So. Assn. Vasular Surgery, Va. Surg. Assn., Cum Laude Soc., Alpha Omega Alpha, Nu Sigma Nu. Contbr. articles to med. jours. Home: 1503 Old Orchard Ln Baltimore MD 21204 Office: Johns Hopkins Hosp Baltimore MD 21205

SMITH, GEOFFREY F. N., life ins. co. exec.; b. Box Hill, Eng., Mar. 11, 1926; s. Sydney A. and Phyllis I. (Elworthy) S.; came to U.S., 1963, naturalized, 1969; B.A., U. Toronto, 1946; m. Marguerite H. Scaife, Sept. 1954; children—G. Lawrence, Craig D., Gail B. Actuarial trainee, then supr. Can. Life Ins. Co., Toronto, 1947-53; successively asst. actuary, actuary, v.p. and actuary Sovereign Life Ins. Co., Winnipeg, Man., 1953-63; v.p., actuary Am. Mut. Life Ins. Co., Des Moines, 1963-67, pres., 1967—, chief exec. officer, 1969—. Chmn. capital fund drive Campfire Girls, 1978; exec. com. Jr. Achievement of Des Moines, 1975—. Fellow Soc. Actuaries, Canadian Inst. Actuaries; mem. Am. Acad. Actuaries. Episcopalian. Clubs: Des Moines, Des Moines Golf and Country. Home: 2005 69th St Des Moines IA 50322 Office: 418 6th Ave Des Moines IA 50307

SMITH, GEORGE DEE, tobacco co. exec.; b. Winston-Salem, N.C., Nov. 23, 1929; s. George Franklin and Vera Virginia (Hilton) S.; A.B., U. N.C., 1951; m. Jeannine Rose Meacham, May 23, 1953; 1 dau., Dee Ann. With R.J. Reynolds Tobacco Co., 1955—, dir., comptroller, 1970—, v.p., 1972, sr. v.p., 1973—; chmn., chief exec. officer Macdonald Tobacco Inc., Montreal, Que., Can., 1974-76; pres., chief operating officer R.J. Reynolds Tobacco Internat., Inc., 1976—; dir. 1st Union Nat. Bank. Chmn. budget com. Winston-Salem United Fund, 1966—, treas., 1967—; bd. dirs. Winston-Salem Goodwill Industries, Montreal Bd. Trade, 1975, Moravian Home, Inc., Excellence Fund of U. N.C., Greensboro; trustee Old Salem, Inc.; mem. bus. adv. council Western Carolina U. Served to lt. USNR, 1951-55. Mem. Nat. Assn. Accountants (pres. Piedmont chpt. 1969, nat. dir. 1973—), Stuart Cameron McLeod Soc. Home: 317 Sherwood Forest Rd Winston-Salem NC 27104 Office: R J Reynolds Tobacco Internat Inc PO Box 2959 Winston Salem NC 27102

SMITH, GEORGE EDWIN, metal distbg. co. exec.; b. Athens, Ga., Aug. 2, 1916; s. Swinney O. and Willie (Crawford) S.; B.S. in Commerce, Ga. State Coll., 1939; m. Evelyn A. Agnew, Oct. 18, 1940; children—Carol Kay, William A. Accounting mgr. J.M. Tull Metals Co., Atlanta, 1936-46, treas., 1946-62, v.p. finance, 1962-65, exec. v.p., 1965-67; pres., chief exec. officer J.M. Tull Industries, Atlanta, 1967—; dir. Trust Co. Ga., Am. Heritage Life Ins. Co., Jacksonville, Fla. Mem. exec. com., treas. Steel Service Center Inst., 1976—. Trustee YMCA, Atlanta, N.W. Ga. council Girl Scouts U.S.A.; v.p. United Way Met. Atlanta; chmn. Atlanta chpt. ARC; trustee J.M. Tull Found., Ga. State U. Found., So. Assn. Schs. and Colls.; bd. visitors Emory U.; mem. adv. bd. Ga. State U. Served with USAAF, 1943-46. Mem. Nat. Assn. Aluminum Distbrs. (pres. 1971-72), Ga. State U. Alumni Assn. (pres. 1975-76). Clubs: Rotary (pres. 1970-71), Capital City (dir.). Home: 5295 London Dr NW Atlanta GA 30327 Office: Old Peachtree Rd Norcross GA 30091

SMITH, GEORGE ELWOOD, physicist; b. White Plains, N.Y., May 10, 1930; s. George Francis and Lillian Alfreda (Voorhies) S.; B.S., U. Pa., 1955; M.S., U. Chgo., 1956, Ph.D., 1959; m. E. Janet Carson, July 6, 19S5 (dec.); children—Leslie Ann, Lauren Lucille, Carson Eric. Mem. tech. staff Bell Telephone Labs., Murray Hill, N.J., 1959-64, head dept. solid state electronic device devel., 1964—. Served with U.S. Navy, 1948-52. Recipient Franklin Inst. Ballantine medal, 1973. Fellow IEEE (Liebmann award 1974), Am. Phys. Soc.; mem. Phi Beta Kappa, Sigma Xi, Pi Mu Epsilon. Club: Toms River Yacht. Contbr. tech. articles to profl. jours. Patentee in field. Home: 65 Summit Rd Murray Hill NJ 07974 Office: Bell Labs 600 Mountain Ave Murray Hill NJ 07974

SMITH, GEORGE EMMETT, lawyer, bus. exec.; b. Glens Falls, N.Y., Aug. 2, 1928; s. George Lester and Mae Julie (O'Connell) S.; B.S. in Econs., Fordham U., 1953, J.D., 1956; M.A. in Econs., N.Y. U., 1959; m. Therese Marie Deschambault, Dec. 28, 1950; children—Mark Christopher, Laura Ann, Claire Louise, Lydia Margaret. Admitted to N.Y. State bar, 1956; atty. Union Carbide Corp., N.Y.C., 1956-67; asst. sec., asst. gen. counsel Xerox Corp., Stamford, Conn., 1967-75; sr. v.p., gen. counsel LTV Corp., Dallas, 1975—. Served with Signal Corps, AUS, 1947-48. Mem. Am., N.Y. State, Dallas bar assns., State Bar Tex. Clubs: Bent Tree Country, Dallas. Home: 10048 Hollow Way Dallas TX 75229 Office: PO Box 225003 Dallas TX 75265

SMITH, GEORGE FRANKLIN, JR., lawyer; b. Sherman, Tex., May 29, 1916; s. George Franklin and Minnie (Philips) S.; LL.B. (Hon. scholar), U. Tex., 1939; D.C.L., Univ. Kings Coll., Halifax, N.S., Can., 1972; m. Winifred Pauline Gill, Nov. 24, 1973; children—Sharon Smith Ginsburg, Elizabeth Smith Merlin, James A., George Franklin. Admitted to D.C., Mass., Tex., U.S. Supreme Ct. bars; practiced in Dallas, 1938; atty. U.S. depts. agr., war, 1940, chief counsel's office Bur. IRS, 1941-42; partner firm Goodman, Rosenbaum & Meacham, 1945-50; partner firms Cross, Murphy & Smith, Washington and Grady, Johnson, Smith & Blakeley, Dallas, 1951-67; of counsel firm Sherburne, Powers & Needham, Boston, 1954-65; counsel Beam Eye Found., Eberhard Faber Found. Bd. dirs. Kings Coll., N.Y.; adminstrv. trustee April Fund. Served to lt. comdr., JAGC, USNR, 1941-45. Mem. Am., D.C., Mass. bar assns., State Bar Tex. Clubs: Lyford Cay (governing com., bd. property owners assn.), Army Navy Country; East Hill (Nassau, Bahamas); Edgartown Yacht, Edgartown Golf, Royal Chappaquiddock Yacht (Mass.); Yale, Deke (N.Y.); Washington Deke (formerly pres.), Washington Golf and Country, Army Navy, Univ. (Washington); Campestre de Golfo (San Luis Potosi, Mex.); Palm Bay (Miami, Fla.). Formerly mem. Tex. Law Rev.; contbr. articles to profl. jours. Concert soloist U. Tex. Symphony, 1933-36; asst. dir., jazz soloist Longhorn Bank, 1933-36. Home: Wincrest Lyford Cay Nassau Bahamas Office: 1128 16th St NW Washington DC 20036. *This was my father's code—written to me the first day I began the practice of law: It is far better to trust ten men and be wrong as to nine than to distrust all and be wrong as to one!*

SMITH, GEORGE MAYNARD, lawyer; b. Cairo, Ga., Oct. 5, 1907; s. John Quincy and Nona (Hathorn) S.; student Castle Heights Mil. Acad., 1923-24; A.B., Mercer U., 1929; m. Helen Miller, Oct. 5, 1936; 1 dau., Helen Maynard. Admitted to Ga. bar, 1933; pros. atty. Grady County (Ga.), 1935-39, 39-42; spl. asst. to U.S. Atty. Gen., 1942-44; law practice, Atlanta, 1947—, mem. firm. Smith, Currie & Hancock, and predecessors; industry mem. Nat. Wage Stblzn. Bd., 1951. Trustee Young Harris Coll. Served as comdr. USN, 1944-46. Recipient Commendation Ribbon (Navy). Mem. Am., D.C., Ga. State, Fulton County bar assns., Sigma Alpha Epsilon. Methodist. Clubs: Kiwanis (dist. gov. 1941, v.p. 1951, pres. 1953), Capital City, Racket, Lawyers, Breakfast (Atlanta); Army-Navy (Washington); Commerce; Peachtree Golf. Home: 3900 Randall Ridge NW Atlanta

GA 30327 Office: 2600 Peachtree Center Harris Tower 233 Peachtree NE Atlanta GA 30303

SMITH, GEORGE PATRICK, II, educator, lawyer; b. Wabash, Ind., Sept. 1, 1939; s. George Patrick and Marie Louise (Barrett) S.; B.S., Ind. U., 1961, J.D., 1964; certificate Hague Acad. Internat. Law, 1965; LL.M., Columbia U., 1975. Kannert teaching fellow Ind. U. Sch. Law, 1964-65; instr. law U. Mich. Sch. Law, 1965-66; admitted to Ind. bar, 1964, U.S. Supreme Ct. bar; practiced in Ind. and Washington, 1965—; legal adviser Fgn. Claims Settlement Commn., Dept. State, Washington, 1966; asst. prof., asst. dean State U. N.Y. at Buffalo Law Sch., 1967-69; vis. asst. prof. law George Washington U., Nat. Law Center, summer 1968; asso. prof. law U. Ark., 1969-71; spl. counsel EPA, Washington, 1971-74; adj. prof. law Catholic U. Law Sch., Washington, 1973-74, prof., 1977—; adj. prof. law Georgetown U. Law Center, 1971-75; asso. prof. law U. Pitts. Sch. Law, 1975-78; Commonwealth fellow in law, sci. and medicine Yale, 1976-77; vis. prof. law U. Conn., 1977; distinguished vis. scholar Kennedy Bioethics Inst., Georgetown U., 1977—; cons. environ. legislation Govt. of Greece, 1977; spl. counsel to Gov. Ark. for environ. affairs, 1969-71; cons. Ark. Planning Commn., 1970-71; mem. Ark. Waterway Commn., 1970-71; chmn. Ark. Com. on Environ. Control, 1970-71; mem. com. on hwy. research NRC, Nat. Acad. Sci., 1971—; project dir. Center for Study Responsive Law, Nader Study of Congress, 1972. Life mem. Ind. U. Found. Univ. fellow Columbia Law Sch., 1974-75; vis. scholar Cambridge (Eng.) U., summer 1975, spring 1978, 79. U. Ark. del. Pacem In Maribus Conf., Malta, 1970. Mem. Nat. Cathedral Assn. Washington, Selden Soc., Am. Bar Assn. (rep. UN Conf. on Human Environment, Stockholm 1972, rep. Law of Sea Conf., UN, N.Y.C. 1976, Switzerland 1979), Ind. Bar Assn., U.S. Supreme Ct. Hist. Soc., Am. Friends of Cambridge U., Am. Law Inst., Alpha Kappa Psi, Phi Alpha Delta, Sigma Alpha Epsilon, Order of Omega. Club: Cosmos (Washington). Author: Genetics, Ethics and the Law, 1980; Restricting the Concept of Free Seas, 1980; contbr. articles to profl. jours. Office: Catholic U Sch Law Washington DC 20064. *Think big, work hard and—above all—have a dream: these are the simple keys to successful living.*

SMITH, GEORGE ROSE, judge; b. Little Rock, July 26, 1911; s. Hay Watson and Jessie Alice (Rose) S.; student Washington and Lee, 1928-31; LL.B., U. Ark., 1933; m. Peg Newton, Dec. 3, 1938; 1 dau., Laurinda Hempstead. Admitted to Ark. bar, 1933, practiced in Little Rock, 1933-49; mem. firm Rose, Dobyns, Meek & House; asso. justice Supreme Ct. of Ark., 1949—. Mem. Ark. Supreme Ct. Com. on Jury Instrns.; mem. faculty Am. Acad. Jud. Edn. Served from 2d lt. to maj., Air Corps, AUS, 1942-46. Mem. Inst. Jud. Adminstrn., Ark. Bar Assn., Sigma Alpha Epsilon, Phi Delta Phi. Author: Arkansas Annotations to Restatement of Trusts, 1938; Arkansas Mining and Mineral Law, 1942. Home: Two Cantrell Rd Little Rock AR 72207 Office: Justice Bldg Little Rock AR 72201

SMITH, GEORGE VAN RIPER, educator, journalist; b. Salem, Mass., Sept. 16, 1937; s. Alfred Henry and Isabelle (Van Riper) S.; B.S. in Bus. Adminstrn., Miami U., Oxford, Ohio, 1959; M.A. in Communications, U. Pa., 1965; m. Elizabeth Mae Mackey, Aug. 15, 1964; children—Douglas, Todd. Market analyst Shell Oil Co., 1959-60; reporter Jacksonville (Fla.) Jour., 1965-67; with Atlanta Jour., 1967-78, columnist and editorial writer, 1968-78; editor Hawkinsville (Ga.) Dispatch and News, 1978; instr., dept. journalism Ga. State U., 1972-75; free-lance writer, 1978—. Bd. dirs. UN Assn. U.S.A., 1977—. Served with USNR, 1960-64. Home and office: Pine Level Apt B Hawkinsville GA 31036

SMITH, GERALD ALLEN, educator, physicist; b. Akron, Ohio, Jan. 8, 1936; s. Harold C. and Lillian (Garforth) S.; B.A. magna cum laude (Ray Edwards physics fellow 1956-57), Miami U. (Ohio), 1957; M.S., Yale U., 1958, Ph.D. (Socony-Mobil fellow), 1961; m. Vonine Sue Klepinger, June 14, 1958; children—Jennifer, Terrill. Physicist, Lawrence Radiation Lab., Berkeley, Calif., 1961-67; asst. prof. U. Calif., Berkeley, 1965-67; prof. physics Mich. State U., East Lansing, 1967—; asso. lab. dir. for high energy physics Argonne (Ill.) Nat. Lab., 1978-79; cons. AEC, 1968-71, Argonne Univs. Assn., 1971-73, NSF, 1973-76. Fellow Am. Phys. Soc.; mem. AAAS, Acacia, Nat. Accelerator Lab. Users Group (exec. com. 1971-74, chmn. 1972-73), Argonne Univs. Assn. (trustee 1976-78), Phi Beta Kappa, Sigma Xi, Sigma Pi Sigma, Pi Mu Epsilon, Omicron Delta Kappa. Contbr. articles to profl. jours. Address: Dept Physics Mich State U East Lansing MI 48824

SMITH, GERALD WAYNE, coll. dean; b. Nutter Fort, W.Va., Dec. 15, 1920; s. Gerald Newton and Eva Ruth (Musser) S.; A.B., Salem Coll., 1941; A.M., W.Va. U., 1949, Ph.D., 1954; m. Mary Regina McGuire, 1940; children—Gerald Wayne, Lawrence Alan, Judith Elaine; m. 2d, Patricia Ann Williamson, Aug. 24, 1952; children—Leslie Diane, Donald Harold, Margaret Ann. Instr. history Marshall U., 1950-51, 52-54, W.Va. U., 1951-52; from asst. prof. to prof. history Fairmont (W.Va.) State Coll., 1954-63; acad. dean Waynesburg (Pa.) Coll., 1963—. Served with USNR, 1945-46. Mem. Am., W.Va. (pres. 1960-61) hist. assn., W.Va. Hist. Soc. (pres. 1961-62), Orgn. Am. Historians, Phi Beta Kappa, Phi Alpha Theta. Democrat. Baptist. Mason, Rotarian (pres. Waynesburg 1967-68). Author: Nathan Goff, Jr., A Biography, 1959. Contbr. articles Colliers Ency., Ency. Brit. Home: 293 1st Ave Waynesburg PA 15370

SMITH, GOFF, steel co. exec.; b. Jackson, Tenn., Oct. 7, 1916; s. Fred Thomas and Mabel (Goff) S.; B.S. in Engring., U. Mich., 1938, M.B.A., 1939; M.S., Mass. Inst. Tech.; m. Nancy Dall, Nov. 28, 1942 (dec.); children—Goff Thomas, Susan K. Schmidt; m. 2d, Harriet Oliver, June 23, 1973. Sales dept. Amsted Industries, Chgo., 1946-55, pres. Griffin Wheel div., Chgo., 1955-60, v.p., 1960-66, exec. v.p., 1966-69, pres., chief operating officer, 1969-74, chief exec. officer, 1974—, pres., 1974-80, chmn., 1980—, also dir.; dir. LaSalle Nat. Bank, Chgo., NALCO Chem. Co., Central Ill. Pub. Service Co., Clark Equipment Co., Gatx Corp. Served to maj., Ordnance Corps, AUS, 1941-46. Office: 3700 Prudential Plaza Chicago IL 60601

SMITH, GORDON APPELBE, artist, educator; b. Eng., June 18, 1919; s. William George and Daisy (Appelbe) S.; student Winnipeg (Man., Can.) Sch. Art, 1934; grad. Vancouver (B.C., Can.) Sch. Art; student Calif. Sch. Fine Arts, Harvard U.; LL.D. (hon.), Simon Fraser U., 1973; m. Marion Katherine, Sept. 15, 1941. Mem. Faculty Edn., U. B.C., Vancouver, 1956—; exhibited in one-man shows: Godard-Lefort Gallery, Montreal, 1968, Martha Jackson Gallery, N.Y.C., 1970, Bau-Xi Gallery, Vancouver, 1973; exhibited in numerous group shows. Recipient 1st prize Biennial Can. Painting, 1955; Baxter award, Toronto, 1960; prize group exhbn., London, Ont.; 2d prize Winnipeg Biennial, 1966; 1st prize Can. Group, Montreal, 1968; prize 3d Santiago Biennial Exhbn. Modern Engraving; also prizes in Vancouver and Victoria anns.; Can. Council sr. fellow, 1960-61. Anglican.

SMITH, GORDON HATFIELD, electronics co. exec.; b. Putnam, Conn., June 16, 1928; s. Otho Francis and Ruth Weston (Hatfield) S.; student U. Va., 1945-46; B.A. in Math., Brown U., 1957; B.S., U.S. Naval Postgrad. Sch., 1962; postgrad. George Washington U., 1969-70, Indsl. Coll. Armed Forces, 1970; m. Mary Alice Johns, Apr. 4, 1970; children—Gordon, Nancy J., Kelly Ann; 1 stepson, Cameron Irons. Commd. officer U.S. Navy, 1945, advanced through grades to rear adm.; chief spl. intelligence sect. UN staff, Korea, 1959-60; mem. staff Office of Sec. of Def., 1970-73; dep. dir. Def. research and engring. for research and advanced tech., 1973-74; mgr. Reconnaissance, electronic warfare, spl. ops. and naval intelligence systems, 1974-76; vice comdr. Naval Electronic Systems Command, Washington, 1976-79; ret., 1979; v.p. engring. NAVCOM systems div. Gould, Inc., El Monte, Calif., 1979—. Decorated D.F.C. (4), 21 air medals, Bronze star, Purple heart, Legion of Merit, others. Mem. Assn. Naval Aviation, Tail Hook Assn., Am. Soc. Naval Engrs., Armed Forces Communications and Electronics Assn. Home: 956 Rancho Circle Fullerton CA 92635 Office: 4323 Arden Dr El Monte CA 91731

SMITH, GORDON HOWELL, lawyer; b. Syracuse, N.Y., Oct. 26, 1915; s. Lewis P. and Maud (Mixer) S.; B.A. Princeton U., 1932-36; LL.B., Yale U., 1939; m. Eunice Hale, June 28,1947; children—Lewis Peter, Susan D., Catherine H., Maud W. Admitted to N.Y. bar, 1939, Ill. bar, 1946; asso. firm Lord, Day & Lord, N.Y.C., 1939-41, firm Gardner, Carton & Douglas, Chgo., 1946-51; partner firm Mackenzie, Smith & Michell, Syracuse, 1951-53, Gardner, Carton & Douglas, 1954-57, 60—; sec., dir. Smith-Corona, Inc., 1951-54, v.p., Syracuse, 1957-60. Bd. dirs. Rehab. Inst. Chgo., chmn., 1974-78; bd. dirs. United Way Met. Chgo.; trustee Crusade of Mercy. Served to lt. comdr. USNR, 1941-46. Mem. Am. Soc. Corporate Secs., Am., Ill., Chgo. bar assns. Clubs: Comml., Execs., Law, Econ., Legal, Chgo., Old Elm (Chgo.); Century (Syracuse). Home: 1300 N Green Bay Rd Lake Forest IL 60045 Office: 1 First National Plaza Chicago IL 60603

SMITH, GORDON HUNT, educator, musician; b. St. Paul, Oct. 27, 1916; s. Victor Gordon and Evangeline (Hunt) S.; B. Sch. Music, Wooster Coll., 1940, B.Mus., 1945; M.A., Mills Coll., 1947; Ph.D., State U. Iowa, 1955; m. Suzanne Mullett, Apr. 18, 1944; children—Victor Hunt, Daisy Mullett, Laurence Svennungsen. Music tchr. Smithville (Ohio) pub. schs., 1940-41, Oakland (Calif.) pub. schs., 1946-47; faculty Am. U., 1947—, prof. music, 1958—, chmn. dept., 1959-62, 68—, lectr. Adviser, Christian Sci. Orgn. The Am. U., 1954-62, 68—. Served with AUS, 1941-45. Recipient Distinguished Service to broadcasting award Am. U., 1962, 63, 65, 66, 67, 68. Mem. Music Library Assn., Music Tchrs. Nat. Assn. (life, pres. D.C. 1952-54), Alpha Psi Omega (hon.), Mu Phi Alpha (hon. patron). Christian Scientist. Composer of following: Preamble to UN Charter, 1947, Carol, 1949, The Man with the Withered Hand, 1960 (all soprano-alto-tenor-bass); Sonata for piano 4 hands, 1948; Drawings for String Quartet, 1949; Intrada, 1949, Four Vignettes, 1950 (both orch.); The Virtuous Woman, Pretty Robin (both soprano-soprano-alto), 1950; The Lamb, Tree Pictures (both soprano), 1950; Concert for Flute and Orchestra, 1951; Sonate for violin and piano, 1951; Concerto for String Bass, 1952; Toccata for piano quartet, 1953; incidental music for Antigone, 1954; Chorale Symphony, 1955; incidental music for Everyman, 1956; Medea, 1957; Anne of a Thousand Days, 1958; Letitia Wanted to Get Married, Grandmother's Gone to the Bar (3 minute operas), 1959; Twelve Shepherds; Chorale Prelude for Keyboard, 1962; score for Woodpainting, 1967; Sound: Notation and Design, 1968; Evolution of Jazz, 1967; Lysistrata, 1976; Ondine, 1977. Producer; Musicians Face the Music; Professor's Choice (weekly radio programs), 1964-68; Evolution of Jazz (radio course), 1968-69. Contbg. critic mags. Home: 4450 Dexter St NW Washington DC 20007

SMITH, GORDON LAIDLAW, JR., mfg. co. exec.; b. Chattanooga, Jan. 29, 1926; s. Gordon Laidlaw and Sara (Simmons) S.; B.S. in Civil Engring., Duke U., 1948; m. Frances Street, Aug. 22, 1951; children—Gordon L., Preston Lowrance, Sara Frances. With Wheland Co., Chattanooga (merged with Gordon Street, Inc., 1961, merged with N.Am. Royalties, Inc., 1969), 1948—, sec., treas. Gordon Street, Inc., 1964-69, sec., treas., bd. dirs. N.Am. Royalties, Inc., 1969-72, v.p. fin., treas., 1972-78, v.p. planning and devel., treas., 1978—, v.p. planning and devel., sec.-treas., 1979—; bd. dirs. Chattanooga Gas Co., 1967-71; 1st Fed. Savs. and Loan Assn. Chattanooga, 1967—, Commerce Union Bank, Chattanooga, 1976—. Trustee McCallie Sch.; bd. dirs. Boys' Club Chattanooga, v.p., 1975-76; chmn. Chattanooga-Hamilton County chpt. ARC, 1962-64, mem. exec. com., 1958-74; mem. met. bd. YMCA, 1966-67. Served with USNR, 1944-46. Mem. Am. Petroleum Inst., U.S. C. of C., Tenn. Mfrs. Assn. (bd. govs.), Greater Chattanooga Area C. of C. (pres. 1975), Chattanooga Mfrs. Assn. (past pres.), Duke U. Alumni Assn. (mem. adv. admissions com.), Phi Delta Theta, Omicron Delta Kappa. Presbyterian. Clubs: Mountain City, Chattanooga Golf and Country, Kiwanis (past pres.). Office: 200 E 8th St Chattanooga TN 37402

SMITH, GORDON PAUL, bus. exec.; b. Salem, Mass., Dec. 25, 1916; s. Gordon and May (Vaughan) S.; B.S. in Econs., U. Mass., 1944; M.S. in Govt. Mgmt. (Sloan fellow), U. Denver, 1948; postgrad. in Polit. Sci., N.Y. U., 1948-50; m. Ramona Chamberlain, Sept. 27, 1969; children—Randall B., Rodney F. Economist, Tax Found., Inc., N.Y.C., 1948-50; with Booz, Allen & Hamilton, 1951-67, partner, San Francisco, 1959-62, v.p., San Francisco, 1962-67, 69-70; partner Harrod, Williams and Smith, real estate devel., San Francisco, 1962—; state dir. fin. State of Calif., 1967-68; pres. Gordon Paul Smith & Co. Mgmt. Cons., 1968-71; pres., chief exec. officer Golconda Corp., 1972-74, chmn. bd., 1974—; pres. Cermetek Corp., 1978—; bd. dirs., exec. com. First Calif. Co.; dir. Eastman & Beaudine, Inc., Groman Corp., Vetter Corp.; adviser task force procurement and contracting Hoover Commn., 1954-55; spl. asst. to pres. Republic Aviation Corp., 1954-55; cons. Hawaii, 1960-61, Alaska, 1963, Wash. Hwy. Adminstrn., 1964. Mem. Calif. Select Com. on Master Plan for Edn., 1971-73. Alumni council U. Mass., 1950-54, bd. dirs. alumni assn., 1964-70; bd. dirs. Alumni Assn. Mt. Hermon Prep. Sch., 1963; v.p., dir. Palo Alto Stanford Med. Center, 1960-62, pres., chmn., 1962-66; chmn. West Coast Cancer Found., 1976—; trustee Monterey Inst. Internat. Studies, 1978—. Served to 1st lt., cav., AUS, 1943-46; ETO. Recipient spl. commendation Hoover Commn., 1955; Alumni of Year award U. Mass., 1963. Mem. Calif. C. of C., Govtl. Research assn., Am. Indsl. Devel. Council, San Francisco Mus. Art. Clubs: San Francisco Golf, Stock Exchange, Family (San Francisco); Los Angeles Country; Glen View (Chgo.); Carmel Valley Country (Calif.); Monterey Peninsula Country. Author articles govt., econs., edn. Home: 17 Ring Ln Carmel Valley CA 93924 Office: Box 923 Carmel Valley CA 93924. *If the quest for personal success is only for an accumulation of prestige. power or wealth, then personal failure will be assured. Genuine personal success can surely be found, however, through a significant and lasting contribution toward helping the progress of others. This is the true mark of leadership.*

SMITH, GORDON ROSS, English scholar, educator; b. Monmouth County, N.J., May 23, 1917; s. Mortimer Dickerson and Elizabeth Clara (Ross) S.; B.S., Columbia U., 1948, M.A., 1949; Ph.D., Pa. State U., 1956; m. Jane Pakenham, Aug. 29, 1948; children—Gordon Ross, Corinna Pakenham. Instr. English, Waynesburg (Pa.) Coll., 1949-50; instr. English, Pa. State U., 1950-56, asst. prof., 1956-59, asso. prof., 1959-63, prof., 1963-66; Folger Shakespeare Library fellow, 1958; Fulbright lectr. Royal U. Malta, 1962-63; prof. English, Temple U., Phila., 1966—. Democratic party committeeman, State College, Pa., 1952-56. Served with AUS, 1943-46. Mem. MLA, Shakespeare Assn. Am., Pa. Hist. Soc., Huguenot Hist. Soc., Internat. Shakespeare Assn. Author: A Classified Shakespeare Bibliography, 1936-58, 1963; Essays on Shakespeare, 1965; cons. editor Jour. History of Ideas; contbr. articles to scholarly jours. Home: 35 Red Oak Rd Oreland PA 19075 Office: English Dept Temple U Philadelphia PA 19122

SMITH, GREGG, musician; b. Chgo., Aug. 21, 1931; s. Howard Bradley and Myrtle (Adee) S.; B.A., M.A., U. Calif. at Los Angeles; m. Rosaline A. Rees, June 18, 1937; children—Darin Scott, Rachel Theora. Founder, The Gregg Smith Singers, 1955, condr., 1955—; composer G. Schirmer, N.Y.C., 1962—; rec. artist on Columbia, Vox, Cri and Everest Records; tchr. U. Calif. at Los Angeles, Ithaca (N.Y.) Coll., Peabody Conservatory, Columbia U. Ford Found. grantee for choral condrs., 1962; recipient Grammy awards for choral recs., 1966, 68, 70; Alice M. Ditson award to condrs. Am. music, 1978. Mem. ASCAP, Am. Choral Dirs. Assn., Assn. Profl. Vocal Ensembles, Am. Fedn. Musicians. Recs. of compositions include Beware of the Soldier, Festival of Carols, Aesops Fables, Jazz Mass. Home and office: 171 W 71st St New York NY 10023

SMITH, GROVER CLEVELAND, educator; b. Atlanta, Sept. 6, 1923; s. Grover C. and Lillian Julia (McDaniel) S.; B.A., Columbia U., 1944, M.A., 1945, Ph.D. (Alexander M. Proudfit fellow), 1950; m. Phyllis Jean Snyder, June 19, 1948 (div. 1965); children—Alice Elizabeth, Charles Grover; m. 2d Dulcie Barbara Soper, Dec. 29, 1965; children—Stephen Kenneth, Julia Margaret. Instr. English, Rutgers U., 1946-48; instr. Yale U., 1948-52; instr. English, Duke U., 1952-55, asst. prof., 1955-61, asso. prof., 1961-66, prof., 1966—; mem. summer faculty CUNY, 1946, 47, 48, Columbia U., 1963, 64, N.Y. U., 1963, Wake Forest U., 1966; vis. lectr. Wake Forest U., 1963-64. Served with U.S. Army, 1943. Guggenheim fellow, 1958; Am. Philos. Soc. grantee, 1965, Am. Learned Socs. grantee, 1965, Nat. Endowment Humanities grantee, 1979. Author: T.S. Eliot's Poetry and Plays: A Study in Sources and Meaning, 1956 (recipient Poetry Chapbook award). Editor: Josiah Royce's Seminar, 1913-1914: As Recorded in the Notebooks of Harry T. Costello, 1963; Letters of Aldous Huxley, 1969. Office: PO Box 6043 College Station Durham NC 27708

SMITH, GUY DONALD, soil scientist; b. Atlantic, Iowa, June 20, 1907; s. Daniel Christian and Hope (Curtis) S.; B.S., U. Ill., 1930, Ph.D., 1940; M.A., U. Mo., 1934; Dr. Sci., U. Ghent (Belgium), 1968; m. Jean Elizabeth Randall, July 5, 1934 (dec.); children—Ann Smith Spurgin, Guy Donald, Gail Elizabeth Smith Brodyaga, Randall Curtis, Arthur Randall; m. 2d, Yolanda Bultynck, 1973. Research asst. U. Ill., 1930-33, asso., then asst. prof., 1935-42; with Resettlement Adminstrn., Champaign, Ill., 1934-35 sr. soil correlator U.S. Dept. Agr., Bur. Plant Industry Soils and Agrl. Engring. 1946-50, prin. soil correlator, 1950-52, dir. soil survey investigations Soil Conservation Service, 1952-72, with Bur. Soils, N.Z., 1976-78; vis. prof. U. Ghent (Belgium), 1972-73, 74-75, U. West Indies, 1973-74; cons. CENIAP, Maracay, Venezuela, 1975-76; Francqui Chair, U. Ghent (Belgium), 1964-65. Served to capt. AUS, 1942-45. Recipient Soil Research award Am. Soc. Agronomy, 1964; Distinguished Service award Dept. Agr. Fellow Am. Soc. Agronomy, Soil Sci. Soc. Am. (pres. 1959, hon. mem.); mem. Royal Flemish Acad. Fine Arts, Letters and Sci. Author: (with F.F. Rieken, R.W. Simonson) Understanding Iowa Soils; Soil Classification, A Comprehensive System, 1960; Lectures on Soil Classification, 1965; (with others) Soil Taxonomy: A Basic System for Making and Interpreting Soil Surveys. Home: Koning Albertlaan 218 9000 Ghent Belgium Office: Geologic Institute Krijgslaan 271 B9000 Ghent Belgium

SMITH, H. EVERETT, banker; b. Woodhaven, N.Y., Apr. 2, 1909; s. Charles R. and Elsie Margaret (Smith) S.; student N.Y. U.; m. Nadine Proctor, Mar. 22, 1946; children—Kendall Carl, H. Everett, Jory-Ellyn, Donald Proctor, Robin Anne. With Mfrs. Trust Co., 1927-41; joined Marine Midland Trust Co. of N.Y.C., 1942, v.p., 1945-52; formerly pres., dir. Boran Corp.; formerly exec. v.p., dir. Cloroben Chem. Corp., Standard Chlorine Chem. Co., Inc., Met. Packaging Corp., Standard Chlorine of Delaware, Inc.; sr. v.p. Marine Midland Trust Co. So. N.Y., Binghamton, 1968-70; v.p. Marine Midland Bank, N.Y.C., 1970-72, sr. v.p., 1972-75; sr. v.p. Am. Nat. Bank & Trust Co. Ft. Lauderdale (Fla.), 1975-78; v.p. loan adminstrn. 1st Bancshares of Fla., Inc., 1976-78; pres., dir. Fleming Mortgage Co., Boca Raton, Fla., 1976-78; v.p. Atlantic So. Group, Inc., Boca Raton, 1978—; dir. Beacon Leasing Co., West Palm Beach, Fla., Fleming Ins. Co. Home: 501 SW 11th Pl Boca Raton FL 33432 Office: 40 SE 1st Ave Boca Raton FL 33432

SMITH, H. RUSSELL, mfg. co. exec.; b. Clark County, Ohio, Aug. 15, 1914; s. Lewis Hoskins and Eula (Elder) S.; A.B., Pomona Coll., 1936; m. Jeanne Rogers, June 27, 1942; children—Stewart Russell, Douglas Howard, Jeanne Ellen. Security analyst Kidder, Peabody & Co., N.Y.C., 1936-37; economist ILO, Geneva, 1937-40; asst. to pres. Blue Diamond Corp., Los Angeles, 1940-46; pres., dir. Avery Internat. Corp., San Marino, 1946-75, chmn. bd., 1975—; dir. So. Calif. Edison Co., Rosemead, Beckman Instruments, Inc., Fullerton, Security Pacific Corp., Security Pacific Nat. Bank, Los Angeles. Bd. dirs., past pres., chmn. Los Angeles Philharmonic Assn.; bd. fellows Claremont Univ. Center; chmn. bd. trustees Pomona Coll., Claremont, Calif.; past chmn. bd. Community TV of So. Calif. (Sta. KCET), Los Angeles. Served with USNR, 1943-46. Home: 1458 Hillcrest Ave Pasadena CA 91106 Office: 415 Huntington Dr San Marino CA 91108

SMITH, H. SHELDON, ret. banker; b. Taunton, Mass., June 4, 1909; s. Harry Newton and Jessie Mable (Etter) S.; S.B., Mass. Inst. Tech., 1931; m. Harriet Fellowes Bent, Dec. 31, 1941; children—Susan Smith Duckworth, David. With Sears Roebuck & Co., 1931-69, asst. zone mgr. New Eng., 1951-54, zone mgr. Mid-Atlantic zone, 1955-57, mgr. Rochester Retail Group, 1957-69; sr. v.p. Marine Midland Bank, Rochester, N.Y., 1970-74, ret. Mem. N.Y. State Bd. Social Welfare, 1970—; mem. budget com. Rochester Community Chest, 1959-68; trustee Columbia Sch., Rochester, 1965-69, treas., 1968-69; bd. dirs. Rochester Gen. Hosp., 1962-75, Cape Cod Family and Children's Service, 1978—; pres. Episcopal Church Home of Rochester, 1967-68; trustee Episc. Diocese of Rochester, 1969-77. Served to capt. Ordnance Corps, AUS, 1942-46. Mem. Rochester C. of C. (pres. 1973), Delta Kappa Epsilon, Tau Beta Pi. Republican. Clubs: M.I.T. (pres. 1962-63), Genesee Valley (Rochester); Acoaxet (Westport Harbor, Mass.). Home: 20 Richards Rd Falmouth MA 02540

SMITH, HADDON HARTUNG, banker; b. Newark, Dec. 2, 1916; s. Charles R. and Grace (Price) S.; B.A., Duke, 1937; m. Betty Martin, Dec. 3, 1944; children—Peter H., David M., Jonathan P., Mark R. Credit analyst Irving Trust Co., N.Y.C., 1937-40, asst. loaning officer, 1946-47; v.p. First Nat. Bank & Trust Co., Summit, N.J., 1947-54; v.p., rep. in N.Y.C. for First Nat. Assos. Fla., 1954-56; asso. investment mgr. Prudential Ins. Co., Newark, 1956-59; v.p. Marine Midland Trust Co. Western N.Y., 1959-62, sr. v.p., 1962-68; exec. v.p., dir. Niagara Frontier Services, Buffalo, 1968-69; exec. v.p. Commerce Bancshares, Inc., Kansas City, Mo., 1969-78; sr. asso. M.J. Swords Assos., Kansas City, Mo., 1978—. Served to lt. col. USMCR, 1940-46, 1950-52; col. Res. (ret.). Republican. Presbyn. Home: 10306 Grant Ln Overland Park KS 66212 Office: 4900 Oak St Kansas City MO 64152

SMITH, HALLETT DARIUS, educator; b. Chattanooga, Aug. 15, 1907; s. Charles Wilson and Elizabeth Russell (Atkinson) S.; A.B., U. Colo., 1928, L.H.D., 1968; Ph.D., Yale U., 1934; m. Mary Elizabeth Earl, Dec. 30, 1931; children—Diana Russell Smith Gordon, Hallett Earl. Instr. English, Williams Coll., Williamstown, Mass., 1931-36, asst. prof., 1937-40, asso. prof., 1940-45, prof., 1946-49; prof. English, Calif. Inst. Tech., Pasadena, 1949-75, chmn. div. humanities, 1949-70; Guggenheim fellow, 1947-48; vis. prof. Columbia U., summer 1949; sr. research asso. Huntington Library, 1970—; Henry W. and Albert A. Berg prof. Eng. lit. N.Y. U., spring 1977. Mem. Commn. English. Trustee Am. Univs. Field Staff, Poly. Sch.; mem. adv. com. Guggenheim Found. Recipient Poetry Chapbook prize Poetry Soc. Am., 1952; Phi Beta Kappa vis. scholar, 1959-60. Fellow Am. Acad. Arts and Scis.; mem. Modern Lang. Assn. Am., Phi Beta Kappa (senator at large). Author: The Golden Hind, 1942; The Critical Reader, 1949; Elizabethan Poetry, 1951; Renaissance England, 1956; Twentieth Century Interpretations of The Tempest, 1970; Shakespeare's Romances, 1972; contbr. articles to ednl. jours. Home: 1455 S Marengo Ave Pasadena CA 91106

SMITH, HALSEY, banker; b. S. Orange, N.J., July 10, 1921; s. Albridge C. and Frances (Halsey) S.; grad. Lawrenceville Sch., 1940; A.B., Princeton, 1944; LL.D. (hon.), U. Maine, 1961; m. Margaret Haskell, Dec. 19, 1942; children-Margaret Coburn, Karen Woodbridge, Halsey, Ellen Barry. With N.Y. Trust Co., N.Y.C., 1946-51, asst. treas., 1950-51; v.p. Casco Bank & Trust Co., Portland, Maine, 1951-55, pres., 1955-69, chmn. bd., 1969-73, also dir.; dir. Center for Research and Advanced Study, U. Maine, 1972-77; pres., chief exec. officer, dir. N.E. Bankshare Assn., Lewiston, Maine, 1977—; dir. Milliken Tomlinson Co., Portland, Hussey Mfg., North Berwick, Maine; mem. adv. bd. Bingham Assoc., 1975—. Chmn., Commn. on Maine's Future, 1974-77; corporator Maine Med. Center; pres. Maine Cancer Research Found., 1977—; trustee Westbrook Coll., Portland. Served with USMCR, 1942-46; PTO. Decorated Bronze Star; recipient Distinguished Service award Portland Kiwanis Club, 1968, Maine Bar Assn., 1978; Brotherhood award Temple Beth El, Portland, 1970. Mem. Maine (past treas.), Greater Portland (past dir., pres.) chambers commerce, Me. Bankers Assn. (past pres.). Republican. Conglist. Home: High View Rd South Freeport ME 04078 Office: 95 Ash St Lewiston ME 04240

SMITH, HAMILTON OTHANEL, microbiologist, educator; b. N.Y.C., Aug. 23, 1931; s. Bunnie Othanel and Tommie Harkey S.; student U. Ill., 1948-50; A.B. in Math., U. Calif., Berkeley, 1952; M.D., Johns Hopkins U., 1956; m. Elizabeth Anne Bolton, May 25, 1957; children—Joel, Barry, Dirk, Bryan, Kirsten. Intern, Barnes Hosp., St. Louis, 1956-57; resident in medicine Henry Ford Hosp., Detroit, 1959-62; USPHS fellow dept. human genetics U. Mich., Ann Arbor, 1962-64, research asso., 1964-67; asst. prof. microbiology Johns Hopkins U. Sch. Medicine, Balt., 1967-69, asso. prof., 1969-73, prof., 1973—; asso. Institut fur Molekularbiologie der U. Zurich, Switzerland, 1975-76. Served to lt. M.C., USNR, 1957-59. Recipient Nobel Prize in medicine, 1978; Guggenheim fellow 1975-76. Mem. Am. Soc. Microbiology, AAAS, Am. Soc. Biol. Chemists. Contbr. articles to profl. jours. Office: 725 N Wolfe St Baltimore MD 21205

SMITH, HARLAN JAMES, educator, astronomer; b. Wheeling, W.Va., Aug. 25, 1924; s. Paul Elder and Anna Persis (McGregor) S.; A.B., Harvard, 1949, M.A., 1951, Ph.D., 1955; D.Phys. Sci. (hon.), Nicholas Copernicus U., Torun, Poland, 1973; m. Joan Greene, Dec. 21, 1950; children—Nathaniel, Sarah (dec.), Julia, Theodore, Hannah. Research asst. astronomy, teaching fellow and research fellow Harvard, 1946-53; from instr. to asso. prof. astronomy Yale, 1953-63; prof. astronomy, chmn. dept., 1963-78, also dir. McDonald Obs., U. Tex., 1963—; mem. Space Sci. Bd., 1977—. Served as weather observer USAAF, 1943-46. George R. Agassiz research fellow Harvard Obs., 1952-53. Mem. Am. (acting sec. 1961-62, chmn. planetary div. 1974-75, council 1975-78, v.p. 1977-79), Royal astron. socs., Am. Geophys. Union, AAAS, Internat. Astron. Union, Internat. Sci. Radio Union, Sigma Xi. Co-editor: Astron. Jour., 1960-63. Home: 2705 Pecos St Austin TX 78703

SMITH, HARLAN WILLIAM, mfg. co. exec.; b. Salamanca, N.Y., Feb. 16, 1934; s. Gerald Harlan and Irene Eva (Mackay) S.; B.S. cum laude, Syracuse U., 1955; m. Colleen M. Sherman, July 29, 1957; children—Teresa, Vallerie, Laura. Reg. rep. Allis Chalmers Co., Portland, Oreg., 1955-58; v.p. Bannock Steel Corp., Boise, Idaho, 1958-61; gen. mgr. Boise Cascade Corp., 1961-70; pres., chief exec. officer Dyneer Corp., Westport, 1970—, also dir. Mem. Young. Pres.'s Orgn. Home: 140 Signal Hill Rd Wilton CT 06897 Office: Riverside Bldg Westport CT 06880

SMITH, HARMON LEE, JR., clergyman, educator; b. Ellisville, Miss., Aug. 23, 1930; s. Harmon L. and Mary (O'Donnell) S.; A.B., Millsaps Coll., 1952; B.D., Duke U., 1955, Ph.D., 1962; m. Bettye Joan Watkins, Aug. 21, 1951; children—Pamela Lee, Amy Joanne, Harmon L. Ordained priest Episcopal Ch., 1972; asst. dean Duke Divinity Sch., Durham, N.C., 1959-65, asst. prof. Christian ethics, 1962-68, asso. prof. moral theology, 1968-73, prof. moral theology, 1973—, prof. community and family medicine, 1974—; cons. med. ethics; vis. prof. U. N.C., 1964, 70, 72, U. Edinburgh (Scotland), 1969, U. Windsor (Ont.), 1974. Lilly Found. fellow, 1960, Gurney Harris Kearns Found. fellow, 1961. Mem. Am. Assn. Theol. Schs., Soc. for Religion in Higher Edn. Author books med. ethics; U.S. regional editor Ethics in Sci. and Medicine, 1973—. Contbr. articles on Christian ethics to various publs. Home: 3510 Randolph Rd Durham NC 27705 Office: The Divintiy School Duke University Durham NC 27706

SMITH, HAROLD, department store chain exec.; b. N.Y.C., June 22, 1924; s. Irving and Jennie (Shulock) S.; B.B.A., CCNY, 1947; m. Muriel G. Ditchik, Jan. 2, 1949; children—Jane Leslie Smith Bagchi, Donna Gail Smith Budoff. Vice pres. Robert Hall Clothes, N.Y.C., 1955-72; pres. Jonna's Outlet, N.Y.C., 1972-78; v.p. Wal-Mart, Bentonville, Ark., 1975-78; pres. Goldblatt Bros., Inc., Chgo., 1978—; dir. State St. Council, Chgo. Pres. Parent Tchr. Orgn., Deerfield, Ill., 1964-66. Served to capt. USAAF, 1942-45. Decorated D.F.C., Air medal with 3 oak leaf clusters, Purple Heart with oak leaf cluster. Office: Goldblatt Bros Inc 333 S State St Chicago IL 60604

SMITH, HAROLD ARMSTRONG, utility co. exec.; b. Lucknow, Ont., Can., Mar. 17, 1919; s. Bertram and Mabel (Barber) S.; B.S., In E.E., Queen's U., 1940, D.Sc. (hon.), 1977; D.Sc. (hon.), McMaster U., 1978; 1 son, Robert James. With Ont. Hydro, Toronto, 1940—, corporate v.p., 1974-77, v.p. spl. assignments, 1977—. Served with Royal Can. Navy Vol. Res., 1943-45. Fellow IEEE, Royal Soc. Can.; mem. Assn. Profl. Engrs. Ont. (Engring. medal 1966). Patentee high speed device for interrupting and completing high voltage power circuits. Home: 1463 Larchview Trail Mississauga ON L5E 3C2 Canada Office: 700 University Ave Toronto ON M5G 1X6 Canada

SMITH, HAROLD BYRON, JR., mfg. co. exec.; b. Chgo., Apr. 7, 1933; s. Harold Byron and Pauline (Hart) S.; grad. Choate Sch., 1951; B.S., Princeton, 1955; M.B.A., Northwestern U., 1957; m. Frederica Herriman, June 12, 1954; children—Stephanie, Carrie, Pauline, Emily. With Ill. Tool Works, Inc., Chgo., 1954—, exec. v.p., 1968-72, pres., 1972—, also dir.; dir. Marshall Field & Co., No. Trust Co., First Nat. Bank & Trust Co. of Barrington (Ill.); trustee Northwestern Mut. Life Ins. Co. Del., Republican Nat. Conv., 1964, 76; mem. Rep. Nat. Com. from Ill., 1976—. Bd. dirs. Adler Planetarium, Chgo. Hist. Soc., Council for Technol. Advancement, Northwestern U., Rush-Presbyn.-St. Luke's Med Center, Newberry Library. Clubs: Chicago, Commercial, Commonwealth, Economic, Northwestern, Princeton University (Chgo.). Home: 284 Donlea Rd Barrington IL 60010 Office: 8501 W Higgins Rd Chicago IL 60631

SMITH, HAROLD COLBY, ret. book mfr.; b. Clifton, Ill., Aug. 28, 1903; s. Weldon Charles and Alice Mary (Colby) S.; A.B., U. Ill., 1927; m. Maude Adams, May 9, 1930; children—Lewis Adams, Carolyn Colby (Mrs. Kent Chambers Davies), Miriam Goodale. With advt. dept. Chgo. Tribune, 1927-30; with J.J. Little & Ives, N.Y.C., 1930-31; with Colonial Press, Inc., Clinton, Mass., 1931-73, pres., dir., 1937-72; pres., dir. C.H. Simonds Co., 1943-61, Colonial Offset, Inc., Clinton, Mass., 1961-68; v.p., dir. Victoreen Leece Neville, Inc., Cleve., 1967-73; treas., dir., exec. com. Rex. Corp., West Acton, Mass., 1955-59; cons. Am. Enka Corp., Ashville, N.C., 1957-67; dir., treas. Nashoba Engring. Co., Inc., Gilbert Harold, Inc.; mem. adv. com. Worcester County Nat. Bank, 1962-68; dir. Freeman, Cooper & Co., San Francisco, 1971—, Colorcon, Inc., West Point, Pa., 1972-78. Finance bd. Town of Concord, 1950-57, bd. selectmen, 1957-61, chmn., 1958-61. Trustee Clinton Hosp. Assn., 1948-70, v.p., 1950-70; trustee Mus. of Sci., Miami, Fla., 1973-78. Served as pvt. Q.M.C., U.S. Army, 1918-19, AEF. Mem. Asso. Industries Mass. (dir. 1960-70), Am. Inst. Graphic Arts, Worcester Metal Trades Assn. (dir. 1947-49), Soc. Colonial Wars, Soc. of Cincinnati, SAR, Phi Kappa Sigma. Republican. Clubs: Rotary (hon.) (Clinton); Social Circle, Concord Country (Concord, Mass.); Bass River Yacht (gov. 1961-65); Key Biscayne Yacht (Fla.) Home: 1045 Mariner Dr Key Biscayne FL 33149

SMITH, HAROLD HILL, geneticist; b. Arlington, N.J., Apr. 24, 1910; s. Frederick Harold and Hilda Niles (Burgess) S.; B.S., Rutgers U., 1931; A.M., Harvard U., 1934, Ph.D., 1936; m. Mary Downing, Feb. 11, 1939; children—Frederick, Lucy Smith Keane, Hilda Smith Hodges, Susan Smith Jurs. Asst. geneticist Dept. Agr., Beltsville, Md., 1935-43; asso. prof., then prof. genetics Cornell U., 1946-56; sr. scientist IAEA, Vienna, Austria, 1958-59; sr. geneticist Brookhaven Nat. Lab., Upton, N.Y., 1956—; adj. prof. N.Y. U., 1977—; vis. prof. U. Calif., Berkeley, U. Buenos Aires; Fulbright lectr. U. Amsterdam, 1953. Served to lt. USNR, 1943-46. Guggenheim fellow, 1953; hon. research asso. Univ. Coll., London, 1966; Nat. Acad. Sci. exchangee with Romanian Acad., 1970. Mem. Am. Genetic Assn. (pres. 1976), Genetics Soc. Am., Bot. Soc. Am., AAAS, AAUP, Tissue Culture Assn., Soc. Developmental Biology, Sigma Phi Epsilon. Clubs: Shoreham Country, Harvard of L.I., Raritan. Editor: Evolution of Genetic Systems, 1972; editorial bd. Jour. Heredity, Mutation Research, Environ. and Exptl. Botany. Contbr. to profl. publs. Home: Tower Hill Rd Shoreham NY 11786 Office: Brookhaven Nat Lab Upton NY 11973

SMITH, HAROLD LEE, advt. agy. exec.; b. Cranford, N.J., Feb. 17, 1935; s. Harold C. and Muriel (Lee) S.; grad. Philips Acad., 1952; B.A., Dartmouth, 1956; M.B.A., Amos Tuck Sch., 1960; m. Margaret Belle Brierre Swanson, Dec. 30, 1957; children—Lee Ann, Sally. Sr. v.p. N.W. Ayer ABH Internat., N.Y.C., 1978—. Served with USN, 1956-59, 61-62. Clubs: Whippoorwill (Chappaqua); Wings, 29 (N.Y.C.). Home: 36 Gray Rock Ln Chappaqua NY 10514 Office: 1345 Ave of Americas New York NY 10019

SMITH, HAROLD PHILIP, rabbi; b. Chgo., Sept. 4, 1915; s. Samuel and Rose (Siegel) S.; B.A., U. Tulsa, 1937; Rabbi, Hebrew Theol. Coll., 1940, D.H.L., 1960; grad. work U. Chgo. Fed. Schs. Theology; m. Lillian Waid, Nov. 14, 1943. Dir. edn., Tulsa, 1937-39; dir. activities Garfield Community Center, Chgo., 1939- 41; rabbi Beth El Synagogue, Gary, Ind., 1941-44; exec. dir. Midwest region Religious Zionist Am., 1944-49; rabbi Congregation Agudath Achim South Shore, Chgo., 1949-69; v.p. Jewish U. Am., Hebrew Theol. Coll., Skokie, Ill., 1969—; lectr. practical rabbinics Hebrew Theol. Coll. Chmn. nat. com. on edn. Rabbinical Council Am., 1947-52, mem. Israel commn., 1976—, mem. publs. com., 1952—, v.p., 1958-60, mem. religious standards com., 1960—, co-chmn. nat. legis. com., 1976—, chmn. Midwest legis. com., 1963-; editor Passover Bull., Chgo. Rabbinical Council, 1950-54, v.p., 1954-58, mem. publs. com., 1956, pres., 1958-60, chmn. exec. bd., 1960—, mem. religious standards com., chmn. legislative com., 1961—, mem. coll. relations com., 1965—; mem. exec. bd. Council Traditional Synagogues, 1956—; mem. Commn. Religion in Pub. Schs., 1956—; mem. exec. com. Chgo. Bd. Rabbis, 1962—, mem. broadcasting commn., chmn. legislative com., 1963—, chmn. Israel affairs com., 1965—, chmn. Israel relations com., 1965-66, v.p., 1976—; mem. exec. com. Chgo. Hebrew Culture Council, 1965-66; ofcl. del. Nat. Conf. Religion and Race, 1963; mem. exec. bd. Chgo. div. Am. Jewish Congress, mem. conv. com., 1963; mem. mediating commn. United Vaad Hakashruth, 1963; mem. exec. United Kashruth Commn. Greater Chgo., 1963—, co-chmn. So. Shore regional com., 1963—; mem. conv. com. Midwest region Union Orthodox Jewish Congregations Am., 1963; mem. pub. affairs com. Jewish Fedn. Met. Chgo., 1978—, mem. Middle East subcoms., 1978—, co-chmn. interfaith relations subcom., 1978—; mem. Speaker's Bur., Combined Jewish Appeal, Bonds for Israel, South Shore Commn. Juvenile Delinquency; rabbinic adv. council Combined Jewish Appeal, Chgo., 1961—; nat. rabbinic adv. council United Jewish Appeal, 1961—, also mem. publs. com. rabbinic adv. council. Mem. Gary Mayor's Youth Commn., 1942-43; chmn. Kosher Law Enforcement Com., 1956—; mem. law enforcement com. South Shore, 1957—; mem. Ill. Com. Equal Job Opportunities, 1959—; mem. Jewish Religious Ct. Chgo., 1963—; spl. emissary Ill. Legislature, 1963. Exec. Jewish Nat. Fund, 1956—; director, Nat. chmn. com. for alumni fund raising Hebrew Theol. Coll. pres. Nat. Rabbinical Alumni Assn., 1964-65; mem. academic com. Jewish U. Am., 1959—, also trustee, mem. president's adv. com. gov. Akiba Jewish Day Sch., 1955—; bd. govs. Chgo. Jewish Acad. Recipient award Chicago Sun-Times, 1954; Clergyman of Year award Chgo. Tribune, 1955; Merit citation Hebrew Theol. Coll., 1956; Spl. Service citation Chgo. Rabbinical Council, 1963; Spl. Service award Jewish Fedn. Met. Chgo., 1963; Community Service award Assn. Torah Advancement, 1963; Jewish United Fund award, 1967; Religious Zionists Man of Year award, 1969; Bonds of Israel award, 1969. Mem. Jewish Fedn. Met. Chgo. (chmn. Rabbinic div. 1962, 63), South Shore Ministerial Assn., Nat. Assn. Jewish Day Schs., League Religious Labor (nat. exec.), Nat. Council Adult Edn., Am. Zionist Council, Ill. Conf. Jewish Orgns., Am. Assn. Higher Edn., Nat. Social Sci. Honor Soc., Anselm Forum (hon.), Hebrew Theol. Coll. Alumni Assn., Internat. Platform Assn., Pi Gamma Mu. Author: A Treasure Hunt in Judaism, 1942; Meaningfulness in Prayer, 1963; Anthology on Sunday Law Legislations, 1963; At Thirteen- -Religious Responsibilities, 1963; Kiddushin Means Sanctity; The Holiness of the Jewish Marriage Vow, 1964; Anthology of State Aid to Non-Public Schools, 1969. Editor The Scroll, 1949—. Compiler, translator; Sidduri, 1940. Translator: History and Spirit of Jewish Homiletics. Contbr. periodicals. Home: 3180 N Lake Shore Dr Chicago IL 60657 Office: 7135 N Carpenter Rd Skokie IL 60076

SMITH, HARRISON, ret. educator; b. Kansas City, Mo., June 1, 1917; B.S. cum laude, Sch. Fgn. Service, Georgetown U., 1939, M.A., 1942, Ph.D., 1950; Phil. D. summa cum laude, Fribourg (Switzerland) U., 1953. Sec. to Congressman Clarence F. Lea, Washington, 1939-40; instr. history Sch. Fgn. Service, Georgetown U., 1940-41; vice consul American embassy, Rio de Janeiro, Brazil and Montevideo, Uruguay, 1941-43; asst. prof. history and govt. U. Md. with NATO armed forces, Greece, Morocco, Italy and Germany, 1951-53; vis. lectr. univs. Geneva and Berne (Switzerland), 1954-55; asso. prof. U. Md. with NATO armed forces, Britain, France, Spain and Turkey, 1955-58; asst. prof. European history Georgetown U., 1958-61; lectr. U. Md. at Munich, Germany, 1961-71, at College Park, Md., 1971-77; vis. lectr. Anne Arundel Community Coll., Arnold, Md., 1971-77, emeritus, 1977—. Served to lt. USNR, 1944-48; India-Ceylon. Decorated Order Merit (Italy); knight grand cross Order St. John (Yugoslavia); Order St. Mark (Greek Orthodox Patriarch); hon. comdr. Chevaliers d'Orient (Grandson Castle Switzerland); recipient Terrapin award U. Md., Munich, 1968-69; taroman, 24th Inf. Div., U.S. Army; sr. vis. Fulbright lectr. Royal U. Malta, 1953-54, hon. prof., 1955. Mem. Byzantine Inst. Oriental Studies (Alexandria, Egypt), Royal Malta Hist. Soc., Royal Commonwealth Soc. (London), Accademia Teatine per le Scienze (Pescara, Italy), English Speaking Union (London). Roman Catholic. Clubs: Union (Malta); Cornell (N.Y.C.); University (Washington). Author: Constitutional Development of Malta in the Nineteenth Century, 1953; Italian Influence on British Policy in Malta, 1954; Order of St. John of Jerusalem and Malta, 1964, rev. edit. (with Storace), 1977; Mussolini and Strickland, 1974. Editor: First the Blade, 1936. Reviewer Am. Cath. Hist. Rev., 1960-77. Contbr. profl. jours. Home: Villa de la Grangette Lens-Lestang 26210 St Sorlin-en-Valloire France also Univ Club 1135 16th St NW Washington DC 20036. *Watch and pray.*

SMITH, HARRISON VENTURE, trust co. exec.; b. N.Y.C., Nov. 26, 1919; s. Oliver Harrison and Claire (Spencer) S.; grad. Lincoln Sch. of Tchrs. Coll., N.Y.C., 1937; A.B., Yale, 1941; m. Marlis de Greve, Jan. 22, 1943; children—Elizabeth, H. Spencer, Claire, Anne, Oliver, Sarah. With J.P. Morgan & Co., Inc. (merged with Guaranty Trust Co. to form Morgan Guaranty Trust Co., 1959), N.Y.C., 1946—, v.p., 1957-67, sr. v.p., 1967-75, exec. v.p., 1975—; dir. Munich Mgmt. Co., N.Y.C., Munich Am. Reins. Co. Pres. Vis. Nurse Service N.Y., 1969-73, chmn., 1973-75; treas. Meml. Sloan Kettering Cancer Center, N.Y.C., 1965-74. Served with U.S. Coordinator Information, 1941-42, USAAF, 1942-46. Episcopalian. Clubs: Links (N.Y.C.); Center Harbor Yacht (Brooklin, Maine). Home: New York City NY Office: 9 W 57th St New York City NY 10019

SMITH, HARRY ALCIDE, pharm. educator; b. Merrimac, Ky., July 8, 1925; s. Harry A. and Sallie Elizabeth (Brown) S.; B.S., U. Ky., 1949, M.S., Purdue U., 1956, Ph.D., 1959; m. Norma Florence Gabhart, Apr. 8, 1951; children—Elizabeth Ann, Harry Alcide. Asst. prof. U. Ky., Lexington, 1957-61, asso. prof., 1961-65, prof., 1970—; asst. dir. Bur. Pharm. Services, U. Miss., Oxford, 1965-70, asso. prof., 1965-70. Bd. dirs., mem. exec. com. Southeastern Christian Coll., Winchester, Ky., 1972-76. Served with U.S. Army, 1950-52. Fellow Am. Found. Pharm. Edn.; mem. Am. Pharm. Assn., Acad. Pharm. Scis., Acad. Pharm. Practitioners, Am. Coll. Apothecaries, Am. Assn. Coll. Pharmacy, Am. Public Health Assn., Common Cause, Sigma Xi, Rho Chi. Mem. Ch. of Christ. Author: Building A Successful Pharmacy Practice: A Case Study, 1972; Principles and Methods of Pharmacy Management, 1975. Home: 2216 Markham St Lexington KY 40504 Office: Coll Pharmacy U Ky Lexington KY 40506. *Talent is a gift of God; use of that talent is an act of the individual and his responsiblity.*

SMITH, HARTMAN WILLIAM, supermarket chain exec.; b. Corpus Christi, Tex., June 18, 1944; s. Laban Conrad and Margaret (Hayes) S.; B.S., Ind. U., 1966; m. Nancy Marie Foster, June 6, 1964; children—Kelly Lynn, Christopher Brock, Megan Marie. Research and devel. adminstr. Ind. Dept. Revenue, Indpls., 1965-65, tax auditor, Bloomington, 1965-66; audit mgr. Arthur Andersen & Co., Indpls., 1966-74; v.p. fin., sec.-treas. Marsh Supermarkets, Inc., Yorktown, Ind., 1974—; asso. faculty mem. accounting Ind. U.-Purdue U. at Indpls., 1972-73. Former mem. Ind. State Office Bldg. Commn. C.P.A.; hon. dep. atty. gen. State of Ind. Mem. Am. Inst. C.P.A.'s, Ind. Assn. C.P.A.'s. Home: 4112 W Riverside Ave Muncie IN 47304 Office: Depot St Yorktown IN 47396

SMITH, HARVEY LISS, sociologist; b. N.Y.C., Dec. 23, 1915; s. Irving Harold and Mathilda (Liss) S.; student Univ. Coll., London U., 1933-34; A.B., U. Chgo., 1941, A.M., 1947, Ph.D., 1949; m. Lillian Kamen, Dec. 18, 1942; children—Robert Harvey, Katherine Anne. Instr., U. Chgo., 1947-49; mem. research staff Russell Sage Found., 1950-52; mem. faculty dept. sociology and Sch. Medicine, U. N.C., Chapel Hill, 1952—, prof., 1958—, dir. social research sect. Div. Health Affairs, 1952—. Served to capt. AUS, 1942-46. Mem. Am. Sociol. Soc., So. Sociol. Soc., AAAS. Office: 103 Miller Hall Univ of NC Chapel Hill NC 27514

SMITH, HASSEL WENDELL, JR., artist; b. Sturgis, Mich., Apr. 24, 1915; s. Hassel Wendell and Helen (Adams) S.; B.S. cum laude, Northwestern U., 1936; postgrad. Calif. Sch. Fine Arts, 1936-38; m. June Myers, 1943 (dec. 1956); m. 2d Donna D. Raffety, Aug., 1957; children—Joseph H., Bruce; stepchildren—Mark Harrington, Stephan Harrington. Case worker Calif. Relief Adminstrn., San Francisco, 1938-39; case worker and camp clk. Farm Security Adminstrn., Arvin, Calif. also Arvin Farm Workers Community, 1942-45; timber scaler U.S. Forest Service, McKenzie Bridge, Oreg., 1945-46; instr. Calif. Sch. Fine Arts, 1946-47, 48-52, San Francisco State Coll., 1946-47, U. Oreg., 1947-48, Presidio Hill Sch., San Francisco, 1952-54, Apple Orchard Sch., Sebastopol, Calif., 1954-58, U. Calif., Berkeley, 1963-65, 77-78, 79-80, UCLA, 1965-66, U. Calif., Davis, 1973, 75, San Francisco Art Inst., summers 1978-79; prin. lectr. in painting Bristol (Eng.) Poly., 1966—. Rosenberg fellow for ind. study, 1941-42. Home: 19 Ashgrove Rd Bristol BS6 6NA England*

SMITH, HEDRICK LAURENCE, journalist; b. Kilmacolm, Scotland, July 9, 1933 (parents Am. citizens); s. Sterling L. and Phebe (Hedrick) S.; grad. Choate Sch., 1951; B.A., Williams Coll., 1955, Litt.D. (hon.), 1975; postgrad. (Fulbright scholar) Balliol Coll., Oxford, Eng., 1955-56; m. Ann Bickford, June 29, 1957; children—Laurel Ann, Jennifer Laurence, Sterling Scott, Lesley Roberts. With U.P.I., Memphis, Nashville, Atlanta, 1959-62; with N.Y. Times, 1962—, temporary corr. in Vietnam, 1963-64, Middle East corr., Cairo, U.A.R., 1964-66, diplomatic news corr., Washington, 1962-64, 66-71, Moscow Bur. chief, 1971-74, dep. nat. editor, 1975-76, Washington Bur. chief, 1976-79, chief Washington corr., 1980—. Served with USAF, 1956-59. Recipient Pulitzer prize for internat. reporting from Soviet Union and Eastern Europe, 1974. Nieman fellow Harvard, 1969-70. Mem. White House Corrs. Assn., Washington Press Club. Phi Beta Kappa, Alpha Delta Phi. Author: The Russians (Overseas Press Club award 1976), 1975; co-author The Pentagon Papers (Pulitzer prize 1972), 1972. Office: 1717 K St St NW Washington DC 20036

SMITH, HENRIETTA TAMAR, educator; b. Huntsville, Ala., Dec. 9, 1925; d. Clifton Conway and Inez Plunkett (Townsend) Smith; B.A., U. Cin., 1946, M.A., 1948; Ph.D., Radcliffe Coll., 1953. Instr., asst. prof. Allen U., Columbia, S.C., 1947-49, 53-54; instr., asst. prof., asso. prof., prof. Vassar Coll., Poughkeepsie, N.Y., 1954—. Mem. small grants com. NIMH, 1970-73. Trustee Marist Coll., 1974—. Mem. Am., Eastern psychol. assns., AAUP, AAAS, Soc. for Research in Child Devel., N.Y. Acad. Scis. Editor: (with L.J. Stone and L.B. Murphy) The Competent Infant, 1973. Contbr. articles to profl. jours. Home: 6 Vassar Lake Dr Poughkeepsie NY 12601

SMITH, HENRY CHARLES, 3D, symphony orch. condr.; b. Phila., Jan. 31, 1931; s. Henry Charles and Gertrude Ruth (Downs) S.; B.A., U. Pa., 1952; artist diploma Curtis Inst. Music, Phila., 1955; m. Mary Jane Dressner, Sept. 3, 1955; children—Katherine Anne, Pamela Jane, Henry Charles IV. Solo trombonist, Phila. Orch., 1955-67; civic music dir., Rochester, Minn., 1967-68; asso. prof. music Ind. U., Bloomington, 1968-71; asso. condr., ednl. dir. Minn. Orch., Mpls., 1971—; founder, mem. Phila. Brass Ensemble, 1956—. Served to 1st lt., AUS, 1952-54. With Phila. Brass Ensemble nominated for Grammy awards, 1967, 76; winner Grammy award for best chamber music rec., 1969—. Mem. Internat. Trombone Assn. (dir.), Music Educators Nat. Conf., Am. Guild Organists, Am. Fedn. Musicians, Acacia Fraternity. Republican. Congregationalist. Composer: Solos for the Trombone Player, 1963; Hear Us As We Pray, 1963; First Solos for the Trombone Player, 1972; Easy Duets for Winds, 1972. Home: 5640 Wooddale St Edina MN 55424 Office: 1111 Nicollet St Minneapolis MN 55403

SMITH, HENRY CLAY, psychologist; b. Catonsville, Md., May 9, 1913; s. Harry C. and Lovell (Figgins) S.; A.B. magna cum laude, St. John's Coll., Annapolis, Md., 1934; Ph.D., Johns Hopkins U., 1939; m. Nancy Woollcott, Aug. 27, 1938; children—David Barton, Woollcott Keston, Barbara Sunderland. Instr. psychology U. Vt. Burlington, 1940-43; dir. tng. and research Western Electric Co., Balt., 1943-45; asso. prof. Knox Coll., Galesburg, Ill., 1945-46; asso. prof. psychology, chmn. dept. Hamilton Coll., Clinton, N.Y., 1946-49; prof. psychology Mich. State U., E. Lansing, 1949—; Fulbright research fellow, Italy, 1955-56; cons. prof. Waseda U., Tokyo, 1960. Fellow Am. Psychol. Assn.; mem. Phi Beta Kappa. Author: Sensitivity Training, 2d edit., 1973, Personality Development, 2d edit., 1974; co-author: Social Perception, 1968, Psychology of Industrial Behavior, 3d edit., 1972. Office: Psychology Dept Mich State Univ East Lansing MI 48423

SMITH, HENRY J., lawyer; b. N.Y.C., Jan. 2, 1919; A.B., Fordham U., 1940; J.D., Harvard U., 1947. Admitted to N.Y. bar, 1948; now with firm McCarthy, Fingar, Donovan, Glatthaar, Drazen & Smith, White Plains, N.Y.; treas. Legal Aid of Westchester (N.Y.), 1962-72, dir., 1964-72, mem. exec. com., 1968-72; spl. counsel Town of Greenburgh, 1963-69, City of White Plains, 1967—, City of New Rochelle (N.Y.), 1969. Bd. dirs. Welserv OEO, 1968-72. Fellow Am. Bar Found.; N.Y. Bar Found., Am. Coll. Trial Lawyers; mem. White Plains (dir. 1957-66), Westchester County (pres. 1963-65, dirs. council 1965—), N.Y. State (exec. com. 1972-79, pres. 1977-78) Am. (ho. of dels. 1978—) bar assns., Am. Judicature Soc. Office: 175 Main St White Plains NY 10601. *Anyone who stays in love with his wife and his work, and particularly in that order, is a happy man. Life reaches the sublime, even in this world, if children one can be proud of are added to that.*

SMITH, HENRY OLIVER, ins. co. exec.; b. Worcester, Mass., May 19, 1923; s. Philip S. and Marion W. (Strout) S.; A.B., Bowdoin Coll., 1947; LL.B., Boston U., 1950, J.D., 1970; m. Mary Dana Lane, Aug. 13, 1949; children—Henry Oliver, Dana Lane, Stoddard Lane. Admitted to Mass. bar, 1951, also U.S. Supreme Ct. bar; mem. firm Proctor & Howard, Worcester, 1950-53; v.p., gen. counsel State Mut. Life Assurance Co. of Am., Worcester, 1953—; pres., chmn. bd. SMA Mgmt. Corp.; exec. com. Life Ins. Assn. Mass.; counsel Worcester Mut. Ins. Co. Served with USNR, 1943-46. Mem. Internat., Am., Worcester County bar assns., Assn. Life Ins. Counsel (pres.-elect), Nat. Assn. Ins. Commrs., Am. Counsel Life Ins. (chmn. subcom. state matters, chmn. com. all lines charters), Alpha Delta Phi. Clubs: Union (Boston); Worcester Country. Home: 74 North St Shrewsbury MA 01545 Office: 440 Lincoln St Worcester MA 01605

SMITH, HERBERT BONNEWELL, educator; b. Iowa City, Iowa, Mar. 14, 1918; s. Earle Samuel and Clara (Bonnewell) S.; B.A., State U. Iowa, 1940, M.A., 1948; Ph.D., U. Calif., Berkeley, 1952; m. July 2, 1952. With Pomona Coll., Claremont, Calif., 1952—, prof. history, 1969—, coordinator Asian Studies, 1970—, chmn. dept. history, 1974-77; Fulbright lectr. Chulalongkorn U., Bangkok, 1958-59; lectr. United Bd. for Christian Higher Edn. in Asia, 1972. Mem. Am. Hist. Assn., Assn. Asian Studies, Siam Soc., Iowa State Hist. Soc., Circus Hist. Soc. Democrat. Home: 777 W 9th St Claremont CA 91711 Office: Pomona College Claremont CA 91711

SMITH, HERBERT LIVINGSTON, III, architect; b. Norfolk, Va., Nov. 10, 1920; s. Herbert Livingston, Jr. and Alla Burtis (Ransom) S.; B.Arch., U. Va., 1949; m. Martha Birdsong Macklin, Aug. 26, 1948; children—Herbert Livingston, Henry Garrett, William Macklin. Asst. naval architect Norfolk Navy Yard, also mech. div. Panama Canal, 1940-42; pres. Oliver, Smith & Cooke, Ltd., architects, Norfolk and Virginia Beach, Va., 1950—; partner Oliver, Smith, Cooke & Lindner, architects, Richmond; important works include Virginia Beach Conv. Center, Southeastern Tng. Center for Mentally Retarded, Chesapeake, Va., Ch. Good Shepherd, Norfolk. Chmn. historic rev. bd. City of Virginia Beach, 1968—, Virginia Beach City Planning Com., 1954-58; pres. Virginia Beach Devel. Council. Registered architect, Va., N.C., S.C., Ga., Fla., Del., Md., Mich. Fellow AIA (pres. Va. chpt. 1958-59; award merits Va. chpt. 1964); mem. Soc. Am. Mil. Engrs., U. Va. Alumni Assn., Pi Kappa Alpha. Episcopalian (trustee 1968—, sr. warden 1968-70. Clubs: Princess Anne Country, Farmington Country, Harbor, Va., Commonwealth. Home: 1228 Crystal Lake Circle Virginia Beach VA 23451 Office: 303 35th St Virginia Beach VA 23451

SMITH, HOBART MUIR, herpetologist, educator; b. Stanwood, Iowa, Sept. 26, 1912; s. Charles Henry and Frances (Muir) S.; A.B., Kans. State U., 1932; M.S., U. Kans., 1933, Ph.D., 1936; m. Rozella Pearl Blood, Aug. 26, 1938; children—Bruce Dyfrig, Sally Frances. Instr. biology U. Rochester (N.Y.), 1941-45; asst. prof. zoology U. Kans., Lawrence, 1945; asst. prof. wildlife mgmt. Tex. A. and M. Coll., College Station, 1946; faculty U. Ill., Urbana, 1947-68, prof. zoology, 1957-68, curator herpetology Mus. Natural History, 1947-68; prof. biology U. Colo., Boulder, 1968—, chmn. dept., 1970-74, co-chmn., 1978-79. Author: Amphibians of Kansas, 1934; Mexican Lizards, Genus Sceloporus, 1939; Handbook of Lizards, 1945; Checklist and Key to Snakes of Mexico, 1945; Checklist and Key to Amphibians of Mexico, 1948; Handbook of Amphibians and Reptiles of Kansas, 1950; Checklist and Key to Reptiles of Mexico, 1951; Evolution of Chordate Structure, 1960; Reptiles and Amphibians: A Guide to Familiar American Species, 1958; Poisonous Amphibians and Reptiles: Recognition and Bite Treatment, 1959; Herpetological Type-Specimens in the University of Illinois Museum of Natural History, 1964; Snakes as Pets, 1965; Laboratory Studies of Chordate Structure, 1966; Herpetology of Mexico, 1966; Early Foundations of Mexican Herpetology, 1969; Analysis of the Literature on the Mexican Axolotl, 1971; Analysis of the Literature on the Mexican Herpetofauna Exclusive of the Mexican Axolotl, 1973; Source Analysis and Index for Mexican Reptiles, 1976; Source Analysis and Index for Mexican Amphibians, 1976; Guide to Mexican Amphisbaenians and Crocodilians, Bibliog. Addendum II, 1977; Laboratory Studies of Cat Structure, 1977; Amphibians of North America, 1978. Home: 1393 Northridge Ct Boulder CO 80302

SMITH, HOMER DUGGINS, JR., internat. logistician; b. Breckenridge, Tex., Feb. 16, 1922; s. Homer D. and Sara Elsie (Snodgrass) S.; B.S. in Chem. Engring., Tex. A&M Coll., 1943; M.S. in Indsl. Econs., Purdue U., 1959; grad. Indsl. Coll. Armed Forces, 1966-67; m. Joan E. Postlewaite, July 13, 1974; children—Lou Ann, Amanda, Clay, Karen. Commd. 2d lt. U.S. Army, 1943, advanced through grades to maj. gen., 1973; asst. dir. supply and maintenance office, dep. chief of staff for logistics Dept. Army, Washington, 1970-71, dir. plans, 1971-72, dir. supply and maintenance, 1972-73; dep. comdg. gen. U.S. Army Materiel Command, Washington, 1973-74; def. attache to Republic of Vietnam, Saigon, 1974-75; dep. chief of staff for logistics U.S. Army Tng. and Doctrine Command, Ft. Monroe, Va., 1975-77; comdg. gen. U.S. Army Logistics Command, Ft. Lee, Va., 1977-79; ret., 1979; dir. logistics internat. staff NATO, Brussels, 1979—. Decorated D.S.M. with 2 oak leaf clusters, Legion of Merit, Air medal, Army Commendation medal with 2 oak leaf clusters. Mem. Assn. U.S. Army, Soc. Logistics Engrs. Episcopalian. Home: 24 Hyelaan 1900 Overijse Belgium Office: NATO Boulevard Leopold III EVERE 1110 Brussels Belgium

SMITH, HORACE LILBURN, JR., cons. engr.; b. Richmond, Va., July 16, 1894; s. Horace Lilburn and Lilly (Monteriro) S.; C.E., Va. Mil. Inst., 1926; m. Mary Echols Overbey, Oct. 28, 1920; children—Horace Lilburn III, Elisabeth R. Smith Woolard. Pres., Thermal Engring. Corp., Richmond, Va., 1934-41, Girdler Corp., 1942, Auto Ramps Corp., Richmond, 1930; mng. dir. Brit. Thermo-Vactor Ltd.; pres. Food Processes, Inc., Richmond, 1951; Chain Belt Co., Milw., 1944-50; now pres. Smitherm Industries, Inc., Richmond. Served to capt. C.E. 1st Div., U.S. Army, 1917-19. Decorated D.S.C.; recipient awards from various orgns. including Inst. Food Technologists, ASME, ASHRAE, TAPPI, Va. Soc. Profl. Engrs. Fellow ASME (life); mem. ASHRAE (life). Presbyterian. Clubs: Country of Virginia, Bull and Bear, Chemist's, Commonwealth, Masons. Patentee. Office: Smitherm Industries Inc 2405 Westwood Ave PO Box 11184 Richmond VA 23230*

SMITH, HOWARD KINGSBURY, news commentator; b. Ferriday, La., May 12, 1914; B.A., Tulane U., 1936, LL.D., 1955; D.Litt., St. Norbert's Coll., 1958; L.H.D., Alfred U., 1959, Theil Coll., 1961, Roosevelt U., 1961, U. Md., at Balt., 1970; LL.D., Centenary Coll., 1971, U. Md. at Coll. Park, 1973; H.H.D., Pikeville (Ky.) Coll., 1973, L.H.D., St. Michael's Coll., 1973, Ripon Coll., 1974; m. Benedicte Traberg, Mar. 1942; children—Jack, Catherine. Studied Nazism, Berlin, 1936; reviewer fgn. dispatches New Orleans Item-Tribune; Rhodes scholar at Merton Coll., Oxford, Eng., 1937, revisited Germany, Russia, Holland and Austria; foreign corr. in London, United Press, 1939; Berlin corr. CBS, Switzerland, 1941; 9th Army War corr. in France, Holland, Germany, 1944; Nuremberg trials in Germany, 1945; chief European corr. and European dir. CBS in London, 1946-57, CBS corr. Washington Bur., 1957-61, chief corr., gen. mgr., 1961-62; news analyst ABC, Washington, 1962-79. Recipient Overseas Press award for best radio reporting from abroad, 1951-54; DuPont award, 1955; Sigma Delta Chi award for radio journalism, 1957; Sylvania award, 1959; George Polk Meml. award for documentary The Population Explosion, 1960; co-recipient George Peabody award, 1960; Emmy, TV Acad. Arts and Scis., 1960; Radio-TV Daily award as commentator of yr., 1960; Am. Jewish Congress award, 1962; Overseas Press award, best radio intepretation fgn. affairs, 1961, best TV interpretation, 1963; Radio-TV News Dirs. Assn. Paul White Meml. award, 1962; DuPont award, 1963; Honor award for distinguished service in journalism U. Mo., 1971; Lowell Thomas award for outstanding electronic journalist of year Internat. Press Assn., 1976; 4th of July speaker Independence Hall, Phila., 1974; addressed Congress, Flag Day, 1975. Author: Last Train from Berlin, 1942; The State of Europe, 1949; Washington, D.C., 1967. Office: 1124 Connecticut Ave Washington DC 20036*

SMITH, HOWARD MCQUEEN, librarian; b. Charlotte, N.C., July 25, 1919; s. Daniel Holt and Pearl Elizabeth (Truitt) S.; B.A., U. Va., 1941; A.B. in L.S., U. Mich., 1946, M. Pub. Adminstrn., 1947; m. Elaine Betty Wiefel June 27, 1949; children—Carol, Steven Holt. Reference asst. Enoch Pratt Free Library, Balt., 1947-49; coordinator library activities Richmond (Va.) Area Univ. Center, 1949-50; exec. asst. to dir. Enoch Pratt Free Library, 1950-53, head films dept., 1953-55; personnel officer Free Library Phila., 1955-59; city librarian Richmond Pub. Library, 1959—. Served to lt. (s.g.) USNR, 1942-46. Mem. A.L.A. Rotarian. Home: 4120 Hillcrest Rd Richmond VA 23225 Office: Richmond Pub Library Richmond VA 23219

SMITH, HOWARD PERSONS, ret. air force officer; b. West Palm Beach, Fla., Nov. 30, 1924; s. Howard Persons and Ruth (Burns) S.; student U. Ga., 1946-47; B.Gen. Edn., U. Nebr., Omaha, 1962; postgrad. Indsl. Coll. Armed Forces, 1963-64; M.B.A., George Washington U., 1964; m. Ethel Bernice Cady, Aug. 19, 1950; children—Leslie Alan, Kimberly, Brian Rockly, Wendelin. Commd. 2d lt. U.S. Army Air Force, 1944, advanced through grades to maj. gen. U.S. Air Force, 1973; with SAC, Joint Chiefs of Staff, Pacific Air Forces, Hdqrs. USAF, Def. Intelligence Agy., Air Force Security Service, 1947-75; served in Vietnam, 1967-68; comdr. Air Force Security Service, 1974-75; dir. intelligence Hdqrs. US European Command, Stuttgart, Germany, 1975-76, ret., 1976; guest lectr. on U.S. and fgn. mil. affairs. Decorated D.S.M. with one oak leaf cluster, Legion of Merit with three oak leaf clusters. Mem. Order Daedalians, Air Force Assn. Author: Mapping by Radar, 1948; Radar Prediction Improvement Program, 1958; contbr. articles to profl. jours. Home: 1826 Laukahi St Honolulu HI 96821

SMITH, HUGH MONTGOMERY, lawyer; b. Florence, S.C., July 29, 1927; s. William Harold and Marjorie Montgomery (Stupp) S.; B.A., Harvard U., 1950; LL.B., Georgetown U., 1954; m. Nancy Douglass, Apr. 4, 1950; children—Douglass St. Clair, Pinckney Moorer, Catherine Forshee. Admitted to S.C. bar, 1954, Tex. bar, 1964; gen. practice, Florence, 1954-57; trial atty. NLRB, 1959-60, supervising atty., 1960-62; partner firm Schoolfield & Smith, Dallas, 1962—. Served with USN, 1945-46; capt. Res. Mem. Tex. Assn. Bus. Methodist. Club: Masons (32 deg.). Home: Glen Rose TX 76043 Office: 1200 Republic Bank Bldg Dallas TX 75201

SMITH, IAN CORMACK PALMER, biophysicist; b. Winnipeg, Man., Can., Sept. 23, 1939; s. Cormack and Grace Mary S.; B.S., U. Man., 1961, M.S., 1962; Ph.D., Cambridge U., England, 1965; m. Eva Gunilla Landvik, Mar. 27, 1965; children—Brittmarie, Cormack, Duncan. Fellow, Stanford U., 1965-66; mem. research staff Bell Telephone Labs., Murray Hill, N.J., 1966-67; sr. research officer div. biol. scis. Nat. Research Council, Ottawa, 1967—; adj. prof. chemistry Carleton U., 1973—, U. Ottawa, 1976—; adj. prof. biophysics U. Ill., Chgo., 1974—. Recipient Barringer award Can. Spectroscopy Soc., 1979. Fellow Chem. Inst. Can. (Merck award 1978), Royal Soc. Can.; mem. Am. Chem. Soc., Biophys. Soc., Canadian Biochem. Soc. (Ayerst award 1978), AAAS. Contbr. chps. to books Contbr. articles in field to profl. jours. Office: Division of Biological Sciences National Research Council Ottawa ON K1A 0R6 Canada

SMITH, IVAN HURON, architect; b. Danville, Ind., Jan. 25, 1907; s. Calvin Wesley and Irma (Huron) S.; student Ga. Inst. Tech., 1926; B.Arch., U. Fla., 1929; m. Sara Butler, Aug. 18, 1972; 1 dau. by previous marriage, Norma Smith Benton. With Ivan H. Smith, architect, 1936-41; partner Reynolds, Smith & Hills, architects and engrs., Jacksonville, Fla., 1941-70; chmn. bd. Reynolds, Smith & Hills, Architects, Engrs., Planners, Inc., Jacksonville, Tampa, Orlando, Merritt Island and Ft. Lauderdale, Fla., 1971-77; partner Lewis and Eaton, architects, engrs., planners, Jackson, Miss., 1969; dir. So. Indsl. Bank, Jacksonville; sec. Jacksonville Bldg. Code Adv. Bd., 1951-68; mem. Duval County Govt. Study Commn., 1966-67; chmn. Jacksonville Constrn. Trades Qualification Bd., 1971. Mem. council Jacksonville U., 1958-76; pres. Jacksonville Humane Soc., 1956-59; bd. dirs. Jacksonville-Duval Safety Council. Served with USNR, 1943-45. Fellow AIA (Outstanding Service award Fla. region 1965, chpt. pres. 1942, 56); mem. Fla. Assn. Architects (dir. 1957), Jacksonville C. of C. (dir. 1957-59), Beta Theta Pi, Phi Kappa Phi, Sigma Tau. Clubs: Gargoyle (U. Fla.); River, Univ., San Jose Country (Jacksonville). Important works include City Hall, Jacksonville, Duval County Ct. House, Jacksonville, Baptist Hosp., Jacksonville; Engring. Bldg., Nuclear Sci. Bldg., Fla. Field Stadium at U. Fla.; dormitories, Music Bldg., Sci. Bldg., Student Center, Council Bldg., Jacksonville U.; fed. bldgs., Jacksonville, Gainesville, Fla.; So. Bell Telephone bldgs.; (with Edward Durell Stone) Fla. State Capitol Center. Home: 10460 Sylvan Ln W Jacksonville FL 32217 Office: 4019 Boulevard Center Dr Jacksonville FL 32201

SMITH, J. ALBERT, JR., banker; b. Indpls.; s. J. Albert and Berenice (Brennan) S.; B.B.A., U. Notre Dame, 1962; M.B.A., N.Y. U., 1966; m. Maribeth Ann Albers, Aug. 20, 1964; children—J. Albert, III, Kathleen, Edward. Asst. sec. Chem. Bank, N.Y.C., 1964-69; v.p., mgr. Ind. div. Am. Fletcher Nat. Bank, Indpls., 1969, sr. v.p., mgr. corp. banking group, 1969-77, exec. v.p., 1977—; pres. Am. Fletcher Mortgage Co. Inc.; exec. v.p. Am. Fletcher Corp.; dir. Ind. Group, Inc. Bd. dirs. St. Vincent Hosp. Found., Jr. Achievement, Crossroads, Christamore House, Little Sisters of the Poor. Served to lt. (j.g.) USN, 1962-64. Mem. Am. Bankers Assn., Mortgage Bankers Assn., Ind. Bankers Assn., Penrod Soc., Ind. Soc. of Chgo. Republican. Roman Catholic. Clubs: Columbia, Meridian Hills Country, Indpls. Athletic. Home: 7524 N Pennsylvania St Indianapolis IN 46240 Office: 101 Monument Circle Indianapolis IN 46277*

SMITH, J(AMES) E(VERETT) KEITH, psychologist, educator; b. Royal, Iowa, Apr. 30, 1928; s. James H. and Naomi Dorothy (James) S.; B.S. in Math., Iowa State U., 1950; A.M. in Psychology, U. Mich., 1952, Ph.D., 1954; m. Greta Standish, Sept. 10, 1949. Staff psychologist Mass. Inst. Tech., Lincoln Lab., Cambridge, Mass., 1954-64; research psychologist Mental Health Research Inst., Ann Arbor, Mich., 1964-67; prof. psychology U. Mich., Ann Arbor, 1964—, prof. statistics, 1977—, chmn. dept. psychology, 1971-76; lectr. Brandeis U., 1960. Hon. Research fellow Univ. Coll., London, Eng., 1972; named to Rev. Panels, NSF, 1972-74, Nat. Inst. Gen. Med. Sci., 1967-71. Fellow Am. Psychol. Assn.; mem. Am. Statis. Assn., Psychometric Soc., Inst. Math. Statis., Sigma Xi, Phi Kappa Phi, Pi Mu Epsilon, Delta Upsilon. Club: Cosmos. Cons. editor: Psychological Bulletin, 1967-70; editor Jour. Math. Psychology, 1971-74. Home: 1160 Heatherway St Ann Arbor MI 48104

SMITH, J. JOSEPH, U.S. judge; b. Waterbury, Conn., Jan. 25, 1904; s. James Emile and Margaret Loretta (Dunn) S.; A.B., Yale, 1925, LL.B., 1927; LL.D. (hon.), U. Hartford, 1979; m. Eleanor M. Murnane, Aug. 16, 1939; children—J. Joseph, Richard P., Mary Eleanor McCarthy, Mary Martha Murphy. Admitted to Conn. bar, 1927; law practice at Waterbury; research fellow Yale Sch. Law, 1927-28; mem. 74th to 77th Congresses (1935-41), 5th Conn. Dist.; apptd. U.S. dist. judge, Conn., 1941; apptd. U.S. circuit judge, 2d circuit, 1960; now sr. U.S. Circuit judge, 2d Circuit, Hartford, Conn. Mem. Am., Conn., Waterbury bar assns., Am. Judicature Soc., Phi Delta Phi. Catholic. Home: 27 Brenway Dr West Hartford CT 06117 Office: 450 Main St Hartford CT 06103

SMITH, J. KELLUM, JR., lawyer, found. exec.; b. N.Y.C., July 18, 1927; s. James Kellum and Elizabeth Dexter (Walker) S.; grad. Phillips Exeter Acad., 1945; A.B. magna cum laude, Amherst Coll., 1950; LL.B., Harvard, 1953; m. Sarah Tod Lohmann, July 22, 1950; children—Alison Andrews, Timothy Kellum, Jennifer Harlow, Christopher Lohmann. Admitted to New York bar, 1955; asso. firm Lord, Day & Lord, N.Y.C., 1953-59; asst. sec. John Simon Guggenheim Meml. Found., 1960-62; mem. staff Rockefeller Found., 1962-75, asst. sec., 1963-64, sec., 1964-74; v.p., sec. Andrew W. Mellon Found., N.Y.C., 1974—. Trustee Nat. Sculpture Soc., 1955-71, Nat. Ins. Archtl. Edn., 1961-69, trustee Brearley Sch., N.Y.C., 1964—, pres., 1973-78; trustee St. Bernard's Sch., N.Y.C., 1968-78; trustee Am. Acad. in Rome, 1964—, treas., 1965-66, 2d v.p., 1968-72, sec., 1973—; trustee Found. for Child Devel., 1968-74. Served with USAAF, 1945-46. Mem. Phi Beta Kappa. Club: Century Association (N.Y.C.). Home: 131 E 66th St New York City NY 10021 Office: Mellon Found 140 E 62d St New York NY 10021

SMITH, J. STANFORD, land resources mgmt. exec.; b. Terre Haute, Ind., Jan. 4, 1915; s. William J. and Forrest Julia (Luther) S.; A.B., DePauw U., 1936, LL.D. (hon.), 1968; LL.D. (hon.), Rose-Hulman Inst. Tech., 1977; m. Elaine Showalter, Dec. 26, 1938; children—Barbara, Carol Smith Witherell, Stephen, Douglas. With Gen. Electric Co., N.Y.C., Schnectady and Hendersonville, N.C., 1936-73; vice chmn. bd. Internat. Paper Co., N.Y.C., 1973, chmn. bd., chief exec. officer, 1974—; dir. Gen. Motors Corp., Eli Lilly & Co., Chase Manhattan Corp., Can. Internat. Paper Co.; dir., mem. exec. and policy coms. U.S.-USSR Council; chmn. Internat. Task Force Bus. Roundtable, 1972—; mem. Bus. Council, 1974—; co-chmn. Pres.'s Adv. Com. for Trade Negotiations, 1978. Vice chmn. bd. trustees DePauw U.; bd. overseers Tuck Bus. Sch., Dartmouth; chmn. bd. trustees Nat. Fund Minority Engring. Students. Mem. NAM (dir.), Phi Beta Kappa, Phi Gamma Delta. Methodist. Clubs: Greenwich (Conn.) Country; Sky (N.Y.C.); No. Lake George Yacht. Office: 220 E 42d St New York NY 10017

SMITH, J. THOMAS, machinery mfr.; b. Arapaho, Okla., Nov. 19, 1905; s. Carl B. and Sally (Hunt) S,; LL.B., Stetson U. 1928; m. Anne Moreland, Sept. 27, 1930; children—Sally A. (Mrs. Kenneth O'Rourke), Gayle T. Smith. Admitted to Mich. bar, 1930, practiced Deland, Fla., 1928-29, Detroit, 1929—; mem. firm Smith & Huffaker, Detroit, 1940-47; asst., U.S. atty., 1936-40; v.p. Dura Corp., 1947-51, pres. 1951-68, chmn. bd., 1968—, dir., 1946—; chmn. bd., dir. Detroit br. Fed. Res. Bank of Chgo., 1958-62. Mem. water adv. bd. EPA, 1973-75. Mem. adv. bd. YMCA; bd. dirs. Grace Hosp., Mich. Employers Assn., Automobile Club Mich., Boys Club Met. Detroit; trustee Nat. Sanitation Found. Mem. Am., Mich., Detroit bar assns. Clubs: Bloomfield Hills Country; Detroit, Detroit Press, Detroit Athletic, Economic (Detroit); Circumnavigators (dir.); Country of Fla.; Delray Beach (Fla.). Home: Martell Dr Bloomfield Hills MI

48013 Office: 26711 Northwestern Hwy Southfield MI 48075. *Don't take life too seriously or be greedy. Be industrious, help others enjoy life, and stop and enjoy God's gifts along the way.*

SMITH, JACK CARL, pub.; b. Cleve., Sept. 11, 1928; s. John Carl and Florence Agnes (O'Rourke) S.; student Baldwin Wallace Coll., 1948-51, postgrad., 1958; B.A., Ohio U., 1954; m. Nannette June Boyd, Dec. 1, 1962; 1 dau., Colleen Wentworth. Rep., Flying Tiger Line, Inc., Los Angeles, 1958-61; prin. Pub. Rep. bus., Cleve., 1961-64; pub. Penton/IPC, Inc., Cleve., 1964—; dir. Central Cleve. Corp., Nat. Distbn. Terminals. Served with USAF, 1954-58. Mem. Am. Mgmt. Assn., Material Handling Inst., Am. Trucking Assn., Nat. Council Phys. Distbn. Mgmt., Family Motor Coach Assn., Recreation Vehicle Industry Assn., Am. Bus. Press, Mag. Pubs. Assn., Sigma Xi. Club: Wings (N.Y.C.). Home: 457 Devonshire Ct Bay Village OH 44140 Office: Penton Plaza Cleveland OH 44114. *Do your best and God will forgive you the rest.*

SMITH, JACK CLIFFORD, journalist, author; b. Long Beach, Calif., Aug. 27, 1916; s. Charles Franklin and Anna Mary (Hughes) S.; student Bakersfield (Calif.) Coll., 1937-38; m. Denise Bresson, June 17, 1939; children—Curtis Bresson, Douglas Franklin. Reporter, Bakersfield Californian, 1937-38, Honolulu Advertiser, 1941-42, UPI, Sacramento, 1943, Los Angeles Daily News, 1946-49, Los Angeles Herald-Express, 1950-52; reporter Los Angeles Times, 1953-58, columnist, 1958—. Served with USMC, 1944-45. Clubs: Sunset, Calcutta Saddle and Cycle (Los Angeles); Santa Monica Yacht. Author: Three Coins in the Birdbath, 1965; Smith on Wry, 1970; God and Mr. Gomez, 1974; The Big Orange, 1976; Spend All Your Kisses, Mr. Smith, 1978. Home: 4251 Camino Real Los Angeles CA 90065 Office: Times Mirror Sq Los Angeles CA 90053

SMITH, JACK FRANCIS, lawyer; b. Woodlawn, Pa., Dec. 6, 1917; s. Frank James and Marie Elizabeth (Plower) S.; J.D., Cleve. Marshall Law Sch., 1954, B.B.A., 1956, LL.M., 1956; m. Betty Ann Wilson, May 30, 1948; children—Mark Kelan, Leslie Ann, Stacy Jane. Admitted to Ohio bar, 1954; prof. Cleve. Marshall Law Sch., Cleve. State U., 1956-66; partner firm Green, Cronquist and Smith, 1966-70; partner firm Cronquist, Smith and Marshall, Cleve., 1970—. Vice-pres. bd. trustees Urban Community Sch., 1974-77. Served with U.S. Army, 1942-45. Mem. Am., Ohio State, Greater Cleve. bar assns., Cleve. Def. Attys. Group, Am. Judicature Soc., Ohio Def. Assn. Republican. Roman Catholic. Club: Cleve. Athletic. Office: Cronquist Smith and Marshall 1133 Ohio Savings Plaza Cleveland OH 44114

SMITH, JACK PRESCOTT, journalist; b. Paris, Apr. 25, 1945; s. Howard Kingsbury and Benedicte (Traberg) S.; B.A. in History, Carnegie-Mellon U., 1971, Oxford (Eng.) U., 1974. Writer-producer Sta. WIIC-TV News, Pitts., 1969-70; producer-reporter Sta. WLS-TV News, Chgo., 1974-76; fgn. corr. ABC-TV News, Paris, 1976—. Served with inf. U.S. Army, 1964-67. Decorated Purple Heart, Army Commendation medal; recipient citation for best mag. reporting in fgn. affairs Overseas Press Club, 1967. Office: ABC News 22 Avenue D'Eylau Paris France 75116

SMITH, JACLYN, actress; b. Houston, Oct. 26; d. Jack and Margaret Ellen S.; student Trinity U., San Antonio; m. Dennis Cole. Worked as model; appeared in numerous TV commls.; movie appearances include: Bootleggers, The Adventurers, 1970; TV films: Escape from Bogen County, 1977, The Users; appeared TV series: Switch, Charlie's Angels, 1976—; other TV appearances include: McCloud, The Rookies, Get Christy Love. Mem. AFTRA. Office: care ABC 1330 Ave of Americas New York NY 10019*

SMITH, JACQUELINE SARAH, television exec.; b. Phila., May 24, 1933; d. Percy and Gertrude (Elman) Feldenkreis; student Antioch Coll., 1950-54; children—David Anthony, Elinor Sara. Producer, writer childrens program KPIX, San Francisco, 1956-58; dir. on-air-promotion WPIX, N.Y.C., 1960-63; exec. producer childrens program CBS-TV Network, 1964-69, dir. spl. programs, 1973-77; dir. spl. projects Warner Bros. TV, 1969-73; v.p. daytime programs ABC Entertainment, N.Y.C., 1977—. Office: ABC Entertainment 1330 Ave of the Americas New York NY 10019

SMITH, JAMES ALBERT, lawyer; b. Rochester, Ind., May 1, 1921; s. Dell G. and Dora (Halterman) S.; B.S., Ind. U., 1942; J.D. cum laude, U. Notre Dame, 1948; m. Lois E. Fields, Apr. 2, 1944; children—Scott J., Nancy J., Gayle E. (Mrs. David E. French), Terrence M. Admitted to Fla. bar, 1949; partner firm Wicker, Smith, Blomquist, Davant, McMath & Tutan, Miami, Fla., 1948—; mcpl. judge City of North Miami, 1952-53. Served with USAAF, 1943-46. Mem. Am. Judicature Soc., Am., Dade County bar assns., Def. Research Inst., Law and Sci. Acad., St. Vincent DePaul Soc. (treas. 1966-67), Internat. Assn. Ins. Counsel, Dade County Def. Bar Assn., Hon. Order Ky. Cols. Republican. Clubs: Notre Dame Greater Miami (pres. 1959-61), LaGorce Country, Miami Shores Country. Home: 672 NE 98th St Miami FL 33138 Office: Biscayne Bldg Miami FL 33130 also 633 SE 3d Ave Fort Lauderdale FL

SMITH, JAMES C., state atty. gen.; b. Jacksonville, Fla., May 25, 1940; s. John Albert and Fannie Elizabeth (West) S.; B.A., Fla. State U., 1962; J.D., Stetson U., 1967; m. Carole Ann Clark, Dec. 29, 1962; children—Kathryn Elizabeth, Robert Scott, James Clark. Admitted to Fla. bar, 1967; exec. asst. to Fla. Sec. of State, 1969-71; exec. asst. to lt. gov. Fla., 1971; dep. Sec. of Commerce, State of Fla., 1971; sr. staff asst. to Gov. of Fla., 1971-72; mem. Fla. Bd. Regents; now atty. gen. State of Fla.; mem. Gov.'s Task Force on Mobile Homes; dir. Andrew Jackson Savs. and Loan, Coral Ridge Collier Properties, Inc. Mem. bd. overseers Stetson Coll.; trustee Univ. Found., Fla. State U. Served to capt. U.S. Army, 1962-64. Mem. Am. Bar Assn., Leon County Bar Assn., Fla. Bar Assn., Am. Judicature Soc. Democrat. Methodist. Home: 1720 Tarpon Dr Tallahassee FL 32303 Office: The Capitol Tallahassee FL 32304

SMITH, JAMES DAVID BLACKHALL, chemist; b. Peterhead, Scotland, Apr. 25, 1940; s. James and Marion (MacQueen) S.; came to U.S., 1968, naturalized, 1974; B.Sc., Aberdeen (Scotland) U., 1962, Ph.D., 1965. Fulbright fellow State U. N.Y., Syracuse, 1965-66; research chemist Laporte Industries, Ltd., Luton, Eng., 1966-68; fellow scientist Westinghouse Research Labs., Pitts., 1968-78, mgr. insulation systems, 1978—. Recipient IR-100 award Indsl. Research mag., 1976. Mem. Am. Chem. Soc., IEEE, Chem. Soc. London, Royal Inst. Chemistry. Republican. Author, patentee in field. Address: 1310 Beulah Rd Pittsburgh PA 15235

SMITH, JAMES FRANCIS, utilities exec.; b. Saugus, Mass., May 15, 1936; s. James Gregory and Marion Irene (Huckins) S.; A.B., Bentley Coll., 1956; m. Margaret Ellen Frame, Nov. 30, 1963; children—Ellen Hawley Anne, James Gregory. Security analyst Boston Safe Deposit & Trust Co., 1956-58; public acct. Robert C. O'Connell, C.P.A., Boston, 1958-60; controller Precision Microwave Co., Saugus, 1960-65; fin. v.p., dir. Bay State Gas Co., Exeter & Hampton Electric Co., Concord Electric Co., Fitchburg Gas & Electric Light Co., Boston, 1965-75; with Orange and Rockland Utilities, Inc., 1965—, v.p., 1969-75, exec. v.p., chief fin. officer, 1975-78, vice chmn. bd., 1978, chmn., 1979—, also dir. Trustee, treas. Tuxedo Meml. Hosp. Served with AUS, 1958-61. Mem. Am. Gas Assn., Edison Electric Inst. (dir.), Fin. Execs. Inst. Clubs: Tuxedo (gov., treas.), Met., Rockland Country. Home: Club House Rd Tuxedo Park NY 10987 Office: Orange & Rockland Utilities Inc One Blue Hill Plaza Pearl River NY 10965

SMITH, JAMES GERALD, banker; b. Queens, N.Y., June 18, 1918; s. Harry G. and Margaret (Buck) S.; grad. Stonier Grad. Sch. Banking, 1953; m. Dorothy Kollmer, Sept. 15,1946; children—Margaret, Madeline, Maureen, Marilyn, Valerie. With Franklin Nat. Bank, N.Y.C., 1943—, sr. v.p., 1965-69, exec. v.p., 1969-70, pres. 1970—, vice chmn., 1972—; sr. v.p. European-Am. Bank & Trust Co., 1974-78, East N.Y. Savs. Bank, Bklyn., 1978—. Home: 7 Jefferson St West Hempstead NY 11552 Office: 925 Hempstead Turnpike Franklin Square NY 11010

SMITH, JAMES HAMMOND, physicist, educator; b. Colorado Springs, Colo., Feb. 2, 1925; s. James Hollingsworth Clemmer and Elizabeth (Hammond) S.; student Rutgers U., 1944; A.B., Stanford, 1946; Ph.D., Harvard, 1951; m. Jeanne Nelson, Sept. 9, 1950 (dec. Feb. 8, 1953); children—Nelson A., Jennifer E.; m. 2d, E. Jean Walker, Feb. 26, 1955; children—Rebecca R., Margaret A. Prof. physics U. Ill. at Urbana, 1951—; asso. head physics dept., 1973-80; vis. prof. Mass. Inst. Tech., 1962-63. Mem. phys. sci. study com. Ednl. Services, Inc., 1955-58. Guggenheim fellow, 1965-66. Fellow Am. Phys. Soc.; mem. Am. Assn. Physics Tchrs., Alpha Kappa Lambda. Author: Introduction to Special Relativity, 1965; also research publs. Home: 1738 Westhaven Dr Champaign IL 61820 Office: Physics Dept U Ill Urbana IL 61801

SMITH, JAMES JOHN, physiologist; b. St. Paul, Jan. 28, 1914; s. James W. and Catherine (Welsch) S.; M.D., St. Louis U., 1937; Ph.D., Northwestern U., 1946; m. Mariellen Schumacher, Mar. 17, 1945 (div.); children—Philip W., Lucy G. Shaker, Paul R., Gregory K. Intern Ancker Hosp., St. Paul, 1937-38, fellow in pathology Cook County Hosp., Chgo., 1938-39; fellow in physiology Northwestern U., Chgo., 1939-41; dean Stritch Sch. Med., Loyola U., 1946-50, asst. prof. physiology dept. exptl. medicine, 1946-50; chief edn. div., dept. medicine and surgery VA, 1950-52; prof., dir. dept. physiology Med. Coll. Wis., Milw., 1952—; Fulbright research prof. U. Heidelberg, Physiology Inst., Germany, 1959-60. Researcher in aviation medicine, U.S. Air Force, 1941-46. Mem. Soc. Exptl. Biology, Am. Physiol. Soc., Sigma Xi. Roman Catholic. Home: 11050 Maple Ln Wauwatosa WI 53225 Office: 561 N 15th St Milwaukee WI 53233

SMITH, JAMES KIRBY, utility exec.; b. Meade County, Ky., Feb. 10, 1916; s. James Kirby and Minnie (Ritchie) S.; student Western Ky. State Tchrs. Coll., 1934-35, Bowling Green (Ohio) Bus. Coll., 1936; m. Marjorie J. Thomas, Feb. 12, 1938; 1 son, James Thomas. Mgr., Fleming-Mason Rural Electric Coop. Corp., Flemingsburg, Ky., 1938-48; exec. mgr. Ky. Rural Electric Coop. Corp., Louisville, 1948-70; gov. Nat. Rural Utilities Coop. Fin. Corp., Washington, 1970-79; chmn. long range study com. Nat. Rural Electric Coop. Assn.; pres. Area Data Processing Corp., St. Louis, Electric Research and Mfg. Coop., Dyersburg, Tenn.; chmn. awards com. Coop. Month, Coop. League USA; cons. rural electrification, Mekong Delta, Thailand, 1965. Leader People-to-People tour, Europe and Russia, 1963; incorporator Ky. com. Partners of Alliance-Ecuador. Recipient Disting. Service award Rural Electrification Adminstrn.; Spl. Recognition award AID, 1966; Coop. Career award Coop. League USA, 1979; award from pres. Ecuador, 1967. Mem. Met. Washington Bd. Trade. Democrat. Methodist. Clubs: Broken Woods Country (Coral Springs, Fla.); Masons (32 deg.). Home: 1953 Coquina Way Coral Springs FL 33065 Office: 1115 30th St NW Washington DC 20007

SMITH, JAMES MORTON, museum adminstr., historian; b. Bernie, Mo., May 28, 1919; B.Ed., So. Ill. U., 1941; M.A., U. Okla., 1946; Ph.D., Cornell U., 1951; m. Kathryn Hegler, Jan. 5, 1945; children—Melissa Jane, James Morton. Editor, Inst. Early Am. History and Culture, Williamsburg, Va., 1955-66; prof. history Cornell U., Ithaca, N.Y., 1966-70, U. Del., Newark, 1976—; dir. State Hist. Soc. Wis., Madison, 1970-76, Winterthur (Del.) Mus., 1976—. Served to lt. USCGR, 1943-45. Mem. Assn. Art Mus. Dirs., Am. Assn. Museums, Am. Hist. Assn., Orgn. Am. Historians, Am. Assn. State and Local History. Author: Freedom's Fetters, 1956; Liberty and Justice, 1958; Seventeenth-Century America, 1959; George Washington: A Profile, 1969; The Constitution, 1971; Politics and Society in American History, 1973. Office: Winterthur Museum Winterthur DE 19735

SMITH, JAMES OSCAR, (Jimmy Smith), jazz organist, music pub. exec.; b. Norristown, Pa., Dec. 8, 1928; s. James and Grace Elizabeth (Weldon) S.; student Ornstein Sch. music, Phila., 1946-49; m. Edna Joy Goins, Mar. 31, 1957; children—James Oscar, Jia Charlene. Jazz organist, 1951—; appeared at Antibes (France) Jazz Festival, 1962, Complain-de-Tour Jazz Festival, Belgium, 1963; owner, dir. Edmy Music Pub. Co., 1962—, Trieste Builders Co., 1962—. Jay Cec. Corp., 1962—; composer, perfrmer background music film Where the Spies Are, 1965; composer music film La Metamorphose de Clopertes, 1965. Recipient Downbeat's Reader and Critics award, 1962, 63, 64. Mem. Broadcast Music Inc., AFTRA, NAACP, Nat. Acad. Recording Arts and Scis. Mason. Composer numerous organ pieces; compiler organ books; numerous recordings. Office: care Lola Smith 6355 Topanga Canyon Rd Suite 307 Woodland Hills CA 91364*

SMITH, JAMES R., tax atty.; b. Ottumwa, Iowa, Feb. 7, 1933; s. Willis J. and Zella (Rush) S.; B.S. in Bus., Iowa State U., 1954; J.D., State U. Iowa, 1958; m. Rosemary L. Goetzman, Oct. 23, 1955; children—Stephen, Nancy, Susan, David. Tax accountant Arthur Andersen & Co., C.P.A.'s, Kansas City, Mo., 1951-61; with Ceco Corp., Cicero, Ill. 1963-70, sec., head legal dept., 1968-70; tax atty. Sears Roebuck & Co., Chgo., 1970-73, mgr. taxes, internat. ops., 1973-79; gen. tax counsel Baxter Travenol Labs. Inc., Deerfield, Ill., 1979—. Served to capt. USAF, 1955-57. C.P.A., Nebr. Mem. Am., Ill., Iowa, Chgo. bar assns., Chgo. Tax Club, Internat. Fiscal Assn., Am. Inst. C.P.A.'s. Home: 392 N Delaplaine Rd Riverside IL 60546 Office: Baxter Travenol Labs Inc Deerfield IL 60015

SMITH, JAMES RAYMOND, ret. furniture mfr.; b. Mount Airy, N.C., Apr. 12, 1895; s. Alfred Edgar and Florence Eugenia (Patterson) S.; A.B., Trinity Coll. (now Duke U.), 1917; m. Annie James Hadley, Apr. 4, 1923; children—Raymond Alfred, James Hadley. Furniture mfr., 1918—; sec.-treas. Nat. Furniture Co., Mt. Airy, 1920-29, pres., treas., 1929-43, pres., sec., treas., 1944-73; ret.; dir., mem. exec. com. Security Life & Trust Co., Atlantic & Yadkin R.R. (name now Intercon Corp.), Highland Container Co.; dir. Northwestern Bank, So. Furniture Exposition Bldg. Mem. N.C. Prison Bd., 1930-33; mem. N.C. Senate, 1943-44; mem. N.C. Hwy. Commn., 1945-49, 65-69; past mem. bd. of aldermen, Mt. Airy. Trustee, Duke U., Children's Home; chmn. bd. trustees Martin Meml. Hosp., Mt. Airy Community Fund. Mem. Pi Kappa Alpha, Omicron Delta Kappa, Theta Nu Epsilon. Club: Twin City. Home: 323 Franklin St Mount Airy NC 27030

SMITH, JAMES ROSWELL, govtl. affairs cons.; b. Sioux Falls, S.D., May 10, 1917; s. Dick Roswell and Edna Marie (Woodruff) S.; A.A., Sioux Falls Coll., 1938; J.D., U. S.D., 1940; m. Arlene P. Skredsvig, Oct. 1, 1941; children—Dick Roswell, Robert Martin, Douglas James. Admitted to S.D. bar, 1940; practiced in Sioux Falls, 1941-42; mgr. Yankton (S.D.) C. of C., 1942-53; v.p., counsel Mississippi Valley Assn., Omaha, 1953-65; marketing mgr. No. Natural Gas Co., Omaha, 1965-69; asst. sec. of interior, Washington, 1969-73; pres. Am. Waterways Operators, Inc., Washington, 1973-78; U.S. commr. Permanent Internat. Assn. Nav. Congresses, 1978—. Pres., Omaha Zool. Soc., 1968-69. Trustee Neb. Resources Found., 1965-69, Neb. Humane Soc., 1967-69. Recipient Ohio Gov.'s Conservation award, 1970, Distinguished Civilian Service award Dept. Army, 1956; named Water Statesman, Nat. Water Resources Assn., 1972. Mem. Propeller Club of U.S., Beta Theta Pi. Republican. Conglist. Mason (32 deg., Shriner). Club: University (Washington). Home: 6408 Cavalier Corridor Falls Church VA 22044

SMITH, JANE FARWELL, civic worker; b. Chgo.; d. John Charles and Jessie Greene (Delaware) Farwell; student U. Chgo., 1925-28; m. Wakelee R. Smith, Feb. 7, 1929; children—Diana Jane Smith Gauss, Carol Louise Smith, Anderson. Pres. Infant Soc. Chgo., Beverly Hills (Ill.) Center, 1949; chmn. Am. heritage com. DAR, Ill., 1963-65, nat. vice chmn. Am. heritage com. 1965-68, chmn. Insignia, Ill., 1966, Ill. treas., 1966-68, mem. nat. Americanism and manual for citizenship com., 1968, Ill. regent, 1969-71, mem. U.S.A. bicentennial commn., 1971-74, nat. corr. sec. gen., 1971-74, 1st. v.p. gen., 1974-75, pres. gen., 1975-77; trustee U.S. Capitol Hist. Soc., 1976—. Mem. Kate Duncan Sch. Bd., Grant, Ala., 1975—, Tamassee Sch. Bd., Tamassee, S.C., 1975-77. Recipient Gold medal of appreciation Ill. chpt. S.A.R., 1970, resolution of congratulation Senate of 80th Assembly of State of Ill., 1977. Mem. Nat. Gavel Soc. (life), DAR Museum (life), Daus. Colonial Wars, Nat. Soc. New Eng. Women. Episcopalian. Clubs: D.A.R. Exec., Nat. Officers, Alden Kindred Am., Colonial Dames Am., Daus. Am. Colonists, Daus. Founders and Patriots, Am. Nat. Soc. Old Plymouth Colony Descs., Soc. Mayflower Descs., Colonial Daus. 17th Century, Colonial Wars Nat. Soc., New Eng. Women. Home: 538 Pamela Circle Hinsdale IL 60521

SMITH, JEAN CHANDLER, ofcl. Smithsonian Instn.; b. Phila., Apr. 13, 1918; d. Chandler White and Philena Pennell (Cheetham) S.; A.B., Bryn Mawr Coll., 1939; M.S., Yale U., 1953; M.L.S., Cath. U. Am., 1973. Reference librarian D.C. Pub. Library, 1939-43; translator, C.Z., 1943-44; librarian Nat. Air Sta., Kaneohe Bay, Oahu, Hawaii, 1944-46; reference librarian, also research asso. Yale U., 1947-58; acting chief acquisitions NIH Library, Bethesda, Md., 1959-63; chief reader services U.S. Dept Interior, Washington, 1964-65; with Smithsonian Instn. Libraries, Washington, 1965—, asst. dir. instn. services, 1972-79, acting dir., 1977-79. Mem. friends of library com. Bryn Mawr Coll., 1975—; bd. dirs., sec. Universal Serials and Book Exchange. Mem. Spl. Libraries Assn., ALA, AAAS. Clubs: Bryn Mawr Washington (chmn. scholarship com.), Yale of Washington, Zonta. Office: Smithsonian Inst Libraries Constitution Ave at 10th St NW Washington DC 20560

SMITH, JEFFREY BORDEAUX, lawyer; b. Des Moines, Nov. 5, 1926; s. Frank Hurd and Emma Agnes (Brouilette) S.; ed. in Pre-law Western Md. Coll., to 1948; LL.B., U. Md., 1951; m. Ninita Barkman, Jan. 29, 1949; children—Jennifer (Mrs. James Houston Brooks), Holly Ellen, Wendy Carol, Jeffrey Bordeaux, Julie Lynn. Admitted to Md. bar; resident trial atty. Liberty Mut. Ins. Co., 1953-58; partner firm Smith, Somerville & Case, Balt., 1958—. Formerly chmn. Sch. Bd. Nominating Conv. of Baltimore County. Formerly bd. dirs. Legal Aid Bur., Balt. Fellow Internat. Soc. Barristers; mem. Am. (ho. of dels. 1976—), Md. (chmn. com. jud. appointments 1978—, bd. govs. 1974-75, 76-78, 79-80) bar assns., Bar Assn. Balt. City (pres. 1975-76), Internat. Assn. Ins. Counsel, Md. Assn. Def. Counsel. Home: 607 Sudbrook Rd Baltimore MD 21208 Office: 100 Light St Baltimore MD 21202

SMITH, JEFFREY GREENWOOD, army officer; b. Ft. Sam Houston, Tex., Oct. 14, 1921; s. Henry Joseph Moody and Gladys Adrienne (Haile) S.; B.S. in Civil Engring., Va. Mil. Inst., 1943; M.S. in Mech. Engring., Johns Hopkins, 1949; M.A. in Internat. Affairs, George Washington U., 1964; m. Dorothy Jane Holland, June 2, 1948; children—Meredith B., Jennifer H., Jeffrey Greenwood, Tracy E., Melissa A., Ashley A. Commd. 2d lt. U.S. Army, 1944, advanced through grades to lt. gen., 1975; service in CBI, Korea, Germany and Vietnam; comdr. 2d Inf. Div., Korea, 1971-73; dep. chief staff ops. Hdqrs. Army Forces Command, Ft. McPherson, Ga., 1973-74, chief staff, 1974-75; comdr. 1st U.S. Army, Ft. Meade, Md., 1975-79; ret., 1979. Trustee, Norwich U., Northfield, Vt. Decorated D.S.M., Silver Star, Legion of Merit with 3 oak leaf clusters, D.F.C., Bronze Star with V device and 2 oak leaf clusters, Air medal with 12 oak leaf clusters, Army Commendation medal with oak leaf cluster, Purple Heart with oak leaf cluster, Combat Inf. badge (2); breast Order Yun Hui (Republic China); Order Security Merit (Korea); Gallantry Cross with silver and gold stars, Army Distinguished Service Order (Vietnam). Mem. Assn. U.S. Army, Kappa Alpha. Home: 8331 Blowing Rock Rd Alexandria VA 22309

SMITH, JESSE GRAHAM, JR., physician, educator; b. Winston-Salem, N.C., Nov. 22, 1928; s. Jesse Graham and Pauline Field (Griffith) S.; B.S., Duke U., 1962, M.D., 1951; m. Dorothy Jean Butler, Dec. 28, 1950; children—Jesse Graham, Cynthia Lynn, Grant Butler. Intern, VA Hosp., Chamblee, Ga., 1951-52; resident in dermatology Duke U., 1954-56, asso. prof. dermatology, 1960-62, prof., 1962-67; resident U. Miami, 1956-57, asst. prof., 1957-60; prof. dermatology Med. Coll. Ga., 1967—, chmn. dept. dermatology, 1967—, acting chmn. dept. pathology, 1973-75; chief staff Talmadge Meml. Hosp., Augusta, Ga., 1970-72; mem. advisory council Nat. Inst. Arthritis, 1975-79. Served with USPHS, 1952-54. Diplomate Am. Bd. Dermatology (dir. 1974—, v.p. 1979-80). Mem. Am. Dermatol. Assn. (sec. 1976—), Soc. Investigative Dermatology (dir. 1964-69, pres. 1979—), Am. Acad. Dermatology (dir. 1971-74), S.E. Dermatological Assn. (sec. 1970-71, pres. 1975-76), Ga. Soc. Dermatology (pres. 1979—), So. Med. Assn. (chmn. sect. dermatology 1973-74), AMA, Assn. Profs. Dermatology (dir. 1976-77), Med. Research Found. Ga. (dir. 1967—, pres. 1974-75), Alpha Omega Alpha. Contbr. chpts. in books. Mem. editorial bd. Archives of Dermatology, 1963-72, Jour. Investigative Dermatology, 1966-67, Jour. AMA, 1974—, So. Med. Jour., 1976—; editor Jour. Am. Acad. Dermatology, 1978—. Contbr. articles in field to profl. jours. Home: 606 Scotts Way Augusta GA 30909 Office: Medical College of Georgia Augusta GA 30912

SMITH, JESSE MORGAN, JR., educator; b. Charleston, W.Va., June 16, 1939; s. Jesse Morgan and Mildred Lucy Smith; B.S. in Bus. Adminstrn., U. Denver, 1965, M.B.A., 1968, also postgrad. Jr. engr. Martin Co., 1958-61; data processor, pub. relations staff Mountain Bell, 1962-67; mgmt. cons. Peat, Marwick, Mitchell, 1968-71; asst. dean, instr. mgmt. U. Denver, 1961-75; mng. dir. Am. Assembly Collegiate Schs. Bus., St. Louis, 1975-77; prof., dept. chmn. mgmt. and fin. Boise (Idaho) State U., 1975; exec. dir. Coll. Placement Council, 1977—; mgmt. cons. Trustee Fox Creek Estates Subdiv., 1973—. Served with AUS. Mem. Am. Mgmt. Assn., Beta Gamma Sigma, Phi

Delta Kappa, Sigma Iota Epsilon. Home: 4425 Jacksonville Rd Bethlehem PA 18017

SMITH, JESSICA, author, editor; b. Madison, N.J., Nov. 29, 1895; d. Walter Granville-Smith and Jessie May (Stout) S.; A.B., Swarthmore Coll., 1915; m. Harold M. Ware, Jan. 1925 (dec. Aug. 1935); 1 son, David Ware; m. 2d, John Abt, Mar. 1937. Writer Phila. N. Am., 1915-16; organizer and speaker Woman's Suffrage movement, 1917-18; exec. sec. Intercollegiate Socialist Soc., 1920-22; famine relief work and publicity Am. Friends' Service Com. in Russia, 1922-24; publicity dir. Russian Reconstr. Farms (Am.), USSR, N. Caucasus, 1926-28; editor Soviet Union Rev., Washington, 1929-33; tour USSR, 1935, 45, 61, 64, 70, 78; editor Soviet Russia Today (Am. mag.), 1936-50; editor New World Rev., 1950-76, editor emeritus, 1977—. Vice chmn. Nat. Council Am. Soviet Friendship, 1960—. Recipient Order of Friendship of Peoples, Govt. of USSR, 1976, Friendship medal Union Socs. Friendship and Cultural Relations, USSR. Author: Woman in Soviet Russia, 1928; War and Peace in Finland (with Bayer and Brody), 1940; People Come First, 1948; Jungle Law and Human Reason, 1949; Soviet Democracy and How It Works, 1969; co-editor: Lenin's Impact on the United States, 1970; Building a New Society, 1977; editor Voices of Tomorrow, 1971; A Family of Nations: The USSR After Fifty Years, 1973; co-editor: Six Decades that Changed the World: The USSR After 60 Years. transl. Over the North Pole (George Baidukov). Home: 444 Central Park W Apt 10-D New York NY 10025 Office: 156 Fifth Ave New York NY 10010

SMITH, JESSIE CARNEY, librarian, author; b. Greensboro, N.C., Sept. 24, 1930; d. James Ampler and Vesona Bigelow Carney; B.S., N.C. A. and T. State U., 1950; student Cornell U., fall 1950; M.A., Mich State U., 1956; A.M., George Peabody Coll. Tchrs., 1957; Ph.D., U. Ill., 1964; m. Frederick Douglas Smith, Dec. 22, 1950 (div.); 1 son, Frederick Douglas, Jr. Head cataloger, instr. library sci. Tenn. State U., 1957-60; teaching asst. U. Ill., 1961-63; coordinator library service, asst. prof. Tenn. A. and I State U., 1963-65; univ. librarian, prof. Fisk U., 1965—, dir. library tng. insts., 1970-79, fed. relations officer, 1976-78; lectr. Peabody Library Sch., George Peabody Coll. for Tchrs., 1969—, Ala. A. & M. U., 1971, U. Tenn., 1973; cons. So. Assn. Colls. and Schs., 1968—, U.S. Office for Civil Rights, 1979—. Sec. COSATI Subcom. on Negro Research Libraries, 1970-73; mem. Biomed. Library Review Com., 1972-76; lectr., cons. black lit. and black collections. Dir. library study Tenn. Higher Edn. Commn., 1974. Bd. dirs. Bethlehem Center, Nashville, 1965-68. Council on Library Resources fellow, 1969. Mem. Am. (mem. council 1969-71), (vis. team com. on accreditation 1973—, com. on program evaluation and services 1973-76, chmn. 1975-76), Southeastern, Tenn. (chmn. coll. and univ. sect. 1969-70) medical library assns., Am. Assn. U. Profs., Assn. Coll. and Research Libraries, Links Inc., Beta Phi Mu, Pi Gamma Mu, Alpha Kappa Alpha. Democrat. Methodist. Author: Black Academic Libraries and Research Collections; compiler: Directory of Significant 20th Century American Minority Women. Editorial bd. Choice, 1969-74. Contbr. articles to profl. jours. Office: Fisk U Library 17th Ave N Nashville TN 37203

SMITH, JIM ALLISON, indsl. co. exec.; b. Sweetwater, Tex., Jan. 21, 1939; s. Terry B. and Patty (Flippen) S.; student Rice U., 1957-58; B.B.A., U. Tex., Austin, 1961; m. Jare Horne, June 17, 1961; children—Stephen Matthew, Amanda. Sr. auditor Arthur Andersen & Co., Dallas, 1962-66; controller, treas., v.p. and treas. TRACOR, Inc., Austin, 1966—, dir., 1974—; dir. Enviroquip, Inc. Bd. dirs. Heritage Soc. Austin, 1976—, Jr. Achievement Central Tex., 1975—, Austin Civic Ballet, 1979—. Served with U.S. Army, 1961-62. C.P.A., Tex. Mem. Am. Inst. C.P.A.'s, Tex. Soc. C.P.A.'s (treas. Austin chpt. 1970, v.p. 1971, pres. 1974, state dir. 1977—), Nat. Assn. Accountants (v.p., dir. Austin chpt. 1968-70, pres. 1971). Presbyn. (elder). Home: 602 E 43d St Austin TX 78751 Office: 6500 Tracor Ln Austin TX 78721

SMITH, JOE DORSEY, JR., newspaper publisher; b. Selma, La., Apr. 6, 1922; s. Joe Dorsey and Louise (Lindsay) S.; B.A., La. Coll. Pineville, 1939-43; m. Margaret Jane Wilson, Nov. 20, 1943; 1 son, Lawrence Dorsey. Gen. mgr. Alexandria (La.) Daily Town Talk, 1958—, publisher, 1965—, pres. McCormich & Co., Inc., Publishers, 1968—; dir., chmn. exec. com. Guaranty Bank & Trust Co., Alexandria; chmn. adv. bd. UPI. Mem. bd. regents for Higher Edn. in La.; vice chmn. Gulf South Research Inst. Served with USAF, 1942-45. Mem. Am. Newspaper Publishers Assn. (dir., exec. com., trustee found., past pres.), Newspaper Advt. Bur. (dir.). Democrat. Episcopalian. Clubs: Alexandria Golf and Country, Boston, New Orleans. Home: 2734 George's Ln Alexandria LA 71301 Office: PO Box 7558 Alexandria LA 71306

SMITH, JOE MAUK, educator; b. Sterling, Colo., Feb. 14, 1916; s. Harold Rockwell and Mary Calista (Mauk) S.; B.S., Calif. Inst. Tech., 1937; Ph.D., Mass. Inst. Tech., 1943; m. Essie Johnstone McCutcheon, Dec. 23, 1943; children—Rebecca K., Marsha Mauk. Chem. engr. Texas Co., Standard Oil Co. of Calif., 1937-41; instr. chem. engring. Mass. Inst. Tech., 1943; asst. prof. chem. engring. U. Md., 1945; prof. chem. engring. Purdue U., 1945-56; dean Coll. Tech., U. N.H., 1956-57; prof. chem. engring. Northwestern U., 1957-59, Walter P. Murphy prof. chem. engring., 1959-61; prof. engring. U. Calif., 1961—, chmn. dept. chem. engring., 1964—; hon. prof. chem. engring. U. Buenos Aires Argentina, 1964—; Fulbright lectr., Eng., Italy, Spain, 1965, and Argentina, 1963, 65, Ecuador, 1970; Mudaliar Meml. lectr. U. Madras (India), 1967; UNESCO cons., Venezuela, 1972—. Guggenheim research award for study in Holland, also Fulbright award, 1953-54. Mem. Am. Chem. Soc., Am. Inst. Chem. Engrs. Wilhelm award 1960, Walker award 1977), Nat. Acad. Engring., Sigma Xi, Tau Beta Pi. Author: Introduction to Chemical Engineering Thermodynamics, 3d edit., 1975; Chemical Engineering Kinetics, 1956, 2d edit., 1970. Home: 760 Elmwood Dr Davis CA 95616

SMITH, JOEL PRITCHARD, univ. adminstr.; b. Toledo, June 30, 1933; s. Lavern Pritchard and Florence (Blish) S.; B.A. summa cum laude, Beloit (Wis.) Coll., 1955, LL.D., 1970; B.A., Oxford (Eng.) U., 1957; J.D., U. Wis., 1961; children—Rebecca, Jennifer. Admitted to Minn. bar, 1961; with firm Cant, Havenstock, Beardsley, Gray & Plant, Mpls., 1961-65; asso. dean of students Stanford U., 1965-67, asso. provost, dean of students, 1967-69, cons. Devel. Office, 1976-77, v.p.-devel., 1977—; pres. Denison U., 1969-76. Mem. Great Lakes Colls. Assn. (chmn. 1972-74), Order of Coif, Phi Beta Kappa, Beta Theta Pi, Phi Delta Phi. Office: 301 Encina Hall Stanford U Stanford CA 94305

SMITH, JOHN BERTIE, art educator; b. Lamesa, Tex., June 5, 1908; s. Bertie Phelps and Mary Etta (Hodges) S.; A.B., Baylor U., 1929; A.M., U. Chgo., 1931; Ed.D. (Arthur W. Dow scholar), Columbia U., 1946; student Sch. of Art Inst. Chgo., evening 1930-31; m. Ellen Capes, Mar. 18, 1933; 1 dau., Elaine Hope. Prin., Cox's Chapel Rural Sch., Tex., 1926-27; prin., tchr. math. and sci. Malakoff (Tex.) High Sch., 1927-30; head dept. art, dir. art in lab schs. Adams State Tchrs. Coll., Alamosa, Colo., 1931-36, 1937-39; head dept. art U. Wyo., 1939-45; part-time instr. art Columbia U., 1945-46; head dept. art U. Ala., 1946- 49; dean Kansas City Art Inst. Sch. Design, 1949-54; head art dept., chmn. humanities Hardin-Simmons U., 1954-60; chmn. dept. art Baylor U., Waco, Tex., 1960-78, prof. fine arts, 1978—; chmn. state curriculum coms. in art Colo. elementary schs., 1936, secondary schs., 1942; mem. survey staff pub. schs., Hartford, Conn., 1937, Laramie, Wyo., 1942, Mobile, Ala. (dir.), 1947; dir. U. Ala. Art Mus.; co-founder San Luis Valley Crafts (Colo.), 1933. Mem. Ala. Art League (pres. 1948-49), Ala. Edn. Assn. (pres. art sect. 1949-50), S.E. Art Assn. (v.p. 1948-49, pres. 1949-50), Nat. Art Edn. Assn. (council), Artists Equity, Coll. Art Assn., Tex. Fine Arts Assn. (pres. 1959-60), Watercolor Soc. Ala., Tex. Art Edn. Assn. (pres. 1969-71), Tex. Watercolor Soc., Alpha Chi, Kappa Pi, Phi Delta Kappa, Kappa Delta Pi. Democrat. Presbyterian. Club: Rotary. Author of articles on art and edn.; editor Tex. Trends Art Edn., 1961-63. Paintings exhibited, 1931—; one-man shows: U. Colo., Mobile (Ala.) Gallery, Southeastern Ann., San Angelo (Tex.) Coll., Big Spring (Tex.) Gallery, Wichita Falls (Tex.) Gallery, Baylor Art Gallery; represented in permanent collection Denver Art Mus. Home: 2109 Charboneau Dr Waco TX 76710. *In making value judgments regarding art and people, I always feel somewhat inadequate. I can never make absolute ones. After making a tentative decision I work to see if it should last.*

SMITH, JOHN BREWSTER, librarian, univ. dean; b. Bryan, Tex., June 26, 1937; s. Elmer Gillam and Sara Roland (Lull) S.; B.A., Tex. A. and M. U., 1960; M.S., Columbia, 1963; m. Ida Hawa, Dec. 28, 1963; children—Susan Helen, Rona Esther. Asst. law librarian Law Sch., Columbia, N.Y.C., 1963-66; asst. library dir. for pub. services Tex. A. and M. U., College Station, 1966-69, dir. libraries, 1969-74; dir. libraries, dean library scis. State U. N.Y. at Stony Brook, 1974—. Named Librarian of Year, Tex. Library Assn., 1972. Mem. Am., Suffolk County library assns., State U. N.Y. Librarians Assn. Home: 121 Gnarled Hollow Rd East Setauket NY 11733 Office: Libraries State U NY Stony Brook NY 11794

SMITH, JOHN BURNSIDE, bus. exec.; b. Indpls., 1931; grad. U. Ind., 1957, postgrad. Sch. Bus. Adminstrn., 1958; m. Barbara J.; children—John S., Lynn B., Nancy L. Pres., dir. Aero Mayflower Transit Co., Indpls.; pres., chief exec. officer, dir. Mayflower Corp., Indpls.; v.p., dir. Hogan Transfer & Storage Co.; pres., dir. Mayflower Transit Co. Ltd. of Can.; dir. Ind. Group, Inc., Ind. Nat. Corp. Trustee, Hanover Coll.; mem. adv. bd. St. Vincent Hosp., Brebeuf Prep. Sch.; bd. dirs. Ind. State C. of C. Office: PO Box 107B Indianapolis IN 46206

SMITH, JOHN BURNSIDE, business exec.; b. Indpls., 1931; grad. U. Ind., 1957, postgrad. Sch. Bus. Adminstrn., 1958. Pres., chief exec. officer Mayflower Corp.; dir. Ind. Group Inc., Ind. Nat. Corp. Trustee, Hanover Coll.; past pres.'s council Jr. Achievement Central Ind.; pres.'s council Brebeuf Prep. Sch.; adv. bd. St. Vincent's Hosp.; past pres. 500 Festival Assos. Mem. Ind. C. of C. (dir.), Indpls. C. of C. (dir.), Am. Movers Conf. (dir.), Household Goods Carriers Bur. (dir.). Office: 9998 N Michigan Rd Carmel IN 46032

SMITH, JOHN EDWIN, educator; b. Bklyn., May 27, 1921; s. Joseph Robert and Florence Grace (Dunn) S.; A.B., Columbia, 1942, Ph.D., 1948; B.D., Union Theol. Sem., N.Y.C., 1945; M.A. (hon.), Yale, 1959; LL.D., U. Notre Dame, 1964; m. Marilyn Blanche Schulhof, Aug. 25, 1951; children—Robin Dunn, Diana Edwards. Instr. religion and philosophy Vassar Coll., 1945-46; from instr. to asst. prof. philosophy and religion Barnard Coll., 1946-52; mem. faculty Yale, 1952—, prof. philosophy, 1959—, chmn. dept., 1961—, Clark prof. philosophy, 1972—; vis. prof. Union Theol. Sem., 1959, U. Mich., 1958; guest prof. U. Heidelberg (Germany), 1955-56; Dudleian lectr. Harvard, 1960; lectr. Am. Week, U. Munich (Germany), 1961; Suarez lectr. Fordham U., 1963; pub. lectr. King's College, Univ. London, 1965; Aquinas lectr. Marquette U., 1967; Warfield lectr. Princeton Theol. Sem., 1970; Fulbright lectr. Kyoto U., Japan, 1971; Sprunt lectr. Union Theol. Sem. (Va.), 1973; Mead-Swing lectr. Oberlin Coll., 1975; H. Richard Niebuhr lectr. Elmhurst Coll. (Ill.), 1977; Merrick lectr. Ohio Wesleyan U., 1977: Roy Wood Sellars lectr. Bucknell Corp., 1978. Mem. adv. com. Nat. Humanities Inst., New Haven, 1974, dir., 1977—. Named hon. alumnus Harvard Div. Sch., 1960; Am. Council Learned Socs. fellow, 1964-65. Mem. Culinary Inst. Am. (dir. New Haven), Am. Philos. Assn., Am. Theol. Soc. (pres. 1967-68), Metaphys. Soc. Am. (pres. 1970-71), Hegel Soc. Am. (pres. 1971). Author: Royce's Social Infinite, 1950; Value Convictions and Higher Education, 1958; Reason and God, 1961; The Spirit of American Philosophy, 1963; The Philosophy of Religion, 1965; Religion and Empiricism, 1967; Experience and God, 1968; Themes in American Philosophy, 1970; Contemporary American Philosophy, 1970; The Analogy of Experience, 1973; Purpose and Thought: The Meaning of Pragmatism, 1978. Translator: (R. Kroner) Kant's Weltanschauung, 1956. Editor: (Jonathan Edwards) Religious Affections, Vol. 2, 1959. Gen. editor, Yale edit. Works of Jonathan Edwards. Editorial bd. Monist, 1962—, Jour. Religious Studies, Philosophy East and West, Internat. Jour. for Philosophy of Religion, Jour. Chinese Philosophy. Home: 300 Ridgewood Ave Hamden CT 06517 Office: 1562 Yale Station New Haven CT 06520

SMITH, JOHN FRANCIS, educator, metallurgist; b. Kansas City, Kans., May 9, 1923; s. Peter Francis and Johanna (Spandle) S.; B.A., U. Mo. at Kansas City, 1948; Ph.D., Iowa State U., 1953; m. Evelyn Ann Ross, Sept. 1, 1947; children—Mark Francis, Letitia Ann. Mem. faculty Iowa State U., also staff Ames Lab. of Dept. Energy, 1953—, prof., 1962—, chmn. dept. metallurgy, 1966-70, chief div. metallurgy Ames lab., 1966-70; cons. in field, 1958—. Served as aviator USNR, 1942-46. Decorated Air medal (2). Mem. Am. Soc. Metals (past chmn. Des Moines chpt. 1957), Am. Crystallographic Assn., Brit. Inst. Metals, Am. Inst. Mining, Metall. and Petroleum Engrs., Am. Legion, Sigma Xi, Phi Lambda Upsilon, Phi Kappa Phi. Catholic. Elk. Author articles and book in field. Home: Rural Route 3 Ames IA 50010

SMITH, JOHN IVOR, sculptor; b. London, Eng., Jan. 28, 1927; s. Albert Sidney and Frances (Warrior) S.; came to Can., 1940, naturalized, 1950; B.S., McGill U., 1948; postgrad. Sch. Art and Design, Montreal (Que.) Mus. Fine Arts, 1952-55; 1 son, Fraser Matthew. Various positions No. Electric Co. Ltd., Montreal, 1950-66; asso. prof. fine arts Concordia U. (formed by Sir George Williams U. merger Loyola Coll. 1974), 1966—. One-man shows Isaacs Gallery, Toronto, 1965, 67, 69, 72, Marlborough-Godard Gallery, Montreal, 1970, Sir George Williams U., 1970; group shows Nat. Outdoor Sculpture, Ottawa, 1960, Exhbn. Contemporary Art, Vancouver, 1961, Nat. Gallery, Can., 1967, Expo '67, Montreal, Survey '70, Montreal, Canadian Sculpture, Paris, France, 1970; represented in permanent collections; major sculpture commns. Expo 67; asso. with Isaacs Gallery, Toronto, Ont., 1964—, Marlborough Godard Gallery, Montreal, 1969—. Can. Council sr. arts fellow 1967, 69, 73. Fellow Royal Can. Acad. Home: 727 Rue Principale Piedmont PQ J0R 1K0 Canada Office: Fine Arts Dept Henry Hall Bldg Concordia U 1455 Blvd de Maisonneuve Montreal PQ H3G 1M8 Canada

SMITH, JOHN J., mfg. co. exec.; b. Woodland, Mich., Dec. 9, 1911; s. Owen Benjamin and Ethyl (Katherman) S.; student Argubright Coll., 1929-31; C.P.A., 1940; m. Elinor S. Lamoreaux, Dec. 10, 1938. Sr. partner Smith & Skutt, C.P.A.'s, 1942-50; pres., gen. mgr., dir. Sparton Corp., now chmn.; chmn. Sparton Can. Ltd., London, Ont.; dir. Lake Odessa Machine Products, Inc. (Mich.), Kent Products, Inc., Grand Haven, City Bank Trust Co., Jackson., Northern States Fin. Corp., City Nat. Bank, Detroit, DU-WEL Metal Products, Inc., Energy Reserves Group, Inc., Wichita, Kan. Mem. Chief Execs. Forum, Mich. Assn. C.P.A.'s, Am. Inst. C.P.A.'s. Clubs: Detroit Athletic, Renaissance (Detroit). Home: 1839 S Walmont Jackson MI 49203 Office: Sparton Corp Jackson MI 49202

SMITH, JOHN JOSEPH, educator, textile co. exec.; b. Fall River, Mass., Feb. 11, 1913; s. John J. and Mabel E. (Reid) S.; B.S. in Chem. Engring., Tufts U., 1935; m. Mary C. Moson, Aug. 8, 1936; children—Nancy S. (Mrs. John Lee Lesher, Jr.), Robert J. With Chicopee Mfg. Corp., New Brunswick, N.J., 1935—, pres., 1959—, chmn., 1971-74; with Chicopee Mills, Inc., N.Y.C., 1959—, pres., 1960—, chmn., 1971-74; mem. exec. com., dir. Johnson & Johnson, New Brunswick, until 1976; prof. Fla. Atlantic U., Boca Raton. Mem. Am. Assn. Tech. Colorists and Chemists, Am. Chem. Soc. Home: 1225 S Ocean Blvd Delray Beach FL 33444

SMITH, JOHN LEE, JR., assn. exec.; b. Fairfax, Ala., Dec. 11, 1920; s. John Lee and Mae Celia (Smith) S.; A.B., Samford U., 1950; student New Orleans Bapt. Theol. Sem., 1950-51, 53; D.D., Ohio Christian Coll., 1967, Birmingham Bapt. Bible Coll., 1979; postgrad. Auburn U., 1956, Baylor U., 1972-73; LL.D., Nat. Christian U., 1974; m. Vivian Herrington, Aug. 15, 1942; children—Vicky Smith Hawkins, Joan Smith Wimberly, Jennifer Lee Smith Ruscilli. Owner, Smith's Grocery Co., Montgomery, Ala., 1945-47; ordained minister Bapt. Ch., 1947; pastor Dolomite Bapt. Ch., Birmingham, Ala., 1947-50, Elim Bapt. Ch., Brewton, Ala., 1950-51, 1st Bapt. Ch., Tallapoosa, Ga., 1951-52, 1st Bapt. Ch., Villa Rica, Ga., 1952-54, Fairfax, Ala., 1954-57, West End Bapt. Ch., Birmingham, 1957-59, Dalraida Bapt. Ch., Montgomery, 1959-66, 1st Bapt. Ch., Demopolis, Ala., 1966-69; asso. exec. dir. Ala. Council Alcohol Problems, Birmingham, 1969-70, exec. dir., 1970-78; tchr., dir. Bessemer Bapt. Inst., 1978—; v.p. Bessemer Bapt. Assn., 1977—, dir. missions, 1978—; exec. dir. Am. Council Alcohol Problems, Washington, 1972-74, sec., 1974—; tchr. Mercer U. extension, Carrollton, Ga., 1953-54, Samford U. extension, Fairfax, Ala., 1955-57; mem. bd. ministerial edn. Bapt. Ch., 1958-59, Christian Life Commn., 1959-60; pres. Bessemer Ministers Alliance, 1979—. Chmn., Marengo County Cancer Soc., 1967-68, Good News Ala. (Jefferson County), 1977-79, Gov.'s Commn. on Pornography, 1970-78, Nat. Temperance and Prohibition Council, 1973—, Nat. Coordinating Council on Drug Edn., 1972-78, Alcohol Drug Problems Assn. Am., 1972-78; exec. dir. Temperance Edn., Inc., Washington, 1972-74; trustee Internat. Reform Fedn., Washington, 1973-74; adv. bd. JCCEO, 1975—. Served to capt. USAAF, 1942-45; ETO. Mem. C. of C., Trident, Phi Kappa Phi. Mason. Contbr. profl. jours. Home: 608 Staffordshire Dr Birmingham AL 35226 Office: 1331 Fairfax Ave PO Box 298 Bessemer AL 35020

SMITH, JOHN LEWIS, JR., U.S. dist. judge; b. Washington, Sept. 20, 1912; s. John Lewis and Claribel (Cassin) S.; grad. Lawrenceville Sch., 1931; A.B. cum laude, Princeton, 1935; LL.B., Georgetown U., 1938, LL.M., 1939; m. Madeline Cotter, Oct. 3, 1940 (dec. 1967); children—John Lewis III, Madeline (Mrs. Lawrence G. Lynn), Joseph Cotter, Janet Ambler (Mrs. David Garabrant), Barbara Cassin (Mrs. Stephen Fennell); m. 2d, Louise Tompkins Parker, Feb. 15, 1974. Admitted to D.C. bar, 1938, also U.S. Supreme Ct.; asst. U.S. atty. D.C., 1940-46; pvt. practice, Washington, 1946-56; mem. D.C. Pub. Utilities Commn., 1956-57; asso. judge D.C. Ct. Gen. Sessions, 1957-59, chief judge, 1959-66; U.S. dist. judge U.S. Dist. Ct. D.C., 1966—. Chmn. Republican Vets Com. for D.C., 1952, Vets. Com. for Eisenhower-Nixon Inaugural, 1953, 57; pres. Rep. Club D.C., 1955-56. Trustee Boys Club Washington, 1965—; bd. dirs. D.C. chpt. A.R.C., 1957—, Washington Heart Assn., 1967—. Served to col. AUS, World War II. Decorated Army Commendation medal; recipient 1st scholarship prizes Georgetown U. Law Sch., 1936, 37, Princeton Class award, 1959, Georgetown U. Alumni Achievement award, 1960. Fellow Am. Bar Found.; mem. Am. Bar Assn., Bar Assn. D.C., Lawyers Club, The Barristers, Am. Judicature Soc., Mil. Order World Wars (gen. staff emeritus). Republican. Catholic. Clubs: Nat. Lawyers (founder mem.), Princeton, Vinson (Washington); Chevy Chase (Md.); Rehoboth Beach (Del.) Country. Home: 2700 Virginia Ave Washington DC 20037 Office: US Dist Ct Washington DC 20001

SMITH, JOHN LUCIAN, JR., beverage co. exec.; b. West Point, Miss., Oct. 24, 1918; s. John Lucian and Sara Eugenia (Cottrell) S.; B.C.S., U. Miss., 1940; m. Claire Davis, Aug. 6, 1953; children—Daniel Davis, Susan Peyton. With Coca-Cola Co., Atlanta, 1940-67, field sales mgr., 1957-61, pres., 1974-79, still dir.; pres. foods div. Coca-Cola Co., Houston, 1967-70; pres. Coca-Cola USA, Atlanta, 1971-74; chmn. bd. Coca-Cola Export Corp., 1976—; dir. Phillips Petroleum Co.; adv. dir. So. Ry. System. Nat. bd. dirs., v.p. Boys' Clubs Am.; trustee Spelman Coll.; mem. adv. bd. Scottish Rite Hosp. Mem. Am. Soc. Corporate Execs., Delta Kappa Epsilon. Clubs: Capital City, Univ. Yacht, Commerce, Piedmont Driving (Atlanta). Home: 3444 Tuxedo Rd NW Atlanta GA 30305 Office: PO Drawer 1734 Atlanta GA 30301

SMITH, JOHN STEVEN, business exec.; b. Winchester, Ont., Can., June 6, 1936; s. Bert and Catherine (Fader) S.; diploma Smiths Falls (Ont.) Collegiate Inst., 1952; m. Mary Lowe Petrie, Apr. 2, 1960. With Royal Bank Can., 1953-57; chief clk. acctg. Can. Oil Companies Ltd., 1957-61; with Russelsteel Ltd., 1961-71, controller, 1969-71; mgr. corp. acctg., then mgr. fin. and adminstrn. Hugh Russel, Inc., Toronto, 1971-75, treas., 1976—. Mem. Cert. Gen. Accountants Assn., Tax Execs. Inst., Can. Tax Found. Club: Port Credit Yacht. Home: 18 Goswell Rd Islington ON M9B 1W6 Canada Office: 8 King St E Suite 1500 Toronto ON M5C 1B5 Canada

SMITH, JOHN SYLVESTER, coll. pres.; b. Phila., Aug. 18, 1914; student Muhlenberg Coll., 1932; B.S., Temple U. Tchrs. Coll., 1937; S.T.B. with honors, 1938; M.A., Drew U., 1940, Ph.D., 1948; postdoctoral study, Columbia; m. Margaret Viola Giebel, Jan. 7, 1939; children—Roy Harold (dec.), Barbara Lynn (Mrs. Thomas Knowles). Ordained to ministry Methodist Ch., 1938; pastor in Bklyn., 1943-46; Protestant chaplain Bklyn. State Hosp., later N.Y.N.G., 1943-46; asst. to pres. Washington Coll., Chestertown, Md., 1946-51; with Ia. Wesleyan Coll., 1951-53, head dept. philosophy and religion, chmn. div. humanities, then dean of coll.; head dept. philosophy and religion, adminstrv. adviser to pres. Bethune- Cookman Coll., Daytona Beach, Fla., 1953, dean, 1953-54, dean and registrar, 1954-58; dean Dillard U., New Orleans, 1958-59; v.p., univ. dean Ill. Wesleyan U., 1959-62; chmn. div. humanities Findlay Coll., 1962-66; acad. dean, v.p. Lake City (Fla.) Jr. Coll. and Forest Ranger Sch., 1966-67; pres. Fla. Keys Coll., Key West, 1967-79; pastor Presbyn. Ch. of the Keys, Marathon, Fla., 1979—. Home: 277 89 St Ocean Marathon FL 33050

SMITH, JOHN WAYNE, librarian; b. Barberton, Ohio, Sept. 26, 1936; s. Dorsie B. and Edna Frances (Cheadle) S.; B.B.A., Tex. Western Coll., El Paso, 1964; M.A. in Librarianship, U. Denver, 1965. With Sears, Roebuck & Co., 1960-62; loan librarian Tex. Western Coll. Library, 1965-67; with El Paso Pub. Library, 1967—, dir., 1967—; cons. Research Assos; mem. Bd. Tex. Library Examiners, 1971—. Adviser to Mayor El Paso on Community Renewal Project, 1970; adv. com. Parents Without Partners, 1970; bd. dirs. El Paso Arts Council, 1969-71. Served with USNR, 1956-60. Mem. Am., Tex. (chmn. dist. VI 1971, pub. libraries div. 1971-72), Border Regional (pres. 1969, Librarian of Year award 1976), Southwestern library assns., Tex. Municipal Librarians Assn. (pres. 1970-71), Arabian Horse Registry Am., Internat., Border (chmn. publicity com. 1969-70, exhibitors banquet 1971, pres. 1973) Arabian horse assns., Asociacion Mexicana de Bibliotecarios. Clubs: Ditch Riders Internat.; El Paso Riding and Driving (treas. 1970-71, dir. 1971-72). Contbr. Ency. Americana. Office: El Paso Public Library 501 N Oregon St El Paso TX 79901*

SMITH, JONATHAN LESLIE, investment cons.; b. Colfax, Wash., Mar. 25, 1940; s. Jasper A. and Emily L. (Lobdell) S.; A.B., Stanford, 1962; m. Elinor Johnston, May 20, 1967; children—Jonathan Quincy, Nicholas Ogden. Partner, Lehman Brothers, N.Y.C., 1964-73; sr. v.p. Mitchell, Hutchins, N.Y.C., 1973—. Mem. Com. for N.Y. Philharmonic, 1975-78. Treas., trustee, mem. exec. com., chmn. investment com. Spelman Coll.; trustee, mem. investment com. Morehouse Coll., Atlanta U. Served to lt. USNR, 1962-64. Clubs: Bond of N.Y., Madison Sq. Garden; Cooperstown Country. Home: 1105 Park Ave New York NY 10028 Office: 1 Battery Park Plaza New York NY 10004

SMITH, JOSEPH ALAND, cons., design, constrn. mgmt. and appraisal services co. exec.; b. Lava Hot Springs, Idaho, Mar. 26, 1930; s. Collis Romer and Verda (Aland) S.; B.A., Coll. of Idaho, Caldwell, 1952; M.B.A., Harvard U., 1956; m. Joanne C. Goul, Aug. 11, 1950; children—Mark B., Eric M., Stephanie A. With systems group TRW, Inc., 1956-68; with Bank Bldg. Corp., St. Louis, 1968—, dir., 1968—, pres., chief exec. officer, 1973-76, chmn. bd., chief exec. officer, 1976—. Trustee Mo. Baptist Hosp., St. Louis, Mo. Bapt. Coll., St. Louis; mem. president's council St. Louis U.; bd. dirs. YMCA Greater St. Louis, Jr. Achievement Mississipi Valley. Served to lt. (j.g.) USNR, 1952-54. Office: 1130 Hampton Ave Saint Louis MO 63139

SMITH, JOSEPH BENJAMIN, phonograph record co. exec.; b. Chelsea, Mass., Jan. 26, 1928; s. Philip and Lillian Esther (Schlafman) S.; B.A., Yale, 1950; m. Dione Greenstone, Aug. 25, 1957; children—Jeffrey Duke, Julie. Radio broadcaster in Va., Pa. and Mass., 1950-61; with Warner Bros. Records, Burbank, Calif., 1961-75, pres., 1971-75; chmn. bd. Elektra/Asylum Records, 1975—; dir. GM Records, WEA Distbg. Co. Pres. community relations for rec. industry, 1968—. Served with AUS, 1945-47. Recipient Industry Exec. of Year award Nat. Assn. Record Merchandisers, 1975; Promotion Exec. of Year award Bill Gavin Report, 1963, 64, 65; named Man of Year, Anti-Defamation League, 1973; Man of Year, Record Industry Promotion Assn., 1969; Exec. of Yr., Radio Broadcasters, 1976. Mem. Country Music Assn. (v.p.). Clubs: Variety (dir.), Hillcrest Country. Office: 962 N La Cienega Blvd Los Angeles CA 90069*

SMITH, JOSEPH EDWARD, mfg. co. exec.; b. Monroe, N.Y., July 12, 1923; s. Howard A. and Emily A. Smith; student Princeton U., 1941-42; m. Elizabeth Bennett, Sept. 6, 1947; 1 son, Joseph Edward. With Investors Diversified Service, Mpls., 1954-56, Bear Stearns & Co., N.Y.C., 1957-64; fin. cons., 1964-68; with Singer Co., N.Y.C., 1968—, sr. v.p., 1974—, chief fin. officer, 1975—, vice chmn. for policy and programs, 1978—, also dir.; dir., mem. exec. com. Penn Central Corp.; dir. Mass. Mut. Corp. Investors. Served with U.S. Army, 1942-45. Clubs: N.Y. Yacht, Rumson Country, Edgartown Yacht, Indian Harbor Yacht. Home: 16 Rockwood Ln Greenwich CT 06830 Office: 30 Rockefeller Plaza New York NY 10020

SMITH, JOSEPH HENRY, lawyer, educator; b. N.Y.C., Sept. 4, 1913; s. Adolph Q. and Agnes (Buchner) S.; A.B., Yale U., 1935; LL.B., Columbia U., 1938; student Inst. Hist. Research U. London, 1938-39; m. Edith C. Stenberg, Jan. 5, 1946; 1 dau., Linda E. (Mrs. Donald G. Price, Jr.). Research asst. Found. for Research in Legal History, Columbia Law Sch., 1938-42; admitted to N.Y. bar, 1940; pvt. practice, N.Y.C., 1946-61; prof. N.Y. Law Sch., 1951-61; prof. Columbia Law Sch., 1961-67, George Welwood Murray prof. legal history, 1967—. Chmn. Found. for Research in Legal History, 1961—; mem. adv. com. Am. Bar Found. Project in Legal History, 1966-77; chmn. com. for Littleton-Griswold Fund, Am. Hist. Assn., 1967-69, mem. com., 1973—; mem. editorial adv. bd. Studies in Legal History, Harvard U. Press, 1970-76, U. N.C. Press, 1977—; spl. asst. to atty. gen. U.S., 1965; chmn. Seminar on 18th Century European Culture, 1977-79. Served with USNR, 1942-45. Mem. Assn. Am. Law Schs. (chmn. legal history sect. 1973), Am. Soc. for Legal History (treas. 1972-73, v.p. 1974-75, pres. 1976-77, dir. 1979—), Selden Soc., Am. Bar Assn. Author: Appeals to the Privy Council from the American Plantations, 1950; Colonial Justice in Western Massachusetts: 1639-1702, 1961; Cases and Materials on the Development of Legal Institutions, 1965; editor (with P.A. Crowl) Court Records of Prince Georges County, Maryland, 1696-1699, 1964. Co-editor Law Practice of Alexander Hamilton, 1974—. Home: 155 Beech St Floral Park NY 11001 Office: Law Sch Bldg Columbia U New York NY 10027

SMITH, JOSEPH JAMES, chemist; b. Bklyn., Apr. 6, 1921; s. Alexander and Amelia (Sax) S.; B.S. in Chemistry and Philosophy, Fordham U., 1943; D.Sc. (hon.), W.Va. State U., 1975, Marshall U., Huntington, W.Va., 1976; m. Rosemary A. Murray, Aug. 10, 1946; children—Joellen, Stephen, Beverly, Virginia, Christopher, Alan, Margaret. With Union Carbide Corp., 1943—, dir. research and devel. for chems. and plastics, S. Charleston, W.Va., 1967—, for polyolefins, 1967-70, for coatings, 1970—, for chem. spltys., 1973-75, exploratory research, 1975-77, for environ. research, 1977—; dir. Belgrove Savs. & Loan Assn., Harrison, N.J., 1955-60. Founder Nomahegan Swim Club, Westfield, N.J., 1962, pres., 1962-63, bd. govs., 1962-66. Named High Sch. Swim Coach of Year, W.Va. Sports Writers, 1970, 72-74. Mem. Am. Chem. Soc. (chmn. regional meeting 1977; Student award 1943), Greater Charleston Swim Assn. Roman Catholic. Club: Charleston Tennis. Author articles infrared spectroscopy, polymer molecular structure, catalysis, coatings, research mgmt., innovation process. Home: 1580 Virginia St E Charleston WV 25311 Office: Union Carbide Tech Center South Charleston WV 25303

SMITH, JOSEPH LECONTE, JR., educator; b. Macon, Ga., Sept. 4, 1929; s. Joseph LeConte and Margaret (Blair) S.; B.S. in Mech. Engring., Ga. Inst. Tech., 1952, M.S., 1954; D.Sc., Mass. Inst. Tech., 1959; m. Sara Luverne Floyd, Mar. 21, 1953; children—Catherine LeConte, Suzanne Blair, Sara Elizabeth. Faculty, Mass. Inst. Tech., Cambridge, 1955—, asst. prof. mech. engring., 1958-63, asso. prof., 1963-69, prof., 1969—, prof. charge Cryogenic Engring. Lab., 1964—. Served to 1st lt., Signal Corps, U.S. Army, 1953-55. Recipient George W. McCarty-ANAK award Ga. Inst. Tech. Alumni Assn., 1964. Mem. Am. Soc. Mech. Engring., Sigma Xi. Home: 28 Powers Rd Concord MA 01742 Office: 41-204 Mass Inst Tech Cambridge MA 02139

SMITH, JOSEPH NEWTON SMITH, III, architect; b. Jacksonville, Fla., July 4, 1925; s. Joseph Newton, Jr. and Oneal (Kemp) S.; B.S., Ga. Inst. Tech., 1948, B.Arch., 1949; m. Gloria Bevis, Aug. 24, 1946; 1 son, Gordon Kemp. Designer and/or draftsman archtl. firms in Miami, Fla., 1949-56; propr. Joseph N. Smith, Architech., Miami, 1956-63; partner firm Smith, Polychrone and Wolfcale, Atlanta, 1966-69; gen. cons. architecture, 1969—; mem. faculty Sch. Architecture, Ga. Inst. Tech., 1963—, prof. architecture, asst. dir. sch., 1971—, asst. dean, 1977—. Served to lt. (j.g.) USNR, 1943-46. Recipient Birch Burdette Long Meml. award Archtl. League N.Y., 1956; award merit S. Atlantic region AIA for Key Biscayne (Fla.) Presbyn. Ch., 1964, for Friendship Center, low income housing, Atlanta, 1970; named Honored Artist of Year, Young Women of Arts, Atlanta, 1970. Fellow AIA. Presbyterian. Home: 2466 Ridgewood Rd NW Atlanta GA 30318 Office: Coll Architecture Ga Inst Tech Atlanta GA 30332

SMITH, JOSEPH VICTOR, educator; b. Crich, Eng., July 30, 1928; B.A. (Hons.), Cambridge (Eng.) U., 1948, M.A., Ph.D., 1951; m. Brenda Florence Wallis; children—Virginia Ann, Susan Hilary. Fellow Carnegie Inst., Washington, 1951-54; demonstrator U. Cambridge, 1954-56; asst. prof. Pa. State U., 1956-57, asso. prof., 1957-60; prof. mineralogy and crystallography U. Chgo., 1960-77, Louis Block prof. phys. scis., 1977—; cons. Linde div. Union Carbide, 1956—; editor X-Ray Powder Data File, 1958-69. Fellow Royal Soc., Mineral Soc. Am. (award 1961, pres. 1972), Geol. Soc. Am., Am. Geophys. Union; mem. Mineral. Soc. London, Am. Crystallographic Assn., Meteoritical Soc., Electron Probe Analysis Soc. Am. Contbr. numerous articles in field to profl. jours. and encys. Home: 5455 S Dorchester Ave Chicago IL 60615

SMITH, JOSEPH WILSON, lawyer; b. Phenix City, Ala., Feb. 12, 1917; s. Ernest Clifford and Essie (Baker) S.; LL.B., U. Ala., 1941; m. Lenora West Coghlan, July 17, 1943; children-Sydney Bowen Smith Smith, Lenora West Smith Gregory, Joseph Wilson, Walter Clifford II. Admitted to Ala. bar, 1941; practice in Phenix City, 1946—; partner firm Smith & Smith, 1946-79; sr. partner firm Smith, Smith & Morgan, 1980—; legal counsel Ala. C. of C., 1969—. Dir., Phenix-Girard Bank. Mem. Ala. Edn. Commn., 1957-58, Phenix City Bd. Edn., 1950-60; chmn. Chattahoochee Valley Airport Commn., 1969—. Mem. Ala. Senate, 1954-58, 62-66, Ala. Ho. of Reps., 1958-62; del. Democratic Nat. Conv., 1956. Served with AUS, 1941-46. Named Young Man of Year, Phenix City Jr. C. of C., 1947; Outstanding Legislator, Ala. Press Assn., 1959. Mem. Am., Ala. bar assns., Am. Legion, Assn. U.S. Army, Omicron Delta Kappa, Phi Alpha Delta, Pi Kappa Alpha. Democrat. Methodist. Home: 3301 14th Ave Phenix City AL 36867 Office: Phenix-Girard Bldg Phenix City AL 36867

SMITH, JOSEPHINE WOOLLEY, advt. agy. exec.; b. Findlay, Ohio, Mar. 15, 1934; d. Walton Douglas and Charlotte Josephine (Bente) Woolley; B.A., Sarah Lawrence Coll., 1954; m. Lawrence Sophian, June 22, 1954; children—Celia, Catherine. Advt. copywriter Batten, Barton, Durstine & Osborn, 1954-62; copy supr. Ogilvy & Mather, N.Y.C., 1962-70, v.p., 1970-73, creative dir., 1973, sr. v.p., 1974—. Office: 2 E 48th St New York City NY 10017

SMITH, JOSHUA LAWRENCE, community coll. pres.; b. Boston, Dec. 11, 1934; s. Joshua and Lorina A. Smith; B.A., Boston U., 1955; M.A. in Teaching, Harvard U., 1959, Ed.D., 1967. Program officer Ford Found., 1970-74; prof. edn., then dean Sch. Edn., City Coll. N.Y., 1974-77; acting pres. Borough of Manhattan Community Coll., pres., 1978—; bd. dirs. Research Found., CUNY, 1978—, N.Y. Statewide Com. Equal Ednl. Opportunities, 1978—; trustee Nat. Humanities Faculty, 1974—, Museums Collaborative, Inc., 1974—, Public Edn. Assn., 1974—; adv. council regents com. N.Y.C. Public Schs. Project, 1977—. Bd. deacons Riverside Ch., N.Y.C., 1976—. Served to capt. USAF, 1955-58. Recipient award appreciation So. Regional Council, 1974, Joshua L. Amith award established, 1974. Life mem. NAACP (co-chmn. edn. com., dir. Mid-Manhattan br. 1979—), ACLU. Author papers, reports in field. Home: 315 W 70th St New York NY 10023 Office: 1633 Broadway New York NY 10019

SMITH, JULIAN CLEVELAND, JR., educator; b. Westmount, Que., Can., Mar. 10, 1919 (parents Am. citizens); s. Julian Cleveland and Bertha (Alexander) S.; B.Chemistry, Cornell U., 1941, Chem. Engr., 1942; m. Joan Elsen, June 1, 1946; children—Robert Elsen, Diane Louise Smith Brook, Brian Richard. Chem. engr. E. I. duPont de Nemours and Co., Inc., 1942-46; mem. faculty Cornell U., 1946—, prof. chem. engring., 1953—, dir. continuing engring. edn., 1965-71, asso. dir. Sch. Chem. Engring., 1973-75, dir., 1975—; vis. lectr. U. Edinburgh, 1971-72; cons. to govt. and industry, 1957—; UNESCO cons. Universidad de Oriente Venezuela, 1975. Fellow Am. Inst. Chem. Engrs.; mem. Am. Chem. Soc., Soc. Chem. Industry, Sigma Xi, Tau Beta Pi, Phi Kappa Phi, Alpha Delta Phi. Clubs: Ithaca Country, Statler (Ithaca). Author: Unit Operations of Chemical Engineering (with W. L. McCabe), 3d edit., 1976; also articles; sect. editor: Perry's Chemical Engineers Handbook, 1963. Home: 711 The Parkway Ithaca NY 14850

SMITH, K(ERMIT) WAYNE, corp. exec.; b. Newton, N.C., Sept. 15, 1938; s. Harold Robert and Hazel K. (Smith) S.; B.A., Wake Forest U., 1960; M.A., (Danforth fellow, Woodrow Wilson fellow), Princeton U., 1962, Ph.D., 1964; postgrad. U. So. Calif., 1965; m. Audrey M. Kennedy, Dec. 19, 1958; 1 son, Stuart W. Instr., Princeton U., 1963; asst. prof. econs. and polit. sci. U.S. Mil. Acad., 1963-66; spl. asst. to asst. sec. def. for systems analysis, Washington, 1966-69; program mgr. def. studies RAND Corp., Santa Monica, Calif., 1969-70; dir. program analysis Nat. Security Council, Washington, 1970-72; group v.p. planning Dart Industries, Los Angeles, 1972-73, group pres. resort devel. group, 1973-76; exec. v.p. Washington Group, Inc., 1976-77; mng. partner Coopers & Lybrand, Washington, 1977—; cons. in field. Mem. vis. com. Brookings Instn., Washington, 1971—; vice-chmn. bd. visitors Wake Forest U., 1974-77, chmn., 1977—. Served to capt. U.S. Army, 1963-66. Mem. Am. Polit. Sci. Assn., Am. Econ. Assn., Council Fgn. Relations, Internat. Inst. Strategic Studies, Am. Mgmt. Assn., Phi Beta Kappa, Omicron Delta Kappa, Kappa Sigma. Methodist. Clubs: Washington Country, Internat., Capitol Hill. Author: How Much is Enough? Shaping the Defense Program, 1961-69, 1971; contbr. articles to profl. jours. Office: 1800 M St NW Washington DC 20036*

SMITH, KATE (KATHRYN ELIZABETH), singer; b. Washington, May 1, 1907. Singer in public since early years; stage debut in Honeymoon Lane, 1926; appeared in road show Hit the Deck; co-starred in Broadway mus. Flying High; made debut on radio in 1931 with own show Kate Smith Sings; helped write lyrics for theme song When The Moon Comes Over The Mountain; star radio program Kate Smith Speaks, 1938-51; introduced song God Bless America, 1938; TV debut in 1950, starred in own show, 1950-54; guest appearances on Ed Sullivan Show, 1955, Jack Paar Show, 1964, Donny and Marie Osmond Show, 1975; TV spls. include The Stars and Stripes Show, 1976, Women of the Year, 1976; appeared in concert at Carnegie Hall, 1963; appeared in numerous motion pictures; made numerous records; introduced over 700 songs which made the Hit Parade, 19 of them have sold over a million copies. Address: care Katz-Gallin Entertainments 9255 Sunset Blvd Suite 1115 Los Angeles CA 90069

SMITH, KEITH A., artist; b. Tipton, Ind., May 20, 1938; s. Vern and Edna (Andrews) S.; B.A., Sch. Art Inst. Chgo., 1967; M.S. in Photography, Ill. Inst. Tech., 1968. Instr. photography UCLA, 1970, Art Inst. Chgo., 1971-75; coordinator printmaking Visual Studies Workshop, Rochester, N.Y., 1975—; one man exhbns. include: Gallerie Civica D'Arte Moderne, Turin, Italy, 1973, Mus. Modern Art, N.Y.C., 1975, Lichtroppen, Agen, W.Ger., 1976, In a Plain Brown Wrapper, Chgo., 1979; group exhbns. include: Mus. Modern Art, 1975; Santa Barbara Mus. Art, 1979, Art Inst. Chgo., 1979; represented in permanent collections: Mus. Modern Art, N.Y.C., Nat. Gallery Can., Gallerie Civica Moderne Art, Torino, Italy. Guggenheim fellow, 1972; Nat. Endowment Arts grantee, 1978. Author: When I Was Two, 1977. Home: 22 Cayuga St Rochester NY 14620 Office: 31 Prince St Rochester NY 14607

SMITH, KENDRICK, fund raising cons.; b. N.Y.C., Jan. 6, 1922; s. Walter Murray and Doramont (Kendrick) S.; B.A., Amherst Coll., 1943; m. Margaret Ross Gray Sturtevant, Nov. 26, 1966; 1 child, K. Tasker; stepchildren—Deborah R. Sturtevant, Thomas C. Sturtevant, Jr., Kristin F. Sturtevant, Susan G. Sturtevant. With Kersting Brown & Co., N.Y.C., 1946-63, v.p., 1955-63, sec., 1960-63, also dir.; cons. fundraising, Wayland, Mass., 1963—; owner Info. Research Service, Execs. in Edn., search orgn.; guest lectr. Harvard U. Sch. Edn., 1975; trustee Beaver Country Day Sch., 1973-75; v.p., bd. dirs. Mass. Children's Lobby, 1975-76; judge Lilly Endowment Competition, 1976, 78. Served as cryptographer USAAF, 1943-46; ETO. Author: Boston-How You Can Plan a Perfect Visit, 1979. Home and Office: 12 Cole Rd Wayland MA 01778

SMITH, KENNETH, bass-baritone; b. Leeds, Eng., Aug. 26, 1922; s. Thomas Henry and Ada (Sedgewick) S.; came to U.S., 1924, naturalized, 1931; student Manhattan Sch. Music, 1945-46, N.Y. Coll. Music, 1946-49; m. Marguerite Prentice, Mar. 3, 1945; 1 son, Eric. N.Y.C. debut NBC-TV Opera Down in the Valley, 1950; with New Eng. Opera Co., 1950; concert debut Town Hall, 1951; with Central City Opera, 1953, Chgo. Lyric Opera, 1955-58, N.Y.C. Opera, 1956, 60, Washington Opera, 1959, also festivals various cities; appeared Am. premiere Billy Budd, NBC-TV, 1951, Gloriana, Cin. May Festival, 1956, Tempest, N.Y. C. Opera Co., 1956, War and Peace, NBC-TV, 1957, world premiere Life of the Mission, San Antonio, 1959; debut with Met. Opera Co., 1963, San Francisco Opera, 1966; with N.Y. Philharmonic, symphony orchs. various cities U.S., also Symphony of the Air; recordings Columbia, RCA-Victor, Concert Hall Soc. records; world premiere opera Cyrano, U. Colo., 1965; world premiere Carry Nation, 1966, My Heart's in the Highlands, Nat. Ednl. TV, 1970; 1st performance with L'Orqueta Sinfoniea Nacional de Venezuela, Caracas, 1968; prof. voice, chmn. voice dept. U. Kans., 1965—, chmn. dept. performance, 1976. Served from 2d lt. to 1st lt., USAAF, 1942-45. Decorated D.F.C., Air medal with clusters. Mem. Actor's Equity, AFTRA, Am. Guild Mus. Artists, Screen Actor's Guild, Pi Kappa Lambda. Home: 514 Pioneer Rd Lawrence KS 66044

SMITH, KENNETH ACTON, mineral resources co. exec.; b. LaCrosse, Wis., Dec. 30, 1921; s. George Kenneth and Mildred Amelia (Acton) S.; B.S. in Chem. Engring., U. Wis., 1944, M.S. in Chem. Engring., 1947, Ph.D. (Wis. Alumni Research Found. fellow), 1948; m. Ruth Vivian Durkee, June 26, 1948; children—Edgar Acton, Harry Kenneth, Arthur Brian. Engr. devel. dept. Sinclair Oil Co., 1944-46, div. head research and devel., 1948-60, mgr. corp. computer services, 1960-64; v.p., jt. venture coordinator Sinclair Petrochems., N.Y.C., 1964-68; mgr. coordination chem. affiliates ARCO Chem. co. div. Atlantic Richfield Co., Phila., 1969-73, v.p., gen. mgr., 1973-77; v.p. environment, health and tech. Anaconda Co., N.Y.C., 1977—, also dir.; v.p. tech. Anaconda Industries, 1978—; instr. chem. engring. U. Wis., 1947; dir. ARCO Polymers Inc., 1973-77. Mem. Am. Inst. Chem. Engrs., Am. Chem. Soc., Am. Petroleum Inst., Indsl. Research Inst., Soc. Chem. Industry, Research Mgmt. Group Phila., Am. Soc. for Metals, Am. Mining Congress, NAM, Metall. Soc. of AIME, Colo. Sch. Mines Research Inst., Newcomen Soc. N.Am., Sigma Xi, Phi Lambda Upsilon, Alpha Chi Sigma, Tau Beta Pi. Contbr. articles to profl. jours. Patentee in field. Home: 1997 Oak Leaf Ln Littleton CO 80121 Office: 555 17th St Denver CO 80217

SMITH, KENNETH ALAN, chem. engr., educator; b. Winthrop, Mass., Nov. 28, 1936; s. James Edward and Alice Gertrude (Walters) S.; S.B., Mass. Inst. Tech., 1958, S.M., 1959, Sc.D., 1962; postgrad. Cambridge (Eng.) U., 1964-65; m. Ambia Marie Olsson, Oct. 14, 1961; children—Kirsten Heather, Edward Eric, Andrew Ian Beaumont, Thurston Garrett. Asst. prof. chem. engring. Mass. Inst. Tech., 1961-67, asso. prof., 1967-71, prof., 1971—, acting head dept., 1976-77; cons. chem. and oil cos. NSF predoctoral fellow, NSF postdoctoral fellow, 1964-65. Mem. Am. Inst. Chem. Engrs., Am. Chem. Soc., AAAS, Sigma Xi, Phi Lambda Upsilon, Tau Beta Pi. Episcopalian. Home: 32 School St Manchester MA 01944 Office: Mass Inst Tech Bldg 66 Cambridge MA 02139

SMITH, KENNETH HUGO, holding co. exec.; b. Winnipeg, Man., Can., May 6, 1917; s. William Alfred and Janie (Hugo) S.; student U. Man., 1939-42; m. Annie Jean Arthur, July 17, 1943; children—Lynda (Mrs. Larry Marshall), Robert Barry, Heather Anne, Roger Kenneth, Craig Arthur. With Dept. Nat. Revenue Taxation Div., Hamilton, Ont., Can., 1946-51; with Eddy Forest Products Ltd. (formerly KVP Co.), v.p., dir., 1969; asst. to v.p. finance George Weston Ltd., Toronto, Ont., 1969-70, sec., 1970—, v.p., 1977—, also officer and dir. serveral subsidiaries. Served with RCAF, 1942-45. Mem. Fin. Execs. Inst., Fin. Execs. Inst. Can. (pres. 1979), Tax Execs. Inst., Inst. Chartered Accountants Ont., Inst. Chartered Accountants Man., Canadian Inst. Chartered Accountants. Mem. United Ch. Can. Home: 1762 Valentine Gardens Mississauga ON Canada Office: 22 St Clair Ave E Toronto M4T 2S7 Canada

SMITH, KENNETH JUDSON, JR., chemist, educator; b. Raleigh, N.C., Sept. 4, 1930; s. Kenneth Judson and Irene (Strickland) S.; A.B., East Carolina U., 1957; M.A., Duke U., 1959, Ph.D., 1961; m. Dorothy Margaret Ratcliffe, Mar. 6, 1953; children—Patricia Lynne Smith Pittman, Pamela Jean. Research chemist Chemstrand Research Center, Durham, N.C., 1961-65, sr. research chemist, 1965-68; asst. prof. polymer research SUNY Coll. Environ. Sci. and Forestry, Syracuse, 1968-70, asso. prof., 1970-73, prof., 1973—, asst. dir. Polymer Research Center, 1971-79, acting dir., 1979—, dir. Organic Materials Sci. Program, 1971-75, chmn. dept. chemistry, 1972—; vis. prof. Instituto di Chimica Industriale, U. Genoa (Italy), 1979; cons. U.S. Army Materials and Mechanics Research Center, Watertown, Mass., 1973, 75. Mem. adv. council Syracuse Met. Transp. Council; mem. adv. bd. confs. in polymer sci. and tech. SUNY, New Paltz, 1978—. Served with USMC, 1951-54. Mem. Am. Chem. Soc. (dir. Syracuse sect. 1977-79, chmn. 1978, councilor 1979—), Am. Inst. Chemists, AAAS, Soc. Plastics Engrs., Am. Chem. Soc., Sigma Xi, Phi Lambda Upsilon, Kappa Delta Pi. Contbr. articles to profl. jours. Home: 108 Scottholm Blvd Syracuse NY 13224

SMITH, KENNETH MYERS, mfg. exec.; b. Sacramento, Jan. 3, 1920; s. Hervey G. and Hazel S. (Myers) S.; student St. Mary's U., Moraga, Calif., 1943, Calif. Poly. Coll., 1944; m. Rosemary Louise Mullen, May 9, 1953; children—Carole K., Suzette C. With Consol. Vultee Aircraft Corp./Convair-Gen. Dynamics Corp., 1939-62, corp. v.p. mktg., 1961-62; v.p. mktg. Consol. Electrodynamics Corp./Bell & Howell Co., 1962-65; v.p., gen. mgr. Aero Comdr. div. Rockwell-Standard Corp., 1965-66; pres. Mgmt. Enterprises, Inc., Oklahoma City, 1966-67; pres., also chief exec. officer Windecker Research, Inc., Midland, Tex., 1967-70; dep. adminstr. FAA, Washington, 1970-72; exec. v.p. E-Systems, Inc., Dallas, 1972-73,

77—, pres. Aircraft Systems Group, Majors Field, Greenville, Tex., 1973-77; exec. v.p. E-Systems, Inc., Dallas, 1977—. Mem. Nat. Security Indsl. Standard (v.p. S.W. region), Nat. Aero. Assn. (v.p., bd.), Air Force Assn., Assn. U.S. Army, Navy League, N.A.M., Am. Inst. Aeros. and Astronautics, Newcomen Soc. N.Am. Mason (Shriner), Rotarian, Assn. of Old Crows. Address: E-Systems Inc PO Box 226030 Dallas TX 75266

SMITH, KENNETH WRIGHT, mfg. co. exec.; b. Newark, Jan. 11, 1916; s. S. Leroy and Irene (Blair) S.; A.B. cum laude, Wheaton (Ill.) Coll., 1937; m. Harriet Barr, Apr. 8, 1938 (dec. Dec. 1975); 1 son, Barry Hamilton; m. 2d, Betty Brohm, May 29, 1976. With Dun & Bradstreet, N.Y.C., 1937-49, Peerless Photo Engraving Co., N.Y.C., 1949-50, Qualitone Press, N.Y.C., 1950-51; v.p. Dade Bros., Mineola, N.Y., 1951-53; pres. Robert Hammond Inc., Venice, Calif., 1953-57; v.p. Field Mfg. Co., El Segundo, Calif., 1957-60; adminstrv. v.p. Security-Columbian Banknote Co., N.Y.C., 1960-65; exec. v.p. U.S. Banknote Corp., N.Y.C., 1965-66, pres., 1966-73, also dir., spl. rep., 1973-76; pres. Corinthian Services, Inc. (doing bus. as Ensign Yachts), Ft. Lauderdale, Fla., 1977—; pres., dir. Chemfilters Ltd. (Can.), Gen. Protein Products, Ltd.; pres., dir. Inorganic Resin Mfg. Co., Inc., IRMCO, Ltd. (Can.); pres. Rolmor Press div., Security-Columbian Banknote Co. div., Security-Columbian-New Eng. div., Twentieth Century-Hamilton div.; pres., dir. U.S. Technical Devels. of Brazil, Inc.; dir. U.S. Banknote Corp. Internat., U.S. Banknote do Brasil, Valcometrix, Inc., Societa Nebitype, S.p.A., Italy. Bd. dirs. Neuroscis. Found., Boston, Camp Berea, Bristol, N.H. Clubs: Sky (N.Y.C.); Indian Harbor Yacht (Greenwich). Home: 936 Intracoastal Dr Suite 15E Fort Lauderdale FL 33304

SMITH, KEVIN MALCOLM, chemist, educator; b. Birmingham, England, Mar. 15, 1942; s. Michael and Doris (Hinley) S.; came to U.S., 1977; B.Sc., U. Liverpool, Eng., 1964, Ph.D., 1967, D.Sc., 1977; m. Josette Madeleine O'Shea, Aug. 14, 1965; children—Kimberley Deborah, Juliette Vanessa. Fellow, Harvard U., 1967-69; lectr. organic chemistry U. Liverpool, 1969-77; prof. chemistry U. Calif., 1977—; cons. Palmer Research Co., U.K., Elsevier Publishing Co., Amsterdam. Recipient Leverhulme prize, 1964; Parke-Davis award, 1967; Fulbright award, 1967-69; Corday-Morgan medallist, prizewinner Chem. Soc. London, 1976. Fellow Royal Inst. Chemistry, Chem. Soc. London; mem. Am. Chem. Soc. Contbr. articles in field to profl. jours. Office: Department of Chemistry University of California Davis CA 95616

SMITH, LACEY BALDWIN, educator, historian, author; b. Princeton, N.J., Oct. 3, 1922; s. E. Baldwin and Ruth (Hall) S.; B.S., Bowdoin Coll., 1946, Litt.D., 1977; M.A., Princeton, 1949, Ph.D., 1951; m. Jean Elizabeth Reeder, June 24, 1961; children—MacAllister Baldwin, Dennison Baldwin, Katherine Chandler Baldwin. Instr., Princeton, 1951-53; asst. prof. Mass. Inst. Tech., 1953-55; mem. faculty Northwestern U., 1955—, prof. history, 1962—, chmn. dept., 1974-77. Mem. Ill. Humanities Council, 1978—. Served with USAAF, 1943-46. Fulbright scholar, 1949-50; Fulbright sr. research scholar, 1963-64; Guggenheim fellow, 1963-64; Nat. Endowment for the Humanities sr. scholar, 1973-74. Fellow Royal Hist. Soc. Fellow Royal Soc. Lit.; mem. Am. Hist. Assn., Conf. Brit. Studies (pres. 1977—). Author: Tudor Prelates and Politics, 1953; A Tudor Tragedy, the Life and Times of Catherine Howard, 1961; This Realm of England, 1399-1689, 1966; The Elizabethan Epic, 1966; Henry VIII: The Mask of Royalty, 1971; Elizabeth Tudor: Portrait of a Queen, 1975; bd. editors Am. Hist. Rev., 1967-72, mem. council, 1979—. Home: 225 Laurel Ave Wilmette IL 60091 Office: Dept History Northwestern University Evanston IL 60201

SMITH, LANTY L(LOYD), lawyer, textile mfg. co. exec.; b. Sherrodsville, Ohio, Dec. 11, 1942; s. Lloyd H. and Ellen Ruth (Newell) S.; B.S. with honors in Mathematics, Wittenberg U., Springfield, Ohio, 1964; LL.B. with honors, Duke U., 1967; m. Margaret Hays Chandler, June 11, 1966; children—Abigail Lamoreaux, Margaret Ellen, Amanda Prescott. Admitted to Ohio bar, 1967; asso. firm Jones, Day, Cockley & Reavis, Cleve., 1967-68, 69-73; partner firm Jones, Day, Reavis & Pogue, Cleve., 1974-77; exec. v.p., sr. gen. counsel, sec. Burlington Industries, Inc., Greensboro, N.C., 1977—. Mem. bd. visitors Duke U. Sch. Law; nat. adv. council Wittenberg U. Served with Office Gen. Counsel, USN, 1968-69. Mem. Am. Bar Assn. Episcopalian. Home: 3100 Saint Regis Rd Greensboro NC 27408 Office: 3330 W Friendly Rd Greensboro NC 27410

SMITH, LAWRENCE LEE, conductor; b. Portland, Oreg., Apr. 8, 1936; s. Lawrence Keller and Bonita Evelyn (Wood) S.; B.S. cum laude, Portland State Coll., 1956; grad. magna cum laude, Mannes Coll. Music, N.Y.C., 1959; m. Kathleen Dale, June 4, 1976; children by previous marriage—Kevin, Gregory; stepchildren—Kristine, John. Mem. faculty Mannes Coll. Music, 1959-62; prof. piano Boston U., 1963-64; asst. condr. Met. Opera, 1964-67; mem. faculty Curtis Inst., Phila., 1968-69, Calif. Inst. Arts, 1970-72, U. Tex., 1962-63; prin. guest condr. Phoenix Symphony, 1970-73; music dir., condr. Austin (Tex.) Symphony, 1971-72, Oreg. Symphony, Portland, 1973—; guest condr. N.Y., Los Angeles philharmonics, Tulsa, Winnipeg (Can.), Minn. orchs. Winner 1st prize Met. Internat. Condrs. competition, 1964. Mem. Am. Fedn. Musicians, Mensa. Buddhist. Club: Rotary. Office: Oregon Symphony Orchestra 1119 SW Park Ave Portland OR 97205•

SMITH, LEE HERMAN, univ. pres.; b. Ector, Tex., Jan. 7, 1935; s. Lee Herman and Willie Mae (Morrison) S.; B.S. in Math., Tex. A. amd M. U., 1957, Ph.D. in Statistics, 1964; M.S. in Engrng. Adminstrn., So. Methodist U., 1961; m. Eva Landers, Feb. 18, 1960; 1 dau., Diette. Engrng. positions in industry, 1957-65; asst. prof. Sch. Bus., U. Tex., Arlington, 1965-66; asso. dean, asso. prof., 1967-68; exec. planning adviser N.Am. Aviation Co., Los Angeles, summer 1966; prof., chmn. dept. quantitative mgmt. sci. U. Houston, 1969-71; dean faculties, prof. mgmt. sci. U. Tex., Dallas, 1971-72, v.p. acad. affairs, prof. mgmt. sci., 1972-74; pres. S.W. Tex. State U., San Marcos, 1974—; cons. in field. Mem. San Marcos Indsl. Team, San Marcos Bicentennial Comm.; sci. adv. com. Callier Hearing and Speech Center, Dallas; mem. Am. Assn. State Colls. and Univs. trip to People's Republic of China, 1975, Republic of China, 1976. Mem. bd. Central Tex. Higher Edn. Authority, 1977-78. Tex. A. and M. Coll. Opportunity scholar, 1953-57; Iowa State U. Research Found. fellow, 1961; Gen. Electric Co. fellow, 1962; Ling-Temco-Vought fellow, 1963-64; U. Tex. travel grantee, 1967. Mem. Am. Statis. Assn. (pres. N.Tex. chpt. 1967-68), Ops. Research Soc. Am., Inst. Mgmt. Scis. (program chmn. meetings), Am. Inst. Decision Scis. (v.p. planning and devel. 1970-71, council 1971-72), S. Tex., San Marcos (dir.) chambers commerce, Delta Sigma Pi, Phi Kappa Phi. Author books, articles, revs. in field. Home: 301 Roanoke St San Marcos TX 78666

SMITH, LEE KEITH, JR., lawyer; b. Grove, Okla., Jan. 20, 1934; s. Lee Keith and Ruth Mae (Butler) S.; B.A., U. Okla., 1955, LL.B., 1957; m. Barbara Jean Bartheld, June 7, 1955; children-Linda Suzanne, Jeanne Ann, Janice Lee. Admitted to Okla. bar, 1957, since practiced in Tulsa; law clk. U.S. Dist. Judge, No. Dist. Okla., 1958-60; atty. Helmerich & Payne, Inc., 1960-61; 1st asst. U.S. dist. atty. No. Dist. Okla., 1961-63; mem. firm Boone, Ellison & Smith, 1963—. Chmn. bd. Guaranty Nat. Bank, Tulsa, 1st State Bank, Catoosa, Okla., Security Bank, Tulsa. Mem. Am., Okla., Tulsa County bar assns., Phi Alpha Delta. Democrat. Presbyn. (deacon). Kiwanian. Club: Southern Hills Country. Home: 6885 S Florence St Tulsa OK 74136 Office: 9th Floor World Bldg Tulsa OK 74103

SMITH, LEMUEL AUGUSTUS, JR., state justice; b. Holly Springs, Miss., Aug. 30, 1904; s. Lemuel Augustus and Louise (Robertson) S.; LL.B., U. Miss., 1926; m. Chesley Thorne, Dec. 2, 1931; children—Caffey (Mrs. Edward E. Litkenhous), Lemuel Augustus III. Admitted to Miss. bar, 1926; practiced in Holly Springs, 1926-66; county pros. atty., 1935-50; atty. Marshall County Bd. Suprs., 1948-65; spl. chancellor 3d Chancery Ct. Dist., Miss., 1958-59; asso. justice Supreme Ct. of Miss., 1965—, presiding justice, 1977—; dir. 1st State Bank, Holly Springs. Pres. bd. dirs. Holly Springs Municipal Separate Sch. Dist., 1946-57. Mem. Miss. Ho. Reps., 1929-36. Served to lt. comdr. USNR, 1942-45. Mem. Am., Miss. (former complaint commr.) Marshall County (pres. 1957) bar assns., Am. Judicature Soc., Soc. Mayflower Descs., Kappa Alpha. Episcopalian (vestryman 1948-60). Clubs: Country (Jackson); Holly Springs; Country; Tennessee (Memphis). Home: 631 Chulahoma Ave Holly Springs MS 38635 Office: Dept of Justice Bldg Jackson MS 39205

SMITH, LEO CLIFFORD, energy co. exec.; b. Santaquen, Utah, June 15, 1932; s. William Clifford and Olive (Taft) S.; B.S. in Chem. Engrng., U. Utah, 1955; grad. advanced mgmt. program Harvard U., 1970; m. Bonnie Garrett, Dec. 26, 1955; children—Julie, Carol, Merianne, Linola, Garrett. Prodn. supr. U.S. Steel Co., Provo, Utah, 1957-64; with Wycon Chem. Co., 1964—, v.p., gen. mgr., Colorado Springs, Colo., 1971-72, pres., 1972—, sr. v.p. Coastal States Gas Corp., Houston, 1974—, pres. subs. So. Utah Fuel Co., 1975—, pres. subs. Wycom Chem. Co., 1972—. Served with Chem. Corps, U.S. Army, 1955-57. Mem. Am. Inst. Chem. Engrs. Republican. Mormon. Office: 9 Greenway Plaza Houston TX 77046

SMITH, LEO EMMET, assn. exec., lawyer; b. Chgo., Jan. 6, 1927; s. Albert John and Celia Gertrude (Dwyer) S.; LL.B., De Paul U., 1950; m. Rita Kathleen Gleason, Apr. 14, 1956; children—Mary Cecilia, Gerianne, Kathleen, Leo A., Maureen. Admitted to Ill. bar, 1950; asso. with law firm, also engaged in pvt. industry, 1950-54; asst. states atty. Cook County, Ill., 1954-57; asst. counsel Traffic Inst., Northwestern U., 1957-60; asst. exec. sec. Comml. Law League Am., Chgo., 1960-61, exec. dir., also editor Comml. Law Jour., 1961—. Mem. Am., Ill. bar assns., World Assn. of Lawyers (founding mem.). Contbr. articles legal jours. Home: 1104 S Knight St Park Ridge IL 60068 Office: 222 W Adams St Chicago IL 60606

SMITH, LEO GILBERT, health care cons.; b. Oroville, Calif., July 29, 1929; s. Leo Paul and Laura Mae (Hoffschulte) S.; B.S.C., U. Santa Clara, 1951; M.P.H., U. Calif., 1958; m. Marcia Elise Ernest, Jan. 26, 1952; children—Matthew Paul, Mara Lee, Bridget Mari, Leo Ernest. Adminstrv. resident San Diego County Gen. Hosp., 1958-59; asst. hosp. adminstr. Santa Clara Valley Med. Center, 1959-67, adminstr., 1967-76, dir. planning, 1976-77; health care cons., 1977—. Bd. dirs. State Children's Home Soc. Calif., chmn. dist. bd., 1969-70. Served in mil., 1952-54. Mem. Central Coast Hosp. Conf. (pres. 1970), Hosp. Council No. Calif. (dir. 1970-73), Am. Coll. Hosp. Adminstrs. Home and office: 11890 Walbrook Dr Saratoga CA 95070

SMITH, LEONARD BINGLEY, musician; b. Poughkeepsie, N.Y., Sept. 5, 1915; s. Frank Roderick and Ethel (Schubert) S.; student Ernest Williams Sch. Music, 1933-36, N.Y. U., 1936-37, Curtis Inst. Music, 1943-45; H.H.D., Detroit Inst. Tech., 1965; m. Helen Gladys Rowe, Apr. 20, 1940; 1 dau., Sandra Victoria. Cornet soloist Ernest Williams Band, 1933-36, The Goldman Band, summers 1936-42; 1st trumpet Barrere Little Symphony, 1935-37, Detroit Symphony Orch., 1937-42, Ford Sunday Evening Hour, 1937-42; condr. The Leonard Smith Concert Band, 1945—, Detroit Concert Band, 1945—, U. Detroit Bands, 1949-50, Moslem AAONMS Band, 1945-57, Scandinavian Symphony Orch. of Detroit, 1959-61; guest condr. Indpls. Symphony Orch., 1967; guest condr., soloist, clinician numerous concerts U.S., Can.; mus. dir. John Philip Sousa documentary for BBC, 1970, Sousa Am. Bicentennial Collection (record series), Blossom Festival Band, Blossom Music Center, 1971—; producer Our Am. Heritage in Music, 1970; pres. Bandland, Inc., 1951-61, Accompaniments Unlimited, Inc. Chmn. music com. Mich. Civil War Centennial Commn., 1961-64; gov. bd. Mac Award. Served with USNR, 1942-45. Recipient spl. medal Mich. Polish Legion Am. Vets., Distinguished Service medal Kappa Kappa Psi; Mich. Minuteman Gov.'s award, 1973; Freedom Found. award, 1975, Gen. William Booth award, 1976; named Alumnus of Distinction, N.Y. Mil. Acad., 1976. Mem. ASCAP, Philippine Bandsmen's Assn. (hon.), Am. Bandmasters Assn., Am. Fedn. Musicians, Internat. Platform Assn. Clubs: Masons (33 deg.), Shriners, K.T., Jesters; Detroit Boat. Author compositions: Treasury of Scales, over 270 pub. compositions. Home: 403 Shore Club Dr Saint Clair Shores MI 48080

SMITH, LEONARD CHARLES, biochemist, educator; b. Spokane, Wash., Jan 31, 1921; s. Leonard Charles and Edith (McLellan) S.; A.B., Mont. State U., 1943; Ph.D., U. Ill., 1949; m. Mary Elaine Rush, Oct. 1, 1945; children—David Evan, Lynn Frederic, Steven Mark, Peter Douglas, Andrew Ian. Instr. biochemistry Northwestern U. Med. Sch., Chgo., 1949-56; asso. prof. biochemistry U. S.D., Vermillion, 1956-61, prof., 1962-66; prof. chemistry Ind. State U., Terre Haute, 1966—; adj. prof. biochemistry Terre Haute Center for Med. Edn., Sch. Medicine, Ind. U., 1972—; vis. lectr. Glasgow (U.K.) U., 1961-62. Research biochemist Hines (Ill.) VA Hosp., 1949-56. Mem. Am. Chem. Soc., Soc. Exptl. Biology and Medicine, Chem. Soc. (U.K.), AMA (affiliate), Sigma Xi, Pi Mu Epsilon, Phi Sigma. Research and publs. on amino acid metabolism. Home: 422 Bluebird Dr Terre Haute IN 47803

SMITH, LESLIE CLARK, banker; b. Mitchell, S.D., Oct. 31, 1918; s. Harry L. and Leah (Grace) S.; B.A. in Bus. Adminstrs., Fresno State Coll., 1940; grad. exec. devel. program, Stanford, 1963; m. Marion E. Shook, July 12, 1942; children—Lesley (Mrs. Douglas Jensen), Randal E., Mark A. With Wells Fargo & Co., 1940—, exec. v.p. retail banking No. Calif. area, 1978—. Pres., Calif. Neighborhood Housing Service Found. Served with USAAF, 1941-46. Mem. Calif. Bankers Assn., Robert Morris Assos. Methodist. Clubs: Menlo Country. Home: Menlo Park CA Office: 464 California St San Francisco CA 94104

SMITH, LESLIE JACK, pipeline co. exec.; b. Calgary, Alta., Can., Apr. 15, 1939; s. J. Walter Smith; chartered accountant U. B.C., 1963; m. Velma Jean Moore, Aug. 5, 1960; children—Carla, Stephen Jason. Articled student Collins & Collins, charter accountants, 1957-62; audit supr. Thorne, Riddell, chartered accountants, 1962-65; asst. comptroller Westcoast Transmission Co. Ltd., Vancouver, B.C., 1968-71, comptroller, 1971-72, treas., 1972-74, v.p. finance, 1974—. Mem. Inst. Chartered Accountants Can., Inst. Chartered Accountants B.C., Fin. Execs. Inst., Pacific Coast Gas Assn. Home: 6111 Wiltshire St Vancouver BC V6M 3M1 Canada Office: 1333 W Georgia St Vancouver BC Canada

SMITH, LESLIE RAYMOND, clergyman; b. York, Nebr., July 16, 1904; s. Ezra Harold and Myrtle (Zook) S.; A.B., Cotner Coll., 1927; B.D., Yale, 1930; student U. Chgo., 1934; D.D., Transylvania Coll., 1949, Culver Stockton Coll., 1953; m. Ruth M. Moss, June 24, 1931; children—Leslie R. Owen, Margaret Joan (dec.), Larry, Sonia (Mrs. James A. Ross). Minister Tabernacle Christian Ch., Lincoln, Nebr., 1930-36, Huntington Park Christian Ch., Calif., 1936-41, Walnut Hills Christian Ch., Cin., 1942-44, Central Christian Ch., Lexington, Ky., 1944-69, minister emeritus. Mem. bd. higher edn. Disciples of Christ, Com. on World Order; rep. Am. div. World Council Chs., 1962-68; mem. planning com. Coll. of Bible, Lexington; chmn. com. on recommendations, Internat. Conv. Disciples of Christ, 1956-58, chmn. program com., 1959-60; pres. Internat. Conventions of Christian chs., 1961-62; mem. com., marriage and home, Nat. Council Chs., 1948-54. Trustee United Christian Missionary Soc.; bd. Disciples' House Yale Univ.; trustee Lexington Theol. Sem.; bd. dirs. Woodhaven Home for Exceptional Children; curator Transylvania Coll. Mem. Internat. Platform Assn., Lexington Ministerial Assn. (pres.). Mason, Rotarian. Author: Understanding Jesus, 1936; On Being Christian, 1937; From Sunset to Dawn, 1945; This Love of Ours, 1947; Two Sides of the Disciple Coin, 1958; Meditations on God's Love, 1960; Four Keys to Prayer, 1962; Four Keys to Adequacy, 1965. Contbr. column, sermons, to religious jours. Home: 395 Redding Rd Apt 106 Lexington KY 40502 Office: PO Box 1354 Central Church Lexington KY 40501

SMITH, LESLIE ROPER, hosp. adminstr.; b. Stockton, Calif., June 20, 1928; s. Austin J. and Helen (Roper) S.; A.B., U. Pacific, 1951; M.S. in Pub. Adminstrn., U. So. Calif., 1956; m. Edith Sue Fincher, June 22, 1952; children—Melinda Sue, Leslie Erin, Timothy Brian. Adminstrv. asst. Ranchos Los Amigos Hosp., Downey, Calif., 1953-57; asst. adminstr. Harbor Gen. Hosp., Torrance, Calif., 1957-65, adminstr., 1966-71; acting regional dir. Los Angeles County Coastal Health Services Region, 1973; exec. dir. San Pedro and Peninsula Hosp., San Pedro, Cal., 1974—, Los Angeles County/U. So. Calif. Med. Center, 1971-73; adminstr. Long Beach (Calif.) Hosp., 1965-66; asso. clin. prof. community medicine and pub. health, also emergency medicine U. So. Calif., 1968-78, instr. Sch. Pub. Adminstrn., 1968; preceptor hosp. adminstrn. U. Calif. at Los Angeles, Sch. Pub. Health, 1964-74; lectr. in field, 1963—; cons. emergency health services HEW, 1970-73; Chmn. com. diaster preparedness Hosp. Council So. Calif., 1966-72, sec., 1971—, pres., 1973; mem. Calif. Assembly Com. on Emergency Med. Services, 1970; mem. Calif. Emergency Med. Adv. Com., 1972-75; mem. Los Angeles County Commn. on Emergency Med. Services, 1975—; mem. adv. com. on emergency health services Calif. Dept. Health, 1974-75; dir., mem. exec. com. Truck Ins. Exchange of Farmers Ins. Group, 1977—. Mem. goals com., Torrance, 1968—; pres. Silver Spur Little League, Palos Verdes, 1969-70. Served with AUS, 1946-48. Recipient Silver Knight award Nat. Mgmt. Assn., 1970, Walker Fellowship award, 1976. Fellow Am. Coll. Hosp. Adminstrs.; mem. Am., Nat. mgmt. assns., Am. (chmn. com. on community emergency health services 1973), Calif. (chmn. com. emergency services 1965—, trustee 1973-76) hosp. assns., County Suprs. Assn. Calif. (chmn. joint subcom. on emergency care 1970), Presbyn. (elder, trustee). Rotarian. Home: 29212 Oceanridge Dr Palos Verdes Peninsula CA 90274 Office: 1300 W 7th St San Pedro CA 90732

SMITH, LESTER MARTIN, broadcasting exec.; b. N.Y.C., Oct. 20, 1919; s. Alexander and Sadie Smith; B.S. in Bus. Adminstrn., N.Y. U., 1940; m. Bernice Reitz, Sept. 28, 1962; 1 son, Alexander. Chief exec. officer Kaye Smith Enterprises, radio stas. in Seattle, Portland, Oreg., Spokane, Kansas City, Mo. and Cin., 1954—; gen. partner 700 Investment Co., Seattle Mariners Profl. Baseball Team, Seattle Sounder Profl. Soccer Team; exec. com., dir. Seattle C. of C.; past chmn. dir. Radio Advt. Bur. Served to maj. U.S. Army, 1942-46. Decorated Bronze Star. Mem. Nat. (past dir.), Oreg. (past pres.) assns. broadcasters, Broadcast Pioneers. Clubs: Rotary, Rainer, Wash. Athletic (Seattle). Address: PO Box 3010 Bellevue WA 98009

SMITH, LEWIS MOTTER, JR., advt. exec.; b. Kansas City, Mo., Nov. 4, 1932; s. Lewis Motter and Virginia Hall (Smith) S.; student Hotchkiss and Darrow Schs., 1947-51, Kenyon Coll., 1951-53, Columbia, 1956-58; m. Alice Allen, June 28, 1975; children—Katherine Allen, Patience Allen. Copywriter mail order div. Grolier Soc., Inc., N.Y.C., 1957-59; free lance copywriter, Santa Fe, N.M., 1960-61; v.p. creative services Grolier Enterprises Inc., N.Y.C., 1962-67; v.p., creative planning dir. Wunderman, Ricotta & Kline, Inc., N.Y.C., 1968-72; exec. v.p., creative dir., 1972—. Bd. dirs. Young Concert Artists, Inc., N.Y.C., 1966-67, Harlem Sch. Arts, 1967-68. Served with U.S. Army, 1953-56. Mem. Delta Phi. Episcopalian. Club: Metropolitan (N.Y.C.). Home: 1 E 62d St New York NY 10021 Office: 575 Madison Ave New York NY 10022

SMITH, LILLIAN MAY, mag. editor; b. Bklyn., June 11, 1918; d. Charles Harold and Kathryn Viola (Martin) Smith; student Sweet Briar Coll., 1935-39, Traphagen Sch. Fashion Design, 1939-40. Mem. media and research staff Young & Rubicam Co., 1941-44; mem. editorial staff Chgo. Daily News Fgn. Service, 1944-48; copy editor The Reporter, 1948-49; media dir. Wildrick & Miller Co., 1949-51; managing editor Mag. Mgmt., N.Y.C., 1951-59; editor Ideal Pubs., N.Y.C., 1959-61; editor Lopez Pubs., N.Y.C., 1961—; editor Movieland TV Time, 1961-75, Day TV, 1975-76, Teen Bag, 1976—. Mem. Nat. Assn. TV, Arts and Scis. Republican. Episcopalian. Office: 23 W 26th St New York NY 10010

SMITH, LINN CHARLES, architect; b. Flint, Mich., Dec. 15, 1917; s. Charles Montgomery and Floy (LeFurgey) S.; B.S. in Architecture, U. Mich., 1942; m. Grace Walker, Sept. 10, 1938; children—Cece Marianne, Linn Charles, Kim Walker. With archtl. firms Lyndon and Smith, Detroit, 1942, Maynard Lyndon, Los Angeles, 1945, Eberle M. Smith Assos., Inc., Detroit, 1945- 54; pvt. practice, Birmingham, Mich., 1954-56; pres. firm Smith, Tarapata, MacMahon, Inc., Birmingham, 1956-59, Linn Smith Assos., Inc., Birmingham, 1959-69, 74-76, Linn Smith, Demiene, Adams, Inc., 1969-74; v.p. architecture Ellis/Naeyaert/Genheimer Assos., Inc., Troy, Mich., 1976—; prin. works include high schs. in area. Mem. city plan bd., Birmingham, 1959-72, chmn., 1963, 68; mem. bldg. code bd. appeals, Birmingham, 1958-63; co-chmn. sch. adv. com., Detroit, 1957; mem. com. sch. bldg. Mich. Dept. Pub. Instrn., 1954; mem. Nat. Archtl. Accrediting Bd., 1963-69, pres., 1968-69. Chmn. architecture scholarship fund U. Mich., 1958—; bd. dirs. Birmingham Community House, 1973-76. Served to lt. (s.g.) USNR, 1942-45. George G. Booth travelling fellow in architecture, U. Mich., 1947; recipient better sch. design award Sch. Exec. competition, 1957, 59, design awards Progressive Architecture, 1957, 58; Gold medal Detroit chpt. A.I.A., 1965; Outstanding Achievement award U. Mich., 1969; Gold medal Mich. Soc. Architects, 1969. Fellow A.I.A. (regional dir. 1959-62); mem. Mich. Soc. Architects (pres. 1953- 54, bd. dirs. 1950-56), Am. Assn. Sch. Adminstrs., Architects Soc. Ohio (hon.), Alpha Rho Chi. Home: 7440 Deep Run Birmingham MI 48010 Office: 3270 W Big Beaver Troy MI 48084

SMITH, LIZ, newspaper columnist; b. Ft. Worth, Feb. 2; d. Sloan and Sarah Elizabeth (McCall) Smith; B.J., U. Tex., 1948. Editor, Dell Publns., N.Y.C., 1950-53; asso. producer CBS Radio, 1953-55, NBC-TV, 1955-59; asso. on Cholly Knickerbocker newspaper column, N.Y.C., 1959-64; film critic Cosmpolitan mag., 1966—; columnist Chgo. Tribune-N.Y. Daily News Syndicate, 1976—; freelance mag. writer, also staff writer Sports Illus. mag. Author: The

Mother Book, 1978. Address: Chicago Tribune-NY News Syndicate Inc 220 E 42d St New York NY 10017*

SMITH, LLOYD, musician; b. Cleve., Dec. 1, 1941; s. Thomas George Russell and Anita May (Speer) S.; Mus.B., Curtis Inst. Music, 1965; m. Rheta R. Naylor, Mar. 30, 1967; 1 son, Peter Eldon. Cellist, Pitts. Symphony, 1965-67, Phila. Orch., 1967—; soloist Indpls. Symphony, 1958, 68, Garden State Philharmonic, 1964, Lansdowne Symphony, 1965; tchr. Settlement Music Sch., 1970-72; mem. Huntingdon Trio, 1974—. Mem. Bryn Athyn Ch. Organ Com., 1970—. Mem. Subud (chmn. Phila. 1967-70, 76—, Am. Soc. Ancient Instruments (asst. artistic dir. 1975—, music dir. 1977—). Home: PO Box 199 2916 Sycamore Rd Bryn Athyn PA 19009 Office: 1420 Locust St Philadelphia PA 19103

SMITH, LLOYD BRUCE, mfg. co. exec.; b. Milw., Oct. 13, 1920; s. Lloyd Raymond and Agnes (Gram) S.; student Sheffield Sci. Sch., Yale, 1938-42; m. Lucy Anne Woodhull, Sept. 22, 1945; children—Robert Lewis, Bruce McGregor, Roger Scott, Nancy Dun. With A. O. Smith Corp., Milw., 1942—, successively asst. to pres., v.p., mgr. home appliance div., asst. gen. mgr., pres., 1951-67, chmn., chief exec. officer, 1967—, also dir.; dir. A.O. Smith-Inland Inc., 1st Wis. Nat. Bank, 1st Wis. Corp., Deere & Co., Goodyear Tire and Rubber Co., Continental Group Inc. Mem. Bus. Council. Bd. dirs. Med. Coll. of Wis.; trustee Hwy. Users Fedn. for Safety and Mobility. Mem. Am. Soc. Metals (distinguished life mem.). Office: 3533 N 27th St Milwaukee WI 53216

SMITH, LLOYD HILTON, ind. oil and gas producer; b. Pitts., July 9, 1905; s. Roland Hilton and Jane (Lloyd) S.; Ph.B., Yale, 1929; m. Jane Clay Zevely, Sept. 7, 1931; children—Camilla; m. 2d, Elizabeth Keith Weiss, May 25, 1940; children—Sandra Keith, Sharon Lloyd, Sidney Carothers. Statistician Biggs, Mohrman & Co., N.Y.C., 1932; mgr. New York office Laird & Co., 1933-34; v.p. Argus Research Corp., 1934-35; chmn., dir. Paraffine Oil Corp., 1949—; dir. Curtiss-Wright Corp., 1st City Nat. Bank Houston, Nat. Rev. Bd. dirs. Houston Symphony Soc., Houston Mus. Sci.; trustee Pine Manor Coll., 1963-74. Served as lt. comdr. USNR, 1942-45. Republican. Clubs: Bayou, Houston, Ramada, Tejas (Houston); Racquet and Tennis, Brook, River (N.Y.C.); Nat. Golf Links of America; Southampton, Meadow. Home: 2 Longfellow Ln Houston TX 77005 Office: 1530 Capital Nat Bank Bldg Houston TX 77002

SMITH, LLOYD HOLLINGSWORTH, physician; b. Easley, S.C., Mar. 27, 1924; s. Lloyd H. and Phyllis (Page) S.; A.B., Washington and Lee U., 1944, D.Sc., 1969; M.D., Harvard, 1948; m. Margaret Constance Avery, Feb. 27, 1954; children—Virginia Constance, Christopher Avery, Rebecca Anne, Charlotte Page, Elizabeth Hollingsworth, Jeffrey Hollingsworth. Intern, then resident Mass. Gen. Hosp., Boston, 1948-50, chief resident physician, 1955-56; mem. Harvard Soc. Fellows, 1952-54, asst. prof. Med. Sch., 1956-63; vis. investigator Karolinska Inst., Stockholm, Sweden, 1954-55, Oxford (Eng.) U., 1963-64; prof. medicine, chmn. dept. U. Calif. Med. Sch., San Francisco, 1964—. Mem. Pres.'s Sci. Adv. Com., 1970-73. Bd. overseers Harvard, 1974—. Served to capt., M.C., AUS, 1950-52. Mem. Am. Acad. Arts and Scis., Am. Soc. Biol. Chemists, Am. Soc. Clin. Investigation (pres. 1969-70), Western Soc. for Clin. Research (pres. 1969-70), Assn. Am. Physicians (pres. 1974-75), Am. Fedn. Clin. Research. Spl. research genetic and metabolic diseases. Home: 309 Evergreen Dr Kentfield CA 94904 Office: University California San Francisco Medical Center San Francisco CA 94143

SMITH, LLOYD PRESTON, mgmt. cons.; b. Reno, Nov. 6, 1903; s. Preston Brooks and Ida (Sauer) S.; B.E.E., U. Nev., 1925; Ph.D., Cornell U., 1930; D.Sc., U. Nev., 1961; m. Florence S. Hunkin, Sept. 16, 1928 (dec.); children—Sandra Lee Reynolds, Jacqueline Sue Sullivan; m. F. Irene Anderson, 1971. Research engr. Gen. Electric Co., Schenectady, 1925-26; Coffin fellow physics Cornell U., 1926-27, instr. physics, 1927-30, asst. prof., 1932-36, prof., 1936-56, chmn. dept. physics, dir. dept. engring. physics, 1946-56, dir. Research Found., 1948-56, chmn. corp. com. Cornell U. Council, mem. council for Coll. Engring., 1956—; faculty mem. bd. trustees Cornell U., 1952-56; NRC fellow Calif. Inst. Tech., 1930-31; Internat. Research fellow U. Munich, U. Utrecht, 1931-32; lectr. Stanford U., 1935; research physicist RCA Labs., Princeton, N.J., 1939, cons. war research, 1941-45, asso. research dir., 1945-46, cons., 1946-55, mem. research planning commn., 1952-55, mem. council Fund for Peaceful Atomic Devel., 1956—; cons. atomic bomb research U. Calif., 1942; cons. Union Carbide Nuclear Co. (formerly Carbide & Carbon Chems. Corp.), Oak Ridge, 1947—, Brookhaven Nat. Labs., Upton, L.I., 1947-49, Haloid Co., 1952-53, Detroit-Edison Co., 1953-56; cons. AVCO Mfg. Corp., 1956, 1959, v.p., dir., 1956-59, pres. research and advanced devel. div., 1956-58; research dir. research lab. Aeronutronic div. Ford Motor Co., 1959-63, v.p., dir. applied research labs. Aeronutronic div. Philco Research Labs., 1964-65; v.p. phys. scis. Stanford Research Inst., Menlo Park, Calif., 1965-69, sr. sci. adviser Office Research Ops., 1969-71; cons. on tech. research and devel. of bus. mgmt., 1965—; pres. Lloyd P. Smith and Assos., 1972—; pres. Desert Research Inst., U. Nev., 1975—; dir. Research Corp. N.Y.; cons. Union Carbide Corp., Douglas Aircraft, Inc., 1959; mem. exec. com. Def. Sci. Bd., 1961-65; adv. panel for physics NSF, 1956-59; mem. adv. com. anti-submarine warfare Nat. Security Indsl. Assn. Pres., bd. dirs. Orange County Philharmonic Soc. Recipient certificate of merit USN, 1947. Mem. Am. Phys. Soc., Am. Assn. Physics Tchrs. (chmn. com. physics engring. edn. 1955-56), Am. Ordnance Assn. (chmn. physics sect. 1959—), Am. Inst. Physics, Am. Soc. Engring. Edn., N.Y. Acad. Scis., Sigma Xi, Theta Chi, Phi Kappa Phi. Clubs: Masons; Cosmos (Washington); Univ. (N.Y.C.); Balboa Bay (Newport Beach, Calif.); Commonwealth of Calif. Author: Mathematical Methods for Scientists and Engineers, 1953; contbr. articles sci. jours. Address: 565 Woodside Dr Woodside CA 94062. *My goal was to teach and contribute new things in the field of science to the best of my ability, day by day. I had the great opportunity of living in an era when the greatest activity and developments took place in physics. It was my privilege to have contact with great scientists such as H.A. Lorentz of Holland, Millikan, Einstein, Robert Oppenheimer, H.A. Kramers, Hans Bethe, Arnold Summerfeld, and many others. To each I owe much inspiration and knowledge which I have earnestly tried to use to contribute to scientific education, government activities—such as the atomic bomb—and to industrial processes and products. But perhaps most of all I am proud of the good students I have had.*

SMITH, M(AHLON) BREWSTER, psychologist; b. Syracuse, N.Y., June 26, 1919; s. Mahlon Ellwood and Blanche Alice (Hinman) S.; student Reed Coll., Portland, Oreg., 1935- 38; A.B., Stanford, 1939, A.M., 1940; Ph.D., Harvard, 1947; m. Deborah Anderson, June, 1947; children—Joshua H., T. Daniel, Rebecca M., J. Torquil. Rantoul scholar Harvard, 1940-41; jr. analyst Office Coordinator of Information, U.S. Govt., 1941; Social Sci. Research Council fellow Harvard, 1946-47, asst. prof. social psychology Dept. Social Relations, 1947-49; prof. psychology, chmn. dept. Vassar Coll., 1949-52; staff Social Sci. Research Council, 1952-56; prof. psychology N.Y. U., 1956-59; prof. psychology U. Calif. at Berkeley, 1959-68, dir. Inst. Human Devel., 1965-68; prof., chmn. dept. psychology U. Chgo., 1968-70; prof. psychology U. Calif. at Santa Cruz, 1970—, vice chancellor social scis., 1970-75; fellow Center Advanced Studies Behavioral Scis., 1964-65. Vice pres. Joint Commn. Mental Illness and Health, 1955-61. Served from pvt. to maj. Adj. Gen. Div., AUS, 1942-46; research officer Information and Edn. div. War Dept., 1943-46; research asso. spl. com. on soldier attitudes Social Sci. Research Council, 1946. Decorated Bronze Star medal. Nat. Endowment for Humanities fellow, 1975-76. Fellow AAAS, Am. Psychol. Assn. (pres. 1978); mem. Soc. Psychol. Study Social Issues (past pres.), Soc. Research Child Devel., Am. Sociol. Assn., Sigma Xi, Phi Beta Kappa. Democrat. Club: Cosmos (Washington). Author: Social Psychology and Human Values, 1969; Humanizing Social Psychology, 1974. Co-author: The American Soldier, vol. 2; Combat and Its Aftermath, 1949; Opinions and Personality, 1956. Contbr. profl. jours. Editor Jour. Social Issues 1951-55, Jour. Abnormal Soc. Psychology, 1956-61. Home: 316 Escalona Dr Santa Cruz CA 95060

SMITH, MAGGIE, actress; b. Ilford, Eng., Dec. 28, 1934; d. Nathaniel and Margaret (Hutton) Smith; ed. Oxford High Sch. Girls; m. Robert Stephens, 1967 (div. 1974); 2 sons; m. 2d, Beverley Cross, 1974. Stage and film actress, 1952—; stage appearances include New Face, N.Y.C., 1956, Share My Lettuce, 1957, The Stepmother, 1958, Rhinoceros, 1960, Strip The Willow, 1960, The Rehearsal, 1961, The Private Ear and The Public Eye, 1962, Mary, Mary, 1961; mem. Old Vic, 1959-60, Nat. Theatre, London, 1963—; productions at Nat. Theatre include The Recruiting Officer, Othello, The Master Builder, Hay Fever, Much Ado About Nothing, Miss Julie, A Bond Honoured, The Beaux Strategem, Hedda Gabler, Private Lives, 1972, Snap, 1973; participant Stratford Festival (Ont., Can.), 1976, 77, 78; Night and Day, London and N.Y.C., 1979-80; Virginia, N.Y.C.; films include Othello, 1966, The Honey Pot, 1967, Oh What a Lovely War, 1968, Hot Millions, 1968, The Prime of Miss Jean Brodie (Oscar award), 1968, Love and Pain and The Whole Damn Thing, 1971, Travels With My Aunt, 1972, Murder by Death, 1976, Death on the Nile, 1977, California Suite (Oscar award for Best Supporting Actress), 1978. Recipient Best Actress award Eve. Standard, 1962, 70; Best Film Actress award Soc. Film and TV Arts U.K., 1968, Film Critics Guild, 1968; named Actress of Year, Variety Club, 1963, 72; decorated comdr. Order Brit. Empire. Address: care Fraser & Dunlop 91 Regent St London W1R 8RU England

SMITH, MALCOLM BERNARD, investment co. exec.; b. Lynn, Mass., May 27, 1923; s. Philip and Ida (Zenis) S.; B.A., Dartmouth, 1944; M.A., Harvard, 1948; m. Betty Booth, June 20, 1948; children—Eric, Daniel. Treas., Gen. Am. Investors Co., Inc., N.Y.C., 1957-59, v.p., 1958-61, pres., 1961—; dir. Group Health, Inc. Trustee, chmn. finance com. N.Y. Found. Served with Signal Corps, AUS, 1943-46. Mem. Assn. Publicly Traded Investment Funds, (dir.), AAAS (chmn. investment and fin. com.), Fedn. Jewish Philanthropies N.Y. (mem. investment com.), Phi Beta Kappa. Club: Harvard. Home: 1248 Hardscrabble Rd Chappaqua NY 10514 Office: 330 Madison Ave New York NY 10017

SMITH, MALCOLM NORMAN, mfg. co. exec.; b. Milw., Feb. 25, 1921; s. Samuel H. and Dorothea (Werner) S.; B.S. in Econs., U. Pa., 1942; m. Muriel J. Foreman, Feb. 14, 1943; 1 dau., Louise K. With Ekco Products Co., Chgo., 1946-50, 56-63, v.p., 1956-63; dir. Platers & Stampers Ltd., Brit. div. Ekco, London, 1950-56; pres., chief exec. officer, dir. Argus, Inc., Chgo., 1963-68; pres. Malcolm N. Smith & Co., Chgo., 1968-70; adminstrv. v.p., cashier Am. Nat. Bank and Trust Co., Chgo., 1971-75; pres., chief exec. officer Macromatic, Inc., 1975—; professorial lectr. U. Chgo. Grad. Sch. Bus. Bd. dirs. The Acorn Fund; mem. citizen's bd. U. Chgo. Served to 1st lt. USMCR, 1942-46. Decorated Silver Star. Clubs: Lake Shore Country (Glencoe, Ill.); Tavern, Econ. (Chgo.); Royal Tennis Court (Eng.). Home: 309 Maple Ave Highland Park IL 60035 Office: 4700 W Montrose Ave Chicago IL 60641

SMITH, MALCOLM SOMMERVILLE, bass; b. Rockville Centre, N.Y., June 22, 1933; s. Carlton Newell and Margaret (Sommerville) S.; B.Music Edn., Oberlin Coll., 1957, B.Mus., 1960; M.A. in Ednl. Adminstrn., Columbia Tchrs. Coll., 1958; student Ind. U. Sch. Music, 1960-62; m. Margaret Yauger, Oct. 4, 1975. Dir. choral music Ramapo Regional High Sch., Wyckoff, N.J., 1958-60; basso Lyric Opera, Chgo., 1961, 63; bass soloist Russian tour Robert Shaw Choral, 1962; leading bass N.Y.C. Opera, 1965-70, Deutsche Oper Am Rhein, Dusseldorf, Germany, 1971—, Vienna State Opera, 1973-74, Met. Opera, Japan Tour, spring 1975, N.Y.C., 1975-77, Paris Opera, 1978, Barcelona Opera, 1978, Sao Paulo, Brazil, 1978, Mexico City, 1979, Berlin Opera, 1979, Montreal Symphony, 1979; maj. soloist Boston Symphony, Minn., Cin., Houston, Utah, Chgo. symphonies, also Cin. Summer Opera, Central City (Colo.) Summer Opera, Festival of two Worlds, Spoleto, Italy. Served with AUS, 1954-56. Conglist. Office: care Thea Dispeker Artists Rep 59 E 54th St New York NY 10022. *Hard work and a sense of humor.**

SMITH, MARGARET CHASE, former U.S. senator; b. Skowhegan, Maine, Dec. 14, 1897; d. George Emery and Carrie (Murray) Chase; student Skowhegan High Sch., 1912-16; m. Clyde H. Smith, May 14, 1930 (dec. 1940). Began as teacher, Skowhegan, 1916; office exec. Independent Reporter, 1919-28; Daniel E. Cummings Co., 1928-30; treas. New Eng. Process Co., Skowhegan, 1928-30. Mem. Rep. State Com., Maine, 1930-36; became mem. 76th Congress, 2d Maine Dist., June 3, 1940; mem. 77th to 80th Congresses (1941-49), 2d Maine Dist.; elected to U.S. Senate, 1948, re-elected, 1954, 60, 66; nominee for Pres. U.S., Rep. Nat. Conv., 1964; vis. prof. Notre Dame U., Pacific Luth. U., De Pauw U., U. of South, Okla. Bapt. U., others; lectr. U. Ala. Law Sch., Syracuse U., Stetson U., U. Pitts., others. Chmn. bd. Freedom House, N.Y.C., 1970-77, chmn. emeritus, 1977—; bd. dirs. Lilly Endowment, Inc., 1976—; chmn. nat. women's bd. Northwood Inst., 1978—; trustee U.S. Supreme Ct. Hist. Soc. Recipient numerous Nat. awards, 85 hon. degrees colls. and univs. Republican. Mem. Am. Acad. Arts and Scis., Theta Sigma Phi, Pi Sigma Alpha, Sigma Kappa, Delta Kappa Gamma, Beta Sigma Phi. Author: Gallant Women, 1968; Declaration of Conscience, 1972; nationally syndicated columnist United Feature Syndicate; columnist McCalls mag.

SMITH, MARION LEROY, coll. dean; b. Sharon, Pa., June 3, 1923; s. Frank M. and Blanche (Bistline) S.; student Purdue U., 1941-43; B.Sc. in Mech. Engring., La. State U., 1944; M.Sc., Ohio State U., 1948; m. Marjorie L. Hoover, June 9, 1944; children—Kristine Ellen, Patricia Ann, Kathryn Sue. Instr. mech. engring. Ohio State U., 1947-50, asst. prof., 1950-55, asso. prof., 1955-58, asso. dean Coll. Engring., 1958—; mem. engring. dept. Cooper-Bessemer Corp., summers 1947, 48, 50; univ. research work miniature engine-generator sets, mechanism of oxidation of pure hydrocarbons, heat transfer in aircraft, dual-fuel diesel engines; on leave Ohio State U. to participate in DuPont engring. dept. Year-In- Industry Program, Wilmington, Del., 1956-57; mem. Ohio Bd. Registration Profl. Engrs. and Surveyors, 1975—. Served from pvt. to 2d lt., ordnance, AUS, 1943-46. Named Tech. Person of Year, Columbus Tech. Council, 1977; registered profl. engr., Ohio. Fellow Am. Soc. M.E. (chmn. Columbus 1953-54, student br. com. region V 1955-56, sects. com. region V 1960-62, mem. policy bd. edn. 1971-76); mem. Am. Soc. Engring. Edn. (chmn. Ohio 1957-58, chmn. continuing engring. studies div. 1965-66, chmn. ann. meeting com.), Soc. Automotive Engrs. (chmn. engring. edn. activity 1965-67), Sigma Xi, Tau Beta Pi, Phi Kappa Phi, Pi Tau Sigma. Methodist. (ofcl. bd., chmn. edn. commn., lay leader). Author: (with K.W. Stinson) Fuels and Combustion, 1952; also articles. Home: 4135 Rowanne Ct Columbus OH 43214

SMITH, MARION PAFFORD, aero. co. exec.; b. Waycross, Ga., Dec. 12, 1925; s. Rossa Elbert and Lillian Solee (Pafford) S.; student Okla. State U., 1944, Yale U., 1945; B.E.E., La. State U., 1949; postgrad. U. So. Fla., 1966-70; m. Esther Pat Davis, Nov. 23, 1952; children—Bryan P., Danton D., Patricia Anne. Engr., Bell Telephone Co., Baton Rouge, 1949-51; mgr. engring. Vitro Labs., Silver Spring, Md., 1952-57; mgr. dept. quality Honeywell Avionics Div., St. Petersburg, Fla., 1957—; vice chmn., dir. Atlantic Bank, Largo, Fla.; cons. U.S. Army Mgmt. Engring. Tng. Agy., 1975-79; U.S. del. Internat. Elec. Tech. Commn., 1965—, chmn., chief U.S. tech. adviser com. on reliability and maintainability, 1975—, v.p., exec. com. U.S. nat. com.; U.S. del. NATO Quality Conf., 1973; mem. White House Summit Conf. on Inflation, 1975; del. White House Conf. on Handicapped, 1977. Mem. Nat. Adv. Council on Developmental Disabilities HEW, 1974-78, Fla. Adv. Council Devel. Disabilities, 1974-78; mem. devel. council Morton Plant Hosp., Clearwater, Fla., 1971-74. Served to 1st lt. Signal Corps, AUS, 1944-45, 51-52. Recipient McDonald award Fla. Rehab. Assn., 1968; Bilgore award Citizen of Year, Clearwater, Fla., 1969; Outstanding Service award Am. Soc. Quality Control, 1968-69; United Comml. Travelers award Most Outstanding Service Retarded, Fla., 1970; named Engr. of Year Fla. W. Coast, 1970; Service to Mankind award Sertoma Clubs, 1977. Fellow IEEE (dir., Nat. Reliability award 1979); mem. Nat. Assn. Retarded Citizens (pres. 1973-75, nat. govt. affairs chmn. 1975—), Am. Assn. Mental Deficiency, Nat. Symposium Reliability Quality Control (gen. chmn.), Sigma Chi. Presbyterian. Club: Kiwanis (Marion P. Smith award established in his honor). Home: 1884 Oakdale Ln N Clearwater FL 33516 Office: 13350 US Hwy 19 Saint Petersburg FL 33733. *True turning points in life are sometimes difficult to recognize, but for those who have become parents of a handicapped child, particularly a mentally retarded child, then that turning point is easy to recognize. After the difficult period of adjustment, one becomes aware of a realization that all persons have human dignity and worth and can make a contribution to humanity and to society.*

SMITH, MARK KERN, JR., mgmt. cons.; b. N.Y.C., Feb. 14, 1928; s. Markwick Kern and Elizabeth (Morning) S.; B.S., Mass. Inst. Tech., 1951, Ph.D., 1954; m. Martia Reed, Mar. 2, 1951; children—Karen, Rebecca, Mark David, Jennifer. Vice pres., then exec. v.p. Geophys. Service Inc., Dallas, 1962-67, pres., 1967-69; v.p. Tex. Instruments, Dallas, 1967-73; mgmt. cons., author, Norwich, Vt., 1973—. Served with USNR, 1946-48. Mem. Nat. Acad. Engring. Congregationalist. Address: PO Box 189 Main St Norwich VT 05055

SMITH, MARSHALL FRANCIS, diversified co. exec.; b. Chgo., Apr. 30, 1929; s. Marshall E. and Suzanne (Vernia) S.; B.S. in Accounting, U. Ill., 1951; postgrad. U. Chgo., 1954, Northwestern U., 1955; m. Catherine A. Kerin, Sept. 9, 1955; children—Thomas, Kathryn, Suzanne, Elizabeth. Div. controller U.S. Steel Corp., N.Y.C., 1966-67; asst. controller Indian Head, Inc., N.Y.C., 1967-68; v.p., asst. gen. mgr. Wayne Corp. div. Indian Head Co., Richmond, Ind., 1969; v.p., controller Indian Head, Inc., N.Y.C., 1969-72, exec. v.p., 1972-74, pres., chief exec. officer, dir., 1974—; bd. mgmt. T-B Inc., 1977—; dir. Madera Glass Co., Hapad, Inc. Mem. adv. council Clarkson Coll., 1978—; mem. U. Ill. Found., 1978—. Mem. Psi Upsilon. Home: 571 River Rd Yardley PA 19067 Office: 1211 Ave of Americas New York NY 10036

SMITH, MARVIN HUGH, judge; b. Federalsburg, Md., Aug. 10, 1916; s. Charles Henry and Jeannette (Brown) S.; A.B., Washington Coll., Chestertown, Md., 1937; LL.B., U. Md., 1941; m. Rebecca Groves, Feb. 21, 1942; children—Melissa (Mrs. Charles O. Waggoner, Jr.), Marvin Hugh, Sarah Jeannette. Admitted to Md. bar, 1941; practice in Denton, 1946-68; asso. judge Ct. Appeals Md., 1968—; asst. atty. gen. Md., 1953-55. Chmn. trustees Client's Security Trust Fund of Bar of Md., 1966-68. Mem. Caroline County Bd. Edn., 1951-53, pres., 1952-53; mem. Commn. to Revise Criminal Law of Md., 1952; del. from Caroline County to Md. Constl. Conv., 1967; mem. exec. bd. Del-Mar-Va Area council Boy Scouts Am., 1967—, v.p., 1969-71, pres., 1971-73. Served with CIC, AUS, 1941-45. Recipient Silver Beaver award Boy Scouts Am., 1968, Distinguished Eagle Scout award, 1975. Mem. Am., Md. (past gov.), Caroline County bar assns., Am. Legion, Omicron Delta Kappa. Methodist. Rotarian (past pres.), Mason (Shriner). Home: 318 Maple Ave Federalsburg MD 21632 Office: PO Box 309 Denton MD 21629

SMITH, MARY LOUISE, former chmn. Republican Nat. Com.; b. Eddyville, Iowa, Oct. 6, 1914; d. Frank and Louise (Jager) Epperson; A.B., U. Iowa, 1935; m. Elmer Milton Smith, Oct. 7, 1934; children—Robert C., Margaret L., James E. Field staff aide Iowa Emergency Relief Adminstrn., 1935-36; vice chmn. Wright County (Iowa) Republican Central Com., 1962-63; mem. Iowa adv. bd. Fedn. Rep. Women, 1961—; alternate del. Rep. Nat. Conv., 1964; del., mem. platform, arrangements coms. Rep. Nat. Conv., 1968, 72, 76; Iowa vice chmn. Rep. Presdl. Campaign, 1964; mem. Rep. Nat. Com. for Iowa, 1964—, co-chmn., 1974, chmn., 1974-77, mem. exec. com., 1969—, mem. Rep. nat. subcom. on conv. reform, 1966, co-chmn. Rule 29, com., 1973-74; vice chmn. Midwest region Rep. Conf., 1969-71; co-chmn. Iowa Com. to Re-elect the Pres., 1972, nat. co-chmn. Physicians Com. to Re-elect the Pres., 1972; vis. fellow Woodrow Wilson Nat. Fellowship Found., 1979—. Mem. U.S. del. 15th session Population Commn. ECOSOC, UN, Geneva, Switzerland, 1969; mem. U.S. del. to 3d extraordinary gen. conf. UNESCO, 1973; mem. Pres.'s. Commn. Observance of 25th Anniversary UN, 1970-71. Pres. Eagle Grove (Iowa) Community Chest, 1952, mem. bd. edn., 1954-58; mem. Iowa Commn. Blind, 1961-63, chmn., 1962-63; mem. Gov. Iowa Commn. Aging, 1962; mem. nat. commn. on observance Internat. Women's Year, 1975-77, del. conf., 1977. Bd. dirs. Mental Health Center N. Iowa, 1962-63; trustee Robert A. Taft. Inst. Govt., 1975—; mem. adv. bd. Nat. Women's Polit. Caucus, 1978—; trustee Herbert Hoover Presdl. Library Assn., Inc., 1979—. Named hon. col. Mil. Staff Gov. Iowa, 1973; named to Iowa Women's Hall of Fame, 1977. Mem. AMA Aux., Am. Women for Internat. Understanding, Planned Parenthood, YWCA, UN Assn., P.E.O. (pres. Eagle Grove chpt. 1959-60, del. supreme conv. 1959), Nat. Women's Polit. Caucus, Kappa Alpha Theta. Home: 654 59th St Des Moines IA 50312

SMITH, MATTHEW JOSEPH, lawyer; b. Columbus, Ohio, Jan. 21, 1905; s. Edward John and Anna (Doyle) S.; B.A., Ohio State U., 1927, J.D., 1929; m. Mary L. Jahnke, Jan. 15, 1936; children—Kathleen (Mrs. Johnson), Edward, Margaret (Mrs. Hicks), Robert. Research asst. Yale, 1929-31, Johns Hopkins, 1931-32; admitted to Ohio bar, 1929, practiced, Columbus, 1932-34, New Philadelphia, 1934—; mem. Smith, Renner, Hanhart, Miller & Kyler. Trustee Union Hosp. Assn., Dover, Ohio, 1958-76, v.p., 1971-72; trustee Ohio State Bar Asso. Found., 1962-66; past trustee, past pres. Tuscarawas Valley Comprehensive Mental Health Center; past trustee Ohio Legal Center Inst. Fellow Am. Coll. Trial Lawyers, Am. Bar Found., Ohio Bar Assn. Found., Am. Coll. Probate Counsel; mem. Am., Ohio (pres. 1960-61), Tuscarawas County (past pres.) bar assns., Internat. Assn. Ins. Counsel, Soc. Hosp. Attys., Am. Judicature Soc., U.S. 6th Circuit Jud. Conf. (life), Order of Coif, Delta Theta Phi. Club: Kiwanis.

Home: 221 Brookside Dr Heritage Village N Dover OH 44622 Office: 405 Chauncey Ave New Philadelphia OH 44663

SMITH, MAURICE EDWARD, lawyer, acct., business cons.; b. Denver, Mar. 30, 1919; s. Edward Daniel and Junie Ardella (Fox) S.; student Brigham Young U., 1938-40; B.S. in Commerce, U. Denver, 1942; LL.B., Stanford U., 1948; m. Gloria Tanner, June 17, 1944; children—Christine, Kathryn, Carol, Daniel. Mem. staff Ralph B. Mayo & Co., Denver, 1949-50; v.p. finance, v.p. and gen. counsel Husky Oil Co., Cody, Wyo., 1950-61; exec. v.p. Central Nat. Ins. Group, Omaha, 1961-65; treas., legal counsel Sunnen Products Co., St. Louis, 1965-69; v.p., treas. Global Marine, Inc., Los Angeles, 1969-78; bus. cons., 1978—. Mem. Cody City Council, 1955-57. Served with USNR, 1942-45. Mem. Am., Calif. bar assns., Colo. Soc. C.P.A.'s. Mem. Ch. Jesus Christ of Latter-day Saints. Home: 5022 Alta Canyada Rd La Canada CA 91011

SMITH, MAURICE FREDERIK, bus. cons., conservationist; b. Fort Wayne, Ind., Nov. 24, 1908; s. George Levi and Lou Emma (Pierce) S.; student U. Mich., 1924-26, Coll. William and Mary, 1927-29, Dayton Art Inst., 1926-30; m. Vivian Weston, 1932; 1 son, Christopher F.; m. 2d, Catherine Hanley, Aug. 22, 1941; children—Michaele, Mark, Frederik, Drusilla, Francesca. Advt. mgr. Hobart Mfg. Co., 1924-26; dir. pub. relations Batten, Barton, Durstine & Osborn, N.Y.C., 1931-36; partner Selvage & Smith, 1937-40; dir. pub. relations Young & Rubicam, 1941-42; v.p. ABC, 1944-45; dir. advt. Simon & Schuster, 1945-46, Book-of-the-Month Club, 1946-48; pres. Fred Smith & Co., N.Y.C., 1948-56; v.p. Prudential Ins. Co., Newark, 1956-64; asso. Rockefeller Family & Assos., N.Y.C., 1964—; dir. Am. Motors, Howard Johnson Co., Perini Corp., George Rogers Constrn. Co., UN Devel. Corp., Grand Teton Lodge Co.; trustee Jackson Hole Preserve Inc.; asst. to sec. Treasury, 1942-44; asst. to U.S. Pres., Bretton Woods Conf., 1944; mem. Nat. Outdoor Recreation Resources Rev. Commn., 1958-60; mem. adv. bd. Nat. Parks Bd., 1945—. Recipient award Trustees of Reservations, 1956. Fellow Rochester (N.Y.) Mus. Republican. Clubs: Explorers, Boone and Crockett, Sky, Rockefeller Center Luncheon, Whitehall, Johns Island. Author: Rufus Woods; The Story of Grand Coulee Dam, 1938; contbr. articles to profl. jours. Home: Apt 14C 20 Sutton Pl S New York NY 10022 Office: Room 5600 30 Rockefeller Plaza New York NY 10020

SMITH, MCNEILL, state senator, lawyer; b. Rowland, N.C., Apr. 9, 1918; A.B., U. N.C., 1938; LL.B., Columbia, 1941; m. Louise Huske Jordan; children—Louise Jordan, Anne Talbott, John McNeill III, Eleanor Huske. Admitted to N.C. bar, 1941, N.Y. bar, 1942; now partner firm Smith, Moore, Smith, Schell & Hunter, Greensboro, N.C. Mem. Fed. Jud. Conf. for 4th Circuit; dir. Central Carolina Legal Services, N.C. Center Public Policy Research, 1978—; chmn. N.C. Civil Rights Adv. Com., 1959-63, exec. com. So. Regional Council, 1965-69; vis. prof. constl. law U. N.C., 1964-65; mem. N.C. Ho. of Reps., 1970-71, N.C. Senate, 1971-78; chmn. State Ethics Bd., 1978—. Sec., Excellence Fund U. N.C. at Greensboro; 1st v.p. N.C. Council Chs.; chmn. N.C. Crime Study Commn., 1975; trustee N.C. Outward Bound Sch. Served to lt. comdr. USNR, 1942-45. Recipient Frank Porter Graham award N.C. Civil Liberties Union, 1975. Mem. Am. (chmn. sect. individual rights and responsibilities 1972-73, mem. ho. of dels. 1976—, chmn. com. on mentally disabled 1979—), Internat., N.C., Greensboro bar assns., N.C. State Bar, Am. Freedom Assn. (pres. 1958-62), Acad. Trial Lawyers, Internat. Assn. Ins. Counsel, Greensboro C. of C. (dir. 1962-63), Phi Beta Kappa, Phi Delta Phi. Home: 2501 W Market St Greensboro NC 27403 Office: NCNB Bldg Greensboro NC 27402

SMITH, MERLIN GALE, assn. exec.; b. Germantown, Ky., May 12, 1928; s. Allen Edward and Gladys Myrtle (Kaiser) S.; B.E.E., U. Cin., 1950; M.E.E., Columbia U., 1957; m. Elinore Klein, Dec. 23, 1955; children—Laurence Robin, Derek Randall, April Rena. With IBM, N.Y.C. and Yorktown Heights, N.Y., 1952—, engring. mgr. large scale integration, Yorktown Heights, 1964-70, research staff mem., 1970—; mem. IEEE, 1946—, sr. mem., 1964, fellow, 1977—, bd. govs. Computer Soc., 1970—, sec., 1972-73, v.p., 1975-76, pres., 1977-78, mem. tech. activities bd., 1977-78. Bd. dirs. Nat. Computer Conf., 1973-77, chmn., 1975, conf. chmn., 1978. Served with Signal Corps, AUS, 1951-52. Mem. Am. Fedn. Info. Processing Socs. (dir. 1977—, exec. com. 1978—), Assn. Computing Machinery. Contbr. articles to profl. jours. Patentee in field. Home: 2485 Trelawn St Yorktown Heights NY 10598 Office: TJ Watson Research Center PO Box 218 Yorktown Heights NY 10598

SMITH, MERVIN GEORGE, educator; b. Corunna, Ind., Apr. 6, 1911; s. John Timothy and Della Susan (Haynes) S.; B.S. with distinction, Purdue U., 1933, Ph.D., 1940; grad. study U. Chgo., 1938; m. Margaret Lydia Schmierer, Aug. 8, 1942 (dec. 1971); m. 2d, Hazel Duncan Townsend, Dec. 9, 1972. Vocat. agr. tchr., Middlebury and Goshen, Ind., 1933-36; research asst. agrl. econs. dept. Purdue U., 1936-39, research asso., summers 1936, 37, 41, instr. agrl. econs., 1939-42; agrl. economist, attache in Mex., Dept. State, 1942-45; research dir. May Seed & Nursery Co., Shenandoah, Iowa, 1945-48; asso. prof. agrl. econs. and rural sociology dept., extension Ohio State U., 1948-50, prof., 1950-53, prof., chmn. dept. Ohio State U. Agrl. Expt. Sta., 1953-66, asst. dean internat. agrl. affairs Coll. Agr. and Home Econs., 1966—, dir. Agrl. Fin. Center, 1965-67. U.S. rep. Internat. Conf. Agrl. Econs., Helsinki, Finland, 1955, Mex., 1961, France, 1964, Brazil, 1973, Kenya, 1976; spl. cons. AID, Latin Am., 1957, 59, 61; vis. prof., cons. Iowa State U., 1960. Mem. AAUP, Am. Farm Econs. Assn., Sigma Xi, Alpha Zeta, Kappa Delta Pi, Theta Alpha Phi, Gamma Sigma Delta, Ceres. Mem. Church of Brethren, also nondenominational ch. Contbr. to profl. publs. Home: 1345 Fishinger Rd Columbus OH 43221

SMITH, MICHAEL BRACKETT, fgn. service officer; b. Marblehead, Mass., June 16, 1936; s. Ralph Leslie and Elizabeth (Brackett) S.; A.B., Harvard, 1958; m. Nancy Pickering Hodgson, Feb. 21, 1959; children—Leslie Sieburg, Eric Brackett. Fgn. service office Dept. State, 1959—, now dep. U.S. trade rep with rank of ambassador. Episcopalian. Home: 11909 Harmony Ln Potomac MD 20854 Office: Office of US Trade Rep Exec Office of President Washington DC 20506 also US Trade Rep Geneva Switzerland Dept State Washington DC 20506

SMITH, MICHAEL TOWNSEND, author: b. Kansas City, Mo., Oct. 5, 1935; s. Lewis Motter and Dorothy (Pew) S.; student Yale U., 1953-55; m. Michele Marie Hawley, 1974; children—Julian Bach, Alfred St. John. Theatre critic Village Voice, N.Y.C., 1959-68, 1970-74, asso. editor, 1962-65; curator, judge Obie awards for theatre, 1962-68, 1970-74; tchr. New Sch. Social Research, 1964-65, Hunter Coll., 1972; playwright mem. Open Theatre, N.Y.C., 1962-66; dir. Theatre Genesis, N.Y.C., 1971-74; arts editor Taos (N.Mex.) News, 1977-78. Recipient creative arts citation in theatre Brandeis U., 1965; Obie award, 1971; Rockefeller Found. award, 1976. Author: (fiction) Getting Across, 1962; Near the End, 1965; Automatic Vaudeville, 1970; (poetry) American Baby, 1975; (plays) I Like It, 1961; The Next Thing, 1963; A Dog's Love, 1965; Captain Jack's Revenge, 1970; Country Music, 1971; Double Solitaire, 1973; Prussian Suite, 1973; A Wedding Party, 1974; Cowgirl Ecstasy, 1976; (translation) Life Is Dream, 1978; (critical jour.) Theatre Trip, 1969; also articles; editor: (anthologies) Eight Plays from Off-Off-Broadway 1966; The Best of Off-Off-Broadway, 1969; More Plays from Off-Off-Broadway, 1971. Address: 91 Water St Stonington CT 06378

SMITH, MONCRIEFF HYNSON, JR., psychologist; b. St. Louis, Sept. 21, 1917; s. Moncrieff Hynson and Nell Drane (Galbraith) S.; A.B., U. Mo., 1940, M.A., 1941; Ph.D., Stanford U., 1947; m. Mary Mildred Devine, June 12, 1960; children—MacKenzie, Laurie; children by previous marriage—Mason A., Virginia D., Parker G. Instr., Harvard U., 1947-49; asst. prof., prof. psychology U. Wash., Seattle, 1949—, chmn. Physiology-Psychology Grad. Tng. Program, 1960—. Served with USAAF, 1942-46. Fellow, Am. Psychol. Assn., AAAS. Contbr. sci. articles to profl. jours. Home: 6003 50th St NE Seattle WA 98115 Office: U Wash Guthrie Hall Seattle WA 98195

SMITH, MONROE G., mfg. exec.; b. Camden, N.J., Dec. 24, 1910; s. Charles E. and Anna (Githens) S.; student prep. sch., Swarthmore, Pa., 1928-29; B.S., U. Pa., 1933; m. Lois A. Wade, June 20, 1936; children—Charles Monroe, Judith Ann, Wade Monroe. Spl. agt. F.B.I., 1943-46; pres., gen. mgr., dir. Silex Co., Hartford, Conn., 1950-52, pres., dir. Silex Co., Ltd., St. John, Que., Can., Hartford Products, Inc., 1950-52; exec. v.p., dir. Rockwood & Co., Bklyn., 1953-55; exec. v.p., dir. Gobelin Co., Inc., 1953-55, Our Mothers, Inc., 1953-55; comptroller, gen. mgr., group v.p. ESB, Inc., Phila., 1955-67; pres., dir. Diagnostic Data Inc., Mountain View, Calif., 1968—; comptroller, dir. Electric Storage Battery Co. (Can.), Ltd., Toronto, Willard Storage Battery Co. (Can.), Ltd., Atlas Mineral Products Co., Mertztown, Pa., pres., dir., Cleve. Electric Vehicle Co.; v.p., dir. Battronic Electric Vehicle Co.; dir. Timely Brands, Inc., Boston, Timely Brands (Can.), Ltd., Jessall Plastics, Inc., New Kensington, Conn., Ohline Co., Inc., Pasadena, Calif., Marketing Services, Inc., Scottsdale, Ariz., Vocon, Inc., Los Angeles, Vitrex, Inc., N.Y., Nutrex, Inc., Atlanta. Mem. Financial Execs. Inst., Am. Def. Preparedness Soc., Newcomen Soc., Am. Soc. Naval Engrs., Nat. Security Indsl. Assn. (pres. 1960-65), Material Handling Inst. (pres. 1964, dir. 1960-67), Nat. Football Found., Am. Mgmt. Assn., Soc. Former F.B.I. Agts., Am. Security Council, Sigma Phi Epsilon, Phi Sigma Chi. Clubs: Merchants and Manufacturers, Seaview Country, Vesper, Manufacturers Country, Sharon Heights Country. Home: 201 Family Farm Dr Woodside CA 94062 Office: 518 Logue Ave Mountain View CA 94043. *It has always been my philosophy that hard work, straightforward honesty, a thoroughness that causes one to look ahead and plan every detail, a good memory and a willingness to admit a mistake are the ingredients that enabled me to overcome my many faults and attain some success.*

SMITH, MORGAN KINMONTH, pub. co. exec.; b. Morristown, N.J., May 10, 1912; s. Morgan Kinmonth and Sarah C. (Boswell) S.; grad. St. Paul's Sch., Concord, N.H., 1930; B.S., Yale, 1934; m. Beatrice Stewart, July 14, 1934; children—Morgan Kinmonth, Helen (Mrs. Brian Taylor), Joan (Mrs. John N. Kidder), Frances deF. (Mrs. Page L. Edwards, Jr.), Nancie C. (Mrs. Robert E. Ash, Jr.). Prodn. asst. Weyerhaeuser Timber Co., Longview and Everett, Wash., 1934-38; with Riverside Press, subsidiary Houghton Mifflin Co., Cambridge, Mass., 1938-71, mng. dir., 1966, pres., 1966-71, v.p. parent co., 1966-71, also dir., 1952-71; with Gambit, Ipswich, Mass., asso. mng. dir., 1971—; dir., v.p. Wolf Composition Co., 1960-71; dir., Concord Bookship Inc., 1967—, treas., 1972—, pres., 1976—; gov. Yale U. Press, 1968—, pres. bd. govs., 1971—. Dir. Book Mfrs. Inst., 1958-69, pres., 1965-67. Mem. Concord Personnel Bd., 1952-65, chmn., 1956-57, 61-62. Trustee Concord Acad., 1947-67, 71-77, pres., 1952-60, v.p., 1971-74; trustee Emerson Hosp., 1947-50, St. Paul's Sch., 1962-66, United Community Services Boston, 1964-67; trustee Douglas Thom Clinic, 1954-73, pres., 1962-64; trustee Little House, 1948-56, pres., 1951-55; trustee Concord Community Chest, 1947-51, pres., 1947-49; bd. govs. Concord Antiquarian Mus., 1976—, pres., 1977—. Served to capt. AUS, 1943-45. Republican. Mem. P.E. Ch. Clubs: Yale (N.Y.C.); Ausable (trustee 1965-68, pres. 1968-73, chmn. 1973-78) (St. Hubert's, N.Y.); Tavern (Boston); Concord Country. Home: 9 Musketaquid Rd Concord MA 01742 Office: 27 Main St Ipswich MA 02116

SMITH, MORTIMER BREWSTER, author, assn. editor, exec.; b. Mt. Vernon, N.Y., Feb. 17, 1906; s. Mortimer Allen and Matilda (Wolfe) S.; ed. pub. schs.; m. Sylvea Shapleigh, June 11, 1932 (div. Nov. 1959); children—Patricia, Stephen, Olea, Shapleigh; m. 2d, Edna Burrows Crilley, Jan. 18, 1962. Formerly asst. to out-of-town dept. mgr. Johnson and Faulkner; author: Evangels of Reform, 1933; The Life of Ole Bull, 1944; And Madly Teach, 1949; William Jay Gaynor, Mayor of New York, 1951; The Diminished Mind, 1954; A Citizen's Manual for Public Schools, 1965; co-author: A Consumer's Guide to Educational Innovations, 1972; contbg. author anthologies and textbooks including Essays on Educational Reform, 1970; Farewell to Schools, 1971; Teaching: A Course in Applied Psychology, 1971; Rhetoric in Thought and Writing, 1972; Controversies in Education, 1973; School: Pass at Your Own Risk, 1974; co-founder Council for Basic Edn., Washington, 1956, editor Council for Basic Edn. Bull., 1957-74, exec. dir., 1960-74, bd. dirs., 1975—. Del. White House Conf. on Edn., 1965, White House Conf. on Children, 1970; Spaulding lectr. Yale, 1966; Dana lectr. Psychiat. Inst. U. Md. Hosp., Balt., 1969; mem. adv. bd. Ency. Brit. Reading Achievement Center, Oak Brook, Ill., 1969-71. Vice pres. Newtown (Conn.) Orchestral Soc., 1936-40; chmn. Rationing Bd., Newtown, 1942-45; chmn. Conn. Regional High Sch. Bd. Number 3, 1945-47. Trustee Booth Library, Newtown, 1940-50, chmn., 1950-60. Club: Nat. Press (Washington). Contbr. numerous articles to profl. jours., popular mags., newspapers. Home: 5014 N 76th Pl Scottsdale AZ 85253

SMITH, MOWRY, mfg. co. exec.; b. Neenah, Wis., Mar. 19, 1918; s. Mowry and Katharine (Ives) S.; B.A., Yale U., 1941; M.B.A., Stanford U., 1947; m. Mary Louise Leach, June 1947; children—Mowry III, Curtis Nolte, Onnie Leach. Pres., dir. Menasha Wooden Ware Co., Neenah; sr. v.p., dir. Menasha Corp., Neenah; dir. 1st Nat. Bank of Neenah, New Eng. Wooden Ware Co. Trustee Lawrence U. Served with U.S. Navy, 1942-46; PTO. Mem. Wis. Taxpayers Alliance (dir.). Clubs: North Shore Golf (pres.), Oshkosh Power Boat, Elks. Co-author: One Third Crew, One Third Boat, One Third Luck: The Menasha Corporation Story, 1849-1974, 1974 (State Hist. Soc. Wis. award 1974). Office: PO Box 367 Neenah WI 54956

SMITH, MYRON GEORGE, ofcl. AID; b. Terrebonne, Minn., June 9, 1920; s. Adrian G. and Marie E. (Crompe) S.; B.S. in Agrl. Econs., U. Minn., 1946; m. Louise J. Hennessey, May 22, 1944; children—Michael, Thomas, John, Patricia, Dennis; m. 2d, Nguyen Anh My, Aug. 30, 1975. Owner, No. Ill. Agrl. Service, 1958-62; with AID, Dept. State, 1962—, chief agrl. div., Indonesia, 1970-74, asst. dir., Vietnam, 1974-75, livestock project mgr., Bamako, Mali, 1976-78, agr. devel. officer, 1978—. Served to 1st lt. USAAF, 1941-44. Decorated Purple Heart, Air medal with 6 oak leaf clusters, D.F.C.; recipient Agr. medal 2d class, Agr. medal 1st class, Labor medal 1st class, Economy medal 2d class (Vietnam). Mem. Am. Fgn. Service Assn. Address: Bamako/Mali Dept State AID Washington DC 20520

SMITH, MYRON JOHN, JR., librarian; b. Toledo, May 3, 1944; s. Myron John and Marion Oliva (Herbert) S.; student Coll. Steubenville, 1962; A.B., Ashland Coll., 1966; M.L.S., Western Mich. U., 1967; M.A., Shippensburg State Coll., 1969; postgrad. U. Wis.; m. Susan Pearl Bullion, June 15, 1968; 1 son, Myron John III. Research librarian G.W. Blunt White Library, Mystic Seaport, Conn., 1967-68; asst. librarian Western Md. Coll., Westminster, 1969-72; library dir. Huntington (Ind.) Pub. Library, 1972-76; asso. prof. history and library sci., dir. libraries Benedum Learning Resources Center, Salem (W.Va.) Coll., 1976—; mem. Am. Com. on History 2d World War. Mem. ALA, U.S. Naval Inst., U.S. Mil. Inst., U.S. Air Force Found., CAP (dir. aerospace edn. W.Va. wing), Beta Phi Mu, Phi Alpha Theta. Club: Optimist. Author: American Naval Bibliography Series, 1972-74; Huntington Centennial Handbook, 1973; The Sophisticated Lady: The Battleship Indiana in World War II, 1973; World War II at Sea: A Bibliography of Sources in English, 1976; (with Robert Webber) Sea Fiction Guide, 1976; The Cloak and Dagger Bibliography, 1976; Air War Chronology 1939-45, 1977; Air War Bibliography Series, 1977—; The Mountain State Battleship: USS West Virginia, 1979; Air War Southeast Asia, 1979; The Rise of the Soviet Navy, 1941-1978, 1979; contbr. articles to various jours. Home: Rt 2 Box 402 Salem WV 26426 Office: Benedum Learning Resources Center Salem Coll Salem WV

SMITH, NATHAN JAMES, physician, educator; b. Cuba City, Wis., Oct. 13, 1921; s. Floyd and Rachel (Calder) S.; B.A., U. Wis., 1943, M.D., 1945; student U. Minn. Grad. Sch., 1945-46; m. Marcella Emma Keller, Feb. 9, 1946; children—Nanette, Douglas, Bradley. Intern pediatrics and pathology U. Minn. Sch. Medicine, 1945-46, grad. fellow, 1946; fellow Children's Med. Center, Boston, 1948-50; Fulbright scholar U. Paris, (France), 1950; instr. pediatrics Temple U. Sch. Medicine, 1951-53; asso. prof. pediatrics U. Calif. at Los Angeles, 1954-57; prof. pediatrics, chmn. dept. U. Wis. Med. Sch., 1957-65, Alfred Dorance Daniels prof., 1957-65; prof. pediatrics U. Wash., Seattle, 1965—, prof. sports medicine, 1975—; spl. asst. for nutrition programs sec. HEW, Washington, 1970—; pediatrics-in-chief King County Hosp. Seattle, 1965-72; vis. prof. UCLA, 1958, hon. mem. faculty medicine U. Chile, Santiago. Served with M.C., AUS, 1946-48. Diplomate Am. Bd. Pediatrics. Mem. Am. Acad. Pediatrics, Am. Pediatric Soc., Soc. Pediatric Research (council 1961—), Western Pediatrics Research Soc., Western, Central socs. clin. research, Soc., Exptl. Biol. and Med., Am. Soc. Hematology, Midwestern Soc. Pediatric Research (pres. 1959), Internat. Soc. Hematology, Chilean, Peruvian pediatrics socs., Am. Coll. Sports Medicine. Home: 6704 Parkpoint Way NE Seattle WA 98115

SMITH, NEAL AUSTIN, elec. engr., educator; b. Norwich, Ohio, Feb. 10, 1919; s. Miner Francis and Bessie Lillian (Shuman) S.; B.E.E., Ohio State U., 1941, M.Sc., 1947; m. Faye Louise Schlupe, June 7, 1942. Elec. engr. Fed. Machine & Welder Co., Warren, Ohio, 1941-43, asst. chief elec. engr., 1943-44; instr. elec. engring. Ohio State U., 1947-54, asst. prof., 1954-60, asso. prof., 1960-65, prof., 1965—. Cons. in elec. power systems, electric shock, fires of elec. origin. Served as lt., j.g., USNR, 1944-46. NSF grantee, 1961-62. Mem. Am. Legion (past post comdr.), Eta Kappa Nu, Tau Beta Pi. Mason. Club: Ohio State U. Faculty. Contbr. articles to profl. jours. Home: 67 Westview Ave Columbus OH 43214 Office: 2015 Neil Ave Columbus OH 43210

SMITH, NEAL EDWARD, Congressman; b. Hedrick, Iowa, Mar. 23, 1920; s. James N. and Margaret M. (Walling) S.; student U. Mo., 1945-46, Syracuse U., 1946-47; LL.B., Drake U., 1950; m. Beatrix Havens, Mar. 23, 1946; children—Douglas, Sharon. Farmer, Iowa, 1937—; admitted to Iowa bar, 1950; practice in Des Moines, 1950—; atty. 50 sch. bds. in Iowa, 1953-64; asst. county atty. Polk Country, Iowa, 1951; mem. 86th-96th Congresses from 4th Dist. Iowa. Chmn. Polk County Bd. Social Welfare, 1954-56; pres. Young Democratic Clubs Am., 1953-55. Served with AUS, World War II. Decorated Air medal with 4 oak leaf clusters, Purple Heart. Mem. Am. Bar Assn., Farm Bur., Farmers Union, DAV. Clubs: Masons, Moose. Home: RFD 1 Altoona IA 50009 Office: 2373 Rayburn House Office Bldg Washington DC 20515

SMITH, NELS JENSEN, rancher, state legislator; b. Newcastle, Wyo., Jan. 29, 1939; s. Peter Franklin and Helen Catherine (Jensen) S.; B.S., U. Wyo., 1961; m. Jeanette Rae Keener, Dec. 21, 1968; children—Douglas, Garrett. Owner, operator cattle ranch and wheat farm, Sundance, Wyo., 1961-76; mgr., gen. partner Smith Ranch, Sundance, 1977—; mem. Wyo. Ho. of Reps. from Crook County, 1963-79, majority floor leader, 1973-74, speaker of house, 1977-78. Bd. dirs. Blue Cross-Blue Shield of Wyo., 1978—; trustee Range Telephone Co-op., 1979. Mem. Wyo. Stockgrowers Assn. (exec. com. 1969—, chmn. transp. com. 1971-75), Am. Nat. Cattlemen's Assn. (transp. com. 1973-75, forest com. 1976—), Wyo. Taxpayers Assn. (exec. com. 1977—). Republican. Home and Office: Sundance WY 82729

SMITH, NORMAN CLARK, museum ofcl.; b. Hartford, Conn., Jan. 2, 1917; s. Raymond W. and Elinor (Smith) S.; A.B., Middlebury Coll., 1939; postgrad. Hartford Coll. Law, Trinity Coll.; m. Mary Alice Beall. Tchr., Loomis Sch., 1945-50, adminstr., tchr., 1952-53, asst. bus. mgr., 1953-55, bus. mgr., 1955-58, controller, 1958-63; treas. Vassar Coll., 1963-64; v.p. devel., planning Emory U., Atlanta, 1964-76; v.p. univ. devel. U. Del., Newark, 1976-79; dir. resource devel. Mystic (Conn.) Seaport Mus., 1979—. Bd. dirs., past chmn. bd. Nat. Soc. Fund Raising Execs; past trustee Loomis Inst., Watkinson Sch.; mem. vis. com. Mystic (Conn.) Seaport. Served to capt. USNR, 1941-45, 50-52. Decorated Navy Cross. Mem. Assn. Devel. Officers Urban Univs., Nat. Soc. Fund Raising Execs., Chi Psi, Omicron Delta Kappa. Rotarian. Clubs: Lincoln, Univ. and Whist (Wilmington, Del.). Home: 161 Pequot Ave Mystic CT 06355 Office: Mystic Seaport Museum Mystic CT 06355

SMITH, NORMAN CUTLER, geologist, bus. exec.; b. Paterson, N.J., Mar. 18, 1915; s. Archibald Nicholas and Ruth (Cutler) S.; student Pennington Prep. Sch., 1930-33, Drew U., 1933-34; A.B. cum laude in Geology and Biology, Washington and Lee U., 1937; postgrad. Harvard, 1940-42, U. Okla., 1947; m. Dorothy Phyllis Barnes, June 12, 1942; children—Roxanne Lorraine, Lee Cutler. Field geologist Standard Oil Co. Venezuela, 1938-40; teaching fellow Harvard Grad. Sch. Geology, 1941-42; geologist Humble Oil & Refining Co., 1946-49; cons. geologist and photo-geol. specialist, 1949-62; mem. Am. Assn. Petroleum Geologists, 1940—, exec. dir., 1963-72; now pres. Resource Devel. Internat., Inc., Operation Central, Inc. Founder, 1st pres. Council Sci. Socs., Dallas-Ft. Worth Area, 1958, chmn. bd., 1960; mem. standing com. Nat. Com. on Geology, 1962-72. Bd. dirs. Tulsa Sci. Found., 1967; trustee Tulsa Sci. Center, 1967-72. Served to lt. (s.g.) USNR, 1942-46; PTO. Fellow Geol. Soc. Am., A.A.A.S.; mem. Am., Tulsa (pres. 1968) socs. assn. execs., Dallas (pres. 1958-59, exec. com. 1956-60, hon. mem.), Tulsa geol. socs., Soc. Petroleum Engrs., Soc. Exploration Geophysicists, Council Engring. and Sci. Soc. Secs. Author articles, chpts. in books in field. Home: 395 Briarwood Ct NE Marietta GA 30067

SMITH, NORMAN OBED, educator; b. Winnipeg, Man., Can., Jan. 23, 1914; s. Ernest and Ruth (Kilpatrick) S.; B.Sc., U. Man., 1935, M.Sc., 1936; Ph.D., N.Y. U., 1939; m. Anna Marie O'Connor, July

1, 1944; children—Richard Obed, Graham Michael, Stephen Housley. Came to U.S., 1950, naturalized, 1958. Teaching fellow N.Y. U., 1936-39; mem. faculty dept. chemistry U. Man., Winnipeg, 1939-50, asst. prof., 1946-49, asso. prof., 1949-50; asso prof. Fordham U., N.Y.C., 1950-65, prof. chemistry, 1965—, chmn. dept. chemistry, 1974-78. Sr. phys. chemist Arthur D. Little, Inc., Cambridge, Mass., 1957; indsl. cons. Fellow Chem. Inst. Can.; mem. Am. Chem. Soc., Asso. Canadian Coll. Organists, Am. Guild Organists (dir. chpt. 1964-66, 79—), Sigma Xi, Phi Lambda Upsilon. Author: (with others) The Phase Rule and Its Applications, 1951; Chemical Thermodynamics, A Problems Approach, 1967; contbr. to Ency. Brit., 1974. Home: 59 Monrovia Blvd Yonkers NY 10707 Office: Dept Chemistry Fordham U New York NY 10458

SMITH, NUMA LAMAR, JR., lawyer; b. Rock Hill, S.C., Nov. 22, 1915; s. Numa Lamar and Grace (Hanes) S.; A.B., Furman U., 1938; LL.B. with distinction, Duke U., 1941; m. Mary Catherine Gray, Mar. 24, 1941; children—Patricia Gray, Elizabeth Hanes, Lamar Douglas. Admitted to N.Y. bar, 1942, D.C. bar, 1946; asso. firm White & Case, N.Y.C., 1941-42; asso. firm Miller & Chevalier, Washington, 1946-49, partner, 1949—; sr. fellow Duke U. Law Sch., 1979-80, bd. visitors, 1973—. Served with U.S. Army, 1942-46, with Judge Adv. Gen. Corps, 1944-46. Recipient Gen. Excellence award Furman U., 1938. Fellow Am. Bar Found.; mem. Am. Bar Assn., Fed. Bar Assn., D.C. Bar Assn., Am. Law Inst., Duke Law Alumni Assn. (pres. 1967-69), Order of Coif, Sigma Alpha Epsilon. Baptist. Clubs: Metropolitan (Washington); Burning Tree (Bethesda, Md.); Washington Golf (Arlington, Va.). Asso. editor Duke Law Jour., 1940-41. Home: 3443 N Venice St Arlington VA 22207 Office: 1700 Pennsylvania Ave NW Washington DC 20006

SMITH, OLIVER, theatrical producer-designer; b. Waupun, Wis., Feb. 13, 1918; s. Larue F. and Nina (Kincaid) S.; B.A., Pa. State U., 1939; Dr. (hon.), Bucknell U., L.I. U. Co-producer, designer plays: On the Town, 1945; Billion Dollar Baby, 1945; No Exit, 1946; Me and Molly, 1947; Gentlemen Prefer Blondes, 1949; Bless You All, 1950; In The Summer House, 1952; Clearing in the Woods, 1957; Time Remembered; Romulus, 1961; The Night of the Iguana; Lord Pengo, 1962; Barefoot in the Park, 1963; 110 in the Shade, 1963; The Girl Who Came to Supper, 1963; Dylan, 1963; The Chinese Prime Minister, 1964; Ben Franklin in Paris, 1964; Luv, 1964; Poor Richard, 1964; Odd Couple, 1965; designer of musicals: Brigadoon, 1946; High Button Shoes, 1946; Miss Liberty, 1949; Paint Your Wagon, 1952; Pal Joey, 1952; On Your Toes, 1955; My Fair Lady, 1956; Candide, 1955; Auntie Mame, 1956; West Side Story (Antoinette Perry award 1958); Jamaica; Destry; Flower Drum Song; Camelot; Beckett; Broadway: First Monday in October; Met. Opera; Traviata, 1958; Martha, 1961; Hello Dolly (Tony award), 1963; I Was Dancing, 1964; Candide, 1971; The Little Black Book, 1972; The Time of Your Life, 1972; Lost in The Stars, 1972; Naughty Marietta, N.Y.C. Opera, 1978; designer movies; Band Wagon, 1952; Oklahoma, 1955; Guys and Dolls, 1955; Porgy and Bess; Sound of Music; designer Unsinkable Molly Brown, 1960; co-dir. Am. Ballet Theatre, 1945—; designer ballets: Rodeo, 1942; Fancy Free, 1943; Fall River Legend, 1946; Swan Lake; Les Noces; exhbns.: Pa. State Coll., Mus. Modern Art, Bklyn. Mus., Chgo. Art Inst., Cocoran Gallery, Yale; produced Natural Affection; Tiger, Tiger; On the Town, London (all 1962-63); master tchr. N.Y. U. Recipient Donaldson award, 1946, 47, 49, 53. Antoinette Perry award, 1957, 58, 60, 61, 64, 65, Shubert award, 1960; Pa. State U. Distinguished Alumni award, 1962; N.Y. Handel medallion, 1975. Mem. Triangle Soc., Acacia, Nat. Council Arts. Address: 70 Willow St Brooklyn NY 11201

SMITH, ORMA RINEHART, judge; b. Booneville, Miss., Sept. 25, 1904; s. Jefferson Davis and Lena (Rinehart) S.; J.D., U. Miss., 1927; m. Margaret Elizabeth Fernandez, June 17, 1930; 1 son, Orma Rinehart. Admitted to Miss. bar, 1927; practice in Corinth, Miss., 1928-68; mem. firm Smith & Smith, 1959-68; U.S. dist. judge No. Dist., 1968—. Dir. Nat. Bank of Commerce of Corinth, 1946-68, Fidelity Fed. Savs. & Loan Assn. of Corinth, 1957-68. Trustee, Corinth Separate Sch. Dist., 1940-55. Fellow Miss. Bar Found.; mem. Am., Alcorn County bar assns., Miss. State Bar (past pres.), U. Miss. Alumni Assn. (pres. 1961-62), Alpha Tau Omega. Baptist (past chmn. bd. deacons.). Mason (33 deg., Shriner, K.T.). Home: 812 Gloster St Corinth MS 38834 Office: Municipal Bldg Corinth MS 38834

SMITH, ORVILLE AUVERNE, educator; b. Nogales, Ariz., June 16, 1927; s. Orville Auverne and Bess (Gill) S.; B.A. in Psychology, U. Ariz., 1949; M.A., Mich. State U., 1950, Ph.D., 1953; m. Clara Jean Smith; children—Nanette, Marcella. Instr. psychology Mich. State U., 1953-54; fellow U. Pa., 1954-56; trainee dept. physiology and biphysics U. Wash., 1956-58; instr. physiology and biophysics, 1958-59, asst. prof., 1959-61, 62-63, asst. dir. Regional Primate Research Center, 1962-69, asso. prof. 1963-67, prof., 1967—, asso. dir. Regional Primate Research Center, 1969-71, dir., 1971—. Mem. Am. Physiol. Soc., Am. Soc. Primatologists (pres. 1977-79), Internat. Congress Physiol. Scis., Am. Assn. Anatomists, AAAS, Pavlovian Soc. N.Am. (pres. 1977-78), Western Psychol. Assn., Internat. Primatological Soc., AAUP, Neurosci. Soc. Contbr. articles to profl. jours. Home: 7521 30th St NE Seattle WA 98115 Office: Regional Primate Research Center SJ-50 U Wash Seattle WA 98195

SMITH, OTIS M., lawyer; b. Memphis, Feb. 20, 1922; s. Samuel M. and Eva Smith; student Fisk U., 1941-42; student Syracuse U., 1946-47, LL.D. (hon.), 1978; J.D., Cath. U. Am., 1950, LL.D. (hon.), 1977; LL.D. (hon.), Western Mich. U., 1973, Southwestern at Memphis, 1978, Morgan State Coll., 1978; m. Mavis C. Livingston, Dec. 29, 1949; children—Vincent, Raymond, Anthony, Steven. Admitted to D.C., Mich. bar; mem. Mallory & Smith, Flint, until 1957; asst. pros. atty. Genesee County, 1954; pub. adminstr. Genesee County, 1955-57; mem. Flint Election Bd., 1956-57; chmn. Mich. Pub. Service Commn., 1957-59; auditor gen. Mich., 1959-61; justice Supreme Ct. Mich., 1961-66; mem. legal staff Gen. Motors Corp., 1967—, asst. gen. counsel, 1973-74, v.p., 1974—, asso. gen. counsel, 1974-77, gen. counsel, 1977—. Bd. dirs. Nat. Urban League, 1973—, sec., 1979—; bd. regents U. Mich., 1967-71; trustee Oakland U., 1971—, chmn. bd., 1972-74; v.p. United Found. Detroit, 1973—; trustee Fisk U., 1973-79, Henry Ford Hosp., 1978—, Cath. U. Am., 1979—. Served with AUS, 1942-46. Recipient Distinguished Service award Flint Jr. C. of C., 1956, Nat. Alumni award for govt. Cath. U. Am., 1961; Silver Beaver award Boy Scouts Am., 1966. Fellow Am. Bar Found.; mem. Adminstrv. Conf. U.S., State Bar Mich. (bd. commrs. 1968-76), Am. Bar Assn. (ho. of dels. 1972-76), Am. Judicature Soc., Omega Psi Phi (Man of Year award 1962). Office: Gen Motors Bldg Detroit MI 48202

SMITH, PATRICIA LILIAN, librarian; b. Otley, Yorkshire, Eng., Oct. 10, 1931; d. Frank Arthur and Ida Jane (Eagles) Smith; A.L.A., Leeds Sch. Librarianship, Yorkshire, 1951-52; B.A. in Gen. Arts, U. Toronto, 1959. Jr. asst. Ipswich pub. libraries, Suffolk, Eng., 1949-50; gen. asst. West Riding County Library, 1950-51; sr. asst. South Yorkshire regional libraries, 1952-55; intern gen. librarian Toronto pub. libraries, 1955-57; br. librarian B.C. Pub. Library Commn., East Kootenay, B.C., 1959-65; dir. N.W.T. Pub. Library Services, 1965—. Mem. Library Assn. U.K., Canadian Library Assn. Address: Box 1733 Hay River NT X0E O4O Canada

SMITH, PAUL, JR., lawyer; b. N.Y.C., Jan. 24, 1923; s. Paul and Barbara Frances (Cronin) S.; B.S., Fordham U., 1943; LL.B., Columbia U., 1946; J.S.D., N.Y. U., 1950; m. Patricia M. Larkin, Feb. 12, 1949; children—Monica Frances, Andrea Patricia, Christopher Paul. Admitted to N.Y. bar, 1946, N.J. bar, 1952, Colo. bar, 1974; asso. firm Davis Polk & Wardwell, N.Y.C., 1946-50; counsel Socony-Vacuum Oil Co., N.Y.C., 1951-59; v.p. Mobil Petroleum Co., 1960-65, also dir.; exec. Mobil Oil Corp., N.Y.C., 1965-68, asst. gen. counsel internat., 1968-73; counsel Hamilton Bros. Oil Co., Denver, 1973-77; individual practice law, Denver, 1977—. Served with U.S. Army, 1942-43. Mem. Am. Bar Assn, Am. Law Inst., Am. Soc. Internat. Law, Internat. Bar Assn., Union Internationale Des Avocats, Assn. Bar City N.Y., Colo. Bar Assn. Republican. Roman Catholic. Club: Univ. (Denver). Editor Columbia Law Rev., 1945-46; mem. editorial adv. bd. Internat. Lawyer, 1979—. Home: 101 S Birch St Denver CO 80222 Office: 620 Sherman St Denver CO 80203

SMITH, PAUL DAVID, educator; b. Warsaw, Ind., Jan. 17, 1928; s. Paul W. and Gladys Adel (Izor) S.; student DePauw U., 1946-47; B.S., Rose Poly. Inst., 1950; M.S., U. Ill., 1952; Ph.D. (NSF Sci. Faculty fellow), U. Denver, 1967; m. Marion Boyce Greenleaf, May 21, 1950; children—Lawrence David, Ronald James, Timothy Jay, Thomas Alan, William Herrick. With Bell Tel. Labs., 1952-54; mem. faculty Rose Poly. Inst., Terre Haute, 1954-60; group leader Denver Research Inst., 1960-65; lectr. U. Denver, 1967; prof. elec. engring. Rose-Hulman Inst. Tech., Terre Haute, 1967—, chmn. dept., 1970-72. Cons. Naval Research Lab., 1951, Farnsworth Electronics, Boeing Airplane Co., Naval Avionics Facility, Indpls., 1958, Tex. Instruments, 1959-60, Denver Research Inst., 1967. Mem. Blue Key, Lambda Chi Alpha, Tau Beta Pi, Eta Kappa Nu. Methodist. Research on spl. frequency synthesizer systems. Home: RFD 25 Box 57 Terre Haute IN 47802

SMITH, PAUL DAVIS, ret. lawyer; b. Rochester, N.Y., May 2, 1916; s. Earle David and Mabel (Andrus) S.; A.B., U. Rochester, 1937; LL.B., Columbia U., 1940; m. Nancy Dudley Hanks, Oct. 17, 1942; children—Paul Davis, David Bradford. Admitted to N.Y. bar, 1940; mem. firm Conboy, Hewitt, O'Brien & Boardman, N.Y.C., 1948-57; v.p., gen. counsel Philip Morris, Inc., 1958-71, also dir. Served from ensign to comdr. USNR, 1941-46. Mem. Phi Beta Kappa. Home: 18 Shirlawn Dr Short Hills NJ 07078

SMITH, PAUL FRANCIS, microbiologist, educator; b. Brookville, Pa., Apr. 3, 1927; s. Leo F. and Josephine (Ferguson) S.; B.S., Pa. State U., 1949; M.S., U. Pa., 1950, Ph.D., 1951; m. Marie D. Rymshaw, July 1, 1951; children—Rebecca, Leigh Ann, Laurie, Graham. Research microbiologist Merck & Co., Inc., Rahway, N.J., 1951-52; faculty U. Pa. Sch. Medicine, Phila., 1952-61, asst. prof., 1956-61; prof., chmn. dept. microbiology U. S.D., Vermillion, 1961—. Cons. USN Med. Research Unit 4, 1965-73. Recipient Lederle Med. Faculty award, 1960. Diplomate Am. Bd. Microbiology. Fellow Am. Acad. Microbiology, Am. Pub. Health Assn., A.A.A.S.; mem. Am. Soc. for Microbiology, Am. Chem. Soc., Sigma Xi, Delta Chi. Mem. editorial bd. Jour. Bacteriology, 1964—. Author: Biology of the Mycoplasmas, 1970. Contbr. articles to profl. jours. Home: 11 N Prentis St Vermillion SD 57069

SMITH, PAUL FREDERICK, economist, educator; b. Mansfield, Ohio, Dec. 21, 1919; s. Phillip Fred and Myrtle Grace (Robinson) S.; A.B., U. Chgo., 1941; A.M., Northwestern U., 1946; Ph.D., Am. U., 1955; m. Margaret Alice Peacock, Oct. 30, 1942; children—Terence James, Barbara Jo Smith Moren. Economist bd. govs. Fed. Res. System, 1947-59; prof. fin. U. Pa., Phila., 1959—, chmn. fin. dept., 1963-67, 72-75, vice-dean, dir. doctoral programs Wharton Sch. Bus., 1976—; asso. staff mem. Nat. Bur. Econ. Research, 1960-70. Served with USNR, 1941-46. Decorated Bronze Star, Purple Heart. Mem. Am. Econs. Assn., Am. Fin. Assn. Author: Consumer Credit Costs, 1949-59, 1964; Economics of Financial Institutions and Markets, 1971. Home: 31 Highview Dr Radnor PA 19087 Office: Dept Fin U Pa Philadelphia PA 19104

SMITH, PAUL LYNGE, banker; b. N.Y.C., Apr. 25, 1918; s. Paul C. and Anna (Lynge) S.; student Kent Sch., 1931-36, Yale, 1937-39; m. Viola Fern Malm, Nov. 5, 1944; children—Susan L., Peter L., Ann W. Supr. accounting stock records and billing Conduit Products div. Gen. Electric Co., Bridgeport, Conn., then mem. corp. controllers staff Schenectady, 1939- 51; comptroller Acme Shear Co., Bridgeport, 1951-56; asst. controller, asst. treas., controller, sec.-treas. Bullard Co., Bridgeport, 1957-61; sr. v.p. charge control service dept., mem. adminstrv. com., central operations com. Security Pacific Nat. Bank, Los Angeles, 1961-68, exec. v.p., mem. mng. com., 1968—; chmn. fin. com., treas. Security Pacific Corp., 1974—, with Office Chief Exec., 1978—; pres., dir. Pacific S.W. Realty Co.; dir. Equitable Trust Co., 1st Small Bus. Investment Co. of Calif., Security Overseas Corp., Security Pacific Internat. Bank. Chmn., chief exec. officer, Children's Hosp., Los Angeles, 1969—, bd. dirs., 1964—; bd. dirs. United Way of Los Angeles. Served to capt. AUS, 1942-46. Mem. Financial Execs. Inst. (chmn. admissions com. Los Angeles chpt., past pres. So. Conn. control), Los Angeles C. of C. Clubs: Annandale Golf (Pasadena, Calif.); Stock Exchange. Home: 1947 San Pasqual St Pasadena CA 91107 Office: 333 S Hope St Los Angeles CA 90017

SMITH, PAUL SAMUEL, coll. adminstr. b. Richmond, Ind., July 3, 1897; s. Harry J. and Louise (Wolfe) S.; A.B., Earlham Coll., 1919; LL.D.; A.M., U. Wis., 1922, Ph.D., 1927; L.H.D., Calif. Coll. Medicine; LL.D., Whittier Coll.; m. Lillian E. McMinn, Aug. 28, 1923; 1 dau., Eleanor Patricia. Fellow in history, U. Wis., 1919-20, teaching asst., 1920-22; prof. Am. history Whittier (Calif.) Coll., since 1923, dir. summer session, 1939-51, coll. pres., 1951-69, chancellor, 1969—. Mem. Am. Revolution Bicentennial Commn. Mem. Am. Hist. Assn., Am. Polit. Sci. Assn., Pi Gamma Mu. Mem. Soc. of Friends. Lectr. on problems on constl. govt. Radio lectr. in series of discussions on problems of democratic govt. Author: American Political Institutions and Social Idealism (booklet), 1928; A New Approach to the American Constitution, 1931; New Approach to the Study of the American Constitution (Pamphlet), Calif. Dept. Edn., 1940; Nixon Analecs, 1975. Contbr. to The Young Nixon, 1977. Home: 14314 Bronte Dr Whittier CA 90602

SMITH, PAUL TRAYLOR, bus. exec., former army officer; b. Burkesville, Ky., June 22, 1923; s. Samuel Joseph and Bonnie (Ferguson) S.; B.A., U. Md., 1960, M.B.A., 1962; m. Elizabeth C. Nolte, July 2, 1942; m. 2d, Phyllis Jean Corbin, Oct. 11, 1975; children—Gregory L., Douglas B., Paula J. Smith Richardson, Mary K. Enlisted in U.S. Army, 1940, advanced through grades to maj. gen., 1975; service in Japan, Ger., Korea, Vietnam; adj. gen. Continental Army Command, 1968-70; comdg. gen. U.S. Army Computer Systems Command, 1973-75; adj. gen. U.S. Army, 1975-77; exec. v.p. Taylor Craft Industries, Inc., Burkesville, Ky., 1977—. Bd. dirs. U.S. Army and USAF Exchange Service, Army Emergency Relief Fund, U.S. Soldiers and Airmens Home; mem. U.S. Olympic Com.; nat. relationships com. Boy Scouts Am. Decorated D.S.M., Legion of Merit with 2 oak leaf clusters, Bronze Star with oak leaf cluster. Mem. Assn. U.S. Army, Conseil Internat. du Sports Militaire (exec. com.), Ret. Officers Assn. Address: Box 607 Burkesville KY 42717

SMITH, PAULETT, pub., editor; b. Istanbul, Turkey, Jan. 3, 1945; d. Francois and Regine (Karasu) Tumay; student Fashion Inst. Tech., 1962-63; children—Nicole Smith, Erik Smith. Asso. editor Public Life, N.Y.C., 1969-72; pub. Twp. Newspaper chain, 1970-75; pub. WomensWeek newspaper, N.Y.C., 1976—; asso. pub. Inside N.Y. mag., 1979; mem. exec. bd. November Communications, Inc. Co-dir. Citizens for Local Democracy, 1970-74. Recipient Big Apple award for journalism N.Y.C. Jr. C. of C., 1978. Office: 145 E 49th St New York NY 10017

SMITH, PETER ALAN SOMERVAIL, educator, chemist; b. Erskine Hill, Eng., Apr. 16, 1920; s. Harold Beaumont and Eva (Barr) S.; came to U.S., 1923, naturalized, 1944; B.S., U. Calif. at Berkeley, 1941; Ph.D., U. Mich., 1944; m. Mary Charmaine Walsh, Apr. 19, 1952; children—Kent Alan Kinloch, Leslie Charmaine. Research asso. Penicillin project OSRD, 1944-45; mem. faculty U. Mich., 1945—, prof. chemistry, 1959—; Fulbright research scholar Auckland U., New Zealand, 1951; cons. in field, 1957—. Bd. dirs. Detroit Waldorf Sch., 1966-67, Rudolf Steiner Inst. Gt. Lakes Area, 1973—. Fellow Royal Philatelic Soc. (London); mem. Am. Chem. Soc., Anthroposophical Soc., Philatelic Soc. Egypt (Am. agt. 1966-78), Gamma Alpha (nat. treas. 1975—), Alpha Chi Sigma. Club: Collectors (N.Y.C.). Author: The Chemistry of Open-chain Organic Nitrogen Compounds, 2 vols., 1965, 66; also chpts. in books, research papers. Book rev. editor Jour. Am. Chem. Soc., 1971—. Home: 811 Mt Pleasant Ave Ann Arbor MI 48103

SMITH, PETER GARTHWAITE, natural gas co. exec., lawyer; b. South Orange, N.J., July 22, 1923; s. Karl Garthwaite and Fannie A. (Jones) S.; A.B., Princeton, 1948; LL.B., Yale, 1951; m. Anne Allerton Ward, Dec. 23, 1950; children—Allerton G., Thomas G., Amy G., Abigail G. Admitted to N.Y. bar, 1951; practiced in N.Y.C., 1951-54; atty. So. Natural Gas Co., Birmingham, Ala., 1955-58, asst. sec., atty., 1958-63, sec., atty., 1963-65, sec., asst. gen. counsel, 1965-66, gen. counsel, sec. 1966-71, v.p., 1967-71, exec. v.p., 1971-76, pres., 1976—, also dir.; exec. v.p., dir. So. Natural Resources, Inc., 1973—; dir. South Ga. Natural Gas Co., chmn. bd., 1975—; pres., dir. So. Energy Co., So. Deepwater Pipeline Co.; dir. 1st Ala. Bank of Birmingham. Bd. dirs. Birmingham Jr. Programs, 1959-61; v.p. Birmingham Festival Arts, 1975-76, pres., 1976-77; trustee Ala. Found. Hearing and Speech, 1965-69, 73-76, pres., 1967-69; bd. dirs. Birmingham council Camp Fire Girls, 1966-68, Birmingham Big Bros., Inc., 1975—; bd. dirs. Better Bus. Bur., 1976—; bd. dirs. Inst. Gas Tech., 1976—, chmn. bd., 1978—; bd. dirs. Gas Devels. Corp., 1976—, chmn. bd., 1978—. Served with USAAF, 1943-46. Mem. Am. Bar Assn., Asso. Industries Ala. (dir. 1974—), Am. (dir. 1976—), So. (dir. 1974-77) gas assns., Mid-Continent Oil and Gas Assn. (dir. 1977—), Interstate Natural Gas Assn. (dir. 1976—), Phi Delta Phi. Episcopalian. Clubs: Mountain Brook; Relay House; Downtown; Princeton (N.Y.C.). Home: 2605 Caldwell Mill Ln Mountain Brook AL 35243 Office: First Nat-So Natural Bldg Birmingham AL 35203

SMITH, PETER JOHN, geographer, educator; b. Rakaia, New Zealand, Sept. 18, 1931; s. Sidney Charles and Ethel May (Pettit) S.; B.A., U. New Zealand, 1953, M.A., 1954; diploma of town and regional planning (Central Mortgage and Housing Corp. planning fellow) U. Toronto, 1959; Ph.D., U. Edinburgh (Scotland), 1964; m. Sheana Mary Lee, May 30, 1959; children—Katrina, Hugh. Tchr. schs., New Zealand and Gt. Britain, 1951-55; research planner Calgary City Planning Dept., 1956-59; mem. faculty dept. geography U. Alta. (Can.), Edmonton, 1959—, prof., 1969—, chmn. dept., 1967-75. Planning cons., 1958—. Recipient certificate of distinction Town Planning Inst. Can., 1959. Leave fellow Can. Council, 1970, 77. Mem. Canadian Assn. Geographers (newsletter editor 1969—, councillor 1966-70, v.p. 1972-73, pres. 1973-74 editor Can. Geographer 1978—), Canadian Inst. Planners, Am. Assn. Geographers, New Zealand Geog. Soc. Author: Population and Production: An Introduction to Some Problems in Economic Geography, rev. edit., 1971; The Edmonton-Calgary Corridor, 1978; editor: The Prairie Provinces, 1972; Edmonton: The Emerging Metropolitan Pattern, 1978. Home: 64 Marlboro Rd Edmonton AB T6J 2C6 Canada

SMITH, PETER WALKER, mfg. co. exec.; b. Syracuse, N.Y., May 19, 1923; s. Stanley Sherwood and Elizabeth Wilkins (Young) S.; B.Chem. Engring., Rensselaer Poly. Inst., 1947; M.B.A., Harvard, 1948; LL.B., Cleve. Marshall Law Sch., 1955; m. Lucile Elizabeth Edson, June 22, 1946; children—Andrew E., Laurie (Mrs. Samuel J. Falzone), Pamela C. (Mrs. Denison W. Schweppe, Jr.), Stanley E. Admitted to Ohio bar, 1955; div. controller Raytheon Co., Lexington, Mass., 1958-66; v.p. finance, indsl. systems and equipment group Litton Industries Inc., Stamford, Conn., 1966-70; v.p. finance, treas. Copeland Corp., Sidney, Ohio, 1970-74; v.p. fin., treas., dir. Instrumentation Lab. Inc., Lexington, Mass., 1974-78; chief fin. officer, treas. Ionics, Inc., Watertown, Mass., 1978—. Served to 1st. lt. AUS, 1943-46, 50-52. Registered profl. engr., Ohio. Mem. Financial Execs. Inst., Accounting Council, Machinery and Allied Products Inst., Rensselaer Soc. Engrs., Sigma Xi, Tau Beta Pi. Home: 155 Monument St Concord MA 01742 Office: Ionics Inc 65 Grove St Watertown MA 02172

SMITH, PHILIP ALAN, clergyman; b. Belmont, Mass., Apr. 2, 1920; s. Herbert Leonard and Elizabeth (MacDonald) S.; B.A., Harvard U., 1942; B.D., Va. Theol. Sem., 1949, D.D., 1970; m. Barbara Ann Taylor, June 12, 1949; children—Sarah Elizabeth, Ann Warren, Jeremy Taylor. Ordained deacon, priest Episcopal Ch., 1949; asst. rector All Saints Ch., Atlanta, 1949-51; rector Christ Ch., Exeter, N.H., 1952-59; asst. prof. pastoral theology Va. Theol. Sem., 1959-62, chaplain, asso. dean student affairs, 1962-70; suffragan bishop Diocese of Va., Alexandria, 1970-73; bishop Diocese of N.H., 1973—. Served to capt. A.A.A., AUS, 1942-46; ETO. Decorated Bronze Star. Home: 122 School St Concord NH 03301 Office: 63 Green St Concord NH 03301

SMITH, PHILIP EDWARD LAKE, archaeologist, educator; b. Fortune, Nfld., Can., Aug. 12, 1927; s. George Frederick and Alice Maggie (Lake) S.; B.A., Acadia U., 1948; M.A., Harvard U., 1957, Ph.D., 1962; postgrad. Universite de Bordeaux, 1958-59; D. Litt. (hon.), Meml. U. Nfld., 1976; m. Fumiko Ikawa, 1959; 1 son, Douglas Philip Edward. Clk., Sun Life Assurance Co., Montreal, Que., Can., 1948-53; lectr. anthropology U. Toronto (Ont., Can.), 1961-63, asst. prof., 1963-65, asso. prof., 1965-66; asso. prof. anthropology Universite de Montreal, 1966-69, prof., 1969—. Can. Council Research grantee, 1969, 71, 74, 77, Leave grantee, 1970; NRC research grantee, 1967. Fellow Royal Soc. Can., Am. Anthrop. Assn.; mem. Internat. Union Prehistoric and Prehistoric Scis. (permanent council), Current Anthropology (asso.), Prehistoric Soc. (Eng.), Can. Soc. for Archaeology Abroad (past pres.), Permanent Council Internat. Union Anthrop. and Ethnol. Scis., AAAS, East Coast Marching, Archaeol. and Chowder Soc., Newfoundland Hist. Soc. Author: Le Solutreen en France, 1966; Food Production and its Consequences, 1976. Contbr. articles to profl. jours. Archaeol. expdn. dir., Egypt, 1962-63, Iran, 1965, 67, 69, 71, 74, 77; other field work in Mex., U.S.A., France, Iraq, French W. Indies, 1954-76. Home: 3955 Ramezay Ave Montreal PQ H3Y 3K3 Canada Office: Universite de Montreal Dept Anthropologie Montreal PQ H3C 3J7 Canada

SMITH, PHILIP GEORGE, educator; b. New Philadelphia, Ohio, Apr. 28, 1917; s. Peter Gee and Forrest (McGrew) S.; A.B., Ohio U., 1940; Ph.D., Ohio State U., 1954; m. Wilanna Smedley Neal, Aug. 12, 1943; children—Philip Neal, David Hunt. Asst. prof. Western Res. U., 1953-55, U. Va., 1955-58; asso. prof. U. Tenn., 1958-61; mem. faculty Ind. U., 1961—, prof. philosophy edn., 1963—, chmn. dept. history, philosophy edn., 1964-76; vis. prof. Wayne State U., 1959, U. Hawaii, 1965. Served to capt., inf., AUS, 1941-44. Mem. Am. Philos. Assn., Philosophy of Edn. Soc. (pres. 1965-66), John Dewey Soc. (exec. bd. 1966-68, 72-74), Am. Assn. U. Profs., Am. Ednl. Research Assn., A.A.A.S., Phi Delta Kappa. Author: Philosophic Mindedness in Educational Administration, 1956; (with H.G. Hulfish) Reflective Thinking-The Method of Education, 1961; Philosophy of Education; Introductory Studies, 1965; Value Theories and Problems of Education, 1970; also articles. Home: 206 S Smith Rd Bloomington IN 47401

SMITH, PHILIP LAWTON, food co. exec.; b. LaGrange, Ga., Dec. 16, 1933; s. Hayden McKinley and Anne Mae (Slaughter) S.; B.B.A. with distinction, U. Mich., 1960, M.B.A. with distinction, 1961; m. Nancy Lou Fagan, Sept. 8, 1956; children—Kevin James, Stephen Eric, Scott Andrew. Account exec. Benton & Bowles, N.Y.C., 1961-65; v.p., account exec. Ted Bates, Inc., N.Y.C., 1965-66; product mgr. Gen. Foods Corp., White Plains, N.Y., 1966, product group mgr., 1966-67, advt. and merchandising div. Jell-O div., 1969-70, v.p. mktg. and devel., 1970-72, exec. v.p., 1972-73, mgr. strategic bus. unit, 1973-74, v.p. Gen. Foods and pres. Pet Foods div., 1974-77, group v.p. U.S. Grocery group and pres. Maxwell House div., 1977-79, exec. v.p. fin. and adminstrn., 1979—. Mem. Bedford (N.Y.) Sch. Bd., 1974-77; trustee World Edn., 1979—. Served to capt., USMC, 1954-58. Office: 250 North St White Plains NY 10625

SMITH, PHILIP RICHTER, banker; b. Mpls., Apr. 23, 1930; s. Clarence Burt and Jessie Elizabeth (Richter) S.; B.B.A., U. Wis., 1952, LL.B., 1957; m. Katherine Lichtfeldt, June 28, 1958; children—Anne, Margaret, Elizabeth. Admitted to Wis. bar, 1957, Ill. bar, 1960; new bus. rep. Continental Ill. Nat. Bank & Trust Co., Chgo., 1957-60; asst. trust officer First Nat. Bank Racine (Wis.), 1960-63; with First Wis. Nat. Bank Madison (Wis.), 1963—, v.p., sr. trust officer, 1969-76, sr. v.p., 1976-77, exec. v.p., 1977—, also dir., mem. exec. com.; lectr. law U. Wis., 1967-70; mem. faculty Nat. Trust Sch., Northwestern U., 1965-75. Pres. Madison Estate Council, 1968. Bd. dirs. Madison Gen. Hosp., 1973—, 2d vice chmn. bd., 1975-77, 1st vice chmn., 1977—; trustee Rotary Found. Served with AUS, 1953-55. Conglist. (trustee). Rotarian (dir. Downtown Madison 1973-75). Clubs: Madison (dir. 1972-75), Maple Bluff Country (dir. 1974-77) (Madison). Contbg. editor Eckhardt's Workbook for Wisconsin Estate Planners, 1965-70. Home: 7009 Applewood Dr Madison WI 53711 Office: PO Box 7900 Madison WI 53707

SMITH, PHILLIP HARTLEY, steel co. exec.; b. Sydney, Australia, Jan. 26, 1927; s. Norman Edward and Elizabeth (Williams) S.; came to U.S., 1950, naturalized, 1960; B.Engring. with 1st class honors in Mining and Metallurgy, U. Sydney, 1950; Metall. Engr., M.I.T., 1952; diploma indsl. relations U. Chgo., 1958; LL.D., Grove City Coll., 1975; m. Martha Frances Dittrich, June 4, 1955; children—Elizabeth Thomas, Johanna, Alice, Margaret, Sarah. Successively trainee, metallurgist, foreman Indiana Harbor, Ind., Inland Steel Co., 1952-55; successively trainee, metallurgist, dir. purchasing and planning La Salle Steel Co., Hammond, Ind., 1956-64; with Copperweld Corp., Pitts., 1964—, pres., 1968-77, chmn., 1973-77; pres., chief exec. officer Bekaert Steel Wire Corp., Pitts., 1979—. Trustee, Grove City (Pa.) Coll., Berea (Ky.) Coll.; chmn. Inroads Inc. Served as cadet officer Australian Mcht. Marine, 1942-43, Royal Australian Fleet Aux., 1943. Recipient Nat. Open Hearth Steelmaking award, 1955. Mem. Sigma Xi. Presbyterian (trustee Ministers Fund; ruling elder). Clubs: Univ. (Chgo.); Duquesne (Pitts.); Fox Chapel Golf, Rolling Rock (Ligonier, Pa.). Editor Am. Inst. Metall. Engrs. Handbook, Mechanical Working of Steel, 1961. Patentee in field. Home: 102 Haverford Rd Pittsburgh PA 15238 Office: One Allegheny Sq Pittsburgh PA 15212

SMITH, PHILLIP NOLAN, JR., lawyer; b. Pittsburg, Tex., Nov. 16, 1943; s. Phillip Nolan and Emma Lee (George) S.; B.B.A., U. Tex., 1966; LL.B., Baylor U., 1968; LL.M., Harvard U., 1970. Admitted to Tex. bar, 1970; partner firm Hughes & Hill, Dallas, 1973—. Home: 4505 Dorset Rd Dallas TX 75229 Office: 1000 Mercantile Dallas Bldg Dallas TX 75201

SMITH, POMEROY, oil prodn. co. exec.; b. Newark, Feb. 2, 1924; s. Van Tuyl and Elmira A. (Spurr) S.; B.S. in Mech. Engring., Princeton U., 1948; m. Betty J. Perry, Feb. 1, 1958; children—Elizabeth Spurr, Pomeroy II, Andrew Albright, Timothy Perry. Ind. oil operator, Midland, Tex., 1954-70; founder Coquina Oil Corp., Midland, 1970, pres., 1970-73, chmn. bd., 1970—, chief exec. officer, 1970—,(Coquina Oil Corp. merged with St. Joe Mineral Corp., 1977). Pres. Midland YMCA, 1968-69; pres. Trinity Sch., 1969-71, trustee, 1963-79; trustee Midland Meml. Hosp., 1976—, BTA Found., 1968—, Museum of S.W., 1979—. Mem. Ind. Petroleum Assn. Am., Am. Assn. Petroleum Landmen, Mid-Continent Oil and Gas Assn., Tex. Mid-Continent Oil and Gas Assn., Midland C. of C. Club: Racquet (pres. 1969-70, trustee 1967-69). Home: 3 Willow Ct Midland TX 79701 Office: Coquina Oil Corp PO Drawer 2960 Midland TX 79702

SMITH, QUENTIN MILLER, JR., educator; b. Cookeville, Tenn., Dec. 14, 1924; s. Quentin Miller and Esmerelda (Robinson) S.; student Vanderbilt U., 1941-43; D.D.S., U. Tenn., 1946; M.P.H., U. Mich., 1957; m. Lois Ann Gann, May 31, 1947; children—Quentin Miller III, Linda Lois. Dental intern John Gaston Hosp., Memphis, 1947; instr. U. Tenn., 1948; commd. asst. dental surgeon USPHS, 1948, advanced through grades to dental dir., 1958, dep. chief Div. Dental Resources, 1954-62, asso. chief Div. Dental Health, 1963-64; chief Office Program Planning and Evaluation, Div. Indian Health, Albuquerque, 1965-66; regional dental cons. Dept. Health, Edn. and Welfare Region IV, Atlanta, 1966-67, asso. regional health dir., 1967-69; ret., 1969; prof. dept. community dentistry U. Fla. Coll. Dentistry, Gainesville, 1969—, chmn. dept., 1969-76; fellow Am. Bd. Dental Pub. Health, pres., 1978. Fellow Am. Pub. Health Assn. Am. Coll. Dentists; mem. Am., Fla. dental assns., Am. Assn. Pub. Health Dentists, Am. Assn. Dental Schs., Kappa Sigma, Delta Sigma Delta, Delta Omega. Democrat. Contbr. numerous articles to profl. jours. Home: PO Box 404 McIntosh FL 32664

SMITH, R. G., corp. exec.; b. Bonham, Tex., Mar. 3, 1923; s. Rainer G. and Angie (Henson) S.; B.S., Austin Coll., 1949; postgrad. So. Meth. U., 1950-51; m. Frances Aderholt, Aug. 2, 1946; 1 stepson, Joe Regian. With M. & P. Bank, Sherman, Tex., 1948-49; auditor U.S. Dept. Agr., 1949-51; with Southland Corp., Dallas, 1951—, controller, 1960—, sec., 1971—, treas., 1973—. Active Richardson Symphony Orch. Served with USAAF, 1941-45. Mem. Richardson C. of C., Adminstrv. Mgmt. Soc., Budget Execs. Inst. Club: Optimist (Dallas). Home: 1204 Cheyenne Pl Richardson TX 75080 Office: 2828 N Haskell Ave Dallas TX 75204

SMITH, RALPH CARLISLE, ednl. cons.; b. West New York, N.J., May 24, 1910; s. Alfred Thomas and Katharine (Haller) S.; Chem.-Engr., Rensselaer Poly. Inst., 1931; J.D., George Washington U., 1939; M.A., U. N.M., 1955, Ph.D., 1962; m. Harriett V. Petersen, May 20, 1954. Chemist, E.I. duPont de Nemours & Co., Inc., 1931-35; engr. U.S. Patent Office, 1935-37, Colgate Palmolive Co., 1938-42; admitted to D.C. bar, 1940, also U.S. Supreme Ct.; patent counsel Manhattan Project, Los Alamos, 1943-47; asst. dir. Los Alamos Sci. Lab., 1946-57; asst. to pres. nuclear electronic div. ACF Industries, 1957-60; mem. faculty N.Mex. Highlands U., 1961—, prof. polit. sci., 1965—, v.p., acad. dean, 1966-70, pres., 1970-73, counsel to pres., 1974-78; mem. law faculty U. N.M., 1950-57; cons. Teaching Machines, Albuquerque, 1961-65, Lytle Corp., Albuquerque, 1960-61. County probate judge, Los Alamos, 1950-55 justice of peace, Los Alamos, 1948-50. Chmn. planning commn., Las Vegas, 1964-78. Republican candidate for Congress, 1956. Served to lt. col., C.E., AUS, 1942-47. Decorated Legion of Merit, Army Commendation medal. Registered profl. engr., N.Mex. Fellow Am. Inst. Chemists; mem. Am. Bar Assn., Am. Chem. Soc., Am. Phys. Soc., Am. Nuclear Soc., Am. Inst. Chem. Engrs., Order of Coif, Sigma Xi, Tau Beta Pi, Phi Kappa Phi. Co-author: The Effects of Atomic Weapons, 1950; History of Los Alamos Scientific Laboratory, 1961. Co-editor: National Nuclear Energy Series, 1951. Patentee in field. Home: 838 Arguello Blvd San Francisco CA 94118

SMITH, RALPH JUDSON, educator; b. Herman, Nebr., June 5, 1916; s. George Andrew and Gwen (Taylor) S.; B.S., U. Calif., 1938, M.S., 1940, E.E., 1942; Ph.D., Stanford, 1945; m. Louise Dally, July 17, 1938; children—Kent Warner, Sheridan Jeffrey, Nancy Carolyn, Elaine Kathryn. Engr., Standard Oil Co. of Calif., 1938-39; partner Walton & Smith, cons. engrs., 1947-56; instr. engring. math. San Jose State Coll., 1940-42, prof. and head engring. dept., 1945-51, chmn. engring. and math. div., 1951-56; asst. prof. elec. engring. Stanford, 1942-44, research asso. elec. engring., 1944-45, prof., 1957—, asso. chmn. dept. elec. engring., 1959-76; adviser on electronics for Philippine Dept. Edn. under ICA, 1957-58, Ministry of Edn., Republic of South Vietnam under AID, 1965. Fellow I.E.E.E.; mem. Am. Soc. Engring. Edn. Author: Engineering as a Career, 1956, 3d edit., 1969; Circuits, Devices and Systems, 1966, 3d edit., 1976; Electronics: Circuits and Devices, 1973. Contbr. articles to profl. jours. Address: Dept Elec Engring Stanford U Stanford CA 94305

SMITH, RALPH LEE, author, musician; b. Phila., Nov. 6, 1927; s. Hugh Harold and Barbara (Schatkin) S.; B.A., Swarthmore Coll., 1951; m. Betty H. Smith, Sept. 1954 (div. Jan. 1963); children—David Bruce, Robert Hugh; m. 2d, Mary Louise Hollowell, 1971 (div. 1977); m. 3d, Shizuko Maruyama, 1977; 1 dau., Lisa Koyuki. Editor, Nat. Better Business Bur., N.Y.C., 1954-58; free lance writer, 1958-73; asso. prof., Sch. Communications, Howard U., 1973-76, dir. telecommunications studies, tech. and econs., 1979—; partner Berner and Smith Assos., 1978-79; folk musician on Appalacian dulcimer, banjo, harmonica; recording artist Elektra, Union, Meadowlands, Skyline. Recipient Russell L. Cecil Distinguished Med. Writing award Arthritis Found., 1963; A.M.A. Jour. award, 1965; Nat. Mag. award Columbia U. Grad. Sch. Journalism, 1971; Bus. and Financial Journalism award U. Mo., 1971. Fletcher Pratt fellow Bread Loaf Writers Conf. Middlebury Coll., 1965; Nelson Poynter fellow in journalism and communications Yale, 1971-72. Author: The Health Hucksters, 1960; The Bargain Hucksters, 1962; The Grim Truth About Mutual Funds, 1963; The New Nations of Africa, 1963; Getting to Know the World Health Organization, 1963; The Tarnished Badge, 1965; At Your own Risk, 1969; The Wired Nation 1970. Recs. include Old Fashioned Dance Music, 1969; Allan Block and Ralph Lee Smith, 1971; Dulcimer: Old Time and Traditional Music, 1973. Home: 1662 Chimney House Rd Reston VA 22090 Office: 204 G St NE Washington DC 20002

SMITH, RANKIN MCEACHERN, ins. co. exec., profl. football team exec.; b. Atlanta, Oct. 29, 1925; ed. Emory U., U. Fla., U. Ga.; married; 5 children. With Life Ins. Co. of Ga., 1943—, agy. asst. v.p., 1954, corp. sec., 1954-57, agy. v.p., 1957-63, exec. v.p., 1963-68, sr. v.p., 1968-70, pres., chief exec. officer, from 1970, later chmn., now dir.; owner Atlanta Falcons football team, 1965—, past pres., now chmn. bd.; dir. Greyhound, Inc., Trust Co. Ga. Assos. Div. chmn. United Way, Atlanta, 1973-74; Ga. sightsaving chmn. Nat. Soc. for Prevention Blindness, 1973-74; mem. exec. com. Central Atlanta Progress, Inc.; mem. exec. bd. Atlanta Area Council Boy Scouts Am. Bd. dirs. Better Bus. Bur. Atlanta; trustee U. Ga. Found., Reinhardt Coll., Waleska, Ga., Lovett Sch., Atlanta. Mem. Atlanta C. of C., Commerce Club, Chi Pi. Methodist. Mason (Shriner). Rotarian. Clubs: Capitol City (gov.), Piedmont Driving. Office: care Atlanta Falcons I-85 and Suwanee Rd Suwanee GA 30174*

SMITH, RANKIN MCEACHERN, JR., profl. football club exec.; b. Atlanta, Aug. 23, 1947; s. Rankin McEachern and Miriam (Wellman) S.; B.B.A., U. Ga., 1971; m. Rebecca Robinson, Sept. 11, 1970; 1 dau., Caroline McEachern. With Life of Ga. Ins. Co., 1971-75; with Atlanta Falcons, 1975—, now pres.; dir. Life of Ga. Ins. Co. Bd. dirs. Atlanta Cerebral Palsy Found., Greater Atlanta USO, Boy Scouts Am. Served with U.S. Army. Methodist. Clubs: Capitol City, Piedmont Driving, Rotary. Office: Suwanee Rd at I-85 Suwanee GA 30174

SMITH, RAY FRED, entomologist, educator; b. Los Angeles, Jan. 20, 1919; s. Ray M. and Elsie E. (Weisheit) S.; B.S., U. Calif. at Berkeley, 1940, M.S., 1941, Ph.D., 1946; D.Agr.Sc. (honors causa), Landbouwhogeschool, Wageningen, 1976; m. Elizabeth J. McClure; children—Donald, Thomas (dec.), Kathrine N. Stark. Tech., lab. asst. U. Calif. at Berkeley, 1941-45, asso. expt. sta., 1945-46, instr. entomology and jr. entomologist expt. sta., 1946-48, asst. prof. entomology, asst. entomologist expt. sta., 1948-54, asso. prof., asso. entomologist expt. sta., 1954-60, prof., entomologist expt. sta., 1960—, chmn. dept. entomology and parasitology, Berkeley-Davis, 1959-63, chmn. dept. entomol. scis., Berkeley, 1963-73; cons. FAO, AID. Guggenheim fellow, 1950-51. Fellow Entomol. Soc. Am. (pres. 1976), Am. Acad. Arts and Sci., AAAS, Entomol. Soc. Can.; mem. Brit. Ecol. Soc., Ecol. Soc. Am., Pacific Coast Entomol. Soc. Home: 3092 Hedaro Ct Lafayette CA 94549 Office: 2288 Fulton Suite 310 U Calif Berkeley CA 94704

SMITH, RAY WINFIELD, educator; b. Marlboro, N.H., June 4, 1897; s. John Henry and Ellen Maria (Stone) S.; B.S., Dartmouth, 1918, L.H.D. (hon.), 1958; m. Bonnie D. Jones, Oct. 20, 1923; children—Michel Frans, Champney Fowlis. With Am. oil interest Belgium, Netherlands, Germany, 1922-36; propr. import-export firm, Houston, 1936-42; govt. ofcl., 1946-55; econ. advisor U.S. comdt., Berlin, Germany, 1951-52; U.S. commr. Mil. Security Bd., Germany, 1952-55; pres. Ray Winfield Smith Found., 1955-73; mem. faculty, mem. supervising com. for Ray Winfield Smith lectures on origins, devel. and future prospects of mankind Dartmouth, 1974—. Dir. Akhenaten Temple Project in U.A.R. 1965-72; dir. research project on City of Isfahan, Iran; cons. Brookhaven Nat. Lab. Bd. visitors Boston Mus. of Fine Arts, 1956-62. Vice pres., exec. dir. Eisenhower-Nixon Club, D.C., 1956; gen. chmn. N.H. Vols. for Nixon-Lodge, 1960; officer of inaugural com., Washington, 1957. Served as 2d lt. Ordnance Dept., AEF, 1918-19; served to lt. col. USAAF, 1944-45. Decorated Purple Heart, Legion Merit; recipient 1st award AIA. Fellow German Archeol. Inst., A.A.A.S. (council member); mem. Internat. Com. Ancient Glass (chmn. 1948-68), Archeol. Inst. Am. (mem. bd. trustees 1957-66, chmn. com. ancient glass 1955-68), Am. Research Center Egypt, Cairo (dir. 1963-65), Sigma Alpha Epsilon. Club: Army and Navy (Washington). Author: Glass from the Ancient World, 1957; numerous articles on ancient glass; bd. editorial rev. Jour. Glass Studies; sr. editor The Akhenaten Temple Project; patentee in fields directional drilling, elevator safety. Attaché for U.S. in Olympic games, Amsterdam, 1928. Home: 3435 Westheimer Rd Apt 501 Houston TX 77027

SMITH, RAYMOND D(ANIEL), pub. co. exec.; b. St. Johnsville, N.Y., Aug. 4, 1912;. Emery Augustus and Ada (Groff) S.; student N.Y. U., 1949; m. Blanche Virginia Wolfram, Feb. 11, 1960; 1 stepson, Charles H. Copeland. Newspaper advt. Union Star, Schenectady, 1929-31; chemist, dispatcher, gen. office Standard Oil N.J., 1934-51; free lance photographer, 1944-50; pub. Cats mag., Washington, 1951—; asso. pub. CATS mag., Japan, 1977—; instr. Henry George Sch. Social Sci., 1948-50. Mem. A.A.A.S., Henry George Found. Am., Am. Cat Fanciers Assn., Crown Cat Fanciers Fedn., Am. Contract Bridge League. Democrat. Presbyn. (elder). Editor: (with Blanche V. Smith) Complete Cat Ency. Contbr. articles to profl. jours., also World Book, other encys.; poetry to In Praise of Cats, other anthologies. Home: 1928 Vernon Pl South Daytona FL 32014 Office: PO Box 37 Port Orange FL 32019. *My life has been shaped by others much more than by myself. My mother and siblings, my religion, my teachers, my employers, my friends, by wife, and for nearly thirty years my employees and business associates, all have contributed generously—knowingly and unknowingly—to my accomplishments in my relatively small world.*

SMITH, RAYMOND G., ins. co. exec.; b. Columbus, Ohio, Nov. 20, 1916; s. Raymond G. and Nellie (Dorbert) S.; student Ohio State U., also mgmt. devel. program, Case Inst. Tech., 1958; m. Louise Lenora Patton, Nov. 3, 1939; children—David R., Donald R., Barbara Louise. With Nationwide Ins. Cos., 1937—; now sr. v.p. fin. Office Pres., Nationwide Mut. Ins. Co., Nationwide Mut. Fire Ins. Co., Nationwide Life Ins. Co., Nationwide Gen. Ins. Co., Nationwide Found., Nationwide Premium Accounts, Inc., Nationwide Transport, Inc., Nationwide Property and Casualty Ins. Co., Automotive Recycling Center, Inc., Nationwide Profl. Services, Inc.; dir. Peoples Travel Service, Inc. Served with AUS, 1943-46. Mem. Am. Mgmt. Assn., Treas.'s Club, Columbus Area C. of C., Fin. Execs. Inst., Fin. Mgmt. Assn. Home: 1280 Fountaine Dr Columbus OH 43221 Office: One Nationwide Plaza Columbus OH 43216

SMITH, RAYMOND LLOYD, profl. assn. exec.; b. Vanceboro, Maine, Jan. 25, 1917; s. Ivan and Genevieve (Gatcomb) S.; B.S. cum laude, U. Alaska, 1943; M.S. in Metall. Engring., U. Pa., 1951, Ph.D. in Metall. Engring., 1953; D.Sc. (hon.), Western Mich. U.; LL.D., No. Mich. U.; m. Beatrice Bennett, Dec. 4, 1943; children—Bennett Charles, Martin Lloyd. Instr. math. U. Alaska, 1946-47, asst. prof. metallurgy, 1948-49; research asso. dept. metallurgy U. Pa., 1949-53; sr. research metallurgist Franklin Inst. Labs., Phila., 1953, sect. chief metallurgy, 1954-56, asso. dir., 1957, tech. dir., 1958-59; prof., head metall. dept. Mich. Technol. U., Houghton, 1959-64, coordinator of research, 1960-64, pres., 1965-79; pres. Am. Soc. Metals, 1979—; mem. adv. com. Gt. Lakes and Marine Waters Center, U. Mich.; mem. materials adv. com. Office Tech. Assessment; mem. Mich. Gov.'s Adv. Panel for Hazardous and Toxic Wastes; mem. Nat. Materials Adv. Bd.; dir. Lake Superior & Ishpeming R.R. Bd. dirs. Lake Shore, Inc.; v.p. bd. trustees Mich. Tech. Fund; bd. govs. Greater Mich. Found. Served with AUS, 1943-46. Recipient Distinguished Alumnus award U. Alaska, Clair M. Donovan award Mich. Tech. U., D. Robert Yarnall award U. Pa. Engring. Sch.; Outstanding Service award Air Force ROTC. Fellow Metall. Soc.; AIME, Mich. Council Coll. Pres.'s, Scabbard and Blade, Blue Key, Tau Beta Pi, Alpha Sigma Mu, Alpha Phi Omega, Phi Kappa Phi, Theta Tau. Lion, Rotarian. Contbr. numerous articles to metall. sci. jours. Home: PO Box 98 Chassell MI 49916

SMITH, RAYMOND THOMAS, ins. analyst; b. Chgo., Jan. 24, 1898; s. Nicholas H. and Mary (Pival) S.; student Northwestern U.; m. Helen Marshall, Aug. 10, 1955. Dir., vice chmn., mem. exec. com. Alfred M. Best Co., Inc., Chgo., pub. Best's Ins. Reports, until 1968; asso. with Alfred M. Best as intermediary in purchase, sale, merger and reinsurance of ins. cos., 1917—; chmn. mng. dir. Life Ins. Investors, Inc., Chgo., 1954-77; chmn bd., dir. Life Stock Research Corp., until 1977. Clubs: Union League, Tower, Executives (past dir.) (Chgo.); Sunset Ridge Country (Northbrook, Ill.); Thunderbird Country (Palm Springs, Calif.). Home: 33 Briar Rd Golf IL 60029 Office: 33 Briar Rd Golf IL 60029

SMITH, RAYMOND THOMAS, educator; b. Oldham, Lancashire, Eng., Jan. 12, 1925; s. Harry and Margaret (Mulchrone) S.; B.A., Cambridge (Eng.) U., 1950, M.A., 1951, Ph.D., 1954; m. Flora Alexandrina Tong, June 30, 1954; children—Fenela, Colin, Anthony. Sociol. research officer govt. Brit. Guiana, 1951-54; research fellow U. W.I., 1954-59, prof. sociology U. Ghana, 1959-62; sr. lectr. sociology, prof. anthropology, U. West Indies, 1962-66; prof. anthropology U. Chgo., 1966—, chmn. dept. anthropology, 1975—; vis. prof. U. Calif. at Berkeley, 1957-58, McGill U., Montreal, 1964-65; mem. com. on child devel. research and public policy NRC. Served with RAF, 1943-48. Fellow Am. Anthrop. Assn.; mem. Assn. Social Anthropologists. Author: The Negro Family in British Guiana, 1956; British Guiana, 1962; co-author: Class Differences and Sex Roles in American Kinship and Family Structure, 1973; contbr. articles to profl. jours. Office: U Chgo 1126 E 59th St Chicago IL 60637

SMITH, RAYMOND WILLIAM, librarian; b. Deposit, N.Y., Sept. 25, 1923; s. Henry William and Jean (Stinson) S.; B.A., Syracuse U., 1950, M.S. in L.S., 1951; m. Evelyn Lewis, Aug. 31, 1946; children—Robert L., Stephen W., Jerrold A. (dec.). Reference asst., br. librarian Schenectady County (N.Y.) Pub. Library, 1952-57; head librarian Eastern Shore Pub. Library, Accomac, Va., 1957-59, 60-61; head readers services State U. Coll. Edn. at New Paltz, N.Y., 1959-60; asst. dir. So. Tier Library System, Corning, N.Y., 1961-65; state librarian Library Commn. Del., 1965-66; asst. dir. Four County Library System, Binghamton, N.Y., 1967-77, dir., 1978—; del. N.Y. State Gov.'s Conf. on Libraries, 1978. Mem. Gov. of Delaware Com. Reading, 1965-66. Served to 1st lt. AUS, 1942-45, 51-52; ETO, Korea. Decorated Combat Infantrymen's badge with star. Mem. A.L.A., N.Y. State Library Assn. (chmn. bookmobile com. 1965, mem. membership com. 1967-75, v.p. 1976-77, pres. pub. libraries sect. 1977-78). Home: 4716 Amherst Ave Binghamton NY 13903 Office: Clubhouse Rd Binghamton NY 13903. *The only significant success in this ephemeral existence is an act of kindness or compassion for one's fellow beings. Peace and happiness are the twin peaks of any worthwhile civilization and it is only when a person tries to bring them within the reach of others that he experiences them himself.*

SMITH, REA T. WATERS, assn. exec.; b. Jamestown, N.Y., Apr. 13, 1918; d. F. Coy and Rena L. (Schultz) Waters; student Allegheny Coll., 1937, Jamestown Bus. Coll., 1938; m. Shirley D. Smith, Nov. 24, 1945. Asst. sec., time study accountant Am. Aviation Co., Jamestown, 1941-45; account exec., public relations counselor, partner Shirley D. Smith & Assos., Memphis, 1947-57; asst. to exec. dir. Public Relations Soc. Am., N.Y.C., 1957-70, v.p. adminstrn.,

1971-74, exec. v.p., 1975-79; exec. dir. Found. for Public Relations Research and Edn., Inc., N.Y.C., 1979—; TV performer, producer, Memphis, 1949-52. Bd. govs. Jacob Riis Settlement House. Mem. Public Relations Soc. Am., Internat. Public Relations Assn.; Women Execs. in Public Relations (treas. 1971-73). Home: 4 Peter Cooper Rd New York NY 10010 Office: 845 3d Ave New York NY 10022

SMITH, RED (WALTER WELLESLEY), sports columnist; b. Green Bay, Wis., Sept. 25, 1905; s. Walter Philip and Ida Elizabeth (Richardson) S.; A.B., Notre Dame U., 1927, LL.D., 1968; m. Catherine Cody, Feb. 11, 1933 (dec. 1967); m. 2d, Phyllis Warner Weiss, Nov. 2, 1968; children—Catherine W. Smith Halloran, Terence F. Reporter Milw. Sentinel, 1927-28; copyeditor, sportswriter, rewrite man St. Louis Star, 1928-36; sportswriter, columnist Phila. Record, 1936-45; sports columnist N.Y. Herald Tribune, 1945-66, World-Jour.-Tribune, N.Y.C., 1966-67, Pubs. Newspaper Syndicate, 1967-71, N.Y. Times, 1971—. Recipient numerous awards. Clubs: Players (N.Y.C.); Louis Norman Newsom. Author books and mag. articles. Home: 510 West Rd New Canaan CT 06610 Office: New York Times 229 W 43d St New York City NY 10036

SMITH, RHOTEN ALEXANDER, ednl. adminstr.; b. Dallas, Jan. 17, 1921; s. Rhoten Alexander and Ruth Elizabeth (Cooke) S.; student Tex. Wesleyan Coll., 1940, U. Tex., 1940- 42; A.B., U. Kans., 1946, M.A., 1948; Ph.D., U. Calif. at Berkeley, 1955; m. Barbara Maria Okerberg, Dec. 24, 1942; children—Susan Jane (Mrs. William W. Warren), Tyler Rhoten. Instr. polit. sci. U. Kans., 1947-49, 51-54, asst. prof., 1954- 57, asso. prof., 1957-58; asso. dir. Citizenship Clearing House, N.Y.C., 1955-56, dir., 1958-61; prof. politics N.Y. U., 1958-61; dean Coll. Liberal Arts, Temple U., 1961-67; pres. No. Ill. U., DeKalb, 1967-71; provost U. Pitts., 1971—. Research asso. Govt. Research Center, U. Kans., 1946-48, 51-58; research cons. Kans. Legisative Council, summer 1954, cons. survey higher edn. in Kans. of council, summer 1957; cons. Kans. Constl. Revision Commn., 1957-58; mem. Pub. Com. for Humanities in Pa., 1973-77. Adviser to chmn. Kans. Democratic Party, 1956-58. Served to 1st lt., pilot USAAF, 1942-45. Fellow A.A.A.S.; mem. Am., Midwest polit. sci. assns. Democrat. Author: The Life of a Bill, rev. edit., 1961; Republican Primary Fight: A Study in Factionalism (with C.J. Hein), 1958. Home: 717 Amberson Ave Pittsburgh PA 15232

SMITH, RICHARD CARLISLE, educator; b. Marietta, Okla., May 13, 1930; s. Richard C. and Sue V. (Brigham) S.; B.A., Austin Coll., 1951; B.D., Louisville (Ky.) Presbyn. Sem., 1954; M.A., U. Ky., 1957; Ph.D., U. Ill., 1961; m. Eddie Lee Embry, June 1, 1954; children—Mark R., Bruce A., Scott D., Brian D. Ordained to ministry Presbyterian Ch., 1954; minister Presbyn. Ch., Troy, Ky., 1954-57, Bement, Ill., 1958-60; asst. prof. history Wis. State U., Superior, 1961-62, Tex. Christian U., Ft. Worth, 1962-65; asst. prof. classics U. Alta., Edmonton, 1965-68, asso. prof., 1969-77, prof., 1977—, dept. chmn., 1975—, dir. Alta. Sch. of Rome, summer 1974, 75, 76, 77, 78; minister Presbyn. Ch. in Can., Edmonton, 1971—. Mem. Classical Assn. Can. West (pres. 1978-79), Classical Assn. Can., Am. Philol Assn., Archaeol. Inst. Am. Home: 3323 108th St Edmonton AB T6J-3C9 Canada Office: U Alta Dept Classics Edmonton AB Canada

SMITH, RICHARD EMERSON (DICK SMITH), make-up artist, sculptor; b. Larchmont, N.Y., June 26, 1922; s. Richard Roy and Coral (Brown) S.; B.A., Yale, 1944; m. Jocelyn De Rosa, Jan. 10, 1949; children—Douglas Todd, David. Founder, dir. makeup dept. NBC-TV, N.Y.C., 1945-59, developed makeup materials, colors and techniques for black and white, and color TV; pioneered use of rubber and plastics in TV makeup; inventor spl. methods to cope with TV quick-changes; creator character masks permitting facial expression; profl. sculptor; freelance makeup artist and cons., 1959—; make-up dir. Talent Assos., Ltd., N.Y.C., 1959-61, make-up dir. numerous films including Requiem for a Heavyweight, 1961, All The Way Home, 1962, The Cardinal, 1963, The World of Henry Orient, 1963, Little Big Man, 1969, Who is Harry Kellerman, 1970, The Godfather, 1971, The Exorcist, 1973, The Godfather, Part II, 1974, The Sunshine Boys, 1975, The Sentinel, 1976, The Heretic, 1976, Altered States, 1978-79; make-up specialist It's a Mad Mad Mad Mad World, 1962; make-up artist TV prodn. Mark Twain Tonight, 1967 (recipient Emmy award 1967), The Strange Case of Dr. Jekyll and Mr. Hyde, 1968; make-up cons. Midnight Cowboy, 1968; Carnal Knowledge, 1970, Taxi Driver, 1975, Marathan Man, 1975, Burnt Offerings, 1975, The Fury, 1978, The Deer Hunter, 1978. Served as 2d lt. F.A., Army U.S., World War II. Contbr. cons. Vogue, Seventeen, other mags. Inventor lipstick applicator. Address: 209 Murray Ave Larchmont NY 10538

SMITH, RICHARD F., mfg. co. exec.; b. Grand Rapids, Mich., Aug. 26, 1938; s. Harry A. and Ann Mary (Grodus) S.; B.S. in Chemistry, Aquinas Coll., 1960; Ph.D. in Organic Chemistry, U. Mich., 1965; m. Sharon Connell, Dec. 28, 1964; children—Matthew, Katherine. asst. to pres. GAF Corp., N.Y.C., 1973-74, v.p. comml. devel., 1974-78, exec. v.p. tech. services, 1978—. Mem. Comml. Devel. Assn., Soc. Chem. Industry, Soc. Plastics Engrs. Club: Rockefeller Center Luncheon. Home: Mount Kemble Lake Morristown NJ 07960 Office: 140 W 51st St New York NY 10020*

SMITH, RICHARD FREDERICK, chemist, educator; b. Lockport, N.Y., Jan. 31, 1929; s. Frederick E. and Dorothy (Iles) S.; B.S., Allegheny Coll., 1950; Ph.D., U. Rochester, 1954; m. Eleanor Dolores Besemer, Nov. 24, 1951; children—Marilyn Elizabeth, Kenneth Richard, Janet Louise. Research chemist Monsanto Chem. Co., 1953-55, Sterling Winthrop Research Inst., 1955-57; asso. prof., then prof. State U. N.Y. at Albany, 1957-65; NSF faculty fellow U. Calif. at Los Angeles, 1962-63; prof. chemistry, chmn. dept. State U. Coll. at Geneseo, 1965-68, prof., 1968-74, Univ. Distinguished Teaching prof., 1974, vis. scholar, 1974—. Recipient Miller Music prize Allegheny Coll., 1950; research grantee Research Found. State U. N.Y., 1958-67, NSF and Petroleum Research Found. of Am. Chem. Soc., 1963-77. Mem. Am. Chem. Soc., Chem. Soc. London, Sigma Xi. Contbr. articles to profl. jours. Home: 20 Oak St Geneseo NY 14454

SMITH, RICHARD GRIFFITHS, lawyer; b. Clinton, N.Y., Sept. 2, 1922; s. Carl Henry and Jane (Williams) S.; A.B., Albion Coll., 1943; J.D., U. Mich., 1950; m. Joyce Loueva Cummings, June 14, 1947; children—Richard Griffiths, Douglas Cummings, Sarah Jane, Carl Henry III. Admitted to Mich. bar, 1950, since practiced in Bay City; judge 18th Jud. Circuit Ct. Mich., 1957-64; mem. firm Smith and Brooker, P.C., 1964—. Mem. Mich. Ho. of Reps., 1953-56; mem. Mich. Civil Service Commn., 1973-74. Served as 1st lt. USMCR, 1943-45. Fellow Am. Coll. Trial Lawyers; mem. Am. Bar Assn., State Bar Mich., Sigma Nu. Elk, Mason. Home: 707 W Ohio St Bay City MI 48706 Office: 703 Washington Ave Bay City MI 48706

SMITH, RICHARD JAY, hand surgeon; b. N.Y.C., June 13, 1930; s. Jacob and Rose (Adelman) S.; B.A., Brown U., 1951; M.D., N.Y. Med. Coll., 1955; m. Jane Grosfeld, Dec. 17, 1955; children—Lisa Jill, Tracey Elizabeth, James Andrew. Surg. intern 3d surg. div. Bellevue Hosp., N.Y.C., 1955-56; resident orthopaedic surgery Hosp. Joint Diseases, N.Y.C., 1957-60, attending orthopaedic surgeon (hand surgery), 1966-72, chief hand surgery, 1968-72; asst. clin. prof. orthopaedic surgery Albert Einstein Coll. Medicine, 1964-72; asso. clin. prof. orthopaedic surgery Mt. Sinai Sch. Medicine, City U. N.Y., 1967-72; co-chmn. hand surg. group Mt. Sinai Hosp., 1967-72; asso. clin. prof. orthopaedic surgery Harvard Med. Sch., 1972—; chief hand surgery Mass. Gen. Hosp., Boston, 1972—. Served as lt. comdr. USPHS, 1960-62. Frauenthal fellow surgery hand, Los Angeles, 1962, Derby, Eng., 1963. Diplomate Am. Bd. Orthopaedic Surgery. Fellow Am. Acad. Orthopaedic Surgery, N.Y. Acad. Medicine, A.C.S.; mem. Am. Soc. Surgery Hand, Am. Orthopaedic Assn., N.Y. Acad. Sci., A.M.A., Caribbean Soc. Surgery Hand, N.Y. Soc. for Surgery Hand, Groupe D'Etude de la Main, Colombian Hand Soc., Alpha Omega Alpha. Contbg. editor Reoperative Surgery, 1964; Understanding Surgery, 1967; Ency. Child Care, 1967; Flynn's Hand Surgery, 1974; Operative Surgery, The Hand, 1977; Vascular Surgery, 1977. Home: 9 Blake Rd Weston MA 02193 Office: Dept Orthopaedic Surg Mass Gen Hosp Boston MA 02114

SMITH, RICHARD JOYCE, lawyer; b. Hartford, Conn., July 28, 1903; s. Clarence H. and Anne M.B. (Horan) S.; B.A., Cath. U. Am., 1924; LL.B., Yale, 1927; LL.D. (hon.), Am. Internat. Coll., 1970; m. Sheila Alexander, Sept. 6, 1932; children—Peter, Timothy, Christopher, Andrew, Wilford, Joyce. Admitted to Conn. bar, 1927, N.Y. bar, 1934; instr., asso. prof. law Yale, 1927-33, vis. lectr., 1945-48; social sci. research fellow, London and Dublin, 1929-30; mem. law firm Whitman & Ransom 1934—; reorgn. trustee New York, New Haven & Hartford Railroad Co. Member Conn. State Board Pardons, 1937-43; member Fairfield bd. edn., 1941-51; Conn. State Bd. Edn., 1951-57; adv. com. U.S. Alien Property Custodian, 1943-44; chief counsel Petroleum Resources Com., U.S. Senate 1944-45. Del., Dem. Nat. Conv., Chgo., 1940. Trustee Nat. Citizens Commn. Pub. Schs., 1951-56; mem. exec. com. Yale Law Sch. Assn.; Mem. Am., Conn., N.Y. State bar assns., Association Bar City N.Y., Phi Delta Phi. Clubs: Graduates (New Haven); Yale, Century Assn. (N.Y.C.); Fairfield Country, Fairfield Hunt; Pequot Yacht; N.Y. Yacht; Cosmos (Washington) Home: 139 Main St Southport CT 06490 Office: 522 Fifth Ave New York NY 10036

SMITH, RICHARD MILLER, steel co. exec.; b. Bethlehem, Pa., Aug. 29, 1925; s. Herman Percy and Bessie Mary (Miller) S.; B.S., Lehigh U., Bethlehem, 1948; grad. Advanced Mgmt. Program, Harvard U., 1972; m. Shirley Ann Druckenmiller, July 9, 1955; children—Leslie Susan, Gregory Miller, Laurie Elizabeth. With Bethlehem Steel Corp., 1948—, treas., 1972-74, exec. v.p., 1974-77, dir., 1974—, vice chmn. bd., 1977—; dir. Girard Bank, Phila., Girard Co.; trustee Com. Econ. Devel. Bd. dirs. Historic Bethlehem; trustee Lehigh U.; exec. com. Greater Bethlehem; mem. Bus. Com. for Arts. Served with USNR, 1943-45. Mem. Am. Iron and Steel Inst., Newcomen Soc. N.Am., Alpha Pi Mu, Tau Beta Pi, Pi Tau Sigma, Phi Gamma Delta. Clubs: Sky (N.Y.C.); Saucon Valley Country (Bethlehem). Office: Bethlehem Steel Corp Martin Tower Bethlehem PA 18016

SMITH, RICHARD SCHIEDT, steel co. exec.; b. Lancaster, Pa., Aug. 25, 1922; s. Howard Persifor and Norma Ruth (Schiedt) S.; A.B., Amherst Coll., 1943; m. Mary Elizabeth Allen, Jan. 24, 1948; children—G.S. Wylie, Richard C., Abby Anne, Laura Elizabeth. With Lionel D. Edie & Co., N.Y.C., 1946-49, Northwestern Mut. Life Ins. Co., Milw., 1949-52; with First Nat. City Bank N.Y., 1952-62, v.p., 1957-62; v.p., treas. M.A. Hanna Co., Cleve., 1962-63; v.p. finance Hanna Mining Co., Cleve., 1963-64; v.p. adminstrn. Nat. Steel Corp., Pitts., 1964-72, group v.p., 1972-77, sr. v.p., dir., 1977—; dir. United Techs. Corp., Advance Investors Corp., Nat.-Southwire Aluminum Co., St. John d'el Rey Mining Co. Served with AUS, 1942-45. Decorated Purple Heart. Bronze Star, Presdl. Unit citation with oak leaf cluster. Mem. Am. Mgmt. Assn. Clubs: Duquesne, Fox Chapel Golf (Pitts.); Laurel Valley Golf (Ligonier, Pa.); Augusta (Ga.) Nat. Golf. Home: 5915 Braeburn Pl Pittsburgh PA 15232 Office: Grant Bldg Pittsburgh PA 15219

SMITH, RICHARD THOMAS, immunologist, pediatrician; b. Oklahoma City, Apr. 15, 1924; s. Harvey T. and Rachel (Grant) S.; M.D., Tulane U., 1950; m. Jean Whisenant, Aug. 7, 1946; children—Mary Schell, Richard T., Joseph, John T., Claudia J. Intern, U. Minn., 1950-51; resident, 1951-53, research fellow, 1953-55, asst. prof., 1955-56; asso. prof. U. Tex., 1957-58; prof. pediatrics, chmn. dept. pediatrics U. Fla., 1958-67, prof. pathology, chmn. dept. pathology, 1967—, sci. dir. C.V. Whitney Marine Lab., 1976—. Served with USN, 1944-46. Named 1 of 10 Outstanding Young Men of Year, U.S. Jr. C. of C., 1959; recipient Josiah Macy Jr. Faculty Scholar award, 1978-79. Mem. Am. Acad. Pediatrics, Fla. Med. Assn., Am. Assn. Immunologists, Am. Assn. Pathologists and Bacteriologists, Am. Soc. Clin. Investigation (emeritus), Am. Soc. Exptl. Pathology, Soc. Exptl. Biology and Medicine, Alpha Omega Alpha. Office: Dept Pathology U Fla Coll Medicine Box J-275 JHMHC Gainesville FL 32610

SMITH, RICHARD THOMAS, engr.; b. Allentown, Pa., June 15, 1925; s. Raymond Willard and Mary (Rau) S.; B.S. with high honors, Lehigh U., 1946, M.S., 1947; Ph.D., Ill. Inst. Tech., 1955; m. Naomi Elsie Anthony, May 26, 1956; children—Cynthia Louise, Carol Ann. Instr., Lehigh U., Bethlehem, Pa., 1947-50; analytical and design engr. Gen. Electric Co., Schenectady, 1952-58; asso. prof. U. Tex., Austin, 1958-61; George Westinghouse prof. elec. engring. Va. Poly. Inst., Blacksburg, 1961-62; project dir. Tracor, Inc., Austin, 1962-64; sr. engr., asst. dir., dir. Southwest Research Inst., San Antonio, 1964-66; Okla. Gas and Electric prof. elec. engring. U. Okla., Norman, 1966-68; prof. elec. machinery Rensselaer Poly. Inst., Troy, N.Y., 1968-70; Alcoa-UMR Distinguished prof. elec. engring. U. Mo., Rolla, 1970-73; inst. engr., dir. Nondestructive Testing Info. Analysis Center, Southwest Research Inst., San Antonio, 1973—; adj. prof. U. Tex., 1974—; cons., reviewer numerous cos. Recipient Excellence Fund, U. Tex., 1959, DuPont Meml. prize Lehigh U., 1946. Registered profl. engr., Mass., Okla., Tex., Gt. Britain. Fellow Am. Inst. Aeros. and Astronautics (asso.), Instn. Elec. Engrs. (Eng.); mem. Am. Soc. Engring. Edn., I.E.E.E. (1st paper prize 1960, 63, sr.), N.Y. Acad. Scis., I.E.E.E. (numerous coms.), Internat. Electrotech. Commn. (adv. group 1971-74), Sigma Xi, Tau Beta Pi, Pi Mu Epsilon, Phi Eta Sigma, Eta Kappa Nu, Phi Kappa Phi. Office: Box 28510 San Antonio TX 78284

SMITH, RICHEY, chem. co. exec.; b. Akron, Ohio, Nov. 11, 1933; s. Thomas William and Martha (Richey) S.; B.S., U. Va., 1956; m. Sandra Cosgrave Roe, Nov. 25, 1961; children—Mason Roe, Parker Richey. Asst. to pres. Sun Products Corp., Barberton, Ohio, 1963-64, v.p., 1964-67, gen. mgr., dir., 1967-69, chmn., dir., chief exec. officer, 1969-76; associated cons. A. T. Kearney Co., Cleve., 1977—. Mem. exec. com. Great Trail council Boy Scouts Am., 1973-75; chmn. capital funds dr. Summit County Planned Parenthood, 1970-71; trustee Old Trail Sch., Barberton Citizens Hosp.; vestryman St. Paul's Episcopal Ch. Served to lt. USNR, 1957-60. Mem. Navy League (pres. Akron council 1972-73), Young Pres.'s Orgn., Chi Psi. Clubs: Rotary (trustee Akron club 1974-75), Portage Country, Akron City, Mayflower (Akron); Ponte Vedra (Fla.). Home: 721 Delaware Ave Akron OH 44303 Office: Investment Plaza Cleveland OH 44114

SMITH, ROBERT, physician; b. Dublin, Ireland, Apr. 2, 1921; came to U.S., 1968; s. William Abraham and Frances (Schultz) S.; B.A., Trinity Coll., Dublin U., 1944, M.B.,B.Ch., B.A.O., 1945, M.A., 1954, M.D., 1957; m. Myfanwy Nurock, Nov. 3, 1947; children—Jennifer Smith Margolis, Alison Jane, Caroline Rachel, Rosemary Frances. Intern, Royal Surrey Hosp., Guildford, Eng., 1947-48; resident Farnborough Hosp., Eng., 1949-51; asst. prof. physiology Trinity Coll., Dublin U., 1945-46; practice family medicine, Stanwell, Eng., 1952-62; dir., founder gen. practice teaching and research unit Guy's Hosp. Med. Sch., London, 1962-68; chmn., founder family medicine dept. U. N.C., Chapel Hill, 1970-75, dir., founder dept. family medicine, Fred Lazarus prof. family medicine U. Cin., 1975—, chmn. curriculum com., 1979—; Whiteside Soc. lectr. U. N.C., 1972. Served as capt. Royal Army Med. Corps, 1946-48. Nuffield grantee, 1966-68; HEW grantee, 1968-80. Fellow Royal Coll. Gen. Practitioners (Research prize 1958), Royal Soc. Medicine (London) (hon. sec. sect. gen. practice 1967-68, Wander lectr. 1970, bd. dirs. Med. Found. 1978); mem. AMA, Brit. Med. Assn. (Charles Hawthorne prize 1958), Am. Acad. Family Physicians, Soc. Tchrs. Family Medicine, Ohio Med. Soc., Ohio Acad. Family Physicians, S.W. Ohio Soc. Family Physicians, Cin. Acad. Medicine, Assn. Chairmen Depts. Family Medicine, Royal Soc. Medicine, Inc. (U.S.A.) (dir.). Club: The Lit. (Cin.). Author books, the most recent being: Scientific Foundations of Family Medicine, 1978; Anglo-American Conference of Health and the Family, 1978; research in pain, health care delivery, migraine. Home: 614 Liddle Ln Cincinnati OH 45215 Office: 231 Bethesda Ave Cincinnati OH 45267

SMITH, ROBERT BRUCE, security co. exec., ret. army officer; b. De Quincy, La., Apr. 22, 1920; s. Malcolm Monard and Jewell (Perkins) S.; B.J., La. State U., 1941; grad. Command and Gen. Staff Coll., 1951-52, Army War Coll., 1958-59; m. Gladys Opal Borel, Feb. 22, 1941; children—Susan, Richard. Commd. 2d lt. U.S. Army, 1941, advanced through grades to maj. gen., 1969; plans and ops. officer 83d Div. Arty., Europe, 1943-45; personnel officer Philippine-Ryukyus Command, Manila, 1947-49; prof. mil. sci. and tactics ROTC, Lanier High Sch., Macon, Ga., 1949-51; chief res. officers sect., procurement br. Dept. Army, 1952-55, chief troop info. Office Chief Info., 1962-63, dep. chief info., 1968-69; comdg. officer 8th F.A. Bn., 25th Inf. Div., Hawaii, 1955-56, G-1, 25th Inf. Div. and U.S. Army Hawaii, 1956-58; mem. staff, faculty Command and Gen. Staff Coll., Ft. Leavenworth, Kans., 1959-62; chief alt. Nat. Mil. Command Center, Office Joint Chiefs of Staff, Ft. Ritchie, Md., 1963-64; dep. dir. ops. Office Joint Chiefs of Staff, Pentagon, 1964-65; asst. div. comdr. 7th Inf. Div., Korea, 1965-66; dep. comdt. Army War Coll., Carlisle Barracks, Pa., 1966-68; dep. comdg. gen., Ryukyus Islands, 1969-72; dep. comdg. gen., 6th U.S. Army, Presidio of San Francisco, 1972-73, ret. reporter, news editor Lake Charles (La.) AP, 1946-47; region adminstrv. mgr. Burns Security Service, Oakland, Calif., 1974-76; partner constrn. co., Napa, Calif., 1976-77, Burns Security Service, 1978—. Mem. Nat. council Boy Scouts Am., 1969-70. Decorated D.S.M. with oak leaf cluster, Legion of Merit with 2 oak leaf clusters, Bronze Star with oak leaf cluster. Home: 350 St Andrews Dr Napa CA 94558

SMITH, ROBERT BRUCE, coll. dean; b. Phila., July 8, 1937; s. Graeme Conlee and Margaret Edith (Moote) S.; B.S., Wheaton (Ill.) Coll., 1958; Ph.D., U. Calif. at Berkeley, 1962; m. Eileen Adele Petznick, Aug. 21, 1959; children—Monica, Sara, Douglas. Asst. prof. chemistry U. Nev., Las Vegas, 1961-66, asso. prof., chmn. dept., 1966-68, prof., dean Coll. Sci., Engring. and Math., 1968—. Mem. Nev. Bd. Examiners Basic Scis., 1970-75, Nev. Bd. Pharmacy, 1972-77. NSF fellow, 1959-61. Mem. Am. Chem. Soc., AAAS, Sigma Xi, Phi Kappa Phi. Home: 1509 Eaton Dr Las Vegas NV 89102 Office: Coll Sci and Engring U Nev Las Vegas NV 89154

SMITH, ROBERT BURNS, newspaper exec.; b. Columbus, Ohio, Feb. 24, 1929; s. Edwin Clyde and Blanche (Burns) S.; B.S., Ohio State U., 1949; m. Marjorie Ann Otten. Reporter, then asst. news editor Ohio State Jour., Columbus, 1948-59; with Columbus Dispatch, 1959—, mng. editor, 1968—; v.p. Dispatch Features, Columbus, 1968—. Sec.-treas. James Faulkner Meml. Fund, Columbus, 1967—; mem. Ohio Privacy Bd., 1977—. Served with USAF, 1951-55. Mem. Blue Pencil Ohio (v.p. 1969, pres. 1970), AP Ohio (v.p. 1974, pres. 1975), Sigma Delta Chi, Delta Tau Delta. Presbyn. Clubs: Masons; Riverview Country (Powell, Ohio) Home: 1456 Sandalwood Dr Columbus OH 43229 Office: 34 S 3d St Columbus OH 43216

SMITH, ROBERT DRAKE, r.r. exec.; b. Ft. Worth, Oct. 26, 1944; s. Kermit Rudebeck and Lynne Grace (Harris) S.; B.A. with honors, U. Puget Sound, 1966; M.B.A., U. Pa., 1968. Planning analyst C. & N.W. Ry. Co., Chgo., 1968, supr. program planning, 1969, mgr. program planning, 1970-73; corporate sec. Chgo. & North Western Transp. Co., Chgo., 1973—; dir. Des Moines & Central Iowa Ry., Ft. Dodge, Des Moines & So. Ry., Mpls. Indsl. Ry., Northwestern Communications Co., Ry. Transfer of Mpls., Oshkosh Transp. Co. Vol., Juvenile Ct. Cook County, 1970—; mem. jr. governing bd. Chgo. Symphony. Mem. Am. Soc. Corporate Secs., Assn. Am. R.R.s, Nat. Investor Relations Inst., Wharton Sch. Alumni Assn. Clubs: Union League, Barclay. Home: 5445 N Sheridan Rd Apt 2812 Chicago IL 60640 Office: Office of Sec C & NW Transp Co Room 616 400 W Madison St Chicago IL 60606

SMITH, ROBERT E. (BUFFALO BOB), TV and radio entertainer; b. Buffalo, Nov. 27, 1917; s. Emil H. and Emma J. (Kuehn) Schmidt; grad. high sch.; m. Mildred C. Metz, Nov. 21, 1940; children—Robin V., Ronald E., Christopher M. Radio entertainer, Buffalo, 1933-46, NBC, N.Y.C., 1946-60; creator Howdy Doody TV Show, 1947-60, owner radio sta. WQDY, Calais, Maine, 1964—, radio sta. WHOU, Houlton, Maine, 1967—; numerous TV and coll. appearances. Bd. dirs. New Rochelle (N.Y.) Hosp., 1957—. TV show recipient Peabody award, 1950. Lutheran (organist, choir dir. 1972). Elk. Address: care WQDY 281 Main St Calais ME 04619*

SMITH, ROBERT EARL, space scientist; b. Indpls., Sept. 13, 1923; s. Harold Bennett and Bernice (McCaslin) S.; B.S., Fla. State U., 1959, M.S., 1960; M.S., U. Mich., 1969, Ph.D., 1974; m. Elizabeth Lee Usak, Jan. 3, 1947; children—Stephanie Lee, Robert Michael, Cynthia Ann, Kelly Andrew. Served as enlisted man U.S. Army Air Force, 1943-44, advanced through grades to maj. U.S. Air Force, 1955; airway traffic controller, Berlin, Germany, 1945; staff weather reconnaissance officer 9th Air Force, 1956; ret., 1963; project scientist Atmospheric Cloud Physics Lab., dep. chief atmospheric scis. div. NASA/Marshall Space Flight Center, Ala., 1963—. Mem. Am. Meteorol. Soc., Pi Mu Epsilon, Sigma Phi Epsilon. Home: 125 Westbury Dr Huntsville AL 35802 Office: Marshall Space Flight Center AL 35812

SMITH, ROBERT ELLSWORTH, investment exec.; b. Webster Groves, Mo., Sept. 9, 1921; s. Stephen and Sarah (Copithorne) S.; B.A., U. Chgo., 1942; J.D., U. Miami (Fla.), 1949; m. Shirley Sharp, May 18, 1946; children—Anthony, Deborah, Heidi. With Pan Am. Airways, 1942-71, asst. v.p., 1957-62, v.p. charge tourist devel. facilities, 1962-70, v.p. devel., 1970-71; v.p. Nat. Bulk Carriers, Inc., 1971-72; pres. Inversiones Cariari, 1973—, also Valores de Centro Am., Maricultura, S.A.; founding organizer SAHSA, Lanica, Lacsa, COPA airlines of Honduras, Nicaragua, Costa Rica and Panama; dir. Worldtech Costa Rica, S.A. Mem. Alpha Delta Phi. Clubs: Univ., Sky (N.Y.C.). Home: Apartado 5255 San Jose Costa Rica Office: Edificio Colón San Jose Costa Rica

SMITH, ROBERT GRAY, (Graysmith), editorial cartoonist; b. Pensacola, Fla., Sept. 17, 1942; s. Robert Gray and Frances Jane (Scott) S.; B.F.A., Calif. Coll. Arts and Crafts, 1965; m. Margaret Ann Womack, Nov. 6, 1963; children—David Martin, Aaron Vincent. Staff artist Stockton (Calif.) Record, 1965-68; editorial cartoonist San Francisco Chronicle, 1968—. Republican. Presbyn. Office: San Francisco Chronicle 901 Mission St San Francisco CA 94103*

SMITH, ROBERT HAROLD, accountant; b. N.Y.C., Oct. 8, 1924; s. Morris and Clara (Gordon) S.; B.S., N.Y. U., 1949; m. Gaye Sandler, Nov. 1, 1952; 1 dau., Victoria. Chief auditor Hughes Aircraft Co., Culver City, Calif., 1955-60; corporate controller, asst. sec. U.S. Chem. Milling Co., Manhattan Beach, Calif., 1960-62; corporate dir. fin. planning Packard Bell Electronics Co., Los Angeles, 1962-64; controller Librascope group Gen. Precision, Inc., Glendale, Calif., 1964-67; treas., dir. H & S Prodns., Inc., Studio City, Calif., 1959-67; corporate controller Internat. Industries, Inc., Beverly Hills, Calif., 1967-70; v.p. adminstrn. and control Envirodyne, Inc., Los Angeles, 1970-73; pres. Robert H. Smith Accountancy Corp.; instr. taxes and acctg. UCLA, 1956—. A founder, dir. Calif. Montessori Soc., Los Angeles, 1962-64; bd. govs. Beverly Hills Municipal League, 1970-75. Served with USAAF, 1943-46. C.P.A., Calif., N.Y. Mem. Fin. Execs. Inst., Am., Calif. insts. C.P.A.'s, Beverly Hills C. of C., N.Y. U. Alumni Assn. (v.p. Los Angeles chpt. 1962-63). Clubs: Masons, Kiwanis, Town Hall, Beverly Hills Men's (dir.), Beverly Hills Bus. and Profl. Men's. Office: 9171 Wilshire Blvd Beverly Hills CA 90210

SMITH, ROBERT HAROLD, communications co. exec.; b. East Orange, N.J., Aug. 17, 1927; s. Harold Taylor and Una (French) S.; B.Sc., Rutgers U., 1948, M.A., 1949; Ph.D., Syracuse U., 1954; m. Ruth Schiela Hatton, Aug 14, 1966. Lectr. econs. U. Pa., Phila., 1956-58; economist Pa. R.R., Phila., 1956-58; mgmt. cons., 1959-66; v.p. finance and adminstrn., treas., dir. Helme Products, N.Y.C., 1966-67; asst. to mng. partner Wertheim & Co., N.Y.C., 1967-68; sr. v.p., exec. asst. to chmn. Internat. Tel. & Tel. Corp., N.Y.C., 1969—.

SMITH, ROBERT I., utilities exec.; b. 1918; B.S., Brown U., 1940; m. With Pub. Service Electric & Gas Co., Newark, 1940—, chief engr., 1965-67, gen. mgr. engring., 1967-68, v.p. elec. operations, 1968-71, exec. v.p., 1971-72, pres., 1972—, chief exec. officer, 1975—, chmn., 1977—, also dir. Address: 80 Park Pl Newark NJ 07101

SMITH, ROBERT JOHN, accounting firm exec.; b. Torrington, Conn., June 28, 1936; s. James M. and Florence H. (Strandberg) S.; B.S., U. Conn., 1958; m. Shirley Wendel, Aug. 13, 1965; children—Randall, Tonya. Mgr. audits Coopers & Lybrand, Denver, 1959-72; v.p., treas. Wyo. Bancorp., Cheyenne, 1972-75; mng. partner Wittler, Smith and Assos., 1975—; founder East 16th Devel. Co., Cheyenne; cons. Traders Publs., Wind-n-Win Ltd., 519 Ltd., 307 Governors Park Ltd., Randall-Pioneer, J.V., 400 J.V.; chmn. bd. Traders Inc., Traders Colo., Inc.; pres. Trading Post Inc., Basic Software and Computers Wyo., Inc. Served to 1st lt. AUS, 1958-59, 61-62. C.P.A., Conn., Colo., Wyo. Mem. Financial Execs. Inst., Am. Inst. C.P.A.'s, Nat. Assn. Accts. (past pres. Colo.-Wyo. border chpt., mem. nat. com. on publs., treas. Rocky Mountain council), Cheyenne Soccer Assn. (v.p.). Republican. Mason (32 degree, Shriner). Club: Cheyenne Country. Office: Rocky Mountain Plaza Cheyenne WY 82001

SMITH, ROBERT JOHN, educator; b. Essex, Mo., June 27, 1927; s. Will Dan and Fern (Jones) S.; B.A. summa cum laude, U. Minn., 1949; M.A., Cornell U., 1951, Ph.D., 1953; m. Kazuko Sasaki, Aug. 22, 1955. Engaged in cultural anthrop. field research, N.S., Can., 1950, Japan, 1951-52, 55, 57-58, Brazil, 1966-67; mem. faculty Cornell U., 1953—, prof. anthropology, 1963-74, Goldwin Smith prof. anthropology, 1974—, chmn. dept. Asian studies, 1961-66, chmn. dept. antropology, 1967-71, 76—; vis. prof. anthropology U. Ariz., 1971, U. Hawaii, 1978. Tng. grantee Social Sci. Research Council, Japan, 1951-52; recipient Individual Exchange award to Japan, Inst. Internat. Edn., 1957-58; Fulbright lectr. Tokyo Met. U., 1962-63; NSF research grantee, 1965-67; Japan Found. grantee, 1979. Served with AUS, 1944-46. Fellow Am. Anthrop. Assn., Royal Anthrop. Inst. Great Britain and Ireland, Soc. Applied Anthropology (editor jour. Human Orgn. 1961-66); mem. Asiatic Soc. Japan. Author: (with Cornell) Two Japanese Villages, 1956; (with Beardsley) Japanese Culture: Development and Characteristics, 1962; Japanese and Their Descendants in Brazil, 1967; editor: Social Organization and the Application of Anthropology, 1974; Ancestor Worship in Contemporary Japan, 1974; Kurusu: The Price of Progress in a Japanese Village, 1951-75, 1978. Home: 107 Northview Rd Ithaca NY 14850

SMITH, ROBERT JUNIUS, educator; b. Snowflake, Ariz., Dec. 25, 1920; s. Samuel Francis and Lulu Jane (Hatch) S.; B.S., Brigham Young U., 1948; M.B.A., Northwestern U., 1949; D.B.A., Ind. U. 1957; m. Lola Nielson, Nov. 5, 1945; children—Junola (Mrs. Charles D. Bush), Lynette (Mrs. Gregory L. Lyman), Lynn Robert, Shirley (Mrs. Stephen D. Ricks), LaRae (Mrs. Benjamin L. Blake), Jeanine (Mrs. Stanley A. Denton), Larry Kay, Sheldon Ray. With Brigham Young U., 1949—, asst. to asso. prof. accounting, 1949-57, prof., 1957—, chmn. dept., 1951-55, 59-62, acting dean Coll. Business, 1963-64, asst. acad. v.p., 1968-70, asso. acad. v.p., 1970-78, fin. v.p., 1978—; partner Burton, Tenney, Smith & Lewis Co., C.P.A.'s, 1961-65; cons. partner Main Lafrentz & Co., C.P.A.'s, 1966-67. Vice pres. Utah County United Fund, 1970-71, pres., 1972. Served with USNR, 1944-46. Recipient gold medal Ill. Soc. C.P.A.'s, 1949, Elijah Watt Sells gold medal Am. Inst. Accountants. Mem. Am. Accounting Assn., Utah Assn. C.P.A.'s, Am. Inst. C.P.A.'s, Alpha Kappa Psi, Beta Gamma Sigma, Beta Alpha Psi, Phi Kappa Phi. Mem. Ch. Jesus Christ Latter-day Saints (ward exec. sec.). Author: Preparing for the CPA Examination, 1960, 2d edit., 1967. Home: 2465 N 820 E Provo UT 84601

SMITH, ROBERT LEE, civil engr., educator; b. Schaller, Iowa, Oct. 31, 1923; s. Lester Martens and Edith (Bright) S.; B.S., U. Iowa, 1947, M.S., 1948; m. A. Lucille Johnson, Sept. 6, 1947; children—Barbara Lucille, Milton (dec.), Deborah Lee. Research asst. Iowa Inst. Hydraulic Research, 1947-48; asst. prof. dept. applied mechanics U. Kans., 1948-52; exec. dir. Iowa Natural Resources Council, Des Moines, 1952-55; exec. sec., chief engr. Kans. Water Resources Bd., Topeka, 1955-62; Parker prof. water resources U. Kans., Lawrence, 1962-66, prof., chmn. dept. civil engring., 1966-72, Deane E. Ackers prof. engring., 1970—. Design engr. Romine, Sonat & Snow, Davenport, Iowa, summer 1947; hydraulic engr. U.S. C.E., Omaha, summers 1949, 50; hydraulic engr. Kans. Bd. Agr., summer 1951; chmn. Inter-Agency Com. Water Resources Research, Office Sci. and Tech., White House, Washington, 1966-67; water resources cons. Black & Veatch Cons. Engrs., Kansas City, Mo., 1968—; cons. various govt. agys., indsl. firms. Chmn. Interstate Conf. on Water Problems, 1961; mem. Gov.'s Econ. Research Adv. Com., 1964-67; chmn. Kans. delegation Kans.-Okla., Arkansas River Compact Com., 1956-65; mem. USGS Adv. Com. Water Data for Pub. Use, 1965—; mem. U.S. Nat. com. for Internat. Hydrological Decade, 1968-71; mem. panel on water and man's life in India, Nat. Acad. Scis., 1971. Bd. dirs. Lawrence Citizens Adv. Com., 1974-76; vice chmn. Kans. Gov.'s Task Force on Water Resources, 1977—. Served with AUS, 1943-46; PTO. Recipient Key Mem. award Kans. Engring. Soc., 1966, Outstanding Engr. award Kans. Engring. Soc., 1967. Fellow ASCE (past pres. Kans. sect.); mem. Nat. Acad. Engring., Nat. Soc. Profl. Engrs., Kans. Engring. Soc., Am. Water Works Assn., Am. Geophys. Union, Am. Soc. Engring. Edn., A.A.A.S., Sigma Xi, Delta Chi, Theta Tau, Tau Beta Pi, Chi Epsilon. Republican. Conglist. Mason. Contbr. articles to profl. jours. Home: 2915 Harvard Rd Lawrence KS 66044

SMITH, ROBERT LEO, ecologist; b. Brookville, Pa., Mar. 23, 1925; s. Leo F. and Josephine Elizabeth (Ferguson) S.; B.S., Pa. State U., 1949, M.S., 1954; Ph.D., Cornell U., 1956; m. Alice Elizabeth Casey, Nov. 15, 1952; children—Robert Leo, Thomas Michael, Pauline Ann, Maureen Elizabeth. Asst. prof. biology SUNY, Plattsburgh, 1956-58; prof. wildlife ecology W.Va. U., Morgantown, 1958—; cons. in ecology to pubs. and govt. Served with U.S. Army, 1950-52. Mem. Ecol. Soc. Am., Am. Ornithologists Union, Wildlife Soc., Am. Soc. Mammalogists, AAAS, Am. Inst. Biol. Scis., Wilson Ornithol. Soc., Cooper Ornithol. Soc., Sigma Xi. Republican. Roman Catholic. Club: Lakeview Country (Morgantown). Author: Ecology and Field Biology, 3d edit., 1980; The Ecology of Man: An Ecosystem Approach, 1976; Elements of Ecology and Field Biology, 1977; contbr. to Ency. Brit. and World Book Ency.; adv. bd. Funk and Wagnalls Ency. Home: Route 7 Box 660 Morgantown WV 26505 Office: Div Forestry WVa U Morgantown WV 26506. *Success, by whatever standard it may be measured, comes only strong motivation, hard work, persistence, a competitive spirit, self-discipline, a willingness to keep current, and an adversion to stagnation. Above all, don't take yourself too seriously.*

SMITH, ROBERT LONDON, ret. air force officer, scientist, educator; b. Alexandria, La., Oct. 13, 1919; s. Daniel Charleston and Lillie (Roberts) S.; B.A., Coll. St. Joseph, 1954; M.A., U. Okla., 1955; Ph.D., Am. U., 1964; m. Jewel Busch, Feb. 5, 1949; children—Jewel Diane, Robert London, Karl Busch. Commd. 2d lt. USAAF, 1941, advanced through grades to lt. col. USAF, 1961; various assignments in aircraft engring., command and logistics, 1941-60; research logistics Hdqrs. Office Aerospace Research, 1960-63; project scientist, adminstr. postdoctoral research program Nat. Acad. Scis., Hdqrs. Office Sci. Research, 1963-65; ret., 1965; asso. prof. polit. sci., head dept. eve. classes and corr. study U. Alaska, College, 1966-68, dean Coll. Bus., Econs. and Govt., 1968-70, prof., head dept. polit. sci., 1966—; mem. govt. panels and planning groups; dir. Arctic 1st Fed. Savs. & Loan Assn.; corporator Mt. McKinley Mut. Savs. Bank. Committeeman, Western region Boy Scouts Am., 1968-73, mem. exec. bd. Midnight Sun council, 1973-74, committeeman-at-large nat. council, 1968—; mem. Alaska Gov.'s Employment Commn.; pres. United Service Orgn. Council, Fairbanks, Alaska; mem. active corps execs. SBA. Recipient Silver Beaver award Boy Scouts Am.; named Outstanding Prof. U. Alaska, 1975. Mem. Nat. Acad. Econs. and Polit. Sci., AAAS, Air Force Hist. Found., Nat. Inst. Social and Behavioral Scis., Nat. Inst. U.S. in World Affairs, Am. Polit. Sci. Assn., Assn. U.S. Army (bd. dirs. Polar Bear chpt.), Alaska C. of C. (edn. com.), Pi Gamma Mu, Pi Sigma Alpha. Author: (with others) Squadron Adminstration, 1951; also publs. on nat. security and nat. def. Contbr. to The United Nations Peace University, 1965. Roman Catholic. Club: Rotary. Home: Smithhaven 100 College Ln Fairbanks AK 99701 also Smithport Harding Lake Box SR 90751-C Fairbanks AK 99701

SMITH, ROBERT LOUIS, constrn. co. exec.; b. Parkersburg, W.Va., Apr. 19, 1922; s. Everett Clerc and Janet (Morrison) S.; B.S. in Civil Engring. Lehigh U., 1944; m. June Irene Odbert, Oct. 25, 1948; children—Peter Clerc, Morrison James, Edna Louise. Design engr. Chrysler Corp., 1944-46; engr. Harrison Constrn. Co., Charleston, W.Va., 1946-47; sr. engr. Creole Petroleum Co., Las Piedras, Venezuela, 1947-55; v.p. Rea Constrn. Co., Charlotte, N.C., 1955-64; exec. v.p. Warren Bros. Co., Cambridge, Mass., 1964-68, pres., 1968-79, also dir.; sr. v.p. Ashland Oil, Inc. (Ky.), 1974-79; pres., dir. Tree Farm Devel. Corp., Cambridge, 1979—; dir. Thompson-Arthur Paving Co., Mac Dougald Warren, Inc., Panasfalto, S.A., Levingston Shipbldg. Co. Fellow Am. Soc. C.E.; mem. Nat. Asphalt Pavement Assn. (dir.), Phi Beta Kappa, Tau Beta Pi, Sigma Chi. Republican. Unitarian. Home: 140 Worthern Rd Lexington MA 02173 Office: 675 Massachusetts Ave Cambridge MA 02139

SMITH, ROBERT MOORS, anesthesiologist; b. Winchester, Mass., Dec. 10, 1912; s. Francis E. and Elsie C. (Davis) S.; A.B., Dartmouth U., 1934; M.D., Harvard U., 1938; m. Margaret Louise Nash, Aug. 7, 1937; children—Jonathan E., Marcia A., Karen E. Rotating intern Faulkner Hosp., Jamaica Plain, Mass., 1938-39, asst. in pathology, 1939; intern in surgery Boston City Hosp., 1939-41; gen. practice medicine, Cohasset, Mass., 1941-42; anesthesiologist Children's Hosp. Med. Center, Boston, 1946—, pres. staff, 1966-68, now dir. anesthesiology; asso. anesthesiologist Peter Bent Brigham Hosp., Boston, 1958—, Boston Lying-In Hosp., 1964—; instr. anesthesia Harvard Med. Sch., Boston, 1948-63, asso. in anesthesia, 1955, asst. clin. prof. anesthesia, 1963-66, asso. clin. prof., 1966—, clin. prof., 1976—. Bd. dirs. Home for Aged, Winchester, Mass., Minuteman council Boy Scouts Am. Served to maj. U.S. Army, 1941-46. Diplomate Am. Bd. Anesthesiology. Fellow Am. Coll. Anesthesiologists (gov. 1952-58); mem. AMA, Mass. Med. Soc., New Eng. (pres. 1966), Mass. (pres. 1955, dir. 1965-68) socs. anesthesiologists, New Eng. Pediatric Soc., Assn. Univ. Anesthesiologists, Am. Acad. Pediatrics (chmn. com. pediatric anesthesiology 1963-64, 76-77), Royal Acad. Surgeons (Ireland) (hon.), Pan Am. Med. Soc. Home: 4 Leslie Rd Winchester MA 01890 Office: 300 Longwood Ave Boston MA 02115

SMITH, ROBERT MYRON, investment cons.; b. Hartford, Conn., Jan. 10, 1930; s. Sterling Bishop and Harriet (Chamberlain) S.; B.A., Wesleyan U., 1951; M.B.A., U. Pa., 1957; m. Ellen Prouty, Mar. 31, 1956; children—Catherine, Allison, Deborah, Elizabeth. Asst. sec. Investors Mgmt. Co., Elizabeth, N.J., 1957-62; asst. v.p. Security Trust Co., Rochester, N.Y., 1962-64; exec. v.p. Keystone Custodian Funds, Boston, 1964-74; sr. v.p. Reliance Ins. Co., Phila., 1974-79; pres. Reliance Capital Advs., Phila., 1979—, also dir.; dir. Reliance Standard Life Ins. Co., Pilot Ins. Co., Cananwill Co., United Pacific Life Ins. Co., London and N.Y. Investments S.A. Mem. fin. com. Town of Cohasset (Mass.), 1973-74. Served with USAF, 1951-53. Mem. Inst. Chartered Fin. Analysts (chartered fin. analyst), Phila. Securities Assn., Fin. Analysts of Phila. Club: Union League (Phila.). Home: 248 Cheswold Ln Haverford PA 19041 Office: 4 Penn Center Philadelphia PA 19103

SMITH, ROBERT NELSON, chemist, educator; b. Long Beach, Calif. Sept. 25, 1916; s. Robert Nelson and Catherine (Davis) S.; B.A., Pomona Coll., 1938; M.S., Stanford, 1940, Ph.D. (Shell Oil Co. fellow 1940-41), 1942; m. Nancy Stahl, Sept. 10, 1938; children—Eric, Roger, Anne. Instr. chemistry Stanford, 1941-42, U. Mo. Sch. Mines and Metallurgy, 1942-44; asso. chemist Manhattan Project, U. Chgo., 1944; group leader Manhattan Project, E.I. duPont de Nemours & Co., Inc., 1944-45; mem. faculty Pomona Coll., 1945—, prof. chemistry, 1956—, Carnegie prof., 1959-69, Blanche and Frank Seaver prof., 1969—; mem. adv. com. grants Research Corp., 1961-68. Guggenheim fellow, 1951-52; Petroleum Research Fund fellow, 1958-59; recipient Wig Distinguished Prof. award Pomona Coll., 1959, 65, award for college teaching Mfg. Chemists Assn., 1961; Research Corp. fellowship, 1965-66. Mem. Am. Chem. Soc. (chmn. San Gorgonio sec. 1958; exec. com. colloid div. 1957-62), Faraday Soc., Calif. Assn. Chemistry Tchrs. (chmn. So. sect. 1964-65), Phi Beta Kappa, Sigma Xi. Author: Chemistry: A Quantitative Approach, 1969; (with W.C. Pierce) General Chemistry Workbook, 4th edit., 1971. Home: PO Box 368 Mount Baldy CA 91759

SMITH, ROBERT NELSON, asst. sec. defense; b. Toledo, Apr. 2, 1920; s. Robert Frederick and Amy Laura (Nelson) S.; student U. Mich., 1938-39; B.S., U.S. Mil. Acad., 1943; M.S., Mass. Inst. Tech., 1945; M.D., U. Nebr., 1952; m. Marilyn Jane Collins, Jan. 26, 1943 (dec.); children—Sandralyn, Sharon, Robert Nelson, Marilyn Anne, Marcia, Elizabeth. Commd. 2d lt. USAAF, 1943; ret., 1948; intern Toledo Hosp., Ohio, 1952-53, resident, 1954-57; anesthesiologist KFC Med. Corp., Toledo, 1954-76; asst. sec. def. for health affairs, Washington, 1976-78; bd. dirs. Ohio Med. Indemnity Corp., Columbus. Chmn., State Health Planning Council, 1974-76; mem. Statewide Health Coordinating Council, until 1976. Recipient Sec. Def. medal for outstanding pub. service, 1977. Diplomate Am. Bd. Anesthesiologists. Mem. AMA (Resolution of Commendation 1977), Ohio Med. Assn. (pres. 1970, Commendation 1977), Am. Soc. Anethesiology. Club: Inverness (Toledo). Home: 3424 Gallatin Rd Toledo OH 43606

SMITH, ROBERT POWELL, ambassador; b. Joplin, Mo., Mar. 5, 1929; s. Powell Augusta and Estella (Farris) S.; B.A., Tex. Christian U., 1954, M.A., 1955; m. Alice Irene Rountree, Aug. 22, 1953; children—Michael Bryan, Steven Powell, Karen Louise, David Robert. Fgn. service officer Dept. State, 1955—; press officer, Washington, 1955, vice-consul, Lahore, West Pakistan, 1956-58, 2d sec., Beirut, Lebanon, 1959-61, consul and prin. officer, Enugu, Nigeria, 1962-65, officer-in-charge Ghanaian Affairs, 1966, officer-in-charge Nigerian Affairs, dep. dir. Office West African Affairs, 1967-69; dep. chief of mission, counselor of embassy, Pretoria, South Africa, 1970-74; ambassador to Malta, 1974-76, to Ghana, 1976-79, to Liberia, Monrovia, 1979—. Served with USMCR, 1946-49, 50-52. Decorated Air medal. Recipient Meritorious Honor award State Dept., 1967. Mem. Am. Fgn. Service Assn. Mem. Disciples of Christ Ch. Office: American Embassy 111 United States Dr Monrovia Liberia

SMITH, ROBERT RUTHERFORD, educator, univ. dean; b. Buffalo, Nov. 18, 1933; s. Thomas Newlands and Mary Jane (Rutherford) S.; B.A. cum laude, U. Buffalo, 1955; M.A., Ohio State U., 1956, Ph.D., 1963; m. Suzanne Louise Stines, June 7, 1958; children—Eric Anthony, Gwendolyn Anne. Prof. communication, chmn. div. broadcasting and film Sch. Pub. Communication, Boston U., 1961-78, prof. Temple U., Phila., 1978—, dean Sch. Communication and Theater, 1978—; cons. RKO-Gen., Westinghouse, Nat. Endowment for Arts, others. Mem. communication commn. Mass. Council Chs., 1971-76. Served with AUS, 1959-61. Mem. Broadcast Edn. Assn., Internat. Communication Assn., AAUP, Speech Communication Assn., Am. Canoe Assn. Unitarian. Clubs: Appalachian Mountain (Boston); Pen and Pencil (Phila.). Author: (poems) Participations, 1972; (criticism) Beyond the Wasteland; editor: TV Quar., 1971, Feedback, 1973-76. Contbr. articles to profl. jours. Home: 7720-B Stenton Ave Apt 107 Philadelphia PA 19118 Office: Sch Communication and Theater Temple U Philadelphia PA 19122

SMITH, ROBERT SELLERS, lawyer; b. Samson, Ala., July 31, 1931; s. Abb Jackson and Rose (Sellers) S.; B.S., U. Va., 1953, LL.B., 1958; m. June Claire West, Feb. 2, 1963; children-Robert Sellers, David West, Rosemary True, Adam Douglas. Admitted to Ala. bar, 1959; asst. counsel spl. com. to investigate campaign expenditures U.S. Ho. of Reps., 1960; counsel U.S. Senate Labor and Pub. Welfare Com., 1961-63; partner firm Smith, Huckaby & Graves, P.A., Huntsville, 1963—; instr. econs., Am. econ. history U. Ala., 1963-64. Mem. industry adv. com., select com. small bus. U.S. Senate; pres. Madison County (Ala.) Legal Aid Soc., 1971-75; pres. North Ala. Estate Planning Council, 1974. Served with U.S. Navy, 1953-57. Mem. Am., Internat., Ala. bar assns. Episcopalian. Author: Alabama Legal Forms Annotated; Modern Office Forms for Lawyers; Handbook of Law Office Forms; Alabama Law for the Layman; Forms Under A.R.C.P.; Lawyer's Model Letter Book. Home: 6004 Macon Ct Huntsville AL 35802 Office: 223 East Side Sq Huntsville AL 35801

SMITH, ROBERT STEEN, gas co. exec.; b. Holdenville, Okla., Oct. 19, 1923; s. William A. and Nell (Ball) S.; B.S., U. Okla., 1949; J.D., U. Tulsa, 1971; m. Patricia Anne Busey, Jan. 11, 1953; children—Robin Anne, Craig Busey. Admitted to Okla. bar, 1971; with Okla. Natural Gas Co., Tulsa, 1949—, v.p., sec., asst. treas., 1971—. Served with USAAF, 1943-46. Mem. Tulsa County, Okla., Am. bar assns., Am., So. gas assns., Okla. Soc. Ins. Mgrs. (pres. 1973), Am. Soc. Corp. Secs., Tulsa, Okla. City chambers commerce, Petroleum Club Tulsa, Theta Xi. Democrat. Methodist. Home: 129 E 26th Ct Tulsa OK 74114 Office: 624 S Boston Ave Tulsa OK 74119

SMITH, ROBERT VIRGIL, clergyman, educator; b. St. Charles, Iowa, Feb. 28, 1920; s. John Guy and Veta (Payne) S.; B.C.S., State U. Iowa, 1941; B.D., Garrett Theol. Sem., 1944; Ph.D., Yale U., 1953; postgrad. Oxford U. (Eng.), 1962, 67-68; m. Rosalind Eldred Walls, June 17, 1945 (dec. Sept. 1978); children—Deborah Gail, Brian Guy, Lisa Margaret. Ordained to ministry Meth. Ch., 1946; instr. philosophy and religion, dir. religious activities Cornell Coll., Mt. Vernon, Iowa, 1947-51; pastor Grace Meth. Ch., New Haven, 1951-52; instr. philosophy and religion, asso. chaplain Colgate U., 1952-55, asst. prof., 1955-58, asso. prof., 1958-63, chaplain, 1957—, prof., 1963—, chmn. dept. philosophy and religion, 1973—; cons., dir. planning Stony Brook Found., 1970-71; fellow Inst. Ecumenical Research, Collegeville, Minn., 1975; mem. No. N.Y. Conf. Meth. Ch. Com. Higher Edn., 1965-69. Mem. Madison County (N.Y.) Democratic Com., 1968-70, 72-74, 75-77; bd. dirs. N.Y. Student Christian Movement; bd. visitors Marcy Psychiat. Center, 1976-77. Grantee Danforth Found. Campus Ministry, 1967-68. Mem. Am. Acad. Religion (pres. 1961), Am. Philos. Assn., AAUP (treas. N.Y. conf. 1972-75), Nat. Assn. Coll. and Univ. Chaplains (editor 1962-63). Contbr. articles to profl. jours. Home: 8 W Kendrick Ave Hamilton NY 13346

SMITH, ROBERT W. (WOLFMAN JACK), disc jockey; b. Bklyn., Jan. 21; m. Lucy Lamb; children—Joy, Todd. Disc jockey, Newport News, Va., Shreveport, La., Sta. XERF, Ciudad Acuna, Mex., 1957-65, also sta. mgr.; disc jockey Sta. XERB, Rosarita Beach, Mex., Sta. KDAY, Los Angeles; disc jockey Sta. WNBC, N.Y.C., 1973—, syndicated to over 1400 U.S. radio stas., 400 overseas stas.; announcer Midnight Spl., NBC-TV, 1973—; host The Wolfman Jack Show, syndicated TV series, 1977; appeared in film American Graffiti, 1973; numerous TV appearances. Office: care NBC Press Dept 30 Rockefeller Plaza New York NY 10020*

SMITH, ROBERT WILLIAM, ins. co. exec.; b. Catskill, N.Y., Apr. 2, 1923; s. Victor and Leda Leone (Cline) S.; B.S. cum laude, Syracuse U., 1948; m. Inez R. Iuzzolino, Jan. 31, 1976; children—Jeffrey, Timothy, Kathy. With Prudential Ins. Co. Am., Newark, 1948—, sr. v.p., 1973—. Mem. adv. council on mgmt. and personnel research Conf. Bd., 1975—, chmn., 1977-78; chmn. LOMA Personnel Council,

1971-72; bus. adminstr. City of Newark, 1970. Trustee, Coll. of Ins. Served to 1st lt. USAAF, 1942-45. Decorated Air medal with 5 oak leaf clusters; C.L.U.; accredited personnel exec. Am. Soc. Personnel Adminstrn., 1977. Mem. Beta Gamma Sigma, Alpha Kappa Psi, Sigma Phi Epsilon. Home: Eleven Lohman Rd Convent Station NJ 07961 Office: Prudential Plaza Newark NJ 07101

SMITH, ROBERTS ANGUS, educator, biochemist; b. Vancouver, B.C., Can., Dec. 22, 1928; s. Alvin Roberts and Hazel (Mather) S.; B.S.A., U. B.C., 1952, M.Sc., 1953; Ph.D., U. Ill., 1957; m. Mary Adela Marriott, Aug. 22, 1953; children—Roberts H.A., James A.D., Eric J.M., Richard I.F. Came to U.S., 1953, naturalized, 1963. Instr. U. Ill., 1957-58; mem. faculty U. Cal. at Los Angeles, 1958—, prof. biochemistry, 1968—. Dir. ICN Pharms. Inc. Bd. dirs., v.p. Julius and Dorothy Fried Research Found. Guggenheim fellow, 1963-64. Mem. Am. Soc. Biol. Chemists, Am. Chem. Soc. Home: 221 17th St Santa Monica CA 90402

SMITH, ROBYN CAROLINE, jockey; b. San Francisco, Aug. 14, 1944; d. Orville L. and June (Pheaffer) Smith; Jockey, Golden Gate Fields, San Francisco, 1970, Belmont (N.Y.) Park Race Track, 1971—. First female jockey to win maj. stakes race; 1st female jockey to ride 3 winners in 1 afternoon. Mem. Jockeys Guild Inc., Screen Actors Guild. Office: Belmont Park Race Track Belmont NY 11003

SMITH, ROGER BONHAM, automotive mfg. co. exec.; b. Columbus, Ohio, July 12, 1925; s. Emmet Quimby and Bess (Obetz) S.; student U. Mich., 1942-44, B.B.A., 1947, M.B.A., 1949; m. Barbara Ann Rasch, June 7, 1954; children—Roger Bonham, Jennifer Anne, Victoria Belle, Drew Johnston. With Gen. Motors, Detroit, 1949—, treas., 1970-71, v.p. charge fin. staff, 1971-73; v.p., group exec. in charge of non-automotive and def. group, 1973-74, exec. v.p., 1974—, vice chmn. fin. com., 1975—. Mem. vis. com. U. Mich. Grad. Sch. Bus. Adminstrn.; trustee Cranbrook Schs., Bloomfield Hills, Mich., Mich. Colls. Found., Detroit; trustee, treas. Automotive Safety Found.; bd. dirs., mem. exec. com., treas. Hwy. Users Fedn. Served with USNR, 1944-46. Mem. Fin. Execs. Inst., Motor Vehicle Mfrs. Assn. (dir., exec. com.), Assos. Harvard U. Grad. Sch. Bus. Adminstrn. (dir.). Clubs: Detroit, Detroit Athletic; Orchard Lake (Mich.) Country; Bloomfield Hills Country; Links (N.Y.C.). Home: Bloomfield Hills MI 48013 Office: 3044 W Grand Blvd Detroit MI 48202

SMITH, ROGER CARLYLE, copper co. exec.; b. Cleve., Dec. 11, 1927; s. Bradford Bixby and Marilyn (Maw) S.; A.B., Princeton, 1950; M.B.A., Harvard, 1952; m. Nell Becherer, Mar. 19, 1955; children—Roger Jeffrey, Jennifer Nell, Stuart Becherer. Asst. to financial v.p. Motorola, Inc., 1952-56, credit mgr., 1958-60, asst. treas., 1960-65, treas., 1965-69, v.p., treas., 1969-71; v.p., dir. Motorola Internat. Devel. Corp., 1968-70, pres., dir., 1970-71; mgr. consumer products financing Motorola Finance Co., 1956-57, asst. gen mgr., 1957-58; v.p. finance Phelps Dodge Corp., 1971—, treas., 1974-79. Bd. dirs. Am. Bur. Metal Statistics. Served with AUS, 1946-48. Republican. Clubs: Skokie Country (Glenco); Quadrangle (Princeton, N.J.); Woodway Country (Darien, Conn.); University (N.Y.C.). Home: 7 Sherwood Ln New Canaan CT 06840 Office: 300 Park Ave New York NY 10022

SMITH, ROGER DEAN, pathologist; b. N.Y.C., Oct. 6, 1932; s. Joseph Leslie and Matilda (Feigelson) S.; A.B., Cornell U., 1954; M.D., N.Y. Med. Coll., 1958; m. Margaret Helen Smith, Apr. 24, 1957; children—Wade Russell, Craig Andrew, Douglas Dean, Roger Len. Asst. prof. dept. pathology U. Ill. Coll. Medicine, Chgo., 1966; cons. renal pathology Presbyn. St. Lukes Hosp., W. Side VA Hosp., Chgo., 1969, asso. prof. dept. pathology U. Ill. Coll. Medicine, Chgo., 1970, dir. ind. study program, asst. dean Coll. Medicine, 1971-72; Mary M. Emery prof., dir. dept. pathology U. Cin., 1972; dir. lab. services Cin. Gen. Hosp., Holmes Hosp.; mem. exec. bd. Cancer Control Council, 1974-77. Served to capt. M.C., U.S. Army, 1959-61. Recipient Hoektoen award Chgo. Pathology Soc.; USPHS pathology research fellow, 1962-66; Am. Cancer Soc. grantee, 1965-68; NIH grantee, 1968-72, 75-79; diplomate Nat. Bd. Med. Examiners, Am. Bd. Pathology. Contbr. research papers to profl. jours. Home: 1238 Hayward Ave Cincinnati OH 45226 Office: Dept Pathology U Cin Coll Medicine Cincinnati OH 45267

SMITH, ROGER HASKELL, editor; b. Detroit, Apr. 25, 1932; s. Demonte Haskell and Catherine (Linn) S.; B.A., Yale, 1954; m. Beverly Chew Bates, Feb. 18, 1956; children—Roger Haskell (dec.), William Boulton. Asst. editor, news editor, exec. editor, contbg. editor Pubs. Weekly, N.Y.C., 1954—; mng. editor Police Athletic League of N.Y., 1976—. Past bd. dirs. Am. Hist. Documents Inst., Washington, 1963-74, Council on Interracial Books for Children, N.Y.C., 1970-74. Mem. P.E.N. Am. Center N.Y.C. (sec. 1973-76, exec. bd.). Clubs: Players (N.Y.C.); Devon Yacht (East Hampton, N.Y.). Author: Paperback Parnassus, 1976. Editor: The American Reading Public, 1963. Home: 92 Grove St New York NY 10014 Office: 1180 Ave of Americas New York NY 10036

SMITH, RONALD BROMLEY, mech. engr.; b. New London, Conn., Oct. 28, 1907; s. Isaac B. and Emma L. (Stone) S.; B.S. cum laude, U. Wash., 1930, M.E., 1933; M.S., U. Pitts., 1937; postgrad. U. Pa., 1933-36, U. Mich., 1935; D.Eng. (hon.), Worcester Poly. Inst., 1964; m. Evelyn F. Miller, Aug. 15, 1936 (dec. 1973); children—Leslie Ann Smith Elger, Marcia Thompson; m. 2d, Janet Morris Bishop, 1977. With Westinghouse Electric & Mfg. Co., 1930-37; with Elliott Co., 1937-48, dir. research, 1941-45, v.p., 1945-48; with M. W. Kellogg Co., N.Y.C., 1948-67, v.p., 1949-61, sr. v.p., 1962-67; dir. Turbonetics Inc., DeLaval Separator Co., Southeastern Public Service Co., Wilson Bros. Mem. U.S. Naval Tech. Mission to ETO, 1945; pvt. practice cons. engring., 1967—. Recipient Disting. Engring. Alumnus citation U. Mich., 1953, U. Pitts., 1967. Mem. Soc. Naval Architects and Marine Engrs. (Linnard prize 1943), ASME (pres. 1963; hon.), Sigma Xi, Tau Beta Pi, Pi Tau Sigma. Clubs: N.Y. Yacht; Riomar Bay (Fla.) Yacht. Contbr. articles to profl. jours.; tech. contbns.: gas turbines, low pressure oxygen, synthetic gasoline from coal; co-patentee ammonia synthesis (Kirkpatrick award).

SMITH, RONALD LEE, univ. adminstr.; b. Indpls., June 10, 1937; s. Emerson Wellman and Dorothy Elizabeth (Schaefer) S.; B.M.E., Gen. Motors Inst., 1960; M.S., Purdue U., 1962, Ph.D., 1967; m. Betty Joan Bobbitt, Aug. 22, 1959; children—Byron Thomas (dec.), Evan Ronald, Deanna Marie, Kathleen Elizabeth. Asst. Prof. humanities Gen. Motors Inst., 1963-67, asso. prof., 1967-68; prof., chmn. dept. communication and organization behavior, 1968-73; prof. mgmt., dean Coll. Bus. Adminstrn. U. Nebr., Lincoln, 1973-77; prof., dean Sch. Bus. Adminstrn., Georgetown U., Washington, 1977—; dir. Minn. Gas Co., 1976—, 1st Greatwest Corp., 1975-78. Mem. Council Communication Socs. (pres. 1978-80), Am. Psychol. Assn., Acad. Mgmt., Eastern Acad. Mgmt., Internat. Communication Assn. (pres. 1971-72), Speech Communication Assn., Beta Gamma Sigma, Delta Sigma Pi, Theta Xi (pres. 1978-80). Republican. Mem. United Ch. of Christ. Mem. editorial bd., cons. editor Jour. Communication, 1973—. Contbr. chpts. to books. Home: 7311 River Rd Bethesda MD 20034 Office: Sch Bus Adminstrn Georgetown Univ Washington DC 20057

SMITH, RONALD LEE, ednl. adminstr.; b. Berwyn, Ill., July 30, 1933; s. Fred B. and Zola Estelle (Bucher) S.; B.S., U. Nebr., 1955, Ed.D., 1966; M.A., Colo. State Coll., 1958; m. Luanne Marie Raun, June 10, 1956; children—Shelley Marie, Zoanne Lee. Classroom tchr., counselor, asst. prin., Pueblo, Colo., 1955-64; exec. asst. Colo. Commr. Edn., 1965-69; exec. dir. Nat. Assn. State Bds. Edn., Denver, 1969-70; prin. Lakewood High Sch., Jefferson County, Colo., 1970-72; dept. dir. Edn. Commn. of States, Denver, 1972-74, dep. exec. dir., 1974—. Mem. Am. Assn. Sch. Adminstrs., NEA, Phi Delta Kappa. Home: 5126 Black Gore Dr PO Box 1871 Vail CO 81657 Office: 1860 Lincoln St #300 Denver CO 80295

SMITH, RONALD LYNN, hosp. adminstr.; b. Algona, Iowa, Sept. 22, 1940; s.Russell M. and Helen Lucille (Gridley) S.; B.S., Iowa State U., 1962; postgrad. U. S.D., 1963; M.A. in Hosp. and Health Adminstrn., U. Iowa, 1965; m. Jacqueline Sue, Dec. 23, 1962; children—Sheri Rene, Gregory Mark, Brenton Allan. Orderly, Mary Greeley Hosp., Ames, Iowa, 1962; with Harris Hosp., Ft. Worth, 1964—, sr. asst. adminstrn., 1971-74, asso. exec. dir., 1974-76, exec. dir., 1977—; bd. dirs. Tarrant County (Tex.) Heart Assn., 1975-77, Tarrant County chpt. Am. Heart Assn., 1977—; mem. adv. com. Brown-Lupton Health Center, 1975-76; v.p. Easter Seal Soc., 1975-77; mem. med. lab. technician adv. com. Tarrant County Jr. Coll., 1976-77; mem. emergency med. services com. Ft. Worth City Council, 1969-77; mem. regional emergency services adv. com. North Central Tex. Council Govts., 1975. Bd. dirs. Ft. Worth Area Council Chs., 1973-75; mem. commn. on edn., fin. com., adminstrv. bd. Univ. United Methodist Ch., Ft. Worth; bd. dirs. Better Bus. Bur., Ft. Worth, 1976—; trustee Tarrant County United Way, 1977-79. Fellow Am. Coll. Hosp. Adminstrs.; mem. Am. Hosp. Assn., Tex. Hosp. Assn., Dallas-Ft. Worth Hosp. Council, Dallas/Ft. Worth Hosp. Adminstr.'s Jour. Club, Electronic Computing Health Oriented, Forum Ft. Worth, South Ft. Worth Bus. Assn. (v.p. 1975-76), Trinity Emergency Services Assn. (sec.-treas. 1975—). Club: Rotary (trustee Ednl. Found.) (Ft. Worth). Home: 7008 Briar Wild Ct Fort Worth TX 76133 Office: 1300 W Cannon St Fort Worth TX 76104

SMITH, ROSS WILBERT, educator; b. Turlock, Calif., Dec. 11, 1927; s. Emor Wilbert and Eugenia (Mobley) S.; A.A., Hartnell Coll., 1947; B.S., U. Nev., 1950; S.M., Mass. Inst. Tech., 1955; Ph.D., Stanford U., 1969; m. Catherine Anne Parsons, Dec. 31, 1955; children—Walter Stillwell, Anne Quinter, Courtney Ross. Mfg. process engr. Portland Cement Assn., Skokie, Ill., 1955-58; project engr. Research Found. Colo. Sch. Mines, Golden, 1958-60; asso. prof. S.D. Sch. Mines, Rapid City, 1960-66; chem. engr. U.S. Geol. Survey, Menlo Park, Calif., 1966-68; prof. chem. and metall. engring. U. Nev., Reno, 1968—, chmn. dept., 1968-78. Served with AUS, 1951-53. Mem. Am. Chem. Soc., AIME, Am. Inst. Chem. Engrs., Sigma Xi. Contbr. articles to profl. jours. Home: 1730 O'Farrell St Reno NV 89503

SMITH, ROY EMERSON, educator; b. Chippewa Falls, Wis., Apr. 28, 1926; s. Henry L. and Delpha (Olson) S.; B.S., Wis. State U., Eau Claire, 1950; M.S. (NSF fellow 1956), U. Wis., 1957; Ph.D., Ohio State U., 1966; postgrad. Northwestern U., 1950, (NSF fellow) Iowa State U., 1959, (NSF fellow) U. Kans., 1962; m. Carol Louise Smith, June 1, 1947; children—Jay Q., Jill R., Jan D. Tchr., Nichols Sch., Evanston, Ill., 1950-51; tchr, Oregon (Wis.) Consol. Schs., 1951-56; mem. faculty U. Wis. Platteville, 1957—, chmn. dept. physics, 1966—; cons. Wis. Mold & Tool Corp., 1957-62. Mem. Tchr. Edn. Council of Coordinating Council Higher Edn. Wis., 1970-71; mem. task force for rev. and planning Master's/Specialist program in tchr. edn. for So. Wis., 1973-75; mem. Wis. System Edn. Professions Adv. Council, 1976—, Wis. System Task Force Profl. Devel. for Ednl. Personnel, 1977—. Scoutmaster, Boy Scouts Am., Evanston, 1950-51. Served with USNR, 1944-46. NSF fellow Ohio State U., 1963, 66. Mem. Wis. Assn. Sci. Tchrs. (pres. 1958), Am. Assn. Physics Tchrs. (pres. Wis. sect. 1961, 72). Mason, Rotarian. Author: U. Wis. Extension Div. High Sch. Correspondence Study in Physics, 1956; Fundamental Experimental Physical Science, 1965. Home: Route 4 Potosi Rd Platteville WI 53818

SMITH, RUSSELL B., lawyer; b. Ft. Worth, Nov. 1, 1936; s. Russell B. and Marie Antonette (Hornick) S.; B.B.A., So. Meth. U., 1959, J.D., 1962; m. Mary Sue Bowling, May 16, 1964; children—Robert Bryan, Donna Sue. Admitted to Tex. bar, U.S. Supreme Ct. bar; practiced in Dallas, 1962—. Mem. devel. bd. Lakewood Bank & Trust Co., 1972-75. Formerly active The 500 Inc., Community Chest, United Fund, Speakers' Bur. Dallas—Ft. Worth Regional Airport, host com. Nat. Conf. Planned Parenthood N.E. Tex.; mem. com. blood donors Wadley Blood Inst., 1964; mem. Trees for Dallas Project, 1966-67; mem. area coordinating com. Citizens Charter Assn., 1967, nominating com. dist. 5, 1969, v.p. dist. 5, 1971; vice chmn. bd. adjustment, Dallas, 1967-71; mem. procedural com. City Planning Commn., Dallas, 1969-71; mem. sch. liaison Neighborhood Coordinating Com. for Goals for Dallas, 1969; chmn. pres's. task force State Fair Tex., 1970—, vice pres. fair, 1973—; mem. panel Community Council Greater Dallas, 1972-74; mem. com. priorities Dallas Health Planning Council, 1974-75; mem. com. pub. safety Nat. League Cities, 1974-75; mem. adv. council St. Paul Hosp., 1974—; chmn. adv. com. Golden Gloves, 1974-75; chmn. com. concessions Byron Nelson Golf Classic, 1975-79; mem. Bi-Centennial Adv. Com., 1976. City councilman, Dallas, 1971-73, dep. mayor pro tem, 1973-75. Bd. dirs. Met. Dallas chpt. March of Dimes, State Fair Tex. Recipient Distinguished Service award as Outstanding Young Man in Dallas, 1967, award for Five Outstanding Young Texans in 1972, Tex. Jaycees, 1972, Service award as Outstanding Man in Dallas, 1975; Ky. col. Mem. Am., Dallas bar assns., State Bar Tex., Am. Judicature Soc., Am., Tex. trial lawyers assns., Am. Bd. Trial Advocates, Dallas Assn. Trial Lawyers, All Sports Assn. (pres. 1975—), Dallas Assn. Retarded Children, Dallas Big Bros., Dallas (chmn's. council 1972-75), East Dallas, Dallas Jr. (Distinguished Service award, pres. 1966-67) chambers commerce, Exhausted Roosters (pres. 1972-73, life), Philippine Assn. Dallas (hon.), Nat. Football Found., Rock Creek Barbecue Club (life), Salesmanship Club of Dallas, Dallas Estate Council, Dallas Assembly, Dallas Forum, Dallas 40, Trinity Improvement Assn., Dallas Tornado Soccer Club (adv. bd.), Phi Alpha Delta. Clubs: Dallas Woods and Waters, Dallas Athletic. Home: 6323 Danbury Ln Dallas TX 75201 Office: 2001 Bryan Tower Suite 2770 Dallas TX 75201

SMITH, RUSSELL EVANS, U.S. judge; b. Butte, Mont., Nov. 16, 1908; s. Ernest Clifford and Florence (Evans) S.; LL.B. cum laude, U. Mont., 1931; m. Mary Ruth Larison, June 21, 1931; children—Sonia Lee (Mrs. Daniel R. Zenk), Russell Evans. Admitted to Mont. bar, 1931; marshal, law clk. Mont. Supreme Ct., 1931-33; practiced in Cut Bank, Mont., 1933-35, Missoula, Mont., 1935-42, 45-66; counsel for Mont., OPA, 1942-43; judge U.S. Dist. Ct. for Mont., 1966—, chief judge, to 1978, sr. judge, 1978—; lectr. U. Mont. Law Sch. Mem. Mont. Bd. Bar Examiners. Served to USNR, 1943-45 Mem. Mont. Bar Assn. (past pres. 1956), Alpha Tau Omega, Phi Delta Phi. Office: PO Box 7219 Missoula MT 59807

SMITH, RUSSELL HUNT, lawyer; b. Mt. Vernon, Mo., Feb. 9, 1922; s. Ivan Louis and Grace (Hunt) S.; student S.W. Mo. State Coll., 1945-47; LL.B., U. Mich., 1950; m. Gloria Warren, Dec. 28, 1947; children—Cynthia Dianne, Windsor Hunt, Diana Marie. Admitted to Okla. bar, 1951, 10th Circuit Ct. Appeals bar, 1951, 7th Circuit, 1962, Mo. bar, 1950; atty. Amerada Petroleum Corp., Tulsa, 1950-55; asst. U.S. atty. No. Dist. Okla., 1955-59, U.S. atty., 1960-61; atty. Cities Service Oil Co., Bartlesville, 1961—, now asst. gen. counsel. Served with AUS, 1940-45. Mem. Am., Okla. bar assns., Mo. Bar. Home: 204 E 21st St Tulsa OK 74114 Office: Cities Service Bldg Tulsa OK 74102

SMITH, RUSSELL JACK, research cons.; b. Jackson, Mich., July 4, 1913; s. Lee C. and Georgia L. (Weed) S.; A.B., Miami U., Oxford, Ohio, 1937; Ph.D., Cornell U., 1941; m. Rosemary Thomson, Sept. 5, 1938; children—Stephen M., Scott T., Christopher G. Asst. instr. English, Cornell U., 1937-41; instr. English, Williams Coll., 1941-45; with OSS, 1945; asst. prof. English, Wells Coll., 1946-47; with CIA, 1947-74, mem. bd. nat. estimates, 1957-62, dir. current intelligence, 1962-66, dep. dir. for intelligence, 1966-71, spl. asst. U.S. embassy, New Delhi, India, 1971-74; research cons., 1975—; assigned Nat. War Coll., 1951-52, U.S. rep. Brit. Joint Intelligence Com., Far East, Singapore, 1954-56. Recipient Nat. Civil Service League award, 1971, Distinguished Intelligence medal CIA, 1974. Mem. Washington Inst. Fgn. Affairs, Phi Beta Kappa, Phi Delta Theta, Omicron Delta Kappa. Club: Federal City. Author: John Dryden, A Study in Controversy, 1941; also articles. Home: 1138 Bellview Rd McLean VA 22102

SMITH, RUTH DABNEY CAMP, librarian; b. Washington, Oct. 10, 1916; d. William Henry and Minerva Gertrude (Taylor) Dabney; A.B., Howard U., 1937; B.S. in L.S., Hampton Inst., 1938; M.L.S., Columbia U., 1948; m. William Ransom Smith, May 28, 1966. Serials librarian Howard U., 1939-41; librarian N.Y. Pub. Library, N.Y.C., 1942-46, asst. br. librarian, 1946-48; head cataloging sect. U.S. Bur. Ships Tech. Library, Washington, 1949-61, head tech. processing sect., 1961-65; thesaurus coordinator, info. systems div., computation and math. dept. U.S. Naval Ship Research and Devel. Center, Bethesda, Md., 1965-68, head info. analysis and processing br., 1968-71; detailed to project LEX, Office of Naval Research, Washington, 1965-67; dir. sci. documentation div. office mgmt. services U.S. Naval Ship Systems Command, Washington, 1971-73; chief library br., div. research services NIH, Bethesda, Md., 1973—. Recipient Navy Meritorious Civilian award, 1973; librarian's profl. life cert., N.Y. Mem. ALA, Am. Soc. for Info. Sci., D.C. Library Assn., Fed. Librarians Assn., Med. Library Assn., Spl. Libraries Assn. (chmn. documentation div. 1977-78), Internat. Fedn. Library Assns. and Instns. (sec. biol. and med. scis. libraries sect. 1977-80). Democrat. Baptist. Clubs: Toastmistress, Order of Eastern Star, Daus. of Isis, Heroines of Jericho, Cyrene Crusaders, Order of Golden Circle. Office: NIH Library 9000 Rockville Pike Bethesda MD 20205

SMITH, RUTH LILLIAN SCHLUCHTER, librarian; b. Detroit, Oct. 18, 1917; d. Clayton John and Gertrude Katherine (Kastler) Schluchter; A.B., Wayne State U., Detroit, 1939; A.B. in L.S., U. Mich., Ann Arbor, 1942; m. Thomas Guilford Smith, Sept. 28, 1946; 1 son, Pemberton, Jr. librarian Detroit Pub. Library, 1942-43; research asst. Moore Sch. Elec. Engring., U. Pa., Phila., 1946-47; librarian Bethesda (Md.) Methodist Ch. Library, 1955-61; ref. librarian, chief reader services Inst. Def. Analyses, Arlington, Va., 1961-65, chief unclassified library sect., 1965-67, head librarian, 1967-75, mgr. tech. info. services, 1975—; leader ch. library workshops, 1960—; speaker profl. meetings; founder, chmn. Com. Info. Hang-ups, 1969—; mem. Depository Library Council to the Pub. Printer, 1975-78. Served to lt. (j.g.), WAVES, USNR, 1943-46. Mem. ALA, Am. Soc. Info. Sci., Ch. and Synagogue Library Assn. (founding mem., life mem., pres. 1967-68), Fedn. Info. Users (v.p. interactive affairs 1973-75), Spl. Libraries Assn. (chmn. aerospace div. 1975-76, chmn. library mgmt. div. 1978-79). Republican. Methodist. Author: Publicity for a Church Library, 1966; Workshop Planning, 1972; (with Claudia Hannaford) Promotion Planning, 1975; Getting the Books Off the Shelves, 1975; Cataloging Books, Step By Step, 1977; Cataloging Made Easy, 1978; Setting up a Library; How To Begin or Begin Again, 1979; contbr. articles to library and religious jours. Home: 5304 Glenwood Rd Bethesda MD 20014 Office: 400 Army Navy Dr Arlington VA 22202

SMITH, SAMUEL BOYD, educator; b. Adams, Tenn., Oct. 23, 1929; s. Carl S. and Annie (Tolleson) S.; student Milligan Coll., 1947-48, U. Tenn., 1948-49, Syracuse U., 1951-52; B.S., Peabody Coll., 1956; M.A., Vanderbilt U., 1960, Ph.D., 1962; m. Martha Sue Fitzsimmons, Dec. 23, 1956; children—David Fitzsimmons, Mark Tolleson, Stephen Boyd. Asst. prof. history U. South Fla., 1961-64; state librarian and archivist, chmn. Tenn. Hist. Commn., 1964-69; lectr. history Peabody Coll., 1965-66; asso. prof. history U. Tenn., 1969-71, prof. history, editor Andrew Jackson Presdl. Papers, 1972—. Served with USAF, 1951-54. Mem. Orgn. Am. Historians, Am., Tenn. hist. assns. Methodist. Democrat. Rotarian. Co-author: This is Tennessee, 1973. Editor and compiler: Tennessee History: A Bibliography, 1974; co-editor: The Papers of Andrew Jackson, vol. I, 1979, vol. II, 1980. Home: 1135 Sewanee Rd Nashville TN 37220 Office: Andrew Jackson Papers The Hermitage Hermitage TN 37076

SMITH, SAMUEL DAVID, educator, artist; b. Thorndale, Tex., Feb. 18, 1918; s. Otto Frank and Jeanette (Joyce) S.; ed. pub. schs.; m. Elizabeth Marie Smith; children—Cezanne, Rembrandt, Michelangelo. Prof. art U. N.Mex., 1956—; one man exhbns. include Corcoran Gallery Art, Washington, 1949, Santa Fe Mus. Art, 1947, Roswell (N.Mex.) Mus. Fine Art, 1953, 64, Goodwell (Okla.) Hist. Mus., 1964, Panhandle Plains Mus., Canyon City, Tex., 1964, Biltomore Galleries, Los Angeles, 1946, First Nat. Bank, Los Alamos, 1968; group exhbns. include Baker Galleries, Lubbock, Tex., 1964-73, Met. Mus., N.Y.C., 1944, Blue Door Gallery, Taos, N.Mex., 1946-53, Galeria del Sol, Albuquerque, 1968-73, Brandywine Galleries, 1972-73. Served as combat artist AUS, 1942-45. Hon. life mem. N.Mex. Art League; mem. Artist Equity Assn. (pres. N.Mex. chpt. 1957-58, 66-67, 70-71). Elk. Illustrator: Roots in Adobe, 1967; Cowboy's Christmas Tree, 1956; also Coronet mag. Home: 213 Utah St NE Albuquerque NM 87108 Office: Gen Del Telluride CO 81435

SMITH, SAMUEL KREIS, automobile fin. co. exec.; b. Knoxville, Tenn., Nov. 5, 1915; s. Benjamin Franklin and Dora Belle (Kreis) S.; grad. U. Tenn., Knoxville, 1940; m. Virginia Marjorie Shephard, Nov. 9, 1947; children—Walter, Sandra, Charles, Roger, Virginia, Donna. With Gen. Motors Acceptance Corp., 1940—, dir., mem. exec. com., 1968—, pres., chmn. exec. com., 1974—; chmn. bd. MIC, 1974—; chmn. bd. and fin. com. MIC Life Ins. Corp., 1975—. Trustee, mem. ins. and pensions com. Lenox Hill Hosp., N.Y.C.; bd. dirs. Hwy. Users Fedn. Safety and Mobility. Served to maj. USAAF, 1941-47. Mem. Econ. Club N.Y.C. Republican. Clubs: Bay Point Yacht and Country (Panama City, Fla.); Country of Darien (Conn.). Office: 767 Fifth Ave New York NY 10022

SMITH, SCOTT MEADOWS, physician; b. Houston, Mo., July 17, 1912; s. Harry R. and Bessie Mae (Scott) S.; A.B., Mo. U., 1937, B.S., 1937; M.D., Louisville U., 1939; m. Mary Wilmoth Pace, Mar. 17, 1934; children—Nancy Jean, Carol Rene. Registered pharmacist, 1934; rotating intern St. Louis City Hosp., 1939-40, surg. resident, 1940-42; asst. in anesthesia U. Minn., 1942-43; asso. clin. prof. and head dept. anesthesiology U. Utah, 1944-54; pvt. practice anesthesiology, Salt Lake City, 1943—; br. sect. chief in anesthesiol. VA Hosps. Diplomate Am. Bd. Anesthesiology (pres. 1958). Fellow Am. Coll. Anesthesiology; mem. Acad. Anesthesiologists (sec. 1958—, pres. 1979-80), Acad. Anesthesiology (exec. com., sec.

1957—), Am. Soc. Anesthesiology (pres. 1956), AMA (chmn. sect. anesthesiology). Internat. Anesthesia Research Soc., Utah Med. Assn. (ho. of dels., treas. 1972-75), Phi Beta Pi. Presbyn. Mason. Clubs: Ambassador Athletic, Rotary. Author articles. Home: 1601 Yalecrest Salt Lake City UT 84105 Office: 223 S 5th E Salt Lake City UT 84102

SMITH, SHERMAN ALLEN, cons. engr.; b. Hamburg, Iowa, Jan. 17, 1920; s. West Floyd and Lillie Margret (Allen) S.; student Iowa State U., 1937-39; m. Mary Elizabeth Uhler, Apr. 9, 1944; children—Sherman Uhler, Sharon Elizabeth, Gregory Allen. Draftsman, designer Clay Equipment Corp., 1940-41; designer, checker Day & Zimmerman Inc., 1941-42; structural designer, phys. plan coordinator blast furnace design Carnegie Ill. Steel Corp., 1946; designer, field supt. housing Penn Constrn. Co., 1947-48; archtl. and structural designer Fed. Engring. Co., 1949-50; project engr. Silas Mason-Mason Hanger, 1951-53; pres. Sherman Smith & Assos., Burlington, Iowa, 1953—, chmn. bd., 1953—. Mem. plan devel. com. Area 5 Iowa Health Systems Agency, 1975—; chmn. Burlington Constrn. Bd. Appeals, 1973—; pres., bd. dirs. Environ. and Pollution Control Council, 1973—; bd. dirs. Des Moines Health Services Council, 1974—; mem. Des Moines County Resource Conservation and Devel. Com., 1974—; mem. regional advisory bd. Iowa-Cedar River Conservancy Dist., 1976—. Served with C.E., U.S. Army, 1942-45. Named to Com. of 100 Cons. Engr. Mag., 1974. Fellow Am. Cons. Engrs. Council (past pres. award 1976, chmn. profl. standards com. 1973-76, chmn. ethical practices com. 1973-77); mem. Nat. Soc. Profl. Engrs. (past chmn. bd. ethical rev.), Am. Water Works Assn., Water Pollution Control Fedn., Am. Soc. Testing Materials, Am. Congress Surveying and Mapping, Iowa Engring. Soc. (Marston award 1960, past pres., Disting. Service award 1978), Cons. Engrs. Council Iowa (prin. rep., past pres., past bd. dirs.). Republican. Mem. United Ch. of Christ. Contbr. articles to profl. jours. Home: 706 S 9th St Burlington IA 52601 Office: 1115 Summer St Burlington IA 52601

SMITH, SHERWOOD DRAUGHON, hosp. adminstr.; b. Durham, N.C., Feb. 12, 1925; s. Cody Hood and Eula (Draughon) S.; B.A., Duke, 1950, M.S., 1952; m. Patricia Ann Collins, Jan. 27, 1952; children—David Cody, Kenneth Heber, Sherwood Allan, Steven Collins, Sarah Amy. Asst. adminstr. Hubbard Hosp., Nashville, 1952-54, adminstr., 1954-56; exec. dir. Lakeland (Fla.) Gen. Hosp., 1956—. Bd. dirs., exec. com. Suncoast Health Council; bd. dirs. Blue Cross Fla.; past pres., bd. dirs. Southeastern Hosp. Conf., del., 1968—; pres. Central Fla. Hosp. Council, 1961-62; mem. Fla. Health Planning Council, 1971—. Mem. Adv. Com. Employment, Lakeland; mem. Polk County Planning Council, 1970—; bishop Ch. of Jesus Christ of Latter-day Saints. Served with AUS, 1942-46. Fellow Am. Coll. Hosps. Adminstrs. (regent dist. III 1970-73); mem. Fla. (pres. 1966, bd. dirs.), Am. (Fla. del. 1967-73, trustee 1975—, chmn. regional adv. bd.) hosp. assns. Rotarian. Home: 1515 Leighton St Lakeland FL 33803 Office: 1400 Lakeland Hills Blvd Lakeland FL 33802

SMITH, SHERWOOD HUBBARD, JR., utilities exec.; b. Jacksonville, Fla., Sept. 1, 1934; s. Sherwood Hubbard and Catherine Gertrude (Milliken) S.; A.B., U. N.C., 1956, J.D., 1960; m. Eva Hackney Hargrave, July 20, 1957; children—Marlin Hamilton, Cameron Hargrave, Eva Hackney. Admitted to N.C. bar, 1960; asso. Lassiter, Moore & Van Allen, Charlotte, 1960-62; partner Joyner & Howison, Raleigh, 1963-65; asso. gen. counsel Carolina Power & Light Co., Raleigh, 1965-70, sr. v.p., gen. counsel, 1971-74, exec. v.p., 1974-76, pres., 1976—, also dir.; dir. Hackney Bros. Body Co., Wilson, N.C. Chmn. Raleigh Civic Center Authority, 1973—; vice chmn. Morehead Scholar Central Selection Com., U. N.C., 1970—; mem. Gov.'s Efficiency Study Commn., 1973; bd. dirs., sec. Bus. Found. N.C., 1977—; trustee Z. Smith Reynolds Found., 1978—; chmn. bd. dirs. N.C. Heart Assn., 1971-74; bd. dirs. United Fund Wake County; vice chmn. trustees Rex Hosp. Served as ensign USN, 1956-57. Mem. Greater Raleigh C. of C. (pres. 1979). Democrat. Episcopalian. Rotarian. Home: 408 Drummond Dr Raleigh NC 27609 Office: PO Box 1551 Raleigh NC 27602

SMITH, SID, publisher; b. Howardsville, Va., June 4, 1938; s. Albert S. and Virginia L. (Bennett) S.; student UCLA; A.A., Los Angeles Trade Tech. Coll., 1963; m. Lois J. McCartney, Aug. 29, 1964; children—Christine A., Michelle A. Prodn. coordinator RCA, 1960-66; mem. pub. relations staff Trans World Airlines, 1966-73; writer, pub. Palyers Internat. Publs., Los Angeles, 1979—; pub. Concepts of Elegance, Inc., Los Angeles, 1979—; exec. dir., chmn. bd. Universe Communications, Los Angeles, 1979—; exec. dir. Black Boar Pub., Los Angeles, 1979—. Author demographic and geographic study on Black Am. Democratic Nat. Com., 1973. Served with USAF, 1954-60. Mem. Air Force Assn. Democrat. Baptist. Author: Jesse; Forgotten, Dangerous and Aimless. Office: 7100 Hillside Ave Apt 602 Los Angeles CA 90046

SMITH, SIDNEY OSLIN, JR., lawyer; b. Gainesville, Ga., Dec. 30, 1923; s. Sidney Oslin and Isabelle (Charters) S.; grad. Middlesex Sch., 1941; A.B. cum laude, Harvard, 1947; LL.B. summa cum laude, U. Ga., 1949; m. Patricia Irwin Horkan, Aug. 4, 1944; children—Charters, Ellen, Sidney Oslin III. Admitted to Ga. bar, 1948; partner firm Telford, Wayne & Smith, Gainesville, 1951-62, Alston, Miller & Gaines, Atlanta, 1974—; asst. solicitor gen. Northeastern circuit Ga., 1951-61; judge Superior Ct. Ga., 1962-65; U.S. judge No. Dist. Ga., 1965-74, chief judge, 1968-74. Mem. Ga. Bd. Bar Examiners, 1961-62. Chmn. Gainesville Bd. Edn., 1959-62. Trustee Gainesville Art Assn., Brenau Coll. Served to capt. AUS, 1943-46. Mem. Am., Ga., Gainesville bar assns., Phi Beta Kappa, Phi Delta Theta, Phi Delta Phi, Phi Kappa Phi. Democrat. Episcopalian. Rotarian. Clubs: Hasty Pudding, Owl (Harvard); Chattahoochee Country (Gainesville); Capital City (Atlanta). Home: 2541 Club Dr NW Gainesville GA 30501 Office: 1200 C & S Bank Atlanta GA 30303

SMITH, STANLEY ROGER, profl. tennis player; b. Pasadena, Calif., Dec. 14, 1946; s. Charles Kenneth and Rhoda (Widmer) S.; B.A., U. So. Calif., 1969; L.H.D., Greenville Coll., 1974; m. Marjory Logan Gengler, Nov. 23, 1974; 1 son, Ramsey Gengler. Profl. tennis player, 1968—; mem. U.S. Davis Cup Team, 1968-78 (only undefeated doubles team in Internat. Davis Cup competition since 1900); adviser Pres.'s Council on Phys. Fitness, 1971-75; writer nationally syndicated newspaper column Stan Smith's Tennis Tips, 1971-72; cons. Fischer G.m.b.H., Austria, Sea Pines Co., Adidas, Landersheim, France. Bd. dirs. Greater Los Angeles Big Bros. Am., 1966-71. Served with AUS, 1970-72. Decorated D.S.M.; named Martini and Rossi Player of Year, 1971, 72; holder 25 U.S. singles and doubles titles, including U.S. Open singles, 1971, U.S. Open doubles, 1968, 74; ranked number one in U.S. doubles, 1968, 69, 1970, 71, 72, 74, number one in U.S. singles, 1969, 71, 72, 73; winner Wimbledon singles title, 1972; winner 6 World championship tennis titles in 1973, including World Championship of Tennis Finals in singles, also Rothman's World Doubles title; ranked world's number one tennis player, 1973; Lebair Sportsmanship Trophy, 1969; Johnston Sportsmanship Trophy, 1968. Mem. Assn. Tennis Profls. (dir. 1972-79), Athletes in Action, Beta Theta Pi. Republican. Presbyterian. Clubs: Sea Pines Plantation; Los Angeles Tennis; All England; West Side Tennis; Century XXI; Balboa Bay. Author: Inside Tennis, 1974; Stan Smith's Six Tennis Basics, 1974; The Executive Tennis Diary 1975, 1974; Stan Smith's Guide to Better Tennis, 1975; (with Bob Lutz) Modern Doubles, 1975; It's More Than Just a Game, 1977. Office: 888 17th St NW Suite 1200 Washington DC 20006. *God has given me certain talents. I feel a great opportunity and responsibility to develop and use these talents to their fullest on and off the tennis courts. I see great potential in our country and especially in our youth today, and I hope to provide some leadership and direction that this youth will need to develop their potential constructively. God has given me a great life so far and I plan to rely on His guidance to take me the rest of the way.*

SMITH, STANTON KINNIE, JR., lawyer, oil, gas and coal co. exec.; b. Rockford, Ill., Feb. 14, 1931; s. Stanton Kinnie and Elizabeth (Brown) S.; B.A. in Econs., Yale U., 1953; J.D., U. Wis., 1956; m. Mary Beth Sanders, July 11, 1953; children—Stanton E., Kathryn Ann, Dana. Admitted to Ill. bar, 1956, Mich. bar, 1976; partner firm Sidley & Austin, Chgo., 1956—; gen. counsel Am. Natural Resources Co., Detroit, 1974—, also dir.; dir. J.L. Clark Mfg. Co., Self-Service Oil Co., Gt. Lakes Gas Transmission Co. Trustee Rockford Coll. Mem. Am. Bar Assn., Ill. Bar Assn., Mich. Bar Assn., Chgo. Bar Assn., Order of Coif. Unitarian. Clubs: Detroit, Detroit Athletic; University (Chgo.); Yale (N.Y.C.). Home: 33 Preston Pl Grosse Pointe Farms MI 48236 Office: 1 Woodward Ave Detroit MI 48226

SMITH, STEPHEN CORY, educator; b. Muncie, Ind., Oct. 21, 1921; s. William Gordon and Mary Winifred (Jessup) S.; B.A., DePauw U., 1943; Ph.D., U. Wis., 1952; m. Megan Marie Fairham, Oct. 1, 1944; children—Gordon Clark, Eric Jessup. Instr., U. Wis., 1949-50; economist TVA, 1950-55; asso. U. Calif. at Berkeley, 1955-62; dir., prof. Colo. State U., 1962-67; asso. dean, prof. sch. natural resources Coll. Agrl. and Life Scis., U. Wis. at Madison, 1967—; cons. Sec. of Army Civil Functions, U.S. Water Resources Council, U.S. Dept. Interior, U.S. Dept. Agr., Argentina, U.S. Ho. of Reps. Mem. Am. Econ. Assn., Am. Agrl. Econs. Assn., Western Econs. Assn., AAAS. Contbr. articles to profl. jours.; author books. Home: 441 Togstad Glen Madison WI 53711 Office: 1450 Linden Dr Madison WI 53706

SMITH, STEWART GENE, retail drug co. exec.; b. Wyandotte, Mich., Feb. 5, 1926; s. William Melvin and Margaret Nichols (Cameron) S.; B.A., U. Mich., 1949, J.D., 1952; m. Veronica Lucille Latta, Apr. 12, 1952; children—Stewart Gregory, Patrick Allen, Paul Donald, Alison Veronica, Alisa Margaret, Glenn Laurence. Admitted to Mich. bar, 1952; tax atty. Detroit Trust Co., 1952; with Cunningham Drug Stores, Inc., Detroit, 1952—, v.p. charge real estate, 1959-62, sr. v.p. adminstrn., 1969—, also dir., mem. exec. com. Chmn. Grosse Isle (Mich.) Municipal Airport Commn., 1971-72. Served with USNR, 1944-46. Mem. Am. Bar Assn., State Bar Mich., Internat. Council Shopping Centers, Am. Legion. Clubs: Detroit Athletic; Grosse Isle Golf and Country. Home: 22225 Balmoral Dr Grosse Ile MI 48138 Office: 1927 12th St Detroit MI 48216

SMITH, STEWART WILSON, JR., geophysicist; b. Mpls., Sept. 15, 1932; s. Stewart Wilson and Laura Georgina (Frost) S.; B.S. in Geology, M.I.T., 1954; M.S. in Geophysics and Math., Calif. Inst. Tech., 1958, Ph.D., 1961; m. Nancy Lee Wright, June 2, 1956; children—Carol Lee, David Stewart, Peter Scott. Geophysicist, Shell Oil Co., Denver, 1954-55; asst. prof. geophysics Calif. Inst. Tech., Pasadena, 1961-65, asso. prof., 1965-69; prof., chmn. dept. geophysics U. Wash., Seattle, 1969—; cons., prin. TERA Corp., 1973-79; dir. Terra Tech. Corp., 1976-79. Served with USAF, 1955-57. Research grantee NASA, NSF, Office Naval Research, U.S. Geol. Survey; registered profl. geophysicist, Calif. Mem. Seismol. Soc. Am. (dir.), Am. Geophys. Union, Earthquake Engring. Research Inst. Prin. research, co-discoverer of free oscillations of the earth, 1961-65; prin. profl. contbr. earthquake hazard evaluation for nuclear power plant sites. Home: 11855 Holmes Point Kirkland WA 98033 Office: U Wash Geophysics AK 50 Seattle WA 98195

SMITH, STEWART WORLAND, JR., pub. utility co. exec.; b. Milw., Nov. 12, 1932; s. Stewart Worland and Elna (Johnson) S.; A.B., U. Mo., 1954, J.D., 1958; M.B.A., Washington U., St. Louis, 1966; m. Betty Lou Hansen, Nov. 26, 1953; children—Stewart Worland III, Sharon Marie. Admitted to Mo. bar, 1958; law clk. U.S. Dist. Ct. Eastern Dist. Mo., 1958-59; with Union Electric Co., St. Louis, 1959—, gen. counsel, 1966—, v.p., 1969—, dir., 1975—. Served to 1st lt. AUS, 1955-57. Mem. Am., St. Louis, Mo. bar assns., Mo., Ill., St. Louis chambers commerce. Home: 511 Antioch Ln Ballwin MO 63011 Office: 1901 Gratiot St St Louis MO 63166

SMITH, STUART SEABORNE, writer, govt. ofcl., union ofcl.; b. N.Y.C., Jan. 27, 1930; s. Purcell Leonard and Elizabeth (Wright) S.; grad. Lawrenceville (N.J.) Sch., 1948; student Princeton, 1948-51, U. Heidelberg (Germany), 1953-54, U. Madrid (Spain), 1954-55, U. Copenhagen (Denmark), 1955-56; m. Birte Moeller Jacobsen, Apr. 27, 1956 (div., 1972); children—Stuart Seaborne, Bjarne Moeller; m. 2d, Editha Maria Fuchs, Jan. 3, 1973; children—Cornelia Gerda, Melanie Karla. Reporter, Balt. Sun, 1957-65, fgn. corr. chief Bonn (Germany) bur., 1965-69; corr. Washington Bur., 1969-70; with Am. Bar Assn., 1970-71, Law Enforcement Assistance Adminstrn., U.S. Dept. Justice, Washington, 1971—. Recipient Spl. award for meritorious service Washington-Balt. Newspaper Guild, 1965. Served with AUS, 1951-53. Mem. Am. Fedn. State, County and Municipal Employees (pres. council 26, chief steward local 2830). Home: 5710 Aberdeen Rd Bethesda MD 20014 Office: Law Enforcement Assistance Adminstrn PIO 633 Indiana Ave NW Washington DC 20531. *I believe in honor and democracy and social justice. I further believe that for the most part we are the ignorant slaves of political and philosophical superstitions, but in the end the truth shall set us free.*

SMITH, TALBOT MERTON, baseball club exec.; b. Framingham, Mass., Sept. 27, 1933; s. Edward B. and Helen Irene (McClure) S.; A.B. in Bus. Adminstrn., Duke U., 1955; m. Jonnie Valeria Adams, June 10, 1956; children—Valerie Jo, Randall Edward. Asst. dir. minor league clubs and scouting Cin. Reds, 1957-60; asst. to gen. mgr. Houston Astros, 1960-61, dir. scouting and minor league ops., 1961-63, asst. to pres., 1963-65, v.p., dir. player personnel, 1965-72, dir. ops., 1972-73, exec. v.p., gen. mgr., 1975-76, pres., gen. mgr., 1976—; exec. v.p. New York Yankees, 1973-75; chmn. bd. Major League Scouting Bur., also mem. adv. com. on player relations. Served to 1st lt. USAF, 1955-57. Republican. Club: Westside Tennis (Houston). Home: 11645 Blalock Forest Houston TX 77024 Office: PO Box 288 Houston TX 77001

SMITH, TERENCE FITZGERALD, newspaper corr.; b. Bryn Mawr, Pa., Nov. 18, 1938; s. Walter W. and Catherine M. (Cody) S.; B.A., U. Notre Dame, 1960; m. Phyllis Ann Charnley, June 20, 1964; children—Elizabeth Reed, Christopher Wellesly. Reporter Stamford (Conn.) Adv., 1960-62, N.Y. (N.Y.C.) Herald Tribune, 1963-65; with N.Y. Times, N.Y.C., 1965—, fgn. corr. Israel, Thailand, Vietnam bur. chief, 1969-70, diplomatic corr. Washington, 1970-72, chief corr. Israel, 1972-76, dep. fgn. editor, 1976-77, chief White House corr., 1978—; lectr., freelance writer, radio, TV appearances. Mem. Overseas Writers Assn., Washington. Home: 33 W Irving St Chevy Chase MD 20016 Office: NY Times 1000 Connecticut Ave NW Washington DC 20036

SMITH, THOMAS CRAMPTON, JR., lawyer; b. Bristol, Va., Feb. 15, 1917; s. Thomas Crampton and Esme (Howell) S.; B.A., U. Tenn., 1940; LL.B., U. Okla., 1946; m. Jane Miller Harris, Oct. 28, 1941; 1 dau., Virginia Howell (Mrs. James Crawford Shaw). Admitted to Okla. bar, 1946; Supreme Ct. U.S. bar; practiced in Oklahoma City, 1946—; mem. firm Howell & Smith, 1948—. Dir., gen. counsel, past pres. Security Fed. Savs. & Loan Assn. of Oklahoma City. Sec., Supreme Ct. Bar Orgn. Com., 1966; chmn. Bd. Adjustment, Oklahoma City, 1961-63. Mem. exec. bd. Last Frontier council Boy Scouts Am. mem. governing bd. Bapt. Med. Center Okla. Served to lt. col. USAAF, 1941-46; col. Res. ret. Decorated Bronze Star, USAF Commendation medal. Mem. Am., Okla., Oklahoma County (past v.p., past dir.), bar assns., Okla. Bar Found. (past pres.), Oklahoma City C. of C. (past dir.), Title Lawyer Group Oklahoma City (past chmn.), Sigma Alpha Epsilon. Republican. Baptist (deacon). Clubs: Uptown Kiwanis (past pres.), Oklahoma City Golf and Country, Whitehall, Mens Dinner (Oklahoma City). Home: 609 NW 40th St Oklahoma City OK 73118 Office: 201 Security Fed Savs Bldg 305 N Harvey St Oklahoma City OK 73102

SMITH, THOMAS HOWARD, historian; b. Crawford County, Ohio, Sept. 16, 1936; s. Harold Edgar and Marian Ernestine S.; B.S. (fellow), Kent State U., Ph.D. (grantee), 1966; M.A., Ohio State U., 1962; m. Joanne Buckey, Aug. 31, 1957; 1 son, Bradley Howard. Tchr., Oak Hills High Sch., Hamilton County, Ohio, 1962-63; instr. history Marietta (Ohio) Coll., 1966-67; asst. prof. Ohio U., 1967-70, asso. prof., 1970-75; dir. Ohio Hist. Soc., Columbus, 1975—; state coordinator Ohio Hist. Records Preservation Adv. Bd., 1975—; cons. Nat. Endowment for Humanities. Mem. council City of Athens (Ohio), 1970-72, mem. bd. zoning appeals; chmn. Athens County Bicentennial Com. Served with USMC, 1958-61. Mem. Orgn. Am. Historians, Am. Assn. Museums, Am. Assn. State and Local History, Ohio Acad. History, Nat. Trust Historic Preservation, State Historic Preservation Officers (dir. nat. conf. 1975). Lutheran. Club: Kit Kat (Columbus). Author: Forest Rose, 1973; An Ohio Reader, 1975; Mapping of Ohio, 1978; editor: Ohio in The American Revolution, 1975. Home: 131 S Lamar St Athens OH 45701 Office: 1982 Velma Ave Columbus OH 43211

SMITH, THOMAS STEVENSON, univ. pres.; b. Hubbard, Ohio, Feb. 8, 1921; s. Thomas and Hazel (Wiseman) S.; A.B., Kenyon Coll., 1947; Ph.D., Ohio State U., 1952; m. Lillyan Beaver, Aug. 22, 1944; children—Lizbeth, Steve, David. Tchr. physics Kenyon Coll., 1941-43, 46-47; instr. per-meteorology program USAAF, 1943-44; tchr. physics Ohio State U., Columbus, 1947-50, research asso., 1950-52; asst. prof. physics Ohio U., Athens, 1952-56, asso. prof. physics, 1956-61, asst. to v.p., prof. physics, 1961-62, v.p. acad. affairs, 1962-67, provost, 1967-69; pres. Lawrence U., Appleton, Wis., 1969—; cons. in field, 1963—; ednl. cons.-examiner for commn. on colls. and univs. N. Central Assn. Colls. and Secondary Schs.; chmn. Wis. State Govt. Bd. Ethics; chmn. Gt. Lakes Dist. Com. Selection Rhodes Scholarships; bd. dirs. Nat. Assn. Ind. Colls. and Univs.; bd. dirs., exec. com. Ind. Coll. Funds Am. Mem. Am. Phys. Soc., Am. Assn. Physics Tchrs., AAAS, Appleton C. of C. (ednl. com.), Phi Beta Kappa, Sigma Xi, Sigma Pi Sigma. Contbr. articles to profl. jours. Office: Lawrence U Box 599 Appleton WI 54912

SMITH, THOMAS TIMOTHY, physician, educator; b. Stuart, Nebr., Aug. 12, 1910; s. Samuel John and Barbara Mary (O'Neill) S.; B.S., Creighton U., 1931, M.S., 1933; M.S., U. Pa., 1943; m. Mildred K. Noziska, May 3, 1935 (dec. Sept. 1976); children—Mary Alice (Mrs. Robert Hiebner), Beverly Ann (Mrs. James Atchison); m. 2d, Cecelia M. Schmit, Dec. 3, 1977. Intern, St. Joseph Hosp., Omaha, 1933-35; resident Thomas Jefferson Med. Sch., Phila., 1940-43; individual practice medicine, Omaha, 1946—, prof. otolaryngology Creighton U., 1949-78, prof. emeritus, 1978—. Served with USNR, 1943-46. Diplomate Am. Bd. Otolaryngology. Fellow A.C.S.; mem. Nebr., Douglas County med. socs., Am. Triological Soc. (pres. sect. 1970-71), Am. Acad. Ophthalmology and Otolaryngology, Am. Soc. Otol. Allergy. Clubs: Omaha, Omaha Country. Contbr. articles to profl. jours. Home: 615 N 65th St Omaha NE 68132 Office: 8601 W Dodge Rd Omaha NE 68114

SMITH, TIMOTHY LAWRENCE, educator, clergyman; b. Central, S.C., Apr. 13, 1924; s. Lester Berry and Intha Delona (McCraw) S.; B.A. with honors, U. Va., 1943; M.A., Harvard, 1945, Ph.D., 1955; Litt.D., Houghton Coll., 1967; m. Anne Densmore Wright, June 26, 1944; children—Karen (Mrs. James Zien), Timothy Lawrence, Susan (Mrs. Bradley Waterman). Pastor, Ch. of the Nazarene, Cliftondale, Mass., 1944-48, Portland, Maine, 1948-49; prof. Eastern Nazarene Coll., 1949-56; pastor Ch. of the Nazarene, Boulder, Colo., 1957-58; prof. history, chmn. dept. East Tex. State Coll., 1958-61; asso. prof., then. prof. history and edn. U. Minn., 1961-68; prof. edn. and history Johns Hopkins, Balt., 1968—; pastor Wollaston (Mass.) Coll. Ch. of Nazarene, 1971-75. Fund for Advancement Edn. fellow, 1960-61. Mem. Soc. Am. Historians, Am. Soc. Ch. History (Frank S. and Elizabeth D. Brewer prize), Orgn. Am. Historians, Am. Hist. Assn., Am. Studies Assn., Am. Ednl. Research Assn. Author: Revivalism and Social Reform: American Protestantism on the Eve of the Civil War, 1957; Called unto Holiness: The Story of the Nazarenes, 1963. Home: 3346 Gilman Terr Baltimore MD 21211 Office: Johns Hopkins 34th at Charles Baltimore MD 21218

SMITH, TOM EUGENE, retail grocery co. exec.; b. Salisbury, N.C., May 2, 1941; s. Ralph Eugene and Cora Belle (Ervin) S.; A.B. in Bus. Adminstrn., Catawba Coll., 1964; m. Catherine Conway Wallace, Oct. 16, 1971; children—Leigh Anne, Nancy Thompson. With Del Monte Sales Co., 1964-70, dir. account mgr., Hickory, N.C., 1967-68, sales supr., Charlotte, N.C., 1969-70; buyer Food Town Stores, Inc., Salisbury, N.C., 1970-74, v.p. distbn., 1974-77, exec. v.p., 1977—, also dir.; dir. N.C. Nat. Bank. Bd. dirs. United Way, Salisbury, 1977-79. Served with USAR, 1968-72. Mem. Nat. Assn. Retail Grocers U.S., Salisbury Sales Exec. (dir. 1974-79). Republican. Lutheran. Clubs: Salisbury Country, Am. Legion, Rotary (dir. club 1975-76). Home: 620 Catawba Rd Salisbury NC 28144 Office: Food Town Stores Inc Harrison Rd Salisbury NC 28144

SMITH, VICTOR EARLE, economist, educator; b. Lansing, Mich., Apr. 9, 1914; s. Earle Baker and Isabelle (Emery) S.; A.B., Mich. State Coll., 1935, M.A., 1936; Ph.D., Northwestern U., 1940; m. E. Margaret French, Nov. 29, 1940; children—David, Michael. Instr. econs. Northwestern U., Evanston, Ill., 1940-42; asst. prof. econs. Yale, 1942-44, Wellesley (Mass.) Coll., 1944-47, Brown U., Providence, R.I., 1947-48; asso. prof. econs. Mich. State U., East Lansing, 1948-53, prof. econs., 1953—, prof. foods nutrition, 1963, chmn. dept. econs., 1974-76; research grantee Inst. Internat. Agr., 1970; vis. prof. econs. U. Mich. at Ann Arbor, 1963; research grantee study Nigerian rural devel., Midwest Univs. Consortium Internat. Activities, East Lansing, 1966-68. Fund Advancement Edn. faculty fellow, 1954-55; Ford Found. research fellow, 1958-59; NSF research grantee, 1965-67; Rockefeller Found. research grantee, 1968-70. Mem. Am. Econ. Assn., Econometric Soc., Midwest Econ. Assn., Inst. Mgmt. Sci., Mich. Acad. Arts Sci., AAUP. Author: Electronic Computation of Human Diets, 1964; Efficient Resource Use for Tropical Nutrition: Nigeria, 1975. Contbr. articles in field to profl. jours. Home: 4378 Keller Rd Holt MI 48842 Office: 206 Marshall Hall Economics Dept Michigan State Univ East Lansing MI 48824

SMITH, VINCENT DACOSTA, artist; b. Bklyn., Dec. 12, 1929; s. Beresford Leopold and Louise Smith; student Art Students League, N.Y.C., 1953, Bklyn. Mus. Sch., 1954-56; m. Cynthia I. Linton, July 15, 1972. Exhbns. include: Hall of Springs Mus., Saratoga, N.Y., 1970, Contemporary Black Am. Artists, Whitney Mus. Am. Art, N.Y.C., 1971, Two Generations, Newark Mus., 1971; Mus. of Sci. and Industry, Chgo., 1975; Bronx Mus. Art, 1977; Bklyn. Mus., 1979; one-man exhbns. include: Lacarda Gallery, N.Y.C., 1967, 68, 70, 73, 75, 77, Paa Ya Paa Gallery, Nairobi, Kenya, 1973, Chemchemi Creative Arts Center, Arusha, Tanzania, 1973, Kibo Art Gallery, Mt. Kilimanjaro, Tanzania, 1973, Portland (Maine) Art Mus., 1974, Reading (Pa.) Public Mus., 1974, Erie (Pa.) Art Center, 1977, Gallery 7, Detroit, 1977; represented in permanent collections: Mus. Modern Art, N.Y.C., Newark Mus., Bklyn. Mus., U. Va. Art Mus.; instr. painting and graphics Whitney Mus. Art, N.Y.C., 1967-76; instr. painting Bklyn. Mus., 1978-79. Served with U.S. Army, 1948-49. Recipient Thomas B. Clark prize N.A.D., 1974; Winslow and Newton prize Nat. Soc. Painters in Casein and Acrylic, 1978; John Hay Whitney fellow, 1959; Nat. Endowment Arts grantee, 1973; Nat. Inst. Arts and Letters grantee, 1968; Cultural Council Found. grantee, 1971. Mem. Nat. Conf. Artists. Illustrator: Folklore Stories from Africa, 1974. Home: 264 E Broadway New York NY 10002 . *I have tried to develop three things which I feel are necessary to achieving some success in one's chosen field: a philosophy in which one keeps physically fit, mentally aware and consistent in one's work. Through a belief in the importance of the work one can constantly strive to grow and reach new heights.*

SMITH, VIRGINIA DODD (MRS. HAVEN SMITH), congresswoman; b. Randolph, Iowa, June 30, 1911; d. Clifton Clark and Erville (Reeves) Dodd; A.B., U. Nebr., 1936; m. Haven N. Smith, Aug. 27, 1931. Nat. pres. Am. Country Life Assn., 1951-54; nat. chmn. Am. Farm Bur. Women, 1954-74; dir. Am. Farm Bur. Fedn., 1954-74, Country Women's Council; world dep. pres. Asso. Country Women of World, 1962-68; mem. Dept. Agr. Nat. Home Econs. Research adv. com., 1960-65; mem. Crusade for Freedom European inspection tour, 1958. Del. Republican Nat. Conv., 1956, 72. Mem. bd. govs. Agrl. Hall of Fame, 1959—. Mem. Nat. Livestock and Meat Bd., 1955-58, Nat. Comm. Community Health Services, 1963-66; adv. mem. Nebr. Sch. Bds. Assns., 1949; mem. Nebr. Territorial Centennial Commn., 1953; mem. Gov.'s Commn. Status of Women, 1964-66; chmn. Presdl. Task Force on Rural Devel., 1969-70; mem. 94th-96th Congresses from 3d dist. Nebr. Vice pres. Farm Film Found., 1964-74. Apptd. admiral Nebr. Navy. Recipient Award of Merit, D.A.R., 1956; Distinguished Service awards U. Nebr., 1956, 60; award for best pub. address on freedom Freedom Found., 1966; Eyes on Nebr. award Nebr. Optometric Assn., 1970; Internat. Service award Midwest Conf. on World Affairs, 1970; Woman of Achievement award Nebr. Bus. and Profl. Women, 1971; selected as 1 of 6 U.S. women Govt. France for 3 week goodwill mission to France, 1969; Outstanding 4H Alumni award Iowa State U., 1973, 74; Watchdog of Treasury award, 1976, 78; Guardian of Small Bus. award, 1976, 78. Mem. AAUW, Delta Kappa Gamma (state hon. mem.), Beta Sigma Phi (internat. hon. mem.), Chi Omega, P.E.O. (past pres.). Methodist. Mem. Eastern Star. Club: Business and Professional Women. Good Will ambassador to Switzerland, 1950. Home: Chappell NE 69129. *As a fifteen-year-old high school valedictorian, I wrote these words in my valedictory message, "There is no excellence without great labor." Almost half a century later, I continue to live by this philosophy.*

SMITH, W. MASON, lawyer; b. Dongan Hills, N.Y., Dec. 31, 1910; s. William Mason and Mary (Evans) S.; A.B., Yale, 1932; LL.B., Harvard, 1935; m. Jane Prouty, June 20, 1935; children—William Mason III, Olivia Mason. Admitted to N.Y. State bar, 1937, since practiced in N.Y.C.; asst. corp. counsel City of N.Y., 1938-41; partner firm Van Vorst, Siegel & Smith, 1946-54, Hatch, Root, Barrett, Cohen & Knapp, 1955-56, Root, Barrett, Cohen, Knapp & Smith, 1956-72, Barrett, Smith, Schapiro & Simon, 1972—; dir. Gold Fields Am. Corp., Consol. Gold Field Ltd., Azcon Corp., Rosario Resources Corp. Bd. dirs. State Communities Aid Assn. Served from ensign to lt. comdr. USNR, 1941-45. Mem. Am., N.Y. State, N.Y. County bar assns., Assn. Bar City N.Y., Council on Fgn. Relations. Clubs: Century, Downtown, River, Univ. Home: 52 E 92d St New York NY 10028 Office: 26 Broadway New York NY 10004

SMITH, WALKER WILLIAM, govt. ofcl.; co. exec.; b. Topeka, Kans., Oct. 6, 1920; s. William Amos and Ada (Walker) S.; A.B., Washburn U., 1942, LL.B., 1948; m. Nita Scheinhaus, Oct. 8, 1944; 1 dau., Merri Jane. Admitted to Kan. bar, 1948, Tex. bar, 1959; practice in Russell, Kan., 1948-52; atty. Stanolind Oil & Gas Co., Oklahoma City, 1953-54; with Am. Petrofina Co. of Tex., Dallas, 1954—, sec., 1970—; dir. K-T Oil Corp. Served with AUS, 1942-46. Mem. Am. Legion. Methodist. Mason, Kiwanian. Home: 3805 Princess Ln Dallas TX 75220 Office: PO Box 2159 Dallas TX 75221

SMITH, WALLACE BUNNELL, physician, ch. ofcl.; b. Independence, Mo., July 29, 1929; s. William Wallace and Rosamond (Bunnell) S.; A.A., Graceland Coll., Lamoni, Iowa, 1948; B.A., U. Kans., 1950, M.D., 1954; m. Anne M. McCullough, June 26, 1956; children—Carolyn, Julia, Laura. Intern, Charity Hosp. of La., 1955; resident in medicine, U. Kans. Med. Center, 1958, resident in ophthalmology, 1959-62; pvt. practice medicine specializing in ophthalmology, 1962-76; ordained to ministry Reorganized Ch. of Jesus Christ of Latter Day Saints, 1945; asso. pastor Walnut Park Congregation, Independence, Mo., 1966-70, Pleasant Heights Congregation, Independence, 1975-76, center stake pres., 1969-71, president-designate Reorganized Ch. of Jesus Christ of Latter Day Saints, 1976-78, pres., 1978—; clin. asso. U. Kans. Med. Center, 1962-76; dir. Pacific Land Devel. Assn. Pres., bd. trustees Independence Sanitarium and Hosp. Served to lt. M.C., USNR, 1955-58. Diplomate Am. Bd. Ophthalmology. Fellow Am. Acad. Ophthalmology, A.C.S.; mem. AMA, Jackson County Med. Soc., Independence C. of C., Phi Beta Pi. Club: Rotary. Home: 3611 Delaware Independence MO 64055 Office: 221 W Lexington Independence MO 64051

SMITH, WALSTEIN BENNETT, JR., educator; b. Frost, Tex., Jan. 31, 1920; s. Walstein B. and Mayme (Dickerson) S.; B.B.A., Baylor U., 1941, J.D., 1942; M.B.A., U. Tex., 1951, Ph.D., 1969; m. Evelyn Box, Aug. 17, 1946; children—Evelyn Elaine, Walstein Bennett III. Admitted to Tex. bar, 1942; asst. dist. atty. McLennan County, Tex., 1946; mem. faculty Baylor U., 1947—, prof. bus. law and real estate, 1968—; asst. prof. U. Tex., 1963-64; pvt. practice law, real estate appraising, 1953—. City commr., mayor pro tem Waco, 1950; chmn. Waco Tax Adv. Council, 1960, 74. Served to capt. AUS, 1942-46. Decorated Bronze Star. Named Realtor of Year, Waco, 1960, 66; Most Popular Bus. Prof., Baylor U., 1966. Mem. Tex., Waco-McLennan County bar assns., Waco Bd. Realtors (pres. 1965-66), Am. Inst. Real Estate Appraisers, Soc. Real Estate Appraisers (dist. gov. 1971-74), Beta Gamma Sigma. Baptist (deacon, trustee). Author articles in field. Home: 5831 Mt Rockwood St Waco TX 76710. *Persistence—Patience—Prayer.*

SMITH, WALTER DOUGLAS, coll. pres.; b. Harriman, Tenn., Nov. 18, 1918; s. Walter Blaine and Jeanetta Mae (Scarborough) S.; B.A., Lincoln Meml. U., Harrogate, Tenn., 1943; M.A., U. Mich., 1947, Ph.D., 1950; m. Rhondda Verle Miller, Apr. 5, 1947; children—Ian Douglas Miller, Walter Henry. Faculty psychology Fla. State U., 1950-59; dean coll., prof. psychology Winthrop Coll., Rock Hill, S.C., 1959-66, v.p. acad. affairs, dean of faculty, 1966-68; pres. Salisbury (Md.) State Coll., 1968-70, Francis Marion Coll., Florence, S.C., 1970—. Served with USNR, 1943-46. Mem. Am. Psychol. Assn. Presbyterian. Home: 724 Fairway Dr Florence SC 29501

SMITH, WALTER HALL, utility co. exec.; b. Wenatchee, Wash., May 13, 1920; s. Walter and Mary (Hall) S.; B.S.C.E., Oreg. State U., 1946; grad. exec. program Stanford U., 1972; m. Mary Louise Jacobson, July 31, 1942; children—Diane, Marcia, Walter F. Engr., W. Larsen Cons. Engr., Albany, Oreg., 1946-48, Calif.-Oreg. Power Co., Roseburg, Oreg., 1948-50; mgr. Oreg. Water Corp., Roseburg, 1950-51; chief engr. Boise (Idaho) Water Corp. and subs's., 1951-54, v.p., mgr., 1954-64, pres., 1964-69; v.p. Intermountain Gas Co., Boise, 1969-79, exec. v.p., chief operating officer, 1979—. Served to capt. C.E., U.S. Army, 1941-45. Mem. Pacific Coast Gas Assn., Am. Gas Assn., Idaho Soc. Profl. Engrs., Nat. Soc. Profl. Engrs. Republican. Episcopalian. Club: Lions. Home: 3604 Mountain View Dr Boise ID 83704 Office: 555 S Cole Rd Boise ID 83707*

SMITH, WALTER JOSEPH, JR., lawyer; b. N.Y.C., Feb. 23, 1936; s. Walter Joseph and Florence (Watson) S.; A.B., Hamilton Coll., Clinton, N.Y., 1958; LL.B., Columbia, 1961; m. Felicitas von Zeschau, Oct. 5, 1968; children—Caroline Patricia, Alexandra Catherine, Christopher Patrick. Admitted to D.C. bar, 1966; partner firm Wilson, Elser, Edelman and Dicker; mem. 1st Jud. Conf. D.C., 1976; guest lectr. Georgetown U. Served to lt. USNR, 1962-67. Elihu Root scholar, 1958. Mem. Am., D.C. bar assns., Am. Arbitration Assn. (panel), The Counsellors. Democrat. Roman Catholic. Author: Let's Look at the Record: A Grandson's Reflections on Alfred E. Smith. Home: 1203 Ina Ln McLean VA 22102 Office: 944 Washington Bldg Washington DC 20006

SMITH, WALTER LEE, univ. adminstr.; b. Tampa, Fla., May 14, 1935; s. Roosevelt and Eva (Lee) S.; B.A., Fla. A. and M. U., 1963, M.Ed., 1966; Ph.D. (African-Am. Inst. scholar 1971, Kellogg fellow 1972, Edn. Profession Devel Act fellow 1972-73), Fla. State U., 1974; m. Jeraldine Williams, June 19, 1971; children—John, Andre, Salesia, Walter Lee, II. Tchr., head dept. chemistry and biology Hillsborough County (Fla.) Schs., 1963-65; adminstrv. asst. to employee devel. dir. IBM, Cape Canaveral, Fla., 1965-66, edn. tng. coordinator subs. Sci. Research Assos., Chgo., 1966-67; edn. program officer Office Edn., Washington and Atlanta, 1967-68; asso. regional dir. NEA, Washington and Atlanta, 1969-70; adminstrv. asst. to exec. sec. Fla. Edn. Assn., Tallahassee, 1970, asst. exec., 1970-73; collegium dir. Hillsborough Community Coll., 1973, dean employee/student relations, 1973-74, provost, 1974; pres. Roxbury Community Coll., 1974-77, Fla. A. and M. U., 1977—; panelist White House Conf. on Youth. Mem. bd. edn. advisers Permanent Charity Found., Boston, 1976-77; mem. Mass. Post Secondary Edn. Commn., 1976-77. Served with U.S. Army, 1953-56. Recipient Red-X award IBM, 1966, Rosena Willis award NEA, 1971, 72, Leadership award in human rights Fla. Edn. Assn., 1973, Scholarly Distinction award Urban League, 1974, Insight award Rosbury (Mass.) Action Program, 1976; Appreciation award Adminstrv. Staff Rosbury Community Coll., 1977, Mass. Bd. Regional Community Colls., 1977; Outstanding Achievement award Bethlehem A.M.E. Ch., Cairo, Ga., 1977, Achievement award Fla. A. and M. U. Gen. Alumni Assn., 1977, award for keynote speaker Tallahassee Urban League, 1977, Recognition award City of Tampa, 1977; HEW grantee, 1963. Mem. Am. Assn. Community, Jr. Colls. (dir. council on black Am. affairs, pres's. acad.), Nat. Council Research and Devel., Phi Delta Kappa. Editor: Teachers Handbook on Human Relations, 1971; Effect and Impact of Black Junior Colleges in Florida, 1957-66. Office: Fla A and M U Tallahassee FL 32307*

SMITH, WALTER RHEA, univ. dean; b. Jackson, Tenn., Feb. 2, 1918; s. Grover Thomas and Carrie Gertrude (Tacker) S.; B.A., Lambuth Coll., 1939; M.A., So. Meth. U., 1940; Ph.D., U. Calif. at Berkeley, 1951. Lectr. English, So. Meth. U., 1940-41, 46-48; mem. faculty Memphis State U., 1951—, prof. English, 1959—, dean Sch. Arts and Scis., 1960—. Fellow Ford Found., 1961. Served to maj. AUS, 1941-46. Methodist. Home: 814 Thistledown Dr Memphis TN 38117

SMITH, WALTER TILFORD, shipbldg. co. exec.; b. Norfolk, Va., Oct. 9, 1907; s. Walter Edmond and Laura Alice (Griffin) S.; B.S. in Civil Engring., N.C. State Coll., 1929; grad. Advanced Mgmt. Program, Harvard, 1955; grad. Coll. Indsl. Armed Forces, 1952; m. Elizabeth Harriet Parrish, Aug. 20, 1933; 1 son, Walter Tilford. With Newport News Shipbldg. & Dry Dock Co. (Va.), 1929—, asst. to pres., 1962-63, v.p. charge prodn., 1963-64, exec. v.p., 1964-66, sr. v.p., 1966-69, sr. v.p. and asst. to pres., 1969—; dir. Central Nat. Bank, Richmond, Va. Vice pres., dir., mem. exec. finance com. Shipbuilders Council Am. Trustee Patrick Henry Hosp., Newport News, Peninsula United Fund; vice chmn. Newport News chpt. A.R.C. Mem. Soc. Naval Architects and Marine Engrs., Am. Soc. Naval Engrs., Navy League U.S., Nat. Def. Transp. Assn. (v.p.), NAM (nat. def. com.), N.C. State Coll. Alumni Assn. (bd. dirs.), Newcomen Soc., Engineer's Club N.Y.C., Scabbard and Blade, Theta Tau, Phi Kappa Phi. Episcopalian. Lion (bd. dirs., past v.p.). Clubs: Propeller U.S. (past pres. Newport News, past nat. v.p.), James River Country (dir., past pres.) Newport News. Home: 129 James River Dr Newport News VA 23601 Office: Newport News Shipbldg & Dry Dock Co Newport News VA 23607

SMITH, WARD, mfg. co. exec., lawyer; b. Buffalo, Sept. 13, 1930; s. Andrew Leslie and Georgia (Ward) S.; student Georgetown U., 1948-49; A.B., Harvard, 1952; LLB., J.D., U. Buffalo, 1955; m. Gretchen Keller Diefendorf, Oct. 29, 1960; children—Jennifer Hood, Meredith Ward, Jonathan Andrew, Sarah Katherine. Admitted to N.Y. bar, 1955, Mass. bar, 1962, Ohio bar, 1977; asso. firm Lawler & Rockwood, N.Y.C., 1959-62; sec., gen. counsel Whitin Machine Works, Whitinsville, Mass., 1962-66; sec., White Consol. Industries, Inc., Cleve., 1966-69, v.p., 1967-69; sr. v.p. 1969-72, exec. v.p., 1972-76, pres., chief adminstrv. officer, 1976—, also dir.; sec., dir. Blaw-Knox Co.; dir. Centran Corp. Trustee Case-Western Res. U., Cleve. Orch., Cleve. Music Sch. Settlement; bd. advisers Notre Dame Coll., Cleve. Served to lt. USNR, 1955-59. Mem. Am., N.Y. State bar assns. Clubs: Pepper Pike, Country (Pepper Pike, Ohio); Union (Cleve.). Home: 2706 Landon Rd Shaker Heights OH 44122 Office: 11770 Berea Rd Cleveland OH 44111

SMITH, WARNER TALIAFERRO, cons. engr.; b. Portsmouth, Va., Oct. 5, 1915; s. William A. and Elizabeth (Johnson) S.; B.S., U. Md., 1938; m. Grace Lewis, Feb. 24, 1940; children—Katharine, Betsy. Dir. telephone tech. staff REA, Washington, 1950-58, mem. tech. staff, 1975-79; dir. def. activities Anaconda Wire & Cable Co., Washington, 1958-60; v.p. engring. Superior Continental Corp., Hickory, N.C., 1960-68, exec. v.p., 1968-70, pres., 1970-73, sr. group v.p., 1973-75; pres. Warner T. Smith Teleconsultants, Reston, Va., 1979—. Served to capt. USMCR, 1942-46. Registered profl. engr., N.C. Mem. IEEE. Home and office: 2045 Durand Dr Reston VA 22091

SMITH, WARREN BRIERLEY, JR., publishing co. exec.; b. Binghamton, N.Y., May 26, 1919; s. Warren Brierley and Mary Isabel (Clark); B.S. in Econs., Wharton Sch., U. Pa., 1940; m. Beatrice C. Noehren, Oct. 6, 1942; children—Warren Brierley, Alison Nancy Noehren, David Addison. With Vick Chem. Co., 1940-42, 46-56; engaged in account mgmt. and service Compton Advt., Inc., N.Y.C., 1956-60; v.p. P.F. Collier Co., 1960-62; dir. marketing Crowell-Collier Pub. Co. (now Macmillan, Inc.), 1961-62, v.p., 1962-66, sr. v.p., 1966-67, exec. v.p., 1967-75 dir., 1962-75, sr. v.p., 1975—. Pres. LaSalle Extension U., 1962-68, 71-75. Trustee Nat. Home Study Council, bd. dirs., 1962-69, 72-75, pres., 1968, 69. Served with AUS, 1943-46. Mem. Beta Gamma Sigma, Pi Gamma Mu, Delta Kappa Epsilon. Club: Union League (Chgo.). Home: 6 Country Rd Westport CT 06880 Office: 866 3d Ave New York City NY 10022

SMITH, WATSON, anthropologist; b. Cin., Aug. 21, 1897; s. Samuel Watson and Olive (Perkins) S.; Ph.B., Brown U., 1919, LL.D., 1964; LL.B., Harvard, 1924; student U. Calif. at Berkeley, 1934-35; m. Lucy May Cranwell, Sept. 30, 1943; 1 son, Benjamin. Admitted R.I. bar, 1925, Ohio bar, 1931; with Hinckley, Allen, Tillinhast & Phillips, Providence, 1924-30; pvt. practice of law, Cin., 1930-33; anthrop. and archeol. research, direction and writing Mus. No. Ariz., 1935-38, 48, trustee, 1956—; staff Rainbow Bridge-Monument Valley Expdn., Ariz., 1935-37; curator Southwestern archeol. Peabody Mus., Harvard, 1936—; research asso. U. Ariz., 1952—; board advisers Arizona-Sonora Desert Mus., Tucson, 1957-60, 74—, trustee, 1960-74, pres., 1968-70. Trustee Brown U., 1950-64, fellow, 1964-70; past trustee Howard Found., Providence, Sch. Am. Research Santa Fe. Served as maj. USAAF, 1942-45. Fellow Am. Anthrop. Assn.; mem. Soc. Am. Archeology, Am. Ethnol. Soc., Sigma Xi. Contbr. articles profl. jours. Home: 2040 E Drachman St Tucson AZ 85719

SMITH, WAVERLY GRAVES, ins. co. exec.; b. Durham, N.C., Jan. 21, 1924; s. George W. and Lyla (Graves) S.; m. Anne Kathleen Williamson, July 30, 1943; children—Cheryl, Allen, Carolyn. With St. Paul Fire & Marine Ins. Co., 1949—, head mktg. div., 1966-69, exec. v.p., 1969-73, pres., 1973-77; pres., chief operating officer St. Paul Cos., Inc., 1978—; dir. Gen. Mills, Mpls. Trustee, vice chmn. KTCA-TV; bd. dirs. Bush Found. Served with USMCR, 1943-46. Mem. Nat. Assn. Property Casualty Execs. (pres.). Home: 11 Evergreen Rd Saint Paul MN 55110 Office: St Paul Cos Inc 385 Washington St Saint Paul MN 55102

SMITH, WAYNE AUGUSTUS, educator; b. Bieber, Calif., Feb. 8, 1915; s. Augustus and Daisy Agnes (Dunlap) S.; student U. Calif., Berkeley, 1934-35; B.S., So. Oreg. Coll., 1947; M.A., Tchrs. Coll., Columbia, 1953, Ed.D., 1954; m. Velma Lena Yeoman, June 3, 1951; 1 dau., Susan Lynn. Tchr., Riverton (Oreg.) Elementary Sch., 1936-37; tchr. Coquille (Oreg.) Jr. High Sch., 1937-40, prin., 1941-50; prin. Bandon (Oreg.) Grade Sch., 1940-41; curriculum coordinator, elementary supr. Coquille pub. schs., 1950-52; mem. staff dept. of adminstrn. Columbia, 1952-54, Inst. Field Studies, 1953-54, instr. elementary adminstrn., summer 1954; prof. edn., dir. dept. early childhood and elementary edn. Tchrs. Coll., Temple U., 1954-61, prof. edn., asst. dean Coll. of Edn., 1961-67, prof. curriculum and instrn., 1967—. Recipient Stauffer award Gen. Alumni Assn. Temple U., 1974; Legion of Honor award Chapel of the Four Chaplains, Phila., 1978. Mem. NEA, Pa. Edn. Assn., Am. Assn. Sch. Adminstrs., Assn. Supervision and Curriculum Devel., AAUP, Phi Kappa Phi, Phi Delta Kappa. Episcopalian. Elk, Lion. Home: 598 Baeder Rd Jenkintown PA 19046

SMITH, WENDELL ROSS, educator; b. Shenandoah, Iowa, Mar. 4, 1911; s. Charles Ross and Emma Mae (Nordstrom) S.; B.S.C., State U. Iowa, 1932, M.A., 1935, Ph.D., 1941; m. Ruth Anne Frudenfeld, Jan. 1, 1935; children—Stephen, Carolyn, Gail. Asst. mgr. Smith Shoe Store, Shenandoah, 1932-34; with U. Iowa, 1934-54, prof., head dept. mktg. Coll. Commerce, 1949-54; cons. Alderson & Sessions, Phila., summers 1952, 53; partner Alderson and Sessions, Phila., 1954-58; v.p. Alderson Assos., Inc., 1958-59; dir. mktg. research and devel. RCA, 1959-60, v.p. mktg. devel., 1960-62; pres. Mktg. Sci. Inst., 1962-68; prof. mktg. U. Pa., 1962-68; dean U. Mass. Sch. Bus. Adminstrn., 1968-74, Commonwealth prof. mktg., 1974-78; Disting. vis. prof. U. Tex. at El Paso, 1978—; adj. prof. Meisei U., Tokyo, 1970—; sr. price specialist OPA, Des Moines, 1942, 43; chmn. Nat. Mktg. Adv. Com., 1966-69. Named to Distbn. Hall of Fame, 1962; Alpha Kappa Psi award, 1957. Mem. Sales and Mktg. Execs., Am. (dir. 1952-53, v.p.), 1956-57, pres. 1958-59), Japan mktg. assns., Order of Artus, Beta Gamma Sigma, Pi Gamma Mu, Phi Kappa Sigma, Delta Sigma Pi, Alpha Delta Sigma. Clubs: Rotary; Nassau (Princeton, N.J.). Author: Public Utility Economics (with C. Woody Thompson), 1941. Contbg. editor Marketing Handbook, 2d edit., 1965; editorial adv. bd. Handbook of Modern Marketing, 1970; mem. editorial bd. Jour. Mktg., 1968-70. Home: 3109 High Point Dr El Paso TX 79904

SMITH, WESLEY SANFORD, ret. govt. ofcl.; b. Saugerties, N.Y., July 6, 1919; s. Robert B. and Grace (Sanford) S.; B.S., Cornell U., 1940, M.S., 1952; m. Gladys B. Klothe, June 1, 1940; children—Dorothy Jeanne (Mrs. Kenneth P. Goldberg), Judith (Mrs. Martin N. Poulin), Russell Wesley. 4-H Club agt. Coop. Fed. Extension Service, Cornell U., 1940-44, 46-56; with AID and predecessors, 1956-74, rural youth adviser, Saigon, Vietnam, 1956-59, sr. extension adviser, 1959-61, asst. food and agr. officer, 1966-67, dep. asst. dir., 1967-68; sr. extension adviser, Ankara, Turkey, 1961-62, agr. adviser, 1962-66, also spl. cons. CENTO, 1964-66; dep. chief agr. div. Bur. for Africa, Washington, 1968-70; provincial food and agr. officer Dacca, East Pakistan, 1970-71, So. Africa regional food and agr. officer Maseru, Lesotho, 1971-73, Mbabane, Swaziland, 1973-74, also attache Am. embassy, 1971-74; cons. Near East Found., 1975, Nat. 4-H Club Found., 1975-76. Served with AUS, 1944-45; ETO. Mem. Am. Fgn. Service Assn., Am. Acad. Polit. and Social Sci., Diplomatic and Consular Officers Ret., Internat. Platform Assn., Alpha Gamma Rho. Republican. Methodist. Mason, Kiwanian. Home: Happy Hill Farm Bluff Point NY 14417

SMITH, WILBUR STEVENSON, cons. engr.; b. Columbia, S.C., Sept. 6, 1911; s. George W. and Margaret Rebecca (Stevenson) S.; B.S., U. S.C., 1932, M.S. magna cum laude, 1933, LL.D., 1963; postgrad. Harvard U., 1936-37; L.H.D., Lander Coll., 1975; m. Sarah E. Bolick, Dec. 22, 1934; children—Sarah, Margaret, Stephanie. Electric hwy. engr. S.C. Hwy. Dept., 1933-34, asst. traffic engr., 1935-37, traffic engr., 1937-42; traffic cons. FBI, 1942-63; chmn., dir. Freeman, Fox, Wilbur Smith & Assos., cons. engrs., London, 1964-71; transp. cons. U.S. Office Civil Def., 1942-43; asso. dir. Yale U. Bur. Hwy. Traffic, 1943-57, research asso., 1957-68; chmn. bd. Eno Found. for Transp., Saugatuck, Conn.; chmn. bd. Wilbur Smith & Assos., Columbia, S.C. and New Haven, 1946—, also Richmond and Falls Church, Va., N.Y.C., Washington, San Francisco, Los Angeles, Houston, Pitts., Lexington, Ky., Denver, Miami, Fla., Toronto, Melbourne, Perth and Brisbane, Australia, London, Hong Kong, Seoul, Singapore, Athens; dir. Koger Properties, Inc., Isle of Palms Beach and Racquet Club, Bankers Trust S.C., Am. Exec. Life Ins. Co., Columbia. Bd. dirs. Nat. Safety Council, Transp. Assn. Am., Fedn. Safety and Mobility; trustee U. S.C.-Bus. Partnership Found., Presbyn. Coll.; chmn. U. S.C. Chair Endowment Club; bd. visitors Sch. Engring., Duke U.; mem. citizens adv. com. Comprehensive Care Center, Duke U. Med. Center. Recipient Disting. Alumni award U.

S.C., 1968. Registered profl. engr., 50 states, D.C. Mem. Internat. Road Fedn., Inst. Engrs. Australia, Inst. Civil Engrs. (U.K.), N.Z. Instn. Engrs., Internat. Bridge, Tunnel and Turnpike Assn., Am. Inst. Cons. Engrs., ASCE (hon.; past chmn. hwy. div. exec. com., past chmn. transp. planning com., past chmn. nat. transp. policy com.), Transp. Research Bd., Inst. Transp. Engrs. (hon., past nat. pres.), Nat. Acad. Engring., Am. Rd. and Transp. Builders Assn. (past pres., dir.), Hong Kong Instn. Engrs., Am. Soc. Safety Engrs., IEEE, Nat., S.C. (Engr. of Yr. 1964), N.Y. socs. profl. engrs., Am. Pub. Works Assn. (hon. mem. Inst. Transp.), Pub. Works Hist. Soc. (trustee), Phi Beta Kappa, Tau Beta Pi, Phi Sigma Kappa, Blue Key. Clubs: Columbia Country, Forest Lake Country, Palmetto, Summit (Columbia, S.C.); Grads. (New Haven); Cosmos (Washington); Miami; Yale (N.Y.C.); St. Stephens (London). Author: (with N. Hebden) State City Relationships in Highway Affairs, 1950; (with T. Matson, F. Hurd) Traffic Engineering, 1955; author tech. bulls., reports, traffic surveys. Home: 1630 Kathwood Dr Columbia SC 29206 Office: Bankers Trust Tower PO Box 92 Columbia SC 29202 also 155 Whitney Ave New Haven CT 06510

SMITH, WILBURN JACKSON, JR., banker; b. Charlotte, N.C., June 13, 1921; s. Wilburn Jackson and Banna (Ostwalt) S.; B.S. in Accounting, U. N.C., 1943; grad. comml. banking Rutgers U. Grad. Sch. Banking, 1953, grad. investments, 1956; m. Terry Mosteller, Jan. 4, 1944; children—Kenneth, Scott (dec.), Wilburn Jackson, Todd. With First Union Nat. Bank, Charlotte, 1946-74, asst. v.p., mgr. credit dept., 1952-53, v.p., 1953-56, sr. v.p., 1956-60, exec. v.p. charge loan and investment div., 1960-64, exec. v.p., 1964-74; exec. v.p. Cameron Fin. Corp., First Union Nat. Bank N.C., 1967-74; pres., mng. trustee Cameron-Brown Investment Group, 1974-78; chmn. loan policy com. N.C. Nat. Bank, Charlotte, 1979—. Trustee Southwestern Baptist Theol. Sem. Served to lt. (j.g.), USNR. Mem. Order U. N.C. Tar Heel 100, N.C. Soc. Fin. Analysts, U. N.C. Gen. Alumni Assn. (past pres.), Newcomen Soc., Order Golden Fleece, Order Holy Grail, Delta Sigma Pi. Baptist. Clubs: Good Fellows, Myers Park Country. Home: 3823 Foxcroft Rd Charlotte NC 28211 Office: PO Box 120 Charlotte NC 28255

SMITH, WILFRED CANTWELL, educator; b. Toronto, Ont., Can., July 21, 1916; s. Victor Arnold and Sarah (Cantwell) S.; B.A. in Oriental Langs., U. Toronto, 1938; postgrad. Westminster Coll., Cambridge, also U. Cambridge (Eng.), 1938-40; M.A. in Oriental Langs., Princeton, 1947, Ph.D., 1948; D.D. (hon.), McGill U., 1973; LL.D. (hon.), Concordia Coll., 1979; Litt.D. (hon.), U. Trent, 1979; m. Muriel McKenzie Struthers, Sept. 23, 1939; children—Arnold Gordon, Julian Struthers and Heather Patricia (twins), Brian Cantwell, Rosemary Muriel. Rep. among Muslims, Canadian Overseas Mission Council, 1941-49; lectr. Indian and Islamic history Forman Christian Coll., Lahore, India, 1941-45; Birks prof. comparative religion McGill U., Montreal, Can., 1949-63, dir. Inst. Islamic Studies, 1951-63; prof. world religions, dir. Center for Study World Religions, Harvard, 1964-73; McCulloch prof. religion, chmn. dept. Dalhousie U., Halifax, N.S., Can., 1973-78; prof. comparative history of religion and chmn. Com. on Study of Religion, Harvard U., 1978—; ordained to ministry United Ch. Can., 1961. Recipient Chauveau medal, 1974. Fellow Royal Soc. Can. (pres. humanities and social sci. sect. 1972-73), Am. Acad. Arts and Scis.; mem. Am. Soc. Study Religion (pres. 1966-69), Middle East Studies Assn. N.Am. (pres. 1977-78), Can. Theol. Soc. (pres. 1978-79). Author: Modern Islam in India, 5th edit., 1978; Islam in Modern History, 4th edit., 1977; The Faith of Other Men, 4th edit., 1972; The Meaning and End of Religion, 1963, 3d edit., 1978; Questions of Religious Truth, 1967; Religious Diversity, 1976; Belief and History, 1977; Faith and Belief, 1979; also numerous articles, pamphlets. Adv. editor The Muslim World, 1956—, Middle East Jour., 1950-79; asso. editor Religious Studies, 1965—; Studies in Religion, 1972—; cons. editor Ency. Brit. Office: Harvard U 1581 Massachusetts Ave Cambridge MA 02138

SMITH, WILFRED IRVIN, govt. ofcl. Canada; b. Port La Tour, Can., May 20, 1919; s. Claude Albert and Deborah (Inglis) S.; B.A., Acadia U., Wolfville, N.S., Can., 1943, M.A., 1946, D.C.L., 1975; Ph.D., U. Minn., 1968; m. Joan Eileen Capstick, Nov. 27, 1946; children—Gordon, Heather, Gail. Lectr., U. Minn., 1948, U. Sask., 1948-50, Carleton U., 1955-60; mem. staff Pub. Archives Can., 1950—, dir. hist. br., 1964-65, asst., then acting dominion archivist, 1965-70, dominion archivist, 1970—; mem. Canadian Nat. Library Adv. Bd., Canadian Permanent Com. Geog. Names, Historic Sites and Monuments Bd. Can, Indian Hist. Manuscripts Commn.; former mem. internat. adv. com. documentation, libraries and archives UNESCO. Served to maj. Canadian and Brit. armies, 1943-45. Decorated Can. decoration; recipient Centennial medal, 1967, Jubilee medal, 1978. Fellow Soc. Am. Archivists (past pres.); mem. Internat. Council Archives (dep. sec. gen.), Canadian Hist. Assn. (past editor hist. booklets), Assn. Canadian Archivists, Soc. Archivists, Am. Antiquarian Assn., Canadian Heraldry Soc. (hon. v.p.), United Empire Loyalists Assn. (hon. v.p.). Contbr. to profl. publs. Home: 655 Weston Dr Ottawa ON K1G 1V7 Canada Office: Room 317 395 Wellington St Ottawa ON K1A 0N3 Canada

SMITH, WILLI DONNELL, fashion designer; b. Phila., Feb. 29, 1948; s. Willie Lee and June Eileen (Bush) S.; student Phila. Coll. Art, 1962-65, Parsons Sch. Design, N.Y.C., N.Y. U., 1965-69. Sketcher, Bobbie Brooks, N.Y.C., 1969; designer Digits, N.Y.C., 1969-75; designer, v.p. Willi Wear, Ltd., N.Y.C., 1976—; lectr. fashion history Fashion Inst. Tech. Recipient Coty award nomination, 1979; named Designer of Year, Internat. Mannequins, 1978. Mem. League in Aid for Crippled Children, Bedford Stuyvesant Children's Assn. Democrat. Designer patterns for Butterick Co., furniture for Kroll Assos., textiles for Bedford Stuyvesant Workshop. Office: 62 W 39th St New York NY 10018

SMITH, WILLIAM ARTHUR, artist; b. Toledo, Apr. 19, 1918; s. Bert Arthur and Catherine Jane (Doan) S.; student Keane's Art Sch., Toledo, 1932-36, U. Toledo, 1936-37, M.A., 1954; m. Mary France Nixon, Sept. 30, 1939 (div. 1946); 1 son, Richard Keane; m. 2d, Ferol Yvonne Stratton, Oct. 10, 1949; children—Kim, Kathlin Alexandra. Newspaper work, 1936-37; established studio, N.Y.C., 1937; instr. Grand Central Art Sch., 1942-43; lectr. Acad. Fine Arts, Athens, 1954, U. Santa Tomas, Manila, 1955, Acad. Fine Arts, Warsaw, 1958; represented in Met. Mus. N.Y.C., Library of Congress, Washington; one-man shows: Toledo Mus. Art, 1942, 52, Bucknell U., 1952, others, many fgn. cities during recent years; executed mural Md. House, 1968; ofcl. del. Internat. Assn. Plastic Arts, Venice, 1954; mem. ofcl. del. to Russia under Cultural Exchange Agreement, 1958; designed numerous U.S. postage stamps. Bd. dirs. Welcome House, v.p., 1966-73. Recipient Silver medal Am. Water Color Soc., 1948, 52, 73, Nat. Acad. award, water color, 1949, 51, Adolph and Clara Obrig Prize for Oil Painting, 1953, Stuart Water color prize Am. Watercolor Soc., 1954, Gold medal and prize, 1957; Am. Artists Group Prize for lithography, Soc. Am. Graphic Artists, 1954; Knobloch prize, 1956, Winslow Homer Meml. prize, 1962; gold medal and grand prize Am. Watercolor Soc., 1965, bronze medal, 1972; Am. Patriots medal, 1974; Postal Commemorative Soc. prize, 1974. Mem. Internat. Assn. Art (U.S. del. 1963, 66, 69, 73, exec. com. 1963-69, v.p. 1966-69, pres. 1973-76, hon. pres. 1976—, pres. U.S. nat. com. 1970-77, hon. pres. 1977—), NAD (council 1975—), Am. (trustee 1949, pres. 1956-57, hon. pres. 1957—), Calif. watercolor socs., Audubon Artists, Phila. Watercolor Club, Nat. Soc. Mural Painters, Dutch Treat Club. Illustrator five books John Day Pub. Co. and others; author, illustrator articles for various mags. Address: Bucks County Pineville PA 18946

SMITH, WILLIAM BURTON, chemist, educator; b. Muncie, Ind., Dec. 13, 1927; s. Merrill Mark and Felice Hoy (Richardson) S.; B.A., Kalamazoo Coll., 1949; Ph.D., Brown U., 1954; m. Marian Louise Roseborough, Aug. 9, 1954; children—Mark W., Frederick D., Mary F. Research asso. Fla. State U., 1953-54, U. Chgo., 1954-55; asst. prof., then asso. prof. Ohio U., 1955-61; R.A. Welch vis. prof. chemistry Tex. Christian U., 1960-61, prof. chemistry, chmn. dept., 1961—. Research participant Oak Ridge Inst. Nuclear Studies, 1956—. Mem. Am. Chem. Soc., Sigma Xi. Author: A Modern Introduction to Organic Chemistry, 1961; Molecular Orbital Methods in Organic Chemistry, 1974; also research articles. Home: 3604 Wedghill Way Fort Worth TX 76133

SMITH, WILLIAM CLIFFORD, oil co. exec.; b. Athens, Tex., Nov. 2, 1909; s. James Leslie and Maggie Virginia (O'Bannon) S.; ed. pub. schs.; m. Erma Lee Butler, Nov. 24, 1934; children—Gail Lee (Mrs. Gerald L. Trahan), Margie Jean (Mrs. Harold Tomlinson). With Lone Star Gas Co., 1928-34, Clint W. Murchison and Wofford Cain interests, 1934-48; v.p. prodn. Delhi Oil Corp., 1948-55; v.p. prodn. Delhi-Taylor Oil corp., 1955-58, sr. v.p., 1958-64; sr. v.p. exploration and prodn. Delhi Internat. Oil Corp., 1958-64, pres., dir., 1964-74, vice chmn. bd., 1974—; dir. 1st Nat. Bank, Athens, 1975—. Mason (Shriner 32, K.T.). Club: Petroleum (Dallas). Home: 5929 Woodland Dr Dallas TX 75225 Office: 3500 1st Internat Bldg Dallas TX 75270

SMITH, WILLIAM DONALD FRASER, television news analyst; b. Canning, N.S., Can., May 29, 1923; s. Donald Fraser and Vera Monro (Hazel) S.; student pub. schs.; m. Maureen Clare Hull, Nov. 6, 1974; children—Jerome, Dawn, Darren, Amber-Leigh, Andrew. Reporter, Halifax (N.S.) Herald, 1945-47; reporter, editor St. John (N.B.) Telegraph Jour., 1947-52; research asst., exec. aide to chmn. Canadian Banking Com., 1952-67; exec. sec. Canadian Centennial Year, 1967; editor Halifax Herald, 1970—; dir. Halifax Herald Co. Ltd. Bd. dirs. Acadia U. Inst., St. John Coll. Devel. Corp.; chmn. U. N.B. Unemployment Commn.; chmn., bd. dirs. St. John Bd. Trade, 1956. Served with Canadian Armed Forces, 1941-45. Mem. Canadian Press, Canadian C. of C., Maritime Provinces Bd. Trade, RCAF Assn., Canadian Legion. Liberal. Anglican. Editor: Champlain, 1952; The River St. John, 1952. Home: 1941 Rosebank Ave Halifax NS B3H 4C6 Canada Office: 190 Victoria Rd Dartmouth NS Canada

SMITH, WILLIAM FRENCH, lawyer, state ofcl. Calif.; b. Wilton, N.H., Aug. 26, 1917; s. William French and Margaret (Dawson) S.; A.B. summa cum laude, U. Calif., 1939; LL.B., Harvard U., 1942, m. Jean Webb, Nov. 6, 1964; children—William French, Stephanie Oakes, Scott Cameron, Gregory Hale. Admitted to Calif. bar, 1942; atty., sr. partner firm Gibson, Dunn & Crutcher, Los Angeles, 1946—. Dir. Pacific Lighting Corp., Los Angeles, Pacific Tel. & Tel. Co., San Francisco, Pacific Mut. Life Ins. Co., Los Angeles, Crocker Nat. Bank, Crocker Nat. Corp., San Francisco, Jorgensen Steel Co., Pullman Inc., Chgo. Mem. U.S. adv. commn. Internat. Ednl. and Cultural Affairs, Washington, 1971—; bd. dirs. Los Angeles World Affairs Council, 1970—, pres., 1975—; mem. Los Angeles Com. Fgn. Relations, 1954-74; chmn. Calif. delegation to Republican Nat. Conv., 1968, del., vice chmn., 1972, 76; mem. exec. com. Calif. Roundtable, 1975—; mem. Mayor's Com. City Finances, Los Angeles, 1975—; trustee Henry E. Huntington Library and Art Gallery, 1971—, Claremont Men's Coll., 1967—, Cate Sch., 1971—, Northrop Inst. Tech., 1973-75; bd. regents U. Calif., 1968—, chmn., 1970-72, 74-75, 76; bd. dirs. Center Theatre Group, Los Angeles Music Center, 1970—, Partnership for Arts in Calif., 1971—, Ind. Colls. So. Calif., 1969-74, Legal Aid Found. Los Angeles, 1963-72, Calif. Found. Commerce and Edn., 1975—; nat. trustee Nat. Symphony Orch., Washington, 1974—; U.S. del. East-West Center Cultural and Tech. Interchange, Hawaii, 1975—; adv. council Harvard U. Sch. Govt., Cambridge, 1977—; adv. bd. Center Strategic and Internat. Studies, Georgetown U., 1978—; mem. Stanton Panel on Internat. Info., Edn. and Cultural Relations, Washington, 1974—; bd. govs. Performing Arts Council, Los Angeles Music Center, 1978—. Served to lt. USNR, 1942-46. Fellow Am. Bar Found.; mem. Am., Los Angeles County bar assns., State Bar Calif., Am. Judicature Soc., Am. Law Inst., Calif. C. of C. (dir. 1963—, pres. 1974-75), Phi Beta Kappa, Pi Gamma Mu, Pi Sigma Alpha. Office: Gibson Dunn & Crutcher 515 S Flower St Los Angeles CA 90071

SMITH, WILLIAM HAROLD, shipbldg. co. exec.; b. Lillington, N.C., Sept. 1, 1928; s. Edgar Soloman and Flora Estelle (Byrd) S.; B.S. in Bus. Adminstrn., Davidson Coll., 1952; M.B.A., U. N.C., 1954; m. Monteen Cameron Bethune, Aug. 18, 1951; children—William H. II, Lisa Michele, Marcia Leanne. With Newport News Shipbldg. & Dry Dock Co. (Va.), 1958—, asst. to treas., 1958-62, asst. treas., 1962-70, treas., 1970, comptroller, Dec. 1970-73, dir. of finance, comptroller, 1973—, also dir.; dir. Employees Credit Union. Bd. trustees Riverside Hosp., Newport News, Va. Coll. Fund; past bd. dirs., past pres. Peninsula United Fund, Va. Ind. Coll. Fund; asst. treas. Hampton Roads Acad. Served to lt. USNR, 1954-58. Mem. Financial Execs. Inst. (dir.), Kappa Sigma. Presbyterian (elder, former deacon). Clubs: Propeller of U.S. (treas., past dir., past pres. Port Newport News), James River Country (fin. com., dir.), Rotary. Home: 200 Country Club Rd Newport News VA 23606 Office: 4101 Washington Ave Newport News VA 23606

SMITH, WILLIAM HENRY PRESTON, telephone co. exec.; b. Pleasanton, Tex., Sept. 8, 1924; s. Sidney Newton and Willie Gertrude (Cloyd) S.; B.J., U. Tex., 1949; m. Frances Dixon, July 1, 1950; children—Juliet, Dixon, David. Reporter, Dallas Morning News, 1949-52; advt. asst. Dallas Power & Light Co., 1952-55; pub. relations dir. Greater Boston C. of C., 1955-58; with New Eng. Tel. & Tel. Co., Boston, 1958—, asst. v.p., 1966-75, corp. sec., 1975—. Bd. dirs., v.p. Mass. Soc. for Prevention Cruelty to Children; bd. dirs. Urban Dynamics Adv. Com.; mem. support policies com. United Way Mass. Served with Paratroops, U.S. Army, 1943-46. Decorated Purple Heart. Mem. Am. Soc. Corp. Secs., Sigma Delta Chi, Delta Kappa Epsilon. Republican. Clubs: Dedham Country and Polo, Down Town. Home: 10 Turtle Ln Dover MA 02030 Office: 185 Franklin St Boston MA 02107

SMITH, WILLIAM JAY, author; b. Winnifield, La., Apr. 22, 1918; s. Jay and Georgia (Campster) S.; student Institut de Touraine, Tours, France, 1938; B.A., Washington U., St. Louis, 1939, M.A., 1941; postgrad. Columbia U., 1946-47; Rhodes scholar, Oxford U., 1947-48; postgrad. U. Florence (Italy), 1948-50; Litt.D., New Eng. Coll., 1973; m. Barbara Howes, Oct. 1, 1947 (div. June 1965); children—David Emerson, Gregory Jay; m. 2d, Sonja Haussmann, Sept. 3, 1966. Asst. in French, Washington U., 1939-41; instr. English and French, Columbia U., 1946-47; lectr. English, Williams Coll., 1951, poet in residence, lectr. English, 1959-64, 66-67; Ford Found. fellow Arena Stage, Washington, 1964-65; writer in residence Hollins Coll., 1965-66, prof. English, 1967, 70—; cons. poetry Library of Congress, Washington, 1968-70, hon. cons. in Am. letters, 1970-76; vis. prof., acting chmn., writing div. Sch. Arts, Columbia U., 1973, 74-75; mem. staff Salzburg (Austria) Seminar, 1975; mem. jury Nat. Book award, 1962, 70, 75, Neustadt Internat. prize for lit., 1978. Mem. Vt. Ho. of Reps., 1960-62. Served to lt. USNR, 1941-45. Recipient Alumni citation Washington U., 1963; prize Poetry mag., 1945, 64; Henry Bellamann Major award, 1970; Russell Loines award Nat. Inst. Arts and Letters, 1972; Nat. Endowment for Arts fellow, 1972 Gold medal of Labor (Hungary), 1978. Mem. Am. Acad. and Inst. Arts and Letters, Am. Assn. Rhodes Scholars, Acad. Am. Poets, Authors Guild, P.E.N. Author: Laughing Time, 1955; Poems 1947-57; The Spectra Hoax, 1961; (with Louise Bogan) The Golden Journey; Poems for Young People, 1965; The Tin Can and Other Poems, 1966; Poems from France, 1967; Mr. Smith and Other Nonsense, 1968; New and Selected Poems, 1970; The Streaks of the Tulip, selected criticism, 1972; Poems from Italy, 1973; Venice in the Fog, 1975; The Telephone, 1977. Home: 1675 York Ave Apt 20 K New York City NY 10028

SMITH, WILLIAM JOSEPH, gas co. exec.; b. McComb, Miss., Feb. 18, 1927; s. Howard C. and Tinie Maureen (Thompson) S.; student Edinburg Jr. Coll., 1946-47; B.S.E.E., Tex. A&M U., 1949; m. Rosemary Jones, Aug. 14, 1946; children—William Carl, David Anderson, Thomas Joseph, Sam Jones, Jeffrey Luther. Prodn. supr. Tex. Electric Service Co., Ft. Worth, 1949-56; utilities systems engr. Gen. Electric Co., Cin., 1956-57; power engr. Dow Chem. Co., 1957-58; project engr. Barnard & Burk Pipeline Engrs., 1958-59; exec. v.p. Fla. Gas Transmission Co., Winter Park, 1959—. Active Little League. Served with USN, 1945-46. Mem. Fla. Natural Gas Assn. (dir., sec.), So. Natural Gas Assn., Am. Gas Assn. Republican. Episcopalian. Home: 696 Berwick Dr Winter Park FL 32792 Office: PO Box 44 Winter Park FL 32790*

SMITH, WILLIAM KEITH, banker; b. Regina, Sask., Can., Oct. 15, 1934; came to U.S., 1960; s. William Givens and Eva Grace (Close) S.; B.Commerce, U. Sask., 1955; M.B.A., U. Western Ont. (Can.), 1960; m. Katherine Adele Woodin, Nov. 19, 1955; 1 dau., Kelly Adele. Acct., Clarkson Gordon & Co., Chartered Accts., Calgary, Alta., Can., 1955-59; mgmt. cons. Haskins & Sells, N.Y.C., 1960-64; v.p. Booz, Allen & Hamilton, Inc., Chgo., 1964-71; vice chmn. Central Nat. Bank, Chgo, 1971—. Bd. dirs. Guild, Lyric Opera Chgo., 1973—. Mem. Can. Inst. Chartered Accts., Fin. Execs. Inst. Presbyterian. Clubs: Chgo., Saddle and Cycle (gov., pres. 1978-80) (Chgo.). Home: 1320 N State Pkwy Chicago IL 60610 Office: 120 S La Salle St Chicago IL 60603

SMITH, WILLIAM LEIGH, retail merchant; b. East Orange, N.J., May 6, 1917; s. Stephen Moore and Mary Catherine (Schwartz) S.; grad. Phillips Exeter Acad., 1935; A.B., Princeton, 1939; m. Margaret Krueger Tobin, Dec. 13, 1942; children—Sherry Leigh, Shelley Baird, Stephen Moore II, William Leigh II. Buyer L. Bamberger & Co., Newark, 1939-40; div. head Amos Parrish & Co., N.Y.C., 1946-49; mng. dir. John Gerber Co., Memphis, 1949- 58; exec. v.p. Basic Econs. Corp., N.Y.C., 1960-61; pres. Bonwit Teller, N.Y.C., 1962-65; pres., dir. Fundamental Co., 1957—; v.p. Paramount Estates, Inc., 1960-65; pres. Hens & Kelly, Inc., Buffalo, 1965-78, also chief exec. officer, dir.; pres., dir. H & K Warehouse, Inc., 1967-78; dir. Marine Midland Bank-Western, WSF Industries. Mem. adv. council U.S. Navy League; mem. bus. adminstrn. council Canisius Coll. Past bd. dirs. Shelby County (Tenn.) chpt. Am. Cancer Soc.; bd. dirs., mem. exec. com. Studio Arena Theatre; bd. dirs. Govt. Research Inst., Greater Buffalo Devel. Found., Buffalo Conv. and Visitors Bur., Downtown Devel. Corp., N.Y. Council Retail Mchts.; asso. Karl Hinke Assos.; pres. C. of C. task force on retail trade; bd. dirs., exec. bd. NCCJ; mem. devel. com. Clergy Economic Found.; mem. corp. Millard Fillmore Hosp. Served to AUS, 1941; to lt. comdr. USNR, 1942-45. Mem. Nat. Retails Mchts. Assn. (past dir.), Gen. Soc. and Mechanics Tradesmen City N.Y. (life), Downtown Mchts. Assn. Buffalo (dir.). Clubs: Cap and Gown (Princeton, N.J.); Buffalo (pres.), Country (gov., v.p.) (Buffalo); Univ., Princeton (N.Y.C.); Orange (N.J.) Lawn Tennis; Pinoak Hunting (Clarendon, Ark.); Automobile of Western N.Y. (dir.). Address: 1088 Delaware Ave Buffalo NY 14209

SMITH, WILLIAM LEWIS, hotel exec.; b. Cleve., Nov. 7, 1925; s. Floyd Holland and Florence (Goebelbecker) S.; student John Carroll U., Kent State U.; m. Dorothy Losch, Aug. 2, 1945; children—Diane, William, Bradley, Tracey. With Halle Bros. Co., Cleve., 1946-58; with Hilton Hotel Corp., various locations, 1958—, gen. mgr. N.Y. Hilton, N.Y.C., 1963-68, Conrad Hilton Hotel, Chgo., 1968-78, Fontainebleau Hilton, Miami Beach, Fla., 1978—; asst. sec. Hilton Hotels Corp., 1971—; lectr. U. Wis.-Stout, 1974, U. Notre Dame, 1975, 76. Dir., Chgo. Conv. and Tourism Bur., 1968-78, Miami Beach Visitor and Conv. Authority, 1978—; mem. Nat. 4-H Service Com., 1969-78; adv. bd. Mercy Hosp. and Med. Center, Chgo., 1973-78; bd. dirs. Met. Fair and Expn. Authority Chgo., 1975-78, Mich. Blvd. Assn., 1968-78, Good Shepherd Manor, Momence, Ill., 1973—, Maur Hill Prep. Sch., Atchison, Kans., 1973. Served with USNR, 1943-45. Recipient Partner-in-4-H award, 1971. Address: 4441 Collins Ave Miami Beach FL 33140

SMITH, WILLIAM MARTIN, educator; b. Flint, Mich., Nov. 24, 1911; s. William Martin and Mertie (Holiday) S.; B.S., Ohio State U., 1934; M.S., Cornell U., 1937, Ph.D., 1942; fellow Merrill-Palmer Inst., 1954-55; m. Ruth Elaine Henderson, Sept. 3, 1938; children—Colborn W., Elaine Y., Maureen B., Deborah G. Extension asst. Ohio State U., 1934-35, mem. staff Community Inst., 1943-45; extension asst. Cornell U., 1935-37, instr. rural sociology extension, 1937-43; asst. prof. U. Ill., 1945-47; mem. faculty Pa. State U., University Park, 1947—, prof. family relations, 1950—, state 4-H leader, 1959-63, asst. dir. family, youth and community devel. coop. extension service, 1963-69, prof. rural sociology, 1969—, chmn. faculty senate, 1971-72; vis. prof. U. Ark., Columbia Tchrs. Coll., Ariz. State Coll. at Flagstaff; Fulbright prof., The Netherlands, 1964-65, research prof., 1973-74. Mem. State Coll. Community Devel. Council, 1948-50; mem. Gov. Pa. Com. Children and Youth, 1963-70; adviser Nat. Assn. Extension Home Economists, 1967-69. Recipient 4-H Alumni award Pa., 1955; fellow Grant Found., 1954-55; hon. mem. Pa. Future Homemakers Assn., 1955. Fellow Am. Sociol. Assn.; mem. Nat. Council Family Relations (pres. 1966-67), Am. Assn. Marriage and Family Therapists, Am. Edn. Assn., Rural Sociol. Soc., AAUP, Phi Kappa Phi, Alpha Zeta, Gamma Sigma Delta, Phi Delta Kappa, Epsilon Sigma Phi, Pi Gamma Mu, Alpha Kappa Delta. Episcopalian (vestry 1950-51). Author: (with Bernard and Buchanan) Dating, Mating and Marriage, 1958; also research bulls. Editor: The Family Coordinator, 1968-70. Home: 428 E Hamilton Ave State College PA 16801 Office: Weaver Bldg Pa State U University Park PA 16802. *Basically my goal as a parent or a teacher or a citizen is to discover and to help create those conditions conducive to the fullest development of people. This means that interpersonal relationships are more important than anything else. Most significant of all relationships are those in the family. If harmony and respect and trust can be nourished there, the rest of the world will be O.K. A corollary of this is that each person finds meaning for his life in his relationships with caring people. He also fills a need for orientation in living as he carries out his responsibilities—first to those around him who make him human, and second to the natural world which supports his existence.*

SMITH, WILLIAM MCFATE, univ. dean, physician; b. Rupert, Idaho, Nov. 1, 1926; s. William Hudson and LeVon (McFate) S.; B.S. in Biology, So. Meth. U., 1947; M.D., U. Chgo., 1951; M.P.H., U. Calif., Berkeley, 1968; m. Ruby Elizabeth Carlson, July 30, 1947; children—Gregory, Marcelyn Smith Daneke, Michele Smith King. Commd. 2d lt. USPHS, 1951, advanced through grades to rear adm., 1970; intern USPHS Hosp., S.I., N.Y., 1951-52, resident in internal medicine, 1954-57, dir. cardiopulmonary lab., 1959-62; chief dept. medicine USPHS Hosp., San Francisco, 1962-68, dir., 1968-70, regional health dir. Region IX, HEW, San Francisco, 1970-73, asst. surgeon gen. USPHS, 1970-73, ret., 1973, chief research br., div. of hosps., 1975—; asso. dean U. Calif., San Francisco, 1973-76; med. dir. San Francisco Gen. Hosp., 1973-75, clin. prof. medicine, 1974—; chmn. Calif. Council for High Blood Pressure Control, 1973-76, San Francisco Council High Blood Pressure Control, 1976—; vice chmn. steering com. Nat. Heart Attack Prevention Program, 1975—. Recipient Meritorious Service award USPHS, 1973. Mem. A.C.P., Am. Coll. Cardiology, Western Soc. Clin. Research, Am. Heart Assn., Calif. Acad. Medicine, Alpha Omega Alpha. Home: 425 Fairway Dr Novato CA 94947 Office: 15th Ave at Lake St San Francisco CA 94118

SMITH, WILLIAM P., univ. dean; b. Superior, Wis., Jan. 5, 1915; s. William Robert and Emaline (Payne) S.; B.E.E., U. Minn., 1936, M.S., 1937; Ph.D., U. Tex., 1950; m. June Phyllis Nickel, Dec. 23, 1942; children—Susan June Smith Pinero, William P., Sally Ward. With U. Minn., 1936-37, Commonwealth Edison Co., 1937-39, Chgo. Tech. Coll., 1939-41; dean instrn. Assn. Colls. Upper N.Y., 1946-48; mem. faculty U. Tex., 1948-50; mem. faculty U. Kan., 1950—, prof. elec. engring., 1953-65, chmn. dept., 1955-65, dean Sch. Engring., 1965—; cons. in field. Served to capt. USNR, 1941-45. Mem. I.E.E.E., Am. Soc. Engring. Edn., Kan. Engring. Soc., Sigma Xi, Delta Tau Delta, Tau Beta Pi, Sigma Tau, Eta Kappa Nu (nat. pres. 1967-68). Home: 1107 W Campus Rd Lawrence KS 66044

SMITH, WILLIAM REECE, JR., lawyer; b. Athens, Tenn., Sept. 19, 1925; s. William Reece and Gladys (Moody) S.; B.S., U. S.C., 1946; J.D., U. Fla., 1949; Rhodes scholar Oxford U., 1949-52; LL.D., U. So. Fla., 1973; m. Marlene Medina, Aug. 8, 1963; 1 son, William Reece III. Admitted to Fla. bar, 1949; mem. firm Carlton, Fields, Ward, Emmanuel, Smith & Cutler, and predecessor firm, Tampa, 1955—, now chmn.; interim pres. U. So. Fla., 1976-77; city atty. Tampa, 1963-72. Asst. prof. law U. Fla., 1952-53; adj. prof. law Stetson U., 1954-59; past pres. Am. Bar Endowment; past pres. Fla. Legal Services, Inc. Past pres. Tampa Philharmonic Assn., Fla. Gulf Coast Symphony, Inc.; sec. Fla. Rhodes Scholar Selection Com., 1969—. Served to ensign USNR, 1943-46. Named Outstanding Young Man of Tampa, 1961; recipient Good Govt. award Fla. Jr. C. of C., 1965, Distinguished Am. award Tampa Chpt. Nat. Football Found., 1977; Humanitarian award B'nai B'rith Found., 1977; Pres.'s award Fla. Assn. Retarded Citizens, 1978. Fellow Am. Coll. Trial Lawyers, Internat. Acad. Trial Lawyers, Am., Fla. (past pres.) bar founds.; mem. Internat. Soc. Barristers, Am. Law Inst., Am. (chmn. jr. bar conf. 1960-61, life, ho. of dels., sec. 1967-71, pres.-elect 1979-80), Inter-Am. (mem. exec. council), Fla. (pres. 1972-73), Hillsborough County (pres. 1963) bar assns., Nat. Conf. Bar Pres.'s (pres.). Methodist. Home: 11 Ladoga Ave Tampa FL 33606 Office: Box 3239 Tampa FL 33601

SMITH, WILLIAM STANFORD, army officer; b. Macon, Ga., Apr. 6, 1919; s. William Stanford and Willie Della (Leggett) S.; A.B. in Journalism, U. Ga., Athens, 1941; m. Martha Louise Cooper, Oct. 4, 1942; children—Marion C. Smith Hills, Mary Elizabeth Smith Wallace, Lucinda L. Smith Warnick. Commd. 2d lt. U.S. Army, 1941, advanced through grades to capt., 1945; inactive duty, 1945-75; recalled as maj. gen., mil. exec. Res. Forces Policy Bd., Office Sec. Def., 1975-79; civilian career as journalist, 1945-75; pres., gen. mgr. Am. Newspaper Pubs. Assn., 1960-75; 1st chmn. Internat. Press Telecommunications Council, London, 1966-68; gov. council Internat. Fedn. Newspaper Pubs., 1960-75. Decorated Def. D.S.M., Legion of Merit, Bronze Star with V device, Combat Inf. badge; officer cross German Order Merit (W. Ger.); Gold medal City of Paris, 1973. Mem. Assn. U.S. Army, Res. Officers Assn., Am. Mensa Soc. Club: Metropolitan (Washington). Home: 5111 8th Rd S Arlington VA 22204 Office: Office Sec Defense (M&RA) The Pentagon Washington DC 20301

SMITH, WILLIAM VICK, physicist; b. Dallas, Dec. 11, 1916; s. Charles Grover and Aurelia (Mayer) S.; A.B. summa cum laude, Harvard, 1937, M.A., 1939, Ph.D., 1941; m. Jeanette L. Pedersen, Apr. 18, 1941; 1 dau., Jeanette Aurelia. Fluorescent lighting research Sylvania Electric Products Co., 1941-42; microwave magnetron research, radiation lab. Mass. Inst. Tech., 1942-45, Raytheon Mfg. Co., 1946; asst. prof., asso. prof. physics, asso. dir microwave spectroscopy lab. Duke, 1946-51; prof. physics, dept. chmn. U. Del., 1951-56, physicist to mgr., physics research labs. IBM, Yorktown Heights, N.Y., 1956-70, mgr. edn. and personnel devel., 1972-74, mgr. tech. assessment to mgr. advanced tech. IBM Fed. Systems Div., Gaithersburg, Md., 1974—; mgr. physics IBM Research Lab., Zurich, Switzerland, 1970-72. Fellow Am. Phys. Soc. (sec.-treas. div. solid state physics 1965-69), AAAS; mem. IEEE (sr.), Am. Optical Soc., Phi Beta Kappa, Sigma Xi, Sigma Pi Sigma, Pi Mu Epsilon. Author: Laser Applications, 1970; Electronic Information Processing-Physical Principles and Materials Technology, 1974. Co-author: Microwave Magnetrons (vol. 6 Rad. Lab. Series), 1948; Microwave Spectroscopy, 1953; The Laser, 1966. Patentee cathodes for fluorescent lights, mech., electronic tuning of magnetrons, atomic clocks, laser deflection and modulation devices. Address: 1997 Lancashire Dr Rockville MD 20854

SMITH, WILLIAM WALLACE, clergyman; b. Lamoni, Iowa, Nov. 18, 1900; s. Joseph and Ada Rachel (Clark) S.; A.A., Graceland Coll., Lamoni, 1922, D.D. (hon.), 1970; A.B., U. Mo., 1924; m. Rosamond Bunnell, Nov. 12, 1924; children—Rosalee (Mrs. Otto Helmut Elser), Wallace Bunnell. Ordained to ministry Reorganized Ch. of Jesus Christ of Latter Day Saints, 1928; asso. pastor Stone Ch. Congregation, Independence, 1929-30; pastor First Ch., Portland, Oreg. 1945-46; mem. council Twelve Apostles, 1947-50; counsellor to pres. Reorganized Ch. Jesus Christ of Latter Day Saints, 1950-58, pres., 1958-78, pres. emeritus, 1978—; asst. editor in chief Saints' Herald, 1950-58, editor in chief, 1958-78, contbg. editor, 1979—; dir. Pacific Land Devel. Assn. Mem. bd. trustees Independence Sanitarium and Hosp. Hon. fellow Harry Truman Library Inst. for Nat. and Internat. Affairs. Mem. Mo. (trustee), Jackson County hist. socs., C. of C., Delta Upsilon. Rotarian. Home: 428 Bellevista Dr Independence MO 64055 Office: PO Box 1059 Auditorium Independence MO 64051

SMITH, WILLIAM YOUNG, air force officer; b. Hot Springs, Ark., Aug. 13, 1925; s. Ray Sammons and Elisabeth Randolph (Young) S.; student Washington and Lee U., 1943-44; B.S., U.S. Mil. Acad., 1948; M.P.A., Harvard U., 1954, Ph.D. in Polit. Economy and Govt., 1961; postgrad. Case Inst. Tech., 1954; grad. USAF Command and Staff Coll., Maxwell AFB, Ala., 1959, Nat. War Coll., Washington, 1965; m. Maria Helene Petschek, May 30, 1957; children—Raymond P., Mark P., Derek P. Commd. 2d lt. U.S. Air Force, 1948, advanced through grades to gen., 1979; pilot trainee, Randolph AFB, Tex., Williams Field, Ariz., 1948-49; jet fighter pilot 20th fighter bomber group, S.C., U.K., 1950, Korea, 1951-52; asso. prof. social scis. U.S. Mil. Acad., 1954-58; mem. staff Pres's Com. to Study Mil. Assistance Program, 1959; planning and programs officer war plans Hdqrs. USAF, Washington, 1960; staff asst. to Gen. Maxwell Taylor, mil. rep. to Pres., White House, 1961-62; asst. to chmn. Joint Chiefs of Staff, mem. staff NSC, 1962-64; dep. chief of staff for ops., policy and negotiations div., chief war plans div., Hdqrs. USAF in Europe, Wiesbaden, Germany, 1965-67; comdr. 603d air base wing, Sembach, Germany, 1967-68; mil. asst. to sec. Air Force, 1968-71; vice comdr. Oklahoma City Air Materiel Area, Tinker AFB, Okla., 1971, comdr., 1972-73; dir. doctrine concepts objectives, dep. chief of staff, plans and ops. Hdqrs. USAF, Washington, 1973-74; dir. policy plans and Nat. Security Council affairs Office of Asst. Sec. Def. for Internat. Security Affairs, Office of Sec. Def., Washington, 1974-75; asst. to chmn. Joint Chiefs of Staff Dept. Def., Washington, 1975-79; chief of staff SHAPE, Belgium, 1979—. Chmn. exploring com. Last Frontier council Boy Scouts Am., 1972-73. Decorated Def. D.S.M., AF D.S.M. with oak leaf cluster, Silver Star, Legion of Merit, Air medal with 3 oak leaf clusters, Joint Service Commendation medal, Purple Heart. Fellow Met. Mus. Art (N.Y.C.) (life); mem. Council Fgn. Relations, Kappa Alpha. Methodist. Home: 32 Chaussee de Binche 7000 Mons Belgium Office: Chief of Staff SHAPE APO New York NY 09055

SMITH, WILLIS ALLEN, food co. exec.; b. Balt., Oct. 26, 1919; s. Willis Alfred and Grace Lee (Roberts) S.; student Johns Hopkins, 1937-41, 46-48, Coll. William and Mary, Norfolk, Va., 1941-42; m. Joann Cobb, Aug. 29, 1970. Clk., Gas & Electric Co., Balt., 1936-41; accountant F. W. Lafrentz & Co., Balt., 1946-51, mgr., Salisbury, Md., 1952-53, partner, Cleve., 1953-62; partner Main Lafrentz & Co., N.Y.C., 1963-74; comptroller CPC Internat. Inc., Englewood Cliffs, N.J., 1974—; mem. bd. Internat. Acctg. Standards Com., 1979—; lectr. Third Commodity Conf., Chgo., 1973. Served with USNR, 1941-45; PTO. C.P.A., Md., Ohio, N.Y. Mem. N.Y. State Soc. C.P.A.'s, Fin. Execs. Inst., Nat. Assn. Accountants, Am. Accounting Assn., Am. Inst. C.P.A.'s, Accountants Club (gov.). Mason (Shriner). Club: Ridgewood (N.J.) Country. Home: 815 Norgate Dr Ridgewood NJ 07450 Office: CPC Internat Inc Internat Plaza Englewood Cliffs NJ 07632

SMITH, WORTHINGTON LEHURAY, ry. exec.; b. Tacoma, Feb. 12, 1925; s. Worthington C. and Doris (LeHuray) S.; B.A., Yale, 1950; M.A., U. Minn., 1953; postgrad. Harvard Bus. Sch., 1967; m. Elizabeth Ann Getzoff, June 30, 1950; children—Worthington R., Scott, Nancy. With Great No. R.R., 1954-70; with Burlington No., Inc., Seattle and St. Paul, 1970-72; pres. C., M., St.P. & P. R.R., Chgo., 1972-79, pres., chief exec. officer, 1979—, also dir. Trustee, Farm Found., Chgo., 1973—. Served with AUS, 1943-46, 51-52. Mem. Nat. Freight Traffic Assn., Am. Soc. Traffic and Transp., Traffic Club Chgo., Western Ry. Club. Club: Met. (Chgo.). Office: 516 W Jackson Blvd Chicago IL 60606*

SMITH, ZACHARY TAYLOR, II, tobacco co. exec.; b. Mt. Airy, N.C., June 15, 1923; s. Eugene Gray and Leonita (Yates) S.; A.B. in Econs., U. N.C., 1947. With R.J. Reynolds Tobacco Co., 1947—, treas., dir., 1970—. Trustee, pres. Z. Smith Reynolds Found.; v.p., bd. dirs. Mary Reynolds Babcock Found.; trustee St. Augustine Coll.; bd. visitors Wake Forest U.; bd. dirs. Med. Found. N.C.; adv. council Duke U. Hosp.; The Carolina Challenge-U. N.C.; past bd. dirs. N.C. Sch. Arts Found., Devotion Found., N.C. Outward Bound Sch., Small Bus. Devel. Com., Winston-Salem Symphony, Citizens Planning Council; past trustee Forsyth Hosp. Authority; past pres., dir. Child Guidance Clinic Forsyth County, YMCA, Red Shield Boy's Clubs; past chmn. indsl. div. Arts Council fund drive, past v.p., dir. Arts Council; past vice chmn., dir. Friends of U. N.C.-Greensboro Library; past v.p., dir. Amos Cottage; past bd. visitors Meredith Coll. Served to lt. USNR, 1943-46. Mem. Winston Salem C. of C. (state and local govt. com.), Order of Tar Heel One Hundred, Co-founders Club Med. Sch. U. N.C. Democrat. Episcopalian. Clubs: Old Town; Bachelor; Rotary. Home: 2548 Forest Dr Winston-Salem NC 27104 Office: RJ Reynolds Tobacco Co Winston-Salem NC 27102

SMITHBURG, WILLIAM DEAN, food mfg. co. exec.; b. Chgo., July 9, 1938; s. Pearl L. and Margaret L. (Savage) S.; m. Alberta Hap, May 25, 1963; children—Susan, Thomas. Pres., dir. Quaker Oats Co., Chgo. Served with USAR, 1959-60. Roman Catholic. Office: 345 Merchandise Mart Plaza Chicago IL 60654*

SMITHDEAL, WILLIAM FRALIN, pharm. mfg. co. exec.; b. Wise, N.C., Jan. 26, 1924; s. Edward Octavius and Cordie Gertrude (Fralin) S.; B.S. in Commerce, U. N.C., 1948; postgrad. U. Richmond, 1948-50; m. Jean McCulloch Boyle, July 31, 1948; children—Leckie, Douglas, Gray. Sr. auditor A.M. Pullen & Co., C.P.A.'s, Richmond, Va., 1951-60; controller Seward Luggage Mfg. Co., Petersburg, Va., 1960-63; controller A.H. Robins Co., Richmond, 1963—. Served with USAAF, 1942-45. Decorated Air medal. C.P.A., Va. Mem. Fin. Execs. Inst. (pres. Va. chpt. 1971, nat. dir. 1972-75, Eastern area v.p. 1974-75). Club: Fishing Bay Yacht (Deltaville, Va.). Office: 1407 Cummings Dr Richmond VA 23220

SMITHERMAN, GUSTAVUS SCOTT, architect; b. Shreveport, Jan. 4, 1921; s. James Emory and Ina Scott (Thompson) S.; B.Arch., U. Pa., 1946; M.Arch., Harvard U., 1947; m. Margaret Louise Burgess, Dec. 30, 1966; children—Gill Scott, Mark Wofford, Torre Clingman, Thomas Marion, John Paul. With firm Neild & Somdal, Shreveport, summers 1937-42, 45; William Riseman & Assos., Shreveport, part-time, 1946-47; partner Somdal Assos. and predecessors, Shreveport, 1947—. Life mem. met. bd. Shreveport YMCA; pres. Children's Service Bur. Shreveport, 1959-60. Served to 1st lt. USAAF, World War II. Decorated Air medal. Fellow AIA (pres. Shreveport 1958, dir. Gulf States region 1962-65, chmn. commn. profl. soc. 1965, trustee found. 1965); mem. La. Architects Assn. (pres. 1961-62). Democrat. Episcopalian. Clubs: Shreveport Country, Shreveport, Shreveport Rotary (pres. 1977-78). Home: 6401 Birnam Wood Rd Shreveport LA 71106 Office: Suite 210 LBT Milam Bldg 316 Milam St Shreveport LA 71101

SMITHSON, JOHN ROYSTON, physicist, educator; b. Norrisville, Md., Sept. 11, 1912; s. Lawrence and Nettie (Strawbridge) S.; B.S., Washington Coll., 1934; M.S., Ind. U., 1940; Ph.D., Catholic U. Am., 1955; m. Dorothy Leitch, Sept. 11, 1937 (dec. Apr. 1965); children—Martha Lynn, Mary Rae; m. 2d, Dorothy Brock, June 21, 1967. High sch. tchr., 1934-40; asst. prof. Ball State U., Muncie, Ind., 1940-43, 46-47; mem. faculty U.S. Naval Acad., Annapolis, Md., 1947—, prof. physics, 1957—, also formerly chmn. dept. Research scientist; lectr. various univs. Mem. Am. Acoustical Soc., Am. Assn. Physics Tchrs., Sigma Xi. Home: 75 Shipwright St Annapolis MD 21401

SMITS, THEODORE RICHARD, newspaperman, publicist; b. Jackson, Mich., Apr. 24, 1905; s. Bastian and Helen (Hull) S.; student Mich. State U., 1922-24; m. Anna Mary Wells, Sept. 10, 1931 (div. 1952); children—Jean Smits Miles, Helen Smits LeCompte, Gerrit (dec.); m. 2d, Pamela Seward, Sept. 22, 1952; 1 son, Richard. State and telegraph editor Lansing (Mich.) State Jour., 1924-29; city editor Internat. News Service, N.Y.C., 1929-31, bur. mgr., Los Angeles, 1931-34; with AP, Los Angeles, 1934-37, chief bur., Salt Lake City, 1937-39, Detroit, 1939-46, gen. sports editor, N.Y.C., 1946-69, charge world coverage 1948 Olympics in St. Moritz and London, 1952 Olympics in Oslo and Helsinki, 1956 Olympics in Cortina, Italy and Melbourne, 1960 Olympics in Squaw Valley, Calif., Rome; 1964 Olympics in Innsbruck, Austria, Tokyo, Japan; 1968 Olympics, Mexico City; editorial adviser Leisure Time Products, AMF, Inc., 1969-74; editor The Armchair Quarterback, 1976—; author: The Game of Soccer; Soccer For The American Boy; editor: The Year in Sports, 1958. Dir., Hertz Neil award, 1977—. Home: 601 E 20th St New York City NY 10010

SMOKER, EDWARD HEISE, utility exec.; b. Columbia, Pa., Dec. 29, 1905; s. Howard Grant and Ella (Heise) S.; B.S., Franklin and Marshall Coll., 1926; M.A., U. Cin., 1927, Ph.D., 1929; m. Dorothy Conner, Sept. 1, 1927; children—Audrey (Mrs. Dominic Salerno), Dorothy (Mrs. Frederick Nielsen). With Nat. Aniline & Chem. Co., Buffalo, 1929-30; with United Gas Improvement Co. (co. name changed to UGI Corp.), Phila., 1930—, beginning as chemist research dept., successively engr. operation dept., operation mgr., v.p., 1953-55, pres., 1955-70, chmn. bd., 1971-79; dir. Quaker Chem. Corp. Gen. chmn. United Fund, 1966. Trustee Delco Meml. Hosp., Franklin and Marshall Coll.; bd. mgrs. Franklin Inst. Profl. engr., Pa. Mem. Chem. Soc. Am. Inst. Chem. Engrs., Am. (pres. 1961-62), Pa. (pres. 1960-61, 63) gas assns., Soc. Gas Lighting, Phi Beta Kappa, Sigma Xi, Alpha Chi Sigma. Clubs: Union League (Phila.). Home: 101 Kershaw Rd Wallingford PA 19086

SMOKLER, JEROLD, mag. art exec.; b. Bklyn., Feb. 10, 1935; s. Reuben and Sophie (Zerlin) S.; B.F.A., Pratt Inst., 1957. Asst. art dir. Seventeen Mag., N.Y.C., 1959-60, Push Pin Studios, N.Y.C., 1960-62, Columbia Records Co., N.Y.C., 1962-64; art dir. Town and Country Mag., N.Y.C., 1964-73; dir. art Harper's Bazaar, N.Y.C., 1973-79; art dir. All in Style/Mainliner Mags., East West Network, N.Y.C., 1979—. Served with AUS, 1955-57. Recipient award Soc. Publ. Designers, 1972, 73, 74. Mem. Art Dirs. Club (award 1963, 65, 66), Am. Inst. Graphic Arts (award 1962). Home: 100 W 57th St New York NY 10019 Office: 488 Madison Ave New York NY 10022

SMOLANOFF, MICHAEL LOUIS, composer; b. N.Y.C., May 11, 1942; s. Irving and Beatrice (Groopman) S.; B.S., Juilliard Sch. Music, 1964, M.S., 1965; Mus.D., Combs Coll., 1975. Research asst. Columbia U., 1965-66; instr. Juilliard Sch. Music, 1966; editor E.B. Marks Music Corp., N.Y.C., 1966-68; instr. Phila. Mus. Acad., 1968-71; prof. music Rutgers U., Camden, N.J., 1971-77; pres. The Music Press, Collingswood, N.J., 1977—; cons. Amherst Electronic Studios. Served with USAF, 1966-70. Recipient ASCAP award, 1975-76; Rutgers Research Council grantee, 1973. Mem. Nat. Assn. Am. Composers and Condrs., ASCAP, Juilliard Sch. Music Alumni Assn., Phi Mu Alpha Sinfonia. Composer: Concerto for Trombone, 1968; String Quartet, 1972; Pages from a Summer Journal, 1974; Celebration, 1975. Home: 20 A Broun Pl Bronx NY 10475. *Music has always been an extension of my every waking hour. For me, it is an abstract set of principles which I use to reflect my life and its surroundings. It is a means of communication when other ways have failed. My goals are to write the best music within me and to have an audience experience these feelings with me.*

SMOLIN, RONALD PHILIP, publisher; b. Phila., Aug. 12, 1941; s. Harry and Frances (Gordon) S.; B.A., Pa. State U., 1963. Staff writer Prudential Ins. Co., Newark, 1964-65; pub. info. officer Newark War on Proverty program, 1965-66; dir. publs. N.Y.C. Human Resources Adminstrn., 1966-75; chmn. Beekman Pubs., Inc., N.Y.C., 1973-77; pres. Internat. Ideas Inc., N.Y.C., 1977—; pub. info. cons. N.Y. region Fed. Disaster Assistance Adminstrn. Mem. Am. Acad. Polit. and Social Scis., New Directions, Space Futures Soc. (treas.), Nat. Space Inst. Editor Space Futures Newsletter. Address: 1627 Spruce St Philadelphia PA 19103

SMOLUCHOWSKI, ROMAN, educator, physicist; b. Zakopane, Austria, Aug. 31, 1910; s. Marian and Sophia (Baraniecka) S.; came to U.S., 1935, naturalized, 1946; M.A., U. Warsaw, 1933; Ph.D., U. Groningen (Holland), 1935; m. Louise Catherine Riggs, Feb. 3, 1951; children—Peter, Irene. Mem. Inst. Advanced Study, Princeton U., 1935-36, instr., research asso. physics dept., 1939-41, prof. solid state scis. head solid state and materials program, 1960-78; research asso., head physics sect. Inst. Metals, Warsaw, 1936-39; research physicist Gen. Electric Research Labs., Schenectady, 1941-46; asso. prof., staff Metals Research Lab., Carnegie Inst. Tech., 1946-50, prof. physics and metall. engring., 1950-56, prof. physics, 1956-60; prof. astronomy and physics U. Tex., Austin, 1978—; vis. prof. Internat. Sch. Solid State Physics, Mol, Belgium, 1963, Faculté des Sciences, Paris, 1965-66; lectr. Sch. Planetary Physics, Super-Besse, France, 1972; Fulbright prof. Sorbonne, Paris, 1955-56; lectr. Internat. Sch. Solid State Physics, Varenna, Italy, 1957, U. Liège, Belgium, 1956; vis. prof. NRC of Brazil, 1958-59, Tech. U. Munich, 1974; mem. solid state panel Research and Devel. Bd., Dept. Def., 1949, sec. panel, 1950-61; mem. tech. adv. bd. Aircraft Nuclear Propulsion, 1950; chmn com. on magnetism Office Naval Research, 1952-56; chmn. com. on solids NRC, 1950-61, chmn. solid state scis. panel, 1961-67, chmn. div. phys. scis. 1969-75; mem. space sci. bd. Nat. Acad. Scis., 1969-75, mem. physics survey, 1963-66, 1969-72; adv. com. metallurgy Oak Ridge Nat. Lab., 1960-62. Chmn. bd. trustees Simon's Rock Coll., 1971-72. Guggenheim Meml. fellow, 1974; fellow Churchill Coll. Cambridge U., Eng., 1974. Fellow Am. Phys. Soc. (chmn. div. solid state physics 1944-46), Am. Acad. Arts and Scis.; mem. AAAS, Internat. Astron. Union, Finnish Acad. Scis. and Letters, Am. Astron. Soc., Brazilian Acad. Scis., Sigma Xi, Alpha Sigma Mu, Pi Mu Epsilon. Author: (with Mayer and Weyl) Phase Transformations in Nearly Perfect Crystals, 1952; (with others) Molecular Science and Molecular Engineering, 1959; editor: (with N. Kurti) Monograph Series on Solid State, 1957; (with E. Burstein) Comments in Solid State Physics; editor-in-chief: Crystal Lattice Defects; editor-in-chief: Semiconductors and Insulators; asso. editor Fundamentals of Cosmic Physics. Contbr. articles to profl. jours. Home: 1102 Claire St Austin TX 78703 Office: U Tex Dept Physics and Astronomy Austin TX 78712

SMOOT, JOSEPH GRADY, univ. pres., clergyman; b. Winter Haven, Fla., May 7, 1932; s. Robert Malcolm and Vera (Eaton) S.; B.A., So. Missionary Coll., 1955; M.A., U. Ky., 1958, Ph.D., 1964; m. Florence Rozell, May 30, 1955 (dec.); m. 2d, Irma Jean Kopitzke, June 4, 1959; 1 son, Andrew Christopher. Tchr., Ky. Secondary Schs., 1955-57; from instr. to asso. prof. history Columbia Union Coll., Takoma Park, Md., 1960-68, acad. dean, 1965-68; prof. history Andrews U., Berrien Springs, Mich., 1968—, dean Sch. Grad. Studies, 1968-69, v.p. acad. adminstrn., 1969-76, pres., 1976—. Ordained to the ministry Seventh-day Adventist Ch., 1973. Bd. dirs. Hinsdale (Ill.) Hosp.; trustee Loma Linda (Calif.) U., Adventist Coll. West Africa, Ilishan, Nigeria, Helderberg Coll., Somerset West, South Africa, Newbold Coll., Bracknell, Eng.; bd. regents, bd. higher edn. Gen. Conf. Seventh-day Adventists; mem. exec. com. Lake Union Conf., Gen. Conf. Seventh-day Adventists. Mem. Am., So. hist. assns., Orgn. Am. Historians, Phi Alpha Theta. Clubs: Econ. Mich., Point O' Woods Country, Rotary. Author: Profile of a Capital Gift Campaign, 1979; contbr. articles to profl. jours. Home: 324 Hillcrest Dr Berrien Springs MI 49103

SMOOT, LEON DOUGLAS, coll. dean; b. Provo, Utah, July 26, 1934; s. Douglas Parley and Jennie (Hallam) S.; B.S., Brigham Young U., 1957; M.S., U. Wash., 1958, Ph.D., 1960; m. Marian Bird, Sept. 7, 1953; children—Analee, LaCinda, Michelle, Melinda Lee. Engr., Boeing Corp., Seattle, 1956; teaching and research asst. Brigham Young U., 1954-57; engr. Phillips Petroleum Corp., Arco, Idaho, 1957; engr., cons. Hercules Powder Co., Bacchus, Utah, 1961-63; asst. prof. Brigham Young U., 1960-63; engr. Lockheed Propulsion, Redlands, Calif., 1963-67; vis. asst. prof. Calif. Inst. Tech., 1966-67; asso. prof. to prof. Brigham Young U., 1967—, chmn. dept. chem. engring., 1970-77, dean Coll. Engring. Scis. and Tech., 1977—; cons. Hercules, Thiokol, Lockheed, Teledyne, Atlantic Research Corp., Raytheon, Redd and Redd, Billings Energy, Ford, Bacon & Davis, Jaycor, Intel Com Radiation Tech., Phys. Dynamics, Nat. Soc. Propellants and Explosives (France), DFVLR (West Germany), Martin Marietta, Honeywell, Nat. Bur. Standards, Eyring Research Inst., Systems, Sci. and Software. Registered profl. engr., Utah. Mem. Am. Inst. Chem. Engrs., Am. Inst. Aeros. and Astronautics, Am. Soc. Engring. Edn., Combustion Inst., Research Soc. Am., Tau Beta Pi, Phi Lambda Epsilon, Sigma Xi. Republican. Mem. Ch. Jesus Christ of Latter-day Saints. Contbr. over 80 articles to tech. jours.; author book on coal combustion. Home: 1811 N 1550 East Provo UT 84601 Office: 270 CB Brigham Young U Provo UT 84602

SMOOT, THURLOW BERGEN, lawyer; b. Glendive, Mont., Dec. 30, 1910; s. Marvin A. and Ivah (Cook) S.; J.D., U. Colo., 1933. Admitted to Ohio bar, 1933; practice in Cleve., 1933-37, 47—; atty., later trial examiner NLRB, 1937-47. Served with AUS, 1942-45; ETO. Mem. Am. (chmn. labor relations law sect. 1967; sect. del. to ho. dels. 1970-71), Cleve., Ohio, Cuyahoga County bar assns., Nat. Trial Lawyers Assn., Ohio Acad. Trial lawyers. Home: 12700 Lake Ave Lakewood OH 44107 Office: Mall Cleveland OH 44114

SMOTHERS, DICK, actor, singer; b. 1939; s. Thomas B. and Ruth Smothers; student San Jose State Coll.; married; children—Susan, Dick, Steven. Night club appearances at Harrah's (Lake Tahoe), Riviera (Las Vegas); former co-star half hour situation comedy TV series Smothers Bros. Show, 1965-66, TV show Smothers Brothers Comedy Hour, 1967-69, 70; co-star weekly variety hour The Smothers Bros. Show, NBC-TV, 1975; appeared on Broadway in I Love My Wife, 1978. Address: care Smothers Internat 260 S Beverly Dr Beverly Hills CA 90212*

SMOTHERS, TOM, actor, singer, comedian; b. 1937; s. Thomas B. and Ruth Smothers; student San Jose State Coll.; 1 son, Tom. Nightclub appearances at Harrah's (Lake Tahoe), Riviera (Las Vegas); co-star half hour TV situation comedy Smothers Brothers Show, 1965-66, Smothers Brothers Comedy Hour, CBS-TV, 1967-69; co-star weekly variety hour the Smothers Brothers Show, NBC-TV, 1975; starred in films Get To Know Your Rabbit, The Silver Bears; starred on Broadway in I Love My Wife, 1978-79. Address: 8489 W 3d St Los Angeles CA 90048

SMOTHERS, WILLIAM JOSEPH, metal products co. exec.; b. Poplar Bluff, Mo., Mar. 17, 1919; s. John William and Ina (Eliot) S.; B.S. in Ceramics Engring., U. Mo., 1940, M.S., 1942, Ph.D., 1944; m. Marjorie Hunter, Sept. 5, 1943; children—John, Bonnie. Research engr. Bowes Seal Fast Corp., Lafayette, Ind., 1944-50; asso. prof. U. Ark., Fayetteville, 1950-54; dir. ceramic research Ohio Brass Co., Barberton, Ohio, 1954-63; sect. mgr. refractories Bethlehem Steel Corp. (Pa.), 1963—. Recipient Toledo Glass and Ceramic award, 1975. Fellow AAAS, Am. Ceramic Soc. (pres. 1971-72, editor 1972—); mem. Am. Chem. Soc. Am. Soc. Metals. Author: Differential Thermal Analysis: Theory and Practice, 1958; Handbook of Differential Thermal Analysis, 1966. Home: 2700 Woodside Rd Bethlehem PA 18018 Office: Bethlehem Steel Corp Bethlehem PA 18016

SMOTRICH, DAVID ISADORE, architect; b. Norwich, Conn., Oct. 6, 1933; s. Max Z. and Ida (Babinsky) S.; A.B., Harvard, 1955, M.Arch., 1960; m. Bernice D. Strachman, Mar. 25, 1956; children—Ross Lawrence, Maura Faye, Hannah. Mem. master planning team Town of Arad, State of Israel, 1961-62; asso. Platt Assos., architects, N.Y.C., 1963-65; gen. partner Smotrich & Platt, architects, N.Y.C., 1965-74, Smotrich Platt & Buttrick, 1975-76, Smotrich & Platt, 1976—. Cons. to Jerusalem Master Plan Office, Israel Ministry of Housing, 1967; mem. planning bd. Town of New Castle, N.Y., 1974—. Mem. exec. bd. Road Rev. League, Bedford, N.Y., 1966-70. Served with AUS, 1955-57. Recipient Bard award, 1969; Archtl. Record award, 1971, 73, 74, 75, 78. Mem. AIA (Nat. Honor award 1969), Assn. Engrs. and Architects in Israel. Club: Harvard (N.Y.C.). Home: 7 Mayberry Close Chappaqua NY 10514 Office: 227 E 45th St New York NY 10017

SMUCKER, PAUL HIGHNAM, food co. exec.; b. Orrville, Ohio, Apr. 21, 1917; s. Willard Earl and Letha (Highnam) S.; B.S. in Bus., Miami U., Oxford, Ohio, 1939; m. Lorraine Evangeline Smith, June 29, 1940; children—Susan Diane (Mrs. Hollis R. Wagstaff, Jr.), Timothy Paul, Richard Kim. With J. M. Smucker Co., Orrville, 1939—, gen. mgr., 1946-61, pres., 1961-70, chmn., pres., 1970—; dir. Kellogg Co., Nat. Bank Orrville. Served to lt. (j.g.) USNR, 1943-46; PTO. Mem. Nat. Preservers Assn. (pres. 1956-57), Grocery Mfrs. Am. (dir.), Am. Mgmt. Assn. Am. Acad. Achievement, Phi Delta Theta. Republican. Office: Strawberry Ln Orrville OH 44667*

SMUCKER, TIMOTHY PAUL, food co. exec.; b. Wooster, Ohio, June 29, 1944; s. Paul Highnam and Lorraine (Smith) S.; B.A. in Econs., Coll. Wooster, 1967; M.B.A. in Mktg., Wharton Sch., U. Pa., 1969; m. Jennifer Coddington, June 22, 1968; children—Mark, Reid, Sarah. With J.M. Smucker Co., Orrville, Ohio, 1969—, v.p. planning and devel., 1975-78, exec. v.p. ops., 1978—, dir., 1975—; dir. Huntington Bancshares Co. Trustee Coll. of Wooster; mem. Wayne County Republican Exec. Com.; mem. Gov. Ohio Devel. Adv. Council. Mem. Air N.G., 1968-72. Republican. Christian Scientist. Home: 2445 Wadsworth Rd Orrville OH 44667 Office: Smucker Co Strawberry Ln Orrville OH 44667

SMUCKLER, EDWARD AARON, physician, educator; b. N.Y.C., Feb. 10, 1931; s. Abraham Franklin and Agnes Lydia (Jacobson) S.; A.B., Dartmouth Coll., 1952; M.D., Tufts U., 1956; Ph.D., U. Wash., 1963; m. Judith Carole Becker, Mar. 28, 1954; children—Cynthia L., Douglas E., Alison L., Elizabeth L., Daniel J. Intern, U.S. Naval Hosp., Bethesda, Md., 1956-57; postdoctoral fellow U. Wash. Med. Sch., Seattle, 1959-61, mem. faculty, 1961-76, prof. pathology, 1969-76; prof., chmn. dept. pathology U. Calif., San Francisco, 1976—; cons. No. State Hosp., Sedro Woolley, Wash., 1961-63, VA Hosp., 1963-76; mem. pathology B study sect. NIH, 1971; nat. adv. toxicology com. FDA, 1975-78; regional med. adviser Nat. Ski Patrol System, 1972—. Served to lt. M.C., USNR, 1956-59. NSF sr. postdoctoral fellow Wennergren Inst., Stockholm, 1965-66; Guggenheim fellow Nat. Inst. Med. Research, London, 1970-71. Mem. A.C.S., AAAS, Biochem. Soc., Am. Soc. Exptl. Pathology, Am. Assn. Pathologists and Bacteriologists, Am. Assn. Cancer Research, Am. Soc. Biol. Chemistry. Home: 137 Geldert Dr Tiburon CA 94920 Office: Dept of Pathology U of Calif San Francisco CA 94143

SMUDSKI, JAMES WILLIAM, dentist, educator; b. Greensburg, Pa., Oct. 31, 1925; s. Stanley James and Clara (Lakin) S.; D.D.S., U. Pitts., 1952, B.S., 1950; M.S., U. Calif. at San Francisco, 1961, Ph.D., 1965; m. Marjorie Louise Anthony, June 4, 1949; children—David, Paul, Jeffrey. Gen. practice dentistry, Greensburg, 1952-58; mem. faculty U. Pitts. Dental Sch., 1963-76, prof., head dept. pharmacology, 1967-76, dir. grad. and postgrad. edn. Sch. Dental Medicine, 1970-72; dean Sch. Dentistry, U. Detroit, 1976—; cons. VA Hosp., Oakland, Pa., 1967-69, Leech Farm, Pa., 1967-76. Served with USNR, 1943-46. Recipient Career Devel. award NIH, 1962-64. Fellow Am., Internat. colls. dentists; mem. ADA, Am. Coll. Dentists, Internat. Assn. Dental Research, Am. Inst. Oral Biology, Am. Assn. Dental Schs., AAAS, Delta Sigma Delta, Omicron Kappa Upsilon. Club: Masons. Home: 712 Berkshire Rd Grosse Pointe Park MI 48230

SMUIN, MICHAEL, dancer, choreographer, ballet co. dir.; b. Missoula, Mont., Oct. 13, 1938; studied with Christensen Bros. and at San Francisco Ballet Sch.; m. Paula Tracy; 1 child, Shane. Dancer, U. Utah Ballet, 1955-57, San Francisco Ballet, 1957-62, 73—, now co-dir.; choreographic debut with San Francisco Ballet, 1961; worked with wife Paula Tracy as free-lance dance couple, and as choreographer, in night clubs and for TV; prin. dancer, choreographer Am. Ballet Theatre, 1969-73; has appeared on Broadway. Office: care San Francisco Ballet 378 18th Ave San Francisco CA 94121*

SMULL, NED WILLITS, physician, assn. exec.; b. St. Francis, Kans., Jan. 4, 1925; s. Charles Ward and Hollis (Harrison) S.; A.B., U. Kans., 1948, M.D., 1951; m. Lois Jane Miller, Apr. 13, 1949; 1 dau., Sarah Jane. Intern, U. Kans., Kansas City, 1951-52, resident, 1952-54; practice medicine specializing in pediatrics, Kansas City, 1954-57, 58-63; dir., prof., chmn. dept. pediatrics Children's Mercy Hosp. U. Mo., Kansas City, 1962-79; asst. dean U. Mo., Kansas City, 1970-74, vice provost for health scis., 1974-78; dir. dept. edn. Am. Acad. Pediatrics, 1979—. Trustee Barstow Sch., Kansas City, 1964—, pres., 1969-70. Served with USAAF, 1943-46. John and Mary Markle scholar, 1957. Mem. Am. Pediatric Soc., Am. Acad. Pediatrics, Phi Gamma Delta, Nu Sigma Nu. Club: Univ., River. Home: 525 Grove St Evanston IL 60201 Office: 1801 Hinman Ave PO Box 1034 Evanston IL 60204. *A constant search for the truth is a fundamental self-discipline for professional competence. Continuing higher education becomes an integral part of that search, as knowledge advances and professional fibre improves.*

SMUTNY, ROBERT JAROSLAV, educator; b. N.Y.C., Mar. 21, 1919; s. Rudolf Vojtech and Elizabeth (Meskan) S.; A.B., Coll. City N.Y., 1940; A.M., Columbia, 1949; Ph.D., U. Calif. at Berkeley, 1953; m. Ernestine Smith, Aug. 30, 1947. Instr. Latin, Manlius (N.Y.) Sch., 1942, 46-49; teaching asst. U. Calif. at Berkeley, 1951-52; asst. prof. classical langs. U. N.M., 1953-55; mem. faculty U. Pacific, 1955—, prof. classics, 1959—, chmn. dept., 1955—. Served with AUS, 1942-46. Mem. Am. Philol. Assn., Archaeol. Inst. Am., Calif. Classical Assn. (pres. no. sect. 1961-62), Philol. Assn. Pacific Coast. Author monographs. Home: 1545 W Mendocino Ave Stockton CA 95204

SMUTZ, MORTON, chem. engr.; b. Twin Falls, Idaho, Jan. 10, 1918; s. Floyd Alonzo and Evelyn (Denman) S.; B.S., Kans. State U., 1940, M.S., 1941; Ph.D., U. Wis., 1950; m. Eleanor Moran, Dec. 27, 1945 (dec. Apr. 1969); m. 2d, Harue Imamiya, May 27, 1970. Chem. engr. Monsanto Chem. Co., St. Louis, 1941; asst. prof. chmn. engring. Bucknell U., 1949-51; asst. prof., then asso. prof. chem. engring. Iowa State U., 1951-55, prof., head chem. engring. dept., 1955-61; asst. dir. Ames Lab., AEC, 1958-64, dep. dir., 1964-69; asso. dir. engring. research U. Fla., Gainesville, 1969-79, also asso. dean, dir. Coastal and Oceanographic Engring. Lab., 1975-78; project mgr. NOAA, Rockville, Md., 1979—. Served from 2d lt. to maj. AUS, 1941-45. Mem. Am. Chem. Soc., Am. Inst. Chem. Engrs., Am. Soc. Engring. Edn., Am. Nuclear Soc., Coastal Soc., Marine Tech. Soc., Am., Fla. shore and beach preservation assns., Oceanic Soc., Sigma Xi, Tau Beta Pi, Phi Kappa Phi. Home: 12000 Old Georgetown Rd Rockville MD 20852

SMYLIE, JOHN EDWIN, educator; b. Memphis, Mar. 11, 1928; s. Theodore Shaw and Mildred (Hutchinson) S.; B.A., Washington U., St. Louis, 1949; B.D., Princeton Theol. Sem., 1952, Ph.D. (grad. fellow ch. history), 1959; postgrad. Cambridge U., Eng., 1952-53; m. Cornelia Crawford Claxton, Sept. 11, 1954; children—Lydia Crawford, Jonathan Claxton, David Hutchinson. Ordained to ministry Presbyn. Ch., 1952; teaching fellow, instr., asst. prof. ch. history Princeton Theol. Sem., 1953-62; chaplain, asso. prof. religion Occidental Coll., 1962-67; pres. Queens Coll., Charlotte, 1967-74; v.p., ednl. cons. Cardinal Assos. Inc., Charlotte, 1974-77; exec. v.p. Automated Tng., Inc., Charlotte, 1977—; vis. lectr. Grad. Sch. Religion, U. So. Calif., 1964, Sch. Theology, Claremont, Calif., 1967. Treas. N.C. Assn. Ind. Colls. and Univs., 1969-70; v.p. So. Assn. Women's Colls., 1969-70, pres., 1970-71; treas. Piedmont Univ. Center, 1972-73; founder, mem. Coalition Women's Colls., Assn. Am. Colls., 1971-74. Pres. N.E. Los Angeles Human Relations Council, 1965; bd. dirs. Charlotte Social Planning Council, Charlotte United Arts Council. Mem. Am. Hist. Assn., Am. Soc. Ch. History, Am. Acad. Religion, AAUP, Charlotte C. of C. (dir.), Newcomen Soc., Phi Delta Theta. Clubs: Charlotte City, Rotary. Home: 2325 Lathrop Ln Charlotte NC 28211 Office: PO Box 34707 Charlotte NC 28234

SMYLIE, ROBERT E., lawyer; b. Marcus, Iowa, Oct. 31, 1914; s. Lorne F. and Ida Mae (Stevens) S.; A.B., Coll. Idaho, 1938, LL.D., 1955; J.D., George Washington U., 1942, LL.D., 1960; LL.D., Gonzaga U., 1966, U. Idaho, 1966; m. Lucille C. Irwin, Dec. 4, 1943; children—Robert William, Richard. Admitted to D.C. bar, 1942, Idaho bar, 1947; practiced in Boise, 1947—; asst. atty. gen. Idaho, 1947, atty. gen., 1947-54; gov. Idaho, 1954-67; sr. partner firm Langroise, Sullivan & Smylie, Boise, 1967-79. Chmn., Republican Gov.'s Assn., 1963-67. Chmn. trustees Coll. Idaho. Mem. drafting commn. Council of State Govts., 1949-50. Served as lt. USCGR, 1942-46. Mem. Am. Legion, VFW, Order of Coif, Phi Alpha Delta. Lectr. Contbr. articles to profl. jours. Home: 117 Locust St Boise ID 83702 Office: 1400 Idaho First Plaza Boise ID 83702

SMYLY, SUSAN VANDERBILT, sculptor; b. Detroit, Oct. 16, 1940; B.F.A., Memphis Acad. Arts, 1963; M.F.A., Cranbrook Acad. Art, 1965. Exhibited in one-artist shows at Forum Gallery, 1977, Mus. Fine Arts, Springfield, Mass., 1978; exhibited in group shows throughout U.S. and Rome; adj. prof. sculpture and drawing Queens Coll., N.Y.C. Recipient Art award Am. Acad. and Inst. Arts and Letters, 1977; Prix de Rome, Am. Acad. in Rome, 1966, 67; Fulbright fellow to Rome, 1966. Office: care Forum Gallery 1018 Madison Ave New York City NY 10021

SMYSER, ADAM ALBERT, newspaper editor; b. York, Pa., Dec. 18, 1920; s. Adam Milton and Miriam (Stein) S.; B.A., Pa. State U., 1941; m. Elizabeth Harrison Avery, Dec. 25, 1943; children—Heidi, Avery. Rewrite man Pitts. Press, 1941-42; with Honolulu Star-Bull., 1946—, city editor, 1953-60, mng. editor, 1960-65, editor, 1966-75, editor editorial page, 1975—; mem. Pulitzer Journalism Awards Jury, 1970. Chmn. temporary commn. on statewide environ. planning, 1973; bd. dirs. Aloha United Fund, Friends of East-West Center, Oahu Cancer Soc., Found. for Study in Hawaii and Abroad, Aloha Week Hawaii, Nat. Council Crime and Delinquency, Goodwill Industries. Served as lt. USNR, 1942-46; PTO. Recipient Distinguished Alumnus award Pa. State U., 1976. Mem. Hawaii C. of C. (dir.), UN Assn. U.S.A., ACLU, Honolulu Acad. Arts, Am. Soc. Newspaper Editors, Sigma Delta Chi, Honolulu Press Club. Former free lance writer Bus. Week, McGraw-Hill mags. Home: 700 Richards St Honolulu HI 96813 Office: 605 Kapiolani Blvd Honolulu HI 96813

SMYTH, BERNARD JOHN, newspaper editor; b. Renovo, Pa., Nov. 16, 1915; s. John Bernard and Alice C. (Russell) S.; grad. Dickinson Jr. Coll., Pa., 1935; m. Eva Mae Stone, Dec. 31, 1936; children—Constance, Joe, Pamela, Lisa. Machinist helper Pa. R.R. Renovo shops, 1936-39; mgr. Smyth Bros., retail jewelry store, 1939-45; editor, pub., owner Renovo Daily Record, 1946-53; owner, editor, pub. Delaware State News, Dover, 1953-70; chmn. bd. Independent Newspapers, Inc., 1970—; pres. Valley Newspapers, Inc., Tempe, Ariz., 1971—. Served with AUS, 1944-45. Mem. Ariz. Newspaper Assn., Sigma Delta Chi. Home: 6149 E Indian Bend Rd Paradise Valley AZ 85253 Office: 2210 W Desert Cove Phoenix AZ 85029

SMYTH, CHARLES EDWARD, ednl. publisher; b. Milton, Mass., July 23, 1931; s. Ralston Blackburn and Eleanor Rogers (Greene) S.; B.A., Ohio Wesleyan U., 1953; M.Ed., Miami U., Oxford, Ohio, 1957; m. Patricia Ann Rhodes, July 4, 1953; children—Cynthia, William, Scott, Judith. Pub. sch. prin. Spring Valley (Ohio) Schs., 1955-57; guidance dir. Upper Arlington (Ohio) City Schs., 1957-60; staff asso. sci. Research Assos., Ohio, Mich., 1960-62; rep. Learning Materials Inc., Chgo., 1961-63; dir. devel. services Ency. Brit., Chgo., 1963-65; v.p. edn. div. Random House, Inc., N.Y.C., 1965-76; v.p. Baker & Taylor, 1976-77; exec. v.p. Macdonald/Raintree, Inc., pubs., Milw., 1977—; instr. Ohio State Guidance Inst., Columbus, Ohio, 1959—. Chmn. Citizens Com. Quality Edn., White Plains, N.Y., 1972—; mem. Com. Sch. Enrollment, White Plains, 1972-74. Served with USAF, 1953-55. Mem. Am. Assn. Publishers (chmn. research com. 1973—, mem. Great Cities Com. 1973-74), Phi Delta Kappa. Home: 2012 N Menomonee River Pkwy Wauwatosa WI 53226 Office: 205 W Highland Ave Milwaukee WI 53203

SMYTH, CRAIG HUGH, educator; b. N.Y.C., July 28, 1915; s. George Hugh and Lucy Salome (Humeston) S.; B.A., Princeton, 1938, M.F.A., 1941, Ph.D., 1956; M.A. (hon.), Harvard, 1975; m. Barbara Linforth, June 24, 1941; children—Alexandra, Edward Linforth. Research asst. Nat. Gallery Art, Washington, 1941-42; officer-in-charge, dir. Central Art Collecting Point, Munich, Germany, 1945-46; lectr. Frick Collection, N.Y.C., 1946-50; asst. prof. Inst. Fine Arts, N.Y. U., 1950-53, asso. prof., 1953-57, prof., 1957-73, acting dir. Inst., acting head dept. fine arts Grad. Sch. Arts and Scis., 1951-53, dir. Inst., head dept. fine arts Grad. Sch., 1953-73; prof. fine arts Harvard, 1973—, dir. Villa I Tatti, Harvard Center Italian Renaissance Studies, Florence, Italy, 1973—. Art historian Am. Acad. in Rome, 1959-60; mem. U.S. Nat. Com. History Art, 1955—; alt. U.S. mem. Comité Internat. d'Historie de l'Art, 1970—; vis. scholar Inst. for Advanced Study, Princeton, N.J., 1971, mem., 1978; vis. scholar Bibliotheca Hertziana, Max Planck Soc., Rome, 1972, 73; mem. vis. com. dept. art and archaeology Princeton, 1956-73. Hon. trustee Met. Mus. Art, N.Y.C., 1968—. Served from ensign to lt. USNR, 1942-46. Decorated Legion of Honor (France). Sr. Fulbright research fellow, 1949-50. Fellow Am. Acad. Arts and Scis.; mem. Accademia Fiorentina della Arti del Disegno (academician), Coll. Art Assn. Am. (dir. 1953-57, sec. 1956), Am. Philos. Soc., Phi Beta Kappa. Club: Circolo Unione Firenze (asso.). Author: Mannerism and Maniera, 1963; Bronzino as Draughtsman, 1971. Editorial adv. bd. Master Drawings. Address: Villa I Tatti Via di Vincigliata Florence Italy

SMYTH, GLEN MILLER, banker; b. Abingdon, Va., July 26, 1929; s. Glen Miller and Kathleen (Dunn) S.; B.A., Yale, 1951; M.S. in Psychology, Rutgers U., 1958; m. Lilian Castel Edgar, Oct. 31, 1968; children—Catherine Ellen, Glen Miller III, Cynthia Allison, Stephanie Castel, Kimberley Forsyth, Lindsay Dunn. Mktg. rep. Wheeling Stamping Co., N.Y.C., 1953-56; personnel dir. Celanese Internat., N.Y.C., 1958-71; mgr. orgn. and Manpower Internat. and Can. group Gen. Electric Co., 1971-73; sr. v.p. human resources Northwest Bancorp., Mpls., 1973—; leader seminars. Chmn. nat. fgn. trade council Internat. Orgn. & Mgmt. Devel. Com., 1972—. Served with AUS, 1951-53. Mem. Am. Bankers Assn. (chmn. internat. personnel com., mem. adminstrv. and exec. coms.), Am. Psychol. Assn., Phi Gamma Delta. Clubs: Yale (N.Y.C.); Wayzata Country. Co-author: International Career Pathing, 1971. Contbr. articles to profl. jours. Home: 1465 Fox St Wayzata MN 55391 Office: 1200 NW Bank Bldg Minneapolis MN 55480

SMYTH, JOEL DOUGLAS, editor; b. Renovo, Pa., Nov. 8, 1941; s. Bernard John and Eva Mae (Stone) S.; student Lycoming Coll., 1959; m. Madonna Robertson, Nov. 29, 1959; children—Deborah Sue, Susan Kelly, Michael Robertson, Patricia Ann, Rebecca Lee, Jennifer Neilia. Reporter, Del. State News, Dover, 1960-62, news editor, 1962-65, mng. editor, 1965-70, editor, pres., 1970-78; editor Del. Sunday News, 1964-65; pres. Ind. Newspapers, Inc., Dover, 1970—; dir. Bowie (Md.) Blade, Inc., Valley Newspapers, Inc. (Ariz.), Sunshine Newspapers, Inc. (Fla.), Crisfield Times, Inc. (Md.). Recipient writing awards. Mem. AP Mng. Editors Assn. (dir.), Am. Soc. Newspaper Editors, Young Pres.'s Orgn., Sigma Delta Chi. Home: 4308 E Lakeside Ln Scottsdale AZ 85253 Office: PO Box 7001 Dover DE 19901

SMYTH, JOSEPH VINCENT, mfg. co. exec.; b. Belfast, Ireland, July 18, 1919; s. Joseph Leo and Margaret M. (Murray) S.; B.S. cum laude, U. Notre Dame, 1941; m. Marie E. Cripe, Mar. 22, 1941; children—Kevin W., Brian J., Ellen M., Vincent P. With Arnolt Corp., Warsaw, Ind., 1946-63, exec. v.p., gen. mgr., until 1963; pres., gen. mgr. Hills-McCanna Co., Carpentersville, Ill., 1963-72; pres., gen. mgr. Lunkenheimer Co., Cin., 1972-79; v.p. Condec Flow Control Group, Chgo., 1979—. Clubs: Kenwood Country, Queen City (Cin.); K.C. Office: 875 N Michigan Ave Chicago IL

SMYTH, REGINALD (REGGIE SMYTHE), cartoonist; b. Hartlepool, Eng., Oct. 7, 1917; s. Richard Oliver and Florence (Ritson) S.; student Galleys Field Sch., 1922-31; m. Vera Toyne, Aug. 13, 1949. With Brit. Civil Service, 1945-54; cartoonist, 1955—; creator Andy Capp daily comic strip, 1956. Served with Brit. Army, 1936-45. Recipient Best Brit. Cartoon award, 1961-65; Premio Cartoon award, Lucca, 1969; Best Cartoonist award, Genoa, 1973; Best Strip Cartoonist award Am. Cartoonists Soc., 1974. Mem. Nat. Cartoonists Soc. Mem. Ch. of Eng. Address: Whitegates Caledonian Rd Hartlepool Cleveland England

SMYTHE, CHEVES MCCORD, physician, univ. adminstr.; b. Charleston, S.C., May 25, 1924; s. Augustine Thomas and Harriott Ravenel (Buist) S.; student Yale U., 1942-43; M.D. cum laude, Harvard U., 1947; m. Isabella Carr Leighton, Aug. 12, 1949; children—Alexander Cheves, James Leighton, Augustine Thomas, Daniel Thompson, St. Julien Ravenel. Intern, Boston City Hosp., 1947-48; resident Boston City Hosp., also Bellevue and Presbyn. hosps., N.Y.C., 1948-55; instr. Med. Coll. S.C., 1955-62, dean Med. Sch., 1962-64; asso. dir. Assn. Am. Med. Colls., Evanston, Ill.,

1966-70; organizer U. Tex. Med. Sch., Houston, 1970—, also sec. liaison com. on med. edn. Mem. Mgmt. Advancement Steering Com., 1973, also prof.; vice chmn. bd. Houston Acad. Medicine-Tex. Med. Center Library; dir. Nat. Library of Medicine, Med. Edn. Network; cons. Served to comdr., M.C., USNR, 1951-54. Recipient Yale Club prize for outstanding scholastic achievement, 1943; research fellow A.C.P., Life Ins. Research Fund; fellow Markle Found. Mem. Assn. Am. Med. Colls. Episcopalian. Contbr. articles to profl. jours. Home: 219 Stoney Creek Houston TX 77030 Office: 6431 Fannin St Houston TX 77025

SMYTHE, MABEL MURPHY, ambassador; b. Montgomery, Ala., Apr. 3, 1918; B.A., Mt. Holyoke Coll., 1937, L.H.D., 1977; M.A., Northwestern U., 1940; Ph.D., U. Wis., 1942; L.H.D., U. Mass., 1979; m. Hugh H. Smythe, July 26, 1939 (dec. 1977); 1 dau., Karen Pamela. Asst. prof. Lincoln U., 1942-45; prof. Tenn. A. and I. U., 1945-46, Bklyn. Coll., 1946-47; instr. Shiga U., Japan, 1951-53; dep. dir. research NAACP Legal Def. and Edn. Fund, 1953; high sch. tchr. and prin., 1954-69; with Phelps-Stokes Fund, 1970-77, dir. research and publs., 1970-72, v.p., 1972-77; U.S. ambassador to United Republic of Cameroon, Yaounde, 1977—; scholar-in-residence U.S. Commn. on Civil Rights, 1973-74; co-dir. African seminar for pres.'s black colls., 1971; mem. Adv. Com. on Ednl. Exchange, 1961-62, Internat. Ednl. and Cultural Affairs, 1962-65; trustee Conn. Coll., 1964-65, 68-77; trustee Mt. Holyoke Coll., 1971-76, vice chmn., 1976; trustee Hampshire Coll., 1971-77, vice chmn., 1975-77; bd. dirs. Nat. Corp. for Housing Partnerships, 1972-77; mem. Dept. State adv. council on African affairs, 1962-69; U.S. del. 13th gen. conf. UNESCO, Paris, 1964; mem. U.S. Nat. Com. for UNESCO, 1965-70. Decorated Grand Dama d'Inore, Order of Royal Crown of Crete (Malta). Mem. Nat. Assn. Black Profl. Women in Higher Edn. (dir. 1975-76), Council Fgn. Relations, Caucus Black Economists, Nat. Council Women U.S. Author: A Slaver's Log Book or 20 Years Residence in Africa, 1976; co-author: The New Nigerian Elite, 3d edit., 1971; Intensive English Conversation, 1954; editor: The Black American Reference Book, 1976; co-editor: Curriculum for Understanding, 1965; contbr. articles to profl. jours. Office: Am Embassy Rue Nachtigal Boite Postale 817 Yaounde Cameroon also Am Embassy Yaounde care Dept State Washington DC 20520

SMYTHE, WILLIAM RODMAN, educator, physicist; b. Los Angeles, Jan. 6, 1930; s. William Ralph and Helen (Keith) S.; B.S., Calif. Inst. Tech., 1951, M.S., 1952, Ph.D., 1957; m. Carol Richardson, Nov. 27, 1954; children—Stephanie, Deborah, William Richardson, Reed Terry. Engr., Gen. Electric Microwave Lab., Palo Alto, Calif., 1956-57; asst. prof. U. Colo., 1958-63, asso. prof., 1963-67, prof., 1967—, chmn. nuclear physics lab., 1967-69. Group leader Rocky Mountain Rescue Group, 1967-68. Mem. Am. Phys. Soc., Am. Assn. Physicists in Medicine. Club: Colo Mountain (Boulder). Inventor negative ion cyclotron, fractional turn cyclotron. Home: 3275 Dover Dr Boulder CO 80303

SMYTHIES, JOHN RAYMOND, physician; b. Naini Tal, India, Nov. 30, 1922; s. Evelyn Arthur and Olive Muriel (Cripps) S.; came to U.S., 1973; M.A., U. Cambridge, 1942, M.D., 1955, M.Sc., 1958, M.B. B. Chir., 1945; M.Sc., U. B.C., 1955; D.P.M., U. London, 1952; postgrad. Worcester (Mass.) Found., 1958-59, U. Cambridge, 1955-57, U. B.C., 1953-55; m. Vanna Maria Grazia Gattorno, Dec. 2, 1950; children—Adrian Greville, Christopher John Evelyn. Sr. resident Maudsley Hosp., London, 1959-61; reader psychiatry U. Edinburgh (Scotland), 1961-73; C.B. Ireland prof. psychiat. research and biochemistry U. Ala. Med. Center, Birmingham, 1973—; cons. WHO, 1963-68. Served with Royal Navy, 1946-48. Nuffield fellow, 1955-57. Fellow Royal Coll. Physicians (London), Royal Coll. Psychiatrists, Am. Psychiat. Assn., Royal Soc. Medicine; mem. Am. Coll. Neuropharmacology, Internat. Soc. Psychoneuroendocrinology (pres. 1971-74), Internat. Brain Research Orgn., Collegium Internationale Neuropsychopharmacologium, Am. Soc. Pharmacology, Soc. Biol. Psychiatry. Episcopalian. Club: Athenaeum (London). Author: Biological Psychiatry, 1968; Brain Mechanisms and Behavior, 1973; (with Arthur Koestler) Beyond Reductionism, 1969; others; editor Internat. Rev. Neurobiology, 1958—; contbr. articles to profl. jours.; patentee in field. Home: 4245 Stone River Rd Birmingham AL 35213 Office: Neuroscience Program U Ala Med Center Birmingham AL 35294

SNADDON, ANDREW WILLIAM, editor; b. Winnipeg, Man., Can., Apr. 28, 1921; s. William James and Christina (Scobie) S.; B.A. in Econs., U. B.C. (Can.), 1943; m. Jocelyn Winifred Sara, Mar. 20, 1948; children—Sara Jane, Elizabeth Andrea. Polit. reporter Calgary (Alta., Can.) Herald, 1945-51, editorial writer, 1954-56, city editor, 1956-57, asso. editor, 1957-62; with Southam News Services, London, 1951-53, Ottawa, Ont., Can., 1953-54; mng. editor The Edmonton (Alta., Can.), Jour., 1962-67, editor, 1967—. Served as sub lt. Royal Can. Navy, 1943-45. Mem. Am. Soc. Newspaper Editors, Alta. Press Council. Home: 11715-91 Ave Edmonton AB T5J 2S6 Canada Office: The Edmonton Jour 101 St and 100 Ave Edmonton AB Canada

SNAKARD, ROBERT F., lawyer; b. Bradford, Pa., Aug. 19, 1910; s. Frank A. and Mary Ellen (Gallagher) S.; student Georgetown U.; LL.B., U. Tex., 1934; m. Mary Lou Hicks, Oct. 19, 1940; children—Charles R., Laura Ellen. Admitted to Tex. bar, 1934; now partner firm Law, Snakard, Brown & Gambill, Fort Worth. Dir. emeritus Tex. Am. Bancshares, Fort Worth Nat. Bank. Past pres. area council Cath. Charities, Fort Worth, Fort Worth Council of Chs., Family Service Assn., Fort Worth; v.p. Ft. Worth council Camp Fire Girls; v.p. bd. govs. Trinity Terr.; Catholic co-chmn. Ft. Worth chpt. NCCJ; trustee St. Joseph Hosp., Fort Worth. Served to maj. USAAF, 1942-46. Fellow Am. Coll. Probate Counsel, Tex. Bar Found.; mem. Fort Worth C. of C. (dir.), Fort Worth Zool. Assn. (v.p.), Am., Fort Worth-Tarrant County (pres. 1954-55) bar assns., State Bar Tex., Am. Judicature Soc., Newcomen Soc. N.Am. Clubs: Serra Internat., Fort Worth (past gov.), Century II (Fort Worth); Shady Oaks Country. Office: Fort Worth Nat Bank Bldg Fort Worth TX 76102

SNAPP, ROY BAKER, lawyer; b. Strang, Okla., May 9, 1916; s. Harry Moore and Verda Mildred (Austin) S.; B.S. in Pub. Adminstrn., U. Mo., 1936; LL.B., Georgetown U., 1941, LL.M., 1942; m. Dorothy Faye Loftis, Jan. 27, 1942; children—Deborah, Bryan Austin, Martha Lynn, Barbara, James. Lawyer with U.S. State Dept., 1941; spl. adviser comdg. gen. Manhattan (Atomic Bomb) Project, 1946; dir. internat. affairs U.S. AEC, 1947, 48-54, sec., 1948-53, asst. to chmn., 1954-55; v.p. atomic div. Am. Machine & Foundry, 1957; v.p. Am. Machine & Foundry Co., Washington office, 1961; dir. Electro-Nucleonics, Inc. Commd. ensign USNR, 1942, assigned secretariat of U.S. Joint Chiefs of Staff and Combined (U.S.-Brit.) Chiefs of Staff; sec., 1943-44, naval mem., 1945, Intelligence Staff of Joint Chiefs Staff and Combined Chiefs Staff; promoted to lt. comdr., 1945. Recipient D.S.M., AEC, 1955. Mem. SCV, NAM (chmn. atomic energy com. 1963-64), Phi Gamma Mu, Delta Theta Phi. Baptist. Clubs: Univ., Columbia Country (Washington). Home: 3518 Raymoor Rd Kensington MD 20795 Office: Suite 300 1747 Pennsylvania Ave NW Washington DC 20006

SNAPPER, ERNST, educator; b. Holland, Dec. 2, 1913; s. Isidore and Henrietta (Van Buuren) S.; M. A., Princeton, 1939, Ph.D., 1941; m. Ethel Lillian Klein, June 1941; children—John William, James Robert. Came to U.S., 1938, naturalized, 1942. Instr., Princeton, 1941-45, vis. asso. prof., 1949-50, vis. prof., 1954-55; asst. prof. U. So. Calif., 1945-48, asso. prof., 1948-53, prof., 1953-55; NSF post-doctoral fellow Harvard, 1953-54; Andrew Jackson Buckingham prof. math. Miami U., Oxford, Ohio, 1955-58; prof. math. Ind. U., 1958-63, Dartmouth, 1963—, Benjamin Pierce Cheney prof. math., 1971—. Mem. Am. Math. Soc., Can. Congress Math., Math. Assn. Am. (pres. Ind. sect. 1962-63), AAUP, AAAS, Société Mathématique De France, Circolo Mathematico Di Palermo, Assn. Princeton Grad. Alumni (governing bd.), Phi Beta Kappa (hon.), Sigma Xi. Home: PO Box 67 Norwich VT 05055

SNAVELY, BRANT RITTENHOUSE, found. exec.; b. Meadville, Pa., June 23, 1908; s. Guy Everett and Ada (Rittenhouse) S.; A.B., Birmingham So. Coll., 1928; postgrad. Columbia U., 1928-31; Sc.D., Catawba Coll., 1977; m. Dorothy Gilliam, Dec. 18, 1931; 1 son, Brant Rittenhouse. So. rep. John Wiley & Sons, pubs., 1931-32; Southeastern rep. Am. Book Co., 1933-40, dir., mem. exec. com., 1958-67; asso. to pres. Salem Coll., Winston-Salem, N.C., 1940-42; sr. v.p. Wachovia Bank & Trust Co., Winston-Salem, 1947-70; exec. dir. N.C. Found. of Ch. Related Colls., 1970-74; pres. Ind. Coll. Fund N.C., 1975—; dir. Key Co.; pres., dir. SPM Corp. Pres., United Fund Forsyth County, 1957, Winston-Salem Gallery Fine Arts, 1956-57; chmn. High Point Library Bd., 1949-51; mem. nat. council USO; bd. dirs., pres. Citizens Planning Council of Forsyth County, 1966-68; bd. dirs. Boys' Club Am., 1965-78, N.C. Sch. of Arts Found., 1971-73, N.C. Indsl. Devel. Found., 1961-66, Mt. Vernon Coll., 1974—; pres. bd. trustees Va. Episcopal Sch., 1970-73; trustee N.C. Outward Bound Sch. Served from lt. to lt. comdr. USNR, 1942-45. Mem. High Point C. of C. (pres. 1950-51), Robert Morris Assos. (past pres. Carolina-Virginias), Sigma Alpha Epsilon, Omicron Delta Kappa, Alpha Kappa Psi. Epscopalian. Club: Old Town. Home: 2501 Woodbine Rd Winston-Salem NC 27104

SNAVELY, TIPTON RAY, economist; b. Jonesville, Va., Nov. 23, 1890; s. William and Jennie (Graham) S.; B.A., Emory and Henry Coll., 1912, LL.D., 1948; M.A., U. Va., 1915, Ph.D., 1919; M.A., Harvard U., 1918; m. Nell Aldred, Aug. 16, 1916 (dec.); 1 son, William Pennington. Prin. high sch., Scott County, Va., 1912-14; spl. investigator U.S. Bur. Labor, 1917; faculty U. Va., 1918-61, prof. econs., 1924-61, prof. emeritus, 1961—, chmn. dept., 1923-56; tchr. econs. U. Tex. Summer Sch., 1924, U. So. Calif., summer 1928; lectr. U. So. Calif. Inst. Pub. Adminstrn., 1928; tchr. summer sessions Harvard U., 1930, 32; econ. adviser to com. on taxation Va. State C. of C., 1925-35; mem. Va. State Milk Commn., 1934-39, 42-49, chmn., 1937-39, 42-49; dir. Citizens Bank & Trust Co., Charlottesville; mem. legis. com. on pub. schs. Va., 1947-48, com. on revenues and expenditures in Va., 1948-50; mem. industry com. shoe mfg., wage and hour div. U.S. Dept. Labor, 1939, also coms. for leather industry, 1939, luggage industry, 1940, com. for converted paper products industry, 1940, several other coms., in 1941-43; spl. investigator Tenn. State Planning Commn., 1936; chmn. Ann. Assay Commn. U.S. Mint, 1940; occupational cons. U.S. Bur. Labor Statistics, 1940-44; mem. 4th regional labor supply com. WPB, 1941-42; econ. cons. U.S. Bd. Investigation and Research in Transp., 1943-44; chmn. Legis. Comm. to study sales and use tax in Va., 1944-45; mem. P.R. Spl. Industry Com. of Wage and Hour Div., 1945. Mem. Internat. Inst. Pub. Fin., Nat. Tax Assn., So. Econ. Assn. (pres. 1931-32), Royal Econ. Soc. Eng., Phi Beta Kappa, Beta Gamma Sigma (grand pres. 1936-39), Alpha Kappa Psi (grand counselor 1923-31). Methodist. Author: The Taxation of Negroes in Virginia, 1917; Conflict Between State Control and Local Self-Government, 1925; Public Utilities (Ency. of Bus.), 1933; (with others) State Grants-in-Aid in Virginia, 1933; A Study of the Fiscal System of Tennessee, 1936; (with others) Report of the Sales and Use Tax Commission in Virginia, 1945; George Tucker as Political Economist, 1964; The Department of Economics at the University of Virginia, 1825-1956, 1967; also articles in field. Home: 1421 Gentry Ln Charlottesville VA 22903

SNAVELY, WILLIAM PENNINGTON, educator; b. Charlottesville, Va., Jan. 25, 1920; s. Tipton Ray and Nell (Aldred) S.; student Hampden-Sydney Coll., 1936-37; B.A. with honors, U. Va., 1940, M.A., 1941, Ph.D., 1950; postgrad. (Bennett Wood Green fellow) Harvard, 1946-47; m. Alice Watts Pritchett, June 4, 1942; children—Nell Lee, William Pennington, Elizabeth Tipton. Mem. faculty U. Conn., 1947-73, prof. econs., 1961-73, chmn. dept., 1966-72, economist econ. edn. workshop, summers 1954, 55, 56; prof. econs., chmn. dept George Mason U., 1973—; cons. Ford Found., Jordan Devel. Bd., Amman, 1961-62, 64-65, Lebanese Ministry Planning, Beirut, 1964-65, Saudi Arabian Central Planning Orgn., Riyadh, 1964-65, Am. U. Beirut, 1969-70, Bahrain Ministry Finance and Nat. Economy, 1974, 75, 76; cons. U.N., Jordan Nat. Planning Council, Amman, 1972; mem. Danforth Workshop, summer 1966; mem. adv. com. Willimantic Trust Co. (Conn.), 1968-73. Served to capt. AUS, 1942-46. Fellow Fund Advancement Edn., Harvard, 1951-52; faculty-bus. exchange fellow Chase Nat. Bank, N.Y.C., summer 1952; fellow Merrill Center Econs., summer 1957; Fulbright research fellow, Rome, 1958-59. Mem. Am., Atlantic, So. econ. assns., Am. Fin. Assn., Assn. Comparative Econs., Contemporary Econs. and Bus. Assn. (pres. 1976—), Va. Assn. Economists (pres. 1979-80), Phi Beta Kappa, Phi Kappa Phi. Author: (with W.H. Carter) Intermediate Economic Analysis, 1961; Theory of Economic Systems, 1969; (with M.T. Sadik) Bahrain, Qatar and the United Arab Emirates, 1972; contbr. articles to jours., Ency. Americana. Home: 10807 Norman Ave Fairfax VA 22030

SNAVELY-DIXON, MARY MARGARET, govt. ofcl.; b. Los Angeles, Sept. 28, 1944; d. William Wayne and Rosewitha (Berger) S.; B.A. in English and Math., Immaculate Heart Coll., 1966; M.S. in Adminstrn. and Mgmt. Sci./Ops., George Washington U., 1974. Asst. team dir. indsl./mgmt. engring team U.S. Navy, Washington, 1967-72, program mgr. mgmt. engring. program, 1972-75, dep. asst. sec. Navy for manpower, 1977—; sr. ops. research analyst Office Sec. Def., Washington, 1975-77. Named An Outstanding Young Woman of Am., 1978. Mem. Ops. Research Soc. Am., Nat. Assn. Female Execs. Roman Catholic. Home: 3206 S Stafford St Arlington VA 22206 Office: Office of Sec of Navy Pentagon Washington DC 20350

SNEAD, GEORGE MURRELL, JR., scientist, army officer; b. San Diego, Nov. 6, 1922; s. George Murrell and Helen (Olsen) S.; B.S., Va. Mil. Inst., 1943; M.S., U. Ill., 1948; Ph.D., U. Va., 1953; m. Kathleen Hill Dawson, Apr. 26, 1947; children—George Murrell III, James M., William M., John P., Edward W. Commd. 2d lt. U.S. Army, 1943, advanced through grades to brig. gen., 1969; Aleutian Sector comdr. Alaska Communication System, 1948-50; sta. at Electronic Warfare Center, Ft. Monmouth, N.J. and Ft. Huachuca, Ariz., 1953-56; student U.S. Army Command and Gen. Staff Coll., 1956-57; signal adviser MAAG, Vietnam, 1957-58; asst. exec. Office Chief Signal Officer, Dept. Army, 1958-60, Advanced Research Projects Agy., 1960; with U.S. Army Satellite Communications Agy., Ft. Monmouth, 1960-63; student Nat. War Coll., 1963-64; div. signal officer 24th Inf. Div., 1964-65; comdg. officer 7th Signal Group, 1965; dir. Communication /ADP Lab., Ft. Monmouth, 1966-68; exec. asst. chief of staff Communications Electronics, Dept. Army, 1968; dir. army research Dept. Army, Washington, 1968-71; dep. commdr., Army Strategic Communications Commd., 1971-73; prin. scientist Gen. Research Corp., McLean, Va., 1973—. Active local Boy Scouts Am., 1958-68. Bd. dirs. Central Youth Summer Activities, Ft. Monmouth, 1960-63. Decorated Legion of Merit with oak leaf cluster, D.S.M., Army Commendation medal with 4 oak leaf clusters. Mem. Assn. U.S. Army, Armed Forces Communications Electronics Assn. (sec. Washington chpt. 1968-69), Sigma Xi, Kappa Alpha. Home: PO Box 3306 Lynchburg VA 24503 Office: Westgate Research Park McLean VA 22101

SNEAD, JESSE CARLYLE, profl. golfer; b. Hot Springs, Va., Oct. 14, 1940; s. Jesse James and Silvia Lucile (Schooler) S.; m. Susan Ramsey Bryant, Apr. 12, 1969; 1 son, Jason Carlyle. Mem. Washington Senators Profl. Baseball Orgn., 1960-64; asst. golf profl. Century Country Club, Purchase, N.Y., 1964-68; tournament player Profl. Golfers Assn., 1968—. Winner golf tournaments: Andy Williams San Diego Open, 1975, 76, Kaiser Internat. Open, 1976, I.V.B. Golf Classic, 1972, Tucson Open, 1971, Dorsal Eastern Open, 1971, Australian Open, 1973. Methodist. Club: Moose. Address: PO Box 1152 Ponte Vedra Beach FL 32082

SNEAD, SAMUEL JACKSON, golfer; b. Hot Springs, Va., May 27, 1912; m. Audrey; children—Samuel Jackson, Terrance. Profl. golfer, 1935—; winner Profl. Golfers' Assn. Championship, 1942, 49, 51, Brit. Open, 1946, Masters Golf Tournament, 1949, 52, 54. Served with USNR, 1942-45. Recipient Vardon trophy Profl. Golfers' Assn., 1938, 49, 50, 55, Player of Year award, 1949, elected to Hall of Fame, 1963. Author: How to Hit a Golf Ball, 1940; How to Play Golf, 1946; (with Al Stump) Education of a Golfer, 1962; The Driver, 1974; Golf Begins at Forty, 1978. Office: care Uni-Managers Internat 10880 Wilshire Blvd Los Angeles CA 90024

SNEATH, WILLIAM SCOTT, mfg. co. exec.; b. Buffalo, Mar. 29, 1926; s. William Henry and Cyrena (Kean) S.; B.A., Williams Coll., 1947; M.B.A., Harvard U., 1950. With Union Carbide Corp., 1950—, pres., 1971-77, chmn. bd., chief exec. officer, 1977—, dir., 1969—. Office: 270 Park Ave New York NY 10017

SNEDAKER, ROBERT HUME, JR., telephone co. exec.; b. N.Y.C., Feb. 13, 1926; s. Robert Hume and Mary Virginia (Fulton) S.; B.S., Dartmouth, 1947, M.E.E., M.E., B.A., 1949; m. Marlene A. Wessel, Nov. 23, 1969; children—Debra L., Robert Hume III, Cynthia C., James W. With N.Y. Telephone Co., 1949-61, A T & T, 1962-64; v.p., gen. mgr. S.W. area Ohio Bell Telephone Co., 1964-71; pres. United Telephone Co. Ohio, Mansfield, 1971-79; exec. v.p. telephone ops. United Telecommunications, Inc., Shawnee Mission, Kans., 1979—. Served with USNR, 1944-46. Registered profl. engr., Ohio. Mem. Phi Beta Kappa, Tau Beta Pi, Phi Kappa Psi. Congregationalist. Club: The Golf (New Albany, Ohio). Home: 4601 W 87 St Shawnee Mission KS 66207 Office: 2330 Johnson Dr Shawnee Mission KS 66205

SNEDDEN, CHARLES WILLIS, newspaper pub.; b. Spokane, Wash., July 20, 1913; s. William Angus and Christine Ann (McLachlan) S.; student Oreg. State Coll., U. Oreg., Wash. State Coll., 1930-33; LL.D., U. Alaska, 1967; m. Helen Elizabeth McNeel, Apr. 11, 1934; 1 son, Duane McLachian. Linotype machinist Columbian and Mergenthaler Linotype Co., 1933-41; pres. CWS Grinding & Machine Works, 1935-44; supr. machinist div. Kaiser Shipyard, 1942-44; propr. Marshal-Wells retail hardware, 1943-49 (all Vancouver, Wash.); ind. newspaper prodn. cons., 1945-50; pub. Fairbanks (Alaska) Daily News-Miner, 1950—, also pres.; pres. Aurora Bldg., Inc., Comml. Printing Co., Inc., Fairbanks Pub. Co., Inc.; dir. Fairbanks Econ. Devel. Corp., Wien Alaska Airlines. Mem. Fairbanks Municipal Utilities Bd., 1951-54, Alaska Employment Security Com., 1954-57, nat. council Nat. Planning Assn., 1959-65. Pres. Fairbanks United Good Neighbors; pres., mem. adv. bd. St. Josephs Hosp.; bd. govs. No. Devel. Adv. Com. Recipient Fairbanks George Nehrbas award, 1962; City of Fairbanks award, 1961; named Boss of Year, Jr. C. of C., 1956. Mem. Fairbanks (past dir.), Alaska (dir., past pres.) chambers commerce, Pacific N.W. Trade Assn. (v.p.), Inland Empire Waterways Assn. Republican. Conglist. Mason (Shriner), Elk, Rotarian. Office: Fairbanks Publishing Co 200 N Cushman St Fairbanks AK 99701*

SNEDDEN, JAMES DOUGLAS, hosp. adminstr.; b. Toronto, Ont., Can., Mar. 4, 1925; s. David Morrison and Sarah Hayton (Monteith) S.; B.Comm., U. Toronto, 1948; C.A., Inst. Chartered Accts. Ont., 1951; m. Elizabeth Ann McCauley, Dec. 20, 1973. With Hosp. for Sick Children, Toronto, 1952—, asst. dir., 1961-67, adminstr., 1967-70, exec. dir., 1970—; dir. Hosp. Computing Services Ont.; bd. dirs. Hosp. Council Met. Toronto. Hon. dir. Woodgreen Community Centre, Toronto, 1963-65, v.p., 1965-67, pres. 1967-69, hon. mem. bd. dirs., 1973—; mem. Bd. Trade Met. Toronto, 1965—. Served with RCAF, 1943-45. Decorated Can. Centennial medal. Fellow Inst. Chartered Accts. Ont.; mem. Am. Coll. Hosp. Adminstrs., Can. Coll. Health Service Execs., Am. Mgmt. Assn. Presbyterian. Club: Univ. of Toronto, Bd. of Trade. Office: 555 University Ave Toronto ON M5G 1X8 Canada

SNEDEKER, JOHN HAGGNER, univ. pres.; b. Plainfield, N.J., May 30, 1925; s. Alfred H. and Anna Marie (Ward) S.; B.S. cum laude, N.Y. U., 1951, M.A., 1951; Ed.D., Ind. U., 1959; m. Noreen I. Davey, Dec. 30, 1950; children—John D., Philip A., Patrick W. Dir. lab. human devel. U. Mont. 1952-56; cons. psychologist research Purdue U., 1955; asso. prof., dir. bur. research Ball State U., 1956-61; instr. higher edn., research asso. Ind. U., 1958; prof., chmn. div. edn. Western Wash. State Coll., Bellingham, 1961-62; pres. Western N.Mex. U., Silver City, 1962—. Exec. bd. Internat. Council Spl. Edn., 1952-56; Rocky Mountain regional rep. Am. Psychol. Assn., 1953-56; mem. Gov. Wash. Research Adv. Com., 1961, Gov. Wash. Com. Licensing Tchr. Edn., 1961, Eash. State Legislature Research Tech. Com., 1961. Bd. dirs. Nat. Sci. Fair; trustee N.Mex. Health Found. Served with AUS, 1943-45. Fellow AAAS; mem. Midwest Psychol. Assn., Inter-Am. Soc. Psychology, Am. Ednl. Research Assn., Holland Soc. N.Y. Author or co-author rating scales, attitude and opinion measurement devices; contbr. jours. Address: Box 680 Silver City NM 88061

SNEED, EARL, lawyer; b. Tulsa, Jan. 19, 1913; s. Earl and Nellie Frances (Johnson) S.; A.B., U. Okla., 1934, LL.B., 1937; LL.M., Columbia, 1948, S.J.D., 1961; m. Cornelia Lynde, Apr. 22, 1935; children—James Lynde, Cornelia Ann, Robert Earl. Admitted to Okla. bar, 1937; asso. Monnet & Savage, Tulsa, 1937-39; partner Biddison & Sneed, Tulsa, 1939-40; sec. civic and legislative dept. Tulsa C. of C., 1940-41; vis. asso. prof. law U. Okla., 1945-46, asso. prof., 1946-48, prof., 1948-65, dean, 1950-65; v.p., asst. to pres., vice-chmn. Liberty Nat. Bank & Trust Co., Oklahoma City, 1965-77; of counsel firm Crowe, Dunlevy, Thweatt, Swinford, Johnson & Burdick, Okalhoma City, 1977—; formerly pres. Liberty Nat. Corp, also dir.; past dir. Comml. Nat. Bank, Comml. Finance Co., Muskogee, 1st Nat. Bank, Norman, Okla., Doric Corp. Mayor, Norman, 1961-65; pres. Okla. Municipal League, 1964, 65; chmn. Central Okla. Parking and Transit Authority. Trustee U. Okla. Found.; former bd. dirs. Am. Heart Assn. Past pres. Okla. Heart Assn., Oklahoma City Symphony; past chmn. Jud. Council Okla. Served as col. USAAF, 1941-45. Decorated Bronze Star; Croix de Guerre. Fellow Am. Bar Found. (trustee); mem. Am., Okla. (pres.-elect), Oklahoma County bar assns., Am. Judicature Soc., Air Force Assn. (past nat. dir.), Am. Legion, Res. Officers Assn., Nat. Municipal

League (past v.p.), Okla. C. of C. (past pres.), Okla. Hall of Fame, Okla. Hist. Soc., Phi Beta Kappa, Phi Delta Phi, Beta Theta Pi, Order of Coif. Episcopalian. Clubs: Oklahoma City Golf and Country, Beacon, Whitehall, Petroleum (Oklahoma City). Home: 1707 Drury Ln Oklahoma City OK 73116 Office: Liberty Tower Oklahoma City OK 73102

SNEED, JOSEPH TYREE, judge; b. Calvert, Tex., July 21, 1920; s. Harold Marvin and Cara (Weber) S.; B.B.A., Southwestern U., 1941; LL.B., U. Tex., Austin, 1947; S.J.D., Harvard, 1958; m. Madelon Juergens, Mar. 15, 1944; children—Clara Hall, Cara Carleton, Joseph Tyree IV. Admitted to Tex. bar, 1948; instr. bus. law U. Tex., Austin, 1947, asst. prof. law, 1947-51, asso. prof., 1951-54, prof., 1954-57, asst. dean, 1949-50; counsel Graves, Dougherty & Greenhill, Austin, 1954-56; prof. law Cornell U., 1957-62; prof. law Stanford Law Sch., 1962-71; dean Duke Law Sch., 1971-73; dep. atty. gen. U.S. justice dept., 1973; judge U.S. Ct. Appeals, 9th Circuit, San Francisco, 1973—. Cons. estate and gift tax project Am. Law Inst., 1960-69. Served with USAAF, 1942-46. Mem. Am. Bar Assn., State Bar Tex., Am. Law Inst., Am. Judicature Soc., Assn. Am. Law Schs. (past pres.), Order of Coif. Author: The Configurations of Gross Income, 1967. Contbr. articles to profl. jours. Address: PO Box 547 San Francisco CA 94101

SNEEN, RICHARD ALLEN, organic chemist; b. Menomonie, Wis., July 19, 1930; s. Emil Andrew and Mildred (Lentz) S.; B.A., St. Olaf Coll., 1952; Ph.D., U. Ill., 1955. Research asso. UCLA, 1955-56; instr. Purdue U., West Lafayette, Ind., 1956-58, asst. prof. organic chemistry, 1958-62, asso. prof., 1962-72, prof., 1972—. Mem. Phi Beta Kappa, Sigma Xi. Research, numerous publs. in field. Home: 5808N 75E West Lafayette IN 47906 Office: Chem 450D Purdue U West Lafayette IN 47907

SNEIDER, RICHARD LEE, former ambassador; b. N.Y.C., June 29, 1922; s. Leopold J. and Frances (Magid) S.; A.B. Brown U., 1943; M.I.A., Columbia, 1948; m. Leah Ruth Tartalsky, Oct. 1, 1944; children—Dena Ann, Daniel Charles, David Abbott. Joined U.S. Fgn. Service, 1955; fgn. affairs officer State Dept., 1948-54; 2d sec., later 1st sect. embassy, Tokyo, Japan, 1954-58; officer charge Japanese affairs State Dept., 1958-61; assigned Nat. War Coll., 1961-62; polit. counselor embassy, Karachi, Pakistan, 1962-65; country dir., Japan, 1966-68; sr. staff mem. Nat. Security Council 1969, dep. chief mission, minister for Okinawa Reversion Negotiations Tokyo, 1969-72; dep. asst. sec. bur. E. Asian-Pacific affairs State Dept., 1972-74; ambassador to Korea, 1974-78; ret., 1978; fellow Inst. Politics, Harvard U., 1978; adj. prof. Columbia U., 1979. Served to 1st lt. AUS, 1943-46. Mem. Asia Soc. (trustee 1979—). Home: 211 Central Park W New York NY 10024

SNELL, ABSALOM WEST, educator; b. Parler, S.C., Apr. 29, 1924; s. Algernon Hutto and Julia (Harvey) S.; B.S. in Agrl. Engring., Clemson U., 1949; M.S. in Agrl. Engring., Iowa State U., 1952; Ph.D., N.C. State U., 1964; m. Sarah Lou Oliver, Jan. 28, 1951; children—Rodney Mark, Nancy Kay, Carla Susan, Janet Elizabeth. Asst. prof., Clemson (S.C.) U., 1949-53, asso. prof., 1953-55, prof., head dept. agrl. engring., 1955-75, chmn. directorate Water Resources Research Inst., 1964-75, asso. dir. S.C. Agrl. Expt. Sta., Coll. Agrl. Scis., 1975—. Cons. Water Resources Com.; del. Univs. Council Water Resources. Chmn. Gov.'s Adv. Com. on Water Resources, 1966-70. Served with USAAF, 1943-46; ETO. Decorated Air medal. Recipient Clark Lindsay McCaslan award Clemson U., 1949. Registered profl. engr., S.C. Mem. Am. Soc. Agrl. Engrs. (chmn. organizational com. S.C. sect. 1957, sec. S.E. region 1958-59, v.p. S.E. region 1959-60, chmn. grad. instrn. com. 1969-70, dir. 1971-73), Am. Water Resources Assn., Am. Soc. for Engring. Edn., Am. Geophys. Union, Sigma Xi, Phi Kappa Phi, Tau Beta Pi, Gamma Sigma Delta, Alpha Zeta. Lion. Home: 116 Lewis Rd Clemson SC 29631 Office: Agrl Expt Sta 104 Barre Hall Clemson U Clemson SC 29631

SNELL, BERNARD, physician; b. Glasgow, Scotland, Aug. 1, 1919; s. Asher and Rebecca (Katz) S.; M.D., U. Glasgow, 1943; D.P.H., U. Edinburgh, 1946; m. Edna Altaras, Sept. 5, 1949; children—Linda, Lauren. Intern, Stobhill Hosp., Glasgow, 1943-44; resident in internal medicine So. Gen. Hosp., Glasgow, 1946-47; resident Monsall Hosp., Manchester, Eng., 1947-49, asst. supt., 1949-51; asst. supt. Lodge Moor Hosp., Sheffield, Eng., 1951-57; asst. med. supt. U. Alta. (Can.) Hosp., Edmonton, 1957-60, med. supt., 1960-65, exec. dir., 1966—, pres., 1976; clin. prof. community med. U. Alta. Pres. United Way of Edmonton area. Served with Brit. Mcht. Service, 1944-46. Fellow Royal Coll. Physicians (Edinburgh), Am. Coll. Hosp. Adminstrs. (regent for Alberta 1973); mem. Alta. Med. Assn., Alta. Hosp. Assn. (pres. 1974), Canadian Coll. Health Service Execs., Royal Coll. Physicians (U.K.) (faculty of community medicine). Home: 88 Quesnell Crescent Edmonton AB Canada Office: U Alta Hosp 112th St and 84 Ave Edmonton 61 AB Canada

SNELL, ESMOND EMERSON, biochemist; b. Salt Lake City, Sept. 22, 1914; s. Heber Cyrus and Hedwig Elaine (Ludwig) S.; B.A., Brigham Young U., 1935; M.A., U. Wis., 1936, Ph.D., 1938; m. Mary Caroline Terrill, Mar. 15, 1941; children—Esmond Emerson (dec.), Richard T., Allan G., Margaret Ann. Research asso. chemistry U. Tex., 1939-41, asst. prof. chemistry, 1941-43, asso. prof., 1943-45, prof. chemistry, 1951-56; prof. biochemistry U. Calif., 1956-76, chmn. dept., 1956-62; prof. microbiology and chemistry U. Tex., Austin, 1976—, chmn. dept. microbiology, 1976—; Guggenheim Meml. Found. fellow Max-Planck Institut für Zellchemie, München, 1962-63, U. Wash., Seattle, Rockefeller U., N.Y.C., Hebrew U., Jerusalem, 1969; asso. prof. biochemistry U. Wis., 1945-47, prof. biochemistry (on leave 1951-53), 1947-53; Walker-Ames prof. biochemistry U. Wash., Seattle, spring 1953; Guggenheim Meml. Found. fellow U. Cambridge, 1954-55. Fellow A.A.A.S.; mem. Nat. Acad. Scis., Japanese Biochem. Soc. (hon.), Biochem. Soc. Eng., Am. Chem. Soc. (Kenneth A Spencer award 1974), Am. Soc. Biol. Chemists (pres. 1961-62), Am. Inst. Nutrition (Meade-Johnson B-Complex award 1946, Osborne-Mendel award 1951), Soc. Am. Bacteriologists (Eli Lilly award in bacteriology and immunology 1945), Author numerous research articles in sci. jours. Editor: Volume III Biochemical Preparations, 1963-64; Chemical and Biological Aspects of Pyridoxal Catalysis, 1963; Pyridoxal Catalysis, Enzymes and Model Systems, 1968. Mem. editorial bd. jour. Am. Chem. Soc., 1948-58, Jour. Biol. Chemistry, 1949-59, Biochemistry, 1961-70, Biochem. and Biophys. Research Communication, 1970—; editor Ann. Rev. Biochemistry, 1969—. Home: 5001 Greystone Dr Austin TX 78731

SNELL, FRANK LINN, lawyer; b. Kansas City, Mo., Dec. 23, 1899; s. Frank Linn and Marie Louise (Genult) S.; LL.B., Kans. U., 1924; m. Elizabeth S. Berlin, Aug. 3, 1927; children—Richard B., Kathryn L. Admitted to Ariz. bar, 1924; practiced in Phoenix, 1927—; sr. mem. firm Snell & Wilmer, 1934—; past dir., chmn. bd. Ariz. Pub. Service Co.; dir. Combined Communications Corp. Chmn. dedication Phoenix Civic Plaza, 1972; past chmn. Phoenix Civic Center Mgmt. Bd.; past chmn. bd., past dir. Am. Grad. Sch. Internat. Mgmt.; hon. bd. dirs. Samaritan Health Services. Recipient Distinguished Service award U. Kans., 1964, Distinguished Alumnus citation, 1973; Man of Year award Phoenix Advt. Club, 1966; Distinguished Achievement award Coll. Bus. Adminstrn., Ariz. State U., 1977. Mem. Phoenix C. of C. (pres. 1934), Ariz. Nat. Livestock Show Inc. (past pres.), Am., Ariz. bar assns., Internat. Solar Energy Soc. (hon. dir.), Phoenix Fine Arts Assn. (past pres.). Republican. Presbyterian. Clubs: Phoenix Kiwanis (past pres.); Paradise Valley Country (past pres.). Home: 5201 E Arroyo Rd Scottsdale AZ 85253 Office: 3100 Valley Center Phoenix AZ 85073

SNELL, FRED MANGET, physician, educator; b. Soochow, China, Nov. 11, 1921 (parents Am. citizens); s. John Abner and Grace (Birkett) S.; A.B. cum laude, Maryville (Tenn.) Coll., 1942; M.D., Harvard U., 1945; Ph.D., Mass. Inst. Tech., 1952; m. Mary Larmour, Mar. 14, 1946; children—Susanna Jean, John Steven, Cynthia Anne. Intern, Children's Med. Center, Boston, 1945-46, asst. resident, 1948-49; profl. asso. com. atomic casualties NRC, 1948; Am. Cancer Soc. fellow Mass. Inst. Tech., 1949-52; Nat. Found. Infantile Paralysis fellow Mass. Inst. Tech. and Children's Med. Center, 1952-54; asso. biol. chemistry, Lowell M. Palmer sr. fellow Harvard Med. Sch., 1954-57, asst. prof. biol. chemistry, 1957-59; prof. biophysics, chmn. dept. State U. N.Y. at Buffalo, 1959-68, dean grad. studies, 1967-69, coll. master, 1968-71, prof. biophys. sci., 1968—; vis. prof. atmospheric scis. Oreg. State U., Corvallis, 1977-78; mem. U.S. nat. com. Internat. Union Pure and Applied Physics-Nat. Acad. Sci.-NRC, 1972—, vice chmn., 1973-74, chmn., 1974-76. Chmn., Niagara Frontier Coalition for a Democratic Alternative, 1968. Served to lt. (j.g.) M.C., USNR, 1946-48. Mem. N.Y. Acad. Scis., Am. Chem. Soc., Biophys. Soc. (council 1962-65, exec. bd. 1962-64, 66-71, pres. 1970-71), Am. Physiol. Soc., Am. Inst. Biol. Scis., AAUP, AAAS, Sigma Xi. Editor: Progress in Theoretical Biology, 1965-76, Biophys. Jour., 1966-69. Home: 53 Royal Pkwy East Williamsville NY 14221 Office: Dept Biophys Sci State U NY at Buffalo Buffalo NY 14226

SNELL, GEORGE DAVIS, geneticist; b. Bradford, Mass., Dec. 19, 1903; s. Cullen Bryant and Katharine (Davis) S.; B.S., Dartmouth, 1926; M.S., Harvard U., 1928, Sc.D., 1930; M.D. (hon.), Charles U., Prague, 1967; Sc.D., Dartmouth, 1974; m. Rhoda Carson, July 28, 1937; children—Thomas Carleton, Roy Carson, Peter Garland. Instr. zoology Dartmouth, 1929-30, Brown U., 1930-31; asst. prof. Washington U., St. Louis, 1933-34; research asso. Jackson Lab., 1935-56, sr. staff scientist, 1957—, emeritus, 1969—, sci. adminstr., 1949-50. NRC fellow U. Tex., 1931-33; NIH health research grantee for study genetics and immunology of tissue transplantation, 1950-73 (allergy and immunology study sect. 1958-62); Guggenheim fellow, 1953-54. Recipient Bertner Found. award in field cancer research, 1962; Griffin award Animal Care Panel, 1962; career award Nat. Cancer Inst., 1964-68; Gregor Mendel medal Czechoslovak Acad. Scis., 1967; Internat. award Gairdner Found., 1976; Wolf Found. prize in medicine, 1978; award Nat. Inst. Arthritis and Infectious Disease-Nat. Cancer Inst., 1978. Fellow AAAS; mem. Nat. Acad. Scis., Transplantation Soc., Genetic Soc. Am., Am. Acad. Arts and Sci., French Acad. Scis. (fgn. asso.), Brit. Transplantation Soc. (hon.), Phi Beta Kappa. Co-author: Histocompatibility, 1976; also sci. papers in field; editor: The Biology of the Laboratory Mouse, 1941; Immunogenetics. Home: 21 Atlantic Ave Bar Harbor ME 04609

SNELL, JOHN RAYMOND, civil engr.; b. Soochow, China, Dec. 9, 1912 (parents Am. citizens); s. John A. and Grace (Birkett) S.; B.E., Vanderbilt U., 1934; M.S., U. Ill., 1936; D.Sc., Harvard U., 1939; m. Florence Moffett, Dec. 8, 1939; children—Dorothea Snell Fenska, Karen Snell Dailey, Martha E., John Raymond, David Moffet. Instr. civil engring. Hangchow U., 1934-35; with Water Supply Fed. Pub. Works Dept., Venezuela, 1939-40; design engr. Metcalf & Eddy, also Fay Spofford and Thorndyke, Stone & Webster, Boston, 1941-42; san. engr., head water and sewage sect. 1st Service Command, Boston, 1942-45; organizer China San. Engring. Services, Inc., 1947; project engr. Burns & Kenerson, Boston, 1948; pres., chief engr. Engring. Services, Inc., Boston, 1948, 51; lectr. Mass. Inst. Tech., 1949-51; prof., head dept. civil and san. engring. Mich. State U., 1952-56; owner John R. Snell & Assos., 1956; sr. prin. Mich. Assos., cons. engrs., 1956-60; pres. John R. Snell Engrs., Inc., 1960-75, Snell Environ. Group, 1975—; joint venturer Snell-Republic Assos., Ltd., Lahore, West Pakistan, 1961—, with Asso. Architects & Engrs., Dacca, Bangladesh, 1965—; pres. Blue Lake Estates, Inc.; founder Trans Mich. Waterway, Inc., Southwest Waterway (Ont.), Ltd., N.Y.; spl. cons. Govt. of Japan on 1st High Rate Compost Plant, 1955-56; cons. (traveled to Orient) WHO, Sept.-Nov. 1956. Chmn. bd. Bootstrap Internat., Inc. Served as maj. USPHS, 1945-47. Recipient Prescott Eddy award, 1944; registered profl. engr., Mass., Mich., Ohio, Ill., Ind., La., Wis., N.Y., Tex., Fla., Idaho, Oreg., Ont., Can.; certified san engr. Diplomate Am. Acad. San. Engrs. Mem. Nat., Mich. (life) socs. profl. engrs., Am. Water Works Assn., Hwy. Research Bd., ASTM, ASCE, Am. Pub. Works Assn., Water Pollution Control Fedn. (life), Mich. Engring. Soc. (life), Cons. Engrs. Council (past dir.), Cons. Engrs. Assn. Mich. (past pres.), Inter-Am. Assn. San. Engrs., Am. Acad. San. Engrs., Tau Beta Pi, Chi Epsilon. Club: Rotary. Author 12 sects. Environment Engineering Handbook; co-author Municipal Solid Waste Disposal; contbr. articles to profl. jours. Home: 918 Rosewood East Lansing MI 48823 Office: 1120 May St Lansing MI 48933

SNELL, RALPH RONALD, med. services co. exec.; b. Memphis, June 12, 1932; s. Ralph Dillon and Ruby Elizabeth (Wheatley) S.; grad. high sch.; m. Karrene Payne, Feb. 2, 1952; children—Ronnye Kay, Ralph Edwin, Ronald Ted. Prosthetist, Snell's Artificial Limb Co., Nashville, 1952-61; pres., mgr. Snell's Limbs & Braces Inc., Memphis, 1961-76; v.p. Durr Fillauer Med., Inc., Montgomery, Ala., 1976—; treas. Guaranty Trust Savs. & Loan Assn., Memphis, 1974—. Sr. research prosthetist/orthotist U. Tenn. Rehab. Engring. Program, 1975—, clin. instr. phys. therapy sch., 1974—; dir. Health Systems Mgmt. Inc. Vice-pres. Tenn. Easter Seal Soc., 1971; mem. rehab. com. Mid S. Med. Center Council, 1974. Served with USNR, 1952-53. Recipient Gov.'s Distinguished Employer award for hiring handicapped, 1972. Mem. Tenn. Rehab. Assn. (dir. 1964), Am. Bd. Certification in Orthotics and Prosthetics (pres. 1969), Am. Orthotic and Prosthetic Assn. (pres. 1975), Am. Acad. Orthotists and Prosthetists (pres. 1971) (recipient Spl. Tribute award as only practitioner to serve as pres. of all 3 latter orgns.). Episcopalian (past vestryman). Mason. Club: Delta Sailing. Home: 3815 Lakehurst Dr Memphis TN 38128 Office: Snell's Limbs and Braces Inc 22 N Pauline St Memphis TN 38105. *In his poem, "Abou Ben Adhem", the author, Leigh Hunt, describes how favorably God looked upon Abou Ben Adhem for loving his fellowmen. It is my hope that I will subscribe well enough to these principles that, like Abou Ben Adhem, you could write of me as one who loves his fellowmen.*

SNELL, RICHARD SAXON, anatomist; b. Richmond, Surrey, Eng., May 3, 1925; s. Claude Saxon and Daisy Lilian S.; came to U.S., 1963; M.B., B.S., Kings Coll., U. London, 1949, Ph.D., 1955, M.D., 1961; m. Maureen Cashin, June 4, 1949; children—Georgina Sara, Nicola Ann, Melanie Jane, Richard Robin, Charles Edward. House surgeon Sir Cecil P.G. Wakeley, Kings Coll. Hosp. and Belgrave Hosp. for Children, London, 1948-49; lectr. anatomy Kings Coll., U. London, 1949-59, U. Durham (Eng.), 1959-63; asst. prof. anatomy and medicine Yale U., 1963-65, asso. prof., 1965-67, vis. prof. anatomy, 1969; prof., chmn. dept. anatomy N.J. Coll. Medicine and Dentistry, Jersey City, 1967-69; vis. prof. anatomy Harvard U., 1970-71; prof. anatomy Coll. Medicine, U. Ariz., Tucson, 1970; prof., chmn. dept. anatomy George Washington U. Med. Center, Washington, 1972—. Med. Research Council grantee, 1959, NIH grantee, 1963-65. Mem. Anat. Soc. Gt. Britain, Am. Soc. Anatomists, Soc. Investigative Dermatology, Alpha Omega Alpha. Club: George Washington U. Author: Clinical Embryology for Medical Students, 1972; Clinical Anatomy for Medical Students, 1973; Atlas of Normal Radiographic Anatomy, 1976; Atlas of Clinical Anatomy, 1978; Gross Anatomy Dissector, 1978; editor Anat. Record, 1974; contbr. articles to med. jours. Home: 33 Liberty St Madison CT 06443 also 7809 Moorland Ln Bethesda MD 20014 Office: 2300 Eye St NW Washington DC 20037

SNELL, WILLIAM N., lawyer; b. Nevada City, Calif., Feb. 23, 1916; s. James and Emma (Nankervis) S.; A.B., Stanford U., 1937, LL.B., 1940; m. Barbara Perry, July 20, 1941. Admitted to Calif. bar, 1940; asso. firm McCutchen, Olney, Mannon & Greene, San Francisco, 1940-41; practice in Fresno, 1941—, partner firm Thomas, Snell, Jamison, Russell, Williamson & Asperger, and predecessor, 1945—; lectr. com. continuing edn. Calif. State Bar, 1958. Vice-pres., dir. Doyle Springs Assn., 1977—. Served to lt. (j.g.) USNR, 1942-45; PTO. Mem. Am. Bar Assn., Am. Law Inst., Am. Judicature Soc., Am. Trial Lawyers Assn., Order of Coif, Delta Theta Phi. Clubs: San Joaquin Country (dir., sec. 1968—); Univ.-Sequoia-Sunnyside (pres. 1960), Downtown (Fresno); Commonwealth (San Francisco). Contbr. articles to profl. jours. Home: 7475 N Valentine Fresno CA 93705 Office: Suite 1000 2220 Tulare St Fresno CA 93721

SNELLGROVE, HAROLD SINCLAIR, educator; b. Meridian, Miss., May 18, 1913; s. Edwin Doty and Laura (Sinclair) S.; B.A., Duke, 1936, M.A., 1940; Ph.D., U. N.Mex., 1948. Instr., Gulf Coast Mil. Acad., 1936-41; teaching fellow U. N.C., 1941-42; instr. history U. N.Mex., 1946-47, vis. prof., summer 1951; mem. faculty Miss. State U., 1947—, prof. history, 1957-78, head dept., 1961-78, prof. and head emeritus, 1978—. Served with AUS, 1942-46. Mem. Mediaeval Acad. Am., Am., So. hist. assns., Phi Kappa Phi, Omicron Delta Kappa, Phi Alpha Theta, Alpha Psi Omega, Pi Delta Phi, Sigma Delta Pi. Republican. Episcopalian. Author: The Lusignanas in England, 1247-1258, 1950; also articles. Home: 404 Myrtle St Starkville MS 39759

SNELLING, GEORGE ARTHUR, banker; b. St. Petersburg, Fla., June 27, 1929; s. William Henry and Eula Hall S.; B.S.B.A., U. Fla., 1951; m. Carolyn Shiver, Mar. 3, 1963; children—George, John S. Partner, Smoak, Davis, Nixon & Snelling, C.P.A.'s, Jacksonville, Orlando, Fla., 1956-66; v.p. planning Barnett Banks of Fla., Jacksonville, 1966-76; exec. v.p. 1st Bancshares of Fla., Boca Raton, 1976-78; exec. v.p. Fla. Nat. Banks of Fla., Jacksonville, 1979—, dir. Served with USAF, 1951-55. Mem. Am. Inst. C.P.A.'s, Assn. Bank Holding Cos., Fla. Bankers Assn. Democrat. Methodist. Home: 7769 Miller Oaks Dr W Jacksonville FL 32217 Office: PO Box 689 Jacksonville FL 32201

SNELLING, RICHARD ARKWRIGHT, gov. Vt.; b. Allentown, Pa., Feb. 18, 1927; s. Walter Otheman and Marjorie (Gahring) S.; student Lehigh U., 1943; A.B., Harvard U., 1948; m. Barbara T. Weil, June 14, 1947; children—Jacqueline, Mark, Diane, Andrew. Chmn. bd. Shelburne Industries, Inc., Barreca Products Co., Inc., Wessel Hardware Co.; mem. Vt. Ho. of Reps., 1959-60, 72-74, 75-76; gov. State of Vt., 1977—. Mem. Vt. Devel. Commn., 1960-62, Adv. Com. on Intergovtl. Relations, 1977—; chmn. Vt. Aeros. Commn., 1968-72; del. Republican Nat. Conv., 1960-68; Rep. nominee for lt. gov. Vt., 1964, for gov. Vt., 1966; chmn. Vt. Rep. Fin. Com., 1974-76. Chmn. bd. dirs. Greater Burlington Indsl. Corp., 1960-62; trustee Med. Center Hosp. of Vt.; mem. steering com. Edn. Commn. of the States, 1977—. Served with AUS, 1944-46; ETO. Mem. Nat. Govs. Assn. (exec. com. 1977—), Chief Execs. Forum, World Bus. Council, Lake Champlain C. of C. (dir. 1962-64). Office: Office of the Governor State House Montpelier VT 05602

SNELSON, KENNETH DUANE, sculptor; b. Pendleton, Oreg., June 29, 1927; s. John Tavner and Mildred F. (Unger) S.; student U. Oreg., 1946-47, Black Mountain Coll., 1948-49, Chgo. Inst. Design, 1950-51, Academie Montmartre, Paris, 1951-52; m. Katherine Eve Kaufmann, May 2, 1972; 1 dau., Andrea Nicole. Numerous one-man shows, U.S. and Germany, Holland, including Portrait of an Atom, Balt., 1979-80; group shows include: Mus. Modern Art, N.Y.C., 1967, Whitney Mus., N.Y.C., 1966, 69, 70, Albright Knox Gallery, Buffalo, 1968, Prospect '68, Dusseldorf, Germany, 1968, Salon International de Galeries Pilotes, Lausanne, Switzerland, 1970, Sammlun Etzold, Kolnischer Kunstverein, Cologne, Germany, 1970, Expo '70, Osaka, Japan, 1970, Fondation Maeght, St. Paul de Vence, France, 1970, Art Inst. Chgo., 1972; represented in permanent collections, including: Mus. Modern Art, Whitney Mus. Am. Art, cities of Hannover and Hamburg, Germany, Rijksmuseum Kroller Muller, Otterlo, Holland, Rijksmuseum, Amsterdam, Holland, Japan Iron, Steel Fedn., Osaka, City of Balt., Hirshhorn Mus., Milw. Art Center, City of Buffalo. Served with USNR, 1945-46. DAAD fellow Berlin Kunstlerprogram, 1976. Subject of articles in art publs.; patentee discontinuous compression structures, model for atomic forms. Home and Office: 140 Sullivan St New York NY 10012. *My art is concerned with nature in its most fundamental aspect; the patterns of physical forces in space.*

SNELSON, ROY, prosthetist; b. Oklahoma City, Sept. 4, 1927; s. Albert B. and Mary (Johnson) S.; student U. Calif. at Los Angeles, 1947-49; m. Bernadette Kowske, Nov. 8, 1947 (div. 1974); 1 son, Daniel B.; m. 2d, Vivian Conklin, Oct. 9, 1976. Clin. instr. prosthetics U. Calif. at Los Angeles Sch. Medicine, 1950-57; chief prosthetic research Rancho Los Amigos Hosp., U. So. Calif. Sch. Medicine, 1957-67; project dir. amputation fracture research, 1967—; pres. Orthopaedic Supplies Co., Inc., Downey, Calif., 1957-70, Orthomedics, Inc., Downey, 1970—, Brea, 1979—; clin. instr. prosthetics U. Wash., 1976—. Mem. com. prosthetic research and devel. Nat. Acad. Sci.; mem. exec. com. med. engring. center U. So. Calif., 1971—; sec.-treas., dir. Am. Bd. for Certification in Orthotics and Prosthetics, 1975-77, pres., 1978. Served with AUS, 1945-47. Recipient Prosthetist of Year award Am. Orthotics and Prosthetics Assn., 1951; Outstanding Contbn. award Soc. Orthotist and Prosthetists, 1957; HEW, grantee, 1970-71. Mem. Am. Orthotic and Prosthetic Assn. (pres. 1970-71). Home: 1001 N Cypress La Habra CA Office: 2950 E Imperial Hwy Brea CA 92621

SNEVA, THOMAS EDSOL, race car driver; b. Spokane, Wash., June 1, 1948; s. Edsol Hilmer and Joan (Giles) S.; B.A. in Edn., Eastern Wash. State Coll., 1970; m. Sharon Setchell, Aug. 17, 1968; children—Joey, Amanda. Tchr., coach, prin. Sprague (Wash.) Sch. Dist., 1970-73; race car driver for Grant King, 1974, for Roger Penske Racing Team, 1975-78, for Jerry Oconell, 1979; won Norton 200, 1975, second Indpls. 500, 1977, 78; winner Schaefer 500 at Pocono Internat. Speedway, 1977, Tex. Grand Prix, 1977. Recipient U.S. Auto Club Rookie of the Year award, 1973, Jimmy Clark award, 1976, Eddie Sachs Scholarship award, 1977, U.S. Auto Club Nat. Champion, 1977, 78, Triple Crown, 1977, Jim Malloy Meml. award, 1977; U.S. Auto Club Champion, 1977, 78. Mem. U.S. Auto Club, Fedn. Internationale de L'Automobile. Lutheran. First driver to officially break 200 MPH (200.535) barrier at Indpls., 1977, current record holder (203.6). Home: N 5526 Forest Blvd Spokane WA 99208

SNIBBE, RICHARD WILSON, architect; b. Balt., Oct. 31, 1916; s. George W. and Mildred (Robinson) S.; B.A., St. Johns Coll., 1939; postgrad. Harvard Sch. Design, 1940-41; m. Miriam Bergman, Jan. 3, 1942 (div. May 1962); children—John Robinson, Paul Clor; m. 2d, Patricia Lois Miscall, Sept. 8, 1962. Asso., Edward D. Stone, architect, N.Y.C., 1951-56; partner Ballard, Todd & Snibbe, N.Y.C., 1957-61; individual practice architecture, N.Y.C., 1962; partner Myller, Snibbe, Tafel, N.Y.C., 1962-67, Snibbe, Tafel, Lindholm, 1967-73, Wilson & Snibbe, architects, planners, engrs., N.Y.C., 1970—; instr. Cooper Union, N.Y.C., 1949; vis. critic Columbia, N.Y.C., 1956, Pratt Inst., N.Y.C., 1962; important works include U.S. embassy, New Delhi, India (as asso.), 1955, Tennis Pavilion, Princeton, 1960, comprehensive campus plan and bldgs. State U. Coll., Geneseo, N.Y., 1962-72, Handloser Project, Future Town, 1973. Brunner scholar N.Y. chpt. AIA, 1957. Fellow AIA (chmn. nat. com. on aesthetics 1963); mem. Harvard Grad. Sch. Design Assn., Am. Arbitration Assn. Author: Small Commercial Buildings, 1956. Patentee for suspended structure, Landspan. Address: 139 E 18th St New York City NY 10003

SNIDECOR, JOHN CLIFTON, educator; b. Washta, Iowa, Oct. 18, 1907; s. George E. and Jessie June (Ferrin) S.; A.B., U. Calif., 1931; M.A., U. Iowa, 1937, Ph.D., 1940; m. Lois Eleanor Allison, Dec. 30, 1929; 1 son, John Carl. Instr., Antelope Valley Jr. Coll., Lancaster, Calif., 1932-33, dean, 1934-35; instr. U. Idaho, 1935-39; instr. Santa Barbara State Coll., 1940-41, asst. prof., 1941-43; asso. prof. speech U. Calif. at Santa Barbara, 1946-48, acting dean applied arts, 1948-50, acting provost, 1955-56, prof. speech, 1948—, dean applied arts, 1950-60. Adv. bd. Santa Barbara County chpt. Am. Cancer Soc.; program com. Soc. Cripped Children and Adults. Served as lt. comdr. USNR, 1944-46. Certified state psychologist, Calif. Fellow Am. Speech and Hearing Assn.; mem. Am. Psychol. Assn., Calif. Speech and Hearing Assn., Sigma Xi. Contbr. articles profl. jours., books. Home: 2705 Verde Vista Santa Barbara CA 93105

SNIDER, DELBERT ARTHUR, educator, economist; b. Fayetteville, Ohio, Jan. 11, 1914; s. Chris Charles and Florence (Berger) S.; A.B., U. Cin., 1936, M.A., 1937; student Geneva (Switzerland) Sch. Internat. Studies, summer 1936; Ph.D., U. Chgo., 1951; m. Helen Nancy Kuller, Sept. 4, 1939; children—Suzanne, Chris. Economist, Treasury Dept., 1940-43, 45-47; mem. faculty Miami U., Oxford, Ohio, 1947-48, 49—, prof. econs., 1953—, chmn. dept., 1963-66; U.S. mem. Greek Currency Commn., Athens, 1948-49; cons. Fed. Res. Bd., 1965; participant vis. prof. program Am. Econ. Assn., 1966—. Served to lt. (j.g.) USNR, 1943-45. Mem. Am., Midwest (pres. 1971-72) econ. assns., Ohio Assn. Polit. Scientists and Economist, AAUP. Author: Introduction to International Economics, 7th edit., 1979; Economics: Principles and Issues, 1962; Economic Myth and Reality, 1965; International Monetary Relations, 1966; Economic Essentials, 1972. Home: 213 Oakhill Dr Oxford OH 45056

SNIDER, EDWARD MALCOLM, profl. hockey club exec.; b. Washington, Jan. 6, 1933; s. Sol C. and Lillian (Bonas) S.; B.S., U. Md., 1955; m. Myrna Gordon, July 11, 1954; children—Craig Alan, Jay Thomas, Lindy Lou, Tina Suzanne. Maj. stockholder, exec. v.p. Edge Ltd., Washington, 1957-63; v.p. Phila. Eagles Football Club, 1964-67; chmn. bd. Phila. Flyers Hockey Club, 1967—, Spectrum Arena, Phila., 1971—, Nat. Hockey League Services, 1968-76; bd. gov. Nat. Hockey League, 1967—, mem. fin. com., 1969-74. Bd. dirs. Hahnemann Cancer Inst., Phila. Assn. Retarded Children, 1971—, Western br. JYC, 1973—, Police Athletic League, 1974—. C.P.A., Md. Office: care Philadelphia Flyers The Spectrum Broad and Pattison Philadelphia PA 19148*

SNIDER, EDWIN WALLACE, assn. exec., lawyer; b. Mt. Rainier, Md., Aug. 18, 1923; s. Clyde Elwood and Marguerite Eunice (Root) S.; student Franklin and Marshall Coll., 1944-45; B.A., Princeton, 1947; J.D. with honors, George Washington U., 1959; m. Leigh Alice Winter, June 16, 1956. Stenographer-clk. Eastern Airlines, Washington, 1941-42; sec. FTC, Washington, 1947; sales corr. Prentice-Hall Pub. Co., N.Y.C., 1947-48; sec. exploration dept. Socony-Vacuum Oil Co. of Venezuela, Anaco, 1948-51; adminstrv. sec. Nat. Geog. Soc., Washington, 1953-63, adminstrv. asst., 1964—, sec. com. research, exploration, 1966—, asst. sec., 1969-77, asso. sec., 1977—, also house counsel; admitted to D.C. bar, 1959. Served with USNR, 1942-46; ETO. Mem. Am. Bar Assn. (copyright com.), D.C. Bar (chmn. com. copyright 1972-74), Phi Kappa Sigma. Club: Princeton of Washington. Home: 6722 Lucy Lane McLean VA 22101 Office: Nat Geog Soc Washington DC 20036

SNIDER, HAROLD WAYNE, educator; b. Puyallup, Wash., Apr. 16, 1923; s. P. Marion and Grace Stevenson (Short) S.; B.A., U. Wash., 1946, M.A., 1950; Ph.D., U. Pa., 1955; m. Isobel Milne Dice, Jan. 20, 1961; stepchildren—Isobel Milne Given, John Kenneth Desmond. Instr. bus. U. Wash., 1952-54; asso. prof. Ill. Wesleyan U., 1954-57; asst. prof. U. Pa., Phila., 1957-64; prof., chmn. dept. ins. and risk Temple U., Phila., 1964—. Served with AUS, 1943-46. S.S. Huebner Found. fellow, 1950-52. Mem. Risk and Ins. Mgmt. Soc., Am. Mgmt. Assn., Am. Risk and Ins. Soc., Phi Beta Kappa, Beta Gamma Sigma. Club: Phila. Aviation Country. Author: Life Insurance Investment in Commercial Real Estate, 1956; (with Denenberg and others) Risk and Insurance, 1964; (with John Adams) The Automobile Accident Problem: Saskatchewan Approach, 1973; contbg. author The Job of Risk Management, 1962. Home: Box 256 Gwynedd PA 19436 Office: Sch Bus Adminstrn Temple U Philadelphia PA 19122

SNIDER, JOHN JOSEPH, lawyer; b. Seminole, Okla., July 25, 1928; s. George Nathan and Katherine (Harris) S.; A.B., U. Okla., 1950, LL.B., 1955; m. Harriet Jean Edmonds, June 14, 1952; children—John Joseph, Dorothy Susan (Mrs. Mark E. Blohm), William Arnold. Admitted to Okla. bar, 1955, since practiced in Oklahoma City; mem. firm Fellers, Snider, Blankenship, Bailey & Tippens, 1964—; mem. Okla. adv. council Nat. Legal Services Corp., 1976-77. Pres., Okla. Soc. for Prevention Blindness, 1965-71; bd. dirs. Hosp. Hospitality House, Okla., 1978—, Nat. Soc. Prevention Blindness, 1971-75; vice chmn. Oklahoma City Crime Prevention Council, 1976-77. Served to 1st lt. USAF, 1950-53. Fellow Am. Bar Found.; mem. Oklahoma City C. of C., Am., Okla., Okla. County bar assns., Am. Judicature Soc., Phi Delta Phi, Phi Kappa Psi. Methodist. Club: Men's Dinner. Home: 2018 Redbud Pl Edmond OK 73034 Office: First Nat Bldg Oklahoma City OK 73102

SNIDER, LAWRENCE K., lawyer; b. Detroit, Dec. 28, 1938; s. Ben and Ida (Hertz) S.; B.A., U. Mich., 1960, J.D., 1963; m. Maxine Bobman, Aug. 12, 1962; children—Stephanie, Suzanne. Admitted to Mich. bar, 1964; since practiced Detroit; partner law firm Jaffe, Snider, Raitt, Garratt & Heuer, Detroit, 1968—; adj. prof. law Wayne State U., Detroit, 1973—. Pres. Jr. Council, Founders Soc. Detroit Inst. Arts, 1973-74. Mem. Am., Mich., Detroit bar assns., Am. Judicature Soc. Contbr. articles profl. publs. Home: 316 Lone Pine Ct B Bloomfield Hills MI 48013 Office: 1800 1st Nat Bldg Detroit MI 48226

SNIDER, ROBERT JOE, coal co. exec.; b. Huntington, W.Va., Jan. 15, 1921; s. Joseph and Madge (Runyon) S.; certificate exec. program U. Chgo., 1951; m. Sarah J. Wake, Sept. 16, 1942; children—Duke W., Robert Richard. With Peabody Coal Co., Chgo., 1940-65, became v.p. fin., 1953, sr. exec. v.p., dir., exec. com.; pres. Piamco, Inc., 1965—. Served with USAAF, 1942-45. Mem. Beta Gamma Sigma. Presbyterian. Clubs: Algonquin Golf; Clayton; Monroe, Chicago (Chgo.). Home: 151 Jefferson Rd Webster Groves MO 63119 Office: Suite 922 Community Federal Center Des Peres MO 63131

SNIDER, ROBERT LARRY, energy co. exec.; b. Muskogee, Okla., Aug. 10, 1932; s. George Robert and Kathryn (Smiser) S.; B.S. in Indsl. Engring., U. Houston, 1955, postgrad., 1956; postgrad. Pomona Coll., 1960; Gerlene Rose Tipton, Nov. 26, 1953; children—Melody Kathryn, Rebecca Lee. Instr. Coll. Engring., U. Houston, 1955-56; sr. indsl. engr. Sheffield Steel Corp., Houston, 1955-59, Kaiser Steel Co., Fontana, Calif., 1959-60; cons. Arthur Young & Co., Los Angeles, 1960-61; mgmt. analyst Iranian Oil Exploration & Producing Co., Masjidi-Suliman, Iran, 1961-62, cons., 1962-64, asso., 1964-65; v.p. operating methods div. Booz, Allen & Hamilton, Inc., Dallas, 1965-67, v.p., mng. officer internat. prodn. and inventory control div., 1967-69; prin., gen. cons. practice Peat Marwick Mitchell, C.P.A.'s, Houston, 1969-71; exec. v.p. mfg. Sterling Electronics Corp., Houston, 1971-72; pres., chief operating officer, 1972-77; pres., chief exec. officer Rapoca Energy Corp., Cin., 1977-79; S.W. mng. partner cons. Coopers & Lybrand, Houston, 1979—. Served with C.E., AUS, 1956. Recipient Outstanding Mil. Engr. award Soc. Mil. Engrs., 1955. Mem. Pres.'s Assn., Soc. Mining Engrs., Am. Mgmt. Assn., Cin. Coal Exchange, So. Coal Conf., Phi Theta Kappa, Phi Kappa Phi. Clubs: Houston, Met. Racquet, City, Bankers. Contbr. articles to Electronic News, Radio TV Weekly, Hosp. mag. Home: 11643 Green Bay Houston TX 77024 Office: Suite 715 1010 Jefferson Houston TX 77002

SNIDER, WILLIAM DAVIS, newspaper editor; b. Salisbury, N.C., June 7, 1920; s. William Marvin and Mildred (Davis) S.; A.B., U. N.C., 1941; m. Florence Lide, June 12, 1948; children—Jane Telfair, Mary Alice Cordon, Florence Lide, Mildred Davis. Reporter, Salisbury Evening Post, 1941-42, 46-48; pvt. sec. Gov. R. Gregg Cherry (N.C.), 1948; adminstrv. asst. Gov. W. Kerr Scott (N.C.), 1949; adminstrv. asst. N.C. Hwy. Commn., 1950-51; asso. editor Greensboro (N.C.) Daily News, 1951-65, editor, 1965—; editor Greensboro Record, 1966—; v.p. Greensboro News Co., 1972—; lectr. U. N.C., 1963-64; pres. Nat. Conf. Editorial Writers, 1969, editor Masthead, 1961-63. Mem. N.C. Constn. Commn., 1957-59; chmn. N.C. Awards Commn., 1963-74; chmn. bd. trustees Greensboro Pub. Library. Served to 2d lt. Signal Corps, AUS, 1942-46; CBI. Mem. Am. Soc. Newspaper Editors, N.C. Press Assn. (pres. 1974-75), Sigma Nu. Democrat. Presbyterian. Club: Greensboro Country. Home: 1405 Briarcliff Rd Greensboro NC 27408 Office: Box 20848 200 E Market St Greensboro NC 27420

SNITZER, ELIAS, physicist; b. Lynn, Mass., Feb. 27, 1925; s. Isaac and Jenny (Sussman) S.; B.S.E.E., Tufts U., 1946; M.S. in Physics, U. Chgo. 1950, Ph.D. in Physics, 1953; m. Shirley Ann Wood, Nov. 22, 1950; children—Sandra, Barbara, Peter, Helen, Louis. Research physicist Honeywell, Phila., 1954-56; asso. prof. physics Lowell Inst. Tech., 1956-58; dir. advanced research Am. Optical Corp., 1959-77; mgr. tech. planning United Techs. Research Center, East Hartford, Conn., 1977—. Served with USN, 1943-46. Mem. Am. Phys. Soc., Optical Soc. Am., IEEE, Am. Ceramic Soc. (George W. Morey award 1971), Nat. Acad. Engring. Research in fiber optics, glass lasers, display devices. Home: 11 Fox Meadow Ln West Hartford CT 06107 Office: United Techs Research Center Silver Ln East Hartford CT 06108*

SNITZER, MARTIN HARRY, advt. agy. exec.; b. Chgo., Oct. 24, 1925; s. Louis A. and Lillian (Councilbaum) S.; B.S., U. Ill., 1948; postgrad. Northwestern U., 1949; m. Rosalie Ruth Lichtenstien, Mar. 30, 1952; 1 son, Thomas A. With Young & Rubicam, Inc., Chgo., 1948-52; account exec., Earle Ludgin & Co., Chgo., 1952-58; chmn. exec. com. Leo Burnett USA, Chgo., dir., 1970-77; dir. Continental Ill. Venture Corp. Bd. dirs. Chgo. Easter Seal Soc., 1958-62. Served with USAAF, 1943-46. Clubs: Standard (Chgo.); Northmoor (Ill.) Country. Office: Prudential Plaza Chicago IL 60601

SNIVELY, HARVEY BOWDEN, JR., citrus prodn. and processing co. exec.; b. Winter Haven, Fla., Dec. 20, 1923; s. Harvey Bowden and Sara May (McKibben) S.; B.S. in Agr., U. Fla., 1948; m. Mary Ann Schock, Nov. 25, 1949; children—Patricia Ann Snively Herndon, Harvey Bowden III, Nancy Carol, Margaret Jane. Prodn. mgr. Lake Hamilton Coop. (Fla.), 1952-67, v.p., 1967-68, pres., 1968—; pres. Orange-Co. of Fla. Inc., Lake Hamilton, 1968—; sr. v.p., dir. Orange-Co. of Columbus (Ohio); dir. First Nat. Bank, Winter Haven, Holiday Bank (Fla.), Citrus Central Coop., Orlando, Fla., Lake Alfred (Fla.) Growers Fertilizer Coop. Served to 2d lt. USAAF, 1943-45. Club: Lake Region Country, Rotary. Home: 694 W Lake Otis Dr Winter Haven FL 33880 Office: PO Box 99 Lake Hamilton FL 33851

SNIVELY, WILLIAM DANIEL, JR., physician; b. Rock Island, Ill., Feb. 9, 1911; s. William Daniel, Sr. and Mary (Wills) S.; student Augustana Coll., 1930-32; A.B., U. Ill., 1934; M.B., M.D., Northwestern U., 1938. Intern, Cin. Gen. Hosp., 1937-38; resident Children's Meml. Hosp., Chgo., 1938-39; pvt. practice limited to internal medicine and pediatrics, Rock Island, 1939-41; med. cons. Mead Johnson & Co., 1947-49, med. dir., 1949-54, v.p., med. dir., 1954-60, exec. v.p., 1960-65, v.p. med. affairs, 1965-69; prof. life scis. U. Evansville, 1970-76, prof. emeritus, 1976—; clin. prof. pediatrics Ind. U., 1973—; staff St. Mary's Hosp., Evansville. Founder, Ohio Wabash Valley Hist. Soc. Served from lt. (j.g.) to comdr. USNR, 1941-46; flight surgeon in Okinawa operation, air war in Japan, later Japanese occupation; resigned comdr. USNR. Recipient Gold medal AMA, 1956; sci. exhibit medal Am. Acad. Gen. Practice, 1965. Fellow Am. Med. Writers Assn. (bd. dirs. 1957-66, pres. 1964), A.C.P.; mem. AMA, Ind. Med. Assn., Vanderburgh County Med. Soc., Ind. Acad., Sigma Xi, Phi Beta Kappa, Phi Kappa Phi. Roman Catholic. Club: Evansville Petroleum. Author: (with others) Fluid Balance Handbook for Practitioners, 1956; Sea Within, 1960; Pageantry of the English Language; Profile of a Manager, 1965; Nurse's Fluid Balance Handbook, 1967, 3d edit., 1978; Satan's Ferryman, 1968; Sea of Life, 1969; (textbook) Pathophysiology, 1973; Healing Beyond Medicine, 1973; also articles in med. and history jours. Editor, contbr. Body Fluid Disturbances, 1962. Home: RFD 10 Box 149 Evansville IN 47712 Office: U Evansville Room 309 Health Scis Bldg Evansville IN 47721. *Time is such a limited commodity that one must develop a sort of sixth sense, which I call the "sense of the significant." Recognizing what is truly significant, the individual can then apportion that precious resource, time, to best advantage.*

SNODDY, JAMES ERNEST, educator; b. Perrysville, Ind., Oct. 6, 1932; s. James Elmer and Edna May (Hayworth) S.; B.S., Ind. State U., 1954; M.Ed., U. Ill., 1961, Ed.D., 1967; m. Alice Joanne Crowder, Aug. 15, 1954; children—Ryan Anthony, Elise Suzanne. Tchr., Danville (Ill.) Public Schs., 1954-57, prin., 1961-64; instr. U. Ill., Champaign, 1965-67; prof. edn. Mich. State U., East Lansing, 1967-72, chairperson dept. elem. and spl. edn., 1972-78, prof. edn., 1978—, dir. Program CORK, 1978—. Served with U.S. Army, 1955-57. Mem. Internat. Reading Assn., Mich. Reading Assn., Am. Assn. Colls. Tchr. Edn., Assn. Supervision and Curriculum Devel., Smithsonian Assos., Lansing Investment Research Assos. Methodist. Home: 3655 Bayou Pl Holt MI 48842 Office: 115 Erickson Hall Mich State U East Lansing MI 48824

SNODDY, JOHN MARTIN, mfg. co. exec.; b. Marion, N.C., May 4, 1924; s. John Martin and Ethel Pearl (Riddle) S.; student N.C. State U., Raleigh; m. R. Marie Griffin, Nov. 24, 1949; children—Elizabeth, Emily. Plant mgr. Reeves Bros. Inc., Greenville, S.C.; sales mgr. Greige Goods div. Reeves Bros. Inc., N.Y.C.; pres. Fabrics div. The Bibb Co., N.Y.C. Served with U.S. Army, 1943-46. Decorated Bronze Star. Office: Fabrics Div The Bibb Co 111 W 40th St New York NY 10018*

SNODGRASS, ALAN CARL, banker; b. Chgo., Mar. 30, 1934; s. Harry Taylor and Louise Anna (Schroeder) S.; B.S. in Commerce, Tex. Christian U., 1954, M.B.A., 1964; diploma Stonier Grad. Sch. Banking, Rutgers U., 1966; m. Patsy Jane Canterbury, June 7, 1956; children—Catherine Lorraine, Julie Louise. With First Nat. Bank Ft. Worth, 1950—, asst. v.p., 1962-65, v.p., 1965-68, sr. v.p., 1968—; dir. Metroplex Nat. Bank, Arlington, Tex. Treas., Dallas-Ft. Worth Regional Airport Bd., 1970-74. Served with AUS, 1956-58. Clubs: Fort Worth, Shady Oaks Country (Ft. Worth). Home: 4108 Tamworth Rd Fort Worth TX 76116 Office: 1 Burnett Plaza Fort Worth TX 76102

SNODGRASS, WILLIAM DEWITT, writer, educator; b. Wilkinsburg, Pa., Jan. 5, 1926; s. Bruce DeWitt and Jesse Helen (Murchie) S.; student Geneva Coll., 1943-44, 46-47; B.A., State U. Iowa, 1949, M.A., 1951, M.F.A., 1953; m. Lila Jean Hank, June 6, 1946 (div. Dec. 1953); 1 dau., Cynthia Jean; m. 2d, Janice Marie Ferguson Wilson, Mar. 19, 1954 (div. Aug. 1966); children—Kathy Anne Wilson (foster dau.), Russell Bruce; m. 3d, Camille Rykowski, Sept. 13, 1967 (div. 1978). Faculty English dept. Cornell U., Ithaca, N.Y., 1955-57, U. Rochester, 1957-58; prof. English, Wayne State U., 1958-68; prof. English and speech Syracuse (N.Y.) U., 1968—; Disting. vis. prof. Old Dominion U., Norfolk, Va., 1978; Disting. vis. prof. English, U. Del., Newark, 1979—; mem. faculty Morehead (Ky.) Writers' Conf., summer 1955, Antioch Writers' Conf., Yellow Springs, Ohio, summer 1958, 59. Recipient Ingram-Merrill award, 1958; Hudson Review fellow in poetry, 1958-59; Longview lit. award, 1959; spl. citation Poetry Soc. Am., 1960; grantee Nat. Inst. Arts and Letters, 1960; Pulitzer prize poems, 1960; Guiness Poetry award, 1961; Miles' Modern Poetry award, 1966; Centennial medal Govt. of Romania, 1977; Guggenheim fellow, 1972-73. Fellow Am. Acad. Poets; mem. Nat. Inst. Arts and Letters. Mem. Soc. of Friends. Author: (poems) Heart's Needle, 1959; After Experience, 1968; Gallows Songs of Christian Morgenstern, 1967; (essays) In Radical Pursuit, 1975; The Führer Bunker, 1977; Six Troubador Songs, 1977; Traditional Hungarian Songs, 1978; If Birds Build with your Hair, 1979. Contbr. essays, poems, translations to lit. mags. Home: RD 1 Erieville NY 13061 Office: English Dept U Del Newark DE 19711

SNODGRESS, CARRIE, actress; b. Chgo.; ed. No. Ill. U.; 1 son, Zeke. Appeared in plays Goodman Theatre, Chgo., in play Vanities, 1977; films include Diary of a Mad Housewife, 1970, Rabbit, Run, 1970, The Fury, 1978; TV appearances include Silent Night, Lonely Night, The Whole World is Watching, The Outside, The Dark Ride, The Solitary Man, The Virginian, Judd for the Defense, Medical Center, Marcus Welby, M.D. Recipient Golden Apple award for New Female Star of Yr., 1970; Golden Globe awards for best actress in comedy/drama, most promising female newcomer, 1971; nominee Acad. award as best actress, 1971. Address: care Creative Artists and Assos 1888 Century Park E Century City CA 90067

SNOKE, HARRY CONWELL, lawyer, ch. ofcl.; b. Phila., July 29, 1905; s. Harry Albert and Bertha (Schultz) S.; A.B., U. Pa., 1927; LL.B., Temple U., 1931; LL.D., Baldwin Wallace Coll., 1961, Lycoming (Pa.) Coll., 1962; m. Alice Foster Hansen, Sept. 6, 1932. Admitted to Pa. bar, 1931, since practiced in Phila. Treas. nat. div. Meth. Ch., 1948-60, gen. sec., 1960-64, gen. treas. bd. missions, 1964-67; pres. Meth. Investment Fund, 1960-70; sec., treas. pension fund Eastern Pa. conf. United Meth. Ch., 1970-73; treas. div. home missions Nat. Council Chs., 1950-60. Bd. dirs. Goodwill Industries Am., 1948—, pres., 1967-71, chmn. bd., 1971-74; treas., trustee William Duncan Trust, Metlakatla, Alaska; sec., trustee George A. Ruck Trust, Phila.; trustee Alaska Meth. U., Spartanburg Jr. Coll., Paine Coll. Mem. Am., Phila. bar assns. Club: Atlantic City Country. Home: 238 Street Rd Southampton PA 18966

SNOOK, JOHN LLOYD, business exec., cons.; b. Troy, Ohio, Nov. 25, 1896; s. Clarence Guy and Anna B. (Counts) S.; Ph.B., Kenyon Coll., 1919; m. Alice V. Winger, June 21, 1923 (dec. Dec. 31, 1967); children—John Lloyd, Elizabeth Anne, Julia Winger, Alice Winger; m. 2d, Mary C. Gayler, Jan. 29, 1972. Sec., treas., plant mgr. Kitchen Aid Mfg. Co., Springfield, Ohio, 1919-24; prof. indsl. research Antioch Coll., Yellow Springs, Ohio, 1924-30; pres., gen. mgr. J.L. Snook Co. (formerly Antioch Shoe Project, Inc.), 1930-60. Cons. SCORE, 1966—. Mem. dist. 11, Fla. Ancillary Manpower Planning Bd.; mem. Lakeland Creative and Performing Arts Council; chmn. Scioto County chpt. A.R.C., 1946-59; chmn. Greater Lakeland (Fla.) chpt., 1965—, life mem., 1970—; mem. nominating com. Am. Nat. Red Cross, 1948-49, mem. Eastern area adv. council, 1950-52, vice chmn. mems. and funds Ohio, 1953-55, mem. nat. bd. govs., 1957-61, mem. Fla. conf. com., 1965—; chmn. Ret. Sr. Vol. Program; mem. Human Services Council; bd. dirs. YMCA, 1957-62, pres. Clay Twp. br., 1960-62; bd. dirs. Lakeland Family YMCA, 1967—, treas., 1973—; chmn. Scioto County Community Chest, 1950; bd. dirs. Scioto County Crippled Children's Soc., 1948-60, pres., 1950-56; active Ohio Soc. Crippled Children, 1949-55, pres., 1951-52; dir. Nat. Soc. Crippled Children, 1951-52; pres. Scioto County Council Social Agys., 1953-55; chmn. Com. for Ministry to Def. Community in Scioto Valley, 1952-56; mem. Portsmouth Town Hall Forum Com., 1942-60, chmn., 1955-59; exec. com. Ohio Citizens Council for Health and Welfare, 1954-59; bd. dirs. United Cerebral Palsy of Polk County, Fla., 1962—, v.p., 1964—; bd. dirs. United Fund of Greater Lakeland, 1964—; bd. dirs. Salvation Army, 1965—, chmn. adv. bd., 1968-70; bd. dirs. Human Relations Council; pres. Lakeland Concert Assn., 1968-71; bd. counsellors Fla. So. Coll. Mem. bishop and chpt. Diocese of So. Ohio, Episcopal Ch., 1956-59, del. ho. of dels., 1955; chmn. dept. stewardship and every mem. canvass Diocese of S. Fla., 1964—, mem. exec. bd., 1966—, chmn. dept. communications Diocese S. Fla.; pres. Portsmouth Assn. Chs., 1949-50; adminstrv. com. Ohio Council Chs., 1954-61, trustee Found., 1961-62; dir. Fla. Council Chs., 1968—. Mem. Portsmouth City Charter Revision Com., 1951-52. Served as ensign, aviation USN, 1918-19; lt. comdr. USNR, 1944-46. Recipient citation for outstanding performance Navy Dept., 1945. Mem. Nat. Mgmt. Assn. (charter), Mid-State Tb and Respiratory Assn. (dir. 1969—), Imperial Polk Mgmt. Assn. (hon. life), Delta Kappa Epsilon. Episcopalian (past sr. warden, vestryman, jr. warden 1966—). Mason, Rotarian (past pres., past dist. gov., dir. 1964-67, 68-71, Coll. Govs. 1963—, Paul Harris Fellow award 1975). Home: 1342 Edgewater Beach Dr Lakeland FL 33801

SNOOK, JOHN ORLA, lawyer, found. exec.; b. Sterling, Kans., Aug. 31, 1902; s. Arthur Jordan and Rachel P. (Dawson) S.; A.B., Sterling Coll., 1924, LL.D., 1963; J.D., Northwestern U., 1928; m. Kathryn Koons, Oct. 14, 1934. Admitted Ill. bar, 1929, since practiced in Chgo.; mem. firm Concannon, Dillon, Snook & Morton, 1937—; bd.

dirs. Kellogg Co., 1965—. Trustee La Rabida Children's Hosp. and Research Center, 1945-79, W. K. Kellogg Found., 1953—. Arbitrator, Am. Arbitration Assn. Mem. Am., Ill., Chgo. bar assns., Pi Kappa Delta. Home: 770 Sheridan Rd Glencoe IL 60022 Office: 111 W Washington St Chicago IL 60602

SNORTLAND, HOWARD JEROME, state govt. ofcl.; b. Sharon, N.D., June 22, 1912; s. Thomas and Aline (Vig) S.; B.A., U. N.D., 1937, M.S., 1958; m. Anna Adeline Anderson, Sept. 1, 1940; children—Jan Signe, Kristi Jo, Howard Jay. Cashier, N.D. Workmen's Compensation Bur., 1937-42, N.D. State Treas.'s Office, 1945-48; with N.D. Dept. Pub. Instrn., Bismarck, 1948—, supt. pub. instrn., 1977—; pres. State Econ. Council, 1978; nat. pres. Com. Ednl. Data Systems, 1965-67. Chmn. Burleigh County A.R.C., 1963-67, bd. dirs., 1946—, vice chmn., 1964—; bd. dirs. Burleigh County Tb Assn., 1950—; stated clk. United Presbyterian Ch., 1942—; pres. N.D. United Christian Campus Fellowship, 1964-67, N.D. Westminster Found., 1963-70; mem. N.D. Synod Council, 1970—. Served with USAAF, 1942-45. Recipient Summit Conf. award for outstanding pub. service, 1976. Mem. NEA, N.D. Edn. Assn., N.D. Sch. Bus. Ofcls., N.D. Assn. Adminstrs., Nat. Assn. Adminstrs., Phi Beta Kappa, Phi Delta Kappa. Club: Kiwanis (dir.). Home: 1324 Meredith Dr Bismarck ND 58501 Office: State Capitol Bismarck ND 58505

SNOW, GEORGE ABRAHAM, educator; b. N.Y.C., Aug. 24, 1926; s. Joseph and Anna (Snow) Ginsberg; B.S., Coll. City N.Y., 1945; M.A., Princeton, 1947, Ph.D., 1949; m. Lila Alpert, June 20, 1948; children—Zachary, Andrew, Sara Ellen. Jr. physicist Brookhaven Nat. Lab., Upton, N.Y., 1948-51, asso. physicist, 1951-55; physicist Naval Research Lab., Washington, 1955-58; vis. prof. dept. physics and astronomy U. Md., College Park, 1957-58, asso. prof., 1958-61, prof., 1961—, acting chmn. dept. physics and astronomy, 1970-71. Mem. Inst. for Advanced Study, Princeton, 1952-53; vis. lectr. U. Wis., Madison, 1955-56; vis. prof. U. Rome, 1965-66, U. Paris (France), Oxford, 1972-73; mem. high energy physics adv. panel AEC, 1970-72; mem. high energy physics vis. com. Argonne Nat. Lab., 1969-71, Princeton-Pa. Accelerator, 1969-70; mem. high energy physics adv. com. Brookhaven Nat. Lab., 1967-69; cons. to physics editor Prentice Hall, Inc., 1971-76. Trustee, URA, 1973-78, vice chmn., 1974, chmn. sci. com., 1975-77. NSF sr. postdoctoral fellow, 1961-62; John S. Guggenheim sr. fellow, Fulbright scholar, 1965-66. Cited by Washington Acad. Scis., 1963. Fellow Am. Phys. Soc. (mem. exec. council div. particles and fields 1968-70, vice chmn. div. particles and fields 1975, chmn. 1976); mem. Fedn. Am. Scientists, Am. Assn. Physics Tchrs., AAAS, Chesapeake Physics Assn., Phi Beta Kappa, Sigma Xi. Home: 4816 Essex Ave Chevy Chase MD 20015 Office: Dept Physics and Astronomy U Md College Park MD 20742

SNOW, GORDON HAROLD, lawyer, ins. co. exec.; b. Chgo., Mar. 14, 1907; s. Ernest Alexander and Augusta (Smith) S.; Ph.B., U. Wis., 1930; postgrad. San Francisco Law Sch., 1937-38; LL.D., J.D., Golden Gate Coll. Law, 1941; m. Dorothy Pride, June 1, 1932; 1 son, Gordon Harold. Admitted to Calif. bar, 1941; practice in San Francisco, 1942—; counsel firm O'Connell & Cook, San Francisco, 1948-72; sr. partner Veatch, Snow, Carlson, Dorsey & Quimby, Los Angeles, 1972—; sr. v.p., dir. Pacific Indemnity Co., Northwestern Pacific Indemnity Co., Tex. Pacific Indemnity Co.; v.p. Chubb & Son, Inc. Chmn. nat. governing bd. Nat. Automobile Theft Bur. Mem. U.S. Power Squadron (legal officer), USCG Aux. (past capt.). Clubs: Jonathan (Los Angeles); Shark Island Yacht (staff commodore) (Newport Beach, Calif.). Home: 19192 Woodford Terr Irvine CA 92715 Office: 3200 Wilshire Blvd Los Angeles CA 90005 also 18952 MacArthur Blvd Irvine CA 92715

SNOW, HANK (CLARENCE EUGENE SNOW), country music entertainer; b. Brooklyn, N.S., Can., May 9, 1914; s. George Lewis and Marie Alice (Boutlier) S.; came to U.S., 1948, naturalized, 1957; m. Minnie Blanche Aalders, Sept. 2, 1935; 1 son, Jimmie Rodgers. Star show Clarence Snow and His Guitar radio sta. CHNS, Halifax, N.S., 1935; rec. star RCA Records, 1936—; performed as The Singing Ranger, U.S. and Can., 1946-50; mem. Grand Ole Opry, Nashville, 1950—; toured Europe, Far East; owner Hank Snow Music Inc., Hank's Music Inc.; assigned as exclusive writer to Hill & Range Songs, Inc., N.Y.C., 1948. Entertainer U.S. Armed Forces, Korea, 1953, Vietnam, 1967. Founder, Hank Snow Internat. Found. for Prevention of Child Abuse and Neglect of Children, Inc., 1978. Named Am.'s Favorite Folk Singer, Song Round-Up mag., Billboard mag., 1954; named Top Country Singer Can., 1940—; named to Songwriter's Hall of Fame, 1978, Can. Hall of Fame, 1979, Country Music Hall of Fame, 1979; recipient numerous citations, plaques, awards for best-selling records. Recorded numerous albums including My Early Country Favorites, Hank Snow Souvenirs, Hank Snow Sings Your Favorite Country Hits, Heartbreak Trail, Gospel Train, My Nova Scotia Home, This Is My Story, Cure for The Blues; also numerous singles. Home: 310 E Marthonna Dr Madison TN 37115 Office: PO Box 1084 Nashville TN 37202

SNOW, HERMAN BERNARD, hosp. adminstr.; b. N.Y.C., Mar. 6, 1909; s. Harry and Sarah (Mistofsky) Snofsky; B.A., Syracuse U., 1929, M.D., 1933; m. Eleanor Frances Howell, Nov. 12, 1934; 1 son, Robert. Intern, Univ. Hosp., Syracuse, 1933-34; resident psychiatrist Binghamton (N.Y.) State Hosp., 1934-36, sr. psychiatrist, 1936-39, supervising psychiatrist, 1939; practice medicine specializing in cons. psychiatry, Binghamton, 1946-48, Utica, N.Y., 1948-54, Ogdensburg, N.Y., 1954-62, Poughkeepsie, N.Y., 1962-79; asst. dir. Utica State Hosp., 1948; med. insp. Dept. Mental Hygiene, Albany, N.Y., 1949-51; dir. St. Lawrence State Hosp., Ogdensburg, 1954-62; psychiat. cons. VA Hosp., Sunmount, N.Y., 1957-62, Postdam (N.Y.) Hosp., 1959-62; dir. Hudson River State Hosp., Poughkeepsie, 1962-79; psychiat. cons. Vassar Bros., St. Francis hosps. Mem. Gov.'s Prison Commn., 1963—. Mem. N.Y. State Bd. Medicine, 1963-75. Served to capt. N.Y. N.G., 1935-39; to lt. col. M.C., AUS, 1940-46. Recipient citations St. Lawrence U., 1958, Congregation Anshe Zophen, 1958, Adolf Meyer award for distinguished service in behalf of improved care and treatment of mentally ill, 1959; named Ky. col., 1963. Diplomate Am. Bd. Psychiatry and Neurology. Fellow Am. Psychiat. Assn. (life, pres. Mid. Hudson br. 1965-66), Am. Coll. Psychiatry (hon.); mem. Med. Soc. State N.Y., Assn. Med. Supts. Mental Hosps. (pres. 1965), AMA, Dutchess County Med. Soc. (pres. 1967). Contbr. articles to profl. jours. Address: Royal Crest Apts 2-C-2 Hyde Park NY 12538

SNOW, JAMES BYRON, JR., physician, med. educator; b. Oklahoma City, Mar. 12, 1932; s. James B. and Charlotte Louise (Andersen) S.; B.S., U. Okla., 1953; M.D. cum laude, Harvard, 1956; M.A. (hon.), U. Pa., 1973; m. Sallie Lee Ricker, July 16, 1954; children—James B., John Andrew, Sallie Lee Louise. Intern Johns Hopkins Hosp., Balt., 1956-57; resident Mass. Eye and Ear Infirmary, Boston, 1957-60; prof., head dept. otorhinolaryngology Sch. Medicine U. Okla., Oklahoma City, 1962-72; prof., chmn. dept. otorhinolaryngology and human communication U. Pa. at Phila., 1972—. Mem. nat. adv. council neurol. and communicative disorders and stroke NIH, 1972-76; chmn. Nat. Com. Research Neurol. and Communicative Disorders, 1979—. Served with M.C., AUS, 1960-62. Recipient Regents award for superior teaching U. Okla., 1970. Diplomate Am. Bd. Otolaryngology (dir. 1972—). Mem. Soc. Univ. Otolaryngologists (pres. 1975), Am. Acad. Otolaryngology (asso. sec.), A.C.S., Am. Laryngol. Rhinol., Otol. Soc., Am. Otol. Soc., Am. Laryngol. Assn., Am. Broncho-esophagol. Assn. (editor trans. 1973-77, pres. 1979), Collegium Otorhinolaryngologicum, Phi Beta Kappa, Alpha Omega Alpha. Contbr. articles in field to sci. and profl. jours. Home: 708 Governors Circle Newtown Square PA 19073 Office: 3400 Spruce St Philadelphia PA 19104

SNOW, PHOEBE, vocalist, musician, composer; b. N.Y.C., 1951; student Shimer Coll.; m. Phil Kearns; 1 dau., Valerie Rose. Formerly recs. for Shelter Records, now with Columbia Records; recs. include (singles) Poetry Man, Harpo's Blues; albums include Phoebe Snow, 1974, Second Childhood, 1975, It Looks Like Snow, 1976, Never Letting Go, 1977, Against the Grain, 1979. Office: care Tiburon Artists Mgmt 19 Main St Tiburon CA 94920*

SNOW, PHYLLIS ROBERTA, former coll. dean; b. Phila., Aug. 26, 1912; d. Lawrence Crosby and Mattie (McArthur) S.; B.A. in Home Econs. Edn., U. Utah, 1934; M.S. in Home Mgmt., Cornell U., 1953, Ph.D. in Food and Home Mgmt., 1956. Emergency relief case worker Fed. Emergency Relief Adminstrn., 1934-35; tchr. gen. home. econs. Jordan Sch. Dist., Midvale, Utah, 1935-39; tchr. foods and nutrition Salt Lake City sch. system, 1939-43; home service dir. Mountain Fuel Supply Co., Salt Lake City, 1943-52; vis. lectr. Brigham Young U., summer 1961, Alta. (Can.) Tchrs. Assn., summer 1962; grad. asst. Cornell U., 1953-56, asso. prof., 1956-61; dean Coll. Family Life, Utah State U., Logan, 1961-78; ret., 1978. Mem. Gov. Utah Com. on Status Women, 1970-76. Mem. AAUW, Inst. Food Technologists, Faculty Women's League, Phi Kappa Phi, Omicron Nu, Phi Upsilon Omicron. Mem. Ch. Jesus Christ of Latter-Day Saints. Contbr. articles to profl. jours. Home: 165 East 1st North Apt E Logan UT 84321

SNOW, WILLIAM HAYDEN, electric co. exec.; b. Shreveport, La., May 7, 1926; s. Lee Harley and Kathleen (Van Hoose) S.; B.S., Centenary Coll., 1948; postgrad. La. State U., 1948-49; M.B.A., Tulane U., 1950; grad. pub. utility exec. course U. Mich., 1962; m. Jo Ann Drake, Jan. 19, 1952; children—James Hayden, Karen Ann. With Southwestern Electric Power Co., Shreveport, La., 1950—, supr. budgets and statistics, 1965-68, asst. controller, 1968-69, controller, 1969—, v.p., 1973—, v.p. fin., 1977—. Mem. Shreveport Park and Recreation Council. Served with USAAF, 1944-46. Recipient L.M. Moffitt award Shreveport Jr. C. of C., 1961-62; Pres.'s Trophy Shreveport chpt. Nat. Assn. Accountants, 1964-65. Mem. Missouri Valley Electric Assn., Edison Electric Inst., Nat. Assn. Accountants (pres. Shreveport chpt. 1969-70, nat. dir. 1974-76), Shreveport C. of C., Shreveport Jr. C. of C. (treas. 1960-61, dir. 1960-62). Presbyterian (deacon). Clubs: Caddo Toastmasters (pres. 1966-67); Shreveport, Shreveport Country. Home: 337 Woodbine Dr Shreveport LA 71105 Office: 428 Travis St Shreveport LA 71156

SNOWBARGER, WILLIS EDWARD, ednl. adminstr.; b. Sylvia, Kans., Aug. 24, 1921; s. Edward William and Mary (King) S.; A.B., Bethany-Peniel Coll., Bethany, Okla., 1942; A.M., U. Okla., 1947; Ph.D., U. Calif., Berkeley, 1950; m. Wahnona Ruth Horger, Jan. 31, 1943; children—Vincent Keith, Delia Mae. Teaching asst. U. Calif., 1947-49; prof. history, chmn. dept. Olivet Nazarene Coll., 1949-65, 70—, coll. dean, 1953-65, 70-76, v.p. charge acad. affairs, 1964-65, 70—; exec. sec. Dept. Edn., Ch. Nazarene, Kansas City, Mo., 1965-70. Served as lt. USNR, 1942-45, PTO. Mem. Am. Hist. Assn., Phi Alpha Theta, Phi Delta Lambda, Kappa Delta Pi. Mem. Church of the Nazarene. Home: 1279 Gertsam Dr Bradley IL 60915 Office: Olivet Nazarene College Kankakee IL 60901

SNOWDEN, FRANK MARTIN, JR., educator; b. York County, Va., July 17, 1911; s. Frank Martin and Alice (Phillips) S.; grad. Boston Latin Sch., 1928; A.B., Harvard, 1932, A.M., 1933, Ph.D., 1944; postgrad. Am. Acad. in Rome, summer 1938; Fulbright research scholar, Italy, 1949-50; LL.D., Bard Coll., 1957; D.Litt., Union Coll., 1979; m. Elaine Hill, June 8, 1935; children—Jane Alice, Frank Martin III. Instr. classics Va. State Coll., 1933-36, Spelman Coll., 1936-40; instr. classics Howard U., 1942-44, chmn. dept., 1942-77, asso. prof., 1944-45, prof., 1945—, dir. Summer Sch., 1942-54, dir. Evening Sch. and Adult Edn., 1942-48, chmn. Humanities Program, 1950-51, dean Coll. Liberal Arts, 1956-68; specialist lectr. Internat. Information Adminstrn., Dept. State, French West Africa, Gold Coast, Nigeria, Libya, Italy, Greece, Austria, 1953; cultural attache Am. embassy, Rome, Italy, 1954-56; vis. lectr. Fgn. Service Inst., 1956-62, 66-68; U.S. specialist in India, lectr., Bombay, New Delhi, Lucknow, Calcutta, Madras areas, 1957; lectr. as U.S. specialist, Brazil, summer 1960; studied higher edn. Soviet Union, 1958; participant internat. seminar University Today, Dubrovnik, Yugoslavia, 1958; mem. U.S. del. UNESCO, Paris, 1958, 60, U.S. nat. commn. for UNESCO, 1958-61; mem. Nat. Humanities Faculty, 1969-70, mem. bd., 1970-73; ann. lectr. Archaeol. Inst. Am., 1970-71, 74-76; vis. scholar U. Center Va. 1971-72; mem. com. Internat. Exchange Persons, 1970-73; mem. jury to select fellows in classics Am. Acad. Rome, 1971-73; mem. com. Folger Fellowship Program, 1972-75; Am. Council Learned Socs. rep. Council on Internat. Exchange of Scholars, 1973-77; mem. D.C. com. on Fulbright scholarships, 1951-54, 68-74; fellow Woodrow Wilson Internat. Center for Scholars, 1977; scholar-in-residence Rockefeller Found., Bellagio, Italy, fall 1977. Mem. D.C. Mayor's Commn. Arts and Humanities, 1972-74; vis. com. bd. overseers dept. classics Harvard Coll., 1977-81. Decorated Medaglia d'Oro for outstanding work Italian culture and edn., Italy, 1958. Am. Council Learned Socs. fellow, 1962-63; Nat. Endowment for Humanities grantee, summer 1970. Mem. Am. Conf. Acad. Deans (sec., editor 1959-62, chmn. 1963-64), Am. Council on Edn., Vergilian Soc. Am. (trustee 1956-60), Am. Philol. Assn. (Charles J. Goodwin award of merit 1973, bd. dirs. 1976-79), Archeol. Inst. Am. (pres. Washington soc. 1971), Classical Soc. Am. Acad. in Rome, Washington Classical Soc. (v.p. 1949-50, pres. 1974-75), Washington Fedn. Chs. (v.p. 1951-53). Clubs: Cosmos, Harvard. Author: Blacks in Antiquity; Ethiopians in the Greco-Roman Experience; co-author: The Image of the Black in Western Art I: From the Pharaohs to the Fall of the Roman Empire (also pub. in French), 1976. Contbr. articles to classical and ednl. jours. Home: 4200 Massachusetts Ave NW Washington DC 20016

SNOWDEN, FREDRICK, educator; b. Brewton, Ala., Apr. 3, 1936; s. Julia Johnson S.; B.S. in Phys. Edn., Wayne State U., 1958, M.S., 1965; m. Maye Boga, July 14, 1962; 1 child, Stacey Shannon. Head basketball and baseball coach Northwestern High Sch., Detroit, 1958-68; asst. basketball coach U. Mich., Ann Arbor, 1968-72; mem. faculty U. Ariz., Tucson, 1972—, head basketball coach, asso. prof. health and phys. edn.; dir. Am. Savs. & Loan, Tucson. Mem. Presdl. Environ. Merit Awards Commn.; co-chmn. Ariz. March of Dimes, 1974. Named Tucson Man of Yr., 1973; Coach of Yr., Western Athletic Conf. and Dist. 7, 1973. Mem. Nat. Assn. Basketball Coaches. Office: McKale Center U Ariz Tucson AZ 85712*

SNOWDEN, LAWRENCE FONTAINE, aircraft co. exec., ret. marine corps officer; b. Charlottesville, Va., Apr. 14, 1921; s. Lawrence Fontaine Snoddy and Beatrice M. (Huffman) S.; student Stetson U., 1938-39; B.S., U. Va., 1942; M.A., Northwestern U., 1950; advanced mgmt. program Harvard U., 1968; grad. Indsl. Coll. Armed Forces, 1967; m. Martha Roselyn Ham, Nov. 17, 1942; children—John Stephen, Brian Fontaine. Commd. 2d lt. USMC, 1942, advanced through grades to lt. gen., 1975; comdr. 7th Marine Regt., Vietnam, 1966; ops. officer III Marine Amphibious Force, Vietnam, 1967; asst. dir. personnel Hdqrs. Marine Corps, Washington, 1968-69, dir. systems support group, 1969-70; dir. Marine Corps Devel. Center, Quantico, Va., 1970-72; former chief of staff Hdqrs. U.S. Forces, Japan. U.S. rep. Japan-U.S. Joint Com.; U.S. rep. UN Bd. in Japan, 1972-75; ret., 1979; v.p. Far East area Hughes Aircraft Internat. Service Co. subs. Hughes Aircraft Co., 1979—. Exec. v.p. Far East council Boy Scouts Am., also mem. nat. adv. council. Recipient Disting. Eagle Scout award Boy Scouts Am.; decorated Legion of Merit (5), Army Commendation medal, Navy Commendation medal, D.S.M., Purple Heart (2); Cross of Gallantry (3) (Vietnam); Second Order of Sacred Treasure (Japan). Mem. VFW, Marine Corps League, Marine Corps Assn., U.S. Naval Inst., Sigma Nu. Office: Hughes Aircraft Internat Central PO Box 1089 Tokyo 100-91 Japan

SNOWDON, JOHN COLIN, physicist; b. London, June 21, 1932; s. Cecil Filis and Norah Cater (Crowhurst) S.; came to U.S., 1956, naturalized, 1965; B.Sc. in Physics and Math., U. London, 1952, B.Sc. in Physics, 1953, D.I.C., Imperial Coll. Sci., 1956, Ph.D., 1956, D.Sc., 1965; m. Anne Joy Vickery, Sept. 8, 1956; children—Jane Louise, Mark Andrew. Research scientist Philco Corp., Phila., 1956-58; research asso. Willow Run Labs., Ann Arbor, Mich., 1958-59, asso. research physicist, 1959-60; vibration engr. Hawker-Siddeley Aviation, Ltd., Eng., 1960-61; asst. prof. engring. research Applied Research Lab., Pa. State U., State College, 1961-64, asso. prof., 1964-67, prof., 1967—; mem. Nat. Acad. Scis.-NRC evaluation panel for Mechanics div. Inst. for Basic Standards, Nat. Bur. Standards, 1970-73, ad hoc panel for acoustics and vibration, 1972-74; chmn., organizer Pa. State U. seminars, 1972-79; program chmn. Inter-Noise 74, Internat. Conf. Noise Control Engring. Fellow Acoustical Soc. Am. (pres. 1977, asso. editor jour. 1966—), Brit. Inst. Physics, Brit. Inst. Acoustics, Am. Acad. Mechanics; mem. ASME (chmn. shock and vibration com. applied mechanics div. 1972-73), Sigma Xi. Episcopalian. Club: Pa. State U. Faculty. Author: Vibration and Shock in Damped Mechanical Systems, 1968. Editor: (with E.E. Ungar) Isolation of Mechanical Vibration, Impact and Noise, 1973; Proceedings of Inter-Noise 74, 1974; bd. editors Dept. Def. Shock and Vibration Digest, 1975—; editorial adv. bd. Jour. Soc. Environ. Engrs., 1975—. Contbr. articles to profl. jours. Home: 251 S Osmond St State College PA 16801 Office: Applied Research Lab PO Box 30 State College PA 16801

SNOWE, OLYMPIA J., congresswoman; b. Augusta, Maine, Feb. 21, 1947; B.A., U. Maine, 1969. Businesswoman; dir. Superior Concrete Co., Inc.; mem. Maine Ho. of Reps., 1973-76; mem. Maine Senate, 1976-78, chmn. com. on health and instl. services; mem. 96th Congress from 2d Maine Dist.; corporator Mechanics Savs. Bank. Mem. Gov.'s Commn. Alcoholism, Drug Abuse and Treatment, Gov.'s Adv. Com. on U. Maine, Gov.'s Positive Action Com.; dir. Kent's Hill Sch.; mem. Bd. of Voter Registration, Auburn, Maine, 1971-73. Mem. Lewiston-Auburn League of Women Voters. Republican. Greek Orthodox. Club: Philoptochos Soc. Office: 1729 Longworth House Office Bldg Washington DC 20515

SNYDER, ARTHUR, publishing co. exec.; b. Valley Stream, N.Y., Feb. 6, 1925; s. Arthur and Kathryn (Staubitzer) S.; B. Metall. Engring., Cornell U., Ithaca, N.Y., 1950, M.B.A., 1952; m. Betty Lain Harper, July 8, 1950; children—Susan, Arthur, Betsy, Jack, Heidi, Bonnie. Mfg. engr. Norton Co., Worcester, Mass., 1952-56, chief accountant, 1956-58, asst. controller, 1958-59, mgr. data processing, 1959-61, controller, 1961-65; exec. v.p. A.M. Best Co., Oldwick, N.J., 1965-67, pres., 1968-70, chmn., 1971—; chmn. bd. Risk Exchange, Inc., Oldwick, N.J., 1978—; dir. Rockaway Corp. Served to 1st lt. 95th Inf. div. AUS, 1942-45. Decorated Bronze Star with oak leaf cluster, Purple Heart. Mem. Fin. Execs. Inst., Cornell Soc. Engrs. Presbyterian. Clubs: Roxiticus Golf (Mendham, N.J.); Baltusrol Golf (Springfield, N.J.); Morris County Golf (Morristown, N.J.); High Meadows Hunt (Far Hills, N.J.); Mendham Valley Gun (Green Village, N.J.). Author: Principles of Inventory Control and Managing Capital Expenditures. Home: Lloyd Rd Bernardsville NJ 07924 Office: Ambest Rd Oldwick NJ 08858

SNYDER, ASA EDWARD, mgmt. cons.; b. McGehee, Ark., May 17, 1923; s. Lucien Edward and Oliva (Richardson) S.; B.S. in Mech. Engring., Swarthmore Coll., 1951; M.S. in Mech. Engring., Princeton, 1952; m. Jean Elizabeth Mosher, Sept. 14, 1946; children—Kim S. Rice, Jon Richardson, Jared Mark, Adam Edward. Engr. Baldwin Locomotive Works, Eddystone, Pa., 1947-48; sr. project engr. Internat. Harvester Co., 1953-55; supr. advanced component design Gen. Electric Co., 1955-58; dir. research clearing div. U.S. Industries, Inc., 1958-60, exec. v.p. tech. center, Pompano Beach, Fla., 1960; v.p. research Pratt & Whitney Co., West Hartford, Conn., 1960-64; dir. tech. planning Colt Industries, 1964-69; founder, prin. Snyder Assos., mgmt. cons., Essex, Conn., 1970—. Instr. engring., evening div. Northeastern U., 1957-58. Pres., Middlesex council Boy Scouts Am. Served as lt. (j.g.) USNR, 1943-46. Mem. Internat. Assn. Exchange Tech. Students (chmn. 1962-70), ASME, Soc. Automotive Engrs., Soc. Internat. Devel., AAAS, Sigma Xi, Sigma Tau. Clubs: Princeton (N.Y.C.); Miles Creek Beach, Pettipaug Yacht; Old Saybrook Racquet. Home: Harbor View East Essex CT 06426 Office: Snyder Assos Essex CT 06426

SNYDER, CHARLES ROYCE, sociologist, educator; b. Haverford, Pa., Dec. 28, 1924; s. Edward D. and Edith (Royce) S.; grad. Hill Sch., 1942; B.A., Yale, 1944, M.A., 1949, Ph.D. 1954; m. Patricia Hanson, June 30, 1951; children—Stephen Hoyt, Christiana Marie, Constance Patricia, Daniel Edward. Mem. staff Yale Center Alcohol Studies, 1950-60; asst. prof. sociology Yale, 1956-60; prof. sociology So. Ill. U., 1960—, chmn. dept., 1964-75; cons. behavioral scis. tgn. com. Nat. Inst. Gen. Med. Scis., NIH, 1962-64; mem. planning com., dep. chmn. program 28th Internat. Congress Alcohol and Alcoholism, 1964—. Mem. theol. commn. United Ch. of Christ, 1964—. Served with USNR, World War II. Fellow Am. Sociol. Assn.; mem. Soc. Study Social Problems (v.p. 1963-64, rep. to council Am. Sociol. Assn. 1964-66), Midwest Sociol. Soc. (dir. 1970—), AAUP. Author: Alcohol and the Jews, 1958. Editor: (with D. J. Pittman) Society, Culture and Drinking Patterns, 1962; mem. editorial bd. Quar. Jour. Studies on Alcohol, 1957—; asso. editor Sociol. Quar., 1960-63. Home: 705 Taylor Dr Carbondale IL 62901

SNYDER, CLAIR ALLISON, banker; b. Reading, Pa., June 12, 1921; s. Augustus M. and Estella G. (Bright) S.; student W.Va. U., 1943-44, U. Mich., 1944-45; m. Jean Doris George, June 27, 1948; children—Joan Marie Snyder Ferguson, Jerry George. With Am. Bank and Trust Co. of Pa., Reading, 1938-43, 46—, exec. v.p., gen. banking, 1973-78, exec. v.p., chmn. credit policy com., 1978—; chmn., pres. Pa. Devel. Credit Corp., Am. Bus. Credit Corp., Am. Venture Capital Corp.; dir. Colonial Berks Real Estate Co. Nat. del. dir. Am. Cancer Soc.; bd. dirs. Pa. div. Am. Cancer Soc., 1965—, chmn. bd. dirs., 1975-77; bd. dirs. Berks County (Pa.) unit Am. Cancer Soc., 1955—, pres. bd. dirs., 1964-66; v.p. Wyomissing Hills (Pa.) City Council. Served with U.S. Army, 1943-46. Recipient Luther Halsey Gulick award Camp Fire Girls, 1966; cert. comml. lender, Am. Bankers Assn. Mem. Pa. Bankers Assn. (group chmn. 1972-73), Robert Morris Assos. (pres. 1972-73). Republican. Mem. United

Churches of Christ. Clubs: Moselem Springs Golf, Wyomissing, Iris, Seaview Country (Atlantic City, N.J.), Am. Legion (post comdr. 1948-49). Home: 4 Northfield Rd Wyomissing Hills PA 19609 Office: 35 N 6th St Reading PA 19601. *My life has been dedicated to personal achievement, but always with the knowledge that mankind's progress can only occur if each of us is willing to commit some of our efforts and resources to the future.*

SNYDER, DANIEL J., JR., fed. judge; b. 1916; B.A., Wooster Coll.; LL.B., U. Pitts. Admitted to Pa. bar, 1941; judge U.S. Dist. Ct. Western Dist. Pa. Mem. Am. Bar Assn. Office: US Dist Ct US Post Office and Courthouse Courtroom 11 10th Floor Pittsburgh PA 15219*

SNYDER, EDWARD PHEATT, banker; b. Toledo, Jan. 9, 1924; s. Ralph O. and Babette (Pheatt) S.; B.A., Oberlin Coll., 1948; student U. Chgo., 1948-51; m. Alice Boston, Aug. 27, 1949; children—Katharine, Ralph. Economist, Treasury Dept., 1951-53, Fed. Res. Bd., 1953-61; economist Treasury Dept., 1961-66, dir. Office Debt Analysis, 1966-76, sr. adviser for debt research, 1976-79; v.p. Nat. Bank Detroit, 1979—. Served with USAAF, 1943-46. Mem. Am. Econ. Assn. Home: 630 Westchester Rd Grosse Pointe Park MI 48230 Office: Nat Bank Detroit Detroit MI 48236

SNYDER, EDWIN KNOWLSON, ret. naval officer, congressional affairs cons.; b. Detroit, Feb. 12, 1922; s. Edwin Stahl and Helen (Knowlson) S.; B.S., U.S. Naval Acad., 1943; M.A., Stanford U., 1957; m. Nancy McCarty, Oct. 19, 1945; children—Stephen W., Thomas E., Charles W., Kathie Ann. Commd. ensign U.S. Navy, 1943, advanced through grades to vice adm., 1974; submarine war patrols, 1943-45; various assignments, 1945-68; comdg. officer U.S.S. Newport News, 1968-70; chief legis. affairs Navy Dept., Washington, 1971-74; comdr. U.S. Taiwan Def. Command, 1974-77; pres. Snyder & Ball Assos., Inc., Arlington, Va., 1977—. Decorated D.S.M. (2), Legion of Merit (3), Bronze Star. Home: 1101 S Arlington Ridge Rd Arlington VA 22202

SNYDER, GARY SHERMAN, poet; b. San Francisco, May 8, 1930; s. Harold Alton and Lois (Wilkie) S.; B.A., Reed Coll., 1951; postgrad. Ind. U., 1951-52, U. Calif. at Berkeley, 1953-56; m. Masa Uehara, Aug. 6, 1967; children—Kai, Gen. Lookout, Mount Baker Forest, 1952-53; research in Japan, 1956-57, 59-64; lectr. U. Calif. at Berkeley, 1964-65. Bollingen fellow, 1966-67; Poetry award Nat. Inst. Arts and Letters; Pulitzer prize for poetry, 1975; Guggenheim fellow, 1968-69. Author: (poems) Riprap, 1959; Myths and Texts, 1960; Six Sections from Mountains and Rivers without End, 1965; A Range of Poems, 1966; The Back Country, 1968; Earth House Hold, 1969; Regarding Wave, 1970; Turtle Island, 1974; The Old Ways, 1977; (prose) He who Hunted Birds in His Father's Village, 1979. Office: care New Directions 333 6th Ave New York NY 10003

SNYDER, GEORGE EDWARD, lawyer; b. Battle Creek, Mich., Feb. 7, 1934; s. Leon R. and Edith (Dullabahn) S.; B.S., Mich. State U., 1957; J.D., U. Mich., 1960; m. Mary Jane Belt, July 27, 1957; children—Sara Lynn, Elizabeth Jane. With Gen. Electric Co., 1957-58; admitted to Mich. bar, 1961; asso. firm Miller, Johnson, Snell & Commisky, Grand Rapids, 1960-62, Goodenough & Buesser, Detroit, 1962-66; partner firm Buesser, Buesser, Snyder & Blank, Detroit and Bloomfield Hills, 1966—; dir. Bill Knapps Mich., Inc. Chmn. E. Mich. Environ. Action Council, 1974-78; pub. mem. inland lakes and streams rev. com. Mich. Dept. Natural Resources, 1975-76. Served as 2d lt. AUS, 1957. Mem. State Bar Mich. (chmn. family law com. 1968-72, mem. rep. assembly 1972-78, chmn. rules and calendar com. 1977-78, mem. family law sect. council 1973-76, prepaid legal services com. 1973—, com. on judicial selection 1974, com. on specialization 1976—), Am., Detroit (chmn. family law com. 1966-68), Oakland County bar assns., Am. Judicature Soc., Am. Arbitration Assn. (panel arbitrators), Delta Upsilon (chmn. trustees, alumni chpt. dep. 1965-70), Tau Beta Pi, Pi Tau Sigma, Phi Eta Sigma. Conglist. Clubs: Detroit Athletic, Square Lake Racquet, Thomas M. Cooley. Home: 454 Yarmouth Rd Birmingham MI 48009 Office: 4190 Telegraph Rd Bloomfield Hills MI 48013 also 100 Renaissance Center Suite 2707 Detroit MI 48243

SNYDER, HAROLD RAY, educator, chemist; b. Mt. Carmel, Ill., May 20, 1910; s. Ira Martin and Sabra (Hobbs) S.; B.S. in Chemistry, U. Ill., 1931; Ph.D. in Organic Chemistry, Cornell U., 1935; m. Mary Jane McIntosh, May 23, 1935 (dec. Apr. 1974); children—Jane McIntosh, John Jerome, Mary Ann; m. 2d, Bonnie McIntosh Adams, May 2, 1975. Asst. chemistry Cornell U., 1931-35; research chemist Solvay Process Co. (N.Y.), 1935-36; mem. faculty U. Ill. at Urbana, 1936—, research prof., asso. dean Grad. Coll., 1960-75. Mem. panel course content improvement programs NSF, 1961-64. Guggenheim fellow, 1951. Fellow A.A.A.S.; mem. Am. Chem. Soc., Soc. Chem. Industry, Sigma Xi, Phi Lambda Upsilon, Phi Eta Sigma. Author: (with R.C. Fuson) Organic Chemistry, 1954; also articles. Editorial bd. Organic Syntheses, 1942-50, adv. editorial bd., 1951—; mem. editorial bd. Organic Reactions, 1941-53, adv. editorial bd., 1954—. Home: 708 W Florida Ave Urbana IL 61801

SNYDER, HARRY MARTIN, state ednl. adminstr.; b. Corbin, Ky., Oct. 22, 1941; s. Harry Martin and Aileen (Edwards) S.; B.S. in Econs. and Bus. Adminstrn., Georgetown (Ky.) Coll., 1963; J.D., U. Ky., 1966; m. Carolyn Witt; children—Paige Edwards, Sara Blake. Fin. aid coordinator fed. programs, legal counsel Georgetown Coll., 1966-68; asst. coordinator program budget U. Ky., 1968-70, asst. budget dir., 1970-73; asso. dir., legal counsel Ky. Council Higher Edn., Frankfort, 1973-75, exec. asst., legal counsel, 1975-76, exec. dir., 1976—; mem. So. Regional Edn. Bd. Served with U.S. Army. Episcopalian. Home: 1712 Fairway Dr Lexington KY 40502 Office: Council Higher Edn US 127 S Frankfort KY 40601

SNYDER, J. HERBERT, educator; b. McCloud, Calif., May 5, 1926; s. Clyde Herbert and Grace Altheda (Peaslee) S.; B.S., U. Calif., 1949, Ph.D., 1954; m. Ruth Margaret Forsyth, Feb. 14, 1948; children—Craig H., Neal R., Roy R. Asst. prof. to prof. agrl. econs. U. Calif. at Davis, 1953—, chmn. dept., 1966-70, chmn. div. resource scis., 1970-71, asst. dean environ. studies, 1971-72, prof., 1971—, dir. Water Resources Center, 1972—. Chmn. Gov.'s Adv. Com. Regional Land Use Info. Systems, 1964-67; com. cons. to Calif. Joint Legis. Com. on Open Space Land, 1967-70; mem. citizens adv. com. to Calif. Assembly Com. on Agrl. Land Use, 1964-67, citizens tech. adv. com. open space land to Calif. Legislature, 1967-71; mem. exec. bd. Univ. Council on Water Resources, 1976-79. Mem. Davis City Planning Commn., 1968-70. Served with USNR, 1944-46. Fellow Soil Conservation Soc. Am.; mem. Am., Western agrl. econs. assns., AAAS, Calif. Soil Conservation Soc., Sigma Alpha Epsilon, Alpha Zeta. Mason. Contbr. articles profl. jours. Home: 1106 Maple Ln Davis CA 95616

SNYDER, JACK O., pub. co. exec.; b. Reading, Pa., Jan. 10, 1942; s. Alvin Hugh and Elizabeth S. (Skoldiski) S.; B.S., Pa. State U., 1963; m. Patricia Mayone, May 2, 1970; 1 dau., Jacqueline. Mgr., Arthur Andersen & Co., N.Y.C., 1963-71; v.p., treas. Academic Press, Inc., N.Y.C., 1971-75, pres., 1975-78; exec. v.p. Harcourt Brace Jovanovich, N.Y.C., 1978—. Mem. Am. Inst. C.P.A.'s, N.Y. State Soc. C.P.A.'s, Am. Mgmt. Assn. Home: 65 Nicholson Dr Chatham Twp NJ 07928 Office: 757 3d Ave New York NY 10017

SNYDER, JAMES (JIMMY THE GREEK) G. (SYNODINOS, DEMETRIOS GEORGE), oddsmaker, columnist; b. Steubenville, Ohio, 1919; married; 4 children. Former gambler, oddsmaker; now syndicated columnist with Pubs.-Hall Syndicate. Jimmy the Greek Snyder-Pub. Relations; sports analyst CBS-TV. Author: Jimmy the Greek, 1975. Office: care Field Newspaper Syndicate 401 N Wabash Ave Chicago IL 60611*

SNYDER, JAMES NEWTON, physicist, computer scientist, educator; b. Akron, Ohio, Feb. 17, 1923; s. Louis Emery and Mary (Sullivan) S.; B.S., Harvard, 1945, M.A., 1947, Ph.D., 1949; m. Betty Jane Cooper, July 28, 1944; 1 son, James Newton. Mem. faculty physics dept. U. Ill. at Urbana, 1949—, asso. prof. Digital Computer Lab., 1957-58, prof., 1958-70, prof. computer sci. and physics, head dept. computer sci., 1970—; head computer div. Midwestern U. Research Assn., Madison, Wis., 1956-57. Mem. Am. Phys. Soc., A.A.A.S., Assn. Computing Machinery, I.E.E.E., Phi Beta Kappa, Sigma Xi. Contbr. articles to profl. jours. Home: 2304 S Vine St Urbana IL 61801

SNYDER, JOAN, painter; b. Highland Park, N.J., Apr. 16, 1940; d. Leon D. and Edythe A. (Cohen) Snyder; A.B. in Sociology, Douglass Coll., 1962; M.F.A., Rutgers U., 1966; m. Laurence Fink, Oct. 12, 1969. One-women exhbns. include Paley and Lowe, New Brunswick, N.J., 1971, 73, Michael Walls Gallery, San Francisco, 1971, Parker 470, Boston, 1972, Los Angeles Inst. Contemporary Art, 1976, Portland (Oreg.) Center Visual Arts, 1976, Carl Solway Gallery, N.Y.C., 1976, Neuberger Mus., Purchase, N.Y., 1978, Hamilton Gallery Contemporary Art, 1978; group exhbns. include Whitney Ann., 1972, Whitney Bienniel, 1974, Corcoran Bienniel, 1975; mem. faculty State U. N.Y., Stony Brook, 1967-69, Yale, 1974, U. Calif., Irvine, 1975, San Francisco Art Inst., 1976, Princeton U., 1975-77. Grantee Nat. Endowment Art, 1974. Address: 105 Mulberry St New York City NY 10013

SNYDER, JOHN JOSEPH, bishop; b. N.Y.C., Oct. 25, 1925; s. John Joseph and Katherine Marie (Walsh) S. Ordained priest Roman Cath. Ch., 1951; asso. pastor St. Mel's Parish, Flushing, N.Y., 1951-57; sec. to archbishops Diocese Bklyn., 1957-72; titular bishop of Forlimpopoli, vicar gen., aux. bishop Diocese Bklyn., 1972-79; bishop of St. Augustine, 1979—. Office: Chancery Suite 1648 Gulf Life Tower Suite 1648 Saint Augustine FL 32207

SNYDER, JOHN WESLEY, corp. exec.; b. Jonesboro, Ark., June 21, 1895; s. Jere Hartwell and Ellen (Hatcher) S.; student Vanderbilt U., 1914-15; hon. degrees 8 U.S. univs.; m. Evlyn Cook, Jan. 5, 1920 (dec. May 1956); 1 dau., Edith Cook Snyder Horton. Banker, Ark. and Mo., 1919-30; nat. bank receiver Office of Comptroller of Currency, Washington, 1931-37; mgr. St. Louis Loan Agy., R.F.C., 1937-43, asst. to dirs. R.F.C., 1940-44; exec. v.p. and dir. Def. Plant Corp., Washington, 1940-43; apptd. fed. loan adminstr., Apr. 1945, resigned; apptd. dir. Office War Mblzn. and Reconversion, July 1945; v.p. First Nat. Bank, St. Louis, 1943-45; sec. treasury, 1946-53; chmn. fin. com., pres. Overland Corp., Toledo, 1953-66, dir., 1953—; del. Internat. Fin. Confs., Mexico City, 1945-52, Rio de Janeiro, 1947, London, 1947, Paris, 1950-52, Ottawa, 1951, Rome, 1951, Lisbon, 1952; adviser U.S. Treasury, 1955-76; mem. Bus. Council, Washington. Mem. council adv. bd. Boy Scouts Am.; mem. Fed. City Council; chmn. Georgetown U. Library Assos.; mem. bd., finance com. Consortium Univs. of Washington Met. Area; chmn. bd. trustees Harry S. Truman Scholarship Found.; chmn. spl. fin. com. Washington Nat. Cathedral; trustee Toledo Art Mus., Harry S. Truman Library; past chmn. bd. regents Georgetown U. Served as capt. 57th F.A. Brigade, 32d Div., World War I, ret. col., U.S. Army, 1955. Mem. Am. Legion, Res. Officers Assn. (past pres. Mo. dept.), Bus. Council, Res. Officers Assn. (life), Omicron Delta Kappa, Alpha Tau Omega. Episcopalian. Clubs: Masons (33 deg.); Rotary (past pres. Toledo, hon. mem. Washington); Mo. Athletic (St. Louis); Chevy Chase, Alfalfa, Metropolitan (Washington). Home: 4 Chalfant Ct Bethesda MD 20016 Office: 2401 Calvert St NW Washington DC 20008

SNYDER, JOHN WILLIAM, educator; b. Denver, Feb. 18, 1924; s. Walter A. and Berenice (Hibbs) S.; student U. Calif. at Berkeley, 1942-43; A.B., U. Minn., 1950, M.A., 1952, Ph.D., 1954, B.D., Northwestern Theol. Sem., 1949; m. Margaret Ann Heetderks, July 10, 1946; children—Mark Alan, Kathryn Dee. Instr. Greek, Bethel Coll., 1953-54; instr. history U. Calif. at Berkeley, 1954-56; asst. prof. Ind. U., Bloomington, 1956-61, asso. prof., 1961-67, prof., 1967-69, asso. dean Coll. Arts and Scis., 1964-65, dean jr. div., 1965-67, v.p., 1967-69; pres. Westmont Coll., 1969-70; exec. vice chancellor U. Calif. at Santa Barbara, 1970-74; exec. v.p., provost Kent (Ohio) State U., 1974-77, prof., 1977—. Mem. Ind. State Scholarship Commn., 1967-69. Served with AUS, 1943-46. Mem. Am. Hist. Assn., Am. Inst. Archaeology, Am. Oriental Soc. Author: Sumerian Economic Texts, 1961; Alexander the Great, 1966; Western Cultural Traditions, 1967. Home: 3143 Dover Rd Cuyahoga Falls OH 44224

SNYDER, JOSEPH JULIEN, corp. exec.; b. Findlay, Ohio, Oct. 29, 1907; s. Paul Julien and Mabel Sarah (Bair) S.; B.S., Carnegie Inst. Tech., 1931; M.B.A., Harvard, 1934; postgrad. Mass. Inst. Tech., 1943-44; m. Helen Torrance Colburn, Apr. 3, 1937; children—Clinton Lytle, Joseph MacGeorge, Susanne Colburn. Dir., v.p. Colonial Mgmt. Assos., Boston, 1945-74, Colonial Fund, Inc., 1954-77; chmn. bd. dirs. Mich. Seamless Tube Co., Detroit, 1942-53, dir., 1940-77; dir. Quanex Corp., Transcontinental Gas Pipe Line Corp., Houston, 1951-78; trustee Boston Five Cents Savs. Bank, 1950-79; dir. Liberty Mut. Ins. Cos., Montagu Boston Investment Trust, London; staff mem. Radiation Lab., Mass. Inst. Tech., 1944-45, asst. treas., 1946-50, v.p., 1951-73, treas., mem. corp., mem. exec. com., 1950-75, life mem. corp., treas. emeritus, financial cons., 1975—, mem. corp. investment com., 1950—. Recipient Army-Navy Certificate Appreciation, 1946. Mem. Am. Acad. Arts and Scis., Am. Inst. Chem. Engrs., Harvard Bus. Sch. Alumni Assn. (pres. 1943-44), Beta Theta Pi. Clubs: Detroit; Downtown, St. Botolph (Boston); University (N.Y.C.). Home: 100 Memorial Dr Cambridge MA 02142 Office: 77 Massachusetts Ave Cambridge MA 02139

SNYDER, LEON CARLETON, educator; b. Shepherd, Mich., Mar. 11, 1908; s. Charles N. and Emiline (Robinson) S.; student Central State Tchrs. Coll., Mt. Pleasant, Mich., 1925-28; B.S., U. Wash., 1931, M.S., 1931, Ph.D., 1935; m. Vera A. Ferch, Mar. 29, 1934; children—Ann Marie, Leon Carleton, Mary Carol, Erva May. Instr. botany U. Wyo., 1935-36; instr. botany S.D. State Coll., 1936-42, asst. prof. horticulture, 1942-45; with U. Minn., 1945—, successively asso. prof., extension horticulturist, prof., head horticulture dept., supt. Fruit Breeding Farm, 1953—, also dir. of Landscape Arboretum, 1969—, prof. emeritus, 1977—; mem. bd. experts Home and Hobby Sect., Mpls. Star & Tribune, 1954—, garden editor, 1966—. Bd. dirs. Minn. Zool. Soc. Recipient Good Neighbor award WCCO Radio, 1968, 69, 76; Greater Mpls. Outstanding Achievement awards; George Robert White medal honor Mass. Hort. Soc., 1974; medal honor Garden Club Am., 1974; Norman Jay Colman award Am. Assn. Nurserymen, 1974; Distinguished Service to Agr. award Gamma Sigma Delta, 1976; Liberty Hyde Bailey medal Am. Hort. Soc., 1976; John Robertson Meml. award S.D. Hort. Soc., 1976; Meritorious Service certificate Epsilon Sigma Phi, 1976; honored by proclamation of Leon C. Snyder Day in State of Minn., dedication of Leon C. Snyder edn. bldg. at Arboretum and establishment Leon C. Snyder Scholarship program, 1976. Fellow Am. Soc. Hort. Sci. (sec. Gt. Plains sect. 1958, pres. 1959, chmn. 1959, chmn. floriculture, ornamental and landscape hort. sect. 1966-67, Am. Hort. Soc. (dir.), Royal Hort. Soc. Eng.; hon. life mem. Minn. Hort. Soc. (exec. bd. 1953; fruit list com. 1945—); mem. Am. Assn. Bot. Gardens and Arboreta (dir. 1960-63, award for arboretum devel. 1974), AAUP, Federated Garden Clubs Minn. (life), Men's Garden Club Am. (Gold medal 1963), Phi Beta Kappa, Sigma Xi, Gamma Sigma Delta, Phi Sigma, Pi Alpha Xi, Epsilon Sigma Phi. Author: Gardening in the Upper Midwest, 1978. Editor garden column Mpls. Star & Tribune. Home: Rt 1 Box 573E Excelsior MN 55331

SNYDER, LEONARD WAYNE, minister; b. Sotuh Charleston, W.Va., Feb. 26, 1931; s. Leonard J. and Erma F. (Duncan) S.; student Queens Coll., Charlotte, N.C., 1954, Sch. Pastoral Care of N.C. Bapt. Hosp., 1960; A.B., Anderson Coll., 1959; postgrad. Miami U., Oxford, Ohio, 1965-68, Cin. Bible Sem., 1976; m. Bettie Jean Petrey, June 12, 1950; children—John Herbert, Karen Forrest. Ordained to ministry Ch. of God (Anderson, Ind.), 1955; pastor 1st Ch. of God, Charlotte, 1955-60, Hamilton, Ohio, 1960—. Chmn. N.C. gen. assembly Ch. of God (Anderson, Ind.), 1953-54, Ohio gen. assembly, 1970-71, 72-73, chmn. Ohio bd. conservation and evangelism, 1966-70, 73; mem. nat. bd. Christian edn., 1961-71, pres. bd., 1964-65; mem. Ohio exec. council, 1966—, mem. nat. exec. council, 1972—; vice chmn. Nat. Gen. Assembly, 1972-74, chmn., 1974—; chmn. Southwestern Ohio dist. Gen. Assembly Ch. of God; mem. Nat. Commn. on Christian Unity, 1978—. Home: 1016 Tiffin Ave Hamilton OH 45015 Office: 501 Woodlawn Ave Hamilton OH 45015

SNYDER, LEWIS EMIL, astrophysicist; b. Ft. Wayne, Ind., Nov. 26, 1939; s. Herman Lewis and Bernice (McKee) S.; B.S., Ind. State U., 1961; M.A., So. Ill. U., 1964; Ph.D., Mich. State U., 1967; m. Doris Jean Selma Lautner, June 16, 1962; children—Herman Emil, Catherine Jean. Research asso. Nat. Radio Astronomy Obs., Charlottesville. Va., 1967-69; prof. astronomy dept. U. Va., Charlottesville, 1969-73, 74-75; vis. fellow Joint Inst. for Lab. Astrophysics, U. Colo., Boulder, 1973-74; prof. astronomy dept. U. Ill., Urbana, 1975—; dir. A.J. Assos., Charlottesville; cons. Mfg. Chemists Assn. NASA-Am. Soc. Engring. Edn. summer fellow, 1972, 73. Mem. Am. Phys. Soc., Am. Astron. Soc., Internat. Astron. Union, Union Radio Scientifique Internationale, Sigma Xi. Lutheran. Co-editor: Molecules in the Galactic Environment, 1973; contbr. articles to sci. jours. Office: 341 Astronomy Bldg U Ill Urbana IL 61801

SNYDER, LOUIS IRVING, JR., newspaperman; b. Stratford, Conn., Mar. 23, 1912; s. Louis Irving and Agnes Ellen (Tilton) s.; B.A., Yale U., 1934. Engaged in adminstrn. and pub. relations Met. Opera, 1934-62; asso. music critic N.Y. Herald Tribune, 1963-66; pub. relations dir. Manhattan Sch. Music, 1966-69; music critic Christian Sci. Monitor, 1969-74; press rep. Opera Co. Boston, 1975-76; co-producer Berkshire Playhouse, Stockbridge, Mass., 1958. Bd. dirs. Marcella Sembrich Meml. Found. Served with AUS, 1939-45. Episcopalian. Author: Community of Sound: Boston Symphony and Its World of Players, 1979. Home: 1880 Hillside Rd Fairfield CT 06430

SNYDER, MARLON GENE, congressman; b. Louisville, Jan. 26, 1928; s. M. G. and Lois (Berg) S.; J.D., U. Louisville, 1951; LL.B. cum laude, Jefferson Sch. Law, Louisville, 1951; 1 son, Mark; m. 2d, Patricia C. Robertson, Apr. 10, 1973; 3 step-children. Admitted to Ky. bar, 1950, D.C. bar, 1970, since practiced in Louisville; farmer, 1957—; city atty. Jeffersontown, 1953-57; magistrate 1st dist. Jefferson County, 1957-61; real estate broker, 1949—; mem. 88th Congress from 3d Ky. Dist.; mem. 90th-96th congresses from 4th Ky. Dist.; v.p. Ky. Magistrates and Commrs., 1958. Vice pres. Jeffersontown Civic Center, 1953-54; pres. Lincoln Republican Club Ky., 1960-61, 1st Magisterial Dist. Rep. Club, 1955-57. Mem. Ky., D.C., Louisville, bar assns., Ky. Farm Bur., Louisville, Kenton-Boone bds. realtors. Clubs: Masons, Shriners, Lions, Optimists (pres. Jeffersontown 1957-58). Home: 8405 Hwy 22 Brownsboro Farms Louisville KY 40222 Office: House Office Bldg Washington DC 20515 also Fed Bldg Covington KY also 125 Chenoweth Ln Saint Matthews KY 40207

SNYDER, MAX MUTSE, ednl. adminstr.; b. Denver, Mar. 13, 1919; s. David and Esther (Rothchild) S.; B.A., Colo. State Coll. Edn., 1941, M.A., 1948; postgrad. U. So. Calif., 1958-61; Ed.D., Wash. State U., 1967; m. Nancy Fitzgerald, June 1, 1944; children—Kathleen Snyder Cox, Michael, Mary Anne Snyder Yount, Sarah Snyder Oxner, Patricia Snyder Henderson, John Vann. Tchr., boy's adv. McLoughlin Jr. High Sch., Vancouver, Wash., 1944-46, prin., 1946-51; asst. supt. Vancouver Public Schs., 1951-53, dep. supt., 1953-57; asst. supt. Inglewood (Calif.) Public Schs., 1957-61; supt. schs. Pullman (Wash.) Public Schs., 1961-70; pres. Spokane Falls Community Coll., 1970-74; supt. Internat. Sch., Manila, Philippines, 1974-76; dist. pres. Wash. Community Coll. Dist. 17, Spokane, 1976—; mem. Wash. State Supts. Adminstrv. Adv. Com., Wash. State Supts. Cert. Adv. Com.; mem. capital projects com. Community Colls. Bd. dirs. Spokane Area Devel. Council; vice chmn. in charge govtl. affairs edn. div. United Way, Spokane, Wash., 1978-79, pres., 1979-80; pres. United Fund, Spokane, 1979-80. Mem. Wash. Assn. Sch. Supts. (pres. 1967-68), Wash. Edn. Assn. (dir. 1954-57), Vancouver Edn. Assn. (pres. 1949-50), Am. Assn. Sch. Adminstrs. (state adv.), Wash. Assn. Community Colls. (sec.-treas. 1971-78, pres. 1978-79), Phi Kappa Phi (pres. 1963-64), Phi Delta Kappa. Clubs: Exchange, Lions (pres. club 1956-57). Home: S5412 Arthur Spokane WA 99203 Office: N200 Greene St Spokane WA 99207

SNYDER, MELVIN HAROLD, clergyman, ch. orgn. exec.; b. Evansville, Ind., Jan. 1, 1912; s. Harold M. and Lucille (Myers) S.; student Frankfort Pilgrim Coll., 1927-31; D.D., Eastern Pilgrim Coll., 1960; m. Eloise May Brown, July 31, 1933; children—Ina Ruth Snyder Buckles, Mary Katherine Snyder McGinnis, Evangeline May Snyder Greves, Harold DeWayne, David Leroy, Margaret Frances Snyder McFrederick, Mark Wesley. Evangelist, 1930-35; ordained to ministry Pilgrim Holiness Ch., 1938; pastor in Marion, Ind., 1935-42; asst. dist. supt. Ind. Pilgrim Holiness Ch., Frankfort, 1942-44, dist. supt. No. Ind. dist., 1944-48, So. Ind. dist., Terre Haute and Bedford, 1948-56, asst. gen. supt., Indpls., 1954-58, gen. supt., 1958-68; gen. supt. Wesleyan Ch., Marion, 1968—; chmn. polity com. Wesleyan Meth. and Pilgrim Holiness Chs., 1962-68; co-chmn. Wesleyan Ch. and Free Meth. Ch. Commn. on Merger, 1970-76; chmn. Wesleyan World Fellowship, 1972-76; pres. bd. trustees Frankfort Pilgrim Coll., 1947-58, Wesleyan Ch. Corp., 1969-72, Houghton (N.Y.) Coll., 1970-72; pres. Pilgrim Holiness Ch. Corp., 1966-68. Recipient Alumni award Frankfort Pilgrim Coll., 1951. Mem. Nat. Holiness Assn. (bd. adminstrn., treas. 1964-69), Nat. Assn. Evangelicals (commn. chaplains 1964-68, bd. administrn. 1966—, exec. com. 1974-78). Contbr., editor Pilgrim Holiness Advocate, 1958-68, Wesleyan Advocate, 1968—, The Preacher's Mag., 1973—, other periodicals. Composer: The Prince of Bethlehem, 1946; Suffer the Children To

Come Unto Me, 1944; There's Music in My Soul, 1942. Home: 5604 S Scott Rd Marion IN 46952 Office: PO Box 2000 Marion IN 46952

SNYDER, MILO F., investment co. exec.; b. Ethan, S.D., Sept. 9, 1902; s. William S. and Anna (Freeman) S.; B.S., Northwestern U., 1925; m. Helen Rae Reed, Jan. 7, 1926; children—Mary (Mrs. George A. Shurtleff), Helen (Mrs. Raymond Replinger), Milo F., William G., Roberta. With Lowei & Co., Inc., Milw., 1932-42, 45—, now sr. v.p., also dir., mem. corp. finance dept.; comptroller, mem. exec. com. Ampco Metal, Inc., 1942-45; dir. Clark Oil & Refining Corp., Indsl. Logistics Consultants, Inc., Assn. Life Ins. Co., Gettys Mfg. Co., Versa-Technologies, Inc. Bd. dirs. Neighborhood House, Milw. Mem. Financial Execs. Inst. Clubs: Milwaukee Athletic (Milw.). Home: 2614 E Newton St Milwaukee WI 53211 Office: 225 E Mason St Milwaukee WI 53202

SNYDER, NATHAN, communications co. exec.; b. Hartford, Conn., Oct. 7, 1934; s. Saul and Betsy (Wand) S.; A.B., Harvard U., 1956; LL.B., Columbia U., 1963; postgrad. N.Y. U. Sch. Bus., 1967-68; m. Geraldine Wolff, Dec. 27, 1964; children—Hannah Abigail, Alexander Lowell Wolff. Admitted to N.Y. bar, 1963; with firm Paul, Weiss, Rifkind, Wharton & Garrison, N.Y.C., 1963-66; v.p., sec. Randolph Computer Corp., Greenwich, Conn., 1966-69, exec. v.p., gen. counsel, dir., 1969-73; exec. v.p., chief operating officer BanCal Tri-State Corp. (holding co. Bank of Calif.), 1974-76; v.p. acquisitions CBS Inc., N.Y.C., 1976—; lectr. Grad. Sch. Mgmt., Golden Gate U., San Francisco. Vol. legal services OEO, 1963; bd. dirs. New Canaan Community Nursery Sch., 1970. Served to lt. USNR, 1956-60. Harlan Fiske Stone scholar, 1964-65. Mem. Am. Bar Assn., Assn. Bar City N.Y., Columbia Law Sch. Alumni Assn. (dir. 1979). Clubs: Harvard (N.Y.C.), Hasty Pudding, Inst. of 1770 (Harvard). Editor Columbia Law Rev., 1962-63. Home: 163 Parish Rd New Canaan CT 06840 Office: 51 W 52d St New York NY 10019

SNYDER, NATHAN WILLIAM, engr., physicist; b. Montreal, Que., Can., Apr. 21, 1918; s. Joseph and Sarah (Catton) S.; came to U.S., 1923, naturalized, 1940; B.S., U. Calif. at Berkeley, 1941, M.S., 1944, Ph.D. in Engring., 1947, postdoctorate study physics, 1951; m. Rosalie Shaw, May 21, 1944; children—Christine Ellen, Lorraine Dale. Test engr. Byron Jackson Co., Los Angeles, 1940; mem. faculty U. Calif. at Berkeley, 1942-58, asso. prof. nuclear engring., chmn. dept., 1955-58; prin. scientist space tech. Inst. Def. Analyses, 1958-61; v.p. research and engring. Royal Research Corp., Hayward, Calif., 1961-62; chief scientist Kaiser Aerospace & Electronics Corp., 1962-64; Neely prof. nuclear and aerospace engring. Ga. Inst. Tech., 1964-68; asst. to sr. v.p. aerospace and systems group N.Am. Rockwell Corp., El Segundo, Calif., 1968-70; pres. N.W. Snyder Assos., 1971-72; chief scientist, tech. dir. Ralph M. Parsons Co., 1973-78, tech. dir., 1978—; cons. bus. devel., tech., 1971—; adj. prof. energy and kinetics U. Calif., Los Angeles, 1973-74; mem. Air Force Sci. Adv. Bd., 1967-71; mem. space tech. panel Pres.'s Sci. Adv. Com., 1964-67; mem. adv. com. isotope and radiation devel. AEC, 1967-69; adv. com. nuclear systems in space NASA, 1960-63, adv. com. space power and electric propulsion, 1967-68, chmn. life support panel, 1969-71, mem. research adv. com. on biotech. and human research, mem. life scis. com., 1970-74; mem. panel on assessment on environ. impacts Am. Inst. Biol. Scis., 1974-78; adviser to mayor Oakland (Calif.) on indsl. devel., 1961-64; mem. Calif. Intersoc. Legis. Adv. Commn., 1977—. Recipient Skylab achievement award NASA, 1973; George Washington award as Engr. of Year, Inst. Advancement of Engring., 1976. Mem. Am. Phys. Soc., Am. Inst. Aeros. and Astronautics (chmn. power sources com. 1960-62), Am. Nuclear Soc., Acoustical Soc. Am., Am. Inst. Chem. Engrs., Phi Beta Kappa, Sigma Xi, Tau Beta Pi. Episcopalian. Club: Berkeley Tennis. Author: Energy Conversion for Space Power, 1961; Space Power Systems, 1961; Energy Recovery and Resource Recycling from Solid Waste Chemical Engineering, 1974; Water from Alaska; also numerous research articles. Home: 14901 La Cumbre Dr Pacific Palisades CA 90272 Office: 100 W Walnut St Pasadena CA 91124

SNYDER, RACHEL FRANCES, editor; b. Topeka, Kans., Feb. 12, 1924; d. Otis F. and Lela Gertrude (Retter) S.; A.B., Washburn U., 1945. Reporter, Topeka (Kans.) Daily Capital, 1943-45; writer Kans. Indsl. Devel. Commn., Topeka, 1946-47; asst. WTOP and Washington Post, Washington, 1948; writer FAO, Washington, 1949; reporter, mgr. Emporia (Kans.) Times, 1950-52; asst. editor Workbasket mag., Kansas City, 1952-56; editor Flower and Garden mag., Kansas City, 1957—. Recipient Profl. Writers award Am. Seed Trade Assn., 1967; Garden Writers award Am. Assn. Nurserymen, 1975. Mem. Women in Communications, Garden Writers Assn. Am., Am. Hort. Soc., Nature Conservancy, Wilderness Soc. Unitarian. Club: Sierra. Author: The Complete Book for Gardeners, 1964. Home: 4200 Oxford Rd Prairie Village KS 66208 Office: 4201 Pennsylvania St Kansas City MO 64111. *Start with the best education you can get, and keep on with it. This is the foundation. Then add persistence, a fixation on high standards, and all the energy you can muster. Along the way you'll need other qualities, but they are all covered by the Golden Rule.*

SNYDER, RICHARD CARLTON, educator; b. Kingston, N.Y., Aug. 21, 1916; s. Carl Warner and Florence (Dedrick) S.; A.B., Union Coll., Schenectady, 1937; M.A., Columbia U., 1939, Ph.D. (Univ. fellow), 1945; m. Marjorie L. Leibel, Mar. 28, 1942. Instr. polit. sci. Am. U., 1941-42; instr. govt. Columbia U., 1942-46; adminstrv. sec. war and peace studies Council Fgn. Relations, 1944-45; asst. prof. politics Princeton U., 1946-50, staff mem. organizational behavior sect., 1951-54, steering com. organizational behavior project, 1950-54, asso. prof. politics, 1950-55, dir. fgn. policy analysis project, 1953-55; prof. polit. sci. Northwestern U., 1955-65, chmn. dept., 1957-65, Benjamin Franklin prof. decision making, 1960-65, Pres.'s fellow, 1963-64, also co-dir. Program Grad. Tng. and Research in Internat. Relations; prof. adminstrn. and polit. sci. U. Calif. at Irvine, 1965-70, dean Grad. Sch. Adminstrn., 1965-67; prof. ednl. devel., polit. sci. and pub. adminstrn. Ohio State U., 1970-79, co-dir. Nat. Program of Ednl. Leadership, 1970-75, dir. Mershon Center, 1970-79; pres. Civic Edn. Assos., 1974—; mem. adv. bd. Inst. for Ednl. Leadership, 1974—; lectr.-cons. Mid-Career Course, Fgn. Service Inst., 1957-59; lectr. Army War Coll., 1958-59; vis. fellow Western Behavioral Scis. Inst., 1963-64; cons. U.S. Office Edn., 1963—; vis. scholar Russell Sage Found., 1967-68; fellow Center for Advanced Study in Behavioral Sci., 1956-57. Trustee Social Sci. Found., U. Denver, 1960-74; chmn. adv. com. Project Michelson, 1960-65, Naval Ordnance Test Sta. Mem. Am. Polit. Sci. Assn. (exec. council 1960-62, v.p. 1966-68, chmn. com. pre-collegiate edn. 1970—), Internat. Studies Assn. (pres. 1971-72), Fgn. Policy Assn. (dir. 1972-74). Mem. adv. com. U.S. Fgn. Relations Series, 1972-76; author: The Most Favored Nation Clause, 1948; (with E.S. Furniss) American Foreign Policy, 1954; (with B.M. Sapin) Role of the Military in American Foreign Policy, 1954; (with J.A. Robinson) National and International Decision-making, 1961; (with Dean Pruitt) Theory and Research on the Causes of War, 1969; others; editor: (with H.H. Wilson) Roots of Political Behavior, 1949; Pub. Opinion Quar., 1950-53; cons. editor Doubleday Studies in Political Science, 1953-55; editorial bd. Ohio State U. Press, 1970—, Jour. Conflict Resolution, 1957-70, Teaching Political Science, 1973-75. Home: 7949 E Vista Dr Scottsdale AZ 85253

SNYDER, RICHARD ELLIOT, pub. co. exec.; b. N.Y.C., Apr. 6, 1933; s. Jack and Molly (Rothman) S.; B.A., Tufts U., 1955; m. Otilie R. Freund, Mar. 17, 1963; children—Jacqueline, Matthew; m. 2d, Joni Evans, May 19, 1978. Asst. mktg. dir. Doubleday & Co., N.Y.C., 1958-60; sales mgr. Simon & Schuster, N.Y.C., 1960-64, dir. sales, 1964-66, dir. mktg., 1967-68, pub., exec. v.p., 1969-75, pres., 1975—, mem. editorial bd., 1968—, dir., 1969—, mem. exec. com. of bd., 1970—. Served with AUS, 1956-58. Mem. Assn. Am. Pubs. (dir. 1976-79). Contbr. articles to profl. jours. Home: The Linden Farm Cross River NY 10518 Office: Simon & Schuster Bldg 1230 Ave of Americas New York City NY 10020

SNYDER, RICHARD LYNNE, librarian; b. Toronto, Ont., Can., Feb. 18, 1927; s. Lester Lynne and Florence (Steece) S.; B.A., U. Toronto, 1949; M.A., Ind. U., 1952; m. Jeanette Sutherland, May 28, 1949; children—Robert Lyle, Carol Lynne. Came to U.S., 1949, derivative citizen. Librarian dept. geology and geol. survey Ind. U., 1953-55, biology librarian, 1955-58, sci. librarian, 1958-59, lectr. lit. sci. and tech., div. library sci., 1955, 58; sci. librarian Mass. Inst. Tech., 1959-62, asso. dir. libraries, 1962-64; lectr. lit. sci. and tech. Simmons Coll. Sch. Library Sci., Boston, 1963-65; dir. libraries Drexel U., 1965—; cons. to industry, 1965-69, rep. to EDUCOM, 1967-73; mem. adv. com. Mid-East Regional Med. Library Program, 1969-73; mem. panel library programs Com. Sci. and Tech. Info., 1971-73; mem. gen. adv. council Ind. U. Grad. Library Sch., 1971-77; mem. vis. com. Tufts U. Library, 1976—; chmn. bd. dirs. PALINET, 1973-75, v.p., 1978—; dir. Q.T. Inc., Boston, 1960-61. Bd. dirs. Unitarian Fellowship, Bloomington, Ind., 1956-57, Concord (Mass.) Band Assn., 1962-63, 63-64; bd. dirs. Union Library Catalogue of Pa., 1969-72, 74-75, mem. com. library cooperation, 1969—, chmn. com., 1972-74; sec. Delaware County Band, 1977—; pres. Delaware County Ostomy Assn., 1975-76. Council on Library Resources fellow, 1971-72. Mem. ALA (chmn. subject specialists sect. 1967-68, mem. urban univs. library com. univ. libraries sect. 1969-72, mem. sci. and tech. reference services com. of reference services div. 1965-68), Spl. Libraries Assn. (chmn. sci.-tech. group Boston 1963-64), Assn. Coll. Research Libraries (chpt. pres. 1969-71, dir. 1968-73), Am. Soc. Info. Sci., AAAS, Ind. U. Grad. Library Sch. Alumni Assn. (dir. 1971-72), Phi Gamma Delta, Archons of Colophon. Compiler: (with Bernadette Shih) International Union List of Communist Chinese Serials, Scientific, Technical and Medical with Selected Social Science Titles, 1963; bd. dirs., treas., acting bus. mgr. Documentation Abstracts, 1966-70. Home: 600 Wilder Rd Wallingford PA 19086 Office: Library Drexel U Philadelphia PA 19104

SNYDER, ROBERT HARVEY, chemist, tire co. exec.; b. Great Falls, Mont., Oct. 11, 1918; s. Harvey and Helen Agnes (Johnson) S.; B.S. in Chemistry, U. Mich., 1940; Ph.D., U. Chgo., 1948; m. Evelyn Adair Kuivinen, Dec. 27, 1945: children—Lucinda Gall, Cornelia Ann, Christine Adair, William David. Jr. chemist Hoffmann-La Roche Co., Nutley, N.J., 1940-42; chemist U.S. Rubber Co., Passaic, N.J., 1942-45, 48-56; with Uniroyal Inc., Detroit, 1956—, research mgr., 1958-63, mgr. product engring., 1963-68, dir. devel., 1968-73, v.p. tire tech., 1973—. Mem. Am. Chem. Soc., N.Y. Acad. Scis., Am. Inst. Chemists, Soc. Automotive Engrs., Akron, Detroit rubber groups. Episcopalian. Contbr. articles to tech. jours.; patentee field polymer chemistry and tire tech. Home: 1367 Balfour Rd Grosse Pointe Park MI 48230 Office: 6600 E Jefferson Ave Detroit MI 48232

SNYDER, ROBERT MARTIN, cons., ret. govt. ofcl.; b. Lahmansville, W.Va., Sept. 6, 1912; s. Noah W. and Maggie M. (Varner) S.; B.S. in Agr., W.Va. U., 1937; m. Gail M. Hiser, Nov. 25, 1937; children—Rebecca J. (Mrs. Walbert Peters), Margaret A. (Mrs. John Bensenhaver), Shirley L. (Mrs. Jerry L. Williams), Robert Martin. Engaged in farming, 1929-34; agrl. extension agt. Nicholas County, W.Va., 1937-41; adminstrn. commodity loans crop ins. and program performance AAA, Morgantown, W.Va., 1941-42, adminstrn. grain and oilseed program E central region U.S., 1942-47; asst. coordinator CCC, U.S. Dept. Agr., 1947-50, coordinator dairy, poultry, fruit and vegetable programs, 1950-52; chief agriculturist U.S. mission to Karachi, Pakistan, FOA, 1952-54; counselor Am. embassy and dir. U.S. mission to Afghanistan, Kabul, ICA, 1955-59; rep. ICA to Brit. East Africa, 1959-60; food and agr. officer West African countries of Ivory Coast, Upper Volta, Niger, Dahomey, 1961-62; acting dir. U.S. AID Mission Ivory Coast, 1962-63, attache U.S. Embassy, food and agrl. officer, Ivory Coast, 1963; agr. adviser, area office rep. AID mission to Rhodesia and Nyasaland, 1964; attache, AID affairs officer, Malawi, Africa, 1964-68; cons. World Bank, IBRD, 1967; detail officer fgn. direct investments Dept. Commerce, 1968; AID affairs officers, Washington, 1968-69; food and agr. officer U.S. AID, Amman, Jordan, 1969-70; planning adviser Ministry Natural Resources Nigeria, 1970-72; cons., 1972—. Mem. del. Gen. Agreements Tariffs and Trade Conf., Torquay, Eng., 1951; mem. Mus. Commn., Library Commn. Served to lt. USNR, 1944-46; PTO. Mem. Fgn. Service Assn., Am. Legion, W.Va. U. Alumni Assn., Am. Acad. Polit. and Social Sci., Soc. Internat. Devel., Internat. Platform Assn., UN Assn., U.S. Nat. Trust for Historic Preservation, Nature Conservancy, Commn. on Aging, Alpha Zeta. Clubs: Masons, Kiwanis, Explorers. Home: Noah Snyder Farm Lahmansville WV 26731. *I feel that any success which I have achieved in life is in direct relationship to my interest in others and my ability to contribute to a better world situation in which each person can develop and achieve a better life for himself or herself and family.*

SNYDER, ROBERT OWEN, magazine pub.; b. Omaha, Sept. 7, 1922; s. William Owen and Gertrude R. (Read) S.; B.S., U. Minn., 1945; m. Frances Mary Marleau, June 21, 1945; children—Gary Steven, Richard Allen, Thomas Owen, James David. Advt. sales W.D. Hoard & Sons Co., Ft. Atkinson, Wis., 1954-64; advt. sales mgr. Webb Co., St. Paul, 1964—, pub. Snow Goer mag., 1974—. Pres. Crookston (Minn.) Jr. C. of C., 1953; v.p. Minn. Jr. C. of C., 1954. Mem. Nat. Agrl. and Mktg. Assn. (chpt. pres. 1968, nat. exec. v.p. 1969). Methodist. Club: Hastings Country (pres. 1974). Home: 1211 Southview Dr Hastings MN 55033 Office: 1999 Shepard Rd St Paul MN 55116

SNYDER, ROY DIETRICH, JR., naval officer; b. Bloomsburg, Pa., Aug. 3, 1927; s. Roy Dietrich and Ida Gardner (Wilson) S.; B.S., U.S. Naval Acad., 1950; M.S., U.S. Naval Postgrad. Sch., 1955; M.S., George Washington U., 1970; m. Ann Marie Lydon, Dec. 29, 1951; children—Mari Katherine, Lisa Marie, Stacy Ann. Commd. ensign U.S. Navy, 1950, advanced through grades to rear adm., 1974; comdg. officer Naval Air Sta., Brunswick, Maine, 1971-74; comdr. patrol wings, Atlantic, 1974-76; commandant 1st Naval Dist., Boston, 1974-76; dir. ocean surveillance div. Office Chief of Naval Ops., Washington, 1976-79; ret., 1979. Home: 3921 Colonel Ellis Ave Alexandria VA 22304

SNYDER, SOLOMON HALBERT, psychiatrist-pharmacologist; b. Washington, Dec. 26, 1938; s. Samuel Simon and Patricia (Yakerson) S.; student Georgetown U., 1955-58, M.D. cum laude, 1962; m. Elaine Borko, June 10, 1962; children—Judith Rhea, Deborah Lynn. Intern, Kaiser Found. Hosp., San Francisco, 1962-63; research asso. NIMH, Bethesda, Md., 1963-65; resident psychiatry Johns Hopkins Hosp., Balt., 1965-68; asso. prof. psychiatry and pharmacology Johns Hopkins Med. Sch., 1968-70, prof., 1970-77, distinguished service prof. psychiatry and pharmacology, 1977—. Served with USPHS, 1963-65. Recipient Outstanding Scientist award Md. Acad. Scis., 1969; John Jacob Abel award Am. Pharmacology Soc., 1970; A.E. Bennett award Soc. Biol. Psychiatry, 1970; Gaddum award Brit. Pharm. Soc., 1974; F.O. Schmitt award in neuroscis. Mass. Inst. Tech., 1974; Nicholas Giarman lecture award Yale U., 1975; Rennebohm award U. Wis., 1976; Salmon award, 1977; Stanley Dean award Am. Coll. Psychiatrists, 1978; Harvey Lecture award, 1978; Lasker award, 1978. Fellow Am. Coll. Neuropsychopharmacology (Daniel Efron award 1974), Am. Psychiat. Assn. (Hofheimer award 1972); mem. Psychiat. Research Soc., Soc. for Neuroscis., Am. Soc. Biol. Chemists, Am. Pharmacology Soc. Author: Uses of Marijuana, 1971; Madness and the Brain, 1973; Opiate Receptor Mechanisms, 1975; The Troubled Mind, 1976; editor: Perspectives in Neuropharmacology, 1971; Frontiers in Catecholamine Research, 1973; Handbook of Psychopharmacology, 1974; contbr. articles to profl. jours. Home: 2300 W Rogers Ave Baltimore MD 21209

SNYDER, TOM, TV journalist; b. Milw., May 12, 1936; student Marquette U.; 1 dau. News anchorman KNBC-TV, Los Angeles, 1970; host Tomorrow Show, NBC, 1973—, Prime Time Sunday, 1979—; news anchorman WNBC-TV, N.Y.C., 1974; newscaster NBC News Update, 1975; anchorman NBC Sunday Night News, 1975; co-host with Barbara Walters of TV spl. Of Women and Men, 1975; anchored TV spl. The Legion Disease: What Happened in Philadelphia, 1976; host TV spl. The National Disaster Survival Test, 1977; co-host The National Love, Sex and Marriage Test, 1978; prin. on-camera reporter Medicine in America: Life, Death, and Dollars, 1978. Winner Emmy award, 1974. Office: care NBC 30 Rockefeller Plaza New York NY 10020*

SNYDER, WAHL JOHN, architect; b. Beaver, Pa., July 5, 1910; s. Wahl John and Frances (Kuhl) S.; B.S., Pa. State U., 1932; m. Jane Roth, Apr. 6, 1946; children—Karen Lynn, Deborah Denman. Owner firm Wahl Snyder & Assos., architects, Miami, Fla., 1937—; prin. works include Zollner residence, Golden Beach, Fla., 1954, Levitz residence, Coral Gables, Fla., 1970, Anchorage Apt., Miami Beach, 1956, Briggs residence, Nassau, 1958, Staley residence, Decatur, Ill., 1968, McArthur Engring. Bldg., U. Miami, 1959, Ski Complex, Beech Mountain, N.C., 1969, also townhouses and condominiums. Mem. bd. dirs. archtl. bd. Inter-Am. Center Authority; bd. dirs. Florida Architecture mag.; pres. Fla. Bd. Arch., 1968. Mem. bd. appeals, Bal Harbour Village, Fla. Served with C.E., AUS, 1942-44. Fellow AIA (pres. Fla. 1957; citation Lanai Apt. design 1956); mem. Fla. Assn. Architects, Com. of 100, Wine and Food Soc., Scarab, Sigma Pi. Presbyterian (elder). Clubs: Bath, Symphony, Vizcayans, Rotary (Miami Shores) (Miami, Fla.). Home: 4765 Lake Rd Bay Point Miami FL 33137 Office: 1177 NE 79th St Miami FL 33138

SNYDER, WILLIAM CORDES, JR., business exec.; b. Snow Shoe, Pa., June 12, 1903; s. William Cordes and Mary Allen (Perry) S.; grad. Lehigh U., 1926, Dr. Engring. (hon.), 1963; m. Virginia Harper, June 4, 1932; children—Virginia, William Cordes. With Wheeling Mold and Foundry Co. (W.Va.), 1925-27, chemist, 1926, metallurgist, 1927; metallurgist and roll maker Lewis Foundry & Machine Co., Pitts., 1927-35, became v.p. in charge sales, 1935, pres., gen. mgr. (co. then a subs. Blaw Knox Co.) until 1937, dir., mem. exec. com., 1937-45; pres., gen. mgr., dir., mem. exec. com. Continental Foundry & Machine Co., 1945-47; v.p. in charge metall. dept. Koppers Co., Inc., also in charge Chile mgmt. and in charge constrn. and operation of completely integrated steel plant Concepción, Chile, 1947-51; pres., chmn., chief exec. officer Blaw-Knox Co., 1951-68, chmn. bd., 1968—; dir. White Consol. Industries, Inc. Mem. fund-raising coms. Community Fund, Red Cross, Salvation Army; bd. dirs. Nat. Indsl. Conf. Bd., Boy Scouts Am., Pitts. YMCA; trustee Sewickley Valley Hosp. Recipient Horatio Alger award, 1956. Mem. Tri-State Indsl. Assn., Am. Iron and Steel Inst., Iron and Steel Engrs., Am. Inst. Mining and Metall. Engrs., Engrs. Soc. Western Pa. Clubs: Duquesne, Univ. (Pitts.); Allegheny Country (Sewickley, Pa.); Rolling Rock, Laurel Valley Golf (Ligonier, Pa.); Met., Internat., Capitol Hill (Washington); Saucon Valley Country (Bethlehem, Pa.); Castalia (Ohio) Trout; Pine Valley Golf; Gulf Stream Golf, Gulf Stream Bath and Tennis (Delray Beach, Fla.). Home: Pine Rd Sewickley PA 15143 Office: 1 Oliver Plaza Pittsburgh PA 15222

SNYDER, WILLIAM COWPERTHWALTE, plant pathologist; b. Berkeley, Calif., July 26, 1904; s. Christopher Henry and Harriet (Runyon) S.; B.S., U. Calif. at Berkeley, 1927; Ph.D., U. Wis., 1932; m. Alice Lindberg, Aug. 20, 1932; children—Margaret L. Snyder Vogt, Katherine H. Snyder Connell, Elizabeth J. Snyder Powell. Nat. Research fellow Berlin-Dahlem (Germany) Biologische Reichsanstalt, 1933-34; plant pathologist U.S. Forest Service, 1947; prof. plant pathology U. Calif. at Berkeley, 1949—, vice chmn. dept., 1959, chmn., 1963-70; cons. plant diseases Ford Found., AID, FAO, U. Bari (Italy), Nat. Sci. Council Taiwan, 1971—; spl. research nature and control diseases vegetable and tropical plant crops and genus Fusarium; mem. NRC, 1961-64; v.p. Internat. Congress Plant Pathology, London, 1968. Rockefeller Found. traveling fellow, Europe, 1954, Australia, 1961, Eng., 1966. Fellow AAAS (pres. Pacific div. 1968), Am. Phytopath. Soc. (Ruth Allen award 1969, award merit Caribbean div. 1970, pres. 1959-60); mem. Mycol. Soc. Am., Bot. Soc. Am., Brit. Mycol. Soc. Contbr. articles to profl. jours.; editor: (with others) Ecology of Soil-Borne Plant Pathogens, 1965; contbr. chpts. to books. Home: 1926 Napa Ave Berkeley CA 94707

SNYDER, WILLIAM L., tile co. exec.; b. Phila., Oct. 28, 1935; s. S. Morris and Florence L. (Conner) S.; B.S. in Bus. Mgmt., Pa. State U., 1957; M.B.A. in Mktg., U. Chgo., 1964; m. Suzanne Opperman, Mar. 25, 1951; children—William L., L. Suzanne. Sales rep. U.S. Gypsum Co., to 1961; with Am. Olean Tile Co., 1961—, v.p. sales ops., Lansdale, Pa., 1974-76, exec. v.p. mktg., 1976—. Served with U.S. Army, 1957. Mem. Am. Mgmt. Assn., Alpha Kappa Psi, Theta Delta Chi. Republican. Methodist. Clubs: Valley Forge Riders and Drivers Assn., Fourth Light Continental Dragoons, Masons. Home: 1630 Thomas Rd Wayne PA 19087 Office: 1000 Cannon Ave Lansdale PA 19446

SNYDER, WILLIAM PENN, III, mfg. co. exec.; b. Pitts., Mar. 11, 1918; s. William Penn and Marie Elise (Whitney) S.; student U. Pitts.; m. Jean Evans Rose, Sept. 30, 1939; children—William Penn, Marie Elise, J. Brandon. With Shenango Furnace Co., Pitts., 1945—, v.p., 1950-57, pres., 1957—; chmn. bd., dir. Shenango, Inc.; pres., dir. Snyder Mining Co.; dir. Salem Corp., Mellon Nat. Bank & Trust Co., H. J. Heinz Co. (all Pitts.), Whitney Nat. Bank, New Orleans, Nat. Forge Co. Bd. dirs. Pa. Economy League; chmn. bd. trustees, dir. Allegheny Gen. Hosp., Pitts.; trustee Carnegie Hero Fund Commn. Western Res. Hist. Soc. Served as lt. (s.g.) USNR, 1942-45. Mem. Am. Iron and Steel Inst. (dir.). Republican. Episcopalian. Clubs: N.Y. Yacht; Duquesne (Pitts.); Laurel Valley Golf, Rolling Rock (Ligonier, Pa.); Allegheny Country (bd. govs., pres.) (Sewickley, Pa.); Boston (New Orleans); Gulf Stream Golf (Delray Beach, Fla.). Home: Blackburn Rd Sewickley PA 15143 Office: One Oliver Plaza Pittsburgh PA 15222

SNYDER, WILLIAM RUSSELL, oil co. exec.; b. nr. Laytonsville, Md., Mar. 11, 1926; s. Russell L. and Mary C. (Allnutt) S.; B.S., U. Md., 1951; m. Ann Lewis, Sept. 10, 1949; children—Kathryn E., Elaine M. With Crown Central Petroleum Corp., Balt., 1951—, dir.

employee relations, 1967-71, sec., dir. employee and pub. relations, 1971-74, sec., mgr. corporate adminstrn., 1974-76, v.p. adminstrn., sec., 1977—. Served with USAAF, 1944-46. Mem. Am. Soc. Corporate Secs., Am. Petroleum Inst., Toastmasters (lt. gov. 1967-68). Republican. Methodist. Club: Hunt Valley Golf. Home: 2426 Hartfell Rd Timonium MD 21093 Office: 1 N Charles St Baltimore MD 21203

SNYDERMAN, REUVEN KENNETH, plastic surgeon, educator; b. Phila., July 6, 1922; s. Harry S. and Anna (Koss) S.; A.B., U. Pa., 1943, M.D., 1946; m. Patricia Dawn Kennedy, June 29, 1955 (div. 1969); children—Peri Lynne, Lisa Mari, Scott R.; m. 2d, Adrienne E. Nordenschild, Dec. 6, 1970. Intern, U.S. Naval Hosp., Phila., 1946-47; resident in gen. surgery Montefiore Hosp., N.Y. U. Med. Center, N.Y.C., 1949-51; resident in plastic and reconstructive surgery Columbia-Presbyn. Med. Center, N.Y.C., 1951-53; resident Meml. Sloan-Kettering Hosp., N.Y.C., 1953; practice medicine specializing in plastic, reconstructive surgery, N.Y.C., 1954-73, Princeton, N.J., 1973—; mem. staff plastic and reconstructive surgery, head of tissue transplantation sect. Sloan-Kettering Inst. Cancer Research, N.Y.C., 1955-73; chief div. plastic surgery Raritan Valley Hosp.; attending surgeon Princeton Hosp.; asso. prof. surgery Cornell U. Med. Sch.; head sect. plastic and reconstructive surgery, prof. plastic surgery Rutgers Med. Sch.; chmn. Plastic Surgery Research Council; spl. cons. Auerbach Corp., Phila. Served with USNR, 1943-45; to lt. (j.g.) USMC, 1947-49. Recipient Honor award N.Y. chpt. Hadassah, 1969. Fellow A.C.S.; mem. AMA, N.Y. Regional (historian), Am. socs. plastic and reconstructive surgery, N.J., Mercer County med. socs., Webster Soc. (sec.-treas.), Am. Assn. Plastic Surgeons, N.Y. Cancer Soc. Author: New Parts for People, 1969; Symposium on Neoplastic and Reconstructive Problems of the Female Breast, 1973; The Breast, 1978; contbr. numerous articles to med. jours. Home: 24 Balcort Dr Princeton NJ 08540 Office: 253 Witherspoon St Princeton NJ 08540

SOARS, HAROLD MARSHALL, JR., machinery mfg. co. exec.; b. Providence, Mar. 28, 1924; s. Harold Marshall and Grace (Munro) S.; grad. Phillips Exeter Acad., 1943; B.S. in Mech. Engring., Yale, 1946; m. Mary Elizabeth Cox, Oct. 5, 1946; children—Harold Marshall III, Robert Lewis. With Sprout, Waldron & Co., Inc., Muncy, Pa., 1946—, v.p. engring. and prodn., 1956-65, pres., 1965-75, with Koppers Co. Inc., metal products div., Sprout, Waldron Operation, 1975—. dir. Muncy Bank & Trust Co. Vice pres., dir. Muncy Jr. C. of C., 1950-54. Mem. Muncy Borough Council, 1946-48. Bd. dirs. Lycoming United Fund, 1956-60. Registered profl. engr., Pa. Mem. West Br. Mfrs. Assn. (dir. 1973—). Republican. Baptist. Rotarian (pres. Muncy 1966-67). Clubs: Williamsport (Pa.) Country: Dunwoody-Big Bear Fish and Game (Lycoming County, Pa.). Home: RD 2 Muncy PA 17756 Office: Koppers Co Inc Metal Products Div Sprout Waldron Operation Muncy PA 17756

SOBEL, BURTON ELIAS, physician, educator; b. N.Y.C., Oct. 21, 1937; s. Lawrence J. and Ruth (Schoen) S.; A.B., Cornell U., 1958; M.D. magna cum laude, Harvard U., 1962; m. Susan Konheim, June 19, 1958; children—Jonathan, Elizabeth. Intern, Peter Bent Brigham Hosp., Boston, 1962-63, resident 1963-64, 66-67; clin. asso., cardiology br. NIH, Bethesda, Md., 1964-66, 67-68; asst. prof. medicine U. Calif. at San Diego, La Jolla, 1968-71; asso. prof. medicine, dir. myocardial infarction research unit, dir. coronary care, 1971-73; asso. prof. medicine Barnes Hosp.-Washington U., St. Louis, 1973-75, prof., 1975—, dir. cardiovascular div., 1973—, program dir. specialied center research in ischemic heart disease, 1975—, program dir. principles in cardiovascular research, 1975—; program dir. Collaborative Clin. Trial Therapy to Protect Ischemic Myocardium, Washington U., 1977. Served to lt. comdr. USPHS, 1964-68. USPHS Career Research Devel. awardee, 1972. Fellow A.C.P.; mem. Royal Soc. Medicine, Am. Fedn. Clin. Research (Councilor 1975—), Am. Heart Assn., Am. Coll. Cardiology, Assn. Univ. Cardiologists, Am. Soc. Clin. Investigation (Councilor 1978—), Assn. Am. Physicians, Am. Physiol. Soc., Cardiac Muscle Soc., Western Soc. for Clin. Research, Alpha Omega Alpha. Asso. med. editor The Heart Bull., 1971-72; editor Clin. Cardiology, 1971-74, mem. circulation bd., 1971—; mem. editorial bd. Circulation Research, 1974—, Annals of Internal Medicine, 1976—, Am. Jour. Cardiology, 1976—, Cardiology Digest, 1976-77; Jour. Continuing Edn. in Cardiology, 1978—; mem. editorial bd., asso. editor Jour. Clin. Investigation, 1977—; asso. editor Am. Jour. Physiology: Heart and Circulatory Physiology, 1978—; Churchill Livingstone editorial advisory bd. Internat. Seminars in Cardiovascular Medicine, 1978—. Home: 444 Baker Ave Webster Groves MO 63119 Office: Barnes Hosp 660 S Euclid Ave Saint Louis MO 63110

SOBEL, EDNA H., pediatric endocrinologist; b. N.Y.C., Nov. 2, 1918; d. Samuel P. and Frances B. (Selkin) S.; A.B. with high honors, U. Wis., 1939, M.A. in Zoology, 1940; M.D. cum laude, Boston U., 1943. Intern, Montefiore Hosp., N.Y.C., 1944; fellow Mass. Gen. Hosp., Harvard Med. Sch., Boston, 1944-50; research and teaching, specializing in pediatrics and endocrinology, Cin., 1950-53, Boston, 1954-56, N.Y.C., 1956—; asst. prof. pediatrics Albert Einstein Coll. Medicine, Bronx, N.Y., 1956-60, asso. prof. pediatrics, 1960-68, prof., 1968—; asst. vis. pediatrician Bronx Municipal Hosp. Center, 1956-60, asso. vis. pediatrician, 1960-68, vis. pediatrician, 1968—. Commonwealth Fund of N.Y. fellow, 1963-64; NIH grantee, 1957—, other grants. Mem. Am. Pediatric Soc., Soc. Pediatric Research (v.p. 1963-64), Am. Fedn. Clin. Research, Endocrine Soc., European Soc. Pediatric Endocrinology, Lawson Wilkins Pediatric Endocrin Soc. (dir. 1976-78), Sigma Xi. Home: 1 Garrett Pl Bronxville NY 10708 Office: Albert Einstein College of Medicine Bronx NY 10461

SOBEL, ELI, educator; b. N.Y.C., Jan. 17, 1915; s. Martin David and Lean (Filenbaum) S.; A.B., U. Ala., 1937, M.A., 1938; Ph.D., U. Calif. at Berkeley, 1947; m. J. Margaret Forster, Dec. 2, 1944; 1 son, Jeffrey Abbott. Instr., U. Ala., 1938-39; teaching fellow U. Calif. at Berkeley, 1939-42; mem. faculty U. Calif. at Los Angeles, 1946—, prof. German, 1957—, asso. dean Coll. Letters and Sci., 1957-64, chmn. faculty, 1975-76, chmn. dept. Germanic langs., 1964—. Cons. Council Grad. Schs. U.S., 1966—, Can. Council, 1970—; mem. sr. accrediting commn. Western Assn. Schs. and Colls., 1965; panelist cons. Nat. Endowment for the Humanities, 1971—. Served to lt. comdr. USNR, 1942-45. Decorated Silver Star, Presdl. citation with bronze star; citation President Philippines; Guggenheim fellow, 1959-60. Mem. Modern Lang. Assn. Am., Renaissance Soc. Am. (a founder), Philol. Assn. Pacific Coast (pres. 1974-75), Medieval Acad., Phi Sigma Delta. Jewish. Author: Sebastian Brant and Ovid, 1952; Alte Newe Zeitung: A Sixteenth-Century Collection of Fables, 1958; The Tristan Romance in the Meisterlieder of Hans Sachs, 1963. Editor: Pacific Coast Philology, 1974-75. Contbr. numerous articles, revs. to jours. Home: 2207 Kelton Ave Los Angeles CA 90064

SOBEL, LESTER ALBERT, editor; b. N.Y.C., Oct. 3, 1919; s. David and Ray Dorothy (Mendelson) S.; B.B.A., Coll. City N.Y., 1942; m. Eileen Lucille Helfer, May 3, 1953; children—Martha Lorraine, Sharon Ruth, Jonathan William. Mem. editorial staff Facts on File, 1946—, editor-in-chief, 1960-73; v.p. Facts on File, Inc., 1964—; editor-in-chief News Year, 1960-63, News Dictionary, 1964-73, Interim History, 1964-75; editor Realty, 1976—. Served with AUS, 1942-45; ETO. Decorated Bronze Star. Jewish. Author: National Issues, 1956; Space: From Sputnik to Gemini, 1965; South Vietnam: U.S.-Communist Confrontation in South-east Asia, Vol. 1, 1966, Vol. 2, 1969; Civil Rights, 1967; Russia's Rulers: The Khrushchev Period, 1971. Home: 226 Porterfield Pl Freeport NY 11520 Office: 119 W 57th St New York City NY 10019. *Success should not be considered an absolute. A person is not either absolutely successful or absolutely unsuccessful. We all struggle somewhere between the two extremes, but we should make honorable efforts to move toward the goal that represents success to us. Progress in this direction is an honest and gratifying form of success although the absolute goal may never be reached.*

SOBEL, WALTER HOWARD, architect: b. Chgo., July 25, 1913; s. Karl B. and Blanche K. (Klein) S.; student in Engring., Northwestern U., 1930-31; B.Arch., Armour Inst. Tech., 1935; m. Betty Debs, Oct. 2, 1943; children—Susan Sobel Kaufman, Richard, Steven, Nancy, Robert. Owner, Walter H. Sobel, Architect, 1938-42; partner Walter H. Sobel-J. Stewart Stein, Architects, Chgo., 1945-60; prin. Walter H. Sobel, F.A.I.A. and Assos., Chgo., 1960—; archtl. cons. Vice-pres. Family Service Center, Wilmette, Ill., 1962-64, pres., 1965; v.p. United Fund, Wilmette, 1965-66; mem. Wilmette Council for Comml. Renewal; mem. Wilmette Planning Commn., 1977; mem. Exec. Mansion Com. State of Ill., 1966—; bd. dirs. Abraham Lincoln Centre, 1968—; mem. Hull House Assn., 1968—. Nat. cons. in field. Served with USNR, 1942-45. Decorated Purple Heart. Fellow AIA (past pres. Chgo. chpt.); mem. Nat. Trust Historic Preservation, Landmarks Preservation Council Chgo., Ill. Assn. Professions (pres. 1970), Ill. Architects-Engrs. Council (past chmn.). Editor (with others) The American Courthouse: Planning and Design for the Judicial Process, 1973; contbr. articles to profl. jours. Home: 507 Lake Ave Wilmette IL 60091 Office: 2 N Riverside Plaza Chicago IL 60606

SOBER, SIDNEY, ret. fgn. service officer; b. N.Y.C., Nov. 12, 1919; s. Isaac and Mary (Krug) S.; B.A., City Coll. N.Y., 1939; M.A., George Washington U., 1964; postgrad. Northwestern U., 1952-53; student U.S. Army War Coll., 1963-64; m. Elizabeth Holmes, Apr. 2, 1947; children—Stephen Holmes, Elizabeth Hahn (dec.). Civilian employee War Dept., 1940-44, 46-47; joined U.S. Fgn. Service, 1947; vice consul Am. consulate, Tananarive, Madagascar, 1947-49; 3d sec. Am. embassy, Prague, Czechoslovakia, 1949-50; 2d sec. Am. legation, Reykjavik, Iceland, 1950-52, Am. embassy, Ankara, Turkey, 1953-56; assigned Dept. State, 1956-60, 64-69, chief S. Asia div., Office Research and Analysis for Asia, 1959-60; consul Am. consulate gen., Bombay, India, 1961-63; dir. regional affairs, staff dir. interdepartmental group for Nr. East and South Asia, Dept. State, 1966-69; minister-counselor Am. embassy, Islamabad, Pakistan, 1969-73; dep. asst. sec. state for Near Eastern and South Asian affairs, 1974-78; vis. prof. Am. U., 1978—. Served to lt. (j.g.) USNR, 1944-46. Mem. Phi Beta Kappa. Address: 5009 Hawthorne Pl NW Washington DC 20016

SOBERON, GUILLERMO, univ. rector, physician, biochemist; b. Iguala, Mexico, Dec. 29, 1925; s. Galo and Carmen (Acevedo) S.; M.D., U. Mexico, Ciudad Universitaria, 1949; Ph.D., U. Wis., 1956; m. Socorro Chavez, July 3, 1952; children—Socorro, Gloria, Guillermo, Mario, Adolfo, Rosario. Intern, Hosp. Enferme de les Nutricion, Mexico, 1949-50; resident internal medicine Inst. Nutrition, Mexico, 1950-52; head dept. biochemistry U. Mexico, 1956-65, dir. Inst. Biomed. Research, 1965-71, sci. coordinator, 1971-73, rector, 1973—. Recipient Sourasky Sci. award Fondo Fomento Educativo, 1968, Elizondo Sci. award Fundación Elizondo, 1974. Mem. Acad. Medicine Mexico, Acad. Sci. Mexico (Acad. award 1965), Am. Assn. Biol. Chemistry, Biochem. Soc. U.K. Home: 64 Nino Jesus Mexico DF 22 Mexico Office: Torre de Rectoria Ciudad Universitaria 20 Mexico DF Mexico

SOBEY, WILLIAM MACDONALD, merchant; b. New Glasgow, N.S., Can., June 9, 1927; s. Frank H. and Irene L. (MacDonald) S.; grad. high sch.; m. Doris C. Cameron, Oct. 1948; children—Frank, Karl, Heather, Ann. Chmn. bd., chief exec. officer, dir. Sobeys Stores Ltd., Stellarton, N.S.; pres., dir. Gulf Services Ltd., Foord Constrn. Ltd.; pres. Food City Ltd., Primrose Mall Ltd.; v.p., dir. Atlantic Motors Ltd., Amleco Leasing Ltd., Sobeys Holdings Ltd., Avalon Mall Ltd., T.R.A. Foods Ltd.; dir. Bank of Montreal, Empire Co. Ltd., Can. Shopping Centres Ltd., Atlantic Shopping Centres. Mayor, Stellarton, 1965-70. Nat. dir. Can. Council Christians and Jews, 1967, Human Relations award, 1971; bd. dirs. N.S. Heart Found., N.S. Tourist Assn.; chmn. Pictou County Heart Found. Mem. Young Pres.'s Assn. Mem. United Ch. of Can. Mason (32 degree, Shriner, Jester). Clubs: Royal N.S. Yacht Squadron; Saraguay; Union (St. Johns); City (New Glasgow); Abercrombie Country; Halifax. Home: 155 Pleasant St Stellarton NS Canada Office: King St Stellarton NS Canada

SOBILOFF, MYER NATHANIEL, business cons.; b. Fall River, Mass., Nov. 2, 1907; s. Israel and Fannie (Gollub) S.; A.B., Harvard, 1928; m. Cilla Sander, July 10, 1932; children—Ellen B., James I. Treas., gen. mgr. Fall River Curtain Co. (Mass.), 1929-47; partner Sobiloff Bros., Inc., Fall River, 1948-66, pres., treas., dir., 1966-77; mem. Logast Syndicate, N.Y.C., 1950-77; chmn. bd., dir. Larchfield Corp., N.Y.C., 1951-77, Marshall-Wells, Internat., Nassau, 1956-77; Eastern Tablet, Albany, N.Y., 1963-77; sr. v.p., dir. Scruggs Vandervoort Barney; chmn. bd. Johnson Stores, Inc.; chmn. bd., dir. Mont. Merc. Co., Larchfield Corp.; v.p., dir. Auto-Lec. Stores, Inc., 1966-77; dir. Johnson Cotton Co., Kilburn Mill, Fall River; business mgmt. cons., 1977—. Mem. Fall River Airport Commn., 1946-52, Fall River Indsl. Commn., 1952-55; 1st v.p. Greater Fall River Devel. Corp., 1952-55; chmn. bd. Greater Fall River chpt. A.R.C., also mem. exec. com., 1947; pres. Community Fund Greater Fall River, 1948; nat. vice chmn. Joint Def. Appeal, 1946-49; mem. Nat. Bd. Joint Distbn., 1950—; 1st v.p. Community Ednl. Found. Fall River, 1959—; exec. com. Fall River Boys Club, 1950—; finance com. Massasoit council Boy Scouts Am., 1951-53, bd. dirs. Nat. council; mem. Nat. Jewish Scouting, 1959—, Greater Fall River Assn. Mental Health, 1959—; exec. com. So. New Eng. region Nat. Conf. Christians and Jews, 1960—; past bd. advisers Stonehill Coll.; hon. trustee Friends Acad., N. Dartmouth, Mass., Union Hosp., Fall River; trustee Ambrook Found., Norwich, Conn.; hon. bd. dirs. B.M.C. Durfee Trust, Fall River; bd. dirs. Soc. Friends of Touro Synagogue Nat. Historic Shrine, Newport, R.I.; a founder Albert Einstein Coll. Medicine. Mem. Mass. N.G., 1942-45, Mass. Militia, 1945-46. Mem. N.A.M., Fall River C. of C., Colonial Navy of Mass., Holstein-Friesian Assn. Am. Plymouth County (Mass.) Breeders Assn. Jewish religion (past v.p., dir. temple). Mason (32, Shriner), K.P., Elk, Rotarian; mem. B'nai B'rith (bd. New Eng. Anti-Defamation League). Clubs: Harvard (Fall River, Boston, N.Y.C. and Cape Cod); Fetherdic Tennis (Fall River). Home: 687 Woodlawn St Fall River MA 02720 Office: PO Box 247 Fall River MA 02722

SOBIN, JULIAN MELVIN, chem. co. exec.; b. Boston, July 14, 1920; s. Irving Maxwell and Selma Helen (Brodie) S.; A.B., Harvard, 1941; m. Leila Ruth Feinburg, May 3, 1942; children—Patricia (Mrs. Jerome Bernard Brightman), Jonathan. Trainee Sobin Chems. Inc., Boston, 1946-48, adminstrv. mgr., 1948-55, mgr. purchasing, 1955-63, v.p.-internat., 1963-68, exec. v.p., 1968-70, pres., 1970—; sr. v.p. Internat. Minerals & Chem. Corp., 1975-77, dir. internat. bus. devel., 1976-77, exec. cons., 1977-78; exec. v.p. IMC Chem. Group, 1975-76; pres. Julian M. Sobin & Assos., Inc., 1977—; chmn. Sobin Chems. Inc., 1978—; treas. Friendship Internat. Corp., 1977—; v.p. Asso. Metals & Minerals Corp., 1978—, dir. Comml. Solvents Corp.; lectr. in field. Corporator South Boston Savs. Bank; mem. Pres's Roster Tech. Specialists for Chem. Products, 1962-63; advisor, cons. to Spl. Rep. of Pres. for Trade Negotiations, Kennedy Round of Tariff Reductions, 1962-63; mem. Mass. Gov.'s Adv. Council on Internat. Trade, 1965-71; mem. Pres.'s Adv. Com. Nat. Trade Policy, 1968-69; mem. adv. com. on East/West trade Dept. Commerce, 1976—; mem. exec. com. Mass. Gov.'s Fgn. Bus. Council, 1977—. Gen. chmn. New Eng. Trade Week, 1959; trustee Nat. Jewish Hosp. and Research Center, Denver, Emerson Coll.; bd. advisors Stonehill Coll., 1975-78; mem. overseers com. to visit dept. fine arts Harvard U., 1968-74, to visit dept. Germanic langs. and lit., 1973-75; mem. Boston Com. on Fgn. Relations; bd. dirs. Nat. Council U.S.-China Trade, 1976-77, World Affairs Council, Internat. Assn. Students in Econs. and Mgmt., East-West Trade Council, Drug, Chem. and Allied Trades; bd. dirs., mem. exec. com. Internat. Trade Center New Eng. Inc.; bd. dirs., chmn. bd. trustees Internat. Mktg. Inst.; trustee Lesley Coll., Boston U. Served to maj. F.A., AUS, 1941-46; CBI. Decorated Legion of Merit; recipient Annual Honor medal Nat. Jewish Hosp. and Research Center, 1975. Mem. Mfg. Chemists Assn., Chlorine Inst., Chemists Club of N.Y., Hong Kong-Am. C. of C., Execs. Club of Greater Boston C. of C., Internat. Mgmt. Devel. Inst. (corp. strategic planning council), Soc. Am. Chem. Industry, Appalachian Mountain Club, Am. Radio Relay League. Clubs: Harvard of Boston, of N.Y.; Univ. of Boston, St. Botolph, Belmont Country. Contbg. author: China, the U.S.S.R. and East Europe—A U.S. Trade Perspective; Doing Business With China—American Trade Opportunities in the 1970s; Future United States Foreign Trade Policy; The China Trader, an audio-album; co-author Ency. of China Today. Contbr. numerous articles to profl. jours. First Am. businessman invited to attend Canton (China) Trade Fair, spring 1972; first Am. businessman invited to Peking, China, spring 1972; several trips to People's Republic of China, 1972—. Home: 790 Boylston St Boston MA 02199 Office: Internat Sobin Chems Corp 1900 Prudential Tower Boston MA 02199

SOBIN, MORRIS, corp. exec.; b. N.Y.C., Aug. 7, 1913; s. Philip and Katie (Schwartz) S.; B.B.A., Coll. City N.Y., 1935; m. Ruth Newmark, Nov. 25, 1936; 1 dau., Louise. Staff, Popper, Katzman & Scheckman, C.P.A.'s, 1935-39; pub. accountant. 1939-42; chief accountant Olympic Radio & TV, 1942-46, v.p., treas., 1946-52, exec. v.p., gen. mgr., 1952, pres., 1953-65, also dir.; v.p. Siegler Corp.; v.p. Lear Siegler, Inc., 1962-65, pres. Data and Controls div., 1962-65; pres., dir., chief exec. officer Pilot Radio, Inc., 1965-66; pres. Pilot Radio-TV Corp., 1966-69; exec. v.p., dir. Regent-Sheffield, Ltd., 1971—; dir. Westall Richardson Ltd., Sheffield, Eng., Suburbia Fed. Savs. & Loan Assn., Garden City, N.J. Mem. Am. Arbitration Assn., N.Y. State Soc. C.P.A.'s, N.Y. Credit and Fin. Mgmt. Assn., Nat. Assn. Cost Accountants, Electronic Industries Assn. (chmn. comsumer products div. 1962, 63, dir. 1965—). Clubs: Masons; Fresh Meadow Country (bd. govs., treas.); Roslyn Country. Home: 56 Shadetree Ln Roslyn Heights NY 11577 Office: 70 Schmitt Blvd Farmingdale NY 11735

SOBKOVIAK, KENNETH RAYMOND, fin. exec.; b. Chgo., Nov. 1, 1944; s. Raymond J. and Emily A. S.; B.B.A., Wis. State U., Whitewater, 1966; m. Sharon M. Uhle, Mar. 2, 1974; 1 dau., Tracy Lynn. Auditor, Arthur Young & Co., Milw., 1966-71; with fin. div. MGIC Investment Corp., Milw., 1971—, now treas. Active Cedarburg (Wis.) Jaycees. Served with USAR. Mem. Nat. Assn. Accts. Office: MGIC Plaza Milwaukee WI 53201

SOBLE, DAVID S., steel service center exec.; b. Chgo., July 3, 1943; s. Morris and Eleanor S.; B.S. in Econs., U. Pa., 1965; m. Marcia Greenstein, Sept. 4, 1966; children—Michael, Jeffrey. With Lesso Steel Co., 1965-69, sales mgr., 1967-69; with Interstate Steel Co., Des Plaines, Ill., 1969—, v.p. sales, 1971-74, exec. v.p., 1974-75, pres., 1975—. Home: 24 Country Ln Northfield IL 60093 Office: 401 Touhy Ave Des Plaines IL 60018

SOBLE, RONALD NORMAN, actor; b. Chgo., Mar. 28, 1928; s. Aaron and Dorothy (Turk) S.; B.A. in Speech, U. Mich., 1951; m. Elynor Fogel, Aug. 10, 1952; children—Laura, Nancy. Appeared in numerous films, including: Navajo Run, 1964, Al Capone, 1959, Cincinnati Kid, 1965, True Grit, 1969, Chisum, 1970, Papillon, 1973, When You Comin' Back, Red Ryder, 1979; appeared in numerous TV series, including The Monroes, 1966-67. Served with U.S. Army, 1946-48, 51-53. Mem. Screen Actors Guild (3d v.p.), AFTRA (mem. nat. bd.), Acad. Motion Picture Arts and Scis. Office: care Stevens Gray Agy 8733 Sunset Blvd Suite 205 Los Angeles CA 90069

SOBOL, DONALD J., author; b. N.Y.C., Oct. 4, 1924; s. Ira J. and Ida (Gelula) S.; B.A., Oberlin Coll., 1948; m. Rose Louisa Tiplitz, Aug. 14, 1955; children—Diane, Glenn, Eric, John. Mem. editorial staff New York Sun, N.Y.C., 1948, L.I. Daily Press, 1949-51; with R. H. Macy's Co., 1953-54; free-lance writer, 1954—; books include: The Amazons of Greek Mythology, 1973; Encyclopedia Brown & the Case of the Dead Eagles, 1975; Encyclopedia Brown & the Case of the Secret Pitch, 1965; Encyclopedia Brown: Boy Detective, 1963; Encyclopedia Brown Finds the Clues, 1966; Encyclopedia Brown Gets His Man, 1967; Encyclopedia Brown Keeps the Peace, 1969; Encyclopedia Brown Lends a Hand, 1974; Encyclopedia Brown Shows the Way, 1972; Encyclopedia Brown Strikes Again, 1973; Encyclopedia Brown Takes the Case, 1973; Encyclopedia Lends A Hand, 1974; Encyclopedia Brown and the Case of The Dead Eagles, 1975; Still More Two-Minute Mysteries, 1975; True Sea Adventurers, 1975; Encyclopedia Brown and The Case of the Midnight Visitor, 1977; Disaster, 1979; Encyclopedia Brown's Record Book of Weird and Wonderful Facts, 1979; Best Animal Stories of Science Fiction and Fantasy, 1979; Encyclopedia Brown Carries On, 1980; syndicated newspaper feature Two Minute Mystery Series; originator comic strip Encyclopedia Brown; author numerous short stories for adults and children. Served with AUS, 1943-46. Mem. Authors League Am., Mystery Writers Am., Soc. Children's Book Writers. Jewish. Office: care McIntosh & Otis Inc 475 Fifth Ave New York NY 10017

SOCHA, WLADYSLAW WOJCIECH, med. researcher; b. Paris, July 3, 1926; s. Tadeusz and Anna (Klara) S.; M.A., Jagellonian U., 1952; M.D., Med. Acad. Cracow (Poland), 1959, teaching cert., 1963; m. Adela Katherine Zacharko, Jan. 3, 1956. Asst. dept. pathology Cancer Inst., Warsaw, Poland, 1952-60; asso. prof. dept. forensic medicine Med. Acad., Cracow, 1955-63; dir. Inst. Pediatrics, Cracow, 1963-69; research prof. dept. forensic medicine Sch. Medicine, chief pathology Lab. Exptl. Medicine and Surgery in Primates, N.Y. U., N.Y.C., 1969—; asso. dir. Primate Blood Group Reference Lab. and WHO Collaborating Center for Hematology of Primate Animals, 1977—. Served with Polish Home Army, 1941-45. Decorated Mil. Cross of Merit, Cross of Valor; recipient Polish Med. Soc. Ann. award, 1959; Polish Surg. Soc. award, 1960; Polish Acad. Sci. Ann. award, 1966. Mem. Am. Soc. Human Genetics, N.Y. Acad. Scis., AAAS, Polish Inst. Arts and Sci. in Am., Polish-Am. Med. Soc., Institut Pyreneen d'Etudes Anthropologiques Toulouse. Author, co-author various med. texts, 1963—; editor Jour. Med. Primatology; contbr. numerous articles on immunology, immunogenetics, pathology and anthropology to profl. jours. Home: 10 Townsend Ave Upper Grandview NY 10960 Office: 550 st Ave New York NY 10016

SOCHEN, JUNE, historian; b. Chgo., Nov. 26, 1937; d. Sam and Ruth (Finkelstein) S.; B.A., U. Chgo., 1958; M.A., Northwestern U., 1960, Ph.D., 1967. Project editor Chgo. Superior and Talented Student Project, 1959-60; high sch. tchr. English and history North Shore Country Day Sch., Winnetka, Ill., 1961-64; instr. history Northeastern Ill. U., 1964-67, asst. prof., 1967-69, asso. prof., 1969-72, prof., 1972—. Nat. Endowment for Humanities grantee, 1971-72. Mem. Am. Studies Assn. Author books including: The New Woman, 1971; Movers and Shakers, 1973; Herstory: A Womans View of American History, 1975. Contbr. articles to profl. jours. Office: Northeastern Ill U 5500 N Saint Louis St Chicago IL 60625

SOCOLOW, ARTHUR ABRAHAM, geologist; b. Bronx, N.Y., Mar. 23, 1921; s. Samuel and Yetta (Solomon) S.; B.S., Rutgers U., 1942; M.A., Columbia, 1947, Ph.D., 1955; m. Edith S. Blumenthal, Apr. 10, 1949; children—Carl, Roy. Jeff. Photogrammetrist, U.S. Geol. Survey, 1942, 46; with Eagle Picher de Mexico, 1947; instr. geology So. Methodist U., 1948-50; dir. geology field camp, Colo., 1948-50; asst. prof. Boston U., 1950-55; asso. prof. U. Mass., 1955-57; econ. geologist Pa. Geol. Survey, 1957-61, dir., chief geologist, 1961—; geologist Def. Minerals Exploration Authority, Alaska, 1952; cons., 1949—; mem. Outer Continental Shelf Adv. Com.; geol. adv. Boston Mus. Sci., 1955-57; lectr. mineral conservation Pa. State U., 1959—; mem. conf. earth sci. source materials NSF, 1959; chmn. ann. field conf. Pa. Geologists; past mem. U.S. Nat. Com. on Tunnelling Tech.; mem. Gov.'s adv. com. Nat. Council on Environ. Quality; chmn. Pa. Water Resources Coordinating Com. Served with USAAF, 1942-46. Fellow Geol. Soc. Am. (sec.-treas. N.E. sect.), Mineral. Soc. Am.; mem. Soc. Econ. Geologists, AAAS (div. bd.), AAUP, Phila. Geol. Soc. (past pres.), Am. Geol. Inst. (com. on manpower), Nat. Assn. Geology Tchrs. (past regional pres.), Pa. Acad. Sci., Am. Meteoritical Soc., Am. Assn. State Geologists (past pres.), Am. Geophys. Union, Am. Commn. Stratigraphic Nomenclature (past chmn.), Harrisburg Geol. Soc., Interstate Oil Compact Commn. (research com., environ. com.), Sigma Xi. Club: Internat. Torch (past pres. chpt.). Editor: Pa. Geology Bull. Contbr. articles to profl. jours. Home: 420 Larry Dr Harrisburg PA 17109 Office: Pa Geol Survey Harrisburg PA 17120. *I have great respect for the individualism of man in the midst of a society and a world where there is an unavoidable interrelationship and interdependence of man upon man, and of man upon his environment. While we strive to maintain our individualism, we are forced to share our common resources and our common aspirations. This is the challenge that makes our lives worth living.*

SOCRANSKY, SIGMUND SYDNEY, periodontist, microbiologist; b. Toronto, Ont., Can., Dec. 2, 1934; s. Ben and Yettie (Fruitman) S.; came to U.S., 1963, naturalized, 1963; D.D.S., U. Toronto, 1957; postdoctoral certificate, Harvard U., 1961; m. June Hutchison, Nov. 4, 1965. Asso. in dental medicine, dept. bacteriology and periodontology Forsyth Dental Infirmary and Harvard Sch. Dental Medicine, Boston, 1961-64, asst. prof. periodontology, 1964—, asso. clin. prof. oral biology, 1976—, sr. staff mem. Forsyth Dental Center, 1968—. Mem. Internat. Assn. Dental Research (Basic Research in Oral Sci. award 1971, Research in Periodontology award 1978), Am. Soc. Microbiology. Contbr. research articles to dental jours. Home: 141 Summit Ave Brookline MA 02146 Office: 140 Fenway St Boston MA 02115

SODERBERG, CARL RICHARD, mech. engr., educator; b. Ulvöhamn, Sweden, Feb. 3, 1895; s. Jonas Axel and Johanna Kristina (Nordquist) S.; naval architect, Chalmers Inst. Tech., Goteborg, Sweden, 1919, Tech. Dr., 1951; fellow Am.-Scandanavian Found., 1919-20; S.B., M.I.T., 1920; D.Eng., Tufts U., 1958; came to U.S., 1919, naturalized, 1927; m. Sigrid Kristina Lofstedt, May 9, 1921; children—Carl Richard, Lars Olof, Barbro Kristina. Devel. engr. for large elec. machinery Westinghouse Electric & Mfg. Co., East Pittsburgh, Pa., 1922-28, chief turbine engr., 1931-38; in charge of turbo generators ASEA, Västeras, Sweden, 1928-30; prof. mech. engring. Mass. Inst. Tech., 1938-59, Inst. prof., 1959-61, Inst. prof. emeritus, 1961, head dept. mech. engring., 1947-54, dean engring., 1954-59. Decorated comdr. Royal Order North Star; recipient Capt. Joseph H. Linnard prize (with Ronald R. Smith), Soc. Naval Architects and Marine Engrs., 1944; Certificate of Appreciation, Army and Navy, 1948, John Ericsson gold medal Am. Soc. of Swedish Engrs., 1952; Exceptional Service award U.S. Air Force, 1955, ASME, 1960; DeLaval medal Royal Swedish Engring. Acad., 1968; Gustaf Dalen medal Chalmers, 1970. Fellow Am. Acad. Arts and Scis., AIAA, ASME (hon.), Royal Swedish Engring. Acad., Nat. Acad. Sci., Nat. Acad. Engring.; mem. A.A.A.S., Brit. Inst. M.E., Svenska Teknologföreningen, Soc. Naval Architects and Marine Engrs. (hon.), Am. Soc. Swedish Engrs. Designer, inventor steam turbines, generators for land and marine applications, aircraft turbo engines. Author numerous monographs in Am. and European jours. on dynamics, vibrations, design of turbines and generators, gas turbines, etc. Address: 100 Memorial Dr Cambridge MA 02142

SODERBERGH, PETER ANDREW, univ. dean, educator; b. Bklyn., Nov. 14, 1928; s. Sven Eric and Mary Margaret (McGowan) S.; B.A., Amherst Coll., 1950; M.A., Harvard U., 1959; Ph.D., U. Tex., 1966; m. Mary Ann Bernard, May 12, 1953; children—Susan, Mary, Peter, Katherine, Steven Charles. Tchr. public schs., Andover, Mass., 1959-60, prin. Andover Jr. High Sch., 1960-61; instr. English, Phillips Andover Acad., summers 1959-61; lectr. in edn. Emory U., Atlanta, 1961-63; asst. prof. edn. U. Tex., Austin, 1966-67; prof. edn. U. Pitts., 1967-73; asso. dean Sch. Edn., U. Va., Charlottesville, 1973-76; dean Coll. Edn., La. State U., Baton Rouge, 1976—. Served with USMCR, 1950-58; Korea. Decorated Purple Heart; Markoe scholar, 1958-59. Mem. Soc. for Cinema Studies, Soc. for Study So. Lit., Phi Delta Kappa, Kappa Delta Pi, Phi Kappa Phi, Alpha Delta Phi. Democrat. Contbr. articles to profl. jours. Home: 437 Carriage Way Baton Rouge LA 70808 Office: Coll Edn La State U Baton Rouge LA 70803

SODERBLOM, LAURENCE ALBERT, geophysicist; b. Denver, July 17, 1944; s. Albert Laurence and Elizabeth Ann (Walters) S.; B.S. in Physics and Geology, N.Mex. Inst. Tech., 1966; Ph.D. in Planetary Sci. and Geophysics, Calif. Inst. Tech., 1970; m. Barbara Barr Maris, July 20, 1968; children—Brian, Eric, Jason. With astrogeologic studies br. U.S. Geol. Survey, Flagstaff, Ariz., 1970—, now chief; dep. leader Voyager Imaging Sci. Team; mem. Viking Orbiter Imaging Sci. Team, Mariner 9 Imaging Team, Galileo Project Team, Venus Orbital Imaging Radar Team. Office: 2255 N Gemini Dr Flagstaff AZ 86001

SODERHOLM, LARS GUSTAV, mag. editor; b. Kvillinge, Sweden, May 7, 1924; s. Nils Gustav and Ebba Augusta (Stenholm) S.; came to U.S., 1927, naturalized, 1939; B.S. in Mech. Engring., Ill. Inst. Tech., 1949; m. Betty Cartwright, Nov. 22, 1951; children—Elin Ann, Robert Gustav. Safety engr. Am. Asso. Ins. Cos., Chgo., 1949-51; design-devel. engr. Whiting Corp., Harvey, Ill., 1951-59; Midwest editor Design News, Cahners Pub. Co., Chgo., 1959-71, editorial dir., Boston, 1971—. Coordinator ann. fluidic seminars Milw. Sch. Engring., 1965-68, recipient Master key for service, 1966; bd. govs. Nat. Conf. Power Transmission, 1978—. Served with AUS, 1943-45. Recipient Cahners award for excellence, 1967. Registered profl. engr., Ill., Ind., Ia., Minn., Mo., Wis. Mem. Nat., Mass. socs. profl. engrs., Am. Soc. Bus. Press Editors (pres. Chgo. 1966-67, nat. pres. 1969-70), Am. Bus. Press (Western editorial bd. 1970-71), Fluid Power Soc., Nat. Fluid Power Assn. (tech. rep.), Nat. Conf. on Fluid Power (exec. com. 1975—), Sigma Delta Chi. Author numerous articles in field. Home: 3 Crestview Dr Southboro MA 01772 Office: 221 Columbus Ave Boston MA 02116

SODERLIND, STERLING EUGENE, newspaperman; b. Rapelje, Mont., Sept. 6, 1926; s. William John and Florence (Longbotham) S.; B.A., U. Mont., 1950; Rhodes Scholar Oxford U. (Eng.), 1950-52; m. Helen Boyce, Apr. 9, 1955; children—Steven, Sarah, Lori. Reporter, Mpls. Tribune, 1952-55; reporter Wall St. Jour., Chgo., 1955-56, Southeastern bur. chief, Jacksonville, Fla., 1956-57, mem. page one editing staff, N.Y.C., 1957-65, asst. mng. editor, 1966-70, mng. editor, 1970; econs. editor Dow Jones & Co., Inc., N.Y.C., 1970-77, asst. to pres., 1975-77, v.p., 1977—. Served with USNR, 1944-46. Congregationalist. Home: 58 Wellington Ave Short Hills NJ 07078 Office: 22 Cortlandt St New York City NY 10007

SOELTER, ROBERT RICHARD, chain store exec.; b. Wamego, Kans., Jan. 3, 1926; s. Erich R. and Vera G. (Brock) S.; B.S. in Econs., Kans. State U., 1949; m. Ruth Morris, Sept. 1, 1947; children—Eric, Michael, Laura. Mgmt. trainee S.S. Kresge Co., 1949; buyer Duckwell Stores, Inc., Abilene, Kans., 1952-70, mdse. mgr., 1970-74; exec. v.p., 1974-77, pres., dir., 1977—. Bd. dirs. Dickinson County Meml. Hosp. Served with AUS, 1943-46. Republican. Episcopalian. Home: 1000 N Buckeye Ave Abilene KS 67410 Office: Duckwall Stores 401 Cottage St Abilene KS 67410

SOENNEKER, HENRY JOSEPH, bishop; b. Melrose, Minn., May 27, 1907; s. Henry and Mary (Wessel) S.; B.A., Josephinum Coll. and Sem., Worthington, O., 1930; J.C.L., Cath. U. Am., 1950. Ordained priest Roman Cath. Ch., 1934; asst. parish of St. Anthony, St. Cloud, Minn., 1934-40, also tchr. Cathedral High Sch., St. Cloud and chaplain VA Hosp.; chaplain Sisters of St. Francis, Little Falls, Minn., 1940-48; spiritual dir. St. John's Major Sem., Collegeville, Minn., 1950-61; bishop Diocese of Owensboro, Ky., 1961—. Office: PO Box 773 Owensboro KY 42301*

SOFAER, ABRAHAM DAVID, judge, educator; b. Bombay, India, May 6, 1938; came to U.S., 1948, naturalized, 1959; B.A. magna cum laude in History Yeshiva Coll., 1962; LL.B. cum laude (Root-Tilden scholar), N.Y. U., 1965; m. Marian Bea Schever, Oct. 23, 1977; children—Daniel E., Michael J. Admitted to N.Y. bar, 1965; law clk. U.S. Ct. Appeals, Washington, 1965-66, to Hon. William J. Brennan, Jr., U.S. Supreme Ct., Washington, 1966-67; asst. U.S. atty. So. Dist. N.Y., N.Y.C., 1967-69; prof. law Columbia U., N.Y.C., 1969-79; Meyer prof. law and social research, 1974-75, adj. prof. law, 1979—; Brainerd Currie lectr. Duke U., Durham, N.C., 1975; hearing officer N.Y. Dept. Environ. Conservation, 1975-76. Bd. dirs. Citizens Union and Moblzn. for Youth Legal Services, 1976-78. Served with USAAF, 1956-59. Mem. Fed. Bar Assn., Am. Bar Assn., N.Y. Bar Assn., Am. Law Inst. Jewish. Author: War, Foreign Affairs and Constitutional Power: The Origins, 1976; contbr. articles to legal jours.; editor-in-chief N.Y. U. Law Rev., 1964-65. Office: US Dist Ct So Dist NY Foley Sq New York NY 10007

SOFAER, ABRAHAM DAVID, judge educator; b. Bombay, India, May 6, 1938; came to U.S., 1948, naturalized, 1959; B.A. in History magna cum laude, Yeshiva Coll., 1962; LL.B. (Root-Tilden scholar) cum laude, N.Y. U., 1965. Admitted to N.Y. bar, 1965; law clk. U.S. Ct. Appeals, Washington, 1965-66; to U.S. Supreme Ct., Washington, 1966-67; asst. U.S. Atty. So. Dist. N.Y., N.Y.C., 1967-69; prof. law Columbia U., 1969-79; adj. prof. law, 1979—. Mem. Am. Bar Assn., N.Y. Bar Assn., Am. Law Inst. Author: War Foreign Affairs and Constitutional Power: The Origins, 1976; contbr. articles to legal jours. Office: US Dist Ct So Dist NY Foley Sq New York NY 10007

SOFFEN, GERALD ALAN, govt. ofcl.; b. Cleve., Feb. 7, 1926; B.A., U. Calif., Los Angeles, 1949; M.S., U. So. Calif., 1956; Ph.D. (USPHS fellow 1958-59), Princeton U., 1960; USPHS fellow N.Y. U., 1960-61; m. 1956. Sr. scientist Jet Propulsion Lab. Calif. Inst. Tech., 1961-79; chief scientist Viking project NASA, Langley Research Center, Hampton, Va.; dir. NASA Life Scis., 1979—. Served with AUS, 1944-46. Mem. AAAS. Office: NASA Hdqrs Code SB Washington DC

SOFFER, ALFRED, physician; b. South Bend, Ind., May 5, 1922; s. Simon M. and Bessie (Rokeach) S.; B.A., U. Wis., 1943, M.D., 1945; m. Isabel M. Weinstraub, July 22, 1956; children—Jonathan Joshua, Gil. Intern, Genesee Hosp., Rochester, N.Y., 1945-46; asst. resident St. Louis Jewish Hosp., 1948-49; fellow physiology U. Rochester Sch. Medicine, 1949; fellow cardiology Genesee Hosp., 1950-51; dir. cardiopulmonary labs. Rochester Gen. Hosp., 1958-62; sr. editor Jour. AMA, 1962-67, editor in chief Chest, 1968—; exec. dir. Am. Coll. Chest Physicians, 1969—; prof. medicine Chgo. Med. Sch.-Univ. Health Scis., 1968—; chief editor Archives Internal Medicine, AMA, 1976—; vis. prof. U. Tel Aviv Sch. Medicine, 1973-74: cons. to dir. Nat. Heart and Lung Inst., Bethesda, Md., 1973-74; cons. to minister of health Israel, 1973-74; pres. Am. Physicians Fellowship, 1970-72; sec. Am. Coll. Cardiology, 1968, trustee, 1968-72. Mem. nat. lecture bur. Hadassah, 1962—. Served to capt. AUS, 1946-48. Author books and articles on cardiology; editor Heart and Lung, 1971—; editorial bd. Respiration. Home: 950 Central Rd Glenview IL 60025 Office: 911 Busse Hwy Park Ridge IL 60068

SOFFER, MILTON DAVID, educator, chemist; b. N.Y.C., Dec. 11, 1914; s. Henry Alfred and Hannah (Kleinman) S.; B.S., U. Ark., 1937; M.A., Harvard, 1939, Ph.D., 1942; m. Rosanne Smith, Feb. 16, 1957; children—Katherine Barns, Roderick Wallace, Frederic David. Fellow Nat. Def. Research Com., Purdue U., 1941-42; mem. faculty Smith Coll., 1942—, prof. chemistry, 1956—, Sophia Smith prof., 1970—; vis. prof. U. Mass., 1962, mem. grad. faculty, 1962—; vis. scientist in residence Hollins Coll., 1963; cons. to industry. Research grantee Research Corp., 1946-52, NSF, 1952-68; Guggenheim fellow Oxford U., 1950-51; NSF sr. postdoctoral fellow, Harvard, 1958-59. Fellow Am. Inst. Chemists; mem. AAAS, AAUP, Am. Chem. Soc., Soc. Harvard Chemists, Sigma Xi. Club: Harvard (Pocumtuck Valley, Mass.). Contbr. profl. jours. Home: Poplar Hill Rd RFD Haydenvile MA 01039 Office: Sabin-Reed Hall Smith Coll Northampton MA 01063

SOFFER, SHELDON, impressario; b. N.Y.C., Aug. 20, 1927; s. Samuel and Bertha (Wissex) S.; B.A., Queens Coll., 1948; M.A., U. Calif., Berkeley, 1950. Conductor Lemonade Opera, 1952-54, Ark. State Opera, 1953-54, Provincetown Symphony, 1955-60; condr. Broadway shows including nat. tour Tea House of the August Moon; mgr. Little Orch. Soc., N.Y.C., 1962-65; with Artists Mgmt., N.Y.C., 1965—, project dir. Am. Dance Festival, 1973—, adminstrv. dir. Am. Choral Found., 1966—; chmn. bd. Young Concert Artists, 1970—; bd. dirs. Nat. Assn. Regional Ballet, 1977—, Dance Notation Bur., 1978—. Mem. adv. bd. Profl. Children's Sch., 1976—; nat. advisory council Chopin Found. U.S.A., 1977—. Named distinguished grad. Queens Coll. Div. Arts, 1977. Address: 130 W 56th St New York City NY 10019

SOFIELD, HAROLD AUGUSTUS, orthopedic surgeon; b. Jersey city, Mar. 27, 1900; s. David and Elvaretta (Brown) S.; student Columbia, 1918-23; M.D., Northwestern U., 1928; m. Ruth Robinson, Apr. 19, 1934; children—David, Julie (Mrs. Otis Tholander). Intern San Francisco Hosp., 1927-28; resident Shriners Hosp. for Crippled Children, Chgo., 1928-30, resident orthopedic surgery, 1928-35, chief surgeon, 1944-65, emeritus, 1965—; chief cons. orthopedic surgery VA for Ill., Ind. and Wis., 1946—; sr. cons. orthopedic surgery VA Hosp., Hines, Ill.; staff orthopedic surgery West Surburban Hosp., past chmn., life trustee; staff Gottlieb Meml. Hosp., Melrose Park, Ill.; asso. prof. dept. orthopedic surgery Northwestern U., 1946-50, prof., 1950-68, emeritus prof., 1968—; cons. Norwegian Am., DuPage County Meml., Westlake Community hosps.; spl. cons. lectr. U.S. Army hosps. in Europe, 1955; rep. adv. com. on phys. therapy edn. Council on Med. Edn. and Hosp.; sec.-treas., co-founder Orthopaedic Research and Edn. Found.; past chmn. sect. orthopedic surgery NRC, Washington; treas. Pub. Health Study and Survey Commn. Ill.; past chmn. bd. trustees Easter Seal Research Found.; trustee Lincoln (Ill.) Acad.; past chmn. exec. com. orthopedics overseas div. Medico-CARE; past med. adv. univ. senate Northwestern U. Served as col. M.C., AUS, World War II; chief cons. orthopedic surgery to S. Pacific Theatre. Decorated Bronze Star, Legion of Merit with 5 battle stars. Diplomate Am. Bd. Orthopedic Surgery (past pres.). Fellow A.C.S., Brit. Orthopaedic Assn. (hon.); mem. A.M.A., Assn. Mil. Surgeons U.S., Clin., Chgo. (past pres.) orthopedic socs., Am. Orthopedic Assn. (past sec.-treas.), Ill. State (past pres.), Chgo. med. socs., Ill. Assn. for Crippled, Chgo. Inst. Medicine, Am. Acad. Orthopaedic Surgeons (pres. 1959), Soc. Med. Cons.'s to Armed Forces, Orthopaedic Research Soc., Australian Orthopaedic Assn. (corr.), Assn. Mil. Surgeons U.S., Internat. Soc. Orthopaedic Surgery, Am. Ret. Physicians Assn. (sec.-treas. 1976—), Am. Legion, Assn. Bone and Joint Surgeons (hon.), Soc. Orthopaedic Surgeons of Chile (hon.), Latin Am. Soc. Orthopaedic Surgery and Traumatology (hon.), Academia Nat. de Medicina of Brazil (hon.), Beta Theta Pi. Mason (33 deg., Shriner, Jester). Clubs: River Forest (Ill.) Tennis; Oak Park (Ill.) Country. Contbr. articles to surg. jours., books. Home: 165 N Kenilworth Ave Oak Park IL 60301. *If a surgeon adds just one new procedure that helps alleviate pain and diminishes physical or mental handicaps he has justified his acceptance into the company of those who serve mankind.*

SOFTNESS, DONALD GABRIEL, mktg. and broadcasting exec.; b. Bklyn., Nov. 14, 1927; s. Burt H. and Ida (Kaiser) S.; A.B., N.Y. U., 1949, M.B.A., 1959; H.H.D., St. John's U., 1979; m. Sydell Meyerson, Apr. 26, 1953; children—Michael, Anita May, Beth. Sr. publicist Sta. WNEW-TV, N.Y.C., 1953-55; dir. promotion H-R TV, Inc., N.Y.C., 1955-59; chmn. Softness Group, Inc., N.Y.C., 1960-79; pres. Don Softness Enterprise, Ltd., N.Y.C., 1979—; v.p., maj. prin. Radio Stas. WVNJ-AM-FM, Newark and N.Y.C.; mem. faculty Advt. Week seminars Advt. Age, 1978. Mem. exercise com. N.Y. Heart Assn. Served with USNR, 1945-46. Mem. Public Relations Soc. Am., Internat. Radio TV Soc., Am. Coll. Sports Medicine, U.S. Power Squadron. Club: N.Y. Yacht. Co-author: Cardiologists' Guide to Health and Fitness Through Exercise, 1979. Contbr. articles to bus. and trade jours. Home: 28 True's Dr West Islip NY 11795 Office: Don Softness Enterprise 251 E 51 St New York NY 10022

SOFTNESS, JOHN, pub. relations exec.; b. Bklyn., Nov. 7, 1930; s. Burt H. and Ida (Kaiser) S.; B.A., U. Miami, 1955; m. Leona Ruth Golden; children—Barney, David, Daniel. Reporter Miami Herald, 1953; reporter Sta. WTVJ, Miami, Fla., 1954; asso. pub. relations dir. aviation dept. Shell Oil Co., N.Y.C., 1958-60; pres., chief exec. officer The Softness Group, Inc., N.Y.C., 1960—. Spl. counselor to Bklyn. Borough pres., 1966-76. Served to capt. USAF, 1955-58. Mem. Pub. Relations Soc. Am., Am. Mktg. Assn., Sigma Delta Chi. Home: Lattingtown Rd Glen Cove NY 11542 Office: 3 E 54th St New York NY 10022

SOGG, WILTON SHERMAN, lawyer; b. Cleve., May 28, 1935; s. Paul P. and Julia (Cahn) S.; A.B., Dartmouth Coll., 1956; J.D., Harvard U., 1959; Fulbright fellow U. London, 1959-60; m. Saralee Frances Krow, Aug. 12, 1962 (div. July 1975); 1 dau., Stephanie. m. 2d, Linda Rocker Lehman, Dec. 22, 1979. Admitted to Ohio bar, 1960, D.C. bar, 1970, Fla. bar, 1970, to practice before U.S. Supreme Ct., U.S. Tax Ct.; asso. firm Gottfried, Ginsberg, Guren & Merritt, 1960-63, partner, 1963-70; partner firm Guren, Merritt, Sogg & Cohen, Cleve., 1970—; trustee, pres. Cleve. Jewish News; adj. prof. Cleve. State Law Sch.; lectr. Harvard Law Sch., 1978—. Trustee Jewish Community Fedn. of Cleve., 1966—; bd. overseers Cleve. Marshall Coll. Law, 1969—, Cleve. State U., 1969—; mem. adv. com. Pres.'s Commn. on The Holocaust. Recipient Kane Meml. award Jewish Community Fedn., Cleve., 1970; named one of 10 outstanding young men Cleve. Jaycees, 1967, 68. Mem. German Philatelic Soc. (nat. dir.), Am., Ohio, Cleve., Cuyahoga County bar assns., Am. Law Inst., Am. Soc. Corp. Secs., Chaine des Rôtisseurs, Phi Beta Kappa. Author: (with Howard M. Rossen) new and rev. vols. of Smith's Review Legal Gems series, 1969—; editor Harvard Law Rev. Contbr. articles to profl. jours. Home: 21175 Shaker Blvd Shaker Heights OH 44122 Office: 650 Terminal Tower Bldg Cleveland OH 44113

SOHLIN, DONNELLY ALLEN, fgn. service officer; b. Lakota, N.D., Nov. 9, 1926; s. Alfred and Alma Engelive (Simons) S.; student Oreg. State Coll., 1944; B.S., U. Calif., 1950. Supervisory auditor Army and Air Force Exchange Service, Japan, 1950-56; chief audit div. I.C.A., Saigon, 1956-59, dep. controller, Vientiane, Laos, 1959-61; controller A.I.D., Conakry, Guinea, 1961-64; area operations officer A.I.D., Washington, 1964-67, dep. asso. dir. financial mgmt., Saigon, 1967-68; asst. dir. finance U.S.O.M., Thailand, also controller A.I.D., Rangoon, Burma, 1969-71; dep. AID affairs officer, controller Am. Embassy, Phnom Penh, Khmer Republic, 1971-74; dep. dir. AID, Khmer Republic, 1974-75; dep. chmn. planning, budgeting, acctg. and reporting Task Force AID, Washington, 1975-76; controller Internat. Narcotics Control Dept. State, 1976-78; pvt. cons. on mgmt. and fin. mgmt., 1978-79; dep. exec. dir. UN Fund Drug Abuse Control, Vienna, 1979—. Served with AUS, 1945-46. Recipient meritorious service award, AID, 1964, superior honor award, 1975; Papal medal Pope Paul VI, 1974. Mem. Am. Acad. Polit. and Social Sci., English Speaking Union, Am. Fgn. Service Assn., Asia Soc., Siam Soc., Alliance Francais, Delta Phi Epsilon. Clubs: Royal Bangkok Sports; Saigon Cercle Sportif, Khmer Cercle Sportif. Address: UNFDAC Vienna Internat Center PO Box 600 A1400 Vienna Austria

SOHMER, BERNARD, educator; b. N.Y.C., July 16, 1929; s. Sol and Florence (Schonfeld) S.; B.A., N.Y. U., 1949, M.S., 1951, Ph.D., 1958; m. Margot Rosette, July 27, 1952; children—Emily, Olivia. Lectr., Coll. City N.Y., 1952-57, faculty, 1958—, prof. math., 1969—, dean students, 1969-72, v.p. student affairs, 1972-75; asst. prof. N.Y. U., 1957-58. Mem. AAUP (pres. Coll. City N.Y. chpt. 1966-67, sec. 1977-78), Am. Math. Soc., Math. Assn. Am., AAAS. Home: 33 45 92d St Jackson Heights NY 11372 Office: 139th and Convent Ave New York City NY 10031

SOHN, LOUIS BRUNO, lawyer, educator; b. Lwów, Poland, Mar. 1, 1914; s. Joseph and Fryderyka (Hescheles) S.; came to U.S., 1939, naturalized, 1943; LL.M., Diplomatic Sc.M., John Casimir U., 1935; LL.M., Harvard U., 1940, S.J.D., 1958; m. Elizabeth Mayo. Asst. to Judge M. O. Hudson, 1941-48; research fellow Harvard Law Sch., 1946-47, lectr. law, 1947-51, asst. prof. law, 1951-53, John Harvey Gregory lectr. in world orgn., 1951—, prof. law, 1953-61, Bemis prof.

internat. law, 1961—; cons. U.S. ACDA, 1960-70, Office Internat. Security Affairs, Dept. Def., 1963-70; asst. to del. Permanent Ct. Internat. Justice, San Francisco Conf. UN, 1945; exec. sec. legal subcom. on atomic energy Carnegie Endowment for Internat. Peace, 1946; asst. reporter on progressive devel. internat. law Am. and Canadian bar assns., 1947-48; cons. UN secretariat, 1948, 69, legal officer, 1950-51; counselor internat. law Dept. State, 1970-71; U.S. del. to UN Law of Sea Conf., 1974—. Recipient World Peace Hero award World Federalists of Can., 1974. Mem. Am. Soc. Internat. Law (exec. council 1954-57, v.p. 1965-66), World Parliament Assn. (legal adviser 1954-64), Internat. Law Assn. (v.p. Am. br.), Am. Law Inst., Am. Bar Assn. (hon.), Fedn. Am. Scientists (vice chmn. 1963, mem. council 1964-65, 68-69), Commn. Study Orgn. Peace (chmn. 1968—). Author: Cases on World Law, 1950; Cases on United Nations Law, 1956, 2d edit., 1967; (with G. Clark) World Peace Through World Law, 1958, 3d edit., 1966; Basic Documents of African Regional Organizations, 4 vols., 1971-72; (with T. Buergenthal) International Protection of Human Rights, 1973; also articles on legal subjects; editor devel. internat. law Am. Bar Assn. Jour., 1947-50; editorial bd. Am. Jour. Internat. Law, 1958—. Home: 780 Boylston St Boston MA 02199 Office: Harvard Law Sch Cambridge MA 02138

SOHN, MICHAEL N(ORMAN), lawyer, govt. ofcl.; b. N.Y.C., May 11, 1940; s. David M. and Dora S. S.; A.B., Columbia U., 1960; LL.B. cum laude, Harvard U., 1963; m. Margaret Ball, July 7, 1978; children—Samantha, Jonathan, Suzannah. Admitted to N.Y. bar, 1964, D.C. bar, 1969; appellate atty. NLRB, Washington, 1964-69; asso. firm Arnold & Porter, Washington, 1969-72, partner, 1972-77; gen. counsel FTC, Washington, 1977—; bd. dirs. Center for Auto Safety, 1974-77; mem. council Adminstrv. Conf. U.S.; mem. exec. com. Regulatory Council U.S. Mem. D.C. Bar Assn., Am. Bar Assn. Author: (with others) The Law and Roadside Hazards, 1974. Office: Office Gen Counsel FTC 6th and Pennsylvania Ave NW Washington DC 20580

SOKAL, JOSEPH EMANUEL, physician; b. Lwow, Poland, Apr. 11, 1917; s. Henry B. and Ethel (Torten) S.; came to U.S., 1924, naturalized, 1928; B.A. with honors, Columbia U., 1936; M.D. cum laude, Yale U., 1940; m. Nancy Branan, Nov. 29, 1947; children—David C., Paul J. Intern in medicine New Haven Hosp., 1941-42, asst. resident, 1946-47; Jane Coffin Childs fellow in pathology and immunology Yale U., New Haven, 1947-50, Markle scholar, 1950-55, instr., 1950-53, asst. prof. medicine, 1953-55; chief cancer research internist Roswell Park Meml. Inst., Buffalo, 1955-79; research prof. physiology State U. N.Y., Buffalo, 1955-79, research prof. medicine, 1970-79; research prof. medicine Duke U., Durham, N.C., 1979—. Served to maj. U.S. Army, 1942-46; PTO; to lt. col., 1950-52. Decorated Bronze Star with 2 oak leaf clusters. Fellow A.C.P.; mem. Am. Physiol. Soc., Soc. Exptl. Biology and Medicine, Endocrine Soc., Am. Assn. Cancer Research, AMA, Am. Fedn. Clin. Research, AAAS, Am. Soc. Hematology, Phi Beta Kappa, Sigma Xi, Alpha Omega Alpha. Contbr. articles to profl. jours. Office: Sch Medicine Duke U Durham NC 27706

SOKATCH, JOHN ROBERT, educator; b. Joliet, Ill., Dec. 20, 1928; s. John Peter and Christina (Yuratik) S.; B.S., U. Mich., 1950, M.S. in Bacteriology, U. Ill., 1952; Ph.D., U. Ill., 1956; m. Carol Koch, June 10, 1957; children—David, Barbara, Karen. Research asso. Wash. State U., 1956-58; asst. prof. microbiology U. Okla. Sch. Medicine, 1958-61, asso. prof., 1961-65, prof., 1967—, prof. biochemistry and molecular biology, 1968—, asst. dean Grad. Coll., Med. Center Campus, 1970-71, asso. dean, 1971—, asso. dir. research adminstrn., 1973, interim dean Coll. Pharmacy, 1976—. Recipient Research Career Devel. award NIH, 1962-72; Am. Soc. Microbiology Pres.'s fellow, 1961; Fulbright Sr. Research scholar Sheffield U., Eng., 1963-64. Mem. Am. Soc. Microbiology, Am. Acad. Microbiology, Am. Soc. Biol. Chemists. Author: Bacterial Physiology and Metabolism, 1969; co-author: Basic Bacteriology and Genetics, 1976. Co-editor: The Bacteria, Vol. 6 and 7. Research on microbial biochemistry including metabolism of branched chain amino acids by bacteria, regulation of catabolic and biosynthetic pathways. Home: 2224 NW 48th St Oklahoma City OK 73112

SOKEL, WALTER HERBERT, educator; b. Vienna, Austria, Dec. 17, 1917; s. Salomon Rubin and Rosa (Popper) S.; came to U.S., 1939, naturalized, 1944; B.A., Rutgers U., 1941; M.A., Columbia U., 1944, Ph.D., 1953; m. Jacqueline R. Printz, Sept. 27, 1961; 1 dau., Shari Maria. Instr. German, Temple U., Phila., 1947-53; instr. German and humanities Columbia U., N.Y.C., 1953-56, asst. prof., 1956-60, asso. prof., 1960-64; prof. German lit. and humanities Stanford (Calif.) U., 1964-73; Commonwealth prof. Germanic lang. and lit. U. Va., Charlottesville, 1973—, Commonwealth prof. German and English lit., 1979—; vis. prof. Harvard U., 1978-79. Nat. Endowment of the Humanities sr. fellow, 1971-72; Am. Council Learned Socs. grantee, 1962-63. Mem. Modern Lang. Assn. Am. (exec. council), Am. Assn. Tchrs. of German, Internat. Comparative Lit. Assn. Author: The Writer in Extremis, 1959; Franz Kafka Tragik und Ironie, 1963; Franz Kafka, 1966; An Anthology of German Expressionist Drama, 1963. Office: Dept German Langs Cocke Hall U Va Charlottesville VA 22903

SOKMENSUER, ADIL, physician, educator; b. Izmir, Turkey, Jan. 24, 1928; s. Cevat and Rukiye (Sun) S.; B.A. with honors, Namik Kemal Lisesi, Izmir, Turkey, 1945; M.D., U. Istanbul (Turkey), 1951; m. Ulku Sakizlioglu, June 22, 1956; children—G. Hakan, Cem Yanki, Kent Halit. Came to U.S., 1956. Intern Loretto Hosp., Chgo., 1956-57; resident Phila. Gen. Hosp., 1957-59; staff physician Central Fla. Tb Hosp., Orlando, 1959; mem. staff A.G. Holley State Hosp., Lantana Fla., 1959—, dir. clin. services, 1963-66, med. dir., supt., 1966-73, cons., 1973—; practice internal medicine specializing in pulmonary medicine, 1973—, clin. asso. prof. chest medicine Sch. Medicine, U. Miami, 1971—. Cons. chest service VA Hosp., Miami, 1969—. Served with Turkish Army, 1951-52. Mem. S.E. Fla., Am. Coll. Chest Physicians, Am., Fla. (pres. elect) thoracic socs. Research chemotherapy of Tb. Home: 267 Dunbar Rd Palm Beach FL 33480 Office: 1411 N Flagler Dr West Palm Beach FL 33401

SOKOL, HERMAN, corp. exec.; b. Bloomfield, N.J., Oct. 14, 1916; s. Joseph and Rose (Mann) S.; B.A., Montclair State Coll., 1937; M.S., U. Mich., 1940; Ph.D. in Organic Chemistry, N.Y. U., 1944; m. Margaret Augusta McCormack, July 4, 1942. Research chemist Rubber Reserve Corp. (OSRD), 1942-44; research chemist, group leader, tech. supt. Heyden Chem. Corp., 1944-50, mgr. antibiotics research div., 1950-53; v.p. research and devel. Heyden Newport Chem. Corp., 1954-58, exec. v.p., dir., 1958-62; pres., dir. Am. Plastics Corp., N.Y.C., 1958-61; pres. Bristol Labs. Internat. Corp., 1963-67; v.p. Bristol-Myers Co., 1963-67, sr. v.p., 1967-76, pres., 1977—, also dir.; trustee East River Savs. Bank, N.Y.C., 1971—; dir. Technicon Corp., Tarrytown, N.Y., 1973—. Mem. Am. Chem. Soc., AAAS, N.Y. Acad. Scis., Pharm. Mfrs. Assn. (dir. 1975—), Sigma Xi, Phi Lambda Upsilon. Home: 870 Fifth Ave New York NY 10021 Office: 345 Park Ave New York NY 10022

SOKOLOW, ANNA, dancer, choreographer, educator; b. N.Y.C. Attended Neighborhood Playhouse Sch. Theatre. Mem. Martha Graham Co.; organizer own co., 1939—, own works include Rooms, Lyric Suite, Dreams: tchr. in Sweden, Switzerland, Germany, Holland, Mexico; tchr., dir. in Tel. Aviv, Israel, 1953—; choreographer for Candide, Regina, Street Scene, Red Roses for Me, Camino Real, choreographer for debut performances of Am. Dance Theater, 1964; mem. dance faculty Juillard Sch. Music, N.Y.C., 1957—; adviser Inbal Dance Co. Address: 1 Christopher St New York City NY 10014

SOKOLOW, MAURICE, physician, educator; b. N.Y.C., May 19, 1911; s. Alexander and Anna (Spiegelman) S.; A.B. cum laude, U. Calif., Berkeley, 1932; M.D., U. Calif., San Francisco, 1936; m. Ethel Schwabacher, June 30, 1941 (dec. 1970); children—Gail Anne, Jane Carol (dec.), Anne May. Intern San Francisco Gen. Hosp., 1935-36; resident U. Calif., San Francisco, 1936-37, New Eng. Med. Center, Boston, 1937-38; research fellow Michael Reese Hosp., Chgo., 1938-39, U. Calif., San Francisco, 1939-40; pvt. practice medicine, San Francisco, 1946-62; mem. faculty cardiovascular div., dept. medicine Sch. Medicine, U. Calif., San Francisco, 1946—, asso. prof., 1952-58, prof. medicine, 1958—, chief electrocardiograph dept., chief hypertension clinic, 1946-78, chief cardiovascular div., 1954-73, program dir. USPHS cardiology tng. grant, 1960-73, sr. mem. Cardiovascular Research Inst., 1957—; cons. in field. Bd. dirs. Fromm Inst Life Long Learning, U. San Francisco. Served to lt. comdr. M.C., USN, 1942-46. Nat. Heart Inst. grantee, 1950-78. Fellow Am. Coll. Cardiology (hon.); mem. Am. Fedn. Clin. Research (v.p. 1948-49), Assn. Univ. Cardiologists, Am. Soc. Clin. Investigation, Brit. Cardiac Soc. (corr.), Am. Heart Assn., San Francisco Heart Assn. (pres. 1950-51). Club: Menlo Circus. Author: Clinical Cardiology. Contbr. articles to med. jours., texts.; mem. editorial bd. Jour. Cardiovascular Medicine, 1975—, Western Jour. Medicine, 1946-68. Home: 3452 Jackson St San Francisco CA 94118 Office: U Calif San Francisco CA 94143

SOKOLSKY, ROBERT LAWRENCE, journalist; b. Boston, May 18, 1928; s. Henry and Lillian (Gorodetzky) S.; A.B., Syracuse (N.Y.) U., 1950; m. Sally-Ann Moss, Aug. 11, 1955; 1 son, Andrew E. Reporter, Springfield (Mass.) Union, 1950; asst. dir. pub. info. ARC, Syracuse, 1952-54; entertainment editor Syracuse Herald-Jour., 1954-61; entertainment editor Buffalo Courier Express, 1961-72; entertainment editor Phila. Bull., 1972—; radio show host; freelance writer; guest lectr. Bd. dirs. Brush Hollow Civic Assn., Evesham Twp., N.J. Served with U.S. Army, 1950-52. Recipient Sigma Delta Chi award for feature writing, 1950. Mem. Am. Newspaper Guild (Page One award for opinion writing), Syracuse Press Club, Greater Buffalo Press Assn., Pen and Pencil Club of Phila. Republican. Jewish. Club: Variety (Buffalo). Contbr. articles to profl. jours. Home: 29 Elmgate Rd Marlton NJ 08053 Office: Phila Bull 30th and Market Sts Philadelphia PA 19101

SOLADAY, CHARLES W., packing co. exec.; b. Lakewood, Ohio, 1922; grad. Ohio U., 1946; married. With Price Waterhouse & Co., until 1965; with Wells Lamont Corp., Chgo., 1965-68; with Hammond Corp., Deerfield, Ill., 1968-72; v.p. fin. and adminstrn. Rath Packing Co., Waterloo, Iowa, 1972-74, v.p., treas., 1974—. C.P.A., Ohio. Home: 334 Progress Ave Cedar Falls IA 50601 Office: Elm and Sycamore Sts Waterloo IA 50703

SOLANDT, OMOND MCKILLOP, research scientist; b. Winnipeg, Man., Can., Sept. 2, 1909; s. Donald McKillop and Edith (Young) S.; B.A., U. Toronto, 1931, M.A., 1933, M.D., 1936, LL.D., 1954; M.A., Cambridge (Eng.) U., 1939; D.Sci., U. B.C., 1947, Laval U., 1948, U. Man., 1950, McGill U., 1951, St. Francis Xavier U., 1956, Royal Mil. Coll., 1966, U. Montreal, 1967: LL.D., Dalhousie U., 1952, Sir George Williams U., 1966, U. Sask., 1968; D. Eng., U. Waterloo, 1968; m. Elizabeth McPhedran, Jan. 25, 1941; children—Sigrid, Andrew, Katharine; m. 2d, Vaire Pringle, 1971. Intern Toronto Gen. Hosp., 1937-38; lectr. physiology Cambridge U., 1939; mem. Joint Mil. Mission to Japan to evaluate effects atomic bomb, 1945; chmn. Def. Research Bd., 1946-56; asst. v.p. research and devel. Canadian Nat. Rys., 1956, v.p., 1957-63; v.p. research and devel., dir. de Havilland Aircraft of Can., Ltd.; vice chmn. Electric Reduction Co. Can. Ltd., 1966-70; dir. Mitchell, Plummer & Co. Ltd., 1971-75, Huyck Corp., Wake Forest, N.C. Chmn. Sci. Council of Can., 1966-72. Chancellor, U. Toronto, 1965-71; pub. gov. Toronto Stock Exchange, 1971-76. Trustee Internat. Centre for Agrl. Research in Dry Areas in Syria and Iran, 1976, Internat. Centre for Wheat and Maize Improvement, Mexico, 1976. Served as col. Canadian Army, 1944-46; dir. S.W. London Blood Supply Depot, 1940, physiol. lab. Armored Fighting Vehicle Sch., 1941; dir. tank sect. Army Operational Research Group, 1942, dep. supt., 1943, supt., 1944. Decorated Order of Brit. Empire, 1946, Medal of Freedom with bronze palm (U.S.), 1947; companion Order of Can., 1970; recipient Gold medal U. Toronto, 1936, Profl. Inst. Can., 1956; Vanier medal Inst. Pub. Adminstrn. Can., 1975. Fellow Royal Soc. Can., Royal Coll. Physicians (London); mem. Engring. Inst. Can. (hon.), Canadian Physiol. Soc., Canadian Operational Research Soc. (pres. 1958-60). Mem. United Church Can. Home: Wolfe Den Rural Route 1 Bolton ON L0P 1A0 Canada Office: Inst for Environ Studies Univ Toronto Toronto ON M5S 1A4 Canada

SOLARZ, STEPHEN JOSHUA, congressman; b. N.Y.C., Sept. 12, 1940; s. Sanford and Ruth (Fertig) S.; B.A., Brandeis U., 1962; M.A., Columbia U., 1967; m. Nina Koldin, Feb. 5, 1967; children—Randy, Lisa. Mem. N.Y. State Assembly from 45th Dist., 1968-74; mem. 94th and 96th Congresses from 13th Dist. N.Y., mem. Fgn. Affairs com., Post Office and Civil Service com.; past faculty Bklyn. Coll., City U. N.Y. Mem. 61st Precinct Community Council, 1968—; mem. Governing Council Am. Jewish Congress; bd. fellows Brandeis U. Mem. N.Y. Americans for Democratic Action (state bd. 1971—). Democrat. Past nat. affairs editor Newsfront; past asso. editor Greater Philadelphia. Office: 1530 Longworth House Office Bldg Washington DC 20515*

SOLBERG, KRISTEN BIRDEAU, clin. psychologist; b. Turner County, S.D., Apr. 13, 1917; s. Knud B. and Anna Camilla (Carter) S.; student Freeman Jr. Coll., 1936-37; B.A., Augustana Coll., 1942; Ed.M., U. S.D., 1950; Ed.D., U. Wyo., 1953; m. Opal Lavina Christopherson, June 18, 1944; children—Kenneth Bruce, Don Alan, Ona Claire. Prin., Centerville (S.D.) High Sch., 1947-51; chmn. dept. psychology Pacific Lutheran U., Tacoma, Wash., 1953-64, dean students, 1960-64; staff psychologist Am. Lake VA Hosp., Tacoma, 1965-69, Ft. Meade (S.D.) VA Hosp., 1969-71; chief psychology service Am. Lake VA Hosp., Tacoma, 1971—; lectr. in field. Bd. dirs. Comprehensive Community Mental Health Center, 1964-66, chmn. 1965; bd. dirs. Greater Lakes Community Mental Health Center, 1965-69. Served with USNR, 1943-46. Mem. Am. Personnel and Guidance Assn., Am., Wash. (pres. div. 1975) psychol. assns., Sons of Norway, Phi Delta Kappa, Psi Chi. Lutheran. Elk. Home: 865 S 173d St Spanaway WA 98387 Office: VA Hosp American Lake Tacoma WA 98493

SOLBERG, MORTEN EDWARD, artist; b. Cleve., Nov. 8, 1935; s. Morten Odvard and Violet Elizabeth (Lamphier) S.; student pub. schs., Cleve.; m. Theresa Lee Lynch, June 25, 1977; children—Morten, Eric, Scott, Brandy, Monet. Art dir. Am. Greetings Corp., Cleve., 1958-68; art dir. Buzza Cardozo Greeting Cards, Anaheim, Calif., 1968-71; painter, Running Springs, Calif., 1971—; tchr., demonstrator seminars; juror art exhbns.; juror Nat. Watercolor Soc. Annual, 1976. Recipient Purchase awards NAD, Am. Bicentennial Gallery. Mem. Nat. Watercolor Soc. (Top award), Am. Watercolor Soc. (awards), Soc. Animal Artists (award). Lutheran. Contbr. articles to SW Art, 1976; artist watercolor page Am. Artist, 1976. Home and studio: PO Box 1317 Running Springs CA 92382

SOLBERG, OSCAR, farmer, state legislator; b. Agate, N.D., May 16, 1911; s. Ole K. and Sophie (Royland) S.; student pub. schs., Bisbee; m. Ida M. Good, June 1, 1944. Farmer, Rolla, N.D., 1966—; mem. N.D. Ho. of Reps., 1949—, speaker, 1977—; mem. N.D. Legislative Council, 1959—. Pres. bd. dirs. Internat. Peace Garden. Mem. Future Farmers Am. Democrat. Lutheran. Clubs: Kiwanis of Rolla; Elks. Home: 415 E Main St Rolla ND 58367

SOLBERG, WINTON UDELL, educator; b. Aberdeen, S.D., Jan. 11, 1922; s. Ole Alexander and Bertha Georgia (Tschappat) S.; A.B. magna cum laude, U. S.D., 1943; student Biarritz (France) Am. U., 1946; A.M., Harvard, 1947, Ph.D., 1954; m. Ruth Constance Walton, Nov. 8, 1952; children—Gail Elizabeth, Andrew Walton, Kristin Ruth. Instr., then asst. prof. social scis. U.S. Mil. Acad., 1951-54; instr., then asst. prof. history Yale, 1954-58, fellow Pierson Coll., 1955-58, Morse fellow, 1958; James Wallace prof. history Macalester Coll., 1958-62; vis. prof. U. Ill., 1961-62, asso. prof. history, 1962, prof., 1967—, chmn. dept. history, 1970-72; research fellow Center Study History of Liberty in Am., Harvard, 1962-63; summer research scholar Henry E. Huntington Library, San Marino, Calif., 1959; dir. Coe Found. Am. Studies Inst., summers 1960-62, lectr., cons. Army War Coll., 1959-62; lectr. U.S. Command and Gen. Staff Sch., 1963-64; Fulbright lectr. Johns Hopkins U. Bologna, 1967-68, Moscow (USSR) State U., 1978. Mem. Ill. Humanities, Council 1973-75. Served to maj. inf. AUS, 1943-46, 51-54; lt. col. U.S. Army Res. Nat. Endowment for Humanities sr. fellow, 1974-75. Mem. Am., So. hist. assns., Orgn. Am. Historians, Am. Studies Assns., AAUP (chpt. pres. 1965-66, mem. council 1969-72, 1st v.p. 1974-76), Phi Beta Kappa. Episcopalian. Author: The Federal Convention and the Formation of the American States, 1958; The University of Illinois, 1867-1894, 1968; Redeem the Time: The Puritan Sabbath in Early America, 1977; also articles. Home: 508 W Delaware Urbana IL 61801 Office: Dept History U Ill Urbana IL 61801

SOLBERT, PETER OMAR ABERNATHY, lawyer; b. Copenhagen, Denmark, Mar. 9, 1919; s. Oscar Nathaniel and Elizabeth (Abernathy) S.; B.A., Yale, 1941; J.D., Harvard, 1948; m. Deborah Kirk, Sept. 8, 1945; children—Leslie, Alan, Elizabeth, Alison, Christopher. Admitted to N.Y. bar, 1948; with firm Davis Polk & Wardwell, and predecessor firm, N.Y.C., 1948-63, partner, 1957-63, 65—; dep. asst. sec. def. internat. security affairs, 1963-65. Bd. dirs. Japan Fund, 1961-63, 66-74; chmn. bd. dirs. Seven Springs Center, Yale U. Served to lt. comdr. USNR, 1941-46. Home: 416 West Neck Rd Lloyd Harbor NY 11978 Office: 1 Chase Manhattan Plaza New York City NY 10005

SOLBRIG, OTTO THOMAS, biologist, educator; b. Buenos Aires, Argentina, Dec. 21, 1930; s. Hans Joachim and Rose Mabel (Muggleworth) S.; student U. La Plata (Argentina), 1954; Ph.D., U. Calif., Berkeley, 1959; M.A. (hon.), Harvard, 1969; m. Dorothy Jane Crosswhite, June 21, 1969; children—Hans Joseph, Heide Frances. Asst. curator Gray Herbarium Harvard U., Cambridge, Mass., 1959-61, asso. curator, 1961-66, dir., 1978—, prof. biology, 1969—, supr. Bussey Instn., 1978—; asso. prof. dept. botany U. Mich., Ann Arbor, 1966-69; dir. structure ecosystems program U.S. Internat. Biol. Program; chmn. com. Nat. Acad. Sci., 1979—. Served with Argentine Army, 1945-48. Recipient Cooley prize Am. Soc. Plant Taxonomy; Congressional medal Antarctic Campaign, 1965-66; Wildenow medal Berlin Bot. Garden. Fellow Am. Acad. Arts and Scis.; mem. Phi Beta Kappa, Sigma Xi (sec.-treas. Harvard-Radcliffe chpt. 1976-79). Author: Evolution and Systematics, 1966; Plant Biosystematics, 1969; Biosystematic Bibliography, 1970; Convergent Evolution in American Deserts, 1977; Introduction to Population Biology and Evolutionary Theory, 1979; Demography and Dynamics of Plant Populations, 1979; Topics in Plant Population Biology, 1979; contbr. articles to biol. jours. Office: 22 Divinity Ave Cambridge MA 02138

SOLDNER, PAUL EDMUND, ceramist, mfg. co. exec.; b. Summerfield, Ill.; s. Grover and Beulah (Geigner) S.; B.A., Bluffton Coll., 1946; M.A., U. Colo., 1954; M.F.A., Los Angeles County Art Inst., 1956; m. Virginia I. Geiger, June 15, 1947; 1 dau., Stephanie. Tchr. art Medina (Ohio) County Schs., 1946-47; supr. art, asst. county supr. Wayne County Schs., Wooster, Ohio, 1951-54; tchr. adult edn. Wooster Coll., 1952-54; vis. asst. prof. ceramics Scripps Coll., 1957-66, prof., 1970—; vis. asst. prof. Claremont (Calif.) Grad. Sch., 1957-66, prof., 1970—; prof. U. Colo., Boulder, 1966-67, U. Iowa, Iowa City, 1967-68; pres. Soldner Pottery Equipment, Inc., Silt, Colo., 1956-77; 93 one-man shows including: Florence Duhl Gallery, N.Y.C., 1976, Contemporary Craft Gallery, Portland, Oreg., 1977, Patricia Moore Gallery, Aspen, Colo.; group shows include: Lica Gallery, Los Angeles, Fellows of Am. Crafts Council, Winston Salem, N.C.; works in permanent collections: Nat. Mus. Modern Art, Kyoto, Japan, Victoria and Albert Mus., London, Smithsonian Instn., Washington; mem. steering com. Internat. Sch. Ceramics, Rome, 1965-77; advisor Vols. for Internat. Assistance, Balt., 1966-75; craftsman, trustee Am. Craft Council, N.Y.C., 1970-74, trustee emeritus, 1976-77; dir. U.S. sect. World Craft Council, 1970-74; cons. in field. Served with U.S. Army, 1941-46. Decorated Purple Heart. Grantee Louis Comfort Tiffany Found., 1966, 72, Nat. Endowment for Arts, 1976. Mem. Nat. Council on Edn. for Ceramic Arts. Originator, Am. Raku philosophy and techniques in ceramics. Patentee in field. Author: Kilns and Their Construction, 1965; Raku, 1964. Contbr. articles to profl. jours. Five films about his work. Home: PO Box 90 Aspen CO 81611

SOLDOW, JAMES JOSEPH, business exec.; b. Berlin, Germany, Jan. 31, 1924; s. Sol Leon and Jenny (Malina) S.; came to U.S., 1938, naturalized, 1941; B.Gen. Edn. with honors, U. Omaha, 1964; m. Edith Burns, Sept. 24, 1950 (dec. July 1974); 1 dau., Brenda L.; m. 2d, Carole A. Brennan, Mar. 16, 1976; 1 dau., Rachel L. Commd. 2d lt. U.S. Army, 1951, advanced through grades to col., 1971; adj. gen. 2d Inf. Div., Korea, 1965-66; asst. dir. for communications Adj. Gen. Office, U.S. Army, Washington, 1966-68; ret., 1971; joined U.S. Fgn. Service, 1971; counselor for adminstrv. affairs U.S. Mission to NATO, 1971-75, Am. embassy. Athens, Greece, 1975-78; asst. to pres. United Technologies (Europe) Inc., Brussels, Belgium, 1978—. Decorated Legion of Merit, Merit Service medal, Army Commendation medal with 2 oak leaf clusters; cited by Govt. of Republic of Korea, 1966; recipient Superior Honor award Dept. State, 1975. Home: 621 11th St Miami Beach FL 33139 Office: United Techs (Europe) Inc 7 Ave Lloyd George Brussels Belgium

SOLECKI, R. STEFAN, educator; b. Bklyn., Oct. 15, 1917; s. Kazimierz John and Mary (Tarnawski) S.; B.Sc., City Coll. N.Y., 1941; M.A., Columbia, 1950, Ph.D. in Anthropology, 1958; m. Rose Muriel Lilien, June 24, 1955; children—John Irwin, William Duncan. Archaeologist, Smithsonian Instn., 1948-54; archaeol. asst. anthropology Columbia, 1954-55; field dir. archaeol. expdn. to Iraq, 1956-57; asso. curator old world U.S. Nat. Mus., 1957-59; mem. faculty Columbia, 1959—, prof. anthropology, 1965—, chmn. dept.,

1975-78; archaeol. expdns. to Iraq, 1950-51, 53, 56-57, 60, 78, Sudanese Nubia, 1961, Turkey and Syria, 1963, 1964-65, Iran, 1968, Lebanon, 1969-73, Alaska, 1949, 61, also Eastern, Midwestern and Western U.S.; Fulbright scholar, Iraq, 1952-53; collaborator in archaeology Smithsonian Instn., 1953; cons. UNESCO, 1959. Served with AUS, 1943-45. William Bayard Cutting travelling fellow Columbia, 1956-57. Fellow Am. Anthrop. Assn., Arctic Inst. Am., N.Y. Acad. Scis. (chmn. anthropology sect. 1977—); mem. N.Y. Archaeol. Assn. (pres. 1960-62), N.Y. Oriental Club (pres. 1965), Soc. Archaeology, Am. Schs. Oriental Research (asso. trustee 1969-71), Prehistoric Soc., Deutsches Archaeologisches Inst., Soc. Préhistorique Français, Archaeol. Inst. Am. (exec. com. 1968-70), Assn. Field Archaeology (pres. 1972-74). Home: 597 Piermont Rd Demarest NJ 07627 Office: Dept Anthropology Schermerhorn Extension Columbia Univ New York City NY 10027

SOLEM, DELMAR E., educator; b. Volin, S.D., Jan. 13, 1915; s. Martin and Anna (Rockne) S.; B.A., Yankton Coll., 1937; M.A., Northwestern U., 1947; Ph.D., 1952; m. Jane Robertson, June 19, 1948; children—Monica, Meredith, Wendy. Teaching fellow Northwestern U., 1949-52, vis. prof., 1956; with Knox Coll., 1949-52, beginning as chmn. dept. speech and drama, 1952-56; chmn. dept. drama U. Miami, Coral Gables, Fla., 1956-68, prof. drama, 1970—; prof. drama, coordinator grad. studies U. Ga., 1968-70; vis. prof. U. Colo., 1952, 54. Short term theatre specialist U.S. Dept. of State, 1967, 68, 70. Served to ensign USNR, 1943-46. Recipient Alumni Achievement award Yankton Coll., 1977. Mem. Internat. Platform Assn., Miami Beach Music and Arts League, Theatre Arts League Greater Miami, Speech Assn. Am., Am. Ednl. Theater Assn., ANTA, Fla., Southeastern theatre confs., Theta Alpha Phi, Pi Kappa Delta, Delta Theta Mu. Contbr. articles to profl. jours. Home: 9390 SW 181 St Miami FL 33157 Office: Drama Dept U Miami Coral Gables FL 33124

SOLENDER, ROBERT LAWRENCE, mktg. exec.; b. Rochester, N.Y., Sept. 1, 1923; s. Samuel S. and Catherine (Goldsmith) S.; B.A., Oberlin Coll., 1943; m. Ellen Van Raalte Karelsen, Nov. 25, 1948; children—Elizabeth, Jefferson, Katherine. Asst. to pres. Craven & Hedrick, Inc., N.Y.C., 1946-49; with Dallas Times Herald, 1949-75, v.p., advt. dir., 1964-69, v.p. sales and mktg., 1969-75; pres. Robert L. Solender Assos., Dallas, 1975—; dir. Northpark Nat. Bank, Dallas. Pres. Dallas Child Guidance Clinic, 1956, Dallas Assn. Mental Health, 1958, Hope Cottage Children's Bur., 1973—; bd. dirs. Dallas Theatre Center, Child Care Assn. Met. Dallas. Served to lt. USNR, 1944-46; PTO. Clubs: 2001, T Bar M, Racquet (Dallas), Dallas Press, Masons. Home: 9131 Devonshire Dr Dallas TX 75209 Office: 13612 Midway Rd Dallas TX 75234

SOLENDER, SANFORD, social worker; b. Pleasantville, N.Y., Aug. 23, 1914; s. Samuel and Catherine (Goldsmith) S.; B.S., N.Y. U., 1935; M.S., Columbia U., 1937; m. Ethel Klonick, June 19, 1935; children—Stephen, Peter, Ellen, Susan. Dir. activities Neighborhood House, Bklyn., 1935-36; asst. headworker Bronx (N.Y.) House, 1936-39; headworker Madison House, N.Y.C., 1939-42; exec. dir. Council Ednl. Alliance, Cleve., 1942-48; dir. bur. personnel and tng., also dir. Jewish community center div. Nat. Jewish Welfare Bd., N.Y.C., 1948-60, exec. v.p. bd., 1960-70; exec. v.p. Fedn. Jewish Philanthropies N.Y., 1970—; past pres. Nat. Conf. Jewish Communal Service; past chmn. planning com. Internat. Conf. Jewish Communal Service; chmn. Task Force on N.Y.C. Crisis, 1976—, Council Inter-Group Relations, N.Y.C., 1978. Recipient Joseph E. Kappel award Nat. Conf. Jewish Communal Service, 1968; Florence G. Heller award Nat. Jewish Welfare Bd., 1972. Pres. Mt. Vernon Bd. Edn., 1953-58; chmn. sec. HEW's ad hoc. com. to study fed. govt. social welfare programs, 1961; adv. council pub. welfare HEW, 1963-65. Mem. Gov. Hugh Carey's Task Force on Human Services, N.Y. State, 1975; bd. dirs. Community Council Greater N.Y., Lavanburg Corner House, Herman Muehlstein Found.; adv. bd. Brandeis U., Hornstein Program in Jewish Communal Service. Mem. Nat. Assn. Jewish Center Workers (past pres.), Nat. Conf. Social Work (past pres.), Nat. Assn. Social Workers, Nat. Conf. Social Welfare (past pres.). Named Most Distinguished Citizen of Mt. Vernon, 1960. Contbr. articles to profl. jours., chpts. in books. Home: 121 Country Ridge Dr Port Chester NY 10573 Office: 130 E 59th St New York City NY 10022

SOLES, WILLIAM ROGER, ins. co. exec.; b. Whiteville, N.C., Sept. 16, 1920; s. John William and Margaret (Watts) S.; B.S. in Commerce, U. N.C., 1947, postgrad., 1956; m. Majelle Marrene Morris, Sept. 22, 1956; children—William Roger, Majelle Janette. With Jefferson Standard Life Ins. Co., Greensboro, N.C., 1947—, v.p., mgr. securities dept., 1962-64, asst. to pres., 1964-66, exec. v.p., mgr. securities dept., 1966, now pres., also dir.; pres., dir. Jefferson-Pilot Corp., Jefferson Standard Life Ins. Co.; chmn. bd. Jefferson-Pilot Fire & Casualty Co., Jefferson-Pilot Title Ins. Co., JP Investment Mgmt. Co., Jefferson-Pilot Equity Sales, Inc.; vice-chmn. bd., dir. Jefferson-Pilot Publs., Inc.; dir. Pilot Life Ins. Co., Jefferson-Pilot Broadcasting Co. Va., Piedmont Natural Gas Co., NCNB Corp., N.C. Nat. Bank. Trustee, High Point Coll., Wesley Long Community Hosp., Independent Coll. Fund N.C. Served with USAAF, 1941-45. Mem. Am. Council Life Ins. (past chmn., dir.), Beta Gamma Sigma. Club: Greensboro Country. Home: 604 Kimberly Dr Greensboro NC 27408 Office: PO Box 21008 Greensboro NC 27420

SOLHEIM, WILHELM GERHARD, II, anthropologist; b. Champaign, Ill., Nov. 19, 1924; s. Wilhelm Gerhard and Ragnhild Risty S.; B.S., U. Wyo., 1947; postgrad. U. Wis., 1943, U. Chgo., 1943-44; M.A., U. Calif., 1949; Ph.D., U. Ariz., 1959; m. Ludy Montenegro, Sept. 10, 1973; children—Gary, Kristina, Valerie, Lisa, Mei Li, Siri, Edwin. Mus. preparator Mus. Anthropology, U. Calif., Berkeley, 1947-49; research asso. Mus. Archaeology and Ethnology, U. Philippines, 1950-54; lectr. U. East, Manila, Philippines, 1950-52; provincial public affairs officer USIA, Manila, 1953-54; asst. prof. anthropology Fla. State U., Talahassee, 1960-61; mem. faculty dept. anthropology U. Hawaii, Honolulu, 1961—, prof., 1967—, asso. archaeologist Social Sci. Research Inst., 1963-67, archaeologist, 1967-70, editor, 1976—; vis. prof. Inst. Advanced Studies, U. Malaya, Kuala Lumpur, Malaysia, 1979-80. Trustee Hawaii Found. for History and Humanities, 1969-74, 1st v.p., 1972, 2d v.p., 1974; bd. dirs. Balih Bahay Project, Inc., Honolulu, 1976—, pres., 1977—; mem. Hawaii Com. for the Humanities, 1978-81. Served with USAF, 1943-46. Fulbright grantee, 1958-59; NSF grantee, 1963-66; Nat. Endowment Humanities fellow, 1967-68. Fellow Philippine Assn. Advancement Sci.; mem. AAAS, Assn. Asian Studies, Soc. Am. Archaeology, Siam Soc., Societe des Etudes Indochinoises, Royal Asiatic Soc., Burma Research Soc., ASsam Sci. Soc., Indian Archaeol. soc., Far-Eastern Prehistory Assn. (pres. 1971-76), Indo-Pacific Prehistory Assn. (pres. 1976-80), Sigma Xi, Phi Kappa Phi, Phi Delta Theta. Author: The Archaeology of Central Philippines, 1964; (with Ernestine Green) Jahore Lama Excavations, 1960; editor: Asian Perspectives, 1957—; Asian and Pacific Archaeology Series, 1967—. Office: Dept Anthropology Univ of Hawaii 2424 Maile Way Honolulu HI 96822

SOLIE, RICHARD JOHN, educator; b. Barron, Wis., Sept. 19, 1933; s. Maurice P. and Rachel (Rassmussen) S.; B.S., Wis. State U. at Superior, 1955; Ph.D., U. Tenn., 1965; m. Elsie Eleanor Granstrom, Dec. 20, 1954; children—Daniel, Richard James, Barry, Joy. Gen. agt. Beneficial Standard Life Ins. Co., Wyo., Colo., Mont. and N.D., 1955-60; asst. prof. Centre Coll. Ky., Danville, 1964-66; asso. prof. econs. U. N.D., Grand Forks, 1966-70; prof., head dept. econs. U. Alaska, Fairbanks, 1970-74, 77—, asso. dean Coll. Bus., Econs. and Govt., 1973-75, acting dean Sch. Mgmt., 1975-76; vis. prof. Indsl. Relations Center, U. Minn., Mpls., 1978-79. NDEA fellow, 1961-64. Mem. Am., So., Western econ. assns., Am. Arbitration Assn. (panel arbitrators), Indsl. Relations Research Assn., Omicron Delta Epsilon, Phi Kappa Phi, Beta Gamma Sigma. Baptist. Club: Rotary. Home: 4549 Wood River Dr Fairbanks AK 99701

SOLIMAN, PATRICIA KATHLEEN BREHAUT (MRS. ANWAR EL SAYED I. SOLIMAN), editor; b. New Rochelle, N.Y., Oct. 11, 1937; d. Ernest Henry and Winnifred (Gatehouse) Brehaut; B.A., Tufts U., 1959; M.A., Stanford U., 1962; m. Anwar el Sayed I. Soliman, Sept. 26, 1964. Editorial asst. Harper & Row, Pubs., Inc., 1962-65; asso. editor Coward, McCann & Geoghegan, Inc., N.Y.C., 1965-68, sr. editor, 1968-71, exec. editor, 1971-72, exec. editor, v.p., 1972-74, v.p., editor-in-chief, 1974-79, pres., pub., 1980—. Woodrow Wilson fellow, 1959. Mem. Phi Beta Kappa. Office: 200 Madison Ave New York NY 10016

SOLINGER, DAVID MORRIS, lawyer; b. N.Y.C., Feb. 17, 1906; s. Morris David and Birdie (Bloch) S.; B.A., Cornell U., 1922-26; student Oxford (Eng.) U., 1925; J.D., Columbia U., 1926-29; m. Hope Alva Gimbel, Sept. 16, 1937 (div. Apr. 1978); children—Faith Solinger Sommerfield, Lynn Solinger Stern; m. 2d, Betty Ann Besch, Jan. 23, 1979. Admitted to N.Y. bar, 1929; mem. firm Solinger & Gordon; lectr. Practising Law Inst. Trustee, Am. Fedn. Arts; trustee, hon. pres. Whitney Mus. Am. Art, pres., 1966-74, chmn., 1974-77; mem. emeritus Cornell U. Council. Served as capt., 1943, maj., 1944, staff of comdg. gen. Eastern Def. Command. Mem. Assn. Bar City of N.Y., N.Y. County, N.Y. State, Am., Fed. Communications bar assns. Clubs: Century Assn., Cornell (N.Y.C.); Century Country (White Plains, N.Y.); Delray Dunes (Fla.). Author articles on TV law Fortune mag.; Unauthorized Uses of Television Broadcasts, Columbia Law Review. Co-author: 1953 Copyright Problems Analyzed. Editor and co-author Television Agreements. Home: 33 E 70th St New York NY 10021 Office: 250 Park Ave New York NY 10017

SOLL, A. IVAN, educator; b. Phila., Mar. 29, 1938; s. Hyman and Betty S.; A.B. summa cum laude (Univ. fellow), Princeton U., 1960, Ph.D. (Univ. fellow), 1966; postgrad. (Woodrow Wilson fellow), Harvard U., 1960-61 (Fulbright fellow) Ludwig Maximilians Universitat, Munich, W. Ger., 1961-62; m. Sandra Levowitz, June 14, 1964; 1 son, Adam. Instr., U. Wis., Madison, 1964-66, asst. prof. philosophy, 1966-69, asso. prof., 1969-72, prof., 1972—; lectr. in field; bd. cons. in humanities World Book Ency.; reviewer Nat. Endowment for Humanities. Am. Council Learned Socs. travel grantee, 1972, 76; Counsel for European Studies travel grantee, 1972; U. Wis. Grad. Sch. grantee, 1966, 67, 70, 72, 74, 76, 78; Nat. Endowment for Humanities younger humanist grantee, 1974. Fellow Inst. for Research in Humanities; mem. Am. Philos. Assn., Internat. Hegel Soc. (adv. bd.), Phi Beta Kappa. Author: An Introduction to Hegel's Metaphysics, 1969; contbr. essays, revs. to profl. jours. Home: 1711 Summit Ave Madison WI 53705 Office: Dept Philosophy 5185 Helen C White Hall U Wis Madison WI 53706

SOLL, DAVID BENJAMIN, ophthalmologist; b. N.Y.C., Aug. 9, 1930; s. Hyman and Sara (Karansky) S.; B.A., N.Y. U., 1951, M.S., 1963; M.D., Chgo. Med. Sch., 1955; m. Jean Shtasel, Dec. 23, 1956; children—Abby, Stephen, Warren, Adam. Intern, Phila. Gen. Hosp., 1955-56; resident Manhattan Eye, Ear and Throat Hosp., N.Y.C., 1957-59; asst. chief EENT, then chief eye dept. USPHS, 1959-61; chief service B, dept. ophthalmology Frankford Hosp., Phila., 1961-65, dir., 1965—; asso. asst. attending ophthalmologist Phila. Gen. Hosp., 1961-75, cons. dept. ophthalmology, 1975-79; attending in ophthalmology VA Hosp., Phila., 1961-79; clin. affiliate, dept. surgery, div. ophthalmology Children's Hosp., Phila., 1961—; dir. dept. ophthalmology Phila. Geriatric Center, 1965—, Rolling Hill Hosp. and Diagnostic Center, Elkins Park, Pa., 1969—; surgeon in ophthalmology Presbyn.-U. Pa. Med. Center, Phila., 1972-79; cons. plastic surgery Pa. Hosp., 1973-75, cons. ophthalmology, 1975—; instr. dept. ophthalmology U. Pa., 1961, asso., 1962-68, asst. prof., 1968-72, asso. prof., 1972-75, lectr., 1975-79; prof., chmn. dept. ophthalmology Hahnemann Med. Coll. and Hosp., Phila., 1974—. Recipient Disting. Alumnus award Chgo. Med. Sch., 1979. Diplomate Am. Bd. Ophthalmology. Fellow A.C.S., Am. Acad. Ophthalmology and Otolaryngology (award of merit 1977), Am. Soc. Ophthalmic Plastic and Reconstructive Surgery (pres. 1978), Phila. Coll. Physicians; mem. AMA, Pa. Acad. Ophthalmology and Otolaryngology, Am. Assn. Cosmetic Surgeons (pres. 1978-79), Am. Acad. Facial Plastic and Reconstructive Surgery, Am. Assn. Ophthalmology, AAUP, Assn. Univ. Profs. Ophthalmology, Robert H. Ivy Soc., Phila. Ophthalmic Club, Phila. Soc. Facial Plastic Surgeons, Am. Intra-Ocular Implant Soc., Assn. for Research in Ophthalmology, Pan Am., Pa., Phila. County med. socs., Am. Soc. Ocularists (adv. com.), Pan Am. Ophthal. Found., Med. Club Phila., U. Pa. Eye Alumni Soc., Alumni Assn. Chgo. Med. Sch., Phi Delta Epsilon. Editor: Management of Complications in Ophthalmic Plastic Surgery, 1976; contbr. articles to med. jours. Home: 1127 Devon Rd Rydal PA 19046 Office: 5001 Frankford Ave Philadelphia PA 19124

SOLLARS, BENJAMIN KEMP, mfg. co. exec.; b. Clinton, Ind., Mar. 24, 1919; s. Ben Warren and Cloa Mae (Payton) S.; B.S. in Mech. Engring., Rose Poly. Inst., 1942; m. Marcella Josephine Lawson, Aug. 24, 1941; 1 dau., Pamela Jo (Mrs. Rick Hott). With Diamond Chain Co., Indpls., 1946—, v.p., 1958-62, pres., 1962—; dir. Amsted-Siemag Kette, Germany, T.I.D.C., India. Bd. dirs. Indpls. Jr. Achievement, 1963-68, Indpls. United Fund, 1964—. Served to capt. AUS, 1942-45. Registered profl. engr., Ind. Mem. Tau Beta Pi. Republican. Baptist. Mason. Clubs: Junto, Rotary, Hillcrest Country, Columbia. Home: 4401 King Arthur Ct Carmel IN 46032 Office: 402 Kentucky Ave Indianapolis IN 46225

SOLLENBARGER, LEE R., transp. co. exec.; b. Hugo, Colo., 1912; married. exec. v.p. Denver-Chgo. Trucking Co., 1938-60; with Transcon Lines, 1960—, pres., chief exec. officer, 1963-73, chmn., 1974—, also dir. Office: Transcon Lines PO Box 92220 Los Angeles CA 90009*

SOLLENBERGER, HOWARD EDWIN, govt. ofcl.; b. N. Manchester, Ind., Apr. 28, 1917; s. Oliver Clark and Hazel (Coppock) S.; B.A., Manchester Coll., 1941, LL.D. (hon.), 1963; m. Agnes Hafner, Dec. 31, 1944; children—David Olaf, Roger Hafner (dec.), Zoe Karin. Relief adminstr. Brethern Services Com., also Am. Friends Service Com., N. China, 1938-40; engaged in civilian pub. service, 1941-44; orientation officer UNRRA, 1945-46, liaison officer, Shanghai, China, 1946-47; with Fng. Service Inst., State Dept. 1947—, dir. Chinese lang. and area sch., Peiping, China, 1947-50, asso. prof. Chinese Studies, Washington, 1950, 55, dean Sch. Lang. and Area Studies, 1956-65, acting dir. Inst., 1965-66, 69-71, asso. dir., 1966-69, dir., 1971-76; cons. internat. edn., 1976—; mem. adv. com. lang. and area programs NDEA, 1962-64; adv. com. Center Applied Linguistics, 1959-62; adviser Georgetown U. Sch. Langs. and Linguistics, 1964—; Unitarian-Universalist rep. Task Force on U.S. Food Policy, 1977—. Pres., McLean (Va.) PTA, 1960; pres. Fairfax Meml. Soc., 1969-74. Recipient Superior Honor award State Dept., 1964, John Jacob Rogers award State Dept., 1976. Mem. Linguistics Soc. Am., Modern Lang. Assn., Assn. Asian Studies, Tau Kappa Alpha. Unitarian (v.p. 1961-62, 66-67). Author: Read Chinese Script, 1949; Chinese Newspaper Syllabus, 1949; Documentary Chinese, 1949. Home: 1287 Berry Pl McLean VA 22102

SOLLO, EUGENE DONALD, mktg. agy. exec.; b. Chgo., Oct. 12, 1931; s. Leonard H. and Ray (Schwartz) S.; student U. Ill., 1948-50, Northwestern U., 1951-53; m. Lenore R. Bronson, Sept 20, 1953; children—Wendy, Tami. Exec. v.p. Ency. Brit., Inc., Chgo., 1955-74; pres. Carlyle Mktg. Corp., 1974—. Mem. Direct Selling Assn., Chgo. Assn. Direct Mktg. (dir., pres.), Pi Sigma Epsilon. Home: 1083 Carlyle Terr Highland Park IL 60035 Office: Carlyle Bldg 5850 N Lincoln Ave Chicago IL 60659

SOLLOWAY, CHARLES ROBERT, forest products co. exec.; b. Vancouver, B.C., Can., May 19, 1935; s. Harold Eugene and Elva Merle (McAllister) S.; B.Commerce, U. B.C., 1959, LL.B., 1960. Admitted to B.C. bar, 1960; practice in Vancouver, 1960-63; asst. to pres. Westcoast Transmission Co. Ltd., Vancouver, 1963-68; v.p., gen. counsel, sec. Weldwood of Can. Ltd., Vancouver, 1968—; dir. Babine Forest Products Ltd. Mem. Can., Vancouver bar assns., Law Soc. B.C., Vancouver Bd. Trade. Anglican. Clubs: Univ., Lawn Tennis and Badminton (Vancouver). Home: 6480 Madrona Crescent West Vancouver BC V7W 2J8 Canada Office: Weldwood of Can Ltd PO Box 2179 Vancouver BC V6B 3V8 Canada

SOLNIT, ALBERT JAY, physician, educator; b. Los Angeles, Aug. 26, 1919; s. Benjamin and Bertha (Pavin) S.; B.A. in Med. Scis., U. Calif., 1940, M.A. in Anatomy, 1942, M.D., 1943; M.A. (hon.), Yale U., 1964; m. Martha Benedict, 1949; children—David, Ruth, Benjamin, Aaron. Rotating intern L.I. Coll. Hosp., 1944, asst. resident in pediatrics, 1944-45; resident in pediatrics and communicable diseases U. Calif. div. San Francisco Hosp., 1947-48; asst. resident dept. psychiatry and mental hygiene Yale U., 1948-49, sr. resident, 1949-50, fellow in child psychiatry, 1950-52, instr. pediatrics and psychiatry, 1952-53, asst. prof., 1953-60, asso. prof., 1960-64, prof., 1964-70, Sterling prof., 1970—, dir. Child Study Center, 1966—; tng. and supervising analyst Western New Eng. Inst. Psychoanalysis, 1962—, N.Y. Psychoanalytic Inst., 1962—; chmn. Center for Study Edn., Instn. for Social and Policy Studies, Yale U., 1971-73; cons. Childrens Bur., HEW; mem. adv. council Erikson Inst. for Early Childhood Edn., 1966—; nat. adviser Children, publ. of Children's Bur., 1965—; mem. com. on publs. Yale U. Press, 1971—; sci. adviser Center for Preventive Psychiatry, White Plains, N.Y., 1970—; mem. adv. bd. Action for Childrens TV, Newtonville, Mass., 1973—; mem. div. med. scis. Assembly Life Scis. NRC, 1974—; cons. div. mental health service program NIMH, 1974—. Bd. dirs. Human Services Inst. for Children and Families, Washington, 1973—; WHO prof. psychiatry and human devel. U. Negev, Beer-Sheva, Israel, 1973—; mem. Conn. Adv. Council Children and Youth Services, 1976—; mem. bd. maternal, child and family health research Assembly Life Scis., NRC, 1976—; mem. nat. adv. council Center for Study Families and Children, Vanderbilt U., 1978—; mem. panel child welfare resource info. exchange Nat. Center Child Advocacy, 1978—; med. adv. council Tourette Syndrome Assn., 1978—. Served with USAAF, 1945-47. Mem. Am. Orthopsychiat. Assn. (editorial bd. jour.), Am. Psychiat. Assn., Am. Psychoanalytic Assn. (past pres., editorial bd. jour. 1972-74), Am. Acad. Child Psychiatry (past pres.), Internat. Assn. Child Psychiatry and Allied Professions (pres. 1974-78), Am. Pediatric Soc., Am. Assn. Child Psychoanalysis (past pres.), Am. Acad. Pediatrics (mem. task force pediatric edn.), AAAS, Internat. Psychoanalytic Assn. N.Y. Psychoanalytic Soc., Soc. Profs. Child Psychiatry. Author: (With M.J.E. Senn) Problems in Child Behavior and Development, 1968; (with A. Freud, J. Goldstein) Beyond the Best Interests of the Child, 1973; editor: (with S. Provence) Modern Perspectives in Child Development, 1963; mng. editor Psychoanalytic Study of the Child, 1971—; editorial bd. Pediatrics, Jour. Acad. Pediatrics, 1968-76, Am. Jour. Psychiatry, 1974—, Jour. Am. Acad. Child Psychiatry, 1975, Psychiatry in Medicine, Internat. Jour. Med. Psychology and Psychiatry in the Gen. Hosp., 1969—; editorial adv. bd. Internat. Ency. Psychiatry, Psychoanalysis and Psychology, 1972—; mem. Am. editorial com. Israel Annals of Psychiatry and Related Disciplines, 1969—; editorial bd. Gen. Hosp. Psychiatry, Psychiatry Medicine and Primary Care, 1978. Home: 30 Short Hill Rd Hamden CT 06517 Office: 333 Cedar St New Haven CT 06510

SOLOFF, LOUIS ALEXANDER, educator, physician; b. Paris, Oct. 2, 1904; s. Abraham and Rebecca (Wagenfeld) S.; came to U.S., 1905, naturalized, 1930; B.A, U. Pa., 1926; M.D., U. Chgo., 1930; m. Mathilde Robin, 1933; 1 dau., Joann Soloff Green. Dir. pathology St. Joseph's and St. Vincent's hosps., Phila., 1933-45; dir. pathology Eagleville Sanitorium, Norristown, Pa., 1933-45; with Temple U. and Hosp., Phila., 1930—, chief div. cardiology, 1956-70, prof. medicine, 1966—, Blanche P. Levy distinguished service prof., 1970—; chief div. cardiology Episcopal Hosp., 1950-56. Mem. A.C.P., AMA, Am. Heart Assn., Am. Fedn. Clin. Research, Pa. Med. Soc., Am. Heart Assn., Council on Clin. Cardiology, AAUP, Assn. Univ. Cardiologists, Sigma Xi, Alpha Omega Alpha. Research, publs. on cardiovascular disease. Home: 1901 Walnut St Philadelphia PA 19103 Office: Temple U Health Scis Center Philadelphia PA 19140

SOLOMON, ALLAN BERNARD, lawyer; b. Brookline, Mass., Feb. 7, 1936; s. Norman R. and Madeline (Newman) S.; B.S. in Econs., U. Pa., 1957; J.D., Boston Coll., 1960; LL.M. in Taxation, N.Y. U., 1961; m. Shirley Fleischer, July 10, 1960; children—Lois, Susan, Marcia, Michael. Admitted to Mass. bar, 1960, Ky. bar, 1961, Fla. bar, 1978; pvt. practice law, Louisville, 1961-64; with Nat. Industries Inc., Louisville, 1964-77, exec. v.p. ops., 1975-77; partner firm Barnett & Algia, Louisville, 1978—. Bd. dirs. Louisville Jewish Community Center; v.p. Louisville Jewish Fedn. Mem. Order of Coif, Beta Gamma Sigma, Beta Alpha Phi. Jewish. Address: 1700 Kentucky Life Bldg Louisville KY 40202

SOLOMON, ANTHONY JOSEPH, state ofcl.; b. Providence, Apr. 1, 1932; student Providence Coll., also R.I. Coll. Pharmacy, 1956; m. Sarah Symia; children—Michael A., Anthony E., Donna M., Sharon A. Mem. R.I. Ho. of Reps. 11th Dist., 1967-76; treas. State of R.I., 1977—; chmn. R.I. Investment Commn., R.I. Unclassified Pay Bd., R.I. State Employee's Retirement Bd.; mem. bd. R.I. Bank Corp. Mem. Nat. Democratic Charter Commn., R.I. Dem. Charter Commn. Recipient Man of Year award Christian Bros. Boys Assn., LaSalle Acad., Providence, 1979. Mem. Nat. Assn. State Treasurers (pres. elect 1980-81), R.I. Pharm. Assn. Roman Catholic. Clubs: K.C. (4 deg.), Lions. Address: Treasury Dept 102 State House Providence RI 02903

SOLOMON, ANTHONY MORTON, banker; b. Arlington, N.J., Dec. 27, 1919; s. Jacob and Edna (Yudin) S.; B.A. in Econs., U. Chgo., 1941; M.A. in Econs. and Pub. Adminstrn., Harvard U., 1948, Ph.D., 1950; m. Constance Beverly Kaufman, Aug. 12, 1950; children—Adam Nicole (dec.), Tracy. Jr. economist OPA, 1941-42; mem. Am. fin. mission to Iran, 1942-46; securities analyst Bache & Co., N.Y.C., 1950-51; pub. Nat. Indsl. Directory Mex., 1951-53; pres. Rosa Blanca Products Corp., Mex., 1954-61; dep. asst. sec. state for Latin Am., also dep. asst. AID adminstr. for Latin Am., 1963-65; asst. sec. state econ. affairs, 1965-69; pres. Internat. Investment Corp. for

Yugoslavia, London, 1969-73; undersec. monetary affairs Treasury Dept., 1977-80; pres., chief exec. Fed. Res. Bank N.Y., 1980—; lectr. Harvard Bus. Sch., 1961-63; chmn. AID mission to Bolivia, 1963; chmn. mission U.S. Trust Ter., Pacific Ocean, 1963; cons. in field, pvt. investor, sculptor; founder a criminal justice system in Washington and Great Falls, Va. Democrat. Jewish. Clubs: Riverbend Country; Harvard (N.Y.C.); Federal City (Washington). Office: Fed Res Bank NY Fed Res PO Sta New York NY 10045

SOLOMON, ARTHUR KASKEL, educator; b. Pitts., Nov. 26, 1912; A.B., Princeton, 1934; M.A., Harvard, 1935, Ph.D. in Phys. Chemistry, 1937; Ph.D. in Physics, Cambridge U. (Eng.), 1947, Sc.D., 1964; married; 2 children. Research asso. in physics and chemistry Harvard, 1939-41; officer Brit. Ministry Supply, 1941-43; mem. staff Radiation Lab., Mass. Inst. Tech., 1945; asst. prof. phys. chemistry Med. Sch., Harvard, 1946-57, asso. prof. biophysics, 1957-68, prof., 1968—; asso. in biophysics Peter Bent Brigham Hosp., Boston, 1950-72; dir. Read's Inc., Balt., 1946-77, pres., 1961-77. Mem. U.S. Nat. Com. for Pure and Applied Biophysics, 1965-72, U.S. Nat. Com. for Biology, 1966-71; mem. U.S. Nat. Com. for UNESCO, 1969-74, mem. U.S. del. to gen. assembly, Nairobi, 1976; mem. vis. com. biology dept. Brookhaven Nat. Lab., 1961-65; mem. NRC com. on radiology, 1957-59, com. on growth, 1954-57; sec. Gen. Internat. Union for Pure and Applied Biophysics, 1961-72; mem. NIH radiation study sect., 1960-63, biophys. sci. tng. com., 1963-68, chmn., 1966-68; mem. U.S. del. Gen. Assembly of UNESCO, Paris, 1978; mem. bd. internat. orgns. and programs Nat. Acad. Scis., 1973—, chmn., 1977—, mem. Commn. on Internat. Relations, 1977—; mem. exec. com. Internat. Council Sci. Unions, 1966-72; U.S. del. 17th Gen. Assembly of Internat. Council Sci. Unions, Athens, 1978; chmn. Harvard com. on higher degrees in biophysics, 1959—; chmn. Harvard Council on the Arts, 1973-76. Trustee, Inst. Contemporary Art, Boston, 1946-76, pres., 1965-71; bd. overseers Boston Mus. Fine Arts, 1978—. Decorated Order Andres Bello (Venezuela). Fellow Am. Acad. Arts and Scis.; mem. Am. Chem. Soc., Am. Physiol. Soc., Biophysics Soc., Soc. Gen. Physiology. Clubs: Cosmos (Washington); St. Botolph (Boston). Mem. editorial bds. Quarterly Revs. of Biophysics, 1972-74, Journal Gen. Physiology, 1958—. Home: 27 Craigie St Cambridge MA 02138 Office: Harvard Medical School 25 Shattuck St Boston MA 02115

SOLOMON, ARTHUR PAUL, educator; b. New Haven, Conn., Aug. 22, 1939; s. Harry Peter and Gladys Bernice (Chasnoff) S.; B.A., Brown U., 1961; M.A., Trinity Coll., 1967; Ph.D., Harvard U., 1971; children—James, Jennifer, Joshua. Dir., manpower and econ. devel. United Planning Orgn., 1965-67; mem. staff White House, 1967-68; prof. econs. and urban studies M.I.T., 1971—, dir. Harvard-M.I.T. Joint Center for Urban Studies, 1975—; cons. U.S. Senate Banking, Housing and Urban Affairs Com., U.S. Ho. Reps. Housing Subcom., HUD, Fed. Home Loan Bank Bd., U.S. Conf. Mayors; mem. econ. adv. bd. Nat. Savs. and Loan League. Ford Found. fellow, 1970-71. Mem. Am. Real Estate and Urban Econs. Assn., Nat. Assn. Bus. Economists, Nat. Housing Conf. Jewish. Author: Property Taxes, Housing and the Cities, 1973; Housing the Urban Poor, 1974; The Nation's Housing, 1975-1985, 1977; The Prospective City, 1980; editor Eton Jour. Real Estate Investment, Jour. Am. Real Estate and Urban Econs., Jour. Am. Inst. Planners. Home: 244 Brattle St Cambridge MA 02138 Office: 53 Church St Cambridge MA 02138

SOLOMON, DANIEL LEE, artist; b. Topeka, July 13, 1945; s. Joseph Hyman and Geraldine I. (McQuilkin) S.; B.Sc., U. Oreg., 1967. Exhibited paintings in one-man shows at Isaacs Gallery, Toronto, Ont., Can., 1970, 71, 73, 74, Mirvish Gallery, Toronto, 1977; exhibited in group show 14 Canadians, Hirshorn Mus., Washington, 1976. Can. Council fellow, 1970, 75. Home: 115 Wolseley St Toronto ON M6J 1K1 Canada

SOLOMON, DAVID HARRIS, educator, physician; b. Cambridge, Mass., Mar. 7, 1923; s. Frank and Rose (Roud) S.; A.B., Brown U., 1944; M.D., Harvard, 1946; m. Ronda L. Markson, June 23, 1946; children—Patricia Jean (Mrs. Richard E. Sinaiko), Nancy Ellen. Intern, Peter Bent Brigham Hosp., Boston, 1946-47, resident, 1947-48, 50-51; fellow endocrinology New Eng. Center Hosp., Boston, 1951-52; faculty U. Calif. at Los Angeles Sch. Medicine, 1952—, prof. medicine, 1966—, vice chmn. dept. medicine, 1968-71, chmn. dept., 1971—; chief med. service Harbor Gen. Hosp., Torrance, Calif., 1966-71; cons. Wadsworth VA Hosp., Los Angeles, 1952—, Sepulveda VA Hosp.; cons. metabolism tng. com. USPHS, 1960-64, endocrinology study sect., 1970-73; mem. dean's com. Wadsworth, Sepulveda VA hosps. Mem. Assn. Am. Physicians, Am. Soc. Clin. Investigation, Am. Fedn. Clin. Research, Am. Physiol. Soc., Western Soc. Clin. Research (councillor 1963-65), Endocrine Soc., Am. Diabetes Assn., Am. Thyroid Assn. (pres. 1973-74), Soc. Exptl. Biology and Medicine, A.C.P., Los Angeles Soc. Internal Medicine (exec. council 1960-62), Inst. Medicine Nat. Acad. Scis., AAAS, Western Assn. Physicians (councillor 1972-75), Phi Beta Kappa, Sigma Xi, Alpha Omega Alpha. Contbr. numerous articles to profl. jours. Home: 863 Woodacres Rd Santa Monica CA 90402 Office: Dept Medicine U Calif at Los Angeles Sch Medicine Los Angeles CA 90024

SOLOMON, EDWARD DAVID, chain store exec.; b. Paterson, N.J., Mar. 3, 1931; s. Charles and Lee (Bernstein) S.; B.S., Wharton Sch. Fin., U. Pa., 1952; m. Regina Ellen Purcell, Mar. 18, 1972; 1 son, David; children by previous marriage—Jerry, Susan. Buyer, Miles Shoes div. Melville Corp., N.Y.C., 1956-59; buyer, mdse. mgr., exec. v.p., then pres. Gallenkamp Stores Co. div. Scoa Industries Inc., Los Angeles, 1959-69; pres. Karl's Shoe Stores Ltd. div. Hartfield Zodys Inc., Los Angeles, 1969-74, pres., chief operating officer Hartfield-Zodys, Inc., Los Angeles and N.Y.C., 1974-76, pres., chief exec. officer, 1977—, chmn., 1978—, also dir.; dir. Three D Depts., Inc. Trustee, City of Hope. Served with USNR, 1953-56. Named man of year, professions and fin. group City of Hope, 1973, man of year Jack Martin Fund, Mt. Sinai Hosp., N.Y.C., 1977. Mem. Volume Footwear Retailers Am. (dir. 1967—, pres.), Nat. Retailers Inst., Mass Retailers Inst. (dir. 1977). Office: Hartfield-Zodys Inc 2525 Military Ave Los Angeles CA 90064

SOLOMON, EZRA, educator, economist; b. Rangoon, Burma, Mar. 20, 1920; s. Ezra and Emily (Rose) S.; A.B. (hons.), U. Rangoon, 1940; Ph.D., U. Chgo., 1950; m. Janet Lorraine Cameron, May 7, 1949; children—Catherine Shan, Janet Ming, Lorna Cameron. Came to U.S., 1947, naturalized, 1951. Instr., U. Chgo., 1948-51, asst. prof. finance, 1951-55, asso. prof., 1955-57, prof., 1957-61; Dean Witter prof. finance Stanford, 1961-71, 73—, also dir. Internat. Center Mgmt. Edn., 1961-64; mem. Council Econ. Advisers, 1971-73; dir. United Financial Corp., Kaiser Aluminum & Chem. Corp., Ency. Brit., Capital Preservation Fund, Foremost-McKesson Inc. Served as lt., Burma div., Royal Naval Vol. Res., 1942-47. Mem. Am. Econ. Assn., Am. Finance Assn. Author: The Theory of Financial Management, 1963; Money and Banking, 5th edit., 1968; The Management of Corporate Capital, 1959; Metropolitan Chicago: An Economic Analysis, 1958; The Anxious Economy, 1975; An Introduction to Financial Management, 2d edit., 1980. Editor Jour. Bus., 1953-57; bd. editors Jour. of Finance, 1965-66, Jour. Bus. Finance, 1969-73, Jour. Quantitative and Financial Analysis, 1969-71. Home: 775 Santa Ynez St Stanford CA 94305

SOLOMON, GEORGE EDWARD, aerospace co. exec.; b. Seattle, July 14, 1925; s. George Henry and Rose Steinum (Borgford) S.; student U. Wash., 1942-43, B.S. in Aeros., 1946-49; M.S., Calif. Inst. Tech., 1950, Ph.D., 1953; m. Betty Jane Day, Mar. 22, 1948; children—George Cleve, Jane Olga. Cons., Los Angeles, 1953-54; with TRW Systems, Los Angeles, 1954-59, Redondo Beach, Calif., 1959—, v.p., dir. systems research and analysis div., 1962-65, v.p., dir. systems labs., 1965-68, v.p., dir. mktg. and requirements analysis, 1968-71, v.p., gen. mgr. TRW Systems, 1971—. Mem. Ames indsl. affiliates U. Calif., San Diego, 1966—; mem. vis. com. U. Wash., 1970—; mem. indsl. adv. group NATO, 1971-74. Served with inf. AUS, 1943-45. Decorated Bronze Star, Purple Heart. Fellow AIAA, Am. Astronautical Soc.; mem. Am. Ordnance Assn., Assn. U.S. Army, Nat. Security Indsl. Assn., VFW, Armed Forces Mgmt. Assn., Electronics Industries Assn., Am. Mgmt. Assn., Nat. Acad. Engring., Phi Beta Kappa, Sigma Xi, Tau Beta Pi. Home: 529 Via Media Palos Verdes Estates CA 90274 Office: TRW Systems 1 Space Park Redondo Beach CA 90278

SOLOMON, GERALD BROOKS HUNT, congressman; b. Okeechobee, Fla., Aug. 14, 1930; s. Seymour and Rlee Eugenia (Hunt) S.; student Siena Coll., Albany, N.Y., 1948-49, St. Lawrence U., Canton, N.Y., 1953-54; m. Freda Frances Parker, Feb. 5, 1955; children—Susan, Daniel, Robert, Linda, Jeffrey. Town supr., chief exec., Queensbury, N.Y., 1967-72; legislator Warren County, N.Y., 1968-73; mem. N.Y. State Assembly, 1972-78, mem. agr., transp., local govts. and social services coms., 1972-78; mem. 96th Congress from 29th N.Y. Dist., mem. pub. works and transp. com., select com. on coms.; founding partner Asso. of Glens Falls (N.Y.), Inc. ins. agy., 1964—. Chmn., Warren County Social Service Com., 1968-72; active, Eastern Adirondack Heart Assn., Adirondack Muscular Dystrophy Assn.; mem. Queensbury Central Vol. Fire Co., 1967—; bd. dirs. Adirondack Park Assn., Glens Falls Area Youth Center, council Boy Scouts of Am. Mem. Queensbury C. of C. (pres. 1972), Queensbury Jaycees (pres. 1964-65). Presbyn. Clubs: Masons, Shriners, K.T., Elks, Kiwanis (dir. Queensbury club 1965-69), Grange. Office: 515 Cannon House Office Bldg Washington DC 20515

SOLOMON, GUS J., judge; b. Portland, Oreg., Aug. 29, 1906; s. Jacob and Rose (Rosencrantz) S.; student Reed Coll., 1923-25, LL.D. (hon.), 1975; Ph.B., U. Chgo., 1926, Columbia U., 1926-27; LL.B., Stanford U., 1929; m. Elisabeth Willer, Mar. 18, 1939; children—Gerald, Philip, Richard. Pvt. practice law, 1929-49; U.S. Dist. judge, 1949—, chief judge, 1959-71, sr. judge, 1971—; dist. judges rep. for 9th Circuit, Jud. Conf. U.S., 1963-66. Mem. bd. visitors Columbia U. Law Sch. Recipient Portland First Citizen for 1970 award. Mem. Dist. Judges Assn. 9th Circuit (pres. 1968-69). Democrat. Jewish. Home: 2323 SW Park Pl Portland OR 97205 Office: US Court House Portland OR 97205

SOLOMON, HAROLD CHARLES, profl. tennis player; b. Washington, Sept. 17, 1952; s. Leonard and Roslyn (Orenstein) S.; student Rice U., Houston. Profl. tennis player; one of final 8 players in Grand Prix Masters, 1978; winner Ceasar's Palace-Las Vegas Tennis Classic, 1978, Louisville Classic, 1978, Balt. Grand Prix Tennis Tournament, 1979; finalist Boston-U.S. Profl. Championships, 1978, Springfield (Mass.) Grand Prix Tennis Tournament, 1978, South African Open, 1978. Mem. Assn. Tennis Profls. Jewish. Address: 1500 S Ocean Blvd Pompano Beach FL 33062

SOLOMON, HENRY, univ. dean; b. Bronx, N.Y., Nov. 28, 1926; s. Max and Tillie (Gilerowitz) S.; B.A., Bklyn. Coll., 1949; M.A., N.Y. U., 1950, Ph.D., 1960; m. Jacqueline Mona Cohen, May 31, 1953; 1 son, Michael Robert. Research asso., then sr. staff investigator and dep. prin. investigator, logistics research project George Washington U., 1950-66, prof. econs., chmn. dept., 1962-74, dean Grad. Sch. Arts and Scis., 1974—; dep. asst. adminstr. econs., acting asst. adminstr. planning, research and analysis SBA, 1966-67; cons. in field. Served with U.S. Army, 1945-46. Recipient Founder's Day award N.Y. U., 1960. Mem. Am., So. econ. assns., Am. Statis. Assn., Econometric Soc. Asso. editor Naval Research Logistics Quar., 1957—. Home: 6311 Stratford Rd Chevy Chase MD 20015 Office: 2000 H St NW Washington DC 20052

SOLOMON, HYDE, artist; b. N.Y.C., May 3, 1911; s. Samuel and Ida (Chasin) S.; student Art Students League, Pratt Inst., Columbia U. One-man shows: Peridot Gallery, N.Y.C., 1954-55, 56, Poindexter Gallery, N.Y.C., 1957, 58, 60, 63, 65, 67, 69, 70, 73, 74, Princeton Art Mus., 1959, Gallery of Modern Art, Taos, N.Mex., 1974, Stables Gallery, Taos, 1978, Mus. Fine Arts, Santa Fe, N.Mex., 1979, Roswell (N.Mex.) Mus., 1979; group shows: Whitney Mus., Carnegie Internat., 1965, 67; artist-in-residence Princeton U., 1959-62; represented in permanent collections: Whitney Mus., N.Y.C., Wadsworth Atheneum, Hartford, Conn., Helena Rubenstein Pavilion, Tel Aviv Mus., Palestine, Newark Mus., Walker Art Centre, Minn., Telfair Acad. Fine Arts, Savannah, Ga., Munson-Williams Proctor Mus., Utica, N.Y., U. Va. Mus., U. Calif. Mus. at Berkeley, Mus. of N.Mex., Santa Fe, Amarillo (Tex.) Area Arts Found., numerous corporate collections. Recipient Purchase award Acad. Arts and Letters, 1970; Mark Rothko Found. grantee, 1973; Grant Adolph and Esther Gottlieb Found. grantee, 1978. Address: PO Box 2538 Taos NM 87571

SOLOMON, IZLER, symphony conductor; b. St. Paul, Jan. 11, 1910; s. Harry Thomas and Eva (Levin) S.; student Mich. State Coll., 1928-31; studied violin, St. Paul and Kansas City to 1924, N.Y. and Phila., 1924-28, Europe, summer 1928; Doctorate (hon.), Pacific U., 1958; LL.D., Ind. Central Coll., 1959; Mus. D. (hon.), Anderson Coll., 1963, Butler U., 1966, Ind. U., 1971; A.F.D. (hon.), Franklin U., 1965; m. Sorelle Melamed, Nov. 26, 1931 (dec. Dec. 1959); children—Joseph (dec.), David; m. 2d, Elizabeth Weems Westfeldt, 1961 (div. 1971). Instr. violin Mich. State Coll., 1928-31; instr., music supr. Lansing Pub. Schs., 1931-35; organized and conducted local orch.; condr. Ill. Symphony Orch., Chgo., 1936-42; condr. Woman's Symphony Orch., Chgo., and presented with this orgn. 26 weekly broadcasts for the Libby-Owens Ford Glass Co., 1940-51; mus. dir. and condr. Columbus (Ohio) Philharmonic Orch., 1941-49, Aspen (Colo.) Music Festival, summer 1956-60, Indpls. Symphony Orch., 1956—; festival music dir., condr. Brandeis U., 1955, Music Assos. Aspen, 1956-57; music dir. Flagstaff (Ariz.) Music Festival, 1966; prof. music Ohio U., 1948-49; resident condr. Buffalo Philharmonic Orch., 1952-53; condr. New Orleans Summer Pops Symphony, 1943-44, 50-52; guest condr. Chgo. Symphony, CBS Symphony, Los Angeles Philharmonic, St. Louis Little Symphony, Los Angeles Chamber Orch., Detroit Symphony, Les Concerts Symphoniques de Montreal, Phila. Orch., Vancouver (B.C.) Symphony Orch., 1945, Buffalo Philharmonic Orch., 1946, Chgo. Grant Park Symphony, 1945, 46, 47, Hollywood Bowl Symphony, 1946-47, NBC Symphony, 1947, Palestine Philharmonic Orch., 1948, Israel Philharmonic, 1948-49, 58 (U.S. tour 1951), Boston Symphony, 1959-60, Houston Symphony, 1959-60, N.Y. Philharmonic, 1961-62, B.B.C., London, 1962, Berlin Philharmonic, 1966, Frankfurt Radio, 1966, Oslo, Norway, Berlin, Frankfurt, Germany, Flagstaff, 1969. Recipient several awards including Alice M. Ditson Award for distinguished service to Am. Music. Recordings for RCA Victor and MGM Record Co. Home: 6437 C Park Central Dr W Indianapolis IN 46260 Office: Clowes Hall 625 W 46th St Indianapolis IN 46208

SOLOMON, JACK AVRUM, JR., automotive distbr., lawyer, art dealer; b. Omaha, Oct. 25, 1928; s. John A. and Matilda (Bienstok) S.; B.S., U. Nebr., 1950, LL.B. cum laude, 1952; LL.M. (Cook fellow), U. Mich., 1953; m. Josephine J. Kleiman, June 1948 (div. Mar. 1971); children—Debra, Alisa, Michael, Rena; m. 2d, Carolyn Summers, Dec. 1973. Admitted to Nebr. bar, 1950, Ill. bar, 1951; practice law, Chgo., 1950—; with firm Stiefel, Greenberg, Burns, Baldridge & Solomon, 1953-66, partner, 1958-66; partner Solomon, Rosenfeld, Elliot, Stiefel & Engerman and predecessor, 1966—, sr. partner, 1966—. Dir. Amco Industries, Inc., Chgo., 1968—, chmn. bd., 1968-69, sec., gen. counsel, 1969—; sec., dir. Mogen David Wine Corp., Chgo., 1964-71; chmn. bd., dir. Arts and Leisure Corp., 1969-76; pres., dir. Circle Fine Art Corp., 1968—; chmn. bd., dir. London House, Inc., 1969-76, Edison Theater Corp., 1970-76, Piper's Alley Corp., 1963-74. Mem. Ill., Nebr. bar assns., Order of Coif. Jewish (pres. temple 1959-61). Club: Nat. Arts (N.Y.C.). Home: 1312 N Sandburg Terr Chicago IL 60611 Office: 30 N LaSalle St Chicago IL 60602

SOLOMON, JOSEPH, lawyer; b. N.Y.C., Mar. 11, 1904; s. Abraham and Rebecca (Rubin) S.; LL.B., N.Y. Law Sch., 1927, LL.D. with honors, 1976; m. Rita Schwartz, Aug. 31, 1929; children—Alan, Diane (Mrs. Bernhard Kempler). Admitted to N.Y. State bar, 1928; with Leventritt, Cook, Nathan & Lehman, N.Y.C., 1919-22, asst. to mng. clk., 1922-28, mem. legal staff, 1928-45; partner firm Lehman, Rohrlich & Solomon and predecessor firms, 1945-63, sr. partner, 1963—. Joseph Solomon chair in wills, trusts and estates named in his honor Columbia U. Sch. Law, 1974, Joseph Solomon chair in law N.Y. Law Sch., 1975, Joseph Solomon chair in medicine Mt. Sinai Sch. Medicine, 1976. Mem. Com. on Character and Fitness of Applicants for Admission to the Bar, Appellate div. First Jud. Dept., 1977—; chmn. Dr. Alfred Meyer Found. Mt. Sinai Hosp., 1951—. Trustee Milton Helpern Library of Legal Medicine. Recipient Horatio Alger award, 1978. Mem. N.Y. County Lawyers Assn. (dir. 1974-78), Assn. Bar City of N.Y., Lawyers Club (gov. 1975—), Phi Delta Phi (hon.). Bd. editors N.Y. Law Jour. Home: 1025 Fifth Ave New York NY 10028 Office: 30 Broad St New York NY 10004. *Mindful of my debt to various institutions and individuals in my formative years, I have constantly sought to make repayment in some small measure by my acts for the betterment of society in general and people in particular.*

SOLOMON, MAYNARD ELLIOTT, recording co. exec.; b. N.Y.C., Jan. 5, 1930; s. Benjamin and Dora (Levine) S.; B.A., Bklyn. Coll., 1950; postgrad. Columbia, 1950-51; m. Eva Georgiana Tevan, Jan. 22, 1951; children—Mark Jonathan, Nina Stephanie, Maury David. Co-founder, 1950, since co-owner Vanguard Rec. Soc., Inc., N.Y.C., 1950. Mem. Phi Beta Kappa. Author: Stephen Crane—a Critical Study, 1956; Beethoven and Bonaparte, 1968; Marxism and Art, 1973; Beethoven, 1977; Myth, Creativity and Psychoanalysis, 1978; asso. editor Am. Imago; contbr. articles to profl. jours. Home: 1 W 72d St New York City NY 10023 Office: 71 W 23d St New York City NY 10010

SOLOMON, NATHAN AARON, physician; b. Bklyn., Oct. 31, 1922; s. Barney W. and Gertrude S.; B.S., CCNY, 1942; M.S., N.Y. U., 1947, Ph.D., 1955; M.D., SUNY, 1959; m. Florence Schneider, Mar. 25, 1944; children—William, Robert, Judith. Chief chemist, chief surg. research Maimonides Med. Center, Bklyn., 1945-55, intern, 1959-60, resident, 1960-63, dir. nuclear medicine, 1964-70; practice medicine specializing in metabolism and nuclear medicine, N.Y.C., 1964—; dir. nuclear medicine State U. N.Y., Bklyn., 1970—, asso. prof., 1977—, prof. Downstate Med. Center, 1977—; cons. Bklyn.-Queens Hosp., VA hosps., Bklyn. and Northport, Maimonides Hosp., Coney Island Hosp., Kings Hwy. Hosp. Recipient A. Cressy Morrison award N.Y. Acad. Scis., 1954; NIH spl. fellow, 1962-63. Mem. AMA, N.Y. Acad. Scis., Am. Assn. Clin. Chemists, Soc. Nuclear Medicine. Contbr. articles to med. jours., chpts. to texts. Office: 1308 E 21st St Brooklyn NY 11210

SOLOMON, NEIL, physician; b. Pitts., Feb. 27, 1932; s. Max Maurice and Clara (Eisenstein) S.; A.B. with honors, Western Res. U., 1954, M.D. with honors (fellow in physiology, Arthritis and Rheumatism Found. fellow), 1961, M.S. with honors, 1961; Ph.D. with honors, U. Md., 1965; m. Frema Rose Sindell, June 26, 1955; children—Theodore C., Scott, Clifford T. Intern, Osler Med. Service, Johns Hopkins Hosp., Balt., 1961-62, asst. resident, 1962-63; trainee in physiology USPHS, 1955-61; practice medicine specializing in endocrinology and metabolism, gerontology, Balt., 1965—; asst. chief medicine Balt. City Hosps., 1963-68, visitant in medicine, 1963-68; asst. sr. surgeon child health and human devel. dept. gerontology NIH, 1964-65; vis. physician VA Hosp., Perry Point, Md., 1963-68; asso. prof. physiology, asst. prof. medicine Sch. Medicine, U. Md., 1965-71; instr. medicine Sch. Medicine, Johns Hopkins U., Balt., 1964-69, asst. prof. psychiatry and behavioral scis., 1971-79; asso. prof. pharmacology Sch. Medicine, U. Miami (Fla.), 1978-79, prof., 1979—; sec. health and mental hygiene State of Md., 1969-79. Sr. researcher Am. Heart Assn., 1965-67; cons. internal medicine and endocrinology VA Hosp., Perry Point, 1963-68. Served to lt. comdr. USPHS, 1963-65. Recipient Lederle award Am. Geriatric Soc., 1962; Schwentker award Johns Hopkins Hosp., 1963. Diplomate Nat. Bd. Med. Examiners. Fellow Am. Heart Assn.; mem. AMA, AAAS, AAUP, Johns Hopkins, Balt. City, Western U. med. socs., Johns Hopkins Med. and Surg. Assn., Med. and Chirurgical Faculty Md., N.Y. Acad. Sci., Md. Soc. Med. Research, Fedn. Am. Soc. Exptl. Biology, Am. Fedn. Clin. Research, Am. Physiol. Soc., Alpha Omega Alpha, Phi Delta Epsilon. Author: Dr. Solomon's Easy No-Risk Diet; The Truth about Weight Control: How to Lose Excess Pounds Permanently; Dr. Solomon's Proven Master Plan for Total Body Fitness and Maintenance; Dr. Solomon's High Health Diet; syndicated columnist Los Angeles Times Syndicate, 1974—; contbr. articles to profl. jours. Address: 1726 Reisterstown Rd Suite 213 Baltimore MD 21208

SOLOMON, RICHARD ALLAN, lawyer; b. N.Y.C., July 29, 1917; s. Herbert Michel and Hermine (Kaufmann) S.; A.B., Harvard, 1939; LL.B., Yale, 1942; m. Elinor Ruth Harris, Mar. 30, 1957; children—Joan, Robert, Thomas. Admitted to N.Y. bar, 1942, D.C. bar, 1969; atty. FCC, 1942-58, asst. gen. counsel, 1952-56; asst. chief appellate sect. antitrust div. Dept. Justice, 1958-62, chief sect., 1961-62; gen. counsel FPC, 1962-69; partner Wilner and Scheiner, Washington, 1969—. Served with USAAF, 1942-46; CBI. Mem. Am., Fed. bar assns., Yale Law Sch. Assn. Washington (pres. 1963). Clubs: Harvard, Nat. Lawyers (Washington). Case editor Yale Law Jour., 1941-42. Home: 6805 Delaware St Chevy Chase MD 20015 Office: 2021 L St NW Washington DC 20036

SOLOMON, RICHARD LESTER, educator; b. Boston, Oct. 2, 1918; s. Frank and Rose (Roud) S.; A.B., Brown U., 1940, M.Sc., 1942, Ph.D., 1947; children by previous marriage—Janet Ellen, Elizabeth Grace. Instr. psychology Brown U., 1946; asst. prof. Harvard U., 1947-50, asso. prof., 1950-57, prof. social psychology, 1957-60; prof. psychology U. Pa., Phila., 1960-74, James M. Skinner prof. sci., 1975—. Staff OSRD, 1942-45. Mem. Am., Eastern (pres.) psychol. assns., Psychonomic Soc. (chmn. governing bd.), Am. Acad. Arts and Scis., Soc. Exptl. Psychologists, AAAS, Nat. Acad. Sci., Phi Beta Kappa, Sigma Xi. Office: 3815 Walnut St Philadelphia PA 19104

SOLOMON, ROBERT, economist; b. N.Y.C., May 2, 1921; s. Sol and Betty (Brownstone) S.; B.A., U. Mich., 1942; M.A., Harvard, 1947, Ph.D., 1952; m. Fern Rice, Sept. 11, 1946; children—Carol Ann, Barbara Betty, Anne Eleanor. With Fed. Res. Bd., 1947-76, asso. adviser research div., 1963-65, adviser research div., 1965, adviser to bd. govs., 1965-76, dir. div. internat. fin., 1966-72; sr. fellow Brookings Instn., Washington, 1976—; vice chmn. deps. of com. of 20 IMF, 1972-74; adj. prof. Am. U., 1962-67; sr. staff economist Council Econ. Advisers, 1963-64. Served to 1st lt. USAAF, 1942-45. Decorated D.F.C., Air medal, officier Legion of Honor (France); recipient Rockefeller Pub. Service award, 1971. Mem. Am. Econ. Assn., Am. Fin. Assn., Council on Fgn. Relations. Club: Cosmos (Washington). Author: The International Monetary System, 1945-76, 1977. Columnist: Jour. Commerce. Contbr. to profl. jours. Home: 8502 W Howell Rd Bethesda MD 20034 Office: Brookings Instn 1775 Massachusetts Ave NW Washington DC 20036

SOLOMON, ROBERT BAILEY, army officer; b. Balt., Dec. 14, 1930; s. Adolphe Robert and Sylvia (Rochkind) S.; A.S., U. Balt., 1950; B.S., U. Md., 1964; M.S., Johns Hopkins U., 1975; postgrad. U.S. Army Command and Gen. Staff Coll., 1967-68, Nat. War Coll., 1974-75; m. Frances S. Nathanson, Apr. 2, 1955; children—Sharon M., Eric J., Leah S. Enlisted in U.S. Army, 1951; commd. 2d lt., 1952, advanced through grades to maj. gen., 1978; dep. chief public affairs Dept. Army, Washington, 1976-77, chief public affairs, 1977-79; dep. chief of staff Pacific Command, Camp H.M. Smith, Hawaii, 1979—; instr. Army Info. Sch., 1961-63. Mem. nat. com. USO, 1978-79. Mem. Assn. U.S. Army, U.S. Armor Assn., Public Relations Soc. Am. Jewish. Club: B'nai Brith. Office: Dept Chief of Staff Pacific Command Camp HM Smith HI 96861

SOLOMON, SAMUEL, scientist, educator; b. Brest Litovsk, Poland, Dec. 25, 1925; s. Nathan and Rachel (Greenberg) S.; B.S. with honors, McGill U., 1947, M.S., 1951, Ph.D. in Biochemistry, 1953; m. Sheila R. Horn, Aug. 11, 1953 (div. 1974); children—David Horn, Peter Horn, Jonathan Simon; m. 2d, Augusta M. Vineberg, July 12, 1974. Research asst. Columbia, 1953-55, asso. in biochemistry, 1958-59, asst. prof., 1959-60; asso. prof. biochemistry and exptl. medicine McGill U., 1960-66, prof., 1967—; dir. endocrine lab. Royal Victoria Hosp., Montreal, Que., 1965—; mem. endocrinology and metabolism grants com. Med. Research Council Can., 1967-71; vis. prof. endocrinology U. Vt., 1964; cons. in field. Mem. bd. govs. McGill U., 1975—. Fellow Chem. Inst. Can., Royal Soc. Can.; mem. Perinatal Research Soc. Am. (pres. 1976). Club: Montreal Amateur Athletic Assn. Co-editor: Chemical and Biological Aspects of Steroid Conugation, 1970. Editorial bd. Endocrinology, 1962; asso. editor Can. Jour. Biochemistry, 1967-71, Jour. Med. Primatology, 1971. Contbr. articles profl. jours. Home: 239 Kensington Ave 603 Montreal PQ H3Z 2H1 Canada Office: Dept Endocinrology Royal Victoria Hosp 687 Fine Ave West Montreal PQ H3A 1A1 Canada

SOLOMON, SAMUEL RANDOLPH, educator; b. N.Y.C., Aug. 24, 1909; s. Henry and Elisa (Copel) S.; A.B., Syracuse U., 1930, A.M. (Maxwell scholar), 1931, Ph.D., 1949; postgrad. Harvard Grad. Sch. Bus., 1944; m. Elizabeth Reading, July 28, 1961; 1 dau., Elizabeth (Mrs. Eldon Van Liere). Case worker, survey dir. Syracuse (N.Y.) Dept. Pub. Welfare, 1933-34; research asst. Gov. Lehman's Com. on Unemployment Relief, 1934-35; instr., chmn. social studies Syracuse Pub. Schs., 1937-42; instr. Maxwell Sch., Syracuse U., 1946-51; asst. prof., vis. prof. State U. N.Y., 1951-59; asst. prof., asso. prof., prof. Eastern Mich. U., Ypsilanti, 1960-79, prof. emeritus, 1979—, chmn. polit. sci. div., 1965-68. Editorial cons. Coll. Blue Book, 1957-66; cons., participant Mich. Forum on State and Local Govt., 1967-68; dir. Town and Gown Series of Lectures on Govt. Served to capt. USAAF, 1942-46; PTO. Mem. Phi Beta Kappa, Phi Kappa Phi, Delta Sigma Rho, Pi Gamma Mu, Kappa Phi Kappa. Author: The Governors of the States, 1900-1974, 1974. Author continuing surveys on govs. of the states, 1931—. Home: 2797 Manchester Rd Ann Arbor MI 48104

SOLOMON, SIDNEY, educator, physiologist; b. Worcester, Mass., Feb. 22, 1923; s. Samuel and Bessie (Grace) S.; B.S. in Chemistry, U. Mass., 1948; Ph.D. in Physiology, U. Chgo., 1952; m. Minnie Libian Kramer, Dec. 28, 1947; children—Anne Fay, Susan Judith. Mem. faculty Med. Coll. Va., 1952-60, 60-63, asso. prof., 1960-63; cons. Phillips Morris, Inc., 1960-63; prof. physiology, chmn. dept. U. N.Mex. Sch. Medicine, 1963-78; spl. asst. NSF, 1978-79; spl. research comparative physiology, renal physiology, active transport; lectr. Czechoslovakia Acad. Scis., 1963; vis. prof. U. Hawaii, 1973, U. Tel-Aviv, 1974-75. Chmn. Va. Acad. Scis., 1954-55; program dir. metabolic biology program NSF, 1968-69; cons. Nat. Bd. Med. Examiners, 1968—. Served with USMCR, 1942-45. Guggenheim fellow, 1962-63. Mem. AAUP, Am. Physiol. Soc., Biophys. Soc., N.Y. Acad. Scis., Soc. Exptl. Biology and Medicine, Sigma Xi (pres. Med. Coll. Va. chpt. 1959-60). Democrat. Author chpts. profl. books. Home: 2406 Morrow NE Albuquerque NM 87106. *Have fun doing what you are doing. Try to do it well. Treat people with dignity. Don't get too shook up when you get kicked in the face.*

SOLOMON, SYD, artist; b. Uniontown, Pa., July 12, 1917; s. Jack E. and Edith (Bennett) S.; student Chgo. Art Inst., 1934. Ecole des Beaux Arts, Paris, 1945; m. Ann F. Cohen, Dec. 29, 1941; children—Michele R., Michael. Dir. Sarasota (Fla.) Sch. Art, 1950—; prof. of art New Coll., Sarasota, 1967-69; mem. of guiding faculty Famous Artists Schs., Inc. Westport, Conn., 1954-70; dir. painting classes Ringling Mus. Art, Sarasota, 1952-60; vis. instr. U. Ill., 1968, Roberson Center of Art, 1969; exhbn.: Met. Mus., 1952, Delgado Mus., New Orleans, 1951-57, Butler Mus., Youngstown, 1954-56, Carnegie Inst., 1956, Dallas Mus., 1954, Houston Mus., 1955, Balt. Mus., 1952, High Mus., Atlanta, 1956, Free State Israel Mus., Jerusalem, 1956; Williams Proctor Inst., Utica, N.Y., 1956. Nat. Acad. Art, 1951-56. Birmingham Mus., 1952-62. Saidenberg Gallery, N.Y., 1959-70, Ringling Mus. Art, 1975, N.Y. Cultural Center, 1975, Tampa Bay Art Center, 1975, Benson Gallery, N.Y., 1975, Adley Gallery, 1978-79; represented in permanent collections: Phila. Mus. Art, Rose Mus., Brandeis U., La. State Mus., Baton Rouge, Guggenheim Mus., Whitney Mus. Am. Art, Wadsworth Athenaeum, Ringling Mus., Birmingham Mus., High Mus., Florida So. Coll., Clearwater (Fla.) Art Mus., Miss. Art Assn., Jackson, Fla. Fedn. Art Miami, Mus. Fine Arts, St. Petersburg, Fla., Miami Dade Collection, Fla., Balt. Mus., Lowe Gallery Mus., Miami, Fla., Cin. Mus. Art, Walter P. Chrysler, Jr. Collections, Dewitt Mus., Joseph Hirschhorn Collection, Delgado Mus., Adelphi U. Mus., Tel Aviv Mus., Norton Mus., Ft. Lauderdale Mus., Polk Pub. Mus., Guild Hall, E. Hampton, N.Y., Mus. of South, Memphis, Tampa Bay Art Center, Tampa, Fla. Camouflage designer Engrs. Bd., Washington, 1942. Recipient Hallmark Internat. award, 1952, purchases prize Fla. Internat., 1952, Lowe Gallery ann. award, 1953. Southeaster ann. award 1953, High Mus. award, 1956, Casein Soc. medal of honor, 1957, Audubon Soc. medal of honor, 1957; 1st purchase watercolor award, Butler Mus. of Art, 1957; 1st purchase prize. Sarasota Art Assn. 1958; Childe Hassam purchase award Am. Acad. Arts and Letters. Mem. Artists Equity. Allied Arts Council. Address: 9210 Blind Pass Rd Sarasota FL 33581 Summer studio: PO Box 16 Sagaponack NY 11962

SOLOMON, VITA PETROSKY, artist; b. Phila., Dec. 16, 1916; d. Harry and Rose (Bobrow) Petrosky; diploma Moore Inst. Art, 1937; B.F.A., Tyler Sch. Fine Arts, Temple U., 1958, B.S. in Edn., 1958, M.F.A., 1960; m. Charles M. Solomon, Apr. 8, 1941; children—Robert Charles, Henry Andrew, Jon David. One-artist shows: Phila. Art Alliance, 1953, 54, 58, Red Door Gallery, 1959, 60, 61, Newman Gallery, 1964, Moore Coll. Art, 1974, Suzanne Gross Gallery, 1979; tchr. art and art history Cheltenham High Sch.; tchr. art and English, Elkins Park Jr. High Sch.; exhibited group shows: United Soc. Artists, London, Pa. Acad. Fine Art, Phila. Art Mus., Detroit Inst. Art, Butler Inst. Art, Silvermine Guild (Conn.), N.A.D., Am. Water Color Soc., Audubon Soc., Royal Acad. Arts, London, Silvermine Guild Conn., Paris Salon, Woodmere Art Gallery, Phila. Art Alliance, Royal Inst. London, Nat. Arts Club (N.Y.), Met. Mus. Art, others; represented in permanent collections: Nat. Portrait Gallery, Phila. Mus. Art, Fed. Res. Bank, Temple U., U. Pa., Phila. City Hall, others, including portraits on commn. J.F. Lewis traveling fellow, Europe, by Moore Inst., 1937; recipient Gross Meml. award Silvermine Guild, 1958; Chendler prize Allied Artists Am., 1960, Nat. Arts Club award, 1974; prizes Moore Inst., 1957, 60, 61; purchase prize Temple U., 1959 (2), 1960, painting prize, 1966; Burdine meml. prize Woodmere Gallery, 1964; painting prize Wharton Art Center, 1964; Lowell Painting prize C.L. Wolfe Club, Nat. Arts Club, 1966; Painting prize Silver medal Paris Salon, 1966; award Phila. Watercolor Club, 1973; Benedictine Art award, 1972; Blumenthal prize Cheltenham Art Center, 1973; Jane Peterson medal Audubon Artists, 1975; Eugenia Atwood purchase prize Phila. Print Club, 1975; Eyre medal Phila. Watercolor Club, 1977; Best Figure Painting prize Woodmere Gallery, 1977. Mem. Am. Watercolor Soc., Cheltenham Twp. Art Centre, Art Alliance, Artists Equity, Phila. Water Color Club, Allied Artists Am. Address: 112 Glenview Ave Wyncote PA 19095

SOLOMON, WILLIAM TARVER, constrn. and mfg. co. exec.; b. Dallas, Aug. 11, 1942; s. Marion Bryant and Margaret (Moore) S.; B.S.C.E., So. Meth. U., 1965; M.B.A. (Baker scholar), Harvard U., 1967; m. Gay Ferguson, Feb. 15, 1964; children—William Tarver, Meredith Margaret. With Austin Industries, Dallas, 1967—, pres., chief exec. officer, 1970—; dir. Republic Nat. Bank, Dallas, Fidelity Union Life Ins. Co. Bd. dirs., chmn. exec. com. So. Meth. U. Found. Sci. and Engrng.; bd. dirs. So. Meth. U. Found. for Bus.; trustee St. Mark's Sch. of Tex., Dallas, Circle Ten council Boy Scouts Am. Mem. Dallas Citizens Council, Dallas Assembly, Salesmanship Club of Dallas, Young Presidents Orgn. (chmn. Dallas chpt. 1977-78), ASCE, Tex. Soc. Profl. Engrs., Dallas C. of C. (dir., mem. exec. com.). Methodist. Clubs: Dallas Country, City. Office: 2949 Stemmons St Dallas TX 75221

SOLOMON, ZACHARY LEON, retail store exec.; b. N.Y.C., July 22, 1934; s. Nathan and Rose S.; B.A., Bklyn. Coll., 1957; M.B.A., N.Y. U.; m. Eve Gerson, Aug. 11, 1957; 3 children. With Abraham & Straus, 1957-72, div. mdse. mgr., 1972; v.p., gen. mdse. mgr. Apparel Buying Assos., Secaucus, N.J., 1972-73; sr. v.p., gen. mdse. mgr. May Co., Los Angeles, 1974-75; exec. v.p. merchandising and sales promotion The Emporium, San Francisco, 1976-77, pres., 1978—. Bd. dirs. Am. Conservatory Theater, Fedn. Jewish Welfare. Mem. San Francisco Retail Dry Goods Assn., Fashion Inst. (dir.). Office: 835 Market St San Francisco CA 94103

SOLOMONS, DAVID, educator; b. London, Eng., Oct. 11, 1912; s. Louis and Hannah (Isaacs) S.; B.Commerce, London Sch. Econs., 1933, D.Sc. in Econs., 1966; m. Kate Miriam Goldschmidt, Sept. 14, 1945; children—Jane, Jonathan. Came to U.S., 1959. Accountant, London, 1936-39, 48. Lectr. accounting London Sch. Econs., 1946-48; reader accounting U. London, 1949-55; prof. accounting U. Bristol (Eng.), 1955-59; prof. U. Pa., Phila., 1959—, chmn. dept. accounting, 1969-75, Arthur Young prof. accounting, 1974—. Vis. asso. prof. U. Calif. at Berkeley, 1954; prof. Imede, Lausanne, Switzerland, 1963-64. Dir. long range inquiry into edn. and tng. for accountancy profession in U.K., Adv. Bd. Accountancy Edn., 1972-74. Bd. regents Inst. Mgmt. Accounting, 1973-76. Served to capt. Royal Army Service Corps, 1939-45. Recipient notable contbrn. to accounting lit. award, Am. Inst. C.P.A.'s, 1970. Fellow Inst. Chartered Accountants Eng. and Wales, Royal Econ. Soc.; mem. Am. Inst. C.P.A.'s (study on establishment accounting principles 1971-72), Am. Accounting Assn. (dir. research 1968-70, pres. 1977-78), Am. Econ. Assn., Nat. Assn. Accountants. Author: Divisional Performance: Measurement and Control, 1965; Studies in Cost Analysis, 1968; Prospectus for a Profession, 1974. Contbr. articles to profl. jours. Home: 205 Elm Ave Swarthmore PA 19081 Office: Wharton School Univ Pa Philadelphia PA 19104

SOLOMONSON, CHARLES D., hospitality co. exec.; b. 1930; B.S., Columbia U., 1954; M.B.A., Harvard U., 1956; m. Sarah B. Auer, 1952; children—Katherine M., Charles W. With Denver Union Stock Yard Co., 1956-60; sec., asst. treas. G. D. Searle & Co., 1960-68; with Jos. Schlitz Brewing Co., 1968-69, treas., 1968-69; v.p. fin. Fairmont Food Co., Omaha, 1969-73, pres., 1973-74, dir., 1972-75; v.p. fin., treas. Hobart Corp., Troy, Ohio, 1975-77, v.p. fin. and Adminstrn., dir., 1977-79; sr. v.p., chief fin. officer Holiday Inns, Inc., Memphis, 1979—; dir. Mut. of Omaha, Protection Mut. Ins. Co. Trustee Nebr. Meth. Hosp., 1973-75, Miami Valley Hosp., Dayton, Ohio, 1977-79. Episcopalian. Home: 2221 Thornwood Ln Memphis TN 38138 Office: 3742 Lamar Ave Memphis TN 38195

SOLOV, ZACHARY, choreographer, ballet artist; b. Phila., Feb. 15, 1923; s. Carl Nathan and Sima (Silnutzer) S.; student Littlefield Ballet Sch., 1937-40, U. of the Dance, 1947. Appeared with Am. Jubilee, N.Y. World's Fair, 1940; tour with Littlefield Ballet, 1941, Am. Ballet, S.A., 1941; with Dance Players, summer quarters, New Hope, Pa., 1942; The Lady Comes Across, N.Y. City, 1942; Ballet Theatre, London, 1946; choreographer ballet master Met. Opera, N.Y. City. Served as staff sgt. A.A.C., 1943-46. Recipient Capezio Dance award. Office: 200 W 58th St New York NY 10019*

SOLOW, MARTIN, advt. exec.; b. Bklyn., May 19, 1920; s. John and Ruth (Nelson) S.; A.B., Franklin and Marshall Coll., 1942; m. Rita Newman, Dec. 12, 1943; children—Ellen, Peter, Michael, Steven. With publicity dept. Greater N.Y. Fund, 1946; asst. editor Nat. CIO News, 1946-47; editor AFL and CIO newspapers, free-lance writer under pseudo Peter Nelson and own name, also ghost writer, 1948-53; asst. to pub. Nation mag., 1953-56; pres. Creative Advt. Promotion Service, N.Y.C., 1956-58, also v.p. Royer and Roger; exec. v.p. Wexton Co. (co. name changed to Solow Wexton, Inc.), N.Y.C., 1958-61, pres., creative dir., 1961-73; v.p., copy chief Kenyon & Eckhardt, N.Y.C., 1973-74; pres. Martin Solow Creative Service, Inc., N.Y.C., 1974—; asso. prof. marketing and advt. Hofstra Coll.; lectr. New Sch., N.Y.C. Served with AUS, 1942-46. Recipient Nat. Ann. award NCCJ. Mem. ACLU, Copy Club N.Y. (past pres.). Author: (with E. Handman) Effective Advertising; Second Love, 1973. Contbr. articles and short stories to various publs. Home: 24 Hemlock Ln Roslyn Heights NY 11577 Office: Martin Solow Creative Service Inc 488 Madison Ave New York City NY 10022

SOLOW, ROBERT MERTON, economist, educator; b. Bklyn., Aug. 23, 1924; s. Milton Henry and Hannah Gertrude (Sarney) S.; B.A., Harvard U., 1947, M.A., 1949, Ph.D., 1951; LL.D., U. Chgo., 1967, Brown U., 1972, U. Warwick, 1976; D.Litt., Williams Coll., 1974, Lehigh U., 1977; Dr. honoris causa, U. Paris, 1975; m. Barbara Lewis, Aug. 19, 1945; children—John Lewis, Andrew Robert, Katherine. Mem. faculty Mass. Inst. Tech., 1949—, prof. econs., 1958—, Inst. prof., 1973—; sr. economist Council Econ. Advisers, 1961-62, cons., 1962-68; cons. RAND Corp., 1952-64; Marshall lectr., fellow commoner Peterhouse, U. Cambridge (Eng.), 1963-64; Eastman vis. prof. Oxford U., 1968-69; sr. fellow Soc. Fellows Harvard U., 1975—; dir. Boston Fed. Res. Bank, chmn., 1979; mem. Pres.'s Commn. on Income Maintenance, 1968-70, Pres.'s Com. on Tech., Automation and Econ. Progress, 1964-65. Bd. dirs., mem. exec. com. Nat. Bur. Econ. Research; trustee Inst. for Advanced Study, Princeton U., 1972-78. Served with AUS, 1942-45. Fellow Center Advanced Study Behavioral Scis., 1957-58; recipient David A. Wells prize Harvard U., 1951. Fellow Am. Acad. Arts and Scis., Brit Acad. (corr.); mem. AAAS (v.p. 1970), Nat. Acad. Scis. (council), Am. Econ. Soc. (exec. com. 1964-66; John Bates Clark medal 1961, v.p. 1968, pres. 1979), Econometric Soc. (pres. 1964, mem. exec. com.). Author: Linear Programming and Economic Analysis, 1958; Capital Theory and the Rate of Return, 1963; The Sources of Unemployment in the United States, 1964; Growth Theory, 1970; Price Expectations and the Behavior of the Price Level, 1970. Home: 528 Lewis Wharf Boston MA 02110 Office: Dept Econs Mass Inst Tech Cambridge MA 02139

SOLOWAY, ALBERT HERMAN, chemist, coll. dean; b. Worcester, Mass., May 29, 1925; s. Bernard and Mollie (Raphaelson) S.; student U.S. Naval Acad., 1945-46; B.S., Worcester Poly. Inst., 1948; Ph.D., U. Rochester, 1951; m. Barbara Berkowicz, Nov. 29, 1953; children—Madeleine Rae, Paul Daniel, Renee Ellen. Postdoctoral fellow Nat. Cancer Inst. at Sloan-Kettering Inst., N.Y.C., 1951-53; research chemist Eastman Kodak Co., Rochester, N.Y., 1953-56; asst. chemist Mass. Gen. Hosp., Boston, 1956-61, asso. chemist, 1961-73; asso. prof. med. chemistry Northeastern U., Boston, 1966-68, prof. medicinal chemistry, chmn. dept., 1968-71, prof. medicinal chemistry and chemistry, chmn. dept. medicinal chemistry and pharmacology, 1971-74, dean Coll. Pharmacy and Allied Health Professions, 1975-77; dean Coll. Pharmacy, prof. medicinal chemistry Ohio State U., Columbus, 1977—; pres. Cambridge (Mass.) Nuclear Corp., 1960-61, v.p., 1961-74, dir., 1960-74. Served with USNR, 1944-45. Mem. Am. Chem. Soc., AAAS, Am. Pharm. Assn., Am. Assn. Coll. Pharmacy, Ohio Pharm. Assn., Am. Assn. Cancer Research. Jewish (trustee temple 1969-77, v.p., 1970-73). Author research medicinal chemistry. Office: 500 W 12th Ave Columbus OH 43210

SOLT, LEO FRANK, educator; b. Waterloo, Iowa, Oct. 12, 1921; s. Harry Earl and Mabel Louise (Schneider) S.; B.A., U. No. Iowa, 1943; postgrad Harvard U., 1943-44; M.A., U. Iowa, 1948; Ph.D. (Lydia Roberts fellow 1948-50, 51), Columbia U., 1955; m. Mary Ellen Bottom, Dec. 22, 1946; children—Catherine Anne, Susan Jane. Teaching asso. U. Iowa, 1947-48; instr. U. Mass., 1952-55; asst. prof. history Ind. U., 1955-60, asso. prof., 1960-64, prof., 1964—, also dean Grad. Sch.; vis. lectr. U. Wis., 1960; vis. prof. Moray House Sch. Edn., Edinburgh, 1972, 74; pres. Midwest Conf. on Brit. Studies, 1968-70. Served to lt. U.S. Navy, 1943-46. Guggenheim fellow, 1961-62; Folger Library fellow, 1966; Henry E. Huntington Library fellow, 1967-79; Am. Philos. Assn. grantee, 1958; Social Sci. Research Council grantee, 1959. Mem. Am. Hist. Assn. (v.p. research); Am. Soc. Church History, Conf. of British Studies. Unitarian. Author: Saints in Arms, Puritanism and Democracy in Cromwell's Army, 1959. Home: 836 Sheridan Rd Bloomington IN 47401 Office: Kirkwood Hall 111 Indiana University Bloomington IN 47406

SOLTI, GEORG, conductor; b. Budapest, Hungary, Oct. 21, 1912; s. Mor Stern and Theres (Rosenbaum) S.; Brit. citizen, 1972; ed. Budapest Music High Sch.; Mus.D., Leeds U., 1971, Oxford U., 1972, DePaul U., Yale U., 1974, Harvard U., 1979; m. Hedi Oechsli, Oct. 29, 1946; m. 2d, Anne Valerie Pitts, Nov. 11, 1967; 2 daus. Musical asst. Budapest Opera House, 1930-39; pianist, Switzerland, 1939-45; gen. music dir. Munich (Germany) State Opera, 1946-52, Frankfurt (Germany) City Opera, 1952-60; mus. dir. Royal Opera House Covent Garden, London, 1961-71, Chgo. Symphony Orch., 1969—, Orchestre de Paris, 1972-75; prin. condr. and artistic dir. London Philharmonic, 1979—; pianist Concours Internat., Geneva, 1942; guest condr. various orchs. including N.Y. Philharmonic, Vienna Philharmonic, Berlin Philharmonic, London Symphony Orch., New Philharmonia, Los Angeles Philharmonic; condr. Salzburg Festival, Edinburgh and Glyndebourne Festivals, Ravinia Festival, Chgo., Vienna State Opera and Philharmonic, N.Y. Philharmonic Orch., Amsterdam, Concertgebouw, orchs. in San Francisco, Hollywood, Los Angeles, St. Louis; Met. Opera condr. concert tours to Europe, 1971, 74, Japan, 1977; prin. guest condr. Paris Opera Bicentennial Tour, 1976; rec. artist for London Records. Decorated Great Cross of the German Republic; comdr. Order Brit. Empire, knight comdr. Order Brit. Empire; comdr. Legion of Honor (France); recipient grand prix du Disque Mondiale, 1959, 62, 63, 64, 66; Grammy award (14). Mailing address: care Chgo Symphony Orch 220 S Michigan Ave Chicago IL 60604

SOLTIS, ANDREW EDEN, JR., reporter; b. Hazelton, Pa., May 28, 1947; s. Andrew E. and Bette Katherine (Eden) S.; B.A. cum laude, Coll. City N.Y., 1969. Copyboy, N.Y. Post, part-time 1967-69, reporter, 1969—, chess columnist, 1972—. U.S. intercollegiate chess champion, 1969; mem. U.S. team World Student Chess Olympiade, 1967-72; winner Internat. Chess Tournament, Reggio Emilia, Italy, 1972, N.Y., 1977, 78. Republican. Methodist. Club: Marshall Chess (v.p.). Author: The Best Chess Games of Boris Spassky, 1969; (with F. Reinfeld) Morphy Chess Masterpieces, 1973; (with A. Bisguier) American Chess Masters—From Morphy to Fischer, 1974; The Great Chess Tournaments and their Stories, 1975; The Art of Defense in Chess, 1975; Pawn Structure Chess, 1977. Home: 69 Fifth Ave New York City NY 10003 Office: New York Post 210 South St New York City NY 10002

SOLTIS, JONAS FRANCIS, educator; b. Norwalk, Conn., June 11, 1931; s. Jonas John and Margaret Irene S.; B.A. with distinction in Philosophy, U. Conn., 1956; M.A.T. (fellow), Wesleyan U., 1958; Ed.D. (fellow), Harvard U., 1964; m. Nancy Lynn Schaal, Sept. 10, 1955; children—Susan L. Soltis Shaw, Robin L. Instr. philosophy, history U. Conn., Waterbury, 1958-60; instr. edn. Wesleyan U., Middletown, Conn., 1962-64; asst. prof. philosophy and edn. Tchrs. Coll., Columbia U., 1964-68, asso. prof., 1968-71, prof., 1971-78, William Heard Kilpatrick prof., 1978—, dir. Tchrs. Coll. div. instrn., 1972-76, dir. div. philosophy and social scis., 1977-79. Served with USAF, 1950-54. Columbia Council for Research in Humanities research fellow, 1966; U.S. Office of Edn. postdoctoral research fellow, 1967-68. Mem. Am. Philos. Assn., Philosophy of Edn. Soc. (pres. 1974-75), Am. Ednl. Research Assn., Nat. Soc. for Study of Edn., Phi Beta Kappa. Author: Seeing, Knowing and Believing: A Study in the Language of Visual Perception, 1966; Moral Education, 1973; An Introduction to the Analysis of Educational Concepts, 1978. Office: Box 202 Tchrs Coll Columbia U New York NY 10027

SOLTOW, JAMES HAROLD, historian, educator; b. Chgo., July 1, 1924; s. Lawrence Milton and Gladys Louise (Combs) S.; A.B., Dickinson Coll., 1948; A.M., U. Pa., 1949, Ph.D., 1954; m. Martha Jane Stough, Sept. 14, 1946. Lectr. Hunter Coll., N.Y.C., 1952-55; research asso. Colonial Williamsburg, Va., 1955-56; instr. history

Russell Sage Coll., Troy, N.Y., 1956-58; asst. to full prof. history Mich. State U., East Lansing, 1959—. Served with AUS, 1943-46. Bus. history fellow Harvard, 1958-59; Fulbright fellow U. Louvain (Belgium), 1965-66. Mem. Am. Hist. Assn., Orgn. Am. Historians, Econ. History Assn. Author: Economic Role of Williamsburg, 1965; Origins of Small Business, 1965. Contbr. articles to profl. publs. Home: 520 Wildwood Dr East Lansing MI 48823 Office: Dept History Mich State U East Lansing MI 48824

SOLZBACHER, WILLIAM ALOYSIUS, linguist, lectr., ret. govt. ofcl.; b. Honnef, Germany, Feb. 1, 1907; s. Carl and Josepha (Schmitz) S.; student U. Bonn, 1926-28; Ph.D., U. Cologne, 1931; m. Regina Reiff, July 27, 1931; children—Josephine, (Mrs. Patrick Evetts Kennon), Irene (Sister Irene of Maryknoll), Regina (Mrs. Richard Oliver Rouse), Eve (Mrs. Richard D. Cuthbert). Came to U.S., 1941, naturalized, 1947. Interpreter, organizer internat. confs., 1925-39; founder, editor La Juna Batalanto (internat. youth mag. in Esperanto), 1926-34; faculty mem. Am. Peoples Coll. in Europe, Oetz, Tyrol, 1932-37; lecture tours, Europe, 1925-40, U.S., 1933; exiled by Nazis; free lance writer, journalist, lectr. in Luxembourg and Belgium, 1933-40; escaped from Nazi-occupied Belgium and France, 1940; asso. editor Cath. Intercontinental Press, N.Y.C., 1942-50, treas., 1947-48, v.p., 1948-49; asst. prof. history and polit. sci. Coll. Mt. St. Vincent, 1950-51; fgn. lang. editor, chief program schedule sect. Voice of Am., Dept. State, 1951-53; ednl. dir. study tours ASSIST, 1953-54; chief Monitoring Staff, Voice of Am., 1954-67, in charge programs in Esperanto, 1960-61, policy officer for Latin Am. and Europe, 1967-77, World Congresses Sociology, Liege, 1953, Amsterdam, 1956, Stresa, 1959, Washington, 1962, Varna, Bulgaria, 1970, World Esperanto Congress, Zagreb, 1953, Copenhagen, 1956, Brussels, 1960, The Hague, 1964, Tokyo, 1965, Madrid, 1968, Helsinki, 1969, London, 1971, Portland, 1972, Belgrade, 1973, Copenhagen, 1975, Athens, 1976, Reykjavik, Iceland, 1977, Varna, Bulgaria, 1978, Stockholm, 1980. Mem. Am. Sociol. Assn., Esperanto Assn. N.A. (past pres.), Internat. Commn. Esperanto and Sociol. (chmn.), World Esperanto Acad. Speakers Research Com. UN, Acad. Political Sci., Modern Lang. Assn., Linguistic Soc. Am., The Polynesian Soc. (Wellington, New Zealand), Internat. Platform Assn., Soc. Sci. Study Religion, Am. Hist. Assn., Am. Acad. Polit. and Social Sci., Am. Assn. Advancement of Slavic Studies. Author: Walther Rathenau als Sozialphilosoph, 1932; Devant Hitler et Mussolini, 1933; Pie Xi contre les Idoles, 1939; Rome en de Afgoden van Onzen Tijd, 1940; Esperanto: The World Interlanguage (with George Alan Connor and Doris T. Connor), 1948, 3d edit., 1966; Say It In Esperanto, 1958. Contbr. encys. Home: 6030 Broad St Washington DC 20016

SOLZHENITSYN, ALEXANDER, author; b. Kislorodsk, Russia, Dec. 11, 1918; corr. student in philology Moscow Inst. History, Philosophy and Lit., 1939-4; degree in math. and physics U. Rostov, 1941; Litt.D., Harvard U., 1978; m. Natalya Reshetovskaya (div.). Imprisoned under Premier Joseph Stalin on unnamed polit. charges, 1945-53; exiled to Siberia, 1953; wrote and taught; freed from exile, 1956; after release taught at secondary sch. in Ryazan; exiled from USSR, 1974; now living in U.S.A. Arty. officer Russian Army, World War II. Recipient Nobel prize for lit., 1970. Mem. Am. Acad. Arts and Scis. Author: (novel) One Day in the Life of Ivan Denisovich, 1962; We Never Make Mistakes, 1963; The First Circle, 1968; The Cancer Ward, 1968; Stories and Prose Poems, 1971; August 1914, 1972; The Gulag Archipelago, 1918-1956, Part I, 1974, Part II, 1975, Part III, 1976; The Oak and the Calf, 1975; Letter to the Soviet Leaders, 1975; From under the Rubble, 1976; Detente: Prospects for Democracy and Dictatorship, 1976; Warning to the West, 1976; (novel) Lenin in Zurich, 1976; The Nobel Lecture, 1973; (narrative poem) Prussian Nights, 1977; (Harvard U. commencement address) A World Split Apart, 1978; (plays) Love-Girl and the Innocent, 1970; Candle in the Wind, 1974. Address: care Harper and Row Publs Inc 10 E 53d St New York NY 10022*

SOMERS, ANNE RAMSAY, educator; b. Memphis, Sept. 9, 1913; d. Henry Ashton and Amanda Vick (Woolfolk) Ramsay; B.A., Vassar Coll., 1935; postgrad. U. N.C., 1939-40; D.Sc. (hon.), Med. Coll. Wis., 1975; m. Herman Miles Somers, Aug. 31, 1947; children—Sara Ramsay, Margaret Ramsay. Ednl. dir. Internat. Ladies Garment Workers Union, 1937-42; labor economist U.S. Dept. Labor, 1943-46; research asso. Haverford Coll., 1957-63; research asso. indsl. relations sect. Princeton, 1964—; prof. community and family medicine Coll. Medicine and Dentistry N.J.-Rutgers Med. Sch., Piscataway, N.J., 1971—; dir. Office Consumer Health Edn., Coll. Medicine and Dentistry N.J., 1972-74; vice chmn. Adv. Council on Edn. for Health, 1978—; dir. Nat. Fund for Med. Edn., 1977—, Nat. Center for Health Edn., 1977—; cons. in health econs., health edn., hosp. adminstrn., related areas. Bd. visitors Duke U. Med. Center, 1972-77. Recipient Elizur Wright award Am. Risk and Ins. Assn., 1962. Fellow Am. Coll. Hosp. Adminstrs. (hon.), Coll. Physicians Phila. (hon.); mem. Inst. Medicine of Nat. Acad. Scis., Indsl. Relations Research Assn., N.J. Pub. Health Assn., N.J. Hosp. Assn., Soc. Tchrs. Family Medicine (hon.). Author: Hospital Regulation: The Dilemma of Public Policy, 1969; Health Care in Transition: Directions for the Future, 1971; (with H.M. Somers) Workmen's Compensation: The Prevention, Rehabilitation and Financing of Occupational Disability, 1954, Medicare and the Hospitals, 1967, Doctors, Patients and Health Insurance, 1961, Health and Health Care: Policies in Perspective, 1977. Home: 31 Scott Ln Princeton NJ 08540 Office: Coll Medicine and Dentistry NJ-Rutgers Med Sch Piscataway NJ 08854

SOMERS, CARIN ALMA, librarian; b. Frankfurt/Main, Ger., Mar. 18, 1934; d. Josef and Helen Josephine (Badham) Stein; B.A., Newton (Mass.) Coll. Sacred Heart, 1955; M.A., Dalhousie U., Halifax, N.S., Can., 1956; B.L.S., U. Toronto, 1961; m. Frank George Somers, Aug. 23, 1958. Registrar, then lectr. French, St. Mary's U., Halifax, 1956-60; with Halifax City Regional Library, 1958-64, librarian tech. services, 1961-64; asst. librarian, then chief librarian Halifax County Regional Library, 1964-73; supr. pub. libraries N.S. Provincial Library, Halifax, 1973-74, dir., 1974—; occasional lectr. Dalhousie U. Sch. Library Service. Decorated Gov. General's medal, Can. (Queen Elizabeth II) Silver Jubilee medal; grantee Province N.S., 1960-61, French Govt., 1956. Mem. Canadian (2d v.p. 1974-75), Atlantic Provinces (past pres.), N.S. library assns., N.S. Bird Soc., Canadian Nature Fedn. Roman Catholic. Club: Royal N.S. Yacht Squadron. Contbr. articles to profl. jours. Home: Box 772 Armdale PO Halifax NS B3L 4K5 Canada Office: NS Provincial Library 5250 Spring Garden Rd Halifax NS B3J 1E8 Canada

SOMERS, GEORGE FREDRICK, plant physiologist; b. Garland, Utah, July 9, 1914; s. George Fredrick and Elizabeth (Sorenson) S.; B.S., Utah State U., 1935; B.A. with honors, Oxford U., 1938, B.Sc., 1939; Ph.D., Cornell U., 1942; m. Beulah Rich Morgan, June 24, 1939; children—Ralph M., Steven J., Gary F. Faculty, Cornell U., 1941-51, asso. prof. biochemistry, 1949-51; plant physiologist U.S. Dept. Agr., 1944-51; asso. dir. Del. Agrl. Expt. Sta., 1951-59; faculty U. Del., Newark 1951—, asso. dean Coll. Agr., 1954-59, chmn. dept. biol. scis., 1959-71, H. Fletcher Brown prof. biology, 1962—; vis. prof. U. Philippines, 1958-59. Union Pacific scholar, 1930, Rhodes scholar, 1936 Henry Strong Denison fellow, 1939. H.C. fellow AAAS; mem. Am. Inst. Biol. Scis., Am. Soc. Plant Physiology, Bot. Soc. Am., Sigma Xi, Phi Kappa Phi. Author: (with J.B. Sumner) Chemistry and Methods of Enzymes, 3d edit., 1953; Laboratory Experiments in Biological Chemistry, 2d edit., 1949; also articles. Editor biochem. sect. Chem. Abstracts, 1968-75. Research on influence of environ. factors on vitamin C content of vegetables; viscoelasticity in plant tissues as related to cell wall properties; chem. properties of algal cell walls; halophytes as food plants. Home: 22 Minquil Dr Newark DE 19713

SOMERS, HAROLD MILTON, economist, educator; b. Toronto, Ont., Can., Sept. 30, 1915; s. Joseph and Elizabeth (Behr) S.; came to U.S., 1937, naturalized, 1947; B.Com., U. Toronto, 1937; Ph.D., U. Calif., 1942; student U. Chgo., 1940; LL.B., U. Buffalo, 1956; m. Claire Rosen, June 12, 1939; children—Joan, Margery, Warren. Teaching asst. in econs. U. Calif., 1937-39; research asst. govt. fin. U. Chgo., 1940; fellow Social Sci. Research Council, 1940-41; mem. research staff Brookings Instn., summer 1941; teaching fellow in econs., U. Mich., 1941-42, instr. in econs., summer 1942; asst. prof. econs. U. Buffalo, 1942-45, asso. prof., 1945-46, prof., 1946-61, dean. sch. bus. adminstrn., 1947-61, lectr. U. Buffalo Sch. Law, 1957-59; prof. econs. U. Calif. at Los Angeles, 1961—, chmn. dept. econs., 1961-66, dean div. social scis., 1967-70; vis. prof. econs. U. Calif. at Berkeley, summer 1947, Columbia, summer 1954, U. B.C., summer 1953; vis. prof. law Yale Law Sch., 1968; econ. affairs officer in fiscal div. UN, summer 1950, cons., 1950-53; cons. to research div. O.P.A., 1943, arbitrator Fed. Conciliation and Mediation Service, 1950—, Am. Arbitration Assn., 1955—, N.Y. State Bd. Mediation, 1952-61, Los Angeles County Employee Relations Commn. Arbitration, 1970-73; cons. U.S. Office Edn., Bur. Higher Edn., 1965-69; mem. Personnel Security bd. AEC, 1957-59; cons. N.Y. State Legis. Com. on Constn., 1957- 58; economist N.Y. State Dept. Commerce, summer 1944, cons., 1944-45; tech. adviser to mayor's full employment com. City of Buffalo, 1945-46, cons. to budget div., 1946-47; chmn. exec. com., fin. subcom. Capital Expenditures Com., 1956-57; chmn. N.Y. State Minimum Wage Bd. for Restaurant Industry, 1956-58; mem seminar adv. com. Fed. Res. Bank, N.Y., 1952; editorial cons. Blakiston Co., Phila., 1947-52; cons. Employment and Youth Opportunities Agy., Los Angeles, 1966; cons. Calif. Adv. Commn. on Tax Reform, 1968. Mem. Am., N.Y. State bar assns., AAUP, Am. (nominating com. 1969, 70), Western econ. assns., Econometric Soc. (session chmn. 1947, 51, program chmn. 1949), Am. Fin. Assn. (dir. pub. fin. 1969-71), Nat. Tax Assn. (mem. sales tax com. 1975-77), Phi Beta Kappa, Alpha Kappa Psi, Beta Gamma Sigma. Author: Public Finance and National Income, 1949; (with others) Industrial Conflict, 1939; American Policies of Postwar Readjustment (monograph), 1944; (with others) Growth of the American Economy, 1944, rev. edit., 1951; (with others) Readings in Business Cycle Theory, 1944; (with others) Readings in the Theory of Income Distribution, 1946; (with others) Taxation and Business Concentration, 1952; (with others) Corporate Tax Problems, 1952; co-author: Taxation of Corporate Income in California, 1964; editor: Estate Taxes and Business Management, 1957; (with others) Taxation of Property in California, 1964; Public Finance and Welfare, 1966; A Search for City Revenue, 1968; (monographs) The Sales Tax, 1964; Capital Gains, Death and Gift Taxation, 1965; editor Western Econ. Jour., 1966-69; editorial bd. Am. Econ. Rev., 1952-54; contbr. articles to Ency. Brit. and econ. and law jours. Home: 152 N Kenter Ave Los Angeles CA 90049 Office: Dept Econs U Calif Los Angeles CA 90024

SOMERS, HARRY STEWART, composer; b. Toronto, Ont., Can., Sept. 11, 1925; s. James Russel and Ruth S.; studied piano and theory with Dorothy Hornfelt, Toronto, 1939-41; studied piano with Reginald Godden, Royal Conservatory Music, Toronto, 1941-43, student theory and composition with John Weinzweig, 1942-43, 46-49, student theory and composition with Weldon Kilburn, 1946-49; studied piano with E. Robert Schmitz, Denver and San Francisco, summers 1947-48; studied composition under Darius Milhaud, Paris, 1949-50; m. Catherine Mackie (dec. 1963). Wrote first string quartet at age 17; formerly worked as taxi driver, music copyist; free-lance composer; has worked as commentator and/or pianist in numerous CBC radio and TV prodns.; composed music for orch., solo instruments, chamber music, piano, voice, string quartet, choir, opera, and ballet, including Movement for Orchestra (Cava dei Tirreni Summer Festival spo. Critic's award 1965). Served with RCAF, 1943-45. Decorated companion Order of Can.; Can. Council sr. arts fellow, 1960. Mem. Can. League Composers.*

SOMERS, HERMAN MILES, educator; b. Bklyn., Apr. 11, 1911; s. Morris and Edna (Chalefont) S.; B.S., U. Wis., 1933, Ph.M., 1934; M.A., Harvard U., 1944, Ph.D., 1947; m. Anne Ramsay, Aug. 31, 1946; children—Sara Ramsay, Margaret Ramsay. Chief statistician Wis. Pub. Welfare Dept., 1934-39; sr. economist Nat. Resources Planning Bd., 1940-41; research asso. com. social security Social Sci. Research Council, 1941-42; sr. economist WPB, 1942; economist Office War Moblzn. and Recon., 1946-47; vis. lectr. govt. Harvard, 1947-48; prof., chmn. dept. polit. sci. Haverford Coll., 1948-63; prof. politics and pub. affairs Princeton, 1963—; vis. prof. N.Y. Sch. Social Work, Columbia U., 1954, 55, 58, U. Calif. at Berkeley, 1956-57, Harvard, summers 1950, 52, 58, U. Wis., summer 1955; vis. research prof. Brookings Instn., 1960-61. Cons. numerous U.S. govt. and state agys. and orgns.; counsellor ILO, Geneva, 1962-63; trustee Inter-Univ. Case Program, 1955—; adv. council on social security HEW, 1963-65; mem. tech. bd. Milbank Meml. Fund, 1970-74, 75-78; chmn. Employment Security Council of N.J., 1964-67. Littauer fellow Harvard, 1937-38, 39-40; fellow Fund for Advancement Edn., 1951-52; Fulbright sr. research fellow U.K., 1955-56; sr. research fellow Social Sci. Research Council, 1960-61; Ford Found. research prof. govtl. affairs, 1965-66. Mem. Pres.'s Task Force on Health and Social Security, 1961, Pres.'s Task Force on Health Legislation, 1964, Health Ins. Benefits Adv. Council of Social Security Adminstrn., 1968-72. Trustee, Hosp. Service Plan N.J., 1964—, Coll. Medicine and Dentistry N.J., 1970-76; bd. mgrs. Haverford Coll., 1975—. Recipient Elizur Wright award Am. Risk and Ins. Assn., 1962; Justin Ford Kimball award Am. Hosp. Assn., 1973; Norman Welch Meml. award Nat. Assn. Blue Shield Plans, 1977. Hon. fellow Am. Coll. Hosp. Adminstrs.; mem. Indsl. Relations Research Assn. (exec. bd. 1959-62), Inst. Medicine, Nat. Acad. Scis., Nat. Acad. Pub. Adminstrn., Phi Beta Kappa (hon.). Club: Cosmos (Washington). Author: Presidential Agency: OWMR, 1950; Workmen's Compensation (with Anne R. Somers), 1954; Doctor, Patients and Health Insurance, 1961; Medicare and the Hospitals (with Anne R. Somers), 1967; The Federal Government Service (with others), 1954; (with Anne R. Somers) Health and Health Care, 1977; also articles. Mem. editorial bd. Health and Soc.-Milbank Meml. Fund Quar., 1971-75. Home: 31 Scott Ln Princeton NJ 08540

SOMERS, LOUIS ROBERT, food co. exec.; b. Pontiac, Mich., Aug. 8, 1926; s. Jay G. and Maggie (Gee) S.; B.S., Mich. State U., 1950; m. Rynda Horinga, July 28, 1950; children—Linda, Laurie. With Kellogg Co., Battle Creek, Mich., 1955—, controller Kellogg Internat., 1967-70, 72-75, fin. dir. Kellogg Gt. Britain Ltd., 1970-72, v.p. fin., treas. Kellogg Co., 1975—. Chmn., Calhoun County chpt. ARC, 1968-69, 76-78; pres. bd. trustees 1st Presbyn. Ch., Battle Creek, 1969, 75; chmn. citizens com. Pennfield Sch. Dist., 1974-75; chmn. budget rev. com. Battle Creek Area United Fund, 1960; chmn. fin. com. Girl Scouts U.S.A., 1965-68. Served with USAF, 1951-55. Office: Kellogg Co Battle Creek MI 49015

SOMERS, STEVEN MARK, dept. store exec.; b. Bklyn., Aug. 4, 1939; s. Al M. and Ann Somers; student U. Bridgeport, 1957-59; B.A., Syracuse U., 1961; m. Susan R. Halpern, Feb. 8, 1964; children—Lisa, David, Jodi. Dept. mgr. Abraham & Straus, Bklyn., 1964-68; br. divisional mgr. and buyer Gimbels, N.Y.C., 1968-74; with Burdine's of Fla., Miami, 1974-79, v.p. merchandising, v.p., gen. mgr. merchandising, 1978-79; pres., chief exec. officer I. Magnin, San Francisco, 1979—. Sec. chmn. United Way, Miami. Home: 2536 Butternut Dr Hillsborough CA 94010 Office: 135 Stockton St San Francisco CA 94108

SOMERS, SUZANNE (SUZANNE MAHONEY), actress; b. San Bruno, Calif., Oct. 16; d. Frank Mahoney: B.A., Lone Mountain Coll.; m. Bruce Somers, Sr. (div.); 1 son, Bruce Somers; m. 2d, Alan Hamel, Nov. 19, 1977. Model; bit parts in movies: Bullitt, 1968, Daddy's Gone A-Hunting, 1969, Fools, 1970, Magnum Force, 1973; speaking movie debut in American Graffiti, 1973, also appeared in Billy Jack Goes to Washington, Yesterday's Hero, 1979; TV movie Sky Heist; appeared in summer stock prodns.: Guys and Dolls, Annie Get Your Gun, The Sound of Music, The Boyfriend; regular TV talk show Mantrap, on TV game shows Anniversary Game, High Rollers; regular Canadian TV series The Sensuous Man and Going, Going Gone (also co-host); regular TV series Three's Company, 1977—; other TV appearances include: Tonight Show, Merv Griffin Show, Lotsa Luck, The Rockford Files, The Streets of San Francisco; co-host The National Love, Sex and Marriage Test, 1978. Mem. AFTRA. Author: (poetry) Touch Me; (poetry) Touch Me Again; Some People Live More Than Others. Office: care ABC 1330 Ave of Americas New York NY 10019*

SOMERSET, HAROLD RICHARD, agribus. co. exec.; b. Woodbury, Conn., Sept. 25, 1935; s. Harold Kitchener and Margaret Mary (Roche) S.; B.S., U.S. Naval Acad., 1957; B.C.E., Rensselaer Poly. Inst., Troy, N.Y., 1959; LL.B., Harvard U., 1967; m. Marjory Deborah Ghiselin, June 22, 1957; children—Timothy Craig, Paul Alexander. Commd. ensign U.S. Navy, 1957, advanced through grades to lt., 1961; service in U.S. and Hawaii; resigned, 1964; admitted to Mass. bar, 1967, Hawaii bar, 1973; with firm Goodwin, Procter & Hoar, Boston, 1967-72; corp. counsel Alexander & Baldwin, Inc., Honolulu, 1972-74, v.p., gen. counsel, 1974-78, group v.p.-sugar, 1978-79, exec. v.p.-agr., 1979—; pres., dir. McBryde Sugar Co., Ltd., East Maui Irrigation Co., Ltd., Kahului Trucking & Storage, Inc.; dir. Calif. and Hawaiian Sugar Co.; dir., mem. exec. com. Alexander & Baldwin Agribus. Corp. Mem. Hawaiian Sugar Planters Assn. (dir.), Am., Mass., Hawaii bar assns. Club: Oahu Country (Honolulu). Home: 4818 Kahala Ave Honolulu HI 96816 Office: 822 Bishop St Honolulu HI 96813

SOMERSET, JOSEPH BERNARD, broadcasting exec.; b. Boston, May 25, 1928; s. Samuel and Etta (Goldstein) S.; student Bowdoin Coll., 1945-46, Boston U., 1956; m. Weymouth S. Sallinger, Apr. 14, 1952; 1 son, Matthew James. Program dir. McLendon Corp., Houston and San Francisco, 1957-59, Sta. WPRO, Providence, 1959-61; with Capital Cities Broadcasting Corp., N.Y.C., 1962-74, sr. v.p., 1968-74; broadcast cons., 1974—; pres. Mercury Broadcasting Corp., 1975—. Trustee Churchill Sch., N.Y.C., 1973—. Home: Church Hill Rd Washington Depot CT 06794 Office: PO Box 205 Washington Depot CT 06794

SOMERVILLE, ORMOND, lawyer; b. Tuscaloosa, Ala., July 20, 1904; s. Ormond and Elizabeth R. (Edgar) S.; B.S., U. Ala., 1924, LL.B., 1926; m. Susan C. Porter, Oct. 24, 1934; children—Jane Devereux (Mrs. O. Randall Braman), Ormond III; m. 2d, Martha McDavid Perry, Apr. 3, 1948; children—James, Martha Hays. Admitted to Ala. bar, 1926, since practiced in Birmingham; mem. firm Lange, Simpson, Robinson & Somerville, 1931—; counsel Birmingham Bd. Edn., 1951—, Samford U., 1973—; counsel, sec. Birmingham Indsl. Water Bd., 1959—; sec., dir. Baggett Transp. Co.; dir. Birmingham Mfg. Co. Asso. justice Ala. Supreme Ct., 1972. Mem. Am., Ala. bar assns., Soc. Colonial Wars, Sigma Nu, Phi Delta Phi. Clubs: Mountain Brook Country, Redstone (Birmingham). Presbyn. (trustee). Home: 3336 Dell Rd Birmingham AL 35223 Office: First Ala Bank Bldg Birmingham AL 35203

SOMERVILLE, THEODORE ELKIN, lawyer; b. N.Y.C., May 12, 1940; s. Gilbert and Eileen Sarah (Elkin) S.; A.B., Brown U., 1961; LL.B., Yale U., 1964. Admitted to N.Y. bar, 1966; asso. firm Donovan, Leisure, Newton & Irvine, N.Y.C., 1964-73; v.p., gen. counsel Alleghany Corp., N.Y.C., 1973—; dir. Investors Syndicate Title & Guaranty Corp. Mem. Am. Bar Assn., Assn. Bar City N.Y. Republican. Episcopalian. Club: Yale (N.Y.C.). Home: 870 UN Plaza New York NY 10017 Office: 350 Park Ave New York NY 10022

SOMERVILLE, WILLIAM B., lawyer; b. Cumberland, Md., Sept. 6, 1916; A.B., Duke, 1938; LL.B., U. Md., 1946. Admitted to Md. bar, 1942; now partner firm Smith, Somerville & Case, Balt. Served with USMCR, 1942-45. Fellow Am. Coll. Trial Lawyers; mem. Am., Md. bar assns., Bar Assn. Balt. (pres. 1968-69), Internat. Assn. Ins. Counsel, Omicron Delta Kappa, Tau Kappa Alpha. Clubs: Merchants, Center, Lawyers' Round Table, Wednesday Law. Address: 100 Light St Baltimore MD 21202

SOMIT, ALBERT, univ. adminstr.; b. Chgo., Oct. 25, 1919; s. Samuel and Mary (Rosenblum) S.; A.B., U. Chgo., 1941, Ph.D., 1947; m. Leyla D. Shapiro, Aug. 31, 1947 (div. June 1978); children—Scott H., Jed L.; m. Nora Post, Aug. 25, 1979. Prof. polit. philosophy N.Y. U., 1945-65; chmn. dept. polit. sci. State U. N.Y. at Buffalo, 1966-69, exec. v.p., 1970—, acting pres., 1976-77; fellow Netherlands Inst. Advanced Study, 1978-79; Nimitz prof. polit. philosophy U.S. Naval War Coll., 1961-62. Served with AUS, 1950-52. Author: (with Joseph Tanenhaus) The Development of American Political Science: From Burgess to Behavioralism, 1967; (with Tanenhaus) American Political Science: A Profile of A Discipline, 1964; Political Science and the Study of the Future, 1974; Biology and Politics: Recent Explorations, 1976; (with others) The Literature of Biopolitics 1963-1977, 1978. Home: SUNY 503 Capen Hall Buffalo NY 14260

SOMJEN, GEORGE GUSTAV, physiologist; b. Budapest, Hungary, May 2, 1929; s. Laszlo and Margit (Ranschburg) S.; came to U.S., 1962; grad. U. Amsterdam Med. Faculty, 1956; M.D., U. N.Z., 1962; m. Eva Herman, 1952 (dec. 1974); children—Monika, Maria, Georgette, Evelyn; m. Amalia Deutsch, 1976. Research asst. Pharmaco-therapeutic Lab., U. Amsterdam, 1953-56; lectr., sr. lectr. dept. physiology U. Otago, Dunedin, N.Z., 1956-62; prof. physiology Duke U., Durham, N.C., 1963—; cons. Nat. Inst. Environ. Health Scis. Recipient research grants NIH, 1964—. Mem. Am. Physiol. Soc., Am. Soc. Pharmacology and Exptl. Therapeutics, Am. EEG Soc. Author: Sensory Coding in the Mammalian Nervous System, 1972; editor: Neurophysiology Studied in Man, 1972. Office: Dept Physiology Duke U Durham NC 27710

SOMMER, ALPHONSE ADAM, JR., lawyer; b. Portsmouth, Ohio, Apr. 7, 1924; s. A.A. and Adelaide (Orlett) S.; A.B., U. Notre Dame, 1948; LL.B., Harvard, 1950; LL.D., Cleve. State U., 1976; m. Storrow Cassin, June 13, 1951; children—Susan, Edward, Nancy. Admitted to Ohio bar, 1951, D.C. bar, 1976; asso. Calfee, Halter, Calfee, Griswold & Sommer, Cleve., 1950-60, partner, 1960-73; commr. SEC, 1973-76;

partner firm Wilmer, Cutler & Pickering, Washington, 1977—. Served with AUS, 1943-46. Contbr. articles to profl. jours. Home: 7105 Heathwood Ct Bethesda MD 20034 Office: 1666 K St NW Washington DC 20036

SOMMER, CHARLES H., chem. co. exec.; b. St. Louis, Sept. 24, 1910; s. Charles Henry and Mary (Steele) S.; B.S. in Chemistry, U. Ariz., 1933; m. Julia McCalla, May 2, 1978; 1 son, Charles Scudder. With Monsanto Co., St. Louis, 1934—, successively asst. gen. mgr. sales, asst. gen. mgr. Organic Chem. div., gen. mgr. Merrimac div., v.p., gen. mgr. organic chems. div., 1954-59, exec. v.p. of co., dir., 1959-60, pres. of co., dir., chmn. exec. com., 1960-68, chmn., 1968-75; dir. St. Louis Union Trust Co., Trans World Airlines. Trustee, St. Louis U. Mem. Am. Chem. Soc., Am. Inst. Chem. Engrs., Bus. Council. Clubs: St. Louis, St. Louis Country; Log Cabin; Links (N.Y.C.). Home: 942 Tirrill Farms Rd Saint Louis MO 63124 Office: 7811 Carondelet Ave Saint Louis MO 63105

SOMMER, ELKE (SCHLETZ, ELKE), actress; b. Berlin, Germany, Nov. 5, 1941; attended schs. in Erlangen, No. Bavaria and Eng., then Univ. in Erlangen; m. Joe Hyams, 1964. At age 17 was au pair girl in Eng., for 7 months; entered films in Germany, 1958, and then made films in Germany, France, Spain, and Italy, including: Friend of the Jaguar, Traveling Luxury, Heaven and Cupid, Ship of the Dead; made debut in Brit. films in 1960; films since 1960 include: Don't Bother to Knock, 1960 (Eng.); The Victors, 1963 (Eng.); The Prize, 1963 (U.S.); A Shot in the Dark, 1964; The Art of Love, 1965; Four Kinds of Love, 1965 (Italy); The Money Trap, 1965 (U.S.); The Oscar, 1966 (U.S.); Boy, Did I Get a Wrong Number, 1966; Deadlier than the Male, 1966 (Eng.); The Venetian Affair, 1966 (U.S.); The Corrupt Ones (The Peking Medallion), 1967; The Wicked Dreams of Paula Schultz, 1968; Frontier Hellcat, 1966; They Came to Rob Las Vegas, 1969; The Wrecking Crew, 1969; Baron Blood, 1972; Percy, 1971; Zeppelin, 1971; Ten Little Indians, 1975; Lisa and the Devil; The House of Exorcism, 1976; It's Not the Size that Counts, 1979; The Swiss Conspiracy, 1979; The Double Maguffin, 1979; The Prisoner of Zenda, 1979; TV movie Top of the Hill, 1979. Office: care George Durgom 9255 Sunset Blvd Los Angeles CA 90069

SOMMER, FRANK HENRY, III, librarian, archeologist, author, educator; b. Newark, July 30, 1922; s. George R. and Abigail Woodruff (Van Horn) S.; B.A., Yale U., 1943, Ph.D., 1950; diploma gen. archeology Cambridge U., 1948. Keeper folk art Wintherthur (Del.) Mus., 1958-63, head of libraries, 1963—; mem. faculty U. Del., 1948—, prof. history of art, 1958—; cons. Nat. Gallery, 1971, Nat. Endowment Humanities, 1978; dir. Furniture Library. Henry fellow, 1947-48. Mem. Am. Assn. Archtl. Bibliographers, Soc. Archtl. Historians. Republican. Roman Catholic. Clubs: Grolier (N.Y.C.); Odd Volumes (Boston); Franklin Inn (Phila.); Elizabethan (New Haven). Contbr. articles to profl. jours. Address: Winterthur Mus Winterthur DE 19735

SOMMER, HOWARD ELLSWORTH, accounting co. exec.; b. Kansas City, Mo., May 1, 1918; s. Frederick H. and Edna O. (Olsen) S.; B.A. magna cum laude, Dartmouth, 1940; M.B.A., Harvard, 1942; m. Sarah Scott McElevey, June 20, 1942; children—Scott E., Paul F. With Wolf & Co., C.P.A.'s, Chgo., 1946-76; chmn. mng. group Wolf & Co., C.P.A.'s, 1960-76; dir. Jockey Internat., Kenosha, Wis., 1959—, sr. v.p., chmn. audit com., 1979—. Counsellor, Chgo. chpt. Boy Scouts Am. Served from 2d lt. to lt. col. AUS, 1942-46. Decorated Bronze Star, Commendation ribbon with oak leaf cluster; Croix de Guerre with palms, Medaille de la Reconnaissance (France). Mem. ASME, Assn. Cons. Mgmt. Engrs. (cert. of Award 1956, v.p. 1970-72), Inst. Mgmt. Cons.'s (cert. mgmt. cons., dir.), Phi Beta Kappa, Chi Phi. Episcopalian (vestryman, warden). Clubs: Univ. (pres., dir. 1959-61), Chgo., Harvard Bus. Sch. (dir. 1958-59) (Chgo.); Indian Hill, North Shore Cotillion (Winnetka); Dartmouth (Chgo. and N.Y.C.); Kishwaukee (past pres.) (Kirkland, Ill.); Singing Hills (Round Lake, Ill.); Masons (32 deg.), Shriners. Author: Procedural Routine for a Business Audit, 1947; also articles. Office: 2300 60 St Kenosha WI 53140

SOMMER, JOHN ROBERT, mfg. co. exec.; b. Brigham City, Utah, Sept. 7, 1913; s. John and Elizabeth (Schmutz) S.; B.S., U. Ill., 1935; m. Evelyn Merrifield, Aug. 9, 1941; children—John Robert, Mitchell Farrar, Floy Lynn, Rex Allen, Daniel Kevin. Metallurgist, Keystone Steel & Wire Co., Peoria, Ill., 1935-40; metallurgist Mid-States Steel & Wire Co., Crawfordsville, Ind., 1940-41, v.p. charge sales, 1946-51, dir., 1948-68; with Nat. Lock Co., Rockford, Ill., 1951—, exec. v.p., 1962-64, pres., 1964-71; pres. Keystone Consolidated Industries Inc., 1971-73, chmn. bd., 1973—, also dir. Trustee Rockford Coll. Served with USAAF, 1941-46. Mem. Delta Phi. Clubs: Masons (32 deg.), Shriners. Home: 190 1st Ave N Naples FL 33940

SOMMERBURG, MIRIAM, artist; b. Hamburg, Germany; d. David and Nanny (Munk) Cahn; student, Hamburg, 1926-29; sculpture pupil Richard Luksch, 1926-29; design pupil Friedrich Adler, Bauhaus, 1926; m. Rudolf Sommerburg, Feb. 10, 1927 (dec.); children—Sascha, Dimitri, Sonia S. Rabin, David P., Gioconda (Mrs. Howard L. Richards). Came to U.S., 1946, naturalized, 1951. Exhbns.: New Delhi, Bombay, Calcutta, Madras, Hyderabad and Baroda, India, 1965-66, Alpes Maritimes, La Napoule, Musée de Cognac, Cannes, France, 1965-66, N.Y. World's Fair, 1965, Vera Cruz, Mexico City and Monterey, Mex., 1964-65, 75, Birmingham, Eng., 1964, Edinburgh, Scotland, 1965, Mus. Modern Art, Rio de Janeiro, 1963, Museo de Bellas Artes, Buenos Aires, Argentina, 1963, S.Am. with USIA, 1963-64, Acad. Arts and Letters (grant candidate), 1960, invitation to participate in Ford Found. grant, 1959, Brussels, Antwerp, Ghent and Ostend, Belgium with USIA, 1956-57, Stedelijk Mus., Amsterdam, Netherlands, 1956, Burlington Galleries, London, 1955, Berlin Acad. Fine Arts, 1954, Whitney Mus., 1951, 54, Bklyn. Mus., 1951, 54, Pa. Acad., 1954, 66, Isaac Delgado Mus., 1947-56, Boston Art Mus., 1954, Audubon Artists, 1948—, Nat. Assn. Women Artists, 1952—, Soc. Am. Graphic Artists, 1947, 48, 51, 59, Am. Soc. Contemporary Artists, 1951—, The Contemporaries, N.Y.C., 1956, 57, Nat. Arts Club, N.Y.C., 1961, 71, 74, 76, Bd. of Trade, N.Y.C., 1968, Union Carbide, N.Y.C., 1970, 72, 75, Jewish Tercentary traveling exhbn., 1954, 55, Soc. Young Am. Artists, 1955, Allied Artists Am., 1949, Grand Central Art Galleries, N.Y.C., 1952, Bergen County Mus., Paramus, N.J., 1974, New Sch. Social Research, N.Y.C., 1955, Calif. Soc. Etchers at Gumps, San Francisco, 1946, Syracuse Mus., 1945, also in Florence and Naples, Italy, 1972, Am. Drawings, Portsmouth, Va., 1976, Lever House, 1977, numerous others; one-woman shows, 1950, 51, 53, 54, 55, 58, 59, 63, 65; represented in permanent collections: Met. Mus., N.Y.C., Norfolk (Va.) Mus., Springfield (Mo.) Mus., Butler Inst. Am. Art, Fla. So. Coll., B'nai B'rith Mus., Inst. Advanced Study, Princeton, N.J., Rose Art Mus., Brandeis U., Assn. Research and Enlightenment, Va. Recipient Audubon Artists prize, 1966, Audubon award, 1978, Nat. Assn. Women Artists award, 1961, 2 awards Design in Hardwoods, Chgo., 1959, Silvermine Guild Artists award, 1959, Am. Soc. Contemporary Artists award 1958, 62, 64, Painters and Sculptors N.J. award, 1949, 55, Knickerbocker Artists award, 1954, Village Art Center award, 1946, 48, 49, 50, 51, 56, 57, 60, Creative Gallery, 1951, Fla. So. Coll., 1952, Internat. Women's Yr. award, 1976. Life fellow Intercontinental Biog. Assn.; mem. Audubon Artists, Nat. Assn. Women Artists, Am. Soc. Contemporary Artists, Print Council Am., Artists Equity Assn. N.Y., Washington Women Artists. Work reproduced in Mosaics and Design Through Discovery. Address: Westbeth Artists Housing 463 West St Apt G227 New York NY 10014. *INTEGRITY, in life and work, never creating anything against my personal convictions; DETERMINATION, to follow through plans, even if considerable efforts are required; INSPIRATION and IMAGINATION, without which no original art could be formed. Working alone, not talking about work in progress, not paying attention to any praise or criticism, I stamp the distinctive single-mindedness of my indivisible identity on each and every work of mine.*

SOMMERFELD, RAYNARD MATTHIAS, accounting educator; b. Sibley, Iowa, Aug. 10, 1933; s. Ernest Robert and Lillian Emma (Matthias) S.; B.S.C., U. Iowa, 1956, M.A., 1957, Ph.D., 1963; m. Barbara Ann Spear, June 9, 1956; children—Andrea Joan, Kristin Elaine. Asst. prof. Grad. Sch. Bus., U. Tex., Austin, 1963-66, asso. prof., 1966-68, prof., 1968-72, Arthur Young prof., 1972-76; partner Arthur Young & Co., C.P.A.'s, 1976-78; John A. White prof. accounting U. Tex., Austin, 1978—. Served with USAF, 1957-60. Mem. Am. Taxation Assn. (pres. 1975-76), Tex. Soc. C.P.A.'s (dir. 1969-72, pres. Austin chpt. 1967-68), Am. Inst. C.P.A.'s, Am. Accounting Assn., Nat. Tax Assn. Lutheran. Club: Austin Yacht. Author: Tax Reform and the Alliance for Progress, 1966; (with H. Anderson, H. Brock) An Introduction to Taxation, 1969, rev. edits., 1972, 76, 77, 78, 79, 80; (with G.F. Streuling) Tax Research Techniques, 1976; The Dow Jones-Irwin Guide to Tax Planning, 1974, rev. edit., 1978. Home: 6018 Mount Bonnell Hollow Austin TX 78731 Office: BEB 203 U Tex Austin TX 78712

SOMMERFIELD, CHARLES MICHAEL, educator, physicist; b. N.Y.C., Oct. 27, 1933; s. Arthur and Ann (Wasil) S.; B.S., Bklyn. Coll., 1953; A.M. Harvard, 1954, Ph.D., 1957; A.M. (hon.), Yale, 1967; m. Linda M. Bartoshuk, May 25, 1969; children—Daniel Arthur, Elizabeth May. NSF postdoctoral fellow U. Calif. at Berkeley, 1957- 58; instr. U. Calif. at Berkeley, 1958-59, Harvard, 1959-61: mem. faculty Yale, 1961—, prof. physics, 1967—. Ford Found. fellow U. Central Venezuela, 1966. Fellow Am. Phys. Soc.; mem. AAAS. Home: 495 Ellsworth Ave New Haven CT 06511

SOMMERS, ALBERT TRUMBULL, research assn. exec.; b. Milford, Conn., July 30, 1919; s. Robert Edward and Isabel (Faust) S.; A.B., Columbia U., 1939; M.A., N.Y. U., 1949; m. Jean Marvin Sommers, Dec. 26, 1946; children—Elizabeth, John. Partner Boni, Watkins, Jason & Co., N.Y.C., 1947-50; with Conf. Bd., N.Y.C., 1950—, dir. econ. research, 1961-72, v.p., 1965-72, sr. v.p., chief economist, 1972—; econ. adviser Ford Found.; dir. Alliance Capital Reserves, Inc., Alliance Govt. Reserves Inc., Glow Group Inc.; trustee Bklyn. Savs. Bank, MassMut. Morgage & Realty Investors. Pres. Port Alert, Inc., Port Washington, N.Y., 1969-71. Served with U.S. Army, 1941-46. Fellow Nat. Assn. Bus. Economists; mem. Am. Econ. Assn., Am. Statis. Assn., Internat. Mgmt. Devel. Inst. (bd. advisers 1976—), Commn. on Law and the Economy, Am. Bar Assn. Democrat. Contbr. articles to profl. jours. Home: 16 Bonnie Heights Rd Manhasset NY 11030 Office: 845 3d Ave New York NY 10022

SOMMERS, HERBERT MYRON, physician, educator; b. Colorado Springs, Colo., Sept. 4, 1925; s. Herbert Manitou and Edna Earl (McReynolds) S.; student U. Colo., 1943, 46-48; B.S., Northwestern U., 1949, M.D., 1952; m. Sarah Mason Shute, Apr. 30, 1955 (div. 1977); children—Mark Stuart, Lee Scott, Keith Eric, Todd Craig. Intern, Chgo. Wesley Meml. Hosp., 1953-54, resident in surgery and pathology, 1954-58; instr. pathology Northwestern U. Med. Sch., Chgo., 1957-61, asso., 1961-62, asst. prof., 1962-66, asso. prof., 1966-71, prof., 1971—; practice medicine specializing in pathology, Chgo., 1958—; mem. staff Northwestern Meml. Hosp. Served with U.S. Army, 1943-46. Chgo. Heart Soc. grantee, 1968-69. Diplomate Am. Bd. Pathology. Mem. Am. Assn. Pathologists, Am. Soc. Clin. Pathology, Coll. Am. Pathologists, Am. Soc. Microbiology, AAAS, Am. Thoracic Soc., Ill. Soc. Microbiology. Club: Wilmette (Ill.) Sailing. Author: (with others) The Biologic and Clinical Basis of Infectious Disease, 1st edit., 1975, 2d edit., 1980; (with others) A Color Atlas and Textbook of Diagnostic Microbiology, 1979; contbr. articles to profl. jours. Home: 643 Walden Rd Winnetka IL 60093 Office: 303 E Chicago Ave Chicago IL 60611

SOMMERS, JAMES BAINBRIDGE, banker; b. Richmond, Va., Apr. 23, 1939; s. John Edward and Nettie (Cates) S.; B.A., U. Va., 1962, M.B.A., 1964; m. Susan Clarke Oast, Apr. 24, 1965; children—Susan Merchant, Ruth Chapman, James Bainbridge. Mgmt. trainee N.C. Nat. Bank, Charlotte, N.C., 1965-67, asst. cashier, asst. v.p., 1967-71, v.p. nat. div., v.p. marketing services exec., 1971-72, sr. v.p., marketing exec., 1972-73, sr. v.p., internat. banking exec., 1973-77, exec. v.p., internat. group exec., 1977—, also dir.; dir. NCNB (Asia) Ltd., Hong Kong, NCNB Internat. Banking Corp. N.Y., Carolina Leasing Ltd., London; mem. adv. com. Pvt. Export Funding Corp., N.Y.C. Campaign coordinator for passage of $23 million bond package for city of Charlotte, 1973. Bd. dirs. Cental Piedmont Community Coll., Charlotte. Served with USCGR. Recipient award of appreciation Charlotte C. of C., 1973. Mem. Bankers Assn. for Fgn. Trade (pres. 1979—). Republican. Episcopalian. Club: Charlotte Country. Home: 226 Huntley Pl Charlotte NC 28207 Office: PO Box 120 Charlotte NC 28255

SOMMERS, LAWRENCE MELVIN, educator, geographer; b. Clinton, Wis., Apr. 17, 1919; s. Emil L. and Inga (Anderson) S.; B.S., U. Wis., 1942, Ph.M., 1946; Ph.D., Northwestern U., 1950; m. Marjorie Smith, Apr. 26, 1948; 1 dau., Laurie Kay. With Mich. State. U., 1949—, successively instr., asst. prof. dept. geography, asso. prof., 1949-55, prof., chmn. dept., 1955-79, prof. Environ. Quality Center, 1979—. Mem. adv. com. geography Office Naval Research and NRC, 1958-61. Fellow Am. Scandinavian Found., Social Sci. Research Council, for research in Norway, 1948; recipient Office Naval Research grant for research in Denmark, 1953, travel grant to Europe, 1960. Served with adj. gen. dept. AUS, 1942-45. Mem. Am. Geog. Soc., Assn. Am. Geographers (exec. council 1967-70, chmn. cons. service 1970-77), Nat. Council Geog. Edn. (exec. bd. 1967-70), Mich. State U. Acad. Council and Grad. Council, AAAS, Mich. Acad. Sci. Arts and Letters, Am. Scandinavian Found., Scandinavian Studies Assn., Phi Kappa Phi, Sigma Xi (pres. Mich. State U. chpt. 1959-60). Co-author: Outside Readings in Geography, 1955; Introduction to Geography-Selected Readings, 1967; Cultural Geography-Selected Readings, 1967; Economic Geography-Selected Readings, 1970; World Regional Geography, 1976; articles on Norwegian, European geography. Editor: Atlas of Michigan, 1977. Home: 4292 Tacoma Blvd Okemos MI 48864 Office: Mich State East Lansing MI 48824

SOMOGI, JUDITH, conductor; b. Bklyn., May 13, 1943; d. Louis J. and Antonina (Lo Biondo) Somogi; B.S., Juilliard Sch. Music, 1963, M.S., 1965. Condr. Am. Symphony Orch., 1972, Spoleto Festival of Two Worlds, 1974, N.Y.C. Opera, 1974, Naumberg Symphony Orch., 1974, Los Angeles Philharmonic, 1975, Syracuse Symphony Orch., 1975, Tulsa Opera, 1976, N.Y. Philharmonic, 1977, Oklahoma City Symphony, 1977, Tulsa Philharmonic, 1977, San Diego Opera, 1977, Milw. Symphony, 1977, San Francisco Opera, 1978, Florentine Opera, 1978, San Antonio Opera, 1979. Home: 150 W 82d St New York City NY 10024 Office: New York City Opera Lincoln Center Plaza New York City NY 10023

SOMOGYI, LASZLO, orch. conductor; b. Budapest, Hungary, June 25, 1908; s. Lajos and Berta (Kohn) S.; student composition Franz Liszt Acad. Music, Budapest; student conducting with Hermann Scherchen; m. Julianne Laub, 1933; 1 son, Andrew George. Violinist, Budapest Opera and Philharmonic Orch.; conductor Chamber Orch. and Chamber Opera Group, Budapest, 1937; founder, chief conductor Hungarian State Orch. until 1957; mus. dir. Hungarian Radio Symphony Orch., 1950; guest conductor Hungarian State Opera; frequent appearances in USSR, Czechoslovakia, E. Germany, Poland, Yugoslavia, Roumania, 1950-56; prof. conducting Franz Liszt Acad. Music, 1959-56; guest conductor major orchs. Europe, Israel, S. Am., U.S., 1956- -; prof. master class conducting Acad. Chigiana, Siena, Italy, 1964; prof. Bartok Seminar, Hungary, 1979-80; condr. mus. dir. Rochester Philharmonic Orch., 1964; festival appearances include Bartok Festivals, Budapest, Spring of Prague, Wiener Musikfest wochen, Athens, Granada, Strasbourg, Ravello, Sagra Musicale in Perrugia and Monreale; recording artist for Qualiton, Ducretet-Thomson, Erato, His Master's Voice, Westminster records. Mem. Hungarian Art Council, 1946-50. Recipient Kossuth prize; named Honored Artist of Hungary. Home: 11 Parc Diru Lipatti 1225 Geneva Switzerland

SOMORJAI, GABOR ARPAD, chemist, educator; b. Budapest, Hungary, May 4, 1935; came to U.S., 1957, naturalized, 1962; s. Charles and Livia (Ormos) S.; B.S. in Chem. Engring., U. Tech. Scis., Budapest, 1956; Ph.D., U. Calif., Berkeley, 1960; m. Judith Kaldor, Sept. 2, 1957; children—Nicole, John. Mem. research staff IBM, Yorktown Heights, N.Y., 1960-64; prin. investigator materials and molecular research div. Lawrence Berkeley (Calif.) Lab., 1964—; mem. faculty dept. of chemistry U. Calif., Berkeley, 1964—, asso. prof., 1967-72, prof., 1972—; Unilever vis. prof. dept. chemistry U. Bristol (Eng.), 1972; vis. fellow Emmanual Coll., Cambridge, Eng., 1969; Baker lectr. Cornell U., 1977. Recipient Emmett award Am. Catalysis Soc., 1977, Kokes award Johns Hopkins U., 1976; Guggenheim fellow, 1969. Fellow Am. Phys. Soc.; mem. Nat. Acad. Scis., Am. Chem. Soc., Catalysis Soc. N. Am. Author: Principles of Surface Chemistry, 1972; Chemistry in Two Dimensions, 1980; contbr. over 200 sci. articles on catalytic reactions and surface studies to sci. jours.; editorial bd. Jour. Solid State Chemistry, 1976—, Progress in Solid State Chemistry, 1973—, Nouveau Jour. de Chimie, 1977-80, Colloid and Interface Sci. Office: Dept Chemistry Univ of California Berkeley CA 94720

SONDAK, NORMAN EDWARD, educator; b. Cornwall, N.Y., Sept. 1, 1931; s. Michel and Sadie (Cohen) S.; B.E., Coll. City N.Y., 1953; M.S., Northwestern U., 1954; D. Engring., Yale, 1958; m. Eileen L. Miller, June 6, 1954; children—Vernon, Emily, Bradley. Sr. technologist Socony Mobil, Paulsboro, N.J., 1957-61; mgr. application services EDP div. R.C.A., Cherry Hill, N.J., 1961-63; v.p. J. Walter Thompson Co., N.Y.C., 1963-68; prof., head computer sci. dept. Worcester Poly. Inst., 1968-78; prof. San Diego State U., 1978—, chmn. info. systems dept., 1978—; research prof. U. Mass. Med. Sch., Worcester; vis. lectr. computer sci. Worcester State Coll.; dir. Worcester Area Coll. Computation Center, 1968-71; prof. math. Clark U. Mem. cooperating staff Worcester Found. for Exptl. Biology. Served as 1st lt., AUS, 1957. Mem. Am. Inst. Chem. Engrs., Assn. Computing Machinery (Worcester chpt. chmn. 1974-76, nat. lectr. 1973, 74, 75, 77), Data Processing Mgmt. Assn., Soc. Indsl. Applied Math. (nat. lectr. 1976, 77), Am. Soc. Information Sci., Sigma Xi, Tau Beta Pi. Author: PL/1 for Programmers, 1970; Layman's Dictionary of Computer Technology, 1973; Microprogramming, 1978. Contbr. articles to profl. jours. Home: 6344 Lake Lomond Dr San Diego CA 92119

SONDEREGGER, JOHN FORSTER, chem. co. exec.; b. Chgo., July 3, 1931; s. Hans H. and Edith M. (Aagaard) S.; student Ill. Inst. Tech., 1949-50; B.S. in Bus. Adminstrn., Drake U., 1957; m. Beatrice E. Morris, June 22, 1957; children—David A., Stephen M. Auditor, Arthur Young & Co., Chgo., 1957-59; with Internat. Minerals & Chem. Corp., Northbrook, Ill., 1959—, v.p., controller, 1974—. Served with USMCR, 1952-54. C.P.A., Ill. Mem. Chgo. Presbytery Functional Unit Camps and Confs., Am. Inst. C.P.A.'s, Ill. Soc. C.P.A.'s., Fin. Execs. Inst. Presbyn. (elder 1971—). Home: 422 E Maude St Arlington Heights IL 60004 Office: 2315 Sanders Rd Northbrook IL 60062

SONDERGAARD, GALE, actress; b. Litchfield, Minn., A.B., U. Minn.; m. Herbert Biberman. Appeared in stage in Strange Interlude, Red Rus, others; appeared in films Anthony Adverse, Maid of Salem, Seventh Heaven, Cat and the Canary, The Life of Emile Zola, The Blue Bird, The Strange Death of Adolph Hitler, Mark of Zoro, Never Say Die, The Letter, The Spider Woman, The Spider Woman Strikes Back, The Climax, The Invisible Man's Revenge, Gypsy Wildcat, Christmas Holiday, Anna and the King of Siam, Road to Rio, Pirates of Monterrey, East Side, West Side, Hollywood on Trial, 1977, others. Recipient Acad. award as best actress in supporting role Anthony Adverse, 1936; Outstanding Achievement award U. Minn., 1968; nominated Acad. award for best actress supporting role for Anna and the King of Siam, 1946. Address: care Roberts/Shiffrim Artists Ltd 8833 Sunset Blvd Suite 406 Los Angeles CA 90069*

SONDHEIM, STEPHEN JOSHUA, composer, lyricist; b. N.Y.C., Mar. 22, 1930; s. Herbert and Janet (Fox) S.; B.A., Williams Coll., 1950. Composer: (incidental music) Girls of Summer, 1956, Invitation to a March, 1961; (lyrics) West Side Story, 1957, Gypsy, 1959; (music and lyrics) A Funny Thing Happened on the Way to The Forum, 1962, Anyone Can Whistle, 1964, Evening Primrose, 1966, Company, 1970, Follies, 1971, A Little Night Music, 1973, The Frogs, 1974; (lyrics) Do I Hear a Waltz, 1965; (film score) Stavisky, 1974; (music and lyrics) Pacific Overtures, 1976, Sweeney Todd, The Demon Barber of Fleet Street, 1979.

SONENBERG, JACK, artist; b. Toronto, Ont., Can., Dec. 28, 1925; s. Solomon and Leah (Saltzman) S.; student N.Y. U., 1949; B.F.A., Washington U., 1951; m. Phoebe Helman, June 7, 1949; 1 dau., Maya. Mem. faculty dept. art Queens Coll., 1970-72, Bklyn. Coll., 1972, Sch. of Visual Arts, 1962-73; mem. faculty Pratt Inst. Bklyn., 1968—, chmn. painting and drawing dept., 1973—; one-man shows: Byron Gallery, N.Y.C., 1965, 68, Hampton Inst., 1968, U. No. Iowa, 1969, Grand Rapids (Mich.) Art Mus., 1968, Flint Inst. Arts, 1972, Fischback Gallery, N.Y.C., 1973; group shows include: Whitney Mus., 1967, 73, Mus. Modern Art, 1974, Art Inst. Chgo., 1975, C. Mollet-Vieveille, Paris, 1977; represented in permanent collections: Guggenheim Mus., Whitney Mus., Washington U., Met. Mus., Bradley U., Nat. Gallery Can., W.Va. U. Ford Found. grantee, 1966; Guggenheim Found. grantee, 1973. Home: 217 E 23d St New York NY 10010 Office: Sch Art and Design Pratt Inst Brooklyn NY

SONENBERG, MARTIN, educator; b. N.Y.C., Dec. 1, 1920; s. Berl and Nellie (Gordon) S.; B.A., U. Pa., 1941; M.D., N.Y.U., 1944, Ph.D., 1952; m. Dellie Madeleine Ellis, Jan. 17, 1956; children—Santha, Andrea. Mem. Sloan-Kettering Cancer Center, N.Y.C., 1965; faculty Cornell U., 1957—, prof. biochemistry, 1967—, prof. medicine, 1972—; chief endocrine service Meml. Hosp. Cancer and Allied Diseases. Mem. biomed. adv. com. Population Council, 1960; mem. adv. com. Am. Cancer Soc., 1971. Recipient Van Meter award Am. Thyroid Assn., 1952; Am. Cancer Soc. scholar, 1952-55; Guggenheim fellow, 1957-58; recipient Sloan award for cancer research, 1968. Mem. Am. Thyroid Assn., Am. Soc. Clin. Investigation, Am. Soc. Biol. Chemists, Endocrine Soc. Mem. editorial bd. of Endocrinology, 1967-75. Contbr. articles to profl. jours. Research on role of pituitary gland in normal and abnormal growth. Office: 1275 York Ave New York City NY 10021

SONENSHEIN, NATHAN, bus. exec., ret. naval officer; b. Lodi, N.J., Aug. 2, 1915; s. H. W. and Sarah Sonenshein; B.S., U.S. Naval Acad., 1938; M.S., Mass. Inst. Tech., 1944; grad. Advanced Mgmt. Program, Harvard U., 1964; m. Ila Nina Baker, May 11, 1941; children—Carol Dale Sonenshein King, William Baker. Commd. ensign U.S. Navy, 1938, advanced through grades to rear adm., 1965; various assignments, U.S. and Japan, 1938-49; dir. navy facilities div. Bur. Ships, 1949-51; engring. officer U.S.S. Philippine Sea, 1951-53; planning and estimating officer N.Y. Naval Shipyard, 1953-56; head hull design br. Bur. Ships, 1956-60; fleet and force maintenance officer on staffs comdr.-in-chief and comdr. service force U.S. Pacific Fleet, 1960-62; dir. ship design div. Bur. Ships, 1962-64, asst. chief for design, shipbldg. and fleet maintenance, 1965; project mgr. Fast Deployment Logistics Ship Project, 1965-66; dep. chief naval material for logistic support, 1967-69; comdr. Naval Ship Systems Command, 1969-72; chmn. NMC Shipbldg. Council, 1972-73; dir. for energy Dept. Def., 1973-74; asst. to pres. Global Marine Devel., Inc., Newport Beach, Calif., 1974—. Decorated Legion of Merit with 2 Gold stars, Navy Commendation ribbon with combat V, also numerous unit and area ribbons. Mem. Am. Soc. Naval Architects and Marine Engrs. (v.p.), Am. Soc. Naval Engrs. (past pres.), Sigma Xi. Home: 1884 Joseph Dr Moraga CA 94556 Office: Box 3010 Newport Beach CA 92663

SONES, CHARLES GAYLON, petroleum co. exec.; b. Marshall, Tex., Feb. 5, 1922; s. Henry Jackson and Roxie (Williams) S.; B.S., Tex. A. and M. U., 1946; m. Lillian Pilat, Sept. 4, 1948; children—Charles R., Kenneth W., Robert A. With Texaco, Inc., Houston, 1947; with ADA Resources Inc., Houston, 1948—, exec. v.p., 1962—, dir., 1970—; dir. Bayou City Barge Lines, Inc., Houston, Plastics Universal Corp., Barbourville, Ky.; v.p., dir. Service Transport Co., Houston; v.p. Adams Petroleum Center, Houston, 1970—. Served to 1st lt. C.E., AUS, 1943-46, to capt., USAF, 1950-52. Decorated Bronze Star. Methodist (trustee 1960-74). Club: Golfcrest Country (Pearland, Tex.). Home: 3012 Country Club Dr Pearland TX 77581 Office: PO Box 844 Houston TX 77001

SONETT, CHARLES PHILIP, physicist; b. Pitts., Jan. 15, 1924; s. Erwin and Helen (Dorner) S.; B.A. in Physics, U. Calif., Berkeley, 1949; M.A. in Physics, U. Calif., Los Angeles, 1951, Ph.D. in Nuclear Physics, 1954; m. Virginia Hooten, June 20, 1948; children—Eric Erwin, Maria Lisa. Asso. physics U. Calif., Los Angeles, 1953-54; head range devel. group Ramo Wooldridge Corp., 1954-57; mem. sr. staff, head space physics sect. Space Tech. Labs., 1957-60; cons. NASA Hdqrs., 1960-73, dep. dir. astronautics Ames Research Center, 1971-73; prof. planetary scis., head dept., dir. Lunar and Planetary Lab., U. Ariz., Tucson, 1973-77, prof. planetary scis., 1977—; lectr. engring. U. Calif., Los Angeles, 1955-58; cons. Jet Propulsion Lab., Rockwell Internat. Served with U.S. Army, 1943-46. Decorated Purple Heart; Guggenheim fellow, 1968-69; grantee NASA, 1959—, recipient Exceptional Sci. Achievement medal, 1969, 72; recipient Space Sci. award Am. Inst. Astronautics and Aeros., 1969. Mem. AAAS, Am. Astron. Soc., Internat. Astron. Union, Am. Geophys. Union, Univ. Space Research Assn. (trustee 1977-80). Editor: Cosmic Electrodynamics, 1970-72; co-editor: Astrophysics and Space Sci., The Moon and the Planets, 1973—; mem. editorial com. Ann. Rev. Earth and Planet Scis., 1973-76. Home: 5745 N Camino Real Tucson AZ 85718 Office: Dept Planetary Scis Lunar and Planetary Lab Univ Ariz Tucson AZ 85721

SONFIELD, ROBERT LEON, JR., lawyer; b. Houston, Oct. 28, 1931; s. Robert Leon and Dorothy Harriett (Huber) S.; B.A., U. Houston, 1956, LL.B., J.D., 1959; Ph.D. (hon.), U. Eastern Fla., 1962; LL.D. (hon.), London Inst. Applied Research, 1973; certificate fed. taxation N.Y.U., 1973; m. Jeanne Margaret Crusemann, July 14, 1969; 1 dau., Sheree. Admitted to Tex. bar, 1959, U.S. Supreme Ct. bar; partner Sonfield & Sonfield, Houston, 1959—. Dir., gen. counsel Am. Assn. Real Estate Bds. Mem. nat. adv. council Nat. Fedn. Ind. Bus. Recipient St. John Garwood award, 1957, Frio-Finnegan Outstanding Alumnus award, 1970-71, citation for outstanding contbn. to legal profession, 1971. Mem. Am. Assn. Tax Lawyers (pres.), Lawyers Soc. Houson, Am. Judicature Soc., Am., Tex. (dist. com. on admission to state bar, chmn. clients security fund com.), Houston (com. chmn.) bar assns., Real Estate Securities and Syndication Inst., Huguenot Soc. of London, Order Stars and Bars, SAR, Sons Confederate Vets., Mil. Order World Wars, Mil. and Hospitaller Order St. Lazarus of Jerusalem, Smithsonian Assos., Houston Heritage Soc., Houston Mus. Fine Arts, Newcomen Soc. N.Am., Phi Delta Phi, Delta Sigma Phi. Clubs: Metropolitan (N.Y.C.); Argyle (San Antonio); Houston; Valley Internat. Country (life) (Brownville, Tex.). Author: Corporate Financing by Sale of Securities to the Public, 1969; Mergers and Acquisitions, 1970; Student Rights, 1971; The Limited Partnership as a Vehicle for Real Estate Investment, 1971; Integration of Partnership Offerings, 1974. Home: 1022 Fountainview Houston TX 77057 Office: 4615 Post Oak Pl Dr Houston TX 77027

SONFIST, ALAN, environ. artist; b. N.Y.C., May 26, 1946. One man shows include: Deson-Zaks Gallery, Chgo., 1971, Finch Coll. Art Mus., 1971, 75, Johnson Mus., Ithaca, N.Y., 1975, Galerie Thelen, Cologne (W.Ger.), 1971, 74, Akron Art Inst., Ohio, 1972, Paley and Lowe Gallery, N.Y.C., 1972, Galerie Cavellino, Venice, Italy, 1976, Centre Cultural Americain, Paris, 1976, Carl Solway Gallery, Cin., 1972, 74, Stefanotty Gallery, N.Y.C., 1975, Boston Mus. Fine Arts, 1977, Light Gallery, N.Y.C., 1977, Neuberger Mus., Purchase, N.Y., 1978, Leo Castelli Gallery, N.Y.C., 1978, Smithsonian Instn., 1978, High Mus. Art, Atlanta, 1979; group shows include: Sch. Visual Arts, N.Y.C., 1969, Mus. Fine Arts, Boston, 1971, Stedelijk Mus., Amsterdam, 1971, Deson-Zaks Gallery, Chgo., 1972, Mus. Fine Arts, Caracas (Venezuela), 1972, Mus. Modern Art, N.Y.C., 1972, 78, Vassar Coll. Art Mus., 1973, 78, Wallraf-Richartz Mus., Cologne, 1974, Hayden Gallery, Mass. Inst. Tech., 1974, Whitney Mus. Am. Art, N.Y.C., 1974, Fine Arts Bldg., N.Y.C., 1975, U. Glassboro (Pa.), 1975; represented in permanent collections: Everson Mus., Syracuse, N.Y., Mus. Modern Art, N.Y.C., Power Inst. Fine Art, Sydney (Australia), Akron (Ohio) Art Inst., Mus. Fine Arts, Boston, Allen Mus. Fine Arts, Oberlin, Ohio, Westherspoon Gallery, U. N.C., also numerous pvt. collections; illustrator Lives of a Cell (Lewis Thomas), 1974; works reproduced in various books and jours. Grantee, Graham Found., 1971, 72, Nat. Endowment for Arts, 1972, 78, Chase Manhattan Found. for Environ. and Fine Art, Nat. Endowment for Art in Pub. Places, 1975, 78, N.Y. State Creative Artist Program, 1977, CitiBank Found., 1978. Author several videotapes.

SONG, PILL-SOON, educator; b. Osaka, Japan, Aug. 5, 1936; s. Jamin and Ocksoon (Kang) S.; B.S., Seoul Nat. U., 1958, M.S., 1960; Ph.D., U. Calif. at Davis, 1964; m. Woosun Choy, July 3, 1963; children—Minn, Young, Linn. Research asso. Iowa State U., Ames, 1964-65; research asst. prof. Tex. Technol. U., Lubbock, 1965-68, research and teaching asso. prof., 1968-69, prof., 1969—, Paul W. Horn prof., 1975—. Mem. U.S. nat. com. for photobiology Nat. Acad. Sci.-NRC, 1973—; mem. biophys. chem. study sect. NIH, 1974—. Served with Korean Army, 1958-60. Research grantee Robert Welch Found., 1966—, NSF, 1967—, HEW, 1971—. Fellow Am. Inst. Chemists; mem. Am. Chem. Soc., Am. Soc. Biol. Chemists, Internat. Soc. Quantum Biology, Biophys. Soc., Am. Soc. Plant Physiologists, Am. Soc. Photobiology, Sigma Xi. Contbr. articles to tech. jours. Asso. editor Photochemistry and Photobiology, 1971-74, editor-in-chief, 1974—. Home: 4806 11th St Lubbock TX 79416

SONKOWSKY, ROBERT PAUL, educator; b. Appleton, Wis., Sept. 16, 1931; s. Paul and Loretta Stella (Nooyen) S.; B.A., Lawrence Coll., 1954; postgrad. U. Rome, 1956-57; Ph.D., U. N.C., 1958; m. Barbara Lou Zierke, June 8, 1956; children—Paul Victor, Steven Robert, Michael Edward, Instr., asst. prof. U. Tex., 1958-61; fellow Inst. Research in Humanities, U. Wis., 1961-62; asso. prof. U. Mo., 1962-63; asso. prof., chmn. dept. classics U. Minn., Mpls., 1963-78, prof., 1963—; actor Wilderness Rd. Theater Co., Berea, Ky., The Confederacy Co., Virginia Beach, Va., summers 1955-58. Mem. St. Paul Sch. Com., 1971—. Mem. Am. Philol. Assn., Classical Assn. Middle West and South, AAUP, ACLU, Phi Beta Kappa (nat. senator 1976—). Contbr. articles to profl. jours. Office: 310 Folwell Hall Dept Classics U Minn Minneapolis MN 55455

SONNABEND, PAUL, hotel exec.; b. Boston, Aug. 15, 1927; s. Abraham and Esther (Lewitt) S.; B.S., Cornell U., 1950; m. Gloria Aisenberg, Jan. 28, 1951; children—Jill, Peter J., Thomas A., Kim. Gen. mgr. Hotel Shelton, Boston, 1950-52; sales mgr., then gen. mgr. Hotel Somerset, Boston, 1953-57; v.p., gen. mgr. Hotels Somerset, Kenmore and Braemore, Boston, 1957-59; v.p. hotel div. Hotel Corp. Am. (co. name changed to Sonesta Internat. Hotels Corp.), 1959-66, exec. v.p. of corp., 1966-70, pres., 1970-77, now dir., mem. exec. com.; pres. Hotel Corp. Am. Internat., 1959-64, Plaza Hotel, N.Y.C., 1960—; pres., dir. Premier Corp. Am., 1963—; a founder Boston Patroits Football Team, 1960: exec. dir. NFL Mgmt. Council; corporator Boston Five Cents Savs. Bank. Bd. dirs. Boston Conv. Bur., Library Presdl. Papers, N.Y., Nat. Center for Voluntary Action, Call for Action Involvement Corps; mem. exec. bd. Boston council Boy Scouts Am.; pres. Bay State Soc. Crippled and Handicapped Children and Adults; treas., dir. Nat. Soc. for Crippled Children and Adults. Bd. incorporators Mass. Meml. Hosp., Boston; trustee Easter Seal Soc. (pres. 1964-66), Beth Israel Hosp., Boston. Mem. Greater Boston C. of C. (dir.; chmn. visitors and tourists bur.), Navy League U.S. (dir. Boston council), Young Pres. Orgn., Am., Mass. hotel assns. Clubs: Charles River Yacht; Belmont (Mass.) Country. Home: 65 Fifer Ln Lexington MA 02173 Office: 540 Madison Ave New York NY 10022

SONNABEND, ROGER PHILIP, hotel co. exec.; b. Boston, Sept. 17, 1925; s. Abraham M. and Esther (Lewitt) S.; B.S., Mass. Inst. Tech., 1946; M.B.A., Harvard, 1949; LL.D., U. N.H., 1969; m. Elsa Golub, July 17, 1949; children—Andrea, Stephanie, Jacqueline, Alan Michael; m. 2d, Joan Snider, Feb. 18, 1971. Engaged in hotel bus., 1946—; with Sonnabend-Operated Hotels, 1950, which became part of Hotel Corp. Am. (named changed to Sonesta Internat. Hotels, 1970), 1956; pres. hotel and motor hotel div. Hotel Corp. Am., 1960-63, pres. of corp., 1963-68, chmn., chief exec. officer, 1968-78, chmn., pres., 1978—. Exec. com. Nat. Alliance of Businessmen, 1968-69. Mem. exec. com., council on arts Mass. Inst. Tech., 1974—; mem. vis. com. on biology and related scis. Harvard U., 1972-77; mem. vis. com. on contemporary art Mus. Fine Arts, Boston; bd. dirs., exec. com. New Eng., NCCJ, 1957, regional co-chmn., 1960-68, nat. v.p., 1961-68; v.p., campaign chmn. Combined Jewish Philanthropies Greater Boston, 1964; trustee Radcliffe Coll.; trustee Inst. Contemporary Art, Boston, 1972—, v.p., 1976—. Mem. Am., Mass., Boston hotel assns., Young Pres. Orgn. (nat. pres. 1961-62, chmn. nat. conv. 1960), World Bus. Council, Chief Execs. Forum. Club: Harvard (Boston). Home: RD 1 Box 177 Chester NH 03036 also Odell Rd Sandown NH 03873 Office: 390 Commonwealth Ave Boston MA 02215

SONNE, CLARENCE MELVIN, JR., economist; b. Titusville, Pa., Dec. 3, 1922; s. Clarence Melvin and Lillian (Carpenter) S.; B.S., U. Pa., 1943, M.A., 1947; M.P.A., Harvard, 1957; m. Eva Melitta Hubert, July 8, 1950; children—Peter Stefan, Phillip Michael, Neil Hubert. Instr. U. Pa., 1945-47; with U.S. Fgn. Service, 1947, serving in Copenhagen, 1947-49, Hamburg, 1949-50, Hanoi, 1950-51, Cd. Juarez, 1951-54, Vienna, 1954-56, U.S. Dept. State, 1957-61, Milan, 1961-65, Jidda, 1966-69; prin. officer Am. consulate, Turin, Italy, 1969-73; personnel officer Dept. State, Washington, 1973-74, spl. asst. for internat. negogiations Bur. Internat. Orgns., 1975-77; dir. Far East div. Dept. Commerce, Washington, 1974-75; dir. internat. econ. research Pharm. Mfrs. Assn., Washington, 1977—; mem. U.S. del. 31st UN Gen. Assembly, 1976. Served to 1st lt. USAAF, 1943-45; PTO. Decorated Air medal, D.F.C. with oak leaf clusters. Mem. Beta Gamma Sigma. Club: Nat. Economists. Home: 1938 Rockingham St McLean VA 22101 Office: Pharm Mfrs Assn 1155 15th St NW Washington DC 20005

SONNEBORN, HARRY LEE, newspaper editor; b. Detroit, June 4, 1919; s. Arthur B. and Lois (Speer) S.; A.B., U. Mich., 1940; m. Jacquelyn V. Panette, July 21, 1943; children—Carolyn Mayr, Susan, Prudence. Reporter, copy editor Grand Rapids (Mich.) Press, 1940-41; mem. staff Milw. Jour., 1941-62, city editor, 1959-62; mng. editor Milw. Sentinel, 1962-77, exec. editor, 1977—; dir. Newspapers, Inc. div. Milw. Jour. Co., 1977—. Served as aviator USNR, 1942-45. Mem. Am. Soc. Newspaper Editors, AP Mng. Editors Assn. (dir. 1964-70, treas. 1970), Milw. Press Club (pres. 1960-61), Sigma Delta Chi (pres. Milw. 1964), Theta Chi. Unitarian. Home: 2683 N Summit Ave Milwaukee WI 53211 Office: 918 N 4th St Milwaukee WI 53201

SONNEBORN, HENRY, III, petroleum-chem. co. exec.; b. Balt., Mar. 11, 1918; s. Henry and Lillian (Hamburger) S.; A.B., Johns Hopkins, 1938, Ph.D., 1941; hon. doctorate Hebrew U. Jerusalem, 1976; m. Clara Louise Lauer, Nov. 12, 1942; 1 son, Peter. Various positions Sonneborn Chem. & Refining Co., N.Y.C., 1941-60; dir. Witco Chem. Corp., N.Y.C., 1960—, exec. v.p., 1971-75, pres., 1975—. Past pres. Am. Friends Hebrew U.; past chmn. bd., trustee Preventive Medicine Inst. Strang Clinic, N.Y.C.; v.p. bd. trustees Hosp. for Joint Diseases, N.Y.C.; trustee Johns Hopkins U., 1977—. Served with USNR, 1941-45. Decorated comdr. Ordre du Mérite Brabançon (Belgium). Home: 110 N Chatsworth Ave Larchmont NY 10538 Office: 277 Park Ave New York NY 10017

SONNEBORN, TRACY MORTON, scientist, educator; b. Balt., Oct. 19, 1905; s. Lee and Daisy (Bamberger) S.; B.A., Johns Hopkins, 1925, Ph.D., 1928, D.Sc (hon.), 1957; D.Sc. (hon.), Université de Genève, Northwestern U., 1975, Ind. U., 1978, U. Münster (W. Ger.), 1979; m. Ruth Meyers, June 6, 1929; children—Lee M., David R. Fellow, NRC, 1928-30; research asst. zoology Johns Hopkins U., 1930-31, research asso., 1931-33, asso., 1933-39; asso. prof. zoology Ind. U., 1939-43, prof., 1943-53, distinguished prof., 1953-76, distinguished prof. emeritus, 1976—, acting chmn. div. biol. scis., 1963-64; vis. prof. U. Wash., Seattle, Battelle Research Center, 1971; vis. researcher U. Paris South, Orsay, France, Laboratoire de Génétique Moleculaire, Gif-sur-Yvette, France, 1973; vis. prof. zoology U. Geneva (Switzerland), 1979. Discoverer of mating types in ciliated protozoa, 1937, roles of genes, cytoplasm and environment, control cell heredity, 1943—. Co-winner Newcomb-Cleveland prize for outstanding research paper AAAS, 1946; Kimber Genetics award Nat. Acad. Scis., 1959; Mendel medal Czechoslovakia Acad. Sci., 1965. Mem. Am. Soc. Naturalists (pres. 1949), Am. Soc. Zoologists (pres. 1956), Genetics Soc. Am. (pres. 1949), Soc. Study Evolution (v.p. 1958), Nat. Acad. Sci. (1946), Am. Philos. Soc. (Phila.), Am. Acad. Arts and Sci. (Boston), Am. Soc. Protozoologists (hon.), Royal Soc. London (fgn.), Am. Soc. Cell Biology, Am. Inst. Biol. Scis. (pres. 1960-61), Phi Beta Kappa (vis. scholar 1969, asso. lectr. 1975—), Sigma Xi (nat. lectr. 1949, 68); hon. mem. Faculdad de Biologia y Ciencias Medicas, Universidad de Chile, Sociedad de Biologia de Santiago de Chile, Sociedad de Biologia de Concepcion (Chile), Sociedad Medica de Concepcion (Chile), French Soc. Protozoology (hon.), Genetics Soc. Japan (hon.). Editor: The Control of Human Heredity and Evolution, 1965; editorial bd. Jour. Morphology, 1946-49; Genetics, 1947-62; Jour. Exptl. Zoology, 1948-60; Physiol. Zoology, 1948-60; editorial com. Ann. Rev. Microbiology, 1954-58; contbr. articles to mags. and chpts. to books on genetics. Home: 1305 Maxwell Ln Bloomington IN 47401

SONNECKEN, EDWIN HERBERT, mfg. co. exec.; b. New Haven, July 22, 1916; s. Ewald and Pauline (Halfmann) S.; B.C.S., Northwestern U., 1938; M.B.A., 1940; m. Elizabeth Gregory, June 3, 1939; children—William H., Richard G., Paul D. With Montgomery Ward & Co., 1940-42, OPA, 1942, B.F. Goodrich Co., 1943-53; dir. consumer research Ford Motor Co., 1953-57; pres. Market Planning Corp., N.Y.C., 1957-61; dir. corp. planning and research Goodyear Tire & Rubber Co., 1961-72, v.p. corp. bus. planning, 1972-80; chmn. Mktg. Sci. Inst., 1980—, also trustee, chmn. research policy com. Pres. Akron (Ohio) chpt. Am. Mktg. Assn., 1950, v.p. Detroit chpt., 1955, nat. v.p., dir., 1957, nat. pres., 1964-65. Served with AUS, 1945-46. Mem. Am. Statis. Assn., Am. Assn. Pub. Opinion Research, Nat. Assn. Bus. Economists, Am. Mktg. Assn., Internat. Mktg. Fedn. (pres.). Home: 550 Hampshire Rd Akron OH 44313

SONNEDECKER, GLENN ALLEN, historian of pharmacy; b. Creston, O., Dec. 11, 1917; s. Ira Elmer and Letia (Linter) S.; B.S., Ohio State U., 1942; M.S., U Wis., 1950, Ph.D., 1952; Dr. Sci. honoris causa, Ohio State U., 1964; D.Phar. honoris causa, Mass. Coll. Pharmacy, 1974; m. Cleo Bell, Apr. 3, 1943; 1 son, Stuart Bruce. Licensed pharmacist. Mem. editorial staff Sci. Service, Washington, 1942-43; editor Jour. Am. Pharm. Assn. (practical pharmacy edit.), Washington, 1943-48; asst. prof. U. Wis., 1952-56, asso. prof., 1956-60, now prof.; sec. Am. Inst. History of Pharmacy, 1949-57, dir., 1957-73, hon. dir., mem. exec. com. and council, 1974—; editor-in-chief RPh, 1978—. Sec., mem. bd. Friends of Hist. Pharmacy, 1945-49. Am. Found. fellow, 1948-51; Horlick fellow, 1948-52; Guggenheim fellow, 1955, Fulbright Research scholar, Germany, 1955-56. Life mem. Am. Pharm. Assn., chmn. com. on pub. relations, 1943-46, sec. Nat. Pharmacy Week com., 1946-48, chmn. com. radio broadcasts, 1943-46, sec. sect. history of pharmacy, 1949-50, vice chmn., 1950-51, chmn., 1951-52, research asso., 1964-65; chmn. Joint Com. on Pharmacy Coll. Libraries, 1960-61; U.S. del. Internat. Pharm. Fedn., Paris, 1953, London, 1955, Vienna, 1962; U.S. del. World Union Socs. History Pharmacy, Paris, 1953, London, 1955, Vienna, 1962 (v.p. 1962-65), Prague, 1971, Paris, 1973, Innsbruck, 1977; U.S. rep. to Middle East Pharm. Congress, Beirut, 1956; sec. sect. hist. pharm. and biochem. Pan-Am. Congress of Pharm. and Biochem., Washington, 1957. Recipient Edward Kremers award (for writings), 1964; nat. award Rho Chi, 1967; Schelenz plaquette Internat. Soc. for History Pharmacy, 1971; Remington honor medal Am. Pharm. Assn., 1972; Urdang medal, 1976. Mem. Wis. Pharm. Assn., Internat. Acad. History Pharmacy (1st v.p. 1970—), Internat. Pharm. Fedn., Am. Assn. History of Medicine (exec. council 1966-69), Internat. Gesellschaft fur Geschichte der Pharmazie (exec. bd. 1965—), History Sci. Soc.; corr. mem. Société d'Histoire de la Pharmacie, Sociedad de Farmacia e Quimica de Sao Paulo, Deutschen Gesellschaft fur Geschichte der Medizin, Naturwissenschaft und Technik; hon. mem. Associazione Italiana di Storia della Farmacia; Cercle Benelux d' Histoire de la Pharmacie; mem. Sigma Xi, Rho Chi (mem. nat. exec. council 1957-59), Phi Delta Chi. Unitarian. Co-author books and contbr. to pharm. and hist. publs. Office: Pharmacy Bldg Madison WI 53706

SONNEKALB, WILLIAM FREDERICK, JR., lawyer; b. Newark, Sept. 26, 1903; s. William Frederick and Meta (Abbe) S.; S.B., Mass. Inst. Tech., 1925; J.D., George Washington U., 1928; m. Jeannette Forsyth, June 22, 1940; children—Anne F. Sonnekalb Iskrant), June F. Sonnekalb Dwyer. Admitted to N.Y. bar, 1929; since practiced in N.Y.C., partner firm Howson & Howson, 1928-65, Davis, Hoxie, Faithfull & Hapgood, 1965—. Trustee Family Service Assn., Summit, N.J., 1964-70. Mem. Am. Bar Assn., Am., N.Y. patent law assns., Phi Beta Epsilon, Theta Tau. Congregationalist (deacon 1971-73). Home: 74 Blackburn Rd Summit NJ 07901 Office: 45 Rockefeller Plaza New York City NY 10020

SONNEMANN, HARRY, elec. engr.; b. Munich, Germany, Sept. 3, 1924; s. Leopold and Emmy (Markus) S.; came to U.S., 1938, naturalized, 1944; B.S., Poly. Inst. Bklyn., 1954; m. Shirley E. Battles, Nov. 25, 1949; children—Carol Jean, Joyce Elaine, Patricia Ann. Research electroence-phalography, 1944-47; asst. to dir. electronics dept., AEC contract, Columbia U., 1947-50, supr. electronics shop Columbia Hudson Labs., 1951-53, head electronics dept., 1954-59, asst. dir. Project Artemis, 1959-64, asst. dir. Hudson labs., 1961-64; asst. dir. field engring. Advanced Research Projects Agy., Nuclear Test Detection Office, 1964-67, acting dep. dir. Nuclear Test Detection Office, 1967-68; spl. asst. in electronics to asst. sec. navy for research and devel. Navy Dept., 1968-76, spl. asst. to asst. sec. navy for research and devel., 1976-77; asst. to chief engr. NASA, 1977-78, dep. chief engr., 1978—; chmn. Dept. Def. Tactical Satellite Exec. Steering Group, 1968-69, chmn. Dept. Def. nav. satellite exec. steering group, 1969-70, 72-73, Treas., Art League. No. Va., 1967-68. Clubs: Washington Figure Skating (dir. 1968-73, treas. 1969-72), Ice of Washington (pres. 1974-76). Home: 8360 Greensboro Dr McLean VA 22102 Office: 600 Independence Ave Washington DC 20546

SONNEMANN, ROGER CHRISTOPHER, mining co. exec.; b. Carlinville, Ill., July 4, 1919; s. Otto Charles and Lucie (Heinemeyer) S.; B.S. in Chem. Engring., U. Ill., 1940; J.D., Boston Coll., 1948; LL.D., Blackburn Coll., Carlinville, 1968; m. Helen L. Arnett, Apr. 25, 1942; children—David B., Judith L. With Monsanto Chem. Co., 1940-51, indsl. relations dir. Merrimac div., 1947-51; dir. personnel McDonnell Aircraft Corp., St. Louis, 1951-59; dir. indsl. relations Hooker Chem. Corp., 1959-62, v.p. indsl. and pub. relations, 1962-68; v.p. adminstrn. and employee relations Amax Inc. (formerly Am. Metal Climax, Inc.), N.Y.C., 1968-79, sr. v.p., 1979—; instr. Univ. Coll., Washington U., St. Louis, 1954-56. Dir. Radiation Tech. Inc., Hawaii Pacific Growth Fund, Mktg. and Systems Devel. Treas. sch. dist. bd. dirs. Kirkwood R-7 Sch., 1956-59. Vice-pres., AMAX Found., 1969—. Mem. Am. Mgmt. Assn., Am. Soc. Personnel Adminstrn., Am. Inst. Chem. Engrs., Mass. Bar Assn., Labor Policy Assn. (dir. 1972—), U.S. C. of C. (dir. 1972-78), N.Y. Indsl. Relations Assn., Phi Kappa Sigma. Republican. Presbyn. Home: 5 Deerfield Rd

Chappaqua NY 10514 Office: Amax Inc Amax Center Greenwich CT 06830

SONNENBLICK, BENJAMIN PAUL, radiation biologist, educator; b. N.Y.C., May 31, 1910; s. Moritz and Esther (Berkowitz) S.; B.S., Coll. City N.Y., 1930; postgrad. U. Mich.,1931-32; M.S., N.Y. U., 1934, Ph.D., 1938; m. Estelle Prussin, Apr. 10, 1939; children—Ruth, Mark; m. 2d, Perle Beegel, Aug. 15, 1966; children—Ellen, Jane. Instr. biology, Guggenheim fellow Queens Coll., 1941-42; asst. prof. Rutgers U., 1947-49, asso. prof., 1949-55, prof. biology, 1955—, chmn. biology dept., 1958-62, chmn. zoology and physiology depts., 1962-65; mem. corp. Marine Biol. Lab., Woods Hole, Mass.; mem. N.J. Commn. on Radiation Protection, 1958; chmn. N.J. Com. on Licensing for Possession and Use Radioisotopes; sci. com. 3 Nat. Council Radiation Protection and Measurements; chmn. adv. com. Nuclear Medicine N.J. Health Dept.; mem. N.J. Bd. Examiners X-Ray Technologists, 1978—. Served from 2d lt. to capt., USAAF, 1943-46. F.A.A.A.S.; mem. Genetics Soc. Am., Radiation Research Soc., Soc. Naturalists, Am. Soc. Human Genetics, Environmental Mutagen Soc., Sigma Xi. Editor: Protection in Diagnostic Radiology, 1959. Author: Low and Very Low Dose Influences of Ionizing Radiations on Cells and Organisms, Including Man: A Bibliography, 1972; mem. editorial bd. Environ. Mutagenesis, 1978—; also articles. Office: Rutgers University 195 University Ave Newark NJ 07102. *My only real success is observing my active children, all deeply imbued with a sense of social justice. They work at this individually, in their fashion.*

SONNENBLICK, EDMUND HIRAM, cardiologist; b. New Haven, Dec. 7, 1932; s. Ira J. and Rosalind H. S.; B.A. summa cum laude, Wesleyan U., Middletown, Conn., 1954; M.D. cum laude, Harvard U., 1958; m. Linda Bland, Dec. 21, 1954; children—Emily, Annie, Charlotte. Intern, resident in medicine Presbyn. Hosp., N.Y.C., 1958-60, 62-63; sr. investigator cardiology br. Nat. Heart Inst., Bethesda, Md., 1963-67; asso. prof. cardiology Harvard Med. Sch., Boston, also dir. cardiovascular research Peter Bent Brigham Hosp., Boston, 1967-75; prof. medicine, chief div. cardiology Albert Einstein Coll. Medicine, N.Y.C., 1975—. Served as sr. surgeon USPHS, 1960-62. Mem. Phi Beta Kappa, Sigma Xi, Alpha Omega Alpha. Clubs: Woods Hole and Noroton Yacht; Harvard (Boston). Author books on cardiovascular topics; contbr. articles to profl. publs.; editor: Progress in Cardiovascular Diseases, 1973—. Home: 138 Goodwives River Rd Darien CT 06820 Office: Albert Einstein Coll Medicine 1300 Morris Park Ave Bronx NY 10461

SONNENFELDT, HELMUT, former govt. ofcl., educator; b. Berlin, Germany, Sept. 13, 1926; s. Walter H. and Gertrude (Liebenthal) S; came to U.S., 1944, naturalized, 1945; A.B., Johns Hopkins, 1950, M.A., 1951; m. Marjorie Hecht, Oct. 4, 1953; children—Babette H., Walter H., Stewart H. With Dept. State, Washington, 1952—, formerly dir. Office Research and Analysis for USSR and Eastern Europe, counselor, 1974-77; lectr. Sch. Advanced Internat. Studies, Johns Hopkins U., 1958-69, vis. scholar, 1977-78; vis. scholar Brookings Instn., Washington, 1978—; sr. mem. Nat. Security Council, 1969-74. Served with AUS, 1945-46. Mem. Am. Assn. Slavic Studies, Am. Polit. Sci. Assn., Inst. Strategic Studies (London), Royal Inst. Internat. Affairs (London), Council on Fgn. Relations N.Y., Pi Delta Epsilon. Home: 4105 Thornapple St Chevy Chase MD 20015 Office: Brookings Instn Washington DC 20520

SONNENFELDT, RICHARD WOLFGANG, broadcasting co. exec.; b. Berlin, July 3, 1923; s. Walter H. and Gertrude (Liebenthal) S.; B.S. in Elec. Engring., Johns Hopkins U., 1949; postgrad. U. Pa., 1953-56; m. Shirley C. Aronoff, Dec. 23, 1949; children—Ann Elizabeth, Lawrence Alan, Michael William. Mgr. engring. and prodn. RCA, 1949-62; gen. mgr. digital systems div. Foxboro Co., 1962-65; pres., dir. Digitronics Corp., 1965-70; v.p. RCA Corp., 1970-79; chmn. bd. Electronic Indsl. Engring. Corp., 1972-75; exec. v.p. ops. and tech. services NBC, N.Y.C., 1979—. Served with AUS, 1942-45. Fellow IEEE; mem. Instrument Soc. Am. (sr.), Tau Beta Pi, Omicron Delta Kappa. Contbr. articles to profl. jours. Home: 13 Hillside Ave Port Washington NY 11050 Office: 30 Rockefeller Plaza New York NY 10020

SONNENREICH, MICHAEL ROY, lawyer; b. N.Y.C., May 5, 1938; s. Emanuel Hirsch and Fay (Rosenberg) S.; A.B., U. Wis., 1960; J.D., Harvard U., 1963; m. Linda Beth Swartz, Sept. 4, 1961; children—Peter Charles, Nina Manya. Admitted to Mass. bar, 1975, U.S. Ct. Mil. Appeals, 1965, U.S. Supreme Ct. bar, 1965; atty. Dept. Justice, Washington, 1966-68; spl. asst. to U.S. Atty. for D.C., 1968-71; dep. gen. counsel Fed. Bur. Narcotics and Dangerous Drugs, Dept. Justice, Washington, 1968-71; exec. dir. Nat. Commn. on Marijuana and Drug Abuse, Washington, 1971-73; sr. partner firm Chayet and Sonnenreich, P.C., Washington, 1973—; dir., chmn. audit com. Penn-Dixie Industries. Pres., Nat. Coordinating Council on Drug Edn., 1973-74; trustee New Eng. Conservatory Music, N.C. State Mus. Art Found., Mus. African Art, Washington; mem. adv. bd. U. Va. Art Mus. Served with U.S. Army, 1963-65. Mem. Am. Bar Assn. Co-author 2 books; contbr. articles to profl. jours. Home: 4720 Linnean Ave NW Washington DC 20008 Office: Suite 720 600 New Hampshire Ave NW Washington DC 20037 also One Federal St 34th Floor Boston MA 02110

SONNENSCHEIN, HUGO, lawyer; b. Chgo., Feb. 22, 1917; s. Hugo and Irene (Plaut) S.; student Swarthmore Coll., 1934-36; B.A., Lake Forest Coll., 1944; LL.B., J.D., U. Va., 1941; LL.M., John Marshall Law Sch., 1945; m. Virginia Bensinger, June 21, 1947; children—Deane (Mrs. Gregory Engstrom), Hugo III. Admitted to Ill. bar, 1942; asst. U.S. atty., Chgo., 1945-46; pvt. practice, Chgo., 1946-54; partner firm Martin, Craig, Chester & Sonnenschein, Chgo., 1954—; instr. labor law Lake Forest Coll., 1947-48; asst. to chief justice Municipal Ct. Chgo., 1956-57; dir. H. Kohnstamm & Co. Trustee, Lake Forest College; pres., trustee Modern Poetry Assn., Library Internat. Relations. Served to capt. USAAF, 1942-45. Mem. Am., Ill. (vice chmn. state taxation com. 1967-68), Chgo. bar assns., Assn. Art Historians (London), Selden Soc., Judge Advocates Assn., Phi Beta Kappa, Delta Upsilon, Delta Sigma Rho. Clubs: Law, Ill. Athletic, Lake Shore Country, Mid-day (Chgo.); Farmington (Va.). Editor Chgo. Bar Record, 1950-66. Home: 809 Lincoln Ave Winnetka IL 60093 Office: 115 S LaSalle St Chicago IL 60603

SONNENSCHEIN, HUGO FREUND, economist, editor; b. N.Y.C., Nov. 14, 1940; s. Leo William and Lillian Irene (Mary) S.; A.B., U. Rochester, 1961; M.S., Purdue U., 1963, Ph.D., 1964; m. Elizabeth Gunn, Aug. 26, 1962; children—Leah, Amy, Rachel. Mem. faculty dept. econs. U. Minn., 1964-70, prof., 1968-70; prof. econs. U. Mass., Amherst, 1970-73; Northwestern U., 1973-76, Princeton U., 1976—; vis. prof. U. Andes, Columbia, 1965, Tel-Aviv U., Israel, 1972, Hebrew U., 1973, U. Paris, 1978, U. Aix-en-Provence, France, 1978. Social Sci. Research Council fellow, 1967-68, NSF fellow, 1970—; Ford Found. fellow, 1970-71; Guggenheim Found. fellow, 1976-77. Mem. Econometric Soc. (mem. council). Editor: Econometrica, 1977—; asso. editor Jour. Econ. Theory, 1972-75; bd. editors Jour. Math. Econs., 1974—, SIAM Jour., 1976—. Contbr. articles to profl. jours. Home: 25 Campbelton Circle Princeton NJ 08540 Office: 215 Dickinson Hall Princeton U Princeton NJ 08540

SONNENSCHEIN, RALPH ROBERT, physiologist; b. Chgo., Aug. 14, 1923; s. Robert and Flora (Kieferstein) S.; student Swarthmore Coll., 1940-42, U. Chgo., 1942-43; B.S., Northwestern U., 1943, B.M., 1946, M.S., 1946, M.D., 1947; Ph.D., U. Ill., 1950; m. Patricia W. Niddrie, June 21, 1952; children—David, Lisa, Ann. Research asst. in physiology Northwestern U. Med. Sch., 1944-46; intern Michael Reese Hosp., Chgo., 1946-47; successively research fellow clin. sci., research asst. psychiatry, research asso. psychiatry U. Ill. Med. Sch., Chgo., 1947-51; mem. faculty U. Calif. Med. Sch., Los Angeles, 1951—, prof. physiology, 1962—; liaison scientist Office Naval Research, London, 1971-72. Served with AUS, 1943-46. Spl. research fellow USPHS, 1957-58; fellow Swedish Med. Research Council, 1964-65; grantee USAF, Office Naval Research, NIH, NSF. Mem. Am. Physiol. Soc., Microcirculatory Soc., Soc. Exptl. Biology and Medicine, AAAS. Author papers on pain, innervation of skin, peripheral circulation. Home: 18212 Kingsport Dr Malibu CA 90265 Office: Dept Physiology Univ Calif Medical Sch Los Angeles CA 90024

SONNINO, CARLO BENVENUTO, elec. mfg. co. exec.; b. Torino, Italy, May 12, 1904; s. Moise and Amelia S.; came to U.S., 1952, naturalized, 1959; Ph.D., U. Milano (Italy), 1927, LL.B., 1928; m. Mathilde Girodat, Jan. 21, 1949; children—Patricia, Frederic, Bruno. Dir. research Italian Aluminum Co., Milano, 1928-34; pres. Laesa Cons. Firm, Milano, 1934-43; tech. adviser Boxal, Fribourg, Switzerland, 1944-52, Thompson Brand, Rouen, France, 1972-76; materials engring. mgr. Emerson Electric Co., St. Louis, 1956-72, staff scientist, 1973—; prof. metall. engring. Washington U., St. Louis, 1960-68, U. Mo., Rolla, 1968—; cons. Monsanto Chem. Co., Wagner Co., other maj. firms U.S., Europe. Decorated knight comdr. Italian Republic. Fellow Am. Soc. Metals, ASTM (hon.), Alpha Sigma Mu. Patentee process for synthetic cryolite; patentee in field of metallurgy, corrosion; mfr. 1st aluminum cans in world, 1940. Home: 7206 Kingsbury Blvd Saint Louis MO 63130 Office: Emerson E and S Div Emerson Electric Co 8100 Florissant St Saint Louis MO 63136. *I have always been guided by the highest ethical standards in professional, business, and civic life, even in the most difficult moments, and by strong dislike for hypocrisy and greed.*

SONNY. see Bono, Sonny Salvatore

SONS, RAYMOND WILLIAM, journalist; b. Harvey, Ill., Aug. 25, 1926; s. William Henry and Gladys Lydia (Steinko) S.; B.A., U. Mich., 1950; m. Bettina Dieckmann; children—David, Pamela (Mrs. William Haan), Ronald. Reporter, mng. editor Murphysboro (Ill.) Daily Independent edit. So. Illinoisan newspaper, 1950-52; asso. news editor Middletown (Ohio) Jour., 1952-53; reporter, asst. city editor, sportswriter, sports editor Chgo. Daily News, 1953-78; sports editor, columnist Chgo. Sun-Times, 1978—; Chgo. corr. Sports Illustrated mag. Served with USAAF, 1945-46. Recipient Best Sports Story in Ill. award U.P.I., 1970, Marshall Field award for outstanding editorial contbn. to Chgo. Daily News, 1972; Best Sports Column, AP Sports Editors, 1979. Mem. Profl. Football Writers Am., Chgo. Press Club. Roman Catholic. Home: 6813 N Seeley Ave Chicago IL 60645 Office: 401 N Wabash Ave Chicago IL 60611

SONTAG, FREDERICK EARL, educator; b. Long Beach, Calif., Oct. 2, 1924; s. M. Burnett and Cornelia (Nicholson) S.; B.A., Stanford, 1949; M.A., Yale, 1951, Ph.D., 1952; m. Carol Ann Furth, June 10, 1950; children—Grant Furth, Anne Burnett. Instr., Yale, 1951-52; mem. faculty Pomona Coll., Claremont, Calif., 1952—, Robert C. Denison prof. philosophy, 1962—, chmn. dept., 1960-67, 76-77; chmn. coordinating com. philosophy Claremont Grad. Sch. and Univ. Center, 1960-65; vis. prof. philosophy Union Theol. Sem., N.Y.C., 1959-60, Pontifical Coll. Sant' Anselmo, Rome, Italy, 1966-67, U. Copenhagen (Denmark), 1972; Japan Found. vis. prof. U. Kyoto, 1974; theologian-in-residence Am. Ch. in Paris (France), 1973; Fulbright vis. lectr., India, Asia, Pacific Areas, 1977-78. Pres. bd. dirs. Claremont Family Service, 1960-64; mem. nat. adv. council Kent Fellowships, Danforth Found., 1963-66; bd. dirs. Pilgrim Place, Claremont, past co-chmn. challenge gift com. Served with AUS, 1943-46. Recipient Wig Distinguished Prof. award Pomona Coll., 1970, 75. Fellow Soc. Religion Higher Edn.; mem. Am. Philos. Assn., A.A.U.P., Metaphys. Soc. Am., Am. Acad. Religion, Phi Beta Kappa. Author: Divine Perfection: Possible Ideas of God, 1962; The Existentialist Prolegomena, 1968; The Future of Theology, 1969; The Crisis of Faith, 1969; Problems of Metaphysics, 1970; The God of Evil, 1970; God, Why Did You Do That?, 1970; How Philosophy Shapes Theology, 1971; (with John Roth) The American Religious Experience, 1972; Love Beyond Pain, 1976; (with John Roth) Sun Myung Moon and the Unification Church, 1977, God and America's Future, 1977; Understanding Kierkegaard, 1979; What Can God Do? And Not Do?, 1979; also articles. Editor: (Kierkegaard) Authority and Revelation, 1966. Office: Dept Philosophy Pomona Coll Claremont CA 91711

SONTAG, FREDERICK H., public affairs and research cons.; b. Breslau, Germany, Apr. 29, 1924; came to U.S., 1937, naturalized, 1943; s. Hugo and Lotte (Laband) S.; grad. Phillips Acad., 1942; A.B., Colby Coll., 1946; grad. student Columbia, 1947-48; m. Edith Virginia Sweeney, Feb. 8, 1958. Asso. Earl Newsom & Co., pub. relations counsel, N.Y.C., 1947-48; asst. dir. Citizens Found., Syracuse, N.Y., 1948-50; pub. relations and advt. cons. Merchants Nat. Bank, Syracuse, 1948-51; central N.Y. corr. Business Week, other McGraw-Hill publs., 1950-51, dir. pub. relations Bus. Week mag., 1951-55; manuscript cons. McGraw-Hill Book Co., 1951-60; spl. cons. to U.S. Sec. Labor, 1954-61, congressman Thomas B. Curtis, 1957-69, Civic Service, Inc., St. Louis and Washington, 1957—, 1960 Winter Olympics, Sec. HEW, 1969, 72, U.S. Internat. Trade Commn. chmn., 1975-77; asso. Anna M. Rosenberg Assos., 1957-60; spl. cons. Monsanto Co., 1962-77; spl. cons. to Edwin J. Putzell, Coburn, Croft, Shepherd, Herzog & Putzell, St. Louis, 1977—, 1st Caribbean Mainland Capital Co., Inc., N.Y.C., San Juan, P.R., 1962; spl. cons. bishop Episcopal Diocese of Springfield (Ill.), 1947-72; program and planning asso. to dir. broadcasting Nat. Council Episcopal Ch., 1956-61; exec. dir. com. increased minority staffing U.S. Ho. of Reps., Washington, 1961-69; dir. Study of Am. Polit. Parties, Cambridge, Mass., also South Orange, N.J., 1969—; vis. lectr. Colby Coll., Waterville, Maine, 1975; lectr., discussion leader John F. Kennedy Sch. Govt., Inst. Politics, Harvard, Brookings Inst., Washington, Woodrow Wilson Internat. Center Scholars, Washington, Am. Assembly, Arden House, Columbia. Analyst-commentator Maine Pub. Broadcasting Network, 1973-75, Suburban Cablevision TV3, East Orange, N.J., 1977—; spl. cons. Pres.'s Com. on Govt. Employment Policy, 1955-60; bd. advisers Husson Coll., Bangor, Maine, 1965-79, trustee, 1979—; cons. Bd. Christian Social Concerns, United Meth. Ch., 1965-71; legis. cons. to N.J. State Senator James H. Wallwork, 1968-79. Recipient certificates achievement Am. Pub. Relations Assn., 1952, 54, Silver Anvil award, 1953; Spl. Achievement award U.S. Internat. Trade Commn., 1976. Mem. Pub. Relations Soc. Am., Am. Polit. Sci. Assn., Am. Assn. Polit Cons. (charter, also dir.), N.J. Conf. Promotion Better Govt., Phi Delta Theta, Phi Gamma Mu. Anglo-Catholic. Club: Overseas Press (N.Y.C.). Co-author: Parties: The Real Opportunity for Effective Citizen Politics, 1972, softcover, 1973. Editorial adv. bd. Electoral Studies Yearbook. Contbr. Op-ed pages N.Y. Times, Los Angeles Times; nat. corr. Am. Ch. News, Witness, Living Ch., Scroll; contbg. writer, reviewer Worrall Newspapers, No. N.J. Home: 764 Scotland Rd South Orange NJ 07079 also Seal Harbor ME 04675

SONTAG, JAMES MITCHELL, exptl. oncologist; b. Denver, Dec. 8, 1939; s. Samuel Henry and Rose Hazel (Silverman) S.; B.S., Lamar State Coll. Tech., Beaumont, Tex.; M.S., U. Ill., 1967; Ph.D. (grad. stipend), Weizmann Inst. Sci., Rehovot, Israel, 1971; m. Evelyne Andrée Karsenti, Mar. 26, 1969; children—Ariella, Eythan. Damon Runyon Meml. Fund Cancer Research postdoctoral fellow, 1971-72; guest worker Nat. Cancer Inst., NIH, Bethesda, Md., 1972-73, staff fellow, 1973-74, exptl. oncologist, 1973-76, mgr. carcinogen bioassay program, asst. to dir. cancer cause and prevention, 1976-80, exec. sec. Clearinghouse on Environ. Carcinogens, 1976—, asst. dir. for interagy. affairs Office of Dir., 1980—. Served with AUS, 1956-59. Beaumont League Women Voters scholar, 1963-65. Mem. Beta Beta Beta. Author, editor in field. Home: 1517 Allview Dr Rockville MD 20854 Office: Nat Cancer Inst Bldg 31 Room 10A06 Bethesda MD 20205

SONTAG, SUSAN, author, film dir. Author: (novels) The Benefactor, 1963; Death Kit, 1967; (stories) I, etcetera, 1978; (essays) Against Interpretation, 1966; Trip to Hanoi, 1968; Styles of Radical Will, 1969; On Photography, 1977; Illness as Metaphor, 1978; (film scripts) Duet for Cannibals, 1970, Brother Carl, 1974; editor, author introduction: Antonin Artaud: Selected Writings, 1976; dir. film Duet for Cannibals, 1969, Brother Carl, 1971, Promised Lands, 1974. Guggenheim fellow, 1966, 75; Rockefeller Found. fellow, 1965, 74; recipient Ingram Merrill Found. award in lit. in field of Am. Letters, 1976; Creative Arts award Brandeis U., 1976; Arts and Letters award Am. Acad. Arts and Letters, 1976; prize Nat. Book Critics Circle, 1978. Mem. Am. Inst. Arts and Letters. Address: care Farrar Straus & Giroux Inc 19 Union Sq W New York NY 10003

SONTHEIMER, MORTON, journalist, pub. relations exec.; b. N.Y.C.; s. Emanuel W. and Sadie (Alderman) S.; student Temple U.; m. Alice Hradecky, July 3, 1948; children—Marcia, Donna Jo. Reporter, Atlantic City Daily Press, Phila. Inquirer, Newark Star-Eagle, feature writer N.Y. Telegram, N.Y.C.; feature writer, city editor, news editor, mng. editor San Francisco News; asst. to pres. Am. Heritage Found., N.Y.C.; pres. Sontheimer and Co., Inc., N.Y.C., 1957—; cons. indsl. and tourism devel. State Dept., 1961, also to govts. of Surinam, Venezuela, Guatemala, Indonesia, Japan, P.R., Jamaica, Kenya, Netherlands Antilles, Taiwan. Served as hist. officer AUS, 1943-45; S.W. PTO. Mem. Am. Soc. Journalists and Authors (past pres.), Sex Info. Edn. Council U.S. (vice chairperson). Author: Newspaperman, 1942; Attention, Comrades, 1955. Contbr. articles and fiction to Esquire, Good Housekeeping, Ladies Home Jour., Look, McCalls Mag., Readers Digest, Redbook, Saturday Rev. Office: Sontheimer and Co Inc 445 Park Ave New York NY 10022

SOONG, TSU-TEH, educator; b. Honan, China, Feb. 10, 1934; s. Tung and Yu-Hsieh (Lee) S.; B.S., U. Dayton, 1955; postgrad. U. Ill., 1955-56; M.S., Purdue U., 1958, Ph.D., 1962; m. Dorothy Yen-Ling Tsai, June 5, 1959; children—Karen, Stephen, Susan. Instr. engring. sci. Purdue U., 1958-62; sr. research engr. Jet Propulsion Lab., Pasadena, Calif., 1962-63; asst. prof. engring. sci. State U. N.Y. at Buffalo, 1963-66, asso. prof., 1966-68, prof., 1968—; part-time lectr. engring. U. Calif. at Los Angeles, 1962-63; part-time research mathematician Cornell Aero. Lab., Buffalo, 1964-67, prin. research mathematician, 1967-70. NSF Sci. Faculty fellow Tech. U. Delft (Netherlands), 1966-67. Mem. Soc. Indsl. and Applied Math., A.A.A.S., N.Y. Acad. Sci., Sigma Xi, Tau Beta Pi. Research in stochastic processes and stochastic differential equations in engring. Home: 218 MacArthur Dr Williamsville NY 14221

SOOY, FRANCIS ADRIAN, physician, educator; b. Coalinga, Calif., July 1, 1915; s. Francis Adrian and Mabel Maleta (Boone) S.; B.A., U. Calif. at Berkeley, 1937; M.D., U. Calif. at Francisco, 1941, postdoctoral tng. surgery and otolaryngology, 1941-42; postdoctoral tng. otolaryngology Washington U. Med. Sch., St. Louis, 1942-44; m. Elizabeth Dean Thompson, Apr. 17, 1944, children—Charles Daniel, Jane Anne, Elizabeth Dean, Frances McAllister, Adrian Thompson. Mem. faculty U. Calif. Sch. Medicine, San Francisco, 1946—, prof. otolarynology, 1961—, dir. audiology and speech clinic, 1953-72, chmn. div. otolaryngology, 1958-67, chmn. dept. otol., 1967-72, chmn. acad. council, chmn. acad. assembly, 1969-70, Univ. chancellor, 1972—. Served with USNR, 1944-46. Mem. otolaryngology tng. grant com. NIH, 1959-63, nat. adv. council neurol. diseases and blindness, 1964-68; bd. dirs. Am. Council Otolaryngology. Diplomate Am. Bd. Otolaryngology (dir. 1968—). Mem. Am. Acad. Ophthalmology and Otalaryngology, Am. Laryngol. Assn., Am. Laryngol., Rhinol. and Otol. Soc. (pres. elect 1977), Am. Otol. Soc., Pacific Coast Oto-Ophthal. Soc. (exec. sec.-treas. 1968—), Collegium ORL Amicitiae Sacrum (pres. 1980). Editorial bd. Annals Otology, Rhinology and Laryngology. Home: 9 5th Ave San Francisco CA 94118

SOPER, ALEXANDER COBURN, educator, author; b. Chgo., Feb. 18, 1904; s. Alexander Coburn and Bertha (Dunlop) S.; B.A., Hamilton Coll., 1925; L.H.D., 1962; M.F.A., Princeton U., 1929, Ph.D., 1944; m. Suzanne Townley Smyth, June 15, 1929; children—Suzanne Soper Clohesy, John Dunlop. Instr., Princeton U., 1929-30, 38-39; Rockefeller Found. fellow, Japan, 1935-38; asso. prof. history of art Bryn Mawr Coll., 1939-48, prof., 1948-62; prof. fine art Inst. Fine Arts, N.Y. U., 1960—, Jayne Wrightsman prof., 1971-73. Served from capt. to maj., USMCR, 1942-46. Mem. Coll. Art Assn. (award for distinguished teaching of art history 1977), Assn. Asian Studies, Am. Oriental Soc., Asia Soc. (trustee 1966-73), Japan Soc. Author: Evolution of Buddhist Architecture in Japan, 1942; Kuo Jo-hsu's Experiences in Painting, 1951; Literary Evidence for Early Buddhist Art in China, 1959: Chinese, Korean, Japanese Bronzes (catalog of the Auriti Collection), 1966; Textual Evidence for the Secular Arts of China in the Period from Liu Sung through Sui, 1967. Contbr. sects. on architecture Pelican History of Art, vol. on Japan, 1956, China, 1956; also articles on Asian art. Editor Artibus Asiae, 1958. Home: 1441 Orchard Way Rosemont PA 19010 Office: 1 E 78th St New York City NY 10021

SOPKIN, GEORGE, cellist; b. Chgo., Apr. 3, 1914; s. Isador and Esther (Sopkin) S.; student with Daniel Saidenberg, Am. Conservatory Music, 1930-32, with Emmanuel Feurermann, in Switzerland, Chgo., Mus. Coll., 1932-34; D.Mus. (hon.), Northland Coll., 1977; m. Thelma Friedman, July 5, 1936; children—Monica, Paula; m. 2d, Carol Borchard Durham, Aug. 30, 1956; children—Edwin, Anthony. Mem. Kansas City (Mo.) Philharmonic Orch., 1933-34, Chgo. Symphony Orch., 1934-40, Pro Arte String Quartet, 1940-42; asso. prof. music U. Wis., 1940-42, artist-in-residence 1963-79, prof., 1967-77, Disting. prof., 1977—; founder, 1946, since mem. Fine Arts Quartet, Chgo.; staff ABC, Chgo., 1946-52; artist-in-residence Northwestern U., 1952-55, U. Wisconsin-Milw., Cleve. Inst.; soloist Kansas City (Mo.) Philharmonic Orch., Chgo. Symphony Orch., Ill. Symphony Orch., Milw. Chamber Orch., Saidenberg Symphonette; frequent TV appearances; artist of film for Ency. Brit. films, Nat. Ednl. TV films; recording artist for Mercury, Decca, Concert-disc, Everest; numerous tours Europe. Bd. dirs. Contemporary Concerts, Inc., Chgo. Served with USAAF, 1943-45. Mem. Lincoln Acad. Address: Newbury Neck Rd Surry ME 04684

SOPRANOS, ORPHEUS JAVARAS, mfg. co. exec.; b. Evanston, Ill., Oct. 4, 1935; s. James Javaras and Marigoula (Papalexatou) S.; A.B., U. Chgo., 1957, M.B.A., 1957; m. Angeline Buches, Dec. 31, 1959; children—Andrew Javaras, Katherine. Mgmt. trainee Ford Motor Co., Chgo., 1958-59; with Amsted Industries, Chgo., 1959—, dir. bus. research, 1966-70, treas., 1970—. Served with U.S. Army, 1958, 61-62. Mem. Am. Inst. C.P.A.'s, Ill. Soc. C.P.A.'s, Risk and Ins. Mgmt. Soc., Fin. Mgrs. Assn. Club: Univ. (Chgo.). Office: 3700 Prudential Plaza Chicago IL 60601

SORAH, BAXTER LEE, JR., labor union exec.; b. Lee County, Va., June 9, 1920; s. Baxter Lee and Laura Mae (Tignor) S.; degree McClungs Bus. Coll., Greensboro N.C., 1942; postgrad. Detroit Inst. Tech., 1950-52; certificate trade union program Harvard U., 1949; m. Eunice G. Gabel, Aug. 19, 1944; children—Sandra, Terry, Janice, Dian, Margaret, Charles, John Scott. Trackman, So. Ry. System, St. Charles, Va., 1940; chief clk.-organizer Southern System div. Brotherhood Maintenance of Way Employees, Greensboro, 1940-47, adminstrv. asst. to pres. Grand Lodge, 1948-70, internat. sec.-treas., 1970—; mem. R.R. Retirement Bd., 1970—; treas. Maintenance of Way Polit. League, 1970—. Served as flight officer USAAF, 1942-45; PTO. Decorated Bronze Star. Mem. AFL-CIO Sec.-Treas. Assn. Club: Lions. Office: 12050 Woodward Ave Brotherhood of Maintenance of Way Employees Detroit MI 48203

SORAUF, FRANCIS JOSEPH, educator; b. Grand Rapids, Mich., May 31, 1928; s. Francis Joseph and Mary Estelle (Norton) S.; B.A., U. Wis., 1950, M.A., 1952, Ph.D., 1953. Instr., then asst. prof. Pa. State U., 1953-61; vis. asso. prof. U. Ariz., 1960-61; mem. faculty U. Minn., 1961—, prof. polit. sci., 1965—, chmn. dept., 1966-69, dean Coll. Liberal Arts, 1973-78; Fulbright lectr., Italy, 1964-65. Mem. Mpls. Library Bd., 1966-69. Social Sci. Research Council fellow, 1958; Guggenheim fellow, 1969-70. Mem. Am. (council 1968-70, chmn. nominating com. 1974-75, v.p. 1976-77, Atherton prize 1962), Midwest (pres. 1973-74) polit. sci. assns., AAUP, Phi Beta Kappa, Phi Kappa Phi. Democrat. Author: Party and Representation, 1963; Political Parties in the American System, 1964; Political Science: An Informal Overview, 1965; Party Politics in America, 1968; The Wall of Separation: The Constitutional Politics of Church and State, 1976; also articles. Home: 3506 Edmund Blvd Minneapolis MN 55406

SORBY, DONALD LLOYD, univ. dean; b. Fremont, Nebr., Aug. 12, 1933; s. Lloyd A. and Orpha M. (Simmons) S.; B.S. in Pharmacy, U. Nebr., 1955; M.S., U. Wash., 1958, Ph.D., 1960; m. Jacquelyn J. Burchard, Nov. 7, 1959; children—Thomas, Sharon. Dir. pharm. services U. Calif., San Francisco, 1970-72; chmn. dept. pharmacy practice Sch. Pharmacy, U. Wash., Seattle, 1972-74; dean Sch. of Pharmacy, U. Mo., Kansas City, 1974—. Asso. fellow Am. Coll. Apothecaries; mem. Am. Pharm. Assn., Am. Assn. Colls. of Pharmacy, Fedn. Internat. Pharmaceutique, Mo. Pharm. Assn., Acad. Pharm. Scis., Sigma Xi. Contbr. articles in field to profl. jours. Home: 14205 W 48th St Shawnee KS 66216 Office: Sch of Pharmacy U Mo Kansas City MO 64110

SOREL, CLAUDETTE MARGUERITE, pianist; b. Paris; d. Michel M. and Elizabeth S.; grad. with top honors Juilliard Sch. Music, 1947, postgrad., 1948; student of Sigismund Stojowski, Sari Biro, Olga Samaroff Stokowski, Mieczyslaw Horszowski, Rudolf Serkin, ensemble with Felix Salmond, musicology with Dr. Robert Tangeman, music history with Marian Bauer; grad. Curtis Inst. Music, 1953; B.S. cum laude in Math., Columbia U., 1954. Debut at Town Hall, N.Y.C., 1943, since appeared in leading cities of U.S.; performed with N.Y. Philharmonic, London Philharmonic, Zurich, Boston, San Antonio, Milw., NBC, Phila., New Orleans and Cin. symphony orchs., Youth Orch. of Am., 200 others; appeared at Aspen, Berkshire, Chautauqua, other festivals; European concert tours, 1956, 57, 58, to Eng., Sweden, Holland, Germany, Switzerland, France; appeared on various radio, TV programs; made recordings for R.C.A. Victor Rec. Co., Monitor Records, Musical Heritage. music faculty, vis. prof. Kans. U., 1961-62; asso. prof. music Ohio State U., 1962-64; prof. music, head piano dept. State U. N.Y., Fredonia, 1964—, Distinguished Univ. prof., 1969—, univ. artist, 1969—, faculty exchange scholar, 1976—; mem. internat. jury Van Cliburn Internat. Piano Competition, Tex., 1966, Que. and Ont. Music Festivals, 1967, 75; 2000 solo appearances, U.S. and Europe. Fulbright scholar, 1951; Ford Found. Concert grantee, 1962; recipient Harry Rosenberg Meml., Frank Damrosch prizes, 1947; winner Phila. Orch. Youth Auditions, 1950, to appear with orch. under direction Eugene Ormandy; Nat. Fedn. Music Clubs Young Artist award, 1951; citation for service to Am. music Nat. Fedn. Music Clubs, 1966; citation Nat. Assn. Composers and Condrs., 1967, Mu Phi Epsilon, 1968. Bd. dirs. Olga Samaroff Found., Jr. com. aux. bd. N.Y. Philharmonic Symphony Orch., N.Y. State Nat. Fedn. Music Clubs; mem. adv. bd. Univ. Library Soc. Mem. Nat. Music Council (dir. 1973—, chmn. performance com.), Pi Kappa Lambda, Mu Phi Epsilon (dir. Meml. Found., nat. chmn. Sterling Staff Concert Series; citation 1968). Author: Compendium of Piano Technique, 1970; Mind Your Musical Manners - Off and On Stage, 1972, 2d edit., 1975; The 24 Magic Keys, 3 vols., 1974; The Three Nocturnes of Rachmaninoff, 1974, 2d edit., 1975; Fifteen Smorgasbord Studies for the Piano, 1975; Arensky Piano Etudes, 1976. Linguist, painter of oil portraits; contbr. articles to profl. mags. Compiler: The Modern Music of Today, 1947; Serge Prokofieff - His Life and Works, 1947; The Ornamentations in Mozart's Music, 1948. Home: 333 West End Ave New York City NY 10023. *The most difficult achievement in life is to try to reach one's goals while keeping one's highest idealism and integrity. If these aims can also be maintained in an atmosphere of freedom and respect for quality in all aspects of life, then the individual is most fortunate.*

SOREL, EDWARD, artist; b. N.Y.C., Mar. 26, 1929; s. Morris and Rebecca (Kleinberg) Schwartz; diploma Cooper Union, 1951; m. Nancy Caldwell, May 29, 1965; children—Jenny, Katherine; children by previous marriage—Madeline, Leo. Co-founder Pushpin Studio, 1953; free-lance artist, 1956—; syndicated Sorel's News Service, 1969-70, King Features; exhibited in Pushpin Studio retrospective at the Louvre, 1970, other European galleries, 1970-71; exhibited one-man show Graham Galleries, N.Y.C., 1973. Recipient awards Soc. Illustrators, also Art Dirs. Club N.Y.; Augustus St. Gauden's medal Cooper Union. Mem. Am. Inst. Graphic Arts, Alliance Graphique International. Author, illustrator: Moon Missing; Making The World Safe for Hypocrisy, 1972. Illustrator: Pablo Paints a Picture, 1961; Gwendolyn the Miracle Hen (N.Y. Herald Tribune Book award for illustration, 1962), 1963; What's Good for a Five-Year-Old, 1969; The Duck in the Gun, 1969; Word People, 1970; Magical Storybook, 1972; Superpen, 1978. Contbr. to nat. magazines; weekly cartoon in The Village Voice.

SORENSEN, ALLAN CHRESTEN, service co. exec.; b. Edson, Alta., Can., Apr. 27, 1938; came to U.S., 1962, naturalized, 1965; s. Henry and Vivien A. (Howie) S.; B.S. in Pharmacy, Drake U., 1961; children—Scott, Jody. Salesman, Hoffman LaRoche Pharm. Co., Kitchener, Ont., Can., 1961-62; salesman Labor Pool of Am., Inc., Chgo., 1962-63, sales mgr., 1963-67, pres., 1967—; with Personnel Pool of Am., Inc., Ft. Lauderdale, Fla., 1962—, pres., 1967—, chief exec. officer, 1978—; dir. H&R Block. Mem. Nat. Assn. Temporary Services (dir.), Exec. Assn. Ft. Lauderdale (dir.). Republican. Club: Rotary. Home: 1500 S Ocean Dr Fort Lauderdale FL 33316 Office: 303 SE 17th St Fort Lauderdale FL 33316

SORENSEN, CLARENCE WOODROW, ret. coll. pres.; b. Loup City, Nebr., Apr. 6, 1907; s. James C. and Anna (Madsen) S.; Ph.D., U. Chgo., 1951; L.H.D., Wittenberg U., 1963, Marycrest Coll., 1970; m. Edna L. Schaus, Aug. 13, 1938. Dir. Pakistan edn. project, 1951-52; asst. prof. Ill. State U., 1949-52, asso. prof., 1952-56, prof. geography, 1956-59, dean Grad. Sch., 1959-62; pres. Augustana Coll., Rock Island, Ill., 1962-75. Bd. dirs. Found. Inter Confessional Research, France, Luth. Sch. Theology, Chgo., 1976—. Recipient Distinguished Service award Quad-Cities Grad. Studies Center, Rock Island, Ill., 1975, Distinguished Community Service award Rock Island Rotary, 1975; named Man of Yr., Quad-Cities chpt. B'nai B'rith, 1975; decorated comdr. Order of North Star (Sweden). Fellow Royal Geol. Soc.; mem. Nat. Council Social Edn. (editorial bd. 1952-55), Phi Beta Kappa, Pi Kappa Delta, Gamma Theta Upsilon. Author: A World View, 1950; Ways of Our Land, 1954; (with H.H. Barrows, E.P. Parker) Our Big World, 1945, Old World Lands, 1948, The American Continents, 1947; co-author vols. published in Urdu: Neighbors in Asia, Europe and North America, The Southern Continents, Pakistan and the World, Regions and Resources, Economic Geography Physical Geography and Geology, 1952-54; also numerous articles, filmstrips in field. Home: 2025 E Lincoln St Bloomington IL 61701

SORENSEN, ERIK PER, cons. civil engr.; b. Copenhagen, Feb. 28, 1914; s. Ejnar A. and Helga (Hansen) S.; came to U.S., 1938, naturalized, 1941: B.S. in Civil Engring., Royal Tech. Coll., Copenhagen, 1937; M.S., Harvard U., 1939; m. Mariann Isler, Apr. 2, 1971; children—Ejnar Per, Erik Paul, Erling Patrick. Project engr. Charles T. Main, Inc., Boston, 1939-42; prin. engr. Inst. Inter Am. Affairs, Washington, 1942-46; overseas mgr., asso. partner Tippetts-Abbett-McCarthy-Stratton, N.Y.C., 1948-67, partner, 1967—. Registered profl. engr., Alaska, N.Y., Va. Fellow ASCE; mem. Nat. Soc. Profl. Engrs., Am. Cons. Engrs. Council. Club: Harvard (N.Y.C.). Home: 51 Craig Ct Fairfield CT 06430 Office: 655 Third Ave New York NY 10017

SORENSEN, GLADYS ELAINE, coll. dean; b. Rockville, Nebr., Oct. 17, 1922; d. Victor and Christine (Heide) Sorensen; B.S. in Nursing, U. Nebr., 1945; M.S. in Nursing, U. Colo., 1951; Ed.D., Columbia, 1964. Head nurse U. Neb. Hosp., 1945-48; evening supr., asst. nursing arts instr. Good Samaritan Hosp., Phoenix, 1949-50; nursing supr. Luth. Hosp., Grand Island, Neb., 1950; asst. prof. nursing, coordinator med.-surg. nursing U. Colo. Sch. Nursing, 1951-57; acting asst. prof. nursing, grad. student on leave U. Wash. Sch. Nursing, 1955-56; asso. prof. nursing U. Colo. Sch. Nursing, 1957-58; prof. nursing U. Ariz. Coll. Nursing, 1958-67, dean coll., 1967—; cons. in field, 1945—. Mem. Def. Adv. Com. on Women in Services. Bd. dirs. Tucson Vis. Nurse Assn. Fellow Am. Acad. Nursing; mem. Nat., Ariz. (v.p. 1958-60) leagues nursing, Am., Ariz. nurses assns., Am. Assn. Colls. Nursing (exec. bd. 1976—). Contbr. profl. jours. Address: 7811 E Lee St Tucson AZ 85715

SORENSEN, LEIF BOGE, physician, educator; b. Odense, Denmark, Mar. 25, 1928; s. Henry V. and Mary (Nielsen) S.; B.S., Odense Katedralskole, 1946; M.D., U. Copenhagen (Denmark), 1953, Ph.D. in Biochemistry, 1960; m. Kari Heggtveit, July 12, 1968; 1 dau., Heidi. Came to U.S., 1955, naturalized, 1963. Intern, Copenhagen County Hosp., Hellerup, Denmark, 1954; resident Copenhagen Municipal Hosp., 1955, U. Chgo. Hosp., 1957-60; practice medicine specializing in metabolic (genetic) disease and rheumatology U. Chgo. Clinics; mem. faculty U. Chgo. and Franklin McLean Meml. Research Inst., 1956—, prof. medicine, 1970—, scientist, 1956—, attending physician dept. medicine, asso. chmn. dept. Pritzker Sch. Medicine, U. Chgo.; cons. FDA, 1972—. Served with M.C., Danish Army, 1951. Fulbright scholar, 1955; Ill. Arthritis Found. grantee, 1970-72. Mem. A.A.A.S., Am. Rheumatism Soc., Am. Soc. Clin. Investigation, Central Soc. Clin. Research, N.Y. Acad. Scis., Danish Med. Assn., Ill. Acad. Gen. Practice. Mem. editorial bd. Jour. Lab. and Clin. Medicine, 1964-70, Arthritis and Rheumatism, 1965-72. Contbr. articles to profl. jours. Home: 5825 S Dorchester Chicago IL 60637

SORENSEN, NEIL CLIFFORD, coll. exec.; b. Vancouver, B.C., Can. June 24, 1932; s. Walter and Anna Ilona (Lehto) S.; B.Sc., Walla Walla Coll., 1958, M.A., 1963; Ed.D., U. So. Calif., 1973; m. Betty Louella Heinrichs; Aug. 26, 1956; children—Melvin Neil, Laura Lynne. Tchr. public elem. schs., Bremerton, Wash., 1958-59; vice prin. Walla Walla Coll. Acad., 1959-61; prin. Pacific Union Coll. Prep. Sch., 1961-63, San Pasqual Acad., Escondido, Calif., 1963-69; asso. dir. edn. Pacific Union Conf. of Seventh-day Adventists, Glendale, Calif., 1969-72; chmn. dept. edn. and psychology Walla Walla Coll., 1972-75, v.p. for acad. affairs, 1975-76, pres., 1976—; co-chmn. Ind. Colls. Washington; bd. dirs. Wash. Friends of Higher Ed., Seattle; registered edd. cons. UN Capital Devel. Funds Program; spl. assignment Peoples Democratic Republic of Yemen, 1977-78. Bd. dirs. Paradise Valley Hosp., National City, Calif., Walla Walla (Wash.) Gen. Hosp., Portland (Oreg.) Adventist Med. Center, United Way of Walla Walla County. NSF grantee, 1963-64. Mem. Am. Assn. Higher Edn., Am. Ass. Sch. Adminstrs., Am. Psychol. Assn., Am. Assn. Colls. Tchr. Edn., Assn. Supervision and Curriculum Devel., Phi Delta Kappa. Club: Rotary. Home: 1030 E Highland Park Dr College Place WA 99324 Office: Pres's Office Walla Walla Coll College Place WA 99324

SORENSEN, PARRY DANIEL, educator; b. Manti, Utah, June 23, 1916; s. E. D. and Ann (Parry) S.; B.S., U. Utah, 1936; postgrad. U. London, 1937; M.S., Northwestern U., 1940; m. Margaret Christensen, July 12, 1941; children-Richard P., Daniel P., Holly Ruth, Michael H., William F. Reporter, Deseret News, Salt Lake City, 1938-39; reporter Washington Post, 1940-41; spl. agt. FBI, 1942-45; reporter Los Angeles Examiner, 1945-46; dir. univ. relations U. Utah, Salt Lake City, 1946-64, exec. asst. to pres., 1964-76, asst. prof. journalism, 1946-52, asso. prof., 1952-64, prof., 1964—, acting chmn. dept. journalism, 1961-62; cons. Assn. Governing Bds. of Colls. and Univs., 1968. Pres., Western Motor Lodge, 1958-67; dir. Deseret Book Co., 1969-74. Mem. gen. bd. Young Mens Mut. Improvement Assn., Latter-day Saints Ch., 1964-71. Recipient Outstanding Young Man award Utah Jr. C. of C., 1947, Silver Anvil award Pub. Relations Soc. Am., 1964. Mem. Pub. Relations Soc. Am. (past pres. Intermountain chpt.), Former Spl. Agts. of FBI (past chmn. Utah chpt.), Am. Coll. Pub. Relations Assn. (pres. 1969-70), Nat. Assn. State Univs. and Land Grant Colls. (past com. chmn.), Sigma Nu, Phi Kappa Phi, Sigma Delta Chi, Kappa Tau Alpha. Mem. Ch. of Jesus Christ of Latter-day Saints (missionary in Gt. Britain 1936- 38). Home: 2349 Logan Circle Salt Lake City UT 84108

SORENSEN, PHILIP CHAIKIN, lawyer; b. Lincoln, Nebr., Aug. 31, 1933; s. Christian Abraham and Annis (Chaikin) S.; B.S. in Law, U. Nebr., 1959, LL.B. cum laude, 1959; m. Janice Lichtenberger, Dec. 20, 1958; children—Rebecca Chaikin, Allan Philip, Karen Maria, Josephine Ann. Admitted to Nebr. Bar, 1959; law clk. to U.S. dist. judge Dist. Nebr., 1959-60; practiced in Lincoln, 1960-65; instr. U. Nebr. Coll. Law, 1960-61; lt. gov. Nebr., 1965-67; lectr. U. Omaha, 1965-66; exec. dir. Irwin-Sweeney-Miller Found., Cummins Engine Found., Irwin Union Found., Columbus, Ind., 1967-70; dir. Migrant Task Force; vis. prof. Ohio State U. Coll. Law, Columbus, 1973-74, prof. law, 1974—, asso. dean, 1979—. Dir. Lincoln Bank South. Mem. Nebr. Gov.'s Human Rights Commn.; chmn. Exec. Reorgn. Commn. State of Ind. Mem. Nebr. Democratic Central Com., 1964. Trustee Tougaloo Coll., Jackson, Miss.; bd. dirs. Council on Founds., Center Community Change. Served with USCG, 1951-54. Mem. Am., Ind., Nebr. bar assns., Order of Coif. Editor-in-chief Nebr. Law Rev., 1957-58. Home: 844 Oxford St Columbus OH 43085

SORENSEN, RAYMOND ANDREW, educator; b. Pitts., Feb. 27, 1931; s. Andrew J. and Dora (Thuesen) S.; B.S., Carnegie Inst. Tech., 1953, M.S., 1955, Ph.D., 1958; m. Audrey Nickols, Apr. 2, 1953; 1 dau., Lisa Kirsten. Mem. faculty Columbia, 1959-61; asso. prof. Carnegie-Mellon U., Pitts., 1961-68, prof. physics, 1968—. NSF sr. postdoctoral fellow, 1965-66. Mem. Am. Phys. Soc. Home: 1235 Murdoch Rd Pittsburgh PA 15217

SORENSEN, ROYAL MILNER, lawyer; b. Pasadena, Calif., Oct. 22, 1914; s. Royal Wasson and Grace (Milner) S.; B.A., Stanford, 1936; LL.B., U. So. Calif., 1939; m. Dorothy Louise Russell, Sept. 1, 1938; children—Eric Russell, Julia Margaret (Mrs. Lee Martin Serjak), Jane Anne (Mrs. Joseph Arnold Thibedeau). Admitted to Calif. bar, 1941; dep. city atty., Pasadena, 1941-43, 46-47; city atty. Santa Monica, Calif., 1947-52; partner firm Burke, Williams & Sorensen, Los Angeles, 1952—; cons., spl. atty. municipalities. Mem. Santa Monica City Council, 1965-69. Served with USNR, 1943-45. Mem. State Bar Calif., Am., Los Angeles County bar assns., League Calif. Cities (dir. 1965-67). Club: Calif. Yacht. Home: 1102 San Vicente Blvd Santa Monica CA 90402 Office: Suite 3300 707 Wilshire Blvd Los Angeles CA 90017

SORENSEN, SVEND OLUF, banker; b. Grenaa, Denmark, Feb. 24, 1914; s. P. and Anna (Jensen) S.; diploma banking Copenhagen Sch. Econs. and Bus. Adminstrn., 1941; m. Karen Vontillius, Nov. 12, 1949; children—Aase Hellemann, Birgit Hoffmeyer. With Den Danske Bank, Copenhagen, 1930—, mng. dir., 1962—; gov. Adela Investment Co. S.A. Adviser banking Govt. Pakistan, 1952-53; mem. bd. Danish Bankers Assn.; mem. bd. Banking Fedn. EEC; chmn. bd. Ship Credit Fund Denmark; chmn. bd. Den Danske Bank Internat. S.A., Luxembourg; mem. bd. Danish Agrl. Real Property Loan Fund; mem. Institut International d' Etudes Bancaires, Internat. Monetary Conf.; internat. counsellor Conf. Bd.; mem. Danish-Am. Trade Council. Mem. bd. Danish nat. com. Internat. C. of C.; mem. com. Fin. Inst. Danish Industry and Handicrafts, Ltd., Danish Soc. Preservation Bldgs. and Landscapes. Decorated comdr. Order Dannebrog (Denmark); knight 1st class Order St. Olav (Norway). Mem. Danish Acad. for Tech. Scis. Rotarian. Clubs: American (Copenhagen); Overseas Bankers (London, Eng.); Rungsted Golf. Home: 11 A Hambros Alle 2900 Hellerup Denmark also 47A Kystvejen 3100 Hornbaek Denmark Office: 12 Holmens Kanal 1092 Copenhagen K Denmark

SORENSEN, THEODORE CHAIKIN, lawyer, former spl. counsel to Pres. U.S.; b. Lincoln, Nebr., May 8, 1928; s. Christian Abraham and Annis (Chaikin) S.; B.S. in Law, U. Nebr., 1949, LL.B., 1951, LL.D., 1969; LL.D., U. Canterbury, 1966, Alfred U., 1969, Temple U., 1969, Fairfield U., 1969; m. Gillian Martin, June 28, 1969; 1 dau., Juliet Suzanne; children from previous marriage—Eric Kristen, Stephen Edgar, Philip Jon. Admitted to Nebr. bar, 1951, N.Y. bar, 1966, D.C. bar, 1971, also U.S. Supreme Court bar; atty. Fed. Security Agy., 1951-52; mem. staff joint com. r.r. retirement U.S. Senate, 1952; asst. to Sen. John F. Kennedy, 1953-61; sec. New Eng. Senators' Conf., 1953-59: spl. counsel to Pres. U.S., 1961-64; mem. firm Paul, Weiss, Rifkind, Wharton & Garrison, N.Y.C., 1966—; mem. Pres.'s Adv. Com. Trade Negotiations, 1978—; commentator nat. affairs Metromedia Channel 5, 1971-73. Democratic candidate for N.Y. Senate, 1970. Named by Jr. C. of C. as one of ten Outstanding Young Men of Year, 1961. Mem. D.C., Nebr. bar assns., Phi Beta Kappa, Order of Coif. Editor Nebr. Law Rev., 1950-51; author: Decision Making in the White House, 1963; Kennedy, 1965; The Kennedy Legacy, 1969; Watchmen in the Night: Presidential Accountability After Watergate, 1975. Office: 345 Park Ave New York NY 10022

SORENSEN, THOMAS CHAIKIN, financial exec.; b. Lincoln, Nebr., Mar. 31, 1926; s. Christian and Annis (Chaikin) S.; B.A., U. Nebr., 1947; m. Mary Barstler, July 5, 1947; children—Ann Christine Sorensen Ketter, Alan Thomas, Jens Christian. Radio announcer, 1943-44; newspaper reporter, 1945-46; asst. night editor Nebr. State Jour., 1946-49; dir. news and pub. affairs radio sta. KLMS, Lincoln, 1949-51; instr. U. Nebr. Sch. Journalism, 1948-50; information officer, press attache Am. embassy, Beirut, Lebanon, 1952-56, Baghdad, Iraq, 1956, Cairo, Egypt, 1957-59; program and policy officer for Near East, USIA, Washington, 1959-61, dep. dir. for policy, 1961-65; v.p. Internat. Tech. Assistance & Devel. Co., 1965-66; v.p. U. Calif., 1966-68; campaign coordinator Robert Kennedy for Pres., 1968, Alan Cranston for U.S. Senator, 1968; sr. fellow Adlai Stevenson Inst., 1968-69; v.p. Leasco Corp., 1969-70; partner Sartorius & Co., N.Y.C., 1971-74; sr. v.p., dir. Advest Inc., 1974-80; pres. Advest Internat., 1974-80; pres. Sorensen & Co., 1980—; dir. Advest Group, Inc., Hartford, Pa. Mut. Fund, N.Y.C., Hyde Park Bank and Trust Co., Public Media Inc., Chgo. Trustee Population Reference Bur. Recipient Arthur S. Flemming award, 1961. Mem. Phi Beta Kappa, Sigma Delta Chi, Delta Sigma Rho. Author: The Word War, 1968. Home: 250 Beverly Rd Scarsdale NY 10583

SORENSEN, VIRGINIA (MRS. ALEC WAUGH), author; b. Provo, Utah, Feb. 17, 1912; d. Claud E. and Helen El Deva (Blackett) Eggertsen; A.B., Brigham Young U., 1934; m. Frederick C. Sorensen, Aug. 16, 1933; children—Elizabeth (Mrs. Christian Anderson), Frederick W.; m. 2d, Alec Waugh, 1969. Guggenheim fellow, 1946-47, 54-55. Author: (novels) A Little Lower Than the Angels, 1942, On This Star, 1946, The Neighbors, 1947, The Evening and the Morning, 1949, The Proper Gods, 1951, Many Heavens, 1954, Kingdom Come, 1960, The Man With The Key, 1974; (children's books) Curious Missie, 1953, The House Next Door, 1954, Plain Girl (recipient award Child Study Assn. Am. 1955), 1955, Miracles on Maple Hill (recipient Newberry award A.L.A. 1956), 1956, Where Nothing is Long Ago, 1963, Lotte's Locket, 1964, Around the Corner, 1970; Companions of the Road, 1977. Mem. Authors Guild, P.E.N. Home: Ave Sidi Mohammed Ben Abdallah 97 Tangier Morocco Office: care Dir Pub Relations Harcourt Brace & Jovanovich 757 3d Ave New York City NY 10017

SORENSON, ALLAN RICHARD, chem. engr., univ. regent; b. Manistee, Mich., Dec. 12, 1919; s. Albert Reinhold and Alberta Europa (Vlach) S.; B.S. in Engring., U. Mich., 1948; m. Edith Claire Harris, Feb. 3, 1950; children—Christopher Allan, Eric Richard. Chem. engr. Dow Chem. Co., Midland, Mich., 1948-65, mgr. process engring. and econ. evaluation, Ludington, Mich., 1972-76; project engr. Dow Chem. Internat., France, Spain and Netherlands, 1965-72, Alta., Can., 1976-80; owner, propr. Averill Nursery (Mich.), 1953-58; dir. Midland Tree Growers Coop. Assn., 1955-57. Mem. bd. control Mich. Tech. U., 1959-61; trustee Mich. Tech. U. Found., 1960-61; vice chmn. Gov. Mich. Commn. Status Women, 1962-63; bd. regents U. Mich., 1962—; chmn. Midland County United Negro Coll. Fund,

1962, Lincoln Township Zoning Commn., 1957-58; vice chmn. Mich. Democratic Bus. and Profl. Assn., 1961. Served with AUS, 1942-46. Registered profl. engr. Mem. Am. Inst. Chem. Engrs., Midland Engrng. Soc., Am. Mus. Natural History, Audubon Soc., Nat. Parks Assn., Midland Music Found., Community Concerts Assn., ACLU, Alpha Chi Sigma. Home: Granville OH Office: Dow Chem Co PO Box 515 Granville OH 43023

SORENSON, RALPH ZELLAR, II, coll. pres.; b. Evanston, Ill., Sept. 20, 1933; s. Ralph Zellar and Verna Mary (Koenig) S.; A.B. magna cum laude, Amherst Coll., 1955; M.B.A. with distinction, Harvard U., 1959, D.B.A., 1967; m. Charlotte Bacon Ripley, June 25, 1960; children—Kristin Elizabeth, Katrina Anne, Eric Ripley. Research asst. IMEDE Mgmt. Devel. Inst., Lausanne, Switzerland, 1959-61; exec. Nestle Alimentana SA, Vevey, Switzerland, 1961-63; prof. Harvard Bus. Sch., 1964-74; pres. Babson Coll., Wellesley, Mass., 1974—; dir. Houghton-Mifflin Co., Foxboro Co., Barry-Wright Corp., Knapp King Size Inc., Gen. Housewares Corp. Served to lt. USAF, 1955-57. Ford Found. fellow; recipient spl. award appreciation Asian Inst. Mgmt., Manila. Mem. Assn. Ind. Colls. and Univs. Mass. (chmn. exec. com.), Amherst Coll. Alumni Soc. (pres. 1974—), Phi Beta Kappa. Clubs: Wellesley Country, Wellesley; Comml. Home: 56 Whiting Rd Wellesley Hills MA 02181

SORGE, WALTER FELIX, artist, educator; b. Forestburg, Alta., Can., Oct. 25, 1931; s. Herman and Augusta (Gensch) S.; B.A., UCLA, 1954, M.A., 1955; Ed.D., Tchrs. Coll., Columbia U., 1964; postgrad. Atelier 17, Paris, 1961-62, 68. Instr. art South Peach Sr. High Sch., Dawson Creek, B.C., Can., 1956-59; head dept. art Ky. So. Coll., Louisville, 1964-69; chmn. dept. art Hardin Simmons U., Abilene, Tex., 1969-70; mem. faculty dept. art Eastern Ill. U., Charleston, 1970—, prof., 1975—. Thirty-five one-man shows of paintings and/or drawings, latest being: Paul Sargent Gallery, Charleston, Ill., 1974, Blackburn Coll., Carlinville, Ill., 1974, Mitchell Mus., Mt. Vernon, Ill., 1975, Am. Embassy in Turkey, 1974-75, J.B. Speed Mus., Louisville, 1976, 77, Hiscock Gallery, Portsmouth, Eng., 1978, Stairways Gallery, Louisville, 1978; also numerous group shows, 1956—; represented in permanent collections: Sheldon Swope Gallery, Terre Haute, Ind., Mobile (Ala.) Art Gallery, Evansville (Ind.) Mus. Arts and Scis. Recipient numerous merit awards, including: Nat. Directions Exhbn., 1972, Mid-States Exhbn., 1973; Can. Council grantee, 1959-61, 70; Huntington Hartford Found. fellow, 1963. Baptist. Home: 6843 Fraser St Vancouver BC Canada Office: Dept Art Eastern Ill U Charleston IL 61920

SORGENTI, HAROLD ANDREW, petroleumand chem. co. exec.; b. Bklyn., May 28, 1934; s. Louis J. and Lucille (Sisti) S.; B.S.Ch.E., CCNY, 1956; M.S., Ohio State U., 1959; m. Ann Rusnack, June 30, 1962; children—Elizabeth, Lucille. Research engr. Battelle Meml. Inst., Columbus, Ohio, 1956-59; with Atlantic Richfield Co., 1959—, v.p. research and engring., products div., 1975-76; sr. v.p., 1978-79; v.p. chem. devel. ARCO Chem. Co., Phila., 1976-78, pres., 1979—. Bd. dirs. Am. Heart Assn., Phila., Internat. Bus. Forum, Phila., Greater Phila. Partnership, Phila. Coll. Art, Jr. Achievement Delaware Valley, Pa. Economy League. Mem. Am. Chem. Soc., Am. Inst. Chem. Engrs., Ohio State U. Alumni Assn., CCNY Alumni Assn., Greater Phila. C. of C. (dir.). Club: Union League (Phila.). Home: 3303 Green Countrie Dr Newtown Square PA 19073 Office: 1500 Market St Philadelphia PA 19101

SORIA, DARIO, music and records cons.; b. Rome, Italy, May 21, 1912; s. Raffaello and Amelia (Padoa) S.; B.A., U. Rome, 1934; postgrad. law U. Ferrara (Italy), 1937-39; m. Dorle Jarmel, July 26, 1942. Came to U.S., 1939, naturalized, 1945. Jr. partner Raffaello Soria & Co., bank, Rome, 1930-39; treas., dir. Buitoni Foods Corp., N.Y.C., 1940-41; announcer Italian programs, dir. Italian and French programs OWI, N.Y.C., 1942-43; asst. dir., then dir. network programs CBS, N.Y.C., 1943-48; dir. radio programs D'Arcy Advt. Agy., N.Y.C. and Hollywood, 1948-50; pres., gen. mgr. Cetra-Soria Records, N.Y.C., 1950-53; pres. EMI Inc. (Angel Records), N.Y.C., 1953-57; adminstrv. dir. Festival of Two Worlds, Spoleto, Italy, 1958; ind. producer Soria Series for RCA Victor, N.Y.C., 1959-61; div. v.p. charge internat. operations and fgn. subsidiaries RCA Records, N.Y.C., 1961-70; mng. dir. Met. Opera Guild, Inc., N.Y.C., 1971-78; adv. dir. Met. Opera Assn., 1978—; producer Met. Opera Historic Broadcasting Rec. Series, 1975—; producer, narrator weekly radio program Festival of Opera, WOR radio, N.Y.C., 1951-56. Served to lt. Italian Alpine Troops, 1933, 35-36. Decorated War Cross of Merit, Ufficiale al Merito della Repubblica (Italy); officier Ordre des arts et des lettres (France). Clubs: Metropolitan Opera, Century. Home: 24 W 55th St New York NY 10019 Office: Met Opera Lincoln Center New York NY 10023

SORKIN, GERALD B., advt. agy. exec.; b. Bklyn., June 20, 1932; s. Nathan and Dora (Butlin) S.; A.B., Dartmouth, 1953; m. Eleanor Smith, Sept. 30, 1956; children—Andrea Joyce, Lynn Harriet, Jessica Lee. Art dir., prodn. mgr. Wesley H. Porter, Advt., Los Angeles, 1953-56; advt. mgr. Plastix Footwear Corp., Los Angeles, 1956-58; mgr. sales promotion, brand mgr. Hunt Foods & Industries, Inc., Fullerton, Calif., 1958-63; prin. G.B. Sorkin & Co., Los Angeles, 1963-64; pres. Sorkin/Hudson, Los Angeles, 1964-67, 69-72; v.p. West Coast, Adams/Dana/Silverstein, Los Angeles, 1967-69; v.p. David W. Evans, Advt., Inc., Los Angeles, 1972-73, pres., 1973-77; ind. mktg. cons., 1977-78; dir. advt. and mktg. Shapell Industries, Inc., Beverly Hills, Calif., 1978-79; dir. sales and mktg. Arvida Primary Housing, Miami, Fla., 1979—; v.p., dir. Rinkled Raisin, Inc., Los Angeles, Diamond Fork Land Cattle Co., Cedar City, Utah; dir. David W. Evans, Inc., Salt Lake City, 1973-77; cons., franchising mktg. Trustee Eddie Cantor Charitable Found., 1972—; commr. Wilshire Blvd. Temple Camps, 1973—. Mem. Am. Assn. Advt. Agencies, Econ. Soc. So. Fla., Builders Assn. S. Fla., Aircraft Owners and Pilots Assn., B'nai B'rith (Service awards 1973, 74, 75, 76). Republican. Jewish. Club: Dartmouth of So. Calif. Author, co-author TV scripts and movies. Home: 11305 SW 134 Ave Miami FL 33186. *To dare to do, then do it, is a wonder and a joy; something all free men should reflect on and help preserve.*

SORKIN, LEONARD, violinist; b. Chgo., Jan. 12, 1916; s. David and Rebecca (Azef) S.; studied Chgo. Musical Coll., Am. Conservatory; D.Mus. (hon.), Northland Coll., 1977; m. Aviva B. Doinick, July 6, 1939; children—Rafael, Naomi (Mrs. David Shapiro). Mem. 1st violin sect. Chgo. Symphony, 1936-43; soloist in recital with orchs., including Chgo. Symphony, Ill. Symphony, Middle West concerts; concertmaster Seidenberg Symphonette, in Chgo. and on tour Midwest; organized Fine Arts Quartet, 1940, ann. series of concerts, 1940-43; reorganized Fine Arts Quartet, joined Staff ABC, 1946-54, quartet in residence Northwestern U., 1953-55, Community Music Sch. of North Shore, Winnetka, 1960-64, 1st violinist of quartet; participant June Music Festival, Albuquerque, 1968-78; pioneer stereophonic recs. Concert Disc Records; ednl. films for Ency. Brit. Films, also ednl. series for Nat. Ednl. and TV Center; European tours, 1958-59, 59-60, 60-61, 62, 63, 70-77; Australia-New Zealand tour, 1961; State Dept. sponsored tour of Orient, 1967; artist-in-residence Sch. Fine Arts. U. Wis.-Milw., 1962—, prof. music, 1967—; distinguished prof., 1977—; laureate, mem. Lincoln Acad. for distinguished service in performing arts, 1967; performer Edinburgh Festival, 1971. Served with AUS, 1943-46. Recipient Wis. Gov.'s award for out-standing contbn. to performing arts, 1968; named Artist of Year, Am. String Tchrs. Assn., 1970. Home: 1027 E Ogden Milwaukee WI 53202 Office: Sch Fine Arts U Wis Milwaukee WI 53201

SORLING, CARL AXEL, lawyer; b. Moline, Ill., Sept. 13, 1896; s. Jacob Axe and Alma Josephine (Lonnegren) S.; LL.B., U. of Mich., 1921, J.D., 1922; m. Winifred Josephine White, Sept. 15, 1921 (dec. Dec. 1960); 1 dau., Sheila Elizabeth; m. 2d, Macon Atnip Johnson, June 4, 1966. Admitted to Ill. bar, 1922; engaged in practice of law; now mem. firm Sorling, Northrup, Hanna, Cullen & Cochran. Served as lt., arty., A.E.F., 1917-19. Mem. Am., Ill., Sangamon County, Chgo. bar assns., Alpha Tau Omega, Phi Delta Phi. Lutheran. Clubs: Illini Country, Sangamo (Sprinfield). Home: 1711 Illini Rd Springfield IL 62704 Office: Ill Bldg Springfield IL 62701

SORNSON, HELEN HENRIETTA, educator; b. Cushing, Wis., Aug. 12, 1908; d. Henry E. and Anne (Hanson) Sornson; B.E., Superior State Coll., 1942; M.A., U. Minn., 1946, Ph.D., 1950. Tchr., St. Croix Falls, Wis., 1927-29, 36-40, Cameron, Wis., 1931-33, Luck, Wis., 1933-36; county supr. elementary schs., Balsam Lake, Wis., 1940-45; prof. elementary edn., supr. student teaching Ball State U., Muncie, Ind., 1947-73; tchr. Eastern Ky. U., Richmond, summers 1974, 76, 77. Bd. dirs. Head Start, Muncie, 1970-73. Recipient 1st Outstanding Educator award Ind. Internat. Reading Council, 1970, 1st Outstanding Tchr. award Ball State U., 1972; Disting. Service award Ind. Assn. Edn. Young Children, 1974. Mem. Assn. Supervision and Curriculum Devel., NEA, Wis. Edn. Assn., Ind. Tchrs. Assn., Assn. Tchr. Edn., Ind. Assn. Childhood Edn., Nat. Assn. Edn. Young Children, Pi Lambda Theta, Delta Kappa Gamma. Home: 412 Shellbark Rd Muncie IN 47304

SOROKIN, PETER PITIRIMOVICH, physicist; b. Boston, July 10, 1931; s. Pitirim Alexandrovich and Elena Petrovna (Baratynskaya) S.; A.B., Harvard U., 1952, M.S., 1953, Ph.D., 1958; m. Anita J. Schell, Oct. 1, 1977. Research physicist IBM Watson Research Center, Yorktown Heights, N.Y., 1957—. Recipient Michelson medal Franklin Soc., 1974; R.W. Wood award Optical Soc. Am., 1978; IBM fellow, 1968—. Mem. Nat., Am., N.Y. acads. sci. Contbr. articles in quantum electronics to profl. jours.; patentee laser devices. Home: PO Box 225 Millwood NY 10546 Office: IBM Watson Research Center PO Box 218 Yorktown Heights NY 10598

SORREL, WILLIAM EDWIN, psychiatrist, educator; b. N.Y.C., May 27, 1913; s. Simon and Lee (Lesenger) S.; B.S., N.Y. U., 1932; M.A., Columbia, 1934, M.D., 1939; Ph.D., N.Y. U., 1963; m. Rita Marcus, July 1, 1950; children—Ellyn Gail, Joy Shelley, Beth Mara. Intern, Madison (Tenn.) Sanitarium and Hosp., 1939; resident physician Alexian Bros. Hosp., St. Louis, 1940; officer instrn. St. Louis U. Sch. Medicine, 1940-41; asst. psychiatrist Central State Hosp., Nashville, 1941; asso. psychiatrist Eastern State Hosp., Knoxville, 1942-44; asso. attending neuropsychiatrist, chief clin. psychiatry Jewish Meml. Hosp., N.Y.C., 1946-59; asso. attending neuropsychiatrist, chief clin. child psychiatry Lebanon Hosp., Bronx, N.Y., 1947-65; psychiatrist-in-chief Psychiatry Clinic, Yeshiva U., 1950-66, asst. prof. psychiatry, 1952-54, asso. prof., 1954-58, prof., 1959-62, psychiatrist-in-chief, asso. dir. Psychol. Center, 1957-67; prof. human behavior Touro U., 1974-79; psychiat. cons. SSS, 1951, N.Y. State Workmens Compensation Bd., 1951—; vis. psychiatrist Fordham Hosp., N.Y.C., 1951; attending neuropsychiatrist, chief mental hygiene service Beth-David Hosp., 1950-60; asso. attending neuropsychiatrist Grand Central Hosp., 1958-66, Morrisania Hosp., 1959-72; psychiatrist-in-chief Beth Abraham Hosp., 1954-60; psychiat. cons. L.I. U. Guidance Center, 1955-60, Daytop Village, 1970-71; asso. psychiatrist Seton City Hosp., 1955; guest lectr. U. London, 1947; vis. prof. Jerusalem, Israel Acad. Med., 1960; vis. lectr. Hebrew U., 1960; mem. psychiat. staff Gracie Sq. Hosp., 1960—; chief psychiatry Trafalgar Hosp., 1962-72; vis. prof. psychiatry Tokyo U. Sch. Medicine, 1964; adj. prof. N.Y. Inst. Tech., 1968; vis. lectr. in psychiatry N.Y. U., 1971-73. Am. del. Internat. Conf. Mental Health, London, 1948; mem. Am. Psychiat. Commn. to USSR, Poland and Finland, 1963. Vice pres. Golden Years Found.; N.Y.C. chmn. Com. Med. Standards in Psychiatry, 1952-54. Qualified psychiatrist, also certified examiner N.Y. State Dept. Mental Hygiene; recipient Sir Wm. Osler Internat. Honor Med. Soc. Gold Key; 3d prize oil paintings, N.Y. State Med. Art Exhibit, 1954; N.Y. Univ. Founders Day award, 1963, others. Fellow Am. Psychiat. Assn. (life, pres. Bronx dist. 1960-61, del. council 1961-63, Gold medal 1974), Am. Assn. Psychoanalytic Physicians (pres. 1971-72, gov. 1972-79); mem. Eastern Psychiat. Research Assn., N.Y. State Soc. Med. Research, Am. Med. Writers Assn., A.M.A., N.Y. State, N.Y. County med. socs., N.Y. Soc. for Clin. Psychiatry, Assn. for Advancement Psychotherapy, Bronx Soc. Neurology and Psychiatry (pres. 1960-61, Silver medal 1970), Pan Am. Med. Assn. (pres. sect. on suicidology), Am. Acad. Psychotherapy, Assn. Research Nervous and Mental Disease, A.A.U.P. Author: (booklets) Neurosis in a Child, 1949; A Psychiatric Viewpoint on Child Adoption, 1954; Shock Therapy in Psychiatric Practice, 1957; The Genesis of Neurosis, 1958; The Prejudiced Personality, 1962; The Schizophrenic Process, 1962; The Prognosis of Electroshock Therapy Success, 1963; Psychodynamic Effects of Abortion, 1967; Violence Towards Self, 1971; Basic Concepts of Transference in Psychoanalysis, 1973; A Study in Suicide, 1972; Masochism, 1973; Emotional Factors Involved in Skeletal Deformities, 1977; Cults & Cult Suicide, 1979; contbr. articles on the psychoses. Home: 23 Meadow Rd Scarsdale NY 10583 Office: 263 West End Ave New York NY 10023. *Very meaningful to me is the matter of professionalism in the practice of my discipline. A helping service to individuals is to add and enhance their contentment of living; especially in a world of turmoil. Medical science has added greatly to the art of my training; and I apply it daily.*

SORRENTINO, GILBERT, poet, novelist; b. Bklyn., Apr. 27, 1929; s. August E. and Ann Marie (Davis) S.; student Bklyn. Coll., 1949-51, 54-56; m. Victoria Ortiz; children—Jesse, Delia, Christopher. In various positions, 1947-70, including reins. clk. Fidelity's Casualty Co., N.Y.C., 1947-48; freight checker, Ace Assembly Agency, N.Y.C., 1954-56; packer Bennett Bros. Inc., N.Y.C., 1956-57, messenger Am. Houses, Inc., N.Y.C., 1948-49; shipping-room supr. Thermo-fax Sales, Inc., Queens, N.Y., 1957-60; editor Grove Press, N.Y., 1965-70; tchr. Columbia U., 1966, Aspen Writers Workshop, 1967, Sarah Lawrence Coll., 1972, The New Sch. Social Research, 1976—, Nat. Endowment for Humanities chair in lit. U. Scranton, 1979; author books: The Darkness Surrounds Us, 1960, Black and White, 1964, The Sky Changes, 1966, The Perfect Fiction, 1968, Steelwork, 1970, Imaginative Qualities of Actual Things, 1971, Corrosive Sublimate, 1971, Splendide-Hotel, 1973, Flawless Play Restored, 1974, A Dozen Oranges, 1976, White Sail, 1977, Sulpiciae Elegidia/Elegiacs of Sulpicia, 1977, The Orangery, 1978, Mulligan Stew, 1979. Served with U.S. Army, 1951-53; Recipient Samuel Fels award in fiction Coordinating Council Lit. Mags., 1974; John Simon Guggenheim Meml. fellow, 1973-74; Creative Artists Public Service Program grantee, 1974-75. Nat. Endowment for Arts grantee, 1975-76, 1978-79. Mem. PEN Am. Center.

SORTOR, HAROLD EDWARD, financial exec.; b. Craig, Nebr., Jan. 18, 1925; s. Harold E. and Ruth (Oldham) S.; B.S., U. Ill., 1949, J.D., 1950; m. Dorothy M. Johnson, Oct. 9, 1954; 1 dau., Georgia Lynn. Admitted to Ill. bar, 1950; tax supr. Ernst & Ernst, Chgo., 1950-56; mem. firm McDermott, Will & Emery, Chgo., 1956-59; tax mgr. Amphenol-Borg Electronics Corp. (name changed to Amphenol Corp. 1965), Oak Brook Ill., 1959-62, asst. controller, 1962-63, treas., 1963-68; treas. Bunker Ramo Corp., 1968; treas. Montgomery Ward & Co., Chgo., 1968-73; sr. v.p. corporate finance CNA Financial Corp., 1973-75; group v.p. finance Pennzoil Co., 1975—. Lectr., Northwestern U., 1954-59. Mem. Sch. Bd. Dist. 25, Cook County, Ill., 1962-67, pres., 1965-67. Bd. dirs. United Charities Chgo., 1971-75. Served with AUS, 1943-46. C.P.A., Ill. Mem. Am. Inst. C.P.A.'s. Office: 1 Pennzoil Place Houston TX 77001

SORVINO, PAUL, actor; b. N.Y.C.; attended Acad. Musical and Dramatic Arts. N.Y.C. stage debut in Bajour, 1964; other stage appearances include: Mating Dance, Skyscraper, That Championship Season, King Lear, An American Millionaire, For My Last Number, We'll Get By, Philemon, The Baker's Wife; film appearances include: Panic in Needle Park, Cry Uncle, Made for Each Other, The Day of the Dolphin, The Gambler, A Touch of Class, I Will, I Will...For Now, Oh, God!, Bloodbrothers, The Brink's Job, Shoot It, Black, Shoot It, Blue, Slow Dancing in the Big City, Lost and Found; star TV series: We'll Get By, 1975, Bert D'Angelo/Superstar, 1976; appeared on TV mini-series Seventh Avenue, 1977; appeared in The Queen of the Star Dust Ballroom, 1975.*

SOSA, DAN, JR., justice Supreme Ct. N.Mex.; b. Las Cruces, N.Mex., Nov. 12, 1923; s. Dan and Margaret (Soto) S.; B.S. in Bus. Adminstrn., N.Mex. State U., 1947; J.D., U. N.Mex., 1951; m. Rita Ortiz, Aug. 31, 1950; 7 children. Tchr., coach, public schs., Mesilla, N.Mex., 1947-48; admitted to N.Mex. bar, 1951; practiced law, Las Cruces, 1952-75; judge Las Cruces City Ct., 1952-55; spl. agt. Office of Price Stblzn., 1951-52; asst. dist. atty., then dist. atty. N.Mex. 3d Jud. Dist., 1956-64; spl. asst. atty. gen. for prosecution capital criminal cases Dept. Justice, 1965-66; justice N.Mex. Supreme Ct., 1975—. Served to 1st lt. AC, U.S. Army, 1942-45. Democrat. Roman Catholic. Office: Supreme Ct N Mex 327 Don Gaspar Ave Santa Fe NM 87501*

SOSA, ERNEST, philosopher, educator; b. Cuba, June 17, 1940; s. Ernesto S. and Maria Julia (Garriga) S.; B.A., U. Miami, Coral Gables, Fla., 1961; M.A., U. Pitts., 1962, Ph.D., 1964; m. Sara M. Saborido, Dec. 21, 1961; children—David, Adrian. Instr., U. Western Ont., London, Ont., Can., 1963-64, asst. prof., 1966-67, vis. prof., summer, 1971; vis. prof. U. Miami, 1970, U. Mich., 1971-72, U. Tex., 1976-77; postdoctoral fellow Brown U., Providence, 1964-66, asst. prof. philosophy, 1966-67, asso. prof., 1968-74, prof., 1974—, chmn. dept., 1970-76. Can. Council grantee, 1964; Carnegie Found. fellow, 1964-66; Am. Council Learned Socs. grantee, 1969; NSF grantee, 1970-72. Mem. Am. Philos. Soc. (sec.-treas. Eastern div. 1974—, mem. nat. bd. officers, mem. exec. com., program com. Eastern div. 1974—). Editor: Causation and Conditionals, 1974; editorial bd. Am. Philos. Quart., 1974—, Philosophy Research Archives, 1975—, Philos. Studies, 1979—. Contbr. articles to profl. jours. Home: 591 Hope St Providence RI 02906 Office: Dept Philosophy Brown Univ Providence RI 02912

SOSCHIN, ETHEL U(MAN), editor; b. Muskogee, Okla., Dec. 21, 1916; d. David and Vera (Grau) Uman; B.A., Tex. A. and I. U., Kingsville, 1940; m. Victor Soschin, May 23, 1942. Librarian, 1944-48; with Russell & Russell, publishers, N.Y.C., 1958—, mng. editor, 1972—. Home: 181 E 161st St Bronx NY 10451 Office: 122 E 42d St New York City NY 10017

SOSHNIK, JOSEPH, investment banker, former univ. adminstr.; b. Omaha, Feb. 14, 1920; s. Ben Nathan and Clara (Lehman) S.; B.S.C. summa cum laude, Creighton U., 1941; M.S. (Alfred P. Sloan fellow), U. Denver, 1943; student U. Colo., 1943-44; Ph.D., U. Nebr., 1952; m. Miriam Saks, June 29, 1941; children—David, Allan, Robert. Instr., asst. prof., asso. prof. Creighton U., 1946-57, auditor, budget cons., 1952-57; with U. Nebr., 1957-71, prof. bus. adminstrn., 1966-71, comptroller, 1957-62, vice chancellor, 1962-68, pres. Lincoln campuses and outstate activities, 1968-71; dir., chmn. exec. com. Kirkpatrick, Pettis, Smith, Polian, Inc., 1971—; dir. Lincoln Mut. Life Ins. Co., 1972—. Chmn. Nebr. Commn. Higher Edn. Facilities Act, 1964-71; trustee Nebr. Council Econ. Edn., 1969—, chmn., 1974-75; trustee Nebr. Ednl. TV Council Higher Edn., 1969-71, Omaha Indsl. Found., 1979—; mem. higher edn. adv. com. Midwest Regional Conf. Council State Govts., 1963-71; mem. Citizens Adv. Com. Omaha Pub. schs., 1954-57. Trustee Lincoln Gen. Hosp. and Lincoln Hosp. Assn., 1963-71, treas., 1963-67; nat. trustee NCCJ, 1978—; bd. dirs. Lincoln Hosp. and Health Council, 1962-69, sec. treas., 1962-64; bd. dirs. Lincoln Community Chest, 1963-69, Child Guidance Center, 1960-63, Nebraskans for Pub. TV, 1972-76, Jewish Fedn. Omaha, 1975-78, Father Flanagan's Boys Home, 1978—; co-chmn. Midlands exec. bd. Nat. Conf. Christians and Jews, 1973—; bd. govs. Omaha Boys' Clubs, 1972-76; mem. Lincoln Found., 1968-71; mem. council bus. execs. Creighton U. Coll. Bus. Adminstrn., 1972—, chmn., 1973-77; mem. pres.'s council Creighton U., 1973—; mem. citizens assembly United Way Midlands, 1975—; bd. visitors Creighton Inst. Bus., Law and Social Research, 1976-78; mem. pres.'s adv. council U. Nebr., 1977—. Served with USNR, 1943-46. Mem. Omaha C. of C., Am. Council Edn., Nat. Assn. State Univs. and Land-Grant Colls. (senate joint com. bus. officers 1959-66), Nat. Assn. Coll. and Univ. Bus. Officers, Omaha C. of C. (dir. 1980—), Beta Gamma Sigma. Alpha Sigma Nu, Innocents Soc., Pi Lambda Phi, Delta Sigma Pi, Delta Sigma Rho, Order of Artus. Jewish (former trustee temple). Mem. B'nai B'rith. Clubs: Highland Country, Omaha. Author articles. Home: 919 S 106th Plaza Apt 202 Omaha NE 68114

SOSIN, SIDNEY, lawyer; b. Chgo., June 7, 1924; s. Jacob and Ida (Weinstein) S.; student Central YMCA Coll., Chgo., 1942-43; B.S., U. Ill., 1949, LL.B., 1950; m. Anita Beatrice Sokol, Apr. 16, 1950; children—Lynne C., Barbara J. Admitted to Ill. bar, 1950, since practiced in Chgo.; atty. SEC, 1950-61, chief br. interpretation and small issues Chgo. regional office, 1959-61; asso. Arvey, Hodes, Costello & Burman, 1961-65, partner, 1966—; dir., sec. Triangle Home Products, Inc. Served with AUS, 1943-45. Recipient certificate of merit for superior achievement SEC, 1956, Wm. A. Jump Meml. Found. Meritorious award for exemplary achievement in pub. adminstrn., 1959. Mem. Fed., Chgo. bar assns., Am. Radio Relay League, Skokie Valley Orchestral Assn. Contbr. chpts. to ICLE Securities Law Practice Handbook, 1973, 79; contbr. articles to profl. jours. Home: 1107 Arbor Ln Glenview IL 60025 Office: 180 N LaSalle St Chicago IL 60601

SOSKIN, THEODORE SAMUEL, broadcasting exec.; b. Vancouver, B.C., Can., Mar. 7, 1926; s. Morris and Rose (Hyams) S.; m. Sybil Stellar, Sept. 8, 1953; children—Sandra Michelle, Susan Fern. Pres., gen. mgr. Sta.-CHQR, Calgary, Alta., Can.; dir. Western Broadcasting Co. Ltd. Mem. Can. Assn. Broadcasters (dir.), Western Assn. Broadcasters (past pres.), Alta. Assn. Broadcasters (past pres.). Club: B'nai B'rith. Office: 830 9th Ave SW Calgary AB T2P 1L7 Canada*

SOSNIK, HARRY, composer, conductor; b. Chgo., July 13, 1906; s. Arnold and Dora Sosnik; student U. Ill., Am. Conservatory Music, Chgo.; student composition with Arthur O. Anderson, Kurt Wanieck, Ernst Toch, Vittorio Giannini; m. Mary Elizabeth Bryant, Nov. 8, 1937. Musical dir. Decca Records, 1937-44; v.p. in charge music Am. Broadcasting Cos., 1967-76; composer original scores, conductor, TV, 1935—; original scores include Producers Showcase series, 1955-56. Playwrights '56 series, Philco TV Playhouse, 1949, also Ford, Coca-Cola, Pontiac and other spectaculars; condr. U.S. Treasury Guest Star programs on radio, 1949—; v.p. charge music for various divs. ABC Inc., N.Y.C., 1967-76. Composer: (popular songs) Lazy Rhapsody, Gavety, Producer's Showcase Theme, Out of the Night, You Stole My Heart; (instrumental orchestral compositions) Three Moods for Orchestra: Tango Chino, Beauty Through Night, Turquoise Waltz; also TV commls. Home: 215 E 68th St New York City NY 10023 Office: 1330 6th Ave New York City NY 10009

SOSNOVKSY, GEORGE, educator; b. Petersburg, Russia, Dec. 12, 1920; s. Nikolai and Akilina (Michailowa) S.; Ph.D., U. Innsbruck (Austria), 1948; m. Margaret Hildegard Christine, July 17, 1944. Postdoctoral fellow, research asso. dept. chemistry U. Chgo., 1956-59; sr. scientist IIT Research Inst., Chgo., 1959-63; asso. prof. chemistry, Ill. Inst. Tech., 1963-66; prof. chemistry U. Wis. at Milw., 1967—. Spl. sr. research fellow USPHS, Univ. Coll., London, Eng., U. Tübingen (Germany), 1967-68. Mem. Am. Chem. Soc., Chem. Soc. London. Author: Free Radical Reactions in Preparative Organic Chemistry, 1964. Editor Synthesis, Internat. Jour. Methods in Synthetic Organic Chemistry, 1969—. Contbr. articles to profl. jours. Address: Dept Chemistry 3210 N Cramer St Milwaukee WI 53201

SOSNOW, LAWRENCE IRA, health care co. exec.; b. Newark, Mar. 7, 1935; s. Emanuel and Edith (Grunt) S.; B.B.A., Upsala Coll., E. Orange, N.J., 1957; student N.Y. U. Grad. Sch. Bus., 1958; m. Ellen N. Rosenthal, May 30, 1965; children—Peter, Meg. Pres., Sosnow & Co., Inc., Newark, 1960-66; chmn., pres. Spade & Archer, N.Y.C., 1966-69; chmn. Gilbert Youth Research, N.Y.C., 1968-69; pres. MIND, Inc., N.Y.C., 1969-74, vice chmn., 1974-75; pres. Patient Care Inc., West Orange, N.J., 1975—. Bd. govs., v.p. Boy's Athletic League, N.Y.C., 1969—. Served with AUS, 1957, 61-62. Mem. Nat. Assn. Home Health Agys. (dir. 1979—). Home: 12 Rochambeau Rd Scarsdale NY 10583 Office: 59 Main St West Orange NJ 07052

SOSTRIN, MOREY, merchant; b. Russia, Jan. 10, 1904; s. Jacob and Anna (Bush) S.; brought to U.S., 1909, citizen by father's naturalization, 1920; student U. Chgo., 1920, Northwestern U., 1921; m. Anne Ferer, Aug. 22, 1964. With Fair Dept. Store, Chgo., 1921; mdse. mgr. J. N. Adam Co., Buffalo, 1924, v.p., 1928; mdse. mgr. Loesers, Bklyn., 1933; pres. McAlpin Co., Cin., 1936; with Younker Bros., Inc., Des Moines, 1938—, v.p., 1942, pres., dir., 1944-69, chmn., 1965—, cons., 1969—. Club: Des Moines. Home: 2295 S Ocean Blvd Palm Beach FL 33480 Office 7th and Walnut Des Moines IA 50306

SOTAK, JOSEPH EDWARD, savs. and loan exec.; b. Cleve., Aug. 31, 1918; s. Joseph Edward and Anna M. (Molitors) S.; B.A. cum laude, U. Notre Dame, 1940; J.D., Cleve.-Marshall Law Sch., 1952; m. Mary Louise Cooper, Sept. 16, 1942; children—Joseph Edward, Nancy Jane, Donald, Mary Ann. With State Savs. & Loan Co., South Euclid, Ohio, 1946—, pres., counsel, 1961, chmn. bd. dirs., 1965—; dir. Ohio Fin. Service Corp., Columbus. Mem. Cleve. Reinvestment Task Force; mem. Greater Cleve. Growth Bd.; trustee Buckeye Area Devel. Corp., Cleve., Neighborhood Housing Services, Cleve.; exec. trustee Savs. and Loan Polit. Action Com. Ohio. Served with USAAF, 1941-45. Mem. U.S., Ohio, N.E. Ohio (past pres.) savs. and loan leagues, Ohio League Savs. Assns. (2d v.p. 1977, 1st vice-chmn. 1978), Ohio Bar Assn., Heights Area C. of C. (dir.). Clubs: Notre Dame (past pres.), Acacia Country (dir.), Mid-day (Cleve.). Home: 32155 Creekside Dr Pepper Pike OH 44124 Office: 4065 Mayfield Rd South Euclid OH 44121

SOTER, GEORGE NICHOLAS, advt. exec.; b. Chgo., May 16, 1924; s. Nicholas A. and Emily (Damascus) S.; student U. Chgo., 1947-51; m. Effie Hartocollis, Feb. 7, 1949; children— Nicholas, Thomas, Peter. Writer, McCann-Erickson, Chgo., 1951-53; with Needham, Louis & Brorby, 1954-62, v.p., N.Y. creative dir., 1958-62; v.p., asso. creative dir. Lennen & Newell, Inc., N.Y.C., 1962-67; dir. Interpub. Product Devel. Workshop, N.Y.C., 1967; v.p., co-dir. creative services, mgmt. supr. Kenyon & Eckhardt, Inc., N.Y.C., 1968-73; exec. v.p., creative dir. Pampuzac-Soter Assos., Inc., N.Y.C., 1974-76; founder Greek Island, Ltd., N.Y.C., 1963, pres., 1963—. Served with AUS, 1943-47; ETO. Home: 404 Riverside Dr New York City NY 10025 Office: 215 E 49th St New York City NY 10017

SOTH, LAUREN KEPHART, journalist; b. Sibley, Iowa, Oct. 2, 1910; s. Michael Ray and Virginia Mabel (Kephart) S.; B.S., Iowa State U., 1932, M.S., 1938; m. Marcella Shaw Van, June 15, 1934; children—John Michael, Sara Kathryn, Melinda. In charge econ. info. Iowa State U., 1934-47; editor Agrl. Situation, Bur. Agrl. Econs., 1936-37; prin. economist OPA, 1942; editorial writer Des Moines Register and Tribune, 1947-54, editor editorial pages, 1954-75. Bd. dirs. Living History Farms. Served as maj. AUS, World War II. Recipient Pulitzer prize for editorial writing, 1956; Headliners Club award, 1956; Disting. Service to Agr. award Mo. Farmers Assn., 1977; Disting. Achievement citation Iowa State U. Alumni Assn., 1970. Fellow Am. Agrl. Econs. Assn.; mem. ACLU, Nat. Conf. Editorial Writers, Nat. Planning Assn. (trustee), Sigma Delta Chi, Alpha Zeta, Gamma Sigma Delta, Phi Kappa Phi, Beta Theta Pi. Episcopalian. Club: Cosmos (Washington). Author: Farm Trouble, 1957; An Embarrassment of Plenty, 1965; Agriculture in an Industrial Society, 1966. Home: 801 State Farm Rd West Des Moines IA 50265

SOTHERN, ANN (FORMERLY HARRIETTE LAKE), actress and singer; b. Valley City, N.D., Jan. 22, 1912; d. Walter J. and Annette (Yde) Lake; ed. pub. schs., Waterloo, Iowa, and Minneapolis; student U. of Wash.; m. Roger Pryor, 1936 (div. 1942); m. 2d Robert Sterling, 1943 (div. 1949); 1 dau., Patricia Ann. First appearance on N.Y. stage, America's Sweetheart, 1932; appeared in musicals, N.Y. City, 1932-34; 1st screen role, Let's Fall in Love, 1935; since starred in Maisie series, 1939-44, Lady Be Good, 1941, Panama Hattie, 1942, Cry Havoc, 1943, Dulcy, 1940, Three Hearts for Julia, 1943, April Showers, 1948, Words and Music, 1948, Letter to Three Wives, 1949, Nancy Goes to Rio, 1950, Death in a Doll's House, Judge Steps Out, 1949, Come Share My Love, Chubasco, 1962, Blue Gardenia, 1953, Sylvia, 1965, Crazy Mama, 1975; in play, Faithfully Yours, 1951, The Manitou, 1978; title role in TV program, Private Secretary, 1954-57; Ann Sothern Show, 1958-61; appeared on stage in The Duchess of Pasadena, 1978; in TV ltd. series Captains and the Kings, 1976. Pres. Vincent Prodns., Inc., Ann Sothern's Sewing Center, Sun Valley, Idaho, Anso Productions, Inc., Los Angeles, Calif. TV show, Ann Sothern Show; owner A Bar S Cattle Co. Address: care Contemporary-Korman Artists Ltd 132 Lasky Dr Beverly Hills CA 90212*

SOTT, HERBERT, lawyer; b. Detroit, Jan. 26, 1920; s. Harry and E. Helen (Nalven) S.; A.B., U. Mich., 1940, M.B.A., 1942, J.D., 1943; m. Dorothy E. Inglis, June 19, 1977; children by previous marriage—Lesley Sott Nickel, Lynne Scott Jackson. Admitted to Mich. bar, 1946; since practiced in Detroit, partner firm Friedman, Meyers & Keys, 1951-68, Barris, Sott, Denn & Driker, 1968—. Active Founders Soc. Detroit Inst. Arts, Detroit Grand Opera Assn., Detroit Symphony Assn., Detroit Zool. Assn.; bd. dirs. Mich. Heart Assn., Jewish Home for Aged, Jewish Family and Children's Service, Jewish Vocat. Service, Frank Meml. Corp., Krohn Found. Served as lt. (j.g.), USNR, 1943-46. Mem. Detroit, Mich., Am. bar assns. Clubs: Detroit, Franklin Hills, Renaissance, Standard. Office: Barris Sott Denn & Driker 2100 1st Fed Bldg Detroit MI 48226

SOTTILE, JAMES, financier, citrus grower; b. Charleston, S.C., Oct. 19, 1913; s. James and Louise (Mohlman) S.; m. Ethel Hooks, June 16, 1936; children—Linda (Mrs. Frank Hammond), James III, Suzanne (Mrs. Charles Guanci), Jeanne (Mrs. Harold Walsh III), John. Pres, dir. Canaveral Indian River Groves, Inc., 1962-70, Brevard Indian River Groves, Inc., 1963-68; pres., dir. Indian River Orange Groves, Inc., 1959-68, chmn. bd., 1968-73; pres., dir. Gulfstream Groves, Inc., 1962-65; pres. Lake Byrd Citrus Packing Co; pres., dir. Valencia Center, Inc.; dir., chmn. bd. Harlan Fuel Co., Goldfield Corp.; dir. No. Goldfield Investments, Inc., Black Range Mining Corp., Detrital Valley Salt Corp., Fla. Transport Corp., Getchell Mining Corp., Goldfield Consol. Mines Co., Mamba Engring. Co., Inc., San Pedro Mining Corp.; pres., dir. Pan Am. Bank of Miami, 1956-58. Trustee U. Miami, 1956-66. Mem. Fla. C. of C. (dir.-at-large). K.C., Elk. Clubs: Country of Coral Gables (Fla.), Riviera Country (Coral Gables); Eau Gallie Yacht (Melbourne, Fla.). Home: 2525 Indian Mound Trail Coral Gables FL 33134 Office: 65 E Nasa Blvd Melbourne FL 32901

SOTTILE, JAMES, III, mining co. exec.; b. Miami, Fla., Aug. 3, 1940; s. James and Ethel (Hooks) S.; B.S. cum laude, U. Fla., 1962; m. Judith Horne, Dec. 5, 1959; children—James IV, Michael, Scott, Thomas, Jennifer. Vice pres. Goldfield Corp., Melbourne, Fla., 1970-71, pres., dir., 1971—; v.p., dir. Canaveral Indian River Groves, Inc., Micco, Fla., 1964-70, Brevard-Indian River Groves, Inc., Micco, 1964-69, Indian River Shores Groves, Inc., 1964; pres., dir. Indian Mound Corp., Micco, 1963-69, Original 51 Corp., Micco, 1966-69, Harlan Fuel Co. (Ky.), 1975—; v.p. Lake Byrd Citrus Packing Co., Melbourne, 1963-71, pres., 1971—, also dir.; v.p. Indian River Orange Groves, Inc., Melbourne, 1963-69, pres., 1969-74, also dir.; pres., dir. Citrus Growers of Fla., Inc., Melbourne, 1970—; v.p., dir. No. Goldfield Investments Ltd., Inc., Melbourne, Fla., 1971-79, pres., 1979—; v.p., dir. Mamba Engring. Co., Inc., Titusville, Fla., 1972—; pres., dir. Black Range Mining Corp., Albuquerque, 1972—, Goldfield Consol. Mines Co., Albuquerque, 1972—, San Pedro Mining Corp., Albuquerque, 1972—; v.p., dir. Valencia Center, Inc., Coral Gables, Fla., 1964—. Supr., sec. San Sebastian Drainage Dist., Melbourne, 1965-78. Mem. Fla. C. of C. (dir. 1972), Young Pres.'s Orgn. Democrat. Roman Catholic. Clubs: Eau Gallie Yacht; Cat Cay (Bahamas). Home: 846 Malibu Ln Indialantic FL 32903 Office: 65 E NASA Blvd Melbourne FL 32901. *Success is achieved only through long days of hard work, awareness of the smallest detail, and total dedication to one's goals.*

SOUBRY, EMILE EDMUND, assn. exec.; b. London, Eng., Mar. 18, 1896; s. Stephen and Alice (Fowler) S.; student Acton Comml. Coll., 1904-11; m. Jennie Bennett, Apr. 2, 1919 (dec.); children—Kenneth William, Moira Barbara (Mrs. J. Michael Esdaile); m. 2d, Renée Mayberry, 1971. Came to U.S., 1941, naturalized, 1948. With Anglo Am. Oil Co., Ltd. (now Esso Petroleum Co., Ltd., affiliate of Standard Oil Co. of N.J.), 1911, chmn. bd. dirs., 1940; fgn. marketing coordinator Standard Oil Co. (N.J.), N.Y.C., 1943, dir., 1949-61, v.p., 1951-58, exec. v.p., 1958-61, mem. exec. com., 1955-61; dir. UN Assn. U.S.A., Inc., 1962—, nat. council, 1973—. Liaison Brit. Trade Com. and U.S. Govt., 1940-43; mem. fgn. petroleum supply com. Petroleum Adminstrn. Def. 1951-56. Mem. Fgn. Policy Assn. (dir. 1958—, chmn. bd. 1962-67). Office: 620 Fifth Ave New York NY 10020

SOUBRY, KENNETH WILLIAM STEPHEN, ins. broker; b. London, Eng., Jan. 15, 1920; s. Emile Edmund and Jennie (Benett) S.; B.A., Jesus Coll., Cambridge (Eng.) U., 1940; m. Irene Makowsky, Sept. 14, 1948. Came to U.S., 1946, naturalized, 1951. With Alexander & Alexander, Inc., N.Y.C., 1948—, dir., 1962—, pres., chief exec. officer, 1963-70, chmn., chief exec. officer, 1970-77, chmn. exec. com., 1977-78, chmn. bd., 1978—. Served with Royal Scots, 1940; to capt. Armoured Corps, Indian Army, 1941-46. Clubs: University, India House (N.Y.C.); Greenwich Country; Shenorock Shore. Home: 425 N Maple Ave Greenwich CT 06830 Office: 1211 Ave of Americas New York City NY 10036

SOUCCAR, JOSEPH EDWARD, glass co. exec.; b. Alexandria, Egypt, Dec. 2, 1933; s. Edward and Becca (Bondi) S.; B.E.E. with honors, U. Leeds (Eng.), 1954; M.B.A., U. Western Ont., London, Can., 1959; immigrated to Can., 1954, naturalized, 1959; children—Debbie, Audrey, Diane. Engr., No. Telecom. Com., Montreal, 1954-58; with Atlas Steels Ltd., 1959-65, dir. mktg., 1964-65; prin. P.R. Ross & Partners, mgmt. cons., Montreal, 1966-69; with Domglas Ltd., Montreal, 1969—, exec. v.p., 1975-76, pres., 1976—, also dir.; dir. Nat. Press Glass Co., Dorchester Electronics Ltd., Twinpak Ltd., Ampak Ltd. Clubs: Montreal Amateur Athletic Assn., Mt. Royal Country. Home: 1390 Pine Ave W Montreal PQ H3G 1AB Canada Office: Domglas Ltd 1080 Beaver Hall Hill Montreal PQ H2Z 1P2 Canada*

SOUDDER, EDWARD WALLACE, JR., newspaper, broadcasting exec.; b. Newark, Dec. 8, 1911; s. Edward Wallace and Katherine (Hollifield) S.; A.B., Princeton, 1935; m. Louise Bagby Fry, Jan. 19, 1945; children—Katherine Allison Soudder Tiballi, Mary Gale, Edward, Robert. Advt. dept. Newark Evening News, 1935, bus. and advt. depts., 1936-42, dir. news, asst. treas. 1938-45, v.p., 1945-50, pres., 1950-70, chmn. bd., 1970-72, pres. Newark Broadcasting, operating Sta. WVNJ, Newark, to 1978; pres. Orange Mt. Communications, Newark. Vice pres. Paper Mill Playhouse, Millburn, N.J. Trustee Newark Mus., Lake Placid (N.Y.) Edn. Found. Served from lt. (j.g.) to lt. comdr. USNR Air Force, 1942-46. Clubs: Rumson (N.J.) Country; Essex (Newark); Short Hills (N.J.). Home: 1 Euclid Ave Summit NJ 07901 Office: 1180 Raymond Blvd Newark NJ 07102

SOUDER, PAUL CLAYTON, banker; b. Greencastle, Ind., Dec. 2, 1920; s. Dewey C. and Julia (Dowell) S.; A.B., DePauw U., 1941; grad. Harvard Grad. Sch. Bus. Adminstrn., 1943, Grad. Sch. Banking, Rutgers U., 1951; m. Doris E. Elliott, Sept. 27, 1941; children—Douglas Paul, Julie Jan. Office mgr. Comml. Credit Corp., 1941; credit mgr. Mich. Nat. Bank, 1946, asst. v.p., 1947-52, v.p. Saginaw bd. dirs., 1952-62, sr. v.p., dir., 1961-71, exec. v.p., 1971-72, pres., dir., 1972—, vice chmn., 1980—; chmn. MNC Outstate Banks, 1980; dir. Auto-Owners Ins. Co., Auto-Owners Life Ins. Co., Wickes Corp., Mich. Nat. Bank, Mich. Nat. Corp., Detroit & Mackinac R.R. Corp., Mich. Nat. Corp., Lake Huron Broadcasting Corp., Homeowners Co., Jameson Corp., Lake Huron Broadcasting Corp., Homeowners Mut. Ins. Co., Garber Buick, Inc., Mich. Capital & Service, Inc., Mich. Bank Midland, Mich. Nat. Bank-West, Mich. Nat. Bank-Michiana, Property Owners Ins. Co., Owners Ins. Co., W.F. McNally Co., Inc. Pres. Greater Mich. Found.; trustee Mich. Wildlife Found., Mich. State U. Devel. Fund; bd. dirs., v.p. Frank N. Anderson Found.; bd. dirs. Woldumar Nature Center. Served from ensign to lt. comdr. USNR, 1942-46. Recipient Distinguished Service awards Saginaw's Outstanding Young Man. Mem. Robert Morris Assos., Am., Mich. bankers assn., Ind. Petroleum Assn., Am., Mich. oil and gas assns., C. of C. (dir.). Methodist. Clubs: Saginaw, Bankers, Econ. (Detroit); Otsego Ski. Author: Financing Oil Production in Michigan, 1951. Home: 2800 Maurer Rd Charlotte MI 48813 Office: 124 W Allegan St Lansing MI 48901

SOUDERS, WILLIAM FRANKLIN, office equipment co. exec.; b. Detroit, July 14, 1928; s. Clifford E. and Julia (O'Brien) S.; B.A. in Econs., Lake Forest Coll., 1952; m. Barbara L. Huskey, Nov. 25, 1950; children—Susan Lynn, Scott William, Sally Anne. In various sales and mktg. positions A.B. Dick Co., Chgo., 1951-63, gen. mgr. subs., 1963-64; with Xerox Corp., 1964—, group v.p., Stamford, Conn., 1973-77, exec. v.p. ops., 1977—, also dir.; dir. Rank Xerox Ltd., Fuji Xerox Co., Ltd., Xerox Can. Inc., Xerox do Brasil, S.A., Xerox de Mex., S.A. de C.V. Charter trustee, mem. exec. com. Lake Forest Coll.; bd. dirs. St. Joseph's Hosp., Stamford; mem. bd. visitors U. Conn. Sch. Bus. Adminstrn. Served with parachute inf. U.S. Army, 1946-47. Clubs: Wee Burn Country, The Landmark, Aspetuck Golf, Oak Hill. Office: Xerox Corp Long Ridge Rd Stamford CT 06904

SOUERS, LOREN EATON, lawyer; b. Canton, Ohio, Jan. 29, 1916; s. Loren Edmunds and Ilka (Gaskell) S.; A.B., Denison U., 1937; J.D., Western Res. U., 1940, postgrad., 1954-55; m. Mildred M. McCollum, June 21, 1941; children—Mary Sue (Mrs. J. James), Loren Eaton. Admitted to Ohio bar, 1940, U.S. Supreme Ct., 1960; asso. Black, McCuskey, Souers & Arbaugh, Canton, 1940—, partner, 1946—, chmn., 1979—; dir. Harter Bank and Trust Co., Harter BanCorp., Phoenix Mfg. Co., Joliet, Ill., Whitacre-Greer Fireproofing Co. Cons., Ohio Supreme Ct. Continuing Com. Admissions, 1957-59; mem. Ohio Bd. Bar Examiners, 1959-64; citizens adv. com. to State Library System. Pres. McKinley Area council Boy Scouts Am., 1954-57, mem. nat. council, 1954-70. Mem. Canton City Council, 1948-49; del. Rep. Nat. Conv., 1948; Rep. city campaign mgr., 1951, 53; mem. Ohio Bd. Edn., 1956-60, v.p., 1958-60; mem. Canton City Bd. Edn., 1962-72, pres., 1965, 68, 71; mem. Canton Recreation Bd., 1964-72; trustee Canton Welfare Fedn., 1965-72; bd. mgrs. Canton YMCA, 1965-79; mem. Canton Planning Commn., 1972-78; trustee Stark County Law Library Assn., 1945-76, pres., 1972-76; trustee Ohio Bar Found., Denison U., 1967—, Ohio Legal Center Inst.; mem. trust com. Hoover Found., 1967—; mem. vis. com. Case Western Res. U. Law Sch., 1968-77. Served to capt. inf., AUS, 1942-45; ETO. Decorated Fourragere (Belgium); recipient research prize in econs. Denison U., 1937, Disting. Service award Canton Jr. C of C., 1950, Silver Beaver award Boy Scouts Am., 1957. Fellow Am. Bar found.; mem. Am., Ohio (exec. com. 1976-79, pres. 1980) bar assns., Am. Legion, Canton Jr. C. of C. (pres.), Canton C. of C. (v.p. 1959-60), Phi Delta Theta, Phi Delta Phi, Omicron Delta Kappa, Tau Kappa Alpha, Pi Delta Epsilon. Baptist (endowment com. Ohio Bapt. Conv. 1962-75) Mason (32 deg.). Clubs: The Canton, Oakwood Country, Brookside Country (Canton). Contbr. to legal publs. lectr. on legal subjects. Home: 135 19th St NW Canton OH 44709 Office: Harter Bank Bldg Canton OH 44702

SOUL, DAVID, actor, singer; b. Chgo., Aug. 28; s. Richard W. Solberg; student Augustana Coll., Sioux Falls, S.D., U. of Americas, Mexico City, U. Minn.; student of Uta Hagen; children—Kristofer, Jon. Movie appearances: Johnny Got His Gun, 1971, Magnum Force, 1973, Mud, Dog Pound Shuffle; TV movies: The Disappearance of Flight 412, Intertect, Movin' On, Starsky & Hutch, Little Ladies of the Night; appeared TV series: Here Come the Brides, 1968-70, Owen Marshall: Counselor at Law, Starsky & Hutch, 1975—; other TV appearances include: Star Trek, The Rookies, The Merv Griffin Show, McMillan and Wife, Circle of Fear, others; TV spl. David Soul & Friends; album: David Soul; concert tour of Eng.; producer, star play Baal, 1975. Mem. AFTRA. Office: care Internat Creative Mgmt 40 W 57th St New York NY 10019*

SOULE, ARTHUR BRADLEY, radiologist, educator; b. St. Albans, Vt., Oct. 22, 1903; s. Arthur Bradley and Minnie (Miller) S.; A.B., U. Vt., 1925, M.D., 1928, D.Sc., 1974; m. June Yale Crouter, June 29, 1931; children—Caroline Yale, Arthur Bradley III. Practice medicine specializing in radiology, Burlington, Vt., 1929-76; chief radiol. service Mary Fletcher Hosp., 1933-70; prof. radiology Coll. Medicine, U. Vt., 1936-70, chmn. dept., 1937-70, prof. emeritus, 1970—, dir. alumni affairs, 1977—, dir. med. alumni affairs, 1976—; mem. com. acad. radiology Nat. Acad. Sci.-NRC; mem. tng. grants com. USPHS. Recipient Excellence in Teaching award Nu Sigma Nu, 1964, Distinguished Service medal U. Vt. Med. Alumni Assn., 1970, Certificate of Honor, A.S.R.T., 1969, Citation of Honor, Council Med. Edn., A.M.A., 1969. Fellow Am. Coll. Radiology (commn. chmn.; Gold medal 1971); mem. Am. Roentgen Ray Soc. (2d v.p. 1957, 68), Radiol. Soc. N.Am., New Eng. Cancer Soc. (pres.). Contbr. articles profl. jours. Home: Shelburne VT 05482 Office: Office of Dean Coll Med U Vt Burlington VT 05401

SOULE, GARDNER BOSWORTH, author, picture editor; b. Paris, Tex., Dec. 16, 1913; s. Edgar Huckabee and Floy DeVore (Perfect) S.; B.A., Rice Inst., 1933; B.S., Columbia, 1935, M.S., 1936; m. Janie Lee McDowell, Sept. 20, 1940. With A.P., N.Y.C., 1936-41, Newspaper PM, 1942; mng. editor Better Homes and Gardens, Des Moines, 1946-50; free-lance writer articles, books, N.Y.C., 1950—. Served to lt. USNR, 1943-46. Mem. Authors League, Sigma Delta Chi, Sigma Nu. Club: Columbia Univeristy (N.Y.C.). Author: The Maybe Monsters, 1963; Tomorrow's World of Science, 1963; Gemini and Apollo, 1964; The Mystery Monsters, 1965; Trail of the Abominable Snowman, 1966; The Ocean Adventure: Science Explores the Depths of the Sea, 1966; Sea Rescue, 1966; UFO's and IFO's, 1967; Undersea Frontiers, 1968; Under the Sea, 1969; Strange Things Animals Do, 1970; Wide Ocean, 1970; The Greatest Depths, 1970; Surprising Facts, 1971; New Discoveries in Oceanography, 1974; Wide Ocean, Brit. edit., 1974; Remarkable Creatures of the Seas, 1975; Men Who Dared The Sea: The Ocean Adventures of the Ancient Mariners, 1976, German edit., 1978; The Long Trail: How Cowboys and Longhorns Opened The West, 1976. Contbr. articles to mags. including Popular Sci. Monthly, Elks mag., United Feature Syndicate, London Express Syndicate, Am. Petroleum Inst., Diner's Club mag., Boys' Life. Address: 517 W 113th St New York City NY 10025

SOULE, GEORGE, coll. pres.; b. New Orleans, Nov. 24, 1896; s. Albert Lee and Anna Sophronia (Cooper) S.; student Isadore Newman Sch., Ga. Mil. Acad. Soulé Coll., La. State U.; m. Mary Brooks Ragland, Feb. 21, 1922; children—George, Evan R., Mary Brooks. Began as clk. and asst. instr., Soulé Coll., 1919, successively tchr. asst. treas. (1926), sec. and mgr. in charge of adminstrn., 1929—, partner in the firm of A. L., E. E. and George Soulé, owners of Soulé Coll., Inc., 1936- 48, pres., 1948—; past v.p. Am. Empire Ins. Co.; dir. Union Savs. & Loan Assn.; dir., past v.p. Bur. Govtl. Research of New Orleans. Past pres. New Orleans chpt. Nat. Officers Management Assn.; former dir. Magnolia Sch. for Exceptional Chidren (pres. 1945, 46): chmn. campaign executives com. United Community and War Chest, 1945; past pres. New Orleans Community Chest; chmn. New Orleans Ednl. Fund; past vice chmn. City Planning and Zoning Commn. of New Orleans; campaign vice chmn. United Fund, 1952,; gen. chmn. Congress Freedom nat. conv., 1963. Served to 2d lt. U.S.

Field Arty., 1917-18. Recipient Americanism award Am. Legion, 1960. Mem. New Orleans C. of C., Young Men's Bus. Club, Discussions Unlimited (hon. life). Episcopalian. Clubs: Boston (hon. life mem.), Pendennis (pres. 1970-71), Gyro (past pres., past dist. gov.) (New Orleans); New Orleans Executive of Louisiana (pres. 2 terms); Juanita (hon. life mem.). Home: 4825 Carondelet St New Orleans LA 70115 Office: 1410 Jackson Ave New Orleans LA 70130 also PO Box 53306 New Orleans LA 70153

SOULE, JOHN DUTCHER, educator; b. Moline, Ill., Oct. 11, 1920; s. Earl Arnold and Laney (Dutcher) S.; A.B., Miami U., Oxford, Ohio, 1942; M.S., U. So. Calif., 1948, Ph.D., 1952; m. Dorothy Louise Fisher, July 3, 1943; children—Patricia Lynn Kendrick, Susan Michele Harrison. Research fellow Allan Hancock Found., U. So. Calif., Los Angeles, 1948-50, instr. Sch. Dentistry, 1950-53, asst. prof. histology, 1953-58, asso. prof., 1958-63, prof., 1963—, chmn. dept. histology-pathology, 1953-67, chmn. dept. histology, 1967-78, asst. dean admissions, 1979—, adj. prof. dept. biol. scis., 1970—, Allan Hancock Found. research asso., 1952—; research asso. Am. Mus. Natural History, N.Y.C., 1961—; research fellow Calif. Inst. Tech., 1958. Served with U.S. Army, 1942-46. Recipient Excellence in Teaching award U. So. Calif. Assos., 1961, Kaplan award for teaching excellence, 1976. Fellow AAAS, Calif. Acad. Sci., So. Calif. Acad. Sci.; mem. Am. Soc. Zoologists, Soc. Systematic Zoology, Am. Microscopy Soc., Internat. Bryozoology Assn. (councilor 1971—, pres. 1977—), Sigma Xi, Phi Sigma, Delta Phi Alpha, Omicron Kappa Upsilon. Contbr. sect. to ency.; numerous publs. in dental histology, marine inverts, fouling, calcification. Home: 2361 Hill Dr Los Angeles CA 90041

SOULES, JACK ARBUTHNOTT, univ. dean; b. Ashtabula, Ohio, Jan. 26, 1928; s. David Lee and Lilly (Pasbjerg) S.; B.Sc. in Physics, Ohio State U., 1948, M.S., 1950, Ph.D., 1954; m. Shirley Emma Buechling, June 15, 1949 (div. 1970); children—Merrie Lee, William Peter, David Brian; m. 2d, Shirley Jean Anderson Barnett, Oct. 16, 1970. Prof. physics N.M. State U., 1955-61, 63-65, 66-68; physicist Office Naval Research, 1961- 63; acad. adminstrn. intern Ohio State U., 1965-66; dean arts and scis. Cleve. State U., 1968—. Home: 1900 E 30th St Cleveland OH 44114

SOUPART, PIERRE, physician, educator; b. Morlanwelz, Belgium, Oct. 1, 1923; s. Arthur and Angèle (Couteau) S.; came to U.S., 1962, naturalized, 1969; M.D., Brussels U., 1949, Ph.D., 1959, hon. prof., 1975; m. Simone Haegeman, July 23, 1949; children—Evelyne, Antoinette, Pascale. Asst. prof. dept. biochemistry Brussels U. Sch. Medicine, 1950-56, asso. prof., 1956-62; head clin. labs. Clinic for Indsl. Accidents, Brussels, 1952-62; prof. biochemistry and human nutrition Province of Brabant Inst. Tech., Brussels, 1959-62; research asso. div. reproductive physiology, dept. Ob-Gyn, Vanderbilt U. Sch. Medicine, Nashville, 1962-63, asst. prof. Ob-Gyn, 1963-66, asso. research prof., 1966—, sr. investigator Vanderbilt Center for Population Research and Studies in Reproductive Biology, 1969—, mem. univ. com. for protection of human subjects, 1973-76; vis. prof. Universidad Catolica de Chile and Universidad de Chile, Santiago, 1976; vis. prof. U. Calif., spring 1979; guest speaker numerous confs.; vis. prof. U. B.C., Vancouver, Can., 1979, Karolinska Inst., Stockholm, 1979, Monash U., Melbourne, Australia, 1979. Served as med. officer Belgian Army, 1949-50. Francqui Found. fellow, 1948, advanced fellow, 1961; Vanderbilt U. Centennial fellow, 1974-75; grantee NSF, March of Dimes, others. Mem. Soc. Study of Reprodn. (chmn. bylaws com. 1973-75), Société Belge de Biochimie, N.Y. Acad. Scis., Soc. Study of Fertility (U.K.), Am. Fertility Soc., Sociedad Latino Americana de Microscopia Electronica, Am. Soc. Andrology (charter), Soc. Cryobiology, Am. Assn. Tissue Banks, Internat. Embryotransfer Soc., Am. Assn. Gynecologic Laparascopists, Sigma Xi, Belgian Dietetic Assn. (hon.). Democrat. Club: Masons (Brussels). Author: Aminoaciduria of Pregnancy, 1959; editorial bd. Advances in Reproductive Biology, 1975—; contbr. articles to profl. jours. Pioneer in in vitro fertilization of human ovum. Office: Vanderbilt U Med Center Dept Ob-Gyn Nashville TN 37232. *In any new situation in his life man is alone. Don't count on any help that wouldn't come first from yourself.*

SOUR, ROBERT BANDLER, musical co. exec.; b. N.Y.C., Oct 31, 1905; s. Bernard and Adele (Somborn) S.; ed. Princeton, 1925; m. Geraldine Scofield, Oct. 24, 1940; children—R. Thomas, Peter, Bonnie (Mrs. Arthur A. Anderson), Victoria Jean (Mrs. John R. Raben, Jr.). With S.W. Straus, real estate, 1925-29; free-lance song writer, 1929-31; mem. Am. Stock Exchange, 1931-37; asso. producer Fed. Theatre, 1937-39; with Broadcast Music, Inc., 1940-70, cons. to pres., vice chmn. bd., 1970—; cons. adv. council dept. music Princeton; cons. Am. Guild Authors and Composers. Bd. dirs. Songwriters Hall Fame, also v.p.; bd. dirs. N.Y. Com. Young Audiences. Mem. Contemporary Music Soc. (dir.). Club: Century Assn., Princeton (N.Y.C.); Innis Arden (Old Greenwich, Conn.). Composer lyrics to Body and Soul, Practice Makes Perfect, Walking By the River, We Could Make Such Beautiful Music Together, I See a Million People. Home: 20 Rocky Point Rd Old Greenwich CT 06870 Office: 40 W 57th St New York NY 10019

SOURASKY, ELIAS, banker; b. Bialystock, Russia, Oct. 10, 1899; s. Jacob and Elka (Slomiansky) S.; Ph.D., U. Tel Aviv, 1971; m. Ida Thau (dec.); 1 dau., Joan Sourasky Constantiner; m. 2d, Cesia Pineles. Founder wool factory, Mex.; land developer, road bldr., Mex.; founder Central de Fianzas, Mex., 1936, Banco de Cedulas Hipotecarias, S.A., Mexico City, 1941—, Banco del Ahorro Nacional S.A., Cia. Mexicana de Seguros La Equitativa, S.A. Recipient Aguila Azteca, Mex., 1968. Established Fondo de Fomento Educativo; established yearly Premio Elias Sourasky for most distinguished person in fields of art, sci., lit. Office: 364 Paseo de la Reforma Mexico 6 DF Mexico

SOURIS, THEODORE, lawyer; b. Detroit, Aug. 5 1925; A.B., U. Mich., 1947, LL.B., 1949; m. Jane Helen Keller, Mar. 27, 1952; children—Christopher, Stephen, Susan. Admitted to Mich. bar, 1949; practiced law, Detroit, 1949-59; circuit Judge 3d Jud. Circuit Mich. (Wayne County), 1959-60; justice Supreme Ct. Mich., 1960-68; partner Bodman, Longley & Dahling, Detroit, 1968—; dir. Community Nat. Bank, Pontiac, Mich.; mem. Mich. State Bd. Ethics, 1973—. Served with USAAF, 1943-45. Fellow Am. Bar Found.; mem. Am., Detroit bar assns., Am. Judicature Soc., Am. Law Inst., State Bar Mich. Clubs: Detroit Athletic, Grosse Pointe. Home: 895 Edgemont Park Grosse Pointe Park MI 48230 Office: 34th Floor 100 Renaissance Center Detroit MI 48243

SOURKES, THEODORE LIONEL, biochemist, educator; b. Montreal, Que., Can., Feb. 21, 1919; s. Irving and Fannie (Golt) S.; B.Sc., McGill U., 1939, M.Sc. magna cum laude, 1946; Ph.D., Cornell U., 1948; m. Shena Rosenblatt, Jan. 17, 1943; children—Barbara, Myra. Asst. prof. pharmacology Georgetown U. Med. Sch., 1948-50; research asso. dept. enzyme chemistry Merck Inst. Therapeutic Research, Rahway, N.J., 1950-53; sr. research biochemist Allan Meml. Inst., Montreal, 1953-65, dir. lab. chem. neurobiology, 1965—; mem. faculty McGill U., Montreal, 1954—, prof. biochemistry, 1965—, asso. dean for research Faculty Medicine, 1972-75. Mem. Que. Med. Research Council, 1971-77; sr. fellow Parkinson's Disease Found., N.Y.C., 1963-66. Fellow Royal Soc. Can., mem. Canadian Biochem. Soc., Pharmacol. Soc. Can., Canadian Soc. Clin. Chemistry, Am. Soc. Biol. Chemists, Am. Soc. Pharmacology and Exptl. Therapeutics, Am. Soc. Neurochemistry, Internat. Soc. Neurochemistry, Internat. Brain Research Orgn., Canadian Soc. Study History and Philosophy Sci., Sigma Xi. Author: Biochemistry of Mental Disease, 1962; Nobel Prize Winners in Medicine and Physiology, 1901-1965, 1967. Mem. editorial bd. Progress in Neuro-Psychopharmacology, Acta Belgica Psychiatrica, Biochemistry Pharmacology and Behavior, Jour. Psychoneuroendocrinology, Essays in Neurochemistry and Neuropharmacology. Research and publs. on drugs for treatment high blood pressure; 1st basic research on methyldopa; elucidation of role of dopamine and other monamines in nervous system; biochem. and histological bases of Parkinson's disease, biochemistry of mental depression. Home: 4645 Montclair Ave Montreal PQ H4B 2J8 Canada

SOURS, JAMES KINGSLEY, former coll. pres.; b. Corydon, Iowa, Sept. 16, 1925; s. James N. and Virginia (Kantor) S.; student Phillips U., 1943; B.A., U. Wichita, 1949; M.P.A. (Adminstration fellow 1949-51), Harvard, 1951, Ph.D., 1954; m. Alice Hyde, July 11, 1947; children—James W., Mary Jan. David Bryan. Adminstrv. aid City Mgr.'s Office, Wichita, 1947-49; mem. faculty U. Wichita, 1951-65; prof. polit. sci., head dept., 1958-62, dean Fairmount Coll. Arts and Scis., 1962-65, chmn. Center Urban Studies, 1957-63; pres. So. Oreg. State Coll., Ashland, 1969-79; ednl. cons. Dankook U., Seoul, 1979-80, Korean Ministry Edn., 1979—; exec. v.p. Am. Coll. Testing Program, Iowa City, 1965-68; vis. prof. polit. sci. U. Istanbul (Turkey), 1968-69; vis. prof. Dankook U., Seoul, Korea, 1976. Vice pres. Nat. Collegiate Athletic Assn., 1959-64. Pres. Urban League Wichita, 1953-56, Wichita City Commn. Human Relations, 1962; treas. Sedgwick County chpt. A.R.C., 1962; chmn. com. nursing edn. Wesley Med. Center, Wichita, 1962-64. Served with USNR, 1943-46. Mem. Am. Polit. Sci. Assn. Democrat. Unitarian. Author: (series) Some Observations on the Management of Large Cities, 1957; also numerous articles. Home: 3100 Payne Rd Medford OR 97501

SOUSA, JOHN PHILIP, III, pub. co. exec.; b. N.Y.C., Oct. 22, 1913; s. John Philip, Jr. and Eileen (Adams) S.; A.B. cum laude, Princeton, 1936; m. Dorothy LaFollette, May 12, 1944; 1 son, John Philip IV; m. 2d, Joy Arnsten, Mar. 15, 1959 (dec.). With Time Inc., 1942-70, dir. pub. affairs Time mag., 1963-64; asst. pub. Fortune mag., 1964-67; dir. planning Time-Life Books 1967-68; dir. research and devel. Books, Arts, Recordings group Time Inc., 1968-70; pres. John Philip Sousa, Inc., 1968—; pub. mem. Fgn. Service Selection Bds., USIA, 1970, insp. team, Korea, 1971; cons. mag. pub. and pub. affairs, 1973—; cons. Am. Heritage Pub. Co., Inc., 1976-77. Trustee, Council Religion Internat. Affairs, 1973—. Roman Catholic. Author: My Family Right or Wrong, 1943; The Psychopathic Dog, 1946. Home and Office: 225 E 57th St New York City NY 10022

SOUTAR, DOUGLAS H., metals co. exec.; b. Oklahoma City, Sept. 2, 1918; s. Richard Gray and Myra (Davidson) S.; Ph.B., U. Wis., 1940, LL.B., 1943; postgrad. George Washington U., 1944; m. Patricia Ann Lockett, June 12, 1940; children—Douglas Lockett, Nancy Jane, Richard Glenn, Clay Ann. Admitted to Wis. bar, 1946, N.Y. State bar, 1950; exec. sec. trucking commn. NWLB, 1943-44; indsl. relations counsel Am. Trucking Assn., 1944-47; counsel Sunshine Biscuits, Inc., 1947-51; with ASARCO, Inc., N.Y.C., 1951—, v.p. indsl. relations and personnel, 1963—. Mem. manpower adv. com. U.S. Dept. Labor, 1971-74; mem. adv. council Cornell U. Sch. Indsl. and Labor Relations; mem. exec. bd. labor-mgmt. relations inst. Pace U.; mem. Fed. Adv. Council on Unemployment Ins.; mem. adv. council Union Coll.; bd. dirs. Automation House. Served to lt. USNR, World War II. Mem. Indsl. Relations Research Assn. (nat. pres. 1973, pres. N.Y.C. chpt. 1968), Indsl. Relations Soc. N.Y.C. (pres. 1963), Labor Policy Assn. (mem. exec. com., dir.), Inter-Am. Safety Council (dir.), NAM (indsl. relations steering com., chmn. subcom. multinat. labor relations), Unemployment Benefit Advisers (pres. 1976), Am. Bar Assn., Wis. Bar Assn., N.Y. State Bar Assn., Bus. Roundtable (chmn. labor-mgmt. com. 1973-75). Clubs: Wall Street (dir.), Univ., Bankers of Am. (pres. 1976-79) (N.Y.C.); Met. (Washington); Belle Haven, Indian Harbor Yacht, Stanwich (Greenwich, Conn.); Dorset Field (Vt.). Home: Belle Haven Greenwich CT Office: 120 Broadway New York NY 10005

SOUTER, DAVID HACKETT, state justice; b. Melrose, Mass., Sept. 17, 1939; s. Joseph Alexander and Helen Adams (Hackett) S.; B.A., Harvard U., 1961, LL.B., 1966; Rhodes scholar, Oxford U., 1961-63. Admitted to N.H. bar; asso. firm Orr & Reno, Concord, 1966-68; asst. atty. gen. N.H., 1968-71, dep. atty. gen., 1971-76, atty. gen., 1976-78; asso. justice Superior Ct. N.H., 1978—. Pres. bd. trustees Concord Hosp.; trustee N.H. Hist. Soc. Mem. N.H. Bar Assn., Phi Beta Kappa. Republican. Episcopalian. Home: Weare NH 03281

SOUTER, ROBERT TAYLOR, banker; b. Melrose, Mass., Feb 17, 1909; s. Walter Wilson and Mary (Taylor) S.; student Harvard, 1934; m. Barbara P. Claybourne, Sept. 7, 1935; children—Scott C., Pamela (Mrs. Edward Reilly). Treas. Braintree Coop. Bank (Mass.), 1937-42, v.p. U.S. Savs. and Loan League, 1942-47; v.p., dir. Coast Fed. Savs. & Loan Assn., Los Angeles, 1947-55; pres., dir. World Savs. and Loan Assn., Oakland, Calif., 1955—; dir. Trans-World Bank, Los Angeles, FHLB, San Francisco, Mem. Fed. Savs. and Loan Adv. Council, Washington. Mem. U.S., Calif. (bd. dirs.) savs. and loan leagues, Nat. League Insured Savs. Assns. Republican. Methodist. Home: 4 Windsor Dr Hillsborough CA 94010

SOUTH, CHARLES SUMNER, airline exec.; b. Phila., June 17, 1915; s. Aaron L. and Bessie S. (Delaney) S.; ed. Asbury Coll., U. Ky.; children—John R., Patricia South Adams; m. 2d, Alice Major, Aug. 23, 1969; 1 son, James M. With Chase Nat. Bank, Panama, 1934-37; with air transp. cos. in C.Am. and S.Am., 1937-46; with Braniff Airways, Inc., Dallas, 1946—, sr. v.p. Latin Am., 1975-76, sr. v.p. internat., 1976—. Clubs: Burning Tree (Bethesda, Md.); Lakewood Country (Dallas). Office: PO Box 61747 Room W308 Dallas/Ft Worth Airport TX 75261

SOUTH, FRANK EDWIN, physiologist, univ. adminstr.; b. Norfolk, Nebr., Sept. 20, 1924; s. Frank Edwin and Gladys (Brinkman) S.; A.B., U. Calif., Berkeley, 1949, Ph.D., 1952; m. Berna Deane Phyllis Casebolt, June 23, 1946; children—Frank Edwin, Robert Christopher. Asst. prof. physiology U. P.R. Sch. Medicine, 1953-54, U. Ill. Coll. Medicine, 1954-61; asso. prof. Colo. State U., 1961-62, prof., 1962-65; prof. U. Mo., 1965-76; prof., dir. Sch. Life and Health Scis., U. Del., Newark, 1976—; mem. governing bd., dir. Hibernation Info. Exchange, 1959—. Bd. dirs. Del. Lung Assn., 1976—, Del. Cancer Network, 1977—; mem. research com. Del. Heart Assn., 1977—; mem. med. adv. bd. A.I. DuPont Inst., Wilmington, Del., 1978—. Served with AUS, 1943-45. Decorated Purple Heart with oak leaf cluster, Silver Star; NIH career devel. awardee, 1961-65. Fellow AAAS, Sigma Xi; mem. Am. Physiol. Soc., Soc. Gen. Physiologists, Soc. Exptl. Biology and Medicine, Internat. Hibernation Soc. (governing bd., dir.), Am. Soc. Zoologists, Cryobiology Soc., U.S. Power Squadron, Oceanic Soc., Soc. Hist. Preservation. Episcopalian. Club: North East River Yacht. Editorial bd. Cryobiology; contbr. numerous articles on physiology of hibernation, temperature regulation, renal function, marine mammals, artificial atmospheres, and sleep to profl. jours. Office: Dir Sch Life and Health Scis U Del Newark DE 19711

SOUTH, JERRY GLOVER, mortgage banker; b. Frankfort, Ky., Dec. 1, 1932; s. Polk and Alice (Alexander) S.; A.B. in Econs., Washington and Lee U., 1954; LL.B., Stanford U., 1958; grad. Advanced Mgmt. Program, Harvard Bus. Sch., 1976; m. Marilyn Jean Page, Jan. 30, 1960; children—Lindsay Page, Alison Phillips, Marian Alexander. Admitted to Calif. bar, 1959, U.S. Supreme Ct. bar, 1969; corporate counsel Bank of Am. NT&SA, 1958-67, sec., counsel, 1968-70, v.p., exec. asst. to pres., 1970-71, v.p. communications, 1971-72; sec. BankAm. Corp., 1969-70; v.p., sec. BankAm. Corp. and Bank of Am. NT&SA and subs., 1972-76; pres. BA Mortgage and Internat. Realty Corp., San Francisco, 1977—; dir. Nat. Bank Americard Inc., 1970-74. Mem. adv. council Calif. region U.S. Forest Service, 1973-77; trustee Washington and Lee U. Served as lt. (j.g.) USNR, 1954-56. Mem. Am., Ky., San Francisco bar assns., Mortgage Bankers Assn., Bar Assn. Calif. Democrat. Club: Bankers (San Francisco). Office: 555 California St Suite 4480 San Francisco CA 94104

SOUTHAM, CHESTER MILTON, physician, educator; b. Salem, Mass., Oct. 4, 1919; s. Walter A. and Elizabeth (Furbish) S.; B.S., U. Idaho, 1941, M.S., 1943; M.D., Columbia U., 1947; m. Anna L. Skow, Sept. 24, 1939; children—Lawrence A., Lenore E., Arthur M.; m. 2d, Gertrude E. Lundin, June 9, 1973. Intern, Presbyn. Hosp., N.Y.C., 1947-48; from research fellow to mem. Sloan-Kettering Inst. Cancer Research, N.Y.C., 1948-70; from clin. fellow to attending physician Meml. Hosp. Cancer, N.Y.C., 1948-71; mem. faculty Cornell U. Med. Coll., 1951-71, asso. prof. medicine, 1958-71; prof. medicine Jefferson Med. Coll., Phila, 1971—, head div. oncology, 1971—; mem. adv. com. research therapy cancer Am. Cancer Soc., 1961-66, 70-74; adv. com. tobacco and health research AMA Edn. and Research Found., 1965- 66; mem. sci. adv. com. Damon Runyon Fund, 1961-68; mem. com. virology and immunology Internat. Union Against Cancer 1966-70; mem. exptl. therapy com., NIH, 1972-76. Trustee Leopold Schepp Found., 1961-67, Strang Clinic and Preventive Medicine Inst., 1963-68; bd. dirs. Nat. Inst. for Seriously Ill and Dying, 1976—. Served with AUS, 1943-46, 53-55. Recipient certificate achievement U.S. Army, 1965. Fellow A.C.P.; mem. Am. Assn. Cancer Research (dir. 1966—, pres. 1968-69), Am. Assn. Exptl. Pathology, Am. Assn. Immunologists, Am. Fedn. Clin. Research, Am. Soc. Tropical Medicine and Hygiene, Am. Soc. Microbiology, Harvey Soc., Soc. Surg. Oncology, N.Y. Acad. Scis., Soc. Exptl. Biology and Medicine, Reticuloendothelial Soc., Tissue Culture Assn., Transplantation Soc., Phi Beta Kappa, Sigma Xi. Office: Jefferson Med Coll 1025 Walnut St Philadelphia PA 19107

SOUTHAM, G(ORDON) HAMILTON, Canadian govt. ofcl.; b. Ottawa, Ont., Can., Dec. 19, 1916; s. Wilson Mills and Henrietta Alberta (Cargill) S.; B.A. with Honors, Trinity Coll., Toronto, Ont., 1939; postgrad. Christ Ch. Coll., Oxford, Eng., 1939; LL.D. (hon.), Trent and Carleton univs.; m. Jacqueline Lambert-David, Apr. 15, 1940 (div. Mar. 1969); children—Peter, Christopher, Jennifer, Michael; m. 2d, Gro Mortensen, May 17, 1969 (div. Jan. 1978); children—Henrietta, Gordon. Reporter, The Times, London, Eng., 1945-46; editorial writer Ottawa Citizen, 1946-47; with Dept. External Affairs Can., 1948-64, ambassador, Warsaw, Poland, 1960-62, head information div., Ottawa, 1962-64; coordinator Nat. Arts Centre, Ottawa, 1964-67, dir. gen., 1967-77; spl. advisor to sec. state, 1977-79; dir. Southam Inc., Toronto. Chmn. organizing com. UNESCO Festival and Seminar on Films on Art, Ottawa, 1963, Colloquium '67, Internat. Theatre Inst., Montreal, Que., 1967; chmn. Nat. Theatre Sch., Montreal, 1979; pres. Can. Archeol. Inst., Athens, 1979; bd. dirs. Can. Opera Co., 1979, Can. Film Inst., 1979. Served with Brit. Army, 1939-40, to capt. Royal Canadian Arty., 1940-45. Decorated officer Order of Can. Mem. Nat. Gallery Assn. (a founder, 1st pres. 1958-59), Clubs: Cercle Universitaire (Ottawa); Reform (London). Home: 327 Buena Vista Rd Ottawa ON K1M 0W1 Canada

SOUTHARD, FRANK ALLAN, JR., economist; b. Cleve., Jan. 17, 1907; s. Frank Allan and May Lucretia (Bowsher) S.; A.B., Pomona Coll., 1927, LL.D., 1976; Ph.D., U. Calif., 1930; m. Mary Isabel Hay, Dec. 27, 1942. Instr., U. Calif., 1930-31; asst. prof., prof. econs. Cornell U., 1931-48, chmn. dept. econs., 1946-48; researcher internat. relations Carnegie Endowment, 1934-35; sr. econ. analyst U.S. Tariff Commn., 1933; Guggenheim fellow to study fgn. exchange policy in S.Am., 1940; asst. dir. monetary research Treasury Dept., 1941-42, dir. office internat. fin., 1947-48; asso. dir. research and statis. in charge internat. sect. Bd. Govs., Fed. Res. System, 1948-49; U.S. exec. dir. IMF and spl. asst. to Sec. Treasury, 1949-62, dep. mng. dir., vice chmn. exec. bd., 1962-74; dir. Atlantic Council, 1974—; alt. gov. (U.S.), bd. govs. Internat. Bank and Monetary Fund., 1949-62. Bd. dirs. Population Crisis Com., Per Jacobsson Found., Washington Internat. Sch. Served to comdr. USNR, 1942-46; fin. adviser Allied Force Hdqrs. in Mediterranean, 1943-45. Decorated Legion of Merit; officer Order Brit. Empire, officer Legion of Honor (France). Mem. Am. Econ. Assn., Council Fgn. Relations, Washington Inst. Fgn. Affairs, Phi Beta Kappa Assos. Republican. Presbyterian. Clubs: Nat. Economists, Internat. (Washington). Author: American Industry in Europe, 1931; Foreign Exchange Practice and Policy, 1940; The Finances of European Liberation, 1946; co-author: Canadian American Industry, 1936; International Monetary System, 1976; The Floating Rate System, 1978; The Evolution of the IMF, 1980. Home: 4620 N Park Ave Chevy Chase MD 20015

SOUTHARD, RUPERT BARRON, JR., govt. ofcl.; b. St. Johnsbury, Vt., Apr. 8, 1923; s. Rupert Barron and Kathleen Wilhemina (Larvey) S.; student U. Rochester, 1943-44; B.C.E., Syracuse U., 1949; m. Jean Frances Scott, July 7, 1945; children—John Scott, Kathleen, Timothy Will, Matthew Barron, Ann, Joseph Rupert. With U.S. Geol. Survey, 1949—, mem. program staff topographic div., 1960-61, 65-70, asso. chief topographic div., 1970-78, chief, 1978—; mem. faculty, cons. U.S. Dept. Agr. Grad. Sch., 1957—; mem. Fed. Mapping Task Force, 1972-73; U.S. mem. commn. on cartography Pan Am. Inst. Geography and History. Served with USMC, 1943-46, 50-52. Recipient Disting. Service award Dept. Interior, 1976; Mt. Southard, Antarctica, named in his honor. Mem. Am. Soc. Photogrammetry, Am. Congress Surveying and Mapping, Am. Soc. Cartographers, Antarctican Soc. Roman Catholic. Contbr. articles to profl. jours. Home: 4203 Burke Station Rd Fairfax VA 22032 Office: US Geol Survey 516 National Center Reston VA 22092

SOUTHARD, SHELBY EDWARD, editor, writer; b. Athens, Ala., Oct. 30, 1914; s. Lorin Samuel and Ada Ethel (Davis) S.; A.B., Birmingham-So. Coll., 1937; A.M., Vanderbilt U., 1938; ind. study and travel on Rosenwald fellowship, 1939. Exec. sec. Ala. Coll., 1939-42; with Office Sec. of War, World War II; editor The Methodist Layman (mag.), Chgo., 1947-59; editor of World Mag., 1959-63; dir. pub. affairs Coop. League U.S.A., 1963—; contbr. religious press, other periodicals. Founding bd. dirs., chmn. transp. com. Consumer Fedn. Am., 1967—; mem. consumer adv. council Underwriters Labs.; mem. Pres.'s Adv. Com. on Trade Negotiations, 1976—. Sec. bd. trustees Ala. Coll., 1939-42; mem. joint dept. stewardship Nat. Council Chs. Mem. Nat. Com. Religious Leaders for Safety, Coop. Editorial Assn. U.S. and Can. (pres. 1962-63), Nat. Com. Support

Pub. Schs., Phi Beta Kappa, Omicron Delta Kappa, Pi Gamma Mu. Methodist (asso. sec. gen. bd. lay activities, cons. mem. curriculum com., interboard com. town and country work of the ch.; mem. TV, radio and film commn. 1953-56). Author: The Schism in American Methodism, 1844; editor: Guidebook of Alabama, 1942. Travel in Alaska, Aleutians, C. Am., S. Am., Caribbean area, Europe, Africa, Middle East. Home: 1711 Massachusetts Ave NW Washington DC 20036 Office: Suite 1100 1828 L St NW Washington DC 20036

SOUTHER, ROY HOBART, cons. research engr-scientist; b. nr. Elkin, N.C., July 25, 1897; s. William A. and Fannie (Norman) S.; B.S. in Chem. Engring. and Chemistry, U. N.C., 1920, postgrad., 1941-42, 44, 56. With Cone Mills Corp., Greensboro, N.C., 1920-59, research dir., 1944-59; sci. and engring. research cons. in water conservation, Greensboro, 1960—. Mem. adv. bd. Inst. Textile Tech., Charlottesville, Va., 1948-51, Textile Research Inst., Princeton, N.J., 1957-60; chmn. chem. processing industries task group Nat. Tech. Task Com. on Indsl. Waste, USPHS, 1959-65. A founder, sec.-treas. Greensboro Evening Coll., 1947-53; mem. adv. bd. Greensboro div. Guilford Coll., 1947—, recipient Coll. Adminstrn. award, 1956; mem. N.C. adv. com. on sci. engring. and specialized personnel SSS, 1957-71. Precinct chmn. Democratic party Guilford County, N.C., 1940-52. Mem. Am. Assn. Textile Chemists and Colorists (chmn. nat. com. stream sanitation tech. 1956-58, 62-64), Water Pollution Control Fedn. (Indsl. Waste medal award 1959), Am. Chem Soc., Am. Soc. Quality Control, N.C. Acad. Sci., Greensboro C. of C., U. N.C. Alumni Assn. (pres. Greensboro chpt. 1949-50), Textile Quality Control Assn. (founding mem.), Civitan Internat., Toastmasters (N.C. Community Service award 1971), Phi Beta Kappa, Alpha Chi Sigma. Presbyn. Mason. Club: Greensboro Writers. Contbr. over 60 articles on research in water conservation, pollution abatement, statis. quality control and textile processing to profl. jours., chpts. to books. Developer innovative prolonged bioaeration systems now used by various industries and municipalities. Home: 3116 Summit Ave Greensboro NC 27405

SOUTHERLAND, LOUIS FENO, JR., architect; b. Trenton, Tex., Apr. 23, 1906; s. Louis Feno and Adelia Pearl (Inzer) S.; grad. Burleson Coll., Greenville, Tex., 1924; student U. Tex., 1924-27; B.Arch., Mass. Inst. Tech., 1930, grad. study, 1931; m. Teresa Jean Reed, Jan. 8, 1941; 1 son, John Robb. Asst. architect R.H. Hunt, Chattanooga, 1928, 31-32, Densmore, Leclear & Robbins, Boston, 1930-31, Ralph Cameron, San Antonio, 1933; partner firm Page, Southerland, Page Architects, Austin, Tex., 1934—, sec. PSP Profl. Corp.; spl. instr. U. Tex., 1953; vice-chmn. bd. J.R. Reed Music Co., Austin. Mem. Tex. Planning Commn., 1953-56; regional chmn., hon. sec. ednl. council Mass. Inst. Tech., 1956-72; pres. Austin Symphony Orch. Soc., 1965-67. Served from lt. to comdr. USNR, 1942-46. Fellow AIA; mem. Tex. Soc. Architects (sec.-treas. 1953-56), Nat. Soc. Profl. Engrs., Austin Found. Baptist (deacon). Clubs: Tarryhouse, Headliners (trustee) (Austin); Argyle (San Antonio). Prin. works include Am. Embassy Office Bldg., Mexico City, Stark Mus. Art, Orange, Tex., Lutcher Theater Performing Arts, Orange, Civic Auditorium, Austin, Sch. Bus. Adminstrn. Bldg. U. Tex.; numerous bldgs. Tex. Woman's U. Home: 2801 Robb's Run Austin TX 78703 Office: 805 Congress Ave Austin TX 78701

SOUTHERN, EILEEN (MRS. JOSEPH SOUTHERN), educator; b. Mpls., Feb. 19, 1920; d. Walter Wade and Lilla (Gibson) Jackson; A.B., U. Chgo., 1940, M.A., 1941; Ph.D., N.Y. U., 1961; M.A. (hon.), Harvard U., 1976; m. Joseph Southern, Aug. 22, 1942; children—April, Edward. Concert pianist, 1940-55; instr. Prairie View U., Hempstead, Tex., 1941-42; asst. prof. So. U., Baton Rouge, 1943-45, 49-51; tchr. N.Y.C. Bd. Edn., 1954-60; instr. Bklyn. Coll., City U. N.Y., 1960-64, asst. prof., 1964-69; asso. prof. York Coll., City U. N.Y., 1969-71, prof., 1972-75; prof. music Harvard U., Cambridge, Mass., 1976—, chmn. dept. Afro-Am. studies, 1976—. Active Girl Scouts U.S.A., 1954-63; chmn. mgmt. com. Queens Area YWCA, 1970-73. Recipient Alumni Achievement award U. Chgo., 1970; Deems Taylor award ASCAP, 1973; Nat. Endowment for Humanities grantee, 1979—. Mem. Internat. Am. (dir. 1974-76) musicol. socs., Renaissance Soc., NAACP, Alpha Kappa Alpha. Author: The Buxheim Organ Book, 1963; The Music of Black Americans: A History, 1971; Readings in Black American Music, 1971; editor, pub. The Black Perspective in Music, 1973—; contbr. articles to profl. jours., encys. Home: 115-05 179th St Saint Albans NY 11434 Office: Harvard U Cambridge MA 02138

SOUTHERN, RONALD DONALD, mfg. co. exec.; b. Calgary, Alta., Can., July 25, 1930; s. Samuel Donald and Alexandra (Cuthill) S.; B.Sc. in Medicine, U. Alta., Edmonton, 1953; LL.D. (hon.), U. Calgary, 1976; m. Margaret Visser, July 30, 1954; children—Nancy, Linda. Pres., chief exec. officer Atco Ltd., Calgary, 1954—; mem. Calgary Exhbn. and Stampede Bd.; gov. Olympic Trust Can.; dir. Alta. Gas Trunkline Co., Ltd., Can. Cement Lafarge Ltd., Canadian Pacific Investments Ltd., Crown Zellerbach Can. Ltd., Mercantile Bank Can., Pacific Western Airlines Ltd., Rothmans of Pall Mall Can. Ltd., Royal Ins. Co. Ltd. Scott & Easton United Securities Ltd. Mem. Young Pres's. Orgn. (charter). Mem. United Church of Can. Clubs: Calgary Petroleum, Earl Grey Golf, U. Calgary Chancellors. Home: 67 Massey Pl SW Calgary AB T2V 2G7 Canada Office: 1243 McKnight Blvd NE Calgary AB T2E 5T2 Canada

SOUTHERN, TERRY, author; b. Alvarado, Tex., May 1, 1924; s. Terry M. and Helen (Simonds) S.; B.A., Northwestern U., 1948; student Sorbonne, Paris, France, 1948-50; m. Carol Kauffman, July 14, 1958; 1 son, Nile. Author: (novels) Fleash and Filigree, 1958, The Magic Christian, 1959, Candy, 1958; (screen plays) (with Stanley Kubrick) Dr. Strangelove (Acad. Award nomination l963; Screenwriters award l963), with Christopher Isherwood) The Loved One, 1964; (with Ring Lardner, Jr.) The Cincinnati Kid, 1965, Barbarella, 1967, Easy Rider (Acad. Award nomination 1968), 1968, End of the Road, 1968, Blue Movie, 1970; (anthology) (with Alex Trocchi) Writers in Revolt, 1960, Red Dirt Marijuana and Other Tastes, 1967; Journal of the Loved One, 1965; also short stories, critical essays. Office: care Sterling Lord Agy 660 Madison Ave New York NY 10022

SOUTHGATE, DONALD FREDERIC, ret. bus. cons.; b. Railroad Mills, N.Y., Aug. 20, 1893; s. William F. and Harriet F. (Edwards) S.; student U. Rochester, 1912-15; m. Edna R. Scutt, June 24, 1919; 1 dau., Betty H. Copywriter, Lyddon & Hanford Advt. Agy., Rochester, 1915-16; asst. advt. mgr. Standard Optical Co., 1917, advt. mgr., 1919-25; with Shur-on Standard Optical Co., Inc., 1925-35, v.p. charge advt., 1935-37, asst. to pres., 1938-40, comptroller, 1941-42, mgr. ophthalmic lens prodn., 1943- 47, v.p. charge sales promotion, 1947-49, sec., 1950-51, v.p., sec., dir., 1952-53, pres., dir., 1954-60; bus. cons., Geneva, N.Y., 1960-67; mem. adv. com. Lincoln Rochester Trust Co. Mem. V.F.W., Am. Legion. Home: Rt 3 Box 87-A Retirement Village Santa Fe NM 87501

SOUTHGATE, MARIE THERESE, physician, med. jour. editor; b. Detroit, Apr. 27, 1928; d. Clair and Josephine Marie (Hoefeyzers) S.; B.S., Coll. of St. Francis, 1948, LL.D. (hon.), 1974; M.D., Marquette U., 1960. Research editor Ill. Inst. of Tech. Research Inst., Chgo., 1951-55; intern St. Mary's Hosp., San Francisco, 1960-61; sr. editor Jour. of the AMA, Chgo., 1962-75, dep. editor, 1975—; mem. editorial bd. Forum, 1978—; mem. ad hoc com. on biol. scis. Ill. Bd. of Higher Edn., 1969-70. Mem. ad hoc com. on lay deacon Archdiocese of Chgo., 1973; trustee Coll. St. Francis, 1978—. Diplomate Nat. Bd. Med. Examiners. Mem. AMA, Am. Med. Women's Assn. (v.p. Chgo. chpt. 1967-68, mem. com continuing med. edn. 1978—), Council of Biology Editors, AAAS. Editor-in-chief Marquette Med. Review, 1959-60. Home: 300 N State Chicago IL 60610 Office: 535 N Dearborn Chicago IL 60610

SOUTHWICK, CHARLES HENRY, educator, zoologist; b. Wooster, Ohio, Aug. 28, 1928; s. Arthur F. and Faye (Motz) S.; B.A., Coll. Wooster, 1949; M.S., U. Wis., 1951, Ph.D., 1953; m. Heather Milne Beck, July 12, 1952; children—Steven, Karen. NIH fellow, 1951-53; asst. prof. biology Hamilton Coll., 1953-54; NSF fellow Oxford (Eng.) U., 1954-55; faculty Ohio U., 1955-61; asso. prof. pathobiology Johns Hopkins Sch. Hygiene and Pub. Health, Balt., 1961-68, prof., 1968-79; prof., chmn. dept. environ., population and organismic biology U. Colo., Boulder, 1979—; mem. primate adv. com. Nat. Acad. Sci.-NRC, 1963—, com. primate conservation, 1974-75. Recipient Fulbright Research award, India, 1959-60. Fellow A.A.A.S., Acad. Zoology, Animal Behavior Soc.; mem. Am. Soc. Zoologists, Ecol. Soc. Am., Am. Soc. Mammalogists, Internat. Soc. Study Aggression. Editor: Primate Social Behavior, 1963; Animal Aggression, 1970; Nonhuman Primates in Biomedical Research, 1975; Ecology and the Quality of Our Environment, 1976. Research, publs. on animal social behavior and population dynamics, influences animal social orgn. on demographic characteristic mammal populations, primate ecology and behavior, estuarine ecology and environmental quality; pioneered primate surveys in India and Malaysia. Home: 4685 Gordon Dr Boulder CO 80303

SOUTHWICK, HARRY WEBB, surgeon; b. Grand Rapids, Mich., Nov. 21, 1918; s. G. Howard and Jessie (Webb) S.; B.S., Harvard U., 1940, M.D., 1943; m. Lorraine Hinsdale, June 27, 1942; children—Harry Webb, Sandra, Charles Howard, Gay. Intern, Presbyn. Hosp., Chgo., 1944-45, surg. resident, 1945-46; surg. resident U. Ill. Research and Ednl. Hosps., 1948-50; now chmn. dept. gen. surgery Rush-Presbyn.-St. Luke's Med. Center, Chgo.; pvt. practice surgery, Chgo., 1950—; clin. asso. prof. surgery U. Ill. Med. Sch., 1957-63, clin. prof., 1963-71; prof. surgery Rush Med. Coll., 1971—. Pres. Chgo. unit Am. Cancer Soc., 1964-66, pres. Ill. div., 1972-73. Served to lt. (j.g.) M.C., USNR, 1946-48. Fellow A.C.S.; mem. Am. Surg. Assn., Pan Am., Minn. (hon.), Western, Central, Chgo. (pres. 1979-80) surg. socs., Soc. Head and Neck Surgeons (sec.-treas. 1956-63, pres. 1964-65), Soc. Surgery Alimentary Tract, Soc. Surg. Oncology, Soc. Univ. Chmn. Clubs: Harvard (Chgo.); Westmoreland Country (Wilmette, Ill.). Contbr. articles to med. jours. Home: 830 Heather Ln Winnetka IL 60093 Office: 1725 W Harrison St Chicago IL 60612

SOUTHWICK, LINUS ELY, banker; b. Lincoln, Nebr., Jan. 4, 1911; s. Homer John and Gladys Rose (Hargreaves) S.; student Grinnell (Iowa) Coll., 1929-31; B.S., U. Nebr., 1936; m. Helen Elizabeth Drummond, Jan. 16, 1937; children—Susan, Janet Southwick Servatius, Linus Ely. With Security Pacific Nat. Bank, 1937-52, br. mgr., Santa Maria, Calif., 1948-52; v.p. First Nat. Bank, Lincoln, 1953-57; pres., dir. Valley Nat. Bank, Glendale, Calif., 1957—; v.p., dir. First Nat. Bank, Friend, Nebr., 1953—; dir. Los Angeles br. Fed. Res. Bank San Francisco, 1971-76. Mem. Ind. Bankers Assn. So. Calif. (past pres.), Phi Kappa Psi. Episcopalian. Clubs: Elks; Oakmount Country, Verdugo (past v.p., dir.) (Glendale). Home: 1101 Olive Ln La Canada CA 91011 Office: 420 N Brand Blvd Glendale CA 91209

SOUTHWICK, PAUL, pub. relations exec.; b. West Newton, Mass., Mar. 27, 1920; s. Alfred and Pauline (Winkler) S.; A.B. cum laude in Econs., Harvard, 1943; m. Susan Barbara Heider, Feb. 24, 1947; children—Thomas Paul, Peter Alfred, Linda Susan. A.P. corr., Concord, N.H., 1947-49; U.P. corr., Washington, 1949-57; profl. staff mem. Ho. of Reps. Govt. Info. subcom., 1957-59; legis. asst., adminstrv. asst. U.S. Senator Long of Hawaii, 1959-62; dep. adminstr. charge accelerated pub. works program Area Redevel. Adminstrn., 1962-63; spl. asst. The White House, 1963-65; spl. asst. for Congl. relations to sec. commerce, 1965-67 v.p. Newmyer Assos., Inc., Washington, 1967—. Served with USNR, 1941-45; PTO. Mem. U.S. Senate Adminstrv. Assts. Assn. Democrat. Presbyn. Clubs: Nat. Press, Federal City (Washington); Bethesda (Md.) Country. Home: 4012 Underwood St Chevy Chase MD 20015 Office: 1000 Vermont Ave NW Washington DC 20005

SOUTHWICK, PHILIP LEE, chemist; b. Lincoln, Nebr., Nov. 15, 1916; s. Phillip Orin and Dorothy (Harpham) S.; A.B., U. Nebr., 1939, M.A., 1940; Ph.D., U. Ill., 1943; m. Helen Louise Cather, Sept. 1, 1942; 1 son, James Philip. Research chemist Merck & Co., Inc., Rahway, N.J., 1943-46; faculty Carnegie-Mellon U., Pitts., 1946—, prof. chemistry, 1955—. Mem. exec. com. Samuel and Emma Winters Found., 1962-75; chmn. organic chemistry com. Health Research and Services Found., 1975—; mem. com. on awards in chemistry Fulbright Act, Nat. Acad. Scis.-NRC, 1960-63. Recipient Carnegie Teaching award, 1953. Fellow N.Y. Acad. Scis., AAAS; mem. Am. Chem. Soc., Pitts. Chemists Club, Pitts. Bibliophiles, Phi Beta Kappa, Sigma Xi, Alpha Chi Sigma. Research, publs. on introduction of methods for synthesis of new organic compounds with physiol. activity, discovered agts. reducing blood presure, affecting some functions of central nervous system or suppressing growth of certain disease organisms. Home: 36 Woodland Farms Rd Pittsburgh PA 15238

SOUTHWICK, WAYNE ORIN, educator, surgeon; b. Lincoln, Nebr., Feb. 6, 1923; s. Philip Orin and Dorothy (Harpham) S.; A.B., U. Nebr., 1945, M.D., 1947; D.Sc. (hon.), 1973; M.S. (hon.), Yale U., 1961; m. Jessie Ann Seacrest, May 6, 1944; children—Frederick, Steven, Marcia. Intern, asst. resident surgery Boston City Hosp., 1947-50; resident orthopaedic surgery Johns Hopkins Hosp., 1954; instr., then asst. prof. surgery Johns Hopkins Med. Sch., 1954-58; chief orthopaedic surgery, prof. Yale Med. Sch., 1958—. Mem. Am. Orthopaedic Assn., Am. Acad. Orthopaedic Surgeons, Sigma Xi, Alpha Omega Alpha. Asso. editor Jour. Bone and Joint Surgery. Research arthritis and injuries to neck, slipped capital femoral epiphysis. Home: Route 5 Old Lyme CT 06371

SOUTHWOOD, JOHN EUGENE, banker; b. Evansville, Ind., Nov. 7, 1929; s. Walter H. and Vera M. Southwood; B.A., Vanderbilt U., 1952; m. Myrna McLain, Dec. 24, 1960; children—Deborah Lynn Southwood Love, John Eugene. With Third Nat. Bank, Nashville, 1952—, asst. v.p., 1963-68, v.p., 1968-72, sr. v.p., 1972-76, exec. v.p., 1976-79, vice chmn., 1979—; now pres. Third Nat. Corp. Mem. Am. Inst. Banking, Bank Adminstrn. Inst., Nashville C. of C. Baptist. Clubs: Richland Country, Temple Hills Country. Home: 7975 Highway 100 Nashville TN 37221 Office: Third Nat Bank Bldg Nashville TN 37244

SOUTHWORTH, HERMAN MCDOWELL, agrl. economist; b. Binghamton, N.Y., Apr. 7, 1909; s. Herman Roy and Grace Marilla (Belknap) S.; A.B., Cornell U., 1930; postgrad. Iowa State Coll., 1938-41; D.Agr., Seoul Nat. U., 1973; m. Carol Louise Treyz, June 29, 1935; children—Edward Gordon, Thomas Roy, Harrison Treyz, Douglas Belknap. Research technician Consumer's Research, Inc., 1934-36, Consumers Union U.S., 1936-38; agrl. economist Bur. Agrl. Econs. and War Food Adminstrn., Dept. Agr., 1940-47; bus. economist Council Econ. Advisers, 1947-50; asst. to asso. chief Bur. Agrl. Econs., Dept. Agr., 1950-52, asst. to dep. adminstr. Agrl. Mktg. Service, 1953-57; prof. agrl. econs. Pa. State U., 1957-66; asso. Agrl. Devel. Council, Inc., N.Y.C., 1966-73; faculty Dept. Agr. Grad. Sch., 1945-57; tng. materials specialist Agrl. Devel. Council, Inc., 1964-65; mem. com. agrl. econs. Social Sci. Research Council, 1955-66, chmn., 1959-66; guest prof. agrl. econs. Seoul Nat. U., 1966-72. Recipient Rockefeller Pub. Service award, 1955. Mem. Phi Beta Kappa, Phi Kappa Phi. Author: Agricultural Marketing for Developing Countries, 1971; co-author: The School Lunch Program and Agricultural Surplus Disposal, 1941; Marketing Policies for Agriculture, 1960; editor: Farm Mechanization in East Asia, 1972; co-editor: Agricultural Development and Economic Growth, 1967; Experience in Farm Mechanization in S.E. Asia, 1974; Agricultural Growth in Japan, Taiwan, Korea, and the Phillipines, 1979. Address: 529 W Nittany Ave State College PA 16801

SOUTHWORTH, WILLIAM DIXON, educator; b. Union City, Tenn., Dec. 28, 1918; s. Thomas and Gertrude (Dyer) S.; Ph.B., Marquette U., 1948, M.Ed., 1950; Ph.D., N.Y. U., 1961; m. Violet Kuehn, July 22, 1944; children—Geoffrey Scott, Linda Jean. Tchr., coach La Follette Sch., Milwaukee County, Wis., 1948-51; teaching dist. prin. Grand View Sch., Milwaukee County, 1951-56; supervising dist. prin. Maple Dale Sch., Milwaukee County, 1956-58; bldg. prin. Main St. Sch., Port Washington, N.Y., 1958-65; asst. supt. for elementary edn. Huntington (N.Y.) pub. schs., 1965-67; asso. prof., acting head, dept. adminstrn. and supervision St. John's U., Jamaica, N.Y., 1967, prof., chmn. dept., 1968-73; ednl. cons. to pub. and pvt. ednl. orgns. Served with USN, 1938-44. Lutheran. Contbr. numerous articles to ednl. jours. Home: 14 Stern Ct Huntington Station NY 11746. *I believe that the good life must balance the elements of service to others and service to self. If there is an imbalance, if service to others dominates, there is a diminishing of the individual, and he becomes only a part of a group, and not an entity in himself. If service to self dominates, there follows a shriveling of the spirit that demeans and narrows the individual, for he never then belongs to anything larger than his own self.*

SOUTTER, LAMAR, physician, educator; b. Boston, Mar. 9, 1909; s. Robert and Helen E. (Whiteside) S.; A.B. cum laude, Harvard U., 1931, M.D., 1935; D.Sc. (hon.), U. Mass., 1975; m. Norah Goldsmith, 1939 (div. 1945); 1 son, Nicholas B.; m. 2d, Mary C. Bigelow, 1946; children—Elizabeth P., Sarah B. Intern gen. surgery Presbyn. Hosp., N.Y.C., 1936-38; intern gynecology Free Hosp. for Women, 1939-40; chief resident 1st surg. div. Bellevue Hosp., 1938-39; 1st asst. resident surgery Mass. Gen. Hosp., 1940-41, organized Blood Bank, 1942, dir., 1942-52; prof. surgery Boston U., 1959-64, dean Sch. Medicine, 1959-61; dean, chancellor Worcester campus, prof. surgery U. Mass., 1964-75; cons. to chancellor State U. and Community Coll. System of Tenn., 1976—; chief surgery Boston Area VA, 1961-63, area cons. thoracic surgery VA; chmn. blood Mass. Civil Def. Agy., 1950-53. Bd. dirs. Nat. Easter Seal Soc., 1971-78, pres., 1975-77. Trustee, Faulkner Hosp., Boston, 1975—; vol. Internat. Exec. Service Corps, 1979. Served to maj. AUS, 1943-45; head surg. team ETO. Decorated Silver Star. Diplomate Am. Bd. Surgery, Am. Bd. Thoracic Surgery. Fellow A.C.S.; mem. Am. Assn. Thoracic Surgery, AMA, AAUP, Bostonian Soc., Suffolk Dist. Med. Soc. (pres. 1960-63), Eastern, New Eng., Boston (exec. council 1957-61) surg. socs., Halsted Soc., Mass. Med. Soc. (pres. 1970-71), Mass. Easter Seal Soc. (pres. 1970-71, 77-79), Sigma Xi, Alpha Omega Alpha. Clubs: Harvard (N.Y.C.); Century, Somerset, Cohasset Yacht. Home: 684 Sudbury Rd Concord MA 01742

SOUTTER, THOMAS D., lawyer; b. N.Y.C., Nov. 1, 1934; s. Thomas G. and Hildreth H. (Callanan) S.; B.A., U. Va., 1955; LL.B., 1962; m. Ginny Hovenden; children—Sam, Andy, Hadley. Admitted to N.Y. State bar, 1962, R.I. bar, 1969; atty. Breed, Abbott & Morgan, N.Y.C., 1962-68; with Textron Inc., Providence, 1968—, v.p., gen. counsel, 1973—. Served to lt. USNR, 1955-59. Mem. Am., N.Y. State, R.I. bar assns. Office: Textron Inc 40 Westminster St Providence RI 02903

SOVERN, MICHAEL IRA, univ. pres.; b. N.Y.C., Dec. 1, 1931; s. Julius and Lillian (Arnstein) S.; A.B. summa cum laude, Columbia, 1953, LL.B. (James Ordronaux prize), 1955; m. Lenore Goodman, Feb. 21, 1952 (div. Apr. 1963); children—Jeffrey Austin, Eilzabeth Ann, Douglas Todd; m. 2d, Eleanor Leen, Aug. 25, 1963 (div. Feb. 1974); 1 dau., Julie Danielle; m. 3d, Joan Wit, Mar. 9, 1974. Asst. prof., then asso. prof. law U. Minn. Law Sch., 1955-58; admitted to N.Y. bar, 1956; mem. faculty Columbia Law Sch., 1957—, prof. law, 1960—, Chancellor Kent prof., 1977—, dean Law Sch., 1970-79; chmn. exec. com. faculty Columbia U., 1968-69, provost, exec. v.p., 1979-80, univ. pres., 1980—; research dir. Legal Restraints on Racial Discrimination in Employment, Twentieth Century Fund, 1962-66; spl. counsel N.Y. State Joint Legislative Com. Indsl. and Labor Conditions, 1962-63, to gov. N.J., 1974-77; cons. NAACP Legal Def. Fund, Time mag. Mem. N.J. Bd. Mediation Panel of Arbitrators: mem. panel arbitrators Fed. Mediation and Conciliation Service. Fellow Am. Acad. Arts and Scis.; mem. Assn. Bar City N.Y., Am. Bar Assn., Internat. Soc. Labor Law, Am. Arbitration Assn. (panel arbitrators), Am. Law Inst., Nat. Acad. Arbitrators. Author: Legal Restraints on Racial Discrimination in Employment, 1966; Law and Poverty, 1969. Home: 32 E 64th St New York NY 10021

SOVEY, LOUIS TERRELL, textile mfg. co. exec.; b. Gainesville, Ga., Apr. 1, 1931; s Louis Terrell and Kathryn Bell (White) S.; B.S. in Indsl. Engring., Ga. Inst. Tech.; m. Anne Smith, June 5, 1952; children—Kathryn Sovey Bishop, Louis Terrell, Myra Jacquelyn. In cost control positions Owens Corning Fiberglas Co.; v.p., gen. mgr. Milliken & Co.; now pres., chief operating officer M. Lowenstein & Sons, Inc., N.Y.C. Served with USN. Republican. Presbyterian. Clubs: N.Y. Union League; Spartanburg (S.C.) Country; Snee Farm Country (Mt. Pleasant, S.C.). Home: 990 Arden Way Spartanburg SC 29302 Office: Lyman SC 29365

SOVIERO, DIANA BARBARA, soprano; b. N.J.; d. Amerigo and Angelina Catani; student Juilliard Sch. Music, Hunter Coll. Opera Workshop; m. Louis Soviero, May 20, 1967. Appearances with opera cos. including Tulsa Opera, Houston Grand Opera, San Diego Opera, Ottawa (Ont., Can.) Opera, Zurich Opera, Goldovsky Opera Theatre, Lake George Opera, New Orleans Opera; now leading soprano N.Y.C. Opera; instr. master classes The Faculty, sch. for actors, Los Angeles. Mem. AFTRA, Am. Guild Musical Artists. Office: Columbia Artists 165 W 57th St New York NY 10019

SOVIK, EDWARD ANDERS, architect; b. Honan, China, June 9, 1918 (parents Am. citizens); s. Edward Anderson and Anna (Tenwick) S.; B.A., St. Olaf Coll., 1939; student Art Students League N.Y., 1939-40, Luther Theol. Sem., 1940-42; M.Arch., Yale U., 1949; m. Genevieve Elaine Hendrickson, June 29, 1946; children—Rolf, Martin, Peter. Pres. Sovik, Mathre, Quanbeck, Inc., and predecessors, Northfield, Minn.; works include chs., coll. and univ. bldgs., instns.; tchr. art St. Olaf Coll.; lectr. on ch. design at various confs., schs., univs.; participant, planner, del. numerous domestic and fgn. confs. on religion and architecture; mem., officer various profl., religious and pub. bds. and commns. Served with USMCR, 1942-45; maj. Res. Decorated D.F.C., Purple Heart, Air medal. Fellow AIA; mem. Minn. Soc. Architects (pres. 1977). Republican. Lutheran. Author: Architecture for Worship. Contbr. numerous articles to mags., anthologies. Patentee in furniture design. Home: 711 Summit Ave Northfield MN 55057 Office: 205 Water St Northfield MN 55057

SOWADA, ALPHONSE AUGUSTUS, bishop; b. Avon, Minn., June 23, 1933; s. Alphonse B. and Monica (Pierskalla) S.; student Onamia (Minn.) Sem., 1947-53; grad. Crosier House of Studies, Ft. Wayne, Ind., 1959; M.A., Cath. U. Am., 1961. Ordained priest Roman Cath. Ch., 1958; arrived in Irian Barat to work among headhunters of Asmat, 1961, selected as mission superior, 1966; ordained bishop Diocese Agats-Asmat, 1969—. Mem. Order of Alhambra, Kappa Delta Gamma. Contbr. to Nat. Geog. Yearbook, 1968, other publs. Address: Crosier Missions Box 789 Hastings NE 68901 also Keuskupan Agats-Asmat Misi Katolik Jayapura Irian Jaya Indonesia*

SOWARDS, GLADE M., state legislator; b. Vernal, Utah, Sept. 9, 1929; s. Harmon S. and Ida Rebecca (Jensen) S.; B.S. cum laude in Accounting, U. Utah, 1954; m. Rachel Elizabeth Farley, May 29, 1952; children—Rebecca Jane, Olivia, H. Scott, J. Farley, Paula, Allen H., Samuel L., G. Michael, Christen Ned; 1 foster dau., Trinidad Madge Ben. With H.S. Sowards & Sons, Inc.; mem. city council, Vernal, 1959-67; mem. Utah Ho. of Reps. from 61st Dist., 1967—, speaker of house, 1977-79; mem. Utah Senate, 1979—; vice chmn. state fed. assembly Nat. Conf. State Legislatures, 1978. Mem. Vernal C. of C. (past pres.). Mormon. Club: Lions (past pres.). Home: 380 W 1st St S Vernal UT 84078 Office: Box 308 Vernal UT 84078

SOWDER, ROBERT ROBERTSON, architect; b. Kansas City, Kans., Dec. 29, 1928; s. James Robert and Agnes (Robertson) S.; B.A., U. Wash., 1953; B.Arch., U. Va., 1958; grad. diploma in Architecture, Ecole Des Beaux Arts, Fontainebleau, France, 1952; m. Joan Goddard, July 26, 1954; 1 dau., Lisa Robertson. Designer, Architects Collaborative, 1958-59; designer Peirce & Pierce, architects, Boston, 1959-63; asso. Fred. Bassetti & Co., architects, Seattle, 1963-67; partner Naramore, Bain, Brady & Johanson, architects, Seattle, 1967—; pres. NBBJ Internat., 1976—; archtl. design critic Boston Archtl. Center, 1961-62. Mem. Seattle Forward Thrust Transit Com., 1968-70, Seattle Central Assn., 1968-73. Served with CIC, U.S. Army, 1954-56. Recipient Premier Prix D'Architecture, Ecole Des Beaux Arts, Fontainebleau, 1951, 52, Prix D'Remondet, Fontainebleau, 1952. Mem. A.I.A., Scarab, Sigma Chi. Episcopalian. Clubs: Seattle Tennis, Rainier. Important works include Ridgeway III Dormitories, Bellingham, Wash. (with Fred Bassetti & Co.), (Dept. Housing and Urban Devel. Honor award), Seattle Rapid Transit (HUD Excellence award), Safeco Ins. Co. Home Office Complex, Seattle, King County Stadium, Balt. Conv. Center. Home: 1120 38th Ave E Seattle WA 98112 Office: 904 7th Ave Seattle WA 98104

SOWERS, GEORGE FREDERICK, civil engr.; b. Cleve., Sept. 23, 1921; s. George Bloomer and Marie (Tyler) S.; B.S. in Civil Engring., Case Inst. Tech., 1942; M.S. in Civil Engring., Harvard, 1947; m. Frances Adair Lott, Apr. 29, 1944; children—Carol Adair, Janet, Nancy, George. Pvt. practice engring. with G. B. Sowers, Cleve., 1939-42; hydraulic engr. TVA, 1942-44, U.S. Navy, 1944-46; chmn. bd. Law Engring. Testing Co., Atlanta, 1947-66, now cons. engr., sr. v.p.; Regents prof. civil engring. Ga. Inst. Tech., 1966—. Cons. Resources Devel. Center of South East Asia, Roorkee, India, 1959, AID, 1966. Trustee, Northside Methodist Ch., Atlanta. Registered civil engr., Ohio, Ga., N.C., Fla., Tenn., Va., Ala.; registered geologist, Ga. Fellow ASCE, Geol. Soc. Am.; mem. Seismol. Soc. Am., Earthquake Engring. Inst., ASTM, U.S. Nat. Soc. Soil Mechanics, Internat. Soc. Soil Mechanics (v.p.), Ga. Acad. Sci., Nat. Soc. Profl. Engrs., Sigma Xi, Tau Beta Pi, Beta Theta Pi, Tau Kappa Alpha, Theta Tau. Author: Soil Laboratory Manual, 1955; Earth and Rockfill Dam Engineering, 1961; co-author: Introductory Soil Mechanics and Foundations, 1951, 4th edit., 1979; Foundation Engineering, 1961; contbr. articles to profl. jours. Home: 3031 Westminster 13508 NW Atlanta GA 30327 Office: 2749 Delk Rd SE Marietta GA 30062

SOWERS, WESLEY HOYT, lawyer, mgmt. counsel; b. Whiting, Ind., Aug. 26, 1905; s. Samuel Walter and Bertha E. (Spurrier) S.; B.S., Purdue U., 1926, M.S., 1927; J.D., DePaul U., 1941; grad. Advanced Mgmt. Program, Harvard, 1960; m. Gladys Krueger, Jan. 21, 1929; children—Penny (Mrs. David Buxton), Wesley Hoyt. Chemist, Shell Oil Co., East Chicago, Ind., 1927-29; sales engr. Nat. Lead Co., St. Louis, 1929-31; admitted to Ill. bar, 1940; lab. supr. patent atty. Pure Oil Co., Chgo., 1932-42; v.p. Bay Chem. Co., New Orleans, 1942-50, Frontier Chem. Co., Wichita, Kans., 1950-57; pres. Frontier Chem. div. Vulcan Materials Co., 1957-65; exec. v.p., dir. Vulcan Materials Co., Birmingham, 1958-65; mgmt. counsel, 1965—; former chmn. bd., dir. Archer Taylor Drug Co., Hershberger Explorations, Inc., Community Antenna TV Wichita, Inc., First Worth Corp.; dir. Fourth Nat. Bank, Coleman Co., Wichita, Gt. Lakes Chem. Co., West Lafayette, Ind. Past chmn. Met. Planning Commn., Wichita and Sedgwick County, 1958; commr. Kans. Econ. Devel. Bd.; chmn. Kansas Com. for Constitutional Revision; chmn. Sedgwick County U.S. Savs. Bonds Sales; past chmn. Kans. Radio Free Europe; mem. adv. com. Kans. Geol. Survey. Mem. Kans. Senate, 1970—. Former mem. engring. adv. council Sch. Engring. and Architecture, Kans. State U.; trustee Wichita State U., Wesley Med. Center, Wichita; bd. dirs. Inst. Logopedics, Quivira council Boy Scouts Am., YMCA; trustee Midwest Research Inst.; former adv. bd. Kans. U. Bus. Sch.; chmn. Kans. Health Care Providers Malpractice Commn.; mem. Kans. Health Care Costs Commn., Kans. Health Coordinating Council. Registered patent atty. and practitioner ICC. Mem. A.A.A.S., Kans. (past pres., past dir.), Wichita (past pres. 1959, past dir.) chambers commerce, Kans. Assn. Commerce and Industry (past pres., dir.), Am. Chem. Soc., Soc. Chem. Industry, Ill., Wichita bar assns., Phi Delta Theta. Rotarian. Patentee in field. Home: 234 S Brookside Dr Wichita KS 67218 Office: 527 Union Center Wichita KS 67202

SOWERS, WILLIAM ARMAND, civil engr.; b. Willis, Va., Apr. 23, 1923; s. Harry Cline and Effie Vivian (Slusher) S.; student Roanoke Coll., 1940-42; B.C.E., Va. Poly. Inst., 1947, B.S. in Archtl. Engring., 1948; m. Gale Johnson, May 20, 1978; children—Jane Dixon, Jean Marie. Asso., Brown, Wells & Meagher, architects, Roanoke, Va., 1948-50; partner R.L. Brown & Assos., architects and engrs., 1950-53, Sowers, Knowles & Rodes, engrs., 1953-59, Sowers, Rodes & Whitescarver, engrs., Roanoke, 1959—; trustee ACEC Health Life Ins., St. Louis, 1975—. Commr. city planning, Roanoke, 1976—. Registered profl. engr., Va. Mem. Am. Cons. Engrs. Council (Service award for serving as nat. pres. 1970-72), Cons. Engrs. Council Va. (Service award 1972), Va. Soc. Profl. Engrs. (Service to Profession award 1971-72), Illuminating Engring. Soc. Clubs: Masons; Hunting Hills Country. Office: PO Box 4038 Roanoke VA 24015

SOWERS, WILLIAM VANCE, lawyer; b. Winnfield, La., July 16, 1916; s. E.H. and Winnie (Vance) S.; A.B., Northwestern State U., 1938; M.A., La. State U., 1942; J.D., U. Mich., 1948; grad. Grad. Sch. Banking of Rutgers U., 1955; m. Cornelia Sturges, July 12, 1944; 1 dau., Laura Alice. Tchr. high sch., La., 1938-40; admitted to Ind. bar, 1948; practice law Coleman & Coleman, Indpls., 1948-50; with Ft. Wayne Nat. Bank (Ind.), 1950-79, vice chmn. bd., dir., to 1978. Mem. Ind. State Probate Study Commn. Trustee YWCA.; bd. dirs. Caylor-Nickel Research Found., Lindwnwood Cemetery, Ft. Wayne Art Mus., Tri-State U., Ind. U.-Purdue U. Found., Ft. Wayne Park Bd. Found., Ft. Wayne Improvement Assn.; trustee Hist. Ft. Wayne, Allen County Soil and Water Conservation Dept. Served to comdr. USNR, World War II. Mem. Ind. (dir.), Allen County bar assns., Am. Inst. Banking, Ft. Wayne Hist. Soc. (pres.), V.F.W., Nature Conservancy (dir. Ind. chpt.). Presbyterian. Mason (33 deg.). Clubs: Fortnightly, Friars, Ft. Wayne Country, Quest (Ft. Wayne). Home: 7323 Covington Rd Ft Wayne IN 46804 Office: 1800 Ft Wayne Nat Bank Bldg Fort Wayne IN 46802

SOWLE, CLAUDE RAYMOND, educator; b. Springfield, Ill., Nov. 27, 1928; s. Claude Raymond and Alyce (Coady) S.; B.S., Northwestern U., 1950, J.D., 1956; D.H.L., Loyola U., Chgo., 1970; m. Kathryn Sharp Dix, Sept. 10, 1955; children—Leslie Ann, Stephen Dix. Admitted to Ill. bar, 1956; with firm Sidley, Austin, Burgess and Smith, Chgo., 1956- 58; mem. faculty Northwestern U., 1958-65, prof. law, 1963-65, asso. dean Sch. Law, 1963-65; dean Coll. Law, U. Cin., 1965-69; pres. Ohio U., Athens, 1969-74; prof. law Ohio State U., Columbus, 1974—. Tng. cons. Chgo. Police Dept., 1961- 62; legal cons. to gov. of Ill., 1961; mem. Mayor Chgo. Com. Organized Crime Legislation, 1964-65; chmn. Com. to Revise Ohio Criminal Code, 1966-68. Bd. dirs. Chgo. Crime Comm., 1964-65. Served with U.S. Navy, 1950-53. Named one of Chgo.'s 10 Outstanding Young Men, 1963; recipient award merit Northwestern U. Alumni Assn., 1970; named hon. alumnus Ohio U., 1971. Mem. Order of Coif, Phi Delta Phi, Acacia. Methodist. Author: (with F.E. Inbau and J.R. Thompson) Cases and Comments on Criminal Justice, 3d edit., 1968; A Concise Explanation of the Illinois Criminal Code of 1961, 1961; Times of Trouble, Times of Hope, 1968. Editor: Police Power and Individual Freedom: The Quest for Balance, 1962. Editor-in- chief Northwestern U. Law Rev., 1955-56, Jour. Criminal Law, Criminology and Police Sci., 1960-65. Home: 111 Price Ave Columbus OH 43201

SOYER, DAVID, cellist, educator; b. Phila., Feb. 24, 1923; s. Samson and Esther (Faggin) S.; student pub. schs., N.Y.C.; D.F.A. (hon.), U. South Fla., 1976; m. Janet Putnam, June 23, 1957; children—Daniel, Jeffrey. Cellist with Bach Aria Group, 1948-49, Guilet Quartet, 1949-51, New Music Quartet, 1954-55, Guarneri String Quartet, N.Y.C., 1964—; prof. cello Curtis Inst. Music, 1967. Served with USNR, 1942-46. Recipient 5 Grammy awards for Guarneri Quartet recs., 1965-74. Mem. Phila. Art Alliance. Jewish. Home: 6 W 77th St New York City NY 10024 Office: care H Beall Mgmt 119 W 57th St New York City NY 10019

SOYER, RAPHAEL, artist; b. Russia, Dec. 25, 1899; s. Abraham and Bella (Schneyer) S.; came to U.S., 1912; student Cooper Union, N.A.D., Art Students League; m. Rebecca Letz, Feb. 8, 1931; 1 dau., Mary. Exhibitor in nat. and internat. shows Corcoran Mus., Washington, Carnegie Internat., Chgo., Phila.; one-man shows since 1929 at following galleries: Daniel, Rehn, Valentine, Macbeth A.C.A., Weyhe, Asso. Am. Artists, Forum Gallery; retrospective exhbn. Whitney Mus. Am. Art, 1967. Mem. Artists Equity Assn., Am. Art Group, Soc. Painters, Sculptors and Gravers, Nat. Inst. Arts and Letters (council), N.A.D. (asso.), Am. Acad. Arts and Letters. Subject of book by Lloyd Goodrich, 1972. Recipient $1000 prize for art, USA, 1959. Author: A Painter's Pilgrimage: Homage to Thomas Eakins, Self Revealment; Diary of an Artist; illustrator: Young Man in Search of Love (Isaac Bashevis Singer); Adventures of Yemima and Other Stories (Abraham Soyer). Home: 88 Central Park W New York City NY 10023 Studio: 54 W 74th St New York City NY 10023

SOZEN, METE AVNI, educator; b. Istanbul, Turkey, May 22, 1930; s. Huseyin Avni and Aysa Saliha S.; came to U.S., 1951, naturalized, 1960; B.S. in Civil Engring., Robert Coll., Istanbul, Turkey, 1951; Ph.D. in Civil Engring., U. Ill., 1956; m. Joan E. Bates, Nov. 22, 1971; children—Tim, Adria, Ayse. Asst. prof. civil engring. U. Ill., 1957-59, asso. prof., 1959-62, prof., 1962—; cons. in field. Mem. ASCE (Research award 1963, Reese award 1971, Moisseif award 1972), Am. Concrete Inst. (Kelly award 1976), Seismological Soc. Am., Nat. Acad. Engring. Home: 503 W Michigan Ave Urbana IL 61801 Office: 3112 CEB University of Illinois Urbana IL 61801

SPACEK, LEONARD PAUL, found. exec.; b. Cedar Rapids, Iowa, Sept. 12, 1907; s. Leo and Emma (Cejka) S.; student Coe Coll., 1926-27, LL.D.; student U. Chgo., 1930-32; L.H.D., Nat. Coll. Edn., Northwestern U.; m. Libbie Smatlan, Jan. 19, 1929; children—Bruce Arnold, Judith Ann (Mrs. Gary Schroeder). With Iowa Electric Light & Power Co., 1925-28; joined Arthur Andersen & Co., Chgo., 1928, mng. partner, 1947-63, chmn., 1963-70, sr. partner, 1970-73; ret., 1973; pres. John L. and Helen Kellogg Found., 1978—; cons. Bur. Budget, Washington, 1964-73; mem. Chgo. panel arbitrators N.Y. Stock Exchange, 1954-65; mem. industry adv. council to sec. Def. Park commr., Wilmette, Ill., 1944-52; bd. edn. New Trier Twp. High Sch., Winnetka, 1952-58; bd. dirs. Jr. Achievement of Chgo., 1953-65; mem. exec. bd. Chgo. Area council Boy Scouts Am., 1963-73; pres. Lyric Opera, Chgo., 1956-59, now life trustee; past trustee Orchestral Assn. Chgo.; adv. bd. YMCA; mem. citizens' com. U. of Ill.; mem. citizens' bd. U. of Chgo.; mem. bd. Chgo. City Coll., 1967-68; treas. Bus. Mgmt. Study Com. Ill., 1966-68; dir. treas. Nat. Alliance of Businessmen; mem. Better Schs. Com.; mem. exec. com. Chgo. Com., 1963-73; trustee Logistics Mgmt. Inst., 1966-73; adv. com. on bus. programs Brookings Instn., 1964-73; adv. bd. House Good Shepherd, 1966-71; asso. Rehab. Inst.; bd. dirs. Inst. Philos. Research, 1955-73; lay bd. consultors Mercy Hosp.; 1966-73; men's adv. com. League Women Voters; sponsoring bd. Travelers Aid Soc. Met. Chgo.; dir. John Crerar Library, 1955-73; mem. exec. com. Taxpayers Fedn., 1953-70; citizens com. Newberry Library, 1964-73; men's adv. com. Vis. Nurse Assn., 1959-74; bd. assos. Chgo. Theol. Sem., 1955-73; asso. Nat. Coll. Edn., 1953-73; fellow Lake Forest (Ill.) Acad., 1949-73, past trustee, treas.; life trustee Northwestern U., Purple Circle; trustee Mus. Sci. and Industry, Coe Coll., Cedar Rapids, Iowa, Lyric Opera Found.; chmn. bd. trustees Better Govt. Assn., 1972-74; bd. dirs. Protestant Found. Greater Chgo., 1964-73. Decorated knight Order St. Olav (Norway); recipient numerous awards and honors, including Spacek chair Northwestern U. Grad. Sch. Mgmt. Mem. Ill. State Soc. C.P.A.'s, Calif., Ind., La., Mich., Mo., Ohio, Tex. socs. C.P.A.'s, Chgo. Assn. Commerce and Industry (dir. 1949-59), Am. Inst. C.P.A.'s (accounting principles bd. 1960-65), Am. Accounting Assn., Nat. Assn. Accountants, Goodwill Industries (dir. 1950-73), Internat. C. of C. (past trustee U.S. council), Chgo. Urban League (mem. bus. adv. council), Beta Alpha Psi, Beta Gamma Sigma. Presbyn. Clubs: Commercial (pres. 1967-68), Chicago (treas. 1959-64), Economic (various coms.), Executives (dir. 1956-59), Mid-Am. (gov. 1958-62), Attic (gov. 1952-70, pres. 1964-66) (Chgo.); Marrakesh Country (Palm Desert, Calif.); Thunderbird Country (Rancho Mirage, Calif.). Home: 73574 El Hasson Circle Palm Desert CA 92260 Office: 69 W Washington St Chicago IL 60602. *I was fortunate in having an innate capability of seeking and stating the truth. It was not an endeavor, I deserve no credit, I only benefitted. In retrospect I realize how grateful I should be.*

SPACEK, SISSY (MARY ELIZABETH), actress; b. Quitman, Tex.; d. Edwin A. and Virginia S.; student Lee Strasberg Theat. Inst. Appeared in films: Prime Cut, 1972, Ginger in the Morning, 1972, Badlands, 1974, Carrie (Acad. award nominee Best Actress), 1976, Three Women, 1977, Welcome to L.A., 1977; Heart Beat, 1980, Coal Miner's Daughter, 1980; TV movies The Girls of Huntington House, 1973, The Migrants, 1973, Katherine, 1975, Verna: USO Girl, 1978; guest host Saturday Night Live, 1977. Named Best Actress by Nat. Soc. Film Critics for Carrie, 1976; Best Supporting Actress by N.Y. Film Critics for Three Women, 1977. Office: care William Morris Agy 1350 Ave of Americas New York NY 10019

SPACH, JULE CHRISTIAN, ch. exec.; b. Winston-Salem, N.C., Dec. 21, 1923; s. Jule Christian and Margaret Stockton (Coyner) S.; student Va. Mil. Inst., 1942-43; B.S. in Chem. Engring., Ga. Inst. Tech., 1949; postgrad. Union Theol. Sem., Richmond, Va., 1951-52, Duke U., 1955-56; M.A. in Ednl. Adminstrn., U. N.C. at Greensboro, 1976; L.H.D. (hon.), Stillman Coll., Tuscaloosa, Ala., 1977; Litt.D. (hon.), Belhaven Coll., Jackson, Miss., 1977; LL.D., King Coll., Bristol, Tenn., 1977; m. Nancy Clendenin, Sept. 18, 1948; children—Nancy Lynn Davis, Margaret Creech, Ann Thomerson, Cecelia, Robert. Salesman, Mengle Corp. subs. Internat. Container Corp., Winston-Salem, 1950-52; prof. scis., athletic dir. Quinze de Novembro Coll., Garanhuns, Pernanbuco, Brazil, 1952-56, pres., 1956-64; edn. dir. Cruzada ABC-Recife, Pernanbuco, 1965-70, pres., 1969-70; exec. sec. Parliamentary Christian Leadership, Brasilia, Fed. Dist., Brazil, 1970-73; exec. dir. Presbyn. Mission in Brazil, Campinas, Sao Paulo, 1973-75; moderator Gen. Assembly of Presbyn. Ch. in U.S., Atlanta, 1976-77; exec. dir. Triad United Methodist Home, Inc., Winston-Salem, 1977—; trustee King Coll., Bristol, Tenn.; bd. dirs. Instituto Gammon, Presbyn. Ch. U.S. Served with USAAF, 1943-45. Decorated Purple Heart. Republican. Clubs: Lions (Brazil); Rotary (Winston Salem). Home: 444 Anita Dr Winston Salem NC 27104 Office: Box 5364 Winston Salem NC 27103

SPACH, MADISON STOCKTON, pediatric cardiologist; b. Winston-Salem, N.C., Nov. 10, 1926; s. Jule Christian and Margaret Elizabeth (Stockton) S.; A.B., Duke U., 1950, M.D., 1954; m. Cecilia Goodson, June 25, 1949; children—Madison Stockton, Joyce Goodson, Susan Statton, David Henry. Intern, Duke Hosp., Durham, N.C., 1954-56, resident, 1956-59; asst. prof. pediatrics Duke U., 1960-64, asso. prof. pediatrics, 1964-67, prof. pediatrics, 1968—, James B. Duke prof. pediatrics, 1977—, prof. physiology, 1978—, chief div. pediatric cardiology, 1960—; mem. NIH Research Tng. Com., 1966-71. Served with USN, 1944-46. USPHS grantee, 1966—. Mem. Am. Heart Assn., N.Y. Acad. Sci., Am. Coll. Cardiology, Am. Acad. Pediatrics, Nat. Soc. Pediatric Research (pres. 1974), N.C. Heart Assn. (pres. 1967-68, Golden Service award 1970), Research, publs. on electrophysiology and electrocardiography in circulation; editorial bd. Circulation Research, 1972—, Circulation, 1973—. Home: 2632 McDowell St Durham NC 27705 Office: PO Box 3090 Duke U Med Center Durham NC 27710

SPADARO, LOUIS MICHAEL, univ. dean; b. N.Y.C., Oct. 11, 1913; s. Joseph and Marianna (Leone) S.; B.A., Coll. City N.Y., 1932, M.S., 1933; Ph.D. in Econs., N.Y. U., 1955; m. Nina Lydia Portale, June 18, 1939; children—Joseph, Anthony, Maryann, Nina. Faculty, Fordham U., N.Y.C., 1938—, prof. econs., 1959—, chmn. dept., 1965-68, dean Grad. Sch. Bus. Adminstrn., 1968-75; pres. Inst. for Humane Studies, 1976—. Mem. Am. Econ. Assn., Am. Statis. Assn., Mont Pelerin Soc. Author: Economics: An Introductory View, 1969. Home: 1670 W 8th St Brooklyn NY 11223 Office: Fordham Univ Bronx NY 10458

SPAETH, EDMUND BENJAMIN, JR., lawyer, judge; b. Washington, June 10, 1920; s. Edmund B. and Lena (Link) S.; A.B. magna cum laude, Harvard U., 1942, LL.B., 1948. Admitted to Pa. bar, 1949; judge Ct. of Common Pleas, Phila., 1964-73, Superior Ct of Pa., Phila., 1973—; lectr. law of evidence U. Pa. Chmn. bd. trustees Bryn Mawr Coll., 1968—; bd. dirs. Diagnostic and Rehab. Center, 1969—. Mem. Am., Pa., Phila. bar assns., Am. Law Inst., Am. Judicature Soc., Order of Coif, Phi Beta Kappa. Home: 635 Westview St Philadelphia PA 19119 Office: Superior Ct of Pa 558 City Hall Philadelphia PA 19107

SPAETH, RAYMOND JULIUS, banker; b. Salina, Kans., Nov. 13, 1907; s. Julius H. and Laura (Lavina) S.; A.B., Am. U., 1930; M.B.A., Harvard, 1932; D.H.L., Ill. Coll. Optometry, 1967; m. Ruth Lee Rinkel, Sept. 3, 1931; children—Raymond Julius, Ruth Lee. Asst. bus. mgr. and adminstrv. asst. to pres. Am. U., 1932-40; bus. mgr. Ill. Inst. Tech., Chgo., 1940-42, exec. sec., treas., bus. mgr., 1942-1950, v.p., treas., 1950-60, 64-70; treas. IIT Research Inst., Inst. Gas Tech., 1964-70; pres. Beverly Bank, Chgo., 1960-64; pres., dir. Lakeside Bank, Chgo., 1965-66, vice chmn., dir., 1966—; v.p., dir. First Security Bank, Cary, Ill., 1971-74; v.p., sec., treas. UARCO, 1963-64. Trustee Jane and Washington Smith Home; chmn. bd., dir. YMCA Hotel, Chgo.; past v.p. Cook County Sch. Nursing; mem. bd. St. Xavier Coll.; trustee, treas. Ill. Coll. Optometry, 1970-78; mem. South Side Planning Bd.; dir. Met. Planning and Housing Council, Am. Inst. Planners. Mem. Lambda Alpha, Sigma Kappa, Pi Gamma Mu. Republican. Methodist. Club: Econ., Union League (Chgo.). Home: 21 Spinning Wheel Rd Hinsdale IL 60521 Office: 2268 S King Dr Chicago IL 60616

SPAGHT, MONROE EDWARD, oil co. exec.; b. Eureka, Calif., Dec. 9, 1909; s. Frederick E. and Alpha (Light) S.; A.B., Stanford, 1929, A.M., 1930, Ph.D., 1933; Internat. Exchange fellow U. Leipzig, 1931-32; Sc.D., Rensselaer Poly. Inst., 1958, Drexel Inst. Tech., 1962; LL.D., U. Manchester, 1964, Calif. State Colls., 1965. Millikin U., 1967, Conn. Wesleyan U., 1968; D.Eng., Colo. Sch. Mines, 1971; children—Pearson Monroe, David Lewis, Sarah Elizabeth Brown. Research chemist, technologist Shell Oil Co., Martinez and Wilmington, Calif., 1933-40, mgr. devel. and mfg., 1940-45; technician U.S. Naval Tech. Mission to Europe, 1945; dir. U.S. Strategic Bombing Survey to Japan, 1945; v.p. Shell Devel. Co., N.Y.C., 1946-49, pres., Emeryville, Calif., 1949-53; exec. v.p., dir. Shell Oil Co., 1953-60, pres., dir., 1960-65, chmn. bd., 1965-70, chmn. exec. com., 1965-70; mng. dir. Royal Dutch-Shell Group Cos., 1965-70; mem. internat. advisory council Wells Fargo Bank; dir. Royal Dutch Petroleum Co., Shell Oil Co., Am. Standard Inc.; advisory bd. Boston Co.; chmn. internat. advisory bd. Chem. Bank. Bd. dirs. Am. Petroleum Inst., Stanford Research Inst., 1953-70; bd. dirs. Inst. Internat. Edn., 1953—, chmn., 1971-74. Trustee Stanford, 1955-65. Decorated Order of Francisco de Miranda (Venezuela), 1968; comdr. Order of Orange-Nassau (Netherlands). Fellow Am. Inst. Chem. Engrs.; mem. Am. Chem. Soc., AAAS, Soc. Chem. Industry (internat. pres. 1963-64), Nat. Acad. Engring., Sigma Xi, Phi Lambda Upsilon, Alpha Chi Sigma, Alpha Kappa Psi (hon.). Clubs: Economic (pres. 1964-65), The Links, Blind Brook, Explorers, Athenaeum, Sunningdale. Author books and tech. papers. Home: 70 Arlington House London SW 1 England Office: Shell Centre London SE 1 England

SPAHN, MARY ATTEA, educator; b. Buffalo, July 16, 1929; d. George H. and Madeline Barbara (Bitar) Attea; student Nazareth Coll., Kalamazoo, 1947; A.B., Nazareth Coll., Rochester, N.Y., 1950; Ed.M., SUNY, Buffalo, 1952, Ed.D., 1966. Tchr., Clarence (N.Y.) Central Schs., 1951-65; reading tchr. Sweet Home Central Schs., Amherst, N.Y., 1965-68; asso. prof. elem. edn. D'Youville Coll., Buffalo, 1968-70; prof. curriculum and supervision SUNY, Buffalo,

1970—; coordinator Sweet Home secondary sch. summer reading program, 1968-70; cons. to Niagara Wheatfield, Clarence Central, Sweet Home schs. Mem. NEA, Internat. Reading Assn. (pres. 1968 Niagara Frontier council), N.Y. State Reading Assn. (sec. 1970), Am. Ednl. Research Assn., United Univ. Profs., Nat. Council Tchrs. English, Phi Delta Kappa. Author: Turning Students on Through Creative Writing, 2d edit., 1979; (poetry) Weep Willow Weep, 1974, Fragments, 1979; Busy Bodies, 1975; contbr. articles to profl. jours. Home: 58 Buffalo Rd East Aurora NY 14052 Office: 1300 Elmwood Ave Buffalo NY 14222. *Persistence, determination, sensitivity, sharing, willingness to take risks and give of myself, plus a faith in God...These are the qualities which have helped me on the road to success.*

SPAHR, BLAKE LEE, educator; b. Carlisle, Pa., July 11, 1924; s. William Alexander and Agnes (Cuddy) S.; A.B., Dickinson Coll., 1947; M.A., Yale U., 1948, Ph.D., 1952; m. Helen Novak, Feb. 2, 1957; 1 stepdau., Amelia. Instr. German, Dickinson Coll., 1946-47, Yale U., 1950-55; mem. faculty U. Calif. at Berkeley, 1955—, prof. German, 1963—, chmn. dept., 1965-70, prof. comparative lit., 1964—, chmn. dept., 1972-74; dir. Studienzentrum U. Calif., Gottingen, Germany, 1974-76. Served to 1st lt. USAAF, 1943-45; ETO. Decorated Air medal with 5 oak leaf clusters; Morse fellow Yale U., 1952-53; Guggenheim fellow, 1962-63. Mem. Pegnesischer Blumenorden, Soc. Internat. Arthurienne, Mediaeval Acad., Raven's Claw, Phi Beta Kappa, Kappa Sigma, Delta Phi Alpha, Omicron Delta Kappa. Author: The Archives of the Pegnesischer Blumenorden, 1960; Anton Ulrich and Aramena, 1966; also articles. Home: 9 Las Piedras Orinda CA 94563 Office: Dept German Dwinelle Hall Univ Calif Berkeley CA 94720

SPAID, JOSEPH SNYDER, banker; b. Syracuse, N.Y., Dec. 22, 1906; s. Clinton A. and Ella (Snyder) S.; certificate Am. Inst. Banking, 1930; m. Mabel Louise Marsh, Sept. 11, 1928; 1 son, Joseph Snyder. With City Bank & Trust Co., Syracuse, 1925-29; accountant, auditor Key Bank Central N.Y. (formerly First Trust & Deposit Co.), Syracuse, 1929-33, personnel officer, asst. treas., 1943-53, v.p., treas., 1953-60, exec. v.p., 1961-62, dir., 1962—, pres., from 1965, chief exec. officer, from 1967, chmn. bd., 1969—; cashier, v.p., dir. Citizens Bank, Clyde, N.Y., 1933-43; pres., dir. Key Banks Inc. (formerly First Comml. Banks Inc.), 1972-77, chmn. bd., 1977—, chmn. exec. com., dir., 1973—; pres., dir. First Securities Corp.; dir. Crouse-Hinds Co., Syracuse Supply Co., Key Trust Co. Mem. Old Erie Canal Park Study Com., 1965-67; mem. Citizens Adv. Bd. Onondaga County; pres. N.Y. State Coll. Forestry Found. Named Man of Year in Syracuse Banking and Finance, 1965; Businessman of Year, 1975; recipient Outstanding Businessman award Syracuse Herald-Jour., Herald-Am., 1975. Mem. Am. Inst. Banking, Newcomen Soc. Episcopalian (trustee). Mason. Clubs: University, Century (Syracuse); Fair Haven (N.Y.) Yacht; Onondaga Golf and Country (Fayetteville, N.Y.); Cavalry (Manlius, N.Y.). Home: 308 E Genesee St Fayetteville NY 13066 Office: 201 S Warren St Syracuse NY 13201

SPAIN, FRANK EDWARD, lawyer; b. Memphis, Oct. 11, 1891; s. John Batt Kennedy and Ida (Lockard) S.; A.B., So. U. (now Birmingham- So.), 1910, LL.D., 1955; LL.B., U. Ala., 1913, LL.D., 1962; m. Margaret Cameron, July 21, 1917 (dec. 1971); children—Margaret C. (Mrs. W. C. McDonald, Jr.), Frances (Mrs. J. C. Hodges, Jr.) (dec.); m. 2d, Nettie Elizabeth Edwards, 1974. Admitted to Ala. bar, 1913, practicing at Birmingham; asst. city atty., 1917; mem. Spain, Gillon, Riley, Tate & Etheredge; dir. emeritus Liberty Nat. Life Ins. Co.; gen. counsel U.S. Fidelity & Guaranty Co. (Ala.); sec. and dir. Odum Bowers & White Corp. Food adminstr. for Jefferson County, 1917; 2d lt., heavy arty., 1918; fair price commr. for Ala., 1919; chmn. Housing Authority of Birmingham Dist., 1938-43. Chmn. Ala. Assn. of Housing Authorities, 1938-43; appeal chmn. Jefferson County Community and War Chest Drive, 1943, Ala. War Chest, 1945. Pres. Community Chest of Birmingham, 1946-47; mem. State Adv. Council Constrn. Mental Retardation Facilities. Mem. Coll. Electors N.Y.U. Hall Fame Gt. Ams.; past dir. U. Ala. Med. Center Found., Ala. Soc. Crippled Children and Adults, Eye Found.; adv. bd. Cumberland Law Sch.; trustee Birmingham-So. Coll.; hon. mem. pres.'s council U. Ala., Birmingham. Decorated chevalier Legion of Honor (France); Gorgas award Ala. Medical Assn., 1964; named to Ala. Acad. Honor, 1973. Pres. Rotary Internat., 1951-52, Birmingham C. of C. (pres. 1953), Ala. Motorists Assn. (pres. 1930-41), Am. (chmn. ins. sect. 1944-46), Ala. State and Birmingham (Man of Year nominee 1973) bar assns.; past mem. Judicial Council Ala.; mem. Assn. Life Ins. Counsel; past chmn. legal section, Am. Life Conv.; mem. Sigma Alpha Epsilon, Phi Beta Kappa, Omicron Delta Kappa. Democrat. Episcopalian. Clubs: Rotary (pres. 1942-43, citation for service above self 1977), Mountain Brook, The Club; The Relay House; Lakeview Country (Greensboro, Ala.); N. River Yacht (Tuscaloosa, Ala.). Home: 3100 Overhill Rd Birmingham AL 35223 Office: John A Hand Bldg Birmingham AL 35203

SPAIN, JAMES DONALD, news service exec.; b. Nashville, June 24, 1938; s. James Willard and Frances Grace (Davis) S.; student Tenn. Sch. Broadcasting, 1956-57; m. Doris Mae Graham, Dec. 18, 1971; 1 son, Jason Donald. Program-news dir. WKRM, Columbia, Tenn., 1957-62, news dir., 1964-66; night news editor WSM-TV, Nashville, 1966-69, asst. news dir., 1972-75; dir. pub. relations Tenn. Dept. Safety, 1969-72; pres., gen. mgr. Tenn. News Service, Inc. and Tenn. Radio Network, Nashville, 1975—; chmn. bd. Tenn. News Service, Inc. Served with U.S. Army, 1962-64. Mem. Nat. Press Photographers Assn., Nat. Assn. State Radio Networks (v.p.), Nashville Press Club (dir.), Sigma Delta Chi. Methodist. Club: Capitol. Home: 705 Harpeth Knoll Nashville TN 37221 Office: Box 23083 Nashville TN 37202

SPAIN, JAMES DORRIS, JR., biochemist, educator; b. Washington, Feb. 3, 1929; s. James Dorris and Frances (Pitkin) S.; student Tulane U., 1947-48; B.S., Mich. Technol. U., 1951; M.S., Med. Coll. Va., 1953; Ph.D., Stanford, 1956; m. Patricia Mann, Oct. 3, 1952; children—James Williamson, Caryn Ann, Mary Alisa. Research fellow biochemistry U. Tex.-M.D. Anderson Hosp. and Tumor Inst., 1955-56; asso. prof. dept. chemistry Mich. Technol. U., Houghton, 1956-62, prof., head dept. biol. scis., 1962-68, prof., 1968—. Chmn. adv. council St. Josephs Hosp. Sch. Nursing, 1967. Trustee, pres. Portage Twp. Sch. Bd., 1968-76; trustee Copper Country Intermediate Sch. Dist., 1975—. Recipient Faculty Research award Mich. Technol. U., 1965. Mem. Am. Inst. Biol. Sci., A.A.A.S., Am. Chem. Soc. (past sect. v.p., chmn.), Assn. Limnology and Oceanography, Sigma Xi, Phi Lambda Upsilon. Episcopalian. Kiwanian. Club: Miscowaubik (gov. 1971-74). Author: Some Computer Programs for Biology, 1970; Biological Simulation Techniques, 1972; Lake Superior Basin Bibliography, 1976; Basic Computer Models in Biology, 1978. Contbr. articles profl. jours. Home: 44 Royalewood St Houghton MI 49931

SPAIN, JAMES WILLIAM, fgn. service officer, educator; b. Chgo., July 22, 1926; s. Patrick Joseph and Mary Ellen (Forristal) S.; M.A., U. Chgo., 1949; Ph.D., Columbia, 1959; m. Edith Burke James, Feb. 21, 1951; children—Patrick, Sikandra, Stephen, William. Cons. sec. army, 1949-50; with U.S. Fgn. Service, 1951-53; researcher, lectr. Columbia, 1955-62; mem. policy planning council State Dept., 1963-64, dir. Office Research and Analysis for Near East and South Asia, 1964-66, country dir. for Pakistan and Afghanistan, 1966-69; charge d'affaires Am. embassy, Rawapindi, 1969; consul gen., Istanbul, Turkey, 1970-72; minister Am. embassy, Ankara, 1972-74; diplomat-in-residence, vis. prof. history and govt. Fla. State U., Tallahassee, 1974-75; ambassador to Tanzania, Dar es Salaam, 1975-79, to Turkey, Ankara, 1980—; adj. prof. polit. sci. Am. U., Washington, 1965-67. Served with U.S. Army, 1946-47; PTO. Fellow Ford Found., 1953-55. Mem. Middle East Inst., Council Fgn. Relations, Royal Central Asian Soc. Club: Cosmos (Washington). Author: The Way of the Pathans, 1962; The Pathan Borderland, 1963. Address: Am Embassy Ankara Dept State Washington DC 20520

SPAINHOWER, JAMES IVAN, state ofcl.; b. Stanberry, Mo., Aug. 3, 1928; s. Elmer Enoch and Stella Irene (Cox) S.; B.A., Phillips U., Enid, Okla., 1950, LL.D. (hon.), 1967; B.D., Lexington (Ky.) Theol. Sem., 1953; M.A. in Polit. Sci., U. Mo., Columbia, 1967, Ph.D., 1971; B.A., U. Ark., 1954, U. Pacific Sch. Religion, Berkeley, Calif., 1958; D.P.A. (hon.), Culver-Stockton Coll., 1973; LL.D. (hon.), Maryville Coll., St. Louis, 1976, Kirksville (Mo.) Coll. Osteo. Medicine, 1977; m. Joanne Steanson, June 10, 1950; children—Janet Dovell, James Jeffrey. Ordained to ministry Christian Ch. (Disciples of Christ), 1950; pastor chs. in Ark. and Mo., 1953-70; mem. Mo. Ho. of Reps. from Saline County, 1963-70; pres. Asso. Med. Schs. Mo., Jefferson City, 1970-72; part-time prof. polit. sci. Lincoln U., Jefferson City, 1970-72; treas. State of Mo., 1973—; trustee Mo. Employees Retirement System; bd. dirs. Mo. Bd. Fund Commnrs.; mem. Mo. Housing Devel. Commn.; exec. bd. Mo. Hist. Soc.; mem. div. higher edn. Disciples of Christ Ch., 1969—; mem. Mo. Council Chs., 1969—. Chmn. Mo. del. Democratic Nat. Conv., 1976. Recipient Mental Health award Mo. Mental Health Assn., 1967, Meritorious Service award St. Louis Globe Dem., 1968, Harry S. Truman award Saline County Young Democrats, 1970, citation of merit Alumni Assn. U. Mo., 1975; named Mo. Lay Educator of Year, Mo. chpt. Phi Delta Kappa, 1968. Author: Pulpit, Pew and Politics, 1979. Home: 2228 Hillsdale St Jefferson City MO 65101 Office: PO Box 210 Jefferson City MO 65101

SPALDING, FRANCIS ODIORNE, lawyer, educator; b. Chgo., July 31, 1929; B.A., Yale U., 1950; J.D., Northwestern U., 1964. Admitted to Ill. bar, 1964; asso. firm Isham, Lincoln & Beale, Chgo., 1964-65; asst. prof., asst. dean Northwestern U., 1965-68, asso. prof. law, 1968-71, prof. law, 1971—, asso. dean, 1972—; dir. Legal Assistance Found. Chgo., 1972-76. Mem. Am. Law Inst., Chgo. Council Lawyers, Am., Ill. State, Chgo. bar assns. Contbr. articles to legal jours. Home: 1000 N State St Chicago IL 60610 Office: 357 E Chicago Ave Chicago IL 60611

SPALDING, JACK JOHNSON, newspaperman; b. Atlanta, Feb. 7, 1913; s. Hughes and Bolling Stovall (Phinizy) S.; student Georgetown U., 1933-34; A.B., U. Ga., 1936; m. Anne Wakefield Gowen, June 25, 1955; children—Charles G., Elizabeth, John, James, Mary. With United Fruit Co., Puerto Barrios, Guatemala, 1936-38; with Atlanta Constitution, 1938-40; reporter Atlanta and N.Y. burs. United Press, 1941-42; account exec. Merrill Lynch, Pierce, Fenner & Beane, Atlanta, 1947-48, Clement A. Evans & Co., Atlanta, 1949-50; staff Atlanta Jour., 1951-78, editor, 1956-78. Vice chmn. Atlanta Arts Alliance, now hon. life trustee; past pres. High Mus. Art; 1st v.p., trustee Atlanta Hist. Soc. Served from ensign to lt., USNR, 1942-46. Mem. Am. Legion, Chi Phi. Roman Catholic. Clubs: Piedmont Driving, Nine O'Clocks. Home: 350 Crosstree Ln Atlanta GA 30328

SPALDING, JAMES STUART, telecommunications co. exec.; b. Edinburgh, Scotland, Nov. 23, 1934; came to Can., 1957, naturalized, 1962; student Edinburgh U., 1951-52, Glasgow U., 1953. Gen. mgr., dir. United Corps. Ltd., Montreal, Que., Can., 1970-72; pension fund mgr. Bell Can., Montreal, 1972-76, sr. asst. treas., 1974-76, treas., 1976—, v.p., 1979—; dir. Resource Service Group Ltd., Nat. Telephone Directory Corp., Tele-Direct Ltd., Maritime Telegraph & Telephone Co., Ltd. Mem. Inst. Chartered Accountants Scotland, Order Chartered Accounts Que., Montreal Soc. Fin. Analysts (past pres.), Fin. Execs. Inst. Home: 35 Thornhill Ave Westmount PQ H3Y 2E1 Canada Office: 1050 Beaver Hall Hill Montreal PQ H3C 3G4 Canada

SPALDING, JOHN ROBERT, JR., air force officer; b. Oak Park, Ill., Aug. 28, 1925; s. John Robert and Mae Helen (Hanrahan) S.; M.B.A., U. Chgo.; m. Elizabeth Theresa Light, Dec. 31, 1974; children—Larry, Trena, Robert. Served as enlisted man U.S. Army Air Force, 1943, commd., advanced through grades to maj. gen., U.S. Air Force; fighter pilot Korean War; mem. Thunderbird Jet Acrobatic Team; comdr. Fighter Squadron, Bomber Squadron; dir. ops. Fighter Wing; comdr. Fighter Wing, Vietnam War; vice comdr. Air Def. Command, Pentagon; comdr. Warner-Robins Air Logistics Center, Robins AFB, Ga. Decorated D.S.M., Legion of Merit, D.F.C., Bronze Star, Air medal (U.S.); Cross of Gallantry (Vietnam). Address: Comdr Warner Robins ALC AFLC Robins AFB GA 31098*

SPALDING, VERNON BENJAMIN, cons. civil engr.; b. Ingram, Wis., Jan. 30, 1922; s. Benjamin Bacon and Cassie Gertrude (Baker) S.; B.C.E., U. Minn., 1949; m. Ardis Adele Engler, Feb. 27, 1943; children—Patricia, Gail, Craig, Thom, Jill, Kay, Chris. Office engr. C.E., Ft. Randall, S.D., 1949; design engr. Consoer, Townsend & Assos., Chgo., 1950-51; chief engr. D.L. Briegal Assos., Detroit, 1952-54; part owner, pres. Spalding, DeDecker & Assos., Madison Heights, Mich., 1955—; also dir.; past dir. Design Profls. Ins. Co. Chmn. Southfield (Mich.) Bldg. Code Bd. Appeals, 1977. Served with USAAF, 1940-45. Fellow Am. Cons. Engrs. Council (dir.); mem. Cons. Engrs. Council Mich. (past pres., dir.), Am. Arbitration (panel arbitrators), ASCE, Am. Water Works Assn. Home: 30000 Marimoor Dr Southfield MI 48076 Office: 655 W Thirteen Mile Rd Madison Heights MI 48071

SPALEK, JOHN M., educator; b. Warsaw, Poland, July 28, 1928; s. Bronislaw and Augusta (Gomse) S.; B.A., Whitworth Coll., 1954; M.A., Stanford, 1957, Ph.D., 1961; m. Dortha Ann Tillman, June 16, 1957; children—Anne Margaret, Frederick Carter. From asst. prof., asso. prof., to prof. U. So. Calif., Los Angeles, 1960-70; prof. German, chmn. dept. Germanic langs. and lits. State U. N.Y., Albany, 1970—. Fulbright grantee, Germany, 1958-59; Andrew Mellon postdoctoral fellow U. Pitts., 1967-68; Nat. Endowment for Humanities grantee, 1972-73, 74-78. Mem. Modern Lang. Assn., Am. Assn. Tchrs. German, The Brecht Soc., The Internat. Arthur Schnitzler Soc. (chmn. research seminar on German lit. in exile). Author: Ernst Toller and His Critics, 1968, 2d edit., 1973; Leon Feuchtwanger, 1972; Medieval Epic to the Epic Theater of Brecht, 1968; Deutsche Exilliteratur nach 1933, Vol. I, 1976. Editor: Ernst Toller, Gesammelte Werke, 5 vols.; Guide to the Archival Materials of the German-Speaking Emigration to the U.S. after 1933, 1979. Home: 23 Pheasant Ln Delmar NY 12054 Office: Dept of Germanic Languages and Literatures Hu 209 State Univ NY at Albany Albany NY 12222

SPANBOCK, MAURICE SAMUEL, lawyer; b. N.Y.C., Jan. 6, 1924; s. Benjamin and Belle (Ward) S.; B.A., Columbia Coll., N.Y.C., 1943; LL.B., Harvard, 1950; postgrad. Christ Ch., Oxford (Eng.) U., 1945; m. Marion Heyman, Nov. 21, 1954; children—Jonathan Harris, Betsy Spanbock Ward. Admitted to N.Y. State bar, 1950, since practiced in N.Y.C.; mem. firm Carro, Spanbock, Londin, Fass & Geller, 1954—. Arbitrator nat. panel arbitrators Am. Arbitration Assn., 1967—. Bd. dirs., sec. Initial Teaching Alphabet Found. Served with AUS, 1943-46. Mem. Am. Bar Assn., Assn. Bar City N.Y., Fed. Bar Council, Democrat. Jewish (pres. synagogue). Contbr. articles to profl. publs. Home: 88 Central Park W New York NY 10023 Office: 1345 Ave of Americas New York NY 10019

SPANEL, ABRAM NATHANIEL, mfr., inventor; b. Odessa, Russia, May 15, 1901; s. Heyman and Hannah (Sarokskaya) S.; ed. U. Rochester; m. Margaret R. Spanel; children—Ann, David Louis. Inventor elec. appliances and pneumatic products; for their manufacture formed Vacuumizer Mfg. Corp., 1926, since serving as pres., chmn. bd.; founded internat. Latex Corp., 1932, since serving as chmn. bd. Chmn. bd. Spanel Found., Inc.; founder, chmn. bd. Playtex Park Research Inst.; founder, pres. Spanel Internat., Ltd., 1976—; bd. assos. Linus Pauling Inst. Sci. and Medicine. Decorated grand officer Legion of Honor (France); recipient Gold Medal of Honor (Paris), 1957, 1st Lafayette Bicentenary medal Com. France-Amerique; decorated comdr. du Merite Postal; hon. citizen Vichy, Chavaniac-Lafayette, Istres, Cherbourg. St. Lo. Le Puy, Pessac and Antibes (all France); comdr. Ordre des Lettres et des Arts; grand cross Condor of the Andes. Mem. Cousteau Soc., Am. Soc. French Legion Honor (v.p.; medal of Honor). Mason (32 deg.). Author: That a Nuclear World War May Be Prevented; Levers to Lift this Hemisphere; But It's Later Than You Think; Not Just France; How Nations Commit Economic Suicide; Inflation's Growth: Economic Cancer; Last Chance for Unity; Lest Freedom Go the Way of the Dinosaurs; Oil Embargoes More Potent Weapons Than Atom Bombs; These Fat Geese May Lose Their Golden Eggs; Sudden Shock of Recognition; Blackmailing Trapped Humans; others. Home: Stockton St Princeton NJ 08540 Office: 250 W 34th St New York NY 10001

SPANFELLER, JAMES JOHN, artist, illustrator; b. Phila., Oct. 27, 1930; s. Joseph John and Marie Regina (Breslin) S.; student Phila. Coll. Art, 1948-52, Pa. Acad. Fine Art, 1954-55; m. Patricia Ann Durkin, May 2, 1953; 1 son, James John. Freelance illustrator, 1957—; illustrator numerous children's books, including O-Sono (by Henry Morgan), 1964, The Malibu and Other Poems (by Myra Cohn Livingston), 1974, 4-Way Stop and Other Poems (by Myra Cohn Livingston), 1976, Doug Meets the Nutcracker (by William H. Hooks), 1977, Beware! These Animals Are Poisonous (by Barbara Brenner), 1979; illustrator for mags., advt. agencies, TV commls.; mem. faculty Parsons Sch. Design. Served with U.S. Army, 1952-54. Named Artist of Year, Artists Guild N.Y., 1964; recipient N.Y. Herald Tribune Children's Book award, 1965; Gold medal Washington Art Dirs. Club, 1967, N.Y. Art Dirs. Club, 1978; Gold medal Soc. Publ. Designers, 1973, Silver medal, 1973. Mem. Soc. Illustrators. Address: Mustato Rd Katonah NY 10536

SPANG, RALPH MCCURDY, radio mfg. exec.; b. Altus, Okla., July 18, 1912; s. Howard M. and Lula (Chapin) S.; B.S., Ohio U., Athens, 1937; student Advanced Mgmt. Inst., Crotenvill, N.Y., 1957; m. Ann E. Wagner, Aug. 20, 1938; children—Ralph W., Bruce P. Accountant, Gen. Electric Co., Bridgeport, Conn., 1937-41, traveling auditor, Schenectady, 1941-46; controller, asst. sec. Hotpoint Co., Gen. Electric Co. affiliate, 1946-52, treas., 1952-56, gen. mgr., 1956-58; controller Zenith Radio Corp., Chgo., 1959—, v.p., 1962-70, treas., 1967-70, sr. v.p. finance, dir., 1970-74, cons., 1974—; dir. Central Nat. Bank Chgo., Movado-Zenith-Mondia Holding Co., LeLocle, Switzerland, Zenith Time, S.A.; pres., dir. Zenith Credit Corp., 1971-74; chmn. bd. dirs. Mich. Adminstrs., Inc., 1974-76; mem. adv. bd. Arkwright-Boston Ins. Bd. dirs. Central DuPage Hosp. Mem. Nat. Elec. Mfrs. Assn., Am. Home Laundry Assn. (dir. 1955-58), Fin. Execs. Inst., Theta Chi. Clubs: Yacht and Country (Stuart, Fla.); Glen Oak Country (Glen Ellyn, Ill.). Home: 3985 SE Clubhouse Pl Stuart FL 33494

SPANGLE, CLARENCE WILBUR, lawyer, computer co. exec.; b. Wilkinsburg, Pa., Feb. 16, 1925; s. Carl C. and Blanche E. S.; B.S.M.E., Yale U., 1945; J.D., George Washington U., 1952; m. Virginia Galliher, Aug. 11, 1951; 1 son, Henry Bryan. With Honeywell Inc., Mpls., 1947—, sr. v.p., 1970-71, exec. v.p., 1971-74, pres. Honeywell Info. Systems, Inc., Mpls., 1974—, also dir. Honeywell Inc.; admitted to Minn. bar, 1952; dir. Gelco Corp., 1st Bank System, Inc., Mpls. Bd. dirs. Guthrie Theater, Mpls. Served with USNR, 1942-46. Methodist. Home: 1720 Bohns Point Rd Wayzata MN 55391 Office: Honeywell Plaza Minneapolis MN 55408

SPANGLER, EARL JONES, chocolate co. exec.; b. Campbelltown, Pa., Dec. 15, 1922; s. Abner C. and Beulah M. (Jones) S.; B.S., Lebanon Valley Coll., 1948; m. Edna Reid, Sept. 25, 1948; children—Stephanie Sue, Susan Beth. With Hershey Chocolate Co. (Pa.), 1950—, asst. plant mgr., 1968-70, dir. distribution, 1970-72, div. v.p., 1972-76, pres., 1976—; dir. Hershey Foods Corp.; chmn. bd. Y&S Candies, Inc. Chmn. Dauphin County Hosp. Authority. Served with USNR, 1943-46. Mem. Harrisburg C. of C. Clubs: Rotary, Masons. Office: 19 E Chocolate Ave Hershey PA 17033

SPANGLER, JOHN ALLEN, educator; b. Morgantown, W.Va., Jan. 1, 1918; s. Robert Clifton and Bessie Virginia (Farley) S.; A.B. in Chemistry, W.Va. U., 1939, Ph.D., 1942; m. Jean Grace Pittman, June 12, 1948; children—Terry, Janet, Neal. Research chemist Am. Viscose Corp., Nitro, W.Va., 1942-44; prof. chemistry San Diego State Coll., 1946-52, 54—, chmn. dept., 1955-58, dir. NSF student sci. tng. program, summers 1967-76. Cons. to chem. industry. Active Boy Scouts Am. as scoutmaster, adviser to Explorer Scouts; mem. community area planning coms. city San Diego Planning Dept. Served with USNR, 1942-44, 52-54; ETO, PTO. Mem. Am. Chem. Soc., Calif. State Employees Assn. (pres. chpt. 1958-59), Assn. State Univ. Profs. (pres. chpt. 1960-61). Patentee in field. Home: 4959 Catoctin Dr San Diego CA 92115

SPANGLER, SCOTT MICHAEL, agribus. co. exec.; b. Toledo, Aug. 4, 1938; s. Walter James and Martha Zoe (Hirscher) S.; B.M.E., U. Cin., 1961; M.B.A., Harvard U., 1963; m. Jean Galt Schmonsees, June 10, 1963; children—Karen Elizabeth, Scott Michael, Andrew Galt. Research asso. M.I.T., 1963-65; fin. exec. Cooper Industries, Inc., Mt. Vernon, Ohio, 1965-68; v.p. indsl. group White Motor Corp., Cleve., 1968-70; pres. Spangler and Co., Houston, 1970-73; pres., chief exec. officer Procor, Inc., Phoenix, 1973—, AZL Resources, Inc., Phoenix, 1978—; dir. First So. Capital Corp., Alamosa Nat. Bank. Mem. Am. Agribus. Council. Republican. Presbyterian. Club: Harvard (N.Y.C.). Home: 7837 N 54th St Paradise Valley AZ 85253 Office: PO Box 29008 Phoenix AZ 85038

SPANIER, EDWIN HENRY, educator; b. Washington, Aug. 8, 1921; s. David H. and Anne (Goldman) S.; A.B. magna cum laude, U. Minn., 1941; M.S., U. Mich., 1945, Ph.D., 1947; m. Anne Hardt Lovas, May 26, 1972; children by previous marriage—Rita (Mrs. Robert Wolenik), Gail, Lawrence. Mathematician, U.S. Signal Corps, Ft. Monmouth, N.J., 1941-44; asst. prof. U. Chgo., 1948-54, asso. prof., 1954-58, prof., 1958-59; prof. math. U. Calif. at Berkeley, 1959—. Cons. Ramo-Wooldridge Corp., System Devel. Corp., 1960-70, McGraw-Hill Book Co., Inc., 1965—. Frank B. Jewett fellow, 1947-48; Guggenheim fellow, 1952-53. Mem. Am. Math. Soc., Math. Assn. Am., Phi Beta Kappa, Sigma Xi. Author: Algebraic

Topology, 1966. Contbr. articles to profl. jours. Home: 6820 Snake Rd Oakland CA 94611

SPANIER, MAURY L., lawyer; b. N.Y.C., Aug. 13, 1916; s. Aaron and Elizabeth (Lesser) S.; B.A., Coll. City N.Y., 1936; LL.B., Columbia, 1939; m. Helen Green, July 9, 1941; children—David, Jonathan. Admitted to N.Y. bar, 1939, since practiced in N.Y.C.; counsel firm Hays, Porter, Spanier & Curtis, and predecessors, 1946—, sr. partner, 1958-77; chmn. exec. com. Baldwin Hills Co.; chmn. bd. United Aircraft Products, Inc. bd. govs. nominating com. Am. Stock Exchange, 1979—. Chmn. bd. D.B. McGonagle Found.; trustee, mem. exec. com. Beth Israel Med. Center. Served with AUS, 1942-46. Mem. Am. Bar Assn., Assn. Bar City N.Y., Columbia Law Alumni Assn. (dir. 1974-77), Phi Beta Kappa. Clubs: Lawyers, City Athletic, Atrium, Maplewood (N.Y.C.). Editor Columbia Law Rev., 1937-39. Home: 37 Beechwood Rd Hartsdale NY 10530 Office: 445 Park Ave New York NY 10022

SPANIOL, JOSEPH FREDERICK, JR., govt. ofcl.; b. Columbus, Ohio, Nov. 11, 1925; s. Joseph Frederick and Anna (McGucken) S.; A.B. cum laude, John Carroll U., 1949; LL.B., Western Res. U., 1951; LL.M., Georgetown U., 1953; m. Viola Mae Montz, July 2, 1949; children—Joseph Frederick III, Robert D., Mary Ellen, Thomas A., Timothy J., David G., Anne E., Margaret M. Admitted to Ohio bar, 1951, also Supreme Ct.; with Adminstrv. Office of U.S. Cts., 1951—, atty., 1951-61, counsel, 1961-65, chief div. procedural studies and statistics, 1965-69, asst. dir. legal affairs, 1969-74, exec. asst. to dir., 1974-77, dep. dir., 1977—. Served with AUS, 1944-46; ETO, PTO. Mem. Am. Law Inst., Am. Judicature Soc., Am., Fed. (pres. D.C. chpt. 1967-68, v.p. D.C. circuit 1969-70) bar assns., Nat. Lawyers Club, Phi Delta Phi. Editor: Fed. Bar News, 1960-62, Fed. Bar Jour., 1968-71. Address: Adminstrv Office US Cts Supreme Ct Bldg Washington DC 20544

SPANJER, RALPH HOWARD, marine corps officer; b. Hillside, N.J., Sept. 20, 1920; s. William Henry and Tillie (Vreeland) S.; student N.Y. U.; B.A. in Bus. Adminstrn. and M.Internat. Relations, George Washington U., 1967; m. Barbara Ann Batterson, Aug. 1, 1953; children—Jan, June, Jill. Commd. 2d lt., USMC, 1942, advanced through grades to maj. gen., 1971; combat pilot, World War II Korea, Vietnam; comdg. gen. 2d Marine Aircraft Wing, Cherry Point, N.C., 1974-76; dep. comdr. Fleet Marine Force Atlantic, 1976-78; supt. Marine Mil. Acad., Harlingen, Tex., 1978—. Decorated Legion of Merit, D.F.C., Air medals (2). Mem. Am. Soc. Performance, Marine Corps Aviation Assn., Harvard Sch. Bus. Alumni Assn., Nat. Jogging Assn. (bd. dirs.), Nat. War Coll. Alumni Assn. Home: 320 Iwo Jima Blvd Harlingen TX 78550 Office: Marine Mil Acad Harlingen TX 78550

SPANN, WILLIAM BOWMAN, JR., lawyer; b. Savannah, Ga., June 10, 1912; s. William Bowman and Annie Elizabeth (Holversen) S.; A.B., Emory U., 1932, LL.D., 1973; LL.B., Harvard, 1935; m. Theodora Lillian Peterson, Feb. 8, 1946; children—William Bowman III, Robert Moseley, Karen Elizabeth Marion. Admitted to Ga. bar, 1935, also U.S. Supreme Ct. bar; practice in Atlanta, 1935—; asso. Alston Foster, Moise & Sibley, 1935-41; partner firm Alston, Miller & Gaines, and predecessors, 1942—; prof. law Woodrow Wilson Coll. Law, 1947-62; adj. prof. labor law Emory U., 1979—; chmn. adv. bd. Fulton County Juvenile Ct., 1953-63. Mem., dir. exec. com. Pres.' Lawyers' Com. Civil Rights under Law, 1963—; commr., mem. exec. com. Uniform State Laws, 1965—. Bd. dirs. Atlanta Legal Aid Soc.; trustee Atlanta Lawyers Found., Loridans Found.; mem. vis. com. U. Chgo. Law Sch., 1976-79. Served to lt. comdr. USNR, 1942-46. Fellow Am. Bar Found., Am. Coll. Trial Lawyers; mem. Internat., Inter-Am., Fed., Am. (bd. govs. 1961-64, state del. 1955-70, chmn. ho. dels. 1970-72, pres. 1977-78, life mem. ho. dels.; labor editor Law Notes 1965—), Ga. (chmn. labor sect. 1964-66), Atlanta bar assns., Am. Law Inst. (vice chmn. joint Am. Bar Assn. com. continuing profl. edn. 1976-77), Am. Judicature Soc., Atlanta Lawyer's Club (past pres.), Phi Beta Kappa, Phi Beta Kappa Assos., Tau Kappa Alpha, Delta Tau Delta, Phi Alpha Delta. Lutheran. Clubs: Capital City, Commerce, Harvard (past pres.), Piedmont Driving. Home: 3415 Habersham Rd NW Atlanta GA 30305 Office: Citizens & So Nat Bank Bldg Atlanta GA 30303. *I firmly believe that it is the obligation of the organized bar and of each lawyer individually to assure the delivery of adequate legal services to all persons regardless of ability to pay or unpopularity of the cause. Equal justice for all is the ultimate goal of professional responsibility. To this goal I am totally dedicated.*

SPANNAUS, WARREN RICHARD, state ofcl.; b. St. Paul, Dec. 5, 1930; s. Albert Carl and Anna (Korner) S.; B.B.A., U. Minn., 1958, J.D., 1963; m. Marjorie Louise Clarkson, Dec. 19, 1964; children—Christine Ann, David Clarkson, Laura Zo. Admitted to Minn. bar, 1963; spl. asst. atty. gen. State of Minn., 1963-65; mem. staff Sen. Walter F. Mondale, U.S. Senate, 1965-66, campaign dir. Sen. Mondale, 1966; chmn. Democratic-Farmer-Labor Party of Minn., 1967-69; atty. gen. State of Minn., St. Paul, 1970—. Bd. dirs. United Cerebral Palsy of Greater St. Paul Inc., Sch. for Social Devel., Mpls. Served with USNR. Mem. Minn., Hennepin County, Ramsey County bar assns., Nat. Assn. Attys. Gen., Midwest Assn. Attys. Gen. (chmn.). Methodist. Office: Office of Atty Gen 102 State Capitol Saint Paul MN 55155

SPANOVICH, MILAN, civil engr.; b. Steubenville, Ohio, Feb. 19, 1929; s. Stanley and Katherine (Komazec) S.; B.S. in Civil Engring., Carnegie-Mellon U., 1956, M.S., 1957; m. Syl via J. Tomko, Apr. 16, 1971. Instr., Carnegie-Mellon U., 1957-60; charter asso. E. D'Appolonia Assos., cons. engrs., Pitts., 1957-61; mem. research staff U. N.Mex., 1961-63; founder, prin. engr. Engring. Mechs., Inc., Pitts., 1963—; mem. U.S. com. Internat. Commn. on Large Dams, 1965—; mem. founds. adv. com. Pitts. Bd. Standards and Appeals, 1968—. Recipient Pitts. Young Civil Engr. of Yr. award, 1969; registered profl. engr., Pa., N.Y., Ohio, Va., W.Va., Mich., N.Mex., Ky., Md., Colo., N.J., Del., Fla. Fellow ASCE (chmn. bldg. code com. Pitts. chpt. 1968—), Am. Cons. Engrs. Council; mem. Cons. Engrs. Council Greater Pitts. (pres. 1972-74), Engring. Soc. Western Pa. (dir. 1972, 77—), Nat., Pa. (pres. Pitts. chpt. 1971, state dir. 1976—) socs. profl. engrs., ASTM (chmn. task com. on relative density of granular soils 1959-63), Am. Concrete Inst., Hwy. Research Bd., Internat. Soc. Soil Mechs. and Found. Engring., Pitts. Geol. Soc., Am. Arbitration Assn., Profl. Engrs. in Pvt. Practice (chmn. 1970-71), Soc. Explosives Engrs. Contbr. articles to soil mechs. to tech. jours.; patentee found. systems. Home: 216 Eton Rd Pittsburgh PA 15205 Office: 4636 Campbells Run Rd Pittsburgh PA 15205

SPANTON, WILLIAM FLOYD, ins. co. exec.; b. Cleve., Aug. 1, 1918; s. William Timothy and Ethel (Schramm) S.; B.A., Yale U., 1939, LL.B., 1942; m. Margaret M. Schleyer, Aug. 19, 1943. Admitted to N.Y. bar, 1946, Del. bar, 1953, Minn. bar, 1965; asso. firm Root, Ballantine, Harlan, Bushby & Palmer, 1946-48; house counsel Gen. Baking Co., 1948-51; asst. counsel, sec. Continental Am. Life Ins. Co., Wilmington, Del., 1953-65; v.p., chief counsel Northwestern Nat. Life Ins. Co., Mpls., 1965-75, sr. v.p., sec., gen. counsel, 1975—; v.p., dir. NWNL Companion Fund, Inc. Served to col. USAAF, World War II, USAF, Korean War. Decorated Bronze Star, Croix de Guerre avec Etoile Vermeil. Mem. Am., Hennepin County bar assns., Assn. Life Ins. Counsel. Republican. Episcopalian. Clubs: Mason, Edina Country. Home: 4816 Roycar Rd Minneapolis MN 55435 Office: 20 Washington Ave S Minneapolis MN 55440

SPARBER, BYRON LEE, lawyer; b. Gary, Ind., Aug. 19, 1932; s. Frank Hyatt and Marian (Sobel) S.; B.B.A., U. Mich., 1954, M.B.A., 1957, LL.B., 1957; m. Sandra Fay Bernstein, Aug. 14, 1955; children—Terri Ann, Michael Samuel. Admitted to D.C., Ind. bars, 1957, Fla. bar, 1958; atty.-advisor U.S. Tax Ct., Washington, 1957-60; partner law firm Sparber, Shevin, Rosen, Shapo & Heilbronner, Miami, Fla., 1965—; lectr. Pres., Friends of Art, Lowe Art Mus., Miami, 1970-71; exec. bd. trustees Players State Theatre, Miami, 1977—; trustee Mt. Sinai Hosp., Miami Beach, 1978—. C.P.A., Ind. Mem. Am., Fla. (exec. council tax sect. 1963-72) bar assns., Greater Miami Tax Inst. (pres. 1979), Estate Planning Council S.E. Fla. (dir. 1973-74). Contbr. articles to profl. taxation jours. Office: One SE Third Ave Suite 3050 Miami FL 33131

SPARGO, BENJAMIN H., educator, renal pathologist; b. Six Mile Run, Pa., Aug. 11, 1919; s. Benjamin H. and Lillian (Rankin) S.; B.S. in Biol. Scis., U. Chgo., 1948, M.S. in Pathology, 1952, M.D. with honors, 1952; m. Barbara Scollard, Mar. 12, 1942; children—Janet, Patricia. Intern Univ. Hosp., Ann Arbor, Mich., 1953-54; resident pathology U. Chgo. Med. Sch., 1954-55, mem. faculty 1954—, prof. renal pathology, 1964—; asso. chmn. dept., 1974—; cons. Armed Forces Inst. Pathology. Served with USAAF, 1941-46. Recipient Research Career award Nat. Heart Inst., 1964. Mem. Internat. Acad. Pathology (chmn. edn. com. 1975-77). Home: 5719 Kenwood St Chicago IL 60637

SPARK, MURIEL SARAH, writer; b. Edinburgh, Scotland; d. Bernard and Sarah Elizabeth Maud (Uezzell) Gamberg; student James Gillespie's Sch. for Girls, Edinburgh; marriage dissolved; 1 son. Gen. sec. Poetry Soc., also editor Poetry Rev., 1947-49. Author: (critical and biographical) Child of Light, a Reassessement of Mary Shelley, 1951, John Masefield, 1953, (With D. Stanford) Emily Bronte: Her Life and Work, 1953; (poems) The Fanfarlo and Other Verse, 1952; (fiction) The Comforters, 1957, Robinson, 1958, The Go-Away Bird, 1958, Memento Mori (adapted for stage) 1964), 1959, The Ballad of Peckham Rye (Italian prize for dramatic radio 1962), 1960, The Bachelors, 1960, Voices at Play, 1961, The Prime of Miss Jean Brodie, 1961 (adapted for stage 1966, for film 1969, for TV 1978), The Girls of Slender Means, 1963 (adapted for TV 1974), The Mandelbaum Gate, 1965 (James Tait Black Meml Prize 1965), The Public Image, 1968, The Driver's Seat, 1970 (adapted for film 1972), Not to Disturb, 1971, The Hothouse by the East River, 1973, The Abbess of Crew, 1974 (adapted as film Nasty Habits 1976), The Takeover, 1976, Territorial Rights, 1979; Collected Stories I, 1967; Collected Poems I, 1967; (play) Doctors of Philosophy, 1963; (children's books) The Very Fine Clock, 1969. Editor: (with D. Stanford) Tribute to Wordsworth, 1950; Selected Poems of Emily Bronte, 1972; The Bronte Letters, 1974; (with D. Stanford) Letters of John Henry Newman, 1957. Decorated Order Brit. Empire. Hon. mem. AAAL. Address: care Harold Ober Assos 40 E 49th St New York NY 10017

SPARKMAN, BRANDON BUSTER, ednl. adminstr.; b. Hartselle, Ala., Aug. 2, 1929; s. George Olen and Mary Louise (Jones) S.; B.S., Florence (Ala.) State U., 1952; M.A., U. Ala., 1958, Ednl. Specialist, 1961; Ed.D., Auburn (Ala.) U., 1970; m. Wanda Phillips, Sept. 13, 1952; children—Ricky Brandon, Rita Sharon, Robert Lee. Tchr., asst. prin. Phillips High Sch., Bear Creek, Ala., 1954-57; prin., Tuscumbia, Ala., 1957-65, asst. supt., 1965-69; ednl. cons. Auburn Center, 1969-70; mem. faculty dept. sch. adminstrn. Auburn U., 1970; asst. supt. for staff personnel devel. Jackson (Miss.) Pub. Schs., 1970-71, supt., 1971-73; supt. Richland County Sch. Dist. 1, Columbia, S.C., 1973-75; asst. supt. instruction Hartselle (Ala.) City Schs., 1975—; bd. advisers So. Educators Life Ins. Co. Bd. dirs. Morgan County chpt. ARC, United Givers Fund, Colbert-Lauderdale Child Study Center, Sheffield-Tuscumbia Credit Union; bd. govs. Jackson Symphony Orch.; adv. bd. Jackson Mental Health Center. Served with AUS, 1952-54. Recipient Human Relations award, Jackson. Mem. Am., Ala. assns. sch. adminstrs., Ala. Assn. Sch. Supts., Assn. Supervision and Curriculum Devel., Florence State U. Alumni Assn. (past pres.). Methodist (ch. sch. tchr., supt., vice chmn. ofcl. bd., chmn. commn. edn.). Club: Rotary. Sr. author: Blueprint for a Brighter Child, 1973; STEPS (System for Teacher Evaluation of Pre-reading Skills), 1974; co-author: Preparing Preschoolers to Read, 1977; Competency Tests for Basic Reading Skills, 1978; author: How Well Does Your Child Read, 1979; editor: The In-Between Years, 1979; creator: CORE (Program Management Through Computer Systems), 1975; editor, contbg. author The Advantaged, A Preschool Program for the Disadvantaged, 1969; contbr. articles to profl. jours. Home: PO Box 1131 Hartselle AL 35640 Office: 101 College St Hartselle AL 35640

SPARKMAN, ROBERT SATTERFIELD, surgeon; b. Brownwood, Tex., Feb. 18, 1912; s. Ellis Hugh and Ola (Stanley) S.; B.A., Baylor U., 1935, M.D., 1935, LL.D., 1974; m. Willie Ford Bassett, Feb. 21, 1942. Intern, Cin. Gen. Hosp., 1935-36, resident in surgery, 1938-40; intern Good Samaritan Hosp., Lexington, Ky., 1936-37; resident in pathology Baylor Hosp., Dallas, 1937-38; practice medicine specializing in surgery, Dallas, 1946—; chief dept. surgery Baylor U. Med. Center, Dallas, 1969—; mem. staff Parkland Meml. Hosp., Dallas; clin. prof. surgery U. Tex. Southwestern Med. Sch., Dallas, 1963—; chief civilian surg. cons. 5th U.S. Army Area, 1950-73; cons. to surgeon gen. U.S. Army, 1950—. Bd. dirs. Friends of Dallas Public Library, 1968—, Assos. of So. Meth. U. Libraries, 1970—; trustee Dallas and Mae Smith Found., v.p., 1971—. Served to col. M.C., AUS, 1940-46; PTO. Decorated Bronze Star medal; recipient Disting. Alumnus award Baylor U., 1976, Coll. Medicine, 1976; diplomate Am. Bd. Surgery. Fellow A.C.S. (bd. govs. 1962-70); mem. Am. Surg. Assn. (2d v.p. 1977-78), So. Surg. Assn. (pres. 1978), Okla. Surg. Assn. (hon.), Tex. Surg. Soc. (pres. 1965), Dallas Gen. Surgeons Soc. (pres. 1961), Internat. Soc. Surgery, AMA, Tex. Med. Assn., Soc. Med. Consultants to Armed Forces, James D. Rives Surg. Soc., Soc. Surgery Alimentary Tract, Soc. Internat. de Chirurgie, Philos, Soc. Tex., Alpha Omega Alpha. Clubs: Chaparral, Petroleum, Dallas Country. Editor, also prin. author: The Texas Surgical Society—The First Fifty Years, 1965; editor: Essays of a Louisiana Surgeon, 1977; Minutes of the American Surgical Association 1880-68, 1972; mem. editorial bd. Am. Jour. Surgery. Contbr. articles to profl. jours. Home: 5351 Wenonah Dr Dallas TX 75209 Office: 1004 N Washington St Dallas TX 75204

SPARKS, CLAUD GLENN, librarian; b. Commerce, Tex., Oct. 21, 1922; s. Claud C. and Mamie (Shoemake) S.; B.S., E. Tex. State Coll., 1943; M.A., Tex. Christian U., 1949; postgrad. U. Okla., 1949-50; M.L.S., U. Tex., 1952; Ph.D., U. Mich., 1967; m. J. Lou Turner, Aug. 20, 1960. Adminstrv. officer VA, Dallas, 1946-48; pub. services librarian Tex. A. and I. Coll., Kingsville, 1951-52; asst. reference librarian U. Ill., 1952-53; librarian Tex. Christian U., 1953-65; dean Sch. Library and Info. Scis., N. Tex. State U., 1967-71; prof. library sci. U. Tex., Austin, 1971-72, prof., dean Grad. Sch. Library Sci., 1972—. Served with AUS, 1943-45. Mem. ALA, Southwestern, Tex. library assns., Phi Beta Kappa. Episcopalian. Address: 4213 Prickly Pear Dr Austin TX 78731

SPARKS, DAVID STANLEY, univ. dean; b. Phila., Dec. 8, 1922; s. Richard Frederick and Grace Dorothy (Tuttle) S.; A.B., Grinnell (Iowa) Coll., 1944; M.A., U. Chgo., 1945, Ph.D., 1951; m. Phyllis Ann Bate, June 12, 1949; children—Robert F., E. Anne. Instr., asst. prof., asso. prof. U. Md., College Park, 1947-65, prof. history, 1965—, asso. dean grad. studies and research, 1967-70, dean, 1970—, acting vice chancellor for acad. affairs, 1976-77, acting v.p. grad. studies and research, 1978-79, v.p. grad. studies and research, 1979—; vis. lectr. dept. history Johns Hopkins, 1965. Recipient research awards Am. Philos. Soc., 1958, Social Sci. Research Council, 1957. Mem. Am., So. hist. assns., Orgn. Am. Historians, Am. Assn. U. Profs. (pres. U. Md. chpt.), Phi Kappa Phi. Club: Cosmos (Washington). Co-editor, author: American Civilization: A History of the United States, 1960; The Making of American Democracy, Readings and Documents, 2 vols., 1962. Editor: Inside Lincoln's Army: The Diary of General Marsena Rudolph Patrick, 1964. Home: 4306 Van Buren St University Park Hyattsville MD 20782 Office: Central Adminstrn U Md Adelphi MD 20783

SPARKS, EARL EDWIN, consumer products co. exec.; b. Topeka, May 6, 1920; s. Earl Edwin and Utah Gertrude (Rice) S.; B.S., Omaha U., 1952 (div.); children—Patrick M., Monty E., Dianne M., Daniel E., Jack D.; m. 2d, Marjorie Joyce Voorhees, Oct. 26, 1974. Enlisted as pvt. USAAF, 1940, advanced through grades to col. USAF, 1963; served in North Africa-Italy 15th Air Force, World War II, as sr. navigator, SAC combat crew mem., guided missile staff officer; dep. chief staff 8th Air Force SAC, Westover AFB, Mass., 1961-63; ret., 1963; with IBM Corp., 1963-66, mgr. market planning and adminstrn. Electronic Systems Center, Owego, N.Y.; with Chamberlain Mfg. Corp., Elmhurst, Ill., 1967-71, sr. v.p. marketing, consumer products, 1969-71; v.p. consumer products Kinkead Industries, Inc., 1972-75, v.p. mktg., 1975—. Decorated Legion of Merit, Soldiers medal with oak leaf cluster, Commendation medal with oak leaf cluster. Mem. Am. Inst. Aeros. and Astronautics, Air Force Assn., Ret. Officers Assn., Am. Marketing Assn., Am. Mgmt. Assn. K.C. Mem. Joint Am.-Brit. Program to set up first operational Ballistics Missile System in free world, THOR, 1958-61. Home: 1323 Tall Oaks Ln Wheaton IL 60187 Office: Kinkead Industries Inc 2801 Finley Rd Downers Grove IL 60515

SPARKS, HARVEY VISE, JR., physiologist; b. Flint, Mich., June 22, 1938; s. Harvey Vise and Ellen Louise (Paschall) S.; student U. Mich., 1956-59, M.D., 1963; m. Barbara M. Taylor, Jan. 17, 1969; children—Matthew Taylor, Catherine Elliott, Wendy Sue, Harvey Vise. Postdoctoral fellow dept. physiology Harvard Med. Sch., Boston and U. Goteborg (Sweden); instr. U. Mich., 1966-67, asst. prof. physiology, 1967-70, asso. prof., 1970-74, prof., 1974-78, asst. to dean Med. Sch., 1970-71, asst. dean, 1971-72; prof., chmn. dept. physiology Mich. State U., 1979—; mem. survey team, liaison com. on med. edn. AMA and Am. Assn. Med. Colls.; mem. site visit teams NIH. Recipient Meritorious Service award Mich. Heart Assn., 1962; Borden award for med. student research, 1963; Mich. Heart Assn. student fellow, 1962-63; John and Mary Markle scholar, 1967-72; USPHS postdoctoral fellow, 1963-66; U. Mich. student research fellow, 1960-61; USPHS grantee, 1963—. Mem. Am. Physiol. Soc. (editorial bd. Am. Jour. Physiology 1974—), AAAS, Microcirculatory Soc., Soc. Exptl. Biology and Medicine, Am. Heart Assn. (council circulation), Mich. Heart Assn., Am. Coll. Sports Medicine, Victor Vaughn Soc., Alpha Omega Alpha, Phi Kappa Phi. Author: Casebook of Physiology, 1973; contbr. numerous articles to profl. jours.; editor: (with others) Vascular Smooth Muscle, Handbook of Physiology, 1979. Home: 7996 Lovejoy Rd Perry MI 48872 Office: Dept Physiology Giltner Hall Mich State U East Lansing MI 48824

SPARKS, HENRY ALVY, naval med. officer; b. Woodland, Calif., Nov. 22, 1924; s. Thomas Albert and Marie (Hamel) S.; student Coll. of Pacific, 1943-44; M.D., U. So. Calif., 1948; m. Betty May Brown, Mar. 2, 1946; children—Mark, Nelson, Sandra, Matthew, Teresa. Commd. lt. (j.g.) U.S. Navy, 1948, advanced through grades to rear adm., 1974; intern U.S. Naval Hosp., Long Beach, Calif., 1948-49; mem. surg. team, Korea, 1950-51; resident internal medicine U.S. Naval Hosp., Bethesda, Md., 1951-53; sucessively staff med. officer U.S. Naval Hosp., San Diego, Tripler Army Hosp., Honolulu and U.S. Naval Hosp., Camp Pendleton, Oceanside, Calif., 1955-63; staff med. officer U.S. Naval Hosp., Bethesda, Md., 1963-66, chief medicine, 1965- 66; chief medicine U.S. Naval Hosp., Oakland, Calif., 1966-70; comdg. officer U.S. Naval Med. Research Unit 3, Cairo, Arab Republic of Egypt, 1970-74; comdg. officer Naval Regional Med. Center, Oakland, Calif., 1974-77, Bur. Medicine and Surgery, Washington, 1977-78, dep. surgeon gen., 1978—. Fellow A.C.P., Royal Soc. Medicine (London), Egyptian Pub. Health Assn.; mem. D.C. Radio Control Club, Am. Soc. Tropical Medicine and Hygiene, Explorers Club, Nu Sigma Nu. Office: 6756 Baron Rd McLean VA 22101

SPARKS, JACK DAVID, appliance co. exec.; b. Chgo., Nov. 24, 1922; m. Fredda Sullivan; children—Suzanne, Cinde Marie, Katherine S., Jack David. With Whirlpool Corp., St. Joseph, Mich., 1940—, beginning as laborer, successively asst. dir. personnel, sales dept. staff, advt. and promotion mgr., sales mgr., gen. sales mgr., dir. mktg., 1940-59, v.p. Whirlpool sales, 1959-66, group v.p., 1966-77, exec. v.p., 1977—, also dir.; dir. Meredith Corp., Des Moines, Appliance Buyers Credit Corp., Peoples State Bank, St. Joseph, Mich., Apeco Corp. Formerly chmn. bd. trustees Olivet Coll. Served frpm pvt. to capt., USSAF, 1941-46. Mem. Mich. Acad. Arts and Scis. Clubs: Racquet (Chgo.); Point O'Woods Golf and Country (Benton Harbor, Mich.). Home: 2721 Highland Ct St Joseph MI 49085 Office: 2000 US 33 North Benton Harbor MI 49022

SPARKS, JOHN C., office furniture mfg. co. exec.; b. 1918; B.S., Ohio U., 1940; married. With Glidden Co., 1940-45; asst. treas. U.S. Ceramic Tile Co., 1945-50, treas., 1950- 64, v.p. finance, 1964-65; treas., asst. sec. GF Bus. Equipment, Inc. (formerly Gen. Fireproofing Co.), Youngstown, Ohio, 1966-67, v.p. finance, treas., 1967—. Office: GF Bus Equipment Inc E Dennick Ave PO Box 1108 Youngstown OH 44501

SPARKS, MORGAN, physicist; b. Pagosa Springs, Colo., July 6, 1916; s. Harry Lysinger and Pearl (Morgan) S.; B.A., Rice U., 1938, M.A., 1940; Ph.D., U. Ill., 1943; m. Elizabeth MacEvoy, Apr. 30, 1949; children—Margaret Ellen, Patricia Rae, Morgan MacEvoy, Gordon K. With Bell Telephone Labs., Murray Hill, N.J., 1943-72, exec. dir. semicondr. components, 1968-69, v.p. tech. info. and personnel, 1969-71, v.p. electronic tech., 1971-72; pres. Sandia Labs., Albuquerque, 1972—. Rockefeller Found. fellow U. Ill., 1940-43. Fellow Am. Phys. Soc., IEEE (Jack A. Morton award 1977), Am. Inst. Chemists; mem. Am. Chem. Soc., Nat. Acad. Engring., Phi Beta Kappa, Sigma Xi, Phi Lambda Upsilon. Contbr. articles on transistors, pn junctions and properties of semicondrs. to profl. jours.; patentee semicondr. electronics. Home: 904 Lamp Post Circle SE Albuquerque NM 87123 Office: Sandia Labs Albuquerque NM 87185

SPARKS, RICHARD KINGSLEY, educator; b. Los Angeles, July 20, 1915; s. William Astor and Mildred (Hopkins) S.; B.A., U. Wash., 1939, Central Wash. State Coll., 1941; M.A., U. Calif. at Berkeley, 1952, Ed.D., 1955; m. Elizabeth Mae Chapman, Jan. 31, 1942; children—Richard Kingsley, Robert Chapman. Tchr., Wash. pub.

schs., 1941-42, tchr., adminstr., 1946-51; research asst. U. Calif. at Berkeley, 1951-53; adminstr. Oxnard (Calif.) pub. schs., 1953-55; asst., then asso. prof. sch. adminstrn., dir. secondary student tng., asst. div. chmn. Calif. State Coll. at Los Angeles, 1955-61; dean Sch. Edn., prof. edn. Fresno State Coll., 1961-71, prof., 1971—; summer tchr. Boling Green State U., Calif. State Coll. at Los Angeles, Occidental Coll. Chmn. Calif. Statewide Commn. Tchrs. Selection, Fresno Citywide Commn. Pub. Sch. Integration, Fresno Citywide Ednl. Design Team, Oreg. Dept. Edn. Chmn. bd. Fresno State Coll. YMCA; bd. dirs. Coll. Religious Center. Served to capt. AUS, 1942-46. Mem. Am., Calif. (dist. bd. govs.) assns. sch. adminstrs., Calif. Council PTA (dist. dir.), Western Schs. and Colls. Assn. (chmn. accreditation coms.), Assn. Supervision and Curriculum Devel., Calif. Council Edn. Tchrs., Fresno Dance Repertory Assn. (pres. 1973-74), Phi Delta Kappa, Phi Kappa Phi (pres. Fresno State U. chpt. 1972-74), Contbr. articles to profl. jours. Home: 2020 W Paul Ave Fresno CA 93711. *To succeed as a human being involves the capacity to find fulfillment in one's work, pleasure and satisfaction in a variety of human relationships, a spiritual foundation that sustains and-perhaps most important of all-the ability to love and to be loved. To succeed as a human being may well be the crowning morality. To fail as a human being may be the final immorality.*

SPARKS, ROBERT DEAN, med. edn. adminstr.; b. Newton, Iowa, May 6, 1932; s. Albert John and Josephine S.; B.A., U. Iowa, 1955, M.D., 1957; D.Humanitarian Service (hon.), Creighton U., 1978; m. Shirley Louise Nichols, Sept. 5, 1954; children—Steven Robert, Ann Louise, John James. Prof. medicine Tulane U. Sch. Medicine, 1967-72, asst. dean, 1964-67, asso. dean, 1967-68, vice dean, 1968-69, dean, 1969-72; chancellor U. Nebr. Med. Center, v.p. univ., 1972-76, also prof. medicine Coll. Medicine, 1972-76; program dir. med. affairs W.K. Kellogg Found., Battle Creek, Mich., 1976—; vis. physician Charity Hosp. New Orleans, 1968-72; cons. in field; mem. La. State Health Planning Council, 1968-72, v.p., 1971-72; mem. AMA com. alcoholism, 1972—. Bd. dirs. Family Health Found., 1970-72; bd. dirs. Creighton-Nebr. Univs. Health Found., 1972-76, pres., 1973-74, 75-76; bd. dirs. C.L. Meyer Children's Rehab. Inst., 1972-76; bd. dirs., mem. exec. com. Health Planning Council Midlands, 1974-76; bd. dirs. Monsour Med. Found., Jeanette, Pa. Recipient award Health Edn. Med Assn. Fellow A.C.P.; mem. AMA, Assn. Am. Med. Colls. (Distinguished Service mem.), N.Y. Acad. Scis., Soc. Health and Human Values, Assn. Acad. Health Centers. Mich., Calhoun County med. socs., Am. Gastroenterology Assn., Health Edn. Med. Assn. (chmn. emeritus bd. dirs. 1973-76), Alpha Omega Alpha, Phi Kappa Psi, Nu Sigma Nu. Editorial bd. Preventive Medicine Mag. Home: 144 Waupakisco Beach Battle Creek MI 49015 Office: 400 North Ave Battle Creek MI 49016

SPARKS, ROBERT WILLIAM, publishing exec.; b. Seattle, Dec. 30, 1925; s. James Donald and Gladys (Simmons) S.; student U. Wash., 1947-50; B.A., U. Hawaii, 1954, M.A., 1965. Editor, various publs., 1947-64; mng. editor U. Hawaii Press, 1964-66, dir., 1967-71, 71—; cons. Jour. Hawaiian History. Mem. adv. bd. to pres. Kamehameha Schs. Served with AUS, 1944-46; PTO. Recipient McInerny editorship, 1953; Pacific House citation Pacific and Asian Affairs Council, 1974. Mem. Assn. Am. Univ. Presses, Assn. Am. Publishers, Internat. Assn. Scholarly Publishers, Hawaiian Hist. Soc., Hawaii Found. History and Humanities, Honolulu Acad. Arts, Bishop Mus. Assn. Home: 3634 Nihipali Pl Honolulu HI 96816 Office: 2840 Kolowalu St Honolulu HI 96822

SPARKS, THOMAS EVERETT, lawyer; b. Crossett, Ark., Aug. 15, 1911; s. Albert Theodore and Clara (Morton) S.; A.B., Hendrix Coll., Conway, Ark., 1932; LL.B., Washington and Lee U., 1935; m. Julia Benton, June 29, 1940; children-Thomas Everett, Julianna Dickey, Helen Benton. Admitted to Ark. bar, 1935, since practiced in Fordyce; mem. Ark. Ho. of Reps., 1967—; sec., treas. Benton Furniture Co., Inc., Benton Realty Co., Inc., Benton Hardware Co., Inc., Benton Casket Mfg. Co., Inc., 1947-60, pres., 1960—; owner Morton Abstract Co. Pres. Dallas County Indsl. Devel. Corp. Served to lt. USNR, 1943-46. Fellow Ark. Bar Found.; mem. Am., Ark. bar assns., Am. Coll. Probate Counsel, Am., Ark. trial lawyers assns., Fordyce C. of C. (past pres.). Democrat. Methodist. Club: Rotary. Home: RFD 2 Fordyce AR 71742 Office: PO Box 784 Fordyce AR 71742

SPARKS, WALTER CHAPPEL, horticulturist; b. New Castle, Colo., Aug. 22, 1918; s. Lester Elroy and Jean Ivene (Murray) S.; student Western State Coll., 1936-37; B.S., Colo. State U., 1941, M.S., 1943; postgrad. U. Minn., 1945, Wash. State U., 1949, 56-57; m. Barbara Ferne Gardner, May 31, 1942; children—Robert, Richard, Eugene. Instr., head dept. agr. Pueblo Jr. Coll., 1941; grad. asst. Colo. State U., 1941-43, instr. horticulture, 1943-44, asst. prof., 1944-47, asso. prof., 1947; asso. horticulturist U. Idaho, Aberdeen, 1947-57, acting supt. Aberdeen br. Agrl. Expt. Sta., 1951, 57, 65, horticulturist, 1957—, research prof. horticulture, 1968—, prin. liaison coordinator for potato program, 1976—; exchange prof. Research Inst., Kolding, Denmark, 1972-73; adviser and lectr. on potato problems to various fgn. govts. Recipient 50th Anniversary medal Fed. Land Banks, 1967; Distinguished Service award for service to Potato Industry of Idaho, Gov. of Idaho, 1967. Eldred L. Jenne research fellow, 1957. Mem. AAAS, Am. Inst. Biol. Scis., Am. Soc. Hort. Sci. (life), European Assn. Potato Research, N.W. Assn. Horticulturists, Entomologists and Plant Pathologists, Idaho Acad. Sci., Potato Assn. Am. (life mem., past pres., dir.), Western Regional Potato Improvement Group (past pres.), C. of C., Scabbard and Blade, Sigma Xi (Outstanding Research Paper award 1974), Gamma Sigma Delta (Outstanding Research Worker award 1977), Alpha Zeta, Beta Beta, Beta, Epsilon Rho Epsilon. Club: Rotary. Contbr. articles to profl. jours. Home: 234 N 1st St Aberdeen ID 83210 Office: U Idaho Research and Extension Center Aberdeen ID 83210

SPARLING, MARY CHRISTINE, art gallery dir.; b. Collingwood, Ont., Can., July 8, 1928; d. Alexander and Catherine Henrietta (MacDonald) Malcolm; B.A., Queen's U., Kingston, Ont., 1949; B.Ed. (Gold medal 1970), St. Mary's Coll., Halifax, N.S., 1970; M.A. in Edn., Dalhousie U., 1978; m. Wintfield Henry Sparling, June 17, 1950; children—Margaret, John. Curator edn. N.S. Museum, Halifax, 1968-73; dir. art gallery Mt. St. Vincent U., Halifax, 1973—; cons. in field; mem. Can. Eskimo Arts Council. Recipient Ohio State award for film script The Artist in Nova Scotia, 1977. Fellow Can. Museums Assn. (pres. 1974-76, council 1972—); mem. Atlantic Provinces Art Gallery Assn., Am. Assn. Museums, Assn. Cultural Execs. Unitarian. Home: 6030 Jubilee Rd Halifax NS B3H 2E4 Canada Office: Art Gallery Mt St Vincent Univ Halifax NS B3M 2J6 Canada

SPARLING, ROBERT JOHN, optical co. exec.; b. Syracuse, N.Y., May 14, 1925; s. Waldo and Lydia Pauline (Casler) S.; B.S., Syracuse U., 1948; M.S., U. Rochester, 1956; m. Patricia G. Ide, Aug. 23, 1952; children—Lynne Gilmour, Laura Casler. With Bausch & Lomb Inc., Rochester, N.Y., 1948-61, 72—, contract mgr., 1952-56, products mgr., 1957-61, pres. sci. optical products div., corporate v.p., 1972—; with Gen. Electric, various locations, 1962-71, mgr. optical engring., Syracuse, 1965-67, mgr. mktg. and tech., 1967-71. Registered profl. engr., N.Y. Served with USNR, 1946-48. Mem. Sci. Apparatus Makers Assn. (dir., chmn. optical sect. 1969-71), Rochester Sales Execs. Club (v.p., dir. 1971-73), Rochester C. of C., Rochester Engring. Soc., Tau Beta Pi. Methodist. Club: Monroe Golf Patentee in field. Home: 237 Mount Airy Dr Rochester NY 14617 Office: 1400 N Goodman St Rochester NY 14602

SPARROW, EPHRAIM MAURICE, engring. scientist, educator; b. Hartford, Conn., May 27, 1928; s. Charles and Frieda (Gottlieb) S.; B.S., Mass. Inst. Tech., 1948, M.S., 1949; M.A., Harvard, 1950, Ph.D., 1956; Doutor Honoris Causa, U. Brazil, 1967; m. Ruth May Saltman, Nov. 2, 1952; 1 dau., Rachel Bernarr. Heat transfer specialist Raytheon Mfg. Co., 1952-53; research scientist Lewis Research Center, NASA, Cleve., 1953-59; prof. mech. engring. U. Minn., 1959—, chmn. fluid dynamics program, 1968—; vis. prof. U. Brazil, 1966-67; cons. in field, 1960—. Pres. 1st Brazilian Symposium Heat Transfer and Fluid Mechanics, 1966; chief AID mission U. Brazil, 1966-67; mem. Solar energy panel Fed. Council on Sci. and Tech., 1972; U.S. sci. committeeman 5th Internat. Heat Transfer Conf., 1973-74. Recipient Ralph Coates Roe award Am. Soc. Engring. Edn., 1978. Fellow ASME (Meml. award outstanding contbns. to sci. heat transfer 1962, Max Jakob award for eminent contbns. to sci. and art of heat transfer 1976); mem. Sigma Xi, Pi Tau Sigma. Author: (with R.D. Cess) Radiation Heat Transfer, 1966. Hon. editorial bd. Internat. Jour. Heat Mass Transfer, 1964—; sr. editor Jour. Heat Transfer, 1972—; hon. editorial bd. Letters in Heat Mass Transfer, 1975—; chmn. editorial adv. bd. Numerical Heat Transfer, 1978—; contbr. numerous tech. papers to profl. jours. Home: 2105 Hoyt Ave W Saint Paul MN 55108 Office: Univ Minn Minneapolis MN 55455

SPARSHOTT, FRANCIS EDWARD, poet, educator; b. Chatham, Eng., May 19, 1926; came to Can., 1950, naturalized, 1970; s. Frank Brownley and Gladwys Winifred (Head) S.; B.A., M.A., Corpus Christi Coll. (Oxford, Eng.), 1950; m. Kathleen Elizabeth Vaughan, Feb. 7, 1953; 1 dau., Margaret Elizabeth. Lectr. dept. philosophy U. Toronto (Ont., Can.), 1950-55, asst. prof. Victoria Coll., 1955-62, asso. prof., 1962-64, prof., 1964—, dept. chmn., 1965-70; vis. asso. prof. Northwestern U., Evanston, Ill., 1958-59; vis. prof. U. Ill., Urbana, 1966. Served with Brit. Army, 1944-47. Am. Council Learned Socs. fellow, 1961-62; Killam sr. research fellow, 1977-78. Fellow Royal Soc. Can.; mem. Can. Philos. Assn. (pres. 1975-76), League Canadian Poets (pres. 1977-79), Am. Soc. for Aesthetics (v.p. 1979), Am. Philos. Assn., Aristotelian Soc., Classical Assn. Can. Author: An Enquiry into Goodness and Related Concepts, 1958; The Structure of Aesthetics, 1963; A Divided Voice, 1965; The Concept of Criticism, 1967; A Cardboard Garage, 1969; Looking for Philosophy, 1972; The Naming of the Beasts, 1979; The Rainy Hills, 1979. Home: 50 Crescentwood Rd Scarborough ON M1N 1E4 Canada Office: Victoria Coll Toronto ON M5S 1K7 Canada

SPATZ, SIDNEY S., dental educator; b. Pitts., Jan. 13, 1924; s. Mendel and Charlotte (Fassberg) S.; B.S., U. Pitts., 1942; D.D.S., Pitts. Sch. Dentistry, 1945; m. Phyllis Cohen, Sept. 1, 1946; children—Hilary Ann, Pamela Lynn, Sandra Sue. Pvt. practice oral surgery, Pitts., 1948—; faculty U. Pitts., 1946—, clin. asso. prof., asso. head dept., 1959-71, prof., chmn. oral surgery, 1971—; chmn. dental div. Montefiore, Eye and Ear, Magee-Womens, Childrens, VA hosps. Mem. United Jewish Fedn. Served to capt., Dental Corps, U.S. Army, 1953-55. Named Letterman of Distinction U. Pitts., 1974. Diplomate Am. Bd. Oral Surgery. Fellow Internat., Am. colls. dentists; mem. Am. Dental Assn., Am., Gt. Lakes, Pa. socs. oral surgeons, Internat. Assn. Oral Surgeons, Omicron Kappa Upsilon, Alpha Omega (pres. 1969). Rotarian. Contbr. articles to profl. jours. Home: 1207 Beechwood Ct Pittsburgh PA 15206 Office: Salk Hall Sch Dental Medicine U Pitts Pittsburgh PA 15261

SPAULDING, ALBERT CLANTON, educator, anthropologist; b. Choteau, Mont., Aug. 13, 1914; s. Thomas Claude and Willie (Clanton) S.; B.A., Mont. State U., 1935; A.M., U. Mich. 1937; Ph.D., Columbia, 1946; m. Charlotte L. Smith, 1931; children—Ronald R., Catherine E. Instr., then asst. prof. anthropology, also asst. curator Kans. U., 1946-47; mem. faculty U. Mich., 1947-61, prof. anthropology, 1960-61, curator archaeology, 1951-61; program dir. anthropology NSF, 1959-63; prof. anthropology, head dept. U. Oreg., 1963-66; prof. anthropology U. Calif., Santa Barbara, 1966—, dean Coll. of Letters and Sci., 1967-71. Fellow Am. Anthrop. Assn. (exec. bd. 1963-66, 73-76); mem. Soc. Am. Archaeology (sec. 1954-56, 1st v.p. 1958-59, pres. 1964-65). Author articles in field. Home: 1220 Dover Rd Santa Barbara CA 93103

SPAULDING, ASA TIMOTHY, ret. ins. co. exec.; b. Whiteville, N.C., July 22, 1902; s. Armstead and Annie Belle (Lowery) S.; student Nat. Tng. Sch., Howard; B.S. magna cum laude, N.Y.U., 1930; M.A., U. Mich., 1932; LL.D., Shaw U., 1958, N.C. Coll., 1960, U. N.C., 1967, Duke, 1969, St. Andrews Presbyn. Coll., 1972, Howard U., 1976; D.B.A., Morgan State Coll., 1961; m. Elna Bridgeforth, June 22, 1933; children—Asa Timothy, Patricia Ann (wife Dr. Oscar J. Moore, Jr.), Aaron Lowery, Kenneth Bridgeforth. With N.C. Mut. Life Ins. Co., 1924-68, asst. sec., 1935-48, dir., 1938—, v.p. controller, 1948-58, actuary, 1933-58, pres., 1959-68; actuary Nat. Negro Ins. Assn., 1934-36, 38-40, 1st v.p., 1940-41, pres., 1941-43, chmn. exec. com., 1943-44; cons. actuary Winston Mut. Life Ins. Co., 1934-48, Dunbar Life Ins. Co. 1938-45; v.p., dir. Mut. Savs. & Loan Assn., Realty Services, Inc.; dir. Mechanics & Farmers Bank; v.p. equal employment opportunity services div., cons., dir. Boyden Internat. Group, 1973-74; producer weekly TV program, Your Community, sta. WTVD, 1956-57; program adv. com. Durham Broadcasting Enterprises, Inc., 1953-54, mgmt. adv. com., 1954-57; spl. cons. Urban Nat. Corp. Boston, 1972—; cons. to pres. Howard U., 1975—. Mem. U.S. delegation inaugural of pres. of Liberia, 1956, U.S. delegation USNECO Gen. Conf., New Delhi, India, 1956; chmn. Durham Bi-Racial Human Relations Com., 1957; vice chmn. N.C. adv. com. Commn. Civil Rights, 1959-64; mem. steering com. Urban Coalition; nat. adv. council Airline Passengers Assn., 1972—; mem. Pres.'s Commn. on Income Maintenance Programs, 1968-70; mem. N.C. State Parks and Forests Commn., N.C. Constn. Study Commn., 1968; mem. bd. County Commrs. Durham County, 1968-72; del., head U.S. delegation to presdl. inauguration, Liberia, 1976. Bd. dirs. John Avery Boys Club, Boys Clubs Am.; past dir. United Fund, Durham, Found. for Human Resources Devel., Inc., Nat. Med. Assn. Found., Inc.; mem. exec. com., finance com., treas. James E. Shepard Meml. Found.; chmn. bd. trustees, mem. finance com., Howard U., to 1975; now emeritus; trustee NCCJ People-to-People Program. Recipient Presdl. citation, 1946; Golden Plate award Am. Acad. Achievement, 1964; John B. Russwurm award Nat. Newspaper Pubs. Assn., 1966; Durham C. of C. Civic Honor award, 1968, Bus. Leadership award U. Mich. Grad. Sch. Bus. Adminstrn., 1971; Free Enterprise Exemplar award Freedoms Found., Valley Forge, Pa., 1971; Madden award N.Y. U. Sch. Bus. and Pub. Affairs, 1972; named admiral U.S. Navy, gov. N.C. Mem. N.C. Council Chs. (mem.-at-large exec. com. 1956-57, 3d v.p. 1957-59), Urban League (past trustee), Presidents Profl. Assn., Conf. Actuaries in Pub. Practice, A.I.M., So. Inst. Mgmt. (founding mem.), N.C. Coll. Alumni Assn. (pres. 1944-51), NAACP, Nat. Planning Assn. (nat. council), Am. Acad. Actuaries (charter), Am. Mgmt. Assn. (dir.), Assn. Integration Mgmt. (adv. council), Iota Sigma Nu (hon.), Beta Gamma Sigma (hon. life), Omega Psi Phi. Baptist (trustee). Contbr. articles to ins. publs. Home: 1608 Lincoln St Durham NC 27701 Office: Box 3804 Durham NC 27702. *There is a wide range between the minimum requirement of holding a job and the maximum possibilities of that job. Add any job or position will expand or shrink to the size of the person holding it.*

SPAULDING, BRUCE, lawyer; b. Spokane, June 16, 1906; s. Frank R. and Catherine (McDonald) S.; LL.B., Willamette U., 1930, A.B., 1931; m. Josephine Albert, May 6, 1933; children—Doris Helen (Mrs. Perry H. Rosen), Jean Holman (Mrs. Gary White). Admitted to Oreg. bar, 1930; practice in Dallas, 1930-43, Salem, 1943-51, Portland, 1951—; dist. atty., Polk County, 1934-43; partner firm Souther, Spaulding, Kinsey, Williamson & Schwabe, and predecessor, 1951—. Nominated for atty. gen. Oreg., 1940, 44; nominated for U.S. Congress, 1945. Fellow Am. Coll. Trial Lawyers; mem. Am. Bar Assn. Home: 2844 S W Hillsboro St Portland OR 97201 Office: Standard Plaza Portland OR 97204

SPAULDING, CHARLES CLINTON, JR., lawyer; b. Durham, N.C., Nov. 10, 1907; s. Charles Clinton and Fannie (Jones) S.; A.B., Clark U., 1930; LL.B., St. Johns U., 1935, J.D., 1968; m. Mae Frances Bass (dec.), Sept. 1, 1936; 1 son, Charles Clinton; m. 2d, Minnie Pearson Turner, June 5, 1960. Admitted to N.C. bar, 1946; with N.C. Mut. Life Inc. Co., Durham, 1936—, spl. rep. investment, 1936-41; asst. to treas. then asst. treas., 1941-46, asst. treas. atty., 1946-51, counsel, 1951-58, gen. counsel, dir., 1958-62, v.p., gen. counsel, 1962-73, mem. salary, nominating and fin. com. of bd. dirs., former chmn. charter and by-laws com., former chmn. mortgage and realty com.; partner firm Malone, Johnson, De Jarmon & Spaulding, Durham, 1973—; dir. Mechanics & Farmers Bank; past cons. legal services div. Office Econ. Opportunity, Washington. Past treas., v.p., pres. Durham County unit Am. Cancer Soc., now bd. dirs.; past chmn. Citizens Adv. Com. Workable Program under HUD. Trustee, corporate sec. St. Augustine's Coll., Raleigh, N.C., 1971-79, N.C. Cancer Inst.; charter mem. N.C. for Better Libraries; mem. N.C. Commn. for Study Cancer, 1972-74, Criminal Code Commn. N.C., 75-78. Recipient award pub. service Durham County unit Am. Cancer Soc., 1968-70; award leadership sales program Balt. N.C. Mut. Life Ins. Co., 1966. Mem. Assn. Life Ins. Counsel (emeritus), Nat. Bar Found., Nat. Bar Assn. (life; past treas., exec. com., C. Francis Stradford award 1973), Am. (past chmn. subcom. in taxation sect.) bar assns. Democrat. Baptist (deacon, trustee, bus. mgr., treas. ch.; award for services 1968). Home: 614 Dupree Durham NC 27701 Office: 705 Kent St Durham NC 27702

SPAUR, GEORGE, cons. forester; b. Roseburg, Oreg., Mar. 14, 1903; s. Frank and Dora Lou (Faubion) S.; B.S., Oreg. State U., 1925, M.S., 1935; diploma Army Engr. Sch., 1942, Indsl. Coll. Armed Forces, 1954; m. Gretia Harrison, Mar. 21, 1928. Staff Umpqua Nat. Forest, U.S. Nat. Forest Service, also engaged in pvt. and pub. engring. forestry, 1925-35; grad. asst., instr. Oreg. State Coll., Zellerbach Paper Co., 1935-37; mgmt. and protection div. State of Oreg. Forestry Dept., 1937-40, dep. state forester, 1946-49, state forester, 1949-50, 52-55; with AID, 1955-67, chief forestry adviser Govt. of Pakistan, 1955-60, Govt. of Turkey, 1960-67; forest cons., 1967—; sec. Oreg. State Bd. Forestry, 1949-55; U.S. rep. Asia-Pacific Forestry Conf., Bandung, Indonesia, 1957; forestry cons. Am. embassy, India, also U.S. Mission to Nepal, 1957; spl. cons. Central Treaty Orgn., 1970. Served from maj. to col. C.E., AUS, 1940-46, col., 1950-52, Decorated Bronze Star; recipient meritorious honor award AID, 1967. Profl. land surveyor, Oreg.; registered profl. forester, Ga., Ala. Mem. Western Forestry and Conservation Assn., Assn. State Foresters (exec. com. 1949-55), Keep Oreg. Green Assn. (dir. 1949-55), Oreg. State Foresters Alumni Assn. (past dir.), Soc. Am. Foresters, Internat. Soc. Tropical Foresters, Scabbard and Blade, Hammer and Coffin, Xi Sigma Pi, Alpha Delta Sigma, Kappa Delta Pi, Chi Phi. Republican. Episcopalian. Mason (32, past master), Shriner, Elk, Lion. Address: 1041 W Calle del Regalo Green Valley AZ 85614

SPAW, LOUIS DAVID, JR., constrn. co. exec.; b. Houston, May 6, 1919; s. Louis David and Margaret Elizabeth (Williams) S.; B.S. in Civil Engring., Rice U., 1940; m. Wanda Louise Hoeneke, July 27, 1941; children—Carol Dianne, Wanda Spaw Niebuhr, Louis D. III, Richard H. Jr. engr. Humble Oil and Refining Co., 1940-42; instr. civil engring. Rice U., 1946; project supt., estimator Farnsworth and Chambers Co., 1946-53; with Spaw-Glass, Inc., Houston, 1953—, pres., 1972—. Dir., Ct. Volunteer Services Harris County, Inc., 1968—. Served with USNR, 1942-45. Registered profl. engr., Tex., Miss. Fellow ASCE (pres. Houston br. 1961-62, dir. Tex. sect. 1963-64); mem. Tex. Soc. Profl. Engrs. (chmn. ethical practices com.), Houston C. of C. Democrat. Methodist. Club: River Oaks Rotary (past pres.). Home: 5614 Inwood St Houston TX 77056 Office: Suite 801 2727 Kirby Dr Houston TX 77098

SPEAKE, MARGARET, tobacco co. exec.; b. Mercer County, Ky., Apr. 10, 1914; d. Worley Lee and Nona Bell (Davenport) S.; B.A., Transylvania U., 1936. Tchr., Mercer County (Ky.) High Sch., 1936-42; with Brown & Williamson Tobacco Corp., Louisville, 1942—, corporate sec., 1976—. Mem. Exec. Women Internat. (chpt. pres. 1977). Democrat. Home: 2845 Hikes Ln Louisville KY 40218 Office: 2000 Citizens Plaza Louisville KY 40202

SPEAKER, FRED, lawyer; b. Williamsport, Pa., Apr. 16, 1930; s. Frederick and Helen (Collins) S.; student U. Pa., 1948-50, 54; LL.B., St. John's U., 1957; m. Jo Ann Dunn, June 7, 1952; children—Mark, Paul, Peter, Joseph, Andrew, Thomas. Admitted to Pa. bar, 1957; counsel to majority leader Pa. Ho. of Reps., Harrisburg, 1967; atty. gen. State of Pa., Harrisburg, 1970-71; partner firm Morgan, Lewis & Bockius, Harrisburg, 1968-70, 71; dir. Office of Legal Services, OEO, Washington, 1971-72; partner firm Pepper, Hamilton & Scheetz, Harrisburg, 1972—. Mem. Pa. State Bd. Edn., 1974-77; bd. dirs. Gaudenzia, 1972-75, Pa. Legal Services Center, 1973—, Defender Assn. Phila., 1973-76; mem. Citizens Com. on Basic Edn., 1972-73; mem. Pa. Joint Council on Criminal Justice System, 1972-74. Served with C.I.C., U.S. Army, 1951-54. Mem. Am. Law Inst. Republican. Roman Catholic. Editor-in-chief: St. John's U. Law Rev., 1954. Home: 506 Colony Rd Camp Hill PA 17011 Office: 10 S Market Sq Suite 400 PO Box 1181 Harrisburg PA 17108

SPEAKES, LARRY MELVIN, pub. relations exec.; b. Cleveland, Miss., Sept. 13, 1939; s. Harry Earl and Ethlyn Frances (Fincher) S.; student U. Miss., 1957-61; m. Laura Christine Crawford, Nov. 3, 1968; children—Sondra LaNell, Barry Scott, Jeremy Stephen. News editor Oxford (Miss.) Eagle, 1961-62; news editor Bolivar Comml., Cleveland, 1962-63, mng. editor, 1965-66; dep. dir. Bolivar County Civil Def., 1963-65; gen. mgr. Progress Pubs., Leland, Miss., 1966-68; editor Leland Progress, Hollandale Herald, Bolivar County Democrat, Sunflower County News; press sec. U.S. Senator J.O. Eastland of Miss., 1968-74; staff asst. Exec. Office of Pres., Mar.-May 1974; press asst. to spl. counsel to Pres., May-Aug. 1974; asst. White House press sec., 1974-76, asst. press sec. to Pres., 1976-77; press sec. to Gerald R. Ford, 1977; v.p. Hill & Knowlton, Inc., internat. pub. relations and pub. affairs counsel, Washington, 1977—. Recipient Gen. Excellence award Miss. Press Assn., 1968. Mem. Sigma Delta Chi, Kappa Sigma, Lambda Sigma, Omicron Delta Kappa. Methodist. Home: 4800 Thiban Terr Annandale VA 22003 Office: One McPherson Sq Vermont at K St NW Washington DC 20005

SPEAKMAN, EDWIN AARON, physicist; b. Gratz, Pa., Aug. 14, 1909; s. Clarence Alexander and Sara Ada (Daniel) S.; B.S., Haverford (Pa.) Coll., 1931; m. Dorothy McClellan, June 29, 1937; children—Suzanne, Patricia. Asst. physics Haverford ford Coll., 1931-33, radio, 1933-34; radio engr., research lab., Philco Corp., Phila., 1934-35, Detroit, 1935-39; physicist Curtis Pub. Co., Phila., 1939-40; physicist Naval Research Lab., 1940-43, asst. supt., radio div., 1943-45, head radio countermeasures br., 1945-49; exec. dir. Com. on Electronics, Research and Devel. Board, Dept. Def., vice chmn., 1951-52; gen. mgr. Fairchild Guided Missiles Div. and v.p. Fairchild Engine & Airplane Corp., Wyandanch, N.Y., 1952-58; mgr. planning Def. Electronics Products, RCA, Camden, 1958-59; v.p. missile range programs RCA Service Co., Camden, N.J., 1960-65; v.p. dir. Center Naval Analyses, Franklin Inst., Arlington, Va., 1966-67; dir. Office Research and Devel., U.S. Dept. Transp., 1967-68; staff adviser sci. and cryptologic affairs U.S. Army Security Agy., Arlington Hall, Va., 1968—; cons. asst. sec. defense. Chmn. Joint Signal and Evaluation Analysis Panel, Joint Chiefs of Staff, 1947-49. Mem. electronic countermeasure panel, Research and Devel. Bd.; mem. U.S. Civil Service Bd. of Examiners for scientific and tech. personnel (Potomac River Naval Command), 1946-49; mem. Civilian Service awards com., chmn. efficiency rating com., Naval Research Lab. Mem. countermeasures com., Inter-Bur. Tech. coordinating Com. Awarded scholarship Autocar Co., of Ardmore, Pa., 1927: recipient Navy's Meritorious Civilian Service award, 1946. Fellow IEEE; asso. fellow Am. Inst. Aeronautics and Astronautics, asso. mem. U.S. Naval Inst.; mem. Soc. Automotive Engrs., Am. Phys. Soc., D.C. Fedn. of Citizens Assn. (del.), Fairfax Village Citizens Assn. (pres., 1947-50), Aircraft Industries Assn. (mem. guided missle com.) Radio amateur, Station W3AUR, 1925—. Inventor photo electric timing system, 1934, telescopic rod antenna system, 1939. Home: 9018 Charles Augustine Dr Alexandria VA 22308 Office: US Army Intelligence and Security Command Arlington Hall VA 22212

SPEAKS, DONALD WESLEY, mfg. co. exec.; b. New Lexington, Ohio, Oct. 7, 1921; s. Otis Vincent and Emma Abigail (Stringfellow) S.; B.S., Ohio U., 1943, M.S., 1948; m. Kathleen Bates, Nov. 22, 1945; children—Susan Speaks Mills, David. Accountant, Owens Corning Fiberglass Co., Newark, 1945-47; cost supr. Anchor Hocking Corp., Lancaster, Ohio, 1947-51; with Standard Products Co., Cleve., 1951—, treas., 1971—, v.p., 1976—. Served to 1st lt. inf. AUS, 1943-45. Decorated Purple Heart. Mem. Fin. Execs. Inst., Cleve. Treas.'s Club. Methodist. Home: 2798 W Asplin St Rocky River OH 44116 Office: 2130 W 110th St Cleveland OH 44102

SPEAKS, RUBEN LEE, bishop; b. Lake Providence, La., Jan. 8, 1920; s. Benjamin and Jessie Bell (Nichols) S.; A.B., Drake U., 1946; M.Div., Drew Theol. Sem., 1949; S.T.M., Temple U., 1952; postgrad. Div. Sch., Duke U., 1961; D.D., Hood Theol. Sem., 1972; m. Janie Angeline Griffin, Aug. 31, 1947; children—Robert Bernard, Joan Cordelia, Faith Elizabeth. Ordained deacon Christian Ch., 1942, elder African Methodist Episcopal Zion Ch., 1947; minister St. Thomas A.M.E. Zion Ch., Somerville, N.J., 1947, Wallace Chapel A.M.E. Zion Ch., Summit, N.J., 1948-50, Varick A.M.E. Zion Ch., Phila., 1950-56, St. Mark A.M.E. Zion Ch., Durham, N.C., 1956-64, 1st A.M.E. Zion Ch., Bklyn., 1964-72, bishop 12th Episcopal Area, Roosevelt, N.Y., 1972—. Bd. dirs. Durham Com. on Negro Affairs, 1958-63, N.Y. Urban League, 1967-72; trustee Lincoln Hosp., Durham; chmn. exec. com. NAACP, 1958-63. Recipient Citizens award City of Durham, 1964, Meritorious Service award N.Y. Urban League, 1968. Mem. Nat. Acad. Sci. and Religion. Author: Higher Catechism for Ministers and Laymen, 1966; The Minister and His Task, 1968; The Church and Black Liberation, 1972. Office: 304 Pennsylvania Ave Roosevelt NY 11575*

SPEAR, HARVEY MILTON, lawyer; b. Providence, May 24, 1922; s. Alfred and Esther (Marcus) S.; A.B., Brown U., 1942; LL.B., Harvard, 1948; M.A., George Washington U., 1949, LL.M., 1952, S.J.D., 1955; m. Ruth Abramson, June 27, 1965; children—Jessica Eve, Elizabeth Anne. Admitted to Mass., D.C. bars, 1948, N.Y. bar, 1954, also U.S. Supreme Ct., bar; asst. U.S. atty. D.C., 1948; legal asst. to chmn., asst. to vice chmn. SEC, 1948-50; spl. asst. to atty. gen., tax div. Dept. Justice, 1951-54; legis. asst. to Senator Pastore of R.I., 1956; pvt. practice law, N.Y.C., Washington, London, 1956—; sr. partner firm Spear & Hill, N.Y.C., 1958-72, counsel, 1972-75; counsel firm Davis & Cox, N.Y.C., 1978—. Treas, N.Y. County Democratic Com., 1963—; del.-at-large Dem. Nat. Conv., 1968, alt.-del.-at-large, 1964. Chmn. nat. council exec. com. Met. Opera Assn., 1964-66, chmn. nat. council adminstrv. com., 1966-67, mem. assn., 1961—. Served to maj. USMCR, 1942-45. C.P.A., Md. Mem. Am., N.Y. State, Fed. bar assns., Bar Assn. City N.Y., Law Soc. Eng. and Wales (hon.), Am. Inst. C.P.A.s, Inst. Club of Inst. Chartered Accountants Eng. and Wales, Delta Sigma Rho. Club: Brown U. (bd. govs. N.Y.C. 1961—, pres. 1965). Contbr. articles to legal jours. Home: 765 Park Ave New York NY 10021 also Hither Ln East Hampton NY 11937 Office: 1 State St Plaza New York NY 10004

SPEAR, LLOYD C., indsl. products mfg. co. exec.; b. Malden, Mass., Mar. 15, 1940; s. Lloyd A. and Caroline M. (McGrath) S.; B.S. in Acctg. cum laude, Syracuse (N.Y.) U., 1961; m. Patricia Ellis, June 2, 1962; children—Deborah, Rebecca, Cheryl. With Coopers & Lybrand, C.P.A.'s, N.Y.C., 1961-65; with Albany Internat. Corp., Menands, N.Y., 1965—, dir. corp. acctg., then controller, 1970-74, v.p. fin., 1974—. Trustee Meml. Hosp., Albany, N.Y.; chmn. Northeastern Red Cross Blood Program; bd. dirs. Albany chpt. ARC. C.P.A., N.Y. Mem. Am. Inst. C.P.A.'s, N.Y. State Soc. C.P.A.'s. Home: 8 Chestnut Hill Loudonville NY 12211 Office: 1 Sage Rd Menands NY 12207

SPEAR, LOUIS LAWRENCE, investment banker; b. Minsk, Russia, Mar. 31, 1915; s. Sam and Lena (Zitlin) S.; came to U.S., 1925, naturalized, 1929; B.A., Central Coll., 1935; J.D., Kent Coll. Law, Chgo., 1938; m. Esther Katz, Oct. 23, 1938; children—Carol, James, Scott. Admitted to Ill. bar, 1938; mem. firm Salzman & Spear, Chgo., 1938-52; pres., dir. Forus Investment Corp., Chgo., 1938—, also chmn. bd.; pres., dir. Spear Enterprises, Inc., 1945-52, Display Advt. Corp., Chgo., 1946-52, ABC Display Corp., Chgo., 1947-52; circulation dir. Chgo. Sun-Times, 1952-64, v.p., 1959-64; v.p. Chgo. Daily News, 1959-64; chmn. bd. Crown Point Paper Products, Inc.; chmn. First Charter Corp.; v.p., dir. Bass Fin. Corp.; dir., chmn. exec. com. Unity Savs. Assn., N. Shore Nat. Bank; chmn. bd. Ermine Corp., 1955-59; cons. Field Enterprises, 1964—, Williams Electronic Corp., Bass Fin. Corp.; Ill. rep. ICC, 1949, chmn. motor carrier div. Ill., 1948-50. Vice chmn. Ill. Young Republican Orgn., 1946-47; chmn. Cook County Young Rep. Orgn., 1950-51; Rep. committeeman 4th Ward Chgo., 1951-52; trustee Roosevelt U., Kent Coll. Law. Jewish. Club: Covenent. Home: 4950 S Chicago Beach Dr Chicago IL 60615 Office: 33 N Dearborn St Chicago IL 60602

SPEAR, WILLIAM WILSON, lawyer; b. Genoa, Nebr., May 8, 1911; s. Edward McGraw and Lucia (Wilson) S.; A.B., U. Neb., 1933; J.D., George Washington U., 1936; m. Louise Boles, Apr. 7, 1942 (div. Mar. 1961); children—William E., Andrew M., Loraine: m. 2d, Sylvia C. Gunnlaugson, Aug. 1963. Admitted to D.C. bar, 1936, N.Y. bar, 1938, Nebr. bar, 1945, W.Va. bar, 1968; atty. Chesapeake & Potomac Telephone Co., Washington, 1936-37, Bklyn. Manhattan Transit Corp., N.Y.C. 1937-40; asst. div. atty. AT&T, Washington, 1946-50; mem. firm Spear, Lamme & Simmons, and predecessors, Fremont, Nebr., 1951-58; sr. atty. Standard Oil Co. (Ind.), 1958-70, v.p., 1970-76, v.p. govt. relations ret., 1976; practice law, Martinsburg, W.Va., 1976—. Mem. Republican Nat. Com., 1954-56, chmn. State Central Com., 1954-56, chmn. call com. 1956 nat. conv.; bd. regents Georgetown U., Washington, 1971—. Served as maj. USAAF, 1942-46. Mem. Phi Alpha Delta, Chi Phi. Clubs: Fed. City, Univ., Capitol Hill (Washington). Home: PO Box 1520 Martinsburg WV 25401 Office: 205 E King St Martinsburg WV 25401

SPEARE, ELIZABETH GEORGE, writer; b. Melrose, Mass., Nov. 21, 1908; d. Harry Allan and Demetria (Simmons) George; student Smith Coll., 1926-27; A.B., Boston U., 1930, M.A., 1932; m. Alden Speare, Sept. 26, 1936; children—Alden, Mary Elizabeth. Tchr. high sch. English, Rockland, Mass., 1933-35, Auburn, Mass., 1935-36. Mem. P.E.N., Authors Guild, Kappa Kappa Gamma. Author: Calico Captive, 1957; The Witch of Blackbird Pond (Newbery award), 1958; The Bronze Bow (Newbery award), 1961; Life in Colonial America, 1963; The Prospering, 1967. Contbr. articles to mags. Home: Bibbins Rd RFD 1 Fairfield CT 06430

SPEARING, JOHN SIDNEY, indsl. minerals distbn. exec.; b. London, Apr. 20, 1923; s. Sidney Walter and Puby Mary (Bell) S.; came to Can., 1951, naturalized, 1958; grad. London Poly., 1942; chartered accountant, 1951; m. F.L. Joyce Emes, June 8, 1946; children—Caroline, Jane, Holly. Vice pres. Slater Steel Industries, Hamilton, Ont., Can., 1953-68; with Steetley Industries Ltd., and predecessor, Hamilton, 1968—, pres., 1969—, chief exec. officer, also dir. and pres., dir. all Canadian subsidiaries; dir. Laidlaw Transp. Ltd.,; chmn. bd. dirs. Nat. Slag Ltd. Bd. dirs., past treas. Jr. Achievement Hamilton. Served with RAF, 1942-46. Fellow Inst. Chartered Accountants Ont.; mem. Hamilton and Dist. C. of C. (pres. 1971-72), Chartered Accountants Inst. Eng. and Wales, Hamilton and Dist. Chartered Accountants Assn. Anglican. Clubs: Hamilton Golf and Country, Hamilton, Rotary (Hamilton); Tamahaac; Pennask Lake Fishing and Game. Home: 134 Uphill Ct Ancaster ON L9G 3R1 Canada Office: PO Box 2029 Station A Hamilton ON L8N 3S9 Canada

SPEARS, ADRIAN ANTHONY, U.S. judge; b. Darlington, S.C., July 8, 1910; s. J. Monroe and Mary Agnes (Moore) S.; student The Citadel, 1927, U. N.C., 1928; LL.B., U. S.C., 1934, J.D., 1971; m. Elizabeth Wylie, June 10, 1937 (div. 1973); children—Sara Elizabeth Spears Hultgreen, Claude Monroe, Thomas Wylie, Carolyn Blakely, James Adrian. Admitted to S.C. bar, 1934, Tex. bar., 1937; individual practice law, Darlington, 1934-36, San Antonio, 1937-61; spl. Tex. dist. judge, 1951; U.S. dist. judge Western Dist. Tex., 1961-62, chief judge, 1962-79; mem. jud. conf. U.S. Com. on Adminstrn. Criminal Law; mem. faculty Seminar for Newly Apptd. Judges, 1971-75; mem. Com. to Consider Standards for Admission to Practice in Fed. Cts. Chmn. bd. adjustment City of Alamo Heights, 1947-49; chmn. charter revision com. City of San Antonio, 1949; del. Democratic nat. convs., 1952, 56, 60; mem. Tex. Dem. Exec. Com., 1950-52; trustee Our Lady of the Lake U., 1975-77. Recipient Rosewood Gavel award St. Mary's U. Law Sch., 1971. Mem. Fed., Am., San Antonio (pres. 1959-60) bar assns., State Bar Tex., State Bar S.C., 5th Circuit Dist. Judges Assn. (pres.) Pi Kappa Phi, Phi Delta Phi, Omicron Delta Kappa. Methodist. Clubs: Masons (33), K.T., Shriners, Rotary, Monday Morning Quarterback (pres. 1961) (San Antonio). Home: 9004 Wickfield San Antonio TX 78217 Office: 655 E Durango Blvd San Antonio TX 78206

SPEARS, ALEXANDER WHITE, III, tobacco co. exec.; b. Grindstone, Pa., Sept. 29, 1932; s. Alexander White and Eva Marie (Elliott) S.; B.S., Allegheny Coll., Meadeville, Pa., 1953; Ph.D., U. Buffalo, 1960; m. Shirley Pierce; 1 son, Craig Stewart. Research asso., then research fellow State U. N.Y., Buffalo, 1956-59; instr. Millard Fillmore Coll., Buffalo, 1958-59; with Lorillard Corp., Greensboro, N.C., 1959—, v.p. research and devel., 1971-74, sr. v.p. ops. and research, 1975-79, exec. v.p. ops. and research, 1979—; asst. prof. Greensboro div. Guilford Coll., 1961-65. Chmn. model sch. task force Greensboro Bd. Edn. and Greensboro C. of C., 1975; bd. dirs. United Way Greensboro, 1975. Served with AUS, 1953-55. Recipient Distinguished Achievement award in tobacco sci. Philip Morris, 1970. Mem. Am. Chem. Soc., Soc. Applied Spectroscopy, Plant Phenolic Group N.Am., Coblentz Soc., Am. Mgmt. Assn., N.Y. Acad. Scis., ASTM, Internat. Coop. Center Sci. Research Relative to Tobacco (sci. commn. 1972), Greensboro C. of C. (dir. 1974-75, chmn. council edn. 1974; Nathanael Greene award 1975). Presbyterian. Past editor Tobacco Sci. Jour. Author, patentee in field. Address: 2525 E Market St PO Box 21688 Greensboro NC 27420

SPEARS, BETTY MARY, educator; b. Clinton, Ind., Jan. 16, 1918; d. Archibald D. Spears and Mary E. (Zell) Spears Shumaker; B.S., Purdue U., 1940; M.S., Wellesley Coll., 1944; Ph.D., N.Y. U., 1956. Instr., Douglass Coll., 1944-47, U. Tex., 1947-49, U. Mich., 1949-50, U. Minn., 1950-52; asst. prof. Bklyn. Coll., 1952-60; from asso. prof. to prof. Wellesley Coll., 1960-72, head phys. edn. for women, 1971-73; prof. phys. edn. U. Mass., 1971-73, prof. sport studies, 1973—; cons. in field. Recipient Recognition award Mass. Assn. Health, Phys. Edn. and Recreation, 1971, Council for Nat. Cooperation in Aquatics, 1972, Eastern Assn. Phys. Edn. Coll. Women, 1971, Eastern Dist. AAHPER, 1975. Mem. Nat. Assn. Phys. Edn. Coll. Women (Eastern dist. pres. 1965, nat. pres. 1975-77), AAHPER. Author books, including (with R. A. Swanson) History of Sport and Physical Activity in the U.S.; contbr. articles to profl. jours.; editor Quest, 1973-75. Home: 56 Van Meter Dr Amherst MA 01002

SPEARS, FRANKLIN SCOTT, justice Tex. Supreme Ct.; b. San Antonio, Aug. 20, 1931; s. Jacob Franklin and Lois Louise (Harkey) S.; student So. Methodist U., 1948-50; B.B.A., U. Tex., 1954, J.D., 1954; m. Rebecca Nell Errington, Dec. 4, 1977; children—Franklin Scott, Carleton Blaise, John Adrain. Admitted to Tex. bar, 1954, U.S. Dist. Ct. bar for Western Dist. Tex., 1956, 5th Circuit Ct. bar, 1961, U.S. Supreme Ct. bar, 1966; practiced law, San Antonio, 1956-68; mem. Tex. Ho. of Reps., 1958-61, Tex. Senate, 1961-67; dist. judge 57th Jud. Dist. Tex., 1968-78; justice Tex. Supreme Ct., 1979—. Exec. com. Alamo Area council Boy Scouts Am., 1964-68. Served with U.S. Army, 1955-56. Mem. San Antonio Bar Assn., Tex. Bar Assn., State Bar Tex., YMCA, Soc. Preservation and Encouragement Barbershop Quartet Singing in Am, SAR. Democrat. Presbyterian. Clubs: Masons, Shriners, Rotary. Office: Box 12248 Capitol Station Austin TX 78711

SPEARS, MARIAN CADDY, educator; b. East Liverpool, Ohio, Jan. 12, 1921; d. Frederick Louis and Marie (Jerman) Caddy; B.S., Case Western Res. U., 1942, M.S., 1947; Ph.D., U. Mo., 1971; m. Sholto M. Spears, May 29, 1959. Chief dietitian Bellefaire Children's Home, Cleve., 1942-53; head dietitian Doctors Hosp., Cleve., 1953-57; asso. dir. dietetics Barnes Hosp., St. Louis, 1957-59; asst. prof. U. Ark., Fayetteville, 1959-68; asso. prof. U. Mo., Columbia, 1971-75; prof., head dept. dietetics, restaurant and instl. mgmt. Kans. State U., Manhattan, 1975—; cons. dietitian for small hosps. and nursing homes; cons. in dietetic edn. Mem. Am. Dietetic Assn., Am. Home Econs. Assn., Am. Sch. Foodservice Assn., Food Systems Mgmt. Edn. Council, Soc. for Advancement of Foodservice Research, Manhattan C. of C., Sigma Xi, Gamma Sigma Delta, Omicron Nu. Contbr. articles to profl. jours. Home: 1423 Beechwood Terr Manhattan KS 66502 Office: 105 Justin Hall Kans State U Manhattan KS 66506

SPEARS, MONROE KIRK, educator, author; b. Darlington, S.C., Apr. 28, 1916; s. James Monroe and Lillian (Fair) S.; A.B., A.M., U. S.C., 1937; Ph.D., Princeton, 1940; m. Betty Greene, Sept. 3, 1941; 1 dau., Julia Herndon. Instr. English, U. Wis., 1940-42; asst. prof., then asso. prof. English, Vanderbilt U., 1946-52; prof. English, U. South, 1952-64; Libbie Shearn Moody prof. English, Rice U., 1964—; vis. prof. U. Wash., summer 1960, U. Mich., summer 1961, Swarthmore Coll., 1961-62; mem. adv. council dept. English, Princeton, 1960-66, Christian Gauss lectr., 1975. Served to capt. AUS and USAAF, 1942-46; ETO. Grantee Am. Philos. Soc. and Carnegie Found., 1949; Rockefeller fellow, 1956; Guggenheim fellow, 1965-66, 72-73. Mem. P.E.N. Democrat. Episcopalian. Author: The Poetry of W.H. Auden: The Disenchanted Island, 1963; Hart Crane, 1965; Dionysus and the City: Modernism in Twentieth Century Poetry, 1970; Space against Time in Modern American Poetry, 1972; The Levitator and Other Poems, 1975. Editor: (with H.B. Wright) The Literary Works of Matthew Prior,, 2 vols., 1959; W.H. Auden: A Collection of Critical Essays, 1964; The Narrative Poetry of Shakespeare, 1968. Editor Sewanee Rev., 1952-61, adv. editor, 1961-73. Home: 413 Ripple Creek Houston TX 77024

SPEARS, ROBERT RAE, bishop; b. Rochester, N.Y., June 18, 1918; s. Robert Rae and Phebe (Wing) S.; A.B., Hobart Coll., 1940, D.D. (hon.), 1969; S.T.B., Gen. Theol. Sem., N.Y.C., 1943, S.T.D. (hon.), 1967; m. Charlotte Lee Luttrell, June 16, 1947; children—Robert Rae, Deborah Wing, Gregory Luttrell. Ordained priest Episcopal Ch., 1944; curate in Olean, N.Y., 1943-44; rector in Mayville, N.Y., 1944-48; canon St. Paul's Cathdral, Buffalo, 1948-50; rector in Auburn, N.Y., 1950-54; vicar Chapel of the Intercession, N.Y.C., 1954-60; rector Trinity Ch., Princeton, N.J., 1960-67; suffragan bishop Diocese West Mo., 1967-70; bishop of Rochester (N.Y.), 1970—. Pres. Met. Interch. Agy., Kansas City, Mo., 1968. Trustee Gen. Theol. Sem., 1955—. Home: 40 Douglas Rd Rochester NY 14610 Office: Episcopal Diocese of Rochester 935 East Ave Rochester NY 14607

SPEARS, ROBERT WRIGHT, coll. pres. emeritus; b. Clio, S.C., Oct. 20, 1912; s. Charlie Otho and Mary Jane (Wright) S.; A.B., Wofford Coll., 1933, D.D., 1952; B.D., Duke U., 1936; m. Mary Blue Smith, Dec. 24, 1935; children—Mary Ann, Nancy Lynn. Admitted to S.C. Methodist Conf., 1935, ordained deacon, 1937, elder, 1939; S.C. Conf. dir. youth work Meth. Ch., 1938-41; dean S.C. Meth. Pastor's Sch., 1942-46; pastor chs., Ruby, Bamberg, Manning, Charleston and Florence, S.C., 1946-51; pres. Columbia (S.C.) Coll., 1951-78, emeritus, 1978—; interim minister Washington St. United Meth. Ch., Columbia, 1978; mem. gen. bd. edn. United Meth. Ch., 1960-72, del. jurisdictional and gen. confs., 1956—, mem. Univ. Senate, mem. World Meth. Council and Confs., 20 years; bd. fellows Interpreters' House, Lake Junaluska, N.C. Chmn. S.C. Gov.'s Adv. Council on Mental Retardation Planning; chmn. S.C. Adv. Com. on Higher Edn. for Titles I, II and VII, 1965—; mem. S.C. Bd. Social Service. Mem. Christian Action Council S.C. (pres.), S.C. Found. Independent Colls. (pres.), Theta Phi. Club: Masons. Home: Lake Junaluska NC 28745

SPEAS, ROBERT DIXON, aviation cons.; b. Davis County, N.C., Apr. 14, 1916; s. William Paul and Nora Estelle (Dixon) S.; B.S., Mass. Inst. Tech., 1940; grad. Boeing Sch. Aero., 1938; m. Manette Lansing Hollingsworth, Mar. 4, 1944; children—Robert Dixon, Jay Hollingsworth. Aviation reporter Winston Salem Jour., 1934; sales rep. Trans World Airlines, 1937-38; engr. Am. Airlines, 1940-44, asst. to v.p., 1944-47, dir. maintenance and engring., cargo div., 1947-48, spl. asst. to pres., 1948-50; U.S. rep. A.V. Roe Can., Ltd., 1950-51; pres., chmn. bd. R. Dixon Speas Assos., Inc., aviation cons., 1951-76, chmn., chief exec. officer Speas-Harris Airport Devel., Inc., 1974-76; chmn. bd., pres. Aviation Consulting, Inc., 1976—. Mem. pres.'s council Planning Research Corp., 1967-76. Recipient 1st award Ann. Nat. Boeing Thesis Competition, 1937; research award Am. Air Transport Assn., 1942. Fellow Am. Inst. Aeros. and Astronautics (treas. 1963-64, council 1963-64), Royal Aero. Soc.; mem. Soc. Automotive Engrs. (v.p. 1955, mem. council 1964-66), Flight Safety Found. (bd. govs. 1958-66, 78—, exec. com. 1979—), Inst. Aero. Scis. (past treas.; council 1959-62, exec. com. 1962), L.I. Assn. Commerce and Industry (mem. bd.), Manhasset C. of C. (pres. 1962), ASME. Club: Wings (pres. 1968-69, council 1966-71, 73—). Author: Airplane Performance and Operations, 1945; Pilots' Technical Manual, 1946; Airline Operation, 1949; Technical Aspects of Air Transport Management, 1955. Home: 591 Park Ave Manhasset NY 11030 Office: 58 Hillsdale Ave Manhasset NY 11030

SPECHT, CHARLES ALFRED, business cons.; b. Passaic, N.J., July 30, 1914; s. Alfred F. and Marian A. (Clarke) S.; B.B.A., Rutgers U., 1938; postgrad. N.Y. Grad. Sch. Bus. Adminstrn., 1939-40; m. Gertrude A. Morris, Sept. 14, 1940; children—Sara Ann, Sandra Morris. Clk., bookkeeper Am. Surety Co., N.Y.C., 1933-37; credit analyst Irving Trust Co., 1937-42; staff accountant Price Waterhouse Co., 1942-44; chief accountant DeLaval Steam Turbine Co., Trenton, N.J., 1944-45; works controller Joy Mfg. Co., Franklin, Pa., 1945-50; controller Chas. Pfizer & Co., Inc., Bklyn., 1950-52, dir., 1952-55, also pres. fgn. trade subsidiaries, 1952-55; fin. analyst Lazard Freres & Co., N.Y.C., 1955-56; pres., dir. Horizons Titanium Corp., 1955-57; v.p., dir. Horizons, Inc., 1955-56; pres., chief exec. officer, dir. Minerals & Chems. Philipp Corp., 1956-63; pres., dir., mem. exec. com. MacMillan Bloedel Ltd., Vancouver, B.C., 1963-68, dir., mem. exec. com., 1963-72; pres., chief exec. officer, dir., mem. exec. com. Consol. Packaging Corp., Chgo., 1968-73; dir. Interpace Corp., Horizons Research Inc.; dir. Hazeltine Corp. Instr. Rutgers U., 1940-45. Mem. Fin. Execs. Inst. Clubs: Univ. (N.Y.C.); Englewood (N.J.); Vancouver (B.C.). Home: 628 Armada Rd S Venice FL 33595 Office: 535 N Michigan Ave Chicago IL 60611

SPECHT, HARRY, educator; b. N.Y.C., Aug. 1, 1929; s. Joseph and Helen (Frankle) S.; B.A., City Coll. N.Y., 1951; M.S. in Social Adminstrn., Western Res. U., 1953; Ph.D., Brandeis U., 1964; m. Riva Geufan, June 5, 1954; children—Daniel Joseph, Eliot David. Dir., Mt. Vernon Hebrew Camps, Inc., 1956-60; dir. Community orgn. Moblzn. for Youth, N.Y.C., 1962-64; asso. dir. Contra Costa Council of Community Services, Walnut Creek, Calif., 1964-67; prof. social welfare U. Calif., Berkeley, 1967—, dean Sch. Social Welfare, 1977—; editor Prentice-Hall, Inc., Englewood Cliffs, N.J. Sr. Fulbright lectr., London, 1973-74. Author: (with Brager) Community Organizing, 1973; (with Gilbert) Dimensions of Social Welfare Policy, 1974, Dynamics of Community Planning, 1978; (with Vickery) Integration Social Work Methods, 1976. Home: 807 Oxford St Berkeley CA 94707 Office: School of Social Welfare University of California Berkeley CA 94720

SPECK, JOHN EDWARD, periodontist; b. Toronto, Ont., Can., May 22, 1925; s. Lloyd William and Edith Ivy S.; D.D.S., U. Toronto, 1949, diploma in periodontics, 1952; m. Yvonne Jewell, Apr. 7, 1952; children—Michael, David. Gen. practice dentistry, Toronto, 1949-51, practice dentistry specializing in periodontics, Toronto, 1952-66; prof. periodontics U. Toronto, 1952—, chmn. dept. periodontics. Fellow

Royal Coll. Dentists of Can. (registrar and sec.-treas. 1966—), Am. Coll. Dentists; mem. Can. Dental Assn., Ont. Dental Assn., Acad. Dentistry Pierre Fauchard Acad., Can. Acad. Periodontology (past pres.), Am. Acad. Periodontology, Anderson Study Group (past pres.). Mem. United Ch. of Canada. Club: Royal Can. Yacht. Contbr. articles to profl. publs. Home: 39 Citation Dr Willowdale ON M2K 1S5 Canada Office: 614 Med Arts Bldg 170 St George St Toronto ON M5R 2M8 Canada*

SPECK, JOHN KING, lawyer; b. Crawford, Tex., Aug. 4, 1904; s. James Malachi and Mary (King) S.; student Okla. State U., 1921-22; B.S., U. Okla., 1928; LL.B., Oklahoma City U., 1941; m. Lavon Evelyn Gildersleeve, July 14, 1929; children—James Stanley, Carolyn Kay Speck Schnorrenberg, Bonnie Jean Speck Schroer (dec.). Mdse. mgr. Central States Power & Light Co., Stillwater, Okla., 1928-31; commd. agt. Continental Oil Co., Stillwater, 1930-33; owner John K. Speck, accountant, Stillwater, 1931-35; auditor income tax div. Okla. Tax Commn., 1935-37; dir. income tax div. Kans. Tax Commn., 1937-40; admitted to Kans., Okla. bars, 1939; practice in Oklahoma City, 1940—; sr. mem. Speck, Philbin, Fleig, Trudgeon & Lutz, Inc., and predecessor cos., 1955—; instr. Oklahoma City U. Law Sch., 1940-41. Past pres. Oklahoma City Estate Planning Council, Oklahoma City Tax Lawyers Group. Mem. exec. com. and trustee Okla. Med. Research Found.; life trustee, mem. exec. com., chmn. sem. council Phillips U.; trustee Okla. Christian Home Apts., Inc., Okla. Ind. Coll. Found.; founder, trustee, former pres. Okla. Halfway House, Speck Homes, Inc. Recipient Service to Mankind award Oklahoma City Sertoma Club, 1977. Mem. Am., Okla. (past chmn. probate and tax sects.), Oklahoma County bar assns., Okla. Inst. Taxation (founder, dir. past pres.), Oklahoma City C. of C., Okla. Poetry Soc., Oklahoma City Econ. Club, Christian Men's Fellowship (past pres. Okla., past mem. nat. adv. bd.). Republican. Mem. Christian Ch. (Disciples of Christ) (past moderator Okla. region; mem. gen. bd., bd. homeland ministries; elder). Clubs: Masons, Shriners (50 year medal), Men's Dinner, Sooner Dinner, Chandelle, Economic, Petroleum, Lions (past dir.), Fortune (past pres.), Quail Creek Golf and Country, Twin Hills Golf and Country (past treas., dir.) (Oklahoma City). Contbr. articles to profl. jours.; lectr. legal and tax subjects various state and regional bar insts. Home: 1609 Glenbrook Terr Oklahoma City OK 73116 Office: City Nat Bank Tower Oklahoma City OK 73102. *Since the tenth grade I've lived, studied and worked in the genuine belief that every healthy American who has the determination to do so can prepare for and attain success in his chosen field. It works!*

SPECK, MARVIN LUTHER, microbiologist, educator; b. Middletown, Md., Oct. 6, 1913; s. John Luther and Pearl Lighter (Wilhide) S.; B.S., U. Md., 1935, M.S., 1937; Ph.D., Cornell U., 1940; m. Jean Moler Critchlow, Sept. 11, 1940; children—Linda Jean, Martha Loraine, Susan Carol. Instr. microbiology U. Md., 1940-41; asst. chief bacteriologist Nat. Dairy Research Labs., Balt., 1941-47; mem. faculty N.C. State U. at Raleigh, 1947—, prof. food microbiology, 1951—, William Neal Reynolds prof. food sci., 1957—; lectr. Am. Inst. Chem. Engrs., 1978-79; spl. con. USPHS, 1950-62, HEW, 1967-70. Recipient J.M. Jarrett award N.C. Pub. Health Assn. Fellow Am. Acad. Microbiology (bd. govs. 1976), Inst. Food Technologists; mem. Am. Soc. Microbiology (vice chmn. 1976-77, chmn. sect. 1977-78), Am. Dairy Sci. Assn. (Borden award dairy mfg. 1959, Pfizer-Lewis award for research on cheese 1967), Nat. Acad. Scis./NRC, N.C. Dairy Products Assn. (Distinguished Service award 1976), Inst. Food Technologists (nat. lectr. 1968), AAAS, Sigma Xi, Phi Kappa Phi, Gamma Sigma Delta, Alpha Zeta. Presbyterian (elder). Author: (with others) Dairy Microbiology, 1957; editor: Methods for the Microbiological Examination of Foods, 1976; editorial bd. Jour. Dairy Sci., 1953-68. Home: 3204 Churchill Rd Raleigh NC 27607

SPECK, ROBERT HURSEY, cons., ret. naval officer; b. Oskaloosa, Iowa, Nov. 22, 1906; s. Harris Bert and Mildred (Redfern) S.; B.S., U.S. Naval Acad., 1927; student ordnance engring. U.S. Naval Postgrad Sch., 1934-37; grad. Naval War Coll., 1949; m. Martha Blanchard Brackett, June 4, 1936 (dec. 1979); 1 son, Robert Hursey. Commd. ensign U.S. Navy, 1927; advanced through grades to rear adm., 1956; various assignments of sea duty, 1927-59; chmn. ship characteristics bd. Office Chief Naval Operations, Navy Dept., 1959-61; comdr. Cruiser-Destroyer Force, Atlantic Fleet, 1961-63; chief Mil. Assistance Adv. Group, Netherlands, 1963-65, comdt. 4th Naval Dist., 1965-68, ret., 1968; gov. U.S. Naval Home, 1970-74; cons., 1968—. Nat. trustee Freedoms Found.; pres. Independence Hall Assn. Decorated Bronze Star (2) with combat V, Legion of Merit; comdr. Order of Merit (Italy). Clubs: New York Yacht; Union League (sec. boys work found.), Merion Cricket (Phila.); Army-Navy (Washington); Army-Navy Country (Alexandria, Va.). Address: 132 Adrienne Ln Penn Valley Wynnewood PA 19096

SPECTOR, JOHANNA LICHTENBERG, educator; b. Libau, Latvia; d. Jacob C. and Anna (Meyer) Lichtenberg; came to U.S., 1947, naturalized, 1954; D.H.L., Hebrew Union Coll., 1950; M.A., Columbia U., 1960; m. Robert Spector, Nov. 20, 1939 (dec. 1941). Research fellow Hebrew U., Jerusalem, 1951-53; faculty Jewish Theol. Sem. Am., 1954—, dir., founder dept. ethnomusicology, 1962—, asso. prof. musicology, 1966-70, Sem. prof., 1970—. Fellow Am. Anthrop. Assn.; mem. Am. Folklore Soc., Am. Musicological Soc., Internat. Folk Music Council, World Union Jewish Studies, Asian (v.p. 1964—, pres. 1974-78), African mus. socs., Soc. for Ethnomusicology (sec.-treas N.Y.C. chapt. 1960-64), Soc. Preservation of Samaritan Culture (founder). Research in field. Author: Ghetto-und KZLieder, 1947: Samaritan Chant, 1965; Musical Tradition and Innovation in Central Asia, 1966; Bridal Songs from Sana Yemen, 1960; (documentary films) The Samaritans, 1971, Middle Eastern Music, 1973; About the Jews of India: Cochin (Cine Golden Eagle 1979), 1976; The Shanwar Telis or Bene Israel of India (Cine Golden Eagle 1979), 1978; contbr. articles to encys., various jours. Editorial bd. Asian Music. Home: 400 W 119th St New York NY 10027

SPECTOR, JOSEPH ROBERT, diversified mfg. co. exec.; b. N.Y.C., Apr. 16, 1923; s. Benjamin and Julia (Wagner) S.; A.B., Dartmouth Coll., 1946; LL.B., Cornell U., 1952. Admitted to N.Y. bar, 1952, Fla. bar, 1953; asst. counsel Equitable Life Assurance Soc., N.Y.C., 1956-64; asst. gen. counsel Gen. Precision Co., Tarrytown, N.Y., 1964-68; corp. counsel Singer Co., N.Y.C., 1968-70; v.p., gen. counsel, sec. UMC Industries, Inc., Stamford, Conn., 1970—. First v.p. Assn. Greenwich Village Homeowners, N.Y.C.; trustee No. Dispensary. Served with USNR, 1942-46. Mem. Am., Fed. bar assns., Assn. Bar City N.Y. Club: Plaza (N.Y.C.). Office: UMC Industries Inc Box 1090 High Ridge Park Stamford CT 06904

SPECTOR, LAWRENCE, advt. agy. exec.; b. Bklyn., Feb. 21, 1929; s. Samuel and Sarah (Goldberg) S.; B.B.A., City Coll. N.Y., 1950; LL.B., Bklyn. Law Sch., 1953; m. Shirley Ellman, Jan. 2, 1954; children—Nancie, David. Admitted to N.Y. bar; pvt. practice law; exec. v.p., treas., sec. Delehanty, Kurnit & Geller, Inc. (co. name changed to DKG, Inc.), N.Y.C., 1958-70, pres., 1970—, chief exec. officer, 1977—. Served with AUS, 1955-57. Home: 105 Wildwood Rd Great Neck NY 11024 Office: 1271 Ave of Americas New York NY 10017

SPECTOR, LOUIS, fed. judge; b. Niagara Falls, N.Y., Apr. 4, 1918; s. Jacob and Gussie (Yochelson) S.; student (N.Y. State scholar) Niagara U., 1936-37; LL.B. with honors, U. Buffalo (later State U. N.Y.), 1940; m. Judith Lee Aland, Sept. 19, 1972; children—Gale Anne Spector Pasternack, Arthur George, James Aland. Admitted to N.Y. bar, 1940, D.C. bar, 1972, U.S. Supreme Ct. bar, 1971, U.S. Ct. Claims bar, 1968; asso. firm Saperston, McNaughton & Saperston, Buffalo, 1941-42; asst. chief legal div. U.S. Army C.E., Buffalo Dist., 1942-43, chief sect. claims appeals and litigation Gt. Lakes Div., Chgo., 1946, chief legal br. and real estate div. Buffalo Dist., 1946-53, mem. Bd. Contract Appeals, Washington, 1954-59; exec. dir. Buffalo Port Authority, 1953-54; chmn. Army panel Armed Services Bd. Contract Appeals, Washington, 1959-62, chmn. Unified Armed Services Bd. Contract Appeals, 1962-68; trial judge U.S. Ct. Claims, Washington, 1968—; lectr., speaker, writer public contracts; Congressional appearances, 1953, 66, 69, 77. Served with C.E., U.S. Army, 1943-46. Recipient Freshman medal Bishop Buffalo Diocese for Niagara U., 1936, Sophomore medal, 1937. Fellow Am. Bar Found.; mem. Am. (chmn. sect. pub. contract law 1967-68, ho. of dels. 1968-70), Fed. (gen. editor jour. 1960-74, nat. chmn. com. govt. contracts and procurement law 1961-63, Distinguished Service award D.C. chpt. 1974) bar assns., Nat. Contract Mgmt. Assn. (nat. bd. advisers 1967—), Scribes, Lincoln Law Soc. (alumni pres. 1951). Club: Cosmos. Contbr. articles to profl. publs. Home: 6219 Beachway Dr Falls Church VA 22041 Office: 717 Madison Pl NW Washington DC 20005. *The concept of justice has been a central concern of my life. It is not a unique concern. Daniel Webster described it as "the great interest of man on earth . . . the ligament which holds civilized beings and nations together." And Reinhold Neibuhr reflected that: "Man's capacity for justice makes democracy possible; but man's inclination to injustice makes democracy necessary." It is a great privilege to seek as part of mankind the same concept of justice required by my oath of office.*

SPECTOR, MELBOURNE LOUIS, cons.; b. Pueblo, Colo., May 7, 1918; s. Joseph E. and Dora (Bernstein) S.; B.A. with honors, U. N.Mex., 1941; m. Louise Vincent, Nov. 23, 1948; 1 son, Stephen David. Intern, U.S. Bur. Indian Affairs, 1941, Nat. Inst. Pub. Affairs, 1941; personnel asst. Office Emergency Mgmt., 1941-42; chief classification div. War Relocation Authority, 1942-43, Hdqrs. USAAF, 1943-45; employment officer UNRRA, 1945-46; pvt. employment, 1946-47; personnel officer Dept. State, 1947-49; dep. dir. personnel ECA, Marshall Plan, Paris, 1949-51, dep. dir., acting dir. personnel Econ. Adminstrn., Mut. Security Adminstrn., FOA, 1951-54, asst., dep. dir. Mission to Mexico, ICA, 1954-57, acting dir., 1957-59; chief C. Am., Mex. and Caribbean div. ICA, 1959-61, dir. Office Personnel Mgmt., AID, 1961-62; exec. dir. Bur. Inter-Am. Affairs, Dept. State, 1962-64; commd. fgn. service officer, 1964; counselor for adminstrv. affairs Am. embassy, New Delhi, India, 1964-66; seminarian Sr. Seminar Fgn. Policy, Dept. State, 1966-67; exec. dir. U.S.-Mex. Commn. for Border Devel. and Friendship, 1967-69; exec. dir. Am. Revolution Bicentennial Commn., 1969-71; mem. policy and coordination staff Dept. State, 1971-73; ret., 1973; cons., 1973—; mem. Fgn. Service Grievance Bd., 1976-77. Mem. Am. Soc. Pub. Adminstrn., Phi Kappa Alpha, Phi Kappa Phi. Home: 6414 Bannockburn Dr Bethesda MD 20034

SPECTOR, NORMAN BERNARD, educator; b. Phila., Jan. 2, 1921; s. Morris and Sophie (Edelman) S.; B.S., U. Pa., 1940, M.S., 1942, Ph.D., 1950; postgrad. U. Paris, 1950-51; children—Robert David, Miriam. Instr. romance langs. U. Pa., 1947-50; instr. romance langs. Northwestern U., Evanston, Ill., 1952-55, asst. prof., 1955-59, prof. French, chmn. dept. French and Italian, 1968-78; asst. prof. romance langs. U. Chgo., 1959-63, asso. prof., 1963-66; vis. asso. prof. Yale, 1964-65; prof. French, chmn. dept. romance langs. Oberlin (Ohio) Coll., 1966-68. Mem. selection com. Woodrow Wilson Nat. Fellowship Found., Region IX, 1962-64, 65-66, Region II, 1964-65. Served with USAAF, 1942-46. Recipient Fulbright award for study in France, 1950-51. U. Pa. Jusserand Traveling fellow in romance langs., 1950-51. Mem. Medieval Acad. Am., Renaissance Soc. Am., AAUP, Modern Lang. Assn. Am., Am. Assn. Tchrs. French. Author: Odet de Turnebe: Les Contens, 1961, rev. edit., 1964; The Romance of Tristan and Isolt, 1973. Contbr. articles to profl. jours. Home: 1925 Sherman Ave Evanston IL 60201

SPECTOR, PHIL, record producer; b. Bronx, N.Y., Dec. 26, 1940; student UCLA; m. Veronica Bennett, 1968 (div. 1974); children—Gary Phillip and Louis Phillip (twins), Donte Phillip. Mem. mus. group Teddy Bears, 1958-59; producer with Atlantic Records, 1960-61; founder Philles Records, 1962; now pres. Warner-Spector Records, Inc., also Mother Bertha Music; producer records for Gene Pitney, Ike and Tina Turner, Ben E. King, the Beatles, Righteous Bros., Checkmates, Crystals, Ronettes, others; producer album A Concert for Bangladesh (Grammy award); composer To Know Him is to Love Him, Spanish Harlem, River Deep, Mountain High, You've Lost That Lovin' Feelin', others; appeared in films Easy Rider, The TNT Movie, TAMI; prod. TV documentary film A Giant Stands 5 Ft. 7 In. Office: care Warner-Spector Records Inc PO Box 69529 Los Angeles CA 90069

SPECTOR, ROBERT DONALD, educator; b. N.Y.C., Sept. 21, 1922; s. Morris and Helen (Spiegel) S.; B.A., L.I. U., 1948; M.A., N.Y. U., 1949; Ph.D., Columbia U., 1962; m. Eleanor Helen Luskin, Aug. 19, 1945; children—Stephen Brett, Eric Charles. Instr., L.I. U., Bklyn., 1948-59, asst. prof., 1959-62, asso. prof., 1962-65, prof. English, 1965—, chmn. dept., 1970-75, dir. humanities and communication arts, 1975—, chmn. senate, 1966-67, 69-70; editor, cons. Johnson Reprint Corp., 1967—. Trustee L.I. U., 1969-70. Served with USCGR, 1942-46. Swedish Govt. travel and research grantee, 1966; fellow Huntington Library, 1974; fellow Folger Library, 1975, Newberry Library, 1976. Mem. Modern Lang. Assn., Am.-Scandinavian Found. (publs. com. 1962—), P.E.N. Author: English Literary Periodicals, 1966; Tobias George Smollett, 1968; Pär Lagerkvist, 1973; Arthur Murphy, 1979; editor: Essays on the Eighteenth Century Novel, 1965; Great British Short Novels, 1970; 9 other vols. English and Am. lit., revs. and articles. Home: 1761 E 26th St Brooklyn NY 11229

SPECTOR, SAMUEL, pediatrician; b. Bklyn., Mar. 11, 1914; s. William Zeidel and Rose (Krapko) S.; B.S., Columbia U., 1934; M.D., L.I. Coll. Medicine, 1937; m. Lillian Hutchinson, July 24, 1943; children—Judith Ann, Susan Yancey Spector Wegelin, Michael Lew. Intern, Beth El Hosp., Bklyn., 1937-38, Kingston Ave. Hosp., Bklyn., 1938; resident Willard Parker Hosp., N.Y.C., 1939-41; resident in pediatrics U. Mich. Hosp., Ann Arbor, 1941-42; instr. pediatrics U. Mich., 1942-43; asst. prof. pediatrics Case Western Res. U., Cleve., 1946-51, asso. prof., 1951-60, prof., 1960-70; dir. pediatrics, research and devel. Children's Hosp., Akron, Ohio, 1967-70; prof. pediatrics U. Chgo., 1970—, chmn. dept., 1973-79; prof. pediatrics U. Calif., San Diego, 1979—; dir. pediatrics Wyler Children's Hosp. U. Chgo. Hosps. and Clinics, 1970-79; dir. LaRabida Children's Hosp. and Research Center, Chgo., 1974-1978; dir. pediatric ed. U. Calif., San Diego Med. Center 1979—. Bd. dirs. Home for Destitute Crippled Children, Chgo., 1974—. Served as lt. M.C., USNR, 1944-46. Recipient McClintock award U. Chgo., 1971. Diplomate Am. Bd. Pediatrics. Mem. Am. Acad. Pediatrics, Soc. Pediatric Research, Chgo. Pediatric Soc., Soc. Human Genetics, Am. Pediatric Soc., Sigma Xi, Alpha Omega Alpha. Contbr. articles to profl. jours. Home: 3310 Via Alicante La Jolla CA 92037. *Motivation, Dedication and Persistence.*

SPECTOR, STANLEY, educator; b. N.Y.C., June 10, 1924; s. Irving and Sophie (Braun) S.; B.S., Coll. City N.Y., 1945; Ph.D., U. Wash., 1953; postgrad. London Sch. Oriental and African Studies, 1950-51; m. Betty Peishan Yue, Mar. 8, 1963; children— Pat Lee, Stephanie Spector Van Denberg, Lee Paul, Jon Marc. Instr. history Coll. City N.Y., 1946; instr. Far Eastern history U. Wash., 1951- 52, asst. prof., 1955; lectr. in history U. Calif., Los Angeles, 1953; lectr. in history, post-certificate class Chung Cheng Chung Hsueh, Singapore, 1954; asst. prof. Far Eastern history Washington U., St. Louis, 1955-58, asso. prof., 1959-64, asso. prof. Chinese history, 1964-65, prof. Chinese studies, 1965—, chmn. dept. Chinese and Japanese, 1964-72, dir. East Asian Lang. and Area Center, 1964, dir. Office Internat. Studies, 1969; vis. prof. Chinese and Japanese history Columbia U., 1962; vis. prof. U. Singapore, summers 1967-69, 71-73, Waseda U., Tokyo, 1966-67, IKIP U., Bandung, Indonesia, summer 1969. Chmn. Seattle chpt. Am. Vets. Com., 1948-49; co-chmn. Citizens for Stevenson, Seattle, 1952. Served with USNR, 1942-43. Social Sci. Research Council fellow, 1950-51, 58-59; Ford Found. fellow, 1953-55; Social Sci. Research Council (Toyo Bunko), 1966-67; Fulbright research scholar, Japan, People's Republic of China, Hong Kong, Singapore, Malaysia, 1966-67, USSR, 1975-76. Mem. AAUP, Midwest Conf. on Asian Studies (pres. 1967-68), Chinese Lang. Tchrs. Assn. (pres. 1971—), Am. Polit Sci. Assn., Assn. Asian Studies, Am. Hist. Assn., Internat. Studies Assn. Author: Li Hung-chang and the Huai Army, 1964; co-editor: Guide to the Memorials of Seven Leading Officials of the 19th Century China, 1955. Home: 50 Arundel Pl Clayton MO 63105 Office: Box 1088 Washington U Saint Louis MO 63130

SPEECE, HERBERT ELVIN, educator; b. Meadowlands, Minn., Oct. 29, 1914; s. Ray M. and Grace (Lytle) S.; A.B., York Coll., 1938; M.A., Tex. Christian U., 1943; M.S., N.C. State U., 1951; Ph.D., U. N.C., 1956; m. Ruth E. Lowrance, July 28, 1945; children—Ray Elvin, Deborah Grace. Tchr. sci. Tivy High Sch., Kerrville, Tex., 1946-47; instr. physics Trinity U., San Antonio, summer 1947; instr. math. N.C. State U., Raleigh, 1947-56, asst. prof., asso. prof. math., 1956-62, prof. math. and sci. edn., 1962—, chmn. dept. math. and sci. edn., 1952—; dir. NSF Acad. Insts., NSF Acad. Earth Sci. Project; dir. engring. concepts curriculum project Implementation Center for Southeast, 1970-73. Chmn. in-service con. Edn. Council State Bd. Edn., 1962—; dir. N.C. Student Acad. Sci.; mem. U.S. subcom. Internat. Center Cybernetics and Systems. Served with USAAF, 1942-45. Recipient W.W. Rankin award N.C. Council Tchrs. Math., 1977. Mem. Math. Assn. Am., Nat. Sci. Tchrs. Assn., Nat. Council Tchrs. Math., N.C. Acad. Sci. (pres. 1970-71), Phi Kappa Phi, Kappa Phi Kappa, Pi Mu Epsilon. Methodist. Mason. Home: 3408 Wade Ave Raleigh NC 27607

SPEED, BILLIE CHENEY (MRS. THOMAS S. SPEED), journalist; b. Birmingham, Ala., Feb. 21, 1927; d. John J. and Ruby (Petty) Cheney; grad. W.Ga. Coll.; children—Kathy Lovell Windham, Donna Lovell, Melanie Lovell Stanco; m. 2d, Thomas S. Speed, July 7, 1968. Reporter, Birmingham News, 1945; sports writer, gen. assignment reporter, ch. editor Atlanta Jour., 1947-53, with promotion dept., 1955-57, ch. editor, 1965—; feature editor Coach and Athlete Mag., 1958, So. Outdoors, 1958. Recipient Sharp Tack award Cumberland dist. Seventh Day Adventists; Spl. Service award Christian Council of Metro Atlanta, 1974; Arthur West award for religious feature writing United Meth. Ch., 1977. Fellow Religious Pub. Relations Council; mem. Nat. Religion Newswriters Assn., Theta Sigma Chi. Methodist. Home: 559 Rays Rd Stone Mountain GA 30083 Office: 72 Marietta St Atlanta GA 30302

SPEED, EDWIN MAURICE, periodontist, coll. dean; b. Enterprise, Miss., Aug. 17, 1918; s. Benjamin Thomas and Lela Alma (Davis) S.; B.A., Birmingham So. Coll., 1950; student Trinity U., 1946-47; D.M.D., U. Ala., 1954, M.S., 1965; postgrad. Cumberland Law Sch., 1965-66; m. Adele Marie House, Aug. 16, 1941; children—Edwin Michael, Ann Marie. Pvt. practice dentistry specializing in periodontics, Birmingham, Ala., 1954—; mem. faculty Sch. Dentistry U. Ala., Birmingham, 1965—, asso. prof., 1968—, asst. dean, 1966—. Pres., S. Hill Corp., real estate devel., Birmingham, 1970—. Active United Appeal. Mem. Park and Recreation Bd., 1960-72; mem. City Council Bestavia Hills, Ala., 1960-72, pres., 1960-64. Bd. dirs. Vestavia Library, 1960-72. Served with USAAF, 1941-45, USAF, 1961-62; col. Res. (ret.). Decorated Air medal with 5 oak leaf clusters and 1 silver cluster. Mem. Ala. Dental Assn. (trustee 1967-69), ADA (council on nat. bd. examiners), Am. Assn. Dental Schs. (pres. 1973-74), Am. Acad. Periodontology, Kappa Alpha, Delta Sigma Delta, Omicron Kappa Upsilon, Omicron Delta Kappa. Roman Catholic. Contbr. to profl. jours. Home: 2134 Lynngate Dr Birmingham AL 35216 Office: School of Dentistry University of Alabama Union Station Birmingham AL 35294 also 1516 Center Point Rd Birmingham AL 35215

SPEER, DAVID GORDON, educator; b. Oak Park, Ill., Nov. 16, 1913; s. George Scott and Dorothy (Niver) S.; B.A., U. Chgo., 1937, M.A., 1939; Docteur d'universite, U. Montpellier (France), 1953; m. Ginette Bastien, Nov. 17, 1945; 1 son, John-Michael. Asst. headmaster Pistakee Bay Sch., McHenry, Ill., 1939-41; instr. modern langs. Miss. State U., 1941-42; head, modern langs. St. Helena Extension, Coll. William and Mary, 1947-48; instr. to asso. prof., chmn. French, Purdue U., 1948-66; prof. fgn. langs. and lits. U. S.C., Columbia, 1966-79, head dept., 1966-72, emeritus prof. French, 1979—; vis. prof. U. Strasbourg (France), 1959. Served from pvt. to maj. AUS, 1942-47. Mem. Am. Assn. Tchrs. French, Modern Lang. Assn., Am. Name Soc., South Atlantic Modern Lang. Assn. Author: (with Ginette Speer) A la belle étoile, 1970; also articles. Home: 6111 Cedar Ridge Rd Columbia SC 29206

SPEER, DAVID JAMES, pub. relations co. exec.; b. Mpls., Apr. 30, 1927; s. Ray Patterson and Grace Elizabeth (Kane) S.; B.A. in Polit. Sci., U. Minn., 1950. Sports reporter Mpls. Tribune, 1945-50; night radio editor AP, Mpls., 1950-51; partner Speer's Publicity Service, Mpls., 1950-59; pres. Sullivan & Speer, Inc., Mpls., 1959-61; sr. v.p. Padilla, Sarjeant, Sullivan & Speer, Inc., Mpls., 1961-71, pres., sec., 1971—; pub. relations cons., Mpls., N.Y.C., Los Angeles, 1961—; pub. relations dir. Minn. State Fair, 1961-68, St. Paul Winter Carnival Assn., 1952-70. Bd. dirs. Mpls. Area Red Cross, St. Paul Chamber Orch., Hennepin County chpt. Am. Lung Assn. Served with USN, 1945-46. Mem. Pub. Relations Soc. Am. (chpt. pres. 1967, mem. midwest jud. panel 1967-71), U. Minn. Alumni Assn. (pres. 1975-76), Psi Upsilon (pres. 1967, dir.). Club: Minn. Press (dir. 1965-66); Mpls. Athletic. Home: 1400 Alpine Pass Golden Valley MN 55416 Office: 224 W Franklin Ave Minneapolis MN 55404

SPEER, EUGENE EAVEN, JR., med. center dir.; b. Decatur, Ala., Nov. 10, 1911; s. Eugene Eaven and Emma (Shoemaker) S.; B.S., Athens Coll., 1937; student U. Ala., 1935-38; m. Jessie M. Pridmore, Mar. 1, 1946 (dec. 1977). Tchr., Decatur (Ala.) pub. schs., 1933-38, prin., 1938-41, vocat. adviser, 1937-38; first aid and water safety field rep. East-Coast Am. Nat. Red Cross, 1941-42; with VA, 1946—, nat. dir. med. adminstrn., 1963-66, hosp. dir., Louisville, 1966-69, Buffalo,

1969-71, Augusta, Ga., 1971—; vis. lectr., preceptor George Washington U. Grad. Sch. Health Care Adminstrn.; preceptor health care adminstrv. residents U. Ottawa; faculty Med. Coll. Ga. Dir. numerous community agy. bds. including bd. dirs. E. Central Ga. Health Services Agy. Served to capt. AUS, 1942-46. Recipient citations V.F.W., Am. Legion, D.A.V., Paralyzed Vets. Am.; named Fed. Civil Servant of Year Greater Kansas City Area, 1962. mem. Fellow Am. Coll. Hosp. Adminstrs.; Am. Legion, D.A.V. (life), Nat. Council Tchrs. Math. (Ala. pres. 1937), Tenn. Valley Council Tchrs. Math., Am., Western N.Y. hosp. assns., Assn. Mil. Surgeons U.S., Fed. Exec. Assn. (pres. 1969, dir. Frontier Niagara chpt. 1970-71), Greater Augusta Hosp. Adminstrs. (chmn.). Kiwanian. Club: Civitan. Home: VA Med Center Augusta GA 30904

SPEER, TALBOT TAYLOR, publisher; b. Pitts., Jan. 7, 1895; s. John L. Dawson and Margaret (Taylor) S.; student Brennens and Bradshaw Schs., Pitts. 1900-07; student Episcopal High Sch., Alexandria, Va., 1907-13, U. Va., 1913-15, U. Md., 1915-16; LL.D., U. Balt., 1974; m. Mary Washington Stewart, Dec. 8, 1920 (dec. 1926); 1 dau., Mary Washington; m. 2d, Louise Pierce Leetch, Nov. 1928 (div.); children—Louise Pierce, Margaret Taylor, Eleanor Talbot; m. 3d, Jane Turner, Oct. 5, 1943; children—Talbot Taylor, J.L. Dawson, Jane Alexander, Ramsey Clarke. Salesman, The Daniel Miller Co., Balt., 1919-21; asst. to pres. Balt. Salesbrook Co., 1922, pres. and chmn. of bd., 1922—; pres., chmn. bd. The Capital-Gazette Press, Annapolis, Md., 1926, pub. since 1926 of Daily Evening Capital, Md. Gazette, So. Md. Times, U.S. Coast Guard Mag., Chesapeake Skipper, Prince George County News (Md.), Capital-Gazette News, Ann Arundel County, Md.; pres. Speer Pubs., 1951—; pub. St. Mary's Beacon, Waldorf Leaf; dir. Union Trust Co. Med., 1947—. Founder, pres. Nat. Ednl. Found, Inc., Balt., pres. Talbot T. Speer Found., Inc., 1951-75. Dir. Balt. Assn. of Commerce, 1935-40, Balt. Conv. Bur., 1946-48, County Taxpayers League, 1945—. Dir. U.S. Naval Acad. Found., 1950-54, mem. higher edn. com. Md., 1945—, prison bd., 1948-50; mem. W.P.B., 1940-45; Indsl. Moblzn. Com. since 1950, U.S. Army Adv. Com. since 1947. Served as 2d lt., U.S. Army, with Am. 1st div. in France, 1917-18; resigned with rank of capt., 1918. Decorated Purple Heart, Silver Star (U.S.) Fourrogere Croix de Guerre (France); cited by U.S. Govt., certificate of merit for services to Nat. War Effort; recipient Certificate Distinguished Citizenship for 40 yrs. outstanding Service as leading newspaper pub., industrialist and philanthropist Gov. Md., 1965, 73, Mayor Balt., 1973. Mem. N.A.M. (sr. dir., rep. Md., 1947-50), Splty. Accounting Supply Mfrs. Assn. dir. Asso. Industries Md. (pres., dir. 1949-51), Newcomen Soc. (award 1961), Mil. Order Fgn. Wars, Salesbook Mfrs. Assn, Alumni Assn. U. Md. (pres. 1950-52), Soc. 1st div. A.E.F., Am. Legion, Mems. of the Purple Heart, Delta Psi. Episcopalian (mem. lay council procathedral of Md. 1925-54). Clubs: Rotary, Maryland, Bachelors Cotillion, Elkridge Kennels, Greenspring Valley Hunt, Carrollton Hounds, Wythmore Hounds, Baltimore Country, Annapolis Yacht, Annapolitan, St. Anthony, Lake Placid, Everglades, Nat. Press, Gulf Stream Golf; Rolling Rock (Ligonier, Pa.); Delray Beach (Fla.) Bath and Tennis. Winner sr. amateur golf championship of Md., 1946. Home: 2817 N Ocean Blvd Delray Beach FL 33444

SPEERS, FRANCIS JOSEPH, fgn. service officer; b. Toronto, Ont., Can., Mar. 2, 1920 (parents Am. citizens); s. Charles Krepps and Kathleen Agnes (Connolly) S.; student Pratt Tech. Inst., 1947; m. Alice Marie Campbell, Aug. 27, 1955; children—Michael Campbell, Mark Christopher. Joined U.S. Fgn. Service, 1947; assigned Bankok Thailand, 1948-50, Rome, Italy, 1950-55, Saigon, Vietnam, 1955-57, Tokyo, Japan, 1957-60, Athens, Greece, 1960-63; with regional mgmt. br. Office Communications, State Dept., 1963-67; assigned Bonn, Germany, 1967-70. Mem. Montgomery County (Md.) Bi-Partisan Com. Pub. Sch. Edn., 1964—; active Leukemia Fund Drive Montgomery County, 1964. Served with AUS, 1942-46. Address: 129 W Orange Grove Ave Arcadia CA 91006

SPEERS, JERROLD BOND, lawyer, state ofcl.; b. Cambridge, Mass., June 5, 1941; s. Ronald Thomas and Shirley Helen (Bond) S.; B.A., Colby Coll., 1963; LL.B., Georgetown U., 1966. Admitted to Maine bar, 1966; asso. firm Ralph M. Clark, Gardiner, Maine, 1966-67, Locke, Campbell & Chapman, Augusta, Maine, 1967-69, Lipman & Gingras, Augusta, 1972-74; partner firm Gingras, Speers & Gasink, Augusta, 1974-79; treas. State of Maine, Augusta, 1979—; sec. Maine Senate, Augusta, 1966-69, senator, 1973-79, majority leader, 1975-79; spl. asst. to asst. sec. ednl. and cultural affairs Dept. State, Washington, 1969-70. Bd. dirs. Maine Law Enforcement Planning and Assistance Agy., 1973-75, mem. grants com., 1974-75; mem. Maine Health Study Commn., 1974, Maine Commn. Interstate Coop., 1975-79, Atlantic States Marine Fisheries Commn., 1975-79; mem. adv. com. Jud. Records, 1975—; chmn. Legis. Council, 1975-77; del. to People's Republic of China, Nat. Conf. State Legislatures, 1976, mem. exec. com., 1977-78; U.S. del. Atlantic Alliance Young Polit. Leaders, NATO, Brussels, 1977; coll. chmn. for Maine, Young Republicans Nat. Fedn., 1961-62, nat. committeeman, 1962-64, nat. officer, 1963-65, nat. auditor, 1965; alt. del. Rep. Nat. Conv., 1964, del., 1968, 72; mem. Rep. Nat. Platform Com., 1972; trustee U. New Eng., 1978—, chmn. bd. trustees, 1979—. Mem. Am. Bar Assn., Kennebec Bar Assn., Am. Judicature Soc. Congregationalist. Club: Lions. Office: State House Augusta ME 04333

SPEERS, ROLAND ROOT, II, corp. exec.; b. Jacksonville, Fla., Oct. 8, 1933; s. Roland Root and Alice (Calkins) S.; B.A. cum laude, U. Calif. at Los Angeles, 1955, J.D., 1958; m. Florence Briscoe, Dec. 18, 1954; children—Kirsten, Guy, Gina Marie. Admitted to Calif. bar, 1958; dep. commr. corps. Calif. Dept. Corps., Los Angeles, 1958-59; sec., gen. counsel Suburban Cos., Pomona, Calif., 1959-64; sec., gen. counsel Amcord, Inc., Los Angeles, 1964-67, asst. to pres., 1967, v.p. corp. devel., 1968, v.p., gen. counsel, Newport Beach, Calif., 1970, sr. v.p., 1971, exec. v.p., 1972-75, pres., 1975-77; individual practice law, Newport Beach, 1977—; practiced in Pasadena, Calif., 1969; dir. Logicon, Inc., Torrance, Calif., Amcord, Newport Beach. Trustee Pitzer Coll., Pomona, 1975—; bd. councillors Center Pub. Affairs U. So. Calif., 1976—; bd. dirs. Newport Harbor Art Mus., 1977—. Mem. State Bar Calif., Los Angeles County Bar Assn., U. Calif. at Los Angeles, U. Calif. at Los Angeles Law Sch. alumni assns., Phi Alpha Delta. Clubs: Big Canyon Country (Newport Beach); Univ. (Los Angeles). Office: 660 Newport Center Dr Suite 1375 Newport Beach CA 92660

SPEIDEL, DAVID HAROLD, educator; b. Pottsville, Pa., Aug. 10, 1938; s. Harold O. and Edith M. (Rosser) S.; B.S., Franklin and Marshall Coll., Lancaster, Pa., 1960; Ph.D., Pa. State U., 1964; m. Margaret Helen Liebrecht, Sept. 8, 1962. Research asso. Pa. State U., 1964-66; asst. prof. to prof. dept. earth and environ. sci. Queens Coll., City U. N.Y., Flushing, 1966—, dean faculty sci., 1970-79; vis. scholar Sr. Specialists div. Congl. Research Service, Washington, 1977-78. Mem. Geol. Soc. Am., Am. Ceramic Soc., Mineral. Soc. Am., Am. Geophys. Union, AAAS, Sigma Xi. Contbr. articles to profl. jours. Home: 141-17 228th St Laurelton NY 11413 Office: Queens Coll Dept Earth and Environmental Scis Flushing NY 11367

SPEIDEL, JOHN JOSEPH, physician, govt. ofcl.; b. Iowa City, Iowa, Sept. 17, 1937; s. Thomas Dennis and Edna (Warweg) S.; A.B. cum laude, Harvard U., 1959, M.D., 1963, M.P.H., 1965; m. Brook Seawell, July 11, 1967; 1 dau., Sabrina Brett. Intern St. Luke's Hosp., N.Y.C., 1963-64; resident N.Y.C. Dept. Health, 1965-67, dep. dir. maternal and infant care project, 1966-67; chief research div. Office of Population, AID, Dept. State, Washington, 1969-76, asso. dir. Office of Population, 1977, dep. dir. office, 1978—; lectr. population and family planning Georgetown U., 1973-75. Served to maj. U.S. Army, 1967-69. Recipient Meritorious Unit citation Office of Population, 1969-71, Arthur S. Flemming award Washington Downtown Jaycees, 1972. Diplomate Nat. Bd. Med. Examiners, Am. Bd. Preventive Medicine. Mem. Am. Pub. Health Assn., Population Assn. Am., Assn. Planned Parenthood Physicians, Soc. Study Reproduction, Internat. Union Sci. Study Population, Soc. Study Fertility, Am. Fertility Soc. Contbr. articles to profl. jours. Editor: (with others) Female Sterilization, 1971; Hysteroscopic Sterilization, 1974; Intrauterine Devices, 1974; Control of Male Fertility, 1975; Advances in Female Sterilization Technology, 1976; Risks, Benefits and Controversies in Fertility Control, 1978. Home: 2531 Eye St NW Washington DC 20037 Office: Office of Population AID Dept State Washington DC 20523

SPEIDEL, RICHARD ELI, univ. adminstr., lawyer; b. Cin., May 27, 1933; s. Russell Frazier and Grace (Jarbo) S.; B.A., Denison U., 1954; J.D., U. Cin., 1957; LL.M., Northwestern U., 1958; m. Dorothy Jean Dennett, Sept. 4, 1954; children—Rae Ann, Richard Scott. Admitted to Ohio bar, 1958, Va. bar, 1968; teaching asso. Northwestern U. Law Sch., 1957-58; asst. prof. law U. Va., 1961-63, asso. prof. law, 63-66, prof. law, 1966-70, Doherty prof., 1970-77; dean, prof. Boston U. Sch. Law, 1977—; vis. prof. U. Calif., Berkeley, 1965-66; sr. Fulbright lectr. in law and and guest prof. U. Vienna (Austria), 1974-75; cons. in field. Trustee, Denison U., 1971—. Served as capt. JAGC, USAR, 1958-61. Decorated D.S.M. Recipient Emil Brown Preventive Law award Emil Brown Found., 1964. Mem. Am. Bar Assn., Am. Law Inst., Order of Coif. Democrat. Methodist. Author: (with E.J. Murphy) Studies in Contract Law, 1970, 2d. revised edit., 1977; (with R.S. Summers and J.J. White) Commercial and Consumer Transactions, 1969, 2d revised edit., 1974; contbr. numerous articles to law jours. Home: 31 Brook St Wellesley MA 02181 Office: 765 Commonwealth Ave Boston MA 02215

SPEIER, CHRIS EDWARD, profl. baseball player; b. Alameda, Calif., June 28, 1950; s. Wesley Howard and Marceen May (Kindred) S.; student U. Calif. at Santa Barbara, 1969-70, Laney Jr. Coll., Oakland, Calif., 1971; m. Aleta Camille Pagnini, Oct. 14, 1972; children—Justin James, Erika Lynne, Luke Wesley. Profl. baseball player with San Francisco Giants, 1970-77, Montreal Expos Baseball Ltd., 1977-79; life ins. salesman, 1974—; marriage encounter tchr. Mem. All-Star team, 1972, 73, 74. Founder, Athletes for Life.

SPEIER, JOHN L., chemist; b. Chgo., Sept. 29, 1918; s. John L. and Mary Jane (Dickman) S.; B.Sc., St. Benedict's Coll., 1941; M.Sc., U. Fla., 1943; Ph.D., U. Pitts., 1947; m. A. Louise Kimmel, Oct. 21, 1944; children—Susan, Genevieve, Dorothy, Margaret, John L., III. Naval Stores research fellow U. Fla., 1941-43; research fellow Mellon Inst., Pitts., 1943, sr. fellow, 1947-56; mgr. organic research Dow Corning Corp., Midland, Mich., 1956-69, scientist in corp. research, 1969-75, sr. scientist in corp. research, 1975—. Named Indsl. Research and Devel. Scientist of Yr., Indsl. Research/Devel. mag., 1978. Mem. Am. Chem. Soc., AAAS, Sigma Xi. Contbr. numerous articles to profl. jours., 1950-78; patentee in field, especially on methods to make organosilicon compounds or new ways to react them to make new products. Office: Dow Corning Corp Midland MI 48640

SPEISER, MARVIN M., mfg. co. exec.; b. N.Y.C., Aug. 22, 1925; s. Julius and Yetta (Booxbaum) S.; B.B.A., Coll. City N.Y., 1941-45; M.B.A., U. Pa., 1946; student Columbia, 1951; m. Laura Green, Nov. 25, 1948; children—Robert, Gregory. Prodn. mgr. Lightolier, Inc., Jersey City, N.J., 1959-62; sr. v.p. Standard Industries, Inc., N.Y.C., New Eng. Industries, Inc., N.Y.C., 1962-68; dir., mem. exec. com., chmn. acquisition com. Lehigh Valley Industries, 1964-68; chmn. bd. Herculite Products, Inc.; chmn. bd., chief exec. officer, dir. Health-Chem Corp.; chmn. bd., chief exec. officer Medallion Group, 1969—. Home: 35 E 84th St New York NY 10028 Office: 1107 Broadway New York NY 10010

SPEISER, STUART MARSHALL, lawyer; b. N.Y.C., June 4, 1923; s. Joseph and Anne (Jonath) S.; student U. Pa., 1939-42; LL.B., Columbia, 1948; m. Mary J. McCormick, Feb. 12, 1950; 1 son, James Joseph. Admitted to N.Y. bar, 1948, since practiced in N.Y.C.; mem. Speiser, Shumate, Geoghan & Krause, 1957-68; mem. firm Speiser, Shumate, Geoghan, Krause & Rheingold, 1968-70, Speiser & Krause, P.C., 1971—. Chmn. bd. Aerial Application Corp., 1968-71, Hydrophilics Internat., 1971-77. Hon. atty. gen., La., 1958—. Pilot USAAF, 1943-46. Fellow Internat. Soc. Barristers; mem. Am. Bar Assn., N.Y. County Lawyers Assn. (chmn. subcom. law outer space 1958—), Am. Trial Lawyers Assn. (chmn. aviation law 1955-64), Am. Inst. Aeros. and Astronautics (asso.). Author: Preparation Manual for Aviation Negligence Cases, 1958; Death in the Air, 1957; Liability Problems in Airline Crash Cases, 1957; Private Airplane Accidents, 1958; Speiser's Negligence Jury Charges, 1960; Speiser's Aviation Law Guide, 1962; Lawyers Aviation Handbook, 1964; Recovery for Wrongful Death, 2d edit., 1975; Lawyers Economic Handbook, 1970, 2d edit., 1979; Attorney's Fees, 1972; Res Ipse Loquitur, 1973; A Piece of the Action, 1977; Aviation Tort Law, 1978; bd. editors Jour. Post Keynesian Econs., 1977—. Home: Westover Ln Stamford CT 06902 Office: Pan Am Bldg 200 Park Ave New York NY 10017

SPEITEL, GERALD EUGENE, cons. environ. engr.; b. Phila., Feb. 4, 1930; s. Edmond Joseph and Lillian M. (Kohlschreiber) S.; B.S., Drexel U., 1963, M.S. in Engring. Mgmt., 1967; m. Rosemarie Noller, Aug. 22, 1953; children—Gerald Eugene, Edmond C. With Dept. Water, City of Phila., 1948-51, Day & Zimmerman, Phila., 1953-54; with John G. Reutter Assos., Camden, N.J., 1954-72, v.p., 1970-72; pres. Gerald E. Speitel Assos., Mt. Laurel, N.J., 1972—; dir. Environ. Measurements and Analysis, Hammonton, N.J., 1979—. Served with C.E., U.S. Army, 1951-53. Fellow Am. Cons. Engrs. Council; mem. ASCE (pres. S. Jersey br. 1978-79, N.J. sect. 1979-80), Nat. Soc. Profl. Engrs., N.J. Soc. Profl. Engrs., Water Pollution Control Fedn., Utility Contractors Assn., Home Builders League So. N.J. (dir. 1976-79, Asso. Mem. award 1977), Cons. Engrs. Council N.J. (pres. 1967-68), S. Jersey Devel. Council, S. Jersey C. of C. Roman Catholic. Clubs: Atlantic City Country, K.C. Home: 117 Ramblewood Pkwy Mount Laurel NJ 08054 Office: Gerald E Speitel Assos Ramblewood Center Route 73 Mount Laurel NJ 08054

SPEIZMAN, MILTON DAVID, educator; b. Milw., July 5, 1918; s. Harry and Anna (Siegel) S.; B.S., U. Wis., 1939, Ph.M., 1941, M.S.W., 1955; Ph.D., Tulane U., 1962; m. Arleen Florence Segall, May 10, 1959; children—Elissa Ruth, Richard Alan, Andrew John. Registration officer Vocat. Rehab. and Edn. div. VA, Milw., 1946-51; dir. Adult Services div. Jewish Community Center, Milw., 1951-59; lectr. to prof. social work Tulane U., 1959-68; prof. social welfare State U. N.Y. at Buffalo, 1968-70; prof. social work and social research Bryn Mawr Coll., 1970—; vis. prof. history So. U., Baton Rouge, 1966; nat. chmn. Social Welfare History Group, 1968-70, 79—, treas., 1970-74. Served to 1st lt. AUS, 1941-46. Sr. Fulbright lectr. U. Sheffield (Eng.), 1967-68. Mem. Nat. Assn. Social Workers, Am. Hist. Assn., Orgn. Am. Historians. Editor: Urban America in the Twentieth Century, 1968. Contbg. author: Comparative Development in Social Welfare, 1972. Contbr. articles to profl. jours. Home: 116 Shawnee Rd Ardmore PA 19003 Office: 300 Airdale Rd Bryn Mawr PA 19010

SPEIZMAN, MORRIS, textile machine co. exec.; b. Lodz, Poland, Aug. 31, 1905; s. David Samuel and Elka (Bornstein) S.; came to U.S., 1905, naturalized, 1938; grad. Phila. Textile Sch., 1927; m. Sylvia Valenstein, Mar. 4, 1934; children—Lawrence Jay, Robert Stephen. Cloth salesman, 1927-30; with family machinery bus., Wilkes-Barre, Pa., 1931-36; organizer, 1936, since pres. Morris Speizman Co., Inc.; organizer Speizman Industries, Inc., Charlotte, N.C., 1936, pres., 1936-70, chmn. bd., 1970—; mem. Charlotte bd. N.C. Nat. Bank. Pres. World Council Synagogues, 1968—, hon. pres., 1975—; v.p. United Synagogue Am., 1965—. Chmn. bd. Mercy Hosp., Charlotte; pres. Mint. Mus. Art, Charlotte, 1973, hon. pres., 1975. Author: This Week's Miracle, 1968; A Little Sense, 1970; Our World to Come; The Jews of Charlotte, N.C., 1978. Home: 435 Colville Rd Charlotte NC 28207 Office: 508 W 5th St Charlotte NC 28231

SPELLACY, WILLIAM NELSON, physician; b. St. Paul, May 10, 1934; s. Jack F. and Elmyra L. (Nelson) S.; B.A., U. Minn., 1955, B.S., 1956, M.D., 1959. Intern, Hennepin County Gen. Hosp., Mpls., 1959-60; resident U. Minn., Mpls., 1960-63; practice medicine, specializing in obstetrics and gynecology, Miami, Fla., 1967-73, Gainesville, Fla., 1973-79, Chgo., 1979—; prof. dept. obstetrics and gynecology U. Miami, 1967-73; prof., chmn. dept. U. Fla., 1974-79; prof., head Abraham Lincoln Sch. Medicine, U. Ill., Chgo., 1979—. Diplomate Am. Bd. Obstetrics and Gynecology. Mem. Am. Gynecol. Soc., Am. Assn. Obstetricians and Gynecologists, Soc. Gynecol. Investigation, Am. Coll. Obstetricians and Gynecologists, Endocrine Soc., Am. Fertility Soc., Assn. Profs. Gynecology and Obstetrics, Am. Diabetes Assn., Perinatal Research Soc., South Atlantic Soc. Obstetrics and Gynecology, Central Assn. Obstetrics and Gynecology. Episcopalian. Club: Rotary. Contbr. articles to med. jours. Home: 600 N McClurg Ct #3909A Chicago IL 60611 Office: 840 S Wood St Chicago IL 60612

SPELLER, EUGENE THURLEY, coll. pres.; b. Charleston, Mo., Jan. 25, 1928; s. William Oliver and Nicula Luvenia (McElvaine) S.; B.S. in Engring., Mich. State U., 1955, M.A. in Edn., 1967; Ph.D. in Ednl. Adminstrn., Union U., Yellow Springs, Ohio, 1975; m. Thelma Wilson, Sept. 4, 1955; children—Barry Eugene, Bernnine Elaine, Michelle Annette. Engr., Sundstrand Hydr-Transmission Co., La Salle, Ill., 1969-71; fellow Nat. Program Ednl. Leadership, Ohio State U., Columbus, 1971-73; dean, campus adminstr. Austin (Tex.) Community Coll., 1973-75; pres. Olive-Harvey Coll., Chgo., 1975—. Founder, pres. Bus. and Profl. Men's Improvement Assn., Waterloo, Iowa, 1958-63; bd. dirs. Roseland Hosp., Chgo., 1978—, 11th South YMCA, Chgo., 1977—, Roseland Area Redevel. Enterprises, 1977—; mem. Calumet Indsl. Commn., 1976—. Served to 1st lt. AUS, 1956-58. Recipient Disting. Citizen award Ill. Valley C. of C., 1971. Mem. Soc. Automotive Engrs. (chmn. engring. edn. com. 1979), Am. Assn. Univ. Adminstrs., Am. Assn. Community and Jr. Colls., Nat. Alliance Black Sch. Educators, Chgo. S. C. of C. (dir.; Achievers award 1978), Phi Delta Kappa. Democrat. Methodist. Contbr. articles to profl. jours. Home: 11256 S Lothair Ave Chicago IL 60643 Office: 10001 S Woodlawn Ave Chicago IL 60628

SPELLING, AARON, writer, producer; b. Dallas, Apr. 22, 1928; s. David and Pearl (Wall) S.; student Sorbonne, U. Paris, France, 1945-46; B.A., So. Meth. U., 1950; m. Carole Gene Marer, Nov. 23, 1968; children—Victoria Davey, Randall Gene. Co-owner with Danny Thomas, Thomas-Spelling Prodns., 1969-72; co-pres. Spelling-Goldberg Prodns., 1972-76; pres. Aaron Spelling Prodns., Inc., Los Angeles, 1977—; writer numerous TV plays and movies; producer numerous TV programs, including Zane Gray Theatre, Honey West, Smothers Brothers Show, Dick Powell Show, Danny Thomas Hour, Burke's Law, Mod Squad, The Rookies, Starsky and Hutch, Family, The Beach Bums, The Love Boat, Vegas, Charlie's Angels, Fantasy Island, Hart to Hart, The B.A.D. Cats, also 80 Movies of the Week for ABC. Served with USAAF, 1942-45. Decorated Bronze Star medal, Purple Heart with oak leaf cluster; recipient Eugene O'Neill awards, 1947, 48, NAACP Image awards, 1970, 71, 73, 75, Man of Year award Publicists of Am., 1971, B'nai B'rith Man of Year award, 1972. Mem. Writers Guild Am. (award 1962), Producers Guild Am., The Caucus, Hollywood Radio and Television Soc., Hollywood Television Acad. Arts and Scis. Democrat. Jewish. Clubs: Friars; Big Brothers of Am. Office: 10201 W Pico Blvd Los Angeles CA 90064

SPELLINGS, JAMES MCINTOSH, banker; b. Marshall, Tex., Mar. 25, 1931; s. L.H., Jr. and Martha (McIntosh) S.; B.B.A. in Mgmt., Tex. Tech. U., Lubbock, 1952; m. Darlene Hunsaker; children—James, Tracy. With First Nat. Bank, Dallas, 1956—, v.p., then sr. v.p., 1962-71, exec. v.p., 1971-79, head multinat. banking div., 1977-79; chmn. trust com. Merc. Nat. Bank, Dallas, 1979—. Bd. dirs. Dallas Child Guidance Bd., 1972-75; mem. devel. bd. U. Tex., Dallas, 1974—; mem. vestry com. St. Michael's and All Angels Episcopal Ch. Served to 1st lt. USAF, 1952-56. Mem. Am. Banking Assn. (exec. com. internat. banking), Dallas Council World Affairs (dir.). Clubs: Dallas Petroleum, Dallas Country. Home: 4217 Windsor Pkwy Dallas TX 75205 Office: PO Box 225415 1704 Main St Dallas TX 75265

SPELLMAN, EUGENE PAUL, lawyer; b. N.Y.C., Sept. 16, 1930; s. Michael Francis and Mary Elizabeth (Loftus) S.; A.A., U. Fla., 1951, B.A., 1953, LL.B., 1955, J.D., 1967; D.H.L., Biscayne Coll., 1977; m. Roberta J. Recht, July 16, 1959; children—James Kevin, Michael Patrick. Admitted to Fla. bar, 1956; research aide to chief judge 3d Dist. Ct. Appeals, Miami, Fla., 1957-58; asst. atty. gen. Criminal Appeals Div., Tallahassee, 1958-59, 60-61; asst. state atty. Dade County (Fla.), also head Rackets and Frauds div., 1959-61; apptd. spl. prosecutor Judge Curtis E. Chillingsworth murder case by Govs. Leroy Collins and Farris Bryant, 1969-70; apptd. spl. asst. atty. gen., 1969-70; gen. counsel Biscayne Coll., 1970—. Chmn., Fla. Council for Blind, 1963-65; pres. Southeastern Inst. Human Devel., 1977; bd. dirs. Marian Center Inc.; mem. South Miami Hosp. Found. Hon. mem. Order St. Augustine, Rome; recipient Outstanding Achievement award Fla. Assn. Rehab. Facilities. Mem. Am., Fla., Dade County bar assns., Am., Fla. trial lawyers assns., Supreme Ct. Hist. Soc., Am. Judicature Soc., Dade County Assn. Retarded Citizens, Fla. Assn. Rehab. Facilities. Democrat. Roman Catholic. Clubs: Two Hundred, Miami Bankers. Office: Penthouse 100 Biscayne Blvd N Miami FL 33132

SPELLMAN, GLADYS NOON, congresswoman; b. N.Y.C., Mar. 2, 1918; d. Henry and Bessie G. Noon; ed. George Washington U., Grad. Sch. U.S. Dept. Agr.; m. Reuben Spellman; children—Stephen Louis, Richard Eric, Dana Spellman O'Neill. Formerly tchr. Prince George's County (Md.) Pub. Schs.; mem. Prince George's Bd. Commrs., 1962-70, chmn., 1966-68; mem. Prince Georges County Council, 1971-74; mem. 94th-96th Congresses from 5th Md. Dist.; mem. Adv. Com. Intergovtl. Relations, 1967-69; mem. Gov.'s Commn. on Law Enforcement and Adminstrn. Justice, Gov.'s Commn. on Functions of Govt.; vice chmn. Gov.'s Commn. to Determine State's Role in Financing Pub. Edn.; chmn. Md. State Comprehensive Health Planning Adv. Council, Washington Suburban Transit Commn., Regional Planning Bd. IV, Fed. Omnibus Crime Control and Safe Sts. Act; bd. dirs. Washington Met. Area Transit Authority; mem.

Democratic Adv. Com. Elected Ofcls.; v.p. Met. Washington Council Govts. Chmn. bd. trustees Prince George's Gen. Hosp., 1962-70. Mem. Md. (past dir., chmn. edn. com.), Nat. (past pres.) assns. counties, Nat. Labor-Mgmt. Relations Service, Nat. Council State Govts. (steering com. of urban affairs com.), Nat. Assn. Regional Councils (dir.). Office: 308 Cannon House Office Bldg Washington DC 20515

SPELLMAN, JAMES WALTER, ins. co. exec.; b. Stamford, Nebr., Sept. 5, 1923; s. James Wesley and Clarice (Barmore) S.; B.S., U. Neb., 1947; M.S., U. Iowa, 1949; m. Virginia Nelle Wheeler, Jan. 8, 1949; children—Barbara, James, David. With State Farm Life Ins. Co., Bloomington, Ill., 1949—, actuary, 1958-64, v.p. actuary, 1964-67, v.p. controller, 1967-73, v.p., 1973—. Served with F.A., AUS, 1943-46; PTO. Fellow Soc. Actuaries, Life Mgmt. Inst.; mem. Coll. Life Underwriters. Republican. Presbyn. (elder). Home: 1306 Stephens Dr Normal IL 61761 Office: 1 State Farm Plaza Bloomington IL 61701

SPELLMAN, MITCHELL WRIGHT, physician, dean, educator; b. Alexandria, La., Dec. 1, 1919; s. Frank Jackson and Altonette Beulah (Mitchell) S.; A.B. magna cum laude, Dillard U., 1940; M.D., Howard U., 1944; Ph.D. in Surgery (Commonwealth Fund fellow), U. Minn., Mpls., 1955; D.Sc. (hon.), Georgetown U., 1974, U. Fla., 1977; m. Billie Rita Rhodes, June 27, 1947; children—Frank A., Michael A., Mitchell A., Maria A., Melva A., Mark A., Manly A., Rita A. Intern, Cleve. Met. Gen. Hosp., 1944-45, asst. resident in surgery, 1945-46; asst. resident in surgery Howard U. and Freedmen's Hosp., Washington, 1946-47, chief resident thoracic surgery, 1947-48, teaching asst. physiology, 1948-49, chief resident surgery, 1949-50, teaching asst. in surgery, 1950-51; asst. prof. surgery Howard U., 1954-56, asso. prof., 1956-60, prof., 1960-68, dir. Howard surgery service at D.C. Gen. Hosp., 1961-68; dean Charles R. Drew Postgrad. Med. Sch., Los Angeles, 1969-77, prof. surgery, 1969-78; asst. dean, prof. surgery Sch. Medicine, U. Calif. at Los Angeles, 1969-78; clin. prof. surgery Sch. Med., U. So. Calif., 1969-78; dean for Med. Services faculty of medicine, prof. surgery Harvard U. Med. Sch., Boston, 1978—; fellow Center for Advanced Study in Behavioral Scis., vis. prof. Stanford, 1975-76. Bd. dirs. Kaiser Found. Hosps., Kaiser Found. Health Plan, Lloyds Bank of Calif. Mem. D.C. Bd. Examiners in Medicine and Osteopathy, 1955-68; mem. Nat. Rev. Com. for Regional Med. Programs, 1968-70; mem. spl. med. adv. group, nat. surg. cons. VA, 1969-73; mem. Commn. for Study Accreditation of Selected Health Ednl. Programs, 1970-72; chmn. adv. com. br. med. devices Nat. Heart and Lung Inst., 1972; Am. health del. to visit People's Republic of China, 1973. Bd. dirs. Sun Valley Forum on Nat. Health; former trustee Occidental Coll.; former bd. overseers com. to visit univ. health service Harvard; former regent Georgetown U.; former vis. com. U. Mass. Med. Center. Markle scholar in med. scis., 1954-59; recipient Distinguished Alumnus award Dillard U., 1963, Distinguished Postgrad. Achievement award Howard U., 1974. Mem. AMA, Nat. Med. Assn. (William A. Sinkler Surgery award 1968), AAAS, AAUP, A.C.S., Soc. Univ. Surgeons, Am. Coll. Cardiology, Am. Surg. Assn., Inst. Medicine. Roman Catholic. Mem. editorial bd. Jour. Medicine and Philosophy, 1977—. Contbr. articles on cardiovascular physiology and surgery, measurement of blood volume, and radiation biology to profl. jours. Office: Office of Dean Harvard U Med Sch 25 Shattuck St Boston MA 02115

SPELTZ, GEORGE HENRY, bishop; b. Altura, Minn., May 29, 1912; s. Henry and Josephine (Jung) S.; B.S., St. Mary's Coll., Winona, Minn., 1932, LL.D., 1963; student theology St. Paul Sem., 1936-40; M.A., Cath. U. Am., 1942, Ph.D., 1944; D.D., Holy See, Rome, Italy, 1963. Ordained priest Roman Cath. Ch., 1940; vice chancellor Diocese Winona, 1944-47, supt. schs., 1946-49, aux. bishop, 1963-66; pastor St. Mary's Ch., Minneiska, Minn., 1946-47; tchr. St. Mary's Coll., 1947-63; rector Immaculate Heart of Mary Sem., Winona, 1948-63; co-adjutor bishop, St. Cloud, Minn., 1966-68, bishop, 1968—. Pres., Nat. Cath. Rural Life Conf., 1970-72. Address: 214 S 3d Ave Saint Cloud MN 56301

SPENCE, ARTHUR MEARNS, publishing co. exec.; b. N.Y.C., May 11, 1917; s. James Williams and Margaret Mary (Mearns) S.; B.S., N.Y. U., 1943; m. Jean Gunnip, Mar. 22, 1941; children—Marilyn, Helen (Mrs. Arnold Tschantre). Various positions Guaranty Trust Co., N.Y.C., 1933-42; regional auditor Reuben H. Donnelley Pub. Co., N.Y.C., 1946-49; controller Geyer-McAllister Publs., N.Y.C., 1949-65, treas., 1965-69, v.p., treas., 1969-72, exec. v.p., 1972-74, pres., 1974—, also dir.; dir. Am. Bus. Press. Served to lt. AUS, 1943-46; ETO. Decorated Purple Heart. Mem. Assn. Second Class Mail Pubs. (past chmn. bd.). Republican. Methodist. Clubs: Univ., Orienta Yacht. Home: 409 Edward Pl Mamaroneck NY 10543 Office: 51 Madison Ave New York NY 10010

SPENCE, CLARK CHRISTIAN, educator; b. Great Falls, Mont., May 25, 1923; s. Christian Edward and Lela (Killian) S.; B.A., U. Colo., 1948, M.A., 1951; Ph.D, U. Minn., 1955; m. Mary Lee Nance, Sept. 12, 1953; children—Thomas Christian, Ann Leslie. Instr., Carleton Coll., Northfield, Minn., 1954-55; instr., then asso. prof. Pa. State U., 1955-60; vis. lectr. U. Calif. at Berkeley, 1960-61; mem. faculty U. Ill. at Champaign, 1961—, prof. history, 1964—, chmn. dept., 1967-70, Center for Advanced Study, 1975; vis. lectr. Yale, summer 1964; vis. prof. U. Colo., summer 1967. Served with USAAF, 1943-46. Fulbright fellow, Eng., 1953-54; Ford Found. fellow, 1963-64; Guggenheim fellow, 1970-71; recipient ann. book award Agrl. History Soc., 1959. Mem. Western History Assn. (pres. 1969-70), Phi Beta Kappa, Phi Alpha Theta. Author: British Investment and the American Mining Frontier, 1958; God Speed the Plow: The Coming of Steam Cultivation to Great Britain, 1960; Sinews of American Capitalism: An Economic History, 1964; The American West, 1966; Mining Engineers in the American West, 1970; Territorial Politics and Government in Montana, 1864-89, 1975; Montana: A Bicentennial History, 1978. Home: 1107 S Foley St Champaign IL 61820

SPENCE, CLYDE WADSWORTH, JR., army officer; b. Waycross, Ga., Sept. 1, 1928; s. Clyde Wadsworth and Doris (Towne) S.; B.S., U.S. Mil. Acad., 1950; grad. Army War Coll., 1968; postgrad. Columbia U., 1961-62, U. Md., 1969-70; m. Marilyn Davis Spence, June 26, 1956; children—Kevin, Holly, Heather. Commd. 2d lt. U.S. Army, 1950, advanced through grades to maj. gen.; arty. battery comdr. Korean War, 1952-53; mem. faculty U.S. Mil. Acad., 1960-63; mem. U.S. Army Staff, Heidelberg, W. Ger., 1963-65; comdr. Arty. Bn., Germany, 1965-66; mem. Dept. of Army Staff, 1968-69, U.S. Army G3 Staff, Korea, 1969-71; dep. brig. comdr. Vietnam War, 1971-72; dir. mgmt. budget Army Test Command, 1972-73; mem. office staff Sec. of Def., 1973-76; asst. div./community comdr., Germany, 1976-78; dep. chief NATO Hdqrs., 1978-79; chief Joint U.S. Mil. Aid Group, Greece, 1979—. Leader troop local Boy Scouts Am., 1967-68, commr. for Greece, Boy Scouts Am., 1979—. Decorated Legion of Merit, Bronze Star, Meritorious Service medal, Air medal, Sec. of Def. Superior Ser. medal, Vietnamese Disting. Service medal. Club: Masons. Home: 6620 22d Way S Saint Petersburg FL 33712 Office: Chief JUSMAG Greece APO NY 09253

SPENCE, FLOYD DAVIDSON, congressman; b. Columbia, S.C., Apr. 9, 1928; s. James Wilson and Addie (Lucas) S.; A.B., U. S.C., 1952, J.D., 1956; m. Lula Hancock Drake, Dec. 22, 1952 (dec.); children—David, Zack, Benjamin, Caldwell. Admitted to S.C. bar, 1956; former partner firm Callison and Spence, West Columbia, S.C.; mem. S.C. Ho. Reps., 1956-62; mem. S.C. Senate, 1966-70, minority leader, 1966-70, chmn. joint com. internal security, 1969; mem. 92d-95th Congresses from S.C.; mem. armed services com., com. on standards ofcl. conduct. Past chmn. Ridge dist. Central S.C. council Boy Scouts Am., 1965-66, exec. bd., 1963—; chmn. Lexington County Mental Health Assn., 1959. Served to capt. USNR. Mem. Am. Legion, VFW, Res. Officers Assn., Navy League. Lutheran. Home: Box 869 Lexington SC 29072 Office: 2001 Assembly St Columbia SC 29201

SPENCE, FRANCIS JOHN, bishop; b. Perth, Ont., Can., June 3, 1926; s. William John and Rose Anna (Jordan) S.; B.A., St. Michael's Coll., Toronto, 1946; postgrad. St. Augustine's Sem., Toronto, 1946-50; J.C.D., St. Thomas U., Rome, 1955. Ordained priest Roman Catholic Ch., 1950; consecrated bishop, 1967; diocesan sec., Kingston, Ont., 1950-52; parish asst., 1955-61; mem. Marriage Tribunal, 1961-66; diocesan dir. hosp. and charities, 1961-66; pastor Sacred Heart Ch., Marmora, Ont., 1966-67; aux. bishop Mil. Vicar Canadian Forces, 1967-70; bishop of Charlottetown, P.E.I., 1970—. Office: Box 907 North River Rd Charlottetown PE C1A 7L9 Canada*

SPENCE, HARRY METCALFE, physician, surgeon; b. San Angelo, Tex., Oct. 2, 1905; s. Joseph Jr. and Fannie Lee (Metcalfe) S.; student U. Ill.; M.D. cum laude, Harvard, 1930; m. Lois G. Ames, Aug. 9, 1940; children—Stephen Ames, Charles Metcalfe. Intern, Free Hosp. for Women, Brookline, Mass., also New Eng. Deaconess Hosp.; surg. and urol. resident Mass. Gen. Hosp., Boston, 1930-34; pvt. practice, Ponca City, Okla., 1934-36; urologist, head dept. Dallas Med. and Surg. Clinic, 1936—; from clin. asst. to clin. prof. urology, past chmn. div. urology Baylor Med. Sch., Southwestern Med. Sch., 1950—; past chief urology service Children's Med. Center, Dallas, 1946-55; chief urology Parkland Meml. Hosp.; attending urologist Baylor U. Hosp.; cons. urology to surgeon gen. Brooke Army Hosp., San Antonio. Served to comdr. M.C., USNR, 1942-46. Diplomate Am. Bd. Urology. Mem. A.C.S. (regent, past bd. govs.), Am. Assn. Genlto-urinary Surgeons (past pres.), Am. Urol. Assn. (sec., past pres. South Central sect.), Clin. Soc. Genitourinary Surgeons (past pres.), Société Internationale D'Urologie, Tex. Surg. Soc., AMA, Alpha Omega Alpha, Nu Sigma Nu. Clubs: Corinthian Yacht, Chaparral (Dallas). Author numerous sci. papers on urology. Home: 4533 Lorraine St Dallas TX 75205 Office: 4105 Live Oak Dallas TX 75204

SPENCE, HARTZELL, writer; b. Clarion, Iowa, Feb. 15, 1908; s. William H. and Ethel Hope (Morris) S.; A.B., State U. Iowa, 1930; D.Litt., U. Foundation, 1943; LL.D., Iowa Wesleyan Coll., 1960; m. Margaret L. Lampert, 1942 (div. 1964); children—Matt, Laurie. With United Press, 1930-41, founder and editor Yank (the Army Weekly), 1942- 43. Served as lt. col. USAAF, 1943-45. Decorated Legion of Merit. Mem. Phi Beta Kappa, Phi Kappa Psi, Sigma Delta Chi. Methodist. Author: One Foot in Heaven, 1940; Radio City, 1941; Get Thee Behind Me, 1943; Vain Shadow 1947; Happily Ever After, 1949; The Big Top (with Fred Branda), 1952; Bride of the Conqueror, 1954; Story of America's Religions, 1960; A Foot in the Door (with A. C. Fuller), 1960; The Clergy and What They Do, 1961; Portrait in Oil, 1962; For Every Tear a Victory, 1964; A Great Name in Oil, 1966; The New York Life, 1845-1968, 1969; Marcos of the Philippines, 1969. Clubs: Old Lyme Country, Essex Yacht. Contbr. to mags. Home: Essex CT 06426

SPENCE, JAMES ROBERT, JR., television sports exec.; b. Bronxville, N.Y., Dec. 20, 1936; s. James Robert and Mary Jeffery (Grant) S.; B.A., Dartmouth Coll., 1958; m. Lynn Chapman, Dec. 25, 1961. Prodn. asst. ABC Sports, Inc. (known as Sports Programs, Inc. through 1966), N.Y.C., 1960-63, asst. to exec. producer ABC's Wide World of Sports, 1963-66, coordinating producer, 1966-70, v.p. program planning ABC Sports, Inc., 1970-78, sr. v.p., 1978—. Served with U.S. Army, 1958-60. Club: Westchester Country (Rye, N.Y.). Office: ABC Sports 1330 Ave of the Americas New York NY 10019

SPENCE, JANET TAYLOR, psychologist; b. Toledo, Aug. 29, 1923; d. John Crichton and Helen (Hodge) Taylor; A.B., Oberlin Coll., 1945; postgrad. Yale U., 1945-46; Ph.D., U. Iowa, 1949; m. Kenneth W. Spence, Dec. 27, 1959; instr. psychology Northwestern U., Evanston, Ill., 1949-51, asst. prof., 1951-57, asso. prof., 1957-60; research psychology VA Hosp., Iowa City, Iowa, 1960-64; prof. psychology and ednl. psychology U. Tex., Austin, 1964—, chmn. psychology, 1969-73, Ashbel Smith prof. psychology, 1979—; fellow Center for Advanced Study in Behavioral Scis., 1978-79. Bd. dirs. Social Sci. Research Council, 1975-77. Recipient Gold medal Hollins Coll., 1970; Ford Found. fellow, 1974-75. Mem. Am. Psychol. Assn. (dir. 1977-79), Psychonomic Soc. (mem. governing bd. 1978—), Soc. Exptl. Social Psychologists, Soc. Exptl. Psychology, AAAS, Southwestern Psychol. Assn. (pres. 1972). Author: (with others) Elementary Statistics, rev. edit., 1976; (with R.L. Helmreich) Masculinity and Femininity, 1978; editor: Learning and Motivation, Vol. I (with K.W. Spence), 1967, Vol. II (with K.W. Spence), 1968, Vol. III (with G. Bower), 1969; (with H.H. Kendler) Essays in Neobehaviorism, 1971; editor Contemporary Psychology, A Jour. of Revs., 1974—. Office: U Tex Austin TX 78712

SPENCE, JOHN DANIEL, ednl. exec.; b. Lethbridge, Alberta, Can., May 18, 1915; s. Benjamin Abner and Clara May (Fullerton) S.; came to U.S., 1915, naturalized, 1943; A.B., Grinnell (Iowa) Coll., 1938; m. Phyllis Saxton Johnson, Feb. 4, 1939; children—Susan Kathleen, John Daniel. With Container Corp. Am., 1938-54, v.p., 1949-54; exec. Lanzit Corrugated Box Co., Chgo., 1954—; v.p. Consol. Paper Co., 1963; dir. devel. Rockford Coll., 1964—, v.p., 1965—, acting pres., 1977-79, cons., 1979—. Pres. Woodcrest Assn., Rockford, 1974-78; mem. adv. com. Forest Preserve Dist., Winnebago County, 1974—; chmn. adv. com. Severson Dells Forest Preserve, 1976—; bd. dirs. John Howard Assn., to 1974-76; trustee Keith Country Day Sch., 1971—, Children's Home of Rockford, 1973-76, Lake Forest Acad., to 1975, Pecatonica Prairie Path, 1975. Mem. Rockford C. of C. (dir. 1966-71, v.p.). Lion. Club: University (Chgo.). Home: 6710 Woodcrest Pkwy Rockford IL 61109

SPENCE, JONATHAN DERMOT, historian, educator; b. Surrey, Eng., Aug. 11, 1936; s. Dermot Gordon Chesson and Muriel (Crailsham) S.; came to U.S., 1959; B.A., Cambridge (Eng.) U., 1959; Ph.D., Yale U., 1965; m. Helen Alexander, Sept. 15, 1962; children—Colin Chesson, Ian Alexander. Asst. prof. history Yale U., New Haven, 1966-71, prof., 1971—, chmn. Council E. Asian Studies, dir. div. humanities. Served with Brit. Army, 1954-56. Recipient Christopher award, 1975; Yale fellow in East Asian Studies, 1962-65, 1968-70. Mem. Assn. Asian Studies. Author: Ts'Ao Yin and The K'Ang-Hsi Emperor, 1966; To Change China, 1969; Emperor of China, 1974; The Death of Woman Wang, 1978; editor Ch'ing-Shih Wen'T'I, 1965-73. Home: Newton Rd Woodbridge CT 06525 Office: History Dept Yale U New Haven CT 06520

SPENCE, RICHARD DEE, r.r. co. exec.; b. Tucumcari, N.Mex., Apr. 7, 1925; s. Andrew Doke and Myrtle Hannah (Roach) S.; B.S., U. Calif. at Los Angeles, 1949; postgrad. Transp. Mgmt. Program, Stanford, 1956, Program for Sr. Execs., Mass. Inst. Tech., 1962; children—Diana, Richard N.; m. 2d, Mary Ames Kellogg, July 24, 1976; children—Mary B., Ames T., Richard T. With So. Pacific Transp. Co., San Francisco, 1946-75, asst. v.p. ops., 1967-69, v.p. ops., 1969-75; pres., chief operating officer Consol. Rail Corp., Phila., 1975-78; pres. L & N R.R. Co., Louisville, 1978—. Served with USNR, 1943-46. Mem. Phi Kappa Sigma. Democrat. Methodist. Clubs: Masons, Union League (Phila.). Home: 3600 Glenview Ave Glenview KY 40025 Office: 908 W Broadway Louisville KY 40203

SPENCE, ROBERT DEAN, educator; b. Bergen, N.Y., Sept. 12, 1917; s. La Vergne Robert and Jennie (Waterman) S.; B.S., Cornell U., 1939; M.S., Mich. State U., 1942; Ph.D., Yale, 1948; m. Helen Holbrook, June 14, 1942; children—John, Elizabeth, Janet, Barbara. Asst. prof. physics Mich. State U., East Lansing, 1947-49, asso. prof., 1949-52, prof. physics, 1952—; vis. prof. U. Bristol (Eng.), 1955-56, Technische Hogesch., Eindhoven, Netherlands, 1964, Rijks universiteit, Leiden, Netherlands, 1970-71. Recipient Distinguished Faculty award Mich. State U., 1963. Guggenheim fellow, 1955-56. Fellow Am. Phys. Soc.; mem. Am. Crystallographic Assn., Nat. Soc. Profl. Engrs., Sigma Xi, Phi Kappa Phi. Research and publs. on math. physics, chem. physics, magnetism. Home: 1849 Ann St East Lansing MI 48823

SPENCE, WISHART FLETT, former Canadian justice; b. Toronto, Ont., Mar. 9, 1904; s. James Houston and Margaret (Hackland) S.; B.A., U. Toronto, 1925; Barrister, Osgoode Hall Law Sch., Toronto, 1928; LL.M., Harvard U., 1929; LL.D. (hon.), York U., Toronto, 1974, U. Toronto, 1976; m. Elizabeth Potvin, Sept. 26, 1936; children—Michael W., Margaret M. Called to bar, 1928; pvt. practice, Toronto, 1936-42; dep. adminstr., then adminstr. Wartime Price and Trade Bd. Can., 1942-50; justice High Ct. div. Supreme Ct. Ont., 1950-63, Supreme Ct. Can., Ottawa, 1963-78. Decorated companion Order of Can., officer Order Brit. Empire. Mem. Canadian Bar Assn. Clubs: Rideau (Ottawa); Lawyers (Toronto). Home: 400 Stewart St Ottawa ON K1N 6L2 Canada

SPENCER, DALE RAY, educator; b. Pocatello, Idaho, Oct. 21, 1925; s. Howard Harris and Eleda (Eastman) S.; student Idaho State U., 1944-45, U. N.Mex., 1945-46; B.J., U. Mo., 1948, M.A., 1955, J.D., 1968; m. Lillian Joy Hodkins, Dec. 21, 1947; children—Melinda Sue, Jennifer Joy. Mem. faculty U. Mo., Columbia, 1950—, prof. journalism, 1971—, chmn. news editorial dept., 1979—, lectr. communications law, 1958—; admitted to Mo. bar, 1969; founder, 1st pres. Mo. Assembly of Faculty in Higher Edn., 1975-76. Bd. dirs. Wonderland Camp for Handicapped Children, 1973—. Served with USNR, 1943-46. Recipient Joyce Swan Disting. Faculty award U. Mo. Journalism Sch., 1967. Mem. Am., Mo. bar assns., Investigative Reporters and Editors, Sigma Delta Chi (nat. v.p. 1951-53), Kappa Tau Alpha, Kappa Alpha Mu. Club: Kiwanis. Editor: Columbia Missourian, 1950-73. Home: 917 LaGrange St Columbia MO 65201 Office: Sch Journalism U Mo Columbia MO 65201

SPENCER, DANIEL LLOYD, economist, educator; b. N.Y.C., Mar. 5, 1916; s. William B. and Florence May (Jones) S.; B.S., Pratt Inst., 1938; A.B., Columbia, 1941; M.A., U. Calif. at Berkeley, 1950; Ph.D., Am. U., 1953; m. Flora Chen, Jan. 9, 1948; children—Betty (Mrs. William Stroder), Priscilla, Desiree. Researcher, Engring. Found., 1940-42; economist Japanese Occupation, 1946-48; lectr. Am. U., 1950-52, asst. prof., 1953-57; economist Renegotiation Bd., 1952-53; asst. prof. Berea (Ky.) Coll., 1953-54; lectr. U. Va., 1955-57; asso. prof. So. Ill. U., Carbondale, 1957-60; prof. econs., chmn. dept. Howard U., 1960-70, chmn. div. social scis., 1962-63; prof. econ. Morgan State U., Balt., 1970—. Vis. lectr. Indsl. Coll. Armed Forces, 1960-66, Washington Internat. Center, 1960-69, Bus. Council Internat. Understanding, 1964, Peace Corps., 1964, Dept. Agr., 1972; cons. planning Indian Statis. Inst., 1959, U. Seven Seas, 1960-65, U.S. Commn. on Govt. Procurement, 1971-72, Md. Dept. Econ. and Community Devel., 1973, Soviet tech. transfer project Batelle Meml. Inst., 1973—; editorial asso. Operations & Policy Research, Inc., 1967—; dir. MANDAT project, 1970—. Served to lt. comdr. USNR, 1943-46. Decorated Croix de Guerre (France). Fulbright lectr., India, 1958-59; Ford Found. fellow, 1962. Mem. Am., So. econ. assns., Assn. Asian Studies, Soc. Internat. Devel., A.A.A.S., Acad. Internat. Bus., A.A.U.P., N.A.A.C.P. (D.C. finance com. 1960-65), Nat. Economists Club, Order Artus, Phi Kappa Phi, Pi Gamma Mu. Author: India: Mixed Enterprises and Western Business, 1959; Transfer of Technology to Developing Countries, 1966; Military Transfer of Technology, 1967; Technology Gap in Perspective, 1970, Japanese transl., 1974; Indian Ocean Territories, 1971. Contbr. articles to profl. jours. Home: 4405 Ridge St Chevy Chase MD 20015 Office: Dept Econs Morgan State U Baltimore MD 21239

SPENCER, DICK, III, magazine publisher; b. Dallas, Jan. 28, 1921; s. Richard and Jessie (Burden) S.; B.A., U. Iowa, 1942; m. Jo Anne Nicholson, July 24, 1943; children—Barbara Jo Spencer Corpolongo, Richard Craig (dec.), Debra Jean (Mrs. Kurt Markus). With promotion dept. Look mag., 1945-47; editor info. service U. Iowa, also instr. Sch. Journalism, 1948-50; publs. editor U. Colo., Boulder, 1950-51; editor Western Horseman mag., Colorado Springs, 1951-69, pub., 1969—. Served with AUS, 1942-45; ETO. Decorated Purple Heart with 2 oak leaf clusters, Bronze Star with oak leaf cluster, Combat Inf. badge, Parachutist badge. Mem. Sigma Delta Chi, Alpha Tau Omega. Methodist. Clubs: Pikes Peak Range Riders; Desert Caballeros. Author: Editorial Cartooning, 1949; Pulitzer Prize Cartoons, 1951; Beginning Western Horsemanship, 1959; Intermediate Western Horsemanship, 1960; Horse Breaking, 1967. Home: 10 Cragmor Village Colorado Springs CO 80907 Office: 3850 N Nevada St Colorado Springs CO 80907. *I feel a man is a success: (1) When he enjoys the work he is doing; (2) when he earns enough money to allow him to live the way he wants; (3) when he lives in the part of the country he likes best; (4) when he has a family that loves and believes in him.*

SPENCER, DONALD CLAYTON, mathematician; b. Boulder, Colo., Apr. 25, 1912; s. Frank Robert and Edith (Clayton) S.; B.A., U. Colo., 1934; B.S., Mass. Inst. Tech., 1936; Ph.D., U. Cambridge (Eng.), 1939, Sc.D., 1963; Sc.D. honoris causa, Purdue U., 1971; m. Mary J. Halley, July 25, 1936; children—Maredith, Marianne; m. 2d, Natalie Robertson Sanborn, July 7, 1951; 1 son, Donald Clayton. Instr. math. Mass. Inst. Tech., 1939-42; asso. prof. Stanford U., 1942-46, prof. math., 1946-50, 63-68; asso. prof. math. Princeton U., 1950-53, prof., 1953-63, 68—, Henry Burchard Fine prof. math., 1972-78, emeritus, 1978—; Fulbright grant for study and lectr. Coll. de France, 1954-55; Scott vis. prof. math. U. Pa., fall 1964; mem. Applied Math. Group, N.Y. U., 1944-45, Recipient (with A.C. Schaeffer) Bocher prize Am. Math. Soc., 1948. Mem. Nat. Acad. Scis., Am. Acad. Arts and Scis., Phi Beta Kappa. Contbr. articles to sci. publs. Home: 943 Country Rd 204 Durango CO 81301

SPENCER, EDGAR WINSTON, educator; b. Monticello, Ark., May 27, 1931; s. Terrel Ford and Allie Belle (Shelton) S.; student Vanderbilt U., 1949-50; B.S., Washington and Lee U., 1953; Ph.D., Columbia, 1957; m. Elizabeth Penn Humphries, Nov. 26, 1958;

children—Elizabeth Shawn, Kristen Shannon. Lectr., Hunter Coll., 1954-57; mem. faculty Washington and Lee U., 1957—, prof. geology, head dept., 1962—. Pres., Rockbridge Area Conservation Council, 1978. NSF sci. faculty fellow, New Zealand and Australia; dir. grant for humanities and pub. policy on land use planning Va. Found., 1975. Fellow Geol. Soc. Am., AAAS; mem. Am. Assn. Petroleum Geologists, Assn. Profl. Geol. Scientists, Am. Geophys. Union, Nat. Assn. Geology Tchrs., Yellowstone-Bighorn Research Assn., Phi Beta Kappa (hon.), Sigma Xi. Author: Basic Concepts of Physical Geology, 1962; Basic Concepts of Historical Geology, 1962; Geology: A Survey of Earth Science, 1965; Introduction to the Structure of the Earth, 1969, 2d edit., 1977; The Dynamics of the Earth, 1972. Home: Route 5 Box 1055 Lexington VA 24450

SPENCER, ELIZABETH, author; b. Carrollton, Miss.; d. James Luther and Mary James (McCain) S.; B.A., Belhaven Coll., 1942; M.A., Vanderbilt U., 1943; Litt.D. (hon.), Southwestern at Memphis, 1968; m. John Arthur Blackwood Rusher, Sept. 29, 1956. Writer-in-residence U. N.C., 1969; Hollins Coll., 1973, Concordia U., 1977-78. Recipient Women's Democratic Com. award, 1949; recognition award Nat. Inst. Arts and letters, 1952; Guggenheim Found. fellow, 1953; Richard and Hinda Rosenthal Found. award Nat. Inst. Arts and Letters, 1956; Kenyon Rev. fellow in fiction, 1957; 1st McGraw-Hill Fiction award, 1960; Bryn Mawr Col. Donnelly fellow, 1962; Henry Bellamann award for creative writing, 1968. Author: Fire in the Morning, 1948; This Crooked Way, 1952; The Voice at the Back Door, 1956; The Light in the Piazza, 1960; Knights and Dragons, 1965; No Place for an Angel, 1967; Ship Island and Other Stories, 1968; The Snare, 1972. Contbr. short stories to mags. and collections. Home: 2300 St Mathieu Montreal PQ Canada

SPENCER, F(REDERICK) GILMAN, editor; b. Phila., Dec. 8, 1925; s. F. Gilman and Elizabeth (Hetherington) S.; student pub. and pvt. schs.; m. Isabel Brannon, July 3, 1965; 1 dau., Isabel; children by previous marriage—Amy, Elizabeth Blair, F. Gilman, Jonathan. Copyboy, Phila. Inquirer, 1947-49; photographer-reporter Chester (Pa.) Times, 1949, 1952-59; photographer, sports editor Mt. Holly (N.J.) Herald, 1949-52; mng. editor Main Line Times, Ardmore, Pa., 1959-63; asst. city editor Phila. Bull., 1963-64; editorial spokesman WCAU-TV, Phila., 1964-67; editor The Trentonian, Trenton, N.J., 1967-75, Phila. Daily News, 1975—; dir. Phila. Newspapers, Inc. Served in USNR, 1943-46. Recipient Pulitzer prize for editorials, 1974. Mem. Am. Soc. Newspapers Editors, Sigma Delta Chi. Office: 400 N Broad St Philadelphia PA 19101*

SPENCER, FRANK COLE, surgeon, educator; b. Haskell, Tex., Dec. 21, 1925; s. Frank Spencer and Lillian Josephine (Cole) S.; B.S. summa cum laude, North Tex. State U., 1944; M.D. (Founder's Medal scholar) Vanderbilt U., 1947; m. Corinne Ewell, Sept. 10, 1946; children—Elizabeth Kay, Patricia Jean, Frank Ewell. Mem. faculty Johns Hopkins Sch. Medicine, 1954-61, U. Ky. Sch. Medicine, 1961-65; prof., chmn. dept. surgery N.Y.U., N.Y.C., 1966, George David Stewart prof., chmn. dept. surgery, 1966—, dir. surg. divs. Bellevue Hosp., 1966—; dir. surgery U. Hosp., N.Y.C., 1966—; cons. Walter Reed Army Hosp., 1957-65, Nat. Heart Inst., NIH, Bethesda, Md., 1958-61, VA Hosp., Lexington, Ky., 1961-65. Recipient Legion Merit award USN, 1953; Markle scholar, 1956-61. Diplomate Am. Bd. Surgery, Am. Bd. Thoracic Surgery. Mem. Am. Assn. Thoracic Surgery, A.C.S., Am. Heart Assn., A.M.A., Am. Surg. Assn., Internat. Cardiovascular Soc., Soc. Clin. Surgeons, Soc. Med. Cons. to Armed Services, Soc. U. Surgeons, Soc. U. Surg. Chmn., Soc. Vascular Surgery. Contbr. articles to profl. jours. Home and Office: 560 1st Ave New York City NY 10016

SPENCER, HAROLD GARTH, educator; b. Avon Park, Fla., May 19, 1930; s. James Edgar and Juanita (Adams) S.; B.S., U. Fla., 1952, M.S., 1958, Ph.D., 1959; m. Mary Dean Wilkes, Mar. 30, 1956; children—Stephen Dale, Susan Gale. Asst. prof. Clemson (S.C.) U., 1959-64, asso. prof., 1964-68, head dept. chemistry and geology, 1966-77, prof., 1968—. Served to 1st lt. USAF, 1952-54. Fellow Am. Inst. Chemists; mem. Am. Chem. Soc., A.A.A.S., S.C. Acad. Sci., Phi Beta Kappa, Sigma Xi, Phi Kappa Phi, Alpha Epsilon Delta. Contbr. articles profl. jours. Home: 103 Wren St Clemson SC 29631

SPENCER, HARRY CHADWICK, clergyman; b. Chgo., Apr. 10, 1905; s. John and Jessie (Chadwick) S.; B.A., Willamette U., 1925, D.D., 1953; M.Div., Garrett Bibl. Inst., 1929; M.A., Harvard, 1932; m. Mary Louise Wakefield, May 26, 1935; children—Mary Grace Spencer Lyman, Ralph. Ordained to ministry Meth. Ch., 1931; pastor Washington Heights Ch., Chgo., 1931-33, Portage Park Ch., Chgo., 1933-35; rec. sec. bd. missions and ch. extension United Meth. Ch., 1935-40, asst. exec. sec., 1940-45, sec. dept. visual edn., 1945-52, exec. sec. radio and film commn., 1952-56, gen. sec. TV, radio and film commn., 1956-68, asso. gen. sec. program council div. TV, radio and film communication, 1968-72, asso. exec. sec. joint com. on communications, 1972, 73, ret.; sec. mass media, world div. Bd. Missions and Ch. Extension, 1964-72; exec. producer TV series The Way, Talk Back, Breakthru, Learning to Live; exec. producer radio series Am. Profile, Night Call; exec. producer motion pictures John Wesley, Hello Up There, Gold Is the Way I Feel, Making a Difference, Symbol of a Bell, Women—Amen! Mem. exec. com. Nat. Council Chs. Broadcasting and Film Commn., 1952-73, chmn., 1960-63; mem. exec. com. Nat. Council Chs., 1960-63, mem. gen. bd., 1967-72, v.p. Central div. communications, 1969-72; chmn. constituting assembly World Assn. for Christian Broadcasting, 1963; mem. constituting assembly World Assn. Christian Communication, 1968, dir. assembly, 1975; mem. adminstrv. com. Ravemco, 1950-70, Intermedia, 1970-72; vis. prof. Garrett Evang. Theol. Sem., 1975; lectr. in field. Trustee, Scarritt Coll., 1967-74, emeritus, 1974—; bd. dirs. Outlook Nashville, 1977, Nashville chpt. UN Assn., 1976—. Recipient award excellence art communications Claremont Sch. Theology, 1973. Mem. Soc. Preservation and Encouragement Barber Shop Quartet Singing in Am., World Assn. Christian Communications. Clubs: Kiwanis, Harvard, Woodmont (Nashville). Contbr. articles on films to ch. publs. Home: PO Box 15063 Nashville TN 37215. *The most precious quality we know is human personality. Unfortunately, innumerable hazards constantly beset people, even from the time before they are born. Nevertheless, each person has inherited many priceless advantages. The ability to store up knowledge and the imagination to foresee future events, which make possible human communication, have enhanced the value of human personality and brightened man's hope for the future—if human beings can now learn the secret of self-discipline and use it to achieve long-range benefits for a world community.*

SPENCER, HARRY IRVING, JR., banker; b. Worcester, Mass., Feb. 3, 1925; s. Harry Irving and Bertha (Johnson) S.; B.A., Clark U., 1950; m. Violet Virginia Bergquist, Sept. 16, 1950; children—Nancy Elaine, Harry Irving III, Carol Helen. With Worcester County Nat. Bank, 1950—, asst. treas., 1954-58, cashier, 1958—, v.p., 1966-69, sr. v.p., 1969-77, exec. v.p., cashier, 1977—; sec., treas., dir. Nobility Hill Realty Corp.; sr. v.p., treas., clk. Worcester Bancorp. Inc.; treas., dir. Worcester Capital Corp., Wornat Devel. Corp., Wornat Leasing Corp., Empire Group, Inc., Wornat Ins. Agy., Inc., Wornat Bancfactors, Inc. Bd. dirs. Worcester Taxpayers Assn. Methodist (trustee). Clubs: Kiwanis; Economic, Plaza (Worcester, Mass.). Home: 79 Birchwood Dr Holden MA 01520 Office: 446 Main St Worcester MA 01608

SPENCER, IVAN CARLTON, clergyman; b. nr. West Burlington, Pa., July 8, 1914; s. Ivan Quay and Annie Minnie (Back) S.; grad. Elim Bible Inst., 1933; D.D., Am. Bible Coll., 1966; m. Elizabeth Garate, Apr. 14, 1935; children—David Carlton, Esther Elizabeth (Mrs. Saied Adour), John Wesley. Ordained to ministry Elim Missionary Assemblies, 1935; pastor various chs., 1935-38; instr. Elim Bible Inst., 1938, campus pastor, 1938-44, pres. 1949—. Gen. sec. Elim Missionary Assemblies (now Elim Fellowship), 1940-54, gen. chmn., 1954—; bd. mem. Nat. Assn. Evangs., 1958—; bd. mem. Pentecostal Fellowship of N. Am., 1961—, treas., 1963-65, 73-80; bd. mem. Evang. Family Service N.Y. State, 1966—. Address: Elim Bible Inst Lima NY 14485

SPENCER, JAMES JACOB, exec.; b. Richmond, Va., July 1, 1934; s. James A. and Wally L. S.; student U. Richmond; m. Joyce Blankenship, Oct. 7, 1955; children—Judith, Jacqueline, James, Jennifer. Parts clk. Fruehauf Corp., 1953-55, service mgr., 1957-59; bookkeeper Braver Pontiac, 1955-57; sr. staff accountant Dalton & Pennel Co., C.P.A.'s, 1959-67; comptroller Best Products Co., Inc., Richmond, Va., 1967-70, dir. fin., 1970-72, asst. treas., 1972-76, treas., 1976—. Baptist. Home: 7803 Yardley Rd W Richmond VA 23229 Office: Hwy 1 N Ashland VA 23005

SPENCER, JOHN FRANKLIN, editor; b. Carey, Ohio, Oct. 18, 1912; s. Charles Guido and Grace (Cover) S.; student Harvard, 1930-34; A.B., Western Res. U., 1953; m. Cordelia Bankson Curtz, July 8, 1942; children—John Franklin, Sarah Howe. Asso. account exec. Fuller & Smith & Ross, 1934-40; tech. writer advt. div. Republic Steel, Cleve., 1945-50, editor, 1952-56; account exec. Lee Donnelley Co., Cleve., 1950-52; account exec., v.p. Lee Donnelley Co. & Clark & Bobertz, 1956-60; asso. editor Material Handling Engring., Cleve., 1960-64, mng. editor, 1965; editor Handling and Shipping Mgmt., Cleve., 1965-70, exec. editor, 1970-77, editor emeritus, 1977—; editor Presdl. Issue, 1968—, Mgmt. Time and Leisure, 1969-70; chmn. Transp. Logistics Inst., 1977—; lectr. phys. distbn. mgmt., 1965—. Served with AUS, 1941-45. Decorated Purple Heart. Mem. Cleve. Coll. Alumni Assn. (pres. 1966-68), Soc. Packaging and Handling Engrs. (past sec. Cleve. chpt.), Am. Soc. Bus. Press Editors. Clubs: Harvard of Cleve., Cheshire Cheese. Home: 2367 Demington Dr Cleveland Heights OH 44106 Office: 1111 Chester Ave Cleveland OH 44114

SPENCER, JOHN HEDLEY, educator; b. Stapleford, Eng., Apr. 10, 1933; s. Thomas and Eva (Johnson) S.; B.Sc., U. St. Andrews (Scotland), 1955, B.Sc. with honours, 1956; Ph.D., McGill U., 1960; m. Magdeliene Vera Kulin, Sept. 18, 1958; children—Robin Anne, David Thomas, Mark Stewart. Came to Can., 1956. Mem. faculty McGill U., Montreal, 1961-78, asso. prof. biochemistry, 1966-71, prof., 1971-78; prof. and head biochemistry Queen's U., Kingston, Ont., 1978—. Montreal Cancer Research Soc. student, 1956-59; Damon Runyon Meml. Fund postdoctoral fellow Columbia U., N.Y.C., 1959-61; recipient Ayerst award Canadian Biochem. Soc., 1972. Mem. Canadian Biochem. Soc. (treas. 1966-69, v.p. 1978-79), Biochem. Soc., Am. Soc. Biol. Chemists, AAAS, Sigma Xi. Author: The Physics and Chemistry of DNA and RNA, 1972. Home: 21 Hillcroft Dr Kingston ON K7L 4E8 Canada

SPENCER, LEWIS DOUGLAS, lawyer; b. Frankfort, Ind., Feb. 6, 1917; s. Clarence D. and Hazel (Ghormley) S.; A.B., DePauw U., 1939; LL.B., Columbia, 1942; student Motorola Exec. Inst., 1969; m. Marcia Jane Maish, Jan. 29, 1947; children—Karen Jane Spencer Redman, Margo Linn Spencer Sgarlata. Admitted to N.Y. bar, 1942, Ind. bar, 1943, Ill. bar, 1947; asso. firm Carter, Ledyard and Milburn, N.Y.C., 1942-43, Barnes, Hickam, Pantzer & Boyd, Indpls., 1943-44, O'Connor & Farber, N.Y.C., 1944-47, Peterson, Rall, Barber, Ross & Seidel, Chgo., 1947-51; atty. Motorola, Inc., and subsidiaries, 1951-77, asst. sec., 1956-74, sec., 1974-77, gen. atty., 1959-73, gen. counsel, 1973-77, v.p., 1965-77; lectr. Loyola U. Sch. Law, Chgo., 1978-79, prof., 1979-80. Mem. Park Ridge (Ill.) Bd. Fire and Police Commrs., 1964-67; mem. Park Ridge Zoning Bd. Appeals and Zoning Commn., 1967-75, chmn., 1968-75; bd. dirs. Park Ridge United Fund, 1966-69, pres., 1968. Mem. Chgo. Bar Assn., Chgo. Tax Club (bd. dirs. 1965-71, pres. 1969), Tax Inst. (treas. 1961, bd. dirs. 1961-64). Mem. Park Ridge Community Ch. (bd. dirs. 1964-72, chmn. congregation 1970-71). Club: Park Ridge Univ. Contbr. articles to profl. jours. Home: 1000 S Broadway Park Ridge IL 60068

SPENCER, LEWIS NEAL, constrn. co. exec.; b. Lander, Wyo., May 9, 1923; s. Clyde Hudson and Mary Neal (McCann) S.; B.S., Oreg. State Coll., 1947; m. Mary Lucille Ikard, Nov. 25, 1949; children—Melissa, Mark. Engring. aide C.E., U.S. Army, Bonneville (Oreg.) Dam, 1947-48; city engr., Ontario, Oreg., 1948; with Morrison-Knudsen Co., Inc., 1948—, v.p., 1968-73, mgr. No. Constrn. Co. div., 1968-71, v.p. charge Canadian and European ops., 1971-72, v.p. charge internat. ops., 1972-73, exec. v.p. internat., Boise, Idaho, 1973—, also dir. Served with C.E., U.S. Army, 1943-46, 51-52. Mem. Asso. Gen. Contractors Am., The Beavers. Clubs: Arid, Hillcrest Country (Boise); Capilano Golf and Country (Vancouver, B.C., Can.); Internat. (Washington); World Trade (San Francisco). Home: 4330 Hillcrest Dr Boise ID 83705 Office: 1 Morrison-Knudsen Plaza Boise ID 83729

SPENCER, MELVIN JOE, lawyer, hosp. adminstr.; b. Buffalo Center, Iowa, Jan. 2, 1923; s. Kenos W. and Jennie (Michaelson) S.; A.B., U. Mich., 1948, J.D., 1950; m. Dena Joyce Butterfield, Mar. 1, 1952; children—Dennis Norman, Gregory Melvin, Shelly Lynn. Admitted to Iowa bar, 1950, Mo. bar, 1950, Okla. bar, 1961; practiced in Kansas City, Mo., 1950-61, Oklahoma City, 1961—; asso., partner Watson, Ess, Marshall & Enggas, 1950-61; partner Miller & Spencer and predecessor firm, 1961-75, of counsel, 1975—; adminstr. Deaconess Hosp., 1975—; dir. Union Bank & Trust Co., Oklahoma City; dir., sec. Hosp. Casualty Co. Gen. counsel Free Methodist Ch. N.Am., mem. bd. adminstrn., also mem. investment com.; mem. constl. council Free Meth. Ch. World Fellowship. Municipal judge, Roeland Park, Kans., 1952. Mem. City Council, Roeland Park, 1954; precinct chmn. Republican Party, 1968—; del. Rep. State Conv., 1968. Bd. dirs. Deaconess Hosp., Oklahoma City Christian Counselling Center, 1973-75; bd. dirs., sec. Met. Hosp. Assn., FMC Ministries, Inc.; bd. dirs. Emergency Med. Services Central Okla., 1975-78; trustee Central Coll., McPherson, Kans., Okla. Hosp. Assn.; mem. adv. bd. Okla. State U. Tech. Inst. Served to capt. USAAF, 1943-46. Mem. Am., Okla., Oklahoma County bar assns., Okla. Heritage Assn., Okla. Hist. Soc., Order of Coif, Phi Beta Kappa, Phi Kappa Phi. Free Methodist (bd. dirs., sec.). Asso. editor Mich. Law Rev., 1949-50. Club: Men's Dinner. Home: 5910 N Shawnee St Oklahoma City OK 73112 Office: 5501 N Portland St Oklahoma City OK 73112

SPENCER, MURLIN BERTRAND, journalist; b. Ft. Morgan, Colo., Nov. 11, 1909; s. Robert B. and Carrie (Eyestone) S.; student U. Colo., 1928-29; B.A., U. Nebr., 1931; m. Christine Sorensen, Aug. 18, 1935 (div. 1970); children—Karen Carver, Cynthia Doherty; m. 2d, Nancy Chinn, July 11, 1970. Editor, Ft. Morgan Times, 1932-36; reporter Spokane Daily Chronicle, 1936-37; newsman AP, Salt Lake City, 1937-39, Sacramento, 1939-41, San Francisco, 1941-42, war corr. AP, Gen. Douglas MacArthur's Hdqrs., 1942-45, chief of bur. Central Pacific, 1945, Tokyo, 1945-46, states of Wash. and Alaska, Seattle, 1946-68; exec. editor Fairbanks (Alaska) Daily News Miner, 1968-71; news editor Anchorage (Alaska) Daily Times, 1971-72, Eugene (Oreg.) Register-Guard, 1972—. Recipient Best Editorial Award Alaska Press Club, 1969. (Disting. Service to Journalism award Wash. chpt. 1968), Mem. Sigma Delta Chi, Phi Gamma Delta. Clubs: Farthest North Press (past pres.) (Fairbanks); Alaska Press (past pres.). Reported surrender ceremony aboard U.S.S. Missouri, Tokyo Bay, 1945. Address: 120 Westbrook Way Eugene OR 97405

SPENCER, RALPH LEE, univ. dean; b. Claremont, N.H., Feb. 21, 1927; s. Albert Lee and Olive (Martindale) S.; B.A., Yale, 1951, M.A., 1953; Ed.D., Cornell U., 1964; m. Marion Chapman, Sept. 2, 1950; children—Robert Lee, Janet Chapman. Tchr., McTernan's Sch., Waterbury, Conn., 1951-53; elementary sch. tchr. Corning (N.Y.) City Sch., 1953-56, asst. elementary sch. prin., 1956-57, elementary sch. prin., 1957-62, elementary coordinator, 1962-63, asst. supt., 1963-65; asso. prof. ednl. adminstrn. Temple U., 1965-68, asso. dean grad. sch., 1968-70; dean div. profl. studies State U. N.Y. at Oswego, 1970—, provost, 1978—; team visitor Nat. Council for Accreditation of Tchr. Edn., 1971; chmn. adv. bd. tchr. certification Regents N.Y. State. Served with USAAF, 1945-46. Recipient Am. Assn. Sch. Adminstrs. S.D. Shankland award, 1962; Cornell U. Julian Butterworth award for research in edn., 1965. Mem. NEA, Am. Assn. Sch. Adminstrs., Am. Assn. Colls. for Tchr. Edn. (pres. N.Y. State), Am. Edn. Research Assn., Am. Sociol. Assn., Am. Acad. Social and Polit. Sci., Phi Delta Kappa. Author: (with James J. Jones and C. Jackson Salisbury) Secondary School Administration, 1969. Home: RD 3 McCracken Ln Oswego NY 13126

SPENCER, RICHARD PAUL, educator, physician, biochemist; b. N.Y.C., June 7, 1929; s. David E. and Frances (Fried) S.; A.B., Dartmouth, 1951; M.D., U. So. Calif., 1954; M.A. (NSF fellow, Helen Hay Whitney fellow), Harvard, 1958, Ph.D., 1961; m. Gwendolyn Enid Williams, Apr. 7, 1956; children—Carolyn Roberts, Jennifer Holt, Priscilla James. Intern, Beth Israel Hosp., Boston, 1954-55; practice medicine specializing in nuclear medicine; mem. faculty biophysics U. Buffalo, 1961-63; chief radioisotope service VA Hosp., Buffalo, 1961-63; asso. prof. nuclear medicine Yale Sch. Medicine, 1963-68, prof., 1968-74; prof., chmn. dept. nuclear medicine U. Conn. Health Center, 1974—. Mem. Am. Physiol. Soc., AAAS, Soc. Nuclear Medicine, Biophys. Soc. Author: The Intestinal Tract, 1960; (with others) Biophysical Principles, 1965; Radionuclide Studies of the Spleen, 1975; Clinical Focus on Nuclear Medicine, 1977; Handbook of Nuclear Medicine, 1977. Contbr. articles to profl. jours. Office: U Conn Health Center Farmington CT 06032

SPENCER, ROBERT C., educator; b. Chgo., Mar. 28, 1920; A.B., U. Chgo., 1943, M.A., 1952, Ph.D. (Univ. fellow 1952-53) in Polit. Sci., 1955; m. 1941; five children. Instr. polit. sci. and sociology St. Michaels Coll., 1949-51, asst., then asso. prof. polit. sci., 1953-60, prof. govt., 1960-63, dir. summer sessions, 1960-61, asst. to pres., 1963-65; prof. polit. sci., chmn. dept., dean summer sessions U. R.I., 1965-67, dean Grad. Sch., 1967-69; founding pres. Sangamon State U., Springfield, Ill., 1969-78, prof. govt. and public affairs, 1978—; research asso. Indsl. Relations Center, U. Chgo., 1952-53; extension lectr. N.Y. State Sch. Indsl. and Labor Relations, Cornell U., 1955-56; vice chmn. West Central Ill. Ednl. Telecommunications Consortium, 1975-77, chmn., 1977-78; chmn. task force personnel Vt. Little Hoover Commn., 1957-58; mem. Ill. adv. com. U.S. Commn. on Civil Rights, 1979—. Bd. dirs. City Day Sch., Springfield, 1979—. mem. Vt. Senate, 1958-62; Nat. Com. faculty fellow, research dir. Democratic Nat. Com., 1962-63. Served to lt. (j.g.) USCGR, 1943-45. Mem. Vt. Hist. Soc., Am. Soc. Pub. Adminstrn., AAUP. Author: (with Robert J. Huckshorn) The Politics of Defeat, 1971. Home: 403 W Jackson St Petersburg IL 62675

SPENCER, SAMUEL, lawyer; b. Washington, Dec. 8, 1910; s. Henry Benning and Katharine (Price) S.; student Milton (Mass.) Acad., 1924-29; A.B magna cum laude, Harvard, 1932, LL.B., 1935; m. Dora White, June 28, 1935; children—Henry B., Janet Spencer Dougherty, Richard A. Admitted to N.Y. bar, 1937, D.C., 1938, U.S. Supreme Ct., 1950; asso. firm Shearman & Sterling, N.Y.C., 1935-37, Covington, Burling, Rublee, Acheson & Shorb, Washington, 1937- 40, 45-47; partner firm Spencer, Whalen & Graham, 1947—; pres. bd. commrs., D.C., 1953-56; pres., chmn. bd. Tennessee R.R. Co., 1956-73; dir. Riggs Nat. Bank, C.N.O. & T.P. Ry. Co. Bd. dirs. Nat. Symphony Orch., 1949-53, Garfield Hosp., 1947-53, 56-62; bd. dirs. Children's Hosp., 1948-53, sec., 1951-53; trustee Potomac Sch., 1947-53; pres. Washington Hosp. Center, 1958-60, dir., 1958-65; mem. Washington Nat. Monument Soc., 1958—. Served from ensign to comdr. USNR, 1940-45. Decorated Bronze Star with combat V. Mem. Am. Bar Assn., Bar Assn. D.C., Am. Cancer Soc. (trustee D.C. chpt. 1951-53), AIA (hon.), Washington Inst. Fgn. Affairs (dir., sec. 1961—), Jud. Council D.C. Circuit (com. on adminstrn. of justice 1966-70), Soc. of Cincinnati, Phi Beta Kappa. Episcopalian (sr. warden). Clubs: Metropolitan of Washington (bd. govs. 1949-53, 56-61; pres. 1959-60); Chevy Chase (Md.). Home: 4814 Dexter St Washington DC 20007 Office: 2000 Massachusetts Ave Washington DC 20006

SPENCER, SAMUEL REID, JR., coll. pres.; b. Rock Hill, S.C., 1919; A.B. summa cum laude, Davidson Coll., 1940, LL.D., 1964; M.A., Harvard, 1947, Ph.D., 1951; m. Ava Clark, 1948; children—Samuel Reid, Ellen Spencer Henschen, Clayton, Frank. With Vick Chem. Co., N.Y.C., 1940; research asst. to Grenville Clark, Dublin, N.H., 1947-48; asst. to pres. Davidson Coll., 1951-54, dean of students, asso. prof. history, 1954, dean of students, prof. history, 1955-57; pres. Mary Baldwin Coll., 1957-68; pres. Davidson (N.C.) Coll., 1968—; dir. Piedmont Bank & Trust Co.; Fulbright lectr. U. Munich, 1965-66; mem. commn. on liberal learning Assn. Am. Colls., 1970-73, mem. commn. instl. affairs, 1974—, chmn., 1975—, bd. dirs., 1976—, chmn. commn. instnl. devel. and nat. affairs, 1979; pres. So. Univ. Conf., 1979-80; mem. commn. govtl. relations Am. Council Edn., 1973-76. Bd. dirs. Grenville Clark Fund at Dartmouth Coll., 1973—, Charlotte-Mecklenburg chpt. Urban League, 1979—; trustee Agnes Scott Coll., 1975—, Warren Wilson Coll. Served to maj. AUS, 1940-45. Austin fellow Harvard, 1947-48, Rosenwald fellow, 1948-49, Kent fellow Nat. Council on Religion in Higher Edn., 1949-51. Mem. Phi Beta Kappa, Omicron Delta Kappa. Presbyn. (bd. Christian edn.). Author: Decision for War, 1917, 1953; Booker T. Washington and the Negro's Place in American Life, 1955. Address: Davidson Coll Davidson NC 28036

SPENCER, THAXTER PARKS, life ins. co. exec.; b. Boston, June 25, 1921; s. Graham Parks and Hope Thaxter (Parks) S.; A.B., Harvard U., 1943, LL.B., 1949. Admitted to Mass. bar, 1949; with New Eng. Mut. Life Ins. Co., Boston, 1949—, counsel, 1963-67, v.p., 1967-78, sec., 1975-78, counsel, 1978—. Bd. dirs., sec. New Eng. Hosp., Boston, Dimock Community Health Center, Boston, Gore Pl. Soc.; dist. chmn. Boy Scouts Am.; trustee Kings Chapel, Boston. Served to capt. USNR, 1943-46, 50-52, 60-61. Mem. Am., Mass. bar assns., Assn. Life Ins. Counsel, Naval Res. Assn. Unitarian. Clubs: Somerset, Harvard, Union Boat (Boston); Cambridge (Mass.) Boat; Wardroom. Co-editor: Federal Taxation of Insured Pensions,

1973-78. Home: 147 W Canton St Boston MA 02118 Office: 501 Boylston St Boston MA 02117

SPENCER, THOMAS ANCRUM, educator; b. Orange, N.J., Mar. 31, 1934; s. Thomas Ancrum and Isabelle (Johnson) S.; B.A., Amherst Coll., 1956; Ph.D., U. Wis., 1960; m. Patricia Ann Judkins, June 22, 1956; children—Karen Elizabeth, Robert Andrew, Jonathan Kirk, Melinda. Research asso. U. Wis., 1960, instr., 1960-62, asst. prof., 1962-65, asso. prof., 1965-69; prof. Dartmouth, Hanover, N.H., 1969—, chmn. dept. chemistry, 1969-73, N.H. prof. chemistry, 1972—. Mem. Cottrell program adv. com. Research Corp., 1972—. A.P. Sloan Research fellow, 1965-68. Mem. Am. Chem. Soc., Phi Beta Kappa. Home: Fox Field Ln Hanover NH 03755

SPENCER, THOMAS MORRIS, jr. coll. pres.; b. Nolan County, Tex., Nov. 30, 1916; s. Thomas Monroe and Della (Whitley) S.; B.S., Sam Houston State U., Huntsville, Tex., 1935, M.A., 1939; Ed.D., U. Houston, 1947; m. Rachel Bradham, Nov. 26, 1936; children—Betty Dell, Thomas Morris, Ann Lou, Vera Sue (dec.), Willie Jo. High sch. prin., Holland, Tex., 1935-37; supt. Thrall (Tex.) public schs., 1937-41, Llano (Tex.) public schs., 1941-42; dep. supt. public instrn. State of Tex., 1942-43; supt. Cypress (Tex.)-Fairbanks public schs., 1943-47; pres. Blinn Coll., Brenham, Tex., 1947-57, S. Plains Coll., Levelland, Tex., 1957-61, San Jacinto Coll., Pasadena, Tex., 1961—; past mem. Gov. Tex. Adv. Com. Post Secondary Ednl. Planning; past pres. Tex. Public Jr. Coll. Assn.; now mem. adv. com. Tex. Statewide Study Continuing Edn., Tex. Council Aerospace Edn.; bd. dirs. Tex. Surplus Property Agy. Active local Salvation Army, YMCA, A.R.C., United Fund; past chmn. bd. elders, past chmn. ofcl. bd. First Christian Ch. (Disciples of Christ), Pasadena. Mem. Assn. Tex. Colls. and Univs (past pres.), Am. Assn. Jr. Colls., Pasadena C. of C. (dir.). Clubs: Rotary (past pres. Pasadena), Lions (past pres. Pasadena), Shriners, Woodmen of World. Address: San Jacinto Coll Pasadena TX 77505

SPENCER, VAINO HASSAN, judge; b. Los Angeles, July 22, 1920; d. Abdul and Nona (Taylor) Hassan; grad. summa cum laude, Los Angeles City Coll., 1949; LL.B., Southwestern Sch. Law, Los Angeles, 1952; m. Lorenzo V. Spencer, Oct. 15, 1949 (div. 1967). Real estate bus., Los Angeles, 1938-47; admitted to Cal. bar, 1952; gen. practice law, Los Angeles, 1952-61; judge Municipal Ct. Los Angeles, 1961-76; judge Superior Ct. Los Angeles County, 1976—. Mem. Calif. Law Revision Commn., 1960-63, Atty. Gen.'s Adv. Com. Constl. Rights, 1959-61, 61-63; chmn. legal redress com. NAACP, 1955-56, exec. bd., 1955-56, mem. life membership com., 1962-64; adviser integrated housing Consol. Realty Bd., 1961-65; bd. dirs. Nat. Com. Against Discrimination in Housing. Mem. adv. com. Bank of Finance, Los Angeles, 1963-67. Mem. Calif. Democratic Central Com., 1958-60, 60-62; exec. bd. Dem. County Central Com., 1958-60; pres. Dem. Minority Conf., 1957-60; exec. bd. Community Groups Polit. Action, 1960-62; mem. Jud. Council Calif., 1979—; mem. Jud. Criminal Justice Planning Commn., 1980—. Dir.-at-large Calif. Mental Health Assn., 1962-64; bd. dirs. So. Calif. chpt. ACLU, 1959-61. Named Woman of Year, Pitts. Courier, 1946, 53, Los Angeles Sentinel, 1952, 57, 62; recipient Civil Rights Service award Dem. Minority Conf., 1960; Equal Opportunities honoree Urban League, 1961; named Distinguished Citizen in Field Civil Rights, Coca Cola Co., 1962; recipient Trailblazer award Nat. Assn. Bus. and Profl. Women, 1962; named hon. citizen Omaha, 1962. Mem. Am., Nat., Los Angeles bar assns., Calif. Conf. Judges, Nat. Assn. Women Judges (pres.-elect), Langston Law Club, Am. Judicature Soc. Office: Superior Court County Court House 111 N Hill St Los Angeles CA 90012

SPENCER, WARREN FRANK, educator; b. Swan Quarter, N.C., Jan. 27, 1923; s. Carroll Baxter and Lucille Gertrude (Mann) S.; student George Washington U., 1942, U. Fla., 1942-43; B.S.S. cum laude, Georgetown U., 1947; M.A., U. Pa., 1949, Ph.D., 1955; m. Elizabeth Jolanda Toth, Sept. 6, 1947; children—Lucille Mann, Carroll Baxter. Instr. history Salem Coll., Winston-Salem, N.C., 1950-53, asst. prof., 1953-56; asst. prof. Old Dominion U., Norfolk, Va., 1956-57, asso. prof., 1957-61, prof., chmn. div. social studies, dept. history, 1961-67; prof. history U. Ga., Athens, 1967—, Sandy Beaver Teaching prof. history, 1978—; vis. scholar Duke U., 1952. Served with AUS, 1943-45. Recipient 1st Ann. Faculty award Old Dominion U., 1961-62, Best History Book Pub. in 1970 award Phi Alpha Theta, 1971; named Outstanding Honors Tchr., U. Ga., 1977; Am. Philos. Soc. fellow, 1958, 70, 75. Mem. Am. Hist. Assn., So. Hist. Assn. (chmn. European History sect. program com. 1970), Ga. Assn. Historians (pres. 1978-80), Soc. French Hist. Studies, Phi Alpha Theta. Democrat. Episcopalian. Co-founder, pres. Norfolk Hist. Soc., 1966-67. Author: (with Lynn M. Case) The United States and France - Civil War Diplomacy, 1970. Contbr. articles to profl. jours. Home: 290 Fortson Dr Athens GA 30606 Office: Dept History Univ Ga Athens GA 30602*

SPENCER, WILLIAM ALBERT, physician; b. Oklahoma City, Feb. 16, 1922; s. Arthur M. and Lillian (Wehremeyer) S.; B.S. cum laude, Georgetown U., 1942; M.D., Johns Hopkins, 1946; m. Helen Margaret Hart, Mar. 29, 1945; children—William Albert, Susan Hart. Intern. asst. resident pediatrics Harriet Lane Home, Johns Hopkins Hosp., 1946-48; instr. pediatrics, asst. prof. physiology Baylor U. Coll., Medicine, 1950—; med. dir. Southwestern Poliomyelitis Respiratory Center, Jefferson Davis Hosp., Houston, 1950-58, dir. regional respirator center Nat. Found. Infantile Paralysis: chmn. medical research study section Vocational Rehabilitation Adminstrn.; asst. prof., depts. physiology and pediatrics Baylor U. Coll. Medicine, 1950-57, prof., chmn. dept. of rehabilitation, 1957—; pres. Inst. Rehab. and Research, Tex. Med. Center, 1958—; cons. spl. med. adv. group VA; cons. Nat. Inst. for Handicapped Research, 1979—, dep. dir., acting dir., 1979; pres. Assn. Research and Tng. Centers. Served as capt. M.C., AUS, 1948-50. Named One of Ten Outstanding Young Men of Am., U.S. Jr. C. of C., 1955; Physician of Year, Pres.'s Com. Employment Handicapped, 1964. Diplomate Am. Bd. Pediatrics. Fellow Am. Acad. Pediatrics; mem. Am., Tex med. assns., Harris County Med. Soc., Houston Pediatric Soc., Am. Congress Rehab. Medicine (chmn. legis. com.), Phi Beta Kappa Sigma Xi, also Phi Beta Pi, also mem. Alpha Omega Alpha. Episcopalian. Author and editor: Treatment of Acute Poliomyelitis, 1954. Home: 2836 Bellefontaine Houston TX 77025 Office: 1333 Moursund Ave Houston TX 77025

SPENCER, WILLIAM COURTNEY, educator; b. Uniontown, Pa., Sept. 15, 1919; s. Clarence Ashley and Hazel (Stark) S.; A.B., Drew U., 1941; A.M., Columbia, 1946, Ed.D., 1952; m. Evelyn Van Cleve Bailey, Aug. 6, 1942; children—Courtney Lloyd, Henry Bailey, Edward Ashley. Tchr., Scarsdale (N.Y.) Pub. Schs., 1946-49; dir. Univ. Sch. Columbia, 1949-52; prof. edn. and adminstrn. U. Del., 1952-55; prof. dir. grad. program tchr. edn. N.Y.U., 1955-59; prof. adminstrn. U. Chile, Santiago, 1959-60; prof. higher edn. and internat. affairs N.Y. U., 1960-61; dir. Interam. affairs Inst. Internat. Edn., also asst. sec. gen. Council Higher Edn. in Am. Republics, 1961-65; asso. dean Grad. Sch. Bus., Columbia, 1965-67, spl. asst. to pres., 1967-69; pres. Western Coll., Oxford, Ohio, 1969-74; pres. The Lindenwood Colls., 1974-79; pres., chief exec. officer Fund for Peace, 1979—; cons. Telesession, Inc. and Trans Internat. Mgmt. Corp., 1979—; cons. UNESCO Latin Am. major project in edn., Chile, 1959-60, project edn. and econ. planning, India, 1962; cons. Am. Council Edn., 1960-61; del. Pan-Am. Assembly on Population, 1965; mem. standing com. on internat. edn. Coll. Entrance Exam. Bd., 1972-74; mem. scholarship bd. Timken Co. Ednl. Fund, 1971-76. Bd. dirs. Internat. Sch. Service, 1963-69, chmn., 1967-69; bd. dirs. Hoff-Barthelson Music Schs., 1965-69, chmn., 1969; mem. Mo. master planning com. Coordinating Bd. Higher Edn., 1975—; pres. Ind. Colls. and Univs. of Mo.; mem. exec. com. Mo. Colls. Fund; bd. dirs. St. Louis Council on World Affairs, 1977-79; bd. dirs., mem. exec. com. Fund for Peace, N.Y.C.; mem. Com. on East-West Accord, Washington. Served to lt. comdr. USNR, 1942-46. Decorated Purple Heart, commendation medals from Royal Navy, U.S. Navy. Mem. Council Fgn. Relations. Clubs: Century Assn. N.Y. Yacht (N.Y.C.); Larchmont (N.Y.) Yacht. Author: Education and World Responsibility, 1965; also articles. Editor: Art and the University, 1964; University and National Development, 1965; Agriculture and the University, 1965. Home: 18 Otter Cove Old Saybrook CT 06475

SPENCER, WILLIAM IRA, banker; b. Grand Junction, Colo., July 24, 1917; s. Eugene William and Nellie (Haviland) S.; B.A., Colo. Coll., 1939; postgrad. Columbia U., 1945; m. Kathryn Marie Cope, June 5, 1943. With Chem. Bank & Trust Co., N.Y.C., 1939-51; asst. v.p. Commodities div. Nat. City Bank (name now Citibank, N.A.), N.Y.C., 1951-54, v.p. petroleum dept., 1954-59, sr. v.p., head spl. industries group, 1959-65, exec. v.p. spl. industries group, 1965-68, exec. v.p. operating group, 1968-70, pres., chief adminstrv. officer, 1970—; dir. Sears, Roebuck & Co., United Techs. Corp., Odyssey Inst., Inc., Bus. Mktg. Corp., Econ. Capital Corp., Asia Pacific Capital Corp., Ltd., Bedford Stuyvesant Devel. and Services Corp.; mem. nat. adv. com. on banking policies and practices. Chmn., N.Y. Blood Center, Inc.; hon. chmn. Berkshire Farm Center and Services for Youth; trustee Colo. Coll., N.Y. U. Med Center, N.Y. Community Trust. Named Man of Yr., Odyssey House, 1976. Mem. Transp. Assn. Am. (dir.), Bond Club of N.Y., Econ. Club of N.Y. Clubs: Augusta Nat. Golf, Blind Brook, Sleepy Hollow Country, Racquet and Tennis, Links, Nat. Golf Links; Boone & Crockett, Camp Fire. Home: 12 Beekman Pl New York NY 10022 Office: 399 Park Ave New York NY 10043

SPENCER, WILLIAM MICAJAH, III, distbn. co. exec.; b. Birmingham, Ala., Dec. 10, 1920; s. William Micajah and Margaret Woodward (Evins) S.; B.S., U. South, 1941; postgrad. Grad. Sch. Bus. Adminstrn., Harvard U., 1947; m. Evalina Sommerville Brown, Sept. 28, 1946; children—Murray Brown Spencer South, Margaret Anne Spencer Smith. Vice pres. Owen-Richards Co. (name changed to Motion Industries, Inc. 1972), Birmingham, 1946-52, pres., 1952-72, chmn. bd., 1972—; dir. First Nat. Bank of Birmingham, Ala. Bancorp., Ala. Gt. So. Ry., Mead Corp., Redfern Foods, Robertson Banking Co., ALTEC, Inc. Pres., Birmingham C. of C., 1963-65, Birmingham Festival of Arts, 1964-65, Bapt. Med. Center Found., Birmingham, Ala. Safety Council, 1979-80. Served to capt. USMC, 1942-46. Decorated Bronze Star. Mem. Blue Key, Phi Beta Kappa, Omega Delta Kappa. Episcopalian. Home: 3035 Cherokee Rd Birmingham AL 35223 Office: PO Box 1477 Birmingham AL 35201

SPENDLOVE, REX S., educator; b. Hoytsville, Utah, Apr. 29, 1926; s. Janus Alburn and Hazel Teresa (Stonebraker) S.; B.S., Brigham Young U., 1951, M.S., 1952; Ph.D., Ohio State U., 1955; m. Reta Bright Allen, May 9, 1949; children—Cheri Lynn, Rex Alan, Debbi Susan, Lisa Janette, Lori Jeanne. Instr. dept. bacteriology U. Conn., 1955-58; research microbiologist Viral and Rickettsial Disease Lab., Calif. Dept. Pub. Health, Berkeley, 1958-66; prof., head dept. bacteriology and pub. health Utah State U., Logan, 1966-73, prof. dept. biology, 1973—; pres. Sterile Systems, Inc. Mem. subcom. Internat. Commn. Nomenclature of Viruses. Served with USNR, 1944-46. Diplomate Am. Bd. Microbiology. Mem. Am. Soc. Microbiology (pres. Intermountain br. 1970), Am. Assn. Immunologists, AAAS, N.A. Acad. Scis., Sigma Xi (pres. chpt. 1974). Editorial bd. Excerpta Medica. Home: 931 Sumac Dr Logan UT 84321

SPENGLER, JOSEPH JOHN, economist, educator; b. Piqua, Ohio, Nov. 19, 1902; s. Joseph Otto and Philomena (Schlosser) S.; A.B., Ohio State U., 1926, M.A., 1929, Ph.D., 1930, L.H.D. (hon.), 1965; L.H.D. (hon.), Alma Coll., Tulane U., 1978; m. Dorothy Marie Kress, Aug. 13, 1927. Scholar in econs. Ohio State U., 1926-27, asst. instr. econs., 1927-28, instr., 1928-30; research fellow Brookings Instn., 1928; asst. prof. econs. U. Ariz., 1930-32, asso. prof., 1933-34; asso. prof. econs. Duke U., 1932-33, 34-37, prof., 1937-55, James B. Duke prof. econs., 1955—; tchr. U. N.C., 1935, 72-73, U. Chgo., 1952, Kyoto U., 1952, U. Malaya, 1956, U. Pitts., 1957; cons. Nat. Resources Planning Bd., 1940- 42; regional price exec., region 4, Office Price Adminstrn., 1942-43, cons. to the Dept. of Agriculture. Served in Ohio N.G., 1922-24. Fellow Am. Statis. Assn., AAAS; mem. Mt. Pellerin Soc., Am. Philos. Soc., Am., World acads. art and scis., Am. (past pres.), So. (past pres.) econ. assns., Am. Population Assn. (past pres.), Atlantic Econ. Soc. (past pres.), Canadian Econ. Assn., Royal Econ. Soc., Social Sci. Research Council, Economic Hist. Assn. (past v.p.), Soc. Gen. Systems Research, History of Econs. Soc. (past pres.), Econ. History Soc., Phi Beta Kappa. Author: The Fecundity of Native and Foreign Born Women in New England, 1930; France Faces Depopulation, 1938, 79; French Predecessors of Malthus, 1942; Indian Economic Thought: A Preface to its History, 1971; Declining Population Growth Revisited; 1971; Population Economics, 1972; Population Change, Modernization, and Welfare, 1974; Population and America's Future, 1975; Facing Zero Population Growth, 1978; co-editor: Economic Growth: Brazil, India, Japan, 1955; Population Theory and Policy, 1956; Demographic Analysis, 1956. Contbr.; Am. Studies in Honor of William Kenneth Boyd, 1940; Evolutionary Thought in America, 1950; World Population and Future Resources 1952; Survey of Contemporary Economics, 1952; Economic Development, Principles and Patterns, 1954; Economics and Public Policy, 1954; Economics of International Migration, 1958; Population and World Politics, 1958; Francois Quesnay et La Physiocratie, 1958; Commonwealth Perspectives, 1958; Essays in Econ. Thought, 1960; Traditions, Values and Socio-Econ. Devel., 1961; Pub. Adminstrn. and Econ. Devel. in India, 1963; Employment, Income and Retirement Problems of the Aged, 1963; Bureaucracy and Political Development The Population Crisis and the Use of World Resources, 1964; The South in Continuity and Change, 1965; Modernization, 1966; Aging and Social Policy, 1966; Social Aspects of Aging, 1966; editor: Natural Resources and Econ. Growth, 1961; contbr. over 250 articles to profl. jours. and symposia. Home: 2240 Cranford Rd Durham NC 27706

SPENGLER, WILLIAM FREDERICK, JR., packaging co. exec.; b. Columbus, Ohio, Sept. 22, 1928; s. William Frederick and Louise Esther (Arehart) S.; B.S. in Bus. Adminstrn., Ohio State U., 1950, M.B.A., 1951; m. Sarah Madeline Burd, Aug. 25, 1951; children—William Frederick III, Mary L., John D., Carolyn S. With Owens-Illinois Inc., Toledo, 1951—, comptroller, 1961-63, v.p. div. glass containers, 1963-66, v.p. corp. planning, 1966-68, mng. dir. United Glass Ltd., Eng., 1968-71, asst. gen. mgr. internat. div. Owens-Ill., Toledo, 1971-73, pres. Internat. group, 1973-74, dir. div., 1974-75, exec. v.p. div., 1975-76, pres., chief operating officer internat. ops., 1976-79, domestic ops., 1979—, also mem. exec. com.; dir. Nat. Petro Chems. Corp., N.Y.C.; dir., mem. audit com. Questor Corp., Toledo. Bd. dirs. United Way, Boys' Club Toledo; mem. sr. adv. group Coll. Bus. Adminstrn., Ohio State U.; trustee Bowling Green State U.; mem. adv. council Grad. Sch. Indsl. Adminstrn., Carnegie-Mellon U. Served with USAF, 1952-54. Mem. Conf. Bd. (internat. council), Internat. Econ. Policy Assn. (dir.), Nat. Planning Assn. (commn. on changing internat. realities), Internat. C. of C. (exec. com., trustee of U.S. council). Republican. Roman Catholic. Clubs: Toledo Country, Inverness, Toledo; Muirfield Village Golf (Columbus). Home: 3532 Ridgewood Rd Toledo OH 43606 Office: PO Box 1035 Toledo OH 43666

SPERAKIS, NICHOLAS GEORGE, artist; b. N.Y.C., June 8, 1943; s. George and Kathren (Lokatas) S.; student Pratt Inst., 1960, NAD, 1960-61, Art Students League N.Y., Pratt Graphic Art Center, 1961-63; m. Lois June Schlosberg, Nov. 16, 1969. Exhibited one man shows at Paul Kessler Gallery, 1963, 64, Provincetown, Mass., Hinckley and Brohel Art Gallery, Washington, 1964, N.Y.C., 1965, Mari Galleries, Woodstock, N.Y., 1966, 67, 68, Larchmont, N.Y., 1967, Eric Schindler Galleries, 1965, Richmond (Va.) Art Gallery, N.Y. U. Student Loeb Center, 1969, L.I. U., 1971, Pratt Inst., 1971, Bienville Gallery, New Orleans, 1972, 74, Pace U., N.Y.C., 1972, Lerner-Heller Gallery, N.Y.C., 1975, 76, Daedal Gallery, Balt., 1976; exhibited group shows: Mercy Hurst Coll., Erie, Pa., 1963, 64, Bklyn. Mus., 1964, 77, Jewish Mus., 1964, Chrysler Mus., 1964, 65, Asso. Am. Artists Galleries, N.Y.C., 1965, Norfolk (Va.) Mus. Arts Scis., 1965, Long Beach (Calif.) Coll., 1969, Am. Acad. and Nat. Inst. Arts and Letters, 1969, 75, print exhbns., France, Italy, Spain, other European Countries, Far East, 1970-71, Lerner-Heller Gallery, 1973, 76, Amherst Coll., 1974, Worcester (Mass.) Mus. Fine Art, 1977, Reading (Pa.) Mus. Art, 1977; represented in permanent collections: Bklyn. Mus., Walter P. Chrysler Mus., Norfolk, Va., Norfolk Mus. Arts and Scis., N.Y.C. Public Library, Phila. Mus. Fine Arts, Worcester Mus. Fine Art, Flint (Mich.) Art Inst., Mus. Modern Art, N.Y.C., U. Conn., Storrs, Amherst Coll., Okla. Fine Arts Center Mus., Am. Acad. and Nat. Inst. Arts and Letters, Detroit Inst. Fine Art; organized (with others) Rhino Horn artist group, N.Y.C., 1970; instr. Sumitt (N.J.) Art Center, 1971, New Sch. Social Research, N.Y.C., 1972—, Fashion Inst. Tech., N.Y.C., 1977—. Recipient First Prize Purchase award Mercy Hurst Coll., 1964; Lawrence and Hinda Rosenthal award Am. Acad. and Nat. Inst. Arts and Letters, 1969; Guggenheim graphics fellow, 1970; McDowell Colony summer residency, 1976. Mem. Soc. Am. Graphic Artists. Address: 245 W 29th St Floor 12A New York City NY 10001. *Art doesn't bring out the voters for candidates X or Z. Art brings forth an experience and enters the knowledge of the viewer, so it helps the individual consider new channels and modes of behavior. One of the reasons there is so much censorship of art is due to the power art has to transform people at the roots not into some action but in a more generalized manner in terms of understanding institutions and traditions for what they really are. I think art changes emotions more than it changes specific ideas.*

SPERANDIO, GLEN JOSEPH, educator; b. Glen Carbon, Ill., May 8, 1918; s. Henry A. and Marjorie (Dunstedter) A.; B.S., St. Louis Coll. Pharmacy, 1940; M.S., Purdue U., 1947, Ph.D., 1950; m. Dorys Bell, June 21, 1946; 1 son, James Glen. Pharmacist, 1936-41; analytical chemist Grove Labs., St. Louis, 1941-43, 45; mfg. pharmacist William R. Warner Co., St. Louis, 1944; instr. Purdue U., 1946-50, asst. prof. pharmacy, 1950-53, asso. prof., 1953-62, prof., 1962—, head dept., 1966-78, asso. dean, 1978—; indsl. cons., 1955—; pharm. cons. VA Hosp., Indpls., 1963-69; mem. blue ribbon com. on standardized bd. exams. Nat. Assn. Bds. Pharmacy, 1969; cons. on clin. pharmacology Surgeon Gen., U.S. Army, 1973—. Served with USCGR, 1944. Named 1st prof. clin. pharmacy in U.S., Distinguished Alumnus, St. Louis Coll. Pharmacy, 1969. Mem. Parenteral Drug Assn. (regional v.p. 1965-67), Nat. Forum, Ind. Soc. Hosp. Pharmacists (pres. 1955-57), Am. Pharm. Assn. (sec.-treas. sect. practical pharmacy 1956), Ind., Tipp County pharm. assns., Internat. Fedn. Pharmacists, Soc. Cosmetic Chemistry, Sigma Xi, Kappa Psi (Nat. Service award 1967, nat. pres. 1963-67), Rho Chi, Phi Lambda Upsilon. Author: Laboratory Manual of Cosmetics, 1956; (with others) Scoville's Art of Compounding, 1959; (with others) Clinical Pharmacy, 1965; author, editor Hosp. Pharmacy Notes, 1959-74. Research in drug, cosmetic formulation. Home: 1306 Northwestern Ave West Lafayette IN 47906 Office: Purdue U Sch Pharmacy Lafayette IN 47907. *A great help in solving problems is to look at the situation from the other person's point of view.*

SPERBER, WILLIAM HENRY, JR., banker; b. Portland, Oreg., Mar. 16, 1933; s. William Henry and Elva (Wood) S.; B.A., B.S., Oreg. State U., 1959; M.B.A., U. Wash., 1963; grad. Stonier Grad. Sch. Banking, 1973; m. Virginia May Reese, Sept. 1, 1957; children—Cheryl Sue, Brian Todd. With Longview Fibre Co., 1959-60, Hughes Aircraft Co., 1961-65; asst. sec.-treas., comptroller Forest Lawn Meml. Park, Glendale, Calif., 1965-67; v.p. Seattle First Nat. Bank, 1967-74; exec. v.p. Rainier Nat. Bank, Seattle, 1975—; dir. NW Automated Clearing House. Bd. dirs., chmn. fin. com. Providence Med. Center. Served with AUS, 1954-56. C.P.A., Wash.; chartered bank auditor; certified internal auditor. Mem. Planning Execs. Inst., Fin. Execs. Inst., Inst. Internal Auditors, Bank Adminstrn. Inst., Mensa. Club: Rainier. Home: 4537 90th St SE Mercer Island WA 98040 Office: 1100 2d Ave Seattle WA 98124

SPERLING, GEORGE ELMER, JR., lawyer; b. Phila., Feb. 5, 1915; s. George E. and Margaret Ethel (Fulton) S.; A.B., Pa. State Coll., 1936, M.A., 1937; J.D., U. Mich., 1940; m. Elizabeth Ruth Smollett, Feb. 3, 1945; children—Mary Elizabeth, Doris Fulton, Patricia Anne. Admitted to Mich. bar, 1940; practice in Ann Arbor, 1940-42; counsel Standard Oil Co., Cleve., 1943-45; counsel Carnation Co., Los Angeles, 1946—, asst. sec., 1951-63, sec., 1963—, mem. jr. bd. dirs., 1952—. Chmn. Wilshire YMCA, 1952—; pres. Brentwood Protective Assn., 1958—. Trustee Bel Air Town and Country Sch. Mem. Navy League, Pa. State Coll. Alumni Assn. of So. Cal. (v.p.), Mich., Ohio, Calif., Wis. bar assns., Brentwood Youth Council (pres. 1959). Presbyn. Clubs: Miracle Mile Kiwanis (pres. dir.), Toastmasters, Riviera Country. Home: 347 25th St Santa Monica CA 90402 Office: 5045 Wilshire Blvd Los Angeles CA 90036

SPERLING, GODFREY, JR., journalist; b. Long Beach, Calif., Sept. 25, 1915; s. Godfrey and Ida (Bailey) S.; B.S., U. Ill., 1937; J.D., U. Okla., 1940; m. Betty Louise Feldmann, June 22, 1942; children—Mary (Mrs. John H. McAuliffe), John Godfrey. Admitted to Ill. bar, 1940; practice in Urbana, Ill., also reporter Champaign-Urbana News-Gazette, 1940-41; mem. staff Christian Sci. Monitor, 1946—, Midwest bur. chief, 1957-62, N.Y. bur. chief, 1962-65, news mgr., asst. chief Washington bur., 1965-73, chief Washington Bur., 1973—, nat. polit. corr., 1970—; lectr. nat. affairs, 1955—; Woodrow Wilson vis. fellow, 1976—. Served to maj. USAAF, 1941-46; col. Res. Mem. Okla., Ill., Mass. bar assns., Congl. Press Corr. Assn., White House Press Corr. Assn., Sigma Delta Chi. Christian Scientist. Clubs: Nat. Press, Overseas Writers, Gridiron of Washington, Sperling Roundtable Breakfast with Godfrey (host) (Washington); Kenwood Country (Bethesda, Md.). Home: 7706 Chatham Rd Chevy Chase MD 20015 Office: 910 16th St NW Washington DC 20006

SPERLING, JAMES EVANS, lawyer; b. Paola, Kans., Aug. 10, 1917; s. Burroughs Lee and Lucretia (Evans) S.; B.A., Washburn U., 1939, LL.B., 1941; m. Betty Montgomery, June 6, 1942; children—Paula, Carol, Jamie. Admitted to Kans. bar, 1941, N.M. bar, 1946; asso. firm Simms, Modrall, Seymour & Simms, Albuquerque, 1946-53; partner firm Modrall, Sperling, Roehl, Harris & Sisk, Albuquerque, 1953—; lectr. Southwestern Legal Found. Oil and Gas Inst., 1958, U. N.Mex. Sch. Law, 1967-68; chmn. exec. com., dir. Albuquerque Nat. Bank. Gen. chmn. Rocky Mountain Mineral Law Inst., 1962, lectr., 1968; mem. N.M. Jud. Standards Commn., 1968—; vice chmn. N.M. Authority, 1963—; rep. Gov. N.Mex., Fed. Pub. Land Law Rev. Commn. Served to capt. USAAF, 1942-45. Mem. Am. Bar Assn. (vice chmn. pub. lands com. 1964-65), State Bar N.Mex., Phi Alpha Delta. Home: 4216 Royene NE Albuquerque NM 87110 Office: Pub Service Bldg Albuquerque NM 87103

SPERO, STANLEY LEONARD, broadcasting exec.; b. Cleve., Oct. 17, 1919; s. Morris B. and Hermine (Harve) S.; B.S. cum laude, U. So. Calif., 1942; postgrad. Cleve. Coll., 1943; m. Frieda Kessler, June 30, 1946; children—Laurie, Lisa, Leslie. Account exec. Radio Sta. WHKK, Akron, Ohio, 1946-48, Radio Sta. KFAC, Los Angeles, 1948-52; account exec. Radio Sta. KMPC, Hollywood, 1952-53, v.p., gen. sales mgr., 1953-68, v.p., gen. mgr., 1968-78; v.p. Golden West Broadcasters, 1978—; dir. Major Market Radio, Los Angeles, 1969—. Pres. permanent charities com. entertainment industry, 1972. Served with U.S. Maritime Service, 1942-43. Mem. So. Calif. Broadcasters Assn. (chmn. 1972), Am. Advt. Fedn. (gov. 1972), Advt. Assn. West, Hollywood C. of C. (dir. 1972—). Clubs: Hollywood Advertising (dir. 1972—, pres. 1960-61). Home: 5027 Hayvenhurst St Encino CA 91316 Office: KMPC 5858 Sunset Blvd Hollywood CA 90028

SPERONI, CHARLES, educator; b. Santa Fiora, Italy, Nov. 2, 1911; s. Edoardo and Aida (Falchi) S.; came to U.S., 1929, naturalized, 1941; A.B., U. Calif. at Berkeley, 1933, Ph.D., 1938; m. Carmela Helen Corica, June 15, 1938. Asso. in Italian, U. Calif. at Los Angeles, 1935-38, instr., 1938-41, asst. prof., 1941-47, asso. prof., 1947-53, prof., 1953—, chmn. dept., 1949-56, dir. summer sessions, 1956-68, acting dean Coll. Fine Arts, 1967-68, dean, 1968—. Decorated Star of Italian Solidarity, Cavaliere Ufficiale della Repubblica Italiana, Commendatore dell'Ordine al Merito della Repubblica Italiana; chevalier dans l'Ordre des Palmes Académiques. Mem. Modern Lang. Assn., Philol. Assn. Pacific Coast, Assn. Am. Tchrs. Italian (pres. 1949), Folklore Soc. Calif., Phi Beta Kappa. Club: University of California. Author: Proverbs and Proverbial Phrases in Basile's Pentameron, 1941; Merbury's Proverbi Vulgari, 1946: (with others) Spoken Italian for Travellers and Students, 1946, Decca's Italian Course, 1947; The Italian Wellerism to the End of the Seventeenth Century, 1953; (with others) Basic Italian, 1958; Panorama Italiano, 1960; Michelangelo Letters, 1960; Wit and Wisdom of the Italian Renaissance, 1964; (with others) Leggendo e ripassando, 1968; The Aphorisms of Orazio Rinaldi, Robert Greene, Lucas Gracian Dantisco, 1968; (with others) L'Italia Oggi, 1976. Asst. editor Modern Language Forum, 1943-47, editor, 1947-49; chmn. bd. editors U. Calif. Press Modern Philology Series, 1949-54; editorial cons. Ency. Britannica's World Lang. Dictionary, 1954. Home: 376 Dalkeith Ave Los Angeles CA 90049

SPERRY, JOHN REGINALD, clergyman; b. Leicester, Eng., May 2, 1924; s. William Reginald and Elsie Agnes (Priest) S.; S.Th., King's Coll., Halifax, N.S., Can., 1956, D.D., 1972; m. Elizabeth Binnie Maclaren, Apr. 24, 1952; children—Angela Elizabeth Sperry Friesen, John. Ordained to ministry Anglican Ch. of Canada, 1950; missionary, Coppermine, N.W.T., Can., 1950-69; rector ch., Ft. Smith, N.W.T., 1969-73, Yellowknife, N.W.T., 1974; bishop of the Arctic, Frobister Bay, Yellowknife, 1974—. Served with Royal Brit. Navy, 1943-46. Translator into Copper Eskimo: Canadian Prayerbook, 1962; Four Gospels and Acts, 1972. Home: PO Box 2009 Yellowknife NT X0E IHO Canada Office: 1055 Avenue Rd Toronto ON M5N 2C8 Canada

SPERRY, ROGER WOLCOTT, neurobiologist; b. Hartford, Conn., Aug. 20, 1913; s. Francis B. and Florence (Kraemer) S.; B.A., Oberlin Coll., 1935, M.A., 1937; Ph.D., U. Chgo., 1941, D.Sc. (hon.), 1977; D.Sc. (hon.), Cambridge U., 1972; m. Norma G. Deupree, Dec. 28, 1949; children—Glenn Tad, Janeth Hope. Research fellow Harvard and Yerkes Labs., 1941-46; asst. prof. anatomy U. Chgo., 1946-52; sect. chief Nat. Inst. Neurol. Diseases of NIH, also asso. prof. psychology U. Chgo., 1952-53; Hixon prof. psychobiology Calif. Inst. Tech., 1954—; research brain orgn. and neural mechanism. Recipient Oberlin Coll. Alumni citation, 1954; Howard Crosby Warren medal Soc. Exptl. Psychologists, 1969; Calif. Scientist of Year award Calif. Mus. Sci. and Industry, 1972; award Passano Found., 1973; Albert Lasker Basic Med. Research award, 1979; co-recipient William Thomas Wakeman Research award Nat. Paraplegia Found., 1972, Claude Bernard sci. journalism award, 1975. Fellow AAAS, Am. Acad. Arts and Scis., Am. Psychol. Assn. (recipient Distinguished Sci. Contbn. award 1971); mem. Royal Acad. (fgn. mem.), Nat. Acad. Scis., Am. Physiol. Soc., Am. Assn. Anatomists, Internat. Brain Research Orgn., Soc. for Study of Devel. and Growth, Psychonomic Soc., Am. Soc. Naturalists, Am. Zool. Soc., Soc. Developmental Biology, Am. Philos. Soc. (Lashley prize 1976), Am. Neurol. Assn. (hon.), Soc. for Neurosci., Internat. Soc. Devel. Biologists, AAUP, Pontifical Acad. Scis., Sigma Xi. Contbr. articles to profl. jours., chpts. to books. Editorial bd. Exptl. Neurology, Exptl. Brain Research, Neuropsychologia, Internat. Jour. Neurosci., Behavioral Biology. Home: 3625 Lombardy Rd Pasadena CA 91107 Office: 1201 E California St Pasadena CA 91125

SPERTI, GEORGE SPERI, research prof.; b. Covington, Ky., Jan. 17, 1900; s. George and Caroline (Speri) S.; E.E., U. Cin., 1923, Baldwin fellow, 1923-24; hon. D.Sc., U. Dayton, 1934, Duquesne U., 1936, Bryant Coll., 1957, Thomas More Coll., 1975, Xavier U., 1978; L.H.D., Caldwell Coll., 1974. Asst. chief meter labs. Union Gas & Elec. Co., Cin., 1922; asst. to research dir. Duncan Electric & Mfg. Co., Lafayette, Ind., 1923; research asst. U. Cin., 1924-25, research prof., also dir. Basic Sci. Research Lab., 1926-35; bd. dirs. Gen. Devel. Labs., Inc., N.Y., 1931-35; chmn. med. and sci. adv. bd. Sperti Drug Corp., 1966—; dir. Sperti Drug Products, Inc., Sperti Lamp Corp. of N.Y., Franklin Corp. Fellow of Grad. Sch., U. Cin.; bd. consultants Basic Sci. Research Lab., U. Cin. Fellow NRC, 1929-31, traveling fellow from Rockefeller Found., 1930-31. Co-founder Basic Sci. Research Lab. Trustee Newman Found., Athenaeum of Ohio; adviser Pax Romana Secretariat for N.Am.; pres. St. Thomas Inst. Advanced Studies (formerly Institutm Divi Thomae); pres., dir. St. Thomas Inst. Advanced Studies; bd. overseers Thomas More Coll. Internat. U., Rome. Chief cons. Sperti Products, Inc., 1937—; prin. cons. WPB, 1942-43; cons. Smaller War Plants Corp., Washington, 1944. Decorated Star of Solidarity 3d class, 1956 (Italy); recipient Cath. Action medal, 1942; Mendel medal, 1943; Christian Culture award, 1947; Internat. U. (Rome) medal, 1958; William Howard Taft medal for notable achievement, Cin. Scientist Engr. of Year, 1970. Mem. Am. Soc. Aged (dir.), Academia Internationale de Philosophie des Sciences, Brussels, Academia de Doctores de Madrid, Emeritus Hall, Pontifical Acad. Sci., Sigma Xi, Eta Kappa Nu, Phi Kappa Theta, Tau Beta Pi, Beta Beta Beta (hon.). Roman Catholic. Club: Newman. Author: Probiotics. Co-author: Bulletin of Basic Science, 1926-35; Quantum Theory in Biology, 1927; Correlated Investigations in the Basic Sciences, 1928. Inventor of K-va meter and of light treatment process and Sperti sunlamps. Discoverer of Biodynes (cellular metabolic factors). Editor-in-chief Studies of the Institutum Divi Thomae. Address: 1842 Madison Rd Cincinnati OH 45206

SPETRINO, RUSSELL JOHN, utility co. exec.; b. Cleve., Apr. 22, 1926; s. John Anthony and Madeline Spetrino; B.S., Ohio State U., 1950; LL.B., Western Res. U., 1954; m. July 17, 1954 (dec.); children—Michael J., Ellen A. Admitted to Ohio bar, 1954; asst. atty. gen. Ohio, 1954-57; atty.-examiner Public Utilities Commn. of Ohio, Columbus, 1957-59; atty. Ohio Edison Co., Akron, 1959-69, sr. atty., 1970-73, gen. counsel, 1973-78, v.p., gen. counsel, 1978—. Served with inf. U.S. Army, 1944-46. Mem. Edison Electric Inst., Ohio Electric Utility Inst., Akron Bar Assn., Ohio State Bar Assn., Am. Bar Assn., Summit County Law Library Assn., Fed. Energy Bar Assn. Republican. Episcopalian. Club: Congress Lake. Home: 867 Lafayette Dr Akron OH 44303 Office: 76 S Main St Akron OH 44308

SPEVACK, MARVIN, educator; b. N.Y.C., Dec. 17, 1927; s. Nathan and Miriam (Propper) S.; B.A., City Coll. N.Y., 1948; M.A., Harvard, 1950, Ph.D., 1953; m. Helga Husmann, May 28, 1962; 1 son, Edmund Daniel. Instr. English, City Coll. N.Y., 1955-61, asst. prof., 1961-63; prof. English, U. Muenster (Germany), 1963—, dir. English Seminar, 1964—, dir. Institutum Erasmianum, 1974—, Fulbright lectr., 1961-62; vis. prof. U. Munich, 1962-63, N.Y. U., summer 1966, Harvard, summer 1973. Served with AUS, 1953-55. Sr. fellow Folger Shakespeare Library, 1970; Guggenheim fellow, 1973-74. Mem. Internat. Assn. U. Profs. English, Modern Lang. Assn. Am., Internat. Shakespeare Assn., Deutsche Shakespeare Gesellschaft W., Phi Beta Kappa. Clubs: Harvard of N.Y.C.; Harvard of Rhein-Ruhr (Germany). Author: Harvard Concordance to Shakespeare, 1973; A Complete and Systematic Concordance to the Works of Shakespeare, 9 vols., 1968-80; also articles and editions. Home: 14 Potstiege 4400 Muenster West Germany Office: 12-20 Johannisstrasse 4400 Muenster West Germany

SPEYER, A. JAMES, mus. curator; b. Pitts.; B.S., Carnegie-Mellon U.; postgrad. Chelsea Polytechnique, London, Eng., Sorbonne, Paris, France; M.A., Ill. Inst. Tech.; studied under Mies van der Rohe. Architect, Chgo., 1946-57; prof. advanced architecture Ill. Inst. Tech., Chgo., 1946-61; curator contemporary art Art Inst. Chgo., 1961—; vis. prof. architecture Nat. U. Athens (Greece), 1957-60; instr. modern art Ford Found. seminar Sch. Art Inst. Chgo.; Chgo. corr. Art News Mag., 1955-57. Address: Art Institute of Chicago Michigan Ave at Adams St Chicago IL 60603

SPEZIALE, ANGELO JOHN, organic chemist; b. Rocky Hill, Conn., Nov. 3, 1916; s. Antonio and Giovina (DiMarco) S.; B.S. in Pharmacy, U. Okla., 1943; M.S. in Organic Chemistry, U. Ill., 1944, Ph.D., 1948; m. Dororhy Baumeister, May 2, 1942; children—Dona Speziale Luedde, Karen Speziale Hutcheson, Wendy. With Monsanto Co., St. Louis, 1948—, sr. scientist agrl. div., 1960-61, dir. research Monsanto Agrl. Products Co., 1963-79; chem., agrl. and indsl. cons., 1979—; vis. lectr. Washington U., St. Louis, 1950-53. Served with U.S. Army, 1944-46. Mem. Am. Chem. Soc. (exec. com. organic div. 1974-76, mem. editorial bd. Jour. Organic Chemistry, 1964-69, lectr. 1970-74; St. Louis sect. award 1973), Weed Sci. Soc. Am. (hon.), AAAS, Sigma Xi. Author publs., patentee synthesis and mechanism action pesticides, phoshporus chemistry, enamines, expoxides, heterocyclics, haloamides. Home: 544 Fairways Circle Creve Coeur MO 63141 Office: 800 N Lindbergh St Saint Louis MO 63166

SPEZIALE, JOHN ALBERT, state supreme ct. justice, chief ct. adminstr.; b. Winsted, Conn., Nov. 21, 1922; s. Louis and Mary (Avampato) S.; B.A. in Econs., Duke U., 1943, J.D., 1947; m. Mary Kocsis, Aug. 12, 1944; children—John Albert, Marcia Jean. Admitted to Conn. bar, 1948; clk. Judiciary Com. of Conn. Gen. Assembly, 1949; judge Municipal Ct., Torrington, Conn., 1949-51; dir. CD, 1951-52; atty. OPS, 1951-52; mem. Conn. State Jud. Council, 1955-59; sr. partner firm Speziale, Mettling, Lefebre & Burns, Torrington, 1958-61; city atty., Torrington, 1957-59; treas. State of Conn., 1958-61; judge Conn. Ct. Common Pleas, 1961-65; judge Conn. Superior Ct., 1965-77, presiding judge Appellate div., 1975-77, chief judge, 1975-77, mem. exec. com., 1975—, chmn. exec. com., 1977—; justice Conn. Supreme Ct., Hartford, 1977—, chief ct. adminstr., 1978—; mem. exec. com. Nat. Conf. State Trial Judges, 1970-74; mem. Conn. Jud. Rev. Council, 1975-77; co-chmn. Conn. Justice Commn., 1975-78; mem. Conn. Commn. on Adult Probation, 1976-77; mem. Advisory Council on Ct. Unification, 1976—; mem. Conn. Bd. Pardons, 1977-78; trustee Conn. Jr. Republic, 1975—. Served to lt. (j.g.) USNR, 1942-46; PTO. Recipient Conn. Trial Lawyers Jud. award, 1977; 1st Unico Nat. Disting. Key award, 1977. Mem. Inst. Jud. Adminstrn., Am. Judicature Soc. (dir. 1978—), Am., Conn., Litchfield County bar assns., Am. Fedn. Musicians (life), Sons of Italy of Am., Phi Beta Kappa. Roman Catholic. Clubs: K.C., Litchfield Country Univ., Torrington Country, Eastlawn Country, Unico (life). Home: 278 Wind-Tree Torrington CT 06790 Office: 231 Capitol Ave Hartford CT 06106

SPEZZANO, VINCENT EDWARD, newspaper publisher; b. Retsof, N.Y., Apr. 3, 1926; s. Frank and Lucy Spezzano; B.A. in Journalism, Syracuse (N.Y.) U., 1950; m. Marjorie Elliott, Dec. 18, 1948; children—Steve, Judy, Mark, Christine. Reporter, Livingston Republican, Geneseo, N.Y., 1950-51, Lynchburg (Va.) News, 1951-54, St. Louis Globe-Democrat, 1954-55; polit. writer, then dir. public service and research Rochester (N.Y.) Times Union, 1955-68; dir. public service, then dir. promotion and public service Gannett Co., Inc., 1968-75; pres., publisher Cape Publns., Inc., Cocoa, Fla., 1975—; asst., then v.p. Gannett/South, Gannett Co., Inc., 1977-79; pres. Gannett Southeast Newspaper Group, Gannett Co., Inc., 1979—; dir. Gannett Co., Barnett Bank, Cocoa; mem. journalism endowment adv. com. U. Fla. Bd. dirs. Wuesthoff Meml. Hosp., Cocoa; trustee Brevard Art Center and Mus., Melbourne, Fla. Served with A.C., USNR, 1944-46. Recipient News Writing award Va. Press Assn., 1953, Citizen of Year award, Citizens Club Rochester, 1960, Disting. Service award for non-members Kiwanis Club, 1960, Public Service Reporting award Am. Polit. Sci. Assn., 1963; named Boss of Year, Cocoa Beach chpt. Nat. Secretaries Assn., 1977. Mem. Internat. Newspaper Promotion Assn. (pres. 1970-71; Silver Shovel award 1975), Am. Newspapers Pubs. Assn., Fla. Press Assn. (dir.), Cocoa Beach Area C. of C. (dir.). Roman Catholic. Editor handbook. Home: 855 S Atlantic Ave Cocoa Beach FL 32931 Office: 308 Forrest Ave Cocoa FL 32922

SPICER, EDWARD HOLLAND, anthropologist; b. Cheltenham, Pa., Nov. 29, 1906; s. Robert Barclay and Margaret Lucretia (Jones) S.; student U. Del., 1925-27, Johns Hopkins, 1927-28; B.A., U. Ariz., 1932, M.A., 1933; Ph.D., U. Chgo., 1939; m. Rosamond Pendleton Brown, June 21, 1936; children—Robert Barclay, Margaret Pendleton, Lawson Alan. Instr. anthropology Dillard U., New Orleans, 1938-39; instr. anthropology U. Ariz., Tucson, 1939-41, asso. prof., 1946-50, prof., 1950—; head, community analysis sect. War Relocation Authority, Washington, 1943-46; vis. prof. anthropology Cornell U., Ithaca, N.Y., 1947-50, U. Calif., Santa Barbara, 1958; dir. Pascua Yaqui Devel. Project OEO, Tucson, 1966-69; cons. Stanford Research Inst., 1954, U.S. Bur. Indian Affairs, 1967-69, Office Edn., 1967-70, Weatherhead Found., 1969-70; mem. Ariz. Commn. Civil Rights, 1961-62, Ariz. Commn. Indian Affairs, 1964-66. Recipient award Best Southwestern Book, S.W. Library Assn., 1965; Guggenheim fellow, 1941-42, 55-56; NSF sr. postdoctoral fellow, 1963-64; Nat. Endowment Humanities sr. fellow, 1970-71. Fellow Am. Anthrop. Assn., (pres. 1974), AAAS, Soc. Applied Anthropology (Malinowski award 1976); mem. Am. Philos. Soc., Nat. Acad. Scis. Democrat. Author: Cycles of Conquest, 1962; A Short History of the Indians of the U.S., 1969; editor: Human Problems in Technological Change, 1952; Perspectives in American Indian Culture Change, 1961; editor Jour. Am. Anthrop. Assn., 1960-63. Home: 5344 E Fort Lowell Rd Tucson AZ 85712 Office: Univ Arizona Dept Anthropology Tucson AZ 85721

SPICER, ERIK JOHN, librarian; b. Ottawa, Ont., Can., Apr. 9, 1926; s. Clifford and Violet (Gundersen) S.; B.A., U. Toronto, 1948, B.L.S., 1949, postgrad. in history, 1949-50; M.L.S., U. Mich., 1959; m. Mary Helen Blair, July 4, 1953; children—Erika Anne, John Blair. Circulation and reference librarian Ottawa Pub. Library, 1948-49, 50-53, U. Mich., 1953-54; dep. librarian Ottawa Pub. Library, 1954-60; parliamentary librarian Library of Parliament, 1960—; Canadian corr. Internat. Centre for Parliamentary Documentation, Inter-Parliamentary Union, Geneva, 1966—, also for parliamentary and adminstrv. libraries sect. Internat. Fedn. Library Assns., The Hague, 1962—, mem. standing adv. com. spl. libraries sect., 1972-76, pres. parliamentary libraries sect., 1972—, mem. standing adv. com., com. on ofcl. publs., 1972-76, voting del. ann. congresses Canadian Library Assn., 1966-72, Ont. Library Assn., 1973-75; observer Canadian Govt. Library Com., 1971—; ex-officio mem. Nat. Library Adv. Council, 1960-69, mem. bd., 1970—. Trustee Ottawa Pub. Library Bd., 1970-73. Served with RCAF, 1944-45. Decorated Can. Forces decoration; recipient Centennial medal, 1967; Queen's Jubilee medal, 1977; Library Service fellow U. Mich., 1953-54; Can. Council fellow, 1959. Life mem. Canadian Library Assn. (councillor 1964-67, alt. del. Canadian Commn. on UNESCO, 1972, pres. 1979—), Ont. Hist. Soc.; mem. Inst. Pub. Adminstrn. Can., Canadian Internat. Polit. Sci. Assn., ALA, Brit., Ont. (pres. 1962-63) library assns., Library Assn. Ottawa (pres. 1955-56), Canadian Assn. Info. Sci., Internat. Assn. Documentalists and Info. Officers (France), Royal Can. Mil. Inst., Guards Assn., Beta Phi Mu, Phi Kappa Phi. Clubs: Country (Aylmer); Ottawa Ski. Home: 2129 Killarney Dr Ottawa ON K2A 1R4 Canada Office: Library of Parliament Ottawa ON K1A 0A9 Canada

SPICER, ROBERT THURSTON, physician; b. Ithaca, N.Y., Feb. 22, 1903; s. Clarence Winfred and Anna Olive (Burdick) S.; A.B., Alfred U., 1925; M.D., Cornell U., 1929; D.Sc. (hon.), Alfred U., 1965; m. Marion Aldine Carter, Nov. 24, 1926 (dec. 1968); 1 dau., Aldine R.; m. 2d, Frances C. Cale, Nov. 16, 1968. Intern Jackson Meml. Hosp., Miami, Fla., 1929-30, resident, 1930-31; practice of obstetrics and gynecology, Miami, 1931-53; dean, prof. obstetrics and gynecology U. Miami, 1953-54. Served from lt. comdr. to capt. M.C., USNR, 1942-46. Mem. Fla. Bd. of Med. Examiners, 1957-61. Trustee City Miami Pub. Libraries System, 1965-70, Fairchild Tropical Garden, 1958—. Diplomate Am. Bd. Obstetrics and Gynecology. Fellow A.C.S., Southeastern Surg. Congress; mem. Am. Coll. Obstetrics and Gynecol. (founder), Am. Soc. Study Sterility, Internat. Fertility Assn., South Atlantic Assn. Obstetricians and Gynecologists, Fla. Obstetric and Gynecologic Soc. (founder, past pres.), Miami Obstet. and Gynecol. Soc. (founder, past pres.), Am., Fla., Dade County (past pres.) med. assns., Miami-Dade County C. of C. (pres. 1957-58). Conglist. Mason. Clubs: Rotary (Miami); Biscayne Bay Yacht. Home: 3855 Gulf Dr Sanibel FL 33957

SPICER, WILLIAM EDWARD, III, educator, physicist; b. Baton Rouge, Sept. 7, 1929; s. William Edward II and Kate Crystal (Watkins) S.; B.S., Coll. William and Mary, 1949; B.S., Mass. Inst. Tech., 1951; M.A., U. Mo., 1953, Ph.D., 1955; D.Tech. (hon.), U. Linköping (Sweden), 1975; m. Cynthia Stanley, June 12, 1951 (div. 1969); children—William Edward IV, Sally Ann; m. 2d, Diane Lubarsky, Apr. 24, 1969; 1 dau., Jacqueline Kate. Scientist, RCA Labs., Lawrence Radiation Lab., U. Calif. at Livermore, 1961-62; mem. faculty Stanford, 1962—, prof. elec. engring. and materials sci. engring., 1965—, prof. by courtesy applied physics, 1976-78, Stanford Ascherman prof. engring., 1978—; dir. Acad. Skills, Inc., Los Altos, Calif., 1971-73; dep. dir. Stanford Synchrotron Radiation Lab., 1973-75, cons. dir., 1975—; cons. to govt. and industry, 1962—; mem. solid state scis. panel Nat. Acad. Sci.-NRC, 1965-73; mem. panel 222.00 atomic and molecular physics div. Nat. Bur. Standards, 1966-73, chmn., 1971-73; mem. adv. group election devices Dept. Def., 1975—; fellow Churchill Coll., Cambridge U. (Eng.), 1979. Bd. dirs. Princeton (N.J.) YMCA, 1960-62. Recipient Achievement award RCA, 1957, 60; Guggenheim fellow, 1978-79. Fellow Am. Phys. Soc.; mem. Am. Vacuum Soc. (chmn. electronics material div. 1978-79), Phi Beta Kappa. Author publs. theory and experiment solid state and surface physics, photoemission, optical properties solids, electronic structure metals, semiconductors, insulators. Home: 785 Mayfield Rd Stanford CA 94305 Office: McCullough Bldg Stanford Univ Stanford CA 94305

SPIEGEL, EDWARD ROZLER, film dir., producer, writer; b. Chgo., July 6, 1922; s. Samuel Joseph and Clara (Rozler) S.; B.A., U. So. Calif., 1948; m. Joann Marie Jersild, Sept. 3, 1967; children—Sanda Jo, Jonathan Paul, Michael Anthony, Carrie Michelle, Nicole Lianne. Cameraman, film editor, 1948-52; writer, dir., producer numerous films, documentary films including: Wild River, 1969, The Incredible Machine, 1975, Nat. Geog. spls., Lincoln: Trial by Fire, 1973, The Yanks are Coming, Am. Heritage spls., 1974, Korean Legacy, Surrender at Appomattox, 1972; co-dir. The Hellstrom Chronicle, 1971; producer, dir., writer Gerald Ford '76 Campaign films. Served with USAAF, 1943-45. Recipient Emmy awards. Mem. Producers Guild Am., Dirs. Guild Am., Writers Guild Am. West, Assn. Cinema Editors. Home: 2739 Nichols Cyn Rd Los Angeles CA 90046 Office: 8489 W 3d St Los Angeles CA 90048

SPIEGEL, EDWIN JOHN, JR., paper co. exec.; b. St. Louis, Oct. 30, 1920; s. Edwin John and Ruth (Hall) S.; A.B., Dartmouth, 1942; m. Doris Dee Naylor, Jan. 30, 1943; children—Carol Ann (Mrs. C.E. Ramey), Edwin John III. Asst. plant mgr. Gaylord Container Corp., Greenville, S.C., 1946-49, mgr. Folding Carton div., St. Louis, 1949-55; asst. v.p., regional mgr. Gaylord Container div. Crown Zellerbach Corp., St. Louis, 1955-65; v.p. Alton Box Board Co. (Ill.), 1965-68, pres., 1968-79, chief exec. officer, 1969-79, chmn. bd., 1975—; dir. Boatman's Nat. Bank, St. Louis, First Nat. Bank & Trust Co. Alton, Laclede Steel Co. Bd. dirs. Jr. Achievement of Mississippi Valley, St. Lukes Hosp., St. Louis, Nat. Center Resource Recovery, St. Louis Municipal Opera, Civic Progress, St. Louis. Served to lt. USNR, 1942-45. Mem. NAM (dir. 1969-76), C. of C. Met. St. Louis, Dartmouth Alumni Assn. (past pres.), Phi Delta Theta. Republican. Congregationalist. Clubs: Mo. Athletic, Bogey, Old Warson Country, St. Louis (St. Louis). Home: 57 Portland Dr Frontenac MO 63131 Office: 401 Alton St Alton IL 62002

SPIEGEL, HART HUNTER, lawyer; b. Safford, Ariz., Aug. 30, 1918; s. Jacob B. and Margaret (Hunter) S.; B.A., Yale U., 1940, LL.B., 1946; m. Genevieve Willson, Feb. 12, 1946; children—John Willson, Claire Margaret, Jennifer Emily. Admitted to Calif. bar, 1946, D.C. bar, 1960, U.S. Supreme Ct. bar, 1955; partner firm

Brobeck, Phleger & Harrison, San Francisco. Asst. chief counsel U.S. Dept. Treasury, chief counsel Internal Revenue Service, 1959-61. Mem. exec. com. Yale Law Sch.; chmn. bd. trustees The Head-Royce Schs., 1967-72. Served to lt. USMC, 1942-46. Decorated Purple Heart, Bronze Star. Fellow Am. Bar Found.; mem. Am. Bar Assn. (mem. council sect. taxation 1966-68), Am. Law Inst., Am. Judicature Soc., State Bar Calif., Bar Assn. San Francisco, Calif. Conf. Barristers (pres. 1953), Barristers' Club San Francisco (pres. 1952), Phi Beta Kappa. Clubs: Pacific-Union, Berkeley Tennis (pres. 1964), Commonwealth, Marines' Memorial. Contbr. articles to profl. jours. Home: 3647 Washington St San Francisco CA 94118 Office: Suite 2900 Spear St Tower One Market Plaza San Francisco CA 94105

SPIEGEL, HERBERT, psychiatrist, educator; b. McKeesport, Pa., June 29, 1914; s. Samuel and Lena (Mendlowitz) S.; B.S., U. Md., 1936, M.D., 1939; m. Natalie Shainess, Apr. 24, 1944 (div. Apr. 1965); children—David, Ann. Intern, St. Francis Hosp., Pitts., 1939-40; resident in psychiatry St. Elizabeth's Hosp., Washington, 1940-42; practice medicine specializing in psychiatry, N.Y.C., 1946—; attending psychiatrist Columbia-Presbyn. Hosp., N.Y.C., 1960—; clin. prof. psychiatry Columbia U. Coll. Physicians and Surgeons, 1960—; mem. faculty Sch. Mil. Neuropsychiatry, Mason Gen. Hosp., Brentwood, N.Y., 1944-46. Mem. profl. advisory com. Am. Health Found.; mem. pub. edn. com., smoking and health com. N.Y.C. div. Am. Cancer Soc.; mem. advisory com. Nat. Aid to Visually Handicapped. Served with M.C., AUS, 1942-46. Decorated Purple Heart. Diplomate Am. Bd. Psychiatry. Fellow Am. Psychiat. Assn., Am. Coll. Psychiatrists, Am. Soc. Clin. Hypnosis, Am. Acad. Psychoanalysis, Internat. Soc. Clin. and Exptl. Hypnosis, William A. White Psychoanalytic Soc., N.Y. Acad. Medicine, N.Y. Acad. Scis.; mem. Am. Orthopsychiat. Assn., Am. Psychosomatic Soc., AAAS, AMA, N.Y. County Med. Soc. Author: (with A. Kardiner) War Stress and Neurotic Illness, 1947; (with D. Spiegel) Trance and Treatment: Clinical Uses of Hypnosis, 1978. Mem. editorial bd. Preventive Medicine, 1972. Contbr. articles to profl. jours. Home: 1065 Park Ave New York NY 10028 Office: 19 E 88th St New York NY 10028

SPIEGEL, JACOB J., lawyer; b. Boston, Nov. 24, 1901; s. Israel and Mollie (Greenbaum) S.; LL.B., Boston U., 1922; J.S.D., Suffolk U., L.H.D., Mass. Coll. Optometry; LL.D. Boston U.; J.D., Portia Law School; m. Peggy Schwarz, Aug. 26, 1941 (div.); 1 dau., Lynne Mara. Admitted to Mass. bar, 1923; pvt. practice, Boston, 1923-61; spl. justice Municipal Ct. Boston, 1939-60; legis. sec. to U.S. Senator Lodge, 1937; 1st asst. atty. gen. Mass., 1945-46; counsel Port of Boston Authority, 1948; justice Supreme Jud. Ct. Mass., 1961-72; chmn. Jud. Council Mass., 1976—. Past dir., gen. counsel Mass. Health Research Inst. Mem. Mass., Am., Boston bar assns., Am. Law Inst. Home: 780 Boylston St Boston MA 02199

SPIEGEL, MELVIN, educator, biologist; b. N.Y.C., Dec. 10, 1925; s. Philip Edward and Sadie (Friedman) S.; B.S., U. Ill., 1948: Ph.D., U. Rochester, 1952; M.A. (hon.), Dartmouth, 1967; m. Evelyn Sclufer, Apr. 16, 1955; children—Judith Ellen, Rebecca Ann. Research fellow U. Rochester, 1952-53, Calif. Inst. Tech., 1953-55, 64-65; asst. prof. Colby Coll., 1955-59; mem. faculty Dartmouth, 1959—, prof. biology, 1966—, chmn. dept. biol. scis., 1972-74; summer investigator Marine Biol. Lab., Woods Hole, Mass., 1954—; sr. research biologist U. Calif. at San Diego, 1970-71; vis. prof. biochemistry Nat. Inst. Med. Research, Mill Hill, London, Eng., 1971; vis. prof. Biocenter, U. Basel, 1979-80; Wilson Meml. lectr. U. N.C., 1975; program dir. developmental biology NSF, 1975-76. Mem. cell biology study sect. NIH, 1966-70. Trustee Marine Biol. Lab. Corp.; mem. exec. com., trustee Marine Biol. Lab., 1978—. Served with AUS, 1943-46; ETO. Decorated Purple Heart with 2 oak leaf clusters, Combat Inf. badge. Fellow AAAS; mem. Am. Soc. Zoologists, Am. Soc. Cell Biology, Soc. Developmental Biology, AAUP, Soc. Gen. Physiologists, Internat. Inst. Embryology, Internat. Soc. Developmental Biologists (sec.-treas. 1977—), Sigma Xi. Editorial bd. Biol. Bull., 1966-70, 71-75, Cell Differentiation, 1979—; contbr. articles to profl. jours. Home: 15 Barrymore Rd Hanover NH 03755

SPIEGEL, SAM, film producer; b. Jaroslau, Austria (now Poland), 1904; ed. U. Vienna. Producer for Universal Pictures, making German and French films in Berlin for European distbn., 1930-33; ind. producer in Europe, 1933-37; producer (with Boris Morris) Tales of Manhattan, 1942; founder (with John Huston) Horizon Pictures, Inc., Calif., 1948, pres., 1948—, co-producer We Were Strangers, 1949; producer films including: The African Queen, 1953, On the Waterfront (Acad. award), 1954, The Bridge on the River Kwai (Acad. award), 1957, Suddenly Last Summer, 1960, Lawrence of Arabia (Acad. award), 1962, The Swimmer, 1968, Nicholas and Alexandra, The Last Tycoon, 1976.

SPIEGEL, WALTER F., cons. engr.; b. Berlin, Germany, Nov. 7, 1922; s. Julian F. and Kaethe H. (Placzek) S.; came to U.S., 1930, naturalized, 1935; B.S., U. Pa., 1948, M.S., 1957; m. Jeanne N. Sundheim, Oct. 8, 1950; children—Walter D., Karen J., James R. Staff engr. Charles S. Leopold, Inc., Phila., 1948-61; founder, pres. Walter F. Spiegel, Inc., Cons. Engrs., Jenkintown, Pa., 1963—; dir. Computer Aided Design Assos., Inc., Jenkintown. Founder, v.p. East Abington Little League, 1960-62; v.p. Abington Twp. Parent Council, 1960-61. Served with inf. AUS, 1943-46. Registered profl. engr., Pa., N.Y., N.J., Del., Va., N.C., D.C. Fellow Am. Soc. Heating, Refrigerating and Air-Conditioning Engrs. (pres. 1972-73); mem. Profl. Soc. for Nuclear Def. (dir. 1966-72), Nat. Council for Energy Conservation (steering com. 1973-74), Internat. Inst. Refrigeration (v.p. commn. E-1, air conditioning 1975—), Nat. Soc. Profl. Engrs., Am. Cons. Engrs. Council, Tau Beta Pi, Sigma Tau. Author: Mechanical and Electrical System Design for Protective Shelters, 1968; (with others) Practical Energy Management in Health Care Institutions; also articles. Home: 405 Lodges Ln Elkins Park PA 19117 Office: 321 York Rd Jenkintown PA 19046

SPIEGELMAN, SOL, biologist, educator; b. N.Y.C., Dec. 14, 1914; s. Max and Eva (Kramer) S.; B.S., Coll. City N.Y., 1939; postgrad. Columbia, 1940-42; Ph.D., Washington U., St. Louis, 1944; D.Sc. (hon.), Rensselaer Poly. Inst., 1966, Northwestern U., 1966, St. Louis U., 1968, U. Chgo., 1970, U. Ill., 1975, N.Y. Med. Coll., 1975, City U. N.Y., 1976; LL.D., U. Glasgow, 1973; D. Philosophy, Hebrew U., Jerusalem, 1975; m. Helen Wahala; children—Willard, George, Marjorie. Lectr. physics Washington U., 1942-44, lectr. applied math., 1943-44, instr. bacteriology Sch. Medicine, 1945-46, asst. prof. bacteriology, 1946-48; USPHS spl. fellow U. Minn., 1948-49; prof. microbiology U. Ill., Urbana, 1949-69, mem. Center Advanced Study, 1964-69; dir. Inst. Cancer Research, prof. human genetics and devel. Coll. Phys. and Surg., Columbia, 1969—, Univ. prof., 1975, Univ. lectr., 1974. Mem. Nat. Cancer Adv. Bd., 1972—; Marrs McLean lectr. Baylor Coll. Medicine, 1974; S. Steven Brodie Meml. lectr. Jewish Meml. Hosp., N.Y.C., 1974. Recipient Pasteur award Ill. Soc. for Microbiology, 1963; Alumni citation award Washington U., 1966; Bertner Found. award in cancer research, 1968; Townsend Harris medal Alumni Assn. City Coll. N.Y., 1972; Lila Gruber Meml. award Am. Acad. Dermatology, 1972; Papanicolaou award for cancer research, 1973; Albert Lasker Basic Med. Research award, 1974; numerous distinguished lectureships. Fellow Am. Acad. Arts and Scis.; mem. Nat. Acad. Scis., Am. Soc. Biol. Chemists, Am. Soc. for Microbiology, N.Y. Acad. Scis. (life), Soc. for Gen. Microbiology (Brit.), Soc. Gen. Physiologists, Internat. Assn. for Promotion Clin. and Exptl. Research in Medicine, Soc. Am. Naturalists, Genetics Soc. Am., German Acad. Sics. Leopoldina, Nat. Acad. Medicine Brazil (fgn.), Phi Beta Kappa, Sigma Xi, Phi Kappa Phi, Tau Pi Epsilon. Contbr. articles to profl. jours. Home: 100 Haven Ave New York City NY 10032 Office: Inst Cancer Research 701 W 168th St New York City NY 10032

SPIELBERG, STEVEN, motion picture dir.; b. Cin., Dec. 18, 1947; B.A., Calif. State Coll., Long Beach, 1970. Won film contest with 40-minute war movie, Escape to Nowhere, at age 13; made film Firelight at age 16, and made 5 films while in coll.; became TV dir. at Universal Pictures at age 20, directed segments of TV series including Night Gallery, Marcus Welby, M.D., Columbo, also TV movies Duel, 1971, Something Evil, 1972; dir. motion pictures: The Sugarland Express, 1974, Jaws, 1975, Close Encounters of the Third Kind, 1977, 1941, 1979; producer film I Wanna Hold Your Hand, 1978. Recipient several Acad. awards. Author: (with Patrick Mann) Close Encounters of the Third Kind. *

SPIELER, FRANCIS JOSEPH, editor; b. Glasgow, Scotland, May 23, 1943; s. Ludwig and Rachel (Neuer) S.; came to U.S., 1955, naturalized, 1974; B.A. in Comparative Lit., City Coll. N.Y., 1967; m. Gene Ellen Bobker. Staff editor N.Y. Times, 1963-73; sr. editor Penthouse Publs., 1973-75; exec. editor Gallery mag., Montcalm Publs. Co., N.Y.C., 1975—; music critic Harper's Monthly, 1976—; adj. prof. journalism N.Y. U., 1975; sr. editor SoHo Weekly News, 1975-76; exec. editor Looking Glass Publs., 1976-77; asso. editor Hosp. Physician mag., 1976-78; sr. editor Celebration Mag., 1978—; editorial cons. Home: 26 Bank St New York NY 10014

SPIELVOGEL, CARL, mktg. and advt. exec.; b. N.Y.C., Dec. 27, 1928; s. Joseph and Sadie (Tellerman) S.; B.B.A., Baruch Coll., 1956; m. Roslyn Bremer, July 29, 1953; children—David Joseph, Rachel Fay, Paul Abram. Columnist, New York Times, 1950-60; with McCann-Erickson, Inc., Interpublic Group of Companies, Inc., N.Y.C., 1960—, vice chmn., 1974—, also dir., chmn. exec. com.; dir. Franklin Corp. Chmn. Com. in the Pub. Interest, 1975; pres. bd. trustees Baruch Coll. Fund; mem. Bus. Com. Arts; exec. com. Bus. Mktg. Corp., N.Y.C.; chmn. com. div. WNET-Pub. Broadcasting; mem. bus. com. Met. Mus. Art. Served with U.S. Army, 1953-55. Recipient Human Relations award Anti-Defamation League, 1972; Achievement award Sch. Bus. Alumni, City Coll. N.Y., 1972. Clubs: Hemisphere, City Athletic (N.Y.C.); Winding Brook Country (Valatie, N.Y.). Home: 605 Park Ave New York City NY 10021 Office: 1271 Ave of the Americas New York City NY 10020

SPIER, PETER EDWARD, artist, author; b. Amsterdam, Netherlands, June 6, 1927; s. Joseph Eduard and Albertine Sophie (Van Raalte) S.; student Ryks Academie Voor Beeldende Kunsten, Amsterdam, 1945-47; m. Kathryn M. Pallister, July 12, 1958; children—Thomas P., Kathryn E. Came to U.S., 1952, naturalized, 1958. Jr. editor Elsevier's Weekly, Amsterdam, 1950-51, Elsevier Pub. Co., Houston, 1952; free-lance author, illustrator, N.Y.C., 1952—; speaker, lectr. schs. and libraries. Served to lt. Royal Netherlands Navy, 1947-50. Runner-up for Caldecott medal, 1960; recipient Christopher award, 1970, Boston Globe award, 1967, Caldecott medal, 1978, Christopher award, 1978, Nat. Religious Book award, 1978, Lewis Carroll Shelf award, 1978. Clubs: Shoreham (N.Y.) Country; Netherlands (N.Y.C.). Author, illustrator 18 books, including The Star-Spangled Banner, 1973; Fast-Slow, High-Low, 1972; Crash! Bang! Boom!, 1972; Tin Lizzie, 1975; Noah's Ark, 1977; Oh, Were They Ever Happy!, 1978; Bored—Nothing to Do, 1978; The Legend of New Amsterdam, 1979; People, 1979; illustrator over 150 books; contbr., illustrator many nat. mags. Address: Warden Cliff Rd PO Box 210 Shoreham NY 17786

SPIER, ROBERT FOREST GAYTON, anthropologist, educator; b. Seattle, June 12, 1922; s. Leslie and Erna (Gunther) S.; B.A., U. Calif. at Berkeley, 1947; M.A., Harvard, 1949, Ph.D., 1954; m. Veva Drake, Mar. 15, 1951; children—Martha, Stephen. Instr. U. Minn., Mpls., 1951-52; mem. faculty U. Mo., Columbia, 1949-51, 52—, prof., 1966—; vis. asso. prof. U. Oreg., Eugene, 1962-63; tchr. summers Portland (Oreg.) State Coll., 1957, U. Wis., Madison, 1958, U. Calif. at Berkeley, 1965, 66, 73, Ind. U., Bloomington, 1967. Pres. Friends of Pub. Library, Columbia, 1969, Columbia Swim Parents Assn., 1970. Mem. Bd. Elec. Examiners Columbia, 1971-77. Served with AUS, 1942-46. NATO fellow, 1960-61. Fellow Am. Anthrop. Assn. Club: Columbia Track. Author: From Hand of Man, 1970; Surveying and Mapping, 1970. Home: 708 Morningside Dr Columbia MO 65201

SPIERS, RONALD IAN, fgn. service officer; b. Orange, N.J., July 9, 1925; s. Tomas Hoskins and Blanca (De Ponthier) S.; B.A., Dartmouth, 1948; M.Pub. Affairs (Woodrow Wilson fellow), Princeton, 1950; m. Patience Baker, June 18, 1949; children—Deborah Bianca Spiers Wood, Peter Anselm, Martha Lucy, Sarah Jane. With AEC, 1950-55, Dept. State, 1955-61; dir. office polit. affairs ACDA, 1961-62; dep. dir. Office of NATO and Atlantic polit. and mil. affairs Dept. State, 1962-65, dir., 1965-66; counselor embassy for politico-mil. affairs Am. embassy, London, Eng., 1966-68, polit. counselor, 1968-69; dep. asst. sec. of state for politico-mil. affairs Dept. State, 1969, dir. Bur. Politico-Mil. Affairs, 1969-73; ambassador to Bahamas, Nassau, 1973-74; minister, charge d'affairs Am. embassy, London, 1974-77; ambassador to Turkey, 1977-80; dir. Bur. Intelligence and Research, Dept. State, 1980—; mem. U.S. del. UN Gen. Assembly, 1955, 56, 57, Disarmament Negotiations, 1960-62, Nuclear Test Ban Negotiations, 1958-61, NATO Ministerial meetings, 1961, 63-66, Summit Conf., 1960, alternate U.S. del. IAEA Prep. Commn., 1956-57; coordinator U.S. del. Conf. IAEA, 1956, 18 Nation Disarmament Conf., 1962, SALT, 1971; U.S. permanent rep. CENTO, 1977-79. Served to lt. (j.g.) USNR, 1943-46. Mem. Internat. Inst. Strategic Studies, Am. Fgn. Service Assn., Council Fgn. Relations. Home: 2315 Kimro St Alexandria VA 22307 Office: Dept State Washington DC 20520

SPIES, CLAUDIO, composer; b. Santiago, Chile, Mar. 26, 1925; s. Mauricio and Gertrudis (Heilbronn) S.; came to U.S., 1942, naturalized, 1966; A.B., Harvard, 1950, M.A., 1954; m. Emmi Vera Tobias, June 10, 1953; children—Caterina, Michael, Tatiana, Leah, Susanna. Instr. music Harvard, 1953-57; lectr. music Vassar Coll., 1957-58; asst. prof. music, condr. orch. Swarthmore Coll., 1958-63, asso. prof., 1964-69, prof., 1969-70; prof. music Princeton U., 1970—; conducted 1st performances of new works Stravinsky, Boston, 1954, Santiago, 1954, Swarthmore Coll., 1963-68, Harvard, 1968; cond. own works Composer's Forum, N.Y.C., 1961, Los Angeles County Museum, 1965, Columbia U. Group for Contemporary Music, 1966. Recipient prize for composition U. de Chile, 1948, 54, 56; recipient Bohemian Club prize Harvard, 1950; John K. Paine Traveling fellow, 1950-51; Lili Boulanger Meml. Fund award, 1956; grantee The Ingram Merrill Found., 1966; Brandeis U. Creative Arts Citation, 1967; sr. fellow Council Humanities, Princeton, spring 1966, fall 1966-67; award Nat. Inst. Arts and Letters, 1969; fellow Nat. Endowment Arts, 1975. Mem. Am. Soc. U. Composers (mem. founding bd.), Internat. Alban Berg/Soc. Ltd. (mem. founding bd.), Phila. Composers' Forum (exec. com. 1966-67), League-ISCM (mem. bd. 1970-73), Phi Beta Kappa. Composer: Music for a Ballet (orch.), 1955; Descanso en jardin (woodwind quartet, tenor and baritone; text by Jorge Guillen), 1957; Il Cantico di Frate Sole (bass. and orch.), 1958; Five Psalms (soprano, tenor and 6 instruments; commd. by Harvard Mus. Assn.), 1959; Verses from the Book of Ruth (women's voices and piano; commd. by Phila. Art Alliance), 1959; Tempi (music 14 instruments; commd. by Fromm Music Found.), 1962; Proverbs on Wisdom (male voices, piano and organ; commd. by Colgate U.) 1964; Animula Vagula, Blandula (4 part chorus, a cappella), 1964; Viopiacem (duo for viola and keyboard instruments), 1965; LXXXV, Eights and Fives (strings and clarinets), 1967; Times Two (horns), 1968; Three Songs on Poems by May Swenson, 1969; Bagatelle for piano, 1970; 7 Enzensberger-Lieder (baritone, 4 instrumentalists), 1972; Shirim le Hathunatham (soprano, 5 instruments), 1975; Five Sonnet-Settings (Shakespeare; vocal quartet and piano), 1976-77; A Between-Birthdays Bagatelle for Roger Sessions' 80th-81st (piano), 1977; Ein Aggregats-Walzerl (piano), 1978; Bagatelle (piano), 1979; Verschieden (piano), 1979. Editorial bd. Perspectives of New Music. Home: 117 Meadowbrook Dr Princeton NJ 08540

SPIESS, FRED NOEL, oceanographer; b. Oakland, Calif., Dec. 25, 1919; s. Fred Henry and Elva Josephine (Monck) S.; A.B., U. Calif., Berkeley, 1941, Ph.D., 1951; M.S., Harvard U., 1947; m. Sarah Scott Whitton, July 25, 1942; children—Katharine Spiess Dallaire, Mary Elizabeth Spiess DeJong, John Frederick, Helen Spiess Shamble, Margaret Josephine. With Marine Phys. Lab., U. Calif., San Diego, 1952—, dir., 1958—, dir. Scripps Inst. Oceanography, La Jolla, 1964-65, prof. oceanography, 1961—. mem. Naval Research Adv. Commn., 1978—, Def. Sci. Bd., 1977—, Nat. Acad. Scis. Ocean Sci. Bd., 1977—. Served with USNR, 1941-46, 53. Decorated Silver Star medal, Bronze Star medal; recipient John Prince Wetherill medal Franklin Inst., 1965; Compass Disting. Scientist award Marine Technol. Soc., 1971; Robert Dexter Conrad award U.S. Sec. of Navy, 1974. Fellow Acoustical Soc. Am.; mem. Am. Geophys. Union, Marine Tech. Soc., Phi Beta Kappa, Sigma Xi. Home: 9450 La Jolla Shore Dr La Jolla CA 92037 Office: Scripps Inst Oceanography U Calif San Diego La Jolla CA 92093

SPIETH, HERMAN THEODORE, educator; b. Charlestown, Ind., Aug. 21, 1905; s. Henry Herman and Lydia (Schulte-Wieking) S.; A.B., Ind. Central Coll., 1926, LL.D., 1958; Ph.D., Ind. U., 1931; m. Evelyn E. Wilkinson, Aug. 30, 1931; 1 son, Philip. Instr. zoology Ind. Univ., 1931-32; successively instr., asst. prof., asso. prof. biology Coll. City N.Y., 1932-53; prof. zoology U. Calif. at Riverside, 1953-64, chmn. div. life scis., 1953-56, provost, 1956-58, chancellor, 1958-64; prof. zoology, chmn. dept. U. of Calif. at Davis, 1964-71; guest investigator U. Tex., 1949-50, 64-65; vis. colleague U. Hawaii, summers 1963, 64, 65, 66, 68, 69, 74; lectr. zoology Columbia U., 1938-52; head marine and fresh water zoology Cold Spring Harbor Biol. Lab., L.I., summers 1931-38; research asso. Am. Mus. Natural History, 1943-62. Served from lt. to capt. USAAF, 1943-45. Fellow A.A.A.S., Animal Behavior Soc., Entomol. Soc. Am., Calif. Acad. Sci.; mem. Am. Inst. Biol. Scis., Soc. Systematic Zoology, Am. Soc. Naturalists, Society for Study Evolution, N.Y. Entomol. Soc., Am. Soc. Zoologists, Am. Soc. Limnology and Oceanography, Sierra Club, Sigma Xi, Delta Chi. Author articles in ephemeropteran taxonomy, evolution and behavior in Drosophila. Home: 1031 Miller Dr Davis CA 95616

SPIKES, JOHN DANIEL, coll. dean, scientist; b. Los Angeles, Dec. 14, 1918; s. John Lawrence and Gladys Alva (Murchison) S.; B.S., Calif. Inst. Tech., 1941, M.S., 1946, Ph.D., 1948; m. Anne Dorland, July 17, 1942; children—John N., Daniel A., Mary Anne. Mem. faculty U. Utah, 1948—, prof. molecular biology, 1955—, head dept., 1954-62, chmn. div. biol. scis., 1957-58, Distinguished Faculty lectr., 1962, Distinguished Research prof., 1972, dean Coll. Letters and Sci., 1964—. Cell physiologist AEC, 1958-60, cons., 1960—; mem panels NSF, 1957—; mem. photobiology com. NRC. Mem. council Smithsonian Institution, 1966-76. Served with M.C., AUS, 1943-46. Mem. AAAS, Biophys. Soc., Am. Chem. Soc., Am. Physiol. Soc., Radiation Research Soc., Am. Soc. Photobiology (pres. 1974), Sigma Xi. Home: 1928 Hubbard Ave Salt Lake City UT 84108

SPILHAUS, ATHELSTAN, meteorologist, oceanographer; b. Cape Town, Union of South Africa, Nov. 25, 1911; s. Karl Antonio and Nellie (Muir) S.; came to U.S., 1931, naturalized, 1946; B.Sc., U. Cape Town, 1931, D.Sc., 1948; M.S., Mass. Inst. Tech., 1933; D.Sc., Coe Coll., 1961, Hahnemann Med. Coll., 1968, U. R.I., 1968; D.Sc., Phila. Coll. Pharmacy and Sci., 1969, Hamilton Coll., 1970, U. S.E. Mass., 1970, U. Durham (Eng.), 1970, U. S.C., 1971, Southwestern U. at Memphis, 1972; LL.D., Nova U., 1970, U. Md., 1978; m. Kathleen Fitzgerald, 1978; children by previous marriage—Athelstan F., Mary Muir, Eleanor, Margaret Ann, Karl Henry. Research asst. Mass. Inst. Tech., 1934-35; asst. dir. tech. services Union of South Africa Def. Forces, Pretoria, 1935-36; research asst. Woods Hole (Mass.) Oceanographic Instn., and Cambridge, Mass., 1936-37, investigator in phys. oceanography, 1938, phys. oceanographer, 1940—; asst. prof. meteorology N.Y. U., 1937, asso. prof., 1937-42, prof., 1942, dir. research, 1946; meteorol. adviser to Union S. Africa Govt., 1947; dean Inst. Tech. U. Minn., 1949-66, prof. physics, 1966-67; pres. Franklin Inst., Phila., 1967-69; pres. Aqua Internat. Inc., 1969-70; fellow Woodrow Wilson Internat. Center for Scholars, 1971-74; now with NOAA, Dept Commerce, Washington. Dir., Sci. Service, Inc., Am. Dynamics Corp., Donaldson Co. (Minn.); trustee Aerospace Corp. (Los Angeles). U.S. commr. Seattle World's Fair, 1961-62; chmn. nat. fisheries center and aquariam adv. bd. U.S. Dept. Interior; mem. adv. coms. for armed forces; mem. nat. com. IGY; mem com. on oceanography, com. on polar research Nat. Acad. Scis.; mem. exec. bd. UNESCO, 1955-58; mem. sci. adv. com. Am. Newspapers & Pubs. Assn. Trustee Woods Hole Oceanographic Instn., St. Paul Inst.; mem. Nat. Sci. Bd., 1966-72; vice chmn. Invest-in-America. Served from capt. to lt. col. USAAF, 1943-46. Decorated Legion of Merit, Exception Civilian Service medal USAF; recipient Patriotic Civilian Service award Dept. Army. Fellow Royal Meterol. Soc., Am. Inst. Aeron. and Astronautics; mem. Am. Soc. Limnology and Oceanography, Am. Soc. Engring. Edn., Minn. Soc. Profl. Engrs., Am. Meteorol. Soc., Royal Soc. So. Africa, A.A.A.S. (pres. 1970, chmn. bd. 1971), Am. Philos. Soc., Am. Geophys. Union, U.S. C. of C. (council trends and perspective), Tau Beta Pi, Sigma Xi, Iota Alpha. Episcopalian. Clubs: Cosmos (Washington); Bohemian (San Francisco). Inventor of Bathythermograph, 1938. Contbr. numerons articles to profl. jours. including Jour. of Marine Research, Jour. of Meterology; author: Workbook of Meteorology; Weathercraft; Meteorological Instruments; Satellite of the Sun, Our New Age, Turn to the Sea, The Ocean Laboratory. Home: PO Box 1063 Middleburg VA 22117 Office: Nat Oceanic and Atmospheric Adminstrn Dept Commerce 3300 Whitehaven St NW Washington DC 20235

SPILKA, CONRAD JOSEPH, surgeon; b. Cleve., Aug. 20, 1913; s. Conrad Joseph and Rose (Copenhagen) Sulzmann; student Western Reserve U., 1935-37, D.D.S., 1941; m. Agnes Anselma Salopek, Aug. 12, 1945; children—Karen, Thomas, Cathy. Practice oral and maxillo facial surgery, Lakewood, Ohio, 1946—; clin prof. oral surgery and anesthesia Case Western Res. U., 1955-79. Served with U.S. Army, 1942-46. Recipient Alumnus award Sch. Dentistry Case Western Res. U., 1977. Fellow Internat. Coll. Dentists, Am. Coll. Dentists; mem. Am. Bd. Oral and Maxillo Facial Surgery, Internat. Assn. Oral Surgeons, Am. Soc. Oral and Maxillo Facial Surgeons, Great Lake

Soc. Oral and Maxillo Facial Surgeons. Roman Catholic. Club: Lakewood Country. Contbr. articles in field to profl. jours. Home: 19565 Beachcliff Blvd Rocky River OH 44116 Office: 14701 Detroit Ave Lakewood OH 44107

SPILKA, MARK, educator; b. Cleve., Aug. 6, 1925; s. Harvey Joseph and Zella (Fenberg) S.; B.A. magna cum laude, Brown U., 1949; M.A., Ind. U., 1953, Ph.D., 1956; m. Ellen Potter, May 6, 1950 (div. Dec. 1965); children—Jane, Rachel, Aaron; m. Ruth Dane Farnum, Jan. 18, 1975; stepchildren—Betsy, Polly. Editorial asst. Am. Mercury, 1949-51; instr. U. Mich., 1954-58, asst. prof., 1958-63; asso. prof. Brown U., Providence, 1963-67, prof., 1967—, chmn. English dept., 1968-73. Summer seminar dir. Nat. Endowment for Humanities, 1974; pres. Conf. Editors of Learned Jours., Modern Lang. Assn., 1974-75; vis. prof. Grad. Inst. Modern Letters U. Tulsa, summer 1975, Hebrew U., Jerusalem, 1972, Ind. U., summer 1976. Served with USAAF, 1944-46. Ind. Sch. Letters fellow, 1961, 63; Guggenheim fellow, 1967-68; Nat. Endowment for Humanities fellow, 1978-79. Mem. Modern Lang. Assn., AAUP, Phi Beta Kappa. Author: The Love Ethic of D.H. Lawrence, 1955; Dickens and Kafka: A Mutual Interpretation, 1963; Virginia Woolf's Quarrel with Grieving, 1980. Editor: D.H. Lawrence: A Collection of Critical Essays, 1963; Towards a Poetics of Fiction: Essays from Novel: A Forum on Fiction 1967-76, 1977; mng. editor Novel: A Forum on Fiction, 1967-77, editor, 1978—. Home: 294 Doyle Ave Providence RI 02906

SPILLANE, MICKEY (FRANK MORRISON), author; b. Bklyn., Mar. 9, 1918; attended Kans. State Coll.; m. 2d, Sherri, Nov., 1965. Author mystery-suspense novels: I, The Jury, 1947 (filmed in 1953); Vengeance is Mine!, 1950; My Gun Is Quick, 1950 (filmed in 1957); The Big Kill, 1951; One Lonely Night, 1951; The Long Wait, 1951 (filmed in 1954); Kiss Me, Deadly, 1952 (filmed in 1955); The Deep, 1961; Day of the Guns, 1964; The Snake, 1964; Bloody Sunrise, 1965; The Death Dealers, 1965; The Twisted Thing, 1966; The By-Pass Control, 1967; The Delta Factor, 1967 (filmed); Survival: Zero, 1970; Tough Guys, 1960; Me, Hood; Killer Mine; The Flier; Return of the Hood, many others; also author The Girl Hunters, 1962, author screenplay, 1963, and starred in role of Mike Hammer; TV series Mickey Spillane's Mike Hammer premiered in 1958. Office: care New Am Library 1301 Ave of Americas New York NY 10019*

SPILLER, EBERHARD ADOLF, physicist; b. Halbendorf, Ger., Apr. 16, 1933; s. Walter Richard and Ruth Elfriede (Radzey) S.; came to U.S., 1968; diploma U. Frankfurt (Ger.), 1960, Ph.D., 1964; m. Marga Dietz, Dec. 18, 1964; children—Michael, Bettina. Asst., U. Frankfurt, 1960-68, mem. faculty, 1966-68; physicist IBM Research Center, Yorktown Heights, N.Y., 1968—. Mem. Am. Optical Soc., German Phys. Soc. Research solid state physics, laser and coherence optics, nonlinear optics, thin films, soft x-rays, x-ray microscopy, lithography. Home: Lakeside Rd Mount Kisco NY 10549 Office: IBM Corp TJ Watson Research Center Yorktown Heights NY 10598

SPILLER, ROBERT EARL, bus. exec.; b. Buffalo, June 5, 1930; s. Earl Alexander and Helen May (Hanford) S.; B.A., Ohio Wesleyan U., 1952; M.B.A., Ind. U., 1953; C.P.A., U. Ill., 1956; m. Ruth Evelyn Currier, Aug. 15, 1953; children—Deborah Jean, Marcia Kay, Rebecca Lynn, Robert Earl, Michael Currier. Staff accountant Price Waterhouse & Co., C.P.A.'s, Chgo., 1953-54, 56-60; asst. to exec. v.p. Cuneo Press, Chgo., 1960-62; asst. to pres. Pabst Brewing Co., Milw., 1962-65, v.p. finance, 1965-69, exec. v.p., 1969—, also dir.; vice chmn., chief operating officer Chock Full O'Nuts Corp., N.Y.C., 1974-75; chmn. Ann Keane Enterprises, Inc., 1975—; pres. Graf's Beverages Inc., Milw. Served with AUS, 1954-56. C.P.A., Ill. Mem. Am. Inst. C.P.A.'s, Am. Accounting Assn., Phi Beta Kappa, Chi Phi, Beta Gamma Sigma, Omicron Delta Kappa, Delta Sigma Rho. Home: N61W30721 Beaver View Rd Hartland WI 53029 Office: 16 W 57th St New York NY 10019 also Gremoor Dr Elm Grove WI 53122 also 917 W Juneau Ave Milwaukee

SPILLER, ROBERT ERNEST, educator; lit. historian; b. Phila., Nov. 13, 1896; s. William G. and Helen Constance (Newbold) S.; B.A., U. Pa., 1917, Harrison fellow, 1919-20, M.A., 1921, Ph.D., 1924; Guggenheim fellow for foreign study, 1928-29; Litt.D., Thiel Coll., 1964, Coll. Wooster, 1968; Dr. phil. h.c., Christian Albrechts U., Kiel, Germany, 1965; Dr. Humane Letters, U. Pa., 1967; m. Mary Scott, June 17, 1922 (dec. Mar. 1971); children—William Scott, Constance Newbold (Mrs. Thomas J. Johnston), Mary Miles; m. 2d, Anna Moss Wright, Mar. 15, 1975. Instr. English, U. Pa., 1920-21; with Swarthmore Coll., 1921-45, prof., English, 1934-45, chmn. Humanities Div., 1935-41, chmn. Curriculum Com., 1942-45; prof. English, summers, Duke U., 1927, Harvard, 1930, Columbia, 1931, 1937, U. So. Calif., 1933, U. Mich., 1936, Bread Loaf Sch. of Eng., 1948, U. Minn., 1951, U. Colo., 1956; vis. prof. U. Oslo, 1950, New Sch. for Social Research, 1943-44, U. London (King's and Bedford Colls.), 1958-59, U. N.C., 1968, U. So. Fla., 1969; prof. English, U. Pa., 1945-61, Felix E. Schelling prof. English, 1961-67, Schelling prof. emeritus, 1967—, chmn. dept. Am. civilization, 1947-49, 51-53, 55-57. Adv. editor to Am. Literature, 1928-31 and 1940-55, editor, 1932-40. Chmn. editorial bd. Am. Quarterly 1951-70. Bd. dirs. American-Scandinavian Found., chmn. com. fellowships, 1966-70; bd. dirs. Swarthmore (Pa.) Pub. Library, 1953-56, pres., 1955, 56; hon. cons. Am. cultural history Library of Congress, 1967-69; chmn. Am. studies adv. com. Am. Council Learned Socs., 1960-66. Served with AEF, World War I. Fellow N.Y. State Hist. Assn. (hon.); mem. Hist. Soc. Pa., Am. Studies Assn. (pres. 1955) Modern Lang. Assn. Am. (chmn. Am. lit. group, 1930, 31, 1st v.p. 1957), Phi Beta Kappa. Clubs: Philobiblon (pres. 1964-68), Franklin Inn (pres. 1961-64) (Phila.); Coffee House (N.Y.). Author: The American in Eng. During The First Half Century of Independence, 1926; Fenimore Cooper, Critic of His Times, 1931, 63; The Roots of National Culture (anthology), 1933, 48; The Cycle of American Literature, 1955, 1956, 67; (with others) Eight American Authors, 1956, The Early Lectures of Ralph Waldo Emerson, 1959, Vol. II, 1964, vol. III, 1971; The Third Dimension: Studies in Literary History. 1965; The Oblique Light, 1968; The Mirror of American Life, 1971; The Philobiblon Club of Philadelphia: The First Eighty Years, 1973; Milestones in American Literary History, 1977; Late Harvest, 1980; editor: Fenimore Cooper, Gleanings in Europe, France, 1928, 70, England, 1930, 70; A Descriptive Bibliography of James Fenimore Cooper (with P.C. Blackburn), 1934; James Fenimore Cooper, Representative Selections, 1936; Satanstoe (with J.D. Coppock), 1937; Esther, by Henry Adams, 1938; Five Essays on Man and Nature (by R.W. Emerson), 1955; American Perspectives, 1961; Social Control in a Free Society, 1960; A Time of Harvest, 1961; chmn. editorial bd. Literary History of The United States, 1948, 4th edit., 1974; Tahiti, by Henry Adams, 1946; The American Literary Revolution. 1783-1837, 1967; The Van Wyck Brooks-Lewis Mumford Letters, 1921-63, 1970; (with A.R. Ferguson) the Collected Works of R.W. Emerson, Vol. 1, Nature, Addresses and Lectures, 1971, 79; asso. editor: Etudes Anglaises (France); Jahrbuch für Amerikastudien (Germany). Contbr. to mags. Home: 526 Telner St Philadelphia PA 19118

SPILLER, ROBERT JAMES, banker; b. Rochester, N.Y., July 2, 1930; s. Charles Albert and Lillian M. (Jack) S.; B.B.A., U. Mass., 1952; grad. with honors, Grad. Sch. Savs. Banking, 1967; m. Elizabeth J. Freeman, Dec. 1, 1962; children—Susan, Elizabeth, Linda, Carol. With Boston Five Cents Savs. Bank, 1956—, asst. v.p., then v.p., 1966-70, exec. v.p., 1970-71, pres., 1971—, also trustee; mng. trustee Cameron-Brown Investment Co. Bd. dirs. Boston Mcpl. Research Bur., Greater Boston Conv. and Tourist Bur.; trustee New Eng. Deaconess Hosp., Boston. Mem. Mortgage Bankers Assn. Am. (bd. govs.), Nat. Assn. Mut. Savs. Banks, Savs. Bank Assn. Mass. (exec. com.). Club: Winchester Country. Home: 25 Prospect St Winchester MA 01890 Office: 10 School St Boston MA 02108

SPILMAN, RAYMOND, indsl. designer; b. Wichita, Kans., Jan. 12, 1911; s. Robert Bruce and Willa (Wood) S.; student Kans. State U., 1933; m. Mary Jordan, May 15, 1937; children—Susan, Alden. Stylist, Gen. Motors Corp., 1935-39; staff designer Walter Dorwin Teague, N.Y.C., 1940-42; chief designer Johnson Cushing & Nevell, N.Y.C., 1942-46; propr. Raymond Spilman Indsl. Design, N.Y.C., 1946—; ednl. adviser, lectr. design and design curriculums. Nat. Endowment for Arts design project fellow, 1977. Fellow Indsl. Design Soc. Am.; mem. Am. Soc. Indsl. Designers (pres. 1960-62, chmn. bd. 1963-64), Human Factors Soc. Am., Inter-Soc. Color Council (dir. 1970-72, 76-77), Phi Delta Theta. Editorial bd. Color Research and Application Quar., 1976—. Home: Althea Ln Darien CT 06820 Office: 217 Bedford St Stamford CT 06901

SPILMAN, ROBERT HENKEL, furniture mfr.; b. Knoxville, Tenn., Sept. 27, 1927; s. Robert R. and Lila (Henkel) S.; B.S. in Textiles, N.C. State Coll., 1950; student N.Y.U. Grad. Sch. Commerce, 1953; m. Jane Bassett, Apr. 2, 1955; children—Robert Henkel, Virginia Sale, Vance H. With Bassett Industries, 1957—, pres., 1966—, chief exec. officer, 1979—, also dir.; pres. 1st Bassett Bank and Trust Co.; dir. Bassett Mirror Co., Roy Stone Trucking Co., Blue Ridge Hardware, NCNB Corp.; mem. Va. adv. bd. Liberty Mut. Trustee W.M. Bassett Community Center; trustee, mem. exec. com. Appalachian State U. Served to lt. airborne inf. AUS, World War II, Korea. Mem. So. Furniture Mfrs. Assn. (pres. 1970 chmn. bd. 1971), Va. Mfrs. Assn. (dir.). Home: Bassett VA 24055 Office: Bassett Furniture Industries Bassett VA 24055

SPINA, ANTHONY J., photographer; b. Detroit; s. Costan and Julia (Perry) S.; B.A., Detroit Inst. Tech., 1939; m. Frances Leto, Mar. 2, 1946; children—Costan, II, Julia, Kathryn. Mem. photog. staff Detroit Free Press, 1946—, chief photographer, 1952—; numerous one-man exhbns. include: Detroit Art Inst., 1976, Los Angeles County Museum, 1976, Vatican Mus., 1968; mem. spl. Free Press team, 1968 (Pulitzer prize). Served with USN, World War II, Korean War. Decorated knight St. Gregory The Great (Pope Paul VI); recipient Gold medallion Pope John XXIII, 1962, Silver medallion, 1962, Bronze medallion, 1962; 482 nat. and internat. photog. awards. Roman Catholic. Author: The Making of the Pope-Pope John XXIII, 1962; The Pope and The Council, 1963; This Was the President—John F. Kennedy, 1964; The Press Photographer, 1968; From A Distant Country—Pope John Paul II, 1979; author weekly photog. questions and answer column for Knight Ridder Newspapers Wire Service. Home: 3525 Squirrel Rd Bloomfield Hills MI 48013 Office: 321 W Lafayette Blvd Detroit MI 48231

SPINDEL, BENJAMIN, linen supply co. exec.; b. N.Y.C., Oct. 26, 1917; s. Samuel and Rose (Moskovitz) S.; B.B.A., Coll. City N.Y., 1937; postgrad. N.Y. U., 1938-39; m. Mildred Smith, Oct. 27, 1940; children—Frederic T., Alan H., Neil E. Accountant, Adams & Co., Real Estate, N.Y.C., 1937-40; controller Holly Style Stores, N.Y.C., 1940-42, Block Drug Co., Inc., Jersey City, 1942-47, Valcort Hosiery Corp., N.Y.C., 1947-60; v.p., treas., dir. Sears Industries, Inc., N.Y.C., 1960—; dir. Economy Merc. Corp. Served with U.S. Maritime Service. Mem. Nat. Assn. Accountants, Am. Soc. Ins. Mgmt., Inc., Textile Rental Services Assn. Am., Am. Mgmt. Assn. Home: 1004 Hancock Ave Franklin Square NY 11010 Office: 800 2d Ave New York NY 10017

SPINDEL, WILLIAM, scientist, educator, adminstr.; b. N.Y.C., Sept. 9, 1922; s. Joseph and Esther (Goldstein) S.; B.A., Bklyn. Coll., 1944; M.A., Columbia, 1947, Ph.D., 1950; m. Louise Phyllis Hoodenpyl, July 30, 1967; children—Robert Andrew, Lawrence Marshall. Jr. scientist Los Alamos Lab, Manhattan Dist., 1944-45; instr. Poly. Inst., Bklyn., 1949-50; asso. prof. State U. N.Y., 1950-54; research asso., vis. prof. Columbia, 1954-57, vis. prof., sr. lectr., 1962-74; asso. prof. then prof. Rutgers U., 1957-64; prof., chmn. dept. chemistry Belfer Grad. Sch. Sci., Yeshiva U., 1964-74; exec. sec., office chemistry and chem. tech. Nat. Acad. Scis.-NRC, 1974—; vis. Am. scientist, Yugoslavia, 1971-72. Served with AUS, 1943-46. Guggenheim fellow, 1961-62; Fulbright Research scholar, 1961-62. Fellow AAAS; mem. Am. Chem. Soc., Am. Phys. Soc. Contbr. articles to profl. jours. Patentee in field. Home: 6503 Dearborn Dr Falls Church VA 22044 Office: Nat Acad Scis 2101 Constitution Ave Washington DC 20418

SPINDLER, FRANCIS EDWARD, elec. mfg. co. exec.; b. Denver, July 2, 1925; s. Frank and Rose Clara (Fagan) S.; B.S. in Elec. Engring., U. Colo., 1948; M.S. in Elec. Engring., U. Pitts., 1952; M.B.A., Harvard, 1956; m. Margaret Anne Weaver, Sept. 11, 1954; children—Susan A., Francis E., Paul M., Stephen J., Mary E., Carol M., Regina C., Clare A. Engr., Westinghouse Electric Corp., East Pitts., 1948-54, planning and marketing positions, Buffalo, 1956-60, Pitts., 1960-63, div. gen. mgr., Buffalo, 1963-67, divs. gen. mgr., 1967-68, group v.p., Pitts., 1968-69, exec. v.p. indsl., 1969-74, exec. v.p. industry equipment and services, 1974—. Trustee Carlow Coll. Served with USNR, 1944-46. Mem. Greater Pitts. C. of C., IEEE, Engrs. Soc. Western Pa. Home: 2053 Hycroft Dr Pittsburgh PA 15241 Office: Westinghouse Bldg Gateway Center Pittsburgh PA 15222

SPINDLER, GEORGE DEARBORN, anthropologist, educator, author, editor; b. Stevens Point, Wis., Feb. 28, 1920; s. Frank Nicholas and Winifred (Hatch) S.; B.S., Central State Tchrs. Coll., Wis., 1940; M.A., U. Wis., 1947; Ph.D., U. Calif. at Los Angeles, 1952; m. Louise Schaubel, May 29, 1942; 1 dau., Sue Carol (Mrs. H. Lloyd Walker). Tchr. sch. in Wis., 1940-42; research asso. Stanford, 1950-51, mem. faculty, 1951—, prof. anthropology and edn., 1960—, exec. head dept., 1963-67; editor Am. Anthropologist, 1962-66; cons. editor Holt, Rinehart & Winston, 1965—. Pres. Peninsula Sch. Bd., Menlo Park, Calif., 1954-56. Served with AUS, 1942-45. Fellow Center Advanced Study Behavioral Scis., 1956-57; recipient Distinguished Alumni award Wis. State U., 1972; Lloyd W. Dinkelspeil award Stanford U., 1978. Fellow Am. Anthrop. Assn.; mem. Southwestern Anthrop. Assn. (pres. 1962-63). Author: Menomini Acculturation, 1955; (with A. Beals and L. Spindler) Culture in Process, 1967, rev. edit., 1973; Transmission of American Culture, 1959; (with L. Spindler) Dreamers Without Power, 1971; Burgbach: Urbanization and Identity in a German Village, 1973. Editor: Education and Anthropology, 1955; (with Louise Spindler) Case Studies in Cultural Anthropology, 1960—; Methods in Cultural Anthropology, 1965—; Case Studies in Education and Culture, 1966—. Editor, contbr.: Education and Culture, 1963, Being An Anthropologist, 1970; Education and Cultural Process, 1974; The Making of Psychological Anthropology, 1978. Home: 489 Kortum Canyon Rd Calistoga CA 94515 Office: Dept Anthropology Stanford Univ Stanford CA 94305

SPINDLER, JAMES WALTER, lawyer; b. Middletown, Ohio, Feb. 24, 1939; s. Walter Herbert and Mayme Laue Spindler; B.A., Cornell U., 1961; LL.B., Harvard U., 1964; m. Mary Allen Griffing, Aug. 29, 1964; children—David Neill, Henry Carlton. Admitted to Mass. bar; asso. firm Hale & Dorr, Boston, 1968-73, partner, 1973-79; sec. Masoneilan Internat., Inc., Norwood, Mass., 1973-79; corp. counsel and asst. sec. Computervision Corp., Bedford, Mass., 1979—. Town rep. for Lincoln, Mass., to subregional planning orgn., 1969-75; mem. Lincoln Bd. Edn., 1977—. Served to capt. Judge Adv. Gen.'s Corps, USMC, 1964-68. Recipient Eastern Collegiate Athletic Conf. award, 1961. Mem. Am. Bar Assn., Mass. Bar Assn., Boston Bar Assn., Phi Beta Kappa, Phi Kappa Phi, Delta Sigma Rho. Episcopalian. Contbr. articles to law jours. Home: Weston Rd Lincoln MA 01773 Office: 201 Burlington Rd Bedford MA 01773

SPINGARN, JEROME H., govt. ofcl.; b. Jersey City, Feb. 27, 1914; s. Herman and Lillie (Presslaff) S.; A.B., Dartmouth, 1935; J.D., Columbia, 1939; m. Natalie Davis, June 14, 1944; children—Jeremy, Jonathan. Admitted to N.Y. bar, 1940, D.C. bar, 1948, also U.S. Supreme Ct., others; research asst. Columbia Law Sch., 1930-40; atty. R.R. Retirement Bd., 1941, FCC, 1942; mem. staff U.S. Senate, 1946-48; asst. to chmn. com. lobbying activities Ho. of Reps., 1949; pvt. practice, Washington, 1948-62; vis. prof., dir. arms control center Fairleigh Dickinson U., 1956-57; professorial lectr. Am. U., Washington; sec. com. security through arms control Nat. Planning Assn., 1957-61; sec. President Kennedy's Task Force on Disarmament, 1961; sr. adviser U.S. Arms Control and Disarmament Agy., 1962-74; sr. cons. Nat. Planning Assn., 1974; admistrv. asst. to Congressman Henry Reuss of Wis., 1975—. Chmn. D.C. Health and Welfare Council, 1966-67; asst. dir. research Democratic Nat. Com., 1952; bd. dirs. Friendship House, Washington. Served to lt. comdr. USNR, 1943-46. Mem. Am. Soc. Internat. Law, Am. Polit. Sci. Assn., Soc. Citizen Edn. in World Affairs (dir.), Arms Control Assn., Internat. Inst. Strategic Studies (London), Internat. Studies Assn. Clubs: International, National Press (Washington). Author articles, pamphlets, revs. Home: 1409 29th St NW Washington DC 20007 Office: 2186 Rayburn Dept Bldg Washington DC 20515

SPINGARN, STEPHEN J., lawyer; b. Bedford, N.Y., Sept. 1, 1908; s. J.E. and Amy Judith S.; ed. Phillips Exeter Acad., 1922-25, Yale U., 1925-27, U. Grenoble, France 1927-28, Rollins Coll., Winter Park, Fla., 1929; A.B., U. Ariz., 1930, LL.B., 1934; Stanford U., 1932. Admitted to Ariz. bar, 1933, D.C. bar, 1947, U.S. Supreme Ct. bar, 1974; atty. U.S. Treasury Dept, 1934-41, spl. asst. to gen. counsel, 1941-42, asst. gen. counsel, 1946-49, functioning as treasury legis. counsel and counsel, U.S. Secret Service; spl. asst. to atty. gen. of U.S., 1937-38; dep. dir. Office of Contract Settlement, 1947-49; asst. to spl. counsel of the President, also became adminstrv. asst. to Pres., functioning as White House legis. counsel, 1950; mem. Codification Bd. which codified all fed. regulations, 1937-38; treasury mem. Interdeptl. Com. on War Legislation, 1941-42; alt. mem. Pres.'s Temp. Commn. on Employee Loyalty, 1946-47; treasury rep. to inter.-Am. Bar Assn. Conf., Lima, Peru, 1947; mem., often acting chmn. FTC, 1950-53. Mem. adv. com. on small bus. Dem. Nat. Com., 1956; dir. spl. activities Dem. vice pres. campaign, 1956. Commd. capt. AUS, 1942, advanced through grades to lt. col., 1944; served 3 years. overseas, N. Africa, Italy, Austria, including service on Salerno and Anzio beachheads; comdg. officer, 5th Army Counter Intelligence Corps. 1943-45; relieved from active duty, 1946; lt. col. Mil. Intelligence Res., 1947-55. Decorated Combat Legion of Merit, 1944, Bronze Star Medal with Valor Emblem, 1945; Invasion Arrowhead; 5 battle stars; recipient Wisdom award Honor, 1971. Mem. D.C., Ariz. bar assns. Democrat. Club: Nat. Press (Washington). Author various articles and papers on counter-espionage. Address: 2500 Q St NW Washington DC 20007

SPINGOLA, JOSEPH PETER, banker; b. Chgo., Nov. 7, 1923; s. Peter John and Catherine Mary (Mesce) S.; B.Sc., DePaul U., 1949, M.B.A., 1962; m. Loretta A. Korenchan, June 26, 1948; children—Janet (Mrs. Thomas Dovidio), Michael, William, Constance, Ronald. Accountant various C.P.A. firms, 1949-52, 55-58; with Steber Mfg. Co., 1958-60, Continental Casualty Co., 1960-62; with Northwest Nat. Bank, Chgo., 1962—, sr. v.p., 1972—, also dir. Area chmn. Cancer Crusade, 1973; co-chmn. Ill. K.C. Retarded Citizen Drive, 1976-78; adv. bd. Banking Research Center, Northwestern U.; lay bd. St. Patrick's High Sch., Chgo.; bd. dirs. North River Commn., Joliet diocese Catholic Charities. Served with AUS, 1943-46. C.P.A., Ill. Mem. Ill. Soc. C.P.A.'s, Am. Inst. C.P.A.'s, Ledger and Quill Soc., Am. Bankers Assn., Ill. Bankers Assn., Am. Inst. Banking, Fin. Execs. Inst., Am. Legion, YMCA, Portage Park C. of C. (pres. 1972-74)/ Roman Catholic (trustee ch. 1970—). K.C. Club: River Forest Country (Elmhurst). Home: 823 Kearsage St Elmhurst IL 60126 Office: 3985 Milwaukee St Chicago IL 60641

SPINK, CHARLES CLAUDE JOHNSON, pub. co. exec.; b. St. Louis, Oct. 31, 1916; s. John George Taylor and Blanche (Keene) S.; student Trinity Coll., 1939; m. Edith Swift Jenkin, Oct. 8, 1949. With Sporting News, St. Louis, 1939—, pub., 1962—; pub. Sporting Goods Dealer, 1962-78, chmn. bd., editor, 1978—. Founder United Sporting Goods Dealers, 1960. Chmn. Youth Fitness Council City of St. Louis; mem. citizens adv. com. Pres.'s Council Phys. Fitness, 1957-59; bd. mem. St. Louis Sports Hall Fame, Buddy Fund, Mun. Opera, Stadium Club, Media Club, St. Louis Symphony; trustee Mo. Bot. Garden. Named Ky. col. Mem. Baseball and Football Writers Am., Sigma Delta Chi. Episcopalian. Clubs: Univ., St. Louis, Stadium, Noonday, Racquet, St. Louis Country, St. Anthony, Media. Home: 9 Log Cabin Dr St Louis MO 63124 Office: 1212 N Lindbergh Blvd St Louis MO 63166

SPINK, WALTER MILTON, educator; b. Worcester, Mass., Feb. 16, 1928; s. Herbert Elmer and Amy Ann (Whitford) S.; A.B. summa cum laude, Amherst Coll., 1949; M.A., Harvard U., 1950, Ph.D., 1954; m. Nesta Frances Rubidge, June 20, 1952; children—David, Philip, Anne. Mem. faculty, dept. art, Brandeis U., Waltham, Mass., 1956-61; mem. faculty dept. art history U. Mich., Ann Arbor, 1961—, prof. Indian art, 1961—, dir. Asian Art Archives, 1963—. Served with M.C., U.S. Army, 1954-56. Fulbright fellow, 1952; Am. Council Learned Socs. grantee, 1959, 63, 72; Rackham grantee, 1962, 68, 74, 77; Bollingen grantee, 1964; Am. Inst. Indian Studies grantee, 1966, 75, 79; Smithsonian grantee, 1971; Nat. Endowment for Humanities grantee, 1976. Mem. Assn. for Asian Studies, Coll. Art Assn., Am. Com. for South Asian Art (pres. 1972-76), Asia Soc., Bharata Itihasa Samshodhaka Mandala (Poona) (life mem.). Democrat. Unitarian. Author: Ajanta to Ellora, 1967; Krishnamandala, 1971; The Axis of Eros, 1973; The Quest for Krishna, 1972; contbr. articles on Indian cave temples to profl. jours. Home: 2 Geddes Heights Ann Arbor MI 48104 Office: Tappan Hall U Mich Ann Arbor MI 48109

SPINK, WESLEY W., physician, educator; b. Duluth, Dec. 17, 1904; s. George Charles W. and Caroline (Kuntz) S.; A.B., Carleton Coll., 1926, D. Sc. (hon.), 1950; M.D., Harvard, 1932; research scholar Harvard Med. Sch., 1932-33; m. Elizabeth Hamilton Hurd, Aug. 29, 1935; children—Helen Gayden (Mrs. Robert DuPont, Jr.), George Wesley (dec.), William Wesley. Intern IV Med. Service (Harvard), 1933-34; resident physician Thorndike Memorial Lab. (both Boston City Hosp.), 1934-37; asst. in medicine Harvard Med. Sch., 1934-37; asst. prof. medicine U. Minn. Med. Sch., 1937-41, asso. prof.,

1941-47, prof., 1947-67, Regents' prof. medicine, 1967-73, prof. comparative medicine, 1970-73 emeritus Regents' prof. medicine and comparative medicine, 1973—. Cons. brucellosis to WHO; dir. Brucellosis Research Center of the U.S., 1951-73, WHO, FAO, UN. Recipient Chapin medal City of Providence, 1964; Distinguished Scholar award Nat. Library of Medicine, 1973. Diplomate Am. Bd. Internal Medicine; charter mem. Am. Bd. Microbiology. Master A.C.P. (bd. regents 1960-66; pres. 1963-64); fellow AAAS; hon. fellow Royal Australasian Coll. Physicians, Am. Vet. Med. Assn., N.Y. Acad. Scis.; mem. Am. Soc. Clin. Investigation (pres. 1949), Am. Clin. and Climatological Assn., Assn. Am. Physicians (emeritus), Am. Assn. Immunologists, Am. Assn. History Medicine, Soc. U.S. Air Force Internists and Allied Specialists (hon.), Central Soc. Clin. Research (pres. 1950), Soc. Exptl. Biology and Medicine, Minn. Acad. Medicine, Harvard Med. Alumni Assn. (pres. 1967-68), Minn. State Med. Assn., Mpls. Soc. Internal Medicine (hon.), Minn. Pathol. Soc. (pres. 1944), Mpls. Acad. Medicine, Phi Beta Kappa, Alpha Omega Alpha. Author: Sulfanilamide and Related Compounds in General Practice, 1941, rev. edit., 1942; Nature of Brucellosis, 1956; Infectious Diseases: Prevention and Treatment in the 19th and 20th Centuries, 1978; contbr. med. publs. Home: 1916 East River Terr Minneapolis MN 55414. *One can fool neither students nor his children, and I have always tried to listen to them, painful though it has been at times.*

SPINKS, LEON, profl. boxer; b. St. Louis; m. Nova; 1 son. Charles. Fought 185 amateur bouts; profl. boxer, 1977—; world heavyweight champion, 1978. Served with USMC, until 1976. Winner Bronze medal World Boxing Championships, Cuba, 1975; Silver medal Pan Am. Games, Mexico City, Mex., 1975; Gold medal as light heavyweight Olympic Games, 1976. Address: care World Boxing Assn 1511 K St NW Suite 843 Washington DC 20005*

SPINNER, FRANK KENNETH, banker; b. St. Louis, Aug. 3, 1929; s. Frank Gregory and Anna Eleanor (Senik) S.; B.S., St. Louis U., 1958; m. Beverly Ann Remspecher, June 21, 1952; children—Frank, David, Steven, Mary, Gregory, Thomas, Michael, Paul. With First Nat. Bank St. Louis, 1947—, sr. v.p. charge investment div., 1967—; pres., chief exec. officer Tower Grove Bank and Trust Co., 1979—, TG Bankshares, Inc., 1979—; mem. faculty numerous banking schs.; mem. municipal rulemaking bd. SEC. Served with AUS, 1951-53. Mem. Dealer Bank Assn. (dir., officer), Am. Bankers Assn. (dir. investment div.). Home: 8846 Pardee Rd Affton MO 63123 Office: PO Box 267 St Louis MO 63166

SPINRAD, BERNARD ISRAEL, educator, physicist; b. N.Y.C., Apr. 16, 1924; s. Abraham and Rose (Sorrin) S.; B.S. with honors, Yale, 1942, M.S., 1944, Ph.D. in Phys. Chemistry, 1945, Sterling fellow postdoctoral research, 1945-46; m. Marion Eisen, June 29, 1951; children—Alexander Abraham, Mark David, Jeremy Paul, Diana Esther. Physicist, Oak Ridge Nat. Lab., 1946-48; mem. staff Argonne Nat. Lab., 1949-67, 70-72, dir. reactor engring. div., 1957-63, sr. physicist applied physics div., 1963-67, 70-72, dir. div. nuclear power and reactors IAEA, Vienna, Austria, 1967-70; prof. nuclear engring. Oreg. State U., Corvallis, 1972—. Adviser U.S. delegation Internat. Conf. Peaceful Uses Atomic Energy, Geneva, Switzerland, 1955, 58; cons. IAEA, 1961, 63, 72, 74; chmn. European-Am. Com. Reactor Physics, 1962-64; mem. com. nuclear and alternative energy systems NRC, 1974—; vis. researcher Internat. Inst. Applied Systems Analysis, Vienna, 1978-79. Named Man of Year, Chgo., 1956, Hinsdale, Ill., 1958. Fellow Am. Phys. Soc., Am. Nuclear Soc. (past dir.); mem. AAAS, Am. Chem. Soc., World Future Soc., Sigma Xi. Author papers, reports in field. Home: 3650 NW Roosevelt Dr Corvallis OR 97330. *I have lived by trying to understand the rich fabric of the world and our lives, and I love the richness. All the elements should be in it, and this means that apparent contradictions are to be harmonized and resolved, rather than set against each other. I find that I have to be selectively moderate, aggressively opposing the nonsense which is bound up with the valid points in polarized ideologies. It is an attitude which is a bit lonely, for it rejects blind loyalty and blind faith, but I value the dignity of it.*

SPINRAD, HYRON, astronomer; b. N.Y.C., Feb. 17, 1934; s. Emanuel B. and Ida (Silverman) S.; A.B., U. Calif. at Berkeley, 1955, M.A., 1959, Ph.D. (Lick Obs. fellow), 1961; m. Bette L. Abrams, Aug. 17, 1958; children—Michael, Robert, Tracy. Studied galaxies U. Calif. at Berkeley, 1960-61; planetary atmospheres work Jet Propulsion Lab., Pasadena, Calif., 1961-63; investigation atmospheres of coolest stars U. Calif. at Berkeley, 1964-70; spl. research water vapor on Mars, molecular hydrogen on Jupiter, Saturn, Uranus and Neptune, temperature measurements on Venus atmosphere, spectra of galaxies and near-infrared observations, 71-72, location of faint radio galaxies, redshifts of galaxies, 1973—. Mem. Am. Astron. Soc., Astron. Soc. Pacific. Home: 7 Ketelsen Dr Moraga CA 94556 Office: Dept Astronomy Univ California Berkeley CA 94720

SPIOTTA, RAYMOND HERMAN, editor; b. Bklyn., Feb. 24, 1927; s. Michael Joseph and Olga Elizabeth (Schmidt) S.; B.M.E., Pratt Inst., 1953; m. Marie Theresa Attanasio, Apr. 17, 1949; children—Michael, Ronald, Mark, Sandra. Mfg. engr. Arma div. Am. Bosch Arma Corp., Garden City, N.Y., 1948-53; mng. editor Machinery mag., N.Y.C., 1953-65; editor Machine and Tool Blue Book, Wheaton, Ill., 1965-74, exec. editor, 1974—. Mem. DuPage County (Ill.) area council Boy Scouts Am., 1966-73. Served with AC, USNR, 1944-48. Mem. Indsl. Mgmt. Soc., Numerical Control Soc., Soc. Bus. Press Editors, Am. Bus. Press, Soc. Am. Value Engrs., Soc. Mfg. Engrs., Am. Inst. Indsl. Engrs. Roman Catholic. Contbr. to Am. Peoples Ency. Yearbook. Contbr. articles to profl. jours. Home: 26W354 Blackhawk Dr Wheaton IL 60187 Office: Hitchcock Bldg Wheaton IL 60187

SPIRO, BENJAMIN PAUL, economist; b. Concise, Switzerland, June 6, 1917; s. Louis and Jeanne (Secretan) S.; Lic.Sc.Pol., U. Lausanne, 1939, Lic.Sc.Ec., 1940, Dr.Sc.Pol., 1941; postgrad. Columbia, 1941-42; m. Nelly Riveros, Oct. 2, 1963; 1 son, Cyril Sven. Came to U.S., 1941, naturalized, 1948. Sec. to Swiss Legation, Washington, 1943-45; with Irving Trust Co., N.Y.C., 1945-46; mem. faculty Duke, 1946-47; with World Bank, 1947-59; pres. Bank-Fund credit union, 1959-60; with Stanford Research Inst., 1959; fgn. econ. and financial cons. to internat. orgns., govts., pvt. cos., San Francisco, 1961—; pres. Benjamin Spiro Assos., Inc., San Francisco, 1962—. Adviser Central Bank and Nat. Bank Econ. Devel., Brazil, 1965-67, Indonesian Devel. Bank, 1968; integrated regional devel. projects in Morocco, 1969-71, Iran, 1972-75, East Africa, 1975-76, Yemen, 1977; promoted small-scale industry devel. in Latin Am., Africa, 1978. Active Boy Scouts Am., 1941-60, recipient Silver Beaver award, 1953. Served with Swiss Army, 1937-41. Mem. Am. Econ. Assn., Nat. Democratic Club. Contbr. articles to profl. lit. Home: Le Mazot 1861 Huemoz Switzerland Office: 24 California St San Francisco CA 94111

SPIRO, HERBERT JOHN, ambassador, educator, polit. scientist; b. Hamburg, Germany, Sept. 7, 1924; s. Albert John and Marianne (Stiefel) S.; came to U.S., 1938, naturalized, 1944; student Wilhelm Gymnasium, Hamburg, 1934-38, San Antonio Jr. Coll., 1942-43; A.B. summa cum laude, (John Harvard scholar 1948-49, Detur prize 1948, Holzer scholar 1949-51), Harvard, 1949, M.A., 1950, Ph.D., 1953; M.A. (hon.), U. Pa., 1971; m. Elizabeth Anna Petersen, June 7, 1958; children—Peter John, Alexander Charles Stiefel. Adminstrv. asst. U.S. War Dept., Vienna, Austria, 1945-46; mem. faculty Harvard, 1950-61, asst. prof., 1957-61; asso. prof. polit. sci. Amherst (Mass.) Coll., 1961-65; chmn. Asian and African Studies Program, Amherst-Smith-Mt. Holyoke colls., U. Mass., 1964-65; prof. polit. sci. U. Pa., Phila., 1965-73; vis. asso. prof. U. Chgo., 1961, Stanford, 1963; Fulbright sr. research prof. U. Coll. Rhodesia and Nyasaland, 1959-60; adv. council polit. sci. Haverford Coll., 1966-71; vis. prof. internat. affairs Woodrow Wilson Sch., Princeton, 1966; affiliated Nuffield Coll., Oxford (Eng.) U., 1967-68; mem. policy planning staff Dept. State, 1970-75; ambassador to Cameroon, 1975-77, Equatorial Guinea, 1975-76; fellow Woodrow Wilson Internat. Center for Scholars, Smithsonian Instn., Washington, 1978; vis. prof. polit. sci. Def. Intelligence Sch., 1979-80; guest lectr. various univs.; resident scholar Rockefeller Found. Study Center, Bellagio, Italy, 1968, 78; participant internat scholarly and diplomatic confs. Cons. Japanese Commn. on Revision Constn., 1962, Brit. Commn. to Rev. Constn. of Fedn. of Rhodesia and Nyasaland, 1960. Served with AUS, 1943-45. Decorated Bronze Star medal with oak leaf cluster, Purple Heart; grand officer Legion of Valor (Cameroon), 1977; recipient Superior Honor award Dept. State. Guggenheim fellow, Fulbright prof., 1959-60, Social Sci. Research Council faculty fellow, 1962, 67-68, Rockefeller Found. fellow, 1958; recipient Bowdoin prize, 1952; Sheldon Travelling fellow Harvard, also Fulbright fellow, 1953-54. Mem. African Studies Assn., Am. (council 1968-70, chmn. election com. 1969), Internat. Polit. Sci. Assn., Am. Soc. Polit. and Legal Philosophy, AAAS, Council Fgn. Relations, Am. Fgn. Service Assn., Phi Beta Kappa, Signet Soc. Club: Harvard (Washington). Author: Politics of German Codetermination, 1958; (with others) Patterns of Government, 1958, 2d edit. rev., 1962; Government by Constitution, 1959; Politics in Africa, 1962, 2d edit., 1975; (with others) Five African States, 1963; World Politics: The Global System, 1966; (with others) Authority, Nomos I, 1958, Responsibility, Nomos III, 1960; Privacy Nomos XIII, 1971; (with others) Why Federations Fail, 1968; Responsibility in Government, 1969; The Dialectic of Representation 1619-1969, 1969; Politics as the Master Science: From Plato to Mao, 1970; (with others) Theory and Politics, 1971; (with others) Between Sovereignty and Integration, 1974; The Theory of Replication, 1979; A New Foreign Policy Consensus? 1979; also articles; editor, contbr.: Africa: The Primacy of Politics, 1966; Patterns of African Development, 1967. Contbr. to Internat. Ency. Social Scis., Ency. Britannica, World Book Ency. Research in theory of constn.-bldg., consensus-formation, devel. politics, policy planning, methodological reintegration of splintered compartments of polit. sci. Home: 3418 Garfield St NW Washington DC 20007 Home: 3418 Garfield St NW Washington DC 20007

SPIRO, HOWARD MARGET, physician, educator; b. Cambridge, Mass., Mar. 23, 1924; s. Thomas and Martha (Marget) B.A., Harvard, 1944, M.D., 1947; M.A., Yale, 1967; m. Marian Freelove Wagner, Mar 11, 1951; children—Pamela Marget, Carolyn Standish, Philip Marget, Martha Standish. Intern, Peter Bent Brigham Hosp., Boston, 1947-48; resident Peter Bent Brigham Hosp., 1948-51, Mass. Gen. Hosp., 1953-55; practice medicine, specializing in gastroenterology, New Haven, 1955—; chief gastrointestinal unit Yale Sch. Medicine, 1955—, prof. medicine, 1967—. Served with USNR, 1943-45, AUS, 1951-53. Mem. Am. Gastroent. Assn., Am. Soc. Clin. Investigation. Clubs: New Haven Lawn, Madison Beach. Author: Clinical Gastroenterology, 1970, 2d edit., 1977. Home: 260 Millbrook Rd North Haven CT 06518 Office: 333 Cedar St New Haven CT 06510

SPIRO, MELFORD ELLIOT, educator; b. Cleve., Apr. 26, 1920; s. Wilbert I. and Sophie (Goodman) S.; B.A., U. Minn., 1941; Ph.D., Northwestern U., 1950; m. Audrey Goldman, May 27, 1950; children—Michael, Jonathan. Mem. faculty Washington U., St. Louis, 1948-52, U. Conn., 1952-57, U. Wash., 1957-64; prof. anthropology U. Chgo., 1964-68; prof., chmn. dept. anthropology U. Calif., San Diego, 1968—. Bd. dirs. Social Sci. Research Council, 1960-62. Fellow Am. Acad. Arts and Scis.; mem. Am. Anthrop. Assn., Am. Ethnol. Soc. (pres. 1967-68), AAAS. Author: (with E.G. Burrows) An Atoll Culture, 1953; Kibbutz: Venture in Utopia, 1955; Children of Kibbutz, 1958; Burmese Supernaturalism, 1967; Buddhism and Society: A Great Tradition and Its Burmese Vicissitudes, 1971; Kinship and Marriage in Burma, 1977; editor: Context and Meaning in Culture Anthropology, 1965. Home: 2500 Torrey Pines Rd LaJolla CA 92037

SPIRO, ROBERT HARRY, JR., univ. pres.; b. Asheville, N.C., Dec. 5, 1920; s. Robert Harry and Eoline Peterson (Shaw) S.; B.S., Wheaton (Ill.) Coll., 1941; postgrad. U. N.C., 1945-46; Ph.D., U. Edinburgh (Scotland), 1950; student Union Theol. Sem., summers 1951-53; postdoctoral Duke U., summer 1956; m. Ruth Suenell Bennett, Jan. 10, 1942; children—Robert Timothy, Elizabeth Susan, James Monroe. Asso., then prof. history King Coll., Bristol, Tenn., 1946-50; prof. history Miss. Coll., 1950-57; pres. Blue Ridge Assembly, Black Mountain, N.C., 1957-60; dean Coll. Liberal Arts, prof. history Mercer U., 1960-64; pres. Jacksonville U. (Fla.), 1964-79, pres., chancellor, 1979—; dir. Voyager Variable Annuity of Fla. Bd. dirs. Nat. Commn. on Accrediting, 1972-75, Fla. Council of 100, Gator Bowl Assn., Fla. Bd. Ind. Colls.; past pres. Fla. Assn. Colls. and Univs.; trustee Southwestern Bapt. Theol. Sem.; mem. Ind. Colls. and Univs. of Fla., 1964—, chmn., 1967; sec.-treas. Assn. Urban Univs., 1968-77. Served to lt. USNR, 1941-45; ret. rear adm. Res. Mem. Am., So., Fla., Jacksonville hist. assns., Miss. Hist. Soc. (asso. editor jour. 1953-57), Navy League U.S., Naval Res. Assn. (nat. adv. council), Res. Officers Assn. Baptist (deacon). Clubs: Rotary, River (Jacksonville, Fla.); Ponte Vedra (Fla.); Deerwood; Biltmore Forest; Hidden Hills. Contbr. articles to profl. publs. encys. Home: President's Home Jacksonville U Jacksonville FL 32211

SPIRO, WALTER ANSELM, advt. and pub. relations agy. exec.; b. Berlin, Germany, Aug. 10, 1923; s. Harry L. and Kate (Loewenstein) S.; came to U.S., 1940, naturalized, 1945; student Athelton Coll., affiliate Cambridge U., Folkestone, Eng., 1938-40; m. Sandee Rosen, Dec. 17, 1971; children by previous marriage—Karen Leslie, Pamela Anne, Paul David, Amy Eloise; stepchildren—Gabrielle Goodman, Charles Goodman. Display dir. Allied Stores, N.Y.C., 1947-51; advt. dir. Gimbel Bros., Phila., 1951-58; exec. v.p. Lavenson Bur. Advt., Phila., 1958-64; pres. Spiro & Assos., Phila., 1964—. Mem. Gov.'s Travel Adv. Commn., 1971—; mem. adv. rev. com. Better Bus. Bur., 1975—; bd. dirs. Walnut St. Theatre, 1972—, mem. exec. com., 1972—; bd. dirs. Pa. Ballet Co., 1973-78, v.p., 1974—; trustee Phila. United Fund, 1973—; bd. dirs., mem. exec. com. Greater Phila. Partnership; founding bd. mem. Consumer Council Greater Phila.; mem. founding group Global InterDependence Center; mem. bd. Public Interest Law Center of Phila. Mem. World Affairs Council Phila. (dir. 1971—, vice-chmn. 1974-78), Phila. Cultural Alliance, Phila. Festival (gov. 1974-78). Mem. Am. Assn. Advt. Agys. (com. of bd. agy. mgmt.). Clubs: Downtown, Urban, Vesper, Peale, Sunday Breakfast. Home: 1921 Panama St Philadelphia PA 19103 Office: 100 S Broad St Philadelphia PA 19110

SPITLER, LEE WILLIAM, bank exec.; b. Racine, Wis., Feb. 14, 1919; s. Marion Albert and Agnes Elizabeth (Lowe) S.; B.S., U. Md., 1956; M.B.A., George Washington U., 1962; Advanced Mgmt. Program, Harvard U., 1963; grad. USAF War Coll., 1958, USAF Command and Staff Coll., 1954; m. Helen Deloris Krejci, Mar. 19, 1949; children—Susan D., Lee William, Anne M., James E. Commd. 2d lt. USAF, 1943, advanced through grades to col., 1954; chief personnel stats. div. Hdqrs. USAF, Washington, 1950-54, asst. dir. statis. services, 1958-63; asst. comptroller Hdqrs. U.S. European Command, Paris, 1955-58; asst. comptroller Hdqrs. Air Tng. Command, Randolph AFB, Tex., 1963-64; ret., 1964; v.p. Computax Corp., El Segundo, Calif., 1965-69; exec. v.p. Irving Bank Corp., Irving Trust Co., N.Y.C., 1969—. Decorated Legion of Merit, Air Force Commendation medal, Army Commendation medal. Mem. Am. Bankers Assn., Am. Mgmt. Assn., Soc. for Mgmt. Info. Systems, Ret. Officers Assn., Nat. Assn. Uniformed Services. Club: Harvard. Home: 1 Hearthstone Way Montvale NJ 07645 Office: Irving Bank Corp 1 Wall St New York NY 10005

SPITZ, BARBARA SALOMON, artist; b. Chgo., Jan. 8, 1926; d. Fred B. and Sadie (Lorch) Salomon; A.B., Brown U., 1947; student Art Inst. Chgo., 1942-43, R.I. Sch. Design, 1945; m. Lawrence S. Spitz, Mar. 19, 1949; children—Thomas R., Linda J., Joanne L. One-woman exhbns. include: Benjamin Galleries, Chgo., 1971, 73, Kunsthaus Buhler, Stuttgart, Ger., 1973, Van Straaten Gallery, Chgo., 1976, Ella London Studio, Montreal, Que., Can., 1977; group exhibitions include: Soc. Am. Graphic Artists-Library of Congress traveling print exhbn., Tokyo, Tokyo Central Mus. Arts, Nat. Acad. Design, N.Y.C., Pratt Graphic Center, Honolulu Acad. Arts, Wadsworth Atheneum, others; represented in permanent collections: Phila. Mus. Art, DeCordova Mus., Okla. Art Center, Milw. Art Center, Art Inst. Chgo. Vice-chmn. Chgo. area Brown U. Bicentennial Drive; treas. Hearing and Speech Rehab. Center, Michael Reese Hosp., 1960. Mem. Artists Equity, Print Club Phila., Boston Printmakers, Arts Club of Chgo. Address: 1106 Somerset Ln Newport Beach CA 92660

SPITZ, CHARLES THOMAS, JR., clergyman; b. Hazard, Nebr., May 26, 1921; s. Charles Thomas and Magdalene (Schneemann) S.; grad. St. Paul's Coll., Concordia, Mo., 1939; A.B., Concordia Sem., St. Louis, 1944, D.D., 1965; D.D., Capital U., Columbus, Ohio, 1967, Muhlenberg Coll., 1967, Gettysburg Coll., 1970; L.H.D., Luther Coll., Decorah, Iowa, 1967; m. Dorothy O. Gross, June 11, 1944; children—Charles Thomas III, Gretchen Ann. Ordained to ministry Lutheran Ch., 1944; pastor in Waterloo, Iowa, 1944-46, Marengo, Iowa, 1947-53; dir. broadcasting Luth. Laymen's League, St. Louis, 1953-66, gen. sec. Luth. Council U.S., 1966-73; pastor in Manhasset, L.I., N.Y., 1974—; exec. asso. Evang. Lutheran in Mission, 1974-76; pres. Luth. Ch. in Mission, 1975—; dir. Assn. Evang. Luth. Chs., 1976—; mem. Commn. Luth. Unity, 1978—. Home: 6 Oakland Dr Port Washington NY 11050

SPITZ, LEWIS WILLIAM, historian; b. Bertrand, Nebr., Dec. 14, 1922; s. Lewis William and Pauline Mary (Griebel) S.; A.B., Concordia Coll., 1944; M.Div., Concordia Sem., 1946; M.A., U. Mo., 1947; Ph.D., Harvard U., 1954; m. Edna Marie Huttenmaier, Aug. 14, 1948; children—Stephen Andrew, Philip Mathew. With U. Mo., Columbia, 1953-60, asso. prof. history, 1958-60; Fulbright prof. U. Mainz, Ger., 1960-61; prof. history Stanford (Calif.) U., 1960—, William R. Kenan Jr. prof., 1974—, asso. dean humanities and scis., 1973-77; vis. prof. Harvard U., Cambridge, Mass., 1964-65; dir. research Center for Reformation Research, Clayton, Mo., summer 1964, mem. bd. control, 1973—; sr. fellow Southeastern Medieval and Renaissance Inst., Duke U., summer 1968. Recipient Harbison award for teaching Danforth Found., 1964; Guggenheim fellow, 1956; Nat. Endowment for Humanities sr. fellow, 1965; Am. Council Learned Socs. fellow, 1971; Huntington Library fellow, 1959; Inst. Advanced Study Princeton fellow, 1979-80. Mem. Am. Soc. Reformation Research (pres. 1963-64), Am. Hist. Assn., No. Calif. Renaissance Soc. (pres. 1964-65), Am. Soc. Ch. History (pres. 1976-77). Author: Conrad Celtis—The German Arch-Humanist, 1957; The Religious Renaissance of the German Humanists, 1963; Life in Two Worlds—A Biography of William Sihler, 1968; The Renaissance and Reformation Movements, 2 vols., 1972. Mem. editorial bd. Soundings, 1973-79; mng. editor Archive for Reformation History, 1968-76. Home: 827 Lathrop Dr Stanford CA 94305 Office: Dept History Stanford U Stanford CA 94305. *College teaching has enabled me to develop a career which coincides perfectly with my inner needs and goals in life, which have more to do with service than with ambition, more with love of people than wish to dominate, more with mind and spirit than with material things.*

SPITZ, SEYMOUR JAMES, JR., fragrance co. exec.; b. Milw., Nov. 17, 1921; s. Seymour James and Marie (Spinette) S.; B.S. in Bus. Adminstrn., Mass. Inst. Tech., 1943; m. Elizabeth Taylor Parks, Feb. 7, 1948 (div. Aug. 1967); children—William Taylor, Elizabeth Seymour, Anne Bellin; m. 2d, Ellen C. Flynn, July 25, 1969; 1 dau., Ellen Christina. With Newport Industries div. Heyden Newport Chem. Corp., Pensacola, Fla., 1946-65, asst. chief engr., 1955-57, asst. v.p., 1957-58, v.p., 1959-60, exec. v.p., 1960-61, pres., 1961-65, v.p. parent co. (name changed to Tenneco Chems., Inc. 1964), 1962-65, became group v.p., 1965, exec. v.p., 1966, pres., 1967-69; sr. v.p. parent co. Tenneco Inc.; pres. Internat. Flavors & Fragrances Inc., N.Y.C. 1970—, also dir.; dir. Foster Wheeler Corp. Mem. M.I.T. Corp. Devel. Com., 1977—. Served from ensign to lt. USNR, 1943-46. Clubs: Econ., Univ. (N.Y.C.); Larchmont (N.Y.) Yacht. Home: 201 E 62d St New York NY 10021 Office: 521 W 57th St New York NY 10019

SPITZBART, ABRAHAM, educator, mathematician; b. N.Y.C., Oct. 13, 1915; s. Elias and Helen (Schwartz) S.; B.S., Coll. City N.Y., 1935; A.M., Harvard, 1936, Ph.D., 1940; m. Evelyn Katz, Apr. 18, 1948; children—Donald R., Gail B. Instr. math. Harvard, 1937-40, Coll. City N.Y., 1940-41, U. Minn., 1942; prof. Coll. St. Thomas, St. Paul, Minn. 1942-45; mem. faculty U. Wis.-Milw., 1945—, prof. math., 1961—. Served with AUS, 1941. Mem. Am. Math. Soc., Math. Assn. Am. Author research papers complex variables, numerical analysis, mathematics textbooks. Home: 7322 N Mohawk Rd Milwaukee WI 53217

SPITZER, FRANK LUDWIG, mathematician, educator; b. Vienna, Austria, July 24, 1926; s. Gustav and Margaret (Herzog) S.; came to U.S., 1945, naturalized, 1951; Ph.D. in Math., U. Mich., 1952; m. Jean Wallach, Aug. 11, 1951; children—Karen, Timothy; m. 2d, Ingeborg Wald, 1975. Instr., Cal. Inst. Tech., 1953-58; asso. prof. U. Minn., 1959-60; NSF fellow Princeton, 1960-61; prof. Cornell U., Ithaca, N.Y., 1961—. Guggenheim fellow, 1965-66. Author: Principles of Random Walk, 1964. Home: 114 Cascadilla Park Ithaca NY 14850

SPITZER, JOHN BRUMBACK, lawyer; b. Toledo, Mar. 6, 1918; s. Lyman and Blanche (Brumback) S.; grad. Phillips Andover Acad., 1935; B.A., Yale, 1939, LL.B., 1947; m. Lucy Ohlinger, May 10, 1941 (dec. Oct. 13, 1971); children—John B., Molly (Mrs. Edmund Frost), Lyman, Adelbert L.; m. 2d, Vondah D. Thornbury, July 3, 1972; step-children—Vondah, Barbara James R. Thornbury. Admitted to Ohio bar, 1947, since practiced in Toledo; clk. to U.S. Supreme Ct. Justice Stanley Reed, 1947-48; partner firm Marshall, Melhorn, Cole, Hummer & Spitzer, 1955—. Pres. Spitzer Box Co., 1955-63; v.p. Spitzer Bldg. Co., 1960—. Pres. Toledo Symphony Orch., 1956-58, v.p., 1958—. Served to maj. AUS, World War II. Congregationalist (mem. bd.). Clubs: Toledo, Toledo Country, Otsego Ski, Belmont

Country. Home: 29620 Gleneagles Rd Perrysburg OH 43551 Office: Nat Bank Bldg Toledo OH 43604

SPITZER, JOHN J., physiologist; b. Baja, Hungary, Mar. 9, 1927; s. Sigmond and Irene (Roheim) S.; came to U.S., 1952, naturalized, 1957; student in medicine U. Budapest (Hungary), 1945-49, U. Vienna (Austria), 1949-50; M.D., U. Munich (Germany), 1950; m. Judy Aranka Gottfried, June 30, 1951; children—Peter Gordon, Juliet Irene. Instr. Dalhousie U., Halifax, N.S., Can., 1951-52; asst. prof. physiology Fla. State U., 1952-54; research scientist N.Y. State Dept. Health, Albany, 1954-57; asst. prof. physiology Hahnemann Med. Coll., 1957-58, asso. prof., 1958-61, prof., 1961-73; prof., head dept. physiology La. State U. Med. Center, 1973—; vis. scientist U. Oxford (Eng.), 1963-64. Recipient Lindback Found. award 1961. Mem. Am. Physiol. Soc., Am. Heart Assn. (council on arteriosclerosis), N.Y. Acad. Scis., Soc. Exptl. Biology and Medicine, Internat. Soc. Cardiology, Shock Soc. (council 1978—), Internat. Soc. Heart Research (council Am. sect. 1979—). Jewish. Contbr. numerous articles to profl. jours., 1952—. Home: 5687 Evelyn Ct New Orleans LA 70124 Office: 1542 Tulane Ave New Orleans LA 70112

SPITZER, LYMAN, JR., astronomer; b. Toledo, June 26, 1914; s. Lyman and Blanche C. (Brumback) S.; A.B., Yale U., 1935, D.Sc., 1958; student Cambridge (Eng.) U., 1935-36; Ph.D., Princeton U., 1938; Nat. Research fellow Harvard U., 1938-39; D.Sc., Case Inst. Tech., 1961, Harvard U., 1975; LL.D., Toledo U., 1963; m. Doreen D. Canaday, June 29, 1940; children—Nicholas, Dionis, Lutetia, Lydia. Instr. physics and astronomy Yale U., 1939-42; scientist Spl. Studies Group, Columbia U. Div. War Research, 1942-44, dir. Sonar Analysis Group, 1944-46; asso. prof. astrophysics Yale U., 1946-47; prof. astronomy, chmn. dept. and dir. obs. Princeton U., 1947-79, Charles A. Young prof. astronomy, 1952—, chmn. research bd., 1967-72, dir. project Matterhorn, 1953-61; chmn. exec. com. Plasma Physics Lab., 1961-66; trustee Woods Hole Oceanographic Inst., 1946-51; mem. Com. on Undersea Warfare, NRC, 1948-51; mem. Yale U. Council, 1948-51; chmn. Scientists Com. on Loyalty Problems, 1948-51; fgn. corr. Royal Soc. Scis., Liège, 1961—. Recipient Rittenhouse medal, 1957; Exceptional Sci. Achievement medal NASA, 1972; Bruce Gold medal, 1973; Henry Draper Gold medal, 1974; James C. Maxwell prize, 1975; Distinguished Pub. Service medal NASA, 1976; Gold medal Royal Astron. Soc., 1978. Fellow Am. Phys. Soc.; mem. Nat. Acad. Sci., Am. Acad. Arts and Scis., Am. Philos. Soc., Am. (past pres.), Royal (asso.) astron. socs., Astron. Soc. Pacific, Am. Geophys. Union, Am. Alpine Club. Unitarian. Author: Physics of Fully Ionized Gases (monograph), 1956, rev., 1962; Diffuse Matter in Space (monograph) 1968; Physical Processes in the Interstellar Medium, 1978; also articles in Astrophysical Jour.; Monthly Notices of Royal Astronomical Society, Phys. Rev. on interstellar matter, space astronomy, stellar dynamics, stellar atmospheres, broadening of spectral lines, conductivity of ionized gases, controlled release of thermonuclear energy. Editor: Physics of Sound in the Sea, 1946. Home: 659 Lake Dr Princeton NJ 08540

SPITZER, ROBERT RALPH, coll. adminstr.; b. Waukesha, Wis., May 4, 1922; s. John and Ruth S.; B.S. in Agr., U. Wis., 1943, M.S. in Animal Nutrition and Biochemistry, 1945, Ph.D. in Animal Nutrition and Med. Physiology, 1947; m. Marie L. Woerfel, 1946; children—John, Jeffrey, Susan. With Murphy Products Co., Burlington, Wis., 1947-75, pres., 1958-74, chmn. bd. 1974-75; coordinator Food for Peace, U.S. Dept. State, Washington, 1975-76; pres. lMilw. Sch. Engring., 1976—; dir. lMirro, Inc., Manitowoc, Wis., Larsen Co. Inc., Green Bay, Wis., Tracy & Sons, Inc., Janesville, Wis.; sr. advisor Allis Chalmers Corp., Milw. Mem. Vocat. Industries Bd. for Handicapped, Walworth County, Wis.; chmn. adv. com. Milw. Billy Graham Crusade, 1979; pres. Nat. 4-H Council, 1975; active Boy Scouts Am.; trustee Farm Found., Nutrition Found., N.Y.C.; bd. dirs. Kearney and Trecker Found., Sci. and Tech. Center, Milw. Public Mus. Recipient Freedom's Found. award, 1964; Coll. Agr. award U. Wis., 1971, Disting. Service award, 1972; Disting. Lectr. award Mich. State U., 1976, others. Mem. Am. Dairy Sci. Assn., Am. Inst. Chemists, Am. Soc. Animal Prodn., Am. Chem. Soc., Am. Poultry Sci. Assn., Sigma Xi, Phi Lambda Upsilon, Alpha Zeta, Phi Eta Sigma, Phi Sigma, Delta Phi Zeta, Phi Kappa Phi, Delta Theta Sigma, Gamma Sigma Delta. Republican. Episcopalian. Clubs: Univ., Washington, Lake Geneva Country, Milw. Athletic, Navy League, Milw. Author: Family Organizer, 1977. lIome: 1134 North Rd Burlington WI 53105 Office: 1025 N lMilwaukee Milwaukee WI 53201. *Peace and freedom from hunger will be a reality in our time with enlightened moral leadership in government and if economic and technical literacy are achieved. Service to our fellow human beings is a privilege and is low cost rent for the space we occupy. If we serve humankind while on earth we are carrying out God's purpose.*

SPITZER, WILLIAM G., physicist, educator; b. Los Angeles, Apr. 24, 1927; s. Max and Mary (Axelband) S.; B.A., U. Calif. at Los Angeles, 1949; M.S., U. So. Calif., 1952; Ph.D., Purdue U., 1957; m. Jeanette Navsky, June 26, 1949; children—Matthew L., Margaret I. Mem. tech. staff Hughes Aircraft Co., 1952-53; research physicist Bell Telephone Labs., 1957-62; sr. scientist Bell & Howell Research Center, 1962-63; prof. elec. engring., materials sci. and physics U. So. Calif., 1963—, chmn. materials sci. dept., 1967-69, chmn. physics dept., 1969-72, 78—, dean natural scis. and math., 1972-73. Served with AUS, 1945-46. Fellow Am. Phys. Soc.; mem. AAUP, Am Inst. Physics, Sigma Xi, Sigma Pi Sigma. Contbr. articles profl. jours. Home: 6231 Lindenhurst Ave Los Angeles CA 90048

SPITZNAGEL, WILLIAM F., transp. co. exec.; b. Fairfield, Ala., July 15, 1926; B.A., Auburn (Ala.) U., 1949. With Roadway Express, Inc., 1950—, chmn. bd., pres., Akron, Ohio, 1978—. Address: Roadway Express Inc 1077 Gorge Blvd Akron OH 44309

SPIVACK, HERBERT DANIEL, assn. exec.; b. N.Y.C., Oct. 27, 1917; s. Samuel and Fannie (Edelman) S.; student U. Ala., 1933-34; A.B., N.Y. U., 1937, M.A., 1938; postgrad. Pa. State Coll., 1938, Columbia, 1940-41; m. Florence Paw Tun, Nov. 26, 1949. Social investigator N.Y.C. Dept. Welfare, 1940-42; chief sect. Office of Censorship, San Juan, P.R., 1942-44; vice consul U.S. Fgn. Service, 1945; 3d sec. Am. embassy, vice consul, Tehran, Iran, 1945-48; 2d sec. Am. embassy, Rangoon, Burma, 1948-50; 2d sec., consul Am. embassy, Paris, France, 1951-54; acting officer in charge econ. br. Office Internat. Econ. and Social Affairs, Dept. of State, Washington, 1954; 1st sec., consul Am. embassy, Rangoon, Burma, 1956-59; foreign service inspector, 1960-62, 70—; counselor of embassy, Phnom Penh, Cambodia, 1962-65; counselor of embassy Am. embassy, New Delhi, 1965-67, minister-counselor, 1967-69; vis. prof. polit. sci. Mich. State U., 1969-70; Am. consul gen., Dacca, East Pakistan, 1971-72; chargé d'affaires, Dacca, Bangladesh, 1972; fgn. service insp., 1972-73; consul gen., Munich, Germany, 1974-76; dir. meetings and studies The Asia Soc., N.Y.C., 1976—. Adviser U.S. delegation 11th Session Econ. Commn. for Asia and Far East, Tokyo, 1955; mem. Internat. Secretariat UN Conf. on Internat. Orgn., San Francisco, 1945; alt. U.S. rep. 24th session Econ. Commn. for Asia and Far East, Canberra, 1968. Mem. Phi Beta Kappa. Office: The Asia Society 112 E 64th St New York City NY 10021

SPIVAK, ALVIN A., pub. relations exec., b. Phila., Nov. 30, 1927; s. Herman and Bella (Haimovitz) S.; B.S., Temple U., 1949; m. Martha Barry, Nov. 26, 1965; 1 dau., Denise. With I.N.S., 1949-58, Senate reporter, also mem. gen. staff, Washington, 1951-58; with U.P.I., 1958-67, White House reporter, 1960-67; pub. affairs dir. Nat. Adv. Commn. on Civil Disorders, 1967-68, Democratic Nat. Com., 1968-70; Washington pub. affairs dir. Gen. Dynamics Corp., 1970—. Served with USAAF 1946-47. Mem. Sigma Delta Chi, Beta Gamma Sigma. Club: Nat. Press, Nat. Aviation, Internat., Federal City (Washington). Home: 9201 Fernwood Rd Bethesda MD 20034 Office: 1745 Jefferson Davis Hwy Arlington VA 22202

SPIVAK, LAWRENCE EDMUND, TV-radio producer, cons.; b. N.Y.C., June 11, 1900; s. William B. and Sonya (Bershad) S.; A.B., Harvard, 1921; LL.D., Wilberforce U.; D.Litt., Suffolk U.; L.H.D., Tampa U.; m. Charlotte Beir Ring; children—Judith Spivak Frost (dec.), Jonathan. Bus. mgr. Antiques Mag., 1921-30; asst. to pub. Hunting and Fishing, Nat. Sportsman mags., 1930-33; bus. mgr. Am. Mercury, 1934-39, pub., 1939-44, editor, pub., 1944-50; founder, pub. until 1954, Ellery Queen's Mystery Mag., The Mag. of Fantasy and Science Fiction; founder Mercury Library-Paperback Books, 1937, Mercury Mystery Books, Bestseller Mysteries, Jonathan Press Books; co-founder, producer, moderator program Meet the Press, 1st radio broadcast, 1945, 1st TV broadcast, 1947; ret., 1975; cons. NBC, 1975—. Recipient 2 Peabody awards; Emmy award for outstanding achievement in coverage of spl. events Nat. Acad. TV Arts and Scis.; Honor awards for distinguished service to journalism U. Mo.; Robert Eunson award for distinguished service to broadcasting A.P. Broadcasters; Mass Media award Inst. of Human Relations of Am. Jewish Com. Home: Sheraton Park Hotel Washington DC 20008 Office: 2660 Woodley Rd NW Washington DC 20008

SPIVEY, HERMAN EVERETT, educator; b. Hemingway, S.C., Aug. 10, 1907; s. James Greer and Julia LeHarp (Baxley) S.; A.B., U. N.C., 1928, A.M., 1929, Ph.D., 1936, LL.D., 1969; Litt.D., Maryville Coll., 1968; m. Havens Edna Taylor, Dec. 15, 1928; children—Herman E., H. Olin, Mark Allan, Margaret Katherine. Instr. U. N.C., 1928-30, 1933-36; instr. to prof. English, U. Fla., 1930-33, 1936-42, 1945-48; head dept. English, U. Ky., 1948-51, dean grad. sch., 1950-60; acad. v.p. U. Tenn., 1960-68; prof. English, U. Fla., Gainesville, 1968—. Fulbright lectr. in Italy, 1955, India, 1956; FOA cons. in Yugoslavia, 1954; Phi Beta Kappa vis. scholar, 1970-71. Bd. dirs. Oak Ridge Asso. Univs., Presbyn. Homes, Inc., Maryville Coll. Served as comdr. USNR with naval air duty in U.S. and South Pacific, 1942-45; VTB operations officer at Guadalcanal, 1943, Miami Naval Air Sta., 1944-45; now capt. USNR. Received Presidential Unit citation, 1943, Commendation Comdr. Air Solomons, 1943. Mem. Modern Lang. Assn. Am., So. Atlantic Modern Lang. Assn. (several offices), Bibliog. Soc. Am., Am. Assn. Land Grant Colls. and Univs. (chmn. council on grad. work 1957-58, sec. council on instrn. 1956-58, mem. exec. com. 1966-68), Tenn. Coll. Assn. (pres. 1965-66), So. Humanities Conf. (vice chmn. 1966—), Conf. So. Grad. Deans (sec. 1954-59), Ky. Council Tchrs. English (mem. exec. com.), Am. Studies Assn., Newcomen Soc. Eng., Phi Beta Kappa, Omicron Delta Kappa. Presbyterian (ruling elder). Kiwanian. Author: Essentials of Correctness in English (with A.C. Morris), 1932; Essays for Better Reading (with Wise, Congleton, Skaggs), 1941; The Meaning in Reading (with Wise, Congleton, Morris), 1943, rev. edit., 1947. Contbr. bibliographies, reviews, articles learned jours., 1938—. Home: 269 Costado St Saint Augustine FL 32084

SPIVEY, ROBERT ATWOOD, coll. pres., educator; b. Suffolk, Va., May 25, 1931; s. Joseph Atwood and Wortley (Roberts) S.; B.A., Duke, 1953; B.D. (Omicron Delta Kappa scholar), Union Theol. Sem., N.Y.C., 1956; postgrad. U. Göttingen (Germany), 1956-57; M.A., Yale, 1958, Ph.D., 1962; m. Martha Emily Crocker, Aug. 21, 1954; children—Hope Crocker, Matthew Lee, Paul Atwood. Asst. in instrn. Yale Div. Sch., 1958-60; asst. prof. religion Williams Coll., 1960-64; univ. chaplain Fla. State U., 1964-65, chmn. religion, 1965-72, asso. prof. religion, 1965-69, prof., 1969-78, provost arts and scis., 1974-77, dean arts and scis., 1977-78; pres. Randolph-Macon Woman's Coll., Lynchburg, Va., 1978—; vis. scholar Cambridge (Eng.) U., 1971-72. Chmn., Fla. Com. Study Religion Pub. Schs., 1965-72. Pres. Tallahassee Council Human Relations, 1966-67; sec., trustee Inst. Continuing Studies Religion, 1968-70; mem. profl. adv. com. Pub. Edn. Religious Studies Center, 1972—. Woodrow Wilson Grad. fellow, 1953-54; Danforth grad. fellow, 1953-60; Fulbright scholar, 1956-57; Cross-Disciplinary fellow Soc. for Religion in Higher Edn., 1971-72. Mem. Soc. Religion Higher Edn. (dir. 1966-78), Am. Acad. Religion (chmn. nat. sect. on acad. study religion 1969-72, editorial bd. Jour. 1969-73, exec. dir., treas. 1972-75), Am. Assn. Colls. (commn. on religion in higher edn. 1971-74), Phi Beta Kappa, Omicron Delta Kappa. Clubs: Torch (pres. 1975-76) (Tallahassee); Rotary (Lynchburg). Author: (with D. Moody Smith, Jr.) Anatomy of the New Testament, 2d edit., 1974; (with Rodney Allen) Guide to The Bible Reader, 1970; A Good Servant: A Study of I Timothy, 1971; (with Edwin S. Gaustad, Rodney Allen) Religious Issues in American Culture, 1972; Religious Issues in Western Civilization, 1974; (with Freeman Sleeper) The Study of Religion in Two-Year Colleges, 1975; Religious Issues in World Culture, 1976; (with Joan Dye and Rodney Allen) Learning About Religion/Social Studies, Levels One, Two, Three, 1977. Home: 2460 Rivermont Ave Lynchburg VA 24503

SPLINTER, WILLIAM ELDON, agrl. engr.; b. North Platte, Nebr., Nov. 24, 1925; s. William John and Minnie (Calhoun) S.; B.Sc., U. Nebr., 1950; M.Sc., Mich. State U., 1951, Ph.D., 1955; m. Eleanor Love Peterson, Jan. 5, 1953; children—Kathryn Love, William John, Karen Ann, Robert Marvin. Instr. agrl. engring. Mich. State U., 1953-54; asso. prof. biology and agrl. engring. N.C. State U., 1954-61, prof., 1961-68; prof., chmn. dept. agrl. engring. U. Nebr., 1968—; cons. engr. Served with USNR, 1946-51. Recipient Massey Ferguson Ednl. award. Fellow Am. Soc. Agrl. Engrs. (pres., adminstrv. council), AAAS; mem. Soc. Automotive Engrs., Am. Soc. Engring. Edn., Instrument Soc. Am., Nat. Soc. Profl. Engrs., Sigma Xi, Sigma Tau, Sigma Pi Sigma, Pi Mu Epsilon, Gamma Sigma Delta, Phi Kappa Phi, Beta Sigma Psi. Contbr. articles tech. jours. Patentee in field. Home: 7105 N Hampton St Lincoln NE 68520

SPOCK, BENJAMIN MCLANE, physician, educator; b. New Haven, May 2, 1903; s. Benjamin Ives and Mildred Louise (Stoughton) S.; B.A., Yale U., 1925; student Med. Sch., 1925-27; M.D., Coll. Physicians and Surgeons, Columbia, 1929; m. Jane Davenport Cheney, June 25, 1927 (div. 1976); children—Michael, John Cheney; m. 2d, Mary Morgan Councille, Oct. 24, 1976. Intern in medicine Presbyn. Hosp., N.Y.C., 1929-31, in pediatrics N.Y. Nursery and Child's Hosp., 1931-32, in psychiatry N.Y. Hosp., 1932-33; practice pediatrics, N.Y.C., 1933-44, 46-47; instr. pediatrics Cornell Med. Coll., 1933-47; asst. attending pediatrician N.Y. Hosp., 1933-47; cons. in pediatric psychiatry N.Y. City Health Dept., 1942-47, Inst. on Personality Devel., 1938-47; cons. psychiatry Mayo Clinic, Rochester, Minn., asso. prof. psychiatry Mayo Found., U. Minn., 1947-51; prof. child devel. U. Pitts., 1951-55, Western Res. U., 1955-67. Presidential candidate Peoples Party, 1972. Served as lt. comdr. M.C., USNR, 1944-46. Author: Common Sense Book of Baby and Child Care, 1946 (reprinted as Pocket Book); A Baby's First Year (with J. Reinhart and W. Miller), 1954; Feeding Your Baby and Child (with M. Lowenberg), 1955; Dr. Spock Talks with Mothers, 1961; Problems of Parents, 1962; Caring for Your Disabled Child (with M. Lerrigo), 1965; Dr. Spock on Vietnam (with Mitchell Zimmerman), 1968; Decent and Indecent, 1970; A Teenagers Guide to Life and Love, 1970; Raising Children in a Difficult Time, 1974. Address: PO Box N Rogers AR 72756

SPOCK, WILLIAM THOMAS, ins. co. exec.; b. Bay Shore, N.Y., Aug. 18, 1929; s. Leslie E. and Estelle C. S.; B.A., Swarthmore Coll., 1951; m. Patricia Ellis, June 12, 1959; children—Susan, Thomas, Jennifer, Jeffrey. Vice pres. data processing and planning Penn Mut. Life Ins. Co., Phila., 1968-74, sr. v.p., 1974-79, exec. v.p. corp. planning and control, 1979—. Bd. dirs. Riddle Meml. Hosp., 1975—. Served with U.S. Army, 1951-53. Fellow Soc. Actuaries; mem. Am. Acad. Actuaries. Club: Granite Run Tennis (dir. 1971—). Office: 530 Walnut St Philadelphia PA 19172

SPODEK, BERNARD, educator; b. Bklyn., Sept. 17, 1931; s. David and Esther (Lebenbaum) S.; B.A., Bklyn. Coll., 1952; M.A., Columbia U. Tchrs. Coll., 1955, Ed.D., 1962; m. Prudence Moy Far Debb, June 21, 1957; children—Esther Yinling, Jonathan Chou. Tchr. nursery, kindergarten and primary grades Beth Hayeled Sch., N.Y.C., 1952-56; elem. tchr. N.Y.C. Bd. Edn., 1956-57; tchr. nursery-kindergarten Early Childhood Center, Bklyn. Coll., 1957-60; asst. prof. elementary edn. U. Wis., Milw., 1961-65; prof. early childhood edn. U. Ill., Urbana, 1965—; dir. NDEA Insts., 1965, 66, 67. Childcraft fellow, 1960-61. Mem. Assn. for Supervision and Curriculum Devel., Assn. Childhood Edn. Internat., Am. Ednl. Research Assn., AAUP, Nat. Assn. Edn. of Young Children (pres. 1976-78), Nat. Soc. Study of Edn., Profs. of Curriculum. Author books including: Teaching in the Early Years, 2d edit., 1978; Early Childhood Education, 1973; Teacher Education, 1974; Teaching Practices: Reexamining Assumptions, 1977; editor: Preparing Teachers of Disadvantaged Young Children, 1966; (with Herbert J. Walberg) Studies in Open Education, 1975, Early Childhood Education: Issues and Perspectives, 1977; book rev. editor Young Children, 1972-74; contbr. articles to profl. jours. Home: 1123 W Charles St Champaign IL 61820 Office: 302 Education Bldg U Ill Urbana IL 61801

SPOFFORD, WILLIAM BENJAMIN, JR., clergyman; b. Bklyn., Jan. 28, 1921; s. William Benjamin and Dorothy (Ibbotson) S.; A.B., Antioch Coll., 1942; B.D., Episcopal Theol. Sch., Cambridge, 1945; M.S.W., U. Mich., 1950; D.D., Ch. Div. Sch. of the Pacific, 1968; m. Pauline Lindall Fawcett, Sept. 9, 1944; children—Timothy, Mark, Andrew and Stephen (triplets), Daniel. Ordained priest Episcopal Ch., 1945; vicar Ch. of Good Shepherd, Boston; asst. sec. Diocesan Social Service, 1945-47; rector St. Thomas Ch., Detroit, 1947-50; asso. Nat. Town-Country Ch. Inst., Parkville, Md., 1950-52, dir. Western Extension Center, Weiser, Idaho, 1952-56; chief pastoral services Mass. Gen. Hosp., Boston, 1956-60; dean St. Michael's Cathedral, Boise, 1960-68; 4th bishop Missionary Dist., Eastern Oreg., Bend, 1969-80; asst. bishop Diocese of Washington, 1980—; instr. Park Coll., Parkville, 1950-53; instr. Episcopal Theol. Sch., Cambridge and Boston U. Sch. Theology, 1956-60. Mem. Boise Little Theater, 1960—. Mem. Am. Assn. Clin. Pastoral Edn. Bd. editors: The Witness and Jour. of Pastor Care, 1965—. Office: Church House Mount St Albans Washington DC 20016

SPOHN, CHARLES L., educator; b. Rochester, Ind., July 1, 1926; s. Charles L. and Valura (Bradway) S.; student Purdue U., 1944; Mus.B., Butler U., 1950; M.A., Ohio State U., 1953, Ph.D., 1959; m. Dorothy Mae McConville, Sept. 23, 1949; children—Charles David, Steven Michael. Instr. percussion Arthur Jordan coll. Music, Butler U., 1948-50; faculty Ohio State U., 1951-70, asso. prof. music, 1961-67, prof., 1967-70, dir. Marching Band, 1963-70, asso. dean Coll. Arts, 1968-70; dean Coll. Fine Arts, Wichita (Kans.) State U., 1970-73; dean sch. fine arts Miami U., Oxford, Ohio, 1973—. Sec. Coll. Band Dirs. research com., 1962-64, chmn., 1967-70; research cons. Nat. Conf. Uses Ednl. Media Teaching Music; mem. new media instrn. com. Music Educators Nat. Conf., 1966—; mem. edn. com. Nat. Alliance for Arts, 1976—; pres. Ohio Alliance for Arts in Edn., 1976—. Chmn. campaign Franklin County Tb Soc., 1966; bd. dirs. Wichita Symphony Soc. Served with AUS, 1944-46. Recipient Archibald Davison Meml. medal Harriet Cohen Internat. Music awards, 1962; Alfred J. Wright award Ohio State U., 1966; Distinguished Service award Franklin Tb Soc., 1966; commended by Ohio Legislature, 1970. Mem. Music Educators Research Council, Ohio Music Educators Assn., Am. Ednl. Research Assn., Phi Mu Alpha Sinfonia, Kappa Kappa Psi, Pi Kappa Lambda, Phi Delta Kappa. Author: Sounds of Music: Ascending Intervals, 1967; Sounds of Music: Descending Intervals, 1967; Sounds of Music: Harmonic Intervals, 1967; The Percussion Instruments, 1967; Comparative Techniques in Movement and Music for Marching Band, 1969. Editorial asso. Jour. Research Music Edn., 1964-70. Home: 721 White Oak Dr Oxford OH 45056

SPOHR, ARNOLD, artistic dir., choreographer; b. Rhein, Sask., Can., Dec. 26, 1927; ed. Winnipeg Tchrs. Coll., 1942-43; LL.D. (hon.), U. Man., 1970. Piano tchr., 1946-51; prin. dancer Royal Winnipeg Ballet, 1947-54, artistic dir., 1958—, dir., tchr. Sch. of Royal Winnipeg Ballet, 1958—; television choreographer, performer CBC, 1955-57; choreographer Rainbow Stage, 1957-60; dir. dance dept. Nelson Sch. Fine Arts, 1964-67; artistic dir. dance dept. Banff Sch. Fine Arts, 1967—; bd. dirs. Canadian Theatre Centre; vice chmn. Bd. Dance Can. Choreographer, Ballet Premier, 1950, Intermede, 1951, E Minor, 1959, Hansel and Gretal, 1960, also 18 musicals for Rainbow Stage. Recipient Can. Council Molson prize for outstanding contbn. to arts, 1970, Order of Can., 1970, Centennial medal Govt. of Can., 1967. Office: Royal Winnipeg Ballet 289 Portage Ave Winnipeg MB R3B 2B4 Canada*

SPOHR, CLIFFORD ERNEST, musician; b. Jamaica, N.Y., Feb. 9, 1940; s. Edward Charles and Rita Edith (Schamberger) S.; B.S. magna cum laude in Music Edn., Ithaca Coll., 1961; Mus.M. in Music Lit., Eastman Sch. Music, U. Rochester, 1963; m. Sandra Page, Dec. 12, 1968; children—Leslie Anne, David Alan. Prin. bass Dallas Symphony Orch.; prof. double bass So. Meth. U., Dallas. Office: Dallas Symphony Orch Music Hall PO Box 26207 Dallas TX 75226*

SPOKANE, EARLE JAY, retail splty. chain exec.; b. Pitts., Feb. 25, 1937; s. Joseph and Minnie S.; B.S. in Econs., Wharton Sch., U. Pa., 1958; M.S. in Bus., Columbia U., 1959; m. Ellen Louise Stein, June 5, 1960; children—David, Howard. Mgr., S.D. Leidesdorf & Co., N.Y.C., 1959-73; dir. acctg. services Quote Me, Inc., N.Y.C., 1973-75; v.p. fin., treas. Miller-Wohl Co., Inc., Secaucus, N.J., 1975—, also dir. Recipient Adam Avarell Ross prize U. Pa., 1958; C.P.A., N.Y. State. Mem. Am. Inst. C.P.A.'s, N.Y. State Soc. C.P.A.'s, Nat. Retail Mchts. Assn. Home: 18 Shenandoah Dr North Caldwell NJ 07006 Office: 915 Secaucus Rd Secaucus NJ 07094

SPOKES, ERNEST MELVERN, educator, mining engr.; b. Phila., Feb. 10, 1916; s. John Frederick and Jane (Martin) S.; B.S. in Mining Engring., Lafayette Coll., 1936, Engr. of Mines, 1946; M.S., U. Ky., 1949; Ph.D., Pa. State U., 1956; m. June Marie Allan, Apr. 12, 1941; children—Patricia May (Mrs. Edgar Snowden IV), Ernest Melvern. With Bethlehem Steel Co., 1936-40, Nat. Lead Co., 1945-48; mem. faculty U. Ky., 1949-63, prof. mining engring., 1957-63; prof. mining engring. U. Mo. at Rolla, 1963—, chmn. dept. mining and petroleum engring., 1963-69, chief of party U.S. AID Mission to Vietnam, Higher Edn.-Engring. U. Mo. at Rolla, 1969-71, head mining engring., 1971—; cons. to govt. and industry; mem. coal research com. Ky. Econ. Devel. Commn., 1963; mem. coal mining panel, interdeptl. energy study Office Sci. and Tech., 1963; trustee Engring. Index, 1975—. Served to capt. AUS, 1940-45, to lt. col. U.S. Army Res., 1937-65. Decorated Purple Heart with oak leaf cluster, Bronze Star with oak leaf cluster. Registered profl. engr., Ky., Mo. Mem. Am. Inst. Mining, Metall. and Petroleum Engrs. (dir. 1965-70, v.p. 1967-70, chmn. council of edn. 1975-76, mem. mineral industry ednl. award com. 1977—, dir. for Soc. Mining Engrs. 1960-63, 67-70, v.p. 1967-70, chmn. edn. com. 1973-76, exec. com. Central Appalachian sect. 1959-63; exec. com. St. Louis sect. 1966-69; exec. com. coal div. 1956-67), Engrs. Council Profl. Devel (dir. 1974-78, council 1974-76), Am. Mining Congress, Ky. Mining Inst., Ill. Mining Inst., Am. Soc. Engring. Edn., Res. Officers Assn., Scabbard and Blade, Tau Beta Pi, Phi Kappa Phi, Sigma Gamma Epsilon, Phi Eta Sigma. Republican. Episcopalian. Office: Dept Mining Petroleum and Geol Engring U Mo-Rolla Rolla MO 65401

SPONG, WILLIAM BELSER, JR., lawyer, educator; b. Portsmouth, Va., Sept. 29, 1920; s. William Belser and Emily (Nichols) S.; student Hampden-Sydney Coll., 1937-40, LL.D. (hon.); LL.B., U. Va., 1947; postgrad. U. Edinburgh (Scotland), 1947-48; m. Virginia Wise Gallford, June 3, 1950; children—Martha Kingman, Thomas Nichols. Admitted to Va. bar, 1947; practice law, Portsmouth, 1949—; mem. Va. Ho. Dels., 1954-55, Va. Senate, 1956-66; mem. U.S. Senate, 1966-73; gen. counsel commn. for conduct Fgn. Policy, 1973-75; lectr. law Coll. William and Mary, 1948-49, 75-76, dean Marshall-Wythe Sch. Law, 1976—; guest scholar Woodrow Wilson Center Smithsonian Instn.; vis. scholar U. Va. Sch. Law, 1973; adj. prof. law U. Richmond, 1974-75. Chmn. Va. Commn. Pub. Edn., 1958-62. Trustee Portsmouth Gen. Hosp., 1956-76, Hampden-Sydney Coll., 1957-76; bd. visitors Air Force Acad., 1970, Naval Acad., 1971. Mem. Va. Bar Assn. (pres. 1976), Portsmouth Bar Assn. (past pres.), Order of Coif, Phi Alpha Delta, Omicron Delta Kappa, Pi Kappa Alpha. Home: 111 Montague Circle Williamsburg VA 23185 Office: Marshall-Wythe Sch of Law Coll of William and Mary Williamsburg VA 23185

SPONSLER, GEORGE CURTIS, III, research adminstr.; b. Collingswood, N.J., Dec. 2, 1927; s. George Curtis and Mary Grace (Hollinberger) S.; B.S. in Engring., Princeton, 1949, M.A., 1951, Ph.D., 1952; m. Bridget Ruth Butcher, Sept. 3, 1955; children—Freda Grace, Naomi Margaret Bride, Curtis Alexander. With Lincoln Lab., Mass. Inst. Tech., 1952-56; liaison officer Office Naval Research, London 1956-58, head spl. projects br., Washington, 1958-59; sr. scientist Hoffman Sci. Center, Santa Barbara, Calif., 1959-60; chief sci., dir. tech, analysis and ops. research U.S. Navy Bur. Ships, 1960-63; dir. advanced planning, fed. systems div. IBM Corp., 1963-66, dir. center exploratory studies, 1966-68; exec. sec. div. engring. Nat. Acad. Sci.-NRC, 1968-70; pres. Internat. Planning Mgmt. Corp., 1970—. Mem. adv. com. to Office Emergency Planning, Nat. Acad. Sci., 1967-72, chmn. subcom. automation, 1966-68, mem. joint adv. com. on electromagnetic pulse, 1970-74; cons. Exec. Office of Pres., 1971-73. Fellow Am. Physics Soc., AAAS (electorate nominating com. 1980—); mem. IEEE (sr.), Phi Beta Kappa, Sigma Xi. Democrat. Episcopalian. Clubs: Cosmos (Washington); Kenwood (Bethesda). Contbr. Harper Ency. Sci. and Tech., also Tech. Innovation. Author articles in field. Home: 7804 Old Chester Rd Bethesda MD 20034

SPOONER, THOMAS CLARENCE, advt. agency exec.; b. Prescott, Ariz., July 29, 1940; s. Leonard Thomas and Lucretia B. Spooner; B.S. in Bus. Adminstrn., U. Ariz., 1964; children—Timothy, Terrie, Tammy. Vice pres., account supr. J. Walter Thompson Co., N.Y.C., 1964-72, v.p., dir. client services, San Francisco, 1972-74; pres. Mktg. Media, Inc., San Francisco, 1974-75; mgr., dir. Barnum Communications Inc., San Francisco, 1975-76; sr. v.p., dir. Vicom Assos., Inc., San Francisco, 1976—. Home: 57 Prince Royal Dr Corte Madera CA 94925 Office: Vicom Assos 901 Battery San Francisco CA 94133

SPOOR, THOMAS RICHARD, fin. exec.; b. Colorado Springs, Colo., Oct. 3, 1934; s. Charles H. and Doris F. (Slaughter) S.; B.A., U. Colo., 1958; m. Ann O'Malley, July 5, 1958; children—Stephanie F., William Todd. With U.S. Trust Co. of New York, 1958-78, exec. v.p., 1972-76, trustee, 1974, vice chmn. bd., 1976-78; mng. dir. Spoor Behrins Campbell & Young, Inc., N.Y.C., 1978—; dir. T. Bartholdi & Co.; mem. investment com. Royal Globe Ins. Co. Bd. dirs. U. Colo. Found.; mem. The Pilgrims; trustee Berkshire Sch., Graham Home. Mem. Council Fgn. Relations, Nat. Inst. Social Scis. Republican. Clubs: Links (N.Y.C.); Fox Meadow Tennis (Scarsdale, N.Y.); Shenorock Shore (Rye, N.Y.). Adv. bd. Trust and Estates Mag. Home: 87 Round Hill Rd Scarsdale NY 10583 Office: 280 Park Ave New York NY 10017

SPOOR, WILLIAM ARTHUR, aquatic physiologist; b. N.Y.C., Dec. 14, 1908; s. William H. and Amy (Toogood) S.; B.S., U. Wash., 1931; Ph.D., U. Wis., 1936; m. Iris Rumburg, Dec. 21, 1934; children—Jane Elizabeth, Richard Dean. Mem. faculty U. Cin., 1936-68, head dept., 1958-64; research aquatic biologist Fed. Water Quality Adminstrn., 1968-72, EPA, 1972—; mem. summer staff F.T. Stone Lab., Ohio State U., 1948-62. Mem. aquatic life adv. com. Ohio River Valley Sanitation Commn., 1952-69; mem. Nat. Tech. Adv. Com. for Fish, Other Aquatic Life and Wildlife, 1966-68. Mem. AAAS, ACLU, Sigma Xi. Home: 515 Valley Dr Duluth MN Office: Environmental Research Lab 6201 Congdon Blvd Duluth MN 55804

SPOOR, WILLIAM HOWARD, food co. exec.; b. Pueblo, Colo., Jan. 16, 1923; s. Charles Hinchman and Doris Field (Slaughter) S.; A.B., Dartmouth Coll., 1949; postgrad. Denver U., 1949, Stanford U., 1965; m. Janet Spain, Sept. 23, 1950; children—Melanie G., Cynthia F., William Lincoln. With Pillsbury Co., Mpls., 1949—, v.p. overseas div., 1962, v.p., gen. mgr. internat. ops., 1968-73, chmn. bd., chief exec. officer, dir., 1973—; dir. Northwestern Nat. Bank, N.W. Bancorp., Dayton Hudson Corp., Honeywell, Inc.; mem. regional export expansion council Dept. Commerce, 1966-74; bd. dirs. Exec. Council Fgn. Diplomats, 1976-78. Bd. dirs. Minn. Orchestral Assn., United Negro Coll. Fund. Served to 2d lt. inf., U.S. Army. Mem. Grocery Mfrs. Am. (sec.-treas., dir. 1973-79), Nat. Fgn. Trade Council (dir. 1973-75). Clubs: University (N.Y.C.); Woodhill, Minneapolis, Lafayette (Mpls.). Home: 622 W Ferndale Rd Wayzata MN 55391 Office: Pillsbury Bldg 608 2d Ave S Minneapolis MN 55402

SPORN, ARTHUR DAVID, lawyer; b. N.Y.C., June 6, 1927; s. Philip and Sadie (Posner) S.; A.B., Harvard U., 1947, LL.B., 1950; m. Muriel Krischer, Nov. 17, 1962; children—Robert, Carolyn. Admitted to N.Y. bar, 1950, Wis. bar, 1958; asst. prof. law U. Wis., 1958-60; partner firm Barrett Smith Schapiro, Simon & Armstrong, N.Y.C., 1960—. Trustee Baron de Hirsch Fund, N.Y.C. Served with USNR, 1945-46. Mem. Am. Law Inst., N.Y. State Bar Assn. (chmn. employee benefit com. Tax sect. 1971-73). Jewish. Contbr. articles to legal jours. Home: 40 E 84th St New York NY 10028 Office: 26 Broadway New York NY 10004

SPORN, MICHAEL BENJAMIN, physician; b. N.Y.C., Feb. 15, 1933; s. Philip and Sadie (Posner) S.; student Harvard U., 1949-52; M.D. with honors, U. Rochester, 1959; m. Catherine Daly, Oct. 11, 1956; children—Thomas, Paul. Intern in medicine and psychiatry U. Rochester, 1959-60; research asso. Lab. Neurochemistry, NIH, 1960-64; commd. officer USPHS, 1962—, sr. staff scientist chemistry br. Nat. Cancer Inst., NIH, Bethesda, Md., 1964-70, head lung cancer unit, 1970-73, chief lung cancer br., 1973-78, chief lab. chemoprevention, 1978—. Mem. Am. Assn. Cancer Research, Am. Soc. Neurochemistry, Am. Inst. Nutrition, Am. Soc. Biol. Chemists, Am. Soc. Pharmacology and Exptl. Therapeutics. Asso. editor Cancer Research, 1977—; mem. editorial adv. bd. Jour. of Neurochemistry, 1975—. Office: Nat Cancer Inst Nat Inst Health Bethesda MD 20014

SPRAGENS, THOMAS ARTHUR, coll. pres.; b. Lebanon, Ky., Apr. 25, 1917; s. William Henry and Lillian (Brewer) S.; A.B., U. Ky., 1938, LL.D., 1964; Maxwell fellow pub. adminstrn. Syracuse U., 1939-40; LL.D., Westminster Coll., Fulton, Mo., 1958; Litt. D., U. Ala., 1967; m. Catharine Smallwood, May 24, 1941; children—Thomas Arthur, Barbara Allen, David William. Research asst. Ky. Dept. Revenue, 1938-39, adminstrv. asst. to commr., 1941-42; adminstrv. analyst U.S. Bur. Budget, 1940-41, sr. analyst, 1942-45; asst. chief food allocations Fgn. Econ. Adminstrn., 1945; asst. to pres. Stanford, 1945-51; sec., treas. Fund for Advancement Edn., 1951-52; pres. Stephens Coll., 1952-57; pres. Centre Coll. of Ky., Danville, 1957—. Mem. Ohio Valley Regional Council, 1973-75; pres. So. Coll. Univ. Union, 1970-74, So. Univ. Conf., 1975. Trustee, Ky. Country Day Sch. Mem. Am. Council Edn. (dir. 1966-69), Phi Beta Kappa, Omicron Delta Kappa. Presbyterian (mem. bd. Christian edn. 1968-73). Clubs: Rotary, Pendennis, Filson (Louisville); University (N.Y.C.). Home: Craik House 763 W Main St Danville KY 40422

SPRAGENS, WILLIAM HENRY, JR., educator; b. Lebanon, Ky., Sept. 20, 1914; s. William Henry and Eleanor Lillian (Brewer) S.; A.B., U. Ky., 1935, M.S. 1938; Ph.D., U. Cin., 1948; m. Edna Mae Pratt, Aug. 14, 1940; children—William Henry III, Edna Louise, Alan Pratt. Tchr., Silver Grove (Ky.) High Sch., 1935-36; instr. math. Bethany (W.Va.) Coll., 1940-43; asso. prof. math. Ga. State Womans Coll., 1943-46, Fla. State U., 1948-50, U. Miss., 1950-56; mem. faculty U. Louisville, 1956—, prof. math., 1959—, head dept., 1959-69. Mem. Math. Assn. Am., Phi Beta Kappa, Sigma Xi. Home: 891 Minoma Ave Louisville KY 40217

SPRAGG, HOWARD EUGENE, church ofcl.; b. Boston, Sept. 15, 1917; s. Lee Hanford and Lillian (Hunter) S.; A.B. summa cum laude, Tufts Coll., 1938; B.D., Chgo. Theol. Sem., 1947, D.D., 1968; D.D., Yankton Coll., 1956, Ursinus Coll., 1973, Northland Coll., 1974, m. Jane Nichols, June 23, 1942; children—Susan E., Peter Hunter, Paul Alexander, Martha Ann, Deborah Townsend. Ordained to ministry Congl. Christian Chs., 1942; pastor in Chgo., 1942-48; gen. dir. P.R. mission Congl. Christian Chs., 1948-52; sec. Bd. Home Missions Congl. and Chrisian Chs., 1952-54, gen. sec. for adminstrn., 1954-58, treas., 1959-69, also treas. ten affiliated corps, including United Ch. Found. Annuity Congl. Ministers, Retirement Fund Lay Workers; treas. United Ch. Bd. Homeland Ministries, 1959-69, exec. v.p., 1969—; fin. v.p. treas. United Church Found.; former mem. governing bd. Nat. Council Chs. Trustee Dillard U., Lemoyne Coll., Talladega Coll., Tougaloo So. Christian Coll., Houston-Tillotson Coll. Mem. Soc. Arts, Religion and Culture (v.p.), Phi Beta Kappa. Club: University (N.Y.C.). Home: Wolf Hill Rd Deering NH 07090 Office: 287 Park Ave S New York NY 10010

SPRAGUE, CHARLES CAMERON, coll. pres.; b. Dallas, Nov. 14, 1916; s. George Able and Minna (Schwartz) S.; B.B.A., B.S., D.Sc., So. Meth. U.; M.D., U. Tex., 1943; m. Margaret Frederica Dickson, Sept. 7, 1943; 1 dau., Cynthia Cameron. Intern, U.S. Naval Med. Center, Bethesda, Md., 1943-44; resident Charity Hosp., New Orleans, 1947-48, Tulane U. Med. Sch., 1948-50; Commonwealth research fellow in hematology Washington U. Sch. Medicine, St. Louis, also Oxford (Eng.) U., 1950-52; mem. faculty Med. Sch. Tulane U., 1952-67, prof. medicine, 1959-67, dean Sch. Medicine, 1963-67; prof., dean U. Tex. Southwestern Med. Sch., Dallas, 1967-72; pres. U. Tex. Health Sci. Center, Dallas, 1972—. Mem. Nat. Adv. Council, 1966-70; mem. adv. com. to dir. NIH, 1973—. Served with USNR, 1943-47. Recipient Ashbel Smith Distinguished Alumnus award U. Tex. Med. Br., 1967; Distinguished Alumnus award So. Meth. U., 1965; recipient Sports Illustrated Silver Anniversary award, 1963. Mem. Assn. Am. Med. Colls. (chmn. council deans 1970, chmn. exec. council and assembly 1972-73), Am. Soc. Hematology (pres. 1968). Office: U Tex Southwestern Med Sch 5323 Harry Hines Blvd Dallas TX 75235*

SPRAGUE, EVERETT RUSSELL, mfg. co. exec.; b. Inwood, N.Y., Aug. 9, 1915; s. Louie and Eva C. (Davison) S.; M.E., Stevens Inst. Tech., Hoboken, N.J., 1936, M.S., 1939; D.C.S. (hon.), Am. Internat. Coll., 1978; m. Karen Olson, Sept. 9, 1967; children—Dian Reed, Linda Kenney, Nancy Chouinard, Russell A. With Tampax Inc., Palmer, Mass., 1936—, pres., chief exec. officer, 1976—, also dir.; dir. Canadian Tampax Corp., Tampax Ltd., Tampax Ireland Ltd., Tampax France S.A., TNB Fin. Corp., Third Nat. Bank Hampden County (Mass.), RLW Inc. Trustee Am. Internat. Coll., Springfield, Mass., Stevens Inst. Tech. Fellow Soc. Advancement Mgmt. (profl. mgr. citation Western Mass. chpt. 1960); mem. ASME, Am. Mgmt. Assn., Phi Sigma Kappa, Tau Beta Pi. Clubs: Monson Rotary; Colony (Springfield); Masons. Home: 33 Green St Monson MA 01057 Office: PO Box 271 Palmer MA 01069

SPRAGUE, GEORGE FREDERICK, geneticist; b. Crete, Nebr., Sept. 3, 1902; s. Elmer Ellsworth and Emily Kent (Manville) S.; B.S., U. Nebr., 1924, M.S., 1926, D.Sc., 1958; Ph.D., Cornell U., 1930. With Dept. Agr., 1924-72, leader corn and sorghum investigations, 1958-72; mem. faculty U. Ill., Urbana, 1973—, now prof. genetics and plant breeding. Recipient Superior Service award Dept. Agr., 1960, Distinguished Service award, 1970. Fellow AAAS, Washington Acad. Scis., Am. Soc. Agronomy (pres. 1960; Crops Research award 1957); mem. Nat. Acad. Scis., Crops Sci. Soc. (pres. 1951), Am. Genetics Assn., Genetics Soc. Am., Am. Soc. Plant Physiologists, Am. Naturalists, Biometrics Soc. Editor: Corn and Corn Improvement, 2d edit., 1977. Contbr. articles to profl. jours. Home: 2212 S Lynn St Urbana IL 61871 Office: Dept Agronomy Univ Ill Urbana IL 61801

SPRAGUE, IRVINE HENRY, govt. ofcl.; b. San Francisco, July 4, 1921; s. Irvine Henry and Claire Dolores (Kelly) S.; B.A., U. Pacific, 1947; student Stockton Coll., 1940-41, U. Ind., 1943; postgrad. George Washington Law Sch., 1957; grad. Advanced Mgmt. Program, Harvard, 1972; m. Margery Eleanor Craw, Nov. 3, 1940; children—Michael Irvine, Terry Earl, Kristine Ann. Reporter, Stockton (Calif.) Record, 1938-56; adminstrv. asst. to congressman, 1957-62; dep. dir. finance State of Calif., 1963-66; asst. to Pres. Lyndon B. Johnson, White House, Washington, 1967-68; dir. FDIC, Washington, 1969-72; adminstrv. asst. U.S. Ho. of Reps. Majority Whip, 1973-76; exec. dir. Ho. of Reps. Steering and Policy Com., 1977-78; chmn. FDIC, 1979—. Del. Nat. Dem. Conv., 1964. Served to 1st lt. AUS, 1943-46; Res., 1946-70, lt. col., ret. Decorated Bronze Star with cluster, Purple Heart, Combat Inf. Badge. Mem. DAV. Home: 9510 William Crossman Dr Great Falls VA 22066 Office: 550 17th St Washington DC

SPRAGUE, JAMES MATHER, med. scientist, educator; b. Kansas City, Mo., Aug. 31, 1916; s. James P. and Lelia (Mather) S.; B.S., U. Kans., 1938, M.A., 1940; Ph.D., Harvard, 1942; A.M. (hon.), U. Pa., 1971; m. Dolores Marie Eberhart, Nov. 25, 1959; 1 son, James B. From asst. to asst. prof. anatomy Hopkins Med. Sch., 1942-50; asst. prof. to prof. anatomy U. Pa. Med. Sch., Phila., 1950—, chmn. dept., 1967-76, Joseph Leidy prof. anatomy, dir. Inst. Neurol. Sci., 1973—, chmn. faculty senate, 1963; vis. prof. Northwestern U., 1948, Rockefeller U., 1955, Cambridge U., 1956, U. Pisa, 1966, 74-75; sci. cons. NIH, 1957-60. Recipient Macy faculty award, 1974-75. Guggenheim fellow, 1948-49. Mem. Am. Assn. Anatomists (v.p. 1976-78), Soc. Neurosci., AAAS. Democrat. Co-editor: Progress in Psychobiology and Physiological Psychology, 1966—; asso. editor Archives Ital. Biologie, 1972, Acta Neurobiol. Exper., 1976. Contbr. articles to profl. jours. Home: 631 Moreno Rd Narberth PA 19072 Office: Sch Med U Pa Philadelphia PA 19104

SPRAGUE, JOHN LOUIS, electric mfg. co. exec.; b. Boston, Apr. 1930; s. Robert Chapman and Florence Antoinette (van Zelm) S.; A.B., Princeton, 1952; Ph.D., Stanford, 1959; m. Mary-Jane Whitney, June 19, 1952; children—John Louis, William Whitney, Catherine van Zelm, David Hyatt. With Sprague Electric Co., North Adams, Mass., 1959—, co-dir. engring. labs., sr. v.p. engring., 1964-65, v.p. research and devel., 1965-66, sr. v.p. research and devel., 1966—, sr. v.p. semi-condr. div., 1967-76, pres. co., 1976—; dir. Hybrid Systems Corp., State Mut. Life Assurance Co. Am. Chmn., Williamstown United Fund-ARC Campaign, 1961; trustee Pine Cobble Sch., 1978. Served to lt. (j.g.) USNR, 1952-55. Mem. IEEE, Electrochem. Soc., Am. Chem. Soc., Sci. Research Soc. Am., Confrerie des Chevaliers du Tastevin, Confrerie de la Chaine des Rotisseurs, Mayflower Hist. Soc., Sigma Xi, Phi Lambda Upsilon. Club: Princeton (N.Y.C.). Home: 175 Bee Hill Rd Williamstown MA 01267 Office: Sprague Electric Co 87 Marshall St North Adams MA 01247

SPRAGUE, JOHN NORTON, fin. exec.; b. N.Y.C., Sept. 30, 1929; s. Talbert Wood and Marjorie Eleanor (Norton) S.; B.A., Yale U., 1951; postgrad. N.Y. U. Grad. Sch. Bus., 1954-55; m. Charlene Ann Patterson, Jan. 30, 1960; children—Valerie, Geoffrey. With N.Y. Life Ins. Co., 1954-68, v.p., 1966-68; v.p., treas. AVNET, Inc., 1968-70, The Singer Co., Stamford, Conn., 1970—; pres., dir. Singer Credit Corp. Library trustee; active Cub Scouts, Boy Scouts Am. Served with CIC, U.S. Army, 1951-53. Clubs: Yale, Rockefeller Center Lunch (N.Y.C.); Landmark (Stamford); Milbrook (Greenwich, Conn.). Office: 8 Stamford Forum Stamford CT 06904

SPRAGUE, L(LOYD) DEAN, editor, lectr.; b. Corning, N.Y., Mar. 21, 1922; s. Lloyd Drummond and Iva (Gorton) S.; B.A. magna cum laude, Amherst Coll., 1943; M.A., Syracuse U., 1950, Ph.D., 1959; postgrad. U. Pa., 1954, U. Pitts., 1958, George Washington U., 1955-57; m. Edna Smith, Dec. 17, 1949; children—Linda Ann, John Lloyd. Instr. polit. sci. Syracuse (N.Y.) U., 1949-52; budget analyst Dept. Navy, Washington, 1952-58; budget officer Office Sec. Def., Washington, 1958-62; planning officer Dept. Def., Washington, 1963-77; exec. editor Budget and Program, 1977—. Asso. professorial lectr. George Washington U., Washington, 1966-69, professorial lectr., 1969—; vis. lectr. Syracuse U., 1966-70. Served with AUS, 1943-46. Mem. Am. Polit. Sci. Assn., Am. Soc. Pub. Adminstrn., Am. Assn. for Budget and Program Analysis, Phi Beta Kappa, Phi Delta Theta. Methodist. Author: The Suppression of Dissent During the Civil War and World War I, 1960; Freedom Under Lincoln, 1965. Home: 11113 Ardwick Dr Rockville MD 20852

SPRAGUE, MILTON ALAN, agronomist, educator; b. Washburn, Wis., June 16, 1914; s. Monroe Horr and Daza (Glover) S.; A.B., Northland Coll., 1936; M.S., U. Wis., 1938, Ph.D., 1941; m. Margarete Hardegen, May 20, 1944; children—Monroe A., Katherine A., Lowell H, Barbara H. Research, teaching forage crop physiology and weed control U. Ark., 1940-42, 46; faculty Rutgers U., 1946—, chmn. dept. farm crops, 1955-61, now prof. and research specialist. Agr. cons. to Peru, Yucatan, 1965-72; agrl. cons. to Am. Heritage Dictionary, 1971. Served to lt. USNR, 1942-46; ret. Res. Recipient Merit certificate Am. Forage and Grassland Council, 1966; No-Till Pioneer award, 1976. Fellow Am. Soc. Agronomy (dir. 1956-59, 74-77, sec.-treas. N.E. br. 70, Research award 1977); mem. Am. Grassland Council (dir. 1958-61, 1969-72), Am. Soc. Plant Physiology, Am. Soc. Dairy Sci., Naval Inst., Sigma Xi. Author: Field Crop Production for the Northeast, rev. edit., 1952; Grasslands, 1959; Forages, rev. edit., 1960. Author research papers. Home: Georges Road Dayton NJ 08810 Office: Rutgers U New Brunswick NJ 08903.
Would that the world might end each day a bit better for my having participated.

SPRAGUE, NORMAN FREDERICK, JR., surgeon; b. Los Angeles, June 12, 1914; s. Norman F. and Frances E. (Ludeman) S.; A.B., U. Calif., 1933; M.D., Harvard, 1937; m. Caryll E. Mudd, Dec. 27, 1941; children—Caryll (Mrs. Mingst), Norman Frederick III, Cynthia (Mrs. Holliday), Elizabeth (Mrs. Day). Intern, Bellevue Hosp., N.Y.C., 1937, house surgeon, 1938-39; pvt. med. practice, Los Angeles, 1946—; asst. clin. prof. surgery U. Calif. at Los Angeles, 1951—; dir. emeritus Western Fed. Savs. & Loan Assn.; chmn. bd. dirs. Western Pioneer Co., 1961-63, Pioneer Savs. & Loan Assn., 1959-63; dir. Arden-Mayfair, Inc 1966-69, also chmn. exec. com.; trustee Mesabi Trust, 1964-76. Chmn. exec. com., v.p. Harvard Sch., 1954-65; mem. Community Redevel. Agy. City of Los Angles, 1966-69, vice chmn. 1967-69; mem. Calif. Regional Med. Programs Area IV Council, 1970-75; bd. dirs., v.p. Calif. Inst. Cancer Research, 1974—, Cancer Assos., 1975—; trustee UCLA Found., Harvey and Mildred Mudd Found., Hollywood Bowl Assn., 1962-66; hon. trustee Calif. Mus. Found.; mem. exec. com., trustee Youth Tennis Found., 1960-70; trustee, v.p., mem exec. com. S.W. Mus.; trustee, chmn. investment com. Harvey Mudd Coll.; chmn. bd. trustees Carylland Norman Sprague Found., 1957—. Served to maj. M.C., AUS, 1941-46. Decorated Bronze Star. Recipient Bishop's award of Merit, Episcopal Diocese Los Angeles, 1966; Highest Merit award So. Calif. Pub. Health Assn., 1968. Mem. Am., Calif., Los Angeles County (pres. jr. sect. 1953) med. assns., SAR, Am. Cattlemen's Assn., Symposium Soc., Tennis Patrons Assn. (dir. 1960-70), Delta Kappa Epsilon. Clubs: Faculty, Calif., Harvard, Lincoln, Los Angeles Country (Los Angeles). Home: 550 S Mapleton Dr Los Angeles CA 90024 Office: 3600 Wilshire Blvd Los Angeles CA 90010

SPRAGUE, PETER FROST, pub. co. exec.; b. N.Y.C., June 27, 1946; s. Lewis Clarence and Helen S.; B.A. cum laude, U. Pa., 1968; M.Ed. with honors, Temple U., 1970; m. Barbara Ann Roma, Aug. 20, 1966; children—Heather, Allison. Dir. ednl. service bur. Dow Jones & Co., Inc., 1972-74, circulation dir. Wall Street Jour., 1974-76; dir. new bus. Chilton Co., Phila., 1976-78, dir. corp. planning; cons. Am. Newspaper Pubs. Assn. Mem. Am. Bus. Press, Mag. Pubs. Assn., Info. Industry Assn. Unitarian. Author: Newspapers in the Social Studies Curriculum, 1975; What Do You Do for a Living, 1975. Home: 519 E Moreland Ave Philadelphia PA 19118 Office: Chilton Co 1 Chilton Way Radnor PA 19089

SPRAGUE, PETER JULIAN, bus. exec.; b. Detroit, Apr. 29, 1939; s. Julian K. and Helene (Coughlin) S.; student Yale, 1961, Mass. Inst. Tech., 1961, Columbia, 1962-64; m. Tjasa Krofta, Dec. 19, 1959; children—Carl, Steven, Kevin, Michael. Chmn. bd. dirs. Nat. Semiconductor Corp., Santa Clara, Calif., Advent Corp., Aston-Martin (Lagonda) Ltd.; dir. Auton Computing Corp. Bd. dirs. Manhattan Eye, Ear, Nose, Throat Hosp.; trustee Strang Clinic, Buckley Sch. Clubs: Yale, Marks. Home and office: 6 Sutton Sq New York NY 10022

SPRAGUE, PHILIP ALLCOCK, mfg. co. exec.; b. Michigan City, Ind., Apr. 26, 1923; s. Phil T. and Marguerite (Allcock) S.; B.A., Beloit Coll., 1946; M.B.A., Harvard, 1948; m. Ruth L. Green, Sept. 8, 1947 (dec. Sept. 1978); children—Shelley Marguerite, Laura Lisbeth, Philip Roy. Research asst. Harvard Bus. Sch., 1948-49; with Hays Corp., Michigan City, 1949-71, advt. mgr., 1949-52, exec. v.p., 1952-57, pres., 1957-68, chmn. bd., 1969-71, also dir.; chmn. bd. Hays Republic div. Milton Roy Co., 1971—; dir. Milton Roy Co., St. Petersburg, Fla. Mem. exchange del. to USSR on automation, 1958; del. Internat. Fedn. Automatic Control World Congress, Moscow, USSR, 1960, Warsaw, Poland, 1969, Paris, France, 1972, Boston, 1976, Helsinki, 1978, also chmn. com. social effects of automation, 1972—. Commr., Michigan City Pub. Housing Authority, 1968-72; asst. adminstr. for mgmt. assistance SBA, Washington, 1979—; Democratic nominee U.S. Congress, 2d dist. Ind., 1970. Bd. dirs. Michigan City YMCA, 1960-70, pres., 1960; bd. dirs., pres. Michigan City Council Health Edn., 1960—; chmn. Michigan City Hosps. United Fulfillment Fund, 1964—; trustee Stanley Clark Sch., South Bend, Ind., 1967-71; trustee Beloit Coll., 1961-62, 66—, vice chmn. bd., 1976; bd. dirs. Found. Instrumentation Edn. and Research, 1960-62, Michigan City Community Scholarship Found., 1961-66, Michigan City Family Welfare Assn., 1966-76, LaPorte County Sheltered Workshop, 1975—; bd. dirs. Michigan City United Fund, 1965-70, chmn. drive, 1964; mem. Ind. Devel. Disabilities Planning and Adv. Bd., 1976—. Served with AUS, 1943-46; ETO. Recipient Distinguished Service citation Beloit Coll. Mem. Instrument Soc. Am. (hon.; pres. 1961-62, chmn. nat. conf. and exhibit 1971), Sci. Apparatus Makers Assn. (pres. 1971-72), Michigan City C. of C. (pres., dir. 1960), Sigma Chi. Democrat. Club: Long Beach (Ind.) Country. Co-author: Productivity and Man, 1975. Home: 2600 Belle Plaine Trail Long Beach Michigan City IN 46360 Office: 742 E 8th St Michigan City IN 46360

SPRAGUE, ROBERT CHAPMAN, mfg. co. exec.; b. N.Y.C., Aug. 3, 1900; s. Frank Julian and Harriet Chapman (Jones) S.; grad. U.S. Naval Acad., 1920 (Class 1921-A); B.S., U.S. Naval Post-Grad. Sch., 1922; S.M., Mass. Inst. Tech., 1924; D. Eng. (hon.), Northeastern U., 1953; D.Sci. (hon.), Williams Coll., 1954, Lowell Technol. Inst., 1959, N. Adams State Coll., 1972, U. Mass., 1975; LL.D. (hon.), Tufts, 1959, U. N.H., 1967; m. Florence Antoinette van Zelm, May 24, 1921; children—Robert Chapman, John Louis. Line officer USN, 1920; constrn. officer Office Naval Constn., Bethlehem Shipbldg. Co., 1924-28; retired from USN, 1928. Founder, Sprague Spltys. Co., Quincy, Mass., 1926 (co. now Sprague Electric Co., North Adams, Mass.), pres., 1926-53, chmn., chief exec. officer, 1956-71, hon. chmn., chmn. exec. com., 1971-76, treas., 1954-65; mem. Asso. Industries Mass., 1951—, pres., 1951-53, hon. chmn., dir., 1976—; chmn. agent, dir. Fed. Res. Bank Boston, 1955-60; chmn. bd. MITRE Corp., 1969-72, trustee, 1958—; chmn. Industry Adv. Co. Electronic Components and Parts, 1944-45; mem. exec. com. Mass. Com. on Postwar Reconversion, 1942-45; mem. Munitions Bd. Electronics Equipment Industry Adv. Com., 1950-53; cons. on continental def. Nat. Security Council, 1954-58; dir. security resources panel sci. adv. com. ODM. Trustee Hudson Inst., 1961-71; trustee emeritus Pine Cobble Sch., Williamstown, Mass.; life mem. corp. Mass. Inst. Tech., Northeastern U.; bd. dirs. Charles Stark Draper Labs., Inc.; bd. govs. Mass. Sci. and Tech. Found., 1970-78. Pres., Radio Electronics TV Mfrs. Assn., 1950-51, chmn. bd., 1950-52, 53-54. Recipient Distinguished Citizenship award Bates Coll., 1958; Man of Year award Hotchkiss Alumni Assn., 1958; Medal of Honor award Radio Electronics TV Mfrs. Assn., 1954; Man of Year award New Eng. Council, 1965; Medal of Honor award Electronic Industries Assn., 1979. Fellow IEEE; mem. Am. Acad. Arts and Scis., NAM, U.S. C. of C. Episcopalian. Clubs: Metropolitan (Washington); Chemists (N.Y.C.); Algonquin, Union (Boston). Contbr. articles on electronics industry to jours. Study of continental defense for preparedness com. of Senate Armed Services Com., 1953-54. Home: 118 Bulkley St Williamstown MA 01267 Office: 87 Marshall St North Adams MA 01247

SPRAGUE, RODERICK, anthropologist, educator; b. Albany, Oreg., Feb. 18, 1933; s. Roderick and Mary Kingsley (Willis) S.; B.A., Wash. State U., 1955, M.A., 1959; Ph.D., U. Ariz., 1967; m. 1975; children—Roderick, Katherine K., Frederick L. Staff archeologist Wash. State U., 1964-67, asst. prof. anthropology U. Idaho, Moscow, 1967-69, asso. prof., 1969-72, prof., 1972—, head dept. sociology and anthropology, 1968—. Served with arty. U.S. Army, 1956-58. Fellow Am. Anthrop. Assn.; mem. Soc. Am. Archeology, AAAS, N.W. Sci. Assn. (past trustee), Soc. Hist. Archeology (past pres., past dir.), Sigma Xi. Editor N.W. Anthrop. Research Notes, 1968—. Home: Route 4 Box 411 Moscow ID 83843

SPRAGUE, WALLACE ARTHUR, publishing co. exec.; b. Ritzville, Wash., Feb. 6, 1918; s. Charles Arthur and Blanche (Chamberlain) S.; A.B. magna cum laude, Oberlin Coll., 1938; M.A., Harvard, 1939; m. Mary Louise Dull, Mar. 17, 1942; children—Charles W., John A. Sec., Statesman Pub. Co., Salem, Oreg., 1939-40; asst. mng. editor Parade mag., 1946, asso. mng. editor, 1947, mng. editor, 1949-56, asst. pub., 1956-60; exec. v.p., This Week mag., 1960-62; exec. v.p., dir. Bowater Paper Co., Inc., N.Y.C, 1962-66, pres., 1966-68; v.p., dir. Whitney Communications Corp., 1968-72; pres. Interior Design Div.; pres. Art in Am., Inc., Harvest Years; pub. Oreg. Statesman, Salem, 1969-74; v.p. Item Pub. Co., Millburn, N.J., 1968—; chmn. Info-Media Inc., Framingham, Mass. Cons. Nat. Nat. Security Council, 1948-49. Chmn., Harvard Grad. Soc. for Advanced Study and Research, 1968. Served as lt. USNR, 1941-45. Mem. Phi Beta Kappa. Clubs: Union League (N.Y.C.); Short Hills; Baltusrol; Pilgrims. Home: 33 Birch Ln Short Hills NJ 07078 Office: 12 E 63d St Suite 4A New York NY 10021

SPRAGUE, WILLIAM WALLACE, lawyer; b. St. Johnsbury, Vt., Dec. 6, 1913; s. Arthur Garfield and Elisabeth (Merrill) S.; A.B., Harvard, 1936; LL.B., Hartford Coll. Law, 1939; m. Julia Ingraham Rankin, Mar. 21, 1947; children—Pauline Elisabeth, Margaret Mather, Julia Ann. Admitted to Conn. bar, 1939, since practiced in Hartford; with firm Butler, Howard; Volpe & Garrity, 1939-41, Davis, Lee, Howard & Wright, 1946-60, Howard, Kohn, Sprague & FitzGerald, 1960—. Dir. Hartford Faience Co. Mem. Bd. Edn., Newington, 1952-58; dep. judge Newington Town Ct., 1953-55; treas. Conn. Assn. Bds. Edn., 1955-57; town atty., Newington, 1958-66. Trustee, St. Johnsbury Acad. Served with AUS, 1941-46. Mem. Am. Judicature Assn., Am., Conn., Hartford County bar assns. Conglist. Clubs: Civitan (Newington); Harvard Northern Conn. Home: 1377 Main St Newington CT 06111 Office: 237 Buckingham St Hartford CT 06106

SPRAGUE, WILLIAM WALLACE, JR., food co. exec.; b. Savannah, Ga., Nov. 11, 1926; s. William and Mary (Crowther) S.; B.S., Yale, 1950; m. Elizabeth Louise Carr, Oct. 3, 1953; children—Lauren and Courtney (twins), William Wallace III, Elizabeth. With Savannah Foods & Industries, Inc. (formerly Savannah Sugar Refining Corp.), 1952—, sales mgr. indsl. products, 1959, asst. sec., 1959-61, sec., 1961-62, v.p., 1962-72, pres., chief exec. officer, 1972—, also dir.; chmn. Jim Dandy Co., Birmingham, Ala.; pres. Everglades Sugar Refinery, Clewiston, Fla.; v.p., dir. Adeline Sugar Factory Co., Ltd., Jeanerette, La.; dir. Citizens & So. Nat. Banks of Ga., Atlanta, U.S. Sugar Corp., Clewiston, Atlantic Towing Co., Savannah, Citizens & So. Nat. Bank, Savannah. Asso. chmn. United Community Appeal, 1970-72. Bd. dirs. YMCA, 1963—, Savannah Port Authority, 1970—. Served with USNR, 1945-46. Mem. Savannah Area C. of C. Clubs: Oglethorpe, Century, Cotillion, Carolina Plantation Soc., Chatham Tennis, Savannah Yacht, Savannah Golf. Episcopalian. Home: 24 E 50th St Savannah GA 31405 Office: PO Box 339 Savannah GA 31402

SPRAYREGEN, JOEL JAY, lawyer; b. Jersey City, Mar. 10, 1934; s. Charles and Genevive (Schatell) S.; B.S., Northwestern U., 1955; LL.B., Yale, 1958; m. Marilyn Mandell, June 5, 1955; children—Michele Beth, Linda Robin, James Howard. Admitted to Ill. bar, 1958; staff counsel Ill. div. ACLU, 1958-60; asso. firm Aaron, Aaron, Schimberg & Hess, Chgo., 1960-66, partner, 1967—; gen. counsel George J. London Meml. Hosp., 1973—. Chmn., Glencoe (Ill.) Democratic Com., 1966; mem. Glencoe Village Caucus, 1968-70; vice chmn. Nat. Conf. on Soviet Jewry, 1973—. Mem. Am. (chmn. subcom. libel and privacy sect. individual rights and responsibilities), Chgo. (chmn. mental health com.) bar assns., Yale Law Sch. Assn. (exec. com. 1969-76, pres. Ill. chpt. 1967), Anti-Defamation League (Chgo. exec. com.), Tau Delta Phi, Sigma Delta Chi. Author: The Paradox of the Professor and the Police and the New Serfdom. co-author: The Night of the Murdered Poets. Home: 775 Sheridan Rd Glencoe IL 60022 Office: 1 First Nat Plaza Chicago IL 60670

SPRECHER, DAVID A., mathematician, univ. adminstr.; b. Saarbrucken, Fed. Republic Germany, Jan. 12, 1930; s. Wolfgang and Karolina (Jung) S.; student Hebrew U., 1952-54; A.B., U. Bridgeport, 1958; Ph.D., U. Md., 1963; m. Betty Oberacker, Aug. 11, 1979; children—Lorrie, Jeannie. Instr. math. U. Md., 1961-63; asst. prof. Syracuse U., 1963-66; asso. prof. math. U. Calif., Santa Barbara, 1966-71, prof., 1971—, chmn. dept., 1972-75, asso. dean Coll. of Letters and Sci., 1975, dean, 1979—. Served with Israeli Army, 1948-50. Mem. Am. Math. Soc., Math. Assn. Am. Contbr. articles to profl. jours. Office: Univ Calif 2217 E Adminstration Bldg Santa Barbara CA 93106

SPRECHER, MELVIN, ret. dairy products co. exec.; b. Honey Creek, Wis., Apr. 27, 1911; s. Andrew and Clara (Schoephorster) S.; student pub. schs. Prairie du Sac, Wis.; m. Della, Feb. 28, 1935; children—Howard, Lucille Sprecher Silvester. Farmer; past pres. Honey Creek Valley Dairy Coop., Wis. Dairies; past chmn. bd. Land O'Lakes, Inc., Mpls. Past pres. Wis. Dairy Fedn.; bd. dirs. Nat. Council Farmer Coops., Agr. Council Am.; past v.p. Wis. Fedn. Coops. Methodist. Home: 209 Spruce St Sauk City WI 53483

SPRECHER, ROBERT ARTHUR, judge; b. Chgo., May 30, 1917; s. A.G. and Lillian (Senick) S.; B.S., Northwestern U., 1938, J.D., 1941; m. Helen J. Szymczak, Aug. 22, 1942; children—Mark, Michael, Robert, Maribeth, Richard. Admitted to Ill. bar, 1942; with firm Crowley, Sprecher, Barrett & Karaba, Chgo., 1942-71; U.S. judge U.S. 7th Circuit Ct. Appeals, Chgo., 1971—. Home: 2315 Asbury Ave Evanston IL 60201 Office: 219 Dearborn St Chicago IL 60604

SPREIREGEN, PAUL DAVID, architect, planner, author; b. Boston, Dec. 12, 1931; s. Jacob Harold and Janet Elaine (Zisman) S.; student CIAM Sch., Venice, 1954, M.I.T., 1952-54, Rensselaer Poly. Inst., 1949-51, Boston Mus. Fine Arts Sch., 1946-49;. m. Rose-Hélène Bester, Oct. 17, 1961. Archtl. designer Studio Architetti BBPR, Milan, Italy, 1954, Uhlin & Malm, Stockholm, 1955, Skidmore Owings & Merrill, N.Y.C., 1956; urban designer Adams Howard & Greeley, Boston, 1958-59, Downtown Progress, Washington, 1960-62; dir. urban design programs AIA, Washington, 1962-66; dir. architecture and environ. arts programs Nat. Endowment for Arts, Washington, 1966-70; architect, planner, author, Washington, 1970—; mem. Fed. Commn. for Reconstrn. and Devel. Alaska, 1964; adv. Study of profl. Edn. of Landscape Architects, Ford Found., 1969-72; dir. Bicentennial for Am. Design, Nat. Endowment for Arts, 1972-75; host weekly radio program Places for People, Nat. Public Radio, 1972—; tchr. Boston Archtl. Center, 1959, Yale U. Sch. Planning, 1966, Catholic U. Grad. Sch. Architecture and Planning, 1967, 77, U. Hawaii, 1968, U. Pa., 1968, U. Tenn., 1969, Harvard U., 1970, Ball State U., 1973-74; Emons Distinguished prof. architecture Ball State U., 1973-74. Mem. vis. com. on arts M.I.T., 1973—. Servd to 1st lt. C.E., U.S. Army, 1956-58. Waid Edn. Fund grantee, 1967; Innisfree Found. fellow, 1966; Fulbright fellow, Italy, 1954-55. Fellow AIA (design citation Potomac chpt. 1974; Student medal 1954; chmn. com. design competitions 1977—, chmn. com. regional devel. and natural resources 1970-74, com. urban design, 1966-74), Am Inst. Interior Designers (hon.); mem. Am. Soc. Landscape Architects (Pres.'s award Potomac chpt. 1968). Author: Urban Design: The Architecture of Towns and Cities, 1965 (also in Japanese and Spanish; editor: The Modern Metropolis: Its Origins, Form, Characteristics, and Planning (Hans Blumenfeld), 1967; On the Art of Designing Cities: Selected Essays of Elbert Peets, 1968; Metropolis and Beyond: Selected Essays of Hans Blumnfeld, 1979; author: (with H. Von Hertzen) Building a New Town: The Story of Finland's New Garden City, Tapiola, 1971; Design Competitions, 1979. Address: 2215 Observatory Pl Washington DC 20007

SPRENGER, GORDON MERRIL, hosp. exec.; b. Albert Lea, Minn., Apr. 30, 1937; s. Feodor M. and Ruth Irene (Schoenrock) S.; B.A., St. Olaf Coll., 1959; M.H.A. (Lutheran. Social Services scholar), U. Minn., 1961; m. Delores Irene Idstrom, Aug. 9, 1961; children—Michael, Kristen, Angela. Asst. adminstr. St. Luke's Hosp., Milw., 1964-67; asst. adminstr. Northwestern Hosp., Mpls., 1967-68, adminstr., 1968-71; exec. v.p. Abbott-Northwestern Hosp., Mpls., 1971-75, pres., chief exec. officer, 1975—; pres. Health Care PAC of Minn., 1979—; clin. instr. U. Minn. Grad. Program in Hosp. Adminstrn., Class agt. St. Olaf Coll., 1975-77; bd. dirs. Community Drug Treatment Program, Bloomington, Minn., 1975-77; pres. Camp Lake Sportsmen Assn., Garrison, Minn., 1976-77. Served with USAF, 1961-64. Decorated Distinguished Service Award; recipient Sabra A. Hamilton award U. Minn., 1961. Mem. Am. Coll. Hosp. Adminstrs., Minn. (dir.), Am. hosp. assns., U. Minn. Alumni Assn. (pres. 1975-77). Club: Rotary. Home: 2303 Sherwood Circle Bloomington MN 55431 Office: 810 E 27th St Minneapolis MN 55406

SPRENKLE, CASE MIDDLETON, educator; b. Cleve., Aug. 18, 1934; s. Raymond E. and Helen K. (Middleton) S.; B.S., U. Colo., 1956; M.A., Yale, 1967, Ph.D., 1960; m. Elaine Elizabeth Jensen, June 22, 1957; children—David, Peter, Amy. Instr. econs. Yale, 1959-60; mem. faculty U. Ill., Urbana, 1960—, prof. econs., 1970—, chmn. econs. dept., 1976—, asst. dean Coll. Commerce, 1962-65; faculty Econs. Inst., Boulder, Colo., 1965, 72; cons. Ill. Revenue Commn., 1962—. Bd. dirs. Champaign-Urbana Symphony, treas., 1972-74, pres., 1975-77; bd. dirs. Champaign County Arts and Humanities Council. Am. Bankers Assn. grantee, 1970-71. Mem. Am. Econs. Assn., Am. Fin. Assn., Omicron Delta Epsilon. Presbyterian (pres. bd. trustees 1970-73). Contbr. numerous articles to profl. jours. on the demand for money. Home: 1913 Harding Dr Urbana IL 61801

SPRIGGS, EVERETT LEE, lawyer; b. Safford, Ariz., July 30, 1930; s. Claude E. and Evelyn (Lee) S.; B.S., Ariz. State U., 1955; J.D., U. Ariz., 1958; m. Betty Medley, Aug. 22, 1953; children—Claudia Lynn, Lee M., Scott B. Admitted to Calif. bar, 1960; city atty. criminal dept., Los Angeles, 1960-61; mem. firm Kinkle & Rodiger, Riverside, Calif., 1961-64; pres. firm Kinkle, Rodiger & Spriggs, P.C., Riverside, 1965—; dir. Mission Bank; mem. Am. Bd. Trial Advocates. Mem. Calif. State Bar, Riverside County Bar Assn., Los Angeles County Bar Assn., Def. Research Inst., So. Calif. Def. Counsel (editorial staff 1970—). Served with AUS, 1951-52. Decorated Bronze Star, Purple Heart. Mem. Am. Bd. Trial Advocates. Home: 1456 Muirfield Riverside CA 92506 Office: 3393 14th St Riverside CA 92501

SPRINCHORN, EVERT MANFRED, educator, writer; b. Jamestown, N.Y., Oct. 7, 1923; s. J. Ulrich and Hertha (Landgren) S.; B.Sc., Drexel Inst., 1948; A.M., Columbia, 1950, Ph.D., 1960. Mem. faculty Vassar Coll., 1956—, prof. drama, 1967—, chmn. dept., dir. Exptl. Theatre, 1969-75; vis. prof. Columbia, 1961-62, Yale Sch. Drama, 1967, City U. N.Y., 1970, 72. Served with AUS, 1943-46. Gustaf V fellow, 1953. Mem. Soc. Theatre Research, Am. Soc. Theatre Research, Internat. Fedn. Theatre Research, Soc. Advancement Scandinavian Studies, Shaw Soc., Strindberg Soc. Author articles in field. Editor: Ibsens's Letters and Speeches, 1964; Richard Wagner on Music and Drama, 1964; Twentieth-Century Plays in Synopsis, 1965. Translator and editor: Genius of the Scandinavian Theatre, 1964; Strindberg's Autobiographical Works, 1966-68. Address: Vassar Coll Poughkeepsie NY 12601

SPRING, BERNARD POLMER, univ. adminstr., architect; b. N.Y.C., July 9, 1927; s. Herman and Rose (Polmer) S.; A.B. cum laude, U. Pa., 1949; M.Arch., Mass. Inst. Tech., 1951; m. Phyllis Tubiolo, Nov. 10, 1951; children—Elin Felice, Jonathan Bernard, Suzanne Rebekah, Deborah Leigh. Naval architect U.S. Bur. Ships, 1951-53; lectr. Royal Acad. Fine Arts, Copenhagen, 1954-55; asst. prof. Mass. Inst. Tech., Cambridge, 1955-59; research dir. Weyerhaeuser Co., Seattle, 1959-61; asst. prof. the Cooper Union N.Y.C., 1961-65; dir. Research Center Princeton Sch. Architecture, 1965-69; dean Sch. Architecture City Coll. N.Y., 1969—; sr. cons. Davis, Brody & Assos., Architects, N.Y.C., 1961-76; cons. architect, 1976—; mem. N.Y. State Bd. Architecture; exec. com., bd. dirs. Citizens Housing and Planning Council; chmn. N.Y.C. AIA Schs. Com.; mem. design examining com. Nat. Council Archtl. Registration Bds. chmn. design awards jury Progressive Architecture, 1979. Fulbright fellow, 1953-54; sr. fellow Council on Humanities, Princeton, 1966-68. Fellow AIA (mem. continuing edn. com.), Assn. Collegiate Schs. Architecture (dir.). Author: Design and the Production of Houses, 1959; Building with Plastics, 1959; A Study of Education for Environmental Design, 1968; Planning and Design Workbook, 1969; tech. editor Archtl. Forum, 1961-65. Home: 619 Harrison Ave Harrison NY 10528 Office: Sch Architecture City Coll NY New York City NY 10031. *Quiet persistence and sympathetic understanding of professional colleagues leads most directly to constructive change.*

SPRING, DAVID, educator; b. Toronto, Ont., Can., Apr. 29, 1918; s. Joseph and Miriam (Gold) S.; B.A., U. Toronto, 1939; A.M., Harvard, 1940, Ph.D., 1948; m. Eileen Jeffries, June 14, 1948. Came to U.S., 1949, naturalized, 1963. Lectr. history U. Toronto, 1946-49; faculty Johns Hopkins, Balt., 1949—, prof. history, 1962—; vis. prof. U. Leicester (Eng.), 1968-69. Conservation chmn. Md. Audubon Soc., 1964-69. Served with Can. Army, 1942-44, Can. Navy, 1944-46. Ford Found. fellow, 1952-53; Guggenheim fellow, 1957-58; Nat. Endowment for Humanities fellow, 1976-77. Mem. Am. Hist. Assn., Econ. History Assn., Phi Beta Kappa. Author: The English Landed Estate in the 19th Century, 1963. Editor: Ecology and Religion in History, 1974; The First Industrial Society, 1975; European Landed Elites in the 19th Century, 1978. Contbr. articles to profl. jours. Home: 5605 Wexford Rd Baltimore MD 21209

SPRING, RAYMOND LEWIS, educator; b. Warsaw, N.Y., Aug. 5, 1932; A.B., Washburn U., 1957, J.D., 1959. Admitted to Kans. bar, 1960, U.S. Ct. Appeals bar, 10th Circuit, 1960; asso. firm Crane, Martin, Claussen & Ashworth, Topeka, 1959-65; Workmen's Compensation examiner State of Kans., 1961-62; asst. prof. law Washburn U., Topeka, 1965-68, asso. prof., 1968-70, asso. prof., acting dean Sch. of Law, 1970-71, prof., dean, 1971-78, Distinguished prof., 1978—; mem. cts. subcom. Kans. Gov.'s Com. on Criminal Adminstrn., 1970-79; dir. Century Savs. Assn., Shawnee Mission, Kans. Bd. Dirs. Topeka Welfare Planning Council, 1964-66; chmn. Shawnee County Young Republicans, 1962-64; bd. dirs. Shawnee council Campfire Girls, 1965-68; leader edn. div. Topeka United Fund, 1972; deacon Central Congregational Ch., 1972-74, 1979—; mem. Kans. Bd. Admissions of Attys., 1979—. Mem. Am., Kans. Topeka bar assns., Barristers, Delta Theta Phi. Author: (with Ryan) Vernon's Kansas Criminal Code Annotated, 1971, Vernon's Kansas Code of Criminal Procedure, 1973. Home: 1616 Jewell St Topeka KS 66604 Office: 1700 College St Topeka KS 66621

SPRING, WILLIAM CHARLES, JR., physician; b. Glen Ridge, N.J., June 22, 1913; s. William Charles and Anna Evelyn (Beeny) S.; student U. Wis., 1931-33; M.D., Duke, 1936; M.P.H., Columbia, 1947; m. Louella Ruth Clark, Aug. 15, 1939; children—William Charles III, Peter, Louanne, Jeffrey. Intern, asst. resident U. Hosps. Cleve., 1936-38; instr. bacteriology Western Res. U., 1938; asst. resident Thorndike Meml. Lab., Boston City Hosp., 1938-39; teaching fellow Harvard, 1938-39; fellow, asst. in animal pathology Rockefeller Inst. for Med. Research, 1939-42; asso. dir. lab. ARC-Harvard Field Hosp. Unit, Salisbury, Eng., 1942; resident pub. health physician N.Y. State Dept. Pub. Health, 1945-46; commr. health Tompkins County, N.Y., 1947-52; DeLamar prof. pub. health practice Columbia, 1952-59; med. dir. Pfizer Labs., Bklyn., 1959-61; dir. dept. drugs, sec. council on drugs AMA, 1961-63; dir. drug information network study Inst. for Advancement Med. Communication, 1963; dir. study human factors in Medlars Indexing, Nat. Library Medicine, 1964; cons. dir. pub. health div. Hoover commn., 1954; chmn. health div., mem. central planning bd. Welfare and Health Council N.Y., 1954-56; study dir. Sch. Health Survey, N.Y.C., 1955-58; staff dir., health life scis. div. U. City Sci. Center. Phila., 1965-68; coordinator Greater Del. Valley Regional Medical Program, 1966-68; dir. Bucks County Health Dept., Doylestown, Pa., 1968-71; med. dir. Aspetuck Valley Health Dist., Westport, Conn., 1971-72; chief high blood pressure control sect., chronic diseases div. Pa. Dept. Health, 1973—. Served from capt. to lt. col. AUS, 1942-46. Fellow Am. Pub. Health Assn., N.Y. Acad. Medicine; mem. Am. Coll. Preventive Medicine, Sigma Phi, Alpha Kappa Kappa. Home: 2619 Cranberry Circle Harrisburg PA 17110

SPRINGER, DOUGLAS HYDE, food co. exec.; b. Englewood, N.J., Jan. 31, 1927; s. Arthur Hyde and Melicent Katherine (Messenger) S.; student Wesleyan U., 1944-45; A.B., Yale, 1947; LL.B., Columbia,

1950; m. Virginia Helen Chouinard, Nov. 23, 1949; children—Susan Compton, Debora Lee. Admitted to N.Y. bar, 1950; atty. Port of N.Y. Authority, 1950-52; legal counsel Worthington Corp., Harrison, N.J., 1953-61, asst. sec., 1956-61; asst. counsel Campbell Soup Co., Camden, N.J., 1961-65, asst. sec., 1965, spl. assignments, 1966, dir. spl. studies, corporate planning, 1966-69, dir. corporate planning frozen foods, 1969-70, asst. treas., 1970-71, treas., 1971-73, v.p. fin. planning, 1973-75, v.p., controller, 1975-78, v.p., treas., 1978—; mem. adv. bd. Pa., Liberty Mut. Ins. Co.; exec. sec. Gov.'s Interstate Adv. Com., 1966; asst. to mem. Pres.'s Commn. on Postal Orgn., 1967-68; spl. asst. to chmn South Jersey Port Corp., 1969-71; mem. N.J. Econ. Devel. Council, 1972-76; trustee INA Capital Bond Trust. Trustee Nat. Food Processors Assn. Retirement Plan and Trust Indenture Fund. Served with USNR, 1944-46. Mem. Am. Bar Assn., Phi Nu Theta, Phi Delta Phi. Republican. Clubs: Yale (Phila.). Home: 709 Iron Post Rd Moorestown NJ 08057 Office: Campbell Soup Co Campbell Pl Camden NJ 08101

SPRINGER, EUSTACE LAURENCE, ednl. cons.; b. Ft. Washington, Md., Nov. 9, 1903; s. Ruter William and Gertrude Mason (Lynch) S.; student Dickinson Coll., 1920-21; B.A., Princeton, 1924, Litt.D., 1959; M.A., U. Buffalo, 1928; m. Elizabeth Randolph Ballard, July 25, 1940 (dec. May 1971); 1 dau., Elizabeth Randolph (Mrs. Marcus T. Munji); m. 2d, Virginia Lindsley Loomis, Oct. 9, 1975. Tchr. history, athletic coach Nichols Sch., Buffalo, 1924-30; headmaster Troy Country Day Sch., N.Y., 1930-35; asso. headmaster Montgomery Sch., Wynnewood, Pa., 1935-36; headmaster Pingry Sch., Elizabeth, N.J., 1936-61; sr. partner Ednl. Partners; ednl. cons. for pvt. ind. schs., 1975—; ednl. cons. Commonwealth of P.R., 1960-61, U.S. Dept. State, 1964. Former chmn. commn. on relations between secondary schs. and higher edn. Nat. Council Ind. Schs.; mem. Coll. Entrance Exam Bd., 1944-61, Ednl. Records Bur.; chmn. Joint Commn. which created Nat. Assn. Ind. Schs., 1962. Past pres. Family and Children's Soc.; mem. Chancellors Assos., U. Calif., San Diego; past v.p. Philharmonic Soc. Elizabeth; bd. dirs. Mus. Arts Soc. of La Jolla, 1963-70; trustee La Jolla Country Day Sch., 1967-73, La Jolla Chamber Music Soc., 1977—, San Diego Center for Children, 1977—. Mem. Country Day Sch. Headmasters Assn. U.S. (past pres.), Headmasters Assn. U.S. (past v.p.), Nat. Council Ind. Schs., Council on Religion in Ind. Schs. (past v.p., trustee), World Affairs Council San Diego (dir.). Rotarian. Clubs: San Diego Yacht; Monday Evening (past pres.); Princeton, Corinthians (N.Y.C.); LaJolla Beach and Tennis, La Jolla Country, Travelers Century. Co-author: The Independent School Trustee, 1964, 3d edit., 1974; author: Independent School Administration, 1967. Home: 2112 Caminito Circulo Sur La Jolla CA 92037. *Always, I have been guided by the ideal of service to others, a strong belief in the inherent worth of each human being, compassion for those with problems, and the conviction that the most vital aspect of education is the development of each individual to his own maximum potential, intellectually, physically, and spiritually. Still active after more than a half century of service, I can say with certainty, that, if I had my life to live over, I would follow the same path, motivated by the same ideals.*

SPRINGER, GEORG FERDINAND, scientist, educator, editor; b. Berlin, Germany, Mar. 1, 1924; s. Ferdinand and Elisabeth (Calvin) S.; B.A., U. Heidelberg (Germany), 1947; M.D., Basel U. (Switzerland), 1951; Woodward fellow in physiol. chem. U. Pa., 1953-54; m. Heather Margaret Bligh, Aug. 11, 1951; children—Martin F.B., Elizabeth A., Julia A. Came to U.S., 1951, naturalized, 1962. Immunologist, Walter Reed Army Med. Center, 1955-56; asso. medicine and pathology U. Pa., 1955-56, asst. prof. microbiology, 1956-61, asso. prof., 1961-62; chief blood bank examiner City of Phila., 1958-63; adviser clin. research center Phila. Gen. Hosp., 1961-63, Established investigator Am. Heart Assn., 1958-63; prof. microbiology Northwestern U., 1962—, prof. surgery, 1977—, Julia S. Michels researcher of surg. oncology, also mem. adv. bd. Cancer Research Center; dir. dept. immuno-chemistry Evanston (Ill.) Hosp., 1963—, also mem. research and edn. com., protection of human subjects com. Chmn. bd. Deerfield State Bank (Ill.); dir. Springer Verlag pub. co.; co-owner 1st Nat. Bank, Northbrook, Ill. Mem. research com. Ill. div. Am. Cancer Soc.; mem. med. adv. bd. Leukemia Research Found.; adv. bd. German Nat. Cancer Research Center; coordinator Polish-Am. Immunology Sci. Collaboration, Fogarty Center, NIH. Recipient Oehlecker prize, 1967; Abbott prize in biomed. research, 1977; Jung prize in medicine, 1977. Fellow AAAS, Inst. of Medicine, Am. Inst. Chemists; mem. Assn. Clin. Scientists, French Immunological Soc., German Soc. for Immunology, Soc. Complex Carbohydrates, Am. Soc. Biol. Chemists, Am. Assn. Immunologists, Ill. Acad. Sci. (hon.), Am. Heart Assn., Am. Chem. Soc., Am. Soc. Microbiology, Internat. Transfusion Soc., N.Y. Acad. Sci., French and German Soc. Immunobiology, German Soc. Blood Transfusion, U.S. Equestrian Team, Am. Horse Show Assn., Am. Wildlife Soc., Nature Conservancy (life). Chief editor: Molecular Biol; Biochem and Biophys, 1964; editor Z. Immforschg.; adv. editor Protoplasmatologia, Transfusion, 1965, Jour. Immunogenetics, Progress in Molecular and Subcellular Biology series; asso. editor Klin Woschrift, 1956. Contbr. numerous articles to profl. jours. Research in blood group, blood disorders, carbohydrates, breast cancer, cell receptors. Home: 20 Country Ln Northfield IL 60093 Office: 2650 Ridge Ave Evanston IL 60201

SPRINGER, GEORGE, educator, mathematician; b. Cleve., Sept. 3, 1924; s. Jack H. and Helen (Finkel) S.: B.S., Case Inst. Tech., 1945: M.S., Brown U., 1946; Ph.D., Harvard U., 1949; m. Annemarie Keiner, Mar. 26, 1950; children—Leonard, Claudia, Joel. C.L.E. Moore instr. Mass. Inst. Tech., 1949-51; asst. prof. Northwestern U., 1951-54; asso. prof., prof. U. Kans., 1955- 64; prof. math. Ind. U., 1964—, chmn. 1967-71, asso. dean for research and devel., 1973—; vis. prof. U. Munster (Germany), 1954-55, Würzburg (Germany), 1961-62, Mackenzie U., Sao Paolo, Brazil, 1961, Imperial Coll., U. London, 1971-72; program dir. for classical analysis, math. scis. sect. NSF, 1978-79. Fulbright grantee, 1954-55, 61-62, Mem. Am. Math. Soc., Math. Assn. Am., AAAS, Sigma Xi. Author: Introduction to Riemann Surfaces, 1957. Editor: Jour. Math. and Mechanics, 1965-70, Ind. U. Math. Jour., 1970-77; cons. editor Blaisdell Pub. Co. series pure and applied math., 1961-71, McGraw Hill Book Co., 1971—. Home: 2001 Southdowns Dr Bloomington IN 47401

SPRINGER, JACK G., assn. exec.; b. Norman, Okla., Sept. 11, 1926; s. Charles S. and Mary A. (Goff) S.; B.S., U. Okla., 1950; m. Doris M. Lebow, Apr. 14, 1945; children—Carol Springer Power, Sheryl Springer Sneske, Jane, Cynthia. With Pauls Valley (Okla.) C. of C., 1950-51, Seminole (Okla.) C. of C., 1951-53; Bryan-Coll. Station (Tex.) C. of C., 1953-61, Galveston (Tex.) C. of C., 1961-63, W. Tex. Regional C. of C., 1963-71; exec. v.p. Okla. State C. of C., Oklahoma City, 1971—. Served with U.S. Army, 1944-46. Mem. Assn. Am. C. of C. Execs., Okla. C. of C. Execs. (dir.), Council State Chambers Commerce (past pres.), U.S. C. of C. (pub. affairs com.). Home: 6224 NW 85th St Oklahoma City OK 73132 Office: 4020 N Lincoln Blvd Oklahoma City OK 73105

SPRINGER, JOHN KELLEY, hosp. exec.; b. Salem, Ohio, May 11, 1931; s. Wilbur Johnson and Nellie Marie (Kelley) S.; A.B., Dartmouth Coll., 1953; M.H.A., U. Mich., 1960; m. Jane Lee Parsons, Oct. 13, 1956; children—Kelley Lynn, Dana Lee, Susan Elizabeth, Nellie Jane. Adminstrv. resident Mary Hitchcock Meml. Hosp., Hanover, N.H., 1959-60, asst. adminstr., 1960-64, asso. adminstr., 1964-69, adminstr. for ops., 1969-71; asso. exec. dir. Hartford (Conn.) Hosp., 1971-73, exec. dir., 1974—, pres., 1977—; mem. separate account com. Hartford Variable Annuity Life Ins. Co., 1978—; pres. Combined Hosps. Alcoholism Program, Inc., 1972-75; lectr. Sch. Pub. Health, Yale U., 1975. Deacon, First Ch. of Christ Congl., West Hartford, 1975—; bd. dirs. Urban League Greater Hartford, 1973-76, Hartford Fund, 1978—; bd. dirs. Greater Hartford chpt. ARC, vice-chmn., 1978—; bd. dirs. Hartford Sem. Found. Served to capt. USMC, 1953-58; col. Res. (ret.). Mem. Am. Coll. Hosp. Adminstrs., New England Hosp. Assembly (pres. 1972), Conn. Hosp. Assn. (chmn. council on govt. 1973—), Am. Hosp. Assn. (council on financing 1975-78, del.-at-large 1979—). Clubs: Hartford; Hartford Tennis, Hartford Golf. Home: 1844 Albany Ave West Hartford CT 06117 Office: 80 Seymour St Hartford CT 06115

SPRINGER, JOHN SHIPMAN, pub. relations co. exec.; b. Rochester, N.Y., Apr. 25, 1916; s. W.A. and Alice Jane (Grosjean) S.; student U. Toronto (Ont., Can.), 1935-37; Ph.B., Marquette U., 1939, recipient Byline award Coll. Journalism, 1970; m. June Alicia Reimer, June 3, 1953; children—Gary, Alicia Ann, Cynthia Lynn. Feature writer Rochester Democrat and Chronicle, 1940-41; head mag. publicity RKO Radio Pictures, 1946-57, 20th Century-Fox Films, 1957-59; v.p. Arthur Jacobs, Pub. Relations, 1959-60; partner Jacobs & Springer, pub. relations, 1960-62; pres. John Springer Assos., Inc., N.Y.C., 1964—. Served with USAAF, 1942-45. Recipient By-line award Marquette U., 1970. Author: All Talking! All Singing! All Dancing!, 1966; The Fondas, 1970; They Had Faces Then, 1975; Forgotten Films to Remember, 1980. Producer/host stage-screen shows starring Bette Davis, Myrna Loy, Sylvia Sidney, Joan Crawford, Rosalind Russell, Debbie Reynolds, Joanne Woodward, Lana Turner, others in N.Y.C., U.S. tour, Australia, Gt. Britain. Office: 667 Madison Ave New York NY 10021

SPRINGER, STANLEY G., lawyer; b. Newburgh, N.Y., Sept. 27, 1927; s. Allen Paul and Mabel (Thorn) S.; B.A., Union Coll., 1949; LL.B. with distinction (1st Fraser scholar), Cornell U., 1953; m. Roberta Gietz, Sept. 14, 1947 (div. 1975); children—Valerie, Beverly, Jeffrey, Gregory, Kimberly, Lindsay; m. 2d, Vallie Strong, July 2, 1979. Admitted to Wis. bar, 1953, Ill. bar, 1958, Tex. bar, 1970; mem. firm Whyte, Hirschboeck, Minahan, Harding & Harland, Milw., 1953-58; atty. Libby, McNeill & Libby, Chgo., 1958-63; gen. counsel, v.p. J.I. Case Co., Racine, Wis., 1963-69; v.p., gen. counsel Mich. Gen. Corp., Dallas, 1969—; dir. J.I. Case Credit Corp., 1963-69, Colt Mfg. Co., Inc., 1967-69. Chmn., Racine Heart Fund campaign, 1964; commr. Racine Redevel. Authority, 1965-69. Served with AC, USNR, 1945-47. Recipient WPB Carey Exbn. 1st prize Cornell U., 1953. Mem. Am., Wis., Tex., Dallas bar assns., Lawyer-Pilots Bar Assn., Order of Coif, Phi Delta Phi, Phi Kappa Phi. Club: Royal Oaks Country. Home: 15912 Archwood Ln Dallas TX 75248 Office: 1100 Dallas Fed Savs Tower 8333 Douglas Ave Dallas TX 75225

SPRINGER, URSULA, publisher; b. Berlin, Aug. 28, 1928; d. Hans and Gerta (Leonhard) Pietzschmann; came to U.S., 1950, naturalized, 1961; student U. Berlin, U. Munich (W. Ger.), U. Bologna (Italy); M.A., U. Minn., 1952; Ph.D., Columbia U., 1964; m. Bernhard Springer, Jan., 1964 (dec. 1970). Prof. edn. Bklyn. Coll., 1961-77, ret., 1977; pres. Springer Pub. Co., N.Y.C., 1970—; adv. bd. Internat. Book Programs, Dept. State, 1976-77; Fulbright guest lectr. U. Berlin, spring 1969. Mem. Domestic Affairs Task Force Democratic Party, N.Y.C., 1975-76. Mem. Am. Assn. Publishers (dir.), Comparative Edn. Soc., Am. Ednl. Research Assn. Author: Curriculum Reform in France, West Germany and Italy, 1967; founder, editor Western European Edn., 1968-71; dir. internat. research project on secondary sch. reforms in eleven European countries, 1968-69. Office: 200 Park Ave S New York NY 10003

SPRINGER, WILLIAM LEE, govt. ofcl., former congressman; b. Sullivan, Ind., Apr. 12, 1909; s. Otha Lee and Daisy Ellen (Tucker) S.; B.A., DePauw U., 1931, LL.D., 1972; LL.B., U. Ill., 1935; LL.D., Millikin U., 1953, Lincoln Coll., 1966, m. Elsie Cora Mattis, May 9, 1942; children—Katherine Curtis (Mrs. Paul Hickey), Anne (Mrs. Paul McKnight), Georgia Mattis (Mrs. William Finger). Admitted to Ill. bar, 1935; asso. Busch & Harrington, Champaign, Ill., 1936-39; states atty. Champaign County, 1940-42; county judge Champaign County, 1946-50; mem. 82d-92nd Congress from 22d Ill. Dist., ranking minority mem., 1964-72, mem. com. on interstate and fgn. commerce, Congl. rep. internat. confs. trade, space communications and energy. Mem. Fed. Power Commn., 1973, vice-chmn., 1974—; mem. Fed. Election Commn., 1976—. Served to lt. USNR, 1942-45. Mem. Am., Champaign County bar assns., Am. Juridical Soc. Republican. Presbyn. Kiwanian, Elk, Mason. Clubs: Champaign County Country; Chevy Chase; Capitol Hill. Contbr. treatises law to profl. jours. Home: 900 W Park Champaign IL 61820 Office: Fed Election Commn 1325 K St NW Washington DC 20463

SPRINGFIELD, JAMES FRANCIS, banker; b. Memphis, Nov. 5, 1929; s. C.L. and Mildred (White) S.; B.A. with distinction in econs., Southwestern at Memphis, 1951; LL.B., U. Memphis, 1960; m. Shirley Burdick, June 1, 1951; children—Sidney, Susan, James Francis. With Union Planters Nat. Bank, Memphis, 1951—, exec. v.p., sr. trust officer, head trust dept., 1968—. Treas. Sigma Nu House Corp., 1966-79; pres. Estate Planning Council of Memphis, 1973-74; mem. pres.'s council U. Southwestern, Memphis; chmn. bd. trustees So. Coll. Optometry, 1978—; trustee Plough Found., Memphis Conf. United Methodist Ch. Found., U. Tenn. Memphis Med. Units Found.; v.p., chmn. fin. com. Hutchinson Sch.; sec. bd. trustees Vision Edn. Found.; bd. regents Tenn. Trust Sch., chmn., 1977. Served with USNR, 1951-54. Mem. Tenn. Bankers Assn. (chmn. legis. com. trust div. 1968-69, treas. trust div. 1972-73, pres. trust div. 1976-77, bd. dirs. 1976-77), Memphis and Shelby County (chmn. moral fitness com. 1972), Tenn. (chmn. interprofl. relations com. 1976) bar assns., Bank Adminstrn. Inst. (mem. trust commn.), Sigma Nu (div. comdr. 1967-68). Methodist (trustee ch.). Club: Balmoral Civic (treas. 1967-68) (Memphis). Home: 8334 Heatherglen Dr Germantown TN 38138 Office: 67 Madison Ave Memphis TN 38147

SPRINGSTEEN, BRUCE, singer, songwriter, guitarist; b. Freehold, N.J., Sept. 23, 1949; s. Douglas and Adele S.; attended community coll. Performed in N.Y. and N.J. nightclubs; signed with Columbia Records in 1972; first album: Greetings from Asbury Park, New Jersey, 1973; nationwide concert tours with The E-Street Band, 1974—; other albums include: The Wild, The Innocent and the E-Street Shuffle, 1974, Born to Run (Gold Record award), 1975, Darkness on the Edge of Town, 1978; songs composed include: Blinded by the Light, Tenth Avenue Freeze-Out, Badlands, The Promised Land, Thunder Road. Office: care Premier Talent Assos Inc 888 7th Ave New York NY 10010*

SPRINGSTEEN, GEORGE STONEY, JR., govt. ofcl.; b. N.Y.C., Jan. 7, 1923; s. George S. and Elsa L. (Otto) S.; B.A., Dartmouth, 1943: M.A., Fletcher Sch. Law and Diplomacy, 1947, M.A.L.D., 1949, Ph.D., 1957; m. Rosalind Sawyer, May 28, 1955; children—George Sawyer, Martha Louise. Part-time tchr. econs., history Tufts Coll., 1947-49; internat. economist Dept. State, 1949-58; finance officer, sr. economist Devel. Loan Fund, 1958- 61; spl. asst. under sec. state for econ. affairs, 1961, spl. asst. under sec. state, 1961-66, dep. asst. sec. state European affairs, 1966-74, exec. sec. Dept. State and spl. asst. to sec. state, 1974-76, dir. Fgn. Service Inst., 1976—. Served to lt. (j.g.) USNR, 1943-46. Home: 5115 Baltimore Ave Washington DC 20016 Office: Dept of State Washington DC 20520

SPRINKEL, BERYL WAYNE, economist, banker; b. Richmond, Mo., Nov. 20, 1923; s. Clarence and Emma (Schooley) S.; student N.W. Mo. State U., 1941-43, U. Oreg., 1943-44; B.S., U. Mo., 1947; M.B.A., U. Chgo., 1948, Ph.D., 1952; L.H.D., DePaul U., 1975; m. Barbara Angus Pipher; children—Gary L., Kevin G., Debra, Pamela. Instr. econs., finance U. Mo., Columbia, 1948-49, U. Chgo., 1950-52; with Harris Trust & Savs. Bank, Chgo., 1952—, v.p., economist, 1960-68, dir. research, 1963-69, sr. v.p., 1968-74, economist, 1968—, exec. v.p., 1974—; cons. Fed. Res. Bd., 1955-59, Bur. of Census, 1962-70, Joint Econ. Com. U.S. Congress, 1958, 62, 67, 71, Ho. of Reps. Banking and Currency Com., 1963, Senate Banking Com., 1975; mem. econ. adv. bd. to sec. commerce, 1967-68; bd. economists Time mag. Pres., Homewood-Flossmoor (Ill.) Community High Sch., 1959-60. Served with AUS, 1943-45. Recipient Alumni Leadership and Service award U. Chgo., 1964; Hamilton Bolton award Fin. Analysts Assn., 1968; U. Mo. Alumni citation merit, 1971. Fellow Nat. Assn. Bus. Economists; mem. Am. Fin. Assn. (dir.), Am. Statis. Assn. (past pres. Chgo. chpt.), Am. Bankers Assn. (chmn. econ. adv. com. 1975-76), U.S. C. of C. (bd. dirs.), Conf. Bus. Economists, Beta Gamma Sigma. Author: Money and Stock Prices, 1964; Money and Markets-A Monetarist View, 1971; co-author Winning with Money, 1977. Editorial adv. bd. Fin. Analysts Jour., 1964—. Contbr. articles to profl. jours. Home: 1705 Brookwood Dr Flossmoor IL 60422 Office: 111 W Monroe St Chicago IL 60690

SPRINKLE, GEORGE WESLEY, architect; b. Sweetwater, Tenn., Oct. 4, 1923; s. George Wesley and Gladys Roberta (Callahan) S.; student East Los Angeles Jr. Coll., 1946-47, U. So. Calif., 1948, 49-50, UCLA, 1948-49; m. Dorothy Ann Cope, May 29, 1953; children—Clifton Wesley, Ann Elizabeth. Archtl. draftsman McCune & McCune, Architects, Tulsa, 1950-51, So. Mill. & Mfg. Co., Tulsa, 1951-53, Santa Barbara Mill & Mfg. Co. (Calif.), 1953-54; project architect Welton Becket & Assos., Los Angeles, 1954-61; office mgr. Guirey, Srnka, Arnold, Sprinkle—Architects and Planners, Flagstaff, Ariz., 1961-70, sr. v.p., sec., 1970—. Mem. Flagstaff Planning Commn., 1966-69, chmn., 1965-67; mem. Flagstaff Water Commn., 1966-68, Flagstaff Environ. Commn., 1966-68, Ariz. Gov.'s Commn. on Environ., 1967-73; mem. nat. panel Am. Arbitration Assn., 1968-76; bd. dirs. Jr. Achievement Central Ariz., 1971-76. Served with USN, 1943-46. Fellow AIA (pres. 1973-74, chmn. nat. com. on architects for justice 1977, nat. office mgmt. com. 1976-77, Western Mountain Region Bradley P. Kidder award 1974, Ariz. Personal Contbns. award 1975, Central Ariz. award for outstanding service to profession 1975; Western Mountain Region Architects' medal 1979), Bldg. Owners and Mgrs. Assn., Ariz. Acad., Sigma Chi. Republican. Episcopalian. Clubs: Kiwanis, Masons. Home: 7671 E Edgemont St Scottsdale AZ 85257 Office: 3122 N 3d Ave Phoenix AZ 85013

SPRINTHALL, NORMAN ARTHUR, psychologist; b. Attleboro, Mass., Aug. 19, 1931; s. William Archie and Edith Jarvis (Clark) S.; A.B. magna cum laude, Brown U., 1954, M.A., 1959; Ed.D., Harvard U., 1963; m. Lois May Theis; children—Douglas, Jane, Carolyn. Dir. fin. aid Brown U., 1955-60; asst. prof., then asso. prof. psychology, program chmn. counseling Harvard, 1963-72; mem. faculty U. Minn., Mpls., 1972—, prof. ednl. psychology, 1973—, program chmn. counseling, 1972-74; cons. Bur. Educationally Handicapped. Fellow Am. Psychol. Assn.; mem. Am. Ednl. Research Assn., Am. Personnel and Guidance Assn. Author: Educational Psychology: Readings, 1969, Guidance for Human Growth, 1971, Educational Psychology: A Developmental Approach, 2d edit., 1977, Value Development as the Aim of Education, 1978; mem. editorial bds. profl. jours. Office: 242 Burton Hall Univ Minn Minneapolis MN 55455

SPRITZER, RALPH SIMON, educator; b. N.Y.C., Apr. 27, 1917; s. Harry and Stella (Theuman) S.; B.S., Columbia, 1937, LL.B., 1940; m. Lorraine Nelson, Dec. 23, 1950; children—Ronald, Pamela. Admitted to N.Y. bar, 1941, U.S. Supreme Ct. bar, 1950; atty. Office Alien Property, Dept. Justice, 1946-51, anti-trust div. Dept. Justice, 1951-54, Office Solicitor Gen., 1954-61; gen. counsel FPC, 1961-62; 1st asst. to solicitor gen. U.S., 1962-68; prof. law U. Pa., Phila., 1968—. Adj. prof. law George Washington U., 1967; cons. Adminstrv. Conf. U.S., Ford Found., Pa. Gov.'s Justice Commn. Recipient Superior Service award Dept. Justice, 1960; Tom C. Clark award Fed. Bar. Assn., 1968. Mem. Am. Law Inst. Served with AUS, 1941-46. Home: 2117 Pine St Philadelphia PA 19103

SPROGER, CHARLES EDMUND, lawyer; b. Chgo., Feb. 18, 1933; s. William and Minnette (Weiss) S.; B.S., B.A. (David Himmelblau scholar), Northwestern U., 1954, J.D., 1957. Admitted to Ill. bar, 1957, since practiced in Chgo.; asso. Ehrlich & Cohn, 1958-63, Ehrlich, Bundesen, Friedman & Ross, 1963-71; partner Ehrlich, Bundesen, Broecker & Sproger, 1971-77, individual practice law, 1977—. Mem. adv. com. curriculum Ill. Inst. Continuing Legal Edn., Chgo., 1971—. Fellow Am. Acad. Matrimonial Lawyers; mem. Am., Ill. (chmn. council family law 1970-71), Chgo. (matrimonial law com. 1968—) bar assns., Decalogue Soc., Phi Alpha Delta. Editor: Family Lawyer, 1962-63. Contbr. articles to legal publs. Home: 2901 S King Dr Chicago IL 60616 Office: 69 W Washington St Chicago IL 60602

SPROLE, FRANK ARNOTT, drug co. exec.; b. Bklyn., Sept. 13, 1918; s. Frank Newland and Eleanor A. (Greenberg) S.; A.B., Yale, 1942; LL.B., Columbia, 1949; m. Sarah Louise Knapp, Sept. 23, 1944; children—Wendy A., Frank J., Anne L., Jonathan K., Sarah E. Admitted to N.Y. bar, 1949; asso. atty. firm Winthrop, Stimson, Putnam & Roberts, N.Y.C., 1949-50; with Bristol-Myers Co., 1950—, sec., 1955-65, v.p. legal, 1965-71, v.p., gen. counsel, 1972, sr. v.p., gen. counsel, 1973—, vice chmn. bd., 1977—, also dir.; dir. The Proprietary Assos., The Knapp Fund. Trustee, Hotchkiss Sch.; chmn. bd. Council on Family Health. Served to lt. USNR, 1942-45; PTO. Mem. Assn. Bar City N.Y., Aurelian Honor Soc., Delta Kappa Epsilon. Clubs: Yale, Links (N.Y.C.); Wee Burn Country (Darien); Bohemian (San Francisco); Mid-Ocean (Bermuda). Home: 118 Delafield Island Rd Darien CT 06820 Office: 345 Park Ave New York NY 10022

SPROTT, DAVID ARTHUR, educator; b. Toronto, Ont., Can., May 31, 1930; s. Arthur Frederick and Dorothy Mary (Barry) S.; B.A., U. Toronto, 1952, M.A., 1953, Ph.D., 1955; m. Muriel Doris Vogel, Dec. 16, 1961; children—Anne, Jane. Research asso. Galton Lab. U. Coll. London, 1956-57; biogeneticist dept. psychiatry and clin. tchr. faculty medicine U. Toronto, 1957-58; asso. prof. U. Waterloo, Ont., 1959-62, prof., 1962—, dean math., 1967-72, chmn. statistics, 1967-75. Fellow Royal Soc. Can., Royal Statis. Soc., Am. Statis. Assn., Royal Photog. Soc. Gt. Britain, Inst. Math. Statistics; mem. Internat. Statis. Inst., Internat. Biometric Soc., Inst. Math. Statistics, Am. Statis. Assn. Editor: (with V.P. Godambe) Foundations of Statistical Inference, 1971. Contbr. articles profl. jours. Home: 295 Ferndale Pl Waterloo ON Canada

SPROUL, JOHN ALLAN, public utility exec.; b. Oakland, Calif., Mar. 28, 1924; s. Robert Gordon and Ida Amelia (Wittschen) S.; A.B., U. Calif., Berkeley, 1947, LL.B., 1949; m. Marjorie Ann Hauck, June 20, 1945; children—John Allan, Malcolm J., Richard O., Catherine E. Admitted to Calif. bar, 1950; atty. Pacific Gas & Electric Co., San Francisco, 1949-52, 56-62, sr. atty., 1962-70, asst. gen. counsel, 1970-71, v.p. gas supply, 1971-76, sr. v.p., 1976-77, exec. v.p., 1977—; gen. counsel Pacific Gas Transmission Co., 1970-73, v.p., 1973-79, chmn. bd., 1979—, also dir.; atty. firm Johnson & Stanton, San Francisco, 1952-56; chmn. bd., dir. Natural Gas Corp. Calif.; dir. Alta. and So. Gas Co. Ltd.; Alta. Natural Gas Co. Ltd. Served to 1st lt. USAAF, 1943-46. Mem. Calif. Bar Assn., Am. Gas Assn., Pacific Coast Gas Assn. Clubs: Engineers, World Trade (San Francisco), Commonwealth, Bohemian, Orinda Country. Home: 8413 Buckingham Dr El Cerrito CA 94530 Office: 77 Beale St San Francisco CA 94106

SPROUL, OTIS JENNINGS, civil engr.; b. Dover Foxcroft, Maine, July 9, 1930; s. Dana Crowley and Dorothy Emma (Vose) S.; B.S., U. Maine, 1952, M.S., 1957; Sc.D., Washington U., St. Louis, 1961; m. Dorothy Ruth Estabrook, June 8, 1952; children—Dana C. (dec.), Bryce Jennings. Instr. civil engring. U. Maine, Orono, 1954-57, asst. prof., 1957-59, asso. prof. and prof., 1961-77; vis. asso. prof. civil engring. Washington U., St. Louis, 1961; prof., chmn. dept. civil engring. Ohio State U., Columbus, 1977—. Served to capt., arty., U.S. Army, 1952-54. Registered profl. engr., Maine. Diplomate Am. Acad. Environ. Engrs. Mem. ASCE (Rudolph Hering award 1971), Water Pollution Control Fedn., Am. Soc. Engring. Edn. (chmn. environ. div. 1969-70), Am. Water Works Assn., Internat. Ozone Inst. (co-founder 1973), AAUP, Internat. Assn. Water Pollution Research, Nat. Soc. Profl. Engrs., Maine Assn. Engrs. (pres. 1973), Sigma Xi, Tau Beta Pi, Phi Kappa Phi, Chi Epsilon. Contbr. articles to profl. jours. Home: 1868 Willow Forge Dr Columbus OH 43220 Office: 470 Hitchcock Hall Ohio State U 2070 Neil Ave Columbus OH 43210

SPROULL, JAMES EDWARD, utility co. exec.; b. Norfolk, Va., Oct. 24, 1924; s. James Thomas and Effie (Bateman) S.; B.B.A., U. Tampa, 1950; m. Anna Viola Melching, Aug. 14, 1948; 1 son, James Edward. Clerk, Tampa Electric Co. (Fla.), 1950-55, accountant, 1955-58, adminstrv. asst., 1958-60, adminstrv. asst. to comptroller, 1960-62, asst. to comptroller, 1962- 63, asst. sec., 1963-71, sec., asst. treas., 1971—. Served with USNR, 1943-46, 50-53. Mem. Am. Soc. Corp. Secs., Naval Res. Assn. Club: Optimist (pres. 1967-68) (Tampa). Home: 5020 Bayshore Blvd #502 Tampa FL 33611 Office: P O Box 111 Tampa Tampa FL 33601

SPROULL, ROBERT LAMB, univ. pres., physicist; b. Lacon, Ill., Aug. 16, 1918; s. John Steele and Chloe Velma (Lamb) S.; A.B., Cornell U., 1940, Ph.D., 1943; m. Mary Louise Knickerbocker, June 27, 1942; children—Robert F., Nancy M. Research physicist RCA labs., 1943-46; faculty Cornell U., 1946-63, prof. physics, 1956-63, dir. lab. atomic and solid state physics, 1959-60, dir. materials sci. center, 1960-63, v.p. for acad. affairs, 1965-68; dir. Advanced Research Projects Agy., Dept. Def., Washington, 1963-65; v.p., provost U. Rochester (N.Y.), 1968-70, pres., 1970—. Prin. physicist Oak Ridge Nat. Lab., 1952; physicist European Research Assos., Brussels, Belgium, 1958-59; lectr. NATO, 1958-59; dir. John Wiley & Sons, Security Trust Co., Sybron Corp., United Technols. Corp., Xerox Corp.; mem. sci. adv. com. Gen. Motors Corp, 1971—, chmn., 1973—. Mem. Naval Research Adv. Com., 1974-76; mem. Sloan Commn. Higher Edn., 1977-79. Fellow Center for Advanced Study in Behavioral Scis., 1973. Chmn., Def. Sci. Bd., 1968-70. Trustee Deep Springs Coll., 1967-75, Cornell U., 1972-77. Fellow Am. Acad. Arts and Scis.; mem. Telluride Assn. (pres. 1945-47). Author: Modern Physics, 1956. Editor Jour. Applied Physics, 1954-57. Home: 692 Mt Hope Ave Rochester NY 14620 Office: U Rochester Rochester NY 14627

SPROUSE, JOHN ALWYN, mcht.; b. Tacoma, Nov. 23, 1908; s. Robert Allen and Jenne (Glaessel) S.; student U. Oreg., 1926-28; m. Mary Louise Burpee, Dec. 27, 1932 (div. June 1954); children—Lucy (Mrs. Clyde B. Fletcher), Robert Allen II, John Edward; m. 2d, Barbara Barker, May 22, 1955. With Sprouse-Reitz Co., Inc., Portland, Oreg., 1928—, asst. to pres., 1945-61, pres., 1961-74, chmn. bd., 1974—. Expert cons. to Q.M. Gen., 1943-45. Mem. U.S. Power Squadron, USCG Aux., Delta Upsilon. Rotarian. Clubs: Yacht, Arlington, Multnomah (Portland). Home: 1745 SW Highland Rd Portland OR 97221 Office: 1411 SW Morrison St Portland OR 97205

SPROUSE, ROBERT ALLEN, II, retail chain store exec.; b. Portland, Oreg., Dec. 25, 1935; s. John Alwyn and Mary Louise (Burpee) S.; student Williams Coll., 1953-57; m. Frances Carolyn Russell, June 22, 1957. With Sprouse-Reitz Co. Inc., Portland, 1957—, buyer, sec., 1963-69, v.p., 1969-73, pres., 1973—, also dir. Republican. Episcopalian. Club: Multnomah Athletic (Portland). Address: PO Box 8996 Portland OR 97208

SPROUT, HAROLD, author; b. Benzonia, Mich., Mar. 14, 1901; s. George Milton and Grace Emily (Hance) S.; A.B., A.M., Oberlin Coll., 1924; postgrad. U. Wis. Law Sch., 1924-25, Western Res. Law Sch., 1925-26; Ph.D. (Carnegie fellow), U. Wis., 1929; m. Margaret Ascenath Tuttle, Aug. 6, 1924; children—Donald Francis, Chastina Elisabeth. Asst. prof. govt. Miami U., Oxford, Ohio, 1926-27; asst. prof. polit. sci. Stanford, 1929-31; instr. politics Princeton, 1931-35, asst. prof., 1935-41, asso. prof., 1941-45, prof., 1945—, chmn. dept. politics, 1949-52, Henry Grier Bryant prof. geography and internat. relations in dept. politics, prof. emeritus, 1969—, research asso. Center Internat. Studies, 1969—. Vis. prof. internat. relations Columbia, 1948-50, U. Denver, summer 1950; vis. lectr. U.S. Army War Coll., 1936-38, 71, U.S. Naval Acad., 1941, U.S. Mil. Acad., 1942, U.S. Nat. War Coll. 1946, U.S. Naval War Coll., 1953, 63, 70; vis. prof. polit. sci. U. Pa., summer 1938; vis. prof. Nuffield Coll., Oxford U., 1955, Rutgers U., 1970; cons. OWI, War Dept., 1943, Dept. State 1944, Navy, 1944-47. Mem. Am. Polit. Sci. Assn., AAAS, Internat. Studies Assn., Naval Hist. Found., Phi Beta Kappa, Congregationalist Author: (with Margaret Sprout) The Rise of American Naval Power, rev. edit., 1967, Toward a New Order of Sea Power, rev., 1943, Foundations of National Power 1946, rev. 1951, Man-Millieu Relationship Hypotheses in Context of International Politics, 1956, Foundations of International Politics, 1962, The Ecological Perspective on Human Affairs, with Special Reference to International Politics, 1965, An Ecological Paradigm for the Study of International Politics, 1968, Toward a Politics of the Planet Earth, 1971, Ecology and Politics in America, 1971; Multiple Vulnerabilities: The Context of Environmental Repair and Protection, 1974, The Context of Environmental Politics, 1978. Contbr. articles to profl. Jours. and encys. Home: 93 McCosh Circle Princeton NJ 08540 Office: Center Internat Studies Corwin Hall Princeton U Princeton NJ 08540

SPROUT, WILLIAM BRADFORD, JR., architect; b. Natick, Mass., Apr. 4, 1900; s. William Bradford and Margaret (Bigelow) S.; A.B., Harvard, 1921, M.Arch., 1928; m. Ruth Wilbur, June 1921; m. 2d, Sybil Vroom, June 16, 1928; children—Wesley B., William Bradford III, Sarah B. Practice architecture, Boston, also Hingham, Mass., 1931—; staff architect, sec. housing com. John Hancock Mut. Life Ins. Co., 1935-65; archtl. cons. Chmn. Hingham (Mass.) Historic Dists. Commn. Fellow AIA; mem. Boston Soc. Architects (former dir., exec. dir. 1961-62), Mass. Assn. Architects (co-founder, dir., sec.-treas. 1943-74), Constrn. Specifications Inst. (past pres. Boston chpt.), Am. Arbitration Assn. (panel mem. for constrn.). Clubs: Cohasset Yacht, Harvard of Hingham, Back Bay Lunch. Home: 235 Rockland St Hingham MA 02043 Office: 10 Newbury St Boston MA 02116

SPROW, HOWARD THOMAS, lawyer; b. Atlantic City, Dec. 4, 1919; s. Howard Franklin and Elizabeth B. (Riley) S.; A.B. cum laude, Colgate U., 1942; J.D., Columbia, 1945; m. Mildred J. Fiske, July 22, 1945; children—Howard Hamilton, Mildred Elizabeth (Mrs. Wilson), Matthew Thomas. Admitted to N.Y. bar, 1946; mem. firm Brown, Wood, Fuller, Caldwell & Ivey, N.Y.C., 1945-70, partner, 1954-70; gen. counsel, v.p. corporate and pub. affairs, sec. Merrill Lynch, Pierce, Fenner & Smith Inc., N.Y.C., 1970-77, Merrill Lynch & Co., Inc., 1973-77; mem. firm Rogers & Wells, N.Y.C., 1977—. Adj. prof. law Fordham U., 1973—; chmn. adv. panel to Law Revision Commn. on Recodification N.Y. State Ins. Law, 1976—. Trustee St. Lawrence U., Canton, N.Y.; trustee, vice chmn. bd. Westminster Choir Coll., Princeton, N.J. Mem. Am., N.Y. State bar assns., Assn. Bar City N.Y., Am. Fgn. Lawyers Assn. Am. Judicature Soc. Editorial bd. Columbia Law Rev., 1944-45. Home: 32 Fair St Cooperstown NY 13326 Office: 200 Park Ave New York NY 10017

SPROWL, CHARLES RIGGS, lawyer; b. Lansing, Mich., Aug. 22, 1910; s. Charles Orr and Hazel (Allen) S.; A.B., U. Mich., 1932, J.D., 1934; m. Virginia Lee Graham, Jan. 15, 1938; children—Charles R., Robert A., Susan G., Sandra D. Admitted to Ill. bar, 1935, pvt. practice, 1934—; partner Taylor, Miller, Magner, Sprowl & Hutchings, 1945—. Dir. Paul F. Beich Co., Busch & Schmitt, Inc., Simmons Engring. Corp., A.H. Ross & Sons Co., Petersen Aluminum Corp. Mem. Bd. Edn., New Trier Twp. High Sch., 1959-65, pres., 1962-65; mem. Glencoe Zoning Bd. of Appeals, 1965-76, chmn., 1966-76; mem. Glencoe Plan Commn., 1962-65. Bd. dirs. Glencoe Pub. Library, 1953-65, pres., 1955-56; trustee Highland Park Hosp., 1959-69; bd. dirs. Cradle Soc. Fellow Am. Coll. Trial Lawyers; mem. Chgo. (bd. mgrs. 1949-51), Ill., Am. bar assns., Juvenile Protective Assn. (dir. 1943-53), Northwestern U. Settlement (pres. 1963-70, dir.), Soc. Trial Lawyers, Delta Theta Phi, Alpha Chi Rho. Presbyn. Clubs: Law (pres. 1969-70), Legal (pres. 1953-54), Univ., Monroe, Skokie Country. Home: 558 Washington Ave Glencoe IL 60022 Office: 120 S LaSalle St Chicago IL 60603

SPRUCE, EVERETT FRANKLIN, painter; b. Faulkner County, Ark., Dec. 25, 1908; s. William Everett and Fannie (McCarty) S.; student Dallas Art Inst., 1925-29; pvt. study with Olin H. Travis, Thomas M. Stell; m. Alice Kramer, Feb. 18, 1934; children—Alice Spruce Swaim and Georgia Spruce Walker (twins), William Everett, Henry Arthur. Gallery asst. Dallas Mus. Fine Arts, 1931-34, registrar, 1935, asst. dir., 1935-40; instr. U. Tex., Austin, 1940-44, asst. prof. art, 1944-47, chmn. dept. art, 1948-50, prof. art, mem. grad. faculty, 1954-74, prof. emeritus, 1974—, dir. grad. studio program dept. art, 1965-73; one-man shows: Dallas Mus. Fine Arts, 1932, 58, Santa Barbara Mus. Art, 1945, McNay Art Inst., San Antonio, 1958; exhibited Hudson D. Walker Gallery, N.Y.C., 1938-39, Levitt Gallery, N.Y.C., 1946, 48, 50, 51, ann. exhbn. painting and sculpture Calif. Palace Legion of Honor, 1940, Mus. Fine Arts, Houston, Carnegie Inst., NAD, Corcoran Gallery, 1946, retrospective exhbn. Ford Found., 1959, ann. exhbn. Am. painting, Whitney Mus. Am. Art, 1959 U. Tex. Art Mus., Austin, 1979; represented in permanent collections: Dallas Mus. Fine Arts, Whitney Mus. Modern Art, Met. Mus., Mus. Modern Art, N.Y., Mus. Modern Art, Rio de Janeiro, Phila. Acad. Fine Arts, Nelson Gallery, Kansas City, Mo., Colorado Springs Fine Arts Center. Recipient 1st prize Midwestern Artists Exhbn., Kansas City, 1937; W. W. Crocker prize Calif. Palace Legion of Honor, 1940, 1st prize Tex. Gen. Exhbn. Paintings and Sculpture, 1946, prize Pepsi-Cola competition NAD, 1946, ann. exhbn. Am. Painting and Sculpture, Carnegie Inst., Pitts., 1946, La Tausca art exhbn. Riverside Mus., N.Y.C., 1946, 1st prize 17th exhbn. Tex. painting and sculpture, 1955, biennial exhbn. Contemporary Am. Painting, Corcoran Gallery Art, 1949, Venice Biennial, 1950, Am. Paintings, Brussels, 1948, Bordighera, Italy, 1954, others; Ford Found. grantee, 1958. Mem. AAUP, Tex. Fine Arts Assn. Paintings reproduced in Everett Spruce, A Portfolio of Paintings, vol. I; Everett Spruce (by John Palmer Leeper), 1959; Texas Gulf Coast, 1979. Home: 15 Peak Rd Austin TX 78746

SPRUGEL, GEORGE, JR., ecologist; b. Boston, Sept. 26, 1919; s. George and Frances Emily (Strong) S.; B.S., Iowa State U., 1946, M.S., 1947, Ph.D., 1950; m. Catharine Bertha Cornwell, Oct. 27, 1945; 1 son, Douglas George. Instr., then asst. prof. zoology and entomology Iowa State U., 1946-54; asst. head biology br. Office Naval Research, 1951-53; spl. asst. to asst. dir., div. biology and medicine NSF, 1953-54, program dir. environ. biology, 1954-64; chief scientist Nat. Park Service, 1964-66; chief Ill. Natural History Survey, 1966—. Cons. in field; mem. adv. com. environ. biology NSF, 1965; dir. program conservation of ecosystems U.S. Internat. Biol. Program, 1969-72; mem. study group on role lunar receiving lab. NASA, 1969-70, mem. life scis. com., 1972-78; mem. ecology adv. com. Bur. Reclamation, 1972-74; mem. Gov. of Ill. Sci. Adv. Com., 1967—, Ill. Environ. Quality Council, 1970-73; mem. environ. studies bd. com. to devel. protocol for toxic substances Nat. Acad. Scis.-Nat. Acad. Engring., 1972-73; mem. NRC, 1968-72. Served as officer USNR, 1940-45, 51-53. Fellow AAAS (council 1961-73, v.p., chmn. sect. biol. scis. 1971); mem. Am. Inst. Biol. Scis. (mem.-at-large gov. bd. 1969-72, exec. com. 1972-75, pres. 1974), Ecol. Soc. Am. (council 1961-78, v.p. 1968), Am. Soc. Zoologists (sec. 1970-72, chmn. div. ecology 1971), Sci. Research Soc. Am., Sigma Xi. Home: 2710 S 1st St Champaign IL 61820 Office: 179 Natural Resources Bldg Urbana IL 61801

SPRUNG, ARNOLD, lawyer; b. N.Y.C., Apr. 18, 1926; s. David L. and Anna (Storch) S.; A.B., Dartmouth Coll., 1947; J.D., Columbia U., 1950; m. Audrey Caire; children—Louise, John, Thomas, Doran, D'Wayne. Admitted to N.Y. State bar, 1950, since practiced in N.Y.C.; atty. Sprung Felfe Horn Lynch & Kramer, and predecessor, 1950—, sr. partner, 1972—. Served to lt. (j.g.) USNR, 1943-46. Home: 339 Cedar Dr W Briarcliff NY 10510 Office: 600 3d Ave New York City NY 10016

SPRUNG, DONALD WHITFIELD LOYAL, physicist, univ. adminstr.; b. Kitchener, Ont., Can., June 6, 1934; s. Lyall McCauley and Doreen Bishop (Price) S.; B.A., U. Toronto, 1957; Ph.D., U. Birmingham (Eng.), 1961, D.Sc., 1977; m. Hannah Sueko Nagai, Dec. 12, 1958; children—Anne Elizabeth, Carol Hanako. Instr., Cornell U., 1961-62; mem. research staff Mass. Inst. Tech., 1964-65; asst. prof. physics McMaster U., Hamilton, Ont., 1962-66, asso. prof., 1966-71, prof., 1971—, dean Faculty of Sci., 1975—; C.D. Howe Meml. fellow Institut de Physique Nucleaire, Orsay, France, 1969-70. Mem. Canadian Assn. Physicists (Herzberg medal 1972), Am. Phys. Soc., Inst. Physics (London). Contbr. numerous articles to physics jours.; mem. editorial bd. Canadian Jour. Physics, 1975—. Home: 15 Little John Rd Dundas ON L9H 4G5 Canada Office: Faculty of Sci GSB-114 McMaster Univ Hamilton ON L8S 4K1 Canada

SPUHLER, JAMES NORMAN, anthropologist, educator; b. Tucumcari, N.Mex., Mar. 1, 1917; s. Frank Jacob and Hettie (Aylesworth) S.; B.A., U. N.Mex., 1940; M.A. (Cutting scholar), Harvard U., 1942, Ph.D. (Nat. scholar), 1946; M.A., Oxford U., 1962; m. Helen Margaret McKaig, Sept. 14, 1946; 1 son, Derek Drake. Instr. anthropology and zoology Ohio State U., 1946-47, asst. prof., 1947-50; faculty U. Mich., 1950-68, prof. anthropology and human genetics, 1960-68, chmn. dept. anthropology, 1959- 67; Leslie Spier prof. anthropology U. N.Mex., 1967—; research fellow Oxford U., 1962-63; vis. prof. anthropology and zoology U. Tex., 1965-66. Cons. NIH, 1955-60, NSF, 1965-67; dir. child health survey Atomic Bomb Casualty Commn., 1959. Served to lt. (s.g.) USNR, 1942-46, 51-52. Fellow Center Advanced Study in Behavioral Scis., 1955-56, 71-72. Fellow Am. Anthrop. Assn. (exec. bd. 1958-60); mem. Genetics Soc. Am., Biometric Soc. (adv. bd. 1951-54), Am. Assn. Phys. Anthropologists (exec. com. 1954-55, sec.-treas. 1955-58, pres. 1975-77), Am. Soc. Human Genetics (dir. 1951- 53, 63-65) Am. Soc. Naturalists, Soc. Study Evolution, Sigma Xi. Author: Genetic Diversity and Human Behavior, 1968; editor and contbr.: Natural Selection in Man, 1958; Evolution of Man's Capacity for Culture, 1959; Yearbook of Physical Anthropology, 1952; (with others) Race Differences in Intelligence, 1975; editor Jour. Anthrop. Research, 1975—; asso. editor: Am. Anthropologist, 1954-55; Human Biology, 1953-74; Am. Jour. Human Genetics, 1955-58; Evolution, 1960-63; Am. Jour. Phys. Anthropology, 1969-73; Am. Naturalist, 1978—. Home: 8720 Rio Grande Blvd NW Albuquerque NM 87114

SPULBER, NICOLAS, economist; b. Brasov, Romania, Jan. 1, 1915; naturalized U.S. citizen; M.A., New Sch. Social Research, 1950, Ph.D. magna cum laude, 1952; m. Pauline, Aug. 5, 1950; 1 son, Daniel Francis. Research asso. Center Internat. Studies, Mass. Inst. Tech., 1952-54; mem. faculty Ind. U., Bloomington, 1954—, prof. econs., 1961—, acting chmn. Inst. E. European Studies, 1956-59, Distinguished prof. econs., 1974—; vis. prof. City Coll., City U. N.Y., 1963-64. Halle fellow, 1951-52; grantee Am. Philos. Soc., 1956, Ford Found., 1962-63; research fellow Ford Faculty Found., 1960-61; sr. fellow Internat. Devel. Research Center, Ind. U., 1969-71. Mem. Am. Econ. Assn., Royal Econ. Soc., AAAS. Author: The Economics of Communist Eastern Europe, 1957, reissued 1976; The Soviet Economy: Structure, Principles, Problems, 2d edit., 1969; Soviet Strategy for Economic Growth, 1964; The State and Economic Development, 1966; Socialist Management and Planning, 1971; Organizational Alternatives in Soviet-Type Economies, 1979; co-author: Quantitative Economic Policy and Planning, 1976; editor, co-editor 5 books; contb. numerous articles to profl. jours. in U.S. and fgn. countries. Address: Dept Econs Ind Univ Bloomington IN 47401

SPUNGIN, GARDNER MAWNEY, pub. co. exec.; b. Providence, R.I., July 2, 1935; s. Abraham and Goldie (Morrison) S.; B.S. in Psychology, Tufts U., 1957; m. Susan Jay King, Oct. 21, 1967; children—Jennifer, Meredith, Jesse. Salesman MacMillan Co., N.Y.C., 1959-61; textbook supr. Ronald Press Co., N.Y.C., 1961-65; editor social scis. Van Nostrand Co., Princeton, N.J., 1965-69; John Wiley & Sons, Inc., N.Y.C., 1969-74; pres., publisher Gardner Press Inc., N.Y.C., 1974—; adj. asso. prof. English, Bklyn. Coll. Mem. Am. Assn. Publishers. Home: 45 E 85th St New York NY 10028 Office: 19 Union Square New York NY 10003

SPURLOCK, ESTELLE ELIZABETH, dancer; b. Jersey City, May 9, 1949; d. Charles Wilbur and Thelma Viola (Lay) S.; B.F.A., Boston Conservatory of Music, 1971. Mem. Alvin Ailey Dance Theatre, 1971—, soloist, 1972—, soloist Ailey 2nd Company, 1973—, choreographer duet Two in One for Ailey Repertory Theatre Co., for Repertory Theatre Co.; choreographer Playing Jealousy? for Dance Kaleidoscope, 1978; toured U.S., Europe, S. Am., Asia for State Dept.; lectr. master classes throughout U.S. Roman Catholic. Home: 236 E 8th Ave Roselle NJ 07203 Office: 1515 Broadway New York NY 10036

SPURLOCK, JEANNE, psychiatrist; b. Sandusky, Ohio, 1921; M.D., Howard U., 1947; grad. Chgo. Inst. Psychoanalysis. Intern, Provident Hosp., 1947-48; resident in psychiatry Cook County Psychopathic Hosp., 1948-50; fellow Inst. Juvenile Research, 1950-51; dir. child psychiatry clinic Michael Reese Hosp., 1960-68 (all Chgo.); clin. asst. prof. psychiatry U. Ill., 1953-59; chmn. dept. psychiatry Meharry Med. Coll., Nashville, 1968-73; vis. scientist NIMH, 1973-74; dep. med. dir. Am. Psychiat. Assn., Washington, 1974—. Diplomate in psychiatry and child psychiatry Am. Bd. Psychiatry and Neurology. Mem. Nat. Med. Assn., Am. Psychiat. Assn. Address: 1700 18th St NW Washington DC 20009

SPURR, GREGORY WATERMAN, JR., banker; b. Rye, N.Y., Dec. 10, 1923; s. Gregory Waterman and Jean Armour (Dunlop) S.; B.A., Yale U., 1948; M.B.A., Dartmouth Coll., 1950; m. Cynthia J. Holmes, Dec. 12, 1953; children—Gregory W., Jeffrey H., Cynthia D., Pamela P. With Bank of N.Y., 1950—, asst. v.p., 1958-62, v.p., 1962-69, sr. v.p., 1969-76, vice chmn. credit com., exec. v.p., 1976—, sr. loan and loan policy officer, 1979—. Mem. Robert Morris Assos. Club: Short Hills Office: Bank of New York 48 Wall St New York NY 10015

SPURR, STEPHEN HOPKINS, educator; b. Washington, Feb. 14, 1918; s. Josiah Edward and Sophie Clara (Burchard) S.; B.S. with highest honors, U. Fla., 1938, D.Sc. (hon.), 1971; M.F. cum laude, Yale U., 1940, Ph.D. (Oberlaender Trust fellow), 1950; m. Patricia Chapman Orton, Aug. 18, 1945; children—Daniel Orton, Jean Burchard. Instr., asst. prof., acting dir. Harvard Forest, Harvard, 1940-50; asso. prof. U. Minn., 1950-52; prof. U. Mich., Ann Arbor, 1952-71, asst. to v.p. acad. affairs, dean Sch. Natural Resources, 1962-65, dean Horace H. Rackham Sch. Grad. Studies, 1964-71, v.p., 1969-71; prof. botany and pub. affairs U. Tex., Austin, 1971—, pres., 1971-74; George S. Long lectr. U. Wash., 1975; Albright lectr. U. Calif., 1966; mem. Pres.'s Adv. Panel Timber and the Environ., 1971-73; bd. dirs., v.p. Capital Broadcasting Co. Chmn., Grad. Rec. Exam. Bd., also chmn. Council Grad. Schs., 1969-71; mem. Commn. on Non Traditional Study, 1971; mem. Nat. Bd. Grad. Edn., 1971-75. Trustee, Inst. Internat. Edn., 1972-77, Carnegie Found. for Advancement of Teaching, Ednl. Testing Service, Carnegie Council for Policy Studies in Higher Edn., Nature Conservancy; mem. council Yale U., 1978—. Sci. faculty fellow NSF, 1957-58; Fulbright research scholar, New Zealand and Australia, 1960; vis. scholar Center for Advanced Studies Behavioral Scis., 1966-67; recipient Wilber Cross medal Yale U., 1978. Fellow Soc. Am. Foresters (mem. council, founding chmn. div. forest mgmt., v.p.); mem. New Zealand Inst. Foresters (hon.), Am. Forestry Assn. (dir. 1972-75), Ecol. Soc. Am., Conf. Biol. Editors (exec. com.), Lake States Forest Tree Improvement Com. (chmn.), Orgn. for Tropical Studies (pres. 1967-68), Mich. Acad. Sci., Arts and Letters (pres. 1968-69), Mich. Soc. Fellows (sr. fellow 1970—), Philos. Soc. Tex., Phi Beta Kappa, Sigma Xi, Phi Eta Sigma, Phi Kappa Phi. Unitarian. Author: Aerial Photographs in Foresty, 1948; Forest Inventory, 1952; Photogrammetry and Photo-Interpretation, 1960; Forest Ecology, 1962; Academic Degree Structures, 1970; American Forest Policy in Development, 1976. Founding editor Forest Sci., 1955-60. Inventor photogrammetric devices. Home: 4007 Sierra Dr Austin TX 78731

SPURRIER, WILLIAM ATWELL, clergyman, educator; b. Newton, Mass., June 19, 1916; s. William A. and Marian (Hunt) S.; B.A., Williams Coll., 1939; B.D., Union Theol. Sem., 1942; m. Helene Messer, June 13, 1942; children—Anthony W., Robert D. Instr. religion Amherst Coll., 1942-43; ordained to ministry Episcopal Ch., 1947; instr. religion Wesleyan U., Middletown, Conn., 1946-49, asst. prof., 1949-54, asso. prof., 1954-57, Hedding Found. prof. religion, 1957—, coll. pastor, 1957-68. Served as chaplain, 69th Inf. Div., AUS, 1944-46; ETO. Decorated Bronze Star. Mem. Ch. Soc. for Coll. Work, Biblical Theologians. Author: Power for Action, 1948; Guide to the Christian Faith, 1952; Guide to the Good Life, 1956. Chpts. in College Teaching and Values, 1953; Modern Canterbury Pilgrims, 1956; Ethics and Business, 1962; Natural Law and The Ethics of Love, 1974. Home: 330 High St Middletown CT 06457

SPURWAY, HAROLD R., retail store exec.; b. 1918; A.B., U. Mich., 1940; married. With Mich. Bell Telephone Co., 1940-41; with Carson Pirie Scott and Co., Chgo., 1945—, successively salesman, asst. dept. mgr., dept. mgr., mdse. mgr., asst. to gen. mdse. mgr., asst. to exec. v.p., asst. to chmn. bd., div. v.p., 1945-69, exec. v.p., dir. real estate, 1969-71, exec. v.p., 1971-72, pres., dir., 1972—; dir. First Fed. Savings and Loan Assn. Wilmette, Edens Plaza State Bank; pres., dir. Randhurst Corp.; trustee Baird & Warner Realty and Mgmt. Investors. Served with USNR, 1941-45. Address: Carson Pirie Scott 1 S State St Chicago IL 60603*

SPYERS-DURAN, PETER, educator, librarian; b. Budapest, Hungary, Jan. 26, 1932; s. Alfred and Maria (Almasi-Balogh) S-D; certificate U. Budapest, 1955; M.A. in L.S., U. Chgo., 1960; Ed.D., Nova U., 1975; m. Jane F. Cumber, Mar. 21, 1964; children—Kimberly, Hilary, Peter. Came to U.S., 1956, naturalized, 1964. Profl. asst. library adminstrn. div. ALA, Chgo., 1961-62; asso. dir. libraries, asso. prof. U. Wis., 1962-67; dir. libraries, prof. Western Mich. U., 1967-70; dir. libraries, prof. library sci. Fla. Atlantic U., 1970-76; dir. library Calif. State U., Long Beach, 1976—; vis. prof. State U. N.Y. at Geneseo, summers 1969-70; cons. publs., library-related enterprises; chmn. bd. internat. confs., 1970—. Mem. Kalamazoo County Library Bd., 1969-70. Bd. dirs. United Fund. Mem. ALA, Fla. Library Assn., Calif. Library Assn., Fla. Assn. Community Colls., Boca Raton C. of C., U. Chgo. Grad. Library Sch. Club (pres. 1973-75). Republican. Methodist. Author: Moving Library Materials, 1965; Public Libraries-A Comparative Survey of Basic Fringe Benefits, 1967. Editor Approval and Gathering Plans in Academic Libraries, 1969; Advances in Understanding Approval Plans in Academic Libraries, 1970; Economics of Approval Plans in Research Libraries, 1972; Management Problems in Serials Work, 1973; Prediction of Resource Needs, 1975; Requiem for the Card Catalog: Management Issues in Automated Cataloging, 1979. Home: 11221 Weatherby Rd Rossmoor CA 90720

SQUADRON, HOWARD MAURICE, lawyer; b. N.Y.C., Sept. 5, 1926; s. Jack H. and Sarah (Shereshevsky) S.; A.B., CCNY, 1946; LL.D., Columbia U., 1947; m. Lorraine Vlosky, Oct. 25, 1953 (dec. Oct. 1967); children—William, Richard, Diane; m. 2d, Anne Helen Strickland, June 6, 1972; son, Seth. Admitted to N.Y. bar, 1948, U.S. Dist. Ct. bar for So. and Eastern Dists. N.Y., 1950; Bigelow teaching fellow U. Chgo., 1947-48; asso. firm Stroock, Stroock & Lavan, 1948-50, firm Phillips, Nizer, Benjamin & Krim, 1952-54; counsel Am. Jewish Congress, 1950-52; sr. partner firm Squadron, Alter & Weinrib and predecessor, N.Y.C., 1954-64, Squadron & Plesent, N.Y.C., 1965-70, Squadron, Ellenoff, Plesent & Lehrer and predecessors, N.Y.C., 1970—; asso. prof. City U. N.Y. Active Am. Jewish Congress, 1950—, sr. v.p., 1976-78, pres., 1978—; mem. governing bd. World Jewish Congress; trustee Soc. Advancement Judaism; chmn. N.Y.C. chpt. UN Assn., 1966-68; chmn. Fifty-fifth St. Dance Theatre Found., N.Y.C.; chmn. exec. com. Found. for Joffrey Ballet, Inc., N.Y.C. Served to capt. Judge Adv. Gen. Corps, USAR, 1948-62. Recipient Disting. Service award CCNY, 1973. Mem. Assn. Bar City N.Y., Am. Bar Assn., N.Y. State Bar Assn. Democrat. Club: Century Assn. Editor Columbia Law Rev., 1946-47. Home: 4930 Goodridge Ave Bronx NY 10471

SQUIBB, ROBERT LESLIE, educator, research scientist; b. Portsmouth, Eng., Nov. 13, 1914; s. William Charles and Francis (Clarke) S.; A.S., Compton Coll., 1935; B.S., U. Calif., 1938; Ph.D., Iowa State U., 1948; m. Adeline B. Ege, June 21, 1937; 1 son, Robert E. Agrl. nutritionist U. Calif., 1938-41, asso. animal husbandry, 1941-43; charge animal program, El Salvador, 1943-44; head dept. animal husbandry Inter-Am. Inst. Agrl. Sci., Costa Rica, 1944-46; head dept. animal husbandry and nutrition Instituto Agropecuario Nacional, Guatemala, 1946-56; prof., chmn. dept. poultry sci. Rutgers U., New Brunswick, N.J., 1957-61, prof. nutrition and head diseases Environ. Stress Labs., 1961—, prof. nutrition dept. food sci., 1978—. Mem. Am. Inst. Nutrition, Am. Soc. Animal Prodn., Dairy Sci. Assn., Poultry Sci. Assn., Inst. Food Technologists, Aircraft Owners and Pilots Assn., A.A.A.S., Sigma Xi, Gamma Sigma Delta. Contbr. research articles to profl. jours. Office: 39 Easton Ave New Brunswick NJ 08903

SQUIER, JACK LESLIE, sculptor, educator; b. Dixon, Ill., Feb. 27, 1927; s. Leslie Lee and Ruth (Barnes) S.; student Oberlin Coll., 1945-46; B.S., Ind. U., 1950, M).F.A., Cornell U., 1952; m. Jane Bugg, June 9, 1950. Instr., Cornell U., 1952, asst. prof. art, 1958-61, asso. prof., 1961-65, prof., 1965—; designer Howatt Pottery Co., N.Y.C., 1953; account exec. Jamian Advt. Co., N.Y.C., 1954-58; asst. prof. U. Calif., Berkeley, 1960; one-man shows: Alan Gallery, N.Y.C., 1956, 59, 62, 64, White Mus., Cornell U., 1959, 68, Instituto de Arte Contemporaneo, Lima, Peru, 1963, Landau-Alan Gallery, N.Y.C., 1966, 69; group shows include: Mus. Modern Art, N.Y.C., 1957, Whitney Mus., N.Y.C., 1952, 54, 56, 58, 62, 67, 78, Hirshhorn Mus., Washington, 1978, Mus. Fine Arts, Boston, 1958, Chgo. Art Inst., 1960, Brussel's Worlds Fair, 1956, competition, Auschwitz, Poland, 1957, Albright-Knox Mus., Buffalo, 1968, Claude Bernard Gallery, Paris, 1957, Hanover Gallery, London, 1958; represented in permanent collections: Mus. Modern Art, N.Y.C., Whitney Mus. Art, Hirshhorn Mus., Instituto de Arte Contemporaneo, Everson Mus., Syracuse, N.Y., Stanford U. Mus., St. Lawrence U. Mus., SUNY at Potsdam, Ithaca Coll., Johnson Mus. at Cornell U.; mem. Internat. Assn. Art, UNESCO, 1964-72, mem. exec. com., 1966-69, v.p., 1969-72. Served with AC, USN, 1945-47. Work pub. in various books, mags., newspapers, slide collections, catalogs. Home: 221 Berkshire Rd Ithaca NY 14850 Office: Dept Art Cornell U Ithaca NY 14850

SQUIRE, ALEXANDER, bus. cons.; b. Dumfrieshire, Scotland, Sept. 29, 1917; s. Frederick John and Lillian (Ferguson) S.; B.S., M.I.T., 1939; m. Isabelle L. Kerr, June 23, 1945; children—Jonathan, David, Deborah, Stephen, Philip, Martha, Timothy, Rebecca, Elizabeth. Research metallurgist Handy and Harman, Fairfield, Conn., 1939-41; devel. metallurgist Sullivan Machinery Co., Michigan City, Ind., 1941-42; head power metallurgy br. Watertown Arsenal Lab. (Mass.), 1942-45; mgr. metall. devel. Westinghosue Electric Corp., Pitts., 1945-50; with Bettis Atomic Power Lab., Pitts., 1950-62; gen. mgr. Westinghouse plant apparatus div., 1962-69; dir. purchases and traffic Westinghouse Electric Corp., 1969-71; pres. Westinghouse Hanford Co., Richland, Wash., 1971-79; bus. cons., Richland, 1979—; dir. Old Nat. Bank of Wash. Mem. adv. com. Wash. State U. Coll. Engring.; bd. dirs. Wash. State Council Econ. Edn. Mem. Nat. Acad. Engring., Am. Nuclear Soc., Am. Soc. Metals, AIME, Am. Def. Preparedness Assn., U.S. Naval Inst. Address: 2138 Hamilton Ave Richland WA 99352

SQUIRE, CHRISTOPHER ANTHONY, diplomat; b. Germany, Dec. 14, 1923; s. Earl C. and Elizabeth M. (Crosse) S.; student Williams Coll., 1941-42; B.S., Yale U., 1948; m. Patricia Cody, Sept. 24, 1949; children—Christopher Anthony, Paul L. C., Marguerite H., Elizabeth M. Engr. trainee Gen. Electric Co., 1948-49; research analyst Library of Congress, 1949-51; commd. fgn. service officer Dept. State; vice consul U.S. consulate, Prague, Czechoslovakia, chief Czech Service, Voice of America; sta. in Budapest, Hungary, Brussels; Hungarian desk officer Dept. State, Washington; sci. attache, econ. counselor U.S. embassy, Moscow; sr. province adv. Pleiku, Vietnam; Sr. Seminar, Washington, also Sr. Officer's Personnel; country dir. U.S. embassy, Australia, N.Z., minister-counselor, dep. chief of mission, Canberra. Served to capt. AC, U.S. Army, 1942-45. Home: 12 Mugga Way Canberra ACT 2603 Australia Office: care Dept State Washington DC

SQUIRE, JAMES ROBERT, publisher; b. Oakland, Calif., Oct. 14, 1922; s. Harry Edwin and Ruby (Fulton) S.; B.A., Pomona Coll., 1947; D.Litt., 1966; M.A., U. Calif. at Berkeley, 1949, Ph.D., 1956; m. Barbara Lyman, Jan. 20, 1946; children—Kathryn Elizabeth, Kevin Richard, David Whitford. Tchr. secondary sch., Oakland, Calif., 1949-54; supr., lectr. English edn. U. Calif. at Berkeley, 1951-59; prof. English, U. Ill., Urbana, 1959-67; exec. sec. Nat. Council Tchrs. English, 1960-67; editor-in-chief, sr. v.p. Ginn & Co., Lexington, Mass., 1968-74, sr. v.p., pub., 1975—; treas. Nat. Conf. Research in English, 1978—. Bd. dirs. Am. Edn. Publ. Inst., 1968-70. Served with AUS, 1943-45. Recipient Creative Scholarship award Coll. Lang. Assn., 1961; Exec. Com. award Nat. Council Tchrs. English, 1967; Ky. col., 1966. Mem. Assn. Am. Pubs. (vice chmn. sch. div. 1971-73, chmn. 1974-76), Modern Lang. Assn., Nat. Council Tchrs. English, Internat. Reading Assn., Coll. Conf. on Composition and Communication, Phi Delta Kappa. Author: (with W. Loban, M. Ryan) Teaching Language and Literature, 1961, 69; (with R.K. Applebee) High School English Instruction Today, 1968; (with B.L. Squire) Greek Myths and Legends, 1967; Teaching English in the United Kingdom, 1969; A New Look at Progressive Education, 1972. Editor: Teaching of English, 76th Yearbook Nat. Soc. Study Edn., 1977. Home: Round Hill Rd Lincoln MA 01773 Office: Ginn & Co 191 Spring St Lexington MA 02173

SQUIRES, ARTHUR MORTON, educator; b. Neodesha, Kans., Mar. 21, 1916; s. Charles Loren and Vera (Moore) S.; A.B. with distinction in Chemistry, U. Mo., 1938; Ph.D. in Phys. Chemistry, Cornell U., 1947. Asst. dir. process design The M.W. Kellogg Co., N.Y.C., 1942-46; asst. dir. process devel. Hydrocarbon Research Inc., N.Y.C., 1946-51, dir., 1951-59; pvt. practice consulting to chem. precess industries, N.Y.C., 1959-67; prof. chem. engring. City Coll. N.Y., 1967-74, chmn. chem. engring., 1971-74, distinguished prof., 1974-76; Frank C. Vilbrandt prof. Va. Polytechnic Inst. and State U., Blacksburg, 1976—, univ. distinguished prof., 1978—. Pres. The Cantata Singers, N.Y.C., 1948-51; pres N.Y. Pro Musica, N.Y.C., 1957-60. Mem. Nat. Acad. Engring., Am. Acad. Arts and Scis., Am. Inst. Chem. Engrs. (Inst. lectureship 1977), Am. Chem. Soc. (recipient Henry H. Storch award 1973), ASME, Am. Inst. Mining, Metall. and Petroleum Engrs., AAAS, Air. Pollution Control Assn., Am. Geographical Soc., Iron and Steel Inst., Inst. Energy. Editor: (with D.A. Berkowitz) Power Generation and Environmental Change, 1971. Contbr. articles in field to profl. jours. Home: 2710 Quincy Ct Blacksburg VA 24060 Office: Department of Chemical Engineering Virgina Polytechnic Institute and State University Blacksburg VA 24061

SQUIRES, DONALD FLEMING, educator; b. Glen Cove, N.Y., Dec. 19, 1927; s. Charles and Freda (Fleming) S.; A.B., Cornell U., 1950, Ph.D., 1955; M.A., U. Kans., 1952; m. Marian N. Steinberg. Asst. curator invertebrate paleontology Am. Mus. Natural History, 1955-59, asso. curator, 1959-61; asso. curator div. marine invertebrates Smithsonian Instn., Washington, 1961-62, curator-in-charge, 1962-64, chmn. dept. invertebrate zoology, 1965-66, dep. dir. Mus. Natural History, 1966-68, research asso., 1965—, asso. natural history information resources, 1968—; prof. biol. scis., dir. Marine Scis. Research Center, State U. N.Y. at Stony Brook, 1968-74. Program dir. N.Y. State Sea Grant Program, 1971-74, dir. N.Y. Sea Grant Inst., 1975—; adj. prof. policy scis. Grad. Sch. Pub. Adminstrn., State U. N.Y. at Albany. Vice chmn. Fire Island Nat. Seashore Adv. Council, 1970-72; chmn. Suffolk County Environ. Quality Council, 1971-72; mem. exec. com. Bahamas Nat. Trust, 1971-75. Served with AUS, 1944-45. Fulbright researh fellow, New Zealand, 1959; recipient Sec.'s Gold medal Smithsonian Instn., 1968, also Exceptional Service award. Mem. AAAS, Am. Inst. Biol. Scis., Am. Soc. Limnology and Oceanography, Soc. Systematic Zoology, Geol. Soc. New Zealand, Marine Tech. Soc., Sigma Xi. Contbr. articles to profl. jours. Office: SUNY 411 State St Albany NY 12246

SQUIRES, JAMES DUANE, judge, educator; b. Grand Forks, N.D., Nov. 9, 1904; s. Vernon Purinton and Ethel Claire (Wood) S.; A.B., U. N.D., 1925, LL.D., 1958; A.M., U. Minn., 1927; Ph.D., Harvard, 1933; m. Catherine Emily Tuttle, Sept. 5, 1928; children—Vernon Tuttle, James Wood. Tchr., Dickinson (N.D.) High Sch., 1925-26; grad. asst. U. Minn., 1926-27; prof. history State Tchrs. Coll., Mayville, N.D., 1927-31; faculty history Colby-Sawyer Coll., New London, N.H., chmn. dept. social studies, 1935-70, chmn. summer forum, 1942-47. Vis. lectr. several colls.; dist. judge Town of New London, 1959-70; hist. cons. Pres., New London Hosp.; active several community orgns. as USO, ARC; mem. regional adv. council Nat. Archives; mem. adv. com. N.H. Library Assn.; mem. N.H. Council for Humanities; pres. N.H. Council Chs. and Religious Edn., 1945-48, Boys Club New London; del. 2d Assembly, World Council of Chs., Evanston, Ill., 1954; pres. N.H. YMCA, 1944-45; pres. N.H. State Bapt. Conv., 1946-49; mem. Bd. Edn. and Publ. Am. Bapt. Conv., 1952-61, del. N.Am. conf. on Faith and Order, Oberlin, 1957. Mem. Citizens adv. com. U.S. Commn. on Govt. Security, 1957; chmn. N.H. Civil War Centennial Commn., 1958—, N.H. Revolutionary War Bicentennial Commn., 1970—; mem. Gov.'s Task Force on State Problems, 1970, Com. for a New Eng. Bibliography, Bicentennial Council 13 Original States. N.H. del.-at-large Republican Nat. Conv., 1952, 56, 64; trustee Cathedral of Pines; vice chmn. bd. dirs. Am. Revolution Bicentennial Adminstrn.; mem. N.H. Preservation Rev. Bd., 1978; chmn. 200th Anniversary Planning Bd. for New London. Recipient George Washington Honor medal, Freedoms Found., 1954; Granite State award U. N.H., 1970; 3d of a Century award New London Service Orgn., 1970; William M. Beall award, 1976; Charles H. Pettee medal U. N.H., 1976; ABC Disting. Service award, 1976; Robert Frost Contemporary Am. award for outstanding service to people of N.H., 1979. Mem. nat., state, local hist. socs., profl. socs., Am. Bapt. Hist. Soc. (pres. 1968-70). Baptist. Author numerous books 1935—, later publs. include: Mirror to America, 1952; Experiment in Cooperation, 1953; Community Witness, 1954; The Granite State: A History of New Hampshire, 1923-1955, 1956; and The Story of New Hampshire, N.Y., 1964; New Hampshire: A Students Guide to Localized History, 1966. Co-author: Western Civilization, rev. edit., 1945. Editor several books, brochures; editorial com. N.H. Hist. Soc. Home: 10 Burpee Ln New London NH 03257. *Of great help to me have been the concepts in a bit of verse I learned more than 50 years ago: "Somebody said it couldn't be done But he with a chuckle replied That maybe it couldn't, but he would be one Who wouldn't say so til he tried. So he buckled right in with a trace of a grin on his face. If he worried, he hid it. He started to sing as he tackled the thing That couldn't be done, and he did it."*

SQUIRES, JAMES RADCLIFFE, educator, critic, poet; b. Salt Lake City, May 23, 1917; s. Edward Frederic and Janet Melvina (McNeil) S.; B.A., U. Utah, 1940; A.M., U. Chgo., 1946; Ph.D., Harvard, 1952; m. Eileen Mulholland, Sept. 19, 1946 (dec. Sept. 1976). Instr., Dartmouth, 1946-48; Fulbright prof. U. Salonica (Greece), 1959-60; mem. faculty U. Mich., Ann Arbor, 1952—, prof. English, 1963—; editor Mich. Quar. Rev., 1971-77. Served with USNR, 1941-45. Author: Cornar, 1940; Where the Compass Spins, 1951; The Loyalties of Robinson Jeffers, 1956; The Major Themes of Robert Frost, 1963; Frederic Prokosch, 1964; Fingers of Hermes, 1965; The Light under Islands, 1967; Allen Tate, 1971; Waiting in the Bone, 1973. Editor: Allen Tate and His Work, 1972. Office: 7616 Haven Hall U Mich Ann Arbor MI 48109

SQUIRES, WILLIAM RANDOLPH, JR., banker; b. Dallas, Sept. 10, 1924; s. William Randolph and Mary Florence (Peterman) S.; B.S., So. Methodist U., 1946; m. Kathleen Walters, Sept. 19, 1975; children by previous marriage—William Randolph III, Roderick, Troy, Evin Ann. Marine ins. underwriter Providence Washington Ins. Co., 1946-50; mgmt. trainee Van Waters and Rogers, Portland, Oreg., 1950-51; with El Paso Nat. Bank, 1951—, sr. v.p. charge trust div., 1971—; pres. Continental Nat. Bank, El Paso. Chmn. El Paso Parks and Recreation Bd., 1960-63, El Paso Internat. Airport Bd., 1971—. Bd. dirs. El Paso YMCA; pres., dir. Southwestern Athletics. Served with USNR, 1943-45. Mem. Tex. Bankers Assn. (pres. trust div. 1970-71), Bank Marketing Assn. Episcopalian. Home: 705 Lakeway El Paso TX 79932 Office: Drawer 5050 El Paso TX 79953

SRB, ADRIAN MORRIS, educator; b. Howells, Nebr., Mar. 4, 1917; s. Jerome Valentine and Viola (Morris) Srb; A.B., U. Nebr., 1937, M.S., 1941, D.Sc., 1969; Ph.D., Stanford, 1946; m. Jozetta Helfrich, July 27, 1940; children—Rosalind (Mrs. Robert Westmoreland Mayberry), Katherine, Jerome. Mem. civilian staff OSRD, 1945-46; asst. prof. Stanford, 1946-47; asso. prof. Cornell U., 1947-51, prof. biology, 1951—, Jacob Gould Schurman prof., 1976—. Mem. genetics study sect. NIH, 1965-69; mem. genetics tng. com. Nat. Inst. Gen. Med. Scis., 1969—; mem. agrl. bd. NRC, 1972—; mem. ednl. adv. bd. John Simon Guggenheim Meml. Found., 1975—; trustee Cornell U., 1975—. Fulbright Research scholar U. Paris, 1953-54; NSF sr. postdoctoral research fellow, 1960-61, U. Edinburgh (Scotland), 1967-68; Guggenheim fellow, 1953-54. Recipient Prof. of Merit award Cornell U., 1967. Fellow Bot. Soc. Edinburgh (hon. fgn.), Am. Acad. Arts and Scis., AAAS, N.Y. Acad. Scis.; mem. Genetics Soc. Am., Nat. Acad. Scis., Bot. Soc. Am., Am. Soc. Naturalists, Chilean Genetics Soc. (hon.), Phi Beta Kappa, Sigma Xi, Gamma Sigma Delta. Author: (with R.D. Owen) General Genetics, 1952, rev. (with R.D. Owen, R.S. Edgar), 1965; Pathways to the Understanding of Genetics, 1953; (with B. Wallace) Adaptation, 1961; (with Owen, Edgar) Facets of Genetics, 1969. Editor: Genes, Enzymes, and Population, 1973. Contbr. numerous research articles to profl. jours. Home: 411 Cayuga Heights Rd Ithaca NY 14850

SREEBNY, LEO M., dentist, educator; b. N.Y.C., Jan. 8, 1922; s. Morris and Lillie (Bogdanoff) S.; B.S., U. Ill., 1942, D.D.S., 1945, M.S., 1950, Ph.D., 1954; m. Mathilda H. Sternfeld, Mar. 9, 1945; children—Oren, Daniel. With dept. periodontics U. Ill., 1948-57, asso. prof., 1956-57; asso. prof., chmn. dept. oral biology U. Wash., Seattle, 1957-60, prof., 1960—, dir. Center for Research Oral Biology, 1967-75; dean Sch. Dental Medicine, SUNY, Stony Brook, 1975-79, prof. dept. oral biology, 1979—; cons. VA Hosp., Seattle, 1960—. Mem. governing bd. Jewish Fedn. and Council Greater Seattle, 1972-74. Served with AUS, 1942-45, USNR, 1946-48. Recipient Internat. Assn. for Dental Research Sci. award, 1969. Mem. Fedn. Dentaire Internat. (chmn. sci. assembly com. 1973—), Internat. Assn. Dental Research, A.A.A.S., N.Y. Acad. Sci., Soc. Exptl. Pathology, Am. Dental Assn. Author (with Julia Meyer): Secretory Mechanisms in Salivary Glands, 1963. Contbr. numerous articles to sci., biol. jours. Home: 35 Gnarled Hollow Rd East Setauket NY 11733 Office: Sch Dental Medicine State U NY Stony Brook NY 11794

SRERE, BENSON M., editor; b. Rock Island, Ill, Aug. 13, 1928; s. Jacob H. and Margaret (Weinstein) S.; B.A. magna cum laude, U. So. Calif., 1949; m. Betty Ann Cerruti, June 20, 1957; children—David Benson, Anne Michele, Peter John. Newsman, U.P., Los Angeles, 1948-56; asso. editor Good Housekeeping mag., N.Y.C., 1956-59, sr. editor, 1959-67, asst. mng. editor, dir. spl. publs. div., 1967-68, mng. editor, 1968-72, exec. editor, v.p., 1972-75, v.p., editorial dir., 1975-76; v.p., gen. mgr. King Features Syndicate, 1976—; v.p. Hearst Metrotone News, 1976—. Trustee Optometric Center of N.Y. Found., 1978-79. Served with U.S. Army, 1950-52. Mem. Am. Soc. Mag. Editors, Phi Beta Kappa, Phi Kappa Phi, Sigma Delta Chi, Phi Eta Sigma. Club: Overseas Press. Home: 44 Witherbee Ave Pelham Manor NY 10803 Office: 235 E 45th St New York NY 10017

SRERE, PAUL ARNOLD, biochemist, educator; b. Davenport, Iowa, Sept. 1, 1925; s. Jacob and Margaret (Weinstein) S.; B.S., UCLA, 1947; Ph.D., U. Calif., Berkeley, 1951; m. Marjorie Laslo, Sept. 1, 1953; children—Margot, Elizabeth Ann, Mark, Hilary. Biochemist, Mass. Gen. Hosp., Boston, 1951-53; asst. prof. biochemistry U. Mich., Ann Arbor, 1956-61, asso. prof., 1961-63; research biochemist Lawrence Radiation Lab., U. Calif., Livermore, 1963-66; prof. biochemistry U. Tex. Health Sci. Center, Dallas, 1966—; chief pre-clin. sci. unit VA Hosp., Dallas, 1966; mem. admissions com. U. Tex. Health Sci. Center, 1969—, U. Tex. coordinator faculty seminar, 1971-72; VA liaison rep. to NIH biochemistry study sect., 1971—. Mem. Town Lake Project Com., 1971-72. Served with USNR, 1944-46. Recipient W.S. Middleton award, 1975; Jane Coffin Childs Fund Med. Research fellow, 1953-54, USPHS fellow, 1954-56; VA research grantee, 1972-73. Mem. Am. Heart Assn. (research com. 1971—), Internat. Union Biochemists (commn. biochem. nomenclature 1971—), Fedn. Am. Socs. for Exptl. Biology, Am. Soc. for Cell Biology, AAUP, Am. Chem. Soc. Editorial bd. Jour. Biol. Chemistry, 1973-79, Biochem. Medicine, 1969—. Contbr. articles on biochemistry to profl. jours. Home: 3600 Lindenwood Dallas TX 75205 Office: 4500 S Lancaster Dallas TX 75216

SRIVASTAVA, JAYA NIDHI, educator; b. Lucknow, India, June 20, 1933; d. Mahabir Prasad and Madhuri (Devi); came to U.S., 1959, naturalized, 1966; M.Math. Stats., U. Lucknow, 1954; statistician's diploma Indian Statis. Inst., Calcutta, 1958; Ph.D., U. N.C., 1961. Agrl. statistician, India, 1954-59; research asso. U. N.C., 1961-63; asso. prof. U. Nebr., 1963-66; prof. math. stats. Colo. State U., Ft. Collins, 1966—, chmn. Disting. Vis. Lectrs. Program in Stats., U.S. and Can., 1973-75; vis. prof. many instns. Fellow Am. Statis. Assn., Inst. Math. Stats.; mem. Indian Soc. Agrl. (pres. 1977, Excellence in Research prize 1960), Internat., Indian statis. insts., Biometric Soc., Bernoulli Soc., Am. Platform Assn., N.Y. Acad. Scis. Author: (with S.N. Roy and R. Gnanadesikan) Analysis and Design of Certain Quantitative Multiresponse Experiments, 1971; co-editor: Survey of

Combinatorial Theory, 1973; editor: Survey of Statistical Design and Linear Models, 1974; mem. editorial bd. Communications in Statistics, 1972, Jour. Multivariate Analysis, Jour. Combinatorics, Info. and Systems Sci., 1976—; chief editor Jour. Statis. Planning and Inference, 1976—; contbr. articles to profl. jours. Office: Dept Stats Colo State U Fort Collins CO 80523

SROGE, MAXWELL HAROLD, advt. co. exec.; b. N.Y.C., Oct. 9, 1927; s. Albert N. and Goldie (Feldman) S.; student Coll. City N.Y., 1946-48, N.Y. U. 1948, New Sch. for Social Research, 1948; m. June Elaine Brand, Apr. 14, 1954; children—Roberta, David, Marc. Dir. sales Bell & Howell Co., Chgo., 1950-60, dir. prodn. planning, 1961-62, pres. Robert Maxwell div., 1962-63; pres. Maxwell Sroge Co., Inc., Chgo., 1965—, pres. Telespand, Inc., Chgo., 1971—; chmn. JUF Communications Industry, 1974-75; pub. Non-Store Mktg. Report. Mem. New Ill. Com., 1965; speakers bur. Percy for Gov., 1964, Citizens for Percy, 1972; co-chmn. Percy for Pres. Exploratory Com., 1974. Mem. regional adv. bd. Nat. Jewish Hosp., 1974-75; mem. devel. com. WTTW-Channel 11, 1975-76; mem. devel. com. NCCJ. Served with USNR, World War II. Mem. Direct Mail Mktg. Assn. (founder, Gold Mail Box award 1978), Am., Ill. quarter horse assns., World Futures Soc. Home: 544 Greenwood Glencoe IL 60022 303 E Ohio St Chicago IL 60611. *To succeed man must stretch himself....his mind, his heart, his grasp. Our capabilities far exceed our accomplishments. Within each of us there is the potential for greatness if we will dig deep enough to find it. Those of us who have been blessed to have discovered success owe a special responsibility to the world around us to make it a better place for all men to live.*

SROKA, FRANCIS THEODORE, bearings distbg. co. exec.; b. Cleve., Feb. 5, 1915; s. Frank T. and Bessie (Podlewski) S.; B.B.A., Cleve. Coll. Western Res. U. (now Case Western Res. U.), 1948; m. Ruth G. Siegman, Aug. 5, 1943; children—Paul F., Mary B., Ruth Ann, Jane E. C.P.A. supr. Ernst & Ernst, C.P.A.'s, 1942, 46-58; comptroller Norwalk Truck Line, Inc. (Ohio), 1958-62, treas., 1962-66; treas. Bearings, Inc., Cleve., 1966—, v.p. finance, corp. and subsidiaries Dixie Bearings, Inc., Cleve., Bruening Bearings, Inc., 1972—, also dir. Served with AUS, 1942-46. C.P.A., Ohio. Mem. Am. Inst. C.P.A.'s, Ohio Soc. C.P.A.'s, Fin. Execs. Inst. Republican. Roman Catholic. Home: 21375 Hilliard Blvd Rocky River OH 44116 Office: 3600 Euclid Ave Cleveland OH 44115

SROLE, LEO, social scientist; b. Chgo., Oct. 8, 1908; s. William and Rebecca (Epstein) S.; B.S., Harvard, 1933; Ph.D., U. Chgo., 1940; m. Esther Hannah Alpiner, Dec. 27, 1941; children—Ira Herschel, Rebecca Yona. Lectr., N.Y. U., 1940-41; prof., chmn. dept. sociology Hobart Coll. (now Hobart and William Smith Colls.). Geneva, N.Y., 1941-42; welfare dir. UNRRA (now UNRWA), Landsberg, Germany displaced persons camp, 1945-46; with bur. applied social research Columbia, 1947-48; research dir. ADL B'nai B'rith, 1948-52; prof. sociology Cornell Med. Coll., 1952-59; research prof. Albert Einstein Med. Coll., N.Y.C., 1959-61; prof. sociology SUNY Downstate Med. Center, 1961-65; prof. social scis. dept. psychiatry Columbia Coll. Physicians and Surgeons, 1965-78; prof. emeritus Center for Geriatrics and Gerontology, Faculty Medicine, Columbia U., 1978—; chief psychiat. research in social scis. N.Y. State Psychiat. Inst., 1966-78; cons. WHO, 1979—. Served with USAAF as mil. psychologist Air Surgeon's Office, 1943-45. Hon. fellow Am. Psychiat. Assn.; mem. Internat., Am. sociol. assns., AAUP, Soc. for Study Social Problems, Gerontol. Soc., Sigma Xi. Author: (with W. Lloyd Warner) Social Systems of American Ethnic Groups, 1945; sr. author: Mental Health in the Metropolis: The Midtown Manhattan Study (designated Citation Classic), 1962, paperback edit., 1975, revised, enlarged edit., 1978; chpts. in symposium vols. Past asso. editor Am. Social Rev., Jour. Social Issues. Contbr. articles to sci., gen. periodicals. Home: 151-39 25th Ave Whitestone NY 11357 Office: 722 W 168th St New York NY 10032

STAAB, WALTER EDWARD, advt. agy. exec.; b. Jersey City, Apr. 12, 1933; s. Edward H. and Edna Margaret (Effler) S.; B.A., Rutgers U., 1955; M.B.A., Fairleigh Dickensen, 1958; m. Diane Dee Thomas, May 27, 1961; children—Pamela Ann, Kristin. Research dir. McCann Erickson, N.Y.C., 1957-61; media group head Kenyon & Eckhardt, N.Y.C., 1961-65; v.p., media dir. Ted Bates & Co., N.Y.C., 1965-68; pres. SFM Media Service Corp., N.Y.C., 1968—. Mem. Am. Assn. Advt. Agys. (bd. com. on consumer mags.), Internat. Radio and TV Soc., Phi Gamma Delta. Contbr. articles to trade publs. Home: 55 E 86th St New York NY 10028 Office: 1180 Ave of Americas New York NY 10028

STAAR, RICHARD FELIX, univ. adminstr.; b. Warsaw, Poland, Jan. 10, 1923 (parents Am. citizens); s. Alfred and Agnes (Gradalska) S.; B.A., Dickinson Coll., 1948; M.A. (Univ. fellow), Yale, 1949; Ph.D., U. Mich., 1954; m. Jadwiga Maria Ochota, Mar. 28, 1950; children—Monica, Christina. Research analyst U.S. Dept. State, Washington, 1951-54; prof. polit. sci. Ark. State Coll., Jonesboro, 1957-58; lectr. overseas program U. Md., Munich, Germany, 1958-59; asso. prof. to prof., chmn. dept. polit. sci. Emory U., 1959-69; asso. dir. Hoover Instn. on War, Revolution and Peace at Stanford, 1969—. Nimitz chair Naval War Coll., 1963-64; prof. polit. affairs Nat. War Coll., 1967-69; cons. Office Sec. Def., 1969-73; adj. prof. USMC Command and Staff Coll., 1971—; sr. advisor to Comdg. Officer Politico-Mil. Affairs USNR, Treasure Island, Calif., 1975—; disting. vis. prof. nat. security affairs Naval Postgrad. Sch., 1979—. Asst. dist. commr. Quapaw Area council Boy Scouts Am., 1954-57; Stanford rep. Am. Cancer Soc., 1973—. Active Profs. for Goldwater, 1964; mem. Reagan for Pres. Com., 1980. Bd. dirs. Friends of Dickinson Coll. Library, San Francisco Council, Navy League of U.S.; mem. nat. adv. council Monterey Inst. Internat. Studies, 1978—. Served to col. USMCR, 1960—. Decorated Gold Cross of Merit. Mem. Am. Polit. Sci. Assn., Marine Corps Res. Officers Assn., World Affairs Council No. Calif., Phi Beta Kappa, Kappa Sigma. Republican. Methodist. Author: Poland, 1944-62: The Sovietization of a Captive People, 1962, reprinted, 1975; Communist Regimes in Eastern Europe, 1967, rev. edit., 1971, 3d rev. edit., 1977; contbg. author and editor: Aspects of Modern Communism, 1968. Editor: Yearbook on International Communist Affairs, 1969—. Contbr. articles to profl. jours. Home: 38 Pearce Mitchell Pl Stanford CA 94305 Office: Hoover Instn Stanford CA 94305

STAAS, DUNSTAN JAMES, transp. equipment and engring. constrn. co. exec.; b. Chgo., May 18, 1926; s. Walter Christian and Grace Irene (James) S.; B.B.A., Northwestern U., 1949; m. Elsbeth Elfriede Zahn, Dec. 26, 1948; children—Kristine Staas Duffin, Karen Staas South, John August, Dunstan James, David Brian. Accountant, Price Waterhouse & Co., Chgo., also Peoria, Ill., 1949-61; comptroller Hiram Walker, Gooderham & Worts, Ltd., Walkerville, Ont., Can., 1961-68; asst. v.p. fin. and adminstrn. White Motor Corp., Cleve., 1968-70; controller Internat. Industries Inc., Beverly Hills, Calif., 1970-72; v.p., controller Pullman Inc., Chgo., 1972—. Served with USAAF, 1944-45, USAF, 1948. C.P.A., Ill. Mem. Am. Inst. C.P.A.'s, Fin. Execs. Inst. Unitarian. Club: Univ. (Chgo.). Home: 1902-B N Mohawk St Chicago IL 60614 Office: 200 S Michigan Chicago IL 60604

STAATS, ELMER BOYD, govt. ofcl.; b. Richfield, Kans., June 6, 1914; s. Wesley F. and Maude (Goodall) S.; A.B., McPherson (Kans.) Coll., 1935, LL.D., 1966; M.A., U. Kans., 1936; fellow Brookings Instn., 1938-39; Ph.D., U. Minn., 1939; D.Pub. Service, George Washington U., 1971; D.Adminstrn., U. S.D., 1973; LL.D., Duke, 1975; m. Margaret S. Rich, Sept. 14, 1940; children—David Rich, Deborah Rich, Catharine Rich Taubman. Research asst. Kans. Legislative Council, 1936; teaching asst. U. Minn., 1936-38; staff Pub. Adminstrn. Service, Chgo., 1937-38; staff mem. U.S. Bur. Budget, Exec. Office Pres., 1939-47, asst. to dir., 1947, asst. dir. charge legislative reference, 1947-49, exec. asst. dir., 1949-50, dep. dir., 1950-53, 58-66; comptroller gen. U.S., Washington, 1966—; research dir. Marshall Field & Co., Chgo., 1953; exec. dir. Operations Coordinating Bd., Nat. Security Council, 1953-58. Professorial lectr. pub. adminstrn. George Washington U., 1944-49; hon. faculty, mem. bd. advs. Indsl. Coll. Armed Forces, 1974-77. Mem. vis. com. John F. Kennedy Sch. Govt., Harvard, 1974—, Grad. Sch. Mgmt., U. Calif. at Los Angeles, 1976—, Com. on Pub. Policy Studies, U. Chgo., 1976—; trustee Nat. Inst. Pub. Affairs, 1969-77, Am. U., 1969—, McPherson Coll., 1969—; bd. govs. Internat. Orgn. of Supreme Audit Instns., 1969—. Recipient Rockefeller Pub. Service award, 1961, Alumni achievement award U. Minn., 1964, Distinguished Service citation U. Kans., 1966, Warner D. Stockberger Achievement award, 1973, Abraham O. Smoot Pub. Service award Brigham Young U., 1975; Person of Yr. award Washington chpt. Inst. Internal Auditors, 1975. Mem. Nat. Acad. Pub. Adminstrn., Assn. Govt. Accountants, Am. Acad. Polit. and Social Sci. (dir. 1966—), Am. Soc. Public Adminstrn. (pres. Washington 1948-49, nat. council 1958-65, pres. 1961-62), Phi Beta Kappa, Pi Sigma Alpha, Beta Gamma Sigma, Alpha Kappa Psi. Methodist. Clubs: Cosmos (Washington); Chevy Chase (Md.). Author: Personnel Standards in the Social Security Program, 1939. Contbr. to Am. Econ. Rev., Pub. Personnel Rev. Am. Polit. Sci. Rev. Home: 5011 Overlook Rd NW Washington DC 20016 Office: Gen Accounting Office 441 G St Washington DC 20548

STAATS, WILLIAM FERDINAND, educator; b. San Antonio, Feb. 9, 1938; s. Willie F.W. and Rena (Hehs) S.; B.S., Tex. Lutheran Coll., 1960; M.B.A., U. Tex., 1961, Ph.D., 1965; m. Esther Elizabeth Streng, July 17, 1960; children—Kristine Elizabeth, Stephen William. Lectr. finance U. Tex., 1961-63; asst. prof. commerce Rice U., 1963-66; with Fed. Res. Bank Phila., 1966-72, sec., 1970-72, v.p., 1971-72; La. Bankers Assn. prof. banking La. State U., Baton Rouge, 1972—; vice chmn. bd. New Brauntels Nat. Bank, 1975—. Kraushaar grad. fellow, 1961. Mem. devel. bd. Tex. Lutheran Coll., 1972-75; bd. dirs. La. Banking Sch. for Supervisory Tng. Recipient Distinguished Alumni award Tex. Luth. Coll., 1976. Mem. Am. Fin. Assn., Am. Econs. Assn., Phi Theta Kappa, Beta Gamma Sigma. Lutheran (trustee 1968-70). Author: The Secondary Market for State and Local Government Bonds, 1972; also articles. Home: 422 Castle Kirk Dr Baton Rouge LA 70808 Office: PO Box 18767 Baton Rouge LA 70803

STABA, EMIL JOHN, educator; b. N.Y.C., May 16, 1928; s. Frank and Marianna T. (Mack) P.; B.S. cum laude, St. John's U., 1952; M.S., Duquesne U., 1954; Ph.D., U. Conn., 1957; m. Joyce Elizabeth Ellert, June 19, 1954; children—Marianna, Joanna, Sarah Jane, John, Mark. Asst. prof. U. Nebr., 1957-60, prof., chmn. dept., 1968; prof., chmn. dept. pharmacognosy U. Minn., 1968—. Cons. drug plants, plant tissue culture U.S. Army Q.M. Corps, NASA, Korean govt., pharm. industry. Served with USNR, 1945-46; PTO. Sr. fgn. fellow NSF, Poland, 1969; Fulbright fellow, Germany, 1970; CSIR-NSF fellow, India, 1973; PCSIR-NSF fellow, Pakistan, 1978. Mem. Am. Soc. Pharmacognosy (pres. 1971-72), Am. Assn. Colls. Pharmacy (chmn. tchrs. sect. 1972-73, dir. 1976-77), Tissue Culture Assn. (pres. plant sect. 1972-74), Am. Pharm. Assn. and Acad. (chmn. pharmacognosy and nat. products 1977—, Soc. Econ. Botany, AAAS, Am. Inst. Biol. Scis. Home: 2840 Stinson Blvd NE Minneapolis MN 55418

STABENAU, JAMES RAYMOND, educator, research psychiatrist; b. Milw., May 24, 1930; s. Walter Frederick and Ruth Emile (Jung) S.; B.S. magna cum laude, Marquette U., 1952, M.D. cum laude, 1955; grad. Washington Psychoanalytic Inst.; m. Joan Clasen Straw, Aug. 29, 1953 (div. Apr. 1976); children—Victoria Ruth, Erik Fowler. Intern, Johns Hopkins Hosp., 1955-56; clin. asso. lab. chem. pharmacology Nat. Cancer Inst., NIH, 1956-58; asst., asso. and chief resident psychiatry U. Rochester Sch. Medicine and Dentistry, Strong Meml. Hosp., 1958-61; research psychiatrist sect. twin and sibling studies adult psychiatry br., clin. investigations NIMH, NIH, 1961-69; research cons. Washington Sch. Psychiatry, 1964-69; prof., chmn. dept. psychiatry U. Conn., Hartford, 1969-73, dir. research, 1973—. Recipient Eben J. Carey Anatomy award Marquette U. Sch. Medicine, 1952, Lakeside prize, 1955, Lt. William Milman award, 1955. Diplomate Am. Bd. Neurology and Psychiatry. Fellow Am. Psychiat. Assn.; mem. Conn. Psychiat. Soc., Washington Artists, Alpha Omega Alpha (v.p. Marquette U. chpt. 1955), Epsilon Phi Chi. Contbr. articles to med. jours. Home: 660 Prospect Ave West Hartford CT 06105 Office: Dept Psychiatry Conn Sch Medicine Farmington CT 06032

STABILE, BENEDICT LOUIS, coast guard officer; b. Bklyn., Dec. 13, 1927; s. Domenic and Vita (Grillo) S.; B.S., U.S. Coast Guard Acad., 1950; Naval Engr's. Degree, M.I.T., 1956; m. Barbara Adele Thompson, June 10, 1951; children—Janet T., Bennett R., Gale V., Roderick T. Commd. ensign U.S. Coast Guard, 1950, advanced through grades to rear adm., 1977; served on Bd. Coast Guard cutters, 1953-56; served at Coast Guard Yard, Curtis Bay, Md., 1956-57; served on bd. Coast Guard Cutter Eastwind, polar icebreaker, out of Boston, 1957-59; mem. engring. staff 8th Coast Guard Dist., New Orleans, 1959-63; insp. Todd Shipyard, Houston, 1963-64; exec. officer Coast Guard Cutter Reliance, Corpus Christi, Tex., 1964-65, comdg. officer, 1965; chief Naval Engring. Br., 5th Coast Guard Dist., Portsmouth, Va., 1965-68; sr. staff asst. to chief Office Engring., Coast Guard Hdqrs., Washington, 1969-70, chief ocean engring. div., 1970-73; chief Office Engring., 1977-79; comdr. Coast Guard Cutter Mellon, Honolulu, 1973-75; comdg. officer Coast Guard Yard, Curtis Bay, Md., 1975-77; dist. comdr. 7th Coast Guard Dist., Miami, Fla., 1979—; mem. Coast Guard Marine Safety Council. Decorated Meritorious Service medal with 2 gold stars, Coast Guard Commendation medal (U.S.); Knight Order of Merit (Italy). Mem. Soc. Naval Architects and Marine Engrs., Am. Soc. Naval Engrs. (council), Soc. Am. Mil. Engrs. (dir.), Marine Tech. Soc. Contbr. articles to Soc. Am. Mil. Engrs. Jour. Office: 7th Coast Guard Dist Fed Bldg 51 SW 1st Ave Miami FL 33130

STABLER, DONALD BILLMAN, business exec.; b. Williamsport, Pa., Dec. 23, 1908; s. George William and Etta Mae (Billman) S.; B.S., Lehigh U., 1930, M.S., 1932, LL.D., 1974; m. Dorothy Louise Witwer, Aug. 10, 1952; 1 dau., Beverly Anne. Owner, Donald B. Stabler, Contractor, Harrisburg, Pa., 1940-55; pres., chmn. bd. Protection Services Inc., Harrisburg, 1955—; chmn. bd. Stabler Constrn. Co., Harrisburg, 1955—; pres., chmn. bd. Stabler Cos. Inc.; chmn. bd. State Aggregates Inc., DBS Transit Co., Harrisburg; chmn. bd. Eastern Industries, Inc., Wescosville, Pa.; dir. Dauphin Deposit Bank & Trust Co., Millers Mut. Ins. Co., Harrisburg. Dir., pres. Road Info. Program, Washington, 1970-74, chmn. bd., 1975-78, chmn. emeritus, 1979—; bd. dirs. Harrisburg Polyclinic Med. Center, Miami Heart Inst., Miami Opera Assn.; trustee Lehigh U. Recipient Silver Hard hat award Constrn. Writers Assn., 1973, Humanitarian award Lions, 1973, Nat. Automobile Dealers award, 1978; decorated Knight comdr. Order St. John of Jerusalem, Knights of Malta. Mem. Am. Rd. and Transp. Builders Assn. (dir., recipient award 1974), Assn. Pa. Constructors (dir., adv. bd., pres. 1949-50), U.S., Pa., Harrisburg (adm. 1960) chambers commerce, Am. Soc. Hwy. Engrs. (Industry Man of Year 1975), Harrisburg Builders Exchange, Nat., Pa. socs. profl. engrs., Com. of 100 Miami Beach, Pa. Soc. N.Y., Lehigh U. Alumni Assn. (pres. 1965-66, L-in-Life award 1972), Navy League Chi Epsilon, Pi Delta Epsilon. Presbyterian. Clubs: Masons, Shriners, Jesters, Elks, Rotary, Tall Cedars, Circus Saints and Sinners; Surf (pres. 1974-76, chmn. bd. govs. 1976-78), Bal Harbour, Beach Colony, Coral Reef Yacht, Indian Creek Country (Miami); Tuesday, Harrisburg Country (Harrisburg); Union League (Phila.); Saucon Valley Country (Bethlehem, Pa.); Le Mirador County (Switzerland). Home: Stray Winds Farm 4001 McIntosh Rd Harrisburg PA 17112 also 236 Bal Bay Dr Bal Harbour FL 33154 Office: 635 Lucknow Rd Harrisburg PA 17110

STABLER, KENNETH MICHAEL, football player; b. Foley, Ala., Dec. 25, 1945; s. Lee Roy and Myrtle Margaret (Osborne) S.; student U. Ala., 1964-68; m. Deborah Ann Fitzsimmons, June 20, 1973 (div.); 1 dau., Kendra Clarke. Profl. football player Oakland (Calif.) Raiders, 1968—; pres. Ken Stabler Sporting Goods, Inc., Selma, Ala. Named NFL Player of Yr., 1974, Oakland Raider Player of Yr., 1973, 74, 77. Office: 7811 Oakport St Oakland CA 94621*

STABLER, LEWIS VASTINE, JR., lawyer; b. Greenville, Ala., Nov. 5, 1936; s. Lewis Vastine and Dorothy Daisy Stabler; B.A., Vanderbilt U., 1958; J.D. with distinction, U. Mich., 1961; m. Monteray Scott, Sept. 5, 1958; children—Dorothy Monteray, Andrew Vastine, Monteray Scott, Margaret Langston. Admitted to Ala. bar, 1961; asso. firm Cabaniss & Johnston, Birmingham, Ala., 1961-67; asso. prof. law U. Ala., 1967-70; partner firm Cabaniss, Johnston, Gardner, Dumas & O'Neal and predecessor firms, Birmingham, 1970—. Mem. Am. Law Inst., Am. Bar Assn., Ala. Bar Assn., Birmingham Bar Assn., Am. Judicature Soc., Am. Assn. Railroad Trial Counsel, Order of Coif. Methodist. Clubs: Country of Birmingham, Rotary. Bd. editors: Mich. Law Rev., 1960-61. Home: 3538 Victoria Rd Birmingham AL 35223 Office: 1900 First National Southern Natural Bldg Birmingham AL 35203

STACEY, CHARLES PERRY, historian, educator; b. Toronto, Ont., Can., July 30, 1906; s. Charles Edward and Pearl (Perry) S.; B.A., U. Toronto, 1927; B.A., M.A., Corpus Christi Coll., Oxford (Eng.) U., 1929; A.M., Princeton, 1931, Ph.D., 1933; LL.D., Mount Allison U., 1959, York U., 1973; D.Litt., U. N.B., 1967, Carleton U., 1974, U. Western Ont., 1977; D.Mil. Sci., Royal Roads Mil. Coll., 1978; m. Doris Newton Shiell, Aug. 26, 1939 (dec. 1969). Instr., then asst. prof. history Princeton, 1934-40; commd. maj. Canadian Army, 1940, advanced through grades to col., 1944; hist. officer Canadian Mil. Hdqrs., London, Eng., 1940-45; dir. hist. sect. Canadian Army, 1945-59, ret., 1959; faculty dept. history U. Toronto, 1959—, univ. prof., 1973—, sr. fellow Massey Coll., 1973. Pres. Can. Writers' Found., 1958-59. Decorated officer Order of Can., officer Order Brit. Empire, Canadian Forces Decoration; recipient Gov. Gen. Can. award, 1948. Mem. Royal Soc. Can. (Tyrrell medal, hon. sec. 1957-59, pres. sect. II 1968-69), Can. Hist. Assn. (pres. 1952-53). Club: Royal Canadian Mil. Inst. (Toronto). Author: Canada and the British Army, 1846-1871, 1936; The Military Problems of Canada, 1940; The Canadian Army 1939-1945, An Official Historical Summary, 1948; Six Years of War, 1955; Records of the Nile Voyageurs, 1959; Quebec, 1759: The Siege and the Battle, 1959; The Victory Campaign, 1960; Arms, Men and Governments, 1970; The Arts of War and Peace, 1914-1945, Vol. 5 of Historical Documents of Canada, 1972; A Very Double Life: The Private World of Mackenzie King, 1976; Mackenzie King and the Atlantic Triangle, 1976; Canada and the Age of Conflict: A History of Canadian External Policies, Vol. I, 1977. Home: 89 Tranmer Ave Toronto ON M5P 1E3 Canada Office: Dept History U Toronto Toronto ON M5S 1A1 Canada

STACEY, WESTON MONROE, JR., nuclear engr.; b. Birmingham, Ala., July 23, 1937; s. Weston Monroe and Dorothy (Toole) S.; B.S. in Physics, Ga. Inst. Tech., 1959, M.S. in Nuclear Sci., 1962; Ph.D. in Nuclear Enging., Mass. Inst. Tech., 1966; m. Helen Culpepper, Sept. 6, 1959; children—Helen, Weston. Nuclear engr. Knolls Atomic Power Labs., Gen. Electric Co., Schenectady, 1962-64, 66-69; head reactor theory Argonne (Ill.) Nat. Lab., 1969-72, asso. dir. applied physics, 1972-77, dir. fusion power program, 1973-77; Callaway prof. nuclear engring. Ga. Inst. Tech., Atlanta, 1977—; sr. U.S. rep. to IAEA Workshop To Define Fusion Reactor INTOR, 1979. Served with USMCR, 1959-61. Fellow Am. Nuclear Soc. (dir. 1974-77, chmn. math. and computing div. 1973-74; Reactor Physics Tech. Publn. award 1971-72); mem. Am. Phys. Soc. (tech. program chmn. 1979), AAAS. Author 3 books, also numerous tech. papers on nuclear fission and fusion reactor theory and design. Home: 2016 Castleway Ln Atlanta GA 30345 Office: Ga Inst Tech Atlanta GA 30030

STACK, EDWARD J., congressman; b. Bayonne, N.J., Apr. 29, 1910; s. William J. and Ann (Fitzmaurice) S.; B.A., Lehigh U., 1931; J.D., U. Pa., 1934; M.A., Columbia U., 1938; m. Jean Pearce, 1944; children—Kathleen, William, John. Instr. econs. Hunter Coll., 1937-47; admitted to N.Y. bar, 1934; practice law, N.Y.C., 1934-56; city commr., mayor, Pompano Beach, Fla., 1965-69; sheriff Broward County (Fla.), 1968-78; mem. 96th Congress from 12th Fla. Dist.; dir., chmn. trust com. Landmark 1st Nat. Bank. Founder, pres. Broward County Comprehensive Drug Rehab. Council; mem. Democratic Nat. Fin. Council, 1976-78; pres. Broward County Community Mental Health Bd., 1972-78, Boys' Clubs Broward County, 1965—; mem. Gov.'s Commn. on Criminal Justice. Served with USCG, 1942-46. Recipient Great Am. Traditions award Internat. B'nai B'rith, 1978. Mem. Fla. Devel. Commn., Fla. Council Crime and Delinquency, Fla. Parole Bd. Selection Com., Broward County Assn. Chiefs Police (past pres.), Am. Legion. Democrat. Roman Catholic. Club: Kiwanis. Office: 1440 Longworth House Office Bldg Washington DC 20515

STACK, J. WILLIAM, JR., mgmt. cons.; b. Lansing, Mich., July 13, 1918; s. Joseph William and Helen (Dodge) S.; B.A., Yale, 1940; m. Wolcott Rorick, Sept. 25, 1948; children—Christopher D., Nathan S., Joseph W., David R., Peter S. With Gen. Motors Corp, 1945-57, dir. mktg. AC Electronics div., 1955-57; v.p. Kurth Malting Co., Milw., 1957-59; gen. sales mgr. Massey Ferguson, Inc., Toronto, Can., 1960-62; pres., founder Stancor Ltd., Toronto, 1963-68; pres. William Stack Assos. Inc., N.Y.C., 1968—. Mem. Navy and Marine Corps Acquisition Rev. Com., 1974-75. Served to lt. comdr. USNR, 1940-45. Republican. Episcopalian. Clubs: Yale, Links, Sky, Blind Brook, Madison Sq. Garden, New Canaan Country, Milwaukee. Home: 1082 West Rd New Canaan CT 06840 Office: 230 Park Ave New York NY 10017

STACK, JAMES KEANE, educator, orthopedic surgeon; b. Duluth, Minn., Nov. 10, 1904; s. James Keane and Mary C. (Larkin) S.; A.B., U. Notre Dame, 1926; M.D., Northwestern U., 1931; m. Mary Solon, Sept. 24, 1932; children—John and James (twins), Christopher. Intern, St. Vicent's Hosp., N.Y.C., 1931-32; resident Bellevue Hosp., N.Y.C., 1932-33; practice orthopedic surgery, Chgo., 1933—; clin. asst. surgery Med. Sch. Northwestern U., 1933-35, instr. surgery, 1935-36, asso. bone and joint surgery, 1936-46, asst. prof. bone and joint surgery, 1946-49, asso. prof., 1949-72, prof., 1972—; attending surgeon orthopedics Cook County Hosp.; attending surgeon orthopedics, pres. med. staff Passavant Meml. Hosp.; chief surgeon C. & N.W. R.R. Served to comdr. M.C., USNR, World War II. Diplomate Nat. Bd. Med. Examiners, Am. Bd. Surgery, Am. Bd. Orthopedic Surgery. Fellow A.C.S. (vice chmn. bd. govs.); mem. A.M.A., Chgo. Surg. Soc., Central Surg. Assn., Chgo. Orthopedic Soc. (pres. 1973-74), Assn. R.R. Surgeons (recorder), Am. Assn. Surgery Trauma (pres. 1959-60), Assn. Am. R.R.'s, Am. Assn. R.R. Surgeons (chmn. exec. com.). Club: Lake Shore (Chgo.). Author: (with Paul B. Magnuson) Fractures, 1949. Editorial bd. Jour. Indsl. Medicine and Surgery, Quar. Bull. Northwestern U. Med. Sch. Contbr. sci. articles to profl. jours. Home: 999 Lake Shore Dr Chicago IL 60611 Office: 233 E Erie St Chicago IL 60611

STACK, JAMES VINCENT, steel co. exec.; b. Gary, Ind., Aug. 28, 1928; s. Bernard A. and Lucille C. (Scofield) S.; B.S.E.E., Purdue U., 1955; postgrad. Cornell U., 1970, Ind. U. Grad. Sch. Bus., 1971-72; m. Joyce Hinchman, Sept. 27, 1951; children—Susan J., Kathy A., R. Norman. With Midwest Steel div., 1959-77, v.p., gen. mgr., 1972-76, pres., 1976-77; pres. Granite City Steel div. (Ill.), 1977—; dir. 1st Granite City Nat. Bank. Bd. dirs. St. Elizabeth Hosp., So. Ill. U. Found. Served with USMC, 1946-47, U.S. Army, 1951-52. Decorated Bronze Star. Mem. Am. Iron and Steel Inst., Assn. Iron and Steel Engrs., Tri City C. of C. (dir.), St. Louis Regional Commerce and Growth Assn. (dir.). Clubs: St. Louis, Old Warson Country, Mo. Athletic. Office: 20th and State St Granite City IL 62040

STACK, MAURICE DANIEL, ins. co. exec.; b. N.Y.C., Dec. 15, 1917; s. Maurice E. and Margaret (Brooks) S.; student U. Notre Dame, 1935-36; B.B.A., Manhattan Coll., 1939; M.B.A., Harvard, 1941; m. Catherine T. O'Connor, Nov. 25, 1943; children—Mary Jane, Eileen, Peter, Clare. Investment analyst Carnegie Corp., N.Y.C., 1946-48; adminstrv. asst. Tchrs. Ins. & Annuity Assn., 1948-49; investment analyst First Nat. Bank N.Y., 1949-54; fin. sec. Atlantic Mut. Ins. Co., N.Y.C., 1954-56, v.p. 1957-60, fin. v.p., trustee, 1961-66, chmn. fin. com., 1966—; dir. Centennial Ins. Co., U.S. and Fgn. Securities Corp.; trustee United Mut. Savs. Bank. Trustee Coll. Mt. St. Vincent, Havens Relief Fund Soc., St. Vincent's Hosp., YWCA; mem. fin. com. Am. Bur. Shipping. Served from 2d. lt. to maj. C.E., AUS, 1941-46. Mem. N.Y. Soc. Security Analysts, Am. Hist. Assn. (trustee). Clubs: Harvard, Wall Street (N.Y.C.). Home: 85 Lynbrook Ave Point Lookout NY 11569 Office: 45 Wall St New York NY 10005

STACK, ROBERT LANGFORD, actor; b. Los Angeles, Jan. 13, 1919; s. James Langford and Elizabeth (Wood) S.; student U. So. Calif., 1937-38; m. Rosmarie Bowe, Jan. 23, 1956; children—Elizabeth Langford, Charles Robert. Pres., Langford Prodns., TV and theatrical films, Los Angeles, 1959—; actor, co-producter TV series, The Untouchables, 1959-63; star TV series The Name of the Game, 1968-71, Most Wanted, 1976-77; numerous motion picture appearances, including: First Love, 1940, The Bullfighter and the Lady, 1950, Bwana Devil, 1952, The High and the Mighty, 1953, Written on the Wind (Acad. Award nomination for best supporting actor), 1956, The Last Voyage, 1959, John Paul Jones, 1959, The Caretakers, 1963, The Corrupt Ones, 1967, Story of a Woman, 1970. Recipient Emmy award for outstanding performance by an actor Acad. TV Arts and Scis. Office: care Rush/Flaherty Agy Inc 10889 Wilshire Blvd Suite 1130 Los Angeles CA 90024*

STACY, GARDNER W., chemist; b. Rochester, N.Y., Oct. 29, 1921; s. Gardner Wesley and May (Roberts) S.; B.S., U. Rochester, 1943; Ph.D., U. Ill., 1946; m. Mary Mullen Heydon, Apr. 1, 1968; children—Marcia Ann (Mrs. Carter Boggs), Donald Gardner, Anne Elizabeth (Mrs. Scott V. Gorham), Robert James, Richard Neal Heydon. Research asst. OSRD antimalarial program U. Ill., Urbana, 1943-46; research fellow Cornell U. Med. Sch., N.Y.C., 1946-48; asst. prof. Wash. State U., Pullman, 1948-55, asso. prof. chemistry, 1955-60, prof., 1960—, mem. faculty exec. com., 1961-64. Recipient Petroleum Research Fund Internat. award, Australia and New Zealand, 1963-64. Fellow Am. Inst. Chemists; mem. Am. Chem. Soc. (councilor Wash.-Idaho border sect. 1957-69, nat., region VI dir. 1970-78, bd. dirs. 1970—, past chmn. council com. chem. edn., chmn. bd. com. edn. and students 1972-75, bd. pub., profl. and mem. relations, com. on publs. 1977-78, nat. pres.-elect 1978, nat. pres. 1979, chmn. various profl. confs), AAUP, AAAS, Phi Beta Kappa, Sigma Xi, Alpha Chi Sigma, Phi Lambda Upsilon. Author: Organic Chemistry: A Background for the Life Sciences, 1975; contbr. articles to profl. jours. Research on antimalarials, corticosteroid analogs, anti-radiation agents, tautomeric systems. Home: NW 1825 Turner Dr Pullman WA 99163 Office: Dept Chemistry Wash State U Pullman WA 99164

STADE, CHARLES EDWARD, architect; b. Des Plaines, Ill, June 28, 1923; s. Chris E. and Martha (Drexler) S.; B.S., U. Ill., 1946; M.F.A., Princeton, 1948; certificate of design, Beaux Art Inst. Design, N.Y.C., 1948; French govt. traveling scholar, 1948; m. Annette B. Grewe, Nov. 7, 1972; 1 dau. (by previous marriage), Ramsey. Architect, W.J. McCaughev, Park Ridge, Ill., 1945, K. Kassler, Princeton, N.J., 1948; propr. Charles Edward and Assos., Park Ridge, Ill, 1948-75; prin. works include instl. and related structures. Served with USAAF, 1942-43. Palmer fellow; Princeton fellow; recipient Howard Crosby Butler prize; medal of Prix-de-Emultation of Group Am., Societes des Architects Par Le Govt. Francais. Fellow in Design Am. Soc. Ch. Architects (pres. 1964-66; designs in permanent exhbt.), AIA (award 1956, 57, 62, 63, 65, 67, Excellence in Masonry Architecture award 1972, Outstanding Lighting award 1973, Nat. award for excellence in design 1974). Author articles in field; 4 design-awarded archtl. projects selected for permanent records by Chgo. Archtl. Archives, 1977. Home: 1020 S Knight St Park Ridge IL 60068 Office: 819 Busse Hwy Park Ridge IN 60068

STADEL, WILLIAM WALTER, govt. med. adminstr.; b. Topeka, Jan. 31, 1912; s. Walter Simon and Ethel Roberta (Taylor) S.; A.B., U. Kans., 1933, M.D., 1936; m. Mary Agnes Vale, Oct. 8, 1935; children—Patricia Ann, Bruce Vale. Intern, then resident Latter Day Saints Hosp., Salt Lake City, 1936-38; pvt. practice, Mariposa, Calif., 1938-40; hosp. adminstrn. Alameda County Instns., Oakland, Calif., 1940-48, asst. med. dir., 1946-48; supt. San Diego County Gen. Hosp., 1948-55, Edgemoor Farm, San Diego County, 1952-55; dir. San Diego County Dept. Med. Instns., 1955-79; med. dir. San Diego County Dept. Health Services, 1979—. Mem. Calif. Bd. Vocat. Nurse Examiners, 1952-62, Nat. Bd. Med. Examiners, 1966-69; commr. Joint Commn. Accreditation Hosp., 1963-69, chmn., 1967; v.p., treas., dir. Helix Land Co., Inc. Bd. dirs. San Diego County Tb and Health Assn., 1950-65; bd. regents Nat. Library Medicine, 1958-61. Mem. Am. (past chmn. com. chronic illness, com. vets. relations), Calif. (pres. 1957) hosp. assns., Am. Coll. Hosp. Adminstrs. (regent com., bd. examiners 1960-64). Home: 3510 Front At Apt 1B San Diego CA 92103 Office: 1700 Pacific Blvd San Diego CA 92101

STADELMAN, WILLIAM JACOB, educator; b. Vancouver, Wash., Aug. 8, 1917; s. William Henry and Eda Wilhelmena (Huber) S.; B.S., Wash. State U., 1940; M.S., Pa. State U., 1942, Ph.D., 1948; m. Margaret Jane Lloyd, Apr. 3, 1942; children—Ralph Lindsay, Paula (Mrs. Lawrence Joseph Jurgonski). Asst. prof. poultry sci. Wash. State U., Pullman, 1948-52, asso. prof., 1952-55; asso. prof. food sci. Purdue U., West Lafayette, Ind., 1955-58, prof., 1958—; cons. to food processors internationally. Dir. research and devel. Assos. for the Armed Services, 1966-69, 72-75. Served with USN, 1942-46; capt. USNR ret. Fellow Inst. Food Technologists (chmn. refrigerated and frozen div. 1974-75), AAAS, Inst. Advanced Sanitation Research Internat., Poultry Sci. Assn. (1st v.p. 1976-77, pres. 1977-78); mem. World's Poultry Sci. Assn., Am. Meat Sci. Assn., Am. Soc. Heating, Refrigerating and Air Conditioning Engrs., Sigma Xi, Alpha Zeta, Gamma Sigma Delta, Alpha Gamma Rho, Phi Tau Sigma (internat. pres. 1972-74). Elks. Editor: (with O.J. Cotterill) Egg Science and Technology, 2d edit., 1977. Contbr. articles to profl. jours. Patentee in field. Home: 1429 N Salisbury West Lafayette IN 47906

STADTLER, BEATRICE HORWITZ, author; b. Cleve., June 26, 1921; d. David and Minnie (Gorelick) Horwitz; m. Oscar Stadtler, Jan. 31, 1945; children—Dona Stadtler Rosenblatt, Sander, Miriam. Sec., Cleve. Dept. Pub. Health and Welfare, 1940; sec., dept. mgr. Fed. Pub. Housing Authority, Cleve., 1943; primary supr. Temple Beth Shalom Religious Sch., Cleve., 1953; registrar Cleve. Coll. Jewish Studies, 1958—; asst. editor Israel Philatelist, 1975—; speaker on holocaust; author: Once Upon a Jewish Holiday, 1963; The Story of Dona Gracia, 1969; The Adventures of Gluckel of Hamlen, 1967; Rescue From the Sky (in Hebrew), 1972; Personalities of the Jewish Labor Movement, 1972; The Holocaust: A History of Courage and Resistance (prize outstanding juvenile book Nat. Jewish Welfare Bd. 1975), 1975; (film strip) The Adventures of Mirkee Pirkee and Danny Dollar (prize Nat. Council Jewish Audio Visual Materials 1963), 1963; also articles, stories. Adviser youth group United Synagogue, 1967-70; planning com. Nat. Conf. Jewish Communal Workers; bd. dirs. Ethnic Heritage Com.; exec. bd. Nat. Council Jewish Edn., Am. Zionist Fedn. Mem. Educator's Assembly, Pioneer Women. Recipient prizes Fedn. and Welfare Funds, Audio Visual Council of Am. Assn. Jewish Edn. Democrat. Author weekly column Cleve. Jewish News, 1964-70, Boston Jewish Advocate, 1970—. Home: 24355 Tunbridge Ln Beachwood OH 44122 Office: 26500 Shaker Blvd Beachwood OH 44122

STADTLER, JOHN WALMSLEY, savs. and loan assn. ofcl.; b. Washington, Sept. 23, 1917; s. John H. and Margaret (Walmsley) S.; B.S. in Bus. Adminstrn., Georgetown U., 1939; m. Katherine E. Brown, May 24, 1941; children—John Walmsley, Michael Graham. With Nat. Permanent Fed. Savs. & Loan Assn., Washington, 1946—, exec. v.p., 1956-58, pres., 1958-78, now chmn. bd.; dir. Investors' Mortgage Ins. Co., Boston, Firemen's Inc. Co., Mortgage Investors Ins. Co. of Washington, C & P Telephone Co., Acacia Mut. Life Ins. Co. Served with USCGR, 1942-46; PTO. Recipient 175th Anniversary Medal of Honor award Georgetown U., 1964, Ann. Awards certificate Georgetown Alumni Club Washington, 1965. Mem. U.S. League Savs. and Loan Assns. (v.p. 1963-64, pres. 1964-65), Internat. Union Bldg. Socs. and Savs. Assns. (pres. 1974-77), Delta Phi Epsilon. Clubs: Columbia Country, Burning Tree, Metropolitan. Home: 4418 Boxwood Rd Bethesda MD 20016 Office: 1775 Pennsylvania Ave NW Washington DC 20006

STADTMAN, EARL REECE, biochemist; b. Carrizozo, N.Mex., Nov. 15, 1919 s. Walter William and Minnie Ethyl (Reece) S.; B.S., U. Calif. at Berkeley, 1942, Ph.D, 1949; m. Thressa Campbell, Oct. 19, 1943. With Alcan Hwy. survey Pub. Rds. Adminstrn., 1942-43; research asst. U. Calif. at Berkeley, 1938-49, sr. lab. technican, 1949; AEC fellow Mass. Gen. Hosp., Boston, 1949-50; chemist lab. cellular physiology Nat. Heart Inst., 1950-58, chief enzyme sect. 1958-62, chief lab. biochemistry, 1962—. Biochemist Max Planck Inst., Munich, Germany, Pasteur Inst., Paris, France, 1959-60; faculty dept. microbiology U. Md.; prof. biochemistry grad. program dept. biology Johns Hopkins; adv. com. Life Scis. Research Office, Am. Fedn. Biol. Sci., 1974-77. Bd. dirs. Found. Advanced Edn. Scis., 1966-70, chmn. dept. biochemistry, 1966-68, biochem. study sect. research grants NIH, 1959-63. Recipient medallion Soc. de Chemie Biologique, 1955, U. Pisa, 1966. Mem. Am. Chem. Soc. (Paul Lewis Lab. award in enzyme chemistry 1952, exec. com. biol. div. 1959-64, chmn. div. 1963-64, Hillebrand award 1969), Am. Soc. Biol. Chemists (publs. com. 1966-70, council 1974—), Nat. Acad. Scis. (award in microbiology, 1970), Am. Acad. Arts and Scis., Am. Soc. Microbiology, Washington Acad. Scis. (award biol. chemistry 1957). Editor: Jour. Biol. Chemistry, 1960-65, Current Topics in Cellular Regulation, 1968—, Circulation Research, 1968-70; exec. editor Archives Biochemistry and Biophysics, 1960—, Life Scis., 1973-75, Procs. Nat. Acad. Sci., 1975—, Trends in Biochem. Research, 1975—editorial adv. bd. Biochemistry, 1969-76. Home: 16907 Redland Rd Derwood MD 20855 Office: Nat Heart and Lung Inst Bethesda MD 20014

STAEBLER, GEORGE RUSSELL, forester; b. Ann Arbor, Mich., Mar. 19, 1917; s. Albert John and Ella Lucretia (Goodell) S.; B.S.F., U. Mich., 1939, M.F., 1951; m. Stellajoe English, Nov. 30, 1943; children—Jo Ann, Gretchen, Rebecca. Project forester WPA in Ohio, 1940-41; research forester TVA, 1941-42, Pacific N.W. Forest and Range Expt. Sta., U.S. Forest Service, 1946-55; asst. prof. silviculture U. Wash., 1954-55; silviculturist Weyerhaeuser Co., Centralia, Wash., 1957-66, dir. forestry research, 1966—. Served to capt. USAAC, 1942-46. Recipient Outstanding Achievement award U. Mich., 1976. Fellow Soc. Am. Foresters (Barrington Moore Meml. award 1969); mem. Canadian Inst. Forestry, AAAS, Forest History Soc. Office: PO Box 420 Centralia WA 98531

STAEBLER, NEIL, bus. exec., former congressman; b. Ann Arbor, Mich., July 11, 1905; s. Edward W. and Magdalena (Dold) S.; A.B., U. Mich., 1926, LL.D.; m. Burnette Bradley, Feb. 8, 1935; children—Elizabeth, Michael. Partner, Staebler & Son, home builders, Ann Arbor, 1926—; pres. Mich. Capital & Service, Inc., 1966-75, dir., 1975—. Mich. congressman-at-large, 88th Congress, 1963-64. Finance dir. Mich. Democratic party, 1949-50; chmn. Dem. Mich. Central Com., 1950-61; mem. Dem. Nat. Com. for Mich., 1961-64, 65-68, 72-75, asso. committeeman, 1968-72; mem. Dem. Charter Commn., 1973-75. Vice chmn. 20th Century Fund Task Force on Financing Congl. Campaigns, 1970; mem. Fed. Election Commn., 1975-78; chief bldg. materials br. OPA, 1942-44; mem. Mich. State Officers Compensation Commn., 1978—. Served as lt. USNR, 1944-45. Mem. Am. Econ. Assn., Nat. Assn. Home Builders, Am. Vets. Com., NAACP, Nat. Municipal League, Nat. Planning Assn., Theta Chi. Unitarian. Club: Economic (Detroit). Author: The Campaign Finance Revolution, 1979; co-author: How to Argue with a Conservative, 1966. Home: 601 Huron View Blvd Ann Arbor MI 48103 Office: Room 308 202 E Washington St Ann Arbor MI 48104

STAEHLE, ROGER WASHBURNE, metall. engr.; b. Detroit, Feb. 4, 1934; s. Haswell E. and Carrie (Washburne) S.; B.S., Ohio State U., 1957, M.S., 1957, Ph.D., 1965; m. Ursula Maria Kruse-Vancienne; children—Elizabeth J., Eric W., Sara L., Catherine E. Researcher, U.S. Navy and U.S. AEC, Washington, 1957-61; research asso. Ohio State U., Columbus, 1961-65, prof. metall. engring., 1965-78, Internat. Nickel prof. corrosion sci. and engring., 1971-76; dean Inst. Tech., U. Minn., Mpls., 1979—; cons. numerous bus. firms; organizer internat. confs.; chmn. corrosion adv. com. Electric Power Research Inst., 1974—; mem. coms. on radioactive wastes NRC; mem. Minn. Cooperation Office; chmn. adv. panel, metall. div. Nat. Bur. Standards, 1975-77. Bd. dirs. Midwest Research Inst., Fontana Corrosion Center of Ohio State U., 1975-79. Recipient Achievement award Coll. Engring., Ohio State U., 1966, 69. Fellow Am. Soc. Metals; mem. Electrochem. Soc., Nat. Assn. Corrosion Engrs., Am. Nuclear Soc., Am. Inst. Mining, Metall. and Petroleum Engrs., ASTM, Am. Soc. Engring. Edn., Fedn. Materials Socs., Sigma Xi, Tau Beta Pi, Phi Eta Sigma, Phi Zeta. Editor: Corrosion Jour., 1973—, Advances in Corrosion Science and Technology, 7 vols.; Handbook on Stress Corrosion Cracking and Corrosion Fatigue of Metals, 1980; contbr. tech. articles to profl. jours. Office: 107 Lind Hall U Minn 207 Church St SE Minneapolis MN 55455

STAERKEL, WILLIAM MAX, coll. pres.; b. Newton, Kans., Apr. 14, 1921; s. Otto and Grace Hazel (Williams) S.; B.A., Bethel Coll., 1942; M.Ed., U. Kans., 1948; Ed.D., Stanford U., 1953; m. Mary Lou Plumb, Apr. 15, 1943; children—Scott William, Richard Plumb. Prin., El Dorado (Kans.) High Sch., 1950-54; supt. schs. Beatrice (Nebr.) public schs., 1954-57; Aracadia (Calif.) Unified Sch. Dist., 1957-60; dir. ednl. services Booz, Allen & Hamilton, Chgo., 1960-67; pres. Parkland Coll., 1967—. Served to lt. USN, 1942-46. Decorated Bronze Star. Mem. NEA, Am. Assn. Community and Jr. Colls., Phi Delta Kappa. Presbyterian. Club: Rotary. Home: 3222 Stoneybrook Dr Champaign IL 61820 Office: 2400 W Bradley Ave Champaign IL 61820

STAFF, GEORGE LEON, textile co. exec., mgmt. cons.; b. N.Y.C., Aug. 7, 1917; s. Leon G. and Regina (Johnson) S.; B.S. in Civil Engring., Coll. City N.Y., 1937, M.S., 1938; m. Betty Redmond, Oct. 12, 1940 (div. Feb. 1960); children—Christopher George, Marcia Phyllis, Marc Leon; m. 2d, Gwendolyn Considine, Dec. 10, 1960. Civil engr. design and constrn. various pub. works, war projects, N.Y.C., 1938-45; engr. Deering-Milliken & Co., Spartanburg, S.C., 1945-48, sales mgr., 1948-55; v.p. Textron-Am., N.Y.C., 1955-56; with Burlington Industries, Inc., N.Y.C. and Greensboro, N.C., 1956-74, v.p., 1966-69, exec. v.p., 1969-74, vice chmn., 1972-74, mgmt. com. mem., 1967-74, dir., 1968-74, mem. exec. com., 1969-74; pres., chief operating officer United Mchts. and Mfrs., 1975-77, also dir., mem. exec. com.; dir. Crompton Co., Inc., Reece Corp. Bd. dirs. Internat. Exec. Service Corps, 1975—. Mem. Nat. Assn. Wool Mfrs. (v.p. 1963-72, dir.), Internat. Wool Textile Orgn. (v.p. 1967-73, chmn. U.S. delegation 1967-71), Woolens and Worsteds Am. (pres. 1964-68, dir.), Am. Inst. Men's and Boys' Wear (dir.). Clubs: Silver Spring Country (Ridgefield, Conn.); Union League (N.Y.C.). Home: 22 Little Ridge Rd Ridgefield CT 06877 Office: Suite 906 One Gulf & Western Plaza New York NY 10023

STAFFORD, CHARLES FREDERICK, state justice; b. Burlington, Wash., June 24, 1918; s. Charles Frederick and Madge (Davis) S.; B.A. with honors in Polit. Sci., Whitman Coll., 1940, LL.D., 1956; LL.B., Yale, 1946; m. Katherine Grimm, Aug. 15, 1943; children—Katherine Anne (Mrs. John Schmidt), Joan Craig (Mrs. David E. Halverstadt). Admitted to Wash. bar, 1947; chief dep. pros. atty., Skagit County, Wash., 1947-52; judge Superior Ct. of Skagit and Island Counties, 1952-69; mem. Wash. Ct. Appeals, 1969-70; justice Wash. Supreme Ct., 1970—, chief justice, 1975-76; mem. faculty Nat. Coll. State Trial Judges, summers, 1968, 69. Mem. Wash. Bench-Bar-Press Com., 1964-67; mem. adv. com. Supreme Ct. Pub. Defender Demonstration Project; chmn. Com. on Juvenile Justice, Wash. Little White House Conf.; mem. Wash. Gov.'s Com. on Criminal Justice, 1979—. Mem. exec. bd. Mt. Baker area council Boy Scouts Am., 1965-70, Tumwater Area council, 1970-73; trustee Wash. State Capital Mus., 1975—; bd. visitors U. Puget Sound Law Sch., Tacoma, 1976-78; bd. overseers Whitman Coll., Walla Walla, Wash., 1976—. Served with AUS, 1942-46. Mem. Wash. State, Am. bar assns., Am. Judicature Soc., Am. Law Inst., Phi Beta Kappa, Delta Sigma Rho, Beta Theta Pi. Methodist. Rotarian. Contbr. articles to legal jours. Home: 2016 Clairemont Circle Olympia WA 98502 Office: Wash Supreme Ct Temple of Justice Olympia WA 98504

STAFFORD, DONALD GENE, educator; b. Valliant, Okla., Oct. 9, 1930; s. Otto Lewis and Rose Lavelle (Osterdock) S.; B.S., U. Okla., 1957, Ph.D., 1969; M.S., Okla. State U., 1961; m. Jane Wright, July 5, 1951; children—Michael Royce, Robert Gene, Joel Dan. Prof. sci. edn. East Central U., Ada, Okla., 1961-73, prof. chemistry, 1973—; adj. prof. U. Okla., Norman, 1970—. Served with AUS, 1948-53. Mem. Am. Chem. Soc., Nat. Sci. Tchrs. Assn., Okla. Sci. Tchrs. (pres. 1973-74, 78-79), Sigma Xi. Author: The Improvement of Science in Oklahoma (7-12), 1970; Guidelines and Successful Practices in Elementary Edn., 1970; Wings for a Dinosaur, 1972; Early Childhood Resource Book, 1972; Teaching Science in the Elementary School, 1973, 3d edit., 1979; Teaching Science in the Secondary School, 1973; Research, Teaching, and Learning with the Piaget Model, 1976; Investigations in Physical Science, 1976; The Learning Science Program (K-6) (7 children's books and 7 tchr.'s guides), 1976. Home: 2202 Fullview St Ada OK 74820

STAFFORD, EDWARD STEPHEN, former surgeon; b. Chgo., Mar. 5, 1906; s. Charles Burke and Mattie (Rose) S.; B.A., Yale, 1927; M.D., Johns Hopkins, 1931; m. Frances Symington Lowell, Sept. 28, 1935; children—Charles B., Marion Stafford Robinson, Barbara (Mrs. Hugh E. Jones), William L., Jane Ellen. Intern, resident surgeon Johns Hopkins Hosp., 1931-39; practice medicine specializing in surgery, Balt., 1939-77; asst. prof. surgery Johns Hopkins, 1939-48, asso. prof., 1948-67, prof., 1967-71, prof. emeritus, 1971—, asso. dean, 1971-73; chief surg. service Union Meml. Hosp., 1956-59; dir. clin. programs Columbia Med. Plan and Columbia Hosp., 1973-74. Trustee Robert Garrett Fund, 1963-77. Served from capt. to lt. col. M.C., AUS, 1942-45. Fellow Am., So. surg. assns., A.C.S.; mem. Soc. U. Surgeons, Soc. Surgery Alimentary Tract, AMA, AAAS, Med. and Chir. Faculty Md., Balt. Acad. Surgery (pres. 1973). Presbyterian (elder). Club: Dunedin Country. Author: Textbook of Surgery for Nurses, 1947. Contbr. articles to profl. jours. Home: 9 Haig Pl Apt 412 Dunedin FL 33528

STAFFORD, ELVIN ANDREW, mfg. exec.; b. Hattiesburg, Miss., July 24, 1927; s. Calvin A. and Ruby Lee (Holloway) S.; B.S. in Chem. Engring., U. Miss., 1950; M.S. in Chem. Engring., La. State U., 1951; m. Shirley Ann Laning, May 7, 1977; children—Richard, Randy, Georgia. Process devel. engr. Esso Labs., Baton Rouge, 1950-51; process devel. engr. Buckeye Cellulose Corp., Memphis, 1952-59, plant mgr., 1960-62, plant mgr., Foley, Fla., 1963-70, mgr. mfg., Memphis, 1970-71; v.p. mfg. Procter & Gamble Cellulose, Ltd., Grande Prairie, Alta., Can., 1971-74; pres. MacMillan Bloedel, Inc., Pine Hill, Ala., 1975-78; area dir. So. ops. Am. Can Co., Butler, Ala., 1979—. Mem. engring. adv. bd. U. Miss. Served with AUS, 1945-46. Mem. Ala. Industry Assn. (bd. dirs.). Home: 408 Old Hwy 5 S Thomasville AL 36784 Office: Am Can Co PO Box 315 Butler AL 36904

STAFFORD, GEORGE MILLARD, govt. ofcl.; b. Valley Falls, Kans., May 7, 1915; s. Clarence Henry and Olive Mae (McCoy) S.; grad. Strickler Bus. Coll.; LL.D. (hon.), St. Benedict's Coll., 1971; m. Lena S. Lamendola, June 26, 1947; children—Clair, George W., Susan Ann. Dep. dir. Kans. Sales Tax Dept., 1939-42; exec. sec. to Gov. Kans., 1947-50; adminstrv. asst. to Senator Frank Carlson, Washington, 1950-67; commr. ICC, Washington, 1967-69, 79— vice chmn., 1969, chmn., after 1970. Exec. dir. Kans. Republican Com.,

1946. Served with AUS, 1942-47. Decorated Bronze Star, Combat Inf. badge, Purple Heart. Mem. VFW, Am. Legion, Delta Theta Phi. Mason. Club: Congressional Country (Washington). Office: 12th St and Constitution Ave NW Washington DC 20423*

STAFFORD, J. FRANCIS, clergyman; b. Balt., July 26, 1932; s. Francis Emmett and Mary Dorothy (Stanton) S.; A.B., St. Mary's Sem., Balt., 1954; S.T.B., S.T.L., Gregorian U., Rome, Italy, 1958; M.S.W., Catholic U. Am., 1964. Ordained priest Roman Catholic Ch., 1957; asst. pastor Immaculate Heart of Mary, Balt., 1958-62; asst. pastor St. Ann's, Balt., 1964-65; chaplain Villa Maria Home for Children, Balt., 1965-69; asst. in sacramental ministry Basilica of the Assumption, Balt., 1969-76; dir. Asso. Cath. Charities, Balt., 1966-76; urban vicar, aux. bishop Archdiocese of Balt., 1976—. Mem. policy bd. Center for Met. Planning and Research, Johns Hopkins U., 1973—; bd. trustees Jenkins Meml. Hosp., 1976—; chmn. bishops' com. on marriage and family life U.S. Cath. Conf.; mem. White House Com. on Families, 1979—. Mem. Nat. Conf. Cath. Bishops (adminstrv. com.). Home: 120 N Front St Baltimore MD 21202 Office: 320 Cathedral St Baltimore MD 21201

STAFFORD, JOHN M., food co. exec.; b. Evanston, Ill., Oct. 25, 1936; s. Charles Marshall and Harriet Helen (Walker) S.; B.A., Yale U., 1958; m. Ardietta Deta H. Ford, June 12, 1958; children—John Marshall, Lisa, Michael. Vice-pres., account supr. Leo Burnett Co., Chgo., 1960-72; sr. v.p. mktg. KFC Corp., Louisville, 1972-75; v.p. mktg., sr. v.p. Green Giant Co., Chaska, Minn., 1975-79, chief operating officer, 1979—, exec. v.p. Pillsbury Co., 1979—. Bd. dirs. Children's Theatre and Sch., Minnetonka, Inc. Served with USMC, 1958-60. Mem. Am. Frozen Food Inst. (dir.). Office: Green Giant Co Hazeltine Gates Chaska MN 55318

STAFFORD, MARTIN DOUGLAS, govt. ofcl.; b. Syracuse, N.Y., Sept. 29, 1933; s. George Edward and Jeannette (Martin) S.; B.S., Cornell U., 1955; m. Virginia H. Dyer, Jan. 21, 1956; children—Martin Douglas, Robert George. Account mgr. IBM, Boston Area, 1959-64; dir. adminstrn. U.S. Peace Corps, Washington, 1964-70; v.p. adminstrn. State U. Coll., New Paltz, N.Y., 1970-72; dir. Problem Oriented Mgmt. Inst., Washington, 1972-75; asst. to exec. dir. Equal Employment Opportunity Commn., Washington, 1975-77; controller U.S. AID, 1977—. Home: 6224 Walhonding Rd Bethesda MD 20016

STAFFORD, PAUL TUTT, educator, mgmt. cons.; b. Liberty, Mo., Sept. 16, 1905; s. Thomas Polhill and Anna Gardner (Tutt) S.; A.B., U. Mo., 1926, A.M., 1930; Ph.D. (Proctor fellow), Princeton, 1933; m. Helen Elizabeth Thomson, Dec. 14, 1951; children—Paul T., Timothy A., Mark T., Todd L.; 1 dau. by former marriage, Lucile Stafford Proctor. Instr. polit. sci. Princeton, 1933-36, asst. prof., 1936-42, asso. prof., 1942-48; exec. dir. N.J. Civil Service Commn., Trenton, 1948-50; exec. sec. to gov. N.J., Trenton, 1951; asst. to dir. personnel and community relations Internat. Shoe Co., St. Louis, 1952-53; prin., dir. Ashton Dunn Assos., N.Y.C., 1955-59; founder, chmn. Paul Stafford Assos., Ltd., Mgmt. Cons., N.Y.C., Chgo. and Washington, 1959—. Served with Naval Intelligence, USNR, 1942-46; comdr. USN (ret.). Mem. Beta Theta Pi. Republican. Presbyterian. Clubs: Apawamis (Rye, N.Y.); Coral Beach (Bermuda); Hillsboro (Pompano Beach, Fla.); Princeton (N.Y.C.). Author: (with W.S. Carpenter) State and Local Goverments in the United States, 1936; Government and the Needy: A Study of Public Assistance in New Jersey, 1941. Contbr. articles on polit. sci. and exec. recruiting to profl. jours. Home: Brookside Ridge St Rye NY 10580 Office: Paul Stafford Assos 45 Rockefeller Plaza New York NY 10020

STAFFORD, REBECCA, sociologist, educator; b. Topeka, July 9, 1936; d. Frank C. and Anne Elizabeth (Larrick) S.; A.B. magna cum laude, Radcliffe Coll., 1958, M.A., 1961; Ph.D., Harvard U., 1964; m. Willard VanHazel, Apr. 12, 1973. Lectr. dept. sociology Harvard U., 1964-69, Sch. Edn., 1969-70, mem. vis. com. bd. overseers, 1973—; asso. prof. sociology U. Nev., Reno, 1970-73, prof., 1973—, chmn. dept. sociology, 1974-77, dean Coll. Arts and Sci., 1977—; mem. site visitation team N.W. Assn. Accreditation; bd. dirs. Council Colls. Arts and Sci. Recipient McCurdy-Rinkle prize for research Eastern Psychiat. Assn., 1970; Am. Council Edn. Inst. Acad. Deans grantee, 1979. Mem. Pacific Sociol. Assn., Am. Sociol. Assn., Nat. Council Family Relations, Council Colls. Arts and Sci., NEA, Phi Beta Kappa, Phi Kappa Phi. Research publs. in field. Office: U Nev 217 Physics Bldg Reno NV 89557

STAFFORD, ROBERT THEODORE, U.S. senator, lawyer; b. Rutland, Vt., Aug. 8, 1913; s. Bert L. and Mable R. (Stratton) S.; B.S., Middlebury Coll., 1935, LL.D., 1960; postgrad. U. Mich., 1936; LL.B., Boston U., 1938, LL.D., 1959; LL.D., Norwich U., 1960, St. Michaels Coll., 1967, U. Vt., 1970; m. Helen C. Kelley, Oct. 15, 1938; children—Madelyn, Susan, Barbara, Dianne. Admitted to Vt. bar, 1938; city prosecutor, Rutland, 1939-42; state's atty. Rutland County, 1947-51; dep. atty. gen. Vt., 1953-54, atty. gen., 1954-56, lt. gov., 1957-58, gov., 1959-60; mem. 87th to 92d Congresses, Vt.-at-large; apptd. U.S. Senate, 1971, elected, 1972—; partner Stafford, Abiatell & Stafford, 1938-46; sr. partner Stafford & LaBrake, 1946-51. Served as lt. comdr. USNR, 1942-46, 51-52; capt. Res. Mem. V.F.W., Am. Legion. Elk, Lion. Home: 3541 Devon Dr Falls Church VA 22042 also 64 Litchfield Ave Rutland VT Office: New Senate Office Bldg Washington DC 20510

STAFFORD, THOMAS PATTEN, transp. co. exec., astronaut; b. Weatherford, Okla., Sept. 17, 1930; B.S., U.S. Naval Acad., 1952; student USAF Exptl. Flight Test Sch., 1958-59; D.Sc. (hon.), Oklahoma City U., 1967; LL.D. (hon.), Western State U. Coll. Law, 1969; D.Communications (hon.), Emerson Coll., 1969; D.Aero. Engring. (hon.), Embry-Riddle Aero. Inst., 1970; m. Faye Laverne Shoemaker; children—Dionne, Karin. Comd. 2d lt. USAF, 1952, advanced through grades to lt. gen.; chief performance br. Aerospace Research Pilot Sch., Edwards AFB, Calif., with Manned Spacecraft Center NASA, Houston, 1962-79, assigned Project Gemini; pilot Gemini VI, command pilot Gemini IX, comdr. Apollo X, chief astronaut office, 1969-71, dep. dir. flight crew operations; comdr. on Apollo-Soyuz flight, 1975, comdr. Apollo flight; comdr. Air Force Flight Test Center, Edwards AFB, Calif. and dep. chief staff research, devel. and acquisition; ret., 1979; exec. v.p. comml. sales and fin. Am. Farm Lines, 1979—; chmn. bd. Omega Watch Co. Am. Decorated D.F.C. with oak leaf cluster; D.S.M. (Air Force). Recipient NASA Distinguished Service medal, 2 NASA Exceptional Service medals, Air Force Command Pilot Astronaut Wings; Chanute Flight award Am. Inst. Aeros. and Astronautics, 1976; V.F.W. Nat. Space award, 1976; Gen. Thomas D. White USAF Space trophy Nat. Geog. Soc., 1976; Gold Space medal Fedn. Aeronautique Internationale, 1976; co-recipient Am. Inst. Aeros. and Astronautics award, 1966, Harmon Internat. Aviation trophy, 1966, Nat. Acad. Television Arts and Scis. spl. Trustees award, 1969. Fellow Am. Astronautical Soc.; mem. Soc. Exptl. Test Pilots, AFTRA (hon. life). Co-author: Pilot's Handbook for Performance Flight Test-Aerodynamics; Handbook for Performance Flight Testing. Address: PO Box 75410 Oklahoma City OK 73147. *As we move through life, each of us has an opportunity to make a contribution to humanity. In this respect, I have been extremely fortunate as I have been privileged to help explore new frontiers in space and aviation technology. But, it is clear to me that the most important element in a successful program is people. Their willingness to discipline their efforts and to work together to achieve important objectives remains the most important factor in a successful operation.**

STAFFORD, WILLIAM EDGAR, educator, author; b. Hutchinson, Kans., Jan. 17, 1914; s. Earl Ingersoll and Ruby Nina (Mayher) S.; B.A., U. Kans., 1937, M.A., 1946; Ph.D., State U. Iowa, 1954; Litt.D., Ripon Coll., 1965; L.H.D., Linfield Coll., 1970; m. Dorothy Hope Frantz, Apr. 8, 1944; children—Bret William, Kim Robert, Kathryn Lee, Barbara Claire. Faculty, Lewis and Clark Coll., Portland, Oreg., 1948—, prof. English, 1960—. Faculty, San Jose (Cal.) State Coll., 1956-57, Manchester (Ind.) Coll., 1955-56; cons. poetry Library of Congress, Washington, 1970. Ednl. sec. civilian pub. service sect. Ch. of Brethren, 1943-44; mem. Oreg. bd. Fellowship of Reconciliation, 1959—. Yaddo Found. fellow, 1956; Guggenheim grantee for creative writing, 1966-67. Recipient short story and poetry prizes Oreg. Centennial, 1959. Mem. AAUP, Modern Lang. Assn., Nat. Council Tchrs. English, War Registers League, Modern Poetry Assn. Author: Down in my Heart, 1947; (poems) West of Your City, 1960; Traveling Through the Dark (Nat. Book award 1963), 1962; (poems) The Rescued Year, 1966, Allegiances, 1970, Someday, Maybe, 1973; Stories That Could Be True, New and Collected Poems, 1977; regular contbr. to periodicals. Home: 1050 Sunningdale Lake Oswego OR 97034 Office: Lewis and Clark Coll Portland OR 97219

STAFFORD, WILLIAM HENRY, JR., U.S. judge; b. Masury, Ohio, May 11, 1931; s. William Henry and Frieda Gertrude (Nau) S.; B.S., Temple U., 1953, LL.B., 1956 (J.D., 1968); m. Nancy Marie Helman, July 11, 1959; children—William Henry, Donald Helman, David Harrold. Admitted to Fla. bar, 1961, U.S. Supreme Ct. bar, 1970, U.S. 5th Circuit Ct. Appeals bar, 1969; asso. firm Robinson & Roark, Pensacola, 1961-64; individual practice law, Pensacola, 1964-67; state atty., Pensacola, 1967-69; U.S. atty., Pensacola, 1969-75; U.S. dist. judge No. Dist. Fla., Tallahassee, 1975—; instr. Pensacola Jr. Coll., 1964, 68. Served to lt. (j.g.) USN, 1957-60. Mem. Am., Tallahassee bar assns., Fla. Bar (chmn. fed. funding com., mem. exec. council trial lawyers sect. 1972-75), Soc. Bar First Jud. Circuit Fla., Sigma Phi Epsilon, Phi Delta Phi. Republican. Episcopalian. Clubs: Masons, Shriners, Rotary, Pensacola Yacht. Home: 3750 Shamrock W Tallahassee FL 32308 Office: US Courthouse 110 E Park Ave PO Box 1731 Tallahassee FL 32302

STAGE, THOMAS BENTON, psychiatrist; b. Marietta, Ohio, July 23, 1926; s. John Douglas and Grace (Shawhan) S.; B.A. cum laude, Marietta Coll., 1949; M.D., Ohio State U., 1952; m. Doris Jeane Weinstock, Dec. 22, 1951; children—Samuel Ray, Amy Elizabeth, James Robert. Intern, Detroit Receiving Hosp., 1952-53; psychiat. resident, fellow Menninger Sch. Psychiatry, Topeka, 1953-56; sect. chief, chief psychiatry VA Hosp., Topeka, 1956-62; adminstr. VA Hosp., Sheridan, Wyo., 1962-66; dir. VA Hosp., Salem, Va., 1967-72; dep. asst. chief med. dir. for ambulatory care VA Central Office, Washington, 1972-74; dir. No. Va. Mental Health Inst., Falls Church, 1974-78; asst. commr. for mental health State of Va., Richmond, 1978-79; dir. clin. services Fairfax-Falls Church Community Services Bd., Vienna, Va., 1979—; instr. Menninger Sch. Psychiatry, 1958-62, U. Wyo. Sch. Nursing, 1963-66; asso. prof. U. Va. Med. Sch., 1972—; cons. Crow-No. Cheyenne USPHS Hosp., 1963-66. Mem. Comprehensive Mental Health Center Com., 1968-73, Gov.'s Adv. Commn. on Mental Health, 1971-74; chmn. Drug Abuse Rehab. Com., 1970-73; cons. adminstrv. psychiatry NIMH, 1975-78; chmn. steering com. Asso. Faculties Program Community Psychiatry, Washington, 1975-77; mem. State Health Coordinating Council, 1976—. Served wtih USNR, 1944-46; PTO. Diplomate Am. Bd. Psychiatry and Neurology. Fellow Am. Psychiat. Assn.; mem. Assn. Med. Supts. Mental Hosps., Neuropsychiat. Soc. Va. Contbr. articles to profl. jours. Home: 8624 McHenry St Vienna VA 22180 Office: Fairfax-Falls Church Community Services Bd 301 Tower 3d Floor 301 Maple Ave W Vienna VA 22180

STAGEBERG, JAMES EDGAR, architect; b. Dawson, Minn., Apr. 29, 1925; s. Edgar Clarence and Ethel (Foss) S.; B.Arch., U. Minn.; M.Arch., Harvard U.; m. Helen Michael, June 12, 1950; children—Beth, Frank, Lucy, Jane, Sally, Anne. Architect, The Hodne/Stageberg Partners, Mpls.; prof. architecture U. Minn., Mpls. Served to 1st lt. AUS, 1944-46. Fellow AIA. Democrat. Roman Catholic. Home: 65 Forest Dale Minneapolis MN 55410 Office: 116 E 22d St Minneapolis MN 55404

STAGG, TOM, judge; b. Shreveport, La., Jan. 19, 1923; s. Thomas Eaton and Beulah (Meyer) S.; B.A., La. State U., 1943, J.D., 1949; m. Margaret Mary O'Brien, Aug. 21, 1946; children—Julie, Margaret Mary. Admitted to La. bar, 1949; with firm Hargrove, Guyton, Van Hook & Hargrove, Shreveport, 1949-53; pvt. practice, Shreveport, 1953-58; sr. partner firm Stagg, Cady & Beard, Shreveport, 1958-74; U.S. dist. judge Western Dist. of La., 1974—. Pres., Abe Meyer Corp., 1960-74, Stagg Investments, Inc., 1964-74; mng. partner Pierremont Mall Shopping Center, 1963-74; v.p. King Hardware Co., 1955-74. Mem. Shreveport Airport Authority, 1967-73, chmn., 1970-73; chmn. Gov.'s Tidelands Adv. Council, 1969-70; del. La. Constl. Conv., 1973, chmn. rules com., com. on exec. dept.; mem. Gov.'s Adv. Com on Offshore Revenues, 1972-74. Active Republican party, 1950-74, del. convs., 1956, 60, 64, 68, 72, mem. Nat. Com. for La., 1964-72, mem. exec. com., 1964-68. Pres., Shreveport Jr. C. of C., 1955-56; v.p. La. Jr. C. of C., 1956-57. Served to capt., inf. AUS, 1943-46; ETO. Decorated Bronze Star, Purple Heart with oak leaf cluster. Mem. Am., La., Shreveport bar assns., Photog. Soc. Am. Home: 4847 Camellia Ln Shreveport LA 71106 Office: US Court House Room 2B15 500 Fannin St Shreveport LA 71101

STAGGERS, HARLEY ORRIN, congressman; b. Keyser, W.Va., Aug. 3, 1907; s. Jacob Kinsey and Frances Winona (Cumberledge) S.; A.B., Emory and Henry Coll., 1931, LL.D., 1953; postgrad. Duke, 1935; LL.D., Davis and Elkins Coll., 1969, W.Va. U., W.Va. Wesleyan Coll., 1971; m. Mary Veronica Casey, Oct. 4, 1943; children—Margaret Ann, Mary Katherine, Frances Susan, Elizabeth Ellen, Harley Orrin, Daniel Casey. Coach, tchr. sci. Norton (Va.) High Sch., 1931-33; head coach Potomac State Coll., Keyser, 1933-35; sheriff Mineral County, Keyser, 1937-41; right-of-way agt., Va. dir. Office Govt. Reports, later OWI, 1942; mem. 81st-96th congresses from 2d W.Va. Dist. Served as lt. comdr. AC, USNR, 1942-46; ATO, PTO. Mem. Am. Legion, V.F.W., D.A.V., Amvets, W.Va. Farm Bur. Democrat. Methodist. K.P., Elk, Moose (past pres. state assn.), Lion (past dist. gov. W.Va.). Home: Keyser WV 26726 Office: 2366 Rayburn Office Bldg Washington DC 20515*

STAGL, JOHN MATTHEW, hosp. adminstr.; b. Chgo., Aug. 1, 1915; s. John and Marie (Schoenherr) S.; student Northwestern U., 1936-41; m. Bernice Lowery, Aug. 14, 1943; children—John Martin, Barry Michael, Thomas William, Richard David. With Comml. Investment Trust Corp., 1934-42; office mgr. Passavant Hosp., Chgo., 1947-53; asst. dir., 1953-61, dir., 1961-70, exec. v.p., 1970-71, pres., 1971-72; pres. Northwestern Meml. Hosp., Chgo., 1972-76; exec. v.p. McGaw Med. Center Norwestern U., 1974-76, pres., 1976—; lectr. hosp. adminstrn. Northwestern U., 1951-60, mem. adv. council Grad. Sch. Mgmt., 1972-78, 1st ann. MacEahern lectr., 1976; mem. Joint Commn. Accreditation of Hosps., 1979—; sec. Ill. Regional Med. Program, 1970-75; pres. Chgo. Hosp. Council, 1965; mem. Ill. Health Facilities Planning Bd., 1974—. Bd. dirs. Community Fund Chgo., 1966-68. Served to capt. AUS, 1943-46. Recipient F.C. Morgan award Am. Assn. Hosp. Accountants, 1960. Fellow Am. Coll. Hosp. Adminstrs.; mem. Am. (past chmn., past trustee), Ill. (past trustee, Disting. Service award 1977) hosp. assns., Hosp. Fin. Mgmt. Assn. (past pres.), Inst. Medicine Chgo. (adminstrv. bd.), Council Teaching Hosps. Home: 134 Wilmette Ave Glenview IL 60025 Office: 339 E Chicago Ave Chicago IL 60611

STAGNER, ROSS, educator, psychologist; b. Waco, Tex., June 15, 1909; s. William Arch and Della (Shumate) S.; B.A., Washington U., St. Louis, 1929; M.A., U. Wis., 1930, Ph.D., 1932; M.A., Dartmouth, 1947; m. Margaret Wieland, Dec. 14, 1928; children—Rhea (Mrs. B.C. Das), Martin William. Faculty, U. Akron (Ohio), 1935-39, Dartmouth, 1939-49; with Koppers Co., Pitts., 1943-45; prof. psychology and labor relations U. Ill., 1949-57; prof. Wayne State U., Detroit, 1957-79, prof. emeritus, 1979—, chmn. dept. psychology, 1957-73. Recipient Pabst Postwar Employment award, 1944. Social Sci. Research Council fellow, 1932-33; NSF fellow, 1962, Ford fellow, 1963-64, Fulbright prof., Italy, 1955-56, Eng., 1965-66; NIMH fellow, 1972-73. Fellow AAAS; mem. Am. Psychol. Assn. (past pres. div. personality, indsl. div.), Peace Research Soc., Psychonomic Soc. Author: Psychology of Personality, 1937, 4th edit., 1974; (with T.F. Karwoski) Psychology, 1952; Psychology of Industrial Conflict, 1956; (with H. Rosen) Psychology of Union-Management Relations, 1965; Dimensions of Human Conflict, 1967; Psychological Aspects of International Conflict, 1967; (with C.M. Solley) Basic Psychology, 1970. Contbr. articles profl. jours. Home: 24845 Towne Rd Apt 510 Southfield MI 48034 Office: Dept Psychology Wayne State U 5980 Cass Ave Detroit MI 48202. *After fifty years' study of human conflicts, I remain convinced that the race has many survival characteristics. However, our species may be destroyed by our extraordinary capacity for denial or distortion of reality. Civilization can be preserved, but only if our young people can learn that what is a "fact" depends upon the person observing; that we must try to understand reality as it is perceived by the other person.*

STAHL, BEN, artist, author; b. Chgo., Sept. 7, 1910; s. Ben F. and Grace (Meyer) S.; student pub. schs.; m. Ella M. Lehocky, Dec. 19, 1940; children—Ben F., Gail, Regina, David. Illustrator, Sat. Eve. Post, other nat. mags., 1933—; mem. founding faculty Famous Artists Schs., Westport, Conn., 1949—; founder v.p. Sarasota Mus. of the Cross (created all paintings and drawings exhibited) (all paintings stolen 1968); exhibitor N.A.D., Chgo. Art Inst., Audubon Mus., others; one man shows Soc. Ill., N.Y.C., 1945, Stevens Gross Galleries, Chgo., 1950, Scarab Club, Detroit, 1951, Sarasota Art Assn., 1950, Chgo., 1969, Bridgeport U., 1969, Ft. Lauderdale, Fla., 1970, Topflight Gallery, 1971, Parker Playhouse Gallery, 1971, Red Piano Gallery, Hilton Head, S.C., 1975, Columbia (S.C.) Mus. Art, 1976, Fenn Galleries Ltd., 1978; painter, exhibitor 14 stas. of cross for Cath. Bible and Cath. Press, Chgo., 1955; illustrator 2 vols. Bible, ltd. edit. Gone With the Wind, 1960, Madame Bovary; condr. TV series Journey into Art with Ben Stahl for S.C. Ednl. TV network, 1976. Mem. Fla. Art Commn., 1965—. Recipient 62 nat. awards for painting and illustration including Saltus gold medal N.A.D., 1949. Author, illustrator: Blackbeard's Ghost, 1965 (Sequoia Book award for best children's book 1966; Walt Disney film 1968); Author: The Secret of Red Skull, 1971. Address: Potranca 19 PO Box 421 San Miguel de Allende GTO Mexico. *It wasn't merely ambition, but an overwhelming desire to prove to someone—anyone, that I had more talent than they realized.*

STAHL, CHARLES DREW, educator; b. Altoona, Pa., Aug. 28, 1923; s. Charles Asher and Anna Mary (Leintof) S.; B.A., Pa. State Coll., 1947; M.A., Pa. State U., 1950, Ph.D., 1952; m. Barbara Marie Morrison, Aug. 14, 1948; 1 son, Kevin M. Faculty, Pa. State U., University Park, 1952—, prof., 1956—, head dept. petroleum and natural gas, 1960—. Cons. Marathon Oil, 1963—, Mobile de Venezuela, 1958-59, Continental Oil, 1962—, State Pa., 1955—. Mem. Am. Inst. Mining Engrs., Sigma Xi, Tau Beta Pi. Republican. Methodist. Club: Bradford (Pa.). Contbr. articles to profl. jours. Home: 209 Norle St State College PA 16801 Office: Dept Petroleum and Natural Gas Pa State U University Park PA 16801

STAHL, DAVID EDWARD, assn. exec.; b. Chgo., Apr. 10, 1934; s. Archie Edward and Dorothy (Berning) S.; B.S., Miami U., 1956; m. Carolyn Downs Stahl, June 23, 1956; children—Stephen, Michael, Kurt, Thomas. Exec. v.p. Republic Realty Mortgage Corp., Chgo., 1963-66; dep. mayor City of Chgo., 1966-70, city comptroller, 1971-73; exec. v.p. Urban Land Inst., Washington, 1973-76; exec. v.p. Nat. Assn. Home Builders, Washington, 1977—. Bd. dirs. Nat. Capital Area, Boy Scouts Am.; bd. dirs. Center for Mcpl. and Met. Research. Served to lt. USAF, 1956-59. Recipient Silver Beaver award Chgo. Area council Boy Scouts Am. Mem. Am. Soc. Assn. Execs., Lambda Alpha. Roman Catholic. Clubs: Wayfarers (Chgo.); Md. Capitol Yacht (Annapolis); Harvard (Fontana, Wis.). Home: 3438 Blair Rd Falls Church VA 22041 Office: 15th and M Sts NW Washington DC 20005

STAHL, FREDERICK ANDREW, publisher; b. N.Y.C., Mar. 15, 1904; s. Andrew and Philippine (Schweitzer) S.; B.S. in Econs., Wharton Sch., U. Pa., 1926; m. Josepha E. Sharlow, June 4, 1926; 1 son, Frederick Andrew. With Standard & Poor's Corp., N.Y.C., 1927—, exec. v.p., dir. 1940-58, pres., dir., 1958-67, chmn. bd. dirs., 1967—; dir. McGraw Hill, Inc., until 1975, ret., 1975. Mem. N.Y. Acad. Scis. Clubs: U. of Penn., Analysts, N.Y. Athletic (N.Y.C.); Meadowbrook Country. Home: 1 Fruitledge Rd Brookville Glen Head NY 11545 Office: 25 Broadway New York NY 10004

STAHL, HENRY GEORGE, lawyer; b. Fremont, Ohio, Apr. 18, 1902; s. John Burton and Florence B. (Fisher) S.; student Tiffin U., 1925, Miami U., Oxford, O., 1923, Bowling Green U., 1924, Ohio No. U., 1926; read law with father; m. Gertrude M. Elmers, Mar. 6, 1926; children—Joyce E. (Mrs. Howard B. Thompson), Florence E. (Mrs. Kenneth Harmon), John B. Admitted to Ohio bar, 1926, since practiced in Fremont; mem. firm Stahl, Stahl & Stahl, 1926-51; practice as H.G. Stahl, 1951—; probate judge Sandusky County, 1932, 33. Mem. Sandusky County C. of C. (past pres.), Am., Ohio, Sandusky County (past pres.) bar assns., Am. Judicature Soc. Mason (past dist. dep.), Elk (past dist. dep.), K.P. (past dist. dep.). Home: 1710 McPherson Blvd Fremont OH 43420 Office: 802 Court St Fremont OH 43420

STAHL, LESLEY R., journalist; b. Lynn, Mass., Dec. 16, 1941; d. Louis and Dorothy J. (Tishler) Stahl; B.A. cum laude, Wheaton Coll., Norton, Mass., 1963. Asst. to speechwriter Mayor Lindsay's Office, N.Y.C., 1966-67; researcher N.Y. Election unit, London-Huntley Brinkley Report, NBC News, 1967-69; producer, reporter WHDH-TV, Boston, 1970-72; news corr. CBS News, Washington, 1972—. Trustee, Wheaton Coll. Recipient Tex. Headliners award, 1973. Office: CBS News 40th and Brandywine St NW Washington DC 20016*

STAHL, SIDNEY, lawyer; b. Dallas, Aug. 28, 1933; s. Isadore Louis and Sarah Hilda (Cohen) S.; B.B.A., So. Meth. U., 1954, LL.B., 1956; children—Lori Ann, Cathy Lynn. Admitted to U.S. Supreme Ct., Tex. bars; mem. firm Geary, Stahl & Spencer and predecessor firms, Dallas,

1958—, now sr. partner; lectr. in field. Past chmn. Greater Dallas Community Relations Commn.; past chmn. community relations council and treas. Jewish Fedn. of Greater Dallas; past v.p. Julius Schepps Community Center; past chmn. S.W. regional adv. bd. Anti-Defamation League of B'nai B'rith; pres. Dallas Park and Recreation Bd., 1975-79; mem. Dallas Assembly; mem. Dallas 40; past mem. young leadership council Nat. Democratic Com.; former mem. bd. dirs. USO, Jewish Family Service; bd. dirs. Dallas chpt. NCCJ, Sr. Citizens of Greater Dallas, Dallas Museum Fine Arts, Dallas Symphony Assn., Dallas Theater Center, Dallas Civic Opera, Dallas Health and Sci. Museum, State Fair Tex., Jewish Fedn. Greater Dallas, Dallas Summer Musicals, Tex. Assembly of Arts Councils; mem. Dallas Municipal Cultural Arts Com., Dallas Environ. Quality Com.; mem. adv. council Jr. League of Dallas. Served with JAG Corps, USAF, 1956-58. Mem. State Bar Tex., Dallas, Am. bar assns., Barristers (past pres. chpt.). Jewish (past v.p., bd. dirs. congregation). Home: 5030 Ravine Dr Dallas TX 75220 Office: 2800 One Main Pl Dallas TX 75250

STAHLER, ALFRED FRANCIS, III, mech. engr.; b. Bayonne, N.J., June 1, 1932; s. Alfred Francis and Linda Blossom (Baldwin) S.; M.E., Stevens Inst. Tech., 1956; M.S. in Mech. Engring., U. Wash., 1961; M.B.A., U. Santa Clara, 1969; m. Kathleen Mary Barrett, Dec. 29, 1956; children—Alfred, Mary, Anne. Sr. research engr. Boeing Co., Seattle, 1956-62; sr. aerodynamicist AiResearch, Los Angeles, 1962-64; corporate cons., mem. research staff Ampex Corp., Redwood City, Calif., 1964-78; v.p. engring. A.F. Stahler Co., Inc., 1978—; cons. gas bearings, tape transports, web handling; cons. antenna design Head adviser San Mateo Jr. Achievers, 1970-71. Served with USNR, 1952-54. Mem. Am. Soc. M.E., Am. Soc. Lubrication Engrs. (Walter D. Hodson award 1965), Am. Radio Relay League, Delta Tau Delta. Clubs: Kena (Santa Clara, Calif.); Lacrosse (Palo Alto, Cal.). Contbr. articles to profls. jours. and ham radio mags. Patentee broadcast video contact duplicator video cassette-automatic transport, battery operated video recorder, water analogue of source-vortex flow, super-stable journal bearing, foil-journal bearing, other electronic equipment, antenna feed systems, magnetic tape burnishing and testing equipment. Home: 5521 Big Oak Dr San Jose CA 95129 Office: PO Box 354 Cupertino CA 95015

STAHMANN, MARK ARNOLD, biochemist, educator; b. Spanish Fork, Utah, May 30, 1914; B.A., Brigham Young U., 1936; postgrad. U. Wis., 1936-42, Ph.D., 1941; m. 1941; 2 children. Asst. chemistry Rockefeller Inst., 1942-44; research asso. organic chemistry Mass. Inst. Tech., 1944-45; faculty U. Wis., Madison, 1946—, prof. biochemistry, 1956—; researcher OSRD, 1944-46. FAO cons. Instituto Biologico, San Paulo, Brazil, 1974. Guggenheim fellow Pasteur Inst., Paris, 1955; Fulbright scholar, Nagoya, Japan, 1967. Mem. AAAS, Am. Soc. Plant Physiologist, Am. Chem. Soc., Soc. for Exptl. Biology and Medicine, Phytopath. Soc., Am. Soc. Biol. Chemists. Home: 939 University Bay Dr Madison WI 53705

STAHMANN, ROBERT F., educator; b. Peoria, Ill., Nov. 26, 1939; s. Fred Soeffner and Mary Emma (Thompson) S.; B.A., Macalester Coll., 1963; M.S., U. Utah, 1965, Ph.D., 1967; m. Kathleen Cook, Dec. 21, 1965; children—Benjamin C., John C., Paul C., Mark C. Research fellow U. Utah, 1966-67; sr. counselor U. Iowa, Iowa City, 1967-71, coordinator counseling service, 1971-72, dir. counseling service, 1972-75, asst. prof. edn., 1967-71, asso. prof., 1971-75; prof. child devel. and family relations Brigham Young U., Provo, Utah, 1975—, dir. marriage and family counseling clinic, 1976—, coordinator program in marriage and family therapy, 1977—. Scoutmaster, Boy Scouts Am., 1969-72, cubmaster, 1976—. Mem. Am. Psychol. Assn., Am. (dir. 1977-79), Utah (pres. 1978-80) assns. marriage and family counselors, Phi Kappa Phi. Mormon. Co-author: Premarital Counseling, 1980; co-editor, contbr.: Counseling in Marital and Sexual Problems: A Clinician's Handbook, 1977; asso. editor Jour. Coll. Student Personnel, 1971-77; editor Jour. Asso. Mormon Counselors and Psychotherapists, 1977-78; contbr. chpts. to books, articles to profl. jours. Home: 1951 South 250 East Orem UT 84057 Office: Brigham Young U Provo UT 84602

STAHMER, HAROLD MARTIN, JR., coll. dean; b. Bklyn., Aug. 7, 1929; s. Harold Martin and Ann Lillian (Truntz) S.; B.A., Dartmouth, 1951; vis. scholar Benedictine Abbey of Maria Laach, 1951-52; B.D., Union Theol. Sem., 1955; Ph.D., Cambridge U. (Eng.), 1955-57; vis. scholar Columbia Law Sch., 1965-66; m. Jean Craig Smith, Sept. 22, 1956; children—Sarah Anne, Jennifer Betsy, Hannah Mary. Instr. religion Barnard Coll., 1957-60, acting dept. chmn., 1958-60, asst. prof., 1961-62; asso. prof. Barnard Coll. and Columbia, 1962-67; chmn. dept. religion Barnard Coll., 1962-68; dir. undergrad. program in religion Columbia, 1962-67, prof., 1967-69; dir. Harvard-Yale-Columbia intensive summer studies program, 1967-69; asso. dean U. Fla. Coll. Arts and Scis., Gainesville, 1969—, asso dir. Center for Gerontol. Studies and Programs, prof. religion and philosophy. Lectr. contemporary western religious trends CBS, 1966. Mem. standing com. ch. and state ACLU, 1960-69; coordinator Gov. Askew's Conf. Higher Edn. Disadvantaged, 1970; mem. Gov.'s Capital Punishment Commn., 1972. Recipient Community Service award B'nai B'rith Rockland County, 1966; E. Harris Harbison Distinguished Teaching prize, 1968. Fellow Am. Council Learned Socs., Soc. Human Values in Higher Edn.; mem. AAUP, Soc. Sci. Study Religion, Am. Acad. Religion, ACLU. Author: Speak That I May See Thee, 1968. Editor: Religion and Contemporary Society, 1963. Home: 101 NW 44th St Gainesville FL 32607

STAHNKE, HERBERT LUDWIG GEORGE, biologist, former educator; b. Chgo., June 10, 1902; s. Albert Herman and Marguerite Stahnke; A.A., LaGrange (Mo.) Coll., 1926; S.B., U. Chgo., 1928; A.M., U. Ariz., 1934; Ph.D., Ia. State Coll., 1939; m. Lydia Leona Stille, June 10, 1929; children—Jo Anne Yvonne, Jerry LeRoy. Biology tchr., head sci. dept. Mesa (Ariz.) Union High Sch., 1928-40; prof. zoology, dir. poisonous animals research lab. Ariz. State U., 1941-73, prof. emeritus, 1972—, head div. life scis., 1940-62. Nat. cons. Surgeon Gen. USAF, 1962. Developer, mfr. anti-scorpion serum, 1948—. Fellow AAAS (life), Ariz. Acad. Sci. (life); mem. Am. Inst. Biol. Scis. (life), Phi Delta Kappa, Sigma Xi. Rotarian. Research on biogeography, taxonomy of scorpions, comparative venomology, systematics and biology of order Scorpionida. Author: Biotic Principles (textbook); Treatment of Venomous Bites and Stings; contbr. articles to profl. jours.; research on scorpion taxonomy and evolution. Home: 2016 E Laguna Dr Tempe AZ 85282

STAHR, ELVIS J(ACOB), JR., educator, conservationist, lawyer; b. Hickman, Ky., Mar. 9, 1916; s. Elvis and Mary Anne (McDaniel) S.; A.B., U. Ky., 1936; B.A., U. Oxford (Eng.) (Rhodes scholar), 1938, B.C.L., 1939, M.A., 1943; diploma in Chinese Lang., Yale, 1943; LL.D., W.Va. Wesleyan Coll., Waynesburg Coll., 1959, Concord Coll., 1960, U. Md., U. Pitts., 1961, La. State U., Tex. Christian U., U. Ky., 1962, U. Notre Dame, 1964, Ind. State U., 1966, Brown U., 1967, Northwestern U., U. Fla., 1968, U. Tampa, 1972, Ind. U., 1976; D.Environ. Sci., Rollins Coll., 1973; Dr.Mil. Sci., Northeastern U., 1962; D.Pub. Adminstrn., Bethany Coll., 1962; D.H.L., DePauw U., 1963, Rose Poly Inst., 1965, Transylvania U., 1973; Litt.D., U. Cin., 1966, U. Maine, 1976; Pd.D., Culver-Stockton Coll., 1966; D.Sc., Norwich U., 1968, Hanover Coll., 1975; m. Dorothy Howland Berkfield, June 28, 1946; children—Stephanie Ann, Stuart Edward Winston, Bradford Lanier. Admitted to N.Y. State bar, 1940, Ky. bar, 1948, U.S. Supreme Ct. bar, 1950; practiced as asso. firm Mudge, Stern, Williams & Tucker, N.Y.C., 1939-41, sr. asso., 1946-47; asso. prof. law U. Ky., 1947-48, prof. law, 1948-56, dean Coll. Law, 1948-56, provost, 1954-56; vice chancellor professions U. Pitts., 1957-58; pres. W.Va. U., Morgantown, 1958-61; spl. asst. Sec. Army, Washington, 1951-52; cons. Dept. Army, 1952-53, Sec. Army, 1961-62; pres. Ind. U., 1962-68; pres. Nat. Audubon Soc., N.Y.C., 1968-79, sr. counselor, 1979—; mem. exec. com. Acacia Mut. Life Ins. Co., 1973—, also dir.; dir. Univ. Assos., Inc., Chase-Manhattan Bank & Corp., Saxon Industries; dir. Fed. Res. Bank Chgo., 1966-68, dep. chmn., 1967, 68. Mem. Constn. Rev. Commn. Ky., 1949-56, Ind., 1967-68; exec. dir. Pres.' Com. on Edn. Beyond High Sch., Washington, 1956-57; mem. U.S. del. Joint U.S.-USSR Com. on Cooperation for Protection of Environment, 1973, Internat. Whaling Commn., 1975, 78; mem. U.S. Aviation Adv. Commn., 1970-73, Nat. Commn. for World Population Yr., 1974; nat. chmn. U.S.O., 1973-76, bd. dirs., 1979—; pub. mem. Nat. Petroleum Council, 1974-79; mem. Citizens' Action Com. to Fight Inflation, 1974-75, Summit Conf. on Inflation, 1974. Mem. Nat. Commn. on Accrediting, 1963-68; trustee Transylvania U., 1969-76, mem. founders bd., 1978—; pres. Midwestern Univs. Research Assn., 1963-66; incorporator Argonne Univs. Assn., 1965, trustee, 1965-67; trustee Univs. Research Assn., 1965, mem. council presidents, 1965-68, chmn., 1968; bd. dirs. Alliance To Save Energy, 1977—, Resolve, 1977—, Council Fin. Aid to Edn., 1966-69; chmn. higher edn. adv. com. Edn. Commn. States, 1966-68; mem. bd. Govtl. Affairs Inst., 1968-72, Pub. Adminstrn. Service, 1970-72, Inst. Services to Edn., 1965-67; chmn. Commn. on Fed. Relations, Am. Council on Edn., 1966-68; mem. exec. com. Nat. Assn. State Univs. and Land Grant Colls., 1965-68; mem. at-large bd. dirs. Am. Cancer Soc., 1970-76; trustee Com. Econ. Devel., 1964—; mem. exec. bd. Nat. Assn. Ednl. Broadcasters, 1969-72; adv. council Electric Power Research Inst., 1973-77, Gas Research Inst., 1977—; trustee Nat. Recreation and Park Assn., 1969-72; bd. dirs. Regional Plan Assn. Greater N.Y., 1970-75, Appalachian Highlands Assn., 1975—; mem. U.S. del. UN Conf. on Human Environment, Stockholm, 1972; mem. bd. Citizens Com. Natural Resources U.S., 1969-78; evaluation panel Nat. Bur. Standards, 1975-77; adv. council Nat. Energy Project, Am. Enterprise Inst. Pub. Policy Research, 1974-76; chmn. Coalition Concerned Charities, 1972-78; mem. exec. bd. Am. Com. for Internat. Conservation, 1978—; mem. adv. council Center for Internat. Environ. Info., 1978-79. Served from 2d lt. to lt. col., inf. AUS, 1940-45. Named One of Am.'s Ten Outstanding Young Men, U.S. Jr. C.of C., 1948. Decorated Spl. Breast Order of Yun Hui (2); Army Navy and Air Force medal 1st class (China); Bronze Star medal with oak leaf cluster (U.S.); Order of Grand Cross (Peru). Recipient Algernon Sydney Sullivan medallion of N.Y. So. Soc., 1936; Meritorious Civilian Service medal Dept. Army, 1953, Distinguished Civilian Service medal, 1971; Distinguished Service awards U. Ky. Alumni Assn., 1961, Res. Officers Assn. U.S., 1962; Kentuckian of Year award Ky. Press Assn., 1961; Sesquicentennial medal U. Mich., 1967; Centennial medal U. Ky., 1965; named Ky. col. and gen.; La. and Neb. adm.; Ind. Sagamore. Mem. Assn. U.S. Army (life, pres. 1965-68, chmn. council trustees 1969-74), Ind. Soc. of Chgo. (hon. life), Jr. C. of C. Internat. (hon. life senator), Assn. Am. Rhodes Scholars, Nat. Inst. Social Scis. (v.p. 1969-77), Sons of Ind. in N.Y., Kentuckians (pres. N.Y.C. 1976-79, life trustee), S.R., SAR, Ky. Bar, Ind. (hon.) bar assns., Disciples of Christ Hist. Soc. (life mem.), Phi Beta Kappa, Order of Coif, Sigma Chi (Balfour Nat. award 1936, Significant Sig 1961, dir. found. bd. 1974—), Omicron Delta Kappa, Phi Delta Phi, Tau Kappa Alpha (Dist. Alumni award 1966), Merton Soc. (Oxford, Eng.); hon. mem. Blue Key, Beta Gamma Sigma, Alpha Kappa Psi, Kappa Kappa Psi. Presbyterian. Clubs: Army-Navy, Cosmos (Washington); Field (Greenwich); Century, Princeton, Explorers (N.Y.C.); Pilgrims of U.S.; Nantucket Yacht; Boone and Crockett. Author: (with others) Economics of Pollution, 1971. Home: Martin Dale Greenwich CT 06830 Office: Audubon Hdqrs 950 3d Ave New York NY 10022 also Audubon Office 1511 K St NW Washington DC 20005. *Focus on getting good results rather than on getting credit for them. Do your best, or let somebody else have the chance if you're too busy.*

STAINBACK, THOMAS NATHANIEL, coll. pres.; b. Saranac Lake, NY., Oct. 19, 1923; s. Ashley Forest and Virginia Sarah (Peacock) S.; student Paul Smith's Coll., 1946-48; B.S. in Edn., Ithaca Coll., 1948-50; m. Aida Di Filippo, Oct. 11, 1958. Exec. sec. Saranac Lake (N.Y.) C. of C., 1950-52, exec. dir., Hazleton, Pa., 1953-55; mng. dir. Battle Creek (Mich.) Area Devel. Corp., 1955-57; with C. of C., 1957—, pres. Jersey City, 1957-64, exec. v.p., Greater Cin., 1965-69, N.Y. C. of C., N.Y.C., 1969-73; pres. N.Y. C. of C. and Industry, Inc., N.Y.C., 1973-76; pres. Paul Smith's Coll. (N.Y.), 1976—. Past trustee N.Y.C. Mission Soc., N.Y. State Labor Mgmt. Adv. Council, N.Y. State Apprenticeship and Tng. Council, N.Y.C. Econ. Edn. Council; past trustee, mem. alumni council Ithaca Coll., chmn. alumni fund, 1970-71; chmn. Brighton Twp. Planning and Zoning Bd. Served with AUS, 1942-46. Mem. Am. Assn. Community and Jr. Colls., Assn. Governing Bds. Univs. and Colls., N.Y. Assn. Jr. Colls., U.S. C. of C. (Disting. Service award, chmn. bd. regents 1963-64), Am. (pres. 1968-69), N.J. (pres. 1962-63), N.Y. (exec. com.) chamber commerce execs. Clubs: Rotary, Masons, Shriners. Office: Paul Smith's Coll Paul Smiths NY 12970*

STAINBROOK, EDWARD, psychiatrist, educator; b. Meadville, Pa., Jan. 24, 1912; s. Charles Cochran and Harriet Elizabeth (Smith) S.; B.A., Allegheny Coll., 1935, D.Sc., 1972; Ph.D. in Psychology, M.D., Duke, 1945; m. Elizabeth Kemp Selden, July 13, 1940; 1 dau., Judith Selden Instr. English, Allegheny Coll., summer 1935; psychologist bur. mental health Pa. Dept. Welfare, 1936-37; instr. Am. history Meadville High Sch., 1937-38; Univ. fellow psychology, chief psychol. examiner, also instr. applied, clin. and abnormal psychology Duke, 1938-42; intern Cornell div. Bellevue Hosp., N.Y.C., 1945-46; resident psychiatry Payne Whitney Clinic, N.Y.C., 1946-47, N.Y. State Psychiat. Inst., 1947-48; from instr. to asso. prof. psychiatry Yale, 1948-52, lectr. psychiatry dept. anthropology, 1950-51; cons. Columbia-N.E. Brazil project, 1950-51; psychiatrist-in-charge Yale Psychiat. Hosp. and Clinic, 1951-52; prof. psychiatry, chmn. dept. Upstate Med. Center, State U. N.Y., 1952-56; prof. psychiatry, chmn. dept psychiatry U. So. Calif. Sch. Medicine, Los Angeles, 1956-68, prof. human behavior, 1968-77, chmn. dept. human behavior, 1968-77, emeritus prof. psychiatry, 1977—; chief psychiatrist Los Angeles County Gen. Hosp., 1956-72; creator CBS-TV ednl. series Troubled Self, Conversations with a Psychiatrist, 1967. Cons. Office Surgeon Gen., U.S. Army, 1955; chmn. tng. coms. NIMH, 1966-67; mem. Gov.'s Commn. on Family, 1966—; mem. behaviorial sci. com. Nat. Bd. Med. Examiners, 1969-73, chmn., 1975—. Fellow A.C.P., Am. Coll. Psychiatrists; mem. Am. Psychiat. Assn. (trustee), Group Advanced Psychiatry, AMA, Nat. Assn. Mental Health (mem. profl. adv. com. 1969-77), Am. Acad. Psychoanalysis, So. Calif. Psychoanalytic Soc., So. Calif. Psychiat. Soc. (pres. 1963). Author numerous articles, chpts. in books, research papers. Co-editor: Psychoanalysis and the Human Situation, 1964. Home: 1277 Parkview Ave Pasadena CA 91103 Office: U So Calif Sch Medicine 2025 Zonal Ave Los Angeles CA 90033

STAIR, CHARLES WILLIAM, service co. exec.; b. Ida Grove, Iowa, Oct. 21, 1940; s. Frederick Cleveland and Eunice (Carlson) S.; B.A., Wheaton Coll., 1963; m. Patricia Ellen Gramley, June 15, 1963; children—Kerry John, Andrew Charles, Melissa Katherine. With Servicemaster Industries, Inc., Downers Grove, Ill., 1963—, exec. v.p., 1972-73, div. pres., 1974-75, group v.p., 1976-77, group pres., 1978—, dir.; chmn. bd. dirs. Tyndale House Pubs., Wheaton, Ill. Mem. Am. Hosp. Assn., Cath. Hosp. Assn., Am. Mgmt. Assn. Office: 2300 Warrenville Rd Wheaton IL 60515. *My goal is to contribute to society as a whole by helping the individual grow and develop.*

STAIR, FREDERICK ROGERS, sem. pres.; b. Knoxville, Tenn., Mar. 7, 1918; s. Fred Rogers and Cristyne (Miller) S.; B.S., Davidson Coll., 1939, D.D., 1960; postgrad. U. Edinburgh, 1945; B.D., Union Theol. Sem., Va., 1947, Th.M., 1948; LL.D., Davis and Elkins Coll., 1969; postgrad. Advanced Mgmt. Program, Harvard, 1972-73; m. Martha Osborne, Dec. 19, 1942; children—Mary Miller, Thomas Osborne. Ordained to ministry Presbyn. Ch., 1943; asst. to pres. Union Theol. Sem., Va., 1948-53; pastor in Hickory, N.C., 1953-59, Atlanta, 1959-67; pres. Union Theol. Sem., Va., 1967—. Fellow Yale Div. Sch., 1972. Trustee, vice chmn. bd. Davidson Coll. Served with inf. AUS, 1942-46. Moses D. Hoge fellow, 1948. Mem. Assn. Theol. Schs. (exec. com.), Phi Beta Kappa, Phi Gamma Delta, Omicron Delta Kappa. Club: Richmond Forum. Home: 1216 Rennie Ave Richmond VA 23227

STAIR, GOBIN, publishing exec., painter, typographic designer; b. S.I., N.Y., July 30, 1912; s. Gobin and Elsie (Wilson) S.; A.B., Dartmouth, 1933; L.H.D., Starr King Sch. for Ministry, 1975; m. Julia Sitterly, Oct. 5, 1933; children—Adrian, Charlotte. With Beacon Press, Boston, 1956-75, dir., 1962-75. Mem Bookbuilders of Boston (pres. 1961-62, William A. Dwiggins award 1965), Boston Soc. Printers. Illustrator: Gulliver's Travels (Swift), 1957; Middle Passage (Coxe), 1960; Old Quotes at Home (Darling), 1965; The King Lear Experience, 1976. Home: Wapping Rd Kingston MA 02364

STAIR, LOIS HARKRIDER, church ofcl.; b. Waukesha, Wis., June 22, 1923; d. Lester Dore and Lola (Brown) Harkrider; B.A., Smith Coll., 1944; L.H.D., Carroll Coll., 1971, Keuka Coll., 1975; D.D., Dubuque C. Coll., 1971; Litt.D., Wilson Coll., 1972; m. Ralph Martin Stair, Oct. 14, 1944; children—Ralph Martin, Stuart Randall. Sec., v.p. Gen. Casting Corp. div. Grey Iron Foundry, Waukesha, 1960-73; moderator various levels Presbyterian Ch., 1966—, for Synod Wis., 1969, for gen. assembly United Presbyn. Ch. U.S., 1971—. Sec. bd. dirs. United Fund, Waukesha, 1960-61; sec. Equal Opportunities Commn., Waukesha, 1966-69; mem. bd. counselors Smith Coll., Higher Ednl. Aids Bd. State of Wis. Bd. dirs. Vis. Nurse Assn., Waukesha, 1962-64, Presbyn. Ministers' Fund, Fund for Theol. Edn.; trustee Carroll Coll., Waukesha, McCormick Theol. Sem.; trustee University Lake Sch., Hartland, Wis., 1964-67. Recipient Civic award UNICO, Waukesha, 1968. Home: 401 NE 19th Ave Apt 74 Deerfield Beach FL 33441

STAKEM, THOMAS EDWARD, JR., corp. exec.; b. Midland, Md., July 28, 1907; s. Thomas Edward and Elizabeth (Mullen) S.; LL.B., Georgetown U., 1933; m. Jeannette Livingstone, Feb. 28, 1933; children—Joan, Brian Edward. Head night auditor Willard Hotel, Washington, 1927-33; admitted to D.C. bar, 1932, Md. bar, 1935; spl. agt. FBI, Washington, Kansas City, Mo., 1934-35, spl. agt. in charge div. investigations Fed. Works and Pub. Works Agys., Kansas City, St. Paul, San Francisco, New Orleans, Washington, 1936-42; staff dir. investigations War Shipping Adminstrn., chief investigator U.S. Maritime Commn., 1943-50; asst. dep. adminstr., then acting dep. adminstr. Maritime Adminstrn., 1951-56, mem. Fed. Maritime Bd., 1956-61, chmn., bd., maritime adminstr., 1961; chmn. Fed. Maritime Commn., 1961-63, vice chmn., 1964; sr. v.p. Delta S.S. Lines, Inc., 1964—; partner law firm Macleav, Lynch, Bernnard & Gregg, 1968-76. Mem. Phi Alpha Delta. Clubs: Congl. Country (Washington), Propeller of U.S.; Oceanside Country (Ormond Beach, Fla.). Home: 8360 Greneboro Dr McLean VA 22102 also Surfside Club North Tower 1155 Ocean Shore Blvd Ormond Beach FL 32074 Office: 1625 K St NW Washington DC 20006

STAKGOLD, IVAR, educator; b. Oslo, Norway, Dec. 13, 1925; s. Henri and Rose (Wishengrad) S.; came to U.S., 1941, naturalized, 1947; B.Mech. Engring., Cornell U., 1945, M.Mech. Engring., 1946; Ph.D., Harvard, 1949; m. Alice Calvert O'Keefe, Nov. 27, 1964; 1 dau., Alissa Dent. Instr., then asst. prof. Harvard, 1949-56; head math. and logistics brs. Office Naval Research, 1956-59; faculty Northwestern U., 1960-75, prof. math. and engring. scis., 1964-75, chmn. engring. scis., 1969-75; prof., chmn. math. U. Del., 1975—; cons. in field; mem. U.S. Army basic research com. NRC, 1977—; vis. faculty Math. Inst., Oxford (Eng.) U., 1973, Univ. Coll., London, 1978. Mem. Soc. Indsl. and Applied Math. (trustee 1976—). Author: Boundary Value Problems of Mathematical Physics, vols. I and II, 1967; Green's Functions and Boundary Value Problems, 1978; asso. editor Am. Math. Monthly, 1975—, Jour, Applicable Analysis, 1977—, Internat. Jour. Engring. Sci., 1977—, Jour. Integral Equations, 1978—; U.S. rep. World Bridge Championships, 1959, 60; holder 7 nat. bridge championships. Home: 13 Fairfield Dr Newark DE 19711

STALCUP, JOE ALAN, lawyer, clergyman; b. Hooker, Okla., Feb. 13, 1931; s. Herbert I. and Ruby (Gantt) S.; B.B.A. cum laude, So. Methodist U., 1951, J.D. magna cum laude, 1959, M.Th. magna cum laude, 1978; m. Nancy Jo Vaughn, Sept. 3, 1950; children—Melinda (Mrs. James L. Lundy Jr.), Sondra Jo (Mrs. David Goodson), Cheri Ann (Mrs. Scott Ehley), Tchr. Dallas Ind. Sch. Dist., 1951-57; admitted to Tex. bar, 1959; asso. mem. firm Locke, Purnell, Boren, Laney & Neely, Dallas, 1959-66; asso. atty., partner firm Geary, Brice & Lewis, Dallas, 1966-67; founder, sr. partner firm Stalcup, Johnson, Meyers & Miller and predecessor firm, Dallas, 1968-75; dean Sch. Theology for the Laity, 1978—. Pres. Dallas County Young Democrats, 1952-54. Bd. dirs., mem. exec. com. N. Tex. Christian Communications Commn., 1972-78; bd. dirs., v.p. Greater Dallas Council Chs., 1972-75. Mem. Am., Tex., Dallas bar assns., Am. Judicature Soc., Phi Alpha Delta. Mem. Christian Ch. (minister). Home: 7594 Benedict Dr Dallas TX 75214 Office: 629 N Peak Dallas TX 75246

STALDER, FRED COLLINS, savs. and loan exec.; b. Okeen, Okla., Oct. 12, 1920; s. Fred Tibbles and Lavinia (Collins) S.; student U. Okla., 1938-41, U. Ind. Grad. Sch. Savs. and Loan, 1961; m. Mary Austin, July 4, 1942 (div. 1967); children—Claudia Ann (Mrs. Robert K. Gault, Jr.), Barbara Lynn (Mrs. Michael M. McDaniel), Steven Austin; m. 2d, Christine Cole Stone, Dec. 29, 1969. Escrow officer Union Title Ins. & Trust, Co., San Diego, 1945-47; with Central Fed. Savs. & Loan Assn., San Diego, 1947—, mgr., 1948—, dir., 1949—, v.p., 1950-57, exec. v.p., 1957-62, pres., 1962—; dir. San Diego Gas & Electric Co. Chmn., Econ. Devel. Corp. San Diego County, 1973; pres. Calif. Savs. & Loan League, 1964, Combined Arts and Edn. Council; mem. Centre City Adv. Bd. San Diego, 1961-64; pres. San Diego County United Community Services, 1965, 66. Past pres., bd. dirs. Armed Services YMCA; past v.p., bd. dirs., exec. com. San Diegoans Inc.; v.p., bd. dirs. San Diego Opera Guild, 1966-70; past v.p., San Diego Taxpayers Assn., San Diego Downtown Assn.; past chmn. San Diego Better Bus. Bur.; bd. overseers U. Calif. at San Diego; bd. dirs. San Diegans, Inc.; trustee San Diego Mus. Art. Served to capt. USAAF, 1941-45. Decorated Air medal. Mem. San Diego C. of C. (dir.), Fine Arts Soc. San Diego, Delta Chi. Republican.

Presbyn. Clubs: Cuyamaca; La Jolla Beach and Tennis, La Jolla Country. Home: 6970 Fairway Rd La Jolla CA 92037 Office: 225 Broadway San Diego CA 92101

STALEY, ALLEN PERCIVAL GREEN, art historian; b. Mexico, Mo., June 4, 1935; s. Walter Goodwin and Martha (Green) S.; B.A., Princeton U., 1957; M.A., Yale U., 1960, Ph.D., 1965; m. Etheleen Lichtenstein, July 26, 1968; children—Oliver, Peter. Lectr., Frick Collection, N.Y.C., 1962-65; asst. curator Phila. Mus. Art, 1965-69; asst. prof. art history Columbia U., N.Y.C., 1969-71, asso. prof., 1971-76, prof., 1976—. Nat. Endowment Humantities fellow, 1976-77. Mem. Coll. Art Assn., Walpole Soc., Victorian Soc. Author: The Pre-Raphaelite Landscape, 1973; contbr. articles to profl. jours. Home: 151 Central Park W New York NY 10023 Office: Dept Art History Columbia Univ New York NY 10027

STALEY, DELBERT CLEO, utility co. exec.; b. Hammond, Ind., Sept. 16, 1924; s. Eugene and Nellie (Downer) S.; student Rose Poly. Inst., 1943-44, Advanced Mgmt. Program, Harvard U., 1962; m. Ingrid Andersen, Mar. 16, 1946; children—Crista Ellis, Clifford, Cynthia Logan, Corrin. With Ill. Bell Telephone Co., 1946-66, 68-76, v.p. state ops., Springfield, 1970-72, v.p. ops., Chgo., 1972-76; comml. systems adminstr. AT&T, N.Y.C. 1966-68; pres. Ind. Bell Telephone Co., Indpls., 1976-78; v.p., AT&T, N.J., 1978-79; pres., chief exec. officer and dir. N.Y. Telephone, N.Y.C., 1979—; dir. Dean Foods Co., Franklin Park, Ill., Horizon Bancorp., Morristown, N.J., Ball Corp., Muncie, Ind., The N.Y. Racing Assn., Inc., Rose-Hulman Inst. Tech., I Love A Clean N.Y. Inc. Mem. Business/Labor Working Group, Econ. Dev. Council, exec. com. ARC of Greater N.Y.; adv. bd. Greater N.Y. div. Salvation Army, Inc. Served with U.S. Army, 1943-46. Mem. IEEE, N.Y. C. of C. Club: Harvard Bus. Sch. of Chgo. Home: Poly Park Road Rye NY 10580 Office: 1095 Ave of the Americas New York NY 10036

STALEY, HENRY MUELLER, mfg. co. exec.; b. Decatur, Ill., June 3, 1932; s. Augustus Eugene, Jr. and Lenore (Mueller) S.; grad. Governor Dummer Acad. 1950; B.S. in Psychology, Northwestern U., 1954, M.B.A. in Finance, 1956; m. Violet Lucas, Feb. 4, 1955; children—Mark Eugene, Grant Spencer. Salesman, Field Enterprises, Chgo., 1953; salesman A.E. Staley Mfg. Co., 1951, mgmt. trainee, 1956-57, ins. mgr., 1957-59, asst. treas., 1959-65, treas., asst. sec., 1965-73, v.p., treas., asst. sec., 1973-77, v.p., 1977—, also dir. Crusade chmn. Macon County unit Am. Cancer Soc., 1964-65, mem. bd. dirs., 1965-71, vice chmn. bd., 1965-66, chmn. bd., 1966-69; bd. dirs. United Way Decatur and Macon County, 1972-74; mem. adv. com. Millikin U., 1968—, chmn. adv. com., 1970-71; mem. Decatur Meml. Hosp. Devel. Council, 1969-71, mem. finance com., bd. dirs., 1970—, mem. long-range planning com., 1976-77, mem. devel. and community relations com., 1977—. Mem. Decatur C. of C. (dir. 1967-72), Sigma Nu. Clubs: Decatur, Decatur Country. Home: 276 Park Pl Decatur IL 62522 Office: AE Staley Mfg Co Eldorado at 22d St Decatur IL 62525

STALEY, THOMAS FABIAN, educator, critic; b. Pitts., Aug. 13, 1935; s. Fabian Richard and Mary (McNulty) S.; A.B., Regis Coll., 1957, B.S., 1957, D.H.L., 1979; M.A., U. Tulsa, 1958; Ph.D., U. Pitts., 1962; m. Carolyn O'Brien, Sept. 3, 1960; children—Thomas Fabian, Caroline Ann, Mary Elizabeth, Timothy X. Asst. prof. English, Rollins Coll., 1961-62; mem. faculty U. Tulsa, 1962—, prof. English, 1969—, dean Grad. Sch., 1969—, dir. Grad. Inst. Modern Letters, Trustees prof. modern lit., 1977—; Fulbright prof., Italy, 1966-67; Fulbright lectr., Italy, 1971; Danforth asso., 1965—. Chmn., Internat. James Joyce Symposium; dir. Grad. Inst. Modern Letters, 1970—; Bd. dirs. Tulsa Arts Council, 1969—; pres. James Joyce Found., 1968—; chmn. bd. Undercroft Montessori Sch., 1968-70, Marquette Sch., 1969-70; bd. dirs. Cascia Hall Prep. Sch.; bd. commrs. Tulsa City-County Library. Recipient Am. Council Learned Socs. award, 1969. Mem. AAUP, Modern Lang. Assn., Anglo-Irish Studies Assn., Am. Com. for Irish Studies, James Joyce Soc., Hopkins Soc., U.S. Tennis Assn. Clubs: Tulsa, Tulsa Tennis. Author: James Joyce Today, 1966; James Joyce's Portrait Of The Artist, 1968; Italo Svevo: Essays On His Work, 1969; (with H.J. Mooney) The Shapeless God; Essays On The Modern Novel, 1968; (with B. Benstock) Approaches to Ulysses: Ten Essays, 1970, Approaches to Joyce's Portrait: Ten Essays, 1977; Jean Rhys: A Critical Study, 1979; editor: Il Punto Su Joyce, 1973; Dorothy Richardson, 1975; Ulysses: Fifty Years, 1974; James Joyce Quar., 1963—; adv. editor Virginia Woolf Quar., Lost generation Jour., Twentieth Century Lit., 1966—. Contbr. articles to profl. jours. Home: 3018 S Trenton Tulsa OK 74114

STALKER, ALFRED JOSEPH, investment banker; b. Holyoke, Mass., July 5, 1906; s. Alfred W. and Geneva (Kay) S.; B.S., Syracuse U., 1928; m. Lydia Porter, May 12, 1934. With Pacific Tel. & Tel. Co., Seattle, 1928-29; with Kidder, Peabody & Co., N.Y.C., 1950—, mgr. dealer relations dept., 1950-57, gen. partner, dir. West Coast div., Los Angeles, 1958-67, v.p., 1967—. Served to lt. comdr. USNR, 1943-46. Mem. Delta Kappa Epsilon. Clubs: Birnam Wood Golf (Santa Barbara, Calif.); Stock Exchange, Los Angeles Country (Los Angeles). Home: 1470 Blue Ridge Dr Beverly Hills CA 90210 Office: 707 Wilshire Blvd Suite 3100 Los Angeles CA 90017

STALL, JAMES LAMAR, utilities exec.; b. Shreveport, La., Sept. 19, 1918; s. Lindon C. and Lillian (Harrison) S.; B.S. in Accounting, La. Tech. U., 1939; postgrad. La. State U., 1939-40; M.S. in Indsl. Mgmt. (Sloan fellow), Mass. Inst. Tech., 1960; m. Johnette Ford Adger, Sept. 23, 1942; children—Lindon Adger, Kathryn. Teaching fellow La. State U., 1939-40; salesman Burroughs Corp., 1940-41; with Southwestern Electric Power Co., Shreveport, 1946—, v.p., controller, dir., 1967-69, exec. v.p., dir., 1969-71, pres., chief exec. officer, dir., 1971—; dir. Central and S.W. Corp., Pioneer Bank & Trust Co. Treas., dir. Shreveport Goodwill Industries, 1957-59. Served with AUS, 1941-45. Recipient Corp. Leadership award Mass. Inst. Tech., 1976, Clyde E. Fant Meml. award for outstanding community service, 1978. Mem. Missouri Valley Electric Assn. (v.p.), Nat. Assn. Accountants (nat. dir. 1968-69, 70—, nat. v.p. 1969-70), Shreveport C. of C. Methodist (mem. ofcl. bd.). Home: 122 Richard St Shreveport LA 71105 Office: 428 Travis St Shreveport LA 71101

STALLARD, RICHARD ELGIN, dentist, health adminstr.; b. Eau Claire, Wis., May 30, 1934; s. Elgin Gale and Caroline Francis (Betz) S.; B.S., U. Minn., 1956, D.D.S., 1958, M.S., 1959, Ph.D., 1962; m. Norma Ann Woock, Oct. 15, 1956 (dec. 1973); children—Rondi Lynn, Alison Judith; m. 2d, Jaxon Shirley Sandlin, May 2, 1974; 1 son, Elgin Sandlin. Co-dir. periodontal research Eastman Dental Center, Rochester, N.Y., 1962-65; prof., head dept. periodontology Sch. Dentistry, U. Minn., Mpls., 1965-68, adj. prof. public health, 1976—; asst. dir. Eastman Dental Center, 1968-70; prof. anatomy, asst. dean Sch. Grad. Dentistry, dir. clin. research center Boston U. Sch. Grad. Dentistry, 1970-74; dental dir., head dept. periodontology Group Health Plan, Inc., St. Paul, 1974-79; exec. v.p., dental dir. Minndent, Inc., Mpls., 1980—; cons. USAF, 1968—, U.S. Navy, 1971-75; mem. tng. grant com. NIH/Nat. Inst. Dental Research, 1969-72; edn. cons. Project Vietnam, AID, Saigon, 1969-74; mem. grants and allocations com. Am. Fund for Dental Health, 1976—. Recipient Meritorious Achievement citation for dental research and edn. Boston U., 1970. Fellow Am., Internat. colls. dentists; mem. Am. Acad. Periodontology (pres. 1974), Am. Acad. Dental Spltys. (pres. 1971-75), Am. Pub. Health Assn., Omicron Kappa Upsilon, Sigma Xi. Club: Alumni (Mpls.). Author preventive dentistry textbook, articles in profl. jours. Home: 4200 W 44th St Edina MN 55424 Office: 7645 Metro Blvd Minneapolis MN 55435

STALLINGS, (CHARLES) NORMAN, lawyer; b. Tampa, Fla., Apr. 3, 1914; s. Otto Pyromus and Minnie Henderson (Mitchell) S.; A.B., U. Fla., 1935; J.D., Harvard U., 1938, LL.M., 1940; m. Mary Phillips Powell, Feb. 6, 1943; children—Charles Norman, Jean Katherine, Mary Anne. Admitted to Mo. bar, 1939, D.C. bar, 1941, Fla. bar, 1941, Ga. bar, 1946; asso. firm Ryland, Stinson, Mag & Thomson, Kansas City, Mo., 1938-39, Sutherland, Tuttle & Brennan, Washington, 1940-41, Atlanta, 1946-49; mem. firm Shackleford, Farrior, Stallings & Evans, Tampa, Fla., 1949—; dir. Jim Walter Corp., Jack Eckerd Corp., SE Banks Trust Co.; chmn. SE Bank of Tampa. Vice chmn. Hillsborough County (Fla.) Aviation Authority, 1955-61. Served to lt. col. U.S. Army, 1941-46; ETO. Decorated Bronze Star, Croix de Guerre avec Palma (Belgium). Fellow Am. Coll. Trial Lawyers; mem. Am., Hillsborough County (past pres.) bar assns., Fla. Bar (past gov.), Phi Delta Phi, Kappa Alpha. Republican. Episcopalian. Clubs: Rotary, Univ. (past pres.), Tampa Yacht and Country (past gov.), Palma Ceia Golf and Country, Ye Mystic Krewe of Gasparilla (past capt. and king). Home: 1901 Ardsley Pl Tampa FL 33609 Office: PO Box 3324 Tampa FL 33601

STALLMAN, ROBERT WOOSTER, educator, author: b. Milw., Sept. 27, 1911; s. Paul Michael and Hazel (Wooster) S.; A.B., U. Wis., 1933, A.M., 1939, Ph.D., 1942; m. Virginia Blume, Aug. 21, 1939; children—William Wooster, Robert Wooster. Part-time instr. U. Wis., 1939-42; instr. R.I. State Coll., 1942-43, Yale, 1943-44, Katharine Gibbs Sch., Boston, 1944-46; asst. prof. English, U. Kans., 1946-49; asso. prof. English, U. Conn., 1949-53, prof., 1953—; Bingham prof. U. Lousville (Ky.), 1966; asso. editor The Western Review, 1946-48; staff mem. Writers' Conf., Kans., summer 1948; lectr. U. Wis., summers 1946, 49, U. Minn., summer 1947; Ford Found. fellow, 1953-54; Fulbright lectr. Am. lit. U. Strasbourg, 1958-59, European univs.; vis. prof., Citizen's chair U. Hawaii, 1970; dir. U. Conn. Writers' Conf., 1950-55; fellow La Fondation Camargo, Cassis, France, 1974-75; lectr. French univs., 1977. Recipient U. Conn. Alumni Assn. Excellence award, 1968. Mem. Phi Beta Kappa. Author: The Houses That James Built and Other Literary Studies, 1961, 77; Stephen Crane: A Biography, 1968, rev. edit., 1973; Stephen Crane: A Critical Bibliography, 1972; The Figurehead and Other Poems, 1978. Editor: Critiques and Essays in Criticism, 1920-48, 1949; The Critic's Notebook, 1950, 77; Stephen Crane: An Omnibus, 1952, 54; Stephen Crane: Stories and Tales, 1955; Seventeen American Poets, 1958; The Ambassadors, 1960; The Art of Joseph Conrad, 1960; The Red Badge of Courage and Other Stories, 1960; Stephen Crane: Sullivan County Tales and Sketches, 1968; The Stephen Crane Reader, 1972. Co-editor: The Art of Modern Fiction, 1949, 56; The Creative Reader, 1954, rev., 1962; Stephen Crane: Letters, 1960; American Literature: Readings and Critiques, 1961; The War Dispatches of Stephen Crane, 1964, 77; The New York City Sketches of Stephen Crane, 1966, 77. Contbr. poems and essays, anthologies and jours.; contbr. to Ency. Brit.; Stephen Crane, 1974; adv. editor Studies in Short Fiction, American Literature Abstracts, Studies in the Novel. Address: 1 Westwood Rd Storrs CT 06268

STALLONE, SYLVESTER ENZIO, actor, writer, dir., producer, novelist; b. N.Y.C., July 6, 1946; s. Frank and Jacquline (Labofish) S.; student Am. Coll. of Switzerland, 1965-67, U. Miami, 1967-69; m. Sasha Czack, Dec. 28, 1974; 1 son, Sage. Usher, fish salesman, horse trainer, delicatessen worker, truck driver, bouncer, zoo attendant, short order cook, pizza demonstrator, phys. edn. tchr., motel supt., bookstore detective; appeared in motion pictures Lords of Flatbush, 1973, Capone, 1974, Rocky, 1976, F.I.S.T., 1978, Paradise Alley, 1978, Rocky II, 1979; now producer, dir. own films. Recipient Oscar for best picture, 1976; Golden Globe award for best picture, 1976; Donatello award for best actor in Europe, 1976; Christopher Religious award, 1976; Bell Ringer award Scholastic Mag., 1976; Nat. Theatre Owners award, 1976; Star of Yr. award, 1977. Mem. Screen Actors Guild, Writers Guild, Stuntmans Assn. (hon.), Dirs. Guild. Author: Paradise Alley, 1977; The Rocky Scrapbook, 1977; (novel) Rocky II. Nomination for two Oscars (acting and writing) in same year (1976) occurred for only 3d time in history. Address: care Herb Nanas Orgn 280 S Beverly Dr Suite 507 Beverly Hills CA 90212. *Once in one's life, for one mortal moment, one must make a grab for immortality; if not, one has not lived.*

STALLONES, REUEL ARTHUR, coll. dean; b. North Little Rock, Ark., Oct. 10, 1923; s. Wilner Leroy and Jet (Wilson) S.; student Visalia Jr. Coll., 1941-42, Ripon Coll., 1943-44, U. Mich., 1944-45; M.D., Case-Western U., 1949; M.P.H., U. Calif. at Berkeley, 1952; m. E. Joyce Graves, Aug. 14, 1945 (div. 1977); children—Jorel, Loran, Jared. Intern, Letterman Hosp., San Francisco, 1949-50; asst. chief dept. epidemiology Walter Reed Army Inst. Research, Washington, 1954-56; lectr., prof. U. Calif. at Berkeley, 1956-68; prof., dean Sch. Pub. Health, U. Tex. at Houston, 1968—. Served with AUS, 1943-46, 49-56. Fellow Am. Pub. Health Assn., Am. Coll. Preventive Medicine; mem. Am. Epidemiology, Assn. Tchrs. Preventive Medicine, Hamann Soc., Delta Omega, Sigma Xi. Home: 9427 Bassoon Houston TX 77025

STALNAKER, ARMAND CARL, ins. co. exec.; b. Weston, W.Va., Apr. 24, 1916; s. Thomas Carl and Alta (Hinzman) S.; B.B.A., U. Cin., 1941; M.A., U. Pa., 1945; Ph.D., Ohio State U., 1951; m. Rachel Pickett, Apr. 26, 1946; children—Timothy, Thomas. Asst. prof. bus. Ohio State U., Columbus, 1946-50; with Prudential Ins. Co., 1950-63; adminstrv. v.p., exec. v.p., pres., chmn. Gen. Am. Life Ins. Co., 1963—, also dir.; dir. Anheuser-Busch, Inc., Brown Group, Inc., Fed. Res. Bank of St. Louis, St. Louis-San Francisco R.R. Co. Bd. dirs. YMCA, St. Louis council Boy Scouts Am., Barnes Hosp., United Way, St. Louis Regional Commerce and Growth Assn., Huebner Found., Washington U. Mem. Am. Psychol. Assn., Am. Econ. Assn., AAAS, Am. Council Life Ins. (dir.), Am. Coll. CLU's (dir.), Civic Progress, Omicron Delta Kappa. Mem. Soc. of Friends. Clubs: Mo. Athletic, Noonday, Media, Bogey, Univ., Old Warson Country, St. Louis, St. Louis Country, N.Y. Yacht. Home: 35 York Dr Saint Louis MO 63144 Office: PO Box 396 Saint Louis MO 63166

STALNAKER, JOHN MARSHALL, educator; b. Duluth, Minn., Aug. 17, 1903; s. William Edward and Sara (Tatham) S.; B.S. with honors, U. Chgo., 1925; A.M. in Psychology, 1928; LL.D., Purdue U., 1956, Centre Coll., 1960; m. Ruth Elizabeth Culp, July 29, 1933 (dec. Apr. 1968); children—John Culp, Robert Culp, Judith S. Weikel; m. 2d, Edna Remmers, Aug. 21, 1969. Tchr. rural sch., Hardisty, Alta., Can., 1922; tchr. math., sci. Harvard Sch. for Boys, 1925-26; instr. psychology, spl. research asst. to pres., 1926-30, asst. prof. edn. and psychology (on leave), Purdue U., 1930-31, dir. attitude measurement, athletic survey U. Minn., 1930-31; examiner (instr.) bd. exams. U. Chgo., 1931-36, asst. prof., 1936-37, asso. prof., 1937-44; prof., Princeton, 1944-45; research asso. Coll. Entrance Exam Bd., 1936-37, cons. examiner, 1937-42; asso. sec., 1942-45; dir. Navy test research unit, 1942-45, contractor's tech. rep. for N.D.R.C. project N-106, 1942-45; dir. Army-Navy Coll. Qualifying Test, 1943-45; dean students, prof. psychology Stanford, 1945-49; prof. psychology, coordinator psychol. scis. and services Ill. Inst. Tech., 1949-51; cons. Fund for Advancement Edn., 1952-55, NSF, 1952-56; dir. studies Assn. Am. Med. Colls., 1949-55; pres. Nat. Merit Scholarship Corp., 1955-69, pres. emeritus, dir., 1969—; mem. bd. North Shore Mental Health Assn., 1967-70; mem. Northfield Twp. Mental Health Adv. Bd., 1978—; mem. Ill. Bd. Higher Edn., 1969-75; trustee, dir. Pepsi-Cola Scholarship Bd. 1945-54; mem. adv. com. Fgn. Service Exam. Dept. State, 1941-51, sci. adv. bd. to Chief of Staff, USAF, 1950-53; mem. bd. fgn. scholarships Dept. State, 1962-67, chmn., 1962-65. Recipient Certificate Merit, Pres. U.S., 1948, Distinguished Civilian Service award Sec. Navy, 1946; citation for outstanding contbn. to edn. Nat. Assn. Secondary Sch. Prins., 1970; Distinguished Service medal Coll. Entrance Exam. Bd., 1976. Fellow Am. Psychol. Assn.; mem. Psychometric Soc., Am. Edn. Research Assn., Phi Beta Kappa Assos., Phi Beta Kappa, Sigma Xi, Tau Kappa Epsilon. Clubs: Univ. (Chgo.); Cosmos (Washington); Century Assn. (N.Y.C.). Contbr. articles to ednl., psychol. jours. Home: 3839 Tangier Terr Sarasota FL 33579

STAM, DAVID HARRY, librarian; b. Paterson, N.J., July 11, 1935; s. Jacob and Deana B. (Bowman) S.; A.B., Wheaton (Ill.) Coll., 1955; postgrad. New Coll., U. Edinburgh, 1955-56; M.L.S., Rutgers U., 1962; postgrad. City U. N.Y., 1963-64; Ph.D., Northwestern U., 1978; m. Deirdre Corcoran, May 15, 1963; children—Julian, Wendell, Kathryn. Asst. editor library publs., reference librarian, manuscript cataloguer New York Pub. Library, 1959-64; librarian Marlboro (Vt.) Coll., 1964-67; head tech. services dept. Newberry Library, Chgo., 1967-71, asso. librarian, 1969-73; librarian Milton S. Eisenhower Library, Johns Hopkins, Balt., 1973-78; Andrew W. Mellon dir. research libraries N.Y. Public Library, N.Y.C., 1978—. Served with USNR, 1956-58. Brit. Acad. Overseas fellow, 1975. Mem. Am. Hist. Assn., ALA. Club: Caxton (Chgo.); Grolier (N.Y.C.). Author: (with Elton F. Henley) Wordsworthian Criticism 1945-1959: An Annotated Bibliography, 1960, Wordsworthian Criticism 1945-1964: An Annotated Bibliography, 1965; Wordsworthian Criticism 1964-1973: An Annotated Bibliography, 1974; (with Rissa Yachnin) Turgenev in English: A Checklist of Works by and about Him, 1960. Contbr. articles to profl. jours. Home: 1 Fraser St Pelham NY 10803 Office: NY Public Library Fifth Ave and 42d St New York NY 10018

STAMAS, STEPHEN, oil co. exec.; b. Salem, Mass., Apr. 26, 1931; s. Theodore and Georgia (Fotopulos) S.; A.B., Harvard, 1953, Ph.D., 1957; B.Phil. (Rhodes scholar), Oxford U., 1955; m. Elaine Heidi Zervas, Apr. 24, 1955; children—Heidi, Theodore. Budget examiner Bur. Budget, Washington, 1957-59; loan officer Devel. Loan Fund, Washington, 1959-60; mgr. internat. div. treasurer's dept. Standard Oil Co. (N.J.), N.Y.C., 1960-63, dep. European financial rep., London, Eng., 1963-64; govt. relations mgr., Esso Europe, 1964-67; petroleum planning mgr. Esso Internat., 1967-68; dep. asst. sec. for financial policy Dept. Commerce, Washington, 1968-69; chief economist Standard Oil Co. (N.J.), N.Y.C., 1969-70, dep. mgr. pub. affairs dept., 1971; now v.p. Exxon Corp. Trustee William H. Donner Found., N.Y.C., World Peace Found., Boston, Overseas Devel. Council, Washington, Asia Soc., N.Y.C., Inst. Internat. Edn., N.Y.C., Internat. House, N.Y.C., French-Am. Found., N.Y.C., Ballet Theatre Found., Inc., N.Y.C.; bd. dirs. Advt. Council, N.Y.C., Nat. Bur. Econ. Research, Cambridge, Mass., Salzburg Seminar in Am. Studies, Cambridge, Am. Council for Arts, N.Y.C.; bd. overseers Harvard Coll. Mem. Council Fgn. Relations (bd. dirs.), Phi Beta Kappa. Club: Harvard (N.Y.C.). Home: 325 Evandale Rd Scarsdale NY 10583 Office: Exxon Corp 1251 Ave of Americas New York NY 10020

STAMBAUGH, ARMSTRONG A., JR., bus. exec.; b. Cleve., Nov. 1, 1920; s. Armstrong Alexander and Beatrice (Snyder) S.; B.A., Dartmouth, 1942; Indsl. Adminstr., Harvard, 1943, M.B.A., 1946; m. Janet Turley Marting, July 26, 1943 (div. 1958); children—Susan Reed (Mrs. Roy H. Beaton, Jr.), Sally Russell (Mrs. Michael H. Huber), Elizabeth Renshaw (Mrs. James W. Ewing); m. 2d, Aagot Hinrichsen Cain, June 10, 1972. Research asst., then instr. bus. adminstrn. Harvard Grad. Sch. Bus. Adminstrn., 1946-48; with Gulf Oil Corp., 1948-66, adminstr. sales devel. marketing hdqrs., Houston, 1962-63, v.p. Eastern marketing region, Phila., 1963-66; exec. v.p. adminstrn. Howard Johnson Co., Inc., 1966-70, exec. v.p. ops. and adminstrn., 1970-79, exec. v.p., asst. to pres., 1979—, also dir. Pres. trustees Fox Chapel Country Day Sch., Pitts., 1955-57; div. vice chmn. Boston United Fund, 1961; bd. dirs. Houston Internat. Trade and Travel Fair, 1962-63, World Affairs Council Phila., 1964-65; bd. overseers Hanover Inn, Dartmouth Coll., 1979—. Served to lt. (j.g.) USNR, 1943-46. Mem. Delta Tau Delta. Clubs: Harvard-Yale-Princeton (Pitts.); Pine Valley Golf (N.J.); Weston (Mass.) Golf; Boston Skating (bd. govs.); Vineyard Haven Yacht (Mass.). Home: 474 Concord Rd Weston MA 02193 Office: 220 Forbes Rd Braintree MA 02184

STAMBAUGH, JOHN HOWLAND, mgmt. cons.; b. Chgo., Sept. 30, 1905; s. Frederick A. and Maude A. (Howland) S.; student U. Chgo., 1923-27; LL.D., Westminster Coll., m. Helen R. Rosenfield, Sept. 15, 1936. Pres., Stambaugh Farm Equipment Co., Inc., Valparaiso, Ind., 1938-53, Wood-Jon Farms, Inc., 1946—, Stambaugh Motors, Inc., 1949-53; pres. Internat. Milk Processing Co., Inc., Chgo., 1949-51, chmn. bd., 1952-53; chmn. bd. Tenn. Book Co., Nashville; dep. dir. Office Materials and Facilities, War Food Adminstrn., 1943-45; asst. to sec. agr., 1951-53; adminstr. TCA, Dept. of State, 1953; asst. fgn. econ. policy White House, 1954-55; dir. Inst. Inter-Am. Affairs, 1953-55; spl. cons. to Pres., 1957-60; vice chancellor Vanderbilt U., 1956-63; sr. asso. Fry Consultants, Inc. Faculty, Center for Grad. Studies in Engring. Mgmt., Vanderbilt U.; lectr. Coll. of Desert. Mem. Gov. Ind. Bd. to Study Brucellosis; mem. Pres.'s Commn. on Internat. Trade and Investment Policy, 1970-71; dir. Internat. Dairy Expdn.; dir., organizer Asso. Retailers Ind., 1940; exec. dir. Joint Fed.-State Action Com. Trustee Glenwood Sch. for Boys, member bd. Vanderbilt Med. Center, Nashville Symphony Orch.; trustee Ensworth Sch., Eisenhower Med. Center. Served as capt. Ordnance Dept., AUS, 1942-43. Mem. U.S. (econ. policy com.), Valparaiso (pres. 1939-41) chambers commerce, Ind. Taxpayers Assn. (v.p.), Nat Retail Farm Equipment Assn. (vice chmn. tax com.), Delta Kappa Epsilon. Clubs: Belle Meade (Nashville); Bohemian (San Francisco); Mid-Day (Chgo.); Eldorado Country (Indian Wells). Co-Instigator successful research in canning whole milk. Home: 45765 Pueblo Rd Indian Wells CA 92260

STAMBROOK, FREDERICK GEORGE, educator; b. Vienna, Austria, Nov. 16, 1929; s. Charles Kenneth and Edith (Weiss) S.: B.A. with honors, Oxford (Eng.) U., 1950; B.Sc. in Econs. with honors, London U., 1951, Ph.D., 1960; m. Elizabeth M. Arnold, Aug. 8, 1955; children—Michael G., David C., Andrew J. Editorial mem. German War Documents project, Whaddon Hall, Eng., 1954-59; lectr., sr. lectr. in history U. Sydney (Australia), 1960-68; asso. prof. history U. Man. (Winnipeg, Can.), 1968-72, prof., 1972—, dean Faculty of Arts, 1977—. Served with Royal Air Force, 1950-52. Mem. Can. Inst. Internat. Affairs, Am. Hist. Assn., Assn. Contemporary Historians, Can. Youth Soccer Assn. (pres. 1975—). Author: European Nationalism in the Nineteenth Century, 1969; (with R.B. Rose and N. Meaney) Worlds Old and New, 1964; also articles. Home: 220 Oak St Winnipeg MB R3M 3R4 Canada Office: Faculty of Arts U of Manitoba Winnipeg MB R3T 2N2 Canada

STAMLER, JEREMIAH, physician; b. N.Y.C., Oct. 27, 1919; s. George and Rose (Baras) S.; A.B., Columbia U., 1940; M.D., State U. N.Y., Bklyn., 1943; m. Rose Steinberg, 1942; 1 son, Paul J. Intern L.I. Coll. div. Kings County Hosp., Bklyn., 1944; fellow pathology L.I. Coll. Medicine, 1947; research fellow cardiovascular dept. Med. Research Inst., Michael Reese Hosp., Chgo., 1948, research asso., 1949-55, asst. dir. dept., 1955-58; investigator Am. Heart Assn., 1952-58; dir. heart disease control program Chgo. Bd. Health, 1958-74, dir. chronic disease control div., 1961-63; asso. dept. medicine Northwestern U. Med. Sch., 1958-59, asst. prof. medicine, 1959-65, asso. prof. medicine, 1965-72, prof., chmn. dept. community health and preventive medicine, 1972—, Harry W. Dingman prof. cardiology, 1973—; chmn. dept. community health and preventive medicine Northwestern Meml. Hosp., 1973, attending physician, 1973—; exec. dir. Chgo. Health Research Found., 1963-72, bd. dirs., 1972—; cons. medicine St. Joseph Hosp., Chgo., 1964—, Presbyn.-St. Luke's Hosp., Chgo., 1966—; professorial lectr. dept. medicine Pritzker Sch. Medicine U. Chgo., 1970—; vis. prof. internal medicine Rush. Presbyn.-St. Luke's Med. Center, 1972—. Served to capt. AUS, 1944-46. Recipient award for outstanding efforts in heart research Am. Heart Assn., 1964; Howard W. Blakeslee award, 1964, award of merit, 1967; Albert and Mary Lasker med. journalism award, 1965; Conrad Elvehjem award Wis. Med. Soc., 1967; others. Fellow Am. Coll. Cardiology, Am. Pub. Health Assn., A.A.A.A.S.; mem. Am. Fedn. Clin. Research, Am. Heart Assn. (past vice-chmn. exec. com., fellow council arteriosclerosis, chmn. council on epidemiology 1979—), Am. Physiol. Soc., Am. Soc. Clin. Investigation, Am. Soc. Study Arteriosclerosis (past dir., past chmn. program com., past sec.-treas.), Am., Chgo. diabetes assns., Assn. Tchrs. Preventive Medicine, Am. Soc. Clin. Nutrition Assn. Clin. Scientists, Middle States Pub. Health Assn., Central Soc. Clin. Research, Chgo. Heart Assn. (chmn. epidemiology com., Coeur d'Or award 1979), Ill. Pub. Health Assn. (mem. exec. com.), Ill. Acad. Scis., Diabetes Assn. Greater Chgo. (dir.), Soc. Exptl. Biology and Medicine (sec. Ill. chpt.), Am. Inst. Nutrition, Chgo. Nutrition Assn., Chgo. Acad. Scis., Inst. Medicine Chgo., Phi Beta Kappa. Author (with L. N. Katz): Experimental Atheroscleroses, 1953; (with others) Nutrition and Atherosclerosis, 1958; (with A. Blakeslee) Your Heart Has Nine Lives-Nine Steps to Heart Health, 1963; (with others) Epidemiology of Hypertension, 1967; Lectures on Preventive Cardiology, 1967. Editorial bd. Circulation, Jour. Chronic Diseases, Preventive Medicine. fgn. cons., editoral bd. Heart Care. Home: 1332 E Madison Park Chicago IL 60615 Office: 303 E Chicago Ave Chicago IL 60611

STAMM, ALAN, lawyer; b. Galesburg, Ill., Nov. 22, 1931; s. Gustave Frederick and Miriam (Simon) S.; student Universidad Nacional de Mexico, summer 1950; A.B., Yale, 1952; J.D., Harvard, 1957; m. Shelley Lynn Ramage, Mar. 19, 1978. Admitted to Calif. bar, 1957; U.S. Supreme Ct., 1963; asso. Thelen, Marrin, Johnson & Bridges, San Francisco, 1957-60; staff atty. Litton Industries, Inc., Beverly Hills, Calif., 1960-66, asst. sec., 1963-66; sec., gen. counsel Internat. Rectifier Corp., Los Angeles, 1966-69, v.p., 1968-69; v.p., gen. counsel Republic Corp., Los Angeles, 1969-71, dir., 1970-71; v.p., gen. counsel Sat. Rev. Industries, N.Y.C., 1971-72; v.p., gen. counsel Mattel, Inc., Hawthorne, Calif., 1972-74, staff cons., 1974-75; of counsel, firm Long & Levit, Los Angeles, 1975—; judge pro tem Municipal Ct. Los Angeles Jud. Dist., 1977—; dir. Synestructics, Inc., Sun Systems, Inc. Trustee Center for Law in the Pub. Interest; adv. trustee Los Angeles Center for Photog. Studies; bd. dirs. Photog. Arts Mus., Inc. Served from ensign to lt. (j.g.) USNR, 1952-54, now lt. comdr. Res. ret. Eagle Scout. Mem. Am., Calif., San Francisco, Los Angeles bar assns., Am. Jewish Com., Far West Ski Assn., Harvard Law Sch. Assn., Los Angeles County Art Mus., Los Angeles World Affairs Council, Am. Arbitration Assn. (nat. panel arbitrators), N.A.A.C.P., UN Assn. U.S.A., Sierra Club, Phi Beta Kappa. Clubs: Yale of So. Calif. (dir.), Harvard of So. Calif. Home: 1613 Manning Ave Unit B-2 Los Angeles CA 90024 Office: 1900 Ave of Stars Los Angeles CA 90067

STAMOS, JOHN JAMES, judge; b. Chgo., Jan. 30, 1924; s. James S. and Katherine (Manolopoulos) S.; LL.B., DePaul U., 1948; m. Helen Voutiritsas, Sept. 3, 1955; children—James, Theo, Colleen, Jana. Admitted to Ill. bar, 1949, since practiced in Chgo.; asst. corp. counsel City Chgo., 1951-54; asst. states atty. Cook County, 1954-61, chief criminal div. States Attys. Office, 1961-64, 1st asst. states atty., 1964-66, states atty., 1966-68; judge Appellate Ct. of State of Ill., 1968—. Mem. Ill. Cts. Commn. Served with AUS, 1943-45. Home: Northbrook IL 60062 Office: Civic Center Chicago IL 60602

STAMP, NEAL ROGER, lawyer; b. Watkins Glen, N.Y., Sept. 19, 1918; s. Nelson Mathews and Mae Emma (Broderick) S.; A.B., Cornell, 1940, J.D., 1942; m. Maja Stina Cavetz, Apr. 24, 1946; children—Thomas G., Gayle E. Admitted to N.Y. bar, 1943: pvt. practice, Rochester, 1946-47; asst. sec. corp., asso. legal counsel Cornell U., Ithaca, N.Y., 1947-59, sec. corp., asso. legal counsel, 1959-62, sec. corp., 1959—, univ. counsel, 1962—, dir. aero. lab., research found. Lectr., Practicing Law Inst.; dir. First Nat. Bank & Trust Co. Ithaca, 1971—, chmn., 1978—. Trustee Tompkins County Meml. Hosp., 1959-66, pres., 1961-62. Served to 1st lt., inf. AUS, 1942-46; MTO. Mem. Am., N.Y. State, Tompkins County bar assns., Assn. Bar City N.Y., Nat. Assn. Coll. and U. Attys. (exec. bd. 1964-68, 72-79, pres. 1976-77). Home: 205 N Sunset Dr Ithaca NY 14850

STAMPER, JOE ALLEN, lawyer; b. Okemah, Okla., Jan.. 30, 1914; s. Horace Allen and Ann (Stephens) S.; B.A., U. Okla., 1933, LL.B., 1935, J.D., 1970; m. Johnnie Lee Bell, June 4, 1936; 1 dau., Jane Allen (Mrs. Ernest F. Godlove). Admitted to Okla. bar, 1935; practice in Antlers, 1935-36, 46—; mem. firm Stamper, Otis & Burrage, 1974—, atty. Pushmataha County, 1946-49; spl. justice Okla. Supreme Ct., 1948. Mem. Okla. Indsl. Commn., 1939-40; pres. Antlers Sch. Bd., 1956-67, Pushmataha Found., 1957—; mem. Okla. Bicentennial Com., 1971—; vice chmn. bd. U. Okla. Law Center, 1975-78; mgr. Okla. Democratic party, 1946, dist. chmn., 1946-50; alt. del. Dem. Nat. Conv., 1952. Served to col. AUS, 1935-46; ETO. Decorated Bronze Star. Fellow Am. Bar Found., Am. Coll. Trial Lawyers; mem. Am. (del. 1974, state del. 1975—, mem. com. on law book pub. practices 1974-76), Okla. (bd. govs. 1969-73, Pres.'s award 1977) bar assns., Okla. Bar Found. (pres. 1977), S.A.R., Mil. Order World Wars, Pi Kappa Alpha. Baptist (deacon). Clubs: Masons (32 deg.), Shriners, Lions (past pres.), Whitehall (Oklahoma City). Home: 1000 NE 2d St Antlers OK 74523 Office: PO Box 100 Antlers OK 74523

STAMPER, MALCOLM THEODORE, aerospace co. exec.; b. Detroit, Apr. 4, 1925; s. Fred Theodore and Lucille (Cayce) S.; student U. Richmond (Va.), 1943-44; B.E.E., Ga. Inst. Tech., 1946; postgrad. U. Mich., 1946-49; m. Marion Philbin Guinan, Feb. 25, 1946; children—Geoffrey, Kevin, Jamie, David, Mary, Anne. With Gen. Motors Corp., 1949-62; with Boeing Co., Seattle, 1962—, mgr. electronics ops., v.p., gen. mgr. turbine div., 1964-66, v.p., gen. mgr. 747 Airplane program, 1966-69, v.p., gen. mgr. comml. airplane group, 1969-71, corp. sr. v.p. ops., 1971-72, pres. Boeing Co., 1972—; dir. Fed. Res. Bank San Francisco, Nordstrom Co. Chmn. Wash. State U.S. Treasury Savs. Bond Campaign, Boy Scouts Am. Devel. Fund State of Wash., Variety Club Handicapped Children Telethon. Candidate, U.S. Ho. of Reps., Detroit, 1952. Trustee Seattle Art Mus. Served to ensign USNR, 1943-46. Named Industrialist of Year, 1967; recipient Educator's Golden Key award, 1970. Mem. Nat. Alliance Businessmen, Phi Gamma Delta. Office: Boeing Co Seattle WA 98124*

STAMPER, WILLSON YOUNG, III, artist; b. N.Y.C., Jan. 5, 1912; s. Willson Young and Marguerita (Malcolm) S.; student Art Students League, 1934; m. Si Si Chu, 1966; children—Kimon, Allen. One-man exhbns. include Cin. Art Mus., 1946, 50, Honolulu Art Acad., 1948, Contemporary Arts Center of Hawaii, 1963, Down Town Gallery, 1977; exhibited in group shows Carnegie Internat., 1952, World's Fair, 1939, various mus. and galleries; represented in permanent collections Cin. Art Mus., Mus. Modern Art, Honolulu Acad. Art; ceramic mural commd. by State of Hawaii, 1975; instr. Cin. Art Mus., 1936-43, Carnegie Found. art course, 1936-39; dir. Art Sch., Honolulu Acad. Art, 1945-62. Recipient 15 1st prizes for nat. mus. exhbns. Mem. Painters and Sculptors of Honolulu; Internat. Inst. for Conservation of Historic and Artistic Works. Works reproduced in numerous books and mags. Home: 224 N Kalaheo Ave Kailua HI 96734. *Work like a dog. Close my ears to all advice except from the immortals. Always remember that I'm an American lad, that my sources and their answers are in the experience of woods, field, streams, shoreline, towns, streets, men, women of the land I live in. To embrace them all and leave intellectual rationales to others.*

STAMPFL, RUDOLF ALOIS, govt. ofcl.; b. Vienna, Austria, Jan. 21, 1926; s. Paul Friedrich and Leopoldine (Kittinger) S.; B.S., Inst. Tech. Vienna, 1948, M.S., 1950, Ph.D., 1953; m. Ursula Maria Frieske, Sept. 17, 1956; children—Susanne Maria, Peter Gerhard. Came to U.S., 1953, naturalized, 1959. Sr. engr. astro electronics br. Army Research and Devel. Labs., Fort Monmouth, N.J., 1953-59; with NASA, Greenbelt, Md., 1959—, asst. dir., 1968-73; dir. aeroelectronics dept. Naval Air Devel. Center, Warminster, Pa., 1973—. Vis. lectr. aerospace instrumentation systems U. Calif. at Los Angeles, 1964-65. Served with German Army, 1944-45. Recipient Harry Diamond award, 1967. Fellow IEEE, Am. Inst. Aeros. and Astronautics (asso.). Author chpts. in books. Designer: Nimbus Spacecraft. Patentee in field. Home: 210 Clover Ln Ambler PA 19002 Office: Naval Air Devel Center Warminster PA 18974. *Those who can look back on a measure of achievement are obligated more so than others to use their wisdom and skill for the benefit of our fellow man. For him we must strive to create the opportunities so that he can achieve material wellbeing and happiness of life as well.*

STAMPP, KENNETH MILTON, educator, historian; b. Milw., July 12, 1912; s. Oscar M. and Eleanor (Schmidt) S.; Ph.B., U. Wis., 1935, M.A., 1937, Ph.D., 1942; m. Katherine Mitchell, Dec. 26, 1939 (div.); children—Kenneth Mitchell, Sara Katherine; m. 2d, Isabel M. Macartney-Filgate, July 4, 1962; children—Jennifer, Michele. Instr. history U. Ark., 1941- 42; asst. prof. history U. Md., 1942-45, asso. prof., 1945-46; asst. prof. history U. Calif. at Berkeley, 1946-49, asso. prof., 1949-51, prof., 1951-57, Morrison prof. Am. history, 1957—; vis. lectr. Harvard, 1955, U. Wis., summers 1945, 46, 49, 52, U. Colo., summer 1958; Fulbright lectr. Amerika-Institut, U. Munich, 1957, 68, 72; Commonwealth Fund lectr. U. London, 1960; Harmsworth prof. Am. history Oxford, 1961-62, vis. fellow All Soul's Coll., 1979. Guggenheim fellow, 1952-53, 67-68. Mem. Am., So. hist. assns., Orgn. Am. Historians (pres. 1977-78), Mass. Hist. Soc., Am. Antiquarian Soc., Am. Acad. Arts and Scis., Phi Beta Kappa. Author: Indiana Politics During the Civil War, 1949; And the War Came: The North and the Secession Crisis, 1950; The Peculiar Institution, 1956; The Causes of the Civil War, 1959; The Era of Reconstruction, 1865-1877, 1965; The Imperiled Union, 1980. Co-author: The National Experience, 1963; also articles hist. publs. Co-editor: A Reconstruction Reader, 1969. Home: 682 San Luis Rd Berkeley CA 94707

STANBURY, JOHN BRUTON, physician; b. Clinton, N.C., May 15, 1915; s. Walter A. and Zula (Bruton) S.; A.B., Duke, 1935; M.D., Harvard, 1939; M.D. (hon.), U. Leiden (Netherlands), 1975; m. Jean F. Cook, Jan. 6, 1945; children—John Bruton, Martha Jean, Sarah Katherine, David McNeill, Pamela Cook. House officer Mass. Gen. Hosp., 1940-41, asst. resident, 1946, chief med. resident, 1948, mem. med. staff, 1949—; research fellow pharmacology Harvard Med. Sch., 1947; vis. prof. medicine U. Leiden, Holland, 1955; prof. exptl. medicine Mass. Inst. Tech., Cambridge, 1966—; cons. Pan Am. Health Orgn., U.S. AEC. Served from lt. (j.g.) to comdr., USNR, 1941-45. Mem. Am. Assn. Physicians, Soc. for Clin. Investigation, Soc. for Human Genetics, Am. Thyroid Assn. (pres. 1969), Am. Acad. Arts and Scis., Endocrine Soc., endocrine socs. of Finland, Colombia, Peru and Argentina. Democrat. Episcopalian. Author: Endemic Goiter: The adaptation of man to iodine deficiency, 1954; Metabolic Basis of Inherited Disease, 4th edit., 1978; The Thyroid and Its Diseases, 4th edit., 1975; Endemic Goiter, 1969; Human Development and the Thyroid, 1972. Home: 43 Circuit Rd Chestnut Hill MA 02167 Office: Mass Inst Tech Cambridge MA 02139 also Warren 807 Mass Gen Hosp Charles St Boston MA 02114

STANCIL, JAMES WHITEHURST, former govt. ofcl.; b. Clayton, N.C., Dec. 26, 1915; s. James William and Pearl Estelle (Jones) S.; LL.B., Southeastern U., Washington, 1941; M.S. in Pub. Adminstrn., George Washington U., 1965; m. Anna Pauline Rogers. Admitted to D.C. bar, 1941; legal cons. bd. vets. appeals VA, 1946-50, dir. appeals ops. service, 1950-52, asso. mem. bd. vets. appeals, 1952-56, vice chmn., 1956-57, chmn., 1957-71. Hon. vice chmn. D.C. Com. for Employment of Physically Handicapped. Served from ensign to lt. USNR, 1942-46. Mem. Fed. Bar Assn., N.C. State Soc., Am. Legion, Martin County Hist. Soc., VFW, Assn. Mil. Surgeons U.S., Washington Urban League. Presbyterian (ruling elder). Home: 3402 SE Court Dr Yacht and Country Club Stuart FL 33494

STANCZAK, JULIAN, artist, educator; b. Borownica, Poland, Nov. 5, 1928; s. Victor and Elizabeth (Cwynar) S.; B.F.A., Cleve. Inst. Art. 1954; M.F.A., Yale, 1956; m. Barbara M. Meerpohl, June 10, 1963; children—Danuta M., Christopher. Came to U.S., 1950, naturalized, 1957. Tchr., Art Acad. Cin., 1957-64, Cleve. Inst. Art, 1965—; exhibited one-man shows Dayton Art Inst., 1964, Martha Jackson Gallery, N.Y.C. 1964, 65, 68, 71, 72, 75, 77 Miami U., Oxford, Ohio, 1965, Feingarten Galleries, Los Angeles, 1966, Kent State U., 1968, Dartmouth, 1968, Akron (Ohio) Art Inst., 1969, Cleve. Inst. Art, 1971, London Arts Gallery, 1971, Cin. Art Mus., 1972, Corcoran Gallery Art, Washington, 1972, Canton (Ohio) Art Inst., 1974, Pollack Gallery, Toronto, 1975, Ohio State U., 1976, IMF and CARE, Washington, 1978; exhibited in group shows Mus. Modern Art, N.Y.C., 1965, Albright Knox Art Gallery, Buffalo, 1965, Detroit Art Inst., 1965, Larry Alrich Mus., 1965, U. Ill., 1965, Gallery Moos, Toronto, 1965, Kranert Art Mus., Urbana, Ill., 1965, San Francisco Mus. Art, 1965, Flint (Mich.) Inst. Art, 1966, Carnegie Inst., Pitts., 1967, Albright-Knox Art Gallery, 1968, Japan Cultural Forum, 1967, Smithsonian Instn., Washington, 1967, 69, Dept. State, Washington, 1968, Cin. Art Mus., 1968, Del. Art Center, 1970, Seibu, Tokyo, 1971, Mansfield (Ohio) Art Center, 1973, Butler Art Inst., Youngstown, Ohio, 1973, Minn. Art Mus., Mpls., 1973, Akron Art Inst., 1975, Indpls. Mus. Art, 1976, Bklyn. Mus. Art, 1976, Cleve. Mus. Art, 1976, 77; represented in permanent collections Albright Knox Art Gallery, Larry Aldrich Mus., Modern Mus., Dayton Art Inst., Butler Inst. Am. Art, Youngstown, Ohio, Cleve. Art Assn., Milw. Art Inst., USIA, N.Y.C., Balt. Mus. Art, Herron Mus. Art, Indpls., Pa. Acad. Fine Arts, Phila., Cleve. Mus. Art, Cin. Art Mus., Tulsa Mus. Fine Arts, Akron Art Inst., Corcoran Art Mus., Nat. Gallery, Washington, Lowe Art Mus., Coral Gables, Fla., San Francisco Mus. Art. Recipient 1st prize Dayton Art Inst., 1964, Butler Inst. Am. Art, 1966, Cleve. Fine Arts prize, 1970, Ohio Arts Council award, 1972; Best of Show award Internat. Platform Assn., 1973-76. Mem. Abstract Artists Am., Internat. Platform Assn. Pioneer optical art. Address: 6229 Cabrini Ln Seven Hills OH 44131

STANDEN, CHARLES RAYMOND, advt. co. exec.; b. Lorain, Ohio, May 22, 1917; s. John Clayton and Netta Elizabeth (Fowl) S.: B.S.C., Ohio U., 1939; m. Maxine Lundgren, May 3, 1941; children—Craig C., Cheryl L., Christy L. With RCA, 1939-43; advt. dir. Ladish Co., Milw., 1946-47; with Tatham-Laird & Kudner, Chgo., 1947—, dir. bus. devel. and client service, 1959-64, pres., chief exec., 1964-69, chmn. bd., 1969-71, chmn. exec. com., 1971-74, chmn. mgmt. com., 1974—. Served to 1st lt. AUS, 1943-46. Clubs: Tavern, Univ. (Chgo.); Hinsdale (Ill.) Golf. Home: 505 N Lake Shore Dr Chicago IL 60611 Office: 625 N Michigan Ave Chicago IL 60611

STANDER, RICHARD WRIGHT, physician, assn. exec.; b. Grand Rapids, Mich., Oct. 22, 1922; s. Leon R. and Florence (Wright) S.; student Mich. State U., 1940-42, U. Colo., 1947; M.D., U. Mich., 1951; m. Henrietta Hudelson, Apr. 9, 1943; children—Shiras, Meredith, Peter Bradley, Alden. Intern, U. Mich. Hosp., 1951-52, resident, 1952-56; instr. obstetrics-gynecology U. Mich. Med. Sch., 1956-57; clin. instr. White Meml. Hosp., Coll. Med. Evangelists, Los Angeles, 1957-58; asst. prof. Ind. U. Med. Sch., 1958-61, asso. prof., 1961-67; prof., chmn. dept. obstetrics-gynecology U. Cin. Med. Center, 1967-75; dir. edn. Am. Coll. Obstetricians and Gynecologists, 1975-79; prof. dept. Ob-Gyn, U. N.Mex. Sch. Medicine, Gynecologists, 1975-79; prof. dept. Ob-Gyn U. Mex. Sch. Medicine, Albuquerque, 1979—. Mem. Am., Central assns. obstetricians and gynecologists, Am. Coll. Obstetricians and Gynecologists, Am. Gynecol. Soc., Sigma Xi. Specialist med. edn. Home: 1519 Wagontrain Dr SE Albuquerque NM 87123

STANDISH, JOHN SPENCER, indsl. textiles co. exec.; b. Albany, N.Y., Apr. 17, 1925; s. John Carver and Florence (Spencer) S.; B.S., Mass. Inst. Tech., 1945; m. Elaine Joan Ritchie, Oct. 20, 1962; children—John Carver, Christine Louise. Asst. to prodn. mgr. Forstmann Woolen Co., Passaic, N.J., 1945-52; with Albany Felt Co. Can., Ltd., 1952-61, exec. v.p., 1957-61; exec. v.p., then pres. Albany Felt Co. (N.Y.), 1961-73; exec. v.p. Albany Internat. Corp., 1973-76, vice chmn. bd., dir., 1976—; dir. Nat. Comml. Bank & Trust Co., Albany, Berkshire Life Ins. Co., Pittsfield, Mass. Chpt. chmn. ARC, 1970-73, bd. dirs., 1966—; bd. dirs. Albany United Fund, 1972—, State U. N.Y. Found., 1973—. Served with AUS, 1946-47. Mem. Am. Mgmt. Assn., Albany C. of C. Clubs: Ft. Orange, Schuyler Meadows, Wolferts Roost Country (Albany). Home: 1 Schuyler Meadows Rd Loudonville NY 12211 Office: Albany Internat Corp PO Box 1907 Albany NY 12201

STANDISH, SAMUEL MILES, oral pathologist, coll. dean; b. Campbellsburg, Ind., July 6, 1923; s. Irvin Arthur and Etta May (Smedley) S.; D.D.S., Ind. U., 1945, M.S., 1956; m. Gertrude Elizabeth Eberle, Aug. 6, 1949; children—Nancy Jo, Linda Sue. Practice dentistry, specializing in oral pathology, Indpls., 1948-58; mem. faculty Sch. Dentistry Ind. U., 1958—, prof. oral pathology, 1967—, chmn. div. clin. oral pathology, 1967—, asst. dean sch., 1969-74, asso. dean, 1974—; cons. Nat. Cancer Inst., 1969-73, Nat. Bd. Dental Examiners, 1966—, ADA, 1971—. Served with USNR, 1945-47. Diplomate Am. Bd. Oral Pathology (dir. 1973—), Am. Bd. Forensic Odontology. Fellow Am. Acad. Oral Pathology (pres. 1972-73); mem. ADA, Internat. Assn. Dental Research, Am. Acad. Forensic Sci., Sigma Xi, Omicron Kappa Upsilon, Xi Psi Phi. Author: (with others) Oral Diagnosis/Oral Medicine, 1978, Maxillofacial Prosthetics: Multidisciplinary Practice, 1972. Home: 4548 Manning Rd Indianapolis IN 46208 Office: Ind U Sch of Dentistry Indianapolis IN 47401

STANEK, JEROME HAMATA, engr., mfg. exec.; b. Milw., Mar. 8, 1915; s. Edward John and Carrie (Hamata) S.; B.S., U. Wis., 1936; m. Jane Rieke, Apr. 17, 1937; children—Margaret Ann Schmid, Elizabeth Jane. With Johnson Service Co., Milw., 1936-39; with Stanek Tool Corp., Milw., 1939—, treas., 1941-48, v.p., dir., 1948-55, pres., dir., 1955-75, chmn. bd., treas., 1975—; pres. Tape Machining Corp., New Berlin, Wis. Mem. tool and die industry adv. com. U.S. Dept. Commerce, 1951, Task Group, 1954. Registered profl. engr., Wis. Mem. Am. Soc. Tool Engrs., Nat. Tool and Die Mfrs. Assn. (treas., dir. 1948-49, trustee 1953-55, pres. 1955), Engrs. Soc. Milw., Tool Die and Machine Shop Assn. Milw. (pres. 1948-49), Pi Kappa Alpha. Club: Blue Mound Golf and Country. Home: 13335 W Watertown Plank Rd Elm Grove WI 53122 Office: 2500 S Calhoun Rd New Berlin WI 53151

STANFIELD, ROBERT LORNE, Canadian legislator; b. Truro, N.S., Can., Apr. 11, 1914; s. Frank and Sarah E. (Thomas) S.; B.A., Dalhousie U., 1936; LL.B. cum laude, Harvard U., 1939; LL.D., U. N.B., 1958, St. Dunstan's U., 1964, McGill U., 1967; m. N. Joyce Frazee, June 5, 1940 (dec. July 1954); children—Sarah, Robert M., Judith, Miriam; m. 2d, Mary M. Hall, May 10, 1957 (dec. Oct. 1977); m. 3d, Anne M. Austin, Aug. 10, 1978. Called to N.S. bar, 1940; Queen's counsel, 1950; privy council, 1967; asst. sec. Acadia Trust Co., Truro, 1940-41; regional rentals officer Wartime Prices and Trades Bd., Halifax, N.S., 1942-45; mem. firm McInnes & Stanfield, Halifax, 1945-57; pres. N.S. Progressive-Conservative Assn., 1947; leader Progressive-Conservative party in N.S., 1948-69; mem. House of Assembly for Colchester, 1949-67; chmn. N.S. Power Commn., 1956-60; minister edn., 1960-67; premier N.S., 1956-67; mem. House of Commons, Can., 1967-76, leader opposition party; leader Progressive Conservative Party Can.; mem. Parliament, 1976-79. Mem. Anglican Ch. Clubs: Halifax; Rideau, Saraguay. Home: 136 Acacia Ave Rockcliffe ON Canada

STANFILL, DENNIS CAROTHERS, business exec.; b. Centerville, Tenn., Apr. 1, 1927; s. Sam Broome and Hattie (Carothers) S.; B.S., U.S. Naval Acad., 1949; M.A. (Rhodes scholar), Oxford U., 1953; m. Therese Olivieri, June 29, 1951; children—Francesca, Michaela, Dennis Carothers. Corporate finance specialist Lehman Bros., N.Y.C., 1959-65; v.p. finance Times Mirror Co., Los Angeles, 1965-69, treas., 1968-69; exec. v.p. 20th Century-Fox Film Corp., 1969-71, pres., 1971, chmn. bd., chief exec. officer, 1971—. Served to lt. USN, 1949-59, politico-mil. policy div. Office Chief Naval Ops., 1956-59. Office: Box 900 Beverly Hills CA 90213

STANFORD, ANN, educator, author; b. LaHabra, Calif.; d. Bruce and Rose (Corrigan) Stanford; B.A., Stanford, 1938; M.A. in Journalism, U. Calif., Los Angeles, 1958, M.A. in English, 1961, Ph.D., 1962; m. Ronald Arthur White, Sept. 18, 1942; children—Rosanna, Patricia, Susan, Arthur Bruce. Asst. prof. English, Calif. State U., Northridge, 1962-66, asso. prof., 1966-68, prof., 1968—, co-founder Calif. State U. Northridge Renaissance Edits., 1969—. Recipient Lit. award Nat. Inst.-Am. Acad. Arts and Letters, 1972; Silver medal Commonwealth Club Calif., 1959, 78; Outstanding Prof. award Calif. State U. and Coll. System, 1974; James D. Phelan fellow, 1938-39; Nat. Endowment for Arts grantee in writing,

1974-75. Mem. Modern Lang. Assn., Poetry Soc. Am. (Shelley Meml. award 1969, DiCastagnola award 1976, v.p. West Coast 1970—), P.E.N. Internat., Wilderness Soc., Phi Beta Kappa. Author: (poetry) In Narrow Bound, 1943, The White Bird, 1949, Magellan: A Poem to Be Read by Several Voices, 1958, The Weathercock, 1966, The Descent, 1970, The Bhagavad Gita: A New Verse Translation, 1970; Anne Bradstreet: The Worldly Puritan, An Introduction to Her Poetry, 1975; In Mediterranean Air, 1977. Editor: The Women Poets in English—An Anthology, 1973; editorial bd. Early Am. Lit., 1971-73. Home: 9550 Oak Pass Rd Beverly Hills CA 90210

STANFORD, DENNIS JOE, archeologist, asso. curator museum; b. Cherokee, Iowa, May 13, 1943; s. William Erle and Mary L. (Fredenburg) S.; B.A., U. Wyo., 1965; M.A., U. N.Mex., 1967, Ph.D., 1972; m. Jeanne Ann Easley, Sept. 11, 1965; 1 dau., Brandy L. Archeologist, asso. curator Smithsonian Instn., Washington, 1972—. Mem. anthropology adv. panel NSF, 1976-78. Mem. Anthrop. Soc. Washington (gov. 1974-77), Soc. Am. Archeology, Am. Quaternary Assn. Author: The Walakpa Site, Alaska, 1975; editor: (with Robert L. Humphrey) Pre-Llano Cultures of the Americas, 1979; research, publs. on Paleo-Indian Studies, North and South Am., especially Western U.S., Arctic. Home: Route 3 Box 634 Front Royal VA 22630 Office: Smithsonian Instn Washington DC 20560

STANFORD, HENRY KING, coll. pres.; b. Atlanta, Apr. 22, 1916; s. Henry King and Annie Belle (Callaway) S.; A.B., Emory U., 1936, A.M., 1940, LL.D., 1961; postgrad. U. Heidelberg, Germany, 1936-37; M.S. in govt. mgmt. (Alfred P. Sloan Found. fellow 1941-43), U. Denver, 1943, LL.D., 1962; Ph.D. (Tax Found. fellow 1943-44), N.Y. U., 1949; D.C.L., Jacksonville (Fla.) U., 1963; LL.D., Loyola U., New Orleans, 1963, U. Akron, 1968, Kyung Hee U., Seoul, Korea, 1968, Rollins Coll., 1977; D.H.L., Tampa, 1969; D. Litt., R.I., 1970; m. Laurie Ruth King, Sept. 19, 1936; children—Henry, Lowry, Rhoda, Peyton. Instr. Emory U., 1937-40; asst. prof. Ga. Inst. Tech., 1940-41; instr. N.Y.U., 1943-46; prof. pub. administrn., also dir. sch. pub. administrn. U. Denver, 1946-48; pres. Ga. Southwestern Coll., Americus, 1948-50; dir. U. Center in Ga., 1950-52; asst. chancellor U. System of Ga., 1952-53; pres. Ga. State Coll. for Women, Milledgeville, 1953-56; chief of party N.Y.U.-Internat. Cooperation Adminstrn. Contract, Ankara, Turkey, 1956-57; pres. Birmingham-So. Coll., 1957-62, U. Miami (Fla.), 1962—. Research asst. Tax Found., N.Y.C., 1943-44; staff N.A.M. com. exec., 1944-46; mem. bd. Jacksonville br. Fed. Res. Bank, Atlanta, 1967-72, chmn., 1969, 72. Chmn. Dade County Community Relations Bd., 1969-71; bd. visitors Air U., Maxwell AFB, Ala., 1963-66. Decorated Star of Africa medal (Liberia); officer Order of Merit Fed. Republic Germany; recipient Eleanor Roosevelt-Israel Humanitarian award, 1965; Outstanding Civilian Service award U.S. Army, 1966; Silver Medallion Fla. region NCCJ, 1968; Disting. Service award Ga. Coll., 1979. Mem. Am. Soc. Pub. Administrn., So. Assn. Colls. and Schs. (chmn. commn. colls. 1960-62, pres. 1972-73), Nat. Assn. Ind. Colls. and Univs. (dir. 1976—), Assn. Caribbean Univs. and Research Insts. (v.p. 1965—), Internat. Assn. Univ. Presidents (exec. com. 1977—), Delta Phi Alpha, Phi Beta Kappa, Omicron Delta Kappa, Phi Sigma Iota, Alpha Kappa Psi, Phi Mu Alpha, Phi Kappa Phi. Methodist. Rotarian. Home: 8565 Old Cutler Rd South Miami FL 33143 Office: U Miami Coral Gables FL 33124

STANGE, GEORGE ROBERT, educator; b. Chgo., Sept. 28, 1919; s. George A. and Dagmar (Ruus) S.; S.B. summa cum laude, Harvard, 1941, Ph.D., 1951; m. Alida Butler, Apr. 13, 1963; children by previous marriage—Maren, Margit, Eric. Tutor history, lit. Harvard, 1947-49; faculty Bennington Coll., 1949-52; asst. prof. English, U. Minn., 1952-55, asso. prof., 1955-60, prof., 1960-67; prof., chmn. dept. English, Tufts U., Medford, Mass., 1967—. Asso. mem. English faculty Cambridge (Eng.), U. 1955; vis. lectr. U. Chgo., 1959-60; cons. Nat. Endowment for Humanities, 1973—. Mem. Am. Council Learned Socs. Fellowship Selection Com., 1964, 69-75; chmn. Fulbright Screening Com. for English, 1966-71. Served to lt. USNR, 1943-46. Ford Found. fellow, 1955-56; Guggenheim fellow, 1961-62. Mem. Signet Soc., Modern Lang. Assn., Phi Beta Kappa. Club: St. Botolph (Boston). Author: Victorian Poetry and Poetics, 2d edit., 1968; Matthew Arnold: The Poet as Humanist, 1967. Contbg. author: Art of Victorian Prose, 1968; The Victorian City, 1973; Carlyle Past and Present, 1976. Editor: Coleridge, 1959; Henry Esmond, 1960. Home: 69 Chestnut St Boston MA 02108 Office: Dept English Tufts U Medford MA 02155

STANGELAND, ARLAN INGHART, Congressman; b. Fargo, N.D., Feb. 8, 1930; s. Inghart and Pearle (Olson) S.; student pub. schs., Moorhead, Minn.; m. Virginia Grace Trowbridge, June 24, 1950; children—David, Beth, Brian, Jean, Todd, Jeffrey, Stuart. Farmer, Barnesville, Minn., 1951—; mem. Minn. Ho. of Reps., St. Paul, From 1966; mem. 95th-96th Congresses from 7th Minn. Dist., mem. public works and transp. com., mem. govt. ops. com. Pres., Barnesville PTA, 1964; sec. Republican Party of Wilkin County (Minn.), 1960-65, pres., 1965-66; mem. Barnesville Sch. Bd., 1976-77. Recipient N.D. State U. Agr. award for community service. Mem. Minn. Shorthorn Assn. (dir.). Lutheran. Home: Route 2 PO Box 32 Barnesville MN 56514 Office: Longworth House Office Bldg Washington DC 20515

STANGELAND, TOR OSCAR, paper co. exec.; b. Quebec, Que., Can., June 13, 1929; s. Karl and Torborg S.; B.A., McGill U., 1950; B.C.L. with honors, 1953; m. Barbara Perry, Dec. 27, 1954; children—Lynne, Eric, Cara. Called to Que. bar, 1954; mem. legal dept. DuPont of Can. Ltd., 1955-58; asst. mgr. real estate and ins. Consol. Bathurst, Inc., Montreal, 1958-59, asst. sec., mgr. real estate and ins., 1959-67, dir. employee and public relations, 1967-71, v.p. personnel, sec., 1971-76, exec. v.p. pulp and paper, 1976—, dir. several subs. Bd. dirs. Unltd. Skills, Inc.; bd. dirs., v.p. Julius Richardson Convalescent Hosps., Inc.; bd. govs. Can. Centre for Occupational Health and Safety. Mem. Que. Forest Industries Assn. (vice chmn.), Bar of Province of Que. Clubs: St. James, Mount Royal (Montreal). Home: 105 Harwood Gate Beaconsfield PQ H9W 3A5 Canada Office: 800 Dorchester Blvd W Montreal PQ H3B 1Y9 Canada

STANGER, FRANK BATEMAN, clergyman, educator; b. Cedarville, N.J., Aug. 31, 1914; s. Francis Albert and Sarah Rush (Bateman) S.; A.B. magna cum laude, Asbury Coll., 1934; Th.B., Princeton Theol. Sem., 1937; S.T.M., Temple U., 1940, S.T.D., 1942; D.D., Philathea Coll., 1953; LL.D., Houghton Coll., 1962; L.H.D., Asbury Coll., 1970; m. M. Mardelle Amstutz, June 2, 1937; children—Marilyn Delle, Frank Bateman, Jane Louise. Ordained to ministry Meth. Ch., 1936; pastor in N.J. chs., 1935-59; prof. pastoral work and preaching Asbury Theol. Sem., Wilmore, Ky., 1959—, exec. v.p. 1959-62, pres., 1962—, Freitas lectr., 1956. Dean, Meth. Summer Assembly, 1943-50, pres., 1950-59; pres. Sunday League, 1950-59; 1st pres., Council Chs. Greater Camden, N.J., 1945; pres. N.J. Conf. Hist. Soc., 1948-59, Northeastern Jurisdictional Hist. Soc. Meth. Ch., 1956-60; del. World Meth. confs., Springfield, Mass., 1947, Oxford, Eng., 1951, Lake Junaluska, N.C., 1956, Oslo, Norway, 1961, London, Eng., 1966, Denver, 1971; del. Gen. Conf. Meth. Ch., Mpls., 1956, Atlanta, 1972, Northeastern Jurisdictional Conf. Meth. Ch., 1952, 56, 60, 64, 68, 72, 76; co-chmn. 125th anniversary com. Meth. N.J. Ann. Con., 1961; vice chmn. curriculum resources com. United Meth. Ch., 1972—. Recipient Distinguished Alumnus award Asbury Coll., 1961; named Ky. col., 1962, One of Outstanding Educators Am., 1972. Mem. Assn. for Professional Edn. for Ministry, Evang. Theol. Soc., Wesleyan Theol. Soc., Theta Phi. Author: The Pauline Doctrine of Conscience, 1940; The Life and Work of the Rev. Joseph Pilmore, 1942; A Workman That Needeth Not to be Ashamed, 1958; God's Healing Community, 1978; editor: The Methodist Trail in New Jersey, 1961. Editor The Herald, 1961—. Contbr. to Ency. of World Methodism, Dictionary of Christian Ethics. Home: 203 Asbury Dr Wilmore KY 40390

STANGER, ILA, writer, editor; b. N.Y.C., Oct. 13, 1940; d. Jack Simon and Shirley Ruth (Nadelson) Stanger; B.A., Bklyn. Coll., 1961. Feature and travel editor Harpers Bazaar, N.Y.C., 1969-75; exec. editor Travel and Leisure mag., N.Y.C., 1975—; free lance writer on arts, features and travel. Mem. New York Travel Writers, Soc. Am. Travel Writers. Home: 115 W 71st St New York NY 10023 Office: Travel and Leisure Mag 1350 Ave of Americas New York NY 10019

STANGER, JOHN WILLIAM, credit co. exec.; b. Boston, Jan. 24, 1923; s. John Sawyer and Lenora (Leo) S.; student Boston U., 1941-43; A.B., Harvard U., 1947; m. Valerie Gudel, Apr. 14, 1951; 1 dau., Pamela Beth. With Gen. Electric Credit Corp. subs. Gen. Electric Co., N.Y.C., 1947—, gen. mgr. comml. and indsl. fin., 1960-62, v.p., gen. mgr. comml. and indsl. fin., 1962-75, pres., gen. mgr., 1975—, also dir.; chmn. Puritan Life Ins. Co., Puritan Ins. Co. Served to capt. USAAF, 1943-45, 51-53. Decorated D.F.C. Mem. Southwestern Area Commerce and Industry Assn. Conn. (chmn.). Elfun Soc. Republican. Clubs: Harvard Lower Fairfield, Greenwich Country, Union League, Landmark. Home: 72 Perkins Rd Greenwich CT 06830 Office: Gen Electric Credit Corp 760 Long Ridge Rd Stamford CT 06902

STANGER, RUSSELL, orch. condr.; b. Arlington, Mass., May 8, 1924; s. Herbert and Mellicent (Stemler) S.; grad. New Eng. Conservatory Music; student Tanglewood; m. Mildred Sheffield, Nov. 21, 1970. Condr., Cecelia Soc. Boston, 1953; organizer Boston Little Orch., 1958; asst. condr. New York Philharmonic, 1960-62, Mpls. Symphony Orch. (now Minn. Orch.), 1964-66; music dir. Norfolk (Va.) Symphony Orch., 1966—; guest condr. leading Am. and European orchs., including Phila. Orch., N.Y. Philharmonic, CBC Symphony, Buffalo Philharmonic, Oslo Philharmonic, Bergen (Norway) Philharmonic, Royal Philharmonic, London philharmonic, Orchestre Symphonique des Reims, Societe des Concerts du Conservatoire (Paris). Served with USNR, 1944-47. Recipient cultural citations, Phila., Norfolk. Mem. Phi Mu Alpha Sinfonia. Club: Lions. Composer: Buffoons (A Merry Overture), 1963; Childhood Images, 1968; Rock Opus (for symphony orch. and optional rock group), 1970; Episodes '76 (dramatic cantata), Op. 4, 1976. Office: PO Box 26 Norfolk VA 23501

STANGER, WESLEY ALLEN, JR., investment banker; b. Evanston, Ill., Apr. 25, 1909; s. Wesley Allen and Jennie M. (Price) S.; B.S. in Econs., U. Pa., 1929; m. Natalie Williams Denman, Jan. 1976; children by previous marriage—William M., Robert A. With Dillon, Read & Co., N.Y.C., 1929-33; gen. partner Riter & Co., members N.Y. Stock Exchange, N.Y.C., 1933-72; chmn. bd. Strong-Cobb & Co., Inc., Cleve., 1947-59, A.S.A. Ltd.; dir. Madison Fund N.Y.C., Talley Industries, Inc., Phoenix, Mackay-Shields Financial Corp., N.Y.C. Bd. govs. N.Y. Curb Exchange, 1942-43. Trustee U. Pa., La Nanapoule Found., Nice, France. Served with USNR, 1943-45. Mem. Phi Gamma Delta. Clubs: Baltusrol Golf (Springfield, N.J.); Sky (N.Y.C.). Home: 10 Highland Dr Summit NJ 07901 Office: 551 Fifth Ave New York NY 10017

STANHOPE, E. RAYMOND, food co. exec.; b. Flint, Mich., Nov. 6, 1932; s. Elmer Ray and Ruth Elois (Schlegel) S.; A.A., Grand Rapids Jr. Coll., 1952; B.A., U. Mich., LL.B., 1956; m. Ann Louise Hunter, Sept. 3, 1955; children—George Raymond, Elizabeth Ann, Mary Ruth. Admitted to Ill. bar, Mich. bar; mem. firm McDermott, Will & Emery, Chgo., 1956-57; partner firm Stanhope & McKee, Grand Rapids, Mich., 1958-59; with Upjohn Co., Kalamazoo, 1959-70; with A.E. Staley Mfg. Co., Decatur, Ill., 1970—, now group v.p.-internat. and adminstrn., corporate sec. Trustee, Portage Twp., Mich., 1961-64. Bd. dirs. Kalamazoo United Fund, 1965. Recipient Distinguished Service award Portage Jr. C. of C., 1962. Mem. Am., Mich., Decatur bar assns., Decatur C. of C. (bd. dirs.). Unitarian. Home: 338 Shoreline Pl Decatur IL 62521 Office: 2200 Eldorado St Decatur IL 62525

STANICK, GERALD, educator, violist; b. Winnipeg, Man., Can., Nov. 9, 1933; s. Bernard and Agnes (Gracel) S.; student viola with David Dawson, Ind. U., 1954-57; student United Coll., Winnipeg, 1962-63; m. Mary Kryschuk, July 3, 1953; children—Lesley, Toni, Laurie. Came to U.S., 1963. Prin. violist Winnipeg Canadian Broadcasting Corp. Orch., 1958-63, Winnipeg Symphony, 1958-63, U. Man. Quartet, Cordyon Trio, 1960-62, numerous solo recitals, orch. appearances, 1953—; violist Fine Arts String Quartet, 1963-68; asso. prof. viola U. Wis. at Milw., 1963-68; mus. dir. Wis. Coll. Conservatory Music, Milw., 1968-74; asso. prof. U. Victoria (B.C., Can.), 1974-77, U. Western Ont., London, 1977—; music Music dir. Ars Musica Chamber Orchestra, Milw.; faculty Sch. Fine Arts, Banff, Alta., Can., summers 1974—, Courtney Youth Music Camp, summers 1976-78; founder Quartet Can., 1976. Home: 877 Riverside Dr London ON Canada

STANISH, JOHN RICHARD, lawyer; b. Chgo., Sept. 16, 1945; s. Marion and Angeline Theresa (Dybel) S.; A.B., DePaul U., Chgo., 1967; J.D., Northwestern U., Chgo., 1970; m. Charmaine Swanson, Dec. 16, 1972. Admitted to Ind. bar, 1970; individual practice law, Hammond, 1970-77; city atty., Hammond, 1976-77; Presdl. pardon atty. Dept. Justice, Washington, 1977—. Pres., Bd. Pub. Works and Safety, Hammond, 1976; bd. dirs. N.W. Ind. Symphony Soc. Mem. Am. Bar Assn., Ind. Bar Assn., Hammond Bar Assn., Am. Correctional Assn. Democrat. Roman Catholic. Home: 2455 Birch Ave Hammond (Whiting PO) IN 46394 Office: Office of Pardon Atty Dept Justice 320 1st St NW Washington DC 20534

STANISIC, MILOMIR MIRKOV, educator, math. physicist; b. Bujacic-Serbia/Yugoslavia, Aug. 19, 1914; s. Mirko V. and Ana (Bujisic) S.; student Mil. Officer Acad., Belgrade, Yugoslavia, 1934-37; Cand. Ing., Belgrade U., 1940; Dipl. Ing., Tech., U. Hanover (Germany), 1946, Dr. Ing., 1949; Ph.D., Ill. Inst. Tech., 1958; m. Miroslava, Oct. 2, 1954 (div. Aug. 1962); children—Ana, Michael, Susana. Came to U.S., 1949, naturalized, 1955. Scientist, Armour Research Found., Chgo., 1950-56; asso. prof. Purdue U., 1956-60, prof., 1960—. Vis. prof. Johns Hopkins, 1966-67. Mem. Soc. Natural Philosophy, Am. Math. Soc., Am. Phys. Soc., AAUP. Research in theory of wing in supersonic motion; thermo-elasticity; magnetohydrodynamics; turbulence and nonlinear phenomena; behavior of the structures under moving masses. Home: 801 Princess Dr West Lafayette IN 47906

STANKARD, FRANCIS XAVIER, banker; b. N.Y.C., Jan. 13, 1932; s. John J. and Margaret (Daly) S.; B.S., Coll. Holy Cross, 1953; m. Elsa C. Hoffmann, Apr. 19, 1959; children—Charles, Peter, John. With Chase Manhattan Bank, N.Y.C., 1955—, asst. treas., 1959-62, asst. v.p., 1962-64, v.p., 1964-70, sr. v.p., 1970—; exec. v.p. Chase Manhattan Corp.; chmn. Chase Manhattan Overseas Banking Corp., Chase Internat. Investment Corp.; dir. Nederlandse Credietbank, N.V., Amsterdam, Banque de Commerce, S.A., Brussels. Bd. dirs. Japan Soc. Pub. affairs fellow Brookings Instn., 1967. Served with USMCR, 1953-55. Home: Autumn Ln Middletown NJ 07748 Office: One Chase Manhattan Plaza New York City NY 10015

STANKIEWICZ, EDWARD, educator; b. Poland, Nov. 14, 1920; s. Stefan and Ida (Grün) S.; came to U.S., 1950, naturalized, 1956; M.A., U. Chgo., 1951; Ph.D., Harvard, 1954; m. Florence Freiser, Nov. 5, 1950; children—Barbara, Steven. From asst. prof. to asso. prof. Ind. U., 1954-60; mem. faculty U. Chgo., 1960-71, prof. Slavic and gen. linguistics Yale, 1971—, chmn. dept. linguistics, 1974-78. Mem. Am. Linguistic Soc., Modern Lang. Assn. Author books and articles in field. Home: 30 Fernwood Rd Hamden CT 06517

STANKIEWICZ, RICHARD PETER, sculptor; b. Phila., Oct. 18, 1922; s. Anton and Rose (Pietrociewicz) S.; student pub. schs.; student Hans Hofmann Sch., N. M.C., 1948-50, Atelier Fernand Leger, Paris, 1950, Ossip Zadkine, Paris, 1950-51; m. Patricia M. Doyle, Sept. 30, 1961 (div. Nov. 1978); children—Peter Alex, Anthony Leslie (adopted). Co-organizer, officer Hansa Gallery, N.Y.C., a co-operative gallery, 1952-58; sculpture exhibited in one-man shows Hansa Gallery, 1952-58, Frumkin Gallery, Chgo., 1958, Stable Gallery, N.Y.C., 1959, 60, 65, Tampa (Fla.) Art Inst., 1965, Galerie Neufville, Paris Galerie Claude Bernard, Frank Watters Gallery, Sydney, Australia, 1969, Nat. Gallery of Victoria (Australia), 1969, Zabriskie Gallery, N.Y.C., 1971, 72, 73, Litchfield, Conn., 1973; two-man show Robert Fraser Gallery, London, 1963; group shows Hansa Gallery, Stable Gallery, Silvermine Guild, Riverside Mus., Smith Coll., Providence Art Club, Art Inst. Chgo., Watters Gallery, Nat. Gallery, Melbourne, Australia, Trend House Gallery, Tampa, Moderna Museet, Stockholm, Sweden, numerous others; biannual show Pa. Acad. Fine Arts, Phila., 1954; represented in collections Mus. Modern Art., N.Y.C., Art Inst. Chgo., Whitney Mus. Am. Art, Guggenheim Mus., N.Y., Mus. Modern Art, George Pompidou Center of Culture and Arts, Paris, others. Lectr. Amherst Coll., U. Miami, 1966; Ford Found. artist in residence Tampa Art Inst., 1965, Amherst Coll., 1970-71; prof. art State U. N.Y., 1967—; Salzman vis. artist Brandeis U., 1973. Mem. Nat. Council Arts and Humanities, Century Assn. Address: Star Route Huntington MA 01050

STANLEY, ARTHUR JEHU, JR., judge; b. nr. Lincoln, Kans., Mar. 21, 1901; s. Arthur and Bessie (Anderson) S.; LL.B., Kansas City Sch. Law (U. Mo., Kansas City), 1928; m. Ruth Willis, July 16, 1927; children—Mary Louise (Mrs. Bob Andrews), Carolyn (Mrs. Richard Lane), Constance (Mrs. Sherman Yunghans), Susan (Mrs. Paul Keith Hoffman). Admitted to Kans. bar, 1928; county atty. Wyandotte County, Kans., 1935-41; U.S. dist. judge Dist. of Kans., Leavenworth, 1958-71, chief judge, 1961-71, sr. U.S. dist. judge, 1971—. Mem. Jud. Conf. U.S. 1967-70, chmn. com. on operation of jury system, 1973-78, mem. bicentennial com., 1975—. Mem. Kans. Senate, 1941. Served with 7th U.S. Cav., Can. Army, World War I; with USN, 1921-25, Yangtze Patrol Force, 1923-25, 9th Air Force, USAAF, 1941-45; disch. to Inf. Res. as lt. col. Fellow Am. Bar Found.; mem. Am., Kans., Wyandotte County (past pres.), Leavenworth County bar assns., Am. Judicature Soc., Kans. Hist. Soc. (pres. 1974-75), Am. Legion. Anglican. Home: 501 N Esplanade Leavenworth KS 66048 Office: Federal Bldg Leavenworth KS 66048. *My goal in life has been to have and deserve the affection of my family and the respect of my professional colleagues.*

STANLEY, BOB, artist; b. Yonkers, N.Y., Jan. 3, 1932; s. Robert and Margaret (Druitz) S.; B.A., Oglethorpe U., 1953; postgrad. Columbia, 1953, Bklyn. Mus. Art Sch., 1954-56; m. Marylin Herzka, 1970. One man exhbns. include Bianchini Gallery, N.Y.C., 1965, 66, Internat. Gallery Orez, The Hague, Holland, 1966, Contemporary Art Center, Cin., 1966, Galerie Ricke, Kassel, Germany, 1966-67, Gegenverkehr, Aachen, Germany, 1969, on 1st, N.Y.C., 1969, Warren Benedek Gallery, 1972, N.Y. Cultural Center, 1974, La. State U. Union Gallery, Baton Rouge, 1976; Hal Bromm Gallery, N.Y.C. & Elizabeth Weiner Gallery, 1978. group exhbns. include 2 man show (with Bart Wasserman) P.S.I. Long Island City, 1977, Antisensitivity Show, Ohio U., 1964, Pop and Circumstance, Four Seasons, N.Y.C., 1965, Contemporary Americans, Art Inst. Chgo., 1965, John G. Powers Collection, Larry Aldrich Mus., Ridgefield, Conn., 1966, Hanford Yang Collection, Larry Aldrich Mus., Ridgefield, 1968, 29th Ann., Art Inst. Chgo., 1969, Aspects of a New Realism, Milw. Art Center, 1969, Ann. Exhbn., Whitney Mus. Am. Art, N.Y.C., 1967, 69, 72, 73, 17th Nat. Print Exhbn., Bklyn. Mus., 1970, Monumental Art, Contemporary Arts Center, Cin., 1970. Recent aquisitions Washington U. Mus., St. Louis, 1967, Obsessive Image, Inst. Contemporary Art, London, Eng., 1968, documenta 68, Kassel, Germany, another aspect of pop, P.S.I. Long Island City, 1978 Milw. Art Center, 1969. Faculty, Sch. Visual Arts, N.Y.C., 1970-72; vis. artist La. State U., 1976. Visiting Artist Syracuse University, 1978. Address: 3 Crosby St New York City NY 10013

STANLEY, C. MAXWELL, cons. engr.; b. Corning, Iowa, June 16, 1904; s. Claude Maxwell and Laura Esther (Stephenson) S.; B.S., U. Iowa, 1926; M.S., 1930; L.H.D., Iowa Wesleyan Coll., 1961; H.H.D. (hon.), U. Manila, 1970; m. Elizabeth M. Holthues, Nov. 11, 1927; children—David M., Richard H., Jane S. Buckles. Structural designer Byllesby Engring. & Mgmt. Corp., Chgo., 1926-27; dept. grounds and bldgs. U. Iowa, 1927-28; hydraulic engr. Mgmt. & Engring. Corp., Dubuque, Iowa, Chgo., 1928-32; cons. engr. Young & Stanley, Inc., 1932-39; partner, pres. Stanley Engring. Co., Muscatine, Iowa, 1939-66; pres. Stanley Cons., Inc., Muscatine, 1966-71, chmn. bd., 1971—; pres. HON Industries, 1944-64, chmn. bd., 1964—; pres. Stanley Cons. Ltd. Liberia, 1959-71, dir., 1971—; mng. dir. Stanley Cons. Ltd. Nigeria, 1960-67, dir., 1967—; pres. Atlas World Press Rev., 1975—. Trustee Iowa Wesleyan Coll., 1951—, chmn., 1963-65; chmn. Strategy for Peace Conf., 1962—, Conf. on UN of Next Decade, 1965—; pres. The Stanley Found., 1956—; bd. dirs. U. Iowa Found., 1966—, pres., 1971-75; mem. Pres.'s Commn. on Personnel Interchange, 1976-78. Recipient Disting. Service award U. Iowa, 1967, Hancher-Finkbine medallion, 1971. Fellow ASCE (Alfred Nobel prize 1933, Collingwood prize 1935), IEEE, ASME, Am. Cons. Engrs. Council (chmn. com. fellows 1975); hon. mem. Iowa Engring. Soc. (John Dunlap prize 1943, Marston award 1947, Distinguished Service award 1962); mem. Nat. Soc. Profl. Engrs. (award for outstanding service 1965, PEPP award 1975), World Federalists U.S.A. (council 1947—, pres. 1954-56, 64-66), World Assn. World Federalists (chmn. council 1958-65), Nat. Planning Assn. (dir. new directions 1976—). Republican. Methodist (past bd. Christian social concerns). Club: Rotary (Paul Harris award 1976). Author: Waging Peace, 1956; The Consulting Engineer, 1961; also articles profl. jours. Home: 115 Sunset Dr Muscatine IA 52761 Office: Stanley Bldg Muscatine IA 52761

STANLEY, CECIL EUGENE, assn. exec.; b. Holstein, Nebr., Feb. 12, 1909; s. Chester Loyd and Hazle Gertrude (McCulla) S.; B.S., Nebr. Wesleyan U., 1931; postgrad. U. Nebr., 1930-31, U. Minn., summer 1941; M.Ed., Colo. State U., 1950; m. Ruth Bilva Rockwell, Aug. 31, 1931; children—Nancy (Mrs. Joe Huckfeldt), Susan (Mrs. James Eno), Priscilla (Mrs. Duane Crithfield). With Nebr. Dept. Edn., Lincoln, 1941-75, dir. distributive edn., 1941-55, asst. commr. for vocat. edn., 1955-69, state commr. edn., 1969-75; exec. sec. Nebr. Vocat. Assn., 1975-79; trustee Nebr. State Colls.; mem. Bd. Commrs. Ednl. TV Nebr. Mem. Nebr. Alcoholic Commn., Nebr. Environ. Commn. Served to lt. USNR, 1944-46. Recipient Alumni Medal of Honor, Nebr. Wesleyan U., 1975; W.A. Robbins Community Service award Lincoln Sch. Commerce. Mem. Am. Vocat. Edn. Assn. (pres. 1954-55), Nat. Assn. State Dirs. Vocat. Edn. (pres. 1968-69), Am. Vocat. Assn. Distributive Edn. (v.p. 1953-54), Nebr. Council Sch. Adminstrs., Lincoln C. of C., Phi Delta Phi, Phi Delta Kappa, Iota Lambda Sigma, Delta Upsilon. Republican. Methodist. Mason (Shriner). Home: 1708 Pawnee St Lincoln NE 68502

STANLEY, EDMUND ALLPORT, JR., communications co. exec.; b. N.Y.C., July 9, 1924; s. Edmund Allport and Emily (Hasslacher) S.; A.B., Princeton U., 1949; m. Jennifer Berger, June 5, 1976; children by previous marriage—Edmund Allport III, Eric V., Lisa. With Bowne & Co., N.Y.C., 1949—, v.p., 1953-56, pres., 1956-74, chmn. bd., 1956—; dir. N.Y. Venture Fund Inc., N.Y.C., Atlas Corp., N.Y.C.; gov. Am. Stock Exchange, N.Y.C. Pres. Robert Bowne Found, N.Y.C.; trustee South St. Seaport Museum, N.Y. State Maritime Mus., N.Y.C., Lawrenceville (N.J.) Sch. Served with AUS, 1943-45. Decorated Bronze Star medal, Purple Heart. Clubs: Bond of N.Y., The Pilgrims. Home: 30 Beekman Pl New York City NY 10022 Office: 345 Hudson St New York City NY 10014

STANLEY, EDWARD LANE, ins. co. exec.; b. Phila., Jan. 19, 1916; s. Edwin C. and Edith (Worsham) S.; grad. Episcopal Acad., 1933; A.B., Williams Coll., 1937; m. Mary Gaylord, June 25, 1938; children—Peter G., Linda. Asst. mgr. mortgage loans Provident Mut. Life Ins. Co., Phila., 1949-58, v.p. mortgage loans and real estate, 1958-67, sr. v.p. fin., 1967-69, pres., dir., 1969-76, chmn., chief exec. officer, 1976-78, chmn. exec. com., 1978—; dir. Provident Nat. Bank, Provident Nat. Corp. Trustee Chestnut Hill Hosp., Williams Coll., Phila. Savs. Fund Soc., Episcopal Acad., Bryn Mawr Coll. Served to lt. USNR, 1943-46. C.L.U., Fellow Life Office Mgmt. Inst. Clubs: Phila. Cricket, Phila., Sunnybrook Golf. Home: 6110 Ensley Dr Flourtown PA 19031 Office: 4601 Market St Philadelphia PA 19101

STANLEY, FREDERICK AUSTIN, publisher; b. Bklyn., Sept. 19, 1925; s. Frank Lawrence and Irene Mary (Schmitt) S.; B. Naval Sci., Holy Cross Coll., Worcester, Mass., 1946, B.S. in Bus. Adminstrn., 1947; m. Joan M. Phillips, Sept. 27, 1952; children—David James, John Austin, Michael Anthony, Thomas Phillips, Elizabeth Jane. Advt. mgr. Am. Inst. Mining Engrs., N.Y.C., 1948-52, Penton Pub. Co., N.Y.C., 1953-56; sales mgr. Am. Soc. Metals, N.Y.C., 1956-65; sales mgr., pub. Chilton Co., Phila., 1965—. Served with USNR, 1943-46. Mem. Bus. Pubs. Assn. Am. (v.p. Phila. 1969-70). Club: St. David's Golf (Wayne, Pa.). Home: 648 Spruce Ln Berwyn PA 19312 Office: Chilton Way Radnor PA 19089

STANLEY, H(ARRY) EUGENE, physicist; b. Norman, Okla., Mar. 28, 1941; s. Harry Eugene and Ruth S.; B.A. in Physics (Nat. Merit scholar), Wesleyan U., 1962; postgrad. (Fulbright scholar) U. Cologne (W. Ger.), 1962-63; Ph.D. in Physics, Harvard U., 1967; m. Idahlia Dessauer, June 2, 1967; children—Jannah, Michael, Rachel. NSF predoctoral research fellow Harvard U., 1963-67; mem. staff Lincoln Lab., M.I.T., 1967-68, asst. prof. physics, 1969-71, asso. prof., 1971-73; Miller research fellow U. Calif., Berkeley, 1968-69; Hermann von Helmholtz asso. prof. health scis. and tech. Harvard U.-M.I.T. Program in Health Scis. and Tech., 1973-76; vis. prof. Osaka (Japan) U., 1975; univ. prof., prof. physics, prof. physiology Sch. Medicine, dir. Center for Polymer Studies, Boston U., 1976—; Joliot-Curie vis. prof. Ecole Supérieure de Physique et Chimie, Paris, 1979. Nat. co-chmn. Com. of Concerned Scientists, 1974-76. Recipient Choice award Am. Assn. Book Pubs., 1972; John Simon Guggenheim Meml. fellow, 1979-80. Fellow Am. Phys. Soc. Author: Introduction to Phase Transitions and Critical Phenomena, 1971; editorial bd. Physica, 1973—. Home: 50 Metacomet Rd Newton-Waban MA 02168 Office: Center for Polymer Studies Boston U Boston MA 02215

STANLEY, JAMES PAUL, printing co. exec.; b. Montreal, Que., Can., Aug. 15, 1915; s. Paul Garton and Florence May (Tooke) S.; B.Engring., McGill U., Montreal, 1938; m. Anne Seymour Raynsford, May 28, 1949; children—Marie, Susan, James, Sarah. Staff engr. Stevenson, Kellogg Ltd., 1938-41; plant mgr. Dow Brewery Ltd., 1947-53; v.p., then pres. Ronalds-Federated Ltd., Montreal, 1954-77, chmn. bd., chief exec. officer, 1977—. Served with RCAF, 1941-46. Fellow Graphic Arts Tech. Found.; mem. Montreal Bd. Trade. Mem. Ch. of Eng. Clubs: St. James's Badmington and Squash (Montreal); Royal St. Lawrence Yacht. Address: Ronalds-Federated Ltd 1801 McGill College Ave Suite 1470 Montreal PQ H3A 2N4 Canada

STANLEY, JULIAN CECIL, JR., educator; b. Macon, Ga., July 9, 1918; s. Julian Cecil and Ethel (Cheney) S.; B.S., Ga. So. Coll., 1937, Ed.M., Harvard, 1946, Ed.D., 1950; m. Rose Roberta Sanders, Aug. 18, 1946 (dec. Nov. 1978); 1 dau., Susan Roberta; m. 2d, Barbara Sprague Kerr, Jan. 1, 1980. Tchr., Fulton and West Fulton high schs., Atlanta, 1937-42; instr. psychology Newton Jr. Coll., 1946-48; instr. edn. Harvard, 1948-49; asso. prof. ednl. psychology George Peabody Coll. Tchrs., 1949-53; asso. prof. edn., 1953-57, prof. edn., 1957-62, prof. ednl. psychology, 1962-67, chmn. dept., 1962-63, dir. lab. exptl. design, 1961-67; prof. edn. and psychology Johns Hopkins, 1967-71, prof. psychology, 1971—, dir. study mathematically precocious youth, 1971—. Mem. research adv. council Coop. Research br. U.S. Office Edn., 1962-64; mem. com. examiners for aptitude tests Coll. Entrance Exam. Bd., 1961-65, chmn., 1965-68. Served with USAAC, 1942-45. Recipient Thorndike award for distinguished psychol. contbns. to edn., 1978. Fellow Social Sci. Research Council Inst. Math. for Social Scientists, U. Mich. summer 1955; postdoctoral fellow statistics U. Chgo., 1955-56; Fulbright research scholar U. Louvain (Belgium), 1958-59; Fulbright lectr. New Zealand and Australia, 1974; fellow Center for Advanced Study in Behavioral Sci., 1965-67. Fellow Am. Psychol. Assn. (pres. div. ednl. psychology 1965-66, div. evaluation and measurement 1972-73), AAAS, Am. Statis. Assn.; mem. Nat. Council Measurement Edn. (pres. 1963-64), Am. Ednl. Research Assn. (pres. 1966-67), Nat. Assn. for Gifted Children (2d v.p. 1977-79), AAUP (past pres. chpt.), Psychometric Soc. (past dir.), Phi Beta Kappa (past chpt. pres.), Sigma Xi. Author: Measurement in Today's Schools, 4th edit. 1964; (with D.T. Campbell) Experimental and Quasi-Experimental Designs for Research, 1966; (with Gene V. Glass) Statistical Methods in Education and Psychology, 1970; (with K.D. Hopkins) Educational and Psychological Measurement and Evaluation, 1972; (with Hopkins, G.H. Bracht) Perspectives in Educational and Psychological Measurement, 1972. Editor: Improving Experimental Design and Statistical Analysis, 1967; Preschool Programs for the Disadvantaged, 1972; Compensatory Education for Children, Ages 2-8, 1973; (with D.P. Keating, L.H. Fox) Mathematical Talent: Discovery, Description, and Development, 1974; (with W.C. George, C.H. Solano) The Gifted and the Creative: A Fifty-Year Perspective, 1977; Educational Programs and Intellectual Prodigies, 1978; (with W.C. George, S.J. Cohn) Educational Acceleration and Enrichment: Alternative Strategies, 1979; adv. editor jours. Home: 3938 Cloverhill Rd Baltimore MD 21218

STANLEY, JUSTIN ARMSTRONG, lawyer; b. Leesburg, Ind., Jan. 2, 1911; s. Walter H. and Janet (Armstrong) S.; A.B., Dartmouth, 1933, A.M. (hon.), 1952; LL.B., Columbia, 1937; LL.D. (hon.), John Marshall Law Sch., 1976, Suffolk U., 1976, Vt. Law Sch., 1977, Norwich U., 1977; m. Helen Leigh Fletcher, Jan. 3, 1938; children—Janet Van Wie Hoffman, Melinda Fletcher Douglas, Justin Armstrong, Harlan Fletcher. Admitted to Ill. bar, 1937, since practiced in Chgo.; asso. Isham, Lincoln & Beale, 1937-48, partner, 1948-66; partner Mayer, Brown & Platt, 1967—; v.p. Dartmouth Coll., 1952-54; asst. prof. law Chgo.-Kent Coll. Law, 1938-43, prof., 1943-46. Dir. Charles H. Shaw Co., Inc. Pub. mem. disputes sect. Nat. War Labor Bd., 1943-44. Trustee Presbyn.-St. Luke's Hosp., Wells Coll., 1960-69, Rockford Coll., 1962-70; trustee Ill. Childrens Home and Aid Soc., pres., 1962-63. Served as lt. USNR, 1944-46. Fellow Am. Bar Found., Am. Coll. Trial Lawyers; mem. Am. (chmn. pub. utility sect. 1970-71, ho. of dels. 1973—, pres. 1976-77), Fed. Energy, Chgo. (past pres.), Ill. bar assns., Alumni Council Dartmouth (pres. 1952), Am. Law Inst., Am. Judicature Soc., Alpha Delta Phi. Episcopalian. Clubs: Chicago, University, Legal, Commercial, Commonwealth, Law (Chgo.); Wausaukee (Wis.); Cosmos (Washington); Univ., Century Assn. (N.Y.C.). Home: 1630 Sheridan Rd Wilmette IL 60091 Office: 231 S LaSalle St Chicago IL 60604

STANLEY, LAWRENCE DELANEY, lawyer; b. Van Wert, Ohio, Dec. 30, 1905; s. John Milton and Lora Rebecca (Mathews) S.; B.A., Ohio State U., 1927; LL.B., Harvard, 1930; m. Sarah Carr Meyer, May 27, 1933, 1 dau., Laura (Mrs. Lee O. Gunnels). Admitted to Ohio bar, 1930, since practiced in Columbus; ret. partner, now of counsel firm Porter, Wright, Morris & Arthur, and predecessors, 1930—; chmn. Massillon, Inc. Mem. Am., Ohio, Columbus bar assns. Home: 1290 LaRochelle Dr Columbus OH 43221 Office: 37 W Broad St Columbus OH 43215

STANLEY, LOWELL, business exec.; b. Long Beach, Calif., Aug. 10, 1906; s. George Tatum and Clara (Graves) S.; A.B., U. Calif. at Los Angeles, 1928; m. Helene Archer, Nov. 21, 1934. With Jergins Oil Co. and predecessor, 1933-52, pres., 1950-51, chmn. bd., 1951-52; chmn. bd., chmn. exec. com. successor, Monterey Oil Co., 1952-55; dir. Petrolane, Inc., 1943—, chmn. bd., 1961-71, chmn. exec. com., 1971—; dir. Beckman Instruments, Inc., Beneficial Standard Corp., Great Western Fin. Corp., Gt. Western Savs. & Loan Assn. Panelist fed. tax policy for econ. growth and stability, joint econ. com. U.S. Senate-Ho. of Reps., 1955. C.P.A., Calif. Mem. Ind. Petroleum Assn. Am. (past dir.), Am. Inst. C.P.A.'s. Club: California (Los Angeles). Office: 1600 E Hill St Signal Hill CA 90806

STANLEY, PAUL ELWOOD, elec. engr., educator; b. Huntington, Ind., Nov. 6, 1909; s. Noah E. and Bertha (Chalmers) S.; A.B., Manchester Coll., 1930; M.A., Ohio State U., 1933, Ph.D., 1937; m. Lucille Klutz, Nov. 27, 1930; children—Mary Louise Johnson, Carol Ann (Mrs. Paul Conrad), Barbara Jean (Mrs. Stephan Grenat). Mem. faculty Purdue U., 1943—, interim head Sch. Aeros. and Astronautics Engring. Scis., 1963-65, prof., 1965-76, prof. emeritus, 1976—, asso. dir. Biomed. Engring. Center, 1973-76. Cons. numerous hosps. and indsl. firms. Asso. fellow Am. Inst. Aeros. and Astronautics; mem. I.E.E.E., Am. Soc. Engring. Edn., Assn. for Advancement Med. Instrumentation, Am. Hosp. Assn. Author: (with Joseph Liston) Creative Product Envolvement, 1940. Contbr. tech. papers to profl. lit. Home: 100 Hideaway Ln West Lafayette IN 47906. *To have a successful, pleasant, and satisfying life, find that which is most interesting and which serves mankind, then give if full effort—keeping in mind that all should be done in accordance with the highest Christian principles and teachings.*

STANLEY, RICHARD HOLT, cons. engr.; b. Muscatine, Iowa, Oct. 20, 1932; s. Claude Maxwell and Elizabeth Mabel (Holthues) S.; B.S. in Elec. Engring., Iowa State U., 1955, B.S. in Mech. Engring., 1955; M.S. in San. Engring., U. Iowa, 1963; m. Mary Jo Kennedy, Dec. 20, 1953; children—Lynne Elizabeth, Sarah Catherine, Joseph Holt. With Stanley Cons. Inc., Muscatine, 1955—, exec. v.p., 1968-71, pres., 1971—, also dir.; dir. Stanley Cons. Ltd., Liberia, HON Industries, Inc.; chmn. Nat. Constrn. Industry Council, 1978; chmn. Com. Fed. Procurement Archtl./Engring. Services, 1979. Pres. Eastern Iowa Community Coll., Bettendorf, 1966-68; mem. adv. council Coll. Engring., Iowa State U., Ames, 1969—, chmn., 1980. Bd. dirs., v.p. Stanley Found., Muscatine; bd. dirs. Muscatine United Way, 1969-75, U. Dubuque (Iowa), 1977—. Served with C.E., AUS, 1955-57. Recipient Young Alumnus award Iowa State U. Alumni Assn., 1966, Distinguished Service award Muscatine Jaycees, 1967; Profl. Achievement citation Coll. Engring., Iowa State U., 1977; named Sr. Engr. of Year Joint Engring. Com. of Quint Cities, 1973. Registered profl. engr., Iowa, other states. Fellow Iowa Acad. Sci., Am. Cons. Engrs. Council (pres. 1976-77); mem. Cons. Engrs. Council Iowa (pres. 1967), Nat. Soc. Profl. Engrs., Am. Nuclear Soc., IEEE (sr.), ASME, ASCE, Am. Soc. Engring. Edn., Iowa Engring. Soc. (John Dunlap-Sherman Woodward award 1967, pres. 1973-74), Muscatine C. of C. (pres. 1972-73), C. of C. of U.S. (internat. com. 1975—, constrn. action exec. com. 1976—), Tau Beta Pi, Phi Kappa Phi. Presbyterian (elder). Club: Rotary. Contbr. articles to profl. jours. Home: 601 W 3d St Muscatine IA 52761 Office: Stanley Bldg Muscatine IA 52761

STANLEY, SCOTT, JR., editor; b. Kansas City, Kans., July 11, 1938; s. Winfield Scott and Irene Mae (Flint) S.; B.A., Earlham Coll., 1960; m. Janice Johns, Aug. 30, 1959; children—Leslie, Scott, Margaret. Mng. editor Am. Opinion mag., Belmont, Mass., 1961—; editor Rev. of The News mag., Belmont, 1965—; mem. nat. bd. dirs. Young Ams. for Freedom, 1960-62; public speaker and univ. lectr., 1962—. Keynote speaker Am. Party Nat. Conv., 1976; pres. Ams. Legal Def. Fund, 1977—; trustee D.C. Law Sch., 1977—. Recipient award of merit Young Ams. for Freedom, 1970, Merwin K. Hart award Nat. Econ. Council, 1972, Freedom award Nat. Congress for Freedom, 1969-79. Mem. John Birch Soc. Congregationalist. Club: Nashawtuc Country. Home: 7 Redwood Rd Acton MA 01720 Office: 395 Concord Ave Belmont MA 02178

STANLEY, STEVEN MITCHELL, paleobiologist, educator; b. Detroit, Nov. 2, 1941; s. William Thomas and Mildred Elizabeth (Baker) S.; A.B. with highest honors, Princeton U., 1963; Ph.D., Yale U., 1968; m. Nell Williams Gilmore, Oct. 11, 1969; Asst. prof. U. Rochester, 1967-69; asst. prof. paleobiology Johns Hopkins U., 1969-71, asso. prof., 1971-74, prof., 1974—; asso. in research Smithsonian Instn., 1972—. Recipient Outstanding Paper award Jour. Paleontology, 1968, Allan C. Davis medal Md. Acad. Scis., 1973. Fellow Geol. Soc. Am. (chmn. Penrose com. 1978); mem. Paleontol. Soc. (councilor 1976-77, Charles Schuchert award 1977), Soc. for Study Evolution. Author: Relation of Shell Form to Life Habits in the Bivalvia, 1970; (with D.M. Raup) Principles of Paleontology, 1971; Macroevolution: Pattern and Process, 1979; editorial bd. Am. Jour. Sci., 1975—, Paleobiology, 1975—, Evolutionary Theory, 1973—. Home: 1110 Bellemore Rd Baltimore MD 21210 Office: Dept Earth and Planetary Scis Johns Hopkins U Baltimore MD 21218

STANLEY, THOMAS BAHNSON, JR., furniture co. exec.; b. Martinsville, Va., Jan. 9, 1927; s. Thomas B. and Anne (Bassett) S.; B.S. in C.E., Va. Mil. Inst., 1946; B.S.C., U. Va., 1948; grad. Advanced Mgmt. Program, Harvard, 1970; m. Ruth Barnes, Sept. 10, 1949; children—Thomas Bahnson III, Susan Walker, Andrew. With Stanley Furniture Co., Stanleytown, Va., 1948—, dir., 1950—, exec. v.p., 1952-62, pres., 1962-71, chmn., 1971—; pres. Mead Interiors, Stanleytown, 1969-74; group v.p. Mead Corp., Dayton, Ohio, 1969-74, also dir.; dir. Fieldcrest Mills, Inc., So. Furniture Expn. Bldg., High Point, N.C., Piedmont Trust Co., Martinsville, Va., Stanley Land & Lumber Co., Drakes Branch, Va., B.C. Forest Products, Ltd., Fieldcrest Ireland, Ltd. Mem. Henry County Sch. Bd., 1957—; chmn. bd. trustees Ferrum Coll. Mem. So. Furniture Mfrs. Assn. (dir., pres. 1966, chmn. 1967). Methodist. Mason (32 deg.). Home: Box 26 Stanleytown VA 24168 Office: Stanleytown VA 24168

STANLEY, TIMOTHY WADSWORTH, assn. exec.; b. Hartford, Conn., Sept. 28, 1927; s. Maurice and Margaret Stowell (Sammond) S.; student Choate Sch., 1943-45; B.A., Yale, 1950; LL.B., Harvard, 1955, Ph.D., 1957; m. Nadia Leon, June 7, 1952; children—Timothy Wadsworth III, Alessandra Maria, Christopher Maurice, Flavia Margaret. Mem. staff Office Sec. Def., 1955; admitted to Conn. bar, 1956, also U.S. Supreme Ct.; teaching fellow Harvard, 1955-56; spl. asst. White House staff, 1957-59; spl. asst. to asst. sec. def. for internat. security affairs, 1959-62; vis. research fellow Council on Fgn. Relations, N.Y.C., 1962-63; div. dir. policy planning staff Office Sec. Def., 1963-64; asst. to sec. def. for NATO force planning, Paris, 1965-67; def. adviser (minister) U.S. Mission to NATO, Paris and Brussels, 1967-69; vis. prof. internat. relations Johns Hopkins Sch. Advanced Internat. Studies, 1969-70; exec. v.p. Internat. Econ. Policy Assn., Washington, 1970-74, pres., 1974—; pres. Internat. Econ. Studies Inst., 1974—. Professorial lectr. George Washington U., 1957-60; cons. to various govt. agys., univs., bus. orgns., 1969-70; research asso. Washington Center Fgn. Policy Research, 1969-71; spl. rep. ACDA in negotiations for East-West Mut. Balanced Force Reductions, 1973-74, cons., 1975—; mem. U.S. Govt. Adv. Com. on Investment, Tech. and Devel. Bd. dirs. Atlantic Council U.S. Served to 1st lt. AUS, 1946-48, 51-52. Recipient Distinguished Civilian Service medal Dept. Def., 1969. Mem. Council on Fgn. Relations N.Y., Inst. for Strategic Studies London. Congregationalist. Clubs: Yale (N.Y.C.); Metropolitan, Federal City (Washington). Author: American Defense and National Security, 1955; NATO in Transition, 1965; Detente Diplomacy, 1970. Co-author: U.S. Troops in Europe, 1971; The United States Balance of Payments, 1972; Raw Materials and Foreign Policy, 1977; Technology and Economic Development, 1979. Contbr. articles to profl. jours. Home: 3025 N St NW Washington DC 20007 Office: 1625 I St NW Washington DC 20006

STANLEY, WILLIAM HUBERT, banker; b. Lake View, S.C., Mar. 14, 1925; s. John Hubert and Ina (Humphrey) S.; student Rutgers U., 1955; m. Ida Robinson, Jan. 15, 1946; children—William Christopher, Marianne. Asst. cashier First-Citizens Bank & Trust Co., Spring Hope, N.C., 1946-50; with Peoples Bank & Trust Co., Rocky Mount, N.C., 1950—, asst. v.p., 1952-53, v.p., cashier, 1953-62, exec. v.p., 1962-68, pres., 1968—, also dir. Treas. Rocky Mount chpt. N.C. Symphony Soc., 1957-61; campaign dir. United Fund, 1967-68; bd. regents Barium Springs Home for Children, 1966-70. Trustee Nash Gen. Hosp., East Carolina U. Served with USNR, 1942-46. Mem. Nat. Assn. Bank Auditors and Comptrollers, N.C. Bankers Assn. (pres. young bankers div. 1962-63, pres. assn. 1967-70), Rocky Mount C. of C. Democrat. Presbyn. Kiwanian (pres. 1964-65). Home: 1708 Lafayette Circle Rocky Mount NC 27801 Office: Corner Franklin & Western Aves Rocky Mount NC 27801

STANLEY, WILLIAM OLIVER, JR., ret. educator; b. Sedalia, Mo., Oct. 26, 1902; s. William Oliver and Minnie (Raymond) S.; A.B., Baker U., 1926; A.M., Columbia U. Tchrs. Coll., 1936; Ph.D., Columbia U., 1951; m. Lola Sizemore, Feb. 4, 1933; 1 son, William Oliver. Tchr. history, high schs. in Kans., Colo., Ill., 1926-35; asst. prof. edn. Madison Coll., 1939-42; asst. prof. edn. U. Ill., 1942-51, asso. prof., 1951-54, prof., 1954-71, prof. philosophy of edn., chmn. dept. history and philosophy of edn., 1963-65, chmn. div. social founds. of edn., 1950-63, emeritus, 1971; prof. U. South Fla., Tampa, 1971-73. Mem. John Dewey Soc. (v.p. 1956; Distinguished Service award 1975), Philosophy Edn. Soc. (pres. 1954), Nat. Soc. Coll. Tchrs. Edn. (pres. 1959-60). Author: Education and Social Integration, 1952; (with B. O. Smith, J. H. Shores) Fundamentals of Curriculum Development, 1950; Social Foundations of Education, 1956; editor: Educational Theory, 1965-71; contbr. numerous articles to ednl. jours. Home: 708 Grovewood Ln The Bluffs Largo FL 33540

STANNERS, WILLIAM JOSEPH, bank exec.; b. New London, Conn., May 11, 1927; s. John H. and Mary M. S.; grad. Stonier Sch. Banking, Rutgers U., 1960; m. Mercedes Ann Picazio, May 16, 1953; children—William Joseph, Donald Charles, Robert Kevin. With Hartford Nat. Bank & Trust Co. (Conn.), 1946—, sr. v.p., mgr. nat. div., 1970-72, sr. v.p., mgr. internat. div., 1972-75, exec. v.p., head comml. banking group, 1975-76, 1st exec. v.p. in charge of all banking areas, 1976—; mem. faculty Williams Sch. Banking, 1970-76; moderator Robert Morris workshops; dir. Equator Bank Ltd. Treas., Town of Old Saybrook (Conn.), 1964-70, mem. bd. fin., 1970-72; treas. NACJ; corporator Mt. Sinai Hosp., Hartford. Served with USN, 1945-46. Recipient Disting. Service award as Man of Yr., Greater New London Jr. C. of C. 1954. Mem. Bankers' Assn. Fgn. Trade (dir.), Old Saybrook C. of C. (pres. 1961-63). Clubs: Hartford, Black Hall Golf, Lymes Racket. Office: 777 Main St Hartford CT 06115

STANNETT, VIVIAN THOMAS, educator; b. Langley, Eng., Sept. 1, 1917; s. Ernest and Dorothy Grace (Rustell) S.; B.S., London Poly., 1939; Ph.D., Poly. Inst. Bklyn., 1950; m. Flora Susanne Sulzbacher, May 30, 1946; 1 dau., Rosemary Anthia. Came to U.S., 1947, naturalized, 1957. Chemist, govt. and industry, Eng., 1939-47; research asso. Mellon Inst., Pitts., 1950-51; research chemist Koppers Co., Pitts., 1951-52; prof. polymer chemistry State U. Coll. Forestry, Syracuse, N.Y., 1952-61; asso. dir. Camille Dreyfus Labs., Research Triangle Inst., Durham, N.C., 1961-67; Camille Dreyfus prof. chem. engring. N.C. State U., Raleigh, 1961—, vice provost, dean Grad. Sch., 1975—. Cons. U.S. Army, 1967—, AEC, 1966-69, NIH, 1970—, Ethyl Corp., 1967—, W.R. Grace Co., 1967—, others. Recipient Borden award Am. Chem. Soc., 1974, Anselm Payen award, 1974. Fellow Royal Inst. Chemistry, TAPPI (Silver medal synthetic div. 1967), N.Y. Acad. Sci., Soc. Plastics Engrs. (Internat. award and gold medal 1978). Author: Cellulose Acetate Plastics, 1950; Handbook of Chemical Technology, 1953. Contbr. articles to profl. jours. Home: 1105 Bancroft St Raleigh NC 27612

STANS, MAURICE HUBERT, former govt. ofcl.; b. Shakopee, Minn., Mar. 22, 1908; s. J. Hubert and Mathilda (Nyssen) S.; student Northwestern U., 1925-28, Columbia U., 1928-30; LL.D., Ill. Wesleyan U., 1954, Northwestern U., 1960, DePaul U., 1960; D.P.A., Parsons Coll., 1960; LL.D., Grove City Coll., St. Anselm's Coll., 1969, U. San Diego, Gustavus Adolphus Coll., 1970, Pomona Coll., 1971, Maryville Coll., 1971, Rio Grande Coll., 1972, Nat. U., 1979; m. Kathleen Carmody, Sept. 7, 1933; children—Steven, Maureen, Theodore, Terrell. Joined Alexander Grant & Co., C.P.A.'s, Chgo., 1928, exec. partner, 1940-55; treas., dir. Moore Corp., stove mfrs., Joliet, Ill., 1938-45, chmn. bd., 1942-45; dir., mem. exec. com. James Talcott, Inc., N.Y.C., 1941-55; fin. cons. to postmaster gen. U.S., 1953-55; dep. postmaster gen. U.S., 1955-57; dep. dir. U.S. Bur. Budget, 1957-58, dir., 1958-61; pres. Western Bancorp., Los Angeles, 1961-62; sr. partner William R. Staats & Co., 1963-64; pres. William

R. Staats Co., Inc., 1964-65, Glore Forgan, William R. Staats, Inc., N.Y.C., 1965-69; syndicated columnist, 1961-62; sec. Dept. Commerce, Washington, 1969-72; vice chmn. United Calif. Bank, 1961-62; dir. Pettibone Corp., Chgo.; dir. 10 listed cos., 1950-78. Founder, pres., dir. Stans Found. Chgo.; chmn. Nixon Finance Com., 1968, Republican Nat. Finance Com., 1968-69, 72-73, Finance Com. to Re-Elect Pres., 1972-73; trustee Pomona Coll., 1962-69. Recipient Great Living Am. award U.S. C. of C., 1961; Tax Found. award, 1960; C.P.A. Mem. NAM (dir. 1968-69), Am. Inst. C.P.A.'s (pres. 1954-55, Pub. Service award 1954), Ill. (dir. 1944-46), D.C. (hon.), Hawaii (hon.) socs. C.P.A.'s, Am. Accounting Assn. (nat. Alpha Kappa Psi award 1952), Fed. Govt. Accountants Assn., Nat. Assn. Postmasters (hon.), Iron Molders and Foundry Workers Union (hon.) Clubs: Union League, Adventurers (Chgo.); Calif. (Los Angeles); Shikar-Safari, East African Profl. Hunters (hon.), Explorers (N.Y.C.); African Safari (Washington); Met. (gov. 1968-69) (N.Y.C.); Jamhuri of Garissa (hon.) (Kenya). Author: The Terrors of Justice, 1978; contbr. numerous articles on govt. fin., fgn. trade and bus. to profl. publs.

STANSBERRY, JAMES WESLEY, air force officer; b. Grafton, W.Va., Dec. 29, 1927; s. William Adrian and Phyllis Gay (Robinson) s.; B.S., U.S. Mil. Acad., 1949; M.B.A., Air Force Inst. Tech., 1956; m. Audrey Mildred Heinz, May 7, 1950; children—Nora G. Stansberry, Amy G. Stansberry Goodhand, Lisa A. Advanced through grades from pvt. to maj. gen. USAF; chief prodn. Kawasaki Gifu Contract Facility, Gifu, Japan, 1956-57; dep. asst. to Sec. of Def. for atomic energy Washington, 1970-71; dep. dir. procurement policy U.S. Air Force, 1972-73; dep. chief staff contracting and mfg. Hdqrs. Air Force Systems Command, Andrews AFB, Md., 1977—. Decorated Legion of Merit with oak leaf cluster. Methodist. Home: 1322-1 Vandenberg Dr Andrews AFB MD 20335 Office: HQ Air Force Systems Command Andrews AFB DC 20334. *The real secrets are enthusiasm and competence, laced with good luck; and it helps immensely to marry a good woman.*

STANSKY, PETER DAVID LYMAN, historian; b. N.Y.C., Jan. 18, 1932; s. Lyman and Ruth (Macow) S.; B.A., Yale U., 1953; B.A., King's Coll., Cambridge (Eng.) U., 1955, M.A., 1959; Ph.D., Harvard U., 1961. Teaching fellow history and lit. Harvard U., 1957-61, instr., then asst. prof. history, 1961-68; mem. faculty Stanford U., 1968—, prof. history, 1973-74, Frances and Charles Field prof., 1974—, chmn. dept. history, 1975-78, 79—; chmn. publs. com. Conf. Brit. Studies, 1970-78; pres. Pacific Coast Conf. Brit. Studies, 1974-76; vis. fellow Wesleyan Center Humanities, Middletown, Conn., 1972, All Soul's Coll., Oxford (Eng.) U., 1979. Guggenheim fellow, 1966-67, 73-74; Am. Council Learned Socs. fellow, 1978-79. Fellow Royal Hist. Soc.; mem. Am. Hist. Assn., Conf. on Brit. Studies, Victorian Soc., William Morris Soc., AAUP. Author: Ambitions and Strategies, 1964; England Since 1867, 1973; Gladstone, 1979; co-author: Journey to the Frontier, 1966; The Unknown Orwell, 1972; Orwell: The Transformation, 1979. Home: 375 Pinehill Rd Hillsborough CA 94010 Office: Dept History Stanford Univ Stanford CA 94305

STANTON, BERNARD FREELAND, educator; b. Westerlo, N.Y., Aug. 3, 1925; s. Rhodell M. and Ethel (Kniffen) S.; B.S., Cornell U., 1949; M.S., U. Minn., 1950, Ph.D., 1953; diploma Agrl. Econ., Oxford (Eng.) U., 1950-51; m. Lara S. Kristjanson, June 25, 1955; children—Margaret Ann, Karen, Randall Jon. Asst. prof. agrl. econs. Cornell U., 1953-56, asso. prof., 1956-62, prof., 1962—, chmn. dept. agrl. econs., 1968-76. Econ. statisician Dept. Agr. 1960-61; cons. Experience, Inc., Mpls., 1965—, Agrl. Devel. Fund of Iran, 1969-70, Econ. Devel. Inst., IBRD, 1970—; vis. prof. Australian Nat. U., Canberra, 1976, Tamil Nadu Agrl. U., Coimbatore, India, 1976. Mem. Lansing (N.Y.) Central Sch. Bd., 1965-66, Ithaca Planning Bd., 1977—; bd. dirs., v.p. Fund for Internat. Conf. Agrl. Econs. Fulbright research scholar U. Helsinki (Finland), 1966-67. Mem. AAAS, Am. Econs. Assn., Am. Agrl. Econs. Assn. (exec. bd. 1974—, pres.-elect 1977-78, pres. 1978-79, chmn. nat. awards program 1972-74), Internat. Assn. Agrl. Economists, Ho-Nun-De-Kah, Alpha Zeta Phi Kappa Phi. Mem. Congregational United Ch. of Christ. Editorial bd. Jour. Farm Econs., 1958-62. Home: 2 Sandra Pl Ithaca NY 14850

STANTON, CURTIS HENDERSON, utilities co. exec.; b. Key West, Fla., June 3, 1918; s. Curtis Harvey and Sarah Belle (Knowles) S.; B.Mech. Engring. with high honors, U. Fla., 1940; m. Claire Ann Tillman, Apr. 4, 1942; children—Claire Sutton, Gail Dyer, Kathryn Jennings. Dir. sales tng. Gen. Electric Co., Schenectady, 1940-47; asst. gen. mgr. Orlando Utilities Commn. (Fla.), 1947-48, exec. v.p., gen. mgr., 1948—; pres. Fla. Electric Power Coordinating Group. Pres., Central Fla. Fair, 1960-62. Mem. Am. Water Works Assn. (pres. 1978-79), IEEE, ASME, Fla. Pollution Control Assn. Democrat. Methodist. Clubs: Country, Univ. (Orlando). Office: 500 S Orange Ave Orlando FL 32802. *Hard work and continuing communication with friends and strangers are mainly responsible for my success.*

STANTON, DONALD SHELDON, coll. exec.; b. Balt., June 8, 1932; s. Kenneth Gladstone and Dorothy Erma (Hettrick) S.; A.B., Western Md. Coll., 1953; M.Div. magna cum laude, Wesley Theol. Sem., 1956; M.A., Am. U., 1960; Ed.D., U. Va., 1965; L.H.D., Columbia Coll., 1979; m. Barbara Mae Hoot, June 25, 1955; children—Dale Richard, Debra Carol, Diane Karen. Ordained to ministry United Methodist Ch., 1956; pastor Balt. and Va. confs. United Meth. Ch., 1953-59; dir. Richmond (Va.) Area Wesley Found., 1959-63; chaplain, dean of students Greensboro Coll., 1963-65; chaplain Wofford Coll., 1965-69; dir. office coll. services United Meth. Div. Higher Edn., Nashville, 1969-75; v.p. for devel. Wesleyan Coll., 1975-78; pres. Adrian Coll., 1978—; adminstr., prof. Internat. Ednl. Programs, summers 1960, 69-71, 73; mem. Council on the Ch.-Related Coll., 1967-70; v.p. Ga. Ednl. Advancement Council, 1978; speaker in field. Bass-baritone soloist for civic, community groups; v.p. Middle Ga. Council on World Affairs, 1978; trustee Ga. Indsl. Home, Macon, 1977-78. Mem. Tau Kappa Epsilon (hon.), Psi Chi. Clubs: Adrian Rotary, Lenawee Country. Contbr. articles, revs. to profl. publs., chpts. to books; editor Faculty Forum, 1972-74. Home: 135 S Madison St Adrian MI 49221 Office: Adrian Coll Adrian MI 49221

STANTON, FRANK (NICHOLAS), corp. dir.; b. Muskegon, Mich., 1908; B.A., Ohio Wesleyan U., 1930; Ph.D., Ohio State U., 1935; m. Ruth Stephenson, 1931. Pres. CBS, Inc., 1946-71, vice chmn., 1971-73; dir. CBS Inc., 1945-78, Atlantic Richfield Co., The (London) Observer Ltd., Pan. Am. World Airways, Inc., Am. Electric Power Co., Inc., New Perspective Fund Inc., N.Y. Life Ins. Co., Interpublic Group, Simplicity Pattern Co.; trustee The Rand Corp., 1956-78, chmn., 1961-67; chmn. ARC, 1973-79; v.p. League of Red Cross Socs., Geneva, Switzerland; chmn. Carnegie Instn. Washington. Chmn. panel on internat. info., edn. and cultural relations Georgetown U., 1974-75; mem. N.Y. State Council on Arts, 1965-70; chmn. Center for Advanced Study in Behavioral Scis., 1953-60; chmn. U.S. Adv. Commn. on Info., 1964-73; hon. mem. Bus. Council; mem. Nat. Portrait Gallery Commn.; mem. governing council Rockefeller Archive Center, 1974-78, Archtl. League N.Y. Bd. dirs. Internat. Design Conf., Aspen, Colo., Lincoln Center Inst., Lincoln Center Performing Arts, Inc.; bd. overseers Harvard Coll. of Harvard U.; trustee Rockefeller Found., 1961-73, Am. Crafts Council, 1957-75, Inst. for Architecture and Urban Studies, 1970-75, Recorded Anthology Am. Music, Inc., Archtl. League, N.Y.C., Nat. Humanities Center; chmn. Bus. Com. for Arts, 1971-73. Fellow Am. Acad. Arts and Scis., AAAS, Am. Psychol. Assn., N.Y. Acad. Sci., Sigma Delta Chi; mem. council Fgn. Relations, IEEE, Radio-TV New Dirs. Assn., Sigma Xi. Clubs: Century Assn., Links (N.Y.C.); Cosmos, Metropolitan (Washington). Author: (with others) Students' Guide—The Study of Psychology, 1938; editor: (with Paul F. Lazarsfeld) Radio Research, 1941, Radio Research, 1942-43, Communications Research, 1948-49. Office: 10 E 56th St New York NY 10022

STANTON, FRANK D., mgmt. cons.; b. Mpls., Aug. 1, 1914; s. Michael D. and Ellen (Flaherty) S.; B.B.A., U. Minn., 1937; m. Elizabeth McGrath, Nov. 21, 1941; children—Michael, Ann Marie, Christopher, Damiel, Mary Ellen. Profl. baseball player, 1937-38; insp. N.W. Fire Underwriters, Mpls., 1938-41; spl. agt. FBI, 1941-47; dir. personnel, then v.p. Farmers Union Grain Terminal Assn., St. Paul, 1947-55; founder, 1955, since pres. Stanton Assos., Inc., mgmt. cons., St. Paul. Chmn. finance com. City of Arden Hills, Minn., 1965-66. Mem. Assn. Mgmt. Cons. (pres. 1974-75; citation appreciation), U. Minn. Alumni Assn. Sch. Bus. Adminstrn. (pres. 1965-66; citation appreciation), Personnel Surveys Inc. (exec. sec. 1956-73; citation appreciation), Twin City Personnel Mgrs. Assn. (pres. 1953-54), U. Minn. M. Club (pres. 1961-62), Inst. Mgmt. Cons. Republican. Roman Catholic. Clubs: St. Paul Athletic; Midland Hills Country; St. Paul Rotary; U. Minn. Alumni Author articles. Home: 1569 Edgewater Ave St Paul MN 55112 Office: 1821 University Ave St Paul MN 55104

STANTON, GERALD ELROY, accounting co. exec.; b. Merrill, Wis., Sept. 7, 1922; s. Robert Ernest and Leona Anna (Plautz) Skofronick; student U. Notre Dame, 1940-43, B.S.C., 1947; student U. Md., 1943, Georgetown U., 1944; postgrad. Wharton Grad. Div., U. Pa., 1947; m. Patricia Sydney Ward, June 2, 1945; children—Robert Ward, Jeffrey Thomas. With Arthur Andersen & Co., Washington, 1947-56, Chgo., 1956—, mng. partner merger and acquisitions assistance, Chgo., 1963-70, vice chmn. adminstr. world hdqrs., Chgo. and Geneva, Switzerland, 1970—. Mem. exec. bd. Auditorium Theatre Council, Chgo.; pres., chmn. bd., bd. mgrs. Child and Family Services, Chgo.; mem. exec. com., trustee Lawrence Hall Sch. for Boys, Chgo.; trustee Episcopal Charities, Chgo.; chmn. Chgo. adv. council Episcopal Ch. Found. Served with U.S. Army, 1943-46. Mem. Am. Accounting Assn., Am. Inst. C.P.A.'s, Ill. Soc. C.P.A.'s, Nat. Assn. Accts., Swiss-Am. C. of C. (dir.). Republican. Clubs: Chgo. Athletic, The Chgo., Chgo. Commonwealth, Econ. of Chgo., Execs. of Chgo., Notre Dame of Chgo.; Inverness Golf; Park Ridge Country; Le Mirador Country. Home: 301 Dover Circle Inverness Palatine IL 60067 also 26 Chemin des Crets-de-Champel 1206 Geneva Switzerland Office: 69 W Washington St Chicago IL 60602 also 18 Quai General-Guisan 1211 Geneva 3 Switzerland

STANTON, JOHN WILLIAM, congressman; b. Painesville, Ohio, Feb. 20, 1924; s. Frank M. and Mary (Callinan) S.; B.A., Georgetown U., 1949; m. Margaret Smeeton, Dec. 3, 1966; 1 dau., Kelly Marie. Pres., J.W. Stanton, Inc., Painesville, 1949-63; commr. Lake County, Ohio, 1956-64; mem. 89th-96th Congresses, 11th Dist. Ohio. Served to capt. AUS, 1942-46. Decorated Bronze Star with oak leaf cluster, Purple Heart. Mem. Painesville Jr. (charter), Painesville (pres. 1952-55) chambers commerce, Am. Legion. Elk, K.C. (4 deg.). Republican. Roman Catholic. Club: Painesville Exchange (pres. 1951). Home: 7 N Park Pl Painesville OH 44077 Office: Rayburn Bldg Washington DC 20515

STANTON, ROBERT LEE, farmer, cattle feeder; b. Hamburg, Iowa, June 8, 1925; s. William J. and Mabel (Garst) S.; student U. Mo., 1942-43; m. Cassalou Fischer, Aug. 17, 1946; Farmer, Rockport, 1943-48; mgr. grain elevators, Watson and Rockport, 1948-61; mgr., v.p. Kawaihae Elevator Co. (Hawaii), 1961-64; farmer, cattle feeder, Rockport, 1964—; pres. Rockport Telephone Co., 1972—, also dir.; dir. Bank of Atchison County, Rockport; asst. sec., dir. MBPXL Corp., Wichita, Kans., 1965—, Bd. dirs. Atchison County Levy Bd., Rockport, 1958—, v.p., 1973—. Presbyterian. Home: 800 Stanton Dr Rockport MO 64482 Office: MBPXL Corp PO Box 2519 Wichita KS 67201

STANTON, ROGER, editor, publisher, sports broadcaster; b. Mpls., Dec. 31, 1928; s. M.E. and Pearl (Lind) S.; B.A., U. Mich., 1951; m. Pamela Elisabeth Kornmeier, Dec. 19, 1970. With advt. pub. relations dept. Fed. Dept. Stores, Detroit, 1951-54; sales promotion mgr. Wolf Detroit Envelope Co., 1954-56; editor employee publs. Nat. Bank Detroit, 1956-64, coordinator employee recreation program, 1957-64; pres. editor, pub. Football News, Detroit, 1962—; pub. Basketball Weekly, 1967—, Big Ten Report, 1972—. Sports dir. Sta. WDTM, Detroit, Sta. WXON-TV; instr. writing pub. relations Sta. WMCA, Detroit, 1960-62; chmn. indsl. publs. for Mich. Week, 1958-63. Bd. dirs. Mich. chpt. Nat. Football Found. and Hall of Fame. Mem. speakers bur. United Found. Active in pub. relations work; mem. exec. bd. Detroit Area council Boy Scouts Am., 1977—; del. Mich. Republican Com. Mem. Nat. Sportswriters and Sports Broadcasters Assn., Basketball Writers Assn., Pro Football Writers Assn., Coll. Sports Info. Dirs. Assn., Sigma Delta Chi. Clubs: Adcraft (publicity chmn.), U. Mich. (mem. bd. govs.), Economic (publicity com.), Lochmoor, Press (Detroit); Palm Bay, Racquet (Miami, Fla.). Home: 7 Stratford Pl Grosse Pointe MI 48230 also Key Biscayne FL Office: 17820 E Warren St Detroit MI 48224. *Each day I wake up happy to be alive and anxious to do something to make the world a better place. I have a positive attitude that problems can be solved and there is something good in all people.*

STANTON, THOMAS JOSEPH, steel co. exec.; b. N.Y.C., Dec. 1, 1921; s. Howard Alfred and Anna (Pitson) S.; student Coll. City N.Y., 1943-48, U. Pa., 1949-53, Dartmouth, summers 1954-56, Columbia, 1968; m. Alice Fugett, June 5, 1943; children—Barbara Anne, Susan Elizabeth. Cashier, Australian Govt. Offices, N.Y.C., 1939-42; supr. credit dept. Hanover Bank & Trust Co., 1943-49; with Carpenter Tech. Corp., Reading, Pa., 1949—, asst. treas. asst. sec., 1964-66, treas., asst. sec., 1966-69, v.p. corporate devel., 1969-71, group v.p. research planning and div. ops., 1971-75, group v.p. corporate devel. and div. ops., 1975-77, group v.p. fabricated products, 1977—; pres., dir. Gt. Valley Savs. Assn., 1959—. Bd. dirs. Shillington (Pa.) Sch. Bd., 1959-65, pres, 1962; bd. dirs. Gov. Mifflin Joint Sch. System, 1959-65, pres., 1964-65; treas., bd. dirs. Reading United Community Service, 1964-70; bd. dirs. St. Joseph's Hosp., Reading; treas., bd. dirs. Berks County Area Vocat. Tech. Sch., 1965-66. Served with USAAF, 1943-46. Mem. Am. Iron and Steel Inst., Indsl. Research Inst., Berks County C. of C. Home: PO Box 346A Rd 4 Reading PA 19606 Office: 101 Bern St Reading PA 19601

STANTON, THOMAS JOYCE, JR., banker; b. Jersey City, Jan. 14, 1928; s. Thomas Joyce and Louise (Lynch) S.; B.A., Georgetown U., 1952; postgrad. N.Y. U. Grad. Sch. Bus. Administrn.; Ph.D. (hon.), St. Peter's Coll.; m. Jane Maloney, Sept. 25, 1954; children—Louise, Thomas, Joyce III, Patricia, Charles, William, Katherine Anne, John, Robert. With First Jersey Nat. Bank, and predecessor, 1954—, asst. cashier, 1956-57, asst. v.p., 1957-60; v.p., 1960-66, exec. v.p., 1966-67, pres., chief exec. officer, 1967-75, chmn., chief exec. officer, 1975—, also dir.; dir. Reliance Ins. Co. Phila., Reliance Group, Inc., N.J. Machine Corp., N.J. Bell Telephone Co., Hennessy Industries, Inc., APL Corp., Brooks Fashion Stores, Inc.; chmn. N.J. Commn. on Budget Priorities. Regional chmn. Nat. Alliance Bus.; bd. dirs. N.J. region NCCJ; trustee Stevens Inst. Tech., Newark Mus., St. Vincent's Hosp., Montclair. Served to capt., arty., World War II and Korea. Mem. Hudson County C. of C. and Industry (dir.), N.J. State C. of C. (treas., dir.), Am. Bankers Assn. (govt. relations council), N.J. Bankers Assn. (legis. and taxation com.). Clubs: Essex Fells Country, Baltusrol Golf (Springfield, N.J.); Bergen Carteret (Jersey City); Seaview Country (Absecon, N.J.); Essex, 200 (Newark). Home: 240 S Mountain Ave Montclair NJ 07042 Office: 1 Exchange Pl Jersey City NJ 07303

STANTON, WILLIAM JOHN, JR., educator; b. Chgo., Dec. 15, 1919; s. William John and Winifred (McGann) S; B.S., Ill. Inst. Tech., 1940; M.B.A., Northwestern U., 1941, Ph.D., 1948; m. Imma Mair, Sept. 14, 1978; 1978; children by previous marriage—Kathleen Louise, William John III. Mgmt. trainee Sears Roebuck & Co., 1940-41; instr. U. Ala., 1941-44; auditor Olan Mills Portrait Studios, Chattanooga, 1944-46; asst. prof., asso. prof. U. Wash., 1948-55; prof. U. Colo., Boulder, 1955—, head mktg. dept., 1955-71, acting dean, 1963-64, asso. dean Sch. Bus., 1964-67. Vis. prof. summers U. Utah, 1946, 1949, U. Calif., Berkeley, 1950, U. Calif., Los Angeles, 1957; mktg. cons. to various bus. firms and govt. agys., 1950—. Mem. Am., So., Southwestern, Western mktg. assns., Beta Gamma Sigma. Roman Catholic. Author: Economic Aspects of Recreation in Alaska, 1953; (with Richard H. Buskirk) Management of the Sales Force, 5th edit., 1978 (also Spanish transl.); (with others) Challenge of Business, 1975; Fundamentals of Marketing, 5th edit., 1978 (also Spanish transl.; Can. edit. with M.S. Sommers and J.G. Barnes); editorial bd. Jour. Mktg. 1963-69. Home: 1445 Sierra Dr Boulder CO 80302

STANTON-HICKS, MICHAEL D'ARCY, physician, educator; b. Adelaide, South Australia, June 3, 1931; s. Cedric and Florence (Haggitt) S.-H.; came to U.S., 1972; M.B., B.S., U. Adelaide, 1961; m. Kristina Litsmark, Sept. 2, 1967; children—Erik, Leif. Intern, Queen Elizabeth Hosp., Adelaide, 1961-62; resident Central Lasarett, Falun, Sweden, 1967; registrar anesthesiology Lasarett Koping, Sweden, 1966-67; registrar anesthesiology Postgrad. Med. Sch., Hammersmith, London, 1967-68; practice medicine specializing in anesthesiology, London, 1967, Stockholm, 1968, Seattle, 1969, Adelaide, 1970, Worcester, Mass., 1975—; asst. dir. anesthesiology Sodersjukhuset, Stockholm, 1968-69; staff anesthesiologist Queen Elizabeth Hosp., Adelaide, 1970-72; instr. anesthesiology U. Wash., Seattle, 1969-70, asst. prof., 1972-75; prof., chmn. anaesthesia U. Mass., Worcester, 1975—. Served as flight lt. Royal Australian Air Force, 1962-65. Fellow Royal Soc. Medicine, Faculty of Anaesthetists; mem. Assn. Anaesthetists of Gt. Britain and Ireland, Australian Soc. Anaesthetists, Societas Anaesthesiologica Sueciae, Australian Med. Assn., Internat. Assn. for Study of Pain, Am. Soc. Anesthesiologists, Mass. Soc. Anesthesiology, Soc. Acad. Anesthesia Chairmen, Am. Soc. Regional Anesthesia, Worcester Dist. Med. Soc. Club: Army, Navy, Air Force. Research in regional anaesthesia, local anesthetics and mechanics of pain. Home: 10 Otsego Rd Worcester MA 01609 Office: U Mass Med Center Worcester MA 01605

STANWICK, TAD, corp. exec.; b. Severn, Md., May 4, 1916; s. Walter L. and Mary Ann (Pfeiffer) S.; student St. John's Coll. Annapolis, Md., 1935, U.S. Naval Acad., 1936; m. Wickliffe Shackleford, Dec. 16, 1941; children—Covington Philip, Wickliffe Mary, Wells Thomas. Asst. to pres. and chmn. bd. Am. Machine & Foundry Co., N.Y.C., 1952-55, v.p., 1955-57; v.p., dir. Cleve. Pneumatic Industries, Inc., 1957-62; pres. Pneumo Dynamics Corp., 1959-62; pres., chmn. bd. Stanwick Corp., 1962—. Mem. adv. bd. Georgetown Visitation Sch. Trustee Religious Educators Found. of Trinity Coll. Served as comdr. USNR, 1940-53 Mem. Philos. Soc. Washington, Soc. Naval Architects and Marine Engrs., Internat. Oceanographic Found., Def. Orientation Conf. Assn., Navy League U.S., Internat. Christian Union Bus. Execs., Am. Soc. Metaphysics, IEEE, Holy Name Soc., Phi Sigma Kappa. Clubs: U.S. Yacht Racing Union; Chesapeake Bay Yacht Racing Assn., Annapolis Yacht. Author: Lacrosse, 1939. Home: 4715 Upton St Washington DC 20016 Office: 1735 K St N W Washington DC 20006

STANWYCK, BARBARA (RUBY STEVENS), actress; b. Bklyn., July 16, 1907; ed. pub. schs., Bklyn.; m. Frank Fay, Aug. 26, 1928; m. 2d, Robert Taylor, May 14, 1939. Began as chorus girl, later scored success in Burlesque, prod. by Arthur Hopkins; motion picture appearances include: The Mad Miss Manton, Stella Dallas, Remember the Night, Ball of Fire, The Lady Eve, Meet John Doe, 1941; The Great Man's Lady, The Gay Sisters, 1942; Double Indemnity, 1944; My Reputations, 1945; Christmas in Connecticut, Two Mrs. Carrolls, 1946; Bride Wore Boots, Strange Love of Martha Ivars, 1947; Cry Wolf, The Other Love, B.F.'s Daughter, 1948; Sorry Wrong Number, File on Thelma Jordon, The Lady Gambles, The Lie, East-Side, West-Side, The Furies, 1949; To Please a Lady, 1950; The Man in the Cloak, 1951; Clash by Night, 1951; Jeopardy, 1952; Titanic, 1952; Executive Suite, Witness to Murder, Escape to Burma, 1955; Cattle Queen of Montana, There's Always Tomorrow, 1956; Maverick Queen, 1956; These Wilder Years, 1956; Crime of Passion, 1957; Trooper Hook, 1957; Walk on the Wild Side, 1962; Roustabout, 1964; The Night Walker, 1965; TV shows: The Barbara Stanwyck Theater, NBC-TV, 1960-61, The Big Valley, ABC-TV; appeared in TV movie The Letters, 1973; guest star numerous TV shows. Recipient Emmy award, 1960-61, 66. Address: 151 El Camino Beverly Hills CA 90212*

STAPEL, PAUL FREDERICK, symphony exec.; b. Muskegon, Mich., Oct. 13, 1940; s. Herman Frederick and Aloha Lorraine (Young) S.; Mus.B., U. Mich., 1969. Ford Found. adminstrv. intern Cin. Symphony Orch., 1969-70; asst. mgr. New Orleans Philharmonic Symphony Orch., 1970-73; gen. mgr. Wichita Symphony Soc., 1973-74, Toledo Symphony Orch., 1974-76; orch. mgr. Dallas Symphony, 1976—. Active Big Bros. Am. Served with U.S. Army, 1959-62. Mem. Am. Guild Organists, Am. Symphony Orch. League. Home: 805 Newell St Dallas TX 75223 Office: PO Box 26207 Dallas TX 75226

STAPERT, JOHN CHARLES, mag. editor; b. Kalamazoo, Sept. 25, 1942; s. Elko M. and Martha Edith (Van Zee) S.; A.B., Hope Coll., Holland, Mich., 1963; B.D., Fuller Theol. Sem., Pasadena, Calif., 1966; M.A., U. Ill., 1968, Ph.D., 1969; m. Barbara Sue Vander Linde, Aug. 17, 1963; children—Craig, Terri. Ordained to ministry Reformed Ch. Am., 1969; asso. prof. psychology Northwestern Coll., Orange City, Iowa, 1969-72; exec. coordinator Synod of West, Reformed Ch. Am., 1972-74, editor Ch. Herald, Grand Rapids, Mich., 1974—. Mem. Am., Midwestern psychol. assns., Evang. Press Assn., Asso. Ch. Press (dir. 1978—). Author articles. Home: 502 Edgeworthe Dr SE Grand Rapids MI 49506 Office: 1324 Lake Dr SE Grand Rapids MI 49506

STAPLEFORD, FREDERICK HAMILTON, publisher; b. Phila., Feb. 14, 1921; s. Edward Townsend and Mabelle Irene (Hamilton) S.; A.B., U. Pa., 1941; m. 2d, Susan Meyerhoff, Sept. 2, 1966; children—Frederick Hamilton, John E., Irene H., Kate T. With Triangle Publs., Phila., 1953-66, promotion dir. TV Guide, 1956-58, advt. dir. Phila. Inquirer, 1960-66; v.p. gen. mgr. Playboy mag. HMH Pub. Co., Inc., Chgo., 1966-68; with Crowell Collier & Macmillan, Inc., N.Y.C., 1968—, publisher This Week, 1968—, pres. profl. mags., 1969—, corp. v.p., 1969—, pres. Stechert Macmillan, Inc., 1975—. Pres. Katharine Gibbs Sch., 1972—. Served with M.I., AUS, World War II, 1942-46; Korea, 1950-52. Decorated Bronze Star medal. Mem. Phi Beta Kappa. Office: Stechert Macmillan Inc 7250 Westfield Ave Pennsauken NJ 08110*

STAPLES, ALBERT FRANKLIN, dentist, educator; b. Sanford, Maine, Sept. 3, 1922; s. Charles Clifton and Bessie Albertina (Small) S.; student Boston U., 1943-44, 46-47; D.M.D., Tufts U., 1951; B.S.D., Baylor U., 1954, Ph.D., 1970; m. Virginia Barker McManus, July 5, 1953; children—SueEllen, Craig Lawrence, Amy Jane, Allen Francis. Resident in oral surgery Parkland Meml. Hosp., Dallas, 1954-57; pvt. practice oral surgery, Corpus Christi, Tex., 1957-61; asst. prof. oral surgery Baylor Dental Coll., Dallas, 1961-63, asso. prof., 1963-67, spl. fellow in physiology, 1967-70; prof., chmn. div. oral surgery Coll. Dentistry, U. Okla., Oklahoma City, 1970—, prof. physiology, biophysics Coll. Medicine, 1970—; cons. oral surgery VA Hosp., Oklahoma City, 1971—. Treas., Dallas-Ft. Worth Area Com. for Project Hope, 1965-66; chmn. faculty appeals bd. U. Okla. Health Scis. Center, 1976-78; bd. dirs. Nueces County unit Am. Cancer Soc., 1959-60. Served with USAF, 1951-53. Lic. dentist, Mass., Tex., Okla.; diplomate Am. Bd. Oral Surgery. Fellow Am. Dental Soc. Anesthesiology; mem. Am. Assn. Dental Schs., Internat. Assn. Dental Research, ADA, Am. Soc. Oral Surgeons, Sigma Xi, Omicron Kappa Upsilon. Contbr. articles to profl. jours. Home: 2713 NW 55th Terr Oklahoma City OK 73112 Office: Coll Dentistry PO Box 26901 Oklahoma City OK 73190

STAPLES, EUGENE LEO, hosp. adminstr.; b. Walker, Minn., Aug. 26, 1926; s. Frank August and Elizabeth Josephine (Leibl) S.; B.A., U. Minn., 1950, M.H.A., 1952; m. Noreen Janice Henry, June 23, 1951; 1 dau., Barbara Elizabeth. Administrv. asst. U. Minn. Hosps., Mpls., 1952-53, asst. to dir., 1953-55, asst. dir., 1955-60; dir. W.Va. U. Hosp., Morgantown, 1960—, asso. prof. Sch. Medicine, 1964-78, clin. prof., 1978—; mem. liaison com. Grad. Med. Edn. Cons. NIH, 1968—; mem. grad. med. edn. nat. adv. com. Health Resources Adminstrn., 1977—; dir. Westover Bank (W.Va.). Bd. dirs. United Fund, 1966-72, Am. Cancer Soc., 1971, Morgantown Hosp. Service, W.Va. Hosp. Service Inc., W.Va. Hosp. Research and Edn. Found., Inc. Served with USNR, 1944-46. Fellow Am. Coll. Hosp. Adminstrs. (regent 1972-75); mem. W.Va. (pres., 1969-71), Am. (ho. dels. 1963-66, 72-78, trustee 1980—) hosp. assns., Southeastern (dir. 1970-72), Ohio Valley (pres. 1965-66, dir. 1960—) hosp. confs., AMA, Am. Assn. Med. Colls. (council teaching hosps. 1972-73). Home: 665 Bellaire St Morgantown WV 26505

STAPLES, JACK ROBISON, investment banker; b. Scranton, Pa., Apr. 29, 1911; s. Reuben and Ann (Williams) S.; A.B., Ohio Wesleyan U., 1934; m. Leah Virginia Gentle, Oct. 23, 1937; children—Jill (Mrs. Duke Winston Thomas), Judith (Mrs. Frederick Standish C. Perry), James George. Salesman, Maynard H. Murch & Co., Cleve., 1934-43, partner, 1945-50; partner Fulton, Reid & Co., Cleve., 1950-56; exec. v.p., dir. Fulton, Reid & Staples, Inc. (formerly known as Fulton, Reid & Co., Inc.), Cleve., 1956-71, pres., chief operating officer, 1971—, vice-chmn., 1975; v.p., dir. Cascade Industries. Bd. govs. Midwest Stock Exchange, 1965-66, 73-77. Capt., United Appeal, Cleve., 1952-55; mem. Juvenile Delinquency Prevention Com., 1961—; treas. Jimmie Lee Found. Served to lt. USNR, World War II. Mem. Securities Industry Assn. Am. (past chmn. No. Ohio Group), Nat. Assn. Securities Dealers (past com. chmn.), Bond Club Cleve. (dir. 1965-68, pres, 1967), Newcomen Soc. N. Am., Alpha Sigma Phi. Clubs: Union, Cleve. Athletic (past pres.), Cleve. Skating (past pres.). Home: 24407 Duffield Rd Beachwood OH 44122 Office: Bond Ct Bldg 1300 E 9th St Cleveland OH 44114

STAPLES, O. SHERWIN, orthopaedic surgeon; b. Boston, May 19, 1908; s. Oscar S. and Nellie E. (Barnes) S.; A.B., Harvard, 1930, M.D., 1935; m. Mable Hughes, Dec. 11, 1945; children—Katherine E., Thomas H. Intern, Boston City Hosp., 1935-37; resident Mass. Gen., Children's hosps., Boston, 1937-39; asst. orthopaedic surgery Mass. Gen. Hosp., 1939-46; asst. orthopaedic surgeon New Eng. Peabody Home Crippled Children, 1939-46; chmn. orthopaedic surgery sect. Hitchcock Clinic and Mary Hitchcock Meml. Hosp., 1946-73 cons. VA Hosp., White River Junction, Vt., 1947-73, chief, orthopedic sect., 1973—; cons. Springfield (Vt.) Hosp., 1954—; asst. orthopaedic surgery Harvard Med. Sch., 1939-46; mem. faculty, chmn. orthopaedic sect. Dartmouth Med. Sch., 1946-73, clin. prof. surgery, 1967-73, emeritus, 1973—. Served from capt. to lt. col. M.C., AUS, 1942-45; MTO. Diplomate Am. Bd. Orthopaedic Surgery (examiner 1964-69). Mem. Aesculapian Club, N.H., Grafton County (pres. 1963) Boylston med. socs., Boston Orthopaedic Club (pres. 1960-61), Am. Acad. Orthopaedic Surgeons, A.C.S., Am. Orthopaedic Assn., New Eng. Surg. Soc., Soc. Internat. de Chirurgie Orthopedique et de Traumatologie, Am. Orthopaedic Foot Soc. (founding), Assn. Orthopaedic Chmn. (founding). Asso. editor Jour. Bone and Joint Surgery, 1961-67. Contbr. articles to med. jours. Home: Hemlock Rd Hanover NH 03755 Office: VA Hosp White River Junction VT 05001

STAPLES, ROBERT INNES, lawyer; b. Atlantic City, Oct. 18, 1915; s. Robert Innes and Emily Stewart (Fisler) Jones; B.S., Lafayette Coll., 1937; LL.B., U. Pa., 1940; m. Dorothy J. Wisener, Sept. 20, 1941; 1 son, Lewis F. Admitted to Pa. bar, 1941, U.S. Dist. Ct., Ct. Appeals, 1941; asso. firm Truscott, Trinkle & Wright, Phila., 1940-42; atty. Atlantic Refining Co., Phila., 1943-47; patent atty. ESB Inc., Phila., 1947-62, asst. sec., 1962-63, group counsel for internat. ops., 1963-70, sec., 1970—, chief counsel, 1975—. Mem. Com. of Seventy, Phila., 1974—. Served with USMC, 1942-43. Mem. Am., Phila. bar assns., Am., Phila patent law assns. Episcopalian. Clubs: Union League, Aronimink Golf. Home: 1865 Mallard Ln Villanova PA 19085 Office: 5 Penn Center Plaza Philadelphia PA 19103

STAPLETON, HARVEY JAMES, educator; b. Kalamazoo, Dec. 22, 1934; s. Herbert James and Viola Delia (Early) S.; B.S., U. Mich., 1957; Ph.D., U. Cal., Berkeley, 1961; m. Joan Eilleen Sylvander, June 22, 1957; children—Patricia Lynne, Susan Joan, Jeffrey Denis. Faculty physics U. Ill., Urbana, 1961—, prof., 1969—. Alfred P. Sloan fellow, 1962-64. Fellow Am. Phys. Soc.; mem. Phi Beta Kappa, Sigma Xi, Phi Sigma Kappa, Phi Kappa Phi, Phi Eta Sigma. Roman Catholic. Contbr. articles to profl. jours. Home: 305 Elmwood Rd Champaign IL 61820 Office: Physics Dept U Ill Urbana IL 61801

STAPLETON, JEAN (JEANNE MURRAY), actress; b. N.Y.C., Jan. 19; d. Joseph E. and Marie (Stapleton) Murray; ed. Hunter Coll., N.Y.C.; m. William H. Putch, Oct. 26, 1957; 1 son, 1 dau. Sec., Greenwood Playhouse, Peaks Island; appeared numerous Broadway plays including: In The Summerhouse, Damn Yankees, The Bells Are Ringing, Juno, Rhinoceros, Funny Girl; numerous summer stock prodns. including: Call Me Madam, The Solid Gold Cadillac, The Miracle Worker, Everybody Loves Opal, others Pocono Playhouse, Mountainhome, Pa., also Cecilwood Theatre, Fishkill, N.Y.; nat. tour Harvey, Come Back, Little Sheba, Time of the Cuckoo, 1974; appeared in numerous motion pictures including: Damn Yankees, Bells Are Ringing, Something Wild, Up the Down Staircase, Cold Turkey, Klute; appeared on TV shows: Camera Three, Danger, Studio One, Philco TV Playhouse, Omnibus, Woman With a Past, Today Is Ours, Naked City, Armstrong Circle Theatre, The Defenders, The Nurses, Eleventh Hour, Dr. Kildare, Dennis the Menace, Jackie Gleason Show, Car 54, Where Are You?; stars in All in the Family. Recipient Emmy award best performance comedy series, 1970-71, 71-72, Golden Globe awards Hollywood Fgn. Press Assn., 1972, 73. Mem. Actors Equity Assn. (council 1958-63), Screen Actors Guild, AFTRA. Address: care Coleman-Rosenberg Agy 850 7th Ave Suite 1201 New York NY 10019*

STAPLETON, KATHARINE LAURENCE, educator, writer; b. Holyoke, Mass., Nov. 20, 1911; d. Richard Prout and Frances (Purtill) Stapleton; A.B., Smith Coll., 1932; postgrad. U. London (Eng.), 1932-33. Registrar, Mass. Pub. Employment Service, 1933-34; faculty Bryn Mawr Coll., 1934—, prof. English and polit. theory, 1948-64, chmn. dept. English, 1954-65, Mary E. Garrett prof. English, 1964—. Mem. bd. sponsors Nat. Com. for an Effective Congress. Smith Coll. Alumnae fellow, 1932-33; Guggenheim fellow, 1947-48; Nat. Endowment for Arts fellow; 1972-73. Mem. AAUP, Modern Lang. Assn., English Assn., Renaissance Soc., Thoreau Soc. Author: Justice and World Society, 1944; The Design of Democracy, 1949; H.D. Thoreau: A Writers Journal, 1960; Yushin's Log and Other Poems, 1969; The Elected Circle: Studies in the Art of Prose, 1973; Marianne Moore: The Poet's Advance, 1978. Home: 229 N Roberts Rd Bryn Mawr PA 19010

STAPLETON, MAUREEN, actress; b. Troy, N.Y., June 21, 1925; d. John P. and Irene (Walsh) S.; student Siena Coll, 1943; m. Max Allentuck, July 1949 (div. Feb. 1959); children—Daniel, Katharine. Debut appearance in Playboy of the Westen World, 1946; other plays include tour with Barretts of Wimpole Street, 1947, Anthony and Cleopatra, 1947, Detective Story, The Bird Cage, Rose Tatoo, 1950-51, The Sea Gull, Orpheus Descending, The Cold Wind and the Warm, 1959, Toys in the Attic, 1960-61, Plaza Suite, 1969, The Gingerbread Lady, 1970, Country Girl, 1972, Secret Affairs of Mildred Wild, 1972, The Gin Game, 1977-78; motion pictures include: Lonely Hearts, 1959, The Fugitive Kind, 1960, A View from the Bridge, 1962, Bye Bye Birdie, 1963, Plaza Suite, 1971, Interiors, 1978, Airport, 1970; TV drama Tell Me Where It Hurts, 1974, Cat On a Hot Tin Roof, 1976. Recipient Nat. Inst. Arts and Letters award, 1969, Tony award for the Gingerbread Lady, 1970. Address: care Internat Creative Mgmt 8899 Beverly Blvd Los Angeles CA 90048*

STAPLETON, WALTER KING, judge; b. Cuthbert, Ga., June 2, 1934; s. Theodore Newton and Elizabeth Grantland (King) S.; B.A. cum laude, Princeton, 1956; LL.B. cum laude, Harvard, 1959; m. Patricia Chappelle Ames, Oct. 27, 1956; children—Russell K., Theodore N., Teryl J. Admitted to Del. bar; asso. mem. firm Morris, Nichols, Arsht & Tunnell, Wilmington, Del., 1959-65, partner, 1966-70; U.S. Dist. judge Del., Wilmington, 1970—. Dep. atty. gen. Del., 1964. Bd. dirs. Am. Bapt. Chs., U.S.A., 1978. Mem. Am., Del. bar assns. Baptist. Office: Federal Bldg Wilmington DE 19801

STAPP, DAN ERNEST, utility exec.; b. New Orleans, July 1, 1934; s. James Frank, Jr. and Marguerite Edna (Joubert) S.; B.B.A., Loyola U., New Orleans, 1955, LL.B., 1957; m. Barbara Allan Wilmot, June 10, 1961; children—Marguerite Wilmot (dec.), Mary Darby, Paul Wilmot, James Andrew. Admitted to La. bar, 1957; with New Orleans Pub. Service Inc., 1958-68, asst. to v.p., 1965-68; with Middle South Services, Inc., New Orleans, 1968—, v.p., sec., asst. treas., 1968—; sec., asst. treas. System Fuels, Inc., New Orleans, 1972—, Middle South Utilities, Inc., New Orleans, 1974—, Middle South Energy, Inc., New Orleans, 1974—. Trustee Mercy Hosp., New Orleans, 1973—, pres., 1975, chmn. bd. devel., 1971-72; mem. pres.'s council Loyola U., 1975—, vice chmn., 1978—; adv. council Coll. Bus. Adminstrn., 1969-70; mem. adv. bd. Asso. Cath. Charities, 1979—; gen. chmn. United Way Greater New Orleans, 1978, trustee, 1978—; past dist. and council Explorer adviser, chmn. sustaining unit fund New Orleans Area council Boy Scouts Am. Served as 2d lt. AUS, 1957. Mem. Am., La., New Orleans bar assns., Loyola U. Alumni Assn. (treas. 1960), New Orleans Area C. of C., Bur. Govtl. Research, Blue Key (past chpt. pres.), Alpha Sigma Nu, Delta Theta Phi. Roman Catholic. Clubs: New Orleans Country, Internat. House (dir. 1976-78), Essex, Pendennis (gov. 1979—), Loyola U. Bus. Alumni (past pres.), Rotary. Home: 401 Bellaire Dr New Orleans LA 70124 Office: 225 Baronne St New Orleans LA 70112

STAPP, JOHN PAUL, former air force officer, surgeon; b. Bahia, Brazil, July 11, 1910 (parents Am. citizens); s. Charles Franklin and Mary Louise (Shannon) S.; B.A., Baylor U., 1931, M.A. cum laude, 1932, D.Sc., 1956; Ph.D., U. Tex., 1939; M.D., U. Minn., 1943; grad. Army Field Service Sch., 1944, Sch. Aviation Medicine, 1945, Indsl. Med. Course, 1946; D.Sc., N.Mex. State U., 1979; m. Lillian Lanese, Dec. 23, 1957. Commd. 1st lt. U.S. Army, 1944, advanced through grades to col. M.C., USAF, 1957; research project officer Aero Med. Lab., Wright Field, Ohio, 1946, chief lab., 1958-60; chief scientist aerospace med. div., Brooks AFB, Tex., 1960-65; chief impact injury br. Armed Forces Inst. Pathology, Washington, 1965-67; chief med. scientist Nat. Hwy. Safety Bur., 1967-70; ret., 1970; cons. Dept. Transp., Washington, 1970—; adj. prof. Safety and Systems Mgmt. Center, U. So. Calif., 1972—. Systems Mgmt. Center, Los Angeles, 1973—; cons. accident epidemiology and pathology Armed Forces, Bur. Standards, NIH, Nat. Acad. Scis., Gen. Services Adminstrn.; research rocket sled expts. reproducing aircraft crash forces to determine human tolerance limits, 1947-51; chief Aero Med. Field Lab., Holloman AFB, Alamogordo, N.Mex., 1953-58; cons. N.Mex. State U. Phys. Scis. Lab., Las Cruces, 1972—. Mem. subcom. on flight safety NACA; permanent chmn. Ann. Stapp Car Crash Conf. Mem. N.Mex. Gov.'s Commn. Internat. Space Hall of Fame, 1974—; mem. N.Mex. Planning Bd., 1975—. Bd. dirs. Kettering Found.; v.p. Internat. Astronautical Fedn., 1959-60. Decorated D.S.M. with bronze oak leaf, Legion of Merit (for crash research) with bronze oak leaf; recipient award for outstanding research by Air Force officer Nat. Air Council, 1951; John Jeffries award for med. research Inst. Aero. Sci., 1953; Air Power award for sci. Air Force Assn., 1954; Flight Safety Found. award for contbns. Air Transp. Safety, 1954; Air Force Cheney award, 1955; Gorgas award Assn. Mil. Surgeons, 1956; Med. Tribune award for automotive safety, 1965; award for contbns. to automotive safety Am. Assn. for Automotive Medicine, 1972; Cresson medal Franklin Inst., 1973; Excalibur award safety research, 1975; Certificate of Achievement, Nat. Space Club, 1976, other awards; named to Internat. Space Hall of Fame, 1979. Diplomate Am. Bd. Preventive Medicine. Fellow Aero. Med. Assn. (Liliencrantz award for deceleration research 1957), Am. Astronautical Soc., Am. Rocket Soc. (pres. 1959, Wyld award 1955, Leo Stevens medal 1956); mem. Soc. Automotive Engrs., U.S. Mil. Surgeons Assn., Internat. Acad. Astronautics, Internat. Acad. Aviation Medicine, Civil Aviation Medicine Assn. (pres. 1968—), Am. Soc. Safety Engrs. (hon.), Sigma Xi. Home: PO Box 553 Alamogordo NM 88310 Office: Phys Scis Lab NM State U Box 3548 Las Cruces NM 88001. *Life is consciousness involved in thinking and doing; it is valued in terms of the quality of resulting contributions to the stream of human advancement. I live in hopes of always doing better and producing more.*

STAPP, OLIVIA BREWER, soprano; b. N.Y.C., May 31, 1940; s. Henry and Jean Brewer; B.A., Wagner Coll.; student Ettere Campogalliani, Oren Brown; m. Henry Pierce Shupe Stapp, III, Jan. 29, 1965; 1 son, Henry Pierce Shupe Stapp IV. Appeared with maj. opera house and symphony orchs. internationally; operas include: Nabucco, Electra, Isolde, Tosca, Turandot. Fulbright scholar, Rome. Mem. Religious Science Ch. Club: Lions (hon.) (Naples, Italy). Office: care Herbert H Breslin 119 W 57th St New York NY 10019*

STARBUCK, JO JO (ALICIA JO), performing artist, athlete; b. Birmingham, Ala., Feb. 14, 1951; d. Hal F. Starbuck and Alice (Plunkett) Starbuck Sells; student Theatre Arts, Long Beach State Coll., 1969-72; m. Terry Bradshaw, June 6, 1976. Mem. U.S. Winter Olympics team, Grenoble, France, 1968, Sapporo, Japan, 1972; figure skater with partner Ken Shelley, Ice Capades, 1972-76; numerous NBC and ABC network appearances, 1967—; figure skating commentator with CBS in U.S., 1976-79, Europe, 1977-79; appeared on numerous TV commls. and talk shows, 1976—; appeared as co-star in Ice Dancing, Minskoff Theater, Broadway, 1978-79; free lance figure skating artist, 1976—. Spl. rep. for Kennedy Found.'s Spl. Olympics, 1973-79; bd. dirs. So. Calif. Olympians, 1978—. Named Athlete of the Year, Helms Found., 1972; recipient various Christian Achievement awards, 1972-79. Mem. U.S. Figure Skating Assn. (Gold Medal award 1967-68), Arctic Blades Figure Skating Club, Los Angeles Figure Skating Club, DAR. Mem. Christian Ch. Author: (with Nina Ball) Jo Jo Starbuck, 1977. World Bronze Medalist in figure skating, Lyon, France, 1971, Calgary, Alta., Can., 1972; U.S. Nat. Pair Champion, 1970-72. . *On a trophy proudly displayed in our living room, my mother kept a little card with a typewritten message that always made me feel better when I was depressed enough to quit everything. It read: "When the going seems easy, check to see if you aren't going downhill."*

STARE, FREDRICK JOHN, nutritionist, biochemist, physician; b. Columbus, Wis., Apr. 11, 1910; s. Fredrick Arthur and Susan (Seidell) S.; B.S., U. Wis., 1931, M.S., 1932, Ph.D., 1934; M.D., U. Chgo., 1941; D.Sc., Suffolk 1963, Trinity Coll. (Dublin), 1964, Muskingum Coll., 1977; m. Joyce Allen, Sept. 14, 1935 (dec. May 1957); children—Fredrick Allen, David, Mary; m. 2d, Helen Haxton Foreman, June 9, 1959 (dec. Feb. 1974); m. 3d, Mary Bartlet Engle, Dec. 30, 1976. Asst. biochemist U. Wis., 1931-34; Nat. Research fellow Washington U. Sch. Medicine, St. Louis, 1934-35; Gen. Edn. Bd. fellow, Cambridge (Eng.) U., 1935-36, Szeged (Hungary), 1936, Zurich, 1937; research asso. Bowman Cancer Found., Wis., 1937-39; intern Barnes Hosp., St. Louis, 1941-42; asst. prof. nutrition Harvard Med. Sch. and Sch. Pub. Health, mem. food and nutrition bd. NRC; prof. nutrition, chmn. dept. nutrition, 1942-76; jr. asso. medicine Peter Bent Brigham Hosp., 1942-44, asso. in medicine, 1944-50, sr. asso. medicine, 1950-60, cons. medicine, 1960—; co-founder syndicated radio program Healthline; dir. Continental Group: former mem. food and nutrition bd. NRC; cons. nutrition Sec. War, USPHS; mem. health adv. com. Fgn. Operations Adminstrn.; com. health Commn. on Inter-govtl. Relations; mem. Nat. Health Edn. Com. Trustee New Eng. Conservatory of Music; bd. dirs. Pathfinder Fund; co-founder, bd. dirs. Am. Council on Sci. and Health; Fellow Am. Pub. Health Assn., Royal Irish Coll. Physicians (hon.); mem. Am. Chem. Soc., Am. Soc. Biol. Chemists, Am. Inst. Nutrition, Biochem. Soc. (Eng.), Am. Soc. Clin. Investigation, Am. Soc. Arteriosclerosis, AMA (Goldberger award 1961), Am. Dietetic Assn. (hon.), Soc. Nutrition Edn., Sigma Xi. Clubs: Harvard (Boston, N.Y.C.); Cosmos (Wasington). Author: Eating for Good Health; Living Nutrition; Scope Manual on Nutrition; Nutrition for Good Health; Panic in the Pantry; Eat OK-Feel OK; nat. syndicated columnist Food and Your Health; former editor: Nutrition Revs. Home: 267 Cartwright Rd Wellesley MA 02181 Office: 665 Huntington Ave Boston MA 02115. *I never expect anyone to work any harder than I do. Be overly generous in giving credit to others. Never ask anyone to do anything you are not willing to do yourself.*

STARER, ROBERT, composer; b. Vienna, Austria, Jan. 8, 1924; s. Nison and Erna (Gottlieb) S.; student State Acad., Vienna, 1938-39, Jerusalem Conservatory, 1939-42; postgrad. diploma Juilliard Sch. Music, 1949; m. Johanna Herz, Mar. 27, 1942; 1 son, Daniel. Came to U.S., 1947, naturalized, 1957. Symphonic works premiered by N.Y. Philharmonic condrs., other leading condrs. in U.S., abroad; ballets commd. by Martha Graham, 1961-63, CBS TV for Anna Sokolow, 1964, Lincoln Center for John Butler, 1967; faculty Juilliard Sch. Music, 1949—; asso. prof. Bklyn Coll., 1963—; prof. Bklyn. Coll. N.Y., 1966—. Served with RAF, 1943-46. Guggenheim fellow, 1957, 63; Fulbright postdoctoral research grantee, 1964; Nat. Endowment for Arts grantee, 1974, 77. Mem. ASCAP, Am. Music Center (dir. 1962-64). Composer: Symphony 1, 1950, Symphony 2, 1951, Piano Concerto 1, 1947, Piano Concerto 2, 1952, Concerto a Tre, 1954, Viola Concerto, 1958, Ariel, 1959, Joseph and His Brothers, 1966, (opera) The Intruder, 1956, Concerto for Violin Cello and Orch., 1967, Six Variations with Twelve Notes, 1967, On The Nature of Things (chorus), 1968, Symphony 3, 1969, (ballets) The Dybbuk, 1960, Samson Agonistes, 1961, Phaedra, 1963, Mutabili, 1965; Third St. Overture, 1970, (opera) Pantagleize, 1971, Concerto Piano 3, 1972, Images of Man, 1973; Stone Ridge Set, Mandala, Profiles in Brass, 1974; The Last Lover (opera), 1975; Journals of a Songmaker (text by Gail Godwin), 1975; The People, Yes (text by Carl Sandburg), 1976; Piano Quartet, 1977; (song cycle) Transformations, 1978; (opera) Apollonia, 1978; also chamber music, choral, piano music, songs. Author: Rhythmic Training.

STARFIELD, BARBARA HELEN, physician, educator; b. Bklyn., Dec. 18, 1932; d. Martin and Eva (Illions) S.; A.B., Swarthmore Coll., 1954; M.D., SUNY, 1959; M.P.H., Johns Hopkins U., 1963; m. Neil A. Holtzman, June 12, 1955; children—Robert, Jon, Steven, Deborah. Teaching asst. in anatomy Downstate Med. Center, N.Y.C., 1955-57; intern in pediatrics Johns Hopkins U., 1959-60, resident, 1960-62, dir. pediatric med. care clinic, 1963-66, dir. community staff comprehensive child care project, 1966-67, dir. pediatric clin. scholars program, 1971-76, asso. prof. pediatrics, 1973—, prof. health care orgn., 1975—; cons. HEW. Recipient Dave Luckman Meml. award, 1958; HEW Career Devel. award, 1970-75. Mem. Nat. Acad. Sci. Inst. Medicine, Am. Pediatric Soc., Soc. Pediatric Research, Internat. Epidemiologic Assn., Ambulatory Pediatric Assn. (pres. elect 1979), Am. Public Health Assn., Sigma Xi, Alpha Omega Alpha. Contbr. articles to profl. jours. Editorial bd. Med. Care, 1977—; Pediatrics, 1977—; Internat. Jour. Health Services, 1978—. Office: 615 N Wolfe St Baltimore MD 21205

STARGATT, BRUCE MARVIN, lawyer; b. N.Y.C., July 8, 1930; B.A., U. Vt., 1951; LL.B., Yale U., 1954. Admitted to N.Y. bar, 1955, Del. bar, 1955, D.C. bar, 1956, U.S. Supreme Ct. bar, 1971; asso. firm Young, Conway, Stargatt & Taylor and predecessors, Wilmington, Del., 1956-59, partner, 1959—; legal officer U.S. Air Force, Dover AFB, Dover, Del., 1954-56; chmn. Gov.'s Com. for Revision of Del. Criminal Laws, 1965-67; mem. 3d Circuit Lawyers Adv. Com., 1979. Recipient Good Govt. citation Com. of 39, 1969. Fellow Am. Coll. Trial Lawyers; mem. Am., Del. bar assns., Am. Law Inst. Office: 1401 Market Tower Wilmington DE 19899

STARGELL, WILVER DORNEL (WILLIE), profl. baseball player; b. Earlsboro, Okla., Mar. 6, 1941; student Santa Rosa Jr. Coll. Mem. Pitts. Pirates (Nat. League), 1962—; player All-Star Game, 1964-66, 71-73, 78. Named Sportsman of Year, Sports Illus. mag., 1979, co-Most Valuable Player, Nat. League, 1979. Office: care Pitts Pirates 3 Rivers Stadium 600 Stadium Circle Pittsburgh PA 15212*

STARGER, MARTIN, ind. motion picture, TV and theatre producer; b. N.Y.C., May 8, 1932; s. Isidore and Rose (Stamler) S.; B.S., City Coll. N.Y., 1953. With Batten, Barton, Durstine & Osborne, Inc., advt., N.Y.C., 1956-66, v.p. TV, 1964-66; with ABC, N.Y.C., 1966-75, pres. ABC Entertainment, 1972-75; pres. Marstar Prodns., Inc., Los Angeles, 1975-78, Marble Arch Prodns., 1978—. Mem. pub. relations com. Multiple Sclerosis Soc. Served with AUS, 1953-55. N.Y. State scholar, 1949-53. Mem. Nat. Acad. TV Arts and Scis., Acad. Motion Picture Arts and Scis., Phi Beta Kappa. Office: 4024 Radford Ave Studio City CA 91604

STARK, BRUCE GUNSTEN, artist; b. Queens, N.Y., Feb. 17, 1933; s. Richard M. and Karen (Gunsten) S.; student Sch. Visual Arts, N.Y.C., 1955-58; m. Joan Patricia Lauer, Nov. 19, 1960; children—Robert, Ronald. Artist, cartoonist N.Y. Daily News, N.Y.C., 1961—; exhibited one-man shows Art Inst. Pitts., 1968, U. Kutztown (Pa.), 1970, N.Y. Bank for Savs., N.Y.C., 1971; group shows Nat. Art Mus. Sport, N.Y.C., 1971; represented permanent collections Everett Dirksen Library, L.D. Johnson Library, Baseball Hall Fame, Cooperstown, N.Y., Basketball Hall Fame, Mass. Served with USNR, 1952-54. Recipient Nat. Cartoonist Soc.'s Rueben Catagory awards for sports, 1966, 75, spl. features, 1968; Page One award for best sports cartoon, 1970, 73, N.Y.C., 71; 3d, 4th, 6th prizes Internat. Salon de Caricatures, Montreal, 1966, 68, 69. Original cartoons requested by Pres. Nixon, Johnson; 1st color cartoon appearing on front page of N.Y. Daily News. Home: 161 Chestnut St Emerson NJ 07630 Office: 220 E 42d St New York City NY 10017

STARK, CAMILLE RENE, data processing co. exec.; b. Schoenenwerd, Switzerland, Sept. 28, 1925; s. Camille Albert and Klara (Widmer) S.; grad. in bus. adminstrn. U. Zurich, 1945; m. Ruth Geissbuehler, Oct. 17, 1971. With Burroughs Corp., 1945—, gen. mgr., Zurich, Switzerland, 1957-59, mng. dir., Paris, 1959-65, Europe-Africa, 1966-74, v.p. Europe-Africa div., Fribourg, Switzerland, 1974-76, treas., Detroit, 1977—. Clubs: Detroit Economic, Rotary, Detroit Athletic, Grosse Pointe. Home: 34 Elm Ct Grosse Pointe Farms MI 48236 Office: Burroughs Pl Detroit MI 48232

STARK, DENNIS EDWIN, banker; b. Springfield, Ill., Dec. 24, 1937; s. Edwin C. and Ida (Fentem) S.; B.S., Ill. Wesleyan U., 1959; Sanxay fellow practical ethics Princeton, 1959-60; M.B.A., Harvard, 1962. Exec. v.p. Old Stone Corp., Providence, 1965—; exec. v.p. Old Stone Bank. Bd. dirs. Found. Repertory Theatre, Providence Preservation Soc.; bd. dirs., pres. R.I. Hist. Soc.; bd. dirs., treas. Ocean State Performing Arts Center; mem. allocations and budget com. United Way Southeastern New Eng.; bd. dirs. United Arts R.I.; vestryman, treas. St. Stephen's Episcopal Ch., chmn. diocesan fin. com., diocesan council; mem. R.I. adv. council Episc. Ch. Found.; mem. investment adv. com. Ill. Wesleyan U. Mem. Fin. Execs. Inst. (dir., v.p. R.I. chpt.), Fin. Analysts Fedn., Am. Econ. Assn., Providence C. of C. (dir.), Harvard Bus. Sch. Assn. R.I. (mem. bd., sec.-treas.), Acacia (co-founder Ill. Wesleyan U. chpt.). Republican. Clubs: Providence Art; Hope (bd. govs., treas.); Univ. (R.I.); Harvard, Met. (N.Y.C.); Harvard (Boston); Agawam Hunt; Dunes. Home: 21 Hersey Rd Cranston RI 02910 also Courtway St Narragansett RI Office: 150 S Main St Providence RI 02903

STARK, ELI H., osteo. physician; b. Monticello, N.Y., Feb. 21, 1926; s. Morris and Celia (Shapiro) S.; D.O., Phila. Coll. Osteo. Medicine, 1951; m. Anita Rothenberg, June 18, 1949; children—Richard, Ira, Jay, Lauri. Exec. dir. Massapequa Gen. Hosp., 1967-73; asst. dean of student affairs N.Y. Coll. Osteo. Medicine, also dept. family medicine, prof. medicine, 1976—, editorial dir. Osteo. Annals, 1973—. Served with U.S. Army, 1944-46. Decorated Bronze Star, Purple Heart (2); diplomate Nat. Osteo. Bd., Am. Coll. Gen. Practitioners (chmn. council edn. and evaluation). Fellow Am. Coll. Gen. Practitioners (pres. 1975), Am. Sch. Health Assn., Royal Soc. Health; mem. Am. Med. Writers Assn., Am. Osteo. Assn. (v.p., trustee, Gen. Practitioner of Yr. award 1977), N.Y. State Osteo. Soc. (pres. 1971-73), Am. Acad. Med. Adminstrs. Editor: Clin. Rev. Series Osteo. Medicine, 1975. Home: 1072 Old Britton Rd North Bellmore NY 11710 Office: 1046 Bellmore Rd North Bellmore NY 11710

STARK, ETHEL, violinist, conductor, educator; b. Montreal, Que., Can., Aug. 25, 1916; d. Adolph and Laura (Haupt) Stark; student McGill U., 1926-28, Curtis Inst. Music, Phila., 1928-34. Appeared as soloist with leading symphony orchs. in Can., U.S. and Europe; guest condr. Toronto Symphony Orch., 1945, N.Y. Civic Orch., 1937; founder, condr. Montreal Women's Symphony Orch., 1940-65, Ethel Stark Symphonietta, 1967, Montreal Women's Symphony Strings, 1969—; condr. series of CBC radio and television programs, which were broadcast throughout Can. and U.S., also S.Am., Central Am.; founder Can. Choir, 1952; condr. Kol Israel Symphony Orch., 1952, Tokyo Asahi Philharmonic, 1960, Nippon Hoso Kyokai, 1960; violin recitals in Japan, Hong Kong, India and other Far Eastern countries; tchr. Concordia U. (Sir George Williams Campus), 1974—, Catholic U., Washington, 1951; prof. violin Provincial Conservatoire de Music, Montreal, 1952-63. Recipient Concert Soc. award, 1976; Outstanding Citizenship award Montreal Citizenship Council, 1977; Can. Council research grantee, 1962. Mem. Musicians Guild (hon.), Sigma Alpha Iota. Home: 5501 Adalbert Ave Apt 1110 Cote St Lue Montreal PQ H4W 2B1 Canada

STARK, FORTNEY HILLMAN, JR., congressman; b. Milw., Nov. 11, 1931; s. Fortney Hillman and Dorothy M. (Mueller) S.; B.S., Mass. Inst. Tech., M.B.A., U. Calif., children—Jeffrey Peter, Beatrice Ann, Thekla Brumder, Sarah Gallun. Teaching asst. Mass. Inst. Tech., 1953-54; prin. Skaife & Co., Berkeley, Calif., 1957-61; founder Beacon Savs. & Loan Assn., Antioch, Calif., 1961; pres., founder Security Nat. Bank, Walnut Creek, Calif., 1963-72; mem. 93d-96th congresses from 9th Dist. Calif.; mem. Ways and Means Com., D.C. Com., Select Com. on Narcotics. Dir. A.C.L.U., 1971; dir. Housing Devel. Corp.; adv. com. Contra Costa County Coalition; dir. Common Cause, 1971. Del. Democratic State Central Com; trustee Calif. Dem. Council; bd. dirs. Starr King Sch. Served to capt. USAF, 1955-57. Mem. Delta Kappa Epsilon. Club: University (San Francisco). Office: House of Representatives Washington DC 20515

STARK, FRANKLIN CULVER, lawyer; b. Unityville, S.D., Apr. 16, 1915; s. Fred H. and Catherine (Culver) S.; J.D., Northwestern U., 1940; A.B., Dakota Wesleyan U., 1937, LL.D., 1959; m. Alice C. Churchill, Sept. 16, 1941 (dec. May 1975); children—Margaret C., Wallace C., Judith C., Franklin Culver; m. 2d, Carlyn Kaiser Saxton, July 18, 1976. Admitted to Ill. bar, 1940, Cal. bar, 1946; asso. Sidley, McPherson, Austin & Burgess, Chgo., 1940-41, Fitzgerald, Abbott & Beardsley, Oakland, Calif., 1946-47; sr. mem. firm Stark, Stewart & Simon, and predecessor firms, Oakland, 1947—. Lectr. comml. law U. Calif. Sch. Bus., 1946-66. Staff, Office Gen. Counsel, OPA, Washington, 1941-42. Bd. dirs. Claremont Sch. Theology, Dakota Wesleyan U., Fred Finch Youth Center, Calif.-Nev. United Meth. Found., Oakland Meth. Found.; chmn. bd. trustees Calif.-Nev. Meth. Homes, 1966-73; pres. Oakland Council of Chs., 1954-56; charter mem. World Peace Through Law Center. Served with USNR, 1942-45. Named Alumnus of Year for notable achievement Dakota Wesleyan U., 1966; certified taxation law specialist, Calif. Mem. Am., Calif., Alameda County bar assns., Oakland C. of C., Am. Legion, Am. Trial Lawyers Assn. (sustaining mem.), Phi Kappa Phi, Pi Kappa Delta, Phi Alpha Delta, Order Coif. Methodist. Mason (Shriner), Elk. Clubs: Athenian Nile (Oakland); Commonwealth (San Francisco). Editor: Ill. Law Rev., 1939-40. Contbr. articles to legal publs. Home: 333 Wayne Ave Oakland CA 94606 Office: Financial Center Building Oakland CA 94612

STARK, JAMES ARTHUR, pub. and printing co. exec.; b. Chgo., June 2, 1933; s. Herbert O. and Florence M. (Bofinger) S.; B.S. in Bus., U. Colo., 1955; m. Sarah Ann Spencer, June 9, 1956; children—Carolyn, James, Janet. Mgr., Arthur Andersen & Co., Chgo., 1958-66; treas. Chicago Musical Instrument Co., Lincolnwood, Ill., 1966-73; exec. v.p. Western Pub. Co., Inc., Racine, Wis., 1973—; dir. M & I Am. Bank & Trust Co., Racine. Bd. dirs. Racine United Way, 1973-76, Racine County Area Found., 1977—, St. Luke's Hosp., 1978—. Served to lt., j.g., USN, 1955-57. C.P.A. Mem. Nat. Alliance Businessmen (dir., vice chmn. 1975—), Am. Inst. C.P.A.'s. Episcopalian. Clubs: Racine Country, Somerset, Chgo. Yacht. Home: 5345 Wind Point Rd Racine WI 53402 Office: 1220 Mound Ave Racine WI 53404

STARK, JAMES GEORGE, telecommunications co. exec.; b. Montreal, Que., Can., June 3, 1928; s. Thomas John and Marjorie Clare (Dart) S.; m. Catherine G. Bulger, Dec. 23, 1950; children—Norman James, Carol Anne. Acct., Touche Ross & Co., Montreal, 1945-52; sr. fin. analyst Aluminium Securities, Ltd., Montreal, 1953; chief fin. officer Alcan Jamaica, Jamaica, 1958-65; dir., v.p. Alcan Ore Ltd., Montreal, 1965-68; v.p., treas. Consol. Edison Co., N.Y.C., 1968-73; partner Lehman Bros., N.Y.C., 1973-74, exec. v.p., chief fin. officer No. Telecom Ltd., 1974-79, exec. v.p. U.S. ops., 1979—; dir. Bell-No. Research Ltd., No. Telecom Systems Corp., No. Telecom, Inc., No. Telecom Can., No. Telecom Internat.; pres. Nevron Investments Ltd. Mem. Can. Inst. Chartered Accts. Anglican. Clubs: Mt. Royal (Montreal); Apawamis (Rye, N.Y.); Wall Street (N.Y.C.). Home: 656 Grandview Ln Lake Forest IL 60045 Office: Box 45 Morton Grove IL 60053

STARK, JOHN EDWIN, mfg. co. exec.; b. St. Albans, W.Va., July 24, 1916; s. Medary Wilson and Sylvia Prudentia (Colcord) S.; A.B., Williams Coll., 1938; m. Louisa Constance Abbe, June 14, 1941; children—Peter M., Michael E. (dec.), Christopher A., Abbe. Personnel mgr. W.R. Grace & Co., 1938-54; cons. McKinsey & Co., 1954-57, personnel dir. R.R. Donnelley & Sons, 1957-60; v.p., indsl. relations Westinghouse Air Brake Co., 1960-70; mgr. corporate indsl. relations Am. Standard, N.Y.C., 1970-74; asso. Boyden Assos., Chgo., 1974—. Served to capt. USAAF, 1943-45. Mem. Am. Mgmt. Assn., Western Pa. Safety Council (dir.), Tristate Indsl. Assn. (dir.), Pitts. Personnel Assn. (past dir.), Delta Upsilon. Home: 10768 Garma Way Turner OR 97392 Office: 120 S Riverside Pl Chicago IL 60606

STARK, KAREN, fashion designer; b. N.Y.C.; d. Maximilian and Tobe (Kafka) Berke; m. Sanford W. Stark, May 17, 1931; 1 son, Stephen H. Creative fashion designer; pres. Karen Stark, Inc. Named one of 10 best designers in Am., Lord & Taylor, 1941; recipient Fashion Critics' award Coty, 1952, citation Phila. Mus. Art, 1953, Men's Fashion Critics award, 1954, Nat. Cotton award, Washington, 1954, Med. Soc. W.Va. award by governor, 1955, citation Phila. Mus. Art, 1957; National Ribbon award, 1958; Designer of Yr. award, 1961; Internat. Fashion award, 1964. Mem. Fashion Group. Club: N.Y. Athletic. Designer inaugural gown, 1969. Home: 25 E 77th St N New York City NY 10021 also East Hampton NY 11937 Office: 530 7th Ave New York NY 10018

STARK, LAWRENCE, physician, educator; b. N.Y.C., Feb. 21, 1926; s. Edward and Frieda (Blatt) S.; A.B., Columbia, 1945; M.D., Albany (N.Y.) Med. Coll., 1948; postgrad. Trinity Coll., Oxford (Eng.) U., 1949-50, Univ. Coll., U. London (Eng.), 1950-51; children—Stefanie, Mathilde, Elizabeth. Intern U.S. Naval Hosp., St. Albans, N.Y., 1948-49; clin. fellow Neurol. Inst., Columbia-Presbyn. Hosp., N.Y.C., 1951-52; instr., then asst. prof. neurology Yale Med. Sch., 1954-60; head neurology sect. Mass. Inst. Tech., 1960-65; prof., chmn. biomed. engring. dept. Presbyn.-St. Luke's Hosp., U. Ill. at Chgo. Circle, 1965-68; prof. physiol. optics and engring. sci. U. Calif. at Berkeley, 1968—; prof. neurology U. Calif., San Francisco, 1974—; dir. Biosystems, Inc., Biocontacts, Inc., Direct Access Corp. Cons. to industry; adviser NSF, NIH, 1967—; mem. vision com. NRC, 1964—. Served with M.C., USNR, 1952-54. Guggenheim fellow, 1968-70. Diplomate Am. Bd. Psychiatry and Neurology. Fellow IEEE (Morlock award in biomed. engring. 1977); founding mem. Biophys. Soc., Biomed. Engring. Soc., Am. Soc. Cybernetics, Soc. Neurosci.; mem. Sigma Xi, Eta Kappa Nu. Clubs: Harvard (Boston); Cliffdwellers (Chgo.). Author: Neurological Control Systems, 1968; Biomaterials, 1969; Biomedical Engineering, 1971; Hering's Theory of Binocular Vision, 1977. Contbr. articles to profl. jours. Home: 9 W Parnassus Ct Berkeley CA 94708

STARK, LELAND WILLIAM FREDERICK, bishop; b. Evanston, Ill., Sept. 5, 1907; s. Rev. Gustaf Knute and Jennie (Peterson) S.; student U. Minn., 1927; B.A., Gustavus Adolphus Coll., St. Peter, Minn., 1932; postgrad. Chgo. Theol. Sem., 1932-34; Th.B., Seabury-Western Theol. Sem., Evanston, Ill., 1935, D.D., 1953; L.H.D., Seton Hall U., South Orange, N.J., 1966; m. Phyllis Wilma Anderson, Sept. 10, 1935; children—Craig Latimer, Leighton Bradley. Ordained priest, deacon P.E. Ch., 1935; vicar Episcopalian chs., New Ulm, Sleepy Eye, St. James, also Windom, Minn., 1935-38; rector Ascension Ch., Stillwater, Minn., 1938-40; dean Calvary Cathedral, Sioux Falls, S.D., 1940-48; rector Ch. of Epiphany, Washington, 1948-53; bishop co-adjutor Episcopal Diocese Newark, 1953-58, bishop, 1958-73. Pres., N.J. Council Chs., 1964-66; pres. council Christ Hosp., N.J., 1953-59; trustee Newark Mus. Decorated Liberian Humane Order African Redemption. Mem. House of Bishops. Clubs: Glen Ridge Country; Rock Spring Golf, Rotary. Home: 153 Morningside Rd Verona NJ 07044 Office: 24 Rector St Newark NJ 07102. *As a Christian I have tried to order my life with all its relationships and duties according to the will of God as I see it in Christ in Scripture, history, and human experience. God knows how many times I fail, but I am given strength to go on by knowing that when I err and then repent, I am forgiven by the love of God in Christ. Thus despite my many failures, I am buoyed up by a power and joy that can meet every exigency of life.*

STARK, NATHAN JULIUS, govt. ofcl.; b. Mpls., Nov. 9, 1920; s. Harold and Anna (Berlow) S.; A.A., Woodrow Wilson Jr. Coll., Chgo., 1940; B.S., U.S. Mcht. Marine Acad., 1943; J.D., Chgo. Kent Coll. Law, 1948; LL.D., Park Coll., 1969; m. Lucile D. Seidler, Nov. 28, 1943; children—Paul S., David H., Robert, Margaret J. Plant mgr. Englander Co., Inc., Chgo., 1949-51; admitted to Ill. bar, 1947, Mo. bar, 1952; partner law firm Downey, Abrams, Stark & Sullivan, Kansas City, 1952-53; v.p. Rival Mfg. Co., Kansas City, Mo., 1954-59; sr. v.p. ops. Hallmark Cards, Inc., Kansas City, 1959-74; pres., chmn. Crown Center Redevel. Corp., Kansas City, 1971-74; vice chancellor Schs. Health Professions, U. Pitts., also pres. Univ. Health Center, 1974-79; undersec. HEW, Washington, 1979—; dir. ERC Corp., 1970-79, Hallmark Continental Ltd., Ireland, 1971-73. Legal counsel Lyric Opera Theatre, Kansas City, Mo., 1958-72; mem. com. undergrad. med. edn. AMA, 1966-73; vice chmn. health ins. benefits adv. com. HEW, 1965-70, sec. task force on Medicaid, 1969-70, chmn. adv. commn. incentive reimbursement experimentation, 1968-70, chmn. capital investment conf. HEW-HRA, 1976; mem. liaison com. Am. Assn. Med. Colls.-AMA, 1970-74; chmn. task force life-long learning opportunities Kellogg Found., 1975-77; chmn. community hosp.-med. staff group practice program Robert Wood Johnson Found., 1974-79; mem. bd. Blue Cross Western Pa., 1975-79, Am. Nurses Found., 1975-77, Health Systems Agy. SW Pa., 1976—. Vice pres. Kansas City Philharmonic Assn., 1954; sec. Eddie Jacobson Meml. Found., 1960—; mem. tech. bd. Milbank Meml. Fund, 1976-78; pres., chmn. Kansas City Gen. Hosp. and Med. Center, 1962-74; trustee Allegheny Found., 1975—, Pitts. Ballet Theater, 1977-79, Pitts. Chamber Opera Theater, 1978—; mem. VA Scholars Bd. Governance, 1979—. Served with U.S. Maritime Service, 1942-45. Recipient Chancellor's medal U. Mo. at Kansas City, 1969; Pro-Meritus award Rockhurst Coll., 1967; Layman award AMA, 1974. Mem. Inst. Medicine of Nat. Acad. Scis. (council 1973-76), Am. Hosp. Assn. (hon. mem.; Trustee award 1968). Contbr. articles to profl. and bus. jours. Home: 5200 Westminster Pl Pittsburgh PA 15232

STARK, RICHARD ALVIN, lawyer; b. Ann Arbor, Mich. Apr. 6, 1921; A.B., DePauw U., 1943; M.B.A., Harvard U., 1947; LL.B., Ind. U., 1948. Admitted to Ind. bar, 1948, N.Y. bar, 1949; asso. firm Milbank, Tweed, Hadley & McCloy, N.Y.C., 1948-57, partner, 1957—. Mem. Am. (securities law com.), N.Y. State (corp. law com.) bar assns. Office: 1 Chase Manhattan Plaza New York NY 10005

STARK, RICHARD BOIES, surgeon; b. Conrad, Iowa, Mar. 31, 1915; s. Eugene and Hazel (Carson) S.; A.B., Stanford, 1936; U. Heidelberg, 1936-37; M.D., Cornell U., 1941; m. Judy Thornton, Oct. 31, 1967. Intern Peter Brent Brigham Hosp., Boston, 1941-42; asst. resident surgery Children's Hospital, Boston, 1942; plastic surgeon Northington Gen. Hosp., Ala., 1945-46, Percy Jones Gen. Hosp., Mich., 1946; postwar fellow anatomy and embryology Stanford, 1946-47; asst. resident and resident surgery, plastic surgery VA Hosp., Bronx, N.Y., N.Y. Hosp., 1947-50; instr. surgery Cornell U., 1950-52; asst. prof., 1952-55, asso. prof., 1955; asst. attending surgeon N.Y. Hosp., 1950-55; asst. prof. surgery Columbia, 1955-58, asso. prof., 1958-73, prof., 1973—; adj. prof. speech pathology and audiology Adelphi U.; asso. attending surgeon St. Luke's Hosp., N.Y.C., 1955-58, attending surgeon, 1958—; artist, exhibited 8 one-man shows paintings and drawings. Chmn. Medico Adv. Bd.; v.p. CARE. Served with AUS, plastic surgeon, 1943-46; ETO. Decorated Bronze Star (U.S.); Medal of Honor (2) (Vietnam); cavallero Order of San Carlos (Colombia). Diplomate Am. Bd. Plastic Surgery (pres. 1967-68). Fellow A.C.S.; mem. Am. Assn. Plastic Surgeons, Am. Soc. Plastic and Reconstructive Surgery (pres. 1966), Found. Am. Soc. Plastic and Reconstructive Surgery (pres. 1961-65), Am. Soc. Aesthetic Plastic Surgery (pres. 1975), Am. Surg. Assn., Soc. U. Surgeons, French, Brasilian, Colombian, Argentina socs. plastic surgeons, Brit. Assn. Plastic Surgery, Peruvian Acad. Surgeons, N.Y. Surg. Soc., N.Y. State Med. Soc. (pres., sec. med. history), Halsted Soc. (pres.), James IV Assn. Surgeons (sec.). Author: Plastic Surgery at the New York Hospital 100 Years Ago, 1953; Plastic Surgery, 1963; Cleft Palate, 1968. Editor: Annals of Plastic Surgery, 1977—. Contbr. numerous chpts. to books, articles to profl. jours. Home: 35 E 75th St New York NY 10021 Office: 115 E 67th St New York NY 10021

STARK, ROBERT EDWARD, business exec.; b. Garfield, N.J., May 9, 1921; s. Joseph Edward and Edith (Stewart) S.; B.S., U.S. Naval Acad., 1942; M.S., Mass. Inst. Tech., 1948; m. Grace Burlingame Cadwell, Mar. 11, 1950; children—Nancy, David, Jonathan. Commd. ensign USN, 1942, advanced through grades to capt., 1962; elec. and fire control officer U.S.S. Philadelphia, 1942-45; design project officer Bur. Ships, Navy Dept., 1953-56, 60-62; design supt. Phila. Naval Shipyard, 1956-60; prof. naval architecture Mass. Inst. Tech., 1965-68; v.p. M. Rosenblatt & Son, Inc., N.Y.C., 1970-72; sr. program mgr. Gibbs & Cox, Inc., 1972-79, asst. v.p., 1979—. Mem. Order of Arrow, Boy Scouts Am., 1968—. Registered profl. engr., N.Y. Mem. Soc. Naval Architects and Marine Engrs. (chmn. New Eng. sect. 1967-68, v.p. 1975-77), Am. Soc. Naval Engrs., Sigma Xi, Tau Beta Pi. Home: 64 Pine Way New Providence NJ 07974 Office: 40 Rector St New York NY 10006

STARK, ROBERT MARTIN, mathematician, civil engr.; b. N.Y.C., Feb. 6, 1930; s. Alexander and Julia (Gross) S.; A.B., Johns Hopkins U., 1951; M.A., U. Mich., 1952; Ph.D., U. Del., 1965; m. Carol LaSage, Jan. 13, 1955; children—Bradley R., Timothy D., Steven M., Candice B. Research scientist Bausch and Lomb, Rochester, N.Y., 1955; instr. Rochester Inst. Tech., 1956-57; asst. dean engring., asst. prof. math. Cleve. State U., 1957-62; instr. U. Del., 1962-64, asst. prof. civil engring., ops. research, 1964-68, asso. prof., 1968-76, prof., 1976—; vis. asso. prof. M.I.T., 1972-73; cons. in field. Office Naval Research grantee, 1974—; NSF grantee, 1966-70; U.S. Army Research Office grantee, 1967-68. Mem. AAAS, Phila. Ops. Research Soc. (pres. 1970), Ops. Research Soc. Am., ASCE, Inst. Mgmt. Sci. Author: (with R.L. Nicholls) Mathematical Foundations for Design: Civil Engineering Systems, 1972; research, publs. ops., applied probability. Home: One Fox Ln Newark DE 19711 Office: U Del Dept Math Sci Newark DE 19711

STARK, ROBERT WILLIAM COREY, landscape painter; b. Sidney, N.Y., Mar. 27, 1939; s. Alva Roland Corey and Ruth Dibble (Banner) S.; B.A., U. Denver, 1964; m. Lucy Clark, Jan. 23, 1972. Propr. Robert Stark Studio, Washington, 1967-69; partner Clark & Stark, Washington, 1970-75; pres. Art Exchange, Inc., Washington, 1973—; mem. D.C. Commn. Fine Arts, 1968-69; one-man exhbns. include Corcoran Gallery Art, 1969, Phillips Collection, Washington, 1979; paintings exhibited State Dept. Art in Am. Embassies, London, Paris, Rome, Peking, Helsinki, Stockholm, Tokyo, Mexico City, Katmandu, Caracas, Brussels, Geneva, Tehran, Sofia, Amman, Lisbon, Tunis, Nassau, 1973—; rep. permanent collections Mus. Modern Art, N.Y.C., Smithsonian Instn., Biblioteque Nationale, Paris, Washington Post. Recipient Best in Show award Everhart Gallery, Scranton, Pa., 1978. Home: Main St Union Dale PA 18470

STARK, RONALD WILLIAM, entomologist; b. Calgary, Alta., Can., Dec. 4, 1922; came to U.S., 1959, naturalized, 1966; s. Robert Donaldson and Christina Glen (Currie) S.; B.Sc.F., U. Toronto, 1948, M.A. in Zoology, 1951; Ph.D. in Forest Entomology, U. B.C., 1958; m. Mary Laurita McMann, Sept. 2, 1944; children—Debra Jeanne, David Ronald. Research entomologist forest biology div. Can. Dept. Agr., 1948-59; asst. prof. forest entomology U. Calif., Berkeley, 1959-61, asso. prof., 1962-66, prof., 1966-70; grad. dean, coordinator research U. Idaho, 1970-77, prof. Coll. Forestry, Wildlife and Range Scis., 1977—; exec. v.p. Idaho Research Found., 1970-77; cons. Deutscher Akademischer Austauschdienst fellow, Germany, 1976; NSF sr. fellow, 1967-68. Served with Can. Army, 1942-44. Fellow Entomol. Soc. Can. (Gold medal 1978); mem. Entomol. Soc. Am., Soc. Am. Foresters, Ecol. Soc. Am., AAAS, Finnish Entomol. Soc.

(hon.), Sigma Xi. Club: Elks. Contbr. numerous articles to profl. publs.; author 3 symposium procs.; co-editor: Theory and Practice of Mountain Pine Beetle Management in Lodgepole Pine Forests, 1978; The Douglas-fir Tussock Moth: A Synthesis, 1979. Office: Dept for Resources Coll Forestry Wildlife and Range Scis U Idaho Moscow ID 83843

STARK, SUSAN ROTHENBERG, journalist; b. N.Y.C., July 9, 1940; d. Albert and Lillian (Landau) Rothenberg; B.A., Smith Coll., 1962; M.A., Harvard, 1963; m. Allan Frederick Stark, July 5, 1968; children—Allana Fredericka, Paula Rose. Story cons. Columbia Pictures Corp., N.Y.C., 1963-64; mem. pub. relations staff Seventeen Mag., N.Y.C., 1964-65, Girl Scouts U.S.A., N.Y.C., 1965-68; film critic Detroit Free Press, 1968-79, Detroit News, 1979—. Mem. Phi Beta Kappa. Home: 8162 E Jefferson Detroit MI 48214 Office: Detroit News 615 Lafayette Blvd Detroit MI 48231

STARKE, WALTER MARCELLUS, gas co. exec., lawyer; b. Birmingham, Ala., Jan. 23, 1935; s. John Metcalfe and Elizabeth (Jones) S.; B.A., U. Ala., 1957, LL.B., 1961; m. Mary Ann Schanbacher, Oct. 6, 1958; children—Walter, Elizabeth, Curran. Admitted to Ala. bar, 1961; pvt. practice in Birmingham, 1961-62; atty. So. Natural Gas Co., Birmingham, 1962-68, asst. sec., atty., 1968-73, sec., atty., 1973-75, asst. v.p. pub. affairs, 1975—. Bd. dirs. Ala. Kidney Found., 1976—, pres., 1979—; bd. dirs. Birmingham Festival Arts, 1976-77, men's com. Birmingham Music Club. Served to 1st lt. U.S. Army, 1958-60. Decorated Army Commendation medal. Mem. Am., Fed. Power, Ala. bar assns., Ala. C. of C., Phi Delta Phi. Republican. Methodist. Clubs: Birmingham Country, Relay House. Home: 913 Crestview Dr Birmingham AL 35213 Office: PO Box 2563 Birmingham AL 35202

STARKER, JANOS, cellist; b. Budapest, Hungary, July 5, 1924; s. Alexander and Margarete S.; ed. Franz Liszt Acad. Music, Budapest, Mus.D. (hon.), 1961; Mus. D., Chgo. Conservatory, Cornell Coll.; m. Eva Uranyi, Nov. 11, 1944 (div.); 1 dau., Gabrielle Edith; m. 2d, Rae Busch Goldsmith, June 22, 1960; 1 dau., Gwen Ann. Came to U.S., 1948, naturalized, 1953. Solo cellist Budapest Opera House and Philharmonic, 1945-46, Dallas Symphony Orch., 1948-49, Met. Opera, 1949-53, Chgo. Symphony Orch., 1953-58; resident cellist Ind. U., 1958—, prof. music, 1961, now Distinguished prof.; concertizing and rec. artist, tchr., lectr. Recipient Grand Prix du Disque, 1948, George Washington award, Yale Sanford award. Mem. Am. Fedn. Musicians. Author: An Organized Method of String Playing, Bach Suites, Concerto Cadenzas. Contbr. articles to mags. Inventor Starker Bridge. Home: 1241 Winfield Rd Bloomington IN 47401. *Predestination, hard work, and unquestioned belief in one's goals and abilities. Goals that are not determined by success but maximum exploitation of talent and self. In art the constant observation of traditional values and principles coupled with the unceasing search for new roads. In education helping others to find themselves.*

STARKEY, PAUL EDWARD, dental educator; b. Fultonham, Ohio, Dec. 9, 1920; s. Charles Henry and Magdalena (Frank) S.; student Wittenberg U., 1937-40; D.D.S., Ind. U., 1943; m. Arlene Doris Luders, Dec. 27, 1942; children—Susan, Scott, Jan, Charles Henry. Pvt. practice pedodontics, Miamisburg and Dayton, Ohio, part-time tchr. Ohio State U. Sch. Dentistry, 1946-59; faculty Ind. U. Sch. Dentistry, 1959—, chmn. clin. div. pedodontics, 1963—, chmn. dept., 1969—. Examining mem. Am. Bd. Pedodontics, 1970—. Served with USNR, 1943-46. Recipient Frederick Bachman Lieber Meml. award distinguished teaching Ind. U., 1968. Mem. Am. Soc. Dentistry Children (founder Dayton study club, 1956, nat. pres. 1966-67), Ohio Soc. Dentistry Children (pres. 1959). Contbr. articles to profl. publs. Home: 1760 E 110th St Indianapolis IN 46280

STARKEY, ROBERT LYMAN, educator; b. Fitchburg, Mass., Sept. 27, 1899; s. Charles W. and Etta C. (Howes) S.; B.S., Mass. Agr. Coll., 1921; M.S., Rutgers U., 1923, Ph.D., 1924; m. Florence Tenney, 1928. Instr. bacteriology U. Minn., 1924-26; asso. prof. soil microbiology Rutgers U., 1926-44, prof. microbiology, 1944-65, emeritus prof., 1966—, head dept. agrl. microbiology, 1954-65; asso. soil microbiologist N.J. Agr. Expt. Sta., 1926-44, research specialist, 1944-65. Participant 1st Internat. Congress Soil Sci., Wash., 1927, 2d Congress, Russia, 1930; sec. sect. agrl. and indsl. microbiology 3d Internat. Microbiology Congress, N.Y.C., 1939, v.p. sect. agrl. microbiology 6th Congress, Rome, Italy, 1953; focal topic chmn. 8th congress, Montreal, Can., 1962; v.p. sect. microbiology, chmn. symposium 9th Internat. Bot. Congress, Montreal, 1959; rep. Soc. Am. Bacteriologists on NRC, 1956-59. Rockefeller fellow, 1937-38. Recipient Distinguished Research award, adv. bd. Research Council Rutgers U., 1958, certificate Office Naval Research, 1967, award Alumni Assn. U. Mass., 1969; Charles Thom award Soc. for Indsl. Microbiology, 1976. Served with SATC, World War I. Fellow AAAS; mem. Am. Soc. Agronomy (exec. com., mem. bd. govs. 1957-58), Theobald Smith Soc. (1st pres. 1941-42), Am. (pres. 1962-63, hon. mem.), Can. (hon.) socs. for microbiology, Associacion Mexican de Microbiologia (hon.), Sigma Xi, Phi Kappa Phi, Phi Sigma Kappa. Republican. Unitarian. Co-author: The Soil and the Microbe. Contbr. articles on microbiology and microbiol physiology and indsl. microbiology to profl. jours. Home: 7 Crest Rd Dewey Heights New Brunswick NJ 08901

STARLING, JAMES HOLT, biologist, educator; b. Troy, Ala., June 28, 1912; s. James Jefferson and Minnie (Radford) S.; B.A., U. Ala., 1933., M.A., 1937; Ph.D., Duke, 1942: student summers Brit. Mus. Natural History, 1953, Oak Ridge Inst. Nuclear Studies, 1961; m. Mary Nell Lewis, Nov. 14, 1936; 1 son, John Lewis. Sci. tchr. Troy High Sch., 1934-39; grad. asst. zoology Duke, 1939-42; faculty Washington and Lee U., 1942—, prof. biology, 1951—, faculty marshall, 1960-74, coordinator premed. studies, 1964—, chmn. dept. biology, 1976-78; vis. prof., cons. NSF Insts., summers 1955-65. Pres., Rockbridge Tb Assn., 1948-50. Bd. dirs. Va. Tb Assn., 1948-50. Served to capt. AUS, 1943-46. Mem. Va. Acad. Sci., AAAS, Southeastern Biologists Assn., Sigma Xi, Alpha Epsilon Delta, Sigma Alpha Epsilon. Presbyterian. (deacon, elder). Contbr. research to profl. publs. Home: 207 Paxton Rd Lexington VA 24450

STARNES, EARL MAXWELL, urban and regional planner; b. Winter Haven, Fla., Sept. 14, 1926; s. Thomas Lowe and Kathryn Maxwell (Gates) S.; student Fla. So. Coll., 1946-48; B.Arch. cum laude, U. Fla., 1951; M.S. in Urban and Regional Planning, Fla. State U., 1973, Ph.D., 1977; m. Dorothy Jean Prather, Aug. 21, 1949; children—Tom, Will, Janet, Patricia. Asso., Courtney Stewart, Architect, Ft. Lauderdale, Fla., 1951-52, William Bigoney, Architect, Ft. Lauderdale, 1952-53, William T. Vaughn, Architect, Ft. Lauderdale, 1953, Alfred B. Parker, Architect, Miami, Fla., 1953-55, Rufus Nims, Architect, Miami, 1955-57; partner Starnes & Rentscher, Architects, Miami, 1957-63, Starnes, Rentscher & Assos., Architects, Miami, 1963-71; dir. div. mass transp. Fla. Dept. Transp., Tallahassee, 1971-72; dir. div. state planning Fla. Dept. Adminstrn., 1972-75; engaged in research and cons. service, Tallahassee, 1975; prof., chmn. urban and regional planning Coll. Architecture, U. Fla., Gainesville, 1976—; instr. architecture U. Miami, 1953; adj. asst. prof. dept. urban and regional planning Coll. Social Scis., Fla. State U., 1971-74; mem. adv. panel B8-15, Nat. Coop. Hwy. Research Program, Transp. Research Bd., NRC-Nat. Acad. Scis., 1974—; mem. adv. bd. Pub. Tech., Inc., 1974—. Co-chmn. Joint Liaison Com. on Div. Responsibility for Urban Services, Dade County, Fla., 1965-71; chmn. joint policy com. U. Miami-Dade County Jackson Med. Center, 1966-71; chmn. Cape Fla. State Park Adv. Council, 1966-69, Dade County Landscape Ordinance Study Com., 1967-70, South Fla. Everglades Area Planning Council, 1969-71; active South Dade Mental Health Study Group, 1967-68, Cape Fla. Acquisition Com., 1966, Dade County Downtown Govtl. Center Com., 1967-71, Miami Downtown Devel. Authority, 1970, Gov.'s Task Force on Resource Mgmt., 1971-72, Nat. Task Force on Natural Resources and Land Use Info. and Tech., 1973-74; county commr. Dist. 7, Dade County, 1964-71; vice mayor, Dade County, 1964, 68; mem. adv. com. Legis. Council Subcom. on Constrn. Industry Study, 1966-68; bd. dirs., chmn. retirement and compensation com. State Assn. County Commrs., 1968-71; mem. Alachua County Budget Study Com., 1978, Fla. Land Use Adv. Com. for Phosphate Lands, 1978-79. Served with USCG, 1944-46. Registered architect, Fla. Fellow AIA (urban design com. 1976-80); mem. Am. Inst. Planners (asso.), Nat. Inst. Bldg. Scis. (steering com. for research 1979—), Gargoyle Soc., Phi Kappa Phi. Democrat. Unitarian. Contbr. articles on land use and urban devel. policies to profl. jours. Important works include First Unitarian Ch., Miami. Office: 431 GPB U Fla Gainesville FL 32611

STARNES, RICHARD, newspaperman; b. Washington, July 4, 1922; s. John Irby and Eveline (Belt) S.; m. Nancy Ely, Mar, 15, 1947. With Scripps-Howard Newspapers, 1938—, copy boy, reporter, asst. city editor, news editor, asst. mng. editor Washington Daily News, corr. Scripps-Howard Newspaper Alliance, 1949-53, mng. editor N.Y. World-Telegram & Sun, 1953-60; daily syndicated columnist, 1960-65; Washington corr. Scripps Howard Newspapers, 1965-79. Author: Requiem in Utopia, 1968; The Flypaper War, 1969. Home: 1404 Gower Ct McLean VA 22101 Office: 777 14th St NW Washington DC 20005

STARNES, STANCIL ROSE, lawyer; b. Aldrich, Ala., Jan. 26, 1922; s. Stancil Rose and Sadie (Patton) S.; student Emory U., 1946; LL.B., U. Ala., 1949; m. Mary Margaret Lee, Aug. 30, 1947; children—William S., Nancylee, James H. Admitted to Ala. bar, 1949; practiced in Oneonta, 1949-53, Birmingham, 1958—; partner firm Nash, Nash & Starnes, 1949-53, Spain, Gillon, Riley, Tate & Ansley, 1958-74, Starnes & Starnes, 1975—. county atty. Blount County, 1950-53; dir. Citizens Bank, Oneonta. Govt. appeal agt. Blount County, U.S. SSS, 1951-53. Bd. dirs. Longview Gen. Hosp. Served with USNR, 1942-45, Fellow Am. Coll. Trial Lawyers; mem. Internat. Assn. Ins. Counsel, Def. Research Inst. (state chmn.), Am., Ala., Birmingham (pres. 1972, past mem. exec. com.), bar assns., Omicron Delta Kappa, Alpha Tau Omega, Phi Delta Phi. Club: Birmingham Country. Home: 3613 Brookwood Rd Birmingham AL 35223 Office: 1701 Daniel Bldg Birmingham AL 35233

STARNES, WILLIAM LOVE, ins. co. exec., ret. army officer; b. Columbus, O., Mar. 23, 1919; s. William Love and Mildred (Richardson) S.; B.S., U.S. Mil. Acad., 1943; M.S., Mass. Inst. Tech., 1947; M.B.A., George Washington U., 1962; postgrad. Indsl. Coll. Armed Forces, 1959-60; m. Mary D. Jay, Jan. 20, 1943; children—William Henry (dec.), Mary Mildred (Mrs. D.E. Saunders), Lucille Love (Mrs. D.M. Calwhite), Susan Rhea (Mrs. G.C. Kaiser). Commd. 2d lt. U.S. Army, 1943, advanced through grades to maj. gen., 1970, ret., 1973; operations officer U.S. Forces in Austria, 1947-50; comdr. 16th Engr. Bn., 1st Armored Div., 1951-52; instr. U.S. Mil. Acad., 1952-55; area engr., Thule, Greenland, 1955-57; dep. corps engr. 18th Airborne Corps, 1958-59; staff officer Joint Chiefs of Staff, 1960-62; dist. engr. Canaveral Engr. Dist., Fla., 1962-66; comdr. 35th Constrn. Group, Vietnam, 1966-67; dep. dir. mil. constrn. Office Chief of Engrs., Washington, 1967-69; asst. for constrn. operations Office Sec. Def., 1969-70; div. engr. Ohio River Div., Cin., 1970-73; sr. v.p. adminstrn. United Services Automobile Assn., San Antonio, 1973-79; engring. cons., 1979—. Chmn. Greater Cin. Fed. Exec. Bd., 1972-73. Bd. dirs. Project Mgrs. Inst. Decorated D.S.M., Legion of Merit with 3 clusters, Bronze Star, Air medal, Army Commendation medal, Purple Heart; Belgium Croix de Guerre; Vietnamese medal honor. Fellow Soc. Am. Mil. Engrs.; mem. Space Pioneers, West Point Soc. Republican. Episcopalian. Home: 4310 Little Ln San Antonio TX 78229 Office: USAA Bldg San Antonio TX 78288

STARR, BENJAMIN FRED, JR., air force officer; b. Atlanta; s. Benjamin Fred and Lida Belle (Miller) S.; student Ga. Inst. Tech., 1945-48; B.A., George Washington U., 1962, M.A., 1963; m. Virginia Anne White, July 17, 1943; children—Rick, Mark, Cindy. Commd. 2d lt. USAF, 1945, advanced through grades to maj. gen., 1975; service in U.K., Thailand, S. Vietnam; comdr. 62d Mil. Airlift Wing, 1973-74, 63d Mil. Airlift Wing, 1974-75; dir. transp. Hdqrs. USAF, 1975-77, 76th Mil. Airlift Wing, Andrews/Bolling AFB, 1977—. Decorated Air Force Commendation medal, Air medal with 8 oak leaf clusters, D.F.C., Bronze Star, Legion of Merit with one oak leaf cluster. Mem. Air Force Assn., Daedaelians. Baptist. Clubs: Masons, Shriners. Home: 78 Westover Ave Bolling AFB DC 20336 Office: Hdqrs 76MAW Andrews AFB MD 20331

STARR, BRYAN BARTLETT (BART), profl. football coach; b. Montgomery, Ala., Jan. 9, 1934, s. Benjamin B. and Lula I. (Tucker) S.; B.S., U. Ala., 1956; m. Cherry Morton, May 8, 1954; children—Bart, Bret. Quarterback, Green Bay Packers, Nat. Football League, 1956-71, asst. coach, 1972, gen. mgr., head coach, 1975—; owner, operator Bart Starr Lincoln-Mercury automobile dealership, Birmingham, Ala. Active in fundraising for numerous charities; mem. bd. 1st Meth. Ch., DePere, Wis. Played in NFL Pro-Bowl after 1960, 61, 62, 66 seasons; NFL Passing Leader, 1962, 64, 66; NFL Player of the year: 1966; Super Bowl Most Valuable Player: 1967, 68; named to Nat. Profl. Football Hall of Fame, 1977. Co-author: Quarterbacking, 1967. Office: Green Bay Packers 1265 Lombardi Ave Green Bay WI 54303*

STARR, CHAUNCEY, research inst. exec.; b. Newark, Apr. 14, 1912; s. Rubin and Rose (Dropkin) S.; E.E., Rensselaer Poly. Inst., 1932, Ph.D., 1935, D.Engring. (hon.), 1964; m. Doris Evelyn Debel, Mar. 20, 1938; children—Ross M., Ariel E. Research fellow physics Harvard, 1935-37; research asso. Mass. Inst. Tech., 1938-41; research physicist D.W. Taylor Model Basin, Bur. Ships, 1941-42; staff radiation lab. U. Calif., 1942-43, Tenn. Eastman Corp., Oak Ridge, 1943-46, Clinton Labs., 1946; chief spl. research N. Am. Aviation, Inc., Downey, Calif., 1946-49, dir. atomic energy research dept., 1949-55, v.p., 1955-66, gen. mgr. Atomics Internat. div., 1955-60, pres. div., 1960-66; dean engring. U. Calif. at Los Angeles, 1966-73; cons. prof. Stanford, 1974—; pres. Electric Power Research Inst., 1973-78, vice chmn., 1978—. Dir. Atomic Indsl. Forum. Decorated Legion of Honor (France). Fellow Am. Nuclear Soc. (past pres.), Am. Phys. Soc., AAAS (dir.); mem. Am. Inst. Aeros. and Astronautics (sr.), Am. Power Conf., Nat. Acad. Engring., Am. Soc. Engring. Edn., Royal Swedish Acad. for Engring. Scis., Eta Kappa Nu, Sigma Xi. Contbr. sci. articles to profl. jours. Home: 95 Stern Ln Atherton CA 94025

STARR, CHESTER G., educator; b. Centralia, Mo., Oct. 5, 1914; s. Chester Gibbs and Nettie (Glore) S.; A.B. with distinction, U. Mo., 1934; M.A., 1935; Ph.D., Cornell U., 1938; m. Gretchen Daub, July 15, 1940; children—Jennifer (Mrs. Michael Johnson), Deborah (Mrs. Gene Sessions), Richard G., Thomas J.J. Faculty, U. Ill. at Urbana, 1940-70, prof., history, 1953-70, chmn. div. humanities, 1953-55, chmn. dept. history, 1960-61; prof. U. Mich., Ann Arbor, 1970—, Bentley prof., 1973—. Cons. World Book, 1963-67, Ency. Americana, 1966—. Served from 1st lt. to lt. col. AUS, 1942-46; MTO. Decorated Bronze Star; Croce di Guerra (Italy). Recipient certificate as distinguished grad. U. Mo., 1963. Am. Acad. in Rome fellow, 1938-40; Guggenheim fellow, 1950-51, 58-59. Mem. Am. Hist. Assn. (chmn. com. on ancient history 1961-67), AAUP (chpt. pres. 1956-57), Socs. for Promotion Roman and Hellenic Studies, Royal Numis. Soc., Assn. Ancient Historians (pres. 1974-78), Phi Beta Kappa, Phi Mu Alpha. Author: Roman Imperial Navy, 1941; From Salerno to the Alps, 1948; Emergence of Rome, 1950; Civilization and the Caesars, 1954; Origins of Greek Civilization, 1961; History of Ancient World, 1965; Rise and Fall of Ancient World, 1965; Awakening of the Greek Historical Spirit, 1968; Athenian Coinage, 480-449 B.C., 1970; Ancient Greeks, 1971; Ancient Romans, 1971; Early Man, 1973; Political Intelligence in Classical Greece, 1974; Economic and Social Growth of Early Greece, 1977. Home: 2301 Blueberry Ln Ann Arbor MI 48103

STARR, DAVID, newspaper editor, publisher; b. N.Y.C., Aug. 1, 1922; s. Aaron and Helen (Simon) S.; B.A., Queens Coll., 1942; m. Marjorie Giffen, Aug. 3, 1943; children—Pamela, Peter. Reporter, rewriteman L.I. Daily Press, 1942-50; exec. editor Nassau Daily Rev. Star, 1950-53; asst. editor Newark Star-Ledger, 1954-56; asso. editor L.I. Press, 1953-54, 56-62, mng. editor, 1962-69, editor, 1969-77; sr. editor Newhouse Newspapers, 1971—; pub. Springfield Union, Daily News, Sunday Republican, 1977—; mem. N.Y. State Fair Trial/Free Press Conf., 1969-77, vice-chmn., 1975-77; pres. Springfield Central, Inc., 1978—. Trustee Nassau Community Coll., State U. N.Y., 1959-66; v.p. United Fund L.I., 1965-70; bd. dirs. Springfield Library and Mus. Assn. Served with U.S. Army, 1943-46. Mem. Am. Soc. Newspaper Editors, Am. Newspaper Pubs. Assn. Office: 1860 Main St Springfield MA 01101

STARR, EUGENE CARL, cons. engr.; b. Falls City, Oreg., Aug. 6, 1901; s. Harie Eugene and Loretta Alice (Hart) S.; B.S. in Elec. Engring., Oreg. State U., Corvallis, 1923, E.E., 1938; m. Oma Mae Herald, Sept. 11, 1950. High voltage research engr. Gen. Electric Co., 1923-27; instr. elec. engring. Oreg. State U., 1927-33, asso. prof., 1934-39, prof., 1939-54; coordinator aircraft precipitation static research OSRD, 1942-45; cons. Bonneville Power Adminstrn., Portland, Oreg., 1939-54, chief engr., dir. div. engring., 1954-61, cons. engr., 1962—; civilian sci. observer Bikini atom bomb tests, 1946; cons. indsl. power AEC, 1953-65; mem. adv. panel on electricity Nat. Bur. Standards, Nat. Acad. Scis.-NRC, 1961-64; mem. U.S. nat. com., U.S. rep. study com. 14, Internat. Conf. Large High Voltage Electric Systems, 1962-78; mem. adv. group tech. coms. 8, 28, 30, Internat. Electrotech. Commn., 1954—; mem. adv. coms. Fed. Power Commn., 1965-67; mem. task force on nuclear safety research Electric Power Research Inst., 1969-75. Mem. Portland Mayor's Utility Underground Conversion Com., 1972-74. Recipient Disting. Service award and Gold medal Dept. Interior, 1958; Engr. of Yr. award, Profl. Engrs. Oreg., 1965; registered profl. engr., Oreg. Fellow IEEE (mem. editorial bd. 1965-66, dir. 1963-64, Habirshaw award 1968), AAAS; mem. Am. Nuclear Soc., Nat. Soc. Profl. Engrs., Nat. Acad. Engring., Sigma Xi, Tau Beta Pi, Sigma Tau, Eta Kappa Nu, Phi Kappa Phi. Contbr. articles to profl. jours. Home: 7830 SW Canyon Dr Portland OR 97225 Office: Federal Bldg PO Box 3621 Portland OR 97208. *The world of sci. and engring. research and devel. presents a challenge to look ever to the future for the benefit of man.*

STARR, HENRY FRANK, JR., physician, ins. co. exec.; b. Greensboro, N.C., Nov. 23, 1926; s. Henry Frank and Virginia Morton (Goode) S.; student U. N.C., 1946; M.D., Jefferson Med. Coll., 1948; m. Ellen Ross Izlar, July 7, 1951; children—Virginia Ellen, Elizabeth Ross, Frances Camille. Intern, surg. resident N.C. Bapt. Hosp. Bowman Gray Sch. Medicine, Wake Forest U., 1948-51; individual practice medicine, Greensboro, 1951-53; asst. med. dir. Pilot Life Ins. Co., Greensboro, 1955-62, med. dir., 1962-67, v.p., med. dir., 1967, sr. v.p., dir., 1968—. Chmn. N.C. Com. Health Ins. Council, 1966-68. Mem. Greensboro Zoning Commn., 1966-73; pres. Guilford County Comprehensive Health Planning Council, 1972. Served to capt. M.C., AUS, 1953-55. Mem. Am. Life Ins. Assn. (chmn. med. sect. 1974-75), Assn. Life Ins. Med. Dirs., AMA, N.C., Guilford County (pres. 1970) med. socs., N.C. (dir. 1971—), Greensboro (pres. 1968-70) heart assns., Middle Atlantic Life Ins. Med. Dirs. Club (chmn. 1965). Episcopalian (sr. warden 1967). Kiwanian (pres. 1965). Club: Sedgefield Country (Greensboro). Home: 3106 Alamance Rd Greensboro NC 27407 Office: PO Box 20727 Greensboro NC 27420

STARR, IRVING SUMNER, univ. dean; b. Quincy, Mass., Mar. 31, 1919; s. Jack and Rose B. (Kuperman) Sclarenco; B.S., Mass. State Coll., Bridgewater, 1941; Ed.M., Boston U., 1949, Ed.D., 1953; m. Irene D. Godgart, June 24, 1945; children—Jay Michael, Richard Mark, Lawrence Alan. Tchr. English, Vets. Regional High Sch., Mass. Dept. Edn. part-time 1946-48; tchr. social studies, English, guidance North Quincy High Sch., Quincy, Mass., 1946-50, tchr. social studies, 1951-52; teaching fellow Boston U., 1950-51; dir. tchr. tng. Hillyer Coll., Hartford, Conn., 1952-55, chmn. div. edn., 1955-58; dean U. Hartford Sch. Edn., 1958—, chmn. council of deans, 1965—. Dir. Edn. Cons. Assos. Mem. bd. edn., adult edn. commn., trustee Emanuel Synagogue, Hartford; past mem. bd. Hartford Jewish Center; mem. Gov.'s Adv. Council Tchr. Edn., 1967-72; chmn. Greater Hartford Conf. Christians and Jews, 1967-69; bd. dirs. Urban League Greater Hartford, 1974—, also chmn. exec. com.; bd. dirs. Hartford Scholarship Found. Served with AUS, 1942-45; maj. Civil Air Patrol, ret. Mem. Am. Assn. Sch. Adminstrs., NEA, NCCJ (v.p. Hartford chpt., exec. com.), Conn. Fedn. Jewish Men's Clubs (chmn. adult edn. council), Conn. Council Tchr. Edn. (past mem. bd.), Conn. Edn. Assn. (bd. higher edn.), Conn. Assn. Colls. and Univs. in Tchr. Edn. (officer) Phi Delta Kappa, Pi Gamma Mu. Clubs: Greater Hartford Probus (pres.), Probus Nat. (sec.), Rotary. Author: Youth Problems Inventory, 1951; Billett-Star Youth Problems Inventories, 1956; (with L.H. Clark) Secondary School Teaching Methods, 1959, 3d edit., 1976. Home: 21 Carlyle Rd West Hartford CT 06117

STARR, JASON LEONARD, physician, educator; b. Chelsea, Mass., Aug. 13, 1928; s. Hyman and Anna (Bernstein) S.; A.B. magna cum laude, Harvard, 1949, A.M., 1949, M.D., 1953; m. Naomi Simckes, Dec. 23, 1951; children—Jonathan E., Alexander P., Andrew M. Intern, Beth Israel Hosp., Boston, 1953-54; resident fellow medicine Mayo Found., 1956-58; fellow in biochemistry Western Res. U., 1958-61. Am. Cancer Soc. fellow, asst. prof. medicine Northwestern U. Med. Sch., 1961-65; asso. prof. U. Tenn., Memphis, 1965-67, prof. medicine, 1967-72; prof. medicine U. Calif. at Los Angeles, 1972-74; chief med. oncology Baptist Meml. Hosp., Memphis, 1974—; clin. prof. medicine U. Tenn., 1974—; sr. investigator Arthritis Found., 1963-68. Bd. dirs. West Tenn. Civil Liberties Union. Served to lt. USNR, 1954-56. Am. Cancer Soc. scholar in cancer research, 1971-72. Mem. Am. Soc. Clin. Investigation, Central Soc. Clin. Investigation, AAUP, Am. Assn. Immunologists, Western Soc. Clin. Research, AMA, Am. Soc. Internal Medicine, Am. Chem. Soc., Phi Beta Kappa, Sigma Xi, Alpha

Omega Alpha. Home: 4761 Eagle Crest Dr Memphis TN 38117 Office: 920 Madison Suite 628 Memphis TN 38103

STARR, LUTHER WADE, lawyer; b. Dallas, Aug. 27, 1928; s. Luther Oldrick and Alice Maybelle (Rutledge) S.; B.B.A., So. Methodist U., 1949, J.D., 1963; m. Joy Y. Turner, Jan. 12, 1963; children—Anita Y. Starr Conner, Dana Clare Starr Stallings. Gen. mgr. A & B Transfer & Storage Co., Dallas, 1950-63; admitted to Tex. bar, 1963, since practiced in Dallas; partner firm Goodstein & Starr. Served with USNR, 1953-55. Mem. Tex. Bar Assn. Democrat. Episocpalian. Home: 977 N Rustic Circle Dallas TX 75218 Office: 5925 Forest Ln Dallas TX 75230

STARR, MANYA GARBAT, author; b. N.Y.C., Jan. 21, 1921; d. Abraham Leon and Rachelle (Lubarsky) Garbat; B.A., Bryn Mawr Coll., 1941; m. Roger S. Starr, Dec. 2, 1945; children—Adam, Barnaby. Freelance radio, television and film writer, 1946—; dir. Encounter Films, N.Y.C. Chmn. bd. N.Y.C. Housing Authority Symphony Orch.; trustee Dalton Sch., 1971-73. Served to lt. (j.g.) USNR, 1942-45. Recipient Outstanding Pub. Service award for television series U.S. Army, 1962, Golden Gate award for NBC spl. film San Francisco Film Festival, 1968. Mem. Acad. Television Arts and Scis. (bd. govs.), Writers Guild Am. (nat. chmn.), Internat. Writers Guild (sec.), Writers Guild East (pres.). Address: 45 E 82d St New York NY 10028. *To do for others is to do for oneself—hard work is the greatest gratification—lucky is the person whose work is his/her choice. Mine has been, and so it has been my greatest enjoyment and purpose. When you've done your best, do a little better! Achieving is never achieved, for there is no end to it.*

STARR, MARK, author; b. Shoscombe, Somersetshire, Eng., Apr. 27, 1894; s. William and Susan (Padfield) S.; grad. St. Julian's Nat. Sch. (Eng.) 1907; London Labour Coll., 1920; m. Helen G. Norton, May 31, 1932; children—John (dec.), Emily. Came to U.S., 1928, naturalized, 1937. Builder's mortar boy, 1907-08; coal miner, 1908-15; tchr. econs., social history South Wales Miners Fedn., 1920-21, Esperanto, London County Council 1923-27; divisional organizer, lectr. Nat. Council Labour Colls., 1921-28; tchr. Brit. labor history and econs. Brookwood Labor Coll., Katonah, N.Y., 1928-33, extension dir., 1933-34; ednl. dir. Internat. Ladies Garment Workers Union, N.Y.C., 1935-60; workers edn. expert Internat. Labour Office, Singapore, 1960-61, Tanganyika, 1961-62, E. Africa, 1962-63; instr. Esperanto, N.Y.C. evening schs., 1961—; UN rep. N.Y. Universala Esperanto-Asocio, 1965—; chmn. Esperanto Information Center, N.Y.C., 1965-72; mem. bd. Operation Open City, Queens, 1967; co-adj. instr. labor studies Rutgers, U., 1974-75. Labor party parliamentary candidate, Wimbledon, Eng., 1924. Labor cons. OWI, Britain, 1943. Mem. U.S. del. London UNESCO Conf., 1945; chmn. U.S. delegation UNESCO Adult Edn. Conf., Denmark, 1949. Mem., vice chmn. U.S. Adv. Commn. Ednl. Exchange, 1948-53; labor edn. cons. SCAP in Japan. 1946; bd. dirs. Nat. Ednl. TV and Radio Center, 1958-61. Mem. exec. bd. League Indsl. Democracy; hon. chmn. Queens County Liberal party. Mem. Am. Fedn. Tchrs. (v.p. 1940-42), UN Assn. U.S.A. (chpt. pres. 1970-71). Author: A Worker Looks at History, 1917; A Worker Looks at Economics, 1925; Trade Unionism Past and Future, 1923; Lies and Hate in Education, 1928; (with Theodore Brameld et al) Workers Education in the United States, 1941; (with H.U. Faulkner) Labor in America 1944, rev., 1955, 57: Labor Looks at Education, 1946; Labor Politics in the U.S., 1949; Creeping Socialism vs. Limping Capitalism, 1954; American Labor Movement, 1972; House of Labor, 1951; co-author: Labor and the American Way, 1952, rev. 1965, 70. Home: 3940 47th St Long Island City NY 11104

STARR, MARTIN KENNETH, educator; b. N.Y.C., May 21, 1927; s. Harry and Melanie (Krauss) S.; B.S., Mass. Inst. Tech., 1948; M.S., Columbia, 1951, Ph.D., 1953; m. Polly Exner, Apr. 3, 1955; children—Christopher Herschel, Loren Michael. Partner, dir. M.K. Starr Assos., 1956-61; prof. mgmt. sci. Columbia, N.Y.C., 1961—, vice dean Grad. Sch. Bus., 1974-75; guest lectr. Am. U., Beirut, 1964, Mass. Inst. Tech., 1964-67, U. Cape Town (S. Africa), 1976, 80; cons. Lever Brothers, R.J. Reynolds, Young & Rubicam, IBM. Mem. Inst. Mgmt. Scis. (pres. 1974-75), Ops. Research Soc. Am., European Soc. for Opinion and Mktg. Research, Acad. of Mgmt. Beta Gamma Sigma. Author: (with Irving Stein) The Practice of Management Science, 1976; Systems Management of Operations, 1971; Management: A Modern Approach, 1971; Product Design and Decision Theory, 1963; Production Management: Systems and Synthesis, 2d edit., 1972; (with David W. Miller) Executive Decisions and Operations Research, 2d edit., 1969, The Structure of Human Decisions, Inventory Control-Theory and Practice, 1962; Operations Management, 1978. Editor: Executive Readings in Management Science, 1965; Management of Production, 1970; (with Milan Zeleny) Multiple Criteria Decision Making, 1977; editor in chief Mgmt. Sci., 1967—; mem. editorial bd. Behavioral Sci., 1970—; editorial adviser Operational Research Quar., 1970—; cons. editor (with Milan Zeleny) Columbia Jour. World Bus., Focus: Decision Making, fall, 1977; cons. editor for Quantitative methods in mgmt. McGraw-Hill Book Co., N.Y.C. Contbr. articles to profl. jours. Home: 20 Waterside Plaza New York NY 10010. *The ability to manage has become the most important capability in the last quarter century of the 1900's. Remarkable growth of interdependencies has occurred since 1950. Energy, ecology and productivity are some examples of critical issues for resolution. Management science combines art and logic to achieve social benefit. Perhaps a new name is needed to describe this effort. By whatever name it is called, the concept of management science will determine the character of the 21st century and will, in turn, be changed by it.*

STARR, MAURICE KENNETH, museum dir.; b. Libertytown, Md., Apr. 28, 1922; s. Maurice Scott and Nellie Gray (Fisher) S.; B.A., Duke, 1945; M.A., Yale, 1947, Ph.D. (Jr. Sterling fellow, Sr. Sterling fellow), 1957; m. Betty Jane Leslie, Dec. 23, 1943; children—Leslie Gray, Maurice Winfield. Prin., Tsingtao (China) Am. Sch., 1947-49; curator Asiatic archeology and ethnology Field Mus. Natural History, 1953-70; dir. Milw. Pub. Mus., 1970—. Lectr., Asian prehistory, dept. anthropology U. Chgo., 1958-73. Grantee Am. Council Learned Socs. and Social Sci. Research Council for research on China ink-rubbings, Taiwan, 1960. Mem. Far-Eastern Prehistory Assn., Am. Assn. Museums (v.p. 1975-78, pres. 1978—, chmn. future objectives com. 1976-78, council 1975—), Internat. Council Museums (exec. bd. 1976—), Assn. Sci. Mus. Dirs. (pres. 1974-76), Assn. Sci.-Tech. Centers (bd. dirs. 1975-77, Midwest Museums Conf. (pres. 1974-76), Wis. Fedn. Museums, Wis. Acad. Scis., Arts and Letters, Phi Beta Kappa, Sigma Xi. Clubs: Caxton (Chgo.); Univ. (Milw.), Rotary. Translator, annotator: Ch'eng-tzu-yai: the Black Pottery Culture Site at Lung-shan-chen in Li-ch'eng-hsien, Shantung Province, 1956. Contbr. articles, revs. to profl. jours. Home: 1043 E Ogden Ave Milwaukee WI 53202 Office: 800 W Wells St Milwaukee WI 53233

STARR, NATHAN, merchandising and distbn. co. exec.; b. Toronto, Ont., Can., Apr. 26, 1927; s. Raphael and Pauline (Greenberg) Storozumnick; C.A., Can. Inst. Chartered Accountants, 1950; m. Toby Menkes, Dec. 10, 1950; children—Noreen, Robert, Howard. Partner, Starr, Klyman & Co., 1950-56; freelance pub. accountant, Toronto, 1956-62; partner Starr, Rumack, Tward, Glustein & Co., 1962-65, Starr, Tward & Co., Toronto, 1965-72; sec.-treas. Acklands Ltd., and subsidiary cos., 1959-64, v.p. finance of co. and subsidiary cos., 1964-66, sec.-treas., 1964-70, exec. v.p., dir., 1966-77; pres. Community Video, Ltd. and affiliated cos., Toronto, 1965-77; also dir.; pres., dir. Acklands Ltd., 1977—, chief exec. officer, 1978—; trustee GHI Mortgage Investors Group; dir. Selkirk Holdings Ltd., Gesco Distbg. Co. Nat. treas. Canadian Assn. for Retarded Children, 1967-68, Canadial Friends of Akim, 1971-76. Bd. dirs. New Mt. Sinai Hosp., 1975—, Baycrest Centre for Geriatric Care, 1975—. Mason; mem. B'nai B'rith. Home: 150 Betty Ann Dr Willowdale ON M2N 1X4 Canada Office: 100 Norfinch Dr Downsview ON M3N 1X2 Canada

STARR, RICHARD CAWTHON, educator; b. Greensboro, Ga., Aug. 24, 1924; s. Richard Neal and Ida Wynn (Cawthon) S.; B.S. in Secondary Edn., Ga. So. Coll., 1944; M.A., George Peabody Coll., 1947; postgrad. (Fulbright scholar) Cambridge (Eng.) U., 1950-51; Ph.D., Vanderbilt U., 1952. Faculty, Ind. U., 1952—, prof. botany, 1960-76, founder, head culture collection algae, 1953-76; prof. botany U. Tex. at Austin, 1976—. Head course marine botany Marine Biol. Lab., Woods Hole, Mass., 1959-63. Trustee Am. Type Culture Collection, 1962-68. Guggenheim fellow, 1959; sr. fellow Alexander von Humboldt-Stiftung, 1972-73. Fellow AAAS, Ind. Acad. Sci.; mem. Nat. Acad. Scis., Am. Inst. Biol. Scis. (governing bd. 1976-77), Bot. Soc. Am. (sec. 1965-69, v.p., 1970, pres., 1971; Darbaker prize 1955), Phycological Soc. Am. (past pres., v.p., treas.), Soc. Protozoologists, Internat. (sec. 1964-68), Brit. phycological socs., Sigma Xi. Algae sect. editor Biol. Abstracts. 1959—; editorial bd. Jour. Phycology, 1965-68, 76—, Archiv für Protistenkunde; asso. editor Phycologia, 1963-69. Contbr. articles to profl. jours. Office: Dept Botany Univ Texas Austin TX 78712*

STARR, RICHARD WILLIAM, banker; b. Phila., Oct. 7, 1920; s. Edwin Bell and Bertha (Aurand) S.; student U. Buffalo, 1946-50, U. So. Calif., eves. 1952-58; B.B.A.; grad. Am. Inst. Banking, 1942, Pacific Coast Sch. Banking, U. Wash., 1968, Stanford Gad. Sch. Credit and Fin. Mgmt., 1958; Harvard Advanced Mgmt. Program, 1975; m. Evelyn Irene Johnson, Aug. 3, 1943; children—David Richard, Daniel Robert. With Marine Trust Co. of Buffalo, 1939-47, mgr. credit dept., 1947-50; with United Calif. Bank, Los Angeles, 1952—, installment credit officer, 1952-53, mgr. credit dept., 1953-58, comml. lending officer, loan adminstr., 1958-61, br. mgr., 1961, asst. cashier, 1955, asst. v.p., 1956-63, v.p., 1963-71, sr. v.p., 1971—, area adminstr. nat. div., 1969-70, br. adminstr., 1970-73, mgr. state div. corp. banking dept., 1973-74, mgr. so. div. Calif. Banking Group, Los Angeles, 1974-76, adminstr. spl. credits div., 1976-79, exec. v.p., adminstr. Calif. div., 1979—. Bd. dirs. Better Bus. Bur. Los Angeles. Served with USCGR, 1942-45, USNR, 1950-52. Mem. Mortgage Banking Assn. (chmn. Orange County 1962—), Robert Morris Assos., Cal. Bankers Assn. (exec. com. 1972), Beta Gamma Sigma. Republican. Clubs: Santa Ana (Calif.) Country; Jonathan (Los Angeles), Masons. Home: 2849 Rustic Gate Way Orange CA 92667 Office: 707 Wilshire Blvd Los Angeles CA 90014

STARR, RINGO (RICHARD STARKEY), musician, actor; b. Liverpool, Eng., July 7, 1940; s. Richard and Elsie (Gleave) Starkey; m. Maureen Cox, Feb. 11, 1965 (div. 1975); children—Zak, Jason, Lee. Drummer, vocalist with mus. group The Beatles, 1962-69; solo performer, 1970—; recs. include Sentimental Journey, Beaucoups of Blues, Ringo, Goodnight Vienna, Ringo the 4th. Appeared in films: A Hard Day's Night, 1964, Help!, 1965, Candy, 1968, The Magic Christian, 1970, Let It Be, 1970, 200 Motels, 1971, Blindman, 1972, Sextette, 1978, others. Decorated Order Brit. Empire; recipient numerous Grammy awards with Beatles. Address: care Portrait Records 51 W 52d St New York NY 10019

STARR, ROBERT M(ORTON), food co. exec.; b. Bklyn., Mar. 11, 1928; s. Jacob and Lydia (Rottenberg) S.; B.A., U. Pa., 1948; m. Barbara Barron, Oct. 28, 1972; children—Ian M., Susan R. Trainee, exec. tng. program Sears, Roebuck & Co., 1948-50; asst. mgr. R.U. Delapenha Co., 1950-51; with B. Manischewitz Co., Jersey City, 1951—, exec. v.p., 1972-77, pres., chief operating officer, 1977—, also dir. Mem. nat. governing council, v.p. N.J. region Am. Jewish Congress. Mem. Presidents Assn., Am. Mgmt. Assn. Office: 340 Henderson St Jersey City NJ 07302

STARR, ROSS MARC, economist; b. Oak Ridge, Nov. 14, 1945; s. Chauncey and Doris E. Starr; B.S., Stanford U., 1966, Ph.D., 1972; m. Susan S. Strauss, July 2, 1967; children—Daniel, Diana. Cons., Rand Corp., summers 1966, 67, Western Mgmt. Sci. Inst., Grad. Sch. Mgmt. UCLA, summers 1967, 71; Cowles Found. staff research economist Yale U., New Haven, 1970, faculty, 1970-74, asso. prof. econs., 1974; asso. prof. econs. U. Calif., Davis, 1975-76, prof. econs., 1976—; vis. lectr. London Sch. Econs., 1973-74; vis. scholar U. Calif., Berkeley, 1978—. NDEA fellow, 1966-69, Yale jr. faculty fellow, 1973-74, John Simon Guggenheim fellow, 1978-79; co-prin. investigator NSF grantee, 1979-81. Contbr. articles in field to profl. jours. Office: Econs Dept U Calif Davis CA 95616

STARR, STEVEN DAWSON, photographer; b. Albuquerque, Sept. 6, 1944; s. Richard Vernon and Carol (Harley) S.; student Antioch Coll., 1962-63, Bethel Coll., 1963-64; B.A., San Jose State Coll., 1967; m. Marilynne Sue Anderson, Aug. 6, 1965; 1 son, Stephen Richard. Photographer, San Jose (Calif.) Mercury-News, 1966-67; photographer, picture editor A.P., 1968-73; audiovisual producer, 1974—. Recipient Pulitzer prize spot news photography, 1970, Nat. Headliners award, 1970, George Polk Meml. award, 1970, Pictures of the Year hon. mention, 1970. Mem. Nat. Audiovisual Assn., Assn. for Multi-Image. Home: 256 Carlisle Dr Miami Springs FL 33166 Office: Starr Photo Prodns Inc 2727 Ponce de Leon Blvd Coral Gables FL 33134

STARR, WILMARTH HOLT, educator; b. Charleston, W.Va., Apr. 27, 1913; s. Charles Holt and Jessie (Wilmarth) S.; A.B., Wesleyan U., 1934; Ph.D., Johns Hopkins, 1937; m. Eva Jones, Dec. 27, 1937 (dec. Oct. 1974); children—Judith Lake, Gail Wheaton, Judson Wilmarth, Christopher Holt, Charles Holt; m. 2d, Nan Everhart, May 14, 1977. Instr. in Romance Languages, Bradley U., summer session, 1937; instr. U. Maine, 1937-41, asst. prof., 1941-44, asso. prof. and acting head dept. modern langs. and classics, 1946-47, prof. of Romance langs. and head dept. fgn. langs. and classics, 1947-61, mem. Grad. faculty, 1946-61, dir. summer Fgn. Lang. Inst., 1959, 60; head all-univ. dept. Romance and slavic langs., lits., N.Y. U., 1961-65, head all univ. dept. Romance langs. and lits., 1965-70, also prof. of Romance langs., dir. N.Y. U. Abroad, 1970-75, ann. prof., dir. studies N.Y. U. in France, 1975-76, univ. prof. emeritus, 1978—; mem. advisory bd. research and grad. edn. Rutgers U., 1969-72; dir. for U.S. for European U.S. Joint Institutes in France and Germany, 1966, 67. Chief edn. office Mutual Security Agy.; spl. tech. and econ. mission to Cambodia, Laos, Viet Nam, 1952-53; chmn. N.E. Conf. on Tchg. Fgn. Langs., 1964-65. Served lt. (j.g.) USNR, 1944, lt., 1946; staff Comdr. 7th Fleet, 1945-46. 1964. Decorated officer Ordre des Palmes Academiques; recipient Letter of Commendation from Comdr. Seventh Fleet; citation Wesleyan U., ann. award N.E. Conf. Teaching Fgn. Langs., 1976. Mem. Am. Assn. Tchrs. French (v.p. Maine chpt. 1950-52), Nat. Fedn. Modern Lang. Tchrs. (chmn. for Maine, Nat. Com. on the Place of Modern Langs. in Am. Edn., 1940-41; chmn. for Maine, Nat. Com. on Tng. and Placement of Modern Fgn. Lang. Tchr. 1951), Modern Lang. Assn. (dir. fgn. lang. testing program 1959-65), U.S. Power Squadrons (navigator), Phi Beta Kappa, Phi Kappa Phi, Sigma Nu. Co-author French and Spanish textbooks. Contbr. articles to profl. jours. Home: 19 Blackwell Pl Palm Coast FL 32037. *I think of each day as a total adventure with unlimited possibilities for growth, experience, and knowledge. I look upon my life's work as teacher, scholar, and educational administrator in the area of international studies as a continuing effort to increase my understanding of life, and as an opportunity to contribute, however modestly, to better understanding between all people.*

STARRS, JOHN RICHARD, lawyer; b. Detroit, Aug. 15, 1913; s. Thomas Charles and Nora Ellen (Command) S.; A.B., U. Detroit, 1934, J.D., 1938; m. Geraldine Leigh Poe, Sept. 26, 1948 (dec. Jan. 1950); 1 son, Thomas; m. 2d, Mabel Angeline Gilchrist, May 26, 1951; children—Mary, Elizabeth, William, Kathleen, Michael, Margaretta, John. Admitted to Mich. bar, 1938, U.S. Supreme Ct. bar, 1943; practiced in Detroit, 1938—; sr. partner Wurzer, Higgins & Starrs. Sec., dir. Traugott Schmidt & Sons; faculty U. Detroit Law Sch., 1949-65; Mich. corr. Selden Soc. Active as trained adult in scouting movement, 1959-66. Founder, past pres. Friends of U. Detroit Library; trustee Catholic Social Services of Wayne County. Served to lt. USNR, 1942-46. Mem. Am., Mich. (hearing panel grievance bd.), Detroit bar assns., Am. Arbitration Assn. (panel arbitrators), Alpha Sigma Nu. Roman Catholic. Contbr. articles profl. jours. Home: 1122 Kensington Rd Grosse Pointe Park MI 48230 Office: 1642 Buhl Bldg Detroit MI 48226

STARRY, DONN ALBERT, army officer; b. N.Y.C., May 31, 1925; s. Don Albert and Edith (Sortor) S.; B.S., U.S. Mil. Acad., 1948; M.S. in Internat. Affairs, George Washington U., 1966; m. Leatrice Hope Gibbs, June 15, 1948; children—Michael, Paul, Melissa, Melanie. Commd. 2d lt. U.S. Army, 1948, advanced through grades to gen., 1977; service in Europe, Korea and Vietnam; assigned Dept. Army Staff, 1970-72; comdr. Armor Center and Ft. Knox, Ky., 1973-76, V Corps, Europe, 1976-77, Tng. and Doctrine Command, Ft. Monroe, Va., 1977—. Decorated Silver Star, Bronze Star, Soldier's medal, Purple Heart, Legion of Merit. Mem. U.S. Armor Assn. Episcopalian. Address: Hdqrs USATRADOC Fort Monroe VA 23651

STARTUP, CHARLES HARRY, airline exec.; b. Middletown, N.Y., Feb. 24, 1914; s. Charles H. and Laura Beatrice (Langan) S.; A.B., Middlebury Coll., 1936; postgrad. U. Cin., 1937-39, m. Jane Butler Williams, June 26, 1942; children—Charles Alan, Ann Elizabeth, Thomas Andrew. Purchasing dept. City Cin., 1937-39; with Am. Airlines, N.Y.C., 1939-63, dist. sales mgr., Balt., 1948-50, Cin., 1950-56, San Francisco, 1956, asst. v.p. customer service, N.Y.C., 1957-59, v.p. passenger sales and service, 1959-61, v.p. passenger sales, 1961-63, mgr. passenger sales, 1964-72, dir. passenger sales planning, 1972-73, dir. consumer relations, dir. admiralty bd., 1973—; v.p. mktg. Nat. Car Rental System, 1963-64. Mem. N.Y. Sales Execs., Sales and Mktg. Execs., Newcomen Soc., Cin. Sales Execs. Council (pres. 1955), Soc. Consumer Affairs Profls. (dir.), Chi Psi. Clubs: Theodore, Marco Polo, Skal (N.Y.C.). Home: 276 1st Ave New York NY 10009 Office: 633 3d Ave New York NY 10017

STARYK, STEVEN, violinist; b. Toronto, Ont., Can., Apr. 28, 1932; s. Peter and Mary (Staryk) S.; student Royal Conservatory Music, Toronto, 1942-48, Harbord Collegiate Inst., 1945-48; m. Ida Elizabeth Busch, May 17, 1963; 1 dau., Natalie Elizabeth. Soloist, concertmaster CBC, 1951-55; concertmaster, soloist Royal Philharmonic Orch., London, Eng., also tchr. and performer chamber music, 1956-59; 1st concertmaster Concertgebouw Orch., Amsterdam, Holland, also prof. Amsterdam Conservatory, 1960-63; concertmaster Chgo. Symphony Orch., 1963-67; prof. violin Oberlin Coll. Conservatory, 1968-72; dir. string dept. Community Music Sch. Greater Vancouver, also vis. prof. violin U. Victoria, from 1972, U. Ottawa; now on faculty Royal Conservatory Music, Toronto, U. Western Ont., London; organizer Quartet Canada; appeared as soloist major European orchs., also recitals, broadcasts, recordings; tchr. Am. Conservatory, Chgo.; vis. prof. violin Northwestern U., 1965-66; solo recs. on EMI-HMV, Everest, Baroque, Virtuoso, RCA, Mus. Heritage Soc., Orion, Columbia, Disque Select, Umbrella, Radio Can. Broadcast Rec. Masters of Bow Hist. Series, Historic Rec. Soc. labels. Recipient numerous awards; Can. Council grantee. Address: 41 Foursome Crescent Willowdale ON Canada

STARZINGER, VINCENT EVANS, educator; b. Des Moines, Jan. 12, 1929; s. Vincent and Genevieve (Evans) S.; A.B. summa cum laude, Harvard, 1950, LL.B., 1954, Ph.D., 1959; A.M. (hon.), Dartmouth, 1968; m. Mildred Hippee Hill, June 16, 1953; children—Page Hill, Evans. Admitted to Ia. bar, 1954; practice with firm Bannister, Carpenter, Ahlers & Cooney, Des Moines, 1954; teaching fellow, then instr. govt. Harvard, 1957-60; faculty Dartmouth, 1960—, prof. govt., 1967—, chmn. dept., 1972-77, Joel Parker prof. law and polit. sci., 1976—. Served with AUS, 1955-56. Sheldon traveling fellow, 1950-51; Social Sci. Research Council fellow, 1958-59; Dartmouth faculty fellow, 1963-64; Am. Philos. Soc. award and Earhart Found. fellow, 1970-71. Mem. Am. Polit. Sci. Assn., Am., Iowa bar assns. Phi Beta Kappa. Author: Middlingness: Juste Milieu Political Theory in England and France, 1815-48, 1965; also articles. Clubs: American, Canadian Alpine; Cambridge (Mass.) Boat; Wellington (London). Home: Elm St Norwich VT 05055 Office: Dept Govt Dartmouth Hanover NH 03755

STARZL, THOMAS EARL, physician, educator; b. Le Mars, Iowa, Mar. 11, 1926; s. Roman F. and Anna Laura (Fitzgerald) S.; B.A., Westminster Coll., 1947, D.Sc. (hon.), 1965; M.A., Northwestern U., 1950, Ph.D., 1952, M.D., 1952; D.Sc. (hon.), N.Y. Med. Coll., 1970; LL.D., U. Wyo., 1971, Westmar Coll., 1974; m. Barbara Brothers, Nov. 27, 1954 (div.); children—Timothy, Rebecca, Thomas. Faculty, Northwestern U. Med. Sch., 1958-61; faculty U. Colo. Med. Sch., Denver, 1962—, prof. surgery, 1964—, chmn. dept., 1972—; mem. staffs Colo. Gen., Denver VA hosps. Recipient award Westminster Coll., 1965, Achievement award Lund U. 1965; Eppinger award Soc. Internat. de Chirurgie, 1965, Freiburg award, 1970; William S. Middleton award for outstanding research in VA system, 1968; Merit award Northwestern U., 1969; Distinguished Achievement award Modern Medicine, 1969; Creative Council award U. Colo., 1971; Colo. Man of Year award, 1967; Brookdale award AMA, 1974; David Hume Meml. award Nat. Kidney Found., 1978. Markle Scholar, 1958. Fellow A.C.S., Am. Acad. Arts and Scis.; mem. Soc. Univ. Surgeons, Soc. Vascular Surgery, Am. Surg. Assn., Transplantation Soc., Deutsche Gesellschaft für Chirurgie, numerous others. Author: Experience in Renal Transplantation, 1964; Experience in Hepatic Transplantation, 1969. Contbr. articles to profl. jours. Office: Dept Surgery U Colo Med Center 4200 E 9th Ave Denver CO 80262

STASACK, EDWARD ARMEN, artist; b. Chgo., Oct. 1, 1929; s. Clifford Clement and Elizabeth Frances (Mallek) S.; B.F.A. with high honors, U. Ill., Urbana, 1955, M.F.A., 1956; m. Mary Louise Walters, June 20, 1953 (div. 1972); children—Caren Marie, Jennifer Elizabeth, John Armen, Michael Clifford. Instr. in art U. Hawaii, 1956-61, prof. art, chmn. dept. art, 1969-72, program chmn. in printmaking, 1975-77; affiliate Downtown Gallery, N.Y.C., 1960-70; one-man shows: Honolulu Acad. Arts, 1961, 66, 69, 76, U.S. embassies, Istanbul and Izmir, Turkey, 1976, Am. Cultural Center, Bucharest,

Rumania, 1976, Cleve. Inst. Art, 1976, Hilo (Hawaii) Coll. Gallery, 1976, Amfac Plaza Gallery, 1978; group shows include: Carnegie Inst., Pitts., 1964, Krakow (Poland) Biennial, 1966, 68, Smithsonian Inst., Washington, 1967, Mexico City Mus. Modern Art, 1968, Leicester Gallery, London, 1965; represented in permanent collections: Honolulu Acad. Arts, Hawaii State Found. Culture and the Arts, Library of Congress, Phila. Mus. Art, Boston Pub. Library; cons. Boise-Cascade, Annaehoomalu, Hawaii. Served with U.S. Army, 1952-54. Recipient numerous prizes, including: Boston Printmakers Mems. prize, 1967, Juror's awards Honolulu Printmakers, 1957, 58, 59, 62, 63, 66, 67, 68, 74, 77, Soc. Am. Graphic Artists prizes, 1956, 57, 61, 62, 63, 68, 73, 78; Tiffany Found. fellow, 1958, 62; Rockefeller Found. grantee, 1959; MacDowell Colony fellow, 1971, 75; Hawaii State and U.S. Bicentennial Commns. fellow, 1975. Mem. Soc. Am. Graphic Artists, Boston Printmakers, Am. Colorprint Soc., Hawaii Arts Council, Hawaii Artists League, Honolulu Printmakers. Author: (with J. Halley Cox) Hawaiian Petroglyphs, 1970. Home: 963 Holoholo St Kailua HI 96734 Office: 2535 The Mall Honolulu HI 96822

STASHOWER, ARTHUR LEWIS, lawyer; b. Cleve., Apr. 12, 1930; s. Joseph George and Tillie (Merlin) S.; A.B., U. Mich., 1951, J.D. with Distinction, 1953; m. Joy Schary, Sept. 1, 1957; children—Keren, Saul, David. Admitted to Mich. bar, 1953, Ohio bar, 1953, Calif. bar, 1956; practiced law Beverly Hills, Calif., 1957-64, Los Angeles, 1967—; asso. firm Kaplan, Livingston, Goodwin & Berkowitz, Beverly Hills, 1957-64; resident counsel 4-Star TV, 1960-63; with United Artists Corp., Los Angeles, 1964-65; v.p. Artists Agy. Corp., Los Angeles, 1966-67; mem. firm Sklar, Coben & Stashower, Inc., Los Angeles, 1974—. Exec. com. Pacific S.W. Anti-Defamation League, 1967-74. Community adv. counsel Roscomare Rd. Sch., 1970-73, pres., 1970-71; alternate sch. counsel Area D, 1973-74, chmn., 1974. Bd. dirs. Area D Alt. Sch. Found., 1974—, pres., 1974—. to lt., USCGR, 1953-57. Mem. Assn. Alt. Pub. Schs., State Bar Calif., Beverly Hills, Am. bar assns., Nat. Labor Panels Am. Arbitration Assn., Fed. Mediation and Conciliation Service, Los Angeles Copyright Soc. Home: 15470 Milldale Dr Los Angeles CA 90024 Office: 6399 Wilshire Penthouse Suite Los Angeles CA 90048

STASHOWER, MICHAEL DAVID, mfg. co. exec.; b. Cleve., July 15, 1926; s. Joseph G. and Tillie (Mirlevitz) S.; B.A., Cornell U., 1947, M.B.A., 1949; m. Gloria Goodstein, Oct. 29, 1950; children—Susan, Deborah, Jonathan. With Ford Motor Co., 1949-57; budget dir. Dodge div. Chrysler Corp., 1957-58, controller Dodge assembly plant, 1958-62; asst. controller Am. Machine & Foundry Co., 1962-67; comptroller Perkin-Elmer Corp., 1967-76, v.p., comptroller, 1976—. Served with USNR, 1944-46. Mem. Fin. Execs. Inst. Home: 14 Cardinal Ln Westport CT 06880 Office: Perkin-Elmer Corp Main Ave Norwalk CT 06852

STASSEN, HAROLD EDWARD, lawyer; b. West St. Paul, Minn., Apr. 13, 1907; s. William and Elsie (Mueller) S.; B.A., U. Minn., 1927, LL.B., 1929; LL.D., Hamline U., 1939, U. Pa., 1948, Princeton U., 1950; L.H.D., Temple U., 1949; m. Esther G. Glewwe, Nov. 14, 1929; children—Glen Harold, Kathleen Esther. Admitted to Minn. bar, 1929, U.S. Supreme Ct. bar, 1932, Pa. bar, 1950; began practice in South St. Paul; dist. and county atty. Dakota County, 1930-38; gov. Minn., 1938-45 (youngest gov. of any state in history U.S.); pres. U. Pa., 1948-53; dir. Mut. Security Adminstrn., 1953, Fgn. Ops. Adminstrn., 1953-55; dep. rep. U.S. on UN Disarmament Commn., 1955; spl. asst. to U.S. Pres., with cabinet rank to direct studies of U.S. and world disarmament, 1955-58; appointed one of U.S. dels. to San Francisco Conf. of UN, 1945, a signer of UN Charter; partner Stassen, Kostos & Mason, and predecessor, 1958—. Served on staff Admiral W. F. Halsey in South Pacific, 1943-45; apptd. asst. chief of staff, 1944. Awarded Legion of Merit and Bronze Star. Delivered Godkind lectures on Human Rights, Harvard U., 1946. Pres. Minn. Young Republicans and del. to Rep. Nat. Conv., 1936; temporary chmn. and keynoter Rep. Nat. Conv., 1940; chmn. Nat. Govs.'s Conf., 1940-42, also Council State Govts., 1940-41; candidate for Rep. Presdl. nomination, 1980. Selected as outstanding young man by Nat. Junior C. of C., 1939. Pres. Internat. Council Religious Edn., 1942-50; v.p. Nat. Council Chs., 1950-52, pres. Div. Christian Edn., 1952-54; nat. chmn. Brotherhood Week, NCCJ, 1946; pres. Am. Bapt. Conv., 1963-64; world chmn. World Law Days, 1965-67. Mem. Grey Friars, Sigma Alpha Epsilon, Delta Sigma Rho, Gamma Eta Gamma. Clubs: Masons, Shriners; Union League, Century (N.Y.C.); Rittenhouse (Phila.). Author: Where I Stand, 1947; (with Amos J. Peaslee) Man Was Meant to be Free, 1955; Proposed Rewriting and Modernizing UN Charter, 1978. Office: 2300 Two Girard Plaza Philadelphia PA 19102 also 33 E Wentworth Ave West Saint Paul MN 55118

STASZESKY, FRANCIS MYRON, utility co. exec.; b. Wilmington, Del., Apr. 16, 1918; s. Frank J. and Ruth (Jones) S.; B.S. in Mech. Engring., Mass. Inst. Tech., 1943, M.S. in Mech. Engring., 1943; m. Barbara F. Kearney, May 30, 1943; children—Francis Myron, John B., Barbara J., Faith A., Paul D. Mech. engr. Union Oil Co. Calif., Los Angeles, 1943-45; with E.I. duPont de Nemours Co., Wilmington, Del., 1946-48, joined Boston Edison Co., 1948, supervising engr. design and constrn., 1948-57, supt. engring. and constrn. dept., 1957-64, v.p., asst. to pres., 1964-67, exec. v.p., 1967-79, pres., chief operating officer, 1979—, dir., 1968—; dir. Shawmut Corp., Shawmut Bank Boston N.A. Fellow ASME; mem. IEEE, Engring. Soc. New Eng. (pres. 1961-62), Greater Boston C. of C. (exec. com., v.p.). Clubs: Engineers, Algonquin (Boston); Brae Burn Country. Office: 800 Boylston St Boston MA 02199

STATLAND, EDWARD MORRIS, lawyer; b. Washington, Aug. 20, 1932; s. Harry and Rebecca (Berman) S.; B.A., George Washington U., 1954, J.D. with honors, 1959; m. Pearl Axelrod, June 1, 1958; children—Stuart J., Carole Beth. Admitted to D.C. bar, 1959, Md. bar, 1959, since practiced in Washington and Md.; partner firm Statland & Zaslav, chartered; asst. corp. counsel D.C., 1960-62. Dir. Bank of Columbia, N.A., Washington. Bd. dirs. Hebrew Home Greater Washington, Rockville, Md. Served with AUS, 1954-56. Mem. Am., Md., Montgomery County (Md.) bar assns., Bar Assn. D.C., Assn. Plaintiffs' Trial Attys., Am. Judicature Soc. Home: 6 Windermere Ct Rockville MD 20852 Office: 1101 17th St NW Washington DC 20036 also 4 Courthouse Sq Rockville MD

STAUB, AUGUST WILLIAM, educator; b. New Orleans, Oct. 9, 1931; s. August Harry and Laurel (Elfer) S.; B.A., La. State U., 1952, M.A., 1956, Ph.D., 1960; m. Patricia Gebhardt, Nov. 22, 1952; 1 dau., Laurel Melicent. Instr., tech. dir. Univ. Theatre, La. State U., 1955; instr., scene designer Eastern Mich. U., 1956-58; asso. dir. Dunes Summer Theatre, Michigan City, Ind., summers 1957-60; asst. prof., asso. dir. Univ. Theatre, U. Fla., 1960-64; asso. prof. U. New Orleans, 1964-66, prof., chmn. dept. drama and communications, 1966-76; prof., head dept. drama U. Ga., 1976—. Asso. editor Speech Tchr., 1966-68; exec. sec. Theatres of La.; v.p. New Orleans Internat. Jazz Festival, 1967-69; pres. S.W. Theatre Conf., 1973-74. Bd. dirs. Council Arts for Children, New Orleans, New Orleans Center Creative Arts. Served to lt. AUS, 1952-54. La. State U. Found. Distinguished Faculty fellow, 1970-71. Mem. Speech Assn. Am. (legis. assembly 1967-69), S.W. Theatre Conf. (pres. 1973-74), Am. Theatre Assn. (dir.), Inst. Theatre Tech., Speech Communication Assn., So. Speech Communication Assn., La. Council Music and Performing Arts, Univ. and Coll. Theatre Assn. (pres. 1974-75), Univ. Resident Theatre Assn., Nat. Council Theatre and Humanities. Author: Lysistrata, 1968; The Social Climber, 1969; A Small Bare Space, 1970; Introduction to Theatrical Arts, 1971; Creating Theatre, 1973; Media and the Small Budget, 1974. Asso. editor So. Speech Communication Jour., 1974-77, Quar. Jour. Speech, 1977—. Home: 400 Ponderosa Dr Athens GA 30605. *How good it is to be able to earn a living doing what one loves to do!*

STAUB, E. NORMAN, banker; b. Newark, Mar. 13, 1916; s. Walter Adolph and Ida (Flury) S.; A.B., Princeton, 1937; M.B.A., Harvard, 1939; m. Mary Ann Dilley, Dec. 28, 1940; children—Susan D., Sandra L. (Mrs. Richard F. Bradbury), Stephen R. Jr. accountant Lybrand Ross Bros. & Montgomery, Boston, 1939-41; treas. Nat. Research Corp., Cambridge, Mass., 1942-53; with No. Trust Co., Chgo., 1953—, became sr. v.p., 1967, now vice-chmn.; dir. U.S. Gypsum Co. Bd. dirs. Chgo. Nursery and Half Orphan Asylum, 1963—; trustee Better Govt. Assn., Mus. Sci. and Industry, Rush-Presbyn.-St. Luke's Med. Center, Orchestral Assn. Chgo.; mem. citizens bd. U. Chgo.; trustee Northwestern U., 1978—. Mem. Am. Inst. Banking, Am. Bankers Assn., Assn. Res. City Bankers, Chgo. Council on Fgn. Relations (vice chmn. bd.). Republican. Mem. Glencoe Union Ch. (treas., dir. 1964-67). Clubs: Princeton (N.Y.C.); Chicago, Econ., Comml., Mid-Am. (Chgo.); Indian Hill (Winnetka, Ill.); Old Elm (Ft. Sheridan). Home: 135 Sheridan N Winnetka IL 60093 Office: 50 S LaSalle St Chicago IL 60690

STAUBACH, ROGER THOMAS, football player; b. Cin., Feb. 5, 1942; s. Robert Joseph and Elizabeth (Smyth) S.; student Roswell (N.Mex.) Mil. Inst., 1960-61; B.S., U.S. Naval Acad., 1965; m. Marianne Jeanne Hoobler, Sept. 4, 1965; children—Jennifer Anne, Michelle Elizabeth, Stephanie Marie. Quarterback, Dallas Cowboy Football Team, 1969—; asst. v.p. Henry S. Miller Co., 1970—; spl. advisor to pres. Aurora, toys and games. Bd. dirs. Jesuit High Sch., Paul Anderson Youth Home, Salvation Army. Served from ensign to lt. USNR, 1965-69. Recipient Heisman Trophy, 1963; played ProBowl, 1971, 76, 78. Mem. Fellowship of Christian Athletes (dir.). Roman Catholic. Author: First Down, Lifetime to Go, 1974. Office: 6116 N Central Expy Dallas TX 75206*

STAUDENBAUR, CRAIG ANTHONY, educator, philosopher; b. Mt. Lake, Minn., Nov. 21, 1932; s. William P. and Wilhelmina Carolina (Diger) S.; B.A., U. S.D., 1954; M.A., Brandeis U., 1956; Ph.D., Johns Hopkins, 1961; m. Marjorie Ann Berridge, Aug. 21, 1957; children—Karl, Lorelei, Heidi. Instr., then asst. prof. philosophy and humanities Reed Coll., Portland, Oreg., 1959-62; mem. faculty Mich. State U., East Lansing, 1962—, prof. philosophy, 1972—, chmn. dept., 1977—. A.O. Lovejoy fellow, 1956-59. Mem. Am. Philos. Assn., Phi Beta Kappa. Contbr. articles to profl. jours. Home: 954 Lilac Ave East Lansing MI 48823

STAUDER, WILLIAM VINCENT, seismologist, educator, univ. dean; b. New Rochelle, N.Y., Apr. 23, 1922; s. William P. and Margaret (Boll) S.; A.B., St. Louis U., 1943, M.S. in Physics, 1948; S.T.L., St. Mary's (Kans.) Coll., 1953; Ph.D. in Geophysics, U. Calif. at Berkeley, 1959. Joined Soc. of Jesus, 1939, ordained priest Roman Catholic Ch., 1952; faculty St. Louis U., 1959—, prof. geophysics, 1966—, chmn. dept. earth and atmospheric scis., 1972-75, acting dean Grad. Sch., 1974-75, dean Grad. Sch., 1975—, dir. univ. research, 1975—, rector Jesuit Community at univ., 1967-73. Trustee Marquette U., 1978—. Fellow Am. Geophys. Union; mem. Seismol. Soc. Am. (bd. dirs. 1962-68, pres. 1965, chmn. Eastern sect. 1964), Soc. Exploration Geophysicists, Phi Beta Kappa, Sigma Xi. Contbr. articles to profl. jours. Home: 3601 Lindell Blvd St Louis MO 63108

STAUDERMAN, BRUCE FORD, advt. agy. exec.; b. Jersey City, Mar. 17, 1919; b. Herbert Henry and Helen Ann (Jacobus) S.; student Syracuse U., 1936-38, TV Workshop, N.Y.C., 1949-50, Sch. TV Technique, 1950; m. Claude Outhier, Mar. 23, 1946. Radio, TV program writer: The Big Story, Columbia Workshop, Captain Video, House of Mystery, 1946-51; writer, producer, dir. WXEL-TV, Cleve., 1951-54; v.p. TV, radio, films Meldrum & Fewsmith, Inc., advt. agy., Cleve., 1954-62, exec. v.p., chmn. plans bd., exec. creative dir., 1973—; v.p., creative dir. Ogilvy & Mather, advt. agy., N.Y.C., 1962-69, Kenyon & Eckhardt, Inc., advt. agy., N.Y.C., 1979—; dir. TV, advt. cons. Intermarco-Elvinger, advt. co., Paris, 1969-73; TV cons. gov. Ohio, 1958; council mem., judge C.L.I.O. Festival, 1960—, chmn. Paris jury, 1969-73; jury mem. Internat. Advt. Film Festival, Cannes, Venice, 1976—. Mem. men's com. Cleve. Playhouse, 1958-62; chmn. TV com. Cleve. United Fund, 1958-59. Served from pvt. to 2d lt. AUS, 1941-46; to 1st lt. N.G. Essex Troop AUS, 1948-50. Mem. Am. Assn. Advt. Agys. (TV and radio adminstrs. com. 1958-62). Club: Cleve. Skating. Home: 80 Broadview Ave New Rochelle NY 10804 Office: 1220 Huron Rd Cleveland OH 44115

STAUDTER, GEORGE F., cosmetics co. fin. exec.; b. N.Y.C., Oct. 17, 1931; s. Clement and Anna (Aulbach) S.; B.B.A., Adelphi U., 1962; postgrad. N.Y. U., 1970-72; m. Cherrill Rusk, Aug. 18, 1978; children—Kurt, Thomas, Robert. With Arthur Andersen & Co., 1962-67, 70-72; asst. controller Sylvania Electric Co., 1967-70; v.p. fin. Worthington Pump Co., 1972-73; v.p., gen. auditor CBS, 1973-77; v.p., treas. Revlon Inc., N.Y.C., 1977—. Served with USMC, 1950-54. Decorated Air medal; C.P.A. Mem. Am. Inst. C.P.A.'s., N.Y. State Soc. C.P.A.'s, Fin. Exec. Inst. (trustee). Roman Catholic. Clubs: N.Y. Athletic, Seaview Country, Water Gap Country. Home: Mount Bethel PA 18343 Office: 767 Fifth Ave New York NY 10022

STAUFFACHER, CHARLES B., pub. co. exec.; b. Karuizawa, Japan, July 13, 1916; s. Albert Daniel and Anna Dorothy (Marty) S.; came to U.S., 1916; student Lingnan U., Canton, China, 1935-36; A.B., Pomona Coll., 1937; A.M., Am U., 1938; A.M., Harvard, 1940; m. Lillian Frances Moss, Dec. 27, 1941; children—Charles D., Lillian S. Gillies. Research asst. Brookings Instn., 1940-41; with Bur. Budget, Washington, 1941-52, exec. asst. dir. bur., 1950-52, on leave as asst. to Dir. Def. Moblzn., 1951-52; lectr. George Washington U.; control officer Continental Can Co., 1952-54, v.p. finance, 1955-58, exec. v.p. paper products group, 1959-65, exec. v.p. finance and adminstrn., 1966-68, sr. exec. v.p., 1969-71, vice chmn., chief adminstrv. and financial officer, 1971-74; pres., chief exec. officer Field Enterprises, Inc., Chgo., 1974—; dir. Lumbermens Mut. Ins. Co., Kemper Corp., FMC, First Charter N.Y., Nat. Blvd. Bank, Chgo., Firestone Tire & Rubber Co., U.S. Gypsum. Trustee Pomona Coll., Com. for Econ. Devel.; bd. dirs. Internat. Exec. Service Corps. Served as lt. USNR, 1943-46. Mem. Am. Mgmt. Assn., Nat. Acad. Pub. Adminstrn., N.Y., Chgo. councils fgn. relations, Phi Beta Kappa. Clubs: Glen View (Ill.) Country; Tavern, Chicago (Chgo.); Greenwich (Conn.) Country; Economic (N.Y.C.); Augusta Nat. Golf; Jupiter Hills Golf. Home: 46 Meadowview Ln Northfield IL 60093 Office: 401 N Wabash Chicago IL 60611

STAUFFER, CHARLES HENRY, educator; b. Harrisburg, Pa., Apr. 17, 1913; s. Charles C. and Hannah (Henry) S.; A.B., Swarthmore Coll., 1934; M.A., Harvard, 1936, Ph.D., 1937; m. Eleanor Ramsdell, July 8, 1939; children—Charles R., Anne Elizabeth, John E. Instr., Worcester (Mass.) Poly. Inst., 1937-43, asst. prof., 1943-52, asso. prof., 1952-58; asso. prof. affiliate Clark U., Worcester, 1941; prof., chmn. dept. chemistry St. Lawrence U., Canton, N.Y., 1958-65; prof. chemistry, chmn. div. natural scis. Bates Coll., Lewiston, Maine, 1965—, Charles A. Dana prof. chemistry, 1968-77, prof. emeritus, 1977—. Dir. chem. kinetics data project Nat. Acad. Scis., 1954-64, mem. adv. com. Office Critical Constants, 1961-64. Fellow AAAS, Am. Chem. Soc. (sec., chmn. No. N.Y. sect., councilor Maine sect.); mem. AAUP, Sigma Xi. Mason. Club: Northport Yacht. Home: 10 Champlain Ave Lewiston ME 04240

STAUFFER, HANS, corp. exec.; b. Germany, 1901; D.Sc. (hon.), Central Coll., 1964; m. Virginia Deimel, 1928 (dec.); children—John E., Patricia Stauffer Benson; m. 2d, Eunice Bennett von Reischach, 1976. Past pres., dir. Stauffer Chem. Co., N.Y.C.; dir. Anderson Devel. Co., Adrian, Mich., MCA, SRS, Inc., Linden, N.J. Sr. mem. Nat. Indsl. Conf. Bd. Decorated insignia, comdr.'s cross German Order Merit (Fed. Republic Germany); recipient 27th Chem. Industry medal Am. sect. Soc. Chem. Industry. Mem. German Am. C. of C. (dir.), Am. Bible Soc. (bd. mgrs.). Clubs: Pinnacle, Links (N.Y.C.); Bohemian (San Francisco); Burlingame Country (Hillsborough, Calif.); Am. Yacht (Rye, N.Y.); Siwanoy Country, Bronxville Field (Bronxville). Home: 5 Courseview Rd Bronxville NY 10708

STAUFFER, OSCAR STANLEY, editor, pub.; b. Hope, Kans., Nov. 26, 1886; s. Solomon Engle and Elizabeth (Conrad) S.; student U. Kans., 1908-10; m. Ethel Lucille Stone, Sept. 7, 1914 (dec. July 1964); children—Betty Stauffer Collinson, Stanley Howard, John Herbert; m. 2d, Cornelia Hardcastle, Conwell, July 15, 1965 (dec. July 1973). Reporter, Emporia Gazette, 1906-08, Kansas City (Mo.) Star, 1910-15; editor, owner Peabody (Kans.) Gazette, 1915-24; editor Arkansas City (Kans.) Traveler, 1924-40; editor, pub. Topeka State Jour. and Topeka Daily Capital; chmn. bd., exec. head Stauffer Publs., pubs. Ark. City Daily Traveler, Pittsburg (Kans.) Morning Sun, Grand Island (Nebr.) Daily Ind., Beatrice (Nebr.) Daily Sun, Maryville (Mo.) Daily Forum, Shawnee (Okla.) News & Star, Nevada (Mo.) Daily Mail, York (Nebr.) News Times, Newton (Kans.) Kans., Independence (Mo.) Examiner, Capper's Weekly, Marshall (Mo.) Democrat News, Brookings (S.D.) Register, Glenwood Springs (Colo.) Post, Hillsdale (Mich.) Daily News, Hannibal (Mo.) Courier-Post; pres. KGFF Broadcasting Co., Shawnee. Okla., WIBW-TV, AM-FM, Topeka, KGNC AM-FM, Amarillo, Tex., KSOK Broadcasting Co., Arkansas City, KRNT-AM-FM, Des Moines; former v.p. A.P. Trustee Washburn U., Menninger Found. Former chmn. Kan. Indsl. Devel. Commn., Kans. State Bd. Regents; past pres. Inland Daily Press Assn. Mem. Am. Soc. Newspaper Editors, Beta Theta Pi, Sigma Delta Chi. Republican. Presbyterian. Clubs: Topeka Country, Scottsdale (Ariz.) Villa Monterey, Rotary. Home: 1320 W 27th St Apt 6-44 Topeka KS 66611 Office: 6th and Jefferson Topeka KS 66607

STAUFFER, PAUL STEPHEN, clergyman; b. Norwood, Ohio, Sept. 5, 1915; s. Clarence Roy and Cora (Coriell) S.; A.B., Transylvania Coll., 1936, D.D., 1954; B.D., Lexington Theol. Sem., 1938; m. Peggy Anne Fowler, Apr. 1, 1938; children—Robert Stephen, William Roy, Paul David. Ordained to ministry Christian Ch., 1933; minister in Maysville, Ky., 1935-38, Clinton, Mo., 1938-41, St. Louis, 1941-43, Franfort, Ky., 1943-54, Louisville, 1954-66, Northwood Christian Ch., Indpls., 1966—. Chmn. bd. dirs. Council Christian Unity, Disciples of Christ Ch., 1964-70, del. to consultation ch. union, 1965—; mem. gen. bd. Nat. Council Chs., 1966-72; pres. Ky. Assn. Christian Chs., 1950, 63, Louisville Area Council Chs., 1958-59; mem. interfaith panel Moral Side of News, sta. WHAS, Louisville, 1963-66; del. 4th Assembly World Council Chs., Sweden, 1968; bd. mem. Ind. Inter-religious Commn. on Human Equality, 1971—; v.p. Ind. Council Chs., 1975-76, pres., 1976—; mem. Disciples of Christ-Roman Cath. 5-year Internat. Commn. for Dialogue, Rome, 1978. Mem. Frankfort Sch. Bd., 1950-53; pres. Frankfort chpt. ARC, 1945; trustee Lexington Theol. Sem., 1944—, chmn. exec. com., 1948-55; trustee Christian Theol. Sem., 1973—, chmn. bd., 1976—. Mem. Pi Kappa Alpha. Club: Rotary. Home: 6124 Brokenhurst Rd Indianapolis IN 46220 Office: 4550 Central Ave Indianapolis IN 46205

STAUFFER, ROBERT ALLEN, research co. exec.; b. Dayton, Ohio, Jan. 26, 1920; s. John G. and Verna G. (Theobald) S.; B.A. in Chemistry, Harvard, 1942; m. Justine M. Wells, Mar. 20, 1943 (div. 1969); children—Susan, Nancy; m. 2d, Ruth Stanley Munro, Oct. 30, 1969. With Nat. Research Corp., Cambridge, 1942-67, gen. mgr. research div., 1949-63, dir., 1954-67, v.p., 1949-67, with Norton Co., Worcester, Mass., 1963-71, v.p. research, 1963-71; v.p., gen. mgr. Norton Research Corp., Cambridge, 1968-71; v.p. NRC Metals Corp., 1955-56; v.p. Environ. Research and Tech., Concord, Mass., 1971—. Mem. Am. Mgmt. Assn., Am. Chem Soc. Clubs: Harvard, Boston Research Dirs. (chmn. 1966-67). Patentee in field. Home: RFD 1 102 Wading Place Rd Mashpee MA 02649 Office: 696 Virginia Rd Concord MA 01742

STAUFFER, SARAH ANN, former mem. Republican Nat. Com.; b. Lancaster, Pa., June 13, 1915; d. Charles F. and Gertrude (Frantz) Stauffer; student Franklin and Marshall Coll., 1957-58, U. Pa., 1958-60. Office mgr. aircraft div. Armstrong Cork Co., 1941-43; mem., then capt. 45th div. Clubmobile unit ARC, 1945; dir. personnel and operations U.S. Occupied Ty. ETO Clubmobile div., 1946; bd. dirs. Lancaster (Pa.) chpt. ARC, 1947-51, treas., 1949-51; past mem. bd. Lancaster Symphony Assn.; mem. exec. com. Pa. Health Council, 1954-55; del.-at-large Community Chest Council, 1958-72; regional dir. Assn. Jr. Leagues Am., 1951-55, treas., 1955-57; del. gov.'s conf. White House Conf. on Children and Youth, 1960; del. to U.S. Dept. Labor Women's Bur. Nat. Conf., 1970. Mem. bd. Young Republicans of Pa., 1937-39, 45-47; mem. Rep. Nat. Com. for Pa., 1964-74; exec. com. Rep. Nat. Com., 1964-68; mem. bd. Pa. Council Rep. Women, 1957—; alt. del. Rep. Nat. Conv., 1960, del.-at-large, 1964, 68, 72. Commonwealth com. Med. Coll. Pa., pres. Commonwealth Bd., 1973-75, exec. com. nat. bd., 1979—; bd. visitors Franklin-Marshall Coll., 1972—; sec. Pa. Electoral Coll., 1972. Named Disting. Dau. of Pa., 1965; mem. Legion of Honor-Chapel of Four Chaplains, 1979. Asso. Acad. Polit. and Social Sci., Acad. Polit. Sci. Clubs: Colony (N.Y.C.); Acorn (Phila.); Soroptimist, Bus./Profl. Women (Lancaster, Pa.). Home: Lime Spring Farm Rohrerstown PA 17603

STAUFFER, STANLEY HOWARD, newspaper and broadcasting exec.; b. Peabody, Kans., Sept. 11, 1920; s. Oscar S. and Ethel L. (Stone) S.; A.B., U. Kans., 1942; m. Suzanne R. Wallace, Feb. 16, 1945 (div. 1961); children—Peter, Clay, Charles; m. 2d, Elizabeth D. Priest, July 14, 1962; children—Elizabeth, Grant. Asso. editor Topeka State Jour., 1946-47; editor, pub. Santa Maria (Calif.) Times, 1948-52; rewrite, copy editor Denver Post, 1953-54; staff mem. AP, Denver bur., 1954-55; exec. v.p. Stauffer Publs., Inc., 1955-69; gen. mgr. Topeka Capital-Jour., 1957-69; pres. Stauffer Communications, Inc., 1969—; mem. adv. bd. UPI; dir. Yellow Freight System, Inc., 1st Nat. Bank Topeka, Home Nat. Bank, Arkansas City, Newspaper Advt. Bur., Kans. Devel. Credit Corp., So. Prodn. Program, Inc. Past pres. William Allen White Found., Topeka YMCA; past chmn. adv. bd. St. Francis Hosp.; vice chmn. Met. Topeka Airport Authority; trustee Midwest Research Inst. Served as officer USAAF, 1943-45. Named Chpt. Boss of Year, Am. Bus. Women's Assn., 1976; Legion of Honor, De Molay, Topeka Phi of Year, 1971. Mem. Kans. (past pres.), Inland Daily press assns., Air Force Assn. (past pres. Topeka), Kans. U.

Alumni Assn., Phi Delta Theta (past chpt. pres.), Sigma Delta Chi (past chpt. pres.). Episcopalian (vestryman, fin. chmn). Clubs: Topeka Country, Topeka Town, Topeka Press (past pres.) (Topeka). Home: 2801 MacVicar Ave Topeka KS 66611 Office: Stauffer Communications Inc 6th and Jefferson Sts Topeka KS 66607

STAUFFER, THOMAS GEORGE, hotel exec.; b. Akron, Ohio, Mar. 4, 1932; s. Caldwell E. and Rose C. (Ortcheidt) S.; B.S., Case Western Res. U., 1954; m. Lois Campsey, June 18, 1960. Pres., Stouffer Hotels, also dir., exec. v.p. Stouffer Corp., Cleve., 1955—. Trustee Ashland Coll., Cuyahoga Community Coll. Recipient Legion of Honor, Order of DeMolay. Mem. Am. Hotel and Motel Assn. (adv. council), Nat. Restaurant Assn. (dir.). Clubs: Masons, Shriners; Cleve. Athletic, Clevelander. Home: 1044 Roy St Lakewood OH 44107 Office: 29800 Bainbridge Rd Solon OH 44139

STAUFFER, WILLIAM ALBERT, telephone co. exec.; b. Maryville, Mo., June 9, 1930; s. Marion W. and Louise (Manglesdorf) S.; B.J., U. Mo., 1952; m. Jean VanSlyck Shanley, Apr. 11, 1953; children—Rebecca, John, Rachel. Gen. mgr. York (Nebr.) Daily News-Times, 1955-61, Grand Island (Nebr.) Daily Ind., 1961-63; with Northwestern Bell Telephone Co., 1963—, sec.-treas., 1970-72, v.p., chief exec. officer, Fargo, N.D., 1972-74, v.p., chief exec. officer-Iowa, Des Moines, 1974—; dir. Iowa-Des Moines Nat. Bank, Nat. By-Products, Inc., Des Moines, Stauffer Communications, Inc., Topeka. Pres. Convalescent Home Children, Des Moines, 1969; v.p. Mid-Iowa council Boy Scouts Am.; pres. Regional Health Care Corp., Omaha, 1971; mem. adv. bd. Mercy Hosp., Des Moines. Bd. dirs., sec. Omaha Symphony Orch. Assn. 1970, Iowa Coll. Found., Des Moines Symphony Orch. Assn., YMCA, Des Moines; bd. dirs. Blue Shield Iowa, Living History Farms. Served with USAF, 1952-54. Mem. C. of C. Des Moines (dir.), Greater Des Moines Com., Phi Delta Theta. Clubs: Wakonda, Des Moines. Home: 4916 Harwood Dr Des Moines IA 50312 Office: 909 High St Des Moines IA 50309

STAVE, THOMAS CLIFFORD, fgn. service officer; b. Arlington, Wash., May 31, 1920; s. Thomas and Clara M. (Hyldahl) S.; B.A., U. Wash., 1943; postgrad. George Washington U., 1946, U. Wash., 1947, Naval War Coll., 1966-67; m. Virginia Irene Searing, Oct. 2, 1945; children—Linda Lorraine (Mrs. Douglas Berg), Alan Bradford, Margaret Louise, Thomas Eric, Juanita Marie. Fgn. service officer, 1950—; assigned to Hesse, Germany, 1950-52, Marseille, France, 1952-55, Washington, 1955-58, Bonn, Germany, 1958-61, Tehran, Iran, 1961-66, Washington, 1967-68, Tokyo, 1968-72; comml. attache Am. embassy, Bangkok, Thailand, 1972-76; comml. counselor Am. embassy, Seoul, Korea, 1977—. Served to capt. AUS, 1943-46. Decorated Purple Heart. Mem. Am. Fgn. Service Assn. Presbyterian. Home: Rt 8 Box 8143 Bainbridge Island WA 98110 Office: American Embassy Seoul Korea

STAVER, LEROY BALDWIN, banker; b. Portland, Oreg., Oct. 1, 1908; s. Herbert LeRoy and Grace (Baldwin) S.; J.D., Northwestern Coll. Law, 1930; grad. Rutgers U. Grad. Sch. Banking, 1937-39; m. Helen M. Matschek, Oct. 16, 1937; 1 son, Roger. Admitted to Oreg. bar, 1929; with U.S. Nat. Bank of Oreg., 1925-74, asst. trust officer, 1936-42, trust officer, 1942-58, v.p., trust officer, 1958—, exec. trust officer, 1959-63, exec. v.p., exec. trust officer, 1963-66, pres., 1966-72, chmn., 1971-74, also dir.; chmn. Commerce Mortgage Co., 1967-74; dir. U.S. Bancorp. Trustee Med. Research Found. Oreg., pres., 1975-76; trustee Williamette U., U.S. Nat. Found., Oreg. Grad. Center for Study and Research; bd. dirs., treas. Western Forestry Center; trustee, v.p. St. Vincent Med. Found. Mem. Am., Oreg. bar assns., C. of C. (pres. 1975), Delta Theta Phi. Clubs: Arlington, Waverley Country, Rotary. Home: 9908 SE Cambridge Ln Portland OR 97222 Office: PO Box 4412 Portland OR 97208

STAVITSKY, ABRAM BENJAMIN, educator, immunologist; b. Newark, May 14, 1919; s. Nathan and Ida (Novak) S.; A.B., U. Mich., 1939, M.S., 1940; Ph.D., U. Minn., 1943; V.M.D., U. Pa. 1946; m. Ruth Bernice Okney, Dec. 6, 1942; children—Ellen Barbara, Gail Beth. Research asst. Cal. Inst. Tech., 1946-47; faculty Case Western Res. U., 1947—, prof. microbiology, 1962—. Mem. expert com. immunochemistry WHO, 1963—; mem. microbiology fellowship com. NIH, 1963-66; mem. microbiology test com. Nat. Bd. Med. Examiners, 1970-73. Vice pres. Ludlow Community Assn., 1964-66. Fellow AAAS; mem. Am. Assn. Immunologists, Am. Soc. Microbioloby, Brit. Soc. Immunology, Sigma Xi. Home: 14604 Onaway Rd Shaker Heights OH 44120 Office: 2119 Abington Rd Cleveland OH 44106

STAVRAKY, GEORGE W., physiologist; b. Odessa, Russia, Feb. 19, 1905; s. Waldemar E. and Olga V. S.; came to Can., 1929, naturalized, 1935; M.D., U. Odessa, 1927; M.Sc., McGill U., Montreal, Que., Can., 1930, M.D., C.M., 1932; m. Marie-Maldelein Gabreille Lefebre; 1 son, Waldo K. Fellow, Montreal Neurol. Inst., 1932-35; demonstrator in physiology McGill U., 1935-36; asst. prof. physiology U. Western Ont., London, 1936-42, asso. prof., 1942-51, prof., 1951-70, prof. emeritus, 1970—; plastic and reconstructive surgeon. Fellow Royal Soc. Can.; mem. Am. Physiol. Soc., Can. Physiol. Soc. Author: Supersensitivity of the Central Nervous System, 1961; contbr. numerous articles on physiology of digestion, circulation, neurophysiology to profl. jours. Home: 250 Cheapside St London ON N6A 2A1 Canada Office: Faculty of Medicine U Western Ont London ON N5Y 2Y1 Canada

STAVROPOULOS, D(IONYSOS) JOHN, banker; b. Vicksburg, Miss., Jan. 19, 1933; s. John Dionysos and Olga (Balodemos) S.; B.S., Miss. State U., 1955; M.B.A., Northwestern U., 1956; m. Alexandra Gatzoyanni, Jan. 10, 1976; children—John, Theodore, Mark, Olga. With trust dept. First Nat. Bank of Chgo., 1956-69, internat. banking dept., 1970-76, sr. v.p. real estate dept., 1976-79, exec. v.p. comml. banking dept., 1979—; v.p., dir. research Bache & Co., N.Y.C., 1969-70; dir. Central Ill. Public Service Co.; mem. Real Estate Adv. Council. Served with U.S. Army, 1951-53. Mem. Mortgage Bankers Assn. Am., Investment Analysts Soc., Res. City Bankers Assn. (mem. Chgo. com.), Chgo. Am. Hellenic Ednl. Progressive Assn. Greek Orthodox. Office: One First Nat Plaza Chicago IL 60670

STAW, HAROLD, retail store exec.; b. Newark, Sept. 4, 1917; s. Adolph and Sara (Soffer) S.; student U. Calif. at Los Angeles, 1934-35; m. Charlotte Shirley Posner, Dec. 29, 1940; children—Nancy Lee (Mrs. Glenn Pollock), Barry Martin. Organizer, ABC Union Stores, 1952, pres. until 1961, co. merged with Sage Internat. Inc., pres., 1961—; pres. Riverside Union Stores, Inc., 1967—; exec. dir. Assn. Vol. Buyers, dealer owned appliance coop., 1975-78. Chmn., Reform Jewish Appeal financial drive Pomona Valley area, 1966; exec. chmn. State of Israel Bond drive Pomona Valley, 1967, chmn. bond dr., 1967-69; trustee So. Calif. Retail Clks. Union Trust Fund (chmn. 1970). Mem. Montclair C. of C. (pres. 1970, dir.). Jewish (dir. temple). Clubs: Kiwanis, B'nai B'rith. Home: 1566 Cabildo Circle Palm Springs CA 92262 Office: 1850 Greenfield Los Angeles CA 90025

STEA, DAVID, urban planner, educator; b. Bklyn., Dec. 12, 1936; s. Armand and Henriette (Lipsky) S.; B.S., Carnegie Inst. Tech., 1957; M.S., U. N.Mex., 1960; Ph.D. (NSF fellow), Stanford U., 1964. Human factors engr. Sandia Corp., Albuquerque, 1957-60; engring. psychologist Lockheed Missiles & Space Corp., Sunnyvale, Calif., 1961; asst. prof. geography and psychology Clark U., Worcester, Mass., 1967-69, asso. prof., 1969-71; asso. prof. architecture, urban design and planning U. Calif., Los Angeles, 1971-74, prof., 1974—; co-founder Miniversity, 1970; cons. Navajo Nation and Pima/Maricopa Salt River Community, 1974—. Community adv. Sawtelle Community area, Los Angeles, 1972-75. NSF grantee, 1961-64; Social Sci. Research Council grantee, 1966-67; Shell Found. grantee, 1969; U.S. Office Edn. grantee, 1968-71. Mem. AAAS, Sociedad Interamericana de Psicología, Sociedad Interamericana de Planificación, Environ. Design Research Assn., Sierra Club, Sigma Xi. Author: Environmental Mapping; co-author: Image and Environment; Maps in Minds; editorial bd. Environment and Behavior, 1969—, Human Ecology, 1971-76, Jour. Environ. Psychology and Non-Verbal Behavior, 1976—. Office: Sch Architecture and Urban Planning U Calif Los Angeles CA 90024

STEAD, EUGENE ANSON, JR., physician; b. Atlanta, Oct. 6, 1908; s. Eugene Anson and Emily (White) S.; B.S., Emory U., 1928, M.D., 1932; m. Evelyn Selby, June 15, 1940; children—Nancy White, Lucy Ellen, William Wallace. Med. intern Peter Bent Brigham Hosp., Boston, 1932-33, surg. intern, 1934-35, asso. medicine, 1939-42, acting physician-in-chief, 1942; research fellow medicine Harvard, 1933-34; asst. resident medicine Cin. Gen. Hosp., 1935-36, resident, 1936-37; instr. medicine U. Cin., 1935-37; resident phys. Thorndike Meml. Lab., asst. medicine Harvard and Boston City Hosp., 1937-39; instr. medicine Harvard, 1938-41, asso., 1941-42; prof. medicine Emory U., physician-in-chief Grady Hosp., Atlanta, 1942-46; dean Emory U., 1945-46; physician in chief Duke Hosp., 1947-67; prof. medicine Duke U. Sch. Medicine, 1947-78; distinguished physician VA, 1978—. Mem. N.C. Med. Soc., Am. Soc. Clin. Research, Assn. Am. Physicians, Alpha Omega Alpha, Sigma Xi, Phi Beta Kappa. Methodist. Editor, Circulation, 1973—. Contbr. numerous articles on various aspects of circulation to med. jours. Home: Route 1 Box 135 Clarksville VA 23927 Office: Dept Medicine Duke U Durham NC 27710

STEAD, WILLIAM WHITE, physician, educator, pub. health adminstr.; b. Decatur, Ga., Jan. 4, 1919; s. Eugene Anson and Emily (White) S.; A.B., Emory U., 1940, M.D., 1943; m. Ethel Barnett, June 14, 1947 (div.); children—Richard Barnett; m. 2d, Joan Jordan DeVore, Apr. 22, 1975. Intern Grady Meml. Hosp., Atlanta, 1944; resident in medicine Emory U., 1944-45, U. Cin., 1946-48, U. Minn., 1948-49, faculty med. schs. U. Minn., 1949-57, U. Fla., 1957-60; prof. medicine Med. Coll. Wis., Milw. County Gen. Hosp., Milw., 1960-72; med. dir. Muirdale Sanatorium, Milw., 1963-72; prof. medicine U. Ark. Med. Sch., 1972—; chief pulmonary diseases service VA Hosp., Little Rock, 1972-73, cons., 1973—; dir. Tb control Ark. Health Dept., Little Rock, 1973—. Cons. VA Hosp., Wood, Wis.; 1960-72. Served to lt. (j.g.) M.C., USNR, 1945-46; capt. M.C., AUS, 1953-54. Research grantee in pulmonary emphysema, 1957-65. Mem. Am. Fedn. for Clin. Research (nat. sec. 1955-58, v.p. 1958-59, pres. 1959-60), Central Soc. Clin. Research, Am. Soc. Clin. Investigation, Am. Thoracic Soc., Am. Coll. Chest Physicians, A.C.P., AAAS, N.Y. Acad. Sci. Author 2 books on Tb, also numerous articles. Designed improved spirometer for testing pulmonary function, 1955; research unitary concept Tb and epidemiology of Tb in prison and chemotherapy of Tb. Home: 1701 Westpark Dr Apt 89 Little Rock AR 72204 Office: State Health Dept 4815 W Markham Little Rock AR 72201

STEADMAN, CHARLES WALTERS, lawyer, corp. exec.; b. Falls City, Nebr., July 25, 1914; s. William Sherman and Marie (Walters) S.; A.B., U. Nebr., 1935; J.D., Harvard, 1938; m. Dorothy Marie Fawick, Feb. 14, 1942 (dec. Sept. 1974); children—Suzanne Louise (Mrs. Stanley O. Hoerr, Jr.) (dec.), Carole Elaine (Mrs. Jerome Frank Kinney III), Charles T.W., Dorothy Marie; m. 2d, Marjorie Tracy Lee, Oct. 10, 1977. Admitted to Ohio bar, 1939, D.C. bar, 1956; partner Marshman, Hornbeck, Hollington, Steadman & McLaughlin, Cleve., 1946-65, Steadman, Jones & Baxter, 1956-70; of counsel Marshman, Snyder & Seeley, Cleve., 1969—. Chmn. bd. St. Regis Hotel Corp., 1960-63; vice chmn. Leaseway Intercontinental, 1961-65; chmn. com. to end govt. waste Nat. Taxpayers Union, 1979; chmn. bd., pres. Steadman Security Corp., Oceanographic Tech. and and Growth Fund, Steadman Investment Fund, Steadman Money Market, Inc.; chmn. trustees, pres. Steadman Asso. Fund, Steadman Am. Industry Fund; pres., dir. Community Telecasters Cleve., chmn. bd., dir. United Securities, Inc.; chief counsel Select U.S. Senate Com., 1956. Bd. govs. Investment Co. Inst., 1969-72. Served as lt. col. AUS, World War II; chief counsel legal div. Cleve. Ordnance Dist. Recipient Distinguished Service award U. Neb., 1960. Mem. Internat., Am. (council corp., banking and bus. law 1956-60), Ohio, Cleve. bar assns., Ohio Bar, Bar Assn. D. C., Am. Law Inst., Am. Judicature Soc. Clubs: City Tavern, 1925 F Street, Georgetown, Internat. (Washington); Union (Cleve.); Beach; Everglades (Palm Beach, Fla.); Harvard, Metropolitan, Racquet and Tennis, Sky (N.Y.C.). Author: Steadman's Revision of the Ohio Civil Practice Manual, 1950; also legal and econ. articles. Editor: Charles W. Steadman Economic Review. Home: 315 S Lake Dr PH-A Palm Beach FL 33480 also 2500 Virginia Ave NW Washington DC 20037 Office: 1730 K St N W Washington DC 20006

STEADMAN, JACK W., profl. football exec.; b. Warrenville, Ill., Sept. 14, 1928; s. Walter Angus and Vera Ruth (Burkholder) S.; B.B.A., So. Methodist U., 1950; m. Martha Cudworth Steinhoff, Nov. 24, 1949; children—Thomas Edward, Barbara Ann, Donald Wayne. Accountant, Hunt Oil Co., Dallas, 1950-54; chief's accountant W.H. Hunt, Dallas, 1954-58; chief accountant Penrod Drilling Co., Dallas, 1958-60; gen. mgr. Dallas Texans Football Club, 1960-63; gen. mgr. Kansas City Chiefs Football Club, 1963-76, exec. v.p., 1966-76, pres., 1976—; pres. Mid-Am. Enterprises (Worlds of Fun), Kansas City, 1972—; v.p. First Fidelity Investment Trust, Kansas City; dir. Gt. Midwest Corp., Kansas City. Mem. Greater Kansas City Civic Council; bd. dirs. Greater Kansas City C. of C., 1976—, chmn. world's fair com., 1976; exec. com., bd. dirs. Starlight Theatre Assn., Kansas City; bd. dirs. Kansas City chpt. Fellowship Christian Athletes, 1976, chmn. finance com., 1977; bd. dirs. Jackson County unit Am. Cancer Soc., Am. Royal Assn.; chmn. corp. div. Heart of Am. United Way, 1978; adv. trustee Research Med. Center, Kansas City; deacon Leawood Bapt. Ch. Clubs: Kansas City Downtown Rotary, Kansas City, 711 Inner, Brookridge Country (Kansas City). Home: 6436 Wenonga Terr Shawnee Mission KS 66208 Office: 1 Arrowhead Dr Kansas City MO 64129

STEADMAN, JOHN MONTAGUE, educator, lawyer; b. Honolulu, Aug. 8, 1930; s. Alva Edgar and Martha (Cooke) S.; grad. Phillips Acad., Andover, Mass., 1948; B.A. summa cum laude, Yale, 1952; LL.B. magna cum laude, Harvard, 1955; m. Alison Storer Lunt, Apr. 8, 1961; children—Catharine N., Juliette M., Eric C. Admitted to D.C. bar, 1955, Calif. bar, 1956, Hawaii bar, 1977, also U.S. Supreme Ct. bar; asso. firm Pilsbury, Madison & Sutro, San Francisco, 1956-63; atty. Dept. Justice, 1963-64; dep. under sec. army for internat. affairs, 1964-65; spl. asst. to sec. and dep. sec. def. Dept. Def., 1965-68; gen. counsel Dept. Air Force, 1968-70; vis. prof. law U. Pa. Law Sch., 1970-72; prof. law Georgetown U. Law Center, Washington, 1972—, asso. dean, 1979—; instr. Lincoln Law Sch., San Francisco, 1961-62, San Francisco Law Sch., 1962-63; vis. prof. U. Mich. Sch. Law, 1976, U. Hawaii Sch. Law, 1977; of counsel firm Pillsbury, Madison & Sutro, Washington, 1979—. Sinclair-Kennedy Traveling fellow, 1955-56. Mem. Am., Fed., Calif., San Francisco bar assns., Phi Beta Kappa, Delta Sigma Rho, Zeta Psi. Democrat. Episcopalian. Club: Outrigger Canoe (Honolulu). Editor: Harvard Law Rev., 1953-55. Home: 2960 Newark St NW Washington DC 20008 Office: 600 New Jersey Ave NW Washington DC 20001

STEADMAN, RICHARD COOKE, bus. exec.; b. Honolulu, Oct. 1, 1932; s. Alva Edgar and Martha (Cooke) S.; A.B., Yale U., 1955; M.B.A., Harvard U., 1957; m. Jane Blaner Nuckolls, Aug. 20, 1955; children—Christopher M., Peter W., Lee H. Intelligence analyst U.S. Govt., Washington, 1957-59; asso., partner G.H. Walker & Co., N.Y.C., 1959-66; dep. asst. sec. def. E. Asia and Pacific affairs, 1966-69; partner J.H. Whitney & Co., N.Y.C., 1969—; chmn., dir. Nat. Convenience Stores Inc.; dir. Storage Tech. Corp., Highline Fin. Services. Trustee Brearley Sch., N.Y.C., Children's TV Workshop, N.Y.C., German Marshall Fund, Washington; chief transition Dept. Def., Carter-Mondale Adminstrn; mem. program com. Am. Ditchley Found. Baker scholar, 1957. Mem. Council Fgn. Relations, Phi Beta Kappa. Democrat. Club: Mid-Atlantic (N.Y.C.). Home: 17 E 79th St New York NY 10021 Office: 630 Fifth Ave New York NY 10020

STEAKLEY, ZOLLIE COFFER, JR., state justice; b. Rotan, Tex., Aug. 29, 1908; s. Zollie Coffer and Frances Elizabeth (McGlasson) S.; B.A., Hardin-Simmons U., 1929, LL.D., 1959; J.D., U. Tex., 1932; LL.D., U. Corpus Christi, 1958; m. Ruth Butler, June 3, 1939. Admitted to Tex. bar, 1932; pvt. practice law, 1932-39, 46-57; asst. atty. gen. Tex., 1939-42; sec. state Tex., 1957-60; justice Supreme Ct. of Tex., Austin, 1961—. Home: 3302 Mt Bonnell Dr Austin TX 78731 Office: Supreme Court Bldg Austin TX 78711

STEAMER, ROBERT JULIUS, educator; b. Rochester, N.Y., Oct. 14, 1920; s. William August and Lotte (Becker) S.; B.A. in Social Sci., Bucknell U., 1947; M.A. in Polit. Sci., U. Va., 1952; Ph.D., Cornell U., 1954; postgrad. law Oxford (Eng.) U., 1968-69; m. Jean Worden, Apr. 12, 1947; children—Gregg Robert, James Worden. Asst. prof. Oglethorpe U., 1952-55, U. Mass., 1955-56; asso. prof. La. State U., 1956-62; prof. polit. sci., chmn. dept. Lake Forest (Ill.) Coll., 1962-72; prof. U. Mass., Boston, 1972—, dean Coll. II, Boston, 1974-76, vice chancellor for acad. affairs, provost, Boston, 1976—; vis. summer prof. Tulane U., 1958, Cornell U., 1960, U. Calif. at Los Angeles, 1965. Staff cons. La. sect. U.S. Commn. Civil Rights, 1961. Served with USAAF, 1942-46. Recipient Gt. Tchr. award Lake Forest Coll., 1965; Lilly Found. Research award, 1967. Mem. Am., Midwest (v.p. 1970-71), New Eng. (pres. 1979-80) polit. sci. assns. Author: (with F.V. Cahill, Jr.) The Constitution: Cases and Comments, 1959; The Supreme Court in Crisis, 1971; The Supreme Court-Constitutional Revision and the New Strict Constructionism, 1973. Contbr. articles to profl. jours. Home: 28 Hartford St Medfield MA 02052

STEANS, HARRISON IRWIN, banker; b. Chgo., July 3, 1935; s. Irwin Wells and Helen Brock (Fowlkes) S.; B.A. cum laude in Econs., Princeton, 1957; m. Lois Mae Morrison, June 22, 1957; children—Jennifer, Heather, Robin. With sales dept. I.B.M. Corp., Chgo., 1960-63, mgmt., 1963-66, adminstrv. asst. to chmn., Armonk, N.Y., 1966-67; chmn. bd. La Salle Nat. Bank, Chgo., 1973—, 1st Nat. Bank Highland Park (Ill.), 1968—, Bank Elk Grove (Ill.), 1970—; chmn. exec. com. Woodfield Bank, Schaumburg, Ill., 1971—. Mem. Deerfield (Ill.) Bd. Edn., 1972. Trustee Monmouth (Ill.) Coll. Served to lt. (j.g.) USNR, 1957-60. Mem. Bankers Club Chgo., Econs. Club Chgo. Club: Tennagua. Republican. Presbyterian. Office: La Salle Nat Bank 135 S La Salle St Chicago IL 60690*

STEAR, EDWIN BYRON, educator; b. Peoria, Ill., Dec. 8, 1932; s. Edwin Joseph and Juanita Blance (Hoffman) S.; B.S. in Mech. Engring., Bradley U., 1954; M.S., U. So. Calif., 1956; Ph.D. (Hughes Staff fellow), UCLA, 1961; m. Lorraine Athena Crist, Aug. 9, 1975; 1 son, Brian Douglas, 1 dau., Linnea Susan. Mem. tech. staff Hughes Aircraft Co., Culver City, Calif., 1954-59; asst. research engr. U. Calif., Los Angeles, 1959-61, asst. prof. engring., 1964-68, asso. prof., 1968-69; mgr. guidance and control research lab. Lear Siegler, Inc., Santa Monica, Calif., 1963-64; asso. prof. elec. engring. and computer sci., U. Calif., Santa Barbara, 1969-73, prof., 1973--, chmn. dept., 1975—; chief scientist USAF, 1979—; mem. Sci. Advisory Bd. USAF, 1971—; cons. to industry and govt., 1964—. Served to 1st lt. USAF, 1961-63. Mental Health Tng. Program fellow, 1972-74. Mem. IEEE, Am. Inst. Aeronautics and Astronautics, AAAS, Internat. Fedn. Automation Control, Sigma Xi, Eta Kappa Nu, Pi Mu Epsilon, Tau Beta Pi, Phi Eta Sigma, Tau Sigma. Editor: (with A. Kadish) Hormonal Control Systems, 1969; mem. editorial bd. Aircraft jour. Am. Inst. Aeronautics and Astronautics, 1974—; contbr. articles to profl. lit. Home: 3104 W Cumberland Ct Westlake Village CA 91361 Office: Dept Elec and Computer Engring U Calif Santa Barbara CA 93106

STEARNS, CHARLES EDWARD, educator; b. Billerica, Mass., Jan. 20, 1920; s. Albert Warren and Frances Matsell (Judkins) S.; A.B., Tufts Coll., 1939; postgrad. Cal. Inst. Tech., 1939-40; A.M., Harvard, 1942, Ph.D., 1950; LL.D., Bradford- Durfee Inst. Tech., 1962; m. Helen Louise Hurley, Dec. 17, 1942; children—Jonathan, Martha Warren, Rebecca Cole, Carola, Jeremie, Kate. Instr. geology Tufts U., 1941, 45, 46-48, asst. prof., 1948-51, asso. prof., 1954-57, prof., 1957—, dean Coll. Liberal Arts, 1954-67, 68-69, acting provost, 1966-67; asst. prof. geology Harvard U., 1951-54. Served from ensign to lt. USNR, 1942-45. Mem. AAAS, Geol. Soc. Am., Am. Acad. Arts and Scis., Colonial Soc. Mass., Phi Beta Kappa, Sigma Xi, Delta Upsilon. Club: Examiner of Boston (sec.). Home: 381 Boston Rd Billerica MA 01821

STEARNS, DAVID W., educator; b. Muskegon, Mich., Mar. 23, 1929; s. Frank Earl and Pearl H. (Alford) S.; B.S., U. Notre Dame (Ind.), 1953; M.S., S.D. Sch. Mines, 1955; Ph.D., Tex. A. and M. U., 1969; m. Martha M. Tirey, Nov. 1, 1975. Research geologist, head sect. Shell Devel. Co., Houston, 1955-67; faculty Tex. A. and M. U., 1967—, asso. prof., 1970—, prof., head dept. geology, 1971—; cons. Amoco Producing Co. Mem. Geol. Soc. Am., Am. Geophys. Union, Am. Assn. Petroleum Geologists. Home: 2128 Kazmeier St Bryan TX 77801 Office: Dept of Geology Tex A and M U College Station TX 77843

STEARNS, GEORGE L., II, business exec., mcht.; b. Williamsport, Pa., Jan. 12, 1899; s. Charles Robert and Martha Jane (Hays) S.; student Dickinson Sem.; student Culver (Ind.) Mil. Acad., 1916-18; m. Eleanor Crooks Whitehead, June 7, 1923; children—Ann Crooks Stearns Mansel, Eleanor Elizabeth Stearns Perciballi, Jane Hays Stearns Smith, Charles Robert. With L.L. Stearns & Sons, dept. store, Williamsport, 1918—, v.p., 1925-37, v.p., gen. mgr., 1937-45, pres., 1945—, gen. mgr., 1945-58; v.p., dir. Williamsport Nat. Bank, 1937—, Williamsport Fed. Savs. & Loan Assn.; dir., mem. exec. com. Pa. Gas & Water Co., Williamsport Hotels Co., dir. Pa. Enterprises, Inc. Past chmn. Pa. Pub. TV Network Commn.; past vice chmn. Williamsport Redevel. Authority; mem. Williamsport Municipal Authority. Past trustee, mem. exec. com. Lycoming Coll.; bd. dirs. Lycoming Found.; past pres. bd. trustees YMCA. Served at 2d lt. U.S. Inf., 89th div., 1918. Recipient Am. Legion Distinguished Service award, citation U.S. Navy, Meritorious Community Service award. Mem. Nat. Retail Mchts. Assn. (past v.p. dir., chmn. pub. relations, fin. coms.), Pa. Retailers Assn. (pres. 1948-52, dir.), U.S. v.p. dir. 1963-71, 1966-67, past chmn. accrediting bd., exec. com., policy com., Can.-U.S. com., past mem. various coms.), Pa. (dir., past pres.) chambers commerce. Presbyterian. Mason (33 deg. Shriner, K.T.), Elk. deg.). Home: 400 Upland Rd Williamsport PA 17701 Office: PO Box 787 Williamsport PA 17701

STEARNS, MARTIN, coll. dean; b. Phila., Aug. 16, 1916; s. Celia (Birdman) S.; B.A., U. Calif. at Los Angeles, 1943, M.A., 1944; Ph.D., Cornell U., 1951; m. Mary Beth Gorman, Sept. 8, 1948; children—Daniel G., Richard G. Jr. scientist Manhattan Project, U. Calif. Radiation Lab., Los Alamos, 1945-46; research physicist Carnegie Inst. Tech., 1951-57; cons. Ramo-Woodbridge Corp., Los Angeles, 1955; staff scientist Gen. Atomic, La Jolla, Calif., 1957-60; chmn. dept. physics Wayne State U., Detroit, 1960-62, dean Coll. Liberal Arts, 1962—. Bd. advisers Wayne State U. Press; v.p. Council of Colls. of Arts and Scis. in State Univs. and Land Grant Colls., 1970-71, pres., 1971-72; mem. commn. on arts and scis. Nat. Assn. State Univs. and Land Grant Colls.; mem. North Central Accreditation Commn. Fellow Am. Phys. Soc.; mem. Detroit Engring. Soc., Phi Beta Kappa, Sigma Xi. Contbr. tech. articles to profl. jours. Home: 30700 Marimoor Birmingham MI 48010 Office: Wayne State U Coll Liberal Arts Detroit MI 48202

STEARNS, MILTON SPRAGUE, JR., financial cons. co. exec.; b. N.Y.C., June 3, 1923; s. Milton Sprague and Katherine (Stieglitz) S.; grad. Phillips Exeter Acad., 1942; B.S. cum laude, Harvard, 1946, M.B.A., 1948; m. Virginia McCormick; children—Virginia Parker (Mrs. Lance King), John Brackett, Barbara Ellison, Kathryn Trowbridge, Elizabeth Sprague (dec.). With The Fidelity Bank, Phila., 1948-72, group v.p. in charge nat. lending div., 1960-72; pres. Charter Fin. Co., Phila., 1972—; chmn. bd. Judson Infrared, Inc., Ft. Washington, Pa.; dir. Nat. Valve & Mfg. Co., Pitts., Peripheral Dynamics, Inc., Safeguard Industries, Inc., King of Prussia, Pa., The West Co., Phoenixville, Pa.; mem. Mid.-Atlantic adv. bd. Am. Mut. Liability Ins. Co. Bd. mgrs. Franklin Inst., 1978—. Served with USNR, World War II; lt. (j.g.) Res. ret. Mem. Robert Morris Assos. (pres. Phila. chpt. 1961-62). Clubs: Spee, Merion Golf, Waynesborough Country, Seaview Country, Phila. Skating and Humane Soc., Racquet, Union League (Phila.); Board Room (N.Y.C.); Delray Beach, Delray Beach Yacht, Delray Dunes Golf and Country; Golfstream Bath and Tennis. Home: 43 Righters Mill Rd Gladwyne PA 19035 Office: Suite 2700 1700 Market St Philadelphia PA 19103

STEARNS, MONTEAGLE, ambassador; b. Cambridge, Mass., Dec. 5, 1924; s. William F. and Gwendolyn (Monteagle) S.; B.A., Columbia U., 1948; m. Antonia Riddleberger, Sept. 25, 1959; children—Joanne, Pamela Clark, Christopher Philip, Jonathan, David Foster, Emily. Mem. editorial bd. Film Forum Rev., Columbia U., N.Y.C., 1948-49; motion picture officer Dept. State, USIS, Istanbul, Turkey, 1949, Ankara, 1949-52; asst. attaché Dept. State, USIA, Washington, 1952-57; polit. officer, Athens, Greece, 1957-62, Kinhasa, Zaire, 1963-65; Greek lang. trainee, Athens, 1958-59; spl. asst. to ambassador-at-large, Washington, 1965-67; polit. officer, London, 1967-69; dep. chief mission, Vientiane, Laos, 1969-72; fellow Center Internat. Affairs, Harvard U., 1972-73; dep. asst. sec. state for East Asian and Pacific affairs Dept. State, Washington, 1973-74; dep. chief mission Am. embassy, Athens, 1974-77; ambassador to Ivory Coast, Ibidjan, 1977—. Served with USMC, 1943-45.

STEARNS, RICHARD BYRON, JR., financial exec.; b. Stamford, Conn., Jan. 30, 1939; s. Richard Byron and Barbara (Johnson) S.; B.A., Colgate U., 1961; M.B.A., Wharton Grad. Sch. Finance, 1963; m. Sharon Gates, Oct. 18, 1968; children—Owen, Hope, Leigh. Vice pres. Chase Manhattan Bank, N.Y.C., 1963-72; v.p. corporate fin. Gulf & Western Industries, 1972-75; treas. Schlumberger, Ltd., N.Y.C., 1975—. Co-chmn. Interracial Council for Bus. Opportunity of N.Y., 1977; bd. dirs. Goodwill Industries Greater N.Y. Mem. Fin. Execs. Inst., Treas.'s Group N.Y. Club: University (N.Y.C.). Office: 277 Park Ave New York NY 10017

STEARNS, RICHARD GORDON, educator; b. Buffalo, Apr. 28, 1927; s. Howard Gordon and Grace (Harvey) S.; A.B., Vanderbilt U., 1948, M.S., 1949; Ph.D., Northwestern U., 1953; m. Jane Smallwood, July 8, 1950; children—Jane, Bruce. Geologist, Standard Oil Co. Calif., 1951-53; asst. state geologist Tenn. Div. Geology, 1953-61; faculty Vanderbilt U., Nashville, 1961—, prof. geology, 1967—, chmn. dept., 1967-76. Served with USNR, 1944-45. Fellow Geol. Soc. Am., AAAS; mem. Am. Geophys. Union, Am. Assn. Petroleum Geologists, Phi Beta Kappa, Sigma Xi. Author: Relationships of Earthquakes and Geology in West Tennessee, 1972. Contbr. articles to profl. jours. Home: 304 Binkley Dr Nashville TN 37211

STEARNS, ROBERT LEO, educator, physicist; b. New Haven, July 28, 1926; s. Carl Leo and Mildred (Booth) S.; B.A. in Physics, Wesleyan U., Middletown, Conn., 1950; M.S., Case Inst. Tech., 1952, Ph.D., 1955; m. Frances E. Fowler, Aug. 30, 1958; children—Marshall Edward, Andrew Barker. Instr., Case Inst. Tech., 1954-55, Queen's Coll., 1955-58; faculty Vassar Coll., 1958—, prof. physics, 1968—, chmn. dept. physics, 1962-64, 65-69; dean of freshmen, 1974-77. Research collaborator Brookhaven Nat. Lab., 1957—, vis. asso. physicist, 1964; vis. scientist CERN, Geneva, Switzerland, 1970; vis. staff Los Alamos Sci. Lab., 1972-78. Served with AUS, 1944-46. Mem. Am. Phys. Soc., Am. Assn. Physics Tchrs., Sigma Xi, Phi Nu Theta. Author: The Fundamentals of Physics and Chemistry, 1968; Basic Concepts of Nuclear Physics, 1968; Atomic Physics, 1969; Mechanics, 1970. Home: 11 Carriage Hill Ln Poughkeepsie NY 12603

STEARNS, RUSSELL BANGS, industrialist; b. Chgo., Feb. 9, 1894; s. Robert Bangs and Emma (Owens) S; B.A., U. Mich., 1916; m. Edna Dilley, June 14, 1918 (dec. Feb. 1950); 1 dau., Virginia S. Gassel; m. 2d, Andree Beauchamp Ryan, June 5, 1958; stepchildren—Anthony H. Ryan, Thomas A. Ryan. Partner, Arthur Perry & Co., 1926-30, pres., 1930-38. Chmn. War Dept. Price Adjustment Bd., Washington, 1942; chmn. U.S. del. OEEC Conf., Paris. 1954. Mem. U. Mich. President's Club. Chmn. Mass. Republican Finance Com., 1944-46, regional vice chmn., 1946-48. Chmn. U.S. delegation OEEC Conf., Paris, 1954. Trustee, hon. vice chmn., mem. exec. com. Northeastern U.; trustee Civic Edn. Found., Tufts U., Boston Hosp. for Women, Trustees of Reservations, Milton; trustee, life mem. exec. com. Mus. Sci., Boston; bd. dirs. Boston Opera Assn.; bd. govs. Mass. Inst. Tech. Endicott House; life mem. Boston Episcopal Charitable Soc. Served as arty. officer U.S. Army, World War I. Mem. Squibnocket Assos. (life), Delta Kappa Epsilon. Clubs: Country (Brookline, Mass.); Down Town, (Boston); Hingham (Mass.) Yacht; Somerset (Boston); Edgartown (Mass.) Yacht; Mill Reef (Antigua, W.I.) Home: 50 Haven St Dedham MA 02026 also Edgartown MA 02539 also Antigua West Indies Office: 24 Federal St Boston MA 02110

STEARNS, STEPHEN RUSSELL, civil engr., educator; b. Manchester, N.H. Feb. 28, 1915; s. Hiram Austin and Elisabeth Scribner (Brown) S.; A.B., Dartmouth Coll., 1937, C.E., Thayer Sch. Engring. 1938; M.S., Purdue U., 1949; m. Eulalie Moody Holmes, Jan. 1 1939; children—Marjorie Elisabeth, Stephen James, Jonathan David. Civil engr. Gannett, Eastman, Fleming, Harrisburg, Pa., 1938-40; marine egr. Bur. Ships, Phila. Navy Yard, 1940-41; engr. Dry Dock Assos., Phila. Navy Yard, 1941-43; instr. Thayer Sch. Engring., Dartmouth, 1943-45, asst. prof., 1945-53, prof. civil engring., 1953—. UN cons. to Poland, 1974, 78; engr. Ops. Research, Inc., Washington. 1962-64; phys. reconnaisance in Alaska, Boston U. Phys. Research Labs. 1953; chief applied snow and ice research br. Snow, Ice, Permafrost Research Establishment, U.S. Army Engrs., 1954-55, mem. Arctic problems team NE Air Command, 1955. Mem. Sch. Bd. Hanover, N.H. 1951-60, chmn., 1957-59; mem. N.H. Gov.'s Transp. Com., 1966-67, Task Force, 1969; mem. sponsoring com. N.H.-Tomorrow, 1970-71; chmn. Lebanon (N.H.) Regional Airport Authority, 1966-69; mem. N.H. Bd. Registration Profl. Engrs., 1975—; mem. Transp. Research Bd. Mem. Am. Soc. Engring. Edn., ASCE (dir. 1978-81), AAAS, AAUP, Sigma Chi. Congregationalist. Home: 10 Barrymore Rd Hanover NH 03755

STEBBINS, GEORGE LEDYARD, educator; b. Lawrence, N.Y., Jan. 6, 1906; s. George Ledyard and Edith Alden (Candler) S.; A.B., Harvard, 1928, A.M., 1939, Ph.D., 1931; m. Margaret Chamberlaine, June 14, 1931 (div. 1958); children—Edith Candler, Robert Lloyd, George Ledyard (dec.); m. 2d, Barbara Jean Brumley, July 27, 1958. Instr. biology Colgate U., 1931-35; jr. geneticist U. Calif., Berkeley, 1935-39, asst. prof. genetics 1939-40, asso. prof., 1940-47, prof., 1947-50; prof. genetics U. Calif., Davis, 1950-73, prof. emeritus, 1973—. Guggenheim fellow, 1954, 60-61; recipient Verrill medal Yale U., 1968; Gold medal Linnean Soc. London, 1973. Mem. Soc. Study of Evolution (pres. 1950), Bot. Soc. Am. (pres. 1962), Am. Soc. Naturalists (pres. 1969), Calif. Native Plant Soc. (pres. 1966-72), Western Soc. Naturalists (pres. 1976), Internat. Union Biol. Scis. (sec. gen. 1959-64), Nat. Acad. Scis., Am. Philos. Soc., Am. Acad. Arts and Scis., Genetics Soc. Am., Royal Swedish Acad. Scis., German Leopoldina Acad., Phi Beta Kappa, Sigma Xi. Democrat. Unitarian. Author: Processes of Organic Evolution, 1966; The Basis of Progressive Evolution, 1969; Chromosomal Evolution in Higher Plants, 1971; Flowering Plants: Evolution above the Species Level, 1974; others. Home: 1009 Ovejas Ave Davis CA 95616 Office: Dept Genetics U Calif Davis CA 95616

STEBBINS, THEODORE ELLIS, JR., museum curator; b. N.Y.C., Aug. 11, 1938; s. Theodore Ellis and Mary Emma Flood S.; B.A., Yale U., 1960; J.D., Harvard U., 1964, Ph.D., 1971; children—Michael Morgan, Theodore Samuel, Susan Ellis. Chester Dale fellow Nat. Gallery Art, Washington, 1967; instr. Smith Coll., 1968; asso. prof. art history and Am. studies, curator Am. painting and sculpture Yale U., New Haven, 1969-77; curator Am. paintings Mus. Fine Arts, Boston, 1977—; lectr. fine arts Harvard U., 1979—; mem. governing bd. Yale U. Art Gallery; mem. vis. com. Fogg Art Mus., Harvard U.; mem. Am. art adv. com. San Francisco Museums; trustee Wyeth Endowment for Am. Art. Mem. Am. Fedn. Arts (trustee). Club: Century Assn. Author: Life and Works of Martin Johnson Heade, 1975; American Master Drawings and Watercolors, 1976; The Oil Sketches of Frederic Edwin Church, 1978; Drawings of Washington Allston, 1979. Office: Museum Fine Arts Boston MA 02115*

STEBER, ALAN BARNES, lawyer; b. Mobile, Ala., July 26, 1940; s. David Nelson and Sydney Cherry (Barnes) S.; B.A. in Polit. Sci. with honors (Dunlap scholar), U. of South, 1962; J.D. (Regional scholar), Tulane U., 1965; m. Charlotte Raymonde Madona, Aug. 7, 1971; 1 dau., Charlotte Madona. Admitted to Tex. bar, 1965; since practiced in Houston; asso. firm Royston, Rayzor & Cook, Houston, 1965-71; partner firm Austin, Arnett, Northrop, Kirkpatrick & Steber, Houston, 1974—. Bd. dirs., chmn. devel. com. Houston Sch. Deaf Children. Served to capt. JAG Corps, USAF, 1966-68. Mem. Am., Houston, Houston Jr. (sec. 1972-74) bar assns., State Bar Tex., Maritime Law Assn., Am. Judicature Soc., Blue Key, Beta Theta Pi (pres. chpt.), Phi Alpha Delta (vice-justice chpt. 1964). Episcopalian. Club: Exchange (pres. Houston chpt. 1974-75, Tex. dist. sec. 1976-78, pres. Tex. dist. 1978-79). Home: 10118 Chevy Chase Dr Houston TX 77042 Office: 1938 Bank of Southwest Bldg Houston TX 77002

STEBER, ELEANOR, soprano; b. Wheeling, W.Va., July 17, 1916; d. William Charles and Ida A. (Nolte) Steber; Mus.B., New Eng. Conservatory Music, 1938, hon. Mus.D.; Mus.D. (hon.), Bethany Coll., U. W.Va., Fla. So. Coll., Temple U., Ithaca Coll.; L.H.D. (hon.), Wheaton Coll., 1966; A.F.D., U. Oklahoma City. Singer, 1935—; won Met. Auditions of Air, spring 1940; with Met. Opera Co., 1940-66, San Francisco Opera Co., 1945, Central City Opera Festival, 1946, Cin. Summer Opera, 5 summers; appeared with all maj. Am. opera cos., and all maj. European festivals including Glynbourne, 1948, Bayreuth, 1953, Florence (Italy), 1954, Salzburg, 1959; sang with 7 opera cos. in Yugoslavia, 1955, Vienna Staats Oper, 1956; soloist with N.Y. Philharmonic, NBC, Boston, Mpls., Chgo., Cin., Kansas City, Denver, Montreal, Phila. Symphony orchs., others; makes radio, TV appearances; star of TV's Voice of Firestone, 10 yrs. Concert tours throughout U.S., Can., Europe, Orient; head vocal dept. Cleve. Inst. Music, 1963-73; voice faculty Juilliard Sch. Music, 1971—, New Eng. Conservatory Music, 1971—, Phila. Music Acad., 1975. Bd. dirs. Bklyn. Opera Co., Opera Soc. Washington; founder, pres. Eleanor Steber Music Found., 1975—. Mem. Delta Omicron, Pi Kappa Lambda. Lutheran. Home: Port Jefferson NY 11777 Office: 2109 Broadway New York NY 10023

STEC, ANNETTE, magazine editor; b. Perth Amboy, N.J., Oct. 13, 1944; d. Anthony and Anne (Lazar) S.; student Douglass Coll., Kean Coll., Newark. Mag. editor News Tribune, Woodbridge, N.J., 1965-72, desk editor family living dept., 1972; articles editor Exploring mag., N. Brunswick, N.J., 1972-75, exec. editor, 1975—; cons., adviser The Kilmer Era, Kilmer Job Corps Center, Edison, N.J. Recipient 1st prize Sci. Writers award ADA, 1977. Mem. N.J. Daily Newspaper Women (dir. 1969-71; 1st prize mag. layout 1971, 1st prize book revs. 1971, 1st prize women's page layout 1973), Nat. Fedn. Press Women, N.J. Press Women, Sigma Delta Chi. Office: Exploring Magazine PO Box 61030 Dallas/Fort Worth Airport TX 75261

STECK, NORMAN MARTIN, merchant; b. Mpls., May 9, 1923; s. Herman Louis and Bessie Theresa (Martinson) S.; B.B.A., U. Minn., 1949; m. Norma Jeannette Dinkins, June 4, 1953; children—Michael, Julie, James. Pub. accountant Price Waterhouse & Co., Chgo., 1949-50; mgr. accounting, treas. Gen. Outdoor Advt. Co., Inc., Chgo., 1950-64; asst. treas. Gamble-Skogmo, Inc., Mpls., 1966-74, treas., 1974—, v.p., 1977—. Served with AUS, 1943-46. Mem. Nat. Assn. Accountants, Fin. Execs. Inst., Alpha Kappa Psi. Republican. Methodist. Home: 2160 Aquila Ave N Golden Valley MN 55427 Office: 5100 Gamble Dr Minneapolis MN 55416

STECK, ROBERT CARL, physician, state ofcl.; b. Herrin, Ill., Jan. 7, 1910; s. Lewis Washington and Lelia (Felts) Steckenrider; M.D., U. Ill., 1942; m. Patricia Lee Dick, Mar. 12, 1949; children—Mary Jane, Susan Lee, Carla Jean, Patricia Gail, Robert Lewis. Intern, St. Margaret's Hosp., Hammond, Ind., 1942-43; pvt. practice medicine, 1943-50; cons. Ill. Dept. Pub. Welfare, 1950; supt. Anna (Ill.) State Hosp., 1950-65, 68—; region 5 adminstr. Ill. Dept. Mental health, 1964—; adj. prof. Rehab. Inst. So. Ill. U.; rehab. cons. Nat. dir. Boy Scouts Am., 1959-60, 61-63; bd. dirs. Union County United Fund, Russell Tuthill Found. Certified mental hosp. adminstr. Mem. AMA, Am. Psychiat. Assn., Nat. Rehab. Assn., Ill. Welfare Assn., Am. Soc. Pub. Adminstrn., Phi Beta Pi. Presbyn. Mason (K.T., 32 deg., Shriner). Address: 1000 N Main St Anna IL 62906

STECKEL, MATTHEW, banker; b. N.Y.C., May 13, 1940; s. Ray and Miriam (Keil) S.; student Stevens Inst. Tech., 1958-60; B.A., Drew U., 1963; M.B.A., Harvard U., 1965; m. Olga Suleiman, July 31, 1973; children—Amy, Steven (twins). Vice pres., Kidder Peabody & Co., Ltd., Beirut, Lebanon, 1970-74; exec. v.p., dir. First Arabian Corp, Beirut and Paris, 1974-76; chmn., chief exec. officer Bank of Commonwealth, Detroit, 1976—. Mem. Detroit Econ. Club (bd. dirs. 1977—). Clubs: Detroit, Detroit Athletic. Home: Grosse Pointe Farms MI 48236 Office: 719 Griswold St Detroit MI 48226

STECKER, RUSSELL LEE, architect; b. Barron, Wis., Aug. 7, 1924; s. George Willard and Ingaborg Bertina (Lee) S.; student Augustana Coll., 1942-43; B.Arch., Cornell U., 1949; m. Flora Caroline Burch, Sept. 8, 1946; children—Susan, Kris, George, Paul, Steven. Draftsman, F.J. Stepnoski & Sons, architects, Fond du Lac, Wis., 1949, Willard Wilkins, architects, Hartford, Conn., 1950-54; partner Wilkins and Stecker, Hartford, 1954-64, Stecker and Colavecchio, Hartford, 1964-70; pres. Stecker and Colavecchio, Architect's, Inc., Bloomfield, Conn., 1970-75, Stecker and Assos., Architects, Inc., Bloomfield, 1975-76, Stecker Labau Architects Inc., Hartford, 1976—. Mem. Simsbury Town Plan Commn., 1960-67, sec., 1963-67; mem. Simsbury Charter Revision Com., 1962-63, Conn. Bldg. Code, 1970-75, Simsbury Public Bldg. Commn., 1975—; mem. Capitol Region Planning Agy., 1967-70, vice chmn., 1970. Mem. Conn. Ho. of Reps., 1967-71. Served with USAAF, 1943-45. Eidlitz fellow, 1953. Fellow AIA (Conn. Honor award 1971); mem. Conn. Bldg. Congress (pres. 1960), Gargoyle, Tau Beta Pi, Delta Phi. Republican. Rotarian (v.p. Hartford club 1974-75, pres. 1975). Home: 25 Rosewood Dr Simsbury CT 06070 Office: Broadcast House Constitution Plaza Hartford CT 06103

STECKLEIN, JOHN ELLSWORTH, educator; b. Denver, Nov. 6, 1923; s. John A. and Ethel M. (Dinger) S.; A.B., Whittier Coll., 1944; M.S., Pa. State Coll., 1947; Ph.D., U. Wis., 1953; m. Helen Ross, Aug. 30, 1952; children—Kenneth Andrew, Mark Ellsworth, Robert Paul, Elizabeth Anne. Instr., Whittier Coll., 1947-49; resident counselor Stanford, 1949-50; research and teaching asst. U. Wis., 1951-52; research asso., asst. prof. Bur. Instnl. Research, U. Minn., 1952-54, asst. dir., acting dir., asst. prof., 1954-56, dir., asso. prof., 1956-60, dir., prof., 1960-71, prof. ednl. psychology, 1971—. Ednl. cons. colls., univs.; cons. exams. North Central Assn. Colls. and Secondary Schs.; chmn. research team of liaison com. Higher Edn. in Minn., 1959-65; project dir., Concepcion, Chile, 1968-69. Mem. Assn. Instl. Research (pres. 1965-66), Am. Statis. Assn., Am. Ednl. Research Assn., Am. Psychol. Assn., NEA, Psychometric Soc., Nat. Council Measurements Edn., Am. Assn. Higher Edn., Phi Delta Kappa, Sigma Pi Sigma, Pi Mu Epsilon. Author: (with James Aliferis) Music Achievement Test Series, 1953-68; (with Ruth E. Eckert) An Exploratory Study of Factors Influencing the Choice of College Teaching as a Career, 1958; How to Measure Faculty Work Load, 1961; (with Logan Dameron) Intercollegiate Athletic and Academic Progress, 1965; (with R. Ward, B. Wasson) Exam Practices Study, 1968; Institutional Research, 1970; (with Han Liu) Foreign Student Employment and Sources of Support, 1974. Contbr. articles to profl. jours., books. Home: 2129 Folwell St St Paul MN 55108 Office: Burton Hall U Minn Minneapolis MN 55455

STECKLER, LARRY, magazine editor; b. Bklyn., Nov. 3, 1933; s. Morris and Ida (Beekman) S.; student Coll. City N.Y., 1951; m. Catherine Coccozza, June 6, 1959; children—Gail Denise, Glenn Eric, Kerri Lynn, Adria Lauren. Asso. editor Radio-Electronics mag., N.Y.C., 1957-62; electronics editor Popular Mechanics mag., N.Y.C., 1962-65; asso. editor Electronic Products mag., Garden City, N.Y., 1965-67; editor Radio-Electronics mag., 1967—; editorial dir. Merchandising 2-Way Radio mag., N.Y.C., 1975-77; v.p., dir. Gernsback Publs., N.Y.C., 1975—. Mem. electronics advisory bd. Bd. Coop. Ednl. Services, Nassau County (N.Y.), 1975—; bd. dirs. Nassau County council Camp Fire Girls, 1971-72. Served with U.S. Army, 1953-56. Recipient Coop. award Nat. Alliance Television and Electronic Services Assns., 1974, 75. Mem. Internat. Soc. Certified Electronic Technicians (chmn. 1974-76, 79—), Nat. Electronics Service Dealers Assn. (rec. sec. N.Y. state 1976—, Man of Yr. award 1975), Am. Mgmt. Assn., Radio Club Am., Internat. Underwater Explorers Soc., Am. Soc. Bus. Press Editors (sr.), Empire State Fedn. Electronic Technicians Assns. Author books, handbooks, articles in field. Home: 158 Whitewood Dr Massapequa Park NY 11762 Office: 200 Park Ave S New York NY 10003. *Do not be afraid to try the unaccepted. Do not be afraid to do the undesirable. Do what you enjoy. . .do it well. . .and after it is done. . .never regret having done it. . .only regret what you have not yet done.*

STECKLER, PHYLLIS BETTY SCHWARTZBARD, pub. co. exec.; b. N.Y.C., May 15, 1933; d. Irwin H. and Bertha (Fellner) Schwartzbard; B.A., Hunter Coll., 1954; M.A., N.Y. U., 1957; m. Stuart J. Steckler, June 3, 1956; children—Randy, Sharon. Editorial dir. R.R. Bowker Co., N.Y.C., 1954-69, Crowell Collier Macmillan Info. Pub. Co., N.Y.C., 1969-71, Holt Rinehart & Winston Info. Systems, N.Y.C., 1971-73; pres., chief exec. officer Oryx Press, Scottsdale, Ariz., 1973-76, Phoenix, 1976—. Mem. ALA, Spl. Library Assn., S.W. Library Assn., Ariz. Library Assn., Calif. Library Assn., Am. Soc. for Info. Sci. Office: Oryx Press 2214 N Central at Encanto Phoenix AZ 85004

STECKLER, WILLIAM ELWOOD, judge; b. Mt. Vernon, Ind., Oct. 18, 1913; s. William Herman and Lena (Menikheim) S.; LL.B., Ind. Law Sch., 1936, J.D., 1937; LL.D., Wittenberg U., Springfield, Ohio, 1958; H.H.D., Ind. Central Coll., 1969; m. Vitallas Alting, Oct. 15, 1938; children—William Rudolph, David Alan. Admitted to Ind. bar, 1936, practiced in Indpls., 1937-50, mem. firm Key & Steckler; pub. counselor Ind. Pub. Service Commn., 1949-50; judge U.S. Dist. Ct. So. Dist. Ind., 1950—, now chief judge. Mem. adj. faculty Ind. U. Law Sch. Mem. Ind. Election Bd., 1946-48; chmn. speakers bur. Democratic State Central Com., 1948. Served with USNR, 1943. Recipient Man of Year award Indpls. Law Sch., 1970. Mem. Am., Fed., Ind., Indpls. bar assns., Am. Judicature Soc. Nat. Lawyers Club, Jud. Conf. U.S. (mem. com. operation jury system), Am. Legion, Order of Coif, Sigma Delta Kappa. Lutheran. Mason (33 deg., Shriner). Club: Indianapolis Athletic. Home: 30 Jurist Ln Lamb Lake Trafalgar IN 46181 Office: Fed Bldg Indianapolis IN 46204

STECKLING, ADRIENNE (ADRI), fashion designer; b. St. Joseph, Mo.; ed. Sch. Fine Arts, Washington U., St. Louis, Parson Sch. Design. Former designer H.B. Wragge; designer Clothes Circuit div. Anne Fogarty, Inc., 1971-72; owner, operator design co., N.Y.C., 1972—; exhibited designs in 2-woman show Smithsonian Inst., Washington, 1971. Mem. Council Fashion Designers Am. Office: 320 E 54th St New York NY 10022*

STEDMAN, MURRAY SALISBURY, JR., educator; b. Pitts., Dec. 2, 1917; s. Murray Salisbury and Viola (Lanich) S.; B.A., Williams Coll., 1939; M.A., Columbia, 1940, Ph.D., 1947; m. Susan Winter, Jan. 3, 1942 (div. 1970); children—Emily, Nancy; m. 2d, Evelyn Dennys, Sept. 29, 1970. Asso. prof. polit. sci. Swarthmore (Pa.) Coll., 1950-57; dir. Office Information, U.P. Ch. U.S.A., N.Y.C., 1957-60; gen. dir. pub. interpretation Nat. Council Chs. of Christ U.S.A., N.Y.C., 1961-64; polit. sci. specialist UNESCO, Paris, France, 1953-54; dir. Religion in Am. Life, 1957-60; lectr. social studies

Columbia Tchrs. Coll., 1961-64; chmn. dept. govt. Trinity Coll., Hartford, Conn., 1964-69; prof. polit. sci. Temple U., Phila., 1969—. Trustee Protestant Radio-TV Center, Atlanta, 1957-60. Served to capt. AUS, 1941-45. Mem. Am. Polit. Sci. Assn., Am. Acad. Polit. and Social Sci., ACLU, Nat. Municipal League. Presbyn. Author: Exporting Arms, 1947; (with Susan W. Stedman) Discontent at the Polls, 1950; (with John P. Roche) Dynamics of Democratic Government, 1954; Religion and Politics in America, 1964; (with Eugene J. Meehan, John P. Roche) Dynamics of Modern Government, 1966; Urban Politics, 1972; State and Local Governments, 1976. Editor: Modernizing American Government, 1968. Contbr. articles to profl. jours. Home: Alden Park Manor Philadelphia PA 19144

STEDMAN, WILLIAM PRESTON, educator; b. Austin, Tex., Feb. 10, 1923; s. Nathan Alexander and Mary Lucille (Sneed) S.; B.A., Tex. Christian U., 1944, Mus.M., 1947; Ph.D., Eastman Sch. Music, 1953; m. Leslie Clark McNeill, June 5, 1971; children by previous marriage—Preston Slessor, Alexander Winship. Asst. bus. mgr. Ft. Worth Civic Opera, 1946-47; asst. dean Tex. Christian U. Sch. Fine Arts, Ft. Worth, 1946-47; asso. prof. music Sul Ross State Coll., Alpine, Tex., 1947-51; asst. prin. viola player El Paso Symphony, 1948-51; instr. music Ind. U., 1953-55; prof. music, chmn. dept. Tex. Coll. Arts and Industries, Kingsville, 1955-66; dean Conservatory Music, U. Pacific, Stockton, Calif., 1966-76; chmn. music dept. Calif. State U., Fullerton, 1976—; exec. dir. Pacific Chamber Orch., 1979—; chmn. Fullerton Cultural and Fine Arts Commn., 1979—. Pres., Kingsville Community Concerts, 1962-64, Greater Stockton Area Arts Council, 1970—; bd. dirs. Sacramento Area Arts Council, Stockton Symphony Assn., Stockton Opera Assn., Stockton Community Concerts, Western Opera Theater, 1977—. Served with USNR, 1943-46. Mem. Assn. Calif. Symphony Orchs. (dir., v.p. 1974—), Calif. Assn. Profl. Music Tchrs. (v.p. 1968-70), Music Tchrs. Nat. Assn. (chmn. theory-composition sect. Southwestern div. 1961-65), Phi Mu Alpha, Alpha Chi. Kiwanian, Rotarian. Author: Compendium of Stylistic Devices, 1954; A Guide to a History of the Symphony, 1976; The Symphony, 1979. Home: 1797 Shady Brook Dr Fullerton CA 92631

STEDMOND, JOHN MITCHELL, educator; b. Leicester, Eng., May 14, 1916; s. John Butler and Margaret Hunter (Mitchell) S.; B.A., U. Sask. (Can.), 1950, M.A., 1951; Ph.D., U. Aberdeen (Scotland), 1953; m. Nona Fay Horne, Sept. 14, 1940 (dec. June 1969). Asst. lectr. English, U. Aberdeen, 1951-52; instr. U. Sask., Saskatoon, 1953-56, asst. prof., 1956-58; asst. prof. English, Queen's U., Kingston, Ont., Can., 1958-60, prof., 1963—, R. Samuel McLaughlin Research prof., 1964-65, chmn. English dept., 1968-77; asso. dir. McGill-Queen's U. Press, 1971-74. Served with Royal Can. Ordnance Corps, 1942-45. Nuffield Overseas grantee, 1960. Fellow Royal Soc. Can.; mem. Humanities Research Council Can. (chmn. 1972), Humanities Assn. Can. (pres. 1972), Modern Lang. Assn., Assn. Can. U. Tchrs. English. Author: The Comic Art of Laurence Sterne, 1967. Editor: Queen's Quar., 1959-63; (with Arthur H. Cash) The Winged Skull: Essays on Laurence Sterne, 1971. Home: 8 Barclay Rd Kingston ON K7M 2S4 Canada

STEED, TOM, congressman; b. nr. Rising Star, Tex., Mar. 2, 1904; m. Hazel Bennett, Feb. 26, 1923; 2 sons (Roger, killed in China May 1947). Connected with Okla. daily newspapers, 20 yrs.; mng. editor Shawnee News & Star, 4 yrs. Mem. 81st to 96th Congresses, 4th Okla. Dist. Served from pvt. to 2d lt. A.A.A., AUS, 1942-44; with OWI, 1944-45; CBI. Democrat. Home: 1904 N Pennsylvania Shawnee OK 74801 Address: House Office Bldg Washington DC 20515

STEEG, CARL WORTH, JR., educator; b. Indpls., Aug. 17, 1922; s. Carl Worth and Marie (Howe) S.; A.B., Depauw U., 1943; Ph.D., Mass. Inst. Tech., 1952; postgrad. Mich. State U., 1943-44; m. Janet Ann Johnson, Sept. 22, 1946; children—James Howe, Carl Kiefer. Research mathematician, dynamic analysis and control lab. Mass. Inst. Tech., Cambridge, 1947-56; mgr. analysis and simulation Aerospace Systems Div., RCA, Burlington, Mass., 1956-63; dir. operations indsl. labs. div. ITT, Ft. Wayne, Ind., 1963-69; prof. elec. engring. Purdue U., Ft. Wayne, lectr. bus. St. Francis Coll., Ft. Wayne, 1969-73; vis. lectr. elec. and electronic engring. Trent Polytechnic, Nottingham, Eng., 1977-78. Exec. dir. Mayor's Commn. for More Efficient City Govt. Operations (BEST), 1972-74. Served with Signal Corps, AUS, 1943-46. Fellow AAAS; mem. IEEE, AAUP, Phi Delta Theta. Mem. Disciples of Christ. Mason (Shriner), Rotarian. Author: (with W.W. Seifert) Control Systems Engineering, 1960. Home: 7419 Leo Rd Ft Wayne IN 46825

STEEGER, HENRY, publisher; b. N.Y.C., May 26, 1903; s. Henry and Adelaide (von Holsten) Steeger II; student Trinity Sch., Horace Mann Sch., N.Y.C.; A.B., Princeton U., 1925; postgrad. U. Berlin, 1926; H.H.D., Wilberforce U.; m. Shirley Meeker, June 1, 1928; children—Henry, Susan Shirley, Nancy Victoria. Editor mags. Dell Pub. Co., N.Y.C., 1927-29; pub., pres. Popular Pubs., 1930-72; pres. Fictioneers, Inc., 1939-58, All-Fiction Field Inc., 1942-58, New Publs., Recreational Reading, Post Periodicals, Inc., 1936-60, L.I. Printing Corp.; asso. prodn. TV spls. Reeves Teletape; real estate operator, N.Y., 1926—. Adv. councilor dept. sociology Princeton U., 1963-70. Pres., Soc. for Rehab. Facially Disfigured, United Seamen's Service; co-founder Ct. of Last Resort; v.p. Madison Sq. Boys Club. Trustee Wilberforce U., Manhattan Eye, Ear and Throat Hosp.; asso. bd. trustees N.Y. U. Med. Center. Mem. exec. com. Young Democrats Am. Served as lt. comdr. USCG (T), World War II; v.p. Army War Shows; mem. comdts. adv. panel USCG. Presbyn. Mem. Authors League Am., Nat. Urban League (past pres.), Mag. Pubs. Assn. (dir., exec. com.), U.S. Lawn Tennis Assn. (chmn. publs. com.). Clubs: Quoque Field, River, Princeton, Explorers, Overseas Press, Dutch Treat (N.Y.C.). Author: You Can Remake America, 1969. Pub. Argosy mag. Contbr. stories to nat. mags. Home: 301 E 79th St New York NY 10021 Office: 420 Lexington Av New York NY 10017

STEEGMULLER, FRANCIS, author; b. New Haven, July 3, 1906; s. Joseph F. and Bertha R. (Tierney) S.; student Dartmouth, 1923-24; B.A., Columbia, 1927, M.A., 1928; m. Beatrice Stein, July 1, 1935 (dec. June 1961); m. 2d, Shirley Hazzard, Dec. 22, 1963. Decorated chevalier French Legion of Honor; recipient Red Badge Mystery prize, 1940; Nat. Book award, 1971. Mem. Nat. Inst. Arts and Letters, Phi Beta Kappa. Writer under own name and pen names Byron Steel, David Keith. Author: O Rare Ben Jonson, 1927; Java-Java, 1928; Sir Francis Bacon, 1930; The Musicale, 1930; (with Marie Dresden Lane) America on Relief, 1938; Flaubert and Madame Bovary, 1939; A Matter of Iodine, 1940; A Matter of Accent, 1943; States of Grace, 1946; French Follies, 1946; Blue Harpsichord, 1949; Maupassant: A Lion in the Path, 1949; The Two Lives of James Jackson Jarves, 1951; The Selected Letters of Gustave Flaubert (transl.), 1953; The Grand Mademoiselle, 1956; Madame Bovary (transl.), 1957; The Christening Party, 1960; Le Hibou et la Poussiquette, 1961; Apollinaire, Poet Among the Painters, 1963; (with Norbert Guterman) Sainte-Beuve, Selected Essays (transl.), 1963; (with N. Guterman) Papillot, Clignot et Dodo, 1964; Flaubert's Intimate Notebook (transl.), 1967; Cocteau, 1970; Stories and True Stories, 1972; Flaubert in Egypt (transl., editor), 1973; Your Isadora: the Love Story of Isadora Duncan and Gordon Craig, 1974; Silence at Salerno, 1978; The Letters of Gustave Flaubert, 1830-1857 (transl.), 1980. Contbr. short stories, articles to New Yorker. Clubs: Century, Coffee House (N.Y.C.). Address: 200 E 66th St New York NY 10021

STEEL, EDWIN DEHAVEN, fed. judge; b. Phila., May 7, 1904; s. Edwin DeHaven and Jennie May (Short) S.; A.B., Dartmouth Coll., 1926; LL.B., Yale U., 1931; m. Martha Field, Dec. 19, 1974. In various positions, retail lumber bus., 1926-29; admitted to Del. bar, 1932, U.S. Supreme Ct. bar, 1936; practice law, Wilmington, Del., 1932—, individual practice, 1932-45, 58—, partner firm Morris, Steel, Nichols & Arsht, 1945-58; judge U.S. Dist. Ct. for Dist. of Del., 1958—, sr. judge, 1970—; gen. counsel War Materials, Inc., 1942-43; dir. Kaumaugraph Co. Bd. dirs. Wilmington Gen. Hosp. Mem. Am. Bar Assn., Del. Bar Assn. (pres. 1952-53), Assn. Bar City N.Y., Am. Law Inst., Del. Hist. Soc. (pres. 1961-62, dir. 1962-65), Phi Beta Kappa, Psi Upsilon. Clubs: Wilmington, Wilmington Country, Soc. Colonial Wars. Office: 844 King St Wilmington DE 19801

STEEL, WILLIAM CARLTON, lawyer; b. Cincinnati, Iowa, Feb. 6, 1916; s. David and Myrtle (Stickler) S.; student Ellsworth Jr. Coll., 1933-35; A.B., Grinnell Coll., 1938; LL.B., Harvard, 1941; m. Margaret M. Gordon, 1940; 1 dau., Jane Steel Fritzmeier. Employed with Am. Surety Co., N.Y.C., 1941-42; admitted to N.Y. bar, 1942, Fla. bar, 1946; practice in Miami, 1946—; asso. Steel, Hector & Davis and predecessor firms, 1946-50, partner, 1951—. Served with AUS, 1943-46. Fellow Am. Coll. Trial Lawyers, Am. Bar Found.; mem. Internat., Am. (ho. of dels. 1962-68), Inter-Am., Dade County (past pres.) bar assns., Fla. Bar, Am. Soc. Internat. Law, Am. Judicature Soc., So. Fla. Interprofl. Council (past pres.). Lutheran. Clubs: Miami, Bankers. Address: 1400 SE First Nat Bank Bldg Miami FL 33131

STEELE, ALLEN MULHERRIN, ins. co. exec. b. Franklin, Tenn., July 8, 1917; s. William Alexander and Genevieve (Lewis) S.; student Davidson Coll., 1935-36; B.A., Vanderbilt U., 1939, LL.B., 1941; m. Damaris Witherspoon, Oct. 7, 1944; children—Damaris, Genevieve, Rachel, Elizabeth, Allen Mulherrin. Admitted to Tenn. bar, 1941; pvt. practice, Nashville, 1941, 45; mem. legal staff Life & Casualty Ins. Co. Tenn., Nashville, 1946—, gen. counsel, 1953—, exec. v.p., 1966—, pres., 1970—, also dir.; dir. Nashville Gas Co., Inc., Murray Ohio Mfg. Co., Nashville, 3d Nat. Bank, Nashville, Tenn. Natural Gas Lines, Inc. Pres., Nashville A.R.C., 1953-54, Nashville Salvation Army, 1958-59; campaign chmn. Nashville United Givers Fund, 1962-63. Pres. trustees Presbyn. Children's Home, Tenn., 1959-61, Leadership Nashville, 1976-77; trustee Battle Ground Acad., Vanderbilt U. Served to capt. USAAF, 1941-45. Decorated D.F.C., Air medal; Colonial medal with Sahara bar (France). Mem. Am., Tenn., Nashville bar assns., Assn. Life Ins. Counsel, Vanderbilt U. Alumni Assn. (pres. 1966-67), Nashville Area C. of C. (pres. 1972), Phi Delta Phi, Sigma Alpha Epsilon. Presbyn. (elder). Clubs: Belle Meade (pres. 1965-66), Cumberland (pres. 1963 Nashville). Home: 1001 Overton Lea Rd Nashville TN 37720 Office: Life & Casualty Tower Nashville TN 37219

STEELE, BETTY LOUISE, banker; b. Sigourney, Iowa, Nov. 20, 1920; d. Otto Orville and Freda Marie Christina (Strohman) Utterback; student pub. schs., Iowa; m. David L. Steele, Jan. 17, 1942; 1 son, David Leroy. With N.W. Des Moines Nat. Bank, 1959-68, v.p., 1966-68; v.p., sec. Brenton Banks, Inc., Des Moines, 1968—, dir., 1976—. Sec. Brenton Found., 1970—. Mem. State Banking Bd., 1977—. Mem. Des Moines C. of C. (Nat. Leadership award 1976), Nat. Assn. Bank Women (pres. 1975-76), Am. Bankers Assn. (govt. relations council 1977-79), Iowa bankers assns. Republican. Mem. Ch. of Christ. Club: Order Eastern Star. Author articles. Home: 1511 68th St Des Moines IA 50311 Office: 2840 Ingersoll Ave Des Moines IA 50312

STEELE, CARROLL MAURICE, electronics engr.; b. Tulsa, Feb. 13, 1926; s. William Alvin and Juanita Kathryn (Poindexter) S.; student So. Meth. U., 1943-44; B.S. in Elec. Engring., U. Tex., 1946; postgrad. U. Calif., 1946-47, U. Calif., Los Angeles, 1949-50; m. Lorraine Lavelle Grossnickle, Feb. 2, 1952; children—Larelle Kay, Therese Gail. Research engr. N. Am. Aviation, Inc., 1947-52, Berkeley Sci. Co., 1952; physicist Calif. Research & Devel. Co., Livermore, Calif., 1952-54; with SRI Internat., Menlo Park, Calif., 1954—, sr. research engr., 1962—. Served in USNR, 1943-46. Mem. U.S. Tennis Assn., U.S. Figure Skating Assn. Republican. Mem. Christian Ch. (Disciples of Christ). Patentee electronic systems. Home: 1979 Scott Ln Los Altos CA 94022 Office: 333 Ravenswood St Menlo Park CA 94025

STEELE, CHARLES GLEN, accountant; b. Faulkton, S.D., July 24, 1925; s. Clifford D. and Emily O. (Hanson) S.; B.B.A., Golden Gate U., San Francisco, 1951, M.B.A., 1962; m. Shirley June Ferguson, Nov. 9, 1947; children—Richard Alan (dec.), Deborah Ann Steele Most. With Deloitte Haskins & Sells, 1951—, partner, 1963—, partner charge Chgo. office, 1973-76, partner charge personnel and adminstrn., N.Y.C., 1976-78, mng. partner, 1978—; instr. evening program Golden Gate U., 1952-58. Served with USNR, 1943-48. Recipient Elijah Watts Sells Gold medal for highest grade in U.S. for C.P.A. exam., 1951. Mem. Am. Inst. C.P.A.'s, N.Y. State Soc. C.P.A.'s, Am. Accounting Assn., Newcomen Soc. Clubs: Greenwich Country, Princeton, Blind Brook, Links, Board Room. Home: Greenwich CT Office: 1114 Ave of Americas New York NY 10036

STEELE, DONALD ERNEST, machinery mfg. co. exec.; b. Edgeley, N.D., Apr. 5, 1923; s. Ernest and Etna Pearl (Jordan) S.; B.S. in Phys. Sci., Whitworth Coll., Spokane, Wash., 1945; B.S. in Mech. Engring., U. Wash., Seattle, 1947; m. Evelyn Jean Davis, Aug. 28, 1946; 1 son, Ronald B. With Allis Chalmers Corp., 1947-72, gen. mgr. large pump and compressor systems div., to 1972; pres. Cooper-Bessemer Co., Mt. Vernon, Ohio, 1972-75; exec. v.p. mktg. and internat. services Cooper Energy Services Co., Mt. Vernon, 1975-79, exec. v.p., gen. mgr., 1979—; chmn. bd., dir. Coberrow Ltd.; dir. First Knox Nat. Bank, Mt. Vernon, Cooper-Vulkan, Cooper Rolls, Inc., Cooper Creusot, Nippon Copper, Cooper Energy Services, Ltd. Mem. Mt. Vernon Community Trust Distbn. Com., 1975-79; trustee Knox Community Hosp., Mt. Vernon, 1977-79; trustee Gay St. United Methodist Ch., Mt. Vernon, 1976-78. Served to lt. (j.g.) USNR, 1943-46. Mem. ASME, Compressed Air and Gas Inst. (dir. 1975-77), Machonery and Allied Products Inst. (internat. council 1976—), Sales and Mktg. Execs. (v.p., dir. Milw. chpt.), Mt. Vernon C. of C. (v.p., dir. 1973-78). Republican. Clubs: Mt. Vernon Country, Rotary. Office: Cooper Energy Services Co N Sandusky St Mount Vernon OH 43050

STEELE, EARL LARSEN, educator; b. Denver, Sept. 24, 1923; s. Earl Harold and Jennie (Larsen) S.; B.S. with honors, U. Utah, 1945; Ph.D., Cornell U., 1952; m. Martha C. Hennessey, June 27, 1953; children—Karl Thomas, Earl Robert, Karen Lynn, Kevin Douglas, Lisa Louise, Colleen Carol. Research physicist Gen. Electric Co., 1952-56; chief device devel. Motorola, Inc., 1956-58; mgr. devel. lab. Hughes Aircraft Co., 1958-64; research scientist N. Am. Rockwell Corp., 1964-69; prof. elec. engring. U. Ky., Lexington, 1969—, chmn. dept., 1971—. Affiliate prof. Ariz. State U., 1956-58, U. Calif. at Irvine, 1966-69; adviser So. Calif. Coll., Costa Mesa, 1963-64; charter mem. Orange County Academic Decathlon (Calif.). Fellow IEEE; mem. Am. Soc. Engring. Edn., Am. Phys. Soc., Sigma Xi, Tau Beta Pi, Eta Kappa Nu (dir. 1974-76). Mormon. Author: Optical Lasers in Electronics. Contbr. articles to profl. jours. Home: 313 Blueberry Rd Lexington KY 40503 Office: 453 Anderson Hall Univ Ky Lexington KY 40506

STEELE, ERNEST CLYDE, ins. co. exec.; b. Corbin, Ky., May 11, 1925; s. J. Fred and Leona (McFarland) S.; B.S. with honors, U. Ky., 1948, M.S., 1950; m. Cora Jones, June 17, 1944; children—Gerald R., David. P. Asst. actuary Peninsular Life Ins. Co., Jacksonville, Fla., 1950-54; actuary Pioneer Life & Casualty Co., Gadsden, Ala., 1955; v.p., actuary Guaranty Savs. Life Ins. Co., Montgomery, Ala., 1956-57; exec. v.p., actuary Am. Investment Life Ins. Co., Nashville, 1958-59; pres., actuary Appalachian Nat. Life Ins. Co., Knoxville, Tenn., 1959-67; sr. v.p., chief investment officer, ops. analyst Coastal States Life Ins. Co., Atlanta, 1968-71, exec. v.p., dir., 1971-74, pres., dir., 1974-79; pres., dir. Occidental Life Ins. Co. of N.C., 1979—. Mem. devel. council U. Ky.; bd. dirs. Ednl. Found., Inc.; past pres. Ga. Assn. Life Ins. Cos. Served to 2d lt. U.S. Army, 1943-45. Fellow Life Mgmt. Inst.; mem. Life Office Mgmt. Assn. (chmn. bd.), U. Ky. Alumni Assn. (past bd. dirs.), Am. Acad. Actuaries, Pi Mu Epsilon. Republican. Baptist. Home: 4701 A Edwards Mill Rd Raleigh NC 27612 Office: 1001 Wade Ave Raleigh NC 27605

STEELE, GEORGE, agrl. co. exec.; b. Pocopson, Pa., Oct. 22, 1918; s. Hugh Exton and Katherine (Stevens) S.; student Pa. State U., 1936-37; m. R. Eleanor Brown, Oct. 18, 1941; children—George B., James R., Richard H. Pres. George Steele and Sons, Inc., dairy farm, 1969—; dir. Pa. Farm Bureau Coop. Assn., 1954-65, v.p., 1963-65; dir. Agway, Inc., Syracuse, N.Y., 1965—, vice chmn., 1970-71, chmn. bd., 1971—; dir. Internat. Life, Buffalo, 1971-73, Farm Credit Banks, Balt. Dist., Md., 1963—, Farmers and World Affairs, Inc., 1961-71. Overseer Pa. Grange; trustee Am. Inst. Coop., 1967—. Mem. Sigma Phi Alpha. Mem. Soc. of Friends. Home: 1140 W Street Rd Pocopson PA 19366 Office: Box 4933 Syracuse NY 13221

STEELE, GRANVILLE GEORGE ERNST, assn. exec.; b. Windsor, Ont., Can., Jan. 11, 1920; s. Ernest and Ethel Isabel (Fordham) S.; B.A. in Polit. Sci. and Econs. with honors, U. Toronto, 1949; postgrad. London Sch. Econs., 1949-51; m. Edith Clare Rutherford, Dec. 18, 1948; children—Michael Ernest, Elizabeth Jean, John Peter, Graham Frederick. Accountant, Simonds Can. Saw Co. Ltd., 1937-41; with Can. Dept. Fin., 1951-68, dep. undersec. state, 1964-68; pres. Grocery Products Mfrs. Can., 1968-78, Can. Assn. Broadcasters, Ottawa, 1978—. Trustee Can. Hunger Found.; bd. govs., vice chmn. U. Ottawa; mem. Commn. Internat. Year of the Child. Served with RCAF, 1941-45. Mem. Inst. Public Adminstrn. Can. Clubs: Rideau, Cercle Univ. d'Ottawa, Five Lakes Fishing. Home: 78 Riverdale Ave Ottawa ON K1S 1R2 Canada Office: 165 Sparks St Ottawa ON K1P 5S2 Canada

STEELE, JACK, journalist; b. N. Manchester, Ind., Sept. 15, 1914; s. Roscoe and Dessie (Wonderly) S.; A.B., Middlebury (Vt.) Coll., 1936; M.S. in Journalism, Columbia, 1937; m. Barbara Louise Lyons, Sept. 30, 1939; children—Jeffrey L., Peter C. Reporter, N.Y. Herald Tribune, 1937-53; chief polit. writer Scripps-Howard Newspaper Alliance, 1953-67, mng. editor, 1967-74, editor, 1974—. Recipient Raymond Clapper award, 1949, Sigma Delta Chi award, 1949, Heywood Broun award, 1951, Ernie Pyle award, 1963. Clubs: Nat. Press, Gridiron (Washington). Presbyn. Home: 5824 Osceola Rd Washington DC 20016 Office: 777 14th St NW Washington DC 20005

STEELE, JACK DONALD, univ. dean; b. Sedalia, Mo., Dec. 7, 1923; s. Elvin Aubrey and Jewel Belle (Scruggs) S.; student Central Mo. State Tchrs. Coll., 1942-43, Mich. State U., 1943-44; B.S., Mo. Valley Coll., 1948; M.B.A., U. Kans., 1951; D.B.A., Harvard U., 1956; children—Jack Donald, Sherie Diane. Co-owner Cavalier Studios, Marshall, Mo., 1948-53; asst. prof. Tex. A. and M., College Station, 1950-53; research asso. Harvard Bus. Sch., Boston, 1954-56; prof. bus. adminstrn. U. Kans., Lawrence, 1956-64; prof. bus. adminstrn. Inst. pour l'etude des methodes de direction de l'entreprise, Lausanne, Switzerland, 1962-63; prof. bus. mgmt. Grad. Sch. Bus., Stanford, 1964-68; gen. mgr. N.Y. ops. Xerox Edn. Group, N.Y.C., 1968-70; dean, prof. mgmt. Coll. Bus. Adminstrn., Tex. Tech. U., 1970-75, Sch. Bus. Adminstrn., U. So. Calif., Los Angeles, 1975—; dir. Rohr Industries, Inc., Chula Vista, Calif., Purex Corp., Lakewood, Calif., Judy's Merchandising Corp., Van Nuys, Calif., Glendale Fed. Savs. & Loan Assn. (Calif.), Kanaly Trust Co., Houston, Foothill Group, Inc., Los Angeles; prof. bus. mgmt. Australian Inst. Mgmt., Sydney, 1966-67, Singapore Inst. Mgmt., 1966; prof. bus. adminstrn. U. Costa Rica, San Jose, 1960-61. Served with AUS, 1943-45. Decorated Purple Heart, Bronze Star, Combat Inf. Badge (U.S.); Order of Maple Leaf (Can.); hon. counsel No. Calif. for Costa Rica, 1967—. Mem. Beta Gamma Sigma, Sigma Iota Epsilon, Sigma Nu. Club: Rotary. Author: Role of Air Freight and Physical Distribution, Part II, 1956; Cases in European Marketing, 1963. Home: 1625 Michael Ln Pacific Palisades CA 90272 Office: Sch Bus Adminstrn U So Calif Los Angeles CA 90013

STEELE, JAMES BRUCE, JR., newspaper reporter; b. Hutchinson, Kans., Jan. 3, 1943; s. James Bruce and Mary (Peoples) S.; B.A., U. Mo., 1967; m. Nancy Saunders, June 25, 1966. Labor writer Kansas City (Mo.) Star, 1962-67; dir. information Laborers' Internat. Union of North Am., AFL-CIO, Washington, 1967-70; urban affairs and investigative reporter Phila. Inquirer, 1970—. Recipient Am. Polit. Sci. Assn. award distinguished reporting pub. affairs, 1971; George Polk Meml. award of L.I. U. for met. reporting, 1971; Sigma Delta Chi award gen. reporting, 1971, Heywood Broun award, 1973, George Polk Meml. award for spl. reporting, 1973, Gavel award Am. Bar Assn., 1973, Sidney Hillman award, 1973, John Hancock award for bus. reporting, 1973, Bus. Journalism award U. Mo., 1973; Pulitzer prize, 1975. Office: 400 N Broad St Philadelphia PA 19101*

STEELE, JAMES HARLAN, educator, former pub. health veterinarian; b. Chgo., Apr. 3, 1913; s. James Hahn and Lydia (Nordquist) S.; D.V.M., Mich. State Coll., 1941; M.P.H., Harvard, 1942; hon. diploma, Hellenic Vet. Soc., Athens, 1977, XXI World Vet. Congress, Moscow, 1979; m. Aina Oberg, 1941 (dec. 1969); children—James Harlan, David; m. 2d, Maria-Brigitte Meyer, 1969. With Ohio Dept. Health, 1942-43; with USPHS, 1943-71, advancing through grades to asst. surgeon gen. for vet. affairs and chief vet. officer; chief vet. pub. health activities Communicable Disease Center, Atlanta, 1947-71; prof. environ. health U. Tex. Sch. Pub. Health, Houston, 1971—; cons. WHO, 1950—, Pan-Am. San. Bur., 1945—, FAO, UN, 1960—; vis. prof. Tex. A&M U., 1976—, U. Guelph (Ont., Can.), U. Ont., 1978, Univs. Ibadan, Ife, Zaria, Benin, Nigeria, 1978; plenary speaker Internat. Congress Hydatidosis, Athens, 1978; pres. Internat. Zoonoses Found., Fedn. World Health Found., Geneva/Houston. Recipient USPHS Order of Merit, 1963; Karl F. Meyer award, 1966; Distinguished Service award USPHS, 1971; Mich. State U. Coll. Vet. Medicine award, 1972; hon. mem. Epidemic Intelligence Service, 1975; German Fed. Health Centennial honoree, Berlin, 1976; James H. Steele Vet. Pub. Health award established in his honor World Vet. Epidemiology Soc., 1975. Fellow Am. Pub. Health Assn. (Bronfman award 1971, Centennial award 1972), Royal Soc. Tropical Medicine and Hygiene; mem. Conf. Pub. Health Vets. (founder), Am. Soc. Tropical Medicine, Am. Bd. Vet. Pub. Health (founder), World (founder, pres. 1971), Am. (pres. 1979—) vet. epidemiology socs., Am. Vet. Med. Assn., AAAS, World Vet. Assn.

(hon.), Philippines Vet. Med. Assn. (hon.), U.S. Animal Health Assn., U.S.-Mex. Public Health Assn., Soc. Epidemiological Research, Mil. Surgeons Assn., Wildlife Disease Assn., Infectious Disease Soc. (trustee 1978), Can. Public Health Assn. (hon.), Internat. Epidemiology Soc., Harvard, Mich. State U. alumni assns., Alpha Psi. Episcopalian. Clubs: Army Navy (Washington); Swedish (Chgo.); University Faculty (Houston). Author: (with J. Arthur Myers) Bovine Tuberculosis Control in Man and Animals, 1969; articles and sects. of books. Editor in chief CRC Zoonoses Handbooks, 1979; mem. editorial bd. Jour. Comparative Immunology and Microbiology, Internat. Jour. Zoonoses, Pan Am. Medicine, Jour. Environ. Health. Home: 10722 Riverview Dr Houston TX 77042. *I have believed firmly throughout my career that I should share my knowledge and expertise with my fellow man, be he American or citizen of the world. Those of us who are more fortunate to be endowed with intellectual advantages have an even greater responsibility to share.*

STEELE, JAMES PATRICK, JR., ret. drug co. exec.; b. Reform, Ala., Feb. 7, 1910; s. James Patrick and Ollie (Lawrence) S.; student Ga. Inst. Tech., 1941-42; m. Mary Dunn, Aug. 28, 1935; children—James Patrick, Elizabeth Steele Turley. Sec., Woods Drugs, Inc., Birmingham, Ala., 1934-39; v.p., treas. Jacobs Pharmacy Co., Inc., Atlanta, 1940-63; v.p., sec.-treas., dir. Haag Drug Co. Inc., Indpls., 1964-68, pres., dir., 1968-72; dir. Affiliated Drug Stores Corp.; dir., treas. Medi-Sav, Inc.; v.p., treas., 1966-72; dir., treas. Donlon Distbg. Inc., 1967-72. Bd. dirs. Ind. Retail Council, 1969-72; pres., bd. dirs. Ga. Retail Council, 1958-60. Named hon. Ky. col., 1974. Republican. Methodist. Home: 1600 N Ocean Blvd Pompano Beach FL 33062

STEELE, JOHN HYSLOP, marine scientist, oceanographic inst. adminstr.; b. Edinburgh, U.K., Nov. 15, 1926; s. Adam and Annie H.; B.Sc., Univ. Coll., London U., 1947, D.Sc., 1963; m. Margaret Evelyn Travis, Mar. 2, 1956; 1 son, Hugh. Marine scientist Marine Lab., Aberdeen, Scotland, 1951-66, sr. prin. sci. officer, 1966-73, dep. dir., 1973-77; dir. Woods Hole Oceanographic Instn. (Mass.), 1977—, vis. research fellow, 1958, lectr. marine biol. lab., 1967; vis. prof. U. Miami, 1961; mem. NSF panel for internat. Decade of Ocean Exploration, 1972-73; mem. Council Marine Biol. Assn. of U.K., 1974-76, Council Scottish Marine Biol. Assn., 1974-78. Served with Brit. Royal Air Force, 1947-49. Recipient Alexander Agassiz medal, Nat. Acad. Sci., 1973. Fellow Royal Soc. Edinburgh, Royal Soc. London. Author: The Structure of Marine Ecosystems, 1974. Contbr. articles to profl. jours. Home: Meteor House Woods Hole MA 02543 Office: Woods Hole Oceanographic Instn Woods Hole MA 02543

STEELE, JOHN LAWRENCE, journalist; b. Chgo., June 9, 1917; s. Leo M. and Helen (Schuhmann) S.; grad. Lake Forest Acad., 1935; A.B., Dartmouth, 1939; Nieman fellow, Harvard, 1951-52; m. Louise V. Stein, June 27, 1940; children—Deborah, John Lawrence, Scott. With Chgo. City News Bur., 1939; staff Chgo. bur. U.P.I., 1939-41; bur. legislative corr. U.P., Washington, 1941-42, 45-53; legislative polit. corr. Time mag., 1953-55; White House corr., 1955-58; chief Washington bur. Time-Life mags., 1958-69; sr. corr. Time-Life News Service, 1969-79; v.p. Time Inc., Washington, 1979—. Mem. alumni council Dartmouth, 1971-74; mem. Native Am. Vis. Com., 1973-78, chmn., 1975-78. Served from ensign to lt., USNR, 1942-45. Clubs: City Tavern, Metropolitan (Washington). Collaborator: (with A.H. Vandenberg, Jr. and Joe A. Morris) The Private Papers of Senator Vandenberg, 1952. Contbr. books in field. Home: 3100 Newark St NW Washington DC 20008 Office: 888 16th St NW Washington DC 20006

STEELE, JOSEPH LEE, educator; b. Houston, Aug. 15, 1934; s. Henry Benton and Doris Anne (Binford) S.; B.A., Rice Inst., 1956; M.S., Mass. Inst. Tech., 1957; Ph.D., U. Tex., 1968; m. Elizabeth A. Koch, Jan. 31, 1976. Prof. econs. Memphis State U., 1960-61; econ. intelligence officer C.I.A., 1961-62; prof. decision scis. Am. U., 1966-67; prof. statistics Tex. Christian U., 1967-70, dean Sch. of Bus., 1971-76, David L. Tandy prof. Am. enterprise mgmt., 1976—; vis. prof. U. Sussex (Eng.), 1975-76. Mem. Confrerie des Chevaliers du Tastevin, 1st Internat. Conf. Operational Research. Ops. research adviser Air Chief of Staff, Pentagon, 1967-69; ops. research adviser Dallas/Ft. Worth Regional Airport Bd., 1968—; cons. Battelle Meml. Inst., Columbus, Ohio. Bd. dirs. Tex. Commn. Vol. Blood Donations. Mem. Insts. Organizational Mgmt., C. of C. of U.S., Ft. Worth C. of C. (dir.). Rotarian. Club: Rolls Royce Owners. Author: The Use of Econometric Models by Federal Regulatory Agencies, 1971. Contbr. articles to profl. jours. Home: 3601 Potomac Ave Fort Worth TX 76107

STEELE, LENDELL EUGENE, research scientist; b. Kannapolis, N.C., May 5, 1928; s. Robert Lee and Ina (Chapman) S.: B.S. in Chemistry, George Washington U., 1950; M.A. in Econs., Am. U., 1959; m. Rowena Miller, Jan. 29, 1949; children—Joyce Lee Steele McCartney, Carol Ann Steele González, Pamela Jane, Linda Kay. Chemist, U.S. Geol. Survey, Washington, 1949, U.S. Dept. Agr. Research Center, Beltsville, Md., 1949-50; analytical chemist U.S. Naval Research Lab., Washington, 1950-51, chemist-research physicist, 1953-58, mgr. sci. research, 1958—; metall. engr. AEC, Germantown, Md., 1966; cons. U.S. Metal Properties Council, 1968-70, 75—; U.S. rep. to Internat. Atomic Energy Agy., Vienna, Austria, 1967—. Served with USAF, 1951-53. Recipient Superior Civilian Service medal U.S. Navy, 1976. Fellow Am. Soc. Metals, D.C. Acad. Sci. (Engring. Sci. award 1966), ASTM (Dudley award and medal 1972, bd. dirs. 1979, award of merit 1979); Metal mem. Research Soc. Am. (Applied Sci. award 1962), Am. Nuclear Soc. (Spl. award and prize 1972), Properties Council, Sigma Xi. Author: Analysis of Reactor Vessel Radiation Effects Surveillance Programs, 1970; Neutron Irradiation Embrittlement of Reactor Pressure Vessel Steels, 1975; contbr. articles to profl. jours. Home: 7624 Highland St Springfield VA 22150 Office: Naval Research Lab Washington DC 20375

STEELE, MARGARET THERESE, programmed instrn. co. exec.; b. Kansas City, Kans., Aug. 2, 1910; d. Edward Francis and Therese (Hensmentle) Murphy; student Conservatory of Music, Kansas City, Mo., 1929-32; B.A., U. Kans., 1933; m. James Warren Steele, Jr., Sept. 12, 1936; children—Judith (Mrs. William J. Springer), James Warren III, Donald E., David E. Editor, Adverette, Kansas City, Mo., 1942-44, Nat. Parliamentarian mag., Kansas City, Mo., 1951-57, asso. editor, 1973-77; pres. J.W. Steele & Co., Kansas City, Mo., 1958-68; v.p. Athena Corp., Bethesda, Md., 1972—. Parliamentary cons., instr. Mount Vernon Unit of Parliamentarians, 1976—. Chmn., Council Standards Registered Parliamentarians, 1963-65. Trustee Oakwood, Mo., 1954-56, 60-62. Registered parliamentarian. Recipient Civic Beautification award Mo. K.C.'s, 1968. Mem. Nat. (Service award 1969, pres. 1965-67), Mo. (pres. 1956-57) assns. parliamentarians, D.C. Registered Parliamentarians (pres. 1976-78), Nat. League Am. Pen Women (pres. 1970-72, Distinguished Service award 1966), Internat. Platform Assn., Am. Rose Soc. (nat. accredited show judge), English Speaking Union. Roman Catholic. Club: Woman's of McLean (pres. 1978—). Home: 1707 Strine Dr McLean VA 22101 Office: 7735 Old Georgetown Rd Bethesda MD 20014

STEELE, RICHARD ALLEN, utilities co. exec.; b. Indpls., Jan. 8, 1927; s. Harry A. and Helen A. (Kaiser) S.; B.S. in Bus. Adminstrn. cum laude, Butler U., 1950; m. Jean Porteous, Mar. 14, 1951; children—Richard A., William H., Carol Elizabeth. Acct., Citizens Gas and Coke Utility, Indpls., 1950-55, internat auditor, 1955-59, data processing mgr., 1959-63, dir. systems and audit, 1963-64, controller, 1964-67, asst. gen. mgr., 1967-73, pres., chief exec. officer, 1973—; dir. Indpls. Life Ins. Co., Ind. Nat. Corp., Mayflower Corp. Bd. dirs. Greater Indpls. Progress Com., v.p., 1973-76; bd. dirs. Indpls. area chpt. ARC, 1971—, United Way, 1973—, Day Nursery Found., 1973—, Ind. State Symphony Soc., 1978—; chmn. bd. trustees Butler U., 1974—, Community Hosp., 1974—; v.p. bd. dirs. Jr. Achievement Central Ind., 1978—; bd. dirs. Park. Tudor Sch., 1979—; trustee Butler U., 1974—, chmn., 1974-78. Served with USNR, 1944-46, 50-52. C.P.A., Ind. Mem. Am. Gas Assn. (dir. 1975—), Ind. Gas Assn. (dir. 1968—, pres. 1971), Am. Coke and Coal Chems. Inst., Indpls. C. of C. (vice chmn., dir., mem. exec. com. 1973—), Sigma Chi. Republican. Presbyterian. Club: Meridian Hills Country. Home: 8068 Bayberry Ct Indianapolis IN 46250 Office: 2020 N Meridian St Indianapolis IN 46202

STEELE, RICHARD CHARLES, newspaper exec.; b. Marlboro, Mass., May 13, 1917; D.Sc. (hon.), Worcester Poly. Inst., 1968; m. Louise Farrar, Aug. 14, 1941; children—Nancy Steele Elwell, Virginia Steele Clayton, Barbara. Gen. mgr., v.p. N.Y. Herald Tribune, 1960-61; pres., pub. Worcester Telegram-Gazette, 1961—; dir., past mem. exec. com. A.P.; dir. Enterprise-Sun, Inc., State Mut. Life Assurance Co. Am., State Mut. Securities. Chmn., Arts Council of Worcester; chmn. bd. dirs., past pres. Am. Newspaper Pubs. Assn. Found.; bd. dirs. Newspaper Advt. Bur.; pres., trustee Worcester Sci. Center; trustee Worcester Found. Exptl. Biology, Worcester Hahnemann Hosp. Mem. New Eng. Daily Newspaper Assn. (past pres.), Am. Newspaper Pubs. Assn. (dir.), Am. Antiquarian Soc. (chmn. newspaper steering com.). Clubs: Worcester, Worcester Country; Wianno (Mass.). Office: Worcester Telegram-Gazette 20 Franklin St Worcester MA 01613*

STEELE, RICHARD HAROLD, educator; b. Buffalo, Aug. 1, 1919; s. Henry Goss and Mary Gail (Newton) S.; B.S., U. Ala., 1948; Ph.D., Tulane U., 1953; m. Iona Wood, June 13, 1952; children—Richard, Scott, Raquel. Vis. Investigator Inst. for Muscle Research, Woods Hole, Mass., 1954-57; tchr. Tulane U. Sch. Medicine, New Orleans, 1957—. Served with AUS, 1941-46. Recipient Lederle Med. Faculty award, 1957-60, Research Career Devel. award NIH, 1960-70. Mem. Am. Soc. Biol. Chemists, Am. Chem. Soc., Sigma Xi. Home: 3905 Cleveland Pl Metairie LA 70003 Office: 1430 Tulane Ave New Orleans LA 70112

STEELE, ROBERT HAMPTON, savs. bank exec., former congressman; b. Hartford, Conn., Nov. 3, 1938; s. Robert L. and Shirley (Hanson) S.; B.A., Amherst Coll., 1960; M.A., Columbia, 1963, certificate Russian Inst., 1963; m. Ann Elizabeth Truex, Aug. 5, 1961; children—Kristen, Alison, Jeffrey, Bradley. Soviet specialist U.S. CIA, Washington and Latin Am., 1963-68; securities analyst Travelers Ins. Co., Hartford, 1968-70; mem. 91st-93d Congresses 2d Dist. Conn.; pres. Norwich Savs. Soc. (Conn.), 1975—. Republican candidate for gov. Conn., 1974. Named One of Ten Outstanding Young Men, U.S. Jaycees, 1971. Home: Wicklow Turn Ledyard CT 06339

STEELE, ROBERT MICHAEL, drama critic; b. Chgo., Jan. 14, 1942; s. Robert M. and Ruth (Blume) S.; student Drake U., 1960-61; B.A., U. Colo., 1964. Journalist, Hutchinson (Kans.) News, 1964-66, Topeka Capital, 1966; drama and dance critic Mpls. Tribune, 1966—; weekly columnist Winnipeg (Can.) Free Press, 1978-79; mem. dance adv. panel Nat. Endowment for Arts, 1971-75; critic N.Y. Theatre Rev. Ford Found. fellow, 1969. Contbr. articles to profl. jours. Home: 1415 Douglas Ave Minneapolis MN 55403 Office: 425 Portland Ave Minneapolis MN 55415

STEELE, THOMAS ALLAN, III, constrn. co. exec., real estate co. exec.; b. Cumberland, Md., May 17, 1940; s. Thomas Allan and Sarabelle (Bleckwell) S.; B.A. magna cum laude, Harvard U., 1962, M.B.A. with distinction (George F. Baker Found. fellow), 1969; m. Mary H. Stewart, Aug. 21, 1963; children—Susan T., Barbara A., Douglas S., Elizebeth M. Exec. asst. MGM, N.Y.C., 1969; asst. to v.p. fin. City Investing Co., N.Y.C., 1970, dir. fin. analysis, 1971; exec. v.p. Westamerica Fin. Corp., Denver, 1972, also dir.; v.p. fin. Perini Corp., Framingham, Mass., 1972-75, group v.p. fin. and real estate, 1975-78, sr. v.p. fin. and adminstrn., 1978—, also dir.; pres., chief exec. officer Perini Land & Devel. Co., Framingham, 1975—, also dir. Bd. govs. Council of Greenburgh (N.Y.) Civic Assns., 1971-72; founder, chmn. Saw Mill Valley (N.Y.) Civic Assn., 1971; mem. Boxboro (Mass.) Fin. Com., 1977—, vice chmn., 1978—. Served to lt. USN, 1962-66. Roman Catholic. Office: 73 Mount Wayte Ave Framingham MA 01701

STEELE, WILLIAM FRANK, educator; b. Quincy, Mass., Mar. 14, 1920; s. John Harrison and Gladys (Chase) S.; student Lincoln Tech. Inst., Boston, 1938-41; A.B., M.A., Boston U., 1952; Ph.D., U. Pitts., 1961; m. Ruth Alice Miller, Sept. 4, 1954; children—John Harlan, Susan Jane. Faculty, Heidelberg Coll., Tiffin, Ohio, 1952—, prof. math., 1963—, chmn. dept., 1952—; lectr. extension U. Pitts., Lima, Ohio, 1958-68. Trustee Tiffin YMCA, 1965-70, treas., 1969; trustee 1st Presbyn. Ch., 1976-78, chmn., 1978. Served with C.E., U.S. Army, 1942-45. Recipient Outstanding Service award Tiffin YMCA, 1968. NSF grantee Mass. Inst. Tech., 1970-71. Mem. Math. Assn. Am., Am. Math. Soc., Soc. Indsl. and Applied Math., Phi Beta Kappa. Republican. Home: 181 Clinton Ave Tiffin OH 44883

STEELE, WILLIAM TAYLOR, JR., bus. exec.; b. Appomattox, Va., Nov. 7, 1908; s. William Taylor and Alice (Burke) S.; B.S. in Agrl. Edn., Va. Poly. Inst., 1930; m. Frances Mary Cover, Jan. 8, 1938; children—William Taylor III, Rusell Cover. Tchr. vocat. agr. Varina High Sch., Richmond, Va., 1931-34; with So. States Coop., Inc., 1935-73, dist. mgr., Lynchburg, Va., 1935-37; mgr. Coop. Fertilizer Plant, Balt., 1937-38, asst. mgr., 1938-43; mgr. Coop. Fertilizer Service, Richmond, 1943-47; dir. So. States Wholesale Services, Richmond, 1947-61, gen. mgr., Richmond, 1961-73; mgmt. counsel parent co., 1973, ret., 1973; pres. Coop. Fertilizer Service, Inc., Richmond, Coop. Mills, Inc., Cin., 1950-73; v.p., mem. bd. exec. com. Texas City Refning, Inc. (Tex.), 1958—; now v.p., dir. Stratton Supply, Inc., Petersburg, Va., So. Industries, Inc., Richmond, Central Bank for Coops., Washington. Mem. fed. farm credit bd. FCA, 1962-68. Mem. Greater Richmond C. of C. (pres.). Episcopalian. Kiwanian. Club: Country of Va. Home: 104 Gun Club Rd Richmond VA 23221 Office: 1700 W Main St Richmond VA 23220

STEELMAN, ALAN WATSON, former congressman, business exec.; b. Little Rock, Mar. 15, 1942; s. Ples C. and Flossie (Watson) S.; B.A., Baylor U., 1964; M.L.A., So. Methodist U., 1971; fellow J.F.K. Inst. Politics, Harvard U., 1972; m. Carolyn Findley, Aug. 29, 1962; children—Robin, Kimble, Alan Watson and Allison (twins). Exec. dir. Dallas County Republican Com., 1966-69; exec. dir. Sam Wyly Found., Dallas, 1969; exec. dir. Pres.'s Adv. Council on Minority Bus. Enterprise, Washington, 1969-71; mem. 93d-94th congresses from 5th Tex. Dist.; dir. cons. activities Alexander Proudfoot Co., Chgo. Research. Mem. Friends of Lyndon B. Johnson Library, Austin, Tex.; bd. dirs. Hunger Project; trustee, bd. dirs. KERA-TV, 1969-72; nat. governing bd., chmn. fin. com. Common Cause. Named as future leader Time mag., 1974, Watchdog of the Treasury, 1974, 76, Guardian of Small Bus., 1974, to Golden Age Hall of Fame, 1975; Woodrow Wilson fellow, 1978. Mem. L.Q.C. Lamar Soc. (dir.), Pi Sigma Alpha, Sigma Phi Epsilon (hon.) Home: Ingleside Farms Trappe MD 21673

STEELY, WILL FRANK, educator; b. Hazel, Ky., Apr. 9, 1925; s. Thomas Munsey and Michie (Vaughan) S.; A.B., U. S.C., 1947; M.A., U. Ky., 1948; Ph.D., U. Rochester, 1956; m. Iosetta Morris, July 8, 1951; children—William Morris, Lisa Elizabeth. Prof. history, chmn. dept. social scis. Blue Mountain (Miss.) Coll., 1951-56; prof. history, chmn. dept. Murray (Ky.) State U., 1956-67; prof. history, acad. dean Clinch Valley Coll. of U. Va., 1967-70; pres. No. Ky. U., Highland Heights, 1970-75, prof. history, 1975—. Asst., Salzburg Seminar Am. Studies, 1948; vis. prof. Coe Found. Inst., Union Coll. (Ky.), 1960. Served with USNR, 1943-46. Mem. Am. Hist. Assn., Phi Beta Kappa. Baptist. Office: No Ky U Campus Highland Heights KY 41076

STEEN, DAVID LLOYD, library adminstr.; b. Swan River, Man., Can., Mar. 8, 1947; s. Lloyd Ferguson and Lavinia Marguerite (Townson) S.; B.A., U. Winnipeg, 1969. Research asst. property tax credit Dept. Fin., Province of Man., 1973; policy analyst planning Secretariat of Cabinet, Province Man., 1975; dir. pub. library services br. Man. Dept. Tourism, Recreation, Cultural Affairs, 1975—. Mem. Canadian, Man. library assns., Man. Library Trustees Assn. Home: 357 Waterloo St Winnipeg MB R3N 0S7 Canada Office: 139 Hamelin St Winnipeg MN R3T 4H4 Canada

STEEN, HUGH FLEMING, former gas co. exec.; b. Eula, Tex., Mar. 28, 1911; s. Preston C. and Maude C. (Fleming) S.; student La. State U., 1931-32; LL.D., N.Mex. State U., 1973; m. Mary Marshall, Aug. 10, 1937; children—Stephen M. (dec.), Stanley H. With El Paso Natural Gas Co., 1931—, supt. field, transmission supt., asst. gen. supt., v.p., gen. supt., 1932-57, v.p., mgr. pipeline ops., 1957-65, vice chmn., chief exec. officer, 1976—, also dir.; pres., chief exec. officer El Paso Co., 1974-78, now adv. dir.; dir. El Paso Natural Gas Products Co., Vallen Indsl. Safety Corp., Nat. Standard Bank, Geosource Inc. Mem. Am., So. (past pres.), Pacific Coast (past pres.) gas assns. Clubs: River Oaks Country. Office: PO Box 2185 Houston TX 77001

STEEN, MELVIN CLIFFORD, lawyer; b. Mpls., Feb. 16, 1907; s. Erick and Annie (Running) S.; J.D., U. Minn., 1929; m. Dorothy M. Wagner, Nov. 4, 1932; m. 2d, Florence W. Rollins, Sept. 13, 1952; children—Gordon R., Leslie A., Deborah R., Erick R. Admitted to Minn. bar, 1931, N.Y. bar, 1931, D.C. bar, 1947; asso. firm Root, Clark, Buckner & Ballantine, N.Y.C., 1929-45, partner, 1944-45; now partner Cleary, Gottlieb, Steen & Hamilton, N.Y.C., Washington, Paris, Brussels, London, Hong Kong; dir. MITE Corp., Fairchild Industries, Inc. Decorated chevalier de la Legion d'Honneur; recipient Outstanding Achievement award U. Minn., 1975. Mem. Internat. Law Assn., Am., N.Y. State bar assns., Assn. Bar City N.Y., Am. Bar Found., N.Y. County Lawyers Assn., Order of Coif, Delta Theta Phi. Clubs: India House, Sky (N.Y.C.); Siwanoy Country (Bronxville, N.Y.); Minnesota (Mpls.). Home: 52 Oakledge Rd Bronxville NY 10708 Office: 1 State St Plaza New York NY 10004

STEEN, PETER, copper co. exec.; b. Johannesburg, S. Africa, Dec. 8, 1930; s. Oscar Jul and Eleen Edward (Brock) S.; came to U.S., 1978; Asso., Camborne (Eng.) Sch. Mines, 1956; m. Norma Valerie Crawford, Feb. 16, 1956; children—Beverley Ann, Gregory Jul, Karen Louise, Michael Rodney. From ofcl. learner to mine supt. Anglo American, Zambia, 1956-68; mine supt. Rio Algom Mines, LaRonge, Sask., Can., 1968-70; gen. mgr. Whitehorse, Copper Mines, Yukon, Can., 1970-73; exec. v.p. Cassiar Asbestos Corp., Vancouver, B.C., Can., 1973-74, pres., chief exec. officer, 1974-78; pres., chief exec. officer Inspiration Consol. Copper Co., Phoenix, 1978—; dir. Apache Powder Co. Mem. Am. Inst. Mining Engrs., Mine Mgrs. Assn. S. Africa, Profl. Engrs. Assn. of Ont., Can. Inst. Mining and Metallurgy. Office: 100 W Washington St Phoenix AZ 85003

STEEN, WILLIAM BROOKS, found. exec., physician; b. Joliet, Ill., July 14, 1904; s. Earl R. and Sarah Lavinia (Brooks) S.; student Joliet Jr. Coll., 1922-24; B.S., U. Chgo., 1925, Ph.D., 1931, M.D., 1931; m. Rose Thacker, Oct. 19, 1942; 1 son, William Brooks. Intern Cook County Hosp., Chgo., 1931-33, resident pathology, 1934; instr. anatomy U. Chgo., 1926-31, asst. medicine, 1934-37; asso. physician Desert San., Tucson, 1937-38; resident physician Pima County Gen. Hosp., 1938-39; physician Tucson Clinic, 1939—; med. dir. Oshrin Hosp., 1952-66, Elks State Assn. Hosp., 1951-67; pres. Nat. Asthmatic Found., 1966—; chief staff St. Mary's Hosp., 1955. Mem. bd. Nat. Found. Asthmatic Children, 1954—, med. dir., 1955—, exec. com., 1954—, pres., 1966—; mem. Hosp. Adv. Survey and Constrn. Council, Ariz., 1957-65; mem. Ariz. Bd. Health, 1965-70, sec., 1966-67, vice chmn. bd., 1968, pres., 1970—. Pres. bd. health City Tucson-Pima County, 1952-56; med. dir., mem. exec. com. Nat. Found. Asthmatic Children, 1954—, v.p., 1965, pres., 1966—; pres. Navajo Health Assn., 1955-56. Served to maj. AUS, 1942-46. Fellow A.C.P., Am. Coll. Chest Physicians (past pres. Ariz.), Am. Acad. Allergy (v.p. 1965-66), Am. Coll. Allergists (sec., bd. regents), AAAS; mem. A.M.A. (del. from Ariz. 1966—), Ariz. (pres. 1963-64), Pima County (past pres.) med. socs., Assn. Physicians and Surgeons, Ariz., Am. Trudeau socs., Ariz. Soc. Internists, Ariz. Soc. Allergy, Ariz. Acad. Sci., S.A.R. (pres. Tucson chpt. 1965-67, pres. state soc. 1967—), Am. Thoracic Soc., Am. Soc. Internal Medicine, Sigma Xi, Beta Theta Pi, Nu Sigma Nu. Presbyterian. Clubs: Tucson Literary (sec. 1967—), Old Pueblo, Rotary, Mountain Oyster. lHome and Office: 3242 E 5th St Tucson AZ 85716

STEER, ALFRED GILBERT, JR., educator; b. Lansdowne, Pa., May 30, 1913; s. Alfred Gilbert and Selma Elizabeth (Taber) S.; A.B., Haverford Coll., 1935; M.A., Duke, 1938; Ph.D., U. Pa., 1954; m. Elizabeth Jean Kell, Sept. 6, 1947; children—Susan Elizabeth, John Thomas. Instr., Washington and Lee U., 1937-41, Haverford Coll., U. Pa., 1947-55; asst. prof., asso. prof. State U. N.Y., Binghamton, 1955-59; asso. prof. Columbia, 1959-67; prof., head dept. Germanic and Slavic langs. U. Ga., Athens, 1967—, chmn. linguistics com., 1969—. Mem. corp. Haverford Coll.; dir. U. System of Ga. Studies Abroad Programs, 1969-70, Prospective Tchr. Fellowship Program, HEW. Served with USNR, World War II; head lang. div. Internat. Mil. Tribunal, Nurnberg, 1945-46. Fellow Am. Philos. Soc., 1965-66, Columbia Council for Research in Humanities. Mem. Modern Lang. Assn., Am. Assn. Tchrs. German (chpt. v.p., pres. 1970-71). Author: (with W.W. Pusey III, B.Q. Morgan) Readings in Military German, 1943; Goethe's Social Philosophy, 1955; Goethe's Science in the Structure of the Wanderjahre, 1979. Contbg. author: Jahrbuch des Freien Deutschen Hochstifts, 1965. Contbr. articles to profl. jours. Home: 215 Bishop Dr Athens GA 30601

STEER, CHARLES MELVIN, educator; b. Midvale, N.J., Feb. 13, 1913; s. Charles Henry and Augusta (Smith) S.; A.B., Columbia, 1933, M.D., 1937, Med.Sci.D., 1942; m. Catherine Quinn, June 29, 1945; children—Elizabeth, Anne. Resident in obstetrics and gynecology Presbyn. Hosp., N.Y.C., 1939-43; practice medicine, specializing in obstetrics and gynecology, Presbyn. Hosp., 1946—; mem. faculty

Coll. Physicians and Surgeons, Columbia, N.Y.C., 1946—, prof., acting chmn. dept. obstetrics and gynecology, 1968-70. Served with M.C., AUS, 1943-46. Fellow A.C.S., Am. Coll. Obstetrics and Gynecology, N.Y. Obstet. Soc. Club: Siwanoy (Bronxville, N.Y.). Author: Evaluation of the Pelvis in Obstetrics. Contbr. profl. jours. Home: 2 Eastway Bronxville NY 10708 Office: 161 Fort Washington Ave New York City NY 10032

STEER, MAX DAVID, educator, speech pathologist; b. N.Y.C., June 14, 1910; s. Charles and Sadie (Hisiger) S.; B.S., L.I. U., 1932, LL.D., 1957; A.M., U. Iowa, 1933, Ph.D., 1938; m. Ruth Pittelman, Aug. 25, 1942. Student tchr. N.Y.C. Pub. Schs., 1931-32; research asst. psychol. and speech clinic U. Iowa, 1934-35; instr. speech, dir. speech clinic Purdue U., 1935-37, asst. prof., 1938-40, asso. prof., 1940-46, prof. speech, dir. speech and hearing clinic, dir. voice sci. lab., dir. Purdue Naval voice communications research program, supr. pub. sch. hearing test service, 1946—, head dept. audiology and speech scis., 1963-70, Hanley Distinguished prof. audiology and speech scis., 1970-76, Distinguished prof. emeritus, 1976—. Cons. speech, hearing problems Ind. Bd. Health, 1954-55, chmn. hearing and speech adv. com., 1956; cons. neurol. and sensory diseases service program USPHS; cons. Ind. Sch. for Deaf, Muscatatuck State Sch. for Retarded, Ft. Wayne State Sch. for Retarded, Pan Am. Health Orgn., WHO, 1972—, U. Bogota, 1974—; mem. nat. research adv. com. Bur. Edn. for Handicapped, U.S. Office Edn., HEW, 1972—; cons., vis. lectr. Nat. Rehab. Inst., Panama, 1974—; cons. various govt. agys., 1965—; mem. Ind. Hearing Commn., chmn., 1958-60, 67—. Bd. dirs. Ind. Soc. Crippled Children, 1947-49, v.p., 1950-51; bd. dirs. Purdue Research Found., 1974—. Pres., Am. Speech and Hearing Found. Served as lt. comdr. USNR, 1942-46. Recipient citation as hon. old master Purdue U., 1975; Kephart award for distinguished service to handicapped, 1974; Sagamore of Wabash citation Gov. Ind., 1976. Diplomate in clin. psychology Am. Bd. Examiners in Profl. Psychology. Mem. Am. Speech and Hearing Assn. (pres. 1951), Internat. Assn. Logopedics and Phoniatrics (v.p. 1959-65, 68—), Speech Assn. Am. (chmn. speech sci. com. 1948), Acoustical Soc. Am., Am. Psychol. Assn., AAAS, Ind. Speech Correction Assn. (pres. 1938, exec. council 1946-49), Ind. Clin. Psychol. Assn., AAUP, Latin Am. Fedn. Logopedics, Phoniatrics and Audiology (cons. 1972—, hon. mem. exec. bd. 1973—, award 1973), Sigma Xi. Contbr. research reports to psychol., speech jours. Home: 222 Forrest Hill Dr West Lafayette IN 47906

STEERE, DAVID D., ins. co. exec.; grad. Hotchkiss Sch., Lakeville, Conn., 1933, Yale, 1937, Harvard Grad. Sch. Bus., 1939; m. Cherrie Perkins; children—Catherine, Shirley, Kenneth, Anne. Chmn. bd., pres. Allied Fin. Co.; chmn. bd. Steere Tank Lines; former sec., chmn. Republic Ins. Co., now chmn. exec., finance coms.; dir. Merc. Nat. Bank, Dallas. Mem. Nat. Consumer Finance Assn. (past dir., past pres. Am. Finance Conf.). Trustee Selwyn Sch., Denton, Tex. Clubs: Terpsichorian, Brook Hollow, Dallas Athletic, Idlewild (Dallas); Bath and Tennis, Everglades (Palm Beach, Fla.); Koon Kreek (Athens, Tex.); N.Y. Yacht (N.Y.C.); Stone Horse Yacht (Harwichport, Mass.); Eastward Ho Country (Chatham, Mass.); St. Petersburg (Fla.) Yacht; Yale Sailing Assos. (New Haven, trustee). Home: 31 Royal Way Dallas TX 75229 also Ayer Ln Harwichport MA 02646 Office: Box 2998 Dallas TX 75221

STEERE, DOUGLAS VAN, educator; b. Harbor Beach, Mich., Aug. 31, 1901; s. Edward Morris and Edith Ruby (Monroe) S.; B.S. in Agr., Mich. State U., 1923; A.M., Harvard U., 1925, Ph.D., 1931; B.A. (Rhodes scholar), Oxford U., 1927, M.A., 1953; D.D., Lawrence Coll., 1950; L.H.D., Oberlin Coll., 1954, Earlham Coll., 1965; S.T.D., Gen. Theol. Sem., 1967; LL.D., Haverford Coll., 1970; m. Dorothy Lou Mac-Eachron, June 12, 1929; children—Helen Horn, Anne Nash. Tchr., Onaway (Mich.) High Sch., 1921-22; faculty philosophy Haverford Coll., 1928—, prof., 1941—, also dir. grad. reconstrn. and relief tng., 1943-45, Thomas Wistar Brown prof. philosophy, 1950-64, Thomas Wistar Brown prof. emeritus, 1964—; Reinicker lectr. Episcopal Theol. Sem., 1938; Ingersoll lectr. Harvard, 1942; William Belden Noble lectr., 1943; Alden Tuthill lectr. Chgo. Theol. Sem., 1943; Carew lectr. Hartford Theol. Sem., 1945; Hoyt lectr. Union Theol. Sem., N.Y.C., 1947; Rauschenbusch lectr. Rochester-Colgate, 1952; Swarthmore lectr., London, 1955; Nitobe lectr., Tokyo, 1954; Dana lectr. Carleton Coll., 1954, 62, Stone lectr. Princeton Theol. Sem., 1957, Emily Hobhouse Meml. lectr., Johannesburg, 1957; Harry Emerson Fosdick vis. prof. Union Theol. Sem., 1961-62, Auburn lectr., 1961; Maurice Webb lectr. U. Natal, South Africa, 1971; Shaffer lectr. Northwestern U., 1976. Organizer Quaker Relief Action, Finland, 1945; chmn., Friends World Com., 1964-70; Quaker observer-del. Vatican Council, 1963-65, Lambeth Conf., London, 1968. Chmn. bd. dirs. Pendle Hill Sch. Religion and Social Studies, 1954-70, dir. summer sch., 5 summers; summer sch. Union Theol. Sem., 1947, 51; trustee John Woolman Meml., chmn. bd. trustees, 1947-54; trustee Walnwright House, East Ridge Center, Lewis M. Stevens Conf. Found. Recipient Alumni award Mich. State U., 1947. Mem. Am. Philos. Assn., Assn. Rhodes Scholars, Am. Theol. Soc. (sec. 1935-42, v.p. 1944-45, pres. 1945-46), AAUP, Internat. Fellowship of Reconciliation (chmn. Am. sect. 1954-66), Phi Beta Kappa. Mem. Soc. Friends (clk. Phila. yearly meeting ministers and elders 1944-47, participant Quaker missions, mem. Fed. Commn. Chs. Commn. Theologians on Relations of Ch. to War, 1944-45, Commn. on Atomic Warfare in Light of Christian Faith, 1945-46, World Council Chs. Commn. on Responsibility of Christian Ch. for Prevention of War in Atomic, 1956-60). Author, editor or translator books relating to field; contbr. to religious publs. Mem. editorial bd. Religion in Life, 1961—. Home: 2 College Circle Haverford PA 19041

STEERE, WILLIAM CAMPBELL, botanist; b. Muskegon, Mich., Nov. 4, 1907; s. James A. and Lois (Campbell) S.; B.S., U. Mich., 1929, A.M., 1931, Ph.D., 1932, D.Sc., 1962; postgrad. U. Pa., 1929-31; D.ès-Sci., Montreal, 1959; m. Dorothy Clara Osborne, June 14, 1927; children—Lois (Mrs. Allen Beattie), Alice (Mrs. Joseph Coulombe), William Campbell. Instr. botany Temple U., Phila., 1929-31; instr. U. Mich., 1931-36, prof., 1946-50, chmn. dept., 1947-50, curator bryophytes, 1945-50; prof. biology (botany) Stanford, 1950-58, dean grad. div., 1955-58; dir. N.Y. Bot. Garden, 1958-70, pres., 1970-72, pres. emeritus, sr. scientist, 1973—, prof. botany Columbia U., 1958-76, prof. emeritus, 1976—. Botanist, U. Mich.-Carnegie Instn. expdn. to Yucatan, 1932; U.S. Cinchona Mission to Ecuador, 1943-44; leader U. Mich. expdn. to Great Bear Lake, N.W. Ty., 1948; exchange prof. U. P.R., 1939-40; botanist U.S. Geol. Survey, Alaska, 1949, Arctic Research Lab., Point Barrow, Alaska, summers 1951-53, 60, 61, 63, 72, 74, Greenland, 1962; program dir. systematic biology NSF, 1954-55; pres. bryol. sect. 8th, 9th Internat. Bot. Congresses, Paris, 1954, Montreal, 1959. Decorated Order of Sacred Treasure (Japan); recipient Liberty Hyde Bailey medal Am. Hort. Soc., 1965; Mary Soper Pope medal Cranbrook Inst. Scis., 1970. Benjamin Franklin fellow Royal Soc. Arts London. Fellow AAAS (v.p. 1949, 66, 67), Calif. Acad. Scis., Am. Geog. Soc.; mem. Am. Fern Soc., Am. Soc. Plant Taxonomists (pres. 1959), Assn. Tropical Biology, Internat. Assn. Bryologists (pres. 1969-75), New Eng., So. Appalachian, Torrey (pres. 1961) bot. clubs, Bot. Soc. Am. (pres. 1959), Inst. Ecuatoriano de Ciencias Naturales (hon.), Finnish (corr.), Calif. bot. socs., Zool. Soc. Vanamo (corr.), Mich. Acad. Sci., Arts and Letters (editor 1936-40), Research Club U. Mich., Sci. Research Club U. Mich. (pres. 1941-42), Soc. Venezolana de Ciencias Naturales (corr.), Brit., Am. (pres. 1936-37) bryological socs., Assn. Sudamericana de Fitotaxonomists, Am. Soc. Naturalists (pres. 1957-58), Soc. for Study Evolution, Arctic Inst. N.Am., Am. (pres. 1968-70), N.Y. State (pres. 1961-62) assns. museums, Sigma Xi. Clubs: Cosmos (Washington); Century Assn., University (N.Y.C.). Editor: Fifty Years of Botany, 1958, Am. Jour. Botany, 1953-57; asso. editor Annales Bryologici, 1936-39; editor-in-chief The Bryologist, 1938-54; co-editor: This is Life, 1962, Evolutionary Biology, 1966—. Author: Liverworts of Southern Michigan, 1940; Lab. Outline for Elementary Botany (with others), 1937; Biological Abstracts-Brosis. The First 50 Years, 1976; numerous tech. articles on cytology and systematics of petunia, musci and hepaticae of Mich., musci of tropical Am., Arctic Am., spl. problems of bryogeog., obits of bryologists, fossil bryophytes from Pleistocene and earlier times, search for and discovery of Cinchona species in No. S.Am. Home: 205 Boulder Trail Bronxville NY 10708 Office: NY Bot Garden Bronx NY 10458

STEERS, NEWTON IVAN, JR., former congressman; b. Glen Ridge, N.J., Jan. 13, 1917; s. Newton Ivan and Claire L. (Herder) S.; grad. Hotchkiss Sch., 1935; A.B. in Econs., Yale, 1939, J.D., 1948; certificate advanced meteorology Mass. Inst. Tech., 1943; m. Gabrielle Irwin, Dec. 29, 1978; children—Newton Ivan III, Hugh A., Burr G. Asst. in plant mgmt. E.I. duPont de Nemours Co., Inc., Parlin, N.J., 1939-40, asst. tech. supt. tests, Seaford, Del., 1940-41; asst. works mgr. Gen. Aniline & Film Corp., 1948-51; asst. to br. chief AEC, 1951, div. dir., 1952, asst. gen. mgr., 1953, commr., 1953; pres., dir. Atomics, Physics & Sci. Fund, Inc., Washington, 1953-65; ins. commr. State of Md., 1967-70; mem. Md. Senate, 1971-76; mem. 95th Congress from Md. Chmn., Md. Republican Com., 1964. Capt. USAF Res. Home and Office: 6601 River Rd Bethesda MD 20034

STEEVES, HARRISON ROSS, educator; b. N.Y.C., Apr. 8, 1881; s. John Francis and Imogene (Upson) S.; A.B., Columbia, 1903, A.M., 1904, Ph.D., 1913, Litt.D., 1972; m. Jessie Hurd, June 16, 1906 (div. 1947); children—Imogene Hurd, Harrison Ross; m. 2d, Edna R. Leake, Jan. 28, 1947. Asst. and instr. English, Columbia, 1905-13, asst. prof., 1913-19, asso. prof., 1919-26; prof. English, 1926-49, now emeritus. Mem. Nat. Conf. on Uniform Entrance Requirements in English (chmn. 1925-31); pres. Coll. Conf. on English of Central Atlantic States, 1919- 20. Mem. Phi Beta Kappa, Theta Delta Chi. Author: Learned Societies and English Scholarship, 1913; The Teaching of Literature (with C.C. Fries, J.H. Hanford), 1926; Literary Aims and Art, 1927; Good Night, Sheriff (fiction), 1941; Before Jane Austen, 1965. Co-author: A College Program in Action 1946. Editor: Representative Essays in Modern Thought (with F.H. Ristine), 1913; Selected Poems of Wordsworth, 1922; Three Eighteenth Century Romances, 1931; Plays from the Modern Theatre, 1931; Anatole France's Penguin Island, 1933; (with Edna L. Steeves) Wild Sports in the Far West (Friedrich Gerstäcker), 1968. Translator: Maurice Donnay's Lovers, 1931. Contbr. articles on edn., lit. to newspapers, mags., scholarly publs. Home: 25 North Rd Kingston RI 02881

STEFAN, JOSEPH, banker, industrialist; b. N.Y.C.; s. Alfred and Elsie (Puer) S.; student N.Y. U., 1938-40, Am. Inst. Banking, 1946-48; m. Gloria Virginia Uher; children—Geoffrey Lance, Lorene Claire, Janyce Lynne. With coll. tng. program 1st Nat. City Bank N.Y., 1946-49, officer, 1950-59; mem. exec. mgmt. group as asst. to group exec., v.p. RCA, N.Y.C. and abroad, 1959-63, v.p. record div., 1963-66, v.p., gen. mgr. magnetic products div., 1967-71; dir. RCA, Ltd., Gt. Britain; chmn. bd., mng. dir. RCA, Ltd., London, 1967-71; exec. v.p., chief adminstrv. officer Security Nat. Bank, N.Y.C., 1972-75; chmn., pres. Miami Nat. Bank (Fla.), 1975-79, Modernage Furniture Co., 1976-79; pres. Essayon Inc., Miami, 1979—. Bd. dirs. United Way L.I., Dade County Pillars Club of United Way; bd. govs. Adelphi U. Sch. Banking; trustee Fla. Internat. U.; founder Players State Theater, Miami; dir. Internat. Film Festival of Greater Miami. Served from pvt. to lt. col. C.E., AUS, 1941-46; col. Res. ret. Decorated Bronze Star with oak leaf cluster and valor device, Purple Heart; Croix de Guerre (France); recipient Nat. Spirit of Life award City of Hope, 1977; Eleanor Roosevelt award State of Israel, 1978. Mem. Dade County C. of C. Clubs: Saint Pierre Golf and Country (Chepstow, Gt. Britain); Belfrey (London); Sleepy Hollow Country (Scarborough-on-Hudson, N.Y.); LaGorce Country (Miami Beach, Fla.); Bankers, Palm Bay, Cricket, Jockey, 200 (Miami). Home: 11111 Biscayne Blvd Miami FL 33161

STEFANCIC, EMIL JOSEPH, univ. librarian; b. Cleve., Sept. 18, 1916; s. Steve and Anna (Sercel) S.; B.A., Miami U., Oxford, Ohio, 1940; B.S. in L.S., Western Res. U., 1941, postgrad., 1946-49; m. Jane Jevnikar, Aug. 23, 1947; 1 dau., Kathleen Mary. Library asst. Cleve. Pub. Library, 1940-41; asst. librarian Fenn Coll. Library, Cleve., 1941-42, 46-55, librarian, 1955-65; librarian Cleve. State U., 1965-70, asso. dir. libraries, 1970—. Active Cleveland Community Chest. Served with USAAF, 1942-45. Decorated Air medal, Purple Heart. Mem. Am., Ohio (chmn. coll. and univ. round table 1963-64) library assns. Roman Catholic (lector). Club: Caterpillar. Home: 25504 Chatworth Dr Euclid OH 44117 Office: Cleve State U Cleveland OH 44115

STEFANELLI, JOSEPH JAMES, artist; b. Phila., Mar. 20, 1921; s. Alessandro and Carmela (Leone) S.; student Graphic Sketch Club, 1934-38, Phila. Mus. Coll. Art, 1938-40, Pa. Acad. Fine Arts, 1940-41, New Sch. for Social Research, 1949-50, Art Students League, N.Y.C., 1950-51, Hans Hoffman Sch. Painting, N.Y.C., 1951-52. One-man shows: Artists Gallery, 1950, New Gallery, 1952, Hendler Gallery, Phila., 1953, Artists Gallery, 1954, Ganymede Gallery, 1956, Poindexter Gallery, 1957, 58, 60, Hacker Gallery, 1962, Thibaut Gallery, 1963, Princeton U., 1964, U. Ark., 1965, Westbeth Galleries, 1971, New Sch. for Social Research, 1972, Bertha Schaeffer Gallery, 1973, 74, Andre Zarre Gallery, 1977; group shows include: Stable Gallery, Kootz Gallery, Poindexter Gallery, Tanager Gallery, Mus. Modern Art, Whitney Mus., Andre Zarre Gallery; ann. shows: Whitney Mus., Pa. Acad., Corcoran Gallery, Carnegie Internat., U. Ill., Albright Mus., Walker Art Center, Chgo. Art Inst., Mus. Modern Art; represented in permanent collections: Balt. Mus., Sarah Lawrence Coll., N.Y. U., Cornell U., U. Calif. Mus., Geigy-Ciba collection, Chase Manhattan Bank, Union Carbide Co., U. Mass., U. Mont., Norfolk Art Mus., Walker Art Center, Whitney Mus., also pvt. collections; faculty U. Calif., Berkeley, summers 1960, 63; vis. critic Cornell U., U. Ark., U. Iowa, U. W.Va., U. Wis., U. N.Mex.; artist in residence Princeton U., 1963-66; faculty Columbia U., 1966-74, New Sch. for Social Research, 1966—, Bklyn. Coll., 1974—; murals include: pub. schs., Bklyn., Manhattan Community Coll. War artist for Yank, Army weekly. Recipient Fulbright award for Rome, 1958-59; Spear Research Fund award Princeton U. for Rome, summer 1965; Am. Research Center in Egypt fellow, 1966-67; N.Y. State Council of Arts award, 1971.

STEFANIAK, NORBERT JOHN, educator; b. Milw., Jan. 12, 1921; s. Peter Stephen and Mary Ann (Schlaikowski) S.; B.B.A., U. Wis., 1948, M.B.A., 1950, Ph.D., 1960; m. Elizabeth Jean Horning, Aug. 27, 1949; children—John, Mary, Jane, Beth, Joel, Peter, James, Thomas, Anne, Jean. Instr., U. Wis., Milw., 1950-53; treas., controller Wauwatosa Realty Co. (Wis.), 1953-56; prof. bus. adminstrn. U. Wis., Milw., 1957-75. Past commr. West Allis (Wis.) Planning Commn. Bd. dirs. Guadalupe Med. and Dental Center; trustee West Allis Meml. Hosp., Sacred Heart Sch. Theology; gen. chmn. Milw. Archdiocese Stewardship Appeal. Served with USAAF, World War II. C.P.A. Mem. Am. Soc. Real Estate Counselors, Am. Real Estate and Urban Econs. Assn. (past pres.), Wis. Realtors Assn. (past dir.), Wis. Real Estate Exam. Bd. (vice chmn.). Author monograph, also articles. Home: 865 S 76th St West Allis WI 53214 Office: 5810 W Oklahoma Ave Milwaukee WI 53219

STEFANO, JOSEPH, author, TV producer; b. Phila., May 5, 1922; s. Dominic and Josephine (Vottima) S.; ed. pub. schs.; m. Marilyn Epstein, Dec. 5, 1953; 1 son, Andrew Dominic. Toured as song and dance man in Student Prince, 1945, Merry Widow, 1946; composer music and lyrics popular songs, night club revues, indsl. shows, others, 1946-57; author original screenplays, The Black Orchid, 1958, The Naked Edge, 1960, Psycho, 1960, Anna di Brooklyn, 1962, Eye of the Cat, 1969, Futz, 1970; author TV drama, Made in Japan, 1959, movies for TV, 1970-78; pres. Villa di Stefano Prodns., 1962—; producer, author The Outer Limits, TV series, 1963-64. Recipient Robert E. Sherwood award for Made in Japan, Fund for Republic, 1959; Edgar Allen Poe award for Psycho, Mystery Writers Am., 1960; Columbian award Federated Italo-Ams. Calif., 1964. Mem. Writers Guild Am., Dirs. Guild Am., Producers Guild Am., Acad. Motion Pictures Arts and Scis., Mystery Writers Am., ASCAP. Home: 10216 Cielo Dr Beverly Hills CA 90210

STEFANSCHI, SERGIU, dancer; b. Komralid, Romania, Mar. 2, 1941; came to Can., 1971, naturalized, 1977; s. Alexander and Lidia S.; diploma Acad. Dance, Leningrad, 1960. Prin. dancer Bucharest (Romania) Opera, 1960-68, Jeunesse Musicale de France, 1969-70, Theatre Francoise de la Dance, Paris, 1970, Nat. Ballet of Can., Toronto, Ont., 1971-78; tchr. Nat. Ballet Sch. and Nat. Ballet of Can., Toronto, 1978—; appeared with Belgrade (Yugoslavia) Opera, 1966, 68, Coob Marieta (Ga.) Ballet, 1976. Recipient Silver medal I, Internat. Ballet Concourse, Varna, Bulgaria, 1964. Mem. Actors Equity Can. Mem. Romania Orthodox Ch. Home: 319 Ave Keewatim Toronto ON M4P 2A4 Canada Office: 111 Maitland St Toronto ON M4Y 1E4 Canada

STEFANY, JOHN EDGAR, architect; b. Orange, N.J., Aug. 16, 1931; s. Frederick Joseph and Helen Augusta (Maull) S.; B.Arch., Syracuse U., 1954; m. Barbara Jean Stefany, May 30, 1953; children—David, Darrell, Kristin. Project architect Sargent, Webster, Crenshaw & Folley, Architects/Engrs., Syracuse, N.Y., 1958-64; prin. Mc Elvy, Jennenein, Stefany & Howard, Architects/Planners, Tampa, Fla., 1964—; cons. environ. edn. Fla. Dept. Edn., 1972-79; cons., mem. and nat. chmn. Artist-in-Schs. Panel, Nat. Endowment for Arts, 1977—. Served to lt. C.E., USN, 1955-58. Lic. architect, N.Y. State, Fla. Fellow AIA; mem. Urban Land Inst. (asso.), Nat. Council Archtl. Registration Bds. (nat. cert.). Democrat. Maj. archtl. projects include Engring. Coll. U. Fla., 1966; USN Recruit Tng. Center, Tng. and Recruit Processing Facilities, Orlando, Fla., 1970; Hillsborough County (Fla.) Sch. Adminstrn. Center, 1979; Whiting Plaza Office Complex, Tampa, 1974. Office: 102 W Whiting St Tampa FL 33602

STEFFEN, WALTER WILLIAM, ins. co. exec.; b. Miller City, Ohio, Mar. 12, 1918; s. Joseph Herman and Barbara (Balbaugh) S.; student U. Toledo, 1936-38; B.A., U. Mich., 1941; m. Elizabeth Hickling, June 21, 1941; children—David Joseph, Kathryn Anne, Barbara Martha, Joseph Walter; m. 2d, Maryella Wilson, June 13, 1975. With Lincoln Nat. Life Ins. Co., Ft. Wayne, Ind., 1941—, asst. v.p., 1954-57, 2d v.p., 1957-63, v.p. charge reins., 1963-67, sr. v.p. reins., 1967-73; ins. cons., Ft. Wayne, 1973-75; v.p., dir. LNL Equity Sales Corp., 1969-73; dir. Am. Commonwealth Financial Corp., Dallas, 1973-75, Gt. Fidelity Life Ins. Co., Evansville, Ind., 1973-75; exec. v.p. Am. Life Ins. Co., Wilmington, Del., 1975-76; v.p., sr. actuary Booke & Co., Indpls., 1976, pres., dir., 1976-79; sr. v.p. Meridian Life Ins. Co., Indpls., 1979—. Pres. bd. dirs. Catholic Social Service, 1967-69. Served with C.E., AUS, 1944-46, Fellow Soc. Actuaries (bd. govs. 1968-71), Am. Acad. Actuaries; mem. Winston-Salem C. of C. Clubs: U. of Mich. (past pres.), Bermuda Run Country, Rotary, K.C. (4 deg.). Home: 406 Bent Tree Ln Indianapolis IN 46260 Office: Meridian Life Ins Co PO Box 1980B Indianapolis IN 46207

STEFFENS, DOROTHY R., orgn. exec.; b. N.Y.C., May 5, 1921; d. Saul M. and Pearl Y. (Reiter) Cantor; B.B.A. (N.Y. C. of C. scholar, N.Y. State Regents scholar), Coll. City N.Y., 1941; M.Ed., Temple U., 1961; postgrad. Howard U., 1961-62; m. Jerome Steffens, Nov. 19, 1940; children—Heidi Sue, Nina Ellen. Economist, Nat. War Labor Bd., Washington, 1941-44, United Elec. Radio Machine Workers, Phila., 1944-46; instr. group dynamics Temple U., Phila., 1955-57; seminar program dir. Soc. Friends, Washington, 1958-61; tng. dir. Nat. Council Negro Women, Washington, 1967-68; edn. cons. Peace Corps, Nigeria, 1969-70; exec. dir. Women's Internat. League for Peace and Freedom, Phila., 1971-77; exec. dir. Fund for Open Info. and Accountability, Inc., 1978—; labor relations cons., Phila., 1946-51; dir. Conf. on Children and Youth, Washington, 1966-67; exec. sec. Nigerian Women's Com., 1968-69; del. African Women's Seminar UN, Accra, Ghana, 1969. Mem. internat. div. exec. com. Ams. Friends Ser. Com., 1977—. Mem. Montgomery County (Md.) Edn. Assn. (officer exec. com. 1965-67). Soc. of Friends. Author: The Day after Summer, 1966. Contbr. to profl. jours., newspapers, mags. Home: 570 N 23d St Philadelphia PA 19130 . *Fundamental change in social, political and economic institutions is the central fact of our time. I use myself as an agent for non-violent change. As teacher and enabler I employ education and organization as tools to develop others, capabilities to discover and build their strengths. I believe that women, racial and ethnic minorities, the world's economically disadvantaged majorities have the wisdom and the capacity to build a world of peace and social justice. We must do it without destroying each other.*

STEFFEY, ALBERT O., former merchandising exec.; b. Basco, Ill., Oct. 26, 1906; s. Chester and Ethel (Priessman) S.; student Northwestern U., 3 yrs.; m. Ethel Williams, June 24, 1928; 1 son, Richard. Mgr. retail store Montgomery Ward & Co., Decatur, Ill., 1938-40, dist. mgr., hdqrs. Decatur, 1940-41, retail mdse. mgr., Chgo., 1942-45, asst. gen. mdse. mgr., 1945-47, retail v.p., Chgo., 1947-49; v.p. Butler Bros., 1949-56, dir., 1950-60, pres., 1956-60; pres., dir. City Products Corp., 1960-69, chmn., 1964-72; dir. Household Finance Corp. Clubs: Skokie Country (Glencoe, Ill.); Eldorado Country (Palm Desert, Calif.); Glenview (Golf, Ill.); Thunderbird Country (Rancho Mirage, Calif.). Home: 1630 Sheridan Rd Wilmette IL 60091 Office: Willow Hill Exec Center 540 Frontage Rd Northfield IL 60093

STEFFY, DAVID LOUIS, hosp. adminstr.; b. Indpls., June 4, 1943; s. Harold D. and Rita (Asa) S.; B.S. in Bus. Adminstrn., Ohio State U., 1965; M.P.A., U. So. Calif., 1971. Grad. research asso. Sch. Pub. Health, U. Calif., Los Angeles, 1968-71; asst. adminstr. U. Cin. Med. Center, 1971-72; dir. hosp. adminstr. Ohio State U. Hosps., 1972-79; adj. asst. prof. Ohio State U.; instr. Coll. Medicine, U. Cin. 1979—; v.p. Hosp. Affiliates Mgmt. Corp. Served with U.S. Army, 1965-66. Mem. Am. Coll. Hosp. Adminstrs., Young Adminstrs. Council Central Ohio (past pres.). Contbr. articles to profl. publs. Home: 6080 Springburn Dr S Dublin OH 43017 Office: 4525 Harding Rd Nashville TN 37205

STEFL, CHARLES ARTHUR, coal co. exec.; b. Dunbar, Pa., Apr. 23, 1920; s. Charles E. and Margaret A. (Stemmler) S.; B.S., Duquesne U., 1951; postgrad. Harvard U., 1964; m. Jane Mellinger, Feb. 1, 1946; children—Charles, Margaret Ann. With Eastern Asso. Coal Corp., Pitts., 1947—, sr. v.p., 1971-75, exec. v.p., 1975-77, pres., 1977—, also dir.; sr. v.p. Eastern Gas & Fuel Assos. Served with AUS, 1942-46. Decorated Bronze Star medal, Purple Heart. Mem. Financial Execs. Inst. Office: Koppers Bldg Pittsburgh PA 15219

STEG, J(AMES) L(OUIS), artist; b. Va., Feb. 6, 1922; s. Albert J. and Clara M. (Manista) S.; student Rochester Inst. Tech., 1939-42; B.F.A., State U. Iowa, 1947, M.F.A., 1949; m. Margaret O'Brien, July 5, 1948; instr. Newcomb Coll. Tulane U., 1951-53, asst. prof. art, 1953-58, asso. prof., 1958-64, prof., 1964—; one-man shows: Associated Am. Artists Gallery, N.Y.C., 1964, U. So. Fla., Tampa, 1964, Weyhe Gallery, N.Y.C., 1945, Phila. Art Alliance, 1955, Cushing Gallery, Dallas, 1966, Ohio State U., 1972; group shows include: Lugano (Switzerland) Exhbn., 1964, Phila. Art Alliance, 1968, Graphic Arts, Russia, 1966, U. Pitts., 1974; represented in permanent collections: Mus. Modern Art, N.Y.C., Library of Congress, Phila. Mus., Fogg Mus. of Harvard U., Cleve. Mus., Malmo Mus., Sweden; retrospective exhbn., New Orleans Mus. Art, 1978; technique cons. Perment Pigments Corp.; mem. staff cultural project High Sch. New Orleans, HEW Project Genesis. Bd. dirs. Urban League New Orleans, 1963. Served with U.S. Army, 1942-45. Recipient prize 8th Lugano Internat. Print Exhbn., 1964; awards Bklyn. Mus., 1948, 52, Phila. Print Club, 1951, 64, Ark. Art Center, 1969; Carnegie-Tulane fellow, 1960. Mem. Color Print Soc. Am. Home: 7919 Spruce St New Orleans LA 70118 Office: Newcomb Art Dept Tulane U New Orleans LA 70118. *I have had two basic standards given to me by my father: "Work for the night is coming!" "Do this while you are resting!"*

STEG, LEO, mfg. co. research and devel. exec.; b. Vienna, Austria, Mar. 30, 1922; s. Jacob and Clara (Gellert) S.; came to U.S., 1941, naturalized, 1946; B.S., City Coll. N.Y., 1947; M.S., U. Mo., 1948; Ph.D., Cornell U., 1951; m. Doreen Ethel Ray, June 12, 1947; children—Paula Jamie, Ellen Leslie, Audrey Leigh. Chief engr. Fed. Design Co., N.Y.C., 1946-47; instr. mech. engring. U. Mo., Columbia, 1947-48; instr. applied mechanics and materials Cornell U., Ithaca, N.Y., 1948-51, asst. prof., 1951-55; systems engr., missile and space div. Gen. Electric Co., Phila., 1955-56, mgr. space sci. lab., 1956—; adj. prof. Drexel. U.; cons. to space scis. bd. Nat. Acad. Scis., other govt. agencies. Asso. trustee U. Pa. Named Engr. of Yr., Phila., 1965; registered profl. engr., Pa. Fellow Am. Inst. Aero. and Astronautics (editor-in-chief jour. 1963-67), AAAS; mem. Phila. Acad. Scis. (founding), N.Y. Acad. Scis., Franklin Inst. Phila. (bd. mgrs.), Long Beach Island Found. Arts and Scis. (past chmn. bd.), Sigma Xi, Phi Kappa Phi. Clubs: Cosmos, Cornell of N.Y. Contbr. articles to profl. jours.; editor 2 books. Home: 1616 Hepburn Dr Villanova PA 19085 Office: PO Box 8555 Philadelphia PA 19101

STEGEMEIER, HENRI, educator; b. Indpls., Aug. 23, 1912; s. Richard William and Minna (Schmidt) S.; student Butler U., 1928-30; A.B. summa cum laude, Ind. U., 1933; postgrad. U. Heidelberg, 1935-36; Ph.D., U. Chgo., 1939; m. Mercedes Kahlert, Feb. 3, 1948; children—Henri K., Henriette C. Instr., U. Chgo., 1933-35, 36-40, Mt. Holyoke Coll., 1940-42; faculty U. Ill., Urbana, 1942—, prof. Germanic langs. and lit., 1948-77, emeritus prof., 1977—. Faculty, Columbia, summers 1948-52; cons. for textbook pubs., jours., govt. agys. Decorated Officers Cross of Order Merit 1st class Fed. Repub. Germany. Mem. Am. Assn. Tchrs. German, Modern Lang. Assn., Renaissance Soc., AAUP, Phi Beta Kappa, Delta Phi Alpha, Sigma Chi (Order of Constantine award). Episcopalian. Author: The Dance of Death in Folksong, 1939. Contbr. articles to profl. jours. Home: 604 Hessel Blvd Champaign IL 61820 Office: Fgn Langs Bldg U Ill Urbana IL 61801

STEGENGA, PRESTON JAY, educator; b. Grand Rapids, Mich., July 9, 1924; s. Miner and Dureth (Bouma) S.; B.A., Hope Coll., 1947; M.A., Columbia, 1948; Ph.D., U. Mich., 1952; m. Marcia Jean DeYoung, July 28, 1950; children—James Jay, Susan Jayne. Instr. history, polit. sci. Berea Coll., Ky., 1948-50, asso. prof., 1952-55; assistantship U. Mich., 1950-52; pres. Northwestern Coll., Orange City, Iowa, 1955-66; chief Cornell U. Project, U. Liberia-U.S. AID Program, Monrovia, W. Africa, 1966-68; coordinator internat. program Calif. State U., Sacramento, 1968-71, dir. Internat. Center, 1971—, acting v.p. acad. affairs, 1974-75, mem. Calif. State Liaison Com. for Internat. Edn.; ednl. cons. to Pres., Republic of Liberia, 1973-74; cons. internat. programs Am. Assn. State Colls. and Univs., 1975—; cons. UN Devel. Programme, 1977—. Vice pres. Sacramento chpt. UN Assn. U.S.A., 1969-71, pres., 1971—, also bd. dirs.; mem. Calif. UN Univ. Adv. Council, 1976—; pres. Tri-State Coll. Conf., 1963-64; Trustee Western Sem., Mich., New Brunswick Sem., N.J., World Affairs Council (v.p. 1976-77). Served with AUS, 1942-45. Decorated Purple Heart; named hon. chief Kpelle Tribe, West Africa, 1973. Mem. Assn. Iowa Coll. and U. Presidents (v.p. 1965-66), NEA, Calif. State U. Student Personnel Assn., Phi Delta Kappa, Phi Kappa Phi. Mem. Ref. Ch. Am. (bd. edn. 1954—). Lion. Author: Anchor of Hope, 1954. Asst. to editor History of Edn. Jour., 1952-54; contbg. editor Internat. Dimensions, 1978-79. Contbr. articles to profl. jours. Home: 545 Mills Rd Sacramento CA 95825

STEGER, BYRON LUDWIG, physician, former army officer; b. Cardington, Ohio, 1910; M.D., Ohio State U., 1933; D.P.H., Johns Hopkins U., 1950. Commd. 1st lt. M.C., U.S. Army, 1933, advanced through grades to maj. gen.; intern Station Hosp., Ft. Sill, Okla., 1935-36; comdg. officer Station Hosp., Camp Crowder, Mo., 1941-42, 51st Gen. Hosp., New Guinea and Manila, 1944-45, Tokyo Army Hosp., 1945-46; asst. chief edn. and tng. div., then chief div. Office Surgeon Gen., 1949-51, 55-58, chief personnel and tng. div., 1958-59; served in Korea, 1952-53; comdg. officer Womack Army Hosp., Ft. Bragg, 1959-61, 97th Gen. Hosp., Frankfurt, Germany, 1961-63; comdg. gen. Madigan Gen. Hosp., Tacoma, 1963-65, Tripler Army Med. Center, chief surgeon U.S. Army, Pacific, 1965-68, Fitzsimons Gen. Hosp., Denver, 1968-69; ret, 1969; exec. dir. Health and Hosp. Corp. of Marion County, Indpls., 1969-71; exec. v.p. Winona Meml. Hosp., Indpls., 1971-75, bd. dirs., 1975—; prof. preventive medicine Ind. U. Sch. Medicine, 1970—; dir. Inter-Agy. Insts. for Fed. Hosp. Adminstrs., 1952-55; prof. mil. sci. and tactics Johns Hopkins U., 1947-49. Decorated Legion of Merit with oak leaf cluster, Bronze Star with oak leaf cluster, D.S.M. with oak leaf cluster; Ulchi medal with silver star (Korea); Red Cross medal (Sweden); Star of Solidarity (Italy); Nat. Order Vietnam (5th class). Diplomate Am. Bd. Preventive Medicine. Fellow Am. Pub. Health Assn., A.C.P., Am. Coll. Hosp. Adminstrs., Am. Coll. Preventive Medicine; mem. AMA, Am. Hosp. Assn., Assn. Mil. Surgeons, Royal Soc. Health. Address: 6434 Vista Butte San Antonio TX 78239

STEGER, MERITT HOMER, lawyer; b. Denison, Tex., Aug. 25, 1906; s. Allen Homer and Alva Delilah (Perkins) S.; A.B., LL.B., U. Tex., 1930; m. Mae Garlington, Nov. 10, 1929; children—Kenneth, Carolyn (Mrs. Carolyn Hiner). Admitted to Tex. bar, 1930, D.C. bar, 1965; U.S. Supreme Ct. bar, 1963; asso. firm Church & Graves, San Antonio, 1930-36; partner firm Church & Steger, 1936-42; dist. rent atty. OPA, San Antonio dist., 1942-44; counsel, bur. supplies and accounts Navy Dept., 1946-50, asst. gen. counsel, 1950-56, dep. gen. counsel of Navy Dept., 1956-60, gen. counsel, 1960-71. Served to lt. USNR, 1944-46. Named Most Outstanding Young Man in San Antonio, 1941. Mem. Fed., Tex., San Antonio (pres. 1941) bar assns., San Antonio Jr. C. of C. (pres. 1941-42). Mason (past master). Home: 3717 Morningside Dr Fairfax VA 22031

STEGER, WILLIAM MERRITT, judge; b. Dallas, Aug. 22, 1920; s. Merritt and Lottie (Reese) S.; student Baylor U., 1938-41; LL.B., So. Meth. U., 1950, m. Ann Hollandsworth, Feb. 14, 1948; 1 son, Merritt Reed. Admitted to Tex. bar, 1951, pvt. practice Longview, 1951-53; apptd. U.S. dist. atty. Eastern Dist. Tex., 1953-59; mem. firm Wilson, Miller, Spivey & Steger, Tyler, Tex., 1959-70; U.S. dist. judge Eastern Dist. Tex., Tyler, 1970—. Republican candidate for gov. of Tex., 1960, for U.S. Ho. of Reps., 1962; mem. Tex. State Republican Exec. Com., 1966-69; chmn. Tex. State Republican Party, 1969-70. Served as pilot with ranks 2d lt. to capt. USAAF, 1942-47. Mem. Am. Bar Assn., State Bar Tex. Mason (32 deg., Shriner). Home: 801 Meadow Creek Tyler TX 75703 Office: PO Box 1109 Tyler TX 75710

STEGLICH, WINFRED GEORGE, educator; b. Giddings, Tex., Sept. 21, 1921; s. Gustav E. and Meta (Behnken) S.; B.A., Concordia Sem., St. Louis, 1942, diploma theology, 1946; postgrad. Washington U., St. Louis, 1942-43; M.A., U. Tex., 1945, Ph.D., 1951; post-doctoral fellow Fla. State U., 1955-56; m. Ruth Edwards, May 30, 1948; children—Carolyn Sue, Catherine Ann, James Edwards. Instr. sociology U. Tex., 1946-48, vis. prof., summer 1961; instr. sociology U. N.Mex., 1948-49; from asst. prof. to asso. prof. sociology Colo. State U., 1949-57; faculty Tex. Tech. U., Lubbock, 1957-68, prof. sociology, chmn. dept., 1959-68; prof., head dept. sociology U. Tex, El Paso, 1968-76; prof., chairperson U. Okla., Norman, 1976—; vis. prof. Calif. State U., Hayward, summer 1973. Pres., Tex. Com. Population Studies, 1963-65. Fellow Am. Sociol. Assn.; mem. Southwestern Social Sci. Assn. (pres. 1975-76), Am. Acad. Polit. and Social Sci., Southwestern (pres. 1962), Pacific, So. sociol. socs., Population Assn. Am. Author: Student Guide to Sociology, 1969. Home: 3926 Briarcrest Dr Norman OK 73069

STEGNER, WALLACE EARLE, author; b. Lake Mills, Iowa, Feb. 18, 1909; s. George Henry and Hilda Emilia (Paulson) S.; A.B., U. Utah, 1930, D.Litt., 1968; A.M., U. Ia., 1932, Ph.D., 1935; postgrad. U. Calif., 1932-33, L.H.D., 1969; D.Litt., Utah State U., 1972; LL.D., U. Sask., 1973; m. Mary Stuart Page, Sept. 1, 1934; 1 son, Stuart Page. Instr. English, Augustana Coll., Rock Island, Ill., 1933-34, U. Utah, 1934-37, U. Wis., 1937-39; instr. English, Harvard, 1939-45; prof. English, Stanford, 1945—, Reynolds prof. humanities, 1969-71; writer, 1934—; editor in chief Am. West, 1966-69. Guggenheim fellow, 1950, 52, 59. Recipient Little Brown & Co. prize for novelette Remembering Laughter, 1937; O. Henry 1st prize for short story, 1950. Mem. Nat. Inst. Arts and Letters, Am. Acad. Arts and Scis. Author numerous books, 1937—, latest publs.: The Women on the Wall, 1950; The Preacher and the Slave, 1950; Beyond the Hundredth Meridian, 1954; The City of the Living, 1956; A Shooting Star, 1961; Wolf Willow (Blackhawk award), 1963; The Gathering of Zion, 1964; All the Little Live Things, 1967 (Commonwealth Club gold medal 1968); The Sound of Mountain Water, 1969; Angle of Repose, 1971 (Pulitzer prize 1972); The Uneasy Chair: A Biography of Bernard DeVoto, 1974; The Spectator Bird, 1976 (Nat. Book award 1977); Recapitulation, 1979. Editor numerous texts and edits. Contbr. articles to mags. Home: 13456 South Fork Ln Los Altos Hills CA 94022

STEHLI, FRANCIS GREENOUGH, educator, geologist; b. Upper Montclair, N.J., Oct. 16, 1924; s. Edgar and Emily (Greenough) S.; B.S., St. Lawrence U., 1949, M.S., 1950; Ph.D., Columbia U., 1953; m. Irene Comfort, June 19, 1948; children—Anne, Robert, John, Edgar. Asst. prof. invertebrate paleontology Calif. Inst. Tech., 1953-56; tech. group supr. research dept. Am. Petroleum Corp., 1956-60; prof. geology, chmn. dept. Case Western Res. U., 1960-73, Samuel St. John prof. earth scis., 1973—, acting dean sci., 1975, acting dean sci. and engring., 1976, dean sci. and engring., 1977—; geol. cons., 1960—. Served with USNR, 1943-46. Fellow Geol. Soc. Am., AAAS; mem. Geochem. Soc., Paleontol. Soc. (pres.), Am. Soc. Engring. Edn., No. Ohio Geol. Soc. Author articles in field. Home: 16432 Stoneridge Rd Chagrin Falls OH 44022 Office: Dept Geology Case Western Res U Cleveland OH 44106

STEIBEL, LEONARD HAROLD, lawyer; b. N.Y.C., Jan. 12, 1915; s. George J. and Phoebe D. (Horwitz) S.; B.A., Coll. City N.Y., 1934; LL.B., St. John's U., Jamaica, N.Y., 1937, LL.M., 1938; m. Marjorie Wenstrom, May 16, 1964; children—Bruce, Pamela. Admitted to N.Y. bar, 1937, since practiced in N.Y.C.; partner firm Smith, Steibel, Alexander & Saskor, 1970—; dir., mem. exec. com. Sears Industries Inc.; chmn. bd. dirs. BSR (USA) Ltd., Wain, Shiell & Son, Inc.; v.p. Burberrys Ltd. (N.Y.); dir. Dunfey Family Corp.; dir., sec. Imero Fiorentino Assos., Inc., Audio Dynamics Corp., Jones & Shipman, Inc. Decorated comdr. Order Brit. Empire. Mem. Am. Bar Assn., N.Y. County Lawyers Assn., Sands Point Acres Beach Assn. (pres. 1957—). Home: 14 Hilldale Ln Sands Point NY 11050 Office: 460 Park Ave New York NY 10022

STEIDEL, ROBERT FRANCIS, JR., educator; b. Goshen, N.Y., July 6, 1926; s. Robert Francis and Edna (Terry) S.; B.S. (Pulitzer Nat. scholar, Regents scholar), Columbia U., 1948, M.S., 1949; D.Eng. (NSF fellow), U. Calif. at Berkeley, 1955; m. Jean Ann McKissick, Nov. 13, 1946; children—John Robert, Mark Howard, David William, Steven James. Instr., asst. prof. mech. engring. Oreg. State U., 1949-52; asst. prof., asso. prof., prof. mech. engring. U. Calif. at Berkeley, 1955—, chmn. dept., 1969-74, U. Calif. rep. Pacific-10 Conf., 1972—, pres., 1973-74; cons. Lawrence Radiation Lab., 1955—, Jet Propulsion Lab., 1962-68; mem. mech. engring. adv. bd. John Wiley & Sons, N.Y.C., 1974—. Served with USNR, 1944-46. Fellow Inst. Mech. Engrs. Gt. Britain; mem. ASME (past chmn. San Francisco), Am. Soc. Engring. Edn. (Western Electric Fund award 1973, Chester F. Carlson award 1974), Sigma Xi, Tau Beta Pi, Pi Tau Sigma. Office: 5138 Etcheverry Hall University of California Berkeley CA 94720

STEIDER, DORIS, artist; b. Decatur, Ill., Apr. 10, 1924; d. Rudy C. and Helen M. (Regan) Sleeter; B.S., Purdue U., 1945; M.A. in Fine Art, U. N.Mex., 1965; m. C.B. McCampbell, May 19, 1972; children by previous marriage—Kristen (Mrs. G. Latham), Robert S., Tim D. Steider. One-man shows include Baker Gallery, Lubbock, Tex., 1967, 69, 70, 71, 73, 76, 78, Brandywine Galleries, Albuquerque, 1970, 71, 72, 73, 74, 76, Triton Mus., Santa Clara, Calif., 1968, DeColores Gallery, Denver, 1975; exhibited in numerous group shows including Smithsonian Instn., Washington, 1963, Witte Mus. Western Art, San Antonio, 1969, Mont. State Hist. Soc. Mus., Helena, 1966, Nat. Alpine Artists Holiday Exhbns., Ourey, Colo., 1966, 67, 75, Mus. of N.Mex., Santa Fe, Ft. Sill Internat. Show, Lawton, Okla., 1974, Ft. Robinson Profl. Western Art Exhbn., Nebr., 1975, Nat. Art Show, La Junta, Colo., 1972, Artists of Rockies invitational, Pueblo, Colo., 1976, Nebraskaland Days Exhbns., North Platte, Nebr., 1971-76, others; represented in permanent collections at Bank N.Mex., Citizen's Bank, 1st Nat. Bank, Fidelity Nat. Bank (all Albuquerque), First Nat. Bank, Mineral Wells, Tex., West Tex. Mus., Lubbock, Holt, Rinehart & Winston. Free lance sign writer, 1945—; theater costume designer Off-Broadway-West, Albuquerque, 1964, 65. Mem. Albuquerque Fine Arts Adv. Bd., 1971-77; chmn. invitational rev. bd. Southwest Arts and Crafts Fair, 1978. Recipient numerous awards including First Prize award N.Mex. Mus., 1960, 64, 65, Purchase Prize award N.Mex. State Fair, 1970, 71, Purchase award N.Mex. Arts and Crafts Fair, 1966, Colo. Sweepstakes prize Uncompahgre Artists Guild Art Festival, 1975, 1st prize, 1976, 1st prize sculpture, 2d prize painting Tri-State Exhbn., Carlsbad, N.Mex., 1977, 1st prize 10th Ann. Nat. Art Show, LaJunta, Colo., 1978; chosen for Am. Artist Mag. Exec. Diary, 1980. Mem. Nat. League Am. Pen Women (Spl. award 1965, dir. 1965), Nat. Artists Equity Assn. Address: Z-61 Rincon Loop Rd Tijeras NM 87059. *I believe that the purpose of life is spiritual growth through learning experiences. My paintings are valid if they are truthfully reflecting these changing understandings.*

STEIG, WILLIAM, artist, author; b. N.Y.C., Nov. 14, 1907; s. Joseph and Laura (Ebel) S.; ed. Coll. City N.Y., 1923-25, NAD, 1925-29; m. Elizabeth Mead, Jan. 2, 1936 (div.); children—Lucy, Jeremy; m. 2d, Kari Homestead, 1950 (div. 1963); 1 dau., Margit Laura; m. 3d, Stephanie Healey, Dec. 12, 1964 (div. Dec. 1966); m. 4th, Jeanne Doron, 1969. Humorous artist, 1930—; drawings in New Yorker, other mags.; water color in collections Bklyn. Mus.; one-man exhibit wood sculpture Downtown Gallery, N.Y.C., 1939; also exhibited drawings and sculpture Smith Coll., 1940. Recipient William Allen White award, 1975. Author: About People (symbolic drawings), 1939; The Lonely Ones, a book of drawings, 1942; All Embarrassed, 1944; Small Fry, 1944; Persistent Faces, 1945; Till Death Do Us Part, 1947; The Agony in the Kindergarten; The Rejected Lovers, a book of drawings, 1951; Dreams of Glory, a book of drawings, 1953; Roland, the Minstrel Pig, 1968; CDB, 1968; Sylvester and the Magic Pebble, 1969 (Caldecott medal 1970); The Bad Island, 1969; An Eye for Elephants, 1970; Amos and Boris, 1971; Male/Female, 1971; Dominic, 1972 (Christopher award 1973); The Real Thief, 1973; Farmer Palmer's Wagon Ride, 1974; Abel's Island (Newbery Honor book), 1976; The Amazing Bone (Caldecott Honor book), 1976; Caleb and Kate, 1977; Tiffky Doofky, 1978; Drawings, 1979. Wood sculpture in collection of R.I. Mus., Providence, Smith Coll. Mus., Northampton, Mass. Home: RFD #1 Box KH2 Kent CT 06757

STEIGER, CHAUNCEY ALLEN, dept. store exec.; b. Westfield, Mass., Feb. 28, 1893; s. Albert and Izetta (Allen) S.; grad. Phillips Exeter Acad., 1914; B.S., Dartmouth, 1917; m. Esther R. Emery, Oct. 3, 1923 (dec.); children—Reynolds E., Elisabeth A.; m. 2d, Hazel Clark, Jan. 3, 1947. With Steiger Co., Springfield, Mass., 1917—, treas., 1932-66, chmn. bd. dirs., 1966—; treas., dir. Hilbridge Corp., Springfield, 1940—; pres. Steiger Investment Co., Springfield, 1971—; hon. dir. Valley Bank & Trust Co., Springfield. Pres. bd. dirs. Albert Steiger Bldg. Trust, 1962—, Steiger Meml. Fund Ind., 1953—, hon. trustee Wesson Meml. Hosp., Springfield, Springfield Coll., Springfield Library and Mus. Assn., Eastern States Expn., Springfield. Served as ensign USN, World War I. Clubs: Longmeadow Country; Springfield Colony, Dartmouth (Springfield); Tequesta (Fla.) Country; Rotary. Home: 232 Overbrook Rd Longmeadow MA 01106 Office: 1477 Main St Springfield MA 01101

STEIGER, FREDERIC, artist; b. Solwutz, Austria, Oct. 21, 1905; s. Michael and Ida (Schaeffer) S.; student Olmouc (Austria) U.; m. Netty Meth, Aug. 5, 1922 (div.); m. 2d, Ruby Eleanor Fevens; children—Trudi, Linda. One man exhbns. include Carroll Galleries, Toronto, Roberts Art Gallery, Toronto, Ont., Can., 1950, Odeon Theatre Gallery, Toronto, 1947, Ho. of Assembly, St. John's, Nfld., Can., 1960, Arts Club, Montreal, Que., Can., 1957, L'Art Francaise Art Gallery, 1957, Montreal Arts and Letters Club, 1960, T. Eaton Art Gallery, Toronto, 1972, 79, O'Keefe Centre Gallery, 1974; exhibited in group shows at Vancouver Art Mus., 1939, Royal Can. Acad., Montreal and Toronto, 1941, 45, Montreal Mus. Art, 1941, Ont. Soc. Artists, Art Gallery Toronto, 1938-40, Cummerford Gallery, N.Y.C., 1962; represented in permanent collections IBM, 40 portraits Nfld. Parliament Bldg., Meml. U. Nfld., St. John's, Hallmark Collection Can. Art, Imperial Oil Ltd., Toronto, Toronto Pub. Library, also pvt. collections; portrait of Hon. William G. Davis, Premier of Ont., 1976. Recipient Bronze medal IBM Corp. Unitarian. Home: 316 The Kingsway Islington ON Canada Studio: 406 Bloor St E Toronto ON Canada. *In my earlier work, I preferred to paint in an impressionistic style relating man to his environment but presently, Light, Color, and Rhythm play an important part in my abstract paintings. Perhaps this represents my own optimistic outlook on life.*

STEIGER, ROD, actor; b. W. Hampton, L.I., N.Y., Apr. 14, 1925; s. Fredrick and Lorraine (Driver) S.; ed. pub. schs., Newark; m. Sally Gracie, 1952; m. 2d, Claire Bloom, Apr. 15, 1959 (div.); 1 dau., Anna Justine; m. 3d, Sherry Nelson, Apr. 1973 (div. 1979). Theatrical appearances include: Night Music, 1951, Enemy of the People, 1953, Rashomon, 1959; motion picture appearances include: On the Waterfront, 1953, Big Knife, 1955, Oklahoma, 1956, Jubal, 1957, Across the Bridge, 1958, Al Capone, 1959, Seven Thieves, 1959, The Mark, 1960, World in My Pocket, 1960, The Tiger Among Us, 1961, The Longest Day, Convicts 4, 1961, The Time of Indifference, 1962, Hands on the City, 1963, The Pawnbroker (Berlin Film Festival award), 1964, The Loved One, 1964, Duck, You Sucker, 1972, Happy Birthday, Wanda June, 1971, In the Heat of the Night (Golden Globe award, Acad. award Best Actor), 1967, Waterloo, 1971, Lolly-Madonna, 1973, Lucky Luciano, 1975, Hennessy, 1975, W.C. Fields and Me, 1976, F.I.S.T., 1978, Dirty Hands, 1978, Love and Bullets, 1979; TV appearance as Marty, 1953 (Sylvania award); appeared in play Moby Dick, 1962. Life mem. Met. Mus. Art, N.Y.C. Served with USNR, 1942-45. Address: care Creative Artists Agy Inc 1888 Century Park E Suite 1400 Los Angeles CA 90067*

STEIGER, WILLIAM A., physician; b. Phila., Oct. 15, 1920; s. William Anthony and Regina (McCann) S.; A.B., U. Pa., 1942, M.D., 1945; m. Nancy Liebert, June 22, 1946; m. 2d, Maria Vaccaro, Dec. 19, 1970. Resident internal medicine Phila. Gen. Hosp., 1948-50, research fellow cardiology, 1950-51; prof. community medicine Temple U. Sch. Medicine, Phila., 1951-70, also chmn. dept.; practice medicine specializing in internal medicine, Virginia Beach, Va., 1970—. Served to capt. M.C., AUS, 1946-48. Fellow A.C.P.; mem. AMA, Coll. Physicians Phila. (sec. 1964-67). Author: Patients Who Trouble You, 1964. Address: 1821 Old Donation Pkwy Suite 11 Virginia Beach VA 23454

STEIGERWALT, ALBERT KLECKNER, educator; b. N.Y.C., Dec. 20, 1919; s. Albert K. and Erma V. (Lorensen) S.; A.B., Wayne State U., 1946; A.M. (Univ. fellow), U. Mich., 1950, Ph.D., 1952; m. Nan Hartmann, Dec. 30, 1940; children—Albert Kleckner III, Susan Patricia. Instr. history Wayne State U., 1946-48; mem. faculty U. Mich., Ann Arbor, 1953-65, prof. bus. history, 1962-65, prof. bus. adminstrn., dean Coll. Bus. Adminstrn., 1965-68, vis. scholar in philosophy, 1975; prof. bus. policy, faculty bus. McMaster U., Hamilton, Ont., Can., 1968-78; prof. bus. and pub. policy Central Mich. U., 1978—; cons. to industry, 1953—. Active Boy Scouts Am. Served with USNR, 1942-44. Recipient citation State Dept., 1960, Universidad de los Andes, Merida, Venezuela, 1964. Mem. Am. Econ. Assn., Am. Hist. Assn., Orgn. Am. Historians (chmn. conf. bus. history 1953-63), Conf. Latin Am. History, Econ. History Assns. Club: University (Ann Arbor). Author: The National Assn. of Manufacturers: 1895-1914: A Study in Business Leadership, 1964;

The Enlightened Manager, 1979. Home: 1050 Wall St Ann Arbor MI 48105

STEIL, GEORGE KENNETH, SR., lawyer; b. Darlington, Wis., Dec. 16, 1924; s. George John and Laura (Donahue) S.; student Platteville State Tchrs. Coll., 1942-43; J.D., U. Wis., Madison, 1950; m. Mavis Elaine Andrews, May 24, 1947; children—George Kenneth, John R., Michelle E., Marcelaine K. Admitted to Wis. bar, 1950, U.S. Tax Ct., 1971; asso. firm J. G. McWilliams, Janesville, 1950-53; partner firm McWilliams and Steil, Janesville, 1954-60; partner firm Brennan, Steil, Ryan, Basting & MacDougall, S.C., and predecessor, Janesville, 1960-72, pres., 1972—; lectr. in law U. Wis., 1974; chmn. bd. First Nat. Bank, Janesville, 1979—. Served with U.S. Army, 1943-45. Fellow Am. Bar Found., Am. Coll. Probate Counsel; mem. Janesville Area C. of C. (pres. 1970-71), State Bar Wis. (pres. 1977-78), Am. Bar Assn. Roman Catholic. Office: One E Milwaukee St Janesville WI 53545

STEIM, JOSEPH MATSON, biophysicist, educator; b. Pitts.; s. Joseph Mefford and Ethel (Matson) S.; B.S., Pa. State U., 1954, B.S., 1956, Ph.D., 1962; M.S., U. Pitts., 1959; M.A., Brown U., 1969; m. Caroline Grace Nittle, Mar. 12, 1955; 1 son, Joseph Michael. USPHS postdoctoral fellow Pa. State U., 1962-65; asst. prof. Brown U., 1966-69, asso. prof., 1969-70, prof. chemistry, 1970—. Contbr. articles to profl. jours. Home: 65 Warren Ave Seekonk MA 02771 Office: Dept Chemistry Brown U Providence RI 02912

STEIMEL, EDWARD JOSEPH, assn. exec.; b. Running Lake, Ark., Jan. 20, 1922; s. George Hubert and Josephine Marie (Zosso) S.; B.A. in English, Ark. State U., 1949; H.L.D., Centenary Coll., 1962; m. Mary Emily Welch, Aug. 18, 1947; children—Phillis Susanne (dec.), Edward, Mary Jo, George. Tchr. public schs., Running Lake, Ark., 1940-42; public relations dir. Ark. State U., 1949; asst. mgr. Baton Rouge C. of C., 1949-51; with Public Affairs Research Council of La., 1951-75, exec. dir., 1954-75; pres. La. Assn. Bus. and Industry, Baton Route, 1975—; lectr. Loyola U., New Orleans, La. State U., Centenary Coll., Shreveport, La. Pres., founder Cerebral Palsy Center of Baton Rouge, 1953-54, dir., 1953—; gen. campaign chmn. United Givers Fund of Baton Rouge, 1956; vice chmn. La. Task Force for Ednl. Fin., 1972-76; chmn. Gov.'s Edn. Study Com., 1974-75; mem. Gov.'s Joint Legis. Com. on Reorganization of Exec. Br., 1975—. Recipient Golden Deeds award Baton Rouge, 1956; Golden Mike award La. Broadcasters Assn., 1970; Distinguished Citizen award Nat. Mcpl. League, 1971; Hornblower award Public Relations Soc. Am., New Orleans chpt., 1973; communications and leadership award Toastmasters Internat., 1977; named Outstanding Young Man of Baton Rouge, Jaycees, 1956, Outstanding Young Man of La., La. Jaycees, 1956. Mem. Govtl. Research Assn. (pres. 1963), Nat. Tax Assn. (exec. com. 1963-66), C. of C. of U.S. Democrat. Roman Catholic. Clubs: Sherwood Forest Country, Baton Rouge City; Internat. House (New Orleans). Home: 10250 Goodwood Blvd Baton Rouge LA 70815 Office: PO Box 3988 201 Lafayette St Baton Rouge LA 70821

STEIMLE, DOUGLAS BRUNING, lawyer; b. Bklyn., Sept. 7, 1902; s. Augustus and Emily (Bruning) S.; A.B., Princeton, 1924; LL.B., Harvard, 1929; m. Hildegarde Gauss, Oct. 5, 1937; children—Hildegarde Gay, Douglas Christian. Admitted to N.Y. bar, 1929, since practiced in N.Y.C.; asso. Shearman & Sterling, 1929-45, partner, 1945—; dir. emeritus Combustion Engring., Inc. Past trustee Wilson Coll., Chambersburg, Pa. Served as lt. comdr. USN, 1943-45. Decorated Bronze Star (2). Clubs: University, Downtown Assn., Princeton, Links. Home: 755 Park Ave New York City NY 10021 Office: 53 Wall St New York City NY 10005

STEIMLE, EDMUND AUGUSTUS, clergyman, educator; b. Allentown, Pa., Sept. 19, 1907; s. Augustus and Emily (Bruning) S.; grad. Phillips Acad., Andover, Mass., 1926; A.B., Princeton U., 1930; B.D., Lutheran Theol. Sem., Phila., 1935; A.M., U. Pa., 1934; D.D., Wagner Coll., 1950, Pacific Luth. U., 1977; Litt.D., Muhlenberg Coll., 1957; LL.D., Roanoke Coll., 1960, Gettysburg Coll., 1962; L.H.D., Hamilton Coll., 1974; m. Rosalind Weinert Ball, Apr. 24, 1936 (dec.); children—Sondra (Mrs. David R. Offord), Rosalind Ball (Mrs. David J. Horn), Edmund Augustus; m. 2d, Eleanor Floyd Wadleigh, Jan. 23, 1971. Ordained to ministry Luth. Ch., 1933; teaching fellow Luth. Theol. Sem., Phila., 1933-35, Hagan prof. practical theology, 1952-61; pastor, Jersey City, 1935-40, Cambridge, Mass., 1940-52; Brown prof. homiletics Union Theol. Sem., N.Y.C., 1961-75, emeritus, 1975—; vis. prof. preaching Louisville Presbyn. Theol. Sem., 1976; adj. prof. preaching Wesley Theol. Sem., Washington, 1976—; Zimmerman lectr. Gettysburg Theol. Sem., 1960; Gray. lectr. Duke Div. Sch., 1966; preacher on radio, 1955-74. Author: Are You Looking for God?, 1957; Disturbed by Joy, 1967; From Death to Birth, 1973; God the Stranger, 1978; (with others) Preaching the Story, 1979. Editor: Renewal in the Pulpit, 1966; cons. editor Preacher's Paperback Library. Home: 710 Americana Dr Annapolis MD 21403

STEIN, BERNARD, stock broker; b. N.Y.C., Nov. 24, 1913; s. Abraham and Fannie (Zoob) S., student Sch. Commerce, N.Y. U., 1930-32; m. Marion Charlotte Holtsberg, Feb. 24, 1946; children—Robert Frederick, Ellen Frances (Mrs. Howard Lazarus). Partner firm Ralph E. Samuel & Co., N.Y.C., 1947-70, Neuberger & Berman, Inc., 1970—; sr. v.p., treas., dir. Energy Fund, N.Y.C., 1962—; v.p., dir. Regency Fund, N.Y.C., 1967—, Neuberger & Berman Mgmt. Co.; treas. Partners Fund, 1975—; pres. Hemisphere Fund, 1979—. Served with USAAF, 1942-45. Club: Quaker Ridge Golf (Scarsdale); Beach Point (Mamaroneck, N.Y.). Home: 8 Split Tree Rd Scarsdale NY 10583 Office: 522 Fifth Ave New York NY 10036

STEIN, BERNARD ALVIN, supermarket chain exec.; b. Winnipeg, Can., June 4, 1923; s. Herman Louis and Rebecca (Harris) S.; m. Dorothy Lock, Jan. 1, 1942; 1 dau., Marilynn Stein Lakein. Vice-pres. food drug div. Giant Food, Inc., Washington, 1951-69; v.p., gen. mgr. Read Drug Stores, Balt., 1969-70; pres. Scotty Stores, div. Sav-A-Stop, Jacksonville, Fla., 1970-71; pres., gen. mgr. Liberal Markets. Dayton, Ohio, 1971-72; pres. Pueblo Supermarkets, San Juan, P.R., 1972-74; pres. Hills Supermarkets, Brentwood, N.Y., 1974-75, pres. Allied Supermarkets, Detroit, 1976-78, Chatham Supermarkets, Detroit, 1978—, also dir. Mem. Presdl. Com. for Emergency Food Controls, 1969. Served with USAAF, 1943-45. Decorated Air medal. Home: 4138 Golf Ridge Dr E Bloomfield Hills MI 48013 Office: 2300 E 10 Mile Rd Warren MI 48091

STEIN, CHARLES, lawyer; b. Riviere-du-Loup, Que., Can., July 6, 1912; s. Charles Adolphe and Alice (Hamel) S.; B.A., Laval U., 1931, Ph.L., 1932, LL.L., 1934, LL.D., 1961; m. Gabrielle des Rivieres, Oct. 15, 1938; children—Michel, Claire (Mrs. Georges Robitaille). Called to bar, Que., 1934, created Queen's counsel, 1947; gen. practice, Quebec City, 1934-38; counsel, asst. dep. minister Dept. Justice Can., Ottawa, Ont., 1938-49; under sec. state, dep. registrar gen., dep. custodian Enemy Property of Can., Ottawa, 1949-61; mem. firm Letourneau & Stein, Quebec, 1961—. Vice pres., dir. Alpin-Otis Elevator Co., Ltd. Mem. Can. del. to UN, 1954. Mem. Province Que. Bar, Internat. Commn. Jurists, Cercle Universitaire Quebec. Roman Catholic. Club: Cap-Rouge (Que.) Golf. Home: 4 Jardins de Merici Apt 302 Quebec PQ G1S 4M4 Canada Office: 65 Ste Anne Quebec G1R 3X5 PQ Canada

STEIN, CLAIRE ALPERN, assn. exec.; b. N.Y.C., Sept. 19, 1923; d. Milton B. and Henrietta (Nathanson) Alpern; B.A., Adelphi Coll., 1944; m. Howard M. Stein, Feb. 15, 1944; children—M. Bradford, Wendy A. Sculptor N.Y.C., 1951—; group shows at North Shore Community Arts Center, 1955-60, Audubon Artists, 1956, Nat. Acad., 1957; represented in pvt. collections; exec. dir. Nat. Sculpture Soc., N.Y.C., 1967—. Bd. dirs. North Shore Community Art Center, N.Y.C., 1954-57. Contbr. articles to profl. publs. Home: 6 Dorchester Dr Manhasset NY 11030 Office: Nat Sculpture Soc 777 3d Ave New York City NY 10017

STEIN, DALE F., tech. univ. pres.; b. Kingston, Minn., Dec. 24, 1935; s. David Frank and Zelda Jane Stein; B.S. in Metallurgy, U. Minn., 1958; Ph.D., Rensselaer Poly. Inst., Troy, N.Y., 1963; m. Audrey Dean Bloemke, June 7, 1958; children—Pam, Derek. Research metallurgist research lab. Gen. Electric Co., Schnectady, N.Y., 1958-67; asso. prof. U. Minn., 1967-71; prof. metall. engring., head dept. Mich. Tech. U., Houghton, 1971-77, head mining engring., 1974-77, v.p. acad. affairs, 1977-79, pres., 1979—; cons. NSF, 1972—. Mem. AIME, Metall. Soc. (pres. elect 1979; inst. Hardy Gold medal 1965), Am. Soc. Metals (Geisler award Eastern N.Y. chpt. 1967), AAAS, Sigma Xi, Phi Kappa Phi, Tau Beta Pi, Alpha Sigma Nu. Mem. United Ch. Club: Houghton Rotary. Contbr. articles to profl. jours. Office: Mich Tech Univ Houghton MI 49931

STEIN, ELLIOT H., investment broker; b. St. Louis, May 10, 1918; s. Samuel and Esther (Bearman) S.; student Washington U., St. Louis, 1939; m. Mary Ann Bleiweiss, July 6, 1947; children—Elliot H., John Samuel, Mary Elizabeth, James David. With Mark C. Steinberg & Co., St. Louis, 1939-41, 46-51; jr. exec. Elliot H. Stein & Co., St. Louis, 1951-53; officer Scherck, Richter Co., Inc. (now Scherck, Stein & Franc, Inc.), St. Louis, 1953—, pres., 1964—; dir. Alvey, Inc., N.Mex. and Ariz. Land Co., W.I. Sugar Co., St. L.-S.F. R.R., Angelica Corp., Gen. Am. Life Ins. Co., Ralston Purina Co., Gen. Dynamics Co., Laclede Gas Co., City Investing Co., Gen. Steel Industries, Inc. Mem. pres.'s council St. John's Mercy Hosp., St. Louis; dir. Arts and Edn. Council St. Louis; bd. dirs. United Way Greater St. Louis, Jewish Hosp., St. Louis; trustee St. Louis Symphony Soc., Washington U., St. Louis. Served with U.S. Army, 1941-46. Jewish. Clubs: Westwood Country, Noonday, Saint Louis (St. Louis); Standard (Chgo.). Home: 9 Maryhill Saint Louis MO 63124 Office: 515 Olive St Saint Louis MO 63101

STEIN, ERIC, educator, lawyer; b. Holice, Czechoslovakia, July 8, 1913 (came to U.S. 1940, naturalized 1943); s. Zikmund and Hermina (Zalud) S.; J.U.D., Charles U., Prague, Czechoslovakia, 1937; J.D., U. Mich., 1942; Dr. honoris causa, Vrije U. Brussels, 1977, U. Libre, Brussels, 1978; m. Virginia Elizabeth Rhine, July 30, 1955. Practiced law Prague, 1937; admitted to Ill. bar, 1946, D.C. bar, 1953; with State Dept., 1946-55, acting dep. dir. Office UN Polit. Affairs, 1955; faculty U. Mich. Law Sch., Ann Arbor, 1956—, prof. internat. law and orgn., 1958-76, Hessel E. Yntema prof. law, 1976—. co-dir. internat. legal studies, 1958-76, dir., 1976—, Vis. prof. Stanford Law Sch., 1956, 77, Law Faculties, Stockholm, Uppsala and Lund, Sweden 1969; lectr. Hague Acad. Internat. Law, summer 1971; vis. prof. Inst. Advanced Legal Studies, U. London, 1975. Adviser, U.S. delegation UN Gen. Assembly, 1947-55; mem. adv. panel Bur. European Affairs, State Dept., 1966-73, cons. 1966-73, cons. U.S. rep. for trade negotiations, 1979; vice chmn. com. Atlantic studies Atlantic Inst., 1966-68; mem. adv. council Inst. European Studies, Free U., Brussels, Belgium, 1965—. Served with AUS, 1943-46. Decorated Bronze Star (U.S.); Order Italian Crown; Italian Mil. Cross. Guggenheim fellow, 1962-63; Social Sci. Research Council grantee; Rockefeller Found. scholar-in-residence, 1965, 73. Mem. Am. Bar Assn., Internat. Law Assn., Council Fgn. Relations, Am. Soc. Internat. Law (exec. council 1954-57, bd. rev. and devel. 1965-67, 70-75), Brit. Inst. Internat. and Comparative Law, Internat. Acad. Comparative Law (asso.). Author: (with others) American Enterprise in the European Common Market-A Legal Profile, vols. I, II, 1960; (with H.K. Jacobson) Diplomats, Scientists and Politicians: The United States and the Nuclear Test Ban Negotiations, 1966; Harmonization of European Company Law— National Reform and Transnational Coordination, 1971; Impact of New Weapons Technology on International Law-Selected Aspects, 1971. Editor: (with Peter Hay) Law and Institutions in the Atlantic Area Readings, Cases and Problems, 1967; (with Peter Hay and Michel Waelbroeck) European Community Law and Institutions in Perspective, 1976. Bd. editors Am. Jour. Internat. Law, 1965—, Common Market Law Rev., 1964—; Legal Issues of European Integration, 1974—. Contbr. articles to profl. jours. Home: 2649 Heather Way Ann Arbor MI 48104

STEIN, FRANCES PATIKY, fashion exec.; b. Huntington, N.Y., Sept. 21, 1937; d. Jack M. and Frieda (Krakower) Patiky; student Smith Coll., 1955-58, Parsons Sch. Design, 1959; m. Ronald Jay Stein, Dec. 23, 1961. Fashion editor Harper's Bazaar, N.Y.C., 1960-62, Glamour Mag., N.Y.C., 1963-68; v.p. Halston, Ltd., fashion design, 1968-69; prin. Frances Patiky Stein Assos., fashion cons., N.Y.C., 1969-72; dir. fashion Vogue Mag., N.Y.C., 1972-76; v.p., dir. design studio for Calvin Klein, Ltd., N.Y.C., 1976-79; prin. Frances Patiky Stein Inc., design agy., N.Y.C., 1979—. Office: 205 W 39th St New York NY 10018

STEIN, GEORGE NATHAN, radiologist, educator; b. Phila., Aug. 11, 1917; s. Samuel M. and Marie B. S.; B.A., U. Pa., 1938; M.D., Jefferson Med. Coll., 1942; postgrad. Sch. Medicine, U. Pa., 1946; m. Hazel Gloria Gould, Aug. 18, 1948; children—Stephen G., Eric J., James M. Asso. radiologist Grad. Hosp. U. Pa., 1948-60, asst. dir. dept. radiology, 1960-71; dir. dept. radiology Presbyn. U. Pa. Med. Center and prof. radiology U. Pa., 1971—. Prof. extraordinaire Javeriana U., Bogota, Colombia, 1960; cons. VA Hosp., Wilmington, Del., 1968-70. Served with M.C., AUS, 1943-46. Fellow Am. Coll. Radiology; mem. Phila. (pres. 1968-69), Am. Roentgen ray socs., Tex. Radiol. Soc. (hon.), Philadelphia County, Pa. State med. socs., Radiol. Soc. N.Am., AMA. Author 3 books. Contbr. numerous articles to profl. jours. Home: 544 Howe Rd Merion Station PA 19066 Office: 51 N 39th St Philadelphia PA 19104

STEIN, HERBERT, economist; b. Detroit, Aug. 27, 1916; s. David and Jessie (Segal) S.; A.B., Williams Coll., 1935; Ph.D., U. Chgo., 1958; m. Mildred Fishman, June 12, 1937; children—Rachel (Epstein), Benjamin. Economist, U.S. Govt., 1938-45; with FDIC, 1938-40, Nat. Def. Adv. Commn., 1940-41, WPB, 1941-44, Office War Moblzn. and Reconversion, 1945; economist Comm. for Econ. Devel., 1945-48, asso. dir. research, 1948-56, dir. research, 1956-66, v.p., chief economist, 1966-67; sr. fellow Brookings Instn., 1967-69; mem. Pres.'s Council Econ. Advisers, Washington, 1969—, chmn., 1972-74; A. Willis Robertson prof. econs. U. Va., Charlottesville, 1971—; weekly columnist The Economy Today, Scripps-Howard and other newspapers, 1974—; bd. contbrs. Wall St. Jour., 1974—; dir. Reynolds Metals Co., Ozma Corp.; cons. Congl. Budget Office, 1976—; mem. Adv. Com. Nat. Growth Policy Processes, 1976-77; mem. Pharm. Reimbursement Adv. Bd., 1976-77; adj. scholar Am. Enterprise Inst., 1975-77, sr. fellow, 1977—, editor AEI Economist 1977—. Co-chmn. Economists for Ford, 1976; mem. vis. com. econs. dept. Harvard U., 1979—; mem. Group of 30, 1978—. Served as ensign USNR, 1944-45. Recipient 1st prize Pabst Post-War Employment awards, 1944; Center Advanced Study in Behavioral Scis. fellow, 1965-66. Mem. Am., So., Va. econ. assns., Nat. Economists Club (chmn., bd. govs. 1969-70). Club: Cosmos. Author: U.S. Government Price Policy during the World War, 1938; (with de Chazeau, Hart, Means, Myers, Yntema) Jobs and Markets, 1946; The Fiscal Revolution in America, 1969; Economic Planning and the Improvement of Public Policy, 1975; (with W. Leontief) The Economic System in an Age of Discontinuity, 1976; (with Benjamin Stein) On the Brink, 1977; (with Benjamin Stein) Money Power, 1980; editor: Policies to Combat Depression, 1956; contbr. to Agenda for the Nation, 1968, Contemporary Economic Problems, 1976, 77, 78, 79. Home: 1704 Yorktown Dr Charlottesville VA 22901

STEIN, HERMAN DAVID, educator; b. N.Y.C., Aug. 13, 1917; s. Charles and Emma (Rosenblum) S.; B.S.S., Coll. City N.Y., 1939; M.S., Columbia, 1941, D. Social Welfare, 1958; L.H.D., Hebrew Union Coll.-Jewish Inst. Religion, Cin, 1969; m. Charmion Kerr, Sept. 15, 1946; children—Karen Lou Gelender, Susan Deborah, Naomi Elizabeth. Family case worker, dir. pub. relations Jewish Family Service, N.Y.C., 1941-45; mem. faculty Columbia Sch. Social Work, N.Y.C., 1945-47, 50-64, prof., 1958-64, dir. research center, 1959-62; dean Sch. Applied Social Scis., Case Western Res. U., Cleve., 1964-68, provost for social and behavioral scis., 1967-71, provost univ., 1969-72, v.p. univ., 1970-72, Univ. prof., 1972—, vis. prof. Sch. Social Work, U. Hawaii, Honolulu, winter 1971-72; fellow center for Advanced Study in Behavior Scis., 1974-75, 78-79. Asst. dir. budget and research dir. welfare dept. Am. Joint Distbn. Com., European Hdqrs., Paris, 1947-50; spl. adviser to exec. dir. UNICEF, 1976—; cons. UNICEF, UN Social Devel. Div., 1960—; adv. com. NIMH, 1959-71; mem. Bd. Human Resources, Nat. Acad. Scis., 1972-74; lectr. Sch. Social Work, Smith Coll., 1950-63. Chmn. Mayor's Commn. on Crisis in Welfare in Cleve., 1968. Recipient Distinguished Service award Nat. Council on Social Work Edn., 1970. Fellow Am. Sociol. Assn.; mem. Nat. Council Social Work Edn. (pres. 1966-69), Internat. Assn. Schs. Social Work (pres. 1968-76), Nat. Assn. Social Workers (chmn. commn. internat. social welfare 1964-66), Internat. Conf. Social Welfare (mem. exec. com. 1976—). Author: The Curriculum Study of the Columbia University School of Social Work, 1960; co-author: The Characteristics of American Jews, 1965. Editor: (with Richard A. Cloward) Social Perspectives on Behavior, 1958; Planning for the Needs of Children in Developing Countries, 1965; Social Theory and Social Invention, 1968; The Crisis in Welfare in Cleveland, 1969. Contbr. to profl. jours. Office: Pardee Hall Case Western Res U Cleveland OH 44106

STEIN, HOWARD, mut. fund exec.; b. 1926; student Julliard Sch. Music, 1944-46. With Seaporcel Metal Inc., 1950-53, Bache & Co., 1952-55; asst., dir. Dreyfus Investment Mgmt. of Dreyfus and Co., also gen. partner, 1955-61; v.p. Dreyfus Fund Inc., 1961-65, pres., chmn. bd., 1965—; pres., dir. Dreyfus Corp., 1965-70, chmn. bd., chief exec. officer, 1970—; pres., dir. Dreyfus Corp. Can., 1965—. Address: 767 Fifth Ave New York NY 10022*

STEIN, HOWARD, educator; b. N.Y.C., Jan. 21, 1929; s. Morris and Fay (Reich) S.; A.B., Columbia, 1947; Ph.D., U. Chgo., 1958; M.S., U. Mich., 1959; m. Lee Sandra Bernstein, July 11, 1948; children—Katherine, David. Asst. natural scis. U. Chgo., 1950-51, instr., 1951-53, asst. prof., 1953-60; instr. math. Brandeis U., Waltham, Mass., 1959-60; systems analyst, electronic data processing div. Honeywell, Inc., 1962-66, computer control div., 1966-67; prof. philosophy Case Western Res. U., Cleve., 1967-73, Columbia, 1973—. NSF sci. faculty fellow, 1958-59, sr. postdoctoral fellow, 1965-66, adv. com. for history and philosophy of sci., 1977-79; John Simon Guggenheim fellow, 1974-75. Mem. Am. Math. Soc., Am. Philos. Assn., Philosophy of Sci. Assn. Home: 454 Riverside Dr New York City NY 10027

STEIN, HOWARD S., banker; b. N.Y.C., Dec. 27, 1939; s. J. Zachary and Adele (Epstein) S.; B.A., U. Mich., 1961; M.B.A., Harvard, U., 1963. Mem. treas.'s staff Gen. Motors Corp., N.Y.C., 1963-69; dep. dir., dir. fiscal ops. Human Resources Adminstrn., City of New York, 1969-71, asst. commr. Manpower and Career Devel. Agy., 1971-72, dep. commr. rent and housing maintenance Housing and Devel. Adminstrn., 1972, dep. adminstr. Human Resources Adminstrn., 1972-74; 1st dep. adminstr. Human Resources Adminstrn., 1974-78; v.p. Citicorp Credit Services Inc., 1979—; dir. Advt. Corp. Am. Holyoke, Mass.; lectr. human resources policy Nova U., Ft. Lauderdale, Fla., 1973-74; field instr. adminstrn. specialization N.Y. U. Sch. Social Work, 1976-77. Mem. adv. council Vol. Urban Cons. Group, Inc.; chmn. bd. dirs. Nova Inst; treas., past pres., bd. dirs. Child Study Assn. Am./Wel-Met, Inc.; past treas., bd. dirs. Career Center for Social Services Greater N.Y., Inc.; treas., past pres. bd. dirs. Cavalier King Charles Spaniel Club U.S.A., Inc.; bd. dirs., sec. Child Welfare Info. Services; bd. dirs. N.Y.C. Health and Hosps., Corp., 1976; mem. corp. Children's Mus., Boston. Clubs: University, Harvard Bus. Sch., Harvard (past mem. admissions com.) (N.Y.C.). Home: 55 E 76th St New York NY 10021 Office: 575 Lexington Ave New York NY 10043

STEIN, IRVIN, orthopaedic surgeon, educator; b. Fayetteville, N.C., Oct. 17, 1906; s. Kalman and Fannie (Berman) S.; A.B., U. N.C., 1926; M.D., Jefferson Med. Coll., Phila., 1930; m. Dorothy Bluthenthal, Aug. 21, 1934; children—Jane (Mrs. Gerald Finerman), Margery (Mrs. James Winer), Katherine (Mrs. Keith Sachs). Intern, Sinai Hosp., Balt., 1930-31; resident surg. pathology Johns Hopkins, 1931-32; resident Phila. Orthopaedic Hosp., 1932-33; resident orthopedic surgery Johns Hopkins Hosp. and Children's Hosp. Sch., 1933-34; chief orthopedic surgery Phila. Gen. Hosp., 1941—; dir. chmn. dept. orthopedic surgery Albert Einstein Med. Center, Phila., 1962-72, emeritus chmn., 1972—; clin. prof. orthopedic surgery emeritus U. Pa. Sch. Medicine, Phila.; cons. dept. health services Phila. Sch. System. Chmn., Phila. Chamber Orch. Soc., 1967-70. Bd. dirs. Phila. Orch.; trustee Acad. Music. Recipient Rehab. Physician of Year award Phila. Easter Seal Soc., 1971. Diplomate Am. Bd. Orthopedic Surgery. Fellow A.C.S., Am. Assn. Study Neoplastic Diseases, N.Y. Acad. Scis., Coll. Physicians Phila., Am. Med. Writers Assn., Internat. Coll. Surgeons (pres. Pa. div. 1971, regent), Phila. Orthopedic Soc. (pres. 1970), Am. Geriatric Assn. Clubs: Philmont Country, Locust. Co-author: Living Bone in Health and Disease, 1955; Clinical Densitometry, 1971. Contbr. numerous articles to profl. jours. Home: 220 W Rittenhouse Sq Philadelphia PA 19103 Office: 1936 Spruce St Philadelphia PA 19103

STEIN, JEROME LEON, educator, economist; b. Bklyn., Nov. 14, 1928; s. Meyer and Ida (Shapiro) S.; B.A. summa cum laude, Bklyn. Coll., 1949; M.A., Yale, 1950, Ph.D., 1955; m. Hadassah Levow, Aug. 27, 1950; children—Seth, Gil, Ilana. Instr., Brown U., Providence, 1953-56, asst. prof., 1956-60, asso. prof., 1960-62, prof., 1962-70, Eastman prof. polit. economy, 1970—; vis. prof. Hebrew U., Jerusalem, 1965-66, 72-73, 78; mem. faculty research grants com. Social Sci. Research Council, 1967-70, chmn., 1971-72. Ford Found. faculty fellow, 1961-62; Social Sci. Research Council grantee, 1965-66; Guggenheim fellow, 1972-73. Mem. Am. Econ. Assn. Author: Nature and Efficiency of the Foreign Exchange Market, Essays in International Finance, 1962; (with G.M. Borts) Economic

Growth in a Free Market, 1964; Money and Capacity Growth, 1971; Monetarism, 1976. Bd. editors Am. Econ. Rev.; asso. editor Jour. of Finance, 1964-70. Home: 77 Elton St Providence RI 02906

STEIN, JESS, publisher, editor; b. N.Y.C., June 23, 1914; s. Elias and Regina (Goldenberg) S.; A.B., Wayne State U., 1933; M.A., U. Chgo., 1934, postgrad., 1934-36; m. Dorothy Gerner, Mar. 7, 1943; children—Regina (Mrs. Bruce H. Wilson), Eric. Editor, Scott Foresman & Co., Chgo., 1934-42; with Office of Censorship, Washington, 1942-45; with Random House, Inc., N.Y.C., 1945—, head coll. and reference depts., 1950-59, v.p., 1959—, dir., 1967-74; v.p. Alfred A. Knopf, Inc., N.Y.C., 1967-74; pres. Jess Stein Assos., 1974—; cons. Internat. Reading Assn., 1976—; dir. L.W. Singer Co., N.Y.C., Random House Can. Ltd., Toronto, RH Sch. and Library Services, Inc. Mem. White Plains (N.Y.) City Democratic Com., 1954-58, Westchester County (N.Y.) Dem. Com., 1956-58 adviser proposed Hall of Fame, Jerusalem, 1976—. Mem. Am. Textbook Publs. Inst. (dir. 1961-64, treas. 1964), Linguistic Soc. Am., Nat. Council Tchrs. English, Coll. Pub. Group (chmn. 1960-61), Modern Lang. Assn., Am. Hist. Assn., Dictionary Soc. Am., Coll. English Assn., Dialect Soc., AAAS, Am. Geog. Soc., NAACP, ACLU, Urban League. Club: Dutch Treat (N.Y.C.). Author: (with R.N. Linscott) Why You Do What You Do, 1956; mng. editor Am. Coll. Dictionary, 1947—; editor, translator (pseudonym Isai Kamen) Tolstoy's The Kreutzer Sonata, 1957, Great Russian Stories, 1959; editor Am. Everyday Dictionary, 1949—, Am. Vest Pocket Dictionary, 1951—, Basic Everyday Ency., 1954—, Vest Pocket Rhyming Dictionary, 1951—, Modern Am. Dictionary, 1957—, Irving's Life of George Washington, 1975, Random House Coll. Dictionary, rev., 1975—; editor-in-chief Random House Dictionary of the English Language, 1966—; editorial dir. Random House Ency., 1977—; RH dictionaries, 1966—; cons. U. Mass. Press, 1975-78. Home: 11 Sherman Ave White Plains NY 10605 Office: 201 E 50th St New York NY 10022

STEIN, JOSEPH, playwright; b. N.Y.C., May 30, 1912; s. Charles and Emma S.; B.S.S., CCNY, 1934; M.S.W., Columbia U., 1937; children by previous marriage—Daniel, Harry, Joshua; m. 2d, Elisa Loti, Feb. 7, 1975. Psychiat. social worker, N.Y.C., 1938-45; writer radio shows, including Raleigh's Room, 1948-49, Henry Morgan Show, 1949-52; writer TV shows, including: Your Show of Shows, 1952-54, Sid Caesar Show, 1954-55; playwright: Plain and Fancy, 1955, Mr. Wonderful, 1957, Juno, 1959, Take Me Along, 1959, Enter Laughing, 1963, Fiddler on the Roof (N.Y. Drama Critics Circle Best Musical award 1965, Am. Theatre Wing Tony award for best musical 1965), 1964, Zorba, 1968, Irene, 1975, King of Hearts, 1978, Carmelina, 1979; screenplays: Enter Laughing, 1970, Fiddler on the Roof, 1972. Mem. Authors League, Screen Writers Guild, Dramatists Guild (council 1970-79). Home: 1130 Park Ave New York NY 10028 Office: 250 W 57th St New York NY 10019

STEIN, JULES, entertainment bus. exec., physician; b. South Bend, Ind., Apr. 26, 1896; s. Louis M. and Rosa (Cohen) S.; student Winona (Ind.) Acad., summers 1911-12, U. W. Va., 1912-13; Ph.B. U. Chgo., 1915; M.D. Rush Med. Coll., Chgo., 1921; postgrad. Eye Clinic, U. Vienna, Austria, 1922; L.H.D., U. Louisville, 1966; LL.D., U. Calif. at Los Angeles, 1968; D.Sc., Med. Coll. Wis., 1975; m. Doris Jones, Nov. 16, 1928; children—Jean Babette, Susan Rosa. Resident staff Cook County Hosp., Chgo, 1921-23; ophthalmologist asst. to Dr. Harry Gradle, Chgo., 1923-25; founded MCA Inc. (Music Corp. Am.), 1924, pres. corp. and affiliated cos., 1924-46, chmn. bd., 1946-73, founder, 1973—. Bus. mgr. Hollywood Canteen, 1942-45, chmn. Hollywood Canteen Found., 1945-66, pres., 1966—; co-founder, chmn. Research to Prevent Blindness; mem. nat. adv. eye council NIH 1969-71. Served as 1st lt. Med. Officer Res. Corps., AUS, 1923-28. Named asso. Knight Order of Hosp. of St. John Jerusalem, Pioneer of Yr., Found. Motion Picture Pioneers, 1978; recipient Migel award Am. Found. for Blind, 1963; Humanitarian award Variety Clubs Internat., 1968; hon. Alumnus award U. Calif. at Los Angeles Alumni Assn., 1972; Albert Lasker Pub. Service award, 1975; Humanitarian award Lions Internat., 1976; Jean Hersholt Humanitarian award Acad. Motion Picture Arts and Scis., 1976; Walt Disney Humanitarian award Nat. Assn. Theatre Owners, 1976. Former fellow Am. Bd. Ophthalmology; hon. fellow Am. Acad. Ophthalmology and Otolaryngology; mem. Assn. for Research in Ophthalmology (hon.). Author: Telescopic Spectacles and Magnifiers as Aids to Poor Vision, 1924. Home: PO Box 30 Beverly Hills CA 90213 Office: 100 Universal City Plaza Universal City CA 91608

STEIN, JUSTIN JOHN, physician, educator, b. Haskell, Tex., Oct. 18 1907; s. Justin John and Annie Minnie (Frederick) S.; M.D., Baylor U., 1933; m. Lillian May Kolar, Oct. 23, 1936; 1 dau. Justine Johanna. Intern, Cin. Gen. Hosp., 1934-35; spl. student Mayo Clinic and Found., 1933-34; tumor surgeon, radiotherapist Edward Hines Jr. VA Hosp., Hines, Ill., 1935-41; cons. Elmhurst (Ill.) Community, West-Lake hosps., Melrose Park, 1938-41; tumor surgeon, radiotherapist Los Angeles Tumor Inst., 1946-52; attending surgeon, mem. tumor bd., malignancy service Los Angeles County Hosp., 1948-59; cons. oncologost VA, West Los Angeles, 1948—; attending surg. staff Calif. Hosp., Los Angeles; dir. Calif. Inst. Cancer Research 1955-76, sec., 1966-75; prof. radiology U. Calif. Sch. Medicine, Los Angeles, 1952-75, prof. emeritus radiol. scis., 1975—, chief div. radiation therapy, dept. radiology, 1955-70, radiologic safety adv. com. (all campuses), 1955-60, acting chmn. dept. radiology, 1960, cancer coordinator, 1955-75, dir. Cancer Research Inst., 1956-70, cons. to lab. nuclear medicine and radiobiology, 1960-64; exec. coordinator for radiation therapy residency tng. program from univ., 1970-75; clin. prof. radiol. scis. U. Calif., Irvine, 1976—; chief radiation therapy VA Hosp., Long Beach, Calif., 1975—; cons.-lectr. Va. hosps., San Diego, Long Beach; exchange prof. Ministry Higher and Specialized Edn. USSR, 1963. Chmn., Gov.'s Emergency Med Adv. Com., 1950-67; dir. Calif. div. Am. Cancer Soc. 1950—, mem. exec. com., 1963-65, dir.-at-large, 1963-65, del. to nat. soc., 1966, pres. Los Angeles br., 1964-65, dir.-at- large, vice chmn. med. and sci. exec. com. N.Y. br., nat. dir.-at-large 1968—, chmn. nat. exec. com. of med. and sci. com., 1970—, v.p. 1972-73, pres., 1973-74, nat. past officer dir., 1976—, pres. Calif. div., 1977; cons. radiotherapy or radiology to various hosps. and health agys.; mem. Calif. Bd. Med. Examiners, 1952-70, v.p., 1955, pres., 1956. Rep. on cancer from Am. Coll. Radiology to A.C.S., 1960-68. Served to lt comdr. M.C., USNR, 1941-46. Diplomate Am. Bd. Radiology (trustee, chmn. com. on recertification), Internat. Bd. Surgery. Fellow Am. Coll. Nuclear Medicine, A.C.S. (exec. com on care of patient with cancer 1967-70), Internat. Coll. Surgeons (pres. So. Calif. chpt. 1952, vice regent 1953-65), Royal Soc. Medicine (Eng); mem. Am. Radium Soc. (pres. 1965-66, mem. exec. com. 1962-69), Pan Pacific Surg. Assn., AASA, Radiation Research Soc., Research Soc. Calif., Soc. Nuclear Medicine, Am. Club Therapeutic Radiologists, Radiol. Soc. So. Calif., Am. Roentgen Ray Soc. (2d v.p. 1965-66) Med.-Dental Vets. Assn. (pres. 1949), James Ewing Soc., Los Angeles Surg. Soc. (sr.), Calif., Los Angeles radiol. socs., Radiol. Soc. N.Am., Am., Los Angeles County (councillor 1950-53), Calif. (ho. of dels. 1950-54, 55-57, 61-63, chmn. com. sci. info. 1964—) med. assns., Dallas So. Clin. Soc. (hon.), Peruvian Cancer Soc. (hon.), Ky. Obstet. and Gynecol. Soc. (hon.), Mil. Order World Wars (surgeon gen. 1954), Kappa Sigma, Phi Chi. Asso. editor Breast. Contbr. numerous sci. articles to med. jours. Home: 3526A Bahia Blanca W Laguna Hills CA 92653

STEIN, LEON, educator, musician; b. Chgo., Sept. 18, 1910; s. Harry and Rebecca (LaZar) S.; Mus.B., DePaul U., 1931, Mus.M., 1935, Ph.D., 1949; m. Anne Helman, Oct. 30, 1937; children—Robert Edwin, Kenneth Erwin. Faculty sch. music DePaul U. Chgo., 1931—, successively instr., asso., prof., prof. chmm. dept. composition and theory, 1948—, dir. grad div. sch. music, 1948—, dean Sch. Music, 1966-76, dean emeritus, 1978—, prof. music, 1976—, dir. DePaul U. Symphony Orch., 1965—; chmn. Coll. Jewish Studies Inst. Music, 1951-57; condr. Community Symphony Orch., Amalgamated Chorus, Skokie Valley Symphony Orch., 1962-66, City Symphony, Chgo., 1965—; founder, condr. DePaul U. Chamber Orch.; guest condr. Ill. Symphony, Kenosha (Wis.) Symphony; mem. conducting class Chgo. Civic Orch., 1937-40. Composer 4 symphonies; Sonatine for Two Violins, 1946; Three Hassidic Dances, 1947; (operas) The Fisherman's Wife, 1953-54, Deirdre, 1955-56; Trio for Trumpets; Quintet for Saxophone and Strings; Sextet for Saxophone and Winds; Quintets for Harp and String Quartet, 1977; Concerto for Violoncello and Orch., 1977; also compositions for violin, cello piano and string quartets, Served as petty officer USNR, 1944-45; condr. concert band and orch. Naval Tng. Center, Gt. Lakes, Ill., also composer, arranger music Meet Your Navy, on Target. Recipient award for Triptych on Three Poems of Walt Whitman Am. Composers Commn. 1950, Symphonic Movement for Orch. award, Midland Music Found. composition prize, 1955; Symphony No. 4 named winner internat. competition Elkhart (Ind.) Orchestral Assn., 1977-78. Mem. Am. Composers Alliance, AAUP, Internat. Soc. Contemporary Music, Music Educators Council, Phi Mu Alpha, Pi Gamma Mu. Author: Racial Thinking of Richard Wagner, 1959; Outline of Music History; Structure and Style (The Study and Analysis of Musical Forms); Anthology of Musical Forms. Recs. include Five String Quartets, 1974. Contbr articles to music publs. Home: 4050 Greenwood Ave Skokie IL 60076

STEIN, MARVIN, physician, educator; b. St. Louis, Dec. 8, 1923; s. Samuel G. and Dora (Kline) S.; B.S., Washington U., St. Louis, 1945, M.D., 1949; grad. Phila. Psychoanalytic Inst., 1959; m. Ann Hackman, May 5, 1950; children—Leslie, David, Lisa. Intern St. Louis City Hosp., 1949-50; asst. resident in psychiatry Barnes Hosp., St. Louis, 1950-51; fellow in psychiatry Hosp. U. Pa., 1953-55; asst. prof., asso. prof. psychiatry U. Pa. Med. Sch., 1956-63; prof. psychiatry Cornell U. Med. Sch., 1963-66; prof., chmn. dept. psychiatry State U. N.Y. Downstate Med. Center, Bklyn., 1966-71; Esther and Joseph Klingenstein prof., chmn. dept. psychiatry Mt. Sinai Sch. Medicine, N.Y.C., 1971—. Mem. fellowships rev. panel NIMH, 1961-64, chmn. mental health extramural research adv. com., 1968-71; mem. research adv. com. VA, 1965-68, mem. research service merit rev. bd. in behavioral sci., 1972—; chmn. Mental Health Research Career Award Com., 1963-67; chmn. bd. dirs. Foundations Fund for Research in Psychiatry, 1967-70. USPHS postdoctoral fellow, 1951-53, mental health career investigator, 1956-61, sr. fellow grantee, 1961-63. Contbr. articles on psychosomatic medicine to med. jours. Home: 5700 Arlington Ave Riverdale NY 10471 Office: Mt Sinai Sch Medicine 100th St and Fifth Ave New York City NY 10029

STEIN, MARVIN LEONARD, educator; b. Cleve., July 15, 1924; s. Carl and Marian (Marks) S.; B.A., U. Calif. at Los Angeles, 1947, M.A., 1949, Ph.D., 1951; m. Ruth Meyerson, July 15, 1944; children—Tamar (Mrs. Abram Edelson), Eugene, Jerome. Mathematician, Inst. Numerical Analysis, U. Calif. at Los Angeles, 1948-52; research engr. Consol.-Vultee Aircraft Corp., San Diego, 1952-55; asso. prof. U. Minn., Mpls., 1956-61, prof., 1961—, dir. Univ. Computer Center, 1958-70, acting head computer sci., 1970-71; vis. prof. Tel Aviv U. and Hebrew U., Jerusalem, 1971-72; cons. in field. Served with AUS, 1943-46. Guggenheim fellow, 1963-64. Mem. Am. Math. Soc., Assn. Computing Machinery, Soc. Indsl. and Applied Math. Mem. Democratic-Farm-Labor party. Jewish (dir. congregation). Co-author: Computer Programming: A Mixed Language Approach; A Fortran Introduction to Computers and Programming; Introduction to Machine Arithmetic; Notes on Structure and Programming of Software Systems. Contbr. articles to profl. publs. Home: 98 Malcolm Ave Minneapolis MN 55414

STEIN, MAURICE ROBERT, educator; b. Buffalo, Sept. 19, 1926; s. Edward and Rebecca (Jaffee) S.; A.B., U. Buffalo, 1949; Ph.D., Columbia, 1958; m. Phyllis Ann Rosenstein, Aug. 29, 1964; children—Paul Radin, Nina Rebecca Rosa. Instr. sociology Dartmouth, 1952-53; asst. prof. Oberlin (Ohio) Coll., 1953-55; mem. faculty Brandeis U., Waltham, Mass., 1955—, prof. sociology, 1967—, chmn. dept., 1966-69; dean Sch. Critical Studies, Calif. Inst. of Arts. Burbank, 1969-71. Mem. internat. reference com. Reevaluation Counseling Communities, Seattle, 1974-75. Served with AUS, 1944-46. Author: Eclipse of Community, 1960; (with A. Vidich) Identity and Anxiety, 1960; Reflections in Community Studies, 1964; Sociology on Trial, 1964; (with others) The Drifters, 1967; (with L. Miller) Blueprint for Counter Education, 1969. Home: 59 Parker St Cambridge MA 02138 Office: Dept Sociology Brandeis Univ Waltham MA 02154

STEIN, MELVIN, life ins. co. exec.; b. Bklyn., Aug. 9, 1931; s. Jack Aaron and Clara (Lichtenstein) S.; A.B., Coll. City N.Y., 1952; LL.B., Yale U., 1955; m. Susan Ramsfelder, Dec. 12, 1964; children—Ellice, Amy Carin. Admitted to N.Y. State bar, 1958; asso. Temporary Commn. on Cts., N.Y. State, 1957-58; asst. dist. atty. N.Y. County, 1958-62; regional counsel HUD, N.Y.C., 1962-67; v.p., asso. gen. counsel Equitable Life Assurance Soc. U.S., N.Y.C., 1967-79, v.p. corp. hdqrs., 1980—. Trustee Congregation B'nai Jehuda, N.Y.C. Served with AUS, 1955-57. Mem. N.Y. State Bar Assn. Co-author: Courts of Terror, 1976. Contbr. articles to profl. jours.

STEIN, OTTO LUDWIG, educator; b. Augsburg, Germany, Jan. 14, 1925 (came to U.S. 1939, naturalized 1944); s. Julius and Margaret (Haas) S.; B.S. with distinction, U. Minn., 1949, M.S., 1952, Ph.D., 1954; m. Diana Borut, June 15, 1958; children—Deborah Lee, Judith Ann, Suzanne Beth, Jonathan Henri Richard. Instr. botany U. Mo. at Columbia, 1955; USPHS research fellow Brookhaven Nat. Lab., 1955-57, research collaborator, 1958-68; asst. prof. botany U. Mont., Missoula, 1957-63, asso. prof., 1963-64; asso. prof. botany U. Mass., Amherst, 1964-70, prof. botany, 1970—, head dept., 1969-74; vis. asst. prof. botany U. Calif. at Berkeley, 1961-62; NATO sr. research fellow, Imperial Coll., London, Eng., 1971-72. Served with AUS, 1944-46. Mem. AAAS, Am. Genetics Assn., AAUP, Bot. Soc. Am. (chmn. developmental sect. 1963-65), Soc. Developmental Biology, Soc. Exptl. Biology, Am. Soc. Cell Biology, Sigma Xi. Gamma Sigma Delta, Alpha Zeta, Gamma Alpha. Home: 140 Red Gate Ln Amherst MA 01002 Office: Dept Botany University Mass Amherst MA 01003

STEIN, RICHARD GEORGE, architect; b. Chgo., Aug. 23, 1916; s. Julius J. and Minnie (Gartenzaun) S.; Certificate in Design, Cooper Union, 1937; B.Arch. magna cum laude, N.Y. U., 1937; M.Arch., Harvard U., 1939; m. Ethel Levy, June 10, 1940; 1 son, Carl J. Draftsman, designer firm Gropius & Breuer, Cambridge, Mass., 1939-41; designer Edward D. Stone, N.Y.C., 1941, Tuttle, Seelye, Place & Raymond, N.Y.C., 1941-43; partner Katz, Waisman, Blumenkranz, Stein, Weber, N.Y.C., 1946-60; propr. Richard G. Stein & Assos., N.Y.C., 1960-76; partner Richard G. Stein & Partners, 1977—; instr., adj. prof. Cooper Union, 1947—; guest critic Syracuse U., 1961. Mem. N.Y. State Bd. Examiners Architecture, 1964-74, chmn., 1970-72; chmn. joint com. on N.Y.C. community dists. of Citizens' Union-Citizens' Housing and Planning Council, 1968—; prin. investigator NSF funded research on energy utilization in schs. (through N.Y.C. Bd. Edn.); mem. Nat. Bur. Standards Task Force on Illumination Performance Standards, 1977. Served with C.E., AUS, 1943-46; PTO. Recipient certificate commendation Parks Assn. N.Y.C., for Stephen Wise Plaza, 1965, Design Steel award for Central Park Music Festival, N.Y.C., 1967, citation Indsl. Design Rev. for Inwood Park, 1970; Merit award N.Y. State Assn. Architects, AIA for Rochdale Park, 1971, 1st place Competition for Affordable House, N.J. Dept. Community Affairs, 1978. Arnold W. Brunner scholar, 1972. Fellow AIA (mem. task force on energy conservation 1972—, pres. N.Y. chpt. 1976-77). Architect for several pub. facilities, including Rochdale Park, Queens, N.Y., 1971; Manhattan Children's Treatment Center, Wards Island, N.Y., 1971, Eleanor Roosevelt campus Wiltwyck Sch. Boys, Yorktown Heights, N.Y., 1966, N.Y.C. Community Coll., 1973—. Author: Architecture and Energy, 1977. Contbr. articles to profl. jours.; also studies for fed., state and local govts. Home: 40 Mt Airy Rd Croton-on-Hudson NY 10520 Office: 588 5th Ave New York City NY 10036

STEIN, RICHARD PAUL, lawyer; b. New Albany, Ind., Sept. 2, 1925; s. William P. and Lillian (Russell) S.; student Miligan (Tenn.) Coll., 1943-44, Duke, 1944-45, J.D., U. Louisville, 1950; m. Mary Charlotte Key, June 22, 1957; children—Richard Paul, William, Patricia. Admitted to Ind. bar, 1950; with Goodyear Engring. Co., Charlestown, Ind., 1951-52; law partner with Herbert F. Naville, New Albany, 1952-61; pros. atty. 52d Jud. Circuit Ind., 1954-61; U.S. atty. So. Dist. Ind., 1961-67; chmn. Pub. Service Commn. of Ind., 1961-70; legis. counsel Eli Lilly Co., Indpls., 1970-74; v.p. pub. affairs Pub. Service Co. Ind., 1974—; dir. Indpls. Indians, Carmel Bank & Trust Co. Co-counsel New Albany-Floyd County Bldg. Authority, 1960-62; mem. State Bd. Tax Commrs. Adv. Bd., Jud. Study Commn. Named Floyd County Young Man of Year, Floyd County Jr. C. of C., 1955. Served to lt. USNR, 1943-46, 50-51; lt. Res. Mem. Ind. Electric Assn. (dir.), Am. Legion, Pi Kappa Alpha, Phi Alpha Delta. K.C. Home: 5517 Surrey Hill Circle Indianapolis IN 46226 Office 1000 E Main St Plainfield IN 46168

STEIN, RICHARD STEPHEN, educator; b. N.Y.C., Aug. 21, 1925; s. Isidor and Florence (Lewengood) S.; B.S., Polytech. Inst. Bklyn., 1945; M.A., Princeton, 1948, Ph.D., 1949; m. Judith Elma Balise, May 27, 1951; children—Linda Ann, Anne Marie, Carol Joan, Lisa Jean. Postdoctoral fellow Cambridge U., 1948-49; research asso. Princeton, 1949-50; asst. prof. U. Mass., Amherst, 1950-57, asso. prof., 1957-59, prof., 1959-61, Commonwealth prof., 1961—, founder, dir. Polymer Research Inst., 1961—; cons. Monsanto Co., Gen. Tire and Rubber Co., Xerox Corp., Upjohn Corp. Recipient Internat. award Soc. Plastics Engrs., 1969, Bingham award Rheology Soc., 1972. Mem. Am. Chem. Soc. (Bordon award 1972), Am. Phys. Soc. (award in high polymer physics 1976), Rheology Soc., AAAS, AAUP, Sigma Xi. Co-editor: Electromagnetic Scattering, 1967; Structure and Properties of Polymer Films, 1973. Author numerous sci. articles. Founder sci. rheo-optics of polymers. Home: 5 Berkshire Terr Amherst MA 01002

STEIN, RITA F., educator; b. Buffalo, July 25, 1922; d. Samuel I. and Mary (Resnick) Fish; diploma Edward J. Meyer Meml. Hosp. Sch. Nursing, 1942; B.S. with distinction in Pub. Health Nursing, U. Buffalo, 1952; M.S. in Pub. Health, State U. N.Y., Buffalo, 1957, Ph.D. with distinction in Social Psychiatry, Med. Sociology (USPHS fellow), 1966; m. Jacob B. Stein, Dec. 21, 1947. Pub. health nurse Vis. Nurse Assn., Hartford, Conn., 1942-43; med., surg., neurol. nurse U.S. Army Nurse Corps, 1943-47; psychiat. nurse Dr. H. E. Favor, 1954-66; psychiat. nursing instr. Buffalo State Hosp., 1959-60; asso. prof., dir. of research Sch. Nursing, Ind. U., Indpls., 1966-67, prof., dir. research, 1968—; cons. in field. Mem. Am. Sociol. Assn., Nat. League Nurses, Am. Nurses Assn., Nat. Assn. Study Edn., Midwest Regional Med. Library and Coop. Info. Services (council) AAUP (mem. exec. com.), Ind. State Nurses Assn. (council on edn.), Am. Pub. Health Assn., Sigma Theta Tau. Jewish. Clubs: Hadassah, Sisterhood of Temple of Hebrew Congregation. Contbr. articles to profl. jours. Home: 4808 Dorkin Ct Indianapolis IN 46254 Office: Ind U Sch Nursing Indianapolis IN 46202

STEIN, ROBERT, publishing co. exec.; b. N.Y.C., Mar. 4, 1924; s. Isidor and Gertrude (Bohrer) S.; B.A., Coll. City N.Y., 1947; postgrad. Columbia; m. Dorothy Price Weichel, Mar. 31, 1956; children—Gregory, Keith, Clifford. Editorial asst. N.Y. Daily News, 1942-43; asst. dir. pub. relations, exec. editor Alumnus mag. Coll. City N.Y., 1947-51; article editor Argosy mag., 1951-53; asso. editor Redbook mag., 1953-54, articles editor, 1954-55, mng. editor, 1955-58, editor-in-chief, 1958-65; editor-in-chief McCall's mag., 1965-67, 72—, dir. book div. 1969-71; exec. asst. to pres. McCall Pub. Co., 1967-70, exec. v.p., 1970—. Chmn. bd. judges Fed. Woman's Award, 1966. Served with inf. AUS, 1943-46 Recipient Neuberger award Soc. Mag. Writers, 1961. Mem. Am. Soc. Mag. Editors (chmn. 1966-67). Author: Media Power, 1972. Contbr. articles to nat. mags. Office: 230 Park Ave New York NY 10017

STEIN, ROBERT ALAN, toy retail co. exec., mfg. co. exec.; b. Chgo., Oct. 18, 1930; s. Manfred and Mildred (Rosenfield) S.; B.A., U. Chgo., 1950, M.B.A., 1953; m. Frances Roslyn Berger, Dec. 25, 1960; 1 dau., Marcia Beth. Sr. auditor Scovell, Wellington & Co., Chgo., 1955-63; supr. corp. acctg. Mack Trucks, Inc., Montvale, N.J., 1963-65; v.p., treas. Lionel Corp., N.Y.C., 1965—. Served with U.S. Army, 1953-55. C.P.A., Ill. Mem. Fin. Exec. Inst., Am. Inst. C.P.A.'s, Am. Acctg. Assn. Home: 32 Stonewall Dr Livingston NJ 07039 Office: 9 W 57th St New York NY 10019

STEIN, ROBERT ALLEN, univ. adminstr.; b. Mpls., Sept. 16, 1938; B.S. in Law, U. Minn., 1960, J.D. summa cum laude, 1961. Admitted to Wis. bar, 1961, Minn. bar, 1967; asso. firm Foley, Sammond & Lardner, Milw., 1961-64; prof. Law Sch., l). Minn., Mpls., 1964—, asso. dean, 1976-77, v.p. adminstrn. and planning, 1978-80, dean Law Sch., 1979—; of counsel firm Mullin, Weinberg & Daly, Mpls., 1970—; vis. prof. UCLA, 1969-70, U. Chgo., 1975-76; mem. Uniform State Laws Commn. Minn., 1973—; acad. fellow Am. Coll. Probate Counsel, 1975—; vis. scholar Am. Bar Found., Chgo., 1975-76; mem. trust com. Northwestern Nat. Bank St. Paul, 1977—. Mem. Am. Bar Assn., Minn. Bar Assn. (mem. exec. council, probate and trust law sect. 1972-77), Hennepin County Bar Assn., Am. Law Inst. Author: Stein on Probate, 1976; Estate Planning Under the Tax Reform Act of 1976, 2d edit., 1978; Probate and Inheritance Tax, 1979, others; contbr. articles to legal jours. Home: 6005 Manchester Dr Minneapolis MN 55422 Office: Law Sch U Minn Minneapolis MN 55455

STEIN, ROBERT JACOB, pathologist; b. Odessa, Ukraine, July 20, 1915; s. Jacob and Esther S.; B.S., L.I. U.; M.D., U. Innsbruck; M.S. in Pathology, Northwestern U.; m. June 8, 1951; children—Ty, Peter. Head dept. pathology and toxicology Abbott Labs., North Chicago, Ill., 1954-61; dir. labs. McHenry (Ill.) Hosp. 1961-76; chief med. examiner Cook County (Ill.), 1976—; prof. dept. pathology Loyola U. Med. Sch., Chgo., Northwestern U. Med. Sch., Chgo. Served with Armed Forces, 1942-46. Diplomate Am. Bd. Pathology. Mem. Coll. Am. Pathologists, Am. Coll. Legal Medicine, Am. Assn. Pathologists,

Am. Soc. Clin. Pathologists, AMA. Jewish. Contbr. articles to med. jours. Home: 2926 Arlington Ave Highland Park IL 60035 Office: Office Cook County Med Examiner 1828 W Polk St Chicago IL 60612*

STEIN, SOL, publisher, writer; b. Chgo., Oct. 13, 1926; s. Louis and Zelda (Zam) S.; B.S.S., Coll. City N.Y., 1948; M.A., Columbia, 1949, postgrad., 1949-51; m. Patricia Day, Mar. 31, 1962; children—Kevin David, Jeffrey Lewelyn, Leland Dana, Robert Bruce, Andrew Charles, David Day, Elizabeth Day. Lectr. social studies Coll. City N.Y., 1948-51; editor ideological adv. staff Voice of Am., U.S. State Dept., 1951-53; gen. editor, originator Beacon Press paperbacks, 1954—; cons. Harcourt Brace Jovanovich, 1958-59; exec. v.p. Mid-Century Book Soc., 1959-62; pres. Stein & Day, book pubs., Briarcliff Manor, N.Y., 1962—. Lectr. dramatic arts Columbia, 1958-60. Exec. dir. Am. Com. for Cultural Freedom, 1953-56; treas. Forensic Found., 1959-62; mem. exec. com. Am. Friends of Captive Nations. Served to 1st lt. AUS, World War II. Playwriting fellow Yaddo, MacDowell Colony. Mem. New Dramatists Com. (council mem.), Playwrights Group, Actors Studio, Internat. Brotherhood Magicians (hon. life). Author: (plays) The Illegitimist, 1954 (first prize Dramatists Alliance), A Shadow of My Enemy, 1957; (novels) The Husband, 1969, The Magician, 1971; Living Room, 1974; The Childkeeper, 1975; Other People, 1979; The Resort, 1980. Contbr. articles to profl. jours., also revs., poetry to lit., scholarly mags. Home: Linden Circle Scarborough-on-Hudson NY 10510 Office: Scarborough House Briarcliff Manor NY 10510

STEIN, STANLEY, apparel mfg. co. exec.; b. N.Y.C., Nov. 29, 1922; s. Harry Samuel and Fanny (Brosowsky) S.; B.S. in Social Sci., City Coll. N.Y., 1942; LL.B., Bklyn. Law Sch., 1951; m. Julia I. Bass, Oct. 11, 1942 (div. July 1963); children—Frederick M., Stephanie L., Deborah C; m. 2d, Roberta Shields, Apr. 11, 1968. Systems analyst Toeppen Co., N.Y.C., 1946-47; controller, dir. Publix Shirt Co., N.Y.C., 1947-58; financial v.p., dir. Manhattan Shirt Co., N.Y.C., 1958-64; exec. v.p. operations, dir. McGregor-Doninger, Inc., N.Y.C., 1964-68; financial v.p. Villager Industries, Inc. (acquired by Jonathan Logan, Inc. 1973), Phila., 1969, exec. v.p., dir., 1969—, pres. Villager div., 1969-79, chmn. Villager div., 1979—. Served with USAAF, 1943-45. Mem. Am. Apparel Mfrs. Assn. (chmn. statis. com., 1966-67), Fin. Execs. Inst. Home: 50 Sutton Pl New York NY 10022 Office: Villager Industries Inc 1411 Broadway New York NY 10018

STEIN, WALTER, artist; b. N.Y.C., Nov. 30, 1924; s. Louis and Fannie (Maidenburg) Peartree; student Art Students League, Cooper Union, 1941, New Sch. Social Research, 1946-47, N.Y. U., 1948; m. Suria-fiica Coogan, 1946 (dec. 1972). Mem. faculty dept. art Cooper Union, 1968-69, Parsons Sch. Design, 1972—; one-man shows: Durlacher Bros. Gallery, N.Y.C., 1951, 53, 55, 57, 59, 61, 63, 65, 67, Graham Gallery, N.Y.C., 1967, 69, Indpls. Mus. Art, 1974, Morristown Unitarian Fellowship (N.J.), 76, 78, Pauline Trigere Showroom, N.Y.C., 1978, Boston Atheneum, 1978, Cathedral Mus., 1979; group shows include: Coe-Kerr, N.Y.C., 1976, Weyhe Gallery, N.Y.C., 1977, 79, Genesis Gallery, N.Y.C., 1977; Maxwell Davidson Art Gallery, N.Y.C., 1979; represented in permanent collections: Boston Mus. Fine Arts, Chgo. Art Inst., Fogg Art Mus., Mus. Modern Art, Phillips Collections, Indpls. Mus. Art, Yale U. Art Gallery, Smithsoni an Instn. Served with AUS, 1942-45. MacDowell fellow, 1977. Democrat. Jewish. Address: 103 Reade St New York NY 10013

STEIN, WALTER, apparel mfg. co. exec.; b. Germany, Nov. 25, 1908 (came to U.S. 1928, naturalized 1933); s. Aron and Flora (Katten) S.; m. Rosemarie J. Trager; 1 son by previous marriage, Walter Rich. With A. Stein & Co., (name changed to Paris Accessories for Men), N.Y.C., 1928—, beginning as stock boy, successively salesman, sales mgr. in charge N.Y. office, staff Chgo. office, exec. v.p., Chgo., 1928-57, pres., 1957—, chmn. bd., 1977—. Mem. Am. Inst. Men's and Boy's Wear (dir.), Anti-Defamation League (exec. bd.). Home: 485 Landreth Ln Northbrook IL 60062 Office: 2150 Frontage Rd Des Plaines IL 60018

STEIN, WILLIAM HOWARD, biochemist; b. N.Y.C. June 25, 1911; s. Fred M. and Beatrice (Borg) S.; grad. Phillips Exeter Acad., 1929; B.S., Harvard, 1933; Ph.D., Columbia, 1938, D.Sc. (hon.), 1973; D.Sc. (hon.), Yeshiva U., 1973; m. Phoebe Hockstader, June 22, 1936; children—William Howard, David F., Robert J. Asst., Rockefeller Inst. Med. Research, N.Y.C., 1938-42, assoc., 1942-49, assoc. mem., 1949-52, mem. staff, 1952; prof. Rockefeller U., 1954—; vis. prof. U. Chgo., 1960, Harvard, 1964. Fellow Am. Swiss Found., 1956; Harvey lectr., 1957; mem. med. adv. bd. Hebrew U. Hadassah Med. Sch., Israel, 1947-61; Phillips lectr. Haverford Coll., 1962; Philip Schaffer lectr. Washington U., St. Louis, 1965; sci. counselor Nat. Inst. Neurol. Diseases and Blindness. Trustee Montefiore Hosp., N.Y.C., 1947-74. Recipient (with Stanford Moore) Kaj Linderstrøm-Lang award, 1972; (with Stanford Moore and Christian B. Anfinsen) Nobel prize in chemistry, 1972; Columbia Grad. Faculty and Alumni Assn. award excellence, 1973. Fellow AAAS; mem. Am. Acad. Arts and Scis., Nat. Acad. Scis., Am. Soc. Biol. Chemists (chmn. editorial com. 1958-61), Am. Chem. Soc. (co-recipient with Stanford Moore Electrophoresis award, Richards medal 1972), U.S. Nat. Com. Biochemistry (chmn. 1965-68), Biochem. Soc. (London), N.Y. Acad. Sci., Harvey Soc., Sigma Xi. Editorial bd. Jour. Biol. Chemistry, 1962-64, asso. editor, 1964-68, editor, 1968-71. Contbr. to sci. jours. Home: 530 E 72d St New York NY 10021 Office: Rockefeller Univ 66th St and York Ave New York NY 10021

STEINBACH, FRANK WARD, lawyer; b. Orange, Tex., July 30, 1931; s. William George and Mildred Jane (Brown) S.; A.A., Del Mar Jr. Coll., Corpus Christi, 1954; B.B.A., U. Tex., 1956, J.D., 1958; m. Mary Lou Heckler, Sept. 25, 1952; children—Frank Ward, Richard Scott, Margaret Virginia, Penny Janice. Admitted to Tex. bar; practice law, Corpus Christi, 1958, 66-77, Dallas; asst. county atty., 1958; with Guaranty Title Ins. Co., 1958-63, Dallas Title Co., 1963-66; partner firm Crozier & Steinbach, 1971-75. Served with USMC and Res., 1947-52. Mem. Dallas, Am. bar assns., State Bar Tex., Am. Trial Lawyers Assn., Am. Judicature Soc., Tex. Surveyors Assn., Tex. Title Assn. (v.p. 1960-61, sec. 1965-66), Praetorian. Methodist (chmn. bd. trustees). Home: 4525 Catina Dallas TX 75229 Office: 1010 W Mockingbird Ln Dallas TX 75247

STEINBACH, HENRY BURR, ednl. adminstr., biologist; b. Dexter, Mich, Oct.7, 1905; s. Henry August and Mary (Laney) S.; A.B., U. Mich., 1928; A.M., Brown U., 1930; Ph.D., U. Pa., 1933; m. Eleanor Parsons, June 9, 1934; children—Alan Burr, Mary Parsons, Joseph Henry, James Burr. Demonstrator physiol. and bio-chemistry Brown U., Providence, 1928-30; instr. zoology U. Pa., 1930-33, U. Minn., Mpls., 1935-37, asst. prof., 1937-38, prof., 1947-57, asst. prof. zoology Columbia, N.Y.C., 1938-42; asso. prof. zoology Wash. U., 1942-46, prof., 1946-47; prof., chmn. dept. zoology U. Chgo., 1957-68; dean Grad. Sch. Woods Hole Oceanographic Inst., 1968-73, cons. MP&OM Program; sci. dir. Harbor Br. Found. Lab., 1973; pres. Oceanic Inst., Makapuu Point, Waimanalo, Hawaii, 1974-76, pres. emeritus, 1976—; asst. dir. NSF, 1952-53; chmn. div. biology and agr. NRC, 1958-62 pres., dir. Marine Biol. Lab., 1966-70. NRC fellow U. Chgo. and U. Rochester med. schs., 1933-35; Guggenheim fellow, 1955-56. Fellow AAAS (dir. 1964-69); mem. Am. Soc. Zoologists (pres. 1957), Soc. Gen. Physiologists (pres. 1953), Am. Physiol. Soc., Sigma Xi. Mason. Club: Cosmos (Washington). Contbr. articles to profl. jours. Address: 1 Bell Tower Ln Woods Hole MA 02543

STEINBERG, ARTHUR G(ERALD), geneticist; b. Port Chester, N.Y., Feb. 27, 1912; s. Bernard Aaron and Sarah (Kaplan) S.; B.S., CCNY, 1933; M.A., Columbia U., 1934, Ph.D. (Univ. fellow), 1941; m. Edith Wexler, Nov. 22, 1939; children—Arthur E., Jean E. Steinberg Shengili. Mem. genetics dept. McGill U., Montreal, Que., Can., 1940-44; chmn. dept. genetics Fels Research Inst., asso. prof. genetics Antioch Coll., Yellow Springs, Ohio, 1946-48; cons. div. biometry and med. stats. Mayo Clinic, Rochester, Minn., 1948-52; geneticist Children's Cancer Research Found. and research asso. Children's Hosp., Boston, 1952-56; prof. biology Case Western Res. U., Cleve., 1956-72, asst. prof. human genetics, dept. preventive medicine, 1956-60, asso. prof., 1960-70, prof. human genetics, dept. reproductive biology, 1970—, Francis Hobart Herrick prof. biology, 1972—, prof. human genetics, dept. medicine, 1975—; lectr. genetics dept. orthodontics Harvard Sch. Dental Medicine, 1956-58; dir. heredity clinic Lakeside Hosp., Cleve., 1958-76; vis. prof. Albert Einstein Med. Coll., N.Y.C., 1962, 64, 66, Ind. U., Bloomington, 1972, N.Y. U. Sch. Medicine, 1977; XIIth Ann. Raymond Dart lectr. U. Witwatersrand, Johannesburg, S.Africa, 1975; mem. permanent com. to arrange IV Internat. Congress Human Genetics; mem. med. adv. bd. Cystic Fibrosis Found. Cleve., 1957-69; mem. sci. adv. bd. Nat. Cystic Fibrosis Research Found., 1961-63; cons. to expert adv. panel on human genetics WHO, 1961, mem. expert adv. panel, 1965—; mem. research adv. com. United Cerebral Palsy Found., 1962-65; mem. med. adv. bd. Nat. Genetics Found., 1966-68, chmn., 1968—; dir. WHO Collaborating Centre for Reference and Research on Genetic Factors of Human Immunoglobulins, 1966-78; cons. study of diabetes in Pima Indians, NIH, 1970—. Bd. dirs. Cleve. Zoo; mem. Cleve. Inst. Art, Cleve. Mus. Art, Cleve. Health Mus., Mlus. Natural History. Fellow Australian Acad. Sci. (sr.), AAAS; mem. Am. Soc. Human Genetics (pres. 1964, dir. 1954-66), Genetics Soc. Am., Am. Assn. Immunologists, Japanese Soc. Human Genetics (hon.), Societe Francaise d'Anthropologie et d'Ecologie Humaine (fgn. mem. sci. counsel 1972), Sigma Xi. Editor Am. Jour. Human Genetics, 1956-61; sr. editor Progress in Med. Genetics, 1960—; mem. internat. bd. editors Human Genetics Abstracts, 1962—; cons. editor Transfusion, 1964—; contbg. editor Vox Sanguinis, 1965-79; contbr. articles to sci. jours. Home: 2196 Delaware Dr Cleveland Heights OH 44106 Office: 403N lMillis Sci Center Case Western Res U Cleveland OH 44106

STEINBERG, DANIEL, physician, educator, biochemist; b. Windsor, Ont., Can., July 21, 1922 (came to U.S. 1922); s. Maxwell Robert and Bess (Krupp) S.; B.S. with highest distinction, Wayne State U. 1941, M.D. with highest distinction, 1944; Ph.D. with distinction (fellow Am. Cancer Soc. 1950-51), Harvard, 1951; m. Sara Murdock, Nov. 30, 1946; children—Jonathan Henry, Ann Ballard, David Ethan. Intern Boston City Hosp., 1944-45; physician Detroit Receiving Hosp., 1945-46; instr. physiology Boston U. Sch. Medicine, 1947-48; joined USPHS, 1951, med. dir., 1959; research staff lab. cellular physiology and metabolism Nat. Heart Inst., 1951-53, chief sect. metabolism, 1956-61, chief of lab. metabolism, 1962-68, lectr. grad. program NIH, 1955, mem. sci. adv. com. ednl. activities, 1955-61, com. chmn., 1955-60; mem. metabolism study sect. USPHS, 1959-61; chmn. heart and lung research rev. com. B, Nat. Heart, Lung and Blood Inst., 1977-79; vis. scientist Carlsberg Labs., Copenhagen, 1952-53, Nat. Inst. Med. Research, London, 1960-61; pres. Lipid Research Inc., 1961-64, adv. bd., 1964-73; prof. medicine, head div. metabolic disease Sch. Medicine, U. Calif., San Diego and La Jolla, also program dir. basic scis. medicine, 1968—. Bd. dirs. Found. Advanced Edn. in Scis., 1959-68, pres. 1956-62, 65-67. Served to capt. M.C. AUS, World War II. Mem. Am. Heart Assn. (mem. exec. com. council on arteriosclerosis 1960-63, 65-73, chmn. council arteriosclerosis 1967-69), Fedn. Am. Scientists (exec. com. 1957-58), Am. Soc. Biol. Chemists, Am. Soc. Clin. Investigation, Assn. Am. Physicians, Am. Fedn. Clin. Research, A.M.A., European Atherosclerosis Discussion Group, Am. Physiol. Soc., Alpha Omega Alpha. Former editor Jour. Lipid Research; editorial bd. Jour Clin. Investigation, 1969-74; exec. editor Analytical Biochemistry, 1978-80; contbr. articles to profl. jours. Home: 7742 Whitefield Pl La Jolla CA 92037

STEINBERG, DAVID, comedian, author, actor; b. Winnipeg, Man., Can., Aug. 9, 1942; s. Jacob and Ruth S.; student Hebrew Theol. Coll., U. Chgo. Writer, actor Second City; actor Little Murders; Broadway appearances include: Carry Me Back to Morningside Heights; star Music Scene; host on Johnny Carson, David Frost and Dick Cavett shows; appearances on Smothers Bros., Flip Wilson, Glen Campbell shows; author spl. This is Sholem Aleichem, Return of Smothers Bros.; rec. on Elektra-David Steinberg Disguised as a Normal Person; starred in film Something Short of Paradise, 1979. Address: care William Morris Agy Inc 151 E Camino Beverly Hills CA 90212*

STEINBERG, ERIC JOSEPH, wholesale and retail food co. exec.; b. Wolfenbuttel, Germany, Oct. 6, 1934; s. Ernest D. and Hannah (Loewe) S.; grad. public schs.; children—Stephen, John, David, Gary, Karen. Came to U.S., 1946, naturalized, 1954. Vice pres. indsl. relations Hills Supermarkets div. Pueblo Internat., Brentwood, N.Y., 1966-70, v.p., asst. to pres., 1970-71; pres., chmn. bd., dir. Asso. Food Stores Inc., N.Y.C., 1971-73; exec. v.p. Royal Food Distbrs., Inc. div. Fleming Cos., Inc., Woodbridge, N.J., 1974-77; pres. Thriftway Foods div. Fleming Foods, Oaks, Pa., 1978—; v.p. Eastern region Fleming Foods Co., 1979—. Served with USAF, 1953-57. Recipient B'nai B'rith Youth Services-Nat. Food Industry Man of Year award, 1972. Home: 1607 Morgan Dr Ambler PA 19002 Office: Oaks PA

STEINBERG, ERWIN RAY, educator; b. New Rochelle, N.Y., Nov. 15, 1920; s. Samuel and Lea (Neumann) S.; student Coll. City N.Y., 1937-38, State U. N.Y. Coll. at Plattsburg, 1938-40; B.S., State U. N.Y. at Albany, 1941, M.S., 1942; Ph.D., N.Y. U., 1956; m. Beverly Mendelson, Aug. 15, 1954; children—Marc William, Alan Jay. Mem. faculty Carnegie—Mellon U., Pitts., 1946—, prof. English, 1961-75, prof. English and interdisciplinary studies, 1975—, head dept. gen. studies, 1955-61, dean Margaret Morrison Carnegie Coll., 1960-73, dean Coll. Humanities and Social Scis., 1965-75, dir. Communications Design Center, 1979—; coordinator project English, U.S. Office Edn., 1963-64; vis. scholar Center for Advanced Study in Behavioral Scis., 1970-71. Mem. commn. of scholars Bd. Higher Edn., State of Ill., 1974—, vice chmn., 1979—; bd. dirs. Action-Housing, Pitts. Served with USAAF, 1943-46. Recipient Carnegie Teaching award, 1946; named Distinguished Alumnus State U. N.Y. at Albany, 1969, Alumnus of Year State U. N.Y. Coll. at Plattsburg, 1971. Mem. Modern Lang. Assn., Nat. Council Tchrs. English, Pitts. Council on Pub. Edn. (pres. 1966), Phi Kappa Phi, Phi Delta Kappa, Kappa Delta Pi. Author: Needed Research in the Teaching of English, 1963; The Stream of Consiousness and Beyond in Ulysses, 1973. Co-author: Communication in Business and Industry, 1960; Communication Problems from Business and Industry, 1961. Editor: The Rule of Force, 1962. Co-editor: Personal Integrity, 1961; Curriculum Development and Evaluation in English and Social Studies, 1964; English Education Today, 1970; English Then and Now, 1970; Stream of Consciousness Technique in the Modern Novel, 1979; gen. editor Insight series, 1968-73. Home: 1376 Sheridan Ave Pittsburgh PA 15206

STEINBERG, JACOB, pub. co. exec.; b. Bklyn., Jan. 31, 1915; s. Meyer and Ida (Shapiro) S.; B.A., Bklyn. Coll., 1936; postgrad. Columbia U., 1936-37, 46-48; m. Claire Bernstein, Jan. 31, 1943; 1 son, Michael Gary. Tchr. secondary schs., N.Y.C., 1937-43; free-lance editor, 1936-43; lectr. Columbia U., N.Y.C., 1947-48; founded Twayne Pubs., Inc. (name now G.K. Hall Co.) N.Y.C., Boston, 1948, pres., 1948-74. Served with AUS, 1943-46. Mem. Assn. Jewish Book Pubs. (pres. 1974—). Editor: Introductions to World Literature Series, 1966; Introduction to Rumanian Literature, 1966. Home: 1044 E 27th St Brooklyn NY 11210 Office: 1 Pennsylvania Plaza New York NY 10001

STEINBERG, JOSEPH SAUL, fin., co. exec.; b. Chgo., Feb. 5, 1944; s. Paul S. and Sylvia (Neikrug) S.; A.B., N.Y. U., 1966; M.B.A., Harvard U., 1970; m. Deborah G. Segal, Feb. 21, 1968; 1 dau., Sarah Aliza. Vol., Peace Corps, Kingston, Jamaica, 1966-68; v.p. Carl Marks & Co., Inc., investment bankers, N.Y.C., 1970-78; pres. Talcott Nat. Corp. and James Talcott, Inc., N.Y.C., 1979—; dir. Atlantic Research Corp., Roberts Consol. Industries, Inc. Club: Harvard (N.Y.C.). Office: 1290 Ave of the Americas New York NY 10019

STEINBERG, LAWRENCE EDWARD, lawyer; b. Dallas, Nov. 25, 1935; s. Oscar J. and Pearl L. (Soloman) S.; B.B.A., U. Tex., 1958; J.D., So. Methodist U., 1960; m. Linda Sue Goidl, Aug. 31, 1967; children—Adam Joseph, Ilana Sara. Admitted to Tex. bar, 1960, since practiced in Dallas; partner firm Steinberg & Luerssen, 1971—. Mem. Urban Rehab. Standards Bd., Dallas, 1975; mem. adv. com. affirmative action program Dallas Ind. Sch. Dist., 1974-76; regional bd. chmn., nat. commr., nat. law com. Anti-Defamation League, B'nai Brith, 1973-77. Served as 2d lt. U.S. Army, 1958-59. Mason (Shriner). Clubs: City, Columbian. Home: 7308 Glendora Dallas TX 75230 Office: 2200 Fidelity Union Tower Dallas TX 75201

STEINBERG, MALCOLM SAUL, educator, biologist; b. New Brunswick, N.J., June 1, 1930; s. Morris and Esther (Lerner) S.; B.A., Amherst Coll., 1952; M.A., U. Minn., 1954, Ph.D., 1956; m. Carol Bruber, Aug. 18, 1956; children—Jeffery, Julie, Eleanor, Catherine. Postdoctoral fellow Carnegie Instn., Washington, 1956-58; asst. prof. Johns Hopkins, Balt., 1958-64, asso. prof., 1964-66; prof. biology Princeton, 1966—, Henry Fairfield Osborn prof. biology, 1975—. Instr.-in-charge embryology course Marine Biol. Lab., 1967-71, trustee, 1969-77. Fellow AAAS; mem. Am. Soc. Zoologists (program officer div. developmental biology 1966-69), Am. Soc. Cell Biology, Internat. Soc. Developmental Biologists, Soc. Developmental Biology (trustee, sec. 1970-73), Am. Inst. Biol. Scis., AAUP. Editorial bd. Jour. Exptl. Zoology, Bioscience. Contbr. articles to profl. jours. Home: 86 Longview Dr Princeton NJ 08540

STEINBERG, MARTIN REMEZ, physician, hosp. adminstr.; b. Russia, June 5, 1904; s. Harry and Rose (Remez) S.; came to U.S. 1907, naturalized 1914; M.Med. Sci., U. Pa., 1931; M.D. Temple U. 1927; m. Cecily J. Kaplan, June 30, 1931; children—Deborah, Howard. Intern, Mt. Sinai Hosp., Phila., 1928-29; resident Grad. Hosp. U. Pa., 1929-31; pvt. practice, Phila., 1929-42; asst. prof. U. Pa. Grad. Med. Sch., 1932-43; chmn. med. adv. bd. Sidney-Hillman Clinic, 1953—; dir. Mt. Sinai Hosp., N.Y.C., 1948—; now prof., chmn. dept. adminstrv. medicine Mt. Sinai Sch. Medicine, also lectr. Sch. Pub. Health, Columbia. Mem. N.Y. State Hosp. Rev. and Planning Council. Served to lt. col. M.C., AUS, 1942-46. Diplomate Am. Bd. Otolaryngology. Fellow Am. Acad. Otorhinolaryngology, N.Y. Acad. Medicine, Am. Coll. Hosp. Adminstrs.; mem. Greater N.Y. Hosp Assn. (bd. govs., past pres.), Hosp. Assn. N.Y. State (trustee pres.) Am. Hosp. Assn. (trustee). Home: 1901 Kennedy Blvd Apt 2421 Philadelphia PA 19103 Office: Mt Sinai Hosp 11 E 100th St New York City NY 10029. *Life is worth its pain if there is love of family and friends—flashes of beauty—literature, music, art—and a dedication to morality and the dignity of all men.*

STEINBERG, MICHAEL, music critic, educator; b. Breslau, Germany, Oct. 4, 1928 (came to U.S. 1943, naturalized 1950); s. Siegfried and Margarethe (Cohn) S.; A.B., Princeton, 1949, M.F.A., 1951; Mus. D. (hon.), New Eng. Conservatory Music, 1966; m. Jane Bonacker, July 26, 1953; children—Peter Sebastian, Adam Gregory. Free-lance writer, 1952—; head history dept. Manhattan Sch. Music, N.Y.C., 1957-64; music critic Boston Globe, 1964-76; dir. publs. Boston Symphony Orch., 1976-79; artistic adviser, publs. dir. San Francisco Symphony, 1979—; vis. mem. faculty Hunter Coll., 1954, U. Sask. (Can.) 1959, Smith Coll., 1964, Brandeis U., 1964-65; faculty New Eng. Conservatory Music, 1968-71, Wellesley Coll., 1971-72, Brandeis U., 1971-72, Mass. Inst. Tech., 1973. Mem. sr. fellowship panel Nat. Endowment for Humanities. Bd. dirs. Handel and Haydn Soc., Boston Musica Viva. Served with AUS, 1955-57. Recipient Sang prize for criticism in arts, 1969; citation for Excellence in Criticism Am. Guild Organists, 1972. Mem. Am, Internat. musicological socs., Harvard Musical Assn. Home: 73 Terra Vista San Francisco CA 94115 Office: 107 War Meml Vets Blvd San Francisco CA 94102

STEINBERG, MORRIS ALBERT, metallurgist, aircraft mfg. co. exec.; b. Hartford, Conn., Sept. 24, 1920; s. Abraham and Rose (Bellow) S.; B.S. (Competitive scholar), M.I.T., 1942, M.S. in Metallurgy (S.K. Wellman fellow), 1946, D.Sc., 1948; postgrad. Harvard Bus. Sch., 1970; m. Natlee Jean Haas, Apr. 29, 1951; children—Laurie Beth, Cathy, James J. Instr. dept. metallurgy M.I.T., Cambridge, Mass., 1946-48; head and dir. Horizons Inc., Cleve., 1948-58; officer and dir. Micrometric Instrument Corp., Cleve., 1949-51; sec., dir. Diwolfram Corp., Cleve., 1950-53; chief metallurgist Horizons Titanium Corp., Cleve., 1951-54; dir. material sci. lab. Lockheed Missiles & Space Co., Palo Alto, Calif., 1958-65; dep. chief scientist Lockheed Corp., Burbank, Calif., 1965-72, dir. tech. application, 1972—; adj. prof. materials dept. Sch. Engring. and Applied Sci., UCLA, 1978—; mem. structures tech. panel for Chief of Staff, USAF, 1971-72, mem. ad hoc com. of B-1 structures, sci. adv. bd., 1972—; mem. Nat. Materials Adv. Bd., NRC, Nat. Acad. Scis., 1976—. Served to capt. USAF, 1942-46; ETO. Registered profl. engr., Calif. Fellow Am. Soc. Metals (mem. public affairs com. 1973-75), Am. Inst. Chemists; mem. Soc. Mfg. Engring. (chmn. engring. materials com. 1969-72), Soc. Automotive Engrs., Aerospace Industries Assn. (chmn. materials and structures com. 1973-74), Nat. Acad. Engring., Soc. Mfg. Engrs. (mem. tech. council 1969-72), AIAA (chmn. materials com. 1962-64, chmn. honors and awards com. Los Angeles sect. 1977-79). Contbr. numerous articles on metallurgy and aerospace materials to engring. jours. Home: 348 Homewood Rd Los Angeles CA 90049 Office: Lockheed Corp PO Box 551 Burbank CA 91520

STEINBERG, PAUL MARTIN, educator; b. N.Y.C., Jan. 29, 1926; s. Abraham and Lena (Schimelman) S.; B.S. with honors, Coll. City N.Y., 1946, M.Sc., 1948; M.H.L., Hebrew Union Coll.-Jewish Inst. Religion, 1949; Ed.D., Columbia, 1961; m. Trudy Strudler, June 15, 1947; children—Alana Wittenberg, Alan. Rabbi, 1949; fellow dept. edn. Coll. City N.Y., 1946-48; lectr. dept. edn. Hebrew U., 1949-50; lectr. Sch. Social Welfare, Jerusalem, 1949-50; dir. Hillel Found., U. Calif. at Berkeley, 1950-52; chaplain FDR VA Hosp., Montrose, N.Y., 1952-57; rabbi Temple Israel, Croton-on-Hudson, N.Y., 1952-58; lectr. Sch. Edn. N.Y.U., 1956; instr. human relations and edn. Hebrew Union Coll., 1955-57, asst. prof., 1957-59, asso. prof., 1959-61, prof. human relations and edn., dean, 1961—, now Eleanor

Sinsheimer distinguished service prof. Jewish religious edn. and human relations; exec. dean HUCBAS, Jerusalem, 1963-70; profl. asso. Richardson, Bellows & Henry, 1958-60, BFS Psychol. Assos., 1961—; expert examiner N.Y. State Civil Service Commn.; lectr. Army Mgmt. Sch. Mem. bd. Council Higher Ednl. Instns. N.Y.C., 1957-73; mem. Commn. on Church Family Fin. Planning; trustee Jewish Braille Inst. Am. Guggenheim fellow for research and travel Israel, 1949-50; N.Y. State Dept. Edn. Research fellow, Israel, 1967. Fellow A.A.A.S.; mem. Central Conf. Am. Rabbis, Am. Psychol. Assn., AAUP, Smithsonian Instn. Assos., Am. Found. for Psychiatry and Religion, Phi Delta Kappa. Jewish. Contbr. articles to ednl. jours. Home: 54 Rutledge Rd Scarsdale NY 10583 Office: Office of Dean and Dept Human Relations and Edn Hebrew Union Coll Jewish Inst Religion One W 4th St New York NY 10012

STEINBERG, RAFAEL MARK, writer, editor; b. Newark, June 2, 1927; s. Isador N. and Polly (Rifkind) S.; A.B. cum laude, Harvard, 1950; m. Tamiko Okamoto, Nov. 21, 1953; children—Summer Eve, Joy Nathania. Editor, pub. Fire Island (L.I.) N.Y. Reporter, summers 1949, 50; war corr. Internat. News Service, Korea, 1951-52; corr. Time mag., Korea, Japan, 1952, contbg. editor, N.Y.C., 1953-55, corr. London bur., 1955-58; Tokyo bur. chief, Far Eastern corr. Newsweek mag., 1959-63, gen. editor, 1970-72, sr. editor, 1972-73, mng. editor internat. edition, 1973; editor Cue mag., 1975-76; free-lance corr., Tokyo, 1963-67, U.S., 1968-70, 73-75. Exec. dir. Acad. and Profl. Alliance for a Responsible Congress, 1970; coordinator Columbia Program in Urban Ecology, 1970. Served with USNR, 1945-46. Mem. Authors Guild. Clubs: Foreign Correspondents (Tokyo); Harvard (N.Y.C.). Author: Postscript from Hiroshima, 1966; Japan (Nations Today series), 1969; Pacific and Southeast Asian Cooking, 1970; Man and the Organization, 1975; Island Fighting, 1978; Return to the Philippines, 1979. Contbr. articles, stories to publs. Home: 1391 Somerset Gate Teaneck NJ 07666 Office: 1841 Broadway New York NY 10023

STEINBERG, SAUL, artist; b. Romanic-Sarat, Romania, June 15, 1914; s. Maurice and Rosa (Jacobson) S.; ed. Bucharest High Sch., 1932; La Bucharest (philosophy), 1932-38; Dottore Archittura, Regio Poltecnico, Faculta de Architettura, Milan, Italy, 1933-40; m. Hedda Lindenberg Sterne, Oct. 11, 1944. Naturalized Am. citizen, 1943. Cartoonist for mag. Bertoldo, Milan, 1936-39; practicing architect, 1939-41; went from Italy to Ciudad Trujillo, Dominican Rep., 1941, to U.S., 1942; free-lance artist, cartoonist, illustrator, mainly for New Yorker, 1941—; artist-in-residence Smithsonian Instn., 1967; exhibited one-man shows: Galerie Mai, Paris, 1953, Kunstmuseum, Basel, Switzerland, 1954, Stedelijk Mus., Amsterdam, 1953, Museo de Arte, Sao Paulo, Brazil, 1952, Galerie Blanche, Stockholm, 1953, Hanover, Germany, 1954, Mus. Modern Art, 1946, Betty Parsons Gallery, 1952, 66, 68, 73, Sidney Janis Gallery, 1952, 66, 73, Galerie Maeght, Paris, 1973, Inst. Contemporary Art, London, 1952, others; represented in permanent collections: Mus. Modern Art, N.Y.C., Met. Mus. Art, N.Y.C., Albright-Knox Gallery, Buffalo, Fogg Mus., Harvard U., Victoria and Albert Mus., London, others. Served to lt. USNR, 1943-45. Recipient Gold medal Am. Acad. Arts and Letters, 1974. Author: All in Line (book of drawings), 1945; The Art of Living, 1949; The Passport, 1954; The Inspector, 1973. Contbr. drawings to nat. mags. Address: care Viking Press 625 Madison Ave New York NY 10022*

STEINBREDER, HARRY JOHN, JR., publishing co. exec.; b. St. Louis, Aug. 21, 1930; s. Harry John and Susan (Fritch) S.; B.A. in History, Washington U., St. Louis, 1952; m. Cynthia Means, Feb. 26, 1955; children—Harry John III, Susan Gay, Gillett, Sarah Cole. With Life SMR, Time, Inc., St. Louis, 1954, advt. salesman Fortune mag., 1955-59, advt. salesman Sports Illustrated, N.Y.C., 1959-66, mgr., 1966-67, advt. dir., 1967-72, asso. pub., 1972-73, pub. Money mag., 1973-76, dir. spl. projects Time mag., 1976—. Bd. dirs. Audubon Soc. Conn., 1965-68, Fairfield County (Conn.) Ducks Unlimited, 1967—, Franklin Coll., Lugano, Switzerland; mem. adv. com. U.S. Ski Team, U.S. Equestrian Team. Served to 1st lt. arty., AUS, 1952-54. Clubs: Fairfield County Hunt, Fairfield Country; Mashomack Fish and Game Preserve (Pine Plains, N.Y.); Seminole-Fla., Ekwanok (Manchester, Vt.). Home: 931 Mine Hill Rd Fairfield CT 06430 Office: Time and Life Bldg Rockefeller Center New York NY 10020

STEINBRENNER, GEORGE MICHAEL, III, shipbuilding co. exec., baseball exec.; b. Rocky River, Ohio, July 4, 1930; s. Henry G. and Rita (Haley) S.; B.A., Williams Coll., 1952; postgrad. Ohio State U., 1954-55; m. Elizabeth Joan Zieg, May 12, 1956; children—Henry G. III, Jennifer Lynn, Jessica Joan, Harold Zieg. Asst. football coach Northwestern U., 1955, Purdue U., 1956-67; treas. Kinsman Transit Co., Cleve., 1957-63; pres. Kinsman Marine Transit Co., 1963-67, dir. 1965—; pres., chmn. bd. Am. Ship Bldg. Co., Cleve., 1967-78, chmn. bd., 1978—; prin. owner N.Y. Yankees, 1973—; dir. Gt. Lakes Internat. Corp., Gt. Lakes Assos., Cin. Sheet Metal & Roofing Co., Nashville Bridge Co., Nederlander-Steinbrenner Prodns. Mem. Cleve. Little Hoover Com., group chmn., 1966; chmn. Cleve. Urban Coalition; vice chmn. Greater Cleve. Growth Corp., Greater Cleve. Jr. Olympic Found. Bd. dirs. Greater Cleve. Growth Assn. Served to 1st lt. USAF, 1952-54. Named Outstanding Young Man of Year Ohio, Cleve. jr. chambers commerce, 1960; named Chief Town Crier, Cleve., 1968; Man of Yr., Cleve. Press Club, 1968; recipient Acad. Achievement Gold Plate award, Dallas, 1960. Office: 911 Bond Court Blvd Cleveland OH 44114*

STEINBRINK, STUART HENRY, lawyer; b. Bklyn., Feb. 5, 1908; s. Meier and Sadie (Bloch) S.; A.B., Princeton, 1927; LL.B., Columbia, 1930; m. Carolyn Strauss, June 18, 1933 (dec. May 1961); children—Richard F., Barbara S. (Mrs. Ira G. Levine); m. 2d, Therese Obermeier Kamins, June 24, 1962. Admitted to N.Y. bar, 1931; asso. firm Rushmore, Bisbee & Stern and successor, N.Y.C. 1930-43, Levien, Singer & Neuburger, N.Y.C., 1943-47; partner firm Levien, Steinbrink & Beaudet and predecessors, N.Y.C., 1947-61; v.p., gen. counsel Universal Am. Corp. N.Y.C., 1962-78; asso. counsel, asst. sec. Gulf & Western Industries, Inc.; asso. counsel Consol. Cigar Co. Mem. Alien Enemy Hearing Bd. for Eastern Dist. N.Y., World War II, panel Am. Arbitration Assn.; asso. govt. appeal agt. SSS, 1951-63; sec., dir. Bklyn. Bur. Community Service; past chmn. Contr.'s Information Bur. Mem. Am., N.Y. State, Fed., Bklyn. bar assns., N.Y. County Lawyers Assn., Am. Judicature Soc., Columbia Law Alumni Assn., Cum Laude Soc., Phi Beta Kappa. Republican. Jewish (former trustee congregation). Mem. B'nai B'rith. Club: Princeton (N.Y.C.). Home: 180 W 58th St New York NY 10019 Office: 1 Gulf and Western Plaza New York NY 10023. *I have always been a fatalist—combining with it a belief that there must be some Supreme Being or Power ordering the Universe—a somewhat inconsistent position, perhaps; but one that has guided my life, nevertheless.*

STEINCROHN, PETER JOSEPH, physician, author; b. Hartford, Conn., Nov. 28, 1899; s. Myer and Pearl (Brownstein) S.; student N.Y. U., 1917-19; M.D., U. Md., 1923; m. Patti Chapin, Feb. 8, 1936; 1 dau., Barbara Jane. Intern, Muhlenberg Hosp., Plainfield, N.J., 1923-25; postgrad. Mass. Gen., Beth Israel hosps., Boston, Mt. Sinai Hosp. N.Y.C.; practice medicine specializing in internal medicine and cardiology, Hartford, 1925—; attending physician Mt. Sinai Hosp., Hartford, 1930-54, chief staff, 1940-41, now cons.; attending physician McCook Meml. Hosp., 1930-54, now cons.; ex-cons. internal medicine, cardiologist Hartford Inst. Living; columinst Bell Newspaper Syndicate, N.Y.C., 1954-68, McNaught Newspaper Syndicate, 1968—; former radio broadcaster health programs WKAT and WINZ, Miami; moderator weekly program WTHS-TV; med. editor WTVJ-TV, Miami, Fla., 1965-67. Med. co-chmn. Hartford Rehab. Soc., 1950-55; adviser Hartford Vis. Nurse Assn., Cerebral Palsy Assn. Served as pvt. U.S. Army, World War I. Fellow A.C.P.; mem. AMA, Conn. (1st v.p. 1940), Hartford County (dir.), Hartford med. socs., Hartford (v.p. 1950), Greater Miami (co-chmn edn. com., dir.) heart assns., Hartford Cancer Soc. (dir.), Hartford Tb Soc. (dir.), Tau Epsilon Phi. Mason. Author: More Years for the Asking, 1940; How to Keep Fit Without Exercise, 1942; Heart Disease is Curable, 1943; How to Stop Killing Yourself, 1950; How to Master Your Fears, 1952; Doctor Looks at Life, 1953; Live Longer and Enjoy It, 1956; You Can Increase Your Heart Power, 1958; Mr. Executive-Keep Well-Live Longer, 1960; Your Life to Enjoy, 1963; Common Sense Coronary Care and Prevention, 1963; You Live as You Breathe, 1967; How to Get a Good Night's Sleep, 1968; How to be Lazy, Healthy and Fit, 1969; Your Heart is Stronger than You Think, 1970; How to Master Your Nerves, 1970; Don't Die Before Your Time, 1971; Antidotes For Anxiety, 1971; Low Blood Sugar, 1972; Questions and Answers About Nerves, Tension and Fatigue, 1973; Medicalettes, 1979; Ask Dr. Steincrohn, 1979; How To Cure Your Joggermania!, 1979. Contbr. articles to nat. mags. and prof. jours. Address: 1430 Ancona Ave Coral Gables FL 33146. *Ben Hecht in his "Charlie" said of his friend Charles Mac Arthur: "He was born without the illusion of permanence." So was I. Often overlooked, life is our most cherished possession. I've tried to keep reminding people to keep it as long as possible.*

STEINEM, GLORIA, writer, editor, lectr.; b. Toledo, Mar. 25, 1934; d. Leo and Ruth (Nuneviller) Steinem; B.A., Smith Coll., 1956; postgrad. (Chester Bowles Asian fellow), India, 1957-58; D. Human Justice, Simmons Coll., 1973. Co-dir., dir., ednl. found. Ind. Research Service, Cambridge, Mass. and N.Y.C., 1959-60; editorial asst., editorial cons., contbg. editor, free-lance writer various nat. and N.Y.C. publs., 1960—; co-founder, contbg. editor New York mag., 1968—; feminist lectr., 1969—; co-founder, editor Ms. mag., 1971—. Active various civil rights and peace campaigns including United Farmworkers, Vietnam War Tax Protest, Com. for the Legal Def. of Angela Davis (treas., 1971-72); active polit. campaigns of Adlai Stevenson, Robert Kennedy, Eugene McCarthy, Shirley Chisholm, George McGovern. Co-founder, chairperson bd. Women's Action Alliance, 1970—; convenor, mem. nat. adv. com. Nat. Women's Polit. Caucus, 1971—; co-founder, mem. bd. Ms. Found. for Women, 1972—; founding mem. Coalition of Labor Union Women, 1974; mem. Internat. Women's Year Commn., 1977. Recipient Penney-Missouri Journalism award, 1970; Ohio Gov.'s award for Journalism, 1972; Bill of Rights award A.C.L.U. of So. Calif., 1975; named Woman of the Year McCall's mag., 1972; Woodrow Wilson Internat. Center for Scholars fellow, 1977. Mem. Nat. Orgn. for Women, AFTRA, Nat. Press Club, Soc. Mag. Writers, Authors' Guild, P.E.N., Phi Beta Kappa. Author: The Thousand Indias, 1957; The Beach Book, 1963. Contbr. to various anthologies. Address: care of Ms Magazine 370 Lexington Ave New York NY 10017*

STEINER, DONALD FREDERICK, biochemist, physician, educator; b. Lima, Ohio, July 15, 1930; s. Willis A. and Katherine (Hoegner) S.; B.S. in Chemistry and Zoology, U. Cin., 1952; M.S. in Biochemistry, U. Chgo., 1956, M.D., 1956; D.Med.Sci., U. Umea, 1973. Intern King County Hosp., Seattle, 1956-57; USPHS postdoctoral research fellow, asst. medicine U. Wash. Med. Sch., 1957-59, asst. medicine, med. resident, 1959-60; mem. faculty U. Chgo. Med. Sch., 1960—, A.N. Pritzker prof. biochemistry and medicine, 1971—, chmn. dept. biochemistry, 1973-79. Jacobaeus lectr., Oslo, Norway, 1970; E.F.F. Copp Meml. lectr., La Jolla, Calif., 1971. Recipient Gairdner award, Toronto, 1971; Hans Christian Hagedorn medal Steensen Meml. Hosp., Copenhagen, Denmark, 1970; Lilly award, 1969; Ernst Oppenheimer award, 1970; Diaz-Cristobal award Internat. Diabetes Fedn., 1973; Banting medal Am. Diabetes Assn., 1976; Passano award, 1979. Mem. Nat. Acad. Scis., Am. Soc. Biol. Chemists, AAAS, Biochem. Soc., Am. Diabetes Assn. (50th Anniversary medallion 1972), Am. Acad. Arts and Scis., Sigma Xi, Alpha Omega Alpha. Club: Innominates (U. Chgo.). Co-editor: The Endocrine Pancreas, 1972. Discoverer proinsulin. Home: 2626 N Lakeview Ave Apt 2508 Chicago IL 60614

STEINER, ERICH ERNST, educator; b. Thun, Switzerland, Apr. 9, 1919; s. Gotthold and Emmy (Schmid) S.; B.S., U. Mich., 1940; postgrad. U. Va., 1940-42; Ph.D., Ind. U., 1950; m. Dorothy White, July 8, 1944; children—Kurt, Karl, Kim. Faculty, U. Mich., Ann Arbor, 1950—, prof. botany, 1961—, chmn. dept. botany, 1968-71, dir. Matthaei Bot. Gardens, 1971-77. Served to 2d lt. AUS, 1943-46. NSF sr. postdoctoral fellow, 1960-61. Mem. Bot. Soc. Am., Genetics Soc. Am., Soc. Am. Naturalists, Soc. Study Evolution, Econ. Botany Soc., Phi Beta Kappa, Sigma Xi. Spl. research evolutionary genetics. Home: 268 Indian River Pl Ann Arbor MI 48104

STEINER, GILBERT YALE, polit. scientist; b. Bklyn., May 11, 1924; s. Isidor Aaron and Fannie (Gelbtrunk) S.; A.B., Columbia, 1945; A.M., 1948; Ph.D., U. Ill., 1950; m. Louise King, July 27, 1950; children—Charles King, Daniel Tod, Paula Amy. Faculty, U. Ill., Urbana, 1950-66, prof. govt., pub. affairs 1959-66, asst. dean Grad. Coll., 1956-58, dir. Inst. Govt. and Pub. Affairs, 1958-66; sr. fellow Brookings Instn., Washington, 1966—, dir. govtl. studies, 1968-76, acting pres., 1976-77. Staff dir. Chgo. Home Rule Commn., 1954-55; research dir. Northeastern Ill. Local Govt. Area Commn., 1957-63; vis. prof. polit. sci. U. Calif. at Berkeley, 1964-65; study dir. Commn. to Recommend Plan for Pub. Higher Edn. in Ill., 1960; spl. asst. to gov. Ill., 1961-63; cons. Bush Found., Edna McConnell Clark Found., Found. for Child Devel. Bd. dirs., vice chmn. Children's Def. Fund; bd. dirs. Manpower Demonstration and Research Corp. Social Sci. Research Council fellow, 1957; Ford Found. fellow, 1961-62. Served with AUS, 1943-46. Author: The Congressional Conference Committee, 1951; Legislation by Collective Bargaining 1951; (with others) Chicago's Government, 1954; (with S.K. Gove) Legislative Politics in Illinois, 1960; Social Insecurity, 1966; The State of Welfare, 1971; The Children's Cause, 1976. Home: 5408 Center St Chevy Chase MD 20015 Office: Brookings Instn Washington DC 20036

STEINER, GITTA HANA, composer, pianist, poetess; b. Prague, Czechoslovakia, Apr. 17, 1932; d. Eric Erhard and Erna (Bondy) S.; came to U.S., 1939, naturalized, 1945; diploma composition (Abraham Ellstein scholar) Juilliard Sch. Music, 1963, Mus.B., 1967, M.S., 1969; studied with Vincent Persichetti, Gunther Shuller, Elliot Carter. Compositions include: Suite for Flute Clarinet and Bassoon, 1958; Suite for Orch., 1958; Three Songs for Medium Voice, 1960; Three Pieces for Piano, 1961; Concerto for Violin and Orch., 1963; String Trio, 1964; Pages From a Summer Jour., 1963; Piano Sonata, 1964; Fantasy for Clarinet and Piano, 1964; Brass Quintet, 1964; Jouissance for Flute and Piano, 1965; Five Choruses, 1965; Movement for Eleven, 1966; Tetrark for String Orch., 1965; Fantasy Piece for Piano, 1966; Two Songs, 1966; Concerto for Piano and Orch., 1967; Refractions for Solo Violin, 1967; String Quartet, 1968; Percussion Quartet, 1968; Three Pieces for Solo Vibraphone, 1968; Concert Piece for Seven, 1968; Interludes for Voice and Vibraphone, 1968; Concert Piece for Seven II, 1968; Trio for Two Percussionists and Piano, 1969; Four Bagatelles for Solo Vibraphone, 1969; Five Poems for Mixed Chorus, 1970; Duo for Horn and Piano, 1970; Four Songs for Medium Voice and Vibes, 1970; Settings for Chorus, 1970; Duo for Cello and Percussion, 1971; Percussion Music for Two, 1971; Trio for Voice Piano and Percussion, 1971; Four Choruses, 1972; Four Settings for A Capella Chorus, 1973; New Poems for Voice and Vibes, 1974; Dream Dialogues for Voice and Percussion, 1974; Cantos, 1975; Dialogue for Two Percussionists, 1975; Music for Four Players, 1976; 8 Miniatures for Vibraphone, Fantasy for Solo Percussion, Night Music for Marimba Solo, 1977; commd. N.Y. Percussion Trio, 1969, mems. Boston Symphony Orch., 1971, various soloists; works included in Lincoln Center Repertoire Project, 1967; performed orchestral, chamber music throughout U.S., abroad; pvt. tchr. piano, 1960—; faculty Bklyn. Conservatory Music, 1963-65; co-dir. Composer's Group for Internat. Performance, 1968. Recipient Gretchaninoff Meml. prize for string orch. work, 1966; Marion Freschl award for vocal works with original texts, 1966-67; Standard Ann. award ASCAP, 1972—; awarded Composer's Forum, Donell Library, 1966; fellow Berkshire Music Center, Tanglewood, 1967. Address: 71-81 244th St Douglaston NY 11362

STEINER, HERBERT MAX, educator, physicist; b. Goeppingen, Germany, Dec. 8, 1927; s. Albert and Martha (Epstein) S.; came to U.S., 1939, naturalized, 1944; B.S., U. Calif. at Berkeley, 1951, Ph.D., 1956. Physicist, Lawrence Berkeley Lab., Berkeley, Calif., 1956—; mem. faculty U. Calif. at Berkeley, 1958—, prof. physics, 1966—; vis. scientist European Center Nuclear Research, 1960-61, 64, 68-69; vis. scientist Max Planck Inst. Physics and Astrophysics, Munich, 1976-77; vis. prof. Japanese Soc. Promotion Sci., 1978. Served with AUS, 1946-47. Recipient Sr. Am. Scientist award Alexander von Humboldt Found., 1976-77. Guggenheim fellow, 1960-61. Mem. Am. Phys. Soc. Author articles in field. Office: Lawrence Berkeley Lab Berkeley CA 94720

STEINER, JOHN EDWARD, aerospace co. exec.; b. Seattle, Nov. 7, 1917; s. George Edwin and Jessie Robertson (Cunningham) S.; B.S. in Aero. Engring., U. Wash., 1940, Summa Laude Dignatus, 1978; M.S. in Aero. Engring., M.I.T., 1941; m. Dorothy Leah Olson, Sept. 5, 1942; children—George Martin, Christine Ellen Steiner Schwager, John Edward. With Boeing Co., Seattle, 1941—, v.p., gen. mgr., v.p. ops., comml., 1970-76, v.p. corp. product devel., 1976—; mem. exec. com., dir. Peoples Nat. Bank Wash.; trustee, mem. exec. com. Pacific Sci. Center. Industry chmn. United Way, Seattle. Recipient Aviation Man of Yr. award Aviation Week publ., 1964, 72, City of Seattle, 1964; Elmer A. Sperry award 1965; Sir Charles K. Smith award Royal Aero. Soc., Australia, 1969; Thulin medal Swedish Soc. Aeros. and Astronautics, Sweden, 1974. Fellow AIAA, Royal Aero. Soc.; mem. ASME, Soc. Automotive Engrs., IEEE, Soc. Naval Architects and Marine Engrs., Nat. Acad. Engring., Tau Beta Phi. Contbr. articles to tech. and econ. jours.; patentee in field. Home: 3425 Evergreen Point Rd Bellevue WA 98004 Office: PO Box 3707 Mail Stop 10-17 Seattle WA 98124

STEINER, KENNETH DONALD, bishop; b. David City, Nebr., Nov. 25, 1936; s. Lawrence Nicholas and Florine Marie (Pieters) S.; B.A., Mt. Angel Sem., 1958; M.Div., St. Thomas Sem., 1962. Ordained priest Roman Catholic Ch., 1962, bishop, 1978; asso. pastor various parishes, Portland and Coos Bay, Oreg., 1962-72; pastor Coquille Ch., Myrtle Point, Powers, Oreg., 1972-76, St. Francis Ch., Roy, Oreg., 1976-77; aux. bishop Diocese of Portland (Oreg.), 1977—; vicar of worship and ministries and personnel dir. clergy personnel Portland Archdiocese. Democrat. Office: 2838 E Burnside St Portland OR 97214

STEINER, KURT, educator, lawyer, polit. scientist; b. Vienna, Austria, June 10, 1912; s. Jacob and Olga (Weil) S.; D.Jurisprudence, U. Vienna, 1935; Ph.D. in Polit. Sci., Stanford U., 1955; m. Josepha, Aug. 26, 1939. Came to U.S. 1938, naturalized 1944. Jud. asst., later atty., Vienna, 1935-38; instr., asst. dir., then dir. Berlitz Schs. Langs., Cleve., Pitts., 1939-43; prosecutor, spl. asst. to chief counsel, prosecution sect. Internat. Mil. Tribunal Far East, Tokyo, Japan, 1948; pros. atty., legal sect. SCAP, Tokyo, 1948-49, legis. atty., later chief civil affairs and civil liberties br., legislation and justice div., legal sect., 1949-51; vis. research scholar Center Internat. Studies, Princeton, 1954-55; faculty Stanford U., 1955—, prof. polit. sci., 1962—, asso. exec. head dept., 1959-63, chmn. com. East Asian Studies, 1964-65, dir. Stanford in Germany, summer 1961, dir. Stanford Center Japanese Studies, Tokyo, 1962. Ofcl. escort Japanese Legal Edn. Mission to U.S. 1950-51. Served with AUS, 1944-48; PTO. Ford fellow, 1953-54. Mem. Am. Polit. Sci. Assn., Assn. Asian Studies, AAUP, Japanese Am. Soc. Legal Studies (councillor 1965—). Author: Local Government in Japan, 1965; Politics in Austria, 1972. Contbr. articles to publs., chpts. to books. Home: 832 Sonoma Terr Stanford CA 94305

STEINER, LEE RABINOWITZ, psychologist; b. Superior, Wis., Nov. 18, 1901; d. Harry and Sarah (Skolnik) Rabinowitz; B.A., U. Minn., 1924; M.S.S. (Commonwealth fellow), Smith Coll., 1929; Ph.D., Union Coll., 1972; m. Alfred Leo Steiner, Apr. 15, 1935 (dec. Sept. 1939); m. 2d, Samuel Melitzer, Apr. 22, 1949. Social worker Michael Reese Clinic, Chgo., psychiat. social worker, supr. Inst. Juvenile Research, Chgo., 1929-33; spl. teaching project U. Chgo., 1932-33; spl. lectr. Ill. Soc. Mental Hygiene, 1933-34; cons. personal problems, N.Y.C., 1935—. Radio broadcaster; lectr.; lectr. Forham U., Rutgers U., Atlanta U., Coll. of William and Mary, Hunter Coll., 1943-48, Queen's Coll., 1948-49; radio broadcaster: Everybody's Personal Problems, 1938, You and Your Problems, 1939-42, Psychologically Speaking, WEVD U. Air, 1949—, What Makes You Tick, 1950-51, Make Up Your Mind, 1953-56. Founder, dir. Inst. for Inter-Personal Research, 1949—; founder, pres. Acad. Psychologists in Marital Counseling, 1959—; dir. research Bio-Phoresis Research Found., 1978—. Mem. Am. Psychol. Assn., AAUP, Am. Women in Radio and TV, N.Y. Soc. Clin. Psychology, Am., N.Y. State, Eastern psychol. assns. Author: Where Do People Take Their Troubles, 1945; A Practical Guide for Troubled People, 1952; Make the Most of Yourself, 1954; Understanding Juvenile Delinquency, 1960; Romantic Marriage: The Twentieth Century Illusion, 1964; Psychic Self-Healing for Psychological Problems, 1977. Address: 302 E 88th St New York NY 10028

STEINER, MICHAEL, sculptor; b. N.Y.C., 1945. Exhibited in one-man shows at Fischbach Gallery, N.Y.C., 1962, Dwan Gallery, N.Y.C., 1966, 68, Marlborough Gallery, N.Y.C., 1970, 72, 74, David Mirvish Gallery, Toronto, Ont., Can., 1970, 76, 78, Mus. Fine Arts, Boston, 1974, Andre Emmerich Gallery, N.Y.C., 1975, 76, 78, 79, Galerie Wentzel, Hamburg, Ger., 1976, 79, Harcus Krakow Gallery, Boston, 1977, Galerie Gerald Piltzer, Paris, 1978, others; exhibited in group shows Light Show, Inst. Contemporary Art, Phila., 1964, Gemeentemuseum, The Hague, 1968, Whitney Mus. Am. Art, N.Y.C., 1970, Mus. Contemporary Art, Montreal, Que., Can., 1973, Edmonton (Alta., Can.) Gallery, 1974, Hayward Gallery, London, 1975, Everson Mus. Art, Syracuse, N.Y., 1976, U.S. Embassy, Ottawa, Ont., 1977, others; works in collections including Storm King Art Center, Boston Mus. Fine Arts, Mus. Modern Art. Instr. Emma Lake Workshop, U. Sask., 1969; vis. artist Cranbrook Art Inst., Bloomfield Heights, Mich., 1969. Recipient Guggenheim award,

1971. Office: care Andre Emmerich Gallery 41 E 57th St New York NY 10022

STEINER, PAUL, pub. co. exec.; b. Vienna, Austria, Jan. 1, 1913; s. Geza and Ilona (Singer) S.; came to U.S., 1939, naturalized, 1945; student U. Vienna, 1938; m. Marianne Esberg, Feb. 15, 1942; 1 son, H. Thomas. Asst. to owner, editor in chief Neue Freie Presse, Vienna, 1934-38; owner, chief exec. Chanticleer Press, Inc., N.Y.C., 1950—; pub. illustrated books in natural history and the arts, pub. Audubon Soc. Field Guide to N.Am. Birds, 2 vols. Home: 936 Fifth Ave New York NY 10028 also Dune Rd Bridgehampton NY Office: 424 Madison Ave New York NY 10017

STEINER, PETER OTTO, educator; b. N.Y.C., July 9, 1922; s. Otto Davidson and Ruth (Wurzburger) S.; A.B., Oberlin Coll., 1943; M.A., Harvard, 1949, Ph.D., 1950; m. Ruth E. Riggs, Dec. 20, 1947 (div. 1967); children—Alison Ruth, David Denison; m. 2d, Patricia F. Owen, June 2, 1968. Instr. U. Calif. at Berkeley, 1949-50, asst. prof. econs., 1950-57; asso. prof. econs. U. Wis., Madison, 1957-59, prof., 1959-68; prof. econs. and law U. Mich., Ann Arbor, 1968—, chmn. dept. econs., 1971-74; vis. prof. U. Nairobi (Kenya), 1974-75. Cons. U.S. Bur. Budget, 1961-62, Treasury Dept., 1962-63, various pvt. firms, 1952—. Served to lt. USNR, 1944-46. Social Sci. Research Council Faculty Research fellow, 1956; Guggenheim fellow, 1960; Ford Faculty Research fellow, 1965. Mem. Am. Econ. Assn., Econometric Soc., AAUP (chmn. com. Z 1970-73, pres. 1976-78). Author: An Introduction to the Analysis of Time Series, 1956; (with R. Dorfman) The Economic Status of the Aged, 1957; (with R.G. Lipsey) Economics, 5th edit., 1978; On the Process of Planning, 1968; Public Expenditure Budgeting, 1969; Mergers: Motives, Effects, Policies, 1975; also articles. Home: 2611 Hawthorne Rd Ann Arbor MI 48104

STEINER, RICHARD LEWIS, educator, urban planner; b. Balt., Nov. 4, 1913; s. Bernard Christian and Ethel (Mulligan) S.; B.E. in Civil Engring., Yale, 1936; M. City Planning, Mass. Inst. Tech., 1939; postgrad. Harvard, Johns Hopkins; m. 2d, Madeline Kelser Sadler, Jan. 17, 1969; children by former marriage—David, Roland, Carol, Stephen (dec.). Cons. Town Planning Bd., Lexington, Mass., 1938; rural road inventory and traffic analyst Conn. Hwy. Dept., Hartford, 1938; project planner U.S. Housing Authority, Washington, 1938-41; dir. Balt. Redevel. Commn., 1946-54; dep. commr. Urban Renewal Adminstrn. HHFA, Washington, 1954-57, commr., 1957-59; dir. Balt. Urban Renewal and Housing Agy., 1959-67; spl. cons. to sec. HUD, 1967-68; prof. city planning Howard U., Washington, 1968-70; vis. prof. community planning Sch. Social Work and Community Planning, U. Md. at Balt., 1970-74, planning asst. to univ. chancellor, 1974-78; urban cons. 1968—; now cons. Nat. Endowment for Arts; past mem. Mt. Vernon Pl. Archtl. Adv. Commn.; vis. lectr. city planning and urban renewal U. Pitts., Johns Hopkins, U. N.C., Mass. Inst. Tech., Md. Inst. Art, Grad. Sch. U.S. Dept. Agr., N.Y. U., Practicing Law Inst. Past bd. dirs. Nat. Housing Conf., Balt. Neighborhoods, Inc., Transitional Living Council Central Md.; bd. dirs. Union Meml. Hosp., Balt.; past pres. Md. Partners of the Alliance; past mem. housing com. Md. Commn. on Aging; mem. Balt. Mayor's Task Force on Population Migration; mem. Balt. Area Housing Council; former mem. adv. commn. Problems Met. Soc. United Presbyn. Ch. of U.S.A.; bd. visitors, mem. exec. com. Md. State Sch. Deaf; hon. trustee Balt. Mus. Art., pres., 1969-71. Served from ensign to lt. comdr. C.E.C., USNR, 1941-45. Registered profl. engr., Md. Fellow ASCE (pres. Md. sect. 1965); mem. Engring. Soc. Balt., Md. Assn. Engrs., Am. Inst. Certified Planners (past pres. Washington and Balt. chpts., Distinguished Service award 1977), Nat. Assn. Housing and Redevel. Ofcls. (past gov., M. Justin Herman Disting. Service award 1975), Am. Planning Assn., Mass. Inst. Tech. City Planning Alumni Assn. (past pres.), Tau Beta Pi, Lambda Alpha; asso. Sigma Xi. Presbyterian. Clubs: 14 W Hamilton Street, Center (Balt.). Home: 6 Wendover Rd Baltimore MD 21218 Office: PO Box 1362 Baltimore MD 21203

STEINER, RICHARD RUSSELL, conglomerate exec.; b. Chgo., Feb. 26, 1923; s. Frank Gardner and Ruth (Cowie) S.; B.A., Dartmouth Coll., 1948; m. Colleen M. Kearns, Dec. 6, 1949; children—Robert C., Kevin K., Sheila M. With Steiner Corp., Salt Lake City, 1948—, divisonal dir., v.p., 1951-59, pres., 1959—; dir. Am. Uniform Co. Served with USAAF, 1942-46. Decorated D.F.C. Mem. Textile Rental Service Assn., Phi Beta Kappa. Clubs: Alta, Salt Lake Country. Office: 505 E South Temple Salt Lake City UT 84102

STEINER, ROBERT FRANK, phys. biochemist; b. Manila, Philippines, Sept. 29, 1926; s. Frank and Clara Nell (Weems) S.; A.B., Princeton U., 1947; Ph.D., Harvard U., 1950; m. Ethel Mae Fisher, Nov. 3, 1956; children—Victoria, Laura. Chemist, Naval Med. Research Inst., Bethesda, Md., 1950-70, chief lab. phys. biochemistry, 1965-70; prof. chemistry U. Md., Balt., 1970—, chmn. dept. chemistry, 1974—; mem. biophysics study sect. NIH, 1976. Served with AUS, 1945-47. Recipient Superior Civilian Achievement award Dept. Def., 1966; NSF research grantee, 1971; NIH research grantee, 1973. Fellow Washington Acad. Sci.; mem. Am. Soc. Biol. Chemists. Club: Princeton (Washington). Author: Life Chemistry, 1968; Excited States of Proteins and Nucleic Acids, 1971; editor Jour. Biophys. Chemistry, 1972—. Home: 2609 Turf Valley Rd Ellicott City MD 21043 Office: 5401 Wilkens Ave Baltimore MD 21228

STEINER, ROBERT LISLE, cons.; b. Tehran, Iran, May 21, 1921 (parents Am. citizens); s. Robert Lisle and Lois (Foresman) S.; grad. Mercersberg (Pa.) Acad., 1938; B.A., Wooster (O.) Coll.; M.I.A., Columbia, 1948; m. Margaret S. Sherrard, June 4, 1944; children—Patricia Jean, Robert Lisle III, William Sherrard, John Scott. Cons., Commn. Chs. on Internat. Affairs, 1948-49; cultural attache Am. embassy, Iran, 1950-52; educationist U.S. Office Edn., 1952-54; program dir. Am. Friends of Middle East, 1954-59; v.p. Vershire Co. (Vt.), 1959-62; dir. Peace Corps, Kabul, Afghanistan, 1962-66. regional dir. North Africa, Near East and South Asia, 1966-69; dir. Washington office Devel. & Resources Corp., 1969-70; dir. Center for Cross-Cultural Tng. and Research, adviser to univ. pres. on internat. affairs U. Hawaii, Honolulu, 1971-72; dir., gen. mgr. Hawaii Pub. Broadcasting Authority, 1972-73; exec. dir. N.J. Edn. Consortium, Princeton, 1973-78; internat. cons., Princeton, 1979—. Tchr., U. Kansas City (Mo.), 1957, Bradford (Vt.) Acad., 1961; poultry cons. Middle East Tech. U., Ankara, Turkey, 1963. Councilman, v.p. Shanks Village Assn., Orangeburg, N.Y., 1948; chmn. Kabul Sch. Bd., 1965. Served as pilot USNR, 1943-46. Mem. Am. Acad. Polit. and Social Sci. Democrat. Presbyterian. Home: 406 Rosedale Rd Princeton NJ 08540 Office: 406 Rosedale Rd Princeton NJ 08540

STEINER, STAN, author, conservationist. Lectr., U. N.Mex., U. Calif., Colo. Coll.; guest prof. U. Paris (France), 1974-75. Author: George Washington: the Indian Influence, 1970; New Indians, 1968; Raza: the Mexican Americans, 1970; The Tiguas: the Lost Tribe of City Indians, 1972; (with Luis Valdez) Aztlan: an Anthology of Mexican American Literature, 1972; (with Shirley Witt) The Way: an Anthology of American Indian Literature, 1972; The Islands: The Worlds of the Puerto Ricans, 1974; (with Maria Teresa Babin) Borinquen: An Anthology of Puerto Rican Literature, 1974; The Vanishing Whiteman, 1976; The Spirit Woman, 1979; Fusang: The Chinese Who Built America, 1979; In Search of the Jaguar, 1979. Address: 1000 Camino Rancheros Santa Fe NM 87501. *Though it has its problems, it is fascinating to live through the fall of the Second Roman Empire; and to await a new, and unknown civilization.*

STEINER, STUART, coll. pres.; b. Balt., July 24, 1937; s. Louis and Lillian (Block) S.; B.S., U. Md., 1959; grad. certificate Fla. State U., 1962; M.S.W., U. Pa., 1963; J.D., U. Balt., 1967; M.A., Tchrs. Coll., Columbia U., 1972; m. Rosalie Weiner, Sept. 12, 1962; children—Lisa, Susan, David, Robyn. Caseworker, then supr. and dir. juvenile ct. services Balt. Dept. Social Services, 1960-64; dir. referral center Health and Welfare Council Met. Balt., 1964; dir. admissions and placement Hartford Jr. Coll., Bel Air, Md., 1965-67; dean of students Genesee Community Coll., Batavia, N.Y., 1967-68, dean of coll., 1968-75, pres., 1975—; pres. SUNY West; mem. Council of Presidents SUNY. Bd. dirs. Genesee County Community Chest, Health Sci. Agy. Western N.Y., N.Y. Spl. Olympics Com.; pres. Genesee County United Way. Heisler scholar, 1960-61; Kellogg fellow, 1971-72; Sigma Delta scholar, 1958-59. Mem. Am. Assn. Higher Edn., Jr. Coll. Council Middle Atlantic States (v.p.), Assn. Presidents Public Community Colls. (v.p.), Am. Coll. Personnel Assn., Batavia C. of C., Club: Rotary. Contbr. articles to profl. jours. Home: 33 Woodcrest Dr Batavia NY 14020 Office: Genesee Community Coll Batavia NY 14020

STEINER, WILFRED JOSEPH, educator; b. Mallard, Iowa, Feb. 9, 1916; s. Albert and Sadie Mary (Hahn) S.; B.A., Loras Coll. 1936; M.A., Harvard, 1938; Ph.D., Ohio State U., 1957; m. Roberta Carson Johnson, July 18, 1944; 1 dau., Josephine. Mem. faculty U. Dayton, 1946—, prof. history, 1960—, chmn. dept., 1949-69, asst. to pres. for institutional studies, 1969—. Bd. dirs. Dayton Sch. Practical Nursing, 1965—. Served with AUS, 1941-45. Fulbright fellow, Rome, 1953-54. Mem. Ohio Conf. Coll. and Univ. Planners, Dayton Council World Affairs (dir. 1958-71, adv. bd. 1971—, v.p. adult program 1958-60, v.p. program services 1964-66, pres. 1969-71), Assn. for Instnl. Research, Dayton Opera Assn. (dir. 1971-77). Club: Harvard (Dayton). Author: (summary cards) American History I, 1960, American History II, 1961, American History III, 1978, World History I, 1963. Editor: (summary cards) History of England, 1962. Contbr. articles to New Catholic Ency., profl. jours. Home: 2512 S Patterson Blvd Dayton OH 45409

STEINERT, ALAN, JR., wholesale trade co. exec.; b. Cambridge, Mass., Apr. 10, 1936; s. Alan and Claire (Hyman) S.; grad. Phillips Exeter Acad., 1954; B.A., Harvard, 1958, M.B.A., 1962; m. Monica Wulff, Mar. 21, 1959; children—Timothy Alexander, John Alan, Alexandra Thomae, Jessica Blair. With Eastern Co. (name now Eastco), Westwood, Mass., 1958—, treas., 1969—, pres., 1972—, also dir. Mem. adv. council Physicians' Asst. Program, Northeastern U., Boston, 1971—; pres. Eastern Charitable Found., 1969-75, treas., 1975—; mem. trustees adv. com. Mass. Hosp. Assn.; mem. Health Hosp. and Welfare Bd., City Cambridge, 1967-69. Bd. dirs. Cambridge Econ. Edn. Opportunity Com., 1968-70 (treas. 1969-70), Health Planning Council Boston, 1969-70, 74-76, Cambridge Mental Health Assn., 1970—; trustee Peter Bent Brigham Hosp., Boston, 1969—, pres., 1974-79, vice chmn., 1979—; trustee Affiliated Hosps. Center Inc., 1974—. Mem. Cambridge C. of C. (bd. dirs. 1971-74). Clubs: Harvard (Boston); Cambridge; Belmont (Mass.) Country. Home: 43 Appleton St Cambridge MA 02138 Office: 26 Dartmouth St Westwood MA 02090

STEINFALS, CHRISTIAN WERNER, hotel exec.; b. Duesseldorf, W. Ger., Jan. 22, 1933; came to U.S., 1964, Can. citizen; ed. Duesseldorf Hotel and Gastronomic Sch., 1948-51. Banquet mgr. Hotel Sonesta, Hartford, Conn., 1964-68; food and beverage mgr. Euclid Charterhouse Hotel, Cleve., 1968-69, Kaanapali Beach Hotel, Maui, Hawaii, 1969-70; dir. food and beverage Carlton Tower Hotel, London, 1970-71; asst. gen. mgr. Sutton Pl. Hotel, Toronto, Ont., Can., 1971-72; gen. mgr. Bristol Pl. Hotel Group, Toronto, 1972-78; exec. v.p. ops. Resorts Internat. Hotel Casino, Atlantic City, 1978—; mem. South Jersey Devel. Council. Mem. Am. Hotel and Motel Assn., Atlantic City Conv. Bur., Atlantic City Hotel Assn., Maitre de Table of Confrerie de la Chaine des Rotisseurs. Office: Resorts Internat Hotel Casino North Carolina ave at Boardwalk Atlantic City NJ 08404

STEINFELD, JESSE LEONARD, physician, med. sch. dean; b. W. Aliquippa, Pa., Jan. 6, 1927; s. Jack and Lena Helen (Klein) S.; B.S., U. Pitts., 1945; M.D., Western Res. U., 1949; LL.D. (hon.), Gannon Coll., 1972; m. Mildred Stokes, July 12, 1953; children—Mary Beth, Katherine Jody, Frances Susan. Sr. investigator Nat. Cancer Inst., Bethesda, Md., 1952-58, dep. dir., 1968-69, cons., 1961-68, 74—; acting chief medicine City of Hope Med. Center, Duarte, Calif., 1958-59; asst. prof. medicine U. So. Calif., Los Angeles, 1959-62, asso. prof., 1962-66, prof., 1967-68; Surgeon Gen. of U.S., Washington, 1969-73; dir. Comprehensive Cancer Center Mayo Clinic, Rochester, Minn., 1973-74; prof. medicine U. Calif., Irvine, 1974-76; dean Sch. Medicine, Med. Coll. Va., Richmond, 1976—; cons., chmn. ad hoc com. on research and smoking Am. Cancer Soc.; chmn. YMCA Phys. Fitness and Health Nat. Policy Bd. Served with USPHS, 1952-58, 69-73. Fellow A.C.P., Royal Soc. Health (hon.); mem. Am. Soc. Clin. Oncology (pres. 1970), Am. Assn. Cancer Research, Soc. Nuclear Medicine, Am. Soc. Hematology. Contbr. articles on cancer chemotherapy, metabolic changes in cancer patients, and smoking and pub. health to med. jours. Home: 308 Long Ln Richmond VA 23221 Office: PO Box 636 MCV Sta Richmond VA 23298

STEINFELD, THOMAS ALBERT, publisher; b. N.Y.C., June 17, 1917; s. Albert and Marjorie (Lesser) S.; grad. Phillips Exeter Acad., 1934; student Harvard, 1934-35; m. Joan Rollinson, July 29, 1945 (dec. Nov. 1973); children—Geoffrey T., Jill R.; m. 2d, Viviane Barkey, June 20, 1977. Salesman, John Orr Products, N.Y.C. 1935-36; asst. advt. mgr. Bloomingdale's N.Y.C. 1936-37; with Playbill mag. N.Y.C., 1937—, pub., 1962-65, pres., 1962-68, now v.p., nat. sales dir. Playbill. Served to capt. AUS, 1942-46; CBI. Club: Aspetuck Valley Country (Weston, Conn.). Home: 83 W Meadow Rd Wilton CT 06897 Office: 151 E 50th St New York City NY 10022

STEINFINK, HUGO, educator; b. Vienna, Austria, May 22, 1924; s. Mendel and Malwina (Fiderer) S.; B.S., Coll. City N.Y., 1947; M.S., Columbia, 1948; Ph.D., Bklyn. Poly. Inst., 1954; m. Cele Intrator, Mar. 21, 1948; children—Dan E., Susan D. Research chemist Shell Devel. Co., Houston, 1948-51, 53-60; prof. chem. engring. U. Tex., Austin, 1960—. Served with AUS, 1944-46. Fellow Am. Mineral. Soc.; mem. Am. Chem. Soc., Am. Crystallographic Soc., Am. Inst. Chem. Engrs., Phi Beta Kappa, Sigma Xi, Phi Lambda Epsilon. Contbr. articles to profl. jours. Home: 3811 Walnut Clay Austin TX 78731

STEINFORT, CHARLES ROY, broadcasting exec.; b. Covington, Ky., Oct. 1, 1921; s. Charles Roy and Elsie (Joering) S.; B.A., U. Ky., 1946; children—Susan Lee Bender, Cissy Ross. Reporter, Courier - Jour., 1946-47; dir. sports info. U. Ky., 1948-49; with Associated Press, 1949-51, 61—, dep. dir. broadcast services, N.Y.C., 1964-74, dir. broadcast services, v.p., 1974—; editor, pub. Aberdeen (Miss.) Examiner, 1951-61. Served with USNR, 1943-45. Mem. Kappa Sigma Delta Chi. Episcopalian. Home: 40 Eureka Terr Stamford CT 06902 Office: Associated Press 50 Rockefeller Plaza New York NY 10020

STEINHARDT, MARTIN, advt. agy. exec.; b. Providence, June 26, 1913; s. Benjamin E. and Ray (Schenker) S.; student Newark Sch. Fine Arts, 1930-32, Nat. Acad. Design, 1933; m. Vivian Rosenthal, Jan. 26, 1941; children—Barbara (Mrs. Steve Anderson), Stephen, John. Asst. advt. dir. Ronson, Inc., 1935-40; advt. mgr. L & R Mfg. Co., 1940-46; chmn. bd. Keyes, Martin & Co., Springfield, N.J., 1974—. Mem. Millburn Scholarship Boosters, 1960-65, Kiwanis Aid to Orphans Com., 1954-56, Millburn Red Cross Fund Drive, 1960-61, Millburn Student Loan Fund, 1960-61. Mem. Indsl. Advt. Group of N.J., Am. Assn. Advt. Agys. Democrat. Mem. B'nai B'rith. Club: Fiddlers Elbow Country. Home: Claridge 11-D East Claridge Dr Verona NJ 07044 Office: 841 Mountain Ave Springfield NJ 07081

STEINHARDT, RALPH GUSTAV, JR., educator, chemist; b. Newark, Sept. 15, 1918; s. Ralph Gustav and Norma (Stein) S.; B.S. in Chemistry, Lehigh U., 1940, M.S. in Chemistry, 1941; B.S. in Chem. Engring., Va. Poly. Inst., 1944; Ph.D. in Chemistry, Lehigh U., 1950; m. Mary Etzler Hawks, Sept. 11, 1946; children—Theresa Ruth, Sarah Jean, Ralph Gustav III. Research fellow Lehigh U., Bethlehem, Pa., 1940-42, from research fellow to asst. prof., 1946-54; mem. staff Los Alamos Lab., 1944-46; asso. prof. Va. Poly. Inst., 1954-56; prof. chemistry Hollins (Va.) Coll., 1956—, chmn. dept., 1956-63, 66-69. Research participant Oak Ridge Nat. Lab., 1958-78; vis. research prof. U. Wis., summer 1960; vis. lectr. chemistry Stanford, 1963-64; cons. Aerospace Research Corp., 1967—; research collaborator Brookhaven Nat. Lab., 1970-71, 78. Served with AUS, 1942-46. Fellow AAAS, Am. Inst. Chemists; mem. Am. Chem. Soc., Va. Acad. Sci. (chmn. chemistry sect. 1962-63), Sigma Xi, Phi Lambda Upsilon. Contbr. numerous articles to sci. jours. Patentee in field. Developer 1st photoelectron spectrometer for chem. studies. Address: Box 9716 Hollins Coll VA 24020. *Learning is vanity unless we exercise our responsibility for its decent and compassionate use, for its ultimate utility in a world that must have all the decency and compassion and love and intelligence that it so desperately needs. We ourselves burn in the candles of our own thoughts, and, once in a while, if we are good and faithful and work decently and well, we may illuminate the whole world in our own well-chosen light.*

STEINHART, ALBERT B., accountant, food co. exec.; b. N.Y.C., Oct. 27, 1930; s. Samuel and Rose (Solomon) S.; B.B.A., Coll. City N.Y., 1952, M.B.A., 1957; m. Lorraine Freiman, May 30, 1953; 1 son, Stephen. Sr. accountant Brach, Gosswein & Lane, C.P.A.'s, 1950-57; v.p. Dellwood Foods, Inc., Yonkers, N.Y., 1957—. Pres. bd. dirs. Edgebrook Coop., Inc., 1963—; asst. treas., bd. dirs. Westchester chpt. ARC, exec. bd., 1978—; mem. United Way of Westchester, 1975—, panel chmn., 1978—. C.P.A., N.Y. State. Mem. Am. Inst. C.P.A.'s, N.Y. State Soc. C.P.A.'s, Risk and Ins. Mgmt. Soc., Yonkers C. of C. (dir. 1978—). Club: B'nai B'rith (exec. bd. 1977—). Home: 62 Lawrence Dr North White Plains NY 10603 Office: 170 Saw Mill River Rd Yonkers NY 10701

STEINHAUS, JOHN EDWARD, physician; b. Omaha, Feb. 23, 1917; s. Emil F. and Pearl (Haynie) S.; B.A., U. Neb., 1940, M.A., 1941; M.D., U. Wis., 1945, Ph.D., 1950; m. Mila Jean Pinkerton, Feb. 21, 1943; children—Kathryn, Carolyn, Barbara, William, Elizabeth. Practice medicine, specializing in anesthesiology, Madison, Wis., 1951-58, Atlanta, 1958—; faculty U. Wis., 1951-58; mem. faculty Emory U., Atlanta, 1958—, prof., chmn. anesthesiology, 1959—; chief anesthesiology service Grady Meml. Hosp., 1959-77, chief anesthesiology service, 1979—. Pres. Anesthesia Found. Diplomate Am. Bd. Anesthesiologists. Mem. Am. (past pres.), So. (past pres.) socs. anesthesiologists, AMA, AAAS, Assn. U. Anesthetists (past pres.), Soc. Pharm. Exptl. Therapeutics, Phi Beta Kappa, Sigma Xi, Alpha Omega Alpha. Contbr. articles to profl. jours. Home: 836 Castle Falls Dr Atlanta GA 30329 Office: 1365 Clifton Rd NE Atlanta GA 30322

STEINHAUSER, FREDRIC ROBERT, educator; b. Lamberton, Minn., July 16, 1918; s. Emil C. and Ella L. (Albright) S.; B.S. with spl. honors, Mankato (Minn.) State Coll., 1949; M.A., U. Chgo., 1951; Ph.D., U. Minn., 1960; m. Joan F. Lenertz, Aug. 27, 1949; children—Mark, Paul, Kurt, Louise. Tchr. rural schs., 1937-40; mem. faculty U. Minn., Mpls., 1957—, prof. social studies, 1960—, head social and behavioral scis., 1979—. Organizer Assn. St. Paul Communities; charter mem. St. Paul's Capital Improvements Com.; chmn. St. Paul Citizens Finance Com., chmn. St. Paul Sch. Bond Com. Bd. dirs. Minn. Resources Project, 1974. Served to lt. col. AUS, 1941-46, 50-54; col. Minn. N.G. Named Man of Year, 1967; recipient Student Service award U. Minn., 1961, Alumni award, 1970, Morse-Amoco Outstanding Tchr. award, 1978; State of Minn. medal for Meritorious Service. Mem. Nat. Council Geog. Edn (coordinator Minn.), Minn. Council Geog. Edn. (pres., dir.), Minn. Acad. Sci. (chmn. geog. sect.). Contbr. articles to publs. Home: 2243 Scudder St St Paul MN 55108 Office: Nicholson Hall Univ Minn Minneapolis MN 55455

STEINHOFF, DAN, educator; b. Spokane, Wash., Dec. 16, 1911; s. Dan and Bertha (Van Os) S.; B.B.A., U. Wash., 1934, teaching diploma, 1939; postgrad. Northwestern U. Coll. Law, 1935-36; M.S., U. Mich., 1941; D.Social Sci. in Econs., U. Havana (Cuba), 1952; m. Jill Hegner, June 1, 1962. Credit exec. Bank of Calif., Portland, Oreg., 1934-37; teaching fellow econs. U. Wash., 1937-39; instr. econs. U. Mich., 1939-41; asst. prof. bus. adminstrn. Antioch Coll., 1941-42; pub. utilities cons., 1946-52; from asst. prof. to prof. mgmt. U. Miami, 1946-50, dean evening div., prof. mgmt., 1950-62, dean div. continuing edn., 1962-63, prof. mgmt., 1963—, chmn. mgmt. dept., 1969-73. Dir. Indsl. Research, Inc. Served with AUS, 1942-45. Mem. Assn. Univ. Evening Colls., Assn. Urban Univs., Southeastern Adult Edn. Assn., Newcomen Soc., Chi Phi, Delta Sigma Pi, Beta Gamma Sigma, Phi Delta Kappa, Artus. Methodist. Club: Exchange (Coral Gables, Fla.). Author: Small Business Management Fundamentals, 1974, 78; Small Business: Cases and Essays, 1975; Developing Managers in Organizations, 1976; World of Business, 1979. Home: 1437 Sopera Ave Coral Gables FL 33134

STEINHOFF, WILLIAM RICHARD, educator; b. Chgo., Feb. 13, 1914; s. William Richard and Nellie (Mulligan) S.; A.B., U. Calif. at Berkeley, 1938, M.A., 1940, Ph.D., 1948; m. Rosannah Jenne Cannon, Jan. 6, 1940. Mem. faculty U. Mich., Ann Arbor, 1948—, prof. English lit., 1963—; vis. prof. U. Aix-Marseilles (France), 1964-65. Mem. exec. com. Coll. Conf. Composition and Communications, 1959-60; chmn. Mich. Commn. Tchr. Certification 1961-62. Served to 2d lt. AUS, 1943-46. Ford fellow, 1954-55. Mem. Modern Lang. Assn., Alliance Francaise. Editor: (with others) Modern Short Stories, 1951; (with others) The Image of the Work, 1952; (With A. Carr) Points of Departure, 1960; George Orwell and the Origins of 1984, 1975 (pub. in Eng. as The Road to 1984). Home: 519 Onondaga St Ann Arbor MI 48104

STEINKE, HERBERT A., JR., communications co. exec. Vice pres., asst. gen. counsel ITT. Office: ITT World Hdqrs 320 Park Ave New York NY 10022*

STEINKRAUS, WARREN EDWARD, educator; b. Boston, Feb. 14, 1922; s. John Herman and Florence Louise (Rabe) S.; A.B., Baldwin-Wallace Coll., 1943, L.H.D., 1975; S.T.B., Boston U., 1946, Ph.D. (Jacob Sleeper fellow), 1952; postgrad. U. Iowa, 1957, Harvard, 1961, Cambridge (Eng.), 1970; m. Barbara Annette Morris, July 15, 1948; 1 dau., Elizabeth. Instr. English lit. Emerson Coll., 1946-49; instr. philosophy Cornell Coll., Mt. Vernon, Ia., 1949-50; instr. Depauw U., 1950-52, asst. prof., 1952-56; asso. prof., chmn. dept. philosophy Iowa Wesleyan Coll., 1956-59; prof., head dept. philosophy Union Coll., Barbourville, Ky., 1959-64; prof. philosophy State U. N.Y. Coll., Oswego, 1964—; vis. prof. philosophy Benares Hindu U., Varanasi, India, 1977-78. Cons. Kraus Reprints, N.Y.C., 1966-68; Faculty Exchange prof. State U. N.Y., 1975—. Active Oswego Civic Orch. and Chorus, 1964—. State U. N.Y. Summer Research fellow, 1966, 67; State U. N.Y. grantee, 1965, 68, 75; Am. Council Learned Socs. Travel grantee, 1972, 75; Nat. Endowment for Humanities Vis. Philosopher grantee, 1972, 73. Mem. Am. Philos. Assn., Metaphys. Soc. Am., Hegel Soc. Am. (v.p. 1968-70, mem. exec. council 1976—), Am. Aesthetics Soc., Fellowship of Reconciliation, Phi Mu Alpha Sinfonia. Democrat. Mem. Troy Conf. Methodist Ch. Author: (with G. R. Malkani) Discussion of Karma, 1966; Philosophy of Art, 1974; contbg. author: Ency. of Philosophy, 1967, The Critique of War, 1969, Hegel & The Philosophy of Religion, 1970, The Abdication of Philosophy, 1976, others; editor: (with K. Schmitz) Art and Logic in Hegel's Philosophy, 1979. Music editor Motive Mag., 1943-46; editor Philos. Forum, 1947; editor and contbr.: New Studies in Berkeley's Philosophy, 1966; editor: New Studies in Hegel's Philosophy, 1971; lit. editor Idealistic Studies 1974—. Contbr. numerous articles to profl. jours. Home: 89 Sheldon Ave Oswego NY 13126 Office: Sheldon Hall State Univ Coll Oswego NY 13126

STEINMAN, JOHN FREDERICK, newspaper pub.; b. Lancaster, Pa., Aug. 21, 1884; s. Andrew Jackson and Caroline Morgan (Hale) S.; Ph.B., Yale U., 1906; LL.D., Elizabethtown Coll., 1957; m. Blanche Lazo, June 3, 1913; 1 dau., Shirley Lazo Steinman Katzenbach; m. 2d, Shirley Watkins, Nov. 25, 1933. Chmn. bd. Lancaster Newspapers, Inc., pubs. Lancaster New Era, Intelligencer Jour., Sunday News; chmn., dir. Steinman Stas., Intelligencer Printing Co. Trustee Lancaster Gen Hosp. Served as civilian, Washington, World War I. Clubs: Porcupine, Nassau, Lancaster Country, Hamilton (Lancaster); St. Elmo (New Haven). Home: Drumore Farm Pequea Rd 1 Lancaster County PA 17565 Office: 8 W King St Lancaster PA 17604

STEINMAN, ROBERT CLEETON, banker; b. Phila., June 11, 1931; s. George Curtis and Kathryn Agnes (Johnstone) S.; B.Sc. in Bus. Adminstrn., Drexel U., 1954, M.B.A., 1970; m. Nancy Badri Pourian, Sept. 24, 1960; children—Shirley Kathryn, Susan Soraya, Robert Mark. Accountant, Main Lafrentz & Co., C.P.A.'s, Phila., 1956-58; asst. treas. Ostheimer and Co., Inc., Phila., 1958-62; controller Biol. Abstracts, Inc., Phila., 1962-64; budget, cost and fin. analysis mgr. PQ Chems. Co., 1964-70; v.p., group controller 1st Pa. Bank, Phila., 1970-78; v.p., comptroller Phila. Savs. Fund Soc., 1978—. Co-founder Briarlin Civic Assn., 1969, treas., 1969-72, pres., 1975—. Bd. dirs. Sigma Pi Nat. Found., treas. frat. Served with AUS, 1954-56. C.P.A., Pa. Mem. Pa. Bankers Assn. (faculty trust tng. sch.), Fin. Execs. Inst., Am. Inst. C.P.A.s, Pa. Inst. C.P.A.s, Sigma Rho, Sigma Pi. Republican. Methodist. Club: St. Albans Swim (dir., fin. adviser, pres. 1974) (Newtown Square, Pa.). Home: 804 Lawrence Lane Newtown Square PA 19073 Office: 1212 Market St Philadelphia PA 19107

STEINMANN, ANNE, clin. psychologist, psychotherapist; b. N.Y.C.; d. Harry and Rebecca (Comer) Gelof; B.A., Hunter Coll., 1927; M.A., N.Y. U., 1953, Ph.D., 1957; m. Herbert R. Steinmann, June 26, 1927; children—Shelley List, Peter, Daniel. Clinic affiliate, psychotherapist, research psychologist N.Y. Clinic Mental Health, N.Y.C., 1958-64; psychotherapist Soc. Psychoanalytic Study and Research, 1958-65; pres., prin. investigator Male-Female Role Research Project, Maferr Found., 1965—; with dept. research Postgrad. Center for Mental Health, N.Y.C., 1969—; clin. psychologist, pvt. practice ind., couple and family psychotherapy, N.Y.C.; clinician problems of sexual dysfunction tng. div. continuing edn. N.Y. Med. Coll., 1974-76, staff, supr. Human Sexuality program, 1976—; clin. psychologist N.W. Ackerman Family Inst., summer 1972; adj. asst. prof. psychology Hofstra Coll., 1958-61; lectr. Human Relations Center, New Sch. for Social Research, 1969—; tchr. English pub. high schs. Co-founder, co-organizer Five Towns Music and Art Found., 1949-53, N.Y. Clinic Mental Health, 1955-58; mem. mayor's com. N.Y. Shakespeare Festival, 1963; sponsor Eleanor Roosevelt Meml. Found., 1964; mem. adv. bd. Internat. Inst. Women Studies. Cert. psychologist, N.Y. State; cert. psychologist Nat. Register Health Providers in Psychology. Fellow AAAS, Internat. Council Psychologists; mem. Am., N.Y. State, Eastern psychol. assns., N.Y. Soc. Clin. Psychologists, Am. Acad. Psychotherapists, Interam. Soc. Psychology, Am. Assn. Sex Educators and Counselors (certified), Easter Assn. Sex Therapy, Am. Personnel and Guidance Assn., Nat. Vocat. Guidance Assn., Nat. Council Family Relations, N.Y. Acad. Scis., Soc. Sci. Study of Sex, N.Y. League Bus. and Profl. Women, AAUW, Soc. Founding Fellows Center for Human Devel. Hebrew U. (Jerusalem), Pi Lambda Theta, others. Author: (with David J. Fox) The Male Dilemma, 1974 (Family Life Book award 1975); (monograph) A Study of the Concept of the Feminine Role in 51 Middle Class American Families, 1963. Contbr. chpts. to New Life Options: The Working Woman's Resource Book, 1976; Women in Society and Sex Roles, 1975; Woman: Dependent or Independent Variable, 1975; Women in Therapy, 1974; New Directions in Mental Health, vol. I, 1969. Contbr. articles to numerous profl. jours., including McCalls, Redbook, London Observer. Research on concept of feminine and masculine roles, 1952—. Home: 9 E 81st St New York NY 10028 Office: 140 W 57th St New York NY 10019. *From almost the beginning of my life as a person, whatever success I have attained in my professional and personal life has been guided by the following: "This above all: to thine own self be true, and it must follow, as the night the day thou canst not them be false to any man." And my belief that "the more one forgets one's self—giving one's self to a cause or another person—the more human he or she is. And the more one is immersed and absorbed in something or someone other than one's self the more one really becomes a person."*

STEINMANN, FREDERICK ROGER, bank holding co. exec.; b. Monticello, Wis., Aug. 25, 1918; s. Fred Herman and Alda Marie (Marty) S.; Ph.B., U. Wis., 1940; certificate Grad. Sch. Bus. Adminstrn., Harvard U., 1943, Central States Sch. Banking, U. Wis., 1958; m. Joyce B. Francke, Jan. 4, 1941; children—Barbara, Jan. Partner, Karlen & Steinmann Lumber Co., 1946-48; auditor M&I No. Bank, Milw., 1948-50, comptroller, 1950-56, asst. v.p., 1956-59, v.p., comptroller, 1959-61; v.p. M&I Marshall & Ilsley Bank, Milw., 1961—; sec. Marshall & Ilsley Corp., Milw., 1962—, M&I Bldg. Corp., Milw., Loujo Co., Milw., Beltower, Inc., Milw., 1st Nat. Leasing Corp., Milw.; sec., dir. M&I Fin. Corp., Milw.; dir. M&I Bank of Mayville (Wis.). Served to 1st lt. U.S. Army, 1942-46. Mem. Psi Upsilon. Lutheran. Club: Blue Mound Golf and Country (Wauwatosa, Wis.). Home: 13405 Wrayburn Rd Elm Grove WI 53122 Office: 770 N Water St Milwaukee WI 53201

STEINMETZ, RICHARD BIRD, JR., mfg. co. exec., lawyer; b. Orange, N.J., Mar. 27, 1929; s. Richard Bird and Charlotte (Quinby) S.; grad. Choate Sch., Wallingford, Conn., 1946; B.A., Yale, 1950; J.D., Harvard, 1955; m. Holly Miller, June 9, 1956; children—Richard Blair, Jonathan Bird, Edward Quinby. Admitted to N.Y. bar, 1955; asso. firm Chadbourne, Parke, Whiteside & Wolff, N.Y.C., 1955-59; atty. legal dept. Anaconda Co., N.Y.C., 1959-67; v.p., counsel, sec. Anaconda Aluminum Co., Louisville, 1967-71; v.p., gen. counsel Anaconda Co., N.Y.C., 1971-79; v.p. Colt Industries Inc., N.Y.C., 1979—. Served as 1st lt. USMC, 1950-52. Mem. Am., N.Y.C. bar assns., Assn. Gen. Counsel. Episcopalian. Republican. Club: Harvard (N.Y.C.). Home: 78 Zaccheus Mead Ln Greenwich CT 06838 Office: 430 Park Ave New York NY 10022

STEINMEYER, ROBERT HENRY, chess player; b. St. Louis, Mar. 10, 1927; s. William Charles and Katherine (O'Connell) S.; A.B., Washington U., St. Louis, 1951. With Valley Line, St. Louis, 1956-62, Nat. Marine Service, Inc. inland river barge line, St. Louis, 1962—. Rated lifemaster U.S. Chess Fedn. Served with AUS, 1945-46. Home: 10078 Sakura Dr St Louis MO 63128 Office: 1750 Brentwood Blvd St Louis MO 63144

STEINMEYER, ROBERT JAY, lawyer; b. Clatonia, Nebr., Aug. 10, 1921; s. William F. and Willie (Davis) S.; B.S., U. Nebr., 1943; postgrad. Albany Law Sch., 1947-48; LL.B., George Washington U., 1949; m. Susie Levicki, Dec. 23, 1948; children—William Bruce, James Jay, Sharon Sue. Devel. engr., patent atty., patent counsel Gen. Electric Co., 1943-57; admitted to D.C. bar, 1950, Calif. bar, 1958; since practiced in Fullerton; patent counsel, gen. counsel Beckman Instruments, Inc., 1957—, now v.p. Mem. Am. Bar Assn., Am. Patent Law Assn., Assn. Corporate Patent Counsel (pres.), Order of Coif, Sigma Tau, Pi Mu Epsilon. Home: 609 Lemon Hill Terr Fullerton CA 92632 Office: 2500 Harbor Blvd Fullerton CA 92634

STEINRUCK, CHARLES FRANCIS, JR., mgmt. cons. lawyer; b. Phila., Apr. 25, 1908; s. Charles Francis and Laura (Crutchley) S.; student U. Pa., 1925-28; LL.B., South Jersey Law Sch. (now Rutgers U.), 1937, J.D., 1972; m. Esther Sophia Schramm, June 1, 1936 (dec. Oct. 1962); children—Carol, Lisa.; m. 2d, Alice Bignell Marchese, Nov. 22, 1967. Accountant, J.S. Timmons, Inc., Phila., 1926-28, merged with Philco Corp., 1928, asst. to sec., 1937-41, asst. sec., 1941-42, sec. 1942-61; asst. sec. Philco-Ford Corp., 1962-68, cons. 1962—; resident v.p. Togotechnique, S.A.R.L., Republique Togolaise, 1979—. Admitted to D.C. bar, 1938. Mem. John W. Westcott Law Soc., Night Watch Sr. Soc. (U. Pa.), Am. Bar Assn., Sigma Kappa Phi, Delta Sigma Pi. Republican. Presbyterian. Clubs: Germantown Cricket (Phila.); Seaview Country (Absecon, N.J.) Address: 1000 New York Rd Absecon NJ 08201

STEINWAY, HENRY ZIEGLER, piano mfr.; b. N.Y.C., Aug. 23, 1915; s. Theodore E. and Ruth (Davis) S.; B.S., Harvard, 1937; m. Polly Zinsser, Aug. 25, 1944; children—William Theodore, Daniel Knowlton, Kate Davis, Henry Engelhard, Susan Zinsser. With Steinway & Sons, 1937—, v.p, 1946-55, pres., 1955-77, chmn., 1977—; dir. Manhattan Life Ins. Co., Pratt Read Corp. Served with U.S. Army, World War II. Home: 141 E 72d St New York NY 10021 Office: Steinway Place Long Island City NY 11105

STEIRMAN, HY, publishing co. exec.; b. Montreal, Que., Can., Nov. 11, 1921; s. Bernard and Rose (Rosen) S.; student McGill U., 1946-48, Columbia, 1948-49; m. Ruth Kravitz, Jan. 2, 1947; children—Beryl Kay, Andrew Robin. Came to U.S., 1948, naturalized, 1958. Editor, Street & Smith, 1948; editorial dir. Stearn Publs., N.Y.C., 1950-53; editor Hillman Periodicals, N.Y.C., 1954-57; pres., pub. Coronet Communications, Inc. (now div. Warner Communications, Inc.), 1958-72, pres. Paperback Library div., 1961-72; chmn., pub. Warner Communications, Inc., 1970-72; editor, pub. Single mag., div. Steirman Communications, Inc., N.Y.C., 1973—; chmn. bd. Ralmar TV Sports Prodns., Family Media, Inc., pubs. Family Health mag., Weight Watchers mag., 1,001 Decorating Ideas mag., 1974—. Vol. tchr. Fox Meadow Sch., 1966-72; mem. sch. system evaluation com. Scarsdale (N.Y.) Sch., 1971; trustee Bronx-Lebanon Hosp. Served with RCAF, 1940-45. Mentioned in dispatches for invention muzzle blast suppressor, 1944. Mem. Warbirds of RAF, Jewish War Vets, Am. Book Assn. Clubs: Overseas Press, Friars (N.Y.C.). Author: Triumph, 1961; Strike Terror, 1968; Good News, Bad News, Agnews, 1969; Cry of the Hawk, 1970. Home: 1 Chesterfield Rd Scarsdale NY 10583 Office: 149 Fifth Ave New York NY 10010

STEIWER, FREDERICK HERBERT, investment banker; b. Pendleton, Oreg., Nov. 8, 1917; s. Frederick and Frieda (Roesch) S.; student George Washington U., 1935-36, Georgetown U., 1936-39; m. Edna Mae Miller, June 28, 1946; children—Frederick, Peter. With Alexander Brown & Sons, N.Y.C., 1939—, office mgr., 1950-66, gen. partner, 1966—; Served from 2d lt. to lt. col., USAAF, AUS, 1941-45; lt. col. Res. Mem. Kappa Alpha, Republican. Clubs: New Canaan (Conn.) Field; Vista Tennis (Lewisboro, N.Y.). Home: Silvermine Norwalk CT 06850 Office: 72 Wall St New York NY 10004

STELLA, CHARLES GUY, JR., newspaperman; b. Cleve., Feb. 24, 1931; s. Charles G. and Josephine Elsie (Sottosanti) S.; B.A., Western Res. U. (now Case Western Res. U.), 1954; m. Evelyn N. Jarzembowski, Nov. 3, 1954; children—Guy, Jeffrey, James. With Cleve. Press, 1954—, now chief editorial writer. Recipient award for best editorial writing Cleve. Newspaper Guild, 1974. Club: City (Cleve.). Home: 3014 Essex Rd Cleveland OH 44118 Office: Cleve Press 901 Lakeside Ave Cleveland OH 44114

STELLA, FRANK, artist; b. Malden, Mass., May 1936; student Princeton U. One man shows: Leo Castelli Gallery, N.Y.C., 1960, 62, 64, 66, 69, 73, 75, Galerie Lawrence, Paris, 1961, 64, Fergus Gallery, Los Angeles, 1963, 65, Kasmin Ltd., London, 1964, 66, David Mirvish Gallery, London, 1966, Pasadena (Calif.) Art Mus., 1966, Seattle Art Mus., 1967, Gallery Modern Art, Washington, 1968, Mus. Modern Art, N.Y.C., 1970; numerous group shows throughout U.S., Europe, 1959—; included in permanent collections: Stedelijk Mus., Amsterdam, Art Inst., Chgo., Detroit Inst. Art, Los Angeles County Mus. Art, Walker Art Center, Mpls., Mus. Modern Art, N.Y.C., San Francisco Mus. Art, Whitney Mus. Am. Art, N.Y.C., Albright-Knox Gallery, Buffalo; artist-in-residence Dartmouth Coll., 1963; lectr. Yale U., 1965, Cornell U., 1965; instr. art U. Saskatchewan, 1967, Brandeis U., 1968. Recipient 1st prize Tokyo Internat. Biennale, 1967. Office: care Lawrence Rubin Gallery 49 W 57th St New York NY 10019*

STELLA, JOHN ANTHONY, environ. control co. exec.; b. Jessup, Pa., Feb. 3, 1938; s. John Anthony and Alda (Parri) S.; B.S., U. Detroit, 1960; M.B.A., N.Y. U., 1965; m. Aurelia M. Arre, Feb. 20, 1965; children—John C., Matthew A., Krista R. Bus. evaluation cons. Allied Chem. Co., N.Y.C., 1965-70; treas. Spinnerin Yarn Co., Hackensack, N.J., 1970-72; treas. Penn-Dixie Cement Corp., N.Y.C., 1972-74; v.p. finance Halecrest Co., 1974-76; treas. Research-Cottrell, 1976—. Served with AUS, 1960. Office: Box 1500 Somerville NJ 08876

STELLAR, ELIOT, educator; b. Boston, Nov. 1, 1919; A.B., Harvard U., 1941; M.Sc., Brown U., 1942, Ph.D., 1947; m. Betty E. Stellar. Formerly asst. prof. psychology Johns Hopkins U.; mem. faculty U. Pa., 1954—, prof. physiol. psychology, dept. anatomy Sch. Medicine, 1960—, dir. Inst. Neurol. Scis., 1965-73, provost univ., 1973-78, co-chmn. devel. commn., 1971-73; cons. Nat. Inst. Gen. Med. Scis. Mem. sci. adv. bd. U. Wash. Nat. Primate Center; mem. coms. NIH, VA Central Office Adv. Com. Research, NIMH, Carnegie Corp. com. Nat. Acad. Scis., Nat. Commn. Protection Human Subjects of Biomed. and Behavioral Research. Mem. Nat. Acad. Scis. (chmn. brain scis. com.), Am. Acad. Arts and Scis., Am. Philos. Soc., Am. Psychol. Assn. (chmn. council editors), AAAS, Soc. Exptl. Psychologists (Warren medal 1967), Am. Assn. Anatomists, Internat. Brain Research Orgn., Phi Beta Kappa, Sigma Xi. Author: (with C.T. Morgan) Physiological Psychology; (with V.G. Dethier) Animal Behavior. Editor (with J.M. Sprague) series Progress in Physiological Psychology, 1966-73. Editor Jour. Comparative and Physiological Psychology, 1969-74. Address: 243 Anatomy-Chemistry Bldg U Pa Med Sch Philadelphia PA 19174

STELLING, HENRY BARTHOLD, JR., air force officer; b. San Francisco, July 9, 1924; s. Henry Barthold and Eva Ruth (Young) S.; B.S., U.S. Mil. Acad., 1948; M.B.A., U. So. Calif., 1965; M.S. in Internat. Affairs, George Washington U., 1969; m. Lucille Celesta Treat, Mar. 26, 1949; children—Henry Barthold III, Sandra A., Mark C., Sharon R. Enlisted U.S. Army, 1943; commd. 2d lt. U.S. Air Force, 1948, advanced through grades to maj. gen., 1976; assigned Armed Forces Spl. Weapons Project, Sandia (N.Mex.) AFB, 1949-53, Directorate Spl. Weapons. Langley (Va.) AFB, 1953-54; navigator SAC, 1955-61; assigned Space and Missile Systems Orgn., Los Angeles, 1962-72; dir. of space Hdqrs. U.S. Air Force, Washington, 1972-76; vice comdr. Electronic Systems. div., Hanscom AFB, Mass., 1976—. Decorated D.S.M., Legion of Merit, D.F.C., Air Force Commendation medal with 3 clusters, Army Commendation medal. Mem. Beta Gamma Sigma. Home: 4 Andrews Dr Bedford MA 01730 Office: Hdqrs Electronic Systems Div Hanscom AFB MA 01730

STELLINGS, ERNEST GEORGE, recreation co. exec.; b. Petersburg, Ind., July 26, 1900; s. George W. and Anna (Link) S.; grad. high sch.; m. Mary Elizabeth Bogan, Feb. 2, 1940; children—Isabel, Princess Anne, Sandra, Everett, Ernest George. Various positions motion picture theatres, Washington, Ind., 1916-20; mgr. theatres, Wilmington, N.C., 1920-39; a founder Everett Enterprise (later Stewart-Everett Theatres), Charlotte, N.C., 1939, pres. 1954—; formed Stelling-Gossett Theatres, 1953; pres. Stellings Investment Co. Dir. amusement div. Am. Heart Assn., Will Rogers Meml. Hosp. Mem. Theatre Owners Am. (lifetime dir., pres. 1956-58), Theatre Owners N.C. and S.C. (dir.), Council Motion Picture Orgns. (dir.), Motion Picture Pioneers Am. Mason. Club: Variety, Myres Park Country (Charlotte); Hounds Ear Golf (Blowing Rock, N.C.). Address: 6714 Constitution Ln Charlotte NC 28210

STELLMAN, SAMUEL DAVID, educator; b. Detroit, Nov. 11, 1918; s. Solomon D. and Fannie (Wiseblum) S.; B.Health and Phys. Edn., U. Toronto (Ont., Can.), 1943; M.S.W., Ohio State U., 1958, Ph.D., 1963; m. Lillian Mandlsohn, July 11, 1943; children—Steven Dale, Leslie Robert. Asso. dir. Columbus (Ohio) Jewish Center, 1950-62; asso. prof. social work Ohio State U., Columbus, 1963-68; prof. social work, chmn. social work extension U. Wis., Madison, 1968-74, first dir. Criminal Justice Inst., 1974-79; exec. dir. Anti-Poverty Program, Franklin County, Ohio, 1965-66. Mem. Columbus Community Relations Commn., 1966-68; Wis. founder drug Help-Lines in Sheboygan, Milw., Kenosha; statewide vol. in probation program, others. Served with Can. Army, 1943-46. Recipient Disting. Service award U. Wis., 1973. Mem. Am. Assn. Criminology, Adult Edn. Council U.S., Wis. Assn. for Vols. in Adult and Juvenile Justice (founder), Wis. Criminal Justice Edn. Assn. (pres.). Initiator rural crime center, deprogramming men who batter women, tng. of divorce counselors, life coping—econ. security for divorced women. Home: 1545 W Fairfield Ct Glendale WI 53209 Office: 2400 E Hartford Milwaukee WI 53201

STELLY, MATTHIAS, assn. exec., editor; b. Sunset, La., Aug. 7, 1916; s. Felix Paul and Louise Adoisca (Guilbeau) S.; B.S. in Agr. and Chemistry, U. Southwestern La., 1937; M.S. in Soil Fertility and Chemistry (research fellow 1937-39), La. State U., 1939; Ph.D. (research fellow 1939-42), Ia. State U., 1942; m. Thelma Louise Thoreson, July 30, 1940; children—Mary Louise, Julia Marie, David Matthias, Carol Anne. Asst. agronomist La. Expt. Sta., 1942-43; asso. prof. soils U. Ga., 1946-49, prof., 1949-57; prof. charge soil testing service La. State U., 1957-59, prof. soil chemistry, 1959-61; exec. sec. Am. Soc. Agronomy and affiliates Soil Sci. Soc. Am. and Crop Sci. Soc. Am., Madison, Wis., 1961-71, now exec. v.p., also sec.-treas., bus. mgr., editor of publs., also liaison Asociación Latinoamericana de Ciencias Agricolas, 1974—; exec. dir. Agronomic Sci. Found., Inc., 1967—; with dept. agr., Kenya, East Africa for Mut. Security Agy., 1952-53. Am. sec. commn. IV, 7th Congress Internat. Soc. Soil Sci., 1958-60. Served to lt. (j.g.) USNR, 1943-46; lt. comdr. Res. ret. Fellow AAAS Am. Soc. Agronomy rep., v.p., chmn. sect. O agr. 1970-72, council del. sect. agr. 1974—), Am. Soc. Agronomy (sec. Ga. sect. 1955, chmn. membership com. So. region 1957-59, nat. membership chmn. 1960-61; program dir. vis. scientist program 1963-72); mem. Soil Sci. Soc. Am. (program dir. translation and printing of Soviet Soil Sci., 1964-69), Am. Registry Certified Profls. in Agronomy, Crops and Soils (treas. 1977—, certified profl. 1977), AAUP (pres. U. Ga., 1954-55), Sigma Xi (pres. U. Ga. 1950-51), Phi Kappa Phi, Gamma Sigma Delta. Roman Catholic. Editor: Agronomy Jour., 1961-70; now editor-in-chief all Am. Soc. Agronomy publs. Contbr. articles to profl. jours. Home: 2113 Chamberlain Ave Madison WI 53705 Office: 677 S Segoe Rd Madison WI 53711. *Perseverance and confidence in the attainment of worthy goals in life have served me well; these have substituted in part for other desirable qualities which may not be fully developed in me.*

STELMACHOWICZ, MICHAEL JOSEPH, JR., coll. pres.; b. St. Louis, Sept. 18, 1927; s. Michael Joseph and Esther Fern (Boylan) S.; A.A., St. John's Coll., 1947; B.Sc., Concordia Tchrs. Coll., 1950; M.Ed., St. Louis U., 1954; B.A., Concordia Sem., St. Louis, 1957; Ph.D., U. Nebr., 1966; m. Betty A. Rivers, June 14, 1949; children—Candyce, Cheryl, Cary, Crystal, Corrie. Tchr., prin. Luth. High Sch., St. Louis, 1957-61; mem. faculty dept. edn. Concordia Tchrs. Coll., Seward, Nebr., 1961-68, dean students, 1966-68; supt. Luth. High Schs., Detroit, 1968-73; pres. St. John's Coll., Winfield, Kans., 1973-78; pres. Concordia Coll., Seward, 1978—. Chmn. bd. Youth Ministry, Luth. Ch.-Mo. Synod, 1971-75. Mem. Mayor's Commn. on Human Relations, Detroit, 1969-70; mem. exec. bd. Quivira council Boy Scouts Am., 1973-78. Mem. Assn. Luth. Secondary Schs. (past pres.), Am. Assn. Higher Edn., Luth. Edn. Assn., Am. Council Edn., Nat. Assn. Ind. Colls. and Univs. Home: 200 Faculty Ln Seward NE 68434 Office: 800 N Columbia Seward NE 68434

STELSON, PAUL HUGH, physicist; b. Ames, Iowa, Apr. 9, 1927; s. Hugh Eugene and Ada May (Woolley) S.; B.S., Purdue U., 1947, M.S., 1948; Ph.D., Mass. Inst. Tech., 1950; divorced; children—Hugh, James, Fred, Ben. Research asso. Mass. Inst. Tech., 1950-52; mem. staff Oak Ridge Nat. Lab., 1952—, sr. physicist, dir. Van de Graaff Lab., 1963-71, asso. dir. physics div. at lab., 1971-73, dir., 1973—; vis. prof. Rice U., Houston, 1962-63; chmn. Internat. Conf. Reactions Between Complex Nuclei, 1974; Ford prof. physics

U. Tenn., 1968—. Served with USNR, 1944-46. AEC predoctoral fellow, 1948-50. Mem. Am. Phys. Soc. (exec. com. Southeastern sect. 1971-75). Author research and rev. articles. Editor: Electromagnetic Lifetime and Properties of Nuclei, 1962; co-editor: Proc. Internat. Nuclear Physics Conf., 1966; asso. editor Jour. Nuclear Physics, 1972. Home: 212 N Purdue St Oak Ridge TN 37830 Office: PO Box X Oak Ridge Nat Lab Oak Ridge TN 37830

STELTENPOHL, JOSEPH ALOYSIUS, utilities co. exec.; b. Louisville, Mar. 10, 1916; s. Joseph Clement and Mary Catherine (Conroy) S.; B.A., U. Louisville, 1949; m. Mary Teresa Hannon, Aug. 20, 1968. With Louisville Gas & Electric Co., 1934—, accounting clk., 1934-42, asst. tax accountant, 1947-48, tax accountant, 1949-61, asst. controller, 1962-68, controller, 1969-73, v.p., controller, 1974—. Dir. Bus. Devel. Corp. Ky. Served to 1st lt. AUS, 1943-46. C.P.A., Ky. Mem. Am. Inst. C.P.A.'s, Ky. Soc. C.P.A.'s. Roman Catholic. Home: 800 S 4th St Louisville KY 40203 Office: 311 W Chestnut St Louisville KY 40232

STELZEL, WALTER TELL, container mfg. co. exec.; b. Chgo., Aug. 23, 1940; s. Walter Tell and Kathryn (Evans) S.; B.S.B.A., Xavier U., 1962; m. Sarah A. Raven, Jan. 21, 1963; children—William, Susan, Michael, Sr. Acct. Ernst & Ernst. Chgo., 1966-69; gen. mgr. div. Fed. Metals Co., Alton, Ill., 1969-71; controller U.S. Reduction Co., East Chicago, Ind., 1971-74; v.p., controller Nat. Can Corp., Chgo., 1974—. Served to 1st lt., arty., USAR, 1963-65. C.P.A., Ill. Office: 8101 W Higgins St Chicago IL 60631

STELZER, IRWIN MARK, economist; b. N.Y.C., May 22, 1932; s. Abraham and Fanny (Dolgins) S.; B.A. cum laude, N.Y. U., 1951, M.A., 1952; Ph.D., Cornell U., 1954; m. Elaine Waldman, June 18, 1950 (div. 1964); 1 son, Adam David; m. 2d, Agnes Sasaki, Aug. 30, 1966 (div. 1976). Fin. analyst Econometric Inst., 1952; teaching fellow Cornell U., 1953-54; instr. U. Conn., 1954-55; researcher Twentieth Century Fund, 1953-55; economist W.J. Levy, Inc., 1955-56; sr. cons., v.p. Boni, Watkins, Jason & Co., Inc., 1956-61; pres. Nat. Econ. Research Assos. Inc., N.Y.C., 1961—. Lectr., N.Y. U., 1955-56, Coll. City N.Y., 1957-58; researcher Brookings Instn., 1956-57, dir. U.S. Nat. Com. World Energy Conf. Chmn. tech. adv. com. on impact of inadequate electric power supply Fed. Power Commn.; mem. adv. com. on revision of rules and practice procedure Fed. Energy Regulatory Commn.; mem. adv. council Electric Power Research Inst.; mem. exec. com., bd. dirs. Pub. Utility Research Center, U. Fla.; mem. energy fin. adv. com. Fed. Energy Adminstrn.; mem. Gov.'s Task Force on Energy; mem. pres.'s econ. adv. panel Nat. Commn. Rev. Antitrust Laws; mem. N.Y.C. Mayor's Energy Policy Adv. Group. Mem. bd. governing trustees Am. Ballet Theatre. Mem. Am. Statis. Assn., Am., So. econ. assns., Cornell U. Council, Phi Beta Kappa. Clubs: Cornell; Harbor View; Wall St.; City Athletic. Author: Selected Antitrust Cases: Landmark Decisions. Contbr. articles to profl. jours. Econs. editor Antitrust Bull. Home: 31 E 79th St New York NY 10021 Office: 80 Broad St New York NY 10004

STEMBLER, JOHN HARDWICK, theatre co. exec; b. Miami, Fla., Feb. 18, 1913; s. George C. and Harriett Elizabeth (Sligh) S.; J.D., U. Fla., 1937; m. Kathrine Jenkins, July 5, 1941; children—John Hardwick, William Jenkins. Admitted to Fla. bar, 1937; mem. firm Carson, Petteway & Stembler, Miami, 1937-41; asst. U.S. atty. So. Dist. Fla., 1941; with Ga. Theatre Co., Atlanta, 1946—, pres., 1954—; dir., chmn. bd., chmn. exec. com. Nat. Bank Ga., Atlanta. Trustee Atlanta Music Festival Assn.; bd. dirs. Ga. div. Am. Cancer Soc. 1957—, pres., gen. chmn. edn.-funds crusade Fulton County unit, 1956; bd. dirs. Atlanta area council Boy Scouts Am., 1953—, pres., 1959-61. Served as lt. col. USAAF, 1941-46; maj. gen. USAF ret. Decorated Air medal with oak leaf cluster, Legion of Merit. Mem. Nat. Assn. Theatre Owners (past pres., chmn. finance com.), Motion Picture Theatre Owners and Operators Ga. (v.p., dir.), Phi Delta Phi, Sigma Alpha Epsilon, Fla. Blue Key. Rotarian. Clubs: Capital City, Commerce, Peachtree Golf, Piedmont Driving. Home: 309 Peachtree Battle Ave NW Atlanta GA 30305 Office: 3445 Peachtree Rd NE Atlanta GA 30326

STEMBRIDGE, VERNIE A(LBERT), pathologist, educator; b. El Paso, Tex., June 7, 1924; s. Vernie Albert and Anna Marie (Lawless) S.; B.A., U. Tex. at El Paso (formerly Tex. Coll. Mines), 1943; M.D., U. Tex., Galveston, 1948; m. Aileen Cofer Marston, June 14, 1944; children—Shirley (Mrs. J.P. Watkins), Ann (Mrs. Donald M. Connell), Vivian (Mrs. R.P. Bays, Jr.). Intern, U.S. Marine Hosp., Norfolk, Va., 1948-49; resident in pathology Med. Br., U. Tex., Galveston, 1949-52, asst. prof. pathology, 1952-54, asso. prof., 1954-56; asso. prof. Southwestern Med. Sch., Dallas, 1959-61, prof., 1961—, chmn. dept. pathology, 1966—; asso. dir. clin. labs. U. Tex. Med. Br. Hosps., 1952-56; sr. pathologist, chief aviation pathology sect. Armed Forces Inst. Pathology, Washington, 1956-59; dir. pathology labs. Parkland Hosp., Dallas, 1966—; cons. VA Hosp., Dallas. Cons. to surgeon gen. USAF; civil air surgeon FAA; chmn. sci. adv. bd. Armed Forces Inst. Pathology. Served with USAF, 1956-59. Decorated Legion of Merit; named Outstanding Alumnus, U. Tex. at El Paso, 1978. Diplomate Am. Bd. Pathology (trustee 1969—, sec. 1976—). Mem. Internat. Acad. Pathology (counsellor 1970-73), Am. Soc. Clin. Pathologists (dir., pres. 1977-78), AMA (residency rev. com. 1972-78, chmn. 1977-78, residency rev. com. nuclear medicine 1972-78), Coll. Am. Pathologists, Am. Assn. Pathologists, Assn. Pathology Chairmen (mem. council, pres. 1979), Am. Assn. Blood Banks, Aerospace Med. Assn., Tex. Soc. Pathologists (pres. 1966, Caldwell award 1967), Tex. Med. Assn. (ho. of dels.), Phi Rho Sigma, Mu Delta, Alpha Omega Alpha. Contbr. articles to med. jours. Home: 10424 Marsh Ln Dallas TX 75229 Office: 5323 Harry Hines Blvd Dallas TX 75235

STEMMLER, EDWARD JOSEPH, physician, univ. dean; b. Phila., Feb. 15, 1929; s. Edward C. and Josephine (Heitzmann) S.; B.A., La Salle Coll., Phila., 1950; M.D., U. Pa., 1960; Sc.D. (hon.), Ursinus Coll., 1977; m. Joan C. Koster, Dec. 27, 1958; children—Elizabeth, Margaret, Edward C., Catherine, Joan. Intern, U. Pa. Hosp., 1960-61, med. resident, 1961-63, fellow in cardiology, 1963-64, chief med. resident, 1964-65, chief med. outpatient dept., 1966-67; chief of medicine U. Pa. Med. Service, VA Hosp., Phila., 1967-73; cons. pulmonary disease VA Hosp., Phila., 1973—, mem. deans com., 1974—; cons. pulmonary disease Phila. Gen. Hosp., 1973-76; NIH postdoctoral research trainee, dept. physiology Grad. Div. Medicine, U. Pa., 1965-67, instr. medicine, 1964-66, asso. in medicine, 1966-67, asso. in physiology Grad. Div. Medicine, 1967-72, asst. prof. medicine, 1967-70, asso. prof., 1970-74, prof., 1974—, asso. dean Univ. Hosp., Sch. Medicine, 1973, asso. dean student affairs, 1973-75, acting dean Sch. Medicine, 1974-75, dean, 1975—; dir. Rorer Group, Inc. Chmn. policy com. on drug abuse and alcoholism Lower Merion Twp. Bd. Sch. Dirs., 1973-74; mem. Gov.'s Com. on Health Edn., 1974-76; mem. ednl. policy com. Nat. Fund for Med. Edn., 1975-77; chmn. Pa. Dean's Com., 1976—; bd. govs. Mid-Eastern Regional Med. Library Services, 1977—, chmn., 1978—. Served with Chem. Corps, U.S. Army, 1951-53. Decorated Commendation medal; recipient Frederick A. Packard award, 1960, Albert Einstein Med. Center staff award, 1960, Roche award, 1960. Diplomate Am. Bd. Internal Medicine. Fellow A.C.P. (treas., chmn. investment com. 1975—); mem. AMA, Phila. County Med. Soc., Am. Heart Assn.. Am., Pa. thoracic socs., Am. Fedn. for Clin. Research, Assn. Am. Med. Colls., Laennec Soc., Am. Clin. and Climatological Soc., John Morgan Soc., Alpha Omega Alpha. Republican. Mem. Christian Ch. Contbr. articles to med. jours. Home: 139 E Wynnewood Rd Merion PA 19066 Office: 36th and Hamilton Walk U Pa Philadelphia PA 19104

STEMPEL, ERNEST EDWARD, ins. exec.; b. N.Y.C., May 10, 1916; s. Frederick Christian and Leah Lillian S.; A.B., Manhattan Coll., 1938; LL.B., Fordham U., 1946; LL.M., N.Y. U., 1949, D.J.S., 1951; m. Phyllis Brooks; children—Diana Brooks, Calvin Pinkcomb, Neil Frederick, Robert Russell. Admitted to N.Y. bar, 1946; with Am. Internat. Underwriters Corp., N.Y.C., 1938-53; v.p., dir. Am. Internat. Co. Ltd., Hamilton, Bermuda, 1953-63, chmn. bd., 1963—; pres., dir. Am. Internat. Assurance Co. (Bermuda) Ltd., Am. Internat. Reins. Co. Ltd., Bermuda, Am. Internat. Comml. Co., Inc., Bermuda, exec. v.p., mem. exec. com., dir. Am. Internat. Group Inc.; dir. C.V. Starr & Co. Inc., N.Y.C., Starr Internat. Co. Inc., Am. Life Ins. Co., Wilmington, Del., Am. Internat. Life Ins. Co., P.R., La Interamericana, S.A., Mexico, Mt. Mansfield Co., Inc., Stowe, Vt., Seguros Venezuela, C.A., Caracas, Underwriters Bank Inc., Bermuda, Australian Am. Assurance Co., Ltd., Malaysian Am. Assurance Co.; chmn. bd., dir. Am. Internat. Assurance Co. Ltd., Hong Kong, Philippine Am. Ins. Cos., Manila; dir. Am. Internat. Underwriters Japan, Inc., Am. Internat. Underwriters (Latin Am.), Inc., Bermuda, Am. Internat. Underwriters Mediterranean, Inc., Bermuda, Del.Am. Life Ins. Co., Wilmington, Pacific Union Assurance Co., Calif., Underwriters Adjustment Co., Panama. Served to lt. (s.g.) USNR, 1942-46. Mem. Am. Bar Assn., N.Y. State Bar, Bermuda C. of C. (mem. exec. com. internat. cos. div.). Clubs: Marco Polo, Lawyers (N.Y.C.); Royal Bermuda Yacht, Mid-Ocean, Coral Beach (Bermuda). Home: Caliban Cove Fairylands Pembroke Bermuda Office: Am Internat Co Ltd PO Box 152 Hamilton 5 Bermuda

STEMPEL, IRVING ROBERT, advt. agy. exec.; b. N.Y.C., Nov. 19, 1919; s. George and Goldie (Theodore) S.; student Bates U., 1936-38, Pratt Inst., 1938-40; N.Y. U.; B.S., New Sch. Social Studies, 1945, M.A., 1945; m. Shirley Klase, June 22, 1941; children—Bruce Denis, Stephanie. Prodn. mgr. New Era mag., N.Y.C., 1945; creative dir. A.W. Lewin, advt., N.Y.C., 1945-47; v.p. Lewin Williams Advt., N.Y.C., 1947; exec. v.p. William Tauder Advt., N.Y.C.; pres. Posner Zabin Advt. (now Loewy Stempel Zabin), N.Y.C., 1955—; pres. Expn. Press, Miami, Fla., 1970—; v.p. Barton Irving Case Printing, N.Y.C., 1960—. Served with 23d Spl. Troops, AUS, 1941-45. Home: 812 Ascan St Valley Stream NY 11580 Office: Loewy Stempel Zabin Advt 801 2d Ave New York City NY 10017

STEMPEL, JOHN EMMERT, journalist, ret. educator, b. Bloomington, Ind., May 6, 1903; s. Guido Hermann and Myrtle (Emmert) S.; A.B., Ind. U., 1923, postgrad. 1926-27; M.S. in Journalism, Columbia, 1928; m. Mary Roberts Farmer, Aug. 30, 1928; children—John Dallas, Thomas Ritter. Reporter on Bloomington Evening World, 1917-19; instr. journalism and director publicity Lafayette Coll., Easton, Pa., 1923-26; part time instr. in journalism, Ind. U., Bloomington, 1926-27, prof. journalism, chmn. dept., 1938-68, prof. emeritus, 1968—; asso. editor Bloomington Star, 1926-27; news editor Columbia Univ. Alumni News, 1927-30; staff New York Sun, 1929-36; news and mng. editor Easton (Pa.) Express, 1936-38; ednl. adviser Def. Info. Sch., Ft. Benjamin Harrison, 1968-69. Past chmn. United Episcopal Charities Diocese Indpls.; past chmn. Ind. Conf. ARC. Named Newspaperman of Yr., Indpls. Press Club, 1968; recipient Distinguished Alumnus award Columbia Sch. Journalism, 1963, Elihu Stout Plaque for distinction in journalism, Vincennes U., 1970, Distinguished alumni award Ind. U., 1972; named to Ind. Journalism Hall Fame, 1970. Mem. Assn. Edn. Journalism, Internat. Typographical Union, Greater Bloomington C. of C. (exec. v.p. 1976, pres.'s award 1977), Phi Kappa Psi, Sigma Delta Chi (past nat. pres. Wells Meml. Key 1936), Mason. Democrat. Episcopalian. Clubs: Rotary (past dist. gov.); Indpls. Press; Univ. (Ind. U.). Author textbooks. Contbr. to journalism publs. Home: 924 Atwater Ave Bloomington IN 47401

STEMPLER, JACK LEON, govt. ofcl.; b. Newark, Oct. 30, 1920; s. Morris and Ida (Friedman) S.; B.A., Montclair (N.J.) State Coll., 1943; LL.B., Cornell U., 1948; m. J. Adelaide Williams, Oct. 28, 1950; children—Mark N., Sandra J., Carrie B. Admitted to N.Y., D.C. bars, 1949; atty. com. uniform code mil. justice Dept. Def., 1948-49, atty. adviser legis. div., 1949-50; asst. counsel Munitions Bd., 1950-53; counsel Armed Forces Housing Agy., 1952-54, Advanced Research Projects Agy., 1958-65; asst. gen. counsel logistics Dept. Def., 1953-65, asst. to sec. def. for legislative affairs, 1965-70; gen. counsel Dept. Air Force, 1970-77; asst. to sec. of def. for legis. affairs, 1977—. Served to 1st lt. USMCR, 1942-46; PTO. Recipient Outstanding Civilian Performance award Dept. Def., 1959, Distinguished Civilian Service award, 1965, Distinguished Civilian Service award with palm, 1969, with 2d bronze palm, 1970; Exceptional Civilian Service award USAF, 1973, 75, 77. Mem. Fed., D.C. bar assns., Cornell Law Sch. Assn., Montclair State Tchrs. Alumni Assn. Home: 4701 Newcomb Pl Alexandria VA 22304 Office: Pentagon Washington DC 20301

STENASON, WALTER JOHN, investments co. exec.; b. Winnipeg, Man., Can., Sept. 24, 1930; s. Walter George and Margaret (Smith) S.; B.Commerce, McGill U., 1952, M.Commerce, 1954; Ph.D. in Econs., Harvard U., 1961; m. Letty Trant Watson, Dec. 24, 1954; children—David James, Robert Walter, William Albert. With Can. Pacific Ltd., Montreal, Que., Can., 1952—, asst. to pres., asst. to chmn., pres., 1961-66, v.p. co. services, 1966-69, v.p. transport and ships, 1969-72, v.p. adminstrn., 1972-74; exec. v.p. Can. Pacific Investments Ltd., Montreal, Que., Can., 1974-79, pres., 1979—; v.p., dir. Gt. Lakes Forest Products Ltd.; dir. Cominco, Vancouver, CP Investments, Montreal, Can. Trust Co., Commandant Properties Ltd., Provident Properties Ltd., Dominion Bridge Co. Ltd., Amca Internat. Corp., Algoma Steel Corp. Ltd., Can. Pacific Securities Ltd., Can. Pacific Hotels Ltd., Marathon Realty Ltd., Cascade Pipeline Ltd., Pancan. Petroleum Ltd., Pacific Logging Co. Ltd., numerous others. Mem. Am., Canadian, Royal econ. assns., Am. Statis. Assn. Author: (with Meyer) Avoidable Costs of Railway Passenger Service, 1957; (with Meyer, Peck, Zwick) Economics of Competition in the Transportation Industries, 1959. Home: 316 Pinetree Crescent Beaconsfield PQ Canada Office: Canadian Pacific Investments Ltd Place du Canada Montreal PQ H3B 2N2 Canada

STENCHEVER, MORTON ALBERT, educator, physician; b. Paterson, N.J., Jan. 25, 1931; s. Harold and Lena (Suresky) S.; A.B., N.Y. U., 1951; M.D., U. Buffalo, 1956; m. Diane Bilsky, June 19, 1955; children—Michael A., Marc R., Douglas A. Intern, Mt. Sinai Hosp., 1956-57; resident obstetrics and gynecology Columbia-Presbyn. Med. Center, N.Y.C., 1957-60; asst. prof., Oglebey Research fellow Case-Western Res. U., Cleve., 1962-66, asso. prof. dept. reproductive biology, 1967-70, dir. Tissue Culture Lab., 1965-70, coordinator Phase II Med. Sch. program, 1969-70; prof., chmn. dept. obstetrics-gynecology U. Utah Med. Sch., Salt Lake City, 1970-77; prof., chmn. dept. obstetrics-gynecology U. Wash. Sch. Medicine, Seattle, 1977—; test com. chmn. for Ob-Gyn, Nat. Bd. Med. Examiners, 1979—. Served to capt. USAF, 1960-62. Fellow Am. Coll. Obstetricians and Gynecologists, Am. Assn. Obstetricians and Gynecologists, Am. Gynecol. Soc.; mem. Assn. Profs. Gynecology and Obstetrics (chmn. steering com. teaching methods in obstetrics and gynecology 1970—, v.p. 1975—), AMA, AAAS, Pacific Northwest Obstetrics-Gynecology Soc., Wash. State Med. Assn., Seattle Gynec. Soc., Am. Soc. Human Genetics, Central Assn. Obstetrics and Gynecology, Soc. Gynecologic Investigation, Wash. State Obstet. Soc., Tissue Culture Assn., N.Y. Acad. Sci., Utah Obstetrics-Gynecology Soc., Utah State Med. Assn. Author: Labor: Workbook in Obstetrics, 1968; Human Sexual Behavior: A Workbook in Reproductive Biology, 1970; Human Cytogenics: A Workbook in Reproductive Biology, 1973; Introductory Gynecology: A Workbook in Reproductive Biology, 1974. Contbr. articles to profl. jours. Home: 8301 SE 83d St Mercer Island WA 98040 Office: Dept Obstetrics and Gynecology U Wash Sch Medicine Seattle WA 98105

STENDAHL, KRISTER, clergyman, educator; b. Stockholm, Sweden, Apr. 21, 1921 (came to U.S. 1954, naturalized 1967); s. Olof and Sigrid (Ljungquist) S.; Theol. Cand., U. Uppsala (Sweden), 1944, Theol. Lic., 1949, Theol.Dr., 1954; studies Cambridge, Eng., Paris, 1951; Litt. D. (hon.), Upsala Coll., 1963, Thiel Coll., 1966; D.D., Colby Coll., 1970, Whittier Coll., St. Olaf Coll., 1971; S.T.D., Carthage Coll., 1971; LL.D., Susquehanna U., 1973; L.H.D. (hon.), Miami U., Oxford, Ohio, 1978; m. Brita Johnsson, Sept. 7, 1946; children—John, Anna, Daniel. Ordained priest Ch. of Sweden, 1944; chaplain to students Uppsala U., 1948-50, instr. O.T., N.T. exegesis, 1951-54, docent, 1954; asst. prof N.T., Harvard Div. Sch., 1954-56, asso. prof., 1956-58, John H. Morison prof. N.T. studies, 1958-63, Frothingham prof. Bibl. studies, 1963-68, dean Div. Sch., John Lord O'Brian prof. div. 1968-79, prof. div., 1979—; pastor Luth. Ch. Am., 1968—; chmn. consultation on ch. and Jewish people World Council Chs., 1975—. Fellow Am. Acad. Arts and Scis.; mem. Nathan Soederblom Soc. Author: The School of St. Matthew, 1954, 2d edit., 1968; The Bible and the Role of Women, 1966; Holy Week, 1974; Paul Among Jews and Gentiles, 1976. Home: 85 Trowbridge St Cambridge MA 02138 Office: Harvard U Div Sch 45 Francis Ave Cambridge MA 02138

STENEHJEM, LELAND MANFORD, banker; b. Arnegard, N.D., May 25, 1918; s. Odin N. And Lillie (Moe) S.; B.S., N.D. State U., 1941; grad. U. Wis. Grad. Sch. Banking, 1948; m. Judith H. Johnson, July 21, 1944; children—Leland Manford, Stephen Leslie, Joan Marie. With First Internat. Bank, Watford City, N.D., 1943—, exec. v.p., 1961-66, pres., 1966—; dir. State Bank Burleigh County, Bismarck, N.D., 1963—. Mem. N.D. Banking Bd., 1958-63; mem. N.D. adv. council Farmers Home Adminstrn., 1957-60. Pres. Good Shepherd Home, 1963—. Bd. dirs. N.D. State U. Alumni Assn., Greater N.D. Assn. Served as 2d lt. USMCR, World War II. Mem. Am. (past mem. exec. council), N.D. (past pres.) bankers assns., Ind. Bankers Assn. Am. (past pres.). Watford City Assn. Commerce (pres.), Alpha Tau Omega. Lutheran. Mason, Elk, Lion (pres. Watford City), Rotarian (pres.). Home: 100 SW 4th St Watford City ND 58854 Office: 100 N Main St Watford City ND 58854

STENGEL, LOUIS C., JR., business exec.; b. Feb. 2, 1915; s. Louis and Ann (McGuigan) S.; L.H.D. (hon.), Villanova U., 1965; m. Ann Beversluis, Feb. 3, 1940; children—Louis C. III, Muriel Ursillo. Chmn. exec. com., dir. Manhattan Industries; mem. adv. bd. Mfrs. Hanover Bank, 1960-68. Mem. adv. com. Dept. Def.-Supply Agy.; chmn. bd. dirs. Nat. Brand Names Found., 1963-65; chmn. Nat. Fathers Day Council, 1959-65. Decorated Knight Order Holy Sepulchre; named Man of Yr., N.Y. Men's Wear Industry, 1965. Mem. Am. Arbitration Assn. (panel). Home: 410 Portsmouth Dr Lakewood NJ 08701 Office: 1271 Ave of Americas New York NY 10020

STENHOLM, CHARLES W., congressman; b. Stamford, Tex., Oct. 26, 1938; grad. Tarleton State Jr. Coll., 1959; B.S., Tex. Tech. U., 1961, M.S., 1962; m. Cynthia Ann Watson; children—Chris, Cary, Courtney Ann. Farmer, Tex.; past pres. Rolling Plains Cotton Growers and Tex. Electric Coops.; mem. 96th Congress from 17th Tex. Dist. Former mem. state Democratic Exec. Com. Mem. Stamford C. of C. (past pres.). Democrat. Lutheran. Office: 1610 Longworth House Office Bldg Washington DC 20515

STENNIS, JOHN CORNELIUS, senator; b. Kemper County, Miss., Aug. 3, 1901; s. Hampton Howell and Cornelia (Adams) S.; B.S., Miss. State U., 1923; LL.B., U. Va., 1928; LL.D., Millsaps Coll., 1957, U. Wyo., 1962; LL.D., Miss. Coll., 1969, Belhaven Coll., 1972, William Carey Coll., 1975; m. Coy Hines, Dec. 24, 1929; children—John Hampton, Margaret Jane (Mrs. Womble). Admitted to Miss. bar; practiced in DeKalb, Miss.; mem. Miss. Ho. of Reps., 1928-32; dist. pros. atty. 16th Jud. Dist., 1931-37; apptd. circuit judge, 1937, elected, 1938, 1942, 1946; mem. U.S. Senate from Miss., 1947—; chmn. armed services com.; mem. appropriations com. Active in promotion farm youth tng. programs; state chmn. Miss. 4-H Adv. Council. Mem. Am., Miss. bar assns., Phi Alpha Delta, Phi Beta Kappa, Alpha Chi Rho. Presbyn. (deacon). Mason, Lion. Home: DeKalb MS 39328 Office: US Senate Washington DC 20510

STENSLAND, ANNA LEE, educator; b. Ashland, Wis., July 25, 1922; d. Arthur John and Effie Belle (Madbury) Stensland; B.A., Northland Coll., 1944; M.A., U. Wis., 1947, Ph.D., 1958. Tchr. high sch., Boyd, Wis., 1944-46, Merrill, Wis., 1947-49; asst. prof. edn. Peru (Nebr.) State Tchrs. Coll., 1949-51; asst. prof. Dakota Wesleyan U., Mitchell, S.D., 1952-57; asst. prof. Stout State Coll., Menomonie, Wis., 1958-60; prof. English, head dept. U. Minn., Duluth, 1975-79. Mem. Minn. Council Tchrs. English (past pres., exec. sec.) Nat. Councils Tchrs. English, Internat. Reading Assn., AAUP. Congregationalist. Contbr. articles to profl. jours. Home: 811 Kenwood Ave Duluth MN 55811 Office: Dept English U Minn Duluth MN 55812

STENSRUD, RUSSELL KENNETH, chem. co. exec.; b. Grand Forks, N.D., June 8, 1927; s. Russell Edward and Leonore Anne (Scheibe) S.; B.S. in Forestry, U. Wash., 1950, M.F., 1957; m. Beatrice Dorraine Sorenson, Oct. 27, 1951; children—Rebecca Lynn, Bradley Russell. Engaged in lumber sales, cost analysis West Waterway Lumber Co., Seattle, 1950-52; with Reichhold Chems., Inc., Seattle, 1952-61, Tacoma, 1961—, nat. product mgr. treated fiber products div., 1965-71, v.p., gen. mgr. treated fiber products div., 1971-72, v.p., mgr. Western region, 1972-78, dir., mem. exec. com., 1972—, exec. v.p., Western regional mgr., 1978—, pres., chief exec. Reichhold Energy Corp., 1978—. Active local civic groups. Served to lt. comdr. USNR, World War II, Korean conflict. Mem. Forest Products Research Soc. (area chmn. industry edn. com.), ASTM, Am. Soc. Quality Control, Soc. Wood Sci. and Tech., Sigma Xi, Xi Sigma Pi. Republican. Episcopalian. Clubs: Washington Athletic (Seattle); Tacoma, Pacific West Racquet. Research, patents, publs. in wood veneer drying, adhesive compositions. Office: 2340 Taylor Way Tacoma WA 98421

STENSVAAG, JOHN MONRAD, educator, clergyman; b. Bergen, Norway, June 1, 1911; s. Hans and Malene (Kjellevold) S.; came to U.S. 1925, naturalized 1935; A.B., Augsburg Coll. and Theol. Sem., 1936, B.Th., 1939; S.T.M., Hartford Sem. Found., 1940, Ph.D., 1941; postgrad. Johns Hopkins, 1941-42, Ind. Theol. Sem. and Univ. Oslo, 1956, Harvard Div. Sch., 1966-67, Union Theol. Sem., Richmond, Va., 1973-74; m. Hannah Ovidia Mehus, Sept. 16, 1939; children—Rebecca Marlene, Ruth Ingrid, John Mark, Saul George.

Ordained to ministry Luth. Ch., 1942; pastor Oak Grove Luth. Ch., Mpls., 1942-46; instr. Augsburg Coll. and Sem., 1942-46, prof. O.T. and religion, 1946-58, 62-63, dean sem., 1953-58; prof. O.T., Luth. Theol. Sem., St. Paul, 1963—; v.p. Luth. Free Ch., 1953-58, pres., 1958-63; bd. dirs. Am. bd. Santal Mission, 1950-64, 69-72, pres. bd., 1955-64; del. Luth. World Fedn. Conv., Helsinki, Finland, 1963; mem. Commn. on Fellowship, Am. Luth. Ch.-Luth. Ch. Mo. Synod, 1969-77. Bd. dirs. Luth. Deaconess Hosp., Mpls., 1949-66, 68—, pres. bd., 1962-66; bd. dirs. Fairview Community Hosps., 1978—. Mem. Am. Schs. Oriental Research, Soc. Bibl. Lit. and Exegesis. Home: 3329 14th Ave S Minneapolis MN 55407

STENT, GUNTHER SIEGMUND, educator, molecular biologist; b. Berlin, Germany, Mar. 28, 1924; s. George and Elizabeth (Karfunkelstein) S.; came to U.S. 1940, naturalized 1945; B.S., U. Ill., 1945, Ph.D., 1948; m. Inga Loftsdottir, Oct. 27, 1951; 1 son, Stefan Loftur. Research asst. U. Ill., 1945-48; research fellow Calif. Inst. Tech., 1948-50, U. Copenhagen (Denmark), 1950-51, Pasteur Inst., Paris, France, 1951-52; asst. research biochemist U. Calif., Berkeley, 1952-56, faculty, 1956—, prof. molecular biology, 1959—, prof. arts and scis., 1967-68. Document analyst U.S. Field Intelligence Agy. Tech., 1946-47; mem. genetics panel NIH, 1959-64, NSF, 1965-68. Merck fellow NRC, 1948-54; sr. fellow NSF, 1960-61; Guggenheim fellow, 1969-70. Fellow Am. Acad. Arts and Scis.; mem. Soc. Neurosci. Author: Papers On Bacterial Viruses, 2d edit., 1966; Molecular Biology of Bacterial Viruses, 1963; Phage and the Origin of Molecular Biology, 1966; The Coming of the Golden Age, 1969; Function and Formation of Neural Systems, 1977; Morality as a Biological Phenomenon, 1978; Paradoxes of Progress, 1978; Molecular Genetics, 2d edit., 1978. Mem. editorial bd. Jour. Molecular Biology, 1965-68, Genetics, 1963-68, Zeitschrift für Vererbungslehre, 1962-68, Ann. Revs. Genetics, 1965-69, Ann. Revs. Microbiology, 1966-70. Contbr. numerous sci. papers to profl. lit. Home: 145 Purdue Ave Berkeley CA 94708

STENVIG, CHARLES S., former mayor Mpls.; b. Mpls., Jan. 16, 1928; s. Selmer and Myrtle (Lee) S.; B.A., Augsburg Coll., 1951; m. Audrey Thompson, Aug. 6, 1951; children—Terri, Tracy, Todd, Thomas. Mem. Mpls. Police Dept. (to lt.), 1956-69; mayor Mpls., 1969-73, 76-78. Organizer mag. Law Officer, 1967; pres. Police Officers Fedn. Mpls., 1965-69. Mem. Air N.G., 1952-53. Served with AUS, 1946-47; PTO. Recipient Law Enforcement commendation S.A.R., 1970, Reverence for Law award Eagles, 1969. Mem. Internat. Conf. Police Assn. (v.p. 1966-69, award 1970), Minn. Police and Peace Officers Assn., VFW (Gold medal of merit 1972, nat. security com.), Sons of Norway, Mil. Order Cootie. Methodist. Mason (Shriner). Home: 5604 35th Ave S Minneapolis MN 55417

STEP, EUGENE (LEE), pharm. co. exec.; b. Sioux City, Iowa, Feb. 19, 1929; s. Harry and Ann (Keiser) S.; B.A. in Econs., U. Nebr., 1951; M.S. in Acctg. and Fin., U. Ill., 1952; m. Hannah Scheuermann, Dec. 27, 1953; children—Steven Harry, Michael David, Jonathan Allen. With Eli Lilly Internat. Corp., 1956-72, v.p. market planning, Indpls., 1971-72, v.p. continental Europe, Middle East and North Africa, Indpls., 1972; v.p. mktg. devel. and planning Eli Lilly and Co., Indpls., 1972-73, pres. pharm. div., Indpls., 1973—. Served to 1st lt. Fin. Corps, U.S. Army, 1953-56. Home: 1131 Pimbury Ct Indianapolis IN 46260

STEPAN, ALFRED CHARLES, JR., chem. mfg. exec.; b. N.Y.C., Apr. 17, 1909; s. Alfred Charles and Charlotte (Corbett) S.; B.A., U. Notre Dame, 1931, hon. degree, 1963; student Northwestern U., 1931-33, Ill. Inst. Tech. 1933-34; m. Mary Louise Quinn, Feb. 10, 1934; children—Marilee (Mrs. Richard Wehman), Alfred Charles, F. Quinn, Stratford, Charlotte (Mrs. Joseph Flanagan), Paul, John. Founder, Stepan Chem. Co., Northfield, Ill., 1932, chmn., chief exec. officer, 1973—; dir. 1st Nat. Bank of Winnetka. Bd. dirs. Ravinia Festival Assn., Lyric Opera of Chgo.; pres. Lyric Opera Sch. Chgo.; mem. vis. com. humanities U. Chgo.; trustee U. Notre Dame. Trustee Orchestral Assn. Republican. Clubs: Arts, Commercial, Chgo., Univ. (Chgo.); Bob O'Link Golf (Highland Park, Ill.); Glen View (Glenview, Ill.); Everglades, Seminole Golf, Bath and Tennis (Palm Beach, Fla.). Home: 76 Woodley Rd Winnetka IL 60093 also 212 Via Palma Palm Beach FL Office: Edens and Winnetka Northfield IL 60093

STEPAN, FRANK QUINN, chem. co. exec.; b. Chgo., Oct. 24, 1937; s. Alfred Charles and Mary Louise (Quinn) S.; A.B., U. Notre Dame, 1959; M.B.A., U. Chgo., 1963; m. Jean Finn, Aug. 23, 1958; children—Jeanne, Frank Quinn, Todd, Jennifer, Lisa, Colleen, Alfred, Richard. Salesman, Indsl. Chems. div. Stepan Chem. Co., Northfield, Ill., 1961-63, mgr. internat. dept. 1964-66, v.p. corporate planning, 1967-69, v.p., gen. mgr. Indsl. Chems. div., 1970-73, pres., 1974—, now pres. Stepan Chem. Co., also dir.; dir. Kona Communications, Inc. Trustee Loyola Acad.; mem. liberal arts council Notre Dame U., South Bend, Ind., 1972—. Served to 1st lt. AUS, 1959-61. Clubs: Econ. (Chgo.); Exmoor (Highland Park, Ill.). Home: 200 Linden St Winnetka IL 60093 Office: Stepan Chem Co Edens and Winnetka Sts Northfield IL 60093

STEPANCHEV, STEPHEN, educator; b. Mokrin, Yugoslavia, Jan. 30, 1915; s. George and Olga (Dobrich) S.; came to U.S., 1922, naturalized, 1938; B.A., U. Chgo., 1937, M.A., 1938; Ph.D., N.Y. U., 1950. Instr. English, Purdue U., 1938-41, N.Y. U., 1946-47, 48-49; mem. faculty Queens Coll., City U. N.Y., 1949—, prof. English, 1964—. Served to 1st lt. AUS, 1941-45. Decorated Bronze Star. Mem. Phi Beta Kappa. Mem. Serbian Orthodox Ch. Author: (poems) Three Priests in April, 1956, Spring in the Harbor, 1967, A Man Running in the Rain, 1969, The Mad Bomber, 1972, Mining the Darkness, 1975, Medusa and Others, 1975; The Dove in the Acacia, 1977; Chapbook of poems: What I Own, 1978; (criticism) American Poetry Since 1945, 1965. Home: 140-60 Beech Ave Flushing NY 11355

STEPHAN, EDMUND ANTON, lawyer; b. Chgo., Oct. 7, 1911; s. Anton Charles and Mary Veronica (Egan) S.; A.B., U. Notre Dame, 1933; LL.B., Harvard, 1939; m. Evelyn Way, July 3, 1937; children—Miriam S. Hucke, Edmund Anton, Martha (Mrs. Robert McNeill), Donald, Christopher, Evelyn, Gregory, Joan. Admitted to N.Y. bar, 1940, Ill. bar, 1945; asso. firm Carter, Ledyard & Milburn, N.Y.C., 1939-42; atty. charge N.Y. office U.S. Alien Property Custodian, 1943-45; asso. firm Mayer, Brown & Platt and predecessors, Chgo., 1945-47, partner, 1947—; dir. Brunswick Corp., Bunker-Ramo Corp., Stepan Chem. Co., Marsh & McLennan Cos. Chmn. bd. trustees U. Notre Dame. Mem. Am., Ill., Chgo. bar assns. Roman Catholic. Clubs: Legal, Mid-Day, Chicago, Law (Chgo.); Michigan Shores, Westmoreland Country (Wilmette, Ill.); Harvard (N.Y.C.); Bob-O-Link Golf (Highland Park, Ill.). Home: 144 Greenwood Blvd Evanston IL 60201 Office: 231 S LaSalle St Chicago IL 60604

STEPHAN, ROBERT DOWNS, constrn. supplies co. exec.; b. Chgo., Feb. 8, 1905; s. John Edward and Lettie A. (Downs) S.; A.B., U. Notre Dame, 1927; m. Virginia Delehanty, Oct. 19, 1929; children—Roxanne (Mrs. R.R. O'Brien), Ellen Virginia (Mrs. R.A. Hunziker), Patricia (Mrs. Lynn Harshbarger), Mary Bob, Penelope (Mrs. Anthony Cuttone). With U.S. Gypsum Co., Chgo., 1934—, dist. mgr., 1939-41, div. sales mgr., 1941-44, mdse. mgr., 1944-48, dealer sales mgr., 1948-53, v.p. 1953—; cons. Cons. in field, 1971—. Clubs: Union League, Notre Dame (Chgo.); Barrington (Ill.) Hills Country. Home: 228 Pine Crest Circle Barrington IL 60010. *My philosophy is this: "Work until the job is done—whatever that takes in effort or time." My priorities are: Love my God; love my family; love my country; do my work; keep a sense of humor.*

STEPHAN, ROBERT TAFT, atty. gen. Kans.; b. Wichita, Kans., Jan. 16, 1933; s. Taft and Julia Stephan; B.A., Washburn U., 1954, J.D., 1957; grad. Nat. Coll. State Trial Judges, U. Pa., 1967; m. Bettie Nell; children—Judy, Marty, Dana, Lisa. Admitted to Kans. Bar, 1957; pvt. practice, 1957-63; judge Wichita (Kans.) Mcpl. Ct., 1963-65, Kans. Dist. Ct., 18th Jud. Dist., 1965-78; atty. gen. State of Kans., 1979—; chmn. Kans. Jud. Conf., 1977. Hon. crusade chmn. Kans. div. Am. Cancer Soc., 1979-80; Kans. state chmn. Muscular Dystrophy Love Run; bd. dirs. Kans. Big Bros.-Big Sisters, Kans. chpt. Leukemia Soc. Am. Named Kans. Trial Judge of Yr., Kans. Trial Lawyers Assn., 1977. Mem. Am. Judges Assn., Am. Judicature Soc., Am. Bar Assn., Am. Cancer Soc. Republican. Clubs: Elks, Moose, Masons (Shriner), Wagonmasters. Office: Office Atty Gen State House Topeka KS 66612

STEPHANOPOULOS, ROBERT GEORGE, clergyman; b. Neochorion, Elis, Greece, Nov. 19, 1934; s. George Charalampos and Anastasia (Mataranga) S.; came to U.S., 1939, naturalized, 1957; B.A., Holy Cross Greek Orthodox Theol. Sch., 1958, B.D., 1959; postgrad. U. Athens Div. Sch., 1959; Ph.D., Boston U., 1970; m. Nikki Gloria Chafos, June 8, 1958; children—Anastasia, George, Marguerite, Andrew. Ordained to ministry Greek Orthodox Ch., 1959; pastor St. Demetrios Greek Orthodox Ch., Fall River, Mass., 1959-66; pastor Ch. of Our Savior, Rye, N.Y., 1966-75; dir. Interchurch Office Greek Orthodox Archdiocese, N.Y.C., 1970-75; pastor Sts. Constantine and Helen Ch., Cleve., 1975—. Vice chmn. Faith and Order Commn., Nat. Council Chs., 1969—, orthodox cons., rec. sec. NCCCUSA, 1970-72; pres. Greater Cleve. Council Orthodox Clergy, 1978—; mem. Adv. Com. on Desegregation and Community Relations of Cleve., 1978—. Trustee Hellenic Coll., Brookline, Mass. Mem. Holy Cross Theol. Sch. Alumni Assn. (pres.), Orthodox Theol. Soc. Am. (sec.), Presbyters Council of Greek Orthodox Archdiocese, Standing Conf. Canonical Orthodox Bishops in Am. (gen. sec., chmn. Ecumenical Commn.), Archdiocesan Pension Com. (chmn.). Contbr. articles to profl. jours. Home: 3352 Mayfield Rd Cleveland OH 44118

STEPHANS, WILLIAM JACOB, JR., banker; b. Jamaica, N.Y., Oct. 24, 1926; s. William Jacob and Elsie Florence Virginia (Mennerich) S.; A.B., Hobart Coll., 1948; postgrad. Grad. Sch. Banking, Rutgers U., 1955-57; m. Margaret Lucille Kingston, Oct. 2, 1948; children—Brent Kingston, Pamela Margaret, Douglas William. Asst. trust officer Marine Midland Bank, Rochester, N.Y., 1948-64, sr. v.p., trust officer, 1970—; v.p., trust officer First Nat. Bank & Trust Co., Ithaca, N.Y., 1965-70; tchr. Am. Inst. Banking. Bd. dirs. United Community Chest, Rochester, Episcopal Ch. Home, Rochester, Jr. Achievement, Rochester. Served with USNR, 1944-47. Mem. N.Y. State Bankers Assn., Theta Delta Chi. Episcopalian. Author: Commercial Bankers Television Guidebook, 1957. Home: 15 Little Brook Dr Pittsford NY 14534 Office: 1 Marine Midland Plaza Rochester NY 14639

STEPHANSKY, BEN SOLOMON, former U.S. ambassador; b. Bogoslav, Russia, Nov. 10, 1913; s. Aaron Harry and Edith Gertrude (Spector) S.; B.A., U. Wis., 1938, M.A., 1939, Ph.D., 1952; m. Anne Edelman, June 7, 1947; children—Evan, Kate Judith, Eric Thomas. Came to U.S., 1915, naturalized, 1926. Asst. U. Wis. Sch. for Workers, 1938-39, mem. faculty, 1938-42, 48-49; exec. asst. Nat. War Labor Bd., 1943-44, ofcl. historian, 1944-45; social sci. faculty Sarah Lawrence Coll., 1945-47; cons. Columbia U. Bur. Applied Social Research, 1946; social sci. faculty U. Chgo., 1947-56; cons. U.S. Dept. Labor, 1950-51; fgn. service officer, 1956—, labor attaché, 1st sec., Am. embassy, Mexico City, 1952-57; labor adviser Bur. Inter-American Affairs, Dept. State, 1957-60; ambassador to Bolivia, 1961-63; dep. asst. sec. Bur. Inter-Am. Affairs, 1963-64; exec. sec. U.S. P.R. Commn. on Status of P.R., 1964-66; ambassador and alt. del. OAS, 1967-68; adminstr. Office Commonwealth of P.R., Washington, 1975-76; dir. Washington Center WE Upjohn Inst Employment Research, 1969-77; sr. asso. Carnegie Endowment for Internat. Peace, 1977—; cons. fgn. labor program to asst. sec. of labor for foreign affairs, 1950. Co-chmn. Democratic Study Group in Latin Am. Trustee, Found. for Coop. Housing, Overseas Edn. Fund, Internat. Vol. Services; chmn. bd. Ideas, Inc. Found. Mem. Caribbean Studies Assn., Am. Econ. Assn., Am. Assn. Indsl. and Labor Relations, Alpha Kappa Delta. Author articles on labor, indsl. relations. Bd. editors Center for Latin Am. Affairs, N.Y.C. Home: 3517 Cummings Ln Chevy Chase MD 20015 Office: Office Dir Washington Center Ave NW Washington DC 20036

STEPHEN, JOHN ERLE, lawyer, business exec.; b. Eagle Lake, Tex., Sept. 24, 1918; s. John Earnest and Vida Thrall (Klein) S.; J.D., U. Tex., 1941; m. Gloria Yzaguirre-Skidmore, May 16, 1942; children—Vida Leslie, John Lauro Kurt. Admitted to Tex. bar, 1946, D.C. bar, 1956; gen. mgr. Sta. KOPY, Houston, 1946; gen. atty., exec. asst. to pres. Hofheinz Enterprises, Houston, 1947-50; partner firm Hofheinz & Stephen, Houston, 1950-57; v.p., gen. counsel TV Broadcasting Co., Tex. Radio Corp., Gulf Coast Network, Houston, 1953-57; spl. counsel, exec. asst. to mayor City of Houston, 1953-56; v.p., gen. counsel Air Transp. Assn. Am., Washington, 1958-71; gen. counsel Amway Corp., Ada, Mich., 1972—; chief protocol City of Houston, 1953-56; advisor Consulates Gen. of Mex., San Antonio, Houston, New Orleans, Washington, 1956-66; vis. lectr. Harvard U. Grad. Bus. Sch., Washington Fgn. Law Soc., Pacific Agribus. Conf.; cons. in field, mem. U.S. del. various treaty confs. Bd. dirs. Houston Mus. Fine Arts, 1953-57, Contemporary Arts Assn., 1953-57. Served to comdr. USNR, 1941-46. Mem. Am. Bar Assn. (past chmn. council, sect. public utility law), World Peace Through Law Center (past chmn. internat. aviation law com.), Fed. Bar Assn., D.C. Bar Assn., Tex. Bar Assn., FCC Bar Assn., Assn. ICC Practitioners, Am. Judicature Soc.; hon. mem. fgn. law socs. Clubs: Internat., Explorers, Houston Polo, Lakeshore, Saddle and Cycle, Breakfast, Nat. Aviation. Author, editor in field. Home: 6884 Ada Dr Grand Rapids MI 49506 Office: 7575 E Fulton Rd Ada MI 49355

STEPHENS, ALBERT LEE, JR., dist. judge; b. Los Angeles, Feb. 19, 1913; s. Albert Lee and Marie (Clarke) S.; A.B. cum laude, U. So. Calif., 1936; LL.B., 1938; m. Barbara McNeil, Sept. 20, 1939; children—Virginia (Mrs. Bing Stevens Newton), Marylee. Admitted to Calif. bar, 1939, U.S. Supreme Ct. bar, 1944; practice law, 1939-59; judge Superior Ct. Los Angeles, 1959-61, U.S. Dist. Ct., Central Calif., Los Angeles, 1961—, now chief judge. Chmn. bd. coun-Dist. Calif., Los Angeles, 1961—. Chmn. bd. councillors Sch. Internat. Relations, U. So. Calif. Served to lt. USNR, 1943-46. Mem. Am., Los Angeles (trustee 1955-57, 59-61) bar assns., Am. Judicature Soc., World Affairs Council, Chancery Club (pres. 1960-61), Town Hall Los Angeles, Nat. Lawyers Club, Phi Kappa Tau, Phi Alpha Delta, Pi Sigma Alpha, Blackstonian (pres.), Skull and Scales (v.p.). Presbyn. Native Son of Golden West. Clubs: Lawyers (bd. govs. 1950, 55, 56), University (Los Angeles). Office: 312 N Spring St Los Angeles CA 90012*

STEPHENS, ARIAL AVANT, librarian; b. Charlotte, N.C., July 23, 1932; s. Leroy Chapman and Ibbie Annie (Lowe) S.; A.A., Charlotte Coll., 1952; B.A. in History, U. N.C., 1960, M.S. in L.S., 1968; m. Laurie Anne Brockmann, Mar. 26, 1960; children—Laurie Reid, Duncan Gray. Library asst. Mecklenburg County Sch. Library Dept., Charlotte, 1947-52; library asst. Public Library, Charlotte and Mecklenburg County, Charlotte, 1960-61, asst. dir., 1962-71, dir. libraries, 1971—. Served with USN, 1952-56. N.C. State Library scholar, 1961-62. Mem. ALA, Southeastern Library Assn. (chmn. public library sect. 1972-74), N.C. Library Assn., Metrolina Library Assn. (pres. 1965-67), Mecklenburg Library Assn. (pres. 1965-66), Community Execs. Congress (pres. 1971-72). Clubs: Rotary, Torch. Home: 810 Sunnyside Ave Charlotte NC 28204 Office: 310 N Tryon St Charlotte NC 28202

STEPHENS, BART NELSON, fgn. service officer; b. Norfolk, Va., May 29, 1922; s. Bart Dannelly and Lura Lee (Cannon) S.; A.B., Duke, 1943; A.M., Harvard, 1947; lang. tng. Fgn. Service Inst., 1962, 66, 76; m. Betty Barrett Krausz, Jan. 7, 1950; children—Tracey Rainier, Schuyler Barrett, Holly Cannon, Sinah Kendall Lee. Divisional asst. U.S. Dept. State, 1948-49; asst. pub. affairs officer, Salonika, Greece, 1950; asst. info. officer Athens, 1950-51; pub. affairs officer, Patras, Greece, 1951-54, Salonika, 1954; dir. Amerika Haus, Nuernberg, Germany, 1955-59; mgmt. analyst USIA, Washington, 1959-61; cultural attache Am. embassy, Warsaw, Poland, 1963-65; dir. Am. Cultural Center, Saigon, Vietnam, 1967-68; 1st sec., regional projects officer Am. embassy, Vienna, Austria, 1968-70; consul, pub. affairs officer Am. consulate gen., Stuttgart, Germany, 1970-73; area coordinator (Europe), USIA, Washington, 1973, seminar-conf. Programming officer, 1973-74; dep. dir. Office Internat. Arts Affairs, Dept. State, 1974-76; cultural affairs officer Am. embassy, Bangkok, Thailand, 1976—. Served to lt. (j.g.) USNR, 1944-46; PTO. Decorated Bronze Star, Purple Heart. Recipient Meritorious Service award USIA, medal for civilian service in Vietnam, 1968. Mem. Am. Fgn. Service Assn., Soc. Lees of Va., Phi Beta Kappa, Omicron Delta Kappa, Pi Kappa Phi. Methodist. Clubs: Westwood Country (Vienna, Va.); Regency Racquet (McLean, Va.); Royal Bangkok Sports. Home: Am Embassy (USICA) Box 48 APO San Francisco CA 96346

STEPHENS, CLARENCE FRANCIS, educator; b. Gaffney, S.C., July 24, 1917; s. Sam and Jeannette (Morehead) S.; B.S., Johnson C. Smith U., 1938, D.Sc. (hon.), 1954; M.S., U. Mich., 1939, Ph.D., 1943; m. Harriette Josephine Briscoe, Dec. 21, 1942; children—Harriette Jeannette, Clarence Francis. Instr., Prairie View A. and M. Coll., 1940-42, prof., 1946-47; tchr. specialist USN, 1942-43; faculty chmn. dept. math. Morgan State Coll., 1947-62; prof. State U. N.Y. at Geneseo, 1962-69; prof., chmn. dept. math. State U. N.Y. at Potsdam, 1969—. Mem. com. math. examiners Coll. Entrance Exam. Bd.; vis. lectr. Math. Assn. Am.; cons. NSF, Middle States Assn.; mem. Inst. Advanced Study at Princeton, 1953-54. Served with USNR, 1943-45. Recipient certificate for distinguished citizenship State of Md., 1962. Ford fellow, 1953-54. Mem. Am. Math. Soc., Math. Assn. Am., AAUP, Pi Mu Epsilon. Contbr. articles to profl. jours. Home: 81 Pierrepont Ave Potsdam NY 12676

STEPHENS, CLAUDE ODELL, engr., ret. diversified corp. exec.; b. Pike County, Miss., Oct. 6, 1908; s. Buford D. and Carrie Madeline (Collins) S.; B.S. in Petroleum Engring., La. State U. 1932; m. Lois Boyd Fairclough, Sept. 3, 1960. Operator driller helper Tex. Gulf Sulphur Co., Inc. (now Texasgulf Inc.), 1932, various positions, 1932-38, field engr., 1938-42, mgr. Wyo. ops., 1948-51, mgr. gas dept., 1951, v.p., 1952, v.p., gen. mgr., to 1957, pres., 1957—, chmn. bd., 1968-73, chief exec. officer, until 1973, now dir., cons., 1973—. Served to maj. AUS, 1942-46; PTO. Decorated Bronze Star medal. Mem. Am. Mining Congress, Am. Inst. Mining, Metall. and Petroleum Engrs., Am. Petroleum Inst., AAAS, Pi Kappa Alpha. Mason. Clubs: Sky, Links (N.Y.C.). Home: Star Brook Farm Kitchawan Rd Ossining NY 10562 Office: TexasGulf Inc High Ridge Park Stamford CT 06904

STEPHENS, DENNY, librarian; b. Kilgore, Tex., Oct. 3, 1932; s. Shuler S. and G. Marie (Tims) S.; B.S. in English, Hardin Simmons U., 1954; M.A. in L.S., Denver U., 1958. Audio-visual librarian Denver Pub. Library, 1950-56; dir. Hutchinson (Kans.) Pub. Library, 1961-65; adminstrv. asst. Colo. State Library, 1965-67; state librarian Kans. State Library, 1967-71; adminstrv. library officer U.S. Office Edn. Region VII, Kansas City, Mo., 1971-77, acting asst. regional commr. for elementary and secondary edn., 1977, adminstrv. library officer Region VI, Dallas, 1978-79, urban resources library specialist, Washington, 1979; asst. dir. Okla. Dept. Libraries, Oklahoma City, 1980—; TV host sta. KTVH, Wichita, 1963-64; lectr. Hutchinson Arts and Scis. Found., 1964. Served with AUS, 1955-56. Mem. ALA, S.W., Tex. library assns. Home: 4621 N Pennsylvania Oklahoma City OK 73119 Office: 200 NE 18th St Oklahoma City OK 73105

STEPHENS, DONALD JOSEPH, architect; b. Albany, N.Y., Apr. 29, 1918; s. Arthur Everett and Evangeline (Cosgrave) S.; B.Arch., Rensselaer Polytechnic Inst., 1941; m. Jean E. Brown Clausen, Apr. 15, 1950; children—Christian, Linda, Suzanne, Marc, Paul, Thomas. Archtl. engr. Watervliet Arsenal, 1941-44; asso. architect Henry L. Blatner, Albany, 1946-56; pres. Stephens Assos. P.C., Architects, Albany, 1956—; mem. N.Y. State Bd. Architecture, 1976-81. Chmn. Taconic Valley Planning Assn., 1967-72; chmn. Town of Berlin (N.Y.) Planning Bd., 1960-79; pres. bd. edn. Berlin Central Sch. Dist., 1971-72. Served with USN, 1944-46; PTO. Fellow AIA (regional dir. 1974-76; mem. N.Y. State Assn. Architects (Matthew Del Gaudio award 1971). Home: Springhill Center Berlin NY 12022 Office: 41 State St Albany NY 12207

STEPHENS, GEORGE GAYLE, physician; b. Ashburn, Mo., Aug. 6, 1928; s. George Lewis and Helen Cleo (Williamson) S.; A.A., Central Coll., McPherson, Kans., 1946; student Greenville Coll., 1947; B.S., U. Mo., 1950; M.D., Northwestern U., 1952; m. Eula Jean Shields, July 10, 1948; children—Lynn, Joel, Scott, Jan, Julie, Ken, Jean. Intern, Wesley Hosp., Wichita, Kans., 1952-53; gen. practice medicine, Wichita, 1955-67; dir. family practice residency Wesley Med. Center, Wichita, 1967-72; prof. family practice, chmn. dept. family practice Wichita State br. U. Kans. Sch. Medicine, 1972-73; dean Sch. Primary Med. Care, U. Ala., Huntsville, 1973-77, prof., chmn. dept. family practice, Birmingham, 1977—. Served with M.C. AUS, 1953-55. Home: 4300 Overlook Rd Birmingham AL 35222 Office: U Ala Sch Medicine 1016 S 18th St Univ Sta Birmingham AL 35294

STEPHENS, JACK EDWARD, engring. educator; b. Eaton, Ohio, Aug. 17, 1923; s. Harry M. and Mary E. (Galloway) S.; B.S., U. Conn., 1947; M.S., Purdue U., 1955, Ph.D., 1959; m. Virginia M. Ives, June 19, 1948; children—Jay Edward, Jerry Edward, Jill Louise, Jana Lynn. Mem. faculty U. Conn., Storrs, 1946-48, 50—, prof. civil engring., 1962—, head dept., 1966-72, acting dir. Transp. Inst., 1974-75. Owner, Jack E. Stephens Soil Testing Lab., 1958—, Asso. Mart, Inc., 1971—; soil found. cons. A.J. Macchi Engrs., 1958—; v.p., sec. Pilot Engring. Co. Inc., 1973-75. Mem. New Eng. Adv. Council Continuing Edn. for Constrn. Industry, 1972-75; mem. coms. Transp. Research Bd. Mem. adv. council Center Real Estate and Urban Econ. Studies. Served with AUS, 1943-46; ETO. Decorated Belgian cross 2d class. Fellow Automotive Safety Found., ASCE (pres. Conn. 1968);

mem. Conn. Soc. C.E. (pres. 1969, H. Jackson Tibbet award 1972), Am. Soc. Engring. Edn. (George Westinghouse award 1974), Am. Road Builders Assn. (dir. edn. div. 1962-66, 72-76, pres. 1977), Am. Congress Surveying and Mapping, Assn. Asphalt Paving Technologists Am. Soc. Photogrametry, ASTM, Conn. Acad. Sci. and Engring., Sigma Xi, Tau Beta Pi, Phi Eta Sigma, Phi Kappa Phi, Chi Epsilon. Home: 270 S Eagleville Rd Storrs CT 06268

STEPHENS, JACK THOMAS, JR., hosp. adminstr.; b. Birmingham, Ala., Apr. 6, 1947; s. Jack Thomas and Ruth Moss (Carroll) S.; B.S. in Bus. Adminstrn., U. Ark., 1969; M.B.A., U. Fla., 1971; m. Peggy Lee Stoia, June 28, 1969; children—Jack Thomas, III, Christopher John. Hosp. adminstr. extern Sparks Regional Med. Center, Ft. Smith, Ark., 1969; adminstrv. resident Meml. Hosp., Sarasota, Fla., 1971; asst. adminstr., asso. adminstr. Broward Gen. Med. Center, Ft. Lauderdale, Fla., 1971-76, adminstr., 1976—. Active United Way Broward County; asso. mem. Health Systems Agency. Mem. Am. Coll. Hosp. Adminstrs., Am., Fla., So. Fla. (dir. 1978—) hosp. assns., Diversified Bus. Assos., Ft. Lauderdale C. of C. Clubs: Rotary (dir.), Lauderdale Yacht. Home: 915 Cordova Fort Lauderdale FL 33316 Office: 1600 S Andrews Ave Fort Lauderdale FL 33316

STEPHENS, JACKSON THOMAS, investment banker; b. Prattsville, Ark., Aug. 9, 1923; s. Albert Jackson and Ethel Rebecca (Pumphrey) S.; B.S., U.S. Naval Acad., 1947; children—Jackson Thomas, Warren A. With Stephens Inc., Little Rock, 1946—, 1947-57, pres., 1957—. Trustee, U. Ark., 1948-58. Office: Stephens Bldg 114 E Capitol Ave PO Box 3507 Little Rock AR 72201

STEPHENS, JACKSON THOMAS, investment exec.; b. Prattsville, Ark., Aug. 9, 1923; s. Albert Jackson and Ethel Rebecca (Pumphrey) S.; grad. Columbia Mil. Acad., Tenn., 1941; student U. Ark., 1941-43; B.S., U.S. Naval Acad., 1946; children—Jackson Thomas, Warren Amerine. Pres., Stephens, Inc., Little Rock, Stephens Prodn. Co.; chmn. bd. Union Life Ins. Co., Little Rock; dir. Wal Mart Stores. Trustee U. Ark., 1948-57. Home: Little Rock AR Office Stephens Bldg Little Rock AR 72201

STEPHENS, JOHN BOYD, newspaperman; b. Elmira, N.Y., May 30, 1905; s. Lee A. and Lula (Boyd) S.; A.B., U. Calif., 1927; m. Dorothy Jarvis, July 2, 1927; 1 son, Eric Paul. Editor, Santa Maria (Calif.) Times, 1927-34; instr. polit. sci. U. Calif., 1933-39; city editor, mng. editor, asso. editor San Diego Sun, 1934-39; city editor Houston Press, 1939-42, mng. editor, 1946-49; instr. journalism U. Houston, 1948-49; news editor N.Y. World-Telegram and Sun, 1949-54; mng. editor Indpls. Times, 1954-60; exec. editor Scripps-Howard News, Cleve., 1960-63, editor, 1963-76. Served with 7th Fleet, USNR, 1942-46; capt. USNR ret. Home: 17105 W Bernardo Dr Apt 207 San Diego CA 92127

STEPHENS, JOHN CALHOUN, JR., educator; b. Augusta, Ga., July 23, 1916; s. John Calhoun and Lillian (Cason) S.; A.B., Emory U., 1937, M.A., 1938; Ph.D., Harvard, 1950; m. Enid Leslie Bryan, June 7, 1947; 1 dau., Anne Howard. Tchr., Dalton (Ga.) High Sch., 1938-39; instr. English, Clemson Coll., 1939-41; faculty Emory U, Atlanta, 1946-73, prof. English, 1960-73, chmn. dept., 1959-61, dean Coll., 1961-73; prof. English, U. Ga., Athens, 1973—, dean Franklin Coll. Arts and Scis., 1973-77; mem. policy Council Undergrad. Assessment Program Ednl. Testing Service. Guggenheim fellow, 1957-58. Served to maj. USAAF, 1941-46, lt. col. USAF Res., ret. Mem. So., Atlantic modern lang. assns., Ch., Ga. Hist. Soc., English-Speaking Union, Modern Lang. Assn. Am., Am. Soc. Eighteenth-Century Studies, Internat. Berkeley Soc., Nat. Council Tchrs. English, Phi Beta Kappa, Sigma Alpha Epsilon, Omicron Delta Kappa. Democrat. Mem. P.E. Ch. (ordained perpetual deacon 1957). Club: Harvard (Atlanta). Author articles, essays, poems, revs. Editor: Longsword, 1957; Georgia, A Poem 1736, 1950; Poems of Zechariah Worrell, 1764-1834, 1958. Home: 1648 E Clifton Rd NE Atlanta GA 30307

STEPHENS, JOHN FRED, ins. co. exec.; b. Dallas, Jan. 26, 1916; s. Thomas Parsons and Albina Calvin (Stanley) S.; B.A. in Math., U. Tex., 1938; m. Ruth Marian Thornton, Sept. 14, 1940; children—Patricia Ann, John Fred, Thomas Thornton. With Employers Casualty Co. and Tex. Employers Ins. Assn., Dallas, 1938—, asst. actuary, 1943-48, actuary, 1948-59, v.p., actuary of cos., 1959-67, sr. v.p., 1967-69, exec. v.p., 1969-72, pres., chmn. bd., 1972—; dir. Rep. Nat. Bank, Dallas. Bd. dirs. United Way of Met. Dallas, Am. Cancer Soc., Dallas Council World Affairs, Central Bus. Dist., Dallas Citizens Council, Tex. Research League; bd. dirs., pres. Dallas Zool. Soc.; pres., mem. exec. bd. Circle Ten council Boy Scouts Am. Served with USMC, 1943-46. Mem. Dallas C. of C. (dir.), Am. Acad. Actuaries, Am. Inst. Property and Liability Underwriters (trustee, bd. govs.), Assn. Fire and Casualty Cos. Tex. (exec. com.), Tex. Ins. Adv. Assn., Dallas C. of C. (dir.). Baptist. Clubs: Citadel (Austin); City, Ins., Northwood Country (Dallas). Home: 3704 Caruth St Dallas TX 75225 Office: 423 S Akard St Dallas TX 75202

STEPHENS, LOUIS CORNELIUS, JR., ins. co. exec.; b. Dunn, N.C., Dec. 19, 1921; s. Louis Cornelius and Agnes (Warren) S.; B.S., U. N.C., 1942; M.B.A., Harvard U., 1947; m. Mary Adams, Sept. 6, 1952; children—Michael W., Mary A., Louis Cornelius III, Anne M., Suzanne G., Joan R., Melanie L., Peter W. With Pilot Life Ins. Co., Greensboro, N.C., 1949—, v.p., treas., 1965-66, mem. exec. com., 1968, sr. v.p., exec. v.p., 1970, pres., 1971—; pres., dir. JP Investment Mgmt. Co.; v.p., dir. Jefferson-Pilot Corp.; dir. Jefferson-Pilot & So. Fire & Casualty Cos., Jefferson-Pilot Title Ins. Co.; treas. JP Growth Fund, Inc. Past pres. United Community Services. Bd. dirs. Excellence Fund U. N.C. at Greensboro, N.C. Leadership Inst., Research Triangle Inst., Salem Coll. and Acad., Ecumenical Inst. Belmont Abbey Coll. Served with USNR, World War II. Mem. N.C., Richmond socs. fin. analysts, Greensboro C. of C. (dir.). Office: Pilot Life Ins Co PO Box 20727 Greensboro NC 27420

STEPHENS, NORVAL BLAIR, JR., advt. agy. exec.; b. Chgo., Nov. 20, 1928; s. Norval Blair and Ethel Margaret (Lewis) S.; B.A., DePauw U., 1951; M.B.A., U. Chgo., 1959; m. Diane Forst, Sept. 29, 1951; children—Jill E., John G., Sandra J. (dec.), Katherine B., James N. Asst. to v.p. ops. Walgreen Drug Co., Chgo., 1953-56; with Needham, Harper & Steers (formerly Needham, Louis & Brorby), N.Y.C., 1956—, v.p., 1964-70, sr. v.p., 1970-72, exec. v.p. internat., 1972-74, exec. v.p., mng. dir. N.Y.C. 1974-75, exec. v.p. Chgo. office, 1975—, also dir.; pres. Deltacom, N.Y.C., 1971-76; dir. USP Needham Australia, Needham, Harper & Steers Can. Mem. Pelham (N.Y.) Bd. Edn., 1972-75; trustee Village of Arlington Heights, Ill., 1961-65; commr., chmn. Plan Commn. Arlington Heights, 1965-67. Trustee Meml. Library, Arlington Heights, 1966-67, Arlington Heights United Fund, 1963-67; bd. dirs. Lake Forest (Ill.) Children's Home, 1966-67, Northwest Community Hosp. Found., Arlington Heights, 1976—, Harper Coll. Ednl. Found., Palatine, Ill., 1977—, Barrington Area Devel. Council, 1978—; bd. visitors, dir. alumni bd. DePauw U., 1979—. Served with USMCR, 1951-53. Named Young Man of Year, Arlington Heights Jaycees, 1964, Rector award DePauw U., 1976. Mem. Internat. Advt. Assn., Chgo. DePauw U. Alumni Assn. (pres. 1977—), Phi Beta Kappa, Delta Tau Delta. Presbyterian (ruling elder). Club: Larchmont Yacht. Home: 107 Fox Hunt Trail Barrington IL 60010 Office: Needham Harper & Steers Inc 401 N Michigan Ave Chicago IL 60611. *I view my life not as a passage but a daily renewing challenge: to be better; to be a better father, husband, brother, son; to return each day an honest day's work; to bear witness to my beliefs and my faith; to serve my fellowman. I seek a whole life and a life of rewarding parts, each a lesson and an experience.*

STEPHENS, OLIN JAMES, II, yacht designer, naval architect; b. N.Y.C., Apr. 13, 1908; s. Roderick and Marguerite (Dulon) S.; student Mass. Inst. Tech., 1926-27; M.S. (hon.), Stevens Inst. Tech.; M.A. (hon.), Brown U.; m. Florence Reynolds, Oct. 21, 1930; children—Olin James III, Samuel R. Draftsman, Henry J. Gielow, N.Y.C., 1927-28, P.L. Rhodes, N.Y.C., 1928; formed with Drake H. Sparkman firm of Sparkman & Stephens, 1928, Inc., 1929, serving as chmn., dir. Yachts designed include: Cherokee, Dorade, 1930; Stormy Weather, 1934; Lulu, Ranger (with W. Starling Burgess), 1937; Baruna, Blitzen, Goose, 1938; Vim, Gesture, 1939; Llanoria, 1948; Finisterre, 1954; Columbia, 1958; Constellation 1964; Intrepid, 1967; Charisma, Morning Cloud, 1971; Courageous, 1974; Enterprise, 1977, Freedom, 1979, others; design agt. U.S. Navy, 1939—. Fellow Soc. Naval Architects and Marine Engrs.; mem. Am. Boat and Yacht Council (pres. 1959, 60), N.Am. Yacht Racing Union, Offshore Racing Council (chmn. internat. tech. mem. 1967-73, 76-79). Clubs: N.Y. Yacht, Manhasset Bay (hon.); Cruising Club of Am.; Royal Ocean Racing (Eng.), Royal Thames Yacht (London). Home: PO Box 346 Putney VT 05346 Office: 79 Madison Ave New York City NY 10016

STEPHENS, RALPH HAYGOOD, publishing exec.; b. Wrens, Ga., Oct. 4, 1910; s. Charles Wynn and Annie May (Barton) S.; B.S., Ga. So. Coll., 1933; M.A., U. Ga., 1939; m. Eugenia Doughtie, Oct. 4, 1948; 1 son, Ralph Haygood. High sch. prin., 1933-36; prof. English, U. Ga., 1939-41, prof. journalism, 1949-50; asst. dir. U. Ga. Press, 1941-43, 45-49, dir., 1950—. Served with AUS, 1943-45. Mem. Assn. Am. Univ. Presses (v.p. 1962), Athens Hist. Soc., South Atlantic Modern Lang. Assn., Ga. Writers Assn., Phi Beta Kappa (treas. U. Ga. chpt. 1964—). Episcopalian. Kiwanian. Club: Athens Country. Home: 235 McWhorter Dr Athens GA 30601 Office: U Ga Athens GA 30602

STEPHENS, ROBERT F., judge; b. Covington, Ky., Aug. 16, 1927; student Ind. U.; LL.B., U. Ky., 1951. Admitted to Ky. bar, 1951; asst. atty. Fayette County (Ky.), 1964-69; judge Fayette County, 1969-75; atty. gen. Ky., Frankfort, 1976-79; justice Supreme Ct. Ky., Frankfort, 1979—. Bd. dirs. Nat. Assn. Counties, 1973-75; 1st pres. Ky. Assn. Counties; 1st chmn. Bluegrass Area Devel. Dist. Served with USN, World War II. Named Outstanding County Judge of Ky., 1972. Democrat. Office: Ky Supreme Ct State Capitol Bldg Frankfort KY 40601

STEPHENS, ROBERT GRIER, JR., ret. congressman, lawyer; b. Atlanta, Aug. 14, 1913; s. Robert Grier and Martha Lucy (Evans) S.; A.B., U. Ga., 1935, M.A., 1937, LL.B. cum laude, 1941; exchange student U. Hamburg (Germany), 1935-36; m. Grace Winston, July 20, 1938; children—Grace Winston (Mrs. D.R. Bianchi), Robert Grier III, Mary Winston, Lawton Evans. Mem. staff dept. history and polit. sci. U. Ga., Athens, 1936-41, 46; admitted to Ga. bar, 1941; practiced in Athens, 1946-61; city atty., Athens, 1947-50; mem. Ga. Senate, 50th Dist., 1951-53, Ga. Ho. of Reps. from Clarke County, 1953-59; mem. 87-94th Congresses, 10th Dist. Ga. Gen. counsel Ga. Press Assn., 1956-61; mem. adv. com. naval affairs 6th Naval Dist., 1959—. Mem. Ga. Democratic Exec. Com. Bd. dirs. Athens YMCA, 1949—. Served with AUS, 1941-46; legal staff Nuremberg Trial, 1945; lt. col. Res. Mem. Ga. Bar Assn., Phi Beta Kappa, Blue Key, Phi Kappa Phi, Omicron Delta Kappa, Kappa Alpha. Presbyn. (elder). Kiwanian (lt. gov.). Home: 435 Woodward Way Athens GA 30606 Office: 304 E Washington St Athens GA 30601

STEPHENS, ROTHWELL CLIFFORD, emeritus educator; b. Kansas City, Mo., Dec. 30, 1906; s. William Franklin and Beulah (McGuire) S.; B.F.A., U. Okla., 1926, B.A., 1927, M.A., 1929; Ph.D., U. Iowa, 1931; postdoctoral Inst. Advanced Study, Princeton, 1939-40; m. Margaret Clark, Sept. 3, 1930; 1 son, John Kirker. Grad. asst. U. Okla., 1928-29, U. Iowa, 1929-31; instr. Knox Coll., Galesburg, Ill., 1931-35, asst. prof. 1935-39, sec. faculty, 1936-46, asso. prof., 1939-40, prof. math., 1940-54, chmn. dept. math., 1944-70, Hitchcock prof., 1954-59, Distinguished Service prof., 1959-75, emeritus, 1975—, registrar, 1946-51; instr. Princeton, 1939-40, vis. fellow, 1952-53, Fund for Advancement Edn. fellow, 1952-53; prof. NSF Summer Inst. State U. N.Y., 1958. Mem. regional selection com. Woodrow Wilson Nat. Fellowship Found. Mem. Am. Statis. Assn., Inst. Math. Statistics, Nat. Council Tchrs. Math. (Outstanding Service in Math. Edn. award 1975), Am. Math. Soc., Math. Assn. Am. (chmn. Ill. sect. 1954-55, chmn. vis. lectr. com. 1958-60, gov. 1959-62), AAUP, Ill. Council Tchrs. Math. (v.p. 1954-55, hon., life), Phi Beta Kappa, Sigma Xi, Delta Tau Delta, Phi Mu Alpha, Pi Mu Epsilon, Gamma Alpha, Blue Key. Episcopalian (lay reader). Author: (with H.G. Ayre) A First Course in Analytic Geometry. Contbr. articles on math. and econs. to profl. jours. Home: 652 Reed Ave Norman OK 73071

STEPHENS, ROY MALCOLM, textile co. exec.; b. Caryville, Fla., Aug. 26, 1914; s. Fred and Clemie C. (Mouring) S.; student indsl. mgmt. LaSalle Extension U., 1938; m. Lucile Balkcom, June 29, 1940; children—Roy Malcolm, Carole, Kay. Plant mgr. standards dept. Bibb Mfg. Co., 1935-37, office mgr., 1937-39, textile overseer, 1939, textile asst. supt., 1939-44, textile gen. supt., 1944-46; asst. div. mgr. Riverside div. Dan River Mills, Inc. (co. name changed to Dan River Inc.), Danville, Va., 1946-49, div. mgr., 1950, asst. gen. supt., 1950-52, supt. grey mfg., 1952-55, v.p., gen. supt., 1955-62, exec. v.p., 1962-66, pres. Danville div., corp. exec. v.p., 1966-71, corp. exec. v.p. mfg., 1971—, also dir.; dir. Norfolk, Franklin & Danville Ry. Co., 1st & Mchts. Corp., Richmond, Va., 1st & Mchts. Nat. Bank. Bd. dirs., past chmn. Nat. Tobacco-Textile Mus.; mem. exec. com., dir. Danville Meml. Hosp.; judge Va. Cultural Laureate Found. Mem. Am. Textile Mfrs. Inst., Newcomen Soc., Va. Mfrs. Assn. (chmn. 1973-74, mem. exec. com.). Home: Dans Hill Danville VA 24541 Office: Dan River Inc Danville VA 24541

STEPHENS, THOMAS MARON, educator; b. Youngstown, Ohio, June 15, 1931; s. Thomas and Mary (Hanna) S.; B.S., Youngstown Coll., 1955; M.Ed., Kent State U., 1957; Ph.D., U. Pitts., 1966; m. Evelyn Kleshock, July 1, 1955. Asso. prof. edn. U. Pitts., 1966-70; prof. edn., chmn. dept. exceptional children, exec. dir. Nat. Center Ednl. Media and Materials for Handicapped, Ohio State U., 1970—; mem. Higher Edn. Consortium for Spl. Edn., chmn., 1976-77; pub., pres. Cedars Press, Inc. U.S. Office of Edn. fellow, 1964-65. Mem. State Dirs. for Gifted (pres. 1962-63), Council Exceptional Children (gov.), Council Children with Behavioral Disorders (pres. 1972-73). Author: Directive Teaching of Children with Learning and Behavioral Handicaps, 2d edit., 1975; Implementing Behavioral Approaches in Elementary and Secondary Schools, 1975; Teaching Skills to Children with Learning and Behavioral Disorders, 1977; Teaching of Children Basic Skills: A Curriculum Handbook, 1978; Social Skills In The Classroom, 1978; dir. Jour. Sch. Psychology, 1965-75; exec. editor The Directive Tchr.; asso. editor Exceptional Children Jour., Behavior Disorder Jour., Viewpoints in Teaching. contbr. articles to profl. jours. Home: 1753 Blue Ash Pl Columbus OH 43229

STEPHENS, WARREN CLAYTON, mfg. co. exec.; b. Mobile, Ala., Apr. 6, 1942; s. Warren Clayton and Ellen Story (Fretz) S.; B.A. in Econs., Notre Dame U., 1964; M.B.A. in Fin., Stanford U., 1966; m. Millicent A. Wynne, Dec. 28, 1963; children—Warren Clayton, III, Brent Christopher, Craig Gordon, Keith Wynne. Second v.p. Chase Manhattan Bank, N.Y.C., 1966-69; corp. v.p., div. pres. Genway Corp., Chgo., 1969-72; v.p. fin. and adminstrn. Wheelabrator Fin. Corp., Hampton, N.H., 1972-74; pres. Wheelabrator Energy Systems, Inc., Hampton, 1974-76; v.p., treas. Wheelabrator-Frye, Inc., Hampton, 1976—, v.p. fin. internat. div., 1979—; bd. dirs., treas. N.H. Bus. and Industry Assn., 1977—. Mem. Treasurers Club New Eng., U. Notre Dame Alumni Assn. (nat. alumni sec. 1964-74), Stanford U. Bus. Sch. Assn. Roman Catholic. Author papers in field. Home: 36 Pine St Exeter NH 03833 Office: Wheelabrator-Frye Inc Liberty Ln Hampton NH 03842

STEPHENS, WILLIAM EDWARDS, educator, physicist; b. St. Louis, May 29, 1912 s. Eugene and Marie P. (Gelwicks) S.; A.B., Washington U., 1932, M.S., 1934; Ph.D., Calif. Inst. Tech., 1938; m. Helen Elizabeth Burnite, Oct. 27, 1942; children—Richard Burnite, William Massie. Westinghouse Research fellow, East Pittsburgh, 1938-40; lectr. physics U. Pitts., 1938-39; instr. Stanford U., 1940-41; instr. U. Pa., Phila., 1941-42, asst. prof., 1942-46, asso. prof., 1946-48, prof., 1948—, chmn. dept. physics, 1955-56, 63-68, dean Coll. Arts and Scis., 1968-74. Vis. prof. U. Zurich, 1957, 69; sci. investigator NDRC, 1942-46; vis. fellow Australian Nat. U., 1974, Princeton U., 1975. Fellow Am. Phys. Soc.; mem. AAUP, AAAS, Am. Inst. Physics, Phi Beta Kappa, Sigma Xi. Author: (With G.P. Harnwell) Atomic Physics, 1955. Editor: Nuclear Fission and Atomic Energy, 1950. Home: 105 Rolling Rd Carroll Park Philadelphia PA 19151

STEPHENS, WILLIAM THEODORE, lawyer, business exec.; b. Balt., Mar. 31, 1922; s. William A. and Mildred (Griffin) S.; student Balt. City Coll., 1939-41, U. Md., 1946-47; A.B., J.D., George Washington U., 1950, postgrad., 1951; m. Arlene Alice Lesti, June 2, 1958; children—William Theodore, Renee Adena. Admitted to D.C. bar, 1951; mem. firm J.L. Green, Washington, 1950-51, J.M. Cooper, Washington, 1952-54; own law firm William T. Stephens, Washington, 1955—; sec. gen. counsel, dir. Exotech, Inc., Gaithersburg, Md., KHI Corp., Fairfax, Va.; dir., prin. owner BARBCO, Inc. (Nev.), Fairfax Racquet Club; gen. counsel, dir. Frat. Housing Corp., Washington; gen. counsel various nat. corps.; mem. adv. bd. Hamilton Bank & Trust Co. Mem. exec. com. Nat. Com. on Uniform Traffic Laws and Ordinances, 1967—. Trustee Ophthalmic Research Found., Washington, Fairfax-Brewster Sch., Falls Church, Va., Am. Bikeways Found., Washington. Served to 1st lt. AUS, 1941-45. Mem. Bar Assn. D.C. (com. taxation 1959-68), Am. (sec. taxation 1959—, sec. corps, banking and bus. law 1960—), Md., Va. bar assns., XVI Corps Assn. (pres. 1967), Kappa Alpha Order, Delta Theta Phi. Clubs: Commonwealth (Calif.); Univ., Capitol Hill (Washington); Army-Navy Country (Arlington, Va.); Regency Racquet (McLean, Va.); Jockey, Racquet Club Internat. (Miami, Fla.); Montego Bay (Jamaica); Cap d'Antibes (France). Home: Unit 1702 1800 Old Meadow Rd PO Drawer BB McLean VA 22101 also 881 Ocean Dr Key Biscayne FL 33149 Office: Regency at McLean 1800 Old Meadow Rd McLean VA 22101 also 1050 17th St NW Suite 900 Washington DC 20036

STEPHENS, WILLIAM THOMAS, paper co. exec.; b. Crosset, Ark., Sept. 2, 1944; s. William Edgar and Vera Inej (Miller) S.; B.S., U. Ark., 1965, M.S., 1966; children—Elizabeth Lee, Vera Ellen. With Olinkraft, Inc., West Monroe, La., 1966—, dir. fin. planning, 1974-76, treas., 1976-78, v.p., 1978—. Mem. Am. Inst. Indsl. Engrs. Republican. Methodist. Clubs: Chauvin Racquet, Lotus. Home: 2304 Hawthorne Monroe LA 71201 Office: PO Box 488 West Monroe LA 71291

STEPHENSON, CHARLES BRUCE, educator, astronomer; b. Little Rock, Feb. 9, 1929; s. Chauncey Alvaro and Ona (Richards) S.; student Little Rock Jr. Coll., 1946-47; B.S. in Math., U. Chgo., 1949, M.S. in Astronomy, 1951; Ph.D., U. Calif., Berkeley, 1955-58; m. Elizabeth Griffith Strong, June 21, 1952. With Army Map Service Lunar occultation Project, U.S. Army, 1953-55; mem. faculty Case Western Reserve U. (formerly Case Inst. Tech.), Cleve., 1958-68, asso. prof. astronomy, 1964-68, prof. astronomy 1968—. Mem. Internat. Astron. Union, Am. Astron. Soc., AAAS. Contbr. to profl. jours. Research on spectral classification procedures for stars by objective prism method; discovered 1st white dwarf stars to be found by the objective prism method; 2d preoutburst spectrum of a nonrecurrent nova (exploding star) to be observed in 40 years; co-discoverer optical counterpart of the Scorpius X-Ray source. Home: 3362 Henderson Rd Cleveland Heights OH 44112 Office: Case Western Res U Dept Astronomy Cleveland OH 44106

STEPHENSON, CHARLES EUGENE, interior designer and decorator; b. Portsmouth, Va., s. C. Eugene and Eva May (Robertson) S.; student Coll. William and Mary; grad. Parsons Sch. Design, N.Y.C. and Paris, France; student camouflage, Pratt Inst., 1942; m. Olive M. Thompson, Nov. 2, 1940. Partner C. Eugene Stephenson Assos., N.Y.C., 1946-70; cons. to Am. mfrs. of home furnishings products on interior decoration, design, lighting and color; head first group of designers to visit Europe under auspices of Am. Inst. Interior Designers, 1955; design cons. to Ladie's Home Jour. on editorial Kitchens, 1945-52; conducted decorating sessions N.Y. Herald Tribune Bride's Sch., 1957-61. Founder, pres. Resources Council Inc., 1958. Co-designer interiors and furnishings House Good Taste, N.Y. World's Fair, 1964-65. Trustee Parsons Sch. Design, 1955-70. Recipient 1961 Am. Inst. Interior Designers Internat. Design award for research and devel., 1961; Nat. Assn. Home Builders award for meritorious service to housing industry; medal Am. C. of C. for Italy, 1955. Fellow Am. Inst. Interior Designers (nat. pres. 1953-55; gov. 1951-60, hon. gov. 1960-74), Am. Soc. Interior Designers (past pres. Conn. chpt. 1975-76, hon. gov. 1975—). Author: (with E. W. Commery) How To Decorate and Light Your Home, 1955. Home: Sugar Hill Jeremy Swamp Rd Southbury CT 06488 Office: Jeremy Swamp Rd Southbury CT 06488

STEPHENSON, DAVID A., hydrogeologist; b. Moline, Ill., July 1, 1936; s. Wilbert A. and Marie E. (Means) S.; student Colo. Sch. Mines, 1954-55; B.A., Augustana Coll., 1958; M.S., Wash. State U., 1961; Ph.D., U. Ill., 1965; m. Maryann Kay Olson, Aug. 28, 1958; children—Laura Ann, Jenny Leigh. Research asso. Desert Research Inst., Reno, 1962-64; geologist Ill. State Geol. Survey, Urbana, 1961, 64-65; prof. geology U. Wis.-Madison, 1965-79; chief water resources sect. Wis. Geol. Survey, Madison, 1977-79; chief water resources sect. Western region office Woodward-Clyde Cons., San Francisco, 1979—; chmn. com. on groundwater resources in relation to coal mining NRC; mem. U.S. Nat. Com. on Sci. Hydrology; mem. U.S. del. UNESCO Com. on Impacts of Man on Hydrologic Cycle. Mem. Assn. Profl. Geol. Scientists, Geol. Soc. Am., Am. Water Resources Assn., Internat. Water Resources Assn., Internat. Assn. Hydrogeologists, Nat. Water Well Assn. Contbr. articles to profl. jours. Home: 5917 Hempstead Rd Madison WI 53711 Office: Suite 700 3 Embarcadero San Francisco CA 94111

STEPHENSON, DONALD EUGENE, lawyer; b. Kansas City, Kans., Dec. 13, 1930; s. George Emmet and Mae (Capps) S.; B.S., U. Kans., 1952, LL.B., 1958; m. Nancy Sue Stephenson, Sept. 26, 1958; children—Jill Diane, Jennifer Dawn, Douglas Eric. Admitted to Kans. bar, 1959, Ariz. bar, 1964, also U.S. Supreme Ct.; asso. mem. firm Weeks, Thomas, Lysaught, Bingham & Mustain, Kansas City, Kans., 1958-63; with Del E. Webb Corp., Phoenix, 1963-77 v.p., sec., gen. counsel, 1966-77; partner firm Jones, Teilborg, Sanders, Haga, Parks & Stephenson, Phoenix, 1977-78; v.p., asso. gen. counsel Sheraton Corp., Boston, 1978-79, exec. v.p., 1979—, also dir. Chmn. Ariz. adv. com., 8 state project Designing Edn. for Future, 1966-69. Bd. dirs. Theodore Roosevelt council Boy Scouts Am., 1971-78, pres. council, 1978; met. bd. dirs. YMCA Phoenix and Valley of Sun, 1975; bd. dirs. Mass. Bay Federated Councils, 1978; trustee Gordon Coll., Lexington Christian Acad., 1979. Served with USNR, 1953-56. Recipient Phi Delta Kappa Outstanding Contbn. to Edn. award, 1968. Mem. Phoenix Met. C. of C. (chmn. edn. com. 1971-73, outstanding service award 1973), Am., Kans., Ariz., Maricopa County bar assns., Am. Judicature Soc., Am. Soc. Corp. Secs., Am. Arbitrarion Assn. (Ariz. adv. council 1970—), Inst. Bus. Planning (nat. edit. adv. bd. 1972-73). Rotarian. Home: 6 Leeland Terr Lexington MA 02173 Office: Sheraton Corp 60 State St Boston MA 02173

STEPHENSON, HAROLD F., advt. exec.; b. N.Y.C., 1915; M.B.A., N.Y. U., 1942; children—Peter, Brian. Exec. v.p. sec., treas., dir. D'Arcy MacManus & Masius, Inc. Bd. dirs. Birmingham Community House. Clubs: Orchard Lake Country, Pauma Valley Country, Bloomfield Open Hunt (dir.), Turtle Creek. Home: 617 N Woodward Birmingham MI 48009 also 74 Turtle Creek Dr Tequesta FL 33458 Office: 10 W Long Lake Rd Bloomfield Hills MI 48013

STEPHENSON, HERMAN HOWARD, banker; b. Wichita, Kans., July 15, 1929; s. Herman Horace and Edith May (Wayland) S.; B.A., U. Mich., 1950; J.D., U. Mo. at Kansas City, 1958; m. Virginia Anne Ross, Dec. 24, 1950; children—Ross Wayland, Neal Bevan, Jann Edith. Admitted to Kans. bar, 1958; mem. fgn. dept. City Nat. Bank, Kansas City, Mo., 1952-54; asst. sec. City Bond & Mortgage Co., Kansas City, Mo., 1954-59; with Bank of Hawaii, Honolulu, 1959—, asst. cashier, 1960-62, v.p., 1962-68, sr. v.p., 1968-72, exec. v.p., 1972—; v.p., treas. Hawaii Bancorp., Inc.; chmn. Hawaii Computer Services; trustee Realty & Mortgage Investors of Pacific; dir. Banque de Tahiti, Bank of Hawaii Internat., Bank of New Caledonia Bankoh Advisory Corp. Chmn. urban renewal com. Oahu Devel. Conf., 1966-68, mem. comprehensive planning com., 1970-71. Trustee, past pres. Tax Found. Hawaii; former trustee Hawaii Conf. Found., United Ch. of Christ; trustee Realty and Mortgage Investors of the Pacific. Served with U.S. Army, 1950-52. Mem. Am. Bankers Assn. (past chmn. exec. com. housing and real estate fin. div., dir. 1976-77, mem. governing council 1976-77), Am., Kans. bar assns., Mortgage Bankers Assn. Hawaii (past pres.), Kappa Sigma, Pi Eta Sigma. Clubs: Rotary, Oahu Country, Pacific, Waialae. Home: 5239 Poola St Honolulu HI 96821 Office: PO Box 2900 Honolulu HI 96846

STEPHENSON, HUGH EDWARD, JR., physician, educator; b. Columbia, Mo., June 1, 1922; s. Hugh Edward and Doris (Pryor) S.; A.B., B.S., U. Mo., 1943; M.D., Washington U., St. Louis, 1945; m. Sarah Norfleet Dickinson, Aug. 15, 1964; children—Hugh Edward III, Ann Dunlop. Mem. faculty U. Mo. Sch. Medicine, Columbia, 1953—, prof. surgery, 1956—, chmn. dept. surgery, 1956-60, chief div. gen. surgery, 1976—. Markle scholar acad. medicine, 1954-60. Named one of Ten Outstanding Young Men of Nation Nat. Jr. C. of C., 1956, James IV Surg. Traveler, Gt. Britain, 1962. Diplomate Am. Bd. Surgery, Am. Bd. Thoracic Surgery. Mem. AMA, A.C.S., Vascular Surgery, Soc. Thoracic Surgeons, So. Thoracic Surg. Assn., Beta Theta Pi (trustee, v.p., pres. gen. frat. 1978-81). Baptist. Author: Cardiac Arrest and Resuscitation, 4th edit.; Immediate Care of the Acutely Ill and Injured, 2d edit., 1974. Contbr. articles to profl. jours. Home: 5 Danforth Circle Columbia MO 65201 Office: 807 Stadium Rd Columbia MO 65201

STEPHENSON, JAMES BENNETT, state ct. justice; b. Greenup, Ky., Jan. 26, 1916; s. Elmer D. and Emabel (Bennett) S.; A.B., U. Ky., Lexington, 1938, LL.B., 1951; m. Elizabeth Campbell Paddison, June 28, 1941; children—Martha Bennett, Jane Marsh. Admitted to Ky. bar, 1939; practice in Pikeville, Ky., 1940-57; circuit judge Div. I 35th Jud. Dist., Pike County, 1957-73; justice Ky. Ct. Appeals, 1973-75; justice Supreme Ct. Ky., 1975—. 1973—. Mem. Jud. Council Ky., 1959-61. Bd. dirs. Meth. Hosp., Pikeville. Served to capt. USAAF, 1942-45. Mem. Sigma Chi, Phi Delta Phi. Democrat. Methodist (chmn. finance com. 1955-70; chmn. ofcl. bd. 1971-72; Ky. Conf. Com. on World Service and Finance 1969-72). Home: 108 Walnut Dr Pikeville KY 41501 Office: 239 State Capitol Frankfort KY 40601

STEPHENSON, MARY RITA, assn. exec.; b. Toronto, Ont., Can., Mar. 27, 1917; d. John Alexander and Marie Josephine (Kennedy) Pickett; student U. Toronto, 1933-36; m. Harald Jon Stephenson, June 19, 1945 (div. 1969); children—Helga Maria, Fridrik Jon, Helen Veronica, Donald Joseph. Advt., sales promotion mgr. Assos. Textiles, Montreal, Que., Can., 1941-45; head pub. relations dept. Cardon Rose Ltd., Montreal, 1968-73; exec. dir., founder Fashion Designers Assn. of Can. Ltd., Montreal, 1974—; v.p. Fashion/Canada; bd. dirs. Can. Colour Service. Mem. Fashion Group Internat., Inst. Assn. Execs. Roman Catholic. Home: 675 Roselawn Ave Toronto ON M5N 1L2 Canada Office: 320 Davenport Rd Toronto ON M5R 1K6 Canada

STEPHENSON, REVIS LINDSAY, engring co. exec.; b. Westboro, Ottawa, Can., Feb. 12, 1910; s. Roy Lindsay and Helen (Scobie) S.; B.S. in Mech. Engring., Clarkson Coll. Tech., 1934; m. Josephine Papa, Oct. 24, 1936; children—Revis L., Carol Roye, Lorne Jae. Mech. engr. L.J. Wing Mfg. Co., N.Y.C., 1934-36; with U.S. Hoffman Machinery Corp., N.Y.C., 1936-61, gen. mgr., 1952-54, v.p., 1954-55, v.p., dir., 1955-57, exec. v.p., dir., also dir. fgn. and export ops., 1957-61; pres., dir. Hoffman Internat. Corp., 1957-63, Belson Corp., N.Y.C., 1963-67; chmn., dir., chief exec. Clarkson Industries, Inc., N.Y.C., and Ridgefield Conn., 1967—; chmn. bd. Atmos Engring. Co., Kenilworth, N.J., 1972—; chmn., dir. Hoffman Air & Filtration Systems, Ltd., Altrincham, Cheshire, Eng., Hoffman Air & Filtration Systems A.G., Zug, Switzerland, Hoffman Air & Filtration Systems (Mexico) S.A. de C.V., Mexico City; pres., dir. Hoffman Air & Filtration Systems S.r.l., Milano, Italy, Hoffman Systems Installation Co., Syracuse, N.Y., Hoffman Industries of Can., Ltd., Toronto, Ont.; exec. v.p., dir. Stanton Foundry, Inc., Solvoy, N.Y.; dir. Hoffman Air & Filtration Systems G.m.b.H., Dusseldorf, Germany, Hoffman Air & Filtration Systems S.A.R.L., Paris France, R. McIvor & Sons Ltd., Stockport Eng., Hoffman do Brasil Sistemas de Ar e Filtragem Ltda., Sao Paulo, Brazil, Nippon Hoffman K.K., Tokyo; bd. govs. Am. Stock Exchange; exec. officer Com. Publicly Owned Cos., N.Y.C. Trustee Clarkson Coll. Tech., Potsdam, N.Y. Mem. Soc. Am. Mil. Engrs., Am. Ordnance Assn., ASME, Assn. Operative Millers, AIM, Am. Mgmt. Assn., Am. C. of C. in France, Am. C. of C. in London, Canadian Soc. N.Y., N.J., Delta. Mason. Onondaga Golf and Country (Syracuse, N.Y.). Home: 432 B Heritage Village Southbury CT 06488 Office: Clarkson Industries 950 3d Ave New York NY 10022

STEPHENSON, ROY L., judge; b. Spirit Lake, Iowa, Mar. 14, 1917; A.B., State U. Iowa, 1938, J.D., 1940; m.; children—Betty Jean, Douglas Lane, Randall. Admitted to Iowa bar, 1940; practiced in Des Moines; mem. firm Fountain, Bridges, Lundy & Stephenson; U.S. atty. for So. Iowa, 1953-60; U.S. dist. judge So. Iowa, 1960-71, chief judge, 1962-71; judge U.S. Court of Appeals, 8th Circuit, 1971—. Chmn. Polk County Republican Central Com., 1951-53. Served to capt. AUS, 1941-46; ETO; brig. gen. ret. Iowa N.G. Decorated Silver Star, Bronze Star. Mem. Am., Iowa, Polk County bar assns., Order of Coif, Gamma Eta Gamma. Clubs: Masons, Shriners, Sertoma. Office: 301 US Courthouse E 1st and Walnut Des Moines IA 50309

STEPHENSON, SAMUEL EDWARD, JR., physician; b. Bristol, Tenn., May 16, 1926; s. Samuel Edward and Hazel Beatrice (Walters) S.; B.S., U. S.C., 1946; M.D., Vanderbilt U., 1950; m. Janet Sue Spotts, May 16, 1970; children—Samuel Edward III, William Douglas, Dorothea Louise, Judith Maria. Intern, Butterworth Hosp., Grand Rapids, Mich., 1950-51; instr. to asso. prof. surgery Vanderbilt U., 1955-67; prof. surgery U. Fla., 1967—; chmn. dept. surgery Univ. Hosp., Jacksonville, 1967-78. Co-chmn. Fla. Burn and Trauma Registry, 1974-77. Served with USNR, 1944-45. Fellow A.C.S.; mem. Am. Coll. Chest Physicians. Mason. Club: Ponte Vedra (Fla.). Asst. editor So. Med. Jour., 1968—. Contbr. articles to profl. jours. Home: 10553 Scottmill Rd Jacksonville FL 32217

STEPP, HOWARD WELLINGTON, co. exec., ret. educator; b. East Haven, Conn., Apr. 26, 1904; s. Charles Timothy and Aline Hope (Palmer) S.; spl. studies Princeton, 1928-36, hon. mem. classes 1939-44; m. Dorothy Louise Taylor, Sept. 9, 1925; children—Leora Aline (Mrs. Everett T. Tower), Howard W. Jr. Asst. swimming coach Yale, 1925-27, head swimming coach Princeton, 1928-53, dir. athletics, 1944-46, registrar, mem. corp., 1946-69, now registrar emeritus, faculty dir. Princeton summer camp for underprivileged children, Blairstown, N.J., 1946-67; v.p. Bunbury Co., Inc., 1969-74, chmn., 1974—; dir. Nassau Broadcasting Co. Phys. activities adviser, Poland, 1937-39, coach, dir. Polish Olympic Swimming Teams. Mem. N.J. Legislature, 1944-45; referee Juvenile and Domestic Relations Ct., Princeton, N.J. Dist., 1947-66. Bd. dirs., chmn. Pocumtuck Found.; chmn. bd. dirs. Windham Found., Vt. Mem. Assn. Collegiate Registrars, Am. Swimming Coaches Assn. (past pres.), Amateur Athletic Union U.S. (past N.J. pres.), Nat. Collegiate Athletic Assn. (chmn. swimming rules com. 1952-54), Am. Olympic Swimming Committee. Clubs: Tiger Inn (Princeton); Nassau. Author: Swimming and Diving, 1937. Contbr. articles on swimming, diving to publs. Home: The Bouwerie 604 Pretty Brook Rd Princeton NJ 08540

STEPTO, ROBERT CHARLES, educator, physician; b. Chgo., Oct. 6, 1920; s. Robert Louis and Grace (Williams) S.; B.S., Northwestern U., 1938-41; M.D., Howard U., 1944; Ph.D., U. Chgo., 1948; m. Ann Burns, Sept. 13, 1942; children—Robert Burns, Jan Kristin. Intern, Provident Hosp., Chgo., 1945, resident obstetrics and gynecology, 1946-48; resident Chgo. Lying-In Hosp., 1946-48; USPHS fellow Michael Reese Hosp., Chgo., 1948-51; asst. prof. Loyola U., Chgo., 1953-56; asst. prof. U. Ill., Chgo., 1956-60, asso. prof., 1960-69; prof., chmn. dept. obstetrics and gynecology Chgo. Med. Sch., 1970-75; prof. Rush Med. Coll., Chgo., 1975-79; prof. U. Chgo., 1979—; dir. obstetrics and gynecology Cook County Hosp., 1972-75, Mt. Sinai Hosp. Med. Center, 1970—. Mem. Chgo. Bd. Health, Chgo. Health Research Found., Am. Cancer Soc., Family Planning Coordinating Council Met. Chgo.; pres. Nat. Med. Fellowships, Bd. dirs. Chgo. Urban League, 1960-63, Mus. Contemporary Art, Lyric Opera; trustee Ill. Children's Home and Aid Soc., 1967-71. Served to capt. AUS, 1951-53. Fellow A.C.S., Internat. Coll. Surgeons, Am. Coll. Obstetrics, Gynecology, Inst. of Med.; mem. Am. Soc. Clin. Pathologists, Am. Soc. Colpscopy, Pan Am. Surg. Soc., AMA, Nat. Med. Assn., Am. Soc. Exptl. Pathology, Central Assn. Obstetrics and Gynecology, Chgo. Gynecol. Soc. (v.p. 1969), Chgo. Pathol. Soc. Clubs: Quadrangle, City (Chgo.). Home: 5201 S Cornell Ave Chicago IL 60615

STERBAN, RICHARD ANTHONY, singer; b. Camden, N.J., Apr. 24, 1943; s. Edward Joseph and Victoria Marie (Giordano) S.; student Trenton State Coll.; m. Sandra Bertha Wilson, June 29, 1964; children—Richard Alan, Douglas Scott, Christopher Patrick. Mem. gospel singing groups; mem. Stamps Quartet; bass singer, partner Oak Ridge Boys, 1972—; co-owner Silverline-Goldline Music Pub. Cos.; partner Nashville Sounds, Greensboro Hornets, baseball teams. Recipient Grammy awards; 12 Dove awards Gospel Music Assn.; named Vocal Group of Year Country Music Assn. Mem. Country Music Assn., AFTRA, Nat. Acad. Rec. Arts and Scis., Acad. Country Music. Office: 329 Rockland Rd Hendersonville TN 37075

STERENBUCH, MARTIN, lawyer; b. N.Y.C., June 26, 1939; s. Leo Turkel and Fay (Weintraub) S.; B.A., Columbia, 1960; LL.B., Harvard, 1963; m. Diane I. Schiffman, Mar. 23, 1969. Admitted to D.C. bar, 1963; since practiced in Washington; clk. U.S. Ct. of Claims, 1963-64; asso. firm Denning & Wahlstetter, 1964-66, Todd, Dillon & Sullivan, 1966-68; partner firm Cake & Sterenbuch, 1968-74, Gajarsa, Liss & Sterenbuch, 1975—. Mem. Am., D.C. bar assns., Am. Soc. Internat. Law, D.C. Bar, Am.-Israel Pub. Affairs Com. Clubs: City Tavern, George Washington U. President's. Home: 3265 P St NW Washington DC 20007 Office: 1700 K St NW Suite 801 Washington DC 20006

STERLING, CHANDLER WINFIELD, bishop; b. Dixon, Ill., Jan. 28, 1911; s. Robert and Mary Eleanor (Chandler) S.; grad. Northwestern U., 1932; B.A., Seabury-Western Sem., 1938, D.D., 1957; m. Catherine Ricker, June 17, 1935; children—Mary, Margaret, Kathy, Ann, Beth, Sarah, Jonathan, Julia. Ordained to ministry P.E. Ch. as deacon, 1938, priest, 1938; minister in Wilmette, Ill., 1938-40, Oak Park, Ill., 1941-42, Milw., 1942-43, Freeport, Ill., 1943-44, Elmhurst, Ill., 1944-50, Chadron, Nebr., 1950-56; bishop Mont., 1956-68; asst. bishop Pa., 1968-76. Mem. staff exptl. programs Western Nebr. Mission Fields; chmn. Youth Commn., Chgo., 1944-50; mem. bd. Nat. Parks Ministry. Recipient Silver Beaver award for citywide work with juveniles Boy Scouts Am., 1947. Author: Little Malice in Blunderland, 1965; The Holroyd Papers, 1969; The Eighth Square, 1969; Arrogance of Piety, 1969; The Icehouse Gang, 1972; Beyond This Land of Whoa, 1973; The Doors to Perception, 1974; The Witnesses, 1975. Contbr. articles to nat. mags. Address: 830 Forest Ct Oconomowoc WI 53066

STERLING, DONALD JUSTUS, JR., newspaper editor; b. Portland, Oreg., Sept. 27, 1927; s. Donald Justus and Adelaide (Armstrong) S.; A.B., Princeton U., 1948; postgrad. (Nieman fellow) Harvard U., 1955-56; m. Julie Ann Courteol, June 7, 1963; children—Sarah, William, John. Reporter, Denver Post, 1948-52; reporter, asst. city editor, asso. editor, editor editorial page Oreg. Jour., Portland, 1952-71, exec. news editor, 1971, editor, 1972—. Pres., Tri-County Community Council, 1972-73; bd. dirs. Oreg. Hist. Soc., pres., 1977-79. Recipient Izaak Walton League Golden Beaver award, 1969; Edith Knight Hill award Women in Communications, 1978. English-Speaking Union traveling fellow, 1959. Mem. Am. Soc. Newspaper Editors, Soc. Nieman Fellows, Phi Beta Kappa, Sigma Delta Chi. Clubs: City (pres. 1973-74), Multnomah Athletic (Portland); Dial Lodge (Princeton). Home: 1718 SW Myrtle St Portland OR 97201 Office: 1320 SW Broadway Portland OR 97201

STERLING, ELWYN FRANKLIN, educator; b. Frankfort, N.Y., June 2, 1925; s. Elwyn Bennett and Hazel (Grundy) S.; B.A., Colgate U., 1950; M.A., Syracuse U., 1952, Ph.D., 1957; m. Grace Madolyn Lloyd, Aug. 11, 1946; children—Sandra Grace, Elwyn Jan. Instr., Colgate U., Hamilton, N.Y., 1950-57, asst. prof., 1957-62, asso. prof., 1962-67, prof., 1967—, chmn. dept. Romance langs. and lits., 1965—, dir. NDEA Summer Lang. Insts., 1963-65; dir. French Group Abroad-U. Dijon, 1967, 71. Served with inf. AUS, 1943-46. Mem. AAUP, Am. Assn. Tchrs. French, Modern Lang. Assn. Home: Preston Hill Rd Hamilton NY 13346

STERLING, JOHN EWART WALLACE, univ. chancellor; b. Linwood, Ont., Can., Aug. 6, 1906; s. William Sterling and Annie (Wallace) S.; came to U.S., naturalized, 1947; B.A., U. Toronto, 1927; M.A., U. Alta., 1930; Ph.D., Stanford U., 1938; LL.D., Pomona Coll., Occidental Coll., 1949, U. San Francisco, U. Toronto, 1950, U. B.C., Northwestern U., U. Calif., 1958, U. Denver, Loyola U., McGill U., 1961, Columbia U., 1962, McMaster U., 1966, Harvard U., 1968, U. Alta., 1970; D.C.L., Durham U., England, 1953; Litt.D., U. Caen (France), 1957, U. So. Calif., 1960; L.H.D., St. Mary's Coll., 1962, Santa Clara U., 1963, Mills Coll., 1967, U. Utah, 1968; m. Anna Marie Shaver, Aug. 7, 1930; children—William W., Susan Hardy (Mrs. Bernard Monjauze), Judith Robinson (Mrs. Frank Morse). Lectr. history Regina (Sask., Can.) Coll., 1927-28; asst. in history, dir. phys. edn. U. Alta., 1928-30; mem. research staff Hoover War Library, Stanford U., 1932-37, instr. history, 1935-37; asst. prof. history Calif. Inst. Tech., 1937-40, asso. prof., 1940-42, prof. history, 1942-45, Edward S. Harkness prof. of history and govt., exec. com., 1945-48, chmn. faculty, 1944-46; news analyst CBS, 1942-48; dir. Huntington Library, 1948-49; pres. Stanford U., 1949-68, lifetime chancellor, 1968; past dir. Fireman's Fund Am. Ins. Cos., Kaiser Aluminum & Chem. Corp., Shell Oil Co., Tridair Industries, Dean Witter & Co. Civilian faculty Nat. War Coll., 1947, bd. cons., 1948-52; bd. visitors U.S. Naval Acad., 1956-58, Tulane U., 1960-74; mem. nat. adv. council Health Research Facilities, HEW, 1956-57; chmn. Commn. Presdl. Scholars, 1965-68; adv. bd. Office Naval Research, 1953-56; chmn Am. Revolution Bicentennial Commn., 1969-70; mem. Ford Internat. Fellowship Bd., 1960; mem. Can.-Am. Com., 1957-54; mem. Am. adv. com. Ditchley Found., Eng., 1962-76; mem. adv. com. fgn. relations U.S. Dept. State, 1965-68; bd. dirs. Council Fin. Aid to Edn., 1967-70; mem. Brit.-N.Am. Com., 1969-74. Decorated knight comdr. Order Brit. Empire, 1976; comdr.'s cross Order Merit Fed. Republic Germany; chevalier Legion d'Honneur (France); 2d degree Imperial Order Rising Sun (Japan), Grand Gold Badge of Honor for Merits (Republic of Austria); Herbert Hoover medal Stanford Alumni Assn., 1964; Clark Kerr award U. Calif., Berkeley, 1969; Uncommon Man award Stanford Assos., 1978; fellow Social Sci. Research Council, 1939-40. Fellow Am. Geog. Soc.; mem. Council on Fgn. Relations, Western Coll. Assn. (pres. 1953), Am., Pacific Coast hist. assns., Assn. Am. Univs. (pres. 1962-64). Clubs: Commonwealth, Bohemian, California, Burlingame Country, Family, Pacific-Union, University (hon.) (Palo Alto, San Francisco, N.Y.C., Los Angeles). Editor: (with H.H. Fisher, X.J. Eudin) Features and Figures of the Past (V.I. Gurko), 1939. Home: 2220 Stockbridge Ave Woodside CA 94062 Office: PO Box 5096 Stanford CA 94305

STERLING, LIONEL N., mfg. co. exec.; b. N.Y.C., May 16, 1937; s. Samuel B. and Fannie (Glazer) S.; B.A., Bklyn. Coll., 1959; M.B.A., N.Y. U., 1960; m. Ann Freeman, Mar. 13, 1971. Various positions fin. staff ITT, N.Y.C., 1961-71; v.p. Donaldson, Lufkin & Jenrette, N.Y.C., 1971-74; sr. v.p. fin. Am Can Co., Greenwich, Conn., 1974—; dir. Simmonds Precision Products, Apcoa Services, Inc. Served with U.S. Army, 1960-64. Mem. Fin. Execs. Inst. Home: 226 Dogwood Ln Stamford CT 06903 Office: Am Can Co American Ln Greenwich CT 06830

STERLING, RICHARD WHITNEY, educator; b. Los Angeles, Feb. 16, 1922; s. Richard Whitney and Frieda (Mueller) S.; B.A., Yale, 1942, M.A., 1947, Ph.D., 1956; postgrad. U. Berlin, Free U. Berlin, 1948-49; m. Lucretia Holt Lincoln, Feb. 11, 1950 (div.); children—Mary Lincoln, John Alva, Richard Whitney, James Brewster; m. 2d, Maud Marie La Rouche, Sept. 1, 1978. Research asst. U.S. Prosecution Staff Nuremberg War Crimes Trials, 1945-46; U.S. fgn. service officer, Germany, 1947-51; research asso. So. Regional Edn. Bd., New Orleans, 1953-54; instr. to asso. prof. Dartmouth, Hanover, N.H., 1954-62, prof. govt., 1962—, chmn. internat. relations program, 1962-68; research asso. Washington Center Fgn. Policy Research, 1959-60. Chmn., Hanover Democratic party, 1956-59. Served with AUS, 1943-46. Rockefeller Research grantee, 1956-57, Rockefeller Found. grantee, 1970. Mem. Am. Polit. Sci. Assn., Council on Fgn. Relations. Episcopalian. Author: Ethics in a World of Power; The Political Ideas of Friedrich Meinecke, 1958; Macropolitics-International Relations in a Global Society, 1974. Home: Union Village Rd Norwich VT 05055

STERLING, ROBERT R., educator; b. Bugtussle, Okla., May 16, 1931; s. Roland Pomeroy and Lillian (Neuman) S.; B.S., U. Denver, 1956, M.B.A., 1958; Ph.D., U. Fla., 1964; children—Robert, Kimberly. Asst. prof. social sci. Harpur Coll., Binghamton, N.Y., 1963-66; Sci. Faculty fellow Yale U., 1966-67; asso. prof., then prof. bus. adminstrn. U. Kans., Lawrence, 1967-70, Arthur Young distinguished prof., 1970-74; dir. research Am. Accounting Assn., 1972-74; Jesse Jones Distinguished prof. Rice U., Houston, 1974—, dean Grad. Sch. Adminstrn., 1976—. Bd. dirs. Nat. Bur. Econ. Research, United Way, Trust Corp. Internat. Recipient Gold medal Am. Inst. C.P.A.'s, 1968, 74; Bicentennial Disting. Internat. lectr., Europe, 1976; Hoover Disting. Internat. lectr., Australia, 1979. Fellow Accounting Researchers Internat. Assn. (pres. 1974—), Am. (v.p. 1975—), S.W. (pres.) accounting assns., Accountants for Pub. Interest (dir.); mem. Nat. Assn. Accountants (dir.), Houston Philos. Soc. (dir.). Author: Theory of the Measurement of Enterprise Income, 1970; (with William F. Bentz) Accounting in Perspective, 1971; Asset Valuation and Income Determination 1971; Research Methodology In Accounting, 1972; Institutional Issues in Public Accounting, 1973. Editor: Accounting Classics Series; editorial bd., dept. editor Accounting Rev.; editorial bd. Abacus; pub., editor Scholars Book Co. Home: 5618 Chaucer St Houston TX 77005

STERMAN, IRVIN, real estate exec.; b. Mpls., July 15, 1929; s. Maurice and Gussie (Grossman) S.; B.S., U. Calif., Los Angeles, 1951; m. Anida Feldman. Mar. 31, 1957; children—Scott, Carole. Controller, System Devel. Corp., Santa Monica, Calif., 1956-59; sec. Shapell Industries, Inc., Beverly Hills, Calif., 1959—, treas., 1970—, fin. v.p., 1973—. Served with AUS, 1953-55. C.P.A., Calif. Mem. Am. Inst. C.P.A.'s, Calif. Soc. C.P.A.'s. Home: 3829 Encino Hills Pl Encino CA 91436 Office: 8383 Wilshire Blvd Beverly Hills CA 90211

STERN, AARON, author, ednl. cons., lectr.; b. Germany, May 20, 1918; s. David and Helen (Schurek) S.; student gymna zium, Plock, Poland, 1933-37, Warsaw U., 1937-38; B.A., Bklyn. Coll., 1956; M.A. Equiv., Columbia U., 1957; student Jewish Theol. Sem. Am.; m. Bella Tcherniawska, Jan. 1940; children—Edith, David. Originator, Total Edn. Submersion Method; conducted sch. based on method in Displaced Persons Camp, Germany, 1948-79; lectr. on method at univs., 1949—; conducted landmark study of Head Start Program for HEW, 1974. Active participant desegregation of pub. facilities, voters registration; active presdl. campaigns senators Eugene McCarthy,

George McGovern. Honored by resolutions City of Miami, 1964, Fla. Legislature, 1965, U.S. Congress, 1974; nominated for Pulitzer prize, 1977; Justinian Lodge scholar; Columbia grantee. Mem. Nat. Soc. Profs., NEA, Authors Guild, Authors League Am., Internat. Platform Assn. Author: Ethnic Minorities in Poland, 1937; Nazi Atrocities in Europe; The Making of a Genius; Principles of the Total Education Submersion Method; The Joy of Learning; 72 sci. papers. Home: 2485 NE 214th St North Miami Beach FL 33180. *My life-long research into the awe-inspiring area of early child development culminated in my daughter, a happy, well-adjusted fifteen-year-old girl, becoming a university instructor, the youngest on record. This feat, which can be replicated, is to be attributed to environment. Unfortunately, we are eager to decode only the physiological needs of a baby, while we ignore its truly insatiable craving for learning. As a matter of fact, intensive work with infants to stimulate their God-given gift of inquiry, will also significantly enhance their socioemotional, as well as physical, progress. Intellectual growth commences at birth, and should cease at death only.*

STERN, ALFRED, educator; b. Passaic, N.J., Feb. 27, 1916; s. David and Rose (Teich) S.; B.S., U. Tex., Austin, 1949, M.A., 1950, Ph.D., 1963; m. Carolyn M. Banks, Oct. 2, 1942. Dir. spl. services Victoria (Tex.) pub. schs., 1950-60; acad. asst. U. Tex., 1961-62, supr. tchrs. exceptional children, 1962-63; vis. lectr. U. N.C., summer 1963; prof., chmn. dept. spl. edn., dir. Spl. Edn. Center, U. New Orleans, 1963—. Vice pres., hon. bd. mem. New Orleans chpt. Assn. for Retarded Children, 1964—, New Orleans chpt. ARC, 1966-68, Emotionally Disturbed, Inc., New Orleans, 1967—. Served with AUS, 1934-45. Recipient Spl. citation Council for Exceptional Children, New Orleans, 1970. Mem. Am., La. psychol. assns., Council Exceptional Children, Phi Delta Kappa, Psi Chi, Alpha Kappa Delta, Phi Theta Kappa. Office: U New Orleans New Orleans LA 70122

STERN, ALFRED PHILLIP, securities broker; b. Los Angeles, May 31, 1933; s. Herman J. and Geraldine (Rosenberg) S.; A.B., Stanford, 1955; M.B.A., 1957; m. Lise Muriel Roch, Nov, 24, 1966; children—Kim Marie, Eric Roch, Claire Phyllis. With Stern, Frank, Meyer & Fox, Inc., Los Angeles, 1957—, co. acquired by Drexel Burnham Lambert Inc., 1977, v.p., 1977—; pres. Spring St. Forum, Los Angeles, 1972-73. Mem. Mayor's Adv. Com. Rapid Transit, chmn. finance subcom.; mem. devel. bd. Studio Watts Workshop Los Angeles, 1970; treas., bd. dirs. Montessori West Los Angeles, 1973-75; chmn. Stanford Bus. Sch. Trust, 1978-80; trustee Beverly Hills Edn. Found., 1979—; chmn. Citizens Advisory Com. Specific Plan for Century City, 1976. Mem. Stanford Bus. Sch. Assn. Los Angeles (v.p. 1965), Securities Industry Assn. (exec. com. chmn. legislation com. Calif. group 1974-77), Kappa Beta Phi. Clubs: Bond (dir. 1974-75, sec. 1976, 77), Stock Exchange (Los Angeles); Stanford Westside (pres. 1971). Home: 427 S Rodeo Dr Beverly Hills CA 90212 Office: 1901 Ave of Stars Suite 1100 Los Angeles CA 90067

STERN, ALFRED R., communications exec.; b. Chgo., Aug. 8, 1922; s. Alfred K. and Marion (Rosenwald) S.; grad. Deerfield (Mass.) Acad., 1941; student U. N.C., 1941-42; m. Joanne Melniker, Feb. 11, 1950; children—Chris, Catherine, Nicholas, Thomas, Margaret Pres., Raymond & Raymond, Inc., N.Y.C., 1949-51; with NBC, Inc., 1952-62, formerly v.p. Enterprises div., also chmn. NBC Internat.; chmn. bd. Television Communications Corp. (now Warner Cable Corp.), 1962-75; sr. v.p. corp. affairs Warner Communications Inc., 1975-77, cons., 1977—; chmn. Bus. Research Publs. Inc., 1979—; dir. Theatre, Inc. (Phoenix Theater); dir. Starwood Corp., N.Y.C. Pres. bd. trustees Dalton Schs., N.Y.C., 1961-69; chmn. Mt. Sinai Med. Center, N.Y.C., Mt. Sinai Med. Sch., Mt. Sinai Hosp., N.Y.; chmn. planetarium com., trustee Am. Mus. Nat. History, N.Y.C., Radcliffe Coll., 1979—; pres. Film Soc. of Lincoln Center, N.Y.C. Served with USAAF, 1943-46. Clubs: Century Country, Century Assn. (N.Y.C.). Home: 993 Fifth Ave New York NY 10028 Office: Warner Communications Inc 75 Rockefeller Plaza New York NY 10019

STERN, ARTHUR CECIL, educator; b. Petersburg, Va., Mar. 14, 1909; s. Harry Abraham and Mary (Rosenstock) S.; M.E., Stevens Inst. Tech., 1930, M.S., 1933, D.Eng. (hon.), 1975; m. Dorothy Henrietta Anspacher, Jan. 16, 1938 (dec.); children—Richard Cecil, Elizabeth Ann (Mrs. Mark Greenwold), Robert Cecil, m. 2d, Katherine Barbour Perlman, Oct. 30, 1976. Dir. N.Y.C. Air Pollution Survey, 1935-38; chief engring. unit div. indsl. hygiene N.Y. State Dept. Labor, 1942-55; chief lab. engring. and phys. scis., div. air pollution USPHS Robert A. Taft San. Engring. Center, Cin., 1955-62; asst. dir. Nat. Center Air Pollution Control, USPHS, Washington, 1962-68; prof. air hygiene U. N.C., Chapel Hill, 1968-78, emeritus, 1978—. Recipient jr. award ASME, 1938. Licensed profl. engr., N.C. Fellow ASME; mem. Am. Indsl. Hygiene Assn., Air Pollution Control Assn. (pres. 1975-76, Richard Beatty Mellon award 1970), Nat. Acad. Engring., Pi Lambda Phi. Editor: Air Pollution, 3d edit., 5 vols. Home: 602 Croom Ct Chapel Hill NC 27514

STERN, ARTHUR LEWIS, lawyer; b. Rochester, N.Y., Apr. 11, 1911; s. Arthur Lewis and Irma (Loveman) S.; grad. St. George's Sch., Newport, R.I., 1929; A.B., Yale U., 1933; LL.B., Harvard U., 1936; m. Molly Jane Stein, Feb. 22, 1934; children—Arthur Lewis III, Timothy Land. Admitted to N.Y. bar, 1936, Fla. bar, 1974; since practiced in Rochester and Fla.; partner firm Dibble, Koff, Lane, Stern & Stern, 1979—. Trustee, mem. exec. com. Rochester Savs. Bank. Mem. corp. Community Chest Rochester and Monroe County. Trustee, mem. exec. com. Rochester Inst. Tech.; hon. bd. dirs. Meml. Art Gallery U. Rochester; bd. govs. Nova U. Law Sch.; adv. council Rochester Philharmonic Orch. Mem. Am., N.Y. State, Monroe County, Fla., Palm Beach County bar assns., Am. Judicature Soc. Clubs: Automobile, Country (Rochester); Genesee Valley (Rochester). Home: 14 Elmwood Hill Ln Rochester NY 14610 (winter) 341 Garden Rd Palm Beach FL 33480 Office: One Exchange St Rochester NY 14614 also 341 Garden Rd Palm Beach FL 33480

STERN, CARL LEONARD, news correspondent; b. N.Y.C., Aug. 7, 1937; A.B., Columbia U., 1958; M.S., 1959; J.D., Cleve. State U., 1966. Admitted to Ohio bar, 1966, D.C. bar, 1968; law corres. NBC News, Washington, 1967—. Recipient Gavel award, 1969, 74; Peabody award, 1974, Emmy award, 1974. Mem. Am. Bar Assn. (vice chmn. criminal justice sect. com. on criminal justice and the media). Home: 2956 Davenport St NW Washington DC 20008 Office: 4001 Nebraska Ave NW Washington DC 20016

STERN, CHARLES, fgn. trade co. exec.; b. Germany, Dec. 2, 1920 (came to U.S. 1940, naturalized 1943); s. Julius and Else (Brand) S.; Matriculation, U. London, Eng., 1937; m. Eve Hamburger, Sept. 20, 1947; children—Enid S., June M. With J. Gerber & Co., Inc., N.Y.C., 1940—, asst. v.p., 1960-63, v.p., 1963-68, exec. v.p., 1968-74, pres., 1974—, also dir. Served with AUS, World War II. Mem. Am. Inst. Imported Steel (past pres.), ASTM. Home: 25 Robins Rd New Rochelle NY 10801 Office: 855 Ave of Americas New York NY 10001

STERN, CLARENCE AMES, historian, educator; b. McClusky, N.D., Jan. 6, 1913; s. Adam M. and Minnie (Krieger) S.; A.B., Eastern Mich. U., 1934; M.A. Wayne State U., 1938; postgrad. LaSalle Extension U., 1947-49; Ph.D., U. Nebr., 1958; m. Kathleen Gober, Feb. 20, 1946. Tchr. pub. schs., Mich., 1934-42, 54-55; asst. prof. history and polit. sci. Coll. Engring., Lawrence Inst. Tech., Detroit, 1946-50; asst. in history U. Neb., 1951-53; asso. prof. history and polit. sci. Wayne State Coll., 1958-65; asso. prof. constl. and polit. history U. Wis.-Oshkosh, 1965—; asso. prof. history U. Wis.-Fond du Lac, 1975—, head dept. history, 1977—, chmn. div. social scis., 1979—; grant proposal reviewer Nat. Endowment Humanities, 1978—. Served with USAAF, 1942-46. Ford Found. grantee, 1962. Fellow Intercontinental Biog. Assn., Internat. Inst. Community Service, Harry S. Truman Library Inst. Nat. and Internat. Affairs (hon.); mem. AAUP (chpt. pres. 1964-65), ACLU, Am. Hist. Assn., Orgn. Am. Historians, Am. Polit. Sci. Assn., Nat. Trust for Hist. Preservation, Smithsonian Assos., Phi Alpha Theta, Pi Gamma Mu, Kappa Delta Pi. Author: Republican Heyday: Republicanism Through the McKinley Years, 2d edit., 1969; Resurgent Republicanism: The Handiwork of Hanna, 2d edit., 1968; Golden Republicanism: The Crusade for Hard Money, 2d edit., 1970; Protectionist Republicanism: Republican Tariff Policy in the McKinley Period, 1971. Home: 1625 Elmwood Ave Oshkosh WI 54901. *As the gateway to a vast reservoir of knowledge essential to a meaningful understanding of the background and complex character of contemporary civilization inside and outside the United States, history courses should be so presented as to foster the development of leadership capability commensurate with the problems involved in an era of domestic drift and international nuclear tension. Instructional emphasis should be placed upon such unique attributes of the study of history as chronology, perspective, the concept of continuity and change. Students should be encouraged to cultivate reflective capacity through involvement in the investigation analysis, correlation, synthesis and interpretation of pertinent historical information. Progress toward greater student independence in the pursuit of educational goals will entail the fostering of awareness in the continuing search for national and international stability, of the need for a more generous infusion of humanitarianism in the promotion of the democratic process, global cooperation, and tolerance. The pioneering, rather than the routinely conformist conception of higher education, will contribute to the advancement of the frontiers of knowledge, an objective justifiably to be regarded as essential to the intellectual life of any college or university.*

STERN, EDGAR BLOOM, JR., corporate exec.; b. N.Y.C., Sept. 1, 1922; s. Edgar Bloom and Edith (Rosenwald) S.; grad. Hotchkiss Sch., 1940; B.S. cum laude, Harvard, 1943; m. Pauline Stewart, May 23, 1947; children—Sandra (Mrs. David A. Steiner), Eric, Monte, Lessing. Chief engr. Offshore Navigation, Inc., radar surveyors, 1946-48; mng. partner WDSU Broadcasting Services, Inc., 1949-50; pres., dir. Royal St. Corp. (formerly WDSU Broadcasting Corp.), New Orleans, 1948—, Royal St. Investment Corp., Royal St. Louis, Inc., New Orleans; chmn. bd. Aspen Music Assos., Inc.; dir. Sears, Roebuck & Co., Chgo., Dir. United Fund Greater New Orleans, 1951-57, treas., 1953, pres., 1954; chmn. pub. relations adv. com. United Community Funds and Councils Am., 1956-59, exec. com., dir., mem. United Fund adv. com., vice chmn. United Community campaigns, 1956-63, v.p., 1958-63; dir. Internat. Trade Mart, Council for A Better La., Internat House, New Orleans; past dir. Council Social Agencies. Trustee U. Chgo., 1972—, Com. Econ. Devel., N.Y.C.; mem. univ. resources com. Harvard, 1963-73; mem. vis. com. Harvard Grad. Sch. Edn., 1963-69, 70-73; bd. adminstrs. Tulane U., 1959-77; bd. govs. Ochsner Found. Hosp., New Orleans, 1959-73. Served as 1st lt. Signal Corps, AUS, 1943-46, 50-52. Home: Box JJ Aspen CO 81611 Office: New Orleans LA 70139

STERN, EDWARD ABRAHAM, educator; b. Detroit, Sept. 19, 1930; s. Jack Munich and Rose (Kravitz) S.; B.S., Calif. Inst. Tech., 1951, Ph.D., 1955; m. Sylvia Rita Sidell, Oct. 30, 1955; children—Hilary, Shari, Miri. Research fellow Calif. Inst. Tech., Pasadena, 1955-57; asst. prof. U. Md., College Park, 1957-60, asso. prof., 1960-64, prof., 1965; prof. physics U. Wash., Seattle, 1966—. Guggenheim fellow, 1963-64; NSF sr. postdoctoral fellow, 1970-71. Fellow Am. Phys. Soc. Contbr. articles to profl. jours. Home: 9536 42d St NE Seattle WA 98115

STERN, FRANK, physicist; b. Koblenz, Germany, Sept. 15, 1928; s. Gustav and Louise (Beiersdorf) S.; came to U.S. 1936, naturalized 1943; B.S., Union Coll., 1949; Ph.D., Princeton, 1955; m. Shayne Nemerson, July 9, 1955; children—David, Linda. Physicist, Nat. Bur. Standards, summers 1949-51; mem. tech. staff Bell Telephone Labs., summer 1952; physicist U.S. Naval Ordnance Lab., White Oak, Md., 1953-62; lectr. physics U. Md., College Park, 1955-58, part-time prof. physics, 1959-62; research staff mem. Thomas J. Watson Research Center, IBM Corp., Yorktown Heights, N.Y., 1962—, mgr. semicondr. electronic properties, 1973—; with IBM Zurich Research Lab., Switzerland, 1965-66. Mem. Pleasantville Conservation Adv. Council, 1972—, chmn., 1976—. Charles A. Coffin fellow, 1949-50; NSF predoctoral fellow, 1952-53. Fellow Am. Phys. Soc.; mem. Am. Vacuum Soc., AAAS, Phi Beta Kappa, Sigma Xi. Home: 6 Robbins Rd Pleasantville NY 10570 Office: Thomas J Watson Research Center IBM Corp Yorktown Heights NY 10598

STERN, FRITZ RICHARD, educator, historian; b. Breslau, Germany, Feb. 2, 1926; s. Rudolf A. and Catherine (Brieger) S.; came to U.S., 1938, naturalized, 1947; B.A., Columbia, 1946, M.A., 1948, Ph.D., 1953; m. Margaret J. Bassett, Oct. 11, 1947; children—Frederick P., Katherine B. Lectr., instr. Columbia, 1946-51, faculty, 1953—, prof. history, 1963—, Seth Low prof. history, 1967—; acting asst. prof. Cornell U., 1951-53. Tchr., Free U. Berlin, 1954, Yale, 1963; permanent vis. prof. U. Konstanz (West Germany), 1966—; Elie Halévy prof. U. Paris, spring 1979; Phi Beta Kappa vis. scholar, 1979-80. Decorated Officer's Cross Order of Merit (Fed. Republic of Germany). Fellow Center Advanced Behavioral Scis., 1957-58, Social Sci. Research Council, 1960-61, Am. Council Learned Socs., 1966-67, Netherlands Inst. for Advanced Study, 1972-73; mem. Nuffield Coll., Oxford, 1966-67, Inst. Advanced Study, Princeton, 1969-70; Guggenheim fellow, 1969-70; Ford Found. grantee, 1976-77. Mem. Am. Hist. Assn., Am. Acad. Arts and Scis., Council Fgn. Relations, Phi Beta Kappa (senator-at-large 1973-78). Club: Century (N.Y.C.). Author: The Politics of Cultural Despair, 1961; Gold and Iron: Bismarck, Bleichroeder and the Bldg. of the German Empire, 1977 (recipient Lionel Trilling award Columbia U.). Editor: The Varieties of History, 1956, 71; (with L. Krieger) The Responsibility of Power, 1967; The Failure of Illiberalism-Essays in the Political Culture of Modern Germany, 1972. Editorial bd. Foreign Affairs, 1978—. Contbr. articles to profl. jours. Reviewer for Fgn. Affairs, 1963—. Home: 15 Claremont Ave New York NY 10027

STERN, GUY, ednl. adminstr.; b. Hildesheim, Germany, Jan. 14, 1922; s. Julius and Hedwig (Silberberg) S.; came to U.S. 1937, naturalized 1943; B.A. in Romance Langs., Hofstra Coll., 1948; M.A. with honors in Germanic Langs., Columbia, 1950, Ph.D. with honors, 1953; m. Judith Edelstein, June 16, 1979; 1 son, Mark. Grad. asst., then instr. Columbia, 1948-55; asst. prof., then asso. prof. Denison U., Granville, Ohio, 1955-63; prof. German, head dept. U. Cin., 1964-73, dean univ., 1973-76; prof., chmn. Germanic and Slavic dept. U. Md., 1976-78; v.p., provost Wayne State U., 1978—, also prof. German; guest prof. Goethe Inst., summers 1963-66, adv. editor for langs. and linguistics Dovers Publs. Bd. dirs. Leo Baeck Inst., 1967—, exec. bd., 1978—; pres. Lessing Soc., 1975-77. Served with AUS, 1942-45. Decorated Bronze star. Fulbright research grantee U. Munich (Germany), 1961-63; Bolingen research fellow, 1962-63. Mem. Am. Assn. Tchrs. German (pres. 1970-72), AAUP, Internat. P.E.N. Club, MLA, South Atlantic Modern Lang. Assn. Co-author: Brieflich Erzaehlt, 1956; Listen and Learn German, 1957; Say it in German, 1958; Uebung macht den Meister, 1959; An Invitation to German Poetry, 1960; Hints on Speaking German, 1961; Quick Change Pattern Drills, vol. I, 1962, vol. II, 1963; Hoer Zu und Rat mit, 1964; author: Efraim Frisch: Zum Verstaendnis des Geistigen, 1964; War, Weimar and Literature, 1971; Alfred Neumann (anthology with biography), 1979. Editor: Konstellationen: Die besten Erzählungen des Neuen Merkur, 1964; co-editor: Nelly Sachs Ausgewaehlte Gedichte, 1968; asso. editor Lessing Yearbook, 1970—; contbr. articles on 18th and 20th century German lit. to profl. jours. Home: 20672 Knob Woods Dr Southfield MI 48076

STERN, HERBERT JAY, judge; b. N.Y.C., Nov. 8, 1936; s. Samuel and Sophie (Berkowitz) S.; B.A., Hobart Coll., 1958; J.D. (Ford Found. scholar), U. Chgo., 1961; LL.D. (hon.), Seton Hall Law Sch., 1973, Hobart Coll., 1974; L.H.D. (hon.), Newark State Coll., 1973; D.C.L. (hon.), Bloomfield Coll., 1973; Litt.D. (hon.), Montclair State Coll., 1973; children—Jason Andrew and Jordan Ezekiel (twins). Admitted to N.Y. State bar, 1961, N.J. bar, 1971; asst. dist. atty. New York County, 1962-65; trial atty. organized crime and racketeering sect. Dept. of Justice, 1965-69; chief asst. U.S. atty. Dist. of N.J., Newark, 1969-70, U.S. atty., 1971-74, U.S. dist. judge, 1974—. Trustee, Chilton Hosp.; mem. adv. com. U. Chgo. Law Sch. Named One of America's 10 Outstanding Young Men, U.S. Jr. C. of C., 1971. Mem. Am., N.J., Fed. (past pres. Newark chpt.), Essex County bar assns., Am. Judicature Soc., Phi Alpha Delta. Office: US Courthouse Federal Sq Newark NJ 07101

STERN, ISAAC, violinist; b. Kreminiecz, Russia, July 21, 1920; s. Solomon and Clara S.; came to U.S., 1921; student San Francisco Conservatory, 1930-37; numerous hon. doctorates; m. Nora Kaye, Nov. 10, 1948; m. 2d, Vera Lindenblit, Aug. 17, 1951; children—Shira, Michael, David. Debuted as guest artist San Francisco Symphony Orch. (Pierre Monteux condr.), 1931; appeared with Los Angeles Philharmonic and concerts in Pacific Coast cities; N.Y. debut, 1937; has since appeared in concerts throughout U.S. and abroad, participated Prades Festivals with Pablo Casals, 1950-52; performed cycle Beethoven chamber works for piano with Eugene Istomin and Leonard Rose, 1970-71; soloist 1st orchestral performance Kennedy Center, Washington, has played with maj. orchs. U.S., Europe; performed in China at invitation of Chinese Govt.; records for Columbia Records; made soundtrack for motion pictures Humoresque (Warner Bros.), Fiddler on the Roof (United Artists); starred in Tonight We Sing (20th Century Fox), Journey to Jerusalem with Leonard Bernstein; pres. Carnegie Hall; chmn. bd. Am.-Israel Cultural Found. Recipient Grammy award, 1971, 73; comdr. Ordre de la Couronne, 1974, officier Legion d'Honneur, 1979. Mem. Original Nat. Arts Council. Address: care ICM Artists Ltd 40 W 57th St New York NY 10019

STERN, JAMES LAWRENCE, educator, arbitrator; b. N.Y.C., Nov. 3, 1920; s. Lawrence and Katherine (Friedman) S.; B.S. in Engring., Antioch Coll., 1943; Ph.D. in Econs., U. Calif. at Berkeley, 1954; m. Joanne Alexander, Dec. 18, 1943; children—Mark, Nina. Internat. rep. U.A.W., Detroit, 1947-49, 54-62; chief productivity sect., labor div. ECA (Marshall Plan), Paris, France, 1949-51; prof. labor edn. and econs. U. Wis., Madison, 1962-65, prof. econs., 1962—, dir. Indsl. Relations Research Inst., 1968-71, 80; vis. prof. Monash U., Melbourne, Australia, 1976, U. Hawaii, 1979. Arbitrator, factfinder Wis. Employment Relations Commn., Am. Arbitration Assn., Fed. Mediation and Conciliation Service. Served from ensign to lt. (j.g.) USNR, 1943-46. Sr. Fulbright research fellow, 1971. Mem. Indsl. Relations Research Assn. (sec.-treas. 1969-70, co-editor 1975-78), Am. Econ. Assn., Nat. Acad. Arbitrators (editor 1978—). Home: 225 S Kenosha Dr Madison WI 53705

STERN, JOSEPH SMITH, JR., investment banker, former footwear mfg. co. exec.; b. Cin., Mar. 31, 1918; s. Joseph S. and Miriam (Haas) S.; A.B., Harvard, 1940, M.B.A., 1943; m. Mary Stern, June 14, 1942; children—Peter Joseph, William Frederick, Peggy Ann Graeter. With R. H. Macy & Co., N.Y.C., 1940-41; with U.S. Shoe Corp., Cin., 1941-68, v.p., 1951-65, pres., 1965-66, chmn. bd., chief exec. officer, 1966, chmn. exec. com., 1966-68, dir., 1956-70; pres. J. S. Stern Jr. & Co., bus. brokers, Cin.; ltd. partner Shearson, Hayden, Stone Inc., N.Y.C.; adj. prof. bus. policy U. Cin. Vice pres. bd. trustees Cin. and Hamilton County Pub. Library; trustee Cin. Music Hall Assn., Cin. Hist. Soc., Children's Hosp. Med. Center, Cin. Symphony Orch., Cin Country Day Sch. 1956-72, Family Service, Cin.; trustee, pres. Cin. Mus. Festival Assn.; pres. bd. trustees Children's Convalescent Hosp., Cin., 1972-75; bd. overseers vis. com. univ. library and univ. resources Harvard. Served to lt. USNR, 1943-46. Mem. Am. Footwear Industries Assn. (life; dir.). Jewish (past pres. temple). Clubs: Literary, Racquet, Harvard (pres. 1965), Queen City, Losantville Country (Cin.); Harvard (N.Y.C.). Home: 3 Grandin Pl Cincinnati OH 45208 Office: Carew Tower Cincinnati OH 45202

STERN, LAURENT, educator; b. Budapest, Hungary, Mar. 22, 1930 (came to U.S. 1952, naturalized 1957); s. Herbert and Eleonora (Strasser) S.; Ph.D., U. Zurich (Switzerland), 1952. Lectr. philosophy Coll. City N.Y., 1959-61; asst. prof. philosophy U. Wash., 1961-66; vis. asso. prof. philosophy Rutgers U., New Brunswick, N.J., 1966-67, mem. faculty, 1967—, chmn. dept. philosophy, 1968-71, prof., 1970—, chmn. New Brunswick dept. philosophy and dir. grad. program in philosophy, 1976-79. Contbr. articles to profl. jours. Office: Van Dyck Hall 2 New Brunswick NJ 08903

STERN, LEAH GORDON (MRS. MORDECAI A. STERN), religious worker; b. Union City, N.J., Nov. 28, 1909; d. Barnet I. and Bessie (Rogosin) Gordon; grad. Hebrew Tchrs. Sem., 1928; student Bklyn Coll., 1952; m. Mordecai Stern, Feb. 7, 1928 (dec. Dec. 1963); children—Ariel, Pnina (Mrs. Henry Grinberg). Pres. women's br. Union Orthodox Jewish Congregations of Am., N.Y.C., 1954-56, exec. v.p., 1962—, pres.'s award, 1978; rep. Leadership Conf. Nat. Jewish Women's Orgns., also Conf. Ch. and Synagogue Women, 1970—; trustee Jewish Braille Inst., 1954-56, Young Israel of Fifth Ave., 1978; organizer L.I. region Am. Mizrachi Women; past nat. pres. Histadruth Harabbonioth; mem. Joint Kashruth Commn., Union Orthodox Jewish Congregations and Rabbinical Council Am. Honoree Women's div. Israel Bonds, 1975. Compiler, editor: A Pesach Sampler. Home: 210 E 15th St New York NY 10003 Office: 84 Fifth Ave New York NY 10011

STERN, LEONARD BERNARD, TV and motion picture prodn. co. exec.; b. N.Y.C., Dec. 23, 1923; s. Max and Esther (Marton) S.; student Sch. Commerce, N.Y. U., 1944; m. Gloria Jane Stroock, Aug. 12, 1956; children—Michael Stroock, Kate Jennifer. Writer, dir. TV, Los Angeles, 1946-53, N.Y.C., 1953-59; founder Price-Stern, Los Angeles, 1959-64; v.p. Price-Stern-Sloan, Los Angeles, 1964-69, dir., 1969—; pres. Heyday Prodns., Los Angeles, 1962-69, 75—; v.p. Talent Assos./Norton Simon, Los Angeles, N.Y.C., 1965-75. Bd. dirs., v.p. Hollywood Presbyn. Med. Center; mem. adv. council Sch. of Arts, N.Y. U. Served with USAAF, 1943-46. Recipient Peabody award U. Ga., Writers' Guild award, 1956, Nat. Assn. TV Arts and

Scis. award, 1956, 66, 1967, Emmy award 1956, 1966. Mem. Writers' Guild Am., Dirs. Guild Am., Caucus for Producers, Writers and Dirs. (co-chmn. steering com.). Author: (with Roger Price) What Not to Name the Baby, 1960. Office: 410 N La Cienega Blvd Los Angeles CA 90048

STERN, LEONARD NORMAN, pet supply mfg. co. exec.; b. N.Y.C., Mar. 28, 1938; s. Max and Hilda (Lowenthal) S.; B.S. cum laude, N.Y. U., 1956, M.B.A., 1957; m. Judith Falk, Jan. 4, 1962; children—Emanuel Theodore, Edward Julius, Andrea Caroline. Pres., dir. Hartz Mountain Corp., N.Y.C., 1959—; pres. Hartz Mountain Industries; mem. adv. bd. Chem. Bank, N.Y.C., 1970—; active real estate constrn., devel. Bd. dirs. Manhattan Day Sch., Jewish Center, N.Y.C.; founder Albert Einstein Coll. Medicine, 1958. Mem. Nat. Assn. Pet Industry. Office: 700 S 4th St Harrison NJ 07029*

STERN, LOUIS WILLIAM, educator, mktg. analyst; b. Boston, Sept. 19, 1935; s. Berthold Summerfield Stern and Gladys (Koch) Cohen; A.B., Harvard, 1957; M.B.A. in Mktg., U. Pa., 1959; Ph.D. in Mktg., Northwestern U., 1962; children—Beth Ida, Deborah Lynn. Mem. staff bus. research and consumer mktg. sects. Arthur D. Little, Inc., Cambridge, Mass., 1961-63; asst. prof. bus. orgn. Ohio State U., Columbus, 1963-64, asso. prof. mktg., 1966-69, prof. mktg., 1970-73; prof. mktg. Northwestern U., Evanston, Ill., 1973-75, A. Montgomery Ward prof. mktg., 1975—, chmn. dept. mktg., 1977—. Mem. staff Nat. Commn. on Food Mktg., Washington, 1965-66; vis. prof. bus. adminstrn. U. Calif. at Berkeley, 1969-70; Distinguished lectr. York U., Toronto, Ont., Can., 1971; Root Distinguished Lectr. Series, La. State U., 1976; distinguished visitor in mktg. U. Minn., 1976; faculty asso. Hernstein Inst., Vienna, Austria, 1976-77, Mgmt. Analysis Center, Inc., Cambridge, Mass., 1977—; disting. visitor York U., 1978; disting. lectr. U. Ky., 1979; cons. to FTC, 1973. Mem. exec. com. Northwest Area Council on Human Relations, Columbus, 1971-72. Ohio State U. research grantee, 1964-73; Mktg. Sci. Inst. research grantee, 1976-77. Mem. Am. Mktg. Assn. (mem. program com. educators conf. 1971, chmn. com. 1978), Am. Econ. Assn., AAUP, Am. Acad. Polit. and Social Sci., Beta Gamma Sigma. Author: Distribution Channels: Behavioral Dimensions, 1969; (with Frederick D. Sturdivant and others) Managerial Analysis in Marketing, 1970, Perspectives in Marketing Management, 1971; (with John R. Grabner, Jr.) Competition in the Marketplace, 1970; (with Adel I. El-Ansary) Marketing Channels, 1977. Contbr. articles on marketing to profl. jours. Mem. editorial bd. Jour. Marketing Research, 1975—, Jour. Marketing, 1978—. Home: 1940 Sherman Ave Apt 401 Evanston IL 60201 Office: Graduate Sch Mgmt Dept of Mktg Northwestern Univ Evanston IL 60201

STERN, MARVIN, mgmt. cons.; b. Bklyn., Jan. 5, 1923; s. David and Regina (Harnik) S.; B.S. in Mech. Engring., Coll. City N.Y., 1943; M.S., N.Y. U., 1947, Ph.D. in Math., 1954; m. June Bronstein Wittlin, Mar. 24, 1945; children—Ellis Roy, Richard Keith; m. 2d, Patricia Wolberg, June 17, 1955; children—Valerie Ann, Gary Allen, Jody Amanda. Corp. staff exec. research, devel. Gen. Dynamics Co., 1958-60; asst. dir. strategic weapons Office Sec. Def., Washington, 1960-61, dep. dir. def. research and engring. Weapons systems, 1961-62; v.p. research, engring. N.Am. Aviation, Inc., El Segundo, Calif., 1962-63; mgmt. cons., Los Angeles, 1963-64; pres. aero. systems div. Gen. Precision, Inc., Wayne, N.J., 1964-66; v.p. Rand Corp., Santa Monica, Calif., 1967-68; pres. Laird Systems, Los Angeles, 1968-70; pres. Marvin Stern & Assos., Ltd., Los Angeles, 1970—; dir. Maul Tech. Corp. Cons. Office Sec. Def., Sec. Transp., Pres.'s Sci. Adv. Com., CIA. Trustee Lycée Français De Los Angeles. Recipient Meritorious Civilian Service medal Sec. Def., 1962. Author: (with George Gamow) Puzzle Math, 1958. Editor: (with Morton Alperin) Vistas in Astronautics, 1958. Address: 2492 Mandeville Canyon Rd Los Angeles CA 90049

STERN, MILTON, mining co. exec.; b. Boston, Apr. 20, 1927; s. Morris and Lily (Colton) S.; B.S., Northeastern U., 1949; M.S. (Alcoa fellow), M.I.T., 1950, Sc.D. (Alcoa fellow), 1952; m. Roberta L. Navisky, July 10, 1949; children—Mark, Lawrence, Brian. Postdoctoral fellow in metallurgy M.I.T., 1952-54; with Union Carbide Corp., N.Y.C., 1954-73, v.p. electronics div., 1968-69, exec. v.p. mining and metals div., 1969-73; v.p. exploration Kennecott Copper Corp., N.Y.C., 1973-76, sr. v.p., 1976-78, exec. v.p., 1978—, also dir. Mem. vis. com. M.I.T., 1972-75; mem. corp. Northeastern U.; mem. White House Task Force on Am. Indian, 1966; bd. dirs. Assn. Am. Indian Affairs. Served with USNR, 1945-46. Recipient Nuodex award Northeastern U., 1949; Sears B. Condit award, 1949. Mem. AIME, Nat. Assn. corrosion Engrs. (Willis R. Whitney award 1963), Am. Soc. Metals, Electrochem. Soc. (Young Authors award 1955, 58, jour. div. editor 1958-61), Sigma Xi, Tau Beta Pi. Clubs: Mining, Sky (N.Y.C.); Rolling Hills (Wilton, Conn.). Contbr. numerous articles in electrochemistry and metallurgy to tech. jours.; patentee in field. Home: 23 Highline Tr S Stamford CT 06902 Office: 161 E 42d St New York NY 10017

STERN, MORT(IMER) P(HILLIP), univ. ofcl.; b. New Haven, Feb. 20, 1926; s. Bernard and Louise Eleanor (Spiro) S.; A.B., U. Ark., 1947; M.S., Columbia, 1949; postgrad. (Nieman fellow), Harvard, 1954-55; Ph.D., U. Denver, 1969; m. Patricia Ruth Freeman, Jan. 10, 1946; children—Susan C., Margaret L. Reporter, Southwest-Am., Ft. Smith, Ark., 1947; night bur. mgr. U.P.I., Little Rock, 1947-48; reporter, polit. writer Ark. Gazette, Little Rock, 1949-51; reporter, rewrite man Denver Post, 1951-53, night city editor, 1953-54, asst. Rocky Mountain Empire editor, 1955-56, mng. editor 1956-58, asso. editor, 1958, editorial page editor, 1958-65, asst. to pub., 1965-70, editorial page editor, 1971-73; dean Sch. Pub. Communication, U. Ala., 1973-74; dean Sch. Journalism, U. Colo., Boulder, 1974-77; lectr. journalism U. Denver, 1953-54, adj. prof., 1970, exec. dir. pub. affairs, 1977-78, exec. asst. to chancellor, 1978—; adj. prof. U. Colo., 1972. Served with USAAF, 1944-45. Mem. Assn. for Edn. in Journalism, Phi Beta Kappa, Omicron Delta Kappa, Sigma Delta Chi. Baptist. Home: 916 Griffith St Georgetown CO 80444

STERN, PHILIP MAURICE, author; b. N.Y.C., May 24, 1926; s. Edgar Bloom and Edith (Rosenwald) S.; A.B. magna cum laude, Harvard, 1947; postgrad. Georgetown U. Law Center, 1975-76; m. Helen Phillips Burroughs Sedgwick, Aug. 30, 1957; children—Henry D., Michael P., Helen P., David M., Eve; m. 2d, Nellie L. Gifford, June 14, 1975. Reporter, editorial writer New Orleans Item, 1948; legislative asst. U.S. Rep. Henry M. Jackson, 1949-50, U.S. Senator Paul Douglas, 1951-52; personal asst. Wilson W. Wyatt, campaign mgr. to Adlai E. Stevenson, 1952; dir. research Democratic Nat. Com., also sr. editor Dem. Digest, 1953-56; editor No. Va. Sun, Arlington, 1957- 60, editor, pub., 1960; dep. asst. sec. of state for pub. affairs, 1961-62; mag. writer, author, 1962—; spl. assignment reporter, nat. staff Washington Post, 1974-75. Mem. Health and Welfare Council Greater Washington Area, 1960; chmn. Va. United Givers Fund, 1960, chmn. Arlington, 1959; dir. Council Founds. and Fair Campaign Practices Com.; pres. Center Pub. Financing of Campaigns, 1975-76. Pres., Stern Family Fund, Philip M. Stern Family Fund. Rockefeller fellow, 1948-49. Mem. Phi Beta Kappa. Club: Federal City. Author: The Great Treasury Raid; The Oppenheimer Case: Security on Trial; (with Helen B. Stern) Oh, Say Can You See: A Bifocal Tour of Washington; (with George de Vincent) The Shame of a Nation; The Rape of the Taxpayer, 1973. Founder: Stern Community Law Firm, Stern Concern. Home: 27 W 67th St New York NY 10023

STERN, PHILIP VAN DOREN, author; b. Wyalusing, Pa., Sept. 10, 1900; s. I.U. and Ann (Van Doren) S.; Litt.B., Rutgers U., 1924, Litt.D., 1940; Litt.D., Lincoln (Ill.) Coll., 1958; m. Lillian Diamond, 1928; 1 dau., Marguerite Louise Robinson. Engaged in advt. work, 1924-33; connected with Alfred A. Knopf, Simon & Schuster, Pocket Books, Inc., 1933-54, gen. mgr. Edits. for Armed Services, 1943-45. Guggenheim fellow for research, 1959-60. Author: An Introduction to Typography, 1932; (with Herbert Asbury) The Breathless Moment, 1935; The Selected Works of Thomas DeQuincey, 1937; The Man Who Killed Lincoln, 1939; The Life and Writings of Abraham Lincoln, 1940; The Midnight Reader, 1942; The Drums of Morning, 1942; The Moonlight Traveler, 1943; The Greatest Gift, 1944; The Portable Library Poe, 1945; (with Bernard Smith) The Holiday Reader, 1947; Travelers in Time, 1947; Lola, 1949; Love is the One with Wings, 1951; Our Constitution, 1953; A Pictorial History of the Automobile, 1953; The Assassination of President Lincoln and the Trial of the Conspirators, 1954; Tin Lizzie, the Story of the Fabulous Model T Ford, 1955; An End to Valor, the Last Days of the Civil War, 1958; Secret Missions of the Civil War, 1959; They Were There: The Civil War in Action as Seen by its Combat Artists, 1959; Prologue to Sumter, 1961; The Confederate Navy: a Pictorial History, 1962; Robert E. Lee, the Man and the Soldier 1963; The Annotated Uncle Tom's Cabin, 1964; When The Guns Roared: World Aspects of the American Civil War, 1965; (with Lillian D. Stern) Beyond Paris: A Touring Guide to the French Provinces, 1967; Prehistoric Europe: from Stone Age Man to the Early Greeks, 1969; The Other Side of the Clock, 1969; The Annotated Walden, 1971; Henry David Thoreau, Writer and Rebel, 1972; Edgar Allan Poe, Visitor From The Night of Time, 1973; The Beginnings of Art, 1973; The Pocket Book of America, 1975. Contbr. articles to nat. mags. Address: 4430 Exeter Dr Apt M202 Longboat Key FL 33548

STERN, RICHARD GUSTAVE, author, educator; b. N.Y.C., Feb. 25, 1928; s. Henry George and Marion (Veit) S.; B.A., U. N.C., 1947; M.A., Harvard, 1950; Ph.D., State U. Ia., 1954; m. Gay Clark, Mar. 14, 1950 (div. Feb. 1972); children—Christopher Holmes, Kate Macomber, Andrew Henry, Nicholas Clark. Faculty, U. Chgo., 1955—, prof. English, 1965—, sec. com. gen. studies in humanities, 1955—. Vis. lectr. U. Venice (Italy), 1962-63, U. Heidelberg (Germany), 1949-50, U. Calif. at Santa Barbara, summer 1964, 68, State U. N.Y. at Buffalo, summer 1966, Harvard, 1969, U. Nice, 1970. Recipient Longwood Found. award, 1960, Friends of Lit. award, 1963, fiction award Nat. Inst. Arts and Letters, 1968. Rockefeller fellow, 1965; Nat. Council Arts and Humanities fellow, 1967-68; Carl Sandburg award for fiction, 1979; Arts Council award, 1979; Guggenheim fellow, 1973-74. Author: Golk, 1960; Europe or Up and Down with Baggish and Schreiber, 1961; In Any Case, 1962; Teeth, Dying and Other Matters, 1964; Stitch, 1965; 1968: A Short Novel, An Urban Idyll, Five Stories and Two Trade Notes, 1970; The Books in Fred Hampton's Apartment, 1973; Other Men's Daughters, 1973; Natural Shocks, 1978; Indirection, 1980; editor: Honey and Wax, 1966. Address: Dept English U Chgo Chicago IL 60637. *The word success is one I could not apply to myself without gross flattery. One is lucky to work where one's small gift is best employed. The rest is not letting what happens to and around one roll off your back; moderate amounts of misfortune are perhaps more precious than much fortune (though I don't know the second firsthand). A few jolts of luck are essential; but one remembers Pasteur's "Luck comes to those prepared for it." Which utterance is enough to tempt the gods to break everything down.*

STERN, RICHARD JAY, investment banker; b. Kansas City, Mo., Sept. 26, 1913; s. Sigmund and Sybil Stern; B.A., Yale U., 1934; M.B.A., Harvard U., 1936. Pres., Stern Brothers & Co., Kansas City, 1936—; dir. Milgram Food Stores, Central Coal & Coke Co., Rival Mfg. Co., Russell Stover Candies. Pres., Lyric Opera of Kansas City; v.p., mem. exec. com. Kansas City Philharmonic Assn., Kansas City Art Inst. Served with USAAF, 1942-45. Address: Stern Brothers & Co 9 W 10th St Kansas City MO 64199

STERN, RICHARD MARTIN, writer; b. Fresno, Calif., Mar. 17, 1915; s. Charles Frank and True (Aiken) S.; student Harvard U., 1933-36; m. Dorothy Helen Atherton, Dec. 20, 1937; 1 adopted dau., Mary Elisabeth Emery (Mrs. Robert Vinton). Gen. advt., radio and newspaper pub. and promotion Hearst Corp., 1936-37; dehydrator foreman Boothe Fruit Co., Modesto, Calif., 1938-39; mfg. engr. Lockheed Aircraft Corp., Burbank, 1940-45; writer short stories and serials for nat. mags. including McCalls, Cosmopolitan, Sat.Eve.Post, This Week, Good Housekeeping, Redbook, 1945—. Mem. Mystery Writers Am. (Edgar award 1959, exec. v.p. 1962-64, pres. 1971), Brit. Crime Writers Assn., Authors Guild. Author: The Bright Road to Fear, 1958; Suspense, 1959; The Search for Tabatha Carr, 1960; These Unlucky Deeds, 1961; High Hazard, 1962: Cry Havoc, 1963; Right Hand, Opposite, 1964; I Hide, We Seek, 1964; The Kessler Legacy, 1967; Merry Go Round, 1969; Brood of Eagles, 1969; Manuscript for Murder, 1970; Murder in the Walls, 1971; You Don't Need An Enemy, 1972; Stanfield Harvest, 1972; Death in the Snow, 1973; The Tower, 1973; Power, 1974; The Will, 1976; Snowbound Six, 1977; Flood, 1979; editorial bd. The Writer. Home: Santa Fe NM 87501 Office: Brandt & Brandt 1501 Broadway New York NY 10036

STERN, ROBERT A. M., architect; b. N.Y.C., May 23, 1939; s. Sidney S. and Sonya (Cohen) S.; A.B., Columbia U., 1960; M.Arch., Yale U., 1965; m. Lynn G. Solinger, May 22, 1966 (div. 1978); 1 son, Nicholas S.G. Program dir. Archtl. League N.Y., 1965-66; designer Richard Meier, Architect, N.Y.C., 1966; cons. Small Parks Program, Dept. Parks N.Y.C., 1966-70; urban designer, asst. to asst. adminstr. housing and devel. adminstrn., N.Y.C., 1967-70; partner Robert A.M. Stern & John S. Hagmann, Architects, N.Y.C., 1969-77; prin. Robert A.M. Stern, Architects, 1977—; asso. prof. architecture Columbia U., 1970—; vis. lectr. Yale, 1972, 73; vis. critic R.I. Sch. Design, 1976, U. Pa., 1977, N.C. State U., Raleigh, 1978; William Henry Bishop vis. prof. architecture Yale U., fall 1978; mem. Mayor's Task Force on Urban Design, N.Y.C., 1966-67. Trustee Am. Fedn. Arts, 1967—; v.p. Cunningham Dance Found., 1969-73, bd. dirs., 1968-75. Mem. AIA (dir. N.Y. chpt.), Soc. Archtl. Historians (dir. 1975-78), Archtl. League N.Y. (pres. 1973-77). Clubs: Century Assn.; Coffee House. Author: New Directions in American Architecture, 1969, 2d edit., 1977; George Howe, Toward a Modern American Architecture, 1975; (with Deborah Nevins) The Architects Eye, 1979; editor: Philip Johnson, Writings, 1979. Home: 177 E 77th St New York NY 10021 Office: 200 W 72d St New York NY 10023

STERN, ROBERT LOUIS, lawyer; b. N.Y.C., Sept. 18, 1908; s. Albert Louis and Alma (Hays) S.; A.B., Williams Coll., 1929; LL.B., Harvard U., 1932; m. Terese Marks, Oct. 16, 1936; children—Lawrence R., Kenneth M., Allan H. Admitted to N.Y. State bar, 1933, Ill. bar, 1954, D.C. bar, 1954; asso. Henry F. Wolff, N.Y.C., 1932-33; atty. Petroleum Adminstrn. Bd., Dept. Interior, Washington, 1933-34, Antitrust div. Justice Dept., 1934-41; with Office Solicitor Gen., Justice Dept., 1941-54, 1st asst., 1950-54, acting solicitor gen., 1952-54; mem. firm Mayer, Brown & Platt, Chgo., 1954—; vis. prof. U. Ariz. Coll. Law, 1972. Mem. Fed. Adv. Com. on Appellate Rules, 1963-68, Ill. Supreme Ct. Rules Com., 1967—; mem. study group on caseload Supreme Ct., 1972. Chmn., Winnetka Community Chest, 1961-62; mem. Winnetka Caucus, 1965-67. Mem. Am. Law Inst., Am. Bar Fellows, Am. (Ross prize essay 1955, council adminstrv. law sect.), Ill., 7th Fed. Circuit, Chgo. bar assns., Am. Coll. Trial Lawyers, Am. Bar Found. (past dir., research com.), Law Club Chgo. Club: 49ers Country (Tucson). Author: (with Gressman) Supreme Court Practice, 5th edit., 1978. Contbr. articles to profl. jours. Home: 1080 Willow Rd Winnetka IL 60093 Office: 231 S La Salle St Chicago IL 60604

STERN, ROBERT MORRIS, educator; b. N.Y.C., June 18, 1937; s. Irving Dan and Nellie (Wachstetter) S.; A.B., Franklin and Marshall Coll., 1958; M.S., Tufts U., 1960; Ph.D., Ind. U., 1963; m. Wilma Olch, June 19, 1960; children—Jessica Leigh, Alison Rachel. Research asso. dept. psychology Ind. U., 1963-65; asst. prof. psychology Pa. State U., 1965-68, asso. prof., 1968-73, prof., 1973—, head dept. psychology, 1978—. Recipient Nat. Media award Am. Psychol. Found., 1978. Mem. Am. Psychol. Assn., Eastern Psychol. Assn., Soc. Psychophysiol. Research. Author: (with W.J. Ray) Biofeedback, 1977; (with W.J. Ray and C.M. Davis) Psychophysiological Recordings, 1980. Contbr. articles in field to profl. jours. Home: 1360 Greenwood Circle State College PA 16801 Office: 417 Moore Bldg Pennsylvania State Univ University Park PA 16802

STERN, RUSSELL THURSTON, JR., fin. services co. exec.; b. Chgo., Apr. 2, 1927; s. Russell T. and Eleanor J. S.; B.A., Princeton U., 1949; m. Carol Larson Stern, July 6, 1949; children—Russell Thurston, William Carl, K. Patricia, Darrell S. With Merrill Lynch Pierce Fenner & Smith Inc., Chgo., 1949—, office mgr., 1969-72, regional v.p., 1972-78, mng. dir. mktg., 1979—. Republican. Episcopalian. Clubs: Econs., Exec. Home: 46 Fox Lan Winnetka IL 60093 Office: 135 S LaSalle St Chicago IL 60603

STERN, SAMUEL ALAN, lawyer; b. Phila., Jan. 21, 1929; A.B., U. Pa., 1949; LL.B., Harvard U., 1952. Admitted to Mass. bar, 1952, D.C. bar, 1958; asso. firm Cox, Langford, Stoddard & Cutler, Washington, 1956-62; partner firm Wilmer, Cutler & Pickering, Washington, 1962—; vis. prof. law Harvard U., 1976; dir. Inst. Internat. and Fgn. Trade Law, Georgetown U., 1971—; asst. counsel Warren Commn., 1974; cons. UN, 1974—. Mem. pres.'s council Tulane U., 1976—. Mem. Am. Law Inst., Am. Soc. Internat. Law, Am., D.C. bar assns. Contbr. articles to legal jours. Home: 3626 Prospect St NW Washington DC 20007 Office: 1666 K St NW Washington DC 20006

STERN, SYDNEY VAUGHN, oil. co. exec.; b. N.Y.C., Aug. 10, 1932; s. Samuel and Edith V. S.; B.S. in Chem. Engring., Ga. Inst. Tech., 1954, M.S. in Chem. Engring., 1960, Ph.D., 1962; grad. mgmt. devel. program Harvard U. Sch. Bus., 1969; m. Marion Shelton Jones, Feb. 27, 1954; children—Adam V., Susan C. With Continental Oil Co., 1962—, dir. project devel., Stamford, Conn., 1970-74, pres. Continental Oil Co. Far East, Tokyo, 1974—; rep. dir. Petrocokes Ltd. (Japan); dir. Nissan-Conoco Corp., Nippon Aluminum Alkyls, Tokyo Continental Carbon. Bd. dirs., trustee Am. Sch. in Japan, Tokyo. Served with USN, 1954-58. Mem. Am. C. of C. in Japan (chmn. civic affairs com. 1976, gov. 1976-77, v.p. 1978), Am.-Japan Soc. Clubs: Tokyo Am., Tokyo Lawn Tennis, Yomiuri Country. Home: Homat President 170 1-3-20 Roppongi Minato-ku Tokyo Japan Office: PO Box 64 Kasumigaseki Bldg Tokyo Japan

STERN, THEODORE, educator; b. Briarcliffe, N.Y., July 27, 1917; s. Stanley W. and Catherine (Sessler) S.; B.A. cum laude, Bowdoin Coll., 1939; M.A., U. Pa., 1941, Ph.D., 1948; m. Mary Capuzzi, Jan. 16, 1942; children—Theodore Andrew, Holly Elizabeth. Research asso. Mus. No. Ariz., 1940; asst. instr. anthropology U. Pa., 1946, instr., 1947-48; asst. prof. U. Oreg., Eugene, 1948-57, asso. prof., 1957-63, prof. anthropology, 1964—, chmn. dept., 1969-72. Served to 1st lt. AUS, 1941-45. Fulbright research fellow, Burma, 1954; NSF fellow, Thailand, 1964. Fellow Am. Anthrop. Assn.; mem. Am. Ethnol. Soc., Burma Research Soc., Siam Soc. Author: The Rubber-ball Games of the Americas, 1950; (with R.F. Spencer, J.D. Jennings et al) The Native Americans, 1965; The Klamath Tribe, 1965. Asso. editor: Jour. Am. Folklore. Research in culture change, ethnolinguistics, folklore, religion, Am. Indians, S.E. Asia. Home: 2055 Fairmount Blvd Eugene OR 97403

STERN, THOMAS, fgn. service officer; b. Karlsruhe, Germany, Aug. 17, 1927; s. Kurt and Gemma (Baer) S.; came to U.S., 1939, naturalized, 1944; A.B., Haverford Coll., 1950; postgrad. Maxwell Grad. Sch., Syracuse U., 1950-51; m. Vivian Margolis, Sept. 27, 1959; children—Michael Lawrence, Kenneth Paul. Budget officer State Dept., 1952-55; mgmt. analyst, personnel officer, program officer ICA, 1955-61; dir. Office Finance, State Dept., 1961-62; dir. Office Near East-S. Asia Mgmt., AID, 1962-63; spl. asst. dep. undersec. State Dept., 1963-66; counselor for adminstrn. Am. embassy, Bonn, Germany, 1966-69; dep. asst. sec. for O and M, Washington, 1969-71, mem. sec.'s planning and coordination staff, 1971-72; sr. seminar Fgn. Service Inst., 1972-73; dep. dir. polit.-mil. bur. State Dept., 1973; dep. chief mission, Seoul, Korea, 1976—. Served with AUS, 1946-47. Recipient Superior Honor award State Dept., 1964. Mem. Am. Soc. Pub. Adminstrn. Address: American Embassy APO San Francisco CA 96301

STERN, THOMAS NOEL, educator; b. Pitts., July 7, 1913; s. Leon Thomas (LeFevre) and Elizabeth Gertrude (Limburg) S.; B.A. with honors, Swarthmore Coll., 1934; postgrad. U. Lyons (France), 1934-35; M.A. in Polit. Sci., U. Pa., 1940, Ph.D. in Polit. Sci., 1942; m. Katherine Frances Kirk, Dec. 28, 1940; children—S. Yolanda, Roland Craig, Ellen Cornog, Joan Thrush. With dept. govt. Boston U., 1945-53; Fulbright prof. U. Rennes, U. Strasbourg, 1952; dir. Foundation des Etats-Unis, U. Paris (France), 1953-56; acting chief UN Pub. Adminstrn. Mission to Ethiopia, 1956-57; dir. research and statistics Pa. Dept. Revenue, 1957-60; pres. West Chester (Pa.) State Coll., 1960-61; research prof. govt. African Studies program Boston U., 1962-63, also chief pub. adminstrn. team, Guinea, West Africa; prof., past chmn. dept. polit. sci. S.E. Mass. U., North Dartmouth, 1964-69, prof., 1969—. Mem. Soc. of Friends, exec. com. Friends Gen. Conf., Phila. Mem. AAUP (past pres. S.E. Mass. chpt.), Am. Polit. Sci. Assn. Mem. editorial bd. Internat. Rev. History and Polit. Sci. Contbr. to Jour. Thought, Social Sci., Peace and Change, Friends Jour., Quaker Life, others. Home: 875 Smith Neck Rd South Dartmouth MA 02748

STERN, WALTER EUGENE, surgeon, educator; b. Portland, Oreg., Jan. 1, 1920; s. Walter Eugene and Ida May (McCoy) S.; A.B. cum laude, U. Calif., M.D., 1943; m. Elizabeth Naffziger, May 24, 1946; children—Geoffrey Alexander, Howard Christian, Eugenia Louise, Walter Eugene III. Surg. intern, asst. resident surgery and neurol. surgery U. Calif. Hosp., 1943-46, asst. resident neurol. surgery and neuropathology, 1948; clin. clk. Nat. Hosp. Paralyzed and Epileptic, London, Eng., 1948-49; Nat. Research fellow med. sci. Johns Hopkins, 1949-50; asst. resident, resident U. Calif. Service, 1951; NIH spl. fellow univ. lab. physiology Oxford U., 1961-62; clin. instr. U. Calif., 1951; asst. prof. neurosurgery U. Calif. at Los Angeles, 1952-56, asso. prof., 1956-59, prof., 1959—, chief div. neurosurgery, 1952—; cons. neurosurgery Wadsworth VA Hosp. Served from lt. to capt. M.C., AUS, 1946-48. Diplomate Am. Bd. Neurol. Surg. (vice chmn.). Fellow A.C.S. (sec.); mem. A.M.A., Am., Pacific Coast surg. assns., Los Angeles Surg. Soc. (pres. 1978), Am. Assn. Neurol. Surgeons (pres. elect), James IV Assn. Surgeons, Brit., Western (past pres.) neurosurg. assns., Soc. Neurol. Surgeons (past pres.), Neurosurg. Soc. Am., Am. Neurol. Assn., Soc. U. Surgeons, Soc. Brit. Neurol. Surgeons (hon.), Phi Beta Kappa, Sigma Xi, Alpha Omega Alpha. Republican. Epsicopalian. Editorial bd. Jour. Neurosurgery. Contbr. articles to sci. jours., chpts. in books. Home: 435 Georgina Ave Santa Monica CA 90402 Office: Sch Medicine University of California Los Angeles CA 90024

STERN, WALTER PHILLIPS, investment exec.; b. N.Y.C., Sept. 26, 1928; s. Leo and Marjorie (Phillips) S.; A.B., Williams Coll., 1950; M.B.A., Harvard U., 1952; m. Elizabeth May, Feb. 12, 1958; children—Sarah May, William May, David May. With Lazard Freres & Co., N.Y.C., 1953-54; asso. Burnham & Co., Inc. (now Lambert Drexel Burnham Group, Inc.), N.Y.C., 1954-60, partner, 1960-71, sr. exec. v.p., 1972-73; vice chmn. Capital Research Co., 1973—, also mng. dir. eastern ops.; chmn. bd. New Perspective Fund, Inc., 1973—, Anchor Growth Fund, 1978—, Fundamental Investors Inc., 1978—; pres., chief exec. officer Capital Strategic Services, Inc., 1974—; dir. Income Fund Am., Inc., Growth Fund Am., Inc., May Corp., Nashville, Capital Research S.A., Capital Guardian Mgmt. Co. Inc.; instr. N.Y. U., 1956-62, 70-73. Pres., bd. dirs. Research Project on Energy and Econ. Policy; mem. fin. com. Hadassah; bd. dirs. Westchester chpt. Am. Jewish Com., Westchester Planned Parenthood; bd. dirs., treas. Am. Friends of Tel Aviv U.; vice-chmn., trustee Hudson Inst.; trustee Tel Aviv U.; trustee, treas. Fin. Accounting Found., Inst. Strategic Studies, Tel Aviv; v.p., trustee Fin. Analysts Research Found.; adv. bd. Ams. for Energy Independence. Served as 1st lt. USAF, 1952-53. Mem. N.Y. Soc. Security Analysts (bd. dirs.), Fin. Analysts Fedn. (pres. 1971-72, bd. dirs.), Inst. Chartered Fin. Analysts (pres. 1976-77), Phi Beta Kappa. Jewish. Clubs: Board Room, Harvard, Williams, Economic (N.Y.C.); Sunningdale Country (Scarsdale N.Y.); California (Los Angeles). Contbr. articles to profl. jours. Home: 450 Ft Hill Rd Scarsdale NY 10583 Office: 280 Park Ave New York NY 10017

STERN, WILLIAM LOUIS, botanist, educator; b. Paterson, N.J., Sept. 10, 1926; s. Abram and Rose (Chrisman) S.; B.S., Rutgers U., 1950; M.S., U. Ill., 1951, Ph.D., 1954; m. Floraet Selma Tanis, Sept. 4, 1949; children—Susan Myra, Paul Elihu. Instr., then asst. prof. Yale Sch. Forestry, 1953-60; curator div. plant anatomy Smithsonian Inst., 1960-64, chmn. dept botany, 1964-67; prof. botany U. Md., College Park, 1967-79; prof., chmn. dept. botany U. Fla., Gainesville, 1979—. Forestry officer FAO, 1963-64; mem. sci. adv. bd. Pacific Tropical Bot. Garden, 1969—; mem. sci. adv. com. Winterthur Mus., 1973—; vis. com. Arnold Arboretum of Harvard, 1971-77, vice chmn., 1973-76; asesor cientifico Universidad de los Andes, Merida, Venezuela, 1975; program dir. systematic biology NSF, 1978, 79. Served with USNR, 1944-46; PTO. Fellow Linnean Soc. of London; mem. Bot. Soc. Am., Am. Inst. Biol. Sci., AAAS, Internat. Assn. Wood Anatomists (hon.; council), Am. Soc. Plant Taxonomists (pres.-elect 1980), Soc. Econ. Botany, Torrey Bot. Club (editor Memoirs 1971-75), Washington Bot. Soc. (pres. 1972), Internat. Soc. Tropical Foresters, Soc. Advancement Research (Philippines), Amigos del Museo Nacional (Panama), Assn. for Tropical Biology, Internat. Wood Collectors Soc. (life), Phi Beta Kappa, Sigma Xi, Delta Phi Alpha, Phi Kappa Phi, Phi Sigma. Editor: Tropical Woods, 1953-60, Plant Sci. Bull., 1962-64, Biotropica, 1968-73; asso. editor BioSci., 1963-65, Econ. Botany, 1966-75; mem. editorial com. Am. Jour. Botany, 1967-69. Office: U Fla Gainesville FL 32611

STERNBACH, LEO HENRYK, medicinal chemist; b. Abbazia, Austria, May 7, 1908; s. Michael Abraham and Piroska (Cohn) S.; naturalized, 1946; M.Pharmacy, U. Cracow, Poland, 1929, Ph.D., 1931; D.Techn. Scis. h.c., Vienna, Austria, 1971; m. Herta Kreuzer, Feb. 7, 1941; children—Michael, Daniel. Research asso. U. Cracow, 1931-37, Swiss Fed. Inst. Tech., Zurich, 1937-40; research chemist Hoffmann LaRoche, Basle, Switzerland, 1940-41, sr. research chemist Hoffmann LaRoche, Inc., Nutley, N.J., 1941-59, group chief, sect. chief, 1959-65, dir. medicinal chemistry, 1966-73; cons. in field, 1973—. Mem. Am. Chem. Soc. (Medicinal Chemistry award 1978, Creative Invention award 1979, Chem. Pioneer award 1979), Swiss Chem. Soc., Internat. Soc. Heterocyclic Chemistry, Chem. Soc. (Gt. Britain), Sigma Xi. Synthesis and discovery of centrally acting 1, 4-Benzodiazepines, Librium, Valium, Dalmane, Clonopin, Mogadon, Rohypnol and others; tech. synthesis of the vitamin Biotin. Contbr. articles to profl. jours.; patentee in field. Home: 10 Woodmont Rd Upper Montclair NJ 07043 Office: Hoffmann La Roche Nutley NJ 07110. *I ascribe my results to my love for chemical research and particularly to my deep interest in organic chemical laboratory bench-work.*

STERNBERG, DANIEL ARLE, musician, condr., coll. dean; b. Lwow, Poland, Mar. 29, 1913; s. Philipp and Eva (Makowska) S.; baccalaureate, Realgymnasium, Vienna, 1931; student U. Vienna, 1931-35; diploma of condr. Vienna State Acad. Music, 1935; composition study with Karl Weigl, 1931-35; conducting with Fritz Stiedry, 1935-36; m. Felicitas Gobineau, July 29, 1936. Came to U.S., 1939, naturalized, 1946. Lectr. Vienna Volkschochschule, 1933-34; condr. Vienna Vets. Orch., 1934-35; asst. condr. Leningrad Philharmonic and Grand Opera, 1935-36; guest condr. Leningrad and Moscow radio orchs., 1936, Dallas Symphony Orch., 1952, 65; music dir. Tiflis State Symphony Orch., Tiflis, Russia, 1936-37; head piano dept. Hockaday Inst. Music, Dallas, 1940-42; dean Sch. Music, Baylor U., Waco, Tex., 1942—; mus. dir. condr. Waco Symphony Orch., 1963—; concert accompanist; lectr. mus. subjects. Recipient Abrams Meml. award for orchestral composition Dallas Symphony Orch., 1948. Mem. AAUP, Music Tchrs. Nat. Assn. (pres. Southwestern div.), Sinfonia, Phi Mu Alpha, Omicron Delta Kappa. Contbr. articles to mags. Home: 3108 Robin Rd Waco TX 76708

STERNBERG, ELI, educator; b. Vienna, Austria, Nov. 13, 1917; s. Philip and Eva (Mackowska) S.; came to U.S., 1939; naturalized, 1945; B.C.E., U. N.C., 1941; M.S. in C.E., Ill. Inst. Tech., 1942, Ph.D. in Mechanics, 1945; D.Sc. (hon.), U. N.C., 1963; m. Rae Shifrin, July 23, 1955; children—Eve Louise, Peter Joshua. Prof. mechanics, Ill. Inst. Tech., Chgo., 1945-56, Brown U., Providence, 1956-64, Calif. Inst. Tech., Pasadena, 1964—. Fulbright fellow, 1956-57, 70-71; Guggenheim fellow, 1963-64. Mem. Am. Acad. Arts and Scis., Nat. Acad. Engring., Nat. Acad. Sci. Editorial com. Archive Rational Mech. Analysis, 1957, Jour. Elasticity, 1971. Contbr. articles to profl. jours. Home: 2052 Pinecrest Dr Altadena CA 91001 Office: California Institute Technology Pasadena CA 91109

STERNBERG, HARRY, artist; b. N.Y.C., July 19, 1904; s. Simon and Rose (Brand) S.; student Art Students League, N.Y.C.; m. Mary Elizabeth Gosney, 1939; 1 dau., Leslie Louise. Exhibited 25 Year Retrospective Exhbn., ACA and Gorezick Galleries, 1953; one man exhbns. ACA Gallery, N.Y.C., 1956, 59, 60, 65, 68, 70, 72, 75, Brigham Young U., 58, 62, 75, Gorelick Gallery, 58, Nat. Inst. Arts and Letters, 1961, Utah State U., 1962, Salt Lake Art Center, Salt Lake City, 1962, Heritage Gallery, Los Angeles, 1964, Gray Gallery, Escondido, 1970, Ulrich Mus.; retrospective exhbns. Walker Art Centre, Mpls., 1973, Wichita State U., 1975, Art Students League, N.Y.C., Asso. Am. Artists, N.Y.C., Art and Design Gallery-Bonsall, 1976, others; represented in permanent collections Mus. Modern Art, Met. Mus., Whitney Mus., Bklyn., Cleve., Phila. museums, Library Congress, Victoria and Albert Mus., London, Bibliothique Nationale, Paris, Syracuse U., H. de Young Meml. Mus., Wichita (Kans.) State Mus., San Francisco, Fogg Mus., Boston, Addison Gallery Am. Art, Boston, Syracuse U. Mus., Library Congress, Washington, N.Y. Pub. Library, U. Minn., Nat. Mus. Tel Aviv, N.Z. Mus. Art, St. Lawrence U., Roberson Art Centre, Binghamton, N.Y., Cleve. Mus. Art, Ulrich Mus., Thorne Mus., Keene State Coll., Hirshorn Mus., Washington; tchr. Art Students League, N.Y.C.; head art dept. Idyllwild Sch. Music and Art, U. Calif. at Los Angeles, U. So. Calif., Idyllwild (Cal.) Arts Found., 1956-63; tchr. graphics San Diego State Coll., 1967-68; artist in residence Palomar Coll., San Marcos, Calif.; producer, dir. motion pictures The Many Worlds of Art, 1960, Art and Reality, 1961. Recipient Guggenheim fellowship, 1936, 1st prize Phila. Print Club, 1942, Audubon Artists graphic prize, 1955, Nat. Inst. Arts and Letters purchase award, 1972. Living Arts Found., grantee, 1960. Mem. Art Students League N.Y.C. (hon.), Artists Guild of Fine Arts Gallery (San Diego). Author: Silk Screen Color Printing, 1942; Modern Methods and Materials of Etching, 1949; Compositions, 1957; Modern Drawing, 1958; Woodcut, 1962. Home: 1606 Conway Dr Escondido CA 92027 Studio: 1718 Valley Pkwy Escondido CA 92025

STERNBERG, HILGARD O'REILLY, geographer, educator; b. Rio de Janeiro, Brazil, July 5, 1917; s. Bruno Ludwig and Johanna Mary O'Reilly (Begg) S.; Bacharel, U. de Brasil, 1940, Licenciado, 1941, Doutor, 1958; Ph.D., La. State U., 1956; Docteur h.c., U. Toulouse (France), 1965; m. Carolina de Silveira Lobo, July 28, 1942; children—Hilgard, Maria Inês (Mrs. Francis Anthony Mangiola), Ricardo, Leonel, Cristina. Faculty, U. Brazil, 1942-64, prof. geography, 1944-64, dir. Center Research in Geography of Brazil, 1951-64; prof. geography U. Calif. at Berkeley, 1964—. First v.p. Internat. Geog. Union, 1956-60; mem. com. research priorities in tropical biology NRC. Decorated comdr. Nat. Order Merit, Order Rio Branco (Brazil); recipient Best Publ. award Nat. Council Geog. Edn., 1966. Mem. Brazilian Acad. Scis., Deutsche Akademie der Naturforscher Leopoldina, Assn. de Géographes Français, Assn. Am. Geographers, Assn. de Geógrafos Brasileiros; hon. mem. Soc. de Géographie (Paris), Gesellschaft für Erdkunde zu Berlin, Soc. Serbe de Géographie; hon. corr. mem. Royal Geog. Soc., Orgn. Tropical Studies (past chmn. com. geography). Author articles, books in field. Spl. research geomorphology, settlement patterns, land-use in Amazonia, N.E. Brazil, West Central Brazil; environ. impact of devel., geography of food. Home: 466 Michigan Ave Berkeley CA 94707

STERNBERG, MARVIN JOHN, state justice; b. Louisville, May 2, 1912; s. Manuel and Christina (Jegen) S.; LL.B., Jefferson Sch. Law, 1933; J.D., U. Louisville, 1933: m. Lillian Marie Rafferty, May 21, 1935; children—Tina Jegen Sternberg VanMeter, Marvine Joan Sternberg Butler. Admitted to Ky. bar, 1933; practiced law, Louisville, Frankfort and Jamestown, Ky.; asst. atty. gen. Commonwealth of Ky., 1944-46; judge Jefferson Circuit Ct., Chancery Br., Second Div., Louisville, 1964-74; justice Ky. Supreme Ct. of Appeals, 1975—. Pres. South End Republican Club, Louisville; bd. dirs. Whittenberg U. Recipient Distinguished Alumnus certificate Law Alumni Assn. U. Louisville, 1975. Mem. Louisville (Jud. award 1974), Ky. State bar assns., Phi Alpha Delta. Clubs: South Park Country, Order Ky. Cols., Ky. Silver Muskie, League Ky. Sportsmen, Iroquois Civic, Beechmont Civic, Kenwood Optimist, Lincoln, Masons, Shriners, DeMolay, Audubon High-Twelve of Louisville, Order Eastern Star. Lutheran. Office: Capitol Bldg Room 245 Frankfort KY 40601*

STERNBERG, PAUL, physician; b. Chgo., Dec. 18, 1918; s. David M. and Sarah (Kopeka) S.; B.S., Northwestern U., 1938, M.D., 1940; m. Dorie Betty Feitler, Dec. 24, 1949; children—Daniel P., Patricia F., Paul, Susan P., David. Intern, Michael Reese Hosp., Chgo., 1940-41; resident ophthalmology Michael Reese Hosp., Ill. Eye & Ear Infirmary U. Ill.; spl. fellow ophthalmology Cornell U. Med. Center, N.Y. Hosp., Wilmer Inst. Johns Hopkins, 1941-44; practice medicine, specializing in ophthalmology, Chgo., 1945—; attending opthalmologist Cook County Hosp., Michael Reese Hosp., Highland Park (Ill.) Hosp., Louis Weiss Meml. Hosp.; prof. opthalmology Chgo. Med. Sch. Fellow A.C.S.; mem. Assn. for Research in Ophthalmology, Am. Assn. Ophthalmology, Am. Acad. Ophthalmology, Chgo. Ophthal. Soc., Pan-Am. Congress Ophthalmology. Clubs: Standard (Chgo.); Lake Shore Country (Glencoe, Ill.). Contbr. sci. articles to med. and ophthal. jours. Home: 359 Surfside Pl Glencoe IL 60022 Office: 111 N Wabash Ave Chicago IL 60602

STERNBERG, THOMAS HUNTER, physician, dermatologist, educator; b. Mt. Pleasant, Iowa, July 25, 1908; s. Walter A. and Elizabeth (Hunter) S.; B.S., Northwestern U., 1932, M.D., 1934; fellow in dermatology and syphilogy U. Pa., 1934-37; m. Mary Magoon, July 25, 1929; children—Thomas J., Richard Walter, James Hunter; m. 2d, Camilla R. Cassity, Jan. 18, 1958. Intern Los Angeles County Gen. Hosp., 1933; resident surgery Passavant Meml. Hosp., Chgo., 1934; affiliated with Los Angeles County Gen. Hosp.; spl. cons. USPHS, 1946—; cons. Dept. Army and Surgeon Gen., 1946—; sr. cons. dermatology VA Hosp., West Los Angeles, 1946—; prof. dermatology Sch. Medicine, U. Calif. at Los Angeles, 1951-71, head postgrad. instrn. med. extension U. Calif., asst. dean post-grad. med. edn. U. Calif. Med. Center, 1955-65, prof. emeritus, 1971—; med. dir. Dermatologic Research Found. Calif., 1971—; sr. cons. dermatology Long Beach VA Hosp.; cons. dermatology Los Angeles County Harbor Gen. Hosp. Mem. com. on venereal diseases NRC, 1946-50; Mem. Commn. on Cutaneous Diseases, Armed Forces Epidemiol. Bd., 1955-59; pres. Internat. Postgrad. Med. Found. Served as lt. col. AUS, 1942-46. Decorated Legion of Merit. Diplomate Am. Bd. Dermatology and Syphilology. Fellow Am. Acad. Dermatology and Syphilology, Soc. Investigative Dermatology (dir.); mem. Am. Dermatol. Assn., Am. Venereal Disease Assn. (pres. 1951-52), AMA, Calif., Los Angeles County med. assns., Nat. Inst. Allergy and Infectious Diseases (grad. tng. grants com. 1958-60), Phi Delta Theta, Nu Sigma Nu; hon. mem. dermatol. assns. France, Germany, Denmark, Israel, Mexico. Contbr. articles to profl. jours. Author: Therapy and Fungus Disease, 1955; More Than Skin Deep, 1970. Sr. editor Modern Dermatologic Therapy 1959. Editor: The Evaluation of Therapeutic Agents and Cosmetics, 1964. Office: Linde Med Plaza 10921 Wilshire Blvd Los Angeles CA 90024

STERNE, AUGUSTUS HERRINGTON, ednl. adminstr., ret. banker; b. Montgomery, Ala., Feb. 28, 1913; s. Adolph Herrington and Sue Evans (Brown) S.; A.B., U. Ga., 1934; student Emory U. Law Sch., 1934-35; m. Helen Hill Hopkins, Apr. 29, 1938; children—Helen (Mrs. James S. Anderson), William A., Carroll P., Augusta H., Nancy Evans. With Retail Credit Co., Atlanta, 1935-36; with Trust Co. of Ga., Atlanta, 1936-78, sr. v.p., 1957-64, pres., 1964-73, chmn., dir., 1973-78, ret., 1978; dean Grad. Sch. Bus. Adminstrn., Atlanta U., 1978—. chmn., dir. Munich Am. Reins. Co.; dir., chmn. exec. com. Atlantic Steel Co.; dir. Trust Co. Ga. Assos., Oxford Industries, Inc., So. Natural Resources, Inc., Lanier Bus. Products, Inc., Internat. Exec. Service Corps. Bd. dirs. United Way Met. Atlanta; bd. dirs. Central Atlanta Progress; bd. dirs. Soc. Center Internat. Studies, Atlanta Bot. Gardens, Inc.; trustee Agnes Scott Coll., Atlanta Arts Alliance, U. Ga. Found. Served with USMCR, 1942-45. Mem. Atlanta C. of C. (dir.), Sigma Alpha Epsilon, Phi Delta Phi. Episcopalian. Clubs: Peachtree Golf, Piedmont Driving, Commerce (dir.), Nine O'Clocks, Capital City, Augusta Nat. Golf. Home: 2655 Rivers Rd NW Atlanta GA 30305 Office: PO Box 4418 Atlanta GA 30302

STERNE, HEDDA, artist; b. Bucharest, Romania; d. Simon and Eugenia (Wexler) Lindenberg; m. Saul Steinberg, Oct., 1944. One-woman exhibitions include: Wakefield Gallery, N.Y.C., 1943, Mortimer Brandt Gallery, N.Y.C., 1945, Betty Parsons Gallery, N.Y.C., 1947, 48, 50, 53, 54, 57, 58, 61, 63, 66, 68, 70, 74, 75, 78, Galleria dell'Obelisco, Rome, 1953, 61, Arts Club of Chgo., 1955, Vassar Coll., 1956, Saidenberg Gallery, 1956, Rizzoli Gallery, 1968, Sneed Gallery, 1971, Guild Hall, East Hampton, N.Y., 1973, Rochester U., 1973, Upstairs Gallery, East Hampton, 1974, Lee Ault & Co., N.Y.C., 1975, Fairweather Hardin Gallery, Chgo., 1976, Montclair Art Mus., 1977; represented in permanent collections: Met. Mus., Modern Art, Whitney Mus., Art Inst. Chgo., Va. Mus., U. Ill., Detroit Inst. Art, Joseph H. Hirshhorn Collection, Albrecht Gallery, Chase Manhattan Bank, Albright-Knox Art Gallery, Pa. Acad. Fine Arts, Toledo Mus. Art, Minn. Mus. Art, Montclair Art Mus., Ford Found., DeMenil Collection, others. Recipient Am. Acad. Arts and Letters award, 1971. Fulbright fellow, 1963. Address: 179 E 71st New York NY 10021

STERNE, JOSEPH ROBERT LIVINGSTON, newspaper editor; b. Phila., Apr. 25, 1928; s. Robert Livingston and Edith Eisner (Heymann) S.; B.A. cum laude, Lehigh U., 1948; M.S., Columbia, 1950; m. Barbara Adele Greene, Feb. 10, 1951; children—Robert Greene, Paul Livingston, Edward Joseph, Adam Heymann, Lee Winslow Greene. Reporter, Salt Lake Telegram, Salt Lake City, 1948-49, Wall Street Jour., N.Y.C., 1950-51, Dallas Morning News, 1951-53; reporter Balt. Sun, 1953-72, editor, 1972—. Mem. Am. Soc. Newspaper Editors, Phi Beta Kappa. Clubs: Center, Hamilton Street (Balt.). Home: 215 Melanchton Ave Lutherville MD 21093 Office: Baltimore Sun Baltimore MD 21203

STERNER, FRANK MAURICE, indsl. exec.; b. Lafayette, Ind., Nov. 26, 1935; s. Raymond E. and Maudelene M. (Scipio) S.; B.S., Purdue U., 1958, M.S., 1959, Ph.D., 1962; m. Elsa Y. Rasmusson, June 29, 1958; children—Mark, Lisa. Sr. staff specialist Gen. Motors Inst., Flint, Mich., 1962-63; dir. personnel and orgnl. research Delco Electronics, Milw., 1963-66, dir. personnel devel. and research, 1966-68; partner Nourse & Sterner, Inc., Milw., 1968-69; pres., 1969-73; asso. dean, prof. Krannert Grad. Sch. of Mgmt., Purdue U., West Lafayette, Ind., 1973-79; v.p. human resources mgmt. and strategic planning Johnson Controls, Inc., Milw., 1979—; dir. Heil Co., Milw., T.A. Chapman Co., Milw., Wausau Homes, Inc., Sterling Custom Homes, Inc. Club: Reamer. Contbr. articles to profl. jours. Home: 141 Colony Rd West Lafayette IN 47906 Office: Johnson Controls Inc 507 N Michigan Ave Milwaukee WI 53202

STERNER, JAMES HERVI, physician, educator; b. Bloomsburg, Pa., Nov. 14, 1904; s. Lloyd Parvin and Nora (Finney) S.; student Pa. State Tchrs. Coll., Bloomsburg, 1925; B.S., Pa. State Coll., 1928; M.D., Harvard U., 1932; m. Frances Elkavich, Apr. 11, 1932 (div. 1971); children—James R., Susan M., John P.; m. 2d, Patricia L. Hudson, 1971. House officer New Eng. Deaconess Hosp., Boston, 1931-32, intern, 1932-34; chief resident physician, Lankenau Hosp., Phila., 1934-36; dir. lab. indsl. medicine Eastman Kodak Co., Rochester, N.Y. 1936-48, asso. med. dir., 1949-50, med. dir. 1951-68; med. dir. Clinton Engring. Works, Tenn. Eastman Corp., Oak Ridge, 1943-45; med. cons. Holston Ordnance Works, Kingsport, Tenn., 1941-43; instr. indsl. medicine and toxicology U. Rochester Sch. Medicine, 1940-50, asso. prof. medicine, 1951-57, clin. asso. prof. medicine, 1958-68, from clin. asso. prof. to clin. prof. preventive medicine and community health, 1951-68; prof. environmental health U. Tex. Sch. Pub. Health, Houston, 1968-75, acting dean, 1968, asso. dean, 1969-70; clin. prof. occupational medicine U. Calif. Coll. Medicine at Irvine, 1975—; acting dir. pub. health City Houston, 1970; vis. lectr. indsl. hygiene Harvard U., 1952-56; vis. lectr. indsl. medicine U. Tex. Postgrad. Sch. Medicine, 1954-58; sr. asso. physician Strong Meml. Hosp.; cons. indsl. medicine Genesee Hosp., 1960-68, Rochester Gen. Hosp., 1963-68; adv. med. bd. in Am., Am. Hosp. of Paris, 1958. Mem. interim med. adv. bd. Manhattan Project AEC, 1945-47; mem. radiol. safety sect. and medicolegal bd. Operations Crossroads (Bikini experiment), 1946; cons. indsl. health AEC, 1948—, mem. adv. com. biology and medicine, 1960-66, mem. gen. adv. com., 1971-74; mem. com. fellowships in indsl. medicine, chmn., 1950-51; mem. com. on toxicol. div. chem. and chem. technol. NRC, 1947-55, 71-74; mem. Nat. Transuranium Registry Adv. Com., chmn., 1969—; spl. cons. USPHS (chmn. com. on radiation studies), 1951-53; mem. cancer control com. Nat. Cancer Inst., 1957-61; expert adv. panel on occupational health WHO, 1951—; cons. Nat. Center Health Statistics, 1966-75; mem. com. occupational safety and health ILO; mem. Nat. Council Radiation Protection and Measurements, 1955-68; mem. N.Y. State Gen. Adv. Com. Atomic Energy, 1959-65; environ. health panel Pres.'s Sci. Adv. Com., 1961-65, Nat. Adv. Disease Prevention and Environ. Control Council, 1964-68; chmn. Nat. Air Conservation Commn., 1966-70; mem. adv. environ. panel U.S. Senate Com. on Pub. Works, 1970-75; mem. sci. adv. panel U.S. Ho. of Reps. Com. Pub. Works, 1973-75; environ. health adv. com. EPA, 1975—. Recipient Indsl. Health award Houston C. of C., 1954, award N.Y. Acad. Preventive Medicine, 1963. Diplomate Am. Bd. Indsl. Hygiene, Am. Bd. Preventive Medicine (chmn. 1961-67). Fellow AAAS, Indsl. Med. Assn. (Knudsen award 1957), Am. Coll. Preventive Medicine (v.p. 1957-58, pres. 1959-60), Am. Pub. Health Assn., Am. Acad. Occupational Medicine (Award of Honor 1959, pres. 1952-53); mem. AMA (chmn. council on occupational health 1961-62, mem. residency rev. com. preventive medicine 1956-61, mem. council environmental and pub. health 1963-73, chmn. 1963-69), Soc. Toxicology, World Med. Assn., Am. Indsl. Hygiene Assn. (Cummings award 1955, pres. 1948-49), Am. Chem. Soc. (councilor, 1949-52), Royal Soc. Health, Assn. Tchrs. Preventive Medicine, Radiation Research Soc., Health Physics Soc., NAM (med. adv. com. 1950-68), Mfg. Chemists Assn. (med. adv. com. 1950-57, chmn. environ. health adv. com. 1966-68), Nat. Health Council (pres. 1961), Nat. Tb Assn. (dir.), Aerospace Med. Assn., Air Pollution Control Assn., Internat. Assn. Occupational Health (U.S. del. permanent commn.), Phi Kappa Phi, Alpha Omega Alpha. Club: Cosmos. Editorial bd. Archives Indsl. Hygiene and Occupational Medicine, 1948-54. Contbr. to text books, jours. Home: 3354-0 Monte Hermoso Laguna Hills CA 92653 Office: Dept Community and Environmental Medicine University of Cal College Medicine Irvine CA 92717

STERNER, MICHAEL EDMUND, govt. ofcl.; b. N.Y.C., Dec. 26, 1928; s. Harold Walther and Leonie (Knoedler) S.; A.B., Harvard, 1951; m. Courtenay Read, Mar. 30, 1957; children—Lucian, Marcelin. Govt. relations rep. Arabian-Am. Oil Co., Dhahran, Saudi Arbia, 1951-54; joined Fgn. Service, 1956; vice consul, Aden, 1957-58; polit. officer, Cairo, 1960-64; desk officer Near Eastern Affairs Dept. State, 1964-70, country dir. Egyptian affairs, 1970-74; ambassador to United Arab Emirates, Abu Dhabi, 1974-76; dep. asst. sec. state for Near East and South Asian affairs, 1976—. Served with

AUS, 1954-56. Home: 2712 36th St Washington DC 20007 Office: NEA Dept State Washington DC 20520

STERNFELD, REUBEN, bank exec.; b. N.Y.C., May 5, 1924; s. Morris A. and Ethel (Kaplan) S.; A.B., U. Md., 1947; postgrad U. Mich., 1949; m. Marcia Katz, June 8, 1967. Asst. chief internat. div. U.S. Bur. of the Budget, 1949-60; spl. asst. to under sec. of state and exec. sec. Pres. Task Force on Fgn. Econ. Assistance, 1960-61; Asso. adminstrn. Alliance for progress AID, 1961-66; alternate U.S. exec. dir. Inter-American Devel. Bank, Washington, 1967-73, exec. v.p., 1974—; asst. dir. Pres. Council Internat. Econ. Policy, 1973-74; teaching asst. U. Md. Served with U.S. Army, 1943-46. Decorated Bronze Star, Purple Heart, Crox de-guerre. Mem. Soc. Internat. Devel., Am. Soc. Public Adminstrn. Home: 2800 Battery Pl Washington DC 20016 Office: 808 17th St NW Washington DC 20577

STERNHAGEN, FRANCES, actress; b. Washington, Jan. 13; d. John Meyer and Gertrude S.; B.A., Vassar Coll., 1951; attended Catholic U. Am., 1952. Profl. stage debut in The Glass Menagerie and Angel Street at Bryn Mawr (Pa.) Summer Theatre, 1948; N.Y.C. stage debut in Thieves' Carnival at Cherry Lane, 1955; other stage appearances include: The Admirable Bashville (Clarence Derwent award, Obie award), The Country Wife, Ulysses in Nighttown, Great Day in the Morning, The Room, A Slight Ache, The Right Honourable Gentleman, The Displaced Person, Blood Red Roses, The Playboy of the Western World, All Over, Mary Stuart, The Sign in Sidney Brustein's Window, Enemies, The Good Doctor, Equus, Angel; film debut in Up the Down Staircase, 1967; other films include: The Tiger Makes Out, 1970, The Hospital, 1971, Two People, 1973, Fedora, 1979; TV debut on Omnibus in The Great Bank Robbery, 1955; appeared on TV serials Love of Life and The Doctors; numerous other TV appearances. Recipient Obie award for performance in The New Pinter Plays, Antoinette Perry (Tony) award for performance in The Good Doctor.*

STERNIG, JOHN MICHAEL, ret. publishing co. exec.; b. Milw., Nov. 13, 1913; s. John and Anna (Sternig) S.; B.S., Wis. State Tchrs. Coll., Milw., 1935; M.A., Northwestern U., 1939; m. Matilda Schwenner, Nov. 25, 1939; children—Amy (Mrs. Richard Schendel), MaryLou (Mrs. Dennis Shelp), Nancy (Mrs. Jerry Head), Betsy (Mrs. John Miller), Barby, Cathy (Mrs. Terry Cammon), John, Laura. Tchr. elementary schs., Cin., 1935-37, Highland Park, Ill., 1937-41, Glencoe, Ill., 1941-48; lectr. Dearborn Obs., Northwestern U., 1949-53; prin. pub. schs. Glencoe, 1948-58, asst. supt., 1958-65; v.p. Field Enterprises Ednl. Corp., Chgo., 1965-76; tchr. summer sessions and workshops Ariz. State Coll., univs. Akron, Ariz., Conn., Neb., Wyo., also Wis. State Coll., Lake Forest Coll., Northwestern U., Butler U., Harvard, Ind. U., Cornell U., Trinity Coll. Mem. adv. bd. Ednl. Policies Commn., Washington, 1950-55; mem. Ill. Curriculum Council, 1963-76, Ill. Aerospace Com., 1954-76; tech. adviser space films Swift Chaplin Studios, Hollywood, 1956-57; cons. Visual Edn. Films, Inc., Highland Park, 1962-63; author, performer 2 TV series on space exploration, 1952, 53; lectr. various groups. Mem. sch. bd. Sacred Heart Sch., Winnetka, Ill., 1964-76, Library Bd. Glencoe, 1967-73. Trustee Chgo. Planetarium Soc., 1963-69; bd. dirs. parents com. Marquette U., Milw., 1966-69; bd. dirs. Friends Chgo. Pub. Library; chmn. edn. com. St. Thomas Parish, Boulder, Colo., 1978—. Fellow AAAS; mem. N.E.A., Ill. Edn. Assn., Nat. Sci. Tchrs. Assn., Brit. Interplanetary Soc., Dept. Elementary Sch. Prins., Assn. Supervision and Curriculum Devel., Elementary Prin.'s Assn., Phi Delta Kappa. Author: Off to School, 1946; Conservation Education, 1949; Science and Industry, vol. 9 Childcraft, 1954; Beginner's Book of Astronomy, 1958; Space Primer for Perplexed Parents, 1958; Trip to the Moon, 1960; Laidlaw Science Series, 1965; also sci. films strips, sci. charts. Editor book reviews Elementary Prin's Jour., 1955-57, N.E.A. Jour., 1960-63, also Sky and Telescope mag. Contbr. profl. jours. Home: Sunburst Jamestown Star Route Boulder CO 80302. *The principles which have guided my actions and behavior on this earth are based on a belief in God as the author of all goodness and a consequent effort on my part to live and act in harmony with His will within the limitations of my human nature.*

STERNIK, HANS GREGORY, hotel co. exec.; b. Vienna, Austria, Jan. 1, 1932; s. Maximilian and Blanka (Hass) S.; student U. Vienna, 1949-50, Union Coll., Schenectady, 1950-51, Vienna Sch. Hotel Mgmt., 1953; m. Lynn Staley, Nov. 11, 1953; children—Laura, Gregory, Alan, Karen. Came to U.S., 1954, naturalized, 1959. Mng. dir. Madison Hotel, Washington, 1962-64; gen. mgr. Hotel Vienna Inter-Continental, 1964-69; pres. Inter-Continental Hotels Corp. and gen. mgr. Hotel Phoenicia Inter-Continental, Beirut, Lebanon, 1969-72, exec. v.p., chief operating officer corp., 1972-74, pres., dir., 1974—. Mem. Young Presidents Orgn., Chaine des Rotisseurs, Internat. Hotel Assn. Address: Inter-Continental Hotels 200 Park Ave New York City NY 10017

STERNLICHT, MANNY, psychologist; b. N.Y.C., July 21, 1932; s. Oscar and Blanche (Sternlicht) S.; B.A., CCNY, 1953, M.A., 1954; Ph.D., Yeshiva U., 1960; m. Madeline Goldstein, Apr. 10, 1954; children—Elliot F., Harold C., Jeffrey M., Riva R. Clin. psychologist intern Kings County Hosp., N.Y.C., 1957-58; asst. prof. psychology Rockford Coll., 1958-60; clin. psychologist Inst. Juvenile Research, N.Y.C., 1959-60; prin. psychologist Willowbrook State Sch., 1960-69, asst. dir., 1969-72, dep. dir., 1973—; pvt. practice psychology, S.I., N.Y., 1962—; prof. psychology Yeshiva U., 1965—; cons. S.I. Aid for Retarded Children, 1961—. Mem. ednl. adv. bd. S.I. Brain-injured Assn., 1966—; bd. dirs. S.I. Family Service. Fellow Am. Psychol. Assn., Am. Assn. Mental Deficiency, Am. Group Psychotherapy Assn. Author: Personality Development and Social Behavior in the Mentally Retarded, 1972; The Psychology of Mental Retardation, 1977; contbr. articles, chpts. to profl. lit. Home: 263 Martin Ave Staten Island NY 10314 Office: Victory Blvd Staten Island NY 10314

STERNLICHT, SANFORD, educator, author; b. N.Y.C., Sept. 20, 1931; s. Irving S. and Sylvia (Hilsenroth) S.; B.S., State U. N.Y. Coll. at Oswego, 1953; M.A., Colgate U., 1955; Ph.D., Syracuse U., 1962; m. Dorothy Hilkert, June 7, 1956 (dec. 1977); children—David, Daniel; m. 2d, Hazel McCatty, Nov. 2, 1979. Grad. preceptor Colgate U., 1953-55; instr. English, State U. Coll. at Oswego, 1959-60, asst. prof., 1960-62, prof. English, 1962-71, prof. theatre, 1971—, chmn. dept. theatre, 1973—. Leverhulme fellow, vis. prof. York (Eng.) U., 1965-66. Served to lt. USNR, 1955-59; comdr. Res. Am. Council Learned Socs. travel grantee, Pakistan, 1969, Australia, 1975. Mem. Poetry Soc. Am. (fellow 1965), Modern Lang. Assn., Naval Res. Assn. Author: Gull's Way, 1961; The Blue Star Commodore, 1961; Love in Pompeii, 1967; (with E.M. Jameson) The Black Devil of the Eaycus, 1970; John Webster's Imagery and the Webster Canon, 1972; John Masefield, 1977; McKinley's Bulldog, 1977; also essays, poems, revs., stories. Home: 1301 E Genesee St Syracuse NY 13210

STERNLIGHT, PETER DONN, banker, economist; b. N.Y.C., May 21, 1928; s. Morris Henry and Pearl (Donn) S.; B.A., Swarthmore Coll., 1948; M.A., Harvard, 1950, Ph.D., 1960; m. Lenore Frane, Oct. 14, 1956; children—Jean Renee, Judith Ann. With Fed. Res. Bank N.Y., 1950-65; aide to under sec. treasury, 1961, asst. v.p. open market ops., 1964; dep. under sec. treasury monetary affairs, 1965-67; with Fed. Res. Bank N.Y., 1967—, v.p. open market ops., 1968-77, sr. v.p., dep. mgr. system account for domestic ops., 1977-79, mgr. system account for domestic ops., 1979—. Served with AUS, 1950-52. Recipient Exceptional Service award Treasury Dept. Mem. Am. Econ. Assn., Am. Finance Assn., Phi Beta Kappa. Home: 301 Garfield Pl Brooklyn NY 11215 Office: 33 Liberty St New York NY 10045

STERNS, SYDNEY S., govt. ofcl.; b. 1917; B.S., N.Y. U., 1943. Mgr., Arthur Andersen & Co., C.P.A.'s, 1946-53; comptroller Ill. Power Co., 1953-65; v.p. finance Cudahy Co., 1966; treas., chief financial officer Interstate Brands Corp., 1967-70; controller Nat. R.R. Passenger Corp. (AMTRAK), Washington, 1971-77; asst. to bd. FDIC, 1977—. Served as lt. USNR, 1943-45. C.P.A. Mem. Am. Inst. C.P.A.'s, Financial Execs. Inst., N.Y. Soc. C.P.A.'s. Home: 6807 Melrose Dr McLean VA 22101 Office: 550 17th St NW Washington DC 20429

STERNSTEIN, JOSEPH PHILIP, clergyman; b. Bklyn., Aug. 20, 1925; s. Charles and Bertha (Milman) S.; B.A., Bklyn. Coll., 1944; J.D., St. John's U., 1943; rabbi, Master Hebrew Letters, Jewish Theol. Sem., 1948; D.Hebrew Letters, 1961; m. Geraldine S. Cohen, Dec. 21, 1947; children—Judith, Rachel, Gerson, Hillel. Rabbi, Temple Tifereth Israel, Glen Cove, L.I., 1948-51, Beth Abraham Synagogue, Dayton, Ohio, 1951-62; nat. dir. Jewish Nat. Fund Am., N.Y.C., 1962-64; rabbi Temple Ansche Chesed, N.Y.C., 1964-69, Temple Beth Sholom, Roslyn Heights, N.Y., 1969—. Dean Women's Inst., Jewish Theol. Sem. Am., 1965—. Vice chmn. rabbinic cabinet Jewish Theol. Sem.; sec. N.Y. Bd. Rabbis, UN del. Synagogue Council Am. Chmn. Montgomery County Mental Health Assn., 1958, speakers bur. Greater Dayton Com., 1958-61. Bd. dirs. Ohio Mental Health Assn., 1954-61, Ohio Civil Liberties Union, 1955-61. Charter fellow Herbert H. Lehman Inst. Talmudic Ethics. Mem. Rabbinical Assembly Am., Zionist Orgn. Am. (nat. pres. 1974-78), World Union Gen. Zionists (exec. com.), Am. Zionist Fedn. (nat. pres.), World Zionist Council (presidium), World Zionist Orgn. (world exec.), Am. Jewish Hist. Soc., Soc. Bib. Lit., Conf. Jewish Social Studies. Author: Theology of the Hassidic Rabbi of Ger, 1961; American Zionism-Diagnosis and Prognosis, 1955; Comparative Studies of Secular and Rabbinic Laws of Inheritance, 1947. Contbr. articles to profl. publs. Home: 320 Locust Ln Roslyn Heights NY 11577 Office: Temple Beth Sholom Roslyn Rd Roslyn Heights NY 11577

STERNSTEIN, SANFORD SAMUEL, chem. engr.; b. N.Y.C., June 19, 1936; s. Benjamin Phillip and Shirley Sarah (Roth) S.; B.S., U. Md., 1958; Ph.D., Rensselaer Poly. Inst., 1961; m. Gail Golden, June 15, 1958; children—Alan Barry, Deborah Ann. Asst. prof. chem. engring. Rensselaer Poly. Inst., Troy, N.Y., 1961-64, asso. prof., 1964-67, prof., 1967-72, William Weightman Walker prof. polymer engring., 1972—; pres. Dynastatics Instruments Corp.; cons. Eastman Kodak, B.F. Goodrich Co. Fellow Am. Phys. Soc.; mem. Soc. Rheology, Am. Chem. Soc., Am. Inst. Chem. Engrs. Jewish. Mem. editorial bd. Jour. Macromolecular Sci., 1970—, Internat. Jour. Polymeric Materials, 1972—. Home: 9 Oak Tree Ln Schenectady NY 12309 Office: Materials Engring Rensselaer Poly Inst Troy NY 12181

STERRETT, SAMUEL BLACK, judge; b. Washington, Dec. 17, 1922; s. Henry Hatch Dent and Helen (Black) S.; student St. Albans Sch., 1933-41; grad. U.S. Mcht. Marine Acad., 1945; B.A., Amherst Coll., 1947; LL.B., U. Va., 1950; LL.M. in Taxation, N.Y.U., 1959; m. Jeane McBride, Aug. 27, 1949; children—Samuel Black, Robin Dent, Douglas McBride. Admitted to D.C. bar, 1951, Va. bar, 1950; asso. law firm Alvord & Alvord, Washington, 1950-56; trial atty. Office Regional Counsel, Internal Revenue Service, N.Y.C., 1956-60; asso. and partner law firm Sullivan, Shea & Kenney, Washington, 1960-68; municipal cons. to office vice pres. U.S., 1965-68; judge U.S. Tax Ct., 1968—. Bd. mgrs. Chevy Chase Village, 1970-74, chmn., 1972-74 1st v.p. bd. trustees, mem. exec. com. Washington Hosp. Center, 1969-79, pres. bd. trustees, 1979—; mem. Washington Cathedral chpt., 1973—; mem. governing bd. St. Albans Sch., 1977—. Served with AUS, 1943, U.S. Mcht. Marine, 1943-46. Mem. Am., Fed., Va., D.C. bar assns., Beta Theta Pi. Episcopalian. Clubs: Chevy Chase (bd. govs. 1979—), Metropolitan Washington; Lake Placid (N.Y.). Home: 8 Magnolia Pkwy Chevy Chase MD 20015 Office: US Tax Ct 400 2d St Washington DC 20217

STERZING, CARL BRUCE, railroad exec.; b. Austin, Tex., May 14, 1933; s. Carl B. and Minna Mae (Maerki) S.; B.A., Tex. A. and M. U., 1954; LL.B., Harvard U., 1962; m. Betty Maas; children—David Scott, Carl Bruce III, Sarah Elizabeth. Admitted to Tex. bar, 1961; asso. firm Naman, Howell, Smith & Chase, Waco, 1961; solicitor, then asst. gen. solicitor, gen. atty. Norfolk & Western Rwy. Co., Roanoke, Va., 1961-70; gen. solicitor, gen. counsel Del. & Hudson Ry. Co., Albany, N.Y., 1970-72, pres., chief exec. officer, 1972-77; gen. mgr. Chgo., Rock Island & Pacific R.R. Co., 1977-78, chief operating officer, 1978—. Served to 1st lt. USMC, 1954-58. Mem. Ry. Fuel and Operating Officers Assn., Chgo. Traffic Club. Episcopalian. Home: 3020 Manor Dr Northbrook IL 60062

STETIN, SOL, labor union ofcl.; b. Poland, Apr. 2, 1910; s. Hyman Joseph and Fanny (Belzen) S.; came to U.S., 1921; L.H.D. (hon.), Rutgers U., 1961; hon. degree William Patterson Coll., 1975; m. Frieda Goldstein, Mar. 15, 1934; children—Sondra (Mrs. Ira Gash), Myra (Mrs. Robert Levine). Textile dye worker, 1930-35; organizer Textile Workers Orgn. Com., CIO, 1937-39; with Textile Workers Union Am., 1939-76, mem. exec. council, 1944-76, gen. sec.-treas., 1968-72, mem. exec. council AFL-CIO, 1973-77; mem. exec. com. indsl. union dept. AFL-CIO, 1968-73, v.p., 1973-78; sr. exec. v.p. Amalgamated Clothing and Textile Workers Union, AFL-CIO/CLC, N.Y.C., 1976—; pres. Textile Workers Union Am., 1972-76; treas. Inter-Am. Fedn. Textile and Garment Workers, 1970-72; exec. com. Internat. Textile, Garment and Leather Workers, Fedn., 1972—; dir. Group Health Ins. N.J., 1975—; mem. N.J. Mediation Bd., 1947-51, N.J. Tax Adv. Com., 1963. Mem. Nat. Community Services Com., 1950-55. Trustee William Paterson Coll., Wayne, N.J., 1967-74; bd. dirs. Am. Arbitration Assn., 1975—. Home: 39 E 39th St Paterson NJ 07514 Office: 770 Broadway New York NY 10003

STETLER, C. JOSEPH, lawyer; b. Wapaconeta, Ohio, May 13, 1917; s. Clarence Henry and Mary Frances (Kavanaugh) S.; LL.B., Cath. U. Am., 1938, LL.M., 1940; postgrad. Benjamin Franklin Sch. Accounting, Washington, 1940-41 m. Mary Norine Delaney, Aug. 16, 1941; children—Joseph James, David John, Mary Catherine, Julia Anne, Norine Teresa and Kathleen Frances (twins). Admitted to D.C. bar, 1940, Ill. bar, 1951; with various agys. U.S. Govt., 1935-51; with A.M.A., 1951-63; gen. counsel, dir. legal and socio-econ. div., 1953-63; exec. v.p., gen. counsel Pharm. Mfrs. Assn., Washington, 1963-65, pres., 1965-79; partner firm Munsey, Samuel & Stetler, 1979—. Mem. staff 2d Hoover Commn., 1953-54; bd. dirs. Project Hope. Served to capt. AUS, 1942-46; PTO. Mem. Am., Ill., D.C., Chgo. bar assns. Roman Catholic. Author: (with Alan Moritz) Doctor Patient and the Law, 1962; Handbook of Legal Medicine, 1964. Home: 9312 Mercy Hollow Ln Potomac MD 20854 Office: 1155 15th St Washington DC 20005

STETLER, JAMES M., credit card co. exec.; b. White Plains, N.Y., Nov. 11, 1931; s. Donovan B. and Boline (Merrifield) S.; B.A., Wesleyan U., 1953; M.B.A., Harvard U., 1955; m. Linda Calkin, July 10, 1954; children—Susan, Joy, James, David. Regional promotion mgr. Grand Union Co., N.Y.C., 1958-65; dir. merchandising, money order div. Am. Express Co., N.Y.C., 1965-67, v.p. mktg. communications, credit card div., 1967-77; exec. v.p. mktg. Diners Club, Inc., N.Y.C., 1977—. Served to lt. (j.g.) USN, 1956-58. Office: 10 Columbus Circle New York NY 10019

STETLER, RUSSELL DEARNLEY, JR., editor; b. Phila., Jan. 15, 1945; s. Russell Dearnley and Martha Eleanor (Schultz) S.; B.A. with honors in Philosophy, Haverford (Pa.) Coll., 1966; postgrad. New Sch. Social Research, 1966-67. Research asst. to Bertrand Russell, 1967; lectr. Hendon Coll., London, 1968-69; pres. Archetype, Inc., Berkeley, Calif., 1971-78; pub. Westworks, Berkeley, 1977—; cons., dir. Ramparts Press, Palo Alto, 1971—; editorial cons. Internews, Berkeley, 1973-79; faculty Caribbean Sch., Ponce, P.R., 1978-80. Research grantee Atlantic Peace Found., 1969-70. Club: Albany-Berkeley Soccer (pres. 1977-78). Author: The Battle of Bogside, 1970; co-author: Echoes of Conspiracy, 1979; editor: The Military Art of People's War, 1970; Palestine: The Arab-Israeli Conflict, 1972. Co-editor: The Assassinations: Dallas and Beyond, 1976. Home: Apartado 16 Adjuntas PR 00601

STETSON, JOHN, architect; b. Ft. Pierce, Fla., June 26, 1915; s. Frank K. and Viorena (Hambleton) S.; student U. Fla.; fgn. studies 8 univs.; m. Josephine DeFina, Oct. 23, 1976; children by previous marriage—Michael, Suzy (Mrs. Douglas Sturmak), Teresa A. (Mrs. Thomas A. Wison). Pvt. practice architecture, Palm Beach, Fla., 1936—; works include: Fed. Office Bldg. and P.O., West Palm Beach; 1st Ch. Christ Scientist, Boca Raton; Fortin residence, Billings, Mont.; Old Port Cove, North Palm Beach; Tamberlain; Tanglewood; Covered Bridge, Sugar Sands. Dir. Home Fed. Savs. & Loan Assn. Chmn., Palm Beach County March of Dimes, 1959; pres. Fla. Coop. Council, 1958, 59, 61; chmn. Gov.'s Hurricane Study Com., 1959, 63; v.p. South Fla. Fair; bd. dirs. Salt Found., 1959-60, Royal Poinciana Chapel, pres., 1966-67. Served with USAAF, 1944-45. Registered architect, Fla., N.Y., Pa., Ill., Ind., Ohio. Fellow A.I.A.; mem. Fla. Assn. Architects (pres. 1959-60), Smithsonian Instn., SAR, Old Guard Soc. Palm Beach. Clubs: Islanders (Palm Beach); Sailfish of Fla.; Beach, Kiwanis. Patentee plumbing connections for rotating bldg. Address: 249 Peruvian Ave Palm Beach FL 33480

STETSON, JOHN BENJAMIN BLANK, anesthesiologist, educator; b. Chgo., Mar. 18, 1927; s. Louis Blank and Dorothy (Cohen) S.; student U. Chgo., 1942-44, 46-47; M.D., Harvard U., 1951; m. Gwyneth Evans, Dec. 22, 1966; children—Diana S., Dana L., Jonathan O. Intern, U. Utah Hosp., 1951-52; resident Mass. Gen. Hosp., Lowell Gen. Hosp., 1952-54; instr. anesthesiology U. Mich., 1954-57; practice medicine, specializing in anesthesiology, Johnson City, Tenn., 1957-59; instr. anesthesiology Harvard Med. Sch., Children's Hosp., 1959-65; asst. prof., dir. vital function lab. U. Ind. Med. Sch., 1965-67; asso. prof., asso. dir. dept. anesthesiology Ohio State U. Sch. Medicine, 1967-68; dir. clin. pharmacology, acting med. dir. Strasenburgh Labs., Rochester, N.Y., 1968-70; asso. anesthesiologist Strong Meml. Hosp., U. Rochester, 1970-76; dir. clin. research Arnar Stone Labs., Inc., Mt. Prospect, Ill., 1976-77; prof. Rush Med. Coll., 1977—; cons. Roswell Park Meml. Inst., Buffalo, 1968—. Served with USNR, 1944-46. FDA grantee, 1973-76; Jackson Johnson research fellow in biochemistry Washington U., St. Louis, 1947—. Diplomate Am. Bd. Anesthesiologists. Fellow Am. Coll. Anesthesiologists; mem. AMA, Can. Anaesthetists Soc., Am. Soc. Clin. Pharmacology and Therapeutics, Assn. Anaesthetists Gt. Britain and Ireland, Am. Soc. Regional Anesthesia, Internat. Anesthesia Research Soc., Soc. Critical Care Medicine, Pan Am. Med. Assn., Am. Soc. Anesthesiologists (past chmn. history and archives com.). Republican. Unitarian. Editor: Cardiovascular Problems, 1963; Ventilation in Anesthesiology, 1965; Metabolism in Anesthesiology, 1967; Prolonged Tracheal Intubation, 1970; (with P.R. Swyer) Neonatal Intensive Care, 1976; contbr. articles to profl. jours. Office: Rush-Presbyterian-St Lukes Med Center Chicago IL 60612

STETSON, JOHN CHARLES, former govt. ofcl.; b. Chgo., Sept. 6, 1920; s. John Charles and Dorothy H. (Eckman) S.; B.S., Mass. Inst. Tech., 1943; postgrad. Northwestern U. Bus. Sch., 1946-48; m. Gayle McDowell, Jan. 1, 1946; children—Sherry, Robert, Susan. Partner, Booz Allen & Hamilton, Chgo., 1951-63; pres. pub. div. Houston Post Co., Houston, 1963-70; pres. A.B. Dick Co., Chgo., 1970-77, also dir.; sec. of the Air Force, Washington, 1977-79; dir. Kemper Corp., Houston Post Co., Belden Corp., Powers Regulator. Trustee Chgo. Symphony Orch., Boys Clubs Am. Served with USNR, 1945-46. Clubs: Glen View; F St; Chgo. Yacht. Home: Watergate West Apt 1505 2700 Virginia Ave NW Washington DC 20037

STETSON, NATHANIEL, govt. ofcl.; b. New Bedford, Mass., Nov. 19, 1916; s. John N. and Florence (Gee) S.; grad. in textile chemistry New Bedford Textile Inst., 1938; B.Chem. Engring., N.C. State Coll., 1940; postgrad. chem. engring. Ill. Inst. Tech., 1940-41; Dr. Comml. Sci. (hon.), Southeastern Mass. Tech. Inst.; m. Helen Elizabeth Casey, Jan. 14, 1943; children—Richard N., Barbara J. (Mrs. Richard D. Brasco), Linda S. (Mrs. L. Thomas Miller), Carol E. Chem. engr. Celanese Corp. Am., 1941-42, Chem. Warfare Service, 1942-43; prodn. supr. Tenn. Eastman Corp., Oak Ridge, 1942-43; sr. engr. Carbide & Carbon Chem. Corp., Oak Ridge, 1945-52; with AEC (now ERDA), 1952—, dep. dir. prodn. div., Washington, 1962-66, mgr. Aiken (S.C.) Savannah River operations office, 1966—. K.C. (past council grand knight past sec. S.C.), Rotarian (past pres.). Home: 4 Longwood Dr Aiken SC 29801 Office: PO Box A Aiken SC 29801

STETTEN, DEWITT, JR., biochemist; b. N.Y.C., May 31, 1909; s. DeWitt and Magdalen (Ernst) S.; B.A., Harvard, 1930; M.D., Columbia, 1934, Ph.D., 1940; D.Sc. (hon.), Washington U., St. Louis, 1974, Coll. Medicine and Dentistry N.J., 1976, Worcester Found. for Exptl. Biology, 1979; m. Marjorie Roloff, Feb. 7, 1941; children—Gail (Mrs. Peter C. Maloney), Nancy (Mrs. Frank Einstein), Mary (Mrs. Michael Carson), George. Intern, 3d med. div. Bellevue Hosp., N.Y.C., 1934-37; instr., asst. prof. biochemistry Coll. Phys. and Surgs., Columbia, 1940-47; asso. medicine Peter Bent Brigham Hosp., Boston, 1947-49; asst. prof. biol. chemistry Harvard Med. Sch., 1947-48; chief div. nutrition and physiology Pub. Health Research Inst. City N.Y., 1948-54; asso. dir. charge research Nat. Inst. Arthritis and Metabolic Diseases, NIH, 1954-62; dean Rutgers Med. Sch., New Brunswick, N.J., 1962-70; dir. Nat. Inst. Gen. Med. Scis., NIH, Bethesda, Md., 1970-74, dep. dir. for sci. NIH, 1974-79, sr. sci. adv. to dir., 1979—; mem. subcom. liver diseases NRC, 1948-49, panel intermediary metabolism, com. on growth, 1948-52, chmn. panel, 1950, mem. exec. bd. div. med. scis., 1965-69; cons. Walter Reed Army Med. Center, 1948-53; chmn. research com. N.Y. Diabetes Assn., 1951-52; cons., study sect. mem. NIH, 1952-53; mem. adv. com. health research facilities and resources; mem. adv. council dept. biology Princeton; chmn. nat. adv. com. Okla. Found. Med. Research, 1966; chmn. nat. sci. adv. com. Roche Inst. Molecular Biology, 1966-70. Trustee N.J. Mental Health Research and Devel. Bd.; bd. dirs. Found. for Advanced Edn. in Scis., pres., 1973; mem. vis. com. Oklahoma City campus U. Okla.; bd. visitors Grad. Sch. Pub. Health, U. Pitts. Recipient Joseph Mather Smith prize Columbia, 1943; Alvarenga prize Phila. Coll. Physicians, 1954; Banting medal Am. Diabetes Assn., 1957; Superior Service award HEW, 1973; gold medal for distinguished achievement in medicine Columbia U. Coll. Phys. and Surg., 1974; Disting. Service award HEW, 1976; Woodrow

Wilson fellow, 1979—. Mem. Nat. Acad. Scis., AAAS (chmn. sect. on medicine and v.p. 1962), Am. Acad. Arts and Scis., Nat. Acad. Scis. (council 1976-79), Am. Chem. Soc., Am. Soc. Biol. Chemists, N.Y. Acad. Scis., Harvey Soc., Soc. Exptl. Biology and Medicine (pres. 1977-79), Washington Acad. Medicine, Med. Soc. N.J., Phi Beta Kappa, Sigma Xi, Alpha Omega Alpha. Author: Principles of Biochemistry (with others), 1954, 59. Mem. editorial bd. Jour. Biol. Chemistry, Physiol. Revs., Am. Jour. Medicine, Metabolism, Jour. Chronic Diseases, Sci. and Perspectives in Biology and Medicine. Contbr. articles to profl. jours. Home: 2 West Dr Bethesda MD 20014 Office: NIH Bethesda MD 20205

STEUERMANN, CLARA, music librarian, archivist; b. Los Angeles, Feb. 10, 1922; d. Samuel and Sarah (Nathanson) Silvers; A.B., U. Calif., Los Angeles, 1943, M.A., 1944; M.L.S., Columbia U., 1964; piano studies with Jakob Gimpel and Edward Steuermann; m. Edward Steuermann, Nov. 11, 1949 (dec.); children—Rebecca, Rachel. Teaching asst. to Arnold Schoenberg, 1943-44: free lance music editor, N.Y.C., 1944-45; music editor Carl Fischer, Inc., 1945-47, Music Pubs. Holding Corp., N.Y.C., 1947-51; adminstrv. asst. Juilliard Sch. Music, Opera Theatre, 1951-56, New York Philharmonic Orch., 1965; asst. librarian Kingsborough Community Coll., Bklyn., summer 1965; cataloguer Juilliard Sch. Music Library, 1965-66; librarian Cleve. Inst. Music, 1966-75; archivist Arnold Schoenberg Inst., Los Angeles, 1975—; co-dir. Music Library Inst., Kent State U., summer 1969, vis. prof. Sch. Library Sci., summer 1970; vis. instr. music dept. Claremont (Calif.) Grad. Sch., spring 1979; cons. State U. N.Y. Purchase Univ. Library, 1972-73, Curtis Inst. Music, Phila., 1973-74. Vice pres., bd. dirs. Cleve. Modern Dance Assn., 1969-74. MacDowell Colony fellow, summer 1973. Mem. Am. Fedn. Musicians (Local 802), Am. Musicol. Soc., Coll. Music Soc., Internat. Assn. Music Libraries, Music Library Assn. (chmn. Midwest Regional chpt. 1969-71, chmn. Music Librarians of Ohio 1971-72, chmn. MLA/NASM Joint Com. 1971-72, dir. 1972-74, pres. 1975-76, rep. Internat. Music Council, Toronto 1975, rep. Internat. Fedn. Library Assns. 1977, rep. Internat. Conf. on New Musical Notation, Belgium, 1974, chmn. Round Table for Music in Libraries, 1978—), Soc. Am. Archivists, Internat. Soc. for Contemporary Music (dir. U.S. sect. 1960). Home: 8529 Saturn St Apt 2 Los Angeles CA 90035 Office: Arnold Schoenberg Inst U So Calif Los Angeles CA 90007

STEVEN, JULIA CLARK. see Krafft, Julia Steven

STEVENS, ANDREW, actor, producer; b. Memphis, June 10, 1955; s. Noble Herman and Stella (Stevens) Stephens; student Immaculate Heart Coll., Los Angeles, 1973-74, West Los Angeles Coll./Los Angeles Valley Coll., 1974-75; m. Kate Jackson, Aug. 23, 1978. Appeared in feature films, including: Vigilante Force, 1976, Day of the Animals, 1977, The Boys in Company C, 1978, The Fury, 1978; appeared in TV Films, including: The Bastard, 1978, Women At West Point, CBS, 1978, The Rebels, 1979, Beggarman Thief, NBC, 1979; exec. producer, actor in TV film Topper, Cosmo Prodn., 1979; co-owner, exec. producer Cosmo Prodns., Beverly Hills, Calif., 1979—; numerous recs. for Warner/Curb Records including: Helpless in Love, 1978, The Party's Not Over (also composer), 1979. Mem. Studio Transp. Drivers-Teamster's Union Local 399 (hon.). Democrat. Office: care Creative Artists Agy Inc 1888 Century Park E Suite 1400 Los Angeles CA 90067 also 415 N Camden Dr Suite 106 Beverly Hills CA 90210

STEVENS, ART, public relations co. exec.; b. N.Y.C., July 17, 1935; B.A., CCNY, 1957; m. Eva Sandberg, Mar. 19, 1972. Public relations dir. Prentice Hall, Inc., Englewood Cliffs, N.J., account exec. William L. Safire Public Relations Inc., N.Y.C., 1966-69, v.p., 1967-68, pres., 1968-69; pres. Lobsenz-Stevens Inc., N.Y.C., 1970—; instr. Fairleigh Dickinson U. Mem. Publicity Club N.Y. (Disting. Service award 1969), Public Relations Soc. Am. Club: Gipsy Trail (Carmel, N.Y.). Contbr. articles to profl. jours. Home: 201 E 21st St New York NY 10010 Office: 2 Park Ave New York NY 10016

STEVENS, ARTHUR WILBER, JR., educator; b. Bklyn., Aug. 16, 1921; s. Arthur Wilber and Isabella Ellen (MacGibbon) S.; A.B., Brown U., 1942; M.A., U. Wash., 1956, Ph.D., 1957; m. Marjorie Athene Rogers, Feb. 15, 1955 (dec. Feb. 1979); children—Arthur Wilber III, Christopher Rivers. Teaching fellow, asso., then instr. U. Wash., Seattle, 1944-54; vis. lectr., then asst. prof. Idaho State U., Pocatello, 1954-60; asso. prof., chmn. dept. English, 1961-64; Fulbright prof. Am. and English lit. U. Mandalay (Burma) and U. Chulalongkorn (Thailand), 1956-57; Fulbright prof. Am. lit. U. Brazil, Rio de Janeiro, 1959; prof., chmn. dept. lit. Park Coll., Parkville, Mo., 1964-66; prof. English, chmn. Center Lang. and Lit. Studies, Prescott (Ariz.) Coll., 1966-69, provost, 1968-71, dir. coll. press, 1968-73, prof. English and comparative lit., 1972-73; dean Coll. Arts and Letters, prof. English and humanities U. Nev., Las Vegas, 1973—; vis. prof. Ariz. State U., Tempe, summer 1968, SUNY, Buffalo, summer 1971, Utah Shakespeare Festival, 1972, Baylor U., summer 1976; dramatic and music critic Billboard, 1947-54, Intermountain, 1954-64, Seattle Home News, 1947-53, Prescott Courier and The Paper, 1966-73, Las Vegas Rev.-Jour., 1973-77, Las Vegas Sun, 1977—, KLAV Radio Sta., The Las Vegan. Del. UNESCO Conf., San Francisco, 1957. Bd. dirs. Orme Sch., Prescott, 1969-73. Frances Wayland scholar, 1940-42. Mem. Modern Lang. Assn., Rocky Mountain Modern Lang. Assn. (pres. 1971), Am. Soc. Aesthetics, Conf. Christianity and Lit., AAUP, Am. Comparative Lit. Assn., Internat. Comparative Lit. Assn., Philos. Assn. Pacific Coast (exec. bd.), Asian Studies Assn., Modern Humanities Research Assn., Beta Theta Pi. Club: Brown (N.Y.C.). Author-editor: Poems Southwest, 1967; Stories Southwest, 1973; co-editor: Anthology of Contemporary Anglo-Indian Poetry, 1979; contbr. poems to anthologies, articles to profl. jours.; editor, pub. lit. mag. Interim, 1944-55. Home: 3770 Forestcrest Dr Las Vegas NV 89121

STEVENS, BARTHOLOMEW MARTIN, bus. machines co. exec.; b. Sioux Falls, S.D., Apr. 15, 1918; s. Bartholomew and Cora Alvina (Martin) S.; student U. S.D., 1936-37; m. Sarah Alice Whitley, Sept. 5, 1942; children—Ronald, Michael. With IBM Corp., 1946—, v.p. ops. Office Products div., 1965-69, pres. Office Products div., 1969-76, sr. v.p., mem. corporate mgmt. com. responsible for corporate ops. staffs—mktg., mfg., service and engring., 1976—; dir. First Nat. Bank N.J.; v.p., trustee N.J. Blue Cross. Mem. advisory bd. Pace U., N.Y.C.; trustee N.J. Coll. Fund Assn. Served from pvt. to maj. U.S. Army, 1940-45. Decorated Bronze Star medal. Episcopalian. Clubs: Arcola Country (Paramus, N.J.); Lost Tree (North Palm Beach, Fla.). Home: 310 Briarly Dr Franklin Lakes NJ 07417 Office: Old Orchard Rd Armonk NY 10504

STEVENS, BOSWELL, agriculturist; b. Macon, Miss., Sept. 4, 1897; s. Nelson and Sallie (Boswell) S.; student Miss. State Coll., 1914-18; m. Sallie Ethel Lovelace, June 30, 1920; children—Arthur Boswell, Katherine (Mrs. George Hollister), Sara (Mrs. Gordon Hazard), Nelson (Mrs. Marlin George). Dairy, cotton, beef cattle and grain farmer, Noxubee County, Miss., 1919—; charter mem. Noxubee County Farm Bur., 1922, pres., 1925-35; bd. dirs. Miss. Farm Bur. Fedn., 1940-43, v.p., 1943-50, pres., 1950—; bd. dirs. Nat. Cotton Council, 1939—, pres., 1959-60, chmn. bd., 1960—; pres. Miss. Fed. Coops., 1949-50, exec. com., 1946—; exec. com., v.p., dir. Am. Farm Bur. Fedn., 1953—. Pres., Miss. Farm Bur. Holding Corp., 1947—, Miss. Farm Bur. Investment Corp., 1947—, Miss. Farm Bur. Mut. Ins. Co., 1953—, Coop. Pub. Co., 1950—, Rural Ins. Agy., 1962—; dir. Miss. Chem. Corp., So. Farm Bur. Casualty Ins. Co., So. Farm Bur. Life Ins. Co., Am. Agr. Mut. Ins. Co., Am. Agr. Ins. Agy., Inc., Farm Bur. Trade Devel. Corp., Forest Owners, Inc. Mem. Miss. Marketing Council; adv. com. local March of Dimes; pres. Miss. Heart Assn., 1965-66, now dir. Trustee Cotton Producers Inst., Instn. Higher Learning. Served with the U.S. Army, World War I. Mem. Am. Dairy Assn. (past pres. Miss., dir., exec. com. 1941-51), Am. Legion, Omicron Delta Kappa, Kappa Alpha. Methodist (steward). Mason. Address: Route 1 Box 42 Macon MS 39341

STEVENS, CAT (STEVEN DEMETRE GEORGIOU), singer, musician, composer; b. London, July 21, 1948; student Hammersmith Coll., Eng. Recs. include albums Mona Bone Jakon, Tea for the Tillerman, Teaser and the Firecat, Matthew and Son, Catch Bull at Four, Foreigner, Buddha and the Choclate Box, Numbers, Izitso. Author: (juvenile) Teaser and the Firecat. Address: care BKM Inc 9076 St Ives Dr Los Angeles CA 90069*

STEVENS, CHARLES EDWARD, vet. physiologist, educator; b. Mpls., June 5, 1927; s. Fred H. and Irene (Lamb) S.; B.S., U. Minn., 1951, D.V.M., 1955, M.S., 1955, Ph.D., 1958; m. Loretta Allen; children—Leslee Marie, Judith Mae, David Edward, Laura Ann, Randy Allen, Karen, Vicki. Research fellow Agr. Research Service, U. Minn., 1955-58, research asso., 1958-60, research physiologist, 1960-61; asso. prof. dept. physiology N.Y. State Coll. Vet Medicine, Ithaca, 1961-66, prof. physiology, 1966—, dept. chmn., 1973—. Dir. comparative gastroenterology tng. program NIH, 1970-76. Mem. AVMA, Am. Physiol. Soc., Am. Soc. Vet. Physiologists and Pharmacologists (pres. 1967-68), Research Workers in Animal Diseases, Am. Gastroenterology Assn., Comparative Gastroenterology Soc. Research and publs. on comparative physiology of digestive system, motility, autonomic regulation and mechanisms of secretion and absorption. Home: 563 Ellis Hollow Creek Rd Ithaca NY 14850

STEVENS, CONNIE, actress, singer; b. Bklyn.; d. Peter and Eleanore (McGinley) Ingolia; grad. high sch.; m. Maurice Elias; m. 2d, Edwin Jack Fisher (div.); children—Joely, Tricia Leigh. Show bus. debut as vocalist with The Three Debs, Hollywood, at age 16; appeared in Finians Rainbow for Hollywood Repertory Co.; appeared in numerous motion pictures, including Dragstrip Riot, Rock-A-Bye-Baby, Parrish, Susan Slade, Two On a Guillotine, Never Too Late, Scorchy; starred in TV series Hawaiian Eye, Wendy and Me; appeared in TV films for ABC-TV Movie-of-the-Week, Call Her Mom, 1972, Playmates, Mister Jericho, Cole Porter in Paris for Bell System Family Theater, The Sex Symbol, 1974; guest star on TV with Bob Hope, Red Skelton, Englebert Humperdinck, Tom Jones, Perry Como and Laugh-In; headliner at Flamingo Hotel, Las Vegas, also Hilton Internat., Sands Hotel, Desert Inn, 1969-76; stage appearances include The Wizard of Oz at Carousel Theatre in So. Calif., Any Wednesday at Melodyland, Anaheim, Calif.; made Broadway debut in Star Spangled Girl, 1967; accompanied Bob Hope around world on his Christmas tour, 1969. Bd. dirs. Center for Plastic and Reconstructive Surgery, South Viet Nam. Office: care Creative Artists Agy Inc 1888 Century Park E Suite 1400 Los Angeles CA 90067*

STEVENS, CRAIG, actor; b. Liberty, Mo.; student U. Kans.; m. Alexis Smith. Actor coll. dramatics; screen debut in Affectionately Yours; other motion pictures include: Since You Went Away, The Doughgirls, Roughly Speaking, Too Young to Know, Humoresque, Lady Takes a Sailor, French Line, Love and Learn, Duel on the Mississippi; The Name's Buchanan; Gunn, 1967; Limbo Line; The Snoop Sisters; star Peter Gun Series, 1959-63, The Invisible Man, 1975-76; TV appearances include; Four Star Playhouse, Lux Video Theater, Schlitz Playhouse, The Millionaire, Name of the Game, The Bold Ones, Killer Bees, The Invisible Man, 1975; TV movies include: Killer Bees, 1973, The Love Boat II, 1977, The Cabot Connection, 1977, many others; also Loretta Young, Dinah Shore, Ernie Ford shows; appeared in play Here's Love, 1963. Address: care Contemporary-Korman Artists Ltd Contemporary Artists Bldg 132 Lasky Dr Beverly Hills CA 90212*

STEVENS, DAVID, educator; b. Burbank, Calif., Jan. 26, 1926; s. Frederick and Alpheus (Parkins) S.; B.A., Whitman Coll., 1947; M.B.A., Stanford U., 1949; 1 son, David Fancher. Asst. prof. Okla. State U., 1949-51; asst. prof. econs. Whitman Coll., Walla Walla, Wash., 1951-54, asso. prof., 1954-56, prof., 1956-67, Roger and David Clapp prof. of econ. thought, 1958—; dean adminstrn., 1954-64; vis. prof. Glasgow U., Scotland, 1964-66; instr. Am. Inst. Banking. Commr. Regional Planning Commn., Walla Walla County, 1960-64; chmn. Walla Walla County chpt. ARC, 1961-63, 75-77; trustee St. George's Sch., Spokane, Wash. Served to lt. J.G., U.S. Navy, 1943-46. Mem. Am. Econ. Assn., Western Econ. Assn., History of Econ. Soc. Episcopalian. Club: Rotary. Author: Adam Smith and the Colonial Disturbances, 1976. Editor: The Wedderburn Manuscript In Adam Smith: Correspondence, 1977. Home: Marcus Whitman Towers Walla Walla WA 99362 Office: Whitman College Walla Walla WA 99362

STEVENS, DENIS WILLIAM, educator, condr.; b. High Wycombe, Buckinghamshire, Eng., Mar. 2, 1922; s. William James and Edith Ruby (Driver) S.; M.A., Jesus Coll., Oxford, 1947; D.H.L., Fairfield U., 1967; m. Sheila Elizabeth Holloway, June 25, 1949; children—Anthony Vincent, Daphne Elizabeth, Michael David; m. 2d, Leocadia Elzbieta Kwasny, Nov. 21, 1975. Violinist, Philharmonia Orch. London, 1948-49; producer music div. BBC, 1949-54, musicological adviser, 1954-61; music critic Gramophone, 1954-64; prof. music Columbia, 1964-74. Vis. prof. music Cornell U., 1955, Columbia, 1956, Royal Acad. Music, 1960, U. Calif. at Berkeley, 1962, Pa. State U., 1962-64, U. Calif. at Santa Barbara, 1974-75; Brechemin distinguished prof. U. Wash., Seattle, 1976, U. Mich., 1977, San Diego State U., 1978; condr. numerous recs. of music of 11th through 19th centuries; guest lectr. radio and TV, U.S. and Europe, also concerts. Pres., artistic dir. Accademia Monteverdiana, 1961—; sec. Plainsong and Medieval Music Soc., 1958-63; fine arts adv. Sta. KCPB-FM, founder, condr. Ambrosian singers. Served with Intelligence, RAF, 1942-46. Fellow Soc. Antiquaries; mem. Worshipful Co. Musicians, Am. Musicological Soc., Coll. Music Soc., Internat. Musicological Soc., Société Française de Musicologie. Author: The Mulliner Book: A Commentary, 1952; Thomas Tomkins, 1957; Tudor Church Music, 1961; Monteverdi: Sacred, Secular and Occasional Music, 1977; Musicology for Musicians, 1980. Editor: The Mulliner Book, 1951; A History of Song, 1960; Monteverdi Vespers, 1961; Orfeo, 1967; Treasury of English Music 1, 1965; Early Tudor Organ Music, 1969; Gabrieli in Ecclesiis, 1971; Machaut Mass, 1973; Monteverdi Madrigals, 1978; Venetian Ceremonial Music, 1978; Monteverdi: Christmas Vespers, 1979; Monteverdi: Collected Correspondence, 1980; asso. editor: History of Music, 1960; Groves Dictionary of Music and Musicians, 1961. Home: 2203 Las Tunas Rd Santa Barbara CA 93103

STEVENS, DWIGHT MARLYN, ednl. adminstr.; b. Wheeler, Wis., May 13, 1933; s. Clifford and Alva Orpha (Follensbee) S.; B.S., Eau Claire (Wis.) State U., 1957; M.S., U. Wis., 1959, Ph.D., 1972; m. Joanne Horky, Feb. 6, 1954; children—Patricia Lee (Mrs. Mark Vanden Heuvel), Jacqueline Ann, Cynthia May, Robert Louis. High sch. speech tchr., Ft. Atkinson, Wis., 1957-61; high sch. prin., Oostburg, Wis., 1961-64; prin. Arrowhead High Sch., Hartland, Wis., 1964-66; dist. adminstr. Arrowhead Sch. Dist., 1966-73; dep. state supt. Wis. Dept. Pub. Instrn., Madison, 1973—. Teaching Sch. plant planning U. Wis., Whitewater, 1971. Dir. Ford Found., Community Planning Project for Chippewa Indians, 1970-71, Nat. Validation Team, Title III, Elementary Secondary Edn. Act; cons. HEW Workshops on Innovation, Eagle River, Wis. Served with U.S. Army, 1953-55. Recipient Outstanding Citizenship award Waukesha County, Wis., 1974. Ford fellow John Hay Fellowship in Humanities, Williams Coll., 1963, Kettering fellow Nat. Seminar on Innovation, Honolulu, summer 1967. Mem. Phi Delta Kappa, Pi Kappa Delta. Club: Hartland Sportsmen's. Author: (with Eye, Netzer and Benson) Strategies for Instructional Management, 1979. Home: Route 1 Box 70-A Deerfield WI 53531 Office: 126 Langdon St Madison WI 53702

STEVENS, EDMUND WILLIAM, journalist; b. Denver, July 22, 1910; s. Edmund William and Florence (Ballance) S.; B.A., Columbia, 1932, postgrad. govt. internat. law, 1932-33; student Russian, Moscow U., 1934; m. Nina Andreyevna Bondarenko, Mar. 14, 1935; children—Edmund, Anastasia (Marchesa Ferrari di Collesape). Began as translator Moscow publishing house, 1935-37, Am.-Russian C. of C., also corr. Manchester Guardian Daily Herald, London, 1937-39; substituted for Reuters, summer 1938; Moscow rep. Cunard-White Star Line, 1938; writer Christian Sci. Monitor from Riga, 1939; covered Finnish war, invasion of Norway, in Rumania, 1940, covered Italo-Greek War, 1940-41, Ethiopian campaign with Wingate, Haile Selassie, 1941, with Brit. 8th Army in Western Desert, 1942-43, accompanied Churchill and Harriman to Moscow as spl. adviser to Gen. Russell Maxwell, Aug. 1942, Wendell Willkie through Mideast, 1942; war corr. in Russia, 1943-44; Moscow corr. Christian Sci. Monitor, 1946-49, chief Mediterranean News Bur., Hdqrs. in Rome, 1949-55; Moscow corr. Look mag., 1955-58; chief Moscow bur. Time and Life, 1958-63; syndicated columnist Newsday, also spl. corr. Soviet affairs Saturday Evening Post, 1963-68; corr. Sunday Times, London, Eng., 1964, London Times, 1973; Giornale nuovo, Milan, die Weltwoche, Zurich, 1978; radio reporter NBC News, 1971. Decorated Africa Star (Britain); recipient citiation War Dept., 1943, Pulitzer prize for internat. reporting, 1950, citation for excellence Overseas Press Club, 1956-58, George Polk Meml. award L.I. U. 1958. Mem. Delta Phi, Associazione della Stampa Estera (Rome). Club: Overseas Press (N.Y.C.). Author: Russia is No Riddle, 1945; This is Russia Uncensored, 1950; North Africa Powder Keg, 1955. Address: Ulitsa Ryleeva 11 Moscow USSR. *Those of us lucky enough to live through World War II, and are now on the threshold of three score and ten, should feel we are living on borrowed time. When we recall the past, we rue the squandered years and missed opportunities. This applies to us not only individually, but as a generation. As we cannot relive the past, we can only hope the coming generation will profit from our experience and avoid our mistakes. Should it fail, it might be the last generation. For the clouds on the horizon are mushroom-shaped.*

STEVENS, FRANKLYN EDWARD, fgn. service officer; b. Portland, Oreg., June 28, 1927; s. Paul George and Eva (Wrenn) S.; B.A., U. Calif., Berkeley, 1955; m. Soonai Chang, Dec. 29, 1960; children—Susan, David. Employment officer Calif. Dept. Employment, Placerville, 1955-56; commd. fgn. service officer Dept. State, 1956; consul gen., Ciudad Juarez, Mexico, 1977—. Served with U.S. Army, 1945-46. Mem. Consular Officers Assn. Office: PO Box 10545 El Paso TX 79995

STEVENS, FREDERICK, bus. exec.; b. Burbank, Calif., June 13, 1922; s. Frederick and Alpheus (Perkins) S.; A.B., Whitman Coll., 1944; M.S. in Elec. Engring., Calif. Inst. Tech., 1947; grad. Advanced Mgmt. Program, Harvard U., 1969; m. Barbara Holmes, Aug. 7, 1945; children—Frederick III, Claire. Chief guidance control, supr. component devel., research engr. Northrop Aircraft Inc., Hawthorne, Calif., 1947-57; mgr. elec. systems and equipment dept. Nortronics, Hawthorne, 1957-60, v.p., mgr., 1960-61; v.p., gen. mgr. Nortronics Research Park, Palos Verdes Peninsula, 1961-69; v.p. Northrop Corp., 1961-77, sr. v.p., group exec. constrn. group, 1977—. Mem. USAF Sci. Adv. Bd., 1959-68. Recipient Meritorious Civilian Service award USAF, 1968. Served with USMCR, 1944-45. Fellow IEEE; mem. Sigma Chi. Registered profl. engr., Calif. Clubs: Cruising of Am., Los Angeles Yacht. Home: 35 Sea Isle Dr Long Beach CA 90803 Office: 1800 Century Park E Los Angeles CA 90067

STEVENS, GEORGE, JR., film exec.; b. Calif., Apr. 3, 1932; B.A., Occidental Coll., 1953; m. Elizabeth Guest, July, 1965; children—Caroline, Michael, David. Prodn. asst., motion picture producer, 1953-54, 56-57, asso. prod., dir., 1957-62; dir. Motion Picture Service, USIA, 1962-67; dir., chief exec. officer Am. Film Inst., 1967—; exec. producer TV spl. A Salute to James Cagney (Emmy award); producer film America at the Movies, 1976; exec. producer The Stars Salute Am.'s Greatest Movies, 1977, The Kennedy Center Honors, 1978; producer, writer America Entertains Vice Premier Deng, 1979; chmn. D.C. Arts Commn., 1969. Trustee Robert F. Kennedy Found., Occidental Coll., 1978—. Served to 1st lt. USAF, 1954-56. Office: Am Film Inst Kennedy Center Washington DC 20566

STEVENS, GEORGE RICHARD, mfg. co. exec.; b. Chgo., Sept. 6, 1932; s. George and Irene (Kaczmarek) S.; B.S. with honors, Northwestern U., 1954; m. Jeanne E. Sowden, Aug. 2, 1957; children—Stacey, Samantha, Pamela. Acct., auditor Arthur Andersen & Co., 1954-78, mng. partner, Brussels, Belgium, 1957-71, partner, Chgo., 1971-78; pres. Daubert Industries, Oak Brook, Ill., 1978—. C.P.A., Ill. Mem. Am. Inst. C.P.A.'s, Ill. Soc. C.P.A.'s, Better Govt. Assn. (dir. 1972—). Clubs: Mid-Am. (Chgo.); Bath and Tennis (Lake Bluff, Ill.). Home: 1598 N Western Ave Lake Forest IL 60045 Office: 1200 Jorie Blvd Oak Brook IL 60521

STEVENS, HALSEY, composer, educator, author; b. Scott, N.Y., Dec. 3, 1908; s. Horace B. and Mary Colenia (Churchill) S.; ed. Syracuse U., U. Cal., pvt. study; Litt.D., Syracuse U., 1966; m. Harriett Elizabeth Merritt, Sept. 2, 1939; children—Christopher, Ann (Mrs. William T. Naftel), Joanna (Mrs. Raymond Shields). Asst. instr. Syracuse U., 1935-37; asso. prof. Dakota Wesleyan U., 1937-41; prof., dir. coll. music Bradley U., 1941-46; prof. U. Redlands, 1946; asst. prof. U. So. Calif., Los Angeles, 1946-48, asso. prof., 1948-51, chmn. composition dept. 1949-74, prof. 1951-76, mem. grad. sch. adminstrv. council, 1961-63, grad. sch. research lectr., 1956, composer in residence, 1972-76, Mellon prof., 1974-76, prof. emeritus, 1976; recipient commns. from Louisville Philharmonic Soc., 1953, 57, U. Redlands, 1953, U. So. Calif., 1955, Fromm Found., 1956, San Francisco Symphony, 1958, Almand Meml. Fund, 1958, Sigma Alpha Iota, 1962, Pi Kappa Lambda (No. Tex. State U.), 1962, Ga. So. Coll., 1967, New Haven Symphony, 1968, Friends and Students of Lee Gibson, 1969, Alchin Fund, 1972, Nat. Endowment for Arts, 1975, Music Tchrs. Nat. Assn., 1975, Draco Found., 1976; program annotator Los Angeles Philharmonic Orch., 1946-51; Phoenix Symphony, 1947-48, Coleman chamber concerts, 1967—; vis. prof. Pomona Coll., 1954, U. Wash., summer 1958, Yale U., 1960-61, U. Cin., 1968, Williams Coll., 1969; resident scholar Rockefeller Found.

Villa Serbelloni, Italy, 1971; composer Symphony 1, Triskelion, Cello Concerto, Double Concerto, Viola Concerto, Ballad Wm. Sycamore, Septet, Sinfonia Breve, Symphonic Dances, A Testament of Life, Magnificat, Te Deum, Ritratti, Clarinet Concerto, Songs from the Paiute, Threnos, other orchestral, chamber, piano, choral music; guest condr. San Francisco Symphony, Los Angeles Philharmonic orchs. Served with USNR, 1943-45. Guggenheim fellow, 1964-65, 71-72. Recipient Sinfonia Nat. award, 1943, 46; Chamber Music award Nat. Fedn. Music Clubs, 1945; Publ. awards Middlebury Coll. Composers Conf., 1946, Soc. Pub. Am. Music, 1948, Nat. Assn. Coll. Wind and Percussion Instrs., 1954; Friends of Harvey Gaul award, 1960; award Nat. Inst. Arts and Letters, 1961; Ramo Distinguished Faculty award U. So. Calif., 1974; Abraham Lincoln award Am. Hungarian Found., 1978. Mem. Nat. Assn. Am. Composers and Condrs. (v.p. So. Calif. chpt.), Nat. Assn. Composers U.S.A. (adv. bd.), Am. Musicological Soc. (v.p. So. Calif. chpt. 1968-70), Am. Liszt Soc. (dir. 1968-78, nat. adv. com. 1978—), Am. Composers Alliance (bd. govs. 1960-61, nat. adv. bd. 1976-79), Music Library Assn., Conf. Bd. Asso. Research Councils (adv. com.), Com. Internat. Exchange Persons (chmn. 1961-63), Phi Beta Kappa, Phi Mu Alpha, Phi Kappa Phi, Pi Kappa Lambda. Author: The Life and Music of Bela Bartok, 1953, rev., 1964. Co-editor: Festival Essays for Pauline Alderman, 1976. Contbr. to World Book, New Cath. Ency., Ency. Brit., East Central Europe: A Guide to Basic Publications; also articles to periodicals. Home: 9631 2nd Ave Inglewood CA 90305 Office: Sch Music U So Calif University Park Los Angeles CA 90007

STEVENS, HARVEY ALONZO, univ. ofcl.; b. West Allis, Wis., Oct. 20, 1913; s. Daniel A. and Genevieve (Kingston) S.; B.S., U. Wis.-Milw., 1939, postgrad., 1946-48; m. Irene Borkowski, June 22, 1940; 1 dau., Patricia Ann. Tchr., South Milwaukee (Wis.) High Sch., 1939-43; prin. No. Wis. Center for Developmentally Disabled, Chippewa Falls, Wis., 1944-46; supr. classes mentally retarded Wis. Dept. Pub. Instrn., Madison 1946-48; supt. So. Wis. Center for Developmentally Disabled, Union Grove, Wis., 1948-55, Johnstone Tng. and Research Center, Bordentown, N.J., 1955-58, Central Wis. Center Developmentally Disabled, Madison, 1958-69; dir. Bur. for Developmentally Disabled, Wis. Dept. Health and Social Services, 1969-72; program adminstr. Waisman Center on Mental Retardation and Human Devel., U. Wis., Madison, 1972-79, program adminstr. emeritus, 1979—; dir. mental retardation services Wis. Dept. Health and Social Services, 1963-66. Cons. Office Spl. Asst. of Pres. for Mental Retardation Internat. Activities, 1963-65; cons. USPHS, hosp. and med. facilities sect., mental retardation br., 1965-67; regional dir. Council Exceptional Children, Madison, 1950-52; rep. Wis. to bd. govs. Council on Exception Children, 1962; spl. adv. Pres.'s Panel on Mental Retardation, 1961-62; chmn. Joint Commn. Internat. Aspects Mental Retardation; past mem. profl. adv. com. mentally retarded and law. Nat. Law Center George Washington U.; mem. Fed. Hosp. Council, 1972-76; mem. Wis. Council Developmental Disabilities, 1977-79; adv. com. U. Ala. Mgmt. Tng. Inst., 1973-79, U. Mo. Career Mgmt. Project, 1978-79. Served with USAF, 1943-44. Recipient Joseph P. Kennedy Found. Internat. Leadership award, 1968; Distinguished Alumni award U. Wis.-Milw., 1968; Distinguished Service award Wis. Acad. Arts, Letters and Dance, 1969. Fellow Am. Assn. Mental Deficiency (Leadership award 1973, pres. 1964-65, mem. profl. adv. com. standards for state residential facilities for mentally retarded); mem. Internat. London Congress for Sci. Study Mental Deficiency (co-chmn. 1960), Am. Assn. Univ. Affiliated Programs for Developmentally Disabled (pres. 1974-75), Mexican (hon. pres.), Venezuelan (hon.), Brazilian (hon. pres.) assns. for study mental deficiency, Internat. Soc. Sci. Study Mental Deficiency. Author: (with Heber) Mental Retardation, a Review of Research, 1964; (with Bathazar) Emotionally Distrubed, Mentally Retarded, 1975; (with Sloan) A Century of Concern: A History of American Association on Mental Deficiency: 1876-1976. Contbr. articles to profl. jours. Home: 606 Morningstar Ln Madison WI 53704

STEVENS, HOLLY, author, editor, former mag. exec.; b. Hartford, Conn., Aug. 10, 1924; d. Wallace and Elsie Viola (Kachel) Stevens; student Vassar Coll., 1941-42, U. Conn., 1951-53; m. John Martin Hanchak, Aug. 5, 1944 (div. Sept. 1951); 1 son, Peter Reed; m. 2d, Duncan Stephenson, Aug. 24, 1957 (div. Dec. 1965). Fire underwriter Aetna Life Affiliated Cos., Hartford, 1942-46; purchasing asst. Trinity Coll., Hartford, 1955-64; sec. Yale, 1966-68; advt. mgr. Yale Rev., 1968-69, bus. mgr., 1969-77; cons. Conn. Public Radio, 1979. Founder, dir. New Eng. Poetry Circuit, 1963-68; founder, dir. Conn. Poetry Circuit, 1968-72, mem. selection com. 1972—; founding mem. Poetry Center Trinity Coll. Bd. dirs. New Haven Symphony Orch., 1975—. Timothy Dwight Coll. fellow, 1971—; Ingram Merrill Found. grantee, 1964, Supplemental award, 1965; Nat. Endowment for Humanities sr. fellow 1972-73. Mem. English Inst. Clubs: Elizabethan, Mory's (Yale). Author: Souvenirs and Prophecies: The Young Wallace Stevens, 1977. Editor: Letters of Wallace Stevens, 1966, 67; The Palm at the End of The Mind: Selected Poems and a Play by Wallace Stevens, 1971; contbr. to So. Rev. Home: Joshua Cove Guilford CT 06437

STEVENS, JOHN HUGH, elec. wire and cable co. exec.; b. Chakrata, India, July 28, 1916; M.A. with honors, Cambridge U. (Eng.). With Can. Wire and Cable Co. Ltd., Toronto, 1948—, project engr., chief quality control engr., chief plant engr., 1949-59, v.p. coordinating sales and engring., 1959-66, exec. v.p., 1966, pres., 1966—, chief exec. officer, 1970—, chmn. bd., 1974—; dir. Noranda Mfg. Ltd., Sidbec-Dosco Ltd., Industrias Conductores Monterrey, S.A. (Mexico), Tolley Holdings Ltd. (N.Z.), Tyree Canada Wire Pty. Ltd. (Australia), others. Served with Royal Engrs., 1936-47. Bd. govs. Canadian Assn. for Latin-Am. Mem. Can. Mfrs. Assn. (dir., mem. exec. com., pres.). Home: 307 Russell Hill Rd Toronto ON M4V 2T7 Canada Office: 147 Laird Dr Toronto ON M4G 3W1 Canada

STEVENS, JOHN PAUL, asso. justice U.S. Supreme Ct.; b. Chgo., Apr. 20, 1920; s. Ernest James and Elizabeth (Street) S.; A.B., U. Chgo., 1941; J.D. magna cum laude, Northwestern U., 1947; m. Elizabeth Jane Sheeren, June 7, 1942; children—John Joseph, Kathryn (Mrs. Edward Jedlicka), Elizabeth Jane, Susan Roberta; m. 2d, Maryan Simon, Dec. 1979. Admitted to Ill. bar, 1949, practiced in Chgo.; law clk. to U.S. Supreme Ct. Justice Wiley Rutledge, 1947-48; asso. firm Poppenhusen, Johnston, Thompson & Raymond, 1948-52; asso. counsel sub-com. on study monopoly power, com. on judiciary U.S. Ho. of Reps., 1951; partner firm Rothschild, Stevens, Barry & Myers, 1952-70; U.S. circuit judge, 1970-75; asso. justice U.S. Supreme Ct., 1975—. Lectr. anti-trust law Northwestern U. Sch. Law, 1953, U. Chgo. Law Sch., 1954-55. Mem. Atty. Gen.'s Nat. Com. to Study Anti-Trust Laws, 1953-55. Served with USNR, 1942-45. Decorated Bronze Star, Mem. Chgo. Bar Assn. (2d v.p. 1970), Am., Ill., Fed. bar assns., Am. Law Inst., Order of Coif, Phi Beta Kappa, Psi Upsilon, Phi Delta Phi. Office: US Supreme Ct 1 First St NE Washington DC 20543

STEVENS, JOHN RICHARD, editor; b. Ithaca, N.Y., May 5, 1930; s. William T. and Helen I. (Howell) S.; B.A., Cornell U., 1951. Asst. editor Outdoor Life mag., 1955-59; copy editor Mademoiselle mag., 1959-64; mng. editor Ladies Home Jour., N.Y.C., 1964—. Served as 1st lt. USAF, 1951-53. Home: 205 W 57th St New York City NY 10019 Office: 641 Lexington Ave New York City NY 10022

STEVENS, KENNETH NOBLE, educator; b. Toronto, Ont., Can., Mar. 23, 1924 (came to U.S. 1948, naturalized 1962); s. Cyril George and Catherine (Noble) S.; B.A.Sc., U. Toronto, 1945, M.A.Sc., 1948; Sc.D., Mass. Inst. Tech., 1952; m. Phyllis Fletcher, Jan. 19, 1957; children—Rebecca, Andrea, Michael Hugh, John Noble. Inst., U. Toronto, 1946-48; faculty Mass. Inst. Tech., Cambridge, 1948—, prof. elec. engring., 1963—, Clarence J. Lebel prof., 1977—. Vis. fellow Royal Inst. Tech., Stockholm, Sweden, 1962-63; cons. to industry, 1952—; vis. prof. phonetics U. Coll., London, 1969-70. Trustee Buckingham Browne and Nichols Sch., 1974—. Guggenheim fellow, 1962. Fellow Acoustical Soc. Am. (exec. com. 1963-66 v.p. 1971-72, pres. elect 1975-76, pres. 1976-77), IEEE. Author: (with A.G. Bose) Introductory Network Theory. Contbr. articles to profl. jours. Home: 46 Foster St Cambridge MA 02138

STEVENS, MARK CHANCELLOR, banker; b. Detroit, Dec. 17, 1906; s. Mark Burnham and Emily M.C.E. (Gilmore) S.; A.B. magna cum laude, Harvard, 1927; B.A. magna cum laude, Trinity Coll., Cambridge U. (Eng.), 1928; m. Betsy Dawson, Apr. 29, 1933 (dec. Dec. 1964); children—Betsy Ann (Mrs. John R. Sutton, III), Mark C., Thomas B.; m. 2d, Serena Ailes, Apr. 3, 1969. With Detroit Bank & Trust Co. and predecessors, 1928-72, successively trust officer, asst. v.p., v.p., 1928-67, officer in charge personal trust dept., 1957-72, sr. v.p., 1967-72; consul, Thailand, 1957—; councilman, Grosse Pointe Farms, Mich., 1965-75. Treas., Alvin M. Bentley Found., 1964-76, v.p., 1978-79, pres., 1979—) trustee, 1964—; trustee Merrill Palmer Inst., 1967-75; trustee Elmwood Cemetery, 1946—, sec.-treas., 1946—; trustee, Detroit Hist. Soc., 1961—, pres., 1969-71. Decorated Order Crown of Thailand. Mem. English Speaking Union (pres. Detroit chpt. 1956-63, now trustee, nat. dir., chmn. nat. travel com. 1976—), Circumnavigators Club (pres. Detroit chpt. 1969-71, internat. pres. 1972), Detroit Com. on Fgn. Relations (chmn. 1966-68), C. of C. Clubs: Detroit; Grosse Pointe; Country; Economic; Consular Corps The Players; Farmington Country (Charlottesville, Va.); Trinity Boat (Cambridge, Eng.). Home: 280 Moross Rd Grosse Pointe Farms MI 48236

STEVENS, MARTIN, educator, coll. adminstr.; b. Hamburg, Germany, Jan. 11, 1927; s. Hans Siegfried and Hertha Paula (Stern-Geiger) S.; came to U.S., 1939, naturalized, 1945; B.A., Western Res. U., 1949, M.A., 1950; Ph.D., Mich. State U., 1956; m. Rose Zimbardo, Nov. 26, 1974; children by previous marriage—Cynthia Jean, Marc, David. Prof. English, Ohio State U., 1964-69; prof., chmn. dept. English, SUNY, Stony Brook, 1973-75; prof. English, dean of humanities Herbert Lehman Coll., CUNY, 1975-79; dean liberal arts and scis. Baruch Coll., CUNY, 1979--; prof. English Grad. Center, CUNY, 1975—. Served with USNR, 1945-46. Guggenheim fellow, 1966-67; Fulbright research scholar 1966-67. Mem. MLA, Mediaeval Acad. Am., Nat. Council Tchrs. English. Jewish. Author works in field; contbr articles to profl. jours. Home: 2600 Netherland Ave New York NY 10463 Office: 17 Lexington Ave New York NY 10010. *As an educator and coll. adminstr., I have been guided throughout my career by a belief in the importance of a liberal edn. made available to all who desire it. Freedom of thought and inquiry and the desire to know and evaluate are the basic requirements of a dem. soc.*

STEVENS, MAY, artist; b. Boston, June 9, 1924; d. Ralph and Alice (Dick) Stevens; B.F.A., Mass. Coll. Art, Boston, 1946; postgrad. Academie Julian, Paris, France, 1948-49; m. Rudolf Baranik, June 5, 1948; 1 son, Steven. One-woman shows Terry Dintenfass Gallery, N.Y.C., 1971, Cornell U., 1973, Douglass Coll., Rutgers U., 1974, Lerner-Heller Gallery, N.Y.C., 1978; exhibited in group shows at Gemeente Mus., The Hague, 1979, Whitney Mus., 1970, Gedok, Kunsthaus, Hamburg, Germany, 1972, Everson Mus., Syracuse, N.Y., 1976; represented in permanent collections at Whitney Mus., Bklyn. Mus., Herbert F. Johnson Mus., Cornell U.; faculty Sch. Visual Arts, N.Y.C., 1964—; sr. vis. critic Cornell U., 1973; lectr. Art Students League, N.Y.C., 1972, U. Wis-Racine, 1973, Coll. Art Assn., Washington, 1975. MacDowell Colony fellow, 1970, 71, 73. Recipient New Eng. Ann. Landscape prize Silvermine Guild, 1958, Childe Hassam Purchase awards Nat. Inst. Arts and Letters, 1968, 69, CAPS award for graphics N.Y. State Council on Arts, 1974. Home: 97 Wooster St New York NY 10012. *To be autonomous and responsible has been the motivation of my work. To be a woman faced with restrictions, limitations, and responsibilities not chosen by me has been the life situation I have had to combat. I feel it has been necessary to rethink and redesign my life and my work, myself as a person, in an existential sense. Certain rights obtain by virtue of my humanness and my particular capabilities, but I have had to seize those rights and insist on them in front of cliché concepts of woman's role. Wholeness, openness, the glad taking-on of freely chosen responsibilities are the keys.*

STEVENS, MILTON LEWIS, JR., trombonist; b. Gt. Barrington, Mass., Nov. 10, 1942; s. Milton Lewis and Edna Laura (Coates) S.; Mus.B., Oberlin Conservatory Music, 1965; Mus.M., U. Ill., 1966; D.M.A., Boston U., 1975; m. Elizabeth Mruk Stevens, June 14, 1966. Instr., Oberlin (Ohio) Conservatory Music, 1967-68; asst. prof. Boston U., 1970-73, Ohio State U., Columbus, 1973-74; prin. trombonist Denver Symphony, 1974-78; prin. trombonist Nat. Symphony Orch., Washington, 1978—. Recipient Albert Spaulding award Berkshire Music Center, 1968. Mem. Internat. Trombone Assn. Home: 3326 Longbranch Dr Falls Church VA 22041 Office: Nat Symphony JF Kennedy Center Washington DC 20566

STEVENS, NORMAN E., lawyer; b. Los Angeles, June 24, 1928; s. E. M. and Florence (Kaufman) Smuckler; B.A., U. Calif. at Los Angeles, 1951, J.D., 1956; postgrad. U. So. Calif. Sch. Law, 1957-58; m. Carole Baskin, Sept. 23, 1956; children—Jeffrey Mark, Curtis Frank, Suzanne Lynn. Admitted to Calif. bar, 1956, U.S. Supreme Ct. bar, 1974; practiced in Los Angeles, 1956—; asso. firm Leland & Plattner, Los Angeles, 1956-57; asso. firm Buchalter, Nemer, Fields & Savitch, Los Angeles, 1957-63, partner, 1963-65; partner firm Meyers, Stevens & Walters, Los Angeles, 1965-69; mem., pres. Meyers, Stevens & Walters, P.C., 1969—. Lectr. edn. of bar U. Calif., 1964-65, 73, 74, 75, 76, 77. Served to capt. USAF, 1952-53. Mem. Financial Lawyers Conf. (pres. 1967, gov.), Bankruptcy Study Group (chmn. 1968), Beverly Hills (chmn. sect. comml. law 1970-71), Los Angeles County (chmn. sect. comml. law and bankruptcy 1975-76, exec. com.), Am. bar assns., State Bar Calif. (subcom. bus. law sect.), Phi Alpha Delta. Editor, Bankruptcy Study Group Bull., 1966-67. Home: 16611 Park Lane Circle Los Angeles CA 90049 Office: 6300 Wilshire Blvd Los Angeles CA 90048

STEVENS, PAUL EDWARD, lawyer; b. Youngstown, Ohio, July 22, 1916; s. Raymond U. and Mary Ann (Pritchard) S.; LL.B., Ohio State U., 1941; m. Janet L. Weisert, Mar. 9, 1946; 1 son, Mark O. Admitted to Ohio bar, 1941; since practiced in Youngstown; partner firm Green, Schiavoni, Murphy & Stevens, 1962-71, Burdman, Stevens & Gilliland, 1971-75, Stevens & Toot, 1976-77, Paul E. Stevens Co., 1977—; prof. law Youngstown Coll. Sch. Law, 1946-60; trial examiner Ohio Civil Rights Commn., 1968—. Gen. counsel Animal Charity League of Ohio, 1965—. Trustee Poland Township, Ohio, 1960-69; Republican candidate for U.S. Congress, 1959; dist. adminstrv. asst. Congressman Charles J. Carney, 19th Ohio dist., 1970; endowment chmn. Welsh Nat. Gymanfa Ganu Assn. Served with AUS, 1942-46. Mem. Am., Ohio (chmn. membership com. 1955), Mahoning County (pres. 1953-54) bar assns., Assn. Trial Lawyers Am., ACLU. Unitarian. Home: 7191 N Lima Rd Poland OH 44514 Office: 808 Wick Bldg Youngstown OH 44503

STEVENS, PAUL IRVING, mfg. co. exec.; b. Lawrence, Kans., Mar. 22, 1915; s. Ira F. and Ida M. Stevens; student bus. adminstrn., Pasadena (Calif.) Coll., 1933-35; m. Artie Faye Womack, Nov. 10, 1935; children—Richard Irving, Constance Irene. Indsl. engr. Consol. Aircraft Co., San Diego, 1940-49; founder, prin. stockholder, pres. United Machine Co., Ft. Worth, 1958-67; exec. v.p. Clary Corp., San Gabriel, Calif., 1962-65; pres., owner Stevens Corp., Ft. Worth, 1965-69; pres., chief exec. officer Waltham Industries, N.Y.C., 1969-71, Stevens Industries, La Jolla, Calif., 1972—, Campbell Industries, San Diego. 1976-79. Pres., chief exec. officer, bd. dirs. San Diego Symphony. Republican. Methodist. Clubs: La Jolla Country, Colonial Country, Canyon Country. Rotary. Home: 2585 Calle Del Oro La Jolla CA 92037 Office: PO Box 950 La Jolla CA 92038

STEVENS, PHINEAS, lawyer; b. Jackson, Miss., Dec. 20, 1917; s. John Morgan and Ethel (Featherstun) S.; B.S.C., U. Miss., 1939, LL.B., 1941, J.D., 1969; m. Patricia Land, Nov. 12, 1949; children—Susan Land, Stuart Phineas. Spl. agt. FBI, 1941-43; admitted to Miss. bar, 1941; since practiced in Jackson; partner firm Butler, Snow, O'Mara, Stevens & Cannada, 1954—; gen. counsel, dir. Miller Transporters, Inc., Jackson; lectr., Miss. Law Inst., 1965, Transp. Law Inst., U. Denver Law Sch., 1968, 78. Pres., Motor Carriers Lawyers Found., 1971-72, Miss. Bar Found., 1978-79. Served to lt. USNR, 1943-46. Mem. Motor Carrier Lawyers Assn. (pres. 1966-67), Am. Bar Assn., Assn. ICC Practitioners, Am. Judicature Soc., Omicron Delta Kappa, Kappa Alpha, Phi Delta Phi. Episcopalian. Contbr. articles to profl. jours. Home: Box 22567 Jackson MS 39205 Office: 17th Floor Deposit Guaranty Plaza Jackson MS 39202

STEVENS, PRESTON STANDISH, architect; b. Pike County, Miss., Jan. 28, 1896; s. Augustin Washburn and Caroline (Ulmer) S.; student Miss. Coll., 1913-15, Ga. Inst. Tech., 1919; m. Hermoine Ross Walkr, Dec. 10, 1928; children—Preston Standish. Practice of architecture, Atlanta, 1919—; hon. chmn. fin. com. Stevens & Wilkinson, architects and engrs., Inc.; prin. works include Ga. Bapt. Hosp., Atlanta, 1920—, Rich's, Inc., Richway Stores, 1950—, E. Rivers Elementary Sch., Atlanta, 1950, Ga. Center for Continuing Edn., Athens, 1958; architect Techwood Housing Project, Atlanta, first slum clearance project in U.S., 1935, Citco office bldg., Tulsa, 1973, Tower Pl., Atlanta, 1975, Bapt. Village, Waycross, Canterbury Ct., Atlanta. Fellow AIA. Clubs: Capital City (life), Piedmont Driving. Contbr. articles to profl. jours. Home: 1599 W Paces Ferry Rd NW Atlanta GA 30327 Office: 100 Peachtree St NW Atlanta GA 30303

STEVENS, RAY (HAROLD RAY RAGSDALE), singer, musician, songwriter; b. Clarkdale, Ga., Jan. 24, 1939; s. Willis Harold and Mary Frances (Stephens) Ragsdale; student Ga. State U., 1957-59; m. Penny Dee Jackson, Mar. 30, 1960; children—Timi Lynn, Suzi. Rec. artist, 1957—; numerous appearances on TV, night clubs, concerts in U.S. and abroad; singer, composer numerous songs, including: Everything Is Beautiful, 1970 (Grammy award best contemporary male vocal); Ahab The Arab, 1962 (BMI Performance award); The Streak, 1974 (BMI Performance award); Mr. Businessman, 1968 (BMI Performance award); Gitarzan, 1969 (BMI Performance award); recs. include Bluegrass version of Misty, 1974, I Need Your Help, 1979; founder, owner Ahab Music Co. Inc., Nashville, 1963—; founder Ray Stevens Music, 1977; host Andy Williams Summer Show NBC-TV, 1970. Built rec. studio, Nashville, 1971. Office: Ahab Music Co Inc 1707 Grand Ave Nashville TN 37212

STEVENS, RAYMOND DONALD, JR., chem. co. exec.; b. Buffalo, Feb. 17, 1927; s. Raymond Donald and Annette (Wells) S.; grad. Nichols Sch., Buffalo, 1945; B.S. in Econs., Wharton Sch. U. Pa., 1951; m. V. Aline Larkin, Aug. 20, 1949; children—Raymond Donald III, Larkin Edgeworth, Courtney Curtis, Hunter Hubbard. With Pierce & Stevens Chem. Corp., Buffalo, 1951—, exec. v.p., 1958-63, pres., 1963-70, chmn. bd., 1970—, also dir.; exec. v.p. Pratt & Lambert, Inc., Buffalo, 1967-70, pres., chief exec. officer, 1970—, chmn., 1970—, also dir.; dir. United Paint Co., Niagara Share Corp., Mfrs. & Traders Trust Co., First Empire State Corp., Ramblewood Mfg. Co. Trustee Buffalo Gen. Hosp. Served with USNR, 1945-47. Mem. Nat. Paint and Coatings Assn. (dir., exec. com. 1977—), Am. Legion (past post comdr.), Friars Sr. Soc., Phi Kappa Sigma. Club: Saturn (Buffalo). Home: 21 Meadow Rd Buffalo NY 14216 Office: 75 Tonawanda St Buffalo NY 14207

STEVENS, RISË, mezzo-soprano; b. N.Y.C.; d. Christian Steenberg; student Juilliard Sch. of Music, N.Y.C., Mozarteum, Salzburg, Austria; studied singing with Mme. Anna Schoen René and Mme. Vera Schwarz; m. Walter G. Surovy, Jan. 6, 1939; 1 son, Nicolas Vincent. Made debut as Mignon, Prague, Czechoslovakia, 1936; 1st appearance with Metropolitan Opera Co. in Mignon, Dec. 1938; has sung at Prague Opera, Vienna State Opera, Teatro Colon, Buenos Aires, Cairo, Egypt, Glyndbourne Mozart Festival, San Francisco Opera Co., Athens, Greece, Paris Grand Opera; created title-role in world premiere of Virgilio Mortari's opera La Figlia del Diavolo at La Scala, Milan, 1954; prin. roles in Mignon, Der Rosenkavalier, Carmen, Samson et Dalila, La Gioconda, Hansel and Gretel, Le Nozze di Figaro, Die Walküre, Cosi Fan Tutte, Orfeo ed Euridice, Khovanchina (Met. opera premiere), Tales of Hoffmann, Die Fiedermaus; created Carmen in new Met. Opera prodn.; in motion pictures The Chocolate Soldier, Going My Way, Carnegie Hall; opened Music Theater of Lincoln Center starring in The King and I, 1964. Co-general mgr. Metropolitan Opera Nat. Co., 1963-66; lectr. New Sch., N.Y.C.; pres. Mannes Coll. of Music, N.Y.C. Traveled extensively with the Hollywood Victory Caravan during World War II; headed own radio programs; starred regularly on TV programs; concertized yearly throughout U.S. and Canada; recordings for Columbia Records and RCA Victor. Mem. music panel Nat. Endowment for Arts. Bd. dirs. Met. Opera Guild. Recipient Citation for U.S. Treasury Dept.; Certificate of Honor from ARC; Citation from Greater N.Y. Fund; Distinguished Service Award, N.Y. Cancer Com.; Box Office Blue Ribbon Award for picture, Going My Way; voted best female vocalist in radio by Motion Picture Daily and Musical America, 1947 and 1948. Established Risë Stevens Scholarship, Adelphi Coll., 1947. Hon. mem. Wagnerian Soc. (Buenos Aires), Sigma Alpha Iota. Address: Metropolitan Opera Association New York City NY 10023

STEVENS, ROBERT BOCKING, coll. pres., lawyer; b. U.K., June 8, 1933; s. John Skevington and Enid Dororthy (Bocking) S.; naturalized, 1971; B.A., Oxford U., 1955, B.C.L., 1956, M.A., 1959; LL.M., Yale, 1958; m. Rosemary Anne Wallace, Jan. 28, 1961; children—Carey, Richard. Barrister-at-law, London, 1956; tutor in law Keble Coll. Oxford U., 1958-59; asst. prof. law Yale, 1959-61, asso. prof., 1961-65, prof., 1965-76; provost, prof. law and history Tulane U., 1976-78; pres. Haverford Coll., 1978—; vis. prof. U. Tex., 1961, U. East Africa, 1962, Stanford, 1966; cons. UN, HEW, U.S. Dept. State. Rockefeller Found. grantee, 1962-64, Ford Found. grantee, 1962-64, 73-74; Nat. Endowment for the Humanities grantee; Nuffield Found. grantee; Russell Sage Found. grantee, 1967-68. Clubs: Oxford and Cambridge (London); Yale (N.Y.C.). Author: Income Security, 1970; Welfare Medicine in America, 1974; In Search of Justice, 1968; The Restrictive Practices Court, 1965; Lawyers and the Courts, 1967; Law and Politics, 1978. Home: 1 College Circle Haverford PA 19041 Office: Office of Pres Haverford Coll Haverford PA 19041

STEVENS, ROBERT DAVID, librarian, educator; b. Nashua, N.H., Aug. 11, 1921; s. David Philip and Ruth (Ackley) S.; A.B. magna cum laude, Syracuse U., 1942; B.S. in L.S. with honors, Columbia, 1947; M.A., Am. U., 1955, Ph.D., 1965; m. Helen Medora Conrad, Jan. 16, 1943; children—Ruth Wilson Robertson, Hope Conrad. With Library of Congress, Washington, 1947-64, coordinator pub. law 480 programs, 1962-64; dir. library East West Center, Honolulu, 1964-65; dean Grad. Sch. Library Studies U. Hawaii, Honolulu, 1966-75; chief cataloging div. Copyright Office, 1975—. Fulbright lectr. U. Indonesia, 1971; U.S. del. Intergovtl. Conf. Planning Nat. Libraries Infrastructures, 1974. Served to lt. USNR, 1943-46. Mem. Hawaii (pres. 1966-67), Am. (mem. council 1967-70, mem. U.S.-Japan adv. com. 1972—, chmn. 1974-76, Relms policy and research com. 1977—), Japan library assns., Phi Beta Kappa, Pi Sigma Alpha. Club: Club 15 (Honolulu). Author: Role of the Library of Congress in International Exchange of Government Publications, 1955; Toshokan Kyoryoku, 1970; Documents of International Organizations, 1974; Japanese and U.S. Research Libraries at the Turning Point, 1977. Contbr. articles to profl. publs. Home: Crystal Plaza 918-N 2111 Jefferson Davis Hwy Arlington VA 22202

STEVENS, ROBERT EDWIN, ins. co. exec.; b. Hartford, Feb. 12, 1927; s. Horace and Anna E. (Lauritzen) S.; B.S., Wesleyan U., 1949; m. Betty L. Hippler, June 30, 1951; children—Paul, Lynn, Peter. Various positions bond and common stock divs. Conn. Mut. Life Ins. Co., Hartford, 1951-71, v.p., treas., 1972-74, sr. v.p., 1974-76, exec. v.p., 1976—; dir. Liberty Bank for Savs., Middletown, Conn. Bd. dirs. Hartford Hosp.; trustee Fox Scholarship Found., Hartford Sem.; corporator Middlesex Meml. Hosp., Middletown, St. Francis Hosp., Hartford, Newington Children's Hosp. Served with USNR, World War II. Mem. Hartford Soc. Financial Analysts. Home: Keighley Pond Rd Cobalt CT 06414 Office: 140 Garden St Hartford CT 06115

STEVENS, ROBERT JAY, mag. editor; b. Detroit, July 25, 1945; s. Jay Benjamin and Louise Ann (Beyreuther) S.; student Huron (S.D.) Coll., 1963-66, Wayne State U., 1968-71; m. Dahlia Jean Conger, Aug. 15, 1970; children—Sandra Lee, Julie Ann. Sr. staff writer Automotive News, Detroit, 1968-71; editor Excavating Contractor mag. Cummins Pub. Co., Oak Park, Mich., 1971-78, Chevrolets, Pro Jour., Sandy Corp., Southfield, Mich., 1978-79; editor Cars and Parts mag. Amos Press, Sidney, Ohio, 1979—; truck editor Automotive Design & Devel. mag., 1971-78; lectr., speaker in field. Served with AUS, 1966-68; Vietnam. Decorated Air medal, Bronze Star, Commendation medal; recipient Alphomega Publs. award, 1965—, Robert F. Boger Meml. award for outstanding constrn. journalism, 1975, U.L.C.C. nat. editorial award Am. Pub. Works Assn., 1978. Mem. Detroit Auto Writers (past dir.), Internat. Motor Press Assn., Soc. Automotive Historians, Antique Automobile Club Am., Contrn. Writers Assn., Am. Motorcycle Assn. Republican. Presbyterian. Author articles, poems. Home: 3696 Mt Vernon Ct Highland MI 48031 Office: PO Box 150 911 Vandemark Rd Sidney OH 45367

STEVENS, ROGER L., theatrical producer; b. Detroit, Mar. 12, 1910; s. Stanley and Florence (Jackson) S.; student Choate Sch., 1928; student U. Mich., 1928-30, D.H.L., 1964; H.H.D. (hon.), Wayne State U., 1960; D.H.L., Tulane U., 1960; LL.D., Amherst Coll., 1968; hon. degrees Skidmore Coll., 1969, U. Ill., 1970, Boston U., 1970, Am. U., 1979; m. Christine Gesell, Jan. 1, 1938; 1 dau., Christabel. Producing partner in more than 200 Broadway shows including West Side Story, Cat on a Hot Tin Roof, Bus Stop, Tea and Sympathy, The Visit, Ondine, Sabrina Fair, Mary, Mary, A Man For All Seasons, The Best Man, Old Times; former real estate broker specializing in hotels and investment properties, 1934-60. Spl. asst. to the Pres. on the arts, 1964-68; chmn. Nat. Council on the Arts, 1965-69; chmn. Nat. Endowment for the Arts, also trustee; pres. Nat. Opera Inst.; chmn. Am. Film Inst., 1969-72; chmn. adv. com. Nat. Book Award, 1970-75; mem. Council for Arts, Mass. Inst. Tech. Chmn. finance com. Democratic Party, 1956. Chmn. bd. trustees John F. Kennedy Center Performing Arts, 1961—; trustee Am. Shakespeare Theater and Acad.; bd. dirs. Met. Opera Assn., Filene Center/Wolf Trap Farm Park for Performing Arts, Peabody Conservatory, Folger Library, Circle in the Square Theatre. Decorated Royal Order of Vasa (Sweden); grand ufficiale Order of Merit (Italy); comdr.'s cross Order of Merit (W. Ger.); recipient award contbn. theatre Nat. Theater Conf., 1970. Fellow Royal Soc. Arts; mem. ANTA (treas. 1951-65), Phi Gamma Delta. Clubs: Bohemian (San Francisco); Racquet and Tennis, Century Assn., Pilgrims (N.Y.C.). Home: 1686 34th St NW Washington DC 20007 Office: John F Kennedy Center for Performing Arts Washington DC 20566

STEVENS, ROLLAND ELWELL, educator; b. St. Louis, Apr. 7, 1915; s. Clair E. and Viola (Foelsch) S.; A.B., Washington U., St. Louis, 1939; B.S. in L.S., U. Ill., 1940, M.S., 1942, Ph.D., 1951; m. Dorothy Zulauf, Aug. 30, 1941; children—Barbara K. (Mrs. Frederick Osgood), Trudi K. (Mrs. Austin Fontenot). Bibliographer, U. Ill., Urbana, 1940-42, prof. Grad. Sch. Library Sci., 1963—; reference librarian, asst. to dir. libraries U. Rochester, 1946-48; acquisition librarian Ohio State U., 1950-53, asst. dir. libraries, 1953-60, asso. dir. libraries, 1960-63. Served with AUS, 1942-46. Mem. ALA, Phi Beta Kappa, Beta Phi Mu (Good Teaching award 1968). Author: Reference Books in the Social Sciences and Humanities, 4th edit., 1977. Editor: University Archives, 1965; Research Methods in Librarianship: Historical and Bibliographical Methods in Library Research, 1971; Supervision of Employees in Libraries, 1979. Home: 305 Burkwood Ct Urbana IL 61801

STEVENS, ROSEMARY ANNE, educator; b. Bourne, Eng.; d. William Edward and Mary Agnes (Tricks) Wallace; B.A., Oxford (Eng.) U., 1957; Diploma in Social Adminstrn., Manchester (Eng.) U., 1959; M.P.H., Yale, 1963, Ph.D., 1968; m. Robert B. Stevens, Jan. 28, 1961; children—Carey Thomasine, Richard Nathaniel. Came to U.S., 1961, naturalized, 1968. Various hosp. adminstrv. positions, Eng., 1959-61; research asso. Yale Med. Sch., 1962-68, asst. prof., 1968-71, asso. prof., 1971-74, prof. pub. health, 1974-76, mistress Jonathan Edwards Coll., 1974-75; prof. dept. health systems mgmt. and polit. sci. Tulane U., New Orleans, 1976-78, chmn. dept. health systems mgmt., 1977-78; prof. dept. history and sociology of sci. U. Pa., 1979—; vis. lectr. Johns Hopkins U., 1967-68; guest scholar Brookings Instn., Washington, 1967-68; acad. visitor London Sch. Econs., 1962-64, 1973-74. Mem. Inst. Medicine, Nat. Acad. Sci., Am. Pub. Health Assn., Sigma Xi. Author: Medical Practice in Modern England: The Impact of Specialization and State Medicine, 1966; American Medicine and the Public Interest, 1971; (with others) Foreign Trained Physicians and American Medicine, 1972; Welfare Medicine in America, 1974; Alien-Doctors: Foreign Medical Graduates in American Hospitals, 1978. Contbr. articles to profl. jours. Home: 1 College Circle Haverford PA 19041 Office: U Pa 215 S 34th St Philadelphia PA 19104

STEVENS, ROY W., distillery exec.; b. Ottumwa, Iowa, Oct. 28, 1924; s. Manley O. and Ruth (Worrell) S.; B.S.C., State U. Iowa, 1948; m. Donna R. Borman, June 7, 1952 (dec. Jan. 1973); children—Katharine Anne (Mrs. Douglas J. Dillon), Thomas W., John M.; m. 2d, Beth A. Murphy, Apr. 20, 1974; children—Carrie Theresa, Elizabeth Mary. With Coca-Cola Co., 1948-54, Gen. Foods Corp., 1954-67; exec. v.p. Riviana Foods, Houston, 1967-73; v.p. mktg. Hiram Walker Inc., Detroit, 1973-75, pres., 1975—. Bd. dirs., chmn. Detroit Met. YMCA; adv. bd. Boys Club Met. Detroit, Met. Detroit council Boy Scouts Am.; bd. dirs. Met. Detroit Conv. and Visitors Bur., Nat. Call for Action; mem. corporate gifts com. United Negro Coll. Fund Mich. Mem. Sales and Mktg. Execs. Detroit (adv. bd.), Met. Detroit C. of C. (dir.), Sigma Alpha Epsilon. Episcopalian. Clubs: Hundred; Renaissance; Detroit Athletic, Country of Detroit. Home: 9 Rose Terr Grosse Pointe Farms MI 48236 Office: PO Box 14100 Detroit MI 48214

STEVENS, RUSSELL BRADFORD, plant pathologist; b. Washington, Oct. 31, 1915; s. Neil E. and Maude (Bradford) S.; student George Washington U., 1933-34, U. Me., summer 1935; B.S., U. Va., 1937; Ph.D., U. Wis., 1940; m. Helen Anne Crumley, June 8, 1949; children—Charles B., Susan C., Sarah L. Spl. agt. Dept. Agr., summer 1938; asst. prof. biology Birmingham-So. Coll., 1940-42; asst. prof. botany U. Louisville, 1946; asso. prof. botany Ala. Poly. Inst., 1947, U. Tenn., 1947-53; exec. sec. Biology Council, NRC, 1954-57; prof. botany, chmn. dept. George Washington U., 1957-66; exec. sec. div. biol. scis. Nat. Acad. Sci.-NRC, Washington, 1964—. Research asst. Conn. Agrl. Expt. Sta., summers 1939-41, 48-49; Served as 1st lt. San. Corps, AUS, 1942-46. Fellow A.A.A.S.; mem. Bot. Soc. Am., Am. Phytopath. Soc., Mycol. Soc. Am., Bot. Soc. Washington (pres.), Assn. Southeastern Biologists, Washington Acad. Scis., Sigma Xi, Gamma Alpha, Phi Sigma. Author: Disease in Plants, 1952; Career Opportunities in Biology, 1956; Plant Disease, 1974; Mycology Guidebook, 1974. Home: 6657 Sorrell St McLean VA 22101 Office: 2101 Constitution Ave NW Washington DC 20418

STEVENS, SINCLAIR MCKNIGHT, lawyer, Can. govt. ofcl.; b. Milton, Ont., Can., Feb. 11, 1927; s. Robert Murray and Anna Bailey (McKnight) S.; B.A. in Journalism, U. Western Ont., 1950; Barrister-at law, Osgoode Hall Law Sch., 1955; m. Noreen M. T. Charlebois, May 17, 1958. Called to bar, created queen's counsel, privy councillor; asso. firm Fraser & Beatty, Toronto, Ont.; partner firm Stevens & Stevens; with Brit. Internat. Fin. (Can.) Ltd., York Center Corp.; pres. Can. Treasury Bd., Ottawa, Ont.; mem. Can. Parliament for York-Simcoe (renamed York-Peel), 1972-74, 74—. Progressive Conservative. Clubs: Canada of N.Y.; Albany of Toronto (asso. dir.). Office: House of Commons Ottawa ON K1A 0A6 Canada

STEVENS, STORY CRANDALL, army officer; b. Dayton, Ky., Feb. 24, 1927; s. Robert L. and Margaret A. (McArthur) S.; B.S. in Chem. Engring., Purdue U., 1954; B.S. in Aero. Engring., Ga. Inst. Tech., 1958, M.S., 1959; grad. Command and Gen. Staff Coll., 1960, Nat. War Coll., 1972; m. Margaret Eleanor Cosby, May 20, 1946; children—David, Robert, Deborah, Richard. Commd. 2nd lt. U.S. Army, 1946, advanced through grades to maj. gen., 1977; instr. dept. mechanics U.S. Mil. Acad., West Point, N.Y., 1960-61, asst. prof., 1961-64; project officer Army Concept Team, Vietnam, 1964-65; aero. engr. Combat Survivability Office, Washington, 1965-66; aircraft weapons systems analyst Office of the Chief of Staff of the Army, Washington, 1966-67, ops. research analyst, 1967, chief aviation systems group, 1967-68, ops. research analyst, 1968-69; bn. comdr. 58th Transp. Bn., Vietnam, 1969-70; asst. to comdr. 34th Gen. Support Group, Vietnam, 1970; chief air systems div., Washington, 1970-71; comptroller Mil. Traffic Mgmt. Command, Washington, 1972-73; comdr. 1st Support Brigade, U.S. Army Europe, Ger. and community comdr., Mannheim, Ger., 1973-74; dep. comdr. Kaiserslautern Army Depot, Ger., 1974-75; dep. comdg. gen. for acquisition U.S. Army Aviation Systems Command, St. Louis, 1975-76, comdr. U.S. Army Aviation Research and Devel. Command, St. Louis, 1977—. Decorated D.F.C., Legion of Merit with two oak leaf clusters, Bronze Star with one oak leaf cluster, Air medals (13), Army Commendation medal. Office: Comdg Gen US Army Aviation Research and Devel Command Saint Louis MO 63166

STEVENS, THEODORE FULTON, U.S. senator; b. Indpls., Nov. 18, 1923; s. George A. and Gertrude (Chancellor) S.; B.A., U. Calif. at Los Angeles, 1947; LL.B., Harvard U., 1950; m. Ann Mary Cherrington, Mar. 29, 1952 (dec.); children—Susan B., Elizabeth H., Walter C., Theodore Fulton, Ben A. Admitted to Calif., Alaska, D.C., U.S. Supreme Ct. bars; mem. firm Northcutt Ely, Washington, 1950-52, Collins & Clasby, Fairbanks, 1953; U.S. atty. Dist. Alaska, 1953-56; legis. counsel Dept. Interior, 1956-58, asst. to sec. dept., 1958-60, solicitor, 1960; pvt. practice law, Anchorage, 1961-68; mem. Alaska Ho. of Reps., 1965-68, majority leader, speaker pro tem, 1967-78; U.S. senator for Alaska, 1968—, now asst. minority leader. Served as 1st lt. USAAF, World War II. Mem. Fed., Am., Alaska, Calif., D.C. bar assns., Am. Legion, VFW. Republican. Club: Rotary. Home: PO Box 879 Anchorage AK Office: Room 260 Russell Senate Office Bldg Washington DC 20510

STEVENS, WARREN, actor; b. Clark's Summit, Pa., Nov. 2, 1919; s. Albert Clifford and Helen Dodd (Blakeslee) S.; student U.S. Naval Acad., 1939-40; m. Barbara Helen Fletcher, Sept. 9, 1969; children—Adam Fletcher, Matthew Dodd; 1 son by previous marriage, Laurence Blakeslee. Appeared on New York stage in Celebration, Gallileo, 1947, Sundown Beach, 1948, Smile of the World, 1949, Detective Story, 1949; appeared in numerous motion pictures since 1950, including Barefoot Contessa, Forbidden Planet; appeared on numerous television shows, including Richard Boone Rep. Served with USN, 1937-40, USAAF, 1942-46.

STEVENS, WHITNEY, textile co. exec.; b. Plainfield, N.J., Nov. 26, 1926; s. Robert TenBroeck and Dorothy Goodwin (Whitney) S.; student Phillips Acad., 1940-44; B.A., Princeton U., 1947; m. 2d, Helene Baldi, Nov. 1, 1961; children—Mark W., David W., Joan. With J.P Stevens & Co., Inc., N.Y.C. 1948—, v.p., 1958-64, exec. v.p., 1964-69. pres., 1969-79, chmn., chief exec. officer, 1980—, also dir., mem. exec. com.; adv. bd. Chem. Bank, N.Y.C. Trustee St. Luke's/Roosevelt Hosp., N.Y.C., Citizens' Budget Commn., N.Y.C. Served with USNR, 1944-46. Mem. Am. Textile Mfrs. Assn. (internat. trade com.), Color Assn. Am. (pres. 1967-71). Clubs: Links (N.Y.C.); Princeton (N.Y.). Office: 1185 Ave of Americas New York NY 10036

STEVENS, WILLIAM DOLLARD, corp. exec.; b. Bayonne, N.J., Aug. 4, 1918; s. William B. and Beatrice (Dollard) S.; B.Mech. Engring., Rensselaer Poly. Inst., 1940; postgrad. Case Inst. Tech., 1958; m. Mary E. King, Oct. 12, 1940; children—Sandra A. (Mrs. Jeffrey N. Melin), Barbara E. (Mrs. Dennis Gallagher), William K. Various engring. and mgmt. positions Babcock & Wilcox Co., N.Y.C., 1940-62; v.p. equipment div. Foster Wheeler Corp., Livingston, N.J., 1962-73, sr. v.p., 1972-74, exec. v.p., 1974-78, chmn. bd., 1978—, also dir.; dir. Forney Engring. Co., Glitsch, Inc., Belco Pollution Control, Inc. Tchr. Pratt Inst., 1946-47. Chmn. fund drive A.R.C., Hackensack, N.J., 1956; planning commr. Hackensack, 1955-58. Trustee Bergen County Mental Health Consultation Center, 1955-58; bd. dirs. Metals Properties Council, 1972-78; bd. overseers N.J. Inst. Tech., 1978—. Served to lt. USNR, 1943-45. Mem. ASME, Sigma Xi, Tau Beta Pi, Phi Kappa Tau. Methodist. Contbr. articles to profl. jours. Patentee in field. Home: 4 Stony Brook Dr North Caldwell NJ 07006 Office: 110 S Orange Ave Livingston NJ 07039

STEVENS, WILLIAM FOSTER, III, educator; b. Detroit, Oct. 7, 1922; s. William Foster and Alice (Knight) S.; B.S., Northwestern U., 1944; M.S., U. Wis., 1947, Ph.D., 1949; m. Lillian Janda Fort, June 29, 1962; children—Francine (Mrs. Charles Derby), Susan (Mrs. James Pierce), Alan, Martha (Mrs. James Freeman), Karin (Mrs. Daniel Friese). Research engr. B.F. Goodrich Co., 1949-51; faculty Northwestern U, Evanston, Ill., 1951—, prof. chem. engring., 1961—, asso. dean Grad. Sch., 1966-72, dir. freshman program, 1972-75, chmn. dept. chem. engring., 1976—. Cons. to govt., industry, 1955—. Served to ensign USNR, 1943-46. Mem. Am. Soc. Engring. Edn., Am. Chem. Soc., Am. Inst. Chem. Engrs., Sigma Xi, Tau Beta Pi, Phi Lambda Upsilon, Delta Tau Delta. Mem. United Ch. Christ. Home: 718 Windsor Rd Glenview IL 60025 Office: Chem Engring Dept Northwestern U Evanston IL 60201

STEVENS, WILLIAM KENNETH, lawyer; b. Chgo., Apr. 19, 1917; s. Ernest James and Elizabeth (Street) S.; A.B. cum laude, U. Calif., Berkeley, 1938; M.A., U. Chgo., 1940; J.D., Harvard U., 1948; m. Anne Hughes, Jan. 4, 1943; children—Anne Elizabeth Stevens Fishman, William Hughes, Mary Carol, Martha Street. Admitted to Ill. bar, 1948, Fla. bar, 1977; with First Nat. Bank Chgo., 1948-74, asst. v.p., 1958-61, v.p., 1961-74; partner firm McDermott, Will & Emery, Chgo., 1974—; chmn. Ill. Inst. Continuing Legal Edn., 1971-72. Pres., Hinsdale (Ill.) Public Library, 1977-79. Served to lt. USNR, 1941-45. lMem. Am. Bar Assn., Am. Law Inst., Chgo. Bar Assn., Ill. Bar Assn. Clubs: Mid-Day, Monroe, Hinsdale Golf; Chikaming Country (Lakeside, Mich.). Author: Illinois Estate Administration, 1968. Home: 314 S Lincoln St Hinsdale IL 60521 Office: 111 W Monroe St Chicago IL 60603

STEVENS, WILLIAM TRISTRAM, actuary; b. Ithaca, N.Y., Mar. 17, 1927; s. William T. and Helen (Howell) S.; B.A., Cornell U., 1950; m. Dorothy Ann Lyon, June 21, 1952; children—Kenneth, Bruce, Laurie. Sr. math. asst. Mut. Benefit Life Ins. Co., Newark, 1965-69; actuary Hartford Life Ins. Co., Boston, 1961-65; actuary, v.p. and actuary, v.p. and chief actuary Interstate Life & Accident Ins. Co., Chattanooga, 1969— also dir., mem. exec. com.; actuary Interstate Fire Ins. Co., also dir., mem. exec. com. Cons. Madison (N.J.) Bd. Edn., 1963-65; active United Fund, 1961-75, Boy Scouts Am., 1961-68; chmn. Heart Fund, Madison, 1968; mem. finance com. Signal Mountain Library, 1970-71. Trustee, chmn. Southeastern Actuarial Sch. Fund. Served with USNR, 1944-46. C.L.U. Fellow Soc. Actuaries (mem. edn. and exam. com. 1966-70); mem. Am. Acad. Actuaries, Southeastern Actuarial Club, Chattanooga C. of C. (chmn. consumer relations task force), Sigma Phi Epsilon. Presbyn. Kiwanian. Clubs: Cornell; Signal Mountain Country. Home: 608 Marr Dr Signal Mountain TN 37377 Office: 540 McCallie Ave Chattanooga TN 37402

STEVENS, WILLIAM WILSON, clergyman, educator; b. Huntington, W.Va., Oct. 30, 1914; s. William Wilson and Ellen Lorena (Rece) S.; B.A. magna cum laude, Marshall U., Huntington, 1937; Th.M., So. Baptist Theol. Sem., Louisville, 1944, Ph.D., 1951; m. Dorothy Leslie Powell, Oct. 31, 1944; children—William Wilson III, David W., John L. Dairy and milk sanitarian City of Huntington, 1938-41; ordained to ministry Bapt. Ch., 1942; pastor First Bapt. Ch., Hodgenville, Ky., 1951-55; prof. Bible, Miss. Coll., Clinton, 1955-67, chmn. div. religion, 1967—. Served as chaplain USNR, 1944-46. Mem. Assn. Bapt. Profs. of Religion (past pres.), Soc. Bibl. Lit., Am. Acad. Religion. Author: That Ye May Believe, 1959; Doctrines of the Christian Religion, 1967; A Guide for Old Testament Study, 1974; Guide for New Testament Study, 1977; The March of Protestantism: The Gospel in Triumph, 1978. Home: Box 12 Clinton MS 39056

STEVENSON, A. BROCKIE, painter; b. Montgomery County, Pa., Sept. 24, 1919; s. Alfred Brockie and Caroline Lansdale (Sill) S.; student Pa. Acad. Fine Arts, 1940-41, Barnes Found., 1946-48, Skowhegan Sch., Maine, 1950; m. Jane Merriman Mackenzie, Dec. 23, 1978. Instr., Sch. Fine Arts, Washington U., St. Louis, 1960-62; asso. prof. design and watercolor, head dept. painting and drawing Corcoran Sch. Art, 1965—; one-man shows: War Paintings, London and Salisbury, Eng., 1944, Instituto Cultural Peruano-Norteamericano, Lima, Peru, 1953, Art Center, Miraflores, Lima, 1958, 60, Association Cultural Peruano-Britanica, Lima, 1959, Mickelson Gallery, Washington, 1970, Pyramid Galleries Ltd., Washington, 1973, No. Va. Community Coll., 1974, Fendrick Gallery, Washington, 1978; group shows include: Nat. Gallery Art, London, 1944, Pa. Acad. Fine Arts, Phila., 1948, 49, 50, 51, Sociedad Bellas Artes del Peru, Lima, 1953, 54, 55, 56, SUNY at Potsdam and Albany, 1971, Columbia (S.C.) Mus. Art, 1971, EXPO '74, Spokane, Wash., 1974; represented in permanent collections, including: Corcoran Gallery Art, Washington, Dept. Def., Washington, Nat. Collection Fine Arts, Washington, Fed. Res. Bank Richmond (Va.), Woodward Found., Washington. Served with U.S. Army, 1941-45; ETO. Office: Corcoran Sch Art 17 E New York Ave NW Washington DC 20006

STEVENSON, ADLAI EWING, III, U.S. senator; b. Chgo., Oct. 10, 1930; s. Adlai Ewing and Ellen (Borden) S.; grad. Milton Acad., 1948; A.B., Harvard, 1952, LL.B., 1957; m. Nancy L. Anderson, June 25, 1955; children—Adlai Ewing IV, Lucy W., Katherine R., Warwick L. Admitted to Ill. bar, 1957; asso. firm Mayer, Friedlich, Spiess, Tierney, Brown & Platt, Chgo., 1958-66, partner, 1966-67; treas. of Ill., Springfield, 1967-70; mem. U.S. Senate from Ill., 1970—. Mem. Ill. Ho. of Reps., 1965-67. Served to capt. USMCR, 1952-54. Home: Hanover IL 61041 Office: 456 Russell Senate Office Bldg Washington DC 20510

STEVENSON, BEN, choreographer; b. Portsmouth, Eng., Apr. 4, 1936; s. Benjamin John and Florence May (Gundry) S.; came to U.S., 1968; grad. Arts Ednl. Sch., London, 1955; m. Joan Toastivine, Jan. 6, 1968. Dancer, Theatre Arts Ballet, London, 1952-54, Sadlers Wells Theatre Ballet, 1955-56, Royal Ballet, 1956-60, London Festival Ballet, 1960-62; appearances in Wedding in Paris, 1954-55, Music Man, London, 1962-63, Half a Sixpence, also Boys in Syracuse, London, 1964; prin. dancer, ballet master London Festival Ballet, 1964-68; artistic dir. Harkness Ballet Youth Dancers, 1968-71; co-dir. Nat. Ballet, Washington, 1971-74; artistic dir. Chgo. Ballet, 1974-75, Houston Ballet, 1976—; prin. ballets choreographed include Three Faces of Eve, 1965, Cast Out, 1966, Sleeping Beauty (full length), 1967, 71, 76, 78, Fervor, 1968, Three Preludes, 1968, Forbidden, 1969, Cinderella (full length), 1969, 71, 73, 74, 76, Bartok Concerto, 1970, Nutcracker (full length), 1972, 76, Symphonetta, 1972, Courant, 1973, Swan Lake (full length), 1977, L, 1978; mem. dance panel Tex. Commn. Arts, 1977. Recipient 1st prize London Choreographic competitions, 1965, 66, 67; 1st prize modern ballet choreography Internat. Ballet competition, Varna, Bulgaria, 1972. Asso. mem. Royal Acad. Dancing (Adeline Genee Gold medal 1955). Home: 3700 Wake Forest St Apt 75 Houston TX 77098 Office: Houston Ballet 2615 Colquitt St Houston TX 77098

STEVENSON, DONALD ROSS, interior designer; b. Litchfield, Ill., Sept. 8, 1926; s. Ross James and Sue B. (Laughlin) S.; B.F.A., U. Ill., 1950; M.F.A., U. Oreg., 1952; m. Ardis Ann Miller, Dec. 19, 1954; children—Lee Cartier, Eve Elizabeth, Jeffry Clay. Interior designer Laidlaw Bros., pubs., Hinsdale, Ill., 1952-54, Raymor Co., N.Y.C., 1954-56, Meier & Frank, Portland, Oreg., 1956-59, Sieberts, Beaverton, Oreg., 1959-62, Velte's, Vancouver, Wash., 1962-63, Director's, Portland, 1962-65; propr. Don Stevenson Interiors, Ltd., and predecessor, Portland, 1965—; mem. faculty U. Oreg., 1952; executed mural in lobby Student Union bldg. U. Oreg., 1952. Served with USNR, 1944-46. Recipient All-Designers Competition award for Organ Grinder Restaurant, Portland, 1974. Fellow Am. Soc. Interior Designers (nat. chmn. edn. 1977-78, nat. chmn. profl. devel., 1979—, nat. conf. workshop coordinator 1979); profl. affiliate mem. AIA; mem. Contemporary Crafts Assn. (dir.), Delta Tau Delta. Republican. Presbyterian. Home: 16830 S Chapin Way Lake Oswego OR 97034 Office: 1205 NW 25th St Portland OR 97210

STEVENSON, ELMER CLARK, educator; b. Pine City, Wash., Aug. 20, 1915; s. Fred James and Lottie (Crosley) S.; B.S., U. Md., 1937; Ph.D., U. Wis., 1942; m. Margaret E. Hammers, Sept. 1, 1939; children—Carol S. Poe, Craig Clark, James Price, Karen Sue Hedrick, Heather J. Jones, Richard Crosley. Asst. in plant pathology U. Wis., Madison, 1938-42; asst. plant pathologist, asso. plant pathologist, plant pathologist U.S. Dept. Agr., 1942-48; asso. prof. horticulture Purdue U., Lafayette, Ind., 1948-53, prof., 1953-67, head dept., 1958-67; asso. dean agr., dir. resident instrn. Oreg. State U., Corvallis 1967—. Fellow Am. Soc. Hort. Sci. Home: 8240 NW Chaparral Dr Corvallis OR 97330

STEVENSON, ERIC VAN CORTLANDT, lawyer, govt. ofcl.; b. N.Y.C., June 27, 1926; s. Harvey and Winifred (Worcester) S.; B.A., Yale, 1947, LL.B., 1950; m. Judith Kittredge Herrick, Nov. 13, 1955; children—Jonathan Herrick, Michael Kirkham, Anne Kittredge, Margaret Low, Philip Eric. Admitted to D.C. bar, 1951, Conn. bar, 1954; with NLRB, 1951; practice in Hartford, Conn., 1954-55, Norwich, Conn., 1957-61; with Electric Boat Co., 1956-57; research asso. Inst. Def. Analyses, 1961-63; with Labor Dept., 1963-65; research dir. George Washington U., 1965-66; gen. counsel Peace Corps, 1966-68; dir. urban affairs Life Ins. Assn. Am., N.Y.C., 1969-72; cons. Ford Found., 1963, Conn. Housing Investment Fund, 1968-69, Carnegie Corp., 1972, HUD, 1976-77, 78—; mortgage banker Sonnenblick-Goldman Corp., Washington, 1973-74, Boykin Corp., 1974-78. Served with USNR, 1944-46, 51-53. Mem. Fed. Bar Assn. Home: 3503 Woodley Rd NW Washington DC 20016 Office: HUD 451 7th St SW Washington DC 20410

STEVENSON, ERNEST VAIL, farmer coop. exec.; b. Streator, Ill., Mar. 18, 1922; s. James Vail and Lucile (Needham) S.; B.S., U. Ill., 1943, postgrad., 1946-47; grad. Advanced Mgmt. Program, Harvard Bus. Sch., 1964; m. Inez Ruth Schoellerman, Sept. 18, 1948; children—Karen (Mrs. Terry Allen Summers), Teresa (Mrs. William J. Murphy), Roger, Linda. Research asst. U. Ill., 1946-47; with FS Services, Inc., Bloomington, Ill., 1947—, sales edn. dir., 1947-49, dist. mgr., 1950-51, mgr. feed div., 1952-55, asst. gen. mgr., 1956-67, v.p. ops., 1967-68, exec. v.p., gen. mgr., 1968—; exec. v.p., gen. mgr. Ill. Grain Corp., 1969—; chmn. bd. CF Industries Inc., 1967-74, dir., 1957-77; pres. St. Louis Grain Corp., 1969—; chmn. bd. Asri-Trans. Corp.; dir. Farmers Export Co., Nat. Council Farmer Coops.; past dir. Internat. Energy Coop., LVO Internat., Nat. Potash Co., Nat. Coop. Refinery, 1st Nitrogen Corp., Central Nitrogen Inc., St. Paul Ammonia Products, Coop. Farm Chems. Past mem. adv. com. Ill. Bd. Higher Edn. Past bd. dirs. U. Ill. Agrl. Alumni Assn. Served as pilot USNR, 1943-45. Recipient award of merit U. Ill. Agrl. Alumni Assn., 1975; hon. state farmer degree Future Farmers Am., 1969. Mem. Assn. Commerce, Farmhouse frat., Phi Kappa Phi, Gamma Sigma Delta, Alpha Zeta, Ma-Wan-Da. Presbyterian. Home: 213 Fleetwood Dr Bloomington IL 61701 Office: 1701 Towanda Ave Bloomington IL 61701

STEVENSON, GEORGE FRANKLIN, pathologist, assn. exec.; b. Ont., Can., Sept. 13, 1922; s. Ralph Waldo and Lavina (Brunk) S.; came to U.S., 1947, naturalized, 1953; B.A., U. Western Ont., 1944, M.D., 1945; m. Joanne Lorraine Larsen, Oct. 9, 1977; children by previous marriage—Mark, Scot. Intern, Ottawa (Ont.) Civic Hosp., 1945-46; resident St. Joseph Hosp., Hamilton, Ont., 1946-47, St. Joseph Hosp., Ft. Wayne, Ind., 1947-48, Cleve. Clinic, 1948-49, Wesley Meml. Hosp., Chgo., 1950; coordinator cancer teaching Northwestern U. Sch. Medicine, 1950-52; dir. labs. St. Joseph Hosp., Chgo., 1952-62, Alexian Bros. Hosp. and St. Vincents Infant Hosp., Chgo., 1958-62, Holy Cross Hosp., Silver Spring, Md., 1963-65; prof. clin. pathology, prof. med. tech. Med. U. S.C., 1966-71, dean Sch. Allied Health Scis., 1966-68; commr. continuing edn. Am. Soc. Clin. Pathologists, Chgo., 1967-72, exec. v.p., 1971-74, sci. dir., 1974—; prof. pathology Northwestern U. 1972—. Served with Canadian Army, 1940-46. Recipient award for distinguished service to continuing med. edn. Am. Soc. Clin. Pathologists, 1976. Mem. AMA, Am. Assn. Pathologists, Coll. Am. Pathologists, Am. Assn. Blood Banks, Assn. Clin. Scientists (pres. 1959-60, Clin. Scientist of Yr. 1961), Internat. Acad. Pathology, Assn. Schs. Allied Health Professions, Assn. Am. Med. Colls., Am. Assn. Med. Soc. Execs., Am. Soc. Clin. Pathologists, Alpha Omega Alpha. Clubs: Cosmos (Washington); Mid-Am. (Chgo.). Contbr. articles to med. jours. Home: 600 N McClurg Ct Apt 3411A Chicago IL 60611 also 3181 Asoleado Circle Las Vegas NV 89121 Office: 2100 W Harrison St Chicago IL 60612

STEVENSON, HAROLD WILLIAM, educator; b. Dines, Wyo., Nov. 19, 1924; s. Merlin R. and Mildred M. (Stodick) S.; B.A., U. Colo., 1947; M.A., Stanford, 1948, Ph.D., 1951; m. Nancy Guy, Aug. 23, 1950; children—Peggy, Janet, Andrew, Patricia. Asst. prof. psychology Pomona Coll., 1950-53; asst. to asso. prof. psychology U. Tex., Austin, 1953-59; prof. child devel. and psychology, dir. Inst. Child Devel., U. Minn., Mpls., 1959-71; prof. psychology, fellow Center for Human Growth and Devel., U. Mich., Ann Arbor, 1971—, dir. program in child devel. and social policy, 1978—. Mem. tng. com. Nat. Inst. Child Health and Human Devel.; 1964-67; mem. personality and cognition study sect. NIMH, 1975-79; chmn. adv. com. on child devel. Nat. Acad. Scis.-NRC, 1971-73; exec. com. div. behavioral scis. NRC, 1969-72; mem. del. early childhood People's Republic of China, 1973. Fellow Center for Advanced Studies in Behaviorial Scis., 1967-68. Mem. Am. (pres. div. developmental psychology 1964-65), Midwestern psychol. assns., Soc. Research Child. Devel. (governing council 1961-67, pres. 1969-71, chmn. long range planning com. 1971-74, social policy com. 1977—), Internat. Soc. Study Behavioral Devel. (exec. com. 1972-77), Phi Beta Kappa, Sigma Xi. Home: 1030 Spruce Dr Ann Arbor MI 48104

STEVENSON, JAMES RUFUS, physicist, educator; b. Trenton, N.J., May 19, 1925; s. Eugene Hendrix and Helen (MacElree) S.; student Ark. Tech., 1946-47, La. State U., 1947-48; B.S., Mass. Inst. Tech., 1950; Ph.D., U. Mo., 1957; m. Adelyn Portice Stegall, June 14, 1955; children—Alicia Love, Mary Helen, Jana Lyn. Asso. prof. Sch. Physics, Ga. Inst. Tech., Atlanta, 1962-68, prof., dir. Sch., 1968—. Vis. prof. Fulbright-Hays Program, U. Sci. and Tech., Kumasi, Ghana, 1965-66; NATO sr. fellow to DESY, Hamburg, West Germany, 1972; cons. U.S. Naval Research Lab. Served with USAAF, 1944-46. Mem. Am. Phys. Soc., Optical Soc. Am., Am. Assn. Physics Tchrs., Am. Soc. Engring. Edn. (chmn. physics div. 1974-76), Sigma Xi, Pi Mu Epsilon, Gamma Alpha. Methodist. Home: 116 Peachtree Circle Atlanta GA 30309

STEVENSON, JOHN, investment banker; b. Airdrie, Scotland, Apr. 10, 1905; s. Andrew Bonar and Agnes Cleland (Dalglish) S.; came to U.S. 1910, naturalized 1921; B.C.S., N.Y. U., 1928; m. Helen Espie, Oct. 9, 1934 (dec.); children—John E., Carol G.; m. 2d, Esther Anne Burke, Feb. 3, 1970. With N.Y. Stock Exchange, 1923-28, examiner stock list dept., 1927-28; lectr. N.Y. Inst. Finance, 1928-37; mgr. statis. dept. Kidder, Peabody & Co., N.Y.C., 1928-34; financial analyst Analytical Research Bur., Inc., N.Y.C., 1934-35; mgr. corporate finance dept. Salomon Bros. & Hutzler, N.Y.C., 1935-54, partner charge corporate finance dept., 1954-68; ltd. partner Salomon Bros., 1968—; pub. Financial Analysts Jour., 1959-66. Recipient Madden Meml. award, 1964; named life mem. Nat. Trust for Scotland. Mem. Inst. Chartered Financial Analysts, N.Y. Soc. Security Analysts, N.Y. U. Finance Club, St. Andrews Soc., Albert Gallatin Assos. N.Y. U. (life), Beta Gamma Sigma, Delta Phi Epsilon. Conglist. Clubs: New York University, Downtown Athletic, University (N.Y.C.); Apawamis, Westchester Country (Rye, N.Y.). Home: 720 Milton Rd Rye NY 10580

STEVENSON, JOHN REESE, lawyer; b. Chgo., Oct. 24, 1921; A.B., Princeton U., 1942; LL.B., Columbia U., 1949, D.J.S., 1952. Admitted to N.Y. bar, 1949, U.S. Supreme Ct. bar, 1964; with firm Sullivan & Cromwell, N.Y.C., 1950—, mem., 1956-69, 75—, of counsel, 1973-75; legal adv. with rank of asst. sec. U.S. Dept. State, 1969-72; ambassador, spl. rep. of Pres., Law of the Sea Conf., 1973-75; U.S. mem. Permanent Ct. of Arbitration, The Hague, 1969-79; U.S. rep. Internat. Ct. Justice, Namibia (S.W. Africa) case, 1970; dir. Adela Investment Co., Bank of N.Y., Bank of N.Y. Co., Inc. Trustee Andrew W. Mellon Found., Rockefeller U.; pres., trustee Nat. Gallery Art. Fellow Am. Bar Assn. (hon.); mem. Am. Soc. Internat. Law (pres. 1966-68), N.Y. State (chmn. com. on internat. law 1963-65), Inter-Am. bar assns., Internat. Law Assn., Institut de Droit Internat., Assn. Bar City N.Y. (chmn. com. on internat. law 1958-61), Am. Arbitration Assn. (chmn. internat. sect. law com. 1973—), Acad. Polit. Sci. (dir.), Council on Fgn. Relations, Am. Law Inst. Author: The Chilean Popular Front, 1952. Contbr. articles to legal jours. Home: 620 Park Ave New York NY 10021 Office: 125 Broad St New York NY 10004

STEVENSON, JOHN SINCLAIR, geologist, educator; b. New Westminster, B.C., Can., Sept. 21, 1908; s. Ben and Emelia (Johnston) S.; B.A., U. B.C., 1929, B.Applied Sci., 1930; Ph.D., Mass. Inst. Tech., 1934; m. Louise Francis Stevens, Jan. 22, 1935; children—John Stevens, Robert Francis. Instr., asst. in geology Mass. Inst. Tech., 1931-34; engr.-in-charge Longacre Longlac Gold Mines, Ont., 1934-35; asst. mining engr. B.C. Dept. Mines, Victoria, 1935-36, asso. mining engr., 1936-41, mining engr., 1941-50; asso. prof. mineralogy McGill U., Montreal, Que., 1950-61, prof., 1961—, chmn. dept. geol. scis., 1966-68, Sir William Dawson prof. geology, 1971—. Canadian fellow Guggenheim Meml. Found., 1947-48; cons. geologist, 1950—; cons. grad. edn., Ont., 1969. Fellow Royal Soc. Can., Geol. Soc. Am., Geol. Assn. Can., Mineral. Soc. Am.; mem. Mineral. Soc. London, Geochem. Soc., Canadian Inst. Mining and Metallurgy, Soc. Econ. Geologists, Mineral. Assn. Can. (past pres.), Sigma Xi. Mem. United Ch. (elder). Clubs: McGill Faculty (Montreal); Hudson (Que.) Yacht Whitlock Golf (Hudson Heights). Home: Box 245 Ridge Rd Hudson Heights PQ Canada Office: Dept Geol Scis McGill U Montreal PQ H3C 3G1 Canada

STEVENSON, JOSEPH DONALD, transp. and power co. exec.; b. Houston, July 2, 1910; s. Joseph R. and Mary Emma Stevenson; m. Mildred Rose Doyle, Nov. 3, 1932; children—Donald Edward, Keith Thomas. With Stewart & Stevenson Services, Inc., Houston, 1927—, pres., 1952-73, chmn. bd., 1973-75, chmn. bd. emeritus, 1975—, also dir.; chmn. bd., dir. C. Jim Stewart & Stevenson, Inc., Stewart & Stevenson Transp., Inc., Stewart & Stevenson Realty Corp.; v.p., asst. treas., dir. Stewart & Stevenson Internat. Corp.; dir. Machinery Acceptance Corp., Stewart & Stevenson Power Inc., Mangone Shipbldg. Co., Internat. Switchboard Corp. Clubs: Elks, Petroleum of Houston, Houston Yacht. Office: PO Box 1637 Houston TX 77001

STEVENSON, LANGDON RIDDLE, investment banker; b. Tarrytown, N.Y., May 11, 1935; s. Stuart Riddle and Irene (Davis) S.; B.A., Princeton U., 1957; m. Mary Harman Biggs, Apr. 22, 1972; children—Charlotte, John, Alexander; stepchildren—Elizabeth, Susannah, Jennifer Smith. Vice pres. Bankers Trust Co., N.Y.C., 1958-69; 1st v.p. Bache & Co., Inc., N.Y.C., 1969-75; 1st v.p., treas. Bache Halsey Stuart Shields Inc., N.Y.C., 1975-78, sr. v.p., treas., 1978—, also dir.; treas. Bache Group Inc., 1978—. Trustee Village of Irvington-on-Hudson, N.Y., 1967-70, mayor, 1970-71; v.p., bd. dirs. Hudson Valley chpt. Nat. Audubon Soc., 1974—, editor newsletter, 1974-78. Served with USAF, 1961-62. Republican. Presbyterian. Clubs: Down Town Assn., Racquet and Tennis (N.Y.C.); Ardsley Country. Home: Field Terr Ardsley-on-Hudson NY 10503 Office: 100 Gold St New York City NY 10038

STEVENSON, LLOYD GRENFELL, physician, educator; b. London, Ont., Can., June 2, 1918, s. Samuel F. and Laura May (Usher) S.; B.A., U. Western Ont., 1940, M.D., 1944, Litt.D., 1961; Ph.D., Johns Hopkins, 1949; Litt.D., McGill U., 1964; M.A. (hon.), Yale, 1963; m. Margaret Jean Campbell, May 18, 1944; children—Peter Campbell, Hugh Grenfell. Intern, Oshawa Gen. Hosp., 1944-45; asst. prof. history medicine U. Western Ont., 1950-52, asso. prof., 1952-54; asso. prof. history medicine McGill U., 1954-56, prof, 1956-63, dean faculty medicine, 1956-63; prof. history medicine, chmn. dept. history of sci. and medicine Yale, 1963-68; William H. Welch prof., dir. Inst. History Medicine, Johns Hopkins Sch. Medicine, Balt., 1968—. Served to capt. M.C., Canadian Army. World War II. Mem. Canadian, Am. assns. med. colls., Am. Assn. History Medicine (past pres.) Canadian Med. Assn., Canadian Physiol. Soc. Author: Sir Frederick Banting, 1946; Nobel Prize Winner in Medicine and Physiology, 1953; The Meaning of Poison, 1959. Editor: Bull. History Medicine, 1968—. Home: 11 Wendover Rd Baltimore MD 21218

STEVENSON, MCLEAN, actor, comedian; b. Normal, Ill., Nov. 14; grad. Northwestern U. Worked at radio sta. and on Dallas TV; later asst. dir. athletics Northwestern U. and salesman hosp. supply house; acting debut in summer stock prodn. of The Music Man, 1962; later joined Upstairs at the Downstairs revue, N.Y.C.; became writer for TV series That Was the Week That Was and The Smothers Brothers Show; regular on TV series: The Doris Day Show, The Tim Conway Comedy Hour, MASH, The McLean Stevenson Show, In the Beginning, Hello Larry; other TV appearances include: The Defenders, The Ed Sullivan Show, That Was the Week That Was, The Tonight Show, also TV commls. Served with USN. Office: care Public Relations TAT Communications Co 1901 Ave of Stars Los Angeles CA 90067*

STEVENSON, MERLON LYNN, physicist, educator; b. Salt Lake City, Oct. 31, 1923; s. Merlon L. and Katie Lynn (Peterson) S.; student Weber Jr. Coll., 1941-43; A.B., U. Cal., Berkeley, 1948, Ph.D., 1953; m. Lois Griffin, July 16, 1948; children—Leslie Ann, Scott Griffin, Jeffrey Lynn, Conrad Joseph, Cybele Marie. Physicist, Lawrence Radiation Lab., Berkeley, 1953—; mem. faculty U. Calif. at Berkeley, 1957—, prof. physics, 1964—. Mem. Phys. Soc., Phi Beta Kappa, Sigma Xi. Contbr. articles to profl. jours. Home: 683 Vincente Ave Berkeley CA 94707

STEVENSON, ROBERT, film dir.; b. London, 1905; came to U.S., naturalized, 1940; ed. Cambridge U. Dir. motion pictures, including: Dishonored Lady, 1947, To the Victor, 1948, To the Ends of the Earth, 1948, Walk Softly, Stranger, 1950, My Forbidden Past, 1951, Las Vegas Story, 1952, Johnny Tremaine, 1975, Old Yeller, 1958, Darby O'Gill and the Little People, 1959, Kidnapped, 1960, The Absent-Minded Professor, 1961, In Search of the Castaways, 1962, Son of Flubber, 1963, The Misadventures of Merlin Jones, 1964, Mary Poppins, 1964, Monkey's Uncle, 1965, That Darn Cat, 1965, The Gnome-Mobile, 1967, The Love Bug, 1969, Bedknobs and Broomsticks, 1971, Herbie Rides Again, 1974, Island at the Top of the World, 1974, One of Our Dinosaurs is Missing, 1975, The Shaggy D.A., 1976; dir. over 100 TV shows, including: Cavalcade of America, Ford Theatre, Playhouse of Stars, G.E. Theatre, Hitchcock Presents, 20th Century-Fox Hour, Gunsmoke, Walt Disney. Served in U.S. Army, 1943-46. Office: Walt Disney Prodns 500 S Buena Vista Ave Burbank CA 91521*

STEVENSON, ROBERT LOUIS, ins. exec.; b. Honolulu, Apr. 10, 1915; s. Frank Irton and Augusta (Beerman) S.; B.S. in Civil Engring., U. Hawaii, 1937; m. Mary M. Fidler, July 9, 1937; children—Babara Jill (Mrs. George Naukana), John. Ins. bus., 1937-40, 47-62, 66—; dir. Bank Hawaii. Chmn., Aloha United Way, 1974-75; joined N.G., 1931, adj. gen. Hawaii, 1962-66, maj. gen. Army N.G., 1963; comdg. gen. Hawaii N.G., dir. Civil Def. Hawaii, 1962-66. Served with AUS, 1940-46. Decorated Silver Star, Legion of Merit, Bronze Star, Purple Heart. Mem. N.G. Assn., Assn. U.S. Army (pres. Hawaii chpt. 1973-74), Hawaii C. of C. (pres. 1969). Mason (Shriner). Clubs: Oahu Country; Kaneohe Yacht, Pacific (hon.). Home: 3541 Woodlawn Dr Honolulu HI 96822 Office: PO Box 2866 Honolulu HI 96803

STEVENSON, ROBERT MURRELL, educator; b. Melrose, N.Mex., July 3, 1916; s. Robert Emory and Ada (Ross) S.; A.B., U. Tex. at El Paso, 1936; grad. Juilliard Grad. Sch. Music, 1938; M.Mus., Yale 1939; Ph.D., U. Rochester, 1942; S.T.B., Harvard, 1943; B.Litt., Oxford (Eng.) U.; Th.M., Princeton. Instr. music U. Tex., 1941-43, 46; faculty Westminster Choir Coll., Princeton, N.Y., 1946-49; mem. faculty to prof. music U. Calif. at Los Angeles, 1949—. Vis. asst. prof. Columbia, 1955-56; vis. prof. Ind. U., Bloomington, 1959-60, U. Chile, 1965-66; cons. UNESCO, 1977. Served with AUS, 1943-46. Decorated Army Commendation ribbon. Recipient Fulbright research awards, 1958-59, 64, 70-71, Carnegie Found. teaching award, 1955-56. Ford Found. fellow 1953-54, Carnegie Found. fellow 1955-56; Gulbenkian Found. fellow 1966; Guggenheim fellow, 1962; Nat. Endowment for Humanities fellow, 1974. Author: Music in Mexico, 1952; Patterns of Protestant Church Music, 1953; La musica en la catedral de Sevilla, 1954; Music before the Classic Era, 1955; Shakespeare's Religious Frontier, 1958; The Music of Peru, 1959; Juan Bermudo, 1960; Spanish Music in the Age of Columbus, 1960; Spanish Cathedral Music in the Golden Age, 1961; La musica colonial en Colombia, 1964; Protestant Church Music in America, 1966; Music in Aztec and Inca Territory, 1968; Renaissance and Baroque Musical Sources in the Americas, 1970; Music in El Paso, 1970; Philosophies of American Music History, 1970; Written Sources For Indian Music Until 1882, 1973; Christmas Music from Baroque Mexico, 1974; Foundations of New World Opera, 1973; Seventeenth Century Villancicos, 1974; Latin American Colonial Music Anthology, 1975; Vilancicos Portugueses, 1976, Josquin in the Music of Spain and Portugal, 1977; American Musical Scholarship, Parker to Thayer, 1978; contbg. editor Handbook Latin Am. Studies, 1976—; editor Inter-Am. Music Rev., 1978—; contbr. to New Grove Dictionary of Music and Musicians Office: 405 Hilgard Ave Los Angeles CA 90024. *American achievements are as nothing unless they are written about and remembered. My mission has been to rescue the musical past of the Americas. Present-day composers are too busy making their own music to worry about their predecessors. As a result, every new generation of composers thinks that they are the first ones to descry Mount Olympus. Not so. The past is a succession of musical and artistic glories.*

STEVENSON, ROGER, ret. naval med. officer; b. Mansfield, Ark., June 2, 1918; s. Roger and Lula (Wills) S.; student Ark. State Tchrs. Coll., 1935-36, summer 1938, Hendrix Coll., 1936-38; B.S., U. Ark., 1940, M.D. (Buchanan award 1941), 1942; m. Patricia Ann Sullivan, Nov. 10, 1965; children by previous marriage—Roger, Nell Elizabeth, Karen Anne, Franklin Theodore. Intern, Santa Rosa Hosp., San Antonio, 1942-43; practice medicine specializing in gen. medicine and anesthesiology, Kerrville, Tex., 1946-52; preceptorship ophthalmology with Dr. K.W. Cosgrove, Little Rock, 1952-54; practice medicine specializing in ophthalmology, Kerrville, 1954-56; commd. lt. (j.g.) M.C., USN, 1942, advanced through grades to capt., 1960; chief eye, ear, nose and throat service U.S. Naval Hosp., Corpus Christi, Tex., 1956-60, U.S. Naval Hosp., Yokosuka, Japan, 1960-62; chief opthalmology service Naval Hosp., Chelsea, Mass., 1962-64, Naval Hosp., Bethesda, Md., 1964-68, dir. prof. div. Bur. Medicine and Surgery, Navy Dept., Washington, 1968-70; sr. med. officer U.S. Naval Acad., Annapolis, Md., 1970-74; adviser ophthalmology to surgeon gen. USN, 1964-74; dir. Dept. Def. med. exam. rev. bd. US Acad., Colo., 1974-78, ret., 1978. Mem. staff Peterson Meml. Hosp., Kerrville, 1949-56; clin. instr. ophthalmology U. Ark. Med. Sch., 1953-54. Decorated Commendation medal, 1945, 70; Meritorious Service medal, 1975; Joint Service medal, 1978. Diplomate Am. Bd. Ophthalmology. Fellow Soc. Eye Surgeons, Internat. Eye Found., A.C.S.; affiliate Royal Soc. Medicine; mem. Nat. Soc. Prevention Blindness, A.M.A. (vice chmn. sect. mil. medicine 1969-71, chmn. 1971-72), Am. Acad. Ophthalmology and Otolaryngology, Assn. Research Ophthalmology, Assn. Mil. Surgeons U.S., Soc. Mil. Ophthalmologists (pres. 1965-66), Res. Officers Assn., Am. Assn. Ophthalmology (contbr. material to corr. course), Phi Beta Pi. Roman Catholic. Contbr. articles to med. jours. Home: 287 Fischer Circle Portsmouth RI 02871. *It has always been my goal to be the best physician, teacher and leader that I could possibly be with the talents given me by the grace of God, and to try to further refine and improve those talents by diligent investment of time. Through the years I have come to be a strong believer in leadership by example and in participatory management, and have attempted to recognize the impact of my administrative decisions on those who work with me.*

STEVENSON, WARD BARKER, bank exec.; b. Mpls., Jan. 19, 1920; s. William John and Stella (Bain) S.; grad. U. Minn., 1941; m. Barbara N. Stevenson; children—Ward Barker, Candis Stevenson Schuster, Pamela Stevenson Courtney. Asst. to indsl. relations mgr., dir. pub. relations, dir. manpower devel. Pillsbury Co., Mpls., 1943-55; v.p. charge pub. relations Benton & Bowles, Inc., N.Y.C., 1955-60, ITT, N.Y.C., 1960-62; v.p. Dudley-Anderson-Yutzy, N.Y.C., 1962-64; v.p., dir. pub. relations First Nat. City Bank, N.Y.C., 1964-70; sr. v.p. W. region Hill and Knowlton, Inc., Los Angeles, 1970-74; sr. v.p. pub. affairs and mktg. Crocker Nat. Bank, San Francisco, 1974—. Served with USNR, 1944-46. Mem. Pub. Relations Soc. Am. (past pres., past treas., chmn. com. standards profl.

practice). Home: 266 Palmetto Dr Pasadena CA 91105 Office: 1 Montgomery St San Francisco CA 94104 also 611 W 6th St Los Angeles CA 90017

STEVENSON, WILLIAM EDWARDS, former ambassador, lawyer, coll. pres.; b. Chgo., Oct. 25, 1900; s. J. Ross and Florence (Day) S.; A.B., Princeton, 1922; M.A. (Rhodes scholar), Balliol Coll. Oxford (Eng.) U., 1925; L.H.D., Case Inst. Tech., 1948, Alfred U., 1969; LL.D., Wooster Coll., 1948, Colo. Coll., 1950, Princeton, 1956, Fairleigh Dickinson U., 1956, Coe Coll., 1958; Oberlin Coll., 1960, San Carlos U., P.I., 1963; Litt.D., Rider Coll., 1974; m. Eleanor Bumstead, Jan. 9, 1926; children—Helen Day (Mrs. Robert B. Meyner), Priscilla (Mrs. Richard McM. Hunt). Admitted as barrister-at-law Inner Temple (Eng.). 1925; admitted to N.Y. bar, 1927; asst. U.S. atty. South Dist. N.Y., 1925-27; asso. with Davis, Polk, Wardwell, Gardiner & Reed, 1927, 29-31; founding partner Debevoise, Stevenson, Plimpton & Page, N.Y.C., 1931-46; pres. Oberlin Coll., 1946-59; U.S. ambassador to Philippines, 1961-64; pres. Aspen Inst. Humanistic Studies, 1967-70. A.R.C. del. Gt. Britain, 1942, North Africa and Italy, 1942-44, vice chmn. bd. govs. nat. orgn., 1965-71; vice chmn. League Red Cross Socs. (Geneva), 1965-73; mem. Pres.'s Com. on Equality of Treatment and Opportunity in Armed Services, 1948-50; ednl. cons. Japan, India, Lebanon, Egypt for Dept. State, 1952-53; chmn. World Bank Econ. Devel. Commn., Tanganyika, 1959-60. Served with USMC, 1918. Decorated Bronze Star; U.S. AAU 440 yard champion, 1921, Brit. AAU champion, 1923; mem. Olympic Championship 1600 Meter Relay Team, 1924. Mem. Am. Acad. Arts and Scis., Phi Beta Kappa. Club: University (N.Y.C.). Address: Box 71 Captiva FL 33924

STEVER, HORTON GUYFORD, sci. cons., corp. dir.; b. Corning, N.Y., Oct. 24, 1916; s. Ralph Raymond and Alma (Matt) S.; A.B., Colgate U., 1938, Sc.D. (hon.), 1958; Ph.D., Calif. Inst. Tech., 1941; LL.D., Lafayette Coll., U. Pitts., 1966, Lehigh U., 1967, Allegheny Coll., 1968, Ill. Inst. Tech., 1975; D.Sc., Northwestern U., 1966, Waynesburg Coll., 1967, U. Mo., 1975, Clark U., 1976, Bates Coll., 1977; D.H., Seton Hill Coll., 1968; D.Engring., Washington and Jefferson Coll., 1969, Widener Coll., Poly. Inst. Bklyn., 1972, Villanova U., 1973, U. Notre Dame, 1974; m. Louise Risley Floyd, June 29, 1946; children—Horton Guyford, Sarah, Margarette, Roy. Mem. staff radiation lab. Mass. Inst. Tech., Cambridge, 1941-42, asst. prof., 1946-51, asso. prof. aero. engring., 1951-56, prof. aero. engring., 1956-65, head depts. mech. engring., naval architecture, marine engring., 1961-65, asso. dean engring., 1956-59, exec. officer guided missiles program, 1946-48; chief scientist USAF, 1955-56; pres. Carnegie-Mellon U., Pitts., 1965-72; dir. NSF, Washington, 1972-76; sci. adviser, chmn. Fed. Council Sci. and Tech., 1973-76; dir. Office Sci. and Tech. Policy, sci. and tech. adviser to Pres., 1976-77; sci. cons., corp. dir., 1977—; dir. TRW; mem. secretariat guided missiles com. Joint Chiefs of Staff, 1945; sci. liaison officer London Mission, OSRD, 1942-45; mem. guided missiles tech. evaluation group Research and Devel. Bd., 1946-48; mem. sci. adv. bd. to chief of staff USAF, 1947-69, chmn., 1962-69, mem. steering com. tech. adv panel on aeros. Dept. Def., 1956-62; chmn. spl. com. space tech. NASA, chmn. research adv. com. missile and spacecraft aerodynamics, 1959-65; mem. Nat. Sci. Bd., 1970-72, mem. ex-officio, chmn. exec. com., 1972-75; mem. Def. Sci. Bd.; mem. adv. panel U.S. Ho. Reps. Com. Sci. and Astronautics; mem. Pres.'s Commn. on Patent System, 1965-67; chmn. U.S.-USSR Joint Commn. Sci. and Tech. Cooperation, 1973-77, Fed. Council Arts and Humanities, 1972-76, Pres.'s com. Nat. Sci. medal, 1973-77. Past trustee Colgate U., Shady Side Acad., Sarah Mellon Scaife Found., Buckingham Sch.; trustee Univ. Research Assn., 1977—; bd. dirs. Saudi Arabia Nat. Center for Sci. and Tech. bd. govs. U.S.-Israel Binat. Sci. Found., 1972-76. Recipient Pres.'s certificate of Merit, 1948, Exceptional Civilian Service award USAF, 1956, Scott Gold medal Am. Ordnance Assn., 1960, Disting. Pub. Service medal Dept. Def., 1969; comdr. Order of Merit (Poland). Fellow Am. Inst. Aeros. and Astronautics (hon.; pres. 1960-62), Royal Aero. Assn., Am. Acad. Arts and Scis., A.A.A.S., Am. Phys. Soc.; mem. Nat. Acad. Engring. (chmn. aero. and space engring. bd. 1967-69), Sr. Exec. Council, Nat. Acad. Scis. (chmn. assembly engring. 1979—), Phi Beta Kappa, Sigma Xi, Sigma Gamma Tau, Tau Beta Pi. Episcopalian. Clubs: Cosmos (Washington); Bohemian (San Francisco); Century Association (N.Y.C.). Author: Flight, 1965. Contbr. articles to profl. publs. Home: 1528 33d St NW Washington DC 20007 Office: Assembly Engring Nat Acad Scis 2101 Constitution Ave NW Washington DC 20418

STEWARD, CLIFFORD LOYD, bus. exec.; b. Balco, Okla., Sept. 14, 1924; s. Ora K. and Ruby Olene (Pearson) S.; B.A., San Francisco State U., 1949; M.B.A., U. Denver, 1951; m. Ida Mae Truitt, Sept. 2, 1945; children—Victoria Rose Steward Meredith, David Clifford. In various fin. and mktg. mgmt. positions Gen. Electric Co., 1952-66; dir. corp. systems Brown & Sharpe Mfg. Co., 1966-68; mgmt. cons. Stanford Research Inst. (Calif.), 1968-78; pres. Energy Group, CP Nat. Corp., San Francisco, 1978—; dir. Pacific Coast Gas Assn., Pacific Coast Elec. Assn., N.W. Electric Light and Power Assn. Served with U.S. Army, 1943-45, USAF, 1951-52. Mem. Am. Mgmt. Assn. Home: 2216 English Ct Walnut Creek CA 94598 Office: 600 Stockton St San Francisco CA 94108

STEWARD, DONN HORATIO, artist, master printer; b. Moose Jaw, Sask., Can., Nov. 26, 1921; s. Roy Denver and Bessie Marie (Anderson) S. (parents Am. citizens); student Boone Jr. Coll., Iowa, 1939-40; B.A., U. Iowa, 1942, M.F.A.,1948; student (Fulbright scholar) Ecole des Beaux Arts, Paris, 1952-53. Instr., U. Iowa, 1948-54; asst. prof. Fla. State U, 1954-57; vis. lectr. Washington U., St. Louis, 1957-58; coordinator Douglas Aircraft, Calif., 1958-64; master printer Universal Ltd. Art Editions, N.Y.C., 1966-74; prin. Donn Steward, Master Printer and Pub., Halesite, N.Y., 1974—; printer-fellow Tamarind Lithography Workshop, Los Angeles, 1965-66; instr. Huntington Township Art League, N.Y., 1975; vis. artist U. Iowa, summer 1978. Served to lt. j.g., USN, 1943-46. Master printer for first etchings: Jasper Johns, 1967-68, Lee Bonterou, 1968, Helen Frankenthaler, 1968—, Robert Motherwell, 1972, Marisol, Barnett Newman, Larry Rivers, Cy Twombley, 1968. Home and Office: One Noyes Ln Apt 7 Halesite NY 11743

STEWART, AL, singer, songwriter, rec. artist; b. Glasgow, Scotland, 1945. Played guitar with Tony Blackburn's band, Bournemouth, Eng.; later performed folk music, London, from 1965; switched to rock music performing, 1974—; albums include: Bedsitter Images, Love Chronicles, Zero She Flies, Orange, Past, Present and Future, Modern Times, Year of the Cat, Time Passages. Named Compagnon de Vordeaux, 1977. Office: Kinetic Prodns 2059 Laurel Canyon Los Angeles CA 90046*

STEWART, ALEXANDER DOIG, bishop; b. Boston, Jan. 27, 1926; s. Alexander Doig and Catherine Muir (Smith) S.; A.B. cum laude, Harvard U., 1948, M.B.A., 1961; M.Div. cum laude, Union Theol. Sem., N.Y.C., 1951; m. Laurel Gale, June 5, 1953. Ordained priest Episcopal Ch., 1951; asst. Christ Ch., Greenwich, Conn., 1950-52; priest-in-charge St. Margaret's Parish, Bronx, N.Y., 1952-53; rector St. Mark's Episc. Ch., Riverside, R.I., 1953-70; bishop Episc. Diocese Western Mass., Springfield, 1970—; mem. faculty Barrington Coll., 1955-70. Mem. budget and program com. Episc. Ch. U.S.A. Chmn. Urban Renewal, E. Providence, R.I., 1967-70; vice chmn. United Fund Springfield, 1972; mem. schs. and scholarship com. R.I. chpt. Harvard Coll., 1960-70. A founder, 1959, since mem. bd. dirs., sec. corp. Health Havens, Inc., E. Providence; trustee Barrington Coll., 1971—, Providence Country Day Sch., 1964-70, Ch. Pension Fund, N.Y.C.; mem. corp. St. Elizabeth's Hosp., Providence, 1954-70, Springfield Hosp., 1970—. Mem. Religious Research Assn. Clubs: Hartford (Conn.); Harvard (R.I. and Springfield, Mass.). Author: Science and Human Nature (Wainwright House award), 1960; The Shock of Revelation, 1967; also articles. Home: 75 Severn St Longmeadow MA 01106 Office: 37 Chestnut St Springfield MA 01103

STEWART, ANDREW, pub. co. exec.; b. N.Y.C., Feb. 8, 1938; s. George and Ethel (Gilbert) S.; B.A., U. Va., 1959; LL.B., Yale U., 1962; LL.M., Columbia U., 1964; m. Martha Helen Kostyra, July 1, 1961; 1 dau., Alexis. Admitted to N.Y. State bar, 1965; asso. firm Webster and Sheffield, N.Y.C., 1963-68; sr. staff atty., anti-trust counsel Bangor Punta Corp., 1969-73; asst. gen. counsel Piper Aircraft Corp., Greenwich, Conn., 1969-73; asst. gen. counsel, Eastern regional counsel, asst. sec. Times Mirror Co., N.Y.C., 1973-75; exec. v.p. Harry N. Abrams, Inc., N.Y.C., 1975, pres., chief exec. officer, 1976—. Mem. Am., N.Y. State bar assns., Assn. Am. Publishers. Clubs: Univ., Fairfield County Hunt. Office: Harry N Abrams Inc 110 E 59th St New York NY 10017*

STEWART, ANNE ENGLISH, librarian; b. Bryan, Tex., Sept. 9, 1934; d. Ralph Thomas and Ernestine S.; B.A., Duke U., 1955; M.L.S., U. Ill., 1956. Reference librarian Fed. Res. Bd., Washington, 1957-60; reference librarian Dept. Army, Washington, 1960-63; librarian Fed. Maritime Commn., Washington, 1963-65; chief library div. Dept. Treasury, Washington, 1965-79. Mem. Treasury Hist. Assn. (dir. 1976-79), Law Librarians Soc. (v.p. 1977-78), Spl. Libraries Assn., Am. Assn. Law Libraries. Presbyterian.

STEWART, BENNETT MCVEY, congressman; b. Huntsville, Ala., Aug. 6, 1914; s. Bennett and Cathleen (Jones) S.; B.A., Miles Coll., 1936; m. Pattye Crittenden, Sept., 1938; children—Bennett Michael, Ronald Patrick, Miriam Kay Stewart Early. Asst. prin. Irondale High Sch., Birmingham, Ala., 1936; asso. prof. sociology Miles Coll., 1938-40; ins. exec. Atlanta Life Ins. Co., 1940-50, dir. Ill., 1950-68; insp. Chgo. Bldg. Dept., 1968; rehab. specialist Chgo. Dept. Urban Renewal, 1968-71; mem. 96th Congress from 1st Ill. Dist.; alderman Chgo. City Council, 21st Ward, from 1971; mem. Democratic Ward Com., Chgo., 1972—. Bd. dirs. Wabash YMCA; mem. Chesterfield Community Council. Mem. Chgo. Ins. Assn. (past pres.), Alpha Phi Alpha (past Chgo. grad. chpt. pres.), Alpha Phi Alpha (bd. dirs.). Christian Methodist Episcopalian. Home: 650 E 88th Pl Chicago IL 60619 Office: 503 Cannon House Office Bldg Washington DC 20515

STEWART, CARL JEROME, JR., lawyer, state rep.; b. Gastonia, N.C., Oct. 2, 1936; s. Carl Jerome and Hazel Alene (Holland) S.; A.B., Duke U., 1958, J.D., 1961; children—Lisa, Julie, Rome, Robert. Partner Stewart & Lowe, Gastonia, N.C., 1962—; mem. N.C. Ho. of Reps., Raleigh, 1966—, speaker, 1977-80; instr. Gastonia Community Coll., 1962-77; dir. Impact Plastics Inc. Bd. dirs. Gastonia Children's Center, 1962-77; mem. advisory bd. Salvation Army, 1962-79; trustee Greensboro Coll.; bd. advs. Belmont Abbey Coll. Maj. N.C. N.G. Named Outstanding Young Man of Year, Gastonia Jaycees, 1965. Mem. Am., N.C., Gaston County bar assns., Phi Beta Kappa. Democrat. Methodist. Clubs: Gaston Country, Optimist, Mason. Home and office: 211 W 3d St Gastonia NC 28052

STEWART, CARLETON M., banker; b. Chgo., 1921; s. Carleton Merrill and Margaret (Lyon) S.; student Stanford U., 1939-42; I.A., Harvard U., 1943, M.B.A., 1947; m. Alicia Dewar; 3 children. With Citibank, 1947-76, v.p., N.Y.C., 1960-67, sr. v.p. in charge of Asia-Pacific area, 1967-69, S. Asia, Middle East and Africa, 1969-73, sr. officer, London, 1973-76, dir. Grindlay's Bank Ltd., London, Banque Internat. pour L'Afrique Occidentale, Paris, 1973-76; chmn. bd., chief exec. officer Am. Security Corp. and Am. Security Bank, Washington, 1976—; dir. Va. Hot Springs, Inc. Trustee, mem. exec. com. Fed. City Council; trustee George Washington U.; gov. Ditchley Found., London; bd. dirs. Nat. Symphony Orch. Assn., Atlantic Council, Hwy. Users Fedn. for Safety and Mobility. Mem. Assn. Res. City Bankers, Econ. Club N.Y. Office: American Security Bank 1501 Pennsylvania Ave NW Washington DC 20013

STEWART, CHARLES DAVID, econ. cons.; b. Detroit, Feb. 17, 1910; s. Alexander Ferguson and Isabel (Forbes) S.; A.B., U. Mich., 1932; M.S.S., New Sch. Social Research, 1937; J.D., Georgetown U., 1953; m. Pearl Blanck, Oct. 1, 1936; children—Diane Isabel, Donald Alexander. Instr. pub. finance Bklyn. Coll., 1937-39; economist Survey of Current Bus., U.S. Dept. Commerce, 1940; staff Bur. Labor Statistics, U.S. Dept. Labor, 1941-55, chief occupational outlook div., 1943-45, Office Program Planning, 1946-47, Office Labor Econs., 1948-49, asst. commr., 1950-55, dep. asst. sec. labor for standards and statistics, 1956-57, research and devel., 1957-63; labor and edn. adv. U.S. Mission to OECD, Paris, France, 1963-67; exec. dir. Econ. Policy Adv. Com., U.S. Dept. Labor, 1967-70; dep. asst. sec. labor for Internat. Affairs, 1970-71, spl. asst., 1971-72; dir. OECD 1973-74, now cons. Mem. U.S. delegation ECOSOC, Geneva, 1950, ILO, Phila., 1944, Geneva, 1950, 58, 60-61, 71; profl. lectr. econs. George Washington U., 1953-55; cons. Nat. Commn. Manpower Policy, Nat. Manpower Inst. U.S. Dept. Labor, 1975—. Fellow Am. Statis. Assn.; mem. Am. Econ. Assn., Indls. Relations Research Assn. Author: (with A.J. Jaffe) Manpower Resources and Utilization, 1951; (with Gösta Rehn) Japanese Employment Policy, 1973; (with Joseph Deroo) Manpower Policy in France, 1973; Recent Europen Manpower Policy Initiatives, 1975; contbg. author: Principles of Economic Development, 1955, Government Statistics for Business Use, 1956, Economic Reconstruction, 1945. Contbr. articles to profl. jours. Home: 7114 Wilson Ln Bethesda MD 20034

STEWART, CHARLES EDWARD, JR., dist. judge; b. Glen Ridge, N.J., Sept. 1, 1916; s. Charles Edward and Eva (Gay) S.; B.A., Harvard, 1938, LL.B., 1948; m. Virginia Louise Browne, Jan. 21, 1941; 1 son, Charles Edward III. Admitted to N.Y. bar, N.J. bar; asso. firm Dewey, Ballantine, Bushby, Palmer & Wood, N.Y.C., 1948-57, partner 1957-72; judge U.S. Dist. Ct., So. Dist. N.Y., N.Y.C., 1972—. Served to capt. AUS, 1942-45. Mem. Assn. of Bar of City of N.Y., N.Y. State, Am. bar assns., N.Y., N.J. fed. bar assns. Club: Harvard N.Y. Home: Hudson House Ardsley-on-Hudson NY 10503 Office: US Ct House Foley Sq New York NY 10007

STEWART, CHARLES JACK, educator; b. Rawlins, Wyo, June 17, 1929; s. William John and Frieda (Swisher) S.; B.A. in Chemistry with distinction, San Diego State Coll., 1950; M.S., Oreg. State U., 1952, Ph.D., 1955; m. Cynthia Crittenden, Feb. 25, 1956 (dec. 1970); children—Diana Frieda, Elizabeth Esther, Carla Jean; m. 2d, Nancy Carmichael, Nov. 20, 1971. Instr., then asst. prof. San Diego State Coll., 1956-61, asso. prof., 1961-65, prof. chemistry, 1965—, chmn. dept., 1966-70. Fulbright grantee U. Frankfurt (Germany), 1954-55. Mem. Am. Soc. Biol. Chemists, Am. Chem. Soc. (chmn. San Diego sect. 1962, 70), AAAS, Sigma Xi. Research on coenzyme A analogs. Home: 6539 Sunny Brae Dr San Diego CA 92119

STEWART, CHARLES LESLIE, apparel mfg. and retail co. exec., lawyer; b. Fayetteville, Ark., Aug. 12, 1919; s. Charles Leslie and Ruth (Want) S.; A.B., U. Ill., 1940; M.A., La. State U., 1941; postgrad. George Washington U. Law Sch., 1944-45; J.D., U. Chgo., 1947; m. Edalee Esther Gastrock, Aug. 30, 1941; children—William Paul, Thomas Alan, Katherine Jean, Robert Edward. Economist, Dept. Agr., 1941-42; adminstrv. asst. OPA, 1942-43, Bd. Econ. Warfare, 1943; exec. dir. Chgo. div. ACLU, 1946-47; admitted to Ill. bar, 1948, also U.S. Supreme Ct.; practiced in Chgo., 1948—; partner firm Mayer, Brown & Platt, Chgo., 1947-67, 70, resident partner charge European office, Paris, France, 1967-70; v.p., sec., gen. counsel Hart Schaffner & Marx, Chgo., 1971—. Served with OSS, AUS, 1943-45. Mem. Am., Ill., Chgo. bar assns., Am. Soc. Corporate Secs., Delta Phi. Mem. Glencoe Union Ch. Clubs: Union League (Chgo.); Skokie Country (Glencoe). Home: 745 Vernon Ave Glencoe IL 60022 Office: 36 S Franklin St Chicago IL 60606

STEWART, CHESTER LARRY, airline exec.; b. St. Paul, Apr. 16, 1920; s. Chester James and Ethel (Haggard) S.; student Macalester Coll., St. Paul; B.B.A., U. Minn., 1942; m. Vera Oman, July 11, 1942; children—Karen Anne, Jeffrey Oman, Ann Elizabeth. Asst. economist U.S. Bd. Investigation and Research, Washington, 1942-43; staff Brookings Instn., Washington, 1943-44; statis. analyst, economist, asst. sec., asst. v.p., then v.p. Northwest Airlines, Inc., St. Paul, 1964-78; sr. v.p. transp. services Nat. Airlines, Miami, 1978—; dir. Mont. Enterprises, Inc. Mem. P.T.A., pres. Mpls. Mem. Am. Mgmt. Assn., Phi Gamma Delta (past chpt. pres., trustee). Home: 6550 SW 100th St Miami FL 33156 Office: Nat Airlines PO Box 592055 AMF Miami FL 33159

STEWART, CORNELIUS JAMES, II, transp. and power co. exec.; b. Houston, June 27, 1925; s. Ross and Catherine (Rial) S.; student U. Tex., 1945-47; m. Gretchen Elizabeth Braun, Nov. 28, 1947; children—Cornelius James, III, Richard Ross, David Rial, Gretchen (Mrs. Stewart Anderson), Catherine Maria. With Stewart & Stevenson Services, Inc., Houston, 1947—, v.p., 1956-73, pres., 1973-75, chmn. bd., 1975—; pres. C. Jim Stewart & Stevenson, Inc., 1956—, Bayou Bldg. Corp., 1948-75, Stewart & Stevenson Realty Corp., 1975—, Internat. Switchboard Corp., 1971—, Stewart & Stevenson Internat. Corp., 1971—, Stewart & Stevenson Transp., Inc., 1976—; v.p., dir. Stewart & Stevenson Power Inc.; dir. Internat. Electric Corp.; dir. Mangone Shipbldg. Co., 1964—; chmn. bd. Machinery Acceptance Corp., 1972—; v.p., sec. Stewart & Stevenson Overseas, Inc., 1973—; dir. Reagan Commerce Bank, 1973-76, So. State Bank, 1973—, Tex. Commerce Bank, 1975—. Chmn. Houston City Planning Commn., 1974—; bd. dirs. Better Bus. Bur. Met. Houston, 1976—, Holly Hall, 1972-76. Served with USAAF, 1943-45. Mem. Purchasing Agts. Assn. Houston (pres. 1959-60, dir. 1961-62), Houston C. of C. (dir. 1969, 76, 78, mem. aviation com. 1976—). Presbyterian. Clubs: Rotary (dir. 1978), Breakfast, Houston (pres. 1973, pension com. 1974—), Houston Country (dir. 1974-76), Ramada (Houston). Address: PO Box 1637 Houston TX 77001

STEWART, DAVID HUGH, educator; b. Ft. Wayne, Ind., Aug. 12, 1926; s. Carey Hugh and Priscilla (Stauffer) S.; A.B. U. Mich., 1947, A.M., 1949, Ph.D., 1959; M.A., certificate of Russian Inst., Columbia, 1954; m. Diane Silva, July 25, 1949; children—Marc Silva, Christopher David. Instr. English, Valparaiso (Ind.) U., 1949-50, U. Oreg. Extension, 1950-52, Eastern Mich. U., 1955-57; instr. Russian, U. Mich., Ann Arbor, 1955-56, asst. prof. English, 1960-63, asso. prof. English, 1963-68; asst. prof. English, Eastern Mich. U., 1957-59, U. Alta., 1959-60; prof., chmn. dept. English, Idaho State U., Pocatello, 1968-72; prof., chmn. dept. English, Pa. State U., University Park, 1972-74; prof., head dept. English Tex. A. and M. U., College Station, 1975—. Served with USNR, 1944-46, U.S. Mcht. Marine, 1947-48. Rackham Research fellow, 1966. Mem. Modern Lang. Assn. (assembly mem. 1971-74, pres. Rocky Mountain chpt. 1969-70), Coll. English Assn. (pres. Pacific N.W. 1968-70), Nat. Council Tchrs. English, Phi Kappa Phi. Author: Mikhail Sholokhov: A Critical Introduction, 1967; The Wiley Reader, 1976, abridged edit., 1979. Contbr. articles to profl. jours. Home: 2304 Bristol St Bryan TX 77801

STEWART, DAVID MARSHALL, librarian; b. Nashville, Aug. 1, 1916; s. David and Mary (Marshall) S.; B.A., Bethel Coll., 1938; B.S. in L.S., George Peabody Coll., 1939; m. Gladys Carroll, June 9, 1947; 1 son, James Marshall. Circulation asst. Vanderbilt U. Library, 1938-39; county librarian Ark. Library Commn., 1939-40; Tenn. supr. WPA library service projects, 1940-42; librarian Memphis State U., 1942-46; spl. asst. to chief card div. Library of Congress, Washington, 1947; librarian CIA, Washington, 1948-60; chief librarian Nashville Pub. Library, 1960—. Instr., Peabody Library Sch., 1966—. Bd. dirs. Council Community Agys. Nashville, Middle-East Tenn. Arthritis Found. (v.p. 1965—), Friends Chamber Music Nashville, Travelers Aid Nashville. Served to lt. comdr. USNR, 1942-46. Mem. Am., Tenn. (chmn. legislative com. 1961-65; v.p., 1965, pres. 1966), Southeastern library assns., Pub. Library Assn. Am. (chmn. standards com. 1964-65, pres. 1966-67), Alumni Assn. Bethel Coll. (dir.). Democrat. Mem. Ch. of Christ. Kiwanian. Club: Coffee House (Nashville). Home: 6342 Torrington Rd Nashville TN 37205 Office: 8th Ave N at Union St Nashville TN 37203

STEWART, DONALD CHARLES, chem. cons.; b. Salt Lake City, Dec. 15, 1912; s. John Caldwell and Nelle (Marsh) S.; A.B., U. Calif. at Los Angeles, 1935; M.S., U. So. Calif., 1940; Ph.D., U. Calif. at Berkeley, 1950; B.S., Va. Poly. Inst., 1944; m. Dorothy Bockhop, Apr. 16, 1948; children—Katharine Ann, Deborah Jean. Asst. sect. chief, chemistry sect. Chicago Metall. Lab., Manhattan Project, 1945-46; observer Bikini Bomb Tests, 1946; asst. div. dir. chemistry Argonne Nat. Lab., 1952-54, asso. dir. chemistry div., 1959-77, ret., 1977; cons., 1977—; staff exchangee to Atomic Energy Research Establishment, Harwell, Eng., 1957-58. Fellow A.A.A.S.; mem. Am. Chem. Soc. (sec. div. nuclear sci. and tech. 1968-71), Sigma Xi. Co-editor: Progress in Nuclear Energy, Series IX, 1963-74. Home: 4549 Lee St Downers Grove IL 60515 Office: 9700 S Cass Ave Argonne IL 60439

STEWART, DONALD EDWIN, publishing exec.; b. Chgo., Aug. 26, 1927; s. Charles I. and Lillian (Lidquist) S.; A.B., U. Chgo., 1950; m. Barbara Jean Fletcher, Oct. 29, 1955; children—Judith Lillian, Jeanne Marguerite. Asst. to mng. editor Ency. Brit., Chgo., 1951-62, asst. to exec. editor, 1963, asso. editor, 1964, mng. editor, 1965-73; asso. exec. dir. for pub. ALA, Chgo., 1974—, asso. editor ALA Yearbook, 1978—, mng. editor ALA World Ency. Library and Info. Services, 1980—. Vice chmn. Chgo. Com. For Sane Nuclear Policy, 1962-65; chmn. Peace and World Affairs Center, Evanston, Ill., 1962-63, dir., 1962-67. Mem. Am. Soc. Info. Sci., ALA, Chgo. Book Clinic (v.p. 1978—). Unitarian (chmn. Lake Shore Unitarian Universalist Soc. 1968-69). Home: 653 Michigan Ave Evanston IL 60202 Office: 50 E Huron St Chicago IL 60611

STEWART, DONALD WILBUR, U.S. senator; b. Munford, Ala., Feb. 8, 1940; B.S., U. Ala., Tuscaloosa, 1962, LL.S., 1965; m. Priscilla Runckle Black; children—Priscilla, Taylor. Admitted to Ala. bar, 1965; partner firm Stewart and Morris, and predecessor firms, Anniston, Ala.; mem. Ala. Ho. of Reps., 1970-74; mem. Ala. State Senate, 1974-78; mem. U.S. Senate from Ala., 1978—. Mem. Am. Bar Assn., Ala. Bar Assn., Calhoun County Bar Assn., Jaycees, Delta Tau

Delta, Phi Alpha Alpha, Omicron Delta Kappa. Democrat. Methodist. Clubs: Civitans, Masons, Shriners. Office: 110 Russell Senate Office Bldg Washington DC 20510

STEWART, DOUGLAS JAMES, classicist; b. Los Angeles, Dec. 31, 1933; s. Eldon and Elizabeth (D'Angelo) S.; B.A., Loyola U., Los Angeles, 1955; M.A., Cornell U., 1959, Ph.D., 1963; m. Dorothy Sicilia, July 8, 1961; children—Devin, Gina, Daniel. Instr., Reed Coll., 1962-64; asst. prof. Emory U., 1964-66; asst. prof. classical and Oreintal studies Brandeis U., Waltham, Mass., 1966-68, asso. prof., 1968-74, prof., 1974—, chmn. dept., 1973-78; vis. prof. U. Calif., San Diego, 1970. Mass. chmn. McCarthy for Pres., 1972. Mem. Am. Philol. Assn., Phi Beta Kappa. Democrat. Author: The Disguised Guest, 1976; contbr. numerous articles, essays to profl. jours. Home: 90 Westminster Rd Newton Centre MA 02159 Office: Dept Classical and Oriental Studies Brandeis U Waltham MA 02254

STEWART, EASTON, civil engr.; b. Wybark, Okla., Sept. 11, 1922; s. Voistes Lee and Zella (Fears) S.; B.S. in Civil Engring., U. Okla., 1953; m. Maralynn E. Robertson, Dec. 29, 1949; children—Stephen, Charles, Barbara, Cheryl. Owner, Easton Stewart & Assos., Cons. Engrs., Baton Rouge; partner Stewart-Kuyrkendall & Assos., Baton Rouge, 1975—. Served with USNR, 1942-45; PTO. Registered profl. engr., Okla., Miss., La., Tenn., Tex. Fellow Am. Cons. Engrs. Council, ASCE; mem. Nat., La. socs. profl. engrs., Am. Public Works Assn., Inst. Transp., Inst. Mcpl. Engrs. Specialist in maj. hwy. design. Home: 11433 Archery Dr Baton Rouge LA 70815 Office: 6717 Goya Ave Baton Rouge LA 70806

STEWART, EDGAR ALLEN, lawyer; b. Selma, Ala., Sept. 1, 1909; s. Edgar A. and Irma (Mallory) S.; B.A., U. South, 1929; LL.B., U. Ala., 1932; m. Mamie V. Packer, Oct. 15, 1938; children—Edgar Allen III (dec.), Martha M. (Mrs. Edward B. Crosland, Jr.). Admitted to Ala. bar, 1932, since practiced in Selma; sr. partner Reeves & Stewart, 1947—; spl. agt. FBI, 1942-45. Dir. 1st Ala. Bank of Selma, N.A., 1st Ala. Bancshares. Trustee Selma Schs., 1956-67; bd. dirs., pres. Selma YMCA, 1952-68. Fellow Am. Coll. Trial Lawyers; mem. Am. Bar Assn., Ala. Bar Commn. (dir. 1970-76), Am. Coll. Probate Counsel, Internat. Assn. Ins. Counsel, Nat. Assn. R.R. Counsel, Am. Counsel Assn., Am. Judicature Soc., Phi Beta Kappa, Phi Delta Theta, Phi Delta Phi. Contbr. articles to profl. jours. Home: 124 Mallory Dr Selma AL Office: PO Box 457 Selma AL 36701

STEWART, EDWARD WILLIAM, lab. adminstr.; b. Cardiff, Md., Sept. 17, 1931; s. Edward William and Mary Eleanor (Williams) S.; B.S. in Chemistry, Washington Coll., Chestertown, Md., 1952; M.S. in Metall. Engring., Lehigh U., Bethlehem, Pa., 1954; m. Nancy Moore Stewart, June 12, 1954; children—Gail, William, Sandra. With E.I. duPont de Nemours & Co., Inc., 1954—, dist. mgr. pigments dept., New Eng., 1967-70, Chgo., 1970-73, dir. Chestnut Run Lab., Wilmington, Del., 1973—. Served with AUS, 1956-57. Mem. Nat. Paintings and Coatings Assn., Sigma Xi. Office: CD4P Dept Tech Service Lab Chestnut Run Wilmington DE 19898

STEWART, EUGENE LAWRENCE, lawyer, trade assn. exec.; b. Kansas City, Mo., Feb. 9, 1920; s. Edmond Dale and Mary Elizabeth S.; B.S. in Social Sci., Georgetown U., 1948, J.D., 1951; m. Jeanne Ellen, Oct. 19, 1945; children—Timothy, Terence, Brian. Admitted to D.C. bar, 1951; practice law specializing in U.S. customs law and U.S. fgn. trade remedies, Washington, 1951—; asso. firm Steptoe & Johnson, 1951-56, partner, 1956-58; exec. dir. Pulp and Paper Machinery Mfrs'. Assn., 1971-78; exec. sec. Trade Relations Council, U.S., Washington, 1974—; adj. prof. law Georgetown U. Law Center, 1955-58, mem. adv. council, 1962-69. Pres., Sursum Corda, Inc., non-profit, low-income housing corp., 1966—. Served with USAF, 1941-45. Decorated Legion of Merit; recipient John Carroll medal Georgetown U. Mem. Am. Bar Assn., Assn. Customs Bar, Bar Assn., D.C., Georgetown U. Alumni Assn. (pres. 1964-66), Phi Alpha Delta. Democrat. Roman Catholic. Club: Manor Country (Rockville, Md.). Author books, the most recent being: American Manufacturer's Contest of Treasury Department Decision Not to Assess Countervailing or Antidumping Duties, 1976. Home: 15000 Carrolton Rd Rockville MD 20853 Office: Room 910 1001 Connecticut Ave NW Washington DC 20036*

STEWART, GEORGE FRANKLIN, educator; b. Mesa, Ariz., Feb. 22, 1908; s. Mahonri Alma and Anna (Metz) S.; B.S., U. Chgo., 1930; Ph.D., Cornell U., 1933; m. Grace Sledge, June 19, 1933; children—Kent, Carol, Jane. Research chemist Ocoma Food, Inc., Omaha, 1933-38; asso. prof. Iowa State Coll., 1938-42, prof., 1942-51, asso. dir. Agrl. Expt. Sta., 1948-51; chmn. dept. poultry husbandry U. Calif. at Davis, 1951-58, exec. editor Inst. Food Technologists, 1958-66, prof. food sci. and tech., 1959—, chmn. food sci., tech., 1959-64, dir. food protection and toxicology center, 1965-70, chmn. agr. toxicology and residue research lab., 1966-68, chmn. dept. environ. toxicology, 1968-70. Past pres. Internat. Union Food Sci. and Tech. Recipient Christie Research award. Fulbright research scholar, Australia, 1957. Fellow AAAS, Poultry Sci. Assn., Inst. Food Technologists (pres. 1967-68, Internat. and Appert awards); mem. Am. Inst. Nutrition, Sigma Xi, Phi Kappa Phi. Co-editor: Advances in Food Research, also Monographs in Food Science and Technology. Home: 814 Cherry Ln Davis CA 95616

STEWART, GEORGE RAY, librarian; b. Birmingham, Ala., Aug. 19, 1944; s. DeWitt and Ann (McCain) S.; B.A., Samford U., Birmingham, 1966, M.A., 1967; M.A., Emory U., 1971; m. Nancy Ann Norton, June 5, 1964; children—Steven Ray, Jeffery Alan. Mem. staff Birmingham Public Library, 1960—, asso. dir., 1970-76, dir., 1976—; part-time instr. U. Ala., Birmingham. Bd. dirs. Red Mountain Museum, 1972-79; bd. dirs. Indsl. Health Council Birmingham, 1972-79, sec., 1979—. Mem. ALA, Southeastern Library Assn., Ala. Library Assn. (scholarship 1968, pres. 1976), Ala. Hist. Assn., Birmingham Hist. Assn. Baptist. Office: 2020 Park Pl Birmingham AL 35203

STEWART, HAROLD BROWN, biochemist; b. Chatham, Ont., Can., Mar. 9, 1921; s. John Craig and Margaret Gertrude (Brown) S.; M.D., U. Toronto, 1944, Ph.D., 1950; Ph.D., Cambridge (Eng.) U., 1955; m. Audrey Pauline Blake, Oct. 14, 1950; 1 dau., Ann Margaret. Prof. biochemistry U. Western Ont., London, 1960—, chmn. dept. biochemistry, 1965-72, dean grad. studies, 1972—; Med. Research Council Can. vis. scientist dept. biochemistry U. Cambridge (Eng.), 1971-72. Served with Royal Canadian Navy, 1945-46. Mem. Canadian, U.K. biochem. socs., Canadian Physiol. Soc., Am. Soc. Biol. Chemists, Am. Assn. Higher Edn., Coll. Physicians and Surgeons of Ont. Contbr. articles in biochemistry to sci. jours. Home: 118 Baseline Rd E London ON N6C 2N8 Canada Office: U Western Ont London ON N6A 5B8 Canada

STEWART, HAROLD LEROY, physician, educator; b. Houtzdale, Pa., Aug. 6, 1899; s. Alexander and Lillie (Cox) S.; student U. Pa., 1919-20, Dickinson Coll., 1921-22; M.D., Jefferson Med. Coll., 1926; grad. Army Med. Sch., Washington, 1929; research fellow Jefferson Med. Coll., 1929-30, Harvard, 1937-39; Med. Sc.D. (hon.), Jefferson Med. Coll., 1964; D.Medicine and Surgery (hon.), U. Perugia, 1965, U. Turku (Finland), 1970; m. Cecelia Eleanor Finn Sept. 30, 1929; children—Robert Campbell, Janet Eileen. Intern, Fitzimmons Gen. Hosp., Denver, 1926-27; instr. to asst. prof. pathology Jefferson Med. Coll., 1930-37; asst. pathologist Jefferson Med. Coll. Hosp., Phila. Gen. Hosp., 1929-37; pathologist Office Cancer Investigations Harvard, USPHS, 1937-39; chief lab. pathology Nat. Cancer Inst., USPHS, Bethesda, Md., 1939-69, chief pathologic anatomy dept. clin. center NIH, 1954-69, organizer Registry Exptl. Cancers, 1970—, Sci. emeritus, 1976—, prin. investigator, head WHO Collaborating Centre for Research on Tumors Lab. Animals, 1976—; clin. prof. pathology Georgetown U., 1965—. Cons. FDA, 1969-71, Nat. Cancer Inst., 1970-76, Armed Forces Inst. Pathology, 1950—; cons., mem. study groups WHO, 1957, mem. expert adv. panel cancer, 1957—. Mem. subcom. oncology NRC, 1947-65, mem. com. pathology, 1958-66, com. cancer diagnosis and therapy, 1951-57, mem. com. animal models and genetic stocks, 1972-75, chmn. com. histologic classification Lab. Animal Tumors, 1975—, chmn. subcom. classification rat liver tumors, 1976—; chmn. U.S.A. Com. Internat. Council Socs. Pathology, 1957-62, 69-75; chmn. U.S. nat. com. Internat. Union Against Cancer, 1953-59, U.S. del., 1952-74. Mem. adv. bd. Leonard Wood Meml., 1961-66; mem. com. to advance world-wide fight against cancer Am. Cancer Soc., 1963-76. Trustee Thomas Jefferson U., Phila., 1969-72. Served as pvt. USMC, 1918-19, lt. M.C., U.S. Army, 1926-29, from maj. to lt. col. M.C., AUS, 1942-46. Recipient Lucy Wortham James award James Ewing Soc., 1967, Alumni Achievement award Jefferson Med. Coll., 1966; Distinguished Service award HEW, 1966. Diplomate Am. Bd. Pathology, Pan Am. Med. Assn. Mem. Am. Soc. Clin. Pathologists (Ward Burdick award 1957), Am. Assn. Cancer Research (pres. 1958-59), Am. Soc. Exptl. Pathology (hon.; pres. 1955), Am. Assn. Pathologists (Gold-headed Cane award 1978), Coll. Am. Pathologists, Md. (pres. 1950-51), Washington (sec.-treas. 1947-51) socs. pathologists, Internat. Acad. Pathology (pres. 1953-55, F.K. Mostofi award 1976), Internat. Union Against Cancer (exec. com. 1952-70, v.p. 1962), Mass. Med. Soc., Internat. Council Socs. Pathology (pres. 1962), Internat. Soc. Geog. Pathology, Colegio Anatomico Brasilerio (hon.), Societa Italiana di Cancerologia (hon.), Inst. Nacional de Cancerologia Mexico (hon.), Sociedad Columbiana de Patologia (hon.), Societe Belge d' Anatomie Pathologique (hon.), Sociedad Peruana Cancerologia (hon.), Soc. Cryobiology, Soc. Pharm. and Environmental Pathologists (hon.), Japanese Cancer Soc. (hon.), Purdy Stout Surg. Pathology Soc. (hon.), others. Editorial bd. Cancer Research, 1941-49, A.M.A. Archives of Pathology, 1957-62; editorial adviser Jour. Nat. Cancer Inst., 1947-56. Contbr. articles to profl. jours. Home: 119 S Adams St Rockville MD 20850 Office: Del Ray Bldg NIH Bethesda MD 20014

STEWART, HARRIS BATES, JR., oceanographer; b. Auburn, N.Y., Sept. 19, 1922; s. Harris B. and Mildred (Woodruff) S.; grad. Phillips Exeter Acad., 1941; A.B., Princeton, 1948; M.S., Scripps Instn. Oceanography, U. Calif., 1952, Ph.D., 1956; m. Elise Bennett Cunningham, Feb. 21, 1959; children—Dorothy Cunningham, Harry Hasburgh. Hydrographic engr. U.S. Hydrographic Office expdn. to Persian Gulf, 1948-49; instr. Hotchkiss Sch., 1949-51; research asst. Scripps Instn. Oceanography, 1951-56; diving geologist, project mgr. Geol. Diving Cons., Inc., San Diego, 1953-57; chief oceanographer U.S. Coast & Geodetic Survey, 1957-65, dept. asst. dir., 1962-65: dir. Inst. Oceanography, Environmental Sci. Services Adminstrn., U.S. Dept. Commerce, 1965-69, dir. Atlantic Oceanographic and Meteorol. Labs., NOAA, 1969-78, cons., 1978—; dir. S.E. Bank of Dadeland; chmn. Fla. Commn. Marine Sci. and Tech.; mem. exec. com., earth scis. div. Nat. Acad. Scis.; chmn. adv. bd. Nat. Oceanographic Data Center 1965-66; chmn. survey panel interagy. com. oceanography Fed. Council Sci. and Tech. 1959-67; chmn. adv. com. underseas features U.S. Bd. Geog. Names 1964-67; mem. sci. party No. Holiday Expdn., 1951; Capricorn Expdn. 1952-53; chief scientist Explorer Oceanographic Expdn. 1960, Pioneer Indian Ocean Expdn., 1964, Discoverer Expdn., 1968, NOAA-Carib Expdn., 1972, Researcher Expdn., 1975; mem. U.S. delegation Intergovtl. Oceanographic Commn., 1961-65; mem. Gov. Cal. Adv. Commn. Marine Resources; chmn. adv. council Dept. Geol. and Geophys. Scis. Princeton; v.p. Dade Marine Inst., 1976-77, pres., 1977-79; trustee, mem. exec. com. Asso. Marine Insts. Bd. dirs. Vanguard Sch., Miami, 1974-76. Served as pilot USAAF, 1942-46; PTO. Decorated comendador Almirante Padilla (Colombia). Recipient Meritorious award Dept. Commerce, 1960, Exceptional Service award, 1965. Fellow AAAS, Geol. Soc. Am., Marine Tech. Soc. (v.p.); mem. Fla. Acad. Scis. (pres. 1978-79), Am. Geophys. Union, Internat. Oceanographic Found. (v.p. 1974—), Zool. Soc. Fla. (pres. 1970-73), Marine Hist. Assn., Old Dartmouth Hist. Soc. Presbyterian. Clubs: Cosmos (Washington); Explorers (N.Y.C.); Ocean Reef (Key Largo, Fla.). Author: The Global Sea, 1963; Deep Challenge, 1966; The Id of the Squid, 1970; Challenger Sketchbook, 1972. Home: 737 N Greenway Dr Coral Gables FL 33134

STEWART, HOMER JOSEPH, educator; b. Elba, Mich., Aug. 15, 1915; s. Earl Arthur and Alta Fern (Stanley) S.; student U. Dubuque, 1932-33; B.Aero. Engring., U. Minn., 1936; Ph.D., Calif. Inst. Tech., 1940; m. Frieda Klassen, June 15, 1940; children—Robert Joseph, Katherine Stanley, Barbara Ellen. Faculty, Calif. Inst. Tech., Pasadena, 1938—, prof. aeros., 1949—, chief research analysis sect. Jet Propulsion Lab., 1945-56, chief Liquid Propulsion Systems Div., 1956-58, spl. asst. to dir., 1960-62, chief Advanced Studies Office, 1963-67, advanced studies adviser, 1967-76; dir. Sargent Industries, Inc., 1964-79; dir. Office Program Planning and Evaluation, NASA, 1958-60; mem. tech. adv. bd. Aerojet-Gen. Corp., 1956-58, 61-70; mem. tech. evaluation group guided missile com. Research and Devel. Bd., 1948-50, chmn., 1951; mem. sci. adv. bd. USAF, 1949-56, 1959-64; mem. sci. adv. com. Ballistics Research Lab., 1959-69, 73-77. Recipient Outstanding Achievement award U. Minn., 1954, NASA Exceptional Service medal, 1970. Mem. Am. Inst. Aeros. and Astronautics, Am. Meteorol. Soc., Sigma Xi, Tau Beta Pi. Author: Kinematics and Dynamics of Fluid Flow, sect. VI Handbook of Meteorology, 1945. Contbr. articles to tech. jours. Home: 2393 Tanoble Dr Altadena CA 91001 Office: Calif Inst Tech Pasadena CA 91109

STEWART, IRELAND J., auto parts mfg. co. exec.; b. Belfast, No. Ireland, Dec. 7, 1934; came to U.S., 1966, naturalized, 1976; s. Ireland and Margaret Stewart; B.S. in Econs., Queen's U., Belfast, 1963; M.B.A. (scholarship 1967, fellowship 1968), U. Chgo., 1968. Asst. dean students Grad. Sch. Bus., U. Chgo., 1968-69; mgmt. cons. Boston Cons. Group, 1969-72; with Maremont Corp., Chgo., 1972—, v.p. internat. div., 1976-78, sr. v.p. internat., 1978—; chmn. bd. Gabriel S. Africa Ltd.; pres. Gabriel Internat. Co.; sec. Gab. de Mex.; dir. Gabriel of India, Fric-Rot, S.A.I.C., Argentina, Gabriel Europe Inc., Van Der Hout & Assos., Can., Gabriel de Venezuela. Mem. Am. Mgmt. Assn., Automotive Market Research Council (Spl. award 1976), Brit. Inst. Mgmt., Mid-west Planning Assn., Chgo. Assn. Commerce and Industry, Machinery and Equipment Mfrs. Assn., Internat. Trade Club, Chgo. Council Fgn. Relations, Planning Execs. Inst. Author papers in field. Home: 235 Willow Ave Deerfield IL 60015 Office: 200 E Randolph St Chicago IL 60601

STEWART, IRVIN, ret. educator, pub. adminstr.; b. Fort Worth, Oct. 27, 1899; s. William Henry and Sarah Aline (Howell) Stewart; student U. Okla., 1917-19; LL.B., U. Tex., 1920, A.B., A.M., 1922; Ph.D., Columbia, 1926; LL.D., Waynesburg, 1946, W.Va. Wesleyan, 1948, W.Va. State Coll., 1948, Marshall Coll., 1953; Litt.D., Bethany Coll., 1954; m. Florence E. Dezendorf, July 31, 1926; 1 son, Richard Edwin. Instr. govt. U. Tex., Austin, 1922-25, adj. prof., 1925-26, asso. prof., 1928-29; asst. solicitor U.S. Dept. State, Washington, D.C., 1926-28; prof., head dept. govt. Am. U. Grad. Sch., Washington, 1929-30; tchr. summer sessions Duke, Columbia, U. Calif. at Los Angeles; in charge elec. communications, treaty div. Dept. State, Washington, 1930-34; mem. Am. delegations internat. radio confs., Washington, 1927, Copenhagen, 1931, Madrid, 1932, Mexico City, 1933, to Pan-Am. Comml. Conf., Washington, 1931, Internat. Telegraph Conf., Madrid, 1932; mem. FCC, Washington, chmn. telegraph div., 1934-37, vice chmn. commn., 1935-37; dir. Com. on Sci. Aids to Learning, 1937-46; exec. sec. Nat. Def. Research Com., 1940-45; exec. sec. OSRD, Com. on Med. Research (Office for Emergency Mgmt.), 1941-45; dep. dir. OSRD, 1946; pres. W.Va. U., Morgantown, 1946-58, prof. govt., 1958-67; cons. Nat. Acad. Pub. Adminstrn., 1967—; on leave as dir. telecommunications mgmt. Exec. Office Pres., 1962-63. Chmn., Pres.'s Communications Policy Bd., 1950; nat. com. Devel. Scientists and Engrs. 1956, nat. adv. com. for Rural Def., 1956; chmn. Am. delegation Internat. Conf. on Orgn. and Adminstrn. Applied Research, 1956; mem. W.Va. Commn. on Constl. Revision, 1957-61. Mem. Bd. Edn. Am. Bapt. Conv., 1952-58. Recipient Pres.'s Medal for Merit, 1948; Humanities award W.Va. B'nai B'rith. Mem. Am. Assn. Land Grant Colls. and State Univs. (pres. 1956), Am. Soc. Pub. Adminstrn., Am. Polit. Sci. Assn., Phi Beta Kappa, Phi Delta Phi, Pi Sigma Alpha. Democrat. Baptist. Clubs: Century (N.Y.C.); Cosmos (Washington). Author: Consular Privileges and Immunities, 1926; Organizing Scientific Research for War, 1948. Editor: Radio, 1929. Home: 2939 Van Ness St NW Washington DC 20008

STEWART, ISAAC MITTON, lawyer, corp. exec., rancher; b. Salt Lake City, Dec. 30, 1904; s. Charles Biekley and Katherine (Romney) S.; student U. Calif. at Los Angeles, 1923-24; J.D., George Washington U., 1928; m. June Woodruff, Dec. 16, 1927; children—Isaac Mitton, Charles Owen, June, Helen (Mrs. Richard B. Bennett), Wilford. Admitted to Utah bar, 1931, D.C. bar, 1933; sec. to Hon. Reed Smoot, U.S. senator from Utah, 1928-32; clk., spl. asst., U.S. Senate Com. Finance, 1926-32; practiced law, Washington, 1933-36; v.p. Union Carbide Corp., 1949-67, cons., 1967; dir., mem. audit com. Consol. Freightways, Inc. Owner Stewart Ranch, Kamas, Utah. Pres. Salt Lake (Mormon) Tabernacle Choir, 1962-75, gen. counsel, 1975—. Mem. adv. com. Senate Interstate and Fgn. Commerce Com. in a study fgn. trade; chmn. bus. and industry com. Nat. Citizens Commn. on Internat. Cooperation. Recipient George Washington U. Alumni Achievement award in law and pub. service, 1965. Mem. Am. Pioneer Trails Assn., Inc. (mem. adv. council), Am. Mothers Com., Inc. (adv. board), Phi Alpha Delta. Mem. Ch. of Jesus Christ of Latter-Day Saints. Clubs: University (Washington; Indian Wells Country. Home: Midway UT also 77-048 Iroquois Dr Indian Wells CA 92260 RFD Kamas UT 84036 also Midway UT 84049 Office: 270 Park Ave New York NY 10017

STEWART, JAMES, ins. broker; b. Germany, Nov. 25, 1912; s. Cecil Parker and Reine Marie Melanie (Tracy) S.; student Harvard U., 1931; m. Martha, May 18, 1970; children—Tracy, James Cecil, Reine Elizabeth, Barry, China. Salesman, Electrolux Co., Los Angeles, Qui Soit Perfume, N.Y.C.; runner, stock clk. statis. dept. Bancamerica Blair Corp., N.Y.C., 1932-33; with classified advt. dept. New York Times; longshoreman, Houston, Los Angeles, San Francisco, 1934; with publicity dept., cruise dir. French Line, N.Y.C., 1934-36; asst. marine mgr., br. mgr., br. supt., supt. ins. Am. Asiatic Underwriters, Shanghai, 1936-39; sec., dir., supt. ins. Cie Franco-Americaine D'Assurances, 1936-39; embassy corr. for Paris-Soir, 1939; v.p., dir. Frank B. Hall & Co., Inc., N.Y.C., 1939-42, dir., corporate partner, chmn. bd., v.p., sec., chmn. and chief exec. officer, now chmn. exec. com., 1945-78, cons., dir., mem. exec. and fin. coms., 1978—; v.p., dir. U.S. Marine & Fgn. Agys.; dir. Am. Mcht. Marine S/S Corp.; dir. Overseas Shipbuilding Group. Served with AUS, 1942; to lt. (j.g.) USNR, 1942-45. Decorated Shanghai medal, Asiatic Pacific medal. Mem. Assn. Average Adjusters of U.S., Am. Shipping Soc. Republican. Clubs: Whitehall; India House; Racquet and Tennis; Deepdale Golf; The Creek; Nat. Golf Links of Am.; Oslo Golf; Portland; Sunnigdale Golf; The Brook; The Travellers; Lyford Cay. Home: 785 Fifth Ave New York NY 10022 Office: Wall St Plaza New York NY 10005. *The chivalry code is what I seek to live by—and, in my book, good for any era: "Fais ce que doit; Advienne que peut; C'est commandé au chevalier."*

STEWART, JAMES MAITLAND, actor; b. Indiana, Pa., May 20, 1908; s. Alexander Maitland and Elizabeth Ruth (Jackson) S.; B.S., Princeton U., 1932; m. Gloria McLean, Aug. 9, 1949; children—Michael, Ronald (dec.), Judy and Kelly (twins). Appeared in N.Y.C. in Goodbye Again, 1932, Yellow Jack, Divided by Three and Page Miss Glory, 1934; motion pictures include: You Can't Take It With You, Made for Each Other, Mr. Smith Goes to Washington, Destry Rides Again, The Shop Around the Corner, Pot O' Gold, Ziegfeld Girl, Come Live With Me, The Stratton Story, Winchester 73, Broken Arrow, Harvey, No Highway in the Sky, The Greatest Show on Earth, Bend of the River, Naked Spur, Glenn Miller Story, Man from Laramie, 1955, Strategic Air Command, 1955, Spirit of St. Louis, 1957, Midnight Story, 1957, Vertigo, 1958, Bell, Book and Candle, 1959, Anatomy of Murder, 1959, The FBI, 1959, Mr. Hobbs Takes a Vacation, 1962, How the West Was Won, 1962, Take Her, She's Mine, 1963, Cheyenne Autumn, 1964, Shenendoah, 1965, The Rare Breed, 1966, Firecreek, 1968, Bandolero, 1968, Cheyenne Social Club, 1970, Fool's Parade, 1971, That's Entertainment, 1974, The Shootist, 1976, Airport '77, 1977, The Big Sleep, 1978, The Magic of Lassie, 1978; TV show The Jimmy Stewart Show, 1971-72, Hawkins, 1973-74. Recipient N.Y. Critics award for best male performance of 1939 in Mr. Smith Goes to Washington; Acad. award for performance in Philadelphia Story, 1940; Berlin Film award, 1962; Life Achievement award Am. Film Inst., 1980. Served to lt. col. Air Corps, World War II. Decorated D.F.C. with oak leaf cluster. Presbyterian. Address: care Chasin-Park-Citron Agy 9255 Sunset Blvd Los Angeles CA 90069*

STEWART, JAMES PENTLAND, former coll. pres., mgmt. cons.; b. Rochester, Pa., Sept. 25, 1906; s. Charles Abner and Ethelyn (Fry) S.; M.E., Cornell U., 1928; LL.D., Rider Coll., 1962; m. Frederica M. Stockwell, Feb. 18, 1933 (dec. Nov. 1974); children—Beverly (Mrs. Stewart-Almgren), Michael, David; m. 2d, Faith Douglas Severance Hackl, June 30, 1976. Sales engr. to asst. dir. comml. research Elliott Co., Jeannette Pa., 1928-43; asst. gen. mgr. B-W Superchargers, Inc. (div. Borg-Warner Corp.), Milw., 1943-45; with De Laval Turbine Inc. (now Transam. DeLaval), Trenton, N.J., 1946-66, v.p., dir., 1949, exec. v.p., 1950, pres., 1951-66, ret. 1966, also dir., chmn. or pres., dir. various subsidiary cos.; mgmt. cons., Princeton, N.J., 1967—; dir. N.J. Nat. Bank, 1953-66, N.J. Bell Telephone Co., 1960-68; cons., dir. Burns & Roe, Inc. and subsidiaries, 1967-77. Pres., Delaware Valley United Fund, 1952, Greater Trenton Council, 1961-64; v.p. N.J. Gov.'s Mgmt. Commn., 1970; chmn. N.J. Citizens Transp. Council, 1966-71. Bd. dirs. Trenton Community Found.; trustee Rider Coll., Briarcliff Coll. (pres. 1968-69), Cornell U., 1965-70; hon. trustee Pace U., 1977—. Life fellow ASME (past chmn. finance and pension com.); mem. NAM (dir. 1964-66), Conf. Bd. (sr.), Hydraulic Inst. (pres. 1951), Compressed Air and Gas Inst. (pres. 1952-53), Machinery and Allied Products Inst. (exec. com. 1951-66), English-Speaking Union,

S.R., N.J. C. of C. (pres. 1959-61, life dir.), Newcomen Soc. (N.J. chmn.), Sigma Chi. Republican. Presbyn. Clubs: Cornell (N.Y.C.); New York Yacht; Devon Yacht; Nassau (Princeton, N.J.). Home: PO Box 411 Princeton NJ 08540

STEWART, JAMES WILLIAM, JR., accountant; b. Winston-Salem, N.C., Mar. 9, 1921; s. James William and Lottie (Hilton) S.; B.S.C., U. N.C., 1942; m. Jean Glover Slaughter, Oct. 9, 1942; children—Jill Glover, Mary Melissa, James William III, Sally Slaughter, Mark Gibbons. With Deloitte Haskins & Sells, C.P.A.'s, Charlotte, N.C., and N.Y.C., 1945—, partner, 1954—, mem. policy com., partner charge client services, 1976—. Vice pres. United Community Service Charlotte and Mecklenberg counties, 1965-67, treas., 1962-63, pres., 1968-69; v.p. Charlotte Area Fund, 1966-67; v.p. United Arts Council Charlotte and Mecklenberg counties, 1972-73, pres., 1973-74. Served to lt. USNR, 1942-45. C.P.A., N.C., S.C., Utah, N.Y., La., Calif. Mem. Am. Inst. C.P.A.'s (council 1962-63, 65-68, 70-72), N.C. Assn. C.P.A.'s (pres. 1962-63), Nat. Assn. Accountants (pres. Charlotte 1955-56), Middle Atlantic State Accounting Conf. (pres. 1963-65). Home: 88 Cherry Hill Rd Greenwich CT 06830 Office: 1114 Ave of the Americas New York NY 10036

STEWART, JARVIS ANTHONY, educator, artist; b. Maryville, Mo., Dec. 28, 1914; s. John Andrew and Ella Joanna (Pryor) S.; student St. Joseph (Mo.) Jr. Coll., 1933, Escuela de Bellas Artes, San Miguel, 1941; B.F.A., Phillips U., 1942; M.A., Ohio State U., 1947, Ph.D. 1951; m. Madge Ella Smith, Jan. 24, 1942; children—Deborah Susan, Peter Michael Anthony (dec.). Mural painter Am. Hotels Corps., 1939; instr. Phillips U., 1942; chmn. dept. fine arts Ohio Wesleyan U., Delaware, 1953-73, Packard prof. fine arts, 1953—; exhbns. include Art USA, 1958, Momentum, 1951: one-man show Columbus (Ohio) Gallery, Bryson Gallery; represented permanent collections Columbus Gallery Fine Arts, Otterbein Coll. Recipient Welch Teaching award, 1974. Great Lakes Colls. Assn. research grantee. Mem. Am. Studies Assn., Okla., N.W. Mo. art assns., Columbus (pres. 1951), Enid Art League, Delta Phi Delta. Home: 61 Westgate Dr Delaware OH 43015. *I try to keep a childlike curiosity so that awareness is always a pleasant surprise. My device is to avoid becoming an authority because specialists are made drudges in their own expertise. Knowledge can become little more than variations on a theme . . . and the surprise fades.*

STEWART, JOHN DAUGHERTY, publishing co. exec.; b. Indiana, Pa., Oct. 16, 1915; s. Ernest Taylor and Caroline (Daugherty) S.; A.B., Princeton, 1937; postgrad. Harvard, 1938-39; m. Helen Gambrill, Sept. 23, 1940 (dec. Jan. 1964); children—Caroline Leigh (Mrs. Carl G. Estabrook, Jr.), Susan (Mrs. James G. Stockard, Jr.); m. 2d, Margret Pahl, Feb. 18, 1967. Instr. Sch. Pub. and Internat. Affairs, Princeton, 1937-38; mem. editorial staff Bur. Nat. Affairs, Inc., Washington, 1939—, v.p., 1947-64, pres., editor-in-chief, 1964, now chmn. bd., editor-in-chief; dir. Tax Mgmt., Inc., Washington, Fisher-Stevens, Inc., Clifton, N.J.; dir. Union Trust Co., Washington; chmn. tripartite industry com. for minimum wage regulation Am. Samoa, V.I., P.R., Office Sec. Labor, 1957-60; chmn. Southeastern Econ. Devel. Found., 1970—; chmn. disputes panel Dept. State, 1973—. Mem. Indsl. Relations Research Assn. (pres. 1953), White House Corrs. Assn. Clubs: River Bend Country; Nat. Press. Editor: The New Labor Law, 1947; The Landrum-Griffin Act, 1959. Home: 2869 Beechwood Circle Arlington VA 22207 Office: 1231 25th St NW Washington DC 20037

STEWART, JOHN DAVID, travel and fin. services co. exec.; b. Arkansas City, Kans., Apr. 17, 1916; s. Thomas W. and Lillian B. (Gilgis) S.; A.B., LL.B., Kans. U., 1940; m. Hannah Taylor, Sept. 6, 1941; children—Eleanor T. (Mrs. William A. Sawyer), Joan G. (Mrs. Jeffrey Novinger), John David. Admitted to Kans. bar, 1940; with FBI, 1940-46; with Am. Express Co., 1946—, sr. v.p., 1968—, treas., 1972—. Trustee, vice chmn. Overlook Hosp., Summit, N.J. Mem. Beta Theta Pi. Presbyterian. Club: Echo Lake Country (Westfield). Home: 811 Cedar Terr Westfield NJ 07090 Office: Am Express Plaza New York NY 10004

STEWART, JOHN HARGER, singer; b. Cleve.; s. Cecil T. and Marian (Harger) S.; B.A., Yale U., 1962, M.A., Brown U., 1969; postgrad. New Eng. Conservatory Music, Boston. Tenor opera companies in Santa Fe, Houston, Ft. Worth, Cin., San Antonio, San Diego, Phila., also N.Y.C. Opera, major U.S. orchs., European opera companies in Frankfurt, Hamburg, Hannover and Duesseldorf, Ger., Brussels, Geneva and The Netherlands; numerous solo recitals; dir. Affiliate Artists, Inc. Club: Yale (N.Y.C.). Home: 54 W 74th St New York NY 10023 also 53 Eppsteiner Strasse 6 Frankfurt/Main 1 Federal Republic of Germany Office: care Columbia Artists Mgmt Inc 165 W 57th St New York NY 10019•

STEWART, JOHN LINCOLN, univ. provost; b. Alton, Ill., Jan. 24, 1917; s. Frederick William and Hilda (Denovan) S.; A.B., Denison U., 1938, D.A. (hon.), 1964; M.A., Ohio State U., 1939, Ph.D., 1947; m. Joan Elsdon Guthridge, Sept. 23, 1939 (div. 1964); children—Leslie Cythera (Mrs. Gerald Chalmers), Ann Guthridge (Mrs. John Nutt); m. 2d, Ruth Peabody Quinn, July 11, 1964; stepchildren—Geoffrey Cornelius, Andrew Dean. Teaching asst., then instr. Ohio State U., Columbus, 1939-47; instr. U. Calif. at Los Angeles, 1947-49; asst. prof., then prof. English, Dartmouth, 1949-64, asso. dir. Hopkins Center Arts, 1961-64; prof. lit. U. Calif. at San Diego, 1964—, provost John Muir Coll., 1965—, dir. Mandeville Center for Arts, 1974-76. Mem. Dartmouth Community Symphony Orch., 1949-58. Pres., La Jolla Friends Sch. Music, 1971-73. Trustee Kinhaven Music Sch., 1960-64, Fla. W. Coast Symphony, 1958; bd. dirs. Theatre and Arts Found. San Diego County, 1970. Served with AUS, 1942-45. Howard Found. fellow, 1953-54; Dartmouth fellow, 1962-63. Democrat. Author: Exposition for Science and Technical Students, 1950; The Essay, 1952; John Crowe Ransom, 1962; The Burden of Time, 1965; (with others) Horizons Circled, 1974. Contbr. articles to publs. Home: 9473 La Jolla Farms Rd La Jolla CA 92037

STEWART, JOHN MATHEWS, ednl. adminstr.; b. Vermillion, S.D., Apr. 5, 1920; s. John Wilson and Irene (Mathews) S.; B.A. U. Mont., 1941; Ph.D., U. Ill., 1944; m. Helen Marie Faulkner, June 2, 1943 (div. 1972); 1 dau., Gayle Ann; m. 2d, Genevra Hall Hauge, 1972. Research chemist WPB, 1943-45, Calif. Research Corp., 1945-46; asst. prof. chemistry U. Mont., Missoula, 1946-50, asso. prof., 1951-55, prof. 1955—, chmn. dept., 1959-67, dean grad. sch., 1968-77, acting acad. v.p., 1975, asst. acad. v.p., 1978—. Mem. Am. Chem. Soc. (councilor Mont. sect.), Western Mont. Fish and Game Assn. (pres. 1955), Sigma Xi, Phi Kappa Phi, Phi Lambda Upsilon, Pi Mu Epsilon, Phi Delta Theta. Contbr. research papers to chem. jours. Patentee in field. Home: 111 Crest Line Dr Missoula MT 59801

STEWART, JOSEPH LESTER, rubber co. exec.; b. Newton, Ala., May 31, 1915; s. Joseph Crawford and Allie (Lester) S.; B.S., Auburn U., 1937; student Nat. War Coll., 1956-57; m. Margaret Hines, Feb. 9, 1946; children—Margaret Allison, Barbara Lynne. Commd. 2d lt. USMC, 1937, advanced through grades to brig. gen., 1962; dep. dir. strategic plans dir. on staff Supreme Allied Comdr., Atlantic, 1957-59; dir. Marine Corps Command and Staff Coll., 1959-61; dep. dir. Marine Corps Ednl. Center, 1961-62; comdg. gen. Marine Corps Base 29, Palms, Calif., 1962-64; dir. Marine Corps Res., 1964-65; ret., 1965; sr. v.p. Armstrong Rubber Co., West Haven, Conn., 1965-71, chmn. bd., 1971—, also dir.; dir. Copolymer Rubber & Chem. Corp., N.H. Savs. Bank. Mem. exec. bd., v.p. Quinnipiac council Boy Scouts Am., 1966-70. Decorated Silver Star medal, Legion of Merit with combat V and 2 Gold Stars, Bronze Star medal with combat V and 1 Gold Star, Air medal; several fgn. decorations. Mem. Greater New Haven C. of C. (dir.), Rubber Mfrs. Assn. (dir.). Episcopalian. Office: 500 Sargent Dr New Haven CT 06507

STEWART, LARRY S., lawyer; b. Ft. Myers, Fla., Nov. 29, 1939; s. Floyd B. and Eleanor (Riebling) S.; B.A., U. Fla., 1960, J.D. with honors, 1963; m. Pat Korodin, June 13, 1970; children—Scott, Todd, Drew. Admitted to Fla. bar, 1963, U.S. Supreme Ct. bar, 1967; asso. firm Frates Floyd Pearson Stewart Richman & Greer, and predecessor, Miami, Fla., 1963-67, mem. firm, 1967—. Mem. Fla., Dade County (Fla.) bars, Am. Bar Assn., Am. Trial Lawyers Assn., Acad. Fla. Trial Lawyers, Fla. Blue Key, Order Coif, Phi Delta Phi. Club: Univ. Office: 25th Floor One Biscayne Tower Miami FL 33131

STEWART, LEROY ELLIOTT (SLAM), string bassist; b. Englewood, N.J., Sept. 21, 1914; s. Elliott Edward and Mary (Harris) S.; student Boston Conservatory Music, 1934-35; m. Claire Louise Wood, Jan. 11, 1969. Appeared in Boston night clubs with Jabbo Jenkins, Dean Earl and Sabby Lewis, 1935-36; joined Peanuts Holland in Buffalo, 1936; formed guitar and bass duo with Slim Gaillard at Jock's Place, N.Y.C., 1935-37; appeared on radio WNEW, N.Y.C., 1937-41; mem. Art Tatum Trio, 1941-56, Benny Goodman Sextet, 1945-47, 73-79; appeared at Monterey Jazz Festival with Slim Gaillard, 1970, with Benny Goodman Sextet at Kennedy Center, Washington, Red Rock Amphitheater, Denver, Wolf Trap Farm Park, Va., Saratoga Performing Arts Theater, Royal Albert Hall, London, Carnegie Hall, Town Hall and Lincoln Center, N.Y.C., also in Dublin, Hamburg, Helsinki, Vienna and Alaska; appeared in movies, on Broadway and television; guest soloist with symphony orchs. and chamber music quartets; faculty State U. N.Y., dir. jazz workshops Newing Coll., Binghamton, 1971—; lectr., performer Roberson Center Ednl. Services. Cons., Roberson Center. Recipient Esquire Silver award, 1945-46, Downbeat award for best bassist of year, 1945, Metronome award for best all-Am. jazz bassist, 1946; Prez award for contribution to jazz N.Y.C. Dept. Cultural Affairs, 1979; Highest Honor award Berklee Coll. Music, 1979. Fellow Yale U., Newing Coll., State U. N.Y., Binghamton. Mem. A.S.C.A.P., Am. Fedn. Musicians. Russian Orthodox. Club: Sertoma. Author: Styles in Jazz Bass, 1944. Composer: Flat Foot Floogie, 1937. Home: 80 Chestnut St Binghamton NY 13905

STEWART, LORAN LASELLS, wood products mfg. co. exec.; b. Cottage Grove, Oreg., Jan. 10, 1911; s. LaSella D. and Jessie (Hills) S.; B.S. in Logging, Oreg. State Coll., 1932; m. Dorothy Elizabeth McDonald, Apr. 3, 1936; children—LaSells McDonald, Steven Kent. With U.S. Forest Service, Lakeview, Oreg., 1933-42; asst. to gen. mgr. Pope & Talbot Lumber Co., Oakridge, Oreg., 1946-49; pres. Bohemia Inc., Eugene, Oreg., 1949-76, dir., 1946—; dir. Nat. Corp. Housing Partnerships, Washington. Mem. Fed. Res. Bd., Portland br., 1973-75, 76-78. Mem. lumber sub-council Nat. Indsl. Pollution Control Council, 1970-72; industry chmn. State Dept./Industry Log Export Meeting, Japan, 1968; chmn. Oreg. Forest Industries Council, 1976-77; dir. Western Forestry Center, 1976—. Mem. Oreg. Ho. of Reps., 1951-55, Oreg. Bd. Higher Edn., 1970-77; chmn. Oreg. Parks and Recreation Adv. Com., 1964—; trustee Oreg. State U.; bd. dirs. Sacred Heart Med. Center; pres. Oreg. Trail council Boy Scouts Am., 1977—. Served to lt. col. F.A., AUS, 1942-46; CBI. Decorated Bronze Star; Grand Star (China). Mem. Nat. Forest Products Assn. (chmn. bd. 1970-71). Home: 85658 Dillard Access Rd Eugene OR 97405 Office: 107-E Oakway Mall Eugene OR 97401

STEWART, MARGARET MCBRIDE, biologist; b. Guilford County, nr. Greensboro, N.C., Feb. 6, 1927; d. David Henry and Mary (Morrow) S.; A.B., U. N.C., 1948, M.A., 1951; Ph.D., Cornell U., 1956; m. George E. Martin, Dec. 19, 1969. Lab. instr. biology U. N.C. at Greensboro, 1950-51; instr. biology Catawba Coll., Salisbury, N.C., 1951-53; research asst. oceanography Cornell U., Ithaca, N.Y., 1953, extension botanist, 1954-56; asst. prof. biology State U. N.Y., Albany, 1956-58, asso. prof., 1958-65, prof. vetebrate biology, 1965—, distinguished teaching prof., 1977—. Recipient State U. N.Y. Grant-in-aid, Research Found., 1958-61, 65-67, 67-69, 70-72, 73-74; Am. Philos. Soc. research grantee, 1975; NSF grantee, 1978. Mem. AAAS, Am. Inst. Biol. Scis., Am. Soc. Ichthyologists, Herpetologists, Am. Soc. Mammalogists, N.C. Acad. Sci., Soc. Systematic Zoology, Nature Conservancy, Herpetologists League, Soc. Study Amphibians and Reptiles (pres.), Herpetol. Assn. Africa, Assn. Tropical Biology, Soc. Study Evolution, Ecol. Soc., Sigma Delta Epsilon, Phi Kappa Phi, Sigma Xi. Author: Keys to the Vertebrates of the Northeastern States, 1965; Amphibians of Malawi, 1967. Contbr. articles to profl. jours. Home: R D 1 Beaver Dam Rd Voorheesville NY 12186

STEWART, MARY FLORENCE ELINOR, author; b. Sunderland, County Durham, Sept. 17, 1916; d. Frederick A. and Mary Edith (Matthews) Rainbow; B.A., Durham U., 1939, M.A., 1941; m. Frederick H. Stewart, 1945. Lectr. in English, Durham U., 1941-45, part-time lectr. English, 1948-56. Author: (novels) Madam, Will You Talk? 1954; Wildfire at Midnight, 1956; Thunder on the Right, 1957; Nine Coaches Waiting, 1958; My Brother Michael, 1959; The Ivy Tree, 1961; The Moonspinners, 1962; This Rough Magic, 1964; Airs Above the Ground, 1965; The Gabriel Hounds, 1967; The Wind off the Small Isles, 1968; The Crystal Cave, 1970; The Little Broomstick, 1971; The Hollow Hills, 1973; Ludo and The Star Horse, 1974; Touch Not The Cat, 1976; The Last Enchantment, 1979; also poems, articles. Fellow Royal Soc Arts; mem. Soc. Authors, Authors' League Am., P.E.N. Address: care William Morrow 105 Madison Ave New York NY 10016

STEWART, MELBOURNE GEORGE, JR., physicist, educator; b. Detroit, Sept. 30, 1927; s. Melbourne George and Ottilie (Tuholke) S.; A.B., U. Mich., 1949, M.S., 1950, Ph.D., 1955; m. Charlotte L. Ford, Jan. 23, 1954; children—Jill K., John H., Kevin G. Research asso. dept. physics AEC, Ames Lab., Iowa State U., 1955-56, asst. prof., 1956-62, asso. prof., 1962-63; prof. Wayne State U., Detroit, 1963—, chmn. dept. physics, 1963-73, asso. provost for faculty relations, 1973—. Served with AUS, 1946-47. Mem. Am. Phys. Soc., A.A.A.S., Sigma Xi, Phi Beta Kappa. Editorial bd. Wayne State U. Press, 1969-73. Home: 415 Bournemouth Rd Grosse Pointe Farms MI 48236 Office: Mackenzie Hall Wayne State U Detroit MI 48202

STEWART, MERYLE RICHARD, oil co. exec., lawyer; b. Seminole, Okla., Aug. 20, 1943; s. Horace Medford and Francis May (Watson) S.; B.A., U. Tex., 1965, J.D., 1967; m. Donna Gayle Moser, Aug. 21, 1964; 1 dau., Michele. Admitted to Tex. bar, 1967, Okla. bar, 1967; staff atty. Phillips Petroleum Co., Oklahoma City, 1967-71, Bartlesville, Okla., 1972-74; staff atty. Tesoro Petroleum Co., San Antonio, 1974-75, sr. atty., 1975-79, v.p., gen. counsel, sec., 1979—. Mem. adv. bd. Internat. Oil and Gas Edn. Center, Southwestern Legal Found.; mem. adv. bd. Internat. and Comparative Law Center, Southwestern Legal Found. Mem. Tex. Bar Assn., Okla. Bar Assn., Am. Bar Assn., San Antonio Bar Assn. Home: 3714 Hunters Point San Antonio TX 78230 Office: 8700 Tesoro Dr San Antonio TX 78286

STEWART, MURRAY EDGAR, corp. exec.; b. Brandon, Man., Can., Sept. 30, 1926; s. William Murray and Mary Elizabeth (Williams) S.; B.Sc. cum laude, U. Alta. (Can.), 1947; M. Com., U. Toronto (Ont., Can.), 1949; m. Muriel Allison Young, Dec. 28, 1949; children—Janet, Arden, Joan, Karen. Engr. Northwestern Utilities, Ltd., Edmonton, Alta., 1949-56, gen. mgr., 1956-60, gen. mgr., v.p., 1960-65; pres., chief exec. officer, dir. Northwestern Utilities & Canadian Western Natural Gas Co., 1965-68, Gen. Waterworks Corp., 1968-70; sr. v.p. IU Internat. Corp., Phila., 1970-72; pres., chief exec. officer, dir. C. Brewer & Co. Ltd., Honolulu, 1972-75; exec. v.p. Alexander & Baldwin, Inc., Honolulu, 1975-78; exec. v.p., dir. Foothills Pipe Lines (Yukon) Ltd., Calgary, Alta., Can., 1978—. Clubs: Mayfair Golf and Country (past pres.) (Edmonton); Calgary Golf and Country, Ranchmens (Calgary, Can.); Oahu Golf and Country, Waialae Country, (Honolulu). Home: 4427 Britannia Dr SW Calgary AB T2S 1J Canada Office: Bow Valley Sq 2 Box 9083 Calgary AB T2P 2W4 Canada

STEWART, OMER CALL, anthropologist, enthnogeographer, educator; b. Provo, Utah, Aug. 17, 1908; s. John R. and Esther (Call) S.; B.S., U. Utah, 1933; Ph.D., U. Calif. at Berkeley, 1939; m. Wanda Clayton, Jan. 22, 1932 (div. 1934); m. 2d, Lenore Thurston, May 26, 1936; children—Ann, Stephen O., Katherine, Carl T. Instr. anthropology U. Tex., Austin, 1939, U. Minn., 1941-42; post doctoral fellow Social Sci. Research Council, 1940-41; with Office Chief Staff, War Dept., 1942-43; export div. Remington Rand, Inc., 1943-45; prof. anthropology U. Colo., Boulder, 1945-74, emeritus, 1974—, also dir. U. Colo. students at U. Bordeaux, 1967-69. Sponsored research, dir. NIMH; field research Pomo and Pit River Indians of Calif., Washo and No. Paiute Indians of Nev. and Calif., No. Palute Indians of Oreg., Ute and So. Paiute Indians of Utah and Colo., Zuni of N.Mex., also Shoshoni, Chippewa and Ottawa Indians. Expert witness before Indian Claims Commn., 1951—, Nat. Am. Ch., Ariz., 1960, 71, Calif., 1962, Colo., 1967, Washington, 1978; mem. Internat. Symposium on Man's Role in Changing the Face of the Earth, 1955. Fellow Am. Anthrop. Assn., AAAS, Soc. Applied Anthropology (pres. 1965-66); mem. Soc. Am. Archaeology, Colo. Archaeol. Soc. (exec. sec., editor 1949-54), Phi Beta Kappa, Sigma Xi, Phi Sigma. Democrat. Unitarian. Author numerous monographs, chpts. in books, articles; contbr. to Ency. Americana, Ency. Brit. Home: 921 5th St Boulder CO 80302

STEWART, PATRICIA CARRY, found. ofcl.; b. Bklyn., May 19, 1928; d. William J. and Eleanor (Murphy) Carry; student U. Paris, 1948-49; B.A., Cornell U., 1950; m. Charles Thorp Stewart, May 30, 1976. Fgn. corr. Irving Trust Co., N.Y.C., 1950-51, Janeway Pub. and Research Corp., 1951-60, sec.-treas., 1955-60; partner Buckner & Co., N.Y.C., 1961-71; v.p., treas. Walker Buckner & Co., Inc., N.Y.C., 1970-71; pres. Knight, Carry, Bliss & Co., Inc., N.Y.C., 1971-73; pres. G. Tsai & Co., Inc., 1973; allied mem. N.Y. Stock Exchange, 1961-73; v.p., sec. Edna McConnell Clark Found., Inc., 1974—; dir. Trans World Airlines, Trans World Corp., Borden, Inc., Continental Corp., Bankers Trust N.Y. Corp., Morton Norwich Products Inc., Bankers Trust Co. voting mem. Blue Cross and Blue Shield Greater N.Y.; mem. arbitration com. Am. Stock Exchange. Mem. N.Y.C. Panel White House Fellows, 1976-78, Inst. Edn. and Research on Women and Work; bd. dirs United Way of Tri-State; trustee, vice chmn. investment com., mem. exec. com. Cornell U.; vice chmn. bd. trustees City U. N.Y.; trustee N.Y. 4-H Found., 1972-78, Internat. Inst. Rural Reconstrn., 1975-79; mem. vis. com. Harvard Grad. Sch. Bus.; bd. advisers Baruch Coll.; bd. dirs., past chmn. Investor Responsibility Research Center. Named to Acad. Women Achievers, YWCA. Mem. Am. Assn. Colls. and Schs. Bus. (accreditation research resource panel), Pi Beta Phi. Clubs: Cosmopolitan (N.Y.C.); Country of Fla. (Delray Beach). Home: 135 E 71st St New York NY 10021 Office: 250 Park Ave New York NY 10017

STEWART, PAUL, actor, producer and dir.; b. N.Y.C., Mar. 13, 1908; s. Maurice D. and Nathalie Caroline (Nathanson) Sternberg; student Columbia, 1927-28, Bklyn. Law Sch., 1928-30; m. Peg LaCentra, Jan. 14, 1939. Actor and dir. theatre, radio, motion pictures and television; actor appearing on Broadway in Subway Express, Wine of Choice, Native Son, Mr. Roberts; stage credits for direction include The Stars Weep, Twilight Walk, Sing Me No Lullaby, View from the Bridge, Witness for the Prosecution (West coast prodns.); appeared as actor in more than 5000 radio broadcasts, 1934-44, including Cavalcade of Am., March of Time, Mercury Theatre on the Air; producer Mercury Theatre on the Air, Campbell Playhouse, U.S. Treasury Dept. War Loan Series; radio dir. on daytime serials for CBS and NBC, 1938-41, Cavalcade of Am., 1944-45; cons. producer, dir. for Sec. of Treasury Henry Morganthau, 1944; motion picture credits as actor include Citizen Kane, Johnny Eager, Mr. Lucky, Champion, The Window, 12 O'Clock High, A Child is Waiting, Greatest Story Ever Told, In Cold Blood; televison guest star in maj. television series, 1950—; television dir. Defenders, Twilight Zone, Peter Gunn, Chrysler Theatre, Checkmate, M-Squad, Hawaiian Eye. Dir. Acoustica Assos., Inc., Los Angeles, 1963-68; v.p. Rod Devel. Corp., Los Angeles, 1963-68. Chmn. communications com. Anti-Defamation League, 1969-71. Served with OWI, 1941-43. Mem. Acad. Motion Picture Arts and Scis. Club: Lambs (N.Y.C.). Home: 8272 Marmont Ln Los Angeles CA 90069 Office: care HR Williams 9405 Brighton Way Beverly Hills CA 90210

STEWART, PETER CLAYTON, corp. exec.; b. W. Vancouver, B.C., Can., July 24, 1915; s. John and Mabel Annabel (Grant) S.; B.A., U. B.C., 1936; postgrad. B.C. Law Sch., 1939; m. Marie Helen Olson, Mar. 28, 1942; children—Donald Grant, Tiffany Jean (Mrs. Laurie P. Wyles). Lqw student firm Compney, Owen & Murphy, Vancouver, then MacInnis & Arnold, 1936-39; called to B.C. bar, 1939; practice in Vancouver, 1939-41; with Cominco, Ltd., Trail, B.C., Montreal, Que. and Vancouver, 1941—, sec., 1972—. Regional sec., pres. Boy Scouts Can. Clk., Municipality of Tadannc, B.C., 1943-56; pres. Roseland-Trail Liberal Assn., 1943-51. Mem. Beta Theta Pi. Kiwanian (lt. gov. N.W. dist. 1957-58). Home: 2337 Marine Dr West Vancouver BC Canada Office: 200 Granville St Vancouver BC Canada

STEWART, POTTER, asso. supreme ct. justice; b. Jackson, Mich., Jan. 23, 1915; s. James Garfield and Harriet Loomis (Potter) S.; student Hotchkiss Sch.; B.A. cum laude, Yale, 1937, LL.B. cum laude, 1941; Henry fellow Cambridge U., Eng., 1937-38; m. Mary Ann Bertles, Apr. 24, 1943; children—Harriet Virkstis, Potter, David Bertles. Admitted to Ohio bar, 1941, N.Y. bar, 1942; pvt. law practice, N.Y.C., 1941-42, 45-47, Cin., 1947-54; U.S. judge Ct. Appeals, 6th Circuit, 1954-58; asso. justice U.S. Supreme Ct., 1958—. Mem. Cin. City Council, 1950-53, vice mayor, 1952-53. Served as lt. USNR, 1942-45. Mem. Am., Ohio, Cin., City N.Y. bar assns., Am. Law Inst., Yale Law Sch. Assn. (hon.), Phi Beta Kappa, Delta Kappa Epsilon, Phi Delta Phi, Order of Coif. Episcopalian. Clubs: Camargo, Commonwealth, Commercial, University (Cin.); University, Chevy Chase (Washington); Century (N.Y.C.); Bohemian (San Francisco). Home: 5136 Palisade Ln Washington DC 20016 Office: Supreme Ct Bldg Washington DC 20543

STEWART, REGINALD, pianist, condr., conservatory dir.; b. Edinburgh, Scotland, Apr. 20, 1902; s. George Watson and Elizabeth (Drysdale) S.; student Gillespie Sch., St. Mary's Coll., Edinburgh, D.Music (hon.); pvt. tutors, Eng., France, Can., music edn. under Arthur Friedheim, Isidor Phillipp, Nadia Boulanger, Mark Hambourg; m. Ruby McLean Glasgow, July 4, 1921; children—Delphine Glasgow, Ursula Drysdale. Pianist, 1919; mus. dir. Canadian Operatic Soc., 1919; tchr. piano Can. Acad. Music, 1920; pianist Hambourg Trio, 1921; dir. Hart House, U. Toronto, 1922; toured as concert pianist, Eng., 1924, Can., 1925; condr. London Symphony Orch., Albert Hall, also soloist, 1930; series of symphony concerts over Can. radio network, 1931; condr. BBC Symphony Orch., piano recitals in Eng., 1932; formed Bach Soc., Toronto, 1933, condr. many cantatas to 1941; formed Toronto Philharmonic Orch., 1934; condr. radio broadcasts Gen. Motors Hour, N.Y.C., 1935; N.Y.C. debut as pianist Town Hall, 1937; condr. Nat. Symphony Orch., Washington, 1938; toured U.S., Can. as pianist, 1938-39; condr. N.Y.C. Orch., Carnegie Hall, 1940, Detroit Symphony Orch., 1940-41; 2 piano recitals Town Hall, N.Y.C., 1940-41; condr. NBC Symphony Orch., N.Y. Philharmonic Orch., soloist with N.Y. Philharmonic, Chgo. Symphony Orchs., 1941; apptd. dir. Peabody Conservatory of Music., Balt., 1941-58; condr. Balt. Symphony Orch., 1942-52; artist-in-residence Music Acad. West, Santa Barbara, Calif., 1962—; Guest condr. London Philharmonia, 1956; Stratford Festival, Can., with leading symphony orchs. C.Am., S.Am., Holland, Switzerland, Mexico, Eng., Italy, Greece. Transcribed many works for orchs.; recs. for Victor, Vanguard and Educo. Clubs: Canadian, Bohemian (N.Y.); Hamilton (Balt.). Home: 655 El Bosque Rd Santa Barbara CA 93108

STEWART, RICHARD BURLESON, lawyer; b. Cleve., Feb. 12, 1940; s. Richard Siegfreid and Ruth Dysert (Staten) S.; A.B., Yale U., 1961; B.A. (Rhodes scholar), Oxford (Eng.) U., 1963; LL.B., Harvard U., 1966; m. Alice Peck Fales, May 13, 1967; children—William, Paul. Admitted to D.C. bar, 1968, U.S. Supreme Ct., 1971; law clk. to Justice Potter Stewart, U.S. Supreme Ct., 1966-67; asso. firm Covington & Burling, Washington, 1967-71; asst. prof. law Harvard U., 1971-75, prof., 1975—; spl. counsel U.S. Senate Watergate Com., Vice chmn. bd. Environ. Def. Fund. Mem. Am. Law Inst. Author: (with J. Krier) Environmental Law and Policy, 1978; (with S. Breyer) Administrative Law and Regulation, 1979. Office: Harvard Law Sch Cambridge MA 02138

STEWART, RICHARD EDWIN, ins. co. exec.; b. Washington, Nov. 4, 1933; s. Irvin and Florence Elsie (Dezendorf) S.; B.A., W.Va. U., 1955; B.A. (Rhodes scholar), Oxford (Eng.) U., 1957, M.A., 1961; J.D., Harvard, 1959; m. Barbara Claire Dunbar, Sept. 24, 1974. Admitted to N.Y. State bar, 1960; with firm Royall, Koegel & Rogers, N.Y.C., 1960-63; asst. counsel to gov. N.Y., 1963-64, 1st asst. counsel, 1965-66; supr. ins. N.Y. State, 1967-70; sr. v.p., gen. counsel First Nat. City Bank, N.Y.C., 1971-72, First Nat. City Corp., N.Y.C., 1971-72; sr. v.p., dir. Chubb & Son Inc., N.Y.C., 1972—, sr. v.p. Chubb Corp., 1973—, chief fin. officer, 1974—; dir. Fed. Ins. Co., Vigilant Ins. Co., Colonial Life Ins. Co., United Life & Accident Ins. Co. Pres., Nat. Assn. Ins. Commrs., 1970; mem. adv. com. HUD, 1968-72. Bd. dirs. Markle Found., Victoria Found. Served with AUS, 1959. Mem. Am. Arbitration Assn. (dir.), Nat. Acad. Pub. Adminstrn., Phi Beta Kappa Assos. Clubs: Cosmos (Washington); Down Town Assn., Century (N.Y.C.). Co-author: Automobile Insurance....For Whose Benefit?, 1970; Watergate: Implications for Responsible Government, 1974; Medical Malpractice, 1977; author Reason and Regulation, 1972; Insurance and Insurance Regulation, 1978. Home: 184 Columbia Heights Brooklyn NY 11201 Office: 100 William St New York NY 10038

STEWART, RICHARD MORE, lawyer, brass co. exec.; b. Silver Creek, N.Y., Mar. 29, 1910; s. Vernon T. and Helen L. (Quale) S.; B.S., Mass. Inst. Tech., 1932; LL.B., N.Y. Law Sch., 1938; m. Eleanor Noel Russell, Sept. 29, 1934; children—Barry Russell, Donald More, Robert Bradley. Research asso. Carlton Ellis of Ellis Labs., instr. Newark Coll. Engring., 1932-35; admitted to N.Y. bar, 1938; with Anaconda Wire & Cable Co., 1935-49; staff legal dept. The Anaconda Co., counsel, 1949-56, dir. indsl. relations, 1956-58; pres. Anaconda Am. Brass Co., 1958-70, chief exec. officer, 1959-70; commr. commerce State Conn., Hartford, 1973-75; v.p., dir. Nacional de Cobre, Mexico City; chmn. bd. Anaconda Am. Brass, Ltd., New Toronto, Ont., Can.; dir., exec. com. Colonial Bank & Trust Co., Waterbury, Conn., Conn. Nuclear Corp., Hartford; trustee, exec. com. Waterbury Savs. Bank; dir. Anaconda Wire & Cable Co., Anaconda Aluminum Co., Atco Industries, Bridgeport, Conn., MacDermid. Inc. (Waterbury, Conn.), Bullard Co. Pres. Conn. Trust for Historic Preservation, 1975—. Chmn. trustees, exec. com. Conn. Pub. Expenditures Council; chmn. Conn. Devel. Authority, Conn. Council Equal Employment Opportunity; mem. Nat. council Boy Scouts Am.; gen. campaign chmn. United Council and Fund Waterbury; mem. Nat. Labor Mgmt. Policy Com.; chmn. Naugatuck Valley Indsl. Council; vice chmn. Gov.'s Commn. on Services and Expenditures; pres., bd. dirs. Conn. Citizens for Jud. Modernization, 1978—; chmn. Gov.'s Com. Against Discrimination; former pres. Waterbury Hosp.; trustee exec. com. Westover Sch., Middlebury; bd. dirs. Am. Shakespeare Theater, Stratford, Conn. Mem. Hwy. Assn. Western Conn. (co-chmn.), Mfrs. Assn. Conn. (dir.), N.Y. Bar, Conn. State Srs. Golf Assn., Phi Delta Phi, Sigma Nu. Clubs: Highfield Waterbury Country, Waterbury; Veteran Motor Car of Am. (v.p.); Veteran Motor Car of Gt. Britain. Home: Central Rd Middlebury CT 06762 Office: One Bridge Ave Stratford CT 06497

STEWART, ROBERT, JR., banker; b. Phila., Nov. 8, 1919; s. Robert and Helen (Anderson) S.; student U. Mich., 1937-39; B.B.A. in Banking and Finance, U. Tex., 1942; m. Edith L. Carter, Nov. 15, 1942 (dec. Aug. 1973); children—William Robert, Edward Gilmore, Stephanie Ann; m. 2d, Helen C. Ney, Nov. 30, 1974. With Bank of Southwest and predecessor, Houston, 1945—, exec. v.p., chief operating officer, 1966-67, pres., 1967-76, vice chmn., 1976—, also dir.; vice chmn., dir. S.W. Bancshares, Inc.; dir. Gt. So. Life Ins. Co., Mosher, Inc.; adv. dir. 1st Nat. Bank, Port Arthur, Tex. Mem. investment adv. com. Employees Retirement System State Tex., Tex. A. and M. U. Trustee Meml. Hosp. System, bd. dirs. Tex. Research League, Salvation Army; mem. devel. bd. U. Tex. Health Sci. Center at Houston. Served to lt. USNR, 1942-45. Mem. Res. City Bankers Assn., Phi Kappa Sigma. Clubs: Houston, Houston Country, Coronado, Petroleum (Houston). Home: 6015 Pine Forest Houston TX 77057 Office: PO Box 2629 Houston TX 77001

STEWART, ROBERT EDWIN, agrl. engr., educator: b. Carthage, Mo., May 4, 1915; s. Harry Adrian and Mary Evaline (Bridges) S.; B.S., U. Mo., 1948, M.S., 1950, Ph.D., 1953; m. Bonnie Ruth Nance, July 3, 1942; 1 dau., Lillian Moore. Instr., then prof. agrl. engring. U. Mo., 1948-61; prof. agrl. engring., chmn. dept. Ohio State U., 1961-68; Distinguished prof. agrl. engring. Tex. A. and M. U., 1968—. Mem. agrl. bd. NRC-Nat. Acad. Scis., 1962—; chmn. Engrs. Joint Council Com. on Engring. Interactions with Biology and Medicine. Served with USAAF, 1941-45. Recipient award for distinguished service in engring. U. Mo., 1970. Registered profl. engr., Mo., Tex. Fellow AAAS, Am. Soc. Agrl. Engrs. (pres. 1970-71); mem. Nat. Soc. Profl. Engrs., Nat. Acad. Engring., N.Y. Acad. Scis., Sigma Xi, Gamma Sigma Delta (award outstanding service to agr. 1959), Tau Beta Pi, Gamma Alpha, Alpha Epsilon. Episcopalian. Club: Briarcrest Country (Bryan, Tex.). Author: History of the American Society of Agricultural Engineers. Contbr. to Ency. Britannica, profl. jours. Home: 1504 Barak Ln Bryan TX 77801 Office: Texas A and M U College Station TX 77843

STEWART, ROBERT FLETCHER, realty corp. exec.; b. Gardner, Mass., Aug. 6, 1927; s. Arlington K. and Edith (Fletcher) S.; B.S., Worcester Poly. Inst., 1950, D.Engring. (hon.), 1978; postgrad. Babson Inst. Bus. Adminstrn., 1950-51, Boston U. Grad. Sch. Bus., 1957-58; m. Joan Marshall, June 23, 1951; children—Carolyn, Eleanor. Pres., Royal Typewriter Co. div. Litton Industries, Inc., Hartford, Conn., 1969-70; group exec. machine tool systems group, corp. v.p. Litton Industries, Inc., Hartford, 1970-71; pres. indsl. products group, corp. v.p. Rockwell Internat. Corp., Pitts., 1971-75; sr. v.p. strategic planning United Techs. Corp., Hartford, 1975-78; pres. Arlen Realty & Devel. Corp., 1978-79; sr. v.p. corp. planning and devel. IC Industries Inc., Chgo., 1979—. Mem. pres.'s adv. council Worcester (Mass.) Poly. Inst. Served with USNR, 1945-46. Recipient Robert H. Goddard award for outstanding profl. achievement Worcester Poly. Inst., 1971. Patentee in field. Home: Gate Field Dr Greenwich CT 06830 Office: 111 E Wacker Dr Chicago IL 60601

STEWART, ROBERT GORDON, museum curator; b. Balt., Mar. 5, 1931; s. Kenneth Elsworth and Ruth (Chambers) S.; student Gilman Sch., 1946-49; B.F.A., U. Pa., 1954. Architect, Ind. Nat. Hist. Park, Phila., 1954, Nat. Park Service, Phila., 1956-57; architect, curator Jefferson Barracks Hist. Park, St. Louis, 1958-61; dir. properties Nat. Trust for Historic Preservation, Washington, 1961-64; curator Nat. Portrait Gallery, Smithsonian Instn., Washington, 1964—; cons. Loyalist Homestead, St. John's, N.B., Can., 1960—; vis. lectr. George Washington U., 1967-70. Dir. Landmarks of St. Louis, 1959-61; adjudicator Jamaican Nat. Art Competition, 1971. Served with U.S. Army, 1954-56. Mem. Md., Dorchester County, Lewes hist. socs., Am. Assn. Museums, AIA, Coll. Art Assn., Zeta Psi. Episcopalian. Author: Nucleus for a National Collection, 1965; Recent Acquisitions, 1966; A Nineteeth-Century Gallery of Distinguished Americans, 1969; Henry Benbridge (1743-1812): American Portrait Painter, 1971; Robert Edge Pine, A British Artist in America 1784-1788, 1979. Contbr. to In the Minds and Hearts of the People: Prologue to the American Revolution, 1974; The Dye Is Now Cast: The Road to Independence, 1975; Abroad in America, Visitors to the New Nation 1876-1914, 1976. Home: 4104 46th St NW Washington DC 20016 Office: Nat Portrait Gallery 8th and F Sts Washington DC 20560

STEWART, ROBERT H., III, banker; b. Dallas, Dec. 3, 1925; s. Robert H. Stewart; B.B.A. in Banking, So. Meth. U., 1949; m. Cynthia Giesecke, 1949; children—Cynthia Caroline, Alice Partee. With Empire State Bank, Dallas, 1949-50; with First Nat. Bank, Dallas, from 1951, v.p., 1953-59, sr. v.p., 1959-60, pres., 1960-65, chmn. bd., from 1965, now dir.; chmn. bd. First Internat. Bancshares, Inc.; dir. Dallas Power & Light Co., Braniff Internat. Corp., Southwestern Life Ins. Co., Pepsico, NCH Corp., Campbell Taggart Inc. (all Dallas). Bd. dirs. Dallas Citizens Council. Served to 1st lt. inf. AUS, 1944-46; also Korea. Clubs: Brook Hollow Golf (dir.), Terpsichorean (dir.), Idlewild (dir.) (Dallas). Office: First Internat Bancshares Inc 1201 Elm St Dallas TX 75270*

STEWART, ROBERT IVEY, life ins. co. exec.; b. Birmingham, Ala., Jan. 12, 1925; s. Manie Clyde and Elna (Ivey) S.; B.A., U. Va., 1944; M.B.A., Harvard U., 1947; m. Ann Richardson Allen, Apr. 28, 1954; children—Margaret Coleman, Hunter Allen, Robert Ivey. Sr. v.p. Liberty Nat. Life Ins. Co., Birmingham, 1950-73, pres., 1976—; pres. Rockford Life Ins. Co. (Ill.), 1973-76, dir., 1973—; dir. Liberty Nat. Fire Ins. Co. Trustee Va. Epis. Sch., Lynchburg. Served with USNR, 1943-49, 50-52. Fellow Life Mgmt. Inst.; mem. Phi Beta Kappa. Episcopalian. Clubs: Birmingham Country, Kiwanis. Home: 3004 Overhill Rd Birmingham AL 35223 Office: PO Box 2612 Birmingham AL 35202

STEWART, ROBERT MURRAY, JR., educator; b. Washington, May 6, 1924; s. Robert Murray and Emily (Smith) S.; student U. Utah, 1941-43; B.S. in Elec. Engring., Iowa State Coll., 1945, Ph.D. in Physics, 1954; m. Patricia Mary Alberding, June 27, 1945; children—Martha Murray, Scott Robert. Faculty, Iowa State U., 1946—, research asso., 1948-53, asst. prof. physics, 1953, asso. prof. physics, elec. engring., 1956-60, prof. physics, elec. engring., 1960—; research scientist AEC, Ames Lab., 1963-73, chief engr. cyclone digital computer, 1956-66; asso. dir. Iowa State U. Computation Center, 1963—, prof. and chmn. computer sci. dept., 1969—; pres. Computer Sci. Bd., 1976-77; cons. Midwest Research Inst., Kansas City, Mo., Collins Radio Corp., Cedar Rapids, Iowa, Dept. Meteorology and oceanography Tex. A. and M. Coll., Nat. Acad. Sci., Electronic Assos., Inc.; vis. scientist NSF, Assn. for Computing Machinery, Coll. Cons. Service. Mgmt. bd. YMCA, Snow Mountain Ranch, 1969-77; pres. Edwards Sch. PTA, 1970. Bd. dirs. Ames Camp Fire Girls, Ames Town and Gown Chamber Music Soc., 1973-77; pres. bd. dirs. Story County Youth and Shelter Service, 1975—. Served as ensign USNR, 1945-46. Mem. Assn. Computing Machinery, Am. Phys. Soc., IEEE (adminstrv. com. profl. group on electronic computers, 1962-64), Iowa Acad. Sci., Osborn Research Club (chmn. 1971), Am. Fedn. Information Processing Socs. (mem. edn. com.), YMCA of Rockies (dir. 1977—), Ames Soc. for Arts (pres. 1970), UN Assn. (bd. dirs. Ames chpt.), Sigma Xi (pres. Iowa State U. chpt. 1974-75). Chief investigator NSF sponsored time sharing computer research, 1968-78; designer, implementer computer control system for expts. Ames Lab. Research Reactor AEC. Home: 3416 Oakland Ames IA 50010

STEWART, ROBERT WILLIAM, physicist; b. Smokey Lake, Alta., Can., Aug. 1923; s. Robert Edward and Florence May S.; B.Sc., Queens U., Kingston, Ont., Can., 1945, M.Sc., 1947; Ph.D., Cambridge (Eng.) U., 1952; D.Sc., McGill U., 1972; LL.D., Dalhousie U., 1974; m. Anne-Marie Robert, Apr. 19, 1973; children—Anne, Brian, Philip, Colin. Research scientist Can. Def. Research Bd., Victoria, B.C., 1950-61; prof. physics and oceanography U. B.C., Vancouver, 1960-71; dir.-gen. Inst. Ocean Scis., Sidney, B.C., Dept. Fisheries and Oceans, 1970—; vis. prof. Dalhousie U., 1960-61, Harvard U., 1964, Pa. State U., 1964; Commonwealth prof. Cambridge U., 1967-68. Recipient Patterson medal award Can. Meteorol. Soc., 1973; Sverdrup Gold medal Am. Meteorol. Soc., 1976. Mem. Internat. Assn. Phys. Scis. of Ocean (pres. phys. oceanographic commn.), Sea Use Council, Internat. Council Sci. Union, Am. Meteorol. Soc. (councillor), Global Atmospheric Research Programme (Can. nat. sci. com.). Contbr. articles to profl. jours. Home: 1145 Cloakehill Rd Sidney BC Canada Office: PO Box 6000 Sidney BC V8L 4B2 Canada

STEWART, RODERICK DAVID, singer; b. North London, Eng., Jan. 10, 1945; m. Alana Collins, Apr. 6, 1979; 1 dau., Alana. Singer with Jeff Beck Group, 1968-69, Faces, 1969-75; solo recs. include: Rod Stewart, Gasoline Alley, Every Picture Tells a Story, Never a Dull Moment, A Night on the Town, Atlantic Crossing, Smiler, Foot Loose & Fancy Free, Blondes Have More Fun. Named Rock Star of Year, Rolling Stone mag., 1971. Office: Warner Bros Records 3300 Warner Blvd Burbank CA 91510*

STEWART, ROMA J., lawyer, govt. adminstr.; b. Chgo., Aug. 10, 1936; d. Sidney A. and Roma (Lawson) Jones; B.A. cum laude, Fisk U., 1957; J.D., Georgetown U., 1972; children—Scott Douglas, Kenneth Anderson. Admitted to D.C. bar; adminstr. Discrimination Complaint Service, D.C. Bar, Washington, 1973-75; asso. firm Hudson, Leftwich & Davenport, Washington, 1975-76; individual practice law, Washington, 1976-79; dir. Office for Civil Rights, HEW, Washington, 1979—; mem. exec. com. Washington Lawyers Com. for Civil Rights Under Law. Mem. Nat. Bar Assn., D.C. Bar, Washington Bar Assn. Office: 330 Independence Ave SW Washington DC 20201

STEWART, SAMUEL B., lawyer, banker; b. Chattanooga, Oct. 5, 1908; s. Samuel B. and Dora (Pryor) S.; A.B., U. Va., 1927; J.D., Columbia, 1930; LL.D., Golden Gate U., 1965; m. Celeste Dorwin, Apr. 2, 1934; children—Linda Celeste (Mrs. James F. Dickason), James Christopher Dorwin (dec.). Admitted to N.Y. bar, 1931, Calif. bar, 1947. Asso. with Cravath, de Gersdorff, Swaine & Wood, 1930-39; partner Blake & Voorhees and successor firm Blake, Voorhees & Stewart, 1939-47; v.p., gen. counsel Bank of Am. Nat. Trust & Savs. Assn., San Francisco, 1947-59, exec. v.p., gen. counsel, 1959-67, exec. v.p., chief exec. officer trust activities, 1962-67, exec. v.p., sr. adminstrv. officer, 1967-69, vice chmn. bd., 1969-70, sr. vice chmn. bd., 1970-73; also dir.; vice chmn. bd. Bank Am. Corp., 1969-70, sr. vice chmn. bd., 1970-73, also dir., chmn. gen. trust com., 1969-79; dir. Longs Drug Stores Inc., Macy's Calif., Montgomery St. Income Securities, Inc., Occidental Petroleum Co.; spl. counsel price adjustment (Truman) Spl. Com of U.S. Senate for investigation Nat. Def. Program, 1943-44; Distinguished vis. prof. San Francisco State U., 1974. Trustee Golden Gate U.; trustee Salk Inst., chmn., 1974—. Mem. Am. Bar Assn. (past chmn. sect. corp. banking and bus. law), Legal Aid Soc. of San Francisco (pres. 1963-65), Bar Assn. San Francisco (v.p. 1967), Greater San Francisco C. of C. (pres. 1969-70, chmn. bd. 1971), Sponsors San Francisco Performing Arts Center (pres. 1973—), Phi Beta Kappa. Presbyn. (elder). Clubs: Bankers, Bohemian, San Francisco Golf, Silverado Country. Editor: The Business Lawyer, 1959-60. Home: 2288 Broadway Apt 2 San Francisco CA 94115 Office: Bank Am Center 550 California St Room 4980 San Francisco CA 94104. *My philosophy of life is very simple. Do as well as you can that which you do best and that which gives you greatest satisfaction. Don't worry! If you have a problem about which you can do something—do it! If you can't do anything about it, worry won't help. My greatest satisfactions have come from doing things others could not—or would not—do, which were helpful to others.*

STEWART, THOMAS JAMES, JR., baritone; b. San Saba, Tex., Aug. 29, 1928; s. Thomas James and Gladys Naomi (Reavis) S.; Mus.B., Baylor U., 1953; postgrad. Juilliard Sch. Music, 1953-54, Berlin Hochschule for Music, 1957-58; m. Evelyn Lear, Jan. 8, 1955; children—Jan Lear, Bonni Lear. Appeared with Met. Opera, Chgo. Opera, San Francisco Opera, Bayreuth Festival, Salzburg Festival, Vienna State Opera, Royal Opera Covent Garden, Grand Opera Paris, Deutsche Oper Berlin, La Scala, Milan, Budapest Opera, Prague Opera, 1960—, also major orchs. throughout the world. Served with USAF, 1945-49. Recipient Kammersaenger of Berlin, 1964; Richard Wagner medal, 1965; Fulbright grantee, 1957-58. Office: care Columbia Artists Mgmt Inc 165 W 57th St New York NY 10019

STEWART, THOMAS JAMES, JR., ret. chem. co. exec.; b. Flat River, Mo., Oct. 18, 1913; s. Thomas James and Margaret Beulah (Fraizer) S.; B.S., U. Mo., 1934, Chem.E., 1969; m. Mary Catherine Peterson, Oct. 20, 1937; children—Mary Jean (Mrs. Gene F. Newman), Barbara (Mrs. James B. Van Loenen), Thomas James III. Chem. engr. Western Cartridge Co., East Alton, Ill., 1934-36; chem. engr. Mo. Portland Cement Co., 1936-37; chem. engr. C.K. Williams Co., East St. Louis, Ill., 1937-52, works mgr., 1952-55, gen. prodn. mgr., 1955-60, v.p., 1960-62, also dir.; gen. prodn. mgr. minerals, pigments and metals div. Pfizer, Inc., N.Y.C., 1963-68, v.p. prodn. and mktg., 1968-69, pres., 1969-70, asst. to chmn. exec. com., 1970-76, ret., 1976; dir. Stoney Point Devel. Co. Pres., Bd. Edn. Sch. Dist. 175, Belleville, Ill., 1948-52; pres. East Side Asso. Industries, 1962; mem. budget com. United Fund, East St. Louis, 1955-57. Registered profl. engr., Ill. Mem. Am. Inst. Chem. Engrs. (pres. St. Louis sect. 1950), Am. Inst. Mining and Metall. Engrs., Am. Mining Congress, Nat. Lime Assn., Newcomen Soc. Republican. Presbyterian. Home: 307 Carmine Dr Cocoa Beach FL 32931 also Rural Route 1 Keyesport IL 62253

STEWART, THOMAS PENNEY, clergyman; b. Auburn, N.Y., May 24, 1927; s. Weir and Margaret (Penney) S.; grad. Hotchkiss Sch., Lakeville, Conn., 1945; A.B., Princeton U., 1951; M.Div., Union Theol. Sem., N.Y.C., 1954; m. Ann Maxwell Field, June 24, 1950; children—Katherine, Elizabeth, Alison. Ordained to ministry Presbyn. Ch., 1954; pastor in Ballston Spa, N.Y., 1954-59, Rosyln (N.Y.) Presbyn. Ch., 1959-71, Westminster Presbyn. Ch., Buffalo, 1971—. Chmn., Commn. on Religion and Race, Presbytery L.I., 1961-66; moderator Synod N.Y., 1968-69; v.p. Religious Communities for Arts, 1974—; treas. Artpark & Co., 1976-78. Bd. dirs. Union Theol. Sem., Buffalo Philharmonic Orch., 1978—; bd. counselors Smith Coll., 1966-71; term trustee Princeton U. Mem. Alumni Assn. Union Theol. Sem. (pres. 1963-65). Home: 39 St George's Sq Buffalo NY 14222 Office: 724 Delaware Ave Buffalo NY 14209

STEWART, WARD, educator, lawyer, former govt. ofcl., pub. adminstrn. cons.; b. Des Moines, Jan. 29, 1913; s. Louis Bassett and Florence Estelle (Crandall) S.; A.B. magna cum laude, Carleton Coll., 1933; A.M. (gen. edn. bd. fellow), U. Chgo., 1934; Ph.D. (Littauer fellow 1937-38), Harvard, 1938; J.D., George Washington U., 1949; m. Maxine Elinor Glad, June 3, 1941 (div. Dec. 1975); children—Richard, Elizabeth, Philip; m. 2d, Antoinette B.F. Friedman, May 30, 1979. Admitted D.C. bar, U.S. Supreme Ct. bar; research asst. T.V.A., Knoxville, Tenn., 1934-36; asst. dir. personnel U.S. Housing Authority, 1938-40; chief personnel officer Nat. Youth Adminstrn. 1940- 41; asst. dir. fgn. funds control U.S. Treasury, 1941-44; dir. personnel Nat. Housing Agy. (now HUD), 1946-47; spl. asst. orgn. and personnel U.S. AEC, 1947-51; dep. chief pub. adminstrn. mission to Colombia, Bogota, 1950-51; dir. reports and secretariat Office Econ. Stablzn. Adminstr., 1951-52; asst. commr. U.S. Office Edn., HEW, 1952-57, specialist in business and public adminstrn., 1957-65, dir. of higher edn. field services, 1965-73; representative U.S. Commr. Edn. to Pres. Com. Edn. Beyond High Sch., 1956-57; chmn. Washington Higher Edn. Group, 1955-56. Profl. lectr. Washington Semester Program and Grad. Edn. Program of Am. U., 1956-58, mem. adv. com., 1956—, adj. prof., 1958—, cons., 1974—, career cons. in residence, 1978—; mem. Carleton Coll. council, Alumni Achievement award, 1959; lectr. dept. agr., Harvard U. Grad. Sch.; mem. U.S. del. Internat. Congress Adminstrv. Scis., 1962, 1965, 68; mem. People-to-People Tennis Teams, Europe, 1976, 77, South Pacific, 1978, Europe, 1979, Far East, 1980. Served from lt. (j.g.) to lt. USNR, 1944-46. Mem. NEA (life mem.), Am. Polit. Sci. Assn. (pres. D.C. assn. 1957), Am. Soc. Pub. Adminstrn. (D.C. chpt. pres. 1960-61), Phi Beta Kappa, Phi Delta Kappa, Delta Sigma Rho. Clubs: Carleton (pres. Washington-Balt. 1954-55), Chicago, Harvard (Washington); Edgemoor (Bethesda, Md.). Author: Graduate Study in Public Administration, 1961; also articles in profl. jours. Address: 4000 Cathedral Ave NW Washington DC 20016

STEWART, WARREN EARL, chem. engr., educator; b. Whitewater, Wis., July 3, 1924; s. Earl Austin and Avis (Walker) S.; B.S. in Chem. Engring., U. Wis., 1945, M.S. in Chem. Engring., 1947; Sc.D. in Chem. Engring., Mass. Inst. Tech., 1951; m. Jean Durham Potter, May 24, 1947; children—Marilyn, David, Douglas, Carol, Margaret, Mary Jean. Project chem. engr. Sinclair Research Labs., Harvey, Ill., 1950-56, cons., 1956—; asst. prof. chem. engring. dept. U. Wis., Madison, 1956-58, asso. prof., 1958-61, prof., 1961—, chmn. dept. 1973-78. Cons., Engelhard Industries, Inc., Newark, 1956-58; instr. spl. courses transport phenomena Chemstrand Corp., Pensacola, Fla., 1962, Nat. U. La Plata (Argentina), 1962, Esso Research & Engring. Co., 1963, 66, Phillips Petroleum Co., 1963, Am. Inst. Chem. Engrs., 1965, 68, 69. Served to ensign USNR, 1944-46. Fellow Am. Inst. Chem. Engrs.; mem. Am. Chem. Soc., Am. Soc. for Engring. Edn., Sigma Xi, Alpha Chi Sigma, Phi Eta Sigma, Tau Beta Pi, Phi Lambda Upsilon, Phi Kappa Phi. Conglist. (deacon, vice moderator). Author: (with R.B. Bird and E.N. Lightfoot) Transport Phenomena, 1960, Special Topics in Transport Phenomena, 1965; (with R.B. Bird, E.N. Lightfoot and T.W. Chapman) Lectures in Transport Phenomena, 1969. Editorial adviser Latin Am. Jour. Chem. Engring. and Applied Chemistry; asso. editor Computers and Chem. Engring. Home: 734 Huron Hill Madison WI 53711

STEWART, WELLINGTON BUEL, pathologist, educator; b. Chgo., June 18, 1920; s. George Ross and Helen Isabel (Skinner) S.; B.S., U. Notre Dame, 1942; M.D., U. Rochester, 1945; m. Helen M. Zimmerman, June 16, 1945; children—Douglas Peter, Thomas Hale, John Gilman. Intern pathology Strong Meml. Hosp., Rochester, N.Y., 1945-46; Rockefeller fellow pathology U. Rochester, 1948-49, Vet. Postgrad. fellow pathology, 1948-50; from asso. pathology to asso. prof. pathology Columbia, 1950-60; prof. pathology, chmn. dept. U. Ky. Coll. Medicine, 1960-70; prof. pathology, dir. med. computer center U. Mo., Columbia, 1970-75, dir. labs., 1975—. Spl. research iron metabolism, erythrocytes, nutritional injury to liver, computer applications in medicine. Served to capt. M.C., AUS, 1946-48. Diplomate Nat. Bd. Med. Examiners, Am. Bd. Pathology (anat. and clin. pathology). Fellow Coll. Am. Pathologists; mem. Am. Assn. Pathologists, Mo. Soc. Pathologists (sec.-treas. 1978—), Harvey Soc., Am. Assn. Blood Banks, Soc. Computer Medicine (pres. 1978), Am. Soc. Exptl. Biology and Medicine, A.M.A., Ky. Soc. Pathologists (pres. 1965-66), Am. Soc. Clin. Pathlogists (chmn. bd. registry med. technologists 1964-67, commr. for med. tech. 1967-71), Sigma Xi, Alpha Omega Alpha. Club: Cosmos. Contbr. articles to sci. publs. Home: 1401 Ridgemont Ct Columbia MO 65201

STEWART, WILLIAM CHARLES, educator; b. Island of Guam, Jan. 10, 1926; s. Charles and Katherine (Snively) S.; B.S., Cornell U., 1946; M.B.A., Drexel Inst. Tech., 1950, M.M.E., 1953; Ph.D., U. Pa., 1965; m. Dolores E. Caputo, Oct. 30, 1954; children—Glenn, Wayne, Pamela. Engr., Philco Corp., Phila., 1946-48; engr. Schutte & Koerting Co., Cornwells Heights, Pa., 1948-51; prodn. engr. Esterbrook Pen Co., Camden, N.J., 1951-57; prodn. supt. SKF Industries, Phila., 1957-60; prodn. mgr. J. Bishop Co., Malvern, Pa., 1960-61; asso. prof. Drexel Inst. Tech., Phila., 1961-67; prof. Temple U., Phila., 1967—, chmn. dept. statistics, 1967-73. Mem. Sch. Bd., Cherry Hill, N.J., 1965-67. Served to lt. (j.g.) USNR, 1943-46. Recipient J. Parker Bursk award U. Pa., 1965. Registered profl. engr., Pa. Mem. Am. Statis. Assn., ASME, AAAS, Phi Kappa Phi, Phi Delta Theta. Author: (with Braverman) Statistics for Business and Economics, 1973; Mathematics with Application, 1979. Contbr. articles to profl. jours. Home: 103 Lane of Trees Cherry Hill NJ 08003 Office: Dept Statistics Temple U Philadelphia PA 19122

STEWART, WILLIAM DONALD, dermatologist, educator; b. Vulcan, Alta., Can., June 25, 1925; s. Francis John and Mary Elizabeth Jeanette (Moore) S.; M.D., U. Wash., 1950; m. Dorothy Jean Saylor, Feb. 10, 1951; children—Kathlyn, Jennifer, Margot, Meredith, Rebecca. Fellow in medicine Cleve. Clinic, 1953-55; fellow N.Y. U., 1955-57; practice medicine specializing in dermatology, Vancouver, B.C., Can., 1957—; mem. faculty div. dermatology U. B.C., Vancouver, 1958—, now prof., chmn. div. dermatology; chmn. div. dermatology Vancouver Gen. Hosp., 1969—, chmn. med. adv. bd. Mem. Royal Coll. Physicians and Surgeons Can. (past chmn. com. dermatology, chief examiner dermatology), Can. Dermatology Found. (dir.), Can. Med. Assn., B.C. Med. Assn., Can. Dermatol. Assn. (past pres.), B.C. Soc. Internal Medicine, Am. Dermatol. Assn., Am. Acad. Dermatology, Pacific Dermatologic Assn. (pres. 1973-74). Presbyterian. Author: Dermatology: Diagnosis and Treatment of Cutaneous Disorders, 4th edit., 1978. Contbr. articles to profl. jours. Home: 4098 Marine Dr West Vancouver BC Canada Office: 865 W 10th Ave Vancouver BC V5Z 1L7 Canada

STEWART, WILLIAM DONALD, educator; b. Tacoma, Sept. 26, 1920; s. William Douglas and Gertrude (Gilman) S.; B.A., U. Puget Sound, 1942, M.A., 1950, B.E., 1951; postgrad. Mich State U., 1943-44; Ph.D., U. Mainz, Germany, 1953; m. Carin Klass, Sept. 18, 1948 (div. July 1956); children—Kimball Donald, Kent David; m. 2d, Sue Muchmore, July 30, 1960. Dep. dir. pub. information div. Office Mil. Govt. for Hesse, Wiesbaden, Germany, 1946-48; lektor Am. studies U. Mainz (Germany), 1951-53; chmn. English dept. Lambuth Coll., Jackson, Tenn., 1953-55; press officer Radio Liberty, Munich, Germany, 1955-56; asst. prof. English, U. Puget Sound, 1956-59, Central Mo. State Coll., Warrensburg, 1959-61; chmn. English dept. Coll. of Emporia (Kans.) 1961-64; chmn. English and speech depts. U. Tampa (Fla.), 1964-68, prof. English, 1964—, chmn. dept. English, 1964-72. Tenor soloist Symphony Orch. Emporia, 1962-64; violinist St. Petersburg (Fla.) Symphony Orch., 1965-66. Served with AUS, 1942-46. Mem. Modern Lang. Assn., Internat. Shakespeare Assn., Theta Chi. Presbyn. (elder). Editor: Our Common Cause, Russian lang. newspaper, 1955-56. Home: 5006 Longfellow Ave Tampa FL 33609

STEWART, WILLIAM FRANKLIN, food store chain exec.; b. Fountain Inn, S.C., June 22, 1930; s. William Franklin and Lucy (Peden) S.; B.S., Clemson U., 1953; m. Pat Shuford, Oct. 5, 1957; children—Elizabeth, Lucinda. With Sealtest Foods div. Kraftco Corp., 1954-70, dist. gen. mgr., 1965-70; v.p. Colonial Stores, Inc., 1970-73, group v.p., 1974-77; pres., 1978-79; pres., chief exec. officer Red Food Stores, Inc., Chattanooga, 1979—. Served to 1st lt. U.S. Army, 1953-54. Republican. Presbyterian. Office: 5901 Shallowford Rd Chattanooga TN 37421

STEWART, ZEPH, educator; b. Jackson, Mich., Jan. 1, 1921; s. James Garfield and Harriet (Potter) S.; grad. Hotchkiss Sch., 1939; A.B., Yale U., 1942; A.M. (hon.), Harvard U., 1955. m. Diana Childers, Dec. 29, 1959; children—Sarah Barton, Christopher Childers, Mary Alden. Jr. fellow Soc. Fellows, Harvard, 1949- 51; mem. faculty Harvard, 1953—, prof. Greek and Latin, 1962—, chmn. dept. classics, 1977—, Allston Burr sr. tutor Adams House, 1955-60, master Lowell House, 1963-75. Trustee Radcliffe Coll., 1972-76, Loeb Classical Library, Hotchkiss Sch., Inst. for Advanced Study, Center for Hellenic Studies; mem. Yale U. Council, 1976—; mem. adv. council dept. classics Princeton U., 1970—; chmn. Harvard U. campaign United Way, 1976. Served to capt. AUS, 1943-47, 51-53. Decorated Legion of Merit; Guggenheim fellow, 1965-66. Fellow Am. Acad. Arts and Scis. (councilor 1972-76); mem. Am. Philol. Assn. (dir. 1977—), Soc. Promotion Roman Studies, Archeol. Inst. Am., Soc. Promotion Hellenic Studies, Tchrs. Classics New Eng. (pres. 1960—), Classical Assn. (U.K), Century Assn., Elizabethan Club, Signet Soc., Phi Beta Kappa, Delta Kappa Epsilon. Author: The Ancient World, 1966. Editor: Studies in Religion and the Ancient World, 1972. Home: 104 School St Belmont MA 02178 Office: Dept Classics Harvard Cambridge MA 02138

STEYERMARK, JULIAN ALFRED, botanist; b. St. Louis, Jan. 27, 1909; s. Leo and Mamie (Isaacs) S.; A.B., Washington U., 1929, M.S., 1930, Ph.D., 1933; M.A., Harvard (grad. scholar), 1931; m. Cora Shoop, Sept. 1, 1937. Rufus J. Lackland research fellow Mo. Bot. Garden, 1932-33, research asst. to Dr. Robert E. Woodson, Jr., mem. expdn. to Panama, 1934-35, hon. research asso., 1948—; instr. biology University City (Mo.) Sr. High Sch., 1935-37; taxonomist, ecologist U.S. Forest Service, summers 1936-37; asst. curator herbarium Chgo. Natural History Mus., 1937-47, asso. curator, 1948-49, curator, 1950-58; botanist Instituto Botanico, Ministerio de Agricultura and Cria, Caracas, Venezuela, 1959—, curator herbarium, 1975—; leader bot. expdn. Guatemala, 1939-40, 41-42, to Venezuela, 1944-45, 53; del. to Conservation Council Chgo., 1939-58; botanist Cinchona Mission to Ecuador for U.S. Govt., 1943, to Venezuela, 1943-44; hon. 1st v.p. First Latin Am. Bot. Congress; co-leader bot. expdn. to Venezuela, 1954-55, expdns. in Venezuela, 1959—; vis. curator N.Y. Bot. Garden, 1961-65, 68-69. Mem. Gov.'s Natural History Adv. Com. for Ill. Beach State Park, 1950; gov. Nature Conservancy, 1953-56, trustee Mo. chpt.; mem. Commn. Preservation Natural Area Venezuela; mem. adv. bd. Audubon Soc. Venezuela, 1976—; cons. Humid Forests of Venezuela, Sierra Club. Decorated Order of Quetzal (Govt. Guatemala); Gold medal Order Merit Work, Order Andres Bello (Venezuela); recipient distinguished service awards; award Amigos Venezuela, 1972. NSF grantee 1958-59; Fellow A.A.A.S.; mem. Bot. Soc. Am., Am. Soc. Plant Taxonomists, Ecol. Soc. Am., Friends of Our Native Landscape (hon.), Venezuela Soc. Natural Sci. (hon.), Ecuador Inst. Natural Scis. (hon.), Barrington Natural History Soc. (pres.), Sigma Xi. Clubs: St. Louis Wild Flower (hon. mem.); Kennicott. Author: Spring Flora of Missouri, 1940; Flora of Guatemala (with Paul C. Standley) 1946-58; Vegetational History of the Ozark Forest; Flora of Missouri; Rubiaceae of the Guayana Highlands; Flora of Auyan-tepui, Venezuela; Flora of the Meseta del Cerro Jaua, Venezuela; Flora of Ptari-tepui, Venezuela; Rubiaceae of Venezuela, 3 vols., 1974; (with Charles Brewer-Carias) Venezuela, 1975. Contbr. to Flora of Venezuela. Address: Apartado 2156 Caracas Venezuela

STIBOLT, HANS PETER, JR., envelope co. exec.; b. Longmeadow, Mass., Sept. 20, 1920; s. Hans Peter and Kirstin (Hansen) S.; ed. Northeastern Coll., Boston, Harvard U., 1964; m. Alma Muriel Loerke, Nov. 15, 1941; children—Nancy Stibolt Newman, Kenneth. With U.S. Envelope Co., Springfield, Mass., 1947—, plant mgr., 1953-57, gen. mgr., 1967-47, pres., 1974—, now chief exec. officer, also dir. Served with AUS, 1943-46, 50-52. Mem. Greater Springfield C. of C. (dir.). Club: Colony (Springfield). Address: US Envelope Corp Memorial Industrial Park Springfield MA 01101*

STICE, JAMES EDWARD, educator; b. Fayetteville, Ark., Sept. 19, 1928; s. F. Fenner and Charlotte (Anderson) S.; B.S., U. Ark., 1949; M.S., Ill. Inst. Tech., 1952, Ph.D., 1963; m. Patricia Ann Stroner, Sept. 22, 1951; children—Susan Emily, James Clayton. Process engr. Visking Corp., North Little Rock, Ark., 1951-53; chem. engr. Thurston Chem. Co. div. W.R. Grace & Co., Joplin, Mo., 1953-54; asst. prof. chem. engring. U. Ark., 1954-57, asso. prof., prof., 1962-68; instr. chem. engring. Ill. Inst. Tech., Chgo., 1957-62; dir. Bur. Engring. Teaching, asso. prof. chem. engring. U. Tex., Austin, 1968-73, prof. engring. edn. in chem. engring., 1973—, dir. Center for Teaching Effectiveness, 1973—, dir. Effective Teaching Inst. U. Tex. System, summer 1970; vis. prof. U. Iberoamericana, Mexico City, summer 1977. Summer cons. E.I. duPont de Nemours & Co., Inc., Savannah River Plant, Aiken, S.C., 1955, Humble Oil & Refining Co., Baytown, Tex., 1956, Universal Oil Products Co., Des Plaines, Ill., 1957, 58, Phillips Petroleum Co., Bartlesville, Okla., 1963, Ethyl Corp., Baton Rouge, 1965, Wis. State U., Eau Claire, 1970—. Registered profl. engr., Ark. Mem. Am. Inst. Chem. Engrs., Am. Soc. Engring. Edn., Instrument Soc. Am. (Jour. award 1966), Scabbard and Blade, Sigma Xi, Delta Sigma, Sigma Chi, Phi Eta Sigma, Pi Mu Epsilon, Alpha Chi Sigma, Tau Beta Pi, Omicron Delta Kappa, Phi Lambda Upsilon, Phi Kappa Phi. Republican. Presbyn. Author: (with B.S. Swanson) Electronic Analog Computer Primer, 1965; Computadoras Analogicas Electronicas, 1971; Expansion of Keller Plan Instruction in Engineering and Selected Other Disciplines. Home: 1503 W 32d St Austin TX 78703

STICHNOTH, DEAN ROGER, lawyer, utilities co. exec.; b. Benton County, Ind., Feb. 21, 1926; s. August and Lulu M. (Laudenslager) S.; B.S., State U. Iowa, 1948, J.D., 1950; postgrad. U. Mich., 1958; m. Emilie Fredericks, Oct. 28, 1950; children—Frederick J., H. Jane, Timothy J., Todd J., James M., John A. With Iowa-Ill. Gas and Electric Co., 1950—, sec., asst. treas., 1960-63, sec., asst. to pres., 1963-69, sec., dir. staff services, 1969-71, v.p., sec., 1971-74, v.p. adminstrn., 1974-75, dir., 1974—, pres., 1975-77, pres., chief exec. officer, 1977—, chmn., 1979—. Bd. dirs. Mercy Hosp., United Way of Rock Island and Scott Counties, 1973-74; trustee Marycrest Coll. Bd. Served with USAAF, 1944-46. Mem. Iowa, Scott County bar assns., Mo. Valley Electric Assn., Midwest Gas Assn. (dir.), Davenport, Bettendorf Chambers Commerce. Republican. Episcopalian. Clubs: Outing, Davenport, Rock Island Arsenal Golf. Office: Iowa-Ill Gas and Electric Co 206 E 2d St Davenport IA 52801*

STICHT, J. PAUL, business exec.; b. Clairton, Pa., 1917; B.A., Grove City Coll., 1939; postgrad. U. Pitts. With U.S. Steel Corp., 1939-44; personnel dir. Trans World Airlines, 1944-48; v.p. Campbell Soup Co., 1949-57, pres. internat., 1957-60; exec. v.p. Federated Dept. Stores, Inc., 1960-65, vice chmn., 1965-67, pres., 1967-72; chmn. exec. com. R.J. Reynolds Industries, Inc., Winston-Salem, N.C., 1972-73, pres., chief operating officer, 1973-78, pres., ehief exec. officer, 1978-79, chmn., chief exec. officer, 1979—; dir. Celanese Corp., Wachovia Corp., Foremost-McKesson, Inc., S.C. Johnson & Son, Inc. Trustee Grove City Coll., Old Salem, Inc., Rockefeller U., Com. for Econ. Devel.; mem. bd. visitors Bowman Gray Sch. Medicine, U. Pitts. Grad. Sch. Bus. Adminstrn., Duke U. Grad. Sch. Bus. Adminstrn.; bd. govs. Corp. Fund for Performing Arts at Kennedy Center. Mem. Conf. Bd. (sr.), Council on Fgn. Relations. Home: 2705 Bartram Pl Winston-Salem NC 27106 Office: R J Reynolds Industries Inc 401 N Main St Winston-Salem NC 27102

STICKLER, GUNNAR BRYNOLF, pediatrician; b. Peterskirchen, Germany, June 13, 1925; s. Fritz and Astrid (Wennerberg) S.; came to U.S., 1951, naturalized, 1958; M.D., U. Munich (Germany), 1949; Ph.D., U. Minn., Mpls., 1957; m. Duci M. Kronenbitter, Aug. 30, 1956; children—Katarina Anna, George David. Resident in clin. pathology Krankenhaus III Orden, Munich, 1950, resident in pathology U. Munich, 1950-51; intern Mountainside Hosp., Montclair, N.J., 1951-52; fellow in pediatrics Mayo Grad. Sch., Rochester, Minn., 1953-56; sr. cancer research scientist Roswell Park Meml. Inst., Buffalo, 1956-57; asst. to staff Mayo Clinic, Rochester, 1957-58, cons. in pediatrics, 1959—, head sect. pediatrics, 1969—, prof. pediatrics, chmn. dept. pediatrics Mayo Clinic and Mayo Med. Sch., 1974—; mem. test com. III, Nat. Bd. Med. Examiners, 1973-75; vis. prof. at various univs and instns., including U. Dusseldorf (Germany) and U. Munich, 1971, Pahlavi U., Iran, 1975, Olga Hosp., Stuttgart, Germany, 1978. Recipient Humanitarian award Chgo. region chpt. Nat. Found. Ileitis and Colitis, 1978, award for excellence of subject matter and presentation So. Minn. Med. Assn., 1978. Diplomate Am. Bd. Pediatrics (ofcl. examiner), Am. Bd. Surgery (spl. competence com. for pediatric surgery 1974-77. Mem. Am. Acad. Pediatrics, Soc. Pediatric Research, Am. Soc. Nephrology, Internat. Soc. Nephrology, Am. Soc. Pediatric Nephrology, Am. Pediatric Soc., Midwest Soc. Pediatric Research (council 1967-69, pres. 1970-71), N.W. Pediatric Soc. (pres. 1973-74). Contbr. numerous articles to med. publs.; editorial bd. Clin. Pediatrics, 1968-76, 79—, European Jour. Pediatrics, 1979. Office: Mayo Clinic Rochester MN 55901

STICKLEY, JOHN LEON, textile exec.; b. Cambridge, Mass., Sept. 6, 1902; s. Leonard and Annie (Saint) S.; m. Jennie Williamson McMichael, Apr. 5, 1928; children—John Leon, Georgiana S. Meginley, Nancy V. (Mrs. Donald A. Grant). Textile mcht., So. mgr. William Whitman Co., Inc., N.Y.C., 1925-49; pres. John L. Stickley & Co., Charlotte, N.C., also N.Y.C., 1950-66, chmn., 1966—; chmn. Stickley Textiles, Inc.; pres. Textile Realty Co.; dir. Engraph, Inc., E.B. Stone Finance Co., Rossville Spinning Mills, Rossville Yarn Processing Co., Inc., Camelot, Inc., Rossville Mills. Mem. N.C. State Bd. Elections. Mem. Internat. Assn. Lion (pres. 1956-57). Baptist. Mason (Shriner). Clubs: Union League (N.Y.C.); Charlotte City; Myers Park Country. Home: 2270 Sharon Ln Charlotte NC 28211 Office: 1615 East Blvd Charlotte NC 28203. ***Life is a stewardship! Into the keeping of every individual God Almighty has entrusted certain talents, abilities, responsibilities, opportunities, and challenges, and some day as we stand figuratively before the Great White Throne, He shall require an accounting. This I believe!***

STIDHAM, WOFFORD H., lawyer; b. Ocala, Fla., Mar. 24, 1930; s. Wade H. and Dorris (Simpson) S.; B.S. in Bus. Adminstrn., U. Fla., 1952, J.D., 1957; m. Betty Faye Biggs, July 30, 1955; children—Jeffrey Wofford, Jonathan Wade. Admitted to Fla. bar, 1957, since practiced in Bartow; with firm Holland & Knight, and predecessors, 1957—, partner, 1961—. Chmn. Bartow Civil Service Bd., 1967-68. Chmn. bd. dirs. Bartow Meml. Hosp., 1968-71; chmn. bd. trustees Polk County Law Library, 1974-75. Served to 1st lt. AUS, 1952-54. Mem. Am., 10th Jud. Circuit bar assns., Fla. Bar (chmn. labor law com. 1961-62), Am. Judicature Soc., Alpha Tau Omega, Phi Delta Phi. Republican. Presbyn. (chmn. bd. deacons 1972, mem. session 1974-75). Kiwanian (pres. Bartow 1966). Clubs: Peace River Country; Tampa University. Home: 1135 Mariposa Ave Bartow FL 33830 Office: 245 S Central Ave Bartow FL 33830

STIEBER, JACK, educator; b. Hungary, Mar. 27, 1919; s. Israel and Clara (Schechter) S.; came to U.S., 1923, naturalized, 1927; B.S.S., City Coll. N.Y., 1940; M.A., U. Minn., 1948; Ph.D., Harvard U., 1956; m. Carolyn Friedman, Dec. 21, 1947; children—Allison, Joan. Labor market analyst U.S. Employment Service, Washington, 1942; labor specialist Office Housing Expediter, 1946-47; research asso. United Steelworkers Am., CIO, Pitts., 1948-50; spl. asst. to dir. manpower Nat. Security Resources Bd., Washington, 1950-51; economist, exec. asst. labor mems. Wage Stblzn. Bd., 1951-52; research asso. Grad. Sch. Bus. Adminstrn., Harvard U., 1954-56; asso. prof. econs., asso. dir. research and planning Labor and Indsl. Relations Center, Mich. State U., E. Lansing, 1956-59, prof. econs., dir. Sch. Labor and Indsl. Relations, 1959—; exec. sec. Presdl. Adv. Com. Labor Mgmt. Policy, 1962; research cons. Internat. Inst. Labor Studies, ILO, 1963-64; vis. prof. in Belgium, Israel, Japan, India, Iran; overseas fellow Churchill Coll., Cambridge (Eng.) U.; chmn. adv. employment relations com. Mich. Civil Service Commn., 1973; chmn. Gov. Mich. Task Force Labor, 1959; mem. Gov. Mich. Com. Economy, 1960; labor arbitrator, 1956—. Served with USAAF, 1942-46. Littauer fellow, 1952-54; Wertheim fellow, 1952-54; recipient Distinguished Faculty award Mich. State U., 1974. Mem. Indsl. Relations Research Assn. (exec. bd. 1966-69), Am. Econ. Assn., AAUP (chpt. pres. 1969-70), Nat. Acad. Arbitrators (chmn. program com. 1969—, chmn. com. overseas corr. 1976—). Jewish. Author: The Steel Industry Wage Structure, 1959; Governing the UAW, 2d edit., 1967; Public Employee Unionism: Structure, Growth, Policy, 1973. Editor: Employment Problems of Automation and Advanced Technology: An International Perspective, 1966; editor, author introduction: Mullinationals, Unions, and Labor Relations in Industrialized Countries, 1977; U.S. Industrial Relations: The Next Twenty Years, 1958. Home: 231 Lexington St East Lansing MI 48823 Office: Sch Labor and Indsl Relations Mich State Univ East Lansing MI 48824

STIEF, LOUIS JOHN, chemist; b. Pottsville, Pa., July 26, 1933; s. Louis Norman and Dorothy Elizabeth (Bassler) S.; B.A., La Salle Coll., 1955; Ph.D., Catholic U. Am., 1960; m. Kathleen J. Talbot, Nov. 30, 1963; children—Andrew, Lorraine. Nat. Acad. Scis.-NRC postdoctoral research asso. Nat. Bur. Standards, Washington, 1960-61; NATO postdoctoral fellow, ind. researcher chemistry dept. Sheffield (Eng.) U., 1961-63; sr. scientist, sr. chemist Melpar, Inc., Falls Church, Va., 1963-68; Nat. Acad. Scis.-NRC sr. postdoctoral research asso. NASA/Goddard Space Flight Center, Greenbelt, Md., 1968-69, astrophysicist, 1969-74, head br. astrochemistry, 1974—; adj. prof. chemistry Cath. U. Am. Fellow Washington Acad. Sci.; mem. Am. Chem. Soc., Chem. Soc. (London), Am. Astron. Soc., Sigma Xi. Research, numerous publs., especially in Jour. Chem. Physics. Office: NASA Goddard Space Flight Center Code 691 Greenbelt MD 20071

STIEFEL, HERBERT JULIUS, advt. agy. exec.; b. N.Y.C., Apr. 18, 1917; s. Gustav and Martha (Heilner) S.; student pub. schs., N.Y.C.; m. Lucy St. Hilaire Hillary, July 9, 1970; children by previous marriage—Philip, Gail (Mrs. Joseph Paul Mitchell); stepchildren—Hillary, Jennifer. With May Co., Balt., 1939-42, asst. advt. mgr., 1941-42; layout man, asst. account exec. Stone-Wright Studios, 1946-61; v.p. Charles W. Hoyt Co., 1961-64; pres. Coordinated Mktg. Agy., 1964-66, Stiefel/Raymond Advt. Inc., 1966—; (all N.Y.C.). Speaker on mktg., merchandising and sales promotion; lectr. advt. and mktg. Adelphi U., Fairleigh Dickinson U., Rutgers U. Scoutmaster, Boy Scouts Am., Greenwich, Conn., also bd. dirs. Greenwich council; founder, pres. Art Barn, Greenwich, Greenwich Student Loan Found.; pres. Am. Field Service, Greenwich; mem. European Econ. Council; mem. exec. com. Regional Export Expansion Council, 1973—. Chmn. bd. dirs. Carl Duisberg Soc. Am. Served to capt., inf. AUS, 1942-46. Recipient Horatio Alger award, 1975. Mem. Advt. Club N.Y. (co-chmn. membership com.), German Am. C. of C., Deutscher Verein. Mem. Marble Collegiate Ch. (lay preacher, Sunday Sch. tchr., communications com., exec. council). Clubs: Rotary (pres. N.Y.C. 1971-72); Milbrook Country; Indian Harbor Yacht; Coral Beach (Bermuda); Point of Woods (Fire Island, N.Y.). Home: Mead's Point Greenwich CT 06830 Office: Chrysler Bldg New York NY 10017

STIEHM, E. RICHARD, pediatrician, educator; b. Milw., Jan. 22, 1933; s. Reuben Harold and Marie Dueno S.; B.S., U. Wis., 1954, M.D., 1957; m. Judith Hicks, July 12, 1958; children—Jamie Elizabeth, Carrie Eleanor, Meredith Ellen. Intern, Phila. Gen. Hosp., 1957-58; fellow U. Wis., 1958-59; resident in pediatrics Babies Hosp.,

N.Y.C., 1961-63; fellow immunology U. Calif., San Francisco, 1963-65; asst. prof. pediatrics U. Wis., 1965-68, asso. prof., 1968-69; asso. prof. UCLA, 1969-72, prof., 1972—, chief div. immunology and allergy, 1969—, co-dir. Center for Interdisciplinary Research in Immunologic Diseases. Served to lt. M.C., USNR, 1959-61. Recipient Ross Research award Western Soc. Pediatric Research, 1971; E. Mead Johnson award for pediatric research, 1974. Diplomate Am. Bd. Pediatrics, Am. Bd. Allergy and Clin. Immunology. Mem. AAAS, Am. Assn. Immunologists, Western Soc. Pediatric Research, Soc. Pediatric Research, Am. Pediatric Soc., Am. Acad. Allergy, Am. Acad. Pediatrics, Am. Soc. Clin. Investigation, Alpha Delta Phi, Phi Beta Kappa, Alpha Omega Alpha. Editor: (with V. Fulginiti) Immunologic Disorders in Infants and Children, 1973. Asso. editor: Pediatrics Update, 1978—. Editorial bd. Pediatrics, 1972-78, Pediatrics in Rev., 1978—, Jour. Allergy and Clinical Immunology, 1976—. Contbr. articles in field to profl. jours. Home: 434 24th St Santa Monica CA 90402 Office: UCLA Center for the Health Sciences Los Angeles CA 90024

STIER, HOWARD LIVINGSTON, food co. exec.; b. Delmar, Del., Nov. 28, 1910; s. Morris Livingston and Ethel Blanche (Karns) S.; B.S., U. Md., 1932, M.S., 1937, Ph.D., 1939; m. Ruth A. Kaldenbach, Nov. 28, 1933 (div. June 1940); 1 dau., Nancy; m. 2d, Patricia M. Willingham, Sept. 1, 1940; children—Howard Livingston, Elizabeth, Susan, John. Agt., Dept. Agr., Beltsville, Md., 1933-35; research asst. U. Md., 1937-39, instr., then asst. prof. horiculture, 1939-41, extension prof. marketing, head dept., 1946-51; dir. div. statistics Nat. Canners Assn., Washington, 1951-61; dir. quality control United Fruit Co., Boston, 1961-71, dir., devel. and prodn. supporting services, 1972; v.p. United Brands Co., Boston and N.Y.C., 1972-79, cons., 1979—; professorial lectr. George Washington U., 1957-61. Chmn. adv. com. marketing Bur. Census, 1957-67; mem. research adv. com. Dept. Agr., 1962-64; adv. com. Dept. Def., 1963; mem. task group quality control of foods Nat. Acad. Sci., 1964. Served to col. AUS, 1941-46. Decorated Legion of Merit. Fellow AAAS, Am. Soc. Quality Control (dir. 1961-62, 70-72, v.p. 1966-69, pres. 1974, chmn. bd. 1975); mem. Am. Mktg. Assn. (dir. 1953-55, 57-58, v.p. 1955-56), Am. Soc. Hort. Sci., Am. Statis. Assn., Biometric Soc., Inst. Food Technologists, U. Md. Agrl. Alumni Assn. (pres. 1956), Sigma Xi, Alpha Zeta, Kappa Phi Kappa, Alpha Gamma Rho. Author: Quality Control in the Food Industry, 1974. Home: 23 Snow Hill Rd S Box 126 Grantham NH 03753 Office: United Brands Co 1271 Ave of Americas New York NY 10020

STIERS, DAVID OGDEN, actor; b. Peoria, Ill., Oct. 31, 1942; s. Kenneth Truman and Margaret Elizabeth (Ogden) S.; diploma drama div. Juilliard Sch., 1973. Actor, Actors Workshop, 1962, Calif. Shakespeare Festival, 1963-68; mem. The Committee, 1968-70, San Francisco (revue)/Broadway season City Center Acting Co., N.Y.C., 1974; featured in Ullysses in Nighttown, Broadway, 1974; co-star The Magic Show, Broadway, 1974-75; regular MASH TV series, 1977—. Voting mem. Nat. Acad. Rec. Arts and Scis. *

STIERS, ROBERT ARCHER, metal products co. exec.; b. Beverly, Ohio, Nov. 26, 1927; s. Forrest C. and Florence (Archer) S.; B.S. in Bus. Adminstrn., Ohio State U., 1951; m. Beverly Lou Cottrill, June 28, 1952; children—Robert Jacob, Thomas Jay. Plant controller Jeffrey Mfg. Co., Columbus, Ohio, 1951-53; mgr. budgeting and estimating Dayton Malleable, Inc. (Ohio), 1954-70, sec., 1970-72, sec.-treas., 1972—. Sec.-treas. Dayton Malleable Found., 1971—. Served with USNR, 1945-47. Home: 4716 Silverwood Dr Kettering OH 45429 Office: 3931 S Dixie Ave Kettering OH 45439

STIEVATER, JAMES EDWARD, office furniture mfg. co. exec.; b. Mishawaka, Ind., Apr. 3, 1934; s. Edward Allen and Anna (Pozzi) S.; B.S., U. Notre Dame, 1956; M.B.A., Mich. State U., 1961; m. Mary Jo Nichols, Feb. 8, 1958; children—Michael, Lisa, Regina. Div. accountant Kroger Co., Grand Rapids, Mich., 1956-60; staff asst. to pres. Lear Siegler Instrument div., Grand Rapids, 1960-65; controller, asst. treas. Rapistan, Inc., Grand Rapids, 1965-70; v.p. finance New Britain (Conn.) Machine div. Litton Industries, controller metal cutting group, 1970-71; treas., dir. finance Leigh Products Inc., Coopersville, Mich., 1971; corporate controller Steelcase Inc., Grand Rapids, 1971—; part-time mem. faculty Aquinas Coll., 1965-69. Unit capt. Grand Rapids United Community Fund drives, 1965, 69; bus. adviser Jr. Achievement, 1959-60; bd. dirs. S.E. YMCA, Grand Rapids, 1977. Mem. Fin. Execs. Inst., Nat. Assn. Accountants, Am. Inst. Corp. Controllers. Roman Catholic (pres. St. Paul The Apostle Sch. Bd. 1973-74). Clubs: Notre Dame Alumni, Mich. State U. Alumni. Home: 2315 Ridgecroft SE Grand Rapids MI 49506 Office: 1120 36th St SE Grand Rapids MI 49508

STIFEL, LAURENCE DAVIS, found. exec.: b. Cleve., Aug. 29, 1930; s. Richard Ernest and Loretta Ann (Davis) S.; A.B. in Econs., Harvard U., 1952, M.B.A., 1954; LL.B., Cleve. Marshall Law Sch., 1960; Ph.D. in Econs., Western Res. U., 1962; L.H.D., Urbana Coll., 1976; m. Dell C. Chenoweth, June 16, 1962; children—Laura Chenoweth, David Calvert. Admitted to Ohio bar, 1960; asst. prof. econs. Willamette U., Salem, Oreg., 1961-62; program economist AID, Rangoon, Burma, 1962-64; econ. adviser Nat. Econ. Devel. Bd., Bangkok, 1964-67; social sci. project leader Rockefeller Found. in Thailand, also vis. prof. econs. Thammasat U., Bangkok, 1967-74; vis. fellow Econ. Growth Center, Yale U., 1969-70; sec. Internat. Agrl. Devel. Service, N.Y.C., 1975-79; sec. Rockefeller Found., N.Y.C., 1974-78, asso. dir. social scis., 1977-78, v.p., sec., 1978—; trustee Gen. Edn. Bd., N.Y.C., 1974—, Princeton-in-Asia, 1976—; mem. governing council Rockefeller Archive Center. Fulbright fellow, Philippines, 1959-60. Mem. Asia Soc. (chmn. Thai council 1975-77), Siam Soc. (council 1969-72), Soc. Internat. Devel. (v.p., co-founder Bangkok chpt. 1968-70), Council Fgn. Relations, Am. Econs. Assn., Assn. Asian Studies. Clubs: Century Assn., Harvard (N.Y.C.). Author: The Textile Industry-A Case Study of Industrial Development in the Philippines, 1963; Reports on the Burmese Economy, 1964; Methodology for Preparation of the Second Economic and Social Development Plan of Thailand, 1967; also articles. Co-editor: Education and Training for Public Sector Management in the Developing Countries, 1977. Home: 60 Lafayette Rd W Princeton NJ 08540 Office: 1133 Ave of Americas New York NY 10036

STIFF, JOHN STERLING, city mgr.; b. McKinney, Tex., Feb. 14, 1921; s. James Harrison and Elva (Boone) S.; student Tex. A. and M. Coll., 1938-41; B.E., Yale, 1947; m. Harriett Raschig, May 21, 1946; children—Mark, Justin. Mgmt. trainee City of Big Spring, Tex., 1938-39, 41-42; city engr., Abilene, Tex., 1947-51; city mgr. Irving, Tex., 1953-57; gen. mgr. Hardee-Pipkin Constrn.Co., Irving, 1957-58; city mgr., Garland, Tex., 1958-63, Amarillo, Tex., 1963—. Served with USNR, 1942-46, 51-52. Registered profl. engr., Tex. Mem. Internat., Tex. (past pres.) city mgrs. assns., Amarillo, Dallas chambers commerce, Garland Home Builders Assn. Methodist. Rotarian. Clubs: Amarillo A. and M., Amarillo Yale. Home: 7100 Dreyfus St Amarillo TX 79106 Office: PO Box 1971 Amarillo TX 79186

STIFF, ROBERT HENRY, dentist, educator; b. Pitts., Apr. 23, 1923; s. Oliver R. and Ruth A. (Goucher) S.; B.S., U. Pitts., 1940, D.D.S., 1945, M.Ed., 1953; m. Margaret J. Raley, Oct. 18, 1945; children—Barry, Dwight, Heather. Engaged in pvt. practice dentistry, Pitts., 1945-59; instr. U. Pitts., 1945-50, asst. prof., 1950-53, asso. prof., 1954-65, prof., head dept. oral medicine and radiology, 1963-76, dir. clinics, 1976—, asst. dean Sch. Dental Medicine, 1979—; lectr., cons. to U. Garyounis, Benghazi, Libya, 1978—. Served to capt. Dental Corps, AUS, 1946-48. Fellow Am. Coll. Dentists; mem. Am. Acad. Oral Pathology, Am. Dental Assn., Orgn. Tchrs. Oral Diagnosis, Pa. Dental Assn., Omicron Kappa Upsilon. Home: 4601 Doverdell Dr Pittsburgh PA 15236

STIFF, ROBERT MARTIN, newspaper editor; b. Detroit, Aug. 25, 1931; s. Martin L. and Gladys (Mathews) S.; B.A. in Radio and Journalism, 1953; m. Janet Carol Kaser, Oct. 10, 1953; children—David Alan, Amy Anne. Reporter, bur. chief, city editor Painesville (Ohio) Telegraph, 1953-61; deskman, asst. city editor, sports editor, city editor, day editor, state editor, asst. mng. editor St. Petersburg (Fla.) Times, 1961-67; editor St. Petersburg Evening Ind., 1967—; dir. St. Petersburg Times Pub. Co., 1969—. Mem. A.P. Assn. Fla. (pres. 1970—), Am. (chmn. ethics com. 1978-79), Fla. (pres. 1975—), socs. newspaper editors, A.P. Mng. Editors Assn., Sigma Delta Chi (pres. West coast chpt. 1970—). Home: 1491 87th Ave N St Petersburg FL 33702 Office: PO Box 1121 St Petersburg FL 33731

STIGLER, GEORGE JOSEPH, economist, educator; b. Renton, Wash., Jan. 17, 1911; s. Joseph and Elizabeth (Hungler) S.; B.B.A., U. Wash., 1931; M.B.A., Northwestern U., 1932; Ph.D., U. Chgo., 1938; Sc.D., Carnegie Mellon U., 1973, U. Rochester, 1974, Helsinki Sch. Econs., 1976, Northwestern U., 1979; m. Margaret Mack, Dec. 26, 1936 (dec. Aug. 1970); children—Stephen, David, Joseph. Asst. prof. econs. Iowa State Coll., 1936-38; asst. prof. U. Minn., 1938-41, asso. prof., 1941-44, prof., 1944-46; prof. Brown U., 1946-47; prof. econs. Columbia, 1947-58; Walgreen prof. Am. instns. U. Chgo., 1958—, dir. Center Study Economy and the State, 1977—; lectr., London Sch. Econs., 1948; vice chmn., dir. Securities Investor Protection Corp., 1971-74. Mem. atty. gen.'s. com. for study anti-trust laws, 1954-55; mem. Blue Ribbon Def. Panel. Trustee Carleton Coll. Guggenheim fellow, 1955; fellow Center for Advanced Study in Behavioral Scis., 1957-58. Fellow Am. Statis. Soc., Econometric Soc., Nat. Acad. Sci.; mem. Am. Econ. Assn. (pres. 1964), Royal Econ. Soc. Am. Philos. Soc., History of Econs. Soc. (pres. 1977), Mt. Pelerin Soc. (pres. 1977-78). Author: Production and Distribution Theories, 1940; The Theory of Price, 1946; Trends in Output and Employment, 1947; Five Lectures on Economic Problems, 1949; (with K. Boulding) Readings in Price Theory, 1952; Trends in Employment in the Service Industries, 1956; (with D. Blank) Supply and Demand for Scientific Personnel, 1957; The Intellectual and the Market Place, 1964; Essays in the History of Economics, 1965; The Organization of Industry, 1968; (with J.K. Kindahl) The Behavior of Industrial Prices, 1970; The Citizen and the State, 1975. Editor: Jour. Polit. Economy, 1972—. Contbr. articles to profl. jours. Office: U Chgo 1101 E 58th St Chicago IL 60637

STIGWOOD, ROBERT, theatre, movie, TV and record producer; b. Adelaide, Australia, 1934; attended Sacred Heart Coll. Worked as copywriter for advt. agy., Adelaide; came to Eng., 1956, held series of jobs, including mgr. provincial theatre and halfway house for delinquents in Cambridge; opened talent agy., London, 1962; first ind. record producer in Eng. with release of single Johnny Remember Me; liquidated firm, 1965, became bus. mgr. for group Graham Bond Orgn.; became co-mng. dir. NEMS Enterprises, 1967; established own firm Robert Stigwood Orgn., 1967; formed RSO Records, 1973; became dir. of Polygram, 1976; producer films, including: Jesus Christ Superstar, Bugsy Malone, Tommy, Saturday Night Fever, Grease, Sergeant Pepper's Lonely Hearts Club Band, Moment by Moment; producer stage musicals in Eng. and U.S., including: Hair, Oh! Calcutta, The Dirtiest Show in Town, Pippin, Jesus Christ Superstar, Evita; TV producer in Eng. and U.S., prodns. include: The Entertainer (dramatic spl.), The Prime of Miss Jean Brodie (dramatic series). Named Internat. Producer of Year, ABC Interstate Theaters, Inc., 1976. Office: Robert Stigwood Orgn Inc 1775 Broadway New York NY 10019*

STILES, JOHN STEPHEN, wholesale distbn. exec.; b. Green Bay, Wis., Mar. 29, 1913; s. Walter Stephen and Leela (McCurdy) S.; A.B., Dartmouth, 1936; m. Mabel Selberg, May 27, 1939; children—Cynthia Lee (Mrs. Donald J. Ross), Stephanie Lynne (Mrs. James E. Sullivan), Christine Laney (Mrs. Charles Bylsma). With Morley-Murphy Co., Green Bay, 1936—, dir., 1942—, pres., 1953-77, chmn., 1974—; mem. exec. com., dir. Employers Ins., Wausau, Wis.; mem. exec. com., dir. Asso. Banc-Corp.; dir. Wis. Pub. Service Corp., Kellogg Citizens Nat. Bank, Green Bay Packers, Inc., Employers of Wausau Ins. Co. (U.K.) Ltd., London. Mem. exec. com. Nat. Assn. Congl. Christian Chs., 1973-76. Bd. dirs. Wis. Taxpayers Alliance; bd. dirs. Bellin Meml. Hosp., Green Bay, 1954-78, vice chmn., 1956-78. Mem. Nat. Wholesale Hardware Assn. (pres. 1957-59), Green Bay C. of C. (v.p. 1958-63), Phi Kappa Psi (exec. council 1935-37). Conglist. Mason (Shriner), Rotarian. Home: 436 Randall Ave DePere WI 54115 Office: 700 Morley Rd Green Bay WI 54303

STILES, NORMAN B., TV story editor and writer; b. N.Y.C., Dec. 4, 1942; s. Joseph and Dolly (Greene) S.; B.A., Hunter Coll., 1964. Writer Merv Griffin Show, N.Y.C., 1969-70; writer Sesame St. show, N.Y.C., 1971-74, head writer, 1974-75; co-creator/story editor When Things Were Rotten, Paramount TV, Los Angeles, 1975—; co-writer Fernwood 2-Night, 1978, America 2-Nite, 1978; co-producer series Bad News Bears, 1979—. Recipient Emmy award for writing Sesame St., 1974; Gold Album for Sesame St. Fever, 1978. Author: (with Daniel Wilcox) Perils of Penelope, 1972; (with Emily Kingsley, Jeffrey Moss and Daniel Wilcox) Sesame Street 1, 2, 3 Story Book, 1973; (with Daniel Wilcox and Jeffrey Moss) Sesame Street ABC Storybook, 1974. Home and office: 8235 Fountain Ave Los Angeles CA 90046

STILL, BAYRD, educator; b. Woodstock, Ill., July 7, 1906; s. Guy E. and Carrie (Bayrd) S.; A.B., U. Wis., 1928, A.M., 1929, Ph.D., 1933. Asst. prof. history U. Wis., Milw., 1932-38; asso. prof. history Duke U., 1938-47; prof. history N.Y. U., 1947-74, head history dept., 1955-70, acting dean Coll. Arts and Sci., 1958-60, acting dean Grad. Sch. Arts and Sci., 1971, dir. Archives Office, 1974—. Vis. prof. history Columbia, 1966-67. Mem. Landmarks Preservation Commn., N.Y.C., 1962-65, Task Force Municipal Archives, N.Y.C., 1966—. Trustee Inst. Early N.Y.C. History. Served as 1st lt. to lt. col. USAAF, 1942-46. Decorated Legion of Merit. Pintard fellow N.Y. Hist. Soc.; Gallatin fellow N.Y. U.; asso. Columbia U. Seminar on the City. Mem. Am. Hist. Assn. (chmn. local arrangements com. ann. conv. 1954), Orgn. Am. Historians, Soc. Am. Historians, Urban History Group, Phi Beta Kappa, Phi Kappa Phi, Delta Upsilon. Author: Milwaukee: The History of a City, 1948, rev. edit., 1965; Mirror for Gotham: New York as Seen By Contemporaries from Dutch Days to the Present, 1956; The West: Contemporary Records of America's Expansion across the Continent, 1607-1890, 1961; Pionniers vers l'Ouest, 1965, 73; New York City, a Student's Guide to Localized History, 1965; Urban America: A History with Documents, 1974; (with Joseph J. Roberto) Greenwich Village: A Brief Architectural and Historical Guide, 1975; contbr. to New York: The Centennial Years, 1976; Essays in the History of New York City, 1978; co-author, participant CBS-TV series America in the Making, 1954-55. Editor: The Official Pictorial History of the A.A.F. (with John T. McCoy), 1947; mem. editorial bd. N.Y.C. Almanac and Guide, 1957, Jour. Urban History, 1973—. Contbr. articles to profl. jours., mags. Home: 2 Fifth Ave New York City NY 10011

STILL, CLYFFORD, artist; b. Grandin, N.D., Nov. 30, 1904; B.A., Spokane U., 1933; M.A., Wash. State Coll.; D.F.A., Md. Inst., Balt., 1967; D.F.A. (hon.), N.D. State U., 1972, San Francisco Art Inst., 1976. Mem. faculty Wash. State Coll., 1935-41, Richmond Profl. Inst. Coll. of William and Mary, 1943-45, Calif. Sch. Fine Arts, 1946-50, (originated) Subject of the Artist, N.Y.C., 1947-48, U. Pa., 1963, Hunter Coll., 1951, Bklyn. Coll., 1952; mem. Yaddo, 1934, 35; exhibited in one-man shows at San Francisco Mus. Art, 1943, Palace of Legion of Honor, San Francisco, 1947 Betty Parsons Gallery, N.Y., 1947, 50, 51, Metart Gallery, San Francisco, 1950, Art of This Century, N.Y.C., 1946, Albright Art Gallery Buffalo, 1959, U. Pa., 1963, Marlborough Gallery, N.Y., 1969, Met. Mus. Art, N.Y.C., 1979, others; exhibited in group shows 15 Americans, Mus. Modern Art, N.Y., 1952, The New Am. Painting, Europe, 1958-69, Documenta II, Kassel, 1959, others; represented in permanent collections Balt. Mus. Art, Albright-Knox Gallery, Buffalo, Kunsthalle Mus., Basel, Switzerland, Mus. Modern Art, N.Y.C., Whitney Mus. Art, N.Y.C., Tate Gallery, London, San Francisco Mus. Modern Art, numerous others. Mem. Am. Acad. Arts and Letters (Gold medal award of merit for painting 1972). Donor paintings to San Francisco Mus. Modern Art, 1975. Address: Box 337 New Windsor MD 21776

STILL, RAY, musician; b. Elwood, Ind., Mar. 12, 1920; s. Roy R. and Lillian (Taylor) S.; student Pacific States U., 1941-42, 43, Juilliard Sch. Music, 1946-47; m. Mary Brock, Oct. 23, 1940; children—Mimi, Thomas, Susan, James. Began study of oboe, 1936; appeared with Kansas City (Mo.) Symphony, 1939-41; solo oboist Buffalo Philharmonic, 1947-49, Balt. Symphony, 1949-53; solo oboist Chgo. Symphony Orch., 1953—, Strauss Concerto, Mozart Oboe Concerto (1st Chgo. Symphony performances), also English horn N.Y. Philharmonic; solo oboist, tchr. Aspen Music Festival, 1960, 75; rec. musician RCA; solo recs. Concertapes-Concertdiscs, Telefunken; soloist Fine Arts Quartet, Tres Corda Trio, N.Y. Woodwind Quintette, Juilliard String Quartet, Vermeer Quartet, Internat. Trio; tchr. oboe Roosevelt U.; prof. Northwestern U.; coach, condr., artist-in-residence Stratford, Ont., Can. Festival Orch.; concertized in Japan, coached woodwinds Japan Philharmonic Orch., 1968, 70, Marlboro Music Festival, 1969-70; prof. Northwestern U. Sch. Music. Served with USAAF, 1943-46. Club: Arts (Chgo.). Home: 585 Hawthorne Pl Chicago IL 60657 Office: Orch Hall Michigan Ave Chicago IL 60604

STILL, RICHARD RALPH, educator; b. Nampa, Idaho, Apr. 19, 1921; s. Ralph Essick and Helen Elizabeth (Casey) S.; B.A., U. Idaho, 1942; M.B.A., Stanford, 1949; Ph.D., U. Wash., 1953; m. Mary Cathern Austin, Dec. 21, 1947; 1 dau., Roberta F. (Mrs. Craig Holland). Instr., U. Wash., 1949-53; asst. prof. U. Rochester, 1953-55; asso. prof. Syracuse U., 1955-60, prof., chmn. marketing dept., 1960-68, dir. Bus. Research Center, 1956-58, faculty dir. Grad. Sch. Sales Mgmt. and Marketing, 1962-64; vis. prof. U. W.I., 1965-66, Cornell U., 1966-68; prof. marketing U. Ga., Athens, 1968—, dir. internat. bus. studies, 1973-77. Cons. Govt. Spain, 1958; vis. prof. U. Calif., 1960; external examiner U. W.I., 1967-79. Served to 1st lt. F.A., AUS, 1942-46. Mem. Am., So. mktg. assns., AAUP, Am. Inst. Decision Scis., Acad. Internat. Bus., Acad. Mgmt., Blue Key, Delta Tau Delta, Beta Gamma Sigma. Democrat. Presbyn. Author: (with E. Cundiff) Sales Management, 1958, 3d edit., 1976; Basic Marketing 1964, 2d edit., 1971; Essentials of Marketing, 1966, 2d edit., 1972; (with C. Harris) Cases in Marketing, 1972; (with E. Cundiff, N. Govoni) Fundamentals of Modern Marketing, 3d edit., 1980. Contbr. to Modern Marketing Handbook, 1970, Marketing Manager's Handbook, 1973, Annual Review of Marketing, 1978. Editorial rev. bd. Jour. Marketing, 1973-78, Jour. Bus. Research, 1978—. Home: 190 Ravenwood Ct Athens GA 30605

STILL, STEPHEN ALLEN, newspaper editor; b. Akron, Ohio, June 2, 1919; s. Emerson Burton and Ruth Irene (Ferrell) S.; student Akron U., 1939-40; m. Constantine M. Stedman, Oct. 2, 1943; children—Michael A., Timothy B., Stephanie D. Reporter, Akron Beacon Jour., 1940-41; reporter, columnist Richmond (Calif.) Ind., 1945-50; editor Oroville (Calif.) Mercury, 1950-53; mem. staff Oakland (Calif.) Tribune, 1953—, mng. editor, 1963—, met. editor, 1977—; dir. public relations St. Mary's Hosp., San Francisco, 1978—. Served with USNR, 1941-45. Decorated knight Order St. Gregory. Roman Catholic. Club: K.C. (past grand knight Richmond). Contbr. articles to profl. jours. Office: St Mary's Hosp 450 Stanyan St San Francisco CA 94117

STILLE, JOHN KENNETH, educator; b. Tucson, May 8, 1930; s. John Rudolph and Margaret Victoria (Sakrison) S.; B.S., U. Ariz., 1952, M.S., 1953; Ph.D., U. Ill., 1957; m. Dolores Jean Engelking, June 7, 1958; children—John Robert, James Kenneth. Instr. organic chemistry U. Iowa, Iowa City, 1956-59, asst. prof., 1959-63, asso. prof., 1963-65, prof., 1965-77; prof. Colo. State U., Ft. Collins, 1977—; guest prof. Royal Inst. Tech., Stockholm, 1969; cons. E.I. duPont de Nemours & Co., Inc. Served to lt. comdr. USNR, 1953-55. Fellow Chem. Soc. London; mem. Am. Chem. Soc. (chmn. polymer div. 1975), Phi Lambda Upsilon, Alpha Chi Sigma, Soc. Sigma Xi. Author: Introduction to Polymer Chemistry, 1962; Industrial Organic Chemistry, 1968. Editor: Condensation Monomers (vol. 27 High Polymers). Asso. editor Macromolecules; editorial bd. Fortschritte der Hochpolymeren Forschung, Macromolecular Synthesis; adv. bd. Jour. Polymer Sci. Home: 1523 Miramont St Fort Collins CO 80521 Office: Dept Chemistry Colo State U Fort Collins CO 80523

STILLER, JERRY, actor; b. N.Y.C., June 8; s. William and Bella Stiller; B.S. in Speech and Drama, Syracuse U., 1950; m. Anne Meara, Sept. 14, 1954; children—Amy, Benjamin. Actor in summer stock, 1951, 52, 53, with nat. co. of Peter Pan, 1951, also at Henry St. Settlement, 1941, Cherry Lane Theatre, N.Y.C., 1949, Billy Barnes Showboat, Chgo., 1950, Erie (Pa.) Playhouse, 1951, 52, Memphis Arena Theatre, 1952, Phoenix Theatre, 1954, 55, 56, Shakespeare Festival Theatre, Stratford, Conn., 1955; mem. Shakespeare Co. in Central Park, N.Y.C., 1957, 71; Broadway appearances include: The Golden Apple, 1954, The Ritz, 1975, Unexpected Guests, 1977; film appearances include The Taking of Pelham, One, Two, Three, 1973, Airport '75, 1975, The Ritz, 1976, Nasty Habits, 1976, Those Lips, Those Eyes, 1979; off-Broadway appearance in Boubouroche, 1971; co-star TV series Joe and Sons, 1975; mem. comedy team with wife Anne Meara, 1961—; night club appearances include Compass Players, St. Louis, 1957, Happy Medium, Chgo., 1960, also Village Gate, Village Vanguard, Blue Angel, Bon Soir and Phase Two, N.Y.C., Mr. Kelly's, Chgo., Hungry I, San Francisco, The Establishment, London, The Sands, Flamingo, Las Vegas, Harrah's Reno and Lake Tahoe; co-star daily TV series Take Five with Stiller and Meara, 1977-78; numerous appearances on TV games and talk shows, specials and variety shows, commercials for TV and radio. Recipient Disting. Alumnus award Syracuse U., 1973, Arents Pioneer Medal, 1979; Entertainment Father of Yr. award, 1977; co-recipient Voice of Imagery award Radio Advt. Bur., 1975. Address: care Janice S Morgan Communications 250 W 57th St New York NY 10019

STILLINGER, FRANK HENRY, chemist; b. Boston, Aug. 15, 1934; s. Frank Henry and Gertrude (Metcalf) S.; B.S., U. Rochester, 1955; Ph.D., Yale U., 1958; m. Dorothea Anne Keller, Aug. 18, 1956; children—Constance Anne, Andrew Metcalf. NSF postdoctoral fellow Yale U., 1958-59; with Bell Telephone Labs., Murray Hill, N.J., 1959—, head chem. physics dept., 1976—; mem. evaluation panel Nat. Bur. Standards. Welch Found. fellow, 1974. Recipient Elliott Cresson medal Franklin Inst., 1978. Fellow Am. Phys. Soc.; mem. AAAS, Sigma Xi. Club: Early Am. Coppers Inc. Contbr. articles to profl. jours. Home: 216 Noe Ave Chatham NJ 07928 Office: 600 Mountain Ave Murray Hill NJ 07974

STILLINGER, JACK CLIFFORD, educator; b. Chgo., Feb. 16, 1931; s. Clifford Benjamin and Ruth Evangeline (Hertzler) S.; B.A., U. Tex., Austin, 1953; M.A. (Nat. Woodrow Wilson fellow), Northwestern U., 1954; Ph.D., Harvard, 1958; m. Shirley Louise Van Wormer, Aug. 30, 1952; children—Thomas Clifford, Robert William, Susan, Mary; m. 2d, Nina Zippin Baym, May 21, 1971. Teaching fellow in English, Harvard, 1955-58; asst. prof. U. Ill., Urbana, 1958-61, asso. prof., 1961-64, prof. English, 1964—, permanent mem. Center for Advanced Study, 1970—. Guggenheim fellow, 1964-65. Mem. Modern Lang. Assn. Am., Keats-Shelley Assn. Am. (editorial bd. Jour.), Byron Soc., Phi Beta Kappa. Author: The Early Draft of John Stuart Mill's Autobiography, 1961; Anthony Munday's Zelauto, 1963; Wordsworth: Selected Poems and Prefaces, 1965; The Letters of Charles Armitage Brown, 1966; Twentieth Century Interpretations of Keats's Odes, 1968; Mill: Autobiography and Other Writings, 1969; The Hoodwinking of Madeline and Other Essays on Keats's Poems, 1971; The Texts of Keats's Poems, 1974; The Poems of John Keats, 1978. Editor: Jour. English and Germanic Philology, 1961-72. Home: 806 W Indiana St Urbana IL 61801

STILLINGS, FRANK STUART, univ. dean; b. London, Ky., Sept. 9, 1921; s. Taylor and Daisy (Gregory) S.; student U. Detroit, 1942-43; B.A. in Math., Berea Coll., 1947; Mus.M., U. Mich., 1949, Ph.D., 1956; m. Jean Boyce Gibbs, July 25, 1942; children—Scott G., Susan Taylor. From instr. to asso. prof. U. Mich., 1951-62; chmn. Kent State U. Sch. Music, 1962-66; dean Sch. Fine and Applied Arts, Central Mich. U., 1966-75, acting v.p. adminstrn., 1975-76, dean, 1976—. Vice pres. U. Mich. Employees Credit Union, 1957-62. Trustee Am. Council for Arts in Edn., exec. sec., 1968, v.p., 1973-75. Research grantee U. Mich., 1958, 61, Kent State U., 1963, 65. Served with AUS, 1942-46. Recipient Friday Nighter award Laurel County Homecoming, 1956. Mem. Nat. Assn. Schs. Music (past trustee), Music Tchrs. Nat. Assn. (v.p. 1965-67), Mich. Acad. Sci., Arts and Letters (pres. 1976), Am. Assn. State Colls. and Univs. (univ. asso. 1975—), North Central Assn. Colls. and Univs. (evaluator 1972—), Phi Kappa Phi. Translator: (F. Gasparini) The Practical Harmonist at the Harpsichord, 1963; transcriber: Handel Choruses for Study and Performance, 1965; Editor: The Sonatas of Beethoven, 1972; Am. Music Tchr., 1961-72. Contbr. to 1 vol. Carnegie Commn. Higher Edn. series, 1973. Contbr. articles on academia and collective bargaining to profl. jours. Home: 907 Glen Ave Mount Pleasant MI 48858

STILLMAN, CHAUNCEY (DEVEREUX), corp. exec.; b. N.Y.C., Nov. 9, 1907; s. Charles Chauncey and Mary (Wight) S.; student St. Bernards' Sch., N.Y. City, 1917-20, Groton Sch., 1920-24, Kent Sch., 1924-25; A.B., Harvard U., 1930; B.Arch., Columbia U., 1935; m. Theodora M. Jay, Jan. 21, 1939 (div. 1949); children—Emily (dec.), Elizabeth (Mrs. Stephen Q. Shafer), Mary. Pres. Free Am. Inc., mag., N.Y.C., 1939-47; chmn. Homeland Found., Inc., N.Y.C., 1939—; spl. adviser Office Sec. of Def., 1947; agy. staff officer under Nat. Security Council, 1948-51. Dir. N.Y. Eye and Ear Infirmary. Apptd. Privy Chamberlain to Pope Paul VI, 1964. Entered USNR, 1942, served on U.S.S. Enterprise and U.S.S. Lexington as squadron air combat intelligence officer, 1944-45; inactive duty as lt. comdr., 1945. Decorated 5 battle stars, Presdl. Unit citation, Navy Unit commendation. Recipient Cardinal Newman award of found., 1965, Caritas medal Niagara U., 1967. Mem. Soc. of Cincinnati, N.Y. Zool. Soc. (trustee). Roman Catholic. Clubs: Tavern (Boston); Knickerbocker, N.Y. Yacht (commodore 1964-66), Harvard (N.Y.C.); Coaching (London and N.Y.C.); Royal Yacht Squadron (Cowes, Eng.). Home: Wethersfield House Amenia NY 12501 Office: 230 Park Ave New York NY 10017

STILLMAN, DONALD DENNIS, union editor and press sec.; b. Tacoma, Wash., Sept. 23, 1945; s. Carl George and Annabelle (Morrison) S.; B.A. in Govt. magna cum laude, U. Redlands, 1967; M.S. in Journalism, Columbia, 1968. Copy editor AP-Dow Jones Econ. Report, N.Y.C., 1967-68, editorial asst. Columbia Journalism Rev., 1967-68; asst. prof. journalism W.Va. U., 1968-71; editor Miner's Voice newspaper Miners For Democracy, Charleston, W.Va., 1969-72; dir. Appalachian Pub. Interest Journalism Group, Charleston, 1971-72; dir. publs., editor jour. United Mine Workers, Washington, 1972-75; press sec. to pres., editor Solidarity, United Auto Workers, Detroit, 1975—. Cons. Youth Project. Mem. Am. Newspaper Guild, Detroit Press Club. Democrat. Contbr. articles to profl. jours., popular mags., including Life mag., Wall St. Jour., Washington Post Book World, Chgo. Daily News, The Progressive. Home: 2984 Iroquois St Detroit MI 48214 Office: 8000 E Jefferson Ave Detroit MI 48214

STILLMAN, RICHARD NOYES, chem. co. exec.; b. Bklyn., Aug. 17, 1918; s. Ernest Samuel and Ella (Dorn) S.; B.S., Roanoke Coll., 1939; postgrad. Grad. Sch. Bus., N.Y. U., 1939-40; m. Lucille Knox, Feb. 14, 1946; children—Richard, Nancy, Robert. Staff accountant Touche, Niven & Co., C.P.A.'s, N.Y.C., 1939-41, Time, Inc., Chgo., 1946-47; controller Wesco Waterpaints, Inc., Berkeley, Cal., 1947-52; comptroller Stauffer Chem. Co., N.Y.C., 1952-70, treas., 1970-74, v.p., treas., 1974—; dir. Poeples Nat. Bank, Piscataway, N.J. Served with AUS, 1942-46. C.P.A., Ill. Mem. Financial Execs. Inst. Club: Landmark. Author: The Strategy of Investment, 1962; Financial Executives Handbook, 1970. Home: 8 Drum Hill Ln Stamford CT 06902 Office: Westport CT 06880

STILLMAN, W. PAUL, banker; b. Newark, Sept. 17, 1897; LL.D., Rider Coll., 1950, St. Lawrence U., 1964, Seton Hall U., 1967, Drew U., 1971, Rutgers U., 1975, Monmouth Coll., 1976. Chmn. bd. Mut. Benefit Life Ins. Co., Newark, 1st Nat. State Bank of N.J. (formerly Nat. State Bank, Newark), 1st Nat. State Bancorp., Newark; dir., mem. exec. com. Union Camp Corp.; dir. Tri-Continental Corp., Food Fair Stores, Inc., C.F. Mueller Co., Becton-Dickinson & Co. Commr., Port Authority of N.Y. and N.J., 1960—, vice chmn., 1974—; trustee United Hosps. Newark; bd. overseers Found. for Advancement Grad. Study in Engring.; chmn. Cancer Inst. N.J.; trustee N.Y. U.; adv. council dept. politics Princeton U.; chmn. N.J. Tercentenary Fund, 1962; pres. N.J. Electoral Coll., 1952; del.-at-large Republican Nat. Conv., 1956. Mem. SAR, N.J. C. of C. (treas., dir.). Home: 27 Cooney Terr Fair Haven NJ 07701 Office: 1st Nat State Bancorp 550 Broad St Newark NJ 07102

STILLWELL, G(EORGE) KEITH, physician; b. Moose Jaw, Sask., Can., July 11, 1918; s. George B. and Muriel (Bolster) S.; came to U.S., 1947, naturalized, 1964; B.A., U. Sask., 1939; M.D., Queen's U., Kingston, Ont., Can., 1942; Ph.D., U. Minn., 1954; m. Mildred Ethel Cameron, Mar. 12, 1943; children—Paul, Craig. Intern, Gen. Hosp., Kingston, 1942-43, resident, 1945; resident U. Minn., Mpls., 1947-51; pvt. practice medicine specializing in phys. medicine and rehab. Mpls., 1951-54; cons. dept. phys. medicine and rehab. Mayo Clinic, Rochester, Minn., 1954-73, chmn. dept. phys. medicine and rehab., 1973—; instr. U. Minn., 1950-54; instr. Mayo Grad. Sch. Medicine, 1955-60, asst. prof. phys. medicine and rehab., 1960-67, asso. prof., 1967-73; prof. Mayo Med. Sch., 1973—; vis. prof. Ohio State U., 1970. Served with M.C., Royal Can. Army, 1943-46. Diplomate Am. Bd. Phys. Medicine and Rehab. Mem. AAAS, AMA, Am. Acad. Phys. Medicine and Rehab. (editorial Bd. Archives Phys. Medicine and Rehab. 1960—, chmn. editorial bd. 1972-77, bd. govs. acad. 1963-70), Am. Congress Rehab. Medicine (Gold Key award 1973), Assn. Acad. Physiatrists, Am. Heart Assn. (stroke council). Unitarian. Contbr. numerous articles to med. publs. Office: Mayo Clinic Rochester MN 55901

STILLWELL, HAMILTON, ret. univ. adminstr.; b. Tennent, N.J., Feb. 21, 1915; s. Oliver Kipp and Grace (Hodapp) S.; B.S., Trenton State Coll., 1937; Ed.M., Rutgers U., 1941; Ed.D., N.Y. U., 1957; m. Agnes Christine Dooney, Apr. 22, 1943; children—Patricia, Richard. Tchr., prin. Cranbury (N.J.) Pub. Sch., 1937-47; prin. Milltown (N.J.) Pub. Sch., 1947-48; asso. prof., extension specialist Rutgers U., 1948-57; dir. Center for Adult Edn., Detroit (Wayne State U., U. Mich.), 1957-64; dean div. Urban Extension, prof. edn. Wayne State U., 1964-70; dean univ. extension div., prof. adult edn. Grad. Sch. Edn. Rutgers U., New Brunswick, 1970-77, prof. emeritus, 1977—. Exec. dir. Detroit Adventure (City Arts Council), 1961-70; chmn. N.J. Com. on Humanities, 1972; pres. Literacy Vols. of N.J., 1979-80. Served to maj. AUS, 1941-46. Recipient Alumni Citation award Trenton State Coll., 1958. Fund for Adult Edn. scholar, 1954. Mem. Adult Edn. Assn. U.S.A. (pres. 1967-68), N.J. (past pres.), Mich. (past pres.) adult edn. assns., Nat. Univ. Extension Assn. (exec. bd. 1975—), Alumni Assn. Trenton State Coll. (past pres.), Nat. Assn. State Univs. and Land Grant Colls. (chmn. council on extension 1972, mem. exec. com. 1973-76), Friends of N.J. Public Broadcasting (bd. dirs.), Phi Delta Kappa, Kappa Delta Pi. Club: Torch (Trenton). Contbr. articles to profl. jours. Home: 222 King George Rd Pennington NJ 08534 Office: Grad Sch Edn Rutgers U 10 Seminary Place New Brunswick NJ 08903

STILLWELL, MARGARET BINGHAM, bibliographer, writer; b. Providence, Jan. 26, 1887; d. Edward Augustus and Mary Elizabeth Bingham (Pindar) Stillwell; spl. student R.I. Sch. Design, 1899-1905; A.B., Brown U., 1909, hon. A.M., 1925, Litt.D., 1942, U. R.I., 1952. Asst., John Carter Brown Library, Providence, 1909-14; cataloguer rare book div. N.Y. Pub. Library, 1914-17; curator, librarian Annmary Brown Meml., 1917-53; prof. emerita bibliography Brown U., 1954—, Pres.'s fellow Brown U., 1951; hon. fellow Pierpont Morgan Library. Lectr., Sch. Library Service Columbia, 1927-31. Mem. Colonial Dames Am., Bibliog. Soc. Am. (v.p. 1935-36, hon.), Providence Preservation Soc., R.I. Hist. Soc., Institut d'Etudes Europeennes et Mondiales (corr. mem.), R.I. Short Story Club (past pres.), Phi Beta Kappa (pres. Women's Sect. R.I. Alpha chpt. 1925-26). Episcopalian. Clubs: Review, Providence Art; Grolier (N.Y.) (hon.), Hroswitha (hon.). Author: The Influence of William Morris and the Kelmscott Press, 1912; The Heritage of the Modern Printer, 1916; Washington Eulogies, 1916; General Hawkins as He Revealed Himself to His Librarian, 1923; The Fasciculus Temporum, 1924; The Annmary Brown Memorial: A Descriptive Essay, 1925; Incunabula and Americana, 1450-1800, A Key to Bibliographical Study, 1931; Gutenberg and the Catholicon, 1936; The Seventeenth Century (in The Dolphin History of the Printed Book), 1938; The Annmary Brown Memorial, A Booklover's Shrine, 1940; Noah's Ark in Early Woodcuts and Modern Rhymes, 1942; Bibliographical Survey; 15th and 16th Century books in The Hunt Botanical Collection, 1958; The Awakening Interest in Science during the First Century of Printing, 1450-1550, 1970; The Beginning of the World of Books, 1450 to 1470, with a Synopsis of the Gutenberg Documents, 1972; Rhythm and Rhymes: The Songs of a Bookworm, 1977; author and illustrator: While Benefit Street Was Young, 1943; The Pageant of Benefit Street Down Through the Years, 1945; Librarians Are Human: Memories In and Out of the Rare Book World, 1907-70, 1973. Editor, compiler: Incunabula in American Libraries, A Second Census, 1940. Home: Royal Manor East Greenwich RI 02818 Office: care of Annmary Brown Memorial Providence RI 02912

STILO, ANTHONY JOSEPH, ins. co. exec.; b. Bklyn., July 11, 1914; s. Arthur V. and Mary (Caridi) S.; student Bklyn. Coll., 1932-34, U. Pa., 1944-45; LL.B., St. John's U., 1949; m. Norma G. Simonetti, Aug. 29, 1943; children—George A., Vivian E. Admitted to N.Y. bar, 1949; v.p., sec. U.S. Life Ins. Co., 1950-70, USLife Corp., 1970-73; pres. USLife Title Ins. Co., N.Y.C., 1973-78; ret., 1978. Served with AUS, 1942-46. Mem. N.Y. State Bar Assn. Home: West Palm Beach FL

STILWELL, RICHARD DALE, baritone; b. St. Louis, May 6, 1942; s. Otho John Clifton and Tressie Fern (Parrish) S.; student Anderson Coll., 1960-62; Mus.B., Ind. U., 1966; m. Elizabeth Louise Jencks, Mar. 21, 1967. With Met. Opera Co., N.Y.C., 1970—; appearances in major roles with Met. Opera, N.Y.C., Washington Opera Soc., Marseilles (France) Opera Co., Sante Fe Opera, San Francisco Opera Co., Paris Opera Co., Teatro Alla Scala, Covent Garden, Hamburg State Opera, Glyndebourne Opera Festival (Eng.), Vancouver (B.C.) Opera Co., Chgo. Opera Co., Tanglewood Festival, others; soloist with Nat. Symphony, Washington, Chgo. Symphony, Am. Symphony, Carnegie Hall, N.Y.C., St. Louis Symphony, Double Arts Chorale at Philharmonic Hall, Met. Opera Studio at Tully Hall, N.Y.C., Boston Symphony, Los Angeles Philharmonic; soloist Presl. dinner in honor of Apollo 11 astronauts, Los Angeles, 1969; rec. artist. Served with AUS, 1966-69. Recipient Nat. Soc. Arts and Letters award, 1963, Young Artist award St. Louis, 1963, Fisher Found. award Met. Opera Auditions, 1965. Mem. Am. Guild Musical Artists. Home: 1969 Rockingham McLean VA 22101

STIMAC, MICHELE FRANCES, educator, counselor; b. Crested Butte, Colo., Sept. 15, 1929; d. Peter and Veronika (Stajduhar) Stimac; student (Scholastic scholar) Loretto Heights Coll., 1947-48; B.A. in Edn., Webster Coll., 1954; M.A. in English, St. Louis U., 1963; Ed.D., Boston U., 1973; m. William F. Roat, Aug. 5, 1978. Mem. Sisters of Loretto, 1948-70; elementary and intermediate sch. tchr., 1950-57; tchr. high sch. English and lit. St. Mary's Acad., Denver, also Newman Central High Sch., Sterling, Ill., 1957-67; instr. English, Webster Coll., St. Louis, summer 1966; engaged in campus ministry Salem (Mass.) State Coll., 1967-70; counselor, instr. psychology Boston U., 1970-73; dir. career counseling Babson Coll., Boston, 1973-75; prof., doctoral program counselor Pepperdine U., Los Angeles, 1975—. Mem. Nat. Assn. for Women Deans, Adminstrs. and Counselors, Am., Calif., Los Angeles personnel and guidance assns., Women Ednl. Leadership, Croatian Acad., Delta Kappa, Gamma, Phi Delta Kappa. Roman Catholic. Contbr. articles in areas of career devel. and humanistic edn. Home: 6225 Canterbury Dr Culver City CA 90230 Office: Pepperdine U 8035 S Vermont Ave Los Angeles CA 90044. *The key to living a large life is found in the art of transcendence.*

STIMMEL, BARRY, physician, univ. dean; b. Bklyn., Oct. 8, 1939; s. Abraham and Mabel (Bovit) S.; B.S., Bklyn. Coll., 1960; M.D., State U. N.Y., Bklyn., 1964; m. Barbara Barovick, June 6, 1970; children—Alexander, Matthew. Resident, Mt. Sinai Hosp., N.Y.C., 1964-65, 67-69; asst. dean admissions and student affairs Mt. Sinai Sch. Medicine, City U. N.Y., 1970-71, asso. dean, 1971—, asst. prof. medicine, 1972-75, asso. prof., 1975—, asso. dean acad. affairs, 1975—, asso. attending physician, 1975—; mem. com. planning, priorities and evaluation N.Y. Met. Regional Med. Program, 1971-73; adv. com. Nat. Center Urban Problems, City U. N.Y., 1970-71; adv. com. methadone maintenance Office of Drug Abuse Services State of N.Y., 1976—; sci. adv. bd. Nat. Council Drug Abuse, 1976—. Served with M.C., USNR, 1965-67. Diplomate Nat. Bd. Med. Examiners, Am. Bd. Internal Medicine. Mem. Am. Assn. Physicians Assts. (adv. bd. 1972-73), Am. Assn. Higher Edn., Soc. Study of Addiction to Alcohol and Other Drugs, Inst. Study of Drug Addiction, Am., N.Y. heart assns., Am., N.Y. State socs. internal medicine, Soc. Internal Medicine County of N.Y. (dir.), AAUP, Am. Coll. Cardiology, Greater N.Y. Coalition on Drug Abuse, Am. Ednl. Research Assn., Am. Fedn. Clin. Research. Author: Heroin Dependency: Medical, Social and Economic Aspects, 1975; Cardiovascular Effects Mood Altering Drugs, 1979. Editorial bd. Am. Jour. Drug and Alcohol, 1974—. Contbr. chpts. to books, articles profl. jours. Office: 100th St and Fifth Ave New York NY 10029

STIMMEL, THOMAS STRIBLING, journalist; b. Vancouver, B.C., Can., Apr. 29, 1925; s. Samuel Robert and Roberta (Tener) S.; A.B., Bethany (W.Va.) Coll., 1949; m. Lois Tugman, 1979. Reporter, Times-Leader, Martins Ferry, Ohio, 1950-53, A.P., Charleston, W.Va., 1953-56, Herald and News, Klamath Falls, Oreg., 1958-60, Oreg. Jour., Portland, 1960-64, Newhouse News Service, Washington, 1964-71, asso. editor editorial page Oreg. Jour., Portland, 1971-73, staff writer, 1973—. Chmn. Oreg. Gov.'s Scenic Waterways Adv. Com., 1977—. Served with AUS, 1944-46. Recipient 1st Pl. award wire news coverage W.Va. Press Assn., 1957. Mem. Phi Kappa Tau. Club: City (Portland, sec. 1974-75). Home: 6029 SE Taylor Ct Portland OR 97215 Office: 1320 SW Broadway Portland OR 97201

STIMPSON, JOHN H., ins. co. exec.; b. Milo, Maine, Nov. 7, 1926; s. Don H. and Dorrice A. (Clark) S.; B.A., U. Maine, 1950; M.B.A., U. Pa., 1952; m. Valerie B. Smith, June 13, 1953; children—Kevin, Karen, Kimberly. Exec. v.p. N.Y. Life Ins. Co., N.Y.C.; chmn. Variable Contracts Corp. C.L.U. Home: 42 W Clinton Ave Irvington-on-Hudson NY 10533 Office: 51 Madison Ave New York NY 10010

STIMSON, FREDERICK SPARKS, Hispanist, educator; b. Newark, Ohio, Jan. 1, 1919; s. Fred Samuel and Leah Kate (Sparks) S.; B.A., Ohio State U., 1940; postgrad. Harvard U., 1940-41; Jr. fellow in Archaeology, Princeton U., 1941-42; M.A., U. Mich., 1948, Ph.D. (Ford Found. grantee), 1952. Dir., Cultural Center for Dept. State, Medellin, Colombia, 1944-46; asst. public affairs officer Am. embassy, San Salvador, El Salvador, 1947; instr. to prof. dept. Spanish, Northwestern U., Evanston, Ill., 1954—, chmn. dept., 1976-79. Mem. Am. Assn. Tchrs. Spanish, MLA, Phi Beta Kappa. Author: Cuba's Romantic Poet, 1964; New Schools of Spanish American Poetry, 1970; Literatura de la America Hispanica, 3 vols., 1971-75; Los poemas mas representativos de Placido, 1976. Home: 9433 Lincolnwood Dr Evanston IL 60203 Office: Kresge 129 Northwestern U Evanston IL 60201

STINCHFIELD, FRANK EDWARD, surgeon; b. Warren, Minn., Aug. 12, 1910; s. Charles Edward and Mary (Frank) S.; B.S., Carleton Coll., 1932; M.D., Northwestern U., 1937; m. Margaret Taylor, Sept. 30, 1939; children—Lee Taylor, Ann. Intern, Wesley Meml.-Passavant hosps., Chgo., 1937-38; resident in surgery Columbia Presbyn.-N.Y. Orthopaedic hosps., N.Y.C., 1939-40; dir., chief surgeon N.Y. Orthopaedic Hosp., 1956-76; mem. staff Presbyn. Hosp., N.Y.C., 1940—, also pres. med. bd., 1971-75. Served to col., U.S. Army, 1942-46. Decorated Legion of Merit, Bronze star. Diplomate Am. Bd. Orthopaedic Surgery (past pres.). Fellow Royal Australasian Coll. Surgeons, Royal Coll. Surgeons (Eng.), Royal Soc. Medicine (Eng.), A.C.S. (past pres.), Am. Acad. Orthopaedic Surgeons (past pres.). Republican. Presbyterian. Clubs: Century Assn. (N.Y.C.); Elkridge Harford Hunt (Balt.). Home: 4997 Henry Hudson Pkwy New York NY 10471 Office: 161 Fort Washington Ave New York NY 10032

STINE, LEO CLAIR, educator; b. Danville, Ill., Oct. 18, 1914; s. Oscar and Della (Sanders) S.; B.Ed., Ill. State U., 1939; A.M., U. Ill., 1943, Ph.D., 1948; m. Margaret Glenn, Aug. 17, 1946; children—Marilyn Jane, Glen Raymond, Donna June, Susan Ann, Alan Charles. Recreation dir. WPA, 1939-40; ednl. adviser CCC, 1940-41; high sch. tchr., Champaign and Tolono, Ill., 1941-43; grad. asst. U. Ill., 1946-48; asso. prof. polit. sci. Milikin U., Decatur, Ill., 1948-52; prof. polit. sci. Western Mich. U., Kalamazoo, 1952-63, asso. dean Sch. Grad. Studies, 1963-69, dean continuing edn., 1969-77, acting dir. Center for Public Adminstrn., 1978-79, disting. prof. polit. sci., 1977-79, disting. emeritus prof., 1979—; chmn. coordinating council Continuing Higher Edn. Mich., 1974-75. Mem. coordinating council Continuing Higher Edn. Mich., 1969-76. Served with AUS, 1943-46. Mem. Am. Soc. Pub. Adminstrn., Kappa Delta Pi, Pi Gamma Mu, Phi Kappa Phi. Methodist. Editor: The New Campus, 1973-76. Contbr. articles to profl. jours. Home: 109 S Lauderdale St Kalamazoo MI 49007. *In my opinion success in my profession demands a much greater than average willingness to support change, sufficient personal security to accept risks and sufficient drive and determination to enable one to accept a position of policy leadership. Learning what to "overlook" is as important as knowing what to "look for". In other words, leadership in higher education involves setting priorities and following through after due consideration for the ideas and opinions of others. Finally, public leadership demands wise compromise.*

STINE, RICHARD DENGLER, ednl. adminstr.; b. Phila., Sept. 9, 1926; s. Harold S. and Alice E. (Dengler) S.; A.B., U. Pa., 1947, Ph.D., 1951; D.Lit., Monmouth (N.J.) Coll., 1973; m. Elizabeth White Leiby, May 18, 1968; children—Nancy Elizabeth, Catherine Morris, John Bower, Elizabeth Deane Leiby, Jane Erica Leiby. Dir. admissions Roanoke Coll., 1951-53, dir. admissions and devel., 1953-54; campaign dir. Tamblyn & Brown, N.Y.C., 1954-56; project dir. devel. U. Pa., 1956-60, dir. med. devel., 1960-67, asst. to v.p. devel. and pub. relations, 1967-68; asso. Heald, Hobson & Assos., N.Y.C., 1968-70; pres. Monmouth (Ill.) Coll., 1970-74; dir. undergrad. programs Wright Inst., Berkeley, Calif., 1974-76; v.p. for devel. Claremont (Calif.) U. Center, 1976—. Mem. corp. Haverford Coll. Club: University (Los Angeles). Home: 383 Blaisdell Dr Claremont CA 91711 Office: Harper Hall Claremont U Center Claremont CA 91711

STINEBRING, WARREN RICHARD, microbiologist, educator; b. Niagara Falls, N.Y., July 31, 1924; s. Clifford Thomas and Signe (Arvidson) S.; B.A., U. Buffalo, 1948; M.S., U. Pa., 1949, Ph.D., 1951; m. Delores Jean Zakes, June 12, 1948; children—Dan R., Beth E., Eric. With U. Pa., Phila., 1949-55, asso., 1953-55; asst. prof. U. Tex. Med. Br., Galveston, 1955-57; asso. research prof. Inst. Microbiology, Rutgers U., New Brunswick, N.J., 1957-60; asst. prof. U. Pitts. Coll.

Medicine, 1960-65, asso. prof., 1965-66; prof., chmn. med. microbiology U. Calif. Coll. Medicine at Irvine, 1966-68; prof. U. Vt. Coll. Medicine, Burlington, 1968—, chmn. med. microbiology, 1968-78; sabbatical leave Royal Postgrad. Med. Sch., London, 1974-75. Served with inf. AUS, 1943-45; ETO. Decorated Purple Heart. Recipient Golden Apple award Student AMA, 1966-67. Mem. AAAS, Tissue Culture Assn. (ednl. com. 1970-72, chmn. 1970-72), Reticuloendothelial Soc., Am. Soc. Microbiology, Am. Soc. Cell Biologists, Am. Soc. Mammalogy, N.Y. Acad. Scis., Soc. Exptl. Biol. Medicine, Brucellosis Research Conf. Research in host-parasite interactions delayed hypersensitivity, interferon stimulation by non-viral agts., brucellosis. Home: 226 Spear St Burlington VT 05401

STINES, FRED, JR., publisher; b. Newton, Iowa, Mar. 16, 1925; s. Fred and Nella (Haun) S.; B.C.S., U. Iowa, 1949; m. Dorothy G. McClanahan, Sept. 5, 1953; children—Steven, Scott, Ann. With Meredith Corp., Des Moines, 1949—, sales promotion and mdse. mgr., 1955-63, advt. dir., 1963-66, pub., 1966—, pub. dir. mag. div., 1973—. 1973-76, v.p., gen. mgr. books and newspapers, 1976—, pres. Meredith Newspapers, 1978; dir. Homesteaders Life Ins. Co.; certified instr. Dale Carnegie courses, 1958-63. Served with AUS, 1946-49. Named Farm Marketing Man of Year, 1972. Mem. Future Farmers Am. Found. (nat. chmn. 1971), Phi Gamma Delta, Alpha Kappa Psi, Alpha Delta Sigma. Club: Des Moines Golf and Country (dir.). Office: 1716 Locust St Des Moines IA 50303

STINGEL, DONALD EUGENE, govt. ofcl.; b. Pitts., Jan. 31, 1920; s. Eugene E. and Ruth I. (Liddell) S.; B.S., Carnegie-Mellon U., 1941; m. Rita Marie Sweeney, June 14, 1942; children—Donald M., Scott M., Janice L. Metall. engr. Union Carbide Corp., Alloy, W.Va., 1941, metall. engr. to works mgr., N.Y.C., 1946-65; pres. Alloys and Carbide div. Airco, Inc., 1965-68; pres. Pullman Swindell, Pitts., 1969-77; dir. Export-Import Bank U.S., Washington, 1977—; dir. Equimark & Equibank Corp., Pitts. Trustee, Carnegie-Mellon U. Served from 2d lt. to maj., Ordnance Dept., AUS, 1941-46; to lt. col., Transp. Corps, U.S. Army, 1950. Mem. Am. Iron and Steel Inst., Am. Inst. Mining and Metall. Engrs., Pitts. C. of C. (vice chmn. 1975-77). Republican. Clubs: Duquesne (Pitts.); Rolling Rock (Ligonier, Pa.); Congressional Country, Army and Navy (Washington). Home: 4200 Massachusetts Ave NW Washington DC 20016

STINNETT, CASKIE, editor; b. Remington, Va., Aug. 25, 1911; s. Harry Lee and Bena (Caskie) S.; A.B., Coll. William and Mary, 1932; m. LeBaron Coleman, 1931 (div. 1941); 1 son, James LeBaron; m. 2d, Edith Sognier, 1941 (div. 1947); 1 dau., Savannah; m. 3d, Loni Sebold Switzer, 1948 (div. 1967); m. 4th, Judith Lane Rand (div. 1968). Reporter, Staunton (Va.) News-Leader; writer Curtis Pub. Co., 1945-63, asst. to editor in chief all publs., 1963; exec. editor Ladies Home Jour., 1964-65; travel editor Holiday mag., 1965-67, editor in chief, 1967-70, editor, pub., 1970; editor-in-chief Travel and Leisure mag., N.Y.C., 1971-76; exec. v.p. Am. Express Pub. Corp.; essayist Atlantic Monthly, 1976—. Club: Bucks (London, Eng.). Author: Back to Abnormal, 1963; Out of the Red, 1959; Will Not Run February 22nd, 1954; Grand and Private Pleasures, 1977; also articles. Home: 318 Beacon St Boston MA 02116 also Hamloaf Island ME 04011

STINNETTE, CHARLES ROY, JR., clergyman, educator; b. Asheville, N.C., June 18, 1914; s. Charles Roy and Grace (Graham) S.; B.S., N.C. State Coll., 1937; B.D., Union Theol. Sem., N.Y.C., 1940; S.T.M., Hartford Theol. Sem., 1943; Ph.D., Columbia, 1950; certificate William Alanson White Inst. Psychiatry, 1948; m. Nancy Virginia Riddle, June 14, 1937; children—Graham Long, Cynthia Lynn. Ordained to ministry, 1941; curate in Hartford, Conn., 1940-43; asst. in N.Y.C., 1946-48; chaplain, prof. religion U. Rochester, 1948-50; rector in Rochester, 1950-52; canon Washington Cathedral, asso. warden Coll. of Preachers, 1952-56; prof. pastoral theology Union Theol. Sem., 1956-62; prof. pastoral theology and psychiatry U. Chgo., 1962-71; prof. theology of ministry Phillips U. Grad. Sem., Enid, Okla., 1971-79, emeritus, 1979—. Vis. prof. Union Theol. Sem.; lectr. clergy confs. mental health assns., theol. schs.; clin. asso. Ill. State Psychiat. Hosp., Chgo., 1965—, Woodlawn Community Mental Health project, 1965—. Mem. Nat. Com. Health and Human Values, convenor of consultation, 1969. Served as chaplain AUS, 1943-46. Decorated Bronze Star. Mem. Am. Acad. Religion (lectr.). Author: Anxiety and Faith, 1955; Faith, Freedom and Selfhood, 1962; Grace and the Searching of our Heart, 1965; Learning in Theological Perspective, 1965. Contbr. articles to profl. jours. Home: 1509 Indian Dr Enid OK 73701

STINSON, DONALD LEO, educator; b. Hominy, Okla., Oct. 8, 1930; s. Clarence Edward and Eva May (Park) S.; student U. Wyo., 1947-49; B.S., U. Okla., 1950; M.S., U. Mich., 1951, Ph.D., 1957; m. Betty Jane Hoehmann, Oct. 11, 1951; children—Ellen Sue, Glen, Roger (dec.), Kathy, Scott, Lee. Research engr. Phillips Petroleum Co., 1953-58; project engr. Gulf Research & Devel. Co., 1958-60; prof., head dept. mineral engring. U. Wyo., 1960-79, prof., head dept. petroleum engring., 1979—. Mem. Wyo. State Bd. Exam. Engrs. Registered profl. engr., Okla., Wyo. Mem. Am. Inst. Chem. Engring., Am. Inst. Mining, Metall. and Petroleum Engrs., Am. Chem. Soc., Am. Soc. Engring. Edn., Nat., Wyo. socs. profl. engrs., Sigma Xi, Tau Beta Pi, Gamma Alpha. Methodist. Mason. Home: 1213 Garfield St Laramie WY 82070

STINSON, GEORGE ARTHUR, lawyer, steel co. exec.; b. Camden, Ark., Feb. 11, 1915; s. John McCollum and Alice (Loving) S.; A.B., Northwestern U., 1936; J.D., Columbia, 1939; LL.D., U. W.Va., Bethany Coll., Theil Coll., Salem Coll.; m. Betty Millsop, May 31, 1947; children—Thomas, Lauretta, Peter, Joel. Admitted to N.Y. bar, 1939; partner firm Cleary, Gottlieb, Friendly & Hamilton, N.Y.C., 1946-61; spl. asst. to atty. gen., acting asst. atty. gen. tax div. Dept. Justice, 1947-48; v.p., sec. Nat. Steel Corp., Pitts., 1961-63, pres., 1963-75, dir., 1963—, chief exec. officer, 1966—, chmn., 1972—; dir. Nat. Bank Detroit, Pitts. Nat. Bank, Iron Ore Co., Can., Hanna Mining Co., Ralston Purina Co.; trustee Mut. Life Ins. Co. N.Y. Bd. regents Northwestern U.; trustee U. Pitts. Mem. Presdl. Commn. on Internat. Trade and Investment Policy, 1970-71; chmn. U.S. Indsl. Payroll Savs. Com., 1976. Served to lt. col. USAAF, 1941-45. Decorated Legion of Merit. Mem. Am. Iron and Steel Inst. (chmn. bd. 1969-71), Internat. Iron and Steel Inst. (dir., chmn. 1975-77), Am. Law Inst., Bus. Council, Bus. Roundtable, Phi Beta Kappa. Clubs: Links, City Midday, Cloud, Blind Brook (N.Y.C.); Duquesne, Laurel Valley Golf (Pitts.); Gulfstream Golf (Delray, Fla.). Home: 420 Oliver Rd Sewickley PA 15143 Office: Grant Bldg Pittsburgh PA 15219

STINSON, HARRY T(HEODORE), JR., geneticist; b. Newport News, Va., Oct. 26, 1926; s. Harry Theodore and Helen Inez (Marable) S.; B.S., Coll. William and Mary, 1947; Ph.D., Ind. U., 1951; m. Jean Ann Magee, June 11, 1949; children—Sara, David, Martha. Asst. prof. biology Coll. William and Mary, 1951-52; asst. and asso. geneticist Conn. Agr. Expt. Sta., New Haven, 1952-60, chief geneticist, 1960-62; prof. genetics Cornell U., 1962—. Office: Sect of Botany Genetics and Devel Cornell U Ithaca NY 14851*

STINSON, LOUIS, JR., lawyer; b. Savannah, Ga., May 19, 1943; s. Louis and Norma H. (Hussey) S.; B.S., U. Fla., 1965, J.D., 1968; 1 child, Iziar J. Admitted to Fla. bar, 1969, U.S. Supreme Ct. bar, 1979; aide to State Senator Dick Fincher, Fla., 1969; mem. firm Helliwell, Melrose & DeWolf, Miami, Fla., 1969—; counsel, sec. Am. Bankers Life Assurance Co. of Fla., 1973—. Mem. Dade County Bar Assn., Fla. State Bar Assn., Am. Bar Assn., Dade County Young Lawyers Assn. (past dir.). Episcopalian. Office: 1401 Brickell Ave 9th Pl Miami FL 33131

STINSON, RICHARD JAMES, editor; b. Gardner, Mass., Apr. 2, 1929; s. Richard and Marguerite Electra (Foye) S.; B.A., U. Chgo., 1956; M.B.A., N.Y. U., 1958; m. Felina Mijares, Sept. 28, 1956; 1 dau., Suzanne. Research analyst Standard & Poor's Corp., N.Y.C., 1957-58; asso. editor Financial World, N.Y.C., 1958-66, mng. editor, 1966-70, editor, 1970-72, sr. editor, 1972—. Served with USAF, 1951-55. Mem. N.Y. Soc. Security Analysts, Fin. Analysts Fedn. Republican. Unitarian. Editor: Money and Credit, 1975. Home: 53 Greenway S Forest Hills NY 11375 Office: Financial World 919 3d Ave New York NY 10022

STIPANOWICH, JOSEPH JEAN, educator; b. Canton, Ill., Apr. 14, 1921; s. Joseph Anthony and LaVada (Sleeth) S.; B.S. in Edn., Western Ill. State Tchrs. Coll., 1946; M.S. in Teaching Math., U. Ill., 1947; Ed.D., Northwestern U., 1956; m. Mary Laura Forsythe, June 28, 1947; children—Thomas Joseph, James William. Faculty, Western Ill. U., 1947—, prof. math., 1958—, head dept., 1958-67, chmn. dept., 1967-68. Mem. adv. com. Ill. Office Supt. Pub. Instrn., 1964-72. Served with USAAF, 1942-45. Recipient Distinguished Teaching award Western Ill. U., 1970, Alumni Achievement award, 1973, Distinguished Alumni award, 1974. Mem. Nat. (exec. com., 1970-71, past mem. yearbook com., chmn. external affairs com. 1971-72, fin. policies com. 1975—), Ill. (pres. 1962-63, Max Beberman Meml. award in math. edn. 1973-74) councils tchrs. math., Central Assn. Sci. and Math. Tchrs. (pres. elementary math. sect.), Math. Assn. Am. (past co-chmn. com. contests and awards Ill. sect.). Mem. Christian Ch. (past bd. chmn., trustee, deacon, elder). Rotarian, Mason. Editor: Number and Operation, 1960; book rev. editor Math. Tchr., 1950-53. Contbr. articles to profl. jours. Home: 613 Memorial Dr Macomb IL 61455

STIPHER, KARL JOSEPH, lawyer; b. Indpls., Oct. 23, 1912; s. Josiah C. and Clara (Fuerst) S.; B.S., Butler U., 1935; student Harvard Law Sch., 1935-36; LL.B., Ind. U., 1938; m. Jean Houghteling, June 22, 1939; children—Richard, Karen (Mrs. John Irby), Stephen. Admitted to Ind. bar, 1938; asso. firm Gilliom & Gilliom, Indpls., 1938-45; dep. atty. gen. Ind., 1945-47; asso. firm Baker & Daniels, Indpls., 1948-50, partner, 1950—. Mem. Ind. Civil Code Study Commn., 1968-71. Bd. dirs. Catholic Social Services, 1968-78, Alcoholic Rehab. Center, Our Lady Grace Acad.; pres., bd. dirs. Domestic Relations Counseling Service; bd. visitors Ind. U. Law Sch., 1974-78; chmn. Indpls. Mayor's Task Force on Public Safety and Criminal Justice; mem. Citizens Ct. Adv. Com.; pres. Ind. Lawyers Commn. Mem. Indpls. (pres. 1973), Ind. (pres. 1975-76), Am., 7th Fed. Circuit Ct. (pres. 1968-69), Inter-Am., Internat. bar assns., Am. Bar Found., Am. Coll. Trial Lawyers, Ind. Soc. Chgo., Nat. Assn. R.R. Trial Counsel. Clubs: Variety, Mud Creek Players, Indpls. Athletic, Indpls. Lit. Home: 7111 Fremont Ct Indianapolis IN 46256 Office: Fletcher Trust Bldg Indianapolis IN 46204

STIPP, JOHN EDGAR, lawyer, fin. cons.; b. Watseka, Ill., Feb. 10, 1914; s. George Y. and Stella M. (Tubbs) S.; J.D., Drake U., 1936; LL.D., Lincoln Coll., 1961; m. Janet E. Miller, June 4, 1938; 1 son, Thomas John. Admitted to bar Ill., Ia., U.S. Supreme Ct.; practiced in Danville, Ill., 1936-50; dir. Bldg. & Loan Dept., Ill. State, 1949; gen. claims atty. Continental Casualty Co., Chgo., 1950; v.p., sec., mem. fin. com., dir. Continental Casualty Co., Continental Assurance Co.; v.p., sec. Transp. Ins. Co., 1950-53, dir., 1951—; pres. Fed. Home Loan Bank of Chgo., 1953-74; fin. cons., 1974—; dir., mem. fin. com. CNA Fin. Corp., Larwin Group; trustee retirement fund Fed. Home Loan Bank System; dir., mem. fin. investment coms. Chgo. Title & Trust Co., Chgo. Title Ins. Co. Mem. Chgo. Crime Commn. Mem. Fed. Savs. and Loan Adv. Council, created by 74th Congress, 1951; commr. Vermillion Co. Airport Authority, 1946-49; bd. govs., sec., treas., chmn. fin. and investment com. Alpha Tau Omega Found., 1978—; bd. dirs. Goodwill Industries, Cook County chpt. ARC; mem. Mayor's Com. on Econ. and Cultural Devel. Chgo. Served as lt. USNR, 1943-45. Mem. Chgo. Hist. Soc., Chgo. Mus. Natural History, Newcomen Soc., Alpha Tau Omega (past nat. treas.). Clubs: Elks; Executives (past pres.), Economic, Tavern, University (Chgo.); Restless Weasels of Lac du Flambeau (Wis.); Wisconsin (Milw.); Minocqua (Wis.) Country. Speaker, author articles on econs., fin. Home and office: 817 Westerfield Sq Wilmette IL 60091 (summer) 9458 Country Club Rd Box 536 Minocqua WI 54548

STIRES, DAVID WARFIELD, publishing co. exec.; b. Canton, Ohio, July 11, 1933; s. Joseph Dorr and Jane Marguerite (Davidson) S.; B.A., Brigham Young U., Provo, Utah, 1959; 1 dau., Rachel Gretna. Ednl. rep., then asso. editor med. div. Little, Brown & Co., Boston, 1959-64; with Appleton-Century-Crofts, N.Y.C., 1964-67, editor-in-chief, then gen. mgr. med. div., 1967-73, gen. mgr. company, 1973-77, pres., 1977—. Served with AUS, 1954-56. Fellow State U. Iowa Writers Workshop, 1961-62. Contbr. poems to revs. and anthologies. Address: care Appleton Century Crofts 292 Madison Ave New York City NY 10017

STITT, CLYDE LEROY, educator; b. Pawnee City, Nebr., Apr. 21, 1918; s. Roy Samuel and Rosa Alice (Nelson) S.; student Drake U., 1940-42; B.S., Columbia, 1949, M.A., 1950; Ph.D., Stanford, 1961; postgrad. Univ. Coll., London, Eng., 1968, Edinburgh U., 1977; m. Inge Liselotte Hess, Dec. 19, 1952 (dec. 1974); children—Gordon LeRoy, René Linda. Radio announcer KTHS, Hot Springs, Ark., 1939-40; stage mgr., actor, Kennebunkport, Maine, 1947-48; rec. supr. Talking Books, Am. Found. for Blind, N.Y.C., 1950-51; prof. speech San Francisco State U., 1952—, chmn. dept., 1965-69. Cons. speech, speech and lang. program Parks Job Corp Tng. Center, Pleasanton, Calif., 1965-67. Served with USMCR, 1942-45; PTO. USPHS research fellow NIMH, 1959. Mem. AAUP, Speech Communication Assn., Internat. Soc. Gen. Semantics, Western Speech Assn., Am., Calif. speech and hearing assns. Christian Scientist. Contbr. articles to profl. jours. Research exptl. phonetics. Home: 2251 Cobblehill Pl San Mateo CA 94402 Office: San Francisco State U San Francisco CA 94132

STITT, DON NELSON, mfg. co. exec.; b. Pitts., Apr. 7, 1927; s. Don Forrest and Jessie Jacqueline (Cramer) S.; B.S., Carnegie-Mellon U., 1950; M.S. (Sloan fellow), M.I.T., 1965; m. Letitia Orr Neal, Oct. 11, 1952; children—Trevor Nelson, Tracy Gretchen, Christopher Allan. With Rockwell Mfg. Co., Pitts., 1954-73, v.p. corp. planning, 1972-73; exec. v.p. Sterling Faucet Co. subs. Rockwell Mfg. Co., Morgantown, W.Va., 1970-72; v.p., gen. mgr. Powers-Fiat div. Mark Controls Corp., Skokie, Ill., 1973-79; exec. v.p., chief operating officer consumer products Chamberlain Mfg. Corp., Elmhurst, Ill., 1979—; dir. E.W. Bowman, Inc., 1969-73. Dir., v.p. Greater Uniontown Indsl. Fund, 1967-70; mem. Pa. Economy League, 1968-70; mem. Uniontown Human Relations Commn., 1968-70. Served with USAAF, 1945-47. Mem. Am. Mktg. Assn., Am. Water Works Assn., Am. Production and Inventory Control Soc. Clubs: Michigan Shores. Home: 235 Warwick Rd Kenilworth IL 60043 Office: 845 Larch Ave Elmhurst IL 60126

STITT, EDWARD SONNY, saxophonist, orch. leader; b. Boston, Feb. 2, 1924; s. Lonnie Wicks (stepfather) and Claudine Thibou; grad. high sch.; m. Pamela W. Gilmore, Dec. 19, 1960; children—Katea Denise, Jason Cesaré. Toured Europe with Jazz at Philharmonic; played with Billy Eckstine Band, Miles Davis Quintet, Dizzy Gillespie Band; appeared Hollywood Bowl; tchr. harmony, mus. theory; 2 world tours with Giants of Jazz, 1970-72. Recipient All Am. award Esquire mag., All Star award Playboy mag., Jazz Poll winner, Am. Legion award, awards Cook County Dept. Corrections, Outstanding Achievement in Field of Music, Artists and Models Creative Music award. Ellington fellow Yale U., 1973. Office: 80 Park Ave New York NY 10016*

STIVENDER, DONALD LEWIS, mech. engr.; b. Chgo., May 8, 1932; s. Paul Macon and Grace (Larsen) S.; B.S. in Engring., U.S. Coast Guard Acad., 1954; M.S., U. Mich., 1959; m. Margaret Ann Lourim, Apr. 14, 1956; children—Anne, Robert, Carole. Research and devel. Research Labs., Gen. Motors Corp., Warren, Mich., 1959—, sr. research engr., 1968—; pres., dir. Sq. Lake Corp., 1974—. Served with USCG, 1950-58. Registered profl. engr. Mem. Soc. Automotive Engrs. (Arch T. Colwell award 1968, 69, 79; governing bd. 1971-73), ASME, Combustion Inst., Engring. Soc. Detroit. Contbr. articles tech. jours. on diesel, gas turbine and spark ignition engine combustion, emission, constrn. and control aspects. Invented internal combustion engines and control systems. Home: 1730 Hamilton Dr Bloomfield Hills MI 48013 Office: Engine Research Dept 12 Mile and Mound Rds Warren MI 48090

STIVENDER, EDWARD DAVID, conductor, chorus master; b. Milw., Sept. 6, 1933; s. Edward Herman and Frances Strauther (Stabler) S.; Mus.B., Northwestern U., 1955. Asst. condr. Lyric Opera Chgo., 1961-65; asst. chorus master Met. Opera Assn., N.Y.C., 1965-73, chorus master, 1973—, condr., 1978—; Fulbright grantee Rome Opera, 1963-65. Served with USN, 1955-57. Research on Mascagni, Emanuele Carnevali. Home: 170 W 81st St Apt 3-A New York NY 10024 Office: Met Opera Assn Lincoln Center Plaza New York NY 10023

STIVERS, WILLIAM CHARLES, forest products co. exec.; b. Modesto, Calif., June 22, 1938; s. William P. and Helen Louise (Cummings) S.; B.A., Stanford, 1960; M.B.A., U. So. Calif., 1963; certificate Pacific Coast Sch. Banking, 1969; grad. Advanced Mgmt. Program, Harvard U., 1977; m. Karen L. Gaspar, Aug. 6, 1961; children—William, Gregory, Michael, Kristy, Kelly, John. Asst. cashier, asst. v.p., v.p. United Calif. Bank, San Francisco and Los Angeles, 1962-70; finance mgr. treas. dept. Weyerhaeuser Co., Tacoma, 1970, asst. treas., 1971, treas., 1972—; treas. Weyerhaeuser Real Estate Co., 1970. Mem. Financial Execs. Inst. Home: 32325 40th Pl SW Federal Way WA 98003 Office: Weyerhaeuser Co Tacoma WA 98477

STIX, THOMAS HOWARD, physicist, educator; b. St. Louis, July 12, 1924; s. Ernest William and Erma (Kingsbacher) S.; B.S., Calif. Inst. Tech., 1948; Ph.D., Princeton U., 1953; m. Hazel Rosa Sherwin, May 28, 1950; children—Susan Sherwin, Michael Sherwin. Mem. staff Plasma Physics Lab. Princeton U., 1953—, co-head exptl. div., 1961-78, asst. dir. acad. affairs, 1978—; prof. astrophys. sci., 1962—. Chmn. Princeton United Jewish Appeal, 1954-55, 63-64, Princeton Hillel Found., 1972-76. Served with AUS, 1942-45. NSF sr. postdoctoral fellow physics Weizmann Inst. Sci., Rehovot, Israel, 1960-61; Guggenheim Meml. Found. fellow, 1969-70. Fellow Am. Phys. Soc. (chmn. div. plasma physics 1962-63); mem. AAUP, Sigma Xi, Tau Beta Pi. Author: The Theory of Plasma Waves, 1962. Adv. bd. McGraw-Hill Advanced Physics Monograph Series 1963-70; bd. editors Physics of Fluids, 1966-68, Internat. Jour. Engring. Sci., 1969-77, Nuclear Fusion, 1975—; asso. editor Phys. Rev. Letters, 1974-77. Home: 231 Brookstone Dr Princeton NJ 08540

STJERNHOLM, RUNE LEONARD, educator; b. Stockholm, Sweden, Apr. 25, 1924; s. Harry Leonard and Anna Margareta (Soderlund) S.; Ph.D. in Biochemistry, Case Western Res. U., 1958; m. Susan Mavourneen Crowe, June 25, 1970; children—Linda, Birgitta. Came to U.S., 1952. Sr. instr. Case Western Res. U., 1958-59, asst. prof., 1959-64, asso. prof., 1964-70, prof., 1970-71; prof., chmn. dept. biochemistry, Tulane Med. Sch., 1971—. Served with Swedish Army, 1945. Predoctoral Dupont fellow, 1956-58; recipient USPHS research career devel. award, 1963-68. Mem. Am. Soc. Exptl. Biology, N.Y. Acad. Sci., Am. Soc. Hematology, Soc. Am. Microbiologists, Am. Chem. Soc., Reticuloendothelial Soc. Home: 3100 Parc Fontaine New Orleans LA 70114

STOCK, CHARLES CHESTER, biochemist; b. Terre Haute, Ind., May 19, 1910; s. Orion Louis and Jessie May (Blood) S.; B.S., Rose-Hulman Inst., 1932, Sc.D. (hon.), 1954; Ph.D., Johns Hopkins, 1937; M.S., N.Y. U., 1941; m. Grace Elizabeth Knipmeyer, June 6, 1936. Instr. bacteriology N.Y. U., 1937-41; vis. investigator Rockefeller Inst. Hosps., 1941-42; tech. aide com. med. research OSRD, 1942-45, dep. chief div. 5, 1945-46, asst. to chmn. insect control com., 1945; tech. aide com. on treatment gas casualties NRC, 1942-45, exec. sec. insect control com., 1945-46; chief div. chemotherapy Sloan-Kettering Inst., 1947—, asso. dir., 1957-60, sci. dir., 1960-61, v.p., 1961-76, v.p. acad. affairs, 1974-76, v.p., asso. dir. adminstrv. and acad. affairs, 1974—; v.p. inst. affairs Meml. Sloan-Kettering Cancer Center, 1974; dir. Walker Lab., Rye, N.Y., 1960—; prof. biochemistry Sloan-Kettering div. Cornell Med. Coll., 1951-76, emeritus, 1976—. Mem. exptl. therapeutics study sect. USPHS, 1949-54; screening panel, chmn. cancer chemotherapy Nat. Service Center, 1955-58, chmn. drug evaluation panel cancer chemotherapy, 1958-59; mem. chemotherapy rev. bd. Nat. Adv. Cancer Council, 1958-59; com. tumor nomenclature and statistics, chmn. panel nomenclature tumors exptl. animals Internat. Cancer Research Commn., 1952-54; mem. U.S. com. Internat. Union Against Cancer, chmn., 1975. Mem. research com. Music Research Found., 1951-55. Bd. dirs. Am. Cancer Soc., 1972—; bd. mgrs. Rose Hulman Inst., 1972-78. Recipient Hemingway medal Rose-Hulman Inst., 1932; Army-Navy Certificate of Merit, 1948; Alfred P. Sloan award in cancer research, 1965; Order Achievement award Lambda Chi Alpha, 1973. Fellow N.Y. Acad. Medicine (asso.), N.Y. Acad. Sci. (v.p. 1962-63); mem. Am. Chem. Soc., Am. Assn. Cancer Research (dir. 1955, 69), Harvey Soc., A.A.A.S., Am. Soc. Biol. Chemists, Soc. Exptl. Biology and Medicine (chmn. N.Y.C. sect. 1960-62), Societa Italiana Di Cancerologia (corr.), Sigma Xi, Tau Beta Pi, Alpha Chi Sigma, Blue Key. Editorial adv. bd. Cancer Research Jour., 1951-58; mem. editorial bd. jour., Medicinal and Pharm. Chemistry, 1958-64, Research Communications in Chem-Pathology and Pharmacology, 1970—. Contbr. to sci. jours., publs. Home: One Gracie Terr New York City NY 10028 Office: 410 E 68th St New York City NY 10021 also 145 Boston Post Rd Rye NY 10580

STOCK, GREGG FRANCIS, museum dir.; b. Kansas City, Mo., Jan. 30, 1925; s. Arthur Robert and Verna Marie (Prawitz) S.; student Rockhurst Coll., 1942, Central Mo. State Coll., 1942-43; B.A. in Journalism, B.S. in Advt., U. Kans., 1948; m. Sarah Ellen Smart, Nov. 8, 1947; children—Gregory Francis, Heidi Frances, Peter Huston. Pres., Wayne-Fastock Equipment Co., Kansas City, Mo., 1953-65; dir. merchandising Automatique, Inc., Kansas City, Mo., 1965-71; dir. Kansas City Mus., 1971—; cons. Inst. Mus. Services of HEW, Nat.

Endowment for Humanities, Mo. Council on Arts. Served to lt. (j.g.) USNR, 1943-46; PTO. Fellow Explorers Club; mem. Soc. Am. Archaelogy, Mo. Archeol. Soc. (v.p.), Kansas City Archeol. Soc. (hon. life; v.p. 1972, J. Mett Shippee award 1976), Am. Assn. of Museums, Westport, Jackson County hist. socs., Native Sons Kansas City (dir.), Midwest Museums Conf., Mo. Museums Assn. (council, pres. 1978—). Clubs: Rockhill, Rotary. Editorial adv. bd. Explorer Mag. Planner, Sci. Mus., Union Sta., Line Creek Archaeol. Mus.; planner, developer Kansas City Regional Hist. Mus. Home: 4311 Rockhill Rd Kansas City MO 64110 Office: 3218 Gladstone Blvd Kansas City MO 64123

STOCKARD, JAMES ALFRED, life ins. co. exec.; b. Lake Dallas, Tex., Aug. 4, 1935; s. Clifford Raymond and Thelma Gladys (Gotcher) S.; B.A. with honors, N. Tex. State U., Denton, 1956; LL.B. magna cum laude, So. Methodist U., 1959; m. Mary Sue Hogan, Aug. 17, 1956; children—Bruce Anthony, James Alfred, Paul Andrew. Admitted to Tex. bar, 1959; pvt. practice, Dallas, 1959-62; with Employers Casualty Co., Dallas, 1962-65; v.p. Southland Life Ins. Co., Dallas, 1965-77, sr. v.p., gen. counsel, dir., 1977—; sr. v.p., gen. counsel Southland Fin. Corp., Dallas, 1978—; dir. Ins. Systems Am., Atlanta; pres., dir. Dallas County Municipal Utility Dist. 1, Irving, Tex. Mem. exec. com., precinct chmn. Dallas County Democratic Party, 1971. Mem. Am., Tex., Dallas bar assns., Assn. Life Ins. Counsel. Methodist. Contbr. legal jours. Home: 4300 Druid Ln Dallas TX 75205 Office: 1109 Southland Center Dallas TX 75201

STOCKDALE, JAMES BOND, univ. pres., ret. naval officer; b. Abingdon, Ill., Dec. 23, 1923; s. Vernon Beard and Mabel Edith (Bond) S.; B.S., U.S. Naval Acad., 1946; M.A., Stanford U., 1962; hon. degrees: U. S.C., U. Mass., Salve Regina Coll., Norwich U., The Citadel, Brown U.; m. Sybil Elizabeth Bailey, June 28, 1947; children—James Bond, Sidney Bailey, Stanford Baker, Taylor Burr. Designated naval aviator, 1950, advanced through grades to vice adm., 1977; comdr. Fighter Squadron 51, U.S.S. Ticonderoga, 1963-64, Carrier Air Wing 16, U.S.S. Oriskany, 1964-65; sr. naval service prisoner of war in Hanoi, 1965-73; comdr. Anti Submarine Warfare Wing, U.S. Pacific Fleet, 1974-76; dir. Stratagy, Plans and Policy division, office of the Chief of Naval Operations, 1976-77; pres. Naval War College, 1977-79, The Citadel, the Mil. Coll. of S.C., 1979—. Trustee, U.S. Naval Acad. Found. Decorated Congl. medal of honor, D.F.C. with oak leaf cluster, D.S.M. with 2 oak leaf clusters, Silver Star medal with 3 oak leaf clusters, Bronze Star medal with oak leaf cluster, Legion of Merit with Combat "V," Purple Heart with oak leaf cluster; recipient John Paul Jones award for inspirational leadership Navy League of U.S., 1973, medal of honor Nat. Soc. DAR, 1975. Mem. SAR, Am. Acad. Achievement, Ends of Earth Soc., Explorers Club N.Y., Am. Mensa Soc., Congl. Medal of Honor Soc. Clubs: Tavern (Boston); Met. (Washington). Home: The President's House The Citadel Charleston SC 29409 Office: The Citadel Charleston SC 29409

STOCKDALE, RONALD ALLEN, wholesale grocery co. exec.; b. Aplington, Iowa, Apr. 28, 1934; s. Carl Robert and Mildred Louise (Gerhardt) S.; student U. Dubuque, 1952-54; B.S. in Commerce, State U. Iowa, 1958; m. Carol Ann Hermeier, Dec. 23, 1956; children—Bryan Ross, Russell Allen, Paul Roderick. Auditor, Arthur Anderson & Co., Chgo., 1958-63; controller Super Food Services, Inc., Bellefontaine, Ohio, 1963-66, Mountain States Wholesale, Boise, Idaho, 1966-69; exec. v.p., sec., dir. W. Coast Grocery Co., Tacoma, 1969—; dir. State Distbg. Co. Wash. Mem. Univ. Pl. Sch. Bd., 1973-75. Served with U.S. Army, 1954-56. C.P.A. Mem. Fin. Execs. Inst., Am. Inst. C.P.A.'s, Wash. Soc. C.P.A.'s. Republican. Presbyterian. Home: 2705 Soundview Dr W Tacoma WA 98466 Office: 495 E 19th St Tacoma WA 98401

STOCKER, ARTHUR FREDERICK, educator; b. Bethlehem, Pa., Jan. 24, 1914; s. Harry Emilius and Alice (Stratton) S.; A.B. summa cum laude, Williams Coll., 1934; A.M., Harvard U., 1935, Ph.D., 1939; m. Marian West, July 16, 1968. Instr. Greek, Bates Coll., 1941-42; asst. prof. classics U. Va., 1946-52, asso. prof. 1952-60, prof., 1960—, chmn. dept., 1955-63, 68-78, asso. dean Grad. Sch. Arts and Scis., 1962-66; vis. asst. prof. classics U. Chgo., summer 1951. Served with USAAF, 1942-46; col. (ret.). Sheldon traveling fellow from Harvard, 1940-41. Mem. classical assns. Va. (pres. 1949-52), Mid. West and South (pres. So. sect. 1960-62, pres. 1970-71), Am. Philol. Assn., Archaeol. Inst. Am., Mediaeval Acad. Am., Poetry Soc. Va. (pres. 1966-69), S.A.R. (chpt. pres. 1972), Huguenot Soc. Va., Raven Soc. (Raven award 1977), Phi Beta Kappa, Omicron Delta Kappa, Republican, Presbyterian (elder). Mason. Clubs: Colonnade, Farmington Country (Charlottesville, Va.); Williams (N.Y.C.); Army and Navy (Washington). Editor: (with others) Servianorum in Vergilii Carmina Commentariorum Editio Harvardiana, Vol. II, 1946, Vol. III, 1965. Home: 1434 Grove Rd Charlottesville VA 22901. *Education at all levels in this country suffers from a very serious lack of clearly understood objectives. As a society, we simply never have decided what mark we wish to place on the young people who pass through its successive stages, and the whole sequence has become for the student little better than a cafeteria line. A strong society has a clear conception of what it wants the citizens of the future to be like, and turns them out in that pattern.*

STOCKER, JULE E(LIAS), lawyer; b. Detroit, Sept. 16, 1906; s. David R. and Hattie V. (Gerber) S.; A.B. magna cum laude, Harvard, 1926, J.D. magna cum laude, 1929; m. Beatrice H. Klipstein, Mar. 26, 1932; children—Maida (Mrs. George S. Abrams), Michael. Admitted to N.Y. bar, 1929, since practiced in N.Y.C.; mem. Chadbourne, Parke, Whiteside & Wolff, 1950-56; asso. counsel, law dept.-investments Equitable Life Assurance Soc. of U.S., 1956-62, 2d v.p., asso. gen. solicitor, 1962-65, v.p., asso. gen. counsel, 1965-70, v.p., gen. atty., 1970-73, cons., 1974-79; of counsel Gruber & Gruber, N.Y.C., 1977—; lectr. Practicing Law Inst., N.Y.C., 1942—. Mem. adv. com. N.Y. State Commn. Estates, 1961-66. Drafting cons. N.Y. Joint Legis. Com. Revision Corp. Laws, 1960-61; project dir. N.Y. State Law Revision Com., Recodification N.Y. Ins. Law, 1979—. Mem. Assn. Bar City N.Y. (chmn. com. real property law 1946-49), N.Y. County Lawyers' Assn. (sec. com. surrogates' ct. 1946-57), N.Y.C. C. of C., Assn. Life Ins. Counsel, Internat., Am., N.Y. State bar assns. (various coms.), Am. Law Inst., Am. Life Ins. Assn. (com. ins. co. fed. income tax 1972-73), Nat. Legal Aid and Defender Assn., Phi Beta Kappa. Author: Wills for Servicemen, 1944; Drawing Wills with Harold Schwarzberg, 1946, rev. edits., 1969, 73. Editor: Harvard Law Rev., 1927-29. Home: 17 W 54th St New York NY 10019 Office: 200 Madison Ave New York NY 10019

STOCKHOLM, CHARLES MITCHELL, banker; b. San Francisco, Feb. 10, 1933; s. Sophus C. and Clarisse M. (Mitchell) S.; A.B. in Econs., Stanford U., 1955; M.Fgn. Trade, Am. Inst. Fgn. Trade, 1956; m. Dawn Smith, Oct. 14, 1961; 1 dau., Lisa. With First Nat. City Bank, N.Y.C., 1956-74, pres., 1971-74, chmn. bd., 1973-76; sr. officer, supr. 5 Edge Act corps. and Citicorp affiliates, 1974-76; sr. v.p. internat. div. Crocker Nat. Bank, San Francisco, 1976, exec. v.p., mgr. corp. banking div., 1976—; dir. Alexander & Baldwin, Inc., Matson Navigation Co., Pacific Resources, Inc.; pres. Am. Assn. Singapore, 1962, Kuala Lumpur, 1965; chmn. Malaysia Council Asia Soc., 1968; pres. Am. Men's Assn., Jakarta, 1969; chmn. Am. Ambassador's Bus. Com., Indonesia, 1970; vice chmn. Pacific-Indonesian C. of C., 1971; pres. World Trade Assn., San Francisco, 1976—. Mem. San Francisco C. of C. (dir. 1979—). Address: 1 Montgomery St San Francisco CA 94104

STOCKING, CLIFFORD RALPH, educator; b. Riverside, Calif., June 22, 1913; s. Clifford Dodge and Laura (Stephenson) S.; B.S. with highest honors in Plant Nutrition, U. Calif. at Berkeley, 1937, M.S. in Plant Physiology, 1939; Ph.D., U. Calif. at Davis, 1943; m. Elsie Irene Taylor, Aug. 31, 1937; children—Kathleen Ann (Mrs. Warren Cropper), Margery Stocking Reddick. Asso. botany U. Calif., Davis, 1939-42, asst. prof. botany, asst. botanist, 1946-52, asso. prof., asso. botanist, 1952-55, prof. botany, botanist, 1958—, chmn. dept. botany and agrl. botany, 1968-74; chemist Pucunelli Packing Co., Turlock, Calif., 1942-45. Merck sr. postdoctoral fellow, 1955-56; NSF fellow, London, 1963-64; NSF sr. postdoctoral fellow Kings Coll., London, 1971-72. Fellow A.A.A.S.; mem. N.Y. Acad. Scis., Soc. Exptl. Biologists, Am. Soc. Plant Physiologists, Phi Beta Kappa. Author: (with A.S. Crafts, H.B. Currier) Water in Physiology of Plants, 1949; (with W. Robbins, T.E. Weier) Botany-An Introduction to Plant Science, 3d edit., 1964; (with T.E. Weier and M.G. Barbour) Botany—An Introduction to Plant Biology, 5th edit., 1974. Address: 837 Oak Ave Davis CA 95616

STOCKING, HOBART EBEY, geologist, educator; b. Clarendon, Tex., Nov. 16, 1906; s. Jerome Daniel and Sarah Maria (Ward) S.; student Clarendon Jr. Coll., 1925-27, U. Tex., 1928; M.A., Johns Hopkins U., 1938; Ph.D., U. Chgo., 1949; m. Helen Berenice Smith, Aug. 25, 1934; children—Sarah Stocking Ben Bouchta, Martha. Topographic engr. Companhia de Petroleo de Angola, Portuguese W. Africa, 1929-31; asst. geologist U.S. Geol. Survey, 1933-34; geologist Shell Petroleum Co., Midland, Tex., 1936-38; asst. prof. W.Va. State U., Morgantown, 1940-43; chief geologist Dist. 1 Petroleum Adminstrn. War, 1943-45; State Dept. vis. prof. U. Costa Rica, 1945-46; prof. geology Okla. State U., Stillwater, 1946-52, 58—; chief geologist Grand Junction div. AEC, 1956-58, chief Argentine Mission, 1958; Disting. lectr. Am. Assn. Petroleum Geologists, 1956; prof. Johns Hopkins U., summers 1962-73. Dist. coordinator Common Cause, 1973-75. Named hon. prof. U. Costa Rica, 1948; scholar Johns Hopkins, 1932. Fellow AAAS, Geol. Soc. Am. Author: The Road to Santa Fe, 1971. Contbr. articles to profl. jours. Home: 108 Berry St Stillwater OK 74074

STOCKLEN, JOSEPH BERNARD, physician, hosp. adminstr.; b. Nelsonville, Ohio, Mar. 26, 1906; s. John Joseph and Gertrude (Jacoby) S.; A.B., Ohio U., 1927; M.D., Western Res. U., 1930; m. Violet Freiler, Dec. 14, 1963. Resident physician Sunny Acres Hosp., Cleve., 1933-37, 40-41, med. supt., 1942-70; intern Met. Gen. Hosp., Cleve., 1937-38, asst. resident physician, 1938-40; pres. med. staff, 1963; acting v.p. community health Cuyahoga County Hosp., Cleve., 1973-75; controller Tb Cuyahoga County, 1942-75, controller chronic illness, 1959-75; asst. clin. prof. medicine emeritus Case-Western Res. U., 1976—, asso. clin. prof. community health emeritus, 1975—. Sec., Forest City Hosp. Assn., 1944-71; bd. examiners nursing home adminstrs. State of Ohio, 1970-75; pres. Mississippi Valley Conf. on Tb, 1959. Trustee, Golden Age Centers, 1974—. Recipient Dearholt medal Mississippi Valley Conf. on Tb, 1957; Will Ross medal Nat. Tb Assn., 1966; Distinguished Service award Acad. Medicine Cleve., 1975; named Med. Alumnus of Yr., Sch. Medicine, Case-Western Res. U., 1973. Fellow Am. Pub. Health Assn.; mem. A.M.A., Ohio Med. Soc., Ohio Tb and Health Assn. (pres. 1945-46, v.p. 1951-52, sec. 1952-79), Am. Thoracic Soc. (pres. 1968-69), Nat. Tb Assn. (v.p. 1970-71), Am. (pres. 1974-75, trustee 1951-75), No. Ohio (pres. 1976-78) lung assns. Contbr. articles to profl. jours. Home: 5897 Bear Creek Dr Bedford Heights OH 44146. *A bout with tuberculosis on graduation from medical school determined that I should spend the major share of my life in the field of public health combating the white plague rather than entering private practice, my original intention. In my opinion I have contributed more to humanity by following a career which was chosen for me by fate.*

STOCKMAN, DAVID ALLEN, congressman; b. Ft. Hood, Tex., Nov. 10, 1946; s. Allen and Carol (Bartz) S.; B.A. in Am. History cum laude, Mich. State U., East Lansing, 1968; postgrad. Harvard U. Div. Sch., 1968-70, fellow Inst. Politics, 1974. Spl. asst. to Congressman John Anderson, 1970-72; exec. dir. Republican Conf., Ho. of Reps., 1972-75; mem. 95th Congress from 4th Dist. Mich., mem. Interstate and Fgn. Commerce Com., Adminstrn. Com.; chmn. Rep. Econ. Policy Task Force, 1977—. Mem. Nat. Commn. on Air Quality, 1978. Address: 1502 Longworth House Office Bldg Washington DC 20515

STOCKMAYER, WALTER HUGO, educator; b. Rutherford, N.J., Apr. 7, 1914; s. Hugo Paul and Dagmar (Bostroem) S.; S.B., Mass. Inst. Tech., 1935, Ph.D., 1940; B.Sc. (Rhodes scholar) Oxford U., 1937; hon. doctorate U. Louis-Pasteur, Strasbourg, France, 1972; m. Sylvia Kleist Bergen, Aug. 12, 1938; children—Ralph, Hugh. Instr., Mass. Inst. Tech., 1939-41, asst. prof. 1943-46, asso. prof., 1946-52, prof., 1952-61; prof. chemistry Dartmouth, 1961-79, prof. emeritus, 1979—; instr. Columbia, 1941-43. Cons. E.I. duPont de Nemours & Co., Inc., 1945—. Guggenheim fellow, 1954-55; hon. fellow Jesus Coll., Oxford, Eng., 1976. Recipient MCA Coll. Chemistry Tchr. award, 1960; U.S. Sr. Scientist award Alexander von Humboldt Found., 1978-79. Fellow Am. Acad. Arts and Scis., Am. Phys. Soc. (Polymer Physics prize 1975); mem. Am. Chem. Soc. (asso. editor Macromolecules 1968-74, 76—, chmn. polymer chem. div. 1968, Polymer Chemistry award 1965, Peter Debye award 1974), Nat. Acad. Scis. (exec. com. assembly math. phys. sci. 1974-77), Sigma Xi. Contbr. articles on phys. and macromolecular chemistry to sci. jours. Club: Appalachian Mountain. Home: Norwich VT 05055

STOCKS, CHESTER LEE, JR., hosp. adminstr.; b. Montgomery, Ala., Oct. 8, 1928; s. Chester Lee and Evelyn (Cooley) S.; B.S., Auburn U., 1949; M.H.A., Washington U., St. Louis, 1955; m. Mary Gwendoline Hase, June 5, 1954; children—Susan, Bradley Hase, Charles Lee, Sally. Resident Baylor U. Med. Center, Dallas, 1954-55, adminstrv. asst., 1955-57, asst. adminstr., 1957-63; exec. v.p. Good Samaritan Hosp. and Med. Center, 1963, Portland, Oreg., 1963—. Preceptor grad. programs in hosp. adminstrn., U. Calif., U. Iowa, Washington U.; lectr., participant programs on health care; mem. exec. com. Oreg. Regional Med. Programs, 1966-74, v.p., 1969-76; mem. Oreg. Commn. on Nursing, 1969-75, Oreg. Health Manpower Commn., 1966-73, Comprehensive Health Planning Assn. Met. Portland, 1969-76, Oreg. Health Commn. Siting Com., 1974-77; dir. Oreg. Med. Polit. Action Com., 1974-77. Oreg. chmn. Wash. U. devel. program, 1967-70. Trustee Fred Hutchison Cancer Center, Seattle, 1972-79, Oreg. Comprehensive Cancer Center, 1973-75, Blue Cross Oreg., 1965-77; pres. Oreg. Hosp. Found., 1979. Served to 1st lt. USAF, 1950-53. Fellow Am. Coll. Hosp. Adminstrs. (regent 1969-75, gov. 1975-78, chmn. 1979); mem. Assn. Western Hosps. (trustee, pres. 1973-74), Oreg. Assn. Hosps. (pres. 1967-68, trustee 1973-76), Portland Council of Hosps. (pres. 1966-67), Portland C. of C. (bd. dirs. 1967-69), Nat. Assn. for Practical Nurse Edn. and Service (trustee 1960—), Nat. League for Nursing, Pi Kappa Alpha. Episcopalian (dir. William Temple House 1965-70). Rotarian. Clubs: Multnomah Athletic, Arlington (Portland). Home: 282 NW Macleay Blvd Portland OR 97210 Office: 1015 NW 22 Ave Portland OR 97210

STOCKS, WILLIAM GEORGE, food co. exec.; b. Mpls., Jan. 28, 1927; s. George F. and Florence A. (Brombach) S.; B.A., St. Thomas Coll., 1953; J.D., Mitchell Coll. Law, 1963; m. Anne Mary Wensman, June 20, 1953; children—Thomas, Jeanne, Robert, John, Paul. Sr. accountant Peat, Marwick Mitchell & Co., Mpls., 1953-56; with Peavey Co., Mpls., 1956—, asst. treas., 1962-67, treas., 1967-68, v.p. fin., 1968-74, exec. v.p., 1974-75, pres., 1975-77, chmn., chief exec. officer, 1978—; dir. Midland Nat. Bank Jennie-O Foods Inc. Bd. dirs. St. Thomas Coll. Served with USNR, 1945-46. Roman Catholic. Clubs: Minneapolis, Minikahda Country. Home: 6715 Apache Rd Minneapolis MN 55435 Office: 730 2d Ave S Minneapolis MN 55402

STOCKTON, DAVID KNAPP, profl. golfer; b. San Bernardino, Calif., Nov. 2, 1941; s. Gail Rufus and Audrey (Knapp) S.; B.S. in Gen. Mgmt., U. So. Calif., 1964; m. Catherine Fay Hales, Feb. 27, 1965; children—David Bradley, Ronald Edwin. Winner 11 tour tournaments including: Profl. Golf Assn., 1970, 76, Los Angeles, 1974, Hartford, 1974, Colonial, 1967, Cleve., 1968, Milw., 1968-73, Pleasant Valley, 1971, Quad Cities, 1974, Haig and Haig Open, 1968; rep. U.S. in 2 World Cups, 1970, 76, Ryder Cup, 1971, 77; shares record for fewest putts for 18 holes (19); mem. Golf's All Am. Team, 1974-76. Republican. Roman Catholic. Elk. Office: 4812 Lakeview Cyn Rd Westlake Village CA 91361

STOCKTON, ERNEST LOONEY, coll. pres.; b. Lebanon, Tenn., Aug. 27, 1917; s. Ernest Looney and Katherine (White) S.; B.A., Cumberland U., 1939, LL.D. (hon.), 1958; M.A., George Peabody Coll., 1947; L.H.D. (hon.), Okla. Christian Coll., 1971; m. Bettye Hatfield, July 10, 1942; 1 dau., Bettye Sharon. Tchr. English, asst. coach Castle Heights Mil. Acad., Lebanon, Tenn., 1939-41, successively English tchr., dir. guidance, dir. admissions, v.p., headmaster, 1945-58; pres. Cumberland Coll., Lebanon, 1958—; bd. dirs. Nat. Council Ind. Jr. Colls.; mem. Nashville regional adv. council Tenn. Higher Edn. Commn.; trustee Cumberland U., 1957-58, Cordell Hull Found. Internat. Edn., 1978—. Pres. Lebanon Jaycees, 1947-48, Tenn. Jaycees, 1949-50; Tenn. chmn. March of Dimes, 1947. Served to lt. USCGR, 1942-45. Paul Harris fellow, 1977. Mem. Am. Assn. Jr. Colls., So. Assn. Community and Jr. Colls. (past pres.), Tenn. Coll. Assn. (pres. 1974-75), Tenn. Council Pvt. Colls. (chmn. 1976-78). Presbyterian. Club: Lebanon Rotary (pres. 1961-62). Address: Cumberland Coll Lebanon TN 37087

STOCKTON, RALPH MADISON, JR., lawyer; b. Winston-Salem, June 22, 1927; s. Ralph Madison and Margaret (Thompson) S.; B.S., U. N.C., 1948, LL.B. cum laude, 1950; m. Frances Bowles, July 15, 1950; children—Mary Ellen, Ralph Madison III, David Anderson, James Alexander. Admitted to N.C. bar, 1950; asso. firm Dwight, Royal, Harris & Caskey, Washington, 1950-51; with firm Hudson, Petree, Stockton, Stockton & Robinson, and predecessors, Winston-Salem, 1951—, partner, 1956—. Mem. jud. conf. 4th Circuit U.S. Ct. Appeals, 1958—. Trustee Winston-Salem State U. 1958—, vice chmn., 1973—; trustee Forsyth County Legal Aid Soc., 1966-70, pres., 1969; trustee Meth. Children's Home, 1966—, chmn. exec. com., 1969-75, pres. bd. trustees, 1975—; bd. mgrs. Meth. Home, Charlotte, N.C., 1967-70. Mem. Am., N.C. (bd. govs. 1957-60, chmn. comml. banking and bus. law com. 1958-60, chmn. appellate rules study com. 1973—, pres. 1976-77), Forsyth County (pres. 1965-66) bar assns., Internat. Assn. Inst. Counsel, Am. Judicature Soc. (dir. 1976—), Am. Coll. Trial Lawyers, Nat. Conf. Bar Presidents, Fellows of Am. Bar Found., Law Alumni Assn. U. N.C. (pres. 1964, dir. gen. 1970—) Order of Coif, Phi Delta Phi. Democrat. Methodist. Rotarian (pres. Winston-Salem 1965-66). Home: 2696 Reynolds Dr Winston Salem NC 27104 Office: Reynolds Bldg Winston-Salem NC 27101

STOCKTON, RICHARD LACLEDE, tennis player; b. N.Y.C., Feb. 18, 1951; graduated from Trinity U., San Antonio; married. Profl. tennis player, 1972—; with Houston E-Z Riders World Team Tennis, 1974. Winner (with Rosemary Casals) World Mixed Doubles championship, 1975; U.S. Pro Indoor Tennis championship, 1977. Address: care US Tennis Assn 51 E 42d St New York NY 10017*

STOCKWELL, BENJAMIN EUGENE, lawyer; b. Oklahoma City, Aug. 28, 1931; s. Benjamin Paul and Anna (Cunningham) S.; B.A., U. Okla., 1952, LL.B., 1956; m. Marjorie Ethel Ribble, Apr. 4, 1952; children-Margaret Lynn, David Alan. Admitted to Okla. bar, 1956; practice in Oklahoma City, 1956-60, Norman, Okla., 1961—; mem. firm Benedum & Stockwell, 1961-62, then Benjamin E. Stockwell, now Stockwell & Pence; asst. prof. law, legal adviser to pres.'s office U. Okla., 1960-61, spl. lectr. Coll. Law, 1971—. Chmn., Cleveland County Bd. Health, 1963-64; mem. Okla. State Bd. Examiners Certified Shorthand Reporters, 1971—, chmn., 1974-76. Bd. dirs. Cleveland County Cancer Soc. Served to 1st lt. AUS, 1952-54. Mem. Okla. (exec. com. 1965-68, v.p. 1969, chmn. spl. com. implementation jud. reform amendments 1967-69), Cleveland County (past pres.) bar assns., Okla. Inst. Justice, Order of Coif, Order of DeMolay Legion Honor, Scabbard and Blade, Phi Delta Phi, Pi Kappa Alpha, Pi Gamma Mu, Order DeMolay. Episcopalian. Mason. Home: 801 A Cardinal Creek Norman OK 73069 Office: 119 E Main St Norman OK 73069

STOCKWELL, CLIFFORD HOWARD, geologist; b. Estevan, Sask., Can., Sept. 26, 1897; s. James Richardson and Alfretta Susannah (Perry) S.; B.A. in Sci., U. B.C., 1924; Ph.D., U. Wis., 1930; m. Annette Elizabeth Johnston, June 3, 1935; children—Laura Evelyn, James Johnston, Norman Edward. Geologist, Geol. Survey Can., Ottawa, Ont., 1927-67, cons. geologist, 1968-70; cons. N.J. Zinc Co., 1951; vis. prof. McGill U., 1947. Served with Can. Royal Air Force, 1917-19. Fellow Royal Soc. Can. (Willet G. Miller medal 1953); mem. Can. Inst. Mining and Metallurgy (Barlow Meml. medal 1945), Geol. Soc. Am., Geol. Assn. Can. (Logan medal 1973). Mem. United Ch. Can. Contbr. articles to profl. jours. Home: 577 Gainsborough Ave Ottawa ON K2A 2Y6 Canada

STOCKWELL, ERNEST FARNHAM, JR., banker; b. Boston, Dec. 18, 1923; s. Ernest Farnham and Beatrice Burr (Beach) S.; grad. Phillips Acad., 1941; B.A., Yale U., 1945; m. Fiona Munro, May 24, 1952; children—Ernest Farnham III, Diana, Elizabeth. Asst. br. mgr. First Nat. Bank Boston, 1950-55, br. mgr., 1955-56, asst. v.p., 1956-60, v.p., 1960-71; pres. Harvard Trust Co., Cambridge, Mass., 1971-77, chief exec. officer, 1973-77; pres. Bay Banks Assos., Inc., 1977-78; v.p. First Nat. Bank Boston, 1978; dir. Wang Labs., Commonwealth Gas Co., High Voltage Engring. Corp., Cambridge Electric Light Co. Trustee Episcopal Div. Sch., Cambridge, Yale Scholarship Trust Boston. Served with USNR, 1943-46. Episcopalian (trustee Diocesan Investment Trust). Clubs: Yale (Boston and N.Y.C.); Dedham (Mass.) Country and Polo. Home: 36 Dover Rd Dover MA 02030 Office: 100 Federal St Boston MA 02110

STOCKWELL, GEORGE LEWIS, lawyer; b. Nortonville, Kans., Sept. 24, 1928; s. J. W. Stockwell; B.A., J.D., Washburn U.; m. Delia Davis, Nov. 22, 1952; children—Gayle, Craig, Barbra, Dan. Mem. legal staff Amortibanc Investment Co., Wichita, Kans., 1954-66; exec. v.p., then pres., dir. 1st Fed. Savs. and Loan Assn., Coffeyville, Kans., 1966-72; sr. v.p., mgr. real estate div. Tex. Bank & Trust Co., Dallas, 1972-75; pres., dir., mem. exec. com. Wynnewood Bank and Trust, Dallas, 1975-78; gen. counsel Republic Nat. Bank of Dallas, 1978—. Cons. housing-related programs, City of Dallas, 1978; bd. dirs.

Neighborhood Housing of Dallas, 1974-79. Served to 1st lt. USAF, 1946-49. Mem. Tex. Bar Assn., Dallas Bar Assn. Home: 7127 Gateridge Dallas TX 75240 Office: Pacific and Ervay Sts Dallas TX 75201

STOCKWELL, IVAMAY (DENNEWILL), clergywoman; b. Indianola, Iowa, July 12, 1914; d. Julius and Iva Docia (Sill) Dennewill; grad. Am. Inst. Bus., Des Moines, 1935. Tchr., Warren County, Iowa, 1932-33; legal sec. firms, including M. Talbert Dick, Des Moines, 1935, Charles B. Cannon, Chgo., 1940-44, Matthew E. Marsh, Chico, Calif., 1971; minister chs., 1940—; ordained to ministry Nat. Spiritualist Assn. of Chs., 1945; spiritualist minister, counselor. Healer, medium. Mem. Calif. State Spiritualist Assn. (sec. 1971-75), Nat. Spiritualist Assn. Chs. (sec. 1975-77), Bus. and Profl. Women's Club of Chico (Calif.). Home: 4371 W Sirius Ave Las Vegas NV 89102

STOCKWELL, OLIVER PERKINS, lawyer; b. East Baton Rouge, La., Aug. 11, 1907; s. William Richard and Lillie Belle (Dawson) S.; LL.B., La. State U., 1932; m. Roseina Katherine Holcombe, June 24, 1936; 1 dau., Angell Roseina (Mrs. William C. Wright). Admitted to La. bar, 1932, since practiced in Lake Charles; partner firm Stockwell, Sievert, Vicellio, Clements & Shaddock and predecessor firm, 1933—. Dir. Lakeside Nat. Bank of Lake Charles; past dir. Gulf States Utilities Co.; past mem. jud. council La. Supreme Ct.; past mem. La. Commn. on Law Enforcement and Adminstrn. Criminal Justice. Pres., Lake Charles Centennial, Council for a Better La. Bd. dirs. Pub. Affairs Research Council La., La. State U. Found.; mem. bd. suprs. La. State U., chmn., 1977-78. Served to lt. USNR, 1943-45. Research fellow Southwestern Legal Found. Fellow Am. Bar Found., Am. Coll. Trial Lawyers, Am. Coll. Probate Counsel; mem. Inter-Am., Internat., Am. (past state chmn. jr. bar sect., mem. spl. com. adoption jud. conduct code), La. (pres.), S.W. La. (pres. 1942) bar assns., Internat. Assn. Ins. Counsel, Fedn. Ins. Counsel, Am. (life mem.), La. (pres.) law insts., Lake Charles C. of C. (past pres., Civic award 1978), State Assn. Young Men's Bus. Clubs (past pres. Lake Charles), La. State U. Law Sch. Alumni, Order of Coif, Lambda Alpha, Omicron Delta Kappa. Kiwanian. Clubs: Pioneer, Lake Charles Country. Home: 205 Shell Beach Dr Lake Charles LA 70601 Office: One Lakeside Plaza Lake Charles LA 70601. *I have approached life with an appreciation of the privilege of having been born in this great country in these times, with the right to follow a profession (law) which brings me satisfaction, a sense of accomplishment, and financial security.*

STOCKWELL, RICHARD E., ret. corp. exec., author, editor; b. Neillsville, Wis., Mar. 12, 1917; s. Arthur Raymond and Ella (Stelloh) S.; B.S., U. Wis., 1940; M.A., U. Minn., 1945; Nieman fellow Harvard U., 1945-46. Farm editor radio sta. WIBA, Madison, Wis., 1939-40; news staff WLW, Cin., 1940-41; program dir. Wis. Network, Wisconsin Rapids, 1941-42; asso. news editor WMT, Cedar Rapids, Ia., 1942-43; asso. news editor WCCO-CBS, Mpls., 1943-45; editorial writer Mpls. Star, 1946-49; editor Aviation Age, N.Y.C., 1949-52, Monsanto Mag., Monsanto Internat. Mag., 1952-54; editorial dir. Am. Aviation Publs., Inc., Washington, 1954-55; cons., mgmt. information analyst Flight Propulsion Lab., Gen. Electric Co., Cin., 1956-58; group dir. pub. relations and advt., electronics, ordnance and aerostructures divs. Avco Corp., Cin., 1958-68, v.p. comml. and indsl. products group, Nashville, 1968-74, v.p. products and research group, 1974-76. Awarded scholarship radio sta. WLW, 1940. Mem. Royal, Am. econs. assns., Am. Polit. Sci. Assn., Aviation Space Writers Assn. Clubs: Wings (N.Y.C.); Nat. Press (Washington). Author: Soviet Air Power, 1956; also numerous mag. articles. Home: 10 Clay St Neillsville WI 54456

STOCKWELL, ROBERT PAUL, educator; b. Oklahoma City, June 12, 1925; s. Benjamin P. and Anna (Cunningham) S.; B.A., U. Va., 1946, M.A., 1949, Ph.D., 1952; m. Lucy Louisa Floyd, Aug. 29, 1946; 1 son, Paul Witten. Instr. English, Oklahoma City U., 1946-48; mem. linguistics staff Sch. Langs., Fgn. Service Inst., State Dept., 1952-56; mem. faculty U. Calif. at Los Angeles, 1956—, prof. English, 1962-66, prof. linguistics, 1966—, chmn. dept., 1966-73. Mem. com. lang. programs Am. Council Learned Socs., 1965-69. Served with USNR, 1943-45. Am. Council Learned Socs. fellow, 1963-64. Mem. Linguistic Soc. Am. (exec. com. 1965-68), Philol. Assn. Great Britain. Author: (with J.D. Bowen) Patterns of Spanish Pronunciation, 1960, Sounds of English and Spanish, 1965; (with J. D. Bowen, J.W. Martin) The Grammatical Structures of English and Spanish, 1965; (with P.M. Schachter, B.H. Partee) The Major Syntactic Structures of English, 1973; Foundations of Syntactic Theory, 1977; (with D.E. Elliott and M. Bean) Workbook in Syntactic Theory and Analysis, 1977; also numerous articles. Editor: (with R.S.K. Macaulay) Linguistic Change and Generative Theory, 1972; asso. editor Language, 1973—. Home: 4000 Hayvenhurst Ave Encino CA 91436 Office: Univ California Los Angeles CA 90024

STODDARD, BRANDON, film and television co. exec.; b. Bridgeport, Conn., Mar. 31, 1937; s. Johnson and Constance (Brandon) S.; B.A. in Am. Studies, Yale U., 1958; postgrad., Columbia U. Law Sch., 1963; children—Alexandra, Brooke. Program asst. Batten, Barton, Durstine and Osborn, N.Y.C., 1960-61; program ops. supr. Grey Advt., N.Y.C., 1962-66, dir. daytime programs, 1966, v.p. in charge of radio and television programs, 1968-70; dir. daytime programs ABC-TV, 1970-72, v.p. daytime programs, 1972-74, v.p. motion pictures for television, 1974-79; pres. ABC Motion Pictures, Los Angeles, 1979—, sr. v.p. ABC Entertainment, 1979—. Served with U.S. Army, 1960-61. Mem. Hollywood Radio and TV Soc., Am. Film Inst., Acad. Motion Pictures Arts and Scis. Episcopalian. Club: Bel Air Bay. Office: 2040 Ave of the Stars 5th Floor Los Angeles CA 90067

STODDARD, BURDETT CLARK, journalist; b. Oxford, Mich., Sept. 9, 1931; s. Clark Hall and Margaret Jane (Hagerman) S.; B.A., U. Mich., 1953; m. E. Adelaide Wiley, Nov. 8, 1957; children—Hagerman, Drucilla, Kate. Reporter, Pontiac (Mich.) Press, 1953-56; gen. reporter Detroit News, 1956-63, Can. corr., 1963, suburban, state, city, asst. mng. editor, 1964-75, mng. editor, 1975-79; exec. editor Naples (Fla.) Daily News, 1979—; lectr. Mercy Coll., Detroit; 1976-78; condr. journalism seminars Central Mich. U., 1977, Adrian (Mich.) Coll., 1978; dir. Mich. AP, 1976-79. Bd. dirs. Big Bros.-Big Sisters Met. Detroit, 1977-79; mem. citizens adv. council U. Mich., Dearborn, 1977-79. Mem. Fla. Soc. Newspaper Editors. Clubs: Detroit Press; Grosse Ile (Mich.) Yacht; U. Mich. of S.W. Fla. Home: 694 Mooring Line Dr Naples FL 33940 Office: 1075 Central Ave Naples FL 33940

STODDARD, CHARLES HATCH, conservation cons.; b. Milw., Apr. 28, 1912; s. Charles Hatch and Eloise (Jackson) S.; B.S. in Forestry, U. Mich., 1934, M.S., 1938; postgrad. U. Wis., 1941; m. Patricia Coulter, June 30, 1956; children—Charles Hatch, Abby Weed, Paul Christopher, Glenn McDonald, Jeffrey Jackson. Economist, U.S. Forest Service, 1934-40, Bur. Land Econs., 1941-43, Resources for the Future, 1955-61; cons. in resources, 1946-55; dir. resources program staff Dept. Interior, 1961-63, dir. Bur. Land Mgmt., 1963-66; exec. dir. Citizens Adv. Com. on Environment, 1966-68; conservation cons. Conservation Found., 1968-72. Chmn. Public Intervenor Adv. Com. on Environment, State of Wis., 1978—; mem. Pres.'s Quetico Superior Adv. Com., 1963-66; adviser on resources to Pres. Kennedy, 1960-61; chmn. U.S. Army C.E. Environmental Adv. Bd., 1970-72. Fellow Charles Lathrop Forestry Found., 1937-38, 46-48. Served as lt. USNR, 1942-46. Recipient Distinguished Service award Nat. Assn. Conservation Dists., 1964. Sr. mem. Soc. Am. Foresters; mem. Wilderness Soc. (pres. 1977-78), Ecol. Soc. Am., Wis. Acad. Sci., Sigma Xi, Beta Theta Pi. Unitarian. Club: Cosmos (Washington). Author: Forest Farming and Rural Employment, 1949; Essentials of Forestry Practice, 1958; (with Clawson, Held) Land for the Future, 1960; The Small Forest, 1961. Home: Wolf Springs Forest Minong WI 54859. *Such success as I may have achieved appears to be the result more from my efforts to advance ideas and proposals beneficial to the public interest than promotion of personal ambition, organizational aggrandizement or material pursuit. If one keeps in mind the observation that every man is as important as the things about which he is concerned, one has a comparative measure of relative success.*

STODDARD, GEORGE DINSMORE, educator; b. Carbondale, Pa., Oct. 8, 1897; s. Eugene Anson and Charlotte (Dinsmore) S.; A.B., Pa. State Coll., 1921; diplome U. Paris, 1923; Ph.D., U. Ia., 1925; Litt.D., Colgate U., 1942; LL.D., St. Lawrence U., Syracuse U., Hobart Coll., 1942, N.Y. U., Skidmore Coll., 1943, Union Coll., 1944; Yeshiva U., 1946, U. Fla., Lake Forest Coll., Washington U., 1948, U. Toledo, 1949, U. Louisville, 1952, U. Ill., 1968; L.H.D., Alfred U., 1943; D.C.L., Shurtleff Coll., 1952; D.F.A., Grinnell Coll., 1959; m. Margaret Trautwein, Dec. 26, 1925 (dec.); children—Philip Hendrick, Arthur Dinsmore, Eleanor, Caroline, Alfred Eugene (dec.). Asso. in psychology, edn. U. Iowa, 1925-26, asst. prof., 1926-28, asso. prof. psychology, 1928-29, prof., 1929-42, also dir. Iowa Child Welfare Research Sta., 1928-42, dean Grad. Coll., 1936-42, head dept. psychology, 1938-39; pres. U. State N.Y., commr. edn., 1942-46; pres. U. Ill., 1946-53; chmn. directing com. Self-Study N.Y. U.; dean N.Y. U. Sch. Edn., 1956-60, chancellor, exec. v.p., 1960-64, Distinguished prof. edn., 1964-67; vice chancellor for acad. affairs L.I. U., 1967-68, chancellor, 1968-69; chmn. Am. Council Edn., 1946-47. Mem. bd. Lincoln Center Performing Arts, 1958-69; dir. Arts Curriculum project JDR 3d Fund, 1969-70. Chmn., U.S. Edn. Mission to Japan, 1946; del. UNESCO gen. confs., London, 1945, Paris, 1946, 48, 51, Mexico City, 1947, Beirut, 1949, Florence, 1950; mem. U.S. Nat. Commn. UNESCO, chmn., 1949-52. Vice chmn. Nat. Com. Mid-century White House Conf. Children and Youth, 1950. 2d lt. F.A.R.C., 1918-23. Fellow AAAS; mem. Am. Psychol. Assn., NEA, Sigma Xi, Phi Beta Kappa, Sigma Pi, Phi Kappa Phi, Delta Sigma Rho, Phi Delta Kappa, Kappa Delta Pi (laureate chpt.). Clubs: Century Assn., Unitarian. Author: Iowa Placement Examinations, 1925; Tests and Measurements in High School Instruction (with G.M. Ruch), 1927; The General Shop (with L.V. Newkirk), 1928; Study Manual in Elementary Statistics (with E.F. Lindquist), 1929; Getting Ideas from the Movies (with P.W. Holaday), 1933; Child Psychology (with B.L. Wellman), 1934; Manual of Child Psychology (with Wellman), 1936; The Meaning of Intelligence, 1943; Tertiary Education, 1944; Frontiers in Education, 1945; On the Education of Women, 1950; Krebiozen, The Great Cancer Mystery, 1955; The Dual Progress Plan, 1961. Editor-in-chief New Wonder World Ency.; The Outlook for American Education, 1974. Home: 434 E 87th St New York City NY 10028. *We are free in all respects save one; we are not free to tolerate the destruction of our freedom.*

STODDARD, GEORGE EARL, investment co. fin. exec.; b. Perry, Oreg., Jan. 7, 1917; s. G. Earl and Elthira (Thomas) S.; A.B., Brigham Young U., 1937; M.B.A., Harvard U., 1939; LL.B., Fordham U., 1959; m. Elma Skelton, Feb. 4, 1942; children—Evan, Jean, Robert, Patricia. Investment analyst Central Hanover Bank & Trust Co., N.Y.C., 1939-42; v.p. investment ops. Equitable Life Assurance Soc. U.S., N.Y.C., 1945-79; chmn. fin. com. W. P. Carey & Co., N.Y.C., 1979—, also dir.; dir. S.W. Forest Industries, Phoenix. Bd. dirs. United Fund of Bronxville-Eastchester, N.Y., 1960-61; pres. Home Sch. Assn., Eastchester, 1962. Served to lt. USNR, 1942-45. Clubs: Harvard, Harvard Bus. Sch. (N.Y.C.). Home: 11 Cedar Pl Eastchester NY 10707 Office: 689 Fifth Ave New York NY 10022

STODDARD, GEORGE EDWARD, educator; b. Boise, Idaho, July 15, 1921; s. William R. and Estella (Hansen) S.; B.S. in Agr., U. Idaho, 1943, M.S., U. Wis., 1948, Ph.D., 1950; m. Corinne Marie Pecora, Aug. 7, 1946; children—Karalee (Mrs. M.D. Salvesen), Douglas G., Steven E., Gary W., Shauna M. Asst. prof. Iowa State Coll., Ames, 1949-52; prof. Utah State U., Logan, 1952—, head dept. dairy sci., 1960-76; pres. Agri Mgmt. Consultants, Inc., 1972-77; mem. staff Agriservices Found., 1975-76; mem. Utah Dairy Commn. Served with USMCR, 1943-46; PTO; now capt. Res. (ret.). Decorated Purple Heart; recipient Faculty Service award Asso. Students Utah State U., 1967; named Hon. State Farmer, Future Farmers of Am., Utah, 1969. Mem. Am. Soc. Animal Scis., Am. Dairy Sci. Assn., AAAS, Utah Acad. Arts and Scis., Am. Dairy Assn. Utah (exec. com.), Utah Dairy Council (ex-officio mem.), Sigma Xi, Alpha Zeta. Mem. Ch. of Jesus Christ of Latter-day Saints (bishop). Contbr. articles to profl. jours. Home: 950 N 4th E Logan UT 84321. *He who inspires others to achieve up to their potential perpetuates his greatness for all future generations.*

STODDARD, JOHN EDWARD, investment banker; b. Bklyn., Aug. 19, 1932; s. Edward John and Marian D. (Kelly) S.; Ph.B. in Commerce, U. Notre Dame, 1954; m. Joan M. Jurek, June 25, 1955; children—John Edward, Kenneth B., Marian J. Mgmt. cons. Lybrand, Roos Bros. & Montgomery (now Coopers & Lybrand), N.Y.C., 1954-63; exec. v.p. Blyth Eastman Dillon & Co., Inc., N.Y.C., 1963—, also dir.; dir. Eastdil Realty Inc., Blyth Eastman Dillon Capital Markets Inc., Blyth Eastman Dillon & Co. S.Am., Blyth Eastman & Co. Internat. Ltd., Hobe Grove, Inc, Hobe Sound, Fla., Harry M. Stevens, Inc., Depository Trust Co., mem. bd. arbitration N.Y. Stock Exchange. Trustee Blyth Eastman Dillon Found.; bd. dirs., trustee Morris Hall Health and Rehab. Center, Lawrenceville, N.J. bd. dirs. Downtown Manhattan Assn. Mem. Fin. Execs. Inst., Am. Inst. C.P.A.'s (advisory bd.), N.Y. Bond Club. Clubs: Bedens Brook (N.J.); University (N.Y.C.); Coral Reef Yacht (Miami, Fla.); Boca Raton (Fla.). Home: 15 W Long Dr Lawrenceville NJ 08648 Office: Blyth Eastman Dillon & Co Inc 1221 Ave of the Americas New York NY 10020

STODDARD, PHILIP ARNOLD, univ. adminstr.; b. Hingham, Mass., Nov. 29, 1917; s. Ralph Clinton and Florence Victoria (Menzies) S.; grad. Phillips Exeter Acad., 1936; S.B., Mass. Inst. Tech., 1940; m. Lucille Hannah Fortna, July 3, 1943; children—Janet Alison, Jeffrey Richard. Asst. to factory comptroller Ingersoll-Rand Co., 1945-47; with Mass. Inst. Tech., 1947—, asst. treas., 1956-57, vice treas., 1957-61, v.p. operations, 1961—. Vice pres., trustee Hingham Instn. Savs.; sec., dir. Harvard Coop. Soc. Served to maj. AUS, 1940-45. Mem. Third Armored Div. Clubs: Mass. Inst. Tech. Faculty; St. Botolph. Home: 6 Leavitt St Hingham MA 02043 Office: Mass Inst Tech 77 Massachusetts Ave Cambridge MA 02139

STODDARD, ROBERT WARING, corp. exec.; b. Trenton, N.J., Jan. 22, 1906; s. Harry Galpin and Janett (Waring) S.; Ph.B., Yale, 1928; postgrad. Harvard, 1929; D.Eng. (hon.), Worcester Poly. Inst., 1952; LL.D., Assumption, 1959; D.Sc., Piedmont Coll., 1966; L.H.D., Central New Eng. Coll. Tech., 1974; m. Helen Esterbrook, Oct. 7, 1933; children—Judith (Mrs. B.A. King), Valerie (Mrs. S.B. Loring). Asst. works mgr. Wyman & Gordon Co., Worcester, Mass., 1936, works mgr., 1938, v.p., dir., 1941. exec. v.p., dir., 1951-55, pres., dir., 1955-67, chmn. bd., 1967—; chmn. bd. Worcester Telegram & Gazette, Inc.; dir. Internat. Paper Co., Worcester County Nat. Bank, 1st Nat Bank Boston, Raytheon Co., L.S. Starrett Co. Dir., past pres. Asso. Industries Mass.; trustee Worcester Poly. Inst.; bd. dirs., past pres. YMCA; trustee Hahnemann Hosp., Art Mus., Found. for Exptl. Biology, Natural History Soc. Mem. Am. Antiquarian Soc. (council Worcester). Clubs: University, Worcester, Worcester Country, Tatnuck Country (Worcester); Federal (Boston); Safari International (Los Angeles); Anglers (N.Y.C.); Algonquin (Boston); Chicago. Home: 19 Monmouth Rd Worcester MA 01609 Office: Wyman-Gordon Co Worcester MA 01603

STODDARD, STEPHEN DAVIDSON, ceramic engr.; b. Everett, Wash., Feb. 8, 1925; s. Albert and Mary Louise (Billings) S.; student Tacoma Coll., 1944, Conn. Coll., 1946; B.S., U. Ill., 1950; m. Joann Elizabeth Burt, June 18, 1949; children—Dorcas Ann, Stephanie Kay. Asst. prodn. supr., asst. ceramic engr. Coors Porcelain Co., Golden, Colo., 1950-52; ceramics-powder metallurgy sect. leader Los Alamos (N.Mex.) Sci. Lab., U. Calif., 1952—; sr. asso. Materials Tech. Assos., Inc. Cons. Ceramic Age Mag., 1958-60, Nuclear Applications for Ceramic Materials, 1958-60. Jury commr. Los Alamos County, 1969; justice of peace, 1956-62; mem. Los Alamos Sch. Adv. Council, 1966; municipal judge, 1976-77; chmn. Los Alamos Ordinance Rev. Com., 1958. Mem. Republican County and State Central Com., 1955—; county commr., Los Alamos, N.Mex., 1966-68; mem. Los Alamos County Planning Commn., 1962-63. Bd. dirs. Sangre de Cristo council Girl Scouts Am., 1965-71. Served with AUS, 1943-46. Decorated Bronze Star medal, Purple Heart, Combat Inf. badge. Fellow Am. Ceramic Soc. (treas. 1972-74, pres. 1976-77), Am. Inst. Chemists; mem. Nat. Inst. Ceramic Engrs. (Pace award 1965), Am. Soc. Metals, Sigma Xi, Alpha Tau Omega. Episcopalian. Clubs: Masons, Elks, Kiwanis (pres. 1963-64, exalted ruler 1967-68, lt. gov. 1968-69), Los Alamos Golf Assn. (dir. 1964-66). Patentee in field. Home: 203 Chamisa Ave Los Alamos NM 87544 Office: PO Box 1663 Los Alamos NM 87545

STODDART, JACK ELLIOTT, publisher; b. Hamilton, Ont., Can., July 24, 1916; s. Henry Elliott and May (Elliott) S.; student Westervelt Coll., U. Toronto; m. Ruth Elizabeth Robb, May 9, 1942; children—Jack Elliott, Susan Elizabeth. With Macmillan Co. of Can., 1936-57; pres. Gen. Pub. Co. Ltd., Don Mills, Ont., 1957—, now chmn., chief exec. officer; chmn., pres. Stoddart Pub. Ltd.; chmn. Musson Book Co.; pres., pub. PaperJacks Ltd.; dir. Nelson Foster & Scott, George J. McLeod, Mercor Pub. Ltd. Served with RCAF. Mem. Assn. Can. Pubs. Conservative. Anglican. Club: Donalda (Don Mills). Contbr. articles in field to various publs. Office: Gen Pub Co Ltd 30 Lesmill Rd Don Mills ON M3B 2T6 Canada

STODDART, JACK ELLIOTT, pub. co. exec.; b. Hamilton, Ont., Can., July 24, 1916; s. Henry Elliott and May (Elliott) S.; student Westervelt Coll., U. Toronto; m. Ruth Elizabeth Robb, May 9, 1942; children—Jack Elliott, Susan Elizabeth. With Macmillan Co. of Can., 1936-57; owner, pres. Gen. Pub. Co., Don Mills, Ont., 1957—, chmn., chief exec. officer, 1977—; owner, chmn. Musson Book Co., Don Mills, 1967—; owner, pres. New Press, 1974—, Simon & Schuster Can. Ltd. 1976— (became PaperJacks Ltd.); chmn., pres. Stoddart Pub. Ltd., Toronto; owner, dir. Nelson Foster & Scott, 1978—, George J. McLeod Ltd., 1978—; dir. Mercor Pub. Ltd. Served with RCAF. Mem. bd. Trade Met. Toronto. Mem. Assn. Can. Pubs. Conservative. Anglican. Contbr. articles to profl. jours. Office: Gen Pub Co Ltd 30 Lesmill Rd Don Mills ON M3B 2T6 Canada

STODDART, JOHN B., JR., ins. co. exec.; b. Malvern, Iowa, Apr. 6, 1919; s. John B. and Kathryn (Mellor) S.; A.B., U. Nebr., 1941; LL.B., U. Mich., 1946; m. Betty Marie Wait, Feb. 3, 1943; children—Susan, John Bergman III, Lynn. Admitted to Ill. bar, 1947, N.J. bar, 1960; asso. firm Brown, Hay & Stephens, Springfield, Ill., 1947-53; asst. states atty. Sangamon County, Ill., 1949-51; U.S. atty. So. Dist. Ill., 1953-58; with Prudential Ins. Co. Am., 1958—, sr. v.p., gen. counsel, 1969—. Chmn. bd. trustees Overlook Hosp., Summit, N.J., 1972-74. Served to maj. USAAF, 1941-45. Decorated D.F.C. Fellow Inst. Jud. Adminstrn. (pres. 1978—), Am. Bar Found.; mem. Am. (council sect. corp. banking and bus. law 1969-72, 75—, sec. sect. 1976, chmn. corp. law depts. com. 1973—, chmn.-elect sect. 1978), Ill., N.J., Essex County bar assns., Fed. Bar Council, Am. Judicature Soc., Beta Theta Pi, Phi Delta Phi. Presbyn. Mason. Club: Baltusrol Golf, Short Hills, Essex, Chatham (Mass.) Beach and Tennis. Home: 45 North Rd Short Hills NJ 07078 Office: Prudential Ins Co Am Prudential Plaza Newark NJ 07101

STOECKER, KARL A., ry. co. exec.; b. Bklyn., Dec. 22, 1915; s. Walter H. and Marie (Sopp) S.; student N.Y. U., 1946, Harvard, 1948; m. Doris Helen Vincent, Apr. 5, 1941; children—Karl R., Richard V. With Standard Oil Co. N.J., 1935- 58; financial dir. Esso Mediterranean Co., Geneva, Switzerland, 1959-65; asst. treas. internat. Continental Oil Co., 1965-67, treas., 1968-70; v.p. fin. So. Ry. Co., Washington, 1970-75, v.p., chief fin. officer, 1975-77, sr. v.p. fin., 1977—. Active local Boy Scouts Am., 1942-54. Home: 4050 52d St NW Washington DC 20016 Office: 920 15th St Washington DC 20005

STOECKER, LEO JOSEPH, editor; b. Chgo., Feb. 18, 1919; s. George J. and Magdalena M. (Schmitt) S.; student St. Norbert Coll., De Pere, Wis., 1936-39; M.S. in Journalism, Northwestern U., 1941; m. Virginia Thayer, Nov. 25, 1945 (dec. 1960); m. 2d, Ruth Mann, Aug. 11, 1967; children—H. Stephen, John T., Daniel G., Timothy A., Douglas A., Catherine M., John A., Philip A. Reporter-photographer La Crosse (Wis.) Tribune, 1941-43; photographer-editor Acme News-Pictures, UPI, Chgo., 1943-45, war corr., Germany, Italy, 1945-46; bur. mgr., Middle East corr. UPI, Rome, Italy, 1946-53, European newspictures editor, London, Eng., 1953-59, newspictures internat. dir., N.Y.C., 1959-73, newspictures editor, 1973-76, editor, mgr. Unislide Service, N.Y.C., 1976—. Recipient Achievement award for outstanding service to journalism St. Norbert Coll., 1968. Mem. Sigma Delta Chi. Home: 23 S Washington St Port Washington NY 11050 Office: UPI 220 E 42d St New York NY 10017

STOEFFLER, FRED ERNEST, minister, educator, United Meth. Ch.; b. Happenbach, W. Ger., Sept. 27, 1911; s. Karl Gottlieb and Maria (Mueller) S.; came to U.S., 1926, naturalized, 1935; B.S., Temple U., 1938, S.T.M., 1945, S.T.D., 1948; B.D., Yale U., 1941; m. Marie Anna Brodbeck, Aug. 26, 1939; children—P. Marie (Mrs. Robert Richards), Linda R. (Mrs. Bernard Giardetti). Ordained deacon United Methodist Ch., 1939, elder, 1941; pastor Columbus Ave. Meth. Ch., New Haven, 1939-42, Girard Ave. Meth. Ch., Phila., 1942-51; asst. prof. Christianity, Temple U., 1951-56, asso. prof., 1956-57, prof., 1957-62, prof. religion, 1962—; mem. seminar for Christian origins U. Pa., Homewood seminar for early Am. studies Johns Hopkins U.; organizer German relief action Meth. Com. for Overseas Relief. Chmn. theol. com., mem. edn. com. Pa. Council Chs.; chmn. nat. pietism study group Am. Acad. Religion. Recipient alumni award Temple U., 1958. Mem. Acad. Polit. Sci., Am. Soc. Ref. Research, Renaissance Soc. Am., Am. Hist. Assn., Am. Soc. 18th Century Studies, Am. Acad. Religion, AAUP, Pa. Council Chs. Author: Mysticism in the German Devotional Literature of Colonial

Pennsylvania, 1949; Rise of Evangelical Pietism, 1965; German Pietism During the Eighteenth Century, 1973. Translator: History of Doctrine (B. Lohse), 1966; editor: Continental Pietism and Early American Christianity, 1976. Home: 1132 Locust Ave Lansdale PA 19446 Office: Temple University Philadelphia PA 19122

STOEHR, KEITH WAYNE, coll. adminstr.; b. Green Bay, Wis., Aug. 20, 1934; s. Phillip M. and Francis (Murdock) S.; B.S., U. Wis.-Stevens Point, 1956; M.A., Mich. State U., 1963; Ed.S., U. Wis.-Stout, 1978; H.L.D. (hon.), Carthage Coll. Kenosha, Wis., 1979; m. Carol Paiser, Aug. 4, 1956; children—Patrick, Jeanne. Driver edn., safety instr. Kenosha (Wis.) Vocat. and Adult Sch., 1956-63; instructional supr. Kenosha Tech. Inst., 1963-67; dist. dir., pres. Gateway Tech. Inst., Kenosha, 1967—; vis. prof. So. State Coll., Springfield, S.D., 1970; cons. in field. Bd. dirs. Kenosha County Blood Donor Club; group co-chmn. United Way, 1976; mem. adv. bd. Kenosha Meml. Hosp., 1967—. Mem. Wis. Assns Vocat. and Adult Edn., Am. Vocat. Assn., Am. Assn. Community and Jr. Colls., Phi Delta Kappa (past sec.). Contbr. articles to profl. jours. Home: 8521 37th Ave Kenosha WI 53142 Office: 3520 30th Ave Kenosha WI 53141

STOEL, THOMAS BURROWES, lawyer; b. Clayton, N.Y., Oct. 27, 1913; A.B., Hobart Coll., 1934; LL.B., Duke; m. Caroline Phillips, May 28, 1938; children—Thomas Burrowes, Caroline M., Peter F., Polly L. Admitted to Oreg. bar, 1937; now partner firm Stoel, Rives, Boley, Fraser & Wyse, Portland. Mem. Am., Multnomah County bar assns., Oreg. State Bar. Unitarian. Clubs: Arlington, University, Multnomah, Waverley. Address: 900 SW 5th Ave Portland OR 97204

STOELTING, VERGIL KENNETH, physician; b. Freelandville, Ind., Feb. 10, 1912; s. Andrew P. and Ethel B. (Jones) B.; B.S., Ind. U., 1936, M.D., 1936; postgrad. anesthesiology Univ. Wis., 1943-44; m. Bernice B. Markus, Sept. 5, 1936; children—Robert, Ann. Intern, Waterbury, Conn. Hosp., 1936-37; practice of medicine, Winchester, Ind., 1938-42, Indpls., 1948—. specializing anesthesiology, 1946—; residency anesthesiology U. Iowa, 1946-47; prof. anesthesiology Ind. U. Sch. Medicine, 1948-78, prof. emeritus, 1978—, also mem. deans com.; dir. dept. anesthesiology Ind. U. Hosp., 1948-78; sr. cons. anesthesiology Vets. Hosp. cons. anesthesiology Marion County Gen. Hosp., Methodist Hosp. and Community Hospital, Indpls.; cons. St. Vincent's Hosp. Served as major, M.C., AUS, 1942-46. Diplomate Am. Bd. Anesthesiology. Mem. A.M.A., Ind. Med. Assn., Am. Soc. Anesthesiology, Ind. Soc. Anesthesiologists, Assn. U. Anesthetists, Sociedade Brasileira de Anesthesiologia (hon.), Aircraft Owners and Pilots Assn., Flying Physicians Assn., Ind. Flying Physicians, Pan Pacific Surg. Assn., Pan Am. Med. Assn., Soc. Academic Anesthesiology Chairmen, Acad. Anesthesiology, Aerospace Med. Soc., Ind. U. Mens Club, Ind. U. Loyalty Club, Ind. U. Alumni Assn., Phi Chi. Presbyn. Mason (Shriner). Club: Hillcrest Country. Home: 4706 Laurel Circle Indianapolis IN 46226 Office: 1100 W Michigan St Indianapolis IN 46202

STOESSEL, WALTER JOHN, JR., ambassador; b. Manhattan, Kans., Jan. 24, 1920; s. Walter John and Katherine (Haston) S.; A.B., Stanford, 1941; student Russian Inst., Columbia, 1949-50, Center Internat. Affairs, Harvard, 1959-60; m. Mary Ann Ferrandou, June 20, 1946; children—Katherine, Suzanne, Christine. Fgn. service officer, 1942—; vice consul, 3d sec. embassy, Caracas, Venezuela, 1942-44, 2d sec., vice consul, Moscow, USSR, 1947-49; polit. officer, Bad Nauheim, also Bad Homburg, Germany, 1950-52; officer charge USSR affairs Dept. State, 1952-56; assigned White House, 1956; 1st sec., consul, Paris, 1956-59; dir. exec. secretariat Dept. State, 1960-61; counselor embassy, Paris, 1961-63; minister-counselor, Moscow, USSR, 1963-65; dep. asst. sec. state, Europe, 1965-68; ambassador to Poland, 1968-72; asst. sec. state for European affairs, 1972-74; ambassador to USSR, Moscow, 1974-76, to Fed. Republic of Germany, Bonn, 1976—. Served with USNR, 1944-46. Mem. Council Fgn. Relations, Phi Delta Theta. Club: Chevy Chase. Office: Am Embassy Mahlemer Ave 5300 Bonn-Bad Godesberg APO New York NY 09080

STOHN, MARY, mfrs. agt., orgn. ofcl.; b. Brookline, Mass., June 4, 1918; d. Edmund J. and Julia M. (Whelan) Casey; grad. Beaver Country Day Sch., Chestnut Hill, Mass., 1937; m. Alexander C. Stohn, Jr., July 12, 1941; children—Alexander, Joanna (Mrs. Joseph T. Fernim), Mary, Penelope, Sara. Treas. A.C. Stohn Assos., Inc., mfrs. agt. for electric utilities, Hingham, Mass. Pres. Beaver Country Day Sch. Alumnae Assn., 1968-70; v.p. Alumni Pres.'s Council Ind. Secondary Schs., 1970-72, pres., 1974-76, chmn. regional conf., San Francisco, 1974, chmn. nominating com., 1977; mem. exec. com. Beaver Country Day Sch. Parent Assn., Chestnut Hill, Mass., 1972-74. Mem. corp. Beaver Country Day Sch., 1972—; bd. dirs. Plymouth Philharmonic Orch. Clubs: Longwood Covered Courts (Chestnut Hill); Pilgrim Tennis (Plymouth, Mass.); Duxbury Yacht (dir.). Home: 58 King Caesar Rd Duxbury MA 02332 Office: 10 Industrial Park Rd Hingham MA 02043. *In these days of the "liberated" woman, I maintain more vehemently that the basis for success is a sound marriage and a family! I have been liberated since the day I married and have a fantastic family and a rewarding career to prove it!*

STOICHEFF, BORIS PETER, physicist, educator; b. Bitol, Yugoslavia, June 1, 1924; s. Peter and Vasilka (Tonna) S.; B.A.Sc., U. Toronto, 1947, M.A., 1948, Ph.D., 1950; m. Lilian Joan Ambridge, May 15, 1954; 1 son, Richard Peter. McKee-Gilchrist postdoctoral fellow U. Toronto (Ont., Can.), 1950-51; postdoctorate fellow Canadian NRC, 1951-53, sr. research officer, 1954-64; vis. scientist Mass. Inst. Tech., 1963-64; prof. physics U. Toronto, 1964—, Univ. prof., 1977—, chmn. engring. sci., 1972-77. I.W. Killam scholar, 1977-79. Fellow Royal Soc. Can., Royal Soc. London, Am. Phys. Soc., Optical Soc. Am. (pres. 1976), Indian Acad. Sci. (hon.); mem. Canadian Assn. Physicists (gold medal for achievement in physics 1974). Contbr. numerous articles to tech. jours. Devel. techniques for nigh resolution Raman spectroscopy of gases and determined geometrical structures many molecules; used lasers in spectroscopic nvestigations including Brillouin and stimulated Raman scattering and two photon absorption; observed stimulated Raman absorption nd stimulated Brillouin scattering resulting in generation of intense ypersonic waves in solids; used Brillouin spectra to measure elastic onstants of rare gas crystals, spectroscopy with tunable coherent VUV radiation. Home: 66 Collier St Apt 6B Toronto ON M4W 1L9 anada Office: Dept Physics Univ Toronto Toronto ON M5S 1A7 anada

TOIK, JOHN LENTIS, oil co. exec.; b. North Battleford, Sask., an., Mar. 5, 1920; s. Mike and Barbara (Hoffmann) S.; B.S. in Chem. ngring., U. Sask., 1947; m. Margaret Mary Marshall, Aug. 23, 1943; ildren—John H., Gary L. With Gulf Oil Can., Ltd., Toronto. Ont., 47—, v.p. refining, 1968-70, sr. v.p., 1974-75, pres., chief exec. icer, dir., 1976—; exec. v.p., chief exec. officer Korea Oil Corp., oul, 1970-74; mem. bus. and industry adv. com. on energy and raw terials OECD; dir. Can. Exec. Service Overseas, ronto-Dominion Bank. Bd. dirs. Toronto Symphony. Served with CAF, 1942-45. Mem. Am. Petroleum Inst., Engring. Inst. Can. nservative. Mem. United Ch. of Can. Clubs: Masons, Granite, nadian, Engrs., St. George's Golf and Country, Toronto (Toronto); Rideau (Ottawa). Home: 74 Forest Heights Blvd Willowdale ON M2L 2K6 Canada Office: 800 Bay St Toronto ON M5S 1Y8 Canada

STOKELY, ALFRED JEHU, food processing co. exec.; b. Newport, Tenn., Mar. 26, 1916; s. James R. and Janie May (Jones) S.; A.B., Princeton, 1938; m. Elizabeth Home, Feb. 24, 1940 (dec. Sept. 1952); children—Alfred J., Randolph H., Barbara Elizabeth; m. 2d, Jeannette Tarkington Danner, Mar. 11, 1953; 1 dau., Martha. Sales statistician Stokely-Van Camp, Inc., Indpls., 1938-40, prodn. supr., 1940-43, adminstrv. asst., 1943-45, asst. to pres., 1945, v.p., 1954-56, exec. v. p., dir., 1956-60, pres., 1960-65, pres., chief exec. officer, 1965-78, chmn., chief exec. officer, 1978—; mem. exec. com., v.p. Stokely Van Camp of Can., Ltd.; dir. Indpls. Power & Light Co., Am. United Life Ins. Co., Am. Fletcher Nat. Bank and Trust Co., Ind. Bell Telephone Co., Hobart Corp. Trustee Butler U., Indpls., Berea (Ky.) Coll. Mem. Phi Beta Kappa. Clubs: Woodstock, University. Home: 8198 N Pennsylvania St Indianapolis IN 46240 Office: 941 N Meridian St Indianapolis IN 46204

STOKELY, MURRAY MARVIN, engring.-archtl. co. exec.; b. Newport, Tenn., May 26, 1914; s. Murray Marvin and Emma Lee (Robinson) S.; B.S.E.E., Clemson U., 1936; m. Merle Wyline Baird, Mar. 10, 1946; children—Wyline, Murray; 1 stepson, Baird Bowman. With J.E. Sirrine Co., 1946—, v.p., head elec. dept., 1956-61, exec. v.p., 1961-65, pres., 1966-75, chief exec. officer, 1973-78, chmn. bd., 1975—; dir. 1st Nat. Bank, Greenville, S.C. Bd. dirs. Clemson U. Found. Served to lt. col. U.S. Army, 1941-46. Mem. TAPPI, Nat. Soc. Profl. Engrs., N.C. State Pulp and Paper Found. (past dir.), IEEE, Tau Beta Pi. Clubs: Kiwanis, Greenville Country, Poinsett. Home: 132 Rockingham Rd Greenville SC 29607 Office: Box 5456 Sta B Greenville SC 29606

STOKELY, WILLIAM BURNETT, III, corp. exec.; b. Los Angeles, Sept. 18, 1940; s. William Burnett and Tamara S.; m. Kay Haslett, July 28, 1962; children—William Burnett, Stacy Ivie, Shelley Kay, Clayton Frank. Now pres., chief operating officer Stokely-Van Camp, Inc.; dir., chmn., chief exec. officer Stokely-Van Camp of Can., Ltd.; dir., chmn., chief exec. officer M.W. Graves & Co., Ltd., Can.; dir., chmn., pres. Stokely-Van Camp of P.R., Inc., Manati; chmn. S.D.I. of Ind., Inc., Lebanon; dir. Industries Portela, C. por A., and Casa Linda, C. por A., Navarrete, D.R., Hoosier Horse Industries, Inc., Carmel, Ind.; dir., chmn. audit com. Mchts. Nat. Bank & Trust Co., Indpls.; mem. food and agr. com., mem. council to reduce govt. paperwork C. of C. U.S. Pres., William B. Stokely, Jr. Found.; bd. dirs., past chmn. water com. Environ. Quality Control, Inc., Indpls.; bd. dirs. Indpls. Conv. and Visitors Bur.; mem. St. Vincent Hosp. Research and Devel. Found., Indpls.; mem. and past chmn. U. Tenn. Devel. Council, Knoxville, mem. bd. visitors Berry Coll.; mem. Brebeuf Sch. Pres.'s Council, Indpls.; mem. bus. adv. council U. Tenn. Mem. Nat. Food Processors Assn., Ind. Canners Assn. (past pres.), Young Pres.'s Orgn., Penrod Soc. Indpls. (past pres.), Indpls. Museum Art, Children's Mus. Indpls., Newcomen Soc. N.Am., Kappa Sigma, Omicron Delta Kappa. Clubs: Econs., Hundred (dir.), Univ., Indpls. Athletic (Indpls.); Crooked Stick Golf, Carmel Racquet (Carmel, Ind.). Office: 941 N Meridian St Indianapolis IN 46206

STOKER, WARREN CADY, ednl. adminstr., b. Union Springs, N.Y., Jan. 30, 1912; s. Ray W. amd Dora Maude (Cady) S.; E.E., Rensselaer Poly. Inst., 1933, M.E.E., 1934, Ph.D., 1938; m. Ruth Eleanor Gabb, Aug. 30, 1934; children—Robert Warren, W. Lance, Lois Ruth. Instr. to asso. prof. elec. engring. Rensselaer Poly. Inst., 1934-51, prof., 1951—, head computer lab., 1952-55, dir. Hartford Grad. Center, 1955-57, dean Grad. Center, 1957-70, asso. dean Grad. Sch., 1957-69, v.p. Rensselaer Poly. Inst. Conn., 1961-74, pres., 1974-75, also trustee; pres. Hartford Grad. Center (formerly Rensselaer Poly. Inst. Conn.), 1975-76, trustee, 1975—; trustee Mechanics Savs. Bank, Hartford, 1974—. Mem. Sci. Research Soc. Am., I.E.E.E., Newcomen Soc. N.Am., Am. Soc. for Engring. Edn., Greater Hartford C. of C., Sigma Xi, Tau Beta Pi, Eta Kappa Nu. Club: Hartford (Conn.). Home: 4 Neptune Dr Groton CT 06340 Office: 275 Windsor St Hartford CT 06120

STOKES, ARNOLD PAUL, educator; b. Bismarck, N.D., Jan. 24, 1932; s. Joel Edward and Elizabeth (Bauer) S.; student St. Martin's Coll., 1949-53; B.S. (RCA scholar), U. Notre Dame, 1955, Ph.D., 1959; m. Gaye Teresa Wims, Oct. 19, 1957; children—Michael, Jonathan, Thomas, Katherine, Christopher, Peter. Mathematician, Research Inst. Advanced Study, Balt., 1958-60; NSF post-doctoral fellow Johns Hopkins U., 1960-61; asst. prof. Cath. U. Am., Washington, 1961-63, asso. prof., 1963-64; prof. Georgetown U., Washington, 1965—, chmn. math. dept., 1967-70. Cons., NASA, Goddard Space Flight Center, Greenbelt, Md., 1962-67, NRC sr. research asso., 1974-75. Trustee Consortium D.C. Univs., 1970-75. Mem. Am. Math. Soc. Research ordinary, functional differential equations. Home: 7708 Meadow Ln Chevy Chase MD 20015 Office: Math Dept Georgetown U Washington DC 20007

STOKES, B. R., assn. exec.; b. Anadarko, Okla., Feb. 20, 1924; s. Robert Allan and Ethel Nan (James) S.; student U. Okla., 1941-44; B.A., U. Calif., Berkeley, 1947; m. Joan Pringle, Oct. 22, 1950; children—Timothy, Leigh, Lindsey, Celia. Reporter, writer Oakland (Calif.) Tribune, 1946-58; dir. info. San Francisco Bay Area Rapid Transit Dist., 1958-61, asst. gen. mgr., 1961-63, gen. mgr., 1963-74; exec. v.p. Am. Public Transit Assn., Washington, 1974—. Served with USNR, 1942-46. Reid Found. fellow, 1954. Recipient Salzberg medal Syracuse U., 1975. Office: 1100 17th St NW Washington DC 20036

STOKES, CARL BURTON, former mayor Cleve., lawyer; b. Cleve., June 21, 1927; s. Charles and Louise (Stone) S.; B.S. in Law, U. Minn., 1954; LL.B., LL.D., Cleve. Marshall Law Sch., 1956; LL.D., Tufts U., U. Cin., St. Francis Coll., Central State U., Wilberforce U., Lincoln U., Union Coll., Livingston Coll., Boston U., Oberlin Coll.; m. Shirley Joann Edwards, Jan. 28, 1958 (div. Oct. 1974); children—Carl Burton, Cordi, Cordell. Admitted to Ohio bar, 1957, N.Y. State bar, 1974; probation officer Cleve. Municipal Ct., 1954-58; asst. prosecutor City Cleve., 1958-62; partner firm Stokes & Stokes, Cleve., 1962-67; commentator WNBC, N.Y.C., 1972—. Mem. exec. com. Nat. League Cities, 1968-71, pres. elect 1970-71; mem. adv. bd. U.S. Conf. Mayors, 1968-71; mem. steering com. Nat. Urban Coalition, 1968—; adv. com. Urban Am., 1969-71. Mem. Ohio Ho. of Reps., 1962-67; mayor Cleve., 1967-71; mem. policy com. Nat. Democratic Com., 1969-71, hon. chmn. 21st Congl. Dist. caucus, 1970-72. Served with AUS, 1945-46: ETO. Recipient numerous awards including Equal Opportunity award Nat. Urban League; fellow Commn. Phila.; Mass. Com. Protestants, Caths. and Jews; Horatio Alger award; Pacesetter award Young People div. Jewish Community Fedn. Chgo.; Chubb fellow Yale. Mem. Gamma Eta Gamma, Kappa Alpha Psi. Elk. Author: Promise of Power; The Quality of Our Environment. Contbr. articles to profl. jours. Home: 1175 York Ave New York City NY 10021 Office: 30 Rockefeller Plaza New York City NY 10020

STOKES, CHARLES JUNIUS, economist, educator; b. Washington, Aug. 17, 1922; s. Francis Warner and Vivienne E. (Cooke) S.; A.B. with honor and distinction, Boston U., 1943, A.M., 1947, Ph.D., 1950; m. Anne Richardson Wood, June 13, 1946; children—Kevin Barrett, Keith Warner. Mem. faculty Atlantic Union Coll., South Lancaster, Mass., 1946-60, dean coll., 1954-56; Charles A. Dana prof. econs. U. Bridgeport (Conn.), 1960—, Chmn. dept., 1960-72. Dir. econ. research, region I, OPS, 1951-53; dir. Latin Am. case studies Brookings Instn., 1963-64; Fulbright prof., Ecuador, 1958-59, Argentina, 1960, Peru, 1964; lectr. Inter-Am. Def. Coll., 1977—; chmn., dir. Monroe Bank & Trust Co.; cons. to industry, founds., govt. Chmn., Lancaster (Mass.) Housing Authority, 1957-61; chmn. econ. com. Greater Bridgeport Regional Planning Agy., 1961-72; asst. dir. U.S. GAO, 1972-73; mem. Instn. for Social and Policy Studies, Yale U., 1977—. Trustee Pioneer Valley Acad., 1966-69, Andrews U., 1967-72, Atlantic Union Coll., 1968-73; mem. Conn. com. Regional Plan Assn., 1977—; bd. dirs. Greater Bridgeport Symphony Soc., 1978—. Served with AUS, 1943-46. Decorated Medal of Honor (Argentina); named to Collegium of Disting. Alumni, Boston U. Coll. Liberal Arts, 1974. Sears Found. Fed. faculty fellow, 1972-73. Mem. Nat. Economists Club, Am. Econ. Assn. (pres. Conn. Valley 1966), Phi Beta Kappa, Phi Beta Kappa Assos., Delta Sigma Rho, Beta Gamma Sigma. Seventh-Day Adventist (elder, exec. com. SNE Conf. 1966-69, mem. bd. regents edn. dept). Author: Crecimiento Economico (Economic Growth), 1964; Transportation and Economic Development in Latin America, 1968; Managerial Economics: A Case Book, 1968; Managerial Economics: A Textbook, 1969; Historic Fairfield County Churches, 1969; Urban Housing Market Performance, 1975; Economics for Managers, 1978; Corporate Capital Budgeting, 1979; also articles to profl. jours.; columns in regional newspapers. Home: Pepper Crossing Stepney CT 06468 Office: Mandeville Hall Univ Bridgeport Bridgeport CT 06602. *Success is fleeting. If only the good remains from what I have done, even that is not mine but God's.*

STOKES, COLIN, former tobacco co. exec.; b. Winston-Salem, N.C., Apr. 4, 1914; s. Henry Straughan and Eloise (Brown) S.; grad. McCallie Sch., Chattanooga, 1931; B.S., U. N.C., 1935; m. Mary Louise Siewers, Jan. 1, 1943; children—Louise Siewers (Mrs. Philip G. Kinken), Henry Straughan, Daniel Shober. With R.J. Reynolds Tobacco Co., 1935-72, asst. to supt. mfg., 1947-53, asst. supt. mfg., 1953-56, supt. mfg. 1956-59, dir., 1957—, v.p., 1959-61, exec. v.p., 1961-70, chmn. bd., 1970-72; pres. R.J. Reynolds Industries, Inc., 1972-73, chmn. bd. dirs., 1973-79, also dir.; dir. Cannon Mills Co., N.C. Nat. Bank, Winston-Salem Savs. & Loan Assn., NCNB Corp., Integon Corp. Bd. dirs. YMCA, 1946-52; campaign chmn. United Fund Forsyth County, 1957, dir., 1957-59; trustee N.C. Bapt. Hosp., chmn. bd. trustees, 1961, 69, 70, chmn. finance com., 1959; chmn. Ind. Coll. Fund N.C., 1979—; bd. dirs. William and Kate B. Reynolds Meml. Park, 1958-64, Child Guidance Clinic, 1959-61; trustee Salem Coll. and Acad., 1966-74; trustee Wake Forest U., 1971-75, 78—, chmn., 1980. Served from pvt. to capt., inf. AUS, 1941-46. Mem. Winston-Salem C. of C. (dir. 1951-55, 68-70), Zeta Psi. Baptist (deacon, mem. finance com.), Kiwanian (dir., pres. 1963). Office: RJ Reynolds Industries Inc Winston-Salem NC 27102

STOKES, DONALD ELKINTON, univ. dean; b. Phila., Apr. 1, 1927; s. Joseph, Jr. and Frances Deborah (Elkinton) S.; A.B., Princeton, 1951; Ph.D., Yale, 1958; m. Sybil Langbaum, May 18, 1955; children—Elizabeth Ann, Susan Carol. Purser, Grace Line, Inc., 1946-47; instr. polit. sci. Yale, 1952-54; prof. polit. sci. U. Mich., Ann Arbor, 1958-74, program dir. Inst. Social Research, 1958-74, chmn. dept. polit. sci., 1970-71, dean Grad. Sch., 1971-74; dean Woodrow Wilson Sch. Pub. and Internat. Affairs Princeton U., N.J., 1974—; vis. prof. Australian Nat. U., U. W.I., 1969. Asso. mem. Nuffield Coll., Oxford, 1963-64. Sr. Fulbright scholar to Britain, 1963; fellow Social Sci. Research Council, 1955-57, Guggenheim Found., 1964-65. Fellow Am. Acad. Arts and Scis.; mem. Nat. Acad. Public Adminstrn., Am. Polit. Sci. Assn. (Woodrow Wilson award 1970), Am. Statis. Assn., Am. Assn. Pub. Opinion Research, Phi Beta Kappa. Mem. Soc. Friends. Co-author: The American Voter, 1960; Elections and the Political Order, 1966; Political Change in Britain, 1969. Home: 150 Fitz Randolph Rd Princeton NJ 08540 Office: Woodrow Wilson School Public and International Affairs Princeton University Princeton NJ 08544

STOKES, DONALD GRESHAM, vehicle co. exec.; b. London, Eng., Mar. 22, 1914; s. Harry Potts and Marie Elizabeth (Yates) S.; grad. mech. engring. Harris Inst. Tech., Preston, Eng., 1933; LL.D., U. Lancaster, 1967; Ph.D. in Tech., U. Loughborough, 1968; D.Sci., U. Southampton, 1969, U. Salford, 1971; m. Laura Elizabeth Courteney Lamb, May 25, 1939; 1 son, Michael Donald. Student apprentice Leyland Motors Ltd., London, 1930, export mgr., 1946-49, gen. sales and service mgr., 1949-53, dir., 1963—, mng. dir., dep. chmn. Brit. Leyland Motor Corp. Ltd., 1967, chmn., mng. dir., 1968-73, chmn., chief exec., 1973-75, pres. Brit. Leyland Ltd., 1975—; chmn. Brit. Arabian Adv. Co. Ltd., 1977—; dir. Nat. Westminster Bank, Ltd., London, 1969—; v.p. Empresa Nacional de Autocamiones S.A., Spain, 1965-73; dir. Metallurgica de Santa Ana S.A., Spain, 1967-76. Dep. lt. for County Palatine of Lancashire. Vice pres. Inst. Sci. and Tech., U. Manchester, 1968-75, pres., 1972-75. Served to lt. col. R.E.M.E., 1939-45. Created knight, 1965, baron (life peer), 1969; decorated Territorial Decoration; officier de l'ordre de la Couronne (Belgium); comdr. de l'Ordre de Leopold II. Fellow Inst. Mech. Engrs. (council, v.p. 1971, pres. 1972), Inst. Motor Industry; mem. Nat. Econ. Devel. Com. (chmn. electronics com. 1966-68), Worshipful Company Carmen, Soc. Motor Mfrs. and Traders (council, pres. 1961-62). Office: Leyland Cars Devonshire House Piccadilly London W1X 6HP England

STOKES, GEORGE ALWIN, coll. dean; b. Winnfield, La., Dec. 29, 1920; s. Alwin and Elizabeth Smith (McIlhenny) S.; A.B., La. State Normal Coll., 1942; M.S., La. State U., 1948, Ph.D., 1954; m. Mary Jane Deahl, June 20, 1945; children—Gordon Michael, Charles William. Mem. faculty Northwestern State U. La., Natchitoches, 1949—, prof. geography and geology, 1961—, dean Sch. Arts and Scis., 1963-67, dean of acad. affairs, 1967—, dean Coll. Liberal Arts, 1968—. Served with AUS, 1942-46. Mem. La. Tchrs. Assn., Sigma Xi, Phi Alpha Theta, Phi Kappa Phi. Contbr. profl. jours., encys. Home: 773 St Maurice Ln Natchitoches LA 71457

STOKES, JOHN LEMACKS, II, clergyman, ednl. adminstr; b. Songdo, Korea, Aug. 23, 1908 (parents Am. citizens); s. Marion Boyd and Florence Pauline (Davis) S.; A.B., Asbury Coll., 1930; postgrad. Asbury Theol. Sem., 1930-31; M.Div., Duke, 1932; Ph.D., Yale, 1936; LL.D., Pfeiffer Coll., 1975; m. Alda Grey Beaman, June 20, 1933; children—John Lemacks III, Mary Anne (foster dau.). Ordained to ministry Meth. Ch., 1931; pastor Meth. chs., Randleman, Franklin and Elkin, N.C., 1936-45, Rock Hill, St. John's, S.C., 1945-50; sec. religion higher edn., div. ednl. instns. Bd. Edn., Meth. Ch., Nashville, 1950-53, del. jurisdictional conf., 1952, 60, 68; pres. Pfeiffer Coll., Misenheimer, N.C., 1953-68; exec. sec. Quadrennial Emphasis, United Meth. Ch., 1968-69; asso. dir. N.C. Bd. Higher Edn., Raleigh, 1969-71, acting dir., 1972; asso. v.p. U. N.C., Chapel Hill, 1972-75, spl. asst. in acad. affairs, 1976—, dir. out-of-state programs in health professions, 1972—; mem. Gov.'s Commn. Citizens for Better Schs. N.C., 1956-60, N.C. Com. on Nursing and Patient Care, 1956-64, N.C. Higher Edn. Facilities Edn., 1964-68; chmn. N.C. adv. com. Farmers Home Adminstrn., 1967-69, Marine Sci. Council, 1969-72; mem. N.C. Com. on Drug Abuse, 1970—, N.C. Com. on Aero. Edn., 1971—; dir. N.C. Inst. for Undergrad. Curricular Reform, 1972-78; coordinator Fort Bragg-Pope Grad. Program, 1973-77; adv. com. Nat. Four-Year Servicemen's Opportunity Coll., 1973-78. Bd. dirs. A.R.C.,

1940-48, YMCA, 1946-50; vice chmn. Western N.C. Conf. Bd. Missions, 1960-64; trustee Asbury Coll., 1945-51. Mem. Aircraft Owners and Pilots Assn., U.S. Lawn Tennis Assn., Am. Assn. for Higher Edn., So. Srs. Golf Assn., N.E.A., Nat. Christian Edn. Assn., So. Philos. Soc., Woman's Soc. Christian Service. Mason (Shriner), Rotarian, Civitan. Clubs: Quail Hollow Country, Waynesville Country. Contbr. articles to religious publs. Address: U NC PO Box 2688 Chapel Hill NC 27514

STOKES, JOSEPH, III, educator; b. Phila., Dec. 2, 1924; s. Joseph and Frances (Elkinton) S.; A.B., Haverford Coll., 1946; M.D. magna cum laude, Harvard, 1949; m. Rita J. Mack, Nov. 29, 1968; children (by previous marriage)—Peter, Margaret, J. Barclay, Joseph. Intern, Johns Hopkins Hosp., 1949-50, asst. resident, 1950-51; resident gen. medicine Mass. Gen. Hosp., 1953-54, clin. asst. medicine, 1954-55, asst. medicine, 1955-61, acting chief infectious disease unit, 1960-61; asst. medicine Johns Hopkins Sch. Medicine, 1950-51; sr. asst. surgeon, heart disease study Nat. Heart Inst., NIH, 1951-53, med. officer Framingham (Mass.) heart program, 1955-60; research asso. preventive medicine Harvard Med. Sch., 1951-53, teaching fellow medicine, 1953-54, instr. preventive medicine, 1954-56, asso. preventive medicine, 1956-61; asst. medicine Peter Bent Brigham Hosp., Boston, 1951-53; chief family health program Harvard Med. Sch.-Mass. Gen. Hosp., 1954-61; heart disease control officer Hawaii Health Dept., 1961-62; dir. med. edn. Queen's Hosp., Honolulu, 1962-64, asst. chief medicine, 1963-64; cons. Tripler Army Hosp., Honolulu, 1963-64; prof. medicine, dean U. Calif. at San Diego Sch. Medicine, 1964-66, prof. community medicine, 1966—, chmn. dept., 1966-75; spl. cons. Time-Life Books, 1972-74. Diplomate Am. Bd. Internal Medicine. Fellow A.C.P., Council on Clinical Cardiology, Council on Epidemiology; mem. Mass. Med. Soc., Assn. Tchrs. Preventive Medicine, Internat. Epidemiologic Club, Am. Fedn. Clin. Research, Am. Soc. Human Genetics, Am. Heart Assn., Am. Cancer Soc. (bd. dirs. San Diego County br.), Western Soc. Clin. Research, Western Assn. Physicians, Assn. Behavioral Scis. and Med. Edn. (pres. 1976—), Am. Soc. Internal Medicine, Harvard Med. Alumni Council, Alpha Omega. Mem. editorial bd. New Eng. Jour. Medicine, 1958-59, Jour. Community Health, 1974-76; editor New Eng. Jour. Medicine Progress Series, 1964-75. Contbr. articles to profl. jours. Home: 399 Stratford Ct Apt 115 Del Mar CA 92014

STOKES, LOUIS, congressman; b. Cleve., Feb. 23, 1925; s. Charles and Louise (Stone) S.; student Western Res. U., 1946-48; J.D., Cleve. Marshall Law Sch., 1953; LL.D. (hon.), Wilberforce U., 1969; m. Jeanette Frances, Aug. 21, 1960; children—Shelley, Louis C., Angela, Lorene. Admitted to Ohio bar, 1953, since practiced in Cleve.; mem. 91st and 93d-95th congresses from 21st Ohio dist., mem. appropriations com., budget com., chmn. select com. on assassinations, former chmn. Congl. Black Caucus; guest lectr., 1960—. Mem. adv. council African-Am. Inst. Internat.; mem. exec. com. Cuyahoga County Democratic Party, Ohio State Dem. Party; bd. dirs. Karamu House; trustee Martin Luther King, Jr. Center for Social Change, Forest City Hosp., Cleve. State U. Served with AUS, 1943-46. Recipient numerous awards for civic activities including Distinguished Service award Cleve. br. NAACP; Certificate of Appreciation U.S. Commn. on Civil Rights. Fellow Ohio State Bar Assn.; mem. Am., Cuyahoga County, Cleve. bar assns., Nat. Assn. Def. Lawyers Criminal Cases Fair Housing (dir.), Urban League, Citizens League, John Harlan Law Club, ACLU, Am. Legion, Kappa Alpha Psi. Clubs: Masons, Plus (Cleve.). Home: Cleveland OH Office: 2465 Rayburn House Office Bldg Washington DC 20515

STOKES, MACK (MARION) BOYD, bishop; b. Wonsan, Korea, Dec. 21, 1911; s. Marion Boyd and Florence Pauline (Davis) S.; came to U.S., 1929; student Seoul Fgn. High Sch., Korea; A.B., Asbury Coll., 1932; B.D., Duke, 1935; postgrad. Boston U. Sch. Theol., 1935-37, Harvard, 1936-37; Ph.D., Boston U., 1940; LL.D., Lambuth Coll., Jackson, Tenn., 1963; D.D., Millsaps Coll., 1974; m. Ada Rose Yow, June 19, 1942; children—Marion Boyd, III, Archie Yow and Elsie Pauline. Resident fellow systematic theology Boston U., 1936-38, Bowne fellow in philosophy, 1938-39; ordained to ministry Meth. Ch., deacon, 1938, elder, 1940; vis. prof. philosophy and religion Ill. Wesleyan U., 1940-41; prof. Christian doctrine Candler Sch. Theology, Emory U., 1941-56, asso. dean, Parker prof. systematic theology, 1956-72, chmn. exec. com. div. of religion of grad. sch., 1956-72, acting dean Candler Sch., 1968-69; faculty mem. Inst. Theol. Studies, Oxford U., 1958. Del., Meth. Ecumenical Conf., 1947, 52, 61, 71, Holston, Gen. confs., S.E. Jurisdictional Conf., 1956, 60, 64, 68, 72; chmn. com. ministry Gen. Conf. Meth. Ch., 1960; nat. com. Nature Unity We Seek, 1956—; mem. gen. com. ecumenical affairs theol. study com. United Meth. Ch., 1968-72, com. on Cath.-Meth. relations, 1969—; bishop United Meth. Ch., 1972—. Trustee, Emory U., Millsaps Coll., Rust Coll., Wood Jr. Coll. Mem. Am. Philos. Assn., Am. Acad. Religion, Metaphys. Soc. Am., Theta Phi (nat. sec.), Pi Gamma Mu. Author: Major Methodist Beliefs, 1956; The Evangelism of Jesus, 1960; The Epic of Revelation, 1961; Our Methodist Heritage, 1963; Crencas Fundamentals Dos Methodistas, 1964; Study Guide on the Teachings of Jesus, 1970; The Bible and Modern Doubt, 1970; Major United Methodist Beliefs, 1971; The Holy Spirit and Christian Experience, 1975; Twelve Dialogues on John's Gospel, 1975; Korean transl.: What Methodists Believe, 1977; Jesus, The Master-Evangel, 1978; Can God See the Inside of an Apple?, 1979; The Bible in the Wesleyan Heritage, 1979. Home: 110 Olympia Fields Dr Jackson MS 39211. *Faith in God and basic trust in people. Knowing the direction in which to go, and moving toward it with persistence, resourcefulness, imagination, and patience.*

STOKES, WILLIAM FORREST, journalist; b. Barron, Wis., Sept. 11, 1931; s. Forrest Peter and Agnes Elizabeth (Helgeland) S.; B.S., U. Wis., 1958; m. Betty Lou Buckley, July 14, 1956; children—Patricia, Larry, Scott, Rick, Michael. Reporter, Stevens Point (Wis.) Daily Jour., 1958-59; reporter-columnist Wis. State Jour., Madison, 1959-69; writer-columnist Milw. Jour., 1969—. Served with U.S. Army, 1951-54. Recipient Ernie Pyle Ann. Writing award Scripps-Howard Found., 1972. Author: Ship The Kids On Ahead, 1969; Slap Shot, 1975; You Can Catch Fish, 1976; Hi Ho Silver, Anyway, 1979. Home: 5604 Hempstead Rd Madison WI 53711 Office: 333 State St Milwaukee WI 53201

STOKLEY, ROBERT WILLSON, economist; b. Denver, Apr. 13, 1918; s. Cecil Inlow and Mary Louise (Willson) S.; A.B., U. Chgo., 1940, postgrad., 1941; postgrad. Indsl. Coll. Armed Forces, 1958-59; m. Dorothy Hannah Phillips, Dec. 18, 1940; children—John Robert, Nancy Louise, Katherine Dorothy. With estimates div. U.S. Bur. Budget, 1941, 43-54; planning officer FCDA, 1954-58; dep. dir. program and policy officer OCDM, 1958-61; dir. program devel. Office Emergency Planning, Washington, 1961-66, spl. asst. to the dir., 1966-68; chief of party Pub. Adminstrn. Service, Bangkok, Thailand, 1968-70; sr. asso. Nat. Program Center for Pub. Personnel Mgmt., Nat. Civil Service League, Washington, 1973-75; cons. econ. planning, Teheran, Iran, 1975-76; study dir. task force on ethics Commn. on Exec., Legis. and Jud. Salaries, 1976; sr. asso. Internat. Center for Emergency Preparedness, Washington, 1976—. Pres. Emergency Com. For Perservation Potomac Palisades, 1965-68. Mem. Phi Beta Kappa. Home: 4617 Clark Pl NW Washington DC 20007

STOKOE, WILLIAM CLARENCE, anthropologist, educator; b. Lancaster, N.H., July 21, 1919; s. William Clarence and Marie (Stafford) S.; A.B., Cornell U., 1942, Ph.D. (fellow), 1946; m. Ruth Adeline Palmeter, Nov. 21, 1942; children—Helen (Mrs. David G. Phillips), James Stafford. Grad. asst., instr. English, Cornell U., 1943-46; asst. prof. English, Wells Coll., 1947-53, asso. prof., 1953-55, chmn. dept., 1952-53; prof., chmn. English dept. Gallaudet Coll., Washington, 1955-72, prof. linguistics, 1968—, dir. Linguistics Research Lab., 1957—; editor, pres. Linstok Press, Inc., Silver Spring, Md. Am. Council Learned Socs. grantee, 1957, 61; NSF grantee, 1962-65, 71—; research fellow Clare Hall Cambridge U., 1977. Fellow AAAS, Am. Anthrop. Assn.; mem. AAUP, Linguistics Soc. Am., Modern Lang. Assn., Nat. Assn. Deaf, Washington Linguistics Club (pres. 1966), St. Andrews Soc. of Washington (pres. 1970-71), Phi Beta Kappa, Phi Kappa Phi. Presbyterian (elder 1966). Clubs: Masons, Cosmos. Author: Sign Language Structure, 2d edit., 1978; The Study of Sign Language, 1970, rev., 1972; Semiotics and Human Sign Languages, 1972; A Dictionary of American Sign Language, 1965, rev. edit., 1976. Editor: Sign Lang. Studies, 1972—; Signs for our Times, Washington. Home: 9306 Mintwood St Silver Spring MD 20901 Office: Linguistics Research Lab Gallaudet Coll 7th St and Florida Ave NE Washington DC 20002

STOKSTAD, EVAN LUDWIG ROBERT, biochemist, educator; b. China, Mar. 6, 1913 (parents Am. citizens); s. Christian and Elsie (Olsen) S.; B.S., U. Calif., 1934, Ph.D., 1937; m. Edith Grandin, Sept. 8, 1934; children—Robert G., Paul Allan. Research chemist Western Condensing Co., 1937-40; Lalor post doctorate research fellow Calif. Inst. Tech., 1940-41; research biochemist, asst. dir. sect. nutrition and physiology research Lederle Labs., Pearl River, N.Y., 1941—; dir. research Agrl. div. Am. Cyanamid Co., 1959-63; prof. dept. nutritional scis. U. Calif., Berkeley, 1963—, chmn. dept., 1979; mem. food and nutrition bd., com. on food standards and fortification policy NRC, 1969-73. Recipient Mead Johnson award for work on folic acid, 1946; Tom Newman award in poultry nutrition, 1951; Borden award for work in poultry sci., 1952; Osborne and Mendel award for nutrition research, 1979. Mem. Am. Chem. Soc., Am. Soc. Biol. Chemistry, Soc. Exptl. Biology and Medicine, Am. Inst. Nutrition (pres. 1975-76), Poultry Sci. Assn., Biochem. Soc. Eng., Sigma Xi. Home: 769 Arroyo Ct Lafayette CA 94549 Office: Dept Nutritional Scis U Calif Berkeley CA 94720

STOKSTAD, MARILYN JANE, educator; b. Lansing, Mich., Feb. 16, 1929; d. Olaf Lawrence and Edythe (Gardiner) Stokstad; B.A., Carleton Coll., 1950; M.A., Mich. State U., 1953; Ph.D., U. Mich., 1957; postgrad. U. Oslo (Norway) 1951-52. Instr., U. Mich., 1956-58; faculty U. Kans., 1958—, asso. prof., 1962-66, prof., 1966-79, Univ. disting. prof. art history, 1979—, chmn. dept. history of art, 1961-72, dir. Mus. Art, 1961-67, research asso., summers 1965-66, 67, 71, 72, asso. dean Coll. Liberal Arts and Scis., 1972-76; fellow Nat. Humanities Inst., Yale, 1976-77. Research curator Nelson Gallery, Kansas City, Mo., 1969-79, cons. curator medieval art, 1979—. Bd. dirs. Internat. Center Medieval Art, 1972-75. Fulbright fellow, 1951-52; grantee Nat. Endowment for Humanities, 1967-68. Fellow AAUW; mem. Archeol. Inst. Am. (Kans. pres. 1960-61), Midwest Coll. Art Conf. (pres. 1964-65), Coll. Art Assn. (dir. 1971-74, sec. 1974-76, pres. 1978—), AAUP (mem. nat. council 1972-75, v.p. Kans. conf.), Soc. Archtl. Historians (chpt. dir. 1971-73), Midwest Art History Assn. (dir. 1976-79). Home: 2603 Strafford Rd Lawrence KS 66044

STOLBER, DEAN CHARLES, motion picture co. exec.; b. Phila., Sept. 2, 1944; s. Solomon and Ruth (Malamed) S.; A.B. cum laude, Harvard Coll., 1966; J.D., N.Y. U., 1969; m. Jacqueline Bertell, Feb. 18, 1967; 1 son, David. With United Artists Corp., N.Y.C., 1969—, dir. bus. affairs, 1977-78, v.p. bus. affairs, 1978-79, sr. v.p. bus. affairs, 1979—, also dir. Office: 729 Seventh Ave New York NY 10019

STOLL, FORREST DUANE, educator, musician; b. Edon, Ohio, Nov. 22, 1921; s. Henry Martin and Zona (Maier) S.; Mus.B., trumpet performers certificate, Eastman Sch. Music, 1944, Mus.M., 1947; Ph.D., Ohio State U., 1960; m. Shirley Jean Minard, Aug. 2, 1947; children—Gregory Preston, Susan Holly. Asst. dir. bands Ohio Sate U., 1947-56; dir. bands U. Utah, 1956—, prof. music, 1966—, chmn. music edn., 1956—, chmn. dept. music, 1965-68, acting chmn. dept. music, 1977-79, asso. chmn. dept. music, 1979—; first trumpeter Columbus (Ohio) Symphony Orch., 1950-56. Served as officer USNR, 1944-46; PTO. Recipient Rochester prize scholarship, 1940-44. Mem. Utah Music Educators Assn. (pres. 1959-61), Coll. Band Dirs. Nat. Assn., Music Educators Nat. Conf., Phi Mu Alpha, Kappa Kappa Psi. Home: 1748 Millcreek Circle Salt Lake City UT 84106

STOLL, REINER GOTTLIEB, chem. engring. cons.; b. Wolfschlugen, Ger., June 5, 1913; came to U.S., 1946, naturalized, 1956; s. Karl Louis and Pauline Rosina (Hoerz) S.; Dipl. Ing., U. Stuttgart, 1936, D.Sc., 1951; m. Christa Maria Schmidt, June 9, 1938; children—Hans R., Dagmar K. Stoll Murphy, Michael H. Mgr. textile lab. Hoechst AG, 1938-46; contractor scientist U.S. Army, 1946-51; with Celanese Corp. Am., 1951-79, v.p., 1967-79; chem. engring. cons., 1979—; mem. adv. bd. sci. and tech. Celanese Corp.; chmn. Fiber Industries, Inc., 1966-72; chmn. Textile Research Inst., 1970-72, hon. fellow, 1978. Bd. dirs. Camile and Henri Dreyfus Found., 1975-79. Recipient Harold de Witt Smith medal, 1968. Mem. Soc. Chem. Industry, Newcomen Soc. N. Am., Sigma Xi. Clubs: Princeton, Deutscher Verein (N.Y.C.). Author papers in field. Home: Deer Run Shores Sherman CT 06784 Office: 300 E 54th St New York NY 10022

STOLL, ROBERT ROTH, educator; b. Pitts., May 19, 1915; s. Harry Bachman and Elisabeth Menkel (Roth) S.; B.S., U. Pitts., 1936, M.S., 1937; Ph.D., Yale, 1942; m. Sarah Donaldson, Sept. 3, 1937; children—Kurt, Nancy, David. Instr., Rensselaer Poly. Inst., 1937-39; grad. asst. Yale, 1939-42; instr., asst. prof. Williams Coll., 1942-46; asst., asso. prof. Lehigh U., 1946-52; prof. math. Oberlin Coll., 1952-71, acting chmn. dept., 1953-54, 60-61, 66-67; prof., chmn. dept. math. Cleve. State U., 1971—. NRC fellow math., 1945-46; NSF sci. faculty fellow, 1958-59, 67-68; Fulbright-Hayes vis. prof. Am. U., Beirut, 1964-65. Mem. Math. Assn. Am. (chmn. Ohio sect. 1954-55, gov. 1961-64), Am. Math. Soc. Author: Linear Algebra and Matrix Theory, 1952; Sets, Logic and Axiomatic Theories, 1961, 2d edit., 1974; Set Theory and Logic, 1963; (with E.T. Wong) Linear Algebra, 1968. Home: 2344 Ardleigh Dr Cleveland Heights OH 44106

STOLL, WILHELM, educator; b. Freiburg, W. Germany, Dec. 22, 1923; s. Heinrich and Doris (Eberle) S.; Ph.D. in Math., U. Tübingen (Germany), 1953, habilitation, 1954; m. Marilyn Jane Kremser, June 11, 1955; children—Robert, Dieter, Elisabeth, Rebecca. Came to U.S., 1960. Asst., U. Tübingen, 1953-59, dozent, 1954-60, apl. prof., 1960; vis. lectr. U. Pa., 1954-55; temp. mem. Inst. Advanced Study, Princeton, 1957-59; prof. math. U. Notre Dame, 1960—, chmn. dept., 1966-68. Vis. prof. Stanford, 1968-69, Tulane U., 1973; adviser Clark Sch., South Bend, Ind., 1963-68. Research complex analysis several variables; publs. in field. Home: 54763 Merrifield Dr Mishawaka IN 46544 Office: Dept Math U Notre Dame Notre Dame IN 46556

STOLLE, JOHN FRED, pub. co. exec.; b. Evanston, Ill., Aug. 26, 1928; s. Erwin Frederick and Evelyn Elizabeth (Park) S.; B.S. in Mech. Engring., Northwestern U., 1949, M.B.A., 1950; m. Frances Erickson, Dec. 28, 1951; children—Susan, Scott, Mark, Elizabeth. Indsl. engr. Inland Steel Co., Milw., 1952-53; supr. costs analysis-trucking div., cost analyst Ford Motor Co., Detroit, 1953-55; partner, then v.p., mng. v.p. Booz-Allen & Hamilton Mgmt. Cons., Chgo., 1955-69; v.p. Internat. Tel. & Tel. Corp., N.Y.C., 1969-75; exec. v.p. Field Enterprises Inc., Chgo., 1975-79; pres., owner Stolle & Co., Chgo., 1979—; dir. Barber-Greene Co., Aurora, Ill. Served with AUS, 1950-52. Mem. Inst. Mgmt. Sci., Nat. Council Phys. Distbn. Mgmt., Alpha Delta Phi. Clubs: Exec. Chgo. Committee, Tavern (Chgo.). Contbr. articles to profl. jours. Office: Stolle & Co 3800 Lake Shore Dr Chicago IL 60613

STOLLER, CLAUDE, architect; b. N.Y.C., Dec. 2, 1921; s. Max and Esther (Zisblatt) S.; student Black Mountain Coll., N.C., 1942; M.Arch., Harvard U., 1949; m. Anna Maria Oldenburg, June 5, 1946 (div. Oct. 1972); children—Jacob, Dorothea, Elisabeth; m. 2d, Rosemary Raymond Lax, Sept. 22, 1978. Architect, Architects Collaborative, Cambridge, Mass., after 1949, Shepley, Bulfinch, Richardson & Abbot, Boston, 1951; co-founder, partner firm Marquis & Stoller, San Francisco, 1956; pvt. practice architecture, N.Y.C. and San Francisco, 1974-78; founder, partner Stoller/Partners, Berkeley, Calif., 1978; mem. faculty Washington U., St. Louis, 1955-56; mem. faculty U. Calif., Berkeley, 1957—, prof. architecture, 1968—, acting chmn., 1965-66; mem. diocesan commn. architecture Episcopal Diocese Calif., 1961—; vis. architect Nat. Design Inst., Ahmedabad, India, 1963; planning commnr. Marin County Planning Commn., 1966-67; mem. pub. adv. panel archtl. services GSA, 1969-71; citizens urban design adv. com. City of Oakland, Calif., 1968—; vis. com. nat. archtl. accrediting bd. U. Minn. and U. Wis., Milw., 1971; council Harvard Grad. Sch. Design Assn., 1976—. Bd. dirs. Mill Valley Library Assn. Served with AUS, 1943-46. Recipient numerous awards including AIA Honor awards, 1963, 64, AIA Bay Region Honor award, 1974, Concrete Reinforced Steel Inst. award, 1976, AIA award, 1976. Fellow AIA. Prin. works include U.S. Embassy, Bangladesh, 1974, Pub. Housing for Elderly, San Francisco, 1974, Learning Resources Bldg., U. Calif., 1975, Menorah Park Housing for Elderly, San Francisco, 1979; 7 Springs Ranch Planned Community, Cupertino, Calif., 1979-80. Home: 2816 Derby St Berkeley CA 94705 Office: 2512 9th St Berkeley CA 94710

STOLLER, EZRA, photographer; b. Chgo., May 16, 1915; s. Max and Esther (Zistblatt) S.; B.F.A., N.Y. U., 1938; m. Helen Rubin, Sept. 23, 1938; children—Erica, Evan, Lincoln. Pres., Esto, Inc., Mamaroneck, N.Y. Guest lectr. U. Okla., U. Kans., U. Notre Dame, 1971, Ga. Inst. Tech., Va. Poly. Inst., 1972, Columbia Coll., 1974, 76, U. N.C., Smithsonian Instn., Harvard U., 1977. Recipient 1st medal for archtl. photography A.I.A., 1960. Mem. Am. Soc. Mag. Photographers (pres.), Archtl. League N.Y. (Gold medal 1955). Home: Kirby Ln N Rye NY 10580 Office: 222 Valley Pl Mamaroneck NY 10543

STOLLER, ROBERT JESSE, physician, educator; b. Bronxville, N.Y., Dec. 15, 1924; s. Benjamin and Bessie (Greene) S.; student Columbia, 1942-43; B.A., U. Calif., Berkeley, 1945; M.D., U. Calif., San Francisco, 1948; m. Sybil A. White, Dec. 28, 1948; children—Richard, Lawrence, Jonathan, Roger. Intern, San Francisco County Hosp., 1949; resident psychiatry Palo Alto (Calif.) VA Hosp., 1950, Los Angeles County Gen. Hosp., 1953, Los Angeles Psychoanalytic Inst., 1961; instr. U. So. Calif. Med. Sch., 1953-54; successively instr., asst. prof., asso. prof., prof. U. Calif. Med. Sch., Los Angeles, 1954—. Served with AUS, 1943-46, USAF, 1950-53. Diplomate Am. Bd. Psychiatry and Neurology. Fellow Am. Coll. Psychiatrists, Am. Psychiat. Assn.; mem. Internat., Am. psychoanalytic assns., Los Angeles Psychoanalytic Soc.-Inst., Royal Coll. Psychiatrists. Author: Sex and Gender, 1968, vol. II, 1975; Splitting, 1973; Perversion, 1975; Sexual Excitement, 1979; also articles. Home: 1100 Rivas Canyon Rd Pacific Palisades CA 90272

STOLLERMAN, GENE HOWARD, physician, educator; b. N.Y.C., Dec. 6, 1920; s. Maurice William and Sarah Dorothy (Mezz) S.; A.B. summa cum laude, Dartmouth, 1941; M.D., Columbia, 1944; m. Corynne Miller, Jan. 21, 1945; children—Lee Denise, Anne Barbara, John Eliot. Clin. tng. Mt. Sinai Hosp., N.Y.C, 1944-46, chief med. resident, 1948; Dazian research fellow microbiology N.Y. U. Med. Sch., 1949-50, mem. dept. medicine, 1951-55; med. dir. Irvington House for Cardiac Children, 1951-55; prin. investigator Sackett Found. Research in Rheumatic Diseases, 1955-64; asst. prof. medicine Northwestern U., 1955-57, asso. prof., 1957-61, prof. medicine, 1961-65; prof., chmn. dept. medicine U. Tenn., 1965—, Goodman prof., 1977—; physician-in-chief City of Memphis Hosps., 1965—. Cons. Bapt. Meml., Meth., St. Joseph's, Le Bonheur Children's hosps. Chmn. research career program com. NIAMD-NIH, 1967-70; mem. commn. Streptococcal and Staphylococcal diseases U.S. Armed Forces Epidemiological Bd., 1956-74; adv. bd. immunization practices Center for Disease Control, 1968-71; expert adv. panel cardiovascular diseased WHO, 1966—; mem. Am. Bd. Internal Medicine, 1967-73, chmn. certifying exam. com., 1969-73, mem. exec. com., 1971-73; chmn. Panel on Bacterial Vaccines, FDA, 1973—. Served as capt. M.C., AUS, 1946-48. Diplomate Am. Bd. Internal Medicine. Fellow A.C.P. (master 1976, bd. regents 1978); mem. Am. Heart Assn. (mem. exec. com., pres. council on rheumatic fever and congenital heart disease 1965-67), Am. Fedn. Clin. Research, Am. Rheumatism Assn., Am., So. socs. clin. investigation, Central Soc. Clin. Research (v.p. 1973-74, pres. 1974-75), Assn. Profs. Medicine (pres. 1975—), Am. Assn. Immunologists, Assn. Am. Physicians, Infectious Disease Soc. Am. (council 1968-70), Sigma Xi, Phi Beta Kappa, Alpha Omega Alpha. Contbr. chpts. to Loeb Textbook of Medicine, Harrison's Textbook of Medicine, Barnett's Pediatrics, others; also articles profl. jours. Editor-in-chief: Advances in Internal Medicine, 1968—; editor Capsule and Comment (Hosp. Practice). Office: 951 Court Ave Room 456 Dobbs Bldg Memphis TN 38163

STOLLEY, ALEXANDER, advt. agy. exec.; b. Coethen Anhalt, Germany, May 12, 1922; s. Mihall and Tatiana (Rainich) Stolarevsky; came to U.S., 1923, naturalized, 1929; M.E., U. Cin., 1948; m. Patricia Martin, June 26, 1944 (dec. Aug. 1970); children—Christopher, Peter, Laura (Mrs. Lawrence Johnson), Annabel (Mrs. Michael Hodesh), Megan; m. 2d, Bette Vogt, June 15, 1973. With Cin. Milacron, Inc., 1941-50, dir. employee relations, 1948-50; with Northlich, Stolley, Inc., Cin., 1950—, exec. v.p., 1959-67, pres., 1967—. Mem. exec. com. Cincinnatus Assn., 1968-73, sec., 1970-71, v.p., 1971-72, pres., 1972-73; mem. Cin. Council on World Affairs, 1969—; chmn. Contemporary Arts Center, Cin., 1966-67; mem. exec. com. Cin. Conv. and Visitors Bur., 1975. Trustee Cin. Speech and Hearing Center, Cin. Chamber Music Soc., Cin. Opera Assn., Cin Symphony Orch., 1969-75. Served to 1st lt. AUS, 1943-46. Mem. Bus., Profl. Advt. Assn. Clubs: Cincinnati Country, Cincinnati Tenni[s] University, Queen City, Gyro, Camargo Racquet. Home: 3 Madiso[n] Ln Cincinnati OH 45208 Office: 200 W 4th St Cincinnati OH 452[0]

STOLLEY, RICHARD BROCKWAY, journalist; b. Peoria, Ill., O[ct.] 3, 1928; s. George Brockway and Stella (Sherman) S.; B.S. [in] Journalism, Northwestern U., 1952, M.S., 1953; LL.D. (hon.), V[...]

Maria Coll., 1976; m. Anne Elizabeth Shawber, Oct. 2, 1954; children—Lisa Anne, Susan Hope, Melinda Ruth, Martha Brockway. Sports editor Pekin (Ill.) Daily Times, 1944-46; reporter Chgo. Sun-Times, 1953; mem. staff Life mag., 1953-73, bur. chief, Los Angeles, 1961-64, Washington, 1964-68, sr. editor, Europe, 1968-70, asst. mng. editor, N.Y.C., 1971-73; mng. editor People mag., N.Y.C., 1974—. Served with USN, 1946-48. Recipient Alumni merit award Northwestern U., 1977. Mem. Am. Acad. Polit. and Social Sci., Nat. Press Club, Overseas Press Club, Kappa Tau Alpha, Sigma Delta Chi. Home: 6 Minerva Pl Old Greenwich CT 06870 Office: Time-Life Bldg New York City NY 10020

STOLLMAN, ISRAEL, city planner; b. N.Y.C., Mar. 15, 1923; s. Philip and Yetta (Strelchik) S.; B.S. in Social Sci., Coll. City N.Y., 1947; M. City Planning, Mass. Inst. Tech., 1948; m. Mary Florence Callahan, Dec. 27, 1953; children—Susan Elisabeth, Katharine Rachel, Sarah Ellen. Planner, Cleve. Planning Commn., 1948-51; lectr. Western, Res. U., 1949-51; planning dir., Youngstown, O., 1951-57; prof., chmn. div. city and regional planning Ohio State U., 1957-68; exec. dir. Am. Soc. Planning Ofcls., 1968-78; exec. dir. Am. Planning Assn., 1978—; pres. Assn. Collegiate Sch. Planning, 1966-67; chmn. Charles E. Merriam Center Pub. Adminstrn. Trustee Alfred Bettman Found.; bd. govs. Met. Housing and Planning Council Chgo., v.p., 1969—. Served with USAAF, 1943-45. Mem. Am. Inst. Cert. Planners (exec. sec.), Internat. Fedn. Housing and Planning. Home: 215 W Menomonee St Chicago IL 60614 Office: 1313 E 60th St Chicago IL 60637 also 1776 Massachusetts Ave NW Washington DC 20036

STOLNITZ, GEORGE JOSEPH, economist; b. N.Y.C., Apr. 4, 1920; s. Isidore and Julia (Jurman) S.; B.A., CCNY, 1939; M.A., Princeton U., 1942, Ph.D., 1952; m. Monique Jeanne Delley, Aug. 26, 1976; children—Cindy, Wendy, Dia. Statistician, U.S. Bur. Census, 1940-41; research asso. Princeton U. Office of Population Research, 1948-56, asst. prof. Princeton U., 1953-56; vis. research scholar Resources for the Future, 1965-67; prof. econs. Ind. U., Bloomington, 1956—, dir. Ind. U. Internat. Devel. Research Center, 1967-72; prin. officer Population and Econ. Devel., UN, N.Y.C., 1976-78; cons. Ford Found., U.S. Congress, Rockefeller Found., UN, HEW, depts. Commerce, Energy and State. Served to capt. USAF, 1942-46. Nat. Service Found. fellow, 1959-60. Mem. Population Assn. Am. (1st v.p.), Am. Econ. Assn., Am. Statis. Assn., Econometric Soc., Internat. Union Sci. Study of Population. Club: Cosmos. Author books, numerous articles in field. Home: 2636 Covenanter Ct Bloomington IN 47401 Office: Dept Econs Ind Univ Bloomington IN 47401

STOLP, LAUREN ELBERT, speech pathologist; b. Sprague, Wash., July 10, 1921; s. Charles Albert and Sarah Christine (Campbell) S.; A.B., Eastern Wash. State Coll., Cheney, Wash., 1946; M.S., Ind. State U., Terre Haute, 1951; m. Nadine McWhorter, Jan. 29, 1946 (dec. 1976); children—Lauren Elyce Stolp Nasseri, Marla Eve Stolp Sullivan; m. 2d, Barbara Duncombe Lang, Mar. 3, 1978. Pvt. practice speech pathology, Houston, 1947-49, Roslyn, Pa., 1968—; instr. spl. edn. Ind. State U., 1949-53; dir. lower and middle schs. Pa. Sch. for Deaf, Phila., 1953-61, prin. middle sch., 1961-68; head speech dept. All Saints' Hosp., Phila., 1970—; dir. Lauren E. Stolp Assos., 1976—; cons. in field. Pres. Upper Moreland High Sch. Home and Sch. Assn., 1964-66. Served with USCGR, 1942-45. Fellow Am. Assn. Mental Deficiency; mem. Am., Pa. speech and hearing assns., Am. Acad. Pvt. Practice Speech Pathology and Audiology, Acoustical Soc. Am., Am. Forestry Assn., Orton Soc., Internat. Assn. Logopedics and Phoniatrics, Kappa Delta Pi, Phi Delta Kappa. Republican. Episcopalian. Lion (pres. Willow Grove, Pa. 1964-65). Address: 14 Laughlin Lane Philadelphia PA 19118

STOLPER, PINCHAS ARYEH, religious orgn. exec., clergyman; b. Bklyn., Oct. 22, 1931; s. David Bernard and Nettie (Rosch) S.; B.R.E., Jewish Theol. Sem. Am. N.Y.C., 1951, postgrad., 1951-52; B.A., Bklyn. Coll., 1952; M.A., New Sch. for Social Research, 1971; m. Elaine Liebman, Nov. 22, 1955; children—Akiva Psachia, Michal Hadassah, Malka Tova. Rabbi, 1956; dir. L.I. Zionist Youth Commn., 1956-57; dir. public relations, adminstrv. dean, adviser to English-speaking students Ponevez Yeshiva, Bnai Brak, Israel, 1957-59, also prin.; instr. English and Talmud, Gimnazia Bnei Akiva High Sch., 1958-59; nat. dir. youth div. Union Orothodox Jewish Congregations Am., Nat. Conf. Synagogue Youth, N.Y.C., 1959-76, editor Jewish Youth Monthly, 1967—; exec. v.p. Union Orthodox Jewish Congregations Am., 1976—; adj. prof. Jewish studies Touro Coll., N.Y., 1975—. Mem. publs., Israel, campus commns., staff mem. responsible for edn., Talmud Torah, day sch. commns., Union Orthodox Jewish Congregations Am., 1965—; del. White House Conf. on Children and Youth, 1961; cons. N. Am. Jewish Youth Conf., 1967—. Bd. dirs. Chaim Berlin Torah Schs.-Mesivta Rabbi Chaim Berlin-Rabbinical Acad., 1965—. Recipient Alumi Amudim award Mesivta Rabbi Chaim Berlin-Gur Aryeh Inst., 1967. Mem. Rabbinical Alliance Am. (mem. nat. exec. bd. 1965-67), Nat. Assn. dir. Nat. Jewish Youth Orgns. Author: Tested Teen Age Activities, 1961, rev. edit., 1964; Day of Delight, 1961; Tefilah, Text and Source Book, 1963; Revelation, What Happened on Sinai, 1966; Prayer, The Proven Path, 1967; The Road to Responsible Jewish Adulthood, 1967; contbr. numerous articles, plays and revs. to Jewish publs. Home: 954 E 7th St Brooklyn NY 11230 Office: Union of Orthodox Jewish Congregations of Am 116 E 27th St New York NY 10016

STOLPER, WARREN HERBERT, lawyer; b. Plymouth, Wis., July 4, 1921; s. Herbert A. and Selma (Reis) S.; B.A., U. Wis., 1944, LL.B., 1948; m. Jane Hoeveler, May 21, 1947; children—Thomas, Daniel, Carolyn. Admitted to Wis. bar, 1948; since practiced in Madison; pvt. practice, 1948-50; partner firm Murphy, Stolper, Brewster & Desmond. 1951—. Dir. Nelson Muffler Corp., Stoughton, Wis., Home Savs. and Loan Assn., Madison; lectr. U. Wis. Law Sch., 1961—, Practising Law Inst., N.Y.C., 1969-70. Served with AUS, 1943-46. Fellow Am. Coll. Probate Counsel; mem. Am., Dane County (past pres.) bar assns., State Bar Wis. (bd. govs. 1967-71), U. Wis. Law Alumni Assn. (past pres.), Phi Delta Phi. Republican. Lutheran. Clubs: Madison, Maple Bluff Country (Madison). Home: 3100 Lake Mendota Dr Madison WI 53705 Office: 2 E Gilman St Madison WI 53701

STOLPER, WOLFGANG FRIEDRICH, economist; b. Vienna, Austria, May 13, 1912; s. Gustav and Paula (Deutsch) S.; came to U.S., 1934, naturalized, 1940; M.A., Harvard U., 1935, Ph.D., 1938; m. Marta Voegeli, Aug. 11, 1938 (dec. July 1972); children—Thomas E., Matthew W.; m. 2d, Margot Kaufman, 1979. Instr., Harvard U., 1936-41; asst. prof. econs. Swarthmore Coll., 1941-48, asso. prof., 1948-49; asso. prof. U. Mich., 1949-53, prof., 1953—, dir. Center for Research on Econ. Devel., 1963-70; guest prof. U. Zurich, summers, 1969—; head econ. planning unit Fed. Ministry for Econ. Devel., Lagos, Nigeria. 1960-62; cons. USAID, Ford Found., IBRD. Guggenheim fellow, 1947-48; Fulbright prof., Heidelberg, 1966. Mem. Am., Nigerian econ. assns. Author: (with P.A. Samuelson) Protection and Real Wages; The Structure of the East German Economy, 1960; Planning Without Facts, 1966. Contbr. articles to profl. jours. Home: 1051 Lincoln Ann Arbor MI 48104 Office: Dept Economics U Mich Ann Arbor MI 48109

STOLTENBERG, CARL HENRY, univ. dean; b. Monterey, Calif., May 17, 1924; s. George L. and Eloise (Hyatt) S.; B.S. U. Calif. at Berkeley, 1948, M.F., 1949; Ph.D., U. Minn., 1952; m. 2d, Rosemary Johnson, Apr. 20, 1973; children from previous marriage—Bruce C., Gail L., Susan I., Paul L., Shirley J.; stepchildren—Michael Johnson, Jillean Johnson. Instr., U. Minn., 1949-51; asst. prof. Duke, 1951-56; forest economist U.S. Forest Service, Washington, 1956; chief div. forest econs. research N.E. Forest Expt. Sta., Forest Service, U.S. Dept. Agr., Upper Darby, Pa., 1956-60; head dept. forestry Iowa State U., 1960-67; dean Oreg. State U. Sch. Forestry, Corvallis, 1967—. Mem. adv. bd. Coop. for Research, U.S. Dept. Agr., 1963-67, mem. adv. com. for state and pvt. forestry, 1970-74; mem. Oreg. Bd. Forestry, 1967—, chmn., 1974—. Served with AUS, 1943-45; ETO. Mem. A.A.A.S., Soc. Am. Foresters (past mem. council, com. chmn.), Forest Products Research Soc., Am. Econ. Assn., Sigma Xi, Xi Sigma Pi. Conglist. Author: Research Planning for Resource Decisions, 1970. Home: 7890 NW Ridgewood Dr Corvallis OR 97330

STOLTZ, CHARLES EDWARD, meat packing co. exec.; b. Dubuque, Iowa, July 31, 1936; s. Edward and Bertha (Klingenberg) S.; B.S. in Bus. Adminstrn., U. Dubuque; M.A., U. Iowa; m. Jean Wahlert, Aug. 20, 1964; children—Jenni, Michael, John. Salesman, Am. Can Co., 1961-62; v.p. Dubuque Packing Co., 1965, exec. v.p., to 1977, pres., 1977—; dir. Dubuque Bank & Trust Co. Trustee U. Dubuque, United Fund, Boys Club. Served with USMC, 1956-58. Office: Dubuque Packing Co 16th and Sycamore Sts Dubuque IA 52001

STOLTZ, MERTON PHILIP, educator; b. Glidden, Wis., Mar. 28, 1913; s. Philip and Frances Anne (Mertig) S.; B.B.A., U. Minn., 1934; A.M., Brown U., 1936; Ph.D., U. Minn., 1941; LL.D. (hon.), Tougaloo Coll., 1977, Brown U., 1978; m. Margaret Ruth Wackerman, June 10, 1939; children—Frances Margaret, Elizabeth Ann. Instr., U. Minn., 1937-40; asst. prof. Brown U., 1940-46, asso. prof., 1946-50, prof., 1950—, chmn. dept. econs., 1956- 64, asso. dean Grad. Sch., 1960-64, dean of univ., 1964-66, provost, 1966-78, acting pres., 1969-70, 76-77. Trustee Tougaloo Coll. Mem. Am. Econ. Assn., Am. Statis. Assn., Econometric Soc. Author: (with Richard K. Gaumnitz) Elements of Statistics, 1939; The Growth and Stability of the Rhode Island Economy, 1955. Contbr. articles to profl. jours. Home: 55 Keene St Providence RI 02906

STOLTZFUS, JAMES LECK, publishing co. exec.; b. Beirut, July 29, 1926; s. William Alfred and Ethel (Leck) S.; A.B. cum laude, Princeton U., 1947; M.B.A., Harvard U., 1951; m. Jeannette Jennings, Dec. 31, 1955; children—James Leck, John Jennings, Robert Lefler. Western advt. mgr. Harvard Bus. Rev., 1953-54; with Reuben H. Donnelley Corp., 1954-75, gen. mgr. Donnelley Internat., Brussels, Belgium, 1967-70, v.p. corp. planning, N.Y.C., 1970-75; exec. v.p. Life Extension Inst., N.Y.C., 1975-76; pres. Funk & Wagnalls, Inc., N.Y.C., 1976—. Served to 1st lt. airborne inf. U.S. Army, 1944-47, 51-53. Republican. Presbyterian. Clubs: N.Y. Athletic; Belle Haven (Greenwich, Conn.). Office: 53 E 77th St New York NY 10021

STOLTZMAN, RICHARD LESLIE, clarinetist; b. Omaha, July 12, 1942; s. Leslie Harvey and Dorothy Marilyn (Spohn) S.; B.M. summa cum laude, Ohio State U., 1964; M.M. magna cum laude, Yale U., 1967; postgrad. Columbia U. Tchrs. Coll., 1967-70; m. Lucy Jean Chapman, June 6, 1976; 1 son, Peter John. Mem. faculty Calif. Inst. Arts, 1970-75; appeared in concerts throughout U.S., Europe, 1976—; recording artist, 1974—; Western regional dir. Young Audiences, Inc., 1972-74, mem. nat. adv. bd. Recipient Horatio Parker award Yale U., 1966; Avery Fisher prize, 1977; Martha Baird Rockefeller award, 1973. Home: 204 Coronado Dr Aptos CA 95003 Office: 201 W 54th St 4 New York NY 10019

STOLZ, BENJAMIN ARMOND, educator; b. Lansing, Mich., Mar. 28, 1934; s. Armond John and Mabel May (Smith) S.; A.B., U. Mich., Ann Arbor, 1955; certificat U. Libre de Bruxelles (Belgium), 1956; A.M., Harvard U., 1957, Ph.D., 1965; m. Mona Eleanor Seelig, June 16, 1962; children—Elizabeth Mona, John Benjamin. Mem. faculty U. Mich., 1964—, prof. Slavic langs. and lits., 1972—, chmn. dept., 1971—; cons. in field. Served to lt. (j.g.) USNR, 1957-60. Recipient Orion E. Scott award humanities U. Mich., 1954; Fulbright scholar, 1955-56; Fgn. Area fellow, Yugoslavia, 1963-64; Fulbright-Hays research fellow, Eng. and Yugoslavia, 1970-71: Am. Council Learned Socs. grantee, 1968-70, 73. Mem. Am. Assn. Advancement Slavic Studies, Am. Assn. Tchrs. Slavic and E. European Langs., Linguistic Soc. Am., Modern Lang. Assn., Midwest Modern Lang. Assn. (pres. 1976), Phi Beta Kappa, Phi Beta Phi. Democrat. Clubs: Huron Valley Tennis, Chippewa Hills Swim and Tennis. Editor: Papers in Slavic Philology, 1977; co-editor, Oral Literature of and the Formula, 1976; co-editor, translator: (Konstantin Mihailovic) Memoirs of a Janissary, 1975. Contbr. articles to profl. publns. Home: 1060 Baldwin Ave Ann Arbor MI 48104 Office: 3040 MLB Univ Mich Ann Arbor MI 49109

STOLZ, MARY SLATTERY, author; b. Boston, Mar. 24, 1920; d. Thomas F. and Mary (Burgery) Slattery; ed. Birch Wathen Sch., Katherine Gibbs Sch., and New Coll.; m. Stanley Burr Stolz, Jan. 5, 1940 (div.); 1 son, William Burr; m. 2d, Thomas C. Jaleski, Apr. 1965. Author stories, novels pub. Ladies Home Jour., Cosmopolitan, Seventeen mags. Recipient Children's Spring Festival award. Mem. Authors League Am. Author: To Tell Your Love, 1951; The Organdy Cupcakes, 1951; The Seagulls Woke Me, 1951; Ready or Not, 1952; In a Mirror, 1953; Pray Love, Remember, 1954; The Leftover Elf, Truth and Consequence, Two by Two, 1954; Rosemary, 1955; The Day and the Way We Met; Hospital Zone, 1956, Because of Madeline, Goodbye My Shadow, 1957; Second Nature, 1958; And Love Replied, 1958; Some Merry-Go-Round Music; A Dog on Barkham Street; Emmitt's Pig; The Beautiful Friend; Belling the Tiger; Great Rebellion, 1961; Pigeon Flight, 1962; Sir the Conquistador, 1963; Bully of Barkham Street, 1963; Who Wants Music on Monday, 1963; The Noonday Friends, 1965; Maxmilian's World, 1966; A Wonderful, Terrible Time, 1967; Say Something, 1968; Juan, 1969; By the Highway Home, 1970; Leap Before You Look, 1971; Lands End, 1973; the Edge of Next Year, 1974; Cat in the Mirror, 1975; Ferris Wheel, 1977; Cider Days, 1978; Go and Catch a Flying Fish, 1979. Address: Roslyn Targ Literary Agy 250 W 57th St New York City NY 10019. *This is a small planet that in the interest of us, the human beings on it, has been and is being irreversibly ravaged. My hope, in writing for children, is to offer them, besides entertainment, an understanding of the needs of the world that cannot speak to us, the world of oceans, creatures, forests. If the children can learn to care about that world, perhaps some of it will yet be saved.*

STONE, ALAN ABRAHAM, psychiatrist; b. Boston, Aug. 15, 1929; s. Julius and Betty (Pastan) S.; A.B., Harvard U., 1950; M.D., Yale U., 1955; grad. Boston Psychoanalytic Soc. and Inst., 1966; m. Sue Smart, June 15, 1952; children—Karen, Douglas, David. Intern, Yale-New Haven Hosp., 1955-56; resident McLean Hosp., Belmont, Mass., 1956-58, James Jackson Putnam Children's Center, Boston, 1958-59, attending psychiatrist McLean Hosp., Belmont, 1975—; asso. psychiatrist Mass. Gen. Hosp., Boston, 1969-77, cons. in psychiatry, 1977—; prof. law and psychiatry Harvard, 1972—. Mem. Mass. Gov.'s Commn. for Revision Criminal Code, 1968-72. Served to capt. USMC, 1959-61. Fellow Am. Psychiat. Assn. (trustee, v.p., pres. 1979-80); mem. Group for Advancement of Psychiatry (chmn. com. on psychiatry and law 1969-72). Author: (with G. Onque) Longitudinal Studies of Child Personality, 1959; (with Sue Stone) The Abnormal Personality Through Literature, 1966; Mental Health and Law: A System in Transition, 1975. Home: 195 Brattle St Cambridge MA 02138 Office: Harvard Law Sch Cambridge MA 02138

STONE, ALAN JAY, coll. pres.; b. Ft. Dodge, Iowa, Oct. 15, 1942; s. Hubert H. and Bernice A. (Tilton) S.; B.A., Morningside Coll., 1964; M.A., U. Iowa, 1966; M.Th., U. Chgo., 1968, D.Min., 1970; m. Caroline L. Crawford, Dec. 23, 1973; 1 dau., Kirsten K. Admissions counselor Morningside Coll., Sioux City, Iowa, 1964-66; dir. admissions, asso. prof. history George Williams Coll., Downers Grove, Ill., 1969-73; v.p. coll. relations Hood Coll., Frederick, Md., 1973-75; v.p. devel. and fin. affairs W.Va. Wesleyan Coll., Buckhannon, 1975-77; dir. devel. U. Maine, 1977-78; pres. Aurora (Ill.) Coll., 1978—; dir. No. Ill. Telecommunications Corp., Aurora Coll. Research Corp.; trustee Stevens-Linen, Inc. Dist. 20 rep. Nat. Assn. Intercollegiate Athletics, 1978—; bd. dirs. Coll. Consortium, Twin Rivers council Boy Scouts Am., Urban League Aurora. Named Outstanding Tchr., George Williams Coll., 1973; U. Chgo. fellow, 1966-70; Nat. Methodist scholar, 1960-64; Mem. Council Advancement and Support of Edn., Am. Assn. Higher Edn., Am. Council Edn., Am. Assn. Colls., Fedn. Ind. Colls. and Univs., Asso. Colls. Ill., Aurora C. of C. Clubs: Rotary Internat., Union League (Aurora). Home: 1307 Marseillaise Aurora IL 60506 Office: Aurora Coll 347 S Gladstone Ave Aurora IL 60507

STONE, ALBERT LYNN, race track exec.; b. New Orleans, Oct. 18, 1925; s. Albert Houston and Julia (McHugh) S.; student U. San Francisco, 1943, Long Beach City Coll., 1945; m. Margaret Sandra Sampson, Aug., 1977; children—Michael A., Patrick L., Stephen W. Gen. mgr. Braves Baseball Orgn., 1950-58; asst. v.p. Liberty Nat. Bank & Trust Co., Louisville, 1959-60; resident mgr. Churchill Downs, Inc., Louisville, 1961-66, v.p., gen. mgr., 1966-70, pres., 1970—. Served with USCG, 1943-46; PTO. Mem. Thoroughbred Racing Assn. (dir., v.p.), Ky, C. of C. (dir. 1960-63), Louisville C. of C. (dir. 1971-73). Clubs: Audubon Country, Pendennis, Jefferson. Office: 700 Central Ave PO Box 8427 Louisville KY 40208

STONE, ARTHUR HAROLD, mathematician; b. London, Sept. 30, 1916; came to U.S., 1959; s. Aurel P. and Rosa (Schekter) S.; B.A., Cambridge (Eng.) U., 1938, M.A., 1939; Ph.D., Princeton U., 1941; m. Dorothy Maharam, Apr. 12, 1942; children—David A., Ellen R. Mem. Inst. Advanced Study, Princeton, N.J., 1941-42; instr. Purdue U., 1942-44; with Geophys. Lab., Washington, 1944-45; fellow Trinity Coll., Cambridge U., 1946-48; lectr. Manchester (Eng.) U., 1948-57, sr. lectr., 1957-61; prof. math. U. Rochester, 1961—; vis. prof. Columbia U., summer 1961, Yale U., 1965-66; vis. research asso. U. Calif., Berkeley, 1971-72; vis. fellow Australian Nat. U., Canberra, 1978. Mem. Am. Math. Soc., Math. Assn. Am., London Math. Soc., AAUP. Jewish. Research, publs. in field, 1940—; inventor flexagons, 1940; editorial adv. bd. Gen. Topology and Its Applications, 1971—. Home: 120 Oakdale Dr Rochester NY 14618 Office: Dept Math U Rochester Rochester NY 14627

STONE, CHARLES BERTODY, III, bus. exec., ret. air force officer; b. Ft. McPhearson, Ga., Mar. 28, 1904; s. Charles Bertody and Katherine (Bonestell) S.; B.S., U.S. Mil. Acad., 1927; grad. Advanced Mgmt. Program, Harvard, 1949; LL.D., Hofstra Coll.; m. Emma Winburn Smalley; children—Gigi, Charles Bertody IV, Claudia. Commd. 2d lt. U.S. Army, 1927, advanced through grades to maj. gen., 1945; grad. A.C. Primary Flying Sch., 1929, Advanced Flying Sch., 1930, Tech. Sch., 1932; chief of staff Eastern Air Command, comdr. 14th Air Force, CBI; comdr. Continental Air Command Mitchel AFB, to 1957; ret. as lt. gen., 1957; chmn. bd., chief exec. officer U.S. Leasing Corp., 1957-60; v.p. Am. Brake Shoe Corp., Oxnard, Calif., from 1960; v.p. Abex Corp.; chmn. bd. Ventura Internat. Inc., 1971—. Bd. overseers Harvard Bus. Sch. Decorated D.S.M. with oak leaf cluster, Legion of Merit, D.F.C., Bronze Star with oak leaf cluster (U.S.); Tashou Cloud Banner, Lo Shu (China); comdr. Order of Bath (Britain). Mem. Harvard Bus. Sch. Alumni Assn. (exec. council, vis. com. 1955-58), U.S. Mil. Acad. Assn. Grads., 14th Air Force Assn. (hon. v.p.), Order Daedalians. Roman Catholic. Club: Los Angeles Country. Home: 10370 Rochester Ave Los Angeles CA 90024 Office: 500 Esplanade Dr Oxnard CA

STONE, CHARLES BRAGDON, corp. exec.; b. Middletown, Conn., July 1, 1901; s. Berkley Charles and Annie (Bragdon) S.; B.S., Wesleyan U., Middletown, 1923; m. Thyra S. Jacobson, Aug. 22, 1925; 1 son, Charles Bragdon. Sales engr. Valley Fuel Oil Heating Co., 1923-25, mgr., 1925-28; mgr. oil heating div. Meech & Stoddard, Inc., 1928-31; pres., dir. C. B. Stone, Inc., 1931-73, treas., 1931—, chmn. bd. dirs., 1973—; dir. Hill Devel. Corp.; mem. adv. bd. Riverside Trust Co., 1950-65. Mem. adv. bd. United Bank & Trust Co., 1965—, chmn. adv. bd., 1974—. Mem. bd. finance Town of Cromwell, 1955-68. Dir. Middlesex County Mfrs. Assn., 1950-52, pres., 1952; dir. Oil Heat Inst. New Eng., 1955-64, 1st v.p., 1958-60, pres. 1960- 62; dir. Conn. Petroleum Assn., 1955-59, New Eng. Fuel Inst., 1964—. Trustee Wesleyan U., Middletown, 1951—, Conn. Valley Hosp., Middletown, 1963-73; corporator Middlesex Meml. Hosp., 1940—. Mem. Alumni Assn. Wesleyan U. (chmn. 1949-51), Psi Upsilon. Clubs: Exchange (pres. Middletown 1948); Madison (Conn.) Beach, Madison Winter; Hartford (Conn.); Home of Meriden. Home: 645 Main St Cromwell CT 06416 Office: 53 Warwick St Middletown CT 06457

STONE, CHARLES RIVERS, apparel mfg. co. exec.; b. Greenville, S.C., July 9, 1936; s. Eugene Earle, III, Allene Lawton (Wyman) S.; indsl. mgmt. degree Clemson (S.C.) U., 1960; m. Frances Patterson Owings, Mar. 6, 1971; children—Charles Rivers, Frances Rebecca, Rosalie Wyman. With Stone Mfg. Co., Greenville, 1960—, pres., 1976—; adv. bd. S.C. Nat. Bank, 1977—; dir. Sea Pines Plantation Co., 1965-69, Greenville Community Corp., 1977—. Bd. dirs. Greenville Charity Bd.; trustee Faith Meml. Episcopal Chapel, Cedar Mountain, N.C.; charter mem. Leadership Greenville. Served with USAF, 1959-60. Mem. Young Pres. Orgn., Am. Apparel Mfrs. Assn., Greenville County Hist. Soc., Greater Greenville C. of C., Exptl. Aircraft Assn., Clemson U. Alumni Assn. Clubs: Cotillion, Poinsett, Met., Greenville Country. Home: 18 Sirrine Dr Greenville SC 29605 Office: 1500 Poinsett Hwy Greenville SC 29608

STONE, CHARLES TURNER, ret. physician; b. Caldwell, Tex., July 24, 1890; s. Wooten Meriwether and Emily Norris (Parkman) S.; A.B., Southwestern U., Georgetown, Tex., 1911; M.D., U. Tex., 1915; postgrad. Harvard Med. Sch., 1925-26, U. Berlin, Germany, 1926; m. Bertha Neubauer, Oct. 21, 1916; 1 son, Charles Turner, Jr. Instr. medicine U. Tex. Med. Br., 1915-18; adj. prof. clin. medicine U. Tex. 1918-23; asso. prof. clin. medicine U. Tex. Med. Br., 1923-26, prof. medicine, 1926-60, emeritus, 1960—, chmn. dept. internal medicine, 1926-58. Recipient Ashbel Smith Distinguished Alumnus award U. Tex. Med. Br. Diplomate Am. Bd. Internal Medicine. Fellow A.C.P. (former mem. bd. regents); mem. Soc. Internal Medicine, Tex. Med. Assn, AMA (former mem. house dels., past chmn. sect. internal medicine, past mem. council med. edn. and hosps.), Endocrine Soc., Am. Thoracic Soc., Am. Heart Assn., A.A.A.S., Am. Geriatrics Soc. (editorial bd.), Phi Delta Theta, Alpha Omega Alpha. Mason (32 deg., Shriner), Rotarian (past pres.). Clubs: Texas Internists; Port Bay.

Contbr. articles on various phases of internal medicine to Am. med. jours. Home: 11 Cedar Lawn N Galveston TX 77550

STONE, CLEMENT, ins. co. exec.; b. Evanston, Ill., June 12, 1928; s. William Clement and Jessie Verna (Tarson) S.; B.S., U. Ill., 1950; Life Ins. Mktg. degree So. Meth. U., 1951; postgrad. Northwestern U., 1963; M.B.A., Harvard U., 1965; m. Barbara Kost, Oct. 26, 1966; children—Deborah, David Charles and Sara Michelle (twins); children by previous marriage—Steven, Sandra, Michael. With Combined Ins. Co. Am., Chgo., 1942—, salesman, 1942-52, dir., 1952—, asst. to pres., 1952-56, exec. v.p. sales, 1956-61, exec. v.p. sales and mktg., resident v.p., mng. dir. U.K., 1966-69, mng. dir. U.K., exec. v.p. European ops., 1969-70, pres. European ops., mng. dir. U.K., 1970-72, pres., chief operating officer, 1972-73, pres., chief exec. officer, chief operating officer, 1973—; v.p., dir. Combined Am. Ins. Co., 1953—, asst. to pres., 1954-62; pres., chief operating officer, dir. Combined Ins. Co. Wis.; 1st v.p., dir. Combined Life Ins. N.Y.; v.p., dir. Combined Registry Co.; vice chmn. bd. Combined Opportunities, Inc. Trustee Coll. Ins., N.Y.C.; bd. dirs., v.p. W. Clement and Jessie V. Stone Found. Mem. Delta Sigma Pi. Clubs: Harvard Alumni Chgo., Met., Mid-Am., Univ. (Chgo.); Michigan Shores (Wilmette, Ill.). Office: 5050 Broadway Chicago IL 60640

STONE, DAVID BARNES, investment cons.; b. Brookline, Mass., Sept. 2, 1927; s. Robert Gregg and Bertha L. (Barnes) S.; grad. Milton (Mass.) Acad., 1945; A.B., Harvard, 1950, M.B.A., 1952; D.C.S. (hon.), Suffolk U., 1969; LL.D., Northeastern U., 1974; m. Sara Cruikshank, June 16, 1951 (div. July 1976); children—David Stevenson, Benjamin Barnes, Peter Cruikshank, Jonathan Fitch, Andrew Hasbrouck. Vice pres. Hayden, Stone Inc. and predecessor, 1962-65, chmn. exec. com., 1965-67; pres. N.Am. Mgmt. Corp., 1968-78, chmn., 1978—; dir. Debson Mill, Inc., Hersey Products, Inc., Stonetex Oil Corp., Dallas, Oceaneering Internat., Inc., Houston. Pres. bd. New Eng. Aquarium, 1959-70, chmn., 1970-76; bd. overseers Boys Clubs Boston, 1956-61, treas., 1961-67. Trustee Charles Hayden Found., Woods Hole Oceanographic Instn. Served with U.S. Mcht. Marine, 1945-47. Mem. Investment Bankers Assn. (chmn. New Eng. group 1963, bd. govs. 1964-67). Clubs: Anglers (N.Y.C.); Kittansett (Marion, Mass.); Country (Brookline, Mass). Home: Great Hill Marion MA 02738 Office: 28 State St Boston MA 02109

STONE, DESMOND, journalist; b. Christchurch, New Zealand, Apr. 26, 1921; s. William F.H. and Dulcie (Black) S.; Nieman fellow, Harvard, 1955-56; came to U.S., 1959, naturalized, 1964; m. Lorraine Anne Howard, Apr. 19, 1947; children—Howard C., Yvonne I. Asst. editor The Southland Times, Invercargill, New Zealand, 1954-58; reporter Rochester (N.Y.) Times- Union, 1959-67; editor editorial page Rochester Democrat and Chronicle, 1967—. Mem. Am. Press Inst. seminar Columbia, 1961, 68. Chmn. information com. Rochester Council Social Agys., 1969—. Served in Royal New Zealand Navy, 1942-45. Recipient award for disting. editorial writing Sigma Delta Chi, 1977. Mem. Soc. Nieman Fellows, Nat. Conf. Editorial Writers, Rochester C. of C. Presbyn. Editor: Verdict on New Zealand, 1959. Home: 75 Lake Breeze Park Rochester NY 14622 Office: 55 Exchange St Rochester NY 14614

STONE, DONALD CRAWFORD, educator, adminstr., cons.; b. Cleve., June 17, 1903; s. Alfred William and Mary Rebecca (Crawford) S.; A.B., Colgate U., 1925, LL.D., 1960; M.S., Syracuse U., 1926; postgrad. U. Cin., 1927-28, Columbia, 1928-30; LL.D., George Williams Coll., 1953; m. Alice Kathryn Biermann, June 10, 1928; children—Nancy Leland Stone Dickinson, Alice Crawford Stone Ilchman, Elizabeth, Donald Crawford. Asst. to city mgr., mem. staff Bur. Govtl. Research, Cin., 1926-28; mem. staff Inst. Pub. Adminstrn., N.Y.C., 1928-29; dir. research Internat. City Mgmt. Assn. and research asso. U. Chgo., 1930-33; exec. dir. Pub. Adminstrn. Service, 1933-39; asst. dir. Bur. of Budget, Exec. Office of Pres., 1939-48; dir. adminstrn. ECA (Marshall Plan), 1948-51, Mut. Security Agy., 1951-53; pres. Springfield (Mass.) Coll., 1953-57; dean Grad. Sch. Pub. and Internat. Affairs, U. Pitts., 1957-69, prof., 1969-74; adj. prof. Carnegie-Mellon U., Pitts., 1975—; Green Honors Chair prof. Tex. Christian U., 1976; partner, deVries & Stone, Cons., 1974—. Exec. dir. Am. Pub. Works Assn., 1934-36; spl. asst. to Fed. WPA adminstr., 1935; lectr. pub. adminstrn. Syracuse U., 1933-37; adj. prof. Am. U., 1943-53; vis. prof. U. So. Calif., 1952; chmn. Internat. Assn. Schs. and Insts. of Adminstrn., 1962—; cons. Fed. PWA, 1932, Civil Works Adminstrn., 1933, Fed. Relief Adminstrn., 1934-36, TVA, 1934, Fed. Social Security Bd., 1936, U.S. Pub. Housing and R.E.A., 1938, Fgn. Ops. Agy., 1954, Nat. Council Chs., 1956, Am. Council on Edn., 1957, OAS, 1957-58, 60-61, Nat. Security Orgn., 1957-58, NASA, 1960, 73, 74-75, Com. for Econ. Devel., 1966-74, UN, 1969-73, NSF, 1974-75, 79-80, OMB, 1974, Saudi Arabia, 1976, Kuwait, 1977-80, GAO, 1977; adviser U.S. del. to UN confs., San Francisco, 1945, London, 1945-46, Lake Success, 1947, Paris, 1948; mem. Gen. Assembly standing com. on budget and adminstrn., 1946-48; U.S. rep. to UNESCO Preparatory Commn., London, 1945-46; chmn. U.S. del. to Internat. Congress Adminstrv. Scis., Berne, 1948, also Oxford, Wiesbaden, Lisbon, Vienna, Istanbul, Madrid, Hague, Warsaw, Copenhagen, Paris, Rome, Caracas, Mexico, Barcelona, Yugoslavia, Ivory Coast, 1956-77. Mem. Commn. on Edn. and Internat. Affairs, Am. Council on Edn., 1954-63, com. on internat. affairs Nat. Council Chs., 1960-67; mem. Am. Consortium for Internat. Public Adminstrn.; trustee Public Adminstrn. Service; mem. trustees vis. com. on public policy U. Chgo. Mem. Am. Polit. Sci. Assn. (v.p. 1949), Am. Soc. for Pub. Adminstrn. (pres. 1950), Nat. Assn. Schs. Pub. Affairs (pres. 1968-69), Internat. City Mgmt. Assn. (hon. life), Am. Pub. Works Assn. (hon. life), Internat. Assn. Chiefs of Police (disting. service life mem.), Nat. Acad. Pub. Adminstrn., Phi Beta Kappa, Delta Upsilon. Episcopalian. Club: Cosmos (Washington). Author books, monographs. Contbr. articles to profl. jours. Home: 3955 Bigelow Blvd Pittsburgh PA 15213 also Old Mission Route 1 Traverse City MI 49684

STONE, DONALD RAYMOND, med. device mfg. co. exec.; b. Madison, Wis., Mar. 6, 1938; s. Donald Meredith and June Dorothy (Graffenberger) S.; B.S. in Physics, U. Wis., 1960, J.D., 1963; m. Dorothy Tetzlaff, June 23, 1962; children—Randall, Brian. Admitted to Minn. bar, 1963; patent atty. Honeywell, Inc., Mpls., 1963-66; patent atty. firm Burd, MacEachron, Braddock, Bartz & Schwartz, Mpls., 1966-68; with Medtronic, Inc., Mpls., 1968—, v.p., then sr. v.p. product assurance and regulation, 1973-77, sr. v.p., sec., gen. counsel, 1977—; condr. seminars, 1974—. Bd. dirs., 1st v.p. East Side Neighborhood Services, Inc., Mpls., 1976—; bd. dirs. Guthrie Theater Found., Mpls., 1976—; mem. allocations com. United Way Mpls., 1979; mem. Citizens League Twin Cities, 1965—. Mem. Am. Soc. Corp. Sec., Am. Bar Assn., Am. Patent Law Assn., Health Industry Mfrs. Assn. (past chmn. legal and regulatory sect., standard sect.), Nat. Elec. Mfrs. Assn. (past chmn. med. electronics sect.), Assn. Advancement Med. Instrumentation, Minn. Bar Assn., Minn. Patent and Trademark Law Assn. (past sec.), Minn. Corp. Counsel Assn., Hennepin County Bar Assn., Order of Coif, Phi Delta Phi, Kappa Sigma. Episcopalian. Clubs: Mpls., Mpls. Athletic. Contbr. articles to profl. jours. Office: 3055 Old Hwy 8 Minneapolis MN 55418

STONE, DOROTHY MAHARAM, educator; b. Parkersburg, W.Va., July 1, 1917; d. Max and Ella (Solovey) Maharam; B.Sc., Carnegie Inst. Tech., 1937; Ph.D., Bryn Mawr Coll., 1940; m. Arthur Harold Stone, Apr. 12, 1942; children—David, Ellen. Vis. prof. math. Wellesley Coll., 1950-51; asst. lectr. U. Manchester (Eng.), 1952-61; prof. math. U. Rochester (N.Y.), 1961—. Sr. Postdoctoral fellow Nat. Acad. Scis., 1965-66. Mem. at large NRC, 1972—. Mem. Am. Math. Soc. (council 1972—), Math. Assn. Am. (com. on undergrad. program in math. 1969-72) AAAS (chmn. Sect. A 1977). Contbr. research articles to math. jours. Home: 120 Oakdale Dr Rochester NY 14618

STONE, EDWARD CARROLL, JR., physicist; b. Knoxville, Iowa, Jan. 23, 1936; s. Edward Carroll and Ferne Elizabeth (Baber) S.; A.A., Burlington Community Coll., 1956; M.S. (NASA fellow), U. Chgo., 1959, Ph.D., 1964; m. Alice Trabue Wickliffe, Aug. 4, 1962; children—Susan, Janet. Research fellow in physics Calif. Inst. Tech., Pasadena, 1964-66, sr. research fellow, 1967, mem. faculty, 1967—, prof. physics, 1976—, Voyager project scientist, 1972—; cons. Office of Space Scis., NASA, 1969—, mem. adv. com. outer planets, 1972-73, editorial bd. Space Sci. Instrumentation, 1975—, mem. high energy astrophysics mgmt. operating working group, 1976—. Sloan Found. fellow, 1971-73. Fellow Am. Phys. Soc. (chmn. cosmic physics div. 1979-80, exec. com. 1974-76); mem. Am. Geophys. Union, Am. Astron. Soc., Am. Assn. Physics Tchrs., AAAS. Office: Dept Physics Calif Inst Tech 1201 E California Blvd Pasadena CA 91125

STONE, EDWARD DURELL, JR., landscape architect; b. Norwalk, Conn., Aug. 30, 1932; s. Edward Durell and Orlean (Vandiver) S.; B.A. in Architecture, Yale U., 1954; M.Landscape Architecture, Harvard U., 1959; m. Jacqueline Marty, Dec. 15, 1954 (div.); children—Edward D. III, Patricia Marty; m. 2d, Jean Herrell Weaver, May 13, 1978. Pres., Edward D. Stone, Jr., & Assos., P.A., Ft. Lauderdale, Fla., 1960—; vis. critic, lectr. U. Fla., U. Mich., U. Ill.; adj. prof. landscape architecture U. Miami (Fla.); vis. critic, lectr. Tex. A&M U.; cons. First Lady's Com. More Beautiful Capital, 1965-68; cons. Fla. Gov.'s. Conf. Environ. Quality, 1968-69; mem. Commn. Fine Arts, Washington, 1971—; landscape archtl. designer; Pepsico World Hdqrs., Purchase, N.Y., 1972; Bal Harbour Shops (Fla.), 1971; El Morro Resort, Puerto La Cruz, Venezuela, 1972—; Bicentennial Park, Miami, Fla., 1976; Profl. Golf Assn. Hdqrs. Master Plan, Palm Beach, Fla., 1978-79. Mem. vis. com. Harvard U. Sch. Design. Served to capt. USAF, 1954-57. Recipient Profl. Landscape Architecture award HUD, 1968, Am. Assn. Nurserymen, 1967, 69, 70, 71, 77. Fellow Am. Soc. Landscape Architects (awards 1963, 70, 73, 74, 76, 78, 79). Office: 2400 E Oakland Park Blvd Fort Lauderdale FL 33306

STONE, EDWARD HARRIS, II, landscape architect; b. Lanesboro, Pa., Aug. 28, 1933; s. Frank Addison and Beth Lee (Brennan) S.; B.S., SUNY, 1955; m. Diane Gertrude Berg, June 11, 1955; children—Randel Harris, Deborah Dee. Landscape architect Harmon, O'Donnell & Henninger, Denver, 1955-56, U.S. Forest Service, Colo., 1958-61; regional landscape architect, Alaska, 1961-64, Colo., 1964-65; chief landscape architect U.S. Forest Service, U.S. Dept. Agr., Washington, 1966—. Served with AUS, 1956-57. Recipient Arthur S. Flemming award for outstanding fed. govt. service U.S. Jr. C. of C., 1969. Fellow Am. Soc. Landscape Architects (pres. 1975-76). Home: 12504 Canfield Ln Bowie MD 20715 Office: Forest Service US Dept Agr Washington DC 20250

STONE, ELHANAN COLEMAN, advt. co. exec., lawyer; b. Norwood, Mass., July 3, 1929; s. Moses J. and Miriam (Cushing) S.; A.B., Harvard Coll., 1952; LL.B., 1955; children—Mark J., Peter B. Admitted to Mass. bar, 1955, U.S. Dist. Ct. Mass., 1957; trial atty. Anti-Trust div. U.S. Dept. Justice, Washington, 1958-62; with Ted Bates & Co., Inc., N.Y.C., 1962—, sr. v.p., gen. counsel U.S. ops., 1976—; instr. advt. law New Sch., N.Y.C. Chmn. zoning bd. appeals City of Stamford, Conn., 1971; mem. Stamford Bd. Edn., 1971—, pres., 1972-73. Served with U.S. Army, 1955-57. Mem. Am. Bar Assn., Assn. Bar City N.Y., Am. Assn. Advt. Agencies (chmn. com. on advt. legal affairs 1973—). Republican. Jewish. Club: Harvard of Fairfield County (bd. govs. 1972—, pres. 1971-72). Home: 91 Strawberry Hill Ave Stamford CT 06902 Office: 1515 Broadway St New York NY 10036

STONE, ELIZABETH WENGER, librarian; b. Dayton, Ohio, June 21, 1918; d. Ezra and Anna Bess (Markey) S.; A.B., Stanford U., 1937, M.A., 1938; M.L.S., Catholic U. Am., 1961; Ph.D., Am. U., 1968; m. Thomas A. Stone, Sept. 14, 1939; children—John Howard, Anne Elizabeth, James Alexander. Tchr. pub. schs., Fontana, Calif., 1938-39; asst. state statistician State of Conn., 1939-40; librarian New Haven Pub. Libraries, 1940-42; dir. pub. relations, asst. to pres. U. Dubuque (Iowa), 1942-46; substitute librarian Pasadena (Calif. Pub. Library System, 1953-60; instr. Cath. U. Am., 1962-63, asst. prof., asst. to chmn. dept. library sci., 1963-67, asso. prof., asst. to chmn., 1967-71, prof., asst. to chmn., 1971-72, prof., chmn. dept., 1972—; exec. dir. Continuing Library Edn. Network and Exchange, 1975—. Mem. ALA (council 1976—), D.C. Library Assn. (pres. 1966-67), Spl. Libraries Assn. (pres. D.C. chpt. 1973-74), Assn. Am. Library Schs. (pres. 1974), Am. Soc. Info. Sci., Cath. Library Assn., Adult Edn. Assn., Phi Sigma Alpha, Beta Phi Mu, Phi Lambda Theta. Presbyterian. Author: Factors Related to the Professional Development of Librarians, 1969; (with James J. Kortendick) Job Dimensions and Educational Needs in Librarianship, 1971; Motivation: A Vital Force in the Organization, (with F. Peterson and M. Choot), 1977; American Library Development 1600-1899, 1977; (with others) Model Continuing Education Recognition System in Library and Information Science, 1979, others; editor D.C. Libraries, 1964-66; contbr. articles to profl. jours. Home: 4000 Cathedral Ave NW Washington DC 20016 Office: Catholic U Am Washington DC 20064

STONE, EUGENE E., III, mfg. co. exec.; b. Greenville, S.C., 1907. Chmn. bd. Stone Mfg. Co., Greenville, Norris Mfg. Co.; dir. Bankers Trust S.C., Columbia, Carolina Fed. Savs. & Loan Assn., So. Weaving Co.; mem. adv. bd. Liberty Mut. Co. Home: Greenville SC 29609 Office: PO Box 3725 Park Pl Greenville SC 29608

STONE, EZRA CHAIM, producer, dir., actor; b. New Bedford, Mass., Dec. 2, 1917; s. Solomon and Rose (Meadow) Feinstone; ed. Oak Lane (Pa.) Country Day Sch., 1928-34, Am. Acad. of Dramatic Arts, N.Y.C., 1934- 35; m. Sara F. Seegar, 1942; children—Josef Seegar, Francine Lida. Actor, Horn & Hardart Children's Hour sta. WCAU, Phila., then Nat. Jr. Theater, Washington, 1931-32; performed minor parts in Theatre Guild's Parade, Ah Wilderness, Oh Evening Star, Three Men on a Horse, and played Bottome in Brother Rat, 1935-38; played over 600 performances as Henry Aldrich in What a Life, 1938-40; created role Henry Aldrich in radio serial Aldrich Family, Sept. 1938-41, 45-51; dir. See My Lawyer, Reunion in New York, 1939; This is the Army, 1942; co-starred film Those Were the Days, 1939; dir. plays on Broadway including January Thaw, 1946, Me and Molly, 1948, At War with the Army, 1949, Mark Twain's, The Man that Corrupted Hadleyburg, 1951, Count Your Blessings, Blue Danube; 1952; Steve Allen in The Pink Elephant, 1953; Loco, 1953; Ezio Pinza in The Play's the Thing, 1953, Comin' Thru the Rye, 1953, 8th Observance of the UN; dir. Tony Randall in To Tell You The Truth, Anna Russell in Half in Ernest; producer, dir. program devel. CBS-TV, 1952-54, also The Hathways, ABC-TV, Affairs in Anatol, CBS-TV, Life With Father and Love That Guy, CBS, 1952, Debbie Reynolds Show, 1970; created Sir Epicure Mammon in the Alchemist, 1949, Tony Lumpkin in She Stoops to Conquer, 1950 for N.Y.C. Center; producer-dir. TV programs for Olsen & Johnson, Aldrich Family, Ed Wynn, Herb Shriner, Danny Thomas, Fred Allen, Martha Raye, Ezio Pinza, others; actor Hawaiian Eye, ABC-TV; star Trial of Urial, NBC-TV; dir. Bachelor Father, Coranado 9, NBC-TV, Angel series, CBS-TV, 1960-61, others; dir. Ann Sothern stage play God Bless Our Bank, Marie Wilson in Fallen Angels; TV dir. My Living Doll series, Karen, The Munsters, Laredo, Pruitts of Southampton, Pistols 'n' Petticoats, Petticoat Junction, Tammy and The Millionaire (feature), Please Don't Eat the Daisies, O.K. Crackerby, Lost in Space, Julia, Flying Nun, Love Am. Style, Sandy Duncan, ABC Circle Films, Dracula—The Vampire King, Finishing Touches, information films for LTV Corp., Southwestern Bell Telephone Co., The James Stewart Show, Lassie; dir. for ednl. TV, Good Morning Freedom; animated feature The Daydreamer; numerous documentaries for IBM; dir. TV shows Bob Hope, Groucho Marx, Bob Cummings; creator, producer, dir. Golden Wedding Anniversary Tribute to the Lunts, 1972; asso. dir. Am. Acad. Dramatic Arts, also exec. dir. postgrad. center; co-star Volpone Music Center Theatre, Los Angeles; appeared TV show Hildergarde Withers, ABC-TV, Diana Rigg Show, Emergency; guest artist tours for U.S. Army Spl. Services; producer, dir. bicentennial documentary The Forty Million; mem. faculty Am. Theatre Wing Vets. Sch., U. Va. Drama Sch.; ednl. TV cons. Ford Found.; gen. dir., cons. IBM, 1962—; lectr., tchr. Am. Coll. Theatre Festival, UCLA, Scott Theatre, Ft. Worth, U. Minn., Ariz. Speech and Drama Assn.; vis. prof. theatre arts Calif. State U. at Long Beach, 1973; guest artist seminar tours U.S. Army Music and Theatre Program; guest lectr., adjudicator at numerous instns. Chmn. radio and TV dept. adv. council U. Judaism; nat. chmn. David Library of the Am. Revolution, 1974; mem. adv. council So. Calif. Ednl. Theatre Assn.; awards dir. Sol Feinstone Environ. Awards, Served as master sgt. AUS, 1941-45. Recipient Grand prize Barcelona Internat. Film Festival, 1971, CINE Golden Eagle award. Mem. Acad. TV Arts and Scis., Actors Equity Assn., Screen Actors Guild, A.F.T.R.A., Soc. Stage Dirs. and Choreographers (sec.), Radio Pioneers, Screen Producers Guild, ANTA (chmn. bd. dirs. ANTA West), AGVA, Am. Ayrshire Breeders Assn., Newtown Reliance Co. Guild, Writers Guild Am., Am. Theatre Assn., Army Theatre Arts Assn., Performing Tree So. Calif., Calif. Theatre Council, Dirs. Guild of Am., Am. Legion, also Am. Vets. Com., Air Force Assn., Pa. First Aid and Rescue Squads Assn. Author: Coming Major, 1945; (with Deems Taylor) Puccini Opera, 1951. Contbr. to mags. Breeder registered Ayrshire Dairy Cattle. Home: 2100 Castilian Dr Hollywood CA 90068 also Stone Meadows Farm Newtown Bucks County PA 18940 Office: Contemporary-Korman Agy 132 Lasky Dr Beverly Hills CA 90212 also David Library of Am Revolution Washington Crossing PA 18977

STONE, FERDINAND FAIRFAX, educator; b. Urbana, Ohio, Dec. 12, 1908; s. Samuel Lukins Pidgeon and Lutie Vella (Ivins) S.; A.B., Ohio State U., 1930, A.M., 1931; B.A. in Juris, (Rhodes scholar Exeter Coll.) Oxford (Eng.) U., 1933, B.C.L., 1934, M.A., 1957; D.Juristic Sci. (Sterling fellow), Yale, 1936; Dr. h.c., U. Grenoble (France), 1966. Mem. legal staff U.S. Supreme Ct. Adv. Com. on Rules Civil Proc., 1935-36; instr. law U. Wyo., 1936-37; vis. prof. law So. Meth. U., summer 1937; asso. prof. law Tulane U., New Orleans, 1937-43, prof. law 1948-63, W.R. Irby prof. law, 1963-79, emeritus, 1979—; dir. Tulane Inst. for Comparative Law, 1949-78; acting prof. law Stanford, 1947-48. Rockefeller Found. grantee comparative law study, Europe, 1955; prof. Asso. de la Faculté de Droit Grenoble, 1960, 66, 76, de l'Institut Universitaire d'Etudes Européenes de Turin, 1960; Fulbright lectr. law King's Coll., U. London, 1957-58; Gastprof. Rechtswissenschaftliches Fakultät, U. Köln, 1962; Fulbright prof. law dept. U. Edinburgh, 1963; vis. Ford prof. Am. law U. London, 1972; vis. Simon prof., laws faculty U. Manchester (Eng.), 1975; vis. prof. Inter-Am. U. of P.R., 1977, 79, U. Coll. Wales Sch. Law, 1978. Served as lt. comdr. USNR, 1943-46. Recipient medal of homage Free U. Brussels, 1958; decorated hon. officer Order Brit. Empire. Mem. Internat. Acad. Comparative Law, Am. Assn. for Comparative Study Law (dir.), La. Bar Assn., Order of Coif, Phi Beta Kappa, Omicron Delta Kappa, Phi Gamma Delta, Phi Delta Phi. Episcopalian. Club: Athenaeum (London). Author: Handbook of Law Study, 1952; Institutions fondamentales du droit des Etats-Unis, 1965; Stone on Louisiana Tort Doctrine, 1977. Contbr. articles to legal jours. Office: Law Sch Tulane U New Orleans LA 70118

STONE, FRANKLIN MARTIN, govt. ofcl.; b. Atlantic, Iowa; s. Fred Martin and Sarah A. (Russell) S.; jr. coll. certificate, Chaffey Coll. Ontario, Cal., 1929; J.D., George Washington U., 1934; 1 son, Franklin Martin. Admitted to D.C. bar, 1934, Minn. bar, 1939, Fla. bar, 1976, U.S. Ct. Appeals for D.C. Circuit, 1940, U.S. Supreme Ct., 1943, U.S. Ct. Claims, 1946, also U.S. Ct. Customs and Patent Appeals, 1973; spl. agt. FBI, 1934-44, adminstrv. asst. to dir., 1940-44; partner firm Stone & Iversen, Waseca, Minn., 1946-55; city atty. Waseca, 1948-54; gen. counsel CAB, 1955-61; trial judge U.S. Ct. of Claims, Washington, 1961-73, sr. trial judge, 1973—. Chmn., Waseca County Republican Com., 1948-54. An incorporator, past sec., dir. Minn. DeMolay Found. Served from capt. to maj. AUS, 1944-46; ETO, CBI. Recipient Legion of Honor (Order DeMolay); Alumni Achievement award George Washington U., 1946; certificate of recognition Minn. Bar Assn., 1947. Mem. Am., Fed., D.C., Minn., Fla., Palm Beach County bar assns., Am. Legion (past comdr.), V.F.W., Sigma Nu. Presbyterian. Clubs: Masons, Shriners (K.T.); National Lawyers, Congressional Country, Capitol Hill (Washington); Kiwanis; Boca Raton Men's Republican. Home: Chalfonte 550 S Ocean Blvd Boca Raton FL 33432 Office: Suite 301 299 Camino Gardens Blvd Rd Boca Raton FL 33432

STONE, FRANZ THEODORE, fabricated metal products mfg. exec.; b. Columbus, Ohio, May 11, 1907; s. Julius Frederick and Edna (Andress) S.; student Phillips Exeter Acad., 1924-25; A.B. magna cum laude, Harvard, 1929; L.H.D., Canisius Coll., Buffalo, 1975, Ohio State U., 1976; m. Katherine Devereux Jones, Feb. 23, 1935; children—Franz Theodore, Thomas Devereux Mackay, Raymond Courtney, Catherine Devereux. Pres., gen. mgr. Columbus McKinnon Corp., Tonawanda, N.Y., 1935—; chmn. Columbus McKinnon, Ltd., Burlington, Ont., Can.; mem. sr. adv. bd. Marine Midland Bank-Western N.Y.; dir. Wheway Watson, Ltd., Glasgow, Scotland, Niagara Share Corp., Buffalo, Roblin Industries, Buffalo, Pitt Waddell Bennett Chain, Ltd., Melbourne, Australia, Utica Mut. Ins. Co. (N.Y.); dir. Columbus McKinnon (France), Argenteuil, France, Columbus McKinnon Zambia Ltd., Kitwe. Bd. dirs. Buffalo Philharmonic Soc., Buffalo Fine Arts Acad., Studio Arena Theatre Sch., Buffalo; trustee, pres. Buffalo and Erie County YMCA, DeGraff Meml. Hosp. Vice chmn. Greater Buffalo Devel. Found.; chmn. Arts Devel. Services; dep. dir. tools div. OPM and WPB, 1941-44; dir. research and devel. OSS, 1944-45; asst. dir. equipment bur. WPB, 1945; asst. adminstr. indsl. and agr. equipment bur. NPA, 1951-52, dep. adminstr., 1952. Mem. Am. Supply and Machinery Mfrs. Assn. (past pres.), Am. Hardware Mfrs. Assn. (past pres.), Asso. Industries N.Y. State (dir.), Am. Mus. Natural History, Buffalo Council World Affairs, Phi Beta Kappa. Clubs: Fort Erie (Ont.) Jockey (dir.); Buffalo, Country of Buffalo, Saturn, Buffalo Tennis and Squash, Harvard of Buffalo, Mid-Town; Genesee Valley Hunt (gov.); Metropolitan (Washington); Columbus (Ohio). Home: Welcome Porterville Rd East

Aurora NY 14052 Office: care Columbus McKinnon Corp Tonawanda NY 14150

STONE, FREDERICK HAMILTON, life ins. co. exec.; b. Springfield, Ill., Mar. 8, 1921; s. Lawrence E. and Adah (Griggs) S.; A.B., Duke, 1947, J.D., 1948; m. Jeanne Lutz, Oct. 13, 1950; children—William, Lawrence, Suzanne, Kim. Admitted to Ill. bar, 1948, since with firm Gillespie, Burke & Gillespie, Springfield; with Franklin Life Ins. Co., Springfield, 1960—, gen. counsel, 1965—, v.p., 1966-69, sr. v.p., dir., 1969—; v.p., gen. counsel, dir. Franklin United Life Ins. Co. Served with USAAF, 1942-45; ETO. Mem. Am., Ill., Sangamon County (pres. 1959) bar assns., Internat. Acad. Trial Lawyers, Assn. Life Ins. Counsel. Home: 2031 Briar Cliff St Springfield IL 62704 Office: Franklin Life Ins Co Franklin Sq Springfield IL 62713

STONE, GALEN LUTHER, ambassador; b. Mass., July 4, 1921; B.S., Harvard, 1946; married. With U.S. Dept. of State, 1947—, dep. dir. office western European affairs, 1962-63, Imperial Def. Coll., London, 1964, counselor polit.-econ. affairs, New Delhi, India, 1965-68, chief, polit. sect., Saigon, Vietnam, 1968-69, dep. chief mission to India, New Delhi, 1969-73, dep. chief mission to France, Paris, 1973-75; dep. rep. with rank of ambassador IAEA, Vienna, Austria, 1976-78; ambassador to Cyprus, Nicosia, 1978—. Served to capt. AUS, 1942-46. Office: Am Embassy FPO New York NY 09530

STONE, GARY K., educator; b. N.D., May 13, 1938; s. Howard L. and Margaret C. Stone; B.A., Hamline U., St. Paul, 1960; M.S., U. Minn., 1962, Ph.D. (S.S. Huebner Found. fellow), U. Pa., 1966; m. Marianne Owens, Dec. 28, 1961; children—Gary Lee, David Allan. Prof. ins. faculty Mich. State U., East Lansing, 1965—; cons. ins. risk and mgmt. C.L.U., 1968. Mem. Risk and Ins. Mgrs. Soc., Am. Risk and Ins. Assn. Author work books, articles, revs. in field. Office: Coll Business Mich State Univ East Lansing MI 48824

STONE, GERALD PAUL, educator; b. Cleve., Dec. 15, 1918; s. Herman and Rose (Simkow) S.; B.Chem. Engring., Coll. City N.Y., 1939; M.Adminstrv. Engring., N.Y. U., 1944, Sc. Engring.D. in Indsl. Engring., 1949; certificate elec. engring. and marine engring. Temple U., 1941; postgrad. Va. Poly. Inst., 1939-40; m. Gladys Meyers, May 20, 1950; children—Donald H., Lawrence J. Marine, indsl. engr. Navy Dept., 1941-52; pres. G.P. Stone Co., cons. mgmt. engrs., product liability and accident investigators for attys., North Bergen, N.J., 1949—; asso. prof. mech.-indsl. engring. Poly. Inst. Bklyn., 1952-64, N.J. Inst. Tech.-Newark Coll. Engring., 1966- -; pres. Pub. Research, N.Y.C., 1964-65, G.P. Stone Hosp. Pub. Co., 1967—. Adj. prof. Coll. City N.Y., Fairleigh Dickinson U., N.Y. U., Pratt Inst., Rutgers U., 1951—. Active local Boy Scouts Am., Inst. Rehab. Medicine; mem. Mayor of North Bergen's Com. to Relocate N. Hudson Hosp.; mem. com. to combat Huntington's disease Beth Israel Med. Center. Bd. dirs. N. Hudson Community Center. Recipient commendation sec. navy, 1949. Registered profl. engr., N.Y., N.J. Mem. N.Y. State (vice chmn. ethical practices com.), Hudson County (chmn. safety com.) profl. engrs. socs., Am. Nat. Standards Inst., AIM, IEEE, AAUP, Am. Inst. Indsl. Engrs. (Greater N.Y. hosp. sect.), Sigma Xi, Phi Lambda Upsilon. Author: Management Engineering for Manufacturing, 1967; Programming and Control for Manufacturing, 1968; Improved Driver Education Curriculum, 1972; Hospital Systems Design, 1975; Hospital Unit Processes, 1976; Hospital Training Management; also radio scripts. Contbr. articles to profl. jours. Home: 8615 5th Ave North Bergen NJ 07047 Office: 323 High St Newark NJ 07102. *I try to follow the way of the Lord—Good work, done diligently, to aid people.*

STONE, GREGORY PRENTICE, educator; b. Olean, N.Y., Oct. 28, 1921; s. Horace Prentice and Sarah Grace (Emerson) S.; B.A., Hobart Coll., 1942; certificate Turkish area and lang., Princeton, 1944; M.A., U. Chgo., 1952, Ph.D., 1959; m. Gladys Ishida, June 9, 1962; children—Mead M., Susan L. Instr., U. Ill., Chgo., 1947-49; asst. prof. Mich. State U., 1949-55; instr. U. Minn., 1955-59; vis. lectr. U. Mo., 1958-59; asst. prof. Washington U., St. Louis, 1959-61; mem. faculty U. Minn., 1961—, prof. sociology, 1963—; guest lectr. 6th Seminar in Honor of George Herbert Mead, U. Tokyo, 1978; cons. in field. Chmn. research com. Gov. Minn. Task Force Mental Retardation, 1966-68. Served with AUS, 1944-45. Recipient all univ. recognition U. Minn., 1967. Fellow Midwest Sociol. Soc. (bd. dirs. 1968-70), Internat., Am. sociol. assns.; mem. Soc. Study Social Problems, Soc. Study Symbolic Interaction (co-founder, co-chmn. 1974-75, pres. 1976-77), Internat. Com. Sociology of Sport (a founder, Am. rep.), AAAS, ACLU. Co-author: Being Urban, 1977. Editor: Internat. Review of Sport Sociology, 1965-71; sr. editor: Social Psychology Through Symbolic Interaction, 1970; editor: Games, Sport and Power, 1971; co-editor, translator Herman Schmalenbach on Society and Experience, 1977. Home: St Croix Cove Route 3 Hudson WI 54016 Office: Social Sci Tower Univ Minn Minneapolis MN 55455

STONE, H. LOWELL, physiologist; b. Baton Rouge, July 22, 1936; B.S., Rice U., 1958; M.S., U. Ill., 1959, Ph.D., 1961; m. Nancy Hunter, Aug. 17, 1957; children—Brenda, Sharon, Donna. Research, teaching asst. U. Ill., 1958-61; postdoctoral fellow dept. physiology U. Miss., 1961-63, asst. prof., 1963-64; research physiologist USAF Sch. Aerospace Medicine, Brooks AFB, San Antonio, 1964-71; prof. physiology U. Tex., Galveston, 1971-77; prof., head dept. physiology U. Okla. Health Center, Oklahoma City, 1977—; cons. cardiologist Emory U., Atlanta. Fellow Am. Coll. Cardiology; mem. Am. Physiol. Soc., Am. Soc. Pharmacology and Exptl. Therapy, Soc. Neurosci., Soc. Exptl. Biology and Medicine. Club: Rotary. Contbr. 200 articles to profl. jours. Home: 5901 Burnham Pl Oklahoma City OK 73132 Office: 940 Stanton L Young Blvd Oklahoma City OK 73190

STONE, HARRY H., mfr. greeting cards; b. Cleve., May 21, 1917; s. Jacob and Jennie (Kantor) Sapirstein: student Cleve. Coll., 1935-36; m. Lucile Tabak, Aug. 10, 1960; children—Philip, Allan, Laurie (Mrs. Parker), James Rose, Douglas Rose. With Am. Greetings Corp., Cleve., 1936—, v.p., 1944-58, exec. v.p. 1958-69, vice chmn. bd., chmn. finance com., chmn audit com., 1969-78, now dir. Mem. Ofcl. U.S. Mission to India and Nepal, 1965; cons. U.S. Dept. Commerce, U.S. Dept. State; adviser on U.S. delegation 24th session UN Econ. Commn. for Asia and Far East, Canberra, Australia, 1968; cons. Nat. Endowment for Arts, Nat. Council on Arts. Treas. Criminal Justice Co-ordinating Council. Trustee emeritus Brandeis U., also univ. fellow. Rotarian. Home: Bratenahl Pl No 2 Suite 9D Cleveland OH 44108 Office: 10500 American Rd Cleveland OH 44144

STONE, I. F. (ISIDOR FEINSTEIN), journalist; b. Phila., Dec. 24, 1907; s. Bernard and Katherine (Novack) Feinstein; student U. Pa., 1924-27, B.A., 1975; L.H.D. (hon.), Amherst Coll., 1970, Reed Coll., 1976; Litt.D., Brown U., 1971; m. Esther M. Roisman, July 7, 1929; children—Celia Stone Gilbert, Jeremy J., Christopher D. Editor, pub. The Progress, Haddonfield, N.J., 1922; reporter Haddonfield Press, Camden (N.J.) Courier-Post, Phila. Record, Phila. Inquirer, 1923-33; editorial writer Phila. Record, 1933, N.Y. Post, 1933-39; asso. editor The Nation, 1938-40, Washington editor, 1940-46; reporter, columnist, editorial writer PM, N.Y. Star, N.Y. Post, N.Y. Daily Compass, 1942-52; editor, pub. I.F. Stone's Bi-Weekly, Washington, 1953-71; Distinguished scholar in residence Am. U., 1975—. Recipient George Polk Meml. award L.I. U., 1970, Journalism award Columbia U., 1971; subject of film I.F. Stone's Weekly by Gerry Brock, Jr. Author: The Court Disposes, 1937; Business as Usual, 1941; Underground to Palestine, 1946; This is Israel, 1948; The Hidden History of the Korean War, 1952; The Truman Era, 1953; The Haunted Fifties, 1964; In a Time of Torment, 1967; The Killings at Kent State, 1970; Polemics and Prophecies, 1971; The Best of I.F. Stone's Weekly, 1973; past contbg. editor N.Y. Rev. Books. Address: 4420 29th St NW Washington DC 20008. *To write the truth as I see it; to defend the weak against the strong; to fight for justice; and to seek, as best I can, to bring healing perspectives to bear on the terrible hates and fears of mankind, in the hope of some day bringing about one world, in which men will enjoy the differences of the human garden instead of killing each other over them.*

STONE, IRVING, author; b. San Francisco, July 14, 1903; s. Charles and Pauline (Rosenberg) Tennenbaum; A.B., U. Calif., 1923, postgrad., 1924-26; A.M., U. So. Calif., 1924, Litt.D., 1965; D.Lit. (hon.), Coe Coll., 1967; LL.D., U. Calif. at Berkeley, 1968; D.Litt., Calif. State Colls., 1971; D.H.L., Hebrew Union Coll., Cin., 1978; m. Jean Factor, Feb. 11, 1934; children—Paula, Kenneth. Instr. econs. U. So. Calif., 1923-24, U. Calif., 1924-26; biographer, novelist, 1926—; prof. creative writing U. Ind., 1948, U. Wash., 1961; lectr. Calif. State Colls., 1966. Chmn., Allan Nevins Meml. Fund, Huntington Library, 1972—; mem. adv. council Nat. Soc. Arts and Letters, 1976—. Decorated Order of Merit, Golden Lily of Florence (Italy); recipient Gold trophy Am. Women in Radio and TV, 1968; Herbert Adams Meml. medal Nat. Sculpture Soc., 1970; Golden Plate award Am. Acad. Achievement, 1971; Alumnus of Year award U. Calif. at Berkeley, 1971; Author of Yr. award Book Bank U.S.A., 1976; named Hon. citizen Athens, Greece, 1972. Editor: Dear Theo (autobiography Vincent Van Gogh), 1937. Author books including: Pageant of Youth, 1933; Lust for Life, (Van Gogh), 1934; Sailor on Horseback (Jack London), 1938; False Witness, 1940; Clarence Darrow for the Defense, 1941; They Also Ran, 1943; Immortal Wife (Jessie B. Fremont), 1944; Adversary in the House (Eugene V. Debs), 1947; Earl Warren, 1948; The Passionate Journey (John Noble), 1949; We Speak for Ourselves (self portrait of America), 1950; The President's Lady (Rachel Jackson), 1951; Love is Eternal (Mary Todd Lincoln), 1954; Men to Match My Mountains, 1956; The Agony and the Ecstasy, 1961; I, Michelangelo, Sculptor, 1962; Lincoln: A Contemporary Portrait, 1962; The Story of Michelangelo's Pieta, 1963; The Irving Stone Reader, 1963; The Great Adventure of Michelangelo, 1965; Those Who Love, 1965; There Was Light, 1970; Passions of the Mind (Sigmund Freud), 1971; The Greek Treasure (Henry and Sophia Schliemann), 1975; Irving Stone's Jack London, 1977. Contbr. to mags. and newspapers; art critic Los Angeles Times Mirror, 1959-60. Vice pres. Eugene V. Debs Found.; adv. bd. U. Calif. Inst. Creative Arts; founder Calif. State Coll Com. for Arts; contbg. mem. Am. Sch. Classical Studies, Athens, Mem. Authors League Am., P.E.N., Soc. Am. Historians, Acad. Motion Picture Arts and Scis., Fellows for Schweitzer (founder, pres.), Western Writers Am., Acad. Polit. Sci., Hist. Soc. So. Calif., Calif. Writers Guild (past pres.), Acad. Am. Poets (founder), Berkeley Fellows (charter mem.). Clubs: Bohemian (San Francisco); Calif. Writers (hon.). Address: care Doubleday & Co 9126 Sunset Blvd Los Angeles CA 90069

STONE, IRVING I., greeting card co. exec.; b. Cleve., Apr. 5, 1909; s. Jacob and Jennie (Canter) Sapirstein; ed. Case-Western Res. U., Cleve. Inst. Art; m. Helen K. Sill, Dec. 12, 1976; children—Hensha (Mrs. Hirsch Gansbourg), Neil, Myrna (Mrs. Harold Tatar), Judith (Mrs. Morry Weiss). With Am. Greetings Corp., Cleve., 1923—, pres., 1960—, chmn. bd., chief exec. officer, 1978—. Chmn. bd. Hebrew Acad. Cleve.; bd. dirs. Cleve. Inst. Art, Young Israel of Cleve., Yeshiva U.; trustee Simon Wiesenthal Center for Holocaust Studies; 1st v.p. Telshe Yeshiva; life mem. bd. dirs. Jewish Community Fedn. of Cleve.; v.p. Am. Assn. for Jewish Edn., Bur. Jewish Edn., Cleve., Am. Friends of Boys Town Jerusalem; founder Kiryat Telshe Stone, Israel. Office: 10500 American Rd Cleveland OH 44144

STONE, J. RALPH, savs. and loan assn. exec.; b. Santa Rosa, Calif., June 11, 1910; s. Grover C. and Mercy Jane (Breaks) S.; B.A., U. Calif. at Berkeley, 1932; m. Lois McMullen, Aug. 18, 1934; children—Robert, Gary. With Stone Co., Santa Rosa, 1931-60; with Santa Rosa Savs. & Loan Assn., 1960-70; exec. v.p. Gt. Western Savs. & Loan Assn., 1970—; v.p. Great Western Financial Corp.; dir. Fed. Home Loan Bank, San Francisco, 1968-74; pres. Tristo, Ltd. Chmn. bd. Sonoma County Retirement Assn., 1965-68. Home: 1925 Alderbrook St Santa Rosa CA 95405 Office: 835 4th St Santa Rosa CA 95403

STONE, JAMES HERBERT, educator; b. Little Rock, Sept. 10, 1918; s. Calvin P. and Minnie Ruth (Kemper) S.; A.B., Stanford, 1939; Ph.D., Yale, 1947; m. Margaret M. Hale, June 22, 1941; children—Judith, Laura, Margaret Ruth, Abigail. Instr. history Stanford, 1947-52, acting asso. prof., 1960-61; mem. faculty San Francisco State U., 1952—, prof. humanities, 1961—, head humanities dept., 1961-64, 73-74, coordinator Am. studies program, 1958-73. Acting instr. U. Calif. at Berkeley, summer 1952; Am. Philos. Soc. grantee-in-aid, 1965; U.S. Office Edn. research grantee, 1965-66. Served to 1st lt. AUS, 1942-46; CBI. Mem. Am. Studies Assn. (pres. No. Calif. 1956-58, Far West regional rep. exec. council, 1973 biennial conv. program chmn.), Calif. Humanities Assn. (co-founder 1969), Coordinating Council Arts and Humanities Calif. (exec. sec. 1969-73), Orgn. Am. Historians, Phi Beta Kappa. Home: 365 Lincoln Ave Palo Alto CA 94301 Office: 1600 Holloway Ave San Francisco CA 94132

STONE, JAMES M., govt. ofcl.; b. N.Y.C., Nov. 12, 1947; s. Henry and Babette Rosmond S.; B.A. with highest honors in Econs., Harvard U., 1969, M.A., 1970, Ph.D., 1973. Lectr. econs. Harvard U., 1973-75; commr. ins. Commonwealth of Mass., 1975-79; chmn. Commodity Futures Trading Commn., Washington, 1979—. Democrat. Author: One Way for Wall Street, 1975. Office: 2033 K St NW Washington DC 20581

STONE, JEREMY JUDAH, assn. exec.; b. N.Y.C., Nov. 23, 1935; s. I.F. and Esther (Roisman) S.; B.S. magna cum laude, Swarthmore Coll., 1957; Ph.D., Stanford U., 1960; m. Betty Jane Yannet, June 16, 1957. Research mathematician Stanford Research Inst., 1960-62; mem. profl. staff Hudson Inst., Croton-on-Hudson, 1962-64; research asso., arms control and disarmament Harvard Center Internat. Affairs, 1964-66; asst. prof. math., lectr. polit. sci. Pomona Coll., Claremont, Calif., 1966-68; dir. Fedn. Am. Scientists, Washington, 1970—. Social Sci. Research Council fellow econs. Stanford, 1968-69; Council Fgn. Relations internat. affairs fellow, 1969-70. Mem. Council Fgn. Relations, Internat. Inst. Strategic Studies, Phi Beta Kappa. Author: Containing the Arms Race; Some Concrete Proposals, 1966; Strategic Persuasion, 1967. Home: 5615 Warwick Pl Chevy Chase MD 20015 Office: 307 Massachusetts Ave NE Washington DC 20002

STONE, JOSEPH, advt. agy. exec.; b. Everett, Mass., Mar. 6, 1920; s. Abraham L. and Pauline (Kurtz) S.; B.S. in Bus. Adminstrn., Boston U., 1941; m. Mildred L. Skollar, Apr. 18, 1958. Vice pres. J. Walter Thompson Co., N.Y.C., 1945-59; v.p., asso. creative dir. McCann-Erickson, N.Y.C., 1960-62, Kenyon & Eckhardt, N.Y.C., 1962-64; sr. v.p., creative dir. Bozell Jacobs (formerly Kastor Hilton), N.Y.C., 1964-65; v.p., creative dir. med. advt. div. Ted Bates, Inc., N.Y.C., 1965-67; pres., dir. creative services Berger, Stone & Ratner, Inc., N.Y.C., 1968—. Bd. dirs. Central Westchester Humane Soc., 1960—, chmn. exec. com., 1970—; bd. dirs. Orienta Point Assn., Mamaroneck, N.Y., 1965-68. Served to 1st lt. USAAF, 1942-45. Decorated Air medal with two clusters; recipient Gold Record award for best radio commls. of year, 1955, 56, 57, 58, 59, numerous best of print and broadcast advt. awards, also nat. outdoor poster awards; named Young Advt. Man of Year, Assn. Advt. Men and Women, 1960. Mem. A.S.C.A.P., Am. Guild Authors and Composers, Boston U. Nat. Alumni Council. Clubs: Boston U. (pres. 1962-63), Friars, Copy (N.Y.C.). Contbr. articles to profl., other mags. Composer: I Just Don't Know, 1957; Kopper Kettle, 1958; Daffodil Feelin', 1959; Red Cross Theme Song, 1960; Ford Theme Song, 1959. Home: Bay Head Mamaroneck NY 10543 Office: 666 Fifth Ave New York City NY 10019

STONE, KENNETH EUGENE, JR., bus. exec.; b. Syracuse, N.Y., Sept. 26, 1926; s. Kenneth Eugene and Hilda H. S.; B.A., Western Res. U., 1958; m. Nicol, Nov. 6, 1947; children—Lizbeth Ann, Kenneth Eugene III, Timothy. Staff asst. to controller White Motor Co., 1959-65; controller Lear Jet Corp., 1965-66; chief fin. officer, Cleve., 1966-70; v.p. fin., chief fin. officer Quanex Corp., Houston, 1970—. Served with AC, US] N, 1944-46. Office: 4801 Woodway Houston TX 77056

STONE, KIRK HASKIN, geographer, educator; b. Bay Village, Ohio, Apr. 27, 1914; s. Charles Henry and Katherine Stockwell (Haskin) S.; B.A., U. Mich., 1935, Ph.D., 1949; M.A., Syracuse (N.Y.) U., 1937; m. Vera Grace Erwin, Nov. 26, 1936; 1 dau., Martha Stone Werth. Asst. prof. geography U. Toledo, 1938-42; prof. geography U. Wis., Madison, 1947-65; research prof. geography U. Ga., Athens, 1965—; Fulbright sr. research fellow, Oslo, 1955-56; geographer U.S. Bur. Land Mgmt., 1941, 45-46, 48; cons. Bur. Census, Dept. Def.; geographer Lincoln Lab. Mass. Inst. Tech., 1952-53. Served to lt., geographer OSS, USNR, 1942-46. Mem. Assn. Am. Geographers (Meritorious Service citation 1965), Am. Geog. Soc., AAAS. Author: Alaskan Group Settlement, 1950; Norway's Internal Migration, 1971; Northern Finland's Post-War Colonizing, 1974; contbr. articles to profl. jours. Home: 220 Tanglewood Dr Athens GA 30606 Office: Dept Geography Univ Georgia Athens GA 30602

STONE, LAWRENCE, educator; b. Epsom, Surrey, Eng., Dec. 4, 1919; s. Lawrence Frederick and Mabel Julia Annie (Read) S.; student Sorbonne, Paris, France, 1938; B.A., M.A., Christ Church, Oxford (Eng.) U., 1946; m. Jeanne Caecilia Fawtier, July 24, 1943; children—Elizabeth Caecilia, Robert Lawrence Fawtier. Came. to U.S., 1963, naturalized, 1970. Bryce research student Oxford U., 1946-47, lectr. Univ. Coll., 1947-50, fellow Wadham Coll., 1950-63; mem. Inst. Advanced Study, Princeton, 1960-61; Dodge prof. history Princeton, 1963—, chmn. dept. history, 1967-70, dir. Shelby Cullom David Center Hist. Studies, 1968—. Served as lt. Royal Naval Vol. Res., 1940-45. Fellow Am. Acad. Arts and Scis.; mem. Am. Philos. Soc. Author: Sculpture in Britain: The Middle Ages, 1955; An Elizabethan: Sir Horatio Palavicino, 1956; The Crisis of the Aristocracy, 1558-1641, 1965; The Causes of the English Revolution 1529-1642, 1972; Family and Fortune: Studies in Aristocratic Finance in the Sixteenth and Seventeenth Centuries, 1973; Family, Sex and Marriage in England 1500-1800, 1977. also numerous articles. Mem. editorial bd. Past and Present, 1959—. Home: 266 Moore St Princeton NJ 08540

STONE, LEON, banker; b. Rockdale, Tex., Feb. 27, 1914; s. Harley J. and Ella (Strelsky) S.; student Blinn Coll., Brenham, Tex, 1932, Sul Ross Coll., Alpine, Tex., 1934, U. Tex., 1935, Rutgers U., 1954; m. Bess Northington, Aug. 39, 1939; children—Pebble Stone Moss, Cherry J. Stone Wallin. With Brown & Root, Houston, 1936-37; Guggenheim-Goldsmith, Austin Tex., 1937-38; with Austin Nat. Bank, 1938—, pres., 1963—, also dir.; dean Southwestern Grad. Sch. Banking, So. Meth. U., Dallas; dir. Lockhart State Bank (Tex.), First State Bank, Burnet, Tex. Vice chmn. Tchr. Retirement System Tex., 1956-77. Bd. dirs. Presbyn. Theol. Sem., 1958—, Seton Hosp., 1966—, Mental Health and Mental Retardation Assn. 1965—. Served to lt. col. U.S. Army, ETO. Named Boss of Year, Credit Women of Austin, 1966. Mem. Am. Bankers Assn. (regional v.p. 1965—, exec. com., 1966—), Tex. Bankers Assn. (pres. 1973), Am. Inst. Banking (past pres.), Austin C. of C. (pres. 1968), Tex. Taxpayers Assn. (pres.). Rotarian, Mason, Shriner (Jester). Office: 501 Congress Ave Austin TX 78701

STONE, MARGUERITE BEVERLEY, univ. dean.; b. Norfolk, Va., June 10, 1916; d. James L. and Clara (Thompson) Stone: B.A. in Chemistry, Randolph-Macon Woman's Coll., 1936; M.A., in Student Personnel Adminstrn., Columbia, 1940, profl. diploma, 1956. Tchr., Norfolk High Sch., 1936-41; instr. Tusculum Coll., 1941-43; asst. dean women U. Ark., 1946-50, asso. dean women, 1952-54, dean women, 1954-55; asst. dean women Purdue U., 1956-67, asso. dean women, 1967-68, dean women, 1968-74, dean students, 1974—. Mem. lay bd. St. Elizabeth's Hosp., Salvation Army. Served with USNR, 1943-46, 52-55. Recipient Outstanding Woman in Edn. award Coalition of Women's Orgns. in Greater Lafayette Area, 1978. Mem. AAUW (past pres. Fayetteville, Ark.), Nat. (treas., chmn. hdqrs. adv. com. 1973-75, mem. hdqrs. adv. com. 1975-79), Ind. assns. women deans and cousellors, Assn. Higher Edn., Women's Equity Action League, Purdue Women's Caucus, Mental Health Assn., Phi Beta Kappa, Kappa Delta Pi, Omicron Delta Kappa, Pi Lambda Theta, Zeta Tau Alpha, Mortar Bd., Alpha Lambda Delta (v.p. 1975—). Methodist. Clubs: Lafayette Country, Purdue Women's, Purdue Univ. Author: (with Barbara Cook) monograph Counseling Women, 1973. Home: 1808 Summit Dr West Lafayette IN 47906 Office: Hovde Hall Purdue Univ Lafayette IN 47907

STONE, MARSHALL HARVEY, educator; b. N.Y.C., Apr. 8, 1903; s. Harlan Fiske and Agnes (Harvey) S.; A.B., Harvard, 1922, A.M., 1924, Ph.D., 1926; postgrad. U. Paris (France), 1924-25; Sc.D., Kenyon Coll., 1939; hon. Dr., Universidad de San Marcos, Lima, Peru, 1943, Universidad de Buenos Aires, 1947, U. Athens, 1954; Sc.D., Amherst Coll., 1954, Colby Coll., 1959, U. Mass., 1966; m. Emmy Portman, June 15, 1927 (div. July 1962); children—Doris Portman, Cynthia Harvey, Phoebe G.; m. 2d, Raviojla Perendija Kostic, Aug. 8, 1962; 1 stepdau., Svetlana Kostic-Stone. Part-time instr. Harvard, 1922-23, instr., 1927-28, asst. prof. math., 1928-31, asso. prof., 1933-37; instr. Columbia, 1925-27; asso. prof. math. Yale, 1931-33; acting asso. prof. Stanford, summer 1933; prof. math. Harvard, 1937-46, chmn. dept., 1942; Andrew MacLeish Distinguished Service prof. math. U. Chgo., 1946-68, chmn. dept. math., 1946-52, mem. com. on social thought, 1962-68, prof. emeritus, 1968—; George David Birkhoff prof. math. U. Mass., 1968-73, prof., 1973—. Walker Ames lectr. U. Wash., summer 1942; vis. lectr. Facultad de Ingenieria, U. Buenos Aires, 1943, U. do Brasil, Rio de Janeiro, 1947, Tata Inst. Fundamental Research, Bombay, 1949-50, Am. Math. Soc., 1951-52, College de France, 1953, Australian Math. Soc., 1959, Middle East Tech. U., Ankara, 1963, Pakistan Acad. Sci., 1964, U. Geneva, 1964; 1st Ramanujan vis. prof. Inst. Math Scis. Madras, 1963; vis. prof. Research Inst. Math. Scis., Kyoto, Japan, 1965; vis. scientist C.E.R.N., Geneva, 1966; Fulbright lectr. Australian Nat. U., 1967; hon. prof. Madurai Kamaraj U. (South India), 1967—; hon. Disting. prof. Tchrs. Coll., Columbia U., 1978—;

cons. to USN Dept. Bur. Ordnance and Office Vice Chief Naval Operations, 1942-43; Civil Service employee U.S. War Dept. office chief of staff, 1944-45, with overseas service CBI, ETO; Cons. State Dept., India, 1961, NSF-AID, India, 1968-69, 73; vis. prof. U. Islamabad (Pakistan), 1968-69; pres. Inter-Am. Com. Math. Edn., 1961-72, hon. pres., 1972—; vice chmn. div. math. NRC, 1951-52. Pres., Internat. Math. Union, 1952-54, Internat. Commn. on Math. Instrn., 1959-62, Inter Union Com. Teaching Sci., Internat. Council Sci. Unions, 1962-65. Mem. Nat. Acad. Scis., Am. Philos. Soc., Union Mathematica Argentine (hon.), Indian Math. Soc. (hon.), Acad. Brasileira de Ciencias, Lund (Sweden) Physiographical Soc., Bologna (Italy) Acad. Author: Linear Transformations in Hilbert Space and Their Applications to Analysis, 1932. Contbr. articles on math. and math. edn. to profl. jours. Home: 260 Lincoln Ave Amherst MA 01002

STONE, MARTIN, business exec.; b. St. Louis, May 5, 1928; s. Sam and Dorothy (Chazen) S.; A.B., U. Calif. at Los Angeles, 1948; J.D., Loyola U., Los Angeles, 1951, LL.D., 1970; LL.M., U. So. Calif., 1962; m. Connie Stone; children—Eric Laurence, Nancy Leigh, Lori Jane, Samuel Gardner. Pres., Monogram Industries, Inc., Los Angeles, 1961-69, chmn. bd., chief exec. officer, 1969—; tchr. law U. So. Calif., Loyola Sch. Law, 1963-68. Mem. nat. steering com. Nat. Urban Coalition, 1970-77; chmn. Los Angeles Urban Coalition, 1969-73; v.p. Los Angeles Recreation and Parks Commn., Los Angeles Colisseum Commn., 1974; mem. nat. council Salk Inst., 1973—. Founding dir. Common Cause; bd. dirs. United Way of Los Angeles; trustee Loyola-Marymount Colls., 1971-74. Office: 100 Wilshire Blvd Santa Monica CA 90401. *On a personal level I am motivated most strongly by the opportunity to overcome challenge. On the social level I am committed to the effort to achieve fairness and equity for all members of society and to preserve maximum amounts of personal freedom and liberty.*

STONE, MARTIN, lawyer, communications exec.; b. N.Y.C., May 26, 1915; s. Frank S. and Bertha (Lenner) S.; B.A., Bard Coll., Columbia, 1935; LL.B., Yale, 1938; m. Lydnel Laura Schwarz, Sept. 2, 1936 (dec.); children—Judith Ann Ain, Richard Elihu. Admitted to N.Y. bar, 1939; law sec. to chief justice N.Y. Ct. Appeals, 1938-41, law sec., 1941-42; atty. Lend-Lease Adminstrn., 1942-44; pvt. practice law, N.Y.C., 1945-57; pres. Stone Assos., TV and motion picture prodns., N.Y.C., 1947-50, 55—; pres. Herald Tribune Radio Network, N.Y.C., 1958-65; chmn. bd. pres. Kagran Corp., TV and motion picture prodn., N.Y.C., 1950-55; v.p. dir. Whitney Communications Corp., 1959-65; pres. dir. VIP Radio, Inc., 1958-65, Suburban Radio Inc., 1958-65, Radio Westchester Inc., 1958-65, Media Enterprises, Inc., 1959-65, Skylark Corp., 1959-64; dir. indsl. sect. N.Y. World's Fair Corp., 1962-65; pres. VIP Broadcasting Corp., 1966—, Mt. Kisco Communications, Inc. (N.Y.), 1969—, Westchester Cable TV, 1974—; v.p. Dreyfus Corp., 1971-73; pres. VIP Guide Corp., 1973—, Dreyfus Cable Develop. Corp., 1973—. Cons. Childrens TV Workshop, 1970, Ford Found., 1978—. Mem. town planning bd., Pound Ridge, N.Y., 1965, chmn., 1972-78. Trustee Bard Coll., 1963-68, No. Westchester Hosp., Mt. Kisco, N.Y., Caramoor Center for Music and Arts, 1975—; bd. dirs. Jackie Robinson Found., 1977—. Served with USNR, 1944-45. Recipient Peabody award for TV programming, 1949, 52. Mem. Assn. Bar City N.Y., Phi Beta Kappa. Club: Yale (N.Y.C.). Editor Yale Law Jour., 1937-38. Office: Radio Circle Mount Kisco NY 10549

STONE, MARTIN LAWRENCE, physician, educator; b. N.Y.C., June 11, 1920; s. Isaac and Margaret (Usoskin) Goldstein; B.S., Columbia, 1941; M.D., N.Y. Med. Coll., 1944, M. Med. Sci., 1949; m. Nancy Gundersen, Sept. 4, 1976; 1 son, Robert Earl. Intern, Flower and Fifth Ave. Hosps., N.Y.C., 1944-45, resident obstetrics and gynecology, 1945-46, 47-49, asst. obstetrician and gynecologist, 1949-52, asst. attending obstetrician and gynecologist, 1952-56, attending, 1956—; dir. dept. obstetrics and gynecology Met. Med. Center, 1956—; instr. obstetrics and gynecology N.Y. Med. Coll., 1949-52, asso. in obstetrics and gynecology, 1952-53, asst. prof., 1953-56, prof., dir. dept. obstetrics and gynecology, 1956—, v.p. for hosp. affairs, 1972-76; asst. vis. Met. Hosp., 1949-52, asso. vis.; 1952-56, vis. obstetrician and gynecologist, 1959—, pres. med. bd., 1963-64, 69-70; prof., chmn. dept. obstetrics and gynecology SUNY Stony Brook, 1978—; vis. gynecologist Bird S. Coler Hosp. and Home; mem. N.Y. State Hosp., Rev. and Planning Council, 1976—, N.Y. State Com. Regionalization Obstet. and Pediatric Practice, 1976—; cons. maternity and newborn div. Dept. Health, N.Y.C., chmn. obstet. adv. com., 1966-67; cons. Fitkin Meml. Hosp., Neptune, N.J. Served to capt. M.C., AUS, 1948, chief female sect. Tilton Gen. Hosp. Diplomate Am. Bd. Obstetrics and Gynecology. Fellow A.C.S., Internat. Coll. Surgeons, N.Y. Acad. Medicine (chmn. obstet.-gynecol. sect. 1961), Am. Coll. Obstetricians and Gynecologists (dist. chmn. 1966-69, mem. exec. bd., sec. 1971-76, pres. 1979, commr. health care delivery 1977—), Am. Soc. Study Sterility, N.Y. Obstet. Soc. (treas. 1967-69, pres. 1971-72), Brazilian Obstet. and Gynecol. Soc. (hon.), Royal Soc. Medicine (asso.), N.Y. Acad. Scis., Am. Gynecol. Soc., Am. Pub. Health Assn.; hon. mem. N.J., N.C. obstet. and gynecol. socs., N.Y. Fertility Soc., Am. Com. Maternal Welfare Assn., Assn. Profs. Gynecology and Obstetrics (v.p., mem. council 1962), Am. Med. colls., N.Y. State, N.Y. County med. socs., A.M.A., Am. Med. Writers Assn., Alpha Omega Alpha, Beta Sigma Rho. Clubs: Harmonie, Columbia University (N.Y.C.). Contbr. articles profl. jours. Home: Water Mill NY Office: Sch Medicine SUNY Stony Brook NY 11794

STONE, MARVIN JULES, physician, educator; b. Columbus, Ohio, Aug. 3, 1937; s. Roy J. and Lillian (Bedwinek) S.; student Ohio State U., 1955-58; S.M. in Pathology, U. Chgo., 1962, M.D. with honors, 1963; m. Jill Feinstein, June 29, 1958; children—Nancy Lillian, Robert Howard. Intern ward med. service Barnes Hosp., St. Louis, 1963-64, asst. resident, 1964-65; clin. asso. arthritis and rheumatism br. Nat. Inst. Arthritis and Metabolic Diseases, NIH, Bethesda, Md., 1965-68; resident in medicine, A.C.P. scholar Parkland Meml. Hosp., Dallas, 1968-69; fellow in hematology, dept. internal medicine U. Tex. Southwestern Med. Sch., Dallas, 1969-70, instr. dept. internal medicine, 1970-71, asst. prof., 1971-73, asso. prof., 1974-76, clin. prof., 1976—, chmn. bioethics com. 1979—; dir. Charles A. Sammons Cancer Center, chief oncology, dir. immunology, co-dir. div. hematology-oncology Baylor U. Med. Center, Dallas, 1976—; adj. prof. biology So. Meth. U., Dallas, 1977—. Chmn. com. patient-aid Greater Dallas/Ft. Worth chpt. Leukemia Soc. Am., 1971-76, chmn. med. adv. com., 1978—; med. v.p. Dallas unit Am. Cancer Soc., 1977-78, pres., 1978-80. Served with USPHS, 1965-68. Named Outstanding Full Time Faculty Mem. Dept. Internal Medicine, Baylor U. Med. Center, 1978. Diplomate Am. Bd. Internal Medicine. Fellow A.C.P.; mem. AAAS, Am. Rheumatism Assn., Reticuloendothelial Soc., Am. Assn. Immunologists, Am. Fedn. Clin. Research, Am. Soc. Hematology, N.Y. Acad. Scis., Council on Thrombosis, Am. Heart Assn. (established investigator 1970-75), Am. Soc. Clin. Oncology, Am. Assn. for Cancer Research, Am. Soc. Preventive Oncology, Fedn. Am. Scientists, So. Soc. Clin. Investigation, Tex. Med. Assn., Dallas County Med. Soc., Phi Beta Kappa, Sigma Xi, Alpha Omega Alpha. Contbr. chpts. to books, articles to profl. jours. Office: Charles A Sammons Cancer Center Baylor U Med Center 3500 Gaston Ave Dallas TX 75246

STONE, MARVIN LAWRENCE, journalist; b. Burlington, Vt., Feb. 26, 1924; s. Samuel and Anita (Abrams) S.; student Emory and Henry Coll., 1943, U. Vt., 1948; B.A., Marshall Coll., 1947; M.S., Columbia U., 1949; Litt.D., Marshall U., 1968; m. Sydell Magelaner, Nov. 20, 1949; children—Jamie Faith, Stacey Hope, Torren Magelaner. Assignment reporter Huntington (W.Va.) Herald-Dispatch, 1941-43, 46-48; European corr. Internat. News Service, 1949-52, Far Eastern dir., 1952-58; Sloan Found. fellow in sci. Columbia U., 1958-59; cons. chief army research and devel., 1959-60; asso. editor U.S. News & World Report mag., 1960-66, gen. editor, 1966-68, asso. exec. editor, 1969-70, sr. asso. exec. editor, 1971-72, exec. editor, 1973-76, editor-in-chief, 1976—, also dir. Sponsor, Atlantic Council; mem. adv. com. U.S. Patent Office, 1976-78; trustee, bd. dirs. Washington Opera; v.p., bd. dirs. U.S. Navy Meml. Found. Served to lt. (j.g.) USNR, 1943-46. Pulitzer traveling fellow (Columbia), Austria, 1950; recipient Columbia Journalism 50th Anniversity Honor award, 1963; Marshall U. Distinguished Alumnus award, 1973; Nat. Distinguished Alumnus award Am. Assn. State Colls. and Univs., 1977; Freedoms Found. award, 1978, 79. Mem. Overseas Writers, White House Corrs. Assn., Am. Soc. Mag. Editors (exec. com.), Nat. Press Club, Overseas Press Club, Sigma Delta Chi. Clubs: Fgn. Corrs. of Japan (pres. 1956-57); Internat., Cosmos, Caribao (Washington). Author: Man in Space. Home: 6368 Waterway Dr Lake Barcroft Falls Church VA 22044 Office: 2300 N St NW Washington DC 20037

STONE, MARVIN N., bus. exec.; b. Chgo., Dec. 30, 1909; s. Joseph H. and Mary (Hefter) S.; ed. Northwestern U.; m. Anita Masover, Aug. 10, 1930; children—Avery J., Roger W. Chmn. exec. com. Stone Container Corp., Chgo., 1926—; exec. v.p. S.C. Industries, Inc., Florence, 1926—. Pres. Jewish Fedn., also Jewish United Fund Met. Chgo., 1976-77; past pres., hon. dir. Mt. Sinai Hosp. Med. Center, Chgo., Jewish Community Centers Chgo. Jewish. Clubs: Standard, Mid-Am., Bryn Mawr Country (Chgo.); Tamerisk Country (Palm Springs, Calif.). Home: 1325 Astor St Chicago IL 60610 Office: 360 N Michigan Ave Chicago IL 60601

STONE, MEAD WILMER, JR., pub. co. exec. b. St. George, N.Y. Oct. 18, 1920; s. Mead Wilmer and Lillie (Seeman) S.; grad. Kent Sch., 1938; B.S., Cornell U., N.Y., 1943. Corr., Daily Racing Form-Morning Telegraph, 1947-48; with McGraw-Hill Book Co., N.Y.C., 1948—, bus. book editor, 1955-60, v.p., 1960-64, v.p. internat. div., 1964-70; pres. McGraw-Hill Internat. Book Co., 1970—. Bd. dirs. Rec. for the Blind, Fund for Overseas Research Grants and Edn. Served to capt. F.A., AUS, 1943-47. Decorated Purple Heart with oak leaf cluster, Bronze Star medal. Mem. Eastern N.Y. Thorobred Breeders Assn., Kappa Alpha. Office: 1221 Ave of Americas New York NY 10020

STONE, MORRIS SAMUEL, greeting card mfr.; b. Cleve., Mar. 15, 1911; s. Jacob and Jennie (Kanter) Sapirstein; m. Maxeen Myerson, May 14, 1960. With Am. Greetings Corp., Cleve., 1928—, now vice chmn. bd., chmn. exec. com., dir. Home: 18803 North Park Blvd Shaker Heights OH 44122 Office: 10500 American Rd Cleveland OH 44144

STONE, NELSON, electronics co. exec.; b. Chgo., Jan. 30, 1923; s. Julius and Clara (Finklestein) S.; student U. Mich., 1943; A.B., U. Cin., 1947, J.D., 1948; m. Dolores Reinlib, Dec. 25, 1957; children—Marla Susan, Julian David. Admitted to Ohio Bar, 1949; atty. adviser U.S. Govt., 1948-52; corp. counsel. dir. contract adminstrn. Gruen Watch Co., 1952-56; with Fairchild Camera & Instrument Corp., 1957—, v.p., 1968—, sec., 1969—; dir. subsidiaries. Served to 1st lt. USAAF, 1943-46. Mem. Fed. Bar Assn. 646 Towle Pl Palo Alto CA 94036

STONE, PATSY RUTH SCHNIBBEN, judge; b. Florence, S.C., July 18, 1930; d. John Herman and Grace Kathryn (Rasberry) Schnibben; student Meredith Coll., 1947-49, Newberry Coll., 1949-50; B.A. in History, Francis Marion Coll., 1977; m. Neal D. Thigpen, May 21, 1977; children—Grace (Mrs. Richard George Irons), John David Poston. Dep. judge Florence County (S.C.) Ct. of Probate, 1962-70, judge, 1970—; mem. com. on uniform probate code S.C. Bar, 1977-79; mem. adv. council S.C. Dept. Mental Health, 1976—. Dir. musical prodns. Florence Little Theatre; mem. Florence County Law Library Commn. Mem. com. on party rules and legislation S.C. Democratic Party; del. nat. mini-conv., 1974; bd. dirs. Florence Little Theatre Guild, 1959—, sec., 1959-62, treas., 1962-68; bd. dirs. Florence County Mental Health Assn.; bd. dirs. Pee Dee Regional Health Systems Agy., 1978, mem. exec. com., 1979; mem. adv. com. John F. Kennedy Center for Performing Arts, 1979—. Named S.C. Style Maker of Year, 1975. Mem. Internat., Nat., S.C. (v.p. 1977-78, pres. 1978-79) assns. probate judges, Nat. Coll. Probate Judges, League of Women Voters, Pi Gamma Mu. Club: Altrusa (Florence). Office: PO Box 965 Florence SC 29501

STONE, PETER H., playwright-scenarist; b. Los Angeles, Feb. 27, 1930; s. John and Hilda (Hess) S.; B.A., Bard Coll., 1951, D.Litt., 1971; M.F.A., Yale, 1953; m. Mary O'Hanley, Feb. 17, 1961. Author: mus. comedies Kean, 1961, Skyscaper 1965, 1776, 1969, Two by Two, 1970, Sugar, 1972; play Full Circle, 1973; motion pictures including Charade, 1963, Father Goose, 1964, Mirage, 1965, Arabesque, 1966, Secret War of Harry Frigg, 1968, Sweet Charity, 1969, Skin Game, 1971, 1776, 1972, Taking of Pelham 123, 1974, Silver Bears, 1977, Who is Killing the Great Chefs of Europe?, 1978; TV scripts The Defenders, Espionage, Studio One, Brenner, Asphalt Jungle, Androcles and the Lion, series Adam's Rib, Ivan the Terrible, and others; novel Charade, 1963. Recipient Acad. award, 1964; Emmy award, 1963; Mystery Writers award, 1964; Tony award, 1969; N.Y. Drama Critics award, 1969; Drama Desk award, 1969; Christopher award, 1973. Mem. Dramatists Guild (exec. council), Authors League, Writers Guild Am. Home: 160 E 71st St New York NY 10021 also Stony Hill Rd Amagansett NY 11930

STONE, PHILIP JAMES, III, educator; b. Chgo., Oct. 6, 1936; s. Philip James, Jr., and Alice (Peterson) S.; B.A., U. Chgo., 1956; Ph.D., Harvard, 1960. Psychologist NIMH, Bethesda, Md., 1958-60; lectr., research asso. dept. social relations Harvard, 1960-67; fellow Center for Advanced Study in Behavioral Scis., Stanford, Calif., 1967-69; asso. prof. social relations Harvard, 1968-69, prof., 1969—; guest prof. U. Koeln, 1974, U. Hamburg, 1975. Mem. coms. Nat. Acad. Scis., Social Sci. Research Council, Council Social Sci. Data Archives. Mem. AAAS. Co-author: The General Inquirer, 1966; Users Manual for the General Inquirer, 1968; Experiments in Induction, 1966; Analysis of Communication Content, 1969; The Use of Time, 1972; Computer Recognition of English Word Senses, 1975. Contbr. articles profl. jours., chpts. in books. Home: Dunster C-24 Cambridge MA Office: William James Hall Harvard U Cambridge MA 02138

STONE, RALPH, cons. civil engr.; b. N.Y.C., Apr. 12, 1921; s. Samuel and Frida (Wahl) S.; B.S. in Engring., U. Calif., Berkeley, 1943, M.S. in Civil Engring., 1944; m. Sunshine C. Anderson, Nov. 4, 1960; children—Marguerita S., Robert W. Research asso. U. Calif., Berkeley, 1943-44; san. engr. USPHS, 1944-46, UNRRA, also WHO, 1946-48, U.S. Inst. Inter Am. Affairs, 1949-51; project engr. Fluor Corp., 1951-53; pres. Ralph Stone and Co., Inc., Los Angeles, 1953—. Pres., founder Friends of Santa Monica Mountains, Parks and Seashore Assn., 1968-72, trustee, 1976—; pres. Brentwood Community Fedn., 1964-66, Crestwood Hills Assn., 1962-63; v.p. Far Eastern art council Los Angeles County Art Mus., 1976-77; rev. panel EPA; mem. Los Angeles County Mulholland Commn., Mayor Los Angeles Adv. Com., Los Angeles Mass Transit Adv. Com., Los Angeles Griffith Park Adv. Com., Calif. Transp. Adv. Com. Recipient James Monroe McDonald award U. Calif., Berkeley, 1943. Fellow ASCE (chmn. environ. engring. div. 1953—; Rudolf Hering award 1953, Samuel A. Greeley award 1976); mem. Am. Acad. Environ. Engrs., Am. Water Works Assn., Fedn. Water Pollution Control Assn., Am. Inst. Planners, Am. Pub. Works Assn., Am. Chem. Soc. Clubs: Riviera Tennis, Los Angeles Athletic. Author, patentee waste recovery processes. Home: 1044 Hanley Ave Los Angeles CA 90049 Office: 10954 Santa Monica Blvd Los Angeles CA 90025

STONE, RICHARD BERNARD, senator; b. N.Y.C., Sept. 22, 1928; s. Alfred and Lily (Abbey) S.; B.A. cum laude, Harvard, 1949; LL.B., Columbia, 1954; m. Marlene Singer; children—Nancy, Amy, Elliot. Former sec. Royal Castle Systems, Inc.; former dir. Eagle Army Navy, Inc.; partner Stone, Bittell, Langer, Blass & Corrigan; city atty., Miami, Fla., 1966-67; mem. Fla. Senate, 1967-70; sec. of state State of Fla., 1971-74; senator from Fla., 1975—. Mem. Dade County, Am., Interam. bar assns., Corp. Banking and Bus. Law Com., Fla. State Bar, Am. Judicature Soc. Jewish. Rotarian. Moose, Elk, K. P., Mason. Office: 1327 Dirksen Senate Office Bldg Washington DC 20510 also 2639 N Monroe Suite 200B Tallahassee FL 32309 also 51 SW 1st Ave Suite 817 Miami FL 33138 also Room 412 Federal Bldg 500 Zack St Tampa FL 33602

STONE, ROBERT ANTHONY, author; b. N.Y.C., Aug. 21, 1937; s. C. Homer and Gladys Catherine (Grant) S.; student N.Y. U., 1958-59, (Stegner fellow) Stanford, 1962; m. Janice G. Burr, Dec. 11, 1959; children—Deidre M., Ian A. Reporter, N.Y. Daily News, N.Y.C., 1958-60; novelist, 1960—; writer-in-residence Princeton, 1971-72. Served with USN, 1955-58. Recipient William Faulkner prize, 1967; Guggenheim fellow, 1971. Mem. P.E.N. Club. Author: A Hall of Mirrors, 1967; Dog Soldiers, 1975 (Nat. Book award 1975); contbg. author: Best American Short Stories, 1970, 1971. Office: care Candida Donadio & Assos 111 W 57th St New York NY 10017*

STONE, ROBERT FREDERICK, advt. agy. exec.; b. Chgo., Sept. 5, 1918; s. Irving John and Tessie Grace (Baier) S.; student Northwestern U., 1936-41; m. Dorothy Hebner, Apr. 17, 1948; children—Karen, Jeffrey, Richard, William, Lawrence. Vice pres. Nat. Research Bur., 1945-60; pres. Nat. Communications Corp., Chgo., 1960-66; pres. Stone & Adler, Inc., Chgo., 1966-70; chmn. bd. Stone and Adler, Inc., Chgo., 1965—; dir. Baldwin Cooke Co., Chgo., Young & Rubicam Affiliates. Mem. Direct Mail Advt. Assn. (trustee Ednl. Found. 1965—), Mail Advt. Chgo. Author: Successful Direct Mail Advertising and Selling, 1955; Successful Direct Marketing Methods, 1975. Feature writer Advt. Age, 1967—. Home: 606 Laurel Ave Wilmette IL 60091 Office: 150 N Wacker Dr Chicago IL 60606

STONE, ROBERT JOSEPH, pub. relations exec.; b. Kingston, N.Y., Aug. 23, 1920; s. Morris and Hattie (Mann) S.; student Rider Coll., Trenton, N.J., 1946-47; m. Shirley C. Siegel, Apr. 11, 1947; children—Barbara, Judith. Dir. pub. relations Schenectady Union Star, 1948-50, Trentonian, Trenton, 1950-51, N.J. Dept. Def. and Div. Civil Def., 1951-52; pub. relations specialist for plant cities Eastern region Ford Motor Co., 1953-58; div. pub. relations dir. Internat. Tel. & Tel. Corp., 1958-60; dir. financial pub. relations dept. Ruder & Finn, Inc., N.Y.C., 1960-63; v.p. operations Monroe B. Scharff & Co., Inc., N.Y.C., 1963-65; sr. v.p., dir. Eastern operations Daniel J. Edelman, Inc., N.Y.C., 1965-70, exec. v.p., dir., 1970-71; pres. Edelman Investor Relations div., 1970-71; pres., chief exec. officer Infoplan Internat., Inc., N.Y.C., 1971; dir. corporate communications Singer Co., N.Y.C., 1973-77; pres. Bus. Orgn., Inc. subs. Carol Byoir & Assos., Inc., v.p. corporate communications and pub. affairs Turbodyne Corp. & Worthington Compressors, Inc., Holyoke, Mass., 1977—. Served with AUS, 1942-46. Mem. Pub. Relations Soc. Am., Internat. Pub. Relations Assn. Club: Overseas Press (N.Y.C.). Office: 104 Lower Westfield Rd Holyoke MA 01040

STONE, ROBERT SAMUEL, coll. dean; b. N.Y.C., Feb. 10, 1922; s. Samuel S. and Ione (Aronson) S.; B.A., Bklyn. Coll., 1942; M.D., State U. N.Y. at Bklyn., 1950; m. Mary Elizabeth Worley, Aug. 14, 1949; 1 dau., Lael Anne. Intern, asst. resident pathology Presbyn. Hosp., N.Y.C., 1950-52; jr. physician pathology VA Hosp., Wadworth, 1952-54; instr. pathology Columbia Coll. Phys. and Surg., 1950-52; from instr. to asso. prof. Sch. Medicine, U. Calif. at Los Angeles, 1952-63; prof. pathology, chmn. dept. U. N.M., 1963-68, asso. dean Sch. Medicine, 1966-68, dean, 1968-73, v.p. health scis., 1970-73; dir. NIH, Bethesda, Md., 1973-75; dean Sch. Medicine, v.p. U. Oreg. Health Scis. Center, Portland, 1975-78; dean Tex. A&M U. Coll. Medicine, 1978—; mem. profl. adv. com. Raleigh Hills Hosp. Chief pathology Atomic Bomb Casualty Commn., Hiroshima, 1959-60; vis. investigator Rockefeller Inst., 1959; cons. VA Hosp., Alburquerque, 1963-73; mem. nat. adv. council on health professions edn. assistance NIH, 1971; vis. prof. Sloan sch. Mass. Inst. Tech., 1972-73. Mem. exec. council Assn. Am. Med. Colls., 1972-73, distinguished service mem. council of deans, 1974—. Served with USNR, 1942-46. Fellow Coll. Am. Pathologists; mem. AMA (del. sect. on med. schs.), Tex. Med. Assn., Alpha Omega Alpha. Editorial Bd. Jour. Med. Edn., 1970-74. Home: Tex A&M U Coll Medicine College Station TX 77843

STONE, ROBERT WINTHROP, banker; b. Danbury, Conn., Nov. 29, 1922; s. Henry D. and Helena (McCauley) S.; B.A., M.A., U. Conn., 1951; Ph.D., U. Va., 1955; m. Lilyan M. Sydenham, Aug. 20, 1954; children—David A., Bradford S., Evan W. Instr. econs. U. Conn., 1949-51; research economist U. Va. Bur. Population and Econ. Research, 1951-53; with Fed. Res. Bank N.Y., 1953-65, economist, 1953-58, mgr. securities dept., 1958-62, asst. v.p., 1962, v.p., mgr. system open market acct., 1962-65; v.p. Nat. Bank of Detroit, 1965-66, sr. v.p., 1966-68; sr. v.p. Irving Trust Co., N.Y.C., 1968-73, exec. v.p., 1973—. Served with USNR, 1942-46. Mem. Pub. Securities Assn. Club: Bond (N.Y.C.). Home: 2 Brook View Ct Ho-HO-Kus NJ 07423 Office: 1 Wall St New York City NY 10005

STONE, ROGER DAVID, orgn. exec.; b. N.Y.C., Aug. 4, 1934; s. Patrick William and Kathleen Mary (Davies) S.; B.A., Yale U., 1955; m. Florence Overall Smith, May 19, 1962; 1 dau., Leslie Burnam. Asst. to publisher Time mag., 1959-61; corr., news bur. chief in San Francisco, Rio de Janeiro and Paris, Time-Life News Service, 1961-68; asst. to pres. Time, Inc., 1968-70; v.p. Chase Manhattan Bank, N.Y.C., 1970-75; pres. Center Inter-Am. Relations, N.Y.C., 1975—; dir. Accion Internat., A.I.T. Found., Inc. Bd. dirs. U.S. appeal World Wildlife Fund, Cintas Found., Americas Found. Served as lt., aviator, USNR, 1956-59. Mem. Council Fgn. Relations. Home: 34 W 88th St New York NY 10024 Office: 680 Park Ave New York NY 10021

STONE, ROGER WARREN, container co. exec.; b. Chgo., Feb. 16, 1935; s. Marvin N. and Anita (Masover) S.; B.S. in Econs., U. Pa., 1957; m. Susan Kesert, Dec. 24, 1955; children—Karen, Lauren, Jennifer. With Stone Container Corp., Chgo., 1957—, dir., 1968-77, v.p., gen. mgr. container div., 1970-75, pres., chief operating officer, 1975-79, pres., chief exec. officer, 1979—; dir. Silvestri Industries,

Internat. Design. Trustee, Michael Reese Hosp., Hadley Sch. for Blind, North Shore Country Day Sch., Glenwood Sch. for Boys. Mem. Econs. Club Chgo., Chgo. Council Fgn. Relations, Young Pres.'s Orgn. Republican. Clubs: Standard; Tavern; Lake Shore Country. Office: 360 N Michigan Ave Chicago IL 60601

STONE, SCOTT CLINTON STUART, author; b. Polk County, Tenn., Aug. 4, 1932; s. Randall and Stella (Beaver) S.; B.S., East Tenn. State Coll., 1956; m. Barbara Miyashiro, Aug. 8, 1953 (div. Aug. 1974); children—Alison Tauhere, Erik Stuart. Reporter, Dayton (Ohio) Daily News, 1956-57, Honolulu Advertiser, 1958-68, Reuters, 1960-74. Served to lt. comdr. USNR. Decorated Kinmen medal (Republic of China). Mem. Naval Res. Assn. Author: The Coasts of War, 1966; A Share of Honor, 1969; Dragon's Eye (Edgar award Mystery Writers Am.), 1969; Pearl Harbor, The Way It Was, 1977; Volcano!!, 1978. Address: care Robert Lewis 500 Fifth Ave Room 905 New York City NY 10036. *There are seasons of the mind, and an inevitability of the mind and the spirit. Man is a transient. I quote Li Po: The peach blossom follows the moving water.*

STONE, SHEPARD, inst. exec.; b. Nashua, N.H., Mar. 31, 1908; s.Simon W. and Anna (Gold) S.; A.B., Dartmouth;, 1929; student U. Heidelberg, 1930; Ph.D., U. Berlin, 1933, prof. h.c., 1978; Dr. h.c., Free U. Berlin, 1954; Dr. rer. pol. h.c., U. Basel (Switzerland), 1967; m. Charlotte Hasenclever, Aug. 15, 1933; 1 dau., Margaret Ann. Writer fgn. affairs, 1933-42; reporter N.Y. Times, 1934-35, editorial asst. Sunday dept., 1935-42, asst. Sunday editor, 1946-49; spl. cons. to U.S. High Commr. for Germany, 1949-50, dir. Office Pub. Affairs, 1950-52; staff Ford Found., 1953, dir. Internat. affairs, 1954-68; pres. Internat. Assn. Cultural Freedom, Paris, 1968-73; dir. Aspen Berlin (Germany) Inst. for Humanistic Studies, 1974—; cons. to State Dept. and ACDA, 1961. Trustee Aspen Inst. for Humanistic Studies, 1972—. Served from lt. to lt. col., G-2 hdqrs., 1st Army, AUS, 1942-46. Decorated Legion of Merit; comdrs. cross Order of Merit (Fed. Republic Germany). Mem. Council Fgn. Relations N.Y.C. Clubs: Century (N.Y.C.); Athenaeum (London, Eng.). Author: Shadow Over Europe, 1938; Editor: (with H.W. Baldwin) We Saw It Happen, 1938. Home: Schleinitzstrasse 1a 1000 Berlin 33 West Germany also 1 Quai aux Fleurs Paris 4 France also South Newfane VT 05351 Office: Aspen Berlin Inselstrasse 10 Berlin 38 West Germany

STONE, THOMAS S., lawyer; b. Reedsburg, Wis., Feb. 23, 1909; s. Charles H. and Edna B. (Bryden) S.; B.A., U. Wis., 1930; LL.B., 1934, S.J.D., 1935; m. Ann Louise Taplin, Sept. 11, 1937; children—Thomas R., William S. Admitted to Wis. bar, 1934, since practiced in Milw.; partner Michael, Best & Friedrich. Mem. Am., Wis., Milw. (mem. citizenship and constn. com., world peace through law com.), bar assns., Am. Soc. Internat. Law, Am. Interprofl. Inst., Milw. County Hist. Soc., Civil War Round Table, S.A.R. (past Wis. Pres., nat. trustee, now Wis. chancellor), Wis. Hist. Soc., Lincoln Fellowship Wis., Benchers Soc., Order of Coif, Alpha Chi Rho, Phi Alpha Delta. Republican. Presbyn. Clubs: Milwaukee Athletic; Kiwanis. Home: Pan Yack Park Route 1 Kansasville WI 53139 Office: 250 E Wisconsin Ave Milwaukee WI 53202

STONE, W. CLEMENT, ins. co. exec., civic leader; b. Chgo., May 4, 1902; s. Louis and Anna M. (Gunn) S.; student Detroit Coll. Law, 1920, Northwestern U., 1930-32; hon. degrees; J.D., Monmouth Coll., 1963; H.H.D., Interlochen Arts Acad., 1964, Whitworth Coll., 1969, S.W. Baptist Coll., Bolivar, Mo., 1970, Lincoln (Ill.) Coll., 1971, L.H.D., De Paul U., 1970, Warner Pacific Coll., Portland, Oreg., 1978; LL.D., Whittier Coll., 1973; Litt.D., Nat. Coll. Chiropractic, Lombard, Ill., 1969; D.Public Service, Salem (W.Va.) Coll., 1974; m. Jessie Verna Tarson; children—Clement, Donna Jessie, Norman Clement. Chmn. bd. Combined Am. Ins. Co. (formerly Am. Casualty Co.), 1939—; organizer Combined Mut. Casualty Co., 1940, pres., 1940-47; pres. Combined Ins. Co. Am. (formerly Pa. Casualty Co.), 1947-69, chmn. bd. dirs., 1969—, chief exec. officer, 1969-73; pres. Combined Ins. Co. Wis. (formerly 1st Nat. Casualty Co.), 1953-73, chmn. bd., chief exec. officer, 1973—; pres., chmn. bd. Combined Life Ins. Co. N.Y., 1971—; chmn. bd. Combined Opportunities, Inc.; dir. Alberto-Culver Co., chmn. bd. Success Unlimited mag. Pres., trustee Religious Heritage of Am., Inc., Washington. Chmn. bd. W. Clement and Jessie V. Stone Found.; mem. John Howard Assn., Chgo.; nat. exec. com. Boys Clubs Am.; life mem. bd. mgrs. Robert R. McCormick Chgo. Boys Club; chmn. bd. Chgo. Boys Clubs, Internat. Council on Edn. for Teaching, Insts. Religion and Health; hon. chmn. Found. for Study Cycles; chmn. bd. trustees Interlochen Arts Acad. and Nat. Music Camp. Mem. Internat. Assn. Health Underwriters, (W.Va.) Coll., 1974; Ill. C. of C., Chgo. Assn. Commerce and Industry, Am. Mgmt. Assn., Sales Marketing Execs. Internat. Presbyn. Mason. Clubs: Executives, Kiwanis, Michigan Shores Country. Author: (with Napoleon Hill) Success Through a Positive Mental Attitude, 1960; The Success System that Never Fails, 1962; (with Norma L. Browning) The Other Side of the Mind, 1964. Office: 5050 Broadway Chicago IL 60640

STONE, WILLIAM EDWARD, ednl. adminstr.; b. Peoria, Ill., Aug. 13, 1945; s. Dean Proctor and Katherine (Jamison) S.; A.B., Stanford U., 1967, M.B.A., 1969. Asst. dean Stanford U., 1969-71, asst. to pres., 1971-77; assn. dir. Stanford Alumni Assn., 1977—. Bd. dirs. North County YMCA, 1975-76; trustee Watkins Discretionary Fund. Mem. Council for Advancement and Support of Edn. Democrat. Club: Stanford Faculty (dir.). Home: 543 Junipero Serra Blvd Stanford CA 94305 Office: Bowman Alumni House Stanford CA 94305

STONE, WILLIAM HAROLD, geneticist, educator; b. Boston, Dec. 15, 1924; s. Robert and Rita (Scheinberg) S.; A.B., Brown U., 1948; M.S., U. Maine, 1949; Ph.D., U. Wis., 1953; m. Elaine Stone, Nov. 24, 1947; children—Susan Joy, Debra M.; m. 2d, Carmen Maqueda, Dec. 22, 1971 1 son, Alexander R.M. Research asst. Jackson Meml. Lab., Bar Harbor, Maine, 1947-48; faculty dept. genetics U. Wis., Madison, 1949—, prof., 1961—, prof. med. genetics, 1964—; NIH fellow Calif. Inst. Tech., 1960-61. Mem. panel blood group experts FAO, 1962—, program dir. immunogenetics research, Spain, 1971—. Recipient I.I. Ivanov medal USSR, 1974. Mem. Am. Inst. Biol. Scis., NRC, Assembly Life Scis., Nat. Acad. Scis. AASA, Am. Soc. Immunologists, Am. Genetics Assn., Am. Aging Soc., Genetics Soc., Am. Soc. Human Genetics, Research Soc. Am., Internat. Soc. Transplant, Am. Soc. Animal Sci., Sigma Xi, Gamma Alpha. Author: Immunogenetics, 1967. Contbr. articles to profl. jours. Home: 3411 Stony Crest Dr McFarland WI 53558 Office: Dept Med Genetics U Wis Madison WI 53706. *Some things are better never than late. We need more education and less legislation. I can't believe I get paid for something I have so much fun doing. Goodness with strength is a virtue, goodness with weakness is stupidity. Quite often, bad luck is really good luck gone unrecognized.*

STONE, WILLIAM OLIVER, screenwriter, dir.; b. N.Y.C., Sept. 15, 1946; s. Louis and Jacqueline Pauline Czezarine (Goddet) S.; student Yale U., 1965; B.F.A., N.Y. U. Film Sch., 1971. Tchr., Cholon, Vietnam, 1965-66; taxi driver, N.Y.C., 1971; screenwriter-dir. films: Seizure, Can., 1972-73, The Hand, Orion Pictures Co., Los Angeles, 1980—; screenwriter various films, including: Midnight Express, London (Acad. award for screenplay adapted from another medium 1978, Writers Guild Am. award for screenplay 1978, Hollywood Fgn. Press award for best screenplay 1978), 1977. Served with U.S. Mcht. Marine, 1966, with inf. U.S. Army, 1967-68; Vietnam. Decorated Purple Heart with oak leaf cluster, Bronze Star. Mem. Writers Guild Am., Dirs. Guild Am. Office: 9025 Wilshire Blvd Suite 301 Beverly Hills CA 90211

STONE, WILLIARD EVERARD, accountant, educator; b. Phila., Aug. 28, 1910; s. Theodore Williard Jr. and Blanche (Patton) S.; A.B., Pa. State U., 1933; M.A., U. Pa., 1950, Ph.D., 1957; m. Louise Cousins Harder, May 19, 1934; children—Theodore Williard III, Donald Edwin, Richard Patton. Auditor, Pa. Liquor Control Bd., 1934-43, U.S. comptroller gen., 1943-47; partner Stone & Fisher, C.P.A.'s, Phila., 1947-50; asst. prof. accounting U. Pa. Wharton Sch. Finance and Commerce, Phila., 1947-57, asso. prof., 1957-60; prof. U. Fla., Gainesville, 1960—, head dept. accounting, 1960-74, bd. mgrs. U. Fla. Press, 1961—. Vis. prof. U. New S. Wales, 1966; Carman G. Blough chair of accounting U. Va., 1972-73; vis. prof. U. Port Elizabeth, 1975, Va. Poly. Inst. and State U., 1976; cons. editor Chilton Book div. Chilton Co., Phila., 1957-61, Holt, Rinehart & Winston, Inc., 1961-70; cons. to U.S. Comptroller Gen., 1963-69. C.P.A., Pa. Mem. Nat. Assn. Accountants (dir. Phila. 1954-55), Am., Fla., Pa. (dir. 1954-55) insts. C.P.A.'s, Am. Accounting Assn. (v.p. 1963), Acad. Accounting Historians, Beta Alpha Psi (past pres), Beta Gamma Sigma. Author (with MacFarland, Ayars) Accounting Fundamentals, 1957. Co-editor: Accounting Historian's Jour. Contbr. articles to profl. jours. Home: 1717 NW 23d Ave Gainesville FL 32605

STONEBURNER, ROGER WHITNEY, geologist, oil and gas co. exec.; b. Cleve., Nov. 16, 1922; s. Whitney E. and Edna Rose (Stauffer) S.; B.A. in Geology, Coll. Wooster, 1946; M.A. in Geology (Sigma Xi fellow), U. Kans., 1948; grad. advanced mgmt. program Harvard U., 1976; m. Jean Lois Kelty, Sept. 6, 1947; children—Susan, Sara, Richard. Geologist, California Co., New Orleans, 1948-55; chief geologist San Jacinto Petroleum Corp., Houston, 1955-57, v.p., 1957-60; mgr. exploration So. Natural Gas Co., Houston, 1960-64; with Union Tex. Petroleum Co., Houston, 1964—, v.p. internat. exploration and prodn., 1974-76, exec. v.p., 1976—, asst. to pres., 1978—. Served with C.E., U.S. Army, 1944-46. Mem. Am. Assn. Petroleum Geologists, Am. Petroleum Inst., Houston Geol. Soc. Republican. Presbyterian. Home: 734 Country Ln Houston TX 77024 Office: One Riverway Houston TX 77056

STONECIPHER, DAVID ALLEN, ins. co. exec.; b. Cleveland, Tenn., Mar. 29, 1941; s. William Oscar and Irene Iola (Kile) S.; B.A., Vanderbilt U., 1962; M.A.S., Ga. State U., 1967; m. Nan Beverly Fuller, June 29, 1963; children—Stephen, Christopher. With Life Ins. Co. of Ga., Atlanta, 1962—, asst. v.p., actuary, 1972-75, v.p., actuary, 1975-77, sr. v.p., actuary, mem. mgmt. com., 1977—. Served with U.S. Army, 1962-64. Mem. Am. Acad. Actuaries, Soc. Actuaries, Beta Gamma Sigma. Republican. Presbyterian. Club: Atlanta Roundtable. Author: (with John M. Bragg) Life Insurance Based on the Consumer Price Index, 1969.

STONEHILL, ROBERT BERRELL, physician, educator; b. Phila., Feb. 14, 1921; s. David Louis and Mary (Herbert) S.; A.B., Temple U., 1942, M.D., 1945; m. Katherine Louise Brown, Mar. 4, 1944 (dec. 1977); children—Susan (Mrs. Ricardo H. D'Alessandro), Mary Elizabeth, Laura Louise; m. 2d, Marjorie P. Leamnson, Sept. 2, 1978. Intern, Jersey City Med. Center, 1945-46; commd. 2d lt. USAAF, 1946, advanced through grades to col. USAF, 1963; ret., 1967; prof. medicine Ind. U., 1967—. Decorated Legion of Merit, Air Force Commendation medal. Diplomate Am. Bd. Internal Medicine (pulmonary disease; recertified 1974), Am. Bd. Preventive Medicine (aviation medicine). Fellow A.C.P., Am. Coll. Chest Physicians (gov. 1965-67), Am. Coll. Preventive Medicine, Royal Soc. Medicine Eng.; mem. Air Force Soc. Physicians, Internat. Platform Assn., Ind. Thoracic Soc. Author: Sophomore Introduction to Clinical Medicine, Pulmonary Course. Contbr. articles to profl. jours. Home: 581 S Century Oaks St Zionsville IN 46077 Office: Ind U Sch Medicine 1300 W Michigan St Indianapolis TN 46232

STONER, BARTINE ALBERT, JR., advt. exec.; b. Trenton, N.J., Apr. 18, 1926; s. Bartine Albert and Estella (Hart) S.; B.S., Princeton, 1948; m. Elizabeth Ann Bond, Mar. 18, 1949 (div. 1973); children—Bartine Albert III, Jonathan West; m. 2d, Madeleine Ruskin, 1973. With Westinghouse Electric Corp., Boston, Newark and Phila., 1948-56; Account exec. N.W. Ayer & Son, Inc., Phila., 1956-65, v.p., dir. account service, 1965-67, dir., exec. v.p., gen. mgr. Phila. region, 1967-73, dir. internat. operations, N.Y.C., 1974-76; pres. Ayer Baker Advt., Seattle, 1974-75; mng. dir. Ayer Barker Hegemann Internat. B.V., London, 1976-79; exec. v.p., gen. mgr., dir. Ayer Pacific, pres., chief exec. officer Ayer, Jorgensen, Macdonald, Los Angeles, 1979—; dir., pres. Settembrini and Tecchio ABH Internat., Milan, Italy; dir. Charles Barker, GmbH, Frankfurt, W. Ger., Moussault ABH Internat., Amsterdam and Antwerp. Bd. dirs. Greater Phila. Movement, 1973-74, Elwyn Inst.-Hosp., 1967-76; bd. pensions U.P. Ch. U.S.A., 1971-76. Served to lt. (j.g.) USNR, 1944-46. Mem. Newcomen Soc., Pa. Soc. Presbyterian (elder). Clubs: Phila. Racquet; Hurlingham (London); Princeton (N.Y.C.). Home: 1778 Palisades Dr Pacific Palisades CA 90272 also 10 Upper Cheyne Row London SW3 England also Stoner Lodge Lake Honnedaga Forrestport NY 13338 Office: 707 Wilshire Blvd Los Angeles CA 90017 also 1345 Ave of Americas New York NY 10019

STONER, JAMES LLOYD, clergyman; b. Point Marion, Pa., Apr. 23, 1920; s. Martin Clark and Bess (Hare) S.; B.S., Bethany Coll., 1941, D.D. (hon.), 1958; B.D., Yale, 1944; m. Janice Faller Evans, Aug. 28, 1943; children—Thomas Clark, James Douglas and Geoffrey Lloyd (twins). Ordained to ministry Christian Ch., 1943; minister in Hamden, Conn., 1942-44; asso. exec. sec. U. Tex., YMCA, 1944-45; dir. Student Christian Fellowship, Bowling Green State U., 1945-47; dir. Univ. Christian Mission, Fed. Council Ch. and Nat. Council Chs., 1947-56; minister North Christian Ch., Columbus, Ind., 1956-66; asst. gen. sec. for exec. operations Nat. Council Chs., 1966-72; sr. minister Central Christian Ch., Austin, Tex., 1972—. Chmn. com. recommendations Internat. Conv. Christians Chs., 1962-65; bd. mgrs. United Christian Missionary Soc., 1956-63; mem. adv. bd. Am. Bible Soc., 1966-72; mem. council Christian unity Christian Ch.; a founder, 1st pres. LINK Award, Ridgewood, N.J., 1966-72; mem. Austin Conf. Chs., pres., 1973-75; rep. Tex. Conf. Chs., 1976—, mem. div. Christian unity, 1976—; a founder, bd. dirs. Fellowship Christian Athletes, Kansas City, Mo., 1956-68; trustee Tougaloo (Miss.) Coll., 1968-74; v.p., mem. exec. com., Ecumenical Center Continuing Edn., Yale, 1966-72; mem. exec. com. Boy Scouts Am., Austin. Mem. Austin Soc. Pub. Adminstrs., Goals Com. Austin Tomorrow, Alpha Psi Omega, Beta Theta Pi. Mason (32 deg.) Rotarian (dir.). Contbr. articles to profl. pubs. Home: 4204 Farhills Dr Austin TX 78731 Office: 1110 Guadalupe Austin TX 78701

STONER, RICHARD BURKETT, mfg. co. exec., mem. Democratic Nat. Com.; b. Ladoga, Ind., May 15, 1920; s. Edward Norris and Florence May (Burkett) S.; B.S., Ind. U., 1941; J.D., Harvard, 1947; LL.D., Butler U., 1975; m. Virginia B. Austin, Feb. 22, 1942; children—Pamela T., Richard Burkett, Benjamin Austin, Janet Elizabeth, Rebecca Lee, Joanne Jeannea. With Cummins Engine Co., Inc., Columbus, Ind., 1947—, various adminstrv., exec. positions 1947-66, exec. v.p., corporate gen. mgr., 1966-69, vice. chmn. bd., 1969—; dir. Am. Fletcher Nat. Bank & Trust Co., Indpls., Kirloskar Cummins Ltd., Am. Fletcher Bank (Switzerland), Am. United Life Ins. Co., Pub. Service Ind., Am. Fletcher Corp. Mem. exec. com. Machinery Allied Products Inst.; del. Democratic Nat. Conv. 1956, 60, 64, 68, 72, 76; Dem. nat. committeeman for Ind. Vice chmn. bd. dirs. Cummins Engine Found.; pres., bd. dirs. Irwin-Sweeney-Miller Found.; trustee Ind. U.; bd. dirs. Christian Found., Columbus. Served to capt. AUS, 1942-46. Mem. Ind. C. of C. (dir.). Office: 432 Washington St Columbus IN 47201

STONESIFER, RICHARD JAMES, educator; b. Lancaster, Pa., June 21, 1922; s. Paul Tobias and Esther (Wittlinger) S.; A.B., Franklin and Marshall Coll., 1946; M.A., Northwestern U., 1947; Ph.D., U. Pa., 1953; m. Nancy Jane Weaver, June 28, 1947; 1 dau., Pamela Ann. Mem. faculty Franklin and Marshall Coll., 1947-63, asso. prof. English, 1954-63, asst. to dean, 1957-60, asst. pres., 1960-63; asst. to provost, also dir. coll. gen. studies U. Pa., 1963-65, asso. prof. communications Annenberg Sch. Communications, 1963-65; dean. Coll. Liberal Arts, prof. English, Drew U., Madison, N.J., 1965-71; pres. Monmouth Coll., West Long Branch, N.J., 1971-79; Woodrow Wilson prof. humanities and social sci. Monmouth Coll., 1979—; moderator TV discussion series, 1954-60. Mem. Pa. Adv. Com. Ednl. Broadcasting, 1963-65. Bd. dirs. Harrisburg Area Center Higher Edn., 1963-65; trustee N.J. Cancer Inst., 1975—. Served with USAAF, 1943-46. Mem. Phi Beta Kappa. Episcopalian. Author: W.H. Davies: A Critical Biography, 2d edit., 1965; also articles in profl. jours. Home: 95 Buttonwood Dr Fair Haven NJ 07701

STONICH, TIMOTHY WHITMAN, transp. equipment mfg. co. fin. exec.; b. Evanston, Ill., July 30, 1947; s. Joseph and Joyce (Whitman) S.; B.A. in Econs., Denison U., 1969; M.B.A. in Fin., U. Chgo., 1972; m. Joy Anne Harrison, June 14, 1969. Comml. banking officer Harris Bank, Chgo., 1969-74; asst. treas. Pullman Inc., Chgo., 1974-77, treas. Pullman Standard div., Chgo., 1977—, v.p. fin. Pullman Leasing Co., Chgo., 1977—. Office: 200 S Michigan Chicago IL 60604

STOOKEY, JOHN HOYT, chem. co. exec.; b. N.Y.C., Jan. 29, 1930; s. Byron and Helen Phelps (Hoyt) S.; student Amherst Coll., 1952, Columbia U., 1955; m. Katherine Elizabeth Emory, Sept. 3, 1954; children—Helen Hoyt, Laura Emory, Hunt Emory, Anson Greene Phelps. Asst. v.p. S.Am. Gold & Platinum Co., N.Y.C., 1956-59; officer, dir. various pvt. corps. for Investor Syndicate, 1959-69; U.S. rep. Financiera Metropolitana S.A., N.Y.C., 1962-75; U.S. rep. Pub. Works Bank of Mexican Fed. Govt., N.Y.C.. 1964-75; pres. Wallace Clark, Inc., N.Y.C.. 1970-75, dir., 1962—; pres. Nat. Distillers & Chem. Corp., N.Y.C., 1975—, dir., 1970—; dir. Riegel Textile Corp., Rexham Corp. Founder, pres. Berkshire Boy Choir, Inc., 1967—; pres. Canterbury Choral Soc., 1968; chmn. health manpower com. United Hosp. Fund, 1966-71; bd. dirs. Assn. For A Better N.Y., 1976—; trustee Boston Symphony Orch., 1969—, Northfield-Mt. Hermon Schs., 1974-79, Council of Ams., 1977—, Bio-Energy Council, 1977—; trustee Coll. for Human Services, 1964—, treas., 1964-75; trustee James Weldon Johnson Community Center, Inc., 1965-70, Oratorio Soc. N.Y., 1965-75, Kodaly Musical Tng. Inst., 1973-75; trustee Stowe Sch., Inc., 1960-76, pres., 1960-73; mem. adv. bd. Grosvenor Neighborhood House, 1970—, Music in Deerfield, 1977. Mem. Council on Fgn. Relations, Alpha Pi Mu, Delta Kappa Epsilon. Clubs: Union, Down Town Assn., Pinnacle, Century Assn., Met. Opera, Pequot Yacht, Center Harbor Yacht, Lenox, Weston Gun. Home: Sasco Hill Rd Southport CT 06490 Office: 99 Park Ave New York NY 10016

STOOKEY, NOEL PAUL, folk singer, composer; b. Balt., Dec. 30, 1937; s. George William and Dorothea (St. Aubrey) S.; student Mich. State U., 1955-58; H.H.D., Husson Coll., 1978; m. Mary Elizabeth Bannard, Sept. 4, 1963; children—Elizabeth Drake, Katherine Darby, Anna St. Aubrey. Released album of songs Birds of Paradise, 1954; sang professionally, master ceremonies events Mich. State U., 1955-58; prodn. mgr. Cormac Chem. Corp., N.Y.C., 1959-60; profl. singer, Greenwich Village, N.Y.C., 1960-61; mem. folk singing group Peter, Paul and Mary, 1961-70; solo rec. artist for Warner Bros., 1971-74; producer folk albums for Scepter Records, Verve/Folkway Records; founder Neworld Media, rec. studio, animation group, film editing, Neworld Records, 1977—; rec. artist Paul And, 1971, One Night Stand, 1972, Real to Reel, 1976, Something New and Fresh, 1978, Band and Bodyworks, 1979. Mem. A.F.T.R.A., Screen Actors Guild, ASCAP, Delta Upsilon. Club: Friars (N.Y.C.). Address: South Blue Hill ME 04615

STOOKEY, STANLEY DONALD, chemist; b. Hay Springs, Nebr.; May 23, 1915; s. Stanley Clarke and Hermie Lucille (Knapp) S.; B.A., Coe Coll., 1936, LL.D., 1959; M.S., Lafayette Coll., 1937; Ph.D. in Phys. Chemistry, M.I.T., 1940; m. Ruth Margaret Watterson, Dec. 26, 1940; children—Robert A., Margaret Ann, Donald Bruce. With Corning Glass Works Research (N.Y.), 1940-79, dir. fundamental chem. research, 1970-79. Recipient Inventor of Year award Am. Chem. Soc., 1971. Fellow Am. Ceramic Soc.; mem. Nat. Acad. Engring., Am. Chem. Soc., Sigma Xi. Republican. Methodist. Club: Rotary. Patentee in field of photosensitive glasses, glass-ceramics, photochromic glasses. Contbr. articles to profl. jours. Home: 12 Timber Ln Painted Post NY 14870

STOPHLET, DONALD VICTOR, univ. adminstr.; b. Oak Park, Ill., Nov. 12, 1918; s. Donald Stirling and Anne (Gilmer) S.; Ph.B., U. Wis., 1941, Ph.M., 1946. Mng. dir. Central City Opera Assn., Central City and Denver, 1948-52; sec. of coll., dir. devel. Rockford (Ill.) Coll., 1952-58; dir. devel. programs U. Pitts., 1958-59; v.p. for devel. Western Res. U., 1959-63; v.p. for devel. affairs Miami (Fla.), 1963-67; v.p. for devel. Fla. Inst. Tech., 1967—. Served as pilot USAAF, 1943-46. Mem. Am. Coll. Pub. Relations Assn., Am. Alumni Council, Nat. Collegiate Players, Alpha Delta Phi. Home: PO Box 595 Melbourne Beach FL 32951

STOPPARD, TOM, playwright; b. Zlin, Czechoslovakia, July 3, 1937; s. Eugene and Martha (Stoppard) Straussler; m. Jose Ingle, 1965 (div.); m. 2d, Miriam Moore-Robinson, 1972; 4 children. Journalist, Western Daily Press, Bristol, Eng., 1954-58, Bristol Evening World, 1958-60; free-lance reporter, 1960-63; playwright, writer, 1963—; author plays: The Gamblers, 1965, A Separate Peace, 1966, Rosencrantz and Guildenstern Are Dead, 1967, Albert's Bridge, 1967, The Real Inspector Hound, 1968, After Magritte, 1970, Dogg's Our Pet, 1971, Jumpers, 1972, Travesties, 1974, Dirty Linen and New-Found-Land, 1976, Night and Day, 1979; author screenplays, including The Romantic Englishwoman, 1975; author radio and TV plays; author novel: Lord Malquist and Mr. Moon, 1966; author short stories. Recipient John Whiting award, 1967; Evening Standard award, 1967, 73, 75; Prix Italia, 1968; Tony award, 1968, 76; N.Y. Drama Critics Circle award, 1968, 76; Ford Found. grantee, 1964. Office: care Kenneth Ewing Fraser and Dunlop Ltd 91 Regent St London WC1 4AE England*

STORER, MORRIS BREWSTER, educator; b. Pitts., Nov. 14, 1904; s. Norman Wilson and Mary Elizabeth Wyman (Perry) S.; B.S., Dartmouth, 1926; postgrad. Columbia, 1930; A.M., U. Chgo., 1929; A.M., Harvard, 1932, Ph.D., 1937; m. Gretchen Geuder Schneider, Aug. 18, 1935; children—John Winthrop, Christopher Martin,

Thomas Perry. Asst. in philosophy U. Chgo., 1927, U. Pitts., 1927-28; corr. N.Mex. State Tribune, 1928; instr. philosophy Lafayette Coll., 1929-30; instr. philosophy, comparative religion Dartmouth, 1932-35; asst. philosophy Harvard, Radcliff Coll., 1935-36; social scientist in field of conf. orgn., discussion leader tng. Bur. Agrl. Econs., Dept. Agr., 1936-41, sr. social scientist extension service, 1941-46, chmn. post-war planning subcom. on agrl.-indsl. relations, 1942-43, acting dir., fgn. student tng. program, 1945-46; dean of instrn. Mt. Vernon Jr. Coll., Washington, 1946-47; prof. humanities and philosophy U. Fla., 1947-73, prof. emeritus, 1973—; pres. Santa Fe Telephone Co., R.E.A. Coop., 1950-52. Served as capt. AUS, 1943-44. Mem. Am., Fla. philos. assns., Am. Fedn. Tchrs. (sec. U. Fla. chpt. 1941-42), Am. Humanist Assn. (dir. 1975—), Humanist Soc. Gainesville (pres. 1975-76), Humanists of Ga., Delta Upsilon. Democrat. Unitarian. Club: Melrose Civic (pres. 1949-50). Author: Toward a Theory of Moral Debt, 1971; Let's Discuss World Peace Organization, other public affairs discussion guides U.S. Dept. Agr., 1940-46; editor: Humanist Ethics, 1979. Home: Swan Lake PO Box 448 Melrose FL 32666 also summer PO Box 66 Sautee GA 30571

STOREY, CHARLES MOORFIELD, lawyer; b. Brookline, Mass., Mar. 4, 1889; s. Moorfield and Anna Gertrude (Cutts) S.; grad. St. Mark's Sch.; A.B., Harvard, 1912, A.M., 1913, LL.B., 1915; m. Susan Jameson Sweetser, June 24, 1913; children— Charles M., Anderson (killed in action, Jan. 17, 1943), Susan Jameson (Mrs. Ronald T. Lyman, Jr.), Gertrude Cutts (Mrs. William M. Bancroft), James Moorfield. Admitted to Mass. bar, 1915; asst. atty., later atty. U.S. Dept. Justice, Washington, 1915-18; asst. commr. Commn. Relating to Prisoners of War, also attache commn. to negotiate peace, U.S. Commn. to Austria-Hungary, Budapest, 1918-19; partner Peabody, Brown Rowley & Storey, Boston, 1920-79; head atty. N.E. regional office WPB, 1942-43; compliance commr. N.E. region, 1943-44; appeal agt. Selective Service, 1941-47, 62-69; cons. (renegotiator) Boston Q.M. price adjustment dist. office U.S. War Dept., 1943-47; chmn. bd. trustees Park Sch. Corp., 1920-30; v.p. Winsor Sch., 1930-32; pres. Mass. Soc. Prevention Cruelty to Children, 1942-49; trustee Mt. Auburn Cemetery, 1932-79; mem. Boston Finance Commn., 1932-35; past chmn.; overseer Harvard, 1945-51. Mem. Am., Mass., Boston (mem. council 1935-36) bar assns., Harvard Alumni Assn. (dir. 1935-37, v.p. 1938), Mass. Hist. Soc., Mass. Soc. Cin. (sec. 1955-72), N.E. Hist. Geneal. Soc. (pres. 1961-63). Clubs: Tavern, Somerset. Home: 17 Old England Rd Chestnut Hill MA 02167 Office: 1 Boston Pl Boston MA 02108

STOREY, CHARLES PORTER, lawyer; b. Austin, Tex., Dec. 4, 1922; s. Robert Gerald and Frances Hazel (Porter) S.; B.A., U. Tex., Austin, 1947, LL.B., 1948, LL.M., So. Methodist U., 1952; m. Helen Hanks Stephens, Oct. 14, 1950; children—Charles Porter, Harry Stephens, Frederick Schatz. Admitted to Tex. bar, 1948; since practiced in Dallas; sr. partner firm Storey, Armstrong, Steger & Martin, 1972—. Dir. Lakewood Bank and Trust Co., United Fidelity Life Ins. Co. Chmn. Internat. Com. YMCA's, 1969-71; mem. nat. bd. U.S. YMCA, 1964-75; pres. Dallas Day Nursery Assn., 1958, Children's Devel. Center, Dallas, 1959, Greater Dallas Council Chs., 1970-71; trustee Southwestern Legal Found., Dallas Found., Baylor Coll. Dentistry. Served to 1st lt., pilot USAAF, 1943-45; ETO. Decorated Air medal. Fellow Am. Coll. Trial Lawyers, Am., Tex. bar founds.; mem. Am., Tex. (dir. 1976—), Dallas (pres. 1975) bar assns., Phi Delta Phi, Phi Delta Theta. Christian (Disciples of Christ). Clubs: Dallas Country, City, Idlewild. Home: 4400 Rheims Pl Dallas TX 75205 Office: 5400 First Internat Bldg Dallas TX 75270

STOREY, FREDERICK GEORGE, theater exec.; b. Columbus, Ga., Nov. 12, 1909; s. Frederick George and Winifred Davis (Bailey) S.; B.S. in Engring., Ga. Inst. Tech., 1933; m. Jean Kingman Lucas, Nov. 20, 1935; children—Margaret (Mrs. Andrew H. Abernathy III) and Winifred (Mrs. Frank T. Davis, Jr.) (twins), Cornelia (Mrs. Thomas T. Richards). Advt. staff Atlanta Jour., 1933-39; advt. staff Clark, Inc., advt. agy., 1939, partner, 1940; staff Ga. Theatre Co., Atlanta, 1946, v.p., 1947-52; organized Storey Theatres, Inc., 1952, now pres.; also dir. theatre cos.; officer, dir. radio and TV firms. Past officer, dir. Community Chest, Boy Scouts Am.; past pres. Family Service Assn. Am.; Trustee Am. Found. for the Blind; past chmn. bd. trustee Ga. Tech. Research Inst.; trustee, pres. Ga. Tech. Found., Holy Family Hosp. Served to comdr. USNR, 1941-46. Recipient Disting. Alumnus award Ga. Inst. Tech., 1979. Mem. Ga. Tech. Nat. Alumni Assn. (past pres., trustee), Family Service Soc. of Atlanta (past pres.), Atlanta C. of C., Nat. Assn. Theatre Owners (dir.), Motion Picture Theatre Owners Ga. (treas. dir.), Kappa Sigma. Roman Catholic. Clubs: Piedmont Driving, Capital City, Peachtree Golf (Atlanta); Rotary (past dist. gov.) Home: 2510 Peachtree St NE Atlanta GA 30305 Office: 572 Morosgo Dr Atlanta GA 30324

STOREY, ROBERT GERALD, ret. lawyer; b. Greenville, Tex., Dec. 4, 1893; s. Frank Wilson and Mary Edith (Thomson) S.; student U. Tex., 1911-14; LL.D., Tex. Christian U., 1947, Laval U., 1953, Drake U., 1954; D.C.L., Chungang U., Korea, 1961, So. Meth. U., 1965; H.H.D., Rikkyo U., Japan, 1961, U. Ryukyus, 1964; m. Frances Hazel Porter, July 26, 1917 (dec. 1962); children—Robert G. (dec.), Charles P.; m. 2d, Jewel Hope Osborn, 1965 (dec. 1978). Admitted to Tex. bar, 1914; city atty., Troup, Tex., 1914-17; asst. atty. gen. Tex., 1921-23; spl. asst. dist. atty., Dallas, 1924; partner Storey, Armstrong, Steger & Martin, ret.; chmn. bd. emeritus Lakewood Bank & Trust Co.; dean law sch. So. Meth. U., 1947-59; pres. Southwestern Legal Found., 1947-72. Mem. New Hoover Commn. to reorganize exec. br. of govt., 1953-55; spl. rep. of State Dept. to conduct seminars among mems. of legal profession of Friendly Free Nations, 1954-55; vice. chmn. U.S. Civil Rights Commn., 1957-63; spl. counsel State Tex. Investigation Pres. Kennedy death, 1963-64; vice chmn. Atlantic-Pacific Interoceanic Canal Study Commn., 1965—; chmn. for U.S., World Peace Through Law Center, 1966—. Chmn. bd. fgn. scholarships Fulbright Bd., 1958-62. Served as 1st lt. U.S. Army, 1918-19; col. AUS, World War II. Decorated Legion of Merit, Bronze Star, Medal of Freedom (U.S.); Legion of Honor (France); Second Order of Merit, Japanese Govt.; recipient Linz civic leadership award, Dallas, 1955; Am. Bar Assn. gold medal, 1956. Served as U.S. exec. trial counsel to Justice Robert H. Jackson in Nuremberg trial of major war criminals, 1945-46. Regent U. of Tex., 1924-29; pres. Park Bd., City of Dallas, 1939-42. Mem. Internat. (council 1950-56), Inter-Am., (pres. 1954-56), Am. (bd. govs. 1949-54, chmn. sect. on legal edn. 1947-49, mem. ho. dels., pres. 1952-53, chmn. electoral coll. Commn. 1966—), Tex. (pres. 1948-49), Dallas (pres. 1934) bar assns., Am. Legion (nat. exec. com. 1920-21), Order of Coif, Phi Beta Kappa, Phi Alpha Delta; hon. mem. Canadian, Peruvian, Mexican, Korean, Cuban, other nat., state bar assns. Mem. Christian Ch. Mason (33 deg., Shriner), Kiwanian (pres. 1927, dist gov. 1931). Club: Dallas Country. Author: Professional Leadership, 1958; Our Unalienable Rights, 1965; The Final Judgement. Office: First Internat Bldg Dallas TX 75270

STOREY, WOODROW WILSON, lawyer; b. Mt. Rainer, Md., Dec. 12, 1912; s. James P. and Etta W. (Martin) S.; J.D., Am. U., 1937, LL.M., 1938, student Sch. Pub. Affairs, 1946-48; m. Margaret Warman, Feb. 18, 1933; children—James A., Lorraine, Woodrow Wilson, Arthur Jay. Admitted to D.C. bar, 1937, Md. bar, 1945, Va. bar, 1969, U.S. Supreme Ct. bar, 1945; comptroller Dept. Def., 1946-59; dir. financial mgmt. Dept. State, 1959-60; dir. contracts Martin Orlando (Fla.), Martin Co., 1961-62; v.p. aerospace div. Martin Marietta Corp., 1963-67; v.p. Vitro Corp. of Am., 1967-68; pres. Storey Assos., govt. marketing cons., 1969-70; practice law, Washington, 1970—. Served to lt. col. AUS, 1941-46. Mem. Am., Fed. bar assns., Am. Def. Preparedness Assn., Am. Legion, Assn. U.S. Army, Sigma Nu Phi. Presbyn. Mason. Club: Eau Gallie Yacht. Home: 1002 Riverside Dr Indialantic FL 32903 Office: Suite 540 1701 Pennsylvania Ave NW Washington DC 20006

STORIN, EDWARD MICHAEL, editor; b. Providence, Dec. 4, 1929; s. Edmund Aloysius and Evelyn Ruth (O'Brien) S.; B.A., U. Miami, 1951; m. Virginia Mae Robak, Feb. 7, 1953; children—Kathy Lynn, Michael, Robert, Edward. With Miami Herald, 1951—, asst. city editor, 1963-64, night exec. sports editor, 1964-68, exec. sports editor, 1968-77, asst. mng. editor, 1977—. Served with USNR, 1952-54. Mem. Iron Arrow, Omicron Delta Kappa, Sigma Delta Chi, Sigma Alpha Epsilon. Home: 5055 SW 83d St Miami FL 33143 Office: 1 Herald Plaza Miami FL 33101

STORIN, MATTHEW VICTOR, newspaper editor; b. Springfield, Mass., Dec. 24, 1942; s. Harry Francis and Blanche Marie S.; B.A., U. Notre Dame, 1964; m. Keiko Takita, Aug. 1, 1975; children by previous marriage—Karen, Aimee, Sean. Reporter, Springfield Daily News, 1964-65; reporter Griffin-Larrabee News Bur., Washington, 1965-69; Washington corr., city editor, Asian corr., nat. editor, asst. mng. editor Boston Globe, 1969—. Recipient award for disting. polit. reporting Am. Assn. Polit. Sci., 1969. Home: 520 Beacon St Boston MA 02215 Office: 135 Morrissey Blvd Boston MA 02107

STORK, GILBERT JOSSE, educator; b. Brussels, Belgium, Dec. 31, 1921; s. Jacques and Simone (Weil) S.; B.S., U. Fla., 1942; Ph.D., U. Wis., 1945; D.Sc. (hon.), Lawrence Coll., 1961; m. Winifred Stewart, June 9, 1944; children—Diana, Linda, Janet, Philip. Sr. research chemist Lakeside Labs., 1945-46; instr. chemistry Harvard, 1946-48, asst. prof., 1948-53; asso. prof. Columbia, 1953-55, prof., 1955-67, Eugene Higgins prof., 1967—, chmn. dept., 1973-76. Vis. lectr. Swiss Am. Found. Sci. Exchange, 1959; Coover lectr., 1958; Folkers lectr.; Bachmann lectr., 1962; Treat B. Johnson lectr.; Frank Burnet Dains lectr., 1964; Kharasch vis. prof. U. Chgo.; Foster lectr. U. Buffalo, 1966; vis. scholar Fisk U., 1967; T. Dale Stewart lectr.; distinguished vis. prof. U. Iowa, 1968; Seydell Wooley lectr. Ga. Inst. Tech.; Karl Pfister lectr. Mass. Inst. Tech.; Robert Gnehm lectr. ETH, Zurich, 1969; Univ. lectr. U. Western Ont., 1974; Phi Lambda Upsilon lectr. Johns Hopkins, 1974; Centenary lectr. Brit. Chem. Soc., 1975; Tishler lectr. Harvard, 1975; John Howard Appleton lectr. Brown U.; Distinguished vis. lectr. U. Rochester; Benjamin Rush lectr. U. Pa., 1976; Royal Australian Chem. Inst. lectr., 1977; McElvain vis. scholar U. Wis., 1977; Debye lectr. Cornell U., 1977; Alexander Todd vis. prof. Cambridge (Eng.) U., 1979; cons. chemistry panel NSF, 1958-61; adv. bd. Petroleum Research Found., 1963-66; cons. NIH, 1967-71, Syntex, Internat. Flavors and Fragrances; chmn. Gordon Steroid Conf., 1958-59; hon. adv. editor Tetrahedron; bd. editors Jour. Organic Chemistry, 1955-61; cons. editor Advanced Chemistry Series McGraw-Hill, 1961-74; com. organic chemistry NRC, 1956-59; com. postdoctoral fellowships, 1959-62. Guggenheim fellow, 1959; recipient Baekeland medal, 1961; Harrison Howe award, 1962; Edward Curits Franklin Meml. award Stanford, 1966; award for creative work in synthetic organic chemistry Am. Chem. Soc., 1967; Gold medal Synthetic Chems. Mfrs. Assn., 1971; Nebr. award, 1973; Roussel prize in steroid chemistry, 1978. Fellow Am. Acad. Arts and Scis., Nat. Acad. Scis.; mem. Chemist Club (hon.), Am. Chem. Soc. (award in pure chemistry 1957, chmn. organic chemistry div. 1967), Chem. Soc. London, Swiss Chem. Soc. Editorial bd. Accounts of Chem. Research, 1968-71. Home: 459 Next Day Hill Englewood NJ 07631 Office: Columbia U New York City NY 10027

STORK, WILLIS WILLIAM, ednl. cons.; b. Enola, Nebr., Dec. 14, 1911; s. William Willis and Fannie Jane (Bryant) S.; A.B., U. Nebr., 1933, M.S., 1935; postgrad. Harvard, summers 1936, 37, U. Mich., summers 1938, 39; m. Helen Baldwin, Aug. 14, 1936; children—William Willis, Cynthia (Mrs. Jay Thomas Gerber). Prin., Mt. Hope High Sch., Meadow Grove, Nebr., 1930-32; tchr. Norfolk (Nebr.) High Sch., 1935-36; prin. West Point (Nebr.) High Sch., 1936-37; headmaster Maumee Valley Country Day Sch. (Ohio), 1937-55, Polytechnic Sch., Pasadena, Calif., 1955-76. Chmn. Nat. Assn. Ind. Schs., 1972-76. Chmn., moderator Toledo Town Meeting of Air, 1946-49; committeeman Pasadena Tournament of Roses Assn., 1960—; mem. Pasadena Cultural Heritage Commn., 1976—; bd. dirs. Toledo Little Repertoire Theatre, 1938-42, Toledo Mental Hygiene Center, 1942-50, Pasadena Child Health Found., 1962-61; trustee Pasadena Library Bd., 1959-64, Pasadena Art Mus., 1960-66. Served with USNR, 1943-46. Mem. Country Day Sch. Headmasters Assn. (pres. 1971-72), Headmasters Assn., Calif. Assn. Ind. Schs. (pres. 1968-70). Rotarian (pres. Toledo 1948-49, Pasadena 1963-64). Clubs: Twilight, Valley Hunt, Breakfast Forum, University. Home: 1586 Oakdale St Pasadena CA 91106

STORKE, WILLIAM FREDERICK JOSEPH, TV exec.; b. Rochester, N.Y., Aug. 12, 1922; s. Legrand Frederick Sommerfeldt and Patricia Louise Storke; B.A. in Econs., U. Cal. at Los Angeles, 1948; children—Victoria Jane, Adam John, William MacKenzie; m. 2d, Georgette MacKenzie Edwards, Feb. 22, 1970. With NBC, 1948—, successivley comml. editor guest relations dept. comml. supr., network sales West Coast, participating program sales, N.Y., dir. participating program sales, dir. program adminstrn., v.p. program adminstrn., 1948-57, v.p. programs East Coast, 1967-68, v.p. spl. programs, 1968—; pres. Claridge Group, Ltd. div. Trent TV Ltd., London, 1979—; mem. theatre and public media panels Nat. Endowment for Arts. Served with USNR, 1943-46. Mem. Acad. TV Arts and Scis., Internat. Radio and TV Soc., Sigma Alpha Epsilon. Club: University (N.Y.C.). Home: 1060 Fifth Ave New York NY 10028 Office: 540 Madison Ave New York NY 10022

STORMANS, RALPH, grocery co. exec.; b. Tacoma, 1908. Chmn. bd. Asso. Grocers, Inc.; pres. Stormans Inc.; dir. Capital Savs. & Loan Assn., Century Service Corp. Home: 600 4th Ave N Tumwater WA 98502 Office: 1908 E 4th Ave Olympia WA 98506

STORMONT, RICHARD MANSFIELD, hotel exec.; b. Chgo., Apr. 4, 1936; s. Daniel Lytle and E. Mildred (Milligan) S.; B.S., Cornell U., 1958; m. Virginia Louellen Walters, Nov. 21, 1959; children—Stacy Lee, Richard Mansfield, John Frederick. Food cost analyst, sales rep. Edgewater Beach Hotel, Chgo., 1957-58, asst. sales mgr. Marriott Motor Hotels, Inc., Washington, 1962-64; dir. sales Marriott Motor Hotel, Atlanta, 1964-68, resident mgr., 1969-71, gen. mgr., Atlanta, 1974-79; pres. Hardin Mgmt. Co., 1979—; gen. mgr. Marriott Hotel, Dallas, 1971-73, Phila., 1973-74; dir. Walters & Co., Cons. to Mgmt. Pres., Atlanta Conv. and Visitors Bur., 1975-76, chmn. bd. 1976-77; bd. dirs. Better Bus. Bur.; exec. com. Central Atlanta Progress, 1979—; exec. council Boy Scouts Am. Served to lt. (j.g.) USNR, 1959-62. Recipient Disting. Salesman of Yr. award Marriott, 1967. Mem. Sales and Mktg. Execs. (exec. v.p. 1969-70, pres. Atlanta 1970-71), Atlanta C. of C. (v.p. 1978-79), Ga. Bus. and Industry Assn. (dir.), Atlanta Hotel Assn. (pres. 1976), Ga. Hospitality and Travel Assn. (dir. 1977-79), Cornell Soc. Hotelmen (pres. Ga. chpt. 1976), Pi Sigma Epsilon, Phi Kappa Psi. Club: Rotary. Home: 495 River Crest Ct Atlanta GA 30328 Office: Marriott Hotel Courtland at International Blvd Atlanta GA 30303

STORMS, CLIFFORD BEEKMAN, lawyer; b. Mt. Vernon, N.Y., July 18, 1932; s. Harold Beekman and Gene (Pertak) S.; B.A. magna cum laude, Amherst Coll., 1954; LL.B., Yale U., 1957; m. Valeria N. Parker, July 12, 1975; children—Catherine E., Clifford Beekman. Admitted to N.Y. bar, 1957; asso. atty. firm Breed, Abbott & Morgan, N.Y.C., 1957-64; with CPC Internat., Inc., Englewood Cliffs, N.J., 1964—, v.p. legal affairs, 1973-75, v.p., gen. counsel, 1975—; trustee Food and Drug Law Inst., 1976—. Mem. Am., N.Y. State bar assns., Assn. Bar City N.Y. (sec., com. on corp. law depts.), Assn. Gen. Counsel, Phi Beta Kappa. Clubs: Yale (N.Y.C.); Milbrook; Board Room. Home: 11 Serenity Ln Cos Cob CT 06807 Office: CPC Internat Inc Internat Plaza Englewood Cliffs NJ 07632

STORMS, LOWELL HANSON, psychologist; b. Schenectady, Feb. 14, 1928; s. Charles Arba and Afton Miriam (Hanson) S.; B.A. in Biostats., U. Minn., 1950, M.S., 1951, Ph.D. in Psychology, 1956; m. Marilyn Isabel Hitchcock, June 16, 1955; children—Christopher, Karen, Bruce. Clin. psychologist Hastings (Minn.) State Hosp., 1954-56; mem. faculty Neuropsychiat. Inst., UCLA, 1957-71, prof. psychiatry, 1970-71, supervising psychologist, 1963-71; prof. psychiatry, head med. psychology Sch. Medicine, U. Calif., San Diego, 1971—; v.p., dir. Clin. Psychol. Services, Santa Monica, Calif., 1972—. Program chmn. Westwood Dem. Club, 1962-65. Served with U.S. Army, 1946-48. Fulbright grantee, 1956-57. Fellow Am. Psychol. Assn., AAAS; mem. Western, Calif. psychol. assns., Internat. Neuropsychology Soc., Sigma Xi. Discoverer priming effect in verbal assns.; co-discoverer behavioral sign of seizure disorders; co-developer theory of schizophrenic behavioral disorganization. Home: Box 1362 Rancho Santa Fe CA 92067 Office: 3350 La Jolla Village Dr San Diego CA 92161. *I try to live with full respect for the depth, richness, beauty and power of nature and with love and respect for my fellow creatures who share with me the human condition.*

STORROW, JAMES J., JR., mag. publisher; b. Boston, May 7, 1917; s. James J. and Margaret (Rotch) S.; grad. Milton (Mass.) Acad., 1936; B.S., Harvard, 1940, postgrad., 1940-41; m. Patricia Blake, June 26, 1940 (dec. May 1962); children—Gerald B., Peter, James J. III, Margaret R.; m. 2d, Linda Eder Jamieson, Dec. 15, 1962. Dir., North Shore Players, Inc., Marblehead, Mass., 1939-41; office mgr., asst. treas. Baush Machine Tool Co., Springfield, Mass., 1941-43; treas. Brooks Green Co., Boston, 1946, Gen. Microfilm Co., Cambridge, Mass., 1947—, The Stamp Show, Inc., N.Y.C., 1953-55, Trident Films, Inc., N.Y.C., 1961—; pres. Henry Thayer Co., Cambridge, 1947-53; pub. The Nation mag., N.Y.C., 1965—; dir. Farrar, Straus & Giroux, Inc., Mid Atlantic Fund Inc. Chmn. Joint Council on Fgn. Affairs, Boston, 1947. Mem. Brookline (Mass.) Democratic Town Com., 1958-61. Bd. dirs. Housing Assn. Met. Boston, 1948-53, Cath. Guild for All the Blind, Newton, Mass., The Med. Found.; trustee New Eng. Coll. Pharmacy, 1956-62. Served with USNR, 1943-45. Clubs: Century, Coffee House (N.Y.C.); Harvard (Boston and N.Y.C.), The Players. Home: 25 East End Ave New York City NY 10028 Office: 333 6th Ave New York City NY 10014

STORRS, ELEANOR EMERETT, research inst. exec.; b. Cheshire, Conn., May 3, 1926; d. Benjamin Porter and Alta Hyde (Moss) S.; B.S. with distinction in Botany, U. Conn., 1948; M.S. in Biology, N.Y. U., 1958; Ph.D. in Chemistry, U. Tex., 1967; m. Harry Phineas Burchfield, Jr., Nov. 29, 1963; children—Sarah Storrs, Benjamin Hyde. Asst. biochemist Boyce Thompson Inst. for Plant Research, Yonkers, N.Y., 1948-62; research scientist Clayton Found. Biochem. Inst., U. Tex., Austin, 1962-65; biochemist Pesticides Research Lab., USPHS, Perrine, Fla., 1965-67; dir. dept. biochemistry Gulf South Research Inst., New Iberia, La., 1967-77; adj. prof. chemistry U. Southwestern La., Lafayette, 1974-77; research prof. biology, head div. comparative mammalogy and biochemistry Med. Research Inst., Fla. Inst. Tech., Melbourne, 1977—; cons. in rehab. and prevention deformities leprosy Pan Am. Health Orgn., WHO, Venezuela, Argentina, Brazil, Mex., 1972—. NIH grantee, 1968—; Center for Disease Control grantee, 1969-73; WHO grantee, 1973—, leprosy program grantee, 1978—; German Leprosy Relief Assn. grantee, 1973—; Nat. Council Episcopal Ch. grantee, 1975-77; recipient plaque La. Health Dept., 1972, Distinguished Alumni award U. Conn., 1975; gold award Am. Coll. Pathologists and Am. Soc. Clin. Pathologists, 1974, Gerard B. Lambert award, spl. recognition, 1975. Fellow AAAS, N.Y. Acad. Scis.; mem. Internat. Leprosy Assn., Am. Chem. Soc., Internat. Soc. Tropical Dermatology, Bot. Soc. Am., Reticuloendothelial Soc., Am. Forestry Assn., Am. Soc. Mammalogy, Am. Assn. Lab. Animal Sci. (Charles A. Griffin award 1975), Wildlife Disease Soc., Sigma Xi. Episcopalian (vestryman). Clubs: Appalachian (Boston); Green Mountain (Bear Mountain, N.Y.); Mystic Krewe of Iberians (mem. ct. 1972, queen 1974). Author: (with H.P. Burchfield) Biochemical Applications of Gas Chromatography, 1962; (with Burchfield, D.E. Johnson) Guide to the Analysis of Pesticide Residues, 2 vols., 1965; also articles, book chpts. Pioneer devel. leprosy in exptl. animal (armadillo). Home: 72 Riverview Terr Indialantic FL 32903 Office: 7725 W New Haven Ave Melbourne FL 32901. *Children display interests early in their lives, and in my life, this early interest - in animals, and the beauty of nature - is one which I have never lost, but one which seems to become more important now with the passing of years. Parents can help mold a child, but should mold the child in the child's interests as my parents did, not in a mold designed by them.*

STORRS, RICHARD S., lawyer; b. Orange, N.J., May 9, 1910; s. Richard S. and Anna (Kingsbury) S.; A.B., Yale College, 1932; LL.B., Harvard, 1935; m. Frances H. Rousmaniere, Apr. 27, 1938; children—Richard S., Mary Ayer, David K., Virginia, Nancy. Practice of law with Sullivan & Cromwell, N.Y.C., 1935, mem. firm, 1945—. Dir. Transatlantic Fund, Inc., Panhandle Eastern Pipe Line Co., Trunkline Gas Co., De Vegh Mut. Fund, Inc., Mass. Mut. Income Investors Inc. Trustee of Village of Cove Neck. Mem. Am., N.Y. State, N.Y.C. bar assns., Phi Beta Kappa, Alpha Delta Phi, Elihu. Clubs: Yale, Down Town Assn. (N.Y.C.); Cold Spring Harbor Beach, Piping Rock. Home: Cove Neck Rd Oyster Bay NY 11771 Office: 125 Broad St New York City NY 10004

STORRS, THOMAS IRWIN, banker; b. Nashville, Aug. 25, 1918; s. Robert Williamson and Addie Sue (Payne) S.; B.A., U. Va., 1940; M.A., Harvard, 1950, Ph.D., 1955; m. Kitty Stewart Bird, July 19, 1948; children—Thomas, Margaret. With Fed. Res. Bank, Richmond, Va., 1934-60, v.p. charge research, 1956-59, v.p. charge Charlotte br., 1959-60; exec. v.p. N.C. Nat. Bank, Charlotte, 1960-67, vice chmn. bd., 1967-69, pres., 1969-73, chief exec. officer, 1973—, chmn. exec. com., 1974-77, chmn. bd., 1977—; pres. NCNB Corp., 1968-73, chmn. bd., 1974—; dir. Black and Decker Mfg. Co., Towson, Md., Cannon Mills Co., Kannapolis, N.C. Pres., FRS Adv. Council, 1974-75; trustee Davidson Coll., U. N.C., Charlotte. Served to lt. comdr. USNR, 1941-45, 51-52. Mem. Assn. of Res. City Bankers (v.p.). Episcopalian. Clubs: Charlotte Country, Charlotte City, Quail Hollow Country (Charlotte). Home: 2633 Richardson Dr Charlotte NC 28211 Office: NC Nat Bank PO Box 120 Charlotte NC 28255

STORRY, JUNIS OLIVER, univ. dean; b. Astoria, S.D., Mar. 16, 1920; s. Ole Jensen and Betsey (Ruttum) S.; B.S. in Elec. Engring., S.D. State U., 1942, M.S., 1949; Ph.D., Iowa State U., 1967; m. Laurel Helen Davis, June 15, 1950; children—Cheryl Ann, David Junis. Engr. trainee Westinghouse Electric Co., 1942; elec. engr. Bur. Ships, Navy Dept., 1942-46, Reliance Electric Co., Cleve., 1946; mem. faculty S.D. State U., Brookings, 1946—, prof. elec. engring., 1955—, dean engring., 1972—. Mem. S.D. Electrical Bd., 1972-77. Mem. founding bd. Assn. Christian Chs. S.D., 1972-73. NSF Sci. Faculty fellow, 1964-65. Registered profl. engr., S.D. Mem. I.E.E.E., Am. Soc. Engring. Edn., Nat. Soc. Profl. Engrs., S.D. Engring. Soc., Illuminating Engring. Soc. Lutheran. Lion. Home: 105 Sunnyview Brookings SD 57006

STORVICK, TRUMAN SOPHUS, educator; b. Albert Lea, Minn., Apr. 14, 1928; s. Carl A. and Ardella C. (Hengesteg) S.; student St. Olaf Coll., 1948-50; B.S., Iowa State U., 1952; Ph.D., Purdue U., 1959; m. Arlyn J. Abrahamson, July 5, 1952; children—Ruth Leigh, Jan Marie, Kris Arlyn, David Olaf. Research engr. FMC Corp., Westvaco div., Charleston, W.Va., 1952-55; instr. Purdue U., 1958-59; asst. prof. to prof. dept. chem. engring. U. Mo., Columbia, 1959-71, Robert Lee Tatum prof. engring., 1971-74, Black and Veatch prof. engring., 1974—. Served with USN, 1946-48, 65-66. NSF Sci. Faculty fellow, Alumni-Faculty Achivement award U. Mo., 1970; Royal Norwegian Council Sci. and Indsl. Research postdoctoral fellow Tech. U. Norway, 1972-73. Mem. Am. Inst. Chem. Engrs., Am. Chem. Soc., Am. Phys. Soc. Presbyn. (elder). Home: 2210 Ridgefield Rd Columbia MO 65201

STOSSEL, JOHN FREDERICK, journalist; b. Chgo., Mar. 6, 1947; s. Otto E. and Anne D. (Tuchmann) S.; B.A., Princeton U., 1969. Reporter, Sta.-KGW-TV, Portland, Oreg., 1969-73, Sta.-WCBS-TV, N.Y.C., 1973—. Recipient George Polk award 1977; Emmy award Nat. Acad. TV Arts and Scis., 1977, 78, 79. Author: Consumer Guidebook, 1980. Office: 524 W 57th St New York NY 10019

STOTHERS, JOHN BAILIE, organic chemist; b. London, Ont., Can., Apr. 16, 1931; s. John Cannon and Florence Louise (Sleigh) S.; B.Sc., U. Western Ont., London, 1953, M.Sc., 1954; Ph.D., McMaster U., 1957; m. Catherine R. Smith, June 6, 1953; children—Marta, Margot. Research chemist Imperial Oil Ltd., Sarnia, Ont., 1957-59; lectr. U. Western Ont., 1959-61, asst. prof. chemistry, 1961-64, asso. prof., 1964-67, prof., 1967—, chmn. dept. chemistry, 1976—. Recipient Merck, Sharp Dohme award, 1971. Fellow Chem. Inst. Can., Royal Soc. Can.; mem. Am. Chem. Soc., Chem. Soc. (London). Club: Sunningdale Country. Author: Carbon-13 NMR Spectroscopy, 1972; research, numerous publs. in field; editor Can. Jour. Chemistry, 1976—. Office: U Western On London ON N6A 5B7 Canada

STOTLAND, EZRA, psychologist, educator; b. N.Y.C., June 9, 1924; s. Isaac and Rose (Chaiken) S.; B.S. in Social Sci., Coll. City N.Y., 1948; Ph.D. in Social Psychology, U. Mich., 1953; m. Patricia H. Joyce, July 12, 1963; stepchildren—Bruce Hilyer, Barbara Chapman, Candace Decorah; 1 dau., Sheila R. Research asso. U. Mich., 1953-57; asst. prof. psychology U. Wash., 1957-61, asso. prof., 1961-64, prof., 1964—, dir. soc. and justice program, 1971—; vis. scientist Battelle N.W., Seattle, 1975-77; cons. VA, VISTA, Crime and Delinquency Center of NIMH. Mgr. campaign Washtenaw County (Mich.) Democratic Com., 1955-56. Bd. dirs. Crisis Clinic of Seattle, 1964-66, Seattle Crime Commn., 1972-74, New Careers, Seattle, 1973-74, Law Enforcement Tng. Bd. of State of Wash., 1978-79, Seattle Mayor's Neighborhood Crime Commn., 1978—. Served to sgt. inf. AUS, 1942-46. USPHS Postdoctoral fellow, 1961-62; Fulbright fellow, 1969-70. Fellow Am. Psychol. Assn.; mem. Soc. Psychol. Study Social Issues (pres. 1976-77), Wash. State Assn. Criminal Justice Edn. (pres. 1976-77). Author: Psychology of Hope, 1969 (Behavioral Sci. Book Club selection); (with L. Canon) Social Psychology, 1972; (with A.L. Kobler) Life and Death of Mental Hospital, 1965; (with A.L. Kobler) End of Hope: A Social-Clinical Study of Suicide, 1964; (with H. Edelhertz, M. Walsh, M. Weinberg) Investigation of White Collar Crime, 1977; (with K. Shaver and S. Sherman) Empathy and Birth Order, 1971; (with R. Mathews, S. Sherman, R. Hansson and B. Richardson(Empathy, Fantasy and Helping, 1978; contbg. author: Advances in Experimental Social Psychology, vol. 4, 1969; (with D. Katz) Psychology: A Study of Science, vol. 3, 1959; (with D. Smith) Urban Policeman in Transition, 1973; Comparative Adminstrative Theory, 1968; Society and War, 1977; Ency. Handbook of Medical Psychology, 1976; Job Stress and the Police Officer, 1976; Internat. Ency. Neurology, Psychiatry, Psychanalysis and Psychology, 1976; (with J. Berberich) Psychology and Criminal Justice. Cons. editor Criminal Justice and Behavior, Jour. Research in Crime and Delinquency. Contbr. numerous articles to profl. jours. Home: 17004 NE 36th St Redmond WA 98052 Office: Society and Justice Program U Wash Seattle WA 98195

STOTLER, ROGER GRANT, investment banker; b. Alamo, Tex., Oct. 19, 1921; s. Charles Clayton and Lula Rita (Grant) S.; B.B.A., U. Tex., 1942; m. Nance Fruit, Feb. 25, 1955; children—David Clayton, Elliott Cason. Exec. v.p. Rowles, Winston & Co., Houston, 1946-72, also dir.; corp. syndicate mgr. Cowen & Co., N.Y.C., 1972—. City councilman, Piney Point Village, Tex. Served with AUS, 1942-45. Methodist. Kiwanian. Clubs: Houston, Houston Country. Home: 339 Tynebridge St Houston TX 77024 Office: Cowen & Co 1100 Milam Bldg Suite 2440 Houston TX 77002

STOTT, ALEXANDER LAW, bus. exec.; b. Boston, July 5, 1908; s. William George and Anne (Law) S.; grad. Boston Latin Sch., 1925; A.B., Harvard, 1929; m. Margaret Whitner, Sept. 12, 1935; 1 dau., Nancy Cleary. With Am. Tel. & Tel. Co., 1929-73, chief statisticians office, 1929-39, with long lines dept., 1940-42, treasury dept., 1945-49, asst. comptroller, 1949-52, asst. treas., 1952, treas., 1952-53, comptroller, 1953-61, v.p. and comptroller, 1961-73; dir., chmn. finance com. Burlington No., Inc., St. Paul, 1973-75, ret., 1975; ret. dir. Northwestern Bell Telephone Co.; dir. Mohasco Industries, Inc., City Trust Conn., Remington Arms Co. Trustee, hon. trustee Com. Econ. Devel.; dir. Conn. Health Plan, 1979; sponsor Ducks Unlimited; ret. trustee Bucknell U., Lewisburg, Pa., 1974—. Served as comdr. USN Bur. Aeros., 1942-43, Office Chief Naval Operations-Air, 1943-45. Mem. Financial Execs. Inst. (trustee Research Found., Inc.), C. of C. U.S. (fiscal policy commn.). Clubs: Harvard (N.Y.C.); Country of Fairfield, Aubichwi Gun (Fairfield, Conn.); Weston (Conn.) Gun; Aspetuck Fish and Game (Easton, Conn.); Conn. Waterfowlers Assn. (Southport). Home: 769 Hillside Rd Fairfield CT 06430

STOTT, DONALD FRANKLIN, geologist; b. Reston, Man., Can., Apr. 30, 1928; s. Franklin Brisbin and Catherine Alice (Parker) S.; B.Sc. with honors, U. Man., 1953, M.Sc., 1954; M.Sc., Princeton U., 1956, Ph.D., 1958; m. Margaret Elinor Hutton, Oct. 8, 1960; children—Glenn, David, Donald. Jr. geologist Consol. Mining and Smelter Co., 1952, Calif. Standard Oil Co., summer 1953; research geologist Geol. Survey Can., 1957-66, head mesozoic stratigraphy sect., 1967-72, head regional geology subdiv., 1972-73, dir. Inst. Sedimentary and Petroleum Geology, Calgary, Alta., 1973—. Fellow Geol. Assn. Can., Geol. Soc. Am.; mem. Can. Soc. Petroleum Geologists (v.p. 1977, pres. 1978), Soc. Econ. Paleontologists, Sigma Xi. Contbr. articles to profl. jours. Office: 3303 33d St NW Calgary AB T2L 2A7 Canada

STOTT, THOMAS EDWARD, JR., engring. co. exec.; b. Beverly, Mass., May 14, 1923; s. Thomas Edward and Mildred (Ayers) S.; B.S., Tufts U., 1945; m. Mary Elizabeth Authelet, Feb. 26, 1944; children—Pamela, Randi, Wendy, Thomas E., Diana. Design engr. Bethlehem Steel, Quincy, Mass., 1956-59, project engr., 1959-64, sr. engr. basic ship design, 1960-63, project coordinator, 1963-64; pres. Stal-Laval, Inc., Elmsford, N.Y., 1964—; dir. Thomas Stott & Co.; trustee Stal-Laval Employees Pension Trust. Trustee Egremont Congregational Ch., 1975-78. Served with USNR, 1944-46. Fellow ASME (chmn. marine com., chmn. gas turbine div. exec. com., chmn. nat. nominating com., exec. sec. gas turbine div.), Soc. Naval Architects and Marine Engrs., Conseil International des Machines a Combustion. Republican. Editor: ASME Gas Turbine Annual Report, 1973-78. Home: PO Box 134 Cummaquid MA 02637 Office: 400 Executive Blvd Elmsford NY 10523

STOTTER, DAVID W., marketing dir.; b. Chgo., May 17, 1904; s. Max and Lena (Wolfson) S.; student U. Chgo., 1925; m. Lucille Guild, Nov. 28, 1930; 1 son, Michael David. Advt. writer Campbell-Ewald Co., Detroit, 1929-34; sr. writer Lord & Thomas, Chgo., 1935-42; v.p., copy dir. MacFarland, Aveyard & Co., Chgo., 1942-51, account exec., 1951-62, sr. v.p., 1959-62; pres., dir. Drewrys Ltd. U.S.A., Inc., S. Bend, Ind., 1962-64; marketing dir. Campbell-Mithun, Inc., Chgo., 1964-65; v.p. Arthur Meyerhoff Assos., Inc., Chgo., 1965—. Bd. dirs. Jewish Welfare Fund Chgo., 1954-61, Alfred Adler Inst., Chgo., 1975—; chmn. pub. relations com. Jewish United Fund, 1969. Home: 330 Diversey Pkwy Chicago IL 60657 Office: 410 N Michigan Ave Chicago IL 60611

STOTTER, HARRY SHELTON, banker; N.Y.C., Aug. 28, 1928; s. Jack and Adele (Sgel) S.; student L.I. U., 1948-49; J.D., St. John's U., 1952; postgrad. N.Y. U. Law Sch., 1956-57; m. Marilyn H. Knight, Nov. 7, 1954; children—Jeffrey Craig, Cheryl Dee. Admitted to N.Y. bar, 1952, N.J. bar, 1974; pvt. practice in N.Y.C., 1952-53, 54-56; atty. Dept. Def., 1953; with trust div. Bank of N.Y., 1956-63; exec. v.p., sr. mgmt. com. United Jersey Bank, Hackensack, 1963—. Former pres. bd. dirs. Bergen County council Girl Scouts U.S.A. Served with USN, World War II; col. Army N.G. Mem. Am. (fed. legis. council), N.J. (exec. com. trust div., pres.) bankers assns., Am., N.J. bar assns., N.Y. Militia Assn., N.Y. County Lawyers Assn., Bergen County Bar Assn. (trustee, former chmn. probate and estate planning com.), Nat. Assn. Bus. Economists.

STOTTLEMYER, DAVID LEE, govt. ofcl.; b. Waynesboro, Pa., June 1, 1935; s. Omar Samuel and Miriam (Noll) S.; A.B., Miami U., Oxford, Ohio, 1959; M. Pub. and Internat. Affairs (NDEA fellow), U. Pitts., 1964, also postgrad.; m. Jane Ann Hembree, Aug. 26, 1961; children—Todd Andrew, Kristen Elizabeth, Kathryn Ann. Program and budget analyst Exec. Office of Pres., Office of Mgmt. and Budget, Washington, 1964-69; sr. mgmt. officer UN, N.Y.C., 1969-70; adviser internat. orgn. affairs U.S. Mission to UN, N.Y.C., 1971-72, counsellor internat. orgn. affairs, 1973-75, counsellor UN resources mgmt., 1976-77, also mem. U.S. del. 26th-31st gen. assemblies, mem. UN Com. on Contbns., 1971, mem. UN Adv. Com. on Adminstrv. and Budgetary Questions, 1973-77; dir. policy mgmt. staff Bur. Internat. Orgn. Affairs, U.S. Dept. State, Washington, 1977—. Served with AUS, 1953-56. Recipient Superior Honor award State Dept., 1975. Mem. Am. Soc. Pub. Adminstrn. Club: Shenarock Shore (Rye, N.Y.). Home: 8608 Nan Lee Dr Springfield VA 22152 Office: 2201 C St NW Washington DC 20520. *Follow the "Golden Rule" by "Doing unto others as you would have others do unto you." Be totally honest with yourself and with others. Take advantage of all opportunities to develop yourself, and then fully apply your talents to the task at hand, commitment to excellence and perseverance in whatever the task might be.*

STOTZ, ELMER HENRY, biochemist, educator; b. Boston, July 29, 1911; s. Herman Gustav and Mary (Hoch) S.; B.S., Mass. Inst. Tech., 1932; Ph.D., Harvard, 1936; m. Doris Mary White, Aug. 22, 1936; children—Cynthia, Gretchen, Lydia, Jonathan, Diana. Buhl fellow U. Pitts., 1936-37; research fellow U. Chgo., 1937-38; dir. labs. McLean Hosp., Waverly, Mass., 1938-43; asso. in biochemistry Harvard Med. Sch., 1938-43; prof. agrl. biochemistry, head dept. food sci. and tech. Expt. Sta., Cornell, 1943-47; prof. biochemistry, chmn. dept. U. Rochester (N.Y.) Sch. Medicine and Dentistry, 1947—. Trustee Asso. Univs. Fellow A.A.A.S.; mem. Am. Soc. Biol. Chemists, Am. Chem. Soc., Biol. Stain Commn. (treas., trustee), Internat. Union Biochemistry (treas. 1955-67), Sigma Xi. Asso. editor Nutrition Revs., 1942—; co-editor: Comprehensive Biochemistry. Home: 240 Doncaster Rd Rochester NY 14623

STOUFFER, GEORGE ANDREW WASHINGTON, JR., univ. dean; b. Mechanicsburg, Pa., Oct. 11, 1911; s. George A.W. and Mary (Keeny) S.; B.S. in Edn., State Coll., Shippensburg, Pa., 1937; M.Ed., U. Pitts., 1939, Ed.D., 1950; m. Anne Kerr Brown, Jan. 19, 1952; children—Mary Jean, Susan Anne, George III, Bruce Brown. Chief clin. psychologist VA, Neuropsychiat. Hosp., Coatesville, Pa., 1946-47; instr. U. Pitts., 1948-50; county supr. spl. edn., Gettysburg, Pa., 1950-55; dean undergrad. studies Indiana U. of Pa., 1955—, now dean emeritus Sch. of Edn.; test author Bobbs-Merrill Co., Indpls.; pres. Psychol. Services Bur., Inc.; vis. lectr. Pa. State U. and St. Francis Coll. Chmn. bd. dirs. Indiana County Guidance Center, 1961—. Served from ensign to comdr. USNR, 1942-46. Fellow Am., Pa. (Disting. Service award) psychol. assns.; mem. Phi Delta Kappa. Contbr. articles to profl. jours. Home: 79 Shady Dr Indiana PA 15701

STOUP, CURRY WARDELL, mfg. exec.; b. Norwalk, Ohio July 29, 1906; s. Delmer W. and Zoe B. (Freeman) S.; grad. Miami U. Sch. Bus., Oxford, Ohio, 1928; Ph.D. (hon.), Miami U., 1976; m. S. Louise Rey, May 14, 1932 (dec.); children—Shirley Ann, Carolyn Rey; m. 2d, Rosalie B. Burgess, July 29, 1965. Account exec. J. Horace Lytle Advt. Agy., 1928-31; asst. advt. mgr. Hobart Mfg. Co., 1931-35; advt. mgr. Skinner Irrigation Co., 1935-36; sales mgr. Kitchen Aid div. Hobart Mfg. Co., 1936-39; account exec. Fuller & Smith & Ross, Inc., 1939-42; advt. mgr. Harry Ferguson, Inc., 1942-45, v.p., sales mgr., dir., 1949-54; account supr. Frigidaire-Foote, Cone & Belding, 1945-49; v.p. Avco Mfg. Co., N.Y.C., pres. New Idea div. 1954-70, agrl. adviser Avco Corp., 1970-72. Past chmn., hon. life mem. Farm and Indsl. Equipment Inst. Past trustee, chmn. bd. Miami U., Oxford, Ohio. Mem. Phi Beta Kappa, Sigma Chi, Beta Gamma Sigma, Delta Sigma Pi. Home: 1717 Gulf Shore Blvd N Naples FL 33940

STOUSLAND, CHARLES EUGENE, JR., architect, educator; b. Galveston, Tex., Aug. 6, 1920; s. Charles Eugene and Emma Ottelia (Rieske) S.; B.A., Coll. William and Mary, 1941; B.Arch., Yale, 1947; M.Arch., Rice Inst., 1949; student Cranbrook Acad. Art, summer 1953; m. Elizabeth Craighead, Feb. 20, 1943; children—Michael Christopher, Gunnar Kyle, Casey. Tchr. archtl. design, history Miami U., Oxford, Ohio, 1947-48, prof. architecture, 1952—, chmn. dept., from 1952; instr. U. Ark., 1949-52; pvt. practice of architecture, Oxford, 1952—; prints, sculpture exhibited Cin. Mus., Butler Art Inst., Serigraph Soc., N.W. Printmakers, Seattle Printmakers, Rice Inst. Registered architect, Conn., Ohio. Mem. AIA, AAUP, Eta Sigma Phi, Delta Phi Delta, Kappa Alpha. Home: 107 E Central Ave Oxford OH 45056

STOUT, ALAN BURRAGE, composer, educator; b. Balt., Nov. 26, 1932; s. Alan Burrage and Elizabeth Archer (Smithson) S.; student Peabody Conservatory, Balt.; B.S., Johns Hopkins U., 1954; postgrad. U. Copenhagen, 1954-55; M.A. in Music and Swedish Lang., U. Wash., 1959. Librarian, Balt. Enoch Pratt Free Library, 1958; mem. theory and composition faculty Northwestern U. Sch. Music, Evanston, 1963—; vis. lectr. Johns Hopkins U., 1968-69, State Coll. Music, Stockholm, 1973, Berkshire Music Center, 1974; composer numerous pieces, including: Passion, 1976; 4 symphonies; Intermezzo for English horn, percussion and strings, 1954; Pieta for string or brass orch., 1957; Nimbus for strings, 1979; Movements for violin and orch., 1962; Pulsar for 3 brass choirs and timpani, 1972; Fanfare for Charles Seeger for orch., 1972; numerous pieces for voice, including ElegiacSuite for soprano and strings, 1962, Laudi, 1961, O Altitudo, 1974, The Great Day of the Lord, 1956; chamber music, including: 10 string quartets; Study in Densities and Durations and Studies in Timbres and Interferences for Organ; other music for organ, for piano, for harpsichord. Mem. Am. Composers Alliance, ACLU, Am.-Scandinavian Found. Home: 2600 1/2 Central St Evanston IL 60201 Office: Northwestern U Sch Music Evanston IL 60201

STOUT, ARTHUR WENDEL, JR., shipbuilding co. exec.; b. Mobile, June 19, 1920; s. Arthur Wendel and Willa (Du Fresne) S.; B. Engring. in Chem. Engring., Tulane U., 1941; m. Rowena K. Lee, June 21, 1946; children—Miriam Mays (Mrs. Golff), Arthur Wendel III, John Bradford. Engr., Tex. Co., 1941-42, Brown Shipbldg. Corp., 1942-43; with Todd Shipbldg. Corp., 1946-55, asst. gen. supt., 1950-55; with Avondale Shipyards, New Orleans, 1955-60, gen. supt., 1957-60; asst. works mgr. N.Y. Shipbldg. Corp., 1960-67, exec. v.p., works mgr., 1963-67; gen. mgr. Houston div. Todd Shipyards Corp., 1967-74, corp. v.p., N.Y.C., 1974-75, pres., dir., 1975; chmn. Designers & Planners Inc., 1975—; pres., dir. Todd Pacific Shipyards Corp., 1977—. Mem. pres.'s adv. council Tulane U., 1976—. Served to lt. USNR, 1943-46; comdr. Res. Mem. Soc. Naval Architects and Marine Engrs., Am. Bur. Shipping, Tau Beta Phi. Home: 20 Canterbury Ln Summit NJ 07901 Office: 1 State St Plaza New York City NY 10004

STOUT, BILL A., agrl. engr.; b. Grant, Nebr., July 9, 1932; s. Homer and Gertrude (Thornton) S.; B.S., U. Nebr., 1954; M.S., Mich. State Coll., 1955; Ph.D., Mich. State U., 1959; m. Rita Lee Hurlburt, June 22, 1951; children—Jo Ellen, Craige. With John Deere Waterloo Tractor Works (Iowa), 1953; faculty Mich. State U., East Lansing, 1954—, prof. agrl. engring., 1966—. Farm power and machinery specialist FAO, Rome, Italy, 1963-64; vis. prof. U. Calif. at Davis, 1969-70, coordinator energy research and extension, 1975—. Registered profl. engr., Mich. Mem. Am. Soc. Agrl. Engrs., Nat. Soc. Profl. Engrs., Sigma Xi. Contbr. articles to profl. jours. Patentee in field. Home: 241 Maplewood Dr East Lansing MI 48823 Office: Agrl Engring Dept Mich State U East Lansing MI 48824

STOUT, FERN DALE, coll. pres.; b. Grady, N.Mex., July 25, 1923; s. George Riley and Claudia Victoria (Rogers) S.; student W. Tex. State U., 1940-41; B.S. in Agr., N.Mex. State U., 1947; M.A. in Edn., Eastern N.Mex. U., 1957; Ed.D. in Adminstrn., U. N.Mex., 1962; m. Leta Mae Fryar, Oct. 31, 1943; children—Roger Dale, Ross Steven. Supt., Grady (N.Mex.) Mcpl. Sch., 1956-60; dir. Peace Corps tng. Calif. Poly. State U., 1962-64; dean student personnel Coll. of the Desert, 1964-73, pres. Coll. of the Desert and supt. Coachella Valley Community Coll., 1973—; regent Eastern N.Mex. U., 1958-62. Mem. N.Mex. Democratic Platform Com., 1958; bd. dirs. World Affairs Council, 1973-79; bd. dirs. Family Y of Desert. Served with inf. U.S. Army, 1944-45, USAAF, 1945-46. Mem. Calif. Community Coll. Assn. (asso.), NEA (life). Mem. Chs. of Christ. Clubs: Rotary (pres. 1969-71), Lions, Red, Red Rose. Home and Office: 43-500 Monterey Palm Desert CA 92260

STOUT, GLYN BOB, bus. mgmt. cons.; b. Amarillo, Tex., Dec. 29, 1937; s. Robert Haskew and Addye Glynne (Council) S.; B.A., Yale U., 1960; M.B.A., Stanford U., 1966; m. Sandra Laden, June 4, 1966 (div. 1976). Adminstrv. mgr. Synergex Corp., Santa Clara, Calif., 1966-70; v.p. corporate planning, 1970-73, pres., 1973-76; prin. Growth Technologies, Los Gatos, Calif., 1976—; dir. Identronix, Inc., Santa Cruz, Calif. Served with USNR, 1960-63. Office: 131 W Main #7 Los Gatos CA 95030

STOUT, GREGORY STANSBURY, lawyer; b. Berkeley, Calif., July 27, 1915; s. Verne A. and Ella (Moore) S.; A.B., U. Calif., 1937, LL.B., 1940; m. Virginia Cordes, Apr. 23, 1948; 1 son, Frederick Gregory. Admitted to Calif. bar, 1940; practice law, San Francisco, 1946, 52—; asst. dist. atty., 1947-52; mem. Penal Code Revision Commn. Calif. Served to master sgt. AUS, 1942-45. Fellow Am. Coll. Trial Lawyers; mem. ACLU (dir. No. Calif. div.), Am., Fed. bar assns., Nat. Assn. Def. Lawyers in Criminal Cases (sec. 1958-59, pres. 1962-63), State Bar Calif. (com. chmn.). Democrat. Episcopalian. Author articles in field. Home: 2389 Washington St San Francisco CA 94115 Office: 235 Montgomery St Suite 1328 San Francisco CA 94104

STOUT, JOHN WILLARD, chemist, educator; b. Seattle, Mar. 13, 1912; s. John Willard and Beatrice Elsie (Edson) S.; student Calif. Poly. Inst., 1925-30; B.S., U. Calif. at Berkeley, 1933, Ph.D., 1937; m. Florence Louisa Parsons, Mar. 20, 1948; 1 son, John Edward. Instr., research asso. U. Calif., 1937-39; instr. chemistry Mass. Inst. Tech., 1939-41; investigator NDRC, U. Calif., 1941-44; group leader Manhattan Dist., Los Alamos, 1944-46; asso. prof. U. Chgo., 1946-54, prof., 1954-77, emeritus prof., 1977—; dir. Calorimetry Conf., 1953-55. Lalor fellow, 1938-39. Fellow Am. Phys. Soc. (council 1972-76); mem. Am. Chem. Soc., AAAS, Phi Beta Kappa, Sigma Xi, Tau Beta Pi, Chi Pi Sigma. Club: Quadrangle. Asso. editor Jour. Chem. Physics, 1954-56, editor 1959—; asso. editor Phys. Rev., 1958-60. Contbr. articles to sci. jours. Home: 5417 S Greenwood Ave Chicago IL 60615 Office: U Chicago Chicago IL 60637

STOUT, MYRON STEDMAN, artist; b. Denton, Tex., Dec. 5, 1908; s. Myron Stedman and Alberta (Inge) S.; B.S., N. Tex. State U., 1930; M.A., Columbia, 1938; student Acad. San Carlos, Mexico City, Hans Hofmann Sch. Art. Cons., Fine Arts Work Center, Provincetown, Mass.; one-man shows include Stable Gallery, N.Y.C., 1954, Hansa Gallery, N.Y.C., 1957, Contemporary Arts Mus., Houston, 1977, Whitney Mus., 1980; exhbns. include Carnegie Inst., 1958, Whitney Mus., 1958, 64, 73, Mus. Modern Art, 1959, travelling show, 1975-77, Inst. Contemporary Art, Boston, 1959, Am. Fedn. Arts travelling show, 1960-61, Jewish Mus., N.Y.C., 1963, Guggenheim Mus., 1964, also travelling, 1964-65, 69, Sidney Janis Gallery, N.Y.C., 1964, Albright-Knox Gallery, Buffalo, 1968, Corcoran Gallery Art, 1969; represented in permanent collections Bklyn. Mus., Carnegie Inst., Guggenheim Mus., Hirshorn Mus., Nat. Gallery, Mus. Modern Art, pvt. collections. Served with USAAF, 1943-45. Recipient award Nat. Found. Arts and Humanities, 1967; Guggenheim fellow, 1969. Address: 4 Brewster St Provincetown MA 02657 also 716 Ector St Denten TX 76201

STOUT, ROBERT DANIEL, univ. dean; b. Reading, Pa., Jan. 2, 1915; s. Harry Herbert and Anna (Guldin) S.; B.S., Pa. State U., 1935; M.S., Lehigh U., 1941, Ph.D., 1944; D.Sc., Albright Coll., 1967; m. Elizabeth Allwein, Aug. 16, 1939; 1 dau., Elizabeth Ann. Metall. engr. Carpenter Steel Co., 1935-39; faculty Lehigh U., Bethlehem, Pa., 1939—, prof. metallurgy, 1950—, dean Grad. Sch., 1960—. Metall. cons. Fellow Am. Soc. Metals (Stoughton Teaching award 1952, White Disting. Teaching award 1974); mem. Am. Welding Soc. (pres. 1972-73, Lincoln gold medal 1943, Adams lectr. 1960, Sparagen award 1964, Thomas award 1973, Jennings award 1974, Am. del. Internat. Inst. Welding 1955—, Houdremont lectr. 1970), Am. Soc. Engring. Edn., Sigma Xi. Author: Weldability of Steels, 1953, 71. Contbr. articles to profl. publs. Home: 135 E Market St Bethlehem PA 18018

STOUT, ROBERT NEWHART, inland waterway transp. co. exec.; b. Pocono Pines, Pa., July 6, 1924; s. Charles Daniel and Bernice (Newhart) S.; B.S. in Acctg., N.Y. U., 1948; m. Dolores M. Zirpoli, July 30, 1959; children—Donna, Robert Newhart, Sharon L., Suzanne M. Sr. auditor Peat, Marwick, Mitchell, N.Y.C., 1948-53; asst. to controller Curtis Wright Corp., Woodridge, N.J., 1953-59; with Ohio River Co., Cin., 1959—, v.p. fin., 1961-74, exec. v.p., 1974—. Served with U.S. Army, 1943-45. Decorated Purple Heart. Mem. Fin. Execs. Inst., Propeller Club. Clubs: Hyde Park Country, Queen City, Cin. Office: 1400 580 Bldg Cincinnati OH 45202

STOUT, WILLIAM JEWELL, dept. store exec.; b. Bloomington, Ind., Dec. 14, 1914; s. Selatie Edgar and Frances M. (Blodgett) S.; A.B., Ind. U., 1937; m. Harriet Cracraft, June 15, 1940; children—David Bruce, Karen Louise. With L.S. Ayres & Co., Indpls., 1937-78, v.p., 1958-64, v.p. operation, 1964-65, exec. v.p., 1965—; pres., dir. Citizens Gas & Coke Utility. Mem. Ind. Personnel Bd., 1952-66; chmn. United Fund drive, 1953. Pres., bd. dirs. Flanner House; bd. dirs. St. Vincent Hosp. Found., pres., 1972-73; bd. dirs. St. Richard's Day Sch. Served to lt. comdr. USNR, 1942-46. Mem. Indpls. Personnel Assn. (past pres.), Nat. Retail Mchts. Assn., Indpls. Mchts. Assn. (pres. 1970—), Ind., Indpls. chambers commerce. Home: 6976 Washington Blvd Indianapolis IN 46220 Office: 1 W Washington St Indianapolis IN 46209

STOUTENBURG, ADRIEN (PSEUDONYM LACE KENDALL), author; b. Dafur, Minn., Dec. 1, 1916; d. Lace Kendall and Madeline (Christy) Stoutenburg; grad. high sch. Free-lance author, 1940—; librarian Hennepin County (Minn.) Library, 1951-52; polit. reporter Richfield (Minn.) News, 1951-53; editor West Coast, Parnassus Press, pub. children's books, 1956-58. Mem. Authors Guild, Poetry Soc. Am. 1961, Edwin Markham award 1961). Author: (poetry) Heroes Advise Us (Lamont Poetry Selection award Acad. Am. Poets), 1964; (juvenile) (with Laura Nelson Baker) Snowshoe Thompson (trans. Norwegian), 1957; Wild Animals of the West, 1958; Good-By Cinderella (transl. German), 1960; (with L.N. Baker Beloved Botanist (transl. Dutch), 1961; Little Smoke (transl. Hindi), 1961; The Blue-Eyed Convertible, 1961; Secret Lions, 1962; Window on the Sea, 1962; (with L.N. Baker) Dear, Dear Livy; Story of Mrs. Mark Twain, 1963; Arctic Challenger; Elisha Kent Kane, 1963; The Mud Ponies, 1963; Time for Dreaming, 1963; Walk Into the Wind, 1964; (poetry) The Things that Are, 1964; Rain Boat, 1965; American Tall Tales, 1966; Greenwich Mean Time, 1979; (with L.N. Baker) Explorer of the Unconscious: Sigmund Freud, 1965; (juvenile) Masters of Magic, 1966; The Crocodile's Mouth, 1966; A Vanishing Thunder, 1967; (adult poetry) Short History of the Fur Trade, 1969; (with Baker) (juvenile) Listen, America, A Life of Walt Whitman; (juvenile) People in Twilight, 1971; Haran's Journey, 1971; Where To Now, Blue?, 1978; numerous others. Home: 2034 Bath St Santa Barbara CA 93105

STOVALL, EDGAR FLETCHER, paper co. exec.; b. Birmingham, Ala., Feb. 5, 1919; s. Edgar F. and Bessie (Camp) S.; student Auburn U., 1938-39; m. Mildred Moore, Dec. 27, 1944. With Birmingham Paper Co., 1939-60, mdse. mgr., 1955-57, regional mgr., 1957-60; div. mgr. St. Regis Paper Co., Los Angeles, 1960-62; with Mead Corp. and subs., Dayton, Ohio, 1962—, group v.p., 1969-78, exec. v.p., chief operating officer-diversified products, 1978—. Bd. dirs. Ohio C. of C., 1976-79. Served to lt. col. USAAF, 1941-45. Decorated D.F.C., Air medal, Purple Heart. Clubs: Country of Birmingham; Moraine Country, Dayton (Dayton). Home: 2230 S Patterson Blvd Dayton OH 45409 Office: Mead World Hdqrs Courthouse Plaza NE Dayton OH 45463

STOVALL, ROBERT H(ENRY), brokerage co. exec.; b. Louisville; B.A. in Econs., Wharton Sch., U. Pa., 1948; postgrad. in polit. economy U. Copenhagen, 1948-49; M.B.A., N.Y. U., 1957; m. Inger Bagger; 4 children. With E. F. Hutton & Co., 1953-67, mgr. dept. investment research, N.Y.C., 1958-60, gen. partner responsible for research, 1961-67, chmn. com. investment policy, 1966-68; research dir. Nuveen Corp., N.Y.C., 1968-69; partner in mktg. and research Reynolds & Co., N.Y.C., 1969, dir. research, 1970-73; 1st v.p., dir. investment policy Dean Witter Reynolds Inc. (merger Reynolds & Co. and Dean Witter & Co.), N.Y.C., 1978—, pub. comments on market column, 1961—; lectr., tchr. in field. Trustee, N.Y. U.; mem. Mountain Lakes (N.J.) Bd. Zoning Adjustment; mem. adv. com. St. Clare's Hosp., Denville, N.J. Served with U.S. Army, World War II; Italy. Mem. Inst. Chartered Fin. Analysts (chartered fin. analyst), N.Y. Soc. Security Analysts (dir., vice chmn. program com.), Mensa. Clubs: Down Town Assn., Union League (N.Y.C.); S.R. Columnist, Forbes, 1968-76, Chgo. Tribune, 1977—, Fin. World, 1979—; contbr. articles to profl. pubs.; panelist Wall St. Week, Public Broadcasting System, 1977—. Office: 130 Liberty St New York NY 10006

STOVALL, S. J., civil engr., mayor; b. Lufkin, Tex., Sept. 26, 1925; s. Sam Jones and Alice Mae (Thompson) S.; student in Petroleum Engring., Tex. A. and M. U., 1942-43, 46-47; m. Mary Margaret Hempel, June 23, 1949; children—Elizabeth, Marc. With C.E., U.S. Army, 1949—, chmn. paving and materials, Ft. Worth, 1960-70, asst. chief Found. and Materials br., Ft. Worth, 1970—; city councilman City of Arlington (Tex.), 1963-77, mayor pro tem, 1970-77, mayor, 1977—; pres. adv. com. central regional wastewater systems Trinity River Authority, 1976-77; mem. steering com. Regional Transp. Policy Adv. Com. Served with USAAF, 1944-45. Named Civil Servant of Yr., Fed. Bus. Assn., 1969. Mem. North Central Tex. Council Govts. (pres. exec. bd. 1977-78), Soc. Am. Mil. Engrs. (v.p. Ft. Worth chpt.), C.E. Employee Credit Union (chmn. bd.). Baptist. Home: 4816 Racquet Club Arlington TX 76015 Office: PO Box 231 Arlington TX 76010

STOVALL, THELMA L., former lt. gov. Ky.; b. Munfordville, Ky., Apr. 1, 1919; d. Samuel Dewey and Addie Mae Howkins; student LaSalle Extention U., Chgo., U. Ky., Eastern State U.; m. Lonnie Raymond Stovall, Sept. 30, 1936. With Brown & Williamson Tobacco Co., 1935-55; sec. Tobacco Workers Internat. Union, Local 185; sec. state Ky., 1956-60, 64-68, 72-75, state treas., 1960-64, 68-72, lt. gov., 1975-79. State chmn. Muscular Dystrophy Assn., 1957-73; v.p. Muscular Dystrophy Assns. of Am., Inc., 1971-75; chmn. com. on employment Gov.'s Commn. on Status of Women; mem. Ky. Commn. on Women; nat. committeewoman Young Democrats Ky., 1956-58, pres.; bd. dirs. edn. dept. Ky. Fedn. Labor. Mem. Nat. Assn. Secs. (rec. sec. 1967, nat. sec. 1968), Bus. and Profl. Womens Club. Baptist. Clubs: Women of Moose; Order Eastern Star.*

STOVER, CARL FREDERICK, found. exec.; b. Pasadena, Calif., Sept. 29, 1930; s. Carl Joseph and Margarete (Müller) S.; B.A. magna cum laude, Stanford, 1951, M.A., 1954; m. Catherine Swanson, Sept. 3, 1954; children—Matthew Joseph, Mary Margaret, Claire Ellen; m. 2d, Jacqueline Kast, Sept. 7, 1973. Instr. polit. sci. Stanford, 1953-55; fiscal mgmt. officer Office Sec. Dept. Agr., 1955-57; asso. dir. conf. program pub. affairs Brookings Instn., 1957-59, sr. staff mem. govtl. studies, 1960; fellow Center Study Democratic Instns. Santa Barbara, Calif., 1960-62; asst. to chmn. bd. editors Ency. Brit., 1960-62; sr. polit. scientist Stanford Research Inst., 1962-64; dir. pub. affairs fellowship program Stanford, 1962-64; pres. Nat. Inst. Pub. Affairs, Washington, 1964-70, Nat. Com. U.S.-China Relations, 1971-72; pres., dir. Federalism Seventy-Six, 1972-74; dir. cultural resources devel. Nat. Endowment for Arts, 1974-78; pres. Cultural Resources, Inc., Washington, 1978—; treas., dir. H.E.A.R. Found., 1976—; pvt. profl. cons., 1970—; cons. to govt. 1953—. Treas., Nat. Com. U.S.-China Relations, 1966-71, bd. dirs., 1966-74, 79—; bd. dirs. Coordinating Council Lit. Mags., 1966-68; trustee Inst. of Nations, 1962-76, Nat. Inst. Pub. Affairs, 1967-71, Kinesis Ltd., 1972—. Fellow A.A.A.S.; mem. Am. Soc. Pub. Adminstrn., Am. Soc. for Cybernetics; Fedn. Am. Scientists, Soc. Internat. Devel., Nat. Acad. Pub. Adminstrn. (hon.), Phi Beta Kappa Assos. (hon.), Phi Beta Kappa. Democrat. Presbyn. Club: City Tavern (Washington). Author: The Government of Science, 1962; The Technological Order, 1963. Founding editor Jour. Law and Edn., 1971-73. Home: 1280 21st St NW Washington DC 20036

STOVER, HARRY MANNING, bldg. products co. exec.; b. Los Angeles, June 9, 1926; s. Harry Manning and Gladys Martha (Cryer) S.; B.S., U. So. Calif., 1947; m. Winifred Nation, Dec. 17, 1949; children—Harry Manning II, Eric, Carina. Chief engr. Raymond Internat. Venezuela, 1948-51; chief project engr. Standard Vacuum Oil Co., Indonesia, 1951-54; v.p. A.P. Green Refractories Co., Mexico, Mo., 1954-71, exec. v.p., 1971-72, pres., 1972—, chmn., chief exec. officer, 1974—; chmn., dir. Bigelow-Liptak Corp., Southfield, Mich., Hollytex Carpet, City of Industry, Calif., Yeso Panamericano, Mex.; group v.p., dir. U.S. Gypsum Co., Chgo. Bd. dirs. Refractories Inst., Pitts. Served as ensign USNR, 1944-46. Episcopalian. Clubs: Garden of the Gods; Chicago; Exmoor Country. Contbr. articles to profl. jours. Home: 2367 Wood Path Highland Park IL 60035 Office: US Gypsum Co 101 S Wacker Dr Chicago IL 60606

STOVER, JAMES HOWARD, real estate exec.; b. Forest Hill, W.Va., Oct. 20, 1911; s. Charles William and Zora (Goode) S.; student Benjamin Franklin U., 1936-38; grad. Advanced Mgmt. Program, Harvard, 1959, Exec. Devel. Program Ind. U. 1960, Inst. Mgmt. Northwestern U., 1960; m. May Simmons, Oct. 21, 1939 (dec.); children—Ann, Robert Bruce; m. 2d, Elizabeth J. Cobb, Dec. 27, 1977. Asst. purchasing agt. Woodward & Lothrop, Washington, 1932-35; asst. chief field supervision div., central accounts office Bur. Accounts, Treasury Dept., 1935-41, asst. chief Treasury Budget sect., 1941-42, fiscal accountant Office Commr. Pub. Debt, 1946-51, chief treasury mgmt. analysis staff, 1951-63, dir. Office Mgmt. and Orgn., 1963-66, regional commr. customs, 1966-72; real estate sales asso., mgmt. cons., 1972-75; pres. Bay Realty of Fla., Inc., 1975—. Chmn., Inter-agy. Mgmt. Analysis Conf., 1958-59; mem. orgn. and mgmt. adv. com. Dept. Agr. Grad. Sch., 1956-63. Chmn. adv. coms. orgn. and procedure and legislative program Arlington (Va.) County Bd., 1958-63; pres. Tuckahoe Recreation Club, 1957; chmn. Greater Miami Fed. Exec. Council, 1968-69; mem. exec. adv. council Coll. Bus. and Pub. Adminstrn., Fla. Atlantic U., 1969—. Served from 2d lt. to maj. AUS, 1942-46. Recipient Rockefeller Pub. Service award, 1959; Spl. Service award Treasury Dept., 1963, Exceptional Service award 1965, other treasury awards, 1969, 70, 71, 72. Baptist. Kiwanian. Club: Harvard of Miami. Home: 707 Vilabella Ave Coral Gables FL 33146 Office: 2335 Biscayne Blvd Miami FL 33137

STOVER, JOHN FORD, educator, historian; b. Manhattan, Kans., May 16, 1912; s. John William and Maud (Ford) S.; A.B., U. Nebr., 1934, M.A., 1937; Ph.D., U. Wis., 1951; m. Marjorie Ellen Filley, Aug. 21, 1937; children—John Clyde, Robert Vernon, Charry Ellen. Instr. social studies Arcadia (Nebr.) High Sch., 1936-37; instr. history and govt. Bergen (N.J.) Jr. Coll., 1937-41; grad. asst. history U. Wis., 1941-42, 46-47, Univ. fellow, 1946; faculty Purdue U., Lafayette, Ind., 1947—, prof. history, 1959-78, prof. emeritus, 1978—, Purdue Research Found. XL grantee, summer 1957, 59, fellow in Coll.-Bus. Exchange Program, I.C. R.R., summer 1962. Chmn. edn. com., mem. exec. com. Ind. Sesquicentennial Commn., 1962-67; hon. mem. Indiana Am. Revolution Bicentennial commn., 1972—; pres. Lafayette Kiwanis Found., 1977-78. Served to capt. USAAF, 1942-46; Res., ret. Fellow Soc. Am. Historians; mem. Ind. Acad. Social Scis., Western History Assn., Bus. History Conf. (trustee 1973-76), Am., So. Ind. (com. on library), Tippecanoe County (pres. 1972-74) hist. assns., Lexington Group (r.r. historians), AAUP, Ind. History Tchrs. Assn. (pres. 1958-59), Orgn. Am. Historians, Newcomen Soc. N.Am., Ry. and Locomotive Hist. Soc. (editorial adv. bd.), Soc. Ind. Pioneers, Phi Beta Kappa (hon.), Phi Alpha Theta, Delta Sigma Rho. Republican. Methodist. Kiwanian (local pres. 1973-74, lt. gov. 1978-79). Clubs: Fortnightly; Wabash Valley Torch. Author: The Railroads of the South, 1865-1900, 1955; American Railroads, 1961; A History of American Railroads, 1967; Turnpikes, Canals and Steamboats, 1969; The Life and Decline of the American Railroad, 1970; Transportation in American History, 1970; History of Illinois Central Railroad, 1975; Iron Road To The West, 1978. Contbr. to hist. jours., book, encys. Home: 615 Carrolton Blvd West Lafayette IN 47906

STOVER, PHIL SHERIDAN, JR., investment cons.; b. Tulsa, Jan. 23, 1926; s. Phil Sheridan and Noma (Smith) S.; student Yale, 1943-44, Denison U., 1944-45; B.S., U. Pa., 1948. With Nat. Bank Tulsa, 1948-70, v.p., 1956-64, sr. v.p., 1964-65, sr. v.p., cashier, 1965-70; owner Phil Stover & Assos., Tulsa, 1970—; pres., treas. Tulsalite, Inc., mag. pubs.; vice chmn., dir. Tulsa Oiler Baseball Club, 1975—, Springfield (Ill.) Redbirds Baseball Club. Chmn., Tulsa County chpt. Nat. Found., 1956-59, Tulsa Met. Water Authority, 1961-70; vice chmn. Tulsa Utility Bd., 1957-70. Treas. adv. bd. Salvation Army. Served with USNR, 1944-46. Named Okla. Jr. C. of C. Outstanding Young Man, 1954. Republican. Presbyn. Address: University Club Tower 1722 S Carson St Tulsa OK 74119

STOVER, WILLIAM RUFFNER, ins. co. exec.; b. Washington, Aug. 31, 1922; s. Daniel I. and Carrie E. (Brubaker) S.; grad. Randolph Macon Acad., 1941; student Northwestern U., 1945; m. Carolyn McKean, July 19, 1947; children—Deborah Ann (Mrs. Dennis Bowgren), Wendi Lee, Sherre Kay. Sales rep. Old Republic Life Ins. Co., Chgo., 1945-49, v.p., 1949-60, sr. v.p., 1960-68, pres., 1968—, dir. 1961—, pres., chmn., past chief exec. officer parent co. Old Republic Internat. Corp.; chief exec. officer Old Republic Life Ins. Co.; also dir. and pres., chief exec. officer subsidiaries Old Republic Life Ins. Co. N.Y., Old Republic Ins. Co., Greensburg, Pa.; pres., chief exec. officer, dir. Motorists Beneficial Ins. Co.; dir., pres. Home Owners Life Ins. Co., Chgo.; dir., v.p. Insured Credit Services, Inc., Chgo., ICS Assurance Co., Phoenix; trustee Barnes Mortgage Investment Trust, Detroit. Mem. Sigma Alpha Epsilon. Office: 307 N Michigan Ave Chicago IL 60601*

STOWE, DAVID HENRY, arbitrator; b. New Canaan, Conn., Sept. 10, 1910; s. Ansel Roy Monroe and Marjorie (Henry) S.; student Washington and Lee U., 1927-30; A.B., Duke, 1931, M. Ed., 1934; m. Mildred Walker, June 7, 1932; children—David H., Richard W. Tchr., N.C., 1931-37; asst. state dir. N.C. state Employment Service, 1937-41; chief examiner Bur. Budget, Washington, 1943-47; dep. to asst. to Pres. U.S., 1947-49, adminstrv. asst. to Pres., 1949-53; arbitrator, Washington, 1953-70; mem. Nat. Mediation Bd., 1970-79, chmn., 1972-75, 78; mem. atomic energy-labor mgmt. relations panel, 1962—; pub. mem. Pres.'s Missile Sites Labor Commn., 1961-67. Recipient distinguished service award Dept. Labor, 1965. Mem. Nat. Acad. Arbitrators, Lambda Chi Alpha, Alpha Kappa Psi. Democrat. Episcopalian. Home: 7402 Glenbrook Rd Bethesda MD 20014

STOWE, DAVID METZ, clergyman; b. Council Bluffs, Iowa, Mar. 30, 1919; s. Ernest Lewellyn and Florence Mae (Metz) S.; B.A., U. Calif. at Los Angeles, 1940; B.D., Pacific Sch. Religion, 1943, Th.D., 1953, D.D. (hon.), 1966; postgrad. Inst. Chinese Studies, Yale, 1945-46; m. Virginia Ware, Nov. 25, 1943; children—Nancy F. (Mrs. Thomas Inui), Elizabeth A. (Mrs. Charles Hambrick-Stowe), Priscilla B., David W. Ordained to ministry Congl. Ch., 1943; asso. minister, Berkeley, Calif., 1943-45, 51-53; missionary, univ. prof., Peking, China, 1947-50; chaplain, chmn. dept. religion Carleton Coll., 1953-56; ednl. sec. Am. Bd. Commnrs. and United Ch. Bd. World Ministries, 1956-62; prof. theology, Beirut, Lebanon, 1962-63; exec. sec. div. fgn. missions Nat. Council Chs., 1963-64, asso. gen. sec. overseas ministries, 1965-70, also gen. bd.; counselor United Bd. Christian Higher Edn. in Asia; exec. v.p. United Ch. Bd. for World Ministries, 1970—. Mem. Commn. on World Mission and Evangelism, 1965-75, Theol. Ed. Fund, 1970-76; del. assemblies World Council Churches, 1961, 68, 76. Mem. Am. Soc. Missiology, Internat. Assn. Mission Studies, Nat. Soc. Values in Higher Edn., Phi Beta Kappa, Pi Gamma Mu, Blue Key. Author: The Churches' Mission in the World, 1963; When Faith Meets Faith, 1963; Ecumenicity and Evangelism, 1970; also articles in religious books and periodicals. Home: 54 Magnolia Ave Tenafly NJ 07670 Office: 475 Riverside Dr New York NY 10027

STOWE, HAROLD CROSBY, textile co. exec.; b. Charlotte, N.C., June 22, 1946; s. George Washington and Kathryn (Crosby) S.; B.S. in Commerce, Washington and Lee U., Lexington, Va., 1968; M.B.A., Harvard U., 1970; m. Claudia Carr Blair, Aug. 4, 1974; children—Harold Crosby, Claudia Blair, Patrick Board. With N.C. Nat. Bank, Charlotte, 1970-77, v.p., corp. banking mgr., 1976-77; fin. analyst Springs Mills, Inc., Ft. Mill, S.C., 1977-78, treas., 1978—. Active local Boy Scouts Am., 1974—; bd. dirs. Community Health Assn. Charlotte, 1977-78. Named Exec. of Year Rock Hill chpt. Nat. Secs. Assn., 1979. Presbyterian. Home: 16 Red Fox Trail Fort Mill SC 29715 Office: PO Box 70 Fort Mill SC 29715

STOWE, LELAND, journalist; b. Southbury, Conn., Nov. 10, 1899; s. Frank Philip and Eva Sarah (Noe) S.; A.B., Wesleyan U., Conn., 1921, hon. M.A., 1936, LL.D., 1944; M.A. (hon.), Harvard, 1945; LL.D., Hobart Coll., 1946; m. Ruth F. Bernot, Sept. 27, 1924; 1 son, Bruce B.; m. 2d, Theodora F. Calauz, June 17, 1952. Reporter, Worcester Telegram, 1921-22, N.Y. Herald, 1922-24; fgn. editor Pathe News, 1924-26; Paris corr. N.Y. Herald Tribune, 1926-35, roving reporter in North and South Am., 1936-39; reporter League of Nations' councils and assemblies, 1927-31, World Disarmament Conf. Geneva, 1932, World Econ. Conf., London, 1933, Reichstag fire trial, Germany, 1933, end of Spanish dictatorship and founding of Spanish Republic 1929-31, Spanish Civil War, 1937-38, Pres. Roosevelt's visit to Brazil and Argentina and Inter-American Peace Conf., Buenos Aires, 1936, Pan-Am. Conf. at Lima, Peru, 1938; war corr. Chgo. Daily News, from London, 1939, in Finland througout Russo-Finnish war, 1939-40, in Norway, 1940, in Hungary, Yugoslavia, Rumania, Bulgaria and Turkey, 1940, in Greece and Albania, 1940-41, in Malaya, Thailand, Indo-China and China, 1941, in Burma, 1942, in Russia, 1942; commentator, Am. Broadcasting Co., 1944-45; war corr. in France, Belgium, Germany, 1944; Italy and Greece, 1945; radio commentator A.B.C. and M.B.S., 1945-46; lectr., free-lance writer 1947-48; fgn. editor The Reporter Magazine, 1949-50; dir. News and Information Service of Radio Free Europe, Munich, 1952-54; roving editor Reader's Digest, 1955-76; prof. journalism U. Mich., 1956-69. Recipient Pulitzer prize, 1930, for coverage of Paris (1929) Reparations Com. and formation of Young Plan and Bank for Internat. Settlements; Legion of Honor (France), 1931; U. of Mo. Sch. of Journalism medal for outstanding war correspondence, 1941; Sigma Delta Chi medal and award for 1940 dispatches revealing German conquest of So. Norway, 1941; awarded Mil. Cross of Greece, 1945; Wesleyan U.'s James L. McConaughty Meml. award, 1963. Author: Nazi Means War, 1933; No Other Road to Freedom, 1941; They Shall Not Sleep, 1944; While Time Remains, 1946; Target: You, 1949; Conquest by Terror: The Story of Satelite Europe, 1952; Crusoe of Lonesome Lake, 1957. Home: 801 Greenhills Dr Ann Arbor MI 48105

STOWE, ROBERT LEE, JR., textile co. exec.; b. Belmont, N.C., Aug. 17, 1902; B.S., Davidson Coll., 1924; m. Ruth Link Harding; children—Robert Lee III, Daniel Harding, Richmond Harding. Pres., treas., dir. Chronicle Mills, Nat. Yarn Mills, Inc., Stowe Spinning Co.; pres., dir. Bank of Belmont, Atlas Real Estate Co., Belmont Syndicate; v.p., treas., dir. Belmont Converting Co.; dir. Stowe Merc. Co., Lakeview Farms. Mem. Belmont City Council, 1953-67; former trustee N.C. Vocational Textile Sch.; mem. nat. adv. bd. MacArthur Meml. Found.; founder Stowe Park. Named Belmont Man of Yr., 1963; Stowe Galleries at Davidson Coll. named in his honor, Robert Lee Stowe, Jr. Tennis House, Davidson Coll., also named in his honor. Mem. Newcomen Soc. N.A., Phi Gamma Delta. Presbyterian (past tchr. Sunday sch.; deacon, later elder). Clubs: Charlotte (N.C.) Country; Dunes Golf and Beach (Myrtle Beach, S.C.). Home: Belmont NC 28012 Office: 100 N Main St Belmont NC 28012. *Try to practice the Golden Rule in all my dealings with my fellowmen.*

STOWE, WILLIAM MCFERRIN, clergyman; b. Franklin, Tenn., Jan. 28, 1913; s. John Joel and Myra Anderson (McFerrin) S.; A.B., Hendrix Coll., Conway, Ark., 1932, D.D., 1956; B.D., Duke, 1935, D.D., 1967; Ph.D., Boston U., 1938, D.D., Oklahoma City U., 1955; L.H.D., Southwestern Coll.; LL.D., So. Meth. U.; LL.D., Baker U., 1966; m. Twila Farrell, July 28, 1943; children—William McFerrin, Twila Gayle (Mrs. Robert Keighley), Martha Elizabeth. Ordained to ministry Meth. Ch., 1937; pastor Meth. Ch., Alta Loma, Tex., 1938-40, Garden Villas Meth. Ch., Houston, 1940-44; mem. staff Bd. Edn., Meth. Ch.; dir. youth work Tex. Cont. Meth. Ch., 1940-44; dir. spl. tng. enterprises, 1944-49, sec. personnel service, 1946-49; sec. vocat. counsel Meth. Ch., 1946-48; pastor First Meth. Ch., Stillwater, Okla., 1949-51, St. Luke's Meth. Ch., Oklahoma City, 1951-64; elected bishop, 1964; bishop The Meth. Ch., Kansas Area, 1964-72, Dallas-Ft. Worth, 1972—; vis. prof. The Iliff Sch. Theol., Denver, summer 1945-47, Scarritt Coll., Nashville, 1944-46, spl. lectr. Boston U. Sch. Theology, 1945, Perkins Sch. Theology, So. Meth. U., 1944-46, Westminster Theol. Sem., 1946-47, Grad. Sch. Religion, U. So. Cal., 1946, Gammon Sch. Theology, 1944-45; dean Okla. Meth. Pastors' Sch. Mem. exec. com. Okla. Council Chs.; pres. Oklahoma City Council Chs., 1955-56; pres. Okla. Conf. bd. edn. The Meth. Ch., mem. exec. com. jurisdictional bd. edn., mem. co-ordinating council, del. to world conf., 1956, 61, 66, 71, jurisdictional conf., 1956, 60, 64, del. gen. conf., 1956, 60, 64, mem. world council; del. World Meth. Theol. Inst., Oxford, Eng., 1958, 62; exec. com. Okla. Meth. Conf. Council; pres. Okla. Conf. Meth. Commn. Christian Higher Edn., 1956-60; mem. exec. com. World Meth. Council; mem. governing bd. Nat. Conf. Chs.; pres. Tex. Conf. Chs., 1976-77. Trustee So. Meth. U., Southwestern U., Huston-Tillotson Coll., Lydia Patterson Inst., Perkins Sch. Theology, Tex. Wesleyan Coll. Recipient Distinguished Alumnus award Boston U. Sch. Theology; Distinguished Service award Baker U., 1972; Recognition award Southwestern Coll., 1972. Mem. Sigma Chi (Significant Sig award 1972). Mason. Club: The Mokus (Boston). Author: Characteristics of Jesus, 1962; Power of Paul, 1963; It All Began With God. Contbr. articles to religious jours. Home: 4123 Echo Glen Dallas TX 75234 Office: PO Box 8124 3300 Mockingbird Ln Dallas TX 75205

STRABLE, EDWARD GEORGE, librarian, advt. exec.; b. Camden, N.J., Feb. 12, 1922; s. Edward E. and Laura (Stevenson) S.; B.S. in Journalism, U. Ill., 1948; M.A., U. Chgo., 1954; m. Jane Sturtevant, Sept. 7, 1946; 1 dau., Jennie Laura Sharp. Advt. copywriter Scantlin & Co., Chgo., 1948-49; exec. asst. Chgo. Pub. Library, 1951-55; library dir. J. Walter Thompson Co., Chgo., 1955-64, mgr. information services, 1968—, v.p., 1972—; exec. sec. Am. Library Trustee Assn. and Reference Services Div., A.L.A., Chgo., 1965-69; vis. lectr. U. Chgo. Grad. Library Sch., 1958-63. Bd. dirs. Ill. Regional Library Council. Served with AUS, 1943-46. Decorated Purple Heart. Mem. Spl. Libraries Assn. (pres. 1972-73). Author: (with Elin B. Christianson) Subject Headings in Advertising, Marketing and Communications Media, 1964. Editor: Special Libraries; A Guide for Management (Spl. Library Assn. Profl. award 1967), 1966, rev. edit., 1974. Home: 5832 Stony Island Ave Chicago IL 60637 Office: 875 N Michigan Ave Chicago IL 60611

STRACHAN, DONALD M., chem. co. exec.; b. Cleve., June 24, 1923; s. Harry Morris and Eva (Maffett) S.; student St. Catherine's Coll., Cambridge (Eng.) U., 1945; B.S. in Econs., U. Pa., 1947; m. Suzanne Merion, June 27, 1953; children—William, Paul. With Ernst & Ernst, C.P.A.'s, 1947-70, staff accountant to mgr., Cleve., 1947-63, partner, Charleston, W.Va., 1964-70; v.p. finance, treas. Cleve. Electronics, Inc., 1970-74; with Barnes, Wendling & Cook, Cleve., 1974-77; treas. McGean Chem. Co. Inc., Cleve., 1977—. Served with AUS, World War II. C.P.A., Ohio, W.Va. Mem. Delta Kappa Epsilon. Methodist. Club: Chagrin Valley Country. Home: 135 Mill Creek Ln Moreland Hills OH 44022 Office: 1250 Terminal Tower Cleveland OH 44113

STRACHAN, JOHN RUPERT, govt. ofcl.; b. N.Y.C., Aug. 5, 1916; s. John and Julia (McDougal) S.; B.S., N.Y. U., 1959, M.A., 1961; children—JoAnn, Jacqueline, John. With U.S. Postal Service, 1941—, clk., 1941-59, supr., 1959-62, chief, employment and placement br., div. personnel N.Y. Region, 1962-66, acting postmaster, 1966-67, postmaster, N.Y.C., 1967—, mgr. N.Y. Met. Center, 1971—; tchr. N.Y.C. Sch. System 1960-62; instr. N.Y. U., 1962-64. Bd. dirs. Cath. Sch. Bd., N.Y.C., 1967—, Assn. Children with Retarded Mental Devel., 1967—; agy. coordinator Combined Fed. Campaign Fund, 1967—; mem. community adv. council Harlem Hosp. Center, 1967—. Bd. dirs., N.Y. County chpt. Nat. Multiple Sclerosis Soc., Cath. Interracial Council N.Y. Served with AUS, 1942-46. Recipient Interracial award Cath. Interracial Council, 1968, Achievement award Nat. Negro Bus. Women, 1968, Man of Year award Am. Legion, 1968, Postmaster of Year award Direct Mail Advt. Assn., 1970. Mem. Columbian Assn. (hon. pres.), Jewish Postal Employees' Welfare League (hon.), Am. Legion, 369th Vets. Assn., Inc., Fed. Bus. Assn., Fed. Exec. Bd., Fed. Personnel Assn., NAACP, Nat. Assn. Postmasters U.S., Nat. League Postmasters, Nat. Urban League, N.Y. U. Alumni Assn., Omega Psi Phi. Office: General Post Office 33d St and 8th Ave New York City NY 10001

STRACHER, ALFRED, educator; b. Albany, N.Y., Nov. 16, 1930; s. David and Florence (Winter) S.; B.S., Rensselaer Poly Inst., 1952; M.S., Columbia U., 1954, Ph.D., 1956; m. Dorothy Altman, July 4, 1954; children—Cameron, Adam, Erica. Asst. prof. State U. N.Y. Downstate Med. Center, Bklyn., 1959-62, asso. prof., 1962-68, prof. biochemistry, 1968—, chmn. dept., 1971—; with Rockefeller Inst. Med. Research, 1956-58, Carlsberg Lab., Copenhagen, Denmark, 1958-59; vis. prof. Oxford U., 1973-74. Nat. Found. for Infantile Paralysis fellow, 1956-59; Health Research Council career scientist, 1961-68; Commonwealth Fund fellow, 1966-67; Guggenheim fellow, 1973-74. Editorial bd. several sci. jours. Contbr. profl. jours. Home: 47 The Oaks Roslyn Estates NY 11576 Office: Dept Biochemistry State Univ NY Downstate Med Center Brooklyn NY 11203

STRACHOTA, BERNARD ARTHUR, banker; b. Milw., Nov. 5, 1922; s. Bernard Adam and Martha Wilhelmina (Wollenzein) S.; student U. Minn., 1942; m. LaVerne Elizabeth Conrad, Feb. 23, 1946; children—Lynn Louise Strachota Fandek, James Conrad, Mark Bernard. Milw. dist. mgr. Miller Brewing Co., 1950-57; gen. sales mgr. Judge & Dolph, Chgo., 1957-58; pres., gen. mgr. Sta. WRIT/WBCS, Milw., 1958-77; v.p. mktg. 1st Bank Midland, Milw., 1977—. Past bd. dirs. Milw. Conv. and Visitors Bur., Charity Epilepsy Center of Mt. Sinai Hosp., Friends of Elm Brook Hosp., St. Anthony Hosp., Greater Milw. Open; past pres., tournament dir. Vince Lombardi Meml. Golf Classic; past v.p., treas. Milw. County Easter Seal Soc.; past pres. Ascension Lutheran Ch., Milw.; past vice chmn. Gov. Wis. Conf. Home and Family; past trustee Warren Spahn Scolarship Found. Served with USAAF, 1943-46. Decorated Air medal with 2 oak leaf clusters; named Vet. of Year, Milw. Allied Council Vets. Orgns., 1967; Communicator of Year, Graphic Arts and Advt. Guild, Milw., 1971. Mem. Wis. Broadcasters Assn. (pres. 1976), Milw. Advt. Club (past dir.), Radio Advt. Bur., Milw. Area Radio Stas., Met. Milw. Assn. Commerce (past chmn.), Am. Legion (pres. Wis. 1968; Neville Dunn Legionnaire of Merit award 1966, Distinguished Service award Cudworth Post 1967). Republican. Clubs: North Hills Country, Variety, Shriners. Home: 11947 W Appleton Ave Milwaukee WI 53224 Office: 201 W Wisconsin Ave Milwaukee WI 53203. *To go through life and not be concerned about your fellow man, would be a complete waste of the gifts that God has given to each one of us. I give thanks that I have been able to contribute something to my community, state and nation even in my small way.*

STRACK, DAVID H., univ. athletic dir.; b. Indpls., Mar. 2, 1923; s. John Augustus and Verna Avis (Bridgford) S.; B.B.A., U. Mich., 1945, M.B.A., 1946; m. Ruth Ann Mayer, Dec. 21, 1946; children—Sarah Strack McElroy, Julie Strack DeWitt, David S., Lucy Strack Singer, Amy. Territory mgr. Firestone Tire & Rubber, Detroit, 1946-48; asst. basketball coach U. Mich., Ann Arbor, 1948-59; head basketball coach U. Idaho, Moscow, 1959-60; head basketball coach U. Mich., 1960-68, asso. dir. athletics, 1968-72; dir. athletics U. Ariz., Tucson, 1972—; dir. Wolverine Mutual Ins. Co. Trustee, Pop Warner Little Scholars. Served with USMCR, 1943-45. Mem. Nat. Assn. Basketball Coaches, Nat. Assn. Collegiate Athletic Dirs. Author: Basketball, 1968. Home: 3924 Calle Casita Tucson AZ 85718

STRACK, HAROLD ARTHUR, ret. air force officer, electronics co. exec.; b. San Francisco, Mar. 29, 1923; s. Harold Arthur and Catheryn Jenny (Johnsen) S.; student San Francisco Coll., 1941, Sacramento Coll., 1947, Sacramento State Coll., 1948, U. Md., 1962, Indsl. Coll. Armed Forces, 1963; m. Margaret Madeline Decker, July 31, 1945; children—Carolyn, Curtis, Tamara. Commd. 2d lt. USAAF, 1943, advanced through grades to brig. gen. USAF, 1970; comdr. 1st Radar Bomb Scoring Group, Carswell AFB, Ft. Worth, 1956-59; vice comdr. 90th Strategic Missile Wing SAC, Warren AFB, Cheyenne, Wyo., 1964; chief, strategic nuclear br., chmn. spl. studies group Joint Chiefs of Staff, 1965-67; dep. asst. to chmn. for strategic arms negotiations Joint Chiefs Staff, 1968; comdr. 90th Strategic Missile Wing, SAC, Warren AFB, Cheyenne, 1969-71; chief Studies, Analysis and Gaming Agy., Joint Chiefs Staff, Washington, 1972-74; v.p., mgr. MX Program electronics div. Northrop, Hawthorne, Calif., 1974—. 1st clarinetist Cheyenne Symphony Orch., 1969-71; mem. Cheyenne Frontier Days Com., 1970-71. Decorated D.S.M., Legion of Merit, D.F.C., Air medal, Purple Heart. Mem. Am. Inst. Aeros. and Astronautics, Inst. Nav., Am. Def. Preparedness Assn., Air Force Assn., Am. Fedn. Musicians, Cheyenne Frontier Days "Heels". Home: 46 Orange Ave Long Beach CA 90802 Office: Northrop Electronics Div 2301 W 120th St Hawthorne CA 90250. *The precepts which have guided me recognize the dignity of the individual and human rights. I believe that living by the Golden Rule contributes to the quality of life by making us better and more useful citizens while favorably influencing others. Integrity, ideals, and high standards reinforce one's own character. While taking pride in accomplishment, show gratitude for opportunity and humility for success. Lead by example and always do your best. Service to humanity and country is the highest calling, and the satisfaction of a job well done, approbation, respect, and true friendship are one's greatest rewards.*

STRADLEY, FRED SILL, lawyer; b. Dallas. Apr. 22, 1931; s. Edward C. and Elva C. (Catto) S.; B.A., U. South, Tenn., 1953; LL.B., So. Meth. U., 1959; children—Mark, Susan, Andrew. Admitted to Tex. bar, 1959; practice in Dallas, 1960—; partner firm Vial, Hamilton, Koch, Tubb, Knox & Stradley, 1965—. Served with AUS, 1953-56. Mem. Am., Tex. bar assns., Am. Bd. Trial Advocates, Kappa Sigma. Episcopalian. Home: 2922 Oxford Terr Dallas TX 75201 Office: 1500 Republic Nat Bank Tower Dallas TX 75201

STRAETZ, ROBERT P., business exec.; b. Hillside, N.J., 1921; grad. U. Chgo.; student Advanced Mgmt. Program at Harvard U. Research chemist Manhattan Project, until 1946; with Textron Inc., 1946—, successively v.p., exec. v.p., pres. Homelite div., until 1974, corp. group v.p., 1974-78, pres., chief operating officer, 1978-79, chmn. bd., chief exec. officer, 1979—. Office: care Textron Inc 40 Westminster St Providence RI 02903

STRAHLER, ARTHUR NEWELL, educator, author; b. Kolhapur, India, Feb. 20, 1918 (parents Am. citizens); s. Milton W. and Harriet (Brittan) S.; A.B., Coll. Wooster, 1938; A.M., Columbia, 1940, Ph.D. (Univ. fellow), 1944; m. Margaret E. Wanless, Aug. 10, 1940; children—Alan H., Marjorie E. Faculty, Columbia, 1941-71, prof. geomorphology, 1958-68, adj. prof. geology, 1968-71, chmn. dept. geology, 1959-62. Fellow Geol. Soc. Am., Am. Geog. Soc.; mem. Am. Geophys. Union, Phi Beta Kappa, Sigma Xi. Author: Physical Geography, rev., 1975; The Earth Sciences, rev. edit., 1971; Introduction to Physical Geography, rev. edit., 1973; Planet Earth, 1971; Environmental Geoscience, 1973; Introduction to Environmental Science, 1974; Elements of Physical Geography, 1976; Principles of Earth Science, 1976; Principles of Physical Geology, 1977; Geography and Man's Environment, 1977; Modern Physical Geography, 1978. Home: 1039 Cima Linda Ln Santa Barbara CA 93108

STRAIGHT, BEATRICE WHITNEY, actress; b. Old Westbury, L.I., N.Y., Aug. 2, 1918; d. Willard and Dorothy (Whitney) Dickerman; studied with Tamara Daykarhanova, with Michael Chekhov at Chekhov Theatre Sch.; m. Peter Cookson, June 2, 1949; 2 sons. Appeared Broadway plays including: Bitter Oleander, 1935, The Possessed, 1939, Twelfth Night, 1941, Land of Fame, 1943, The Wanhope Bldg., 1947, Eastward in Eden, 1947, Macbeth, 1948, The Heiress, 1948, The Innocents, 1950, The Grand Tour, 1951, Heartbreak House, 1952, The Crucible (Tony award), 1953, Sing Me No Lullaby, 1954, The River Line, 1957, Twelfth Night, King Lear, Phèdre, 1966, A Streetcar Named Desire, 1967, 69-70, Everything in the Garden, 1967, The Palace at 4 A.M., 1972, Ghosts, 1972, All My Sons, 1974; toured in The Right Honourable Gentleman, 1971; mem. L.I. Festival Repertory Co., 1968; film appearances include: Phone Call for a Stranger, 1952, Patterns, 1956, The Silken Affair, 1957, The Nun's Story, 1959, The Young Lovers, 1964, Network (Acad. award for best supporting actress), 1976; TV performances include: The Magnificent Failure, 1952, The Borrowers, 1973, The Garden Party, 1974, Strangers in the Homeland, 1976, mini-series The Dain Curse, 1978, also guest roles on Mission: Impossible, Playhouse 90, Kraft Television Theatre, Studio One, Ben Casey, The Nurses, Lamp Unto My Feet; regular on TV series Beacon Hill, 1975. A founder Theatre, Inc., producing orgn., 1945; operates Young World Found., producing children's plays, including Who Am I?, 1971-73; conducted own radio program on Sta. WMCA, N.Y.C., during World War II. Mem. Actors Equity, AFTRA, Screen Actors Guild. Office: care STE Representation Ltd 155 N La Peer Dr Los Angeles CA 90048*

STRAIN, DOUGLAS CAMPBELL, precision instrument co. exec.; b. Spokane, Wash., Oct. 24, 1919; s. Clayton Preston and Edith (Crockatt) S.; B.S. in Elec. Engring., Calif. Inst. Tech., 1948; H.H.D. (hon.), Internat. Coll. of Caymans, 1978; m. Leila Cleo Karicofe, June 13, 1943; children—James Douglas, Barbara Joanne, Gordon Campbell. Design engr. Nat. Tech. Labs., Beckman Instruments, South Pasadena, Calif., 1948-49; v.p. research and engring. Brown Electro Measurements Corp., Portland, Oreg., 1949-53; pres. Electro Sci. Industries, Inc., Portland, 1953—, Sunset Sci. Park, Inc., Portland, 1963-70. Chmn., Tri-County Colls. for Oregon's Future, 1964-68, treas., 1968—; mem. City Club Portland research bd., 1967-69; mem. Gov.'s Adv. Council for Oreg. Tech. Services, 1966-70; chmn. adv. panel to electricity div. Nat. Bur. Standards, Nat. Acad. Sci., 1971-74; mem. nat. metric adv. panel Commerce Dept., 1969-70; trustee internat. Coll. of Caymans, 1971—; asso. Calif. Inst. Tech., 1975—, chmn. Oreg. Alumni Fund, 1975—. Bd. dirs. Vols. Internat. Tech. Assistance; trustee Pacific U.; past pres., trustee Scientists of Tomorrow. Recipient Silver Knight of Mgmt. award Nat. Mgmt. Assn., 1961; Bausch & Lomb Sci. award, 1938, Reed Coll. award, 1975; Wildhack award Nat. Conf. Standards Labs., 1977. Registered profl. engr., Oreg. Fellow Instrument Soc. Am. (nat. pres. 1970-71), Menninger Found., Linus Pauling Inst.; mem. IEEE (sr.), Sci. Apparatus Makers Assn. (chmn. indsl. instrument sect. 1966-68, dir. 1973-76), Nat. Mgmt. Assn. (pres. Portland chpt. 1956-57, v.p. West Coast 1962-63), AAAS, Western Electronic Mfrs. Assn. (dir. 1956-57), Nat. Soc. Profl. Engrs., Precision Measurement Assn. (sr.), Electron Microscopic Soc. Am. Club: City, Multnomah (Portland). Patentee optical and electronic devices. Home: Route 1 Box 19-D Forest Grove OR 97116 Office: 13900 NW Science Park Dr Portland OR 97229

STRAIN, JAMES TERRY, broadcasting co. exec.; b. London, Ont., Can., July 9, 1938; s. Andrew James and Helen Margaret (Torrance) S.; m. Susan Hagarty, July 4, 1964; children—Jennifer, Laura, Andrew. Pres., James Terry Ltd., Toronto, 1960; media supr. Spitzer, Mills & Bates Advt., Toronto, 1958-59, 61; media dir. Colgate Palmolive, Toronto, 1962-63; sr. media supr. MacLaren Advt., Toronto, 1963-64; nat. sales account exec. Standard Radio, Toronto, 1965-66; nat. sales account exec. All Can. Radio and TV, Toronto, 1966-74; gen. mgr., dir. Edmonton (Alta.) Broadcasting Co. Ltd., 1974-76, pres., gen. mgr., dir., 1977—. Mem. mgmt. bd. Edmonton Gen. Hosp.; vice chmn. Red Shield Appeal, 1979; dir. Jr. Achievement, 1977-79; mem. adv. bd. Salvation Army; mem. adv. bd. No. Alta. Inst. Tech. Mem. Western Assn. Broadcasters, Alta. Assn. Broadcasters, Can. Assn. Broadcasters, Bur. Broadcast Mgmt., Young Pres.'s Orgn., Edmonton C. of C. Clubs: Edmonton; Toronto Cricket, Skating and Curling. Home: 13720 101 Ave Edmonton AB T5N 0J7 Canada Office: 10230 108 St Edmonton AB Canada

STRAIN, ROBERT CHARLES, pub. co. exec.; b. Kearney, Nebr., Sept. 23, 1928; s. Richard H. and Hazle L. (Adcock) S.; A.B., Washington U., 1950; m. Eleanor F. Rowland, May 14, 1960; children—Sally, Robert C., Susan, Marion, David. With C.V. Mosby Co., St. Louis, 1963—, v.p., 1967-73, pres., 1973—. Served with USAF, 1950-51. Home: 33 Log Cabin Dr St Louis MO 63124 Office: 11830 Westline Industrial Dr St Louis MO 63141

STRAITON, ARCHIE WAUGH, educator; b. Arlington, Tex., Aug. 27, 1907; s. John and Jeannie (Waugh) S.; B.S. in Elec. Engring., U. Tex., 1929, M.A., 1931, Ph.D., 1939; m. Esther McDonald, Dec. 28, 1932; children—Janelle (Mrs. Thomas Henry Holman), Carolyn (Mrs. Stanley Walter Cameron). Engr., Bell Telephone Labs., N.Y.C., 1929-30; from instr. to asso. prof. Tex. Coll. Arts and Industries, 1931-41, prof., 1941-43, head dept. engring., 1941-43; faculty U. Tex., Austin, 1943—, prof., 1948—, dir. elec. engring. research lab., 1947-72, Ashbel Smith prof. elec. engring., 1963—, chmn. dept., 1966-71, acting v.p., grad. dean, 1972-73. Fellow IEEE; mem. Nat. Acad. Engring., Sigma Xi, Tau Beta Pi, Eta Kappa Nu. Contbr. articles to profl. jours. Home: 4212 Far West Blvd Austin TX 78731

STRAKA, LASZLO RICHARD, pub. co. exec.; b. Budapest, Hungary, June 22, 1934; s. Richard J. and Elisabeth (Roeck) S.; came to U.S., 1950, naturalized, 1956; B.A. cum laude, N.Y. U., 1959; m. Eva K. von Viczian, Jan. 20, 1962; children—Eva M., Monika E., Viktoria K. Accountant, Greatrex Ltd., N.Y.C., 1952-53; partner Hambar Co., accountants, N.Y.C., 1953—; with Pergamon Press, Inc., Elmsford, N.Y., 1954—, v.p., 1964-68, exec. v.p., treas., 1968-74, pres., 1974-75, chmn. bd., 1975-77, vice chmn. bd., 1977—, also dir.; treas. Brit. Book Centre, Inc., N.Y.C., 1956-67; chmn. bd. Microforms Internat. Mktg. Corp., 1971—; dir. Pergamon Press GmbH, Frankfort, Germany, Pergamon of Can., Ltd., Toronto, Ont., Pergamon Press Ltd., Oxford, Eng., European Printing Corp., Dublin, Ireland. Bd. dirs., sec. Szechenyi Istvan Soc., N.Y.C., 1967—. Mem. Phi Beta Kappa. K.C. Home: 1289 Pickens Ct Yorktown Heights NY 10598 Office: Pergamon Press Inc Fairview Park Elmsford NY 10523

STRAKA, RONALD ALBERT, architect, urban designer; b. Cleve., July 11, 1937; s. Albert James and Mary Julia (Karabinos) S.; B.S. in Architecture, U. Cin., 1961; M.S., Ohio State U., 1979; m. Judith Ann Rice, Feb. 20, 1960; children—Mary Susan, Robert James, Nancy Ann. Asso., project designer Schafer, Flynn & Van Dijk Architects, Cleve., 1966-70; dir. design Dalton, Dalton, Little & Brubaker/Branot Inc., Columbus, Ohio, 1971; partner, dir. design Group 4/Design, Denver, 1972-73; prin. Ronald A. Straka, FAIA, Boulder, Colo., 1973—; lectr., dir. Center New Towns and Urban Growth, U. Colo., Boulder, 1972-74, asso. prof., 1973-74, 77-78; vis. prof. Kent (Ohio) State U., 1969-70, Ohio State U., Columbus, 1971, 78, 79, Kans. State U., Manhattan, 1977; mem. evaluation team Nat. Archtl. Accreditation Bd., 1977; project designer Blossom Music Center, Northampton (Ohio) Twp., 1969-70; chief designer, dir. designer State Office Bldg. and Supreme Ct. Bldg. Ohio, Columbus, 1970-73. Mem. Gov. Colo.'s Task Force on Colo. Futures, 1975, Boulder Centennial-Bicentennial Com., 1976; mem. Task Force/Goals for Beaumont (Tex.), 1979. Recipient numerous awards for design. Fellow AIA (Edward C. Kemper award 1977); chmn. urban planning and design com. 1976-77, chmn. urban design assistance team program 1974, 75); mem. Nat. Trust Historic Preservation. Contbg. editor: Symposia mag. Address: Sunshine Canyon Salina Star Route Boulder CO 80302

STRAKE, GEORGE W., JR., state ofcl.; b. Houston, June 10, 1935; s. George W. and Susan (Kehoe) S.; A.B., U. Notre Dame, 1957; M.B.A., Harvard U., 1961; m. Annette Dewalch, 1959; children—George W., Stephen D., Michele M., Melanie, Gregory P., Melissa A. Independent Producers and Royalty Owners Assn., 1976—; chmn. candidates recruiting com. Harris County (Tex.) Republican Party, 1964-65, mem. fin. com., 1975-77; alt. del. Republican Nat. Conv., 1976; sec. of State of Tex., 1979—. Served with U.S. Navy, 1957-59. Office: Office of Secretary of State 105 State Capitol Bldg Austin TX 78711*

STRALEM, PIERRE, stock broker; b. Chappaqua, N.Y., Oct. 17, 1909; s. Casimir Ignace and Edithe (Neustadt) S.; A.B., Princeton, 1932; m. Nancy Lou D.A. Coffyn, June 11, 1936. With Hallgarten & Co., mems. N.Y. Stock Exchange, 1933—, partner, 1941-74; v.p., dir. Moseley Hallgarten Estabrook & Weeden Inc., 1974—; dir. Atlantic Gulf Petroleum. Bd. dirs. George Jr. Republic. Kips Bay Boys Club. Clubs: Court (Princeton, N.J.); Princeton, Stock Exchange Lunch (N.Y.C.). Home: 1000 King St Chappaqua NY 10514 Office: 1 New York Plaza New York NY 10004

STRALEY, H. W., III, geologist; b. Princeton, W.Va., May 12, 1900; s. H.W., II and Rosa Lee Beauregard (Walthall) S.; B.A., Concord Coll., 1923; Ph.D., U. Chgo., 1939; Ph.D., U. N.C., 1938; m. Garnet Brammer, July 24, 1928; children—H.W., IV, William Forest. Asst. prof. Baylor U., 1938-41; geologist, chief supply and resources sect. U.S. Bd. Econ. Warfare, 1941-46; cons. geologist Damas & Moore, Atlanta, 1946—; prof. geology Ga. Inst. Tech., 1949-66, Morehead State U., 1969-72; speaker Royal Astron. Soc. symposium on extra-terrestrial depressions, London, 1966; past pres. Boone-Lewis Devel. Co. Registered profl. engr., W.Va.; registered geologist, Del. Mem. Am. Assn. Petroleum Geologists, Am. Geophys. Union, Am. Inst. Mining Engrs. (com. chmn.), Geol. Soc. Am., Soc. Econ. Geophysicists (com. chmn.), Yorkshire Geol. Soc. (Eng.). Baptist. Club: Princeton Lawn Tennis (past pres.). Contbr. sci. articles to profl. jours. Home and office: 5910 Riverwood Dr NW Atlanta GA 30328

STRAM, HANK LOUIS, profl. football coach, TV commentator; b. Chgo., Jan. 3, 1923; s. Henry L. and Nellie (Boots) S.; grad. Purdue U., 1948; m. Phyllis Marie Pesha, Nov. 27, 1953; children—Henry Raymond, Dale Alan, Stuart Madison, Julia Anne, Gary Baxter, Mary Nell. Offensive football coach, head baseball coach Purdue U., 1948-55; offensive football coach So. Meth. U., 1956, Notre Dame U., 1958, U. Miami, 1959; head football coach Kansas City Chiefs, 1960-74, New Orleans Saints, 1976-77; color commentator CBS Sports, N.Y.C., 1978—. Served with USAAF, 1943-46. Recipient Big 10 medal for athletes and scholarship Big 10 Conf., 1948; named Profl. Football Coach of Year, Knute Rochne Club Am. and Ft. Lauderdale Touchdown Club, 1962. Office: care CBS Sports 51 W 52d St New York NY 10019*

STRAND, CURT ROBERT, hotel exec.; b. Vienna, Austria, Nov. 13, 1920; s. Victor and Enit (Zerner) S.; came to U.S., 1937, naturalized, 1943; B.S., Cornell U., 1943; m. Fleur Lillian Emanuel, June 14, 1946; 1 dau., Karen. Supt. service Plaza, N.Y.C., 1947-49; asst. to v.p. Hilton

Hotels Corp., 1949-53; v.p. Hilton Internat. Co., N.Y.C., 1953-64, exec. v.p., 1964-67, pres., 1967—; sr. v.p., dir. Trans World Airlines, Inc.; vice chmn. Hilton Service Corp. Lectr., Cornell U. Sch. Hotel Adminstrn. Served with M.I., AUS, 1943-46. Mem. Cornell Soc. Hotelmen. Home: 340 E 64th St New York City NY 10021 Office: Waldorf Astoria Park Ave New York City NY 10022

STRAND, KAJ AAGE GUNNAR, astronomer; b. Hellerup, Denmark, Feb. 27, 1907; s. Viggo Peter and Constance (Malmgreen) S.; A.B., M.Sc., U. Copenhagen, 1931, Ph.D., 1938; m. Ulla Nilson, Mar. 11, 1943; 1 dau., Kristina Ragna Strand Miller; m. 2d, Emilie Rashevsky, June 10, 1949; 1 dau., Constance Vibeke. Came to U.S., 1938, naturalized, 1943. Geodesist, Royal Geodetic Inst., Copenhagen, Denmark, 1931-33; asst. to dir. Univ. Obs., U. Leiden (Netherlands), 1933-38; fellow Am. Scandinavian Found., 1938-39; research asso. in astronomy Swarthmore (Pa.) Coll., 1938-42; research astronomer, 1945-46; fellow Danish Rask Oersted Found., 1939-40, John Simon Guggenheim Found. (Europe), 1946; asso. prof., astronomer U. Chgo., 1946-47; prof. astronomy Northwestern U., dir. Dearborn Obs., 1947-58; dir. astrometry and astrophysics div. U.S. Naval Obs., 1958-63, sci. dir., 1963-77; research asso. U. Chgo., 1947-67; vis. prof. astronomy U. Copenhagen, 1954; cons., mem. adv. bd. on astronomy NSF, 1953-56; mem. adv. bd. on astronomy Office of Naval Research, 1954-57, chmn., 1956-57. Served from pvt. to capt. USAAF, 1942-45. Decorated knight cross 1st class Royal Order Dannebrog (Denmark); honor cross 1st class Literis et Artibus (Austria); recipient Distinguished Civilian Service award Dept. Navy, 1973. Mem. Am. Astron. Soc., Astron. Soc. Pacific, Internat. Astron. Union, Royal Danish Acad. Scis. and Letters, Sigma Xi. Club: Cosmos. Asso. editor Astron. Jour., 1954-58. Contbr. articles to Am., fgn. astron. jours. Home: 3202 Rowland Pl NW Washington DC 20008

STRAND, KENNETH T., economist; b. Yakima, Wash., June 30, 1931; s. A.O. and Margaret (Thomson) S.; B.A., Wash. State Coll., 1953; M.S., U. Wis., 1956, Ph.D., 1959; m. Elna K. Tomaske, Dec. 22, 1960. Asst. exec. sec. Hanford Contractors Negotiation Com., Richland, Wash., 1953-55; asst. prof. Wash. State U., 1959-60, Oberlin Coll., 1960-65 (on leave 1963-65); economist Orgn. Econ. Coop. and Devel., Paris, France, 1964-66; asso. prof. econs. and commerce Simon Fraser U., Burnaby, B.C., Can., 1966-68, prof., 1968—, acting pres., 1968-69, pres., 1969-74. Woodrow Wilson fellow, 1955-56; Ford Found. fellow, 1957-58. Mem. Indsl. Relations Research Assn., Am., Can. econs. assns., Internat. Indsl. Relations Assn. Author: Jurisdictional Disputes in Construction: The Causes, The Joint Board, and the NLRB, 1961. Home: Rural Route 1 Group Box 9C Bedwell Bay Rd Port Moody BC V3H 3C8 Canada Office: Dept Econs and Commerce Simon Fraser U Burnaby BC V5A 1S6 Canada

STRAND, MARK, poet; b. Summerside, P.E.I., Can., Apr. 11, 1934; s. Robert Joseph and Sonia (Apter) S.; B.A., Antioch, 1957; B.F.A., Yale, 1959; M.A., U. Iowa, 1962; m. Antonia Ratensky, Sept. 14, 1961 (div. June 1973); 1 dau., Jessica, m. 2d, Julia Rumsey Garretson, Mar. 15, 1976. Came to U.S., 1938. Instr. English, U. Iowa, 1962-65; asst. prof. Mt. Holyoke Coll., 1967; vis. prof. U. Wash., 1968; vis. lectr. Yale, 1969-70, U. Va., 1976, Calif. State U., Fresno, 1977, U. Calif., Irvine, 1979; adj. asso. prof. Columbia U., 1969-72; asso. prof. Bklyn. Coll., 1971-72; Bain-Swiggett lectr. Princeton, 1973; Hurst prof. poetry Brandeis U., 1974-75; author: Sleeping with One Eye Open, 1964; Reasons for Moving, 1968; Darker, 1970; New Poetry of Mexico, 1970; The Contemporary American Poets, 1969; 18 Poems for the Quechua, 1971; The Story of Our Lives, 1973; The Owl's Insomnia, 1973; The Sargentville Notebook, 1973; Another Republic, 1976; The Monument, 1978; The Late Hour, 1978. Recipient award Nat. Acad. Arts and Letters and Nat. Inst. Arts and Letters, 1975; Edgar Allen Poe prize, 1974. Fulbright scholar to Italy, 1960-61; Fulbright lectr. U. Brazil, 1965-66; Ingram Merrill fellow, 1966; Nat. Endowment for Arts fellow, 1967-68, 78-79; Rockefeller fellow, 1968-69; Guggenheim fellow, 1975. Office: care Harry Ford Atheneum Publishers 122 E 42d St New York NY 10017

STRANDJORD, PAUL EDPHIL, physician; b. Mpls., Apr. 5, 1931; s. Edphil Nels and RuBelle Pearl (Corneliusen) S.; B.A., U. Minn., 1951, M.A., 1952; M.D., Stanford U., 1959; m. Margaret Thomas, June 27, 1953; children—Thomas Paul, Scott Nels. Intern, U. Minn., Mpls., 1959-60, resident, 1960-63, dir. div. chemistry, dept. lab. medicine, 1963-69, asso. dir. clin. labs. dept. lab. medicine, 1967-69; asso. prof. lab. medicine U. Wash., 1969, prof., chmn. dept. lab. medicine, 1969—; cons. VA Hosps. Served with USN, 1952-55. Recipient Borden award Stanford U., 1959, Watson award U. Minn., 1962, Gerald T. Evans award Acad. Clin. Lab. Physicians and Scientists, 1976. Mem. Acad. Clin. Lab. Physicians and Scientists (pres.), Am. Assn. Clin. Chemistry, Am. Chem. Soc., Am. Fedn. Clin. Research. Club: Corinthian Yacht (Seattle). Author: (with E. S. Benson) Multiple Laboratory Screening, 1969; (with G. Schmer) Coagulation-Current Research and Clinical Applications, 1973. Home: 9410 NE Lake Washington Blvd Bellevue WA 98004 Office: Dept Lab Medicine U Wash SB-10 Seattle WA 98195

STRANDNESS, DONALD EUGENE, JR., surgeon; b. Bowman, N.D., Sept. 22, 1928; s. Donald Eugene and Merinda Clarine (Peterson) S.; B.A., Pacific Luth. U., 1950; M.D., U. Wash., 1954; m. Edith Victoria Olund, June 30, 1957; children—Erik, Tracy, Jill, Sandra. Rotating intern Phila. Gen. Hosp., 1954-55; resident U. Wash. Sch. Medicine Integrated Program, 1955-57, 59-62; research fellow Nat. Heart Inst., 1959-60; clin. investigator VA Hosp., Seattle, 1962-65, NIH Career Devel. awardee, 1965-68; pvt. practice medicine specializing in surgery, Seattle 1962—; instr. surgery Sch. Medicine, U. Wash., Seattle, 1962-63, asst. prof., 1963-66, asso. prof., 1966-70, prof. 1970—, head peripheral vascular div., 1971. Served with USAF, 1957-59. Fellow A.C.S.; mem. Internat. Soc. Thrombosis and Haemostasis, Am. Surg. Assn., N. Pacific Surg. Assn., Soc. Vascular Surgery, Soc. Univ. Surgeons, Internat. Cardiovascular Soc. Co-author: Hemodynamics for Surgery, 1975; Ultrasonic Techniques in Angiology, 1975. Editor: Collateral Circulation in Clinical Surgery, 1960; Peripheral Arterial Disease—At Physiologic Approach, 1969; asso. editor Jour. Vascular Surgery, 1979. Home: 105 Cedar Crest Ln Bellevue WA 98004 Office: 1959 NE Pacific St Seattle WA 98195

STRANDNESS, THEODORE BENSON, educator; b. St. Paul, Mar. 23, 1915; s. Theodore Andrew and Hilda Theresa (Benson) S.; B.A., Jamestown Coll., 1937; M.A., U. Minn., 1942; Ph.D., Mich. State U., 1951; m. Laura Thorleifson, Oct. 23, 1943; children—Jean Theresa, Linda Ellen, Patricia Lynn. Tchr. pub. schs., N.D., Minn., 1937-42; prof. English, Mich. State U., East Lansing, 1946—, chmn. dept. Am. thought and lang., 1962-67. Served to lt. (j.g.) USNR, 1942-45. Mem. AAUP, Coll. English Assn., Modern Lang. Assn. Nat. Council Tchrs. English, Am. Studies Assn. Author: The Experience of Writing, 1958; Curriculum Building in General Education, 1960; The American Identity, 1962; Language, Form and Idea, 1963; Samuel Sewell; A Puritan Portrait, 1967. Editor, U. Coll. Quar., 1955-61, 67-72. Home: 635 Sunset Ln East Lansing MI 48823

STRANG, CHARLES DANIEL, marine engine mfg. co. exec.; b. Bklyn., Apr. 12, 1921; s. Charles Daniel and Anna Lincoln (Endner) S.; B.M.E., Poly. Inst. Bklyn., 1943. Mem. mech. engring. staff Mass. Inst. Tech., 1947-51; v.p. engring., exec. v.p. Kiekhaefer Corp. div. Brunswick Corp., Fond du Lac, Wis., 1951-64; v.p. marine engring. Outboard Marine Corp., Waukegan, Ill., 1966-68, exec. v.p., 1968-74, pres., gen. mgr., 1974—, also dir. Bd. dirs. Poly. Inst. N.Y. Served with USAAF, 1944-47. Mem. Am. Power Boat Assn. (past pres.), Soc. Automotive Engrs., Union Internat. Motorboating (v.p.), Sigma Xi. Club: Waukegan Yacht. Contbr. research papers to sci. publs. Patentee engine design and marine propulsion equipment. Home: 1576 Tara Ln Lake Forest IL 60045 Office: 100 Seahorse Dr Waukegan IL 60085

STRANG, MARIAN BOUNDY, librarian; b. Gibson City, Ill., May 5, 1918; d. Ralph Edward and Edna Blackburn (Washburn) Boundy; B.A., U. Wis., 1940, M.L.S., 1941; m. Tom H. Strang, Sept. 27, 1943; children—Terry H., Bruce B., David R. Librarian, Richland Center, Wis., 1941-42; children's librarian Dearborn (Mich.) Pub. Library, 1942-43; asst. librarian Rapides Parish Library, Alexandria, La., 1943-45, Beloit (Wis.) Pub. Library, 1945-46, Fort Knox (Ky.) Library, 1952-54; librarian Sukiran Library, Okinawa, 1962-64; chief librarian Fort Leonard Wood, Mo., 1964-70; med. librarian U.S. Gen. Wood Army Hosp., Fort Leonard Wood, 1970—. Mem. ALA, Mo. Library Assn., Fed. Librarian's Assn., Med. Library Assn., Bus. and Profl. Women, Delta Zeta. Home: 1101 Hawthorne St Waynesville MO 65583 Office: Medical Library General Leonard Wood Army Hospital Fort Leonard Wood MO 65473

STRANG, RUTH HANCOCK, physician; b. Bridgeport, Conn., Mar. 11, 1923; s. Robert Hallock Wright and Ruth (Hancock) S.; B.A., Wellesley Coll., 1944, postgrad., 1944-45; M.D., N.Y. Med. Coll., 1949. Intern, Flower and Fifth Ave Hosp., N.Y.C., 1949-50, resident pediatrics, 1950-52; mem. faculty N.Y. Med. Coll., N.Y.C., 1952-57; fellow cardiology Babies Hosp., N.Y.C., 1956-57, Harriet Lane Cardiac Clinic, Johns Hopkins Hosp., Balt., 1957-59, Children's Hosp., Boston, 1959-62; mem. faculty U. Mich., Univ. Hosp., Ann Arbor, 1962—, prof. pediatrics, 1970—; dir. pediatrics Wayne County Gen. Hosp., Eloise, 1965—; mem. staff Univ. Hosp., Wayne County Gen. Hosp., Westland, Mich.; mem. med. adv. com. Wayne County chpt. Nat. Found., 1966—; chmn. med. adv. com. Nat. Cystic Fibrosis Research Found., Detroit, 1971-78; cons. cardiology Plymouth (Mich.) State Home and Tng. Sch., 1970—. Mem. citizen's adv. council to Juvenile Ct., Ann Arbor, 1968-76; mem. med. adv. bd. Ann Arbor Continuing Edn. Dept., 1968-77; mem. Diocesan Com. for World Relief, Detroit, 1970-72; trustee Episcopal Med. Chaplaincy, Ann Arbor, 1971—. Diplomate Am. Bd. Pediatrics. Mem. Am. Acad. Pediatrics, Am. Coll. Cardiology, Detroit Pediatric Soc., Mich., Washtenaw County med. socs., AMA, N.Y. Acad. Medicine, N.Y. Acad. Scis., Am., Mich. heart assns., Women's Research Club (membership sec. 1966-67), Ambulatory Pediatric Assn., Am. Assn. Child Care in Hosps., AAAS, Assn. Am. Med. Colls., Assn. Faculties of PNA/Practitioners Programs (pres. 1978—), Northside Assn. Ministries (pres. 1975-76, 79-80). Episcopalian (mem. bishop's com. 1966-69, sec. 1966-68, mission vestry 1973-76, 78— sr. warden 1975-76, 78—). Author: Clinical Aspects of Operable Heart Disease, 1968; contbr. numerous articles to profl. jours. Home: 4500 E Huron River Dr Ann Arbor MI 48104 Office: Dept Pediatrics Wayne County Gen Hosp Westland MI 48185

STRANG, WILLIAM GILBERT, mathematician; b. Chgo., Nov. 27, 1934; s. William Dollin and Mary Catherine (Finlay) S.; S.B., Mass. Inst. Tech., 1955; B.A. (Rhodes scholar), Oxford (Eng.) U., 1957; Ph.D. (NSF fellow), U. Calif., Los Angeles, 1959; m. Jillian Mary Shannon, July 26, 1958; children—David, John, Robert. Asst. prof. mathematics Mass. Inst. Tech., 1959-63, asso. prof., 1963-66, prof., 1966—. Recipient Chauvenet prize Math. Assn. Am., 1977; Sloan fellow, 1966-67. Club: Maugus (Wellesley, Mass.). Author: An Analysis of the Finite Element Method, 1973; Linear Algebra and Its Applications, 1976. Home: 7 Southgate Rd Wellesley MA 02181 Office: Room 2-240 Mass Inst Tech Cambridge MA 02139

STRANGE, JACK ROY, educator; b. Dallas, Feb. 13, 1921; s. Anthony L. and Katherine (Nabers) S.; Asso. Sci., Arlington State Coll., 1941; B.A., So. Meth. U., 1943, M.A., 1947; student Army Intelligence Japanese Lang. Sch., U. Mich., 1943-44; Ph.D., Johns Hopkins, 1950; m. Sallie Minter, Apr. 18, 1947; children—Richard, Audrey. Instr. psychology So. Meth. U., 1946-48, prof., 1959—, chmn. psychology dept., 1953-57, 59-62, 67—; instr. psychology Johns Hopkins, 1948-50; vis. prof. San Francisco State Coll., 1961. Served as Japanese interpretor AUS, 1944-46. Mem. Am., Southwestern, Tex. (pres. 1967), Dallas psychol. assns., Phi Beta Kappa, Sigma Xi, Psi Chi. Author: Abnormal Psychology: Understanding Behavior Disorders, 1965; Psychology: Understanding Human Behavior, rev. edit., 1973; Study Guide for Psychology: Etc., rev. edit., 1973; Readings in Physiological Psychology, 1966; Reading for Meaning, 1972. Home: 3614 Lindenwood St Dallas TX 75205

STRANGWAY, DAVID WILLIAM, geologist, univ. adminstr.; b. Can., June 7, 1934; B.A. in Physics and Geology, U. Toronto, 1956, M.A. in Physics, 1958, Ph.D., 1960. Sr. geophysicist Dominion Gulf Co. Ltd., Toronto, 1956; chief geophysicist Ventures Ltd., 1956-57, sr. geophysicist, summer 1958; research geophysicist Kennecott Copper Corp., Denver, 1960-61; asst. prof. U. Colo., Boulder, 1961-64, M.I.T., 1965-68; mem. faculty U. Toronto, 1968—, prof. physics, 1971—, chmn. dept. geology, 1972—, v.p., provost, 1980—; chief geophysics br. Johnson Space Center, NASA, Houston, 1970-72, chief physics br., 1972-73, acting chief planetary and earth sci. div., 1973; vis. prof. geology U. Houston, 1971-73; interim dir. Lunar Sci. Inst., Houston, 1973; vis. com. geol. scis. Brown U., 1974-76, Meml. U., St. John's, Nfld., 1974-79; v.p. Can. Geosci. Council, 1977; chmn. proposal evaluating team Univs. Space Research Assos., 1977-78, Ont. Geosci. Research Fund, 1978—; Pahlavi lectr. Govt. of Iran, 1978; cons. to govt. and industry, mem. numerous govt. and sci. adv. and investigative panels. Recipient NASA Exceptional Sci. Achievement medal, 1972; hon. mem. Can. Soc. Explotation Geophysicists. Fellow Royal Astron. Soc., Royal Soc. Can.; mem. Soc. Exploration Geophysicists (Virgil Kauffman Gold medal 1974), Geol. Assn. Can. (pres. 1978-79), Can. Geophys. Union (chmn. 1977-79), Am. Geophys. Union (sect. planetology sect. 1978—), European Assn. Exploration Geophysicists, Soc. Geomagnetism and Geoelectricity Japan, Can. Geosci. Council (pres. 1980), AAAS, Can. Exploration Geophysicists. Author numerous papers, reports in field. Address: Dept Geology Univ Toronto Toronto ON M5S 1A1 Canada

STRASBERG, LEE, theatrical dir.; b. Budzanow, Austria, Nov. 17, 1901; s. Baruch Meyer and Ida (Diner) S.; student Boleslavsky-Ouspenskaya, Am. Laboratory Theatre; m. Nora Z. Orecaun (dec.); m. 2d, Paula Miller, Mar. 16, 1934 (dec.); children—Susan, John; m. 3d, Anna Mizrahi, Jan. 7, 1968; children—Adam Lee Baruch, David Lee Isaac. Came to U.S., 1909, naturalized, 1936. Made first appearance as dir., actor Chrystie Street Settlement House N.Y.C., 1925; began profl. career, 1925; actor Processional, Theatre Guild, also Garrick Gaieties I, 1925; stage mgr. Garrick Gaieties II, 1926; asst. stage mgr. to Alfred Lunt-Lynne Fontanne, The Guardsman; actor in Red Rust, Green Grow the Lilacs; founder Group Theatre, N.Y.C., 1930, dir., 1930-37, including House of Connelly, Night Over Taos, Success Story, Men in White (Pulitzer prize winner), Gold Eagle Guy, Johnny Johnson; director of All The Living, also Clash by Night, Fifth Column; co-producer Country Girl, 1950; director The Big Knife, 1949, Skipper Next to God, 1948; artistic dir. Actors' studio, N.Y.C., 1948—, Actors' Studio Theater, Inc., 1962-66; artistic dir. The Silent Partner, Felix; dir. The Three Sisters, 1964; film debut in The Godfather, Part II, 1974; other film: And Justice for All, 1979, Going in Style, 1979, The Cassandra Crossing, Boardwalk; TV movie The Last Tenant; lectr. Harvard U., Brown U., Yale, Brandeis U., Northwestern U. Established Lee Strasberg Inst. of Theatre, N.Y.C. and Los Angeles, 1969. Recipient Kelcey Allen award, N.Y.C., 1961; Centennial Gold medal award for excellence in dramatic arts Boston Coll., 1963. Author: articles on the theatre. Contbr. Ency. Brit., Ency. Spettacolo, Ency. Funk and Wagnall, Ency. Americana. Address: Actors Studio Inc 432 W 44th St New York NY 10036*

STRASBERG, SUSAN, actress; b. N.Y.C., May 22, 1938; d. Lee and Paula (Miller) S.; m. Chris Jones, Sept. 25, 1965. Stage debut off-Broadway prodn. Maya, 1952; appeared in role of Juliet, TV prodn. Romeo and Juliet, 1953, role of dau. TV series The Marriage, 1953, also Omnibus prodn. Duchess and the Smugs, 1953, (with Helen Hayes) Dear Brutus, 1954; film debut Cobweb, 1954, also appeared motion pictures: Picnic, 1954; Adventures of a Young Man, 1962; High Bright Sun, 1965, Psych-Out, 1968, Roller Coaster, 1977, The Manitou, 1978, In Praise of Older Women, 1979; created role of Anne, Diary of Anne Frank, 1955-56; appeared in Stagestruck, 1957; Time Remembered, 1957-58; Shadow of a Gunman, 1958, The Lady of the Camillias, 1962; co-star with Franchot Tone, Time of Your Life, Brussels World's Fair; Kapo; Scream of Fear; The Brotherhood; appeared TV series Toma, 1973-74; numerous other TV appearances include: The Rockford Files, Night Gallery, Owen Marshall. Address: care Arco Embassy Pictures 6601 Romaine St Los Angeles CA 90038*

STRASBURGER, JOSEPH JULIUS, lawyer; b. Albia, Iowa, Aug. 29, 1913; s. Joseph and Elsa (Gottlieb) S.; A.B., Knox Coll., 1934; J.D., Harvard, 1937; m. Lucile C. Lapidus, Oct. 11, 1957; 1 dau., Susan A. (dec. Jan. 1970). Admitted to Ill. bar, 1937; asso. firm Moses, Kennedy, Stein & Bachrach, Chgo., 1938-39; asso. gen. counsel's office Middle West Service Co., Chgo., 1939-44; partner firm Altheimer & Gray, and predecessor firms, Chgo., 1944—. Sec., dir. Equitable Finance Corp., 1960—, Vitamins, Inc., 1956—. Chmn. lawyer's handbook editorial com. Jewish Fedn. Chgo., 1968-73; mem. adv. council Ill. Inst. Continuing Legal Edn., 1970-76, exec. com., 1971-76, chmn., 1974-75; lectr. probate and tax subjects. Mem. Knox Coll. devel. com., 1964-70; trustee Latin Sch. Chgo., 1978—. Fellow Am. Coll. Probate Counsel; mem. Am., Ill., Chgo. (chmn. probate practice com. 1960-61, chmn. continuing legal edn. com. 1968-69, chmn. legal edn. com. 1972-73) bar assns., Chgo. Estate Planning Council (pres. 1975-76), Phi Beta Kappa, Delta Sigma Rho, Beta Theta Pi. Jewish. Clubs: Tavern, Harvard (Chgo.). Contbr. articles to legal jours. Home: 1335 N Astor St Chicago IL 60610 Office: One IBM Plaza Chicago IL 60611

STRASFOGEL, IAN, opera dir.; b. N.Y.C., Apr. 5, 1940; s. Ignace and Alma (Lubin) S.; B.A., Harvard, 1961; m. Judith Hirsch Norell, Feb. 15, 1973. Adminstrv. asst. N.Y.C. Opera, 1962-64; chmn. opera dept. New Eng. Conservatory, Boston, 1968-72; artistic dir. Augusta (Ga.) Opera Co., 1967—; dir. music theatre project Tanglewood Festival, Lenox, Mass., 1971-73; gen. dir. Opera Soc. Washington, 1972-75; artistic cons. Phila. Lyric Opera, 1973; stage dir. N.Y.C. Opera Co., 1964—, Netherlands Opera Co., 1973—, Kansas City Lyric Theatre, 1970-71, Balt. Civic Opera, 1965-66; tchr. Juilliard Sch. Music, 1965-66; tchr. music Augusta Coll., 1967-68; dir. New Opera Theatre, Bklyn. Acad. Music, 1976—. Served with AUS, 1966-68. Recipient Henry Russell Shaw traveling fellowship, 1961-62; Ford Found. internship performing arts, 1962-64; Internat. Inst. Edn. grantee, 1965. Mem. Phi Beta Kappa. Editor: Ba-Ta-Clan, 1970. Home: 915 West End Ave New York City NY 10025

STRASFOGEL, IGNACE, condr.; b. Warsaw, Poland, July 17, 1909; s. Ludwig and Salomea (Goldberg) S.; student Staatliche Akademische Hochscule für Musik, Berlin; m. Alma Lubin, July 23, 1934; children—Ian, Andrew Leigh. Came to U.S., 1933, naturalized 1937. Accompanist, Joseph Szigeti, world tour, 1927-28, Carl Flesch, 1928-30; coach, condr. Opera of Municipal Theatre, Duesseldorf, Germany, 1929-30; asst. to chief condrs. Kleiber and Blech, State Opera, Berlin, 1930-31; composer, condr. incidental music Fourberies de Scapin, Berlin, 1930; Puenktchen und Anton, Deutsches Theater, Berlin, 1931; mus. dir. Europa A.G., Theater am Kurfuerstendamn, Berlin, 1932; ofcl. pianist N.Y. Philharmonic Symphony Orch., 1935-44, asst. condr., 1944-45; resigned, 1945; apptd. condr. Drs. Orchestral Soc., N.Y.C., 1946; guest condr. Nat. Symphony Orch., Washington, Phila., Buffalo, 1946, Group Theatre prodn., Johnny Johnson, 1936; accompanist, solo pianist with Lauritz Melchior, 1935-43; broadcast chamber music programs Perole and Stradivarius Quartets, Blaisdell Woodwind Emsemble, NBC network; piano soloist New Friends of Music Orch., Carnegie Hall, 1939; guest condr. Ballet Russe, Naumberg Concerts, summer 1945; mus. dir. Polonaise (musi-Am. tour), 1942, N.Y.C., 1945; condr. reading rehearsals new Am. works N.Y. Philharmonic Symphony, 1944-45; condr. N.Y. Philharmonic, Carnegie Hall, 1945, Lewisohn Stadium concerts, 1944, 45, in New Orleans, Chgo., Toronto, N.Y.C.; mus. dir. Brigadoon, coast-to-coast tour, 1949-50; asst. condr. Met. Opera Assn., 1951-60, asso. condr., 1960—; regular condr. Cin. Summer Opera Festival, 1959; condr. Met. Opera auditions of Met. Opera, 1951-55, Met. Opera auditions of air, 1954-57; condr. Met. Opera spring tour, 1957, 69—; asso. dir. Kathryn Long opera courses Met. Opera, until 1972, dir., 1972—; prin. condr. Opera du Rhin, Strasbourg, France, 1974—; debut Met. Opera conducting Eugene Onegin, 1959; condr. Met. Opera Summer Concerts, 1965, 68, 70, 71, L.I. (N.Y.) Festival, summer 1965, Vanessa; guest condr. Grand Theatre, Geneva, Switzerland, 1968; condr. Carmen, St. Paul, 1970, Augusta (Ga.) Opera Co., 1969-71, orchestral concerts Purbech Festival, Eng., 1969, 72; vis. lectr. New Sch. Social Research, N.Y.C., 1980—. Recipient State Mendelssohn prize for compostion, Germany, 1926. Made mus. preparations for Max Reinhardt's prodn. Tales of Hoffman, Grosses Schauspielhaus, Berlin, 1931, Offenbach's La Perichole, 1956-57. Contbr. articles to mags. Home: Apt 17S 30 Lincoln Plaza New York NY 10023 Office: care Joseph Taubman 159 W 53d St New York NY 10019

STRASMA, JOHN DRINAN, economist; b. Kankakee, Ill., Mar. 29, 1932; s. Roy and Charlotte Wilkins (Deselm) S.; A.B., DePauw U., 1953; A.M., Harvard U., 1958, Ph.D., 1969; m. Judith Feaster, Mar. 18, 1956; children—Anne, Patricia, Susan, Kenneth, Mary. Research asst. Fed. Res. Bank of Boston, 1958-59; prof. Econs. Inst., U. Chile, Santiago, 1959-72; economist UN Secretariat, 1964-65; advisor Ministry of Economy and Fin., Lima, Peru, 1970; prof. econs. and agrl. econs. U. Wis., Madison, 1972—; cons. in field. Vice-pres., dir. Latin Am. Scholarship Program of Am. Univs., 1970-74; chmn. fin. com. Wesley Found. of Wis., 1978—; public mem. Wis. Legis. Council Com. on Mining, 1975—. Served with U.S. Army, 1954-56. Danforth fellow, 1956-60. Recipient Outstanding Public Service award Wis. Environ. Decade, 1978. Mem. Am. Econs. Assn., Am. Agrl. Econs. Assn., Internat. Agrl. Econs. Assn., Latin Am. Studies Assn., Am. Inst. Mining Engrs., Soc. Internat. Devel., Chile Planning Assn. Democrat. Methodist. Author: State and Local Taxation of Manufacturing Industry, 1969. Office: 427 Lorch St U Wis Madison WI 53706

TRASSENBURG, ARNOLD ADOLPH, physicist, educator; b. ictoria, Minn., June 8, 1927; s. Otto A. and Minna T. (Techter) S.; S., Ill. Inst. Tech., 1951; M.S., Calif. Inst. Tech., 1953, Ph.D., 1955; . Louise Henderson, June 11, 1949 (dec. Jan. 1979); iildren—Jeffrey, Sandra Strassenburg Paquette, Gary. Asst. prof. iysics U. Kans., Lawrence, 1955-61, asso. prof. physics, 1961-66, of., 1966; staff physicist Commn. Coll. Physics, Rosemont, Pa., and nn Arbor, Mich., 1963-65; prof. physics State U. N.Y. at Stony rook, 1966—; dir. edn. and manpower div. Am. Inst. Physics, Y.C., 1966-72; exec. officer Am. Assn. Physics Tchrs., Stony Brook,)72—; head materials and instrn. devel. sect. higher edn. div. NSF, 'ashington, 1975—. Served with USNR, 1945-47. Recipient lillikan award Am. Assn. Physics Tchrs., 1972. Fellow A.A.A.S.; em. Nat. Sci. Tchrs. Assn. Author: (with others) An Approach to iysical Science, 1974. Office: Grad Physics Bldg SUNY Stony Brook Y 11794

TRASSER, GABOR, mgmt. cons.; b. Budapest, Hungary, May 22,)29; s. Rezso and Theresa (Seiler) S.; B.C.E., City Coll. N.Y., 1954; I.S., U. Buffalo, 1959; P.M.D., Harvard, 1968; m. Linda Casselman emble, Aug. 16, 1958 (div. 1976); children—Claire Margaret, ndrew John; m. 2d, Joke Verhoeff, Feb. 2, 1978. Research engr. Bell ircraft Co., Buffalo, 1956-61; project leader Boeing Airplane Co., eattle, 1961-62; dept. head Mitre Corp., Bedford, Mass., 'ashington, 1962-68; v.p. Urban Inst., Washington, 1968-69; tech. st. to pres.'s sci. adviser White House, 1969-71, exec. sec. pres.'s sci. id tech. policy panel, 1970-71; dir. planning Battelle Meml. Inst., olumbus, Ohio, 1971-73; pres. Strasser Assos., Inc., Washington,)73—. Served to 1st lt., C.E., AUS, 1954-55. Recipient 1st nat. ward Gravity Research Found., 1952. Mem. Am. Inst. Aeros. and stronautics, IEEE, AAAS (chmn. indsl. sci. sect. 1974), Sigma Xi. lubs: Cosmos, Harvard (Washington). Author, editor: Science and echnology Policies-Yesterday, Today, Tomorrow, 1973. Contbr. ticles to profl. jours. Office: Gabor Strasser 2616 Pine Knot Dr ienna VA 22180

TRASSER, MICHAEL WILLIAM, educator; b. Milw., Feb. 19,)20; s. Michael and Ida (Biebritz) S.; B.S., St. Louis U., 1947; M.A., . Toronto (Can.), 1949, Ph.D., 1963; m. Erica A. Klemens, Apr. 27,)46; children—Christopher, Michael J., Stephen, Mary Elizabeth, eter, Paul, Thomas. Asst. instr. philosophy St. Louis U., 1947-48; em. faculty Duquesne U., Pitts., 1951—, asso. prof., 1963—, prof., so. chmn. dept., 1966-70; co-dir. Seminar in Ecumenism, Duquesne . and Pitts. Theol. Sem., 1967-68. Treas., Greater Pitts. Fair Housing iovement, 1965-67; faculty recruiter Tutorial Program for isadvantaged Students, Pitts., 1968. Served with AUS, 1942-46. em. Western Pa. Philos. Soc. (past pres.), Am., Am. Catholic philos. ssns., Soc. Ancient Greek Philosophy, Am. Assn. U. Profs. (past p.). Home: 3303 Mt Royal Blvd Glenshaw PA 15116

TRASSER, WILLIAM CARL, JR., educator; b. Washington, Feb. 1930; s. William Carl and Minnie Elizabeth (Saxton) S.; B.A., U. d., 1952, M.A., 1954, Ph.D., 1961; Carnegie postdoctoral fellow in ill. adminstrn., U. Mich., 1961-62; m. Jeanne Carol Peake, Sept. 17,)54 (div.); children—Sheryl Lynn, Keith Edward, Robert Carl; m. l, Jane Ann Gunn, Nov. 25, 1978. Asst. dean, asst. prof. Sch. Edn., ate U. N.Y. at Buffalo, 1962-64; specialist ednl. adminstrn. U.S. ffice Edn., Washington, 1964-65; asst. dir. profl. personnel ontgomery County (Md.) Pub. Schs., 1965-66; acting pres., exec. ean Montgomery Community Coll., Rockville, Md., 1966-67, pres.,)67-79, prof., 1978—; vis. scholar U. Calif., Berkeley, 1977-79; vice es. Md. Council Community Coll. Presidents, 1971-72, 75-77; pres., p. Jr. Coll. Council Middle Atlantic States, 1969-72; founder ouncil Chief Exec. Adminstrs., 1973-75; mem. exec. com. Pres.'s cad., 1975-77; mem. Gov.'s Adv. Council, Md. Higher Edn. acilities, 1977-79. Del. UNESCO Conf. on Africa, 1961; participant th Anniversary Conf. Fgn. Policy Assn. U.S., 1968; mem. Congl. iternship Adv. Com., 1969-78; chmn. Montgomery County ommunity White Ho. Conf. on Aging, 1971; cons. Middle States ssn. Colls. and Secondary Schs., 1975—. Served with AUS, 1954-55. ecipient Gov. Md. Cert. Disting. Citizenship, 1979. Danforth ound. study grantee 1972, Ford Found. grantee, 1974-75. Mem. Am. ssn. Jr. Colls. (chmn. nat. comm. on instrn. 1969-71, mem. nat. ssembly 1973), AAUP, Am. Assn. Higher Edn., Montgomery ounty C. of C. (Disting. Service award 1979), Phi Kappa Phi, micron Delta Kappa, Pi Delta Epsilon, Phi Eta Sigma, Phi Delta appa. Unitarian-Universalist. Democrat. Rotarian. Contbr. poetry id articles to jours. Office: Montgomery College Germantown MD)767. *Aspire to do the undone, with empathy, compassion, vitality, id wisdom; and take care to reflect on whether what has been done as been done justly.*

TRASSMEYER, MARY, newspaper reporter; b. Cleve., Aug. 5,)29; d. Frederick H. and Katherine (Mullally) Strassmeyer; A.B., otre Dame Coll., 1951; postgrad. Toledo U., 1952, Cleve. Marshall oll. Law, Cleve. State U., 1976-80. Reporter, Cleve. News, 1956-60; ontbr. Cleve. Plain Dealer, 1957-60, feature writer, 1960-65, beauty litor, 1963-65, travel writer, 1963—, society editor, 1965—;)-creator syndicated cartoon Sneakers; columnist, 1977-80. Mem. oc. Am. Social Scribes (founder, 1st pres.), Notre Dame Coll. lumnae Assn., Women in Communications. Club: Press (Cleve.). uthor: Coco: The Special Delivery Dog, 1979. Home: 2059 roadview Rd Cleveland OH 44109 Office: 1801 Superior Ave leveland OH 44114

TRATAS, TERESA, soprano; b. Toronto, Ont., Can., May 26, 1939; Emanuel and Argero (Teregis) S., student Royal Conservatory lusic with Irene Jessner, 1955-59; student U. Toronto, 1959. Radio ebut, 1953, TV debut, 1954, operatic debut as Mimi in La Bohème, anadian Opera Co., 1958; Am. debut with Houston Symphony rch., 1958; winner Met. Opera auditions, 1959; Met. Opera debut s Poussette in Manon, 1959; appeared as Mimi at Covent ardens-Royal Opera House, London, 1961; appeared with mphony orchs. in Houston, Toronto, Montreal, Ottawa, Detroit; atured role in motion picture The Canadians, 1960; title role world remiere opera Nausica, Herod Atticus Theatre, Athens, Greece,)61; appeared as Madame Butterfly, Vancouver Internat. Festival,)60; operatic debut in Atlantida, La Scala Opera, 1962; starred in m prodns. of Otello, Salome, Eugene Onegin, La Rondine, The artered Bride. Office: Met Opera Co 186 S Broadway New York NY)023*

TRATER, HENRY (MIKE), artist; b. Louisville, Jan. 21, 1896; s. harles Godfrey and Adeline (Helme) S.; student Princeton, 1916-17, cad. Julien, Paris, 1919, Art Students League, 1919, Pa. Acad. Fine rts, 1920, Royal Acad., Spain, 1921, Edouard Vuillard, Paris, 1922; Margaret Y. Conner, June 26, 1920 (div. 1942); children—David, artha, Michael Henry, Nicholas Appleby; m. 2d, Janet M. Orr, June 1942 (div. 1946); 1 son, Jeremy Meacham; m. 3d, Lois A. iompson, Aug. 5, 1951 (div. 1967); children—Pompe Ann, William Matthew Helme. One-man shows include Montross Gallery, Y.C., 1931, 32, 34, 36, 38, 40, Speed Mus., Louisville, 1936, 64, rtland (Me.) Mus., 1938, Bowdoin Coll., 1940, 50, Horne Gallery, ston, 1939, Abbot Acad., 1940, Gov. Dummer Acad., 1940, Ind. 1951, Louisville Arts Club, 1952, 62, Art Mus., Princeton, 1951, Frank Rehn Gallery, N.Y.C., 1961, 63, 65, 68, 70, Thieme llery, Palm Beach, Fla., 1961, 62, 64, U. Louisville, 1951, Norton Gallery, Palm Beach, Fla., 1962, 67, Mus. Art of Ogunguit, 1963, 74, 77, Lawrenceville (N.J.) Sch., 1965, Swope Gallery, Indpls., 1964, Butler Inst. Am. Art, 1966, First Nat. Bank, Palm Beach, 1967, 69, 71, 73, 75, Heath Gallery, Atlanta, 1967, Ogunquit (Maine) Gallery, 1970, Lighthouse Gallery, Fla., 1971, Allentown (Pa.) Art Mus., 1971, Art Mus. Palm Beaches, 1977, Gallery Gemini, Palm Beach, 1977, Ariz. State U., 1979; exhibited in group shows including Salon d'Automne, Paris, 1922, also 150 others; represented in public and pvt. collections museums, univs. and schs. in U.S., also Am. embassy, London; exhibiting mem. Whitney Studio Club, 1926; supervising architect Ogunquit Mus. Art, 1950-51, trustee, 1952-73, dir., 1960—; numerous appearances radio and TV. Trustee Ogunquit Pub. Library; trustee York (Maine) Hosp., 1938-73, pres., 1958-72. Recipient 2d prize Golden Gate Exhbn., 1939; citation for achievements in the arts and humanities Gov. of Maine, 1975. Episcopalian. Clubs: Princeton; Sailfish of Fla.; York Harbor Reading Room; Everglades; Players (N.Y.C.). Subject documentary film, 1975, also books. Home: Shore Rd Ogunquit ME 03907. *Faced with the choice of a lifetime career as an artist or as a writer, 60 years ago I made the never-regretted decision that I would prefer to spend my life with a lovely woman in front of me, rather than a typewriter.*

STRATON, JOHN CHARLES, JR., investment banker; b. Warwick, N.Y., Apr. 18, 1932; s. John Charles and Helen (Sanford) S.; diploma Peddie Sch., 1950; B.A., U. Va., 1954; m. Sally M. Strawhand (div. Mar. 1970); children—John Charles III, Sara; m. 2d, Marion S. Holder, Feb. 18, 1974; 1 child, Ashley Holder Straton. With Jas. H. Oliphant and Co., N.Y.C., 1956—, gen. partner, 1962—, 1st v.p., 1972-75; account exec. Spencer Trask & Co., Inc., N.Y.C., 1975-77; v.p. Hornblower, Weeks, Noyes & Trask, N.Y.C., 1977-78, Loeb Rhoades, Hornblower & Co., 1978-79, Shearson Loeb Rhoades, 1979—. Assessor, Village Tuxedo Park, 1963-70. Trustee, Emergency Shelter, 1975—. Served with AUS, 1954-56. Mem. U. Va. Alumni Assn. N.Y. (pres. 1973—), Mil. Order Fgn. Wars, Pilgrims of U.S., Sigma Phi Epsilon. Clubs: Tuxedo Park (N.Y.); Farmington Country (Charlottesville, Va.). Home: Ledge Rd Tuxedo Park NY 10987 Office: 299 Park Ave New York NY 10017

STRATTNER, LAWRENCE WENZ, JR., life ins. co. exec.; b. Mechanicville, N.Y., Nov. 28, 1917; s. Lawrence Walderman and Marie (Wenz) S.; A.B., State U. N.Y. at Albany, 1939, A.M., 1941; m. Ruth Marie Dillon, Aug. 28, 1941; children—Lawrence J., Gregory P., Timothy J., Martha M., Anthony O., Maria A. High sch. tchr., Akron, N.Y., 1940-44; with Reader's Digest, 1946-48; with Prudential Life Ins. Co., 1948-55; with Berkshire Life Ins. Co., Pittsfield, Mass., 1955—, sr. v.p., 1963-67, pres., 1967—, also dir.; Bd. dirs. Mass. Taxpayers Found., 1971—; bd. overseers Boston Symphony Orch., 1979—; chmn. Pittsfield United Fund campaign, 1964. Bd. govs. Berkshire Med. Center, 1967—; bd. dirs. Albany Med. Coll. Served with USNR, 1944-46. Mem. Am. Soc. C.L.U.'s, State U. N.Y. at Albany Alumni Assn. (dir.), Central Berkshire C. of C. (dir.). Roman Catholic. Office: 700 South St Pittsfield MA 01201

STRATTON, HAROLD DUANE, utilities exec.; b. Cookson, Okla., Jan. 12, 1924; s. George Congrave and Ellen Josephine (Ballew) S.; student Okla. State U., 1940-42, George Washington U., 1942; LL.B., U. Okla., 1948; m. Thelma Marie Waggoner, Jan. 23, 1947; children—Harold Duane Jr., Linda Kay. Admitted to Okla. bar, 1948; pvt. practice in Muskogee, 1948-56; atty. Okla. Gas & Electric Co., Oklahoma City, 1956—, sr. v.p. law, 1978—. Served to capt. USAAF, 1943-46. Decorated Air medal, Bronze Star medal. Mem. Am., Okla., Oklahoma County bar assns., Phi Delta Phi. Kiwanian. Clubs: Whitehall, Quail Creek Golf and Country. Home: 11800 Camelot Dr Oklahoma City OK 73120 Office: 321 N Harvey St Oklahoma City OK 73102

STRATTON, JAMES DAVID, physician; b. Cowansville, Pa., Jan. 22, 1913; s. James McGowan and Anna (Aikman) S.; A.B., W.Va. U., 1934, B.S., 1935; M.D., U. Chgo., 1937; m. Hila Edsall Richards, Oct. 14, 1939; children—Anne (Mrs. E. Lloyd Gardiner), Alice (Mrs. Hill B. Wellford, Jr.), James Willard, Robert David. Intern, West Pa. Hosp., Pitts., 1937-38; eye residency Ill. Eye and Ear Hosp., 1945-47; gen practice medicine, Brackenridge, Pa., 1938-40; practice ophthalmology, Charlotte, N.C., 1947—; mem. staff Charlotte Meml., Presbyn., Mercy hosps. Past pres. Charlotte Nature Mus. Served to maj. M.C., AUS, 1940-46; ETO. Fellow Am. Acad. Ophthalmology and Otolaryngology; mem. AMA, Med. Soc. N.C., Mecklenburg County Med. Soc. (pres. 1974-75), N.C. Soc. Ophthalmology (past sec., pres.), Internat. Assn. Secs. Ophthal. and Otolaryng. Socs. (pres. 1968). Republican. Presbyterian (deacon 1952-58, elder 1960-65, 68-73, 76—). Lion. Club: Myers Park (Charlotte). Home 2165 Sharon Ln Charlotte NC 28211 Office: 3535 Randolph Rd Charlotte NC 28211

STRATTON, JULIUS ADAMS, educator; b. Seattle, May 18, 1901; s. Julius A. and Laura (Adams) S.; student U. Wash., 1919-20; S.B., Mass. Inst. Tech., 1923, S.M., 1926; Sc.D., Eidgenossische Technische Hoschshule, Zurich, 1928; D.Eng. (hon.), N.Y. U., 1955; Sc.D. (hon.), St. Francis Xavier, 1957, Coll. William and Mary, 1964, Carnegie Inst. Tech., 1965, U. Leeds (Eng.), 1967, Heriot-Watt U., Edinburgh, Scotland, 1971, Cambridge (Eng.) U., 1972; LL.D., Northeastern U., 1957, Union Coll., 1958, Harvard, 1959, Brandeis U., 1959, Carleton Coll., 1960, U. Notre Dame, 1961, Johns Hopkins, 1962; L.H.D., Hebrew Union Coll., 1962, Oklahoma City U., 1963, Jewish Theol. Sem. Am., 1965; m. Catherine N. Coffman, June 14, 1935; children—Catherine N., Ann Cary, Laura A. Research asso. in communications Mass. Inst. Tech., 1924-26, asst. prof. elec. engring., 1928-31, mem. staff radiation lab., 1940-45, dir. research, lab. electronics, 1945-49, asst. prof. physics, 1931-35, asso. prof. physics, 1935-41, prof., 1941-51, provost, 1949-56, v.p., 1951-56, chancellor, 1956-59, acting pres., 1957-59, pres., 1959-66, emeritus, 1966—; chmn. bd. Ford Found., 1966-71. Expert cons. Sec. War, 1942-46; chmn. Commn. on Marine Sci., Engring. and Resources, 1967-69; mem. Nat. Adv. Com. on Oceans and Atmosphere, 1971-73. Life mem. corp. Mass. Inst. Tech.; life trustee Boston Mus. Sci. Decorated officer French Legion Honor; comdr. Order of Boyaca (Colombia); knight comdr. Order of Merit (Germany); recipient medal for merit, 1946; medal of honor Am. Inst. Radio Engrs., 1957; Faraday medal Inst. Elec. Engrs. (London); hon. fellow Manchester (Eng.) Coll. Sci. and Tech., 1963. Fellow Am. Acad. Arts and Scis., Am. Philos. Soc., Am. Phys. Soc.; mem. IEEE, Nat. Acad. Scis. (v.p. 1961-65), Council Fgn. Relations, Nat. Acad. Engring., Sigma Xi, Eta Kappa Nu, Tau Beta Pi, Zeta Psi. Clubs: Century Assn., University (N.Y.C.); St. Botolph (Boston). Home: 100 Memorial Dr Cambridge MA 02142 Office: Mass Inst Tech Cambridge MA 02139

STRATTON, SAMUEL STUDDIFORD, congressman; b. Yonkers, N.Y., Sept. 27, 1916; s. Paul and Ethel Irene (Russell) S.; grad. Blair Acad., Blairstown, N.J., 1933; A.B., U. Rochester, 1937; M.A., Harvard, 1940; LL.D., Hartwick Coll., 1967, Coll. St. Rose, 1974, Union Coll., 1978; m. Joan H. Wolfe, Dec. 17, 1947; children—Lisa (Mrs. Martin Gonzalez), Debra, Kevin, Kim, Brian. Exec. sec. to Mass. congressman, 1941-42; dep. sec.-gen. Far Eastern Commn., 1946-48; lectr. Union Coll., Schenectady, Rensselaer Poly. Inst., 1948-54; TV and radio news commentator, Schenectady, 1950-56; mem. 86-87th Congresses from 32d Dist. N.Y., 88th-91st Congresses from 35th Dist. N.Y., 92d Congress from 29th Dist. N.Y., 93d-96th Congresses from 28th Dist., mem. Com. Armed Services, chmn. Subcom. on Investigations. Hon. trustee U. Rochester. Councilman, Schenectady, 1950-56, mayor, 1956-59. Served from ensign to capt. USNR, World War II, Korea; capt. Res. ret. Mem. Res. Officers Assn., Am. Legion, V.F.W., Amvets, Navy League, Phi Beta Kappa, Psi Upsilon. Democrat. Mason. Home: 244 Guy Park Ave Amsterdam NY 12010 Office: Rayburn House Office Bldg Washington DC 20515

STRATTON, THOMAS OLIVER, investment banker; b. Los Angeles, Feb. 14, 1930; s. Oliver Clarke and Ethel (Savage) S.; student Taft Sch., 1946-48, Stanford, 1948-50; B.S., U. Calif. at Los Angeles, 1956; M.B.A., Boston U., 1960; m. Carol Joyce Wilson, Feb. 21, 1953; children—Brentley Clarke, James Morris, Thomas Oliver. With Security First Nat. Bank, Los Angeles, 1955-56; security analyst New Eng. Mut. Life Ins. Co., Boston, 1956-60; exec. v.p., dir. Bankers Leasing Corp., Boston, 1960-64; treas. Montgomery Ward & Co., Chgo., 1964-67; pres. Investco Assoc., Inc., 1967-75, Monterey Capital, Inc., 1975—; dir. Charter Group, Inc., McFarland Mgmt. Co. Trustee Hadley Sch. for Blind. Served with AUS, 1952-55. Republican. Congregationalist. Clubs: University, Economic (Chgo.); Indian Hill (Winnetka), World Trade (San Francisco). Home: PO Box 3713 Carmel by the Sea CA 93921 Office: PO Box 7370 Carmel by the Sea CA 93921

STRATTON, WALTER LOVE, lawyer; b. Greenwich, Conn., Sept. 21, 1926; s. John McKee and June (Love) S.; student Williams Coll., 1943; A.B., Yale U., 1948; LL.B., Harvard U., 1951; m. Helen Marie Elting, Sept. 11, 1954; children—John, Michael, Peter, Lucinda. Admitted to N.Y. bar, 1952; asso. firm Casey, Lane & Mittendorf, N.Y.C., 1951-53; asso. firm. Donovan, Leisure, Newton & Irvine, N.Y.C., 1956-63, partner, 1963—; asst. U.S. atty. So. Dist. N.Y., N.Y.C., 1953-56. Served with USNR, 1945-46. Fellow Am. Coll. Trial Lawyers; mem. N.Y. County Lawyers Assn., Am., N.Y. bar assns. Clubs: Round Hill (Greenwich, Conn.); Fairfield County Hunt (Westport, Conn.). Home: Round Hill Rd Greenwich CT 06830 Office: 30 Rockefeller Plaza New York NY 10020

STRAUB, CARL BENTON, coll. dean; b. Carlisle, Pa., Apr. 17, 1936; s. Ellwood Benjamin Franklin and Olivia Louise (Baum) S.; B.A., Colgate U., 1958; S.T.B., Harvard, 1961, Ph.D., 1971. Teaching fellow Harvard, Cambridge, Mass., 1963-65; instr. religion and culture Bates Coll., Lewiston, Maine, 1965-69, asst. prof., 1970-74, asst. dean faculty, 1970-74, acting dean faculty, 1974-75, asso. prof., dean faculty, 1975—. Chmn. bd. dirs. Maine Lyceum; trustee Maine Audubon Soc. Mem. Colgate U. Nat. Council, AAUP, Am. Acad. Religion, Am. Soc. Christian Ethics, ACLU, Nat. Resources Council Maine, Phi Kappa Tau, Pi Delta Epsilon. Home: 163 Wood St Lewiston ME 04240 Office: Lane Hall Bates College Lewiston ME 04240

STRAUB, CHESTER JOHN, lawyer; b. Bklyn., Mar. 12, 1937; s. Chester and Ann (Majewski) S.; A.B., St. Peter's Coll., 1958; LL.D., U. Va., 1961; m. Patricia Morrissey, Aug. 22, 1959; children—Chester, Michael, Christopher, Robert. Admitted to N.Y. State bar, 1962, U.S. Supreme Ct. bar, 1978; asso. firm Willkie, Farr & Gallagher, N.Y.C., 1963-71, partner, 1971—. Mem. N.Y. State Assembly, 1967-72, N.Y. State Senate, 1973-75; mem. Democratic Nat. Com., 1976—; vice chmn. N.Y.C. Dem. Com., 1974—; co-chmn. platform com. N.Y. State Dem. Com., 1975-76; mem. Cardinal's com. of Laity for Cath. Charities N.Y., 1974—; vice chmn. Bklyn. Community Dist. Planning Bd.; chmn. fin. com. Eastern dist. com. Boy Scouts Am.; bd. dirs. Bklyn. Legal Services Corp.; trustee N.Y. League for Histadrut, Greenpoint YMCA. Served with U.S. Army, 1961-63. Mem. Am. Bar Assn., N.Y. State Bar Assn., Assn. Bar City N.Y., Greenpoint-Williamsburg Health Council, Pulaski Bus. and Profl. Men's Assn., Kosciuszko Found., Assn. Sons of Poland. Office: Willkie Farr and Gallagher 1 Citicorp Center 153 E 53d St New York NY 10022

STRAUB, PETER THORNTON, lawyer; b. St. Louis, Mar. 27, 1939; s. Ralph H. and Mary Louise (Thornton) S.; A.B., Washington and Lee U., 1961, J.D., 1964; m. Wendy B. Cubbage, Dec. 29, 1964; children—Karl Thornton, Philip Hamilton, Ellen Elizabeth. Admitted to Mo. bar, 1964, Va. Supreme Ct. Appeals bar, 1964, Mo. Supreme Ct. bar, 1964, U.S. Dist. Ct. Eastern Dist. Mo. bar, 1967, U.S. Circuit Ct. Appeals, 8th Circuit bar, 1969, U.S. Circuit Ct. Appeals, D.C. Circuit bar, 1971, Ct. Mil. Appeals bar, 1970, Tax Ct. U.S. bar, 1971, U.S. Supreme Ct. bar, 1970; mem. firm Evans & Dixon, St. Louis, 1966-68; asst. pub. defender, St. Louis, 1968-69; asst. U.S. atty., St. Louis, 1969-71; trial atty. internal security div. Dept. Justice, Washington, 1971-72, atty.-adviser office of dep. atty. gen., 1972-73, dir. office criminal justice, 1974; counsel com. on judiciary U.S. Ho. of Reps., Washington, 1973-74; gen. counsel SSS, Washington, 1974-76; individual practice law, 1976—. Served to lt. M.P., AUS, 1964-66. Recipient certificate of award Dept. Justice, 1970; certificate of appreciation Law Enforcement Assistance Adminstrn., Dept. Justice, 1974. Mem. Am., Fed., Va., St. Louis County, St. Louis Met. bar assns., Am. Judicature Soc., Am. Trial Lawyers Assn. Republican. Congregationalist. Club: Mo. Athletic. Home: 3207 Cameron Mills Rd Alexandria VA 22302 Office: Parc East 103 1225 Martha Custis Dr Alexandria VA 22302

STRAUBEL, JAMES HENDERSON, assn. exec.; b. Green Bay, Wis., Apr. 11, 1915; s. Otto C. and Alice (Henderson) S.; A.B., Lawrence U., 1937; m. Bette Lee, May 9, 1942; 1 dau., Gay; m. 2d, Arlene Hanon, Sept. 9, 1955; children—Jean, Judi. Reporter, Green Bay Press Gazette, 1937-40, Milw. Jour., 1940; mag. editor Am. Aviation mag., 1941; editor, pub. dir. Air Force mag., 1947-57, pub., 1957-78; exec. dir. Air Force Assn., Washington 1958—, Aerospace Edn. Found., 1954—. Mem. nat. bd. govs. USO, 1976. Served with USAAF, 1941-46. Mem. Phi Delta Theta. Editor: Official Guide to AAF, 1944; Air Force Diary, 1947. Home: 12200 Fairfax Station Rd Fairfax Station VA 22039 Office: 1750 Pennsylvania Ave NW Washington DC 20006

STRAUBINGER, O. PAUL, educator; b. Vienna, Austria, Oct. 16, 1910; s. Ernst and Henrietta (Kopetzky) S.; Absolutorium, U. Vienna, 1934; postgrad. (Internat Exchange fellow) U. Calif. at Berkeley, 1934-35; Ph.D. (Univ. fellow), U. Calif. at Los Angeles, 1946; m. Jean Kasper, Jan. 26, 1939; children—Susan (Mrs. Michael S. Adams), Ann (Mrs. William DeWolfe). Came to U.S. 1934, naturalized, 1941. Instr. German, classical langs. Occidental Coll., 1935-41, instr. math Navy V-12 program, 1943-45; lectr. U. Calif. at Los Angeles, 1945-46; instr. German, U. Calif. at Berkeley, 1946, asst. prof., 1946-53; asst. prof. German, U. Calif. at Riverside, 1953-54, asso. prof., 1954-61, prof., 1961—, vice chmn. div. humanities, 1961-63, chmn. dept. fgn. langs., 1963-65, chmn. dept German and Russian, 1969. Mem. Am. Assn. Tchrs. German, Am. Name Soc., Grillparzer Gesellschaft (Vienna), Phi Beta Kappa, Delta Phi Alpha, Sigma Alpha Epsilon. Author: Elementary German Science Reader, rev. editor, 1960. Contbr. articles on 19th Century German lit., comparative lit., onomastics to profl. jours. Home: 3580 Castle Reagh Pl Riverside CA 92506

STRAUCH, CHARLES SCUREMAN, mfg. co. exec.; b. Ardmore, Pa., May 21, 1935; s. Charles and Arvilla S.; B.S., Lehigh U., 1957; m. Margaret Nan Young, Sept. 20, 1957; children—Wendi, Charles

Scureman, Laura, Amy, Katherine. With Union Carbide Co., 1957-64, mgr. comml. research, new enterprises dept., chems. div., South Charleston, W.Va., 1962-63, gen. mgr. Durox ops., N.Y.C., 1963-64; asst. to pres. First Nat. Bank of St. Paul, 1964-66; cons. mgmt., St. Paul, 1966-67; with Gould, Inc., 1967-79, group v.p. instrument and controls group, Rolling Meadows, Ill., 1975-77, exec. v.p., 1977-79; exec. v.p. Memorex Corp., Santa Clara, Calif., 1979—; corp. dir. Buckbee Mears Co.; mem. bus. adv. council for Calif. Dist. 12. Served with U.S. Army, 1957-65. Office: Memorex Corp San Tomas at Central Expy Santa Clara CA 95052

STRAUCH, KARL, educator, physicist; b. Germany, Oct. 4, 1922; s. Georg and Carola (Bock) S.; came to U.S., 1939, naturalized, 1944; A.B. in Chemistry and Physics, U. Calif. at Berkeley, 1943, Ph.D. in Physics, 1950; m. Maria Gerson, June 10, 1951; children—Roger A., Hans D. Jr. fellow Soc. Fellows, Harvard, 1950-53; faculty Harvard, 1953—, prof. physics, 1962—, dir. Cambridge Electron Accelerator, 1967-74, George Vasmer Leverett prof. physics, 1976—. Served with USNR, 1944-46. Mem. Am. Phys. Soc., Am. Assn. Physics Tchrs., Am. Acad. Arts and Scis., Phi Beta Kappa, Sigma Xi. Contbr. articles to profl. jours. Research in high energy physics. Home: 81 Pleasant St Lexington MA 02173 Office: Physics Dept Harvard Cambridge MA 02138

STRAUS, DONALD BLUN, assn. exec.; b. Middletown, N.J., June 28, 1916; s. Percy S. and Edith (Abraham) S.; A.B., Harvard, 1938, M.B.A., 1940; m. Elizabeth Allen, Sept. 7, 1940; children—David Allen, Robert Beckwith, Sara Elizabeth. Vice pres. Mgmt.-Employee Relations, Inc., consultants, 1946-53; vice chmn. nat. rev. com. WSB, 1952; exec. dir. labor relations panel AEC, 1948-53; v.p. Health Ins. Plan of Greater N.Y., 1953-61; pres. Am. Arbitration Assn., 1963-72, pres. research inst., 1972—. Mem. N.Y. State Bd. Mediation, 1956-59. Chmn. bd. Planned Parenthood Fedn. Am., 1962-65, chmn. exec. com., 1965-68; mem. Western Hemisphere exec. com. Internat. Planned Parenthood, 1975—, treas., 1978—; mem. overseers vis. com. Harvard U. Press, 1941-72, Harvard Sch. Pub. Health, 1965-72, Harvard Grad. Sch. Pub. Adminstrn., 1956-62; pres. Ednl. Alliance, settlement house, 1954-58 mem. Commn. Ednl. Issues, 1975-78, Com. on profl. liability Am. Bar Assn., 1975—. Bd. dirs. State Communities Aid Assn., Inst. for Mediation and Conflict Resolution, Internat. Council Comml. Arbitration, Projects for Population Action, Fund for Peace; trustee Carnegie Endowment for Internat. Peace, Inst. Advanced Study, Princeton, Coll. of Atlantic, Milton (Mass.) Acad., 1962-75. Recipient Stanley Isaacs award, 1965; Sylvan Gotshal award, 1972; Rockefeller Found. fellow, 1974. Fellow Am. Pub. Health Assn.; mem. Soc. Profls. in Dispute Resolution (charter), Internat. C. of C. (vice chmn. commn. internat. arbitration 1970-78), Council Fgn. Relations. Club: Century Assn. Home: 66 E 79th St New York NY 10021 Office: 140 W 51st St New York NY 10020

STRAUS, ELLEN SULZBERGER, radio sta. exec.; b. N.Y.C., Mar. 11, 1925; d. David Hays and Louise (Blumenthal) S.; B.A., Smith Coll., 1945; m. R. Peter Straus, Feb. 6, 1950; children—Diane Straus Tucker, Katherine, Jeanne, Eric. Program sec. N.Y.C. LWV, 1945-48; asst. dir. public info. U.S. AEC, 1948-49; asst. mgr. Herbert Lehamn for Senate, 1949; fgn. corr. No. N.Y. newspapers, 1950-55; editor McCall's mag., 1972-74; dir. spl. projects Sta. WMCA, N.Y.C., 1973-76, v.p., 1976-77, pres. and gen. mgr., 1977—; co-pub. Cranford (N.J.) Citizen & Chronicle, 1976-77. Founder, Vol. Profl., Inc., N.Y.C., 1970; pres., chairperson Nat. Call for Action, Inc., 1969-75; aux. police person Mounted, Central Park precinct, N.Y.C., 1974-77; mem. nat. steering com. Election of Carter-Mondale, 1976; co-chairperson Women United for N.Y., 1976—. Recipient Nat. Council of Women Woman of Conscience award, 1970; Am. Jewish Congress Louise Waterman Wise award, 1971; Smith Coll. medal of honor, 1971; Nat. Council Jewish Women Hannah G. Solomon award, 1972; named Ladies Home Jour. Woman of Year, 1973; Am. Inst. Public Service award, 1974; B'nai B'rith Women Dist. One award, 1976; Caveat Emptor Mag. Consumer Crusader award, 1978. Democrat. Jewish. Club: Century Country. Author: A Smith College Mosaic, 1974; A Survival Kit for New Yorkers, 1973; The Volunteer Professional: What You Need to Know, 1972; Women's Almanac, 1976; monthly column McCall's mag., 1972-74.

STRAUS, GLADYS GUGGENHEIM (MRS. ROGER W. STRAUS), b. Elberon, N.J., Aug. 15, 1895; d. Daniel and Florence (Schloss) Guggenheim; student Finch Sch., Rosemary Hall, Greenwich, Conn., 1910-13; m. Roger W. Straus, Jan. 12, 1914; children—Oscar S. II, Roger W., Florence S. (Mrs. Max A. Hart). Vice pres., asst. editor Gourmet mag., 1940-50. Nutrition commr. for met. area from N.Y. State, 1943-45, 1947-48. Hon. trustee Mt. Sinai Hosp.; trustee Inst. on Man and Sci., Rensselaerville, N.Y., Mt. Sinai Med. Sch. Chmn., Roger Williams Straus Meml. Found.; chmn. Daniel and Florence Guggenheim Found.; mem. council N.Y. State Coll. Home Econs., 1943-46. Vice pres. bd. govs. Women's Nat. Republican Club, 1936-51. Clubs: Cosmopolitan, Woman Flyfishers. Author: My Favorite Recipes; More Recipes. Home: 1 E 66th St New York NY 10021

STRAUS, JACK ISIDOR, dept. store exec.; b. N.Y.C., Jan. 13, 1900; s. Jesse I. and Irma (Nathan) S.; A.B., Harvard U., 1921; LL.D. (hon.), Adelphi Coll., 1955; D.C.S. (hon.), N.Y. U., 1958; m. Margaret Hollister, Apr. 29, 1924 (dec. Apr. 8, 1974); children—Kenneth Hollister, Patricia Straus Harrah, Pamela Straus Haber; m. 2d, Virginia Megear, Jan. 11, 1975. With R. H. Macy & Co., N.Y.C., 1921—, v.p., 1933-39, acting pres., 1939-40, pres., chief exec. officer, 1940-56, chmn., chief exec. officer, 1956-68, chmn. exec. com., 1968-76, hon. chmn. and dir. emeritus, 1977—; mem. N.Y. Stock Exchange, 1964-68, N.Y.C. Econ. Devel. Council, 1965-76. Trustee, Roosevelt Hosp., N.Y.C., 1944-74, chmn. bd. trustees, 1965-74; bd. overseers Harvard U., 1950-54, mem. vis. com. Sch. Bus. Adminstrn., 1938-65, mem. vis. com. Univ. Resources, 1964-67; mem.-at-large, bd. dirs. Empire State Found., 1952-72; bd. dirs. Police Athletic League, N.Y.C., 1961-75, v.p., 1964-75; bd. dirs. United Way N.Y.C., 1969—; bd. govs. Hundred Year Assn. N.Y., 1961-74; trustee St. Luke's-Roosevelt Hosp., 1979—. Served with ROTC, 1918, to 2d lt. U.S. Army, 1919. Decorated cross of officer Order Leopold II (Belgium); chevalier Order Legion of Honor (France); Stella della Solidariety Italiana de 2d classe, commendatore Order of Merit (Italian Republic). Clubs: Harvard (N.Y.C.); Piping Rock, Creek (Locust Valley, N.Y.). Home: 19 E 72d St New York NY 10021 Office: R H Macy & Co Inc 151 W 34th St New York NY 10001

STRAUS, JOSEPH PENNINGTON, lawyer; b. Phila., May 30, 1911; s. M. Franklin and Ella (Pennington) S.; A.B., U. Pa., 1932, LL.B., 1935; m. Ruth Wolstenholme, June 24, 1933 (dec. Dec. 1977); children—Anne S. (Mrs. John M. Rusk), Susan S. (Mrs. William H. Rorer III), Helen H. (Mrs. Alexander Stephens Clay IV); m. 2d, Rosemary Teresa Ioele, Dec. 30, 1978. Admitted to Pa. bar, 1935; counsel RFC, 1938-42; partner firm Schnader, Harrison, Segal & Lewis, Phila., 1948—; dir. Precision Tube Inc. Alt. U.S. rep. Internat. Conf. Wills, U.S. State Dept., 1973. Pres. Chestnut Hill Community Assn., 1957-58, mem. bd., 1960-66; exec. com. Com. of Seventy, 1960—, chmn., 1962, 66; exec. com. Citizens Council on City Planning, 1961-64; vice chmn. Citizens Charter Com., 1956-64; bd. govs. Settlement Music Sch., Phila., vice chmn., 1962-67, mem. central bd. trustees, 1967—; bd. mgrs. All Saints Hosp., Phila.; Phila. co-chmn. White House Conf. on Children and Youth, 1970; mem., past chmn. bd. govs. Heart Assn. S.E. Pa.; bd. dirs., treas. Theodore F. Jenkins Meml. Law Library, 1974—; past vestryman St. Martin-in-the Fields; trustee Police Athletic League Phila., Phila. Bar Found., Epis. Community Services, Diocese of Pa. Served to lt. USNR, 1944-46. Fellow Am. Bar Found., Internat. Acad. Estate and Trust Law; mem. Mil. Order World Wars, Navy League, Am. Bar Assn. (ho. of dels. 1974-78, past chmn., council sect. real property, probate and trust law), Pa. Bar Assn. (past chmn. sect. real property, probate trust law), Phila. (bd. govs. 1968-71), Am. Judicature Soc., Juristic Soc., Pa., Germantown hist. socs., Pa. Acad. Fine Arts, Am. Coll. Probate Counsel (past pres.), Am. Law Inst. (co-chmn. joint editorial bd. uniform probate code, adv. com. Pa. joint state govt. commn. 1971—), World Assn. Lawyers, Newcomen Soc., Welcome Soc. Pa., Colonial Soc. Pa., Phi Beta Kappa. Clubs: Racquet, Phila. Cricket, Peale, Phila. Aviation, Urban. Contbr. articles to profl. publs. Home: 719 Glengarry Rd Philadelphia PA 19118 Office: Packard Bldg Philadelphia PA 19102

STRAUS, KENNETH HOLLISTER, dept. store exec.; b. N.Y.C., Feb. 18, 1925; s. Jack Isidor and Margaret (Hollister) S.; grad. Milton Acad., 1943; student N.Y. U. Sch. Retailing, 1947; grad. Advanced Mgmt. Program Harvard, 1957; m. Elizabeth Browne, Apr. 14, 1945; children—Melinda, Timothy. With R.H. Macy & Co., Inc., 1947—, v.p. men's and boy's wear, 1963-67, sr. v.p. domestic and internat. corp. buying, 1967-78, pres. corp. buying, 1978—, also dir.; dir. Stralem Fund, Inc. Hon. dep. commr., trustee honor emergency fund N.Y.C. Fire Dept. Served with AUS, 1943-45. Clubs: Piping Rock (Locust Valley, N.Y.); Harvard (N.Y.C.); Seawanhaka Corinthian Yacht (Centre Island, Oyster Bay, N.Y.). Home: 149 E 73d St New York NY 10021 Office: 151 W 34th St New York NY 10001

STRAUS, MURRAY ARNOLD, sociologist, educator; b. N.Y.C., June 18, 1926; s. Samuel and Kathleen (Miller) S.; A.B., U. Wis., 1948, M.S., 1949, Ph.D., 1956; m. Jacqueline Harris, Feb. 28, 1948; children—Carol Marie (Mrs. Robert Broderson), John Samuel. Lectr. sociology U. Ceylon, Colombo, 1949-52; asst. prof. sociology Wash. State U., 1954-57, U. Wis., 1957-59; asso. prof. Cornell U., 1959-61; prof., chmn. dept. family social sci. U. Minn., 1961-68; prof., dir. Family Research Lab., U. N.H., Durham, 1968—. Vis. prof. U. Bombay (India), 1964-65, U. Ky., 1966, U. York (Eng.), 1973-74, cons. NSF, Nat. Inst. Mental Health, Nat. Inst. Child Health and Human Devel.; founding editor Teaching Sociology, 1973-76. Served with AUS, 1944-46. Recipient Ernest W. Burgess award for research on family, 1977. Fulbright Hays program sr. research fellow, 1964-65; NIH grantee, 1960—, NSF grantee, 1963-64. Mem. Nat. Council Family Relations (pres. 1972-73, dir. 1963-70), Am. Sociol. Assn. (sec.-treas. research methods sect. 1966-71, chmn. family sect. 1978-79, award for teaching 1979), Eastern Sociol. Soc. (v.p. 1976-78), Assn. Asian Studies (chmn. Ceylon studies com. 1969-70), Rural Sociol. Soc. (council 1970—), A.A.A.S. (council 1970-72). Author: Sociological Analysis: An Empirical Approach Through Replication, 1968; Family Analysis: Readings and Replications of Selected Studies, 1969; Family Problem Solving, 1971; Violence in the Family, 1974; Family Measurement Techniques, 2d edit., 1978; The Social Causes of Husband-Wife Violence, 1980; Behind Closed Doors: Violence in The American Family, 1980. Mem. editorial bd. Jour. Marriage and the Family, 1960-69, Am. Sociol. Rev., 1968-69, Rural Sociology, 1964-69, Sociol. Abstracts, 1957-59, Jour. Family Issues, 1979—. Contbr. articles to profl. jours. Home: 33 1/2 Mill Rd Durham NH 03824 Office: Dept Sociology U NH Durham NH 03824

STRAUS, OSCAR S., II, business exec.; b. N.Y.C., Nov. 6, 1914; s. Roger Williams and Gladys (Guggenheim) S.; A.B., Princeton, 1936; postgrad. U. Dijon, summer 1936, Sch. Bus. Adminstrn. Harvard, 1938; m. Marion Miller Straus, 1941; 1 son, Oscar S. III. Pvt. sec. Internat. Labor Office, Geneva, Switzerland, 1937-38; U.S. fgn. service officer, 1940-42; divisional asst. Dept. State, 1942-43, 44-45; treas., dir., v.p., chmn. finance com. Am. Smelting & Refining Co., 1945-59; partner Guggenheim Bros., 1959—; pres., dir. Guggenheim Exploration Co., Inc., 1963-73; gen. partner Straus Minerals, 1973—; dir. Dry Dock Savs. Bank, Anglo Co. Ltd., Companion Life Ins. Co. Trustee Am. Mus. Natural History, Mystic Seaport (Conn.); chmn. Inst. on Man and Sci.; bd. dirs., pres. Daniel and Florence Guggenheim Found., Fred L. Lavanburg Found. (pres.); adv. council dept. econs. Princeton U. Served as lt. (j.g.) USCGR, 1943-44. Mem. Council Fgn. Relations. Jewish (trustee congregation). Clubs: Chester (N.S.) Yacht; Royal Nova Scotia Yacht Squadron; New York Yacht, Cruising of Am., City Midday, Downtown Execs., River, Megantic Fish and Game. Home: 228 E 62d St New York NY 10021 Office: 120 Broadway New York NY 10005

STRAUS, R. PETER, educator, former broadcasting exec., govt. ofcl.; b. N.Y.C., Feb. 15, 1923; s. Nathan and Helen (Sachs) S.; B.A. cum laude, Yale, 1943; m. Ellen Louise Sulzberger, Feb. 6, 1950; children—Diane Straus Tucker, Katherine, Jeanne, Eric. Chief sec. manpower div. U.S. Office Mil. Govt., Berlin, Germany, 1946-47; pub. relations exec. Edward L. Bernays, N.Y.C., 1947-48; program dir. spl. features radio sta. WMCA, N.Y.C., 1948-50; exec. asst. to dir. gen. ILO, Geneva, Switzerland, 1950- 55, dir. U.S. office, 1955-58; pres. Straus Broadcasting Group, 1958-67; asst. adminstr. for Africa, AID, 1967-69; pres. Straus Communications Inc., 1970-77, Radio Sta. WMCA, N.Y.C., 1970-77; dir. Voice of Am., 1977-79; mem. faculty Johns Hopkins U. Sch. Advanced Internat. Studies, Washington, 1979—; pub. Straus Editor's Report, 1970-72, Cranford (N.J.) Citizen and Chronicle, 1976-78. Spl. cons. USIA, 1966. Co-chmn. Interracial Council Bus. Opportunity N.Y., 1966-67; chmn. Com. Constl. Issues, N.Y., 1966-67; mem. N.Y.C. Commn. on State-City Relations, 1972-73; advisory com. Ministry of Tourism, Israel, 1972-75, N.Y.C. Aux. Policeman, 1974-77; lectr. Boston U. Sch. Pub. Communication, 1975-76; host internat. radio program Hotline, 1974-77. Chmn., N.Y. State Democratic Campaign Com., 1964; N.Y. del. Nat. Dem. Convs., 1960, 64; mem. fgn. affairs task force Dem. Nat. Com., 1975-77. Served to 1st lt. USAAF, 1943-45. Decorated Air medal with 5 oak leaf clusters; recipient award Harlem Lawyers Assn., 1964. Mem. Council Fgn. Relations, Nat. News Council (charter 1974-77), N.Y. State Broadcasters Assn. (pres. 1964). Jewish religion. Clubs: Federal City, Nat. Press (Washington); Century Country, Yale (N.Y.C.). Author: How To Keep Albany from Milking The City Dry, 1968; Is The State Department Color Blind, 1971; The Buddy System in Foreign Affairs, 1973; The Father of Anne Frank, 1975; The Risks and Rewards of Candor, 1979. Office: Johns Hopkins Sch Advanced Internat Studies 1740 Massachusetts Ave NW Washington DC 20036

STRAUS, ROBERT, educator; b. New Haven, Jan. 9, 1923; s. Samuel Hirsh and Alma (Fleischner) S.; B.A., Yale, 1943, M.A., 1945, Ph.D., 1947; m. Ruth Elisabeth Dawson, Sept. 8, 1945; children—Robert James, Carol Martin, Margaret Dawson, John William. Asst. prof. Yale, 1948-51, research asso. applied psychology, 1951-53; acting dir. Conn. Child Study and Treatment Home, New Haven, 1952-53; asso. prof. preventive medicine State U. N.Y. Upstate Med. Center, 1953-56; prof. med. sociology U. Ky., Lexington, 1956-59, prof., chmn. dept. behavioral sci. Coll. Medicine, 1959—, vis. fellow Yale, 1968-69; vis. prof. U. Calif., Berkeley, 1978; sec. Com. Med. Sociology, 1955-57; chmn. Coop. Com. Study Alcoholism, 1960-67, chmn., 1961-63; chmn. Nat. Adv. Com. on Alcoholism, 1966-69; mem. behavioral scis. study sect. NIH, 1964-68; cons. Nat. Inst. Mental Health, 1959-70; chmn. health service research tng. com. Nat. Center for Health Services, Research an Devel., 1970-71, mem. study commn. on pharmacy, 1973-75; cons addiction research center Nat. Inst. on Drug Abuse, 1974-78; mem Inst. Medicine, Nat. Acad. Sci., 1975—. Mem. Am. (chmn. med sociology sect. 1967-68), Eastern, So. sociol. socs., Soc. Health an Human Values, AAAS, Assn. Behavioral Scis. and Med. Edn. (pres 1974), Am. Pub. Health Assn., Assn. Med. Colls., Phi Beta Kappa Author: Medical Care for Seamen, 1950; (with S.D. Bacon) Drinkin in College, 1953; Alcohol and Society, 1973; Escape From Custody 1974. Co-editor: Medicine and Society, 1963. Mem. editorial bd. Jou of Studies on Alcohol. Home: 511 Ridge Rd Lexington KY 40503

STRAUS, ROBERT KENNETH, publisher; b. N.Y.C., Oct. 22 1905; s. Jesse Isidor and Irma (Nathan) S.; A.B., Harvard, 1927 M.B.A., 1931; m. Barbara Joan Tuckey, Mar. 6, 1947 children—Penelope Ann, Christopher Jesse. Asst. exec. dir. Temp Emergency Relief Adminstrn., State N.Y., 1931-32; dep. adminstr NRA, Washington, 1933-35; dept. dir. Resettlement Adminstrn 1935-36; treas., pub. Omnibook Mag., N.Y.C., 1938-52; chmn Mission Publ., Inc., Van Nuys, Calif., Sun Litho, Inc., Van Nuys 1958—. Vice pres. Santa Barbara Mus. Art. Mem. N.Y.C. Counci 1938-42. Served as maj. AUS, 1942-46. Trustee Inst. Gen. Semantics Internat. Soc. Gen. Semantics. Mem. Council Fgn. Relations Democrat. Clubs: Harvard, Valley, Birnam Wood (Montecito, Calif.) Home: 457 Boundary Dr Montecito CA 93108 Office: Box 2280 Sant Barbara CA 93102

STRAUS, ROGER W., JR., editor, pub.; b. N.Y.C., Jan. 3, 1917; s Roger Williams and Gladys (Guggenheim) S.; student Hamilton Coll 1935-37; B.J., U. Mo., 1939, Litt.D. (hon.), 1976; m. Dorothe Liebmann, June 27, 1938; 1 son, Roger W. III. Reporter, Dail Reporter, White Plains, N.Y., 1936, feature writer, 1939-40; editoria writer, reporter Columbia Missourian, 1937-39; editor, pub. Asterisk 1939; editorial asst. Current History, 1940, asso. editor, 1940-45; asso editor Forum, 1940-45; pres. Book Ideas, Inc. 1943-46; founde Farrar, Straus & Co., Inc. (now Farrar, Straus & Giroux, Inc.), 1945 now pres.; pres. L.C. Page & Co., Boston, 1957—, Noonday Press Inc., 1960—, Octagon Books, 1968—, Hill & Wang, 1971—; dir. U Mo. Press; chmn. adv. bd. Partisan Rev. mag. 1959-69. Vice pres. Fre L. Lavanburg Found. Bd. dirs. Harry Frank Guggenheim Found Manhattanville Coll., 1970-76, John Simon Guggenheim Found Center for Inter-Am. Relations. Served to lt. USNR, 1941-45. Mem P.E.N., Emerson Lit. Soc., Union Am. Hebrew Congregations (pub com. 1955-65), Sigma Delta Chi. Clubs: Lotos, Westchester Country Players. Co-editor; The Sixth Column, 1941; War Letters fron Britain, 1941; The New Order, 1941. Chmn. publ. bd. Am. Judaism mag., 1955-65. Office: 19 Union Sq West New York NY 10003

STRAUSBERG, MARC, investor; b. N.Y.C., Mar. 22, 1935; s Benjamin and Rose (Lorber) S.; B.A., Muhlenberg Coll., 1956 postgrad. Columbia; m. Susan J. Gordon, Nov. 18, 1966 children—Lisa Beth, Laura. Asst. to pres. Plenum Pub., N.Y.C 1969-77; pres. MSS Info. Corp., N.Y.C., 1977—; gen. partner SJ Assos., N.Y.C., 1978—. Home: 830 Park Ave New York NY 1002 also Lily Pond Ln East Hampton NY Office: 505 Park Ave New Yor NY 10021

STRAUSS, BERNARD S., educator, geneticist; b. N.Y.C., Apr. 18 1927; s. Joseph and Kate (Silk) S.; B.S., Coll. City N.Y., 1947; Ph.D Calif. Inst. Tech., 1950; postdoctoral fellow U. Tex., 1950-52; m Carol Maxine Dunham, Sept. 8, 1949; children—Leslie Joan Travis David Wilson, Paul Leonard. Teaching asst. Calif. Inst. Tech 1947-48; asst. prof. Syracuse U., 1952-56, asso. prof., 1956-60 research asso. Brookhaven Nat. Lab., 1954-55; asso. prof. U. Chgo 1960, prof., 1965—, chmn. com. genetics, 1962-76, chmn. dept microbiology, 1969—; vis. prof. U. Sydney, 1967, Hadassah Med Sch., Hebrew U., Jerusalem, 1975. Mem. genetics tng. com. NIH 1962-66, 70-73. Served with U.S. Mcht. Marine, 1945-47. Fulbright Guggenheim fellow Osaka U. (Japan), 1958-59. Mem. Am. Soc. Biol Chemists, Genetics Soc. Am., Am. Soc. Microbiology, Environ Mutagen Soc. (councilor 1975-78), Phi Beta Kappa, Sigma Xi. Home 5431 S Ridgewood Ct Chicago IL 60615

STRAUSS, ELLIOTT BOWMAN, econ. devel. cons., ret. nava officer; b. Washington, Mar. 15, 1903; s. Joseph and Mary (Sweitzer S.; B.S., U.S. Naval Acad., 1923; student Imperial Def. Coll., London m. 2d, Beatrice Phillips, Feb. 12, 1951; children by previou marriage—Elliott MacGregor, Armar Archbold, Lydia S. (Mme Delaunay); 1 son, Christopher Joseph. Commd. ensign USN, 1923 advanced through grades to rear adm., 1955; assigned ships at sea 1923-30, 32-35; asst. naval attache, London, 1935-37; staff comdr Atlantic Squadron, 1937-40; spl. naval observer, London, 1941; staf Chief Brit. Combined Ops., 1942-43; U.S. operations officer Allie Naval Comdr.-in-Chief for Normandy Invasion, 1944; comdr. Attac Transport, Pacific, 1944-45; naval adviser 1st Gen. Assembly UN staff, Mil. Staff Com., UN, 1946; comdg. officer U.S.S. Fresno 1946-47; staff div. strategic plans Office Chief Naval Operations 1948-51; comdr. Destroyer Flotilla 6, 1951-52; dir. def. programs div Office Spl. Rep. in Europe, Dept. Def. rep. econ. def., 1952-55; ret 1955; dir. engring. Bucknell U., 1956-57; dir. U.S. Operations Missio to Tunisia, 1957-60; spl. asst. to dir., ICA, 1960; dir. U.S. operation missions to Malagasy Republic, 1960-63; pub. mem. Fgn. Servic Inspection Corps, 1965; asso. Laidlaw & Co., N.Y.C., 1963-66 economic devel. cons. Gen. Electric Co., 1966—; chmn. bd. Interplan Corp., 1969—.; rep. overseas of Interplan. Dir. First Multi Fund o Am. Cons. to Dept. State, 1970. Bd. dirs. Am. Econ. Found Decorated Bronze Star; comdr. Order Brit. Empire; Croix de Guerre with palm (France). Mem. U.S. Naval Inst. Mem. Ch. of England Clubs: The Pilgrims; Army-Navy, Chevy Chase, Metropolitan (Washington); New York Yacht; Bucks', Bath (London). Author prof articles. Home: 2945 Garfield Terr Washington DC 20008 Office Interplan 100 N Hope Ave Santa Barbara CA 93110

STRAUSS, HERBERT LEOPOLD, educator; b. Aachen, Germany Mar. 26, 1936; s. Charles and Joan (Goldschmidt) S.; came to U.S 1940, naturalized, 1946; A.B., Columbia U., 1957, M.A., 1958, Ph.D 1960; postgrad Oxford U., 1960-61; m. Carolyn North Cooper, Apr 24, 1960; children—Michael Abram, Rebecca Anne, Ethan Edward With U. Calif., Berkeley, 1961—, prof. chemistry, 1973—, vice chmn dept. chemistry, 1975—; vis. prof. Indian Inst. Tech., Kanpur 1968-69. Alfred P. Sloan fellow, 1966-70. Mem. Am. Chem. Soc Am. Phys. Soc., AAAS, Sigma Xi, Phi Beta Kappa, Phi Lambd Upsilon. Author: Quantum Mechanics, 1968. Asso. editor: Annua Review of Physical chemistry, 1976—; editorial bd. Vibrationa Spectra and Structure, 1972—. Home: 2447 Prince St Berkeley CA 94705 Office: Department of Chemistry University of Californ Berkeley CA 94720

STRAUSS, JOHN, pub. relations exec.; b. N.Y.C., Apr. 2, 1913; Nathan and Bertha Dorothy (Heineman) S.; B.A., Yale U., 1935; Renee Valensi, Oct. 15, 1947; children—Susan Strauss Fryer, Jo Jay. Securities analyst Mabon & Co., N.Y.C., 1935-41; sales re Warner Bros. Pictures, Buffalo, 1941-45; publicist Warner Br Studios, Burbank, Calif., 1945-46, Columbia Studios, Hollywoo Calif., 1946-48; founder Cleary, Strauss & Irwin, 1948-64; pr McFadden, Strauss & Irwin, Inc., 1964-75, ICPR, Los Angel

1975—. Mem. Acad. Motion Picture Arts and Scis., Acad. TV Arts and Scis. Home: 4205 Stansbury Ave Sherman Oaks CA 91423 Office: 9255 Sunset Blvd Los Angeles CA 90069

STRAUSS, KARL MARTIN, brewer; b. Minden, Germany, Oct. 5, 1912; s. Albrecht and Mathide (Lilienfeld) S.; grad. Munich Inst. Tech. Sch. Brewing Tech., 1933; student U. Calif. at Los Angeles, 1955-56; m. Irene Vollweiler, Jan. 31, 1939 (dec. Mar. 1978). Came to U.S., 1939, naturalized, 1944. Various positions breweries and malt houses, Germany, to 1939; with Pabst Brewing Co., Milw., 1939—, asst. to gen. supt. Milw. plant, asst. supt. brewing and malting, asst. supt. indsl. products div., Peoria, Ill., 1st asst. supt. brewing and malting, Milw., plant supt., Los Angeles, 1939-57, coordinator plant ops. and planning, tech. dir. and v.p. prodn., Milw., 1959—. Bd. dirs. Katahdin Found. Mem. Master Brewers Assn. Am. (past pres., past dist. pres., hon. pres.), Am. Soc. Brewing Chemists, Mpls. Grain Exchange, Malting Barley Improvement Assn. (hon. dir.), U.S. Brewers Assn. (mem. tech. com.). Clubs: Palm Springs (Calif.) Racquet; Los Angeles Athletic. Home: 8515 N Manor Ln Milwaukee WI 53217 Office: 917 W Juneau Ave Milwaukee WI 53201

STRAUSS, PETER, actor; b. Croton-on-Hudson, N.Y., 1947; student Northwestern U. Film debut in Hail Hero, 1969; other films include: Soldier Blue, 1970, The Trial of the Catonsville Nine, The Last Tycoon, 1976; appeared in ltd. TV dramatic series Rich Man, Poor Man, 1976, Rich Man, Poor Man-Book II, 1976-77; TV spl. The Man Without a Country, 1973; TV movies The FBI Story: The FBI Vs. the Ku Klux Klan, 1975, Young Joe, the Forgotten Kennedy, 1978, The Jericho Mile (Emmy award), 1979. Office: care Creative Artists 1888 Century Park E Suite 1400 Los Angeles CA 90067

STRAUSS, ROBERT SCHWARZ, lawyer, politician; b. Lockhart, Tex., Oct. 19, 1918; s. Charles H. and Edith V. (Schwarz) S.; LL.B., U. Tex., 1941; m. Helen Jacobs, 1941; children—Robert A., Richard C., Susan. Admitted to Tex. bar, 1941, D.C. bar, 1971; partner firm Akin Gump Strauss Hauer & Feld, Dallas, 1945-77; pres. Strauss Broadcasting Co., 1964; Democratic nat. committeeman from Tex., 1968-72, mem. exec. com. Dem. Nat. Com., 1969-77, treas., 1970-72, chmn., 1972-77; spl. rep. for trade negotiations with rank of ambassador Office of Pres., 1977-79; chmn. Pres. Carter's reelection campaign, 1979—; Pres.'s personal rep. for Middle East negotiations, 1979—; spl. agt. FBI, 1941-45. Mem. Am., Dallas bar assns., State Bar Tex. Jewish. Office: Exec Office of Pres 1600 Pennsylvania Ave NW Washington DC 20500*

STRAUSS, SIMON DAVID, mfg. exec.; b. Lima, Peru, July 24, 1911; s. Lester W. and Bertha (Miller) S.; student Mackay Sch., Valparaiso, Chile, 1919-21, Townsend Harris Hall, N.Y.C., 1924-27; m. Elaine Ruth Mandle, Sept. 1, 1936; children—Peter Lester, Susan Dee (Mrs. Samuel Carson Orr). Asst. editor Engring. and Mining Jour., 1927-32; editor Madison (N.J.) Eagle, 1932-34; economist Standard Statistics Co., 1935-41; asst. to dep. adminstr. Fed. Loan Agy., 1941; asst. v.p., v.p. Metals Res. Co., 1942-45; sales dept. Am. Smelting & Refining Co., 1946, sales mgr., 1947-71, v.p., 1949-71, exec. v.p., 1971-77, vice chmn., 1977-79, also dir.; dir. Indsl. Minera Mexico, S.A., Mexico City, Mines Trading Co., Ltd., London, So. Peru Copper Corp. Gov., N.Y. Commodity Exchange Inc., 1947-63; dir., mem. exec. com. Zinc Inst., 1953-77, pres., 1957-59, 73-75. Cons., Def. Materials Procurement Agy., 1951-52, Office Def. Moblzn., 1954-55; mem. adv. coms. Munitions Bd.; mem. advisory com. Nat. Growth Policies, 1976; vis. lectr. M.I.T., 1977—; lectr. Pa. State U., 1978, Poly. Inst. N.Y., 1978, U. Ariz., 1979. Trustee Manhattan Sch. Music, 1958-79, v.p., 1966-79; bd. dirs. Internat. Copper Research Assn. Mem. Lead Industries Assn. (pres. 1964-66, exec. com., dir., v.p. 1967-69, pres. 1970-71), Silver Inst. (dir., pres. 1971-73, chmn. bd. 1974-76), Am. Bur. Metal Statistics (chmn. 1975-77), Copper Club (pres. 1967-68), Mining and Metall. Soc. Am., Am. Inst. Mining and Metall. Engrs., Council Fgn. Relations. Clubs: Mining, Downtown Exec., Stockbridge Golf. Author: (with L.H. Sloan), Two Cycles of Corporation Profits, 1936; (with E.H. Robie) Mineral Economics, 1959; (with W.H. Vogeley) Mineral Economics, 1976. Contbr. articles on mining to trade jours. Office: 120 Broadway New York NY 10005

STRAUSS, ULRICH PAUL, educator, chemist; b. Frankfurt, Germany, Jan. 10, 1920; s. Richard and Marianne (Seligmann) S.; A.B., Columbia, 1941; Ph.D., Cornell U., 1944; m. Esther Lipetz, June 20, 1943 (dec. Sept. 1949); children—Dorothy, David; m. 2d, Elaine Greenbaum, Nov. 23, 1950; children—Elizabeth, Evelyn. Sterling fellow Yale, 1946-48; faculty Rutgers U., New Brunswick, N.J., 1948—, prof. phys. chemistry, 1960—, also dir. Sch. Chemistry, 1965-71, chmn. dept. chemistry, 1974—. NSF sr. fellow Nat. Center Sci. Research, Strasbourg, France, 1961-62; Guggenheim fellow U. Oxford, Eng., 1971-72. Fellow AAAS, Am. Inst. Chemists, N.Y. Acad. Scis.; mem. Am. Chem. Soc. (chmn. phys. chemistry group N.J. sect. 1956, councillor 1961—). Contbr. articles to profl. jours. Home: 227 Lawrence Ave Highland Park NJ 08904 Office: Dept Chemistry Rutgers U New Brunswick NJ 08903

STRAUSS, WALTER ADOLF, educator; b. Mannheim, Germany, May 14, 1923; s. Ludwig and Fanny (Haas) S.; brought to U.S., 1936, naturalized, 1944; B.A., Emory U., 1944; M.A., Harvard, 1948, Ph.D., 1951; m. Lilo Teutsch, Sept. 8, 1946 (div. 1966); children—Robert D., Joan E., Charles L.; m. 2d, Nancy Reed Shirley, Oct. 18, 1966; children—Philip R., Matthew C. Instr. Romance langs. and gen. edn. Harvard, 1951-54; mem. faculty Emory U., 1954-70, asso. prof. Romance langs., 1958-63, prof., 1963-70; William C. Treuhaft prof. Case Western Res. U., Cleve., 1970—. Served with AUS, 1944-47. Guggenheim fellow, 1962-63; Bollingen Found. fellow, 1962-63. Mem. Modern Lang. Assn., Dante Soc., AAUP, Phi Beta Kappa. Author: Proust and Literature, 1957; Descent and Return, 1971. Home: 2861 Berkshire Rd Cleveland Heights OH 44118 Office: Dept Modern Langs and Lit Case Western Res U Cleveland OH 44106

STRAUSZ, LAWRENCE EUGENE, ins. co. exec.; b. Spokane, Wash., Dec. 8, 1915; s. Charles O. and Josephine S. (Shull) S.; B.A., Wash. State U., 1941; m. Willene Beaudry, Sept. 14, 1941; children—William, Sally Jo. Controller, Farmers New World Life Ins. Co., Seattle, 1954-58, v.p., 1958-63, v.p., treas., 1963-65, v.p., gen. mgr., 1965-67; pres., dir. Investors Guaranty Life Ins. Co., Los Angeles, 1968—. Served to lt. col. USAAF, 1941-45. Fellow Life Office Mgmt. Assn.; mem. Fin. Exec. Inst., Alpha Kappa Psi. Office: 4680 Wilshire Blvd Los Angeles CA 90054

STRAUSZ-HUPE, ROBERT, ambassador, author; b. Vienna, Austria; Mar. 25, 1903; s. Rudolph and Doris (Hedwig) Strausz-H.; A.M., Ph.D., U. Pa., 1944; m. Eleanor deGraff Cuyler, Apr. 26, 1938 (dec. 1978). Came to U.S., 1923, naturalized, 1938. Investment banking, 1927-37; asso. editor Current History, 1939-41; asso. prof. polit. sci. U. Pa., 1946-52, prof., 1952—, spl. lectr., 1940-46, dir. Fgn. Policy Research Inst., 1955-69; U.S. ambassador to Ceylon, 1970-72, to Belgium, 1972-74, to Sweden, 1974-76, to NATO, 1976-77. Lectr., Air War Coll., 1953. Served to lt. col. AUS. Fellow Royal Geog. Soc.; mem. Council Fgn. Relations, Atlantic Council U.S. Lutheran. Clubs: Merion Cricket (Haverford, Pa.); Interalliés (Paris); Brook (N.Y.C.); Met. (Washington). Author: The Russian-German Riddle, 1940; Axis-America, 1941; Geopolitics, 1942; The Balance of Tomorrow, 1945; International Relations, 1950; The Zone of Indifference, 1952; Power and Community, 1956; (with Kintner, Cottrell, Dougherty) Protracted Conflict, 1959; (with W. Kintner, Stefan Possony) A Forward Strategy for America, 1961; (with others) Building the Atlantic World, 1963; In My Time, 1967; (with others) Dilemmas Facing the Nation, 1979. Editor; The Idea of Colonialism, 1958; Orbis, 1957-69. Home: White Horse Farms Goshen and Grubbs Mill Rds Newtown Square PA 19073

STRAW, H. THOMPSON, geographer; b. Antigo, Wis., Mar. 21, 1907; s. Harold Parker and Clara A. (Thompson) S.; B.A., Hillsdale Coll., 1930; M.A., U. Mich., 1934, Ph.D., 1936; m. Hilda Smith Jackson, Dec. 16, 1932. Teaching fellow geography U. Mich., 1934-36; asst. prof. geography Middle Tenn. State U., Murfreesboro, 1936-37, asso. prof. geography, 1937-39; prof. geography Western Mich. U., 1939-47; vis. prof. George Washington U., 1945, Mich. State U., 1946; chief Africa sect. topographic detachment G-2, Dept. of Army, Washington, 1947-50; geographer Reconnaissance Br. AFCIN, Hdqrs. USAF, Washington, 1950-51, dep. for research and geography, 1951-55, dep. chief photog. intelligence utilization sect., 1955-57, chief photog. intelligence utilization sect. Reconnaissance Br. AFCIN, 1957-59; pvt. research and publs., 1959—; lectr. Strategic Intelligence Sch., Dept. Def., 1947-59; Air Force mem. Bd. on Geographic Names, 1950-58, chmn., 1954-58. Air Corps ground instr. maps and charts, 1943-44, chief cartographic sect. hist. br. G-2, 1944-45. Town councilman, Hillsboro, Va., 1960-66. Grantee Social Research Council, 1940, NRC, 1941. Fellow AAAS; mem. Am. Geog. Soc., Assn. Am. Geographers, Mich. Acad. Sci. Arts and Letters (chmn. geog. sect. 1942-43), Nat. Council Geography Edn., Sigma Xi, Chi Gamma Phi, Epsilon Delta Alpha. Author: Battle Creek Michigan—A Study in Urban Geography, 1939. Episcopalian (past vestryman, treas.). Contbr. articles to profl. mags. Home: 1213 Stafford Ave Fredericksburg VA 22401. *"All excellent things are as difficult as they are rare." (Baruch Spinoza: Ethics). All one can do is one's best to achieve them.*

STRAW, RICHARD MYRON, educator; b. St. Paul, July 25, 1926; s. Myron George and Emma Aglen (Hesli) S.; B.A., U. Minn., 1949; Ph.D., Claremont U. Coll., 1955; m. Dorothy Jane Johnson, Nov. 19, 1949; children—Richard, Michael, Martha, Robert, Maija. Asst. prof. Deep Springs (Calif.) Coll., 1955-56; asst. prof. Calif. State U., Los Angeles, 1956-60, asso. prof., 1960-64, prof. biology, 1964—, dir. curricular planning, 1964-66, asso. dean Sch. Letters and Sci., 1970-75, asso. dean acad. planning, 1975-78; Fulbright lectr., Peru, 1963-64; cons. for sci. and math. Peace Corps, Malaysia, 1966-68. Served with AUS, 1944-46, 50-52. NSF research grantee, 1957-62. Mem. Am. Soc. Naturalists, Soc. Study Evolution, Am. Assn. Plant Taxonomists, Internat. Assn. Plant Taxonomy, AAAS. Republican. Episcopalian. Home: 3942 LaMarada Klamath Falls OR 97601

STRAW, WILLIAM HENRY, fin. exec.; b. Meadville, Pa., Feb. 1, 1933; s. David and Charlotte (Lavier) S.; B.S.B.A., Northwestern U., 1954; Ph.D., Harvard U. Grad. Sch. Bus., 1965; m. Marilyn Joy Hoblick, June 4, 1955; children—William Henry, Michael F., Robert A., Thomas M. Sr. auditor Price Waterhouse, Chgo., 1955-60; v.p., treas., Hammermill Paper Co., Erie, Pa., 1960-72; v.p. fin. Meredith Corp., Des Moines, 1972—; dir. Blue Cross Iowa. Served with U.S. Army, 1957-59. C.P.A. Mem. Am. Inst. C.P.A.'s, Fin. Execs. Inst. Republican. Lutheran. Home: 929 39th St West Des Moines IA 50265 Office: 1716 Locust St Des Moines IA 50336

STRAWBRIDGE, DENNIS WINSLOW, natural scientist; b. Reading, Pa., Oct. 10, 1920; s. Harold E. and Bessie M. S.; B.S., Albright Coll., 1942; M.S., Syracuse U., 1948; Ph.D., U. Chgo., 1953; m. Margaret A. Wade, Dec. 22, 1946. Asst. prof. U. Pa., 1953-56; prof. natural sci. Mich. State U., East Lansing, 1956—. Served with AUS, 1942-46. Mem. Rocky Mountain Biol. Lab., Norwegian Elkhound Assn. Am., Ingham County Kennel Club. Sigma Xi. Democrat. Contbg. author: Molecules to Man, 1961; editor, contbg. author: The Search for Explanations: Studies in Natural Science, 3 vols., 1967. Home: 48 Sherwood Rd Williamston MI 48895 Office: 132 Brody Hall Mich State U Dept Natural Sci East Lansing MI 48823

STRAWBRIDGE, G. STOCKTON, merchandiser; b. Phila., Dec. 17, 1913; s. Francis R. and Anna Estes (Hacker) S.; grad. William Penn Charter Sch., 1933; m. Mary Tilghman Lowry, Dec. 6, 1935; children—Peter Stockton, Susan Sayres, Steven Lowry, Michael, Arthur Lowry, Mary Tilghman. With Strawbridge & Clothier, Phila., 1935—, beginning as clk. and salesman, successively asst. buyer, asst. to mdse. mgr. ready to wear div., buyer ready to wear dept., divisional mdse. mgr., v.p. charge merchandising and publicity, exec. v.p., 1935-55, pres., 1955-67, chmn., chief exec. officer, 1967-79, chmn. exec. com., 1979—, dir., 1948—; dir. Phila. Electric Co., Nat. Sugar Refining Co., Phila. Nat. Bank, Phila. Sav. Fund Soc., Asso. Merchandising Corp., Old Phila. Devel. Corp. Bd. dirs. United Fund, Phila Div. Sch.; bd. mgrs. Pa. Hosp.; mem. adv. com. Greater Phila. Council Chs. Served as officer USNR, 1941-46. Mem. Nat. Retail Mchts. Assn., Better Bus. Bur. Phila. (dir.), Phila. Mchts. Assn. (dir.). Episcopalian (vestryman). Clubs: Merion Cricket; Phila., Racquet, Radnor Hunt, Downtown (Phila.); Wings (N.Y.C.). Office: 801 Market St Philadelphia PA 19105*

STRAWBRIDGE, HERBERT EDWARD, dept. store exec.; b. Niagara Falls, N.Y., Jan. 15, 1918; s. Russell E. and Martha (Long) S.; B.S., Purdue U., 1939; m. Marie Smith, Mar. 28, 1944; children—Holly, Leigh. Buyer, Montgomery Ward & Co., 1939-53; with Turton Assos., consultants, 1953-54; sales promotion exec. Modern Venetian Blinds, Inc., 1954-55; with Higbee Co., Cleve., 1955—, v.p., treas., 1959-62, vice chmn., treas., 1962-66, pres., 1966-71, chmn., 1968—; dir. Asso. Merchandising Corp., Cleve. Trust Co., Cleve. Electric Illuminating Co., Norcom, Inc. Trustee Vocat. Guidance and Rehab. Cleve., Hiram Coll.; hon. trustee Heart Assn. Northeastern Ohio; bd. dirs. No. Ohio Regional Info. Center; trustee Ursuline Coll., chmn., 1969-80. Served to lt. comdr. USNR, 1942-45. Mem. Nat. Retail Mchts. Assn. (past chmn., dir.), World Soc. Ekistics, Ohio Retail Council (dir.), Cleve. Growth Assn., Mus. Arts Assn. (trustee), No. Ohio Opera Assn., Greater Cleve. United, Phi Delta Theta. Clubs: Cleveland Country, Union, Pepper Pike Country. Office: 100 Public Sq Cleveland OH 44113

STRAWSER, NEIL EDWARD, broadcasting news reporter; b. Rittman, Ohio, Aug. 16, 1927; s. Joseph E. and Mamie Rice Christian S.; B.A., Oberlin Coll., 1951; M.A. in History, George Washington U., 1958; children—Neil Edward, Chris, Jay, Stuart, Clara. Disc jockey, announcer local news radio sta. WEOL, Elyria, Ohio, 1950-51, radio sta. WATG, Ashland, Ohio, 1951-52; editorial research asst. CBS News, Washington, 1952-56, corr., 1956—. Served with USNR, 1945-48. Clubs: Congressional Country; Washington Press. Home: 211 C St NE Washington DC 20002 Office: CBS 2020 M St Washington DC 20036

STRAYER, JOSEPH REESE, educator; b. Balt., Aug. 20, 1904; s. George Drayton and Cora (Bell) S.; A.B., Princeton, 1925; M.A., Harvard, 1926, Ph.D., 1930; postgrad. U. Paris, 1928-29; LL.D., Caen U., 1957; L.H.D., Lehigh U., 1976; m. Lois Curry, Sept. 12, 1929; children—Charles Drayton, Elizabeth Anne Strayer Corson. Instr. history Stevens Inst. Tech., 1929-30; instr. history Princeton, 1930-35, Shreve fellow, 1935-36, asst. prof., 1936-40, asso. prof., 1940-42, Henry Charles Lea prof. history, 1942-49, Dayton-Stockton prof. history, 1949-73, prof. emeritus, 1973—, chmn. dept., 1941-61. Councilman of Borough of Princeton, 1964-67. Fellow Am. Acad. Arts and Scis., Brit. Acad., Mediaeval Acad. Am. (pres. 1966-69); mem. Am. Philos. Soc., Am. Hist. Assn. (pres. 1971), Am. Council Learned Socs. (bd. dirs. 1948-51), Phi Beta Kappa. Club: Cosmos (Washington). Author: Western Europe in the Middle Ages, 1954; Feudalism, 1965; The Medieval Origins of the Modern State, 1970; Les Gens de Justice du Languedoc, 1970; The Albigensian Crusades, 1971; Medieval Statecraft and the Perspectives of History, 1971. Author, co-author or editor books relating to field; contbr. to mags. Home: 57 Balsam Ln Princeton NJ 08540

STREAM, ARNOLD CRAGER, lawyer; b. N.Y.C., Feb. 8, 1918; s. Mervyn and Sophia (Hyams) S.; B.A., Coll. City N.Y., 1936; LL.D., St. Lawrence U., 1940; m. Barbara Bloom, Oct. 1, 1967; children by previous marriage—Richard, Raymond, Jane, Abigail. Admitted to N.Y. bar, 1940, D.C. bar, 1942; asst. U.S. atty. N.Y. Dist., 1940-43; author short stories, book revs., tax series, series on constl. law; partner firm Amen, Weisman & Butler, N.Y.C., 1948-55; exec. v.p., gen. counsel C & C TV Corp., 1955-60, Hazel Bishop, Inc., 1955-60; trial lawyer, 1960—; sr. partner firm Monasch, Chazen & Stream, N.Y.C., 1973—; gen. counsel Stein and Day Inc. Counsel, cons. advt. industry, 1969—; trial cons. Gulfstream Am. Corp.; counsel French embassy, N.Y.C., 1965-72; spl. cons. to TV industry. Served to lt. col. AUS, 1943-46. Mem. Bar Assn. City N.Y., N.Y. County Bar Assn., Nat. Trial Lawyers Conf. Contbr. articles to profl. jours. Home: 33 Deepdale Dr Great Neck Estates NY 11021 Office: 777 3d Ave New York City NY 10017. *A lawyer standing in the courtroom provides the ultimate balance between excess government and excess liberty.*

STREAN, BERNARD M., ret. naval officer; b. Big Cabin, Okla., Dec. 16, 1910; s. Ralph Lester and Maude (Hopkins) S.; B.S., U.S. Naval Acad., 1933; grad. Armed Forces Staff Coll., 1949, Nat. War Coll., 1958; m. Janet Lockey, June 12, 1935; children—Bernard M., Richard Lockey, Judy (Mrs. William S. Graves). Commd. ensign U.S. Navy, 1933, advanced through grades to vice adm., 1965; designated naval aviator, 1935; assigned U.S.S. Pennsylvania, 1933-35, Naval Air Sta., Pensacola, Fla., 1935-36, U.S.S. Saratoga, 1936-38, San Diego Naval Sta., 1938-39, Hawaii, 1939-40, Naval Air Sta., Jacksonville, Fla., 1940-42; comdg. officer VF-1, U.S.S. Yorktown, 1943-44, Air Group 98, 1944-45, Air Group 75, 1945-46; head tech. tng. program sect. Office Chief Naval Ops., 1950-51; comdg. officer Air Transp. Squadron 8, 1951-54, Naval Sch. Pre-Flight Sch., 1954-56, U.S.S. Kenneth Whiting, 1956-57, U.S.S. Randolph, 1958-59; chief staff, aide to comdr. Naval Air Force, U.S. Atlantic Fleet, 1959-60; comdr. Fleet Air Whidbey, 1960-61, Patrol Force 7th Fleet, also U.S. Taiwan patrol force, 1961-62; asst. chief naval ops. for fleet ops., 1962-64; comdr. Carrier Div. 2, Atlantic Fleet, 1964-65; comdr. World's 1st all-nuclear naval task force, 1964; dep. asst. chief for personnel Bur. Naval Personnel, Dept. Navy, Washington, 1965-68; chief naval air tng. Naval Air Sta., Pensacola, Fla., 1968-71; ret., 1971; v.p. O.S.C. Franchise Devel. Corp., 1971-75; chmn. bd. Solaray Corp., 1975—; v.p. Huet-Browning Corp., Washington. Bd. dirs. U.S. Olympic Com., 1965-68; trustee No. Va. Community Colls., also found. Decorated Navy Cross, D.F.C. with 2 gold stars, Air medal with 7 gold stars, Legion of Merit, D.S.M., numerous area and campaign ribbons; Distinguished Service medal (Greece); medal of Pao-Ting (Republic China). Mem. Am. Def. Preparedness Assn., Internat. Platform Assn., Mil. Order World Wars, Order Daedalians, Loyal Order Carabao, Early and Pioneer Naval Aviators Assn. (pres. 1977-79), Arlington County Tax Assn. (vice chmn. 1978—), Md. Aviation Hist. Soc. (founder, dir. 1978—). Clubs: Army Navy (Washington); N.Y. Yacht; Washington Golf and Country (Arlington). Address: 5028 N 30th St Arlington VA 22207

STREATOR, EDWARD JAMES, JR., diplomat; b. N.Y.C., Dec. 12, 1930; s. Edward James and Ella (Stout) S.; A.B., Princeton U., 1952; m. Priscilla Craig Kenney, Feb. 16, 1957; children—Edward James, III, Elinor Craig, Abigail Merrill. Commd. fgn. service office Dept. State, 1956; assigned ICA, 1956-58; 3d sec. embassy, Addis Ababa, Ethiopia, 1958-60; 2d sec. embassy, Lome Togo, 1960-62; intelligence research specialist Office Research and Analysis for Africa, Dept. State, Washington, 1962-63, staff asst. to sec. state, 1964-66; chief polit.-mil. affairs unit U.S. mission to NATO, 1966-67, dep. dir. Office Polit.-Mil. Affairs, 1967-68, dep. dir. polit. affairs, 1968-69; dep. dir. Office NATO and Atlantic Polit.-Mil. Affairs, Dept. State, 1969-73; dir. office, 1973-75; dep. U.S. permanent rep. to NATO, dep. chief U.S. Mission, Brussels, 1975-77; minister, dep. chief of mission U.S. embassy, U.K., London, 1975—; mem. U.S. dels. to NATO Ministerial Meetings, 1964, 66, 69-75, 10th SEATO Council Ministers Meeting, 1965, 2d spl. Inter-Am. Conf., 1965, Conf. Security and Coop. in Europe, 1973. Served to lt. (j.g.) USNR, 1952-56. Episcopalian. Clubs: Met. (Washington); Brooks (London). Address: US Embassy London FPO NY 09510

STREEP, MERYL (MARY LOUISE STREEP), actress; b. Summit, N.J.; d. Harry II and Mary S.; B.A., Vassar Coll.; M.A. in Fine Arts, Yale U., 1975; m. Donald J. Gummer, 1978; 1 son, Henry. Appeared with Green Mountain Guild, Quechee, Vt.; off-Broadway debut in Trelawny of the Wells, 1975; theatrical appearances include: 27 Wagons Full of Cotton (Theatre World award), A Memory of Two Mondays, Henry V, Secret Service, The Taming of the Shrew, Measure for Measure, The Cherry Orchard, Happy End, Wonderland, Taken in Marriage; movie appearances include: Julia, 1977, The Deer Hunter (Best Supporting Actress award Nat. Soc. Film Critics), 1978, Manhattan, 1979, The Seduction of Joe Tynan, 1979, Kramer vs. Kramer (N.Y. Film Critics' award, Los Angeles Film Critics' award, both for best actress), 1979; TV film: The Deadliest Season, 1977; TV mini-series: Holocaust (Emmy award), 1978; TV dramatic spls.: Secret Service, 1977, Uncommon Women and Others, 1978. Recipient Mademoiselle award, 1976. Office: care Internat Creative Mgmt 8899 Beverly Blvd Los Angeles CA 90048*

STREET, CLARENCE PARKE, constrn. contractor; b. Cadiz, Ky., Nov. 11, 1900; s. Edward Roberts and Mary (Grinter) S.; A.B. magna cum laude, Vanderbilt U., 1922; m. Ruth Howerton Wallace, Dec. 3, 1925; children—Ruth Wallace (Mrs. Charles E. Ide, Jr.) (dec.), Mary Grinter (Mrs. George E.N. Montague), Jane Harrison Liles, Edward Robert. With McDevitt-Fleming Co., Chattanooga, 1922-25, J.J. McDevitt Co., Charlotte, N.C., 1925-41; with McDevitt & Street Co., 1941—, sec., gen. mgr., 1941-60, pres., 1961-66, chmn. bd. dirs., 1966—. Mem. Airport Adv. Bd. Charlotte, 1946-75. Trustee, mem. exec. com. Queens Coll., 1948—, chmn. bd. trustees, 1967-74; trustee Presbyn. Hosp. Mem. Asso. Gen. Contractors Am. (treas. Carolinas br. 1939-41, 45-51, v.p. 1942-43, pres. 1944, chmn. nat. pub. relations com. 1944-49, vice chmn. bldg. div. 1947, chmn. 1948, nat. v.p. 1952, nat. pres. 1953), Cons. Constructors Council Am., Vanderbilt Alumni Assn., Nat. Planning Assn., Newcomen Soc. N.Am., Phi Beta Kappa, Phi Delta Theta. Presbyterian (elder). Home: 2633 Richardson Dr Charlotte NC 28211 Office: PO Box 32755 Charlotte NC 28232

STREET, DANA MORRIS, orthopedic surgeon; b. N.Y.C., May 7, 1910; s. William Dana and Elizabeth (Clark) S.; B.S., Haverford Coll., 1932; M.D., Cornell U., 1936; m. Elna Alice Clare, June 18, 1940; children—Rosalyn Clare (Mrs. David R. Sprague), Dana Clark,

Steven Morris, William Milo. Intern pathology Duke Hosp., 1936-37, orthopedics, 1937-38; asst. resident phys. medicine Albany (N.Y.) Hosp., 1938-39; fellow Nemour Found., 1939-40; intern orthopedics Boston City Hosp., 1940; asst. resident surgery Albany Hosp., 1940-41; intern, asst. resident orthopedics Johns Hopkins Hosp., 1941-42; fellow N.Y. Orthopedic Hosp., 1942; chief orthopedic sect. Kennedy VA Hosp., Memphis, 1946-59; prof. surgery, chief orthopedic div. U. Ark. Med. Coll., 1959-62; prof. surgery in residence U. Calif. at Los Angeles Med. Coll., 1962-75; head orthopedic div. Harbor Gen. Hosp., Torrance, Calif., 1962-75, Riverside (Calif.) Gen. Hosp., 1975-77; chief orthopedic sect. Jerry L. Pettis Meml. Hosp., Loma Linda, Calif., 1977—; prof. orthopedics Loma Linda U., 1975—. Served to maj. M.C., USAAF, 1942-46. Diplomate Am. Bd. Orthopedic Surgery. Mem. Am. Acad. Orthopedic Surgeons, Am. Orthopaedic Assn., Western Orthopedic Assn., Assn. Bone and Joint Surgeons (treas. 1953-56, v.p. 1956-58, pres. 1959), Am. Fracture Assn. Presbyn. (elder, deacon, clk. sessions). Contbr articles on medullary nailing to med. jours. Home: PO Box 1195 Running Springs CA 92382 Office: Jerry L Pettis Meml Vets Hosp Loma Linda CA 92357

STREET, EDWARD ROBERT, constrn. co. exec.; b. Charlotte, N.C., Nov. 15, 1938; s. Clarence P. and Ruth W. S.; B.S., Davidson Coll., 1959; B.C.E., Ga. Inst. Tech., 1962; married (dec.); children—Linda Brady, Margaret Atkinson, Edward Robert, V. With McDevitt & Street Co., Charlotte, 1962—, asst. sec., 1967-72, v.p., 1970-72, pres., chief exec. officer, 1972—; dir. Wachovia Bank, McGuire Properties. Com. mem. Charlotte Country Day Sch.; chmn. bd. Mary Dore Center, Charlotte. Mem. Asso. Gen. Contractors. Clubs: Charlotte Country, Quail Hollow Country. Office: PO Box 32755 Charlotte NC 28232

STREET, FRANK TANDY, JR., constrn. co. exec.; b. Henderson, Ky., July 22, 1923; s. Frank Tandy and Anne Elizabeth (Smith) S.; student Marion (Ala.) Mil. Inst., 1941-42; student U.S. Naval Acad., 1942-45; m. Juanita H., June 25, 1965; children—Larry, Anne, Kimberly. With McDevitt & Street Co., Charlotte, N.C., 1947—, pres., treas. Tandy Constrn. Co., subs., Charlotte, 1973-78, exec. v.p. Tandy div., 1978—. Civil engr. adv. com. Central Piedmont Community Coll., 1971-79. Served with USN, 1942-47. Mem. Profl. Constrn. Estimators Assn. (pres. 1966-67). Baptist. Club: Charlotte Country. Home: 3729 Pelham Ln Charlotte NC 28211 Office: 145 Remount Rd Charlotte NC 28203

STREET, JAMES HARRY, educator; b. New Braunfels, Tex., Nov. 17, 1915; s. James William and Kate (Goldenbagen) S.; B.A. magna cum laude, U. Tex., 1940, M.A., 1947; Ph.D., U. Pa., 1953; D.Econ. Scis. (hon.), Nat. U. Asuncion (Paraguay), 1955; M.A. (hon.), U. Cambridge (Eng.), 1972; m. Mabel Carroll, Jan. 16, 1944; children—John William, Janet Pauline. Reporter, editor New Braunfels Herald, 1933-36; social sci. analyst U.S. Bur. Agr. Econs., Washington, 1941-43; civilian pub. service employee U.S. Forest Service, Cooperstown, N.Y. and Phila., 1943-46; instr. econs. U. Pa., Phila., 1946-48; asst. prof. econs. Haverford (Pa.) Coll., 1948-52; asst. prof. Rutgers U., New Brunswick, N.J., 1952-55, asso. prof., 1955-59, prof. econs., 1959-76, disting. prof. econs., 1976—, chmn. econs. dept., 1977—; vis. prof. Nat. U. Asuncion, Paraguay, 1955; vis. lectr. various univs. in Argentina, 1957-58; Fulbright lectr. U. San Marcos, Peru, 1963; econ. specialist Central Am. social studies seminars, summers 1965-72; Fulbright lectr. Nat. U. Mex., 1970; vis. scholar U. Cambridge, 1972-73. Bd. dirs. Metuchen Free Pub. Library, 1963-68. Mem. Am. Econ. Assn., Assn. Evolutionary Econs., Conf. Latin Am. History, Latin Am. Studies Assn., Royal Econ. Soc., Council Internat. Exchange Scholars, Phi Beta Kappa (chpt. pres. 1967-68). Editor: Ideas and Issues in the Social Sciences, 1950; author: The New Revolution in the Cotton Economy, 1957; (with others) Technological Progress in Latin America, 1979; contbr. articles to profl. jours. Home: 11 Lexington Dr Metuchen NJ 08840 Office: 77 Hamilton St New Brunswick NJ 08903

STREET, JOHN CHARLES, educator; b. Chgo., Apr. 3, 1930; s. Charles Larrabee and Mary Louise (Rouse) S.; B.A., Yale, 1951, M.A., 1952, Ph.D., 1955. Asst. prof. English, Mich. State U., 1957-59; asst. prof. linguistics and Mongolian langs. Columbia, 1959-62; vis. asst. prof. linguistics U. Wash., 1962-63; asso. prof. linguistics U. Wis., Madison, 1963-65, prof. linguistics, 1965—. Research asso. Am. Council Learned Socs., 1959-62. Served with AUS, 1955-57. Mem. Linguistic Soc. Am., Am. Oriental Soc., Societas Uralo-Altaica, Mongolia Soc., Phi Beta Kappa. Author: The Language of the Secret History of the Mongols, 1957; Khalkha Structure, 1963. Office: U Wis Dept Linguistics Madison WI 53706

STREET, ROBERT ELLIOTT, educator; b. Belmont, N.Y., Dec. 11, 1912; s. Louis Hollingsworth and Harriet Helen (Elliott) S.; B.S. in Physics, Rensselaer Poly. Inst., 1933; A.M., Harvard, 1934, Ph.D., 1939; m. Alice Mary Lee, Oct. 9, 1969; children by previous marriage—David R., Eleanor (Mrs. Frank Hungate II). Instr. math. Rensselaer Poly. Inst., 1937-41; asso. physicist Langley (Va.) Field, 1941-43; asst. prof. physics Dartmouth, 1943-44; engr. Gen. Electric Co., 1944-48; asso. prof. physics U. N.Mex., 1948-49; mem. faculty U. Wash., Seattle, 1949—, prof. aero. and astronautics, 1955—; cons. in field. Sci. faculty fellow NSF, 1964-65. Asso. fellow Am. Inst. Aero. and Astronautics; mem. Math. Assn. Am., Soc. Indsl. and Applied Math., U.S. Power Squadrons. Club: Seattle Yacht. Co-editor proc. 1962 Heat Transfer and Fluid Mechanics Inst. Home: 2818 Boyer E Apt 10 Seattle WA 98102 Office: Guggenheim Hall Univ of Wash Seattle WA 98195

STREET, ROBERT LYNNWOOD, civil and mech. engr.; b. Honolulu, Dec. 18, 1934; s. Evelyn Mansel and Dorothy Heather (Brook) S.; M.S., Stanford U., 1957, Ph.D. (NSF grad. fellow 1960-62), 1963; m. Norma Jeanette Ensminger, Feb. 6, 1959; children—Deborah Lynne, Kimberley Anne. Mem. faculty Stanford U. Sch. Engring., 1962—, prof. civil engring., asso. chmn. dept., 1970-72, prof. fluid mechanics and applied math., chmn. dept., 1972—, asso. dean research Sch. Engring., 1971—, acting vice provost, dean research, 1979; vis. prof. U. Liverpool (Eng.), 1970-71; chmn. audit com. Univ. Corp. Atmospheric Research; cons. in field. Served as officer USNR, 1957-60. Sr. postdoctoral fellow Nat. Center Atmospheric Research, 1978-79. Mem. Am. Soc. Engring. Edn., ASCE (chmn. publns. com. hydraulics div. 1978-80; Walter Huber prize 1972), ASME, Am. Geophys. Union, Phi Beta Kappa, Sigma Xi, Tau Beta Pi. Author: The Analysis and Solution of Partial Differential Equations, 1973; co-author: Elementary Fluid Mechanics, 5th edit., 1975; asso. editor Jour. Fluids Engring., 1978-81; author articles in field, mem. editorial bds. profl. jours. Office: Dept Civil Engring Stanford Univ Stanford CA 94305

STREET, TISON, composer, violinist; b. Boston, May 20, 1943; S. Jabez Curry and Leila Fripp (Tison) S.; A.B., Harvard U., 1965, M.A., 1968. Violinist, composer, 1968—; vis. lectr. U. Calif., Berkeley, 1971-72. Recipient Naumberg Rec. award, 1972, Nat. Inst. Arts and Letters award, 1973. Mem. Soc. Fellows Harvard, 1968-71; Rome (Italy) prize fellow, 1973. Compositions include String Quartet, 1972; So Much Depends, 1973; Three Sacred Anthems, 1974; String Quintet, 1974. Home: 381 Commonwealth Ave Apt 4 Boston MA 02115

STREET, WILLIAM EZRA, educator; b. Benfranklin, Tex., Apr. 12, 1901; s. William Dan and Josie (Cook) S.; B.S. in Elec. Engring., Tex. Tech. U., 1930, M.A., 1933; D.Eng. Edn., Harding Coll., 1947; m. Clara Johnson, June 21, 1924; children—William Elvin, Clara Louise (Mrs. Charles Beagle). Tchr. pub. schs., Tex., 1920-25; instr. Tex. Tech. U., 1928-32, asst. prof., 1932-38, asso. prof., 1938-41; prof., head engring. graphics dept. Tex. A. and M. U., College Station, 1941-65; prof. La. State U., Baton Rouge, 1965—, head dept., 1965-72. Ind. expert Sinclair Oil & Refining Co., Waco Constrn. Co., Lockheed Vega Aircraft Co., Gen. Dynamics. Recipient Gen. Dynamics Convair award for excellence in engring. teaching Tex. A. and M. U., 1961, named outstanding tchr. during first 100 years; Halliburton award for excellence in engring. teaching La. State U., 1969. Registered profl. engr., Tex. Mem. La. Engring. Soc., Am. Soc. Engring. Edn. (chmn. engring. design graphics div. 1955-56; Distinguished Service award graphics div. 1961), Tau Beta Pi, Phi Kappa Phi. Rotarian (dist. gov. 1954-55). Editor: Jour. Engring. Design Graphics Jour., 1944-46. Author numerous books including: Drafting Fundamentals I, 1965; Design and Engineering Graphics Problems, 1965; Drafting Fundamentals II, 1969; Engineering Graphics Design and Analysis Problems, 1970; Design Drafting Problems I, 1973; Descriptive Geometry Problems, 1973; Design Fundamentals, 1975. Home: Box 223 Nashville AR 71852

STREET, WILLIAM SHERMAN, mfg. co. exec.; b. Oakland, Calif., Sept. 30, 1904; s. William Schwerdt and Mary Elizabeth (Smith) S.; student U. Calif. at Berkeley, 1923-24; m. Janice Kergan, Sept. 16, 1925; children—Georgann (Mrs. Phillip M. Evans), William K., John S. Gen. mgr. Hale Bros., San Francisco, 1933-35; gen. mgr. mdse. Herzfeld-Phillipson, Milw., 1935-38; gen. mgr. mdse. Frederick & Nelson, Seattle, 1938-43, pres., 1946-62; gen. mgr. retail and suburban stores Marshall Field & Co., Chgo., 1943-46, exec. v.p., 1954-62, also dir.; pres. United Pacific Corp., Seattle, 1963-64, chmn., 1965-66; vice chmn. Univar Corp., Seattle, 1967-70, chmn., 1970-74, also past dir.; chmn. bd., chmn. exec. com. Univar Corp.; past dir. Seattle-First Nat. Bank, Nat. Airlines, Inc., Pacific Telephone Co., Pacific N.W. Bell Telephone Co.; dir. Ostrom Mushroom Co.; past trustee Wash. Mut. Savs. Bank. Asso. field collector Field Mus. Natural History, Chgo., co-leader expdns. faunal surveys, Iran, 1962, 63, 68, Afghanistan, 1965, Nepal, 1972, Peru, 1976, N.W. Australia, 1976; past dir., chmn. Seattle World's Fair-Century 21. Trustee U. Puget Sound Mus. Natural History. Mem. Explorers Club, Alpha Sigma Phi. Clubs: Rainer, Harbor (Seattle); Commercial (Chgo.). Office: 1600 Norton Bldg Seattle WA 98104

STREETER, DANIEL DENISON, JR., biomechanicist; b. Bklyn., Feb. 8, 1925; s. Daniel Denison and Gladys Marie (Rudolph) S.; S.B., Mass. Inst. Tech., 1946, S.M., 1951; Ph.D., Catholic U. Am., Washington, 1969; m. Patricia Ann Engle, Aug. 10, 1956; children—Ann Megrath, Daniel Denison. Draftsman Douglas Aircraft Co., El Segundo, Calif., 1947; maintenance and constrn. engr. Lago Oil & Transport Co. Ltd., Aruba, Netherlands W.I., 1948-50; research asst. Cavitation Lab., Mass. Inst. Tech., 1950-51, teaching asst., in charge High Temperature Torsional-Creep Lab., 1951-52; vis. prof. mech. engring. U. Rangoon (Burma) on Mass. Inst. Tech.-Dept. State Fgn. Aid contract, 1952-54; instr. engring. scis. div. Purdue U., 1954-55; stress analyst Boeing Co., Seattle, 1955-65; USPHS trainee, spl. fellow Cardiovascular Tng. Program, U. Wash. Sch. Medicine, Seattle, 1965-66, research fellow pathology dept., 1969-71, research asso., 1971-76, project dir. left ventricular fiber geometry unit, 1971-76, on spl. assignment cardiology div. Children's Orthopedic Hosp., Seattle, 1976—; chmn. Inst. of Sci., Seattle, 1979—; USPHS trainee Nat. Heart Inst., Bethesda, Md., 1966-68. Engring. cons. Union of Burma Govt., Am. embassy, Burma, Knappen, Tippetts, Abbetts & McCarthy, Engrs., N.Y.C., 1952-54. Active Boy Scouts Am., 1948-52, 69—. Served with USNR, 1943-45. Recipient Order of Arrow, Boy Scouts Am., 1939, Eagle Scout, 1943. Registered profl. engr., Wash. Fellow The Explorers; mem. ASME, Am. Acad. Mechanics (a founder), Am., Wash. (research fellow 1969-70) heart assns., The Mountaineers (trustee, sec. 1959-60), Vedanta Soc. Western Wash. (pres. 1972—), Wyckoff Soc. Am., Tau Beta Pi. Republican. Congregationalist. Contbr. articles on muscle structure of heart to profl. jours. Patentee in field. Home: 4201 51st Ave NE Seattle WA 98105. *It's important to like your work. Then it isn't work—it's play. And you can go on playing till you're dog tired and not want to stop. You can like your work if you want. Just dress it up in your imagination as something that turns you on. Then turn on.*

STREETER, DONALD VINTON, savs. and loan assn. exec.; b. Saugatuck, Mich., Mar. 13, 1933; s. Paul Horace and Norma (Lentz) S.; student U. Fla., U. Miami; M.B.A., Fla. Atlantic U., 1976; m. June 6, 1962; children—Maxine Karl, Jami-Kay, Dina Donnell, Donald V. Pres., Atlantic Fed. Savs. and Loan Assn., Fort Lauderdale, Fla. Served with U.S. Army, 1953-55. Republican. Roman Catholic. Club: Coral Ridge Yacht, Tower. Home: 1311 Seminole Dr Fort Lauderdale FL 33304 Office: 1750 E Sunrise Blvd Fort Lauderdale FL 33304

STREETER, ROBERT EUGENE, educator; b. Williamsport, Pa., Dec. 7, 1916; s. Allyn Anson and Anna Mary (Stover) S.; A.B., Bucknell U., 1938, L.H.D., 1960; A.M., Northwestern U., 1940, Ph.D., 1943; m. Ruth Parker, Apr. 10, 1941; children—Janette Frear, Robert Allyn. State news editor Williamsport Gazette and Bull., 1938-39; instr. English, Bucknell U., 1942-46, asst. prof., English, 1946-47; prof. English, Am. adviser to head English dept. Seoul (Korea) Nat. U., 1946-47; asst. prof. English, U. Chgo., 1947-53, asso. prof. English, 1953-57, prof. English, 1957—, Edward L. Ryerson Distinguished Service prof., 1973—, dean coll., 1954-59, acting dean div. humanities, 1962-63, dean, 1963-73. Trustee Bucknell U. Mem. Modern Lang. Assn., Am. Studies Assn., Phi Beta Kappa. Co-editor: Province of Prose, 1956; Critical Inquiry, 1976—. Home: 22 Circle Dr Chesterton IN 46304

STREETER, TAL, sculptor; b. Oklahoma City, Aug. 1, 1934; s. Paul Waller and Pauline Viola (Roberts) S.; B.F.A., U. Kans., 1956, M.F.A., 1961; m. Dorothy Ann Sheets, June 26, 1957; 1 dau., Lissa. Exhibited in one-man shows, N.Y.C., yearly 1965—; exhibited in group shows at N.Y. World's Fair, 1965, Whitney Mus., N.Y.C., 1965, Larry Aldrich Mus., Ridgefield, Conn., 1968, 70, Sheldon Art Mus., Lincoln, Nebr., 1970; represented in permanent collections including Mus. Modern Art, N.Y.C., San Francisco Mus. Art, Nat. Fine Arts Collection at Smithsonian, Washington, Wadsworth Atheneum, Newark Mus., Smith Coll. Mus. Art, High Mus., Atlanta, Storm King Art Center, Ark. Art Center, Little Rock, Milw. Art Center; vis. artist-in residence Dartmouth, 1963, U. N.C., 1970, 72, 73, Penland Sch. of Crafts, 1974, 75, 76; prof. State U. N.Y. at Purchase, 1973—. Fulbright lectr., Korea, 1971. Collaborations in Art, Sci. and Tech./N.Y. State Council on Arts grantee, 1976; Artpark artist, Lewisboro, N.Y., 1978. Author: The Art of the Japanese Kite, 1974. Home: Old Verbank School Millbrook NY 12545

STREETMAN, BEN GARLAND, educator; b. Cooper, Tex., June 24, 1939; s. Richard E. and Bennie (Morrow) S.; B.S., U. Tex., 1961, M.S., 1963, Ph.D., 1966; m. Lenora Ann Music, Sept. 9, 1961; children—Paul, Scott. Fellow, Oak Ridge Nat. Lab., 1964-66; asst. prof. elec. engring. U. Ill., 1966-70, asso. prof., 1970-74, prof., 1974—, research prof. Coordinated Sci. Lab., 1970—; dir. Eltek Corp.; cons. in field. Mem. IEEE, Electrochem. Soc., Tau Beta Pi, Eta Kappa Nu, Sigma Xi. Author: Solid State Electronic Devices, 1972. Home: 2901 Rolling Acres Dr Champaign IL 61820 Office: Coordinated Science Laboratory University of Illinois Urbana IL 61801

STREETMAN, JOHN WILLIAM, III, museum ofcl.; b. Marion, N.C., Jan. 19, 1941; s. John William, Jr. and Emily Elaine (Carver) S.; B.A. in English and Theatre History, Western Carolina U., 1963; m. July 15, 1967 (div.); children—Katherine Drake, Leah Farrior, Burgin Eaves. Founding dir. Jewett Creative Arts Center, Berwick Acad., South Berwick, Maine, 1966-70; exec. dir. Polk Pub. Mus., Lakeland, Fla., 1970-75; dir. Mus. Arts and Sci., Evansville, Ind., 1975—; instr. origins of contemporary painting Evansville Mus., 1976—; chmn. mus. adv. panel Ind. Arts Commn. Mem. Am. Assn. Museums. Episcopalian. Office: 411 SE Riverside Dr Evansville IN 47713

STREETT, ALEXANDER GRAHAM, lawyer, b. Camden, Ark., Feb. 21, 1939; s. Johnson Bruce and Gertrude (Sanderson) S.; student Henderson State Tchrs. Coll., 1957-58; J.D., U. Ark., 1965; m. Sue Stephanie Heidgen, Nov. 27, 1965; children—Stephanie, Bridgette, Mary, Alexander Graham, James Albert. Admitted to Ark. bar, 1965; law clk. Ark. Supreme Ct., Little Rock, 1965-66; practiced in Russellville, Ark., 1966—; pros. atty. 5th Jud. Dist. of Ark., Russellville, 1970—. Bd. dirs. Ark. region NCCJ, 1971-74. Served with AUS, 1959-61. Mem. Am., Ark., Pope-Yell County bar assns., Ark. Pros. Atty. Assn. (v.p. 1975, pres. 1976), Am., Ark. trial lawyers assns., Pi Kappa Alpha. Roman Catholic. Rotarian, K.C. Home: Skyline Dr Russellville AR 73801 Office: 107 W Main St Russellville AR 72801

STREHLOW, ROGER ALBERT, chemist, educator; b. Milw., Nov. 25, 1925; s. Elmer John and Edna (Schmidt) S.; B.S., U. Wis., 1947, Ph.D., 1950; m. Ruby M. Miller, Aug. 21, 1948; children—John C., James E. Phys. chemist Ballistic Research Labs., Aberdeen Proving Ground, Md., 1950-58, chief physics br. Interior Ballistics Lab., 1958-60; vis. prof. aero. engring. U. Ill. at Urbana, 1960-61, prof. aero. and astronautical engring., 1961—. Chmn. bd. advisers Central States sect. Combustion Inst., 1966-78. Fellow Am. Phys. Soc., Am. Inst. Aeros. and Astronautics (asso.); mem. Am. Chem. Soc., Am. Inst. Chem. Engring., Nat. Fire Protection Assn., Sigma Xi, Alpha Chi Sigma. Author: Fundamentals of Combustion, 1968. Dep. editor Combustion and Flame. Home: 505 S Pine St Champaign IL 61820

STREIBICH, HAROLD CECIL, lawyer; b. Baton Rouge, June 19, 1928; s. Frederick Franklin and Margaret Rose (Foley) S.: B.A., U. Tenn., 1949; LL.B., U. Va., 1953; Spl. Honors, Memphis State U., 1972; m. Theresa Ann Grimes, Apr. 25, 1973; 1 dau., by previous marriage, Margaret Ann; stepchildren—John B. Snowden, IV, Kathryn Snowden. Admitted to Miss. bar, 1954, Tenn. bar, 1960; partner firm Harsh, Moriarty, Crawford & Streibich and predecessor firm, Memphis, 1960—; vis. lectr. Vanderbilt U. Sch. Law, 1968-74, Brigham Young U., summer 1971; prof. music, prof. entertainment law Memphis State U., 1973—; bd. mem., nat. treas. Nat. Acad. Recording Arts and Scis. Inst., 1978-79, nat. pres., 1979—. Chmn., Tenn. Athletic Commn., 1970, 74. Served with U.S. Army, 1945-47, 50-52. Recipient World Boxing Assn. award as outstanding commr., 1972, Gov.'s award Nashville chpt. Nat. Acad. Recording Arts and Scis., 1972, various civic awards for Easter Seal, Heart Fund. Mem. Am., Tenn. (ho. of dels. 1978—, chmn. copyright, entertainment and sports law sect. 1979), Miss., Memphis and Shelby County (dir. 1975-76) bar assns., Am. Judicature Soc., Internat. Assn. Music Pubs., Kappa Sigma, Omega Delta Kappa, Phi Delta Phi. Democrat. Roman Catholic. Clubs: Petroleum, Summit (Memphis). Home: 5475 Crescent Ln Memphis TN 38117 Office: Suite 1590 One Commerce Sq Memphis TN 38103

STREIBIG, KENNETH CARL, coll. dean; b. Danbury, Conn., Apr. 16, 1917; s. Edward Lewis and Mae Ruth (Nordell) S.; B.E., Tchrs. Coll. Conn., 1940; M.A., Tchrs. Coll. Columbia, 1947, Ed.D., 1949. Dean, Weylister Coll., U. Bridgeport, 1947-49, Highland Manor Jr. Coll., West Long Branch, N.J., 1949-50, 54-55, Quinnipiac Coll., New Haven, 1950-54, Monmouth Coll., West Long Branch, N.J., 1955—. Bd. mgrs. Monmouth Meml. Hosp.; bd. Long Branch Community Concert Soc., Monmouth County chpt. Am. Assn. UN. Pres. N.J. Jr. Coll. Assn. Served with USNR, 1942-46. Hon. fellow Yale, 1953. Mem. N.J. Assn. Colls. and Univs., Assn. Higher Edn. N.E.A., Middle States Assn. Deans and Advisers of Men. Kiwanian. Home: 1 Calvin Terr Oakhurst NJ 07755 Office: Monmouth Coll West Long Branch NJ 07764

STREICHLER, JERRY, educator; b. N.Y.C., Dec. 8, 1929; s. Samuel and Minnie (Waxman) S.; spl. courses certificate Newark Coll. Engring., 1951; B.S. magna cum laude, Kean Coll. N.J., 1956; M.A., Montclair State Coll., 1958; Ph.D., N.Y. U., 1963; m. Rosalind Fineman, Feb. 25, 1951; children—Stuart Alan, Seth Ari, Robin Cheryl. Cons. machine designer to Time Savers Inc., Montclair, N.J., 1950-63, Bristol Equipment Co., Hamilton Equipment Co., 1952-67; mem. faculty dept. indsl. edn. Montclair (N.J.) State Coll., 1958-65, Trenton (N.J.) State Coll., 1965-67; prof., chmn. dept. indsl. edn. and tech. Bowling Green (Ohio) State U., 1967-78, dir. Sch. Tech., 1978—. Vis. prof. S.I. Community Coll., Coll. City N.Y., 1965, Rutgers U., 1967, U. Mo., 1967, U. Mich., Saginaw, 1971; Cons., tchr. Newaygo Vocat. Center, Saginaw Career Opportunities Center, 1971; cons. indsl. tng., pub. schs., colls. Founding com. chmn. Ohio Council on Indsl. Arts Tchr. Edn., 1968-69. Served with USAF, 1951-52. Univ. honors scholar, 1963; recipient Laureate citation Epsilon Pi Tau, 1972. Mem. Am. Edn. Research Assn., Am. Indsl. Arts Assn., Am. Vocat. Assn., NEA, Am. Soc. for Tng. and Devel., Miss. Valley Indsl. Tchr. Edn. Conf., Epsilon Pi Tau (exec. sec. 1976—, editor jour.), Omicron Delta Kappa, Phi Delta Kappa, Kappa Delta Pi. Jewish (past temple trustee). Asst. editor Jour. Indsl. Tchr. Edn., 1968-70; co-editor The Components of Teacher Education, 20th yearbook Am. Council on Indsl. Arts Tchr. Edn. Contbr. articles to profl. jours. Home: 1302 Charles St Bowling Green OH 43402

STREIGHT, JACK MILTON, lawyer, lodge potentate; b. New Westminster, B.C., Can., Jan. 24, 1910; s. Harvey Milton and Alice (Daniels) S.; B.A., U. B.C., 1931; grad. Osgoode Hall Law Sch., Toronto, 1934; m. Isabel Bews, Mar. 16, 1940; children—Barbara, Jean (Mrs. Blackman). Called to B.C. bar, 1934, Canadian bar, 1934; created Queen's Counsel, 1969; practiced in New Westminster, 1934—; spl. prosecutor Dept. Justice, 1940; ofcl. adminstr. County of Westminster, 1938—. Chmn. adv. bd. Salvation Army; bd. dirs. YMCA Found., 1966; bd. dirs. St. Mary's Hosp., 1967; trustee Shriners Hosps.; bd. govs. Winnipeg, Spokane, Portland, Honolulu and San Francisco units Shriners Hosps. for Crippled Children. Named Man of Yr. in Vancouver, 1955. Mem. Canadian, B.C. bar assns., Phi Delta Theta. Mason (Shriner, Jester; imperial potentate N. Am. 1974—), Rotarian (past pres.), Elk. Club: Westminster. Home: 327 3d St New Westminster BC Canada Office: 607 Columbia St New Westminster BC Canada

STREISAND, BARBRA JOAN, singer, actress; b. Bklyn., Apr. 24, 1942; d. Emanuel and Diana (Rosen) S.; student Yeshiva of Bklyn.; m. Elliott Gould, Mar. 1963 (div.); 1 son, Jason Emanuel. N.Y. theatre debut Another Evening with Harry Stoones, 1961; appeared Broadway musical I Can Get It for You Wholesale, 1962, Funny Girl,

1964-65; rec. artist Columbia Records; motion pictures include: Funny Girl, 1968, Hello Dolly, 1969, On a Clear Day You Can See Forever, 1970, The Owl and the Pussy Cat, 1970, What's Up Doc?, 1972, Up the Sandbox, 1972, The Way We Were, 1973, For Pete's Sake, 1974, Funny Lady, 1975, The Main Event, 1979; star, producer film A Star is Born, 1976; TV spls. include: My Name is Barbra (5 Emmy awards), 1965, Color Me Barbra, 1966; Gold record albums include: People, 1965, My Name is Barbra, 1965, Color Me Barbra, 1966, Stoney End, 1971, Barbra Joan Streisand, 1972, The Way We Were, 1974, A Star is Born, 1976, Superman, 1977, The Stars Salute Israel at 30, 1978, Wet, 1979. Recipient Acad. award as best actress of 1968 (Funny Girl); Georgie award AGVA, 1977; Grammy awards for best female vocalist and best song writer (with Paul Williams), 1978. Address: care Jon Peters 4000 Warner Blvd Burbank CA 91522*

STREISINGER, GEORGE, biologist; b. Budapest, Hungary, Dec. 27, 1927; s. Andor and Margit (Freund) S.; B.S., Cornell U., 1950; Ph.D., U. Ill., 1953; m. Lotte Sielman, June 12, 1949; children—Lisa, Cory. Asso. geneticist Carnegie Instn. of Washington, Cold Spring Harbor, N.Y., 1956-60; asso. prof. dept. biology U. Oreg., Eugene, 1960-65, prof., 1965—, co-chmn. dept., 1968-71, research asso. Inst. Molecular Biology, 1960—, acting dir., 1967-68; mem. genetics study sect., div. research grants NIH, 1976—. Nat. Found. for Infantile Paralysis research fellow Calif. Inst. Tech., 1953-56, Med. Research Council Unit for Molecular Biology, Cambridge, Eng., 1957-58, Guggenheim fellow, 1971-72. Mem. Nat. Acad. Scis. Contbr. articles to profl. jours. Office: Inst Molecular Biology U Oreg Eugene OR 97403

STREIT, CLARENCE KIRSHMAN, author; b. California, Mo., Jan. 21, 1896; s. Louis Leland and Emma (Kirshman) S.; A.B., U. Mont., 1919, LL.D., 1939; postgrad. Sorbonne, 1919; Rhodes scholar, Oxford U., 1920-21; LL.D., Colby Coll., 1941; D.Litt., Oberlin, 1940, Hobart Coll., 1941; L.H.D., Ill. Coll., Jacksonville, 1966; m. Jeanne Defrance, Sept. 26, 1921; children—Travan Pierre Defrance (dec.), Jeanne (Mrs. Felix Rohatyn), Colette (Mrs. René Perret). With Phila. Pub. Ledger, 1920-24, Paris Bur., 1920, 24, Turko-Greek War, 1921, Rome corr., 1921-23, Constantinople corr., 1923-24; with N.Y. Times, 1925-39, at Carthage excavation, Riff war, 1925, Vienna corr., 1925-27, N.Y. staff, 1927-28, League of Nations corr., 1929-39, Washington bur., 1939. Pres., Federal Union, Inc., 1939—; editor Freedom & Union 1946—; mem. bd. Atlantic Union Com., 1949-62, pres. Internat. Movement for Atlantic Union, 1958—. Served with U.S. Army, 1917-19; AEF. Recipient Kefauver Union of Free award, 1968. Mem. Phi Beta Kappa, Sigma Delta Chi, Sigma Chi. Author: Where Iron Is, There is The Fatherland, 1920; Hafiz-The Tongue of the Hidden (Rubaiyat), 1928, rev. as Hafiz in Quatrains, 1946; Union Now, 1939, rev., 1948; Union Now With Britain, 1941; Freedom Against Itself, 1954; Freedom's Frontier, Atlantic Union Now, 1960; co-author The New Federalist, 1950. Home: 2853 Ontario Rd NW Washington DC 20009 Office: 1875 Connecticut Ave NW Washington DC 20009

STREITWIESER, ANDREW, JR., chemist; b. Buffalo, June 23, 1927; s. Andrew and Sophie (Morlock) S.; A.B., Columbia, 1949, M.A., 1950, Ph.D., 1952; postgrad. (AEC fellow), Mass. Inst. Tech., 1951-52; m. Mary Ann Good, Aug. 19, 1950 (dec. May 1965); children—David Roy, Susan Ann; m. 2d, Suzanne Cope Beier, July 29, 1967. Faculty, U. Calif. at Berkeley, 1952—, prof. chemistry, 1963—; cons. to industry, 1957—. Recipient Humboldt Found. Sr. scientist award, 1976, Humboldt medal, 1979. Mem. Am. Chem. Soc. (Cal. sect. award 1964, award in Petroleum Chemistry 1967), Chem. Soc. London, AAAS, Nat. Acad. Scis., Am. Acad. Arts and Scis., Phi Beta Kappa, Sigma Xi. Author: Molecular Orbital Theory for Organic Chemists, 1961; Solvolytic Displacement Reactions, 1962; (with J.I. Brauman) Supplemental Tables of Molecular Orbital Calculations, 1965; (with C.A. Coulson) Dictionary of Pi Electron Calculations, 1965; (with P.H. Owens) Orbital and Electron Density Diagrams, 1973; (with C.H. Heathcock) Introduction to Organic Chemistry, 1976; also numerous articles. Co-editor: Progress in Physical Organic Chemistry, 11 vols., 1963-74. Research on organic reaction mechanisms, optically active deuterium compounds, isotope effects, application molecular orbital theory to organic chemistry, effect chem. structure on carbon acidities, rare earths organometallic chemistry. Office: Dept Chemistry U Calif Berkeley CA 94720

STREMBITSKY, MICHAEL ALEXANDER, supt. schs.; b. Smoky Lake, Alta., Mar. 5, 1935; s. Alec and Rose (Fedoretz) S.; B.A., U. Alta., 1955, B.Ed., 1958; M.A., Tchrs. Coll., Columbia U., 1968, M.Ed., 1972; m. Victoria Seminiuk, Aug. 12, 1954; children—Michael, William John. Classroom tchr. Edmonton (Alta.) Pub. Schs., prin., supr., dir., asst. to supt., dep. supt., now supt. Mem. Can. Coll. Tchrs., Can. Edn. Assn., Conf. Alta. Sch. Supts., Am. Assn. Sch. Adminstrs., Can. Soc. for Study Edn., Assn. Sch. Bus. Ofcls., Edmonton Edn. Soc., Edmonton C. of C., Phi Delta Kappa. Office: Edmonton Pub Sch Bd 10010 107A Avenue Edmonton AB T5H 0Z8 Canada*

STRENG, WILLIAM PAUL, lawyer, educator; b. Sterling, Ill., Oct. 17, 1937; s. William D. and Helen Marie (Conklen) S.; B.A., Wartburg Coll., 1959; J.D., Northwestern U., 1962; m. Louisa Bridge Egbert, July 8, 1967; children—Sarah, John. Admitted to Iowa, Ill. bars, 1962, Ohio bar, 1964, Tex. bar, 1975; law clk. to U.S. circuit judge Lester L. Cecil, Cin., 1963-64; asso. firm Taft, Stettinius & Hollister, Cin., 1964-70; atty.-advisor Office Sec. Tax Policy, Office Tax Legis. Counsel, Dept. Treasury, Washington, 1970-71; dep. gen. counsel Export-Import Bank U.S., Washington, 1971-73; prof. law Sch. Law, So. Methodist U., Dallas, 1973-80; vis. prof. Coll. Law Ohio State U., Columbus, 1977; partner firm Bracewell & Patterson, Houston, 1980—; lectr. various Am. Law Inst., Practising Law Inst. and World Trade Inst. confs. Served with USMC, 1962. Lutheran. Author: Estates, Gifts and Trust-Planning, 1979; International Business Transactions—Tax and Legal Handbook, 1978. Contbr. articles to profl. publs. Home: 3917 Amherst St Dallas TX 75225 Office: 2900 S Tower Pennzoil Pl Houston TX 77002

STRICHMAN, GEORGE A., business exec.; b. Schenectady, 1916; B. Chem. Engring., Rensselaer Poly. Inst., 1937. Engr., mfg. exec., 1937-48; various exec. positions Gen. Electric Co., 1948-58; dir. mfg. Raytheon Co., 1959; pres. ITT Kellogg div. ITT, 1959-62; pres., chief exec. officer, dir. Faibanks Whitney Corp. (name changed to Colt Industries Inc.), 1962, chmn. bd., pres., 1963-68, chmn. bd., chief exec. officer, 1968—. Trustee Renssalaer Poly. Inst. Office: 430 Park Ave New York City NY 10022

STRICK, LOUIS, publisher; b. Bklyn., Mar. 9, 1926; s. Charles M. and Rosalind H. (Rosen) S.; B.A., Cornell U., 1948; M.A., Columbia U., 1949; m. Elizabeth McGavin, Aug. 18, 1972; children—Ivy, Wesley, Charlotte. Pres., H.M. Storms Co., Bklyn., 1956-68, Pentalic Corp., N.Y.C., 1968—, Taplinger Pub. Co., N.Y.C., 1977—. Served with U.S. Army, 1944-46. Home: 8 E 83d St New York NY 10028 Office: 200 Park Ave S New York NY 10003

STRICKERT, ROLAND RUDOLF, ins. co. exec.; b. Jackson, Mo., Apr. 21, 1927; s. Henry J. and Minna (Rook) S.; B.S., SE Mo. State U., 1951; M.S., State U. Iowa, 1952; m. Waneta M. Strackbein, June 6, 1952; children—Andrew, Claudia, Sarah, Emily. Actuarial asst. Nat. Life & Accident Ins. Co., Nashville, 1952-58, asst. actuary, 1958-64, asso. actuary, 1964-66, v.p., comptroller, 1966-77; comptroller NLT Corp., 1972-77, v.p., comptroller, 1978—. Served with AUS, 1946-47. Fellow Soc. Actuaries; mem. Fin. Execs. Inst., Acad. Actuaries, Nashville Actuarial Club (past pres.). Home: 4704 Belmont Park Terr Nashville TN 37215 Office: National Life Center Nashville TN 37250

STRICKLAND, BONNIE RUTH, psychologist, educator; b. Louisville, Nov. 24, 1936; d. Roy E. and Billie P. (Whitfield) Strickland; B.S., Ala. Coll., 1958; M.A., Ohio State U., 1960, Ph.D. (USPHS fellow), 1962. Research psychologist Juvenile Diagnostic Center, Columbus, Ohio, 1958-60; asst. prof. psychology Emory U., Atlanta, 1962-64, dean of women, 1964-67, asso. prof., 1968-73; prof. psychology U. Mass., Amherst, 1973—, chmn. dept. psychology, 1976-77, 78—. Diplomate clin. psychology Am. Bd. Examiners in Profl. Psychology. Recipient Outstanding Faculty award Emory U., 1968-69. Fellow Am. Psychol. Assn.; mem. Workshop Inst. for Living Learning, Sigma Xi. Adv. editor Jour. of Cons. and Clin. Psychology, 1973—, Professional Psychology, 1976—. Contbg. author texts personality theory. Contbr. of numerous articles on social personality and clin. psychology to profl. jours. Home: 454 Gulf Rd Belchertown MA 01007 Office: Dept of Psychology Tobin Hall Univ of Massachusetts Amherst MA 01002

STRICKLAND, CHARLES RUTAN, architect; b. Brookline, Mass., Oct. 12, 1907; s. Sidney Talbot and Elsie (Rutan) S.; B.F.A. in Architecture, Yale U., 1930; student Ecole des Haut Beaux Arts, Fountainbleau, France, summer 1928, Ecole de Beaux Arts, Paris, 1931-32. Partner, Strickland and Strickland, Boston, 1932-54, Strickland, Brigham and Eldredge, Boston, 1958-69; practice architecture, Boston, 1954-58; cons. on restorations, Plymouth, Mass., 1969—; pres. Boston Archtl. Center; chmn. Plymouth Hist. Dist. Com.; mem. Brookline (Mass.) Bldg. Commn.; trustee Pilgrim Soc., Plymouth; pres. Richard Sparrow House Inc., Plymouth; curator, mem. exec. com. Pilgrim John Howland Soc., Plymouth; chmn. Mass. Bd. Registration for Architects. Served to maj. USAAF, 1941-46. Fellow AIA (nat. com. for hist. preservation commn. on restoration of octagon in Washington); mem. Boston Soc. Architects (dir.), Nat. Trust Hist. Preservation (charter mem., bd. advs.), Nat. Trust for Places of Natural or Hist. Beauty in Eng., Wales and No. Ireland (council), Trustees of Reservations (pres. Mass.), Colonial Soc. Mass., Bostonian Soc., Soc. Preservations N.E. Antiquities. Excavator Abbay de Cluney (France), various Pilgrim house sites, Plymouth; restorations: Plimoth Plantation, Old North (Christ) Ch., Boston, Paul Revere House, Boston. HoKe: 3 Clifford Rd Plymouth MA 02360

STRICKLAND, EUGENE LEE, air force officer; b. Richland Springs, Tex., May 18, 1917; s. John Hester and Annie Laura (Brown) S.; asso. in sci. and civil engring. North Tex. Agrl. Coll., 1937; grad. Armed Forces Staff Coll., 1948, Air War Coll., 1951, Nat. War Coll., 1957; m. Marion Davis, Sept. 1, 1945; children—Eugene Lee, Donald W., Leslie Jo. Commd. 2d lt. USAAF, 1939, advanced through grades to brig. gen. USAF; various assignments, U.S. and China, 1939-47; ops. officer 20th Air Force, Okinawa, 1952-54; comdr. air def. wing McGuire AFB, N.J., 1954-56; with war plans div. USAF and Joint Chiefs Staff, 1957-60; comdr. 81st Tactical Fighter Wing, Eng., 1960-62; dep. comdr. 3d Air Force, London, Eng., 1962-63; chief Middle East, Africa, and South Asia region Office Sec. Def., 1963-65; dir. internat. staff Inter-Am. Def. Bd., 1965-67; vice comdr. 4th Air Force, Hamilton AFB, Calif., 1967—; exec. v.p. HOMCARE (HCI) Internat. Decorated Legion of Merit with oak leaf cluster; D.F.C. with oak leaf cluster; Air medal with 3 oak leaf clusters; Air Force Commendation medal; Purple Heart. Mem. Air Force Hist. Soc., Air Force Assn., 14th Air Force Assn. Methodist. Lion. Home: 4101 E San Miguel Ave Phoenix AZ 85018 Office: 2227 S 48th St Tempe AZ 85282

STRICKLAND, HAROLD ALLISON, JR., mfg. co. exec.; b. Detroit, Feb. 5, 1915; s. Harold A. and Mary (Pugh) S.; B.S. in Mech. Engring., B.S. in Elec. Engring., U. Mich., 1936; M.B.A., Harvard, 1938; m. Ruth Voigt, May 29, 1940; children—Stephanie Mellon (Mrs. Donald Pfaff), Leslie Crandall, Harold Allison III. Exec. engr. Budd Wheel Co., also Budd Co., 1938-50; v.p. Gen. Electric Co., 1950-64; pres. Gen. Signal Corp., Stamford, Conn., 1964—, also dir.; dir. Edwards Co., Inc., O.Z. Gedney Co., Inc., Henschel Corp., Regina Corp., Axel Electronics, Inc., Cin. Time Recorder Co., Gen. Ry. Signal Co., Kinney Vacuum Co., Gen. Signal Can. Ltd., Gen. Signal Appliance Corp., NYAB Internat., Marsh Instrument Co. (Can.) Ltd., Gen. Signal Internat., Gen. Signal Mfg. Corp., Mixing Equipment Co., Inc., GRS Trading, Perolin Co., Inc., Ceilcote Co., Precise Gear Co., N.Y. Air Brake Co. of Can. Ltd., Cross & Trecker Corp., BIF Accutel Inc., SolaBasic Industries, Leeds & Northrup Co. Mem. IEEE, Soc. Automotive Engrs., Machinery and Allied Products Inst., Delta Upsilon. Republican. Congregationalist. Clubs: University (N.Y.C.), Indian Harbor Yacht. Patentee in field. Home: 70 Oneida Dr Greenwich CT 06830 Office: High Ridge Park Stamford CT 06904

STRICKLAND, HUGH ALFRED, lawyer; b. Rockford, Ill., May 3, 1931; s. Hugh and Marie (Elmer) S.; A.B., Knox Coll., 1953; J.D., Chgo. Kent Coll. Law, 1959; m. Donna E. McDonald, Aug. 11, 1956; children—Amy Alice, Karen Ann. Admitted to Ill. bar, 1960; partner firm McDonald, Strickland & Clough, Carrollton, Ill., 1961—; asst. atty. gen. Ill., 1960-67, spl. asst. gen. Ill., 1967-69; pres. McDonald Title Co. Mem. Greene County Welfare Services Com., 1963—, Ill. Heart Assn., 1961-65. Trustee Thomas H. Boyd Meml. Hosp., 1972—. Served with AUS, 1953-55. Recipient award for meritorious service Am. Heart Assn., 1964. Mem. Ill. Jr. C. of C. (past pres.), Ill., Am., Greene County (past pres.) Southwestern (past pres.) bar assns., Ill. Def. Counsel, Am. Judicature Soc., Def. Research Inst., Phi Delta Theta, Phi Delta Phi. Methodist (trustee). Elk. Club: Westlake Country (v.p. 1968-70, dir.). Home: 827 S 7th St Carrollton IL 62016 Office: Public Sq 522 NW Main St Carrollton IL 62016

STRICKLAND, JAMES TYLER, judge; b. Bastrop, La., Oct. 22, 1926; s. James M. and Annie (Turner) S.; B.S., U. Ala., 1950, LL.B., 1952; m. Joan Elizabeth Keeler, June 21, 1952; children—Wayne Tyler, Mary Ann. Admitted to Ala. bar, 1952; asst. dist. atty. Mobile County, Ala., 1955-65; juvenile ct. judge, Mobile County, 1965-70; circuit ct. judge, Mobile, Ala., 1971—. Mem. Juvenile Correctional Study Com. Ala. Chmn. Region Six; mem. advisory bd. Ala. Law Enforcement Planning Agy., also mem. state supervisory and exec. bds.; vice chmn. Ala. Dept. Youth Services; mem. Judge's Advisory Com. Juvenile Justice; mem. Manpower Planning Com.; mem. Mobile County Rehab. Bd. Served with AUS, 1944-46. Mem. Am. Legion, V.F.W., Nat. Council Juvenile Ct. Judges (police action com.), Ala. Council Juvenile Ct. Judges (pres.). Mason (Shriner). Clubs: Bienville, Optomist. Home: 11 Ashley Dr Mobile AL 36608 Office: Mobile County Court House Mobile AL 36602 also Mobile County Youth Center 2315 Costarides St Mobile AL 36617

STRICKLAND, MAURICE ALEXANDER, physician; b. Moultrie, Ga., Sept. 25, 1910; s. Matthew Lee and Mary (Nesbitt) S.; B.S., U. Ga., 1935; M.A., N.Y. U., 1936, Ph.D., 1939; M.D., Emory U., 1948; diploma Cambridge (Eng.) U., 1974; m. Irma Surovy, Mar. 5, 1938 (dec. Mar. 1970); children—Daniel Matthew, Maurice Henry, John Arthur. Grad. asst. econs. N.Y. U., N.Y.C., 1937-39; instr. Coll. Engring., U. N.C. at Raleigh, 1939-40; asso. prof. statistics Ga. Inst. Tech., Atlanta, 1940-43; intern U.S. Marine Hosp., Stapleton, N.Y. 1948-49; resident surgery Atlanta VA Hosp., 1949-50; asst. resident surgery Nassau Hosp., N.Y.C., 1951-52; sr. resident surgery Buffalo VA Hosp., 1954-55; staff surgeon Bay Pines (Fla.) VA Hosp., 1955-56; staff surgeon Columbia (S.C.) VA Hosp., 1956-57; practice medicine specializing in surgery, Atlanta, 1957-60; resident and matriculate in cancer and dermatology N.Y. U. Postgrad. Hosp. and Bellevue Hosp., N.Y.C., 1960-62; practice medicine specializing in dermatology and cancer surgery, Bakersfield, Cal., 1963-64, Houston, 1965—; sect. chief, dermatology dept. Bellaire Gen. Hosp., Houston; mem. staff dermatology skin cancer surgery sect. Meml. Hosp. System Houston, Sharptown Gen. Hosp.; attending physician Houston Social Hygiene Clinic; mem. staff Ben Taub Gen. Hosp., Houston; pres. Maurice A. Strickland & Assos., Inc.; instr. dermatology Baylor U. Med. Sch. Served to surgeon USPHS, 1953. Recipient Wisdom award of honor Wisdom Soc. Diplomate Am. Bd. Surgery, Am. Bd. Dermatology. Fellow A.C.S., Am. Geriatric Soc., Societas Internat. Dermat. Tropicae, Internat. Acad. Cosmetic Surgery, Royal Soc. Medicine (Eng.); mem. Am. Coll. Dermatology (life), Am., So., Tex. med. assns., Harris County Med. Soc., Harris County Acad. Medicine, Acad. Dermatology (asso.), Houston Dermatol. Soc., Pub. Health League, Bellaire C. of C., Beta Gamma Sigma, Delta Mu Delta. Rotarian. Home: 6801 Bellaire Blvd Houston TX 77074 Office: Bellaire Triangle Bldg Suite 100 Bellaire TX 77401

STRICKLAND, NELLIE B., librarian; b. Belmont, Miss., Dec. 12, 1932; d. Edward Spencer and L. Kathleen (Moore) S.; B.S., Murray State U., 1954; M.L.S., George Peabody Coll., 1971. Reference librarian Murray State Coll., 1954; asst. librarian Dept. Army, Ft. Stewart, Ga., 1955-56; field librarian U.S. Army, Japan, 1957-59, area librarian U.S. Army Europe, 1960-66; staff librarian U.S. Army So. Command, C.Z., 1966-67; area librarian U.S. Army, Vietnam, 1967-68, staff librarian, 1971-72; chief librarian, Ft. Benning, Ga., 1970-71; dir. library program U.S. Army Pacific, 1973-74; dir. Army Library Program, Washington, 1974—. Recipient Outstanding Performance award Ft. Benning, 1970; Dept. Army Tng. grantee, 1971. Mem. ALA, Am. Microfilm Assn., Kappa Delta Phi, Alpha Sigma Alpha. Home: 203 Yoakum Pkwy Apt 614 Alexandria VA 22304 Office: DA TAGCEN Attn: DAAG-MSL Forrestal Bldg Washington DC 20314

STRICKLAND, ROBERT, banker; b. Atlanta, May 20, 1927; s. Robert M. and Jessie (Dickey) S.; grad. Marist Coll., 1944; B.S., Davidson Coll., 1948; LL.B., Atlanta Law Sch., 1953; m. Telside Matthews, July 24, 1953; children—Robert Marion, Douglas Watson, William Logan, Walter Dickey. With Trust Co. of Ga., Atlanta, 1948—, v.p., 1959-67, group v.p., 1967, sr. v.p., 1968-72, sr. exec. v.p., 1972-73, pres., 1973—, chmn. bd. dirs., 1974—; pres. Trust Co. Ga., 1976—, chmn. bd., 1978—; dir. Equifax, Inc., Trust Co. Ga. and Trust Co. Bank, Life Ins. Co. Ga., Ga. Power Co. Bd. dirs., past pres. United Way Met. Atlanta; chmn. finance com., v.p. bd. dirs. Piedmont Hosp.; bd. dirs. Fulton County unit, bd. dirs. Ga. div. Am. Cancer Soc.; trustee emeritus Westminster Schs.; chmn. bd. trustees Emory U.; trustee Davidson Coll., Morehouse Coll.; chmn. bd. Central Atlanta Progress, Inc. Served with AUS, 1950-52. Mem. Assn. Res. City Bankers, Am. (past state v.p.), Ga. (past pres.) bankers assns., Atlanta C. of C. (dir.), Sigma Alpha Epsilon; asso. mem. Am. Textile Mfrs. Inst., Ga. Textile Mfrs. Assn., Atlanta Arts Alliance (past chmn. bd.). Methodist. Rotarian. Clubs: Piedmont Driving (past pres.), Capital City, Commerce (dir.), Peachtree Golf (Atlanta); Augusta Nat. Golf. Home: 94 Brighton Rd NE Atlanta GA 30309 Office: 1 Park Pl NE Atlanta GA 30302

STRICKLAND, ROBERT LOUIS, corporate exec.; b. Florence, S.C., Mar. 3, 1931; s. Franz M. and Hazel (Eaddy) S.; A.B., U. N.C., 1952; M.B.A. with distinction, Harvard, 1957; m. Elizabeth Ann Miller, Feb. 2, 1952; children—Cynthia Anne, Robert Edson. With Lowe's Cos., Inc., North Wilkesboro, N.C., 1957—, sr. v.p., 1970-76, exec. v.p., 1976-78, chmn. bd., 1978—, also mem. office pres., exec. com., 1970-78, dir., 1962—; founder Sterling Advt., Ltd., 1966; v.p., mem. adminstrv. com. Lowe's Profit-Sharing Trust, 1961—, chmn. operations. com., 1972—; dir. Revelstoke Cos. Ltd., Calgary, Can.; panelist investor relations field, 1972—. Mem. N.C. Ho. Reps., 1962-64; mem. exec. com. N.C. Republican Party, 1963-73. Bd. dirs., v.p. Nat. Home Improvement Council, 1972-76; bd. dirs. N.C. Sch. Arts Found., 1975-79, N.C. Bd. Natural and Econ. Resources, 1975-76, Home Center Inst.; trustee, sec. bd. Wilkes Community Coll., 1964-73. Served with USN, 1952-55, lt. Res., 1955-62. Named Wilkes County N.C. Young Man of Yr., Wilkes Jr. C. of C., 1962; recipient Bronze Oscar of Industry award Financial World, 1969-74, 76, 77, Silver Oscar of Industry award, 1970, 72, 73, 74, 76, 77, Gold Oscar as best of all industry, 1972; certificate of distinction Brand Names Found., 1970, Retailer of Yr. award, 1971, 73, Distinguished Mcht. award, 1972. Mem. Nat. Assn. Over-the-Counter Cos. (bd. advisers 1973-77), Newcomen Soc., Scabbard and Blade, Phi Beta Kappa, Pi Alpha Kappa. Clubs: Twin City (Winston-Salem, N.C.); Forsyth Country (Winston-Salem); Hound Ears (Blowing Rocks, N.C.); Roaring Gap (N.C.). Author: Lowe's Cybernetwork, 1969; Lowe's Living Legend, 1970; Ten Years of Growth, 1971; The Growth Continues, 1972, 73, 74; also articles. Home: 226 N Stratford Rd Winston-Salem NC 27104 Office: PO Box 1111 North Wilkesboro NC 28659

STRICKLAND, THOMAS JOSEPH, artist; b. Keyport, N.J., Dec. 27, 1932; s. Charles Edward and Clementine Maria (Grasso) S.; student Newark Sch. Fine and Indsl. Arts, 1951-53, Am. Art Sch., 1956-59, Nat. Acad. Sch. Fine Arts with Robert Philipp, 1957-59; m. Debrah J. Ponn, Jan. 15, 1977. Exhibited in one man shows at Hollywood (Fla.) Art Mus., 1972-76; Elliott Mus., Stuart, Fla., 1974, others; exhibited in group shows at Am. Artists Profl. League, N.Y.C., 1958, 61, Exposition Intercontinentale, Monaco, 1966-68, Salon Rouge du Casino Dieppe, 1967, 7e Grand Prix Internat. de Peinture de la Cote d'Azur, Cannes, 1971, Hollywood Art Mus., 1972-76, Art Guild of Boca Raton, 1973, Am. Painters in Paris, 1975; represented in permanent collections St. Vincent Coll., Elliott Mus., Hollywood Art Mus., Salem Coll., Winston-Salem, N.C., St. Hugh Catholic Ch., Fla.; judge local and nat. art shows; television guest; instr. painting and pastels Grove House; lectr. Served with AUS, 1953-55. Recipient Digby Chandler prize Knickerbocker Artists, 1965, Best in Show Blue Dome Art Fellowship, 1972, Blue Ribbon award Cape Coral Nat. Art Show, 1973, 1st prize Hollywood Art Mus., 1973, Charles Hawthorne Meml. award Nat. Arts Club Exhbn., 1977, 1st prize Miami Palette Club, 1978, others. Mem. Blue Dome Art Fellowship, Pastel Soc. Am., Nat. Soc. Lit. and Arts, Grove House, Miami Palette Club. Roman Catholic. Contbr. articles to profl. jours. Home: 2598 Taluga Dr Miami FL 33133. *My aim in life has been to find, capture, and communicate the beauty I see in the world to others by means of painting in my Impressionistic style. To achieve this goal I have developed my talent, been dedicated to art and its disciplines. I have been uncompromising in my choice of what I paint as I paint only what I want to, preferring people and always striving to do my best.*

STRICKLAND, WILLIAM ALEXANDER, JR., educator; b. Dover, Ark., July 25, 1923; s. William Alexander and Kathleen (Turner) S.; student Ark. Poly. Coll., 1940-41; B.S., U. Tenn., 1944;

M.S., U. Wis., 1952, Ph.D., 1955; m. Wanda Green, June 2, 1946; children—William Alva, Robert Allen, David Arnold. Salesman, Upjohn Co., 1946-50; mem. faculty U. Ark. Sch. Pharmacy, 1952-67; prof. Sch. Pharmacy, U. Mo., Kansas City, 1967—, dean, 1967-73; project adminstr. Western Mo. Area Health Edn. Center, Kansas City, 1974-75, dir. Outreach, 1975-77; asst. dean Sch. Medicine, U. Mo., Kansas City, 1977-79; cons. product devel. Parke, Davis & Co., 1956-67. Served with USNR, 1944-45. Mem. Am. Coll. Apothecaries (chmn. pharm. edn. com. 1975-77), Am. Assn. Colls. Pharmacy (mem. exec. com. 1972-73, chmn. pub. affairs com. 1976-78), Am., Mo. pharm. assns., AAAS, Acad. Pharm. Scis., Sigma Xi. Presbyterian. Mason (32 deg.). Home: 9959 Goddard St Overland Park KS 66214 Office: 5100 Rockhill Rd Kansas City MO 64110

STRICKLER, IVAN K., dairy farmer; b. Carlyle, Kans., Oct. 23, 1921; s. Elmer E. and Edna Louise (James) S.; B.S., Kans. State U., 1947; m. Madge Lee Marshall, Aug. 7, 1949; children—Steven Mark, Thomas Scott, Douglas Lee. Owner, mgr. dairy farm, Iola, Kans., 1947—; tchr. farm tng. to vets. World War II, 1947-54; judge 1st and 2d Nat. Holstein Show, Brazil, 1970-71, Internat. Holstein Show, Buenos Aires, 1972; dairy leader 4-H Club, 1962-75. Trustee Allen County Community Jr. Coll.; mem. agr. edn. and research com. Kans. State U. Served with USNR, 1943-46; PTO. Recipient Top Dairy Farm Efficiency award Ford Found., 1971; Master Farmer award Kans. State U. and Kans. Assn. Commerce and Industry, 1972; Gold award Holstein Friesian Assn. Argentina, 1972; Silver award Holstein Friesian Assn. Brazil, 1969; named Man of Yr., World Dairy Exposition, 1978; portrait in Dairy Hall of Fame, Kans. State U., 1974. Mem. Mid Am. Dairymen (sec. corporate bd. 1971-75), Holstein Friesian Assn. Am. (nat. dir. 1964-72), Dairy Shrine (nat. dir. 1971), United Dairy Industry Assn. (dir. 1971—), Nat. Holstein Assn. Am. (pres. 1979-80), Alpha Gamma Rho. Mem. Christian Ch. (deacon, bd. mem.). Club: Nat. Dairy Shrine (pres. 1977-78). Home: RFD 2 Iola KS 66749

STRICKLER, JAMES CALVIN, physician, educator; b. Wilkinsburg, Pa., 1927; M.D., Cornell U., 1953. Intern N.Y. Hosp., 1953-54, asst. resident medicine, 1956-58, chief resident, 1958-59, physician out-patient dept., after 1962, also asst. attending physician; USPHS fellow dept. physiology and medicine Cornell U., 1959-62; career investigator Health Research Council, N.Y.C., after 1962; asst. prof. medicine Cornell U., 1962-67; asso. prof. medicine, asso. dean, then prof. medicine, dean Sch. Medicine Dartmouth, 1967—; cons. medicine Mary Hitchcock Meml. Hosp., 1967—, VA Hosp., White River Junction, Vt., 1967—. Served to lt. M.C. USNR, 1954-56. Address: Dartmouth Coll Med Sch Hanover NH 03755

STRICKLER, THOMAS DAVID, physicist, educator; b. Ferozepur, Punjab, India, Nov. 11, 1922 (parents Am. citizens); s. Herbert Johnson and Martha Theresa (Stewart) S.; student Lehigh U., 1943-44; B.A., Wooster Coll., 1947; M.S., Yale, 1948, Ph.D., 1953; m. Mildred Laing Martin, June 19, 1948; children—Dennis Johnson, Howard Martin, Frances Laing, Susan Elizabeth. Instr. physics Yale, 1952-53; asst. prof. physics Berea (Ky.) Coll., 1953-56, asso. prof., 1956-61, prof., chmn. dept., 1961—, Charles F. Kettering prof. sci., 1962—; vis. scientist Oak Ridge Nat. Lab., 1965-66; Fulbright lectr. U. Sri Lanka, 1973-74 research participant Oak Ridge Inst. Nuclear Studies, 1955-56, guest lectr. mobile radioisotope lab., 1962-64; NSF faculty fellow U. Wis., 1960-61; cons. NSF summer insts. for Indian coll. physics tchrs., Chandigarh, Punjab, 1966, Gauhati, Assam, 1967, Calcutta, Bengal, 1968. Served with Signal Corps, AUS, 1943-46. Recipient Seabury award for excellence in teaching, Berea Coll., 1973. Mem. Am., Ky (past v.p., pres.) assns. physics tchrs., AAUP, Sigma Xi, Phi Kappa Phi, Sigma Pi Sigma. Home: 114 Van Winkle Grove Berea KY 40403

STRICKMAN, ARTHUR EDWIN, ladies apparel retail chain exec.; b. N.Y.C., July 12, 1924; s. Samuel W. and Lee (Light) S.; B.A. in Bus. Adminstrn., Duke U., 1945; m. Rosemary C. Lawson, Sept. 13, 1947; children—Ellen Sue, Wendy Lee, Nancy Ann. Exec. tng., asst. buyer Bloomingdales, 1946-47; sr. dress buyer Bond Stores, N.Y.C., 1948-50; pres. Sandra Post, N.Y.C., 1951-58; with Lerner Stores, N.Y.C., 1959—, v.p. mdse., 1973-74, exec. v.p., 1975-79, pres., 1980—, also dir. Served as officer USN, 1942-46; PTO. Office: Lerner Stores Corp 460 W 33d St New York NY 10001

STRIDER, ROBERT EDWARD LEE, II, ret. coll. pres.; b. Wheeling, W.Va., Apr. 8, 1917; s. Robert Edward Lee and Mary Manning (Holroyd) S.; A.B., Harvard, 1939, A.M., 1940, Ph.D., 1950; L.H.D., U. Me., 1963, Bates Coll., 1968, St. Francis Coll., 1974; H.H.D., Nasson Coll., 1963; LL.D., Concord Coll., 1961, Bowdoin Coll., 1967, Ricker Coll., 1974; D.Sc. Bus. Adminstrn., Bryant Coll., 1967; D.Ed., Suffolk U., 1968; Litt.D., Colby Coll., 1979; m. Helen Bell, Sept. 9, 1941; children—Mary Holroyd, Robert Edward Lee III, William Bell, Elizabeth Greer. Asst. English, Harvard, also Radcliffe Coll., 1941-42; instr. English, Conn. Coll., 1946-51, asst. prof., 1951-57; dean faculty, prof. English, Colby Coll., 1957-60, pres., 1960-79, prof. emeritus, 1979—. Chmn. Episcopal Commn. Coll. Work in Conn., 1953-57; mem. Episcopal Nat. Commn. Coll. Work, 1956-60; mem. guild of scholars Episcopal Ch., 1965—; mem. bd. edn., New London, 1955-57; pres. Faculty Conf. Theology, 1957-58; pres. New Eng. Colls. Fund, 1962-64; chmn. standing com. on instns. higher edn. New Eng. Assn. Colls. and Secondary Schs., 1960-63, v.p., 1963-65, pres., 1965-66; chmn. com. on liberal learning Assn. Am. Colls., 1965-68, treas., 1968-72, chmn., 1973-74; mem. Maine Adv. Com. Civil Rights, 1962-71; chmn. Maine Gov.'s Task Force on Regional and Dist. Orgns., 1977-78; chmn. Select Commn. on Profl. Responsibility, 1978; chmn. Merit Adv. Panel for Recommending Fed. Judges in Maine, 1979. Chmn., Vols. for Stevenson, New London, Conn., 1952-56; civilian aide for Me. to sec. of army, 1965-69. Trustee Gen. Theol. Sem., 1966-71, Westbrook Coll., 1972-78, United Student Aid Funds. Served as lt. USNR, 1942-46. Recipient Disting. Service award Maine Bar Assn., 1979. Fellow Am. Acad. Arts and Scis.; mem. Modern Lang. Assn. Am., Milton Soc. Am., AAUP, ACLU, Renaissance Soc. Am., Phi Beta Kappa. Democrat. Episcopalian. Clubs: Rotary; Century Assn. (N.Y.C.); Author's (London); Union, Tavern (Boston). Author: Robert Greville, Lord Brooke, 1958. Address: care Colby Coll Waterville ME 04901

STRIEDER, JOHN WILLIAM, thoracic surgeon; b. Boston, June 6, 1901; s. Joseph William and Elizabeth Merritt (Robinson) S.; S.B., Mass. Inst. Tech., 1922; M.D., Harvard, 1926; m. Helen Lucille Roberts, Aug. 17, 1935 (dec. Feb. 1961); children—Alison Tennant (Mrs. John S. Mayher), Helen Roberts (Mrs. Martin Linsky), Elizabeth Merritt (Mrs. John J. Atwood); m. 2d, Denise Jouasset, Aug. 7, 1962. Intern, Boston City Hosp., 1927-29; resident Univ. Hosp., Ann Arbor, Mich., 1933-35; practice medicine specializing in thoracic surgery, Boston, 1927-30, 35—, Trudeau Sanatorium, N.Y., 1930-33, Ann Arbor, 1933-35; house surgeon Boston City Hosp., 1927-29, dir. thoracic surgery, 1946-67; house surgeon Boston Lying-in Hosp., 1929-30; asst. resident Trudeau Sanatorium, 1930-33; instr. thoracic surgery U. Mich. Hosp., 1933-35; instr. surgery Harvard Med. Sch., 1936-40; pvt. practice, 1935—; cons. thoracic surgery Univ. Hosp., Boston, Newton-Wellesley Hosp., Newton, Mass. Soldiers Home, Chelsea, Mass.; sr. surgeon New Eng. Bapt. Hosp., New Eng. Deaconess Hosp.; surgeon-in-chief Boston Sanatorium, Mattapan, Mass., 1946-66; prof. clin. surgery emeritus Boston U. Sch. Medicine. John Alexander Meml. lectr., Ann Arbor, 1967; vis. prof. thoracic surgery U. Pa., 1977. Trustee Elizabeth Carleton House; bd. dirs. Found Study and Treatment Thoracic and Related Diseases. Recipient Leonard Wood medal, 1967, Henry Chadwick medal, 1975. Diplomate Am. Bd. Surgery, Am. Bd. Thoracic Surgery (founder's group; chmn. 1964-66). Mem. AMA (residency rev. com. thoracic surgery), A.C.S., Am. Assn. for Thoracic Surgery (pres. 1971-72), Soc. Thoracic Surgeons (exec. com.), Am. Cancer Soc., Am. Heart Assn., Am. Thoracic Soc., Am. Lung Assn., New Eng. (v.p. 1966), Boston surg. socs., Sigma Xi, Lambda Chi Alpha. Clubs: Aesculapian, Harvard (Boston); Country (Brookline, Mass.). Mem. editorial bd. Alexander Monograph Series, 1956—. Contbr. articles to profl. jours. Home: 143 Laurel Rd Chestnut Hill MA 02167 Office: 2000 Washington St Newton Lower Falls MA 02162

STRIGHT, I. LEONARD, ednl. cons.; b. Mercer, Pa., May 7, 1916; s. Fred L. and Martha (Dight) S.; B.A., Allegheny Coll., 1935, M.A., 1938, LL.D., 1978; Ph.D., Case-Western U., 1946; postgrad. U. Chgo., 1963; m. Virginia Minser, July 24, 1940; children—Suzanne (Mrs. L. David York), Robert, William (dec.). Math. tchr. Freedom (Pa.) High Sch., 1935-39, Indiana (Pa.) Joint High Sch., 1939-42; prof. math. Baldwin-Wallace Coll., Berea, Ohio, 1942-46, No. Mich. U., Marquette, 1946-47; prof. math. Indiana (Pa.) U., 1947-57, dean Grad. Sch., 1957-71; acad. v.p. Ohio No. U., 1971-78; cons. in higher edn., 1978—. Mem. Nat. Council Tchrs. Math., Am. Assn. U. Profs., N.E.A., S.A.R., Phi Delta Kappa, Phi Kappa Phi, Delta Tau Delta. Methodist. Kiwanian (pres. 1960), Mason. Contbr. articles profl. jours. Home: 600 Noble Blvd Carlisle PA 17013

STRIKER, CECIL LEOPOLD, archaeologist; b. Cin., July 15, 1932; s. Cecil and Delia (Workum) S.; B.A., Oberlin Coll., 1956; M.A., N.Y. U., 1960, Ph.D. (Am. Research Inst. in Turkey fellow), 1968; M.A. (hon.), U. Pa., 1972; m. Ute Stephan, Apr. 27, 1968. Instr., asst. prof. Vassar Coll., 1962-68; asso. prof. U. Pa., Phila., 1968-78, prof. history of art, 1978—; field archaeologist Dumbarton Oaks Center for Byzantine Studies, 1966—, fellow, 1972-73; dir. survey and excavation Myrelaion, Istanbul, 1965-66; co-dir. Kalenderhane Archaeol. Project, Istanbul, 1966-78; co-dir. Aegean Dendrochronology Project, Greece, 1977—. Served with U.S. Army, 1954-57. Fulbright grantee in Germany, 1960-62; art historian in residence Am. Acad. in Rome, 1973. Mem. Archaeol. Inst. Am., Assn. for Field Archaeology, Coll. Art Assn., Am. Research Inst. in Turkey (pres. 1978—), Turkish Studies Assn., U.S. Nat. Com. for Byzantine Studies, Oriental Club of Phila. Office: Dept History of Art G-29 Fine Arts Bldg U Pa Philadelphia PA 19104

STRINER, HERBERT EDWARD, coll. dean; b. Jersey City, Aug. 16, 1922; s. Harry and Pearl (Strynar) S.; A.B., Rutgers U., 1947, M.A., 1948; Ph.D. (Maxwell fellow 1949-50), Syracuse U., 1951; m. Erma Steinert, Dec. 9, 1943 (div. 1970); children—Richard Alan, Deborah Jane; m. 2d, Iona V. Meredith. Asst. prof. Syracuse U., 1951; economist Interior Dept., 1951-54; program dir. NSF, 1954-55, Nat. Planning Assn., 1955-57; sr. analyst Operations Research Office, Johns Hopkins, 1957-59; program dir. Brookings Inst., 1959-61; program dir. Stanford Research Inst., 1961-62; dir. Upjohn Inst., Washington, 1962-69; dean Coll. Continuing Edn., Am. U., Washington, 1969-72, dean Sch. Bus. Adminstrn., 1974—; chief planning and policy NIH, 1972-73; pres. U. Research Corp., 1973-74. Mem. rev. panel Pres.'s Cabinet Com. Juvenile Delinquency, 1961-63, D.C. Youth Employment Com., 1963, Pres.'s Task Force Am. Indians, 1967, White House Conf. Aging, 1971. Bd. dirs. Opportunities Industrialization Center, N.A.A.C.P., Washington. Served with inf. AUS, 1943-46. Decorated Govt. China medal of merit, 1945. Author: Toward a Fundamental Program for the Training, Employment and Economic Equality of the American Indian, 1968; Continuing Education as a National Capital Investment, 1972; co-author: Local Impact of Foreign Trade, 1960; Civil Rights, Employment and the Social Status of American Negros, 1966. Contbr. profl. jours. Home: 4979 Battery Ln Bethesda MD 20014 Office: Sch Bus Adminstrn Am Univ Washington DC 20016

STRINGFIELD, HEZZ, JR., corp. and fin. co. exec.; b. Heiskell, Tenn., Oct. 4, 1921; s. Hezz and Cecil Willie (Williams) S.; grad. bus. adminstr., Draughon Coll., 1939; student finance and bus., U. Tenn.; m. Helen Louise Hinton, Mar. 20, 1939; children—Carolyn Mae Joyce (Mrs. James M. Corum), Don Wayne, Gail Louise (Mrs. John D. Gamble), Debra June (Mrs. Patrick T. Cassidy). Finance and bus. adminstrn. exec. Clinton Engr. Works, E.I. duPont de Nemours & Co., 1943-44, Manhattan Dist. metall. project, U. Chgo., 1944-45, Monsanto Chem. Co., 1945-48, nuclear div. Union Carbide Corp., 1948-77; ind. bldg. contractor, real estate developer, 1946—; cons. gen. bus., real estate financing, 1946—; pres. FBF, Inc., 1977—; with U.S. AID Mission to Middle East; cons. with industry, govt. and edn. in developing nations, 1965. Bd. dirs. Found. Mgmt. Edn., Advanced Mgmt. Council, Council for Internat. Progress in Mgmt., Inc., Found. for Internat. Progress in Mgmt.; mem. Adv. Council Univs. and Colls. Fellow Soc. Advancement Mgmt. (Profl. Mgr. citation 1963, v.p. 1958-62, exec. v.p. 1962-63, pres. 1963-64, chmn. bd. 1964-65); mem. Am. Mgmt. Assn., Am. Inst. Accountants, Methodist. Home: 5000 Trent Ln Concord Knoxville TN 37922 Office: 1201 Hilton Rd Knoxville TN 37921

STRINGHAM, JAMES HARRINGTON, food and feed co. exec.; b. Woodstock, Ont., Can., Nov. 30, 1937; s. Lloyd Harrington and Frances Mary (Tabor) S.; B.A. in Econs. and Bus., McMaster U., Hamilton, Ont., 1959; m. Mildred June Shirton, Aug. 1, 1959; children—Kent, Gayle. Sales rep. Steel Co. of Can., Hamilton, 1959-61; with Ralston Purina Can. Inc., Toronto, Ont., 1961—, exec. v.p., 1970-74, sr. exec.v.p., 1974—; dir. Dist. Trust Co., London, Ont. Bd. dirs. Can. Nat. 4H Council. Home: 60 Erindale Crescent Brampton ON L6W 1B5 Canada Office: 2700 Finch Ave Toronto ON M9W 5P5 Canada

STRINGHAM, LUTHER WINTERS, health planner; b. Colorado Springs, Colo., Dec. 14, 1915; s. Luther Wilson and Fern (Van Duyn) S.; B.A. summa cum laude, U. Colo., 1938, M.A. in Econs., 1939; Rockefeller fellow pub. adminstrn. U. Minn., 1939-40, Nat. Inst. Pub. Affairs, 1940-41; m. Margret Ann Pringle, Dec. 1, 1942; 1 dau., Susan Jean. Economist, Dept. Commerce, also OPA, 1941-43; intelligence officer War Dept., 1946-51; program analysis officer Office of the Sec. HEW, 1956-63, chmn. sec.'s com. mental retardation, 1961-63; exec. dir. Nat. Assn. for Retarded Children, 1963-68; intergovtl. relations officer HEW, 1968-77; planning dir. Central Va. Health Systems Agy., 1977—. Mem. President's Com. Employment Handicapped, 1963-68; pres. Music for People, Inc., 1971-74; lectr. City U. N.Y., 1971-76. Mem. Nat. council Boy Scouts Am., 1963—. Served to capt. AUS, 1943-46, to lt. col. USAFR, 1946-56. Mem. Va. Pub. Health Assn., Am. Public Health Assn., Am. Assn. Health Planning, Phi Beta Kappa, Pi Gamma Mu, Delta Sigma Rho. Home: 3101 Mt Hill Dr Midlothian VA 23113 Office: 2015 Staples Mill Rd Richmond VA 23230

STRISIK, PAUL, artist; b. Bklyn., Apr. 21, 1918; s. Abraham Rodger and Reine Rose (Rehbock) S.; student Art Students League, N.Y.C., 1946-48; m. Nancy Susan Samaras, Nov. 16, 1968; children—Peter, John Catherine, Ellen. One-man exhbns. include Grand Central Art Galleries, N.Y.C., 1960-70, Doll & Richards, Boston, 1965, 76, Rockport (Mass.) Art Assn., 1964-69, 75, Andover (Mass.) Gallery Fine Arts, 1969, Gordon Coll., Wenham, Mass., 1972, Johnson-Welch Gallery, Kansas City, Mo., 1978; group exhbns. include Nat. Acad. Art, 1960, 71-72, 73-79, Allied Artists Am., N.Y.C., 1955-78, Salmagundi Club, N.Y.C., 1962-78, Knickerbocker Artists, N.Y.C., 1963-77, Am. Watercolor Soc., N.Y.C., 1963-77, Rockport Art Assn., 1956-79, N. Shore Arts Assn., Gloucester, Mass., 1956-79, Am. Artists Profl. League, N.Y.C., 1960-79; rep. permanent collections Parrish Mus. Art, Southampton, N.Y., Percy H. Whitney Mus., Fairhope, Ala., Naugatuck (Conn.) Mus., Utah State U.; tchr. workshops, lectr. throughout U.S. and Europe; mng. dir. Hall Line Co., Highland Mills, N.Y., 1937-40; dir. Empire Twine & Yarn Co., N.Y.C., 1945-69. Bd. govs. Rockport Bd. Trade, 1958-60. Served with USN, 1941-45. Recipient over 125 awards including Windsor and Newton award Knickerbocker Artists, 1965, medal of merit, 1972; FAS award Allied Artists Am., 1965, Lehrer Meml. award, 1970; Wick award Salmagundi Club, 1967, Chandler award, 1967, AWS award, 1970, Salmagundi award, 1970-73; gold medal Marsh ann. exhbn., 1967, 71; gold medal Rockport Art Assn., 1967, 72; Best in Show award Am. Artists Profl. League grand. nat., 1968, 72; A. Dedn award Am. Watercolor Soc., 1969, Lehman award, 1970; gold medal Hudson Valley Art Assn., 1970; Ray Jones Gold medal Am. Vets. Soc. Artists, 1970; Watercolor prize Nat. Arts Club, 1970, bronze medal, 1960; Obrig prize Nat. Acad., 1972; silver medal Arts Atlantic, Mass., 1972; Gold medal Gallery Am. Art, 1974; Arthur T. Hill Meml. award Salmagundi Club, 1974; Helen Gould Kennedy award Acad. Artists Ann., 1974; Claude Parsons Meml. award, Am. Artists Profl. League, 1975; Grumbacher award Acad. Artists, 1975; Philip G. Shumaker award Rockport Art Assn., 1975, Elizabeth Schlemm award, 1975; Canelli Gold Medal for oils, 1975. Mem. N.A.D. (asso.), Nat. Acad. Western Art, Rockport Art Assn. (pres. 1968-71), Am. Watercolor Soc., Allied Artists Am., Knickerbocker Artists, Am. Artists Profl. League, N. Shore Arts Assn. Club: Salmagundi. Address: 123 Marmion Way Rockport MA 01966

STRITTMATTER, CORNELIUS FREDERICK, IV, biochemist, educator; b. Phila., Nov. 16, 1926; s. Cornelius Frederick and Christine (Frey) S.; B.S., Juniata Coll., 1947; Ph.D., Harvard, 1952; m. Carol Marie Entz, Aug. 29, 1955; 1 dau., Clare Elise. Instr. biol. chemistry Harvard Med. Sch., 1952-54, asso., 1955-58, asst. prof., 1958-61; research fellow Oxford U., Eng., 1954-55; Odus M. Mull prof. biochemistry Bowman Gray Sch. Medicine, Winston-Salem, N.C., 1961—, chmn. dept. biochemistry, 1961-78; cons. New Eng. Deaconess Hosp., 1958-61; mem. fellowship com. NIH, 1967-70, 74. Lalor fellow, 1952, 60; USPHS research fellow, 1954-55; USPHS sr. research fellow, 1961. Mem. Am. Soc. Biol. Chemists, Am. Chem. Soc. (past sect. chmn.), Assn. Med. Sch. Depts. Biochemistry (council 1975-77, sec. 1977-78, rep. to Council Acad. Socs. 1975-77), Biochem. Soc. (Eng.), Soc. for Developmental Biology, Soc. for Exptl. Biology and Medicine, Sigma Xi. Contbr. articles profl. jours. Home: 817 Clovelly Rd Winston-Salem NC 27106

STRNAD, JAMES JOHN, mfg. co. exec.; b. Cleve., Apr. 3, 1925; s. James F. and Jennie D. (Holecek) S.; B.S. in Engring., Mass. Inst. Tech., 1945; m. Edna L. Dawley, Apr. 7, 1951; children—James F. II, Lyse Stuart, Nina Phelps. With Lempco Industries, Inc., Cleve., 1946—, v.p., gen. mgr., 1951-53, pres., gen. mgr., 1953—, pres., chmn. bd., 1968—; pres., chmn. bd. Lempco Internat., Inc., Bedford, Ohio, 1953—, Lempco Can., Ltd., Montreal, Que., 1961—. Del., White House Conf. Export Expansion, 1963; mem. Chief Execs. Forum, 1974. Trustee Cleve. Southeast YMCA, U. Sch. for Boys, Shaker Heights, Ohio. Served to lt. (j.g.) USNR, 1943-46. Mem. Wine and Food Soc. Clubs: Cleveland, Union, Skating (Cleve.); Pine Lake Trout, Shaker Heights Country, Kirtland. Contbr. articles to profl. jours. Home: 2963 Courtland Blvd Shaker Heights OH 44122 Office: care RA Korpowski Lempco Industries 5490 Dunham Rd Cleveland OH 44137

STROBEL, FREDRIC ANDREW, ballet dancer; b. Chgo., Nov. 7, 1935; s. Fred G. and Ella Emma (Zierer) S.; grad. high sch. Prin. dancer Royal Winnipeg (Man., Can.) Ballet, 1957-66; prin. dancer, ballet master Nat. Ballet, Washington, 1966-74; instr. Washington Ballet, 1974-76, Houston Ballet, 1976—; performed on CBC-TV, Winnipeg and Toronto, 1958-65; appeared in summer stock, Louisville and Winnipeg, 1958-65; soloist Chgo. Opera Ballet, 1959-60. Home: 3119 Broadmead Houston TX 77025 Office: Houston Ballet 2615 Colquitt Houston TX 77098

STROBEL, HOWARD AUSTIN, educator, chemist; b. Bremerton, Wash., Sept. 5, 1920; s. Frank Edward and Emma Lena (Scheurer) S.; B.S., Wash. State U., 1942; Ph.D. (Charles A. Coffin fellow), Brown U., 1947; m. Shirley Lou Holcomb, Aug. 26, 1953; children—Paul Austin, Gary Dent, Linda Susan, Jr. chemist Manhattan Project, 1943-46; postdoctoral appointment Brown U., 1947-48; instr. Duke, Durham, N.C., 1948-51, asst. prof., 1951-58, asso. prof., 1958-64, prof. chemistry, 1964—, asst. dean Trinity Coll., 1956-64, asso. dean Trinity Coll., 1964-66, coordinator fedn. programs, 1975—, sec. undergrad. faculty council, 1956-58, 60-66, chmn. com. for study of student residential life, 1968-69; dean Baldwin Fedn., 1972-75, faculty fellow, 1975—; vis. prof. U. Leicester, 1971-72. Recipient Asso. Students Duke U. Outstanding Prof. award 1969. Mem. Am. Chem. Soc. (chmn. N.C. sect. 1962), Chem. Soc., Phi Beta Kappa, Sigma Xi, Alpha Kappa Lambda, Omicron Delta Kappa. Democrat. Baptist. Author: Chemical Instrumentation, 2d edit., 1973. Home: 1119 Woodburn Rd Durham NC 27705

STROBEL, JAMES WALTER, univ. pres.; b. Jefferson County, Ohio, Oct. 31, 1933; s. Walter John and Caroline McCausland (McConnell) S.; A.B., Ohio U., 1951; Ph.D., Wash. State U., 1959; m. Donna Marie Rogers, June 18, 1955; children—Cynthia, James Walter. Research asst. Wash. State U., 1955-59; asst. prof. plant pathology U. Fla., 1959-66, asso. prof., 1966-69, prof., 1969—), dir. research and edn. center, Bradenton, 1968-70, head dept. ornamental horticulture, Gainesville, 1970-74; head dept. hort. sci. N.C. State U., Raleigh, 1974-77; pres. Miss. U. for Women, 1977—; mem. spl. task force groups. Recipient Spl. Research award U. Fla. Hort. Soc., 1972, Fla. Fruit and Vegetable Assn., 1969. Mem. Am. Soc. Hort. Scis., Am. Assn. State Colls. and Univs., Am. Phytopathol. Soc., Miss. Educators Assn., Phi Beta Kappa, Sigma Xi, Phi Eta Sigma, Phi Kappa Phi, Gamma Sigma Delta, Pi Alpha Xi. Democrat. Presbyterian. Clubs: Rotary, Civitan. Research, numerous articles on devel. of eight disease-resistant tomato varieties for Southeastern U.S., genetic relationships, 1961-70. Home: 1217 College St Columbus MS 39701 Office: Office of Pres Miss Univ for Women Columbus MS 39701

STROBLE, FRANCIS ANTHONY, mfg. co. exec.; b. St. Louis, Aug. 20, 1930; s. Frank J. and Loraine L. (Michel) S.; B.S. in Commerce, St. Louis, 1952, M.S. in Commerce magna cum laude, 1960; postgrad. Northwestern U., 1968; m. Ruth M. O'Neill, Feb. 14, 1953; children—Deborah, Mark, Susan, Matthew, Karen. Auditor, Hochschield, Bloom & Co., St. Louis, 1954-56; with Monsanto Co., St. Louis, 1956—, dir. data processing, then v.p., controller, 1973-79, v.p. fin., 1979—; dir. Mfrs. Bank & Trust Co.; mem. profl. adv. bd. U. Ill. Mem. lay adv. bd. St. Mary's Health Center, St. Louis. Served to 1st lt. USAF, 1952-54. Mem. Am. Inst. C.P.A.'s, Fin. Execs. Inst.

Home: 7640 S Rockhill Rd Saint Louis MO 63123 Office: 800 N Lindbergh Blvd Saint Louis MO 63166

STROBOS, ROBERT JULIUS, educator, neurologist; b. The Hague, Holland, July 2, 1921; s. Harm and Anna (Ritzenhofer) S.; B.A., U. Amsterdam (Holland), 1941, M.D., 1945; m. Virginia L. Gaskin, Feb. 10, 1967; children—Semon, Jur, Carolyn, Katharine, Eben. Came to U.S., 1949, naturalized, 1959. Rotating intern Univ. Hosp., Amsterdam, 1945-47; physician Lago Oil Co., Aruba, N.W. I., 1947-49; resident neurology and psychiatry Montefiore Hosp., N.Y.C., Neurol. Inst., N.Y.C., Nat. Hosp., London, Eng. and N.Y. Hosp., White Plains, 1950-54; asst. prof., asso. prof. neurology Bowman Gray Sch. Medicine, Winston-Salem, N.C., 1954-60; prof. neurology, chmn. dept. N.Y. Med. Coll., 1960—; attending neurologist Lincoln, Met., Bird S. Coler hosps., N.Y.C. Westchester County Med. Center, Valhalla, N.Y. Fellow Am. Acad. Neurology; mem. Assn. Research Nervous and Mental Diseases, Am. Epilepsy Soc., Am. EEG Soc., A.M.A., Assn. U. Profs. Neurology. Contbr. profl. jours. Home: 253 W 99th St New York NY 10025 Office: NY Med Coll Munger Pavilion Valhalla NY 10595

STRODE, WILLIAM HALL, III, photojournalist; b. Louisville, Aug. 6, 1937; s. William Hall and Margaret (Diehl) S.; B.S., Western Ky. U., 1959; m. Elizabeth Ann Wheeler, Nov. 26, 1960 (div. 1973); children—Alissa Michelle, Erin Hall; m. 2d, Hope Powel Alexander, Nov. 12, 1977. News photographer Courier Jour. and Louisville Times, 1960-64, asst. dir. photography, 1968-75; photographer Courier Jour. mag., 1964-77; formed William Strode Assos., photog. and pub. co., Louisville, 1978—; exhbns. include Fine Arts III, 1961, Profile in Poverty, Smithsonian Inst., 1966, Documerica in Corcoran Gallery, Washington, 1972, 73, Picture of Year Travelling Exhibits; one man show Speed Mus. Active local Boy Scouts Am.; founder, Nat. Press Photographers Found., 1975. Served with AUS, 1959. Recipient Headliners best photojournalism award, 1965; award for excellence for best mag. photog. reporting Overseas Press Club, 1967; named One of 10 Outstanding Young Men Louisville, Jr. C. of C., 1966; co-recipient Pulitzer Prize for pub. service (Courier Jour.), 1967, for feature photography, 1976. Mem. Nat. Press Photographers Assn. (Photographer of Year award 1966, Newspaper Mag. Picture Editor of Year 1968, nat. ednl. chmn. 1966-68, v.p. 1973, pres. 1974), Sigma Chi, Sigma Delta Chi, Kappa Alpha Mu. Methodist. Author: Barney Cowherd Photographer, 1973. Home and office: 1008 Kent Rd Prospect KY 40059

STRODEL, ROBERT CARL, lawyer; b. Evanston, Ill., Aug. 12, 1930; s. Carl Frederick and Imogene (Board) S.; B.S., Northwestern U., 1952; J.D., U. Mich., 1955; m. Mary Alice Shonkwiler, June 17, 1956; children—Julie Ann, Linda Lee, Sally Payson. Admitted to Ill. bar, 1955, U.S. Supreme Ct. bar, 1970; mem. firm Davis, Morgan & Witherell, Peoria, Ill., 1957-59; pvt. practice law, Peoria, 1959-69; prin. Strodel & Kingery Assos., Peoria, Ill., 1969—; asst. state's atty., Peoria, 1960-61; instr. bus. law Bradley U., Peoria, 1961-62; lectr. Belli seminars, Denver, 1969, Miami, 1970, 73, Portland, 1971, St. Louis, 1972, others. Gov. appointee Ill. Dangerous Drugs Advisory Council, 1970-73; gen. chmn. Peoria-Tazewell Easter Seals, 1963, Cancer Crusade, 1970; pres. Peoria Civic Ballet, 1969-70; mem. Mayor's Commn. on Human Relations, 1962-64; chmn. City of Peoria Campaign Ethics Bd., 1975; sec. Peoria County Republican Party, 1970-74; campaign chmn. Gov. Richard Ogilvie, Peoria County, 1972, Sen. Ralph Smith, 1970; bd. dirs. Crippled Children's Center, 1964-65, Peoria Symphony Orchestra, 1964-68. Served with AUS, 1956-57. Named Outstanding Young Man Peoria, Peoria Jr. C. of C., 1963. Mem. Am., Ill. trial lawyers assns., Am., Ill. (Lincoln awards for legal writing, 1961, 63, 65) bar assns, Am. Coll. Legal Medicine, Am. Soc. Law and Medicine. Mason (Shriner). Author articles in med.-legal field. Home: 3908 N Pinehurst Ct Peoria IL 61614 Office: 900 First Nat Bank Bldg Peoria IL 61602. *The pursuit of professional excellence has been a lifetime goal, coupled with contributions to public, political and civic affairs. He who takes from his community must also contribute to it.*

STROGOFF, ALFRED, food service co. exec.; b. Chelsea, Mass., Mar. 15, 1928; s. Hyman and Ruth (Brush) S.; B.S. in Mech. Engring., Worcester Poly. Inst., 1949; m. Elaine Harriet Kaplan, Oct. 22, 1950; children—Jody, Nancy, Michael, Lauren, James. Exec. v.p. Adler Electronics Co., New Rochelle, N.Y., 1949-63; group pres. Amecon div. and edn. group Litton Industries, White Plains, N.Y., 1963-70; exec. v.p. corporate services and ops. Sun Chem. Corp., N.Y.C., 1970-76; pres., chief exec. officer Internat. FoodService Corp., Los Angeles, 1976—. Home: 6 Rue Cannes Newport Beach CA 92660 Office: 1065 E Walnut St Carson CA 90746

STROHM, JOHN LOUIS, author, editor, radio commentator, bus. exec.; b. nr. West Union, Ill., June 22, 1912; s. Charles Gottlieb and Nellie Ethel (Davidson) S.; B.S., U. Ill., 1935; m. Lillian Ann Murphy, Sept. 8, 1941; children—Terry John, Karen Nell, Robert, Cheryl Ann, David, Colleen. Publicity, Owens-Ill. Glass Co., 1935-36; around the world as journalist, free lance writing, 1937-38; field editor Prairie Farmer, 1938-41; traveled in Latin America, gathered material for writing and radio, 1941; asst. editor Prairie Farmer, 1941-43, mng. editor 1943-46; traveled in Europe extensively, 1946, writing for farm mags., NANA broadcasting for CBS; traveled in Soviet Union extensively, 1946, broadcasting, writing stories for NEA syndicate; pres. No. Ill. Publs., Inc., 1945-50; now pres. Publs., Inc., editor Nat. Wildlife, Internat. Wildlife Mag.; mgr. Nat. Corn Husking Contest, 1941; chmn. 1952 Nat. Rural Electrification Conf.; conducted radio program, World Neighbor, WLS, 1944-46; fgn. corr., Europe, Middle East, 1948, S.E. Asia, 1950, Europe, 1954; ofcl. escort to Russian farm ofcls. on U.S. trip, 1955; worked for Pres. Eisenhower, Washington, 1956; first Am. corr. with State Dept. permision to travel in Red China for NEA syndicate, Readers' Digest, NBC, Look mag., 1958; pres. John Strohm Assos., Inc.; sec., dir., organizer Terra Chems. Internat., Inc., Sioux City, Iowa; organizer World Seeds, Inc.; cons. to sec. agr. Mem., v.p. U. Ill. Found. Recipient Sigma Delta Chi Distinguished Service award, 1947, 59; Overseas Press Club award, 1959; Pres.'s award, 1978. Mem. Pan.-Am. Council (past pres.), Nat. Corn Husking Contest Assn. (pres.), U. Ill. Alumni Assn. (dir.), U. Ill. Journalism Alumni Assn. (dir.), Am. Agrl. Editors Assn. (sec.; pres. 1946), Overseas Press Club, Chgo. Press Club. Clubs: Players (N.Y.C.); Cliff Dwellers, Adventurers (Chgo.). Author: I Live With Latin Americans, 1943; Just Tell the Truth, 1947; editor: Ford Almanac; asso. editor Country Gentleman, 1947-55; contbr. Readers' Digest. Home: 515 W Jackson St Woodstock IL 60098

STROHMEIER, WILLIAM DENGLER, advt. co. exec.; b. Newton, Mass., Mar. 20, 1916; s. Bertram Augustus and Edith Newlin (Dengler) S.; grad. Monson Acad. (Mass.), 1932; B.S., Amherst Coll., 1936; m. Beatrice Torrey Chesterman, Dec. 7, 1940; children—Peter, Judith. Sales promotion mgr. Piper Aircraft Corp., Lock Haven, Pa., 1936-41; pres. Strohmeier Assos., N. Y.C., 1945-50, Davis, Parsons & Strohmeier, Inc., N.Y.C., 1950-69; vice chmn. Friedlich, Fearon & Strohmeier, advt., N.Y.C., 1969-73; sr. v.p. internat. Wilson Haight & Welch Advt., Greenwich, Conn., 1973-78; sr. v.p. deGarmo, Inc., N.Y.C., 1979—. Served with USAF, 1941-45. Mem. Quiet Birdmen, Alpha Delta Phi, Wings Club. Author: (with Beverly Howard) You Can Learn to Fly, 1946; (with Robert Fogg) Seaplane Flying and Operations, 1947. Clubs: Tokeneke (Darien, Conn.); Mishaum Point Yacht (South Dartmouth, Mass.). Home: 8 Partridge Ln Darien CT 06820 Office: 605 3d Ave New York NY 10016

STROHMEYER, JOHN, publishing co. exec.; b. Cascade, Wis., June 26, 1924; s. Louis A. and Anna Rose (Saladunas) S.; student Moravian Coll., 1941-43; A.B., Muhlenberg Coll., 1947; M.A. in Journalism, Columbia, 1948; m. Nancy Jordan, Aug. 20, 1949; children—Mark, John, Sarah. With Nazareth Item, 1940-41; night reporter Bethlehem (Pa.) Globe-Times, 1941-43, 45-47; investigative reporter Providence Jour.-Bull., 1949-56; editor Bethlehem Globe-Times, 1956—, v.p., 1961—, dir., 1963—; African-Am. journalism tchr. in Nairobi, Freetown, 1964. Trustee Moravian Coll.; bd. dirs. Hawk Mountain Sanctuary, Historic Bethlehem, Inc. Served to lt. (j.g.), USNR, 1943-45. Pulitzer Traveling fellow, 1948; Nieman fellow, 1952-53; recipient Comenius award Moravian Coll., 1971; Pulitzer prize for editorial writing, 1972. Mem. Am. Press Inst. (seminar leader 1961—), Am., Pa. (pres. 1965-66) socs. newspaper editors. Club: Hiawatha Hunting and Fishing (E. Stroudsburg, Pa.). Contbr. articles on press and morality in govt. to mags. Home: 262 W Langhorne Ave Bethlehem PA 18017 Office: 202 W 4th St Bethlehem PA 18016

STROKE, GEORGE WILHELM, educator, physicist; b. Zagreb, Yugoslavia, July 29, 1924; s. Elias and Edith Mechner (Silvers) S.; B.Sc., U. Montpellier (France), 1942; Ing. Dipl., Inst. Optics, U. Paris (France), 1949; Ph.D. in Physics, Sorbonne, Paris, 1960; m. Masako Haraguchi, Feb. 5, 1973. Came to U.S., 1952, naturalized, 1957. Mem. research staff and def. research staff Mass. Inst. Tech., 1952-63, lectr. elec. engring., 1960-63; asst. research prof. physics Boston U., 1956-57; NATO research fellow U. Paris, 1959-60; prof. elec. engring., head electro-optical sci. labs. U. Mich., 1963-67; prof. elec. scis. and med. biophysics State U. N.Y. at Stony Brook, 1967—; vis. prof. Harvard U. Med. Sch., 1970-73, Technische U. München, 1978. Adviser laser task force USAAF Systems Command, 1964; govt. sci. Cons. U.S. and abroad, 1964—; cons. NASA Electronics Research Center, Cambridge, Mass., 1966—; mem. commn. I, Internat. Radio Sci. Union, Nat. Acad. Scis., 1965—; cons. Am. Cancer Soc., 1972—; mem. NSF blue ribbon task force on ultrasonic imaging, 1973-74. Recipient Humboldt prize, 1978. Fellow Optical Soc. Am., Am. Phys. Soc., IEEE. Club: Explorers. Author: An Introduction to Coherent Optics and Holography, 1966; also numerous articles, chpts. in books. Co-originator interferometric servo control method of grating ruling; originator several methods of holography, digital and optical image, also bank-automation document-image storage, retrieval and processing, both digital and optical; image deblurring in electron microscopy and space imaging applications (including detection of oil and natural gas resources); three-dimensional image and structure reconstructions in X-ray crystallography, electron microscopy, X-ray and ultrasonic diagnostic imaging. Address: State U NY Stony Brook NY 11790

STROKE, HINKO HENRY, educator, physicist; b. Zagreb, Yugoslavia, June 16, 1927; s. Elias and Edith (Mechner) S.; brought to U.S., 1943, naturalized, 1949; B.E.E., Newark Coll. Engring., 1949; M.S., Mass. Inst. Tech., 1952, Ph.D., 1954; student Columbia U., 1947; m. Norma Bilchick, Jan. 14, 1956; children—Ilana Lucy, Maria Tamar. Research asst. physics Mass. Inst. Tech., 1950-54; research asst. Princeton, 1954-57, research asso., 1957; mem. research staff. Sponsored Research div., lectr. dept. physics Mass. Inst. Tech., 1957-63; asso. prof. physics N.Y. U., 1963-68, prof., 1968—; professeur associé U. Paris, 1969-70, École Normale Supérieure, 1978; prof. d' échange U. Paris and Centre Nat. de la Recherche Scientifique, summers 1971-74; vis. scientist U. Paris, summer 1975, U. Munich, 1977-78; cons. Atomic Instrument Co., Mass. Inst. Tech. Sci. Translation Service, Tech. Research Group, Cambridge Air Force Research Center, Am. Optical Corp., Scripta Technica, Acad. Press, I.T.T. Fed. Labs., Majestic Bolting Cloth Corp., NASA, others; mem. com. on line spectra of elements Nat. Acad Scis.-NRC, 1976-79. Mem. Chorus Pro Musica, Boston, 1951-54, 57-63, Munchener Bach-Chor, Munich, 1977-78; mem. Collegiate Chorale, N.Y., 1964—. Served with AUS, 1946-47. Recipient Sr. U.S. Scientist award Alexander von Humboldt Found., 1977; NATO sr. fellow in sci., 1975. Fellow Am. Phys. Soc.; mem. AAAS, European Phys. Soc., European Group Atomic Spectroscopy, Optical Soc. Am., Société Française de Physique, Tau Beta Pi, Sigma Xi, Omicron Delta Kappa. Contbg. author: Nuclear Physics, 1963; Atomic Physics, 1969; Hyperfine Interactions in Excited Nuclei, 1971; Francis Bitter: Selected papers, 1969; Atomic Physics 3, 1973; Nuclear Moments and Nuclear Structure, 1973; A Perspective of Physics, Vol. 1, 1977. Editor Comments on Atomic and Molecular Physics. Adv. editorial bd. Physica. Home: 271 Old Army Rd Scarsdale NY 10583 Office: Dept Physics NYU 4 Washington Pl New York City NY 10003

STROLL, AVRUM, educator, philosopher; b. Oakland, Calif., Feb. 15, 1921; s. Harry and Dina (Wolf) S.; A.B., U. Calif. at Berkeley, 1943, M.A., 1948, Ph.D., 1951; m. Mary Elizabeth Swensen, June 3, 1955; children—Robin Emily, Susan Elizabeth, Theodore Josef, Betsy Noelle. Mem. faculty U. Oreg., 1951-52, U. B.C., 1952-54, 55-63; vis. prof. U. Iowa, 1954-55; mem. faculty U. Calif. at San Diego, 1963—, prof. philosophy, 1960—. Served with USMCR and AUS, 1942-46. Guggenheim fellow, 1972-73. Mem. Am. Philos. Assn., Mind Soc., Aristotelian Soc. Author: The Emotive Theory of Ethics, 1954; Reason and Religious Belief, 1958; (with R.H. Popkin) Introduction to Philosophy, 1961. Editor, contbr.: Epistemology, New Essays in The Theory of Knowledge, 1967. Home: 1750 Valdez Dr La Jolla CA 92037

STROM, EVERALD HANSON, clergyman, ch. pres.; b. Wahpeton, N.D., June 7, 1921; s. Erwin M. and Bertha C. (Hanson) S.; B.A., Augsburg Coll., 1942; M.A., N.Y. U., 1948; B.D., Northwestern Theol. Sem., 1956; m. Sylvia E. Kilde, June 5, 1943; children—Edward, David. Ordained to ministry Ch. Lutheran Bretheren, 1944; pastor Bethany Lutheran Ch., S.I., N.Y., 1944-47; pastor Ebenezer Lutheran Ch., Mpls., 1947-60, Faith Lutheran Ch., Briarcliff Manor, N.Y., 1960-64, Triumph Lutheran Ch., Moorhead, Minn., 1964-68; pres. Ch. Lutheran Brethren, Fergus Falls, Minn., 1968—. Mem. bd. edn. Lutheran Brethren Schs., Fergus Falls. Bd. dirs. Lutheran Evangelistic Movement, Mpls. Mem. Nat. Assn. Evangelicals. Republican. Kiwanian. Home: 203 Everett Ave E Fergus Falls MN 56537 Office: Box 655 Fergus Falls MN 56537

STROM, LYLE ELMER, lawyer; b. Omaha, Jan. 6, 1925; s. Elmer T. and Eda (Hanisch) S.; student U. Neb., 1946-47; A.B., Creighton U., 1950, J.D. cum laude, 1953; m. Regina Ann Kelly, July 31, 1950; children—Mary Bess, Susan Frances, Amy Clare, Kathleen Ann, David Kelly, Margaret Mary, Bryan Thomas. Admitted to Nebr. bar, 1953; asso. firm Fitzgerald, Brown, Leahy, Strom, Schorr & Barmettler and predecessor firm, Omaha 1953-60, partner, 1960-63, gen. trial partner, 1963—; dir. World of Sleep, Inc., Unpainted Furniture Center, Inc. Instr. law Creighton U., 1959—; mem. com. pattern jury instrns. and practice and proc. Nebr. Supreme Ct., 1965—; spl. legal counsel Omaha Charter Rev. Commn., 1973. Mem. exec. com. Covered Wagon council Boy Scouts Am., 1955-57. Chmn. bd. trustees Marian High Sch., 1969-71. Served as ensign USNR and with U.S. Maritime Service, 1943-46. Fellow Am. Coll. Trial Lawyers, Internat. Acad. Trial Lawyers; mem. Citizens for Edn. Freedom, Am., Nebr., Omaha (pres.-elect 1979-80) bar assns., Am. Judicature Soc., Midwestern Assn. Amateur Athletic Union (pres. 1976—), Alpha Sigma Nu (pres. alumni chpt. 1970-71). Republican. Roman Catholic. Rotarian. Home: 2206 S 91st St Omaha NE 68124 Office: Woodmen Tower Omaha NE 68102

STROM, STEPHEN ERIC, astronomer; b. Bronx, N.Y., Aug. 12, 1942; s. Albert William and Beatrice (Reisinger) S.; A.B., Harvard, 1962, A.M., Ph.D., 1964; m. Karen Marie Lewallen, Mar. 31, 1960; children—Robert Charles, Kathy Marie, David Michael, Julie Eileen. Lectr., Harvard, 1964-68; astro-physicist Smithsonian Astrophysical Obs., Cambridge, Mass., 1964-68; asso. prof. astronomy State U. N.Y., Stony Brook, 1969-71, prof., 1971-72, coordinator astronomy and astrophysics, 1969-72; astronomer Kitt Peak Nat. Obs., Tucson, 1972—, chmn. galactic and extragalatic program, 1975-79; asso. mng. editor Astrophys. Jour., 1979—. Recipient Bok prize Harvard, 1970; Warner prize Am. Astronom. Soc., 1975. Woodrow Wilson fellow (hon.), 1962; Sloan Found. fellow, 1970-72. Mem. Am. Astronom. Soc., Astronom. Soc. Pacific, Internat. Astron. Union, AAAS, Phi Beta Kappa, Sigma Xi. Home: 4201 E Poe Tucson AZ 85711 Office: 950 N Cherry St Tucson AZ 85726

STROMBERG, ARTHUR HAROLD, profl. services co. exec.; b. Los Angeles, July 17, 1928; s. Walter John and Ingfrid Christine (Olsen) S.; B.A. in Econs., U. So. Calif., 1952; m. Fredna B. Copeland, Aug. 29, 1953. Salesman, Francis I. duPont & Co., San Francisco, 1953-59; partner Glore Forgan & Co., San Francisco, 1959-67; v.p., dir. Eaton & Howard, San Francisco, 1967-70; pres., chief exec. officer, chmn. bd. URS Corp., San Mateo, Calif., 1970—. Served with USNR, 1945-48. Mem. Security Analysts Soc. San Francisco, Nat. Council Profl. Services Firms in Free Enterprise (founding dir.). Republican. Clubs: Bohemian, Olympic. Office: 155 Bovet Rd San Mateo CA 94402

STROMBERG, MELVIN WILLARD, educator; b. Quamba, Minn., Nov. 2, 1925; s. Gust and Emma (Westman) S.; student Gustavus Adelphus Coll., 1948-50; B.S., U. Minn., 1952, D.V.M., 1954, Ph.D., 1957; m. Beatrice E. Palm, Dec. 21, 1948; children—Peter, Andrew, Elizabeth, Arnold, John, Maija. Asst. prof. vet. anatomy U. Minn., 1957-59, asso. prof., 1959-60; asso. prof. vet. anatomy Purdue U., Lafayette, Ind., 1960-62, prof., 1962-63, prof., head dept. vet. anatomy, 1963—; adj. prof. anatomy Ind. U. Sch. Medicine, Indpls., 1973—; vis. prof. dept. anatomy Sch. Medicine, U. Munich (W. Ger.), 1978-79. Chmn., Lutheran Student Found., Lafayette, 1965-67, 73-76. Served with Signal Corps, AUS, 1946-48. NIH Spl. fellow dept. anatomy Karolinska Inst., Stockholm, Sweden, 1970-71. Mem. Am. Assn. Vet. Anatomists (pres. 1965-66), Am. Assn. Anatomists. Lutheran. Author: (with R. Hebel) Anatomy of the Laboratory Rat, 1976. Contbr. chpt. to Anatomy of the Dog, 1979. Home: 120 W Lutz St West Lafayette IN 47906 Office: Dept Anatomy Sch Vet Medicine Lafayette IN 47907

STROMBERG, ROLAND NELSON, historian; b. Kansas City, Mo., July 5, 1916; s. Clarence Roland and Harriet (Ridgell) S.; A.B., U. Kansas City, 1939; M.A., Am. U., 1946; Ph.D., U. Md., 1952; m. Mary R. Gray, June 10, 1939; children—Eric, Juliet. With U.S. Dept. Justice, 1940-45; instr., then asst. prof., asso. prof., prof. U. Md., College Park, 1949-66; prof. So. Ill. U., Carbondale, 1966-67; prof. history U. Wis., Milw., 1967—, acting chmn. dept. art history, 1977-78. Rockefeller Found. grantee, 1957-58; recipient Disting. Alumnus award U. Mo., Kansas City, 1966; fellow Woodrow Wilson Internat. Center for Scholars, 1974. Mem. Am. Hist. Assn., Soc. for History Edn., Soc. Historians of Am. Fgn. Relations. Author: Collective Security and American Foreign Policy, 1963; An Intellectual History of Modern Europe, 1966, 75; After Everything, 1975; Religious Liberalism in Eighteenth Century England, 1954; Heritage and Challenge of History, 1971; A History of Western Civilization, 1963; 2d edit., 1969; Realism, Naturalism, Symbolism, 1968; Arnold J. Toynbee, 1972; Europe in the Twentieth Century, 1979, others. Home: 7033 N Fairchild Circle Fox Point WI 53217 Office: Holton Hall U Wis Milwaukee WI 53201. *It would be more edifying to say that, as historian, I have sought an understanding of the past in order to help mankind master its future. It is probably truer to say that I have simply been fascinated by the amazing record of human actions and thoughts, and by the problem of making sense of them.*

STROME, CHARLES BOWMAN, JR., ins. co. exec., lawyer; b. Worcester, Mass., Sept. 18, 1928; s. Charles Bowman and Anne Boyce (Geddes) S.; student Wyo. Sem., 1944-46; A.B., Syracuse U., 1950; LL.B., U. Pa., 1953; m. Margaret Elaine Strayer, Oct. 17, 1954; children—Mary Lee, Charles Bowman III, Arthur Llewellyn. Admitted to Pa. bar, 1954, N.Y. bar, 1968: asst. counsel Provident Mut. Life Co., Phila., 1956-67; v.p., dep. gen. counsel Equitable Life Assurance Soc. U.S., N.Y.C., 1967—: dir. Ins. Fedn. Pa., N.Y. Life Ins. Guaranty Corp., Bradford Trust Co. Mem. planning bd. Briarcliff Manor (N.Y.) Village, 1973-77, trustee, 1977—; mem. corporate advisory council Syracuse U. Served with USAF, 1954-56, 62; Korea, Cuban Missile Crises. Mem. Assn. Life Ins. Counsel, N.Y. State Bar Assn. (chmn. com. on life, health and accident ins.), Am. Arbitration Assn., Soc. Mayflower Descs., Pa. Soc. Sons of Revolution. Republican. Roman Catholic. Club: Sleepy Hollow Country. Home: 290 Macy Rd Briarcliff Manor NY 10510 Office: 1285 Ave of the Americas New York NY 10019

STRONACH, WILLIAM CHARLES, med. soc. exec., lawyer; b. Rochester, N.Y., Jan. 12, 1920; s. Charles Harrison and Helen Catherine (Seward) S.; B.S., Northwestern U., 1941, LL.B., 1947, J.D., 1970; m. Harriet Ann Austin, Feb. 6, 1943 (div. Dec. 1973); children—Karen Ann, Adrienne Austin; m. 2d, Judith Glanz Chandler, Jan. 2, 1978. Asst. exec. sec. Am. Coll. Radiology, 1947-48, exec. sec., 1948-56, exec. dir., 1956—. Mem. adv. com. to exec. v.p. A.M.A., 1968-75; exec. adminstr. Council Med. Splty. Socs., 1970-76; mem. task force on profl. standards rev. Orgns. of Am. Assn. Founds. for Med. Care, 1972—. Served as capt., adj. A.A.A., AUS, 1942-46. Mem. Chgo. Med. Soc. Execs. Assn. (v.p. 1959, pres. 1960), Am. Assn. Med. Soc. Execs. (pres. 1973), Am. Soc. Assn. Execs., Am. Bar Assn., Phi Kappa Psi, Phi Delta Phi. Club: Tower (Chgo.). Home: 353 Ingram St Northfield IL 60093 Office: 20 North Wacker Dr Chicago IL 60606

STRONG, CARTER BRUCE, architect; b. Jackson, Mich., Feb. 9, 1924; s. Gerald D. and Ruth (Carter) S.; student La. State U., 1943; B.Arch., U. Mich., 1950; m. Margaret M. Collins, July 25, 1952; children—Carter C., Brian E., Nancy Ruth. Archtl. draftsman Harford Field, 1950-56, partner Harford Field & Assos., 1956-58; partner Strong, Drury & Cunningham, 1958-68; architect Gourdie, Miller, Fraser & Assos. Traverse City, Mich., 1968-74, Strong, Drury & Elkins, 1974—. Mem. City Commn., Traverse City, 1963-67, mayor, 1966-67; mem. zoning bd., Traverse City, 1959-63, Planning Commn., 1966-67. Served with AUS, 1943-46; ETO. Decorated Bronze Star; named Boss of Year Jr. C. of C., 1967. Mem. A.I.A., Mich. Soc. Architects (dir. 1971-72), Res. Officers Assn., Long Lake Preservation Assn. (pres. 1978-80), Alpha Rho Chi. Republican. Christian Scientist. Rotarian (dir. 1958-59). Prin. archtl. works include Cardinal Lecaro N.Am. Liturgical Conf. competition (2d prize), 1965, St. Hubert's Ch. design, Higgins Lake, Mich., Riverview

Terr. apt. hi-rise, Traverse City. Home: 204 W 19th St Traverse City MI 49684 Office: 129 S Union St Traverse City MI 49684

STRONG, CHARLES WILBUR, JR., banker; b. Mpls., Sept. 20, 1929; s. Charles Wilbur and Birdine (Moore) S.; B.A. in Econs., Stanford U., 1951; m. Marcia Ross, June 14, 1953; children—Richard Curtis, Carol Ross. Exec. v.p. Ralph C. Sutro Co., Los Angeles, 1954-75; pres., chief exec. officer Rainier Mortgage Co., Seattle, 1975-78; pres. Rainier Bancorp., Seattle, 1978—, also dir.; vice chmn. Rainier Nat. Bank, Seattle, 1978—, also dir. Trustee N.W. Hosp., Seattle, Wash. State U. Found. Served with USN, 1951-54. Mem. Calif. Mortgage Bankers, Wash. Mortgage Dankers, Mortgage Bankers Assn. Am., Am. Bankers Assn., Lambda Alpha. Clubs: Seattle Tennis, Broadmoor Golf and Country, Wash. Athletic, Rainier. Office: Rainier Nat Bank PO Box 3966 Seattle WA 98124

STRONG, EARL POE, educator; b. Loundonville, Ohio, June 19, 1910; s. Otto and Louellen (Bassett) S.; B.A., Rider Coll., 1930; B.S., Indiana U. Pa., 1934; M.A., Ohio State U., 1937; Ed.D., N.Y. U., 1943; m. Mildred Julius, June 15, 1937; 1 dau., Lou Ellen. Dep. collector in control sect. U.S. Treasury Dept., Cleve., 1930-32; tchr., head comml. dept., Manasquan (N.J.) High Sch., 1934-37; instr. bus. Coll. Commerce, U. Iowa, Iowa City, 1937-39, acting head bus.-tchr.-tng. dept., 1938-39; teaching fellow bus. edn. Sch. Edn., N.Y. U., 1939-40; head D.C. Dept. Bus. in Pub. Schs., 1940-41; sr. tng. cons. U.S. Civil Service Commn., Washington, 1941-42, dir. exec. devel. programs, 1952; research agt. in bus. edn. Vocational Edn. Div., U.S. Office Edn., Washington, 1942-45; dir. utilization dept. Remington Rand, Inc., N.Y.C., 1946-48, cons. on mgmt. problems, 1946-52; prof. mgmt., dir. bus. mgmt. service Coll. Commerce and Bus. Adminstrn., U. Ill., Urbana, 1948-52 (pioneer in orgn. mgmt. aids and adv. service as univ. ednl. program of direct aid businessmen); prof. mgmt., asst. dean, dir. exec. devel. programs Coll. Bus. Adminstrn., Pa. State U., 1954-70, prof. emeritus mgmt., 1970—; prof. mgmt., dir. exec. devel. programs Temple U., 1971-72, prof. emeritus, 1972; v.p. productivity and research Am. Corp. Cons., Buffalo, also pres., dean faculty Gibraltar Inst., Derby, N.Y., 1974-77; dir., acad. dean South Hills Bus. Sch., State College, Pa. Lectr. pub. adminstrn., Am. U., 1952-53; instr. evening and summer sessions, Sch. Edn., U. Md., 1940-41, bus. edn. and research adv. in bus. edn. Tchrs. Coll., Columbia, 1941, grad. sch. Dept. Agr., Washington, 1941-43. Served as lt. USNR, 1943-46; comdr. Res. ret. Mem. Am. Mgmt. Assn., Am. Assn. Univ. Profs., Soc. Personnel Adminstrn., Delta Sigma Pi, Kappa Delta Pi, Pi Omega Pi, Gamma Rho Tau, Phi Sigma Pi, Phi Delta Kappa. Republican. Presbyterian (elder). Club: Masons (32 deg.). Author or co-author textbooks and manuals in field of bus. mgmt. Home: 1337 S Garner St State College PA 16801 Office: 707G Coll Bus Adminstrn Bldg Pa State U University Park PA 16802. *Not only does one need to set definite achievement goals in life but perhaps of even greater importance is the compulsion to complete with excellence those tasks and endeavors that result in ultimate success.*

STRONG, FREDERICK SMITH, JR., army officer; b. Orchard Lake, Mich., May 16, 1887; s. Frederick Smith and Alice Marion (Johnston) S.; B.S., U.S. Mil. Acad., 1910; grad. Engrs. Sch., Washington, D.C., 1912; m. Marjorie Lee Ward, Oct. 9, 1912 (dec. Feb. 1970); children—Frederick Smith III, John Ward (dec.), Marjorie (Mrs. William A. Richardson), Rosamond (Mrs. Wm. L. Fisher). Commd. 2d lt. C.E., U.S. Army, 1910, advanced through grades to brig. gen., 1944; served with 7th and 2d divs., France, 1918; with Service of Supply, 1918-19, resigned, 1919; commd. col., Q.M. Res., U.S. Army, 1941; zone constructing quartermaster, IV Zone, Atlanta, 1941; War Dept. Gen. Staff, 1942; Office of Chief of Engrs., 1942-43; chief engr., Service of Supply, China-Burma-India, 1943; in hosp. on sick leave, 1943-44; comdg. officer Northwest Service Command, 1944-45; hdqrs. A.S.F. to 1945; comdg. U.K. base, 1945. Reverted to inactive status 1946. Exec. dir. com. on artificial limbs NRC, 1946-55, chmn. prosthetics research board, 1955-59; engaged in real estate and land devel. bus., Orchard Lake, Mich., 1919—; v.p., dir. Ind. Limestone Co., Chgo., 1926-27; with Booth Investment Co., Detroit, 1927-41, successively v.p., pres., gen. mgr. and dir. Commr. Village of Orchard Lake, Mich., 1928-40; pres. 1941, resigning to re-enter active mil service; council member at City of Orchard Lake Village, Mich., 1964. Decorated D.S.M., Legion of Merit. Mem. Am. Soc. Mil. Engrs., West Point Soc. Mich. (pres. 1975—). Clubs: Army and Navy (Washington); Orchard Lake (Mich.) Country. Home: Orchard Lake MI 48033. *Be guided by the precepts of a basic philosophy or religion, avoiding rigid ideologies per se. I have found four helpful: Charity (agape), Excellence, Liberty, Self-discipline. Be flexible: accept opportunities for service in order to do some good in the world. In old age follow Grandma Moses' advice: "Keep busy, keep smiling, keep young company."*

STRONG, GEORGE GORDON, business exec.; b. Vancouver, B.C., Can., Dec. 28, 1913; s. Charles Edmund and Lillian St. Clair (Grant) S.; B. Commerce, U. B.C., 1933, B.A., 1934; M.B.A., Northwestern U., 1935; grad. study U. Cal. 1935-36; J.D., U. Toledo, 1940; m. Jean Boyd McDougall, Aug. 7, 1935; children—George Gordon, Jeanne Adele (Mrs. Richard Derby Williams). Came to U.S., 1934, naturalized, 1940. Asst. prof. U. Toledo, 1936-40; exec. dir. Hosp. Services Assn. (Blue Cross), 1940-42; dir. accounting A.R.C., 1943-45; bus. mgr., treas. Toledo Blade Co., 1946-51; gen. mgr., dir. Brush-Moore Newspapers, Inc., 1952-54, pres., gen. mgr., 1954-64, pres., pub., 1964-68; pres., pub., dir. Thomson-Brush-Moore Newspapers, Inc., 1968-77; chmn. bd. Thomson Newspapers, Inc., 1972-77; pres. Oakland (Calif.) Tribune, 1977—; pres., dir. Weirton Newspapers, Inc. (W.Va.), 1963-68, Salisbury Times, Inc., 1959-68, Penn-Mar Pub. Co., 1958-68, Oxnard Pub. Co. (Calif.), San Gabriel Valley Tribune, Inc., West Covina, Calif., v.p., dir. Humbolt Newspaper, Inc., Eureka, Calif., 1966-67, pres., dir., 1968-77; dir. Great Lakes Paper Co., Mut. Ins. Co., Hamilton, Bermuda, Island Press, Bermuda Sun. Trustee Hiram (Ohio) Coll., 1972-77, United Fund Greater Canton, 1952-61; treas. Blue Cross, Toledo, 1946-51. Mem. Am. Cancer Soc. (pres., dir. Lucas County chpt. 1948-51), VFW, Am. Newspaper Pubs. Assn. (dir., dir. research inst. 1959-64, past chmn. bur. advt.), Beta Gamma Sigma, Beta Alpha Psi, Delta Upsilon (past nat. trustee), Sigma Delta Chi. Presbyn. Mason (Shriner), Rotarian. Clubs: National Press (Washington); Royal Bermuda Yacht, Mid-Ocean (Bermuda); Claremont Country, Athenian Nile (Oakland) Commonwealth of Calif., Oakland Athletic; University (N.Y.C.). Office: 409 13th St Oakland CA 94612

STRONG, HENRY, found. exec.; b. Rochester, N.Y., Oct. 6, 1923; s. L. Corrin and Alice (Trowbridge) S.; A.B., Williams Coll., 1949; m. Malan Swing, June 30, 1951; children—Sigrid Anne, Barbara Kirk, Dana Elizabeth, Henry Lockwood. Joined Fgn. Service, 1950; with State Dept., 1950-51; vice consul The Hague, 1951-54, Washington, 1954-55; 2d sec. U.S. Embassy, Copenhagen, 1955-58; polit. analyst State Dept., 1958-62; 2d sec., Djakarta, Indonesia, 1962-64; resigned, 1968; dir. Nat. Savs. & Trust Co.; pres. Hattie M. Strong Found. Mem. D.C. Commn. Arts, 1968-75; mem. D.C. Bd. Higher Edn., 1973-76; trustee J.F. Kennedy Center for Performing Arts; bd. dirs. Nat. Symphony Orch., Mt. Vernon Coll., Pomfret Sch. Served as lt. (j.g.) USNR, 1943-46. Republican. Episcopalian. Clubs: Chevy Chase; Metropolitan (Washington); International; Gibson Island (Md.). Home: 5039 Overlook Rd NW Washington DC 20016 Office: Hattie Strong Found Cafritz Bldg Suite 409 1625 I St NW Washington DC 20006

STRONG, JACK PERRY, pathologist; b. Birmingham, Ala., Apr. 27, 1928; B.S., U. Ala., 1948; M.D., La. State U., 1951; m. Patricia Powers; four children. Rotating intern Jefferson Hillman Hosp., Birmingham, 1951-52; practice medicine, specializing in pathology, New Orleans, 1952—; cons. pathology Southwest Found. for Research and Edn., 1954-55; assigned to Prof. J.N. Morris social medicine research unit Med. Research Council, London, Eng., 1962-63; asst. vis. pathologist Charity Hosp. of La., 1952-53, 55-58, vis. pathologist, 1958-66, sr. vis. pathologist, pathologist-in-chief La. State U. div., 1966—; asst. dept. pathology La. State U. Sch. Medicine, 1952-53, instr. pathology, 1955-57, asst. prof., 1957-60, asso. prof., 1960-64, prof., 1964—, head dept. pathology, 1966—, chmn. med. center planning and devel. com., 1969—, faculty promotion com. Med. Sch., 1969-71, pub. health and preventive medicine evaluation com., 1973; mem. Pathology A study sect. USPHS, 1965-67, chmn., 1967-69; mem. WHO Atherosclerosis Project, 1962-63; cons. VA Hosp., New Orleans, 1967—; research affiliate Tulane U., Delta Regional Primate Research Center, 1975—; mem. epidemiology and biometry adv. com. NIH, 1971-78; mem. sci. adv. bd. cons. Air Force Inst. Pathology, 1971-78; mem. panel on geochemistry of water in relation to cardiovascular disease U.S. Nat. Com. for Geochemistry, Nat. Acad. Scis., 1976-79. Mem. ofcl. bd. Munholland Methodist Ch., 1965; pres. Bissonet Elem. PTA, 1961; v.p. Jefferson Com. for Better Schs., 1964; mem. exec. bd. Grace King PTA, 1969. Served to capt., M.C., USAF, 1953-55. Recipient Research Career Devel. award USPHS, 1962-64. USPHS sr. research fellow, 1957-62. Diplomate Am. Bd. Pathology (trustee at large 1980—). Fellow Am. Soc. for Study Arteriosclerosis, Am. Heart Assn. (council on epidemiology, chmn. com. on myocardial and coronary artery lesions Council on Arteriosclerosis 1970); mem. Internat. Acad. Pathology (council 1976-78), Internat. Soc. Cardiology, Internat. Acad. Pathology (council 1968, v.p. 1976-77, pres. 1978 U.S.-Can. div.), AMA (alternate del. 1978—, rep. residency rev. com. pathology 1977—), Am. Assn. Pathologists and Bacteriologists (asst. sec. 1959-62), Am. Soc. Exptl. Pathology, Am. Soc. Clin. Pathologists (councilor for La. 1966), Coll. Am. Pathologists, Assn. of Pathology Chairmen, Inc. (v.p. 1969, pres. 1970), La. Heart Assn. (vice chmn. research com. 1964-71, bd. dirs. 1967—), Phi Beta Kappa, Alpha Omega Alpha, Phi Kappa Phi. Mem. editorial bd. Exptl. and Molecular Pathology, 1977—. Contbr. articles to med. jours. Office: La State U Sch Medicine 1542 Tulane Ave New Orleans LA 70112

STRONG, JOHN DONOVAN, physicist, educator; b. Riverdale, Kans., Jan. 15, 1905; s. Fred and Anna Laura (Bennett) S.; student Friends U., 1921-22; A.B., Kans. U., 1926; M.S., U. Mich., 1928, Ph.D., 1930; D.Sc. (hon.), Southwestern at Memphis, 1962; m. Bethany June McLaughlin, Sept. 2, 1928; children—Patricia Ann, Virginia Marie. Nat. research fellow physics Rockefeller Found., Calif. Inst. Tech., 1930-32, research fellow on 200-inch telescope project, Palomar Mountain, 1932-37; asst. prof. physics and astrophysics Calif. Inst. Tech., 1937-42; research fellow Harvard, 1942-45; prof. physics Johns Hopkins, 1945-52, prof. exptl. physics, 1952-67, dir. lab. of astrophysics and phys. meteorology; prof. physics and astronomy U. Mass., 1967—. Cons., Libbey-Owens Ford Corp. Fellow Franklin Inst. (life, Longstreth medal 1939, Levy medal 1942), Am. Acad. Arts and Scis.; mem. Société Royale des Scis. de Liège (corr.), Optical Soc. Am. (pres. 1959; Ives medal 1956), Internat. Acad. Astronautics, Phi Beta Kappa, Sigma Xi. Republican. Author: Procedures in Experimental Physics, 1938; Concepts of Classical Optics, 1958. Home: 136 Gray St Amherst MA 01002

STRONG, JOHN WILLIAM, educator; b. Iowa City, Iowa, Aug. 18, 1935; s. Frank Ransom and Gertrude Elizabeth (Way) S.; B.A., Yale U., 1957; J.D., U. Ill., 1962; postgrad U. N.C., 1966-67; m. Margaret Waite Cleary, June 16, 1962; children—Frank Ransom, Benjamin Waite. Admitted to Ill. bar, 1963, Oreg. bar, 1976, asso. firm LeForgee, Samuels, Miller, Schroeder & Jackson, Decatur, Ill., 1963-64; asst. prof. law U. Kans., 1964-66; asso. prof. Duke U., 1966-69; prof. U. Oreg., 1969-75; legal counsel Oreg. Task Force of Med. Malpractice, 1976; prof. U. Nebr., 1977—, dean, 1977—; dir. NCLE, Inc.; cons. Nat. Judicial Coll. Served with U.S. Army, 1957-59. Mem. Ill. Bar Assn., Oreg. Bar Assn., Am. Bar Assn., Lincoln Bar Assn., Am. Law Inst., Phi Delta Phi. Republican. Methodist. Club: Univ. (Lincoln, Nebr.). Author: Handbook on Evidence, 1972; (with Cleary) Cases on Evidence, 2d edition, 1975. Home: 2925 Woodsdale St Lincoln NE 68502 Office: College of Law University of Nebraska Lincoln NE 68583

STRONG, LEONELL CLARENCE, cancer research scientist; b. Renova, Pa., Jan. 19, 1894; s. Clarence A. and Ella (Mead) S.; B.S., Allegheny Coll., 1917, Sc.D., 1939; Ph.D., Columbia, 1922; M.D. (hon.), U. Perugia, Italy, 1957; m. Katherine Bittner, June 27, 1919; children—Leonell Clarence, Wilson W. Asso. prof. St. Stephen's Coll., 1921-25; research fellow Harvard Med. Sch., 1925-27; research asso. U. Mich., 1927-30, Roscoe B. Jackson Meml. Lab., 1930-33; research asso. cancer Yale Med. Sch., 1933-53; dir. biol. sta. Roswell Park Meml. Inst., Springville, N.Y., 1953-64; vis. fellow Salk Inst. Biol. Studies, San Diego, 1964-68; dir. Leonell C. Strong Research Found., 1968—; Belgium-Am. Found. and Anna Fuller Fund lectr., Europe, 1948; guest lectr. Internat. Gerontology Congress, St. Louis, 1951, London, 1954, Venice and Merano, Italy, 1957, Karolinska Inst., Stockholm, 1955, San Francisco, Mammary Cancer Symposium, Perugia, 1957, 61, 65, 69, 73, 77, Internat. Cancer Congress, Atlantic City, 1939, St. Louis, 1947, London, 1958; research prof. U. Buffalo Grad. Sch., 1964. Mem. NRC com. gastric cancer Nat. Adv. Cancer Council. Mem. Royal Soc. Medicine (London), Genetics Soc. Am., Am. Assn. Cancer Research, French Assn. Cancer Research (asso.), Sigma Xi, Phi Beta Kappa. Mason (Shriner), Rotarian. Author: Biological Aspects of Cancer and Aging, 1970; also numerous articles on cancer research. Developed C3H and other inbred mouse strains; determined genetic factors underlying growth and rejection of transplanted tumors; detected regulatory function of nucleosides on cancer growth; research on effects of aging and maternal age descent on cancer. Home: 8533 Sugarman Dr La Jolla CA 92037

STRONG, MAURICE FREDERICK, resource co. exec., former UN ofcl.; b. Oak Lake, Man., Can., Apr. 29, 1929; s. Frederick Milton and Mary (Fyfe) S.; numerous hon. degrees including U. Toronto, 1972, Acad U., 1972, LaSalle Coll., 1972, U. Alta., 1973, Brandon U., 1973, Springfield Coll., 1973, Yale, 1973. m. Pauline Olivette Williams, July 29, 1950; children—Frederick Maurice, Maureen Louise, Mary Anne, Kenneth Martin. Fin. analyst James Richardson & Sons, Winnipeg, Man., and Calgary, 1948-51, asst. to pres., 1951-52; mktg. asst. Caltex (Africa) Ltd., Nairobi, Kenya, 1953-54; v.p., treas. Dome Petroleum Ltd., Calgary, 1955-59; pres., Canadian Indsl. Gas Ltd., Calgary, 1959-64, Power Corp. Can., Montreal, 1962-66, Canadian Internat. Devel. Agy. Ottawa, 1966-70; exec. dir. environment program UN, also sec.-gen. UN Conf. Human Environment; N.Y.C., 1971-75; chmn. bd. Petro-Can., 1975-78; chmn. Internat. Devel. Research Centre, 1977-78, Procor, Inc.; chmn. AZL Resources Inc., Phoenix; chmn. Internat. Union for Conservation of Nature and Natural Resources. Mem. advisory bd. York U., Toronto, 1969-70, vis. prof. govt. adminstrn., 1969; alt. gov. Internat. Bank for Reconstrn. and Devel., Asian Devel. Bank, 1968-70, Caribbean Devel. Bank, 1970; gov. Internat. Devel. Research Centre, 1970-71, 77—; bd. dirs. Centre D'Etudes Industrielles, Geneva, Switzerland, Aspen Inst. Humanistic Studies; trustee Rockefeller Found. Pres. Nat. Council YMCA's Can., 1967-68; chmn. com. extension and inter-movement aid World Alliance YMCA's, 1963-65; mem. joint com. soc. justice peace World Council Chs., Vatican, 1969-71; Montague Burton prof. Internat. Relations, U. Edinburgh, 1973. Decorated officer Order of Can., 1976. Mem. Century Assn. Clubs: Mount Royal (Montreal); Rideau (Ottawa); Century, Yale, Metropolitan. Office: AZL Resources Inc PO Box 29008 Phoenix AZ 85038

STRONG, MERLE EDWARD, educator; b. Deerfield, Ohio, Aug. 16, 1923; s. Albert Henry and Belle Helena (McCoughney) S.; B.S., Kent State U., 1946, M.A., 1948; Ph.D., Ohio State U., 1968; m. Ruth Naomi Beutler, Sept. 2, 1945; children—Jeffrey, Larry, Gary, Jane, Nancy, Douglas, Linda, Diana. Tchr. pub. schs., 1946-55; specialist tchr. tng. and research U.S. Office Edn., Washington, 1959-64, asst. dir. program services br., 1964-67, dir., 1967-68; prof. ednl. adminstrn. U. Wis., 1968—, chmn. dept., 1970-72, also dir. Center Studies in Vocational and Tech. Edn. Served with USAAF, 1943-46; ETO. Recipient centennial award Ohio State U., 1970. Mem. Am. Vocational Assn. (life, contbr. 4th ann. yearbook), Adult Edn. Assn. Wis., Am. Assn. Jr. Colls., Wis. Assn. Sch. Dist. Adminstrs., Am. Assn. Sch. Adminstrs., Nat. Council Local Adminstrs. Vocational, Tech. Edn. and Practical Arts. Mason. Author: Industrial, Labor and Community Relations, 1969; (with Carl Schaeffer) Introduction to Trade, Industrial and Technical Education, 1975. Editor: Accident Prevention Manual; Developing the Nation's Work Force. Contbr. articles to profl. jours. Home: 6637 Gettysburg Dr Madison WI 53705

STRONG, ROBERT LYMAN, educator; b. Hemet, Calif., May 30, 1928; s. Horace Thomas and Beryl (Jarmon) S.; student U. Utah, 1945-46, Tex. A. and M. U., 1946; B.S., U. Calif. at Berkeley, 1950; Ph.D., U. Wis., 1954; m. Lillian Wilhelmina Oliversen, June 9, 1951; children—Stuart Lyman, Sharon Ann, Julie Ellen, Allan Leif. Research fellow Nat. Research Council, Ottawa, Ont., Can., 1954-55; asst. prof. Rensselaer Poly. Inst., Troy, N.Y., 1955-59, asso. prof., 1959-62, prof. phys. chemistry, 1962—. Mem. Averill Park Bd. Edn., 1964-73, pres., 1967-70; pres. Rensselaer County Sch. Bds. Assn., 1970-72. Served with AUS, 1945-47. Mem. Am. Chem. Soc. (chmn. eastern N.Y. sect. 1967-68), Am. Assn. U. Profs., A.A.A.S., Sigma Xi, Alpha Chi Sigma. Home: Rural Delivery 1 Sheer Rd West Sand Lake NY 12196 Office: Dept Chemistry Rensselaer Poly Inst Troy NY 12181

STRONG, WILLIAM AUGUSTUS, landscape architect; b. Joliet, Ill., Dec. 15, 1891; s. George Woodworth and Laurabel (Wallace) S.; B.A., U. Ill., 1914, B.S., 1916; M.L.A., Harvard U., 1920; m. Lucy Drinkwater Wensley, Oct. 28, 1920; children—Ruth Strong Hammerstrom, William Augustus, Dorcas Wensley. Draftsman, acting sec. Cleve. City Planning Commn., 1920-22; designer Albert D. Taylor, Cleve., 1922-25; partner Alexander & Strong, Cleve., 1925-44; pvt. practice, Cleve., 1944—; partner firm Strong & Hill, Cleve., 1961-76; asst. town planner, Greenhills, Ohio, 1955-57; site and planting planner Kent (Ohio) State U., 1936-68, Holden Arboretum, Mentor, Ohio, 1950-76, Lake View Cementery, Cleve., 1951-77; trustee Regional Assn. Cleve., 1937-71; mem. Cuyahoga County Planning Commn., 1934-47, Cleveland Heights City Planning Commn., 1951-71, Forest Hill Park Adv. Commn., 1951-77; cons. Fine Arts Garden Commn., Cleve., 1950-78; cons. in field. Trustee Hubbard Ednl. Trust, Boston, 1953—. Fellow Am. Soc. Landscape Architects (trustee 1940-44, 45-51; medal Ohio chpt. 1975). Club: Rockwell Springs Trout (Castalia, Ohio). Chmn. publ. bd. Landscape Architecture mag., 1948-62. Home: 13700 Fairhill Rd Shaker Heights OH 44120 Office: 4614 Prospect Ave Cleveland OH 44103

STRONG, WILLIAM LEE, mfg. co. exec.; b. Jacksonville, Fla., Sept. 17, 1919; s. William M. and Hedwig C. (Ulm) S.; A.B. in Econs., Occidental Coll., 1942; M.B.A. with distinction, Harvard, 1947; m. Betty Jean Stream, Dec. 13, 1941; children—William Lee, Thomas B., Robin E. Budget dir. Byron-Jackson div. Borg-Warner Corp., Los Angeles, 1954-56, controller, 1956-57; budget dir. Consol. Freightways, Inc., Menlo Park, Calif., 1957-60, treas., chief fin. officer, 1960-62; v.p. fin., treas., dir. Packard-Bell Electronics Corp., Los Angeles, 1962-65; treas. Allis-Chalmers Mfg. Co., Milw., 1965-68; v.p., treas. Continental Can Co., Inc. (now Continental Group Inc.), 1968-75; sr. v.p., chief fin. officer Firestone Tire and Rubber Co., Akron, Ohio, 1976-77, exec. v.p., dir., 1978—; dir. US Life Corp., Transatlantic Fund; mem. midtown advisory bd. Mfrs. Hanover Trust Co., N.Y.C. Guest lectr. various grad. bus. schs., other groups. Served to lt. comdr. USN, 1942-54; PTO; capt. Res. Mem. Am. Mgmt. Assn. (fin. planning council), Treas. Club N.Y., Fin. Execs. Inst. (trustee research found.), Conf. Bd. (council fin. execs.), Phi Gamma Delta. Clubs: Harvard Business School (N.Y.); Portage Country. Home: 1033 Bunker Dr Akron OH 44313 Office: 1200 Firestone Pkwy Akron OH 44317

STRONGIN, THEODORE, journalist; b. N.Y.C., Dec. 10, 1918; s. Isadore and Ida (Slevin) S.; student Harvard, 1935-37; A.B., Bard Coll., 1941; postgrad. Juilliard Sch. Music, summers 1940, 41, fall 1946, Columbia, 1947-49; m. Ruth Klein, Aug. 13, 1947 (dec. 1954); children—Deborah (Mrs. Edward Randolph, Jr.), Daniel Otto; m. 2d, Harriet Stern Rosenberg, Oct. 4, 1969. Dir. music East Woods Sch., Oyster Bay, N.Y., 1947-54; mem. music faculty Bennington (Vt.) Coll., 1954-56, Dartmouth, spring 1955; arts editor Chattanooga Times, 1957-61, Albany (N.Y.) Knickerbocker News, 1961-63; music critic, reporter, record reviewer N.Y. Times, 1963-65, music critic, reporter, recs. editor, 1965-71; columnist East Hampton (N.Y.) Star, 1972—. Cons. Music in Our Time series, N.Y.C., 1972-73, N.Y. State Council on Arts, 1970, various art instns., 1971—. Mem. Amagansett Village Improvement Soc., 1974—; bd. dirs. Amagansett Residents Assn., 1975—, pres., 1975-77. Dir. pub. relations Ind. Voters of East Hampton, 1971. Served to capt. AUS, 1941-46. Recipient Broude Publ. prize for piano piece, 1948. Mem. Music Critics Assn. (v.p. 1960), Casey Key Protective Assn. Democrat. Composer: Suite for Unaccompanied Cello, 1951, Quartet for Oboe and Strings, 1952. Author: Casals, 1966. Address: 2413 Casey Key Rd Nokomis FL 33555

STRONSKI, VICTOR, lawyer, corp. exec.; b. N.Y.C., June 27, 1932; s. Victor Anthony and Clara Veronica (Quinn) S.; A.B., Queen's Coll., 1954; LL.B., N.Y. U., 1960; m. Margaret M. Dwyer, Aug. 24, 1957; children—James Kevin, Neil Patrick, Paul Michael. Admitted to N.Y. bar; counsel Gen. Counsel's Office N.Y. Central R.R., N.Y.C., 1960-63; asst. counsel Diamond Internat. Corp., N.Y.C., 1963-69, corporate counsel, 1969-71, v.p., gen. counsel, 1971—. Served to lt. USAF, 1954-57. Mem. Am., N.Y., N.Y.C. bar assns. Republican. Roman Catholic. Club: Seven Bridges Field. Home: 35 Winthrop Rd Chappaqua NY 10514 Office: 733 Third Ave New York City NY 10017

STROOCK, ALAN MAXWELL, lawyer; b. N.Y.C., Nov. 12, 1907; s. Solomon Marcuse and Hilda (Weil) S.; A.B. magna cum laude, Harvard, 1929; LL.B. cum laude, Yale, 1934; LL.D., Jewish Theol. Sem. Am., 1961; m. Katherine Wyler, June 12, 1931; children—Robert, Mariana (Mrs. Lawrence W. Leighton), Daniel.

Admitted to N.Y. bar, 1934; law clk. for Justice Benjamin N. Cardozo, U.S. Supreme Ct., 1934-36; asso. Stroock & Stroock, N.Y.C., 1936-37, partner 1939-42, Stroock & Stroock & Laven, 1942—; asst. corp. counsel N.Y.C., 1938. Mem. bd. trustees N.Y. U., 1955-79, life trustee, 1979—; chmn. bd. Jewish Theol. Sem. Am., 1947-63, pres. of corp., 1963-75, chmn. exec. com., 1975—. mem. com. visitors Harvard, dept. history, 1951-56, 58-64, 67-71, dept. philosophy, 1956-62, mem. overseers com. on univ. resources, 1974-77. Mem. U.S. Nat. Commn. UNESCO, 1965-67. Trustee Horace Mann Sch. for Boys, 1946-59; v.p. Am. Jewish Com., 1948-51, 55-58, chmn. adminstrv. com., 1958; trustee at large Fedn. Jewish Philanthropies of N.Y., 1960-74, life trustee, 1974—; trustee N.Y. U. Law Center Found.; chmn. bd. dirs. Am. Friends of the Alliance Israelite Universelle, Inc. Mem. N.Y. County Lawyers Assn., N.Y. Law Inst., Am. Bar Assn., Assn. Bar City of New York (mem. grievance com. 1951-54, 60-63), Order of Coif, Phi Beta Kappa. Clubs: Lawyers, Harmonie (N.Y.C.). Home: 875 Fifth Ave New York NY 10021 also 60 Kerry Ln Chappaqua NY 10514 also Starwood Aspen CO 81611 Office: 61 Broadway New York NY 10006

STROOCK, DANIEL WYLER, mathematician; b. N.Y.C., Mar. 20, 1940; s. Alan Maxwell and Katherine (Wyler) S.; A.B., Harvard Coll., 1962; Ph.D., Rockefeller U., 1966; m. Lucy Barber, Nov. 21, 1962; children—Benjamin, Abraham. Vis. mem. Courant Inst., N.Y. U., 1966-69, asst. prof., 1969-72; asso. prof. math. U. Colo., Boulder, 1972-75, prof., 1975—, chmn. dept. math, 1979—. Guggenheim fellow, 1978-79. Mem. Am. Math. Soc. (editor trans. 1975-78), Sigma Xi. Democrat. Jewish. Author: (with S.R.S. Varadhan) Multidimensional Diffusion Processes, 1979; editor Ill. Jour. Math., 1976—; contbr. articles on probability theory to profl. jours. Home: Sugar Loaf Rd Star Route Boulder CO 80302 Office: Math Dept U Colo Boulder CO 80309

STROOCK, MARK EDWIN, 2D, public relations co. exec.; b. N.Y.C., Nov. 6, 1922; s. Irving Sylvan and Blanche (Loeb) S.; B.A., Bard Coll., 1947; m. Hanna Marks Eiseman, Juen 24, 1945; children—Mark E., Carolyn E. Reporter, The New York Journal of Commerce, 1947-50; writer Barrons, N.Y.C., 1950-51; mng. editor Fairchild Publication, N.Y.C., 1952-53; bus. editor World Mag., N.Y.C., 1953-54; contbg. editor Time Mag., N.Y.C., 1954-56; with Young & Rubicam Inc., N.Y.C., 1956—, sr. v.p., dir. corporate relations, 19—, also dir. Bd. trustee N.Y. Urban League, 1971-78, Alvin Ailey Dance Theatre, N.Y.C., 1977—, Friends of the Theatre Mus. City N.Y., 1977—, Covenant House, N.Y.C., 1978—. Served with U.S. Army, 1943-46. Mem. Public Affairs Council. Democrat. Jewish. Home: 24 Clubway St Hartsdale NY 10530 Office: 285 Madison Ave New York NY 10017

STROTHER, GEORGE B., educator; b. Kansas City, Mo., May 4, 1918; s. George B. and Helen Mae (Tappan) S.; A.B. with distinction, U. Mo., 1938, M.A., 1939; Ph.D., U. Ind., 1942; LL.D., Northland Coll., 1960; m. Mildred Elizabeth Dawson, Nov. 10, 1945; children—George B. 4th, Stephen Vance, Jeffrey Tamm. Asst. prof. psychology U. Minn., Duluth, 1947-51 acad. v.p., dean Northland Coll., Ashland, Wis., 1953-57; prof. Grad. Sch. Bus., U. Wis.-Madison, 1957—, asso. dir. Center for Health Care Fiscal Mgmt., 1977—, chmn. dept. mgmt., 1976—, vice chancellor extension, 1965-74, acting chancellor extension, 1970-71, mem. exec. com. Indsl. Relations Research Inst., 1957-70; profl. Nat. Agrl. Extension for Advanced Study, 1957-60; asst. prof. psychology head U. Mo. Counseling Bur., 1946-47. Mem. personnel com. Village of Shorewood Hills, 1959-69; chmn. 4-County Econ. Devel. Group No. Wis., 1955-57; mem. Bd. Harbor Commrs., City of Ashland, 1954-57; chmn. Wis. Council on Extension, 1970-74; mem. exec. com. Wis. Gov.'s Council on Econ. Devel., 1970-75. Bd. dirs. Personnel Dept. State Wis., 1960-63. Served with USNR, 1942-46, from lt. to lt. comdr., 1951-53. Mem. Nat. U. Extension Assn. (chmn. central midwest dist. 1969-70), Nat. Assn. State Univs. and Land Grant Colls. (council on extension 1968-74), A.A.A.S., A.A.U.P. (v.p. U. Minn., Duluth chpt. 1949-50, pres. 1950-51), Phi Beta Kappa, Sigma Xi., Psi Chi. Fellow Am. Psychol. Assn. Co-author: Social Sciences of Organization, 1963. Editor: Social Science Approaches to Business Behavior, 1962; (monograph) Individual Performance and Corporate Purpose, 1962; contbr. to Internat. Ency. Higher Edn., 1977. Home: 105 N Yellowstone Dr Madison WI 53705

STROTHMAN, DALE ROY, mortgage banker; b. Miami, Fla., Apr. 7, 1939; s. Felix Alvin and Le Vonda Strothman; student Miami Dade Jr. Coll., also U. Miami, part-time 1959-64; divorced; children—Laurie, Jill, Dale Roy. Engring. aide Dade County Parks Dept., Miami, 1959; land evaluator II, Dade County Tax Assessor's Office, Miami, 1960-72; staff appraiser U.S. Park Service, Miami, 1972; comptroller, chief appraiser Mortgage Corp. Am., N. Miami, 1972—, treas., 1976—; sec.-treas. MCANY, Inc., 1976; instr. real estate appraisal State of Fla. Distributive Edn. Program. Asso. mem. Am. Soc. Appraisers. Democrat. Lutheran. Clubs: Miami Snow Ski, Shriners. Office: 1125 NE 125th St North Miami FL 33161

STROTHMAN, MAURICE HENRY, JR., lawyer; b. Mpls., May 22, 1909; s. Maurice Henry and Frances E. (Durham) S.; B.A., U. Minn., 1930, LL.B., 1932; m. Anne Healy, Aug. 29, 1935; children—John Henry, Jean Anne, Charles Healy, Lynne Frances. Admitted to Minn. and Tex. bars, 1932; gen. practice law, Mpls., 1932-41, 74—; with Fed. Res. Bank Mpls., 1942-74, v.p., 1951-63, gen. counsel, 1959-63, 1st v.p., 1964-74. Banking cons. Republic Liberia, 1961. Pres., bd. dirs. Community Health and Welfare Council, 1973-75; mem. Mpls. Commn. Human Relations, 1963-70, chmn., 1966-68. Mem. community planning and research div. United Way of Mpls. Area. Mem. Am., Minn. bar assns., U.S. Yacht Racing Union, U. Minn. Alumni Assn., Phi Delta Phi, Psi Upsilon. Clubs: Lafayette, Minnetonka Yacht. Home: 21035 Minnetonka Blvd Excelsior MN 55331 Office: 1114 Title Ins Bldg Minneapolis MN 55401

STROTHMANN, FRIEDRICH WILHELM, ret. educator; b. Elberfeld, Germany, Oct. 25, 1904; s. Henrich and Elisabeth (Leich) S.; came to U.S., 1930, naturalized, 1936; Ph.D., U. Cologne, 1929; m. Luise Conrad, July 1, 1931; children—Hildegard and Sigrid (twins). Mem. faculty Stanford U., 1930—, prof. German, 1945-70, prof. emeritus, 1970—. Recipient Lloyd W. Dinkelspiel award Stanford U., 1960. Mem. Modern Lang. Assn. Author: Die Gerichtsverbandlung als literaisches Motiv, Jena, 1930; German Reading Grammer (with Stanley L. Sharp), 1941; Reading German (with Bayard Quincy Morgan), 1943; Reading German-Alternate (with B.Q. Morgan), 1950; German, A Structural Approach (with Walter F.W. Lohnes), 1968; editor: (with B. Q. Morgan) Middle High German Translation of the Summa Theologica (Thomas Aquinas), 1950. Home: 526 Rhodes Dr Palo Alto CA 94303

STROTZ, ROBERT HENRY, univ. pres.; b. Aurora, Ill., Sept. 26, 1922; s. John Marc and Olga (Koerfer) S.; student Duke, 1939-41; B.A., U. Chgo., 1942, Ph.D., 1951; LL.D. (hon.), Ill. Wesleyan U., 1976; LL.D., Millikin U., 1979; m. Helen Berry, July 24, 1961; children—Vicki, Michael, Frances, Ellen, Ann. Mem. faculty Northwestern U., Evanston, Ill., 1947—, prof. econs., 1958—, dean Coll. Arts and Scis., 1966-70, pres. univ., 1970—. Dir., chmn. Fed. Res. Bank Chgo., Ill. Tool Works, Inc., Norfolk and Western Ry. Co., Peoples Gas Co., U.S. Gypsum Co., Mark Controls Corp. Bd. dirs., vice chmn. Nat. Merit Scholarship Corp.; bd. dirs. McGaw Med. Center Northwestern U., Northwestern Meml. Hosp.; trustee Field Mus. Natural History, Mus. Sci. and Industry Served with AUS, 1943-45. Fellow Econometric Soc.; mem. Am. Econ. Assn., Econometric Soc. (mem. council 1961-67), Am. Statis. Assn., Royal Econ. Soc. Clubs: Comml., Economic, Execs., Univ., Standard, Tavern, Chgo. (Chgo.); Old Elm (Ft. Sheridan, Ill.); Glen View (Glenview, Ill.); Bohemian (San Francisco). Mng. editor Econometrica, 1953-68; econometrics editor Internat. Ency. Social Scis., 1962-68; editor Contributions to Economic Analysis, 1955-70. Home: 639 Central St Evanston IL 60201 Office: 633 Clark St Evanston IL 60201

STROUD, JOE HINTON, newspaper editor; b. McGehee, Ark., June 18, 1936; s. Joseph Hilliard and Marion Rebecca (McKinney) S.; B.A., Hendrix Coll., Conway, Ark., 1957; M.A., Tulane U., 1959; LL.D. (hon.), Eastern Mich. U., 1977; m. Janis Mizell, Aug. 21, 1957; children—Rebecca McKinney, Joseph Scott, Alexandra Jane. Reporter, then editor editorial page Pine Bluff (Ark.) Comml., 1959-60; editorial writer Ark. Gazette, Little Rock, 1960-64; editorial writer then editor editorial page Winston-Salem (N.C.) Jour.-Sentinel, 1964-68; asso. editor Detroit Free Press, 1968-73, editor, 1973—, sr. v.p., 1978—; corp. mem. Merrill Palmer Inst., 1975—. Mem. gen. bd. publns. United Methodist Ch., 1975-76; adv. bd. Mich. Christian Advocate, 1975-79; bd. govs. Cranbrook Inst. Sci., 1978—; bd. dirs. S.E. Mich. chpt. A.R.C., 1972—, Detroit Symphony, 1978—; chmn. adv. com. Service to Mil. Families, 1974-77, chmn. program evaluation com., 1978-80. Recipient N.C. Sch. Bell award, 1967; Mich. Sch. Bell award, 1973; William Allen White award Inland Daily Press Assn., 1973, 76, 77; citation Overseas Press Club, 1974; Paul Tobenkin award Columbia U., 1976. Mem. Am. Soc. Newspaper Editors, Nat. Conf. Editorial Writers (program chmn. 1978), Detroit Econ. Club, Detroit Com. Fgn. Relations, Sigma Delta Chi. Clubs: Detroit, Renaissance, Pine Lake Country; Nat. Press. Home: 1614 Keller Ln Bloomfield Hills MI 48013 Office: 321 W Lafayette St Detroit MI 48231

STROUD, JOHN FRED, JR., lawyer; b. Hope, Ark., Oct. 3, 1931; s. John Fred and Clarine (Steel) S.; student Hendrix Coll., 1949-51; B.A., U. Ark., 1959, LL.B., 1960; m. Marietta Kimball, June 1, 1958; children—John Fred III, Ann Kimball, Tracy Steel. Admitted to Ark. bar, 1959, since practiced in Texarkana; partner Stroud & McClerkin, 1959-62; legislative asst. to U.S. senator John L. McClellan, 1962-63; partner Smith, Stroud, McClerkin, Dunn & Nutter, 1962—; city atty. Texarkana, 1961-62; spl. justice Ark. Supreme Ct.; chmn., Texarkana Airport Authority, 1966-67, TexarKana United Way Campaign; v.p. Caddo Area council Boy Scouts Am., 1969-71, pres., 1971-73. Mem. exec. com. Democratic party Ark., 1969-70. Served to Lt. Col. USAF, 1951-56. Recipient award of exceptional accomplishment Ark. State C. of C., 1972, Silver Beaver award Boy Scouts Am.; named Outstanding Young Man of Texarkana, 1966, one of Outstanding Young Men of Ark., 1967. Mem. Am., Ark., Miller County (pres.) bar assns., Ark. Bar Found. (pres.), Am. Coll. Probate Counsel, Texarkana C. of C. (pres.). Methodist (chmn. ofcl. bd., chmn. council ministries). Rotarian (pres.). Home: 208 Georgian Terr Texarkana AR 75502 Office: State First Nat Bank Bldg Texarkana AR 75502

STROUD, MALCOLM HERBERT, otolaryngologist; b. Sutton, Gold Field, Eng., May 17, 1920; came to U.S., 1957, naturalized, 1962; M.B., Ch.B., U. Birmingham (Eng.), 1945; L.R.C.P., Royal Coll. Physicians and Surgeons, Eng., 1946; postgrad. U. London, 1948-49; m. Edwina Barbara; children—Jane, Nigel, Honor. House surgeon Queen Elizabeth Hosp., Birmingham, 1945-46, Kidderminster Gen. Hosp., Eng., 1946, Dudley Rd. Hosp., Birmingham, 1950-51; registrar Ear and Throat Hosp., Birmingham, 1950-51, Royal Nat. Ear, Nose and Throat Hosp., London, 1952-53; first asst. to prof. ear, nose and throat studies U. London, 1953-55; cons. surgeon Birmingham Dudley Rd. Group Hosps. with duties as clin. tutor U. Birmingham, 1954-57; asst. prof. medicine Washington U., St. Louis, 1957-65, asso. prof., 1965-72, prof., 1972—. Served with M.C., Royal Army, 1946-48. Diplomate Am. Bd. Otolaryngology. Fellow A.C.S., Royal Coll. Surgeons (Eng.); mem. Am. Acad. Ophthalmology and Otolaryngology, St. Louis Ear, Nose and Throat Club (sec.), St. Louis Soc. Medicine, Am. Triological Soc. (exec. council, asst. editor jour.), Am. Otological Soc., Am. Univ. Otolaryngologists, Royal Soc. Medicine, Barany Soc., Neuro-Otology Group (pres.), Pan Am. Assn. Oto-Rhino-Laryngology and Broncho-Esophogology. Contbr. numerous articles to med. publs. Office: 517 Euclid St Saint Louis MO 63110

STROUD, PETER ANTHONY, artist, educator; b. London, Eng., May 23, 1921; s. Lewis Henry and Dora (Harrington) S.; student U. London, Tchr. Tng. Coll., Central and Hammersmith schs. art; m. Marian Beatrice Sheen, June 22, 1956; 1 dau., Kathryn Sarah. Came to U.S., 1963. Vis. instr. Middlesex and London County Councils, 1952-62; coordinator of studies Maidstone Coll. Art, 1962-63; mem. faculty Bennington Coll., 1963-68, prof. visual studies, chmn. art dept., 1965-66; vis. lectr. Hunter Coll., N.Y.C., 1966-67; prof. grad. painting Rutgers U., 1968—; one man shows include Inst. Contemporary Art, London, 1961, Bennington Coll., 1964, Marlborough-Gerson Gallery, N.Y.C., 1966, Nicholas Wilder Gallery, Los Angeles, 1967, Axiom Gallery, London, 1968, Gertrude Kasle Gallery, Detroit, 1969, Max Hutchinson Gallery, N.Y.C., 1970, 72, 74, Hoya Gallery, London, 1973, Union Coll., N.J., 1977; represented in permanent collections Tate Gallery, London, Guggenheim Mus.; Pasadena (Calif.) Art Mus., Detroit Mus. Art, Fleming Mus., Whitworth Mus., Manchester, Eng., Leverkusen (Germany) Mus., Los Angeles County Art Mus., N.J. State Mus., Trenton. Served with Brit. Army, 1939-46; prisoner of war in Italy, 1941-43, in Germany, 1943-45. Address: 311 Church St New York City NY 10013

STROUD, ROBERT MALONE, SR., physician; b. St. Louis, Mar. 12, 1931; s. Carliss Malone and Frances Elizabeth (Glascock) S.; B.S., Harvard U., 1952, M.D., 1956; m. Gloria June Flowers, June 19, 1955; children—Robert Malone, Katherine Ware. Intern, Cook County Hosp., Chgo., 1956-57; resident in internal medicine Barnes Hosp., St. Louis, 1959-61; Helen Hay Whitney Found. fellow Johns Hopkins U. Sch. Medicine, Balt., 1962-65, instr. dept. microbiology, 1963-65; dir. rheumatology and rheumatology research Ga. Warm Springs Found., 1965-66; asst. prof. dept. medicine U. Ala., Birmingham, 1966-69, prof., 1971—, prof. microbiology, 1976—; on leave for research in food allergy Brookhaven Hosp., Dallas; mem. subcom. on immunology in cancer cause and prevention NIH, also allergy and immunology rev. com., mem. VA merit rev. bd. Served with M.C., U.S. Army, 1957-59. NIH, VA research grantee; diplomate Am. Bd. Allergy and Immunology, Am. Bd. Internal Medicine. Fellow A.C.P., Am. Acad. Allergy; mem. Infectious Disease Soc. Am., Am. Rheumatism Assn., Am. Assn. Immunologists, Am. Soc. for Clin. Investigation, So. Soc. for Clin. Investigation, Sigma Xi. Contbr. sci. articles to med. jours. Home: 9221 Heatherdale St Dallas TX 75243 Office: Div Clin Immunology U Ala Birmingham AL 35294

STROUP, ATLEE LAVERE, educator, sociologist; b. Homeworth, Ohio, Nov. 3, 1918; s. Earl W. and Carrie (Sutton) S.; B.S. in Edn., Kent State U., 1942; M.A., Ohio State U., 1946, Ph.D., 1950; postdoctoral trainee marriage council dept. psychiatry, U. Pa., 1952; student Inst. Research Social Sci., U. N.C., 1957; m. Twyla Schmucker, Aug. 26, 1944; children—Richard Atlee, Carrie Lee, Glenda Fay, William Wesley. Mem. faculty Coll. Wooster, 1948—, prof., chmn. dept. sociology, 1954—; research leaves U. N.C., 1961-62, Washington U., St. Louis, 1966-67; vis. summer prof. U. N.C., 1957, 62, Vanderbilt U., 1958, 64, Pa. State U., 1963, Boston U., 1965, U. Md., 1973; part-time marriage cons., 1950—. Pres. Wayne County Mental Health Assn., 1961. Bd. dirs. Tri-County Guidance Center, 1965-70. Danforth Asso., 1954-58; named hon. Outstanding Alumnus, Kent State U., 1960. Fellow Am. Sociol. Assn.; mem. N. Central Sociol. Soc. Ohio Council Family Relations (v.p. 1977), Nat. Council Family Relations, Am. Assn. Marriage Counselors. Author: Marriage and Family—A Development Approach, 1966; also articles. Home: 1636 Gasche St Wooster OH 44691

STROUP, HERBERT HEWITT, educator; b. Phila., May 1, 1916; s. William Valentine and Margaret (Hewitt) S.; A.B., Muskingum Coll., 1937; M.Div., Union Theol. Sem., N.Y.C., 1940; Dr. Social Sci., grad. faculty of polit. and social sci. New Sch. for Social Research, 1942; m. Grace Evelyn Guldin, May 20, 1939 (dec. Nov. 1963); children—Timothy, Trudi. Dir. Camp Gould, Bantam Lake, Conn., also houseparent The Sheltering Arms, N.Y.C., 1940-42; tutor, instr., asst., then asso. prof. Bklyn. Coll., 1942-54, prof. sociology, 1954—, chmn. dept. student service, 1954-68, dean students, 1954-68. Mem. dept. com. Ch. World Service, 1959-73; v.p. bd. homeland ministries United Ch. Christ, 1962-73; program bd. div. overseas ministries Nat. Council Chs., 1959-73; Danforth asso., 1952—. Dir. Greece, Congl. Christian Service Com., Athens, 1953-54; cons. personalization edn. Danforth Found., 1965. Trustee Ripon Coll., Taraknath Das Found. Fellow Soc. for Religion in Higher Edn., Nat. Council on Religion and Higher Edn.; mem. Am. Sociol. Soc., Am. Personnel and Guidance Assn., Am. Coll. Personnel Assn., Lutheran Welfare Conf. Am., Grange, Kappa Delta Pi, Alpha Kappa Delta, Pi Gamma Mu. Author: Symphony of Prayer, 1944; Jehovah's Witnesses, 1945; Social Work: An Introduction to the Field, 1948, rev. 1960; Community Welfare Organization, 1952; Toward a Philosophy of Student Activities, 1965; Bureacracy and Higher Education, 1966; Church and State in Confrontation, 1967; Four Religions of Asia, 1968; The Future of the Family, 1969; Like a Great River: An Introduction to Hinduism, 1972; Founders of Living Religions, 1974. Mem. Jour. Contemporary Psychotherapy. Home: 171 Fairlawn Ave West Hempstead NY 11552 Office: Bklyn Coll Brooklyn NY 11210

STROUPE, HENRY SMITH, univ. dean; b. Alexis, N.C., June 3, 1914; s. Stephen Morris and Augie (Lineberger) S.; student Mars Hill Jr. Coll., 1931-33; B.S., Wake Forest Coll., 1935, M.A., 1937; Ph.D., Duke, 1942; m. Mary Elizabeth Denham, June 2, 1942; children—Stephen Denham, David Henry. Faculty, Wake Forest U., Winston-Salem, N.C., 1937—, asso. prof. history, 1949-54, prof., 1954—, chmn. dept. history 1954-68, dir. evening classes, 1957-61, dir. div. grad. studies, 1961-67, dean grad. Sch., 1967—. Vis. prof. history Duke, summer 1960. Mem. N.C. Civil War Centennial Commn., 1959-60. Served from ensign to lt. USNR, 1943-46. Mem. Am. Hist. Assn., N.C. Hist. Soc. (pres. 1965), N.C. Lit. and Hist. Assn. (pres. 1974), Phi Beta Kappa, Omicron Delta Kappa. Democrat. Baptist. Author: The Religious Press in the South Atlantic States, 1802-1865; An Annotated Bibliography with Historical Introduction and Notes, 1956. Mem. editorial bd. N.C. Hist. Rev., 1963-69. Home: 2016 Faculty Dr Winston-Salem NC 27106

STROUSE, CHARLES, composer; b. N.Y.C., June 7, 1928; s. Ira and Ethel (Newman) S.; Mus. B., Eastman Sch. Music, 1947; m. Barbara Siman, Sept. 23, 1962; children—Benjamin, Nicholas, Victoria, William. Composer (Broadway musicals) Bye Bye Birdie (Tony award), 1959; All American, 1961; Golden Boy, 1963; Superman, 1966; Applause (Tony award), 1970; Annie (Tony award), 1977; London: I and Albert, 1972; Flowers for Algernon, 1978; (films) Bonnie and Clyde, 1967; The Night They Raided Minskey's, 1968; There Was A Crooked Man, 1970. Mem. ASCAP, Am. Guild Am. Composers Dramatists Guild, Composers and Lyricists Guild Am. Home: 171 W 57th St New York NY 10019

STROUT, RICHARD LEE, newspaperman; b. Cohoes, N.Y., Mar. 14, 1898; s. George Morris and Mary Susan (Lang) S.; A.B., Harvard, 1919, M.A., 1923; m. Edith R. Mayne, June 21, 1914 (dec. Jan. 1932); children—Alan Mayne, Phyllis Mayne, Nancy Ewing; m. 2d, Ernestine Wilke, Sept. 4, 1939; children—Elizabeth Wilke, Mary Newman. Began newspaper work with Sheffield (Eng.) Independent, 1919; reporter Boston Post, 1921; with Christian Science Monitor, 1921—, with Washington Bur., 1925—; TRB column The New Republic, 1944—. Commd. 2d lt. inf. U.S. Army, World War I; war corr. World War II. Recipient George Polk award Nat. Reporting, 1958; award for journalism U. Mo., 1974; Sidney Hillman award, 1974; Fourth Estate award Nat. Press Club, 1975; Pulitzer Spl. citation, 1978. Fellow Sigma Delta Chi (hon.). Clubs: Nat. Press, Overseas Writers, Cosmos. Author: (with E.B. White) Farewell to Model T, 1936. Editor: Maud, 1939; TRB: Views and Perspectives on the Presidency, 1979. Home: 4517 Garfield St NW Washington DC 20007 Office: 910 16th St NW Washington DC 20006

STROUT, SEWALL CUSHING, JR., educator; b. Portland, Maine, Apr. 19, 1923; s. Sewall Cushing and Margaret Deering S.; B.A., Williams Coll., Williamstown, Mass., 1947; M.A., Harvard U., 1949, Ph.D., 1952; m. Jean Philbrick, June 12, 1948; children—Nathaniel Cushing, Benjamin Philbrick, Nicholas Lockey. Instr. English and history Williams Coll., 1949-51; instr. history Yale U., 1952-56, asst. prof., 1956-59; asso. prof. humanities Calif. Inst. Tech., 1959-62, prof., 1962-64; faculty Cornell U., 1964—, Ernest I. White prof. Am. studies and humane letters, 1975—. Trustee Wells Coll., Aurora, N.Y. Served with U.S. Army, 1943-46. Morse fellow, 1956-57; Am. Philos. Soc. grantee, 1961; Fulbright fellow, spring 1967; Soc. Humanities fellow, 1971-72; resident scholar Rockefeller Study and Conf. Center, Bellagio, Italy, 1978. Mem. Am. Studies Assn., Am. Hist. Assn., Phi Beta Kappa. Author: The Pragmatic Revolt in American History: Carl L. Becker and Charles A. Beard, 1958; The American Image of the Old World, 1963; The New Heavens and New Earth: Political Religion in America, 1974. Home: 204 Cayuga Heights Rd Ithaca NY 14850 Office: Cornell University Ithaca NY 14853

STRUBBE, JOHN LEWIS, food chain store exec.; b. Cin., June 27, 1921; s. John August and Emma Katherine (Coleman) S.; B.S. in Gen. Engring., U. Cin., 1947, J.D., 1948; m. Nancy Richards Baer, Sept. 16, 1950; children—William Burrows, Laura, John Charles, Mary. Admitted to Ohio bar, 1948, U.S. Supreme Ct. bar, 1960, U.S. Patent Office, 1950; asso. firm Wood, Arey, Herron & Evans, Cin., 1948-50; with Kroger Co., Cin., 1950—, sec., 1959-65, gen. atty., 1956-62, v.p., 1961-77, group v.p., 1977—. Gen. chmn. United Appeal Greater Cin., 1967; mem. Food Industry Productivity Task Force, 1972; past pres. Dan Beard council Boy Scouts Am.; past trustee Meth. Union; bd. dirs. Christ Hosp. Served with USMCR, 1943-46, 50-52. Recipient U. Cin. Distinguished Alumnus award, chmn. award for devel. new food tech. Supermarket Inst., 1976. Mem. Cincinnatus Assn. (past pres., dir.), Uniform Grocery Products Code Council (past chmn., pres.), Delta Tau Delta. Methodist. Clubs: Queen City (bd. govs.), Cincinnati

Country (Cin.); Commonwealth. Home: 3570 Bayard Dr Cincinnati OH 45208 Office: 1014 Vine St Cincinnati OH 45202

STRUBBE, THOMAS R., ins. holding co. exec.; b. Ft. Wayne, Ind.. Mar. 30, 1940; s. Rudolph C. and Maverne E. (Wagoner) S.; B.S., Ind. U., 1962; J.D., Tulane U., 1965; m. M. Theresa Hoog, Apr. 29, 1967; children—Tracy Lynn, Patrick Thomas. Admitted to Ind. bar, 1965, Ill. bar, 1969; atty. Lincoln Nat. Life Ins. Co., Ft. Wayne, 1965-66, asst. counsel, 1967-68; with Washington Nat. Corp., Evanston, Ill., 1968—, gen. counsel, 1973-79, sec., 1970—, v.p.. 1975-79, sr. v.p., 1979—, also dir., mem. exec. com.; v.p. Washington Nat. Ins. Co. Bd. dirs. Glencoe (Ill.) Union Ch.; v.p., bd. dirs., exec. com. Chgo. chpt. Epilepsy Found. Am., 1975-79. Served to lt. USNR, 1965-71. Lincoln Found. grantee, 1964. Mem. Assn. Life Ins. Counsel. Am. Soc. Corp. Secs., Am., Ind., Ill., Chgo. bar assns. Club: Skokie Country (Glencoe). Address: 230 Fairview Rd Glencoe IL 60022

STRUBEL, RICHARD PERRY, mfg. co. exec.; b. Evanston, Ill., Aug. 10, 1939; s. Arthur Raymond and Martha (Smith) S.; B.A., Williams Coll., 1962; M.B.A., Harvard U., 1964; m. Linda Jane Freeman, Aug. 25, 1961 (div. 1974); children—Douglas Arthur, Craig Tollerton; m. 2d Ella Adelaide Doyle, Oct. 23, 1976. Asso. Fry Cons., Chgo., 1964-66, mng. prin., 1966-68; with N.W. Industries, Inc., Chgo., 1968—, v.p. corp. devel., 1969-73, chmn. bd., pres. Buckingham Corp., N.Y.C., 1972-73, group v.p., 1973-79, exec. v.p., 1979—. Bd. dirs. Better Govt. Assn., Chgo. Presbyterian. Club: Racquet of Chgo., Mid-Day, Met. Home: 180 E Pearson St Chicago IL 60611 Office: 6300 Sears Tower Chicago IL 60606

STRUBY, CHESTER ALBERT, JR., newspaper pub.; b. Macon, Ga., Jan. 19, 1917; s. Chester Albert and Julia Riley S.; A.B. in Journalism magna cum laude, 1938; m. Jane Whitfield Spearman, May 24, 1947; children—Cynthia Jane, Neil Albert. Reporter, Macon Telegraph, 1938-40; state editor, 1940-41; state editor, asst. city editor Macon News, 1946-47; exec. editor Macon Telegraph and Macon News, 1947-57, editor, The Telegraph, 1954-57, exec. v.p., gen. mgr. Macon newspapers, 1957-78, pres., pub. Macon Telegraph and Macon News, 1978—. Chmn. bd. trustees Mercer U., 1978—; chmn. trustees So. Ednl. Reporting Service, 1962-64; pres. Macon United Way, 1979; chmn. truste Macon Housing Authority, 1976-77; trustee Sen. Richard Russell Found., 1970—; v.p. Ga. Boy Scouts Am., 1978—; pres. Forward Macon, 1977; pres. Ga. State Fair Assn., 1975. Served with USNR, 1941-46. Recipient Silver beaver award Boy Scouts Am., 1967. Mem. So. Newspaper Pubs. Assn. (past pres., chmn. bd. trustees So. Newspaper Pubs. Assn. Found. 1967-69), Ga. Asso. Press (past chmn.), Am. Newspaper Pubs. Assn., Ga. Press Assn., Navy League, Air Force Assn., Greater Macon C. of C. (pres. 1974), Sigma Delta Chi, Phi Delta Theta. Democrat. Baptist. Clubs: Rotary, Idle Hour Golf, River North Country, Elks. Office: PO Box 4167 Macon GA 31208

STRUC, ROMAN SVIATOSLAV, univ. adminstr.; b. Mikuliczyn, Ukraine, Oct. 18, 1927; s. Volodymyr and Helen (Bizak) S.; absolutorium U. Innsbruck, 1949; M.A., U. Wash., 1958, Ph.D., 1962; m. Ursula Renate Oppenberg, May 29, 1965; children—Irene, Andrew. Instr. German, U. Wash., Seattle, 1961-62, asso. prof. German and comparative lit., 1966-70; asst. prof. Washington U., St. Louis, 1962-66; prof., head dept. Germanic and Slavic studies U. Calgary (Alta.), 1970—, vice dean acad. affairs Faculty Arts and Scis., 1975-76. Served with AUS, 1953-55. Mem. Modern Lang. Assn. Am., Am. Assn. Advancement Slavic Studies; corr. mem. Ukrainian Acad. Arts and Scis. U.S. Author (with E. Behler) Friedrich Schlegel: Dialogue on Poetry Pennsylvania, 1968. Contbr. articles to Modern Lang. Quar., Monatshefte, Slavic and East European and Slavic Jour., others. Home: 2118 23d Ave SW Calgary AB Canada Office: Dept Germanic and Slavic Studies U Calgary Calgary AB Canada

STRUCHEN, J MAURICE, banker; b. Cleve., Oct. 5, 1920; s. Jay M. and Eoline (Miller) S.; B.B.A. cum laude, Fenn Coll., 1943; M.B.A. with distinction, Wharton Grad. Sch., U. Pa., 1947; m. Arlene Ann Meifert, July 18, 1943; 1 dau., Deborah Lynne. With Nat. City Bank Cleve., 1947-69, exec. v.p., 1967-69; pres., dir. Soc. Nat. Bank, 1969—, chmn. bd., chief exec. officer, 1974—; exec. v.p., dir. Soc. Corp., 1969-70, pres., 1970-76, chmn. bd., chief exec. officer, 1976—. Exec. bd. Greater Cleve. council Boy Scouts Am. Trustee Cleve. Zool. Soc., Ohio No. U.; pres. Fairview Gen. Hosp.; pres. Cleve. State U. Devel. Found.; treas. Bluecoats. Served to lt. USNR, 1943-46; PTO. Recipient Outstanding Alumni award Fenn Coll., 1956. Mem. Cleve. State U., Pa., Wharton Grad. Sch. alumni assns. Methodist (ofcl. bd.). Clubs: Pepper Pike Country, Westwood Country, Clevelander, Union, Tavern, Clifton (Cleve.). Home: 2175 Valley View Dr Rocky River OH 44116 Office: 127 Public Sq Cleveland OH 44114

STRUCHTEMEYER, ROLAND AUGUST, agronomist; b. Wright City, Mo., Jan. 4, 1918; s. Robert Henry and Ida Louise (Jaspering) S.; B.S.A., U. Mo., 1939, M.A., 1940; Ph.D. Agr., Ohio State U., 1951; m. Helen LaVone Renfrow, Sept. 15, 1940; children—Karen Elaine, Robert Roland. Grad. asst. Ohio State U., 1940-42; foreman bomb plant Certainteed Corp., Amarillo, Tex., 1942-43; asst. prof. agronomy U. Maine, Maine Agrl. Expt. Sta., 1946-49, asso. prof., 1949-51, prof., head dept. agronomy, 1951-63, head dept. plants and soils, 1964-71, prof., 1971—; soil fertility specialist with IRI Research Inst., Brazil, 1966-67. Served with Ordnance Dept., AUS, 1943-46. Fellow Am. Soc. Agronomy; mem. Soil Sci. Soc. Am., Soil Conservation Soc. Am., Am. Potato Assn., Internat. Soil Sci. Soc., Sigma Xi, Alpha Zeta, Gamma Delta. Home: 378 College Ave Orono ME 04473

STRUCKHOFF, EUGENE C(HARLES), assn. exec., lawyer; b. St. Louis, Nov. 14, 1920; B.A. magna cum laude, Colby Coll., 1946; LL.B., Harvard U., 1949; m. Ruth Norma Brewer, Jan. 4, 1943; children—Eugene C., III, Laura Lee Struckhoff Cline. Admitted to N.H. bar, 1949, U.S. Supreme Ct. bar, 1970; asso. firm Orr and Reno, Concord, N.H., 1949-55, partner, 1955-71; v.p. Council on Founds., Inc., N.Y.C., 1971-78, pres., 1979—, also dir.; founding mem. Asso. Found. Greater Boston, Affiliated Trusts N.H. Charitable Fund; cons. in field. Exec. sec. Spaulding-Potter Charitable Trusts, Concord, 1959-72; councilman-at-large City of Concord, 1957-61, 63; v.p., fin. chmn. Daniel Webster council Boy Scouts Am., 1958-60; trustee U. N.H., 1964-67; mem. exec. com. N.H. Higher Edn. Loan Plan, 1966-70; co-chmn. Citizens Council for a Better N.H., 1968-70, editorial chmn. book-mag., 1968; nat. chmn. Citizens' Scholarship Found. Am., 1962-68, bd. dirs., 1962-75; trustee Colby Coll., 1967-70; mem. vis. com. Harvard U. Med. Sch. and Sch. Dental Medicine, 1970-73. Served to 1st lt. USAAF, 1942-45. Decorated Air medal with 4 oak leaf clusters, D.F.C.; recipient Condon medal Colby Coll., 1946. Mem. N.H. Mcpl. Assn. (founding), Phi Beta Kappa. Author: The Handbook for Community Foundations: Their Formation, Development, and Operation, 2 vols., 1977. Office: Council on Founds 1828 L St NW Washington DC 20036

STRUCKLE, JOE J., univ. adminstr.; b. Bryant, Okla., June 29, 1933; s. Louis and Caroline (Luzar) S.; B.S., East Central Okla. U., 1959; M.S., Okla. State U., 1964; Ed.D., Tulsa U., 1968; m. Barbara Ann Mitchell, Aug. 1, 1958; children—Jay, Jeff. Tchr. pub. schs., Shidler, Okla., 1959-60, Ponca City, Okla., 1960-64; mem. NDEA guidance inst. Okla. State U., 1964-65; dean of men Northwestern State U., Alva, Okla., 1965-68, dean of students, prof. psychology, 1968-75, pres., 1975—. Served with U.S. Army, 1953-55. Mem. NEA, Am., Okla. personnel and guidance assns., Am. Assn. State Colls. and Univs., Okla. Edn. Assn. Club: Rotary. Office: Northwestern State U Alva OK 73717*

STRUCKMEYER, FREDERICK CHRISTIAN, JR., state chief justice; b. Phoenix, Jan. 4, 1912; s. Frederick C. and Inez (Walker) S.; LL.B., U. Ariz., 1936; m. Margaret Mills, Apr. 17, 1948; children—Frederick C. III, Jan Holly Struckmeyer Zeluff, Karl, Kent. Admitted to Ariz. bar, 1936; pvt. practice law, Phoenix, 1936-49; asst. county atty. Maricopa County, 1938-41; judge Superior Ct., 1949-54; justice Ariz. Supreme Ct., 1955—, chief justice, 1960-61, 66, 71, 80—. Served from 2d lt. to 1st lt., inf. AUS, World War II. Decorated Silver Star, Bronze Star. Mem. Sigma Nu, Phi Delta Phi. Democrat. Episcopalian. Office: Capitol Bldg Phoenix AZ 85007

STRUDLER, ROBERT JACOB, bldg. co. exec.; b. N.Y.C., Sept. 22, 1942; B.S. in Indsl. and Labor Relations, Cornell U., 1964; LL.B., Columbia U., 1967; m. Ruth Honigman, Aug. 29, 1965; children—Seth, Keith, Craig. Admitted to N.Y. bar, 1967; asso. firms in N.Y.C., 1967-71; with U.S. Home Corp., Clearwater, Fla., 1972—, v.p., chmn. operating com., 1976-77, v.p. ops., 1977-79, sr. v.p. ops., Houston, 1979—. Mem. Am., N.Y. State, Fla. bar assns. Home: 11110 Greenbay Rd Houston TX 77024 Office: 1177 West Loop S Houston TX 77001

STRUELENS, MICHEL MAURICE JOSEPH GEORGES, fgn. affairs cons., writer, lectr.; b. Brussels, Belgium, Mar. 10, 1928; came to U.S., 1960, naturalized, 1966; B.A., Coll. St. Pierre, Brussels, 1944; M.A., Antwerp (Belgium) U., 1949; Ph.D., Am. U., Washington, 1968; m. Godelieve de Wilde, Aug. 2, 1949; children—Alain, Patricia, Brigitte, Bernard, Jean Paul (dec.). Insp. econ. affairs Congo Govt., Leopoldville, 1950-54, chief ins. econ. affairs, 1954-55, dep. commr. transp., 1955-57; dir. Info. and Public Relations Office for Congo, Brussels, 1957-58, Congo Tourism Pavillion, Internat. World's Fair, Brussels, 1958-59; dir. gen. Belgian Congo and Ruanda Urundi Tourist Office, Congo, 1959; chmn. African Commn. Internat. Union Ofcl. Travel Orgns., Geneva, 1959-60; ofcl. Katanga rep. in U.S., N.Y.C., 1960-63; dir. gen. Internat. Inst. for African Affairs in Can., 1963-64; spl. asst. to prime minister Democratic Republic Congo, fgn. affairs minister, adviser to Congo UN del., adviser Congo embassy, Washington, N.Y.C., 1964-66; dir. Eurafrica, Consultants on Fgn. Affairs, Washington, 1966—; prof. polit. sci., French, internat. bus. Am. U., 1968—, dir. Center Research and Documentation on European Community, 1971—, E.C. Inst. in Europe, 1978—, U. Antwerp Exchange Program, 1979—; investment adviser, 1977—. Adminstr., Congo Touring Clubs, Brussels, Leopoldville, 1959-78; adminstr. French parish, exec. v.p. Eglise Saint Louis Corp., French-Speaking Union, Washington, 1974-75. Recipient Internat. Union Ofcl. Travel Orgns. Poster award, Brussels, 1958, Etoile de Service en Argent, King of Belgium, 1956; chevalier de l'Ordre Royal du Lion, 1957; Faculty award for outstanding contbn. to acad. program devel. Am. U., Coll. Bus. Adminstrn., 1979. Mem. Phi Sigma Alpha. Clubs: Rotary, Bukavu Royal Sports (founder Congo 1950, pres. 1951-54, hon. pres. 1957). Author: (with Inforcongo) Congo Belge et Ruanda-Urundi, 1958; (monograph) Le Canada à l'Heure de l'Afrique, 1964; The United Nations in the Congo - or ONUC and International Politics, 1976. Address: 1374 Woodside Dr McLean VA 22102. *"Ad Augusta per Angusta." Using Latin, French writer Victor Hugo said it all! Nothing comes easy and "success," a very personal perception indeed, requires a great deal of luck, perseverance and hard work. True success, though, is directly related to the pursuit of happiness, which in turn is a state of mind. If and when I reach eternity, I'll then be able to tell how successful I was during my passage on earth.*

STRUEVER, STUART MCKEE, educator; b. Peru, Ill., Aug. 4, 1931; s. Carl Chester and Martha McKee (Scobee) S.; A.B., Dartmouth, 1953; M.A., Northwestern U., 1960; Ph.D., U. Chgo., 1968; m. Alice Russell Melcher, Aug. 21, 1956; children—Nathan Chester, Hanna Russell. Dir., Found. for Ill. Archeology, Chgo., 1956-58, now chmn. bd.; instr. anthropology U. Chgo., 1964-65, lectr., 1969—; instr. Northwestern U., Evanston, Ill., 1965-68, asst. prof., 1968-69, asso. prof., 1969-72, prof., 1972—, chmn. dept., 1975-78, also dir. Archeol. Program; pres. Center Am. Archeology, 1980—. Mem. anthrop. adv. panel NSF; mem. accreditation com. N.Central Assn. (Commn. on Instns. Higher Edn.); mem. bd. archeol. cons. TVA, 1976—. Research grantee NSF, Nat. Geog. Soc., Nat. Endowment Humanities, Nat. Park Service, Am. Philos. Soc., Wenner-Gren Found. for Anthrop. Research, Ill. Dept. Conservation. Mem. Soc. for Am. Archeology (exec. com. 1970-72, pres. 1975-76), Soc. Profl. Archaeologists (exec. bd. 1976-77), Am. Anthrop. Assn., Ill. Archeol. Survey (dir.). Club: Adventurers (Chgo.). Author: Koster: Americans in Search of their Prehistoric Past. Editor: Prehistoric Agriculture, 1971; Acad. Press series Studies in Archeology. Home: 2000 Sheridan Rd Evanston IL 60201

STRUGGLES, JOHN EDWARD, mgmt. cons.; b. Wilmette, Ill., Nov. 29, 1913; s. William George and Sarah Adell (Chambers) S.; student Miami U., Oxford, Ohio, 1932-34; m. Dorothy Eloise Goetz, Oct. 23, 1937; children—Stephanie Struggles Garcia, John Kirk. Supt., Consol. Biscuit Co., Chgo., 1934-37; sales rep. Pillsbury Mills, Chgo., 1937-41; various personnel and operating positions Montgomery Ward & Co., Chgo., Kansas City, Denver, 1941-50, v.p. personnel, 1950-53; co-founder, co-chmn. Heidrick & Struggles, Inc., Chgo., 1953—; dir. Internat. Surplus Lines Ins. Co., Chgo., Internat. Ins. Co., Chgo., L.W. Biegler Co., Chgo., Square D. Co., Chgo., Ziegler Co., West Bend, Wis. Served with USNR, World War II. Republican. Home: 505 Sheridan Rd Winnetka IL 60093 Office: Heidrick Struggles Inc 125 S Wacker Dr Chicago IL 60606

STRUM, GARY JEROME, mutual fund exec.; b. N.Y.C., Dec. 9, 1937; s. Joseph and Bess (Cohen) S.; B.B.A. cum laude, City Coll. N.Y., 1958; LL.B., Harvard U., 1961; m. Sandra Loube, June 20, 1965; 1 dau., Gillian. Admitted to N.Y. bar, 1961; with SEC Spl. Study Securities Markets, Washington, 1961-64, N.Y. State Spl. Commn., 1964-65; spl. asst. to supt. banks, 1st asst. counsel N.Y. State Banking Dept., 1965-69; counsel, dir. dept. retirement and fin. planning Lord, Abbett & Co., N.Y.C., 1969—; v.p. Affiliated Fund, Inc., Lord Abbett Income Fund, Lord Abbett Bond-Debenture Fund, Lord Abbett Developing Growth Fund, Lord Abbett Cash Res. Fund; mem. pension, tax and state liaison coms. Investment Co. Inst.; panel arbitrators Nat. Assn. Securities Dealers. Home: 51 Vine Rd Larchmont NY 10538 Office: 63 Wall St New York NY 10005

STRUNK, OLIVER, educator; b. Ithaca, N.Y., Mar. 22, 1901; s. William Jr., and Olivia Emilie (Locke) S. student Cornell, 1917-19, 27, U. Berlin, 1927-28; Litt.D., U. Rochester, 1936; L.H.D., U. Chgo., 1970; pvt. study music; m. Mildred Altemose, June 23, 1930 (dec. 1973). Staff music div. Library of Congress, 1928-37, chief, 1934-37; lectr. music Cath. U. Am., 1934-37; mem. faculty Princeton, 1937-66, prof. music, 1950-66, prof. emeritus, 1966—, acting chmn. dept., 1942-43, 51-52, 60; lectr. music Columbia, summer 1948, U. Mich., summer 1952, Harvard, fall 1974-75; editorial bd. Monumenta Musicae Byzantinae, Copenhagen, Denmark, 1958—, dir., 1961-71. Mem. Inst. Advanced Study, 1944, Internat. Congress for Sacred Music Rome, 1950. Recipient award distinguished scholarship in humanities Am. Council Learned Socs., 1961, Derek Allen prize British Acad., 1977; traveling fellow Am. Council Learned Socs., 1934; Guggenheim fellow, 1951; Fulbright scholar, 1961-62. Fellow Medieval Acad. Am.; corr. fellow Brit. Acad.; mem. Royal Danish Acad., Music Library Assn. (pres. 1935-37), Am. Musicol. Soc. (pres. 1959-60, jour. editor 1947-48; hon. mem.), Am. Acad. Arts and Scis., Internat. Musicological Soc., Royal Mus. Assn. (hon. fgn.), Dansk selskab for Musikforskning, Gesellschaft für Musikforschung, Vereniging voor Nederlandse Muziekgeschiedenis, Societá italiana di musicologia. Author: State and Resources of Musicology in the United States, 1932; Source Readings in Music History, 1950; Specimina notationum antiquiorum, 1966; Essays on Music in the Western World, 1974; (with Enrica Follieri) Triodium Athoum, 1975; Essays on Music in the Byzantine World, 1977. Editor: Music from the Days of George Washington (with Carl Engel, U.S. Bi-centennial Commn.), 1931. Home: Villa Letizia Grottaferrata I-00046 Rome Italy Office: Am Acad Via A Masina 5 I-00153 Rome Italy

STRUNK, ORLO CHRISTOPHER, JR., educator; b. Pen Argyl, Pa., Apr. 14, 1925; s. Orlo Christopher and Katherine Elizabeth (Glasser) S.; certificate Churchman Bus. Coll., Easton, Pa., 1948; A.B., W. Va. Wesleyan Coll., Buckhannon, 1953; S.T.B., Boston U., 1955, Ph.D., 1957; m. Mary Louise Reynolds, July 3, 1947; children—Laura Louise, John Christopher. Exec. sec. Inst. Pastoral Care, Mass. Gen. Hosp., 1955-57; grad. asst. Boston U., 1955-57, instr. psychology of religion, 1956, instr. Sch. Theology, 1957-58, 62; asso. prof. psychology W. Va. Wesleyan Coll., 1957-60, dean, prof. psychology, 1959-69; prof. psychology of religion Boston U., 1969—, also faculty counselor Albert V. Danielsen Pastoral Counseling Center; asso. dir., staff psychologist Ecumenical Counseling Service, Inc., Melrose, Mass. Research cons. Religion in Edn. Found., Cal. Served with USAAF, 1943-46. Decorated Air medal with five oak leaf clusters. Fellow Mass. Psychol. Assn., Am. Psychol. Assn.; mem. Soc. Sci. Study Religion, W.Va. Assn. Acad. Deans (pres.). Methodist (elder). Author: Readings in the Psychology of Religion. 1959; Religion: A Psychological Interpretaton, 1962; Mature Religion: A Psychological Study, 1965; The Choice Called Atheism, 1969; The Psychology of Religion, 1971; Dynamic Interpersonalism for Ministry, 1973; The Secret Self, 1976. Home: 15 Stearns Rd Scituate MA 02066. *It is my conviction that life is a mystery to be lived more than it is a problem to be solved. As such, I have tried to develop a style of life which permits me to be open to a wide range of experiences guided by a simple principle which requires me to do battle with all those conditions which disrupt my and others freedom to live an authentic life of openness and continuous growth. The central principle guiding the openness to life is found in the spirit of Jesus Christ which includes love of Self, others, and my God. The task of working out these abstractions in a concrete manner is difficult and mysterious - but never, never dull!*

STRUPP, HANS HERMANN, psychologist, educator; b. Frankfurt am Main, Germany, Aug. 25, 1921; s. Josef and Anna (Metzger) S.; came to U.S., 1939, naturalized, 1945; A.B. with distinction, George Washington U., 1945, A.M., 1947, Ph.D., 1954; m. Lottie Metzger, Aug. 19, 1951; children—Karen, Barbara, John. Research psychologist Human Factors Ops. Research Labs., Dept. Air Force, Washington, 1949-54; supervisory research psychologist, personnel research br. Adj. Gen.'s Office, Dept. of Army, Washington, 1954-55; dir. psychotherapy research project Sch. Medicine, George Washington U., Washington, 1955-57; dir. psychol. services, dept. psychiatry U. N.C. Sch. Medicine, Chapel Hill, 1957-64, asso. prof. psychology, 1957-62, prof., 1962-66; prof. dept. psychology Vanderbilt U., Nashville, 1966-76, dir. clin. tng., dept. psychology, 1967-76, Disting. prof., 1976—. Recipient Helen Sargent meml. prize Menninger Found., 1963; Alumni Achievement award George Washington U., 1972; Disting. Profl. Achievement award Am. Bd. Profl. Psychology, 1976, others; diplomate in clin. psychology Am. Bd. Profl. Psychology; licensed clin. psychologist, Tenn. Fellow Am. Psychol. Assn. (mem. exec. council 1964, exec. bd. 1969-72, council of reps. 1970-73, chmn. com. on fellows div. psychotherapy 1970-74, pres. div. clin. psychology 1974-75, recipient Disting. Profl. Psychologist award 1973, Disting. Scientist award 1979), Tenn. Psychol. Assn., AAAS; mem. Eastern Psychol. Assn., Southeastern Psychol. Assn., Am. Psychopathol. Assn., Soc. for Psychotherapy Research (pres. 1972-73), Psychologists Interested in Advancement of Psychoanalysis, Am. Acad. Psychoanalysis, Phi Beta Kappa, Sigma Xi. Mem. editorial adv. bd. Psychotherapy: Theory, Research and Practice, 1963—, Jour. Cons. and Clin. Psychology, 1964—, Jour. Nervous and Mental Disease, 1965—, Jour. Am. Acad. Psychoanalysis, 1972—, Jour. Contemporary Psychotherapy, 1972—, Psychiatry Research, 1979—, Jour. Profl. Psychology, 1976—, others. Contbr. chpts. to books, articles and revs. to profl. jours. Home: 5058 Villa Crest Dr Nashville TN 37220 Office: Dept Psychology Vanderbilt U Nashville TN 37240. *Scientific and professional work is a very personal endeavor. It is the pursuit of meaning and the search for answers to the existential questions that have occupied mankind through the ages. Thus, the motivation to do one's best within one's limited powers is nothing altruistic although it counts as a great reward to kindle a spark in others. As a refugee from Nazi Germany, I remain deeply grateful for the opportunities my adopted country has provided me.*

STRUTHERS, SALLY ANNE, actress; b. Portland, Oreg., July 28, 1948; d. Robert Alden and Margaret Caroline (Jernes) S.; student Pasadena Playhouse Coll. Theatre Arts, 1967; m. William C. Rader, Dec., 1977. Actress TV shows including Smothers Brothers Summer Show, Tim Conway Comedy Hour, All in the Family, 1971-78; TV movie Hey I'm Alive, 1975; films include Five Easy Pieces, The Getaway, Intimate Strangers (TV movie), 1977, others. Recipient Emmy for best supporting actress on a comedy TV series, 1972; Emmy, 1979. Office: care Segal-Goldman 9200 Sunset Blvd Suite 1000 Los Angeles CA 90069*

STRUVE, GUY MILLER, lawyer; b. Wilmington, Del., Jan. 5, 1943; s. William Scott and Elizabeth Bliss (Miller) S.; A.B. summa cum laude, Yale U., 1963; LL.B. magna cum laude, Harvard U., 1966; m. Catherine Tolstoy Arapoff, June 12, 1965; children—Andrew Hardenbrook, Catherine Tolstoy. Admitted to N.Y. State bar, 1967, U.S. Supreme Ct. bar, 1971, U.S. Ct. Appeals bars, 1969, 73, 76, U.S. Dist. Ct. bars, 1970, 73, 79; law clk. Hon. J. Edward Lumbard, Chief Judge United States Ct. Appeals for 2d Circuit, 1966-67; asso. firm Davis Polk & Wardwell, 1967-72, partner, 1973—. Mem. Am. Bar Assn., N.Y. State Bar Assn., Assn. Bar City N.Y., Am. Law Inst. Roman Catholic. Home: 1225 Park Ave New York NY 10028 Office: 1 Chase Manhattan Plaza New York NY 10005

STRUYK, RAYMOND JAY, economist; b. Ann Arbor, Mich., Sept. 5, 1944; s. Jack Howard and Margaret Hazel (McGarry) S.; B.A., Quincy Coll., 1965; M.A., Washington U., 1967, Ph.D., 1968; m. Joan M. Klaski, June 15, 1968; children—Pieter, Zachary. Mem. staff urban studies group Nat. Bur. Econ. Research, N.Y.C., 1968-72; vis. asst. prof. econs. Rice U., Houston, 1971-72; mem. staff Housing Studies Group, Urban Inst., Washington, 1972-74, mgr. housing market behavior project, 1974-77; dep. asst. sec. for research Office of Policy Devel. and Research, HUD, Washington, 1977—; cons. to Republic of Korea, 1975-76. Served with U.S. Army, 1969-71. Mem. Am.

Econ. Assn. Author books in field; contbr. articles to profl. jours. Home: 13 W Oak St Alexandria VA 22301 Office: 7th and D Sts SW Washington DC 20410

STRYCULA, THOMAS FRANCIS, ret. educator, ct. adminstr.; b. Sobieski, Wis., Feb. 25, 1911; s. John and Antonina (Rosinska) S.; student U. Wis., 1928-29, summer 1931, U. Wash., 1929-30; B.A., U. Ala., 1932; postgrad. U. Calif. Extension Confs. and Insts. Div., Berkeley, also San Francisco, 1940-62; M.A., San Jose State U., 1967; m. Maribel Knowles, Sept. 17, 1936; children—Susan Knowles (Mrs. Ronald Lanphere), Thomas James. Social worker San Francisco Welfare Dept., 1933-40; sr. probation officer San Francisco Juvenile Ct., 1940-47, asst. chief probation officer, 1947-55, chief probation officer, 1955-67; tchr. Campbell Union High Sch. Dist., Calif., 1967-76, ret., 1976. Mem. San Francisco Com. on Youth, 1960-66; mem. social planning com. San Francisco United Community Fund, 1960-67; mem. probation services adv. com. to Calif. Youth Authority, 1962-66; mem. bd. Central YMCA, Salvation Army/Red Shield Youth Assn. Com., 1957-67; mem. Explorers planning com. Boy Scouts Am., San Francisco, 1959-67. Served to 1st lt. AUS, 1942-46; maj. Res., ret. Decorated Bronze Star. Mem. Chief Probation Officers Calif. (pres. 1965-66), Calif. Probation Parole and Correctional Assn. (pres. 1963), Cal. Congress Parents and Tchrs. (hon. life mem. 2d dist.), San Francisco Municipal Execs. Assn., County Supr. Assn. Calif. (chmn. law enforcement and probation adv. com. 1964-65). Club: Golden Gate Breakfast (San Francisco). Home: 148 Colton Ave San Carlos CA 94070

STRYER, LUBERT, biochemist, educator; b. Tientsin, China, Mar. 2, 1938; B.S. with honors, U. Chgo., 1957; M.D. magna cum laude, Harvard, 1961. Helen Hay Whitney fellow Harvard, also Med. Research Council Lab., 1961-63; from asst. prof. to asso. prof. biochemistry Stanford U., 1963-69; prof. molecular biophysics and biochemistry Yale, 1969-76; Winzer prof. cell biology, chmn. dept. structural biology Stanford U. Sch. Medicine, 1976—; cons. NIH, Space Sci. Bd. of Nat. Acad. Scis., NRC. Recipient Am. Chem. Soc. award in biol. chemistry Eli Lilly & Co., 1970. Fellow Am. Acad. Arts and Scis.; mem. Am. Chem. Soc., Am. Soc. Biol. Chemists, Biophys. Soc., Phi Beta Kappa. Mem. editorial bd. Jour. Molecular Biology, 1968-72; asso. editor Annual Revs. Biophysics and Bioengineering, 1970-76. Office: Fairchild Center Stanford Sch Medicine Stanford CA 94305

STRYKER, CLINTON EVERETT, mfg. co. exec.; b. Chgo., Feb. 27, 1897; s. Norman U. and Lina (Ehrensing) S.; B.S., Armour Inst. Tech., 1917, E.E., 1924; m. Sarah Hassel, May 18, 1918; children—Juel Irene, Phyllis (Mrs. William A. Thompson). Asst. prof. elec. engring. Armour Inst. Tech., 1920-24; chief engr. Fansteel Metall. Corp., Chgo., 1923-35; partner McKinsey, Kerney & Co., Chgo., 1936-40; v.p., asst. to pres. Nordberg Mfg. Co., Milw., 1940-46; pres. Adel Precision Products Corp., Burbank, Cal., 1946-48, Maysteel Products, Inc., Milw., 1948-64; pres., dir. Maysteel Products Corp., Milw., 1964-73, Maypro, Inc., Milw., 1964—; dir. Falk Corp., Koehring Corp. (both Milw.). Bd. dirs. United Community Funds & Councils Am., 1957-63, v.p., 1962-63; bd. dirs. United Community Services Milw., 1953-65, pres., 1954-56, chmn. bd., 1956-57; bd. dirs. YMCA Milw., 1951—, rec. sec., 1956—; bd. dirs. Goodwill Industries Am., also Milw. mem. adv. bd. St. Mary's Hosp., Milw., 1953—; trustee Armour Inst. Tech., 1938-40, Ill. Inst. Tech., 1962-65. Registered profl. engr., Wis. Fellow I.E.E.E.; mem. Am. Metal Stamping Assn. (pres. 1957-58, bd. dirs. 1958-62), Soc. Automotive Engrs., Eta Kappa Nu, Theta Xi. Congregationalist. Clubs: Masons, Milwaukee, Milwaukee Country, University (Milw.). Home: 7032 N Barnett Ln Milwaukee WI 53217 Office: 800 N Marshall St Milwaukee WI 53202

STRYKER, SHELDON, educator, sociologist; b. St. Paul, May 26, 1924; s. Max and Rose (Moskevitz) S.; B.A. summa cum laude, U. Minn., 1948, M.A., 1950, Ph.D., 1955; m. Alyce Shirley Agranoff, Sept. 7, 1947; children—Robin Sue, Jeffrey, David, Michael, Mark. Mem. faculty Ind. U., 1951—, prof. sociology, 1964—, dir. Inst. Social Research, 1965-70, chmn. dept. sociology, 1969-75. Cons. in field; chmn. social scis. research rev. com. NIMH, 1976-79. Served with AUS, 1943-46. Postdoctoral fellow Social Sci. Research Council, 1959-60; Fulbright research scholar, Italy, 1966-67. Mem. Am. Sociol. Assn. (nat. council 1965-67, chmn. social psychology sect. 1978-79), Ohio Valley Sociol. Soc. (council 1965-67), North Central Sociol. Assn. (pres. 1978-79), Sociol. Research Assn. (council 1978—), Phi Beta Kappa. Author monographs, articles, chpts. in books. Editor Sociometry, 1966-69, Rose Monograph Series of Am. Sociol. Assn., 1971-73, asso. editor Social Problems, 1957-59. Home: 1000 Pleasant Ridge Rd Bloomington IN 47401

STRYPE, FREDERICK CULVER, JR., paper mcht.; b. Bklyn., Nov. 25, 1918; s. Frederick Culver and Claire (Williams) S.; student U. Maine, 1940, U. Pa., 1937-41, Harvard, 1941; m. Louise Marie Schweinler, Oct. 25, 1947; children—Susan, Elizabeth, Kathleen Marie, Frederick, Margaret. Sec., Fred C. Strype, Inc., N.Y.C., 1946, pres. and treas., 1960—. Cons. paper and pulp div. ECA, Wash., 1950-51. Pres. Dem. Club, Ho-Ho-Kus, 1964-67. Served as lt. comdr. Supply Corps, USN, 1941-46. Mem. U.S. Paper Exporters Council (v.p. 1950-52, pres. 1952-54, 69-70). Ky. Col. Roman Catholic. Clubs: Pathfinders (London, Eng.); Channel, Monmouth Beach (trustee) (N.J.). Co-author: Guide for the Export Packing of Paper, 1949. Home: 141 Foster Terr Ridgewood NJ 07450 Office: 60 Glen Ave Glen Rock NJ 07452

STUART, DOUGLAS BAILEY, banker; b. S.I., N.Y., Dec. 22, 1916; s. Frederick Goat and Helen (Bailey) S.; B.A., Wesleyan U. (Conn.), 1940; postgrad. Rutgers U., 1952; m. Elsie Evelyn Sandberg, Aug. 16, 1941; children—Dona (Mrs. David Kerezsi), Drew, Roger, Kent, Duncan. Sr. v.p., sec. Am. Savs. Bank, N.Y.C., 1940—. Commr., South Brunswick Municipal Utilities Authority, 1968-70. Served with inf. AUS, 1941-45. Decorated Silver Star medal. Mem. Investment Officers Assn. of Savs. Banks of N.Y. State. Episcopalian. Home: 24 Sturgis Rd Kendall Park NJ 08824 Office: 335 Broadway New York City NY 10013

STUART, DWIGHT LYMAN, food co. exec.; b. Seattle, Sept. 27, 1924; s. Elbridge Hadley and Nan (Fullerton) S.; student U. Wash., 1947; children by former marriage—Dwight Lyman, William W., Bruce F.; m. 2d, Kathleen Gallant, Oct. 27, 1958; children—Douglas F., Gregory M. With Carnation Co., 1947-48, 50—, asst. v.p., 1957-64, v.p., after 1964, exec. v.p., until 1973, pres., 1973—; self employed as mfrs. rep., 1948-50; dir. E. A. Stuart Co. Served to lt. (j.g.) USNR, 1943-46. Mem. Phi Delta Theta. Club: Los Angeles. Office: 5045 Wilshire Blvd Los Angeles CA 90036*

STUART, EDWARD BERNARD, educator; b. Swissvale, Pa., Aug. 31, 1924; s. Albert Joseph and Mary C. (Conley) S.; B.S. in Chem. Engring., U. Pitts., 1948, M.S., 1949, Ph.D., 1955; m. Geraldine Julia McQuillen, Feb. 2, 1948; children—Suzanne Marie, David Guy, Andrew Laird, Brian Edward, James Gordon. Prof. chem. engring. U. Pitts., 1963—, chmn. dept., 1965—, asso. dean Sch. Engring., 1977—. Guest lectr. U. W.Va., 1949; propr. cons. firm, Pitts., 1959—; cons. in field. Trustee Pa. Engring. Found. Served to 2d lt. USAAF, 1943-45. Registered profl. engr., Pa. Mem. Am. Inst. Chem. Engrs., Am. Chem. Soc. (chmn. nat. task force on energy and environ. 1974—), AAAS, Nat. Soc. Profl. Engrs. (pres. Pa. 1971-72), Am. Soc. Engring. Edn., Soc. Petroleum Engrs., Sigma Xi, Tau Beta Pi, Sigma Tau (Pyramid award 1956), Omicron Delta Kappa, Omega Chi Epsilon, Pi Kappa Alpha, Druids. Author: (with J. Coull)) Equilibrium Thermodynamics, 1964; (with others) A Critical Review of Thermodynamics, 1969. Home: 3264 Nottingham Dr Pittsburgh PA 15235. *Teaching others gives everyone rewards. A little dedication is not enough.*

STUART, GEORGE ROGERS CLARK, lawyer; b. Abingdon, Va., Aug. 31, 1924; s. William A. and Ellen (Bodley) S.; student Hampden-Sydney Coll., 1941-43; B.A., Williams Coll., 1947; B.A., Oxford (Eng.) U., 1949, M.A., 1955; LL.B., U. Va., 1951; m. Mary Baker; children—Lane S., Ellen B. Admitted to Va. bar, 1951; asso. firm Burns & Lively, Lebanon, Va., 1951-52; partner firm Penn, Stuart, Eskridge & Jones and predecessor, Abingdon, 1952—. Chmn., Washington County Democratic Com., 1962-66; mem. Va. Ho. of Dels., 1969-74. Served with AUS, 1943-46. Mem. Va. Bar Assn. (pres. 1968-69), Washington County C. of C. (pres. 1963-64), Order of Coif, Eta Sigma Phi, Alpha Delta Phi. Kiwanian. Home: 225 E Main St Abingdon VA 24210 Office: 208 E Main St Abingdon VA 24210

STUART, GRAHAM H., polit. scientist; b. Cleve., Jan. 27, 1887; s. Graham W. and Annie J. (Gill) S.; A.B., Western Res. U., 1908, LL.D., 1948; student Alliance Francaise, Paris, France, 1911, Ecole Libre des Sciences Politiques, Paris, 1914; A.M., U. Wis., 1918, Ph.D., 1919; m. Agnes Wright, Aug. 27, 1918; children—Jean, Ann. Prof. polit. sci. Stanford, 1924-52, spl. lectr., 1962, 63; vis. prof. Sch. Advanced Internat. Studies, Johns Hopkins, 1952-53; Stuart Chevalier prof. diplomacy and world affairs Occidental Coll., Los Angeles, 1957—; acting asso. prof. polit. sci. U. Chgo., summer 1926; acting prof. U. Wash., summer and fall 1927, summers, 1932-40; vis. Carnegie prof. internat. relations, Toulouse, Poitiers and Montpelier, 1929-30, U. Hawaii, summer and fall 1930, summer 1953; vis. prof. Hague Acad. Internat. Law, summer 1934; acting prof. summers U. Minn., 1936, N.Y. U., 1937, Western Res. U., 1938, Duke, 1939, U. Utah, 1941; lectr. Grad. Inst. Internat. Studies, Geneva, spring 1937, 51; lectr. Salzburg Seminar Am. Studies, summer 1954. Analyst, cons. Bd. Econ. Warfare, 1942-43; cons. Dept. State, 1943-45, 52-53, served on selection bds., 1956, mem. adv. com. Fgn. Service Inst.; adviser Am. Minister, Tangier, Morocco, 1946; dir. Inst. World Affairs, Riverside, Calif., 1946, 48, 51, panel chmn. assembly, Pasadena, 1962; del. 3d Pan-Am. Sci. Congress, Lima, Peru, 1925; leader round table, Harris Inst. Politics, U. Chgo., 1926. Bd. Hoover Library, Stanford, del. Am. Assembly Arden House, N.Y., 1960, San Diego, 1962. Graham H. Stuart room at Stanford named in his honor, 1967; Graham H. Stuart endowed professorship of internat. relations established at Stanford in his honor, 1978. Mem. Stanford Emeriti Profs. (pres. 1961, 62), Am. Polit. Sci. Assn., Am. Soc. Internat. Law, Phi Beta Kappa, Alpha Tau Omega, Phi Kappa Phi, Pi Sigma Alpha. Republican. Club: Cosmos (Washington). Author: American Diplomatic and Consular Practice, 1952; Latin America and the United States, rev. edit., 1954, (with James L. Tigner), 1975, Portuguese edit., 2 vols., 1977; The International City of Tangier, 1955; others. Home: 450 Santa Rita Palo Alto CA 94301

STUART, HAROLD CUTLIFF, lawyer, business exec.; b. Oklahoma City, July 4, 1912; s. Royal Cutliff and Alice (Bramlitt) S.; J.D., U. Va., 1936; m. Joan Skelly, June 6, 1938; children—Randi Stuart Wightman, Jon Rolf. Admitted to Okla. bar, 1936, D.C. bar, 1952; partner Doerner, Stuart, Saunders, Daniel & Anderson, Tulsa; judge Common Pleas Ct., 1941-42; asst. sec. of air force, 1949-51; chmn. bd. Southwestern Sales Corp. (radio, oil, real estate and investments), Tulsa; Norwegian consul for Okla. and Ark.; dir. 1st Tulsa Bancorp., Inc., Tulsa, 1st Nat. Bank & Trusk Co., Tulsa, Getty Oil Co., Los Angeles Greyhound Corp., Phoenix, Armour and Co., Phoenix, Greyhound Support Services, Phoenix, Morrison-Knudsen Co., Boise. Spl. cons. to sec. of air force, 1961-63, Okla. Hwy. Commn., 1959-63. Trustee emeritus Lovelace Found., Albuquerque; chmn. bd. Air Force Acad. Found.; bd. dirs. Internat. Petroleum Expn. Served from 1st lt. to col. USAAF, 1942-46; ETO. Decorated Bronze Star (U.S.); Order of St. Olav (Comdr.), King Haakon 7th Victory Medal, Medal of Liberation (Norway); Croix de Guerre (Luxembourg). Mem. Am., Okla., D.C. bar assns., Air Force Assn. (dir.), Tulsa C. of C., Delta Kappa Epsilon. Democrat. Clubs: Southern Hills Country, The Tulsa (Tulsa); Burning Tree (Washington). Home: 2930 S Yorktown Tulsa OK 74114 Office: 3701 S Peoria PO Box 1349 Tulsa OK 74101

STUART, JAMES ALEXANDER, corp. exec.; b. New Deer, Scotland, Sept. 9, 1925; s. George Alexander and Jessie Isabella (Porter) S.; ed. Glasgow Sch. Accountancy, 1950; m. Dorothy Mary Moir, Nov. 29, 1952; 1 dau., Heather Mary. Came to U.S., 1960. Sec.-treas. Craig Stores (Aberdeen) Ltd., 1954-57; sales mgr. Alex Whyte (Aberdeen) Ltd., 1957-60; with Dynalectron Corp., Washington, 1960—, treas., 1970-77, asst. v.p. risk mgmt., 1977—. Served with Brit. Royal Navy, 1943-46. Mem. Risk and Ins. Mgmt. Soc., Financial Execs. Inst. Mason, Elk. Home: 10215 Edgewood Ave Silver Spring MD 20901 Office: 1313 Dolley Madison Blvd McLean VA 22101

STUART, JESSE HILTON, author: b. W-Hollow, nr. Riverton, Ky., Aug. 8, 1907; s. Mitchell and Martha (Hilton) S.; A.B., Lincoln Meml. U., Harrogate, Tenn., 1929, D.H.L. (hon.), 1950; student Vanderbilt U., 1931-32, Peabody Coll.; D.Litt., U. Ky., 1944, Marietta (Ohio) Coll., 1952; LL.D. Baylor U., Ball State U.; D.Litt. (hon.), Morris Harvey Coll., 1959, Marshall U., 1962, No. Mich. U., 1964, Eastern Ky. State Coll., 1964, Morehead State U., 1974; Dr. Pedagogy (hon.), Murray State U., 1968, Pfeiffer Coll., 1969; Litt.D. (hon.), Berea Coll., 1966; L.H.D. Honoris Causa, U. Louisville, 1974; m. Naomi Deane Norris, Oct. 14, 1939; 1 dau., Jessica Jane (Mrs. Julian Juergensmeyer). Tchr. Sch., lectr. Colls. and Univs. 1940—; supt. city schs., Greenup, Ky., 1941-43; vis. lectr., prof. Am. U., Cairo, 1960-61; tchr. Grad. Coll. Edn., U. Nev., summer 1958; writer in residence Eastern Ky. U., 1965-69; dir. creative writing workshops Murray State U., summers 1969-72, 75-76; author short stories, poetry, articles. Specialist Dept. State, USIS, 1962-63; Am. rep. Asian Writers' Conf., 1962; mem. group to revise Ky. State Constrn., chmn. health, welfare and edn. com.; bd. dirs. Ky. Heart Assn., state chmn., 1964. Served as apprentice seaman, USN, 1944, commd. lt. (j.g.), 1944, 75, 76. Recipient Jeanette Sewal Davis Poetry prize, 1934; $5000 prize, Acad. of Arts and Scis., 1941; $5000 prize Acad. Am. Poets, 1961. Guggenheim fellow for European travel, 1937. Mem. Poetry Soc. Am. Author: Man With a Bull-Tongue Plow (poems), 1934; Head O' W-Hollow (stories), 1936; Beyond Dark Hills (autobiography), 1938; Trees of Heaven (novel), 1940; Men of the Mountains (stories), 1941; Taps for Private Tussie (Thomas Jefferson Southern Award $2500; Book-of-the-Month, Dec. 1943); Mongrel Mettle (autobiography of a dog), 1944; Album of Destiny (poems),1944; Foretaste of Glory (novel), 1946; Tales From the Plum Grove Hills (Stories), 1946; The Thread That Runs So True, 1949 (NEA selection as best book 1949); Hie to the Hunters, 1950; Clearing in the Sky, 1950; Kentucky Is My Land (poems), 1952; The Good Spirit of Laurel Ridge, 1953; The Beatinest Boy, 1953; A Penny's Worth of Character, 1954; Red Mule (juvenile), 1954; The Year of My Rebirth, 1956; Plowshare in Heaven (collection short stories), 1958; The Rightful Owner, 1960; God's Oddling, 1960; Andy Finds A Way, 1961; Hold April, 1962; A Jesse Stuart Reader, 1963; Save Every Lamb, 1964; Daughter of the Legend (novel), 1965; My Land Has A Voice, 1966; Ride with Huey the Engineer (Jr. book), 1966; Mr. Gallion's School, 1967; Come Gentle Spring (story collection), 1969; To Teach to Love, 1969; Old Ben (novel), 1970; Come Back to the Farm (non-fiction), 1971; Come to My Tomorrow Land, 1971; Dawn of Remembered Spring, 1972; The Land Beyond The River (novel), 1973; Thirty-Two Votes Before Breakfast, 1974; My World, 1975; The World of Jesse Stuart: Selected Poems, 1975; The Seasons: Autobiography in Verse, 1976; Dandelion On The Acropolis, 1978. Author of short stories in anthologies: Best Short Stories, O. Henry Meml. Collection. Co-editor: Outlooks Through Literature (textbook), Contbr. to Harpers, Atlantic Monthly, Esquire, Ladies' Home Journal, Poetry, others. Republican. Methodist. Home: W-Hollow Greenup KY 41144

STUART, JOHANNES, govt. ofcl.; b. Sheldon, Iowa, Nov. 1, 1907; s. Frederick and Mary (Kuyper) S.; B.A., U. Mich., 1929; M.A., U. Chgo., 1931; Ph.D., U. Calif. at Berkeley, 1939. Social sci. analyst U.S. Dept. Labor, San Francisco, 1938-40; pub. health adviser Venereal Disease br. USPHS, Washington, 1940-57, spl. asst. to dep. surgeon gen., 1957-62, spl. asst. to dep. chief Bur. State Services, 1962-67, asso. dir. Center for Disease Control, Rockville, Md., 1967—. Exec. sec. Exchange Visitor Waiver Rev. Bd., Dept. Health, Edn. and Welfare, Washington, 1963-66. Mem. U.S.-Mexico Border Pub. Health Assn., Internat. Good Neighbor Council. Home: 5400 Pooks Hill Rd Bethesda MD 20014 Office: Parklawn Bldg 5600 Fishers Ln Rockville MD 20852

STUART, JOHN MCHUGH, JR., pub. relations cons., ret. fgn. service officer; b. Albany, N.Y., Apr. 21, 1916; s. John McHugh and Marie (Fitzgerald) S.; student U. Santa Clara, 1934-35; B.A., Georgetown U., 1939; M.A., George Washington U., 1966; grad. Air War Coll., 1966; m. Ruth Sherman, June 24, 1944 (dec. May 1977). Reporter, editor, 1938-44; fgn. service officer USIA, 1954-71; press attache Am. embassy, New Delhi, 1962-65; pub. affairs officer U.S. Mission in Geneva, 1956-61; fgn. corr. Voice of Am., Korea and Germany, 1950-56; press counselor Am. embassy, Saigon, 1966-67; sr. adviser pub. affairs U.S. Mission to UN, N.Y.C., 1968-71, spl. adviser U.S. del. 26th UN Gen. Assembly, 1971, spokesman, U.S. del. conf. on human environment, Stockholm, 1972, adviser 31st Gen. Assembly, 1976, 3d UN Law of Sea Conf., N.Y., 1977, VIth Spl. Gen. Assembly on Disarmament, 1978; now sr. cons. internat. pub. affairs Michael W. Moynihan Assos., N.Y.C., also Washington; adviser European Security Conf., USIA, 1973. Served with SHAEF, World War II. Mem. Nat. Press Club. Home: 180 West End Ave New York City NY 10023 Office: 730 Fifth Ave New York City NY 10019

STUART, JOHN THOMAS, III, banker; b. Dallas, Aug. 12, 1936; s. John Thomas, Jr.; B.A., U. Tex., Austin, 1958; m. Barbara Kay White, Aug. 10, 1957; children—llichael, Melissa. With Tenn. Gas Transmission Co., 1958-59; with Republic Nat. Bank of Dallas, 1961—, v.p., 1966, sr. v.p., 1966-71, exec. v.p., 1971—; pres. Republic Nat. Mortgage Corp.; faculty Southwestern Grad. Sch. Banking, 1970-73. Coach YMCA Youth Program, 1968-70, 73; committeeman Troop 70 Boy Scouts Am., 1970-73; active Park Cities North Dallas YMCA Membership Drive, 1964—, Community Council, 1971-72, Dallas Symphony Orch., Dallas Symphony Fund Drive; chmn. Bond Info. Com., City of University Park, 1973, cons. to Bd. Commrs., 1972-73; bd. dirs. Dallas Assn. for Retarded Children, 1968-74, pres., 1971-73; bd. dirs. Greater Dallas Community Relations, 1975, Dallas Assembly, 1976—; trustee Franklin Lindsay Student Aid Fund; chmn. adv. council Sch. Bus. Adminstrn., U. Tex., Arlington, 1971-72; mem. advisory bd. Aubrey Costa Inst. Mortgage Bank, So. Meth. U., 1973-74. Served with U.S. Army, 1959-61. Mem. Mortgage Bankers Assn. Am. (bd. govs. 1975—), Tex. (exec. com. 1971-72, dir. 1973-76), Dallas mortgage bankers assns., Tex. Bankers Assn. (chmn. real estate and mortgage finance sect. 1975), Robert Morris Assos., Home and Apt. Builders Assn., Met. Dallas Area (dir. 1970), Ex-Students Assn. U. Tex. (exec. council 1969—, exec. com. 1971—, chmn. bus. and finance com. 1972—, chmn. bd. dirs Campus Service, Inc. 1973—), Newcomen Soc., Salesmanship Club Dallas, Delta Tau Delta, Phi Eta Sigma. Republican. Presbyterian. Clubs: Royal Oaks Country (bd. govs. 1971-73, pres. 1974), City; Dallas Country; 2001 (dir. 1974—); Dallas Country; Dervish; Tex. Cowboys. Home: 3325 Southwestern St Dallas TX 75225 Office: PO Box 5961 Dallas TX 75222

STUART, JOSEPH, TV producer and dir.; b. N.Y.C., Feb. 4, 1936; B.B.A., CCNY, 1957; m. Alice Sperling, May 19, 1957; children—Keith, Adam, Douglas. Producer, The Doctors, NBC, 1973-75 (Emmy award 1974); dir. Daytime TV, ABC, N.Y.C., 1975-77; producer One Life To Live, ABC, N.Y.C., 1977—.

STUART, JOSEPH MARTIN, artist, educator; b. Seminole, Okla., Nov. 9, 1932; s. Arch William and Lillian (Lindsey) S.; B.F.A., U. N.Mex., 1959, M.A., 1962; m. Signe Margaret Nelson, June 18, 1960; 1 dau., Lise Nelson. Profl. artist. 1959—; rep. permanent collections Salt Lake Art Center, Coll. Idaho. U. N.Mex. Art Mus., Sioux City (Iowa) Art Center; dir. S.D. Meml. Art Center, Brookings, 1971—; asso. prof. art history S.D. State U., Brookings, 1971—; past mem. Brookings Area Arts Council; bd. dirs. Upper Midwest Art Conservation Center, Mpls. Served with USN, 1951-55. Recipient certificate appreciation S.D. Bicentennial Commn., 1976; various awards and prizes for art. Mem. Artists Equity, Am. Assn. Museums, Assn. S.D. Museums, Phi Kappa Phi. Democrat. Unitarian. Club: Rotary. Author: The Art of South Dakota, 1974. Editor: Index of South Dakota Artists, 1974. Home: 719 8th St Brookings SD 57006 Office: SD Memorial Art Center Brookings SD 57007

STUART, KENNETH JAMES, illustrator, art dir.; b. Milw., Sept. 21, 1905; s. William Pope and Jennie (Ballinger) S.; student Pa. Acad. of Fine Arts, 1924-25; pupil Arthur Carles, 1925-26; student Academie Colarossi, Paris, France, 1929-30; m. Katharine Moos, June 12, 1937; children—Kenneth James, William Alan, Jonathan. Illustrator mag. covers, cartoonist, 1930-43; art editor Sat. Eve. Post, Phila., 1943-62; art. dir. Reader's Digest Assn., 1962-77, cons. for graphics, new pub. ventures, 1977—; cons. art dir. to Country Gentleman, 1949, Ahlen and Akerlunds (Stockholm) 1949, NSRB, 1950. Recipient Salmagundi Gold medal award, 1960; numerous others. Clubs: The Players, Dutch Treat, Sky, Coffee House. Home: 295 Ridgefield Rd Wilton CT 06897

STUART, LYLE, pub. co. exec.; b. N.Y.C., Aug. 11, 1922; s. Alfred and Theresa (Cohen) L.; student pub. schs., N.Y.C.; m. Mary Louise Strawn, Sept. 26, 1946; children—Sandra Lee, Rory John. Reporter, Internat. News Service, 1945, Variety, 1945-46; script writer Dept. State, Voice of Am., 1946; editor Music Bus. mag., 1946-48; founder Expose, 1951; bus. mgr. MAD mag., 1952-54; pres. Lyle Stuart, Inc., Secaucus, N.J., 1954—, Citadel Press, 1954, University Books, Inc.; producer Chinese Festival Music, 1952-62; author: God Wears A Bowtie, 1949, The Secret Life of Water Winchell, 1953, Mary Louise, 1970, Casino Gambling for the Winner, 1978. Founder North Bergen (N.J.) Pub. Library. Served with AUS, 1942-44. Mem. Am. Booksellers Assn., Silurians, ACLU. Home: 1530 Palisade Ave Fort Lee NJ 07024 Office: 120 Enterprise Ave Secaucus NJ 07094

STUART, MARY, actress; b. Miami, Fla., July 4; d. Guy M. and Mary (Stuart) Houchins; student pub. schs., Tulsa, Okla., m. Richard Krolik, Aug. 1, 1951 (div.); children—Cynthia, Jeffrey M. Appears in leading role Search For Tomorrow, CBS-TV, N.Y.C., 1951—; songwriter, singer Columbia Records, 1956, Bell Records, 1973. Mem. AFTRA, Screen Actors Guild, ASCAP. Episcopalian.

STUART, MEL, film dir.; b. N.Y.C., Sept. 2, 1928; s. Edgar and Cecille Solomon; B.A. in Music, N.Y. U., 1949; postgrad. Columbia U., 1949-50; m. Harriet Dolin, Aug. 13, 1956; children—Madeline, Peter Andrew. Film researcher CBS, 1957-59; v.p. Wolper Prodns., 1960-76; ind. producer-dir., Los Angeles, 1976—; dir. various films, including: Making of the President, 1960, 64, 68, If It's Tuesday, It Must Be Belgium; occasional instr. in film UCLA. Recipient 9 Emmy awards Am. Acad. TV Arts and Scis. Mem. Dirs. Guild Am., Writers Guild Am. Home and Office: 11508 Thurston Circle Los Angeles CA 90049*

STUART, RICHARD KENNETH, economist; b. Belmont, Mass., June 2, 1916; s. Everett Kenneth and Elsie Louise (Gowey) S.; B.S., U. R.I., 1938, M.S., 1940; Ph.D., U. Pa., 1956; m. Lucia Ann Jones, June 21, 1941; children—Bruce Cameron, Nancy Adams Stuart Munsey. Instr. econs. U. Maine, 1940-46, asst. prof., 1948-53, asso. prof., 1958, prof., 1959-60; instr. U. Pa., 1946-48; prof. Whitman Coll., 1960—. Home: 560 University St Walla Walla WA 99362 Office: Whitman Coll Walla Walla WA 99362

STUART, ROBERT, container mfg. co. exec.; b. Chgo., Aug. 3, 1921; s. Robert S. and Marie (Vavra) Solinsky; B.S., U. Ill., 1943; m. Lillian C. Kondelik, Dec. 5, 1962 (dec. May 1978). Sec.-treas., gen. mgr. Warren Metal Decorating Co., 1947-49; asst. to gen. mgr. Cans, Inc., 1950-52; asst. to v.p., then v.p. Nat. Can Corp., Chgo. 1953-59, exec. v.p., 1959-63, pres., 1963-69, chief exec., 1966-69, chmn. bd., chief exec. officer, 1969-72, chmn. bd., 1972—; dir. LaSalle Nat. Bank, Chgo., Chgo. Community Ventures Inc. Past chmn. Nat. Assn. Citizens Crime Commn.; past chmn. Nat. Minority Purchasing Council. Past pres. of Chgo. area United World Federalists, Inc.; past chmn. bd. Can Mfr.'s Inst. Past pres. Chgo. Crime Commn.; bd. dirs. U. Ill. Found., Nat. Com. Prevention Child Abuse, Protestant Found. Greater Chgo.; v.p., exec. com., bd. dirs. United Republican Fund of Ill.; vice chmn. Nat. Council on Crime and Delinquency; citizens council U. Chgo.; mem. bus. adv. council Chgo. Urban League; trustee Ill. Masonic Med. Center, Provident Hosp., Chgo., Chgo. Goodwill Industries; trustee emeritus Nat. Jewish Hosp.; co-chmn. Grand Council Am. Indian Center Chgo.; chmn. World Federalists Assn.; adv. council Coll. Bus. Adminstrn. U. Ill. at Chgo. Circle; trustee Central Ch. Chgo. Congregationalist; numerous other civic activities. Served to capt. AUS, 1943-46. Mem. Am. Mgmt. Assn., Presidents Assn. Alpha Kappa Lambda (past pres., past chmn. exec. council), C. of C. U.S. (dir.), Beta Gamma Sigma. Rotarian (past commodore internat. yachting fellowship). Clubs: Capitol Hill (Washington); Rotary (past pres., dist. gov.), Chicago, Economic, Commercial, Chgo. Yacht, Metropolitan (Chgo.); Little Ship (London, Eng.). Home: 400 E Randolph St Chicago IL 60601 Office: 8101 Higgins Rd Chicago IL 60631

STUART, ROBERT DOUGLAS, JR., food co. exec.; b. Hubbard Woods, Ill., Apr. 26, 1916; s. Robert Douglas and Harriet (McClure) S.; B.A., Princeton, 1937; J.D., Yale, 1946; m. Barbara McMath Edwards, May 21, 1938; children—Robert Douglas III, James McClure, Marian Pillsbury, Alexander Douglas. With Quaker Oats Co., Chgo., 1947—, now chmn. bd., chief exec. officer, dir.; dir. United Airlines, Inc., 1st Nat. Bank Chgo., Deere & Co. Served to maj. AUS, 1942-45. Mem. Grocery Mfrs. Am. (dir.), Bus. Council. Home: 1601 Conway Rd Lake Forest IL 60045 Office: Quaker Oats Co Merchandise Mart Chicago IL 60654

STUART, ROBERT MARVIN, bishop; b. Paulina, Iowa, Nov. 22, 1909; s. Robert Lee and Josia Lena (Conner) S.; A.B., Taylor U., 1931, D.D., 1944; S.T.B., Boston U., 1934, S.T.M., 1935; m. Mary Ella Rose, June 8, 1933; 1 son, Robert Lee. Ordained to ministry Methodist Ch., 1933; pastor in Shideler, Ind., 1931-32, Woods Hole, Mass., 1932-35, El Cerrito, Calif., 1935-38, San Francisco, 1938-42, Palo Alto, Calif., 1942-64; bishop Denver area Meth. Ch., 1964-72, San Francisco area, 1972—; mem. bd. discipleship Meth. Ch., del. gen. confs., 1952-56, 60-64; pres. council bishops United Meth. Ch., 1978-79. Trustee Pacific Sch. Religion, U. of Pacific. Home: 22 Los Altos Sq Los Altos CA 94022 Office: 330 Ellis St San Francisco CA 94101

STUART, THOMAS JOSEPH, automotive parts co. exec.; b. Detroit, July 22, 1935; s. Ray F. and Miriam S. (Smith) S.; B.S., U. Detroit, 1957; postgrad. Harvard Sch. Bus., 1974; m. Dorothy J. Kreiter, June 28, 1958; children—Michael, Thomas Joseph, Charles, Melissa. Agt., reviewer IRS, Detroit, 1957-65; tax mgr. McCord Corp., Detroit, 1965-68, asst. treas., 1968-72, sec., 1972—. Mem. Detroit C. of C., NAM, Am. Soc. Corporate Secs., Engring. Soc. Detroit. Roman Catholic. Club: Elks. Home: 2428 Eaton Gate Rd Lake Orion MI 48035 Office: 2850 W Grand Blvd Detroit MI 48202

STUART, WALTER BYNUM, III, banker; b. Baton Rouge, Oct. 5, 1922; s. Walter Bynum and Rosa (Gauthreaux) S.; B.S., La. State U., 1943; m. Rita Kleinpeter, May 20, 1944; children—Walter Bynum IV, Robert, Douglas, Ronald, Scott. Adminstrv. mgr. Kaiser Aluminum & Chem. Corp., 1946-63; v.p. First Nat. Bank Commerce, New Orleans, 1963-65, sr. v.p., 1965, exec. v.p., 1965-73, vice chmn. bd., dir., 1973—; exec. v.p. 1st Commerce Corp., New Orleans, 1972-73, pres., 1973-75, vice-chmn. bd., 1975-78, dir., 1973-78; pres. Am. Bank & Trust Co., Lafayette, La., 1978—; v.p., dir. 1st Commerce Real Estate Corp., 1st Investment Advisors, Inc.; chmn. bd. First Money, Inc.; dir. 1st Bankcard, Inc. Asso. dir., mem. faculty Sch. Banking La. State U., 1973-75, dir., 1975-78; mem. Faculty Assemblies for Bank Dirs. Campaign group chmn. industry com., mem. United Fund for Greater New Orleans Area, 1974; mem. research com. Pub. Affairs Research Council La., 1973-76, v.p., trustee, 1973-76; bd. dirs. Bur. Govtl. Research, 1973—, Council Better La., 1975—; pres. New Orleans Indsl. Devel. Bd., 1973-75. Served to lt. (j.g.) USNR, 1943-46. Mem. C. of C. of Greater New Orleans Area (v.p. 1973-75, bd. dirs., Am., La. (pres. 1977) bankers assns., Am. Mgmt. Assn., Kappa Alpha, Delta Sigma Pi, Beta Gamma Sigma. Democrat. Roman Catholic. Home: 104 Nickerson Pkwy Lafayette LA 70501 Office: Jefferson at Lee Lafayette LA 70501. *Recognizing that life is the experiencing of reality, and that reality is simply a continuing series of problems, I long ago decided that I would treat a problem as an opportunity. Every incident of difficulty has always invited my intense interest as a challenge, and my thoughts have been immediately marshalled for positive effort. My life has been most rewarding because I believe that "a problem is an opportunity!"*

STUART, WILLIAM CORWIN, judge b. Knoxville, Iowa, Apr. 28, 1920; s. George Corwin and Edith (Abram) S.; B.A., State U. Iowa, 1940, J.D., 1942; m. Mary Elgin Cleaver, Oct. 20, 1946; children—William Corwin II, Robert Cullen, Melanie Rae, Valerie Jo. Admitted to Iowa bar, 1942; practice in Chariton, 1946-62; city atty., Chariton, 1947-49; mem. Iowa Senate from Lucas-Wayne Counties, 1951-61; justice Supreme Ct. Iowa, 1962-71. Judge U.S. Dist. Ct., So. Dist. of Iowa, Des Moines, 1971—. Served as aviator USNR, 1943-45. Mem. Am., Iowa bar assns., Am. Legion, All For Iowa, Order of Coif, Omicron Delta Kappa, Phi Kappa Psi, Phi Delta Phi. Presbyn. Mason (Shriner). Home: 216 S Grand St Chariton IA 50049 Office: US Court House Des Moines IA 50309

STUART-STUBBS, BASIL FREDERICK, librarian; b. Moncton, N.B., Can., Feb. 3, 1930; s. Thomas Edward and Amy (Jefferson) Stuart-S.; B.A., U. B.C., 1952; B.L.S., McGill U., 1954; m. Nancy Page Ballard, June 18, 1955; children—Megan Page, Kathleen. Reference librarian McGill U., 1954-56; with library U. B.C., 1956—, univ. librarian, 1964—. Mem. Am., Canadian, B.C. library assns. Home: 1750 Maple St Apt 104 Vancouver BC Canada

STUBBERUD, ALLEN ROGER, univ. dean; b. Glendive, Mont., Aug. 14, 1934; s. Oscar Adolph and Alice Marie (LeBlanc) S.; B.S. in Elec. Engring., U. Idaho, 1956; M.S. in Engring., U. Calif., Los Angeles, 1958, Ph.D., 1962; m. May B. Tragus, Nov. 19, 1961; children—Peter A., Stephen C. Asso. prof. engring. U. Calif., Los Angeles, 1962-69; prof. elec. engring. U. Calif., Irvine, 1970—, asso. dean engring., 1970-78, dean engring., 1978—. Fellow IEEE, AIAA (asso.); mem. Ops. Research Soc. Am., Sigma Xi, Sigma Tau, Tau Beta Pi, Eta Kappa Nu. Author: Analysis and Synthesis of Linear Time Variable Systems, 1964; (with others) Feedback and Control Systems, 1967. Home: 19352 Sierra Soto Rd Irvine CA 92715. *Intelligence is no substitute for honesty and hard work.*

STUBBINS, HUGH A., JR., architect; b. Birmingham, Ala., Jan. 11, 1912; s. Hugh Asher and Lucile (Matthews) S.; B.S. Arch., Ga. Inst. Tech., 1933; M.Arch., Harvard, 1935; m. Diana Hamilton Moore, Mar. 3, 1938 (div. 1960); children—Patricia, Peter, Hugh 3d, Michael; m. 2d, Colette Fadeuilhe, Sept. 1960. Designer architect's office, Boston, 1935-38; formed a partnership, 1938-40; in architect's office, Birmingham, Ala., 1940; asso. prof. Grad. Sch. of Design, Harvard, 1946-52, chmn. dept. architecture, 1953; pvt. practice of architecture, Boston, 1941—, pres., chmn. bd. Hugh Stubbins & Assos., Inc. Vis. critic in residence, Yale, 1948-49, U. Oreg., 1950; sec. Rotch Traveling Scholarship, 1971—; hon. mem. Boston Archtl. Center. Chmn. design adv. com. Boston Redevel. Authority, 1964—; mem. design rev. panel Worcester Redevel. Authority, 1966—; Thomas Jefferson prof. architecture U. Va., 1979. Bd. dirs. Benjamin Franklin Found.; vis. com. Grad. Sch. Design, Harvard, 1958-72; adv. council Sch. Architecture, Princeton; mem. arts and archtl. com. Kennedy Meml. Library; mem. Harleston Parker Medal Com., 1973; mem. Fgn. Bus. Council, Commonwealth of Mass., 1978—; mem. nat. adv. bd. Ga. Inst. Tech., 1978—. Trustee Tabor Acad., 1974; mem. adv. bd. Whitney Library of Design, 1976—. Recipient Alpha Rho Chi medal, 1933; 3d prize Nat. Smithsonian Gallery of Art competition 1939; Progressive Architecture First Design award, 1954; Arcadia Achievement award, 1957; silver medal N.Y. Archtl. League, 1958; Rodgers and Hammerstein award, 1961; award Am. Inst. Steel Constrn., 1970; award Archtl. Record, 1971; award Prestressed Concrete Inst., 1971; award of merit Inst. So. Affairs and So. Acad. Letters, Arts and Scis., 1973; citation Am. Assn. Sch. Adminstrs., 1974, award environ. design, 1975; award of merit, Library Bldgs. award for Nathan Marsh Pusey Library, Harvard U., AIA and ALA, 1976; Spl. Energy award for Shiraz Tech. Inst., Am. Assn. Sch. Adminstrs. and AIA, 1978; AIA honor award for Citicorp Center, 1979; Thomas Jefferson Gold medal for architecture, 1980. Fellow Am. Acad. Arts and Sci., A.I.A. (v.p. 1964-65; jury fellows 1974-75; Nat. Honor award 1966, 79, award of merit 1970), Mexican Soc. Architects (hon.); mem. N.A.D. (academician), Mass. Assn. Architects, Boston Soc. Architects (pres. 1969-70), Boston Archtl. Center (hon.), Archtl. League N.Y., Beta Theta Pi, Omicron Delta Kappa. Clubs: Harvard (Boston); Laurel Brook; Beverly Yacht (Marion, Mass.); Century (N.Y.C.). Architect, Berlin Congress Hall (Germany), Consulate-Gen. (Tangier, Morocco); designer Countway Library of Medicine, Harvard, Fed. Res. Bank of Boston U. Va. Law Sch., Citicorp Center, N.Y.C., St. Peter's Ch., N.Y.C., and numerous other bldgs.; exec. architect Phila. Stadium. Home: 199 Brattle St Cambridge MA 02138 Office: 1033 Massachusetts Ave Cambridge MA 02138

STUBBLEFIELD, PAGE KINDRED, banker; b. Bloomington, Tex., Aug. 28, 1914; s. Edwin Page and Vinnye L. (Kindred) S.; student Southwestern U., Georgetown, Tex., 1931; B.B.A., U. Tex., Austin, 1936; m. Dorothea Mock, July 7, 1940; children—Edwin Mark, Bob Lynn. Mgr., Page Stubblefield Gen. Mdse., 1936-42; owner-operation P.K. Stubblefield Ins. Agy., 1946-51; asst. v.p. pub. relations pres. Victoria (Tex.) Bank & Trust Co., 1951-52, v.p., 1952-58, sr. v.p., 1958-69, pres., 1969-77, chmn. bd., 1977—, also dir.; pres., dir. Victoria Bankshares, Inc.; dir. Central Power & Light Co.; br. dir. Fed. Reserve Bank Dallas, Houston. Bd. dirs. Detar Hosp., Victoria, Tex. Research League. Served with finance dept. USAAF, 1942-45. Mem. Am. Bankers Assn., Newcomen Soc. in N.Am. Methodist (chmn. bd. trustees). Club: Executive's Dinner. Home: 2402 N DeLeon St Victoria TX 77901 Office: 120 S Main St Victoria TX 77901

STUBBS, DONALD STEWART, lawyer; b. Mulvane, Kan., Jan. 26, 1908; s. James Edwin and Florence (Stewart) S.; LL.B., U. Colo., 1932; m. Esther Louise Anderson, Aug. 26, 1935; children—Donald Stewart, Patricia Lucile (Mrs. John M. Bailey). Admitted to Colo. bar, 1932; practiced in Montrose, Colo., 1932-42, Denver, 1943—; gen. partner Bryant & Stubbs, 1933-42, Davis, Graham & Stubbs, 1943—; Montrose County atty., 1935-39; dep. dist. atty., 1940-42. Dir. Ideal Basic Industries, Inc., Denver. Mem. Colo. Bd. Law Examiners, 1969—. Mem. adv. bd. Salvation Army, 1971—, Denver Bd. Pub. Welfare, 1963—. Chmn. Montrose County Republican Com., 1936-40. Served to lt. (j.g.) USNR, 1944-46. Recipient Alumni award Colo. U., 1975, Knous Meml. Law Alumni award, 1978. Fellow Am. Bar Found.; mem. Am., Colo. (pres. 1974-75), Denver bar assns., Law Club Denver, Order of Coif, Delta Tau Delta. Clubs: Rotary (past pres.) (Montrose); Denver, Denver Country. Home: 3460 E Kentucky Ave Denver CO 80209 Office: 2600 Colo Nat Bldg Denver CO 80202

STUBBS, HAROLD LEROY, educator, mathematician; b. Newport, R.I., July 27, 1918; s. George Francis and Marguerite (Greason) S.; A.B., Harvard, 1939; M.A., Columbia Tchrs. Coll., 1946; Ph.D., Boston U., 1954; m. Lucille Frances Benedetti, Nov. 16, 1945; children—Susan Lee, Deborah Ann. Mem. faculty Northeastern U., 1945—, prof. math., 1957—, Robert G. Stone prof. math., 1972—, chmn. dept., 1957-69. Served with USAAF, 1942-45. Mem. Math. Assn. Am., Inst. Math. Statistics, Sigma Xi. Contbr. articles on applied math. to tech. jours Home: 355 S Main St Sharon MA 02067 Office: Northeastern U Boston MA 02115

STUBBS, JAMES CARLTON, hosp. adminstr.; b. MaGee, Miss., Jan. 26, 1924; s. James Sylvester and Katie Lucille (Grayson) S.; m. Essie Geraldine Shows, June 17, 1949; 1 son, James Hilton. Mgr., R. & A. Appliance Store, MaGee, 1950; field insp. Miss. Mental Instm. Bd., Jackson, 1950-52; dir. Miss. Eleemosynary Bd., Jackson, 1952-75, Miss. State Hosp., Whitfield, 1975—; chmn. Miss. Reimbursement Commn., 1965—; pres. Jackson-Vicksburg Hosp. Council, 1977-79, pres., 1979—. Served with U.S. Army, 1944-46, 50-51; Korea. Charter mem. Sports Hall of Fame, U. So. Miss. Mem. Nat. Assn. Reimbursement Officers, Epilepsy Found., Miss. Public Health Assn., Assn. Mental Health Adminstrs., Am. Acad. Health Adminstrn., Miss. Hosp. Assn. (fin. com., dir.). Democrat. Baptist. Clubs: Colonial Country; Quarter Century; M, Big Gold (U. So. Miss.). Office: Miss State Hosp Whitfield MS 39193

STUBBS, JANET HELENA, mezzo soprano; b. Toronto, Ont., Can., Apr. 21, 1945; d. Edward Martin and Ida Aletha (Hinds) S.; B.A., U. Toronto, 1966, LL.B., 1969, diploma in operatic performance, 1975. Called to Ont. bar, 1971; practiced law, Toronto, 1971-72; debut as Carmen with Can. Opera Co. at Royal Alexandra Theatre, Toronto, 1979, and as Cinderella, 1979; other appearances include: Edmonton (Alta., Can.) Opera Assn., Festival Ottawa (Ont.), Guelph (Ont.) Spring Festival, and maj. Can. orchs., including Toronto Symphony, Nat. Arts Centre Orch., Ottawa, Calgary (Alta.) Symphony, Hamilton (Ont.) Philharm. Mem. Can. Actors Equity Assn. (1st v.p.), Assn. Can. TV and Radio Artists, Law Soc. Upper Can. Mem. United Ch. Can.

STUCKEMAN, HERMAN CAMPBELL, engr.; b. Pitts., Aug. 7, 1914; s. Herman Sydney and Alma (Campbell) S.; B.S. in Architecture, Sch. Engring. Pa. State U., 1937; m. Margaret Eleanor Rockwell, Aug. 28, 1940; children—Ellen Campbell, Alan Rockwell, Joyce Thayer. Architect, Edward B. Lee, Pitts., 1938-39, Gen. State Authority, Harrisburg, Pa., 1940-41, Prack & Prack, Texarkana, Tex. and Pitts., 1941-42; partner Delta Mfg. Co., Milw., 1942-45, gen. mgr., 1945-50; v.p. Rockwell Mfg. Co., Pitts., 1950-73; dir. real estate Rockwell Internat. Corp. (merger Rockwell Mfg. Co. and N.Am. Rockwell), 1973-75; pres., chmn. Precise Corp., 1975—; chmn. bd. Pitts. Testing Lab.; dir. Devon Corp., Rox Enterprises, Inc., Nat. Gas and Oil Corp. Clubs: Duquesne, Pittsburgh Athletic, Longvue, Rotary (Pitts.). Home: 17 Churchill Rd Pittsburgh PA 35208

STUCKEY, WALTER JACKSON, JR., physician; b. Fairfield, Ala., Mar. 6, 1927; s. Walter Jackson and Lena (Brackin) S.; B.S., U. Ala., 1947; M.D., Tulane U., 1951; m. Mildred Creel Roberts, Nov. 27, 1952; children—Walter Jackson, III, John Hamlin, James Allan. Intern, Charity Hosp. La., New Orleans, 1951-52; resident in gen. practice Lafayette (La.) Charity Hosp., 1952; resident in internal medicine Tulane med. service Charity Hosp. La., VA Hosp., New Orleans, 1955-57; fellow, instr. dept. medicine Tulane U. Sch. Medicine, 1958-60, asst. prof., 1960-62, asso. prof., 1962-68, prof., 1968—, chief dept. hematology, 1963—, sr. vis. physician, 1968—; active staff Tulane Med. Center Hosp.; practice medicine specializing in hematology, New Orleans; cons. VA, USPHS, Meth., Mercy hosps., Hotel Dieu, New Orleans, East Jefferson Hosp., Touro Infirmary. Served with USNR, 1952-54. Fellow A.C.P.; mem. AAAS, Am. Assn. Cancer Edn., A.M.A., Am. Soc. Internal Medicine, La., Orleans Parish med. socs., New Orleans Acad. Internal Medicine, N.Y. Acad. Scis., Internat. Soc. Hematology, Am. Soc. Hematology, Am. Soc. Clin. Oncology. Methodist. Home: 7325 Cameo St New Orleans LA 70124 Office: 1430 Tulane Ave New Orleans LA 70112

STUCKI, ROLAND, cons.; b. Santa Clara, Utah, Feb. 24, 1907; s. Christian and Mary (Gubler) S.; student Dixie Jr. Coll., 1926-28; B.S., Brigham Young U., 1930; M.S., U. Utah, 1932; M.B.A. (Henry Newell scholar), Stanford, 1935; Ph.D. (Henry D. White fellow), Cornell U., 1943; m. Rhea Taylor, June 23, 1932; children—Larry Roland, Grant Taylor (dec.), Leon George. Partner, Dixie Fruit Co., Ely, Nev., 1930-33; research dir. Utah Edn. Assn., Salt Lake City, 1935; instr., asst. prof., asso. prof., prof. U. Utah, Salt Lake City, 1935-76, prof. emeritus, 1976—, chmn. dept. finance, 1947-57, 68-72, chmn. dept. mgmt., 1957-68, coordinator European M.B.A. programs in Germany, Eng. and Spain, 1972-73, dir. M.B.A. and Human Resource Mgmt. grad. programs in Germany, Eng., Spain, Greece, 1974-76; cons. Ralph J. Pomoray & Assos., Phoenix, 1959; head bank operations unit, div. research and statistics Fed. Deposit Ins. Corp., Washington, 1950-51, cons., 1952, 66-76; cons., case writer Grad. Sch., U. Tehran, Iran, 1961; vis. prof. Coll. City N.Y., summer 1958; cons. Granite Nat. Bank, Dixie State Bank; pvt. cons., 1977—. Mem. loan com. U. Utah Employees Credit Union, 1956-74. Trustee Consumer Credit Counseling Service Utah. Mem. Am., Western econ. assns., Am., Western finance assns., Alpha Kappa Psi, Beta Gamma Sigma, Phi Kappa Phi. Author: (with J. Whitney Hanks) Money, Banking and National Income, 1956; Analysis of Installment Financing Legislation and Practices in Utah, 1956; Commercial Banking in Utah, 1847-66, 1967; (with Roger H. Nelson) Evaluation of Impact of the Small Business Administration's Financial Program in Utah, 1954-60, 1962; Installment Financing Legislation, State of Utah, 1968; Utah Uniform Consumer Credit Report, 1970; Utah Consumer Credit Code Report, Vol. II, 1972, Vol. III, 1974, Vol. IV, 1977. Contbr. Ency. Britannica, 1964, 68—. Editor, contbr. Personal Finance, rev. edit., 1961. Home: 1766 S 2600 E Salt Lake City UT 84108

STUCKY, KENNETH JOSEPH, business exec.; b. Woodburn, Ind., Oct. 9, 1914; s. Joseph and Della (Kirchhofer) S.; B.S. in Bus. Adminstrn., Ind. U., 1937; m. Dorothy E. Powley, Jan. 18, 1942; children—Elizabeth Jean, Lisa Ann. Partner, Stucky Bros., home appliances, Ft. Wayne, Ind., 1943-47, sec.-treas. Stucky Bros., Inc., 1947-71, chmn. bd., 1965—; pres. S.K.M. Inc., 1949—, Satisfactory Finance Corp., 1959-70, Stuckys Food Service Inc., 1959-65; sec. treas. KVM Realty Co., Inc., 1949-78. Mem. Mart mag. dealer adv. bd., 1960-66. Mem. YMCA bus. com., 1958. Bd. dirs. Brand Names Found., 1962-64. Recipient spl. award Nat. Appliance and Radio TV Dealers Assn., 1956; named Retailer of Year in appliance category Brand Names Found., 1957. Mem. Am. Marketing Assn., Am. Mgmt. Assn., Life Appliance Dealers Marketing Council, Nat. Appliance Radio-TV Dealers Assn. (pres. 1957, mem. exec. com. of bd. dirs.; hon. life), Ft. Wayne Better Bus. Bur. (dir. 1960-63), Ft. Wayne C. of C. (bd. dirs. 1967-69, chmn. retail co-ordinating com. 1967), Ft. Wayne Credit Bur. (dir. 1957-60). Conglist. (past trustee, deacon 1960-63). Mason (Shriner), Rotarian (dir. Ft. Wayne 1967-70). Home: 4410 Vance Ave Fort Wayne IN 46805 Office: 5601 Coldwater Rd Fort Wayne IN 46825

STUCKY, MARVIN WAYNE, automotive exec.; b. Decatur, Ind., Oct. 22, 1932; s. Ivan N. and Hilda (Beeler) S.; B.S. in Agr., Purdue U., 1954; M.B.A., Harvard U., 1959; m. Patricia Louise Lockhart, May 24, 1958; children—William Vincent, David Brian, Eric Randall. With purchasing dept. Ford Motor Co., Dearborn, Mich., 1959p67; v.p. purchasing Am. Motors Corp., Detroit, 1967-70, v.p. Jeep product devel., 1970-73, v.p. product engring., 1973-75, v.p. product group, 1975-79, v.p. govtl. affairs and corp. planning, 1979—. Served to lt. Transp. Corps, AUS, 1954-56. Named outstanding young man of year Outstanding Ams. Found., Chgo., 1968. Mem. Soc. Automotive Engrs., Beta Theta Pi, Alpha Zeta. Club: Harvard Bus. Sch. (Detroit). Office: 14250 Plymouth Rd Detroit MI 48232

STUCKY, RONALD LEON, educator; b. Decatur, Ind., Oct. 24, 1927; s. Ivan N. and Hilda (Beeler) S.; B.S. with highest distinction, Purdue U., 1949, Ph.D. in Econs., 1954; M.B.A. with distinction, Harvard, 1951; m. Patricia Ann Watson, Nov. 23, 1970; children by previous marriage—Carol Alene, Richard Martin, Robert Bruce, Barbara Ann, James Thomas, Jane Clare. Mem. faculty Purdue U., 1951-64, asso. dean Krannert Grad. Sch. Indsl. Adminstrn., 1960-64; prof. bus. adminstrn. Santa Clara (Calif.) U., 1966—, chmn. mktg. dept., 1969-75, dir. Inst. Agribus., 1974—; engaged in real estate devel., San Jose, 1964-66; partner Robert F. Fields Co., Lafayette,

Ind., 1952-64; chmn. bd. Alloy Crafts Co., Delphi, Ind., 1961-64; founder Electro-Numerics Co., Santa Clara, 1968-69; Founder Interdesign, Inc., Sunnyvale, Calif., 1971, Jav-Art Enterprises, San Jose, 1973—. Served with USNR, 1945-47. Mem. Beta Gamma Sigma, Alpha Zeta. Episcopalian. Home: 19123 Vineyard Ln Saratoga CA 95070

STUDDEN, WILLIAM J., mathematician; b. Timmins, Ont., Can., Sept. 30, 1935; Ph.D. in Statistics, Stanford U., 1962; married. Faculty dept. statistics Purdue U., 1964—, prof. statistics and math., 1970—. Fellow Inst. Math. Statistics. Co-author book. Home: 140 Knox Dr Lafayette IN 47906 Office: Statistics Dept Purdue U Lafayette IN 47907

STUDDS, GERRY EASTMAN, congressman; b. Mineola, N.Y., May 12, 1937; s. Eastman and Beatrice (Murphy) S.; grad. Groton Sch., 1955; B.A., Yale, 1959, M.A.T., 1961. Fgn. service officer, State Dept., Washington, 1961-63; exec. asst. to presdl. cons. for a nat. service corps, White House, 1963; legislative asst. to Sen. Harrison Williams, 1964; tchr. St. Paul's Sch., Concord, N.H., 1965-69; mem. 93d-96th congresses from 12th Dist. Mass.; candidate U.S. Congress, 1970. Del. Democratic Nat. Conv., 1968. Home: 16 Black Horse Ln Cohasset MA 02025 Office: House of Representatives Washington DC 20515

STUDENROTH, CARL WILSON, labor union ofcl.; b. Columbia, Pa., Apr. 14, 1915; s. Frederick Melvin and Priscilla Mary (Crist) S.; student Pa. State Coll., 1933-35; m. Apr. 10, 1937; children—Wanda Faye, Donna Marie. Laborer, Pa. R.R., 1935-36; molder and foundry worker Grinnell Corp., 1936-44; organizer, dist. rep., v.p. Internat. Molders and Allied Workers Union, AFL-CIO-CLC, Cin., 1944-55, pres., 1976—; mem. exec. bd. Indsl. Union Dept., AFL-CIO, Metal Trades AFL-CIO; adv. various govt. commns.; pres. Labor Adv.; mem. labor sector adv. Strauss Trade Commn. Democrat. Lutheran. Office: 1225 E McMillan St Cincinnati OH 45206

STUDER, WILLIAM JOSEPH, library exec.; b. Whiting, Ind., Oct. 1, 1936; s. Victor E. and Sarah G. (Hammersley) S.; B.A., Ind. U., 1958, M.A., 1960, Ph.D. (Univ. fellow), 1968; m. Rosemary Lippie, Aug. 31, 1957; children—Joshua E., Rachel Marie. Grad. asst. div. Library Sci., Ind. U., 1959-60, reference asst., 1960-61; spl. intern Library of Congress, 1961-62, reference librarian, sr. bibliographer, 1962-65; dir. regional campuses Ind. U., Bloomington, 1968-73, asso. dean, dir. regional campuses, 1973-77; dir. libraries Ohio State U., Columbus, 1977—; mem. Library Services and Constrn. Act Adv. Com. of Ind., 1971-76, Adv. Council on Fed. Library Programs in Ohio, 1977—, ARL Office Mgmt. Studies Adv. Com., 1977—, ARL Task Force on Nat. Library Network Devel., 1978—; trustee OCLC, Inc., 1977-78, OHIONET, 1977—. Treas., Monroe County Mental Health Assn., 1968—; active Mental Health Social Club, 1971-73, budget rev. com. United Way, 1975-77; bd. dirs. Mental Health Assn. Recipient citation for participation MARC Insts., 1968-69; Louise Maxwell award Ind. U., 1978. Mem. ALA, Ohio Library Assn., Assn. Coll. and Research Libraries (dir. 1977), Am. Soc. for Info. Sci., Nat. Micrographics Assn., AAUP, Acad. Library Assn. Ohio, Phi Kappa Phi, Phi Eta Sigma, Alpha Epsilon Delta, Beta Phi Mu. Contbr. articles to profl. jours. Home: 724 Olde Settler Pl Columbus OH 43214 Office: 106F Main Library 1858 Neil Ave Mall Columbus OH 43210

STUDIER, MARTIN HERMAN, chemist; b. Leola, S.D., Nov. 10, 1917; s. Emil and Mathilda (Mueller) S.; B.A., Luther Coll., 1939; student Iowa State Coll., 1939-42; Ph.D., U. Chgo., 1947; m. Eleanor Chrissinger, Dec. 31, 1944; children—James, Anne, John, Paul. Mem. staff Argonne (Ill.) Nat. Lab., 1943—, sr. chemist, 1948—; co-discover elements einsteinium and fermium, 1952; spl. research nuclear chemistry heavy elements. mass spectrometry with spl. application to chemistry noble gases and organic matter in meteorites, the chemical nature of coals. Served with Signal Corps and C.E., AUS, 1943-46. Recipient U. Chgo. award for disting. performance at Argonne Nat. Lab., 1978. Mem. Am. Phys. Soc., Am. Chem. Soc., A.A.A.S., Research Soc. Am. Lutheran. Home: 4429 Downers Dr Downers Grove IL 60515 Office: Argonne Nat Lab Argonne IL 60439

STUDSGAARD, ANKER CHRISTIAN, banker; b. Mpls., Feb. 16, 1919; s. Jens Erik and Marie (Sorensen) S.; B.B.A., U. Minn., 1940; m. Dorothy Jane Lenzen, Sept. 21, 1946; children—Deborah, Anker Christian. Audit mgr. Arthur Andersen & Co., Seattle, Paris, France, Cleve., 1940-42, 46-56; comptroller Nat. City Bank of Cleve., 1956-73, v.p., 1963-73, sr. v.p., 1973-75, exec. v.p., 1976—; dir. N.E. Bldg., Inc., Third Nat. Bank, Sandusky, Ohio, Motor Discount Corp., Cleve., 1st Nat. Bank, Ashland, Ohio, 1st Nat. Bank, Dayton, Ohio. Mem. Am. Inst. C.P.A.'s, Ohio Soc. C.P.A.'s, Greater Cleve. Growth Assn. Home: 110 Aspenwood Dr Chagrin Falls OH 44022 Office: 623 Euclid Ave Cleveland OH 44101

STUEART, ROBERT D., coll. dean, librarian, educator; B.A., So. Ark. U., 1956; cert. Russian lang., 1958; M.S.I., La. State U., 1962; library sci. advanced cert. U. Pitts., 1969, Ph.D., 1971. Library asst. in reference and cataloging So. State Coll., Magnolia, Ark., 1953-56; librarian, tchr. Desha County (Ark.) Public Schs., 1956-57; library asst. microforms room, serials and Russian cataloging La. State U. Library, 1960-62; with U. Colo. Libraries, 1962-66, head circulation dept., 1964-65, instr., adminstrv. asst. to dir. libraries, 1965-66; asso. prof. library sci., asst. dir. libraries for systems and processes Pa. State U., 1966-68; vis. lectr. U. Pitts. Grad. Sch. Library and Info. Scis., 1968-71; vis. lectr. Coll. Librarianship Wales, 1971-72; asso. prof., asst. dean U. Denver Grad. Sch. Librarianship, 1972-74; dean, prof. library and info. sci. Simmons Coll. Sch. Library and Info. Sci., Boston, 1975—; cons., speaker in field. Mem. com. on media edn. steering com. New Eng. Ednl. Media Assn., 1975—; chmn. personnel standards com. Mass. Dept. Edn. Bur. Library Extension, 1975—; mem. Mass. Gov.'s Planning Com. for White House Conf. on Libraries, 1976—. Mem. Assn. Am. Library Schs. (dir. 1976-79), AAUP, ALA, Assn. Coll. and Research Libraries (editorial bd. Coll. and Research Libraries 1973-74, council 1978—), Library Adminstrn. and Mgmt. Assn. (chmn. stats. com. for library edn. 1978—, pres. library adminstrn. div. 1977-78), Research Roundtable, Am. Soc. Info. Scis., Colo. Library Assn., Spl. Libraries Assn., New Eng. Library Assn., Mass. Library Assn. Author: The Area Specialist Bibliographer: An Inquiry Into His Role, 1972; (with John T. Eastlick) Libraries Unlimited, 1977; editor: Collection Development, 1980; (with Richard Johnson) New Horizons for Academic Libraries, 1979; contbr. articles and revs. to profl. publs. Office: Simmons Coll Sch Library Sci 300 The Fenway Boston MA 02115

STUEBNER, ERWIN AUGUST, investment banker; b. St. Joseph, Mo., Nov. 17, 1905; s. August and Anna S. (Dankers) S.; B.S., U. Pa., 1927; m. Frances B. Quinn, Dec. 6, 1930; children—James, Anne, Mary Lee, Erwin August. Asst. treas. Guaranty Trust Co. of N.Y., 1927-29; v.p. Phila. Nat. Co., 1929-34; mgr. Phila. officer Kidder, Peabody & Co., 1934-38, resident partner Chgo. office, 1949-64; pres. Kidder, Peabody & Co., Inc., 1964-77, vice chmn., 1977—. v.p. Fidelity-Phila. Trust Co., 1938-47; dir. Am. Investment Co. Ill., United Telecommunications, Inc., Uarco, Inc. Served as lt. col. USAAF, 1942-45, overseas. Commr., Lower Merion Twp. Montgomery Co., Pa., 1945-49. Pres. bd. trustees The Lankenau Hosp., Phila., 1946-49; pres. bd. dirs. Hosp. Council, Phila., 1947-49, Passavant Meml. Hosp., 1963-66; pres. Northwestern U. Med. Center, 1967-72, chmn., 1972—. Bd. dirs. Women's Hosp. and Maternity Center Chgo., Northwestern Meml. Hosp.; trustee Village of Kenilworth, 1957-65. Mem. Investment Bankers Assn. Am. (gov.), Midwest Stock Exchange, Beta Theta Pi, Beta Gamma Sigma. Clubs: Indian Hill; Bond, Chicago, Attic. Home: 1500 Sheridan Rd Wilmette IL 60091 Office: 125 S Wacker Dr Chicago IL 60606

STUEHR, JOHN EDWARD, biophys. chemist, educator; b. Cleve., Aug. 30, 1935; s. Sherman John and Alice Gertrude (Cubel) S.; B.A., Western Res. U., 1957, M.S., 1959, Ph.D., 1961; m. Gail Anne Featheringham, Sept. 1, 1962; children—Laura, David, Eric, Andrea. NIH Postdoctoral fellow, 1962-63; asst. prof. chemistry Western Res. U., 1964-69, asso. prof. Case Western Res. U., 1969-74, prof., 1974—, chmn. dept., 1977—. Cons. Durrum Corp. Recipient Career Devel. award NIH. Mem. Am. Chem. Soc., Am. Fedn. Biol. Chemists, Phi Beta Kappa, Sigma Xi (sec. chpt. 1975-77). Contbg. author of 3 book chpts. Contbr. articles on kinetics, thermodynamics to profl. jours. Home: 2183 Demington Ave Cleveland Heights OH 44106 Office: Dept of Chemistry Case Western Res U Cleveland OH 44106

STUFFLEBEAN, JOHN HOWARD, civil engr.; b. Brookfield, Mo., Oct. 7, 1918; s. John Sylvester and Floy (Frakes) S.; B.S. in Civil Engring., U. Mo., 1945; m. Marguerite Hill, Oct. 3, 1942; 1 son, John Edward. Jr. engr. Mo. Hwy. Dept., also C.B. & Q. R.R., 1940-42; sr. engr. S.P. R.R., 1945-46; office engr. Blanton & Co., engrs., Tucson, 1946-48, chief engr., prin., 1948-66, exec. v.p., 1966-69, pres., 1969—. Chmn. Ariz. Bd. Tech. Registration; adv. com. to county engr., Pima County, 1958-64; adviser asst. sec. def. for civil def., 1961-66; mem. Tucson Regional Plan Bd., 1966—. Chmn. trustees Blanton & Co. Profit Sharing Trust. Served to 1st lt. AUS, 1942-44. Recipient Honor award U. Mo.-Columbia, 1976; Distinguished Citizen award U. Ariz., 1976. Registered profl. engr., Ariz., Calif., Mo., Tex., Nev., N.Mex. Mem. Nat. (pres. 1963-64, rep. to engring. edn. and accreditation com. Engrs. Council Profl. Devel. 1974—), Ariz. (Outstanding Service award 1961) socs. profl. engrs., Am. Inst. Civil Engrs., Am. Soc. C.E., A.A.A.S., Am. Soc. Engring. Edn., Am. Water Works Assn., Water Pollution Control Fedn., Tau Beta Pi, Kappa Alpha. Republican. Presbyn. (elder). Elk, Mason, Kiwanian. Author articles, bulls. Home: 4117 E Kilmer St Tucson AZ 85711 Office: 1 W Paseo Redondo Tucson AZ 85702

STUHLINGER, ERNST, physicist; b. Niederrimbach, Germany, Dec. 19, 1913; s. Ernst and Pauline (Werner) S.; Ph.D., U. Tuebingen, Germany, 1936; m. Irmgard Lotze, Aug. 1, 1950; children—Susanne, Tilman, Hans Christoph. Came to U.S., 1946, naturalized, 1955. Research cosmic rays, nuclear physics, 1934-41; asst. prof. Technische Hochschule, Berlin, Germany, 1936-41; guidance and control equipment rocket Devel. Center, Peenemuende, Germany, 1943-45; with Guided Missile Devel. Office, Ft. Bliss, Tex., 1946-50; physicist Ordnance Missile Labs., Huntsville, Ala., 1950-56; physicist Army Ballistic Missile Agy., 1956-60; dir. Space Scis. Lab., George C. Marshall Space Flight Center, NASA, Huntsville, Ala., 1960-68, asso. dir. for sci., 1968-76; sr. research scientist, adj. prof. U. Ala. at Huntsville, 1976—. Served with German Army, 1941-43; Russian Campaign. Fellow Am. Astronautical Soc., Am. Rocket Soc. (dir.), Am. Inst. Aeros. and Astronautics (tech. dir.), Brit. Interplanetary Soc.; mem. Internat. Acad. Astronautics, Von Braun Astron. Soc. (dir.), Austrian Astron. Soc. (hon.), Am. Optical Soc., Deutsche Roentgengesellschaft (hon.), Soaring Soc. Am., Deutsche Physikalische Gesellschaft, Deutsche Gesellschaft Fuer Raketen Technik und Raumfahrt (hon.), Hermann Oberth Gesellschaft (hon.), Assn. U.S. Army. Author: Ion Propulsion for Space Flight, 1964; co-author Skylab, A Guidebook, 1973; Projeck Viking, 1976. Feasibility and design studies elec. propulsion systems for space ships, also artificial earth satellites, lunar and planetary exploration projects, space astronomy, 1954—, user testing of electronic automobiles. Home: 3106 Rowe Dr Huntsville AL 35801 Office: U Ala Huntsville AL 35807

STUHR, EDWARD PHILLIP, banker; b. Bklyn., May 11, 1905; s. Edward and Dora (Lendell) S.; B.C.S., N.Y. U., 1926; m. Theresa Cherney, May 29, 1930; children—Edward Philip, David Paul. Research dir. Callaway, Fish & Co., investment bankers, N.Y.C., 1928-41; research officer Fiduciary Trust Co. of N.Y., investment mgrs., N.Y.C., 1945-46, v.p., 1947-55, 1st v.p., dir. research, 1956-64, chmn. exec. com., dir. research, 1965-69, chmn. exec. com., 1969—, now hon. dir.; dir. Detroit & Can. Tunnel Co., Groov Pin Corp., Nat. Trust Bank of St. Petersburg (Fla.). Mem. Am. Acad. Polit. Sci. Clubs: Stock Exchange Luncheon, Economic (N.Y.C.). Home: 20 Cleverdon Rd Ho-Ho-Kus NJ 07423 Office: 2 World Trade Center New York City NY 10048

STULL, RICHARD JOHN, univ. adminstr.; b. Washington, Pa., Sept. 17, 1916; s. Dr. John and Bertha (Kensley) S.; A.B., Duke, 1940, certificate hosp. adminstrn., 1942; m. Mary Elizabeth May, Dec. 21, 1937; children—Cynthia, Richard John II, Deborah May. Asst. purchasing agt. Duke, 1942; adminstr. Phoenixville (Pa.) Hosp., 1942-44; supt. Norfolk (Va.) Gen. Hosp., 1944-46; cons. hosp. adminstrn. Calif. Dept. Pub. Health, 1946-50; Western rep. James A. Hamilton & Assos., 1947-48; dir. hosps. and infirmaries, clin. prof. hosp. adminstrn. U. Calif., 1948—, v.p., 1955-60; dir. div. health and med. adminstrn. Booz, Allen & Hamilton, San Rafael, Calif., 1960-61; v.p. marketing Aloe Med. div. Brunswick Corp., St. Louis, 1961-64, v.p. health and sci. div., 1964—; exec. v.p. Am. Coll. Hosp. Adminstrs., Chgo., 1965-72, pres., 1972—. Mem. gov.'s adv. com. mental health, 1955; cons. Dept. State in Indonesia; survey Australian Teaching Hosps.; chmn. med. edn. study tech. adv. com. Western Interstate Commn. Higher Edn.; pres. Hosp. Industries Assn., 1964-65; condr. health system studies, Can., Australia, Japan, Europe, 1966-75; cons. Health Resources Adminstrn., HEW, 1977—. Bd. visitors Med. Center, Duke. Recipient Humanitarian of Yr. award Nat. Assn. Health Services Execs., 1975. Fellow Am. Coll. Hosp. Adminstrs. (v.p. 1965, pres. 1973, Silver medal 1977); mem. Nat. League Nurses (adv. com.), Am. (hon. mem.; councils adminstrv. practice and research, Disting. Service award 1978), Western, Va.-Carolina, Calif., Ill. hosp. assns., Am. Pub. Health Assn., Assn. Am. Med. Colls., Australian Inst. Hosp. Adminstrs. (hon.), Assn. U. Programs in Hosp. Adminstrn., Am. Assn. Hosp. Cons. (hon. 1974), Hosp. Industries Assn. (pres.), Delta Omega, Sigma Xi. Contbr. articles profl. jours. Home: 717 Concorde Dr Highland Park IL 60035 Office: 840 N Lake Shore Dr Chicago IL 60611

STULMAN, JULIUS, author; b. N.Y.C., Apr. 11, 1906; s. Joseph and Ida (Goldstein) S.; student N.Y. U., 1923-25; m. Janis Eleanor Dremann, Dec. 26, 1956; children—Stephen Lloyd, Joan Leslie, (Mrs. Phil E. Gilbert, Jr.). With Lumber Industries Inc., N.Y.C., now chmn. bd.; chmn. bd. Lumber Exchange Terminal, Inc., N.Y.C.; dir. Found. Life Ins. Co. Am.; pres. Green Street Terminal Corp., N.Y.C.; dir. World-Wide Press Co., 1953-60; pub. Fields Within Fields ... Within Fields, N.Y.C. Pres. World Inst. Council, N.Y.C.; v.p. Center Integrative Edn., N.Y.C.; mem. adv. council Soc. Gen. Systems Research, Washington, consortium on peace research, edn. and devel. Inst. Behavioral Scis., Boulder, Colo. Mem. adv. bd. Calif. Inst. Asian Studies, Internat. Cooperation Council. Fellow World Acad. Art and Sci.; mem. Poetry Soc. Am., World Med. Assn. (life), Am. Cycle Assn. Club: Masons. Author: He Who Is Prepared, 1939; Energy Theory with Regard to Human Relations, 1944; Containerization Concept formerly presented Cargo City, 1947; Toward a Better Life in a Better Society, 1950; India Report, 1951; Western Aid to Asia's Subcontinent, 1951; Mutual Aid and Development of Underdeveloped Countries, 1951; A Pattern for Life, 1951; The Challenge to American Initiative, 1952; What Underdeveloped Countries Need Most, 1954; New Formula for World Peace and Prosperity, 1955; Applying New Thinking to Current Problems, 1955; A New Look at Aid for Underdeveloped Countries, 1955; The Importance of Distribution in Our Economy, 1955; More Needy than Money, 1956; Looking back to the Future from the Year 2000, 1956; World-Wide Trends and Insights series, 1956-57; Urban Renewal, 1960; Executive Center, 1960; Urban Satellite, 1960; Vertical Dwelling Clusters, 1960; World Cultural Center, 1960; World Economic Development, 1961; Mankind City, 1966; Evolving Mankind's Future, 1967; Man, Mankind, The Universe, 1968; Economic Fluctuations, 1968; Climbing to Mankind Solutions, 1968; World Brain: New Formula for World Peace and Prosperity, 1969; Beyond Crises: A 'Creative Ladder' for Oncoming Generations, 1970; Creative Systems in Housing, 1971; The Methodology of Pattern, 1972; Awakening Consciousness in Education, 1972; (with E. Laszlo) Emergent Man, 1972; The Third Industrial Revolution, 1973; The World Institute: Key to Mankind's Emergence, 1974; also papers. Address: World Inst Council Green and West Sts Brooklyn NY 11222

STULTS, ALLEN PARKER, banker; b. Chgo., June 13, 1913; s. Elmer E. and Minnie (Parker) S.; student U. Ill., 1931-32; diploma Northwestern U., 1941; student Loyola U., 1941-42; certificate Rutgers Grad. Sch. Banking, 1945; m. Elizabeth Van Horne, Aug. 19, 1939; children—Laurence, Shirley, John, James. With Fed. Res. Bank, 1933; asst. cashier Am. Nat. Bank & Trust Co. of Chgo., 1942-45, asst. v.p., 1946-48, v.p., 1949-56, chmn. loan com., 1954-68, exec. v.p., 1956-63, pres., 1963-69, dir., 1957—, chief exec. officer, 1968, chmn. bd. dirs., 1969—; pres. Walter E. Heller Internat. Corp., also dir.; dir. McDonald's Corp. Pub. adviser Midwest Stock Exchange, 1964-65. Mem. bd. finance com. Chgo. Area council Boy Scouts Am.; pres. council Nat. Coll. Edn.; mem. council Grad. Sch. Bus., U. Chgo. Bd. govs. Citizens Greater Chgo.; trustee Alice Lloyd Coll., Pippa Passes, Ky., Nat. Jewish Hosp., Denver, 1973-76; bd. dirs. Lyric Opera Chgo. Mem. Am. (pres. 1971-72), Ill. (pres. 1968-69) bankers assns., Chgo. Assn. Commerce and Industry (dir.), Ill. C. of C., Res. City Bankers Assn., Chgo. Clearing House Assn., Newcomen Soc. N.Am., Phi Gamma Delta, Skull and Crescent. Conglist. Clubs: Bankers (v.p.), Chicago Athletic Assn., Economic, Executive (dir. 1956), Robert Morris Associates (pres. 1952-53), Commercial (exec. com.), Chicago; Sunset Ridge Country (pres. 1956-57) (Winnetka, Ill.); Mid-America (pres. 1974-75); Tucson Nat. Golf. Home: 1420 Sheridan Rd Wilmette IL 60091 Office: 33 N LaSalle St Chicago IL 60690

STUMP, BOB, Congressman; b. Phoenix, Apr. 4, 1927; s. Jesse Patrick and Floy Bethany (Fields) S.; B.S. in Agronomy, Ariz. State U., 1951; children—Karen, Bob, Bruce. Mem. Ariz. Ho. of Reps., 1957-67; mem. Ariz. Senate, 1967-76, pres., 1975-76; mem. 95th-96th Congresses from 3d Ariz. Dist., 1976—. Active Com. for Survival of Free Congress, Citizens Com. for Right to Keep and Bear Arms. Served with USN, 1943-46. Mem. Am. Legion, Ariz. Farm Bur., Gun Owners Am. Democrat. Seventh-day Adventist. Office: 211 Cannon House Office Bldg Washington DC 20515*

STUMP, FOREST J., mfg. co. exec.; b. Akron, Ohio, July 30, 1920; s. Forest M. and Olga (Franks) S.; student Wooster Coll., 1946-47; B.A. in Bus. Adminstrn., Ashland Coll., 1948; m. Ardelle Wimmer, June 15, 1941 (dec. Nov. 1970); children—Kristine, James. Engaged as builder, mortgage banker, 1952-63; pres. U.S. Steel Homes div. U.S. Steel Corp., 1963-72; chief exec. officer, chmn. bd. Mid Am. Housing, Inc., 1972-73; chmn. bd. Fed. Property Mgmt., Inc., Mobile World, 1973—. Mem. English Speaking Union, Navy League. Mason. Clubs: Pendennis (Louisville); Trailside. Home: 2100 Camargo Rd Louisville KY 40207 Office: 200 W 5th St Dayton OH 45402

STUMP, JOHN SUTTON, lawyer; b. Clarksburg, W.Va., Aug. 7, 1929; s. John Sutton and Helen (Mannix) S.; student Washington and Lee U., 1946-47, LL.B., 1957; B.S. in Commerce, U. N.C., 1951; m. Elaine Claire Scammahorn, Sept. 14, 1968; children—John Sutton IV, James Felix. Admitted to W.Va., Va. bars, 1957; asso. Jackson, Kelly, Holt & O'Farrell, Charleston, W.Va., 1957-58, Boothe, Dudley, Koontz & Boothe, Alexandria, Va., 1958-61; asso. Boothe, Dudley, Koontz, Blankingship & Stump, Fairfax and Alexandria, Va., 1962-63, partner, 1963-71; partner Boothe, Prichard & Dudley, 1971—. Served to lt. comdr. USNR, 1951-54, 61-62. Mem. Am. Law Inst. Home: 8329 Weller Ave McLean VA 22101 Office: 4103 Chain Bridge Rd Fairfax VA 22030

STUMPF, PAUL KARL, educator; b. N.Y.C., Feb. 23, 1919; s. Karl and Annette (Schreyer) S.; A.B. magna cum laude, Harvard, 1941; Ph.D., Columbia, 1945; m. Ruth Electa Rodenbeck, June 13, 1947; children—Ann Carol, Kathryn Lee, Margaret Ruth, David Karl, Richard Frederic. Instr. epidemiology U. Mich., 1946-48; asst. prof. to prof. biochemistry U. Calif. at Berkeley, 1948-58, chmn. dept. agrl. biochemistry, 1953-58; chmn. dept. biochemistry U. Calif. at Davis, 1958-62, 65-68, 70-71. Mem. physiol. chemistry study panel NIH, 1959-64; mem. metabolic biology panel NSF, 1965-68, mem. evaluation panel grad. fellowships in biochemistry, 1971-73; mem. NRC, 1967—. Mem. City of Davis Planning Commn., 1967-68. Sr. postdoctoral fellow USPHS, 1954-55; travel grantee NSF, 1958; NSF Sr. Postdoctoral fellow, 1961, 68; Guggenheim fellow, 1962, 69; U.S. sr. scientist fellow Alexander von Humboldt Found., 1976. Mem. Am. Soc. Biol. Chemists, Biochem. Soc. London, Am. Soc. Plant Physiologists (exec. bd. 1974-76, pres.-elect 1978, Stephen Hale award 1974), Am. Oil Chemist Soc. (lipid chemistry prize 1974), Nat. Acad. Sci., Royal Danish Acad. Sci. (fgn. mem.). Co-author: Outlines of Enzyme Chemistry, 1st and 2d edits., 1955, 58; Outlines of Biochemistry, 1st edit., 1963, 2d edit., 1966, 3d edit., 1972, 4th edit., 1976. Author numerous research papers. Editor: Archives Biochemistry and Biophysics, 1960-65, exec. editor, 1965-79; editor Analytical Biochemistry, 1969-78, Lipids, 1976—. Home: 764 Elmwood Dr Davis CA 95616

STUMPF, SAMUEL ENOCH, educator; b. Cleve., Feb. 3, 1918; s. Rev. Louis and Elizabeth (Jergens) S.; B.S., U. Calif. at Los Angeles, 1940; B.D., Andover Newton Theol. Sch., 1943; postgrad. Columbia, 1946; Ph.D., U. Chgo., 1948; m. Jean Goodman, July 3, 1943; children—Paul Jergens, Mark Howard, Samuel Enoch. Asst. prof. ethics Vanderbilt U., 1948-49, asso. prof., 1949-52, prof. philosophy, chmn. dept., 1952-67, vis. prof. med. ethics Med. Sch., 1973-74, research prof. jurisprudence Law Sch., 1974-77, research prof. med. philosophy Med. Sch., 1974—, prof. law, 1977—, also asst. to chancellor, 1966-67; pres. Cornell Coll., Mt. Vernon, Iowa, 1967-74; Gates lectr. Grinnell Coll., 1951; Keese lectr. U. Chattanooga, 1962; Decell lectr. Millsaps Coll., 1963; Louttit-George lectr. Washington Coll., 1967; Willson lectr. Southwestern U., 1970. Trustee Food Safety Council, 1976—, Food and Drug Law Inst., 1978—. Served as lt. USNR, 1943-46. Carnegie research grantee, 1949; Ford fellow, Harvard, 1955-56; Rockefeller fellow Oxford (Eng.) U., 1958-59. Mem. Am. Council on Legal and Polit. Philosophy, Am. Philos. Assn., Phi Beta Kappa. Author: A Democratic Manifesto; Socrates to Sartre;

Morality and the Law, Philosophy: History and Problems; Philosophical Problems; Elements of Philosophy. Contbr. articles to profl. jours. Home: 424 Page Rd Nashville TN 37205

STUNDZA, THOMAS JOHN, editor; b. Lawrence, Mass., Mar. 4, 1948; s. John Anthony and Matilda (Stanulonis) S.; B.A., Merrimack Coll., 1970; M.A., Valparaiso U., 1975; m. Patricia Jurewicz, Mar. 27, 1971. Reporter, Eagle-Tribune, Lawrence, 1968-70; reporter Post-Tribune, Gary, Ind., 1970-73, bus. editor, 1974-78; steel editor Am. Metal Market, Pitts., 1978—; instr. journalism Valparaiso (Ind.) U., 1976. Pres., Porter County (Ind.) Youth Service Bur., 1976-78. Recipient Honor Roll award U.S. Izaak Walton League, 1973, Paul Tobenkin award Columbia, 1974; Pub. Affairs Reporting award Am. Polit. Sci. Assn., 1971; Ind. Reporting award A.P. Mng. Editors, 1976; Newswriting awards Ind. Pub. Health Assn., 1972-74; Amos Tucker Media award Dartmouth Coll., 1977. Mem. Soc. Am. Bus. and Econ. Writers, Pitts. Press Club, Econ. Club Pitts., World Affairs Council Pitts., Lithuanian-Am. Council Pitts. Home: 332 Newburn Dr Pittsburgh PA 15216 Office: 1006 Empire Bldg Pittsburgh PA 15222

STUNKARD, ALBERT JAMES, educator, physician; b. N.Y.C., Feb. 7, 1922; s. Horace Wesley and Frances (Klank) S.; B.S., Yale, 1943; M.D., Columbia, 1945. Intern medicine Mass. Gen. Hosp., Boston, 1945-46; resident physician psychiatry Johns Hopkins Hosp., 1948-51, research fellow psychiatry, 1951-52; research fellow medicine Columbia U. Service, Goldwater Meml. Hosp., N.Y.C., 1952-53; Commonwealth research fellow, then asst. prof. medicine Cornell U. Med. Coll., 1953-57; mem. faculty U. Pa., 1957-73, 76—, prof. psychiatry, 1962-73, 76—, chmn. dept., 1962-73, Kenneth Appel prof. psychiatry, 1968-73; prof. psychiatry Stanford Med. Sch., 1973-76. Served to capt., M.C., AUS, 1946-48. Fellow Center for Advanced Study in Behavioral Scis., 1971-72. Mem. Am. Psychiat. Assn., Am. Psychosomatic Soc. Contbr. articles psychol. and physiol. aspects obesity. Address: U Pa Dept Psychiatry Philadelphia PA 19104

STUNZI, JACQUES RALPH, cons.; b. Lancaster, Pa., May 16, 1920; s. Jean J. and Lilly (Handchin) S.; B.A., Yale, 1942; m. Barbara A. McAdams, Apr. 19, 1949; children—Jacques Ralph, Ann, Elise, Paul, Eric. Asst. v.p. Hanover Bank, N.Y.C., 1946-55; v.p., treas., dir. Celanese Internat. Corp., N.Y.C., 1955-59; v.p. Am. Express Co., N.Y.C., 1959-62; exec. v.p., dir. Continental Bank Internat., N.Y.C., 1962-68; vice chmn. Allied Bank Internat., N.Y.C., 1968-73; financial cons., 1973-74; v.p., mgr. Mfrs. Hanover Trust Co., Tokyo, Japan, 1974-79, v.p., regional mgr. Europe and Can., N.Y.C., 1979—; dir. Dubied Machinery Co.; mem. fgn. exchange com. Fed. Res. Bank N.Y., 1968—. Bd. dirs. Ridge Acres Assn., Darien, Conn. Served to lt. USNR, 1942-45. Recipient Bolivarian medal, 1968. Mem. Am. Mgmt. Assn. (mem. World Planning Council, dir.), Bolivarian Soc. U.S. (v.p., dir.), Am. C. of C. in Japan (bd. govs., exec. com., treas. 1977-79). Clubs: Intercom, Sky (N.Y.C.). Author: The Commercial Banker in International Operations, 1963; Financing in Latin America, 1968. Home: 64 Crooked Trail Rowayton CT 06853 Office: 350 Park Ave New York NY 10022

STUPAR, BRANKO, lawyer; b. Washington, Pa., Nov. 24, 1922; s. Mile and Ann (Orlosky) S.; student Ohio Wesleyan U., 1943-44; B.A., Muskingum Coll., 1947; J.D., Am. U., 1951; m. Helen Marie Amundson, May 24, 1952; children—Peter R., Marlys Jo, David Roald, Brian Christopher. Admitted to D.C. bar, 1952; practiced in Washington, 1952—; atty. on staff to investigate windfall profits FHA, Washington, 1954; partner firm Faulkner, Shands, Stupar & Tucker, Washington, 1954—; dir. Applied Systems Tech. Inc. Lectr. Naval Intelligence Mgmt. Course, Washington, 1973-74. Active mission work Nat. Bapt. Ch., Washington, 1972—. Republican nominee U.S. Congress 26th Pa. Dist., 1954. Served to lt. (j.g.) USNR, 1943-46; PTO, Okinawa. Mem. Counsellors, Am., Fed. bar assns., D.C. Bar, Mil. Order Carabao, Washington Assembly. Sigma Nu Phi. Orthodox Catholic. Clubs: University (Washington); Congressional Country (Bethesda, Md.). Home: 9115 Harrington Dr Potomac MD 20854 Office: 910 16th St NW Washington DC 20006

STURC, ERNEST, economist; b. Bekescaba, Hungary, Jan. 12, 1915; s. Jindrich Jan and Regina (Atlas) S.; J.D., Comenius U., Bratislava, Czechoslovakia, 1938; postgrad. U. Chgo., 1939-42; m. Hilda Sirluck, Dec. 26, 1946; children—Marta Elizabeth, John Henry. Fgn. service officer of Czechoslovakia, 1939-46; dep. dir. Czechoslovakia Govt. Information Service, 1942-46; with IMF, 1946—, dir. exchange and trade relations dept., 1965—. Del. Czechoslovakia to Bretton Woods Conf. Internat. Monetary Coop., 1944, to San Francisco Conf. on UN, 1945. Mem. Am. Econ. Assn. Home: 3406 Q St NW Washington DC 20007 Office: Internat Monetary Fund 700 19th St NW Washington DC 20431

STURDIVANT, FREDERICK DAVID, educator; b. Whitewright, Tex., Oct. 17, 1937; s. Wyatt A. and Juanita P. (Phillips) S.; B.S., San Jose State Coll., 1959; M.B.A., U. Ore., 1960; Ph.D., Northwestern U., 1963; m. Patricia A. Robinson, Dec. 22, 1959; children—Kaira, Lisha, Brian. Asst. prof. U. So. Calif., 1964-67; asso. prof. U. Tex. at Austin, 1967-70; asso. prof. Harvard, 1970-72; M. Riklis prof. bus. and its environment Ohio State U., Columbus, 1972—. Prin., Mgmt. Analysis Center, Inc., Cambridge, Mass.; dir. Progressive Corp., Cleve., State Savs., Columbus, Ohio. Mem. Task Force on Mktg. and Low-Income Consumers, Nat. Mktg. Adv. Com., Dept. Commerce, 1967-70; cons. Office Calif. Atty. Gen., 1966, Sen. Charles Percy, 1968; mem. adv. council on urban affairs to lt. gov. Tex., 1969-70. Recipient CBA Teaching Excellence award, 1968, Jack G. Taylor Teaching Excellence award, 1969, Cactus Teaching Excellence award, 1970. Mem. Am. Mktg. Assn., Assn. for Consumer Research, Southwestern Social Sci. Assn., Bus. and Society Initiative Council, Acad. of Mgmt., Beta Gamma Sigma. Democrat. Author: (with others) Competition and Human Behavior, 1968; The Ghetto Marketplace, 1969; (with others) Managerial Analysis in Marketing, 1970; Growth Through Service: The Story of American Hospital Supply Corporation, 1970; (with others) Perspectives in Marketing Management, 1971; (with O. Smalley) The Credit Merchants: A History of Spiegel, Inc., 1973; Business and Society: A Managerial Approach, 1977; (with L. Robinson) The Corporate Social Challenge, 1977; (with A. Andreasen) Minorities and Marketing: Research Challenges. Contbr. articles to profl. jours. Home: 2500 Stonehaven Ct S Columbus OH 43220 Office: 1775 S College Rd Columbus OH 43210

STURGEON, CHARLES EDWIN, chem. co. exec.; b. Cherryvale, Kans., May 30, 1928; s. William Charles and Lucile Myrtle (Gill) S.; A.A., Independence Jr. Coll., 1948; B.S., U. Kans., 1951; postgrad. U. Tulsa Grad. Sch., 1953-56; grad. Advanced Mgmt. Program, Harvard Bus. Sch., 1977; m. Barbara Ann Flinn, June 12, 1954; children—Carol Ann, John Randolph, Richard Steven. Research engr. Standard Oil and Gas, Tulsa, 1953-56; production supr. Vulcan Materials Co., Wichita, Kans., 1956-62, maintenance supt., 1962-64, mgr. tech. services, 1964-69, plant mgr., Newark, N.J., 1970-71, gen. mktg. mgr., v.p. mktg., Wichita, 1971-73, v.p. mfg., Birmingham, Ala., 1974-77, pres. chem. div., 1977—. Served with U.S. Army, 1951-53. Mem. Am. Inst. Chem. Engrs., Nat. Mgmt. Assn., Chlorine Inst., Chem. Mfg. Assn. Republican. Presbyterian. Clubs: Vestavia Country, Relay House. Home: 2204 Tanglewood Circle Birmingham AL 35216 Office: PO Box 7689 Birmingham AL 35223

STURGEON, THEODORE HAMILTON, author; b. S.I., N.Y., Feb. 26, 1918; s. Edward and Christine (Dicker) Waldo; m. Wina Bonnie Golden, Apr. 16, 1969; 1 son, Andros; children by previous marriage—Patricia (Mrs. Dana Shires), Cynthia (Mrs. J.W. Pegram), Robin, Tandy, Noel, Timothy. Author short stories, novels, 1938—; TV script writer for Star Trek, The Invaders, Wild Wild West, others. Recipient Argosy award, 1949, Internat. Fantasy award, 1954, Nebula award, 1970, Hugo award, 1971. Mem. Writer's Guild Am. W. Author: (novels) Killdozer, 1944; The Dreaming Jewels, 1950; More Than Human, 1954; Some of Your Blood, 1961; The Joyous Invasions, 1965; Starshine, 1968; Caviar, 1968; E Pluribus Unicorn, 1970; Beyond, 1970; Sturgeon is Alive and Well, 1971; The Worlds of Theodore Sturgeon, 1972; More Than Human, 1972; Case and The Dreamer, 1974; The Synthetic Man, 1974. Book editor Galaxy mag. Address: care Kirby McCauley 60 E 42d St New York NY 10017

STURGES, JOHN ELIOT, film dir. and producer; b. Oak Park, Ill., Jan. 3, 1910; s. Reginald Rowe and Grace Delafield (Sturges) Carne; student Marin Jr. Coll., 1930-32 junior certificate, 1932; m. Dorothy Lynn Brooks, Jan. 5, 1945 (div.); children—Deborah Lynn, Michael Eliot. With art dept. RKO Studio, Hollywood, Calif., 1932-34, film editor, 1936-42; production asst. David Selznick Productions, 1934-36; film dir. Columbia Pictures, Metro-Goldwyn-Mayer, Paramount Pictures, Warner Bros., 1945-58; producer, dir. Mirisch Co., Hollywood, Calif., 1958-70; producer, dir., pres. Alpha Corp., North Hollywood, Calif., 1958—; films directed include: Bad Day at Black Rock, 1954, Gunfight at the OK Corral, 1956, The Old Man and the Sea, 1958; prod. and directed: The Magnificent Seven, 1960, The Great Escape, 1963. Served to capt. USAAF, 1942-45. Decorated Bronze Star. Mem. Dirs. Guild Am. (dir.), Writers Guild Am. West, Producers Guild Am., Dramatists Guild Am., Acad. Motion Picture Arts and Scis., Brit. Acad. Film and TV Arts. Democrat. Address: 13063 Ventura Blvd North Hollywood CA 91604

STURGES, RICHARD BARRETT, food co. exec.; b. Mansfield, Ohio, Aug. 7, 1919; s. Paul E. and Helen (Sullivan) S.; B.S.S., Georgetown U., 1941; postgrad. Mich. U., 1941-42; m. Polly Morrissey, June 1, 1946; children—Barry, Jeffrey. Pres., Central Fruit & Grocery Co., Mansfield, 1950-62; v.p., dir. Food Marketing Corp., Ft. Wayne, Ind., 1962-66, exec. v.p., gen. mgr., dir., 1966-72, pres., 1972—; dir. Republic Franklin Ins. Co., Columbus, Ohio, Ind. Bank & Trust Co., Tokheim Corp. Vice chmn. United Fund, 1968-71; pres. United Way Agys., 1973-74. Bd. dirs. YMCA, Boy Scouts Am., Better Bus. Bur., Conv. Bur., United Way of Allen County, Ft. Wayne Found., Ft. Wayne Found. Charities, Jr. Achievement of Ft. Wayne, Taxpayers Research Assn. Named Boss of Year, Ft. Wayne Jr. C. of C., 1970. Served with USAAF, 1943-45; PTO. Mem. C. of C. (dir.). Rotarian. Clubs: Quest, Fort Wayne Country (dir. 1974-77), Mad Anthony (dir. pres. 1977), 100 percent (Ft. Wayne). Home: 6750 Covington Creek Trail Fort Wayne IN 46804 Office: PO Box 1198 Fort Wayne IN 46801

STURGIS, ROBERT SHAW, architect; b. Boston, July 8, 1922; s. George and Rosamond Thomas (Bennett) S.; grad. St. Mark's Sch., Southboro, Mass., 1939; A.B., Harvard, 1947, M.Arch., 1951; m. Chiquita Mitchell, Dec. 20, 1947; children—Susanna, Roger Bennett, John Hanson, Ellen Shaw. Architect, Kilham, Hopkins, Greeley & Brodie, 1952-55, Shepley, Bulfinch, Richardson & Abbott, 1955-64, Robert S. Sturgis, 1964-68 (all Boston); partner Feloney & Sturgis, architects, Cambridge, 1969-75, Robert Sturgis, FAIA, 1975—. Head critic Boston Archtl. Center, 1955-66; vis. lectr. Va. Poly. Inst., Blacksburg, 1970, Boston U., Yale U., 1975; urban design cons. Haverhill, Lynn and Cambridge, Mass., also Atlanta. Mem. overseers' vis. com. Sch. Design Harvard, 1965-70; chmn. Gov.'s Task Force Arts and Cultural Facilities, 1972. Served with USAAF, 1942-45. Fellow A.I.A. (chmn. urban planning and design com. 1970); mem. Boston Soc. Architects (pres., 1972, chmn. civic design com., 1959-68). Prin. works include Cotting House, Harvard Bus. Sch., 1968; Architects' Plan for Boston, 1961; AIA Urban Design Assistance Team Program, 1967; Weymouth (Mass.) Central Jr. High Sch., 1954. Contbr. articles to profl. jours. Home: 5 Doublet Hill Rd Weston MA 02193 Office: 2 Central Sq Cambridge MA 02139

STURM, ALBERT LEE, educator; b. Appalachia, Va., Aug. 5, 1911; s. Albert Lee and Pearl Agnes (Wingate) S.; A.B. magna cum laude, Hampden-Sydney Coll., 1933; M.A., Duke U., 1940, Ph.D., 1942; m. Virginia Frye Butts, Dec. 27, 1941. Pub. schs. tchr. in Va. and W.Va., 1933-38; instr. polit. sci. U. Mich., 1941-42; asso. prof., then prof. W.Va. U., 1946-62; prof. pub. adminstrn. N.Y. U. group U. Ankara (Turkey), 1957-59; prof. govt. Fla. State U., 1962-68, dir. Inst. Govtl. Research, 1962-67; univ. research prof. polit. sci. Va. Poly. Inst. and State U., Blacksburg, 1968-78, Univ. research prof. public affairs Center for Public Adminstrn. and Policy, 1978—, dir. univ. self-study, 1975-77; vis. prof. Duke, Pa. State Coll., U. Mich., U. Nebr.; chmn. So. Pub. Adminstrn. Research Council, 1963-68; cons. on state constl. revision; cons. in field. Chmn. bd. dirs. Monongalia County (W.Va.) chpt. ARC, 1950-52, 56-57. Duke-Brookings fellow, 1940-41. Served to lt. comdr. USNR, 1942-46. Mem. Am., So. (v.p. 1964-65), Internat. polit. sci. assns., Am. Soc. Pub. Adminstrn. (past chpt. pres.), Nat. Municipal League, AAUP (past chpt. pres.), Va. Social Sci. Assn. (exec. com. 1975-78, pres. 1977-78), So. Assn. Colls. and Schs., Phi Beta Kappa (past chpt. pres., chpt. pres. 1977-79), Pi Sigma Alpha, Pi Gamma Mu, Chi Beta Phi, Epsilon Chi Epsilon. Author: Methods of State Constitutional Reform, 1954; Constitution-Making in Michigan, 1963; Major Constitutional Issues in West Virginia, 1961; co-author: Implementing A New Constitution: The Michigan Experience, 1968; Thirty Years of State Constitution Making, 1938-1968, 1970; (with others) West Virginia State and Local Government, 1963. Contbr. chpts. to books, author articles, monographs. Home: Apt 1100G Terrace View Apts Blacksburg VA 24060 Office: Va Poly Inst and State Univ Blacksburg VA 24061

STURM, DOUGLAS EARL, educator; b. Batavia, N.Y., Apr. 22, 1929; s. Fred William and Louise (Gillette) S.; A.B., Hiram Coll., 1950; D.B., U. Chgo., 1953, Ph.D., 1959; postgrad. Harvard, 1964-65; m. Margie Jean Anderson, Sept. 13, 1953; children—Hans Martin, Rolf Anderson. Exec. sec. Christian Action, N.Y.C., 1954-55; asst. prof. religion Bucknell U., Lewisburg, Pa., 1959-64, asso. prof. religion, 1964-67, asso. prof. religion and polit. sci., 1967-70, prof. religion and polit. sci., 1970—, Presidential prof., 1974—, dir. honors council, 1970-72. Vis. prof. Perkins Sch. Theology, summer 1963; vis. tutor Grad. Inst. in Liberal Edn., St. John's Coll., Santa Fe, summer 1972; vis. prof. social ethics Andover Newton Theol. Sch., Newton Centre, Mass., 1972-73; vis. prof. ethics and soc. U. Chgo., 1976-77. Bd. dirs. Inst. Study of Human Values, 1966-67. Recipient Bishop James C. Baker Grad. award, 1957-58, Lindback award for excellence in teaching, 1966; study fellow Am. Council Learned Soc., 1964-65; Cross-disciplinary fellow Soc. Religion in Higher Edn., 1967-68. Mem. Am. Soc. Legal and Polit. Philosophy, Am. Polit. Sci. Assn., Soc. Sci. Study Religion, AAUP, Council on Religion and Law (bd. dirs. 1977—), Am. Soc. Christian Ethics (dir. 1963-67, exec. sec. 1968-72), Council Study Religion (exec. com. 1971-77, vice chmn. 1974-76, chmn. 1976-77), Ams. for Dem. Action, Am. Acad. Religion, A.C.L.U., La Societe Europeenne de Culture. Cons. editor Bucknell Press, 1971—; bd. consultants Jour. Religion, 1972—; asso. editor JRE Studies in Religious Ethics, 1974—. Contbr. articles to profl. jours. and books. Home: 37 S Water St Lewisburg PA 17837

STURM, FREDERICK CHARLES, III, lawyer; b. Phila., Oct. 23, 1948; s. Frederick Charles and Frances (Schisselbauer) S.; A.B., Boston U., 1970; J.D., Temple U., 1973, M.B.A., 1973; m. Andrea M. Ellenhorn, Oct. 10, 1971. Admitted to Pa. bar, 1973; asst. sec., asst. gen. counsel Union Corp., Verona, Pa., 1973-75; sec., gen. counsel Agar Food Products Co., Chgo., 1975-78, Bluebird Inc., Phila., 1975—, Patrick Cudahy Inc., Cudahy, Wis., 1975-78, Bluebird Food Products Co., Phila., 1975-78, Mid-South Packers Inc., Tupelo, Miss., 1975-78; pres., chief legal officer Legal Ins. Inc., Phila., 1978—. Mem. Am., Pa., Phila., Allegheny County bar assns., Am. Soc. Corp. Secs. Home: 2320 Parrish St Philadelphia PA 19130 Office: 2001 Hamilton St Philadelphia PA 19130

STURMAN, JOSEPH HOWARD, lawyer; b. Chgo., Apr. 21, 1931; s. Benjamin A. and Rose (Spitzner) S.; B.S., U. Calif. at Los Angeles, 1953, J.D. (De Garmo scholar), 1956; 1 son, Lee David. Admitted to Calif. bar, 1956; practiced in Beverly Hills, 1957-65, Los Angeles, 1965—; research asst. Calif. Supreme Ct., San Francisco, 1956-57; partner firm Balter & Sturman, Los Angeles (and predecessor firm), 1965-79, firm Murchison & Cumming, 1979—. Residential chmn. United Crusade, Monterey Park, Calif., 1967; mem. long-range planning com. City of Monterey Park, 1966-67, chmn. exec. com. teen center, 1967-68. Mem. exec. com. Calif. Democratic Central Com., 1966-68; mem. Los Angeles County Dem. Central Com., 1966-68; mem. Calif. Dem. Council, 1956-68, controller, 1965-67. Recipient Outstanding Service award United Crusade, 1967. Mem. Wilshire (bd. govs. 1972—, pres. 1978), Los Angeles County bar assns., Am. (dir. 1973—), Calif. (pres. 1977) assns. attys.-C.P.A.'s, Calif. Soc. C.P.A.'s, A.C.L.U. (dir. So. Calif. chpt. 1973-75), Order of Coif, Phi Beta Kappa, Beta Gamma Sigma. Jewish religion. Mem. law rev. U. Calif. at Los Angeles, 1954-56. Home: 3107 Glendon Ave Los Angeles CA 90034 Office: 680 Wilshire Pl Los Angeles CA 90005

STURTEVANT, BRADFORD, educator; b. New Haven, Nov. 1, 1933; s. Julian Munson and Elizabeth (Reihl) S.; B.Engring., Yale U., 1955; M.S., Calif. Inst. Tech., 1956, Ph.D., 1960; m. Carol Elmore, Mar. 28, 1958; 1 dau., Victoria. Research fellow aeros. Calif. Inst. Tech., 1960-62, mem. faculty, 1962—, prof. aeros., 1971—, exec. officer for aeros., 1971-76; cons. to industry. Mem. AAAS, AAUP, Am. Inst. Aeros. and Astronautics. Soc. Automotive Engrs. Acoustical Soc. Am., Am. Phys. Soc. (sec. treas. div. fluid dynamics 1974, 78), Sigma Xi. Home: 1419 E Palm St Altadena CA 91001 Office: 301-46 California Inst Tech Pasadena CA 91125

STURTEVANT, BRERETON, govt. ofcl., lawyer; b. Washington, Nov. 24, 1921; d. Charles Lyon and Grace (Brereton) Sturtevant; B.A., Wellesley Coll., 1942; J.D., Temple U., 1949. Research chemist E.I. duPont DeNemours & Co., 1942-50; gen. practice law, Wilmington, Del., 1950-57; partner Connolly, Bove & Lodge, Wilmington, 1957-71; examiner-in-chief U.S. Patent Office Bd. Appeals, Washington, 1971—. Adj. prof. law Georgetown U., 1974—. Trustee Holton-Arms Sch., Washington. Mem. Am., Del. bar assns., AAUW, Patent Office Soc., Govt. Patent Lawyers Assn., Exec. Women in Govt. (charter mem., chmn. 1978-79). Episcopalian. Clubs: Nat. Press, Wellesley College. Home: 1227 Morningside Ln Alexandria VA 22308 Office: US Patent and Trademark Office Washington DC 20231

STURTEVANT, JUDD, broadcaster, developer; b. Oakland, Calif., Jan. 30, 1916; s. Andrew Judson and Rhoda (Mitchell) S.; B.A., Stanford U., 1939; m. Margaret Marsh, July 18, 1942; children—Peter, Michael, Brook, Craig, Anne. part owner, pres., gen. mgr. sta. KFAX, San Francisco, 1960—; part owner sta. KGMS, Sacramento, 1962—, KAGO, AM-FM, Klamath Falls, Oreg., 1962—, KSFM, Woodland, Calif., 1972—; farmer, San Joaquin Valley, Calif., 1942—; gen. mgr. Empire Sturtevant Co., Modesto, Calif., 1963—; partner, developer Tully Apts., Modesto, 1963—, Ulrich Shopping Center, Modesto, 1962-72, Chinese Cultural Center Bldg., San Francisco, 1965—; chmn. bd. Western Bus. Funds, 1964—, Western Growth Funds, 1972—, Bay Venture Mgmt., 1975—, Biovation, Inc., 1976—, San Francisco Venture Capital Co.'s. Home: PO Box 452 Modesto CA 95353 Office: 1470 Pine St San Francisco CA 94109

STURTEVANT, JULIAN MUNSON, educator; b. Edgewater, N.J., Aug. 9, 1908; s. Edgar Howard and Bessie Fitch (Skinner) S.; A.B., Columbia, 1927; Ph.D., Yale, 1931; D.Sc. (hon.), Ill. Coll., 1962, U. Regensburg (W. Ger.), 1978; m. Elizabeth Caroline Reihl, June 8, 1929; children—Ann (Mrs. John Ormsby), Bradford. Instr. chemistry Yale, 1931-39, asst. prof., 1939-43, asso. prof. chemistry, 1946-52, prof., 1952—, prof. chemistry and molecular biology, 1963-77, prof. emeritus, sr. research scientist, 1977—; asso. dir. Sterling Chemistry Lab., 1951-59, chmn. dept. of chemistry, 1959-62; mem. staff Radiation Lab., Mass. Inst. Tech., 1943-45; vis. fellow Battelle-Seattle Research Center, 1972-73; vis. prof. U. Calif., San Diego, 1966-67, 69-70; vis. scholar Stanford, 1975; cons. Socony-Vacuum Labs., 1946-55, Socony-Mobil Labs., 1956-66. Fulbright scholar Guggenheim fellow U. Cambridge, Eng., 1955-56; Fulbright scholar U. Adelaide, Australia, 1962-63; chmn. Calorimetry Conf. U.S., 1972-73. Recipient Huffman Meml. award Calorimetry Conf. U.S., 1964, sr. scientist award von Humboldt-Stiftung, W.Ger., 1977-78. Fellow N.Y. Acad. Scis., AAAS, Am. Acad. Arts and Scis.; mem. AAUP, Am. Chem. Soc., Am. Soc. Biol. Chemists, Nat. Acad. Scis., Sigma Xi, Alpha Chi Sigma. Home: Indian Neck Point Branford CT 06405 Office: 225 Prospect St New Haven CT 06520

STURTEVANT, WILLIAM CURTIS, anthropologist; b. Morristown, N.J., July 26, 1926; s. Alfred Henry and Phoebe (Reed) S.; B.A., U. Calif. at Berkeley, 1949; Ph.D., Yale, 1955; m. Theda Maw, July 26, 1952; children—Kinthi D.M., Reed P.M., Alfred B.M. Instr. dept. anthropology, asst. curator anthropology Peabody Mus., Yale, 1954-56; ethnologist, gen. anthropologist Bur. Am. Ethnology, 1956-65, curator N.Am. ethnology dept. anthropology Nat. Mus. Natural History, Smithsonian Instn., Washington, 1965—. Fulbright lectr. U. Oxford, 1967-68; adj. prof. anthropology Johns Hopkins U., 1974—; ethnol. fieldwork, Seminole, Fla., 1950-67, Burma, 1955, 63-64, Iroquois, 1952-65, others. Trustee, Mus. Am. Indian, Heye Found., N.Y.C., 1976—. Served with USNR, 1945-46. Fellow Royal Anthrop. Inst. Gt. Britain and Ireland, Am. Anthrop. Assn. (book review editor 1962-66, exec. bd. 1974-77, pres. 1981); mem. A.A.A.S. (del. council 1974-77, mem. com. council affairs 1974-75), Societe des Americanistes(Paris), Am. Soc. Ethnohistory (pres. 1965-66), Council Mus. Anthropology (pres. 1979-81), Am. Ethnol. Soc. (pres. 1976-77) Fla. Anthrop. Soc., Linguistic Soc. Am., Soc. Am. Archaeology, Polynesian Soc., Soc. Hist. Archaeology. Author monographs, chpts. in books. Gen. editor: Handbook of N.Am. Indians. Contbr. articles to profl. jours. Home: 7009 Florida St Chevy Chase MD 20015 Office: Smithsonian Instn Washington DC 20560

STUTZ, HERBERT WALTER, newspaperman; b. Irvington, N.J., Aug. 28, 1929; s. Gustave Frank and Rose Amelia (Engemann) S.; student Rutgers U., 1947-49; m. Esther Gayk, June 28, 1952; children—Jean Carol, Kenneth Mark. With Newark News, 1947-51, 53-64, scholastic sports editor, 1957-64; with Phila. Bull., 1964—, asst. sports editor, 1969-72, sports editor, 1972—; lectr. sports seminars. Served with AUS, 1951-53. Mem. AP Sports Editors Assn. (past regional chmn.), N.J. (past pres.), Phila. (past pres.) sports writers assns. Baptist. Home: 16 Charles Ln Cherry Hill NJ 08003 Office: Phila Bull 30th and Market Sts Philadelphia PA 19101

STUTZMAN, LEROY FRANKLIN, educator; b. Indpls., Sept. 5, 1917; s. Paul Franklin and Alesa (Limp) L.; B.S. in Chem. Engring., Purdue U., 1939; M.S., Kan. State U., 1940; Ph.D., U. Pitts., 1946; m. Lillie Ann Knight, Mar. 20, 1939; children—Paul Franklin, Donald Lee (dec.), Judith Ann (Mrs. Bernard Geaghan), Research fellow Mellon Inst. Indsl. Research, Pitts., 1941-43; prof., chmn. chem. engring. Northwestern U., 1943-56; dir. research Remington Rand Univac, 1956-59; prof., chief of party in Chile, U. Pitts., 1959-61; pres. Tronchemics Research, Inc., Mpls., 1961-63, now dir.; prof., head dept. chem. engring. U. Conn., Storrs, 1963—. Cons., Control Data Corp., Mpls., 1961—, dir., 1975—; vis. prof. U. Vienna, 1976-77. Mem. standing com. on accreditation State of Conn., 1970-71; mem. Mansfield Planning and Zoning Commn., 1966-68. Mem. Am. Inst. Chem. Engrs., N.Y. Acad. Scis., Am. Chem. Soc., Am. Soc. Engring. Edn., AAAS. Optimist. Contbr. articles to profl. jours. Home: 26 Lynwood Rd Storrs CT 06268

STUTZMAN, VERNON CHARLES, health cons.; b. Ransom, Kans., Dec. 16, 1918; s. Charles Melvin and Lura Elizabeth (Vermilion) S.; A.B., Ft. Hays (Kans.) State U., 1940; M.Th., So. Meth. U., 1943; M.S. in Hosp. Adminstrn., Columbia, 1948; m. Evelyn LeNora Smithey, Dec. 14, 1946; children—Charles, Susan, Hugh. Chaplain Gallinger Municipal Hosp., Washington, 1944-46; adminstrv. resident Jewish Hosp., Bklyn., 1947-48; asst. dir., 1948-50; adminstr. S.I. Hosp., 1950-53; exec. dir. Meth. Hosp., Bklyn., 1953-75; spl. cons. div. health and welfare United Meth. Ch., 1975—; lectr. in field. Mem. Gen. Bd. Health and Welfare Ministries United Meth Ch., Gen. Bd. Social Concerns, 1964-72. Fellow Am. Coll. Hosp. Adminstrn. (mem. council regents); mem. Am. Protestant Hosp. Assn., Am. Hosp. Assn., Am. Pub. Health Assn., Hosp. Soc. N.Y., Pi Gamma Mu, Phi Kappa Phi. Clubs: Kiwanis, Municipal (Bklyn.). Home: 1019 N Main St Rutherfordton NC 28139

STUVER, FRANCIS EDWARD, ry. car co exec.; b. Greenville, Pa., Aug. 22, 1912; s. Willard Seeley and Anna Katherine (Henry) S.; grad. high sch.; m. Jessie Lucile Bright, Jan. 26, 1938; children—Robert Edward, Nancy (Mrs. Randolph Patrick Mutdosch). With Greenville Steel Car Co., subsidiary Pitts. Forgings Co., 1937—, chief accountant, 1944-46, asst. treas., 1946-54, asst. sec., 1948-56, treas., 1956-61, v.p., 1956-61, exec. v.p., dir., 1961-75, ret., 1975; pres., dir. Greenville Savs. & Loan Assn., Pitts. Forgings Co. Bd. dirs. Municipal Authority Borough Greenville, 1975-79, treas., 1946-73; bd. dirs., mem. exec. com. Mercer County br. Pa. Economy League, 1949-64; bd. dirs., treas., chmn. finance com. Greenville Hosp., 1953-59. Mem. Am. Ry. Car Inst. (dir. 1964-75). Mason, Elk, Moose, K.P. Club: Greenville Country. Home: 46 Chambers Ave Greenville PA 16125 Office: Foot of Union St Greenville PA 16125

STYAN, JOHN LOUIS, educator; b. London, Eng., July 6, 1923; s. Louis and Constance Mary (Armstrong) S.; came to U.S., 1965; B.A., Cambridge (Eng.) U., 1947, M.A., 1948; m. Constance W. M. Roberts, Nov. 15, 1945; children—Leigh, Day Campbell, Kim, Valentina. Staff tutor lit., drama U. Hull (Eng.), 1950-63, sr. staff tutor, 1963-65; prof. English, U. Mich., Ann Arbor, 1965-74, chmn. dept. English, 1973-74; Andrew Mellon prof. English, U. Pitts., 1974-77; Franklyn Bliss Snyder prof. English lit. Northwestern U., 1977—. Served to lt. Royal Arty., Eng., 1941-45. Mem. Guild Drama Adjudicators, Brit. Drama League, Modern Lang. Assn. Am., Shakespeare Assn. Am., World Center for Shakespeare Studies. Author: The Elements of Drama, 1960; The Dark Comedy, 1962; The Dramatic Experience, 1965; Shakespeare's Stagecraft, 1967; Chekhov in Performance, 1971; The Challenge of the Theatre, 1972; Drama Stage and Audience, 1975; The Shakespeare Revolution, 1977. Address: Northwestern Univ Dept English 633 Clark St Evanston IL 60201

STYCOS, JOSEPH MAYONE, educator, demographer; b. Saugerties, N.Y., Mar. 27, 1927; s. Stravos and Clotilda (Mayone) S.; A.B., Princeton, 1947; Ph.D., Columbia, 1954; m. Maria Nowakowska, Nov. 25, 1964; children—Steven Andrew, Christina Mayone (by previous marriage), Marek. With Bur. Applied Social Research, Columbia, 1948-50; lectr. sociology Columbia, 1951-52; project co-dir. U. P.R., 1952-53; postgrad. PC fellow U. N.C., 1954-55; asso. prof. sociology St. Lawrence U., 1955-57; faculty Cornell U., Ithaca, N.Y., 1957—, prof. sociology, 1963—, chmn. dept., 1966-70, dir. Latin Am. program, 1962-66, dir. internat. population program, 1962—; Fulbright-Hayes Disting. prof. U. Warsaw (Poland), 1979; external examiner U. Ife (Nigeria), 1973. Cons. AID, 1962-64; sr. cons. Population Council, 1963-74, 77—; cons. Airlie Found., 1972-73, Inst. for Research in Social Behavior, 1974, Clapp & Mayne, Inc., 1974, Ford-Rockefeller Population Program, 1977, Nat. U. Costa Rica, 1979, U. P.R., 1979; trustee Population Reference Bur., 1964-68, cons., 1968-74; mem. exec. com. Internat. Planned Parenthood Fedn., West Hemmis, 1965-71, cons., 1971-77; adv. com. population and devel. OAS, 1968-70; mem. bd. Population Assn. Am., 1968-71, editorial cons. demography, 1965-69; adv. panel population Nat. Inst. Child Health and Human Devel., Dept. Health, Edn. and Welfare, 1969; co-chmn. population task force U.S. Nat. Commn. for UNESCO, 1972-73; adv. council, interdisciplinary communications program Smithsonian Instn., 1974-76; cons. Pan Am. Health Orgn., WHO, 1975; mem. steering com., acceptability task force WHO, 1978—; cons. UNESCO, 1978-79. Mem. council Cornell U. Editorial bd. Human Orgn., 1962-64; gen. editor Irvington Population and Demographic Series, 1974—; cons. editor Studies in Family Planning, 1977—; mem. adv. com. Estudios de Poblacion, 1980—. Home: 28 Twin Glens Rd Ithaca NY 14850 Mailing address: Uris Hall Internat Population Program Cornell U Ithaca NY 14853

STYLES, WILLIAM BREWSTER, journalist; b. Cambridge, Mass., July 4, 1923; s. Humphrey Aubrey and Bertha (Hills) S.; student U. Vt., 1942-43; B.J., U. Mo., 1949; m. Corinne Janice Moore, Feb. 14, 1946. With Palladium-Item, Richmond, Ind., 1949-53; mem. staff Cin. Post, 1953—, bus. editor, 1957-72, asst. city editor, 1972-73, bus. editor, 1974—. Served with USAAF, 1943-46. Mem. Sigma Phi, Sigma Delta Chi (v.p. Cin. 1966, pres. 1971-72). Home: 4428 Blue Rock Rd Cincinnati OH 45239 Office: 800 Broadway Cincinnati OH 45202

STYNE, JULE, composer, producer; b. London, Eng., Dec. 31, 1905; s. Isadore and Anna (Kertman) Stein; student Chgo. Mus. Coll., Northwestern U., 1927-31; m. Margaret Brown; children—Stanley, Norton, Nicholas, Katharine. Came to U.S., 1912, naturalized, 1916. Composer: (scores for films) Anchor's Aweigh, West Point Story, Don't Fence Me In, Pink Tights, My Sister Eileen, Living It Up, others; (for N.Y. stage prodns.) High Button Shoes, Gentlemen Prefer Blondes, Two on the Aisle, Peter Pan, Bells are Ringing, Say Darling, Gypsy, Do Re Mi, Subways Are For Sleeping, Funny Girl, Fade Out-Fade In, Lorelei, Sugar, and others; (songs) The Party's Over, Everything's Coming Up Roses, Small World, Make Someone Happy, I Don't Want to Walk Without You Baby, I'll Walk Alone, It's Been a Long Long Time, Every Day I Love You, Papa Won't You Dance With Me, Bye Bye Baby, Diamonds are a Girl's Best Friend, Hold Me, Hold Me, Hold Me, How Do You Speak to an Angel, Money Burns a Hole in My Pocket, People, others. Producer: (theatre) Make a Wish, Pal Joey, Hazel Flagg, Will Success Spoil Rock Hunter, (with George Abbott) In Any Language, Mr. Wonderful, Say, Darling; (TV) Anything Goes, Panama Hatti, Show Stoppers. Recipient Acad. award (with Sammy Cahn) for song Three Coins in the Fountain; Donaldson award and Critics award for prodn. Pal Joey, 1954; Tony award as co-writer best score, co-music and lyrics best musical, Halleujah Baby, 1968. Mem. ASCAP, Dramatist Guild Council, Acad. Motion Picture Arts and Sci. Club: Friars. Office: 237 W 51st St New York City NY 10019

STYNES, STANLEY KENNETH, chem. engr.; b. Detroit, Jan. 18, 1932; s. Stanley Kenneth and Bessie Myrtle (Casey) S.; B.S., Wayne State U., 1955, M.S., 1958; Ph.D., Purdue U., 1963; m. Marcia Ann Meyers, Aug. 27, 1955; children—Peter Casey, Pamela Kay, Suzanne Elizabeth. Lab. asst. U. Chgo., 1951; instr. Purdue U., 1960-63; asst. prof. Wayne State U., Detroit, 1963-64, asso. prof., 1964-71, prof. chem. engring., 1971—, dean engring., 1972—; dir. Energy Conversion Devices, Inc., Troy, Mich.; cons. Schwayder Chem. Metallurgy Co., 1965, chemistry dept. Wayne State U., 1965-66, Claude B. Schneible Co., Holly, Mich., 1968. Mem. council on environ. strategy S.E. Mich. Council Govts., 1976—; v.p. Program for Minorities in S.E. Mich.; sec.-treas. Mich. Ednl. Research Info. Triad; mem. Midwest Program for Minorities in Engring., Com. for Instl. Cooperation. Ford Found. fellow, 1959-63, DuPont fellow, 1962-63, Wayne State U. faculty research fellow, 1964-65. Mem. Am. Chem. Soc., Soc. for Engring. Edn., Am. Inst. Chem. Engrs. (past chmn. Detroit sect.), AAAS, Mich. (v.p.), Detroit (exec. com.) engring. socs., Argonne Univs. Assn. (del.), Sigma Xi, Tau Beta Pi, Omicron Delta Kappa, Phi Lambda Upsilon. Presbyterian. Contbr. engring. articles to profl. jours. Home: 35260 Scone St Livonia MI 48154 Office: Coll Engring Wayne State U Detroit MI 48202

STYRON, WILLIAM, author; b. Newport News, Va., June 11, 1925; s. William Clark and Pauline Margaret (Abraham) S.; A.B., Duke, 1947, Litt.D., 1968; m. Rose Burgunder, May 4, 1953; children—Susanna Margaret, Paola Clark, Thomas, Claire Alexandra. Fellow Am. Acad. Arts and Letters at Am. Acad. in Rome, 1953; fellow Silliman Coll., Yale, 1964—. Hon. cons. Library of Congress. Mem. Am. Acad. Arts and Scis., Nat. Inst. Arts and Letters, Signet Soc., Harvard, Phi Beta Kappa. Democrat. Author: (novels) Lie Down in Darkness, 1951; The Long March, 1953; Set This House on Fire, 1960; The Confessions of Nat Turner, 1967 (Pulitzer prize 1968, Howells medal Am. Acad. Arts and Letters 1970); Sophie's Choice, 1979; In the Clap Shack (play), 1972; also articles, essays, revs. Editor: Best Stories from the Paris Review, 1959; adv. editor Paris Rev., 1953—. Editorial bd. The Am. Scholar, 1970-76. Address: RFD Roxbury CT 06783

SUAREZ, RALEIGH ANTHONY, JR., univ. adminstr.; b. Plaquemine, La., Jan. 2, 1925; s. Raleigh Anthony and Mary (Polizzotto) S.; B.S., La. State U., 1948, M.A., 1949, Ph.D., 1954; m. Ellen Turcan, Dec. 29, 1946. Tchr. adult edn. program La. Sch. Bd., Iberville Parish, 1949-51; instr. La. State U., 1951-55; asso. prof. history McNeese State U., Lake Charles, La., 1955-57, prof. history, head dept. social scis., 1957-61, dean Sch. Humanities, 1961-72, v.p. for acad. affairs, 1972-77, v.p., univ., provost, 1977—. Adminstrv. asst. to sec. state La.; research cons. La. Archival Survey, 1953-55; mem. La. Commn. on Higher Edn., 1955-57; chmn. President's Council La. Colls. and Univs. Com. on Afro-Am. Studies, 1969-70, 72, mem. Com. on Civil Rights, 1969-70; mem. exec. com. La. Com. for Humanities; chmn. tchr. certification appeals com. La. State Bd. Edn., 1975—. Bd. dirs. Friends of the Cabildo, 1964-65; mem. policy bd. Lake Charles-McNeese Urban Obs., 1975-78. Served to lt. (j.g.) USNR, 1942-46. Mem. Am., So., La. (chmn. publs. com. 1958-63, dir., 1958-68, v.p., 1964-65, pres., 1965-66) hist. assns., Phi Kappa Phi. Democrat. Roman Catholic. Contbr. articles to profl. jours. Home: 114 Prospect St Lake Charles LA 70601

SUAREZ, ROBERTO J., pub. co. exec.; b. Havana, Cuba, May 5, 1928; s. Miguel A. and Esperanza (De Cardenas) S.; B.S. in Econs., Villanova Coll., 1949; m. Miriam Campuzano, Nov. 5, 1950; children—Robert, Miriam, Elena, Tony, Miguel, Carlos, Armando, Raul, Teresa, Gonzalo, Esperanza, Ana. Partner, real estate firm and constrn. co., Havana, 1950-58; pres., chmn. bd. Financiera Nacional de Cuba, Havana, 1959-61; with Miami Herald Pub. Co., 1961-69, controller subs. ops., until 1969; owner, operator instnl. equipment co., Honduras, 1969-72; controller Knight Pub. Co., Charlotte, N.C., after 1972, now v.p., gen. mgr. Treas. Charlotte Symphony Orch., 1976-79; bd. dirs. Spirit Square, 1978-79, Family and Children's Services, 1978-79; bd. advisers Belmont Abbey Coll., 1977-79. Mem. Greater Charlotte C. of C. (v.p. 1976-78), Greater Charlotte Urban League (dir. 1979). Clubs: Charlotte City, Carmel Country. Home: 615 Hermitage Ct Charlotte NC 28207 Office: Knight Pub Co 600 S Tryon St Charlotte NC 28202

SUAREZ-MURIAS, MARGUERITE C., educator; b. Havana, Cuba, Mar. 23, 1921; d. Eduardo R. and Marguerite (Vendel) S.-M.; came to U.S., 1935, naturalized, 1959; A.B., Bryn Mawr Coll., 1942; M.A., Columbia U., 1953, Ph.D., 1957. Lectr. in Spanish, Columbia U., 1954-56; pub. relations officer med. div. Johns Hopkins U., 1957-58; asst. prof. Spanish and French, Sweet Briar Coll., 1958-59, Hood Coll., 1960-61; lectr. Cath. U., 1960-63, asst. prof. summers 1960-62, asso. prof., summer 1964-66; asst. prof. dept. langs. and linguistics, Am. U., 1961-63, asso. prof., 1963-66; prof. dept. classical and modern langs. Marquette U., Milw., 1966-68; prof. Spanish and Portuguese, U. Wis., Milw., 1968—, chmn., 1972-75. Mem. Modern Lang. Assn., Am. Assn. Tchrs. Spanish and Portuguese, North Central Council Latin Americanists, Instituto Internacional de Literature Iberoamericana, Caribbean Studies Assn. Roman Catholic. Author: La novela romántica en Hispanoamérica, 1963; Antología estilística de la prosa moderna española, 1968; also various articles to profl. jours.; editor: Gironella's Los cipreses creen en Dios, 1969. Home: 3904 Saint Paul St Baltimore MD 21218 Office: U Wis Milwaukee WI 53201

SUBA, ANTONIO RONQUILLO, surgeon; b. Philippines, Apr. 25, 1927; s. Antonio Mesina and Valentina Cabais (Ronquillo) S.; came to U.S., 1952, naturalized, 1961; M.D., U. St. Thomas, Philippines, 1952; m. Sylvia Marie Karl, June 16, 1956; children—Steven Antonio, Eric John, Laurinda Ann, Gregory Karl, Timothy Mark, Sylvia Kathleen. Intern, St. Anthony's Hosp., St. Louis, 1952-53; resident St. Louis County Hosp., St. Louis, 1953-57; trainee Nat. Cancer Inst., Ellis Fischel State Cancer Hosp., Columbia, Mo., 1957-59; chief surg. services U.S. Army, Bremerhaven, Germany, 1959-61; practice medicine specializing in gen. and hand surgery, St. Louis, 1961—; pres., prin. ARS, P.C., 1971—. Diplomate Am. Bd. Surgery. Fellow A.C.S.; mem. AMA, Pan-Pacific, Mo. surg. assns., St. Louis Surg. Soc., Am. Assn. Hand Surgery. Club: K.C. Contbr. feature articles to Philippine publs., 1946-51, articles to med. jours. Home: 12085 Heatherdane St Saint Louis MO 63131 Office: 141 N Meramec St Clayton MO 63105

SUBAK, JOHN THOMAS, chem. co. exec.; b. Trebic, Czechoslovakia, Apr. 19, 1929; s. William John and Gerda Maria (Subakova) S.; came to U.S., 1941, naturalized, 1946; A.B., Yale U., 1950, LL.B., 1956; m. Mary Corcoran, June 4, 1955; children—Jane, Kate, Thomas, Michael. Admitted to Pa. bar, 1957; asso., then partner firm Dechert, Price & Rhoads, Phila., 1956-76; v.p., gen. counsel Rohm & Haas Co., Phila., 1976-77, group v.p., gen. counsel, 1977—, also dir., mem. exec. com.; dir., mem. exec. Milton Roy Co. Served as lt. (j.g.) USN, 1950-53. Mem. Am. Bar Assn. Democrat. Roman Catholic. Clubs: Merion Cricket, Racquet, Down Town. Editor Bus. Lawyer, 1972—. Home: Seven Springs Rd Radnor PA 19087 Office: Rohm & Haas Bldg Independence Mall W Philadelphia PA 19105

SUBECK, STANTON IRWIN, ins. co. exec.; b. Quincy, Ill., Aug. 25, 1949; s. Milton and Esther (Reister) S.; B.A. in Math., U. Ill., 1971; m. Aug. 28, 1969; children—Lisa, Scott. Actuarial mgr., then dir. mgmt. services CNA/Ins. Co., Chgo.; v.p., actuary Am. Res. Corp., Chgo., now chief fin. officer. Asso. mem. Soc. Actuaries. Home: 2625 Corinth St Olympia Fields IL 60461 Office: 55 E Monroe St Chicago IL 60603

SUBLETT, HENRY LEE, JR., educator; b. Danville, Va., Nov. 8, 1926; s. Henry L. and Freya H. (Cramer) S.; student Randolph-Macon Coll., 1947-49; A.B., Duke U., 1951; M.Ed., U. Va., 1953, Ed.D., 1959; m. Barbara Annette Mishalanie, May 24, 1975; 1 son by previous marriage, Henry Lee. Tchr., Bay County (Fla.) public schs., 1951-52; prin. Charlottesville (Va.) public schs., 1954-58; asso. prof. edn. Madison Coll., Harrisonburg, Va., 1958-61; asst. prof. edn. W.Va. U., 1961-62; asst. prof. edn. Duke U., Durham, N.C., 1962-64, asso. prof., 1964-74, dir. undergrad. studies, 1970-74; prof. edn. Coll. Edn., U. Md., College Park, 1974—, chmn. dept. early childhood-elem. edn., 1974-79; cons. in field. Served with USN, 1944-46. Mem. N.C. Assn. Tchr. Educators (past exec. com.), S.E. Regional Assn. Tchr. Educators (past program chmn.), Md. Assn. Tchr. Educators (co-chmn. program com. 1975-76), NEA, Delta Sigma Phi, Phi Delta Kappa, Kappa Delta Pi. Methodist. Club: Masons. Cons. editor Ednl. Research Quar., 1977-78; contbr. articles to profl. jours. Home: Oakton 83 Farragut Rd Annapolis MD 21403 Office: Coll Edn U Md College Park MD 20742

SUBOTNICK, MORTON, composer, clarinetist; b. Los Angeles, 1933; A.B., U. Denver; M.A., Mills Coll.; pupil of Milhaud and Kirchner. Formerly mem. Denver and San Francisco symphonies; chamber and solo performances; asst. prof., also co-founder Mills Coll. performing group; co-founder San Francisco tape center; formerly mus. dir. Repertory Theatre, Lincoln Center, also with intermedia program Sch. Arts, N.Y. U.; now asso. dean, dir. electronic music Sch. Music, Calif. Inst. of Arts; vis. prof. composition U. Md.; worked with magnetic tape, 1960—; creator Play Number 4, combinating music, theatre and cinema, game-playing, light-shows and ritualistic phenomena suggestive of contemporary society into a new total art form (happenings) and based on indeterminacy; composed Silver Apples of the Moon for electronic music synthesizer especially for Nonesuch Records, 1967; composer The Wild Bull, for electronic music synthesizer, 1968; 2: Game for Two Players and No Audience, 1973; 2 Butterflies for Amplified Orch., The Balance Room; Before the Butterfly (commd. by Los Angeles Philharmonic, Boston Symphony, N.Y. Philharmonic, Phila. Orch., Chgo. Symphony, Cleve. Symphony); Liquid Strata for piano and electronic ghost score, 1977; electronic music Score for Ice Floe, 1978; A Sky of Cloudless Sulphur, 1978. Guggenheim fellow, 1975; NEA grantee, 1976. Address: care Calif Institute of the Arts Valencia CA 91355

SUCHOFF, BENJAMIN, educator; b. N.Y.C., Jan. 19, 1918; s. Aaron and Sadie (Leishin) S.; B.S., Cornell U., 1940; postgrad. Juilliard Sch. Music, 1940-41, 46-47; M.A., N.Y. U., 1949, Ed.D., 1956; m. Eleanor Rosen, Nov. 16, 1949; children—Michael Alan, Susan Carol, Deborah Ann. Dir. music Hewlett-Woodmere Union Free Sch. Dist., Hewlett, N.Y., 1950-78; dir. spl. collections and computer program Center for Contemporary Arts and Letters, SUNY, Stony Brook, 1973—, prof. arts and letters; lectr. Columbia Tchrs. Coll., 1973; cons. computer applications for music research. Dir. N.Y. Bartok Archive, Lynbrook, N.Y., 1953—; trustee Estate of Bela Bartok, Cedarhurst. Served to capt. AUS, 1941-45. Recipient Founders Day award N.Y. U., 1954; Am. Council Learned Socs. grantee in aid computerized music research, 1966. Mem. ASCAP, Am. Musicol. Soc., Soc. for Ethnomusicology, NEA, Coll. Music Soc., Assn. for Computing Machinery, Internat. Folk Music Council, Internat. Music Soc., N.Y. State Sch. Music Assn., Bartok Soc. Am. (dir.), Internat. Bartok Soc. (sec.-gen.). Author: Guide to the Mikrokosmos of Bela Bartok, 1970; Curriculum Guide to Electronic Music, 1973; Electronic Music Techniques, 1975; editor: Rumanian Folk Music (Bartok), vols. 1-3, 1967, vols. 4, 5, 1976; Turkish Folk Music from Asia Minor (Bartok), 1975; Bela Bartok Essays, 1976; Yugoslav Folk Music (Bartok), vols. 1-4, 1978. Composer, arranger works for choruses, symphonic band, orch., instrumental ensemble. Home: 2 Tulip St Cedarhurst NY 11516 Office: Center for Contemporary Arts and Letters SUNY Stony Brook NY 11794

SUCHORS, WILLIAM JAMES, mfg. co. exec.; b. Auburn, N.Y., Apr. 11, 1913; s. Samuel David and Antonina (Tyhaneck) S.; B.S., Pa. State U., 1934; M.S., Mass. Inst. Tech., 1935; m. Nancy Vining, Feb. 24, 1938; children—William W., Cynthia, Cheryl R. Asst. div. sales mgr. Fla. Power and Light Co., Daytona Beach, 1938-42; mgr. product planning IBM, N.Y.C., 1946-55; gen. sales mgr. UARCO Inc., Chgo., 1955-59; v.p. product devel. Sperry Rand Corp., N.Y.C., 1960-65; exec. v.p. domestic ops. Sunbeam Corp., Oak Brook, Ill., 1966—, also dir. Served to maj. U.S. Army, 1942-46. Decorated Bronze Star. Clubs: Tavern, Butterfield Country. Home: 1535 Kirkwood Dr Geneva IL 60134 Office: 2001 S York Rd Oak Brook IL 60521

SUCK, RICHARD LEWIS, hosp. adminstr.; b. Parkersburg, W.Va., July 18, 1917; s. Cecil Augustus and Summer (Leach) S.; student Muhlenberg Coll., 1940; m. Joyce E. Stewart, May 4, 1946; 1 dau., Bonnie Lee Suck Andrews. With Pa. Power & Light Co., Allentown, 1939-44; mem. adminstrv. staff St. Luke's Hosp., Bethlehem, Pa., 1944—, adminstr., 1955—, also exec. v.p., 1971-73, pres., 1973—; dir. Pelsa Corp. Bd. dirs. Hosp. Bur. N.Y.C., 1960-67, Totts Gap (Pa.) Med Center; trustee St. Luke's Hosp. Recipient Distinguished Service award Bethlehem Jr. C. of C., 1953. Fellow Am. Coll. Hosp. Adminstrs., Am. Pub. Health Assn., Royal Soc. Health (Gt. Britain). Home: 1244 Moffitt Ave Bethlehem PA 18018 Office: 801 Ostrum St Bethlehem PA 18015

SUDAN, RAVINDRA NATH, physicist; b. Chineni, Kashmir, India, June 8, 1931; s. Brahm Nath and Shanti Devi (Mehta) S.; came to U.S., 1958, naturalized, 1971; B.A. with first class honors, U. Punjab, 1948; diploma Indian Inst. Sci., 1952; diploma Imperial Coll., London, 1953; Ph.D., U. London, 1955; m. Dipali Ray, July 3, 1959; children—Rajani, Ranjeet. Engr., Brit. Thomson-Houston Co., Rugby, Eng., 1955-57, Imperial Chem. Industries, Calcutta, India, 1957-58; research asso. Cornell U., Ithaca, N.Y., 1958-59, asst. prof. elec. engring., 1959-63, asso. prof., 1963-68, prof., 1968-75, IBM prof. engring., 1975—, dir. Lab. Plasma Studies, 1975—; cons. Lawrence Livermore Lab., Los Alamos Sci. Lab., Sci. Applications Inc., Physics Internat. Co.; vis. research asso. Stanford U., summer 1963; cons. U.K.

Atomic Energy Authority, Culham Lab., summer 1965; vis. scientist Internat. Center Theoretical Physics, Trieste, Italy, 1965-66, summers 1970, 73, Plasma Physics Lab. Princeton U., 1966-67, Inst. for Advanced Study, Princeton, N.J., spring 1975; head theoretical plasma physics group U.S. Naval Research Lab., 1970-71, sci. adviser to dir., 1974-75; chmn. Ann. Conf. on Theoretical Aspects of Controlled Fusion, 1975, 2d Internat. Conf. on High Power Electron and Ion Beam Research and Tech., 1977. Fellow Am. Phys. Soc., IEEE; mem. Sigma Xi. Patentee (with S. Humphries, Jr) intense ion beam generator; mem. editorial bd. Nuclear Fusion, 1976—, Physics of Fluids, 1973-76; Comments on Plasma Physics, 1973—; contbr. articles to sci. jours. Office: 308 Upson Hall Cornell Univ Ithaca NY 14853

SUDARSHAN, ENNACKAL CHANDY GEORGE, physicist; b. Kottayam, Kerala State, India, Sept. 16, 1931; s. Ennackal Ipe and Kaithayil (Achamma) Chandy; came to U.S., 1955; B.Sc., Madras Christian Coll., Tambaram, Tamil Nad, 1951; M.A., U. Madras, 1952; Ph.D., U. Rochester, 1958; m. Lalita Rau, Dec. 20, 1954; children—Pradip Alexander, Arvind Jewett, Ashok John. Demonstrator, resident tutor in physics Madras Christian Coll., 1951-52; research asst. Tata Inst. Fundamental Research, Bombay, 1952-55; teaching asst. U. Rochester, 1955-57, asst. prof., 1959-61, asso. prof., 1961-63; corp. fellow Harvard U., 1957-59; prof., dir. research program in elementary particle physics Syracuse U., 1964-69; prof. physics U. Tex., Austin, 1969—, dir. Center for Particle Theory, 1970—; dir. Centre for Theoretical Studies, Indian Inst. Sci., Bangalore, India, 1972—; co-dir. NSF Coop. Research Program, U. Warsaw, Poland and U. Tex., Austin; pres. SKM, Inc.; mem. adv. bd. Maharishi European Research U., Switzerland. Decorated Order of Lotus (India); recipient Honors award Assn. Indians in Am., 1976; Outstanding Service award Internat. Meditation Soc., 1977. Fellow Indian Nat. Sci. Acad. (Bose award 1977), Am. Phys. Soc., Indian Acad. Sci. Author: (with R.E. Marshak) Elementary Particle Physics, 1965; (with J.R. Klauder) Fundamentals of Quantum Optics, 1968; (with N. Mukunda) Classical Dynamics, 1974; editorial bd. Jour. Math. Physics, 1966-68, 75—, Jour. Math. and Physics, 1967—, Reports on Math. Physics, 1970—, Letters in Math. Physics, 1975—; contbr. sci. articles to tech. jours. Home: 7012 Northledge Dr Austin TX 78731 Office: Center for Particle Theory Physics Dept U Tex Austin TX 78712

SUDARSKY, JERRY M., industrialist, corp. exec.; b. Russia, June 12, 1918; s. Selig and Sara (Ars) S.; came to U.S., 1928, naturalized, 1934; student U. Iowa, 1936-39; B.S., Poly. Inst. Bklyn., 1942; D.Sc. (hon.), Poly. Inst. N.Y., 1976; m. Mildred Axelrod, Aug. 31, 1947; children—Deborah, Donna. Founder, chief exec. officer Bioferm Corp., Wasco, Calif., 1946-66; cons. to Govt. of Israel, 1966-67; founder, chmn. Israel Chems., Ltd., Tel Aviv, Israel, 1967-70; chmn. I.C. Internat. Cons., Tel Aviv, 1971-73; vice chmn. Daylin, Inc., Los Angeles, 1974-77, also dir.; chmn. Nutri-Gen. Inc., Los Angeles, 1978—; dir. Unico Investment Co., Tel Aviv, 1974—. Bd. govs. Hebrew U., Jerusalem, hon. treas., 1968—; chmn. bd. govs. Bezalel Art Acad., Jerusalem, 1974—; trustee Polytechnic Inst. N.Y., 1976—. Served with USNR, 1943-46. Mem. Am. Chem. Soc., Sigma Xi. Clubs: Brentwood Country (Los Angeles); Canyon Country (Palm Springs, Calif.); Caesarea Country (Israel). Patentee in field of indsl. microbiology. Home: 2220 Ave of the Stars Los Angeles CA 90067

SUDERBURG, ROBERT CHARLES, composer; b. Spencer, Iowa, Jan. 28, 1936; s. Robert Suderburg; B.Mus. summa cum laude, U. Minn., 1957; M.Mus., Yale U., 1960; Ph.D., U. Pa., 1966; m. Elizabeth Pipcorn, 1959; children—Erika, Jonathan. Tchr., condr. Bryn Mawr Coll., 1960-61, U. Pa., 1961-65, Phila. Mus. Acad., 1963-66; tchr., condr. U. Wash., Seattle, 1966-74, co-founder Contemporary Group, 1966-74; chancellor N.C. Sch. Arts, Winston-Salem, 1974—; mem. music adv. panel Nat. Endowment Arts; bd. dirs. Eastern Music Festival, N.C. Dance Theatre, Southeastern Center Contemporary Art, N.C. Shakespeare Festival; composer works for orch., cantatas for voice and chamber orch., chamber music, also works for piano, band and choir. Grantee Houston Symphony, 1967, Rockefeller Found., 1968, Broadcast Music Inc., 1961, ASCAP, 1968—, Am. Music Center, 1969, Hindemith Found., 1971, Nat. Found. Arts, 1973, Guggenheim Found., 1968, 74. Mem. ASCAP. Clubs: Yale, Century (N.Y.C.); Winston-Salem Rotary. Home: 28 Cascade Ave Winston-Salem NC 27107 Office: 200 Waughtown St Winston-Salem NC 27107

SUDLER, LOUIS COURTENAY, realtor, baritone; b. Chgo., Feb. 25, 1903; s. Carroll H. and Susan B. (Culbreth) S.; grad. Hotchkiss Sch., 1921; B.A., Yale U., 1925; D.Mus. (hon.), Southwestern Coll., Winfield, Kans., 1963, Augustana College, Rock Island, Ill., 1964; D.Mus. (hon.), DePaul U., 1972; L.H.D., Lake Forest (Ill.) Coll., 1972; D. Fine Arts, Northwestern U., 1973; m. Mary L. Barnes, Feb. 2, 1929; 1 son, Louis Courtenay. Leading baritone Chgo. Civic Opera Co., 1945-47; internat. appearances, 1946—; guest soloist symphony orchs., oratorio socs., radio and TV. Chmn. Sudler & Co., real estate, Chgo.; dir., officer numerous real estate corps., Chgo.; chmn. Dearborn Fin. Conf.; dir. Upper Ave. Bank of Chgo. Founder, host of Artist Showcase, WGN-TV, chmn. emeritus, 1966-75. Past pres. Chgo. Symphony Orch., now chmn. emeritus. Recipient Distinguished Service medal State of Ill., Order of Lincoln. Mem. Soc. Colonial Wars. Clubs: Chicago, Economic, Cliff Dwellers, Saddle and Cycle, Carlton, Tavern (v.p. 1955-56), Arts, Casino (dir. 1955—), Commercial Commonwealth, Mid-Am. (Chgo.); Little Harbor; Delray Beach. Office: Sudler & Co 875 N Michigan Ave Chicago IL 60611. *The main purpose of my life has been to foster the closer understanding and relationship between those engaged in the performance of the musical arts and those involved in providing the necessary financial assistance for their support.**

SUEDFELD, PETER, educator, psychologist; b. Budapest, Hungary, Aug. 30, 1935; s. Leslie John and Jolan (Eichenbaum) Field; came to U.S., 1948, naturalized, 1952; student U. Philippines, 1956-57; B.A., Queens Coll., 1960; M.A., Princeton, 1962, Ph.D., 1963; m. Gabrielle Debra Guterman, June 11, 1961; children—Michael Thomas, Joanne Ruth, David Lee. Research asso. Princeton, lectr. Trenton State Coll., 1963-64; vis. asst. prof. psychology U. Ill., 1964-65; asst. prof. psychology Univ. Coll. Rutgers U., 1965-67, asso. prof., 1967-71, prof., 1971-72, chmn. dept., 1967-72; prof., head dept. psychology U. B.C., Vancouver, 1972—; cons. in field. Served with U.S. Army, 1955-58. NIMH grantee, 1970-72; Can. Council grantee, 1973; Nat. Research Council Can. grantee, 1973. Fellow Can., Am. psychol. assns.; mem. AAAS, Psychonomic Soc., Soc. Exptl. Social Psychology, Phi Beta Kappa, Sigma Xi. Editor: Attitude Change: The Competing Views, 1971; Personality Theory and Information Processing, 1971; The Behavioral Basis of Design, 1976; Jour. Applied Social Psychology, 1975—. Contbr. articles to profl. jours. Office: Dept Psychology U BC Vancouver BC Canada

SUENHOLZ, HERMAN HARRY, banker; b. Jamaica, N.Y., Aug. 6, 1924; s. Herman and Johanna (Gassler) S.; B.S. magna cum laude, Fairleigh Dickinson U., 1959; postgrad. N.Y. U., 1960-64; m. Helen J. Andrews, July 10, 1948; children—Elaine, Robert, Mary Jo, Claire, Margaret, Laura. With 1st Jersey Nat. Bank, Jersey City, 1953—, cashier, 1962-65, v.p., 1965, sr. v.p., cashier, 1966-67, exec. v.p., 1967-75, pres., 1975—, also dir.; pres. First Jersey Nat. Corp.; pres., dir. 1st Jersey Nat. Bank; dir. Guardian Comml. Corp., TTEE. Trustee N.J. Council Econ. Edn.; trustee, chmn. Jersey City State Coll. Served with USNR, 1943-46. Mem. Greater Newark C. of C. (dir.). Home: 160 Lowell Rd Glen Rock NJ 07452 Office: 1 Exchange Pl Jersey City NJ 07303

SUER, MARVIN DAVID, architect; b. Phila., Apr. 4, 1923; B. Arch., U. Pa., 1950; m. Gertrude Litvin, 1947; children—Marsha Clark, Sharon, Deborah. Partner Suer & Livingston, 1961-62, Suer, Livingston & Demas, 1962-69; dir. tech. prodn. Eschbach, Pullinger, Stevens & Bruder, Phila., 1969-74; asso. Ballinger, Phila., 1974-79, Bartley Long Mirenda, Phila., 1979—. Chmn. bd. trustees Phila. Architects Charitable Trust. Works include State Hosp. for Crippled Children addition, 1964, Huey Elementary Sch., Phila., 1964, Dist. No. 4 Health Center, Phila., 1967, Stephen Smith Towers, 1969, Foxchase Br. Library, 1969; lectr. refresher courses A.I.A. Served with C.E., AUS, 1943-46. Registered architect, N.J., Pa. Fellow A.I.A. (pres. Phila. chpt. 1968); mem. Tau Sigma Delta. Home: 305 Overlook Ave Willow Grove PA 19090 Office: 841 Chestnut St Philadelphia PA 19107

SUERSTEDT, HENRY, JR., electronic co. exec.; b. Berkeley, Cal., Oct. 14, 1920; s. Henry and Cecilia Vivien (Reiter) S.; A.A., San Francisco City Coll., 1940; student USN Gen. Line Sch., 1950, Armed Forces Staff Coll., 1955; B.S., U. Md., 1957; m. Mary Josephine Bass, Apr. 13, 1946; children—Candace Cecilia, Cynthia Marie. Commd. ensign USN, 1941, advanced through grades to rear adm., 1969; comdr. Torpedo Squadron 100, 1945, comdr. Escort Carrier Air Group 84, 1946; comdr. Attack Squadron 213, 1948-49; comdr. Fighter Squadron 54, 1953; air officer, navigator U.S.S. Sicily, 1953-55; head Aircraft Conventional Weapons Br., research and devel. Bur. Ordnance, 1955-58; air operations officer Carrier Div. 5, 1958-59; staff CINCPAC, 1959; dir. Strike Warfare Div., initiator, project mgr. A7A Corsair II attack aircraft Bur. Weapons, 1960-63; comdg. officer U.S.S. Union, 1964; comdg. officer U.S.S. Tripoli, 1965-67; asst. comdr. for logistics and fleet support Naval Air, 1968-69; dep. comdr. U.S. Naval Forces Vietnam, 1970; comdr. Joint Task Force 8, 1970; dep. comdr. plans and programs, comptroller Naval Air Systems Command, Washington, 1971-72; comdr. Naval Weapons Center, China Lake, Calif., 1972-73; dir. Western region PRD Electronics, Inc., 1973—. Decorated Silver Star, Legion of Merit with combat V and 3 gold stars, D.F.C. with gold star, Bronze Star with combat V, Air medal with silver and 4 gold stars, Navy Commendation medal with Combat V and gold star. Mem. Soc. Logistic Engrs., Naval Inst., Am. Inst. Aeros. and Astronautics, Nat. Security Indsl. Assn., Navy League. Home: 2 The Inlet Coronado Cays Coronado CA 92118 Office: 591 Camino de la Reina San Diego CA 92108

SUGAR, BERT RANDOLPH, author, editor; b. Washington, June 7, 1937; s. Harold Randolph and Anne Edith (Rosensweig) S.; B.S., U. Md., 1957; M.B.A., U. Mich., 1959, LL.B., 1960, J.D., 1960; Ph.D. candidate, Am. U., 1961; m. Suzanne Davis, Nov. 22, 1960; children—Jennifer Anne, John-Brooks Randolph. Admitted to D.C. bar, 1961; practiced in Washington, 1961; pub., editor Baseball Monthly, 1961-62; account exec. McCann-Erickson, N.Y.C., 1963-64; account rep. J. Walter Thompson, N.Y.C., 1964-65; account supr., v.p. Papert, Koenig, Lois, 1965-66; dir. mktg., v.p. D'Arcy, MacManus, Masius, N.Y.C., 1967-70; pres., pub., editor Champion Sports Pub. Co., 1970-73; editor-in-chief Argosy, Imported Car Performance mags., N.Y.C., 1973-76; sr. v.p. Baron, Costello & Fine Advt., N.Y.C., 1976-77; editor, pub. Ring mag., 1979—. Recipient Media award Media Scope, 1968, certificate of merit Internat. Advt. Assn., 1977; founder Joe Lapchick award, 1972; co-founder Black Athletes Hall of Fame, 1972. Mem. Boxing Writers Assn., Am. Soc. Mag. Editors, Am. Polit. Items Collectors Assn., Football Writers Assn., Basketball Writers Assn., Alpha Delta Sigma, Beta Alpha Psi. Republican. Conglist. Author: Where Were You When the Lights Went Out?, 1976; (with Jose Torres, Norman Mailer) Sting Like a Bee, 1971; (with Floyd Patterson) Inside Boxing, 1974; The Sports Collectors Bible, 1975; The Assassination Chain, 1976; The Horseplayer's Guide to Winning Systems, 1976; Who Was Harry Steinfeldt? And Other Baseball Trivia Questions, 1976; The Life and Times of Harry Houdini, 1976; Classic Baseball Cards, 1977; The Thrill of Victory, 1977; Hit the Sign and Win a Free Suit of Clothes from Harry Finklestein, 1978; The Book of Sports Quotes, 1978; The Nostalgia Collectors Bible, 1979; The Rivalry, 1979; The Scrapbook History of Boxing, 1979; contbr. articles to mags. Home: 6 Southview Rd Chappaqua NY 10514 Office: 120 W 31st St New York NY 10001

SUGAR, OSCAR, physician, educator; b. Washington, July 9, 1914; s. Nathan and Bertha (Miller) S.; B.A., Johns Hopkins, 1934; M.A., George Washington U., 1937, M.D., 1942; Ph.D., U. Chgo., 1940; m. Dorothy Josephine Cohn, Feb. 7, 1944; children—Lawrence Daniel, Ruth Louise, David Morris. Intern, Hosp. U. Ill., 1942-43, resident neurol. surgery, 1946-48; practice medicine specializing in neurol. surgery, Chgo., 1948—; faculty Coll. Medicine U. Ill., 1948—, prof. neurol. surgery, 1956—, head dept. neurosurgery, 1971—. Served to capt. M.C., USAAF, 1943-46. Diplomate Am. Bd. Neurol. Surgery (dir. 1964-70). Mem. Am. Neurol. Assn., Am. Assn. Neurol. Surgeons (v.p. 1968-69), Chgo. Neurol. Soc. (past pres.), Soc. Neurol. Surgeons (v.p. 1973-74). Contbr. articles to med. jours. Home: 3750 N Lake Shore Dr Chicago IL 60613 Office: 912 S Wood St Chicago IL 60612

SUGAR, PETER FRIGYES, historian; b. Budapest, Hungary, Jan. 5, 1919; s. Peter F. and Margit (Pongor) S.; B.A., City Coll. N.Y., 1954; M.A., Princeton, U., 1956, Ph.D., 1959; m. Sally Bortz, June 18, 1955; children—Steven P., Klari A., Karen L. Instr. history Princeton U., 1957-59; asst. prof. history, U. Wash., Seattle, 1959-63, asso. prof., 1963-69, prof., 1969—, asso. dir. Inst. Comparative and Foreign Area Studies. Guggenheim Found. fellow, 1964-65; Woodrow Wilson fellow, 1954-55. Mem. Am. Hist. Assn., Am. Assn. Advancement of Slavic Studies, Western Slavic Assn., Am. Assn. Study of Hungarian History. Author: The Industrialization of Bosnia-Hercegovina, 1878-1919, 1963; Southeastern Europe under Ottoman Rule, 1354-1804, 1977, and others. Mem. editorial bd. Slavid Rev., Austrian History Yearbook. Home: 2540 NE 98th St Seattle WA 98115 Office: Dept History U Wash Seattle WA 98195

SUGARMAN, ALAN WILLIAM, educator; b. Boston, Sept. 26, 1924; s. Henry and Dorothy (Adams) S.; B.S., Boston U., 1948; M.A., Columbia, 1949, Ed.D., 1967; postgrad. State U. N.Y. at Oneonta, 1954-55, State U. N.Y. at Albany, 1954-56; m. Alice Mulhall, 1974; children—Michael, Susan, Ellen, William, Jane, James. Entrance examiner Boston U., 1947-48; tchr. pub. schs., Hudson, N.Y., 1950-54, prin. jr. high sch., 1954-56, prin. sr. high sch., 1956-61; prin. Spring Valley (N.Y.) Sr. High Sch., 1961-67; dir. secondary edn. Ramapo Central Sch. Dist. No. 2, Spring Valley, 1967-69; asst. supt. instruction, 1969-73; supt. schs. Connetquot Central Sch. Dist. Islip, Bohemia, N.Y., 1973—; adj. prof. N.Y. U., N.Y.C., U. P.R., Rio Piedras, Hofstra U., 1967—; prin. Ramapo sr. High Sch., Spring Valley, 1969; prof. Fordham U., N.Y.C., 1969. Athletic dir. East River Day Camp, N.Y.C., summer 1949; group worker St. John's Guild, N.Y.C., summer 1950; asst. dir. Tenn. Work Camp Unitarian Service Com., summer 1951; dir. spl. activities Hudson Youth Bur., Hudson, N.Y., summer, 1952; exec. dir. Jewish Community Center, Hudson, N.Y., 1953-56; chmn. vis. coms. Middle States Commn. Colls. and Secondary Schs., 1958-76. Chmn. County Leadership Training Com., mem. Rockland County exec. council Boy Scouts Am., 1956; corr. sec. Rockland County Negro Scholarship Fund, Inc.; pres. Spring Valley Youth Activities Com., 1956-58. Bd. dirs., past campaign co-chmn. Greater Hudson Community Chest; bd. dirs., 2d v.p. Hudson Youth Recreation Center, 1958-61; bd. dirs. Rockland County Br. Am. Cancer Soc., 1958-61, Columbia Meml. Hosp., 1959-61; chmn. Town of Islip Health Usage Com., 1973. Served with AUS, 1944-46; ETO. Recipient Distinguished Service award Hudson Jr. C. of C., 1960. Mem. Nat. Honor Soc. Secondary Schs. (hon.), Nat. PTA (hon. life), Am. Assn. Sch. Adminstrs., Assn. for Supervision and Curriculum Devel., Nat. Sch. Pub. Relations Assn., Assn. Sch. Bus. Ofcls., Nat. Soc. for Study Edn., DAV, VFW, Jewish War Vets., Phi Delta Kappa, Kappa Delta Pi, Pi Gamma Mu. Jewish (bd. edn.). Rotarian (dir.). Home: Mount Grey Rd Setauket NY 11785 Office: 780 Ocean Ave Bohemia NY 11716

SUGARMAN, GEORGE, artist; b. N.Y.C., May 11, 1912; s. Herman and Rachel S.; B.A., CCNY, 1935. One-man shows: Widdifield Gallery, N.Y.C., 1958, Radich Gallery, N.Y.C., 1961, 64, 65, 66, Phila. Art Alliance, 1965, Dayton's Gallery 12, Mpls., 1966, Galerie Schmela, Dusseldorf, Germany, 1967, Galerie Ziegler, Zurich, Switzerland, 1967, 70, Kaiser Wilhelm Mus., Krefeld, Germany, 1969, Staditsches Mus., Leverkusen, 1969, Kunsthalle, Basel, Switzerland, 1970, Haus Am Waldsee Mus., Berlin, 1970, Stedelijk Mus., Amsterdam, 1970, Gallery 118, Mpls., 1971, Zabriskie Gallery, N.Y.C., 1974, Dag Hammarskjold Plaza Sculpture Garden, N.Y.C., 1974, Robet Miller Gallery, N.Y.C., 1977, 78, Galerie Liatowitsch, Basel, 1979; group shows include: Sao Paulo (Brazil) Biennale, 1963, Whitney Mus. Am. Art, N.Y.C., 1966, Los Angeles County Mus. Art, 1967, Internat. Pavilion, Biennale, Venice, Italy, 1968, Mus. Modern Art, N.Y.C., 1969, Whitney Mus., 1976; represented in permanent collections: Walker Art Center, Mpls., Kunstmuseum, Zurich, Mus. Modern Art, Whitney Mus. Am. Art, Art Inst. Chgo.; sculpture commns.: World Trade Center, Brussels, Albert M. Greenfield Sch., Phila., Empire State Mall, Albany, N.Y., Fed. Ct. Bldg., Balt., Akron (Ohio) Public Library, Lincoln Nat. Life Found., Ft. Wayne, Ind., Internat. Airport, Miami, Fla., Detroit Gen. Hosp.; adj. prof. art Hue Hunter Coll., 1961-68, also Yale U., Princeton U. Served with USN, 1941-45. Recipient 2d prize Pitts. Internat., 1961-62; Longview Found. grantee, 1961, 62, 63; Ford Found. grantee, 1965; Nat. Found. Arts grantee, 1966. Home: 21 Bond St New York NY 10012

SUGARMAN, JULE M., govt. ofcl.; b. Cin., Sept. 23, 1927; s. Melville Harty and Rachel Wolf (Meyer) S.; student Western Res. U., 1945-46; A.B. with highest distinction, Am. U., 1951; m. Sheila Mary Shanley, May 20, 1956; children—Christopher, Maryanne, Jason, James. Dir. Office Child Devel., HEW, 1969-70; adminstr. Human Resources Adminstrn., N.Y.C., 1970-73; chief adminstrv. officer City of Atlanta, 1974-76; vice chmn. CSC, Washington, 1977-78, dep. dir. Office Personnel Mgmt., 1979—; vis. prof. Cornell U., 1972-73, New Sch. for Social Research, 1973, Southeastern U., 1976-79, U. So. Calif., 1977. Pres., Fairfax County Fedn. Citizen's Assns., 1959-60, The Children's Lobby, 1971—. Served with U.S. Army, 1946-48. Recipient Meritorious Service award Dept. State, 1963, Alumni Service award Am. U., 1977. Mem. Nat. Acad. Pub. Adminstrn. Home: 1719 Melbourne Dr McLean VA 22101 Office: 1900 E St NW Washington DC 20415

SUGARMAN, NATHAN, educator, chemist; b. Chgo., Mar. 3, 1917; s. Barnett and Tessie (Fischer) S.; B.S., U. Chgo., 1937, Ph.D., 1941; m. Goldie G. Greenberg, Aug. 22, 1940; children—Tanya, Barry. With Metall. Lab., 1942-45, Los Alamos, Sci. Lab., 1945-46; prof. chemistry U. Chgo., 1946—. Recipient Quantrell award for excellence in undergrad. teaching U. Chgo., 1966. Mem. Am. Chem. Soc., Am. Phys. Soc., A.A.A.S., Fedn. Am. Scientists. Home: 1236 E Madison Park Chicago IL 60615

SUGARMAN, NORMAN ALFRED, lawyer; b. Cleve., Sept. 12, 1916; s. Simon and Esther (Goldstein) S.; A.B., Case Western Res. U., 1938, J.D., 1940; m. Joan Katherine Green, Oct. 20, 1940; children—Joel, Janet, Elaine, Nancy, Laurence. Admitted to Ohio bar, 1940, also D.C. bar; atty. Office of Chief Counsel, Bur. Internal Revenue, 1940-49, spl. asst. to chief counsel, 1949-51, asst. head mgmt. staff, 1951-52, asst. commrs., supervising tech. tax work, 1952-54; partner law firm Baker & Hostetler, Cleve., with offices in Columbus, Ohio, Orlando, Fla. and Washington, 1954—; lectr. law, law sch. George Washington U., 1950-52, U. Miami, 1976—; lectr. in law insts. and tax forums. Spl. counsel on community found. matters Council on Founds., Inc.; gen. counsel Jewish Community Fedn. Cleve., 1971-75; chmn. nat. endowment fund devel. com., mem. bd. dirs. Council Jewish Fedns., N.Y.C. Trustee Dyke Coll., 1966-72, 75-76, Case Western Res. U., 1977—. Served with F.A., AUS, France and Germany, 1943-45. Mem. Am. Bar Assn. (mem. tax sect. com. on exempt orgns., spl. com. on simplification, planning com.), Tax Club Cleve. (pres. 1967). Editor Fed. Bar Jour., 1950-52. Contbr. to various legal and tax publs. Home: 2500 Virginia Ave Washington DC 20037 Office: 818 Connecticut Ave Washington DC 20006

SUGARMAN, ROBERT JAY, lawyer, ofcl. Internat. Joint Commn.; b. Meriden, Conn., May 29, 1938; s. Lester Holman and Ruth Frieda (Kalman) S.; A.B., Brown U., 1960; postgrad. (Ford Found. fellow) Stanford U., 1960-61; LL.B. magna cum laude, Harvard U., 1964; children—Karen Elizabeth, Kenneth John. Partner firm Dechert Price and Rhoads, Phila., 1964-65, 66-78; law clk. to Hon. Abraham L. Freedman, U.S. Ct. Appeals, Phila., 1965-66; U.S. chmn. Internat. Joint Commn., U.S. and Can., Washington, 1978—; lectr. in environ. law; adj. prof. planning; legal cons. Nat. Water Quality Commn. Mem. exec. com., sec. Phila. Council Community Advancement, 1969-78; bd. dirs. Pennypack Watershed Assn., 1974—; mem. nat. staff Carter Presdl. Primary Campaign; chmn. SE Pa. chpt. Americans for Democratic Action, 1972-73; bd. dirs., mem. exec. com. Public Interest Law Center Phila., 1975-78; bd. dirs. Community Legal Services, Inc., 1976-78. Mem. Phila. Bar Assn. (chmn. public service com. 1976-77), Environ. Def. Fund, Inc. (legal adv. com. 1970-76), Am. Bar Assn. Author: (with T. Reiner) The Crosstown Expressway: A Case Study, 1970; editor Harvard Law Rev., 1963-64. Office: 1717 H St NW Washington DC 20440

SUGARMAN, SAMUEL LOUIS, oil transp. and trading co. exec.; b. Montague, Mass., Apr. 18, 1927; s. Julius William and Minnie S.; B.S., U.S. Merchant Marine Acad., 1947; postgrad. N.Y. State Sch. Indsl. and Labor Relations, Cornell U., 1950; M.B.A. with distinction, Harvard U., 1953; m. Marlene Rodenz, Mar. 3, 1958; children—Jord Ann, Shawn, Jay Scott, Robin. Dir. market research and spl. projects Gulf Oil U.S., Houston, 1968-70; mgr. new venture investments Gulf Oil Corp., Pitts., 1972-74; exec. v.p. Gulf Trading & Transp. Co., Pitts., 1974—. Served with USNR, 1953-55. Mem. Am. Petroleum Inst. Clubs: Duquesne, Downtown, Sewickley Heights Golf. Office: Gulf Trading & Transp Co Gulf Bldg Pittsburgh PA 15230

SUGASKI, LLOYD JOHN, banker; b. Elyria, Ohio, Nov. 21, 1923; s. John Daniel and Genevieve (Klingshirn) S.; B.S., U. Colo., 1948; M.B.A., U. Pa., 1949; postgrad. Harvard, 1968; m. Susan Kathleen Whalen, June 12. 1948; children—Catherine Sugaski Heilig, Michael, Kevin, Mary Sugaski French. With Bank of Am., Los Angeles, 1949—, asst. v.p., 1959-61, v.p., 1961-69, sr. v.p., 1968-76, exec. v.p.,

1976—, also chmn. gen. loan com.; chmn. bd., dir. Small Bus. Enterprises Co., Bank Am. Capital Corp. Served with USNR, 1941-46. Mem. Phi Gamma Delta, Delta Sigma Pi. Club: California (Los Angeles), Bankers. Office: 555 California St San Francisco CA 94137

SUGERMAN, ABRAHAM ARTHUR, psychiatrist; b. Dublin, Ireland, Jan. 20, 1929; s. Hyman and Anne (Goldstone) S.; came to U.S., 1958, naturalized, 1963; B.A., Trinity Coll., 1950, M.B., B. Chir., B.A.O., 1952; D.Sc., SUNY, Bklyn., 1962; m. Ruth Nerissa Alexander, June 5, 1960; children—Jeremy, Michael, Adam, Rebecca. House officer Meath Hosp., Dublin, 1952-53, St. Nicholas Hosp., London, 1953-54; sr. house physician Brook Gen. Hosp., London, 1954; registrar in psychiatry Kingsway Hosp. Derby and Kings Coll. Med. Sch., Newcastle, Eng., 1955-58; clin. psychiatrist Trenton (N.J.) Psychiat. Hosp., 1958-59; cons. psychiatry, 1964—; research fellow Downstate Med. Center, Bklyn., 1959-61; chief investigative psychiatry sect. N.J. Bur. Research, Princeton, 1961-73; cons. research, asso. psychiatrist Carrier Clinic, Belle Mead, N.J., 1968-72, 78—, dir. outpatient services, 1972-74, 77-78, med. dir., 1974-77; dir. research Carrier Found., Belle Mead, 1972-79; cons. psychiatry Med. Center, Princeton, N.J., 1972—; clin. asso. prof. psychiatry Rutgers Med. Sch., New Brunswick, N.J., 1972-78, clin. prof., 1978—; vis. prof. Rutgers Center for Alcohol Studies, 1977—, Hahnemann Med. Coll., Phila., 1978—; contbg. faculty Grad. Sch. Applied and Profl. Psychology, Rutgers U., 1974-78. Bd. dirs. N.J. Mental Health Research and Devel. Fund, Princeton, 1968-74; v.p. Jewish Family Service, Trenton, 1972-78; 1st v.p. Trenton Hebrew Acad., 1972-75; mem. bd. sci. advisers Found. Thanatology. Diplomate Am. Bd. Psychiatry and Neurology. Fellow Am. Psychiat. Assn., Am. Coll. Neuropsychopharmacology, Am. Coll. Clin. Pharmacology, AAAS; mem. Am. Coll. Psychiatrists, Royal Coll. Psychiatrists, AMA, Brit. Med. Assn., Soc. Biol. Psychiatry, Assn. Research Nervous and Mental Diseases, Eastern Psychol. Assn., Soc. Gen. Systems Research. Editor: (with Ralph E. Tarter) Alcoholism: Interdisciplinary Approaches to an Enduring Problem, 1976, Expanding Dimensions of Consciousness, 1978; contbr. articles to profl. jours. Home: 125 Roxboro Rd Lawrenceville NJ 08648 Office: Carrier Found PO Box 147 Belle Mead NJ 08502

SUGG, JOHN LOGAN (JACK), advt. exec.; b. Hillsboro, Ill., June 2, 1914; s. Norman J. and Clythera (McDavid) S.; B.A., Lake Forest Coll., 1938; m. Jean Ellen Morrison, Feb. 7, 1942; children—Michael L., Patrick M., Terry Jean. Engaged in newspaper work, 1938-41; with Cole & Weber, Inc., 1946—, pres., 1968-72, chmn. bd., 1972-76, chmn. exec. com., 1976—. Pres., Asso. Oreg. Industries, 1968-69. Bd. dirs. Emanuel Med. Center Found.; chmn. bd. dirs. Portland Better Bus. Bur., 1975—. Named Oreg. Advt. Man of Year, 1965. Mem. Portland C. of C. (dir.), Am. Assn. Advt. Agys. (chmn. Western region 1970-71). Clubs: Arlington (pres. 1975—); Multnomah Athletic; Portland Golf. Home: 2415 SW Timberline Dr Portland OR 97225 Office: 220 SW Morrison St Portland OR 97204

SUGG, ROBERT PERKINS, justice; b. Eupora, Miss., Feb. 21, 1916; s. Amos Watson and Virgie Christian (Cooper) S.; student Wood Jr. Coll., 1933-34, Miss. State U., 1935-37, Jackson Sch. Law, 1939-40; m. Elizabeth Lorraine Carroll, June 23, 1940; children—Robert Perkins, Charles William, John David. Admitted to Miss. bar; practice law, 1940-51; chancery judge, 1951-71; asso. justice Miss. Supreme Ct., 1971—; county pros. atty., Webster County, Miss., 1949-50. Mem. adv. council Nat. Center for State Cts., 1973—. Bd. govs. Miss. Jud. Coll., 1973—. Served with USAAF, 1942-43. Named Outstanding Citizen, Eupora Jr. C. of C., 1970, Alumnus of Year, Wood Jr. Coll., 1973; recipient Service to Humanity award Miss. Coll., 1976. Mem. Miss. State Bar, Am. Judicature Soc., C.A.P. (Miss. Wing, squadron comdr. 1974—), Am. Legion (post comdr. 1950). Democrat. Baptist (chmn. bd. deacons 1964). Home: 1067 Meadow Heights Dr Jackson MS 39206 Office: PO Box 117 Jackson MS 39205

SUGGS, JOHN THOMAS, lawyer; b. Denison, Tex., Dec. 22, 1904; s. John Thomas and Ruby Edna (Bunch) S.; B.B.A., U. Tex., 1925, LL.B., 1927; m. Mary Hope Robinson, Jan. 31, 1929; children—Ann Lee, Mary Shelly. Admitted to Tex. bar, 1927; gen. practice of law, Dallas, 1927-38; State Dist. judge 1938-44; ret. pres., chmn. bd. T. &P. Ry.; dir. State Nat. Bank of Denison, First Nat. Bank of Van Alstyne, Tex.; practicing law; cattel raiser. Instr., So. Methodist U. Law Sch. Mem. initial bd. dirs. State Bar of Tex., 1940-41. Fellow Tex. Bar Found.; mem. Dallas Citizens Council, Am. Bar Assn., State Bar Tex., Sigma Alpha Epsilon. Democrat. Episcopalian. Mason. Clubs: City, Dallas Country (Dallas). Home: 4206 Fairfax Dallas TX 75205 Office: 3033 First International Bldg Dallas TX 75270

SUGIHARA, JAMES MASANOBU, educator, chemist; b. Las Animas, Colo., Aug. 6, 1918; s. William B. and Takeyo (Kubota) S.; A.A., Long Beach Jr. Coll., 1937; B.S., U. Calif. at Berkeley, 1939, postgrad., 1939-41; Ph.D., U. Utah, 1947; m. May Murakami, June 5, 1944; children—John, Michael. Faculty, U. Utah, 1946-48, 49-64; research asso. Ohio State U., 1948-49; dean Coll. Chemistry and Physics, N.D. State U., Fargo, 1964-73, prof. chemistry, 1964—, dean Grad. Sch., 1975—; cons., Sun Oil Co., 1964-70, Esso Research and Engring. Co., 1972. Mem. Am. Chem. Soc., Sigma Xi, Phi Kappa Phi. Author: Laboratory Exercises in Organic Chemistry, 1961; also articles. Research on carbohydrate chemistry, application carbohydrate derivatives in interpreting mechanisms of organic reactions, characterization metal compounds in crude oils, Gilsonite, related materials. Home: 1001 Southwood Dr Fargo ND 58103

SUGIHARA, THOMAS TAMOTSU, educator, scientist; b. Las Animas, Colo., June 14, 1924; s. William Bansaku and Takeyo (Kubota) S.; A.B., Kalamazoo Coll., 1945; S.M., U. Chgo., 1951, Ph.D., 1952; m. Fumi Anraku, Mar. 15, 1952; children—Sara Toshi, Edna Michi. Research asso. chemistry Mass. Inst. Tech., 1952-53; mem. faculty Clark U., 1953-67, prof. chemistry, 1962-67, chmn. dept., 1963-67; prof. chemistry Tex. A & M 1967—, dir. Cyclotron Inst., 1971-78, dean of sci., 1978—; asso. geochemistry Woods Hole Oceanographic Instn., 1954-70; vis. scientist Lawrence Radiation Lab., Berkeley, Calif., summer 1964, Brookhaven Nat. Lab., Upton, N.Y., summer 1965, Oak Ridge Nat. Lab., 1977. Served with AUS, 1945-46. Guggenheim fellow, 1961-62. Fellow AAAS, Am. Phys. Soc.; mem. Am. Chem. Soc., AAUP, Sigma Xi, Delta Kappa Epsilon, Phi Beta Kappa. Contbr. articles on nuclear chemistry, nuclear physics, geochemistry, analytical chemistry to tech. jours. Office: Coll of Sci Tex A & M U College Station TX 77843

SUGIOKA, KENNETH, educator; b. Hollister, Calif., Apr. 19, 1920; s. Seigiro and Kameno (Takeda) S.; B.S., U. Denver, 1945; M.D., Washington U., St. Louis, 1949; m. Mary Trabue Hinternhoff, June 18, 1966; children—Stephanie, Colin, Kimi (by previous marriage), Nathan, Brian. Intern, resident U. Iowa, 1949-52, instr. anesthesiology, 1952; asst. prof. surgery N.C. Meml. Hosp., Chapel Hill, 1958-62, asso. prof. surgery, 1962—; prof. surgery, chmn. div. anesthesiology U. N.C., 1964-69, prof., chmn. dept. anesthesiology, 1969—; vis. prof. Physiol. Inst., U. Göttingen (Germany), 1963, Kings Coll. Med. Sch., London, Eng., Max-Planck Inst. Physiology, Dortmund, Ger., 1976-77. Dir. Morgan Creek Land Co. Mem. adv. com. on anesthetic and life support drugs FDA. Served to capt., M.C., USAF, 1952-54. Recipient spl. research fellowship NIH, 1961-62. Mem. Soc. Acad. Anesthesia Chairmen (past pres.). Author textbook outline of clin. anesthesiology. Contbr. articles to profl. jours. Home: Route 7 Bayberry Dr Chapel Hill NC 27514

SUGRUE, JOHN JOSEPH, engring. and constrn. co. exec.; b. N.Y.C., Feb. 19, 1934; s. Timothy J. and Ellen M. (Walsh) S.; B.B.A., Manhattan Coll., 1961; m. Suszn B. Keckeissen, June 9, 1956; children—Timothy J., Catherine M., John F., Amy T., Christopher J., Gail M. Sr. auditor Arthur Andersen & Co., Hartford, Conn., 1961-65; controller CE Indsl. Group, Windsor, Conn., 1966-70; pres. CE Eastwood Nealley Co., Belleville, N.J., 1970-71; v.p. fin. and adminstrn. CE Minerals Co., King of Prussia, Pa., 1971-72; treas. Lummus Co., Bloomfield, N.J., 1972-73; v.p. fin. Lummus Group Inc., Bloomfield, 1973—, also dir.; dir. Bloomfield Savs. Bank. Served with U.S. Army, 1953-55. C.P.A., Conn. Mem. Am. Inst. C.P.A.'s. Home: 566 Dorchester Dr River Vale NJ 07675 Office: 1515 Broad St Bloomfield NJ 07003

SUHL, HARRY, educator; b. Leipzig, Germany, Oct. 18, 1922; s. Bernhard and Klara (Bergwerk) S.; came to U.S., 1948, naturalized, 1957; B.S.C., U. Wales, 1943; Ph.D., U. Oxford, 1948, D.Sc., 1970. Temporary exptl. officer Brit. Admiralty, 1943-46; tech. staff Bell Labs., Murray Hill, N.J., 1948-60; prof. physics U. Calif., San Diego, 1961—; cons. Aerospace Corp., Bell Labs. Guggenheim fellow, 1968-69; NSF fellow, 1971. Fellow Am. Phys. Soc., Nat. Acad. Scis., Calif. Catalysis Soc. Editor: (with others) Magnetism, 1961-74; (with others) Solid State Communications, 1961—. Office: Physics Dept U Calif San Diego La Jolla CA 92093

SUHLER, JOHN STUART, publisher; b. Des Moines, May 10, 1943; s. Lester F. and Irene (Holmberg) S.; B.S., U. Kans., 1965; m. Charlotte Kay Thompson, Dec. 30, 1966; children—Ashley Thompson, Courtney Ruth, Brooke Thompson. Co-owner Dalton (Mass.)-Hinsdale News, 1965-66; promotion writer Look mag., Des Moines, 1965-66; cons. Benson, Stagg & Assos., N.Y.C., 1966-68; salesman Metromail div. Metromedia, N.Y.C., 1968-69; circulation dir. Psychology Today, CRM div. Boise Cascade, Del Mar, Calif., 1969-70, asso. pub., 1970-71, pub., 1971-73, v.p., pub. Psychology Today Pub. Group, 1973-74; pres. CBS Publs., Consumer Pub. div. CBS Inc., N.Y.C., 1974-79, pres. CBS/Pub. Group, v.p. CBS Inc., 1979—. Pub. Univ. Daily Kansan, 1964-65. Trustee Darien Library, William Allen White Found. Mem. Mag. Pubs. Assn. (dir.), Sigma Chi, Alpha Delta Sigma. Club: Tokeneke. Office: 51 W 52d St New York NY 10036

SUHR, DONALD CARL, mfg. co. exec.; b. Chgo., Apr. 30, 1916; s. Charles J. and Minnie (Glienke) S.; B.S., Ill. Inst. Tech., 1937; student U. Detroit, 1949-50, Detroit Inst. Tech., 1951-52; m. Sylvia Forsgren, Jan. 1, 1942. Gen. mgr. Defiance Alloyed Products Co., 1943-46; asst. mgr. mgmt. services div. Ernst & Ernst, C.P.A.'s, Detroit, 1947-52; v.p. mfg. Allen Industries, Inc., 1952-58; pres., treas., dir. Avis Indsl. Corp., 1958-60; pres., dir. Clinton Engines Corp., 1960-61, 63-67; gen. mgr. microstatics div. SCM Corp., 1967-71; pres., dir. Birmingham Plastics, Inc., Troy, Mich., 1971—; chmn. bd. A.P.I., Inc., Walled Lake, Mich., 1972—; pres., chief exec. officer, dir. ITL Industries, Ltd., Windsor, Can., 1972—, ITL Industries, Inc., Newark, Ohio, Rayolite Inc., Huntington Beach, Calif., 1972—; mgmt. cons., 1961-63; dir. Cadillac Steel Products Co., 1951-55, Keystone Mfg. Co., 1959-60. Exec. sec. St. John Woods Home Owners Assn., 1955—; bd. dirs. Barton Hills Improvement Corp., 1962—. Bd. dirs. Mich. State U. Conf., 1950, Wayne State U. Conf., 1951. Registered profl. engr., Mich. Mem. Engring. Soc. Detroit, Nat. Assn. Accountants, Nat. Soc. Profl. Engrs., Alpha Sigma Phi. Clubs: Forest Lake Country (Bloomfield Hills, Mich.); Barton Hills Country (Ann Arbor, Mich.); Davenport (Iowa) Country. Home: 16034 Martincoit Poway CA 92064

SUHRE, WALTER ANTHONY, JR., indsl. mfg. co. exec.; b. Cin., Jan. 17, 1933; s. Walter A. and Elizabeth V. (Heimbuch) S.; B.S. in Bus. Adminstrn., Northwestern U., 1956; LL.B. with honors, U. Cin., 1962; m. Judy Lee Carrington, June 7, 1975. Admitted to Ohio bar, 1962; asso. firm Taft, Stettinius & Hollister, Cin., 1962-65; with Eagle-Picher Industries, Inc., Cin., 1965—, asst. sec., 1968-74, gen. counsel, 1970-74, v.p., gen. counsel, 1974—. Served with USMC, 1956-59. Mem. Am., Ohio bar assns. Republican. Presbyterian. Clubs: Queen City, Bankers (Cin.). Home: 2691 Saddleback Dr Cincinnati OH 45244 Office: Eagle-Picher Industries Inc PO Box 779 Cincinnati OH 45201

SUINN, RICHARD MICHAEL, psychologist; b. Honolulu, May 8, 1933; s. Maurice B. C. and Edith (Wong) S.; student U. Hawaii, 1951-53; B.A. summa cum laude, Ohio State U., 1955; M.A. in Clin. Psychology, Stanford U., 1957, Ph.D. in Clin. Psychology, 1959; m. Grace D. Toy, July 26, 1958; children—Susan, Randall, Stacy, Bradley. Counselor, Stanford U., 1958-59, research asso. Med. Sch., 1964-66; asst. prof. psychology Whitman Coll., 1959-64; asso. prof. U. Hawaii, 1966-68; prof. Colo. State U., Ft. Collins, 1968—, head dept. psychology, 1973; cons. in field; psychologist U.S. Ski Teams, 1976 Olympic Games; reviewer NIMH, 1977—. Mem. City Council, Ft. Collins, 1975-79, mayor, 1978-79. Recipient cert. merit U.S. Ski Team, 1976; NIMH grantee, 1963-64; Office Edn. grantee, 1970-71. Fellow Am. Psychol. Assn., Behavior Therapy and Research Soc. (charter); mem. Assn. Advancement Behavior Therapy, Phi Beta Kappa, Sigma Xi. Author: The Predictive Validity of Projective Measures, 1969; Fundamentals of Behavior Pathology, 1970, 2d rev. edit., 1975; The Innovative Psychological Therapies, 1975; The Innovative Medical-Psychiatric Therapies, 1976; Psychology in Sport: Methods and Applications, 1980; editorial bd. Jour. Cons. and Clin. Psychology, 1973—, Jour. Counseling Psychology, 1974—, Behavior Therapy, 1977—, Behavior Modification, 1977-78, Jour. Behavioral Medicine, 1978—, Behavior Counseling Quar., 1979—; author tests: Suinn Test Anxiety Behavior Scale, Math. Anxiety Rating Scale. Home: 808 Cheyenne Dr Fort Collins CO 80525 Office: Dept Psychology Colo State U Fort Collins CO 80523

SUITER, GRANT, clergyman; b. Black Bear, Idaho, Jan. 26, 1908; s. Elmer Marshall and Winifred Rosaland (Handson) S.; m. Edith Rettos, May 12, 1956. Ordained to ministry Oct. 10, 1926; dir. Watch Tower Bible and Tract Soc. Pa., 1938—, asst. sec.-treas., 1943-47, sec.-treas., 1947; dir. Watchtower Bible and Tract Soc. N.Y., 1947—, asst. sec.-treas., 1944-47, sec.- treas., 1947. Address: 124 Columbia Heights Brooklyn NY 11201

SUITOR, JESSE HALE, naval officer; b. Memphis, Feb. 19, 1914; s. Charles M. and Jessie (Faircloth) S .; B.S., Memphis State U., 1935; M.D., U. Tenn., 1938; m. Jessie Bishop Kerr, Feb. 2, 1942; children—Roscoe F., David H. Rotating intern Monmouth Meml. Hosp., Long Branch, N.J., 1938-40; commd. lt. (j.g.), M.C., U.S. Navy, advanced through grades to capt., 1955; assigned U.S. Naval Hosp., Charleston, S.C., 1940-41; grad. Sch. Aviation Medicine, Pensacola, Fla., 1941; assigned various aviation units Central and S. Pacific, World War II; sr. med. officer Marine Corps Air Sta., El Toro, Cal., 1945; med. officer Destroyer Div. 18, 1941-42; U.S.S. Prince William, 1946, U.S.S. Leyete, 1947-49; resident ophthalmology U.S. Naval Hosp., Phila., 1949-52; chief ear, eye, nose and throat dept. U.S. Naval Hosp., Memphis, 1952-57; chief eye, ear, nose and throat dept. U.S. Naval Hosp., Newport, R.I., 1957-62, exec. officer, 1959-62; exec. officer U.S. Naval Hosp., Yokosuka, Japan, 1962-65; comdg. officer U.S. Naval Hosp., Camp Lejeune, 1965-69; med. officer Marine Corps Recruit Depot, San Diego, 1969-71; ret. 1971; health dir. Onslow County, N.C., 1975—. Diplomate Am. Bd. Ophthalmology. Mem. AMA. Home: 109 Sea Gull Way Hubert NC 28539

SUITS, BERNARD HERBERT, educator; b. Detroit, Nov. 25, 1925; s. Herbert Arthur and Helen Dorothy (Carlin) S.; B.A., U. Chgo., 1944, M.A., 1950; Ph.D., U. Ill., 1958; m. Nancy Ruth Berr, July 3, 1952; children—Mark, Constance. Investigator venereal disease USPHS, 1950-51; personnel officer Detroit Civil Service Commn., 1952-54; instr. philosophy U. Ill., Urbana, 1958-59; asst. prof. Purdue U., 1959-66; asso. prof. U. Waterloo (Ont.), 1966-72, prof. philosophy, chmn. dept., 1972—. Served with USNR, 1944-46. Mem. Canadian, Am. philos. assns., Philos. Soc. for Study of Sport (pres. 1975—). Author: The Grasshopper: Games, Life, and Utopia, 1978. Contbr. to profl. jours. and books. Office: Dept Philosophy U Waterloo Waterloo ON Canada

SUITS, DANIEL BURBIDGE, economist; b. St. Louis, June 27, 1918; s. Hollis Emerson and Dorothy Dandridge (Halyburton) S.; A.B. in Philosophy, U. Mich., 1940, M.A. in Econs., 1942, Ph.D. in Econs., 1948; m. Adelaide Evens Boehm, Feb. 14, 1942; children—Evan Halyburton, Holly Boehm Suits Kazarinoff. Asst. prof. econs. dept. U. Mich., 1950-55, asso. prof., 1955-59, prof., dir. research seminar in quantitative econs., 1959-69; prof. econs. U. Calif., Santa Cruz, 1969-74, Mich. State U., East Lansing, 1974—; cons. to various state and fed. agys. Served alt. mil. duty, 1942-46. Sr. fellow East-West Population Inst., 1978, 79. Fellow Econometric Soc., Am. Statis. Assn.; mem. Am. Econ. Assn. Quaker. Author: Statistics: An Introduction to Quantitative Economic Research, 1963; Theory and Application of Econometric Models, 1963; Principles of Economics, 1970, rev. edit., 1973. Home: 931 Hockey Ln Ann Arbor MI 48103 Office: Econs Dept Mich State U East Lansing MI 48823

SUKI, WADI NAGIB, physician; b. Khartoum, Sudan, Oct. 26, 1934; s. Nagib Khalil and Fahima (Hariz) S.; B.S., Am. U. Beirut, 1955, M.D. with distinction, 1959; m. Lailah Janet Stephan, May 6, 1967; children—Leila, Ramzy, Lenora, Wade. Came to U.S., 1959, naturalized, 1964. Fellow in exptl. medicine U. Tex. Southwestern Med. Sch., Dallas, 1959-61; resident in internal medicine Parkland Meml. Hosp., Dallas, 1961-63; fellow in nephrology Southwestern Med. Sch., 1963-65, instr., 1965-66, asst. prof. internal medicine, 1966-68; asso. prof. medicine Baylor Coll. Medicine, Houston, 1968-71, prof., 1971—, chief renal sect., 1968—; practice medicine specializing in internal medicine, kidney diseases, Dallas, 1965-68, Houston, 1968—; chief renal sect. Meth. Hosp., Houston; cons. medicine VA Hosp., Houston; attending physician Ben Taub Gen. Hosp., Houston. Chmn. med. adv. bd. Kidney Found. Houston and Greater Gulf Coast, 1969-71; chmn. nat. med. adv. council Nat. Kidney Found., 1971-73, mem. sci. adv. bd., 1972—, sec., 1977-78, pres., 1979-80; mem. exec. com. council on kidney in cardiovascular disease Am. Heart Assn., 1971-75; cons. in nephrology Wilford Hall USAF Med. Center, Lackland AFB, Tex.; mem. gen. medicine B study sect., div. research grants NIH, USPHS, 1975-79. NIH, USPHS research and tng. grantee, 1968—. Fellow A.C.P.; mem. Internat. Soc. Nephrology, Am. Soc. Nephrology, AAAS, Am. Fedn. Clin. Research, Am. Physiol. Soc., Am. Soc. Clin. Investigation, So. Soc. Clin. Investigation (past pres.), European Dialysis and Transplantation Assn. (asso.), Alpha Omega Alpha. Editor: Kidney in Systemic Disease, 1976; mem. editorial bd. The Kidney, 1970-76, Jour. Clin. Investigation, 1975—, Kidney Internat., 1976—, Mineral and Electrolyte Metabolism, 1977—, Renal Physiology, 1978—, Nephron, 1979—. Contbr. articles to profl. jours. Home: 2330 N Braeswood St Houston TX 77030 Office: 6535 Fannin St Houston TX 77030. *I came from humble beginnings, a modest family. I was an unknown and America gave me a chance. I could only respond by working to my full potential, my maximum capacity. No task was too difficult, no mission was impossible. I was afforded the opportunity to achieve my goals without regard to my name, creed, ethnic background or religion. To America I shall be ever grateful.*

SULCER, FREDERICK DURHAM, advt. exec.; b. Chgo., Aug. 28, 1930; s. Henry Durham and Charlotte (Thearle) S.; B.A., U. Chgo., 1949, M.B.A., 1963; m. Dorothy Wright, May 2, 1953; children—Thomas W., Ginna M., David T. Reporter, U.P. Assn., Chgo., 1945-46; reporter A.P., 1947; with Needham, Harper & Steers Advt., Chgo., 1947-78, dir., 1965-78, sr. account dir., 1965-66, mem. exec. com., 1966-78, exec. v.p., 1967, dir. N.Y. div., 1967-78, pres., 1974-75, chmn. bd. NH & S Internat., 1975-76; pres. Sulcer Communication Co., Inc., 1977-78; group exec., dir. Benton & Bowles, advt., 1978—. Served to capt. C.E., AUS, 1950-53. Mem. Am. Assn. Advt. Agys. (bd. govs. N.Y. chpt.), Internat. Advertisers Assn., Alpha Delta Phi. Home and office: 34 Avon Rd Bronxville NY 10708

SULGER, ALDEN HARWOOD, JR., advt. agy. exec.; b. Rochester, N.Y., Apr. 18, 1928; s. Alden Harwood and Harriet (Remington) S.; B.A., Yale U., 1951; m. Marie R. Connors, Sept. 15, 1956; children—Jennifer Remington, Alden Harwood III, Thomas Connors, Sarah Phillips. Territorial mgr. internat. div. Richardson-Merrell Inc., 1951-53; account exec. Biow Co., 1953-55; account exec. Grey Advt., N.Y.C., 1955-60, v.p. mgmt. supervision, 1963-68; v.p., account supr., Ted Bates Co., 1960-63; sr. v.p. mgmt. supervision, dir. Ogilvy & Mather Inc., N.Y.C., 1968-77, exec. v.p., 1977—. Served with U.S. Army, 1945-47. Republican. Episcopalian. Office: 2 E 48th St New York NY 10017

SULKIN, SIDNEY, editor; b. Boston, Feb. 2, 1918; s. Frank Sam and Celia (Glazer) S.; grad. Boston Pub. Latin Sch., 1935; B.A. cum laude, Harvard Coll., 1939; m. Naomi Ann Levenson, Oct. 4, 1950; 1 son, Jonathan Leigh. Editorial asst. Howell-Soskin Pub. Co., N.Y.C., 1940-41; chief World Wide English Programs, Voice of Am., N.Y.C., 1943-44; chief news Am. Broadcasting Sta. in Europe, SHAEF, London, 1945; dir. No. and Eastern Europe, U.S. Internat. Book Assn., N.Y.C. and Stockholm, 1945-47; spl. Scandinavian corr. CBS-News, Stockholm, 1945-47; commentator Sta. WCCO, Mpls., 1947; chief Washington bur. Voice of Am., 1949-53; editorial dir. Nat. Issues Com., Washington, 1953-55; asso. editor Changing Times Mag., Washington, 1955-62, sr. editor, 1962-71, mng. editor, 1971-75, editor, 1975—; dir. Kiplinger Washington Editors. Mem. Authors Guild, Nat. Press Club, P.E.N. Club, Internat. Club Washington, Am. Soc. Mag. Editors, Acad. Am. Poets. Democrat. Jewish. Club: Harvard. Author: (novel) The Family Man, 1962; Complete Planning for College, 1962, rev. edit., 1968; (play) Gate of Lions, 1975. Co-editor: For Your Freedom and Ours, 1943. Co-translator: Matthew the Young King (by Korczak), 1945. Contbr. short stories, articles, poetry to Harpers, Saturday Rev., New Republic, N.Y. Times, other revs. and mags. Home: 5012 Elsmere Pl Bethesda MD 20014 Office: 1729 H St NW Washington DC 20006

SULLAM, EDWARD, architect; b. N.Y.C., Dec. 20, 1925; s. Benveniste and Florence (Scialom) S.; student Coll. City N.Y., 1945; B.Arch., Carnegie Inst. Tech., 1950; m. Fredda Reich, Dec. 21, 1946; children—Brian Eliot, Steven Albert, Paul Jeffrey. Archtl. designer, Los Angeles, 1950-52, Pasadena, Calif., to 1955; asso. architect

Vladimir N. Ossipoff & Assos., Honolulu, 1955-58; prin. architect Edward Sullam & Assos., Honolulu, 1958—. Served with USNR, 1942-45. Licensed architect, Calif., Hawaii. Fellow AIA (Hawaii chpt. award for design 1961, 66, 76, 78, nat. Homes for Better Living award 1965, pres. Hawaii chpt. 1967); mem. Nat. Council Archtl. Registration Bds. (certified 1970). Designer: Temple Emanu-El, Honolulu, Kaimuki Profl. Bldg., Honolulu, Kailua Profl. Center, Honolulu, Waimea-Kohala Airport Additions, Waimea, Hawaii, Koko Head Dist. Park Recreation Center, Wailea (Hawaii) Town Center, Waianae Neighborhood Community Center. Home: 1612 Kuhilani St Honolulu HI 96821 Office: 1109 12th Ave Honolulu HI 96816

SULLIVAN, ADÈLE WOODHOUSE, orgn. ofcl.; b. Trenton, N.J.; d. William and Adaline Dearth (Fox) Woodhouse; student Rider Coll., 1925-27; L.H.D., Lincoln Meml. U., 1968; m. Harold E. Erb, May 27, 1929 (dec. Nov. 1957); 1 dau., Nancy Elizabeth (Mrs. Joseph P. Thorne); m. 2d, William H. Sullivan, Jr., Mar. 17, 1960. Mem. D.A.R., 1930—, regent N.Y. State, 1953-56, nat. rec. sec. gen., 1956-59, 1st v.p. gen., 1959-62, nat. pres. gen., 1965-68; pres. Nat. DAR Exec. Club, 1962-64, hon. life regent N.Y. State, 1956—, hon. pres. gen. for life, 1968—; trustee D.A.R. schs., Grant, Ala., Tamassee, S.C., also Crossnore, N.C. Sec., Air Corps office Keystone Aircraft Corp., 1927-29; sec., treas. Power Machinery Corp., N.Y.C., 1961-65. Pres. Woodhull Day Sch. PTA, Hollis, N.Y., 1942-44; chmn. student loan fund women's aux. ASME, 1946-48; v.p. N.Y. colony New Eng. Women, 1963-65. Mem. Women's Nat. Adv. Commn. for Nixon, 1968; chmn. N.Y. Women for Buckley, 1970; chmn. Women's Nat. Rep. Campaign Com., 1972. Bd. dirs. Nat. Symphony Orch. Assn., 1965-68, Friends of Historic St. George's Ch., Hempstead, L.I., 1960-67; bd. dirs., exec. v.p. nat. affairs Cultural Laureat Found., Inc., 1973—. Mem. awards jury Freedoms Found., 1966-67; mem. nat. honors com. Women's Hall of Fame, Inc.; program chmn. Women's Soc., Scarsdale Community Bapt. Ch., 1977-80. Recipient commendation award U.S. Navy for work with D.A.R., World War II; Award for outstanding service to nation Am. Coalition Patriotic Socs., 1967; Freedom Found. medal of honor, 1967; Gold medal Nat. Soc. New Eng. Women, 1969; Nat. Capital U.S.O. Distinguished Service certificate, 1968. Mem. Am. Friends of Lafayette, Hon. Soc. Ky. Cols., Ams. for Patriotism, Inc. (organizing past pres.), D.A.R. (pres. Nat. Officers Club 1978—). Club: Scarsdale Women's. Home: 10 Scarsdale Ave Scarsdale NY 10583. *To aid in promoting a sense of responsible citizenship through education. To do each task undertaken to the best of my ability. To endeavor to do unto others as I would have them do unto me. To have the satisfaction of having a young woman say she had been favorably influenced by me.*

SULLIVAN, BARBARA BOYLE, mgmt. cons.; b. Scranton, Pa., Apr. 12, 1937; d. Edmund F. and Mary R. (O'Connell) Boyle; B.S. in Bus. Adminstrn., Drexel U., 1958; Ph.D. (hon.), Newton Coll., 1975, Gwynedd Mercy Coll., Pa., 1975; m. John L. Sullivan, Jr. With IBM Corp., 1959-72, systems engring. mgr. Eastern and Central Europe, Vienna, 1967-70, mgmt. devel. mgr., 1970, mgr. spl. programs, 1970-71, sales mgr., asst. br. mgr., 1971-72; pres. Boyle/Kirkman Assos., N.Y.C., 1972—; trustee Equitable Gas Co.; cons. maj. corps. on human resource devel. programs and affirmative action programs, condr. exec. awareness seminars Harvard Bus. Sch., Internat. Mgmt. Conf., several nat. confs. on equal opportunity. Mem. pres.'s adv. com. Gwynedd Mercy Coll.; mem. adv. com. Coll. Bus. Adminstrn., Drexel U.; trustee Marymount Manhattan Coll., N.Y. Named Bus. Person of Year, St. Johns U., 1973; named to Drexel U. Hall of Fame. Featured in numerous mags., books, radio and TV programs, including Time mag. and CBS 60 Minutes. Mem. NOW, AAUW. Home: 16195 Greenwood Ln Los Gatos CA 95030 Office: 230 Park Ave New York NY 10017

SULLIVAN, CARL ROLLYNN, JR., assn. exec.; b. Marietta, Ohio, Feb. 20, 1926; s. Carl Rollynn and Grace Roberta (Bengel) S.; B.S. in Forestry, W.Va. U., 1950; M.S., Ohio State U., 1953; m. Dolores Marion Cortes, Sept. 12, 1950; children—Carl R., Michael D., Peter A. Asst. chief fish div. W.Va. Conservation Commn., 1951-55; land mgr., public relations mgr. Ravenswood Works, Kaiser Aluminum & Chem. Corp., 1955-62; exec. dir. W.Va. Centennial Commn., 1962-63; dir. Alaska Purchase Centennial, Anchorage, 1964-67; owner, mgr. Sullivan Services, Advt. and Public Relations, 1968-72; exec. sec. Sport Fishing Inst., 1972-75; exec. dir. Am. Fisheries Soc., Bethesda, Md., 1975—, editor Fisheries mag., 1976—. Served with U.S. Army, 1944-46. Mem. Am. Fisheries Soc., Wildlife Soc., Am. Soc. Assn. Execs., Council Engring. and Sci. Soc. Execs., Am. Oceanic Orgn., Izaak Walton League Am., Mason Dixon Outdoor Writers, Nat. Shellfish Assn., Renewable Natural Resource Found., Sport Fishing Research Found. Methodist. Contbr. articles to profl. jours. Home: Box 58 Rt 2 Charles Town WV 25414 Office: 5410 Grosvenor Ln Bethesda MD 20014

SULLIVAN, CHARLES ANDREW, investment co. exec.; b. Washington, Nov. 3, 1920; s. Michael Francis and Gertrude Lavinia (Miller) S.; student George Washington U., 1938-42, Cambridge U., 1943-44; m. Margaret Mary Bailer, Mar. 31, 1979. Comml. specialist Dept. Treasury, 1940-43; economist RFC, War Assets Adminstrn., 1946-48; internat. economist Munitions Bd., 1948-51; staff Office Sec. Def. for Internat. Security Affairs, 1951-57, chief Far East div., 1951-52, chief Western hemisphere, Far East and South Asian affairs, 1952-53, dir. Office Fgn. Politico-Mil. Policy, 1953-55, dir. Office Internat. Affairs, 1955-57; asst. dir. ODM, 1957-59; dep. spl. asst. to sec. of state for disarmament and atomic energy, 1959-60; spl. asst. to under sec. of state Dept. State, 1960-61; asst. to Sec. of Treasury, 1961-66; pres., chmn. bd. dirs. Hispano Corp. Am., 1967-71; pres. Charles A. Sullivan Assos., Inc., 1970—. Chmn. indsl. moblzn. com. NATO, 1950-51; def. adviser to delegations ANZUS, NATO and SEATO councils, 1952-57, fgn. minister's confs. in Berlin, 1954, Geneva, 1954, 55, 59, Summit Conf., Geneva, 1955, Tripartite Heads of Govts. Conf., Bermuda, 1957; mem. Presdl. Base Rights Survey Group, 1956-57. Served with U.S. Army, 1943-45. Home: Forge Run Farm Route 1 Box 19 Lovettsville VA 22080

SULLIVAN, DANIEL JOSEPH, mfg. co. exec.; b. Milw., Mar. 1, 1940; s. Joseph Daniel and Bernice Leone Sullivan; B.A., U. Wis., 1965, LL.B., 1969; m. Karen Jean Comte, Sept. 12, 1964; children—Daniel J., Michael J., Margaret A., Sean S., Erin M. Admitted to Wis. bar, 1969; with Monsanto Corp., St. Louis, 1969-72; dir. venture capital Page Mill Group, San Francisco, 1972—; pres. Savoy Industries, Inc., N.Y.C., 1974—, Hanover Capital Co., N.Y.C., 1974—, Nytronics, Inc., Phoenix, 1976—, Bastian Blessing Co., Phoenix, 1976—; dir., officer Empire of Carolina, N.Y.C.; dir. Change Wares Ltd., U.K., Audiotronics Holdings, U.K. Adv. bd. Mexican Mus., San Francisco. Mem. Am. Bar Assn., Wis. Bar Assn. Office: 633 Battery St Suite 612 San Francisco CA 94111

SULLIVAN, DANIEL JOSEPH, journalist; b. Worcester, Mass., Oct. 22, 1935; s. John Daniel and Irene (Flagg) S.; A.B., Holy Cross Coll., 1957; postgrad. U. Minn., 1957-59; U. So. Calif., 1964-65, Stanford U., 1978-79; m. Helen Faith Scheid, 1965; children—Margaret Ann, Benjamin, Kathleen. Reporter, Worcester (Mass.) Telegram, 1957, Red Wing (Minn.) Republican Eagle, 1959, St. Paul Pioneer Press, 1959-61; reporter Mpls. Tribune, 1962, drama and music critic, 1962-64; music writer N.Y. Times, 1965-66, asst. drama critic, 1966-68; drama critic Los Angeles Times, 1969—. Dramaturg, Eugene O'Neill Theater Center, 1972-73, mem. faculty, 1977-78. Mem. Los Angeles Drama Critics Circle (pres. 1970), Am. Theater Critics Assn. (dir. 1974-78). Office: Times-Mirror Sq Los Angeles CA 90053

SULLIVAN, DONALD, coll. pres.; b. Bklyn., Oct. 22, 1930; s. John T. and Catherine (Lane) S.; B.A., Fordham U.; M.A., N.Y. U.; Ph.D., St. John's U. Former asst. prof., dean students St. Francis Coll., Bklyn., now pres. Mem. Bklyn. Ednl. and Cultural Alliance, Commn. Ind. Colls. and Univs. Mem. C. of C. (dir.). Clubs: Brooklyn, Wheatley Hills Golf. Address: 180 Remsen St Brooklyn NY 11201

SULLIVAN, DONALD GEORGE, advt. agy. exec.; b. Davenport, Iowa, Mar. 11, 1941; s. Wayne B. and Georgia P. (Sickmon) S.; B.S., Northwestern U., 1963, M.B.A., 1965; m. Suzanne H. Hoskins, Feb. 1, 1964; children—Deborah Anne, Heather Joan, Patrick James. Brand mgr. Simoniz div. Texize, Chgo., 1965-67; v.p. Tatham-Laird & Kudner, Chgo., 1967-74; pres., chief exec. officer Botsford Ketchum, Inc., San Francisco, 1974—; dir. KMG Internat., Inc., Pitts. Mem. vestry St. John's Episcopal Ch., Ross, Calif. Mem. Am. Assn. Advt. Agencies, San Francisco Advt. Club. Home: 124 Upland Rd Kentfield CA 94904 Office: 55 Union St San Francisco CA 94111

SULLIVAN, EDWARD CUYLER, brewing co. exec.; b. Balt., Aug. 15, 1906; s. Charles Francis and Emma (Burgess) S.; B.A., Cath. U. Am., 1927; m. Eileen Flanigan, Apr. 20, 1936; 1 son, Pierce Edward. Trainee, then buyer Hutzler Bros., Balt., 1927-33; v.p. O'Neill's Dept. Store, Balt., 1933-41; dir. controls and operations Allied Stores Corp., N.Y.C., 1941-43; exec. v.p. Joskes Dept. Store, San Antonio, 1943-56; pres. Sterling Lindner Dept. Store, Cleve., 1956-59; pres. Wolff & Marx Dept. Store, San Antonio, 1959-65; pres., dir. Lone Star Brewing Co., San Antoniio, 1965—; dir. Merc. Bank & Trust, San Antonio. Pres. Tex. Brewers Inst. Pres., Research and Planning Council, San Antonio, 1963-65; pres. San Antonio Symphony Soc. Bd. dirs. Nat. council U.S.O., S.W. Found. Research and Edn.; v.p., bd. dirs. Tex. Tourist Council; bd. dirs. San Antonio-Air Force Community Council, San Antonio Livestock Expn.; trustee Our Lady of the Lake Coll. Recipient Golden Deeds award San Antonio Exchange Club, 1978. Clubs: San Antonio Argyle, San Antonio Country; Gibson Island (Gibson Island, Md.). Home: 700 E Hildebrand San Antonio TX 78212 Office: 600 Lone Star Blvd San Antonio TX 78297

SULLIVAN, EDWARD DANIEL, educator; b. Boston, Dec. 9, 1913; s. William Patrick and Ella Patience (Hackett) S.; grad. Phillips Exeter Acad., 1932; A.B. summa cum laude, Harvard, 1936, A.M., 1938, Ph.D., 1941; m. Eleanor Harrold, Sept. 15, 1940; children—Barry Michael, Brian Philip. Instr. French, Harvard, 1938-42, Radcliff Coll., 1941-42; asso. French, George Washington U., 1945-46; instr. French, Princeton, 1946-47, asst. prof., 1947-50, asso. prof., 1950-58, prof., chmn. dept. Romance langs. and lit., 1958-66, dean coll., 1966-72, Avalon prof. humanities, 1972—, chmn. council humanities, 1974—; cons. Am. Council Life Ins., Nat. Endowment for Humanities, Careers in Bus. Program. Served from ensign to lt. USNR, 1942-46, 50-51. Fulbright research scholar, Sorbonne, Paris, France, 1956-57; Decorated officier Palmes Academiques, chevalier Legion of Honor (France). Mem. Modern Lang. Assn. of Am., Am. Assn. Tchrs. French, Am. Council Life Ins. (chmn. univ. adv. council 1967—). Author: (editor with W. N. Locke) La Guerre Moderne, 1942; Maupassant the Novelist, 1954; Maupassant: The Short Stories, 1962. Editor: (with Albert Sonnenfield) Témoins de l'homme: nouvelles et récits (1889-1959), 1965—. Home: 475 Lake Dr Princeton NJ 08540

SULLIVAN, EDWARD GERALD, hotel exec.; b. Pocatello, Idaho, July 21; s. Gerald and Vella (Lockyer) S.; B.S. in Bus. Adminstrn., Idaho State U.; m. Phyllis J. Carlson, Aug. 12, 1949; children—Michael, Teresa Ann, Shauna Marie. With Sun Valley (Idaho) Ops. Co., 1950-55, Western Internat. Hotels, Seattle, 1955-62; with Hyatt Corp., 1962—, opened Hyatt Regency, Atlanta, 1966, Hyatt on Union Sq., San Francisco, 1971, Hyatt Regency Waikiki, Honolulu, 1976, corp. v.p., 1967—. Trustee Donald N. Pritzker Found. Served with USNR, 1944-46. Mem. Hawaii Hotel Assn. (dir.). Roman Catholic. Clubs: Skal, Olympic, Oahu, Outrigger Canoe. Address: 2424 Kalakaua St Honolulu HI 96815

SULLIVAN, EUGENE JOHN JOSEPH, mfg. co. exec.; b. N.Y.C., Nov. 28, 1920; s. Cornelius and Margaret (Smith) S.; B.S., St. John's U., 1942, D.Commerce, 1973; M.B.A., N.Y. U., 1948; m. Gloria Roesch, Aug. 25, 1943; children—Eugene John Joseph, Edward J., Robert C., Elizabeth Ann. With chem. div. Borden, Inc., N.Y.C., 1946—, beginning as salesman, successively asst. sales, 1957-58, exec. v.p., 1958-64, pres. Borden Chem. Co. div. Borden, Inc.; v.p. Borden, Inc., 1964-67; exec. v.p., 1967-73, pres., chief operating officer, 1973-79, chmn., pres., chief exec. officer, 1979—; dir. Borden Co., Borden Co. Ltd. of Eng., Bank of N.Y.; trustee Emigrant Savs. Bank, Atlantic Mut. Ins. Co.; adj. prof. St. John's U. Bd. dirs. St. Francis Hosp., Roslyn, N.Y.; trustee St. John's U.; bd. dirs. C.Y.O., N.Y.C. Served as lt. USNR, 1942-46; lt. Res. Mem. Mfg. Chem. Assn. (dir.), Soc. Plastics Industry (dir.), Knights of Malta, Knights of Holy Sephlecur. Clubs: University, Sky, Plandome Country, Manhasset Bay Yacht. Office: 277 Park Ave New York NY 10007

SULLIVAN, FRANCIS CHARLES, educator; b. Chgo., Jan. 14, 1927; s. Frank Colby and Mary Cecilia (Burke) S.; B.S., Loyola U., Chgo., 1947, J.D., 1949; LL.M., N.Y. U., 1961; m. Dolores Gray, June 11, 1955; children—Brian, Eugene, Laurence. Admitted to Ill. bar, 1950; partner firm McKinley, Price & Appleman, Chgo., 1949-56; prof. law Loyola U., Chgo., 1956-66; prof. La. State U., 1966—, asso. dean, 1970-77, dean, 1977—; disting. vis. prof. law U. Okla., 1979; dir. La. Jud. Coll.; cons. in field. Served with U.S. Army, 1945-46, 50-52. Named Papal Knight of Holy Sepulchre. Travel fellow, 1958-59; Ford Found. fellow, 1959-61. Mem. Baton Route Bar Assn., Chgo. Bar Assn., Ill. Bar Assn., La. Bar Assn., Am. Bar Assn. (recipient award 1978), Council La State Law Inst., Am. Law Inst. Roman Catholic. Clubs: City of Baton Rouge, Nat. Lawyers, N.Y. U. Alumni, Bocage, Camelot. Author: The Adminstration of Criminal Justice, 1965, 2d edit., 1968; Evidence, 1969; contbr. articles to profl. jours. Home: 1457 Pollard Pkwy Baton Rouge LA 70808 Office: Louisiana State University Law Center Baton Rouge LA 70803

SULLIVAN, FRANCIS COPELAND, lawyer; b. Duluth, Minn., July 17, 1902; s. Francis W. and Ellen (Copeland) S.; A.B., Georgetown U., 1924; LL.B., Harvard, 1927; m. Rosemary Kenney, Jan. 27, 1934; children—Ann (Mrs. Christopher Houghton), Judith (Mrs. Leonard A. Sarvela, Jr.), Christopher. Admitted to Minn. bar, 1928, since practiced in Duluth; counsel firm Hanft, Fride O'Brien & Harries and predecessor firms. Served to maj. AUS, 1942-46. Home: 3800 London Rd Duluth MN 55804 Office: Alworth Bldg Duluth MN 55802

SULLIVAN, FRANK E., life ins. co. exec.; b. Lowell, Mass., Aug. 17, 1923; s. William H. and Vera Sullivan; B.S., Notre Dame U., 1949; m. Colette Cleary, June 11, 1949; children—Frank E., Mary, Anne, Robert. Adminstrv. asst. to football coach Notre Dame U., 1946-52; gen. agt. Am. United Life Ins. Co., South Bend, Ind., 1953-74; pres. Mut. Benefit Life Ins. Co. N.J., 1977—; dir. St. Joseph Bank & Trust Co., South Bend, Clow Corp., Chgo.; pres. Million Dollar Round Table, 1967; panelist, lectr. in field. Past pres. South Bend United Fund, United Community Services South Bend, Health Found. No. Ind., St. Joseph County (Ind.) Urban Coalition. Served with USNR, World War II. C.L.U. Author: Delling Life Insurance for Deferred Compensation, 1962; Setting Goals for Million Dollar Production, 1968; The Critical Path to Sales Success, 1970. Past chmn. bd. editors C.L.U. Jour. Office: Mut Benefit Life Ins Co 520 Broad St Newark NJ 07101

SULLIVAN, FRED R., business exec.; b. Ft. Wayne, Ind., 1914; B.S. Rutgers U., 1938; M.B.A., N.Y. U., 1942; m.; children—Nancy, Judith, Fred A. Factory cost clk. Monroe Calculating Machine Co., 1934, advanced to pres., 1953 (co. merged with Litton Industries), sr. v.p. Litton, 1961-64; chief exec. officer, dir. Walter Kidde & Co., Inc., 1963—, pres., 1964—, chmn., chief exec. officer, 1966; dir. Sun Chem. Corp., N.Y.C., Dictaphone Corp., Rye, N.Y., Supermarkets Gen. Corp., Woodbridge, N.J. Midlantic Banks, Inc., West Orange, N.J., Midlantic Nat. Bank, Newark, Technicolor, Inc., Hollywood, Calif., Mass Mut. Corporate Investors, Inc., Springfield, Mass., City Investing Co., N.Y.C., Adobe Oil & Gas Corp., Midland, Tex., Becton, Dickinson & Co., Rutherford, N.J., Richton Internat. Corp., N.Y.C., Flintkote Co., Stamford, Conn.; trustee C.I. Realty Investors, Boston. Trustee Found. Coll. Medicine and Dentistry N.J., Newark, Newark Mus., Lenox Hill Hosp., N.Y.C.; adv. bd., policy com. Coalition Northeastern Govs.; bd. overseers Rutgers U. Found. Mem. N.J. State C. of C. Office: 9 Brighton Rd Clifton NJ 07015

SULLIVAN, GEORGE EDMUND, editorial and mktg. co. exec.; b. N.Y.C., Feb. 3, 1932; s. Timothy Daniel and Helen Veronica (Danaher) S.; B.A., Iona Coll., 1957; M.Ed., Rutgers U., 1961; Ed.D., Walden U., 1980; m. Carole Ann Hartz, Sept. 4, 1954; children—Patricia Lynn, George Edmund, Michael Frank. Tchr. English, Holmdel Twp. and Keyport (N.J.) Pub. Schs., 1957-62; field mgr. regional mktg. Harcourt, Brace & World, Inc., N.Y.C., 1962-69; v.p. sales Noble & Noble, Publishers, Inc., 1969-72, sr. v.p., chief exec. officer, 1972-78; pres. Sullivan Ednl. Assos., Inc., Long Branch, N.J., 1978—; ednl. mktg. cons. Hammond, Inc. 4-H leader, 1957-59. Served with USAF, 1950-52. Mem. Assn. Am. Publishers (ofcl. rep. 1972—), Keyport Edn. Assn. (pres. 1960-62). Author: The Hammond Reading Skills Series; Proficiency in Written English; The English Sentence and Paragraph. Home: 325 Bath Ave Long Branch NJ 07740. *The world is full of people who don't really care. Any person who chooses a worthy activity and really cares about doing it the right way, the best way, the most perfect way despite all adversity, will succeed. Really caring is the fuel that generates miracles.*

SULLIVAN, GEORGE MURRAY, mayor Anchorage; b. Portland, Oreg., Mar. 31, 1922; s. Harvey Patrick and Viola (Murray) S.; student pub. schs.; m. Margaret Eagan, Dec. 30, 1946; children—Timothy M., Harvey P., Daniel A., Kevin Shane, Colleen Marie, Georrge, Michael J., Shannon Margaret, Casey Eagan. Line driver Alaska Freight Lines, Inc., Valdez-Fairbanks, 1942-44; U.S. dep. marshal Alaska Dist., Nenana, 1946-52; mgr. Alaska Freight Lines, 1952-56; Alaska gen. mgr. Consol. Freightways Corp. of Del., Anchorage, 1956-67; mayor of Anchorage, 1967—; exec. mgr. Alaska Bus. Council, 1968; dir. 1st Fed. Savs. & Loan, Alaska Internat. Air, Inc.; mem. Nat. Adv. Com. on Oceans and Atmosphere, 1975—; mem. Joint Fed.-State Land Use Planning Commn.; chmn. 4-state region 10 adv. com. OEO; Fairbanks City Council, 1955-59, Anchorage City Council, 1965-67; mem. Greater Anchorage Borough Assembly, 1965-67; mem. Alaska Ho. of Reps., 1964-65. Bd. dirs. Western council Boy Scouts Am., 1958-59. Served with U.S. Army, 1944-46. Mem. Nat. Def. Transp. Assn. (life mem., pres. 1962-63), Nat. League Cities (dir.), Pioneers of Alaska, Alaska Mcpl. League (past pres.), Anchorage C. of C. (exec. com. 1963-65, treas. 1965-66, dir.), Alaska Carriers Assn. (exec. com.), Alaska Transp. Conf. (chmn.), Q.M. Assn., VFW (comdr. Alaska 1952). Club: Elks. Home: 1345 12th Ave Anchorage AK 99501 Office: Office of Mayor 524 W 4th Ave Anchorage AK 99501 also Pouch 6-650 Anchorage AK 99502. *America is truly the land of opportunity, and I feel that the success with which God has blessed my life attests to this fact. I have been twice blessed. Not only was I born in America, but I have lived my life in Alaska.*

SULLIVAN, GEORGE RAYMOND, lawyer; b. Stevens Point, Wis., May 23, 1908; s. Eugene J. and Margaret (Thielen) S.; B.S. in Law, Northwestern U., 1931, J.D., 1935; m. Margaret V. Kilroy, Jan. 6, 1945 (dec. May 1971); children—Mark Eugene, Michael Peter; m. 2d, Dorothy Failer Binyon, Aug. 31, 1975. Admitted to Ill. bar, 1935, Ohio bar, 1947; with Addressograph Multigraph Corp., Cleve., 1935-72, sec., 1961-72, v.p., 1965-72; practice law, Cleve., 1972—. Mem. Cleve. Com. on Fgn. Relations. Served to maj. USAAF, 1942-46. Mem. Am., Ohio, Cleve. bar assns., Am. Soc. Corp. Secs., First Cleve. Cav. Assn., Alpha Sigma Phi, Phi Alpha Delta. Home: 2618 W Park Blvd Shaker Heights OH 44120 Office: 3570 Warrensville Center Rd Shaker Heights OH 44122

SULLIVAN, GEORGE WILLIAM, JR., business exec.; b. Medford, Mass., Sept. 22, 1932; s. George William and Helen Dixon S.; B.S.B.A., Boston U., 1954; m. Sylvia Anne Caron, July 2, 1955; children—Tracy Anne, Susan Elizabeth, Michael Joseph. With Collins-Rockwell Internat., 1959-79, pres. Comml. Telecommunications Group, 1974-79; pres., chief exec. officer No. Telecom, Inc., Nashville, 1979—. Dir., So. Meth. U. Found. for Bus. Adminstrn.; nat. dir. exec. com. Dallas Symphony Orch., vice chmn., 1975-79. Served with U.S. Army, 1955-59. Mem. Nat. Alliance of Bus. (chmn. metro Dallas 1975-77, nat. dir. 1977-79). Named Citizen of Day award Dallas, 1978, Citizen of Day award Dallas County, 1978. Mem. Electronic Industries Assn. (past chmn., now gov. communications div.). Club: Bent Tree Country (Addison, Tex.). Home: 5840 Meadowcreek Dr Dallas TX 75248 Office: International Plaza Nashville TN 37217

SULLIVAN, GLENN RAY, ret. air force officer, assn. exec.; b. McCaysville, Ga., June 5, 1923; s. James William and Minnie (Nichols) S.; student Young Harris Coll., 1940-41; m. Jaunita Nadine Miller, May 5, 1946; 1 son, Glenn Ray. Commd. 2d lt. USAAF, 1944, advanced through grades to brig. gen. USAF, 1972; asst. dep. chief of staff for operations 15th Air Force, 1968-69; comdr. 22d Bomb Wing, SAC, 1970-72, comdr. 17th Air Div., Thailand, 1972-73; comdr. Aerospace Rescue and Recovery Service, MAC, Scott AFB, Ill., 1973-74, ret., 1976; exec. dir. Okaloosa County United Way, Ft. Walton Beach, Fla., 1976—. Decorated D.S.M. with oak leaf cluster, Legion of Merit, Air medal with 2 oak leaf clusters. Mem. Jolly Green Pilots, Air Force Assn., Ret. Officers Assn., Order Daedalians. Club: Kiwanis. Home: 583 Mooney Rd Ft Walton Beach FL 32548 Office: 105 Santa Rosa Blvd Fort Walton Beach FL 32548

SULLIVAN, HAROLD JOSEPH, lawyer; b. Maysville, Okla., Nov. 26, 1909; s. Dr. Ernest and Mary Queen (Colley) S.; A.B., Washington and Lee U., 1932; LL.B., U. Okla., 1935; LL.M., Georgetown U., 1949; grad. Judge Adv. Gen. Sch., 1943; m. Mabel Gurney Wilkes, Apr. 14, 1949; children—Linda Alcott, Gurney Bartlett, Harold Joseph, Stewart Jeffress. Admitted to Okla. bar, 1935, U.S. Supreme Ct., 1947, Republic of Korea bar, 1954; practice of law, Oklahoma City, 1935-42, 65—; commd. 2d lt. U.S. Army, advanced through grades to col. USAF, 1952; judge. adv. Fifth Air Force and Far East Air Forces, 1943-45; chmn. bd. rev. Judge Adv. Gen., USAF, 1948-51, staff judge adv. Eighth Air Force, 1951-53, Fifth Air Force, Korea, 1954, Mobile Air Materiel Area, 1955-58, Eastern Air Def. Force, 1958-60, Oklahoma City Air Materiel Area, 1960-65; ret. 1965. Decorated Bronze Star. Fellow Am. Bar. Found.; mem. Am. (chmn. com. Am. Citizenship 1958, mem. com. continuing edn. 1958-59, 63-68, 74-80, ho. of dels. 1976-78), Okla. (bd. govs. 1968, exec. dir. 1969-75, dir. continuing legal edn. 1975-77) bar assns., Am. Law Inst., Beta Theta Pi, Phi Delta Phi. Democrat. Baptist. Clubs: Army and Navy (Washington); Men's Dinner; Beacon. Home: 800 NW 40th St Oklahoma City OK 73118

SULLIVAN, HENRY PAUL, utility exec., lawyer; b. Ambler, Pa., Aug. 5, 1925; s. Jeremiah John and Dorothy (Stark) S.; B.S. in Econs., U. Pa., 1948, LL.B., 1951; m. Joan Grosvenor Blair, Jan. 2, 1954; children—Jeremiah John IV, Graham Grosvenor, Henry Paul. Admitted to Pa. bar, 1952; asst. counsel Phila. Electric Co., 1951-56, asst. gen. counsel, 1959-67; asst. U.S. atty., Phila., 1957-59; asst. gen. counsel Consol. Natural Gas Co., Pitts., 1967-69, gen. counsel, 1969—, v.p., 1971—; trustee Dollar Savs. Bank, Pitts., 1973—. Served to lt. (j.g.) USNR, 1943-46. Mem. Navy League U.S. (pres., dir. Phila. council 1965-67), Am. (mem. council pub. utility law sect. 1970-73), Pa., Allegheny County, Fed. Energy bar assns., Am. Gas Assn. (chmn. legal com. 1975-78), NAM, Sphinx Honor Soc. Clubs: Allegheny Country, Edgeworth (Sewickley); Merion Cricket (Haverford); Bras d'Or Yacht (N.S.); Mask and Wig (U. Pa., chmn. undergrad. club). Home: 609 Academy Ave Sewickley PA 15143 Office: 4 Gateway Center Pittsburgh PA 15222

SULLIVAN, HERBERT PATRICK, educator; b. Detroit, May 27, 1932; s. Herbert Luke and Gertrude Lennie (Hosking) S.; student Highland Park (Mich.) Coll. 1949-50, N.Mex. Highlands U., 1950-51; B.D., U. Chgo., 1956, Ph.D., U. Durham (Eng.), 1960; m. Joyce Ann Robinson, June 24, 1960; children—Bridget Mary Magdalene, Siobhan Marie Clare. Research asst. Indsl. Relations Center, U. Chgo., 1951-54; research scholar Sch. Oriental Studies, U. Durham, 1956-60; instr. religion Duke U., 1960-62, asst. prof., 1962-64, asso. prof., 1964-70; prof. Vassar Coll., 1970—, dean faculty, 1978—. Fulbright-Hays fellow, 1965-66. Fellow Royal Asiatic Soc.; mem. Am. Oriental Soc., Am. Soc. Study of Religion, Internat. Congress Orientalists, Internat. Assn. History of Religions. Contbr. to Ency. Brit., contbr. chpts. to books and articles to profl. jours. Home: The Dean's House Vassar College Poughkeepsie NY 12601 Office: Box 4 Vassar College Poughkeepsie NY 12601

SULLIVAN, JAMES FRANCIS, educator, physician; b. Peoria, Ill., Feb. 17, 1924; s. James Francis and Edna (Burkey) S.; B.S., Eureka Coll., 1949; M.D., St. Louis U., 1951; m. Jean Heighway, June 3, 1944; children—James, Mary, Patrick, Terrence, Margaret, Anne, Andrew. Mem. faculty St. Louis U., 1955-61, asst. prof. clin. medicine, 1959-61; mem. faculty Creighton U., Omaha, 1961—, prof. medicine, 1964—, asst. chmn. dept. medicine, 1961-69, acting chmn., 1969-72; chief medicine Omaha VA Hosp., 1966—. Fellow A.C.P.; mem. Central Soc. for Clin. Research, Am. Inst. Nutrition, Alpha Omega Alpha. Contbr. articles profl. jours. Home: 5212 Webster St Omaha NE 68132

SULLIVAN, JAMES FRANCIS, univ. adminstr.; b. Pitts., Sept. 15, 1930; s. Francis P. and Leona C. (Patterson) S.; B.A., Dartmouth Coll., 1953; M.S., U. Colo., 1956; Ph.D., U. Pitts., 1965; m. M. Carol Rea, Sept. 10, 1955; children—Leslie Ann, Daniel Paul. Asst. city mgr., Monterey, Calif., 1957-60; city mgr., Ojai, Calif., 1960-62; asst. prof. U. Pitts., 1962-66; vice-chancellor U. Calif. at Riverside, 1966-74, asso. prof. Grad. Sch. Adminstrn., 1970-78, asso. dir. Dry Lands Research Inst., 1974-78; vice chancellor U. Calif. at Davis, 1978—. Served with USAF, 1954-55. Mem. Am. Soc. for Public Adminstrn. Home: 612 Marina Circle Davis CA 95616

SULLIVAN, JAMES H., artist; b. Providence, Apr. 1, 1939; s. James Henry, Jr. and Frances Winifred (Welch) S.; B.F.A., R.I. Sch. Design, 1961; postgrad., Stanford, 1962-63. One-man shows Paley and Lowe Gallery, N.Y.C., 1971, 73, Henri Gallery, Washington, 1974, Fischback Gallery, N.Y.C., 1974, Willard Gallery, 1978; exhibited in group shows including Whitney Mus., Mus. Modern Art, Columbus Gallery Fine Arts, Worcester Art Mus.; asso. prof. art Bard Coll., Annandale-on-Hudson, N.Y., 1966—. Recipient Hinda and Richard Rosenthal award Am. Acad. Arts and Letters, 1973; Stanford grantee, 1962-63; R.I. Sch. Design European Honors program, Rome, 1960-61; Fulbright fellow, Paris, 1961-62; Guggenheim fellow, 1972-73. Home: 59 Wooster St New York City NY 10013 Office: care Bard College Annandale on Hudson NY 12504

SULLIVAN, JAMES HALL, hosp. adminstr.; b. Glasgow, Scotland, Oct. 27, 1918; s. James Hall and Joana (Macgonigal) S.; came to U.S., 1923, naturalized, 1933; B.A., Mich. State U., 1950; M. Hosp. Adminstrn., U. Mich., 1957; m. Pantha June Selsor, Dec. 18, 1971; children by previous marriage—E. Sonja, James Hall, Norman C., Nancy C. Adminstr. McPherson Community Health Center, Howell, Mich., 1951-65; coordinator health facilities mgmt. program Mich. State U., 1965-67; asso. coordinator Wis. Regional Med. Program, 1967-71; adminstr. Max C. Starkloff Hosp., St. Louis, 1971—; lectr. Washington U. Sch. Medicine, St. Louis, 1971—; adj. prof. medicine Lindenwood Coll., 1976—. Mem. President's Commn. on Aging, 1962-66. Bd. dirs. Found. Preservation Health, Aid to Victims of Violent Crime. Served with USNR, 1941-45. Mem. Am. Coll. Hosp. Adminstrs., Mo. Hosp. Assn. Mason. Author: The McPherson Experiment, 1969. Home: 5670 Arsenal St St Louis MO 63139 Office: 1515 Lafayette St St Louis MO 63104

SULLIVAN, JAMES LENOX, clergyman; b. Silver Creek, Miss., Mar. 12, 1910; s. James Washington and Mary Ellen (Dampeer) S.; B.A., Miss. Coll., 1932, D.D., 1948; Th.M., So. Bapt. Theol. Sem., 1935; m. Velma Scott, Oct. 22, 1935; children—Mary Beth (Mrs. Bob R. Taylor), Martha Lynn (Mrs. James M. Porch, Jr.), James David. Ordained to ministry of Baptist Ch., 1930; pastor, Baptist Ch., Boston, Ky., 1932-33, Beaver Dam, Ky., 1933-38, Ripley, Tenn., 1938-40, Clinton, Miss., 1940-42, First Bapt. Ch., Brookhaven, Miss., 1942-46, Belmont Heights, Nashville, 1946-50, Abilene, Tex., 1950-53; exec. sec., treas. Bapt. Sunday Sch. Bd., Nashville, 1953-73, pres., 1973-75; exec. sec. Broadman Press, 1953-75, Convention Press, 1955-75; pres. So. Bapt. Conv., 1976—. Trustee Union U., Cumberland U., So. Bapt. Theol. Sem., Hardin-Simmons U., Midstate (Tenn.) Bapt. Hosp., Hendrick Meml. Hosp. (Tex.). Recipient E.Y. Mullins Denominational Service award, 1973. Mem. Baptist World Alliance (exec. com., v.p., 1975—). Clubs: Rotary (Ripley, Tenn.); Lions (Brookhaven, Miss.); Kiwanis (Abilene, Tex.). Author: Your Life and Your Church, 1950; John's Witness of Jesus; Memos for Christian Living; Reach Out; Rope of Sand with Strength of Steel; God Is My Record. Contbr. articles to religious publs. Address: PO Box 167 Hermitage TN 37076

SULLIVAN, JAMES LEO, city adminstr.; b. Somerville, Mass., Dec. 11, 1925; s. James Christopher and Anna Agnes (Kilmartin) S.; B.S. in History and Govt. cum laude, Boston Coll., 1950, M.Ed. in Adminstrn. and Fin., 1958; m. Anne Dorothy Hevner, Jan. 20, 1951; children—Maura, Mark, Lianne, Christopher. Asst. town mgr. Town of Arlington (Mass.), 1957-62; town mgr. Town of Watertown (Conn.), 1962-65; chief adminstrv. officer Town of Milton (Mass.), 1965-68; city mgr. City of Cambridge (Mass.), 1968-70, 74—, City of Lowell (Mass.), 1970-74; sr. research asst. M.I.T., 1970-71; chmn. Mass. Gov.'s Local Govt. Adv. Com., 1978; del. to Orgn. Econ. and Cooperative Devel., Paris, 1979. Served with USN, 1943-46. Mem. Mass. League of Cities and Towns (pres. 1978), Mass. Mayors Assn., Internat. City Mgmt. Assn., Nat. League Cities. Home: 28 Rindo Park Dr Lowell MA 01851 Office: 795 Massachusetts Ave Cambridge MA 02139

SULLIVAN, JAMES PATRICK, opera exec.; b. Binghamton, N.Y., Sept. 4, 1936; s. Patrick Joseph and Ellen S.; student Le Moyne Coll., 1954-55, Syracuse U., 1956, Harpur Coll., 1957-59; B.Mus. cum laude, M.Mus., Ithaca Coll.; m. Marilyn Scaff, Dec. 14, 1975; children—Julian, Katherine, Peadar. Founder, gen. dir. Ariz. Opera Co., Tucson, 1971—; guest condr. San Diego Ballet. Served with USAR, 1957. Home: 4001 E 4th St Tucson AZ 85711 Office: 412 N 6th Ave Tucson AZ 95705*

SULLIVAN, JAMES STEPHEN, bishop, Roman Catholic Ch.; b. Kalamazoo, July 23, 1929; s. Stephen James and Dorothy Marie (Bernier) S.; ed. St. Joseph Sem,; B.A., Sacred Heart Sem.; postgrad. St. John Provincial Sem. Ordained priest Roman Catholic Ch., 1955; asso. pastor St. Luke Ch., Flint, Mich., 1955-58, St. Mary Cathedral, Lansing, Mich., 1958-60; sec. to bishop, 1960-61; asso. pastor St. Joseph Ch., St. Joseph, Mich., 1961-65; sec. to bishop, 1965-69; asso. pastor, Lansing, 1965; vice chancellor, 1969-72; consecrated bishop, 1972; aux. bishop, vicar gen. Diocese of Lansing, 1972—, diocesan consultor, 1971—; now pastor St. Thomas Aquinas Parish, East Lansing, Mich. Mem. Nat. Conf. Cath. Bishops (bishop's liturgical commn.). Home: 955 Alton Rd East Lansing MI 48823 Office: 300 W Ottawa St Lansing MI 48933

SULLIVAN, JEREMIAH DAVID, physicist, educator; b. Norwood, Mass., Nov. 15, 1938; s. Jeremiah Francis and Doris Ellen (Nutton) S.; B.S., Carnegie Inst. Tech., 1960; M.A. (NSF fellow), Princeton, Ph.D. (NSF fellow), 1964; m. Mary Sheila Bonar, June 12, 1962; children—Maureen Elizabeth, Jeremiah James. Research asso. Stanford Linear Accelerator Center, 1964-67, acting asst. prof. Stanford, 1966-67; asst. prof. physics U. Ill., Urbana, 1967-69, asso. prof., 1969-73, prof., 1973—; cons. in field. A.P. Sloan Research fellow, 1968-70; mem. high energy physics advisory panel ERDA, 1975-78. Mem. Am. Phys. Soc., Am. Assn. Physics Tchrs., Fedn. Am. Scientists, Sigma Xi. Contbr. numerous articles to profl. jours. Home: 604 Burkwood Ct E Urbana IL 61801 Office: Physics Dept U of Ill Urbana IL 61801

SULLIVAN, BROTHER JEREMIAH STEPHEN, coll. pres.; b. Boston, June 25, 1920; s. John Joseph and Bridget Claire (Quirke) S.; B.A., Catholic U. Am., 1943, S.T.L., 1957, S.T.D., 1959; M.A. in Classics, Manhattan Coll., 1950; M.A. in Philosophy, Boston Coll., 1955; LL.D. (hon.), La Salle Coll., 1979. Tchr., St. Peters High Sch., S.I., N.Y., 1943-48, St. Marys High Sch., Waltham, Mass., 1948-53; instr. theology and classics De La Salle Coll., Washington, 1953-59; asst. prof. theology Manhattan Coll., N.Y.C., 1959-63, asso. prof., 1963, acad. v.p., 1963-70, exec. v.p., provost, 1970-75, pres., 1975—. Mem. Coll. Theology Soc. (dir., nat. treas. 1960-71), Cath. Theol. Soc. Am., Cath. Bibl. Assn., Nat. Cath. Ednl. Assn., Am. Assn. Higher Edn., AAUP, Phi Beta Kappa, Delta Mu Delta. Contbr. articles to profl. jours. Address: Manhattan Coll New York City NY 10471

SULLIVAN, JOAN WILSON, TV producer; d. John Harlan and Esther (Stanton) Wilson; student Grinnell Coll.; B.A., U. Wis.; D.F.A. (hon.), Salem (Mass.) State Coll., 1979, Grinnell Coll., 1980; m. Jeremy Brett, Nov. 22, 1977; children—Caleb, Rebekah. Producer, Sta. WGBH-TV, Boston, 1967—, producer nat. series Mystery!, 1980—, Classic Theatre: The Humanities in Drama, 1975-76, Masterpiece Theatre, 1973—, Piccadilly Circus, 1976-77, weekly series Elliot Norton Revs., 1971-74, nat. spl. Growing Up Female, 1974, local spl. To Be Irish in Boston, 1974, local series Kitchen Sync, 1973; asso. producer nat. spl. Godspell Goes to Plimoth Plantation for Thanksgiving with Henry Steele Commager, 1972, nat. series on art Eye to Eye, 1971; asso. project dir., producer, actress nat. radio series The WGBH Radio Drama Development Project, 1967-69; charter mem. com. Harvard Theatre Collection. Recipient (as series producer for Masterpiece Theatre) 9 Emmy awards, Christopher award, Peabody award. Mem. AFTRA, Nat. Acad. TV Arts and Scis., Am. Film Inst., NOW. Unitarian-Universalist. Office: WGBH-TV 125 Western Ave Boston MA 02134

SULLIVAN, JOHN, JR., architect; b. Cin., Aug. 25, 1912; s. John Lawrence and Catherine (Finnerty) S.; student Univ. Sch., Cleve., 1930-31; B.Arch., Cornell U., 1936; M.Arch., Mass. Inst. Tech., 1938; m. Frances Law Pogue Ricketts, 1943; children—Frances Law Pogue, Stephanie Spahr. Archtl. staff Frederick W. Garber, Cin., Russ & Harrison, Indpls., to 1950; partner W. Ray Yount & John Sullivan Jr., architects and engrs., Dayton, Ohio (became Yount, Sullivan & Lecklider, 1956, Sullivan, Lecklider, & Jay), 1950-76; projects include terminal bldg. and facilities James M. Cox Dayton Municipal Airport, 1961, Charles F. Kettering Meml. Hosp., Dayton; Library, Two dormitories, Student Center at Wright State U., 1969-73. Trustee Dayton Art Inst., 1955—, pres. bd. trustees, 1957-68; trustee Grandview Hosp., 1963-66; bd. dirs. Living Art Center, Dayton Found.; sec., asst. treas. Ednl. and Music Arts, Inc.; chmn. Patterson Meml. Center Commn., Dayton; council Cornell U. Mem. AIA (treas. Dayton 1948, pres. 1949-51), Montgomery County Hist. Soc. (sec. 1967, now chmn. bd.), Gargoyle, Phi Delta Theta, Tau Beta Pi. Clubs: Engineers (Dayton); Cincinnati Country; Buzfuz, Racquet, Miami Valley Hunt and Polo (Dayton). Home: 1500 Runnymede Rd Dayton OH 45419 Office: 1395 Winters Tower Dayton OH 45423

SULLIVAN, JOHN DANIEL, publisher, assn. exec.; b. Boston, June 26, 1929; s. John G. and Mary (Moriarty) S.; A.B., Boston Coll., 1950; M.Ed., Mass. State Coll., 1954; D.Ed., Harvard U., 1960; m. Virginia M. Callahan, July 25, 1959. Tchr., Boston Pub. Schs., 1951-54; dir. curriculum Walpole (Mass.) Pub. Schs., 1954-59; dir. New Eng. Office, NEA, 1959-67, exec. pub., Washington, 1967—; dir. Gt. Plains Nat. ITV Library, Rainbow, Inc. Mem. Mag. Pubs. Assn., Am. Soc. Assn. Execs., Nat. Assn. Ednl. Broadcasters, NAACP, Nat. Assn. for Bilingual Edn., Am. Advt. Fedn., Assn. for Supervision and Curriculum Devel., Ednl. Press Assn. Am., Nat. Cath. Edn. Assn., Nat. Press Club, Phi Delta Kappa. Democrat. Roman Catholic. Clubs: Capitol, Cummaquid Golf. Publisher, Todays Edn., 1967—. Home: 3001 Veazey Terr NW Washington DC 20008 Office: 1201 16th St NW Room 714 Washington DC 20822

SULLIVAN, JOHN EDWARD, surgeon; b. Spangle, Wash., May 21, 1900; s. M.H. and Alice (Meagher) S.; student U. Wash.; M.D., Columbia, 1927; m. Gretchen Brehm, 1926; 1 dau., Anne. Intern, Mary Imogene Bassett Hosp., Cooperstown, N.Y., 1927; intern Bellevue Hosp., N.Y.C., 1928-30, now vis. surgeon; fellow surgery Hosp. Ruptured and Crippled, N.Y.C., 1930-32; instr. surgery Columbia, 1932-36; attending surgeon Hosp. Spl. Surgery; instr. surgery N.Y. U.- Bellevue Med. Coll.; cons. surgery V.A. Hosp., Kingsbridge N.Y.C.; attending surgeon Fifth Ave. Hosp., St. Vincents Hosp.; asso. clin. prof. surgery N.Y. Med. Coll., 1949-56, N.Y. U., 1956—; mem. staff as asst. surgeon New York Hosp.; cons. surgeon Bellevue Hosp., Hosp. for Spl. Surg. Mem. bd. dirs. Doctors Hosp., 1953-67. Chmn. bd. Am. Rehab. Com. to 1956, pres., 1956—. Served as col. AUS, World War II. Decorated Legion of Merit. Diplomate Am. Bd. Surgery. Fellow Am. Assn. Surgery of Trauma; mem. AMA, N.Y. Surg. Soc., Soc. U.S. Med. Cons. World War II, Pan-Pacific Surg. Soc., Aerospace Med. Assn. Contbr. articles to med. jours. Home: 137 E 66th St New York City NY 10021 Office: 121 E 60th St New York City NY 10022

SULLIVAN, JOHN FRANCIS, lawyer; b. Omaha, Apr. 25, 1914; s. John Lawrence and Elizabeth (Coyne) S.; student No. Ariz. U. and U. Ariz., 1932-35; J.D., Georgetown Law Sch., 1939; m. Anne Evelyn Fisher, Sept. 25, 1939; children—Frances (Mrs. David Areghini), John Joseph, Kevin Lawrence, Mark. Examiner, U.S. Housing Authority, 1937-40; admitted to Ariz. bar, 1940, also U.S. Supreme Ct.; practice in Phoenix, 1940—; mem. firm Sullivan & Sullivan, 1940-42; dep. county atty., Maricopa County, 1942; reporter of decisions Supreme Ct. Ariz., 1946-47; partner Sullivan, Mahoney and Tang and predecessor firm, 1965-77; judge pro tem Superior Ct. of Ariz., 1973—; commr. superior ct.; mem. Citizens Criminal Justice Planning Advisory Commn., 1973-77. Commr., Housing Authority, Phoenix, 1950-52, 67-70; chmn. Urban Renewal Commn., 1957-59; mem. Employment Security Commn. Ariz., 1966-67. Councilman, Phoenix City Council, 1952-56. Bd. dirs. St. Monica's Hosp., 1946-49; mem. adv. bd. St. Joseph's Sch. Nursing. Served to lt. USNR, 1942-45. Mem. Am., Ariz., Maricopa bar assns., Res. Officers Assn., DAV, VFW. Democrat. Roman Catholic. K.C. (past state dep.). Clubs: Serra (past internat. trustee), Arizona. Home: 1616 W Flower Circle S Phoenix AZ 85015 Office: 201 W Jefferson St Phoenix AZ 85003

SULLIVAN, JOHN FRANCIS, JR., shipbldg. co. exec.; b. Pasco, Wash., June 23, 1924; s. John Francis and Ellen Elizabeth (Makins) S.; B.S. in Chem. Engring., U. Wash., 1945, M.S., 1949; m. Glenna Jane McIlraith, June 18, 1949; children—John Kelly, Thomas Kevin, Mary Elizabeth. Various positions Gen. Electric, N.Y.C., Schenectady and Bridgeport, Conn., 1949-66, mgr. advanced systems group, 1966-68; pres. E.F. Houghton Co., Phila., 1968-72; exec. v.p. ops. Hayes Albion Co., Jackson, Mich., 1972-75; pres., chief exec. officer Bath Iron Works Corp. (Maine), 1975—; dir. Canal Nat. Bank. Bd. dirs. Mich. Space Center, 1973-75, Shipbuilders Council Am., Am. Bur. Shipping, Maine Maritime Mus., Maine Maritime Acad., Bath Meml. Hosp.; mem. exec. bd. Pine Tree council Boy Scouts Am.; U.S. Savs. Bonds vol. chmn. State of Maine; Maine chmn. Nat. Com. for Employer Support of Guard and Res. Served to lt. (j.g.) USNR, 1943-46; PTO. Mem. Licensing Exec. Soc. (charter), Soc. Automotive Engrs. (gov. bd. Detroit 1974-75), Soc. Naval Architects and Marine Engrs., Am. Soc. Naval Engrs., Navy League U.S., Brunswick C. of C. (dir.). Home: High Head South Harpswell ME 04079 Office: Bath Iron Works Corp 700 Washington St Bath ME 04530

SULLIVAN, JOHN JOSEPH, bishop; b. Horton, Kans., July 5, 1920; s. Walter P. and Mary (Berney) S.; student Kenrick Sem., St. Louis, 1941-44. Ordained priest Roman Catholic Ch., 1944; parish priest Archdiocese of Oklahoma City, 1944-61; nat. dir. extension lay vols. Extension Soc., Chgo., 1961-68; parish priest, Tulsa, 1968-72; bishop Diocese of Grand Island (Nebr.), 1972-77, of Kansas City-St. Joseph, Mo., 1977—. Vice pres. Extension Soc., Chgo. Address: PO Box 1037 Kansas City MO 64141*

SULLIVAN, JOHN LAWRENCE, lawyer; b. Manchester, N.H., June 16, 1899; s. Patrick Henry and Ellen J. (Harrington) S.; A.B., Dartmouth 1921, LL.D., 1949; LL.B., Harvard, 1924; LL.D., Duquesne U., 1948, U. N.H., 1949, Loyola U., 1949, U. Portland (Ore.); m. Priscilla Manning, Dec. 28, 1932; children—Patricia, Charles Manning, Deborah. Admitted to N.H. bar, 1923, and began practice in Manchester, 1924, as mem. firm Sullivan & White; county solicitor, Hillsborough Co., 1929-33; partner Sullivan & Sullivan, 1930, became sole owner, 1931; now sr. partner Sullivan & Wynot, Manchester, N.H., also Sullivan & Beauregard, Washington; dir. emeritus Nat. Savs. & Trust Co. Apptd. asst. to commr. of internal revenue, 1939; asst. sec. of treasury, 1940-44; asst. sec. Navy for Air, 1945; undersec. of navy, 1946-47; sec. of navy, 1947-49. Trustee Daniel Webster council Boy Scouts Am., hon. mem. nat. council; trustee Naval Hist. Found. Served with U.S. Navy, 1918. Mem. D.C., N.H. bar assns., Navy League of the U.S. (dir.), Am. Legion (comdr. N.H. Dept. 1937), Chi Phi, Delta Sigma Rho. Democrat. Roman Catholic. K.C. Clubs: Clover (Boston); Burning Tree (Bethesda, Md.); Chevy Chase (Md.); Metropolitan (Washington). Home: 1330 Union St Manchester NH 03104 also 4871 Glenbrook Rd Washington DC 20016 Office: 875 Elm St Manchester NH 03104 also 1800 M St NW Suite 925 Washington DC 20036

SULLIVAN, JOHN MCGRATH, govt. ofcl.; b. Bklyn., Dec. 18, 1924; s. Eugene L. and Marguerite (McGrath) S.; B.S. in Engring., U.S. Naval Acad., 1946; m. Mary Maxine Williamson, 1946; children—Stephen F., M. Karen, James E., Louann, J. David, Joseph M. Commd. 2d lt. U.S. Navy, 1946; resigned, 1954; sales engr. Dollin Corp., Irvington, N.J., 1954-61; founder, pres. John M. Sullivan Co., Jenkintown, Pa., 1961-77; pres., owner Haug Die Casting Corp., Kenilworth, N.J., 1969-77; adminstr. Fed. R.R. Adminstrn., Dept. Transp., Washington, 1977—. Mem. Soc. Die Casters. Democrat. Roman Catholic. Club: Racquet (Phila.). Office: Room 5424 Nassif Bldg 400 7th St SW Washington DC 20590*

SULLIVAN, JOHN PATRICK, educator; b. Liverpool, Eng., July 13, 1930; s. Daniel and Alice (Long) S.; B.A., St. John's Coll., Cambridge (Eng.) U., 1955, M.A., 1957; M.A., Oxford (Eng.) U., 1957; m. Mary Frances Rock, July 20, 1954 (div. 1963); m. 2d, Judith Patrice Eldridge, Apr. 7, 1967 (div. Apr. 1972); m. 3d, Judith Lee Godfrey, Apr. 21, 1973. Came to U.S., 1961. Jr. research fellow Queen's Coll., Oxford U., 1954, fellow, tutor classics Lincoln Coll., 1955-62, dean, 1960-61; vis. prof. U. Tex., 1961-62, asso. prof. classics, 1962-63, prof. classics, 1963-69, chmn. dept. 1963-65; sr. fellow. Nat. Endowment for the Arts and Humanities, 1967-68; prof. arts and letters SUNY, Buffalo, 1969-78, provost arts and letters, 1972-75; prof. classics U. Calif. at Santa Barbara, 1978—; vis. fellow Clare Hall, Cambridge (Eng.) U., 1975-76, Gray lectr., 1978; vis. prof. U. Hawaii, 1977; Martin lectr. Oberlin Coll., 1976. Served with Brit. Army, 1948-49. Author: Ezra Pound and Sextus Propertius: A Study in Creative Translation, 1964; The Satyricon of Petronius: A Literary Study, 1968; Propertius: A Critical Introduction, 1976; The Jaundiced Eye (poems), 1977; also various classical and lit. articles. Editor: Critical Essays on Roman Literature; Elegy and Lyric, 1962; Critical Essays on Roman Literature: Satire, 1963; Ezra Pound, 1970; Arion mag., 1961-70, Arethusa Mag., 1972-75. Address: 1020 Palermo St Santa Barbara CA 93105. *Initial dedication to scholarship and education must eventually go beyond the writing of books and articles that disseminate one's ideas. Eventually, at some stage in one's life, it must be translated into political and, perhaps, administrative terms. If an idea is worth fighting for on paper, then it must be fought for also in councils, committees, and the public media. Where intellectual reform is necessary, it must be backed by more than paper proposals: by the hard work of persuasion and detailed planning. This is why everyone who has intellectual reforms which he wishes to prosper must be prepared to do more than advocate them from his study; he* *must fight for them in the public arena. Administration is too important a chore to be left to mere administrators.*

SULLIVAN, JOHN STEPHEN, banker; b. Lawrence, Mass., Apr. 19, 1914; s. Michael F. and Mary A. (O'Connor) S.; A.B., Dartmouth, 1936, M.C.S., Amos Tuck Sch., 1937; m. Evelyn Dwyer, Apr. 19, 1939; children—John Michael, Mary Susana (Mrs. Stephan Bamford). With Shawmut Bank Boston N.A., 1937-76, v.p. charge adminstrv. div., 1963-71, exec. v.p., 1972-76; sr. v.p. Arlington Trust Co., Lawrence, Mass., 1976—; dir. New Eng. Automated Clearing House, Boston, 1972-78. Chmn. ops. com. Boston Clearing House, 1964-71. Mem. Andover (Mass.) Sch. Com., 1959-65, chmn., 1964-65; mem. Mass. Bd. Edn., 1966-76, vice chmn., 1971-75, chmn., 1975-76. Mem. Bank Adminstrn. Inst. (chmn. ops. commn. 1962-64). Clubs: Dartmouth (Merrimack Valley); Lanam (Andover, Mass.). Home: 50 Sunset Rock Rd Andover MA 01810 Office: 305 Essex St Lawrence MA 01842

SULLIVAN, JOHN VINCENT, life ins. co. exec.; b. Malden, Mass., Feb. 11, 1929; s. John Vincent and Jennie Helen (Marshall) S.; student Burdett Coll., 1947-49, Williams Coll., 1968; m. Mildred E. Goddard, Aug. 21, 1971; children—John, Patricia, Richard, Charles, Alyssa. Purchasing clk. City of Revere (Mass.), 1950; office mgr., bookkeeper Monroe Products, Chelsea, Mass., 1951; with John Hancock Mut. Life Ins. Co., Boston, 1951—, asso. controller, 1966-68, 2d v.p., 1969-74, v.p., 1975—; dir. John Hancock Variable Life Ins. Co.; adviser to Gov.'s Task force on Capital Formation for Econ. Devel., 1976-77. Chmn. fin. com. Town of Saugus (Mass.), 1963-65, treas. Saugus Housing Authority, 1962-64; pres. Saugus PTA, 1961-63. Mem. Life Ins. Assn. Mass. (treas. 1975—, mem. exec. com. 1975—, chmn. 1978-79), Mass. Taxpayers Found. (dir.), Blair Industry Tax Discussion Group, Am. Council Life Ins., Life Office Mgmt. Assn. (chmn. panel 1971), Am. Mgmt. Assn. (chmn. and panel mem. at seminar 1973). Home: 10 Eugley Park W North Reading MA 01864 Office: PO Box 111 Boston MA 02117. *I am probably more optimistic than most about the outcome of events, but not so much so that I allow things to happen totally by themselves.*

SULLIVAN, JOHN W., bus. exec.; b. 1934; B.A., Georgetown U., 1956, M.B., Northwestern U., 1959; married. With Skil Corp. (merged with Emerson Electric Co., 1979), Chgo., 1957—, later v.p., then pres., now chmn. Office: 4801 W Peterson Ave Chicago IL 60646

SULLIVAN, JOSEPH B., judge; b. Detroit, May 30, 1922; s. Joseph A. and Winifred R. (Bruin) S.; Ph.B., U. Detroit, 1947, J.D., 1957; m. Mary Sullivan, June 6, 1946; children—Kathleen (Mrs. Thomas Lewand), Timothy. Admitted to bar; mem. firm Sullivan, Sullivan, Ranger & Ward, Detroit, after 1958; head criminal div. Atty. Gen.'s Office, State of Mich., 1963-64; exec. sec. to Mayor, City of Detroit, 1962; commr. purchasing City of Detroit, 1967-69; clk. Wayne County, 1970-74; judge Wayne Circuit Ct., 1975—. Mem. Detroit Charter Revision Com., 1970-73. Bd. dirs. Mercy Coll., Detroit. Served with AUS, 1943-46. Mem. Mich., Detroit bar assns., Catholic Lawyers Assn., Univ. Detroit Alumni Assn. Democrat. Home: 842 Park Ln Grosse Pointe MI 48230 Office: 1801 City County Bldg Detroit MI 48226

SULLIVAN, JOSEPH CHARLES, lawyer; b. N.Y.C., Feb. 6, 1927; s. Christopher M. and Sophye (Roeber) S.; B.E.E., Manhattan Coll., 1950; LL.B., St. John's U., 1954; LL.M. N.Y. U., 1958; m. Ellen E. Manion, Sept. 15, 1956; children—Ellen M., Jenifer A., Joseph C., David C., Pamela, Marina. Design engr. Ford Instrument Co., 1950-54; admitted to N.Y. bar, 1955; patent atty. Control Instrument Co., 1954-55; asso. firm Kane, Dalsimer & Kane, N.Y.C., 1955-60; partner firm Kane, Dalsimer, Kane, Sullivan & Jurucz, N.Y.C., 1960—. Arbitrator, Am. Arbitration Assn. Home: 82 Eton Rd Garden City NY 11530 Office: 420 Lexington Ave New York City NY 10017

SULLIVAN, JOSEPH EDWARD, diversified services mfg. co. exec.; b. Chgo., Jan. 30, 1934; s. Joseph Frances and Rosemary Ann (McCann) S.; B.S., John Carroll U., 1956; exec. program U. Calif. at Los Angeles, 1972; m. Clare Ann Hoynes, June 16, 1956; children—Timothy, Mary, Maureen. With Ernst & Ernst, Cleve., 1959-65; asst. controller, then controller, treas., dir. Curtis Mfg. Co., Cleve., 1965-70; v.p., sec., chief acctg. officer, corp. controller Wyle Labs., El Segundo, Calif., 1970—. Bd. dirs. St. Jeanne de Lestonnac Home-Sch. Assn., 1973-76, pres., 1974, treas., 1973; bd. dirs. Villa Park Property Owners Assn., 1974-77, pres., 1977; mem. Villa Park City Council, 1978—. Served to 1st lt. AUS, 1957-59. C.P.A., Calif., Ohio. Mem. Am. Inst. C.P.A.'s Ohio, Calif. socs. C.P.A.'s, Am. Soc. Corp. Secs. Home: 9601 Christine Circle Villa Park CA 92667 Office: 128 Maryland St El Segundo CA 90245

SULLIVAN, JOSEPH PATRICK, chems., fertilizers and dental supplies co. exec.; b. Newton, Mass., Apr. 10, 1933; s. Joseph Patrick and Ruth Ann (Kelter) S.; B.A. cum laude, Harvard U., 1954, M.B.A., 1956; m. Jeanne Marie Baldi, Oct. 19, 1957; children—Deirdre, Barbara, Mark. With Swift & Co., Chgo., 1959-73, pres. Swift Chem. Co., 1972-73; pres. Estech Inc., Chgo., 1973—; dir. Consol. Fertilisers, Ltd., Brisbane, Australia; mem. bus. adv. com. Coll. Commerce and Bus. Adminstrn., U. Ill. Bd. dirs. Schwab Rehab. Hosp., Chgo., Chgo. Opera Theater, Am. Refugee Com.; trustee Mundelein Coll.; trustee, mem. fin. com. Farm Found., Oak Brook, Ill.; past pres. trustees Latin Sch., Chgo., 1977—; co-chmn. Emergency Task Force for Indochinese Refugees. Served with AUS, 1956-59. Mem. Presidents Assn. Roman Catholic. Club: Chicago, Economic, Union League (Chgo.); Harvard (Boston). Home: 6145 N Sheridan Rd Chicago IL 60660 Office: 30 N LaSalle St Chicago IL 60602

SULLIVAN, JOSEPH TIMOTHY PATRICK, lawyer; b. N.Y.C., Nov. 17, 1895; s. Timothy Patrick and Hannah (McCarthy) S.; Ph.B., Yale, 1916; LL.B., Fordham U. 1924; m. Grace Darby, Jan. 25, 1933 (dec. 1940); children—Sally (Mrs. David Fox), Maureen (Mrs. Joseph R. Rollins, Jr.), Timothy Patrick. Admitted to N.Y. bar, 1925, since practiced privately in N.Y.C. Pres., Sullivan Enterprises, Inc., N.Y.C., 1950—. Foreman emeritus 2d Panel Sheriff's Jury. N.Y. County; co-founder Just One Break, Inc. Del., del. Democratic Nat. Conv., 1952, 56, 60. Mem. Am., N.Y. State bar assns., Bar Assn. City N.Y., Am. Irish Hist. Soc. (pres. gen. emeritus), Knight of Malta. Clubs: Yale, Brook (N.Y.C.); California (Los Angeles). Office: Yale Club 50 Vanderbilt Ave New York NY 10017

SULLIVAN, JOSEPH V., bishop; b. Kansas City, Mo., Aug. 15, 1919; s. John L. and Anastasia Agnes (Prosser) S.; S.T.D., Cath. U., 1949. Ordained priest Roman Cath. Ch., 1946; bishop of Baton Rouge, 1974—; aux. bishop of Kansas City-St. Joseph, Mo., titular bishop of Tagamuta, 1967-74. Office: PO Box 2028 Baton Rouge LA 70821*

SULLIVAN, KENNETH JAMES, banker; s. Frank C. and Genevieve (Connell) S.; m. Blanche Gribble; children—Barbara Mary, Robert James, Kenneth Joseph, Nancy Ann (Mrs. John D. Taylor). With Continental Bank & Trust Co., Salt Lake City, 1930—, pres., 1962-78, vice chmn. bd., 1978—. Pres., Salt Lake City Clearing House Assn. 1961. Mem. Utah Bankers Assn. (pres. 1959-60), Salt Lake City C. of C. (v.p. 1964). Clubs: Salt Lake City Country, Alta, Ambassador Athletic (pres. 1952) (Salt Lake City). Office: 200 S Main St PO Box 30177 Salt Lake City UT 84125

SULLIVAN, KEVIN IRVING, banker; b. Boston, Aug. 24, 1932; s. F. Francis and Kathryn (Perault) S.; A.B., Dartmouth, 1954; postgrad. Stonier Grad. Sch. Banking, 1966-67; student Am. Inst. Banking; m. Virginia W. Darling, Mar. 26, 1955; children—Kevin Irving, Keith Franklin. With Mfrs. and Traders Trust Co., Buffalo, 1957-71, v.p., sec., 1967-71; sec., dir. M. & T. Capital Corp., M. & T. Discount Corp., until 1971; sec. First Empire State Corp., until 1971; pres., dir. Bank of Buffalo, 1971-76; exec. v.p., dir. Western region Bank N.Y., 1976-78, pres., chief exec. officer, dir., 1978—; sec. Buffalo Clearing House Assn. Bd. dirs., past pres., past v.p., treas., chmn. personnel com., chmn. finance com., chmn. nominating com. Gateway-Methodist Home Children; area enrollment dir., formerly dist. enrollment dir. Western N.Y. for Dartmouth; chmn. Buffalo area exec. com. Dartmouth 3d Century Fund; area coordinator Colby Jr. Coll. 50th Anniversary Fund; past chmn. pres.'s scholarship dinner Daemen Coll.; past chmn., mem. exec. com. Western N.Y. United Negro Coll. Fund; past mem. adv. bd. Buffalo Braves profl. basketball team; mem. Millard Fillmore Hosp.; past mem. Dartmouth Alumni Council; chmn. bd. trustees, past mem. adv. council Medaille Coll.; mem. ho. of dels., past chmn. bus. div. United Way of Buffalo and Erie County; gen. chmn. WNED-TV Auction, 1973-74. Bd. dirs., past v.p. Psychiat. Clinic, Inc.; bd. dirs. Child and Family Services, Jr. Achievement Niagara Frontier; bd. dirs., sec.-treas. Arts Devel. Services, Inc.; bd. dirs., v.p. N.Y. Bus. Devel. Corp., NYBDC Capital Corp.; trustee, treas., chmn. community adv. bd. Western N.Y. Ednl. TV Assn. (WNED-FM-TV, WEBR); trustee Children's Found. Erie County; mem. trustees com. Buffalo Found.; mem. Downtown Core Coalition, Consumer Mortgage Rev. Com.; mem. adv. bd. Salvation Army; bd. dirs. Greater Buffalo Devel. Found., Amherst Symphony Orch. Assn. Served with USAF, 1954-57. Mem. Am. Inst. Banking, Buffalo Area C. of C., Buffalo and Erie County Hist. Soc., Buffalo Zool. Soc., Jack Kemp Assos., Buffalo Soc. Natural Scis., Chi Phi. Republican. Methodist (past chmn. adminstrv. bd., past chmn., Council of Ministries, personnel com., finance com., asso. lay leader). Clubs: Four Seasons Racquet; Buffalo Country, Executive Suite, Buffalo; Dartmouth Western N.Y. (dir.); Coral Beach and Tennis (Bermuda). Home: 81 Lehn Springs Dr Williamsville NY 14221 Office: 17 Court St Buffalo NY 14202

SULLIVAN, LAWRENCE ANTHONY, educator; b. Flushing, N.Y., May 27, 1923; B.A. with distinction, UCLA, 1948; J.D. magna cum laude, Harvard U., 1951; m. Ralda Meyerson; children by previous marriage—Lawrence B., Mark, Neil P. Admitted to Mass. bar, 1952; law clk. 1st Circuit U.S. Ct. Appeals, 1951-52; asso. Foley, Hoag & Eliot, Boston, 1952-55, 1957-60, partner, 1960-67; acting prof. law U. Calif., Berkeley, 1955-57, prof., 1967-79, Earl Warren prof. public law, 1979—, dir. Earl Warren Legal Inst., 1977—; mem. Nat. Commn. Rev. Antitrust Law and Procedure, 1978-79. Guggenheim fellow, 1978-79. Fellow Inst. Advanced Legal Studies of London (Eng.) U. Author: Handbook on the Law of Antitrust, 1977; contbr. articles to profl. jours. Office: University of California School of Law Berkeley CA 94720

SULLIVAN, LEONARD, JR., def. and transp. policy cons.; b. N.Y.C., Dec. 2, 1925; s. Leonard and Marjorie (Dodd) S.; grad. St. Paul's Sch., Concord, N.H., 1943; B.S., M.S., Mass. Inst. Tech., 1949, Aero. Engr., 1950; m. Margo Murray Blackley, Mar. 5, 1960; children—M. Dianne, L. Jason. Asst. chief preliminary design Grumman Aircraft Engring. Corp., 1954-57, chief preliminary design, 1957-62, mgr. advanced systems, 1962-64; dep. asst. dir. tactical warfare program Office Dir. Def. Research and Engring., Dept. Def., 1964-65, asst. dir., 1965-66, dep. dir. S.E. Asia matters, 1966-72, prin. dep. dir., 1972-73, dir. Def. Program Analysis and Evaluation, 1973-74, asst. sec. def., program analysis and evaluation, 1974-76; def. and transp. policy cons., 1976—. Chmn. planning bd. Village of Old Field, N.Y., 1962-64. Served with USMC, 1944-46. Decorated knight of Vietnam; recipient Def. Distinguished Civilian Service medal, 1973, Def. Distinguished Pub. Service medal, 1976. Mem. Delta Psi (pres. Tau chpt. 1948-49), Sigma Xi. Clubs: St. Anthony (N.Y.C.); Chevy Chase (Md.); Mass. Inst. Tech. (Washington). Home: 3601 49th St NW Washington DC 20016 Office: Suite 1700 SPC 1500 Wilson Blvd Arlington VA 22209

SULLIVAN, MARGARET PATRICIA, physician; b. Lewistown, Mont., Feb. 7, 1922; B.A., Rice Inst., 1944; M.D., Duke, 1950. Intern Duke Hosp., Durham, N.C., 1950-51, asst. resident pediatrics, 1951-52; asst. resident St. Louis Children's Hosp., 1952-53; pediatrician Atomic Bomb Casualty Commn., Hiroshima and Nagasaki, Japan, 1953-55; asst. resident pediatrics Tex. Children's Hosp., Houston, 1955; asst. pediatrician U. Tex. M.D. Anderson Hosp. and Tumor Inst., Houston, 1956-61, asso. pediatrician, 1961-74, pediatrician, prof. pediatrics, 1973—; asst. prof. pediatrics U. Tex. Postgrad. Sch. Medicine, 1956-61, asso. prof., 1961-73; participant internat. seminars. Diplomate Am. Bd. Pediatrics. Mem. Am. Acad. Pediatrics, AAAS, Am. Assn. Cancer Edn., Am. Assn. Cancer Research, AMA, Am. Med. Women's Assn. (pres. 1974), Am. Soc. Clin. Oncology. Harris County Med. Soc., Houston Pediatric Soc., N.Y. Acad. Scis., So. Soc. Pediatric Research, Tex. Med. Assn., Phi Beta Kappa, Sigma Xi. Editorial bd. Year Book of Cancer, 1959—. Contbr. articles to profl. jours. Address: U Tex M D Anderson Hosp and Tumor Inst 6723 Bertner-Texas Med Center Houston TX 77030

SULLIVAN, SISTER MARIE CELESTE, hosp. adminstr.; b. Boston, Mar. 18, 1929; d. Daniel John and Katherine Agnes (Cunniff) Sullivan; B.B.A., St. Bonaventure U., Olean, N.Y., 1965. Joined Order Franciscan Sisters. Roman Cath. Ch., 1952; bus. mgr. St. Joseph's Hosp., Providence, 1954-62; asst. adminstr. St. Joseph's Hosp., Tampa, Fla., 1965-70, adminstr., 1970—; bd. dirs. St. Francis Hosp., Miami Beach, Fla.; trustee St. Anthony's Hosp., St. Petersburg, Fla.; mem. Fla. Gulf Health Systems Agy. Adv. Council Hillsborough County, Emergency Med. Planning Council Hillsborough County; adv. com. Hillsborough County Sch. Practical Nursing. Recipient Humanitarian award Judeo-Christian Coalition Clinic, Tampa, 1977. Fellow Am. Coll. Hosp. Adminstrs.; mem. Fla. Hosp. Assn. (trustee), Am. Mgmt. Assn., Greater Tampa C. of C., Royal Soc. Health. Home: 3001 W Buffalo Ave Tampa FL 33607 Office: PO Box 4227 Tampa FL 33677. *I believe success is guaranteed when there is dedication to high standards, when there is respect for the dignity and worth of the human person, and when one believes in the goodness of God.*

SULLIVAN, MARK, JR., investment banker; b. N.Y.C., May 13, 1911; s. Mark and Marie McMechen (Buchanan) S.; B.A., Princeton, 1932; m. Martha Sinclair Davidge, Jan. 11, 1938 (dec. Apr. 1978); children—Mark III, John Davidge, Richard Buchanan. With Auchincloss, Parker & Redpath, Washington, investment bankers and brokers, 1933-70, co-mgr. investment adv. dept., 1937-50, gen. partner, 1950-70; sr. v.p., dir., mem. exec. com. Thomson McKinnon Securities, Inc., 1970—; dir. Steadman Investment Fund, Inc., 1953-65, Garfinckel, Brooks Bros., Miller & Rhoads, Inc., Washington; commr. of D.C., 1960-61. Past mem. Citizens Adv. Council D.C.; mem. D.C. Govt. Bd. of Library Trustees, 1969-72. Chmn. bd. Beauvoir Sch., Washington, 1947-53; dir. Vis. Nurse Assn., Washington (pres. 1968-69), Health and Welfare Council, 1962-65; pres. D.C. United Givers Fund, 1961-63; trustee Fed. City Council; bd. dirs. Met. Washington Bd. Trade, 1963-69; Washington Center for Met. Studies, 1962-70. Trustee George Washington U., Washington. Served with USNR, 1942-45. Mem. Phi Beta Kappa. Clubs: Metropolitan, Princeton (pres. 1952-54), Alfalfa (Washington); Chevy Chase (pres. 1952-54). Home: 5200 Partridge Ln NW Washington DC 20016 Office: 1705 H St NW Washington DC 20006

SULLIVAN, MARK A., asso. justice N.J. Supreme Ct.; b. Jersey City, Aug. 11, 1911; s. Mark A. and Lila E. (Ward) S.; A.B., Georgetown U., 1932; LL.B., Harvard U., 1935; m. Mary Josephine Hamilll, Mar. 28, 1940; 1 son, Mark A. Admitted to N.J. bar, 1936; judge Second Dist. Ct. of Jersey City, 1945-49, Hudson County (N.J.) Dist. Ct., 1949-53, Superior Ct. of N.J., 1953-73, appellate div., 1959-73; asso. justice N.J. Supreme Ct., 1973—. Served with USN, 1942-45. Democrat. Roman Catholic. Club: Spring Lake Golf. Office: 601 Bangs Ave Asbury Park NJ 07712*

SULLIVAN, MAX WILLIAM, mus. dir.; b. Fremont, Mich., Sept. 27, 1909; s. James Timothy and Gertrude Maude (Clark) S.; A.B., Western Mich. U., 1932; M.A. in Teaching, Harvard 1941; LL.D., Providence Coll., 1950; m. Jeannette Stuart Todd, June 21, 1939 (div. 1974); children—Todd, Timothy Clark, William Shaun, Michael Towle, Caleb Kendall; m. 2d, Ruth Lois Wilkins, Aug. 31, 1975. Instr. arts and crafts Cranbrook Sch., Bloomfield Hills, Mich., 1933-35; condr. summer play sch., 1933-37; instr. arts and crafts Middlesex Sch., Concord, Mass., 1935-38; head art dept. Groton (Mass.) Sch., 1938-42; cons. art edn., sch. edn. Harvard, 1940-42; dir. exhbn. contemporary N.E. handicrafts Worcester (Mass.) Art Mus., 1942-43; cons. Met. Mus., N.Y.C., 1943-44, conducted survey recreational therapy in mil. hosps.; dir. edn. Mus. of Art, R.I. Sch. Design, Providence, 1944-45, dean edn., 1945-47, pres. of corp., 1947-55; dir. Portland Art Assn.-Mus. and Art Sch., 1957-60; dir. Everson Mus. Art of Syracuse and Onondage County, 1961-71; program dir. Kimbell Art Mus., Fort Worth, 1971-74, dir. adminstrv. services, 1974-76; adj. prof. art, dir. Univ. Art Gallery U. Tex. at Arlington, 1976—. Mem. Council Museums and Edn. in the Visual Arts, 1973-78. Trustee, pres. Internat. Center for Arts, Todi, Italy and Boston, 1974—. Mem. AIA. Club: Harvard. Home: 4500 Westridge Ave Apt 1 Fort Worth TX 76116 Office: University Art Gallery Fine Arts Bldg Arlington TX 76019

SULLIVAN, MICHAEL, educator; b. Toronto, Ont., Can., Oct. 29, 1916; s. Edward Alan and Elizabeth (Hees) S.; B.A., Cambridge (Eng.) U., 1939, M.A., 1949, Litt.D., 1966; B.A. (honours), U. London (Eng.), 1950; Ph.D., Harvard, 1952; D.Litt., Oxford (Eng.) U., 1973; m. Khoan Ngo, July 20, 1943. Asst. curator W. China U. Mus., Chengtu, 1942-45; prof. Ginling Coll., Chengtu, 1945-46; lectr. history art, also curator art mus. U. Singapore, 1954-60; lectr. Asian art U. London, 1960-66; Christensen prof. Oriental art Stanford, 1966—; Slade prof. fine art Oxford (Eng.) U., 1973-74. Guggenheim Found. fellow, 1974; Nat. Endowment for the Humanities fellow, 1976-77; vis. fellow St. Antony's Coll. Oxford (Eng.) U., 1976-77; fellow St. Catherine's Coll., Oxford U. Fellow Royal Soc. Arts; mem. Am. Acad. Arts and Scis. Author: Chinese Art in the Twentieth Century, 1959; An Introduction to Chinese Art, 1961; The Birth of Landscape Painting in China, 1962; Chinese Ceramics, Bronze and Jades in the Collection of Sir Alan and Lady Barlow, 1963; Chinese and Japanese Art, 1966; A Short History of Chinese Art, 1967; The Cave Temples of Maichishan, 1969; The Meeting of Eastern and Western Art, 1973; The Arts of China, 2d edit., 1977; Chinese Art: Recent Discoveries, 1973; The Three Perfections, 1974; Symbols of Eternity: The Art of Landscape Painting in China, 1979; Chinese Landscape Painting: The Sui and T'ang Dynasties, 1980; also numerous articles. Address: Dept Art Stanford Univ Stanford CA 94305

SULLIVAN, MICHAEL PATRICK, lawyer; b. Holyoke, Mass., July 6, 1948; s. William Joseph and Dorothy Gertrude (Griffin) S.; B.A. cum laude, St. Anselm's Coll., 1970; J.D. cum laude, Suffolk U., 1975; m. Anne-Marie Hurley, Apr. 18, 1971; children—Katherine Anne, Michael Patrick. Admitted to Mass. bar, 1975, Fed. Dist. Ct. Mass. bar, 1977, 1st Circuit Ct. Appeals bar, 1978, U.S. Supreme Ct. bar, 1979; corp. dept. asst. New Eng. Gas & Electric Assn. Service Corp., Cambridge, Mass., 1975-76; sec. New Eng. Gas and Electric Assn. and clk. of subs. cos., Cambridge, 1976—; bd. dirs. New Eng. Gas and Electric Assn. System Pension Plan, Savs. Plan, Tax Reduction Act Stock Ownership Plan. Recipient Mass. Practice and Procedure award Suffolk U. Law Sch., 1975. Mem. Am. Soc. Corp. Secs., Am. Bar Assn., Mass. Bar Assn., Boston Bar Assn., Pi Gamma Mu (Nat. Social Sci. award). Home: 2 Williams St North Quincy MA 02171 Office: 675 Massachusetts Ave PO Box 190 Cambridge MA 02139

SULLIVAN, MORTIMER ALLEN, lawyer, ret. transp. co. exec.; b. Sodus Point, N.Y., Mar. 20, 1901; s. Mark L. and Martha (Allen) S.; grad. Lawrenceville Sch., 1920; A.B., Cornell U., 1924; LL.B., 1926; m. Gertrude B. Hinkley, Sept. 1, 1928; children—Mortimer Allen, Martha Allen. Admitted to N.Y. bar, 1926; trial lawyer with Ward, Flynn, Spring & Tillou, attys., Buffalo, 1926-28; ind. counsel various bus., trucking, ins. cos., 1928—; gen. counsel Asso. Transport, Inc., N.Y.C., 1941-72, chmn. bd., 1966-72, chmn. exec. com., 1959-66, mem. finance com., 1950-72, dir., 1948-72; pres., dir. Keystone Transp. Co., Huntington, W. Va., 1962-72; dir. System Realty Co. of Mich., System Equipment of Mich., J.P. & M. Sullivan, Elmira, N.Y., J.P. & M. Sullivan Corning Corp., Corning, N.Y. Mem. Buffalo Draft Bd., 1939-72. Served as squadron comdr. Civil Air Patrol, 1941-46. Mem. Am., N.Y. State, Erie County bar assns. Clubs: Saturn (Buffalo), Wanakah Country. Home: Erewhon Farms 8931 Versailles Rd Angola NY 14006 Office: Walbridge Bldg Buffalo NY 14202

SULLIVAN, PATRICIA CLARE, hosp. adminstr.; b. Cortland, Nebr., July 2, 1929; R.N. diploma Mercy Hosp. Sch. Nursing, Denver, 1954; B.S.N., Coll. St. Mary, Omaha, 1955; M.H.A., St. Louis U., 1971, cert. for internal resources for renewal, 1971; cert. in gerontology U. Nebr., Omaha, 1976. Instr. Mercy Hosp. Sch. Nursing, Des Moines, 1955-58, dir., 1960-64; nursing supr. pediatrics Mercy Hosp., Des Moines, 1955-58, adminstr., 1977—; coordinator rural hosp. nursing, nursing supr. ob-gyn, Mercy Hosp., Durango, Colo., 1958-60; nursing supr. Mercy Hosp., Williston, N.D., 1964-65; adminstr. St. Joseph's Mercy Hosp., Centerville, Iowa, 1965-69; Resident Peter Bent Brigham Hosp., Boston, 1970-71; in organizational renewal Province of Omaha, 1971-74; dir. community relations Archbishop Bergan Mercy Hosp., Omaha, 1974-77; mem. Province of Omaha Health Services Council, 1958—; provincial chpt. del. Province Omaha, 1970—; Province Omaha del. Gen. Chpt. Provinces, 1970—; bd. dirs. Mercy Hosp., Devils Lake, N.D., 1974—, Sub-Area IV, Iowa Health Systems Agy., 1977—, NCCJ, 1979, Health System of Mercy, 1979; regional rep. Diocesan Pastoral Council, 1978—; dir. Central Nat. Bancshares, 1979. Mem. Nat. League for Nursing, Iowa League for Nursing (pres. 1966-69), Omaha League for Nursing (dir. 1976-77), Am. Hosp. Assn. Club: Zonta. Dir. film depicting tornado strike to Archbishop Bergan Mercy Hosp., 1975 (numerous showings, including at Congl. hearing at Pentagon). Office: Mercy Hosp 6th and University Sts Des Moines IA 50314

SULLIVAN, PHILIP BURT, journalist; b. Mulberry, Tenn., Apr. 22, 1921; s. David Christopher and Eliza (Ashby) S.; m. Edith Murray, Mar. 14, 1938; children—Nicholas M., Victoria (Mrs.

Ronald Anderson), Elizabeth Ann. Reporter, The Tennessean, Nashville, 1945-55, city editor, 1955-62, editorial writer, 1962-73, chief editorial writer, 1973—. Served with USAAF, 1943-45. Home: 944 Colfax Dr Nashville TN 37214 Office: 1100 Broadway Nashville TN 37201

SULLIVAN, R. PARKER, former telephone co. exec.; b. Frankfort, Ky., Feb. 7, 1914; s. James A. and Nora (Parker) S.; grad. Notre Dame U., 1937; m. Ila Graves, Sept. 21, 1944; 1 dau., Jane Parker (Mrs. Larry R. Jones). Formerly with Lexington (Ky.) Telephone Co., to 1953; operating v.p. Gen. Telephone Co. S.W., San Angelo, Tex., 1953-56; v.p. mktg. Gen. Telephone Corp., N.Y.C., 1957-62; traffic mgr. Gen. Telephone Co. Ind., Inc., Gen. Telephone Co. of Ky.; traffic mgr., v.p. ops. Gen. Telephone Co. of the Southwest; pres. Gen. Telephone Co. of Upstate N.Y., Inc., Johnstown, 1956; pres., chief exec. officer Gen. Telephone Co. Calif., Santa Monica, 1962-78; Santa Monica Bank, Transcon Lines; mem. Pacific Stock Exchange. Active Gt. Western council Boy Scouts Am., Jr. Achievement, So. Calif. chpt. Nat. Multiple Sclerosis Soc., NCCJ; mem. adv. council Coll. Bus. Adminstrn. U. Notre Dame; nat. adv. bd. Nat. Alliance Family Life; mem. U. So. Calif. Assn., Pepperdine Assn.; bd. dirs. St. John's Hosp. and Health Center Found., Industry-Edn. Council Calif., City of Hope, Greater Los Angeles Visitors and Conv. Bur. Mem. U.S. Ind. Telephone Assn., Telephone Pioneers Am., Ind. Telephone Pioneer Assn., Calif. (dir.), Los Angeles area chambers commerce, Nat. Alliance Businessmen. Rotarian. Address: 100 Wilshire Blvd Santa Monica CA 90401

SULLIVAN, RICHARD CYRIL, R.R. exec.; b. Erie, Pa., Oct. 25, 1928; s. Cyril and Nancy (Williams) S.; B.A. in Polit. Sci., Allegheny Coll., 1950; M.A. in Polit. Sci., U. Pa., 1951; m. Harriet Walters, June 13, 1953; children—Elizabeth, Nancy, Richard, Harriet, Matthew. With Port Authority N.Y. and N.J., 1951-56, 59-74, dir. World Trade Center, N.Y.C., 1961-67, dir. public affairs, N.Y.C., 1967-74; with U.S. Dept. State, 1957-58; v.p. public and govtl. affairs U.S. Ry. Assn., Washington, 1974-76; v.p., sec. Consol. Rail Corp., Phila., 1974—. Trustee Ridgewood (N.J.) Bd. Edn., 1971-74. Served with U.S. Army, 1946-47. Home: 1 Browns Ln Villanova PA 19085 Office: Room 1808 6 Penn Center Plaza Philadelphia PA 19104

SULLIVAN, RICHARD EUGENE, educator, coll. dean; b. Doniphan, Nebr., Mar. 27, 1921; s. Eugene Michael and Iva Mae (Kingston) S.; A.B., U. Nebr., 1942; M.A., U. Ill., 1947, Ph.D., 1949; m. Vivian Carol Johnson, Nov. 6, 1943; children—Elizabeth, Katherine, Mary Michele. Grad. asst. U. Ill., 1947-49; prof. history N.E. Mo. State Coll., 1949-54; prof. history, adminstr. Mich. State U., East Lansing, 1954-67, chmn. dept. history, 1967-70, dean Coll. Arts and Letters, 1970—. Served with USAAF, 1942-46. Guggenheim fellow, 1961; Fulbright Research fellow to Belgium, 1961; Harbison Distinguished Tchr. award Danforth Found., 1968. Mem. Am. Hist. Assn., Mediaeval Acad. Am., Phi Beta Kappa. Author: A Short History of Western Civilization, 4th edit., 1975; The Coronation of Charlemagne, 1959; Heirs of the Roman Empire, 1960; Aix-La-Chapelle in the Age of Charlemagne, 1963. Contbr. articles to profl. jours. Home: 1182 Bryant Dr East Lansing MI 48823

SULLIVAN, RICHARD HOWARD, found. exec.; b. Arcanum, Ohio, Nov. 1, 1917; s. Henry Lee and Margery (Penn) S.; A.B., Harvard, 1939, A.M., 1940; LL.D., Pacific U., 1960; D.H.L., Hebrew Union Coll., 1962, Manhattan Coll., 1968; LL.D., Reed Coll., 1967, Coll. Notre Dame of Md., 1967, Lycoming Coll., 1968, Occidental Coll., 1968; H.H.D., Central Coll., 1967; Litt.D., Beaver Coll., 1967, Marietta Coll., 1968; m. Jean Elizabeth Fox, Dec. 20, 1941; children—Barbara Lee (Mrs. Lish Whitson), Mary Jean (Mrs. James J. Ragen, Jr.), Richard Penn. Asst. dean Harvard, 1941-42; adminstrv. asst., coll. entrance exam. bd. Princeton, 1946, asst. dir., 1946-48, asst. treas. Ednl. Testing Service, 1948-49, exec. v.p., treas., 1949-56; pres. Reed Coll., Portland, Oreg., 1956-67; pres. Assn. Am. Colls., 1967-69; mng. dir. Am. Book Pubs. Council, 1969-70; asst. to pres. Carnegie Corp. N.Y., 1970-76, treas., 1976—. Sec., Carnegie Found. for Advancement Teaching, 1974-76, treas., 1976—. Trustee, mem. finance com. Coll. Entrance Exam. Bd., 1961-66; mem. Nat. Sci. Bd., 1966-72. Mem. bd. edn. Princeton Twp., N.J., 1956; chmn. Oreg. Colls. Found., 1958. Trustee Oreg. Grad. Center Study and Research, 1963-66, Coll. Retirement Equities Fund, 1963-66, Com. Econ. Devel., 1964-70; trustee Found. Center, 1967-73, chmn., 1970-73; trustee, mem. investment com., mem. exec. com. Common Fund; bd. dirs. John and Mary R. Markle Found., 1965-71, Investor Responsibility Research Center. Served from ensign to lt. USNR, 1942-46. Mem. Phi Beta Kappa, Phi Beta Kappa Assos. Clubs: Harvard (N.Y.C.) (N.J.). Home: 159 Philip Dr Princeton NJ 08540 Office: 437 Madison Ave New York City NY 10022

SULLIVAN, ROBERT EDWIN, lawyer, educator; b. Helena, Mont., Aug. 1, 1917; s. Stephen and Elma M. (Barnes) S.; A.B., U. Notre Dame, 1940, J.D., 1946; LL.D., Carroll Coll. (Mont.), 1965; m. Eleanor M. Laux, July 6, 1943; children—David Patrick (dec.), Sheila, Ellen, Maureen, Kathleen, Bridget, Shannon, Kerry. Admitted to Mont. bar, 1942, Ohio bar, 1946, N.D. bar, 1952; practice law, Ohio, 1946-47; prof. law U. Notre Dame, 1947-54; research fellow Warren Petroleum Corp., Tulsa, summers 1950, 51; prof. law U. Mont., 1954—, dean Law Sch., 1955-78; gen. counsel Mont. Power Co., 1979—; dir. 1st Trust Co. Mont. Mem. legal com. Interstate Oil Compact Commn., 1953-74; commr. Nat. Conf. on Uniform State Laws, 1957—, v.p., 1970-71; chmn. Mont. adv. com. Pres.'s Commn. Civil Rights, 1959-61; chmn. Gov.'s Com. Revise Marriage and Div. Laws; co-chmn. Gov.'s Com. to Revise Mont. Corp. Law; mem. adv. com. Ind. Dept. Conservation, 1953-54. Bd. dirs. Continuing Legal Ed. Mont., Rocky Mountain Mineral Found.; trustee Carroll Coll., Helena, State Bar Mont., 1979—; pres. adv. bd. St. Patrick Hosp.; pres. Cath. High Sch. Bd. Edn. Served with Mont. N.G., 1934-36; maj. USAAF, 1942-45; adjudicator VA, 1946. Recipient Borromeo award Carroll Coll., 1961. Mem. Am. (editor Newsletter sect. mineral and natural resources law 1966-70), Mont. bar assns., Am. Judicature Soc. (dir. 1973-76). K.C. Author: Handbook of Oil and Gas Law, 1955; Conservation of Oil and Gas-A Legal History 1948-58, 1959. Contbg. editor Oil and Gas Reporter, Oil and Gas Taxes. Contbr. articles industry periodicals. Home: 112 Hillcrest Dr Missoula MT 59801

SULLIVAN, ROBERT FRANCIS, newspaperman; b. Lackawanna, N.Y., Aug. 14, 1913; s. John J. and Anna T. (Eustace) S.; B.A., Canisius Coll., Buffalo, 1934; M.S. in Journalism, Columbia, 1937; m. Evelyn Mae Gannon, Feb. 7, 1944; children—Michael, Patrick, Sean. Reporter, copy editor Buffalo Times, 1937-39; copy editor N.Y. Sun, 1939-41, asst. cable editor, 1945-46; with Cleve. Press. 1946-78, asst. mng. editor, 1968-76, mng. editor, 1976-78; ret., 1978. Served to lt. comdr. USNR, 1941-45. Home: Green Valley AZ 85614

SULLIVAN, ROGER MICHAEL, lawyer; b. Los Angeles, Oct. 27, 1926; s. Richard Barry and Anna (Purcell) S.; A.A., Occidental Coll., 1945; J.D., Loyola U., Los Angeles, 1952; m. Jayne Ann Colgan, Feb. 13, 1960; children—Kathleen, Theresa, Maureen, Mary, Carolyn, Michael. Admitted to Calif. bar, 1952; atty. Pacific & Electric Ry. Co., Los Angeles, 1952-57; asst. sec. So. Pacific Pipe Line Co., Los Angeles, 1955-57; partner Thorpe, Sullivan, Workman, Thorpe & O'Sullivan and predecessor firms, Los Angeles, 1957—. Adviser, Uniform Law Commrs., 1973-74; faculty mem. Am. Law Inst.-Am. Bar Assn. Eminent Domain course, 1975; guest lectr. civil trial advocacy course Loyola Law Sch. Gen. chmn. So. Calif. regional bd. dirs. NCCJ, 1955-56, sec., 1965; pres. Right to Life League So. Calif., 1977. Pres. bd. dirs. Family Service of Los Angeles, 1961-62, Hiroshima-Gakuin Found. Served as ensign A.C., USNR, 1947. Mem. Am. Bd. Trial Advs. (sec. Los Angeles chpt. 1975—), Am. (chmn. condemnation com., real property sect. 1976-77), Los Angeles County (chmn. condemnation procedures com. 1970-71) bar assns., State Bar Calif. (v.p. Conf. Barristers 1957, chmn. com. on govtl. liability and condemnation 1975), Am. Right of Way Assn. (Los Angeles chpt.). Rotarian. Clubs: Los Angeles Serra (pres. 1967-68), Los Angeles Country, Los Angeles Athletic. Home: 333 25th St Santa Monica CA 90402 Office: 800 Wilshire Blvd Los Angeles CA 90017

SULLIVAN, ROGER WINTHROP, govt. ofcl.; b. Boston, Nov. 22, 1929; s. Richard Wesley and Monica (McCoy) S.; A.B., Bowdoin Coll., 1952; postgrad. Woodrow Wilson Sch., Princeton U., 1970-71; m. Marguerite Cecelia Barry, Dec. 26, 1953; children—Catherine, Michael, Siobhan, Peter, Marie. Commd. fgn. service officer Dept. State, 1956; U.S. consul., Medan, Indonesia, 1967-70; dep. dir. People's Republic China affairs Dept. State, 1971-73, dir. Taiwan affairs, 1973-74, polit. adv. comdr.-in-chief, Pacific, 1974-76; dep. prin. officer Am. embassy, Hong Kong, 1976-77; dep. chief mission, Taipei, Taiwan, 1977-78; dep. asst. sec. State for East Asian and Pacific affairs, Washington, 1978—. Served with U.S. Army, 1952-56. Office: East Asian and Pacific Affairs Dept State 2201 C St NW Washington DC 20520

SULLIVAN, SELBY WILLIAM, holding co. exec.; b. Houston, Oct. 8, 1934; s. John Francis and Lois Blanch Selby S.; B.A., Rice U., 1956; postgrad. Stanford U., 1956-57; LL.B. with honors, U. Tex., 1963; m. Sandra Lee Huey, Mar. 30, 1972; children—Selby William, Tricia, Lisa, Terry, Jack. Admitted to Tex. bar, 1963, Fla. bar, 1971; practice law, Houston, 1963-72; partner firm Andrews, Kurth, Campbell & Jones, Houston, 1971-72; v.p., gen. counsel, dir. Fla. Gas Co., Winter Park, 1972-73, pres., 1973—, chief exec. officer, 1974—, chmn. bd., 1977—; exec. v.p., chief fin. and adminstrv. officer, dir., mem. exec. office Continental Group Inc., N.Y.C., 1979—; dir. Sun Banks of Fla. Bd. dirs. Orange Bowl Com., 1975, Fla. Bus. Forum, 1974, Fla. Tech. U. Found., Inc., 1974—, Fla. Council 100. Mem. Fla., Tex., Am. bar assns., Young Pres.'s Orgn., Interstate Natural Gas Assn. Am. (dir. 1975-79), Am. Natural Gas Assn. (dir. 1978-78, So. Gas Assn. (dir. 1976-79, Fla. C. of C. Home: 174 Rosebrook Rd New Canaan CT 06840 Office: Continental Group 1 Harbor Plaza Stamford CT 06902

SULLIVAN, THOMAS CHRISTOPHER, coatings co. exec.; b. Cleve., July 8, 1937; s. Frank Charles and Margaret Mary (Wilhelmy) S.; B.S., Miami U., Oxford, Ohio, 1959; m. Sandra Simmons, Mar. 12, 1960; children—Frank, Sean, Tommy, Danny, Kathleen, Julie. Div. sales mgr. Republic Powdered Metals, Cleve., 1961-65, exec. v.p., 1965-70; pres., chmn. bd. RPM, Inc., Medina, Ohio, 1971-78, chmn. bd., 1978—; dir. Overly-Hautz Co., Cleve., NPCA, Washington. Bd. dirs. Culver Ednl. Found. Served to lt. (j.g.) USNR, 1959-60. Mem. Nat. Paint and Coatings Assn. (dir.), Young Pres. Orgn. Roman Catholic. Office: 2628 Pearl Rd Medina OH 44256

SULLIVAN, THOMAS FRANCIS, life ins. co. exec.; b. Evanston, Ill., Dec. 29, 1939; s. Robert F. and Loretta C. (Crawford) S.; B.S., Xavier U., Cin., 1961; J.D., DePaul Coll., Chgo., 1964; m. Ann Miles, May 20, 1964; children—David, Meg, Bradley, Colette. Admitted to bar; atty. Ceco Corp., 1965-70; v.p. United Ins. Co. Am., 1970-71; v.p., sec., gen. counsel Ryan Ins. Group, Inc., Chgo., 1977-79; pres. subs. Globe Life Ins. Co., Chgo., 1979—. Mem. Ill. Bar Assn., Chgo. Bar Assn. Clubs: Butler Nat., Cress Creek Country. Address: Ryan Ins Group Inc 222 N Dearborn St Chicago IL 60601

SULLIVAN, THOMAS JAMES, metals co. exec.; b. Franklin, N.H., Mar. 26, 1923; s. James J. and Helen (Mullin) S.; A.B., Holy Cross Coll., 1947; J.D., Harvard Law Sch., 1949; m. Anne Clark, Aug. 31, 1963. With Gen. Dynamics Corp.,1949-61, asst. div. mgr., 1959-61; sr. asso. Harbridge House, Cambridge, Mass., 1961-63; with Hydraulic Research & Mfg. Co., Valencia, Cal., 1963-71, v.p., 1964-68, exec. v.p., 1968-69, pres., 1969-71; v.p. Textron, Inc., Providence, 1971-73; pres. Walker/Parkersburg Co., Parkersburg, W. Va., 1973—. Served with USAAF, 1943-46. Fellow Nat. Contract Mgmt. Assn. Home: 2516 Plum St Parkersburg WV 26101 Office: 620 Depot St Parkersburg WV 26101

SULLIVAN, THOMAS MICHAEL, civil engr.; b. Wellsville, N.Y., Apr. 28, 1913; s. Daniel Vincent and Catherine Theresa (McCarthy) S.; B.A. in Architecture, B.S. in Structural Engring., Okla. State U., 1935; m. Margaret Louise Neptune, Aug. 5, 1939; children—Thomas Patrick, Kathleen Ann. Dir. internat. properties, then asst. sec. Trans World Airlines, 1940-47; asst. airport engr., then 1st dep. dir. aviation Port N.Y. Authority, 1947-68; exec. dir. Dallas/Ft. Worth Regional Airport, 1968-75; dir. mktg. ground transp. Vought Corp., Dallas, 1975--; mem. Presdl. Aviation Adv. Commn., 1970-72; mem. Dallas/Ft. Worth Airport Bd.; cons. airports throughout world. Hon. v.p. State Fair Tex. Recipient Distinguished Service medal Port N.Y. Authority for design Kennedy Airport, 1957; Engr. of Year award Am. Pub. Works Assn., 1972; Headliner of Year award Press Club of Dallas, 1974; Safety award Air Line Pilots Assn., 1973; registered profl. engr., Tex. Mem. Airport Operators Council Internat., Am. Pub. Transit Assn., ASCE (James Laurie prize 1975), Am. Helicopter Soc., Tex. Soc. Profl. Engrs., Tex. Soc. Architects, Knights of Malta. Roman Catholic. Clubs: K.C., Kiwanis, Northwood. Contbr. profl. jours. Home: 7045 Helsem Way Dallas TX 75230 Office: PO Box 5907 Dallas TX 75222

SULLIVAN, THOMAS PATRICK, lawyer, govt. ofcl.; b. Evanston, Ill., Mar. 23, 1930; s. Clarence M. and Pauline (DeHaye) S.; student Loras Coll., Dubuque, Iowa, 1947-49; LL.B. cum laude, Loyola U., Chgo., 1952; m. Susan Kreyer, June 30, 1962; children—Margaret Mary, Timothy Joseph, Elizabeth Ann. Admitted to Ill. bar, 1952, asso. firm Jenner & Block, Chgo., 1954-62, partner, 1963-77: U.S. atty. for No. Dist. Ill., Chgo., 1977—. Served with U.S. Army, 1952-54. Decorated Bronze Star. Recipient medal of excellence Loyola U. Law Sch., 1965; Ill. Pub. Defender Assn. award, 1972. Fellow Am. Coll. Trial Lawyers; mem. Am., Ill., Fed. Seventh Circuit, Chgo. bar assns., Am. Law Inst., Am. Judicature Soc., Chgo. Council Lawyers. Contbr. articles to profl. jours. Office: 219 S Dearborn St Chicago IL 60604*

SULLIVAN, TIMOTHY JOHN, state justice; b. White Plains, N.Y., Jan. 28, 1917; s. John T. and Dora (Egan) S.; B.A., Fordham U., 1939, LL.B., 1948, LL.D., 1968; m. Henrietta Hasey, Jan. 12, 1947; children—Nancy P., Loretta M., Timothy J., Stephen J., Cynthia Ann, Patricia Ann, Michael J. Admitted to N.Y. bar, 1948; asso. McCarthy & Gaynor, White Plains, 1951-53; mem. firm McCarthy Fingar, Gaynor, Sullivan & Donovan and predecessor firms, White Plains, 1954-70, sr. partner, 1960-70; adminstrv. judge Westchester County Ct., 1970-73; justice N.Y. State Supreme Ct., 1976-79. Mem. local bd. SSS, 1962-69, chmn., 1964-69. Mem. adv. bd. Coll. of White Plains, Pace U., Pace U. Sch. Law. Served with AUS, 1941-45. Decorated Purple Heart, Bronze Star with 2 oak leaf clusters. Mem. Fordham U. Law Alumni (past pres.), N.Y. State, Westchester County (v.p. 1968—, dir.) bar assns. Republican. Roman Catholic. K.C., Elk. Clubs: Fordham University (N.Y.C.); University, Westchester Hills Golf (White Plains). Home: 6 Cedarwood Rd White Plains NY 10605 Office: NY State Supreme Ct Chambers Courthouse 111 Grove St White Plains NY 10601

SULLIVAN, WALTER FRANCIS, bishop; b. Washington, June 10, 1928; s. Walter Francis and Catherine Jeanette (Vanderloo) S.; B.A., St. Mary's Sem. U., Balt., 1947, S.T.L., 1953; J.C.L., Catholic U., Washington, 1960. Ordained priest Roman Catholic Ch., 1953; asst. pastor St. Andrews Ch., Roanoke, St. Mary's, Star of Sea, Ft. Monroe, 1956-58; sec. Diocesan Tribunal, 1960-65; chancellor Diocese of Richmond, Va., from 1965; rector Sacred Heart Cathedral, Richmond, from 1967; ordained aux. bishop of Richmond, 1970; bishop of Richmond, 1974—. Office: PO Box 2 G Richmond VA 23203*

SULLIVAN, WALTER SEAGAR, editor, author; b. N.Y.C., Jan. 12, 1918; s. Walter Seager and Jeanet E. (Loomis) S.; B.A., Yale, 1940, H.L.D., 1969; H.L.D., Newark Coll. Engring., 1973; D.Sc., Hofstra U., 1974, Ohio State U., 1977; m. Mary E. Barrett, Aug. 17, 1950; children—Elizabeth Anne, Catherine Ellinwood, Theodore Loomis. Mem. staff N.Y. Times, 1940—, fgn. corr. Far East, 1948-50, UN corr., 1951-52, fgn. corr., Germany, 1952-56, chief sci. writer, 1960-62, sci. news editor, 1962-63, sci. editor, 1964—. Served to lt. comdr. USNR, 1940-46; PTO. Recipient George Polk Meml. award in journalism, 1959; Westinghouse-AAAS award, 1963, 68, 72, Am. Inst. Physics-U.S. Steel Found. award, 1969; James T. Grady award Am. Chem. Soc., 1969; Bradford Washburn award Boston Mus. Sci., 1972; Ralph Coats Roe medal ASME, 1975; Sci. in Soc. journalism award Nat. Assn. Sci. Writers, 1976; Disting. Public Service award NSF, 1978. Fellow Arctic Inst. N.Am.; mem. Am. Geog. Soc. (councillor, Daly medal 1973), Am. Polar Soc. (v.p.). Author: Quest for a Continent, 1957; White Land of Adventure, 1957; Assault on the Unknown, 1961; We Are Not Alone, 1964 (Internat. Non-Fiction Book prize 1965); Continents in Motion, 1974; Black Holes, the Edge of Space, the End of Time, 1979. Editor: America's Race for the Moon, 1962. Office: NY Times Times Sq New York NY 10036

SULLIVAN, WARREN, pub. co. exec.; b. N.Y.C., May 19, 1922; s. Warren and Pauline (Dickinson) S.; B.A., Dartmouth, 1943; m. Madeleine Schmidt, June 27, 1947; children—Kathleen, Peter, and William and Jeffrey (triplets). With John Wiley & Sons, 1947-61, v.p. marketing, dir., 1955-61; v.p. Crowell- Collier Co., pres. Macmillan Co., 1961-64, chmn. bd. dirs., 1964-66; pres., chief exec. officer Barnes & Noble, Inc., from 1966; now pres. Halsted Press, N.Y.C., also editor, dir. Trustee Englewood (N.J.) Boys Sch. Served to lt. (j.g.) USNR, World War II. Clubs: Field, Men's (Englewood); Players, Salmagundi (N.Y.C.). Office: Halsted Press 605 3d Ave New York NY 10016*

SULLIVAN, WILLIAM ALBERT, JR., surgeon, univ. dean; b. Nashville, Apr. 6, 1924; s. William Albert and Eleanor Katherine (Allen) S.; student U. of South, Sewanee, Tenn., 1941-43; M.D., Tulane U., 1947; M.S. in Surgery, U. Minn., 1956; m. Theresa Margaret Battaglia, Dec. 15, 1949; children—William Albert III, Timothy Allen. Intern, resident surgery U. Minn., Mpls., 1947-55, dir. Cancer Detection Center, 1955-58, dir. dept. continuation med. edn., 1958-68, asso. dean for admissions and student affairs Med. Sch., 1968—. Served with USNR, 1941-46; to capt. M.C., AUS, 1951-53. Mem. Am., Minn., Ramsey County med. assns., A.C.S., Central Surg. Soc., Sigma Alpha Epsilon, Phi Chi. Episcopalian. Club: University (St. Paul). Home: 1978 Portland Ave St Paul MN 55104 Office: U Minn Med Sch Minneapolis MN 55455

SULLIVAN, WILLIAM DANIEL, educator, biochemist; b. Boston, Nov. 18, 1918; s. William Patrick and Delia (Larkin) S.; A.B., Boston Coll., 1944, M.A., 1945; M.S., Fordham U., 1948; Ph.D., Cath. U. Am., 1959. Joined Soc. Jesus, 1938, ordained priest Roman Catholic Ch., 1951; tchr. Cranwell Prep. Sch., Lenox, Mass., 1945-46, Fairfield (Conn.) Prep. Sch., 1946-47, Cheverus High Sch., Portland, Me., 1952-53, Fairfield (Conn.) U., 1957-58; mem. faculty Boston Coll., 1958—, chmn. biology dept., 1958-69, prof. biology, 1963—, dir. Cancer Research Inst., 1958—; cons. WHIS-TV. Recipient Community Leaders Am. award, 1969. Fellow Am. Inst. Chemists; mem. N.Y., New Eng. (treas.) socs. electron microscopy, Soc. Parasitology, Soc. Am. Bacteriology, N.Y. Acad. Scis., AAUP, Am. Soc. Zoologists, Soc. Protozoologists, AAAS, Am. Polar Soc., Am. Micros. Soc., Am. Soc. Cell Biology, Am. Genetic Assn., Mass. Soc. Zoologists, Nat. Geog. Soc., N.E. Biology Soc., Am. Assn. Jesuit Scientists, Am. Internat. Biol. Soc., Albertus Magnus Guild (pres. 1970—), Sigma Xi (pres. Boston Coll. Club 1961-63), Phi Sigma. Contbr. articles to profl. jours. Address: Boston Coll Chestnut Hill MA 02167

SULLIVAN, WILLIAM FRANCIS, assn. exec.; b. Nashua, N.H., Oct. 8, 1913; s. William Francis and Mary Elizabeth (Thomas) S.; student Phillips Exeter Acad., 1930-33; A.B., Harvard, 1938; LL.B., 1941; m. Helen B. Dolan, Feb. 27, 1943; children—Christine B., William, Mary. Admitted Mass. bar, 1941, and practiced with firm of Ropes, Gray, Best, Coolidge & Rugg, specializing in labor law practice, Boston, 1941-50; treas., pres. Nat. Assn. Cotton Mfrs. 1950—; pres. No. Textile Assn., 1959—. Mem. N.H., Boston bar assns. Roman Catholic. Home: 30 Fieldmont Rd Belmont MA 02178 Office: 211 Congress St Boston MA 02110

SULLIVAN, WILLIAM HALLISEY, JR., football league exec.; b. Lowell, Mass., Sept. 13, 1915; s. William H. and Vera F. Sullivan; A.B., Boston Coll., 1937, postgrad., 1938-39; postgrad. Harvard, summer 1938; m. Mary K. Malone, Dec. 29, 1941; children—Charles W., Kathleen Marie, Mary Jeannie, Nancie Vera, William Hallissey III, Patrick Jerone. Publicity dir. Boston Coll., 1938-40; spl. asst. to dir. athletics U. Notre Dame, 1941-42; dir. pub. relations U.S. Naval Acad., 1942-46, Boston Braves, 1946-52; owner All Star Sports, Inc., 1952-55; asst. to pres. Met. Coal & Oil Co., Dorchester, Mass., 1955-56, v.p., 1956-58, pres., 1958-76; group v.p. Met. Petroleum Co., 1977—; pres. Am. Football League, 1963-69, chmn. TV com., merger com. of Nat. and Am. football leagues; pres. Petroleum Heat & Power Co., Frost Coal & Oil Co., Crystal Coal & Oil Co.; owner, pres. New Eng. Patriots Football Club, 1975—; dir. Commonwealth Nat. Bank Boston, Allied Concrete Co., Vol. Coop. Bank, Better Home Heat Council, Kiddle Kamp Corp., Better Bus. Bur. Met. Boston, Nat. Football League Properties, Inc., Nat. Football League Film, Inc.; incorporator Union Savs. Bank. Chmn. Greater Boston Stadium Authority, 1962—; chmn. Christmas Seal campaign Mass. Tb Assn., 1963-64. Bd. dirs. Catholic Counseling Service, Mass. Eye Research Corp., Stonehill Coll.; mem. Pres.'s Council Boston Coll. Served with USNR, 1942-46. Mem. New Eng. Fuel Dealers Assn. Knight of Malta. Clubs: Indian Creek Country; Hundred of Mass. (dir.); Algonquin (Boston); Woodland Golf; Vesper Country; Fort Hill; Oyster Harbors. Office: care New Eng Patriots Schafer Stadium Route 1 Foxboro MA 02035*

SULLIVAN, WILLIAM JAMES, univ. exec.; b. Freeport, Ill., Dec. 20, 1930; s. Arlend Eugene and Bessie (Burton) S.; B.A. in Philosophy, St. Louis U., 1954, M.A. in Philosophy, 1957, Ph.L., 1957; S.T.L., Faculté de Theologie, Lyons, France, 1962; M.A., Yale U., 1966, M.Phil. in Religious Studies, 1967, Ph.D. in Religious Studies, 1971;

D.D. (hon.), Concordia Sem. in Exile, 1977. Tchr. classical lang. Creighton Prep. Sch., 1955-58; asst. prof. theology Marquette U., 1967-71; dean Sch. Div., St. Louis U., 1971-75; provost Seattle U., 1975-76, pres., 1976—; bd. dirs. Am. Council Edn., Internat. Fedn. Catholic Univs., U. San Francisco, Campion High Sch., Maryville Coll.; founder, bd. dirs. Wash. Student Loan Guaranty Assn. Bd. dirs. Pacific Sci. Center, Seattle, 1976—, Pvt. Sector Initiatives, Seattle, 1975—, World Without War Council, Seattle, 1978—, Seattle United Way, 1979—; mem. adv. bd. Seattle Opportunities Industrialization Center, 1978—. Recipient Edmund Campion award Campion High Sch., 1970; Pope John XXIII award Viterbo Coll., 1979. Mem. Assn. Cath. Colls. and Univs., Nat. Assn. Ind. Colls. and Univs., AAUP, Assn. Jesuit Colls. and Univs., Wash. Friends Higher Edn., Ind. Colls. Wash., Seattle C. of C. (dir. 1979—). Catholic. Clubs: Rainier, Seattle Yacht, Coll., Rotary (Seattle). Contbr. articles on theology, edn. and cultural topics to profl. jours., popular publs. Home and Office: Seattle U Seattle WA 98122

SULLIVAN, WILLIAM JAMES, ins. co. exec.; b. Effingham, Ill., July 8, 1919; s. William James and Norma (Underriner) S.; A.B., Ill. Coll., 1941; postgrad. Inst. Meteorology, U. Chgo., 1941-42; m. Charlotte Ann Williams, Aug. 3, 1942; children—Sue Sullivan Shepple, Stephen J., Mary Jo Sullivan Fitzgerald, Margaret L. Sullivan Price, Mark W., Catherine L. Sullivan Dunwiddie, Timothy P. Meteorologist, Chgo. & So. Airlines, Memphis, 1945-46; with State Life Ins. Co., Indpls., 1946—, v.p., actuary, 1959-66, dir., 1963—, pres., 1966-68, chmn., pres., 1968—; dir. Citizens Gas & Coke Utility. Bd. dirs. St. Vincent Hosp. Found., Central Ind. Better Bus. Bur.; trustee Ill. Coll.; mem. admissions com. Indpls. United Way. Served to maj. USAAF, 1941-46. Fellow Soc. of Actuaries; mem. Am. Council LIfe Ins. (Ind. v.p.), Phi Beta Kappa. Democrat. Roman Catholic. K.C. Clubs: Highland Golf and Country; Indianapolis Athletic. Home: 5425 N Delaware St Indianapolis IN 46220 Office: 141 E Washington St Indianapolis IN 46205

SULLIVANT, ROBERT SCOTT, univ. adminstr.; b. Williams, Ariz., Jan. 23, 1925; s. Alexander Scott and Gladys (Hackett) S.; A.B., U. Cal. at Los Angeles, 1947, M.A., 1948; Ph.D., U. Chgo., 1958; postdoctoral exchange scholar, Moscow State U., 1961; m. Enid Marie Olsen, Dec. 27, 1952; children—Wayne Arthur, Stephen Scott, Barbara Kay, Cynthia Lynn. Instr. polit. sci. U. S.D., 1951-54; sr. research analyst, research project Georgetown U., 1954-59; asso. prof. polit. sci. DePauw U., 1959-65; vis. asso. prof. U. Chgo., 1962-63; asso. prof., chmn. polit. sci. dept. U. Mo.-St. Louis, 1965-69, prof. polit. sci., dean Grad. Sch., dir. research, 1969-73; prof. polit. sci., exec. v.p. U. Toledo, 1973—; cons. Atlantic Research Corp., 1967-68. Served with USAAF, 1943-46. Fellow Am. Council Learned Socs., 1969; Samuel MacClintock fellow, 1948-49; fellow U. Chgo., 1949-50; NDEA fellow, 1960; fellow Russian Research Center, Harvard, 1969, Inst. for Ednl. Mgmt., 1972; recipient award Inter-Univ. Com. Travel Grants, 1960, Social Sci. Research Council, 1961. Mem. Am., Midwest, Mo. (pres. 1969-70) polit. sci. assns., AAUP, Am. Assn. Advancement Slavic Studies, Phi Beta Kappa, Pi Sigma Alpha, Phi Kappa Phi. Author: Soviet Politics and the Ukraine, 1917-57, 1962. Home: 2145 Fordway Rd Ottawa Hills OH 43606

SULOWAY, IRWIN JEROME, univ. adminstr.; b. Chgo., Aug. 11, 1921; s. Louis I. and Esther (Gail) S.; B.E., Chgo. Tchrs. Coll., 1943; M.A., Northwestern U., 1948, Ph.D., 1951; m. Elaine Shirley Fox, Oct. 20, 1946; children—Stephen David, Ann Elizabeth. Instr. English, Kelly High Sch., Chgo., 1946-47; lectr. English, Northwestern U., 1948-50; asst. editor English Jour., 1950-51; prof. English, asst. dean charge publs. Ill. Tchrs. Coll., 1951-65, mng. editor Chgo. Schs. Jour., 1955-63; prof. English, dean arts and scis. Chgo. State U., 1965-68, dean faculty, 1968-72, prof. English, 1972-75, acting v.p. acad. affairs, 1975-76, prof. English, 1976—. With AID program, Vietnam, 1963-65. Mem. Citizens Schs. Com., Chgo., 1956-77; sec. Joint Council on Higher Edn., 1969-71. Bd. dirs. Oak Park (Ill.) Library, 1971-75. Served with USAAF, 1943-46. Mem. Nat. Council Tchrs. English (dir., 1952-61, asst. sec.-treas. 1950-51, elementary sect. governing com., 1958-60, conv. chmn. 1960, chmn. com. on promising practices 1963-65), North Central Assn. Colls. and Secondary Schs. (asso. leadership tng. projects 1961-62), Am. Coll. Pub. Relations Assn., Am. Fedn. Tchrs. (chmn. com. on ednl. trends 1955), Chgo. Tchrs. Union (exec. bd., chmn. edn. com. 1954-56), Ednl. Press Assn. Am., Am. Acad. Polit. and Social Sci., AAUP. Jewish. Clubs: The City (Chgo.). Contbr. articles to profl. jours. Home: 3500 N Lake Shore Dr Chicago IL 60657 Office: 284 Williams Hall Chgo State U Chicago IL 60628. *In retrospect it appears that the most important understanding I acquired was the need for balance (perhaps I should say compromise) between the ideal and reality. The religious and the secular ideals early instilled in me were and are important; without them society would be an impossible jungle. And it's relatively easy to pinpoint the means through which I acquired them. It's much more difficult to recollect just how and when I learned that ideals were to be striven for rather than attained and that one must be able to compromise ideals with reality (the art of the possible?) without relinquishing those ideals as goals. These latter ideas seem to be the hard ones to come by. Too many people either cannot accommodate themselves to reality or embrace reality so willingly that they become self-centered cynics.*

SULSER, JACK ARNOLD, fgn. service officer; b. Moline, Ill., Sept. 11, 1925; s. Raymond Jacob and Vera Adele (Swanson) S.; A.B. summa cum laude, Augustana Coll., 1949; M.A., U. Wis., 1950; m. Helen C. Dulemba, Jan. 26, 1952; children—J. David, Julie, Carol. Commd. fgn. service officer, Dept. State, successively vice consul, London, vice consul, Newcastle upon Tyne, Eng., info. officer, Bologna, Italy, consul, Duesseldorf, W. Ger., spl. asst. to dir. of personnel ops., Dept. State, Washington, polit. officer, Vienna, London, dep. prin. officer, Frankfurt, polit. counselor, London, now consul gen., Rotterdam, Netherlands. Past treas. Lincolnia Hills Civic Assn., Alexandria, Va.; past vice chmn. bd. Am. Internat. Sch., Vienna; bd. dirs. Rotterdam Internat. Sch. Served with U.S. Army, 1943-50. Decorated Bronze Star, Purple Heart. Mem. Am. Fgn. Service Protective Assn. (sec.-treas.). Office: American Consulate General Rotterdam APO NY 09159

SULTAN, PAUL EDWARD, educator; b. Vancouver, B.C., Can., Jan. 26, 1924; s. John Edward and Selma (Erickson) S.; B.A., U. B.C., 1947; M.A., Cornell U., 1949, Ph.D., 1950; m. Charlene Barbara Schaeffer, Feb. 15, 1961; children—Cathy (Mrs. Richard Chapin), Laura, Jennifer, Kristen, Deborah. Came to U.S., 1947, naturalized, 1955. Asst. prof. indsl. relations U. Buffalo, 1950-54; asso. prof. finance U. So. Calif., 1954-59; prof. econs. Clarement (Calif.) Grad. Sch., 1959-73, chmn. dept. econs., 1969-73; prof. Sch. Bus., So. Ill. U., Edwardsville, 1973—; vis. lectr. Salzburg (Austria) seminar Am. Studies, summer 1951, U. Calif. at Los Angeles, 1964, Simon Fraser U., Burnaby, B.C., 1970; cons. Can. Dept. Manpower and Immigration, 1970-72. Chmn. Calif. sect. labor com. NCCJ, 1967-70. Served with RCAF, 1943-45. Recipient brotherhood citation NCCJ, 1968. Mem. Am., Western econ. assns., Indsl. Relations Research Assn. Contbr. articles to profl. jours. Home: 1307 Randle St Edwardsville IL 62025

SULZBERGER, ARTHUR OCHS, newspaper exec.; b. N.Y.C., Feb. 5, 1926; s. Arthur Hays and Iphigene (Ochs) S.; B.A., Columbia, 1951; LL.D., Dartmouth, 1964, Bard Coll., 1967; L.H.D., Montclair State Coll., 1972; m. Barbara Grant, July 2, 1948 (div. 1956); children—Arthur Ochs, Karen Alden; m. 2d, Carol Fox, Dec. 19, 1956; 1 dau., Cynthia Fox; adopted dau., Cathy. With N.Y. Times Co., N.Y.C., 1951—, asst. treas., 1958-63, pres., pub., 1963—, also dir.; dir. Times Printing Co., Chattanooga, Gapesia Pulp and Paper Co., Ltd., Chandler, Can. Bd. dirs. N.Y. Conv. and Visitors Bur. Trustee Columbia, Met. Mus. Art. Served to capt. USMCR, World War II, Korea. Mem. Bur. Advt. (dir.), S.A.R. Clubs: Overseas Press, Explorers (N.Y.C.); Metropolitan, Federal City (Washington); Century Country (Purchase, N.Y.); Rockrimmon (Stamford, Conn.). Office: 229 W 43d St New York City NY 10036

SULZBERGER, CYRUS LEO, author; b. N.Y.C., Oct. 27, 1912; Harvard, 1934; m. Marina Tatiana Lada, Jan. 21, 1942; children—Marina Beatrice (Mrs. Adrian Berry), David Alexis. Columnist, N.Y. Times, until 1979. Recipient Pulitzer Prize citation, 1951; award for best consistent reporting from abroad Overseas Press Club Am., 1951, citations for excellence, 1957, 70, award for best book on fgn. affairs, 1973. Clubs: Metropolitan (Washington); Morfontaine (Paris, France). Author: Sit-Down with John L. Lewis, 1938; The Big Thaw, 1956; What's Wrong with U.S. Foreign Policy, 1958; My Brother Death, 1959; The Test-DeGaulle and Algeria, 1962; Unfinished Revolution, 1965; History of World War II (Am. Heritage History), 1966; A Long Row of Candles, 1969; The Last of the Giants, 1970; The Tooth Merchant, 1973; Unconquered Souls, 1973; An Age of Mediocrity, 1973; The Coldest War, 1974; Postscript with a Chinese Accent, 1974; Go Gentle into the Night, 1976; The Fall of Eagles, 1977; Seven Continents and Forty Years, 1977; The Tallest Liar, 1977; Marina, 1979. Address: Spetsais Greece

SULZBERGER, MARION BALDUR, physician, dermatologist; b. N.Y.C., Mar. 12, 1895; s. Ferdinand and Stella (Ullmann) S.; student Harvard, 1912-13; studied medicine, France, Switzerland, Germany, 1920-29; degree of basic med. sci., U. Geneva, Switzerland, 1921; M.D., U. Zurich, Switzerland, 1926; m. Edna F. Lowenstein, 1915; 1 dau., Margaret L. (Mrs. Francis Dobo); m. 2d, Kathryn Mullen Conway, Oct. 23, 1933; m. 3d, Roberta Zechiel Merrill, Sept. 1958. Miscellaneous activities, 1913-20; intern Kantonspital, Zurich, 1925-26; asst. dermatology and syphilis Dermatologic U. Clinic (Bruno Bloch, dir.), 1926-29; in U. Clinic (J. Jadasshon, dir.), Breslau, Germany, 1929; asst. clin. prof. dermatology and syphilology Columbia, 1935-46, asso. clin. prof., 1946-47; George Miller Mackee prof. dermatology and syphilology N.Y. U. Bellevue Med. Center; prof. emeritus N.Y. U. Sch. Medicine; chmn. dept. dermatology and syphilology Post-Grad. Med. Sch., N.Y. U., 1954-60, now prof. emeritus dermatology and syphilology; now clin. prof. dermatology U. Calif. at San Francisco; cons. dermatology and syphilology VA Hosp., Univ. Hosp., N.Y. U. Med. Center, Bellevue Hosp. Asso., dermatology. Montefiore Hosp., N.Y.C., 1931-46; cons. dermatology and syphilology, French Hosp., 1938; attending dermatologist and syphilologist, skin and cancer unit, N.Y. Post-Grad. Hosp., Columbia, 1938-46; dir. N.Y. Skin and Cancer Unit, N.Y. U. Hosp., 1949-60; research asso. Cornell U. Med. Coll., 1942, Spl. cons. USPHS, USN, several other orgns.; pres. Internat. League Dermatologic Socs., 1957-62; mem. gen. medicine study sect. NIH, USPHS, 1957-59; tech. dir. research U.S. Army Med. Research & Devel. Command, Office Surgeon Gen., 1961-64; tech. dir. research Letterman Gen. Hosp., San Francisco, 1964-68; past sci. adviser Letterman Gen. Hosp. and U.S. Army Med. Research Unit, Presidio. Pilot USNR, lt. (j.g.), 1917-19; lt. comdr. MC USNR 1940, comdr. 1943, capt. 1945. Decorated Legion of Merit (U.S.); comdr. Cross of Anjouan, Legion of Honor (France); recipient Meritorious Civilian Service medal Army Dept., 1970. Fellow N.Y. Acad. Medicine, Am. Acad. Allergy, Am. Acad. Dermatology and Syphilology, A.C.P.; mem. Am. Dermatol. Assn. (pres. 1959-60); mem. or hon. mem. fgn., nat. and state profl. socs. Editor: (with Dr. Fred Wise) Yearbook of Dermatology and Syphilology, 1931-42, sr. editor, 1943-55; editor numerous other tech. works. Author: Dermatologic Allergy; Dermatologic Therapy in General Practice (with Dr. Jack Wolf), 1940; Manual of Dermatology, 1942; (with others) Office Imunology 1947. Contbr. sci. articles to jours. Home: 2785 Jackson St San Francisco CA 94115. *Don't waste pity on yourself as long as you can find someone who deserves that pity more. Every occupation, no matter how exciting and satisfying it may be, has intermissions of frustration and deadly boredom. Continue steadfastly and, almost surely, excitement and success will come again. Until you have gotten and weighed all the obtainable facts, try to form no adverse opinion—and, above all, try to express no adverse opinion. Even then, before you judge, put yourself in the place of the other fellow. If you follow these precepts, the poor opinions you express and the enemies you make will both be few. Remember to be grateful for your genes and to those who endowed you with these most essential elements of success. I have accomplished nothing alone. Therefore, I have tried to give credit to my predecessors and co-workers whenever I knew their names.*

SULZBY, JAMES FREDERICK, JR., business exec.; b. Birmingham, Ala., Dec. 24, 1905; s. James Frederick and Annie (Dobbins) S.; ed. Howard Coll., Birmingham, 1925-26; A.B., Birmingham-So. Coll., 1928; grad. Am. Inst. Banking, 1934; Litt.D., Athens Coll.; m. Martha Belle Hilton, Nov. 9, 1935; children—James Frederick III, Martha Hilton (Mrs. Robert J.B. Clark). With trust dept. First Nat. Bank of Birmingham, 1929-43; partner Sulzby Realty Co., 1943—; dir. Home Fed. Savs. & Loan Assn.; dir. Birmingham Real Estate Bd., pres. 1953; pres. Norwood Gardens, Inc. (housing project). Trustee Rushton Lectures, Birmingham Civic Symphony Assn.; bd. dirs. Birmingham Sunday Sch. Assn.; mem. Birmingham Planning Commn., chmn., 1948-61; mem. adv. com. Civil War Centennial Commn.; historian 75th anniversary celebration for Birmingham, 1946; treas., mem. adv. bd. Nat. Hist. Records; treas., mem. exec. com. Southside Bapt. Ch.; pres. Ala. Bapt. Young Peoples Union, 1932-33; bd. govs. Civic Theatre Birmingham, 1946-48; chmn. Jefferson County Nat. Found. Infantile Paralysis, 1951-52, Jefferson County Hist. Commn. Recipient Lit. award A.L.A., 1962; mem. Ala. Hall of Fame. Mem. Newcomen Soc. N.Am. (dir., mem. Ala. com.), Ala. Hist. Assn. (pres. 1947-49, sec. 1950—), Ala. Bapt. Hist. Soc. (pres. 1947-49), Birmingham-Jefferson Hist. Soc., Birmingham Hist. Soc. (sec. 1945-50, trustee 1950—), Avondale Civic Assn. (pres. 1946), Am. Planning and Civic Assn., (dir.), Ala. Assn. Realtors (pres. 1952), Ala. Writers Conclave (pres. 1950), Nat. Assn. Real Estate Bds. (dir. 1952-56), Ala. Acad. Sci. (pres. 1965, trustee), Phi Beta Kappa, Phi Alpha Theta, Omega Tau Rho, Delta Sigma Phi, Omicron Delta Kappa. Democrat. Baptist. Clubs: Filson; Mountain Brook; Univ. (Tuscaloosa, Ala.). Author: Birmingham As It Was in Jackson County, 1944; Birmingham Sketches, 1945; Annals of the Southside Baptist Church, 1947; Historic Alabama Hotels and Resorts, 1960; Arthur W. Smith, A Birmingham Pioneer, 1855-1944, 1961. Home: 3121 Carlisle Rd Birmingham AL 35213 Office: Massey Bldg Birmingham AL 35203

SUMMER, ALBIOUN F., atty. gen. Miss.; b. Pelahatchie, Miss., Nov. 2, 1921; s. Sydney Lamar and Iva Lee (Hardy) S.; diploma Hinds Jr. Coll., 1942; student U. Miss. Sch. Law, 1946-47; LL.B., Jackson Sch. Law, 1950; m. Mary Lois Campbell, June 9, 1945; 1 son, Carl Bennison. Admitted to Miss. bar; town atty. Town of Pelahatchie, 1950-51; practiced law, 1965-68; mem. Miss. Bd. Vet. Affairs, 1957; exec. asst., legal adviser to Gov. Miss., 1958; chancery judge Miss. 5th Dist. Ct., 1958-61; chief asst., legal adviser Gov. Miss., 1968-69; atty. gen. State of Miss., Jackson, 1969-80; v.p., gen. counsel Paine Enterprises, 1953-58, Underwood Homes, Inc., 1960-65; pres. First Realty Co., 1965, Law Research of Miss., Inc., 1966-68. Mem. Am. Legion, VFW, Aircraft Owners and Pilots Assn., Am., Miss., Hinds County bar assns., Nat. Assn. Attys. Gen. (pres. 1975-76, exec. com. 1971-72, 76-79), Phi Delta Theta, Beta Theta Pi. Democrat. Office: Office Atty Gen State Capitol Jackson MS 39205

SUMMER, CHARLES EDGAR, educator; b. Newton, Miss., June 13, 1923; s. Charles Edgar and Emily (O'Rourke) S.; B.A., Coll. William and Mary, 1948; M.B.A., U. Pa., 1949; Ph.D., Columbia, 1957; m. Carol Carlisle, Feb. 21, 1968. Dir. research Booz, Allen & Hamilton, N.Y.C., 1950-54; economist Texaco, Inc., N.Y.C., 1949-50; prof. bus. adminstrn. Columbia, 1957-69; prof. bus. adminstrn. U. Wash., Seattle, 1969—; distinguished vis. prof. U. So. Calif., 1962; cons. corps., hosps. and trade assns. on orgn. and exec. devel. Served as pilot USAAF, World War II. Mem. Acad. Mgmt. (pres. 1973; editorial bd. jour. 1960—), Council Internat. Progress Mgmt. (bd. dirs. 1964—), Inst. Mgmt. Scis. Author: The Managerial Mind, 1977; The Process of Management, 1972; Organizational Behavior, 1978; Strategic Behavior, 1980. Home: 2342 43d Ave E Seattle WA 98112 Office: Grad Sch Bus Adminstrn U Wash Seattle WA 98195

SUMMER, DONNA (LA DONNA ANDREA GAINES), singer, actress, model; b. Boston, Dec. 31, 1948; d. Andrew Gaines; m. Helmut Sommer (div.); 1 dau., Mimi. Singer and model, 1967—; appeared German stage production Hair; resided in Europe, 1967-75, appearing in Vienna Folk Opera prodns. of Showboat and Porgy and Bess, also German prodns. of Godspell and The Me Nobody Knows; appeared in TV show Donna Summer Special, 1980; recorded numerous albums, including Love to Love You Baby, A Love Trilogy, The Four Seasons of Love, I Remember Yesterday, Once Upon A Time; helped create current disco style. Named best rhythm and blues female vocalist of 1978, Nat. Acad. Rec. Arts and Scis.; Disco Singer of Yr., Billboard Mag., 1978; best disco single, disco album, Am. Music Awards, 1979, numerous others. Address: care Munao Mgmt 1220 N Vine St Los Angeles CA 90038

SUMMER, VIRGIL CLIFTON, JR., utility co. exec.; b. Spartanburg, S.C., Aug. 21, 1920; s. Virgil Clifton and Maude Summer (High) S.; M.S., U. S.C., 1968; H.L.D., Newberry Coll., 1978; m. Vera Boland, Nov. 2, 1944; children—Brenda Summer Nunamaker, Michael, Kenneth. With S.C. Electric & Gas Co., 1937—, plant supt., 1955-60, supt. prodn., 1960-62, mgr. prodn. ops. engring. and constrn., 1962-67, sr. v.p., 1967-77, pres., chief operating officer, 1977-79, pres., chief exec. officer, 1979—. Trustee, Lowman Home; mem. Columbia adv. bd. S.C. Nat. Bank. Fellow ASME; mem. Nat. Soc. Profl. Engrs., S.E. Electric Exchange (past chmn. engring. operating div.). Lutheran. Club: Masons. Office: PO Box 764 Columbia SC 29218

SUMMERALL, GEORGE (PAT), sportscaster; b. Lake City, Fla.; degree in Russian History, U. Ark.; m. Katherine Summerall; children—Susan, Jay, Kyle. Football player Detroit Lions, 1952-53, Chgo. Cardinals, 1953-57, N.Y. Giants, 1958-61; with CBS Sports, 1962—, sports dir. WCBS Radio, N.Y.C., 1964-71, host WCBS's morning program, 1966-67, with CBS Radio Network, as sportscaster Sports Time, Predictions, Profiles, also sportscaster early news WCBS-TV, N.Y.C., and sportscaster CBS-TV, host CBS Sports Spectacular. Named Sportscaster of Yr., 1977. Office: care CBS sports 51 W 52d St New York NY 10019*

SUMMERFIELD, MARTIN, physicist; b. N.Y.C., Oct. 20, 1916; s. Jacob and Augusta (Tobias) S; B.S., Bklyn. Coll., 1936; M.S., Calif. Inst. Tech., 1938, Ph.D., 1941; m. Eileen Budin, Aug. 31, 1945; 1 dau., Jacqueline. Asst. chief Air Corps Jet Propulsion Project, Calif. Inst. Tech., 1940-43, chief, rocket research div., 1945-49; chief, rocket devel. div., Aerojet Engring. Corp., Azusa, Calif., 1943-45; mem. subcom. on fuels NACA, 1948-49, subcom. on combustion, 1949-50; prof. jet propulsion Princeton U., 1951—, tech. dir. Project Squid, 1949-51; chief scientist Flow Industries Inc., Princeton Combustion Labs., 1977—; editor Aeros. Publ. Program, 1949-52; editor-in-chief Jour. Am. Rocket Soc., 1951-57; editor Jet Propulsion, also tech. editor Astronautics, 1957-63; editor series on Progress in Astronautics, 1960—; editor-in-chief Astronautica Acta, 1964—. Cons., U.S. Army Research Office, 1968—; mem. adv. com. on chem. propulsion NASA, 1968—. Recipient Pendray award, 1954. Fellow AAAS, Inst. Aero. Scis. (asso.); mem. Am. Rocket Soc. (pres. 1962-63), Internat. Acad. Astronautics, Am. Phys. Soc., ASME, Am. Inst. Aeros. and Astronautics (v.p. 1963-65), Internat. Astronautical Fedn. (v.p. 1963-65), Sigma Xi. Patentee on rocket motors and related devices. Office: Dept Aero Engring Princeton U Princeton NJ 08540*

SUMMERFORD, BEN LONG, artist, educator; b. Montgomery, Ala., Feb. 3, 1924; s. Ben Long and Ollie Jo (Gilchrist) S.; student Birmingham-Southern Coll., 1942-43; B.A., Am. U., 1948, M.A., 1954; student Ecole des Beaux Arts. Paris. 1949-50; m. Christene Morris, Jan. 30, 1951; children—Jeffrey, Rebecca, James. Fellow Acad. Time, 1947, Fulbright fellow to France, 1949-50; staff art dept. Am. U., 1950—, chmn. dept., 1957-66, 70—, prof., 1960—; one-man shows include: Balt. Mus. Art, Goucher Coll., Franz Bader Gallery, Washington, Jefferson Place Gallery, Washington; represented in permanent collection Watkins Gallery, Phillips Gallery Art, Corcoran Gallery Art (all Washington); numerous group shows of paintings. Served to ensign USNR, 1943-46. Home: 10216 Brown's Mill Rd Vienna VA 22180 Office: American University Washington DC 20016

SUMMERLIN, SAM, editor, syndication exec., TV producer, author; b. Chapel Hill, N.C., Jan. 1, 1928; s. Irl Whitaker and Adolpha (Askew) S.; B.A., U. N.C., 1948; m. Cynthia Clare Cyr, Apr. 10, 1952; children—Sandi Claire, Thomas Anthony. State reporter A.P., Raleigh, N.C., 1949-51, fgn. corr., Tokyo and Korea, 1951-54, acting chief bur., Manila, 1953, chief corr. Caribbean and C.Am., Havana, Cuba, 1954-55, chief of bur., Buenos Aires (Argentina) with assignments in Brazil, Chile, Uruguay, Bolivia, Paraguay, 1955-63, chief of bur., New Orleans, 1963-65, Latin Am. editor, 1965-70, dep. world news editor, N.Y.C., 1970-75; asst. editor, asst. gen. mgr. N.Y. Times News Service, 1975-79, gen. mgr., 1979—; v.p. N.Y. Times Syndication Sales Corp., 1978-79, exec. v.p., 1979, pres., 1979—. Served to lt. (j.g.) USNR, 1949-63. Recipient Bronze Hugo, Chgo. Internat. Film Festival; Maria Moors Cabot award Columbia, 1975. Mem. Nat. Assn. TV Program Execs., Am. Soc. Journalists and Authors, Phi Beta Kappa, Sigma Delta Chi, Phi Gamma Delta. Episcopalian. Clubs: Shenorock Shore (Rye, N.Y.); Nat. Press (Washington); Overseas Press (past gov.) (N.Y.C.). Author: (with William L. Ryan) The China Cloud, 1968; (with Bruce Henderson) 1:33 In Memoriam John F. Kennedy, 1968; Latin America: The Land of Revolution, 1972; (with Bruce Henderson) The Super Sleuths, 1976. Producer TV documentaries China: An Open Door, 1972; Oscar: The Story Behind the Statue, 1972; Olympics: The Eternal Torch, 1972; The World in 1974: History As We Lived It, 1975; The

Torch of Champions (Winter and Summer Olympics), 1976, 80; Portraits of Power: Those Who Shaped the 20th Century, 1978; Filmmakers Salute Oscar, 1978, 79, 80; Olympic Champions series, 1980. Home: 420 E 72d St New York NY 10021 also 132 Dearborn Ave Rye NY 10580 Office: NY Times News Service 229 W 43d St New York NY 10036 also NY Times Syndication Sales Corp 200 Park Ave New York NY 10017

SUMMERS, CAROL, artist; b. Kingston, N.Y., Dec. 26, 1925; s. Ivan Franklin and Theresa (Jones) S.; B.A., Bard Coll., 1951, D.F.A. (hon.), 1974; m. Elaine Smithers, Oct. 2, 1954 (div. Aug. 1967); 1 son, Kyle, m. 2d, Joan Ward, May 6, 1974. Represented in permanent collections at Mus. Modern Art, Bklyn. Mus., N.Y. Pub. Library, Library of Congress, Nat. Gallery, Victoria and Albert Mus. (London), Bibliotheque Nationale (Paris), Kunstmuseum (Basil), Lugano (Switzerland) Art Mus., Grenchen (Switzerland) Art Mus., Malmo (Sweden) Mus., Los Angeles County Mus., mus. Phila., Balt., Seattle, Boston, Art Inst. Chgo., Am. embassies Russia, Can., India, Thailand, Federal Republic of Germany, Eng.; traveling exhibit Mus. Modern Art, 1964-66; retrospective exhbn. Brooklyn Mus., 1977; tchr. Hunter Coll., Sch. Visual Arts, Haystack Mountain Sch. Crafts, Bklyn. Mus. Art Sch., Pratt Graphic Art Center, Chelterham Twp. Art Center, Valley Stream Community Art Center, U. Pa., Columbia, Coll. Art Study Abroad, Paris; USIS workshop tour, India, 1974. Served with USMCR, 1944-48; PTO. Italian Govt., study grantee, 1954-55; Louis Comfort Tiffany Found. fellow, 1955, 60, John Simon Guggenheim Found. fellow, 1959, Fulbright fellow Italy, 1961. Mem. Print Council Am., Phila. Print Club. Address: 133 Prospect Ct Santa Cruz CA 95065

SUMMERS, CLYDE WILSON, educator; b. Grass Range, Mont., Nov. 21, 1918; s. Carl Douglas and Anna Lois (Yontz) S.; B.S., U. Ill., 1939, J.D., 1942; LL.M., Columbia, 1946, J.S.D., 1952; LL.D., U. Louvain (Belgium), U. Stockholm, 1978; m. Evelyn Marie Wahlgren, Aug. 30, 1947; children—Mark, Erica, Craig, Lisa. Admitted to N.Y. bar, 1951; mem. law faculty U. Toledo, 1942-49, U. Buffalo, 1949-56; prof. law Yale, 1956-66, Garver prof. law, 1966-75; Jefferson B. Fordham prof. law U. Pa., 1975—. Hearing examiner Conn. Commn. on Civil Rights, 1963-71. Chmn., Gov.'s Com. on Improper Union Mgmt. Practices, N.Y. State, 1957-58; chmn. Conn. Adv. Council on Unemployment Ins. and Employment Service; mem. Conn. Labor Relations Bd., 1966-70. Guggenheim fellow, 1955-56; Ford fellow, 1963-64; German-Marshall fellow, 1977-78; Nat. Endowment for Humanities fellow, 1977-78. Mem. Am. Arbitration Assn., Am. Bar Assn., Internat. Soc. Labor Law and Social Legislation. Congregationalist. Author: Labor Cases and Material, 1968; co-author: Rights of Union Members, 1979. Co-editor: Labor Relations and the Law, 1953; Employment Relations and the Law, 1959. Home: 753 N 26th St Philadelphia PA 19130 Office: U Pa Philadelphia PA 19104

SUMMERS, EARL TALIAFERRO, elec. supply distbg. co. exec.; b. Dallas, Nov. 5, 1913; s. Earl Taliaferro and Fannie (Van Slyke) S.; student pub. schs., Dallas; m. Patricia Nichols, Jan. 15, 1944; children—Stephen, Sharon, James, Tom, Marianne. Vice pres. Beckett Electric Co., Dallas, to 1943; founder, 1943, since chmn. bd., pres., now dir. Summers Electric Co., Dallas; (dir. Town North Bank, Dallas. Mem. Nat. Assn. Elec. Distbrs., Dallas C. of C. Republican. Clubs: Preston Trail (past pres., dir.), Northwood (Dallas); Broadmoor Golf (Colorado Springs, Colo.); El Dorado Country (Palm Desert, Calif.). Home: 5103 Southbrook Dr Dallas TX 75209 Office: 4255 LBJ Expressway Suite 155 Dallas TX 75234

SUMMERS, EDWARD LEE, accountant; b. Houston, Aug. 24, 1937; s. Elmer L. and Elizabeth B. S.; B.A., Rice U., 1959, B.S. in Chem. Engring. (Hohenthal scholar), 1960; M.B.A. (Univ. fellow), U. Tex., 1962, Ph.D. (Ford Found. fellow), 1965; m. Kathryn Frances Beke, 1963; children—Michael, Pamela. Staff accountant Haskins & Sells, Houston, 1962; asst. prof. accounting Rice U., 1965-68; asso. prof. U. Tex. Grad. Sch. Bus., 1968-71, prof., 1971—, Arthur Young Distinguished prof. accounting, 1977—, chmn. dept. accounting, 1975—. Recipient Best Article award Witte Found., 1970, Distinguished Faculty award U. Tex. Ph.D. Students in Bus. Adminstrn., 1971; Arthur Andersen Faculty fellow, summer 1965; Rice U. grantee, 1967; C.P.A. Mem. Am. Inst. C.P.A.'s, Tex. Soc. C.P.A.'s, (editorial advisory bd. 1971-75, Austin chpt. C.P.A. of Yr., 1976), Am. Accounting Assn. (chmn. Southwestern sect. 1968-69), Beta Alpha Psi, Beta Gamma Sigma (pres. U. Tex. chpt. 1969), Phi Kappa Phi. Author: (with K. E. Knight) A Study of Knowledge Used in Management Advisory Services by Accounting Profession, 1977; contbr. articles, revs. to profl. publs.; editorial bd. Accounting Rev., 1969-70. Office: U Tex Austin Coll Bus Adminstrn Austin TX 78712

SUMMERS, FRANK WILLIAM, librarian; b. Jacksonville, Fla., Feb. 8, 1933; s. Frank Wesley and Kathleen (Gilreath) S.; B.A., Fla. State U., 1955; M.A., Rutgers U., 1959, Ph.D., 1973; m. Marie Elizabeth Marjenhoff, Nov. 27, 1957; 1 son, William Wesley. Librarian, Jacksonville Pub. Library, 1955, 57; sr. librarian Linden (N.J.) Pub. Library, 1958-59; dir. Cocoa (Fla.) Pub. Library, 1959-61; asso. librarian Providence Pub. Library, 1961-65; state librarian Fla. State Library, 1965-69; research fellow Rutgers U., 1969-70; asst. dean, prof. Coll. Librarianship, U. S.C., 1971-76, dean., 1976—. lectr. U. R.I. Library Sch., 1964-65; library surveys in Fla. and Ohio; mem. bd. internat. consultants Pahlavi Nat. Library, Tehran, Iran, 1975. Mem. R.I. Bd. Library Commrs., 1964-65. Served to lt. (j.g.) USNR, 1955-57. Mem. A.L.A., R.I. Library Assn. (pres.), Beta Phi Mu. Contbr. profl. jours. Home: 315 Tyler St Columbia SC 29205 Office: Coll of Librarianship U SC Columbia SC 29208

SUMMERS, FRANK WYNERTH, chief justice La. Supreme Ct.; b. Abbeville, La., Sept. 5, 1914; s. Clay Ralph and Esther (LeBlanc) S.; B.A., U. S.W. La., 1938; LL.B., Tulane U., 1938; m. Beverly Miller, June 22, 1940; children—Frank Wynerth II, Preston Miller, Susan Priscilla, Clay James, William Charles, Beverly Marie. Admitted to La. bar, 1938; practice in Abbeville, 1938-41, 46-52, 55-60; dist. judge 15th Jud. Dist. Ct. La., 1952-54; justice Supreme Ct. La., 1960—, chief justice, 1979—; engaged in rice and cattle farming, Vermilion Parish, 1947—. Chmn. fund campaign Vermilion Parish chpt. ARC, 1947-48, past chmn. chpt. 1949; chmn. Vermilion dist. Boy Scouts Am., 1956, pres. Evangeline area council, 1958-60; chmn. Vermilion Parish, U.S. Savs. Bonds. Served to lt. comdr. USNR, 1941-46. Mem. Am., La. bar assns., Am. Judicature Soc., Am. Legion (past post comdr.), V.F.W., Order Coif, White Inn (Tulane U.), Blue Key, Phi Delta Phi, Phi Kappa Sigma. Democrat. Roman Catholic. Clubs: Abbeville Country (past pres.); New Orleans Country, Pickwick, (New Orleans). Mem. bd. adv. editors Tulane U. Law Rev. Office: Supreme Court Bldg New Orleans LA 70112

SUMMERS, GENE RUDOLPH, architect, builder; b. San Antonio, Tex., July 31, 1928; s. Frank Leslie and Etta (Nelson) S.; B.Arch., Tex. A. and M., 1949; M.S. in Arch., Ill. Inst. Tech., 1951; m. Anna Eble O'Bannon, Aug. 17, 1951; children—Blake, Karen, Scott. Asst. to Mies van der Rohe, Chgo., 1950-66; partner in charge of design C.F. Murphy Assos., Chgo., 1967-73; pres., Ridgway Ltd., Newport Beach, Calif., 1973—. Served with U.S. Army, 1953-55. Recipient Best Design award McCormick Place, Steel Inst., 1973. Mem. Am. Inst. Architects (design award 1972). Home: 851 Diamond St Laguna Beach CA 92651 Office: 22600 Lambert St El Toro CA 92630

SUMMERS, HOLLIS, educator, writer; b. Eminence, Ky., June 21, 1916; s. Hollis S. and Hazel (Holmes) S.; A.B., Georgetown Coll., 1937, Litt.D., 1965; M.A., Middlebury Coll., 1943; Ph.D., State U. Iowa, 1949; m. Laura Clarke, June 30, 1943; children—Hollis III, David Clarke. Tchr., Georgetown Coll., 1944-49, U. Ky., 1949-59, Ohio U., 1959—. Staff, Writers Confs., Bread Loaf, Vt., Antioch, Ohio, Morehead, Ky., Grinnell, Iowa, others; adviser Ford Found. conf. on writers in Am., 1958; lectr. arts program Assn. Am. Colls., 1958-63; Danforth lectr., 1963-66, 71; Fulbright lectr. U. Canterbury, Christchurch, N.Z., 1978; mem. Ohio Council for Humanities. Named Distinguished Prof. of Year U. Ky. Coll. Arts and Scis., 1959, Distinguished Prof., Ohio U., 1964; recipient Poetry award Sat. Rev., 1959; Ohio Arts Council award, 1976; Nat. Endowment for Arts fellow, 1974, grantee, 1975. Author: (novels) City Limit, 1948, Brighten the Corner, 1952, The Weather of February, 1957, The Day After Sunday, 1968, The Garden, 1972, (with James Rourke) Teach You A Lesson, 1955; (poetry) The Walks Near Athens, 1959, Someone Else, 1962, Seven Occasions, 1965, The Peddler and Other Domestic Matters (Ohloana Poetry award 1968), 1967, (poetry) Sit Opposite Each Other, 1970; Start from Home, 1972; (short stories) How They Chose the Dead, 1973; (poetry) Occupant Please Forward, 1976. Editor: Kentucky Story, 1954; (with Edgar Whan) Literature: An Introduction, 1960; Discussions of the Short Story, 1963; (poetry) Dinosaurs, 1977. Home: 181 N Congress St Athens OH 45701

SUMMERS, JAMES IRVIN, advt. exec.; b. Lexington, Mo., July 10, 1921; s. William E. and Elizabeth (Hoeflicker) S.; m. Priscilla Barstow West, Jan. 15, 1958; children—Susanne Cornelia, Elizabeth Barstow, James Irvin, Daniel Edward. With Harold Cabot & Co., Inc., Boston, 1946—, exec. v.p., 1960-77, pres., 1977—, also dir. Mem. exec. com., bd. dirs., v.p. and chmn. Public Info. Com., Mass. Bay United Way, 1979—; chmn. Swampscott Republican Finance Com., 1964—; trustee Mass. Eye and Ear Infirmary, also mem. bd. mgrs., exec. com.; trustee Family Service Assn. Greater Boston. Served with USAAF, 1941-45. Decorated Bronze Star. Clubs: Bay, Madison Square Garden (Boston); Tedesco Country (Marblehead, Mass.); Edgartown (Mass.) Golf. Home: 66 Phillips Ave Swampscott MA 01907 Office: 10 High St Boston MA 02110

SUMMERS, JAMES WARFIELD, trucking co. exec.; b. Coatesville, Pa., Aug. 14, 1942; s. Kennell George and Mary Virginia (Warfield) S.; B.S. in Bus. Adminstrn., Susquehanna U., Selinsgrove, Pa., 1964; m. Barbara Irene Evans, Aug. 26, 1967; children—Michelle Lynn, Tricia Ellen. Gen. practice mgr. Coopers & Lybrand, C.P.A.'s, Phila., 1965-74; v.p. fin. Burgmeyer Bros., Inc., Reading, Pa., 1974-77; treas. Smith's Transfer Corp., Staunton, Va., 1977—. Mem. Pa. N.G., 1964-70. C.P.A., Pa. Mem. Am. Inst. C.P.A.'s, Fin. Execs. Inst., Nat. Accth. and Fin. Council, Am. Trucking Assn. (chmn. fin. reporting and info. com. 1979-80). Methodist. Club: Rotary. Home: 603 Woodmont Dr Staunton VA 24401 Office: PO Box 1000 Staunton VA 24401

SUMMERS, JOHN BENJAMIN, trade assn. exec.; b. Upton, Mass., Oct. 21, 1930; s. William R. and Mary E. (Van Riper) S.; B.A., St. Bonaventure U., 1952; LL.B., Georgetown U., 1959; m. Gloria June Hinman, Jan. 29, 1955; children—Stephanie, John F., Stacy. Admitted to D.C. bar, 1960; analyst CIA, Washington, 1955-60; atty. Office of Gen. Counsel FCC, Washington, 1960-67; asst. gen. counsel Nat. Assn. Broadcasters, Washington, 1967-70, gen. counsel, 1970-76, exec. v.p., gen. mgr., 1976—. Served with U.S. Army, 1952-55. Mem. Am. Bar Assn., Fed. Communications Bar Assn., D.C. Bar Assn. Roman Catholic. Home: 12805 Willow Wind Circle Oxon Hill MD 20022 Office: 1771 N St NW Washington DC 20036

SUMMERS, JOSEPH HOLMES, educator; b. Louisville, Feb. 9, 1920; s. Hollis Spurgeon and Hazel (Holmes) S.; A.B. magna cum laude, Harvard, 1941, M.A., 1948, Ph.D. in English, 1950; m. U.T. Miller, Sept. 24, 1943; children—Mary Elliott, Hazel Lincoln, Joseph Holmes. Teaching fellow history and lit. Harvard, 1945-48; instr. lit. Bard Coll., 1948-50; asst. prof. U. Conn., 1950-55, asso. prof., 1955-59; prof. English Washington U., St. Louis, 1959-66, acting chmn. dept., 1960-61, chmn., 1963-64; prof. Mich. State U., 1966-69; prof. U. Rochester (N.Y.), 1969-76, Roswell S. Burrows prof. English, 1976—; vis. prof. Amherst Coll., 1962-63, U. Kent, Canterbury, Eng., 1972. Fund for Advancement Learning fellow, Italy, 1952-53; Guggenheim fellow, 1957-58; Fulbright lectr Oxford U., vis. fellow All Souls Coll., 1966-67; sr. fellow Folger Shakespeare Library, Washington, 1976. Mem. Modern Lang. Assn. Am., Internat. Assn. Univ. Profs. English, Phi Beta Kappa. Episcopalian. Author: George Herbert-His Religion and Art, 1954; The Muse's Method-An Introduction to Paradise Lost, 1962; The Heirs of Donne and Jonson, 1970. Editor: Andrew Marvell-Selected Poems, 1961; The Lyric and Dramatic Milton, 1965; George Herbert-Selected Poetry, 1967. Home: 179 Crosman Terr Rochester NY 14620

SUMMERS, RAY, clergyman, educator; b. Allen, Tex., Feb. 21, 1910; s. Luther Clarence and Alice (Holley) S.; A.B., Baylor U., 1933; Th.M., Southwestern Bapt. Theol. Sem., 1938, Th.D., 1943; grad. study U. Edinburgh, U. Basel (Switzerland), 1954; m. Jester Hilger, June 20, 1934; children—David Ray, Mary Lois, Sarah Nell. Ordained to ministry Baptist Ch., 1928; pastor, Rosamond, Tex., 1928-33, Chilton, Tex., 1934-35, Krum, Tex., 1935-38, Sycamore Heights Ch., Fort Worth, 1938-41; prof. N.T. Greek, Southwestern Bapt. Theol. Sem., 1938-59. Prof. evangelism, 1949-53, dir. Sch. Theology, 1949-53; prof. So. Bapt. Theol. Sem., Louisville, 1959-64, dir. grad. studies, 1960-64; chmn. dept. religion Baylor U., Waco, Tex., 1964—. Mem. Am. Acad. Religion, Soc. for N.T. Studies, Am. Assn. Theol. Schs. Lion. Author: Essentials of New Testament Greek, 1950; Worthy is The Lamb, 1951; The Life Beyond, 1959; Ephesians; Pattern for Christian Living, 1960; The Secret Savings of the Living Jesus, 1968; Broadman Commentary, 1 and 2 Peter and Jude 1970; A Commentary on Luke, 1972; Behold the Lamb, 1979. Contbr. articles to profl. jours. Home: 213 Harrington Ave Waco TX 76706

SUMMERS, ROBERT, educator; b. Gary, Ind., June 20, 1922; s. Frank and Ella (Lipton) Samuelson; B.S., U. Chgo., 1943; Ph.D., Stanford, 1956; postgrad. (Social Sci. Research Council fellow) King's Coll., U. Cambridge (Eng.), 1951-52; m. Anita Arrow, Mar. 29, 1953; children—Lawrence Henry, Richard Fredric, John Steven. Instr., Stanford, 1949-50; mem. faculty Yale, 1952-59, asst. prof., 1956-59; staff mem. Cowles Found., 1955-59; economist RAND Corp., Santa Monica, Calif., 1959-60, cons., 1960—; mem. faculty U. Pa. Wharton Sch., 1959—, prof., 1967—, chmn. grad. group in econs., 1967-70, 73-76. Served with AUS, 1944-46. Ford Found. Faculty Research fellow London Sch. Econs., 1966-67; NSF Research grantee, 1957-59, 63-66. Mem. Am. Econs. Assn., Econometric Soc., Am. Statis. Assn., AAUP. Author: (with Lawrence R. Klein) The Wharton Index of Capacity Utilization, 1966; (with others) Strategies for Research and Development, 1967; (with others) A System of International Comparisons of Gross Product and Purchasing Power, 1975; (with others) International Comparisons of Real Product and Purchasing Power. Contbr. articles to profl. jours. Home: 641 Revere Rd Merion Station PA 19066 Office: Dept Econs U Pa Philadelphia PA 19104

SUMMERS, ROBERT SAMUEL, lawyer, author, educator; b. Halfway, Oreg., Sept. 19, 1933; s. Orson William and Estella Belle (Robertson) S.; B.S. in Polit. Sci., U. Oreg., 1955; postgrad. (Fulbright scholar) U. Southampton (Eng.), 1955-56; LL.B., Harvard U., 1959; postgrad. Oxford (Eng.) U., 1964-65, 74-75; m. Dorothy Millicent Kopp, June 14, 1955; children—Brent, William, Thomas, Elizabeth, Robert. Admitted to Oreg. bar, 1959, N.Y. bar, 1974; asso. firm King, Miller, Anderson, Nash and Yerke, Portland, Oreg., 1959-60; asst. prof. law U. Oreg., 1960-63, asso. prof., 1964-68; vis. asso. prof. law Stanford U., 1963-64; prof. U. Oreg., 1968-69; prof. Cornell U., 1969-76, McRoberts prof. law, 1976—; vis. prof. Ind. U., 1969, U. Mich., 1974, U. Warwick (Eng.), 1975, U. Miami (Fla.), 1976-78, U. Sydney (Australia), 1977; cons. Cornell Law Project in public schs., N.Y., 1969-74, Law in Am. Soc. project Chgo. Bd. Edn., 1968-69; instr. Nat. Acad. Jud. Edn., 1976—. Social Sci. Research Council fellow, 1964-65. Mem. Am. Law Inst., Assn. Am. Law Schs. (chmn. sect. jurisprudence, 1972-73), Am. Soc. Polit. and Legal Philosophy (v.p. 1976-78), Internat. Assn. Philosophers of Law, Phi Beta Kappa. Republican. Congregationalist. Author: (with Howard) Law, Its Nature, Functions and Limits, 1972; (with Speidel and White) Teaching Materials on Commercial Transactions, 1974; (with White) The Uniform Commercial Code, 1980; (with Hubbard and Campbell) Justice and Order Through Law, 1973; (with Bozzone and Campbell) The American Legal System, 1973; American Legal Pragmatism—A Critique of the Leading Ideas, 1980; contbr. articles to scholarly jours.; contbr. book revs. to profl. jours.; editor: Essays in Legal Philosophy, 1968; More Essays in Legal Philosophy, 1971. Home: 116 McIntyre Pl Ithaca NY 14850 Office: Cornell Law Sch Ithaca NY 14853

SUMMERSELL, CHARLES GRAYSON, educator; b. Mobile, Ala., Feb. 25, 1908; s. Charles Fishweek and Sallie Rebecca (Grayson) S.; A.B., U. Ala., 1929, A.M., 1930; Ph.D., Vanderbilt U., 1940; m. Frances Sharpley, Nov. 10, 1934. Instr. history U. Ala., 1935-40, asst. prof., 1940-46, asso. prof., 1946-47, prof. history, 1947—; head dept. history, 1954-71; radio commentator, Tuscaloosa and Selma, Ala., 1941-43. Mem. Ala. Hist. Commn., Ala. State Records Commn., Ala. Bicentennial Commn., 1971—, Tannehill Furnace and Foundry Commn., Tuscaloosa County Preservation Authority, 1973. Served from lt. (j.g.) to lt. comdr. USNR, 1942-46; PTO; comdr. 1954; officer charge Naval Intelligence Sch., Norfolk, Va., 1951-53; mem. steering com. organized Tuscaloosa Unit of Organized Res. Navy, 1947. Recipient Letter of Commendation, USNR, 1945. Mem. Orgn. Am. Historians, English Speaking Union, So., Am., Ala. (pres. 1965-56) hist. assns., U.S. Naval Inst., Naval Hist. Found., S.A.R. (pres. Ala. Soc. 1957-58), Am. Assn. State and Local History (Southeastern area chmn. regional awards com.), Newcomen Soc. N.Am., Soc. Nautical Research (London, Eng.), Hakluyt Soc. (London), Phi Beta Kappa (pres. Ala. chpt. 1953-54), Phi Alpha Theta. Democrat. Clubs: University; Tuscaloosa Country; Army-Navy (Washington). Author: Historical Foundations of Mobile, 1949; Mobile History of a Seaport Town, 1949; Alabama History for Schools, 1957, rev. edit., 1961, 70; Alabama Past and Future (with Howard W. Odum and G. H. Yeuell), 1941, rev. edit. (with G. H. Yeuell & W. R. Higgs), 1950; (with Frances C. Roberts) Exploring Alabama, 1957, rev. edit., 1961; (with Frances S. Summersell) Alabama History Filmstrips, 1961; (with Rembert Patrick and Frances S. Summersell) Florida History Filmstrips; (with W.T. Chambers and Frances S. Summersell) Texas History Flimstrips, 1965; The Cruise of CSS Sumter, 1965; (with Jerome Hausman and Frances Summersell) Ohio History Filmstrips, 1966; (with Andrew Rolle and Frances S. Summersell) California History Filmstrips, 1967; (with Robert Sutton and Frances S. Summersell) Illinois History Filmstrips, 1971. Editor: The Journal of George Townley Fullam, Boarding Officer of the Confederate Sea Raider Alabama, 1973; editor; author introduction Colonial Mobile, 1975; editorial adv. bd. American Neptune, 1946—, editorial bd. The Ala. Rev., 1964-71. Contbr. articles and revs. to encys. and profl. jours. Address: 1411 Caplewood Dr Tuscaloosa AL 35401. *Early each morning I write an agenda for that day's work. This list is based upon a fresh evaluation of the importance of each item, and the importance is appraised by the possible service to others and the satisfaction to myself in solving these daily problems. This is a daily balance between what is desirable and what is possible in a personal chronology.*

SUMMERS-GILL, ROBERT GEORGE, physicist, educator; b. Wadena, Sask., Can., Dec. 22, 1929; s. Herbert Reginald and Margaret (Robson) S.-G.; B.A., U. Sask., 1950, M.A., 1952; Ph.D., U. Calif. at Berkeley, 1956. Faculty, McMaster U., Hamilton, Ont., Can., 1956—, prof. physics, 1966—; vis. scientist Lincoln Lab., Mass. Inst. Tech., Lexington, 1960. Mem. Am. Phys. Soc., Optical Soc. Am., Inst. Physics (London, Eng.), Canadian Assn. Physicists (registrar 1959-65), Sigma Xi. Contbr. articles to profl. jours. Home: 101 King St E Dundas ON Canada Office: Dept Physics McMaster U Hamilton ON Canada

SUMMIT, ROGER KENT, info. systems and services co. exec.; b. Detroit, Oct. 14, 1930; s. Paul Maurice and Mildred Suzanne Summit; A.B., Stanford U., 1952, M.B.A., 1957, Ph.D., 1965; m. Virginia Buckhorn, Aug. 8, 1964; children—Jennifer Lee, Scott Wesley. Research scientist Lockheed Research Lab., Palo Alto, Calif., 1965-72; mgr. DIALOG info. retrieval service Lockheed Corp., Palo Alto, 1972-77; dir. Lockheed Info. Systems, Palo Alto, 1977—; mem. sci. and tech. info. working group Dept. Commerce and M.I.T.; mem. public-pvt. sector relations task force Nat. Commn. on Libraries and Info. Sci.; trustee Engring. Index, Inc. Served to lt. (j.g.) USN, 1952-55. Recipient Spl. Invention award Lockheed Corp. Mem. Info. Industry Assn. (dir.; Info. Product of Year award 1975), Assn. Info. and Dissemination Centers, (v.p. 1975-76), Am. Soc. Info. Sci., IEEE. Contbr. to profl. publs. Inventor aerospace bus. environment simulator, DIALOG info. retrieval lang. Office: 3251 Hanover St Palo Alto CA 94304

SUMMITT, (WILLIAM) ROBERT, chemist, educator; b. Flint, Mich., Dec. 6, 1935; s. William Fletcher and Jessie Louise (Tilson) S.; A.S., Flint Jr. Coll., 1955; B.S. in Chemistry, U. Mich., 1957; Ph.D. (Union Carbide Chems. fellow), Purdue U., 1961; m. Nancy Jo Holland, Apr. 2, 1956; children—Elizabeth Louise, David Stanley. Research asso., instr. chemistry Mich. State U., 1961-62, asst. prof. metallurgy, mechs. and materials, 1965-68, asso. prof., 1968-73, chmn. dept. metallurgy mechs. and materials sci., 1972-78, prof., 1973—; research chemist Corning Glass Works, 1962-65; cons. in field. NRC Sr. Research asso. Air Force Materials Lab., Fairborn, Ohio, 1974-75. Leader Chief Okemos council Boy Scouts Am., 1973-76. Mem. Am. Chem. Soc., Am. Phys. Soc., Am. Soc. Metals, Nat. Assn. Corrosion Engrs., Inter-Soc. Color Council, Detroit Soc. Coatings Tech., Sigma Xi. Research, publs. in optical properties of materials, spectroscopy, corrosion and color sci. Home: 5424 Blue Haven Dr East Lansing MI 48823

SUMNER, BILLY TAYLOR, cons. civil engring. and planning co. exec.; b. Chgo., July 13, 1923; s. Lawton Taylor and Adele (Shelton) S.; B.E. magna cum laude, Vanderbilt U., 1946; m. Mary Sue Williams, Nov. 23, 1951; children—Kimberly Suell, Shelton Williams. Resident engr. Polk, Powell & Hendon, Nashville, 1946-51; Southeastern engring. rep., mgr. Nashville plant Universal Concrete Pipe Co., Columbus, Ohio, 1951-53; cons. Dixie Poultry Processors, Franklin, Tenn., 1953-54; resident mgr. Nashville office Geo. P. Rice, New Orleans, 1954-55; prin. firm Barge, Waggoner, Sumner & Cannon, cons. civil engrs. and planners, Nashville, Knoxville, and Morristown, Tenn., 1955—. Pres. Tenn. Bot. Gardens and Fine Arts Center, 1967-69; chmn. architect-engr. div. United Givers Fund, 1972; mem. steering com. Middle Tenn. Young Life Campaign, 1973-74. Trustee, v.p. Children's Mus., Nashville. Served with U.S. Army, 1943-46. Mem. ASCE, Am. Water Works Assn., Water Pollution Control Fedn., Am. Pub. Works Assn., Soc. Am. Mil. Engrs., Am. Inst. Cons. Engrs. (councilor 1972-73, v.p. 1973), Am. Cons. Engr. Council (v.p. 1973-74, pres. 1975-76), Nat. Soc. Profl. Engrs. (vice chmn. 1967-69, chmn. 1969-70), Tau Beta Pi, Sigma Nu. Presbyterian. Rotarian. Clubs: Belle Meade Country, Nashville City, Cumberland (Nashville). Home: 801 Robertson Academy Rd Nashville TN 37220 Office: 404 James Robertson Pkwy Nashville TN 37219

SUMNER, ERIC EDEN, utility co. exec.; b. Vienna, Austria, Dec. 17, 1924; came to U.S., 1940, naturalized, 1945; B.M.E., Cooper Union, 1948; M.A. in Physics, Columbia U., 1953, profl. degree in elec. engring., 1960; m. Anne-Marie Wiemer, May 24, 1974; children—Eric Eden, Hilary C., Erika, Trevor Anson. With Bell Telephone Labs., Inc., Whippany, N.J., 1955—, dir. underwater systems lab., 1962-67, exec. dir. div. transmission media, 1967-71, exec. dir. div. loop transmission, 1971—; mem. adv. bd. Ga. Inst. Tech. Sch. Elec. Engring.; chmn. adv. council Cooper Union Sch. Engring. Mem. North Caldwell (N.J.) Sch. Bd., 1962-68; pres. Civic Assn., North Caldwell, 1969-71. Fellow IEEE (Alexander Graham Bell medal 1978); mem. Communications Soc. (v.p. tech. affairs), Tau Beta Pi, Pi Tau Sigma. Patentee communications systems, circuits, apparatus. Home: 12 Washington Sq N New York NY 10003 Office: 1 Whippany Rd Whippany NJ 07981

SUMNER, JAMES DUPRE, JR., lawyer, educator; b. Spartanburg, S.C., Nov. 30, 1919; s. James DuPre and Frances Grace (Harris) S.; A.B., Wofford Coll., 1941; LL.B., U. Va., 1949; LL.M., Yale, 1952, J.S.D., 1955; m. Evvie Lucille Beach, Apr. 1, 1945 (dec.); children—Chery Erline (Mrs. Horacek), James DuPre III; m. 2d, Doris Kaiser Malloy, Oct. 20, 1972. Admitted to Va. Bar, 1948, Cal. bar, 1957; practice law, Los Angeles, 1957—; instr. law U. S.C., 1949-52; asso. prof. U. Calif. at Los Angeles, 1952-55, prof., 1955—; distinguished vis. prof. Instituto Luigi Sturzo, Rome, 1959; vis. prof. U. Tex., 1962, U. So. Calif., 1971; lectr. Calif. Bar Rev. Served from 2d lt. to lt. col. inf. AUS, 1941-46; ETO. Decorated Silver Star, Purple Heart with oak leaf cluster. Mem. Calif., Va., Westwood Village (pres.) bar assns., Friends of Scochow (sec.). Republican. Methodist. Club: Westwood Village Rotary; Los Angeles Country, Braemar Country. Co-author: Complete Guide to a Profitable Law Practice; An Anatomy of Legal Education. Contbr. articles to profl. jours. Home: 10513 Rocca Pl Los Angeles CA 90024

SUMNER, THEODORE BYNUM, JR., banker; b. Asheville, N.C., July 9, 1928; s. Theodore Bynum and Lovie (Winn) S.; B.S., Davidson Coll., 1950; m. Ruth Moser, Jan. 6, 1951; children—Stacy Ann, Theodore Bynum III. With First Union Nat. Bank, 1953—, city exec. charge Gastonia (N.C.) office, 1964-66, exec. v.p., city exec., Greensboro, N.C., 1966-69, regional exec. v.p. No. Piedmont region, from 1972, now chmn., Charlotte, also dir.; dean Carolina Sch. Banking U. N.C., 1974-75. Vice chmn. United Way Campaign, 1975; chmn. Council on Fin. and Adminstrn., Western N.C. Conf. of Meth. Ch. Served to 1st lt. cav. AUS, Korean War. Mem. N.C. Bankers Assn. (past pres. young bankers div., dir.), Assn. Res. City Bankers, Charlotte C. of C. (dir.), Methodist. Clubs: Country of N.C. (Pinehurst); Quail Hollow; Charlotte. Home: Charlotte NC 28288

SUMSER, RAYMOND JOSEPH, govt. ofcl.; b. Canton, Ohio, July 3, 1930; s. Raymond Joseph and Emily Elizabeth (Ludlam) S.; B.A., U. Utah, 1952; m. Anne Carolyn Miller, June 7, 1952; children—John Raymond, Brion David, Michael Clark, Anne Marie. Mgmt. intern Labor Dept., Washington, 1959-61, placement specialist, 1961-62, chief div. investigations and security, 1962-64, chief central personnel services, 1964-66, program analyst, 1966-67; Mid-Career fellow Woodrow Wilson Sch. Pub. and Internat. Affairs, Princeton U., 1966; chief manpower utilization div. NASA, Goddard Space Flight Center, Greenbelt, Md., 1967-73, dir. personnel NASA, Washington, 1973-76; dep. asst. sec. for personnel HEW, Washington, 1976—. Served with USNR, 1952-59. Office: Office Personnel Adminstrn HEW 200 Independence Ave SW Washington DC 20201

SUNDARAM, SWAMINATHA, educator; b. India, Oct. 22, 1924; s. Swaminathan and Soundararajan (Subbalakshmi) S.; came to U.S., 1957, naturalized, 1969; B.Sc. with honours, Annamalai U., Annamalainagar, India, 1945, M.A., 1947, Ph.D., 1957, D.Sc., 1960; M.S. in Mech. Engring., Ill. Inst. Tech., 1960; m. Sundaresan Janaki, Feb. 6, 1946; children—Ananthanarayanan, Mangalambal. Lectr., Annamalai U., 1945-57; instr. Ill. Inst. Tech., 1957-59; research asso. U. Chgo., 1959-60; research physicist B.C. Research Council, Vancouver, Can., 1960-61; asso. prof. mech. engring. U. Sask., 1961-62; asso. prof. physics Ill. Inst. Tech., 1962-65; prof. physics U. Ill. at Chgo. Circle, 1965—, head dept., 1967-76; cons. IIT Research Inst., 1964-65. Recipient Outstanding Citizen of Year award Chgo. Council Citizenship, 1969. Fellow Am. Phys. Soc. Author papers in field. Home: 1264 W Elmdale Ave Chicago IL 60660

SUNDBERG, ALAN CARL, state supreme ct. justice; b. Jacksonville, Fla., June 23, 1933; s. Robert Carl and Gertrude Harriet (Rudd) S.; B.S., Fla. State U., 1955; LL.B., Harvard U., 1958; m. Barbara Lou Lester, Aug. 18, 1956; children—Allison, Angela, Laura, Alan, William. Admitted to Fla. bar, 1958; practiced in St. Petersburg, 1958-75; justice Supreme Ct. Fla., 1975—. Mem. Salvation Army Adv. Bd.; chmn. bd. trustees Canterbury Sch. Fla., Inc.; bd. dirs. Fla. Gulf Coast Symphony, St. Petersburg Symphony; trustee Pinellas County Law Library. Mem. Fla. Bar Found. (past 2d v.p.), St. Petersburg, Am., Fla. Bar assns., Pinellas Trial Lawyers Assn., Phi Beta Kappa, Phi Kappa Phi, Omicron Delta Kappa, Phi Delta Phi. Democrat. Episcopalian. Clubs: Dragon, Suncoasters (St. Petersburg). Office: Supreme Ct Bldg Tallahassee FL 32304

SUNDBERG, CARL OSCAR, steel co. exec.; b. East Cleveland, Ohio, June 8, 1916; s. Oscar C. and Victoria (Green) S.; B.S., Va. Poly. Inst., 1939; m. Lela Margaret Rhodes, Sept. 6, 1941. Process metallurgist, research metallurgist, chief metallurgist, sr. engr., chief engr., v.p. engring., v.p. Diamond Chain Co. div. AMSTED, Indpls., 1946-62; mng. dir. AMSTED Siemag Kette GmbH, Betzdorf, Germany, 1962-66; v.p. South Bend Lathe Co. div. AMSTED (Ind.), 1966-67, pres., 1967-70; pres. Am. Steel Foundries div. AMSTED, Chgo., 1970-77; ret., 1977. Bd. dirs. United Community Services, South Bend, 1967; mem. exec. com. Indsl. Council, 1966-70. Served to lt. (j.g.) USNR, 1943-46. Registered profl. engr., Ind. Fellow Am. Soc. Metals (past chmn. Indpls. chpt.); mem. Am. Mgmt. Assn., Steel Founders Soc. Am. (dir. 1974-77), Cast Metals Fedn. (Ill. co-chmn. govtl. affairs conf. 1973-74), Ry. Progress Inst. (adv. com. on research; chmn. project steering com., railroad truck safety, research and test project, also mem. project steering com., railroad coupler safety research and test project Assn. Am. Railroads Coop. Program), N.A.M. (pres.'s council), ASME, Phi Kappa Phi, Tau Beta Pi, Omicron Delta Kappa. Club: Palmetto-Pine Country. Home: 5381 Coral Ave Cape Coral FL 33904

SUNDBERG, R. DOROTHY, educator, physician; b. Chgo., July 29, 1915; d. Carl William and Ruth (Chalbeck) Sundberg; student U. Chgo., 1932-34; B.S., U. Minn., 1937, M.A., 1939, Ph.D., 1943, M.D., 1953; student, instr. Wayne U., 1939-41; m. Robert H. Reiff, Dec. 24, 1941 (div. 1945). Instr., asst. prof. anatomy U. Minn., 1939-53, asso. prof., 1953-60, prof., 1960-63, prof. of lab. medicine and anatomy, 1963-73, prof. lab. medicine, pathology and anatomy, 1973—, hematologist, dir. Hematology Labs., 1945-74, hematologist, co. dir., 1974—. Recipient Lucretia Wilder award for research in anatomy, 1943. Diplomate Am. Bd. Pathology. Fellow N.Y. Acad. Sci.; mem. Am. Assn. Anatomists, Internat., European, Am. socs. hematology, Soc. Exptl. Biology and Medicine, Minn. Soc. Clin. Pathologists, Am. Assn. Pathologists, Am. Soc. Cell Biology, Sigma Xi. Editorial bd. Soc. Exptl. Biology and Medicine, until 1975; mem. editorial bd. Blood, 1960-67, asso. editor, 1967-69. Contbr. articles to med. jours. Home: 5503 Lakeview Dr Edina MN 55424

SUNDERLAND, RAY, JR., ret. ins. co. exec.; b. N.Y.C., Nov. 12, 1913; s. Ray and Rose (Goehl) S.; grad. Sch. Profl. Accountancy Practice, Pace Coll., 1948; grad. Exec. Program Bus. Adminstrn. Columbia U., 1968; m. Melva Joyce Mace, June 13, 1943; 1 son, Joel Wayne. With comptroller's dept. Brown Bros. Harriman & Co., N.Y.C., 1934-40; sr. auditor Price Waterhouse & Co., N.Y.C., 1940-50; with N.Y. Life Ins. Co., N.Y.C., 1950-79, gen. auditor, 1969-71, comptroller, 1971—, v.p., 1971-75, sr. v.p., 1975-79, comptroller N.Y. Life Fund, Inc., 1972-79. Pres. community scholarship fund local sch. dist., Locust Valley, N.Y., 1958-62, pres. parents club, 1958-62. Served to capt. USAAF, 1942-45. C.P.A. Mem. Am. Inst. C.P.A.'s, Am. Council Life Ins. (Fin. reporting principles com. 1977-78), Columbia U. Grad. Sch. Bus. Exec. Alumni Assn. Home: 3 Wood Ln Locust Valley NY 11560

SUNDERLAND, THOMAS ELBERT, lawyer, business exec.; b. Ann Arbor, Mich., Apr. 28, 1907; s. Edson R. and Hannah Dell (Read) S.; student in Eng. and France, 1924-25; A.B. summa cum laude, U. Mich., 1928, student Law Sch., 1927-29; J.D., U. Calif. at Berkeley, 1930; postgrad. advanced mgmt. program Harvard Grad. Sch. Bus. Adminstrn., 1948; m. Mary Louise Allyn, Dec. 21, 1946; children—Louise Allyn, Anne Read, Thomas Edson (dec.), Mary Compton, Alice Elizabeth (dec.). Admitted to Mich. bar, 1930, N.Y. bar, 1933, D.C. bar, Ill. bar, 1948, Mass. bar, 1962, Ariz. bar, 1969; practiced law, Detroit, 1930-31, N.Y.C., 1931-48, Chgo., 1948-59; with firm Cadwalader, Wickersham and Taft, 1931-33, Milbank, Tweed, Hope and Webb, 1933-35, Townley, Updike and Carter, 1935-40, Snell & Wilmer, Phoenix, 1969-79; gen. counsel Pan Am. Petroleum and Transport Co., Am. Oil Co., 1940-48; dir., mem. exec. com. Pan Am. Petroleum and Transport Co., Am. Oil, 1947-54; v.p., gen. counsel, dir. Standard Oil Co. (Ind.), 1948-60; pres., chief exec. officer, chmn. bd., dir. United Fruit Co., 1959-68; dir. First Nat. Bank of Boston, Nat. Cash Register Co., Liberty Mut. Ins. Co., Johns-Manville Corp. Mem. com. on pub. affairs Am. Petroleum Inst., 1948-59, bd. dirs., 1954-59. Nat. trustee Lake Forest Coll.; trustee Lawrence Hall of Sci., U. Calif. at Berkeley, Boston Hosp. for Women, Winsor Sch., Boston; v.p., trustee Phoenix Symphony, pres., 1979—; mem. corp., Northeastern U.; vis. com. Stanford Law Sch., Palo Alto, Harvard Bus. Sch., Harvard Law Sch. and Sch. Pub. Health, Law Sch. U. Mich., U. Chgo. Law Sch. Bd. dirs. Nat. Merit Scholarship Corp.; trustee Phoenix Country Day Sch. Served from 1st lt. to lt. col. USAAF, 1942-46; ETO. Decorated Bronze Star. Recipient Bus. Leadership award U. Mich., 1966, also Outstanding Achievement award, 1970. Mem. Am. Law Inst., Council on Fgn. Relations, Am. Bar Assn. (com. on jurisprudence and law reform 1940-41, chmn. sect. antitrust law 1956-57), Ill., Chgo., Ariz. bar assns., Assn. Bar City N.Y., Nat. Indsl. Conf. Bd. (sr. mem.), Squadron A Assn. (N.Y.C.), Phi Beta Kappa, Phi Delta Phi, Phi Gamma Delta, Phi Kappa Phi. Clubs: Wianno (Cape Cod, Mass.), The Beach (Cape Cod, Mass.); Bohemian (San Francisco); Phoenix Country; The Country (Brookline); Chicago; Glenview (Golf, Ill.); Metropolitan (Washington); Union League (N.Y.C.); Paradise Valley Country (Scottsdale, Ariz.). Home: 5840 E Starlight Way Paradise Valley Scottsdale AZ 85253 summers: 66 Fernwood Rd (Brookline) Chestnut Hill MA 02167 Office: Suite C-103 6991 E Camelback Rd Scottsdale AZ 85251

SUNDERLIN, CHARLES EUGENE, cons.; b. Reliance, S.D., Sept. 28, 1911; s. Glen Eugene and Frances (Smith) S.; A.B., U. Mont., 1933; B.A., M.A. (Rhodes scholar), Oxford U., 1935; Ph.D., U. Rochester, 1939; m. Sylvia Alice Sweetman, July 8, 1936; children—Ann Elizabeth, Mary Cornelia, Katherine Patricia, William Dana. Instr. chemistry Union Coll., 1938-41; instr., asst. prof. U.S. Naval Acad., 1941-43, 45-46; sci. liaison officer U.S. Office Naval Research, London, 1946-47, dep. sci. dir., 1948-49, sci. dir., 1949-51; dep. dir. NSF, 1951-57; dep. dir. Union Carbide European Research Assos., S.A., Brussels, Belgium, 1957-62; research mgr. def. and space systems dept. Union Carbide Corp., 1962-65; spl. asst. to pres. Nat. Acad. Scis., Washington 1965-69; v.p., sec. Rockefeller U., N.Y.C., 1969-76; spl. asst. Nat. Sci. Bd., Washington, 1976-78; exec. sec., staff dir. Com. on 10th Nat. Sci. Bd. Report, 1976-78. U.S. del. 6th and 7th Gen. Assemblies, Internat. Council Sci. Unions, Amsterdam, 1952, Oslo, 1955, Working Party on Establishment of Internat. Adv. Com. on Sci. Research, Paris, 1953, Meeting of Dirs. Nat. Research Centers, Milan, 1955, Symposium on Orgn. and Adminstrn. Applied Research, Vienna, 1956; mem. Com. Experts on Scientists' Rights, Paris, 1953; mem. Nat. Acad. Scis. Workshop on Indsl. Devel. on Taiwan, Republic of China, 1968; chmn. Am. Inst. Aeros., and Astronautics/ASME 9th Structures, Structural Dynamics and Materials Conf., 1968. Treas., bd. dirs. Engrs. and Scientists Com., Inc., People to People Program. Served from lt. (j.g.) to lt. USNR, 1943-45. Fellow AAAS, Chem. Soc. (London); mem. Am. Chem. Soc., Faraday Soc., Royal Instn. Gt. Britain, Soc. Chem. Industry, AIAA, Wadham Assn. U.S., Sigma Alpha Epsilon. Episcopalian. Clubs: United Oxford and Cambridge University (London); International (Washington). Home: 3036 P St NW Washington DC 20007 also 137 E Main St Cambridge NY 12816

SUNDERMAN, FREDERICK WILLIAM, physician, educator; b. Altoona, Pa., Oct. 23, 1898; s. William August and Elizabeth Catherine (Lehr) S.; B.S., Gettysburg Coll., 1919, Sc.D. (hon.), 1952; M.D., U. Pa., 1923, M.S., 1927, Ph.D., 1929; m. Clara Louise Baily, June 2, 1925 (dec. 1972); children—Louise (dec.), F. William, Joel B. (dec.). Intern, then resident Pa. Hosp., 1924-26, asso. charge chemistry div., physician, then chief metabolic clinic A and physician, 1935-47; mem. faculty U. Pa. Sch. Medicine, Phila., 1925—, now asso. prof. research medicine, also lectr.; acting head med. dept. Brookhaven Nat. Lab., Upton, N.Y., 1947-48; chief chem. div. William Pepper Lab. Clin. Medicine, U. Pa. Med. Sch., 1933-57; dir. Temple U. Lab. Clin. Medicine, 1947-48, also prof. clin. pathology; med. dir. govt. explosives lab. Carnegie Inst. Tech. and Bur. Mines, 1943-46; head dept. clin. pathology Cleve. Clinic Found., 1949-51; dir. clin. research M.D. Anderson Hosp. Cancer Research, Houston, 1949-50; dir. clin. labs. Grady Meml. Hosp., Atlanta, 1949-51; chief clin. pathology Communicable Disease Center, USPHS, Atlanta, 1950-51; med. adviser Rohm & Haas Co., 1950-71; med. cons. Redstone Arsenal, U.S. Army Ordnance Dept., Huntsville, Ala., 1947-49; cons. clin. pathology St. Joseph's Hosp., Tampa, Fla., 1965-66; prof. clin. medicine Emory U. Sch. Medicine, 1949-51; attending physician Jefferson Hosp., Phila., 1951—, dir. div. metabolis research, 1961-67, clin. prof. medicine, dir. Inst. Clin. Sci., 1965—; prof. pathology, co-chmn. dept. lab. medicine Hahnemann Med. Coll., 1970—. Trustee Gettysburg Coll., 1967-79, chmn., 1972-74, hon. life trustee, 1979—; bd. dirs. Musical Fund Soc., 1938-78. Recipient Naval Ordnance Devel. award, 1946; certificate appreciation War Dept., 1947; medal of honor Armed Forces Inst. Pathology, 1964; named Distinguished Alumnus, Gettysburg Coll., 1963. Diplomate Am. Bd. Pathology (life trustee). Mem. Am. Assn. History Medicine, Am. Diabetes Assn., AMA, Am. Soc. Clin. Investigation, Royal Soc. Health, AAUP, Endocrine Soc., Am. Assn. Biol. Chemistry, A.A.A.S., Am. Chem. Soc., Am. Assn. Clin. Chemists, Coll. Am. Pathologists (founding gov.; Pathologist of Yr. award 1962), Am. Soc. Clin. Pathology (pres. 1951; Ward Burdick award 1975, Continuing Edn. Distinguished Service award 1976), Assn. Clin. Scientists (pres. 1957-59, dir. edn. 1959—; diploma honor 1960, ann. goblet award 1964, Gold-headed cane 1974), Brit. Assn. Clin. Biochemists (hon.), Soc. Pharm. and Environ. Pathologists (hon.), Phi Beta Kappa, Sigma Xi, Alpha Omega Alpha, Phi Sigma Kappa, Alpha Kappa Kappa. Episcopalian (vestryman, accounting warden). Club: Union League (Phila.). Author 24 books on clin. pathology, also over 250 articles. Editor Annals of Clin. and Lab. Sci., 1971—. Home: 1833 Delancey Pl Philadelphia PA 19103

SUNDERMANN, JUSTUS DANIEL, univ. adminstr.; b. Cin., Jan. 2, 1934; s. Louis William and Velma Loretta (Kline) S.; B.Sc., Ohio State U., 1955; M.Ed., U. Cin., 1959, Ed.D., 1965; m. Sally Lynette Pounds, Sept.12, 1954; children—Cindy Lynette, Deborah Ruth, Justus F. II, Sarah Loretta. Asst. to sr. v.p. and dean of univ. adminstrn. U. Cin., 1957-65; charter dean of student services Monroe County Community Coll., 1965-72; pres. Glen Oaks Community Coll., 1972-76, Anne Arundel Community Coll., 1976-79; dean Ohio U., Zanesville, 1979—; lectr. Catholic U. Am. Bd. dirs. Anne Arundel County (Md.) Cancer Soc., Monroe County (Mich.) Mental Health Soc. Recipient Spl. Tribute, Mich. Legislature, 1976, Congressional award, 1978, award for community service United Way of Central Md., 1978, Disting. Service award Anne Arundel Community Coll., 1978, citation of honor Mich. Minuteman, 1971. Mem. Ohio Hist. Assn., Am. Assn. Higher Edn. Am. Assn. Community and Jr. Colls., Zanesville C. of C., Phi Delta Kappa, Kappa Delta Pi. Unitarian. Club: Rotary (pres. club 1972), Monroe Exchange. Home: 713 Convers Ave Zanesville OH 43701 Office: 1425 Newark Rd Zanesville OH 43701

SUNDLUN, BRUCE GEORGE, bus. exec. b. Providence, Jan. 19, 1920; s. Walter I. and Jane Z. (Colitz) S.; B.A., Williams Coll., 1942; LL.B., Harvard, 1949; student Air Command and Staff Sch., 1948; m. Joyanne T. Carter, Aug. 5, 1974; children by previous marriage—Tracy, Stuart, Peter, Michael R.E. Carter, Cintra Ellis Carter. Admitted to R.I. and D.C. bars, 1949; asst. U.S. atty., Washington, 1949-51; spl. asst. to U.S. atty. gen., Washington, 1951-54; partner firm Amram, Hahn & Sundlun, and predecessor, Washington, 1954-72, Sundlun, Tirana & Scher, 1972-76. Vice pres., gen. counsel, dir. Outlet Co., Providence, 1960-76, pres., chief exec. officer, 1976—; pres. Exec. Jet Aviation, Inc., Columbus, Ohio, 1970-76, chmn. bd., 1976—; dir. Quest Research, Worthington Industries; incorporator, dir. Communications Satellite Corp., 1962—. Chmn. Inaugural Medal Com., Washington, 1961, 65; vice chmn. Inaugural Parade Com., Washington, 1961; pres. Washington Internat. Horse Show, 1970-75, trustee, 1975—; bd. visitors USAF Acad., 1978—; chmn. Ocean State Performing Arts Center, 1978—. Del. Democratic Nat. Conv., 1964, 68. Served to capt. USAAF, 1942-45; col Res., ret. Decorated D.F.C., Air medal with oak leaf cluster, Purple Heart; chevelier Legion d'Honneur (France). Mem. Greater Providence C. of C. (dir. 1976—, 1st v.p. 1978—), Delta Upsilon. Clubs: Hope, Squantum Assn., Univ., Turks Head, Spouting Rock Beach, Ida Lewis Yacht (R.I.); Federal City, 1925 F St (Washington); Fauquier, Middleburg (Va.) Tennis Assn.; Orange County Hunt (The Plains, Va.), Saratoga Reading Room. Home: Salamander Farm The Plains VA 22171 also 1539 27th St Washington DC 20007 also 33 Power St Providence RI 02903 Office: Outlet Co 176 Weybosset St Providence RI 02902 also 600 New Hampshire Ave Washington DC 20037

SUNDQUIST, JAMES LLOYD, polit. scientist; b. West Point, Utah, Oct. 16, 1915; s. Frank Victor and Freda (Carlson) S.; student Weber Coll., 1932-34, Northwestern U., 1934-35; B.S., U. Utah, 1939; M.S. in Pub. Adminstrn., Syracuse U., 1941; m. Beth Ritchie, Dec. 25, 1937; children—Erik L., Mark L., James K. Reporter, Salt Lake Tribune, 1935-39; adminstrv. analyst U.S. Bur. Budget, 1941-47, 49-51; reports and statistics officer Office Def. Moblzn., 1951-53; dir. mgmt. control European Command, U.S. Army, Berlin, 1947-49; asst. to chmn. Democratic Nat. Com., 1953-54; asst. sec. to gov. N.Y. State, 1955-56; asst. to U.S. Senator Clark, 1957-62; dep. under sec. agr., 1963-65; sr. fellow Brookings Instn., 1965—, dir. govtl. studies, 1976-78; adj. prof. Smith Coll., 1975-78. Sec. platform com. Dem. Nat. Conv., 1960, 68. Recipient Exceptional Civilian Service award War Dept., 1945; Sr. Research fellow U. Glasgow (Scotland), 1972-73. Mem. Nat. Acad. Pub. Adminstrn., Am. Polit. Sci. Assn., Am. Soc. Pub. Adminstrn. Author: Politics and Policy: The Eisenhower, Kennedy and Johnson Years, 1968; Making Federalism Work, 1969 (Louis Brownlow award for best pub. adminstrn. book); Dynamics of the Party System, 1973; Dispersing Population: What America Can Learn from Europe, 1975. Editor: On Fighting Poverty: Perspectives from Experience, 1969. Home: 3016 N Florida St Arlington VA 22207 Office: 1775 Massachusetts Ave NW Washington DC 20036

SUNDQUIST, WESLEY BURTON, educator; b. Christine, N.D., Dec. 28, 1927; s. Joel Lars and Ellen Hilda (Nelson) S.; B.S., N.D. State U., 1952; M.S., U. Ky., 1954; Ph.D., Mich. State U., 1957; m. Marcia May Gillespie, Dec. 6, 1958; children—Wesley I., Derek G. Asst. agrl. economist U. Ky., 1953-54; research economist Dept. Agr. at Mich. State U., 1956-58, at U. Minn., 1958-65; dir. Farm Prodn. Econs. div. Dept. Agr., Washington, 1965-70, dep. adminstr. Econ. Research Service, 1970-71; prof., head dept. agrl. and applied econs. U. Minn., St. Paul, 1971—; chmn. social sci. dept. Dept. Agr. Grad. Sch., Washington, 1968-71. Served with AUS, 1946-47. Recipient Superior Service award Dept. Agr., 1969. Mem. Am. Agri. Econs. Assn. (dir. 1970-73), Internat. Assn. Agrl. Economists. Mem. United Ch. of Christ. Co-author: Economics of Foot and Mouth Disease; contbr. articles to profl. jours. Home: 2009 Evergreen Ct Saint Paul MN 55113

SUNDSTROM, FRANK LEANDER, distillery cons.; b. Massena, N.Y., Jan. 5, 1901; s. Charles and Nora (Vandevener) S.; A.B., Cornell U., 1924; m. Jean Ross Johnstone, Dec. 26, 1936; children—Jean R., Frank L. Vice pres. Schenley Industries, Inc., N.Y.C., 1955-69; v.p., dir. Shenley Distillers, 1954-69; ltd. partner Burton, Dana & Co., stockbrokers, N.Y.C., until 1968; exec. Tobacco Inst., Washington, 1969-74; cons. Am. Distillery Co., Inc., 1974—. Mem. U.S. Ho. of Reps., 11th Dist. N.J., 1943-49. Named to Cornell U. Hall of Fame, 1978, Nat. Football Hall of Fame, 1978. Mem. Sigma Delta Chi. Phi Kappa Psi. Republican. Home: 19 Country Club Dr Chatham NJ 07928

SUNDSTROM, VIRGIL GLENN, petroleum co. exec.; b. Sask., Can., Mar. 12, 1928; m. Margaret J. Gelder, Sept. 4, 1950; children—Eric, Gail, Katherine, Barbara. Vice pres. mktg., then group v.p. mfg. and mktg. Pacific Petroleums Ltd., 1972-79; group v.p. mfg. and mktg. Petro Can. Ltd., Calgary, Alta., 1979—. Bd. dirs. Provincial Cancer Soc., Provincial Cancer Hosp., Banff Sch. Advanced Mgmt. Office: 700 6th Ave SW Calgary AB Canada

SUNLEY, EMIL MCKEE, economist; b. Morgantown, W.Va., July 30, 1942; s. Emil McKee and Nelle Berniece (Traer) S.; B.A., Amherst Coll., 1964; M.A., U. Mich., 1965, Ph.D., 1968; m. Judith Evelyn Steere, Dec. 23, 1966; children—Rachel Anne, Gillian Traer, Neil Steere. Economist office tax analysis Dept. Treasury, Washington, 1968-73, asso. dir. office tax analysis, 1973-75, dep. asst. sec. for tax policy, 1977—; sr. fellow Brookings Instn., Washington, 1975-77. Mem. Am. Econ. Assn., Nat. Tax Assn. Tax Inst. Am. (dir.), Internat. Inst. Public Fin., Internat. Fiscal Assn. Episcopalian. Home: 5421 Duvall Dr Washington DC 20016 Office: Dept Treasury Washington DC 20220

SUNSHINE, DONALD RAYMOND, architect; b. Chgo., May 1, 1933; s. Raymond Nelson and Gladys Martha (Bols) S.; B.A. with honors, U. Ill., 1957, M.A., 1970; m. JoAnne Ruck, Jan. 28, 1956; children—Ruck, Ryan, Donn. With John Carl Warneke, San Francisco, 1958-60; pvt. archtl. practice, Park Ridge, Ill., 1960-74; mem. firm Sunshine, Jaeger, Kupritz & Assos., 1968-73; mem. faculty dept. architecture U. Ill. Circle Campus, 1973-76; prof. architecture Hampton (Va.) Inst., 1976—, Va. Poly. Inst. and State U., Blacksburg; 1976—; cons. City of Park Ridge Citizens Planning Adv. Com.; works include Helen McCorkle Sch., Chgo., Bish Creative Display Office Bldg., Northbrook, Ill., various churches, other bldgs. Recipient numerous archtl. awards, 1961—, Honor award and exhibit Va. chpt. AIA Va. Mus. Fine Arts, 1974. Francis J. Plym fellow, Europe, 1967—; NASA grantee to design solar energy house, 1973—. Registered architect Ill., Va., Nat. Council Archtl. Registration Bds. Mem. AIA, Gargoyle. Author: Perspective Drawing, 1972. Contbr. numerous articles to profl. jours. Address: RFD 1 Box 341-1A Blacksburg VA 24060

SUOJANEN, WAINO W., educator; b. Maynard, Mass., Jan. 12, 1920; s. Waino I. and Milma (Lindroos) S.; B.S., U. Vt., 1942; M.B.A., Harvard, 1946; Ph.D., U. Calif. at Berkeley, 1955; m. Doris G. Stinson, Dec. 24, 1948; children—Wayne William, James Norman. Asst. prof. Sch. Bus. Adminstrn., U. Calif. at Berkeley, 1950-59; asso. prof. U.S. Naval Postgrad. Sch., Monterey, Calif., 1959-61; dir. research and devel. mgmt. program Air Proving Ground Center, Eglin AFB, Fla., 1961-64; prof., chmn. dept. mgmt. U. Miami (Fla.), 1964-70, prof. mgmt. Ga. State U., Atlanta, 1970—. Adv. editor Chandler Pub. Co., 1965-71; mem. mgmt. adv. panel NASA, 1968-71; cons. U.S. Army Mgmt. Engring. Tng. Agy., 1955—, U.S. Civil Service Commn., 1964—. Treas. Alameda County Mental Health Assn., 1953-56. Bd. dirs. Vol. Atlanta, 1971-76. Served to capt. AUS, 1943-46. Recipient McKinsey Found. Book award, 1966. Mem. Acad. Mgmt, AAAS, Phi Beta Kappa, Alpha Kappa Psi, Beta Alpha Psi, Beta Gamma Sigma, Pi Gamma Mu, Sigma Iota Epsilon. Author: The Dynamics of Management, 1966; (with others) The Operating Manager-An Integrative Approach, 1974; (with others) Perspectives in Job Enrichment and Productivity, 1975. Home: 11 Olde Ivy Sq Atlanta GA 30342

SUOZZO, FRANK VINCENT, ins. co. exec.; b. New Haven, Mar. 14, 1928; s. Harry and Lina (Del Grippo) S.; B.A., U. Conn., 1952; m. Cecilia Margaret Honan, Oct. 22, 1955; children—Frank Vincent, James Harry, Edward John, Elizabeth. With U.S. Life Ins. Co., N.Y.C., 1952—, 2d v.p., 1970-74, treas., 1974—, v.p., 1976—. Active local Boy Scouts Am., Little League Baseball. Served with AUS, 1946-47. Recipient Scouters award Boy Scouts Am., 1971. C.L.U. Fellow Life Office Mgmt. Inst.; mem. Inst. Mgmt. Acctg. Roman Cath. Author papers in field. Home: 171 Dewey Ave Staten Island NY 10308 Office: 125 Maiden Ln New York NY 10038

SUPER, DONALD E., educator, psychologist; b. Honolulu, July 10, 1910; s. Paul and Margaret Louise (Stump) S.; B.A., Oxford U., 1932, M.A., 1936; Ph.D., Columbia, 1940; m. Anne Margaret Baker, Sept. 12, 1936; children—Robert Marion, Charles McAfee. Asst. employment sec. YMCA, Cleve. 1932-35; dir. Cleve. Guidance Service, 1935-36; asso. prof. psychology Clark U., Worcester, Mass., 1938-42; asso. prof. edn. Tchrs. Coll. Columbia, 1945-49, prof. psychology and edn., 1949-75, prof. emeritus, 1975—, dir. div. psychology and edn., 1965-74, chmn. dept. psychology, 1970-74, internat. coordinator Work Importance Study with Nat. Inst. Careers Edn. and Counseling, Cambridge, Eng., 1979—; hon. dir., sr. fellow Nat. Inst. For Careers Edn. and Counselling, fellow Wolfson Coll., Cambridge U., 1976-79; vis. prof. psychology U. Paris (René Decartes), 1976—. Lectr. in guidance, summer schs. U. Buffalo, 1937-40, in guidance and measurement, Harvard, 1941-42; vis. prof. U. Calif., summer 1953; cons. psychologist, Am. Inst. for Research 1946-76; cons. Mil. Occupational Classification Project, Dept. Def., 1950-51, Human Factors Operations Research labs. USAF, 1951-54; cons. VA, 1951-74, USAF Personnel and Tng. Research Lab., 1954-56, Stephens Coll., 1952-54, 64-65, Ford Found., Poland, 1960, U.S. Civil Service Commn., 1961-64, AID, 1962-64, U.S Office Edn., 1965—, IBM, 1966—, Gen Elec. Co., 1970—, Young Pres' Orgn., 1970-71, U. Keele, Staffordshire, Eng., 1966—, U. East Anglia, Norwich, Eng., 1976—, Nat. Inst. Edn., 1972—, Appalachia Regional Lab., 1973-75, Am. Tel. & Tel., 1973-76, project Discover, 1974—, Orgn. for Econ. Cooperation and Devel., 1975—; Am. specialist State Dept., Japan, 1961. Mem. Bd. Edn., Montclair, N.J., 1960-66, pres., 1965-66. Served as aviation psychologist, maj. USAAF, 1942-45. Fulbright lectr. U. Paris, 1958-59. Diplomate Am. Bd. Examiners in Psychology. Fellow AAAS, Am. Psychol. Assn. (pres. div. of cons. psychology 1947-48, pres. div. counseling psychology 1951-52), British Psychol. Soc.; mem. Nat. Vocat. Guidance Assn. (profl.; pres. 1969-70), Am. Personnel and Guidance Assn. (pres. 1953-54), Internat. Vocational Guidance Assn. (v.p. 1959-75, pres. 1975—), Am. Ednl. Research Assn., Spanish Psychol. Soc. (hon.), Internat. Assn. Applied Psychology (dir.). Congregationalist (pres. Ch. bd. trustees 1970-73). Clubs: Oxford and Cambridge Univ. (London); Princeton (N.Y.C.). Author: Avocational Interest Patterns, 1940; Dynamics of Vocational Adjustment, 1942; Appraising Vocational Fitness, rev. 1962; Opportunities in Psychology, rev. 1975; The Psychology of Careers, 1957; Vocational Development, 1957; Vocational Maturity of Ninth Grade Boys, 1960; La Psychologie des Intérêts, 1964; The Professional Preparation of Counseling Psychologists, 1964; Occupational Psychology, 1970; Computer-Assisted Counseling, 1970; Measuring Vocational Maturity, 1974. Contbr. articles to psychol. and ednl. jours. Home: 124 Stonebridge Rd Montclair NJ 07042 Office: NICEC Bateman St Cambridge England also Teachers Coll Columbia U New York NY 10027

SUPER, ROBERT HENRY, educator; b. Wilkes-Barre, Pa., June 13, 1914; s. John Henry and Sadie (Rothermel) S.; A.B., Princeton, 1935, Ph.D., 1941; B.Litt., U. Oxford (Eng.), 1937; m. Rebecca Ragsdale, Jan. 25, 1953; children—David Allen, Paul Eric. Instr. English, Princeton, 1938-42; asst. prof. Mich. State Normal Coll., Ypsilanti, 1942-47; from asst. prof. to prof. U. Mich., Ann Arbor, 1947—; vis. prof. Rice U., 1965-66, U. Chgo., summer 1954, U. Calif. at Los Angeles, 1967, U. Calif. at Berkeley, 1973; field intelligence officer Fgn. Econ. Adminstrn., 1945; Harris Found. lectr. Northwestern U., 1968. Fulbright research fellow, 1949-50; Am. Council Learned Socs. fellow, 1959-60; Guggenheim fellow, 1962-63, 70-71; Nat. Endowment for Humanities fellow, 1978-79. Author: Walter Savage Landor: A Biography, 1954; The Publication of Landor's Works, 1954; The Time- Spirit of Matthew Arnold, 1970. Editor: The Complete Prose Works of Matthew Arnold, 11 vols., 1960-77. Home: 1221 Baldwin Ave Ann Arbor MI 48104

SUPPES, PATRICK, educator; b. Tulsa, Mar. 17, 1922; s. George Biddle and Ann (Costello) S.; B.S., U. Chgo., 1943; Ph.D. (Wendell T. Bush fellow), Columbia, 1950; LL.D., U. Nijmegen (Netherlands), 1979; m. Joan Farmer, Apr. 16, 1946 (div. 1970); children—Patricia, Deborah, John Biddle; m. 2d, Joan Sieber, Mar. 29, 1970 (div. 1973); m. 3d, Christine Johnson, May 26, 1979. Instr., Stanford, 1950-52, asst. prof., 1952-55, asso. prof., 1955-59, prof. philosophy, statistics, edn. and psychology, 1959—. Served to capt. USAAF, 1942-46. Recipient Nicholas Murray Butler Silver medal Columbia, 1965, Disting. Sci. Contbr. award Am. Psychol. Assn., 1972, Tchrs. Coll. medal for disting. service, 1978. Center for Advanced Study Behavioral Scis. fellow, 1955-56, NSF fellow, 1957-58. Fellow Am. Psychol. Assn., AAAS, Am. Acad. Arts and Scis.; mem. Math Assn. Am., Psychometric Soc., Am. Philos. Assn., Assn. Symbolic Logic, Am. Math Soc., Académie Internationale de Philosophie des Scis. (titular), Nat. Acad. Edn. (pres. 1973-77), Nat. Acad. Scis., Am. Psychol. Assn., Internat. Inst. Philosophy, Finnish Acad. Sci. and Letters, Internat. Union History and Philosophy of Sci. (div. logic, methodology and philosophy of sci., pres. 1975-79), Am. Ednl. Research Assn. (pres. 1973-74), Sigma Xi. Author: Introduction to Logic, 1957; Axiomatic Set Theory, 1960; Sets and Numbers, books 1-6, 1966; Studies in the Methodology and Foundations of Science, 1969; A Probabilistic Theory of Causality, 1970; Probabilistic Metaphysics, Vols. 1-2, 1974; (with Davidson and Siegel) Decision Making, 1957; (with Richard C. Atkinson) Markov Learning Models for Multiperson Interactions, 1960; (with Shirley Hill) First Course in Mathematical Logic, 1964; (with Edward J. Crothers) Experiments on Second-Language Learning, 1967; (with Max Jerman and Dow Brian) Computer-assisted Instruction, the 1965-66 Stanford Arithmetic Program, 1968; (with D. Krantz, R.D. Luce and A. Tversky) Foundations of Measurement, Vol. 1, 1971; (with M. Morningstar) Computer-Assisted Instruction at Stanford, 1966-68, 1972; (with B. Searle and J. Friend) The Radio Mathematics Project: Nicaragua 1974-75, 1976.

SUPPON, CHARLES RICHARD, fashion designer; b. East St. Louis, Ill., Jan. 12, 1949; s. Charles George and Myra Louise (Sova) S.; B.F.A., U. Chgo. and Sch. of Art Inst. Chgo., 1971. Asst. to Mr. Klein, Calvin Klein, Ltd., N.Y.C., 1971-76; designer Intresport, N.Y.C., 1976—; vis. instr. fashion Parsons Fashion Inst. Tech., 1977-79. Recipient Coty award, 1979; Menswear nomination; 1979. Mem. Fashion Council Am. Methodist. Office: 12 7th Ave New York NY 10018

SURAWICZ, BORYS, physician, educator; b. Moscow, Russia, Feb. 11, 1917; s. Josef and Mathilda (Soloweczyk) S.; M.D., Stafan Batory U., Wilno, Poland, 1939; m. Frida G. Van Klaveren, July 19, 1946; children—Christina M., Nina M., Tanya S., Serge J. Came to U.S., 1951, naturalized, 1956. Mem. staffs hosps. Germany, Norway, 1945-49; staff De Goesbriand Meml. Hosp., Burlington, Vt., 1951-53, Phila. Gen. Hosp., 1953-55; instr. cardiology U. Pa., Phila., 1954-55; instr. U. Vt., Burlington, 1955-57, asst. prof. clin. and exptl. medicine, 1957-62; chief div. cardiology U. Ky. Coll. Medicine, Lexington, 1962—, asso. prof. medicine, 1962-66, prof., 1966—. Cons. VA Hosp., Lexington, Ireland Army Hosp., Ft. Knox, Ky. Mem. AMA, A.C.P., Am. Heart Assn., Soc. U. Cardiologists, Am. Coll. Cardiology, Am. Physiol. Soc., Sigma Xi. Editor: (with E.D. Pellegrino) Sudden Cardiac Death, 1964; (with C. Fisch) Digitalis, 1969. Contbr. articles profl. jours. Home: 806 Overbrook Circle Lexington KY 40502

SURBECK, LEIGHTON HOMER, lawyer; b. Jasper, Minn., Oct. 8, 1902; s. James S. and Kathryn (Kilpatrick) S.; B.S., S.D. State Sch. Mines, 1924; J.D. magna cum laude, Yale, 1927; L.H.D., S.D. Sch. Mines and Tech., 1957; LL.D., Central Coll., 1973; m. Margaret H. Packard, 1976. Admitted to N.Y. bar, 1929; law sec. to Chief Justice Taft, 1927-28; asso. Hughes, Schurman & Dwight, N.Y.C., 1928-34, mem. firm, 1934-37; mem. firm Hughes, Hubbard & Reed, N.Y.C., 1937—. Trustee Pacific Sch. Religion, Berkeley, Calif., 1962—, Golden Gate U., San Francisco, 1979—, Central Coll., Pella, Iowa, 1966-78, Collegiate Boy's Sch., N.Y.C., 1975-78; chmn. Yale Law Sch. Fund, 1971-75. Served as col. AUS, 1942-45; chief econ. br. M.I., 1944-45. Recipient Yale medal Yale Alumni, 1975, Distinguished Service award Yale Law Sch., 1976; Horatio Alger award, 1977. Mem. Am., N.Y. State, N.Y. County bar assns., Assn. Bar City N.Y., Order of Coif, Sigma Tau., Delta Theta Phi. Mem. Marble Collegiate Ch. (elder 1962-78). Clubs: Down Town Assn., Siwanoy Country; Masons, University (N.Y.C.); Menlo Country (Woodside, Calif.). Home: 88 Faxon Rd Atherton CA 94025 Office: 1 Wall St New York NY 10005. *Every honest, best effort to a noble purpose beyond self always pays off handsomely ultimately at the most unexpected time, in the most unexpected ways, and from the most unexpected sources.*

SURDAM, JOHN LEWIS, chem. co. exec.; b. N.Y.C., May 16, 1915; s. Lewis J. and Hazle S. (Strickland) S.; ed. Williams Coll., 1937; m. Susan Rumsey Fiske, Sept. 7, 1940; children—Susan Surdam Johnston, Lewis J., II, Manson F. Pres., Fairbanks-Morse Coal Stoker Dealership-Western N.Y. State, 1937-38; with Osmose Wood Preserving Co. of Am. Inc., Buffalo, 1938-43, 49—, exec. v.p., 1949-52, pres., 1952—; pres. Firestone Distbr., Western. N.Y. State, 1947-48; trustee Erie Savs. Bank, Buffalo City Cemetery Assn.; dir., mem. exec. com. First Empire Corp.; dir., mem. exec. com., mem. audit com. Mfrs. & Traders Trust Co. Commr., Niagara Frontier Transp. Authority, 1967-77, treas., 1977. Served with USN, 1943-46. Mem. Am. Wood Preservers Assn., Soc. Am. Wood Preservers. Republican. Presbyterian. Clubs: Saturn, Country of Buffalo. Home: 76 Lincoln Pkwy Buffalo NY 14222 Office: 980 Ellicott St Buffalo NY 14209

SURDAM, ROBERT MCCLELLAN, banker; b. Albany, N.Y., Oct. 28, 1917; s. Burke and LeMoyne (McClellan) S.; B.A. cum laude, Williams Coll., 1939; m. Mary Caroline Buhl, July 8, 1946; children—Peter Buhl, Robert McClellan, Mary Caroline. With Nat. Bank Detroit, 1947—, exec. v.p., 1964-66, pres., 1966-72, chmn. bd., 1972—; dir. Internat. Bank Detroit, Bundy Corp., Bank of Tokyo and Detroit (Internat.) Ltd., Burroughs Corp. Mem. Res. City Bankers Assn. Clubs: Detroit, Detroit Athletic, Country of Detroit, Yondotega, Renaissance (Detroit); Links (N.Y.C.); Metropolitan (Washington). Home: 396 Provencal Rd Grosse Point MI 48236 Office: PO Box 116 Detroit MI 48232

SURDOVAL, DONALD JAMES, financial exec.; b. N.Y.C., Aug. 26, 1932; s. Donald J. and Catherine A. (Slevin) S.; B.B.A., Manhattan Coll., 1954; m. Patricia Fitzpatrick, May 28, 1955; children—Donald, Lisa, John, Catherine, Brian. Mgr., Rouche Ross & Co., 1956-63; treas. Mohican Corp., 1963-65; asst. controller, then v.p., controller Litton Industries, 1965-68; v.p., controller Norton Simon Inc., N.Y.C., 1968—; dir. Fuller O'Brien Paint Co. Bd. dirs. Calvary Hosp., N.Y.C. Served to 1st lt. USMCR, 1954-56. C.P.A., N.Y. Mem. Fin. Execs. Inst. Club: Hackensack Golf. Home: 87 Winding Way Woodcliff Lake NJ 07675 Office: 277 Park Ave New York NY 10017

SURETTE, WILLIAM FEDERHEN, corp. exec.; b. Boston, Jan. 19, 1928; s. Philip L. and Frances (Bullard) S.; B.S. in Bus. Adminstrn., Boston U., 1950; m. Margaret Patricia Ann Stegmaier, Aug. 22, 1950; children—William P., Susan Jeaninne Surette Honstein, Sharon F., Jonathan R. With Gen. Electric Co., 1950-71, mgr. fin. distbn. transformer dept., 1965-67, gen. mgr. medium voltage switchgear dept., Phila., 1967-71; v.p., controller Magnavox Corp., 1972-73; v.p. fin. Union Pacific Corp., N.Y.C., 1973-78, sr. v.p. fin., 1979—; dir. subs. Served with USMC, 1945-46. Mem. Fin. Execs. Inst., Council Fin. Execs. (mem. conf. bd.). Clubs: Wee Burn Country (Darien, Conn.), Sky (N.Y.C.). Home: 34 Crooked Mile Rd Darien CT 06820 Office: 345 Park Ave New York NY 10022

SURFACE, JAMES RICHARD, univ. chancellor; b. Salina, Kans., Feb. 26, 1921; s. Richard Jacob and Lucile (Gary) S.; A.B., U. Kans., 1942, M.A., 1948; M.B.A. with distinction, Harvard, 1950. D.C.S., 1956; m. Mary Ellen Shaver, Nov. 28, 1942; children—Mary Lucile, Richard, Daniel, John, Thomas. Life ins. rep., Salina, 1946-47; asst. instr. U. Kans., Lawrence, 1947-48, dean Sch. Bus., 1957-62, vice chancellor, dean faculties, 1962-66, provost, dean of faculties, 1966-69; prof. Grad. Sch. Mgmt., Vanderbilt U., Nashville, 1969-71, 78—, exec. vice-chancellor, 1972-78; research asso., instr. Harvard Bus. Sch., 1950-53, asst. prof., 1953-57, vis. prof., 1967-68. Served from pvt. to 1st lt. USMCR, 1942-45. Mem. Beta Theta Pi, Beta Gamma Sigma. Contbr. articles to bus. publs. Home: 1215 Otter Creek Rd Nashville TN 37215

SURFACE, RICHARD EUGENE, automotive parts mfg. co. exec.; b. Franklin, Ind., Nov. 6, 1924; s. Earl and Dora L. (Snyder) S.; B.B.A., U. Toledo, 1948; m. Mary Jeanne Barrett, June 17, 1948; children—Steven James, Christy Lynn Surface Schwalbe. Asst. to pres. office products div. IBM, 1948-64; gen. mgr. Dura Bus. Machines, Madison Heights, Mich., 1964-66; with Champion Spark Plug Co., Toledo, 1967—, v.p., dir. organizational planning, 1969-78, exec. v.p., dir. ops, 1978—, mem. exec. com. and bd. dirs., 1969—; dir. Champion subs. cos. in Mexico, Australia, Belgium, South Africa, Eng.; pres., dir. Arman S.p.A. (Italy); v.p., dir. Champion subs. cos. in Venezuela, Can. and Hellertown Mfg. Co. (Pa.), Iowa Industries, Inc., Burlington, Anderson Co. of Ind., Gary; mem. exec. com., dir. Champion-owned Baron Drawn Steel Corp., Toledo; dir. Archambel, S.A. (Belgium); mem. adv. com. DeVilbiss Co. div. Champion, Toledo. Bd. dirs. ARC, Toledo, U. Toledo Corp.; pres. U. Toledo Alumni Found., 1970-74; v.p. Toledo Area Govtl. Research Assn. Served with U.S. Army, 1943-45. Mem. Soc. Automotive Engrs., Phi Kappa Psi. Republican. Clubs: Inverness, Toledo, Belmont Country (Toledo). Home: 10591 Cardiff Rd Perrysburg OH 43551 Office: 900 Upton Ave PO Box 910 Toledo OH 43661

SURFACE, THOMAS JAMES, lawyer, author; b. Riner, Va., Mar. 21, 1906; s. George Thomas and Mary Vernon (Shelburne) S.; student Antioch Coll., Yellow Springs, Ohio, 1925-27; LL.B., U. Ga., 1929; student U. Louisville, 1929-30, J.D., 1969; LL.B., Webster U., 1931, LL.D., 1934; LL.B., Cumberland U., 1936; A.M. (hon.), Capitol City Coll., 1946; hon. degrees St. Andrews U., Trinity Coll, Maranatha Bible Sem.; m. Elizabeth Abbott, June 23, 1928 (dec.); children—Shelburne, James; m. 2d, Ruth Andrew, Nov. 22, 1971. Admitted to Va. bar, 1931, since practiced in Roanoke; atty. for Craig County, Va., 1972—; pres. Franklin Pub. Co., Inc., Roanoke, Franklin Credit Sch.; chmn. bd. Expert Publs., Inc. Mem. U.S.N.G., 1923-25; aide-de-camp to gov. Ky., 1935-37. Named Ky. Col. Mem. U.S. Supreme Ct., Roanoke bar assns., Va. Trial Lawyers Assn., Va. State Bar, Democrat. Mem. Christian Ch. (elder, chmn ofcl. bd. 1962-64). Lion, K.P. Mason (32 deg., Shriner). Club: Jamestown Soc. Author: Credit Reporting, 1945, Collection law, 1946, Legal Pitfalls, 1946, Collection Psychology, 1946, Highlights of the Law of Contracts, Torts, Agency and Sales, Tracing and Investigating, 1946, Canadian Collection Law; syndicated column: Washington Letter. Contbr. articles to nat. mags. Home: 2414 Lincoln Ave SW Roanoke VA 24015 Office: 501 13th St SW Roanoke VA 24016

SURGENOR, DOUGLAS MACNEVIN, educator, biol. chemist; b. Hartford, Conn., Apr. 7, 1918; s. William Hume and Flora E. (MacNevin) S.; A.B., Williams Coll., 1939; M.S., U. Mass., 1941; Ph.D., Mass. Inst. Tech., 1946; hon. degree Nat. U. Asuncion (Paraguay), 1969; m. Lois Hutchinson, Nov. 2, 1946; children—Peter, Sara, Jonathan, Timothy, Stephen. Asst. prof. phys. chemistry Harvard Med. Sch., 1950-55, asso. mem. lab. phys. chemistry related to medicine and pub. health, 1950-54, asst. prof. biol. chemistry 1955-60, vis. prof. pediatrics, 1977—; sr. investigator Protein Found., Boston, 1956-60; prof. biochemistry, head dept. U. Buffalo Sch. Medicine, 1960-62; dean Sch. Medicine, State U. N.Y. Buffalo, 1962-68, provost faculty of health scis., 1967-70, prof. biochemistry, 1962-77, research prof. mgmt., 1971-77; pres. N.E. region ARC Blood Services, Boston, 1977—; vis. prof. pediatrics Harvard Med. Sch., 1977—; chmn. adv. com. Nat. Blood Resource Program, 1970-73; mem. commn. Plasma Fractionation and Related Processes, 1964—, chmn, 1967—; chmn. Internat. Com. Hemostasis and Thrombosis, 1970-72; mem. N.Y. State Pesticide Bd., 1967-70; trustee, mem. exec. com. Comprehensive Health Planning Council Western N.Y., 1968-72. Pres. Center for Blood Research, Boston, 1972—; trustee, bd. govs., mem. exec. com. Children's Hosp. Med. Center, Boston, 1975—. Recipient Spl. citation Distinguished Service to Research Am. Heart Assn., 1967. Mem. Am. Soc. Biol. Chemists, Am. Soc. Hematology, AAAS, Internat. Soc. Thrombosis and Haemostasis, Council on Thrombosis, Am. Heart Assn. Club: St. Botolph (Boston). Editor: The Red Blood Cell, 2d edit., 1974. Mem. editorial bd. Circulation Research, 1966-69, Microvascular Research, 1971-74. Home: 213 Indian Hill Carlisle MA 01741 Office: American Red Cross Blood Services NE Region 812 Huntington Ave Boston MA 02115

SURIANO, RAFFAELE, dentist, univ. dean; b. Kenosha, Wis., May 4, 1921; s. Joseph and Katherine (Manefredi) S.; D.D.S., Loyola U., Chgo., 1944; m. Ruth Crowe, Jan. 10, 1947; children—Patricia, Margaret, Mary. Commd. 2d lt. U.S. Army, 1943, advanced through grades to col., 1964; ret., 1973; dean Sch. Dentistry, Loyola U., Maywood, Ill., 1973—. Decorated Legion of Merit with oak leaf cluster. Fellow Am. Coll. Dentists, Internat. Coll. Dentists, Royal Acad. Surgeons, Am. Acad. Implants; mem. ADA, Chgo. Dental Soc. Home: 160 E Linden Ave Lake Forest IL 60045 Office: Loyola University 2160 S 1st Ave Maywood IL 60153

SURMAN, WILLIAM ROBERT, architect; b. Chgo., May 10, 1926; s. Charles F. and Frances M. (Kadala) S.; B.S., Rice Inst., 1945; B.S. in Civil Engring., Northwestern U., 1948; m. Joan Marie Jeffers, May 5, 1956; children—William Robert, Robert, Julie, Mary, Thomas. Architect, Pace Assos., 1957-60, Shaw-Metz & Assos., 1960-63; pvt. practice architect, 1963-65; chief architect Graham, Anderson, Probst & White, Chgo., 1965-67, v.p., 1967-68, exec. v.p., 1968-70, pres., chmn. bd., from 1970; now pres., architect Probst and White, Chgo. Mem. Glencoe (Ill.) Plan Commn. Served to ensign USNR, 1943-46; PTO; to lt., 1951-53. Mem. AIA, Nat. Council Archtl. Registration Bds., Chgo. Assn. Commerce and Industry, Ill. C. of C.

Clubs: Econ. (dir.), Arts, Execs. (dir. 1973-79, pres. 1976-77) (Chgo.); Skokie Country (Glencoe). Office: 17 East Erie St Chicago IL 60611

SURMEYAN, HAZAROS ARTUR, dancer; b. Skopje, Jugoslavia, Jan. 21, 1943; s. Artur and Radmila S.; student Ballet Sch. of Skopje; m. Sept. 14, 1968. Dancer, Nat. Ballet of Skopje, 1960, Mannheim (Germany) State Opera, 1961; partner Rosella Hightower in Vichy and Cannes, France, 1962; prin. dancer Cologne (Germany) Opera Ballet, 1963-66; guest artist in Munich, Germany, 1966; prin. dancer Nat. Ballet of Can., Toronto, Ont., 1966—; first danced Benvolio in Romeo and Juliet, 1960, Don Quixote, 1960, Kostchei in L'oiseau de feu, 1960, Giselle pas de deux, 1960, Casse-noisette pas de deux, 1961, Colas in La fille mal gardee, 1961, St. Francis in Nobilissime visione, 1961, Argon pas de deux, 1961, Solo boy in The Bitter Weird, 1963, Etudes, 1963, Romeo in Romeo and Juliet, 1966-67, Le corsaire pas de deux, 1966-67, Adagio cantabile, 1966-67, Prince in Casse-noisette, 1966-67, Prince Siegfried in Le lac des cygnes, 1967, Solor in La bayadiere, 1967, Concerto barocco, 1967, Serenade, 1967, Prince in Cinderella, 1968; danced in Le corsaire pas de deux CBC TV, 1967; master of ceremonies Le lac des cygnes (Bruhn, Festival, CBC), 1967. Office: Nat Ballet 157 King St E Toronto ON M5C 1G9 Canada*

SURRENCY, ERWIN CAMPBELL, librarian, educator; b. Jesup, Ga., May 11, 1924; s. H.W. and Mary (Campbell) S.; student N.Ga. Coll., 1940-41; A.B., U. Ga., 1947, LL.B., 1948, M.A., 1949; M.A. in Library Sci., George Peabody U., 1950; m. Ida E. Winn, Sept. 2, 1945; children—Robert Erwin, Ellen Gwinn. Law librarian Temple U., Phila., 1950-78, asst. prof. law, 1951-54, asso. prof., 1954-60, prof., 1960-72, asst. dean, law librarian, 1972-78; prof. law, law librarian U. Ga., Athens, 1979—; vis. prof. Queen's U., Belfast, No. Ireland, 1963-64; library cons. Am. Bar Found., 1953-54; cons. Nigerian Inst. Advanced Legal Studies, 1975-76. Mem. Am. Soc. Internat. Law, Seldon Soc., Spl. Libraries Assn., Ga. Hist. Soc., Am. Assn. Law Libraries (v.p. 1972-73, pres. 1973-74), Am. Hist. Assn., Am. Soc. Legal History (pres. 1957-58, 66-69), Brit. Inst. Internat. and Comparative Law. Author: The Marshall Reader, 1955; (with Carrol C. Moreland) Research in Pennsylvania Law, 1953, 2d edit., 1965. Editor: Am. Jour. Legal History, 1957—. Home: 360 Hickory Hill Dr Watkinsville GA 30677 Office: Univ George Athens GA 30602. *It is imperative that a successful person avoid superficiality and approach all duties presented him meticulously, with humility and with a faith in his own ability to cope with these challenges and with an abiding faith in the future.*

SURREY, MILT, artist; b. N.Y.C., Mar. 18, 1922; s. Leopold and Pauline (Zipper) Schleifer; student Coll. City N.Y., 1939-42; m. Eleanor Gallant, Sept. 15, 1946; children—Elaine (Mrs. Edward Werz), Robert, David. Represented in permanent collections Allentown (Pa.) Art Mus., Butler Inst. Am. Art, Youngstown, Ohio, Cin. Art Mus., Coll. Mus., Hampton (Va.) Inst., Columbia (S.C.) Mus. Art, Davenport (Iowa) Mus., Detroit Inst. Arts, Evansville (Ind.) Mus. Art, Hickory (N.C.) Mus. Art, Jacksonville (Fla.) Art Mus., Lowe Art Center, Syracuse (N.Y.) U., Massillon (Ohio) Mus., Miami (Fla.) Mus. Modern Art, Springfield (Mo.) Art Mus., Telfair Acad. Arts and Scis., Savannah, Ga., Holyoke (Mass.) Mus. Natural History, Theodore Lyman Wright Art Center, Beloit (Wis.) Coll., Treat Gallery, Bates Coll., Lewiston, Maine. Served with AUS, 1942-45. Mem. Am. Fedn. Arts. Home: 7 Bridle Path Dr Old Westbury NY 11568 Office: 201 Montrose Rd Westbury NY 11590

SURREY, PHILIP HENRY, artist, educator; b. Calgary, Alta., Can., Oct. 8, 1910; s. Henry Philip and Kate Alice (de Guerin) S.; student Winnipeg (Man., Can.) Sch. Art, 1927-29, Vancouver (B.C., Can.) Sch. Art, 1930-33, Art Students' League, N.Y.C., 1936-37. Exhibited numerous one man shows, Montreal, Toronto, Ottawa, Quebec and Windsor, Ont., including retrospective Musée d'Art Contemporain, Montreal, 1971, Canadian Cultural Centre, Paris, France, 1972; represented in permanent collections Nat. Gallery Can., Ottawa, Art Gallery Ont., Toronto, Musée du Quebec, other pub., pvt. collections. Mem. Royal Can. Acad. Club: Montreal Press. Home: 478 Grosvenor Ave Montreal PQ H3Y 2S4 Canada

SURREY, STANLEY STERLING, lawyer, educator; b. N.Y.C., Oct. 3, 1910; s. Samuel and Pauline (Sterling) S.; B.S. magna cum laude, Coll. City N.Y., 1929; LL.B., Columbia, 1932; m. Dorothy Mooklar Walton, June 6, 1938; 1 son, Scott Stanley. Admitted to N.Y. bar, 1933, Mass. bar, 1951; research asst. Columbia Law Sch., 1932-33; atty. Proskauer, Rose & Paskus, N.Y.C., 1933; with NRA, Washington, 1933-35, NLRB, Washington, 1935-37, U.S. Treasury Dept., Washington, 1937-44, 46-47; vis. prof. Calif. Sch. Law, Berkeley, summer 1940; vis. lectr. Columbia Law Sch., summer 1947; prof. law. U. Calif., Berkeley, 1947-50; prof. law Harvard, 1950-61, Jeremiah Smith prof. law, 1958-61, 1969—, also dir. program for internat. taxation, 1953-61; chief reporter Am. Law Inst. income tax project, 1948-61, supr., 1975—; asst. sec. for tax policy Treasury Dept., 1961-69, cons., 1977—; Mem. Am. Tax Mission to Japan, 1949, 50; spl. counsel U.S. House ways and means King subcom. on internal revenue adminstrn., 1951-52; cons. Treasury Dept., P.R., 1954; spl. adviser UN Expert Group Tax Treaties. Bd. overseers Florence Heller Sch. Brandeis U., Coll. of V.I.; trustee TIAA, 1972-78. Served as lt. (j.g.) USNR, 1944-46. Decorated Order Sacred Treasure (Japan). Fellow Am. Acad. Arts. and Scis.; mem. Am. Bar Assn. (council taxation sect. 1958-60), Nat. Tax Assn. (v.p. 1978-79), Phi Beta Kappa. Author casebooks in fed. taxation field; (with others) Federal Income Taxation, Cases and Materials, 2 vols., 1972, 73; Federal Wealth Transfer Taxation, Cases and Materials, 1977; Pathways to Tax Reform, 1973. Contbr. articles to legal periodicals. Home: 54 Buckingham St Cambridge MA 02138

SURREY, WALTER STERLING, lawyer; b. Denver, July 24, 1915; s. Samuel and Pauline (Sterling) S.; student Coll. City N.Y., 1932-34; B.S., U. Va., 1936; LL.B., Yale, 1939; m. Dana E. O'Conor; children—Richard Sterling, Elizabeth Sterling Adams. Admitted to N.Y. bar, 1939, D.C. bar, 1950, U.S. Supreme Ct. bar, 1955; atty. Dept. Justice, Washington, 1940-41; research asst. Randolph Paul, Lord, Day & Lord, N.Y., 1939-40; atty. Bd. Econ. Warfare, Washington, 1941-43; attache charge econ. warfare, Am. Legation, Stockholm, Sweden, 1943-45; chief div. econ. security controls Dept. State, Washington, 1945-47, asst. legal adviser, 1947-50; cons. ECA, 1950-52, 59; now sr. partner firm Surrey, Karasik & Morse, Washington; professorial lectr. George Washington U. Law Sch., 1962-63; bd. visitors Fletcher Sch. Law and Diplomacy, Tufts U., Boston, 1976—; dir. Envirotech Corp. Mem. U.S. delegation negotiating on German external assets Switzerland, Sweden, Spain, Portugal, 1945-46; U.S. mem. spl. com. on German property of Inter-Am. Econ. and Social Council; mem., acting chmn. Nat. Conf. Internat. Econ. and Social Devel., 1963-65; bd. dirs., gen. counsel, ex-officio mem. exec. com. Nat. Council for U.S.-China Trade; gen. counsel, mem. Iran-U.S. Bus. Council. Mem. Am. Law Inst., U.S. C. of C. (mem. internat. com.), Am. Soc. Internat. Law (exec. council 1962-68, v.p., pres. 1976-78), Nat. Planning Assn. (chmn., dir., gen. counsel). Clubs: Yale, Federal City, Cosmos (Washington). Co-editor: A Lawyers Guide to International Business Transactions, Vol. 1, 2d edit., 1977. Contbr. articles to profl. jours. Home: 5171 Manning Pl NW Washington DC 20016 Office: 1156 15th St NW Washington DC 20005

SURSA, CHARLES DAVID, banker; b. Muncie, Ind., Nov. 5, 1925; s. Charles Vaught and Ethel (Schukraft) S.; B.S. in Chem. Engring., Purdue U., 1946; M.B.A., Harvard, 1948; m. Mary Jane Palmer, Feb. 2, 1947; children—Ann Elizabeth, Janet Lynne, Charles Vaught, Laura Jane. With Indsl. Trust & Savs. Bank, Muncie, 1948—, chmn., pres., 1951—, also dir.; dir. Old Republic Life Ins. Co., Chgo., N.Y., Standard Locknut & Lockwasher, Inc., Indpls., Muncie Ind. Indsl. Park, Inc., Old Republic Internat. Corp., Chgo., Old Republic Ins. Co., Greensburg, Pa. Dir. and treas., Muncie Symphony Assn., 1949-62, pres. 1962-72, 2d v.p., dir., 1978—; dir. Ball Meml. Hosp., Muncie, Children's Mus., Inc., Muncie; campaign chmn. United Way Del. County, 1967-68, dir., mem. exec. com., 1968-70; mem. Ind. Arts Commn., 1969-73; mem. Ind. Dept. Fin. Instns., 1971-74; pres. Muncie Family Counseling Service, 1959, Muncie YMCA, 1963-64, Community Services Council of Del. County, Ind., Inc., 1973-74. Recipient Outstanding Young Man award Ind. Jr. C. of C., 1956. Mem. Muncie C. of C. (pres. 1959-60), World Bus. Council, Phi Gamma Delta. Republican. Presbyterian. Odd Fellow, Rotarian (pres. 1964-65), Elk. Clubs: Torch, Delaware Country (pres., dir. 1964). Home: 3410 W University Ave Muncie IN 47304 Office: 117 E Adams St Muncie IN 47305

SURTEES, ROBERT LEE, motion picture photographer; b. Covington, Ky., Aug. 9, 1906; s. James Daniel and Besse Ranton (Sayers) S.; grad. high sch., Cin.; m. Maydell Powell, Sept. 17, 1930; children—Nancy Lee (Mrs. Walter Corby), Bruce, Linda, Thomas. With EFA Studio, also UFA Studio, Berlin, Germany, 1928-30; with Metro-Goldwyn-Mayer Studio, Culver City, Calif., 1942—, dir. photography motion picture prodns., 1941—. Recipient Look mag. award for King Solomon's Mines, 1950; Fgn. Corr. award for King Solomon's Mines, 1950, for Quo Vadis, 1951; Academy award for King Solomon's Mines, 1951, Bad and the Beautiful, 1953, Ben Hur, 1960; Acad. award nominations, 1944, 50, 51, 52, 55, 59, 62, 67 (2), 71 (2), 73, 75, 76, 77, 78. Home: 25535 Hacienda Pl Carmel CA 93923

SUSKIND, RAYMOND ROBERT, physician; b. N.Y.C., Nov. 29, 1913; s. Alexander and Anna (Abramson) S.; A.B., Columbia, 1934; student medicine, Edinburgh, Scotland, 1938-39; M.D. (Mitchell prize 1943), L.I. Coll. Medicine, 1943; m. Ida Blanche Richardson, Dec. 27, 1944; children—Raymond Robert, Stephen Alexander. Intern, Cin. Gen. Hosp., 1944, resident in dermatology, 1944-46, 48-49; research asst. bacteriology N.Y. U., 1934-36; research asst. pharmacology, 1936-37; practice medicine specializing in dermatology, Cin., 1949-62; mem. faculty U. Cin., 1948-62, asso. prof. dermatology, 1952-62, dir. dermatol. research program, Kettering Lab., 1948-62, prof., chmn. dept. environ. health, dir. Kettering Lab., Cin., 1969—, now Jacob G. Schmidlapp prof. environ. health, prof. medicine; prof., head, div. environ. medicine, prof. dermatology U. Oreg. Med. Sch., 1962-69. Cons. FDA, 1976—; cons. occupational medicine Surgeon Gen. Dept. of Navy, 1975—; chmn. standards adv. com. on cutaneous and eye hazards OSHA, 1978; mem. sci. mgmt. adv. team for toxic hazards research unit U. Calif. and USAF, 1977—; Gehrmann lectr. Am. Acad. Occupational Medicine, 1977. Mem. Nat. air quality adv. com. EPA, 1970-73; adv. com. Health Scis. Research Lab., ERDA, Los Alamos, N.Mex., 1976—. Mem. Cin. Air Pollution Bd., 1972-76, chmn., 1974-75. Served to capt. M.C., AUS, 1946-48. Diplomate Am. Bd. Toxicology. Fellow A.C.P.; mem AMA (chmn. com. cutaneous health and cosmetics, 1962-65), Am. Occupational Med. Assn. (chmn. dermatology com. and policy group 1958-66; dir. 1969-75, Health Achievement in Industry award 1977), Soc. Investigative Dermatology (dir.), Am. Acad. Dermatology (chmn. edn. com.), Assn. Am. Med. Colls., Cin. (past pres.), Ore. dermatol. socs., Nat. Acad. Scis. (com. cutaneous system 1958-65, com. air pollutants 1970), N.Y. Acad. Scis., Am. Indsl. Hygiene Assn., Soc. for Occupational and Environ. Health (councillor), AAAS, Am. Dermatol. Assn., Soc. Toxicology, Japanese Dermatol. Assn. (hon.), Sigma Xi, Alpha Omega Alpha. Contbr. chpts. to books, articles to profl. jours. Office: Dept Environ Health U Cincinnati Coll Medicine 3223 Eden Ave Cincinnati OH 45267

SUSLAK, HOWARD ROBINSON, co. exec.; b. N.Y.C., Apr. 24, 1920; s. Sigmund and Estelle (Robinson) S.; grad. Juilliard Sch. Music, 1942; B.A. magna cum laude, N.Y.U., 1942; M.B.A., Wharton Sch., U. Pa., 1943; m. Adele Barnett, June 19, 1949; children—Brian Edward, Neil Scott, Valerie Estelle, Pamela Simone. Asst. to pres. E.R. Squibb & Sons, N.Y.C., 1945-46; v.p. Metacan Mfg. Co., Bklyn., 1946-47; with MacDonald & Co., N.Y.C. 1947—, mgr. N.Y.C., 1948, in charge offices, Chgo., Pitts., Boston, Detroit, 1949-54, gen. partner, 1954—, v.p., 1956-58, exec. v.p., 1958-62, pres., 1962—; chmn., mng. dir. Indsl. Mgmt. Cons., Ltd., London, Eng., 1949—; dir. George Hopkinson, Ltd., Schweber Electronics Corp., Marine Protein Corp. Mem. N.Y.C Planning Commn., 1965-66. Trustee Eddie Cantor Camp Commn. Surprise Lake Camp; bd. dirs. Weizmann Inst. Sci., Purchase Community House, Purchase Assn., Opera Orch. N.Y., Sch. Weber Electronics. Served with AUS, 1943-44. Mem. Am. Mgmt. Assn., Newcomen Soc. N.Am., Phi Beta Kappa Assos. Clubs: Economics, Harmonie, Phi Beta Kappa Alumni (N.Y.C.); Royal Automobile (London); Royal Automobile Country (Epsom, Eng.); Windham Mountain Ski; Ski Verein (St. Moritz, Switzerland). Home: Convent Ln Rye NY 10580 Office: 532 Madison Ave New York City NY 10022

SUSMAN, LELAND STANFORD, newspaper cartoonist; b. San Francisco, July 27, 1917; s. Leo Henry and Mildred (Tonn) S.; student Calif. Sch. Fine Arts, also Acad. Advt. Arts; m. M. Eileen Everly, Feb. 7, 1953. With San Francisco Call-Bull., 1939; mem. staff Oakland (Calif.) Tribune, 1946—, editorial sports cartoonist, 1950—. Dep. sheriff, Alameda County, Calif., 1958. Served with USNR, 1940-45. Recipient Joseph R. Knowland award Oakland Tribune, 1953. Home: 4374 Arden Pl Oakland CA 94602 Office: 13th and Franklin Sts Oakland CA 94604

SUSMAN, STEPHEN DAILY, lawyer; b. Houston, Jan. 20, 1941; s. Harry and Helene Gladys (Daily) S.; B.A. magna cum laude, Yale U., 1962; LL.B. summa cum laude, U. Tex. Austin, 1965; m. Karen Lee Hyman, Dec. 26, 1965; children—Stacy Margraeta, Harry Paul. Admitted to Tex. bar, 1965, U.S. Supreme Ct., 1960; law clk. Chief Judge 5th Circuit, 1965-66, to Asso. Justice Hugo Black, U.S. Supreme Ct., 1966-67; partner firm Fulbright & Jaworski, 1966-75; spl. cons. atty. gen. Tex., 1975; partner firm Mandell & Wright, Houston, 1975—; vis. prof. law U. Tex., Austin, 1975. Bd. dirs. Jewish Family Service, 1967-75, Am. Jewish Com., 1967—. Recipient Leon Green Outstanding Ex Editor award U. Tex. Law Sch., 1970; research fellow Southwestern Legal Found., 1975—. Mem. Am. Law Inst., Am. Bar Assn., Tex. Law Rev. (dir.). Clubs: Yale (Houston and N.Y.C.), Houston Athletic. Home: 9211 Kenilworth St Houston TX 77024 Office: 806 Main St 21st Flr Mandell & Wright Houston TX 77002

SUSS, FREDRIC THOMAS, state ofcl., lawyer; b. New Britain, Conn., Jan. 27, 1915; s. George J. and Rose Mary (Coussa) S.; student Holy Cross Coll., Springfield (Mass.) Coll., J.D., Northeastern U., 1942; postgrad. Georgetown U.; m. Hilda McGuire, Mar. 10, 1951; children—Susan, Christopher, Jonathan, Fredric, Jane, Rosemary, Madeline, Jennifer Admitted to Mass. bar, 1942; practiced in Springfield, 1942-50; counsel labor subcom. Welfare and pension funds U.S. Senate, 1954-55; legal adviser FTC, 1956, spl. asst. to exec. dir. anti-trust trial atty., 1956-61; gen. counsel Small Bus. Adminstrn., 1961-65; practiced in Washington, 1965-74; adminstrv. law judge N.Y. State Pub. Service Commn., Albany, 1974—. Cons., Atomic Safety and Licensing bd. AEC, 1972—; cons. on antitrust law AEC, 1972—. Served with USNR, World War II and Korea. Mem. Am., Fed. (mem. nat. council 1963—), D.C. bar assns. Home: 248 State St Albany NY 12210 Office: Bldg 3 Empire State Plaza Albany NY 12223

SUSSER, MERVYN WILFRED, educator; b. Johannesburg, South Africa, Sept. 26, 1921 (came to U.S. 1965); s. Solomon and Ida Rose (Son) S.; M.B., B. Ch., U. Witwatersrand (South Africa), 1950; diploma pub. health, London Conjoint Bd., 1960; m. Zena Athene Stein, Mar. 28, 1949; children—Ida, Ezra, Ruth. Med. officer, later supt. Alexandra Health Centre and Univ. Clinic, Johannesburg, 1952-55; successively lectr., sr. lectr., reader, head dept. social and preventive medicine Manchester (Eng.) U., 1957-65, also med. officer div. mental health, Salford, Eng.; prof., chmn. div. epidemiology Columbia U. Sch. Pub. Health, N.Y.C., 1966-78; Gertrude H. Sergievsky prof. epidemiology, dir. Sergievsky Center, Columbia U., 1977—; cons. WHO, 1962 66-72. Served with South African Army, 1940-45. Belding scholar Assn. Aid Crippled Children, 1965-66; Guggenheim fellow, 1972. Fellow Royal Coll. Physicians (Edinburgh), N.Y. Acad. Medicine, Internat. Epidemiological Assn., World Psychiat. Assn., Am. Pub. Health Assn., Soc. Epidemiological Research, Physicians Forum. Author: (with W. Watson) Sociology in Medicine, 2d. edit., 71; Community Psychiatry; Epidemiologic and Social Themes, 1968; Causal Thinking in the Health Sciences, 1972; concepts and strategies of Epidemiology; (with others) Famine and Human Development: Studies of the Dutch Hungerwinter 1944-45, 1975. Home: 21 Oakdale Dr Hastings-on-Hudson NY 10706 Office: 600 W 168th St New York City NY 10032

SUSSEX, JAMES NEIL, psychiatrist, educator; b. Northcote, Minn., Oct. 2, 1917; s. Rollo and Florence (Bartholomew) S.; A.B., U. Kans., 1939, M.D., 1942; m. Margaret Ann Garty, Apr. 25, 1943; children—Margaret Eileen, Mary Patricia, Barbara Lorraine, Teresa Virginia. Commd. lt. (j.g.), M.C., U.S. Navy, 1943, advanced through grades to comdr., 1955; intern Naval Hosp., Chelsea, Mass., 1942-43; resident psychiatry Naval Hosp., Vallejo, Calif., 1946-49; fellow child psychiatry Phila. Guild Guidance Clinic, 1949-51, asst. chief neuropsychiatry Naval Hosp., Bethesda, Md., 1951-55; resigned, 1955; mem. faculty Med. Coll. Ala., 1955-68, prof. psychiatry, chmn. dept., 1959-68; psychiatrist-in-chief U. Ala. Hosps. and Clinics, 1959-68; faculty U. Miami (Fla.) Sch. Medicine, 1968—, prof. psychiatry, chmn. dept., 1970—. Mem. adv. bd. Nat. Psychiat. Residency Selection Plan, 1965—; mem. Med. Adv. Bd. Ednl. Film Prodn., 1966—; cons. Bur. Research, U.S. Office Edn., 1966-72; dir. Ala. planning for Mental Retardation, 1964—; psychiatry tng. rev. com. Nat. Inst. Mental Health. Diplomate Am. Bd. Psychiatry and Neurology (dir. for child psychiatry 1966-70, dir. 1974—). Mem. Assn. Soc. Profs. Psychiatry (chmn. 1967), Am. (ho. dels. 1966), So. (chmn. sect. neurology and psychiatry 1965-66) med. assns., Am. Assn. Psychiat. Services for Children (council 1966—, pres. 1972-74), Ala. Assn. Mental Health (dir.), Ala. Alcoholic Commn. (dir.), Phi Beta Kappa, Nu Sigma Nu. Editor Jour. Ala. Soc. Med. History, 1957-63; editorial bd. Jour. Am. Acad. Child Psychiatry, 1966—. Home: 6950 SW 134th St Miami FL 33156

SUSSKIND, CHARLES, educator, engr.; b. Prague, Czechoslovakia, Aug. 19, 1921; came to U.S. 1945, naturalized 1946; s. Bruno B. and Gertruda (Seger) S.; student Northampton Poly. (London, Eng.), 1939-40; B.S., Calif. Inst. Tech., 1948; M.Engring., Yale, 1949, Ph.D., 1951; m. Thelma Gabriel, May 1, 1945; children—Pamela Gertrude Susskind Pettler, Peter Gabriel, Amanda Frances. Research asst. Yale, 1949-51; research asso. Stanford, 1951-55, lectr., asst. to dir. Microwave Lab., 1953-55; mem. faculty U. Calif., Berkeley, 1955—, prof., 1964—, asst. dean Coll. Engring., 1964-68, also statewide adminstr. U. Calif., 1969-74; Vis. prof. U. London (Eng.), 1961-62, U. Geneva (Switzerland), 1968-69; cons. electronics industry, govt., publishers; dir. San Francisco Press, Inc. Served with USAAF, 1942-45. Fellow I.E.E.E.; mem. Bioengring. Soc., A.A.A.S., History of Sci. Soc., Soc. for History of Tech., Instn. Electronic and Radio Engrs. (London), Sigma Xi (pres. Berkeley chpt. 1972-73), Tau Beta Pi. Clubs: Yale (N.Y.C.); Commonwealth (San Francisco). Author: (with M. Chodorow) Fundamentals of Microwave Electronics, 1964; (with L. Schell) Exporting Techical Education, 1968; Understanding Technology, 1973, 74; Twenty-five Engineers and Inventors, 1976; (with F. Kurylo) Ferdinand Braun, 1980; editor: (with M. Hertz) Heinrich Hertz: Memoirs, Letters, Diaries, bilingual edit., 1977; editor-in-chief Ency. Electronics, 1962. Office: Coll of Engineering U Calif Berkeley CA 94720

SUSSKIND, DAVID HOWARD, television, motion picture and theatre producer; b. N.Y.C., Dec. 19, 1920; s. Benjamin and Frances (Lear) S.; B.S., Harvard U., 1942; m. Phyllis Briskin, Aug. 23, 1939; children—Pamela, Diana, Andrew; m. 2d, Joyce Davidson, Apr. 22, 1966; 1 dau., Samantha. With publicity dept. Warner Bros., also Universal Picture Corp., 1946-48; talent agt. Century Artists also, Music Corp. Am., 1949-52; co-owner, pres. TV, theatre and motion picture prodns. Talent Assos., Ltd., N.Y.C. (merged with Time-Life Films, Inc. 1977), 1952—; producer Broadway shows A Very Special Baby, 1956, Rashomon, 1959, Kelly, 1965, All in Good Time, 1965, Brief Lives, 1967; producer motion pictures Edge of the City, 1956, Raisin in the Sun, 1960, Requiem for a Heavyweight, 1961, All the Way Home, 1963, Lovers and Other Strangers, 1970, Pursuit of Happiness, 1971, Alice Doesn't Live Here Anymore, 1974, All Things Bright and Beautiful, 1976, Buffalo Bill and the Indians, 1976; moderator TV discussion program Open End, 1958-67, The David Susskind Show, 1967—; TV producer duPont Show of Month, Philco Playhouse, Kraft Theatre, Armstrong Circle Theatre, Art Carney Show, Kaiser Aluminum Hour, Play of the Week, Festival of Performing Arts, East Side, West Side, The Crucible, Death of a Salesman, The Price (Hallmark Hall of Fame), 1971, Look Homeward Angel, 1972, Straw Dogs, 1972, All the Way Home, 1972, If You Give a Dance, You Gotta Pay the Band, 1972, Harvey, 1972, The Shenyang Acrobatic Troupe Special, 1973, The Glass Menagerie, 1973, The Magic Show, 1975, Caesar and Cleopatra, 1976, Eleanor and Franklin (12 Emmy awards), 1976, Truman at Potsdam, 1976, Harry S. Truman: Plain Speaking, 1976, Richard Rodgers: The Sound of His Music, 1976, Eleanor and Franklin: The White House Years (TV Critics Circle award for best drama of year; Emmy awards), 1977, Johnny We Hardly Knew Ye, 1977, The TV Critics Circle Awards Show, 1977, The War Between the Tates, 1977, Goldenrod, 1977, World of Darkness, 1977, Breaking Up, 1977, Tell Me My Name, 1977, also TV series Alice, 1976, On Our Own, 1977. Served to lt. (s.g.) USNR, 1942-46. Recipient Peabody TV award, 1960; Sylvania TV awards, 1959, 60; Robert Sherwood award, 1957, Newspaper Guild award, 1958, Christopher award, 1954, 55, 57, 58, 59. Office: Time-Life Films Inc Rockefeller Center New York NY 10022*

SUSSKIND, LEONARD, physicist; b. N.Y.C., June 16, 1940; s. Benjamin and Irene (Meltz) S.; B.S., Coll. City N.Y., 1966; Ph.D., Cornell U., 1965; m. Maxine Y. Weinberg, June 19, 1960; children—Elana, Yve, Jennifer, Joshua. NSF postdoctoral fellow U. Calif., Berkeley, 1965-66; prof. physics Belfer Grad. Sch. Sci., Yeshiva U., 1967—, Tel Aviv U., 1970—, Stanford U.; Loeb lectr. Harvard U.,

1977. Recipient Boris Pregel award N.Y. Acad. Scis., 1975. Jewish. Address: 950 Mears Ct Stanford CA 94305

SUSSKIND, WALTER, orch. condr.; b. Prague, Czechoslovakia, May 1, 1913; s. Bruno and Gertrude (Seger) S.; grad. State Conservatorium, Prague, 1931, Acad. Music, Prague, 1931; Hum.D., U. So. Ill.; D.F.A., Washington U., St. Louis. Coach, Asst. condr. German Opera, Prague, 1935-38; prin. condr. English opera cos., Royal Carl Rosa, Sadler's Wells and Glyndbourne, 1940-46; mus. dir. Scottish Nat. Orch., 1946-52; music dir. Festival in Aspen, Colo., 1961-68; founder Nat. Youth Orch. Can., 1958; guest condr. symphony orchs. throughout world; prin. condr. Victoria Symphony Orch., Melbourne, Australia, 1953-55, Toronto Symphony Orch., 1956-65; concert pianist, composer, 1944—; music dir. St. Louis Symphony Orch., 1968-75; music advisor Cin. Symphony Orch., 1978—; faculty Washington U., St. Louis, U. So. Ill. Composer, arranger piano works for orch.; recs. for Columbia, H.M.V., Parlaphone, Everest, Pye, Angel, Capitol, Vox, others; lectr. on conducting and contemporary music. Mem. Am. Inst. Orchestral Conducting. Address: care Columbia Artists Mgmt 165 W 57th St New York NY 10019

SUSSMAN, AARON, advt. exec.; b. Odessa, Russia, Dec. 10, 1903 (came to U.S., 1906, naturalized); s. Saul and Adella (Borinef) S.; student Coll. City N.Y., 1921-22, N.Y. U., 1922-24, Mechs. Inst., 1924-25; m. Caryl Wallack Arden, May 14, 1925; 1 son, Leon Arden. News staff Bklyn. Eagle, 1924, N.Y. Daily News, 1925; advt. mgr. G.P. Putnam's Sons, Pubs., N.Y.C., 1925-28, Boni & Liveright, N.Y.C., 1928-29; editor, advt. mgr. Claude Kendall, Pubs., 1930-33; copy chief Franklin Spier, Inc., Advt., N.Y.C., 1933; copy chief, exec. officer Franklin Spier & Aaron Sussman, Inc., Advt., N.Y.C., 1934-43; pres., chief exec. officer Sussman & Sugar, Inc., Advt., N.Y.C., 1944—. Tchr. book advt. and pub. practice Columbia, 1945-50, N.Y. U., 1951-62, U. Pa., Phila., 1963-69; author booklets on civil def., Washington, 1942. Mem. Book Table, Fortean Soc., Soc. of Silurians, Photog. Soc. Am. Clubs: Overseas Press; Princeton, Publishers Ad. Author: Amateur Photographer's Handbook, 8th rev. edit., 1973; (with Ruth Goode) The Magic of Walking, 5th rev. edit., 1980; (with Dr. David Seabury) The Art of Selfishness, rev. edit., 1974. Contbr. articles to mags. Home: 8269 164th Pl Hillcrest Jamaica LI NY 11432 Office: 24 W 40th St New York NY 10018

SUSSMAN, ALFRED SHEPPARD, univ. dean; b. Portsmouth, Va., July 4, 1919; s. Morris and Celia (Rabinowitz) S.; B.S., U. Conn., 1941; A.M., Harvard, 1948, Ph.D., 1949; m. Selma Feinman, Nov. 28, 1948; children—Jean, Paul, Harold. Instr. microbiology Mass. Gen. Hosp., Boston, 1948-49; mem. faculty U. Mich., Ann Arbor, 1950—, prof. botany, 1961—, chmn. dept., 1963-68, asso. dean Coll. Lit. Sci. and the Arts, 1968-70, acting dean, 1970-71, asso. dean H.H. Rackham Sch. Grad. Studies, 1972-74, dean, 1974—, acting v.p. for acad. affairs, 1979. Cons. etiology panel Am. Cancer Soc.; cons. NSF panel devel. biology, 1963-65; commr. Commn. on Undergrad. Edn. in Biol. Scis., 1966-69; vis. scientist Brookhaven Nat. Labs., summers 1950-51; examiner North Central Assn., 1971—; mem. panel for grad. record exam. in biology Ednl. Testing Service, 1973-78, mem. grad. record exam. bd., 1978—. Served to capt. AUS, 1942-46. NRC fellow, 1949-50; Lalor Found. summer fellow, 1956; NSF sr. fellow Calif. Inst. Tech., 1959-60; Atkins fellow Atkins Bot. Garden, Soledad, Cuba, summer 1949. Mem. Am. Inst. Biol. Scis. (chmn edn. com. 1967-69, mem. steering com. biol. sci. curriculum study 1961-63, mem. governing bd.), Soc. for Study Growth and Devel., Am. Acad. Microbiology, Am. Soc. Microbiologists, AAUP, Am. Soc. Biol. Chemists, Argonne Univs. Assn. (mem. biology com. 1969-72, trustee 1973), Bot. Soc. Am., Phi Beta Kappa, Sigma Xi. Author: (with Steiner and Wagner) Botany Laboratory Manual, 2d edit., 1965; Biology Through Microbes, 1961; Microbes: Their Growth, Nutrition and Interaction, 1964. Editor: (with G.C. Ainsworth and F.K. Sparrow) The Fungi, 4 vols., 1965-73; (with H.O. Halvorson) Spores: Their Dormancy and Germination, 1966. Editorial bd. Am. Jour. Botany, 1960-63, Am. Soc. Plant Physiology, 1968—, Mycologia, 1963-66, Developmental Biology, 1968-72. Contbr. articles to profl. jours. Home: 1615 Harbal Dr Ann Arbor MI 48105

SUSSMAN, BARRY, journalist; b. N.Y.C., July 10, 1934; s. Samuel and Esther (Rosen) S.; B.A., Bklyn. Coll., 1956; m. Peggy Earhart, Jan. 20, 1962; children—Seena Gilda, Shari Leigh. Reporter, Bristol (Va.) Herald Courier, 1960-62, mng. editor, 1962-65; editor Washington Post, 1965-70, city editor, 1971-73, spl. Watergate editor, 1972-74, editor for survey reporting, 1974—; tchr. Sch. Gen. Studies N.Y.U., 1958-59. Recipient Drew Pearson award for investigative reporting, 1972; 1st pl. award nat. reporting and Editor of Year award Washington Newspaper Guild, 1973. Mem. Am. Newspaper Guild. Author: The Great Coverup: Nixon and the Scandal of Watergate, 1974. Home: 11016 Gainsborough Rd Potomac MD 20854 Office: Washington Post 1150 15th St NW Washington DC 20071

SUSSMAN, BERNARD JULES, surgeon, educator; b. N.Y.C., Jan. 4, 1926; s. Irving and Sally (Schanzer) S.; M.D., N.Y. U., 1950; m. Clare Ann Stein, Aug. 17, 1956. Intern Bellevue Hosp., 1950-51; resident neurology N.Y. Neurol. Inst., 1951-53, instr., 1953; resident neurosurgery Beth Israel Hosp., N.Y.C., 1953-54, Mt. Sinai Hosp., N.Y.C., 1954-56, Montefiore Hosp., N.Y.C., 1956-57; practice medicine specializing in neurol. surgery, Plainfield and Perth Amboy, N.J., 1957-67; lectr. Coll. Medicine Howard U., 1967-69, asso. prof. neurol. surgery, 1969-72, prof., 1972—; attending neurol. surgeon D.C. Gen. Hosp., 1978-79, Howard U. Hosp., 1978-79. Lectr. Georgetown U., spring 1972, George Washington U., 1972; cons. project dir. Knoll Pharm. Corp., U.S.A. and internat., 1973-75; cons. neurol. surgeon U.S. V.I., 1978-79; vis. prof. U. Goteborg (Sweden), Columbia, 1976. Served with AC, AUS, 1944-46. Recipient Honors Achievement award Angiology Research Found., 1965, citation research com. Howard U., 1974; Am. Heart Assn. grantee, 1972-73. Diplomate Am. Bd. Neurol. Surgery. Fellow Council on Stroke of Am. Heart Assn.; mem. Harvey Cushing Soc., Internat. Coll. Angiology, N.J. Neurosurg. Soc., AMA, Am. Electroencephalographic Soc., Internat. Soc. Psychiat. Surgery (founding mem.), Internat. Med. Soc. Paraplegia, Washington Acad. Neurosurgery. Contbr. articles to profl. jours. Developed the method for dissolving thrombi in cerebral vessels with enzyme fibrinolysin, 1958; developed, patented the method for removing herniated intervertebral discs with enzyme collagenase, 1967-75; testified in opposition to clin. trial of drug chymopapain in disc disease before FDA and Congl. Oversights Com., 1975. Prin. ct. case setting nat. precedent protecting right of qualified physicians to staff privileges. Home: 2400 Tilden St NW Washington DC 20008

SUSSMAN, GERALD, pub. co. exec.; b. Balt., Feb. 21, 1934; s. Hyman Jacob and Sylvia (Applebaum) S.; B.A., U. Md., 1956; m. Arla Ilene Ellison, Aug. 25, 1963; children—Daniel Leonard, Andrew Louis. Co-founder, prin. Investors Service of Md., Balt., 1956-60; coll. traveller Oxford U. Press, Inc., N.Y.C., 1961-62, coll. sales mgr., 1962-69, gen. advt. mgr., 1970-73, v.p., dir. mktg., 1974-79, sr. v.p., dir. mktg., 1979—. Mem. Assn. Am. Pubs. (chmn. mktg. com.), Pubs. Advt. Club, Phi Alpha Theta. Democrat. Jewish religion. Home: 8 Opatut Ct Edison NJ 08817 Office: 200 Madison Ave New York NY 10016

SUSSMAN, JERRY, resort hotel operator; b. N.Y.C., Mar. 20, 1922; s. Louis J. and Bessie (Levinson) S.; B.B.A., Coll. City N.Y., 1942; m. Esther Waldman, Mar. 20, 1946; children—Kenneth, Marc, Lester, David. Asst. mgr. Tamarack Lodge, Greenfield Park, N.Y., 1936-42; gen. mgr. Ritz Plaza Hotel, Miami Beach, Fla., 1946-49, Sorrento Hotel, 1949-52; mng. partner Johnina Hotel, Miami Beach, 1952-57, Crown Hotel, Miami Beach, 1957-59; exec. dir. Carillon Hotel, Miami Beach, 1959-74, Holiday Inn at Calder, 1974-75; partner, exec. dir. R.S.M. Mgmt. Corp., 1974—; adv. bd. Jefferson Nat. Bank, Miami Beach; partner Dunes Motel, Miami Beach, Howard Johnson Motor Lodges, Pompano Beach, St. Petersburg Beach, Treasure Island and Hollywood Beach, Fla., Gateway Inn, Archway Inn, Orlando, Fla. Mem. Miami Beach Planning Commn., 1968—; chmn. Gov. Fla.'s Tourism adv. com., 1972-76. Bd. dirs. United Fund Dade County. Served to 1st lt. AUS, 1942-46. Elected to Hotel Hall of Fame, 1968. Mem. Miami Beach C. of C. (pres. 1968-70), South Fla. Hotel and Motel Assn. (pres. 1971-75), Beta Gamma Sigma. Jewish religion (v.p. temple 1949-59; v.p. United Synagogue Am. 1969—). Mem. B'nai B'rith. Home: 1576 Daytonia Rd Miami Beach FL 33141 Office: 300 71st St Suite 415 Miami Beach FL 33141. *I like to believe my business decisions are based on my Jewish religious principles—"To do justly and to love mercy, and to walk humbly with thy God". (Micah 6:8) Our ethics teach us that our task is not to complete the work of humanity, but neither are we absolved from the responsibility of doing all we can to further the work of making life more meaningful and more wholesome for all mankind.*

SUSSMAN, LEONARD RICHARD, found. exec.; b. N.Y.C., Nov. 26, 1920; s. Jacob and Carrie (Marks) S.; A.B., N.Y. U., 1940; M.S. in Journalism, Columbia, 1941; m. Frances Rukeyser, May 9, 1942 (div. 1958); m. 2d, Marianne Rita Gutmann, May 28, 1958; children—Lynne, David William, Mark Jacob. Copy editor N.Y. Morning Telegraph, also news editor radio sta. WQXR, 1941; cable editor San Juan (P.R.) World Jour., also corr. Business Week mag., 1941-42; editor fgn. broadcast intelligence service FCC, 1942; press sec. to gov. P.R., 1942-43; dir. information in N.Y. for Govt. P.R., 1946-49; regional dir., then nat. exec. dir. Am. Council Judaism, 1949-66; pub. affairs cons. Nationwide Ins. Cos. and indsl. subsidiaries, 1955-57; mem. editorial com. Council Liberal Chs., 1956-59; exec. dir. Freedom House, 1967—, Willkie Meml. Bldg., 1970—; organizer, 1968, since dir. Freedom House/Books USA, 1968—; editor Freedom at Issue, bimonthly, 1970—; organizer acad. confs.; participant Internat. Conf. on Press Freedom, Venice, Italy, 1976, 77, Cairo, 1978. Trustee Internat. Council on Future of Univ., 1973—; bd. dirs. World Press Freedom Com., 1977—; chmn. Friends of Survey Mag. Charitable Trust, 1978—; mem. U.S. Nat. Commn. for UNESCO, 1979—. Served with AUS, 1943-46. Decorated Legion of Merit. Mem. Internat. Press Inst., Internat. Inst. Communication. Club: Century (N.Y.C.). Author: American Press—Under Siege?, 1973; Mass News Media and the Third World Challenge, 1977; contbr. sects. to books, articles to profl. jours. Project dir. Big Story-How The American Press and Television Reported and Interpreted The Crisis of Tet-1968 in Vietnam and Washington, 1977. Editor textbook series, also quar. mag. Issues, 1953-66. Home: 215 E 73d St New York NY 10021 Office: 20 W 40th St New York NY 10018

SUSSMAN, MARTIN VICTOR, engr., educator; b. N.Y.C.; s. Samuel and Selma (Bagno) S.; B.S., Coll. City N.Y.; M.S., Columbia, 1952, Ph.D., 1958; m. Jeanne Fowler, Aug. 22, 1953; children—Ann M., Eve Leslie, David Fowler. Instr., research asso. chem. dept. Fordham U., N.Y.C., 1949-50; research fellow chem. engring. dept. Columbia, 1951-53; sr. engr., research engr. Pioneering Lab., DuPont, Del., 1953-58; co-founder dept. chem. engring. Robert Coll., Istanbul, Turkey, 1958-61; prof. chem. engring. dept. Tufts U., Medford, Mass., 1961—, dept. chmn., 1961-71. Cons. engring. edn. U.S. AID, Brazil and Uruguay, 1963, Ethiopia, 1965, Ford Found., India, 1971, 72, 73, 74, 79; coordinator engring. edn. NSF, New Delhi, India, 1967-68; vis. prof. Mass. Inst. Tech., 1976. Mem. Town Meeting, Lexington, Mass., 1971—. Served with U.S. Martime Service, 1945-47. NIH Spl. Research fellow, 1968; AEC fellow, 1951; Fulbright Hays lectr. award, 1977. Registered profl. engr. Mass. Mem. Am. Inst. Chem. Engrs., Am. Inst. Chemists, Am. Chem. Soc., Sigma Xi, Tau Beta Pi (eminent engr. 1974). Author: Elementary General Thermodynamics, 1972. Editor Chem Engring. Applied Sci. series, 1975—. Patentee in field. 1361 Massachusetts Ave Lexington MA 02173 Office: Dept Chem Engring Tufts U Medford MA 02155

SUSSMAN, MARVIN BERNARD, sociologist, educator; b. N.Y.C., Oct. 27, 1918; s. Louis M. and Gertrude (Clar) S.; B.A., N.Y.U., 1941; M.S., George Williams Coll., 1943; M.A., Yale, 1949; Ph.D., 1951; m. Ruth Annette Strahler, Aug. 15, 1942; children—Stuart Daniel, Martha Jean, Kenneth Brittan, Nancy Louise; m. 2d, Kris Jeter, Aug. 12, 1979. Chmn. dept. sociology Union Coll., Schenectady, 1952-54; vis. asst. prof. U. Chgo., 1954-55; asso. prof. sociology Case Western Res. U., 1955-62, prof. sociology, 1962-71, chmn. dept. sociology, 1962-71, Selah Chamberlain prof. sociology, after 1971; dir. Inst. on Family and Bureaucratic Soc., 1969-76, chmn., prof. dept. med-social scis. Bowman Gray Sch. Medicine, Winston-Salem, N.C., 1976-79; Unidel prof. human behavior U. Del., 1979—; pres. Groves Conf. Marriage and the Family, 1968-72. Fellow Am. Sociol. Assn. (chmn. family sect. 1968-69; council sect. social psychology 1974-76), Soc. Study Social Problems (pres. 1962-63), Am. Pub. Health Assn.; mem. Ohio Valley Sociol. Soc. (pres. 1962-63), Ohio Council Family Relations (pres. 1962-63), Nat. Rehab. Assn., Sociol. Research Assn. AAUP, Author: (with others) Social Class, Maternal Health and Child Care, 1957; (with R. Clyde White) Hough Area, Cleveland, Ohio: A Study of Social Life and Change, 1959; (with others) Rehabilitation and Tuberculosis; (with others) The Walking Patient: A Study in Outpatient Care, 1966; (with others) The Family and Inheritance, 1970. Editor: Sourcebook in Marriage and the Family, 4th edit., 1974; Community Structure and Analysis, 1959; Sociology and Rehabilitation, 1966; (with B.E. Cogswell) Cross-National Family Research, 1972; Non-traditional Family Forms in the 1970's, 1972; (with Ethel Shanas) The Family, Beaucracy and the Elderly, 1977; Author's Guide to Journals in Sociology and Related Fields; 1978; Family Anthology, 1979; editor Marriage and Family Rev., 1977—; editor Jour. Marriage and The Family, 1963-69, asso. editor, 1975—; mem. editorial bd. Jour. Family History, 1975—, Jour. Marriage and Family Counseling, 1974—, Jour. Marriage and Family, 1969—. Home: 146 Dallam Rd Newark DE 19711 Office: Coll Human Resources U Del Newark DE 19711

SUSSMAN, SIDNEY X., accountant; b. N.Y.C., July 5, 1919; s. Jacob F. and Anna (Liebowitz) S.; B.B.A., Coll. City N.Y., 1941; J.D., U. Toledo, 1958; m. Sylvia Blumenthal, Sept. 12, 1948 (dec. Sept. 1968); children—Diane, Philip, Gloria; m. Sally Bleim, Nov. 24, 1973. With I.R. Miller & Co., C.P.A.'s Toledo, 1948-70, partner, 1954-70; partner J. K. Lasser and Co., Toledo, 1970; partner Lublin, Sussman, Rosenberg & Damrautor, Toledo, 1970—; dir. Hickory Farms of Ohio Inc.; tax lectr., 1960—. Admitted to Ohio bar, 1958. Pres. Lucas County Assn. Retarded Children, 1962-63; chmn. budget and finance com. Ohio State Assn. Retarded Children, 1964-66, treas., 1966-68; mem. citizens adv. bd. N.W. Ohio Devel. Center, 1979. Served with AUS, 1942-45. Recipient of certificate of service from the Ohio Assn. Retarded Children, 1966. C.P.A., Ohio. Mem. Am. Inst. C.P.A.'s, Ohio Soc. C.P.A.'s. Home: 6065 Barkwood Sylvania OH 43560 Office: 3166 N Republic Blvd Toledo OH 43615

SUSSNA, EDWARD, economist, educator; b. Phila., Nov. 26, 1926; s. Louis and Manya (Prytzycka) S.; B.A., Bklyn. Coll., 1950; M.A., U. Ill., 1952, Ph.D., 1954; m. Sylvia Fishman, Mar. 8, 1953; children—Audrey Francine, Ellen Sondra. Instr., U. Ill., 1952-54; asst. prof. Lehigh U., 1956-57; prof. bus. adminstrn. and econs. U. Pitts., 1957—, dir. Center for Econ. Edn., Grad. Sch. Bus., 1978—; vis. Fulbright prof. U. Tehran (Iran), adviser, 1972-73; cons. Bur. of Budget, Dept. Health, Edn. and Welfare, Dept. Transp., UN Indsl. Devel. Orgn., Bell Telephone Co., Alcoa, others; vis. prof. UCLA, 1970, Ecole Superieure des Scis. Economiques et Commerciales, Paris, 1976-77. Served with U.S. Mcht. Marine, 1944-47, AUS, 1954-56. Vis. prof. under Ford Found. fellowship Harvard, 1960-61; guest scholar under Ford Found. fellowship Brookings Instn., Washington, 1962-63. Mem. Am. Econ. Assn., Am. Fin. Assn., Evaluation Research Soc., Econometric Soc., Inst. Mgmt. Scis., Beta Gamma Sigma, Omicron Delta. Contbr. articles to profl. jours. Home: 1217 Denniston Ave Pittsburgh PA 15217

SUTCLIFFE, ERIC, lawyer; b. Calif., Jan. 10, 1909; s. Thomas and Annie (Beare) S.; A.B., U. Calif. at Berkeley, 1929, LL.B., 1932; m. Joan Basché, Aug. 7, 1937; children—Victoria, Marcia, Thomas. Admitted to Cal. bar, 1932; mem. firm Orrick, Herrington, Rowley & Sutcliffe, San Francisco, 1943—. Trustee San Francisco Law Library. Fellow Am. Bar Found; mem. Am.(chmn state regulation securities com. 1960-65) San Francisco (chmn. corp. law com. 1964-65) bar assns., San Francisco C. of C. (past treas., dir.), State Bar Calif., Phi Gamma Delta, Phi Delta Phi, Order of Coif. Clubs: Pacific Union, Bohemian, Commonwealth (San Francisco). Home: 260 King Ave Piedmont CA 94610 Office: 600 Montgomery St San Francisco CA 94111

SUTER, CARY GRAYSON, neurologist, educator; b. Bridgewater, Va., Oct. 9, 1919; s. David I. and Elizabeth (Dundore) S.; A.B., B.S., Hampden-Sydney Coll., 1943; M.D., U. Va., 1947; m. Anna Deane Carr, May 3, 1947; children—Cary Carr, Anna Deane. Instr. pathology U. Va., Charlottesville, 1947-48; intern U. Ala., 1948-49; resident in internal medicine Cleve. Clinic, 1949-51; resident in neurology-psychiatry U. Va., 1951-54; resident in neurology Mayo Clinic, 1957-59; asst. prof. neurology-psychiatry U. Va., 1954-57; 1st dir. Va. Epilepsy Clinic for Children, 1954-57; asst. prof. Med. Coll. Va., Va. Commonwealth U., Richmond, 1959-62, asso. prof., 1962-65, prof., chmn. dept. neurology, 1965—, dir. EEG Lab. and Epilepsy Clinic, 1959—, chief staff neurology service coll. hosp., 1959—; cons. VA Hosp., Richmond, Va.; individual practice medicine, Richmond. Fellow Am. Acad. Neurology; mem. AMA, Am. Epilepsy Soc., So. EEG Soc., Am. EEG Soc. Am. Neurol. Assn., Soc. Electromyography and Electrodiagnosis, Phi Beta Kappa, Alpha Omega Alpha. Episcopalian. Home: 833 Arlington Circle Richmond VA 23229 Office: Box 698 Med Coll Va 1200 E Broad St Richmond VA 23298

SUTER, EMANUEL, assn. exec., physician; b. Basel, Switzerland, Feb. 7, 1918 (came to U.S. 1949, naturalized 1955); s. Fritz and Clara (Vischer) S.; M.D., U. Basel, 1944; m. Elsi Reinhard, Aug. 30, 1945 (div. 1962); m. 2d, Joanne F. Potter, May 26, 1962; children—Bradley, Brooke, Jere Q. Research fellow Inst. Hygiene, U. Basel, 1945-48; asst. Rockefeller Inst. Med. Research, N.Y.C., 1949-52; asso. dept. bacteriology and immunology Harvard Med. Sch., 1952-53, asst. prof., 1953-56; prof. microbiology, head dept. U. Fla. Coll. Medicine, Gainesville, 1956-65, prof. microbiology, 1965-72, dean Coll. Medicine, 1965-72; dir. div. edn. resources and programs Assn. Am. Med. Colls., Washington, 1972—. Markle scholar med. scis., 1954-59. Home: 860 Sconset Ln McLean VA 22102

SUTERA, SALVATORE PHILIP, educator, mech. engr.; b. Balt., Jan. 12, 1933; s. Philip and Ann (D'Amico) S.; B.S. in Mech. Engring., Johns Hopkins, 1954; student U. Paris (France), 1955-56; M.S., Cal. Inst. Tech., 1955, Ph.D., 1960; M.A. (hon.), Brown U., 1965; m. Celia Ann Fielden, June 21, 1958; children—Marie-Anne, Annette Nicole, Michelle Cecile. Asst. prof. mech. engring. Brown U., Providence, 1960-65, asso. prof., 1965-68, exec. officer div. engring., 1966-68; prof., chmn. dept. mech. engring. Washington U., St. Louis, 1968—. Vis. prof. U. Paris VI, 1973. Fulbright fellow Paris, 1955. Mem. ASME, Internat. Soc. Biorheology, Am. Soc. Artificial Internal Organs, Am. Soc. Engring. Edn., AAAS, Tau Beta Pi, Pi Tau Sigma. Republican. Roman Catholic. Editorial bd. Circulation Research, 1975—. Research in fluid mechanics, heat transfer, blood flow, rheology of suspensions. Home: 830 S Meramec Ave Clayton MO 63105

SUTHERLAND, DONALD, actor; b. St. John, N.B., Can., July 17, 1934; ed. U. Toronto; m. Shirley Douglas (div.). Theatre appearances include: The Male Animal, The Tempest, August for People (London debut), On a Clear Day You Can See Canterbury, The Shewing Up of Blanco Posnet, The Spoon River Anthology; films include: The Castle of the Living Dead, Dr. Terror's House of Horrors, The Dirty Dozen, Oedipus the King, Interlude, Joanna, The Split, Start the Revolution Without Me, The Act of the Heart, MASH, Kelly's Heroes, Little Murders, Alex in Wonderland, Klute, Steelyard Blues, Alien Thunder, The Master, Don't Look Now, Lady Ice, SPYS, The Day of the Locust, Casanova, The Eagle Has Landed, The Great Train Robbery, Murder By Decree, Invasion of the Body Snatchers, Animal House, A Man, A Woman and A Bank; TV appearances Marching to the Sea, The Death of Bessie Smith, Hamlet at Elsinore, The Saint, The Avengers, Gideon's Way, The Champions; formerly with London Acad. Music and Dramatic Art, Perth Repertory Theatre, Scotland, also repertory at Nottingham, Chesterfield, Bronley, Shieffield. Office: care Avco-Embassy Pictures 6601 Romaine St Los Angeles CA 90038*

SUTHERLAND, DONALD MARSHALL, book publisher; b. Toronto, Ont., Can., June 22, 1916; s. Donald Linus and Agnes Marshall (Tilt) S.; B.A., Trinity Coll., U. Toronto, 1950; postgrad. Coll. Chinese Studies Peking; m. Gwen Evans, June 27, 1952; children—Sheila Catherine, Christina Margaret, Donald Alexander, John Dugald. Asst. curator Far Eastern Art, Royal Ont. Mus., Toronto, 1952-54; coll. traveller Oxford U. Press, Toronto, 1954-57; trade sales mgr. MacMillan of Can., 1958-63, mgr. trade div., dir., sec. co., 1964-74; pres., dir. McGill-Queen's Univ. Press, Montreal, Que., Can., 1974—. Served with Royal Canadian Navy, 1940-45. Mem. Assn. Canadian Univl Presses (v.p. 1977-78, pres. 1979-80). Anglican. Club: Arts and Letters. Office: 1020 Pine Ave W Montreal PQ H3A 1A2 Canada

SUTHERLAND, DONALD WAYNE, historian, educator; b. Sioux Falls, S.D., Jan. 24, 1931; s. Donald Wayne and Kathleen Gertrude (Bickert) S.; B.A., Swarthmore Coll., 1953; D.Phil., Oxford U., Eng., 1957; m. Janet Meager, July 27, 1957; m. 2d, Judith Lynne Cleveland, Dec. 17, 1961; children—Anne, Jean, Kathleen, Ian James. Instr. dept. history U. Iowa, Iowa City, 1958-60, asst. prof., 1960-64, asso. prof., 1964-67, prof., 1967—. Served with AUS, 1956-58. Research fellow Am. Council Learned Socs., 1964-65, Social Sci. Research Council, 1964-65, Nat. Endowment for Humanities, 1971-72, Guggenheim Found., 1973-74. Mem. Medieval Acad. Am., Royal

Hist. Soc., Conf. on Brit. Studies, Am. Soc. for Legal History, Midwest Medieval History Conf., Selden Soc. Lutheran. Author: Quo Warranto Proceedings in the Reign of Edward I, 1278-1294, 1963; The Assize of Novel Disseisin, 1973. Home: 725 W Benton St Iowa City IA 52240

SUTHERLAND, IVAN EDWARD, computer scientist; b. Hastings, Nebr., May 16, 1938; s. Robert Alexander and Annie (Barclay) S.; B.S. in Elec. Engring., Carnegie-Mellon U., 1959; M.S. in Elec. Engring., Calif. Inst. Tech., 1960; Ph.D., Mass. Inst. Tech., 1963; m. Marcia Hermina Getting, Aug. 29, 1959; children—Juliet Belle, Dean Fulton. Asso. prof. Aiken Computer Lab., Harvard U., 1966-68; prof. computer scis. dept. U. Utah, Salt Lake City, 1968-73; v.p., chief scientist Evans & Sutherland Computer Corp., Salt Lake City, 1968-74; sr. tech. staff mem. Rand Corp., Santa Monica, Calif., 1974-76; prof. computer sci. Calif. Inst. Tech., Pasadena, 1976—; cons. in field. Mem. Def. Sci. Bd.; mem. Naval Research Adv. Com., 1968-75. Served with U.S. Army, 1963-65. Recipient 1st Zworykin award Nat. Acad. Engring., 1972. Mem. IEEE, Assn. Computing Machinery, Nat. Acad. Scis., Nat. Acad. Engring., Sigma Xi, Tau Beta Pi, Eta Kappa Nu. Home: 125 Wadsworth Ave Santa Monica CA 90405 Office: Computer Sci Dept 256-80 Calif Inst Tech Pasadena CA 91125

SUTHERLAND, JOAN, coloratura soprano; b. Sydney, Australia, Nov. 7, 1926; d. McDonald Sutherland; student Royal Coll. Music, London, 1951; m. Richard Bonynge, 1954; 1 son. Appeared concert and oratorio performances, Australia; appeared in opera Judith, Syndey Conservatory of Music; debut Covent Garden in Magic Flute, 1952; other operatic performances include Lucia di Lammermoor, La Traviata, La Sonnambula, Handel's Acis and Galatea, heroine roles operas by Bellini and Donizetti; Italian debut in Handel's Alcina, Teatro la Fenice, Venice, 1960; appeared in Bellini's Puritani, Glyndebourne Festival, Sussex, Eng., 1960, Bellini's Beatrice di Tenda, La Scala, 1961, Rossini's Semiramide, La Scala, 1962, Meyerbeer's Les Huguenots, La Scala, 1962; N.Y. debut, Carnegie Hall, 1961; Opera debut, Lucia, 1961; opened Sutherland-Williamson Opera Co. tour, Australia, 1965, appeared Handel's Julius Caesar, Hamburg Co. tour, Australia, 1965, appeared Handel's Julius Caesar, Hamburg Opera, 1969, Bellini's Norma, Met Opera, 1970; opened Lyric Opera Chgo. with Semiramide, 1971, San Francisco Opera with Norma, 1972, San Francisco Opera with Trovatore, 1975, Met. Opera with I Puritani, 1976, Met. Opera with Esclamode, 1976, Vancouver Opera with Le Roi de Lahore, 1977; premiered new prodn. Met. Opera in Tales of Hoffmann, 1973; premiered 1st prodn. in Am. in 80 years, Esclarmonde, Massenet, San Francisco Opera, 1974. Winner Sun Aria competition; recipient Mobil Quest award, 1951; decorated comdr. Order Brit. Empire, Order Australia. Address: care Colbert Artists Mgmt 111 W 57th St New York NY 10019

SUTHERLAND, MALCOLM READ, JR., clergyman, educator; b. Detroit, Nov. 11, 1916; s. Malcolm Read and Edith Ione (Osborne) S.; A.B., Miami (Ohio) U. 1938; M.S., Western Res. U., 1941; B.D., Fed. Theol. Faculty U. Chgo. 1945; L.H.D., Meadville-Lombard Theol. Sch., 1975; LL.D., Emerson Coll., 1963; m. Mary Anne Beaumont, Dec. 23, 1943; children—Malcolm Read III, Maryanne B. Dir. boys work Goodrich Social Settlement, Cleve., 1938-40; housing mgr. Cleve. Met. Housing Authority, 1940-41; regional housing supr. Farm Security Adminstrn., 1941-42; housing mgmt. supr. FPHA, 1942-43; ordained to ministry Unitarian Ch., 1945; pastor in Ill., Va., Mass., 1944-60; exec. v.p. Am. Unitarian Assn., 1959-60; Robert Collier prof. ch. and soc., pres., dean faculty Meadville Theol. Sch. of Lombard Coll., Chgo., 1960-75; minister Harvard (Mass.) Unitarian Ch., 1975—. Former dir. Unitarian Universalist Service Com., Beacon Press; chmn. editorial adv. bd. Christian Register, 1955-60; field rep. Unitarian Service Com., Mexico, 1950-51; mem. sr. secretariat World Conf. Religion and Peace, Kyoto, 1970, Louvain, 1974, Princeton, 1979; lectr., del. Japan-U.S. consultation on peace Internat. Assn. for Religious Freedom, 1970; Thomas Minns lectr. Boston, 1955, Charlottesville, Va., 1978; Berry St., lectr. Boston, 1956. chmn. common council Chgo. Cluster of Theol. Schs., Inc., 1970-74; pres. Inst. on Religion in an Age of Sci., 1969, 75-77. Bd. govs. Manchester Coll., Oxford, also hon. fellow, 1974—; trustee Senexet Retreat Inc. Recipient Distinguished Service award Charlottesville (Va.) Jr. C. of C., 1949, Internat. Assn. Religious Freedom, 1975, Konko Kyo Chs. Am., 1975. Mem. Unitarian Universalist Ministers Assn., Center for Advanced Study of Religion and Sci. (dir.), Phi Delta Theta, Phi Mu Alpha, Alpha Kappa Delta, Omicron Delta Kappa. Clubs: Quadrangle (U. Chgo.); Bucks Harbor Yacht (Maine) (commodore 1979—). Author: Personal Faith, 1955; Creators of the Dawn, 1979. Co-chmn. publs. bd., editorial adv. bd. Zygon (jour. religion and sci.). Contbr. articles to publs. Home: Woodside Rd Harvard MA 01451

SUTHERLAND, ROBERT LOUIS, engring. co. exec., educator; b. Fellsmere, Fla., May 15, 1916; s. John Alexander and Georgia Myrtle (Legg) S.; B.S., U. Ill., 1939, M.S., 1948; m. Mary Alice Reed, May 18, 1945; children—Robert Hynes, Wayne Muzzy, Connie Anne, Nancy Lee, John Gary. Devel. engr. Firestone Tire & Rubber Co., Akron, Ohio, 1939-41; research engr. Borg & Beck div. Borg-Warner Corp., Chgo, 1941; test engr. Buick Motor Div. Gen. Motors Corp., Melrose Park, Ill., 1942-43; sr. engr. research dept. Aeronca Aircraft Corp., Middletown, Ohio, 1943-45; research asso. Coll. Engring., U. Ill., 1945-48; asst., then asso. prof. mech. engring. State U. Ia., Iowa City, 1948-58; city engr., Coralville, Ia., 1950-53; prof. mech. engring. U. Wyo., Laramie, 1958—, head dept., 1960-70; pres. Skyline Engring. Co. Inc., Laramie, 1972—; research engr. Collins Radio Co., Cedar Rapids, Iowa, summer 1954, cons. engr., 1950-56; staff engr. Environ. Test Lab., Martin Co., Denver, summer 1960; dir. Hunter Mfg. Co., Iowa City, 1955-58, sec. bd., 1956-58. Bus. adviser mfg. group Jr. Achievement, Middletown, 1943-44; mem. Iowa City Sch. Study Council, 1956-58. Mem. Civil Air Patrol, Chgo., 1941-43. Co-recipient Richard L. Templin award ASTM, 1952. Registered profl. engr., Ill., Iowa, Wyo. Fellow ASME (regional v.p. 1965-67); mem. Soc. Automotive Engrs., Sigma Xi, Sigma Tau, Pi Tau Sigma, Tau Beta Pi. Methodist (steward, chmn. ofcl. bd. 1964-65, trustee 1966-69, pres. bd. 1967-69, lay leader 1969-72, chmn. council ministries 1973-75, chmn. finance com. 1975—). Kiwanian (dir. Laramie chpt. 1963-65, pres. 1966, div. lt. gov. 1970-71) Author: Engineering Systems Analysis, 1958. Contbr. articles to profl. jours. Home: 1420 Sanders St Laramie WY 82070

SUTHERLAND, RONALD ROY, planetarium adminstr.; b. Pitts., Dec. 28, 1931; s. Roy Elmer and Dellia (Abbatti) S.; B.S., U. Pitts., 1956; grad. U.S. Army Transp. Sch., 1956, U.S. Army Chem., Biol. and Radiol. Warfare Sch., 1957; m. Dorothy May Chinovski, Mar. 5, 1965. Planetarium astronomer Buhl Planetarium, Pitts., 1958-60, asst. to dir., 1960-62; asst. dir. McDonnell Planetarium, St. Louis, 1962-66, planetarium dir., 1966—; pres. Technamics Co., St. Louis, 1970—. Astronomy subject dir. St. Louis Area council Boy Scouts Am., 1967—. Served with U.S. Army, 1956-58. Mem. Royal Astron. Soc., St. Louis Astron. Soc., Internat. Planetarium Soc., Nat. Geog. Soc., Mo. Acad. Sci., Pacific Planetarium Assn., Planetarium Assn. Can., Adult Edn. Council St. Louis, Am. Mus. Nat. History, Smithsonian Assos. Home: 6307 Winona St St Louis MO 63109 Office: McDonnell Planetarium St Louis MO 63110

SUTHERLAND, WILLIAM ANDERSON, lawyer; b. Oct. 4, 1896; s. Phocion Leonidas and Jennie (Mattox) S.; student U. Fla., 1911-12; A.B., U. Va., 1914; LL.B., Harvard, 1917; A.M., U. Wis., 1919; m. Sarah Hall, June 5, 1923; children—Mary Johnston (Mrs. Robert L. Strong), Margaret Copeland (Mrs. James E. Coleman, Jr.), Sarah Hall (Mrs. Frank R. Stoner, III). Legal sec. to justice Brandeis of Supreme Court of U.S., 1917-19; admitted to D.C. bar, 1919, Ga. bar, 1921; atty. and examiner for Fed. Trade Commn., Washington, 1919-20; practiced in Atlanta and Washington, 1921—; sr. partner firm of Sutherland, Asbill & Brennan and predecessor firms, 1924—; gen. solicitor T.V.A., 1933-34. Bd. dirs. Am. Bar Endowment, 1949-74, sec., 1963-67, v.p., 1967-69, pres., 1969-71, bd. dirs. emeritus, 1974—. Served briefly in 2d O.T.C. World War I. Andrew Wellington Cordier fellow, 1977. Fellow Am. Bar Found. (award for distinguished service to legal profession 1976); mem. Am. Bar Assn. (mem. fed. taxation com. 1935-39, taxation sect. council 1939-44; vice chmn. 1944-46; chmn., 1946-48, ho. of dels, 1951-54, 56-71), Nat. Tax Assn. (pres. 1950-51, hon. mem.), Ga. State, Atlanta, Fed., D.C. bar assns. Clubs: Lawyers, Piedmont Driving, Commerce (Atlanta); Harvard, Recess (N.Y.C.); Chevy Chase, Metropolitan, University (Washington). Home: 2101 Connecticut Ave NW Washington DC 20006 also 300 W Peachtree St NE Atlanta GA 30308 Office: 1666 K St NW Washington DC 20006 also 1st Nat Bank Tower Atlanta GA 30303

SUTHERLUND, DAVID ARVID, lawyer; b. Stevens Point, Wis., July 20, 1929; s. Arvid E. and Georgia M. (Stickney) S.; B.A., U. Portland, 1952; J.D., U. N.Mex., 1957; postgrad., U. Wis., 1957. Admitted to D.C. bar, 1957, U.S. Supreme Ct. bar, 1961; atty. ICC, Washington, 1957-58; counsel Am. Trucking Assn., Washington, 1958-62; asso. firm Morgan, Lewis & Brockius, Washington and Phila., 1962-65, partner, 1965—; counsel firm Turney & Turney, Washington, 1972-75; partner firm Fulbright & Jaworski, Washington and Houston, 1975—; exec. dir. Film, Air & Package Carriers Conf., Washington, 1962-72; dir., gen. counsel Nat. Film Service, 1962-75. Vice chmn. Nat. Capitol Area council Boy Scouts Am., 1975-78. Served with U.S. Army, 1952-54. Mem. Am., Fed., D.C. bar assns., Motor Carrier Lawyers Assn., ICC Practioners Assn., Am. Arbitration Assn., Am. Judicature Soc., Clubs: Nat. Lawyers; N.Y. Lawyers; Lakewood Country; Internat. (Washington). Founder, chmn. bd. govs. Transp. Law Jour., 1969-74. Home: 2130 Bancroft Pl NW Washington DC 20008 Office: 1150 Connecticut Ave NW Washington DC 20036

SUTMAN, FRANCIS XAVIER, educator; b. Newark, Dec. 20, 1927; s. Joseph L. and Ella (Joyce) S.; A.B., Montclair State Coll., 1949, M.A., 1952; Ed.D., Columbia, 1956; m. Mabel Ranagan, Apr. 1, 1956; children—Frank J., Catherine J., Elizabeth A. Instr. pub. secondary schs., N.J., 1949-55; instr. chemistry Upsala Coll., 1954-56; asst. prof. Paterson Coll., 1955-57; chmn., asso. prof. natural scis. Inter-Am. U. P.R., 1958-62; prof. gen. edn., chmn. State U. N.Y. at Buffalo, 1958-62; prof. sci. edn., chmn. dept. secondary edn. Temple U., 1962—; mem. tech. research staff Esso Engring. & Research Lab., Linden, N.J., 1955—; vis. lectr. Rutgers U.; cons. India AID Project; vis. prof., scientist, cons. Hebrew U., Israel; del. Council Sci. Edn. and Culture, 1971; cons. Environ. Edn. Conf. Environ. Protection Service, Jerusalem, 1975, also numerous sch. dists. govt. agys.; dir. Bilingual Edn. Center, 1976. Mem. bd. edn., Haddonfield, N.J. Gen. Electric fellow, 1954; NSF-AEC fellow, 1960. Mem. Am. Chem. Soc., Assn. Higher Edn., Nat. Assn. Research Sci. Tchrs. (pres.), Nat. Sci. Tchrs. Assn., Smithsonian Instn. Assn., Phi Delta Kappa. Author 3 books. Contbr. numerous articles to sci. and edn. jours. Home: 249 W Summit Ave Haddonfield NJ 08033 Office: 997 Ritter Hall Temple U Philadelphia PA 19122. *Success comes after one accepts the paradoxes of life. Absolute success only comes when one is uncompromising and willing to give of one's self for his cause. Even then the times must be right or the giving of one's self will not result in absolute success. Any level of success I have achieved results from a mixture of the two conditions described above.*

SUTNICK, ALTON IVAN, coll. dean, physician; b. Trenton, N.J., July 6, 1928; s. Michael and Rose (Horwitz) S.; A.B., U. Pa., 1950, M.D., 1954; postgrad. studies in biomed. math., Drexel Inst. Tech., 1961-62; postgrad. studies in biometrics Temple U., 1969-70; m. Mona Reidenberg, Aug. 17, 1958; children—Amy, Gary. Rotating intern Hosp. U. Pa., 1954-55, resident in anesthesiology, 1955-56, resident in medicine, 1956, USPHS postdoctoral research fellow, 1956-57; asst. instr. anesthesiology, then asst. instr. medicine U. Pa. Sch. Medicine, 1955-57; resident in medicine Wishard Meml. Hosp., Indpls., 1957-58, chief resident in medicine, 1960-61; resident instr. medicine Ind. U. Sch. Medicine, Indpls., 1957-58; USPHS postdoctoral research fellow Temple U. Hosp., 1961-63; instr., then asso. in medicine Temple U. Sch. Medicine, 1962-65; mem. faculty U. Pa. Sch. Medicine, 1965-75, asso. prof. medicine, 1971-75; clin. asst. physician Pa. Hosp., 1966-71; research physician, then asso. dir. Inst. Cancer Research, Phila., 1965-75; vis. prof. medicine Med. Coll. Pa., Phila., 1971-74, prof. medicine, dean, 1975—, sr. v.p., 1976—; dir. clin. devel. Am. Oncologic Hosp., Phila., 1973-75; attending physician Phila. VA Hosp., 1967—, Hosp. Med. Coll. Pa., 1971—; cons. in field. Mem. U.S. nat. com. Internat. Union Against Cancer, 1969-72; mem. Nat. Conf. Cancer Prevention and Detection, 1973, Nat. Workshop Profl. Edn. in High Blood Pressure, 1973, Nat. Cancer Control Planning Conf., 1973; vice chmn. Gov. Pa. Task Force Cancer Control, 1974-76, chmn. com. cancer detection, 1974-76; mem. health research adv. bd. State of Pa., 1976—; mem. diagnostic research adv. group Nat. Cancer Inst., 1974—; chmn. coordinating com., comprehensive cancer center program Fox Chase Cancer Center, U. Pa. Cancer Center, 1975; cons. WHO, 1979; mem. Nat. Conf. on Med. Edn. Bd. dirs. Phila. Council Internat. Visitors, 1972-77; adv. commn. Internat. Participation Phila. '76, 1973-76. Served to capt. M.C., AUS, 1958-60. Recipient Arnold and Marie Schwartz award in medicine, 1976. Diplomate Am. Bd. Internal Medicine. Fellow A.C.P., Coll. Physicians Phila. (censor 1977—, councillor 1977—); mem. Am. Fedn. Clin. Research (pres. Temple U. chpt. 1964-65), Am. Assn. Cancer Research, Am. Soc. Clin. Oncology, Assn. Am. Cancer Insts., Assn. Am. Med. Colls., Am. Cancer Soc. (vice chmn. service com. Phila. div. 1974-76, chmn. awards com. 1976), Am. Lung Assn., AMA, AAAS, Am. Heart Assn., Pan Am. Med. Assn., Phila. Coop. Cancer Assn., N.Y. Acad. Scis., Pa. Heart Assn., Heart Assn. Southeastern Pa., Pa., Phila. County (chmn. com. internat. med. affairs 1964-72) med. socs., Pa. Lung Assn., Soc. des Medecins Militaires Francais, Phi Beta Kappa, Sigma Xi, Alpha Omega Alpha (councillor 1963-65). Author numerous articles in field. Asst. editor Annals Internal Medicine, 1972-75; editorial bd. other med. jours. Discovered assn. of hepatitis B surface antigen with hepatitis. Home: 2135 St James Pl Philadelphia PA 19103

SUTPHEN, HAROLD AMERMAN, JR., paper co. exec.; b. Verona, N.J., Feb. 13, 1926; s. Harold Amerman and Marion Esther (Mason) S.; grad. Phillips Exeter Acad., 1944; B.S. in Mech. Engring., Princeton, 1950; m. Greta May Peterson, June 24, 1950; children—Judith Amerman, Peter Lehmann, Pamela Torrance. With Universal Oil Products Co., Chgo., 1950-51, Texaco, Inc., 1951-52; bus. research analyst Arthur D. Little, Inc., 1952-56; asst. div. mgr. adminstrn., fine papers div. W.Va. Pulp and Paper Co. (name now changed to Westvaco Corp.), 1956-60, v.p., 1967—, mgr. fine papers div., 1974—, dir., 1975—; v.p., treas. U.S. Envelope Co., Springfield, Mass., 1960-62, pres., chief exec. officer, 1962-67, chmn. bd., 1967-74, also dir. Served with AUS, 1944-46. Mem. Holland Soc. N.Y., Phi Beta Kappa. Clubs: Country of Fairfield (Conn.); Weston (Conn.) Gun; Princeton, Board Room (N.Y.C.) Home: 33 Hill Brook Ln Fairfield CT 06430 Office: Westvaco Bldg 299 Park Ave New York City NY 10017

SUTPHIN, SAMUEL REID, paper co. exec.; b. Indpls., Dec. 28, 1911; s. Samuel Brady and Agatha (Reid) S.; A.B., Yale, 1934; student Inst. Paper Chemistry, Appleton, Wis., 1934-36; LL.D. (hon.), Franklin Coll., Ind. State U.; m. Lisa Polk Spilman, Oct. 30, 1948; children—Agatha Reid, Lisa (dec.), Samuel Brady II. With Kimberly-Clark, 1936-38; with Beveridge Paper Co., Indpls., 1938-69, successively chief chemist, sec., 1938-47, v.p. prodn., 1947-52, exec. v.p., 1952-58, chmn. 1958-69; chmn., dir. Tecnifax Corp. 1964-68; chmn., dir. Plastic Coating Corp., Holyoke, Mass., 1958-68, chmn. adv. bd., 1968-69; v.p. Scott Paper Co., 1965-69, dir., 1965—; pres. Madeira Enterprises, 1971—, dir. Ind. Bell Telephone Co., Ind. Nat. Bank of Indpls., Norfolk and Western Ry. Co., Ind. Nat. Corp., Crane Co., Medusa Corp. Trustee, Indpls. Mus. Art; trustee emeritus Nat. Trust Hist. Preservation; chmn. Ind. State Scholarship Commn., 1965-66; bd. dirs. Nat. Audubon Soc. Served to comdr. USNR, 1941-46. Decorated Legion of Merit with Combat V. Republican. Episcopalian. Clubs: Links (N.Y.C.); Nantucket (Mass.) Yacht; Univ., Woodstock, Indpls. Athletic (Indpls.); The Travellers, Conseil International de la Chassé (Paris). Home: Rural Route 3 Box 91 Zionsville IN 46077 Office: PO Box 23 Zionsville IN 46077

SUTRO, JOHN ALFRED, lawyer; b. San Francisco, July 3, 1905; s. Alfred and Rose (Newmark) S.; A.B., Stanford, 1926; LL.B., Harvard, 1929; m. Elizabeth Hiss, Oct. 16, 1931; children—Caroline (Mrs. Gerald F. Mohun), Elizabeth Sutro Mackey, John A., Stephen (dec.). Admitted to Calif. bar, 1929, since practiced in San Francisco; with firm Pillsbury, Madison & Sutro, 1929—. partner, 1935—. Adv. dir. Bank of Calif. N.A., BanCal Tri-State Corp.; dir. Consultants Inc., Kaiser Steel Corp., 1972-75. Mem. Calif. Commn. on Uniform State Laws, 1968, Calif. Commn. on Interstate Cooperation, 1968. Chmn. exec. com. Friends of Stanford Law Library; v.p. San Francisco Airports Commn., 1970-74. Bd. councilors U. So. Calif. Law Center; trustee Hastings Center Law Found., 1976—; bd. visitors U. Santa Clara Sch. Law; pres., trustee San Francisco Law Library: bd. dirs. St. Luke's Hosp. Served as comdr. USNR, 1940-45. Recipient Navy Distinguished Pub. Service award, 1958, ann. award St. Thomas More Soc., 1971, brotherhood award NCCJ, 1975. Fellow Am. Bar Found. (chmn. 1973); mem. Am. Judicature Soc. (dir. 1964-70, exec. com. 1967-70, Herbert Harley award 1974), Navy League (nat. v.p. and dir. 1954-67, mem. nat. adv. council), Calif. Acad. Scis. (vice chmn. trustees), Am. Law Inst., Am. Bar Assn. (standing com. fed. judiciary 1968-74, chmn. 1973-74, chmn. com. jud. selection and tenure 1975-78, vice chmn., dir. Nat. Jud. Coll. 1975—, mem. exec. com. lawyers conf. jud. adminstrn. div. 1977—), State Bar Calif. (bd. govs. 1962-66, pres. 1965-66), Bar Assn. of San Francisco (pres. 1962), San Francisco C. of C. (pres. 1973), Phi Alpha Delta. Clubs: Family, Commonwealth (bd. govs. 1957-59) (San Francisco). Office: 225 Bush St San Francisco CA 94104

SUTTER, CAROLYN OPTHOFF, librarian, adminstr.; b. Kalamazoo, Oct. 9, 1942; d. John Martin and Lorraine Eleanor (Kloosterman) Opthoff; B.S., Calvin Coll., 1964; M.S., Western Mich. U., 1970; M.P.A., Calif. State U., Long Beach, 1980; children—Chandra, Stephan. Dir., Library System of Southwestern Mich., 1974-76; asso. dir. Long Beach (Calif.) Public Library, 1977-79; dir. library and mus. services, City of Long Beach, 1979—. Chairwoman Mich. 4th Dist. Tricounty Women's Polit. Caucus, 1972-76. Mem. ALA, Public Library Execs. Assn. So. Calif., Calif. Library Assn., Urban Libraries Council, Long Beach C. of C. (dir. women's council). Office: Long Beach Public Library 101 Pacific Ave Long Beach CA 90802

SUTTER, MORLEY CARMAN, med. scientist; b. Redvers, Sask., Can., May 18, 1933; s. Christian Benjamin and Amelia (Duke) S.; M.D., U. Man., 1957, B.Sc., 1957, Ph.D., 1963; m. Virginia Frances Mary Laidlaw, June 29, 1957; children—Gregory Robert, F. Michelle, Brent Morley. Intern Winnipeg (Man.) Gen. Hosp., 1956-57, resident, 1958-59; teaching fellow pharmacology U. Man., 1959-63; supr. Downing Coll., Cambridge U., 1963-65; asst. prof. pharmacology U. Toronto, 1965-66; asst. prof. pharmacology U. B.C., 1966-68, asso. prof., 1968-71, prof., head dept. pharmacology, 1971—; mem. active staff Vancouver (B.C.) Gen. Hosp., Shaughnessy Hosp., St. Paul's Hosp. Mem. Minister of Health's Adv. Com. on Drugs, Province of B.C., 1971—. Recipient Gov. Gen. medal, 1950; Med. Research Council of Can. fellow, 1959-63; Wellcome Found. Travelling fellow, 1963; Imperial Chem. Industries fellow, 1963-65; Med. Research Council scholar, 1966-71. Mem. Pharmacol. Soc. Can. (treas. 1969-72), British Pharmacol. Soc., Am. Soc. Pharmacology and Exptl. Therapeutics, Can. Med. Assn. Contbr. articles to sci. jours. Office: Faculty Medicine Dept Pharmacology U BC Vancouver BC Canada

SUTTER, WILLIAM PAUL, lawyer; b. Chgo., Jan. 15, 1924; s. Harry Blair and Elsie (Paul) S.; A.B., Yale U., 1947; J.D., U. Mich., 1950; m. Helen Yvonne Stebbins, Nov. 13, 1954; children—William Paul, Helen Blair. Admitted to Ill. bar, 1950, Fla. bar, 1977; asso. firm Hopkins, Sutter, Mulroy, Davis & Cromartie and predecessor, Chgo., 1950-57, partner, 1957—; mem. Ill. Supreme Ct. Atty. Registration Commn., 1975—. Chmn. Winnetka Caucus Com., 1966-67; precinct capt. New Trier Twp. (Ill.) Republican Party, 1960-68; asst. area chmn. New Trier Rep. Orgn., 1968-72; trustee Gads Hill Center, pres., 1962-70, chmn., 1971—. Served to 1st lt. AUS, 1943-46. Fellow Am. Bar Found., Am. Coll. Probate Counsel (bd. regents 1977—); mem. Am. (ho. dels. 1972—, chmn. com. on income estates and trusts, taxation sect. 1973-75), Ill. (bd. govs. 1964-75, pres. 1973-74), Chgo. (chmn. probate practice com. 1963-64) bar assns., Am. Law Inst., Am. Judicature Soc., Ill. LAWPAC (pres. 1977—), Chgo. Assn. Commerce and Industry (govt. affairs div.), Am. Arbitration Assn., Order of Coif, Phi Beta Kappa, Phi Delta Phi, Chi Psi. Episcopalian. Clubs: Chicago, Mid-Day, Indian Hill, Law, Legal, Economic (Chgo.). Contbr. articles on estate planning and taxation to profl. jours. Home: 96 Woodley Rd Winnetka IL 60093 Office: Hopkins Sutter Mulroy Davis & Cromartie 1 First Nat Plaza Chicago IL 60603

SUTTLE, DORWIN WALLACE, fed. judge; b. Knox County, Ind., July 16, 1906; s. William Sherman and Nancy Cordelia (Hungate) S.; LL.B., U. Tex., 1928; m. Anne Elizabeth Barrett, Feb. 1, 1939 (dec.); children—Stephen Hungate, Nancy Joanna Suttle Walker (dec.); m. 2d, Lucile Cram Whitecotton; stepchildren—Fred and Frank Whitecotton. Admitted to Tex. bar, also U.S. Supreme Ct., 1960; practiced law, Uvalde, Tex., 1928-64; U.S. dist. judge Western Dist. Tex., 1964—. Fellow Tex. Bar Found., Am. Judicature Soc.; mem. Am., Tex., San Antonio bar assns., Tex. Law Rev. Assn., Tex. Law Rev. Assn. Democrat. Methodist. Home: 911 Eventide Dr San Antonio TX 78209 Office: 655 E Durango St San Antonio TX 78206. *The Word is "Integrity."*

SUTTLE, WILLIAM WAYNE, lawyer, assn. exec; b. Marion, N.C., Dec. 4, 1933; s. Edgar Wayne and Ruth (Kincaid) S.; student U. N.C., 1952-55, LL.B., 1958; children—William Eugene, John Reginald. Admitted to N.C. bar, 1958; individual practice, also solictor County

Criminal Ct. Marion, N.C., 1958-65; with N.C. Nat. Bank, Greensboro., 1965-66; pres. U.S. Jr. C. of C., 1966-67, chmn. bd., 1967-68; spl. asst. to dir. Office Econ. Opportunity, 1967-68, dir. S.E. region, Atlanta, 1968-70; exec. cons. U.S. Research and Devel. Corp., N.Y.C., 1970-72; counsel, v.p. Am. Ins. Assn., Atlanta, 1972-79, Washington, 1979—. Bd. dirs. Project Concern. Mem. Theta Chi, Delta Theta Phi. Democrat. Home: 3737 Peachtree Rd NE Apt D-14 Atlanta GA 30319 Office: 1025 Connecticut Ave NW Washington DC 20236

SUTTLES, WILLIAM MAURRELLE, clergyman, univ. adminstr.; b. Ben Hill, Ga., July 25, 1920; s. Wiley Maurrelle and Eddie Lou (Campbell) S.; B.C.S., Ga. State U., 1942; M.R.E., Emory U., 1953, M.Th., 1947; M.Div., Yale, 1946; Ed.D., Auburn U., 1958; D.D., Mercer U., 1972; D.Hum., Tift Coll., 1978; m. Julia Lanette Lovern, Jan. 28, 1950. Asst. registrar Ga. State U., 1942-44, asst. prof. English and speech, 1946-55, asso. prof. speech, 1955-57, prof., 1957—, prof. ednl. adminstrn. and higher edn., 1970—, also chmn. dept. speech, 1955-62, dean students, 1956-62, v.p. acad. affairs, 1964-69, exec. v.p., provost, 1970—; ordained to ministry Baptist Ch., 1938; pastor Haralson (Ga.) Bapt. Ch., 1950—, Luthersville (Ga.) Bapt. Ch., 1951-62; v.p., personnel dir. Rich's, Inc., Atlanta, 1962-64; dir., exec. com. Ga. Fed. Savs. and Loan Assn., 1st Ga. Bank. Chmn. Joint Citizens Adv. Com. To Study Atlanta and Fulton County Govts., 1967-69; mem. southeastern regional manpower adv. com. U.S. Dept. Labor, 1972—. Trustee John and Mary Franklin Found., Tift Coll., Hillside Cottages, Ga. State U. Found., George M. Sparks Scholarship Fund. Served with USNR, 1944-46. Named Rural Minister of Year for Ga., Progressive Farmer mag. and Emory U., 1959; Clergyman of Year for Ga. region NCCJ, 1971; One of 300 Who Have Shaped Atlanta, Atlanta mag., 1976; recipient Medal of St. Paul, Greek Orthodox Archdiocese of N. and S. Am., 1976. Mem. Atlanta C. of C., Ga. State U. Athletic Assn. (trustee 1962—), Ga. State U. Alumni Assn. (dir. 1963-73), Phi Kappa Phi, Beta Gamma Sigma, Phi Eta Sigma, Omicron Delta Kappa, Alpha Kappa Psi, Kappa Phi Kappa, Phi Delta Kappa, Kappa Delta Pi, Sigma Pi Alpha, Sigma Tau Delta, Sigma Nu, Alpha Lambda Delta. Mason (Shriner); Kiwanian. Club: Commerce (Atlanta). Home: 2734 Piney Wood Dr East Point GA 30344 Office: Ga State U Atlanta GA 30303

SUTTON, ALBERT ALTON, educator; b. Minneapolis, Kans., Aug. 14, 1906; s. Samuel B. and Mona Belle (Pawling) S.; B.S., Kans. State Tchrs. Coll., Emporia, 1929; A.M., U. Kans., 1936; Ph.D., Northwestern U., 1943; m. Lenore Wheeler, June 1, 1930; children—Albert Alton, David Benjamin. Reporter, Minneapolis, (Kans.) Messenger, 1923-26, Emporia (Kans.) Gazette, 1926-29; head, English dept. Cherryvale (Kans.) High School, 1929-32; instr. Wichita (Kans.) High Sch. East, 1932-35; instr. journalism U. Kans., 1935-36; asst. prof. dept. printing and rural journalism S.D. State Coll., 1936-37; asst. prof. Sch. Journalism, U. Okla., Norman, 1937-40; asst. prof. Medill Sch. Journalism, Northwestern U., Evanston, Ill., 1941-44, asso. prof., 1944-47, prof. 1947—, chmn. dept. advanced studies, 1960-74. Mem. Assn. for Edn. Journalism, Pi Alpha Mu, Sigma Delta Chi, Phi Delta Chi. Methodist. Club: University (Evanston). Author: Education for Journalism in the United States from Its Beginning to 1940, 1945; Design and Makeup of the Newspaper, 1948; Concepión y Confección de un Periódico, 1963. Contbr. articles to periodicals. Home: 1440 Sheridan Rd Wilmette IL 60091

SUTTON, BARRETT BOULWARE, ins. co. exec.; b. Forsyth, Ga., July 6, 1927; s. James Phinazee and Katherine Woodward (Boulware) S.; A.B., Vanderbilt U., 1949, LL.B., 1950; m. Mary Terecia Wade, Sept. 1, 1948; children—Katherine (Mrs. John P. Apel), Barrett Boulware, Wade. Admitted to Tenn. bar, 1950; with Life and Casualty Ins. Co. Tenn., Nashville, 1950—, gen. counsel, 1970—, sr. v.p., 1972—, also dir. Pres. Nashville Council Community Services, 1968-70, Nashville Travelers Aid Soc., 1970-72; chmn. Nashville U.S.O. Com., 1960-62; vice-chmn. Nashville United Way Campaign, 1975. Served with USNR, 1945-46. Mem. Assn. Life Ins. Counsel, Am., Tenn., Nashville bar assns., Order of Coif, Phi Beta Kappa. Presbyn. (elder). Club: Nashville Exchange. Home: 750 Greeley Dr Nashville TN 37205 Office: Life and Casualty Tower Nashville TN 37219

SUTTON, BERRIEN DANIEL, soft drink co. exec.; b. Axson, Ga., Jan. 24, 1926; s. Frank and Commie (Brooker) S.; B.B.A., U. Ga., 1948; m. Verda Lee Adams, June 6, 1953; 1 dau., Kathryn. From traveling auditor to St. Louis dist. mgr. Coca-Cola Co., 1948-62; from v.p. sales to pres., gen. mgr. Coca-Cola Bottling Co., St. Louis, 1962-66; pres. Asso. Coca-Cola Bottling Co., Inc., Daytona Beach, Fla., 1966—; past mem. pres.'s adv. council Coca-Cola Co.; dir. Security 1st Fed. Savs. and Loan Assn., Daytona Beach, Fla. Past gen. campaign chmn., v.p., dir., mem. exec. com. United Fund East Volusia County; mem. Civic League Halifax Area; bd. counselors Bethune Cookman Coll. Served with USNR, 1944-46. Mem. Coca-Cola Bottlers Assn. (bd. govs., pres.), 49ers, Young Presidents Orgn. Methodist. Rotarian dir., treas.). Club: Oceanside Country (Ormond Beach). Home: 250 Landmark Circle Ormond Beach FL 32074 Office: 320 Orange Ave Daytona Beach FL 32015

SUTTON, CHARLES WILLIAM, lawyer; b. Rochester, N.Y., Apr. 29, 1913; s. Clyde T. and Mary (McLaughlin) S.; A.B. U. Rochester, 1935; J.D., Cornell U., 1938; m. Alice Earl Taylor, June 17, 1941; children—Judith (Mrs. Daniel W. Drake), John Taylor, Edward Dixon, Mary Ogden. Admitted to N.Y. bar, 1938, since practiced in Rochester; partner firm Sutton, Deleeuw, Clark & Darcy, and predecessors, 1939—. Dir. Columbia Banking Savs. & Loan Assn., 1940—, sec., 1940-65; dir. Monroe Abstract & Title Corp., 1959—. Served with AUS, World War II; ETO. Decorated Croix de Guerre with palm, (France). Mem. Monroe County Bar Assn. (trustee 1964-66), Phi Delta Phi. Republican. Presbyn. (elder). Mason (Shriner). Home: 225 Alpine Dr Rochester NY 14618 Office: 31 E Main St Rochester NY 14614

SUTTON, DAVID B., steel co. exec.; b. Phila., Jan. 17, 1939; s. George David and Dorothy Helen (Dobush) S.; B.S., U. Md., 1962; C.P.A., U. State N.Y., 1968, U. Ill., 1971; M.B.A., Bradley U., 1974; m. Margaret Alice Kerr, June 25, 1960; children—Robert Worthington, Mary Anne. Accountant, Peat, Marwick, Mitchell & Co., Rochester, N.Y., 1962-63, Lybrand, Ross Bros. & Montgomery (currently Coopers & Lybrand), Syracuse, N.Y., 1963-68; controller Wickwire div. Keystone Consol. Industries, Inc., Cortland, N.Y., 1968-70; mgr. corporate accounts Keystone Consol. Industries, Inc., Peoria, Ill., 1970-72, controller, 1972-75, v.p., controller, 1975-77; v.p., controller Keystone Group, 1977-79; pres. Nat. Lock Fastener, 1979—. Bd. dirs. YMCA, Cortland, 1968-70, Jr. Achievement Central Ill. C.P.A., N.Y., Ill. Mem. Am. Inst. C.P.A.'s, N.Y., Ill. socs. C.P.A.'s, Nat. Assn. Accountants (dir. Ithaca-Cortland chpt. 1969-70), Am. Iron and Steel Inst., U. Md. Alumni Assn., Delta Sigma Pi. Republican. Presbyn. Home: 2429 Clinton Rd Rockford IL 61103 Office: 4500 Kishwaukee St Rockford IL 61109

SUTTON, DONALD HOWARD, baseball player; b. Clio, Ala., Apr. 2, 1945; ed. Miss. Coll., Clinton, Whittier (Calif.) Coll. With Los Angeles Dodgers, 1966—; Nat. League player in All-Star Game, 1972, 73, 75, 77. Author: How to Throw a Curve, 1977. Office: care Los Angeles Dodgers 1000 Elysian Park Ave Los Angeles CA 90012*

SUTTON, GEORGE EDWIN, univ. dean; b. Blandville, W. Va., June 3, 1923; s. Samuel Brady and Idel Elizabeth (Willis) S.; student Marshall State U., 1939-41; B.S., W.Va. U., 1948; M.S., U. Fla., 1952; Ph.D., Mich. State U., 1957; m. Marilyn Coral Gillette, Aug. 15, 1959; children—Dana Willis, Jeremy Donald. With Indsl. Engring. & Constrn. Co., Fairmont, W.Va., 1948; faculty U. Fla., Gainesville, 1949-55; U. Ariz., Tucson, 1957-59; Ariz. State U., Tempe, 1959-61; prof., chmn. mech. engring. dept. U. Nev., Reno, 1961-73; dir. profl. services Nat. Council Engring. Examiners, Seneca, S.C., 1973-76; dean William Rayen Sch. Engring., Youngstown State U., 1976—; engring. cons. Naval Weapons Center, China Lake, Calif., Sierra Pacific Power Co., Reno. Served with RCAF, 1941-43; with USNR, 1943-46, 52-53. Registered profl. engr., Nev., Ariz., Fla., Ohio. Mem. Nat. Soc. Profl. Engrs. (pres. Reno chpt. 1964), ASME. Club: South Reno Sertoma (pres.). Contbr. articles to profl. jours. Home: 2602 Algonquin Dr Poland OH 44514

SUTTON, GEORGE MIKSCH, ornithologist, bird artist; b. Bethany, Neb., May 16, 1898; s. Harry Trumbull and Lola Anna (Miksch) S.; student Tex. Christian U., Ft. Worth, 1913-14; B.S., Bethany (W.Va.) Coll., 1923, Sc.D., 1952; Ph.D., Cornell U., 1932; Mem. staff Carnegie Mus., Pitts., 1919-25; Pa. state ornithologist, 1925-29; curator of birds Cornell U., Ithaca, N.Y., 1931-45; mem. of expdns. for Carnegie Mus. to Labrador, 1920, 28, to Hudson Bay, 1923, 26; solo expdn. to Southampton Island, Hudson Bay, 1929-30; expdn. to Churchill, Hudson Bay, 1931 (discovered eggs of Harris's sparrow); expdns. since 1930 to Sask., So. states of U.S. (for ivory-billed woodpeckers), Western Okla., Rio Grande Valley, B.C., Hudson Bay, Mexico, Iceland, Victoria Island, Bathurst Island, Galápagos Islands; devoted much time to painting birds, furnishing illustrations for H. H. Bailey's Birds of Florida, Allen's American Bird Biographies and Golden Plover and Other Birds, Burleigh's Georgia Birds, Pettingill's Guides to Bird Finding, Vale's Wings, Fur, and Shot, Todd's Birds of Western Pa., Birds of Santa Marta, Colombia, and Birds of Labrador Peninsula, Meyer de Schauensee's Birds of Colombia and Birds of South America, Van Tyne and Berger's Fundamentals of Ornithology, Burgess's Seashore Book, Roberts' Birds of Minnesota, bird sect. World Book Ency., Brandt's Arizona Birdlife, Phillips, Monson, and Marshall's Birds of Arizona; now George Lynn Cross research prof. zoology and curator of birds emeritus U. Okla. Adviser to Arctic Inst. N.Am. Served to maj., USAAF, 1942-45. Decorated knight cross Icelandic Order Falcon. Mem. Am. Ornithologists Union, Wilson Ornithol. Soc. (past pres.), Cooper Ornithol. Soc., Okla. Zool. Soc. (dir.), Okla. Ornithol. Soc. (dir.), Biol. Soc. Washington, Cranbrook Inst. Sci., Southwestern Assn. Naturalists, Arctic Inst. N.Am., Am. Polar Soc., Am. Geog. Soc., Am. Falconers Assn., Phi Beta Kappa, Sigma Xi, Phi Kappa Phi, Beta Theta Pi. Hon. trustee Oglebay Inst., Wheeling, W.Va. Author: Introduction to Birds of Pennsylvania, 1928; Exploration of Southampton Island, Hudson Bay, 1932; Eskimo Year, 1934; Birds in the Wilderness, 1936; Mexican Birds, 1951; Iceland Summer, 1961 (recipient John Burroughs medal 1962); Oklahoma Birds, 1967; High Arctic, 1971; At A Bend in a Mexican River, 1972; Mexican Bird Portraits, 1975; Fifty Common Birds of Oklahoma, 1977; To a Young Bird Artist, 1979; (autobiography) Bird Student, 1980. Contbg. editor Audubon Mag. Ornithology editor Am. Coll. Dictionary, Ency., Arctica. Home: 818 W Brooks St Norman OK 73069 Office: Stovall Mus Sci and History 1335 Asp Ave Norman OK 73019

SUTTON, GEORGE WALTER, research lab. exec.; b. Bklyn., Aug. 3, 1927; s. Jack and Pauline (Aaron) S.; B. Mech. Engring., Cornell U., 1952; M.S., Calif. Inst. Tech., 1953, Ph.D. magna cum laude, 1955; m. Evelyn D. Kunnes, Dec. 25, 1952; children—James E., Charles S., Richard E., Stewart A. Research scientist Lockheed Missle Co., 1955; research engr. Space Sci. Lab., Gen. Elec. Co., 1955-61, mgr. magnetohydrodynamic power generation, 1962-63; vis. Ford prof. Mass. Inst. Tech., 1961-62; sci. adviser directorate devel. plans, Hdqrs. USAF, 1963-65; with Avco Research Lab., 1965—, dir. laser devel., 1971—, v.p. Avco Everett Research Lab., Everett, Mass., 1972—; spl. cons. Energy Agy., 1977—; lectr. magnetohydrodynamics U. Pa., 1960-63, Stanford, 1964; spl. research on ablation of heat protection for ICBM re-entry and high energy lasers. Served with USAAF, 1945-47. Recipient Arthur Flemming award for outstanding govt. service, 1965. Fellow Am. Inst. Aeros. and Astronautics (chmn. plasmadynamics tech. com.); mem. Symposium Engring. Aspects Magnetohydrodynamics (pres.), Am. Soc. M.E., Am. Inst. Physics, A.A.A.S. Author: Proceedings 4th Symposium Engineering Aspects of Magnetohydrodynamics, 1964; (with A. Sherman) Engineering Magnetohydrodynamics, 1965; Direct Energy Conversion, 1966. Editor-in-chief Jour. Am. Inst. Aeros. and Astronautics, 1967—. Contbr. articles to profl. jours. Home: 37 Winthrop Rd Lexington MA 02173 Office: 2385 Revere Beach Pkwy Everett MA 02149

SUTTON, HARRY ELDON, geneticist; b. Cameron, Tex., Mar. 5, 1927; s. Grant Edwin and Myrtle Dovie (Fowler) S.; B.S. in Chemistry, U. Tex., Austin, 1948, M.A., 1949; Ph.D. in Biochemistry, 1953; m. Beverly Earlene Jewell, July 7, 1962; children—Susan Elaine, Caroline Virginia. Biologist, U. Mich., 1952-56, instr., 1956-57, asst. prof. human genetics, 1957-60; asso. prof. zoology U. Tex., Austin, 1960-64, prof., 1964—, chmn. dept. zoology, 1970-73, asso. dean Grad. Sch., 1967-70, 73-75, v.p. for research, 1975-79; mem. adv. council Nat. Inst. Environ. Health Scis., 1968-72, council sci. advs., 1972-76; com. mem. Nat. Acad. Scis.-NRC, 1969-74; cons. in field; bd. dirs. Associated Univs. for Research in Astronomy, 1975-79, Argonne Univs. Assn., 1975-79, Univ. Corp. for Atmospheric Research, 1975-79, Associated Western Univs., 1978-79. Trustee, S.W. Tex. Corp. Public Broadcasting, 1977-80, sec., 1979-80; bd. dirs. Austin Civic Gallet, 1978—. Served with U.S. Army, 1945-46. Mem. Am. Soc. Human Genetics (dir. 1961-69, pres. 1979), Genetics Soc. Am., Am. Soc. Biol. Chemists, Am. Chem. Soc., Tex. Genetics Soc. (pres. 1979), Environ. Mutagen Soc., AAAS, Am. Genetics Assn. Club: Headliners (Austin). Author: Genes, Enzymes, and Inherited Disease, 1961; An Introduction to Human Genetics, 1965; editor: First Macy Conference on Genetics, 1960; Mutagenic Effects of Environmental Contaminants, 1972; research, pubis. in human genetics; editor Am. Jour. Human Genetics, 1964-69. Home: 1103 Gaston Ave Austin TX 78703 Office: Dept Zoology U Tex Austin TX 78712

SUTTON, HORACE ASHLEY, mag. editor, writer; b. N.Y.C., May 17, 1919; s. Herman and Belle (Chodorov) S.; grad. Lawrenceville Sch., 1936; student U. Pa., 1936-38, Columbia, 1938-41; m. Nancy Waring, May 7, 1950; 1 son, Andrew Charles; m. 2d, Patricia Anne Diamond, June 8, 1958; children—Miranda, Patrick. With N.Y. Sun, 1938-39; with N.Y. Post, 1939-41, travel editor, 1946-47; travel editor Sat. Rev., 1947-61, asso. editor, 1961-72, editorial dir., 1975—; editorial dir. World Mag., 1972-73, Saturday Review/World, 1973-74; syndicated newspaper travel columnist Of All Places, 1952—; contbg. travel editor Sport Illustrated, 1954-61; contbg. editor McCalls mag., 1961-65, asso. editor, 1967-68, mng. editor, 1969, contbg. editor, 1971; editorial dir. Paradise of Pacific, 1963-66; contbg. columnist Bon Appetit mag., 1979—; radio-TV commentator and panelist. Served to capt. inf. AUS, 1941-46; ETO. Decorated Bronze Star Medal (U.S.); Croix de Guerre (France); Star of Solidarity (Italy); recipient Travel Journalism award Am. Soc. Travel agts., 1951, Journalism award for mags. Trans-World Airlines, 1951, for newspapers 1959, for mags., 1970, Asia mag. Overseas Press Club award, 1968, French Medaille du Tourisme, Nat. Fedn. Syndicate d'Initiative, 1973. Mem. Travel Writers Assn. (past pres.). Club: Overseas Press (bd. govs. 1960-62) (N.Y.C.). Author: Footloose in France, 1948; Footloose in Canada, 1950; Footloose in Italy, 1950; Footloose in Switzerland, 1951; Confessions of a Grand Hotel, 1952; Sutton's Places, 1954; Aloha, Hawaii, 1967. Office: Saturday Review 1290 Ave of Americas New York City NY 10022

SUTTON, JOAN M., journalist; b. Mimico, Ont., Can., Nov. 30, 1932; d. Frederick Edward and Anna May (Taylor) Treble; student U. Toronto, 1951-53; m. Walter J. Sutton, Feb. 1955 (div. 1979); children—Walter John, Deborah Anne. Pres. Joan Sutton & Assos., Ltd., 1960—; fashion editor Toronto Telegram, 1972; lifestyle editor, daily columnist Sutton's Place, Toronto Sun, 1972-79; columnist Toronto Star, 1979; daily comentator Sta. CFRB, Toronto, 1974-77; syndicated radio commentator, 1975—; dir. Ont. Pl. Recipient Judy award Garment Salesmen Ont., 1964; named Man of Year, Women's Wear Bur., 1965. Mem. Fashion Group Inc. Toronto. Author: Lovers and Others, 1974; Once More with Love, 1975; Clothing and Culture, 1975; Lovelines, 1979. Office: 1 Yonge St Toronto ON Canada

SUTTON, JOHN FLOYD, JR., sch. ofcl., rancher, lawyer; b. Alpine, Tex., Jan. 26, 1918; s. John F. and Pauline (Elam) S.; J.D., U. Tex., 1941; m. Nancy Ewing, June 1, 1940; children—Nancy Joan Sutton Parr, John E. Admitted to Tex. bar, 1941; asso. firm Brooks, Napier, Brown & Matthews, San Antonio, 1941-42; spl. agt. FBI, 1942-45; asso. firm Matthews, Nowlin, Macfarlane & Barrett, San Antonio, 1945-51; partner Sutton, Steib & Barr, San Angelo, Tex., 1951-57; faculty law U. Tex., Austin, 1957—, prof. 1957-77, Joseph C. Hutcheseon prof. law, 1977—, dean Sch. Law, 1979—. Mem. Am. Bar Assn., State Bar of Tex., Tex. Bar Found., Tex. Law Rev. (dir., sec. 1972—), Philos. Soc. Tex., Order of Coif. Democrat. Presbyterian. Club: North Austin Rotary (pres. 1967). Author: (with Frank Elliott, Charles T. McCormick) Cases and Materials on Evidence, 1971. Home: Route 1 Box 36C Buda TX 78610 Office: Sch Law U Tex 2500 Red River St Austin TX 78705

SUTTON, JOHN PAUL, lawyer; b. Youngstown, Ohio, July 24, 1934; s. Howard Ellis and Lucy Dell (Dennison) S.; B.A., U. Va., 1956; J.D., George Washington U., 1963; m. Jane Williamson, Aug. 20, 1958; children—Julia, Susan, Elizabeth. Patent examiner U.S. Patent Office, Washington, 1956, 59-62; law clk. U.S. Ct. Customs and Patent Appeals, Washington, 1962-64; admitted to Calif. bar, 1965; asso. firm Flehr, Holbach, Test, Albritton & Herbert, San Francisco, 1964-68; partner firm Limbach, Limbach & Sutton, San Francisco, 1969—; adj. instr. Practicing Law Inst., 1968-69, continuing edn. program Calif. State Bar, 1972, 75, U. Calif. Law Sch., Berkeley, 1975. Served with USNR, 1956-59. Mem. Calif. (pres. 1975), San Francisco (pres. 1976) patent law assns., State Bar Calif. (exec. com. patent sect. 1975-77), Am. Chem. Soc. Democrat. Episcopalian. Club: World Trade (San Francisco). Contbr. articles to legal jours. Home: 2421 Pierce St San Francisco CA 94115 Office: Limbach Limbach & Sutton 2001 Ferry Bldg San Francisco CA 94111

SUTTON, JONATHAN STONE, architect, landscape architect; b. Columbus, Ohio, July 31, 1944; s. Charles Reuel and Theodora (Stone) S.; B.A., Amherst Coll., 1966; M.Arch., M.Landscape Architecture, U. Pa., 1970; m. Karen Marie Johnson, May 21, 1970; children—Eva Marie, Theodore Stone. Draftsman, Pierre Zoelly, Architect, Zurich, Switzerland, 1966; designer Weissman/Spohn, Phila., 1967; research asst., regional planning br. Delaware River Port Authority, Phila., 1969; research asst. computer applications group Center Ecol. Research in Planning Design, U. Pa., Phila., 1970, instr. landscape architecture studio Grad. Sch. Fine Arts, 1972-73, dir. urban design studio Grad. Sch. Fine Arts, 1973-79; partner Adaptive Design, Phila., 1970; architect, landscape architect Wallace, McHarg, Roberts & Todd, Phila., 1971—, asso. partner, 1973—; prin. Historic Devel. Corp., 1978—; adj. asst. prof. Drexel U. Sch. Architecture, 1976—; affiliated Wallingford Community Arts Center. Mem. Citizens Council Delaware County (Pa.). Mem. Am. Soc. Landscape Architects (Brad Williams medal 1974, 76, Merit award 1971), AIA, Am. Inst. Planners. Democrat. Presbyterian. Contbr. articles to profl. jours. Home: 355A Plush Mill Rd Wallingford PA 19086

SUTTON, JOSEPH THOMAS, univ. ofcl.; b. Jacksonville, Fla., Dec. 5, 1922; s. George Thomas and Arena Janet (Carson) S.; B.A. magna cum laude, Stetson U., 1948; M.A., Vanderbilt U., 1956, Ph.D., 1958; m. Frances L. Collins, Aug. 29, 1947; children—William Thomas, Nancy Lou, Robert Carson. State psychologist Tenn. Dept. Edn., Nashville, 1951-52; asst. prof. psychology Austin Peay State Coll., 1952-57; asso. prof. psychology Auburn U., 1957-59; prof. psychology Stetson U., 1959-66; dir. instl. research U. Ala., 1966-69, v.p. instl. studies and services, 1969-76, v.p. planning and ops., 1976—. Bd. dirs. Tuscaloosa County United Fund, Jones Law Inst. Served with AUS, 1943-46. Mem. Assn. Instnl. Research (pres. 1972-73), Soc. Coll. and Univ. Planning, Am. Assn. Higher Edn., Assn. Ednl. Data Systems, Tuscaloosa C. of C. (dir.). Home: 18 Woodridge Tuscaloosa AL 35401 Office: Admininstration Bldg University AL 35486

SUTTON, LEONARD VON BIBRA, lawyer; b. Colorado Springs, Colo., Dec. 21, 1914; s. Benjamin Edmund and Anne (von Bibra) S.; B.A., Colo. Coll., 1937; fellow Nat. Inst. Pub. Affairs, 1937-38; J.D., U. Denver, 1941; grad. Inf. Officers Sch., Ft. Benning, Ga., 1942. Admitted to Colo. bar, 1941, U.S. Supreme Ct., 1953, U.S., D.C. Circuit Ct., Tax Ct., Dist. Ct. Colo. and D.C., Ct. of Claims, Customs Ct., U.S. Army Ct. Mil. Rev.; practiced law, Colorado Springs, 1941-42, 46-56; justice Colo. Supreme Ct., 1956-68, chief justice, 1960, 66; chmn. Fgn. Claims Settlement Commn. U.S., 1968-69; pvt. practice law, Denver and Washington, 1969—. Chmn. Colo. Statute Revision Com., 1964-67; del. various nat. and internat. bar assn. confs.; lectr.; past vice chmn. com. internat. cts. World Peace Through Law Commn. Wash.; past chmn. Colo. World Peace through Law Com., World Habeas Corpus; hon. mem. N.J. World Trade Com., 1976—; mem. Colo. Democratic Central Com., 1948-56, mem. exec. com.. 1948-58, chmn. rules com., 1955-56; del. Dem. Nat. Conv., 1952. Hon. trustee Inst. Internat. Edn., N.Y.C.; regent Dana Coll., Blair, Nebr., 1976-78. Served from pvt. to capt., AUS, World War II. Mem. Colo. (Jr. Bar past chmn.), Internat., Inter-Am. (council), Am. (past chmn. com. on internat. cts., former mem. council sect. internat. law), Denver, D.C. bar assns., Mexican Acad. Internat. Law, Am. Arbitration Assn., Washington Fgn. Law Soc. (pres. 1970-71, now hon. mem.), Royal Danish Guards Assn. Calif., Consular Law Soc. N.Y. (hon.), Phi Delta Phi, Episcopalian. Clubs: Wyoming One Shot Antelope Past Shooter's; Colo. Harvard Bus. Sch. (asso.); Masons, Shriners; Garden of Gods, Kissing Camels Golf (Colorado Springs); Cosmos (Washington). Author: Constitution of Mexico, 1973. Contbr. articles on law, jud. adminstrn. and internat. relations to jours. Home: 3131 E Alameda Ave Apt 1908 Denver CO 80209

SUTTON, OTTIS ALTON, oil exec.; b. Dubberly, La., Oct. 27, 1906; s. Henry Otis and Nettie (Warren) S.; student Centenary Coll., 1926-29; m. Neva Anderson, Oct. 1, 1954; children—Dianne, Mike.

Various exec. positions Air Reduction Co., 1930-39; founder The O. A. Sutton Corp., Inc., Wichita, Kans., 1940, Alloys Foundry, Inc., 1943-47; partner Sumac Oil & Gas Co.; oil operator under name O. A. Sutton; chmn. bd. Kans. State Bank, Wichita, 1957-61; owner Bar S Ranch, Eureka, Kans., Carter-Raymond Mines, Gunnison, Colo., Sutton Pl., Wichita; pres., chmn. bd. Oasis Petroleum, Inc., Wichita, 1969-73, Atlantic Bldg. Corp., Boynton Beach, Fla., 1973—; chmn. bd. First Bank & Trust, Boynton Beach, 1968—, First Bank, Delray Beach, Fla., 1973—, First Bank West, Lake Worth, Fla., 1973—, 1st Bank & Trust of Palm Beach County, Delray Beach, Fla. Mem. bd. govs. Am. Royal; pres., mem. bd. dirs. Wichita Community Chest and United Fund. Mem. NAM (dir.), Wichita C. of C. (past mem. bd. dirs.), Alpha Kappa Psi. Methodist. Mason (Shriner). Clubs: Wichita Country, Wichita, Petroleum (Wichita, Kans.); Pine Tree Golf (Delray Beach); La Coquille (Palm Beach, Fla.); N.Y. Yacht (N.Y.C.); Bob'O'Link Golf (Highland Park, Ill.); Boynton Beach. Home: 4518 Turnberry Ct Pine Tree Country Club Estates Boynton Beach FL 33436 Office: PO Drawer 850 Delray Beach FL 33444. *In retrospect, I feel the greatest contributing factor to my success has been a willingness to work harder than the other fellow, along with an avid self-educating hunger and an eagerness to see a project through to a successful conclusion, despite obstacles and hardships.*

SUTTON, PETER ALFRED, bishop; b. Chandler, Que., Can., Oct. 18, 1934; B.A., U. Ottawa, 1960; M.A. in Religious Edn., Loyola U., Chgo., 1969. Ordained priest Roman Catholic Ch., 1960, bishop, 1974; oblate of Mary Immaculate; high sch. tchr. St. Patricks, Ont., 1961-63, London (Ont.) Cath. Central Sch., 1963-74; bishop of Labrador-Schefferville, Que., Can., 1974—; mem. social affairs com. Can. Conf. Cath. Bishops; mem. Indian and Inuit pastoral com. Conf. Que. Bishops. Contbr. religious articles to newspapers. Address: PO Box 700 303 AP Low St Schefferville PQ G0G 2T0 Canada

SUTTON, RICHARD LAUDER, lawyer; b. Dover, Del., July 4, 1935; s. Richard and Anna Kimber (Massey) S.; A.B. with distinction, U. Del., 1957; LL.B., Yale U., 1960; m. Violette Witwer, June 25, 1960; children—Jane Valentine, Richard Mohler. Admitted to Del. bar, 1961; law clk. to Judge Edwin D. Steel, U.S. Dist. Ct., Wilmington, Del., 1960-61; asso. firm Morris Nichols Arsht & Tunnell, Wilmington, 1961-65, partner, 1966—; mem. antitrust and trade regulation com. U.S. C. of C., 1976—. Chmn. Del. Gov.'s Higher Edn. Commn., 1976; dir., mem. exec. com. Greater Wilmington Devel. Council; trustee Wilmington Public Library; bd. dirs., mem. exe. com. Grand Opera House, Inc. Mem. Am. Bar Assn., Del. Bar Assn., Confrerie des Chevaliers du Tastevin, Phi Beta Kappa, Phi Kappa Phi, Omicron Delta Kappa, Phi Delta Phi. Clubs: Wilmington, Wilmington Country, Pine Valley Golf, Bidermann Golf. Home: 10 Barley Mill Dr Wilmington DE 19807 Office: PO Box 1347 Wilmington DE 19899

SUTTON, ROBERT GEORGE, educator, geologist; b. Rochester, N.Y., June 17, 1925; s. George F. and Flora (Stilwell) S.; A.B., U. Rochester, 1948, M.S., 1950; Ph.D., Johns Hopkins, 1956; m. Frances Elizabeth Parker, Feb. 23, 1946; children—Marsha Ann (Mrs. Kevin Brennan), Sandra Hope (Mrs. Juan Ortega). Instr. geology Alfred (N.Y.) U., 1950-52; mem. faculty U. Rochester, 1954—, prof. geology, 1966—, chmn. dept. geol. scis., 1964—. Served with AUS, 1946-47. NSF postdoctoral fellow, 1962-63. Fellow Rochester Acad. Sci., Geol. Soc. Am.; mem. Paleontol. Soc. Am., Soc. Econ. Mineralogists, AAAS, Internat. Assn. Sedimentologists, Sigma Xi. Research on stratigraphy of Devonian Catskill Delta, N.Y., also sedimentology in Lake Ontario. Home: 141 Furlong Rd Rochester NY 14623

SUTTON, ROBERT MIZE, educator; b. Bunker Hill, Ill., Dec. 15, 1915; s. Robert E.L. and Mary (Mize) S.; A.B., Shurtleff Coll., 1937; A.M., U. Ill., 1938, Ph.D., 1948; H.L.D., Wheaton Coll., 1971; m. Elizabeth Blair, June 19, 1942; children—Sarah M., William R., David B., Mary E. Instr. high sch., Bunker Hill, 1938-42; faculty history U. Ill., Urbana, 1948—, asso. prof., 1957-63, prof., 1963—, chmn. dept. history, 1972-74, asst. dean Coll. Liberal Arts and Scis., 1956-58, asso. dean Grad. Coll., 1958-65. Dir. Ill. Hist. Survey, 1964—; chmn. heritage com. Ill. Bicentennial Commn. Trustee No. Baptist Theol. Sem. Served with USAAF, 1942-46. Mem. Ill. Hist. Soc. (past pres., dir.), Orgn. of Am. Historians, Am. Hist. Assn., Am. Assn. for State and Local History, Phi Kappa Phi. Baptist. Club: Exchange (Urbana). Author: A History of Illinois in Paintings, 1968; The Heartland: Pages from Illinois History, 1975; co-author: Lincoln Images, 1960; Manuscripts Guide to Collections of the University of Illinois at Urbana-Champaign, 1976. Contbr. chpts. to books. Home: 1207 S Busey Ave Urbana IL 61801

SUTTON, ROGER BEATTY, educator, physicist; b. Lloydminster, Saskatchewan, Can., Sept 14, 1916 (came to U.S. 1939); s. Alan Ernest and Eva Mary (Holland) S.; B.Sc., U. Saskatchewan, 1937, M.Sc., 1939; Ph.D., Princeton, 1942; m. Caroline Craig, Feb. 18, 1946; children—Judith, Ann. Physicist, Manhattan Project, Los Alamos Lab., 1942-46; asst. prof. to prof. physics Carnegie-Mellon U., Pitts., 1946—. Fellow Am. Phys. Soc.; mem. Am. Assn. Physics Tchrs., AAUP, Sigma Xi. Contbr. sci. papers on nuclear and particle physics to profl. jours. Home: 1235 Wightman St Pittsburgh PA 15217

SUTTON, WALTER, educator; b. Milw., Jan. 25, 1916; s. Walter Evender and Maud (Farrington) S.; B.A., Heidelberg Coll., 1937; M.A., Ohio State U., 1938, Ph.D., 1946; m. Vivian Irene Ryan, Dec. 22, 1941; 1 dau., Catherine Beth. Instr. English, U. Rochester, 1946-47; successively asst. prof., asso. prof., prof. English, dir. grad. studies, chmn. dept. English Syracuse (N.Y.) U., 1948—, now distinguished prof. humanities, 1971—. Vis. prof. U. Minn., summer 1960; vis. prof., sr. vis. fellow Council Humanities Princeton, 1960-61; vis. prof. U. Wash., summer 1966, Colgate U., 1967, U. Hawaii, summer 1968. Mem. com. examiners advanced lit. test Grad. Record Exam., 1962-72. Served with USCGR, 1942-45. Recipient Ohioana Book award, 1963. Howald fellow Ohio State U., 1947-48. Mem. AAUP, Am. Soc. Aesthetics, Am. Studies Assn., Modern Lang. Assn. Am. Author: The Western Book Trade, 1961; Modern American Criticism, 1963; American Free Verse: The Modern Revolution in Poetry, 1973. Editor: Ezra Pound: A Collection of Critical Essays, 1963; (with Richard Foster) Modern Criticism: Theory and Practice, 1963; (with Vivian Sutton) Plato to Alexander Pope: Backgrounds of Modern Criticism, 1966; (with others) American Literature: Tradition and Innovation, 1969-74; editorial bd. Am. Lit., 1973-76. Office: Dept English Syracuse U Syracuse NY 13210

SUYDAM, FREDERICK HENRY, educator; b. Lancaster, Pa., July 30, 1923; s. William F. and Emily (Hardy) S.; B.S., Franklin and Marshall Coll., 1946; Ph.D., Northwestern U., 1950; m. Janet M. Bechtold, Sept. 24, 1944; children—Fred L., Carol Ann, Michael H. Research chemist Armstrong Cork Co., Lancaster, Pa., 1946; instr. Franklin and Marshall Coll., 1946-47, asst. prof., 1952-55, asso. prof., 1955-62, prof., 1962-69, Charles A. Dana prof. chemistry, 1969—; research fellow Northwestern U., 1947-50; instr. Johns Hopkins, 1950-52. Served to lt. USNR, 1943-46. Mem. Am. Chem. Soc., Phi Beta Kappa, Sigma Xi, Phi Lambda Upsilon. Research in field. Home: 442 N President Ave Lancaster PA 17603

SUZIEDELIS, VYTAUTAS A., engring. corp. exec.; b. Kaunas, Lithuania, June 22, 1930; s. Simas and Antanina S.; B.S., Northeastern U., 1954; M.S., N.Y. U., 1955; m. Birute O. Orintas, Jan. 1, 1959. With Stone & Webster Engring. Corp., Boston, 1956—, chief power engr., 1972-74, v.p., 1974-76, sr. v.p., 1976-79, exec. v.p., 1979—, dir., 1975—. Mem. ASME, Aircraft Owners and Pilots Assn., Atomic Indsl. Forum, Pi Tau Sigma (hon.). Republican. Roman Catholic. Club: University (Brockton, Mass.). Home: 36 Westwood Ave Brockton MA 02401 Office: Stone & Webster Engring Corp 245 Summer St Boston MA 02107

SUZUKI, HIDETARO, violinist; b. Tokyo, June 1, 1937; s. Hidezo and Humi (Sakai) S.; came to U.S., 1956, permanent resident, 1979; student Toho Sch. Music, Tokyo, 1953-56; diploma Curtis Inst. Music, 1963; m. Zeyda Ruga, May 16, 1962; children—Kenneth Hideo, Nantel Hiroshi, Elina Humi. Concertmaster Quebec (Que. Can.) Symphony Orch., 1963-78), Indpls. Symphony Orch., 1978—; prof. violin Conservatory Province Que., Quebec, 1963-79, Laval U., Quebec, 1971-77; active as concert violinist, Can., U.S., USSR, Eastern and Western Europe, Cuba, Japan, 1951—; guest condr. orchs. in numerous concerts, broadcasts, 1968—; rec. artist. Recipient prize Tchaikowsky Internat. Competition, Moscow, 1962, Queen Elisabeth Internat. Competition, Brussels, 1963, 67, Montreal (Que.) Internat. Competition, 1966. Office: Indpls Symphony Orch Clowes Meml Hall 4600 Sunset Ave Indianapolis IN 46208

SUZUKI, MICHIO, educator; b. Chiba, Japan, Oct. 2, 1926 (came to U.S., 1952); s. Kyosuke and Taka (Saito); B.S., U. Tokyo, 1945-48, Ph.D., 1951; m. Naoko Akizuki, Nov. 11, 1952; 1 child Kazuko. Asst. prof. math U. Ill. at Urbana, 1955-57, asso. prof., 1958, prof., 1959—, prof. Center Advanced Study, 1968—; research asso. Harvard, 1956; vis. prof. U. Chgo., 1960; mem. Inst. Advanced Study, Princeton, N.J., 1962, 68. Recipient Acad. prize Japan Acad., 1974. Guggenheim fellow, 1962. Mem. Am. Math. Soc. (council 1962-71), Math. Soc. Japan. Home: 2406 Melrose Dr Champaign IL 61820 Office: Dept Math U Ill Urbana IL 61801

SUZY (AILEEN MEHLE), columnist; b. El Paso, Tex; m. Roger Mehle (div.); 1 son, Roger; m. 2d, Kenneth Frank (div.). Soc. columnist syndicated in 101 newspapers. Formerly known as Suzy Knickerbocker. Address: care Milton Fenster Assos 540 Madison Ave New York NY 10022*

SVEC, HARRY JOHN, chemist; b. Cleve., June 24, 1918; s. Ralph Joseph and Lilian Josephine (Pekarek) S.; B.S., John Carroll U., 1941; Ph.D. in Phys. Chemistry, 1949; m. Edna Mary Bruno, Oct. 23, 1943; children—Mary, Peter, Katherine, Jan, Thomas, Jean, Benjamin, Daniel, Lillian. Asst. chemist Iowa State U., 1941-43, research asso. Inst. Atomic Research, 1946-50, asst. prof. chemistry, 1950-55, asso. prof., 1955-60, prof., 1960—, Disting. prof. in scis. and humanities, 1978—, asso. chemist Ames Lab., 1950-55, chemist, 1955-60, sr. chemist, 1960—, program dir., 1974—; jr. chemist Manhattan Project, 1943-46; lectr. in field. NSF grantee, 1972—; EPA grantee, 1974—; AEC grantee, 1950-74; ERDA grantee, 1974-77; Dept. Energy grantee, 1977—; Am. Water Works Assn. grantee, 1977-79. Fellow Chem. Soc.; mem. Am. Chem. Soc., AAAS, ASTM, Geochem. Soc., Am. Soc. Mass Spectroscopy (charter; v.p. 1972-74, pres. 1974-76), Sigma Xi, Alpha Sigma Nu, Phi Lambda Upsilon, Alpha Chi Sigma. Roman Catholic. Author lab. manual in phys. chemistry; contbr. numerous articles to profl. publs.; editor Internat. Jour. Mass Spectrometry and Ion Physics, 1968—. Home: 905 Douglas Ave Ames IA 50010 Office: 21 Gilman Hall Iowa State U Ames IA 50011. *Success in anything we choose to do requires a commitment. The degree of one's success depends directly on the kind of commitment that is made.*

SVEDA, MICHAEL, scientist, mgmt. and research cons.; b. W. Ashford, Conn., Feb. 3, 1912; s. Michael and Dorothy (Druppa) S.; B.S., U. Toledo, 1934; Ph.D. (Eli Lilly research fellow), U. Ill., 1939; m. Martha Augusta Gaeth, Aug. 23, 1936; children—Sally Anne, Michael Max. Tchr. chemistry U. Toledo, 1932-35, U. Ill., 1935-37; research, sales and product mgmt. positions E.I. du Pont de Nemours & Co., Inc., 1939-54; mgmt. counsel, Wilmington, Del., 1955-59; dir. acad. sci. projects NSF, 1960-61; corp. asso. dir. research FMC Corp., 1962-64; mgmt. and research counsel to academia, industry and govt., 1965—; lectr. univs., 1961—, fed. govt., groups, 1965—. Named Outstanding Alumnus, U. Toledo, 1954. Mem. Am. Chem. Soc., AAAS, Sigma Xi, Phi Kappa Phi, Alpha Chi Sigma, Phi Lambda Upsilon. Patentee chems. and processes in polymers, pesticides, chem. intermediates; synthesizer, discoverer cyclamates, sweetening agts., 1937; deviser new concepts and patentee 3 dimensional models complex orgns., selection key personnel; new approach to diets, taking off human fat; new use Boolean algebra, theory of sets in people problems; active drive to have cyclamate sweeteners reinstated, 1973—. Home: West Ln Revonah Woods Stamford CT 06905 Office: PO Box 3086 Stamford CT 06905. *Basic capacity for intelligence is given to us through inheritance. Knowledge—and stupidity—we acquire or develop. My objective has been to minimize my acquisition of, or contribution to, stupidity, while developing as much new knowledge as possible for mankind.*

SVENDSEN, LEROY WILLIAM, JR., air force officer; b. Chgo., Dec. 26, 1928; s. LeRoy William and Ella M. (Johansen) S.; B.S. in Indsl. Mgmt., Fla. State U., 1965; grad. U.S. Army War Coll., 1971; m. Doris I. Scott, Nov. 20, 1971; children—Randy, Lance, Kristi. Enlisted in U.S. Navy, 1944; commd., 1948; joined USAF, advanced through grades to maj. gen., 1977; fighter pilot 335th Fighter Squadron, Langley AFB, Va., 1949-50; served with 41st Fighter Squadron, Johnson Air Base, Japan, 1950; flight comdr. 8th Fighter-Bomber Squadron, Taegu Air Base, Korea, 1951; served with 166th Fighter-Interceptor Squadron, Lockbourne AFB, Ohio, 1951-52, 62d Fighter-Interceptor Squadron, O'Hare AFB, Ill., 1952-56; participant test program for F-102, USAF Flight Test Center, 1956; flight comdr. 323d Fighter-Interceptor Squadron, Truax Field, Wis., 1956-59; chief Fighter-Interceptor Br., Hdqrs. Fifth Air Force, Fuchu Air Sta., Japan, 1959-62; assigned to Eglin AFB, Fla., 1962-66, dir. ops. 1st Air Commando Wing, 1962-66; plans officer Warfare Div., Directorate of Plans, Hdqrs, U.S. Air Force, Pentagon, Washington, 1966-67; liaison officer for U.S. Ho. of Reps., Office Sec. Pentagon, 1967-70; assigned U.S. Army War Coll., 1970-71; dep. comdr. for ops. Laredo AFB, Tex., 1971, comdr. 38th Flying Tng. Wing, 1971-72; asst. dep. chief of staff for ops. Hdqrs Air Tng. Command, Randolph AFB, Tex., 1972-74; comdr. 29th Flying Tng. Wing, Craig AFB, Ala., 1974-75; def. attache to Egypt, Cairo, 1975-77; asst. dep. chief of staff Manpower and Personnel for Mil. Personnel, Hdqrs. USAF and comdr. Air Force Manpower and Personnel Center, Randolph AFB, Tex., 1977—. Decorated D.S.M., Legion of Merit, D.F.C., Bronze Star, Meritorious Service medal, Air medal with 9 oak leaf clusters, Air Force Commendation medal with oak leaf cluster; named to Air Commandos Hall of Fame, 1966. Flew Pima Paisano B-24, World War II aircraft, from India to U.S., 1968, Bendix Air Race, 1957. Home: 5 Military Plaza Randolph AFB TX 78148 Office: AFMPC/CC Randolph AFB TX 78148

SVENDSEN, LOUISE AVERILL (MRS. THORALF SVENDSEN), museum curator; b. Old Town, Me., Nov. 22, 1915; d. Albert Guy and Louise Norris (Pierce) Averill; B.A., Wellesley Coll., 1937; M.A., Yale, 1941, Ph.D., 1949; m. Thoralf Svendsen, July 3, 1950. Docent, Met. Mus. Art, N.Y.C.; lectr. dept. edn. Boston Mus. Fine Arts, 1941-42; instr. history of art Duke, 1943-45; instr., asst. prof. history of art Goucher Coll., 1945-50; asst. prof. history of art Am. U., Washington, 1950-51; lectr. Solomon R. Guggenheim Mus., N.Y.C., 1954—, asso. curator, 1962-66, curator, 1966-78, sr. curator, 1978—. Decorated knight 1st class Royal Norwegian Order St. Olav. Mem. Am. Assn. Museums. Home: 16 Park Ave New York NY 10016 Office: 1071 Fifth Ave New York NY 10028

SVENSON, BO, actor; b. Sweden, Feb. 13, 1941; s. Birger Ragnar and Lola Iris Viola (Johansson) S.; came to U.S., 1958; student U. Meiji, 1960-63, U. Calif., Los Angeles, 1970-74; m. Lise Hartmann-Berg, Dec. 30, 1966; children—Pia, Maja. Starring roles in motion pictures include: Maurie, 1974, The Great Waldo Pepper, 1974, Part II Walking Tall, 1975, Breaking Point, 1975, Special Delivery, 1976, Final Chapter Walking Tall, 1976, Our Man in Mecca, 1977; Son of the Sheik, 1978, Snow Beast, 1978, Gold of the Amazon, 1978, North Dallas Forty, 1979. Served with USMC, 1959-65. Former profl. hockey player, race car driver; holder 3d degree black belt in judo; Far East heavy weight div. judo champion, 1961. Office: Agency for Performing Arts 9000 Sunset Blvd Suite 315 Los Angeles CA 90069

SVETLOVA, MARINA, ballerina, choreographer, educator; b. Paris, France, May 3, 1922; d. Max and Tamara (Andreieff) Hartman; student Vera Trefilova, Paris, France, 1930-36, L. Egorova and M. Kschessinska, Paris, 1936-39, A. Vilzak, N.Y.C., 1940-57. Debut Paris Opera, 1932; baby ballerina original Ballet Russe de Monte Carlo, 1939-41; guest ballerina Ballet Theatre, 1942; prima ballerina Met. Opera 1943-50, N.Y.C. Opera, 1950-52; own concert group under mgmt. Columbia Artists Mgmt., 1944-58, Nat. Artists Corp., 1958-59; toured Far East, Middle East, Europe, S. Am., U.S.; guest ballerina London's Festival Ballet, Teatro dell Opera, Rome, Nat. Opera, Stockholm, Sweden, Suomi Opera, Helsinki, Finland, Het Nederland Ballet, Holland, Cork Irish Ballet, Paris Opera Comique, London Palladium, Teatro Colon, Buenos Aires, others; starred in Paganini, Les Sylphides, Bluebeard, Balustrade, Giselle, Pas de Quatre, Protee, Swan Lake, Graduation Ball; also various classical ballets; choreographer Dallas Civic Opera, 1964-67, Seattle Opera, Houston Opera, Kansas City Performing Arts Found., Ft. Worth Opera, 1967—; ballet dir. So. Vt. Art Center, 1959-64; dir. Svetlova Dance Center, Dorset, Vt., 1965—; prof. ballet dept. Ind. U., Bloomington, 1969—; choreographer The Fairy Queen, 1966, L'Histoire du Soldat, 1968; choreographer, dancer ballet sequences for Samson & Delilah, Aida, Traviata, Romeo and Juliet, Die Fleder-maus, Carmen, Faust, Rigoletto, Masked Ball, The Ballad of Baby Doe, Haensel & Gretel, others. Mem. Am. Guild Mus. Artists (bd.), Conf. on Ballet in Higher Edn., Nat. Soc. Arts and Letters. Contbr. articles to N.Y. Times, Dance mag., Opera News, others. Home: Dorset VT 05251 Office: 2100 Maxwell Ln Bloomington IN 47401 also 25 W 54th St New York NY 10019

SVIKHART, CLIFFORD MILES, banker; b. Chgo., July 23, 1926; s. Miles Leopold and Helen Agnes (Bynerd) S.; grad. Mercersburg Acad., 1943; B.A., Wesleyan U., Middletown, Conn., 1949; m. Winifred T. Steinthal, Sept. 13, 1958; children—Winifred, Elizabeth, Miles, John, Martin, Ann. With Arrow-Hart-Hegeman Electric Co., 1949-51, Time, Inc., 1951-52; with Irving Trust Co., N.Y.C., 1952—, asst. sec., 1957-59, asst. v.p., 1959-62, v.p., 1962-69, sr. v.p., 1969—. Served with AUS, World War II. Home: 1 S Cherry Ln Rumson NJ 07760 Office: 1 Wall St New York City NY 10015

SVIRIDOFF, MITCHELL, found. exec.; b. New Haven, Nov. 4, 1918; s. Solomon and Bella (Brochin) S.; m. Doris Gordon, Aug. 5, 1940; children—Karen, Michelle. Regional dir. New Eng. United Auto Workers, 1946-61; pres. AFL-CIO, Conn., 1946-61; spl. asst. Latin Am. AID program, 1961-62; exec. dir. Community Progress, Inc., New Haven, 1962-66; adminstr. Human Resources Adminstrn., City of N.Y., 1966-67; v.p. div. nat. affairs Ford Found., N.Y.C., 1967—. Pres., New Haven Bd. Edn., 1955-62; mem. Nat. Commn. on Employment and Unemployment Stats., 1978—. Office: 320 E 43d St New York NY 10017

SWABB, LAWRENCE EDWARD, JR., research and devel. co. exec.; b. Dayton, Ohio, Oct. 25, 1922; s. Lawrence Edward and Cora M. S.; B.S., U. Cin., 1948, M.S., 1949, Ph.D., 1951; m. Gertrude Louise Frazon, June 26, 1944; children—Edward A., Richard J., Eileen L. With Esso Research Labs., Humble Oil & Refining Co., Baton Rouge, 1951-66, asst. dir., 1958-63, dir. labs., 1964-66; mgr. new areas planning and coordination Esso Research and Engring. Co., Florham Park, N.J., 1966-67, coordinator personnel devel., 1967-68, v.p. petroleum research, 1968-74, v.p. synthetic fuels research, 1974-80, v.p. corp. services, 1980—; mem. fossil energy adv. com. Dept. Energy, 1976—; mem. NRC Com. on Chemistry of Coal Utilization. Served to 1st lt. U.S. Army, 1943-46. Mem. Am. Inst. Chem. Engrs., AAAS, Am. Petroleum Inst., Nat. Acad. Engring. Contbr. articles to profl. patentee petroleum processing. Home: 92 Addison Dr Short Hills NJ 07078 Office: 181 Park Ave Florham Park NJ 07932

SWACKHAMER, WILLIAM D., sec. state Nev. Mem. Nev. Assembly, 1946-71, speaker, majority leader, chmn. ways and means com., taxation com., chmn. Cow County Caucus, mem. Legis. Commn.; sec. state Nev., 1973—. Democrat. Office: Office Sec State State Capitol Carson City NV 89710*

SWADOS, ELIZABETH A., writer, composer, dir.; b. Buffalo, Feb. 5, 1951; d. Robert O. and Sylvia (Maisel) S.; B.A., Bennington Coll., 1972. Composer, mus. dir. Peter Brook, Paris, Africa, U.S., 1972-73; composer-in-residence La Mama Exptl. Theater Club, N.Y.C., 1977—; compositions include: Medea, 1972, Elektra, 1973, Conference of the Birds, 1973, Sylvia Plath Song Cycle, 1973, Trojan Women, 1974, Nightclub Cantata, 1977, Agamemnon, 1977, Runaways, 1978, Alice in Wonderland In Concert, 1978, Dispatches, 1979; composer CBS Camera 3 Shows, 1973-74, NBC film Too Far to Go, 1978, CBS films Ohms, Gauguin, 1979, PBS Short Story Series, 1978-79; author: Girl With The Incredible Feeling, 1976; mem. faculty Carnegie-Mellon U., 1974, Bard Coll., 1976-77, Sarah Lawrence Coll., 1976-77. Recipient Obie award Village Voice, 1972, 77, 78, Outer Critics Circle award, 1977. Creative Artists Service Program grantee, 1976; N.Y. State Arts Council playwriting grantee, 1977—; Guggenheim fellow. Mem. Broadcast Music Inc., Actors Equity. Jewish. Home: New York NY 10011

SWAIMAN, KENNETH FRED, pediatric neurologist, educator; b. St. Paul, Nov. 19, 1931; s. Lester J. and Shirley (Ryan) S.; B.A. magna cum laude, U. Minn., 1952, B.S., 1953, M.D., 1955, postgrad., 1956-58, (fellow pediatric neurology) Nat. Inst. Neurologic Deseases and Blindness, 1960-63; m. Sheila Hershfield, 1973; children by previous marriage—Lisa, Jerrold, Barbara, Dana. Intern, Mpls. Gen. Hosp., 1955-56; resident pediatrics U. Minn., 1956-58, neurology, 1960-63; asst. prof. pediatrics, neurology U. Minn. Med. Sch., Mpls., 1963-66, asso. prof., 1966-69, prof., dir. pediatric neurology, 1969—, exec. officer, dept. neurology, 1977—, mem. internship adv. council exec. faculty, 1966-70. Cons. pediatric neurology Hennepin County Gen. Hosp., Mpls., St. Paul-Ramsey Hosp., St. Paul Children's Hosp.

Chmn. Minn. Gov.'s Bd. for Handicapped, Exceptional and Gifted Children, 1972—; mem. human devel. study sect. NIH, 1976-79, guest worker NIH, 1978-79. Served to capt. M.C., U.S. Army, 1958-60. Diplomate Am. Bd. Psychiatry and Neurology, Am. Bd. Pediatrics. Fellow Am. Acad. Pediatrics, Am. Acad. Neurology (rep. to nat. council Nat. Soc. Med. Research); mem. Soc. Pediatric Research, Central Soc. Clin. Research, Central Soc. Neurol. Research, Internat. Soc. Neurochemistry, Am. Neurol. Assn., Minn. Neurol. Soc., AAAS, Midwest Pediatric Soc., Am. Soc. Neurochemistry, Child Neurology Soc. (1st pres. 1972-73), Internat. Assn. Child Neurologists (exec. com. 1975-79), Profs. of Child Neurology (pres. 1978—), Phi Beta Kappa, Sigma Xi. Author (with Francis S. Wright) Neuromuscular Diseases in Infancy and Childhood, 1969, Pediatric Neuromuscular Diseases, 1979; (with Stephen Ashwal) Pediatric Neurology Case Studies, 1978. Editor: (with John A. Anderson) Phenylketonuria and Allied Metabolic Diseases, 1966; (with Francis S. Wright) Practice Pediatric Neurology, 1975; mem. editorial bd. Annals of Neurology, 1977—, Neurology Update, 1977—, Pediatric Update, 1977—. Contbr. articles to sci. jours. Home: 420 Delaware St SE Minneapolis MN 55455 Office: U Minn Med Sch Dept Pediatric Neurology Minneapolis MN 55455

SWAIN, EDWARD PARSONS, JR., lawyer; b. Willimantic, Conn., Nov. 4, 1935; s. Edward Parsons and Olga Rachel (Haigis) S.; B.A., Williams Coll., 1957; postgrad. Harvard Law Sch., 1961-64; m. Sue Ellen Swain, Feb. 7, 1976; children—Kaersten Teal, Erik Parsons, Courtney Taryn, Alison Michelle. Admitted to Wash. bar, 1964; atty. Ferguson & Burdell, Seattle, 1964-65; asso. gen. counsel, asst. sec. Boise Cascade Corp. (Idaho), 1965-69, asst. sec., gen. counsel engring. and constrn. group, N.Y.C., 1970-71; pres. Athens Gen. Corp., Washington and Seattle, 1971-79, chmn., chief exec. officer Campbell Indsl. Supply Co., Seattle, 1971-79; chmn., chief exec. officer Airport Machinery Co., Inc., Anchorage, 1973-79; sec. Ebasco Services, Inc., Chem. Constrn. Corp., Walter Kidde Constructors; sec., dir. Miramichi Timber Resources, Ltd., N.B., Can., 1969-71; of counsel Ferguson & Burdell, 1975-79, partner, 1979—. Served to lt. USNR, 1957-60. Mem. Am., Wash. bar assns., Phi Beta Kappa. Office: 1700 Peoples Nat Bank Bldg Seattle WA 98171

SWAIN, FREDERICK MORRILL, JR., educator, geologist; b. Kansas City, Mo., Mar. 17, 1916; s. Frederick M. and Lurline (Hughes) S.; A.B., U. Kans., 1938, Ph.D., 1943; M.S., Pa. State U., 1939; m. Frances Blair, Oct. 1, 1938; children—Marshall W., Suzanne F., Annette F. Geologist, Phillips Petroleum Co., 1941-43; asst. prof. Sch. Mineral Industries, Pa. State U., 1943-46; mem. faculty U. Minn., Mpls., 1946—, prof. geology, 1956—, asso. chmn. dept., 1957-59; geologist U.S. Geol. Survey, Washington, 1944-51; research geologist U.S. Geol. Survey, St. Paul, 1962—; prof. geology U. Del., part time, 1970—. Recipient Erasmus Haworth award U. Kans., 1957. Fellow Geol. Soc. Am. (rep. Am. commn. stratigraphic nomenclature 1965-68, chmn. 1956 meeting), Paleontol. Soc. Am.; mem. Am. Assn. Petroleum Geologists (regional rep. 1959-61; pres's. award 1949), Soc. Econ. Paleontologists and Mineralogists (chmn. com. recent ostracoda 1963-67 research com. 1965-68), Soc. Econ. Geologists, Am. Soc. Limnology and Oceanography, Soc. Internat. Limnologiae, Sigma Xi. Author: Stratigraphy and Micropaleontology of Jurassic System, 1944-49, 79—; Organic Geochemistry of Lake Sediments, 1954-66; Carbohydrate Geochemistry, 1960—; Fossil and Recent Ostracoda, 1939—; Non-Marine Organic Geochemistry, 1970—; Geochemistry of Marsh Gases, 1971-75; Precambrian Volatiles, 1974-78; Geochemistry and Micropaleontology of Deep Sea Deposits, 1974—. Home: 1625 E River Terr Minneapolis MN 55414

SWAIN, HENRY HUNTINGTON, pharmacologist, educator; b. Champaign, Ill., July 11, 1923; s. Joseph Ward and Margaret (Hatfield) S.; A.B., U. Ill., 1943, B.S., 1949, M.S., 1951; M.D., 1951; m. Victoria Prodan, June 26, 1948; children—Carol Diana, David Neville. Intern, Cook County Hosp., Chgo., 1951-52; instr. pharmacology U. Cin., 1952-54; instr. U. Mich. Med. Sch., Ann Arbor, 1954-57, asst. prof., 1957-62, asso. prof., 1962-67, prof., 1967—, acting chmn. dept. pharmacology, 1971-74. Mem. research com. Mich. Heart Assn., 1963-73. Served to capt. AUS, 1943-46. Recipient Elizabeth C. Crosby award for outstanding teaching U. Mich. Med. Sch., 1960. Mem. Am. Soc. Pharmacology and Exptl. Therapeutics, Phi Beta Kappa, Alpha Chi Sigma, Phi Chi, Phi Kappa Phi. Conglist. Cardiovascular field editor Jour. Pharmacology and Exptl. Therapeutics, 1966-72. Home: 2338 Haisley Dr Ann Arbor MI 48103

SWAIN, JAMES OBED, ret. educator; b. Greenfield, Ind., Dec. 31, 1896; s. Ashbell Willard and Laetitia (Lambert) S.; A.B., Ind. U., 1921, A.M., 1923; Ph.D., U. Ill., 1932; postgrad. U. Madrid, summer 1933, U. Chile, 1951-52; m. Nancy Jane Cox, June 19, 1923; children—James Maurice, Juan Robert. Mem. faculty Mich. State Coll., 1931-37, asst. prof. modern fgn. langs. then prof. U. Tenn., Knoxville, 1937-64, chmn. dept., 1937-58; vis. prof. modern fgn. langs. U. Ky., 1964-66; vis. prof. Spanish, Appalachian State Tchrs. Coll., summer 1966; vis. prof. French, Maryville (Tenn.) Coll., 1966; vis. prof. Romance langs. Roanoke (Va.) Coll., 1967; vis. prof. Lee Coll., Cleveland, Tenn.; guest dir. summer langs. sch. Western Colo. Coll., 1937; guest lectr. Am. lit. U. Chile, summer 1952; guest lectr. U. Madrid, summer 1958. Served with C.E., U.S. Army, 1918-19. Mem. Modern Lang. Assn. Am. (sectional officer various times), Central So. States Modern Lang. Assn., South Atlantic Modern Lang. Assn. (pres. 1948-49), Am. Assn. Tchrs. Spanish (mem. exec. com. 1949-52), Am. Assn. Tchrs. French, Am. Assn. Tchrs. Italian, Instituto de Literatura Iberoamericana, Sigma Delta Pi (exec. sec. 1947-62, nat. hon. pres. 1979—). Methodist (deacon). Author: Rumbo a Mexico, 1942; Ruedo Antillano, 1946; joint author Funcción y Alcance de las Escuelas de Temporada, 1955; Juan Marin—Chilean, The Man and His Writings, 1971. Asso. editor Hispania, 1936-42; asst. bus. mgr. Modern Lang. Jour., 1938-51. Home: 414 Forest Park Blvd Knoxville TN 37919. *Having received inspiration and help from hundreds of the generations before mine, I feel that I must not miss any opportunity to pass on to following generations some small part of this inspiration and help.*

SWAIN, O.E., food co. exec.; b. 1917; married. Salesman Ozburn & Abstow Parts Co., 1937-39; with Kraftco Corp., 1939—, salesman Kraft Foods div., 1939-45, dist. sales mgr., 1945-49, product sales mgr., 1949-51, asst. to div. gen. mgr., 1951-55, asso. div. mgr., 1955-57, div. mgr., v.p., 1957, asso. gen. mgr. Kraft Foods Ltd. (Can.), 1957-58, pres., gen. mgr., dir. Kraft Foods Ltd., 1958-68, pres. Kraft Foods div., 1968—, corporate exec. v.p., 1968—, chmn. retail food group, 1976—, chmn. dairy group, 1979, also dir. Address: Kraft Inc Kraft Ct Glenview IL 60025

SWAIN, ROBERT, painter; b. Austin, Tex., Dec. 7, 1940; s. Robert O. and Beth (Brower) S.; B.A., Am.U., 1964; m. Annette Carol Leibel, Oct. 4, 1969. One-man shows: Thenan Gallery, N.Y.C., 1965, Fischbach Gallery, N.Y.C., 1968-69, Everson Art Museum, N.Y.C., 1974, Susan Galdwell Gallery, N.Y.C., 1974, 75, 78, Tex. Gallery, Houston, 1975, Columbus (Ohio) Gallery Fine Arts, 1976, Nina Freundenhein Gallery, Buffalo, 1978; group shows include: Mus. Modern Art, N.Y.C., 1968, Grand Palais, Paris, 1968, Kunsthaus, Zurich, Switzerland, 1969, Tate Gallery, London, 1969, Corcoran Gallery Art, Washington, 1969, Whitney Mus. Am. Art, N.Y.C., 1971, Albright-Knox Gallery, Buffalo, 1971, Mus. Modern Art Internat. Circulating Exhbn.-Latin Am., 1974-75; represented in permanent collections: Corcoran Gallery Art, Walker Art Center, Mpls., Va. Mus. Fine Arts, Richmond, Everson Art Mus., Columbus Gallery Fine Arts, Detroit Inst. Art, Albright-Knox Mus.; works include archtl. installations: Am. Republic Ins. Co., Des Moines, 1969, N.K. Winston Corp., N.Y.C., 1969, Schering Labs., Bloomfield, N.J., 1970, Skidmore, Owings and Merrill, N.Y.C., 1970, Kahn & Mallis Assos., N.Y.C., 1972, Harris Bank, Chgo., 1977, Powell/Kleinschmidt Chgo., 1977, Travenol Labs., Deerfield, Ill., 1977, Skidmore, Owings and Merrill, Chgo., 1977; asso. prof. fine arts Hunter Coll.; vis. artist to various schs., univs., including Bklyn. Mus. Art Sch., 1975, 77, 78, dept. architecture Harvard U. Grad. Sch. Design, 1977. John Simon Guggenheim Meml. Found. fellow, 1969; Nat Endowment for Arts grantee, 1976. Home and Office: 57 Leonard St 4th Floor New York NY 10013

SWALES, WILLIAM EDWARD, oil co. exec.; b. Parkersburg, W.Va., May 15, 1925; s. John Richard and Ellen (South) S.; B.A. in Geology, W.Va. U., 1949, M.S. in Geology, 1951; grad. advanced mgmt. program Stanford U., 1968; m. Lydia Eugena Mills, Dec. 26, 1948; children—Joseph V., Susan Eugena, David Lee. With Marathon Oil Co., 1954-70, 74—, mgr. Western Hemisphere and Australia div., Findlay, Ohio, 1967-70, spl. asst. to sr. v.p. prodn., internat., 1974, v.p. prodn., internat., 1974-77, sr. v.p. prodn., internat., 1977—, also dir.; exec. v.p. Oasis Oil Co. of Libya, Inc., Tripoli, 1970-72, pres., 1972-74. Served with USN, 1943-45. Mem. Am. Petroleum Inst., Am. Assn. Petroleum Geologists, Soc. Petroleum Engrs., Am. Geol. Inst. Office: 539 S Main St Findlay OH 45840

SWALIN, BENJAMIN FRANKLIN, orch. condr.; b. Mpls. Mar. 30, 1901; s. Benjamin N. and Augusta (Johnson) S.; B.S., Columbia, 1928, M.A., 1930; Ph.D., U. Vienna, 1932; diplomas Inst. of Mus. Art, N.Y.C., 1926, 28; fellow study in Europe, Inst. Internat. Edn., 1930-32; diplomas, Hochschule für Musik, Vienna, 1932; D.F.A. (hon.), U. N.C., 1971; D.H.L. (hon.), Duke U., 1979; m. Martha Maxine McMahon, Jan. 1, 1935. Violinist, Mpls. Symphony Orch. (now Minn. Orch.), 1919-21; prof. violin and theory DePauw U., Greencastle, Ind., 1933-35; asso. prof. music U. N.C., Chapel Hill, 1935-49; dir. N.C. Symphony Orch., Chapel Hill, 1939-72, now condr. emeritus. Recipient N.C. Achievement in Fine Arts award, 1966, Morrison award for achievement in the performing arts, 1968. Mem. Am. Musicol. Soc., MacDowell Colony, Delta Chi, Phi Mu Alpha Sinfonia. Clubs: Princeton; Torch (Durham, N.C.); Golden Fleece (U. N.C.). Author: The Violin Concerto; A Study in German Romanticism, 1941, 73. Contbr. articles to music assn. jours. and books: composer several orchestral works and compositions for violin and piano, and chamber music. Guest dir. in Guadalajara and Mexico City, Stavanger, Norway. Home: PO Box 448 Carrboro NC 27510. *Great music, like great art, can bring to us a world of beauty. Music is virtually the only international language that exists in the world today and as such it may become a factor for peace and understanding among people. We should also realize that the potentialities of a human being are immense; and talent constitutes the true wealth of a nation. All over the world, ears will be listening!*

SWALIN, RICHARD ARTHUR, co. exec.; b. Mpls., Mar. 18, 1929; s. Arthur and Mae (Hurley) S.; B.S. with distinction, U. Minn., 1951, Ph.D., 1954; m. Helen Marguerite Van Wagenen, June 28, 1952; children—Karen, Kent, Kristin. Research asso. Gen. Electric Co., 1954-56; mem. faculty U. Minn., Mpls., 1956, prof., head Sch. Mineral and Metall Engring. 1962-68, asso. dean Inst. Tech., 1968-71, dean, 1971-77, acting dir. Space Sci. Center, 1965; v.p. tech. Eltra Corp., N.Y.C., 1977—; guest scientist Max Planck Inst. für Phys. Chemie, Göttingen, Germany, 1963, Lawrence Radiation Lab., Livermore, Cal., 1967. Cons. to govt. and industry. Dir. Medtronic Corp., Buckbee-Mears Corp., Donaldson Co. Trustee Midwest Research Inst., Sci. Mus. Minn. Recipient Distinguished Teaching award Inst. Tech., U. Minn., 1967; NATO sr. fellow in sci., 1971. Mem. AAAS, Am. Phys. Soc., Fedn. Am. Scientists, Am. Soc. Metals, Am. Soc. Engring. Edn., Sigma Xi, Tau Beta Pi, Phi Delta Theta, Gamma Alpha. Author: Thermodynamics of Solids, 2d edit., 1972. Contbr. articles to profl. jours. Home: 264 Oak Ridge Ave Summit NJ 07901 Office: Eltra Corp Two Pennsylvania Plaza New York City NY 10001

SWALL, ROSS FORREST, hosp. adminstr.; b. Walla Walla, Wash., Feb. 3, 1918; s. Charles Edwin and Katie Ester (Maloney) S.; B.S., Oreg. State U., Corvallis, 1945; M.H.A., Baylor U., 1958; m. Zenaida, Dec. 28, 1972; children—Nancy Sue, Ross Forrest, David, Roxanna. Asst. to exec. dir. Assn. Mil. Surgeons U.S., Washington, 1964-65; adminstr. Pakistan Med. Research Center, Lahore, 1965-67; asst. adminstr. Providence Meml. Hosp., El Paso, Tex., 1967, asso. adminstr., 1970-75, adminstr., 1975-78, exec. v.p. bd., 1978—; adv. com. blood services, chmn. El Paso Hosp. Council, 1976-77. Served with M.S.C., U.S. Army, 1960-64. Decorated Purple Heart, Bronze Star. Mem. Am., Tex. hosp. assns., Am. Coll. Hosp. Adminstrs., El Paso C. of C. Clubs: El Paso Country, Masons. Home: 6719 Mariposa Dr El Paso TX 79912 Office: 2001 N Oregon St El Paso TX 79902

SWAMY, SRIKANTA M. N., elec. engr., univ. dean; b. Bangalore, India, Apr. 7, 1935; s. M.K. Nanjundiah and M.N. Mahalakshamma (Kashipathaiah) S.; B.Sc. with honours, Mysore U., 1954; diploma Indian Inst. Sci., Bangalore, 1957; M.Sc., U. Sask., 1960, Ph.D., 1963; m. Leela Sitaramiah, June 5, 1964; children—Saritha, Nikhilesh, Jagadish. Research asst. dept. elec. engring. U. Sask., Saskatoon, 1959-63, lectr. math., 1961-63; scientist Indian Inst. Tech., Madras, 1963-64; asst. prof. math. U. Sask., Regina, 1964-65; asst. prof. elec. engring. N.S. Tech. Coll., Halifax, 1965-66, asso. prof., 1966-67, prof., 1967-68; prof. U. Calgary (Alta.), 1969-70; prof. Concordia U., Montreal, Que., 1968-69, prof., chmn. dept. elec. engring., 1970-77, dean of engring., 1977—. Fellow Instn. Engrs. (India); mem. Am. Soc. Engring. Edn., IEEE (sr.), Math. Assn. Am., Am. Math. Soc., Eta Kappa Nu. Asso. editor Fibonacci Quar., Circuits and Systems, 1974; contbr. articles to profl. jours. Home: 275 Des Landes Saint Lambert PQ Canada Office: Dean of Engring Concordia U Montreal PQ Canada

SWAN, CLARA LINCOLN, coll. adminstr.; b. Princeton, Maine, Apr. 28, 1912; d. Andrew Coburn and Grace (Coffin) S.; tchr. tng. diploma Husson Coll., 1933; B.S., Am. Internat. Coll., 1939; M.Ed., U. Maine, 1951; Ped. D., Fort Lauderdale U., 1971. Tchr., Mexico (Maine) High Sch., 1933-35, Foxcroft (Maine) Acad., 1935-38; faculty Husson Coll., Bangor, Maine, 1939—, dir. summer session, 1941-69, dir. dept. secretarian sci., 1941-51, exec. dir., 1946-53, 3rd v.p., 1954-59, 1st v.p., 1959-68, v.p. academic affairs, 1968-72, v.p., asst. to pres., 1972-73; v.p., dir. Casco Bay Coll., Portland, Maine, 1973-75, pres., 1975—. Bd. dirs. Portland United Way, 1976-79. Recipient Sports Hall of Fame award Bangor Daily News, 1960. Mem. United Bus. Schs. Assn., AAUP, Nat. Judges Women's Basketball, Nat. Assn. Coll. and U. Summer Sessions (audit com. 1965-67), Eastern Bus. Tchrs. Assn. (state membership chmn. 1963-69), New Eng. Bus. Educators Assn. (1st v.p. 1965-66, pres. 1966-67), Bangor Execs. Club, Pi Rho Zeta (gov. gen. 1968—). Club: Altrusa (1st v.p. 1972-74, pres. 1974-76)(Bangor). Home: Mounted Route C Box 42B Bangor ME 04401 also 11 Depot Rd Falmouth ME 04105

SWAN, HENRY, II, physician; b. Denver, May 27, 1913; s. Henry and Carla (Denison) S.; grad. Phillips-Exeter, 1931; A.B. magna cum laude, Williams Coll., 1935, D.Sc., 1959; M.D. cum laude, Harvard, 1939; m. Mary Fletcher Wardwell, June 25, 1936; children—Edith, Henry III, Helen, Gretchen; m. 2d, Geraldine Fairchild, Mar. 21, 1964. Fellow pathology U. Colo. Med. Sch., Denver, 1939-40; Intern surgery Peter Bent Brigham-Children's Hosp., Boston 1940-42; surg. resident Children's Hosp. Boston, 1942-43; asst. surgery Harvard, 1942-43; asst., later asso. prof. surgery U. Colo. Med. Sch., 1946-50, prof., head dept., 1950-61, clin. prof., 1961—; also prof. surgery (research) Colo. State U., 1963—; courtesy staff St. Luke's Presbyn., Gen. Rose Meml. hosps; cons. staff Children's Hosp.; cons. surgery various hosps. Served to maj. M.C., AUS, 1943-45. Recipient Henry Ashbury Christian prize Harvard, 1939, Hektoen Gold Medal for original research AMA, 1955, Mark Allam Lectureship award, 1973. Diplomate Am. Bd. Surgery (dir. 1958-64). Fellow A.C.S. N.Y. Acad. Sci.; mem. Internat. Cardiovascular Soc., Internat. Soc. Surgery, AAAS, Soc. for Cryobiology, Am. Heart Assn., Halsted Soc., Am. Assn. Thoracic Surgery, Soc. Univ. Surgeons, Soc. Vascular Surgery, Soc. Clin. Surgery Am., Central, Western surg. assns., Am. Coll. Vet. Surgeons (hon.), Assn. Costarricense de Cirugia, Soc. Chilena de Angiologia, Soc. de Chirujanos de Chile, Surgery Assn. Chile and Costa Rica, Sociedad Mexicana de Pediatria, Phi Beta Kappa, Alpha Omega Alpha. Author: Thermoregulation and Bioenergetics: Patterns of Vertebrate Survival, 1974. Contbr. articles to profl. publs. Home: 6700 W Lakeridge Rd Lakewood CO 80227

SWAN, JAMES WESLEY, newspaper publisher; b. Des Moines, Nov. 29, 1934; s. Joyce Alonzo and Pauline (Snider) S.; A.B., Princeton, 1957; m. Esther Lavina Freyborg, Nov. 9, 1963; children—James Alan, Nancy Joyce. Computer programmer, systems analyst, salesman Honeywell Electronic Data Processing, Mpls., 1961-63; display salesman Mpls. Star and Tribune, 1963-65; asst. pub. Great Falls Tribune, 1965-68; v.p., pub. Rapid City Jour., 1968-74, pres., pub., 1974—. Bd. dirs. Salvation Army, West River Mental Health Center; pres. Rapid City United Fund; mem. Citizens Adv. Council on Future of S.D. Served to lt. (j.g.) Supply Corps, USNR, 1957-61. Mem. Great Falls (Mont.)-Rapid City C. of C. (dir. 1973-76). Office: 507 Main St Rapid City SD 57701

SWAN, KENNETH CARL, physician and surgeon; b. Kansas City, Mo., Jan. 1, 1912; s. Carl E. and Blanche (Peters) S.; A.B., U. Oreg., 1933, M.D., 1936; m. Virginia Grone, Feb. 5, 1938; children—Steven Carl, Kenneth, Susan. Intern, U. Wis., 1936-37; resident in ophthalmology State U. Iowa, 1937-40; practice medicine specializing in opthalmology, Portland, Ore., 1945—,; staff Good Samaritan; asst. prof. ophthalmology State U. Iowa, Ames, 1941-44; asso. prof. U. Oreg. Med. Sch., Eugene, 1944-45, prof. and head dept. ophthalmology, 1945—. Chmn. sensory diseases study sect., NIH; mem. adv. council Nat. Eye Inst., also adv. council Nat. Inst. Neurol. Diseases and Blindness. Recipient Proctor Research Medal, 1953; Distinguished Service award U. Oreg., 1963; Meritorious Achievement award U. Oreg. Med. Sch., 1968, Aubrey Watzek Pioneer award Lewis and Clark Coll., 1979; named Oreg. Scientist of Yr., Oreg. Mus. Sci. and Industry. Diplomate Am. Bd. Opthalmology (chmn. 1960-61). Mem. Assn. Research in Ophthalmology (trustee), Am. Acad. Ophthalmology (v.p. 1978), Soc. for Exptl. Biology and Medicine, AAAS, AMA, Am. Ophthal. Soc. (Howe medal for distinguished service 1977), Oreg. Med. Soc., Sigma Xi, Sigma Chi (Significant Sig award 1977). Contbr. articles on ophthalmic subjects to med. publs. Home: 4645 SW Fairview Blvd Portland OR 97221 Office: Univ Oregon Med Sch Portland OR 97201

SWAN, ROY CRAIG, anatomist; b. Bklyn., June 7, 1920; s. Roy Craig and Ruth (Paxton) S.; A.B., Cornell U., 1941, M.D., 1947; m. Marian Evalyn Morse, Mar. 26, 1949 (div. 1970); children—R. Craig, Kyle, Brian; m. 2d, Beatrice Gremaud, May 27, 1977; 1 dau., Chantal. Intern, then asst. resident medicine N.Y. Hosp., 1947-49, resident endocrinology and metabolism, 1949-50; research fellow medicine Harvard Med. Sch., 1950-52; asst. medicine Peter Bent Brigham Hosp., Boston, 1950-52; research asso. physiology Cambridge (Eng.) U., 1955-56; mem. faculty Cornell U. Med. Coll., N.Y.C., 1952—, prof. anatomy, chmn. dept., 1959-78, Hinsey prof. anatomy, 1966—, mem. univ. council, 1961-70; vis. prof. anatomy Boston U. Sch. Medicine, 1977-78; cons. USPHS, 1960-64, Office Sci. and Tech., 1964-65; cons. Health Research Council City N.Y., 1960—, mem., 1965—. Mem. Nat. Bd. Med. Examiners, 1971—, mem. exec. com. and dir., 1979—. Served to lt. (j.g.), Submarine Service, USNR, 1943-46; PTO. Markle scholar med. scis., 1954-59. Mem. Am. Physiol. Soc., Am. Soc. Clin. Research, Am. Assn. Anatomists, Assn. Anatomy Chairmen (sec.-treas. 1974-77), Am. Assn. Med. Colls. (council acad. socs. 1974—, adminstrv. bd. 1976-77), Alpha Omega Alpha. Contbr. articles to profl. jours. Mem. editorial bd. Physiol. Revs., 1964-70, Circulation Research, 1965-70; sect. editor Biol. Abstracts, 1970—. Home: Tweed Blvd Nyack NY 10960 Office: 1300 York Ave New York NY 10021

SWANBERG, RANDALL, lawyer; b. Washington, Nov. 13, 1909; s. Alfred V. and Clara E. (Moore) S.; student U. So. Calif., 1927-31; m. Helen I. Gorham, July 14, 1936; children—Gorham E., Chandler A. Admitted to Mont. bar, 1935, ICC bar, 1945; practice law, Great Falls, Mont., 1935—; mem. firm Swanberg, Koby, Swanberg & Matteucci, and predecessor firm, 1935—; dep. county atty., 1937-41; asst. U.S. atty., Mont., 1942-43. Dir. Rocky Mountain Fire & Casualty Co.; sec., dir. Rice Truck Lines; sec. Med. Arts Bldg. Co., 1963—. Dir. Nat. Council Crime and Delinquency, 1958-65; chmn. Mont. Council Correction, 1958-64. Mem. Great Falls Sch. Bd., 1944-56; mem. Mont. Constl. Conv. Commn., 1971-72. Trustee Mont. Deaconess Hosp., Mont. Hist. Soc. Member Am. Trial Lawyers Assn., Am. Mont., Cascade County (pres. 1951) bar assns., Mont. Sch. Bds. Assns. (pres. 1952), Am. Judicature Soc. Home: 207 3d Ave N Great Falls MT 59401 Office: Montana Bldg Great Falls MT 59401

SWANBERG, WILLIAM ANDREW, author; b. St. Paul, Nov. 23, 1907; s. Charles Henning and Valborg (Larsen) S.; B.A., U. Minn., 1930; postgrad. N.Y. U., 1944; m. Dorothy Upham Green, Mar. 21, 1936; children—John William, Sara Valborg, Editor, Dell pub. Co., N.Y.C., 1935-44; field rep. OWI, Europe, 1944-45; free lance writer, 1945—. Mem. Newtown Library Bd. Recipient Christopher award, 1959, Frank Luther Mott Research prize, 1962, Van Wyck Brooks award for non-fiction, 1968. Guggenheim fellow, 1960. Fellow Soc. Am Historians; mem. Authors League Am., Internat. P.E.N. Author: Sickles the Incredible, 1956; First Blood-The Story of Fort Sumter, 1957; Jim Fisk, 1959; Citizen Hearst, 1961; Dreiser, 1965; Pulitzer, 1967; The Rector and The Rogue, 1968; Luce and His Empire, (Pulitzer prize for biography 1973), 1972; Norman Thomas: The Last Idealist (Nat. Book award for biography 1977), 1976. Office: care Dir Pub Relations Charles Scribner's Sons 597 Fifth Ave New York City NY 10017. *I am concerned at the failure of a large part of the public to study politics and to vote in this nuclear era when wise government may make the difference between existence and annihilation. And wise government means earnest negotiation, not necessarily more bombs.*

SWANEY, HUGH FRANTZ, book mfg. co. exec.; b. Meadville, Pa., Mar. 1, 1925; s. Hugh Frantz and Evadine Belle (Joyce) S.; B.S., U. Cal., Berkeley, 1946; postgrad. Cornell U., 1964; m. Natalie Ida Jones,

Mar. 10, 1948; 1 dau., Michele Elaine. With U.S. Gypsum Co., 1946-71, prodn. mgr. S.W., 1959-66, mfg. mgr. South, 1966-69, pres., gen. mgr. Mexico operations, 1969-71; pres., chief exec. officer Kingsport Press, Inc. (Tenn.), 1971—; v.p., group exec. Arcata Nat. Corp., 1973—; pres. Fairfield Graphics Inc. (Pa.), 1976—; bd. dirs. Book Mfg. Inst., Stamford, Conn.; dir., exec. com. 1st Nat. Bank of Sullivan County. Bd. dirs. Tenn. Council Econ. Edn., Holston Valley Community Hosp., Tenn. Taxpayers Assn., Jr. Achievement, Kingsport; past mem. devel. council U. Tenn. Served with USNR, 1943-46. Mem. Tau Beta Pi. Clubs: Ridgefields Country (Kingsport); Hounds Ears (N.C.); Elks, Eagles. Office: 1201 Eastman Rd Kingsport TN 37660

SWANEY, RUSSEL ALGER, assn. exec.; b. Detroit, June 24, 1907; s. Clark Albert and Mae Eva (Perkins) S.; student Grand Rapids (Mich.) Jr. Coll.; student banking U. Wis. financial pub. relations Northwestern U.; m. Marian Theresa Chinnick, Sept. 11, 1930; children—Shirley Anne (Mrs. Gene P. Eyler), Russel Perkins, Sandra Lou (Mrs. Courtney A. Lecklider), William Chinnick, Richard George. Security salesman Chase Securities Corp., Chgo., 1929-30; investment banker, Grand Rapids, Mich., 1931-40; asst. to pres. and dir. Vento Steel Products Co., Muskegon, Mich., 1941-42; dep. mgr. war finance div. U.S. Treasury, Detroit, 1943-45; Mich. rep. Fed. Res. Bank of Chgo. 1945-48, asst. cashier, 1948-52, asst. v.p., 1952-53, v.p. charge Detroit br., 1953-68, sr. v.p. in charge, 1968-69; treas., dir. Econ. Club Detroit 1953-67, sr. v.p., dir., 1968-69, pres., dir., 1969—, leader 6 study tours meeting with bus. and govt. leaders in 40 countries; dir. No. States Bancorp., Detroit, Market Opinion Research Inc. Bd. dirs., United Found. Detroit; gen. chmn. Mich. Week. 1956; chmn. study com. Birmingham (Mich.) Sch. System, 1970; past pres. bd. dirs. YMCA Met. Detroit, trustee Children's Hosp. Mich., Mich. Blue Cross-Blue Shield; bd. dirs. Overseas Adv. Inc., Detroit. Mem. Fin. Analysts Soc., Newcomen Soc. N.Am., Alpha Kappa Psi. Episcopalian. Rotarian Clubs: Holland Country, Macatawa Bay Yacht (Holland, Mich.); Circumnavigators, Detroit Athletic, Detroit, Renaissance, Bankers (pres. 1956-57, Detroit). Home: 753 S Shore Dr Holland MI 49423 Office: 920 Free Press Bldg Detroit MI 48226

SWANK, BEN R., lawyer; b. Mo., Feb. 21, 1910; LL.B., U. Mo.; m. Helen Slagle; children—Allen Noel, Ben Reid, Ruth Ann (Mrs. Balmer), Helen May (Mrs. Kilker). With Gen. Am. Life Ins. Co., St. Louis, 1935-75, v.p., gen. counsel, to 1975; of counsel Slagel and Bernard, Attys., Kansas City, Mo., 1975—. Mem. Am., Mo. St. Louis bar assns., Life Ins. Counsel, Lawyers Assn. Kansas City. Home: 9408 Outlook Dr Overland Park KS 66207 Office: Suite 500 127 10th St Kansas City MO

SWANK, EMORY COBLENTZ, assn. exec.; b. Frederick, Md., Jan 29, 1922; s. George Phillip and Mary Ruth (Coblentz) S.; A.B., Franklin and Marshall Coll., 1942; A.M., Harvard, 1943; m. Margaret Katherine Whiting, May 12, 1949. With U.S. Dept. State, 1946-75, vice consul, Shanghai, China, 1946-48, Tsingtao, China, 1948-49, 2d sec. Am. embassy, consul, Djakarta, Indonesia, 1950-51, Moscow, U.S.S.R., 1953-55, polit. analyst, fgn. service officer, Washington, 1956-57, conselor of legation, Bucharest, 1958-60, spl. asst. to sec. of state, 1961-63, assigned Nat. War Coll., Ft. L.J. McNair, Washington, 1963-64, counselor of embassy, dep. chief of mission Am. embassy, Vientiane, Laos, 1964-67, minister Am. embassy, Moscow, USSR, 1967-67, dep. asst. sec. state for European affairs, 1969-70; ambassador to Cambodia, 1970-73; polit. adviser to CINC, Atlantic, and Supreme Allied Comdr., NATO Atlantic Forces, 1973-75; pres., chief exec. officer Cleve. Council on World Affairs, 1977—. Served with AUS, 1943-46. Decorated Bronze Star medal; recipient Superior Honor award Dept. of State, 1973; Alumni Citation award Franklin and Marshall Coll., 1973. Mem. Phi Beta Kappa. Address: One Bratenahl Pl Suite 809 Lake Shore Blvd Cleveland OH 44108

SWANK, RAYNARD COE, educator; b. Butler, Ohio, Dec. 20, 1912; s. Harry Melvin and Cora Lucretia (Wigton) S.; A.B., Coll. Wooster, 1934; B.L.S., Western Res. U., 1937; Ph.D. U. Chgo., 1944; m. Ethel Louise Mershon, June 7, 1938 (div. June 1968); children—Damon, Barry, Martin, Diana; m. 2d, Portia Hawley Griswold, July 20, 1970 (div. Oct. 1977). Mem. staff U. Colo. Library, 1937-41; chief catalog librarian and asst. prof. library sci. U. Minn., Mpls., 1944-46; librarian U. Oreg., 1946-48; dir. univ. libraries Stanford, 1948-62; dean, prof. Sch. Librarianship, U. Calif. at Berkeley, 1962-71, prof., 1971—; vis. prof., 1953-54, 57; acting dir. U. Calif. Library Research Inst., 1964-66; library cons. U. Philippines, 1954, 63, 64, 66, U. Singapore, 1963, 64, U. Malayia, 1963, 64, Chinese U. Hong Kong, 1964, Asian Inst. Econ. Devel. and Planning, Bangkok, 1966; dir. internat. relations office ALA, 1959-61. Mem. Assn. Am. Library Schs., ALA (chmn. internat. relations com. 1961-64), Spl. Libraries Assn., Assn. Coll. and Research Libraries, Calif. Library Assn., Am. Soc. for Information Sci. Club: Roxburghe (San Francisco). Author: Soviet Libraries and Librarianship, 1963; also articles and library surveys. Home: 206 Park Lane Richmond CA 94803

SWANK, RICHARD BRUCE, publisher; b. Ames, Iowa, Apr. 20, 1931; s. Frederick Charles and Florence Ovanda (Batman) S.; student Johns Hopkins U., 1949-50; B.A., Iowa U., 1953; m. Jean Florence Goodspeed, Dec. 30, 1955; children—Scott, Mark, Andrew, Steven. Various exec. positions Reuben H. Donnelly Corp., N.Y.C., 1963-70, v.p. staff, 1970-72, v.p., Phila., 1975-78, exec. v.p., N.Y.C., 1978—; v.p., chmn. R.H. Donnelley Internat., Ltd., London, 1972-75; dir. Reuben Donnelley Ltd., London, Thomson Yellow Pages, Ltd., Farnborough, Eng. Served as lt. AUS, 1953-55. Mem. Am. Mgmt. Assn., Dirs. Inst. (London), Delta Epsilon. Episcopalian. Clubs: Univ. (N.Y.C.); Phila. Country; Apawamis Country; Manursing Island. Office: 825 3d Ave New York NY 10022

SWANK, ROY LAVER, educator, physician, inventor; b. Camas, Wash., Mar. 5, 1909; s. Wilmer and Hannah Jane (Laver) S.; student U. Wash., 1926-30; M.D., Northwestern U., 1935. Ph.D., 1935; m. Eulalia F. Shively, Sept. 14, 1936; children—Robert L., Susan Jane (Mrs. Joel Keizer), Stephen (dec.). Research in neuroanatomy, 1930-35; investigation vitamin deficiencies, 1936-41; investigation multiple sclerosis, 1948—, platelet-leukocyte aggregation in stored blood and in hypotensive shock; low-fat diet in multiple sclerosis; inventor, developer 1st microemboli filter; prof. neurology Oreg. Med. Sch. 1954-74, prof. emeritus, 1974—, also former head div. neurology; pres. Pioneer Filters. Served to maj. M.C., AUS, 1942-46; Recipient Oreg. Gov.'s award for research in multiple sclerosis, 1966. Mem. Am. Physiol. Soc., Am. Neurol. Assn., Western Soc. Clin. Investigation, European Microcirculation Soc., Sigma Xi. Research of phys. chem. changes in blood after fat meals and during surg. shock. Home: 2211 SW 1st Ave Apt 1105 Portland OR 97201

SWANKE, ALBERT HOMER, architect; b. Thomasville, Ga., Nov. 22, 1909; s. John Christian and Stella (Williams) S.; B.S., Ga. Inst. Tech., 1930; student Beaux Arts Inst. Design, N.Y.C., 1931; m. Margaret Anne Twaddell, Aug. 11, 1936 (dec. 1968); 1 son, Albert Homer; m. 2d, Dorothy Pratt Williams, Feb. 7, 1969. Trainee, Flagg, Embury and Ballard, N.Y.C., 1931-35; architect N.Y. State Ins. Dept., 1936-42, Alfred Easton Poor, 1946; asso. Walker & Poor, Architects, 1947-52; partner Office of Alfred Easton Poor-Architects/Engrs., N.Y.C., 1952-71; partner Poor and Swanke & Partners, N.Y.C., 1972-75; mng. partner Poor, Swanke, Hayden & Connell, Architects, 1975-79; sr. partner Swanke, Hayden, Connell & Partners, 1979—; dir. 565 Park Avenue Corp.; works include extension of East Front of U.S. Capitol, James Madison Meml. Library of Congress Bldg., also restoration Supreme Ct. and Senate Chambers, Washington; Fed. Office Bldg. and Customs Ct., N.Y.C., Home Ins. Co., N.Y.C.; Grumman Aircraft Engring. Plant and facilities, Calverton, L.I., N.Y.; NATO Airbases at Dreux and Evreux, France; Queens County (N.Y.) Courthouse and Prison; addition to Chgo. Bd. of Trade Bldg.; also numerous banking facilities in U.S.; chmn. archtl. rev. bd. Historic Savannah Found.; mem. Village of Larchmont Archtl. Bd. Review, 1963-69, chmn., 1968-69; trustee Larchmont Manor Park Soc., 1962-69, Architects Emergency Com., 1969-76; mem. bd. design Extension of Capitol Project, Washington, 1956-79; alt. mem. coordinating bd. Additional House Office Bldg. Project, Capitol Hill, 1955-60; alt. mem. archtl. adv. bd. Johns Hopkins U., 1961-70. Trustee, exec. com. N.Y. Med. Coll., Flower and 5th Ave. Hosps., 1963-79, Westchester Med. Center Devel. Bd., 1969-73; bd. mgrs., v.p. Am. Soc. Prevention Cruelty to Animals, 1976-79. Served as lt. comdr. USNR, 1943-45. Registered architect, N.Y., Ala., Ariz., Colo., Conn., Del., D.C., Fla., Ga., Idaho, Ill., Ind., Iowa, Kans., Ky., La., Md., Mass., Mich., Minn., Miss., Mo., Mont., N.J., N.Mex., N.C., N.D., Ohio, Pa., R.I., S.C., Tenn., Tex., Utah, Va., W.Va., Wis., Wyo.; registered profl. planner, N.J. Fellow AIA, Am. Soc. Registered Architects; mem. NAD, (asso.), N.Y. Soc. Architects, N.Y. Bldg Congress, Soc. Archtl. Historians, Navy League U.S., English-Speaking Union, Phi Sigma Kappa, Pi Delta Epsilon. Republican, Presbyn. Clubs: Century Assn., University (N.Y.C.); Chatham, Oglethorpe, Savannah Yacht (Savannah, Ga.); Boston (New Orleans); Capitol Hill, Met. (Washington). Home: 416 E Charlton St Savannah GA 31401 also 565 Park Ave New York NY 10021 Office: 400 Park Ave New York NY 10022 also 1333 New Hampshire Ave NW Washington DC 20036 also 2 Illinois Center Chicago IL 60601

SWANKIN, DAVID ARNOLD, lawyer, consumer rep.; b. Boston, Jan. 18, 1934; s. Max and Anne (Rotefsky) S.; A.B., Brandeis U., 1954; M.S., U. Wis., 1957; J.D., George Washington U., 1962; 1 dau., Sheryl. Mgmt. intern U.S. Dept. Labor, Washington, 1957-60, spl. asst. to asst. sec. labor, 1961-63, dep. asst. sec. labor, 1967, dir. Bur. Labor Standards, 1967-68; exec. sec. Pres.'s Consumer Adv. Council, Washington, 1964; exec. dir. Pres's Com. on Consumer Interests, Washington, 1965-66; Washington rep. Consumer's Union, 1969-71; exec. dir. Consumer Interests Found., 1971-73; sr. partner Swankin & Turner, 1973—; cons. U.S. Dept. Labor. Mem. Pres.'s Council, Brandeis U., 1968-69. Served with AUS. 1954-56. Recipient Jump award U.S. Govt., 1969. Mem. Am. Bar Assn., Ombudsman Com. Home: 300 N Cherry St Falls Church VA 22046 Office: Cafritz Bldg 1625 Eye St NW Washington DC 20006

SWANN, FREDERICK LEWIS, organist, choral dir.; b. Lewisburg, W.Va., July 30, 1931; s. Theodore Magruder and Mary Fields (Davis) S.; Mus.B., Northwestern U., 1952; M.Sacred Music, Union Theol. Sem., 1954. Dir. music, organist Riverside Ch., N.Y.C., 1958—; chmn. organ dept. Manhattan Sch. Music, 1972—; cons. on organ design; organ recitalist throughout U.S., Can. and Europe. Served with U.S. Army, 1956-58. Recipient award French Nat. Acad. Arts and Scis. for promotion French organ music, 1972, Merit award Northwestern U. Alumni, 1970. Mem. Am. Guild Organists (award for promotion Am. choral and organ music), Hymn Soc. Am., Phi Beta Kappa, Phi Kappa Lambda. Episcopalian. Clubs: St. Wilfrid, Bohemian (N.Y.C.). Contbr. articles to profl. jours. Home: 1 Horizon Rd Fort Lee NJ 07024 Office: 490 Riverside Dr New York City NY 10027

SWANN, LYNN CURTIS, profl. football player; b. Alcoa, Tenn., Mar. 7, 1952; s. Willie and Mildred (McGarity) S.; B.A., U. So. Calif., 1974. Wide receiver Pitts. Steelers Profl. Football Team, 1974—. Named All Pro, 1977, 78, Most Valuable Player in Super Boxl X, 1975. Mem. Screen Actors Guild, AFTRA. Address: 300 Stadium Circle Pittsburgh PA 15212*

SWANSON, A. HERBERT, publishing co. exec.; b. Chgo., Feb. 21, 1926; s. Otto W. and Ellen M. (Nelson) S.; B.S., U. Ill., 1949; m. Lucille M. Rozek, June 13, 1953; children—Glen, Karen. Audit mgr. Arthur Andersen & Co., C.P.A.'s, Milw., 1949-50, 51-62; v.p. fin. Consol. Foundries & Mfg. Co., Chgo., 1962-70, Scott, Foresman & Co., Chgo., 1970—. Served with USAAF, 1944-46, USAF, 1950-51. C.P.A., Wis. Mem. Am. Inst. C.P.A.'s, Fin. Execs. Inst. Home: 985 Grove St Winnetka IL 60093 Office: 1900 E Lake St Glenview IL 60025

SWANSON, ALFRED BERTIL, orthopaedic surgeon; b. Kenosha, Wis., Apr. 16, 1923; s. O.P. and Esther (Person) S.; B.S., U. Ill., 1944, M.D., 1947; children—Karin Louise, Miles Raymond; m. 2d, Genevieve deGroot, Dec. 27, 1969; 1 son, Eric Alfred. Intern, St. Luke's Hosp., Chgo., 1947; spl. tng. orthopaedic surgery Ill. Crippled Children's Hosp. Sch., Chgo., 1948, St. Luke's Hosp., 1949, Northwestern U. Med. Sch., 1950, Ind. U. Med. Center, 1951; practice medicine specializing in orthopaedic surgery, Grand Rapids, Mich., 1954—; chief orthopaedic and hand surgery tng. program Blodgett and Butterworth hosps. and research dir. Blodgett Meml. Hosp., 1958—; chief of staff Mary Free Bed Children's Hosp. and Orthopaedic Center, Juvenile Amputee Clinic; clin. prof. surgery Mich. State U., Lansing; nat. and internat. lectr. in field. Served with USNR, 1944-45; served to capt. M.C., AUS, 1952-54. Diplomate Am. Bd. Orthopaedic Surgery. Decorated medal of Honor (S. Vietnam), 1967; recipient Profl. Medicine award Mich. Internat. Council, 1977. Fellow A.C.S.; mem. Am. Med. Writers Assn., AMA (Disting. Service award 1966, 69), Am. Acad. Orthopaedic Surgeons, Pan Am. Med. Assn., Assn. Mil. Surgeons, Am. Acad. Cerebral Palsy, Brit. Club Surgery of Hand, Italian Soc. Surgery of Hand, Caribbean Hand Soc., Internat. Fedn. Socs. Surgery Hand (sec.-gen. 1978—), Groupe d'Etude de la Main, Am. Soc. Surgery Hand (pres. 1979-80), Am., Clin., Mich., Lamplighter's orthopaedic socs., Turkish Assn. Orthopaedic Surgery and Traumatology, Mich. Med. Soc. (Disting. Service award 1966, Nat. Pres.'s award 1979), Internat. Soc. Orthopaedics and Traumatology, Assn. Orthopaedic Chairmen, Rheumatoid Arthritis Surg. Soc., S.African Hand Soc., Fla. Orthopaedic Soc., Orthopaedic Letters Club, Brazilian, Latin Am., Chilean, Argentinian socs. orthopaedic surgery and traumatology, Internat. Soc. Rehab. Disabled, Airplane Owners and Pilots Assn., Mid Mich. Soaring Soc. Conglist. (past bd. trustees). Rotarian. Club: Blythefield Country (Grand Rapids). Author: Implant Resection Arthroplasty in the Hand and Extremities, 1973. Contbr. numerous articles in field; producer teaching films. Inventor implants for replacement arthritic joints. Home: 2945 Bonnell St SE Grand Rapids MI 49506 Office: Blodget Profl Bldg 1900 E Wealthy St Grand Rapids MI 49506

SWANSON, ALVIN DE VERN, elec. engr.; b. Stromsburg, Neb., June 20, 1922; s. Alvin Gothard and Esther Mabel (Cedarberg) S.; student U. Colo., 1943-44; S. in Elec. Engring., U. N.Mex., 1946; m. Bonna Vea Brion, Oct. 21, 1945; children—Lynette Eileen, Brion Lee. Design and test engr. Gen. Electric Co., Ft. Wayne, Ind., 1946-47; design engr. W. D. Pratt, Cons. Engr., Denver, 1947-48; design, constr. engr. Pearson Electric Co., Denver, 1948-49; prin. A. D. Swanson, Elec. Engr., Denver, 1949-52; cons. engr., pres., dir. Swanson-Rink & Assos., Denver, 1952—; mem. exec. com., dir. Winter Park Recreational Assn.; dir., chmn. bd. TERCo. Mem. U. Colo. Devel. Council, 1965-75, chmn., 1973-75; mem. rep. and long range plan com. Denver Area Council Churches; elder ch. St. James Presbyn. Ch., Englewood, Colo. Served with USNR, 1942-46. Recipient Alumni Recognition award U. Colo., 1974, Distinguished Engring. Alumnus award, 1975. Fellow Am. Cons. Engrs. Council; mem. Cons. Engrs. Council Colo. (charter; Service award 1960), Colo. Engring. Council (certificate of honor 1976), Rocky Mountain Elec. League (Elec. Industry Relations award), Illuminating Engring. Soc., Nat. Soc. Profl. Engrs., Profl. Engrs. Colo. (Outstanding Engr. award 1967), Cons. Mech., Elec. Engrs. Colo. Club: Lakewood Country. Home: 4700 S Downing St Englewood CO 80110 Office: 1640 Boulder St Denver CO 80211. *I have learned and believe that a right relationship with God and people; as set forth in the bible, is the foundation for my personal, social and professional principles.*

SWANSON, AUGUST GEORGE, physician, assn. exec.; b. Kearney, Nebr., Aug. 25, 1925; s. Oscar Valderman and Elnora Wilhelmina Emma (Block) S.; B.A., Westminster Coll., Fulton, Mo., 1951; M.D., Harvard, 1949; m. Ellyn Constance Weinel, June 28, 1947; children—Eric, Rebecca, Margaret, Emilie, Jennifer, August. Intern, King County Hosp., Seattle, 1949-50; resident internal medicine U. Wash. Affiliated Hosp., 1953-55, neurology, 1955-57; resident neurology Boston City Hosp., 1958; dir. pediatric neurology, then dir. div. neurology U. Wash. Med. Sch., Seattle, 1958-67, asso. dean acad. affairs, 1967-71; dir. dept. acad. affairs Assn. Am. Med. Colls., Washington, 1971—; vis. fellow physiology Oxford (Eng.) U., 1963-64. Cons. in field. Served with USNR, 1943-46, 50-53. Markle scholar medicine, 1959-64. Mem. Inst. Medicine, Nat., N.Y. acads. scis., Am. Neurol. Assn., Western Soc. Clin. Research, Am. Acad. Neurology. Author articles brain function, physician edn., med. manpower. Home: 4841 Tilden St NW Washington DC 20016 Office: 1 Dupont Circle NW Washington DC 20036

SWANSON, BERNET STEVEN, educator; b. Chgo., Nov. 20, 1921; s. Bernet Stephanie and Emma (Conrad) S.; B.S., Armour Inst. Tech., 1942; M.S., Ill. Inst. Tech., 1944, Ph.D., 1950; m. Lucile A. Clapham, June 12, 1948; children—Brian Bernet, David Herbert. Mem. faculty Ill. Inst. Tech., Chgo., 1950—, prof. chem. engring., 1960—, head dept., 1967—; cons. engr., 1944—. Mem. Am. Inst. Chem. Engrs., Instrument Soc. Am., Am. Soc. Engring. Edn., Sigma Xi, Alpha Chi Sigma, Phi Lambda Upsilon. Author: Electronic Analog Computer, 1965. Home: 2N151 Swift Rd Lombard IL 60148 Office: 3300 S Federal St Chicago IL 60616

SWANSON, BERT ELMER, educator; b. Tacoma, Wash., Aug. 15, 1924; s. Lars M. and Enis (Ronman) S.; B.A., George Washington U., 1951; M.A., U. Ore., 1956, Ph.D., 1959; m. Jean Mills, Jan. 28, 1950; m. 2d, Edith Pinkus, Nov. 4, 1969. Instr. polit. sci. U. Oreg., 1958-59, Hunter Coll., N.Y.C., 1959-61; vis. prof. Pratt Inst., 1961-64, Bklyn. Coll. 1964-65, N.Y. U., 1965-66; prof. polit. sociology Sarah Lawrence Coll., Bronxville, N.Y., 1961-71, chmn. social sci. faculty, 1963-64, dir. Inst. Community Studies, 1965-69; co-dir. Consortium on Community Crises, Cornell U., Ithica, N.Y., 1969-71; prof. polit. sci. and urban studies U. Fla., Gainesville, 1971—; sr. cons. Inst. Man and Sci., 1973—. Research cons. N.Y. State Commn. Govt. Ops. of N.Y.C., 1959-60, Inst. Pub. Adminstrn., 1960-61, Office City Adminstr. of N.Y.C., 1963-64, Nat. Commn. Community Health Services, 1963-66, Office of Mayor N.Y.C., 1967; exec. dir. adv. com. decentralization Bd. Edn., N.Y.C., 1967-68. Asst. to U.S. Senator Richard L. Neuberger, 1955-57. Mem. Am. Polit. Sci. Assn. (Woodrow Wilson Book award 1965), Am., Sociol. Soc., Soc. Gen. Systems Research, Pi Sigma Alpha. Author: The Rulers and the Ruled, 1964; The Struggle for Equality, 1966; Black-Jewish Relation in New York City, 1970; The Concern for Community, 1970; (with wife) Small Towns and Smalltowners in America, 1979, Discovering the Community, 1977; editor: Current Trends in Comparative Community Studies, 1962. Home: 1419 NW 48th Terr Gainesville FL 32601

SWANSON, CARL PONTIUS, botanist; b. Rockport, Mass., June 24, 1911; s. Richard and Anna Pauline (Nordstrand) S.; B.S. U. Mass., 1937, Sc.D. (hon.), 1957; A.M. (Thayer fellow), Harvard, 1939, Ph.D., 1941; m. Dorothy Jane Noggle, June 14, 1941; children—Michael Warren, Ann. Asst. prof. botany, Mich. State Coll., 1941-43; asso. biologist NIH, Bethesda, Md., 1946; asso. prof. botany Johns Hopkins, 1946-48, prof. botany, 1948-56, William D. Gill prof. biology, 1957-71, vice chmn. faculty of philosophy, 1960-65, asso. dean undergrad. studies, 1966-71; prof. botany U. Mass., Amherst, 1971-75, Ray Ethan Torrey Prof. botany, 1976—, asso. dir. Inst. for Man and Environment, 1971-75; AEC research Oak Ridge Nat. Lab., 1952-53. Exec. com. mem. NRC Div. Biology and Agr., 1958-62; mem. genetic biol. panel NSF, 1960-63; chmn. NRC Council Com. Photobiology, 1961-65; mem. cell biology panel NIH, 1962-66; pres. Internat. Com. on Photobiology, 1964-68. Mem. sci. adv. council Wesleyan U., 1964-65. Served to USNR, 1943-46 Austin fellow, 1940, Sheldon Traveling fellow, 1941. Guggenheim fellow, 1953-54. Fellow Am. Acad. Arts and Scis.; mem. Am. Inst. Biol. scis. (exec. com., mem. bd. govs. 1957-65), Genetics Soc. Am., AAAS, Phi Beta Kappa, Sigma Xi, Phi Kappa Phi. Asst. editor Quar. Rev. Biology, 1950-57, asso. editor 1958. Co-editor biol. series Prentice-Hall, Inc., 1958-78. Home: 77 Morgan Circle Amherst MA 01002

SWANSON, CARROLL ARTHUR, educator, botanist; b. Burlington, Iowa, Sept. 6, 1915; s. Frank Arthur and Fidelia (Holmen) S.; A.B., Augustana Coll., 1937; M.Sc., Ohio State U., 1938, Ph.D., 1942; m. Betty Marker, June 15, 1941; children—Richard Marker, Nancy Joan. Mem. faculty Ohio State U., 1940—, prof. botany, 1956—, chmn. dept., 1967-68, chmn. faculty organismic and developmental biology, 1968-69, asso. dean Coll. Biol. Scis., 1969-70; research asso. Manhattan Project, 1943-46, Oak Ridge Inst. Nuclear Studies, 1952, Argonne Nat. Lab., 1954. Program dir. spl. projects in sci. edn. NSF, 1959-60, mem. nat. panel regulatory biology, 1964-66. Mem. Am. Soc. Plant Physiologists (exec. com. 1973—), Scandinavian, Canadian socs. plant physiologists, Bot. Soc. Am., AAAS, Ohio Acad. Sci. (joint adminstrv. bd. 1967—), Sigma Xi. Author: (with others) Laboratory Plant Physiology, 1955. Editorial com. Ann. Revs. Plant Physiology, 1954-60; editorial bd. Plant Physiology, 1969—. Contbr. articles to profl. jours. Home: 719 Lauraland Dr S Columbus OH 43214

SWANSON, CHARLES ANDREW, educator; b. Bellingham, Wash., July 11, 1929; s. Clarence Otto and Esther (Hougen) S.; B.A., U B.C., 1951, M.A., 1953; Ph.D., Cal. Inst. Tech., 1957; m. Carolyn Marie Dennis, Aug. 5, 1957; children—Laird Randall, Denise Claire. Prof. U. B.C., Vancouver, 1957—. Mem. Am. Math. Soc., Math. Assn. Am., Canadian Math. Congress. Author: An Introduction to Differential Calculus, 1962; Comparison and Oscillation Theory of Linear Differential Equations, 1968. Asso. editor: Canadian Jour. Math. Contbr. articles to tech., profl. jours. Office: U British Columbia Dept Math Vancouver BC V6T 1W5 Canada

SWANSON, CHARLES EDMUND, educator; b. Oceanside, Calif., Aug. 16, 1911; s. Charles August and Marie (McCarty) S.; B.A., San Diego State Coll., 1941; M.A., State U. Iowa, 1946, Ph.D., 1948; m.

Madelyn Jeraldine Hall, Aug. 17, 1935; 1 dau., Gleam Patricia (Mrs. Evan Rhys Powell). Reporter, desk editor Long Beach (Calif.) Press-Telegram, 1927-32, San Diego Union, 1936-42; instr., asst. prof. San Diego State Coll., 1938-42; instr., asst. prof. Sch. Journalism, State U. Iowa, 1946-49; asst. pub. Daily Iowan, Iowa City, 1948-49; asso. prof., prof. Sch. Journalism U. Minn., 1949-52; research prof. Inst. Communications Research, asst. dean div. communications U. Ill., 1952-54; research exec. Curtis Pub. Co., N.Y.C., 1954-61, research dir., 1961-64, v.p., 1962-64; prof. Grad. Sch. Bus. Adminstrn., N.Y. U., 1965-68; prof. Sch. Bus., Calif. State U., Fresno, 1968-73, 76—, acting v.p. for acad. affairs, 1973-74, v.p. for acad. affairs, 1974-76; profl. research cons.; dir. Nat. Analysts, Phila. Bd. mgrs. Central YMCA Phila.; bd. dirs. Central Valley YMCA, Fresno. Served with USMC, 1932-36; to comdr. USNR, 1942-45. Mem. Am. Psychol. Assn., Am. Statis. Assn., Am. Mktg. Assn. (past dir.), Am. Assn. Public Opinion Research, AAAS, AAUP. Republican. Episcopalian. Club: Rotary. Contbr. articles to profl. jours. Home: 805 E Alamos St Fresno CA 93704

SWANSON, CHARLES ELROY, publishing co. exec.; b. Elgin, Ill., Nov. 14, 1927; s. Clarence E. and Florence T. (Nitchman) S.; B.S. in Indsl. Engring., Northwestern U., 1951; M.B.A., U. Chgo., 1956; m. Barbara J. Loveday, Mar. 31, 1955; children—Mark, Kimberly, Bradford. Mgr. econ. and financial research Elgin Nat. Watch Co., 1951-57; mgr. estimating pricing Curtiss-Wright Corp., 1957-58; prin. Arthur Young & Co., Chgo., 1958-62; with Ency. Brit., Inc., Chgo., 1962—, exec. v.p., 1966-67, pres., 1967—. Bd. dirs. Chgo. Better Bus. Bur., 1967—. Served with AUS, 1946-47. Mem. Assn. Am. Pubs. (dir. 1970), Young Presidents Orgn., Direct Sell Assn. (dir.), Sigma Chi. Clubs: Mid Am., Chicago, Economic (Chgo.); Knollwood. Office: 425 N Michigan Ave Chicago IL 60611

SWANSON, DANIEL CRAMER, educator; b. Pratts Hollow, N.Y., Dec. 9, 1901; s. Theodore and Della (Cramer) S.; B.S., Hobart Coll., 1923; S.B., Mass. Inst. Tech., 1929; Ph.D., Cornell U., 1938; m. Dorothy Foster, Sept. 12, 1935; 1 son, David Louis. Tchr., Elmira Heights High Sch., N.Y., 1924-27; instr. U. Fla., Gainesville, 1929-36, asst. prof., 1938-41, asso. prof., 1941-49, prof. physics, 1949-71, prof. emeritus, 1971—. Fellow AAAS; mem. Am. Phys. Soc., Am. Assn. Physics Tchrs., Fla. Acad. Sci., Phi Beta Kappa, Sigma Xi, Phi Kappa Phi, Sigma Pi Sigma. Home: 1606 N W 12th Rd Gainesville FL 32605

SWANSON, DAVID HEATH, agrl. indsl. co. fin. exec.; b. Aurora, Ill., Nov. 3, 1942; s. Neil H. and Helen J. (McKendry) S.; B.A., Harvard U., 1964; M.A., U. Chgo., 1969; m. Elizabeth Farwell, June 19, 1963; children—Benjamin Heath, Matthew Banford. Account exec. 1st Nat. Bank Chgo., 1967-69; dep. mgr. Brown Bros. Harriman & Co., N.Y.C., 1969-72; asst. treas. Borden, Inc., N.Y.C., 1972-75; v.p., treas. Continental Grain Co., N.Y.C., 1975-77, v.p. chief fin. officer, 1977-79, gen. mgr. European div., 1979—; dir. gen. Finagrain, Geneva, Switzerland, 1979—; mem. bd. advs. Banco Popular de P.R., 1973-75. Mem. Council Fgn. Relations. Republican. Congregationalist. Clubs: Am. Alpine, Scottish Deerhound of Am., New Canaan (Conn.) Field, Fairfield County Striders. Home: 125 Fox Run Rd New Canaan CT 06840 Office: 277 Park Ave New York NY 10017

SWANSON, DON RICHARD, univ. dean; b. Los Angeles, Oct. 10, 1924; s. Harry Windfield and Grace Clara (Sandstrom) S.; B.S., Calif. Inst. Tech., 1945; M.A., Rice U., 1947; Ph.D., U. Calif., Berkeley, 1952; m. Patricia Elizabeth Klick, Aug. 22, 1976; children—Douglas Alan, Richard Brian, Judith Ann. Physicist, U. Calif. Radiation Lab., Berkeley, 1947-52, Hughes Research and devel. Labs., Culver City, Calif., 1952-55; research scientist TRW, Inc., Canoga Park, Calif., 1955-63; prof. Grad. Library Sch., U. Chgo., 1963—, dean, 1963-72, 77—; mem. Sci. Info. Council, NSF, 1960-65; mem. toxicology info. panel Pres.'s Sci. Advisory Com., 1964-66; mem. library vis. com. Mass. Inst. Tech., 1966-71; mem. com. on sci. and tech. communication Nat. Acad. Scis., 1966-69. Trustee, Nat. Opinion Research Center, 1964-73. Research fellow Chgo. Inst. for Psychoanalysis, 1972-76. Served with USNR, 1943-46. Mem. Assn. Am. Library Schs., Am. Soc. for Info. Sci. Editor: The Intellectual Founds. of Library Education, 1965; co-editor, Operations Research: Implications for Libraries, 1972, Management Education: Implications for Libraries and Library Schools, 1974; mem. editorial bd. Library Quarterly, 1963—. Contbr. chpt. to Ency. Brit., 1968—. Contbr. sci. articles to profl. jours. Home: 5550 Dorchester Ave Apt 809 Chicago IL 60637 Office: Grad Library Sch U Chgo 1100 E 57th St Chicago IL 60637. *Problems I wish I could solve: how the universe got started, how volition arose in a heap of molecules, how to find information in a library, and how to sum up life in a sentence or two.*

SWANSON, DONALD FREDERICK, food co. exec.; b. Mpls., Aug. 6, 1927; s. Clayton A. and Irma (Baiocchi) S.; B.A., U. Minn., 1948; m. Virginia Clare Hannah, Dec. 17, 1948; children—Donald Frederick, Cynthia Hannah Lindgren, Janet Clare Webster. With Gen. Mills, Inc., 1949—, div. v.p., dir. marketing flour, dessert and baking mixes, 1964-65, v.p., gen. mgr. grocery products div., 1965-68, v.p., corporate adminstrn. officer consumer foods group, fashion div., transp. and purchasing depts., advt. and marketing services, 1969, exec. v.p. craft, game and toy group, fashion group, direct marketing group, travel group, dir., 1968-76, sr. exec. v.p. consumer non-foods, 1976—, chief financial officer, 1977—; dir. 1st Nat. Bank Mpls., Graco, Inc., Soo Line R.R. Co. Bd. dirs. Met. Econ. Devel. Assn., Minn. Orchestral Assn.; chmn. Minn. adv. bd. United Negro Coll. Fund; bd. overseers U. Minn. Coll. Bus. Adminstrn.; mem. exec. bd. Viking council Boy Scouts Am.; mem. financial com. United Way Mpls. Served with AUS, 1946-47. Mem. Phi Kappa Psi. Clubs: Lafayette, Minneapolis, Wayzata Country; Sky. Home: 19500 Cedarhurst Wayzata MN 55391 Office: 9200 Wayzata Blvd Minneapolis MN 55426

SWANSON, DWIGHT HAROLD, utility co. exec.; b. Princeton, Minn., Aug. 13, 1919; s. Arthur B. and Signe C. (Odelius) S.; B.S. in Elec. Engring., Purdue, 1948; m. Audrey C. Myers, May 30, 1946; children—Mark Alan, Nancy Joan. With Central Ill. Electric & Gas Co., 1939-42; various positions including field engr., div. engr. Commonwealth Edison Co., Chgo., 1948-60; div. v.p., then marketing v.p. Pub. Service Ind., Kokomo and Plainfield, 1961-69; pres., chief exec. officer, dir. Iowa Power & Light Co., Des Moines, 1969-70, pres., chmn. bd., 1970—; dir. Bankers Trust Co., Des Moines, Bankers Life, Des Moines. Past chmn. Farm Electrification Council. Mem. adv. council Iowa State U. Engring. Coll.; mem. pres.'s council Purdue U.; bd. dirs. Central Baptist Theol. Sem., NCCJ, Iowa Methodist Med. Center, Des Moines; bd. govs. Living History Farms Found. Iowa, Iowa State U. Found.; trustee Drake U., Des Moines Served with USNR, 1942-46. Mem. Edison Electric Inst. (pres. 1978), Greater Des Moines C. of C., Missouri Valley Electric Assn. (pres. 1972), Iowa Engring. Soc., Kokomo Fine Arts Assn. (pres. 1967). Rotarian (pres. Kokomo 1967-68). Home: 3131 Fleur Dr Apt 202 Des Moines IA 50321 Office: 666 Grand Ave Des Moines IA 50309

SWANSON, EDWARD WILLIAM, bus. exec.; b. Cleve., Oct. 24, 1935; s. Edward William and Margaret Nellie (Kirkpatrick) S.; B.A., Miami (Ohio) U., 1957; M.B.A., Carnegie Tech. Inst., 1967; m. Lois R. Ladley, May 20, 1961; children—Edward, David, Kristen, Jonathan. Sales rep. IBM, Cin., 1960-65; cons., dir. corp. info. services Booz, Allen & Hamilton, Chgo., 1967-68; mgr. corp. acquisitions, dir. corp. analysis Gen. Mills Co., Mpls., 1968-72, corp. v.p., mng. dir. Smiths Food Group, London, 1972-75; gen. mgr. leisure group Parker Pen Co., Janesville, Wis., 1975, exec. v.p., 1976, pres., chief operating officer, 1977—, dir.; dir. Manpower, Inc., M&S BanCorp, Warner Electric Brake and Clutch Co. Trustee, Beloit Coll., 1977—; bd. dirs. United Way of North Rock County, 1979—. Served with USN, 1957-60. Clubs: Janesville Country, University (Milw.). Office: Court and Division Sts Janesville WI 53545

SWANSON, ELWELL EPHRAIM, mfg. co. exec.; b. Mpls., Mar. 25, 1914; s. Sigfried Otto and Dena (Holmgren) S.; B.S., U. Minn., 1936, M.A., 1940; m. Golda Beatrice Glenn, Oct. 2, 1943; 1 dau., Linda Suzanne. Tchr. high sch. in Minn. and Tenn. pub. schs., 1936-42; standard cost accountant Tenn. Eastman Co., Kingsport, 1942-47, Properties mgr. div. Clinton Engr. Works, Oak Ridge, 1943-45; asst. controller McCloud River Lumber Co. (Calif.), 1947-53; controller M and M Wood Working Co., Portland, Oreg., 1953-56; asst. controller Simpson Timber Co., Portland, 1956-61; controller Tektronix, Inc., Portland, 1961—; chmn. seminars internat. finance Am. Mgmt. Assn., San Francisco, 1967, Chgo., 1967, Bus. Internat., San Francisco, 1973. Mem. accounting council Machinery and Allied Products Inst., 1970—; mem. Oreg. Math. Edn. Council, 1971-78; mem. accounting policy bd. Sch. Bus. Adminstrn., Oreg. State U., 1973-77. Asst. chmn. agy. relations com. United Good Neighbors for Tri-County area, Portland, 1967-68, mem. bd. dirs., 1968-72, chmn. agy. relations. com., 1969, 70, 71. Mem. Financial Execs. Inst. (pres. Portland 1967-68), Nat. Assn. Accountants (bd. dirs. Portland 1964-65), Phi Delta Kappa. Republican. Baptist (trustee 1958-61, 69-72, chmn. 1971-72, adv. bd. 1958-61, 65-68, 69-72, chmn. Christian edn. com. 1965-68). Club: Multnomah Athletic. Mason (K.T., Shriner). Home: 7375 S W Sharon Ln Portland OR 97225 Office: 14150 S W Karl Braun Dr Beaverton OR 97005

SWANSON, FRANK, newspaper pub.; b. Edmonton, Alta., Can., Apr. 11, 1917; s. Frank and Clara (Olson) S.; B.A., U. Alta., 1937; M.S., Columbia, 1938; m. Vera Gowing, Dec. 2, 1944; 1 son, David. With London (Eng.) bur. Southam Newspapers of Can., 1945-48; parliamentary corr. Ottawa Citizen, 1948, 56-60, asso. editor, 1956-60, editor, 1960-62; v.p., pub. The Calgary (Alta.) Herald, 1962—. Served to maj. Canadian Army, 1940-45. Mem. Canadian War Corr. Assn. Clubs: Rideau (Ottawa); Ranchmen's, Calgary Petroleum, Calgary Golf and Country, Glencoe (Calgary). Home: Banff Coach Rd Rural Route 2 Calgary AB Canada Office: Herald Bldg Calgary AB Canada

SWANSON, GLEN OWEN, television dir.; b. Chgo., Apr. 25, 1936; s. Harold Allen and Gurlie Emilie (Johanson) S.; B.A., U. Denver; m. Nadina Bucaria, June 8, 1958; children—Glen Alan, Helne Emilie, Joanne Corin. Television dir. numerous series, pilots and television movies including: Dinah and Friends, Make Me Laugh, Sports Challenge, Movie Game. Recipient Emmy awards, 1975, 76. Advisor Sta. KCSN- Public Radio. Methodist. Home: 9800 Vanalden St Northridge CA 91324

SWANSON, GLORIA (GLORIA MAY JOSEPHINE SWANSON), actress; b. Chgo., Mar. 27, 1899; d. Joseph T. and Adelaide (Klanowski) S.; student pub. schs., Chgo.; m. Wallace Beery, Feb. 1916 (div.); m. 2d, Herbert K. Somborn (div. 1923); 1 dau., Gloria (Mrs. Wilfrid Augustin Daly); m. 3d, Marquis de la Falaise de la Coudray, 1925 (div. 1931); m. 4th, Michael Farmer, Aug. 16, 1931 (div.); 1 dau., Michelle Bridget (Mrs. Robert Amon); m. 5th, William N. Davey, 1945 (div. 1948); 1 son, Joseph (adopted); m. 6th, William Dufty, 1975. Actress on screen since 1913; began with Essanay Studios, Chgo., later with Mack Sennett Comedies, Calif., Triangle Prodns., C.B. DeMille, Famous Players, Lasky-Paramount; formed own co., Gloria Swanson Prodns., 1926, dissolved, 1932; starred in motion pictures, including: Don't Change Your Husband, The Impossible Mrs. Bellew, Male and Female, Bluebeard's Eighth Wife, Zaza, Manhandled, Madame Sans Gene, Sadie Thompson, Tonight or Never, Music in the Air, Father Takes a Wife, Sunset Boulevard, 1950, Airport 1975; 1st picture to record her speaking and singing voice The Trespasser, 1929; stage appearances Reflected Glory, 1942, Let's be Gay, 1943, A Goose for the Gander, 1945, Twentieth Century, 1950-51, Nina, 1951-52; star Gloria Swanson TV Show, 1948-49; narrator, actress TV series, 1953; appeared in film Nero's Big Week-End (Italian), 1956; TV film Killer Bees, 1974; on tour Red Letter Day, 1959-60, Between Seasons, 1961-62, The Inkwell, 1962-63, Reprise, 1967; appeared on Broadway and on tour in Butterflies are Free, 1970-72. Introduced Gloria Swanson Fashions, 1952. Commr. youth and phys. fitness City N.Y., 1975; mem. nutrition com. Dist. 9, N.Y.C. Schs., 1976. Recipient Neiman-Marcus Fashion award, 1955. Office: GS Enterprises 920 Fifth Ave New York NY 10021*

SWANSON, GORDON MERLE, food co. exec.; b. Chgo., Oct. 22, 1930; s. Carl Elmer and Edith Marie (Bergeson) S.; B.S., Northwestern U., 1958, M.B.A., 1961; m. Ann Louise Johnson, July 5, 1958; children—John, Robert. Supr. advt. services finance Quaker Oats Co., Chgo., 1958-62; controller Ansul Co., Marinette, Wis., 1962-70; controller Amtel, Inc., Providence, 1971-78; v.p. fin. Ravenhorst, Bellows & Assos., Inc., Olivia, Minn., 1978-79; v.p. fin. Marshall Foods, Inc. (Minn.), 1979—. Served with USAF, 1951-55. Mem. Am. Inst. C.P.A.'s. Home: 5 Pheasant Lawn Olivia MN 56277 Office: 800 E Southview Dr Marshall MN 56258

SWANSON, GUSTAV ADOLPH, biologist; b. nr. Willmar, Minn., Feb. 13, 1910; s. Gustaf Alfred and Pauline Elizabeth (Hagman) S.; student Macalester Coll., St. Paul, 1926-27, U. Mich., summer 1931; B.S., U. Minn., 1930, A.M., 1932, Ph.D., 1937; m. Evadene Burris, Apr. 11, 1936; children—Hildegarde, Evadene, Arthur. Biologist, Soil Conservation Service, U.S Dept. Agr., 1935, Minn. Conservation Commn., 1935-36; asst. prof. game mgmt. U. Maine, 1936-37; asst. prof econ. zoology U. Minn., 1937-41, asso. prof., 1942-44; asso. regional insp. U.S. Fish and Wildlife Service Mpls., 1941-42, biologist, 1944-46, chief wildlife research div., Washington, 1946-48; head dept. conservation Cornell U., 1948-66, exec. dir. Lab. Ornithology, 1958-61, dir. Field Biol. Sta., 1955-66; head dept. fishery and wildlife biology Colo. State U., 1966-75, emeritus, 1975—; prof. conservation U. Mont., Bozeman, summers 1950, 51, Havre, 1953; on leave Scandinavian countries and Eng., 1954-55; Fulbright lectr. Aarhus U., Denmark 1961-62, U. New Eng., Armidale, N.S.W., Australia, 1968; distinguished vis. prof. N.Mex. State U., Las Cruces, 1976; mem. coms. agrl. land use-wildlife relationships, agrl. pest control, and Yellowstone grizzly bears, Nat. Acad. Sci.-NRC, 1965-70, 73-74, mem. bd. on agr. and renewable resources, 1974-77; program dir., editor The Mitigation Symposium, 1979; cons. N.Y. Joint Legis. Com. Revision of Conservation Law, 1956-64. Fellow Rochester Mus., AAAS; mem. Wildlife Soc. (pres. 1954-55, Aldo Leopold meml. medal 1973), Am. Soc. Mammalogists, Am. Ornithologists Union, Wilson Ornithol. Soc. (treas. 1938-42), Nat. Audubon Soc. (dir. 1950-56), Am. Inst. Biol. Scis., Internat. Assn., Fish and Wildlife Agys. Clubs: Rotary, Cosmos (Washington). Author: (with T. Surber and T.S. Roberts) Mammals of Minnesota, 1946; Fish and Wildlife Resources on the Public Lands. 1969; Water Law in Relation to Environmental Quality, 1974. Sectional editor Wildlife Mgmt., Biol. Abstracts, 1943-46; editor Jour. Wildlife Mgmt., 1948-53. Home: 620 Mathews St Apt 115 Fort Collins CO 80524

SWANSON, GUY EDWIN, social scientist, educator; b. Warren, Pa., Oct. 6, 1922; s. Guy Edwin and Minnie Katherine (Haslett) S.; A.B., U. Pitts., 1943, M.A., 1943; Ph.D., U. Chgo., 1948; m. Eliane Marie Aerts, Aug. 19, 1977; children—Emily Gray, Elisabeth Huntley, Mary Alice, Sarah Catherine. Instr., Boston U., 1945-46, Ind. U., 1946-47, U. Chgo., 1947-48; mem. faculty U. Mich., 1948-69, fellow Center Advanced Study Behavioral Scis., 1957-58, prof., 1959-69, chmn. dept. sociology, 1961-64; prof. sociology U. Calif., Berkeley, 1969—; dir. Social Sci. Research Council, 1961-64. Guggenheim fellow, 1964-65. Fellow Am. Sociol. Assn., Am. Psychol. Assn., A.A.A.S. (v.p. 1968-69). Author: (with Daniel R. Miller) The Changing American Parent, 1958, Inner Conflict and Defense, 1960; The Birth of the Gods, 1960; Religion and Regime, A Sociological Account of the Reformation, 1967; Rules of Descent, Studies in the Sociology of Parentage, 1969; Social Change, 1971. Home: 176 Ardmore Rd Kensington CA 94707

SWANSON, HOWARD PAUL, paper co. exec.; b. N.Y.C., May 7, 1926; s. Max and Gertrude (Handsman) S.; A.B., Bklyn. Coll., 1949; LL.B., Harvard, 1952; m. Sylvia Senturia, June 13, 1954; children—Linda, Richard. Admitted to Ill. bar, 1955; tax accountant S.D. Leidesdorf & Co., Chgo., 1952-55, U.S. Gypsum Co., 1955-56; with M.W. Kellogg Co., N.Y.C., 1956-62. successively asst. tax mgr., tax mgr., 1956-60, asst. treas., mgr. tax dept., 1960-62; dir. tax adminstrn. NBC, N.Y.C., 1962-63; treas. Trans World Airlines, Inc., N.Y.C., 1963-66, v.p., treas., 1966-68; sr. v.p. finance and legal Hudson Pulp & Paper Corp. N.Y.C., 1968—; dir. Tex. Internat. Airlines, 1972—. Mem. Financial Execs. Inst., Tax Exec. Inst., Am., Ill. bar assns., Internat. Fiscal Assn. Clubs: Harvard, Harbor View (N.Y.C.). Contbr. articles on tax. Home: 56 Hampton Rd Scarsdale NY 10583 Office: 477 Madison Ave New York City NY 10022

SWANSON, JOEL OLIVER, food co. exec.; b. Mobile, Ala., Oct. 19, 1921; s. Joel Arvid and Edna Helen (Delchamps) S.; student U. Tex., 1939-42; m. Marilyn Morris, Sept. 25, 1943; children—Joel Craig, Jan Katherine, Kirk Alfred. Announcer Sta. KRIC, Beaumont, Tex., 1946; chief announcer to comml. mgr. Sta. KPAC, Port Arthur, Tex., 1946-51; with Delchamps, Inc., Mobile, Ala., 1951—, advt. mgr., 1951-58, dir. advt. and pub. relations, 1958-63, v.p. advt. and pub. relations, 1963-68, v.p. sales and merchandising, 1968-72, v.p., sec., 1972—, also dir. Pres., Mulherin Custodial Home, 1954, Mobile Mental Health Center, 1959, 76, Mobile County Mental Health Assn., 1967. Served with USAAF, 1942-46. Recipient M.O. Beale Scroll of Merit, Mobile Press-Register, 1962. Mem. Pub. Relations Council Ala. (pres. 1976), Am. Advt. Fedn. (gov. 7th dist. 1970-72, recipient Otis Dodge Meml. award 1973), Food Mktg. Inst. (govt. affairs council), So. Pub. Relations Fedn. Methodist. Clubs: Mobile Advt. (pres. 1964, recipient Silver medal 1962), Mobile Lions (pres. 1958), Internat. Trade, Skyline Country. Home: 4113 Briarcliff Ct Mobile AL 36609 Office: PO Box 1668 Mobile AL 36601

SWANSON, JOHN WILLIAM, banker; b. N.Y.C., Aug. 23, 1919; s. John and Janet (Laidlaw) S.; B.B.A., Pace Coll., 1952; standard certificate Am. Inst. Banking, 1953; certificate Grad. Sch. Savs. Banking, Brown U., 1964; m. Doris May Fischer, Dec. 29, 1945; children—Gladys May, Carol Anne. Asst. mgr. Mfrs. Hanover Trust Co., to 1951; sr. examiner N.Y. State Banking Dept., 1951-60; auditor Anchor Savs. Bank, Bklyn., 1960-66; v.p. br. adminstrn., auditor Emigrant Savs. Bank, N.Y.C., 1966—; faculty N.Y.C. chpt. Am. Inst. Banking, 1956—. Served to 1st lt. USAAF, 1942-45. Mem. Savs. Bank Auditors and Comptrollers Forum State N.Y. (pres.). Methodist. Mason. Home: 9 Roxbury St Farmingdale NY 11735 Office: 5 E 42d St New York NY 10007

SWANSON, KARL THOR WALDEMAR, educator; b. Ogden, Iowa, Jan. 22, 1922; s. Carl Wilhelm and Alma (Erickson) S.; B.A., U. Iowa, 1943. M.A., 1947; Ph.D., Syracuse U., 1953; m. Dorothy Elizabeth Neiman, Sept. 2, 1950; children—Greta Elizabeth, Karl Thor Carolus. Instr. polit. sci. Syracuse U., 1949-51; mem. faculty Wash. State U., Pullman, 1951—, prof. polit. sci., 1966—, chmn. dept., 1968-72; vis. asst. prof. Syracuse U., summer 1956; staff fellow Nat. Municipal League, 1956-57; spl. asst. to Gov. Egan of Alaska, 1963-64; sr. resident scholar U.S. Adv. Commn. on Intergovtl. Relations, 1972-73; cons. in field. Mem. Pullman City Council, 1959-63, Pullman Planning Commn., 1959-63. Served to lt. (j.g.) USNR, 1943-46. Mem. Am., Western, Pacific Northwest polit. sci. assns., Am. Soc. Pub. Adminstrn., Am. Assn. U. Profs. (pres. Wash. State U. chpt. 1960-61). Co-author: American National Government, 7th edit., 1970; American State and Local Government, 5th edit., 1972; The Government and Politics of Washington State, 1978. Home: NE 1055 Creston Lane Pullman WA 99163

SWANSON, LAWRENCE WILBUR, ret. govt. ofcl., cons.; b. Canon City, Colo., Nov. 26, 1904; s. Charles and Lillie (Powell) S.; B.S., Colo. State U., 1926; m. Hazel Ruth Graves, Oct. 13, 1930; 1 son, Robert Lawrence. Commd. ensign U.S. Coast and Geodetic Survey, 1927, advanced through grades to capt., 1957; jr. officer in various survey ships, 1927-37, in charge Balt. photog. office, 1937-42, chief triangulation field party, 1949-53, asst. chief div. photography, 1953-54, chief div. photography, 1954-61, asst. dir. phys. scis., 1961-64, mgr. world geometric-geodetic satellite triangulation program, 1965-72; cons. tidal boundary surveys, 1972—. Recipient Dept. Commerce Exceptional Service medal of award, 1957; Colbert award Soc. Am. Mil. Engrs., 1963; Distinguished Citizen award Canon City, Colo., 1965; award for adminstrn. and program mgmt. Nat. Oceanic and Atmospheric Adminstrn.; 1971; citation Engring. News-Record, 1968; named Honor Engring. Alumnus, Colo. State U., 1976. Mem. Am. Soc. Photogrammetry (nat. pres. 1966-67, hon. mem. 1972—), Soc. Am. Mil. Engrs. (hon.) Am. Congress Surveying and Mapping, Sigma Chi. Clubs: Masons, Cosmos. Pioneer devel. geometric satellite triangulation, color aerial photography, analytic photogrammetry, tidal boundary surveys, photogrammetric survey methods. Home: 4225 Franklin St Kensington MD 20795

SWANSON, LEONARD ARCHIE, oil co. exec.; b. Beaukiss, Tex., July 9, 1917; s. Nils and Ellen (Olson) S.; B.S., U. Tex., 1941; M.S. in Mech. Engring., U. Calif., 1946; m. Mary Jane Pace, June 10, 1942; children—Leonard Dale, Randall Wayne. Chief engr., mgr. prodn. dept. Standard Oil Co. Tex., 1949-56; prodn. v.p., dir. Calif. Standard Co., Calgary, Alta., Can., 1956-62; pres. Standard Oil Co. Tex., Houston, 1962-66; v.p. prodn. Standard Oil Co. Calif., San Francisco, 1966—. Served with USAF, 1942-47. Decorated D.F.C., Air medal. Mem. Am. Petroleum Inst., Soc. Petroleum Engrs., AIME. Republican. Office: 225 Bush St San Francisco CA 94104

SWANSON, LLOYD OSCAR, savs. and loan assn. exec.; b. Mpls., June 26, 1913; s. Carl G. and Ellen (Peterson) S.; student U. Minn., 1930-31; B.A., Gustavus Adolphus Coll., 1935, L.H.D. (hon.), 1968; m. Eileen E. Hedlof, Mar. 29, 1958; children—Marcia L. (Mrs. Joseph Massee), Paul L. J. Bradley, Craig R. Dir. admissions and pub. relations Gustavus Adolphus Coll., 1935-37; spl. agt. John Hancock Life Ins. Co., Mpls., 1937-42; gen. agt. Nat. Life Ins. Co., Mpls., 1942-62; pres. First Fed. Savs. and Loan Assn., Mpls., 1962-77, chmn. bd., 1967—; chmn. bd., dir. The Security Corp.; dir. Soderberg Optical

Co., St. Paul, Reginald Bishop Forster & Assos., Title Ins. Co. Minn.; mem. investment adv. com. Mpls. Tchrs. Retirement Fund. Trustee Fairview-Southdale Hosp., Mpls.; chmn. bd. trustees Fairview Community Hosps., Mpls.; trustee, treas. Mpls. Kiwanis Found.; sec.-treas. Greater Gustavus Fund, 1962—, mem., 1952—. Mem. Savs. League Minn. (dir. pres. 1970). Kiwanian. Clubs: Athletic, Minneapolis (Mpls.); Interlachen Country (past mem. bd. govs.); Imperial Golf (Naples, Fla.). Home: 249 Interlachen Rd Hopkins MN 55343 Office: 77 S 7th St Minneapolis MN 55402

SWANSON, ROBERT DRAPER, coll. pres.; b. Sioux City, Iowa, Aug. 6, 1915; s. Alfred and Tida Ruth (Draper) S.; A.B., Park Coll., 1937; student U. Iowa, 1937; B.D., McCormick Theol. Sem., 1941; D.D., James Millikin U., 1950; L.H.D., Tusculum Coll. 1966, Olivet Coll., 1971; LL.D., Hillsdale Coll., 1968; m. Roberta B. Clements, May 5, 1941 (dec. Oct. 1975); children—Sara Louise, Mark Robert; m. 2d, Dorothy B. Howe, Aug. 4, 1979. Dir. athletics, phys. edn. Park Coll., 1937-38; ordained to ministry Presbyn. Ch., 1941; pastor Second Presbyn. Ch., Tulsa, 1941-45; dean of students McCormick Sem., 1946-47, v.p., prof. preaching, 1948-56; pres. Alma Coll., 1956—. Dir. Gen. Telephone Co. Mich. Served as lt. (j.g.), Chaplain's Corps, USNR, 1945-46. Club: Rotary (Alma). Home: 4105 Riverview Dr Alma MI 48801

SWANSON, ROBERT KILLEN, bus co. exec.; b. Deadwood, S.D., Aug. 11, 1932; s. Robert Charles and Marie Elizabeth (Kersten) S.; B.A., U. S.D., 1954; M.A., U. Melbourne, Australia, 1955; m. Nancy Anne Oyaas, July 19, 1958; children—Cathryn Lynn, Robert Stuart, Bart Killen. With Gen. Mills, Inc., Mpls., 1955-58, 71-79, v.p., 1971-73, group v.p., 1973-77, exec. v.p., 1977-79; pres., chief operating officer Greyhound Corp., Phoenix, 1979—; with Marathon Oil Co., Findlay, Ohio, 1958-60; sr. v.p., dir. Needham, Harper & Steers, Inc., Chgo., 1961-69; joint mng. dir. of bd. S.H. Benson (Holdings), Ltd., Eng., 1969-71; dir. Data Card Internat. Bd. dirs. Guthrie Theater, Mpls. Served to 2d lt. U.S. Army, 1955-56. Fulbright scholar, 1954-55, Woodrow Wilson scholar. Mem. U.S. Council Fgn. Relations, U.K. Dirs. Inst., Econ. Club Chgo., U.S. Internat. Scholars Assn. Episcopalian. Clubs: Masons; Mpls., Lafayette. Office: Greyhound Corp Greyhound Tower Phoenix AZ 85077

SWANSON, ROY ARTHUR, educator; b. St. Paul, Apr. 7, 1925; s. Roy Benjamin and Gertrude (Larson) S.; B.A., U. Minn., 1948, B.S., 1949, M.A., 1951; Ph.D., U. Ill., 1954; m. Vivian May Vitous, Mar. 30, 1946; children—Lynn Marie (Mrs. Gerald A. Snider), Robin Lillian, Robert Roy (dec.), Dyack Tyler, Dana Miriam. Prin., Maplewood Elementary Sch., St. Paul, 1949-51; instr. U. Ill., 1952-53, Ind. U., 1954-57, asst. prof. U. Minn., Mpls., 1957-61, asso. prof., 1961-64, acting chmn. classics, 1963-64, prof. classics, chmn. comparative lit., 1964-65; prof. English, Macalester Coll., St. Paul, 1965-67; co-ordinator humanities program, 1966-67; prof. comparative lit. and classics U. Wis.-Milw., 1967—, chmn. classics, 1967-70, chmn. comparative lit., 1970-73, 76—. Cons. St. Paul Tchrs. Sr. High Sch. English, 1964. Bd. dirs. Lutheran Studies, Inc. Served with AUS, 1944-46. Decorated Bronze Star; recipient Disting. Teaching award U. Minn., 1962, U. Wis.-Milw., 1974. Mem. Am. Philol. Assn., Am. Comparative Lit. Assn., Modern Lang. Assn., Soc. for Advancement Scandinavian Study, Phi Beta Kappa (pres. chpt. 1975-76), Phi Kappa Phi. Author: Odi et Amo: The Complete Poetry of Catullus, 1959; Heart of Reason: Introductory Essays in Modern-World Humanities, 1963; Pindar's Odes, 1974. Editor, Minn. Rev., 1963-67, Classical Jour., 1968-73. Contbr. articles to profl. jours. Home: 11618 N Bobolink Ln Mequon WI 53092 Office: U Wis-Milw Dept Comparative Lit PO Box 413 Milwaukee WI 53201

SWANSON, ROY PAUL, lawyer; b. Kansas City, Mo., Apr. 6, 1896; s. Charles and Christina (Nelson) S.; student Park Coll., 1915-17; LL.B., Mo. U., 1923; children—Charles L., Paula (Mrs. Charles E. Bloczynski). Admitted to Mo. bar, 1923, since practiced in Kansas City; sr. partner firm Swanson, Midgley, Gangwere, Thurlo & Clarke, 1956—; dir. U.S. Supply Co.; mem. fed. ct. martial bd. Gt. Lakes Naval Tng. Center. Mem. bd. police commrs. Kansas City, Mo., 1960-64; pres. Naturalization Council Kansas City, Mo., 1958-59; mem. Jackson County Park Bd., Kansas City, Mo., 1953-55; gen. counsel Order DeMolay. Trustee Liberty Meml. Assn. Served as ensign U.S. Navy, 1917-18. Recipient Citation of Merit, U. Mo. Law Sch. Mem. Am., Kansas City bar assns., Mo. Bar (pres. 1962-63, award of merit), Lawyers Assn. Kansas City (pres. 1950-51), S. Central Bus. Assn. (past pres.), Phi Delta Phi, Kappa Alpha. Conglist. Mason (Shriner). Club: University. Home: 1007 W 66th Terr Kansas City MO 64113 Office: Commerce Bank Bldg Kansas City MO 64106

SWANSON, RUNE E., bldg. material co. exec.; b. Chgo., Aug. 9, 1919; s. John E. and Emma C. (Carlson) S.; B.S. in Commerce (Univ. scholar), Northwestern U., 1943; m. Lenore Reed, Mar. 18, 1944; children—Deborah, Cynthia, Patricia. Asst. controller U.S. Gypsum Co., Chgo., 1946-56; controller Internat. Minerals & Chem. Corp., Chgo., 1956-60, Mobil Chem. Co., N.Y.C., 1960-66; v.p. fin., treas. Nat. Gypsum Co., Dallas, 1966—; instr. Northwestern U. Bd. dirs. Skokie (Ill.) YMCA. Served to lt. USNR, 1943-46; PTO. Mem. Fin. Execs. Inst. Am. Mgmt. Assn., U.S. C. of C., Dallas C. of C., Newcomen Soc. Republican. Lutheran. Clubs: Northwood Country, City (Dallas). Office: Nat Gypsum Co 4100 First Internat Bldg Dallas TX 75270

SWANSON, VERNON ANDREW, lawyer; b. Plum City, Wis., Nov. 13, 1902; s. John S. and Agnes (Brunner) S.; LL.B., U. Wis., 1931; m. Florence M. Hammerstrand, June 18, 1932; children—Mary F., Ann E. (Mrs. William H. Vanderbilt Jr.). Admitted to Wis. bar, 1932, also U.S. Supreme Ct.; partner firm Foley & Lardner, Milw., 1943—; dir. emeritus Wis. Gas Co.; dir. Lake Shore, Inc., Iron Mountain, Mich. Bd. dirs. Chgo. Symphony Assn. Milw. Mem. Order of Coif, Phi Alpha Delta. Clubs: Milw. Country, Univ. (pres. 1968-69) (Milw.). Home: 726 Daisy Ln Milwaukee WI 53217 Office: 777 E Wisconsin Ave Milwaukee WI 53202

SWANSON, WALLACE MARTIN, lawyer; b. Fergus Falls, Minn., Aug. 22, 1941; m. Marvin Walter and Mary Louise (Lindsey) S.; B.A. with honors, U. Minn., 1962; LL.B. with honors, So. Methodist U.. 1965; m. Janet Middleton, Jan. 21, 1964; children—Kristen Lindsey, Eric Munger. Admitted to Tex. bar, 1965, since practiced in Dallas; partner firm Hewett Johnson Swanson & Barbee, 1970—. Served with USNR, 1960-65. Mem. Am., Dallas bar assns., State Bar Tex. Methodist. Club: City (Dallas). Home: 3648 Stratford Ave Dallas TX 75205 Office: 4700 First Internat Bldg Dallas TX 75270

SWANSON, WILLIAM FREDIN, JR., mfg. co. exec., lawyer; b. Phila., Sept. 10, 1928; s. William Fredin and Anna Ida (Moore) S.; B.A., U. Pitts., 1950; J.D., Harvard, 1953; m. Marjorie Beatrice Davis, Aug. 13, 1955; children—Karen Beth, William Fredin III, Susan Davis, Lauren Lynn. Asso. firm Moorhead & Knox, Pitts., 1953-58; asst. counsel PPG Industries, Pitts., 1959-67; asst. gen. counsel Rockwell-Standard Corp., 1967; asst. gen. counsel comml. products group N.Am. Rockwell Corp. (merger Rockwell-Standard Corp. and N.Am. Aviation Inc., name changed to Rockwell Internat. Corp. 1973), Pitts., 1967-68, gen. counsel comml. products group, 1968-71, staff v.p., asso. gen. counsel, 1971—, sec., 1975—. Vice pres. U. Pitts. Alumni Council Gen. Alumni Assn., 1966-68, group chmn. Ann. Giving Fund, 1978—; mem. Wake Forest U. Parents' Council, 1975-77; trustee Athalia Daly Home, 1974-77. Served with AUS, 1946-47. Mem. Allegheny County, Pa., Am. bar assns., Am. Soc. Corp. Secs. (treas. Pitts. regional group), Mid-Atlantic Legal Found. (legal adv. com.), Delta Tau Delta, Omicron Delta Kappa, Phi Eta Sigma, Delta Sigma Rho. Presbyn. (elder, presbytery bd. missions and ch. planning). Mason. Clubs: Duquesne, Edgewood Country. Home: 358 Braddsley Dr Pittsburgh PA 15235 Office: 600 Grant St Pittsburgh PA 15219

SWANSTROM, EDWARD ERNEST, bishop; b. N.Y.C., Mar. 20, 1903; s. Gustave A. and Mary A. (Cronin) S.; A.B., Fordham U., 1924, Ph.D., 1938, LL.D., 1953; M.A., St. John's Sem., Bklyn., 1928; grad. diploma N.Y. Sch. Social Work, 1933; D.D., Rome, 1960; LL.D., Iona Coll., 1961, St. Johns, 1962; D.H.L., Cath. U., 1965. Ordained priest Roman Catholic Ch.; 1928; asst. dir. Cath. Charities, Diocese Bklyn., 1933-43; asst. exec. dir. Cath. Relief Services-Nat. Cath. Welfare Conf., N.Y.C., 1943-47, exec. dir., 1947—; curate St. James Pro-Cathedral, Bklyn., 1934-60; consecrated aux. bishop N.Y., 1960. Office: 350 Fifth Ave New York NY 10001*

SWANTZ, ALEXANDER, ret. govt. ofcl.; b. Buckley, Wash., May 9, 1919; s. Stephen W. and Sarah H. (Maliniak) S.; B.S., Wash. State Coll., 1941; M.S., U. Minn., 1949, Ph.D., 1951; postgrad. Princeton U., 1965-66; m. Elizabeth Josephine Appleford, Apr. 6, 1941; children—Richard Alexander, Tamara Lynn Swantz Dierman. Various positions indsl., farm mgmt., 1941-48; research economist Agr. Mktg. Service, Dept. Agr., 1948-54, dairy mktg. specialist, 1954-56, dep. dir. consumer and mktg. service, dairy div., 1962-66, economist Office of Adminstr., 1966-67, asst. dep. adminstr., 1967-68, fed. milk market adminstr., Spokane, Wash. and Denver, 1956-62; asso. adminstr. Commodity Exchange Authority, Washington, 1968-74; pres. dir. WCC Land Corp., 1969-74; mem. statis rev. bd. Dept. Agr., 1967-68, Outlook and Situation Bd., 1966-68, Agrl. Statistics Yearbook com., 1967-74. Bd. dirs. Fairfax County (Va.) Symphony Orch., 1969-71. Served to capt. USNR, 1943-46. Princeton fellow in pub. affairs, 1965; recipient certificate merit Dept. Agr., 1964. Mem. Am. Agrl. Econs. Assn., Am. Econ. Assn., Alpha Gamma Rho, Alpha Zeta, Wash. State U. Alumni Assn. (dir. 1971-76, 78—). Club: Westwood Country (past pres.; bd. govs. 1966-69, 76—). Author in field. Home: 1003 Fairway Dr NE Vienna VA 22180

SWARTHOUT, GLENDON FRED, author; b. Pinckney, Mich., Apr. 8, 1918; s. Fred Harrington and Lila (Chubb) S.; A.B., U. Mich., 1939, A.M., 1946; Ph.D., Mich. State U., 1955; m. Kathryn Blair Vaughn, Dec. 28, 1940; 1 son, Miles. Books include: Willow Run, 1943, They Came to Cordura, 1958, Where the Boys Are, 1960, Welcome to Thebes, 1962, (with Kathryn Swarthout) The Ghost and the Magic Saber, 1967, The Cadillac Cowboys, 1967, (with Kathryn Swarthout) Whichaway, 1966, The Eagle and the Iron Cross, 1966, Loveland, 1968, (with Kathryn Swarthout) The Button Boac, 1969, Bless the Beasts and Children, (with Kathryn Swarthout) TV Thompson, 1972, The Tin Lizzie Troop, 1972, Luck and Pluck, 1973, The Shootist, 1975, (with Kathryn Swarthout) Whales to See The, 1975, The Melodeon, 1977, Skeletons, 1979; contbr. short stories to mags. including: Cosmopolitan, Esquire, Sat Eve. Post, New World Writing. Served with U.S. Army, 1943-45; ETO. Recipient Playwriting award Theater Guild, 1947; Hopwood award in fiction, 1948; O. Henry Prize Short Stories, 1960; Gold medal Nat. Soc. Arts and Letters, 1972; Spur award for best western novel Western Writers Am., 1975. Home: 5045 Tamanar Way Scottsdale AZ 85353

SWARTHOUT, HERBERT MARION, ins. exec.; b. Sioux Falls, S.D., Aug. 29, 1900; s. Earl Beagle and Jennie Laura (Aldrich) S.; student Nebr. U., 1920-21, Washington U., 1922; grad. Am. Coll. Life Underwriters, 1942; m. Lila Ellen Sosamon, Dec. 21, 1926; 1 dau., Joan Swarthout Wahlstedt. Has been in life ins. bus., 1928—, specializing in estate planning; rep. Mut. Benefit Life Ins. Co. of N.J., 1947—; founder Uniformed Services Benefit Assn., exec. dir., 1959-75; pres. Herrick Fin. Services, Inc. Sponsor activities YMCA; pres., gen. chmn. Heart Am. Meml. Torch Ceremony, 1963-64. Mem. Nebr. U. Alumni Assn. (past pres. Kansas City chpt.), Life Underwriters Assn., Kansas City, Million Dollar Round Table (life and qualifying), Nat. Assn. Life Underwriters, Am. Soc. Chartered Life Underwriters, Assn. Advanced Life Underwriters, Five Million Dollar Forum, Top of the Table, Mut. Benefit Nat. Assos. Hall of Fame, S.R. (pres. Kansas City 1956—, pres. Mo. soc. 1958-59), Assn. U.S. Army (liaison chmn.), Advt. and Sales Execs. Club, Kansas City Art Inst. Mem. Christian Ch. (deacon). Clubs: Masons, Shriners, DeMolay (hon. legion of honor), Rotary, Kansas City, Carriage, Eleven-Eleven (Kansas City, Mo.). Home: 850 W 55th St Kansas City MO 64113 Office: 1221 Baltimore Ave Kansas City MO 64105

SWARTZ, DONALD EVERETT, TV exec.; b. Mpls., Mar. 7, 1916; s. Albert L. and Sara (Shore) S.; grad. high sch.; m. Helen Gordon, Mar. 24, 1940; children—Stuart, Lawrence, Gary. Owner, Ind. Film Distbrs., 1940-53, Tele-Film Assos., 1953-57; pres., gen. mgr. TV sta. KMSP, Mpls., 1957—; pres. United TV, Inc. subs. 20th Century Fox Film Corp., operating KMSP-TV, KTV4, Salt Lake City, KMOL-TV, San Antonio, 1975—. Vice pres. Twin City Broadcast Skills Bank (scholarship program), St. Paul Arts and Sci. Inst.; pres. U. Minn. Heart Hosp.; mem. Gov.'s Commn. Bicentennial. Bd. dirs. Mpls. United Jewish Fund and Council. Mem. Mpls. Inst. Arts, Mpls., St. Paul chambers commerce, Minn. Orch. Assn., Citizens League, U. Minn. Alumni Assn. Jewish (pres. temple). Mem. B'nai B'rith. Clubs: Press, Advertising Standard (Mpls.); Hillcrest Country (St. Paul); Variety. Home: 627 Mt Curve Blvd Saint Paul MN 56116 Office: 6975 York Ave S Minneapolis MN 55435

SWARTZ, DONALD PERCY, physician; b. Preston, Ont., Can., Sept. 12, 1921; s. Simon Wingham and Lydia (Ethell) S.; B.A., U. Western Ont., 1951, M.D. cum laude, 1951, M.S. cum laude, 1953; m. Norma Mae Woolner, June 24, 1944; children—Ian Donald, Rhonda Swartz Peterson. Intern, Victoria Hosp., London, Ont., 1951-52; resident Johns Hopkins U., Balt., 1954-58; asst. prof. Ob-Gyn., U. Western Ont., London, 1958-62; prof. Columbia U. N.Y.C., 1962-72, dir. Ob-Gyn., Harlem Hosp.; prof., chmn. dept. Albany (N.Y.) Med. Coll., 1972—. Vice pres., pres. Assn. Planned Parenthood Physicians, 1972-74. Served with RCAF, 1942-45. NRC Can. fellow, 1952-53; Am. Cancer Soc. fellow, 1956-57; Markle scholar, 1958-63. Fellow Royal Coll. Surgeons Can., Am. Coll. Obstetricians and Gynecologists, Am. Gynecologic Soc., Am. Fertility Soc., Royal Soc. Health. Asso. editor Advances in Planned Parenthood. Home: 24 Devon Rd Delmar NY 12054 Office: 47 New Scotland Ave Albany NY 12208

SWARTZ, HOWARD MARSHALL, lawyer; b. Bellevue, Pa., Oct. 30, 1909; s. Carl and Lorena Rosalie (Hunzeker) S.; A.B., Harvard, 1930; J.D., U. Pitts., 1933; m. Lila I. Smith, Oct. 6, 1945; 1 son, Howard Marshall. Admitted to Pa. bar, 1933; asso. firm Rose & Eichenauer, Pitts., 1933-39; atty. Philadelphia Co. and subsidiaries, Pitts., 1939-58; with West Penn Power Co., Greensburg, 1958-74, v.p., 1959-70, exec. v.p., gen. mgr., 1970-74; pres. Allegheny Pittsburgh Coal Co., West Penn West Va. Water Power Co., West Va. Power & Transmission Co., 1970-74; counsel firm Rose, Schmidt, Dixon, Hasley, Whyte & Hardesty, Pitts., 1974—; v.p., dir. Beech Bottom Power Co. Mem. citizens sponsoring com. Allegheny Conf. on Community Devel., 1970-74. Bd. dirs. Western Pa. Conservancy, 1963—, Westmoreland County Mus. Art, 1970—; trustee Found. Ind. Colls. Pa., 1970-74. Mem. Allegheny County, Westmoreland County, Pa., Am. bar assns., Pa. Electric Assn. (past pres., exec. com. 1964-74). Clubs: Duquesne (Pitts.); Rolling Rock, Laurel Valley (Ligonier, Pa.). Home: 230 Maple Dr Maplewood Terr Greensburg PA 15601

SWARTZ, ROBERT DALE, publisher; b. Flint, Mich., Dec. 2, 1925; s. Harry Corneilius and Mattie Blitze (Jespersen) S.; student Flint Jr. Coll., 1947; m. Idamae Katherine Stiehl, Nov. 2, 1946; children—Timothy J., Mary F., Kathleen A., Dale R. Advt. salesman Flint Jour., 1949-57, controller, 1960-63, pub., 1978—; advt. mgr. Grand Rapids (Mich.) Herald and Press, 1958-60; mgr. Grand Rapids Press, 1964-78. Bd. dirs. Butterworth Hosp., Grand Rapids, 1968-78, Kent Med. Found., Grand Rapids, 1976-78; pres. Grand Rapids C. of C., 1969-70, Jr. Achievement, Grand Rapids, 1969; chmn. bd. Salvation Army, Grand Rapids, 1971, Health System Agy. Western Mich., 1976-78. Served with AC, U.S. Army, 1944-46. Recipient award Jr. Achievement, 1971, Fourth Estate award Am. Legion, 1973, Others award Salvation Army, 1979. Mem. Mich. Newspaper Pubs. Assn., Inland Daily Press Assn., Mich. Daily Press Assn. Episcopalian. Clubs: Rotary, Flint Golf, Univ., Pres, Flint City. llome: 1603 Apple Creek Tr Flint MI 48507 Office: 200 E 1st St Flint MI 48502

SWARTZ, RODERICK GARDNER, librarian; b. Fairbury, Nebr., May 25, 1939; s. E. Wayne and Dorine B. (Gardner) S.; B.A., U. Nebr., 1961; M.A., 1962; M.A., U. Chgo., 1963; m. Marianna Moore, Sept. 1, 1972. Asst. to exec. sec. library adminstrn. div. ALA, 1963-64; library cons. Mo. State Library, 1964-66; asst. dir. Tulsa City-County Library, 1966-70, asso. dir., 1970-72; dep. dir. Nat. Commn. on Libraries and Info. Sci., 1972-74; state librarian Wash. State Library, Olympia, 1975—; mem. faculty U. Okla., 1969-72, U. Denver, 1970, Cath. U. Am., 1972-74, Inst. Library and Info. Sci., Tampere, Finland, 1975. Fulbright fellow, 1975; Council on Library Resources fellow, 1975. Mem. ALA, Washington Library Assn. Office: Washington State Library Olympia WA 98504

SWARTZ, STEPHEN ARTHUR, banker, lawyer; b. Boston, Oct. 7, 1941; s. Norman and Frances (Feinstien) S.; B.A. in Polit. Sci., U. Mass., 1963; LL.B., Boston U., 1966; postgrad. in fin. and mgmt. Boston Coll., 1968-70; m. Louise D. Crosby, June 23, 1963; children—Marti Anne, Nanci Beth, Lori Ellen. Admitted to Mass. bar, 1967, N.Y. State bar, 1971; asst. counsel Fed. Res. Bank Boston. 1968-70, Irving Trust Co., N.Y.C., 1970-74; counsel, asst. sec. Charter N.Y. Corp., N.Y.C., 1974-77, v.p., asst. dir. investor communications, 1977-79; v.p., dir. investor communications Irving Bank Corp., N.Y.C., 1979—. Served to capt. AUS, 1966-68; Vietnam. Decorated Bronze Star (2), Army Commendation medal (2), Air medal (2); Vietnamese Honor medal 1st class. Mem. Am., Mass., N.Y. State bar assns., Bedford Riding Lanes Assn., Dandie Dinmont Terrier Club. Home: The Hook Rd Bedford NY 10506 Office: 1 Wall St New York NY 10005

SWARTZ, WILLIAM JOHN, transp. resources co. exec.; b. Hutchinson, Kans., Nov. 6, 1934; s. George Glen and Helen Mae (Prather) S.; B.S.M.E., Duke U., 1956; J.D., George Washington U., 1961; M.S. in Mgmt. (Alfred P. Sloan fellow), M.I.T., 1967; m. Dorothy Jean Parshall, June 5, 1956; children—John Christopher, Jeffrey Michael. With AT & SF Ry., 1961-78, asst. v.p. exec. dept., 1973-77, v.p. adminstrn., 1977-78; exec. v.p. Santa Fe Industries, Chgo., 1978—. Served with USMC, 1956-59. Mem. Am. Bar Assn., Chgo. Assn. Commerce and Industry, Western Ry. Assn., Republican. Methodist. Clubs: Chgo. Athletic Assn., Mid-Am. Home: 190 N Sheridan Rd Lake Forest IL 60045 Office: 224 S Michigan Ave Chicago IL 60604*

SWARTZBURG, GARY BENNETT, artist; b. San Francisco, Nov. 26, 1939; s. Charles J. and Marian Sylvia (Weiner) S.; B.A., San Francisco State U., 1962, postgrad., 1962-64; postgrad. U. Calif. at Los Angeles, 1964-65. Shows include Telegraph Hill Gallery, San Francisco, 1957, 60, Triangle Gallery, San Francisco, 1958, Pandora's, San Francisco, 1958, William Sawyer Gallery, San Francisco, 1959, San Francisco State U., 1959, Maxwell Gallery, San Francisco, 1959, Billy Pearson Gallery, San Francisco, 1960, Firehouse Gallery, San Francisco, 1962, Grete Williams Gallery, San Francisco, 1963-64, Artist Coop., San Francisco, 1964-67, Julie Dohan Gallery, Beverly Hills, 1968, Playhouse Gallery, San Francisco, 1968, Golden Gateway Center, 1972-73; exhibited in group shows including San Francisco Mus. Modern Art, 1961-62, painting ann. San Francisco Art Inst., print and drawing ann. San Francisco Art Assn., Art in Jazz exhbn., Monterey Internat. Jazz Festival, 1968, Sonora exhbn., 1965, Theater Arts Calif., 1960, Oakland Mus. Art, 1963-67; art instr. Antelope Valley Unified Sch. Dist., 1964, 66, San Francisco Unified Sch. Dist., 1966—; theater designer San Francisco Playhouse Theatre, 1957, CBS-TV, 1964, Abraham Lincoln Center, San Francisco for Owl and Pussycat, 1971, Lovers and Others Strangers, 1971, Man Who Came to Dinner, 1972, Auntie Mame, 1973, Bye, Bye Birdie, 1974. Mem. Artists Coop., 1964-70, v.p., 1969-70. Spl. award winner for Film as Art, San Francisco Internat. Film Festival, 1963; named Outstanding Art Instr., Japan Week, San Francisco, 1969; Outstanding Art Instr., Am. Cancer Soc. poster award, San Francisco, 1970. Home: 1701 Hyde St San Francisco CA 94109 Office: 135 Van Ness Ave San Francisco CA 94107. *"To see the world in a way no one has viewed it before, and in so doing, help others to enter my vision." Perhaps this is what creativity is all about! Anyway, it's ruled my life.*

SWARTZENDRUBER, DALE, soil physicist, educator; b. Parnell, Iowa, July 6, 1925; s. Urie and Norma (Kinsinger) S.; B.S., Iowa State U., 1950, M.S., 1952, Ph.D., 1954; m. Kathleen Jeanette Yoder, June 26, 1949; children—Karl Grant, Myra Mae, John Keith, David Mark. Instr. sci. Goshen (Ind.) Coll., 1953-54; asst. soil scientist U. Calif., Los Angeles, 1955-56; asso. prof. soil physics Purdue U., West Lafayette, Ind., 1956-63, prof., 1963-77; prof. soil physics U. Nebr., Lincoln, 1977—; vis. prof. Iowa State U., 1959, Ga. Inst. Tech., 1968, Hebrew U. Jerusalem at Rehovot, 1971; vis. scholar Cambridge (Eng.) U., 1971. Fellow Soil Sci. Soc. Am. (Soil Sci. award 1975), Am. Soc. Agronomy; mem. Am. Geophys. Union, AAAS, Internat. Soc. Soil Sci., Council for Agrl. Sci. and Tech. Mennonite. Contbr. articles on soil physics to profl. jours.; asso. editor Soil Sci. Soc. Am. Proc., 1965-70; mem. editorial bd. Geoderma (Amsterdam), 1975—; cons. editor Soil Sci., 1976—. Home: 707 D St Box 374 Milford NE 68405 Office: Dept Agronomy 133 Keim Hall East Campus Univ Nebraska Lincoln NE 68583

SWARZ, SAHL, sculptor; b. N.Y.C., May 4, 1912; s. Samuel and Ida (Fass) S.; student Clay Club, N.Y.C., 1928-34, Art Students League, N.Y.C., 1930-31; m. Naoco Kumasaka, May 1978. Asso. Dir. Clay Club, and successor, Sculpture Center, 1938-54; creative sculpture in Italy, 1951-63; residence Am. Acad. in Rome, 1955-57; one man exhbns. Sculpture Center, 1954, 57, 60, 62, 66, 71, 74, 78, Art Alliance, Phila., 1958, Fairweather-Hardin Gallery, Chgo., 1963, Brandeis U., Waltham, Mass., 1964; retrospective exhbn. Fair Lawn (N.J.) Pub. Library, 1977; group shows include Fairmont Park Internat., Phila., 1948, Whitney Mus. Am. Art, 1948, 58, 60, 62, 64,

Pa. Acad., 1948, 52, 54, 57, 60, 62, 66, Bklyn Mus., 1935, Detroit Inst. Fine Arts, 1957, San Francisco Mus., 1955, U. Ill., 1960, 62, others; rep. permanent collections Norfolk (Va.) Mus., Whitney Mus. Am. Art, Ball State Tchrs. Coll., Williams Coll. Mus., Ford Found., Mpls. Inst. Fine Arts, Va. Mus. Fine Arts, Richmond, Newark Mus., N.J. State Mus. at Trenton, Vatican Mus. Collection Modern Religious Art, Rose Art Mus., Brandeis U., Stamford (Conn.) Mus., Columbia U., others; bronze group The Guardian at Brookgreen (S.C.) Gardens Mus., terra cotta wall sculpture Linden, (N.J.) Post Office, sculptural designs Fed. Courthouse, Statesville, N.C., equestrian monument Gen. Bidwell, Buffalo; fountain commn. N.J. State Park at Spruce Run, Mall sculpture, Pittsfield, Mass.; asst. prof. Sculpture Columbia U., 1970-78; instr. Pratt Inst., Bklyn., 1964; vis. asso. prof. fine arts Brandeis U., 1964; instr. New Sch. for Social Research, 1965, 1966; vis. lectr. in art U. Wis. 1966; lectr. sculpture Columbia U., 1966-68. Chmn. sculpture panel N.J. Council on the Arts. Grantee Am. Acad. Arts and Letters, 1955; Guggenheim fellow, 1955, 58. Served with AUS, 1941-45. Author, illustrator; Blueprint for the Future of American Sculpture, 1943; also monograph. Address: Kumasaka-Swarz 2195 Kugenuma Fujisawa Kanagawa 251 Japan. *The essence of creativity is in the searching after the form. Search leads to revelation, understanding, knowledge. Realization of one's ignorance is the first step to the attainment of wisdom. A wise man makes a work of art out of life itself.*

SWARZTRAUBER, SAYRE ARCHIE, naval officer; b. Zion, Ill., June 23, 1929; s. Archie Douglas and Eleanor Miriam (Sayrs) S.; B.S. cum laude, Maryville (Tenn.) Coll., 1951; M.A., Am. U., 1964, Ph.D., 1970; m. Beryl Constance Stewart, June 27, 1953; children—Sayre Archie, Beryl Ann, Heidi, Holly. Commd. ensign U.S. Navy, 1952, advanced through grades to rear adm., 1976; comdr. River Squadron 5, Vietnam, 1968-69, U.S.S. Decatur, guided missile destroyer, 1970-71, Navy Recruiting Area 4, 1974-76; dep. chief staff Supreme Command Atlantic (NATO), 1976-79; co-dir. U.S.-Spanish Combined Staff, Madrid, 1979—; lectr. strategic naval matters, 1973—. Ruling elder Presbyterian Ch. U.S.A., 1965—. Decorated Legion of Merit (2), Meritorious Service medal, Navy Commendation medal, Def. Superior Service medal; Cross of Gallantry (Vietnam); recipient Alfred Thayer Mahan award Navy League, 1974. Mem. U.S. Strategic Inst., Am. Soc. Internat. Law, U.S. Naval Inst., VFW, Phi Kappa Phi, Pi Gamma Mu, Pi Sigma Alpha, Theta Alpha Phi. Clubs: Kiwanis, Mensa. Author: The Three-Mile Limit of Territorial Seas, 1972; contbr. articles, essays and revs. to profl. jours. Home: Oquendo 12 Madrid 6 Spain Office: US-Spanish Combined Staff APO NY 09285. *Most of the distinguished citizens in these volumes got here by hard work and a driving sense of purpose. That, I believe, is how it should be—a natural process in a free society. America was literally driven to the forefront among nations by great numbers of hard-driving workers. But those with these attributes are an endangered species. As their numbers decline, there are more tasks left for them to do. And not the least of these tasks is to help reverse the trend, and keep America in the Who's Who of Nations.*

SWATEK, FRANK EDWARD, educator; b. Oklahoma City, June 4, 1929; s. Clarence Michael and Bessie (Doubek) S.; B.S. in Zoology, San Diego State Coll., 1951; M.A. in Microbiology, U. Calif. at Los Angeles, 1955, Ph.D., 1956; m. Mary Frances Over, Jan. 28, 1951; children—Frank Edward, Lorraine Beth, Martha Lynn, Susan Ann, Cheryl Lee. Mem. faculty Calif. State U. at Long Beach, 1956—, prof. microbiology, 1963—, chmn. dept., 1960—; cons. to industry, 1953—; cons. dept. dermatology Long Beach VA Hosp., 1956—; lectr. postgrad. medicine U. So. Calif., 1958—. Mem. fuel sect. Coordinating Research Council, 1961—. Fellow Royal Soc. Health, Am. Acad. Microbiology; mem. Am. So. Microbiology (Carski Found. Distinguished Teaching award 1974), Internat. Platform Assn., Sigma Xi, Lambda Xi Alpha, Phi Kappa Phi. Club: Long Beach Aquatic (pres. 1963-65). Author: Textbook of Microbiology, 1967; Laboratory Manual and Workbook for General Microbiology, 1969. also articles. Research on med. mycology. Home: 812 Stevely St Long Beach CA 90815

SWAYZE, JOHN CAMERON, SR., news commentator; b. Wichita, Kans., Apr. 4, 1906; s. Jesse Ernest and Mary Christine (Cameron) S.; student U. Kans., 1925-27, Dramatic Sch., N.Y.C., 1928-29; m. Beulah Mae Estes, Oct. 29, 1932; children—John Cameron, Suzanne Louise. Mem. editorial staff Kansas City (Mo.) Jour. Post, news commentator Stas. KMBC and WHB, 1930-40, feature editor, 1940; mem. news staff Sta. KMBC, 1940-45; news and spl. events dir. Western network NBC, Hollywood, Calif., 1946-47, radio and television news commentator NBC, N.Y.C., 1947-56, also radio news programs on ABC, and TV programs, including role of host on Sightseeing with the Swayzes (with wife, son and daughter). Mem. Legion of Honor, Order De Molay. Presbyn. Clubs: Woodway Gun (Darien): Lambs, Players (N.Y.C.); Nat. Press (Washington); Greenwich (Conn.) Country. Author: The Art of Living, 1979. Home: 491 Riversville Rd Greenwich CT 06830. *I am a firm believer in luck and personal contact. The old cliche, "being at the right place at the right time," is 110 percent right. The equally venerable saying, "It's not what you know, but who you know," is only 50 percent correct. The "who you know" is dead center but the rest is bunk.*

SWEANY, GORDON HAMILTON, ins. exec.; b. Curtis, Wash., May 8, 1913; s. Charles H. and Eliza (Harris) S.; LL.B. cum laude, U. Wash., 1934; m. Alta M. Showalter, Sept. 8, 1934; 1 son, Garett Gordon. Admitted to Wash. bar, 1934; with Gen. Am. Corp., Gen. Ins. Co., SAFECO Ins. Co. and affiliate cos., 1934—, successively law clk., atty., chief atty., gen. counsel, 1934-52, v.p., gen. counsel, 1952-66, pres., dir., 1966—; chief exec. officer Safeco Corp. and affiliates, 1970-78, chmn. bd., 1977—; dir. Security Title Ins. Co., Los Angeles, PACCAR, Inc., Wash. Mut. Savs. Bank. Past pres. Found. for Internat. Students; gen. campaign chmn. Seattle-King County United Way, 1974, pres., 1978; regional chmn., bd. dirs. Nat. Alliance of Businessmen, 1976; bd. dirs. Virginia Mason Hosp., pres., 1978; bd. dirs. Ins. Info. Inst., Ins. Inst. Am., Econ. Devel. Council (pres. 1979), Pacific Legal Found., Am. Trauma Soc. Mem. Am., Wash., Seattle bar assns., Seattle C. of C., Property and Casualty Ins. Council (chmn. 1979), Internat. Assn. Ins. Counsel, Order of Coif. Clubs: Rotary, Wash. Athletic, Rainier, Seattle Golf. Home: 13030 39th Ave NE Seattle WA 98125 Office: Safeco Plaza Seattle WA 98185

SWEARER, HOWARD ROBERT, coll. pres.; b. Hutchinson, Kans., Mar. 13, 1932; s. Edward Mays and Elloise (Keeney) S.; A.B., Princeton, 1954; M.A., Harvard, 1956, Ph.D. 1960; m. Janet Lois Baker, June 19, 1954; children—Nicholas Baker, Howard Randolph, Richard William. Prof. polit. sci. U. Calif. at Los Angeles, 1960-67; program officer-in-charge office European and internat. affairs Ford Found., N.Y.C., 1967-70; pres. Carleton Coll., Northfield, Minn., 1970-77; pres. Brown U., Providence, 1977—; dir. Textron Inc. Bd. dirs. A Better Chance, Inc., German Marshall Fund U.S., Am. Council on Edn. Served to 1st lt. AUS, 1958-59. Mem. Council Fgn. Relations, Phi Beta Kappa (senator). Home: 55 Power St Providence RI 02906 Office: Brown U 79 Waterman St Providence RI 02919

SWEARINGEN, EUGENE LAURREL, banker; b. Grant, Nebr., Aug. 21, 1920; s. Laurrel Brooks and Edna Ruth (Frank) S.; B.S., Okla. State U., 1941, M.S., 1948; Ph.D., Stanford, 1955; postgrad. Harvard Grad. Sch. Bus., Williams Coll., Dartmouth, U. Calif.; LL.D. (hon.), Okla. Christian Coll.; m. Aasalee Chace, Sept. 19, 1941; children—Linda Sue, Sandra Kay, Sherry Jean. Field scout exec. Boy Scouts Am., 1941-43, 46-47; instr. econs. Okla. State U., 1948-51, asst. prof., 1951-56, asso. prof., 1956-57, prof., 1957-66, dean Coll. Bus., 1957-65, v.p. univ. devel., 1964-66, v.p. bus. and fin., 1966-67; pres. U. Tulsa, 1967-68; pres., dir. Nat. Bank of Tulsa (now Bank of Okla.), 1968-69, pres., chief exec. officer, 1969-73, chmn. bd., chief exec. officer, 1973-78, chmn. exec. com., 1978—; sr. asso. Kidder & Co., Cambridge, Mass., 1959-61; mem. panel arbitrators Fed. Mediation and Conciliation Service, 1960-66; dean So. Methodist U. Grad. Sch. Banking, Dallas; mem. Okla. State Regents for Higher Edn.; pres. Okla. Council Econ. Edn., 1959. Pres. Downtown Tulsa Unltd., 1972, 73; pres. Indian Nations council Boy Scouts Am., 1976-77; campaign chmn. Tulsa Area United Way, 1978. Served with USNR, 1943-46. Recipient Mktg. Man of Yr. award Tulsa chpt. Am. Marketing Assn., 1971; named Man of Yr., Downtown Tulsa Unltd., 1969; inducted into Hall of Fame, Coll. Bus., Okla. State U., 1970; named to Okla. Hall of Fame, 1973. Mem. Am. Econ. Assn., Financial Execs. Inst., Nat. Council Small Bus. Mgmt. Devel. (pres. 1964-65), Southwestern Assn. Bus. Sch. Deans (chmn. 1964-65), Met. Tulsa C. of C. (pres. 1975), Phi Kappa Phi, Beta Gamma Sigma, Omicron Delta Kappa, Beta Alpha Psi, Delta Sigma Pi. Democrat. Methodist. Clubs: Southern Hills Country, Tulsa (Tulsa). Co-editor: Business Policy Cases with Behavioral Science Implications, 1963. Home: 2650 E 66th St Tulsa OK 74136 Office: PO Box 2300 Tulsa OK 74192

SWEARINGEN, JOHN ELDRED, oil exec.; b. Columbia, S.C., Sept. 7, 1918; s. John Eldred and Mary (Hough) S.; B.S., U. S.C., 1938, LL.D., 1965; M.S., Carnegie-Mellon U., 1939; D.Eng., S.D. Sch. Mines and Tech., 1960, Mont. Coll. Mining Sci. and Tech., 1979; LL.D., Knox Coll., 1962, DePauw U., 1964, Ill. Coll., 1968, Butler U., 1968, Samford U., 1973, Calumet Coll., 1976; D.Bus.Mgmt., Ind. Inst. Tech., 1973; D.L.H., Nat. Coll. Edn., 1967; m. Bonnie L. Bolding, May 18, 1969; children (by previous marriage)—Marcia L. Swearingen Pfleeger, Sarah K. Swearingen Origer, Linda. Chem. engr. research dept. Standard Oil Co. (Ind.), Whiting, Ind., 1939-47; various positions Amoco Prodn. Co., Tulsa, 1947-51; gen. mgr. prodn. Standard Oil Co. (Ind.), Chgo., 1951, dir., 1952, v.p. prodn., 1954, exec. v.p., 1956, pres. 1958, chief exec. officer, 1960—, chmn. bd., 1965—; dir. Lockheed Corp., Chase Manhattan Corp. Mem. adv. bd. Hoover Instn. on War, Revolution and Peace, 1967—; trustee Carnegie Mellon U., DePauw U., Chgo. Orchestral Assn.; bd. dirs. McGraw Wildlife Found., 1964-75; bd. dirs. Automotive Safety Found., 1959-69, chmn., 1962-64; bd. dirs. Hwy Users Fedn. for Safety and Mobility, 1969-75, Northwestern Meml. Hosp. Decorated Order of The Taj (Iran); commendatore Dell'Ordine Del Merito Della Repubblica Italiana. Fellow Am. Inst. Chem. Engrs.; mem. Am. Petroleum Inst. (dir. 1958—, chmn. 1978—), Nat. Petroleum Council (chmn. 1974-76), Am. Inst. Mining, Metall and Petroleum Engrs., Conf. Bd. (sr.), Am. Chem. Soc., Nat. Acad. Engring., Phi Beta Kappa, Sigma Xi, Omicron Delta Kappa, Tau Beta Pi. Clubs: Mid-Am., Execs., Chgo., Racquet, Econ., Comml. (Chgo.); Links (N.Y.C.); Bohemian (San Francisco); Eldorado Country (Palm Springs); Old Elm (Lake Forest, Ill.); Glen View (Ill.) Golf. Home: 1420 Lake Shore Dr Chicago IL 60610 Office: 200 E Randolph Dr Chicago IL 60601

SWEARINGEN, LAWSON LEWIS, ins. co. exec.; b. Tex., Dec. 22, 1919; s. Henry Declouit and Annie Marie (Estlinbaum) S.; B.S. in Bus. Adminstrn., La. Tech. U., 1947; m. Jean Cadwallader, Feb. 2, 1940; children—Carolyn, Sharon, Lawson Lewis. Vice pres. William A. Marbury & Co., Ruston, La., 1947-63; with Commml. Union Assurance Corp., 1963—, sr. v.p., Boston, 1973-75, pres., chief exec. officer, 1975—, also dir. Mem. La. North-South Expressway Commn., 1967, La. Polit. Edn. Commn., 1968-72; bd. dirs. Gordon Coll., Wenham, Mass., 1974—. Served as officer AUS, 1944-46, 50-51. Named Outstanding Alumnus of Year, La. Tech. U., 1973. Mem. Am. Ins. Assn. (dir.), Ins. Info. Inst. (dir.). Baptist. Club: Kiwanis (chpt. pres. 1957). Office: 1 Beacon St Boston MA 02108

SWEENEY, ARTHUR HAMILTON, JR., metal mfg. co. exec., ret. army officer; b. Charleston, W.Va., Nov. 9, 1920; s. Arthur Hamilton and Neva Pauline (Davies) S.; S.B., Mass. Inst. Tech., 1942; M.B.A., Harvard, 1947; m. Veronica Frances Donovan, Dec. 27, 1952. Advanced through grades to maj. gen. U.S. Army; comdg. officer U.S. Army Springfield (Mass.) Armory, 1965-67, U.S. Army Watervliet (N.Y.) Arsenal, 1967-68; dep. comdg. gen. U.S. Army Weapons Command, Rock Island, Ill., 1968-70; comdg. gen. Quinhon Support Command, Vietnam, 1970, DaNang Support Command, Vietnam, 1970-72; comdg. gen. White Sands Missile Range, N.Mex., 1972-74; comdg. gen. U.S. Army Materiel Mgmt. Agy., Europe, 1974-76; dep. chief of staff for logistics U.S. Army Forces Command, 1976-78; ret., 1978; spl. asst. to chmn. bd. Reynolds Metals Internat., Richmond, Va., 1978—. Decorated D.S.M. with oak leaf cluster, Legion of Merit with oak leaf cluster, Joint Services Commendation medal, Army Commendation medal. Home: 2602 Liberty St Parkersburg WV 26101 Office: Reymolds Metals Internat Richmond VA 23161

SWEENEY, ASHER WILLIAM, justice; b. Canfield, Ohio, Dec. 11, 1920; s. Walter William and Jessie Joan (Kidd) S.; student Youngstown U., 1939-42; LL.B., Duke U., 1948; m. Bertha M. Englert, May 21, 1945; children—Randall W., Ronald R., Garland A., Karen M. Admitted to Ohio bar, 1949; practiced in Youngstown, Ohio, 1949-51; judge adv. gen. Dept. of Def., Washington, 1951-65; chief Fed. Contracting Agy., Cin., 1965-68; corporate law, 1968-77; justice, Ohio Supreme Ct., Columbus, 1977—. Democratic candidate for Sec. of State Ohio, 1958. Served with U.S. Army, 1942-46, col. Res., 1951-68. Decorated Legion of Merit, Bronze Star. Mem. Ohio Bar Assn., Phi Delta Phi. Democrat. Home: 6690 Drake Rd Cincinnati OH 45243 Office: 30 E Broad Columbus OH 43215

SWEENEY, BEATRICE MARCY, educator; b. Boston, Aug. 11, 1914; d. Henry Orlando and Eleanor Hunniwell (Nichols) Marcy; A.B., Smith Coll., 1936; Ph.D., Radcliffe Coll., 1942; m. Paul Lee, Nov. 3, 1961; children—Eleanor DeMarco, Sara Constans, Randolph Sweeney, Jay Sweeney. Research biologist Scripps Inst. Oceanography, La Jolla, Calif., 1948-61; lectr. Yale, 1961-67; prof. biology U. Calif. at Santa Barbara, 1967—; cons. NASA; dir. Biol. Scis. Curriculum Study, 1975-77; mem. com. photobiology NRC, 1973-76. NSF grantee, 1958—. Mem. AAAS, Am. Inst. Biol. Scis. (dir. 1975—, pres.-elect 1978), Am. Soc. Plant Physiologists, Phycol. Soc. Am., Am. Soc. Photobiology (pres.-elect 1978), Phi Beta Kappa, Sigma Xi. Author: Rhythmic Phenomena in Plants, 1969. Contbr. articles to profl. jours. Home: 6877 Del Playa Goleta CA 93017 Office: Dept Biol Scis Univ Calif Santa Barbara CA 93106

SWEENEY, CLAYTON ANTHONY, lawyer, mfg. co. exec.; b. Pitts., Oct. 20, 1931; s. Denis Regis and Grace Frances (Roche) S.; B.S., Duquesne U., 1957, LL.B., 1962; m. Sally Dimond, Oct. 4, 1958; children—Sharon, Lorrie, Maureen, Clayton Anthony, Tara, Megan. Supr. transp. claims H.J. Heinz Co., Pitts., 1955-57; mgr. market research Murray Corp. Am., Pitts., 1957-62; admitted to Pa. bar, 1962, Supreme Ct. bar, 1965; partner firm Buchanan, Ingersoll, Rodewald, Kyle and Buerger, Pitts., 1962-78; sr. v.p. Allegheny Ludlum Industries, Inc., Pitts., 1978—, also dir.; dir. Wilkinson Match, Ltd. (U.K.), 2d Fed. Savs. and Loan Assn., Liquid Air N. Am., adj. prof. law Duquesne U. Sch. Law; lectr. Pa. Bar Inst. Bd. dirs. Met. Pitts. Public Broadcasting, Inc., Diocesan Sch. Bd., Roman Catholic Diocese Pitts., Toner Inst., Christian Assos. of Southwestern Pa.; mem. St. Thomas More Sch. Bd., Bethel Park, Pa. Served with U.S. Army, 1953-55. Named one of 100 Most Disting. Living Alumni, Duquesne U. Century Club, 1978. Mem. Acad. Trial Lawyers Allegheny County, Am. Bar. Assn., Pa. Bar Assn., Allegheny County Bar Assn., St. Thomas More Soc. Home: 4972 Highland Ave Bethel Park PA 15102 Office: 2700 Two Oliver Plaza Pittsburgh PA 15222

SWEENEY, FRANCIS JOSEPH, JR., physician, hosp. exec.; b. Phila., Dec. 20, 1925; M.D., Jefferson Med. Coll., 1951; m. Helen Marie Drueding, June 16, 1951 (dec.); children—Margaret Ann Sweeney Boova, Eileen Marie Sweeney Brazitis, Maureen, Francis Joseph III, Michael William. Intern, Jefferson Med. Coll. Hosp., Phila., 1951-52, resident, 1952-53, 55-58, asso. prof. medicine, 1967—, attending physician, 1969—; v.p. health services, dir. Thomas Jefferson U. Hosp., 1972—; v.p. health services Children's Heart Hosp. Phila., 1972—; cons. Chestnut Hill Hosp. Bd. dirs. Health Systems Agy. Southeastern Pa.; mem. Delaware Valley Hosp. Council, Hosp. Assn. Pa. Recipient Lindback award for distinguished teaching Jefferson Med. Coll., 1963. Fellow A.C.P. (regent); mem. Infectious Disease Soc. Am. Home: 931 Cedar Grove Rd Wynnewood PA 19096 Office: Thomas Jefferson U Hosp 11th and Walnut Sts Philadelphia PA 19107

SWEENEY, JAMES DANIEL, food co. exec.; b. Ladonia, Tex., Apr. 17, 1917; s. Albert Earl and Julia Lawson (Nunn) S.; B.B.A., U. Tex., 1939; m. Edith Fly Jarrell, Nov. 18, 1947; children—Thomas Jarrell, Anita. Systems engr. IBM, San Antonio, 1940-43, br. mgr., San Antonio, 1946-48; exec. v.p. Sweeney & Co., Inc., San Antonio, 1948-62; exec. v.p. Waples-Platter Cos., Ft. Worth, 1962-70, pres., 1970—, also dir.; dir. White Swan, Inc., Graphic Arts, Inc., Ranch Style, Inc., Service Stores, Inc. Served to capt. A.C., U.S. Army, 1943-46. Mem. Nat. Am. Wholesale Grocers Assn. (gov. 1970—, mem. exec. com. 1975—, chmn. bd. govs. 1977—), Nat. Assn. Wholesale Distbrs. (trustee), Food Mktg. Inst., Newcomen Soc. Episcopalian. Clubs: Order Alamo, River Crest Country, San Antonio Country, Ft. Worth, Century II, Exchange, Lubbock (Tex.), Argyle. Home: 1101 Hidden Rd Fort Worth TX 76107 Office: PO Box 1350 Fort Worth TX 76101

SWEENEY, JAMES FRANCIS, JR., textile mill exec.; b. Providence, Sept. 5, 1922; s. James Francis and Anne S.; B.S., Providence Coll., 1947; M.B.A., U. Conn., 1970; m. Helen Bertha Brennen, Sept. 23, 1950; children—Paul, James, William, Edward, Maureen. With Crompton Co., Inc., N.Y.C., 1949—, now sec., asst. treas. Mem. Nat. Assn. Accountants, Am. Soc. Personnel Adminstrn., Am. Soc. Corporate Secs., Am. Textile Mfrs. Assn. Home: 37 Raymond Terrace East Norwalk CT 06855 Office: 1071 Ave of Americas New York City NY 10018

SWEENEY, JAMES JOHNSON, writer, museum dir.; b. Bklyn., May 30, 1900; s. Patrick M. and Mary (Johnson) S.; A.B., Georgetown U., 1922, L.H.D., 1963; student Jesus Coll., Cambridge, Eng., 1922-24, Sorbonne, Paris, 1925, U. Siena (Italy), 1926; D.F.A. (hon.), Grinnell Coll., 1957, U. Mich., 1960, U. Notre Dame, 1961; Arts D., Ripon (Wis.) Coll., 1960; L.H.D., Rollins (Fla.) Coll., 1960, Coll., Holy Cross, U. Miami, Georgetown U., 1963; A.F.D. (hon.), U. Buffalo, 1962; LL.D., Nat. U., Dublin, 1978; m. Laura Harden, May 17, 1927; children—Ann Sweeney Baxter, Sean, Siadhal, Tadhg, Ciannait Sweeney Tait. N.Y. corr. Chgo. Evening Post Art World, 1931-32; dir. exhbn. 20th Century Painting and Sculpture, U. Chgo., 1933-34; lectr. on fine arts Inst. Fine Arts, N.Y. U., 1935-40; vis. scholar U. Ga; 1950, 51; lectr. fine arts Harvard U., 1961; dir. exhbn. African Negro Art, Mus. Modern Art, N.Y.C., 1935, dir. exhbn. of work by Joan Miro, 1941, exhbn. of sculpture and constructions by Alexander Calder, 1943, Alfred Stieglitz exhbn., 1947, dir. dept. painting and sculpture, 1945-46; dir. Picasso exhbn. Art Gallery Toronto, 1949; dir. commentary film Henry Moore, 1948; dir. exhbns. 12 Am. Painters, Dublin, 1963; dir. Va. Biennial Exhbn.; 1950; resident scholar U. Ga., 1950-51; dir. Sculpture by Alexander Calder, Mass. Inst. Tech., 1950-51; Masterpieces of XXth Century, Musée d'Art Moderne, Paris and Tate Gallery, London, 1952; installation U.S. Pavillon Biennale, Venice, Italy, 1952; mem. jury Carnegie Internat. July, 1958, 76; Message on the Plastic Arts, Brussels Exposition, 1958; mem. jury Internat. Biennal Exhbn. of Prints, Tokyo, 1966, Rosc Exhbn., Dublin, Ireland, 1967, UNESCO Prize, Venice, 1968; dir. Burlington Mag., London, 1952-61, mem. cons. com., 1961—; dir. Alexander Calder Exhbn. Tate Gallery, London, 1962, Signals in the Sixties, Honolulu Acad. Arts, 1968; contbg. critic New Republic, 1952-53; art adv. com. Chase Manhattan Bank, N.Y.C., 1958—; adv. com. The Arts Center Program, Columbia U., adv. council art and archaeology; mem. curriculum adv. bd. art adn. dept. N.Y. U. Mem. adv. com. Bennington (Vt.) Coll.; trustee Bauhaus-Archive, Am. Acad. in Rome, 1962; mem. art com. Addison Gallery; mem. W.B. Yeats Meml. Com., Dublin; mem. Am. Revolution Bicentennial Commn., 1967-69; bd. dirs. Am. Irish Found.; mem. vis. com. on fine arts Fogg Mus., Harvard; hon. pres. Fedn. Internationale du Film d'Art, Paris; dir. Mus. Fine Arts (Houston), 1961-68, cons. dir., 1968—; gallery cons. Nat. Gallery, Canberra, Australia, 1968—; art adv. com. U. Notre Dame, 1968—; art adviser Israel Mus., Jerusalem, 1972—; adviser on purchase Arts Council N. Ireland, Belfast, 1970. Decorated chevalier Legion d'Honneur, 1955; officer de l'ordre des Arts et des Lettres, 1959; knight comdr. Order of Isabel la Catolica (Madrid), 1977; recipient Art in Am. award, 1963. Fellow Am. Acad. Arts and Scis., Royal Soc. Antiquaries of Ireland (Dublin); mem. Assn. Art Mus. Dirs., Edward MacDowell Assn. (pres. 1955-62, counselor 1964—), Internat. Assn. Art Critics (pres. 1957-63, dir. 1963—), Buffalo Fine Arts Inst. (hon.), Iran Am. Soc. (dir. 1964—), Société Europeéne de la Culture, Mediaeval Acad. Am. (councillor), Art Council Dublin, Nat. Council Arts, Internat. Council Mus. Modern Art (hon.), Yeats Assn. Dublin (hon.), Nat. Council Arts, Soc. Internat. des Arts Chretiens (v.p.), Liturg. Arts Soc. (dir.), Phi Beta Kappa. Clubs: Century, Grolier, Players, Brook, River (N.Y.C.); Cosmos (Washington); Athenaeum (London); Kildare St., Univ., Hibernian United Service, Stephen's Green (Dublin). Author, co-author or editor: Alexander Calder, 1951; African Folk Tales and Sculpture (with Paul Radin), 1952, rev. 1965; Burri, 1955; Antoni Gaudi (with José Luis Sert), 1960, Atmosphere Miro, 1959, AFRO, 1961; Irish Illuminated Manuscripts, 1965; Vision and Image, 1968; Alexander Calder, 1971; Joan Miro, 1970; Eduardo Chillida, 1970; Pierre Soulages, 1972; Contemporaries and Predecessors, 1973; asst. editor Partisan Rev., 1948-63. Home: 120 East End Ave New York NY 10028

SWEENEY, JAMES RAYMOND, lawyer; b. Chgo., Feb. 19, 1928; s. John Francis and Mae J. (McDonald) S.; B.S., U. Notre Dame, 1950; J.D., Northwestern U., 1956; m. Joan T. Machen, Sept. 14, 1957; children—Margaret Elizabeth, John Francis, Thomas Edward. Admitted to Ill. bar, 1956; with firm Schroeder, Hofgren, Brady & Wegner, Chgo., 1956-61; partner Hofgren, Wegner, Allen, Stellman & McCord, Chgo., 1962-71, Coffee, Wetzel, Sweeney, Chgo., 1971-72, Coffee & Sweeney, 1972-76, Mason, Kolehmainen, Rathburn & Wyss, Chgo., 1976—; commr. for disbarment matters Ill. Supreme Ct., 1963-73. Chmn. hearing div. disciplinary com. Supreme Ct. Atty. Registration Commn., 1975-77. Bd. dirs., sec. Highland Park (Ill.) Hosp., 1972-79. Served as lt. (j.g.) USN, 1950-53; lt. comdr. Res. Mem. Am. (council patent, trademark and copyright sect.), Ill., Chgo.

(sec. 1977-79) bar assns., Am., Chgo. patent law assns., U.S. Trademark Assn., Bar Assn. 7th Circuit, Internat. Patent and Trademark Assn., Patent Law Assn. Chgo. (pres. 1974), Am. Judicature Soc. Clubs: Skokie (Ill.) Country; Legal, Chicago Curling, Tower (Chgo.). Home: 690 Carlisle Ave Deerfield IL 60015 Office: 20 N Wacker Dr Chicago IL 60606

SWEENEY, JOSEPH MODESTE, lawyer; b. Phila., Sept. 6, 1920; s. Joseph Patrick and Marie-Louise (Grand) S.; Baccalaureat, U. Grenoble (France), 1938, Licence en Droit, 1945; LL.B., Harvard, 1948; Dr. honoris causa, U. Lyon (France), 1969; m. Barbara M. Cooper, June 27, 1948; children—Marly, Anne-Marie, Pamela, Jacqueline, Patrick. Admitted to D.C. bar, 1948, U.S. Supreme Ct. bar, 1953; with Legal Adviser's Office, State Dept., 1948-56; from asso. prof. to prof. law, dir. Inst. Comparative Law, N.Y.U. Law Sch., 1956-68; dean Tulane U. Law Sch., 1968-77, prof. law, 1977—. Served with AUS, 1942-45. Mem. Am. Law Inst., Am. Soc. Internat. Law. Author: (with Noyes E. Leech and Covey T. Oliver) The International Legal System, Cases and Materials, 1973. Author papers in field. Home: 6028 Pitt St New Orleans LA 70118

SWEENEY, KEVIN BRENDAN, broadcasting exec.; b. Los Angeles, Dec. 22, 1916; s. Edward E. and May R. (Salvant) S.; A.B., U. So. Calif., 1938; m. Marguerite Taylor, Mar. 22, 1941; children—Dennis Gregory, Sheila Meghan, Melissa Ann. Sales promotion dept. CBS, 1938-41; asst. to v.p. Western div. ABC, 1941-44; mgr. HPL programs Fletcher Wiley Prodns., then for CBS, 1945-48; gen. sales mgr. KFI, KFI-TV, Los Angeles, 1948-51; v.p. Radio Advt. Bur., Inc. (formerly Broadcast Advt. Bur., Inc.), 1951-54, pres., 1954-63; pres. John Poole Broadcasting Co., KBIQ, Inc., Los Angeles, 1963-64, v.p., 1964-68; broadcast sta. cons., 1965—; pres. Young Adult Marketing Inc., 1969—, MRS Devel. Inc., 1969—; pres. Danton Books, Inc., 1966-71, Night and Day Formal Wear, Inc., 1968-71, Bridal Fair, Inc., 1968-69, dir., 1968-71. Served as lt. (j.g.) USNR, 1944-45. Home: 20055 Wells Dr Woodland Hills CA 91364 Office: PO Box 1673 Thousand Oaks CA 91360

SWEENEY, (CHARLES) LEO, educator; b. O'Connor, Nebr., Sept. 22, 1918; s. John Michael and Ellen Theresa (McDowell) S.; B.A., St. Louis U., 1941, M.A., 1945, Licentiate in Philosophy, 1943, Licentiate in Theology, 1951; Ph.D., U. Toronto, 1954. Joined Jesuit Order, 1936, ordained Roman Catholic priest, 1949; prof. dept. philosophy St. Louis U., 1954-68; research prof. dept. philosophy Creighton U., Omaha, 1968-70; vis. prof. Cath. U. Am. Sch. Philosophy, Washington, 1970-72; prof. dept. philosophy Loyola U., Chgo., 1972—. Am. Council Learned Socs. fellow, 1963-64; research grantee Creighton U., 1968; research grantee humanities devel. program U.S. Office Edn., 1969-70. Mem. Metaphys. Soc. Am., Mediaeval Acad. Am., Société Internationale pour l'Étude de la Philosophie Médiévale, Jesuit Philos. Assn. Am. (editor Procs. 1960-63, sec. 1960-63, pres. 1965-66), Am. Philos. Assn., Soc. Medieval and Renaissance Philosophy, Am. Maritain Assn., Soc. Christian Philosophers, Am. Cath. Philos. Assn. (exec. council 1968-71, 79-82, v.p. 1979-80, pres. 1980-81), Soc. Ancient Greek Philosophy, Internat. Soc. Neoplatonic Studies. Author: A Metaphysics of Authentic Existentialism, 1965; Infinity in the Presocratics, 1972. Editor: Wisdom in Depth, 1966. Contbr. articles to profl. jours. Address: Loyola U 6525 N Sheridan Rd Chicago IL 60626

SWEENEY, LEO PATRICK AUGUSTINE, ophthalmologist; b. Ardoch, N.D., Oct. 11, 1899; s. James Joseph and Annie (Bogan) S.; B.S., U. N.D., 1922; student U. Chgo. Med. Sch., summer 1922; M.D., Loyola U., Chgo., 1925; m. Elaine Frances Dunphy, Apr. 20, 1927; children—Leo Patrick Augustine, James Joseph II, Lois (Mrs. L. Sweeney Kluck), Merry Carol (dec.). Intern Mercy Hosp., Chgo., 1924-25, mem. attending staff, 1926—, mem. attending free dispensary, 1924-33; mem. attending staff Ill. Eye and Ear Infirmary, 1933-48, St. Francis Hosp., Blue Island, Ill., 1926-30, Little Company of Mary Hosp., Evergreen Park, Ill., 1930—, attending ophthalmologist Ill. State Penitentiary, Joliet, 1938-41; mem. faculty Stritch Sch. Medicine, Loyola U., 1930-74. Trustee Ill. Med. Service (Blue Shield), 1953-77, sec., 1954-59, v.p., 1959, pres., chmn. bd., 1960-70, emeritus, 1970—; bd. dirs. Nat. Assn. Blue Shield Plans, 1963-70, Med. Indemnity of Am., 1964-77, chmn. bd., 1968-75. Bd. dirs. Chgo. USO, 1969-78. Served with U.S. Army, 1918; to col. M.C., AUS, 1941-46. Decorated Legion of Merit; Order of Crown, Order of St. Etienne (Italy); named Man of Year, Intern-Resident Alumni Assn. Mercy Hosp., 1960; recipient Sioux award U. N.D., 1966. Fellow Miss. Valley Med. Soc.; mem. Am. (ho. dels. 1956-71), World med. assns., Ill. (councillor 1946-48, 50-51, pres. 1952), Chgo. (councillor 1938-58, trustee 1958-66, pres. Calumet br. 1939) med. socs., Assn. Mil Surgeons, Ill. Assn. Professions, Constantinian Med. Soc. (councillor 1966-70), Am. Legion, Order Lafayette, Mil. Order World Wars (surgeon Chgo. chpt. 1970—), Conf. Presidents and Other State Med. Soc. Officers (pres. 1969), Phi Beta Pi. K.C. (4 deg.). Roman Catholic. Home: 11301 S Lothair Chicago IL 60643 Office: 3759 W 95th St Evergreen Park IL 60642

SWEENEY, RICHARD THOMAS, library adminstr.; b. Atlantic City, Jan. 22, 1946; s. Harry A. and Margaret (McArdle) S.; B.A. in Humanities, Villanova U., 1967; M.A. in Librarianship, Glassboro State Coll., 1970; M.L.S. in Library and Info. Sci., Drexel U., 1972; m. Virginia Beschen, Aug. 26, 1967; children—Meghan, Moira, Thomas. Tchr., Holy Spirit High Sch., Absecon, N.J., 1967-69; librarian Central Jr. High, Atlantic City, 1969-70; mem. faculty Glassboro State Coll. Grad. Sch. Library Sci., 1973-74; dir. Atlantic City Free Public Library, 1971-76, Genesee County (Mich.) Library, 1976-79; exec. dir. Public Library of Columbus and Franklin (Ohio), 1979—; chmn. personnel com. Thomas A. Edison Coll.; mem. adv. bd. Atlantic Community Coll. Sec. Jaycees of Greater Atlantic City, 1971-72, 74, v.p., 1973. Mem. South Jersey Librarians, Mich. Library Assn., N.J. Library Assn., Cape-Atlantic Consortium, ALA, State Library Ohio. Clubs: Rotary, (Flint, Mich.); Kiwanis (dir.) (Atlantic City). Home: 6571 Borr Ave Reynoldsburg OH 43068 Office: 28 S Hamilton Rd Columbus OH 43213

SWEENEY, ROBERT JOSEPH, oil co. exec.; b. Montpelier, Vt., Oct. 23, 1927; s. Robert Joseph and Glenna Ethylin (Little) S.; B.S., Auburn U., 1948; M.S., La. Tech. U., 1961; m. Hazel Miller, Mar. 7, 1947; children—Robert Joseph, III, Theodore C., James Bradford. With Murphy Oil Corp., El Dorado, Ark., 1952—, pres., chief operating officer, 1972—. Pres. El Dorado Boys Club, 1968, 74-78. Served with USNR, 1945-46. Mem. AIME. Club: K.C. Home: 1502 N Euclid St El Dorado AR 71730 Office: 200 N Jefferson St El Dorado AR 71730

SWEENY, HENRY WARE ALLEN, financial exec.; b. Kansas City, Mo., May 10, 1934; s. Arthur Cary and Winifred (Allen) S.; B.S., U. Kans., 1956; M.B.A., Harvard, 1961; m. Petrea Lee Doty, Oct. 21, 1956 (div.); children—Peter, Christine, Catherine, David. Mgr. capital budget div. Esso Colombiana, Bogota, 1957-59; financial analyst Standard Oil Co. N.J., 1963; asst. controller Esso Argentina, Buenos Aires, 1964-67; mgr. bus. analysis Esso Chem. Co., N.Y.C., 1967-69; treas., controller internat. Standard Brands, Inc., N.Y.C., 1969—, v.p. fin., 1977—; lectr. bus. adminstrn. Norwalk (Conn.) Community Coll., 1968-69. Pres. Brookside P.T.A., Norwalk, 1969-70. Mem. Norwalk Bd. Estimate and Taxation, 1971—. Mem. Financial Execs. Inst., Phi Gamma Delta, Beta Gamma Sigma, Omicron Delta Kappa. Republican. Conglist. (chmn. bd. deacons 1969-70). Author: Accounting Fundamentals for Non Financial Executives, 1972; (with others) Budgeting Fundamentals for Non-Financial Executives, 1975. Home: 760 Park Ave New York NY 10021 Office: 9 W 57th St New York NY 10019

SWEET, BERNARD, airline exec.; b. Cin., Dec. 6, 1923; s. William B. and Elizabeth (Krent) S.; B.A., U. Wis., 1947; m. Betty Sweet, May 29, 1946; 1 dau., Laurie Narda. Chief accounting dept. VA Hosp., Madison, Wis., 1947-48; with N. Central Airlines (now Republic Airlines), 1948—, pres., dir., 1969—, chief exec. officer, 1976—; dir. G & K Services, Inc., S.E. Rykoff & Co., Los Angeles. Mem. Minn. Dept. Econ. Devel. Adv. Commn. Served with USAAF, 1943-46. Mem. Air Transport Assn. Am. (dir.), Assn. Local Transport Airlines. (dir.). Office: 7500 Airline Dr Minneapolis MN 55450

SWEET, CODY, performing artist; b. Chgo., Nov. 12, 1939; d. Charles and Alice (Grush) Sweet; B.S., Northwestern U., 1963, Ph.D., 1972; M.S., Northeastern U., 1969; postgrad. Harvard U., 1972, N.Y. Bur. Movement Research, 1973; m. James Alexander Thom, May 16, 1975. Pres., Nonverbal Communications Inc., Bloomington, Ind., 1972—, Contact, Inc., Ink, Inc.; internat. platform speaker, seminar leader, author How To Recognize Yourself in a Crowd; nat. TV talk show personality; columnist Sweet Talkin' for Post Scripts mag., pub. Sat. Eve. Post Co.; cons. Health-Tex Corp. Address: 9560 W Mallory Rd Bloomington IN 47401

SWEET, DAVID EMERY, coll. pres.; b. Holyoke, Mass., July 9, 1933; s. Adrian John and Elsie King (Jocelyn) S.; A.B., Drury Coll., 1955; M.A., Duke U., 1958, Ph.D., 1967; m. Arleene Pachl, June 4, 1954; children—Karen Joy, Jocelyn Sue. Instr., Ohio U., 1959-60; asso. prof. polit. sci. Ill. State U., 1960-69, asst. to v.p. acad. affairs, 1968-69, spl. asst. to pres., 1965-69; vice chancellor acad. affairs Minn. State U., St. Paul, 1969-71; founding pres. Met. State U., St. Paul, 1971-77; pres. R.I. Coll., 1977—. Bd. dirs. R.I. Philharmonic, Providence. Named Adminstr. of Yr., Minn. chpt. Am. Soc. Public Adminstrn., 1975; Woodrow Wilson fellow, 1955-56; Commonwealth Studies fellow, 1958-59. Mem. Council for Advancement and Support Edn. (chmn. com. govt. relations), Assn. Am. Colls. (dir.), Am. Assn. State Colls. and Univs., Greater Providence C. of C. Christian Scientist. Author monographs; contbr. numerous articles to profl. publs. Office: 404 Roberts Hall 600 Mount Pleasant Ave Providence RI 02908

SWEET, JOHN HOWARD, publisher; b. Emerson, Man., Can., Mar. 21, 1907; s. Henry Charles and Hannah (Mooney) S.; student U. Manitoba, 1923-26; m. Lillian Flora Martin, Sept. 11, 1926; 1 son, John Allan; m. 2d, Anne Ethel Wallace, Oct. 4, 1940; children—Anthony Howard, Elizabeth Anne. Asst. circulation mgr. A.M.A., 1926-29; circulation mgr. Traffic World, 1929-37; v.p. Poor's Publishing Co., 1937-40, Dickie Raymond, Inc., 1940-42; circulation mgr. World Report, 1946-48; with U.S. News and World Report, 1948—, circulation dir., 1948-51, exec. v.p. 1951-59, pres., 1959—, pub., 1951-78, chmn. bd., chief exec. officer, 1973—. Served as lt. comdr. USNR, 1943-45. Mem. Conf. Bd., Mag. Pubs. Assn. (dir.). Presbyn. (trustee). Clubs: Princess Anne Country (Virginia Beach); Nat. Press, Army and Navy, Congressional Country, Metropolitan (Washington). Office: 2300 N St NW Washington DC 20037

SWEET, NORMAN LELAND, fgn. service officer; b. Stockton, Calif., Mar. 5, 1933; s. Max and Fannie Frances (Forman) S.; B.A., Stanford U., 1954; M.I.A., Columbia, 1956; m. Joan Hunter Drew, May 25, 1959 (div. Oct. 1974); children—Gerald, Arden, Allison; m. 2d, Huynh Kim Huong, Mar. 24, 1975; children—Robert, Ruth. Internat. affairs officer Office Sec. of Def., 1956-58, 60-62; officer in charge Laos desk AID, 1962-63; program and econ. affairs officer AID, Laos, 1963-67; program officer Spl. Assistance Mission to Tunisia, 1968-70; dir. plans, policy and programs CORDS, Vietnam, 1970-72, dir. CORDS, 1972, dir. plans, policy and evaluation SAAFO, 1973; dir. Office of Laos and Thailand Affairs, AID, Washington, 1973-74, dir. Office of Vietnam Affairs, 1974, acting dep. asst. adminstr. East Asia Bur., 1974-75, acting mission dir., Cambodia, 1975, sr. civil coordinator Inter-agy. Task Force for Indo-China Refugees, Guam, 1975, dir. Office Middle East Affairs, 1975-77; mem. U.S. Govt. Exec. Seminar, 1977-78; dir. AID Mission, Zaire, 1978—; bus. mgr. to pres. Inst. Internat. Relations, Stanford. Fellow internat. affairs Columbia; UN intern, 1954; recipient Outstanding Service award Office Sec. Def., 1961. Served with AUS, 1958-60. Mem. Pi Sigma Alpha. Home: 1602 N McKinley Rd Arlington VA 22205

SWEET, PHILIP W.K., JR., banker; b. Mt. Vernon, N.Y., Dec. 31, 1927; s. Philip W.K. and Katherine (Buhl) S.; A.B., Harvard, 1950; M.B.A., U. Chgo., 1957; m. Nancy Frederick, July 23, 1950; children—Sandra H., Philip W.K. III, David A.F. Pres., dir. The No. Trust Co., Chgo., 1953—, No. Trust Corp., Chgo. Alderman City of Lake Forest (Ill.), 1972-74. Vice chmn. United Negro Coll. Fund; bd. govs. Ill. Council Econ. Edn.; adv. council U. Chgo. Grad. Sch. Bus.; trustee Lake Forest (Ill.) Improvement Trust; bd. dirs. Lake Forest Hosp., United Way Met. Chgo., J.R. Bowman Health Center for the Elderly. Served with USNR, 1950-53. Mem. Assn. Res. City Bankers, Soc. Colonial Wars (gov. Ill. chpt.). Episcopalian (vestryman 1971-74). Clubs: Chgo. Sunday Evening (trustee, treas.), Bankers, Bond, Econ., Commercial, Chgo., Attic, Commonwealth (Chgo.); Old Elm, Onwentsia (Lake Forest, Ill.); Shoreacres (Lake Bluff, Ill.). Home: 990 Ringwood Rd Lake Forest IL 60045 Office: 50 S LaSalle St Chicago IL 60675

SWEET, ROBERT WORKMAN, dist. judge; b. Yonkers, N.Y., Oct. 15, 1922; s. James Allen and Delia (Workman) S.; B.A., Yale U., 1944, LL.B., 1948; m. Adele Hall, May 12, 1973; children by previous marriage—Robert, Deborah, Ames, Eliza. Admitted to N.Y. State bar, 1949; asso. firm Simpson, Thacher & Bartlett, 1948-53; asst. U.S. atty. So. Dist. N.Y., 1953-55; asso. firm Casey, Lane & Mittendorf, 1955-65, partner, 1957-65; counsel Interdepartmental Task Force on Youth and Juvenile Delinquency, 1958-78; dep. mayor City of N.Y., 1966-69; partner firm Skadden, Arps, Slate, Meagher & Flom, N.Y.C., 1970-77; mem. hearing office N.Y.C. Transit Authority, 1975-77; U.S. dist. judge So. Dist. N.Y., N.Y.C., 1978—. Pres., Community Service Soc., 1961-78; trustee Sch. Mgmt. Urban Policy, 1970—, Law Sch., 1948, Taft Sch.; vestryman St. Georges Epis. Ch., 1958-63. Served to lt. (j.g.) USNR, 1943-46. Recipient various awards, citations for service as dept mayor N.Y.C. Mem. Assn. Bar of City N.Y., N.Y. Law Inst., N.Y. County Lawyers Assn., Am. Bar Assn., N.Y. State Bar Assn., Am. Legion (comdr. Willard Straight Post). Clubs: Quaker Hill Country, Century Assn., Merchants. Office: US Dist Ct 410 US Courthouse Foley Sq New York NY 10007

SWEET, WALDO EARLE, educator; b. Hartford, Conn., Apr. 26, 1912; s. Henry Lewis and Alice Marion (Barlow) S.; grad. Phillips Exeter Acad., 1930; A.B., Amherst Coll., 1934; M.A., Columbia, 1935; A.M. (Westcott fellow), Princeton, 1943, Ph.D., 1943; m. Elizabeth Osborne Smith, Nov. 6, 1943; children—Deborah Page, Holly Barlow. Tchr., Eaglebrook Sch., Deerfield, Mass., 1935-37, Millbrook (N.Y.) Sch. 1937-40, Phillips Andover (Mass.) Acad., 1942-43, William Penn Charter Sch., Phila., 1946-53; asso. prof. Latin and teaching of Latin, U. Mich., Ann Arbor, 1953-61, prof., 1961—. Dir. Carnegie Corp. Latin Workshop, summers 1952-53; mem. vis. faculty State U. Iowa, summer 1951, U. Wash., summer 1961. Served with AUS, 1943-46. Rockefeller grantee, 1950, 51. Mem. Am. Philol. Assn., Linguistic Soc. Am., Am. Classical League, Joint Assn. Classical Tchrs. (Eng.), Phi Gamma Delta. Democrat. Clubs: Sierra; Barton Boat, University. Author: Latin: A Structural Approach, 1957; Artes Latinae (multi-media programmed course including Latin: Levels One and Two, Lectiones Primae, Lectiones Secundae), 1966-71; also articles. Home: 1905 Pontiac Trail Ann Arbor MI 48105

SWEETING, GEORGE, clergyman, editor; b. Haledon, N.J., Oct. 1, 1924; s. William and Mary Roger (Irving) S.; pastors course diploma, Moody Bible Inst., Chgo., 1945; B.A., Gordon Coll., Wenham, Mass., 1948; D.D. (hon.), Gordon-Conwell Theol. Sem., South Hamilton, Mass., 1970; H.H.D. (hon.) Azusa (Cal.) Pacific Coll., 1971; LL.D. (hon.), Tenn. Temple Coll., Chattanooga, 1971; m. Margaret Hilda Schnell, June 14, 1947; children—George David, James Douglas, Donald William, Robert Bruce. Pastor, Grace Ch., Clifton, N.J., 1948-50; world-wide evangelist, 1951-61; pastor Madison Ave. Bapt. Ch., Paterson, N.J., 1961-66, Moody Ch., Chgo., 1966-71; pres. Moody Bible Inst., Chgo., 1971—, Moody Inst. Sci., 1971—, Moody Press, 1971—; editor Moody Monthly mag., 1971—. Club: Union League (Chgo.). Author: The City-A Matter of Conscience, 1972; How to Solve Conflicts, 1973; Love is the Greatest, 1974; How to Begin the Christian Life, 1975. Office: Moody Bible Inst 820 N LaSalle St Chicago IL 60610*

SWEETSER, ALBERT GIBBY, educator, publisher; b. Boston, Oct. 16, 1915; s. Albert Edwin and Alice (Gibby) S.; A.B., Harvard, 1937; M.B.A., N.Y. U., 1942; Ph.D., Am. U., 1961; postgrad. Boston U., 1942; m. Ruth J. Whitney, Sept. 5, 1953. Credit analyst Mfrs. Trust Co., N.Y.C., 1937-42; fgn. air transport economist CAB, Washington, 1942-45; internat. editor Am. Aviation Mag., Washington, 1945; instr. finance Boston U., 1945-46; asst. prof. econs. Wesleyan U., Middletown, Conn., 1946-48; prof., chmn. div. bus. edn. Nasson Coll., 1949-50; dir. summer session Portland U., 1950; organizer Coll. Bus. Adminstrn., U. Maine, Portland, 1950; lectr. accounting and finance Northeastern U., 1951-53; asso. prof. econs., bus. adminstrn. Westminster Coll., 1953-56, Wis. State U. at Eau Claire, 1956- 59; prof. finance, chmn. dept. Duquesne U., Grad. Sch. Bus. Adminstrn., Pitts., 1959-67; prof. finance Sch. of Bus., State U. N.Y. at Albany, 1967—, chmn. dept., 1967-71; Va. Bankers Assn. prof. bank mgmt. McIntire Sch. Commerce, U. Va., Charlottesville, 1979. Chartered fin. analyst. Mem. Eastern Finance Assn. (founder, pres. 1965-67, exec. dir. 1965-74, trustee 1975—), A.A.U.P., Am. Econ. Assn., Am. Finance Assn., Inst. Chartered Financial Analysts, Coll. for Financial Planning (regent 1971-73), Financial Analysts Fedn., Financial Mgmt. Assn. (founder, exec. dir. 1970-75, trustee 1970—), Pitts. Soc. Financial Analysts. Republican. Conglist. Club: Harvard (N.Y.C.). Author, pub. Bank Loans Secured by Field-Warehouse Receipts, 1957; author Financing Goods, rev. 1963. Asso. editor Jour. Financial Edn., 1974—. Contbr. articles profl. jours. Office: Dept Finance Sch Bus State U NY at Albany Albany NY 12222

SWEETSER, EDWARD HORATIO, life ins. co. exec.; b. Bklyn., Oct. 6, 1919; s. Edward Rowe and Nellie (Willoughby) S.; m. Elizabeth D. McKnight, Aug. 20, 1943; 1 son, Edward Rowe. With N.Y. Life Ins. Co., 1937—, 2d v.p., 1956-64, v.p. charge underwriting, 1964-71, sr. v.p., 1971—. Served with USAAC, World War II. Mem. Soc. Actuaries, Am. Acad. Actuaries, Home Office Life Underwriters Assn., Actuarial Club N.Y., Internat. Actuarial Assn., Harvard Advanced Mgmt. Assn. Home: Harbor Rd Harbor Acres Sands Point NY 11050 Office: NY Life Ins Co 51 Madison Ave New York City NY 10010

SWEIGART, JOHN WINFIELD, JR., coll. dean; b. Lancaster, Pa., July 18, 1927; s. John Winfield and Florence (Krenz) S.; A.B., Lafayette Coll., 1950; Ph.D. (Fels Found. fellow), U. Pa., 1959; m. Josephine Frances Neumoyer, May 21, 1949 (div. 1967); children—John Winfield III, Joy Hollis, Joel Charles, Judson Barry, Jefferson Palmer; m. 2d, Elizabeth Marie Karg, July 3, 1967. Internal auditor Prudential Ins. Co., Newark, Jacksonville, Fla., 1950-55; instr. U. Pa., 1956-58; asst. prof. philosophy Jacksonville U., 1959-62, asso. prof., div. chmn., 1962-63; asso. prof., dept. head Cedar Crest Coll., Allentown, Pa., 1963-67; asso. prof., head philosophy dept. U. Me., Portland, 1967-68, chmn. humanities div., 1968, dean acad. affairs, 1968-70, prof. philosophy, 1969-70; dean Grad. Sch., prof. philosophy James Madison U. (formerly Madison Coll.), Harrisonburg, Va., 1970-72, head dept. philosophy and religion, 1972-73, dean Sch. Arts and Scis., 1973—; vis. asso. prof. Lafayette Coll., summers 1963-64; guest lectr. U. Pa., 1965; mem. Philos. Studies Summer Inst. of Carnegie Found., 1966. Asso. Danforth Found. Served with USNR, 1945-46. Recipient Outstanding Prof. award Jacksonville U., 1963. Mem. Am. Philos. Assn., Am. Assn. U. Profs. (past chpt. pres.), Phi Beta Kappa, Phi Kappa Psi. Club: Torch (past chpt. pres.) (Lehigh Valley). Contbr. articles profl. jours. Home: Route 2 Box 57 Bridgewater VA 22812

SWENSON, BIRGER, ret. pub. exec.; b. Averstad, Skattkarr, Sweden, July 31, 1895; s. Sven and Johanna (Spetz) Svensson; came to U.S., 1912, naturalized, 1918; A.B., Augustana Coll., 1924, LL.D., 1958, student Theol. Sem., 1925-26; student Northwestern U., summer 1923; m. Lyal E. Westerlund, Aug. 14, 1943. Field rep. Augustana Book Concern, Rock Island, Ill., 1926, circulation mgr., 1927-42, sales mgr., 1942-44, acting mgr., 1944-45, gen. mgr., treas., 1945-62; asso. exec. sec. Fortress Press, Bd. Publ. Lutheran Ch. Am., Rock Island, 1962-63; exec. bd. Ill. Synod Luth. Ch. Am., 1965-71; dir. Graphic Arts Industry, Mpls., 1946-66. Bd. missions Augustana Luth. Ch., 1941-50; pres. Rock Island YMCA, 1957-59. Mem. Rock Island Bd. Zoning Appeals, 1965-75. Bd. dirs. Luth. Hosp., Moline, Ill., 1943-48, 63-65; trustee Augustana Luth. Found., 1930-62; trustee, pres. Augustana Annuity Trust, 1942—. Served with U.S. Army, 1918- 19; AEF. Decorated knight Order of Vasa 1st class, 1951. (Sweden). Mem. Augustana Luther League Council (treas. 1933-37), Am. Fedn. Luth. Brotherhoods (treas. 1939-43), Augustana Coll. Alumni Assn. (pres. 1938-39), Internat. Council Religious Edn. (nat. pres. publs. sect. 1950-51), Luth. Men Am., Protestant Church-Owned Pubs. Assn. (past pres.), Nat. Council Chs. Christ U.S. (bd. mgrs. central dept. publs. and distbn. 1950-54), Augustana, Swedish Pioneer, Ill. hist. socs., Am.-Scandinavian Found., Am. Swedish Hist. Found., Augustana Swedish Inst., Nat. Luth. Pubs. House Mgrs. Assn. (treas. 1933-63), Rock Island County Hist. Soc., Rock Island C. of C., Am. Legion. Republican. Clubs: Union League (Chgo.); Kiwanis, Quad City Athletic. Author: (autobiography) My Story. Editor: Augustana Almanac, 1930-47; co-editor Augustana Ann., 1948-62; mem. editorial com. Am.-Swedish Handbook, vols. 1, 2, 4, 5, 6, 7, 8. Home: 1209 21st Ave Bldg C-314 Rock Island IL 61201

SWENSON, CLAYTON A., educator, physicist; b. Mpls., Nov. 11, 1923; s. Nels and Anna (Roth) S.; B.S., Harvard, 1944; Ph.D., Oxford U., 1949; m. Heather M.F. Gell, Sept. 2, 1950; children—Anna, Paul, Wendy. Mem. staff Los Alamos Sci. Lab., 1944-46; instr. Harvard, 1949-52; Div. Indsl. Cooperation staff mem. Mass. Inst. Tech., 1952-55; prof. physics, chmn. dept. physics, sr. physicist Ames Lab., U.S. Dept. Energy, Iowa State U., 1955—. Fellow Am. Phys. Soc.;

mem. Am. Assn. Physics Tchrs., A.A.A.S., Phi Beta Kappa, Sigma Xi. Research, publs. in solid state physics with emphasis on low temperature and high pressure and combinations of these; publs. on understanding of elementary solids (inert gases and alkali metals) at low temperatures, devel. temperature scales below 30K. Home: 2102 Kildee Ave Ames IA 50010

SWENSON, ERIC PIERSON, publishing co. exec.; b. South Orange, N.J., Sept. 21, 1918; s. Svante Magnus and Dorothy Wharton (Mendelson) S.; grad. magna cum laude, St. Paul's Sch., Concord, N.H., 1937; B.A. with high orations, Yale, 1941; m. Patricia Morgan, Sept. 14, 1945 (div. June 1965); children—Juliet Morgan (Mrs. Peter Carter) (dec.), Karen Rosamond (Mrs. William McCollum), Dana Graham, Hilary Lloyd; m. 2d, Ann Brooke Kirkland, Aug. 5, 1965; 1 dau., Alexandra Brooke. Publicity asst., editor Pocket Books, Inc., N.Y.C., 1945-47; publicity, editor William Sloane Assos., N.Y.C., 1947-51; exec. editor, vice chmn., dir. W.W. Norton & Co., N.Y.C., 1951—; dir. SMS Ranch Co., Stamford, Tex. Bd. dirs. Internat. Devel. Found., N.Y.C. Served with USNR, 1941-45. Clubs: Players, New York Yacht; Cruising of Am.; Royal Cork Yacht; Saugatuck Harbor Yacht; Yale; Storm Trysail. Author: The South Sea Shilling, 1952. Home: 99 Eleven O'Clock Rd Weston CT 06883 Office: 500 Fifth Ave New York NY 10036

SWENSON, GARY LEE, investment banker; b. Kenmare, N.D., May 30, 1937; s. Orville K. and Lillien R. (Anderson) S.; B.A., U. Wis., 1959, M.B.A., 1961; m. Jannette Dye, July 27, 1963; children—Charlotte, Kimberly. With First Boston Corp., N.Y.C., 1963—, exec. v.p., dir., 1976—. Served to lt. U.S. Army, 1961-63. Recipient VFW Scholastic award, 1955. Mem. N.Y. Soc. Security Analysts, Am. Petroleum Inst. Clubs: Board Room, Union League; Riverside Yacht. Contbr. articles in field to profl. publs. Home: 42 Owenoke Way Riverside CT 06848 Office: 20 Exchange Pl New York NY 10005

SWENSON, GEORGE WARNER, JR., electronics engr., radio astronomer, educator; b. Mpls., Sept. 22, 1922; s. George Warner and Vernie (Larson) S.; B.S., Mich. Coll. Mining and Tech., 1944, E.E., 1950; M.S., Mass. Inst. Tech., 1948; Ph.D., U. Wis., 1951; m. Virginia Laura Savard, June 26, 1943 (div. 1970); children—George Warner III, Vernie Laura, Julie Loretta, Donna Joan; m. 2d, Joy Janice Locke, July 2, 1971. Asso. prof. elec. engring. Washington U., St. Louis, 1952-53; prof. U. Alaska, 1953-54; asso. prof. Mich. State U., 1954-56; faculty U. Ill., Urbana, 1956—, prof. elec. engring. and astronomy, 1958—, acting head dept. astronomy, 1970-72, head dept. elec. engring., 1979—, dir. Vermilion River Obs., 1968—. Vis. scientist Nat. Radio Astronomy Obs., 1964-68; cons. to govt. agys. and other sci. bodies. Fellow IEEE, AAAS; mem. Nat. Acad. Engring., Am. Astron. Soc., Internat. Sci. Radio Union (mem. U.S. nat. com. 1965-67), Internat. Astron. Union, Sigma Xi, Eta Kappa Nu, Tau Beta Pi, Phi Kappa Phi. Author: Principles of Modern Acoustics, 1953. Contbr. articles to profl. jours. Home: 1107 Kenwood Rd Champaign IL 61820 Office: U Ill Urbana IL 61801

SWENSON, HARRY WILLIAM, airline exec.; b. Orange, N.J., Aug. 15, 1930; s. Carl Henric and Judit (Igelstrom) S.; B.B.A. in Accounting, Upsala Coll., 1952; M.B.A., Rutgers U., 1958; m. Grace Ann Leonardis, Dec. 27, 1953; children—Karen, Susan, Harry, Teresa. With Price Waterhouse & Co., 1954-59; treas., asst. sec. Chipman Chem. Co., Bound Brook, N.J., 1959-67; v.p. fin. Pacific Air Lines, San Francisco, 1967-68; asst. v.p. Air West, Inc., San Francisco, 1968-70; treas., controller Hughes Air Corp., San Francisco, 1971-72, v.p. fin., treas., 1973—, also dir. Bd. dirs. Govtl. Research Council San Mateo County (Calif.), 1976—. Served to sgt. U.S. Army, 1952-54. Mem. N.J., Calif. state socs. C.P.A.'s, Am. Inst. C.P.A.'s. Home: 11198 Magdalena Ave Los Altos Hills CA 94022 Office: Hughes Airwest San Francisco Internat Airport San Francisco CA 94128

SWENSON, JOHN WILLIAM, govt. ofcl.; b. Worcester, Mass., Nov. 9, 1917; s. Andrew W. and Ellen M. (Lindstrom) S.; B.S., Mass. State Coll., 1940; m. Priscilla A. Atwood, Feb. 7, 1941; children—Peter J., Susan A. (Mrs. Niederjohn). Personnel mgr. Leland-Gifford Co., Worcester, 1944-46; with VA, 1946—, personnel adminstr. Rutland Heights (Mass.) VA Hosp., 1946-65; personnel dir. VA Hosp., Northampton, Mass., 1965-66; asst. adminstr. The Meml. Hosp., Worcester, Mass., 1966-70, SBA, Boston, 1970—. Mem. Nat. Health Council, 1961—. Bd. dirs. U. Mass. Found., 1950-52; chmn. alumni fund U. Mass., 1968-70. Served to capt. AUS, World War II. Mem. Worcester County Health Assn. (pres. 1962-64), Mass. Tb and Respiratory Disease League (pres. 1964-66), Nat. Tb Assn. (sec. 1964-68) U. Mass. Alumni Assn. (pres. 1950-52), Nat. Tb and Respiratory Disease Assn. (v.p. 1968-70), Internat. Personnel Mgmt. Assn., Am. Arbitration Assn. (panel of arbitrators 1970—), Lambda Chi Alpha (pres. local chpt. 1939-40). Home: 5 Richardson Terr Worcester MA 01602 Office: 60 Battery March Boston MA 02110

SWENSON, KAREN, poet, educator; b. N.Y.C., July 29, 1936; d. Howard William and Dorothy (Trautman) Swenson; B.A., Barnard Coll., 1959; M.A., N.Y. U., 1971; m. Michael Shuter, 1958 (div. 1971); 1 son, Michael. Mem. faculty City Coll. City N.Y. Judge CAPS grants, 1975, Walt Whitman award Acad. Am. Poets, 1976. Author: An Attic of Ideal, 1974. Home: 430 State St Brooklyn NY 11217

SWENSON, MAY, poet; b. Logan, Utah, May 28, 1919; d. Dan Arthur and Anna M. (Helberg) S.; B.A., Utah State U., 1939. Poet, 1949—; editor New Directions, N.Y.C., 1959-66; poet-in-residence Purdue U., 1966-67, U. N.C., 1968-69, Lothbridge U., Alta., Can., 1970; author poetry books: Another Animal, 1954, A Cage of Spines, 1958, To Mix With Time, 1963, Poems to Solve, 1966, Half Sun, Half Sleep, 1967, Iconographs, 1970, More Poems to Solve, 1971, New and Selected Things Taking Place, 1978; author: The Floor, 1966 (play), The Contemporary Poet as Artist and Critic, 1964 (essays); translator: Windows and Stones, 1972 (selected poems of Tomas Transtromer); Lucy Martin Donnelly fellow Bryn Mawr Coll., 1968. Recipient William Rose Benet prize, 1959, Longview Found. award, 1959, Creative Arts award Brandeis U., 1966, Disting. Service Gold medal Utah State U., 1967, Shelley Meml. award, 1968; Rockefeller fellow, 1955, 67; Breadloaf Robert Frost fellow, 1957; Guggenheim fellow, 1959; Amy Lowell travelling fellow, 1960; Ford fellow, 1964. Fellow Acad. Am. Poets; mem. Nat. Inst. Arts and Letters (award 1960). Office: care Little Brown and Co 34 Beacon St Boston MA 02114*

SWENSON, MAY, poet; b. Logan, Utah, May 28, 1919; d. Dan Arthur and Margaret (Hellberg) S.; B.S., Utah State U. Editor New Directions Press, 1959-66; poet in residence Purdue U., Lafayette, Ind., 1966-67, U. N.C., Greensboro, 1968-69, 75, Lethbridge U., Alta., Can., 1970, U. Calif. at Riverside, 1973. Author: Another Animal, 1954; A Cage of Spines, 1958; To Mix with Time, 1963; Poems to Solve, 1966; Half Sun Half Sleep, 1967; Iconographs, 1970; More Poems to Solve, 1971; (translated from Swedish) Windows & Stones (Tomas Tranströmer), 1972; The Guess and Spell Coloring Book, 1976; (poetry) New and Selected Things Taking Place, 1978. Recipient Nat. Inst. Arts and Letters award, 1960, Brandeis U. award, 1967, Shelley Meml. award Poetry Soc. Am., 1968, Distinguished Service Gold medal Utah State U., 1967; Guggenheim fellow, 1959; Amy Lowell Travelling scholar, 1960; Ford Found. fellow, 1965; Rockefeller Found. fellow, 1967-68, Lucy Martin Donnally fellow Bryn Mawr Coll., 1968-69; Nat. Endowment for Arts grantee, 1974; mem. staff Breadloaf Writers Conf., 1976. Mem. Nat. Inst. Arts and Letters. Home: 73 Boulevard Sea Cliff NY 11579

SWENSON, MELVIN JOHN, physiologist, educator; b. Concordia, Kans., Jan. 14, 1917; s. John S. and Ida G. (Anderson) S.; D.V.M., Kans. State U., 1943; M.S., Iowa State U., 1947, Ph.D. (Am. Vet. Med. Assn. fellow 1946-49), 1950; m. Mildred L. Rockey, June 26, 1947; children—Myron John, Pamela Joyce, Brita Christine. Instr., La. State U., 1943; asst. prof. Iowa State U., 1949- 50; from asst. prof. to asso. prof. Kans. State U., 1950-56; prof. Colo. State U., 1956-57; head dept. vet. physiology and pharmacology Iowa State U. Sci. and Tech., 1957-73; prof. Iowa State U., 1973—. Mem. Am. Physiol. Soc., Am., Iowa vet. med. assns., Conf. Research Workers in Animal Diseases, Soc. Exptl. Biology and Medicine, Sigma Xi, Phi Kappa Phi, Phi Zeta, Phi Lambda Upsilon, Gamma Sigma Delta. Club: Masons. Home: 306 Westwood Dr Ames IA 50010

SWENSON, ORVAR, surgeon; b. Halsingborg, Sweden, Feb. 7, 1909; s. Carl Albert and Amanda (Johnson) S.; derivative citizenship; A.B., William Jewell Coll., 1933; M.D. Harvard, 1937; Dr. h.c., U. Aix, Marseilles, France, 1975; m. Melva Criley, Sept. 11, 1941; children—Melva, Elsa, Wenda. Intern Peter Bent Brigham and Children's hosps., Boston, 1939-41; resident Peter Bent Brigham Hosp., 1944-45; Arthur Tracy Cabot fellow Harvard Med. Sch., 1941-44; surgeon Children's Hosp., Boston, 1947-50; surgeon-in-chief Boston Floating Hosp. Infants and Children, 1950-60; asso. surgery Harvard Med. Sch., 1947-50; prof. pediatric surgery Tufts U. Med. Sch., 1957-60; surgeon-in-chief Children's Meml. Hosp., Chgo., 1960-73; prof. surgery Northwestern U. Med. Sch., 1960-73; prof. surgery U. Miami (Fla.), 1973—. Recipient Mead Johnson award, 1952; Ladd award Surg. sect. Am. Acad. Pediatrics, 1969; Achievement award Modern Medicine mag., 1971. Diplomate Am. Bd. Surgery. Hon. fellow Royal Coll. Surgeons (Dublin, Ireland); mem. A.C.S., Am. Surg. Assn., Soc. Univ. Surgeons, Am. Pediatric Surg. Assn. (pres. 1973), Brit. Assn. Pediatric Surgery (hon.; Dennis Brown medal 1979). Author: Pediatric Surgery, 1958. Home: Main St Rockport ME 04856

SWENSON, WENDELL MONSON, psychologist; b. Marinette, Wis., Dec. 6, 1920; s. Emil and Sadie Wilhelmina (Monson) S.; B.A., Gustavus Adolphus Coll., 1942; M.A., U. Minn., 1950, Ph.D., 1958; m. Constance Elizabeth Jane Norman, Apr. 2, 1943; children—Wendell Norman, David Erik, Stephen Scott. Instr. in psychology Gustavus Adolphus Coll., 1946-49, asso. prof., chmn. dept. psychology, 1957-59; chief clin. psychologist St. Peter (Minn.) State Hosp., 1949-56; clin. psychologist Mayo Clinic, Rochester, Minn., 1959-65, head sect. psychology, 1968—; asst. prof. psychology Mayo Grad. Sch. Medicine, 1959-65, asso. prof., 1965-70, prof., 1970—; dir. Mut. of Omaha Ins. Co.; bd. dirs. Northwestern Theol. Sem.; fellow Inst. in Social Gerontology U. Conn., hfjkm958; del. White House Conf. on Aging, 1961, 71; mem. com. on mental health and illness of elderly, mem. pres.'s. tech. adv. com. on aging research, HEW; mem. Minn. Gov.'s Council on Aging. Served with USN, Mem. bd. pensions Lutheran Ch. in Am. Served with USN, 1942-46; PTO. Fellow Am. Psychol. Assn., Gerontol. Soc., Acad. Psychosomatic Medicine (v.p., dir.); mem. Am. Psychopathol. Assn., Sigma Xi. Author: A User's Guide to the Mayo Clinic Automated MMPI Program, 1967; An MMPI Source Book: Basic Item, Scale, and Pattern Data on 50,000 Medical Patients, 1973; editorial bd. Jour. Gerontology, 1979—, Psychosomatics, 1979—; research in automated personality assessment. Home: 2067 Lenwood Dr SW Rochester MN 55901 Office: Mayo Clinic Rochester MN 55901

SWERHONE, PETER EDWARD, hosp. exec.; b. Canora, Sask., Can., May 30, 1931; s. Daniel and Marie (Zabinsky) S.; B.A., B. Commerce, U. Sask., 1953; diploma hosp. adminstrn., U. Toronto, 1955; m. Genevieve Miller, Dec. 27, 1956; children—Lorna M., Danielle K., Michelle A., Edward D.P., Patricia M. Adminstrv. asst. Calgary Gen. Hosp., 1953-56; asst. adminstr. Notre Dame Hosp., North Battleford, Sask., 1957-58; asst. adminstr. Winnipeg Gen. Hosp., 1958-63, adminstr., 1963-67, exec. dir., 1967-72; pres. Health Scis. Centre, Winnipeg, 1972—; asso. prof. pub. health U. Man., 1967—; vis. prof. U. Alta., 1967—; mem. survey team Canadian Council Hosp. Accreditation, 1970—. Dir. United Health Ins. Corp., Winnipeg, 1970—, mem. exec. bd., 1973—; dir. Med. Products Inst., Inc., Man., 1973—. Dir., pres. Red River Exbn., Winnipeg, 1960-67. Bd. dirs. Holy Family Nursing Home, Winnipeg, Fellow Am. Coll. Hosp. Adminstrs. (gov. 1972—, Gold medal 1976); mem. Canadian (dir. 1968-, pres. elect 1972-73), Man. (pres. 1966-67, dir. 1962-66) hosp. assns., Assn. Canadian Teaching Hosps. (pres. 1971), Hosp. Research and Devel. Inst. (dir. 1967—). Editorial bd. Health Devices, 1970—. Home: 306 Laidlaw Blvd Winnipeg MB R3P 0K5 Canada Office: Health Scis Centre 800 Sherbrook St Winnipeg MB R3A 1M4 Canada

SWERLING, PETER, electronics co. exec.; b. N.Y.C., Mar. 4, 1929; s. Jo and Florence (Manson) S.; B.S. in Math., Calif. Inst. Tech., 1947; B.A. in Econs., Cornell U., 1949; M.A. in Math., UCLA, 1951, Ph.D., 1955; m. Judith Ann Butler, July 11, 1958; children—Katherine, Elizabeth, Carole, Steven. Mem. electronics dept. Rand Corp., Santa Monica, Calif., 1948-61; head West Coast ops. Conductron Corp., Inglewood, Calif., 1961-64; chmn. bd. Tech. Service Corp., Santa Monica, 1966—; vice chmn. bd. Allied Tech., Inc., Dayton, Ohio, 1978—; chmn. bd. K/Tronic, Inc., Santa Clara, Calif., 1978—; adj. prof. elec. engring. U. So. Calif., 1965-68; cons. on radar systems, 1964-66; mem. Dept. Def. Com. on AWACS ECM Vulnerability, 1974-75, Def. Sci. Bd. Com. on Patriot System Vulnerability, 1976-77. Founding mem. bd. trustees Crossroads Sch. Arts and Scis., Santa Monica, 1970—. Fellow IEEE; mem. Nat. Acad. Engring., Am. Def. Preparedness Assn., Phi Beta Kappa, Sigma Xi, Pi Mu Epsilon. Office: 2811 Wilshire Blvd Santa Monica CA 90403

SWERN, DANIEL, educator; b. N.Y.C., Jan. 21, 1916; s. Philip and Ida (Sternfield) S.; B.S., Coll. City N.Y., 1935; M.A., Columbia, 1936; Ph.D., U. Md., 1940; m. Ann Ruth Siegel, Aug. 14, 1938; children—Harriet Ellen (Mrs. Stuart Solomon), Dorothy Jane (Mrs. Jay Federman). Research chemist Eastern regional research lab. U.S. Dept. Agr., Phila., 1940-48, research supr., 1948-63; prof. chemistry, sr. research investigator Temple U., 1963—; adj. prof. Drexel Inst. Tech., 1954-63; cons. Armstrong Cork Co., Mobil Research and Devel. Corp. Recipient Arthur S. Flemming award U.S. Jr. C. of C., 1955, Lipid Chemistry award Am. Oil Chemists Soc., 1968. Mem. Phila. Organic Chemists' Club (past chmn.), Am. Chem. Soc. (chmn. 1968), Am. Oil Chemists' Soc., AAAS, AAUP, Am. Assn. Cancer Research, Sigma Xi, Phi Beta Kappa. Author: Industrial Oil and Fat Products, 1964; Organic Peroxides, vol. I, 1970, Vol. II, 1971; Vol. III, 1972. Contbr. to profl. jours. Patentee in field. Home: 7700 B Stenton Ave Philadelphia PA 19118

SWESNIK, ROBERT MALCOLM, geol. engr.; b. Chgo., Jan. 8, 1916; s. Harry Benjamin and Celia (Antler) S.; B.S., U. Okla., 1938, M.S., 1945; m. Lillian Rose, Apr. 16, 1939; children—Marcia Ellen, Hyla Beth, Sherry Kay. With Kingwood Oil Co., 1938, Tex-Harvey Oil Co., 1939, Sun Oil Co., 1944, Gulf Oil Corp., 1944-45; Okla. geol. survey, 1945; with Anderson-Prichard Oil Corp., 1946-50; with Gen. Am. Oil Co. of Tex., 1950—, v.p. fgn. operations, 1953—, vice chmn. bd., 1970—, also mem. exec. com.; pres., dir. Gen. Am. Oils, Ltd., GAO of Spain, Inc., GAO Can. Ltd., GAO Eng. Ltd., GAO (UK) Ltd., Excalibur Oil Corp., Excalibur Oil Co. (UK) Ltd., GAO Netherlands, Inc., GAO Ethiopia, Inc., Gen. Am. Oil Italia, Inc., GAO North Sea Ltd., GAO North Sea EXploration; dir. Premier Petrochem. Co., Brit. Columbia Oil Transmission Co. Served as capt., Armored F.A., AUS, 1942-44. Mem. Geol. Soc. Am., Am. Assn. Petroleum Geologists, Dallas Geol. Soc., Oklahoma City Geol. Soc., Sigma Xi, Tau Beta Pi, Sigma Gamma Epsilon, Sigma Alpha Mu. Mason (Shriner, 32). Clubs: City, Engineers, Cipango 21, Columbian (Dallas). Contbr. articles to profl. jours. Home: 6335 W Northwest Hwy Dallas TX 75225 Office: Meadows Bldg Dallas TX 75206

SWETNAM, MONTE NEWTON, petroleum exploration co. exec.; b. Alexandria, La., Oct. 9, 1936; s. Montreville Morris and Margaret Elizabeth (Cullison) S.; student Johns Hopkins, 1955-58; B.S. in Geology, U. Wyo., 1960, M.S. in Geology, 1961; M.B.A. in Bus. Adminstrn., Pepperdine U., 1978; m. Elaine Adelia Taylor, Dec. 21, 1957; children—Scott David, Robert Troy. Exploration geologist Amerada Petroleum Corp., Durango, Colo., 1961-63; exploration geologist Tenneco Oil Co., Durango, 1963-65, dist. project geologist, Bakersfield, Calif., 1965-69, div. staff geologist, Bakersfield, 1969; partner Argonaut Oil & Gas Cons., Denver, 1969-71; internat. exploration mgr. Tesoro Petroleum Corp., San Antonio, 1971-73, v.p. internat. exploration, 1973-74, sr. v.p. exploration, 1974—; pres. Tesoro-Bolivia Petroleum Co., 1975—, Tesoro-Egypt Petroleum Co., 1975—; pres. Canyon Marinas, Inc., San Antonio. Mem. Nat. Ski Patrol, 1962-72, chief sect., 1966-67. Registered geologist, Cal. Mem. Am. Assn. Petroleum Geologists, Geol. Soc. Am., Rocky Mountain Assn. Geologists, So. Tex., San Joaquin geol. socs., Am. Petroleum Inst., Sigma Xi. Republican. Clubs: Alamo Yacht, Lake Canyon Yacht. Contbr. articles to profl. jours. Home: 201 Fleetwood Dr San Antonio TX 78232 Office: 8700 Tesoro Dr San Antonio TX 78286

SWETS, JOHN ARTHUR, scientist; b. Grand Rapids, Mich., June 19, 1928; s. John A. and Sara Henrietta (Heyns) S.; B.A., U. Mich., 1950, M.A., 1953, Ph.D., 1954; m. Maxine Ruth Crawford, July 16, 1949; children—Stephen Arthur, Joel Brian. Instr. psychology U. Mich., Ann Arbor, 1954-56; asst. prof. Mass. Inst. Tech., Cambridge, 1956-60, asso. prof., 1960-63; v.p. Bolt Beranek & Newman Inc., Cambridge, 1964-69, sr. v.p., 1969-74, gen. mgr. research, devel. and cons., dir., 1971-74, chief scientist, 1975—. Mem. corp. Edn. Devel. Center, Newton, Mass., 1971-75. Bd. dirs. Unitarian Cooperative Nursery Sch., Lexington, Mass., 1958-59; trustee Lexington Home for Aged, 1966-69. Vis. research fellow Philips Labs., Netherlands, 1958; Regents' prof. U. Calif., 1969. Mem. vision com., com. on hearing and bioacoustics Nat. Acad. Sci.-NRC. Fellow AAAS, Acoustical Soc. Am. (exec. council, 1968-71), Am. Psychol. Assn.; mem. Psychonomic Soc., Psychometric Soc., Sigma Xi, Sigma Alpha Epsilon. Clubs: Winchester Country, Cosmos. Conglist. (moderator). Author: (with D.M. Green) Signal Detection Theory and Psychophysics, 1966. Editor: Signal Detection and Recognition by Human Observers, 1964; (with L.L. Elliott) Psychology and the Handicapped Child, 1974. Office: 50 Moulton St Cambridge MA 02138

SWETT, ALBERT HERSEY, business exec.; b. Medina, N.Y., Feb. 18, 1923; s. Raymond Fuller and Marion (Hersey) S.; grad. The Hill Sch., 1941; B.Engring., Yale, 1944; LL.B., Harvard, 1949; m. Mary Stewart, Oct. 10, 1944; children—Marion Hersey Swett Robinson, Margaret Stewart Swett Haskell, Albert Louis. Admitted to N.Y. bar, 1949; asso. firm Harris, Beach & Wilcox, Rochester, N.Y., 1949-56, mem. firm, 1957-66; v.p., gen. counsel Xerox Corp., Stamford, Conn., 1966-75; v.p., gen. counsel Coca-Cola Co., Atlanta, 1975-78, v.p., counsel to chmn., 1978—. Trustee Practising Law Inst. Served with USNR, 1942-46. Mem. Am., N.Y. State bar assns., Assn. Bar City N.Y., Assn. Gen. Counsel, Tau Beta Pi. Republican. Baptist. Rotarian (pres. 1966-67), Mason. Clubs: Capital City, Peachtree Golf (Atlanta); Country (Rochester); Yale (N.Y.C.). Home: 2876 Wyngate NW Atlanta GA 30305 Office: 310 North Ave NW Atlanta GA 30313

SWEZEY, ROBERT DWIGHT, lawyer; b. Somerville, Mass., Sept. 27, 1906; s. Arthur Dwight and Elizabeth (Thompson) S.; student Cambridge Latin Sch., 1923, postgrad., 1924; A.B., Harvard, 1928, LL.B., 1931; spl. courses George Washington U., 1936-37, Southeastern U., Washington, 1938, Columbia, 1939, N.Y.U., 1940; m. Helen Hyde Brereton, Apr. 29, 1938; children—Robert Dwight, Maria, William Denny. Admitted to Mass. bar, 1932, N.Y. bar, 1940, D.C. bar, 1961; practiced law with Dana T. Gallup, Boston, 1932-33; with Warner, Stackpole and Bradlee, Boston, 1933-34; legal asst. in research Chem. Bank & Trust Co., N.Y.C., 1934; atty. RFC, N.Y.C., 1934; atty., legal advisor to treas. Home Owner's Loan Corp., Washington, 1934-38; atty. Pub. Works Adminstrn., Washington, 1938- 39, NBC, N.Y.C., 1939-42; gen. counsel, sec. Blue Network Co. (now ABC), N.Y.C., 1942-44; v.p., gen. mgr. Mut. Broadcasting System, N.Y.C., 1944-48; exec. v.p., gen. mgr. WDSU Broadcasting Corp., 1949-60; spl. asst. to sec. of labor Dept. Labor, 1960-62; dir. Code Authority, Nat. Assn. Broadcasters, Washington, 1962-64; sec.-treas. Corp. Pub. Broadcasting, 1968-70; pres. MCI Mid-Atlantic Communications, Inc., 1970-73; country dir. Internat. Exec. Service Corps, Riyadh, Saudi Arabia, 1974-75; dir. M.C.I. Communications Corp., 1975—. Mem. Bar Assn. City N.Y., Am., Fed. Communications, Boston bar assns., N.Y. County Lawyers' Assn., Am. Arbitration Assn. Methodist. Clubs: Harvard, Lambs, Radio Executives (pres. 1946), Players (N.Y.C.); Broadcasters, Nat. Lawyers', University (Washington). Home: Autre Temps Box 1631 Leesburg VA 22075

SWID, STEPHEN CLAAR, bus. exec.; b. N.Y.C., Oct. 26, 1940; s. David and Selma (Claar) S.; B.S., Ohio State U., 1962; m. Nan Goldman, Mar. 1, 1963; children—Robin, Scott, Jill. Mgmt. trainee Alside Aluminum Co., Akron, Ohio, 1962-63; securities analyst Dreyfus Fund, N.Y.C., 1963-66; sr. investment officer Oppenheimer Fund, N.Y.C., 1966-67; gen. partner City Assos., 1967-69, Swid Investors, N.Y.C., 1970-78; vice chmn. bd. Gen. Felt Industries Inc., Saddle Brook, N.J., 1974—; chmn. bd. Knoll Internat., 1977—. Mem. N.Y. Soc. Security Analysts. Office: 153 E 53d St New York NY 10022

SWIDLER, JOSEPH CHARLES, lawyer; b. Chgo., Jan. 28, 1907; s. Abraham and Dora (Cromer) S.; ed. Chgo. pub. schs., U. Ill., U. Fla.; Ph.B., U. Chgo., 1929, J.D., 1930; m. Gertrude Tyrna, 1944; children—Ann, Mark. Pvt. law practice, Chgo., 1930-33; asst. solicitor U.S. Dept. of Interior, 1933; mem. legal dept. TVA, 1933-57; gen. counsel, sec., chmn. bd. TVA Retirement System, 1945-57; counsel Alien Property Bur., 1941, Power Div., WPB, 1942; pvt. practice law, Knoxville and Nashville, 1957-61; chmn. Fed. Power Commn., 1961-65; mem. Water Resources Council, 1964-65; mem. law firm Swidler & Belnap, Washington, 1965-70; chmn. N.Y. State Pub. Service Commn., Albany, 1970-74; dir. Inst. for Pub. Policy Alternatives, State U. N.Y., Albany, 1974-75; partner firm Leva, Hawes, Symington, Martin & Oppenheimer, Washington, 1975—; mem. bd. Nat. Regulatory Research Inst.; adv. council Electric Power Research Inst., Gas Research Inst. Mem. Nat. Acad. Pub. Adminstrn., Served with USNR, 1943-45. Home: 5405 Potomac Ave Washington DC 20016

SWIFT, A. DEAN, retail trade exec.; b. 1918; B.A., U. Ill., 1940; married. With Sears, Roebuck & Co., 1940—, store mgr., 1949-64, product mgr., 1964-69, v.p. so. territory, 1969-73, pres., 1973—, also dir.; dir. Commonwealth Edison Co., First Chgo. Corp., Sears Roebuck Acceptance Corp., Allstate Ins. Co., Homart Devel. Co. Address: Sears Roebuck & Co Sears Tower Chicago IL 60684*

SWIFT, AL, congressman; b. Tacoma, Sept. 12, 1935; student Whitman Coll., 1953-55, Central Wash. U., 1956; 57; m. Paula Jean Jackson, 1956; children—Amy, Lauri. Broadcaster; public affairs dir. Sta. KVOS-TV; adminstrv. asst. to U.S. rep. Lloyd Meeds, 1965-69; mem. 96th Congress from 2d Wash. dist. Mem. Bellingham (Wash.) City Charter Revision Com.; chmn., mem. Bellingham Citizens Adv. Com.; mem. Bellingham Housing Authority. Democrat. Office: 1511 Longworth House Office Bldg Washington DC 20515

SWIFT, CLIFFORD J., JR., lawyer; b. Columbus, Ga., Sept. 28, 1911; A.B., U. Ga., 1933; LL.B., 1936; m. Barbara Parker, June 30, 1937; children—Clifford J. III, Barbara (Mrs. Gabrielsen), Lucile Woodruff (Mrs. Miller). Admitted to Ga. bar, 1936; mem. firm Page, Scrantom, Harris, McGlamry & Chapman, P.C. Served to lt. comdr. USNR, 1942-46. Fellow Am. Coll. Probate Counsel; mem. Am., Ga., Columbus bar assns., Phi Beta Kappa, Phi Kappa Phi, Phi Delta Phi. Address: 1815 Carter Ave Columbus GA 31906

SWIFT, DAVID EVERETT, educator; b. Miles City, Mont., Mar. 17, 1914; s. Charles Rufus and Ellen (Runner) S.; B.A., Yale, 1936; Ph.D., 1947; m. Jane Hastings Nichols, July 5, 1941; children—Jonathan Gordon, James Everett, Gordon Nichols, Ellen Shepard. From asst. prof. to prof. religion Lincoln (Pa.) U., 1947-51; personnel dir. Am. Friends Service Com., 1951-55; mem. faculty Wesleyan U., Middletown, Conn., 1955—, prof. religion, 1960—. Mem. Phi Beta Kappa. Author: Joseph John Gurney: Banker, Reformer and Quaker, 1962. Home: 390 Coleman Rd Middletown CT 06457

SWIFT, EDWARD FOSTER, III, business exec.; b. Chgo., Nov. 1, 1923; s. T. Philip and Elizabeth (Hoyt) S.; grad. Hotchkiss Sch., 1941; B.A., Yale, 1945; m. Joan McKelvy, July 2, 1947; children—Theodore Philip II, Edward McKelvy, Lockhart McKelvy, Elizabeth Hoyt; m. 2d, Carol Coffey Whipple, June 21, 1968. With Esmark, Inc. (formerly Swift & Co.), 1947-75, asst. to v.p. charge meat packing plants, 1958, asst. v.p., 1958-59, v.p. for provisions, fgn., casings and storage, 1959-64, exec. v.p., 1964-75; vice-chmn., dir. Chgo. Corp., 1975—; dir. Ill. Tool Works, Santa Fe Industries. Chmn. So. Ind. chpt. United Negro Coll. Fund, 1956. Bd. dirs. Evansville (Ind.) Community Fund, 1956; trustee Northwestern U., Evanston, Ill., Ill. Inst. Tech.; bd. dirs. Northwestern Meml. Hosp., Chgo. Served to capt. F.A., AUS, 1942-46. Mem. Chgo. Assn. Commerce and Industry (dir.), Delta Kappa Epsilon, Scroll and Key, Aurelian Honor Soc. Clubs: Chicago, Racquet, Economic, Chicago Commonwealth, Commercial (Chgo.); Onwentsia (Lake Forest); Old Elm. Home: 1501 N State Pkwy Chicago IL 60610 Office: 208 S La Salle St Chicago IL 60045

SWIFT, FRANK MEADOR, lawyer; b. N.Y.C., Dec. 27, 1911; s. Frank Meador and Alberta (Rankin) S.; student Emory U., 1930-32; LL.B., U. Ga., 1935; m. Harriet Elizabeth Simpson, May 30, 1944; children—Frank Meador, Thomas Lamar. Admitted to Ga. bar, 1935; partner law firm Swift, Currie, McGhee & Hiers, Atlanta, 1965—. Served to comdr. USNR, 1942-46. Mem. Am., Ga. bar assns., Lawyers Club Atlanta, Am. Judicature Soc. Republican. Presbyn. Clubs: Piedmont Driving, Commerce (Atlanta) Riomar Bay Yacht (Vero Beach, Fla.). Home: 1960 Brookview Dr NW Atlanta GA 30318 Office: 771 Spring St NW Atlanta GA 30308

SWIFT, GEORGE HASTINGS, JR., salt co. exec.; b. Boston, Jan. 24, 1919; s. George Hastings and Lucile (Casey) S.; grad. Deerfield Acad., 1938; student Harvard, 1938-39; grad. Advanced Mgmt. Program, 1953; m. Byrd Worthington Littlefield, Jan. 24, 1942; children—Byrd G., Silvia L., George Hastings III, Ann Swift Robinson. With N.E.D.M. & W., Somerville, Mass., 1939-40; with Swift & Co., Chgo., 1940-42, 46-50, mgr., Evansville, Ind., 1950-52, asst. v.p. Chgo., 1952-58, v.p. beef, lamb, veal, hides and wool, 1958-60, v.p. assisting pres., coordinator future planning and comml. research, 1960-61, v.p. assisting pres. purchasing, transp., pub. relations, agr. relations, bus. research, printing, patents, 1965-68, also dir. all Swift & Co. ins. affiliates, until 1968; mng. partner Independent Salt Co., Kanopolis, Kans., 1969—; owner, breeder thoroughbreds Augean Stable, Chgo., Quail Run Farm, Middleburg, Va.; hon. chmn. Park Travel Agy.; dir. Cia Minera Internat. Ltd. Mem. Chgo. Crime Commn. Served from pvt. to capt. Q.M.C., AUS, 1942-46. Mem. S.A.R., Soc. Mayflower Descs., Soc. Colonial Wars State Ill., Order Founders and Patriots Am. Episcopalian. Clubs: Rotary, Harvard, Onwentsia, Economic, Chicago, Mid-Day. Home: 505 N Lake Shore Dr Chicago IL 60611 Office: 120 S LaSalle St Chicago IL 60603

SWIFT, HEWSON HOYT, educator, biologist; b. Auburn, N.Y., Nov. 8, 1920; s. Arthur L., Jr. and Hildegarde (Hoyt) S.; A.B., Swarthmore Coll., 1942; M.S., State U. Ia., 1945; Ph.D., Columbia, 1950; m. Joan Woodcock, June 6, 1942; children—Deirdre Anne, Barbara Jean. Curator spiders U.S. Nat. Museum, Washington, 1945-46; lectr. zoology, Columbia, 1948-49; mem. faculty U. Chgo., 1949—, prof. zoology, 1958-70, Distinguished Service prof. biology and pathology, 1971-77, chmn. dept. biology, 1972-77, George Wells Beadle Disting. Ser. prof. biology and pathology, 1977—; vis. prof. Harvard, 1970-71; vis. sr. scientist CSIRO, Canberra, Australia, 1977-78; mem. cell biology study sect. NIH, 1958-62; mem. devel. adv. panel NSF, 1962-65; adv. panel etiology of cancer Am. Cancer Soc., 1965-70; mem. adv. panel Nat. Cancer Inst., 1972-75. Recipient Quantrell award for excellence in teaching U. Chgo., 1977. Fellow A.A.A.S., Am. Acad. Arts and Scis., Nat. Acad. Scis. (chmn. sect. on cellular and developmental biology); mem. Am. Soc. Cell Biology (pres. 1964; editorial bd. of Jour.), Histochem. Soc. (pres. 1973, editorial bd. jour.), Internat. Soc. Cell Biology, Genetics Soc. Am. Home: 5628 S Blackstone Ave Chicago IL 60637

SWIFT, JOHN FRANCIS, health care advt. co. exec.; b. N.Y.C., June 15, 1935; s. John F. and Mary Veronica (Kehoe) S.; B.S. in Bus. Adminstrn., Seton Hall U., 1960, postgrad., 1961-62; postgrad. City Coll. N.Y., 1960-61; m. Eleanor H. Cunniff, Oct. 10, 1964; children—John Francis, Sharon Ann. Mktg. research mgr. Lederle Labs. div. Cyanamid Internat., 1960-63; account exec. Robert A. Becker, advt. agy., N.Y.C., 1963-66; mgr. new products Chesebrough Ponds Co., N.Y.C., 1966-68; v.p. Frohlich Intercon Co., N.Y.C., 1968-72; pres. Lavey/Wolff/Swift, Inc., N.Y.C., 1972—, Frank J. Corbett, Inc., Chgo., 1977—, BBDO Health & Med. Communications Inc., 1977—. Served with USN, 1955-57. Mem. Pharm. Advt. Council (pres. 1979), Bio-Med. Mktg. Assn. Clubs: Fairmount Country (Chatham, N.J.); Skytop (Pa.); Marina Bay (Ft. Lauderdale, Fla.); Boca Raton (Fla.) Country, Boca West Country; N.Y. Athletic. Home: 32 Peppermill Rd Chatham Township NJ 07928 also 3309 Bridgewood Dr Boca Raton FL Office: 488 Madison Ave New York NY 10022

SWIFT, LELA, TV dir. and producer; b. U.S.; d. Jack and Ida Siwoff; student Hunter Coll.; m. Gilbert Schwartz, Feb. 21, 1950; children—Stuart Leslie, Russell Seth. Dir. various TV shows, 1954—, including: Studio One, Purex Spls., Dupont Show of Week, Dark Shadows; dir. Ryan's Hope; cons. ABC-TV. Recipient Emmy award for best dir. daytime TV, 1977, 79; named Dir. of Yr., Am. Women in Radio and TV, 1979. Mem. Dirs. Guild Am. (exec. bd. Dir.'s Council). Home and Office: Spring Lake Rd Sherman CT 06780

SWIFT, RICHARD, composer, educator; b. Middlepoint, Ohio, Sept. 24, 1927; s. Lisle Rusell and Josephine (Ladd) S.; M.A., U. Chgo., 1956; m. Dorothy Zackrisson, Feb. 10, 1951; children—Jeremy, John, Joel. Asso. prof. music U. Calif. at Davis, 1956-67, prof., 1967—, chmn. dept., 1963-71; vis. prof. Princeton U., 1977. Served with AUS, 1950-52. Recipient award Rockefeller Found., 1956, 68; award Fromm Found.; Composers String Quartet award, 1973; award Nat. Endowment for Arts, 1976; Inst. award Am. Acad. and Inst. Arts and Letters, 1978. Fellow Inst. Creative Arts; mem. Am. Music Center, A.S.C.A.P. Composer: A Coronal, 1954; String Quartet I, 1956, II, 1958, III, 1964; Sonata for Clarinet and Piano, 1957; Trio for Clarinet, Cello and Piano, 1957; Sonata for Solo Violin, 1958; Eve., 1959; Stravaganza III for Clarinet, Violin and Piano, 1960; Concerto for Piano and Chamber Ensemble, 1961; Extravaganza for Orchestra, 1962; Domains, I, II, III, 1963; Bucolics, 1964; Trial of Tender O'Shea (opera), 1964; Concerto for Violin and Chamber Ensemble, 1967; Music for A While, 1969; Thanatopsis, 1971; Prime, 1973; Quartet IV, 1973; Specimen Days, 1976. Home: 568 S Campus Way Davis CA 95616

SWIG, BENJAMIN HARRISON, hotel owner and operator; b. Taunton, Mass., Nov. 17, 1893; s. Simon and Fanny (Levy) S.; ed. pub. schs., Taunton; LL.D. (hon.), U. Santa Clara, 1962, Carroll Coll., 1968, Gonzaga U., 1979 L.H.D., Hebrew Union Coll., 1964, Brandeis U., 1966, John F. Kennedy U., 1979; H.H.D., Norwich U., 1967; m. Mae Aronovitz, Dec. 24, 1916 (dec.); children—Melvin M., Betty S. (Mrs. Richard S. Dinner), Richard L. Engaged in real estate, Boston and N.Y.C., 1925-45; chmn. bd. Fairmont Hotel Co. Del., Democratic Nat. Conv., 1956, 60, 64. Vice pres. Western States region Am. Friends of Hebrew U.; founder, chmn. bd. dirs. Careers Unltd. for Women; vice chmn., bd. govs. West Coast U. Judaism; soc. founders, trustee Calif. sch. Hebrew Union Coll.-Jewish Inst. Religion; hon. gov., hon. fellow Hebrew U., Jerusalem; chmn. bd. trustees, life mem. bd. founders U. Santa Clara; bd. dirs., bd. overseers Jewish Theol. Sem. Am., also hon. fellow soc. fellows; bd. dirs. Israel Devel. Corp., Israel Investors Corp.; mem. nat. adv. bd. PEC Israel Econ. Corp.; hon. chmn. No. Cal., mem. exec. com. State of Israel Bonds, San Francisco; mem. nat. council Am. Jewish Joint Distbn. Com.; pres. Greater Western region Jewish Nat. Fund; nat. bd. trustees Nat. Jewish Hosp./Nat. Asthma Center; mem. fund com. U.S. Mil. Acad.; hon. nat. chmn., co-chmn. West Coast region, mem. exec. com. United Jewish Appeal; mem. nat. com., West Coast chmn., vice chmn. soc. Founders Albert Einstein Coll. Medicine; nat. council, hon. vice chmn. West Coast div. Yeshiva U.; chmn. No. Calif. region Am.-Israel Cultural Found.; bd. dirs. Am. Friends Tel Aviv U., Brandeis Camp Inst. West, Brandeis Youth Found., Catholic Youth Orgn., Coast Guard Acad. Found., Nat. Realty Com., St. Anthony Dining Room, Exec. Council on Fgn. Diplomats; mem. adv. council Anna Head Sch., Israel Edn. Fund, Mary's Help Hosp.; hon. bd. dirs. Blackfeet Art Found., Jewish Welfare Fedn. San Francisco, Marin County and the Peninsula; financial adviser Blackfeet Indians, Browning, Mont.; mem. pres.'s council, mem. devel. council Carroll Coll.; v.p., bd. dirs. Columbia Park Boys Club; mem. adv. bd., pres. men's guild Convent of Good Sheperd; mem. nat. council, hon. chmn. Western State Joint Def. Appeal; mem. nat. adv. council Nat. Inf. Museum Devel. Program, Synagogue Council Am.; life mem. San Francisco adv. bd. Salvation Army; mem. vis. com. Stanford Sch. Medicine' alternate mem. bd. govs. Technion-Israel Inst. Tech.; nat. vice chmn. combined campaign, life hon. trustee Union Am. Hebrew Congregations; numerous other civic and charitable activities. Decorated comdr.'s cross Order of Merit of Fed. Republic of Germany; comdr. Order of Merit of Italian Republic, Star of Solidarity (Italy); knight Order St. Sylvester; recipient numerous other fgn., nat. and local awards including: Outstanding Civilian Service medal Dept. Army, 1960, 67, 71; certificates of honor Bd. Suprs. City and County of San Francisco, 1968, 69; Silver Keystone award Boys Clubs Am., 1970; Stephen S. Wise award Am. Jewish Congress, 1970; Gold award N.A.A.C.P., 1971; citation Brandeis U., 1971; Meritorious Pub. Service award U.S. Coast Guard, 1972; Silver medal City of Paris (France), 1972; Prime Minister's medal State of Israel Bonds, 1972; St. Francis of Assisi award City of San Francisco, 1972. Mem. Am. Soc. for Technion (nat. council), Am. Jewish Com. (nat. exec. council, nat. bd. dels., adv. com. San Francisco chpt.), Zionist Orgn. Am. (dir.), Civic League Improvement Clubs and Assns. (dir.), NCCJ (San Francisco adv. bd.), John Carroll Soc. (charter mem.), Soc. Hon. Fellows City of Hope, San Francisco C. of C. (chmn. mil. affairs com.), West Point Soc. San Francisco Bar Area (hon.). Jewish. Mason (33 deg.). Address: Fairmont Hotel San Francisco CA 94106

SWIGART, THEODORE EARL, oil exec.; b. Arroyo Grande, Calif., June 2, 1895; s. Frank W. and Mattie (Rice) S.; A.B., Stanford, 1917, Engr., 1918; spl. officers tng. course U.S. Naval Acad., 1918; m. Erna Patery, Sept. 28, 1918; 1 dau., Patricia (Mrs. James H. Pittman, Jr.). With pipe line dept. Standard Oil Co. (Calif.), 1913-14, Martinez refinery Shell Oil Co. (Calif.), 1915, exploration dept., 1916, prodn. dept., 1917; petroleum engr. U.S. Bur. Mines, Bartlesville, Okla., 1919-20, asst. to chief petroleum engr., Washington, supt. petroleum sta., Bartlesville, 1923; cons. petroleum engr. Steel Bros. & Co., Ltd., London, Attock Oil Co., Ltd., Rawalpindi, Punjab, India, Indo-Burma-Petroleum Co., Ltd., Yenangyaung, Burma, 1923-24; chief prodn. engr. Shell Oil Co. (Calif.), 1924-28; asst. gen. field supt. in charge prodn., 1928-32; v.p. in charge Tex., N.M., La., Ark., Shell Petroleum Corp. (now Shell Oil Co.), 1932-40; pres. Shell Pipe Line Corp., Houston, 1940-54; petroleum adviser Morgan Stanley & Co.; chmn., dir. N. Central Oil Corp., 1955-72; pres., dir. Ednl. Found., Inc.; past dir. Pilot Fund, Commerce Fund, Impact Fund, Industries Trend Fund Inc. Past pres., treas. Houston Museum Fine Arts: trustee United Fund Houston and Harris County; past pres. Community Chest and Council of Houston and Harris Co., Tex.; dir., past chmn. Houston Symphony Soc. Mem. Tex. Mid-Continent Oil and Gas Assn. (dir., Distinguished award), Am. Petroleum Inst. (past dir., past v.p.), Am. Inst. Mining and Metall. Engrs., Am. Assn. Petroleum Geologists, Tex. Soc. S.A.R. Clubs: Tejas, Bayou, River Oaks Country, Eagle Lake Rod and Gun, 25 Year Club of Petroleum Industry. Contbr. articles to tech. jours., govt. publs. Home: 2011 Bellmeade Rd Houston TX 77019 Office: 1300 Main St Houston TX 77002

SWIGERT, JAMES MACK, lawyer; b. Carthage, Ill., Sept. 25, 1907; s. James Ross and Pearl (Mack) S.; student Grinnell Coll., 1925-27; S.B., Harvard, 1930, LL.B., 1935; m. Alice Francis Titcomb Harrower, July 7, 1931; children—Oliver, David Ladd, Sally Harper (Mrs. Hamilton). Admitted to Ill. bar, 1935, Ohio bar, 1937; with firm Campbell, Clithero & Fischer, Chgo., 1935-36; with firm Taft, Stettinius & Hollister, Cin., 1936-47, partner, 1948—; dir., mem. exec. com. Union Central Life Ins. Co., 1963-79; dir. Philips Industries. Past bd. dirs. Cin. Symphony Orch., 1976-78. Republican. Presbyterian. Clubs: Queen City (past dir.), Cincinnati Country (dir.), Queen City Optimists, Tennis (past pres.), Recess (past pres.), Harvard (Cin.). Author articles labor relations labor law. Home: 196 Green Hills Rd Cincinnati OH 45208 Office: Dixie Terminal Bldg Cincinnati OH 45202

SWIGERT, JOHN LEONARD, JR., former astronaut, business exec.; b. Denver, Aug. 30, 1931; s. John Leonard and Virginia Swigert; B.S. in Mech. Engring., U. Colo., 1953; M.S. in Aerospace Sci., Rensselaer Poly. Inst., 1965; M.B.A., U. Hartford, 1967; D.Sc. (hon.), Am. Internat. Coll., 1970, Western Mich. U., 1970; LL.D., Western State U., 1970. Former engring. test pilot N.Am. Aviation, Inc., Pratt and Whitney Co., 1957-64; astronaut NASA, 1966-73, mem. support crew for Apollo 7 mission, mem. Apollo 13 backup crew, later command module pilot, 1970; exec. dir. Com. on Sci. and Tech., U.S. Ho. of Reps., Washington, 1973-79; v.p. Profl. Services Corp., McLean, Va., 1979—. Recipient Presdl. Medal for Freedom, 1970, Distinguished Service medal NASA, Distinguished Alumnus award U. Colo., 1970, gold medal City of N.Y., 1970, City of Chgo., 1970, Medal for Valor, City of Houston, 1970, Antonian gold medal, 1972. Fellow Am. Astronautical Soc. (co-recipient Flight Achievement award 1970), Soc. Exptl. Test Pilots (asso.), Am. Inst. Aeros. and Astronautics (asso., Octave Chanute award 1966, Haley Astronautics award 1971); mem. Quiet Birdmen, Phi Gamma Delta, Pi Tau Sigma, Sigma Tau. Home: 3150 S Tamarac Dr Suite B103 Denver CO 80231 Office: BDM Corp 7915 Jones Branch Dr McLean VA 22101

SWINARTON, ROBERT WALLACE, investment banker; b. Bronx, N.Y., July 22, 1926; s. Herbert Lincoln and Florence (Stein) S.; B.S. summa cum laude, Washington and Lee U., 1950; m. Rosamond W. Harrison, June 25, 1949; children—Patrice, Robert Wallace, Susan, Scott. Account exec. Dean Witter & Co., N.Y.C., 1950-57, municipal bond mgr., 1958-60, sales mgr. partner, 1961-63, nat. dir. research, 1963-68, dir. transaction service, 1969—, also vice chmn., 1972—, dir., mem. exec. com. v.p. Adventures in Recreation Corp.; pres., dir. InterCapital Income Securities Inc., 1977—, InterCapital Liquid Asset Fund Inc., 1977—. Mem. Nat. Market Adv. Bd. Mem. Soc. Valley Hosp.; trustee Washington and Lee U., 1979—. Served with USAAF, 1944-46. Mem. Nat. Assn. Security Dealers (exec. com. 1974-76, chmn. bd. 1976—, dir., dist. vice-chmn.), Securities Industry Assn. Am., Alpha Kappa Psi, Omicron Delta Epsilon, Beta Gamma Sigma. Clubs: Bond (treas. 1975-76), Municipal Bond, Bankers of Am. (gov.) (N.Y.C.); Upper Ridgewood Tennis (Ridgewood, N.J.) (pres. 1966-67, trustee 1968-70); Winding Brook Country (pres. 1977); Arcola Country. Home: 501 Knollwood Rd Ridgewood NJ 07450 Office: 130 Liberty St New York NY 10005

SWINDELLS, WILLIAM, JR., mfg. co. exec.; b. Oakland, Calif., Sept. 16, 1930; s. William and Irene (Gerlinger) S.; student Amherst Coll., 1948-50; B.S. in Indsl. Engring., Stanford U., 1953; postgrad. Harvard U. Sch. Bus. Adminstrn., 1960; m. Ann Johnston, Mar. 12, 1955; children—William, Jean, Leslie, Charles. With Willamette Industries, Inc., Portland, Oreg., 1953—, exec. v.p., 1974—, pres. bldg. materials group, 1974—; dir. Omark Industries. Bd. dirs. Oreg. Symphony; trustee Willamette U. Served to 2d lt. USAF, 1953. Mem. Oreg. Hist. Soc. (dir.). Clubs: Multnomah, Waverley Country, Arlington. Home: 5056 SW Hilltop Ln Portland OR 97221 Office: 1300 SW 5th Ave Portland OR 97201

SWINDLER, WILLIAM FINLEY, lawyer, educator; b. St. Louis, Oct. 24, 1913; s. Merton Clay and Pearl (Traller) S.; A.B., B.S. Washington U., 1935; A.M., U. Mo., 1936. Ph.D., 1942; LL.B., U. Neb., 1958; m. Benetta Rollins, Oct. 7, 1939 (dec. Apr. 1978); children—Elizabeth Pearl Henrietta, William Rollins Clayton. Reporter, St. Louis Star-Times, 1933, editorial writer, 1936-38; spl. corr. St. Louis Post-Dispatch, 1938-40; instr. in journalism U. Mo., 1938-40; asst. prof. journalism U. Idaho, 1940-44, head dept. journalism, 1941-46, asso. prof., 1944-45, prof., 1945-46; prof. journalism U. Nebr., 1946-58, dir. Sch. Journalism, 1946-56; spl. corr. Columbia Broadcasting System, 1952; prof. law and dir. devel. Coll. William and Mary, 1958-65, prof. law, 1965-74, John Marshall prof. law, 1974—; distinguished vis. prof. law Okla. U., 1974; prof. law Summer Sch. Law in Eng. (Exeter), 1970, 73, 78; admitted to Nebr., D.C., Va., U.S. Supreme Ct. bars. Mem. Am. Soc. Legal History (dir. 1960-62, v.p. 1962-64), Am. Judicature Soc. (dir. 1972-75), Am. Bar Assn., Am. Law Inst., Hist. Soc. Mo. (life), Supreme Ct. Hist. Soc. (dir. publs.), Order of Coif, Phi Delta Phi, Sigma Delta Chi, Kappa Tau Alpha (nat. sec. 1948-50, nat. pres. 1950-52). Democrat. Episcopalian. Author: A Bibliography of Law on Journalism, 1947; Problems of Law in Journalism, 1955; Common Law in America 1959; Magna Carta: Legend and Legacy, 1965; Court and Constitution in the 20th Century: The Old Legality, 1889-1932, 1969, The New Legality, 1932-68, 1970, The Modern Interpretation, 1974; Magna Carta (for high schools), 1968; The Constitution and Chief Justice Marshall, 1978. Editor: Justice in the States, 1971; Sources and Documents of U.S. Constitutions, 1972-79; series editor: Studies on Bicentennial of American Legal Education, 1978. Home: 20 Cole Ln Williamsburg VA 23185 Office: Sch Law Coll William and Mary Williamsburg VA 23185

SWINERTON, WILLIAM ARTHUR, bldg. and constrn. co. exec.; b. San Francisco, Dec. 12, 1917; s. Alfred Bingham and Jane Thomas (Hotaling) S.; B.S., Yale, 1939; postgrad. Stanford, 1940; m., June 5, 1943; children—Leslie Engelbrecht, Susan McBaine, James B., Sarah. With Swinerton & Walberg Co., San Francisco, 1940—, chmn., 1977—. Served with USMCR. 1940-46. Decorated Bronze Star. Clubs: Pacific Union; Burlingame Country. Home: 279 Albion St Woodside CA 94062 Office: 100 Pine St San Francisco CA 94111

SWINFORD, JOHN WALKER, lawyer; b. Stillwater, Okla., May 2, 1909; s. William Braden and Velma (Walker) S.; A.B., U. Okla., 1939, LL.B., 1933; m. Lois Steele, Jan. 19, 1938; children—William Steele, John Walker. Admitted to Okla. bar, 1933, since practiced in Oklahoma City; partner in firm Chandler, Shelton, Fowler & Swinford, 1938-42; partner firm Crowe, Boxley, Dunlevy, Thweatt, Swinford, Johnson & Burdick, and predecessor firm, 1947-76, of counsel, 1976—; past dir. Liberty Corp., Liberty Nat. Bank and Trust Co., Oklahoma City. Pres. Legal Aid Soc., 1963-64. Served to maj. USAAF, 1942-46. Mem. Am., Okla., Oklahoma County bar assns., Oklahoma City C. of C. Home: 837 N W 41st St Oklahoma City OK 73118 Office: Liberty Tower Oklahoma City OK 73102

SWING, GAEL DUANE, coll. pres.; b. LaPorte County, Ind., Mar. 13, 1932; s. William Edward and Dorothy Ruth (Jessup) S.; A.B., Franklin (Ind.) Coll., 1954; M.S., Ind. U., 1963; m. Sandra Sue Scott, Apr. 13, 1957; children—Scott, Kristie, Janet. Sales rep. Burroughs Corp., Indpls., 1954; successively dir. placement and admission counselor, dir. admissions, bus. mgr., v.p. devel. Franklin Coll., 1954-69; dir. spl. program services Office Devel., Washington U., St. Louis, 1969-73; exec. v.p. North Central Coll., Naperville, Ill., 1973-75, pres., 1975—; mem. Ill. Bd. Higher Edn. Non-Pub. Adv. Com. Trustee Franklin Coll. Recipient Alumni citation Franklin Coll., 1975. Mem. Am. Coll. Pub. Relations Assn., Fedn. Ind. Ill. Colls. and Univs. (exec. com.), Council W. Suburban Colls. (dir.), United Methodist Found. (dir.), Asso. Colls. Ill. (exec. com.). Club: Naperville Country. Home: 329 S Brainard St Naperville IL 60540 Office: North Central Coll Naperville IL 60540

SWING, PETER GRAM, educator; b. N.Y.C., July 15, 1922; s. Raymond and Betty (Gram) S.; A.B., Harvard, 1948, A.M., 1951; postgrad. U. Utrecht (Netherlands), 1951-52; Ph.D., U. Chgo., 1969; m. Elizabeth Ann Sherman, May 27, 1948; children—Pamela Sherman, Timothy Gram, Bradford Scott. Instr., asso. choirmaster

Rollins Coll., 1952-53; instr. U. Chgo., 1953-55; mem. faculty Swarthmore Coll., 1955—, asso. prof., 1959-69, prof., 1969—, dir. Coll. Chorus, 1955—, chmn. dept. music, 1958-74; mem. faculty Berkshire Music Center, Lenox, Mass., 1962—; Nat. Humanities Faculty, 1969-70; vis. com. music U. Chgo., 1971-77. Served with USNR, 1942-46. Fulbright grantee, Netherlands, 1951-52; Fulbright Sr. Research grantee, Belgium, 1970-71. Mem. Am. Musicol. Soc. (chmn. Phila. chpt. 1969-70), Coll. Music Soc., Renaissance Soc., Vereniging voor Nederlandse Muziekgeschiedenis, AAUP, Phi Beta Kappa (hon.). Research in early 16th century music. Home: 614 Hillborn Ave Swarthmore PA 19081

SWING, WILLIAM LACY, ambassador; b. Lexington, N.C., Sept. 11, 1934; s. Baxter Dermot and Mary Frances (Barbee) S.; A.B., Catawba Coll., 1956; Th.M., Yale U., 1960; postgrad. Oxford (Eng.) U., U. Tuebingen (Germany), 1961; 1 son, Brian Curtis. Vice consul Am. consulate, Port Elizabeth, South Africa, 1963-66; internat. economist Bur. Econ. Affairs, Dept. State, 1966-68; consul, chief consular sect. Am. consulate gen., Hamburg, Germany, 1968-72; internat. relations officer, desk officer for Fed. Republic of Germany, Dept. State, Washington, 1972-74; dep. chief of mission, counselor Am. embassy, Bangui, Central African Republic, 1974-76; fellow Center for Internat. Affairs, Harvard U., 1976-77; alt. dir. Office Central African Affairs, Dept. State, 1977-79; U.S. ambassador People's Republic of the Congo, 1979—. Recipient Meritorious Honor award USIA, 1971. Mem. Am. Fgn. Service Assn. Club: Lions. Co-editor: Education for Decision, 1963. Office: US Embassy BP 1015 Brazzaville People's Republic of the Congo*

SWINTON, STANLEY MITCHELL, journalist; b. Charlevoix, Mich., Sept. 1, 1919; s. Roy Stanley and Jane Ann (Mitchell) S.; A.B., U. Mich., 1940; m. Helen Meek, Feb. 16, 1955; children—Scott, Donald, Neil. Editor A.P., Detroit, 1940-41, corr., Philippines, Indonesia, Indochina, 1945-47, chief of bur., Southeast Asia, 1947-48, Middle East, 1948-50, war corr., Korea, 1950-51, chief of bur., Italy, 1951-57, gen. news editor Asso. Press World Service, 1957-60, dir. world services div., 1960-64, asst. gen. mgr. and dir. world services, 1964—, v.p., 1972—, vice-chmn. AP, Ltd., 1964—. Former pres., chmn. exec. center Corrs. Fund. Am. Served as sgt. AUS, 1941-45; combat corr. Stars and Stripes, North Africa, Italy, France, Austria. Recipient Regents' Outstanding Achievement award U. Mich., 1966, Sesquicentennial award, 1967; award for Outstanding Contbn. to Journalism, Ohio U., 1979. Mem. Council Fgn. Relations, Silurians, Phi Gamma Delta, Sigma Delta Chi, Michigamua. Episcopalian. Clubs: Edgewood (Tivoli, N.Y.); Dutch Treat, Century Assn. Contbg. author: Heartbreak Ridge, 1951; The Stars and Stripes, 1961; How I Got That Story, 1967. Home: 14 Sutton Pl S New York NY 10022 also Dales Bridge Farm Germantown NY Office: 50 Rockefeller Plaza New York NY 10020

SWINTOSKY, JOSEPH VINCENT, educator; b. Kewaunee, Wis., Dec. 14, 1921; s. Joseph Frank and Mary (Paul) S.; B.S., U. Wis., 1942, Ph.D., 1948; m. Dorothy Ann Zevnik, June 13, 1953; children—Joseph Vincent, Denise Claire, Michael David, Steven J., John, Paul, Robert, Damian, David Andrew, Daniel Frank. Instr. U. Wis. Sch. Pharmacy, 1946-49, asst. prof., 1949-53; sr. sci. Smith, Kline & French Labs., Phila., 1953-54, unit head tabletting, 1954-57, group leader pharm. tech., 1957- 59, prin. research pharmacist, 1959-64, head pharm. research sect., 1964-67; adj. prof. pharmacy Temple U.; dean Coll. Pharmacy, U. Ky., Lexington, 1967—. Recipient Ebert award, 1958. Fellow A.A.A.S. (vice chmn. 1960, chmn. pharmacy sect. 1960), Am. Pharm. Assn. (v.p. Phila. br. 1960-61, chmn. sci. sect. 1964-65, found. award 1964, Indsl. Pharm. Tech. award 1975); mem. Am. Chem. Soc., Acad. Pharm. Sciences (pres. 1967-68), N.Y. Acad. Scis., Am. Inst. History of Pharmacy, Am. Pub. Health Assn., Internat. Pharm. Fedn. (steering com. gen. practice sect. 1975—, U.S. coordinator acad. sect. 1976), Assn. Pharmacy Tchrs. of India (hon.). Author numerous sci. research papers. Editorial adv. bd. Jour. Pharm. Scis., 1964—. Home: 303 S Main St Nicholasville KY 40356 Office: Washington and Gladstone Sts Lexington KY 40506

SWINYARD, CHESTER ALLAN, physician, educator; b. Logan, Utah, Oct. 21, 1906; s. William and Bertha E. (Halverson) S.; B.S., Utah State U., 1928, M.S., 1929; Ph.D., U. Minn., 1934; M.D., State U. N.Y., 1951; m. Vivian Redford, June 12, 1929; children—Sharon Joan (Mrs. David B. Sutton), Marilyn (Mrs. Ruddy Havill). Teaching fellow zoology U. Minn., 1929-31, teaching fellow anatomy, Coll. Medicine, 1931-34; Charlton research fellow Tufts U. Med. Coll., 1935-36, instr. anatomy, 1936-37; asst. prof. anatomy Med. Coll. S.C., 1937-40; asso. prof. anatomy U. Utah Coll. Medicine, 1940-44, prof. anatomy, 1944-58, med. dir. Rehab. Center, 1955-58; vis. prof. Med. Coll. State N.Y., 1949-50; lectr. surg. anatomy Maimonides Hosp., Bklyn., 1950-51; fellow phys. medicine and rehab. N.Y.U.-Bellevue Med. Center, 1953-56, asso. dir., children's div. Inst. Phys. Medicine and Rehab., 1958-60; asso. prof. phys. medicine and rehab. N.Y. U. Sch. Medicine, 1958-66, prof. rehab. medicine, 1966—, dir. pediatric rehab. research, 1967-75, vis. prof. emeritus surgery Stanford Med. Center, 1975—; staff asso. Assn. Aid Crippled Children, 1958-72. Mem. Am. Acad. Cerebral Palsy (pres. 1964-65), Am. Acad. Neurology (asso.), Am. Assn. Anatomists, Am. Assn. Electromyography and Electrodiagnosis, Am. Congress Phys. Medicine and Rehab., A.M.A., Am. Soc. Human Genetics, Internat. Soc. Rehab. Disabled, Teratology Soc., Nat. Rehab. Assn., N.Y. County, N.Y. State med. socs., Sigma Xi. Contbr. articles to profl. jours., chpts. to textbooks. Home: 2 White Oak Ct Menlo Park CA 94025 Office: 520 Willow Rd Palo Alto CA 94304

SWINYARD, EWART AINSLIE, coll. dean, pharmacologist; b. Logan, Utah, Jan. 3, 1909; s. William and Bertha (Halverson) S.; B.S., Utah State U., 1932; B.S. in Pharmacy, Idaho State Coll., 1936; M.S., U. Minn., 1941; Ph.D. (univ. fellow, Winthrop Research fellow) U. Utah, 1947; m. Grace Chatterton Parkinson, June 19, 1934 (dec. 1973); children—Emma Lou (Mrs. Rodger David Kasteler), Richard Ewart. Mem. faculty Idaho State Coll., Pocatello, 1936-47; lectr. pharmacology U. Utah Coll. Medicine, Salt Lake City, 1945-67, prof. pharmacology, 1967-76, prof. emeritus pharmacology, 1976—; prof. pharmacology U. Utah Coll. Pharmacy, 1947-76, prof. emeritus pharmacology, 1976—, Disting. Research prof., 1968-69, dir. research, 1947-78, dir. Sch. Alcohol Studies, 1962-78, head dept. biopharm. scis., 1965-70, dean, 1970-76, dir. Center for Early Pharmacol. Evaluation of Antiepileptic Drugs, 1975—; Rennebohm lectr. U. Wis., 1960; George Beecher Kaufmann lectr. Ohio State U., 1963; vis. scientist Utah Acad. Sci., 1962—, Am. Assn. Colls. Pharmacy, 1962-70. Recipient Research Achievement award in pharmacodynamics Am. Pharm. Assn. Found., 1965; award and medal for distinguished research and edn. in alcoholism Am. Med. Soc. on Alcoholism, 1977. Fellow Am. Coll. Apothecaries; mem. Am. Soc. for Pharmacology and Exptl. Therapeutics (editorial bd. 1965-68), Am. (chmn. physiol. testing com. 1955, 57, 59), Utah (hon. life) pharm. assns., Utah Acad. Sci., Arts and Letters, Am. Coll. Neuropsychopharmacology, N.Y. Acad. Scis., Am. Assn. Colls. Pharmacy (sec.-treas. dist. 8, 1953-71), Sigma Xi, Phi Kappa Phi, Phi Delta Chi, Rho Chi. Editor: Remington's Pharmaceutical Sciences, 11th-15th edits.; edits.; editorial adv. bd. Jour. Pharm. Scis., 1953-60; editorial bd. Epilepsia, 1978—. Contbr. to Pharmacological Basis of Therapeutics, 3d, 4th, 5th edits.; articles to profl. jours. Home: 2055 Michigan Ave Salt Lake City UT 84108

SWISHER, SCOTT NEIL, physician, educator; b. LeCenter, Minn., July 30, 1918; s. Scott Neil and Edna (Stenlund) S.; B.S., U. Minn., 1943, M.D., 1945, postgrad., 1948-49; m. Edna Lenora Briese, Sept. 5, 1944; children—Scott Neil III, Edward Allan. Intern, resident U. Rochester Med. Center, 1945, 47-48; practice medicine, specializing in internal medicine, Rochester, N.Y., 1949-67, Lansing, Mich., 1967—; from instr. to prof. medicine, head hematology unit U. Rochester Sch. Medicine and Dentistry, 1950-67; prof., chmn. dept. medicine Coll. Human Medicine, Mich. State U., 1967-77, asso. dean research, 1978—; cons. NIH, Dept. Def. research and engring. div., NASA Manned Spacecraft Center and Hdqrs.; chmn. med. adv. com. ARC Nat. Blood Program, 1973-76, bd. govs., 1976—; chmn. NRC Com. on Blood, 1958-63; chmn. panel 6 Bur. Biologics, FDA, 1975-79. Served from 1st lt. to capt. AUS, 1945-47. Mem. Am. Soc. Clin Investigation, Assn. Am. Physicians, Am. Bd. Internal Medicine, Alpha Omega Alpha. Contbr. articles to profl. jours. Home: 1290 Whittier Dr East Lansing MI 48823

SWIT, LORETTA, actress; b. Passaic, N.J., Nov. 4; student Am. Acad. Dramatic Arts, N.Y.C. Stage appearances include: Any Wednesday, The Odd Couple, Mame, The Apple Tree, Same Time Next Year; films include: Stand Up and Be Counted, 1972, Freebie and the Bean, 1974, Race with the Devil, 1975; regular TV series MASH, 1972—; TV movies: Shirts/Skin, Coffeeville, Superman, Mirror, Mirror, Valentine, The Walls Came Tumbling Down; other TV appearances include: Gunsmoke, Mannix, Hawaii Five-O, Mission Impossible, The Doctors, Cade's County. Mem. AFTRA. Office: care Internat Creative Mgmt 8899 Beverly Blvd Los Angeles CA 90048*

SWITZER, BARRY, football coach; b. Crossett, Ark., Oct. 5, 1937; ed. U. Ark.; m. Kay, 1963; children—Greg, Kathy, Dove. Asst. football coach U. Ark., 1960-65; asst. football coach U. Okla., 1966-72, head coach, 1973—. Served with U.S. Army. Named Coach of Year, 1973. Office: Athletic Dept U Okla 180 W Brooks St Room 201 Norman OK 73019*

SWOFFORD, EDWARD EMERY, airline exec.; b. Terre Haute, Ind., Mar. 11, 1918; s. Evert Washington and Pearl Aurella S.; A.A., Riverside City Coll.; m. Karen Sakai, Jan. 30, 1973; children—Reece Gregory, Susan Diana, Hayden Edward. With Pan Am. World Airways, 1943-66, dir. Pacific N.W. and Alaska, to 1966; v.p. mktg. Northeast Airlines, 1966-70; divisional v.p. Pacific Pan Am. World Airways, 1970-77; pres., chief exec. officer Aloha Airlines, Honolulu, 1977—, dir. Mem. Hawaii Visitors Bur. (chmn. 1978-79), Seattle Visitors and Conv. Bur. (pres. 1966), Air Transport Assn. (dir.). Democrat. Clubs: Plaza, Outrigger Canoe, MidPacific Country, Wings, Masons, Shriners. Office: PO Box 30028 Honolulu HI 96820

SWORD, CHARLES HEGE, computer co. exec.; b. Whittier, Calif., Jan. 1, 1924; s. Charles Greenhill and Helen (Hege) S.; A.B., Stanford, 1947, J.D., 1949, M.B.A., 1951; m. Lois M. Beebe, Jan. 13, 1957; children—Charles Hege, David Loy, Helen Claire. Admitted to Calif. bar, 1950; mgr. Minuteman contracts and controls, autonetics div. N.Am. Aviation Co., 1952-61; dir. space and electronics programs, asst. dir. engring., aero. div. Philco Ford Corp., 1961-69; v.p., sec. Calif. Computer Products, Inc., Anaheim, 1969—. Mem. Alpha Kappa Lambda, Phi Alpha Delta. Republican. Presbyn. (elder). Mason. Home: 2741 Pebble Dr Corona Del Mar CA 92625 Office: 2411 W La Palma Ave Anaheim CA 92801

SWORDS, RAYMOND JOSEPH, ednl. adminstr., clergyman; b. Springfield, Mass., Feb. 9, 1918; s. Raymond L. and Josephine (Noonan) S.; A.B., Coll. Holy Cross, 1938; M.A., Boston Coll., 1943; M.A. in Math., Harvard, 1947; S.T.L., Weston Coll., 1951; LL.D., Clark U., 1967, U. Mass., 1967; D.Sc., Lowell Inst. Tech., 1967, Worcester Poly. Inst., 1969; Litt.D., Suffolk U., 1969; L.H.D., Stonehill Coll., 1970. Ordained priest Roman Catholic Ch., 1950; instr. math. Coll. Holy Cross, Worcester, Mass., 1943-45, dir. admissions, 1953-55, chmn. dept. math., 1955-60, pres., 1960-70; pres. Cranwell Sch., Lenox, Mass., 1972-76; pres. Regis High Sch., N.Y.C., 1976—. Address: 53 E 83d St New York City NY 10028

SWYGERT, LUTHER MERRITT, judge; b. Miami County, Ind., Feb. 7, 1905; s. Irven W. and Catherine (Hoover) S.; LL.B. magna cum laude, Notre Dame U., 1927; LL.D., Valparaiso Sch. Law, 1964, U. Notre Dame, 1969; m. Mildred Kercher, Oct. 10, 1931 (dec. Jan. 1969); m. 2d, Mrs. Gari Pancoe, July 1, 1969; children—Robert L. (dec.), Michael I. Admitted to Ind. bar; in law practice, 1927-31; dep. pros. atty., Lake Co., Ind., 1931-33; asst. U.S. atty., No. Dist. Ind., 1934-43; U.S. dist. judge No. Dist. Ind., 1943-61, chief judge, 1954-61, judge U.S. Circuit Ct. Appeals, 1961—, chief judge, 1970-75. Mem. Am., Ind. bar assns. Office: 219 S Dearborn St Chicago IL 60604

SYAPIN, JOHN JAMES, gas and oil co. exec.; b. Los Angeles, May 10, 1923; s. James Peter and Mary Helen (Galitzen) S.; B.S. in Accounting, U. So. Cal., 1949; m. Mary Anne Teckenoff, Sept. 5, 1948; children—David James, Michael John. Staff accountant Robert Krost & Assos., Pasadena, Cal., 1949; accountant, mgr. Price Waterhouse & Co., Los Angeles, 1949-63; v.p., treas. Sante Fe Internat. Corp., Orange, Calif., 1963—. Served with AUS, 1943-46. C.P.A., Calif. Mem. Fin. Execs. Inst., Am. Inst. C.P.A.'s, Calif. Soc. C.P.A.'s, Beta Gamma Sigma, Beta Alpha Psi. Republican. Presbyn. Clubs: University of Los Angeles. Home: 9204 Otto St Downey CA 90240 Office: PO Box 1401 Orange Commerce Center Orange CA 92668

SYER, WARREN BERTRAM, mag. publisher; b. Somerville, Mass., Mar. 9, 1923; s. C. Bertram and Mabel (Stevens) S.; student Northeastern U., U. Ky.; A.B., Antioch Coll., 1946; m. Barbara Anne Gould, May 18, 1946; children—Deborah Anne, Kurt Warren, Diane Barbara, Cassandra Gould. With Credit Bur. Greater Boston, 1946-47; spl. rep. Nat. Concert Bur., 1948; pub. relations specialist Sears, Roebuck & Co., 1948-53; with Billboard Pub. Inc., N.Y.C., 1953-74, v.p., dir., gen. mgr. consumer publs. High Fidelity, Musical Am., Stereo Quarterly, The Buyers Guide, Four Channel Directory, Test Report Book, Protect!, Massachusetts, Photo Weekly, Modern Photography mags.; gen. mgr. High Fidelity Cable TV, 1954-74, formerly dir. BP Inc.; pres. ABC Leisure Mags. Inc., Great Barrington, Mass. and N.Y.C., 1975—. Served with USAAF, 1942-46. Decorated D.F.C., Air medal with cluster, Purple Heart. Mem. Mag. Pubs. Assn. Club: Wyantenuck Country. Home: 82 West Ave Great Barrington MA 01230 Office: Publishing House Great Barrington MA 01230 also 1330 Ave of the Americas New York NY 10019 also 130 E 59th St New York NY 10022

SYKES, ABEL BAXTON, JR., coll. pres.; b. Wyandotte County, Kans., June 1, 1934; s. Abel Baxton and Grace S.; student Sacramento Jr. Coll., 1953-54, Kansas City Jr. Coll., 1956-57; B.A., U. Mo., 1960, M.A., 1960; postgrad. San Diego State Coll., 1960-67; Ed.D., U. Calif. at Los Angeles, 1971; m. Sylvia Thierry; children—Dawn, Daphne, Leslie. Mem. faculty San Diego Unified Schs., 1959-64, Grossmont Jr. Coll., 1964-68; dean instrn. Compton Coll., 1968-69, pres., supt., 1969—. Bd. dirs. Am. Assn. Community and Jr. Colls.; chmn. Council Black Am. Affairs; vice chmn. Council Chief Exec. Adminstrs. Served with USAF, 1952-56. Mem. Urban League San Diego, Open Forum, Family Services Assn., Planned Parenthood Am. Presbyn. (elder). Home: 1600 Tartar Ln Compton CA 90221

SYKES, CONWELL SHOUP, banker; b. N.Y.C., Jan. 22, 1906; s. Eugene Lanier and Jane Prewett (Shoup) S.; B.A., U. Ala., 1926; LL.B., U. Miss., 1928; m. Frances Gordon Shelton, Apr. 26, 1935; children—Marian Gordon (Mrs. Robert Heard Alexander), Eugenia Lanier (Mrs. Eugene Michael Bogen). Admitted to Miss. bar, 1928; practiced in Aberdeen, 1928-30; v.p. Bank of Clarksdale, Miss., 1930-40, exec. v.p., 1940-47; pres. Comml. Nat. Bank, Greenville, Miss., 1947-75, chmn., 1976—; dir. Planters Mfg. Co., Clarksdale, Henderson & Baird Hardware Co., Greenwood. Former mem. Greenville Port Commn.; past pres. Washington County chpt. A.R.C., Cancer Soc.; past trustee Greenville Sch., Kings Daus. Hosp., Greenville. Mem. Miss. Bankers Assn. (past pres.), Phi Beta Kappa, Delta Kappa Epsilon, Phi Delta Phi, Omicron Delta Kappa. Episcopalian. Rotarian. Author: Bank Manual on Articles Four and Nine Mississippi Uniform Commercial Code, 1967, rev. edit., 1978. Home: 704 S Washington Ave Greenville MS 38701 Office: 604 Washington Ave Greenville MS 38701

SYKES, GRESHAM M'CREADY, sociologist, educator; b. Plainfield, N.J., May 26, 1922; s. M'Cready and Beatrice (Evans) S.; A.B., Princeton, 1950; Ph.D. (Woodrow Wilson fellow 1950-51, Univ. fellow 1951-52), Northwestern U., 1953; M.A. (hon.), Dartmouth, 1961; m. Carla Adelt, July 13, 1946. Instr. sociology Princeton, 1952-54, asst. prof., bicentennial preceptor, 1954-58; asso. prof. Northwestern U., Evanston, Ill., 1958-60; prof. sociology Dartmouth, Hanover, N.H., 1960-63, chmn. dept., 1961-63; exec. officer Am. Sociol. Assn., 1963-65; research prof. law and sociology, dir. adminstrn. of justice program U. Denver, 1965-72, chmn. dept. sociology U. Houston, 1973; prof. sociology U. Va., Charlottesville, 1974—, chmn. dept., 1978—; vis. prof. U. Iowa, 1973-74. Bd. advisers N.J. Prison, 1955-58; adviser N.J. Gov.'s Com. Prisons, 1958; mem. curriculum com. Am. Council Learned Socs., 1961-62; cons. N.H. Dept. Edn., 1962—. Served to capt., C.E., AUS, 1942-46; ETO. Mem. Am. (asso. editor rev. 1960-62), Eastern (exec. com.) sociol. assns. Author: Crime and Society, rev. edit., 1967; The Society of Captives, 1958; Law and the Lawless, 1969; Social Problems In America, 1971; Criminology, 1978. Criminology editor Jour. Criminal Law, Criminology and Police Sci., 1959-64; editor Scott Foresman Series in Institutions and Modern Social Problems, 1968—; asso. editor Contemporary Sociology. Contbr. articles and revs. to Ency. Brit., publs. Home: Cedarcroft Keswick VA 22947 Office: Dept Sociology U Va Charlottesville VA 22903

SYKES, LYNN RAY, geophysicist; b. Pitts., Apr. 16, 1937; s. Lloyd Ascutney and Margaret (Woodburn) S.; B.S., M.S. (Proctor and Gamble scholar 1956-60), M.I.T., 1960; Ph.D. in Geology (Edward John Nible Leadership award 1960-61), Columbia U., 1964. Phys. sci. aide U.S. Geol. Survey, summer 1956; researcher marine geophysics Woods Hole (Mass.) Oceanographic Instn., summers 1959-60; research asst., then research asso. seismology Lamont-Doherty Geol. Obs., Columbia, 1961-66; research geophysicist earth scis. labs. Environ. Sci. Services Adminstrn., Dept. Commerce, 1966-68; adj. asst. prof. geology Columbia U., 1966-68, head seismology group, 1972—, Higgins prof. geology, 1978—; organizing sec. Internat. Symposium Mech. Properties and Processes of the Mantle, 1970; mem. Vetelsen award com. Columbia U., 1972—, chmn. adv. bd. Lamont-Doherty Geol. Obs., 1975—; vis. prof. Earthquake Inst., Tokyo U., 1974; cons. in field, mem. numerous adv. coms., del. internat. meetings. Recipient H.O. Wood award Carnegie Instn., 1970; Sloan fellow, 1969-71. Fellow Am. Geophys. Union (pres. sect. tetonophysics 1972-74; Macelwane award 1970, Walter H. Bucker medal 1975), Geol. Soc. Am., Royal Astron. Soc.; mem. Nat. Acad. Scis., Am. Acad. Arts and Scis., N.Y. Acad. Scis. (pres. geol. sect. 1970-71), seismological Soc. Am. (dir. 1969-72). Author numerous papers in field; asso. editor Jour. Geophys. Research, 1968-70. Home: Washington Spring Rd Palisades NY 10964 Office: Lamont-Doherty Geol Obs Columbia Univ Palisades NY 10964

SYKES, LYNN RAY, geologist, educator; b. Pitts., Apr. 16, 1937; s. Lloyd Ascutney and Margaret (Woodburn) S.; B.S. (Proctor & Gamble scholar) and M.S., Mass. Inst. Tech., 1960; Ph.D. in Geology, Columbia, 1964. Phys. sci. aide geophys. lab. U.S. Geol. Survey, Silver Spring, Md., summer 1956; participant summer coop. program Geophys. Service Inc., Dallas, 1958; Summer Research fellow Woods Hole (Mass.) Oceanographic Inst., 1959; research asst. Lamont-Doherty Geol. Observatory Columbia, 1961-64, research asso. in seismology, 1964-66, adj. asst. prof. geology Columbia, 1966-68, asst. prof., 1968-69, asso. prof., 1969-73, prof., 1973-78, Higgins prof. geology, 1978—, mem. univ. com. on acad. priorities, 1977-79; research geophysicist earth scis. labs. U.S. Dept. Commerce, 1966-68. Mem. panel polar geophysics Nat. Acad. Scis., 1968, adv. com. to ESSA Research Labs., 1968-69; mem. subcom. geodesy and cartography applications steering com. NASA, 1968-70; mem. com. on world-wide standardized network Nat. Acad. Scis./NRC, 1969, com. seismology, 1972-73, panel earthquake prediction, 1973-75; organizing sec. Internat. Symposium Mech. Properties and Processes of Mantle of Internat. Upper Mantle Com., 1970; mem. panel on deep crustal drilling in marine areas JOIDES, 1970-71; advisor N.Y. State Geol. Survey and N.Y. State Environ. Protection Agy., 1970—; mem. U.S. Geodynamics Panel on Mid-Atlantic Ridge, 1971-72; mem. working group U.S./USSR Joint Program for Earthquake Prediction, 1973-77; mem. U.S. Del. on Earthquake Prediction to USSR, fall, 1973; mem. adv. com. on proposals for earthquake prediction U.S. Geol. Survey, 1974, adv. panel earthquake hazards program, 1977—; mem. U.S. Tech. Del. for talks on treaty on Threshold Limitations Underground Nuclear Explosions, Moscow, USSR, summer, 1974; mem. rev. panel earth scis. NSF, 1974-77; mem. study groups on plate interiors and Cocos and Caribbean plates U.S. Geodynamics Com.; mem. U.S. Seismology Group to People's Republic of China, fall, 1974; vis. prof. Earthquake Research Inst. of Tokyo (Japan) U., fall 1974; mem. com. acad. priorities Columbia U., 1977-78. Pres. Far West 77th St. Block Assn., N.Y.C., 1973-74. Recipient H. O. Wood award in seismology Carnegie Instn. of Washington, 1967-70, Edward John Noble Leadership award during first three years grad. study; Sloan fellow, 1969-71; NSF grantee; AEC grantee; Air Force Office Sci. Research, NASA, N.Y. State Sci. and Tech. Found. grantee; N.Y. State Atomic and Space Devel. Authority grantee; U.S. Geol. Survey, Sloan Found. grantee. Fellow Am. Geophys. Union (Macelwave award to Outstanding Young Geophysicist for 1970, Walter H. Bucher medal for original contbns. to basic knowledge of Earth's crust 1975 pres. sect. tectonophysics 1972-74), Seismol. Soc. Am., Geol. Soc. Am.; mem. Nat. Acad. Scis., Am. Acad. Arts. and Scis., Royal Astron. Soc., Soc. Exploration Geophysicists, N.Y. Acad. Scis. (pres. geol. sect. 1970-71). Contbg. author: History of the Earth's Crust, 1968; Geodynamics of Iceland and the North Atlantic Area, 1974; Encounter with the Earth, 1975. Asso. editor Jour. Geophys. Research, 1968-70. Contbr. numerous articles to profl. jours. Research includes maj. contbns. on plate tectonics, earthquake prediction and discrimination of underground nuclear explosions from earthquakes. Home: Washington Spring Rd Palisades NY 10964 Office: Lamont-Doherty Geol Observatory Columbia U Palisades NY 10964

SYKES, MELVIN JULIUS, lawyer; b. Balt., Jan. 9, 1924; s. Philip Louis and Sara (Klein) S.; grad. Balt. City Coll., 1940, Balt. Hebrew Coll., 1941; A.B. with honors, Johns Hopkins, 1943; LL.B. magna cum laude, Harvard, 1948; m. Judith Janet Konowitz, Sept. 24, 1950; children—David K., Rachel A., Daniel E., Israel J. Law clk. to Hon. Morris A. Soper U.S. Ct. Appeals, Fourth Circuit, 1948-49; admitted to Md. Ct. Appeals bar, 1949, U.S. Ct. Appeals, Fourth Circuit bar, 1949, U.S. Dist. Ct. Md. bar, 1950, U.S. Supreme Ct. bar, 1955; practice law, Balt., 1949—. Draftsman Md. Dept. Legis. Reference, 1949-50; research cons. Md. Commn. Adminstrv. Orgn., 1951-52; reporter Md. commns. to study judiciary, 1953, to revise laws relating to pub. service commn., 1953-55; mem. standing com. on rules of practice, procedure, Ct. Appeals, 1954-72, 78—; mem. Legis. Council Commn. on Revision Condemnation Laws, 1961-63; mem. Balt. Charter Revision Commn., 1962-63; pres. Bar Library of Balt., 1962-63; mem. Md. Constl. Conv. Commn., 1966-67; cons. Gov. Md. Commn. to Revise Testamentary Laws, 1967-69; mem. Gov. Md. commns. to study state aid to nonpub. edn., 1969-71, on annotated code Md., 1970—. Mem. governing council Am. Assn. Jewish Edn., 1968—; vice pres. Balt. Jewish Council, 1970-72, now mem. bd. dirs. Balt. chpt. Am. Jewish Com., Balt. Neighborhoods Inc.; formerly chmn. bd. trustees Balt. Hebrew Coll. Served with USAAF, 1943-45. Fellow Am. Coll. Trial Lawyers, Am. Coll. Probate Counsel; mem. Am. Law Inst., Balt. City, Md. (lectr. continuing edn. programs), Am. bar assns., Md. Bar Found. (vice chmn.), Am. Jewish Congress, Zionist Orgn. Am., Phi Beta Kappa. Democrat. Jewish. Mem. B'nai B'rith. Co-author: West's Maryland Procedural Forms, 1964. Home: 3811 Fords Lane Baltimore MD 21215 Office: 906 Munsey Bldg Baltimore MD 21202

SYKES, WALTER HENRY, former chem. co. exec.; b. N.Y.C., June 22, 1921; s. Howard C. and Laura P. (Lyon) S.; B.Sc., Yale U., 1943; m. Barbara Martin, Feb. 10, 1945; 1 son, Walter H. IV. Sales mgr., sec.-treas., exec. com., dir. Western Newspaper Union, 1946-54; asst. to treas. Allied Chem. Corp., N.Y.C., 1955-64, asst. treas., 1964-66, treas., 1966-67, v.p. fin., 1967-79. Mem. U.S. Navy Audit Adv. Com., 1972-75. Served with Royal Canadian Armored Corps, 1942-46. Mem. Fin. Execs. Inst., Treasurers Club, Pilgrims Soc., Delta Psi. Republican. Clubs: Anglers, Knickerbocker Country (Englewood, N.J.). Home: 114 Highwood Ave Tenafly NJ 07670

SYKES, WEATHERS YORK, ins. co. exec.; b. Pond, Miss., May 13, 1927; s. Weathers and Irene Berniece (Lehman) S.; B.S., U. Wis., 1950; m. Carol Elaine Williams, Sept. 4, 1960; children—Michael Gregory, Lori Denise, Stephen York. Asst. claims mgr. Supreme Live Ins. Co. of Am., Chgo., 1962-65, asst. sec., mgr. actuarial dept., 1965-68, v.p. adminstrv. services, 1968-71, sr. v.p. adminstrv. services, 1971-76, also dir., 1973-76; sr. v.p. adminstrn. Chgo. Met. Mut. Assurance Co., 1976—, also dir.; dir. Heritage/Pullman Bank & Trust Co. Cons., Ill. Dept. Welfare. Mem. Chgo. Crime Commn., 1974—. Vice pres., trustee Michael Reese Research Found.; trustee Michael Reese Med. Center, Ravinia Festival Assn., Community Renewal Soc.; pres. Michael Reese Health Plan, 1976—; mem. vis. com. Div. Sch. U. Chgo.; vice chmn. Joint Negro Appeal, 1976; Bd. dirs., mem. exec. com. Mental Health Assn. Greater Chgo.; bd. dirs. Chgo. State U. Found. Served with AUS, 1944-46. Mem. Chgo. Forum (co-chmn. 1968-70), Sci. Research Soc. N.Am., Sigma Xi. Roman Catholic. Clubs: Executives, Original Forty (Chgo.). Mem. editorial adv. bd. Chgo. Reporter, 1975—. Home: 7429 S Constance Ave Chicago IL 60649 Office: 4455 S King Dr Chicago IL 60653

SYKES, WILLIAM MALTBY, artist; b. Aberdeen, Miss., Dec. 13, 1911; s. William McQuiston and Eleanor Raymond (Johnston) S.; studied under Wayman Adams, 1934, Diego Rivera, 1935-36, John Sloan, 1937, Fernand Leger, 1951: m. Marjorie Tyre, Dec. 24, 1961. One-man exhbns. include Montgomery (Ala.) Mus. Fine Arts, 1957, 68, Auburn U., 1967, 73, 75, Columbus (Ga.) Mus. Arts and Crafts, 1958, 68, U. Ala., 1970, New Orleans U., 1972, U. Miss., 1975; group exhbns. include Am. Watercolors, Drawings and Prints, Met. Mus. Art, 1952, Curators Choice Exhbns., Phila. Print Club, 1956; represented in permanent collections at Mus. Modern Art, N.Y., Stedlijk Mus., Amsterdam, Boston Mus. Fine Arts, Phila. Mus. Art; prof., artist-in-residence Auburn U., 1942-77, prof. emeritus, 1977—. Served with USAF, 1944-45. Nat. Endowment for the Arts grantee, 1965-66. Mem. Soc. Am. Graphic Artists, Scarab, Phila. Print Club, Am. Color Print Soc., Omicron Delta Kappa, Phi Kappa Phi. Episcopalian. Author: The Multimetal Lithography Process, Artist's Proof, vol. 8, 1968. Contbr. to Am. Prize Prints of the 20th Century, 1949, Printmaking Today, 1972, Art of the Print, 1976. Home: 712 Brenda Ave Auburn AL 36830 Office: Art Dept Auburn U Auburn AL 36830

SYLK, HARRY STANLEY, drug chain exec.; b. Phila., Apr. 6, 1903; s. Benjamin and Lena (Hunn) S.; m. Gertrude Bardy, Jan. 5, 1930; children—Norma (Mrs. Larry Berman), Robert F., Leonard. Vice pres. Nevins Drug Co., 1935; pres. Sun Ray Drug Co., Phila., 1949-59, chmn. bd. Consol. Sun Ray Inc., 1959—. Gen. chmn. Allied Jewish Appeal, 1954-56; bd. nat. cabinet United Jewish Appeal; bd. dirs. United Fund, Boy Scouts Am., Einstein Med. Center, Phila. Coll. Osteopathy, Golden Slipper Square Club Camp for Children, Villanova U. (all Phila.), City of Hope, Los Angeles; v.p. Federated Charities Phila. Mem. Nat. Assn. Chain Drug Stores. Mason. Clubs: Green Valley Country, Locust (Phila.). Home: 350 N Highland Ave Merion PA 19066

SYLVESTER, GEORGE HOWARD, air force officer; b. Riverside, N.J., Aug. 10, 1927; s. Ralph Davis and Dorothy Clarisse (Mealley) S.; B.S., U.S. Mil. Acad., 1949; M.A., Georgetown U., 1956; m. Elaine Ruth Winderling, June 7, 1949; children—Wendy, Susan, David. Commd. 2d lt. U.S. Air Force, 1949, advanced through grades to lt. gen., 1976; pilot, 1949-54; asst. prof. social scis. U.S. Mil. Acad., 1956-60; long-range planner, 1961-64; mil. asst. to sec. def., 1964-66; squadron comdr. F-4 squadron, Vietnam, 1966; comdr. Danang Air Base, Vietnam, 1967; dir. test Eglin AFB, Fla., 1968-70; asst. dir. tactical systems test and evaluation Office Sec. Def., 1970-73; dep. for systems ASD, Wright-Patterson AFB, Ohio, 1973-74, vice comdr. ASD, 1974-76, comdr. ASD, 1976-79; vice comdr. AF Systems Command, Andrews AFB, Md., 1979—. Decorated D.S.M., Legion of Merit with 2 oak leaf clusters, D.F.C., Air medal with 7 oak leaf clusters, Air Force Commendation medal with 2 oak leaf clusters; Vietnamese Medal of Honor. Lutheran. Home: 1508 Arkansas Rd Andrews AFB MD 20335 Office: Vice Comdr AFSC Andrews AFB MD 20335

SYLVESTER, NORBERT A., banker; b. 1927; student U. Detroit, 1947-50; married. With Mfrs. Nat. Bank Detroit, 1952—, v.p., 1964-69, sr. v.p., 1969-72, exec. v.p., 1972—. Served with USNR, 1945-46. Office: 100 Renaissance Center Detroit MI 48243

SYLVESTRE, JEAN GUY, nat. librarian of Can.; b. Sorel, Que., Can., May 17, 1918; s. Maxime Arthur and Yvonne Marie (Lapierre) S.; B.A., U. Ottawa, 1939, B.Ph., 1940, M.A., 1942, D.L.S. (hon.), 1969, D.Litt. (hon.), 1970, LL.D. (hon.), 1974, 75; m. Francoise Poitevin, Feb. 27, 1943; children—Marie, Jean, Paul. Translator, Dept. Canadian sec. state, 1942-44; editor Wartime Information Bd., 1944-45; asst. pvt. sec. to minister of justice, 1945-47; pvt. sec. to sec. of state for external affairs, 1947-48; pvt. sec. to prime minister, 1948-50; adminstrv. officer Dept. Resources and Devel., 1950-53; asst. librarian Library of Parliament, Ottawa, Ont., 1953-56, asso. parliamentary librarian, 1956-68, nat. librarian, 1968—. Chmn., Gov. Gen.'s Lit. Awards, 1960-62; organizer, chmn. World Poetry Conf., Expo, 1967; chmn. Can. Council Com. on Aid-to-Publs., 1960-68; lectr. U. Ottawa Library Sch., 1954-71; v.p. Canadian Library Week Council, 1965-67. Bd. dirs. Canadian Writers Found., pres., 1960-61. Fellow Royal Soc. Can. (hon. sec. 1959-62, pres. sect. I 1963-64, hon. librarian 1969—, pres. 1973); mem. Académie canadienne-francaise, Société des Ecrivains canadiens, Canadian Library Assn. (life), Library Assn. Ottawa. Author: Louis Francoeur, journaliste, 1941; Situation de la poésie canadienne, 1941; Anthologie de la poésie canadienne-francaise, 1943, 58, 64, 66, 68, 74; Poétes catholiques de la France contemporaine, 1944; Sondages, 1945; Impressions de théâtre, 1950; Amours, délices et orgues, 1953; Panorama des lettres canadiennes-francaises, 1964; Canadian Writers, 1964; Literature in French Canada, 1967; A Century of Canadian Literature, 1967; also articles to profl. jours., encys. Editor: A Canadian Errant (J.P. Manion), 1960; Canadian Universities Today, 1961; Structures sociales du Canada francais, 1967. Clubs: Le Cercle Universitaire (Ottawa); Rivermead Golf (Lucerne, Que.). Home: 1870 Rideau Garden Dr Ottawa ON K1S 1G6 Canada Office: 3 95 Wellington St Ottawa ON KIA ON4 Canada

SYME, SHERMAN LEONARD, educator; b. Dauphin, Man., Can., July 4, 1932; s. Robert and Rose (Bay) S.; came to U.S., 1950, naturalized, 1955; B.A., UCLA, 1953, M.A., 1955; Ph.D., Yale U., 1957; m. Marilyn E. Egenes, Sept. 10, 1954; children—Karen B., David M., Janet E. Sociologist heart disease control program USPHS, Washington, 1957-60, from asst. chief to chief field and tng. sta. heart disease control program, San Francisco, 1962-68; exec. sec. Human Ecology Study Sect. NIH, Bethesda, Md., 1960-62; prof. epidemiology Sch. Public Health, U. Calif., Berkeley, 1968—, prof. dept. biomed. and environ. health scis., Fellow Am. Heart Assn., Am. Sociol. Assn., Am. Public Health Am. Epidemiol. Soc. Author: Social Stress and Cardiovascular Disease, 1967; contbr. articles to profl. jours. Home: 141 La Cuesta Orinda CA 94563 Office: U Calif Sch Public Health Berkeley CA 94720

SYMES, GEORGE JAMES, ins. co. exec.; b. Omaha, Dec. 22, 1928; s. Harry B. and Laurel M. (Clark) S.; B.B.A., U. Wash., 1951; M.B.A., So. Methodist U., 1963; m. Norma J. Fields, May 22, 1954; children—Sandra J., Susan G., Scott E. Sr. acct. Peat, Marwick, Mitchell & Co., San Antonio, 1955-58; adminstrv. accountant Frito-Lay, Dallas, 1958-60; mgr. accounting Varo, Inc., Garland, Tex., 1960-62; chief accountant So. Union Gas Co., Dallas, 1962-64; controller Pioneer Am. Ins. Co., Ft. Worth, 1964-67; v.p., controller Nat. Western Ins. Co., Austin, Tex., 1967-68; controller Life and Casualty Ins. Co., Nashville, 1968-71, v.p., controller, 1971-79; v.p., gen. auditor Am. Gen. Ins. Co., Houston, 1979—; dir. J.Y. Schoonmaker Co. Inc., Dallas. Mem. K.T. Edn. Found. Served to 1st lt. USAF, 1951-55. C.P.A., Tex., C.L.U. Fellow Life Mgmt. Inst.; mem. Tex., Tenn. socs. C.P.A.'s, Am. Inst. C.P.A.'s, Financial Execs. Inst. (pres. Nashville chpt. 1974-75), Life Office Mgmt. Assn., Am. Soc. C.L.U.'s, Leadership Nashville, Toastmasters Internat., Tau Kappa Epsilon. Baptist. Mason (32 deg., Shriner). Home: 1714 Chimney Vine Ln Humble TX 77338 Office: 2727 Allen Pkwy Houston TX 77019

SYMINGTON, JAMES WADSWORTH, lawyer, former congressman; b. Rochester, N.Y., Sept. 28, 1927; s. Stuart and Evelyn (Wadsworth) S.; grad. Deerfield (Mass.) Acad., 1945; B.A., Yale U., 1950; LL.B., Columbia U., 1954; m. Sylvia Caroline Schlapp, Jan. 24, 1953; children—Julia Hay, Jeremy Wadsworth. Admitted to Mo. bar, 1954, D.C. bar, 1960, U.S. Supreme Ct. bar, 1962; asst. city counselor, St. Louis, 1954-55; with firm Cobbs, Armstrong, Teasdale & Roos, St. Louis, 1955-57; asso. D'Arcy Advt. Co., St. Louis, 1957-58; asst. to U.S. ambassador to Great Britain, 1958-60; asso. firm Arnold, Fortas & Porter, Washington, 1960-61; dep. dir. Food for Peace, Washington, 1961-62; adminstrv. asst. to atty. gen. Dept. Justice, 1962-65; exec. dir. Pres.'s Com. on Juvenile Delinquency and Youth Crime, 1965-66; chief protocol of U.S., 1966-67; mem. 91st-94th Congresses from 2d Dist. Mo.; partner firm Smathers, Symington & Herlong, Washington, 1977—. Mem. Met. St. Louis Youth Commn., 1955-58. Served with USMCR, 1945-46. Recipient Distinguished Service award NSF, 1977. Mem. Am., Fed. bar assns., Mo. Bar, D.C. Bar, Phi Delta Phi. Episcopalian. Author: The Stately Game. Author articles, stories. Office: 1700 K St NW Washington DC 20006

SYMINGTON, LLOYD, lawyer; b. N.Y.C., Sept. 28, 1913; s. Charles J. and Elizabeth (Lloyd) S.; A.B. cum laude, Princeton, 1936; LL.B., U. Va., 1939; m. Nancy E. Glover, Sept. 6, 1941; children—Lloyd, Donald, Marion, Nicholas. Admitted to D.C. bar, 1941; with Office Gen. Counsel, WPB, 1942-46; partner Fowler & Symington now Leva, Hawes, Symington, Martin & Oppenheimer, 1946—. Sec. Fiat-Roosevelt Motors, 1966-70. Mem. chpt. Washington Cathedral, 1953-73. Del., Democratic Nat. Conv. from D.C., 1968. Bd. dirs. Nat. Symphony Orch. Assn. (pres. 1968-70). Mem. Am., Fed., D.C. bar assns., Defenders of Wildlife (dir. 1947-77, gen. counsel), Order of Coif, Phi Beta Kappa. Clubs: Federal City, Metropolitan (Washington). Home: 3030 Chain Bridge Rd NW Washington DC 20016 Office: 815 Connecticut Ave NW Washington DC 20006

SYMMERS, WILLIAM GARTH, lawyer; b. Bronxville, N.Y., Nov. 30, 1910; s. James Keith and Agnes Louise (Shuey) S.; grad. Lawrenceville (N.J.) Sch., 1929; A.B., U. Va., 1933, J.D., 1935; m. Marina Baruch, Apr. 25, 1936; children—Benjamin Keith, Ann (Mrs. Edward L. Read); m. 2d, Anne H. Ellis, Mar. 20, 1946; children—Barbara (Mrs. Thomas M. Bancroft), Susan (Mrs. Harold J. Friedman), Deborah. Admitted to N.Y. bar, 1937, D.C. bar, 1953; asso. Bigham, Englar, Jones & Houston, N.Y.C., 1935-37; sr. mem. Symmers, Fish & Warner, and predecessor firm, N.Y.C., 1956—; asst. counsel, sr. admiralty atty. U.S. Maritime Commn., 1937-40, counsel to naval affairs com. Ho. of Reps., in investigation loss of SS Normandie (USS Lafayette), 1942; U.S. del., v.p. Antwerp Conf. Internat. Maritime Com., also del. Maritime Law Assn. U.S. to succeeding confs., Amsterdam, 1949, Brighton, 1952, Madrid, Spain, 1955, N.Y.C., 1966, Tokyo, Japan, 1968, Rio de Janeiro, 1977; titulary mem. Internat. Maritime Commn.; mem. adv. com. admiralty rules, U.S. Supreme Ct. 1962-71. Mem. N.Y. State Bar Assn., Am. Soc. Internat. Law, Am. Bar Assn., Bar Assn. City N.Y. (chmn. admiralty com. 1953-56), Maritime Law Assn. (chmn. com. revision U.S. Supreme Ct. admiralty rules 1952-56, mem. exec. com. 1958-61, 1st v.p. 1964-66), Internat. C. of C. (U.S. rep. internat. com. on maritime arbitration), Phi Delta Theta, Phi Delta Phi. Clubs: Downtown Assn., N.Y. Yacht (N.Y.C.); Field (Greenwich); Chevy Chase University (Washington). Contbr. articles to maritime publs. Home: 636 Steamboat Rd Greenwich CT 06830 Office: 345 Park Ave New York NY 10022

SYMMES, HARRISON MATTHEWS, museum dir.; b. Wilmington, N.C., Nov. 11, 1921; s. Harrison Matthews and Mary (Harriss) S.; B.A., U. N.C., 1942; M.A., George Washington U., 1948; LL.D., Our Lady of the Lake Coll., 1974; D.Hum., Bridgeport Engring. Inst., 1975; m. Joan Margaret Shanahan, June 28, 1947; children—Mary, Rebecca, Peter. Fgn. service officer State Dept., 1947-74; ambassador to Jordan, 1967-70; dep. asst. sec. state for congl. relations, 1970-72; dep. insp. gen. Fgn. Service, 1972-74; pres. Windham Coll., Putney, Vt., 1974-76; resident dir. Mt. Vernon, 1977—. Mem. bd. advs. Dickinson Coll., Carlisle, Pa.; bd. dirs. Am. Boxwood Soc. Served as 2d lt. inf. AUS, 1942-46. Fellow, Harvard U. Center for Internat. Affairs, 1962-63. Mem. Phi Beta Kappa. Clubs: Harvard (N.Y.C.); City Tavern, Dacor (Washington). Home: Mt Vernon VA 22121

SYMMS, STEVEN DOUGLAS, congressman; b. Nampa, Idaho, Apr. 23, 1938; s. Darwin and Irene (Knowlton) S.; B.S., U. Idaho, 1960; m. Frances E. Stockdale, 1959; children—Dan, Susan, Amy, Katy. With Symms Fruit Ranch, Inc., Caldwell, Idaho, 1963-72; mem. 93d-96th congresses from 1st Idaho Dist.; mem. Interior and Insular Affairs Com., Agr. Com. Vice chmn. Republican Study Com.; mem. task force on fgn. policy Rep. Research Com. Served with USMC, 1959-63. Mem. Am. Conservative Union (treas.). Office: 2244 Rayburn House Office Bldg Washington DC 20515

SYMON, JAMES GORDON, advt. exec.; b. Aylesbury, Eng., Dec. 25, 1928; s. William George and Christina (Paton) S.; LL.B., Univ. Coll., U. London, 1954; m. Sheila Grace Skinner, July 9, 1957; children—William, Geraldine, James, Victoria. Came to U.S., 1957. With R.H. Macy Co., 1959-60, Interpublic Co., advt., 1960-65, Doyle, Dane, Bernbach, advt., 1965-66; partner firm Jack Tinker & Partners, N.Y.C., 1966-69, Kurtz & Symon, Inc., N.Y.C., 1969-77, James Symon, Inc., N.Y.C., 1977-78, Symon, Thomas & Hilliard, Inc., N.Y.C., 1978—. Served with Brit. Army, 1947-49. Home: 351 Elm Rd Briarcliff Manor NY 10510 Office: Symon Thomas & Hilliard Inc 850 3d Ave New York NY 10022

SYMON, KEITH RANDOLPH, educator; b. Ft. Wayne, Ind., Mar. 25, 1920; s. James Jefferson Keith and Claribel (Crego) S.; B.S., Harvard, 1942, M.A., 1943, Ph.D., 1948; m. Mary Louise Reinhardt, July 3, 1943; children—Judith Elizabeth (Mrs. Edward Arendsen), Keith Joseph, James Randolph, Rowena Louise. Radio physicist U.S. Naval Research Lab., Washington, 1943-46; successively instr., asst. prof., asso. prof. physics Wayne U., Detroit, 1947-54; successively asst. prof., asso. prof., prof. physics U. Wis., Madison, 1955—; physicist Midwestern Univs. Research Assn., Madison, 1954-66, tech. dir., 1957-60. Mem. Vis. Scientists Program, Am. Inst. Physics; pres. Wis. Horizons Unlimited; mem. high energy physics adv. panel U.S. AEC, 1967-69. Served with USNR, 1944-45. Ford Found. fellow CERN, Geneva, Switzerland, 1962-63. Fellow Am. Phys. Soc.; mem. Am. Assn. Physics Tchrs., Vets. for Peace. Author: Mechanics, 3d edit., 1971. Contbr. to Ency. Brit., 1965. Patentee in field. Home: 1816 Vilas Ave Madison WI 53711

SYMONS, JAMES MARTIN, educator; b. Jacksonville, Ill., May 7, 1937; s. James Lyndall and Stella Pauline (Barton) S.; B.A., Ill. Coll., 1959; M.A., So. Ill. U., 1964; Ph.D., Cornell U., 1970; m. Judith White, Nov. 14, 1959; children—Tracy, Kelly, Carrie. Announcer, Sta. WLDS, Jacksonville, 1953-59; leading actor Off-Broadway prodn. Shakuntala, 1959; asst. prof. drama Yankton (S.D.) Coll., 1964-67; chmn. speech dept. Colls. of St. Catherine and St. Thomas, St. Paul, 1971-74; chmn. theatre dept. State U. N.Y., Albany, 1974-77; prof. dept. speech and drama Trinity U., San Antonio, 1977—, chmn. dept., 1977—. Served with USNR, 1960-63. Mem. Speech Communication Assn., Am. Theatre Assn. Author: Meyerhold's Theatre of the Grotesque (George Freedley Meml. award 1972), 1971. Office: Dept Speech and Drama Trinity U 715 Stadium Dr San Antonio TX 78284. *The great Russian poet, Alexander Pushkin, wrote, "Habit to us is given from above; it is a substitute for happiness." I believe in the life which refuses to accept that substitute, even while realizing that happiness may only be an illusion.*

SYMONS, THOMAS H.B., educator; b. Toronto, Ont., Can., May 30, 1929; s. Harry Lutz and Dorothy Sarah (Bull) S.; B.A., U. Toronto, 1951; B.A., Oxford U., 1953, M.A., 1955; postgrad. univs. Paris, Leyden, Rome, 1953-54, Harvard, 1956; LL.D., Waterloo Lutheran U., 1971, U. N.B., 1972, York U., 1973, Ottawa U., 1974, Trent U., 1975, Laurentian U., 1977; m. Mary Christine Ryerson, Aug. 17, 1963; children—Mary, Ryerson, Jeffrey. Dean men, tutor history Trinity Coll., U. Toronto, 1954-56, dean Devonshire House, 1956-63; founding pres., vice chancellor, prof. modern history Trent U., Peterborough, Ont., 1963-72. Mem. adv. com. on confedn. to prime minister Ont., 1965-72; chmn. Ministerial Commn. on French Lang. Edn., 1971-72; bd. dirs. Assn. Univs. Brit. Commonwealth, 1970—, pres., 1971-72; chmn. Nat. Commn. on Canadian Studies, 1972-79, Ont. Human Rights Commn., 1975-78; pres. Canadian Assn. in Support Native Peoples, 1972-73; v.p. Social Scis. and Humanities Research Council Can., 1978—. Bd. dirs. Can. Council, 1976—, Trinity Coll., 1963-74, Lakefield (Ont.) Coll., 1964—, Sir Sandford Fleming Coll., Peterborough, 1964-69, Upper Can. Coll., Toronto, 1969—, Simcoe Found., Toronto, 1972-76, Ont. Arts Council, 1974-76, Ont. Med. Found., 1975—, Pearson Coll. of the Pacific, 1976—, Robert and Mary Stanfield Found., 1976—; trustee Oriel Coll., Oxford U., 1975—. Decorated officer Order of Can., 1977; recipient Canadian Centennial medal, 1967, Civic award City of Peterborough, 1969; Queen's Silver Jubilee medal, 1977. Massey fellow, 1951; Rockefeller grantee Harvard, 1956. Fellow Royal Soc. Can., Royal Soc. Arts; mem. Assn. Univs. and Colls. Can. (dir. 1969-72), Ont. Ednl. Research Found. (dir. 1964—), Canadian Soc. Study Higher Edn. (founding dir. 1969—), World Univ. Service Can. (founding dir.), Canadian Hist. Assn., Canadian Polit. Sci. Assn., Inst. Pub. Adminstrn. Can., Champlain Soc. (council 1972—), Assn. Canadian Studies in U.S. (council 1973—). Clubs: Peterborough; Rideau (Ottawa); Univ., (Toronto); Athenaeum (London, Eng.). Author: (with others) Confederation Challenge, 2 vols., 1967, 70, One Country or Two, 1971, Life Together, A Report on Human Rights in Ontario, 1977; Report of the Commission on French Language Education, 1972; To Know Ourselves, Report of the Commission on Canadian Studies, 4 vols., 1975-79; also articles. Office: Trent University Peterborough ON Canada

SYNAN, EDWARD ALOYSIUS, JR., former univ. pres., clergyman; b. Fall River, Mass., Apr. 13, 1918; s. Edward Aloysius and Mary F. (McDermott) S.; A.B., Seton Hall Coll., 1938; student U. Louvain (Belgium), 1938-40, Immaculate Conception Sem., Darlington, N.J., 1940-41; S.T.L., Cath. U. Am., 1942; L.M.S., Pontifical Inst. Mediaeval Studies, Toronto, 1951; M.A., Ph.D., U. Toronto, 1952. Ordained priest Roman Cath. Ch., 1942; curate Immaculate Conception Ch., Montclair, N.J., 1942-44; prof. philosophy, chmn. dept. Seton Hall U., South Orange, N.J., 1952-59; prof. history of mediaeval philosophy Pontifical Inst. Mediaeval Studies, U. Toronto, 1959-73, 79—, pres., 1973-79. Served as capt. (chaplain) USAAF, 1944-48. Mem. Am. Cath. Philos. Assn., Mediaeval Acad. Am., Renaissance Soc. Am., Am. Soc. Polit. and Legal Philosophy. Author: The Popes and The Jews in the Middle Ages, 1965; The Works of Richard of Campsall, vol. I, 1968. Asso. editor, contbr. The Bridge, Yearbook of Judaeo-Christian Studies, 1955-62; adv. bd. Speculum, 1971-74. Contbr. chpts. to books, articles and revs. to publs. Address: 59 Queen's Park Toronto ON M5S 2C4 Canada

SYNAN, JOSEPH ALEXANDER, SR., clergyman; b. Pocahontas, Va., Feb. 18, 1905; s. Thomas Sylvester and Maude (Sherratt) S.; student pub. and corr. schs., pvt. study; D.D. (hon.), Holmes Theol. Sem., 1958; m. Minnis Evelyn Perdue, Aug. 12, 1926; children—Evelyn Maurine, Maurice Edwin, Joseph Alexander, Harold Vinson, Hubert Vernon, Doris Jean, Ronald Kay. Ordained to ministry Pentecostal Holiness Ch., 1926; pastor numerous chs., 1926-34; supt. E. Va. Conf. Pentecostal Holiness Ch., 1934-41, asst. gen. supt., 1941-45, gen. supt., 1945-69, sr. bishop, 1950—, chmn. gen. bd. adminstrn. and gen. conf., 1950-69, chmn. gen. bd. edn., 1945-53, chmn. bd. publs., 1966-69. Chmn. Pentecostal Fellowship of North Am., 1950-52, 63-65, mem. bd. adminstrn.; chmn. presidium Pentecostal World Conf., Jerusalem, Israel, 1961, mem. adv. com., 1967-70. Trustee Holmes Theol. Sem., Greenville, S.C., Southwestern Bible Coll., Oklahoma City, 1946-69, Falcon (N.C.) Orphanage, 1943-69; trustee Emmanuel Coll., Franklin Springs, Ga., 1941-69, mem. adv. bd. Sch. Christian Ministries, 1974—, chmn., 1974-76. Mem. Nat. Assn. Evangs. (mem. bd. adminstrn. 20 years). Author: The Good Minister of Jesus Christ, 1951; Christian Life in Depth, 1964; The Shape of Things to Come, 1969; articles in religious publs. Address: PO Box 1477 Hopewell VA 23860

SYNAR, MIKE LYNN, congressman; b. Vinita, Okla., Oct. 17, 1950; s. Edmond and Virginia Anne (Gann) S.; B.B.A., U. Okla., 1972, J.D., 1977; M.A. in Econs., Northwestern U., 1973; postgrad. U. Edinburgh, 1972-73. Farmer, rancher, Muskogee, Okla.; real estate broker, Muskogee, 1968—; mem. 96th Congress from 2d Okla. Dist. Del. White House Conf. on Aging, 1971. Democrat. Episcopalian. Home: 503 1/2 N 15th St Muskogee OK 74401 Office: 1338 Longworth Bldg Washington DC 20515

SYNDERGAARD, PARLEY REX, educator; b. Mt. Pleasant, Utah, Mar. 3, 1918; s. Parley Pratt and Ada (Kay) S.; B.A., Westminster Coll., Fulton, Mo., 1940; M.A. (Van Blarcom scholar), Washington U., St. Louis, 1941; Ph.D., St. Louis U., 1951; m. Patricia Jane Graf, June 10, 1941; children—Susan, Mary Kay, Sally, Martha. Mem. faculty Murray (Ky.) State Coll., 1946-54, asso. prof. history, 1949-54, dean of men, 1948-49; mem. faculty Eastern Ill. U., Charleston, 1956—, prof. history, 1962—, chmn. dept., 1961-70; editor Daily Breeze-Courier, Taylorville, Ill., 1954-56. Served with F.A., AUS, 1943-45; ETO. Newberry Library fellow, 1966; Truman Library fellow, 1962. Mem. Am. Hist. Soc., Omicron Delta Kappa, Alpha Kappa Lambda. Home: 540 Hall Ct Charleston IL 61920

SYNHORST, MELVIN D., sec. state Iowa; b. Orange City, Iowa, Jan. 21, 1914; s. Hugo and Ethel (Lucas) S.; B.A., J.D., U. Iowa; m. Alice Rossing, May 31, 1942; children—Robert B., William J. Sec. state State of Iowa, Des Moines, 1948-64, 66—. Served to lt. j.g. USNR, World War II. Recipient Outstanding Citizenship award Am. Heritage Found., 1961. Mem. Nat. Assn. Secs. State (past pres.), Alpha Tau Omega, Gamma Eta Gamma, Am. Legion. Clubs: Masons, Shriners. Mem. Am. Ref. Ch. Office: Office Sec State State Capitol Des Moines IA 50319

SYNNOTT, RICHARD MAURICE, banker; b. Fall River, Mass., Dec. 28, 1940; s. William Joseph and Marie Aurora (Labrie) S.; B.S., U. Conn., 1967; m. Elizabeth Ann Mockus, Sept. 25, 1965; children—Julie, Christine, Robert, Patrick. Sr. accountant Ernst & Ernst, C.P.A.'s, Hartford, Conn., 1967-70; v.p., auditor Colonial Bank & Trust Co., Waterbury, Conn., 1970-76; loan officer Calif. 1st Bank, San Diego, 1977—. Home: 10059 Ashdale Ln Santee CA 92071 Office: 530 B St San Diego CA 92112

SYPHERD, PAUL STARR, microbiologist; b. Akron, Ohio, Nov. 16, 1936; s. Pearle Clinton and Mary Mildred (Flanick) S.; B.S., Ariz. State U., 1959; M.S., U. Ariz., 1960; Ph.D., Yale U., 1963; m. Mary Jo Moore, June 8, 1954; children—David Paul, Mary Denise, Gregory Dean, Cynthia Jean. NIH postdoctoral fellow U. Calif., San Diego, 1962-64; asst. prof. U. Ill., Urbana, 1964-68, asso. prof., 1968-70; asso. prof. microbiology U. Calif. Coll. Medicine, Irvine, 1970-72, prof., 1972—, chmn. dept., 1974—; mem. NIH study sect., 1977—. NSF sr. fellow, 1970. Mem. Am. Soc. Microbiology, Am. Soc. Biol. Chemists, AAAS. Editor: Jour. Bacteriology, 1979—, mem. editorial bd., 1969-74. Contbr. articles to profl. jours. Home: 1948 Port Dunleigh Newport Beach CA 92660

SYRETT, HAROLD COFFIN, coll. adminstr., editor; b. N.Y.C., Oct. 22, 1913; s. Frank H. and Dorothy (Provost) S.; A.B., Wesleyan U., 1935; M.A., Columbia, 1938, Ph.D., 1944; m. Patricia D. McCarthy, June 19, 1937; children—David, John, Matthew. Tchr. Harvey Sch., Hawthorne, N.Y., 1936-39; instr. history U. Maine, 1941; instr. history Columbia, N.Y.C., 1941-46, asst. prof., 1946-50, asso. prof., 1950-54, prof., 1954-61; exec. editor Alexander Hamilton Papers, 1955—; dir. grad. studies Queens Coll., Flushing, N.Y., 1961-62, dean faculty, 1962-65, acting pres., 1964; exec. dean grad. centers State U. N.Y., 1965-66, vice chancellor univ., 1967-68; pres. Bklyn. Coll., 1968-69; prof. history City U. N.Y., 1969-79; vis. prof. history Manhattan Sch. Music, 1946-48, Yeshiva U., 1954-55. Mem. Mass. Hist. Soc., Am., N.Y. (trustee) hist. assns., Orgn. Am. Historians, Phi Beta Kappa. Author: The City of Brooklyn, 1865-1898, 1944; (with others) A History of the American People, 1952; Andrew Jackson, 1953; Papers of Alexander Hamilton, 26 vols., 1961-79. Editor: The Gentleman and the Tiger (autobiography of George B. McClellan, Jr.), 1956; (with others) A Short History of New York State, 1957; American Historical Documents, 1960; contbr. articles to profl. jours. Home: Box 127 Craryville NY 12521

SYRKIN, MARIE, editor; b. Bern, Switzerland, Mar. 22, 1899; s. Nachman and Batya (Osnos) S.; B.A., Cornell U., 1920, M.A., 1922; hon. doctorates Jewish Tchrs. Sem., 1976, Brandeis U., 1979; m. Charles Reznikoff, May 27, 1930; 1 son, David. Came to U.S., 1907, naturalized, 1915. Tchr. English, N.Y. high schs., 1925-50; faculty, dept. humanities Brandeis U., Waltham, Mass., 1950-66, prof. emeritus, 1966—; editor Herzl Press, N.Y.C., 1971—. Mem. exec. World Zionist Movement, 1965-69; hon. pres. Labor Zionist Movement U.S., 1965-70. Recipient Woman of Year award Jewish War Vets Women's Aux., 1964; Woman of Year Univ. Women-U. Judaism, 1973; Lit. award Pioneer Women-25th Anniversary Israel award, 1973; Myrtle Wreath award Hadassah, 1976. Mem. Am. Profs. for Peace in Middle East (exec. 1968—). Author: Your School, Your Children, 1944; Blessed Is the Match, The Story of Jewish Resistance, 1957; Nachman Syrkin: A Memoir, 1960; Golda Meir: A Biography, 1969; Gleanings: A Diary in Verse, 1979. Editor: Jewish Frontier, 1950-71. Contbr. articles and essays to various publs. Home: 1008 2d St Santa Monica CA 90403

SYSE, GLENNA MARIE LOWES, drama critic; b. Weyburn, Sask., Can.; d. Norman John and Marie (Cunningham) Lowes; B.A., U. Man., 1949; postgrad. U. Minn., 1949-50; tchrs. degree music, Royal Conservatory Music, Toronto, 1946; hon. D. Letters, Rosary Coll., River Forest, Ill., 1974. Critic, TV columnist Seattle Times, 1952-54; reviewer Chgo. Sun-Times, 1954-58, drama and dance critic, 1958—; weekly critical Commentary WBBM radio, Chgo. Mem. Pulitzer Prize drama jury, 1973-75, Tony award nominating com., 1978-79. Recipient spl. award excellence coverage arts Am. Newspaper Guild, 1970. Office: 401 N Wabash St Chicago IL 60611

SYTSMA, JOHN FREDERICK, union ofcl.; b. Paterson, N.J., July 22, 1921; s. Frederick J. and Alice (Hutchinson) S.; student Coll. Paterson, N.J., 1939-41; m. Phyllis Stingle, Sept. 11, 1942; children—Ruth Ann (Mrs. Bruce Lubbers), Jacqueline (Mrs. Floyd Pruitt, Jr.). Clk., Am. Surety Co., N.Y.C., 1939-41; locomotive fireman, engr. N.Y.S. & W. R.R., 1941-56; office mgr. Brotherhood Locomotive Engrs., Cleve., 1956-62, gen. sec.-treas., 1962-74, 1st v.p., 1974-76, internat. pres., 1976—; pres. Locomotive Engrs. Bldg. Assn., Locomotive Engrs. Mut. Life and Accident Ins. Assn. Served with AUS, World War II; PTO. Mem. Fraternal Investment Assn. Mem. Dutch Reformed Ch. Author: Ahrens-Fox, A Pictorial History of a Great Name in Fire Apparatus, 1971; Ahrens-Fox Album, 1973; 100 Favorite Fire Rigs, 1978. Home: 3280 Country Club Dr Medina OH 44256 Office: Engrs Bldg 1365 Ontario St Cleveland OH 44114

SYVERSON, ALDRICH, educator; b. Glenwood, Minn., Mar. 25, 1914; s. Julius and Anna (Arenson) S.; student U. Chgo., 1931-32; B.S. in Chem. Engring., U. Minn., 1938, Ph.D. (Hormel Research Found. fellow), 1942; m. Eleanor Marie Wall, June 16, 1942; children—Elizabeth Anne (Mrs. Douglas Elden Shaw), William Richard. Research engr. B.F. Goodrich Co., Akron, Ohio, 1942-44; mgr. organic chems. devel. B.F. Goodrich Chem. Co., Akron, 1944-45, mgr. Avon Lake (Ohio) Exptl. Sta., 1945-48; asso. prof. chem. engring. Syracuse (N.Y.) U., 1948-50; asso. prof. chem. engring. Ohio State U., Columbus, 1950-54, prof., 1954-59, 60-78, prof., chmn. chem. engring. dept., 1968-76, prof. emeritus, 1978—; dir. research O.M. Scott Co., Marysville, Ohio, 1959-60. Named Tech. Man of Year, Columbus Tech. Council, 1974. Fellow Am. Inst. Chem. Engrs.; mem. Am. Chem. Soc., Am. Soc. Engring. Edn., A.A.A.S., Sigma Xi, Tau Beta Pi, Phi Lambda Upsilon. Lutheran. Contbr. articles to profl. jours. Home: 890 Blind Brook Dr Worthington OH 43085 Office: 140 W 19th Ave Columbus OH 43210

SYVERTSON, CLARENCE ALFRED, govt. ofcl.; b. Mpls., Jan. 12, 1926; s. Alfred and Esther Louise (Goertemiller) S.; B. Aero. Engring., U. Minn., 1946, M.S., 1948; postgrad. Stanford U., 1950-57; grad. Advanced Mgmt. Program, Harvard U., 1977; m. Helen Hammond Gonnella, May 4, 1953; children—Marguerite Louise. Research scientist Ames Aero. Lab., NACA, Moffett Field, Calif., 1948-58; exec. dir. Joint Dept. Transp./NASA Civil Aviation Research and Devel. Policy Study, 1970-71; with Ames Research Center, NASA, Moffett Field, 1958—, dep. dir., 1969-78, dir., 1978—. Served with U.S. Army, 1946-47. Recipient invention and contbn. award NASA, 1964, Exceptional Service medal, 1971. Fellow AIAA (Lawrence Sperry award 1957), Am. Astronautical Soc. Home: 15725 Apollo Heights Ct Saratoga CA 95070 Office: Ames Research Center NASA Moffett Field CA 94035

SZABAD, GEORGE MICHAEL, lawyer, mayor; b. Gorki, Russia, Feb. 21, 1917; s. Michael and Nita (Szereszewski) S.; B.S., Columbia, 1937, LL.B., 1939; m. Shirley Meyers, Nov. 8, 1938; children—Peter James, Ellen Jo (Mrs. Ljung). Admitted to N.Y. bar, 1940; participated reorgn. Asso. Gas & Electric System, 1940-42; with Dept. Labor, 1942-47, chief appellate sect., 1944-47; with Dept. State, 1945-46; with firm Blum, Haimoff, Gersen, Lipson, Slavin & Szabad, N.Y.C., 1947—, partner, 1949—. Sr. v.p., sec., dir. Burndy Corp.; dir. York Research Corp.; former mayor Village of Scarsdale (N.Y.). Served with USCG, 1943, OSS, U.S. Army, 1945. Mem. Am. Arbitration Assn. (panel), Assn. Bar City N.Y., Am., Fed. bar assns., Consular Law Soc. Clubs: Scarsdale Town; Mamaroneck Beach; Yacht. Home: 16 Continental Rd Scarsdale NY 10583 Office: Burndy Corp Norwalk CT 06856 also 270 Madison Ave New York NY 10016

SZABO, ALBERT, educator, architect; b. N.Y.C., Nov. 7, 1925; s. Benjamin and Jane (Margolies) S.; student Bklyn. Coll., 1942-48, Inst. Design, Chgo., 1947-48; M.Arch., Harvard, 1952; m. Brenda Dyer, Dec. 25, 1951; children—Ellen, Stephen, Rebecca, Jeanette. Apprentice, Marcel Breuer, architect, 1947-48; instr. Inst. Design, Chgo., 1951-53; prof. architecture Grad. Sch. Design, Harvard, 1954—, chmn. dept. archtl. scis., 1964-68, asso. chmn., head tutor dept. visual and environ. studies, 1968-70, prof. visual and environ. studies, chmn. dept. visual and environ. studies, 1970-72, sec. faculty of design, 1964-74, prof. visual and environ. studies, 1974—; vis. prof. Rensselaer Poly. Inst., 1967-68; archtl. design practice with Brenda Dyer Szabo, Chgo. and Cambridge, 1953—; partner Solton/Szabo Assos, Inc., 1967-71. Fulbright cons. to municipality of Tehran, Iran, also Fulbright Hayes lectr., 1972; Fulbright-Hayes lectr. architecture Kabul (Afghanistan) U., 1974-76; cons. U.S. AID, Afghanistan, 1974-76, to Govt. of Afghanistan, 1974-76; acting curator Loeb Fellowships in advanced environ. studies, 1974. Served with USAAF, 1944-45. Recipient Alpha Rho Chi medal Harvard, 1952. Wheelwright travelling fellow in architecture Harvard, 1963; Tozier fund research grantee, Harvard, 1963, Milton Fund research grantee, 1966, 72, 77, Faculty research grantee, 1978; Nat. Endowment for Arts project design fellow, 1980. Asso. Boston Soc. Architects; mem. AIA, Assn. Collegiate Schs. Architecture (N.E. regional dir. 1969-70). Author: (with others) The Shape of Our Cities, 1957; Housing Generated by User Needs, 1972; (with B. D. Szabo) Indigenous Architecture of Afghanistan, 1978. Home: 126 High St Brookline MA 02146 Office: Gund Hall and Carpenter Center Harvard Cambridge MA 02138

SZABO, DANIEL, govt. ofcl.; b. Budapest, Hungary, Mar. 23, 1933; s. Alexander and Maria (Berger) S.; came to U.S., 1950, naturalized, 1954; B.A., Coll. City N.Y., 1957; M.A., Johns Hopkins, 1959; m. Corinne Holiber, July 3, 1955; children—Nancy Beth, Peter Stuart. Internat. economist U.S. Tariff Commn., 1959-60; desk officer for Vietnam, Cambodia and Laos, U.S. Dept. Commerce, 1960-63; spl. asst. to U.S. Senator Jacob K. Javits, 1963-69; dep. asst. sec. state for Inter-Am. Affairs, Washington, 1969-74; sr. adviser Inter-Am. Devel. Bank, Washington, 1974—. Mem. alumni council Sch. Advanced Internat. Studies, Johns Hopkins, 1965-75. Served with U.S. Army, 1954-56. Mem. Am. Econ. Assn., for Internat. Devel., Inter Am. Luncheon Group (chmn. steering com.), Tau Delta Phi, Omicron Chi Epsilon. Home: 11600 Danville Dr Rockville MD 20852 Office: Inter-Am Devel Bank Washington DC 20577. *In approaching life I wanted my work to represent a service to our society. I preferred taking risks to job security. I have been attracted to new ideas and new ways of approaching and solving old problems.*

SZABO, DENIS, criminologist, educator; b. Budapest, Hungary, June 4, 1929; s. Jens and Catherine (Zsiga) S.; Doctorate in Social and Polit. Scis., U. Louvain (Belgium), 1956; diploma in criminology Sorbonne, Paris, 1958; m. Sylvie Grotard; children—Chaterine, Marianne. Asst. in sociology U. Louvain, 1951-56; lectr. sociology Cath. Univs., Paris, Lyon, 1956-58; mem. research group Centre Nat. de la Recherche Scientifique, Paris, 1954-58; asst. prof. sociology U. Montreal, 1958, asso. prof., 1959-66, founder, dir. dept. criminology, 1960-70, prof., 1966—, founder, dir. Internat. Center for Comparative Criminology, 1969—. Fellow Royal Soc. Can., Am. Sociol. Soc., Am. Soc. Criminology (exec. council); mem. Internat. Soc. Criminology (pres. 1978—), Can. Soc. Criminology (v.p. 1962-64), Soc. de criminologie du Quebec (sec.-gen. 1960-70), Internat. Assn. Sociology. Roman Catholic. Author, editor: Canadian Criminal Justice System, 1977; Criminologie et Politique Criminelle, 1978. Home: 4742 Roslyn Montreal PQ Canada Office: 3150 Jean Brillant Montreal PQ H3C 3J7 Canada

SZABO, GABOR, guitarist, sitarist, composer; b. Budapest, Hungary, Mar. 8, 1936; escaped to U.S., 1956. Former Hungarian freedom fighter; with Chico Hamilton's quintet, 1961-65, Gary McFarland combo, 1965, Charles Lloyd quartet, 1965—; played at Monterey Festival, Newport Jazz Festival, 1970-73, Fillmore West with Jimmy Hendrix and Janis Joplin; command performance London Palladium; gave Carnegie Hall concert, 1974; rec. artist albums including Spellbinder, Jazz Raga, Sorcerer, Watch What Happens, Wind, Sky and Diamonds. Nightflight, Faces, Femme Fatale; produced record Lena & Gabor; composer score for Repulsion (Roman Polanski); wrote Gypsy Queen (for Santana); wrote and recorded Breezin.' Named No. 1 New Star, Down Beat Critics Poll, 1964. Office: care Artists Internat 2214 Canyon Dr Hollywood CA 90028

SZABO, STEPHEN LEE, photographer; b. Berwick, Pa., July 17, 1940; s. Steve John and Mary (Basala) S.; student Pa. State U., 1958-62, Art Center Sch., Los Angeles, 1964-66. Staff photographer Washington Post Co., Washington, 1966-71; asso. prof. photography Am. U., 1977—; instr. Corcoran Gallery Art, Washington, 1978—; one-man shows: Balt. Mus. Art, 1977, Madison (Wis.) Arts Center, 1979; group shows include Internat. Mus. Photography, George Eastman House, 1979, Vinci 1840 Paris, 1978; represented in permanent collections: Mus. Modern Art, N.Y.C., Library of Congress, Inst. Mus. Photography, Rochester, N.Y., Corcoran Gallery Art, Washington, and others. Served with USAR, 1962. Author and photographer: The Eastern Shore, 1976.

SZARKOWSKI, THADDEUS JOHN, museum adminstr.; b. Ashland, Wis., Dec. 18, 1925; s. Julius ano Rose (Woychik) S.; B.S., U. Wis., 1948; hon. degrees, Phila. Coll. Art, 1972; Mpls. Coll. Art and Design, 1974; m. Jill Anson, Oct. 14, 1963; children—Nina, Alexander, Natasha. Photographer, Walker Art Center, Mpls., 1948-51; instr. in photography U. Minn., 1950, Albright Art Sch., U. Buffalo, 1951-53; dir. dept. photography Mus. Modern Art, N.Y.C., 1962—. Served with U.S. Army, 1945-46. John Simon Guggenheim Meml. Found. fellow, 1954, 61. Club: Century Assn. Author: The Idea of Louis Sullivan, 1956; The Face of Minnesota, 1958; The Photographer and the American Landscape, 1963; The Photographer's Eye, 1966; Walker Evans, 1971; Looking at Photographs, 1973; Mirrors and Windows, American Photography Since 1960, 1978. Home: 1165 Fifth Ave New York NY 10029 Office: 11 W 53d St New York NY 10019

SZASZ, THOMAS STEPHEN, psychiatrist, educator, writer; b. Budapest, Hungary, Apr. 15, 1920 (came to U.S. 1938, naturalized 1944); s. Julius and Lily (Wellisch) S.; A.B., U. Cin., 1941, M.D., 1944; D.Sc. (hon.), Allegheny Coll., 1975; m. Rosine Loshkajian, Oct. 19, 1951 (div. 1970); children—Margot Claire, Susan Marie. Intern 4th Med. Service Harvard, Boston City Hosp., 1944-45; asst. resident medicine Cin. Gen. Hosp., 1945-46, asst. clinician internal medicine div. out-patient dispensary, 1946; asst. resident psychiatry U. Chgo. Clinics, 1946-47; tng. research fellow Inst. Psychoanalysis, Chgo., 1947-48, research asst., 1949-50, staff mem., 1951-56; practice medicine, specializing in psychiatry, psychoanalysis, Chgo., 1949-54, Bethesda, Md., 1954-56, Syracuse, N.Y., 1956—; prof. psychiatry State U. N.Y., Syracuse, 1956—; vis. prof. dept. psychiatry U. Wis., Madison, 1962, Marquette U. Sch. Medicine, Milw., 1968; holder numerous lectureships, including C.P. Snow lectr. Ithaca Coll., 1970, E.S. Meyer Meml. lectr. U. Queensland Med. Sch., Lambie-Dew orator Sydney U., 1977; Mem. nat. adv. com. bd. Tort and Med. Yearbook; cons. com. mental hygiene N.Y. State Bar Assn.; mem. research adv. panel Inst. Study Drug Addiction; adv. bd. Corp. Econ. Edn., 1977—. Served to comdr., M.C., USNR, 1954-56. Recipient Stella Feiss Hofheimer award U. Cin., 1944, Holmes-Munsterberg award Internat. Acad. Forensic Psychology, 1969; Wisdom award honor, 1970; Acad. prize Institutum atque Academia Auctorum Internationalis, Andorra, 1972; Distinguished Service award Am. Inst. Pub. Service, 1974; Martin Buber award Midway Counseling Center, 1974, others; named Humanist of Year, Am. Humanist Assn., 1973. Hon. fellow Postgrad. Center for Mental Health, 1961. Diplomate Nat. Bd. Med. Examiners, Am. Bd. Psychiatry and Am. Psychiat. Assn.; mem. Am., Internat. psychoanalytic assns., Western N.Y. Psychoanalytic Soc., Am. Assn. Abolition Involuntary Mental Hospitalization (founding dir.), Am. Humanist Assn. Author: Pain and Pleasure, 1957; The Myth of Mental Illness, 1961; Law, Liberty and Psychiatry, 1963; Psychiatric Justice, 1965; The Ethics of Psychoanalysis 1965; Ideology and Insanity, 1970; The Manufacture of Madness, 1970; The Second Sin, 1973; Ceremonial Chemistry, 1974; Heresies, 1976; Karl Kraus and the Soul-Doctors, 1976; Schizophrenia: The Sacred Symbol of Psychiatry, 1976; Psychiatric Slavery, 1977; The Theology of Medicine, 1977; The Myth of Psychotherapy, 1978. Editor: The Age of Madness, 1973; cons. editor of psychiatry and psychology Stedman's Medical Dictionary, 22d edit., 1973; contbg. editor Reason, 1974—, Libertarian Rev., 1976—, Inquiry, 1977—; editorial bd. Psychoanalytic Rev., 1965—, Jour. Contemporary Psychotherapy, 1968—, The Humanist, 1971—, Law and Human Behavior, 1977—, Jour. Libertarian Studies, 1977—, Children and Youth Services Rev., 1978—. Home: 4739 Limberlost Ln Manlius NY 13104 Office: 750 E Adams St Syracuse NY 13210

SZATHMÁRY, LOUIS ISTVÁN, II, restaurateur; b. Rakospalota, Hungary, June 6, 1919; s. Louis Istvan and Irene (Strauss) S.; Ph.D., U. Budapest, 1944; m. Sadako Tanino, May 9, 1960; 1 dau., Magda. Came to U.S., 1951, naturalized, 1963. Chef, New Eng. Province Jesuits, Manresa Island, Conn., 1952-55; exec. chef Mut. Broadcasting System, N.Y.C., 1955-58; plant supt. Reddi Fox, Inc., Darien, Conn., 1958-59; exec. chef Armour & Co., Chgo., 1959-64; chef, owner Bakery Restaurant, Chgo., 1964—; owner Louis Szathmary Assos.; pres. Lou D'Or, Inc., Transworldtaste, Inc.; adj. prof. Pa. State U. Food columnist Chgo. Sun-Times. Mem. Chgo. Acad. Scis. (trustee), Nat. Restaurant Assn., Soc. Profl. Mgmt. Cons., Council on Hotel, Restaurant and Instl. Edn., Instl. Food Editorial Council, Screen Actors Guild, Acad. Chefs U.S.A., Japan Am. Soc., Nat. Space Inst. (bd. govs.). Clubs: Grolier (N.Y.C.); Caxton, Cliff dwellers, Chgo. Press. Author: The Chefs Secret Cookbook; American Gastronomy; The Chefs New Secret Cookbook; author-editor Cookery Americana, 16 vols. Office: 2218 N Lincoln Ave Chicago IL 60614. *I always enjoyed my work so much that it was embarrassing to receive payment for what I did with gusto and zest. I love to live - so I hope, that when I die, the world will be a little bit better than it was, when I was born - and my life and work contributed - if not more, then a teeny weeny little bit - to this improvement.*

SZE, MORGAN CHUAN-TUAN, chem. engr.; b. Tien Tsin, China, May 27, 1917; s. Sao Chiang Thomas and E. Toh-Chi (Sun) S.; S.B., M.I.T., 1939, Sc.D., 1941; m. Agnes Chi-Chen Lin, Apr. 7, 1945; children—Karl Chia-Tsen, Arthur Chia-Chang, Morgan Chia-Wen. Engr., Universal Trading Corp., 1941-42; process engr. E.I. Du Pont de Nemours & Co., Belle, W.Va., 1942-44; process engr. Hydrocarbon Research, Inc., 1944-45, sr. process engr., 1947-53, dir. process engring., 1953-59, tech. dir., 1959-61; mgr. engring. devel. center Lummus Co., Bloomfield, N.J., 1961-72, v.p. research and devel., 1972—. Mem. Nat. Acad. Engring., Am. Inst. Chem. Engrs., Am. Chem. Soc., AAAS, Sigma Xi. Presbyterian. Club: Bradford Bath and Tennis. Contbr. articles to profl. jours. Patentee in field. Home: 18 Skytop Terr Upper Montclair NJ 07043 Office: 1515 Broad St Bloomfield NJ 07003

SZE, TSUNG WEI, educator; b. Shanghai, China, Sept. 13, 1922; (came to U.S. 1945, naturalized 1962); s. Chia Sun and Sun (Shih) S.; B.S. in Elec. Engring., U. Mo., 1948; M.S. in Elec. Engring., Purdue U., 1950; Ph.D., Northwestern U., 1954; m. Frances Tung, Aug. 29, 1952; children—David, Deborah, Daniel. Instr., Northwestern U., 1952-54; asst. prof. U. Pitts., 1954-56, asso. prof., 1956-60, prof., 1960—, Fessenden prof., 1957-62, Westinghouse prof., 1962-65, asso. dean engring., 1970—, acting dean engring., 1973-74, dir. Pattern Recognition Lab., 1977—; cons. to industry, 1956—; Served to maj. Chinese Nationalist Army, 1941-45. NATO Sr. fellow NSF, 1967. Mem. I.E.E.E. (Prize Paper award 1962), Am. Soc. Engring. Edn., Assn. Computing Machinery, Sigma Xi, Eta Kappa Nu, Tau Beta Pi. Author: Switching Circuit Fundamental, 1962; A Primer of PITT Time-Sharing System, 1970; (with M.H. Mickle) Optimization in System Engineering, 1971; Introduction to A Time-Sharing System, 1972; Introduction to DEC System-10: Time-Sharing and Batch, 1974. Contbr. articles to profl. jours. Research in logical design, digital computing systems, image processing and pattern recognition. Home: 563 Sandrae Dr Pittsburgh PA 15243

SZEBEHELY, VICTOR G., aero. engr.; b. Budapest, Hungary, Aug. 10, 1921; s. Victor and Vilma (Stockl) S.; M.E., U. Budapest, 1943, Ph.D. in Engring., 1945; m. Jo Betsy Lewallen, May 21, 1970; 1 dau., Julia. Asst. prof. U. Budapest, 1945-47; research asso. State U. Pa., 1947-48; asso. prof. Va. Poly. Inst., 1948-53; research asso. model basin U.S. Navy, 1953-57; research mgr. Gen. Electric Co., 1957-62; asso. prof. astronomy Yale U., 1962-68; prof. aerospace engring. U. Tex., Austin, 1968—, chmn. dept., 1977—, L.B. Meaders prof. engring., 1978—; cons. NASA-Johnson Space Center. Decorated Knight by Queen Juliana of Netherlands, 1956. Fellow AIAA, AAAS; mem. Am. Astron. Soc. (Brouwer award div. dynamical astronomy 1977), Internat. Astron. Union (pres. commn. on celestial mechanics). Author 11 books; contbr. numerous articles on space research, celestial mechanics and ship dynamics to profl. jours. Home: 2501 Jarratt Ave Austin TX 78703 Office: Dept Aerospace Engring and Engring Mechanics U Texas Austin TX 78712

SZEGO, CLARA MARIAN, scientist; b. Budapest, Hungary, Mar. 23, 1916; d. Paul S. and Helen (Elek) Szego; came to U.S., 1921, naturalized, 1927; A.B., Hunter Coll., 1937; M.S. (Garvan fellow), U. Minn., 1939, Ph.D., 1942; m. Sidney Roberts, Sept. 14, 1943. Instr. physiology U. Minn., 1942-43; Minn. Cancer Research Inst. fellow, 1943-44; research asso. OSRD, Nat. Bur. Standards, 1944-45; research asso. Worcester Found. Exptl. Biology, 1945-47; research instr. physiol. chemistry Yale U. Sch. Medicine, 1947-48; mem. faculty U. Calif. at Los Angeles, 1948—, prof. zoology and biology, 1960—. Named Woman of Year in Sci., Los Angeles Times, 1957-58. Guggenheim fellow, 1956. Fellow A.A.A.S.; mem. Am. Physiol. Soc., Am. Soc. Cell Biology, Endocrine Soc. (CIBA award 1953), Soc. for Endocrinology (Gt. Britain), Biochem. Soc. (Gt. Britain), Internat. Soc. Research Reprodn., Phi Beta Kappa (pres. UCLA chpt. 1973-74), Sigma Xi (pres. UCLA chpt. 1976-77). Research and numerous publs. on steroid protein interactions, mechanisms of hormone action and lysosome participation in normal cell function. Home: 1371 Marinette Rd Pacific Palisades CA 90272 Office: U Calif Dept Biology Los Angeles CA 90024

SZEKELY, JULIAN, educator; b. Budapest, Hungary, Nov. 23, 1934; s. Gyula and Ilona (Nemeth) S.; B.Sc., Imperial Coll., London, 1959, Ph.D., D.I.C., 1961, D.Sc. (Eng.), 1972; m. Elizabeth Joy Pearn, Mar. 2, 1963; children—Richard J., Martin T., Rebecca J., Mathew T., David A. Came to U.S., 1966, naturalized, 1975. Lectr. metallurgy Imperial Coll., 1962-66; asso. prof. chem. engring. State U. N.Y. at Buffalo, 1966-68, prof., 1968-76; dir. Center for Process Metallurgy, 1970-76; prof. materials engring. Mass. Inst. Tech., 1976—; cons. to govt. and industry. Recipient Jr. Moulton medal Brit. Inst. Chem. Engrs., 1964; Extractive Metallurgy Div. Sci. award Am. Inst. Mining and Metall. Engrs., 1973, also Mathewson Gold medal, 1973, Howe Meml. lectr., 1979; Sir George Beilby Gold medal Brit. Inst. Chem. Engrs.-Soc. Chem. Industry-Inst. Metals, 1973; Curtis McGraw research award Am. Soc. Engring. Edn., 1974; Profl. Progress award Am. Inst. Chem. Engrs., 1974. John Simon Guggenheim fellow, 1974. Author: (with N.J. Themelis) Rate Phenomena in Process Metallurgy, 1971; (with W.H. Ray) Process Optimization, 1973; (with J.W. Evans and H.Y. Sohn) Gas-Solid Reactions, 1976; Fluid Flow Aspects of Helds Processing. Editor: Ironmaking Technology, 1972; The Steel Industry and the Environment; The Steel Industry and The Energy Crisis, 1975; The Future of the World's Steel Industry, 1976; Alternative Energy Sources for the Steel Industry, 1977. Contbr. articles to profl. jours. Office: Room 4-117 Dept Materials Sci and Engring Mass Inst Tech Cambridge MA 02139

SZENBERG, MICHAEL, educator, economist; b. Sosnowiec, Poland, Apr. 8, 1934; s. Henry and Sara (Rosensaft) S.; came to U.S., 1961, naturalized, 1966; student Bar Ilan U., Israel, 1959-61; B.A. summa cum laude, L.I. U., 1963; Ph.D., City U. N.Y., 1970; m. Miriam Silverstein, Sept. 2, 1962; children—Naomi, Avi. Faculty, L.I. U., 0, Bklyn. Center, 1965—, prof. econs., 1974—; adj. prof. Hunter Coll., 1970-76, Pace U., 1975—; asso. editor Am. Economist, 1973-75, editor-in-chief, 1975—; cons. in field. Founder, dir. Lecture Bur. Econs., 1973; chmn. 1st Met. Grad. Conf. Econs., 1973; asso. mem. Center Tech. Assessment, Newark Coll. Engring., 1973. Served with Israeli Air Force, 1956-59. Grantee Dept. Labor, 1975, Israel Diamond Inst., 1970; fellow econs. City U. N.Y., 1963; fellow Internat. Honor Soc. in Econs., 1972. Recipient Irving Fisher Monograph award, 1971; Dean Abelson award City U. N.Y., 1963; Am. Coll. Abroad award, 1962; Dean Hudson award L.I. U., 1962. Mem. Eastern, (regional dir.), Am. econ. assns., Internat. Honor Soc. Econs. (exec. bd. 1975—, regional dir., 1971-74), Optimates Soc. (pres. 1972—). Author: Economics of the Israeli Diamond Industry, 1973; The Welfare Effects of Grade Restrictions: A Case Study of the United States Footwear Industry, 1977. Contbr. chpts. to books, articles to profl. jours. Home: 1442 E 9th St Brooklyn NY 11230

SZENT-GYORGYI, ALBERT, biochemist; b. Budapest, Hungary, Sept. 16, 1893; s. Nicholas and Josephine (Lenhossek) S.-G.; M.D., U. Budapest, 1917; Ph.D., Cambridge (Eng.) U., 1927; 1 dau., Cornelia Szent-Gyorgyi Pollit. Came to U.S., 1947, naturalized, 1955. Prof. med. chemistry, Szeged, 1931-45; prof. biochemistry U. Budapest, 1945-47, sci. dir. Nat. Found. Cancer Research, Marine Biol. Labs., 1947—. Recipient Nobel prize in medicine, 1937, 55; Lasker award Heart Assn., 1954. Mem. Acad. Scis. Budapest (pres.), Nat. Acad. Budapest (v.p.), Nat. Acad. Scis., Council of Edn. (chmn.). Author: Oxidation, Fermentation, Vitamins, Health and Disease, 1939; Muscular Contraction, 1947; The Nature of Life, 1947; Contraction in Body and Heart Muscle, 1953; Bioenergetics, 1957; Submolecular Biology, 1960; Bioelectronics, 1968; The Crazy Ape, 1970; What Next?, 1971; The Living State, 1972; Electronic Biology and Cancer, 1976; The Living State and Cancer, 1978. Office: Marine Biol Labs Box 187 Woods Hole MA 02543

SZEP, PAUL MICHAEL, editorial cartoonist; b. Hamilton, Ont., Can., July 29, 1941; s. Paul Joseph and Helen (Langhorne) Szep; came to U.S., 1966, A.O.C.A., Ont. Coll. Art, 1964, hon. degree, 1975; hon. degree Framingham State Coll., 1975; m. Angela Diane Garton, Feb. 27, 1965 (div. 1976); children—Amy, Jason. Sports cartoonist Hamilton Spectator, 1958-61; graphics designer Financial Post, Toronto, Ont., 1965-66; editorial cartoonist Boston Globe, 1966—; also syndicated cartoonist, Universal Press Syndicate; lectr. various univs. Served with F.A., Royal Canadian Army, 1957-58. Recipient Pulitzer prize, 1974, 77; award Sigma Delta Chi, 1974, 77; Toyl award Boston Jaycees, 1976; Headliners award, 1977; Reuben award for best editorial cartoonist Nat. Cartoonist Soc., 1979. Clubs: Hatherly Golf and Country, Kittansett. Author: In Search of Sacred Cows, 1967; Keep Your Left Hand High, 1969; At This Point in Time, 1973; The Harder They Fall, 1975; Unvote for a New America, 1976; Them Damned Pictures, 1977; Warts and All, 1979. Home: 191 Buckminster Rd Brookline MA 02146 Office: Boston Globe Boston MA 02107

SZERYNG, HENRYK, violinist; b. Zelazowa Wola, Poland, Sept. 22, 1918; Mexican citizen, 1946; s. Szymon and Aline Woznicka Z.; studied with Carl Flesch, Gabriel Bouillon, Nadia Boulanger; attended Sorbonne, U. Paris. Made first concert tour in 1933, performing in Warsaw, Bucharest, Vienna, and Paris; during World War II acted as liaison officer and interpreter for Gen. Wladyslaw Sikorski, prime minister of Polish govt.-in-exile and comdr. of Free Polish Army, also performed over 300 concerts in mil. camps and hosps.; Carnegie Hall debut, 1943; became dir. string dept. Nat. U., Mexico City; numerous concert tours; apptd. goodwill ambassador by Mexican govt., 1956; named cultural adv. to Mexican del. UNESCP and Mexican Fgn. Ministry; recorded for RCA, Philips, CBS and Mercury labels. Decorated knight comdr. Order Polonia Restituta; officer Order Arts and Letters (France),; comdr. Order Lion (Finland); recipient Grand prix du Disque, Grammy award, Silver medal City of Paris, 1963. Reconstructed and gave first performance in modern times of Paganini's Concerto No. 3, London, 1971. Office: care Shaw Concerts Inc 1995 Broadway New York NY 10023*

SZESKO, LENORE RUNDLE, artist; b. Galesburg, Ill., Mar. 13, 1933; d. James Urvin and Helen (Crawford) Rundle; B.F.A., Art Inst. Chgo., 1961, M.F.A., 1966; m. Robert Stanley, May 2, 1961. Exhbtd. group shows Audubon Artists, 1969-76, Nat. Acad. Design, N.Y.C., 1968-74, Woodcut U.S.A., 1967, Mercyhurst Coll., 1969, 70, Boston Printmakers, 1968, 72, 74, Print Club Albany, N.Y., 1967, 69, 71, Miniature Painters, Sculptor and Gravers Soc., Washington, 1967-66, Hunterdon Co. Print Exhbn., 1967, 70-76; 300 group shows maj. cities U.S.; exhbt. regularly Art Inst. Chgo. Sales and Rental Gallery, Caulfield Gallery, Binghamton, N.Y.; represented in permanent collections including Jayell Pub. Co., Fla., Springfield Coll., Mass., The N.J. State Mus., pvt. collections; travelling exhbn. New Bergen Art Guild's Contemporary American Graphics, 1970-71, 72, 73, 74, 75, 76, 77, 78-79. Recipient Nat. Acad. Design N.Y.C. prize, 1970. Mem. Miniature Art Soc. of N.J., Miniature Art Soc. of Fla., The Boston Printmakers, The Painters and Sculptors Soc. of N.J., Audubon Artists, La. Watercolor Soc., Delta Phi Delta. Home: 835 S Ridgeland Ave Oak Park IL 60304. *Any achievement of an artist may well be transitory, and what is important is the quality of the picture, not the status, ego, or success of the individual designer of it. In a culture obsessed with objects as mere merchandise symbolized by an imaginary monetary value, I have tried to remember that real art cannot be bought and paid for—it belongs to all the people of its time. As a snake leaves his skin behind him, we leave our artwork behind us, to remind the people of the future that their skins and ours are the same.*

SZLAZAK, ANITA CHRISTINA, govt. ofcl. Can.; b. Eng., Jan. 1, 1943; d. Jan and Christina (Matecz) S.; B.A. in Econs., U. Toronto, 1963; cert. of advanced European studies Coll. of Europe, Bruges, Belgium, 1964. Research economist Devel. Centre, Orgn. for Econ. Coop. and Devel., Paris, 1964-67; fgn. service officer Can. Dept. External Affairs, Ottawa, Can., 1967-72; dep. dir. gen. internat. telecommunications Can. Dept. Communications, Ottawa, 1972-73, dir. gen., 1973-76; commr. Pub. Service Commn. of Can., Ottawa, 1976—. Mem. Inst. Pub. Adminstrn. Can. (mem. exec. com. 1976-80), Can. Equestrian Fedn., Can. Combined Tng. Assn. Club: Rockcliffe Lawn Tennis. Office: 300 Laurier Ave W Ottawa ON K1A 0M7 Canada

SZMANT, ALINA MARGARITA, marine biologist; b. Dayton, Ohio, June 18, 1946; d. Herman Harry and Adelina (Mesa) Szmant; B.S., U. P.R., 1966; M.S. in Marine Biology, Scripps Instn. Oceanography, 1970; m. Philip N. Froelich, Jr., Dec. 1971; 1 dau., Celina Marie. Research asst. U. Miami, summer 1965, teaching asst. U. P.R., summer 1966; NSF research traineeship U. Hawaii, summer 1967; Tektite II scientist-Aquanaut St. John's, Virgin Islands, summer 1970; research asso. dept. marine sci. U. P.R., 1970-71, P.R. Nuclear Center, 1971-73; scientist-researcher Raytheon Environmental Services Center, Portsmouth, R.I., 1973-74; research asso. Grad. Sch. Oceanography, U. R.I., Kingston, 1974—. Recipient Conservation award Dept. Interior, 1970, Meritorious Service award Los Angeles County Museum Natural History, 1970, Meritorious Service award, Los Angeles County Bd., 1970, Outstanding Young Woman of Am. award, 1972; named hon. citizen of Chgo., 1970. Mem. A.A.A.S., Marine Biol. Assn. U.K., Internat. Oceanographic Found., Am. Soc. for Limnology and Oceanography, Ecol. Soc. Am., Western Soc. Naturalists. Democrat. Address: Dept Oceanography Fla State U Tallahassee FL 32306

SZOKA, EDMUND CASIMIR, bishop; b. Grand Rapids, Mich., Sept. 14, 1927; s. Casimir and Mary (Wolgat) S.; B.A., Sacred Heart Sem., 1950; J.C.B., Pontifical Lateran U., 1958, J.C.L., 1959. Ordained priest Roman Catholic Ch., 1954; asst. pastor St. Francis Parish, Manistique, Mich., 1954-55; sec. to bishop, Marquette, Mich., 1955-57, 59-62; chaplain St. Mary's Hosp., Marquette, 1955-57; tribunal, notary, defender of bond, Marquette, 1960-71; asst. chancellor Diocese of Marquette, 1962-69, chancellor, 1970-71; pastor St. Pius X Ch., Ishpeming, Mich., 1962-63, St. Christopher Ch., Marquette, 1963-71; bishop Diocese of Gaylord (Mich.), 1971—; sec.-treas. Mich. Cath. Conf., Lansing, 1972-77; chmn. region VI, Nat. Conf. Cath. Bishops, 1972-77, now mem. nat. adminstrv. com.; mem. adminstrv. bd. U.S. Cath. Conf.; mem. budget and fin. com. Nat. Conf. Cath. Bishops/U.S. Cath. Conf. Mem. Canon Law Soc. Am. Address: PO Box 700 Gaylord MI 49735

SZULC, TAD, journalist, commentator; b. Warsaw, Poland, July 25, 1926; s. Seweryn and Janina (Baruch) S.; student U. Brazil, 1943-45; m. Marianne Carr, July 8, 1948; children—Nicole, Anthony. Came to U.S., 1947, naturalized, 1954. Reporter, AP, Rio de Janeiro, 1945-46; corr. at UN for UPI, 1949-53; mem. staff N.Y. Times, after 1953, corr. Latin Am., 1955-61, Washington bur., 1961-65, 69-72, Spain and Portugal, 1965-68, Eastern Europe, 1968-69; commentator fgn. policy, 1972—. Recipient Maria Moors Cabot gold medal Columbia U.; award for best book on fgn. affairs, 1979. Clubs: Federal City (Washington); Overseas Press (award for best mag. interpretation fgn. affairs 1976; citations 1966, 74, 75, 77, 78) (N.Y.C.). Author: Twilight of the Tyrants, 1959; (with Karl E. Meyer) The Cuban Invasion, 1962; The Winds of Revolution, 1963; Dominican Diary, 1965; Latin America, 1966; Bombs of Palomares, 1967; United States and the Caribbean, 1971; Czechoslovakia since World War II, 1971; Portrait of Spain, 1972; Compulsive Spy: The Strange Career of E. Howard Hunt, 1974; The Energy Crisis, 1974; Innocents at Home, 1974; The Illusion of Peace, 1978. Address: 4515 29th St NW Washington DC 20008

SZURSZEWSKI, JOSEPH HENRY, physiologist; b. Pitts., May 25, 1940; s. Henry Joseph and Genevie (Rudzka) S.; B.S. in Zoology, Duquesne U., 1962; Ph.D. in Physiology (Univ. fellow 1962-63, 64-65, NIH fellow 1965-66), U. Ill., 1966; postgrad. (Fulbright-Hays scholar) Monash U., Clayton, Australia, 1969-70; B.Sc. in Pharmacology (Burn fellow), Oxford (Eng.) U., 1971; m. Cecelia Johnson, Aug. 24, 1963; children—Joseph, Marie. Grad. teaching asst. U. Ill., 1963-65, NSF summer research fellow, 1963; asso. cons. in physiology Mayo Grad. Sch. Medicine, Rochester, Minn., 1971-73, cons., 1973—; asst. prof. physiology Mayo Med. Sch., Rochester, 1971-75, asso. prof. physiology, 1975-77, prof. physiology, 1977—, asst. prof. pharmacology, 1971-76, asso. prof. pharmacology, 1976—; NSF summer research fellow Duquesne U. 1961. Served with ROTC. NIH research fellow, 1966-68. Mem. Am. Physiol. Soc., Brit. Physiol. Soc., Am. Gastroenterol. Assn., AAAS, Council on Basic Sci., Soc. Neurosci., Sigma Xi. Research, numerous publs. in field. Home: 913 11 1/4 St Rochester MN 55901 Office: 200 1st St SW Rochester MN 55901*

SZYBALSKI, WACLAW, educator, molecular geneticist; b. Lwów, Poland, Sept. 9, 1921 (came to U.S. 1950, naturalized 1957); s. Stefan and Michalina (Rakowska) S.; Chem. Engr., Poly. Inst. Lwów, (Poland) 1943; D.Sc., Poly. Inst., Gdansk, 1949; m. Elizabeth Hunter, Feb. 5, 1955; children—Barbara A., Stefan H. Asst. prof. Poly. Inst., Gdansk, 1946-50; mem. staff Cold Spring Harbor (N.Y.) Biol. Labs., 1951-55; asso. prof. Inst. Microbiology, Rutgers U., New Brunswick, N.J., 1955-60; prof. oncology McArdle Lab., U. Wis., Madison, 1960—. Recipient Karl A. Forster lecture award U. Mainz, 1970; mem. recombinant DNA adv. com. NIH, 1974-78. Recipient A. Jurzykowski Found. award in biology, 1977. Mem. Am. Soc. Biochemists, Genetic Soc. Am., Am. Soc. Microbiologists (chmn. virology div. 1972-74, chmn. div. IV 1974-75), AAAS, European Molecular Biology Orgns. (lectr. 1971, 76), Polish Soc. Microbiologists (hon.), Italian Soc. Exptl. Biology (hon.), Polish Med. Alliance (hon.). Author numerous papers, revs., abstracts and books in field. Editor-in-chief Gene; mem. editorial bd. Jour. of Virology, Cancer Research, Progress in Molecular Cell Biology, CRC Handbook of Biochemistry and Molecular Biology, others. Home: 1124 Merrill Springs Rd Madison WI 53705. *The profession should also be the hobby and a constant source of enjoyment and satisfaction.*

SZYMANSKI, FREDERICK JOHN, educator, physician; b. Rochester, N.Y., May 16, 1915; s. Joseph L. and Anastasia (Drzewucki) S.; student U. Buffalo Coll. Arts and Scis., 1933-35, M.D., 1939; m. Frances G. Myers, Aug. 1, 1940; children—Peter J., Steven P., Frederick John Jr., Michael W., John R. Intern St. Mary's Hosp., Rochester, 1939-40, resident, 1940-42; gen. practice medicine, Rochester, 1940-42; fellow dermatology and syphilology U. Ill. Coll. Medicine, 1946-49; pvt. practice medicine, specializing in dermatology, Chgo., 1948—; mem. faculty U. Ill. Coll. Medicine, 1949—, clin. prof. dermatology and syphilology, 1965—; clin. prof. dermatology Rush Presbyn.-St. Luke's Med. Coll., 1970—. Served with USNR, 1942-46. Mem. Chgo. Dermatol. Soc. (pres. 1958), Am. Acad. Dermatology (v.p. 1962), Am. Dermatol. Assn. (historian 1962—), Soc. Investigative Dermatology, Am. Dermatopathology Soc., A.M.A. Clubs: Evanston (Ill.) Golf; Northbrook Racquet; North Shore Racquet. Contbr. articles to sci. jours. Home: 525 Woodlawn St Glencoe IL 60022 Office: 55 E Washington St Chicago IL 60602

SZYMANSKI, HERMAN ALOWISIOUS, educator; b. Toledo, Ohio, Sept. 24, 1924; s. Joseph John and Magdeline (Szczublewska) S.; B. Chem. Engring., U. Toledo, 1948; Ph.D., U. Notre Dame, 1952; m. Alice Irene Rospond, Apr. 3, 1948; children—Diane, Herman, Paul, Joseph, Mark, John, Mary. Chmn. dept. natural sci. Loyola U., Chgo., 1952-54; chmn. dept. chemistry Canisius Coll., Buffalo, 1954-68; dean Cecil Community Coll., North East, Md., 1971-72; dean coll. Alliance Coll., Cambridge Springs, Pa., 1969-71, pres., 1972-77; tchr. chemistry Purdue U., N. Central Campus, 1977—. Chmn., Coll. Pres.'s N.W. Pa. for Ednl. TV, 1974—. Adv. bd. Villa Maria Coll., Buffalo, 1968-69. Served with Seabees, USNR, 1943-46. P.C. Reilly fellow U. Notre Dame 1950, 51. Mem. Soc. Applied Spectroscopy (pres. 1967), Assn. Advancement of Polish Studies (sec. 1973-75). Author, editor books in field. Contbg. author books, contbr. articles to profl. jours. Home: Route 1 Box 398 Three Oaks MI 49128

SZYMANSKI, RICHARD FRANK, profl. football exec.; b. Toledo, Oct. 7, 1932; s. Joseph Frank and Helen Sophie (Domalski) S.; B.S., U. Notre Dame, 1955; m. Patricia Ann Kennedy, Aug. 29, 1964; children—Debra Ann, Michael Patrick. Profl. football player Balt. Colts, 1955-68, football scout, 1969-73, asst. personnel dir., 1973, dir. profl. personnel and offensive line coach, 1974-77, v.p., gen. mgr., 1977—; played in Coll. All Star Game, 1955, Nat. Football League Pro Bowl Game, 1955, 62, 64. Served with U.S. Army, 1956-57; Germany. Roman Catholic. Club: Towson Golf and Country. Office: Exec Plaza III Suite 1200xHunt 1200 Hunt Valley MD 21031

TAAFFE, EDWARD JAMES, educator, geographer; b. Chgo., Dec. 11, 1921; s. Edward James and Julia Loretta (Murphy) T.; B.S. in Journalism, U. Ill., 1945; B.S. in Meteorology, N.Y. U., 1944; S.M. in Geography, U. Chgo., 1949, Ph.D., 1952; m. Marialyce Dunne, Sept. 8, 1948; children—Maura Joan, Edward James, Michael Robert, Julie Ann, Susan Deirdre, Brian Thomas, Karen Elizabeth, David Matthew. Instr. geography undergrad. div. U. Ill., Chgo., 1948-51; asst. prof. econ. geography Loyola U., Chgo., 1951-56; asst., then asso. prof. geography Northwestern U., 1956-63; prof. geography Ohio State U., 1963—, chmn. dept., 1963-75. Dir. Insts. application quantitative methods geography, NSF, summers 1961, 62, 65; cons. City Chgo., 1962-63; editorial bd. cons. World Book Atlas, 1962-69; mem. com. geography earth sci. div. Nat. Acad. Scis.-NRC, 1964-71. Bd. dirs. Social Sci. Research Council, 1971-75. Served with USAAF, 1943-46. Mem. Assn. Am. Geographer (mem. council 1966-69, v.p. 1970-71, pres. 1972-73), Commn. Coll. Geography, Am. Geog. Soc., Regional Sci. Assn., Sigma Xi. Author: The Air Passenger Hinterland of Chicago, 1952; The Peripheral Journey to Work: A Geographic Consideration, 1963; Geography, 1970; Geography of Transportation, 1973. Address: 4314 Olentangy Blvd Columbus OH 43214

TAAFFE, JAMES GRIFFITH, ednl. adminstr.; b. Cin., Sept. 15, 1932; s. Griffith C. and Mary (Ropp) T.; A.B., Columbia, 1954; M.A., Ind. U., 1956, Ph.D., 1960; m. Donna Click, June 8, 1955; children—Lauren Kathleen, Patrick Michael. Instr. English, Williams Coll., Williamstown, Mass., 1959-62; asst. prof. English, Vassar Coll., 1962-64; from asst. prof. to prof. English, Case Western Res. U., Cleve., 1964—, chmn. dept. English, 1969-72, asst. to pres., 1971-72, dean grad. studies, 1972-74, v.p. for undergrad. and grad. studies, 1974—, chmn. advanced placement in English, 1968-73. Mem. Joint Council, East Cleve. Sch. Dist., 1970—. Newberry Library fellow, 1964; Am. Philos. Soc. fellow, 1967, 69; NEH fellow, 1971. Mem. Modern Lang. Assn., Milton Soc., Dante Soc. Co-author: A Milton Handbook, 1970. Editor: Abraham Cowley, 1970; co-editor: Poems on Poetry, 1965; Reading English Poetry, 1971. Home: 2595 Norfolk Rd Cleveland OH 44106

TAAFFE, ROBERT NORMAN, educator; b. Chgo., Sept. 20, 1929; s. Edward James and Julia (Murphy) T.; student U. Wis., 1948-50; B.A., M.A., Ind. U., 1952; Ph.D., U. Chgo., 1959; m. Mahaut Jacqueline Mauvier, Aug. 25, 1962; children—Clarisse, Denis, Sabine,

Colombe. Asst. prof. dept. geography Ind. U., Bloomington, 1959-63, prof., chmn. dept., 1971—; asso. prof. U. Wis. at Madison, 1963-67, prof., chmn. dept., 1968-71. Mem. screening com. Inter-Univ. Com. of Travel Grants, 1962-68; mem. joint Slavic com. Am. Council Learned Socs. and Social Sci. Research Council, 1967-70; mem. publs. com. Assn. Am. Geographers, 1971-74. Served with AUS, 1953-55. Inter-Univ. Com. advanced grad. study grantee Moscow (U.S.S.R.) U., 1958-59, Bulgaria Acad. Sci., Sofia, 1964, Ford Found. research grantee, 1966. Mem. Assn. Am. Geographers, Am. Assn. Advancement Slavic Studies, Regional Sci. Assn. Author: Rail Transportation and the Economic Development of Soviet Central Asia, 1959; (with Robert C. Kingsbury) An Atlas of Soviet Affairs, 1965, 2d rev. edit., 1980. Editor: Integrated Transport Development in the USSR, 1958; series regional geographies Prentice-Hall Co., 1969-75; (with John Odland) Geographical Horizons, 1978. Home: 619 S Ballantine Rd Bloomington IN 47401

TAAPKEN, ALBERTUS, banker; b. Holland, Feb. 10, 1916; s. G. and Louise de Lang (Evertsen) T.; ed. in Holland; m. Dorothy M. Winternitz, July 5, 1941; children—Edward, Louise, John. Various positions with Nationale Handelsbank, Amsterdam, Holland, 1933-51; with Crocker Nat. Bank, San Francisco, 1951-76; exec. advisor Internat. Bank N.S., 1976—. Home: 1851 Alameda Diablo Diablo CA 94528 Office: 315 California St San Francisco CA 94104

TABACCHI, FRED LAWRENCE, mfg. co. exec.; b. Kelly, N.Mex., Aug. 10, 1917; s. Carlo F. and Dora M. (Katzenstein) T.; ed. pub. schs.; m. Laura Mae Doebbeling, Dec. 23, 1944; children—Loretta (Mrs. Leroy Johndrow), Larry W., Terri Beth (Mrs. Philip Gardner). With Hoover Co., 1937—; sr. v.p., 1964-66, exec. v.p., 1966-75, pres., chief operating officer, 1975—, also dir.; pres., chief operating officer Hoover Worldwide Corp., 1975-78, vice chmn., 1978—; pres., dir. Hoover Co., Ltd. (Can.), 1975—; pres., dir. Hoover Mexicana, S.A. de C.V., 1975—; dir. Hoover Ltd. U.K., 1974—; pres., dir. Hoover Indsl. y Comml. S.A., 1976—, Chemko Comml. Products, Inc., 1979—. Bd. dirs. Mount Union Coll., Alliance, Ohio. Mem. U.S.-Mex. C. of C. (pres., chmn. bd. 1977—), Vacuum Cleaner Assn. Am. (pres. 1973-75). Office: 101 E Maple St North Canton OH 44720

TABACKIN, LEWIS BARRY, jazz musician; b. Phila., Mar. 26, 1940; s. Isadore and Sarah (Skolnick) T.; student Phila. Conservatory Music, 1958-62; m. Toshiko Akiyoshi, Nov. 3, 1969; 1 child, Michiru Mariano. Tenor saxophone and flute player, 1956—; mem. various bands including Les & Larry Elgart, 1965-66, Cab Calloway, 1966, Maynard Ferguson, 1967, Duke Pearson, 1967-72, Thad Jones & Mel Lewis, 1966-70, Clark Terry, 1967-72, NBC Orch., 1972-77, Doc Severinsen, 1969-76, ABC Orch., 1970-72, Shelly Manne Quartet, 1976—; co-leader Toshiko Akiyoshi-Lew Tabackin Big Band, Los Angeles, 1972—; recorded various albums. Served with U.S. Army, 1963-65. Recipient 1st place award Downbeat Critics Poll, 1976, Album of Year award Stereo Rev., 1976, Gold award Swing Jour., 1976, 1st place reader's poll Swing Jour., 1977, 1st place reader's poll in big band category Downbeat, 1978; named Best Big Band, Downbeat Readers Poll, 1978, Downbeat Critics Poll, 1979. Mem. Am. Fedn. Musicians, Nat. Assn. Jazz Educators. Address: 12823 Friar St North Hollywood CA 91606. *My life is dedicated to perpetuating the spirit and essence of jazz music, and it will be spent in the perfection of my art.*

TABAKOFF, WIDEN, engring. educator; b. Stakevzi, Bulgaria, Dec. 14, 1919, came to U.S. 1958, naturalized 1963); s. Ilia and Rada (Jivova) T.; Dipl. Ing. in Mech. Engring., U. Prague (Czechoslovakia), 1941; Dipl. Ing. with High Honors in Aero. Engring., U. Berlin, 1946, Dr. Ing., 1945; m. Gunhild Rombusch, Sept. 17, 1943; children—Irina Austin, Felicitas. Designer, Aero Talleres Argentino, 1948-50; tech. dir. Helamet S.R.L., Cordoba, Argentina, 1948-56; research dir. Knapsack Grisheim A.G., Cologne, Germany, 1956-58; prof. U. Cin. Coll. Engring., 1958—. NASA grantee, 1965—; U.S. Army Research grantee, 1968—; honor of recognition NASA, 1977. Mem. Am. Inst. Aeros. and Astronautics, Am. Soc. Engring. Edn., AAUP, German Rocket Soc., Sigma Xi, Tau Beta Pi, Sigma Gamma Tau. Contbr. articles to profl. jours. Home: 421 Deanview Dr Cincinnati OH 45224

TABATZNIK, BERNARD, physician; b. Mir, Poland, Jan. 8, 1927; (came to U.S. 1959, naturalized 1966); s. Max and Fay (Ginsberg) T.; B.Sc., U. Witwatersrand (South Africa), 1945, M.B., B.Ch., 1949; m. Marjorie Turner, Jan. 8, 1956; children—Darron Mark, Keith Donald, Ilana Wendy. Intern Baragwanath Hosp., Johannesburg, South Africa, 1950-51, Hillingdon Hosp., Ashford Hosp., also research unit Canadian Red Cross Meml. Hosp., Taplow, Eng., 1951-54; med. registrar Ashford Hosp., 1954-56, Johannesburg Gen. Hosp., 1956-58; physician Baragwanath Hosp., 1958-59; fellow medicine Johns Hopkins Sch. Medicine, 1959-60, fellow cardiology, 1960-61, asst. prof. medicine, 1966—; head cardiopulmonary div. Sinai Hosp., Balt., 1961-72, asso. chief medicine, 1964-72; chief cardiology dept. North Charles Gen. Hosp., Balt., 1972, also dir. med. edn., dir. Postgrad. Inst., coordinator ambulatory services; cons. Balt. City Hosp. Mem. Royal Coll. Physicians (London), South African Cardiac Soc., Am., Md. (chmn. health careers 1964-66) heart assns., Laennec Cardiovascular Sound Group. Contbr. articles to profl. jours. Home: 2209 Ridge Rd Route Reisterstown MD 21136 Office: North Charles Gen Hosp North Charles St Baltimore MD 21218

TABELL, ANTHONY, financial analyst; b. Bklyn., Aug. 5, 1931; s. Edmund Weber and Margaret (Suydam) T.; grad. St. Luke's Sch., New Canaan, Conn., 1948; A.B., Colgate U., 1952; student N.Y. U., 1957-65; m. Ellen Margaret Molwitz, May 23, 1953; children—Margaret Ellen, Roberta Jane, Sarah Elizabeth. With Walston & Co. Inc., 1954-70, v.p., 1961-65, sr. v.p., dir., 1965-70; asso. Delafield, Harvey, Tabell div. Janney, Montgomery Scott, Inc., 1970—, v.p. parent co., 1971—. Served with AUS, 1952-54. Mem. N.Y. Soc. Security Analysts, Market Technicians Assn. (pres. 1975-76). Episcopalian. Clubs: Broad Street (N.Y.C.); Nassau (Princeton, N.J.). Home: 76 Crooked Tree Ln Princeton NJ 08540 Office: 909 State Rd Princeton NJ 08540

TABER, GLADYS, author; b. Colorado Springs, Colo., Apr. 12, 1899; d. Rufus Mather and Grace (Raybold) Bagg; B.A., Wellesley Coll., 1920; M.A., Lawrence Coll., 1921; student Columbia, 1931-33; m. Frank Albion Taber, Jr., June 10, 1922; 1 dau., Constance Ann. Tchr. English, Lawrence Coll., 1921, Randolph-Macon Women's Coll., 1925-26; profl. writer, 1932—; tchr. profl. short story writing Columbia, N.Y.C., 1936—; columnist Ladies Home Jour., 1937-58, asst. editor, 1946-58; columnist Family Circle, 1959—, The Oracle, Orleans, Mass. Writer of plays, among them a one-act play which received Little Theater award in nat. contest, 1925. Mem. Authors League Am., Nat. P.E.N., Pen and Brush Club, Kappa Alpha Theta. Author numerous books, the latest being: Especially Father, 1949; Stillmeadow Seasons, 1950; Stillmeadow Kitchen, 1951; When Dogs Meet People, 1952; Flower Arranging for American Home, 1952; (with Barbara Webster) Stillmeadow to Sugarbridge, 1953; Stillmeadow Daybook; What Cooks at Stillmeadow, 1958; Mrs. Daffodil, 1958; Stillmeadow Sampler, 1959; Spring Harvest, 1959; Road to Stillmeadow, 1960; Another Path, 1963; Gladys Taber's Favorite Stillmeadow Recipes, 1965; Stillmeadow Calendar A Countrywoman's Journal, 1967; Especially Dogs-Especially at Stillmeadow, 1968; Flower Arranging, A Book to Begin On, 1969; Stillmeadow Album, 1969; Amber A Very Personal Cat, 1970; Reveries at Stillmeadow, 1970; (short stories) One Dozen and One; My Own Cape Cod, 1971; My Own Cookbook, 1972; Country Chronicle, 1974; Harvest of Yesterdays, 1976; The Best of Stillmeadow, 1976; Conversations with Amber, 1977. Contbr. to mags. in U.S., Eng., Sweden, Australia. Home: Orleans MA 02653 also Stillmeadow Farm Southbury CT 06488 Office: Brandt and Brandt 101 Park Ave New York NY 10017. *My success as an author is based on a lifelong passion to communicate with others what I keep learning about the world we live in, possibly to widen the horizons and add new perceptions about people and nature. My principles all have to do with the belief that men are created equal, that love for our fellowmen is the one saving grace for the world. I believe war is always a defeat for winner and loser.*

TABER, ROBERT CLINTON, ret. army officer; b. Ithaca, N.Y., Oct. 11, 1917; s. Laurence Sebring and Ethel (Lanning) T.; B.S., Cornell U., 1938; grad. Army War Coll., 1958; m. Jane Feeter, July 20, 1940; 1 son, John Robert. Commd. 2d lt. U.S. Army, 1940; advanced through grades to lt. gen.; comdg. gen. Joint U.S. Mil. Adv. Group, Cambodia, 1963; asst. div. comdr. 82d Airborne Div., 1964-65; asst. comdt. U.S. Army Command and Gen. Staff Coll., Leavenworth, Kans., 1965-66; chief of staff U.S. Army, Vietnam, 1967-68; dir. doctrine and systems Dept. Army, 1968-69; comdg. gen. 3d Inf. Div., Germany, 1970-71; prin. dep. asst sec. def. manpower and res. affairs, 1971-74. Decorated D.S.M. with 2 oak leaf clusters, Legion of Merit with 3 oak leaf clusters, Joint Commendation medal, Bronze Star, Army Commendation medal with 2 oak leaf clusters, Purple Heart, Air medal with two oak leaf clusters. Mem. Annapolis Yacht, U.S. Naval Acad. Sailing Squadron (vice commodore), Va. Foxhound (exec. com.). Home: 3B1 The Point Annapolis MD 21403

TABIN, JULIUS, patent lawyer, physicist; b. Chgo., Nov. 8, 1919; s. Sol. and Lillian (Klingman) T.; B.S., U. Chgo., 1940, Ph.D. in Physics, 1946; LL.B., Harvard, 1949; m. Johanna Krout, Sept. 7, 1952; children—Clifford James, Geoffrey Craig. Jr. physicist metall. lab. U. Chgo., 1943-44; physicist Los Alamos Sci. Lab. (U. Calif.), N.Mex., 1944-45, Argonne Nat. Lab., AEC, Chgo., 1946; staff mem., group supr. Inst. Nuclear Studies, Mass. Inst. Tech., 1946-49; admitted to Calif., D.C. bars, 1949; patent examiner U.S. Patent Office, Washington, 1949-50; admitted to Ill. bar, 1950; asso. firm Fich, Even, Tabin, Flannery & Welsh, Chgo., 1950-52, mem. firm, 1952—; lectr. U. Chgo., 1959. Mem. Am., D.C., Calif., Ill., Chgo. bar assns., Sigma Xi. Home: 162 Park Ave Glencoe IL 60022 Office: 135 S LaSalle St Chicago IL 60603

TABLER, LEVI EARL, JR., engring. and constrn. co. exec.; b. Council Bluffs, Iowa, Feb. 19, 1927; s. Levi Earl and Anna Katherine (Risney) T.; B.S. in Civil Engring., State U. Iowa, 1952; m. Violet Louise Nivin, Aug. 19, 1950; children—Brenda Carol, Laura Lynn. With Dravo Corp., Pitts., 1952—, planning and scheduling supr. engring. and constrn. div., 1958-69, project engr., 1969-71, mgr. planning and scheduling, 1971-77, mgr. project controls, 1977—. Mem. 100,000 Pennsylvanians for Promotion Econ. Growth, 1965—. Served with USNR, 1945-46. Fellow ASCE (Thomas Fitch Rowland prize, 1966, chmn. exec. com. constrn. div. 1972); mem. Assn. Cost Engrs., Am. Arbitration Assn., Theta Tau. Home: 115 Sandralayne Dr Coraopolis PA 15108 Office: 1 Oliver Plaza Pittsburgh PA 15122. *I want to accomplish all things that are within my capabilities and are pleasing in the sight of both God and man. My ultimate goal is to have the world just a little better for my having been here.*

TABLER, WILLIAM BENJAMIN, architect; b. Momence, Ill., Oct. 28, 1914; s. Clyde Lyeth and Frances Beatrice (Ridley) T.; B.S. cum laude, Harvard U., 1936, B.Arch., 1939, M.Arch., 1939; m. Phyllis May Baker, June 12, 1937; children—William, Judith Tabler Kelsey. Architect specializing in hotels; prin. works include Hilton hotels in N.Y.C., Dallas, Pitts., San Francisco, Toronto, Rye Town, N.Y. and Washington; Intercontinental hotels in Lahore, Rawapindi, Jamaica, Ras Al Khaimah, Jeddah, Nairobi, Lusaka, Dacca, Amman, Karachi and Jerusalem; Marriott Phila.; Sheraton Universal City, New Orleans, Brussels and Sheraton Centre, Toronto; Othon Palace in Rio and Bahia; Registry in Bloomington and Scottsdale; Hosts of Houston and Tampa; Sonesta Bermuda; Radisson Duluth; New Otani L.A., Chosen, Korea; Stouffers St. Louis; Bonaventure Montreal; Hanover, Woodstock and Princeton Inns; 15 Hospitality Motor Inns; also Harper and Stony Brook Coll. Dormitories; many others; mem. bldg. constrn. adv. council N.Y.C. Bldg. Dept., 1967—. Bd. dirs. Manhattan Eye, Ear and Throat Hosp., Community Hosp., Glen Cove. Served to lt. USNR, 1943-46; PTO. Recipient Horatio Alger award Am. Schs. and Colls. Assn., 1958; 1st prize for excellence in design Internat. Hotel, Queens (N.Y.) C. of C., 1958; Producers Council award, 1967. Fellow AIA (nat. chmn. bldg. codes com.; pres. N.Y. chpt. 1967-68); mem. ASCE, Royal Inst. Brit. Architects, Bldg. Research Inst., N.Y. Bldg. Congress, N.Y. U. Hotel and Restaurant Soc., Producers Council (N.Y. chpt.), Illuminating Engring. Soc., Am. Nat. Standards Inst. (exec. com., constrn. standards bd.), Nat. Fire Protection Assn. (chmn. sect. com. on residential occupancies, com. on safety to life), Ave. of Americas Assn. (dir.). Club: Harvard (bd. mgrs., exec. com., chmn. ho. com. N.Y.C.). Home: 44 Wolver Hollow Rd Glen Head NY 11545 Office: 401-415 7th Ave New York City NY 10001

TABOR, HERBERT, biochemist; b. N.Y.C., Nov. 28, 1918; s. Edward and Henrietta (Tally) T.; A.B., Harvard U., 1937, M.D., 1941; m. Celia White, Apr. 8, 1946; children—Edward, Marilyn, Richard, Stanley. Intern, Yale U. and New Haven Hosp., 1942; chief Lab. Biochem. Pharmacology, Nat. Inst. Arthritis, Metabolism and Digestive Diseases, Bethesda, Md.; med. dir. USPHS. Mem. Am. Soc. Biol. Chemistry, Nat. Acad. Sci., Am. Acad. Arts and Scis., Am. Soc. Pharm. and Exptl. Therapeutics, Am. Chem. Soc. Editor-in-chief Jour. Biol. Chemistry. Contbr. articles to profl. jours. Office: Bldg 4 Room 110 NIH Bethesda MD 20025

TABOR, JAMES HAMILTON, lawyer, bus. cons.; b. Checotah, Okla., May 3, 1916; s. Britton Hamilton and Bessie Catherine (Duncan) T.; student U. of South, 1933-34, Harvard, 1936, Columbia Law Sch., 1937-38; A.B., U. Okla., 1937, LL.B., 1939; m. Troy Elmore, Aug. 8, 1939 (div. Jan. 1977); children—James Hamilton II, Troy Elizabeth (Mrs. Frank W. Davis II), Stanley Duncan. Auditor firm Young, Lamberton & Pearson, Honolulu, 1939-40; admitted to Okla. bar, 1939, Hawaii bar, 1940; with Smith, Wild, Beebe & Cades, Honolulu, 1940-42; from legal analyst to sec. Hawaiian Pineapple Co., Ltd. (now Dole Pineapple Co.), 1942-57; exec. v.p. Honolulu Iron Works Co., 1957-58, pres., 1958-62; v.p. Theo. H. Davies & Co., Ltd., Honolulu, 1957-58, pres., dir., 1958-62, also former pres. and dir. subsidiary firms; former v.p., dir. Pacific Constrn. Co., Ltd.; now practicing atty., bus. cons., Honolulu; v.p., dir. E & B Ltd.; dir. 1st Hawaiian Bank, Pantheon Co. Ltd., Pacific Devel. Co., Inc. Past pres. Hawaii Sugar Planters Assn. Mem. gov's adv. com. on taxation, 1953; pres., bd. dirs. Found. for Study in Hawaii and Abroad; past pres. Social Sci. Assn. Honolulu. Exec. com., bd. dirs., former pres. Aloha council Boy Scouts; past mem. bd. govs., mem. corp., v.p. Hawaii Prep. Acad.; past pres., bd. dirs. Bishop Mus. Assn.; bd. dirs., past pres. Honolulu Community Theatre, Tax Found. of Hawaii; former bd. dirs. Maunalani Hosp. and Convalescent Home, Honolulu Community Chest, Hawaii Planned Parenthood Assn., Honolulu council Nat. Council of Crime and Delinquency, Health and Community Services Council Hawaii; past mem. bd. dirs., former chancellor Episcopal Ch. in Hawaii. Chmn. Comml. Real Property Control Commn., Hawaii, World War II. Recipient Silver Beaver, Silver Antelope awards Boy Scouts Am. Mem. Okla. Bar Assn., Bar Assn. Hawaii, Newcomen Soc. N.Am., Pacific and Asian Affairs Council, Order of Coif, Phi Beta Kappa, Delta Sigma Rho, Delta Tau Delta, Phi Delta Phi. Episcopalian. Clubs: Pacific (Honolulu); Pacific Union (San Francisco). Home: 1022 Prospect St Honolulu HI 96822 Office: Alexander Young Bldg Bishop and King Sts Honolulu HI 96813

TABOR, JOHN KAYE, lawyer; b. Uniontown, Pa., Apr. 19, 1921; s. Edward Otto and Marguerite B. (Kaye) T.; B.A., Yale U., 1943; B.A. (Henry fellow), Corpus Christi Coll., Cambridge, Eng., 1947, M.A., 1950; LL.B., Harvard U., 1950; D.H.L., Alliance Coll., 1974; m. Kate Hill Williams, Dec. 13, 1952; children—John Kaye, William H. Admitted to N.Y. bar, 1950, Pa. bar, 1953, D.C. bar, 1976; asso. firm Winthrop, Stimpson, Putnam & Roberts, N.Y.C., 1950-53; asso. firm Kirkpatrick, Pomeroy, Lockhart & Johnson, Pitts., 1953-58, partner, 1958-63; partner firm Kirkpatrick, Lockhart, Johnson & Hutchison, Pitts., 1970-73, Purcell & Nelson, Washington, 1976—; sec. commerce State of Pa., 1963-67, sec. internal affairs, 1967-68, sec. labor and industry, 1968-69; chmn. Pa. Indsl. Devel. Authority, 1963-67; sec. Pa. Gen. State Authority, 1967-69; under sec. U.S. Dept. Commerce, Washington, 1973-75; chmn. housing task force and housing strike force Allegheny County Health and Welfare Assn., 1970-73. Trustee Masaryk Publs. Trust, Atwood Scholarship Trust, Yale; vestryman St. John's Ch., Georgetown, 1977—. Served to lt. USNR, 1943-46; PTO. Mem. Am. (corp. laws com.), D.C., Pa., Allegheny County bar assns., Am. Legion, Phi Beta Kappa. Clubs: Federal City, Pitts. Golf. Home: 1616 34th St NW Washington DC 20007 Office: 1776 F St NW Washington DC 20006

TABOR, NEIL, lawyer; b. Balt., Aug. 17, 1928; s. Samuel Louis and Alice Jesse (Sugar) T.; A.B., U. Md., 1949, LL.B., 1951; LL.M., Harvard U., 1952; m. Rhona Lee Brenner, Jan. 24, 1954; children—Steven, Nancy. Admitted to Md. bar, 1952; since practiced in Balt., partner firm Tabor & Rottman, 1977—; asst. reporter standing com. rules of practice and procedure Md. Ct. Appeals, 1956-65, mem. standing com. rules of practice and procedure, 1975—. Served with AUS, 1952-55. Elizabeth Maxwell Carroll Chestnut scholar, 1951; Grad. Law fellow Harvard, 1952. Mem. Md. Bar Assn., Bar Assn. Balt., Order of Coif. Democrat. Jewish. Editor Md. Law Rev., 1950-51; contbr. articles to legal jours. Home: 6812 Cherokee Dr Baltimore MD 21209 Office: 1808 Charles Center S 36 S Charles St Baltimore MD 21201

TACKABERRY, THOMAS HOWARD, army officer; b. Los Angeles, Sept. 6, 1923; s. Thomas Howard and Bessie (Brown) T.; B.A. in Humanities, Gonzaga U., 1956; M.S. in Psychology, Tulane U., 1960; M.S. in Internat. Affairs, George Washington U., 1966; m. Lilian (Kiefer; children—Burt S., Kief S., Thomas H., Richard R., Lilian E., Steven S. Served as enlisted man U.S. Army, 1942-45, commd. 2d lt. 1945, advanced through grades to lt. gen., 1977; comdg. officer 2d Bn., Vietnam, 1966-67, asst. chief of staff 1st Cavalry div., Vietnam, 1967; dep. dir. Office of Asst. to Sec. of Def. for Legis. Affairs, Washington, 1967-68; comdg. officer 196th Infantry Brigade, Vietnam, 1969, chief of staff Americal div., 1969-70; dep. dir. individual tng. for ROTC affairs, dep. chief of staff for personnel Dept. of Army, Washington, 1970-72; chief of legis. liaison Office of Sec. of Army, 1972-74; comdg. gen. 82d Airborne div., Fort Bragg, N.C., 1974-76; dep. comdg. gen. VII Corps, Germany, 1976-77; U.S. mil. rep. Central Treaty Orgn., Turkey, 1977-79; comdg. gen. XVIII Airborne Corps and Fort Bragg, N.C., 1979—. Decorated D.S.C. with two oak leaf clusters, D.F.C., Legion of Merit with 2 oak leaf clusters, Bronze star medal with two oak leaf clusters, Silver Star with four oak leaf clusters, Air medal with 53 oak leaf clusters, Purple Heart, and numerous others. Office: HQ XVIII Airborne Corps and Fort Bragg Fort Bragg NC 28307

TACKER, EDGAR CARROLL, educator; b. Savannah, Tenn., Sept. 26, 1935; s. William Henry and Lue Marjorie (Wagner) T.; B.S. in Elec. Engring. with distinction, U. Okla., 1960; M.S.E.E., N.Y. U., 1962; Ph.D. (Ford Found. fellow), U. Fla., 1964; m. Florence Evelyn Maine, Jan. 20, 1956; children—Donna Carol, Karen Gail, Lara Ruth, David Franklin William. Systems engr. Bell Telephone Labs., N.Y.C., 1960-62; asst. prof. elec. engring. U. Ark., Fayetteville, 1964-67, dir. Analog/Hybrid Computer Lab., 1964-67; asso. prof. depts. systems sci. and elec. engring., computer Sci., Mich. State U., East Lansing, 1967-69, dir. Hybrid Simulation and Control Lab., 1967-69; asso. prof. depts. elec. engring., chem. engring. and engring. sci., dir. Coll. Engring. Hybrid Simulation Lab., Baton Rouge, 1969-74; prof. systems and elec. engring. U. Houston, 1974—, dir. systems engring. program, 1974-77; vis. asso. prof. U. Wis., Madison, 1973-74; systems engring. cons., 1970—. Communications Devel. Tng. Program fellow Bell Telephone Lab., 1960-62, NASA Am. Soc. Engring. Edn. fellow, 1965; Air Force Office Sci. Research grantee, 1973-74, NSF grantee, 1975—. Mem. IEEE. Asso. editor Large-Scale Systems Jour.; contbr. articles to profl. jours. Home: 24203 Norchester Way Spring TX 77379 Office: Cullen Coll Engring U Houston Houston TX 77004

TACKER, WILLIS ARNOLD, JR., physician, educator; b. Tyler, Tex., May 24, 1942; s. Willis Arnold and Willie Mae (Massey) T.; B.S., Baylor U., 1964, M.D./Ph.D., 1970; m. Martha Jane McClelland, Mar. 18, 1967; children—Sarah Mae, Betsy Jane, Katherine Ann. Intern, Mayo Clinic, Rochester, Minn., 1970-71; instr. physiology Baylor U. Coll. Medicine, Houston, 1971-73, asst. prof., 1973-74; asst. prof. physiology Purdue U., W. Lafayette, Ind., 1974-75, asso. prof., 1976-79, prof., 1979—. Mem. Am. Physiol. Soc., Am. Heart Assn. (dir. Ind. 1974-77), Sigma Xi. Baptist. Home: 2901 Wilshire St West Lafayette IN 47906 Office: Purdue U West Lafayette IN 47907

TADE, GEORGE THOMAS, univ. dean; b. Casey, Ill., Dec. 17, 1923; s. Thomas Clement and Lena (Myers) T.; B.S., Ind. State U., 1945, M.S., 1946; Ph.D., U. Ill., 1955; m. Wilma Jean Daily, July 7, 1946; children—Mitzi Jean Tade Mills, Terry Nan. Asst. prof., then asso. prof. speech Greenville (Ill.) Coll., 1946-53, dean coll., prof. speech, 1953-59; dean coll., prof. speech Chapman (Calif.) Coll., 1959-62; prof. speech, chmn. dept., chmn. div. humanities Tex. Christian U., Ft. Worth, 1962-72, acting dean Sch. Fine Arts, 1972-73, dean, 1973—; ordained to ministry Disciples of Christ Ch., 1946; cons. communication to pvt. and govt. agy.; coordinator liberal arts study N. Central Assn. Colls., 1959. Councilman-at-large, Greenville, Ill., 1956-59; trustee Tex. Boys' Choir; mem. bd. Van Cliburn Internat. Piano Competition, Granbury Opera House Assn.; exec. bd. Arts Council Ft. Worth and Tarrant County. Mem. Speech Communication Assn., So. Speech Assn. (exec. council 1972-75), Western Coll. Deans Assn. (sec. 1960-62), Internat. Council Fine Arts Deans, Internat. Communication Assn., Tex. Council on Arts in Edn. (v.p. 1975-77, pres. 1978—), Tex. Speech Communication Assn. (pres. 1973-74), Pi Kappa Delta, Gamma Theta Upsilon, Sigma Alpha Eta. Mem. Christian Ch. (chmn. gen. bd., trustee 1973-75). Club: Ridglea Country. Contbg. author: Careers for Christian Youth, 1956; contbr. numerous articles to profl. jours. Home: 3705 Arbor Lawn Dr Fort Worth TX 76109

TAENI, JOHN IGNATIUS, investment banker; b. Lemberg, Austria, May 18, 1901 (came to U.S. 1938, naturalized 1942); s. Henry and Berthe (Reich) T.; D.Polit. and Econ. Sci., LL.D., U. Vienna, 1922; m. Madeleine Renata Weigner, Nov. 6, 1952. Stock broker Vienna and Paris exchanges, 1923-38; asso. Josephthal & Co., N.Y.C., 1945-63; mgr. fgn. dept. Gregory & sons, 1963-68; dir., chmn. finance com. Seeman Bros., Inc., N.Y.C.; mgr. fgn. dept. Gregory & Sons, 1963-68; mgr. Taeni internat., sr. v.p. Weis, Voisin & Co., Inc., N.Y.C., 1968-71; vice chmn., dir. Bernard Aronson, Taeni, N.Y.C., 1971-74; pres. Taeni Internat. div., ltd. partner Bruns, Nordeman, Rea & Co., N.Y.C., 1974-75; pres. Taeni Internat. div. D.H. Blair & Co., Inc., N.Y.C., 1975—; vice chmn., dir., mem. exec. com. Hygrade Food Product Corp., Detroit, 1968—; vice chmn. Eastern Air Devices, Inc., Luxembourg; exec. com. Seabrooks Foods, Inc., Seabrooks Farms Co., Inc.; dir., mem. exec. com. Eastern Air Devices, Inc., Dover, N.H., Peerless Fabrikkerne A/S, Copenhagen, Denmark, Bretton S.A., Cluses, France. Mem. Royal Soc. Autograph Collectors (hon.). Contbr. articles to financial publs. Owner extensive manuscript and autograph collection. Home: 5271 Nautilus Dr Cape Coral FL 33904 also 5271 Nautilus Dr Cape Coral FL 33904 Office: 44 Wall St New York NY 10005

TAENI, MADELEINE RENATA WEIGNER (MRS. JOHN TAENI), investment banker; b. Vienna, Austria (brought to U.S. 1941, naturalized 1946); d. Rudolph and Olga (Malgaj) Weigner; B.A., Barnard Coll., 1949; M.A., Stanford, 1950; m. John I. Taeni, Nov. 6, 1952. Broker Josephthal & Co., N.Y.C., 1961-63; co-mgr. fgn. dept. Gregory & Sons, N.Y.C., 1963-64, gen. partner, 1964-68; sr. exec. v.p., dir. Weis, Voisin & Co., N.Y.C., 1968-71, also established Taeni Internat. div.; chmn. exec. com., dir. Bernard Aronson, Taeni Inc., N.Y.C., mems. N.Y., Am. stock exchanges, 1971-74; exec. v.p. Taeni Internat. div., ltd. partner Bruns, Nordeman, Rea & Co., N.Y.C., 1974-75; exec. v.p. Taeni Internat. div. D.H. Blair & Co. Inc., N.Y.C., 1975—. Home: 177 E 77th St New York NY 10021 also 5271 Nautilus Dr Cape Coral FL 33904 also 4280 SE 20th Pl Cape Coral FL 33904 Office: 44 Wall St New York NY 10005

TAEUBER, CONRAD, educator, former govt. statistician; b. Hosmer, S.D., June 15, 1906; s. Richard Ernst and Emmy (Mussgang) T.; A.B., U. Minn., 1927, M.A., 1929, Ph.D., 1931; student U. Heidelberg (Germany), 1929-30, U. Wis., 1930-31; m. Irene Barnes, July 26, 1929; children—Richard Conrad, Karl Ernst. Instr. U. Wis., 1930-31; asst. prof. Mt. Holyoke Coll., 1931-33; asso. econ. analyst Fed. Emergency Relief Adminstrn., 1934-35; agrl. economist Bur. Agrl. Econ., Dept. Agr., 1935-40, sr. social scientist, 1940-42, prin. social sci., acting head div. of farm population and rural welfare, 1942-43; head agrl. economist Bur. Agrl. Econ., 1943-46; statistician Food and Agrl. Orgn. of UN, 1946-51; asst. dir. Bur of Census, 1951-68, asso. dir., 1968-73. Joseph F. Kennedy Sr. prof. demography Kennedy Inst., Georgetown U., Washington, 1973—. Recipient U. Minn. award, 1951, Exceptional Service award Dept. Commerce, 1963. Fellow Am. Statis. Assn., A.A.A.S., Am. Sociol. Assn; mem. Population Assn. Am. (former pres.), Inter-Am. Statis Inst. (past pres.), Rural Sociol. Soc., Internat. Statis. Inst. Sociol. Research Assn. Club: Cosmos (Washington). Contbr. articles to social science jours. Author: Rural Migration in the United States (with C.E. Lively), 1939; (with Irene B. Taeuber) The Changing Population of the United States, 1958; (with Irene B. Taeuber) People of the United States in the 20th Century, 1972. Home: 4222 Sheridan St Hyattsville MD 20782

TAEUBER, KARL E(RNST), educator; b. Washington, Mar. 31, 1936; s. Conrad F. and Irene (Barnes) T.; B.A., Yale, 1955; M.A., Harvard, 1957, Ph.D., 1960; postgrad. U. Chgo., 1958-59; m. Alma Ficks, Mar. 17, 1960; children—Shawn Eric, Stacy Robin, Wendy Kim. Sociologist, Nat. Cancer Inst., 1959-61; mem. faculty U. Chgo., 1961-63, U. Calif. at Berkeley, 1963-64; prof. sociology U. Wis., Madison, 1964—, chmn. dept. sociology, 1970-73; on leave with Rand Corp., 1969-70; fellow Inst. for Research on Poverty, 1966—, asst. dir., 1978—. Bd. dirs. Social Sci. Research Council, 1970-75, Fund for Open Soc., 1978—. Served with USPHS, 1959-61. Mem. Population Assn. Am. (dir. 1966-69). Author: (with Alma F. Taeuber), Negroes in Cities, 1965; also research articles on migration, population trends, sch. desegregation. Home: 1911 Vilas Ave Madison WI 53711

TAFEL, EDGAR, architect; b. N.Y.C., Mar. 4, 1912; s. Samuel and Rose (Chary) T.; student N.Y. U., 1930-32. Sr. fellow Frank Lloyd Wright's Taliesin Fellowship, Spring Green, Wis., 1932-41; practice architecture in N.Y.C., 1946—; lectr. architecture, 1946—; lectr. USIS, Eng., Israel, India, Netherlands, 1972-73; lectr., dir. secondary sch. archtl. awareness program New Sch. for Social Research, N.Y.C., 1974; faculty Smithsonian Instn., 1978. Bd. dirs. N.Y.C. Mission Soc. Served with AUS, World War II; CBI. Recipient award of merit for Presbyn. Ch. Fifth Ave. Assn., N.Y.C., service citation State U. N.Y. Coll. at Geneseo, 1970. Mem. AIA (exec. com. N.Y. chpt.), Washington Sq. Assn. (pres.). Contbr. articles to profl. jours. Prin. works include: Protestant Chapel at Kennedy Airport, 1964, First Presbyn. Ch. Addition, 1959, De Witt Ch., 1958 (all N.Y.C.); Fine Arts Bldg., State U. N.Y. at Geneseo, 1967; Fulton-Montgomery Community Coll., Johnstown, N.Y., 1969; Grace Ch., White Plains, 1970; Allentown (Pa.) Art Mus. addition, 1975; Columbia-Greene Community Coll., Hudson, N.Y., 1974; Salvation Army Corps Community Centers, master plans for State Coll. at Geneseo, York Coll., N.Y.C., Cadet Corps Hdqrs., Bronx, N.Y. Author: Apprentice to Genius. Home and Office: 14 E 11th St New York NY 10003

TAFF, CHARLES A., educator; b. Hoisington, Kans., Mar. 25, 1916; s. Charles Riley and Maude (Nimocks) T.; B.C.S., U. Iowa, 1937, M.A., 1941; Ph.D., U. Md., 1952; m. Glatha M. Rutenbeck, Sept. 17, 1938; children—William. Rosemary, Barbara. Instr., Va. Poly. Inst., 1941-42; asst. prof. Kent State U., 1946-49; prof. transp. U. Md., College Park, 1949—, head dept. bus. adminstrn., 1962-73; cons. Dept. Def., 1950-62, Council Econ. Advisers, 1958-69, Dept. Transp., 1972-75; mem. U.S. tolls com. St. Lawrence Seaway Devel. Corp., 1955-58, 61-66; mem. St. Lawrence Seaway Joint Tolls Adv. Bd., 1959-64; mem. Nat. Council Phys. Distbn. and Mgmt. Served as officer USNR, 1942-45. Mem. Am. Soc. Traffic and Transp., Transp. Research Forum, Am. Econ. Assn., Order of Artus, Beta Gamma Sigma, Phi Kappa Phi, Delta Sigma Pi, Delta Nu Alpha. Club: Masons. Author: Management of Physical Distribution and Transportation, 6th edit., 1978; Commercial Motor Transportation, 5th edit., 1975; Operating Rights of Motor Carriers, 1953; co-author: Elements of Business Enterprise, 3d edit., 1971; editor Transp. Jour., 1963-79. Home: 7100 Eversfield Dr Hyattsville MD 20782 Office: Coll Bus and Mgmt U Md College Park MD 20742

TAFF, PAUL KENNETH, TV exec.; b. Belleville, Ill., Jan. 21, 1920; s. Benjamin H. and Louise A. (Wehmeier) T.; B.A., Millikin U., 1941; M.A., Northwestern U., 1948; m. Dawn H. Odell, July 13, 1941; children—Paul K., Richard D. Asst. program dir. radio sta. KFUO, St. Louis, 1945-47; program dir. radio sta. WBEZ, Chgo., 1948-51; dist. mgr. Ency. Brit. Films, Wilmette, Ill., 1951-53; asst. mgr. TV sta. WTVP, Decatur, Ill., 1953-54; mgr. TV sta. WMVS, Milw., 1954-60; dir. program operations N.E.T., N.Y.C., 1960-70; pres., gen. mgr. Conn. Ednl. Telecommunications Corp., Hartford, 1970—; vice chmn. Eastern Public Radio Network; trustee Eastern Ednl. TV Network; bd. mgrs. Pub. Broadcasting Service; mem. adv. bd. Am. Shakespeare Theatre, Conn. Ednl. Seminar; mem. Conn. Commn. for Higher Edn., Commn. on Ednl. and Informational Uses of Cable Telecommunications; co-chmn. media task force Consortium for White House Conf. on Families; cons. U. Conn.; bd. advisers Children's TV Workshop, Sesame St.; del. White House Conf. on Children and Youth, 1970; chmn. adv. bd. Prix Jeunesse Found., Munich, W. Ger.; mem. media studies adv. com. Sacred Heart U., Bridgeport, Conn.; mem. Gov.'s State Police Adv. Com.; bd. dirs. Conn. Council on Freedom of Info. Served with AUS, 1942-45. Recipient Nat. Ednl. award for excellence, 1970; Alumni Merit award Millikin U., 1976. Mem. Nat. Assn. Ednl. Broadcasters, Greater Hartford C. of C. (dir.), Asia Soc. (mem. New Eng. regional China Council), Phi Kappa Phi. Editor First Internat. Workshop TV Producers, 1968. Home: 101 Tall Timbers Ln Glastonbury CT 06033 Office: 24 Summit St Hartford CT 06106

TAFT, CHARLES KIRKLAND, educator; b. Cleve., July 24, 1928; s. Kingsley Arter and Louise (Dakin) T.; B.A., Amherst Coll., 1951; B.S. in Mech. Engring., Mass. Inst. Tech., 1953; M.S., Case Inst. Tech., 1956, Ph.D., (Charles W. Bingham fellow), 1960; m. Carolyn Nancy Eggers, Aug. 25, 1951; children—Charles K., Fredrick D., Richard K. Research engr. Warner and Swasey, Cleve., 1953-58, chief servo engr., 1960-61; asst. prof. Case Inst. Tech., Cleve., 1961-64, asso. prof., 1964-67; prof. mech. engring. U. N.H., Durham, 1967—; cons. Warner and Swasey, Ford Motor Co., duPont Co., Curtiss Wright, TRW. Recipient Charles J. Stosacker Teaching award Case Inst. Tech., 1966, Nat. Fluid Power Assn. Achievement award, 1966. Mem. Am. Soc. M.E. (past chmn. No. New Eng. sect.), I.E.E.E., Instrument Soc. Am. (chmn. fluidics com.), Sigma Xi, Pi Tau Sigma, Tau Beta Pi. Co-author: Introduction to Dynamic Systems. Contbr. articles to publs. Patentee in field. Home: 25 Woodridge Rd Durham NH 03824

TAFT, CHARLES PHELPS, lawyer; b. Cin., Sept. 20, 1897; s. William Howard and Helen (Herron) T.; B.A., Yale U., 1918, LL.B., 1921; LL.D., U. Toledo, 1934, U. Rochester, Miami U., Ohio Wesleyan U., Yale U., 1952; D.C.L., Union Coll.; D.H.L., Hebrew Union Coll.; m. Eleanor K. Chase, Oct. 6, 1917 (dec. 1961); children—Eleanor Kellogg Taft Hall, Sylvia Howard Taft Lotspeich, Seth Chase, Lucia (dec.), Cynthia Taft Morris, Rosalyn (dec.), Peter R. Admitted to Ohio bar, 1922, since practiced in Cin.; pros. atty. Hamilton County (Ohio), 1927-28; mem. Cin. City Council, 1938-42, 48-51, 55-77; mayor of Cin., 1955-57. Pres Fed. Council Chs. Christ Am., 1947-48, Friends World Council Chs.; dir. U.S. Community War Services, Fed. Security Agy., 1941-43; dir. Wartime Econ. Affairs, Dept. State, 1944, dir. Transport and Communications Policy, 1945; Republican candidate for gov. Ohio, 1952; trustee Twentieth Century Fund, Carnegie Instn. Washington, Com. Econ. Devel. Served to 1st lt. U.S. Army, 1917-18; AEF in France. Mem. Am., Ohio, Cin. bar assns., Beta Theta Pi, Phi Delta Phi. Republican. Episcopalian. Author: City Management: The Cincinnati Experiment, 1933; You and I and Roosevelt, 1936; Why I Am for the Church, 1947; Democracy in Politics and Economics, 1950. Home and Office: 1071 Celestial St Cincinnati OH 45202

TAFT, DUDLEY SUTPHIN, broadcasting co. exec.; student Yale U., 1959-62; LL.B., U. Va., 1966. Admitted to Ohio bar, 1966; asso. firm Koteen & Burt, Washington, 1966-67; atty., dir., sec., v.p. corporate devel., exec. v.p. Amusement Park Group, now pres. Taft Broadcasting Co., Cin., 1967—; pres. Family Leisure Centers, Inc.; dir. UMC Industries, Inc., Stamford, Conn., Union Central Life Ins. Co., Cin. Pres., Semple Found.; trustee Cin. Opera Assn., Boys Club Greater Cin., Hamilton County Regional Airport Authority. Served with USMC, 1963-68. Mem. Ohio Bar Assn., Ohio C. of C. (dir.). Address: 1906 Highland Ave Cincinnati OH 45219

TAFT, FREDERICK LOVETT, ret. educator and librarian; b. Cleve., Aug. 15, 1906; s. Frederick Lovett and Mary Alice (Arter) T.; B.A., Amherst Coll., 1928; Ph.D., Western Res. U., 1942; m. Eleanor Dale Barnes, Dec. 30, 1931; children—Morgan Barnes, Eleanor Dale (Mrs. R. Bruce King, Jr). Engaged in bus., Cleve., 1928-33; part-time instr. English, Adelbert Coll., Western Res. U., Cleve., 1935-38; instr. English, Case Sch. Applied Sci., 1938-43; from asst. prof. to prof. English, Case Inst. Tech., Cleve., 1946-67, dir. library, 1959-67; acting dir. libraries Case Western Res. U., 1967-68, asso. dir. libraries, 1968-71, emeritus, 1971—. Dir. Colton Chem. Co., Cleve., 1950-53. Served to 1st lt. USAAF, 1943-46. Mem. Modern Lang. Assn., Internat. Assn. Technol. U. Libraries (sec. 1967-70), Am. Soc. Engring. Edn., Friends of Case Western Res. U. Library (sec. 1972—), Amherst Coll. Alumni Assn. (v.p. 1972-73), Phi Beta Kappa, Phi Kappa Psi. Editor: John Milton's Apology for Smectymnuus, 1953. Home: 20849 Byron Rd Shaker Heights OH 44122

TAFT, HENRY WATERS, ednl. co. exec.; b. N.Y.C., July 5, 1926; s. Walbridge S. and Elizabeth (Clark) T.; B.A., Yale U., 1947; M.B.A., Harvard U., 1949; m. Sylvia Babcock, July 10, 1949 (div. Aug. 1958); children—Charlotte, Henry, Laurie; m. 2d, June Clark, Sept. 9, 1961 (div. Oct. 1976); m. 3d, Jan B. Porter, July 30, 1977. With Plastic Mfrs., Inc., Stamford, Conn., 1949-51; asst. treas. Doubleday and Co., Inc., N.Y.C., 1953-57, treas., dir., 1957-59; treas. Bristol-Myers Co., N.Y.C., 1962-66, v.p., 1966-69, exec. v.p. products div., 1969-73; pres. Outward Bound Inc., Greenwich, Conn., 1973—; dir. Intext, Inc. Pres. bd. trustees Rye Country Day Sch., 1969-74, trustee, 1974-76; trustee Taft Sch. Served to lt. USNR, 1944-46, 51-53. Clubs: N.Y. Yacht, Explorers. Home: Taylor's Ln Mamaroneck NY 10543

TAFT, HORACE DWIGHT, educator, physicist; b. Cin., Apr. 2, 1925; s. Robert A. and Martha (Bowers) T.; B.A., Yale, 1950; M.S., U. Chgo., 1953, Ph.D., 1955; m. Mary Jane Badger, Sept. 9, 1952; children—John Godfrey, Hugh Bancroft, Horace Dutton. Faculty, Yale, 1956—, prof. physics, 1964—, master Davenport Coll., 1966-71, dean Yale Coll., 1971-79. Chmn. bd. trustees Taft Sch., Watertown, Conn., 1975—. Served with AUS, 1943-46. Mem. Am. Phys. Soc. Home: 403 Saint Ronan St New Haven CT 06511

TAFT, PAUL E., broadcasting co. exec.; b. Wallingford, Vt., Sept. 2, 1915; s. Raymond Chauncey and Maude Caroline (Eberhart) T.; student U. Vt., 1932-33; B.S. in Mech. Engring., U.S. Naval Acad., 1938; m. Bette Lynn Hamilton, Nov. 15, 1963. Asst., Duncan Coffee Co., Houston, 1938-51; pres., founder Gulf TV Co., Galveston, Tex., 1952-58; pres. Taft Broadcasting Corp., Houston, 1958—. Served with USN, 1942-45; PTO. Home: 3442 Overbrook Ln Houston TX 77027 Office: 4808 San Felipe Rd Houston TX 77056

TAFT, RICHARD GEORGE, lawyer; b. Ann Arbor, Mich., Mar. 13, 1913; s. George J. and Wilhemina (Voigt) T.; B.S., U. Okla., 1935, LL.B., 1940; m. Pauline Joyner, Sept. 1942 (dec.); 1 son, Richard George (dec.); m. 2d, Margaret Gessner, Sept. 1946 (div. Aug. 1949); m. 3d, Louise Hutto, 1953 (div. Feb. 1960); m. 4th, Louise Holmberg, Dec. 30, 1960; 1 stepdau., Jamy Coulson. With FCA, 1935-37; admitted to Okla. bar, 1940, since practiced in Oklahoma City; asso. firm Campbell, Randolph, Mahin & Mosteller, 1940-41, Mosteller & McElroy, 1946-48; asso. firm Billups, Wood & Champlin, C.P.A.'s, 1948-51; partner McAfee, Taft, Mark, Bond, Rucks & Woodruff, and predecessors, 1951—. Mem. Norman Planning Commn., 1966-69; pres. Okla. Bd. Corrections, 1967-69; mem. Presbyn. Med. Center Found., St. Anthony's Hosp. Found.; trustee Oklahoma County Med. Soc. Community Found.; mem. adv. bd. U. Okla. Law Center. Served to lt. col. USAAF, 1941-45. C.P.A., Okla. Mem. Am., Okla. bar assns., Am. Inst. C.P.A.'s, Am. Judicature Soc. (trustee), U.S. Supreme Ct. Hist. Soc., Phi Delta Phi, Phi Gamma Delta. Republican. Home: 603 Okmulgee St Norman OK 73069 Office: 100 Park Ave Oklahoma City OK 73102

TAFT, ROBERT, JR., lawyer, former U.S. senator; b. Cin., Feb. 26, 1917; s. Robert A. and Martha (Bowers) T.; B.A., Yale U., 1939; LL.B., Harvard U., 1942; m. Blanca Noel, 1939 (dec.); children—Robert A., Sarah B. Taft Jones, Deborah, Jonathan D.; m. 3d, Joan M. Warner, 1978. Admitted to Ohio bar; asso. firm Taft, Stettinius & Hollister, Cin., 1946-51, partner, 1951-63, 77—; mem. Ohio Ho. of Reps., 1955-62, majority floor leader, 1961-62; mem. 88th Congress at-large from Ohio; mem. 90th-91th Congresses from 1st Ohio Dist.; U.S. senator from Ohio, 1971-76; practice law in Washington and Cin., 1976—. Trustee Children's Home Cin., Inst. Fine Arts. Served with USNR, 1942-46. Mem. Am., Ohio, Cin. bar assns. Republican. Clubs: Camargo, Racquet, Lit., Queen City (Cin.); Alibi; Burning Tree. Home: 4300 Drake Rd Cincinnati OH 45243 Office: 1800 Massachusetts Ave NW Washington DC 20036 also 600 Dixie Terminal Cincinnati OH 45202

TAFT, ROBERT STEPHEN, lawyer, educator; b. N.Y.C., Nov. 1, 1934; s. Harold A. and Mae Vivian (Gray) T.; B.A., Dartmouth U., 1956; LL.B., Columbia U., 1959; LL.M., N.Y. Law Sch., 1960; m. Marlene Rosalie Medwin, June 22, 1958; children—Leslie Ann, Peter Stephen. Admitted to N.Y. State bar, 1959, Fla. bar, 1978; practiced in N.Y.C., 1960—; asso. firm Reid and Priest, 1960-67; partner firm Hatfield, Brady and Taft, 1967-77, Miller, Montgomery, Sogi, Brady & Taft, 1977—; lectr. N.Y. U. Tax Inst., N.Y.C., 1973—; prof. law N.Y. Law Sch., 1972—. Pres. Gt. Neck (N.Y.) Grace Ave. Sch. PTA, 1971-72; mem. adv. bd. Odyssey House, 1970—, bd. dirs., 1976—; trustee Practicing Law Inst. Found., 1970—. Mem. Am. Bar Assn., N.Y. State Bar Assn., Nassau County Bar Assn., Soc. Am. Magicians. Author: (with Arnold S. Anderson) New York Practice-Personal Taxes, 1975; contbr. articles to legal jours.; tax columnist N.Y. Law Jour., 1972—. Home: 85 Nassau Dr Great Neck NY 11021 Office: 200 Park Ave New York NY 10017

TAFT, WILLIAM HOWARD, educator; b. Mexico, Mo., Oct. 24, 1915; s. Raymond E. and Ferrie (Dains) T.; A.B., Westminster Coll., 1937; B. Journalism, U. Mo., 1938, M.A., 1939; Ph.D., Western Res. U., 1951; m. Myrtle Marie Adams, Jan. 18, 1941; children—Marie, William Howard, Alice. Pub. relations dir. Hiram (Ohio) Coll., 1939-40, 47-48; asst. prof. Youngstown (Ohio) Coll., 1946-48; prof. Defiance (Ohio) Coll., 1948-50; asso. prof. Memphis State Coll., 1950-56; prof. journalism U. Mo., Columbia, 1956—; yearbook cons., 1957—. Served with USAAF, 1941-45. Recipient Faculty-Alumni citation U. Mo., 1979; research fellow Washington Journalism Center, 1967. Mem. Am. Hist. Assn., Assn. Edn. Journalism, Orgn. Am. Historians, Am. Acad. Polit. and Social Sci., Delta Tau Delta, Pi Delta Epsilon, Kappa Tau Alpha (chief central office, nat. treas 1962—, editor yearbook 1962—), Republican. Methodist. Mason, Kiwanian. Author: Let's Publish That Top-Rated Yearbook, 1961; (with others) Modern Journalism 1962; Missouri Newspapers, 1964; Missouri Newspapers, When and Where, 1808-1962, 1964; American Journalism History, 1968, rev. edit., 1977; Newspapers as Tools for Historians, 1970; Mass Media and the National Experience, 1971; Donrey Media: A Low Profile Group, 1976; mem. editorial bd. Journalism History. Contbr. articles to profl. Jours., encys. Home: 107 Sondra Ave Columbia MO 65201

TAGATZ, GEORGE ELMO, obstetrician, gynecologist, educator; b. Milw., Sept. 21, 1935; s. George Herman and Beth Elinore (Blain) T.; A.B., Oberlin Coll., 1957; M.D., U. Chgo., 1961; m. Susan Trunnell, Oct. 28, 1967; children—Jennifer Lynn, Kirsten Susan, Kathryn Elizabeth. Rotating intern Univ. Hosps. of Cleve., 1961-62, resident in internal medicine, 1962-63; resident in ob-gyn State U. Iowa, 1965-68; sr. research fellow in endocrinology U. Wash. dept. obstetrics and gynecology, 1968-70; asst. prof. ob-gyn U. Minn. Med. Sch., 1970-73, asso. prof., 1973-76, prof., 1976—, asst. prof. internal medicine, 1970-73, dir. div. reproductive endocrinology, 1974—. Served with M.C., U.S. Army, 1963-65. Diplomate Am. Bd. Obstetricians and Gynecologists (lectr. endocrinology postgrad. course 1975-76, examiner bd. reproductive endocrinology 1976—). Mem. AMA, Minn., Hennepin County med. socs., Minn. Obstet. and Gynecol. Soc., Endocrine Soc., Internat. Soc. Advancement Humanistic Studies in Gynecology, Am. Fertility Soc., Central Assn. Obstetricians and Gynecologists, U. Iowa Ob-Gyn Alumni Soc. Ad hoc editor Am. Jour. Ob-Gyn, 1976, Fertility and Sterility, 1976-79, Chest, 1976. Contbr. articles to profl. publs. Home: 6708 Sioux Trail Edina MN 55435 Office: PO Box 395 Mayo U Minn Minneapolis MN 55455

TAGGART, GLEN LAIRD, govt. ofcl.; b. Lewiston, Utah, Jan. 16, 1914; s. James and Valeria (Laird) T.; B.S., Utah State Coll., 1940; Ph.D. in Sociology, U. Wis., 1946; m. Phylls Paulsen, Sept. 3, 1940; children—Stephen (dec.), Edward, Elaine. With Dept. Agr., 1943-53, chief tech. collaboration div. Office Fgn. Agrl. Relations, 1952-53; prof. sociology and anthropology Mich. State U., 1953-56, dean internat. programs, 1956-68; pres. Utah State U., Logan, 1968-79; chief div. instnl. and human resources devel. AID, Washington, 1979—; mem. adv. com. on sci., tech. and devel. White House Office Sci. Tech. Policy, 1979—. Vice chancellor U. Nigeria, 1964-66; cons. in field to govt., ednl. instns., founds. Mem. com. instl. projects abroad Am. Council Edn., 1960-64, mem. overseas liaison com., 1969—, mem. com. edn. in tropical Africa. NRC-Nat. Acad. Scis., 1961-62; mem. inter-univ. bd. pub. affairs internship program in Asia and Africa, Maxwell Center Study Overseas Operations, Syracuse U., 1961-63; mem. com. ednl. exchange policy Inst. Internat. Edn., 1961-63; chmn. internat. affairs com. Nat. Assn. State Univs. and Land-Grant Colls., 1970-75; mem. joint com. instl. devel. Nat. Assn. State Univs. and Land-Grant Colls.-AID; mem. univ. ct. U. Sierra Leone, 1973—. Bd. dirs. Midwest Univs. Consortium for Internat. Activities, 1962-68, Internat. Vol. Services, Inc., 1965-73. Mem. AAAS, Am., Rural sociol. socs., Internat. Assn. Univs. (rep. Mich. State U. 1960-68). Office: Div Instnl and Human Resources Devel AID Washington DC 20523

TAGGART, JOSEPH HERMAN, cons. economist; b. Wakefield, Mass., Dec. 29, 1902; s. David and Josephine (Jess) T.; Ph.B., Yale, 1924; M.B.A., Harvard, 1927; Ph.D., Columbia, 1938; LL.D., L.I.U., 1964, U. Lagos, Fed. Republic Nigeria, 1968. Instr. Lehigh U., 1927-28; from asst. prof. to prof. econs. U. Kans., Lawrence, 1928-46; prof. finance Rutgers U., New Brunswick, N.J., 1947-52, prof. econs., 1952-56; prof. finance Grad. sch. Bus. Adminstrn., N.Y. U., 1956-71, asso. dean, 1956-59, dean, 1959-70, exec. dean schs. of bus, 1962-70, spl. cons. to pres. for univ. affairs, 1970-71, dean emeritus, prof. finance emeritus, 1971—; econ. cons., 1971—; dir. Fed. Paper Board Co., Inc.; trustee Hubbard Real Estate Investments. Pub. gov. Am. Stock Exchange, 1966-72; economist, bus. cons. Dept. Commerce, 1941-42, chief of finance and tax research unit, 1945; econ. adviser commr. in Europe, also dir. planning Fgn. Liquidation Commn., Washington, 1945-46; econ. adviser chmn. munitions bd. Dept. Def., 1946-52; U.S. rep. Western Union Mil. Supply Bd., London, 1949-50; cons. Def. Prodn. Adminstrn., 1951-52; mem. U.S. delegation

Internat. Conf. Am. States, Bogota, Colombia, 1948. Served to maj. AUS, 1942-45. Mem. Am. Econ. Assn., Am. Finance Assn., Am. Assn. U. Profs., Alpha Sigma Phi, Alpha Kappa Psi, Beta Gamm Sigma. Independent. Conglist. Club: University (Washington). Author: Federal Reserve Bank of Boston, 1938. Home: 37 Washington Sq W New York City NY 10011

TAGGART, KENNETH DALE, diversified mfg. co. exec.; b. Montclair, N.J., Oct. 10, 1935; s. John A. and Elizabeth J. (Kinley) T.; B.S. in Bus. Adminstrn., Rutgers U., Newark, 1957; m. Mary Ellen Hickey, June 25, 1960. Mgr., Arthur Young & Co., N.Y.C., 1958-68; with Indian Head Inc., N.Y.C., 1968—, controller, v.p., 1973-76, exec. v.p., 1976—. Mem. Am. Inst. C.P.A.'s, N.J. Soc. C.P.A.'s, Rutgers Sch. Bus. Alumni Assn. Club: N.Y. Athletic. Home: 65 Oakridge Rd Verona NJ 07044 Office: 1211 Ave of the Americas New York City NY 10036

TAGGART, LESLIE DAVIDSON, lawyer; b. Glasgow, Scotland, Aug. 28, 1910; came to U.S. 1920, naturalized, 1934; s. Frederick James and Petrina W. (Paterson) T.; A.B., Columbia U., 1931, LL.B., 1934; m. Mary Mason Kerr, Sept. 27, 1940; children—Georgia M. Taggart Brackett, William K., Patricia A., Douglas G. Admitted to N.Y. bar, 1934, since practiced in N.Y.C.; sr. partner Watson, Leavenworth, Kelton & Taggart; lectr. Practising Law Inst. Past sec., bd. mgrs. St. Andrews Soc. N.Y. State. Mem. Am. (past dir.), N.Y. (past dir.) patent law assns., U.S. Trademark Assn. (past dir.), Am. Bar Assn., Am. Coll. Trial Lawyers, Phi Beta Kappa, Phi Sigma Kappa. Congregationalist. Clubs: Univ., Columbia U. (past treas., gov.) (N.Y.C.); Patterson (Fairfield, Conn.). Home: 2 Melwood Ln Westport CT 06880 Office: 100 Park Ave New York NY 10017

TAGGART, ROSS EDGAR, museum curator; b. New Brighton, Pa., July 28, 1915; s. Ross Edgar and Leah Edgel (Segar) T.; B.A., Geneva Coll., Beaver Falls, Pa., 1936; M.A., Harvard, 1941, Sheldon Traveling fellow, 1940-41; Belgian-Am. Edn. Found. fellow, U. Brussels, summer 1939; m. Kathleen Lothrop Nelson, Nov. 3, 1945; children—Ross Campbell, Jonathan Whittier. Cataloguer prints and drawings Houghton Library, Harvard, 1945-47; mem. staff Nelson Gallery Art, Kansas City, Mo., 1947—, sr. curator 1959-72, chief curator, 1972—. Organizer spl. mus. exhbns., 1950—; research asso. art history U. Mo., 1962—; lectr. Williamsburg Antiques Forum, 1956, 59, Wedgwood Internat. Seminar, 1958, 62, Midwest Antiques Forum, 1960; Cockafair lectr. U. Mo. at Kansas City; cons. historic restorations Old Tavern at Arrow Rock, Mo., Old Jail and Marshall's House, Independence, Mo.; chmn. George Caleb Bingham Sesquicentennial Exhbn., 1961, Wedgwood Internat. Seminar, 1963; lectr. art history U. Kans., 1974—. Exec. bd. Jackson County Hist. Soc.; mem. Mo. Mansion Preservation Commn., 1975—; bd. govs. Wedgwood Internat. Seminar, 1960—. Served with C.E., AUS, 1941-45. Mem. English, Am. (trustee) ceramic circles, Assn. Am. Museums, Mo. Hist. Soc. Author: The Burnap Collection of English Pottery, 1953; The Lipton Collection of Antique English Silver, 1955; George Caleb Bingham, 1961; also numerous articles. Editor: Handbook of the Nelson Gallery, 1951, 2d edit., 1973; also bulls., exhbn. catalogues. Home: 440 E 55th St Kansas City MO 64110 Office: 4525 Oak St Kansas City MO 64111

TAGGART, WALTER JOHN, lawyer, educator; b. N.Y.C., Aug. 4, 1943; s. Walter J. and Agnes C. Taggart; B.A., Belmont Abbey Coll., 1965; J.D., Villanova U., 1968; m. Joell Thomas, July 6, 1970; 1 son, Andrew. Admitted to Pa. bar, 1968; law clk. to judge U.S. Dist. Ct. for Eastern Dist. Pa., 1968-70; asst. prof. law Villanova Law Sch., 1970-72, asso. prof., 1972-74, prof., 1974—; asso. reporter, adv. com. on bankruptcy rules of Jud. Conf. U.S., 1972-75, co-reporter, 1979—; cons. Commn. on Bankruptcy Laws U.S., 1972-73. Mem. Am. Bar Assn., Nat. Bankruptcy Conf., Am. Law Inst., Order of Coif. Roman Catholic. Contbg. editor: Moore's Federal Practice, 1972, Collier on Bankruptcy, 1979. Home: 26 Aldwyn Ln Villanova PA 19085 Office: Villanova Law Sch Villanova PA 19085

TAGIURI, RENATO, educator, social scientist; b. Milan, Italy, Apr. 28, 1919; s. Giulia and Corrado T.; B.Sc., McGill U., 1945, M.Sc., 1946; Ph.D., Harvard U., 1951; m. Consuelo Keller, May 5, 1946; children—Robert, Peter, John. Mem. faculty Harvard U., Cambridge, Mass., 1951—, prof. social sci. Grad. Sch. Bus. Adminstrn., 1962—; cons. to govt., pvt. orgns., 1951—. Fellow Am. Psychol. Assn. Author: (with Petrullo) Person Perception, 1958; (with Litwin) Organizational Climate, 1968; (with Lawrence, Barnett and Dunphy) Behavioral Science Concepts in Case Analysis, 1968; (with Glover and Hower) The Administrator, 5th edit., 1973; contbr. chpts. to books and encys., articles to publs. Home: 432 Concord Rd Weston MA 02193 Office: Harvard U Boston MA 02163

TAGLIACOZZO, DAISY MARGOT, educator; b. Berlin, Germany, Mar. 26, 1923; d. Botho and Luise (Meinecke) Lilienthal; came to U.S., 1946, naturalized, 1951; B.A., Boston U., 1950; Ph.D., U. Chgo., 1956; m. Luigi Tagliacozzo, May 12, 1955 (dec.). Tchr., Wright Jr. Coll., Chgo., 1956-59; lectr. adult edn. U. Chgo. and U. Ill., 1959-61; asso. prof. sociology Ill. Inst. Tech., Chgo., 1961-66, prof., 1966-71, chmn. dept. polit. and social sci., 1964-66; prof. sociology U. Mass., Boston, 1971—, dean coll., 1971-75. Dir. NSF Acad. Year Inst. in Sociology, 1965-71; prin. investigator NIH grant nurse-patient edn. and patterns of compliance, 1966-71; mem. nat. bd. cons. NIH, 1975—; mem. Social Sci. Edn. Consortium, 1978—. Mem. Am. Sociol. Assn. (com. chmn.). Home: 770 Boylston St Boston MA 02199 Office: Harbor Campus Boston MA 92116

TAGUE, BARRY ELWERT, stock broker; b. Phila., June 17, 1938; s. Edward James, Jr., and Eleanor May (Elwert) T.; student Bucknell U., 1956-59; m. Dorothy Elizabeth Beausang, May 14, 1960; children—Kimberly, Nancy, Barry Elwert, Edward James. Parter, E.J. Tague & Co. Phila., 1959-68, Barry E. Tague & Co., Phila., 1968—; exec. v.p., vice chmn. Raymond, James & Assos., Inc., Phila., 1968-76; pres., dir. Tague Securities Corp., Phila. and Bryn Mawr, Pa., 1976—; chmn. bd. The Bryn Mawr Corp., 1977—; pres., dir. The Bryn Mawr Group, 1977—; mem. several investment partnerships, several industry coms. bd. govs. Phila.-Balt.-Washington Stock Exchange, Phila., 1967-77, vice chmn. bd., 1973-74, chmn. bd., 1974-76, bd. trustees, 1973-76; dir. Stock Clearing Corp. Phila., 1973-76. Active, Little League Baseball, 1961-65, 76—; pres. Ithan Sch. PTA, 1971-72. Served with USMCR, 1959-65. Mem. Securities Industry Assn. (nat. market com.), Kappa Sigma. Republican. Episcopalian. Clubs: Waynesborough Country (Paoli, Pa.); Le Mirador (Switzerland). Office: 931 Haverford Rd Bryn Mawr PA 19010

TAGUE, CHARLES FRANCIS, engring. co. exec.; b. N.Y.C., Aug. 16, 1924; s. Charles and Isabelle (Carey) T.; B.S., Fordham U., 1952; m. Alicia Patricia Murtha, Aug. 6, 1949; children—Patrick, Charles, Thomas, Mary Alicia, James, Beth Anne. Auditor Scovell, Wellington & Co., N.Y.C., 1951-57; comptroller Chem. Constrn. Corp., N.Y.C., 1957-75; controller Burns and Roe, Inc., Oradell, N.J., 1975—; domestic and fgn. tax cons. Mem. Colts Neck (N.J.) Sports Found.; active Boy Scouts Am. Served with USNR, 1943-46, PTO, ETO, NATOUSA. Mem. Controllers Inst., Nat. Contract Mgmt. Assn., Assn. Govt. Accountants. Democrat. Roman Catholic (officer Holy Name Soc.). Home: 328 E Saddle River Rd Upper Saddle River NJ 07458 Office: 550 Kinderkamack Rd Oradell NJ 07649

TAIBLESON, MITCHELL HERBERT, educator; b. Maywood, Ill., Dec. 31, 1929; s. Albert Abraham and Leona (Chankin) T.; S.M., U. Chgo., 1960, Ph.D., 1962; m. Charlotte Sybil Patinkin, Aug. 21, 1949; children—Judith, David, Michael. Asst. prof. math. Washington U., St. Louis, 1962-66, asso. prof., 1966-69, prof., 1969—, chmn., 1970-73; mem. Inst. for Advanced Study, Princeton, N.J., 1966-67; research prof. math. in psychiatry Washington U. Med. Sch., 1973—; cons. systems analysis. Mem. Am. Math. Soc., Math. Assn. Am., A.A.A.S. Author: Fourier Analysis on Local Fields, 1974. Research on theory of Lipschitz spaces of distbns. on Euclidean N-Space; harmonic analysis on n-dimensional vector spaces over local fields; methodology and mathematical models in psychiatry. Home: 7539 Cromwell Dr Clayton MO 63105 Office: Washington U St Louis MO 63130

TAIBLESON, W.B., packaging co. exec.; b. Oak Park, Ill., Oct. 25, 1922; s. Albert and Leona (Chankin) T.; B.S.A., Walton Sch. Commerce, 1941; m. Clare Weiner, Dec. 3, 1944; children—Roy, Anne, James, Sally. Accountant firm Glabman Bros., Chgo., 1941-44, Katz Wagner & Co., Chgo., 1944-51; controller United Mfg. Co., Chgo., 1951-58; sr. v.p., chief financial officer Nat. Can Corp., Chgo., 1958—, also dir.; dir. Sonderling Broadcasting Corp., Miami, Fla., Exchange Nat. Bank, Chgo. C.P.A., Ill. Mem. Am. Mgmt. Assn. (finance council), Am. Inst. C.P.A.'s, Financial Execs. Inst., Lyric Opera Chgo. (pres.'s com.). Club: Econ. of Chgo. Home: 849 Highland Pl Highland Park IL 60035 Office: 8101 W Higgins Rd Chicago IL 60631

TAIRA, KOJI, economist; b. Hirara-shi, Okinwawa, Nov. 7, 1926; s. Kimiko Taira; came to U.S., 1950, naturalized, 1975; B.A., U. N.Mex., 1953; M.A., U. Wis., 1954; Ph.D., Stanford U., 1961; m. Setsuko Miyagi, 1957; children—Shinya Karl, Henry Tatsuya. Lectr. econs. Ryukyu U., 1954-57; vis. scholar Stanford (Calif.) U., 1957-61; asst. prof. U. Wash., Seattle, 1961-62; ofcl. ILO, Geneva, 1962-66; asso. prof. Stanford U., 1966-70; prof. econs. U. Ill., Urbana, 1970—; expert OECD, 1965, ILO, 1974. Recipient Eliot Jones award Western Econ. Assn., 1961; 1st prize in Newcomen award Harvard U. Bus. Sch., 1970. Mem. Am., Mo. Valley, Ill. econ. assns., Assn. Asian Studies, Indsl. Relations Research Assn., Soc. Internat. Devel., Midwest Conf. Asian Affairs. Author: Economic Development and The Labor Market in Japan, 1970; (in Japanese) A Tract on the Constitution of Japan, 1974; also articles. Home: 2309 S Cottage Grove St Urbana IL 61801 Office: 504 E Armory Ave Champaign IL 61820

TAISHOFF, LAWRENCE BRUCE, publishing co. exec.; b. Washington, Aug. 30, 1933; s. Sol Joseph and Betty (Tash) T.; A.B., Duke U., 1955; m. Nancy Lee Stuckey, Sept. 21, 1962; children—Robert Paul, Randall Lawrence, Jonathan Bradford. Asst. dir. Sta. WTOP-TV, Washington, 1955-56; with Broadcasting Publs., Inc., Washington, 1958—, pres., pub., 1971—, also dir.; v.p. Jolar Corp., Washington, 1952-72, dir., 1958-72; partner Jolar Assos., Washington, 1972—; chmn. bd. Graphictype, Inc., 1976—, also dir.; mem. Met. Washington Bd. Trade, 1970—. Team capt. pubs. div. United Givers Fund drive, 1965; mem. admissions adv. com. Duke Alumni Assn., 1968-70. Served with AUS, 1956-58. Mem. Advt. Club Washington, Internat. Radio and TV Soc., Sigma Delta Chi, Zeta Beta Tau. Jewish. Clubs: Nat. Press, White House Corrs. Assn., Nat. Broadcasters, Internat. (Washington); Woodmont Country (Rockville, Md.); Mumford Landing Yacht and Tennis (Ocean City, Md.). Home: 6679 Fairfax Rd Chevy Chase MD 20015 Office: 1735 DeSales St Washington DC 20036

TAISHOFF, SOL JOSEPH, publishing co. exec.; b. Minsk, Russia, Oct. 8, 1904; s. Joseph and Rose (Order) T.; ed. pub. schs., Washington; m. Betty Tash, Mar. 6, 1927 (dec. Nov. 1977); children—Joanne Taishoff Cowan (dec. Dec. 1977), Lawrence Bruce. Copy boy Washington bur. AP, 1920-21, successively telegraph operator, mem. news staff, 1922-26; reporter U.S. Daily (now U.S. News and World Report), Washington, 1926-31; radio editor Consol. Press (pen name Robert Mack), 1927-34; mng. editor, co-founder Broadcasting Pub., Inc., 1931—, editor, 1933—; v.p., treas. Broadcasting mag., 1931-34, pres., editor, pub., 1944-71, chmn., editor, 1971—; v.p., dir. Telecommunications Reports, Inc.; partner Jolar Assos. Bd. dirs. Washington Journalism Center. Recipient Distinguished Service in Journalism award U. Mo., 1953, Distinguished Service award Nat. Assn. Broadcasters, 1966, Paul White Meml. award Radio-TV News Dirs. Assn., 1967, Spl. citation Internat. Radio and TV Soc., 1975, Disting. Communications medal So. Bapt. Conv. Radio-TV Commn., 1976; Disting. Service award Nat. Religious Broadcasters, 1977. Mem. IEEE (sr.), Broadcast Pioneers (past nat. pres.), Sigma Delta Chi (past nat. pres.; journalism fellow 1964). Clubs: Nat. Press, Overseas Writers, Woodmont Country, Nat. Broadcasters (Washington). Home: 4200 Massachusetts Ave NW Washington DC 20016 Office: 1735 DeSales St Washington DC 20036

TAIT, EDWARD THOMAS, lawyer; b. Indiana, Pa., Apr. 9, 1920; s. William and Edith (Marley) T.; B.S., U. Pitts., 1942, LL.B., 1949; m. Betty L. Weaver, May 25, 1942; children—Betsy, Marley, Carol, Edward Thomas. Admitted to Pa. bar, 1949; law clk. to Judge W. Heber Dithrich, Pa. Superior Ct., 1949-50; trust adminstr. Pitts. Nat. Bank, 1950-51; asso. firm Kountz, Fry & Meyer, Pitts., 1951-53; exec. asst. to chmn. SEC, 1953-55, exec. dir., 1955; spl. asst. to Pres. Eisenhower, 1955-56; mem. FTC, 1956-60; partner firm Whitlock, Markey and Tait, 1960-70, partner Reed, Smith, Shaw & McClay, 1970—; dir. Henry B. Gilpin Co. Trustee Child Devel. Center. Served to maj. AUS, World War II. Mem. Am. Pa., D.C., Allegheny County bar assns., U. Pitts. Law Rev., Order of Coif, Phi Alpha Delta, Pi Kappa Alpha, Omicron Delta Kappa. Episcopalian (vestryman). Clubs: Metropolitan (Washington); Sankaty Head Country (Nantucket). Home: 26 Kalorama Circle NW Washington DC 20008 also Prince Frederick MD Office: 1150 Connecticut Ave NW Suite 900 Washington DC 20036

TAIT, JAMES M., corp. exec.; b. 1920; married. With Butler Bros., 1938-60; with City Products Corp., 1960—, pres. Ben Franklin Stores div., 1967-70, exec. v.p. parent co., 1970, pres., chief operating officer, 1971, pres., chief exec. officer, 1971, also dir.; dir. Household Finance Corp., Snap-On-Tools Corp. Address: City Products Corp Wolf and Oakton Sts Des Plaines IL 60018

TAIT, JOHN WATTERSON, flour mill exec.; b. Moncton, N.B., Can., Oct. 18, 1915; s. John L. and Jean S. (Smith) T.; student McGill U., 1933; chartered accountant, 1938; m. Eleanor Raymond, Jan. 25, 1941; children—Pamela, John, James, Ruth, David. Exec. v.p., dir. Ogilvie Flour Mills, 1959-66, pres., 1966-79, chmn., chief exec. officer, 1979—; exec. v.p., dir. Catelli Food Products, 1960-66, pres., 1966—; dir. McGavin Bakeries Ltd., John Labatt Ltd. Home: 70 Montclair Ave Toronto ON M5P 1P7 Canada Office: Ogilvie Flour Mills Co Ltd 1 Place Ville Marie Montreal PQ Canada

TAJO, ITALO, bass; b. Pinerolo, Italy, Apr. 25, 1915; s. Luigi and Adele T.; m. Inelda Meroni; 1 dau., Cecilia. Debut in Rheingold, Turin, 1935; since performed at maj. opera houses throughout world; debut as stage dir. Mozart and Salieri, Naples, Italy, 1954; prof. voice and opera, basso-in-residence U. Cin. Conservatory of Music; dir. Internat. Opera Festival, Barga, Italy, 1970—; rec. artist HMV, RCA, Telefunken, Cetra-Soria records. Mem. Nat. Opera Assn., Coll. Coll. Music Soc., McDowell Soc. Roman Catholic. Office: care Press Relations Met Opera 1865 Broadway New York NY 10023*

TAKACS, LAJOS FERENC, educator, mathematician; b. Maglod, Hungary, Aug. 21, 1924 (came to U.S. 1959, naturalized 1965); s. Lajos and Maria (Leiti) T.; Ph.D., Tech. U., Budapest, Hungary, 1948, Dr. Math. Sci., 1957; m. Dalma Sarolta Horvath, Apr. 9, 1959; children—Judith, Susan. Mathematician, Tungsram Research Lab., Budapest, Hungary, 1945-55, Research Inst. Math., Hungarian Acad. Scis., 1950-58,; asso. prof. Eötvös U., Budapest, 1953-58, Columbia, 1959-66; prof. math. Case Western Res. U., Cleve., 1966—. Fellow Inst. Math. Statistics, Royal Statis. Soc.; mem. Am. Math. Soc., Math. Assn. Am., Sigma Xi. Author: Combinatorial Methods in the Theory of Stochastic Processes 1967; Stochastic Processes, 1960; Introduction to the Theory of Queues, 1962. Home: 2410 Newbury Dr Cleveland Heights OH 44118 Office: Dept Math Case Western Res Univ Circle Cleveland OH 44106

TAKAHASHI, YASUNDO, educator; b. Nagoya-Shi, Japan (came to U.S. 1958); s. Sakunosuke Seisen and Teruko (Umemura) T.; Bachelor's Degrees in Engring., U. Tokyo, 1935, Doctor's Degree in Engring., 1946; hon. degree U. Grenoble (France), 1978; m. Kuwako Kusunoki, Apr. 9, 1939; 1 dau., Yuri. Design engr. Japanese Govt. Rys., Tokyo, 1935-37; asst. prof. Yokohama (Japan) Tech. Coll., 1937-40, Nagoya (Japan) U., 1940-44; prof. U. Tokyo, 1944-58; prof. engring. U. Calif., Berkeley, 1958-79, emeritus, 1979—; prof. Toyohashi U. Tech., 1979—; cons. to industry, 1950—. Fellow ASME (chmn. control div. 1967-68, Oldenburger medal 1978; life); mem. Japan Soc. Mech. Engrs. (dir. 1950-54; citation of merit 1967) Instrument Soc. Am., Japan Soc. Control and Instruments. Author: Systems and Control, 1958; Control, 1970; Introducing Systems and Control, 1974; also articles. Home: 135 York Ave Berkeley CA 94708

TAKAL, PETER, artist; b. Bucharest, Romania, Dec. 8, 1905 (came to U.S. 1939, naturalized 1944); s. Gustave and Renee (Vassal) T.; student schs. of Paris, France, also Berlin, Germany; m. Charlotte Tournerie, 1933; 1 dau., Anne; m. 2d, Susy Laytha, 1945; 1 son, Kim; m. 3d, Jean Mali Noyes, Aug. 8, 1956; 1 son, Pierre. One-man shows various cities, including Berlin, Paris, Morocco, Chgo., Los Angeles, San Francisco, Sacramento, N.Y.C., Boston, Mass., Dallas, Tex., Phila., Pitts., also Florence, Geneva, Cleve., Mexico City, 1932—; one-man travelling show, Smithsonian Instn., 1959-60, Kestner Mus. Hanover throughout West Germany, 1961-62; group exhbn. White House, 1966, 70; retrospective exhbn., Geneva, 1970; works permanent collections Berlin, Bremen, Zurich, Geneva, Florence, Montreal, Hamburg, Copenhagen, Stockholm, Hanover, Stuttgart, Hagen, Darmstadt, Saarbrucken, Karlsruhe, Grenoble, Oran, Fort Worth, St. Louis, USIS, Cleveland Mus. Art, Met. Mus., Chgo., Hunt Bot. Library, Pitts., Art Inst., Chgo., Kassel, San Francisco, Los Angeles, Met. Mus. Art, Pa. Acad. Fine Arts Nat. Gallery, Washington, Victoria and Albert Mus., London, Whitney Mus. Am. Art, Mus. Modern Art, Bklyn. Mus., Phila. Mus. Art, E.B. Crocker Art Gallery, Sacramento, Dallas Mus. Fine Art, Balt. Mus. Art, John Herron Art Inst., Indpls., Musee de l'Art Moderne of Paris, others; Ford Found. grant as artist in residence in museums Beloit (Wis.) Coll., 1965. Recipient award for drawing, biennial exhbn. Bklyn. Mus., 1954, 8th ann. Knickerbocker art exhbn. Riverside Mus., N.Y.C., 1955, Ball State Tchrs. Coll., 1958, Print Club award; Ford Found. grantee to Tamarind Workshop, 1963; drawing prize Providence Print Club, 1963. Mem. Am. Color Print Soc., Artists Equity, Soc. Am. Graphic Artists. Author: (portfolio drawings and poems) Takal, 1945; others. Contbr. illustrations to mags., U.S., Paris, Stockholm. Home: 40 Rue du Mole CH 1201 Geneva Switzerland also 116 E 68th St New York NY 10021 Office: care Weyhe Gallery 794 Lexington Ave New York NY 10021 also Gallery Benador 1204 Geneva Switzerland

TAKASUGI, ROBERT MITSUHIRO, fed. judge; b. Tacoma, Sept. 12, 1930; s. Hidesaburo and Kayo (Otsuki) T.; B.S., U. Calif., Los Angeles, 1953; LL.B., J.D. (Harry J. Bauer scholar), U. So. Calif., 1959; m. Dorothy O. Takasugi; children—Jon Robert, Lesli Mari. Admitted to Calif. bar, 1970; practiced law, Los Angeles, 1960-73; judge East Los Angeles Municipal Ct., 1973-75, adminstrv. judge, 1974, presiding judge, 1975; judge Superior Ct., County of Los Angeles, 1975-76; U.S. dist. judge U.S. Dist. Ct. for Central Dist. Calif., 1976—; legal counsel Japanese-Am. Welfare Rights Orgn., Asian-Am. Soc. Blind; nat. legal counsel Japanese Am. Citizens League; guest lectr. law seminars, Harvard U. Law Sch. Careers Symposium; commencement speaker; mem. Criminal Justice Standards Rev. Com., Com. for Standards for Admission to Fed. Practice; bd. dirs. East Los Angeles Coll. Found.; chmn. magistrates com. U.S. Dist. Ct., Central Dist. Calif.; mem. Legion Lex U. So. Calif. Law Center. Bd. dirs. East Los Angeles-Montebello YMCA. Served with U.S. Army, 1953-55. Recipient U.S. Mil. Man of Yr. award for Far East Theater, U.S. Army, 1954; certificate of merit Japanese-Am. Bar Assn., other awards. Mem. U. So. Calif. Law Alumni (dir.). Club: Optimists (hon. dir. local club) (Los Angeles). Mem. editorial bd. U. So. Calif. Law Rev.; contbr. articles to profl. jours. Office: US Dist Ct US Courthouse 312 N Spring St Los Angeles CA 90012

TALALAY, PAUL, pharmacologist, physician; b. Berlin, Germany, Mar. 31, 1923; came to U.S. 1940, naturalized, 1946; s. Joseph Anton and Sophie (Brosterman) T.; S.B., Mass. Inst. Tech., 1944; student U. Chgo. Sch. Medicine, 1944-46; M.D., Yale U., 1948; D.Sc. (hon.), Acadia U., 1974; m. Pamela Judith Samuels, Jan. 11, 1953; children—Antony, Susan, Rachel, Sarah. House officer, asst. resident surg. services Mass. Gen. Hosp., Boston, 1948-50; asst. prof. surgery U. Chgo., 1950-51, asst. prof. biochemistry, 1955-57, asso. prof., then prof., 1957-63, asst. prof. Ben May Lab. Cancer Research, 1951-57, asso. prof., then prof., 1957-63; John Jacob Abel prof., dir. dept., pharmacology and exptl. therapeutics Johns Hopkins Sch. Medicine, 1963-75, John Jacob Abel Distinguished Service prof., 1975—, Am. Cancer Soc. prof., 1958-63, 77—; sr. asst. surgeon USPHS, 1951-53; vis. prof. Guy's Hosp. Med. Sch., London, 1970, 74-76; nat. adv. cancer council USPHS, 1967-71; vis. com. dept. biology Mass. Inst. Tech., 1964-67; bd. sci. advisers Jane Coffin Childs Meml. Fund for Cancer Research, 1971—; bd. sci. consultants Sloan-Kettering Inst. Cancer Research, 1971—. Recipient Premio Internationale La Madonnina, Milan, 1978; Med. Alumni Disting. Service award U. Chgo., 1978. Am. Cancer Soc. scholar, 1954-58, Guggenheim Meml. fellow, 1973-74. Fellow Am. Acad. Arts and Scis.; mem. AAAS (Theobald Smith award med. scis. 1957), Am. Soc. Biol. Chemists, Am. Soc. Clin. Investigation, Biochem. Soc., Am. Chem. Soc., Am. Soc. Pharm. and Exptl. Therapeutics, Phi Beta Kappa, Sigma Xi, Alpha Omega Alpha. Hon. editorial adv. bd. Biochem. Pharmacology, 1963-68; editorial bd. Jour. Biol. Chemistry, 1961-66, Molecular Pharmacology, 1965-68, 71—, editor-in-chief, 1968-71. Office: Johns Hopkins U Sch Medicine Baltimore MD 21205

TALARICO, SAMUEL JOSEPH, labor union ofcl.; b. Chgo., Sept. 20, 1913; s. Joseph and Jennie (Astorino) T.; student U. Wis. Sch. for Workers, 1945-46, Roosevelt U. Labor Edn. Div., 1946-47, Trade Union Program, Harvard U., 1958-59; m. Rita F. De Traglia, June 12, 1937; children—Joseph C., Samuel Joseph, Louis C. Hog and cattle butcher Gold lMedal Packing Co., Utica, N.Y., 1930-33; steward, committeeman Packinghouse Local 13, Utica, 1933-36; internat. rep.

Meat Cutters Union, Utica, 1940-53; pres. local 1, Utica, 1953-60; internat. v.p. Amalgamated lHeat Cutters Union, Utica, 1960-76, internat. sec.-treas. Amalgamated Meat Cutters Union, AFL-CIO, 1976-79; internat. sec.-treas. United Food and Comml. Workers Internat. Union, AFL-CIO, 1979—; dir. Bank of Utica. Recipient Contemporary Ams. award Marist Coll., 1968; Israeli Labor award, 1973. Mem. NAACP (life). Democrat. Roman Catholic. Club: Ft. Schuyler Men's (Utica). Office: 1775 K St NW Washington DC 20006. *Early in my youthful years I discovered a very basic fact, which is, that life is never a one-way street. You get out of it exactly what you put into it. In other words, if you are constantly concerned about the well-being of others—especially those least able to defend and protect themselves—you will always have a clear conscience. My philosophy of life is therefore, "Give to the world the best you have and the best will come back to you."*

TALBERT, ANSEL EDWARD MCLAURINE, mag. editor; b. Washington, Jan. 6, 1912; s. Ansel D. and Lily (McLaurine) T.; grad. Landon Sch., Bethesda, Md., 1930; A.B., Columbia, 1934, Litt.B., 1935, M.S. (Henry Woodward Sackett fellow), 1935; spl. student McGill U.; m. Marlene Zimmer, 1951 (div. 1969). N.Y. corr. Sci. Service, 1935-36; with N.Y. Herald Tribune, 1936-58, spl. assignment Europe, 1939, Far East, 1940, Korean war corr., chief Tokyo bur., 1950-51, assigned Middle East, Japan, Korea, Alaska, Eng., France, 1951-53, Thule, Greenland, Ice Island T-3, North Pole, 1954, operation Deep Freeze, McMurdo Sound, Antarctica, also four flights over South Pole, 1956, Soviet Union, 1956, Scandinavia, Pakistan, Iran, 1957, mil. and aviation editor, 1954-58; writer nationally syndicated column Def. and Aviation; exec. editor publs., v.p. Flight Safety Found., 1959-67, mng. editor Air Transport World mag., 1967-70, exec. editor, from 1970; now sr. editor Travel Agt. mag., Travel Agt. Internat., Interline Reporter. Panelist, CBS-TV show Longines Chronoscope, 1952-54; spl. broadcasts aerospace, mil. devels. WQXR, 1960-61, WRUL-Worldwide Broadcasting System, 1962-63; mem. exec. com. Editorial Opinion Research, from 1970. Trustee, past mem. adv. com. Harmon Internat. Aviation Trophies, past mem. Collier Trophy Com. Served from pvt. to lt. col. AUS, 1941-46; chief ultra intelligence for 8th Air Force, Eng. Decorated chevalier Legion of Honor (France); Royal Yugoslav War Cross of St. Andrew; Medal of Merit of Santos Dumont (Brazil); recipient James J. Strebig trophy for outstanding writing on aviation, 1957; Gold medal Adventures Club, 1959; TWA Nat. award for outstanding mag. writing on bus. subjects, 1970. Mem. Aviation Space Writers Assn. (past pres.), Am. Polar Soc., Arctic Inst. N. Am., Elbeetian Legion, S.A.R., Am. Legion (past post comdr.), Woodmen of World, Air Force Assn., Civil War Round Table, Columbia U. Alumni Assn., Vet. Corps Artillery N.Y., V.F.W., Zeta Psi. Clubs: Wings (past v.p.), Adventurers (past pres.), Dutch Treat, St. Hubert's Soc., N.Y. Athletic, Overseas Press (N.Y.C.); National Press (Washington). Author: Famous Airports of the World, 1953; Newsbreak, 1977. Co-author: How I Got That Story, 1967; The Grand Original - A Biography of Randolph Churchill, 1971, Mem. editorial bd. Mil. Pub. Inst., 1958-65. Home: Bridgeport CT Office: Am Traveler Inc 2 W 46th St New York NY 10036

TALBERT, ERNEST WILLIAM, educator; b. San Jose, Calif., Apr. 3, 1909; s. Franklin Lilburn and Edith Blake (Leach) T.; A.B., San Jose State Coll., 1929; M.A. (Grad. scholar), Stanford U., 1931, Ph.D. (Victor fellow, Univ. fellow), 1936; m. Marion Katherine Tuttle, Dec. 22, 1934; children—Peter Scott, Katherine Talbert Gerritsen. Instr., Compton (Calif.) Dist. Jr. Coll., 1934-36, U. Idaho, 1936-38, U. Tex., 1938-42; asst. prof., then asso. prof. English, Duke U., 1942-49; prof. English, U. N.C., Chapel Hill, then Alumni Distinguished prof., 1949-74, emeritus, 1974—, mem. administrv. bd. Grad. Sch., 1965-70, dir. grad. studies English, 1966-69; bd. govs. U. N.C. Press, 1961-74. Carnegie grantee, 1947, 48; Folger fellow, 1950; sr. fellow S.E. Inst. Medieval and Renaissance Studies, 1965; Kenan research grantee, 1968. Mem. Acad. Lit. Studies, Modern Lang. Assn., Renaissance Soc. Am., S.E. Renaissance Conf. (past pres.). Democrat. Episcopalian. Author: Problem of Order: Elizabethan Political Thought and an Example of Shakespeare's Art, 1962; Elizabethan Drama and Shakespeare's Early Plays, 2d edit., 1973; also numerous articles; co-author: Classical Myth and Legend in Renaissance Dictionaries, 2d edit., 1973; Critical Approaches to Six Major English Works: Beowulf through Paradise Lost, 2d edit., 1973; Manual of Writings in Middle English, 1050-1500, II, 1970; editor: Recent lit. of English Renaissance, Recent lit. of Renaissance in Studies in Philology, 1948-53; Studies in Philology, 1969-74. Address: 2116 Golden Rain Rd No 8 Walnut Creek CA 94595

TALBERT, PRESTON TIDBALL, chemist, educator; b. Washington, Feb. 17, 1925; s. James Loraine and Grace Anna (Johnson) T.; B.S. cum laude, Howard U., 1950, M.S., 1952; Ph.D., Washington U., St. Louis, 1955; m. Rebecca L. Chandler, Aug. 8, 1956. Postdoctoral fellow U. Wash., Seattle, 1955-59; asst. prof. Howard U., Washington, 1959-63, asso. prof., 1963-70, prof., 1970—, asso. chmn. dept. bio-organic chemistry, 1966—. Mem. nat. needs postdoctoral fellowships panel NSF, 1978-79. Served with USAF, 1943-46. Nat. Heart Inst. fellow, 1957-59. Mem. Am. Chem. Soc., AAUP, AAAS, N.Y. Acad. Scis., Beta Kappa Chi. Democrat. Methodist. Contbr. articles to profl. jours. Home: 400 Old Stone Rd Silver Spring MD 20904 Office: Dept Chemistry Howard U Washington DC 20059

TALBOT, GERALD EDGERTON, printing compositor, state legislator; b. Bangor, Maine, Oct. 28, 1931; s. Wilmot Edgerton and Arvella L. (McIntyre) T.; grad. high sch.; m. Anita Joan Cummings, July 24, 1954; children—Renee, Rachel, Regina, Robin. Printing compositor Guy Gannett Pub. Co., Portland, Maine, 1967—; mem. Maine Ho. of Reps., 1972—; corporator Portland Savs. Bank, 1975—. Vice pres. Portland br. NAACP, 1957, pres., 1964-66, 71-72, 79, 3d v.p. New Eng. Conf., 1967-72, del. 55th Nat. Conv., Washington, 1964, co-chmn. 29th Ann. New Eng. Conf., 1967, del. 58th Nat. Conv., Boston, 1967, co-chmn. Portland br. awards banquet, 1969, del. 65th Nat. Conv., New Orleans, 1974, 66th Nat. Conv., Washington, 1975, del. New Eng. Conf., 1965-74, 66th Nat. Conv., Memphis, 1976, 67th Nat. Conv., St. Louis, 1977, life mem.; mem. Portland Adv. Com. to City Council, 1965, Gov.'s Task Force on Human Rights, 1968, Maine Com. on Aging, 1969; v.p. New Sch. Workshop, 1969; mem. U.S. Commn. on Civil Rights, 1972—, Greater Portland Federated Labor Council, Portland Typog. Union, Rescue, Inc., Maine Assn. Black Progress, Maine Conf. on Human Services, Maine White House Conf. Handicapped Individuals, State Interim Adv. Council Mental Health, Advocates for Developmentally Disabled, Portland Neighborhood Foster Grandparents Adv. Bd., NOW; mem. adv. bd. Ingraham Vols., Inc.; justice of peace, 1969—; mem. nat. hon. adv. com. Voices in Vital Am.; del. 58th Ann. New Eng. Conf. Typog. Unions, Manchester, N.H., 1970; chmn. press and publicity 1st and 2d Ann. Miss Black Teen-Age Pageant, 1971-73; adv. council Maine Dept. Manpower Affairs; mem. City Mgrs. Policy Adv. Com.; mem. Democratic City Com., 1970—; candidate Portland City Council, 1971; del. Maine Dem. State Conv., Waterville, 1972, alt. del., Bangor, 1974; mem. Maine Ho. of Reps., 1974, 76; area legis. chmn. Maine, N.H., Vt., New Eng. Conf., NAACP, 1974—; bd. dirs. Maine chpt. Epilepsy Found. Am., 1975—. Served with AUS, 1953-56. Recipient Golden Pin award Portland br. NAACP, 1967, Portland br. award, 1969, certificate of permanent membership New Eng. Conf., 1969, Hall of Fame certificate Laurel, Miss., 1970, Outstanding Service to Community and State plaque Bangor br., 1973; certificate of appreciation Nat. Multiple Sclerosis Soc., Portland, 1974, certificate of recognition and appreciation Voice in Vital Am., 1974; named Citizen of Week, Radio Sta. WLOB, 1964. Home: 132 Glenwood Ave Portland ME 04103 Office: 390 Congress St Portland ME 04103. *Don't miss any opportunity to let the world see the smile on your face or the peace and love in your heart.*

TALBOT, JAMES LAWRENCE, geologist; b. Surrey, Eng., Sept. 6, 1932; s. Herbert Lawrence and Lillian (Lee) T.; B.A., U. Cambridge (Eng.), 1954; M.A., U. Calif. at Berkeley, 1957; Ph.D., U. Adelaide (Australia), 1963; m. Margot Hardenbergh, Nov. 15, 1957; children—Katrin, Gretchen, Susan. Came to U.S., 1970. Lectr., U. Adelaide, 1958-63, sr. lectr., 1963-67; asso. prof. Lakehead U., Thunder Bay, Ont., Can., 1967-70; prof., chmn. dept. geology U. Mont., 1970-75, acting acad. v.p., 1975-76; v.p. acad. affairs, provost Western Wash. U., Bellingham, 1976—; cons. geologist. Alexander von Humboldt fellow, Bonn, W.Ger., 1963-64. Mem. geol. socs. Am., Australia. Editor: Northwest Geology, 1972-75; author: (with R.W. Nesbitt) Geological Excursions in the Fleurieu Peninsula; contbr. articles to profl. jours. Home: 135 S Garden Bellingham WA 98225 Office: Western Wash U Bellingham WA 98225

TALBOT, JOHN MAYO, physician, former air force med. officer; b. Sebastopol, Calif., May 8, 1913; s. John and Florence (Mayo) T.; A.B., U. Oreg., 1935, M.D., 1938; postgrad. U. Calif. at Berkeley, 1947-48; m. Margaret Jane Illingworth, Nov. 3, 1946; children—John Michael, Mark Stuart, Neil Charles. Intern, U.S. Marine Hosp., New Orleans, 1938-39; commd. 1st lt. M.C., U.S. Army, 1939, advanced through grades to brig. gen. M.C., USAF, 1964; assigned 8th Air Force, 1943-45, USAF Sch. Aviation Medicine, 1946-51, Air Research and Devel. Command, 1951-56; comdr. 7112 Central Med. Group, Germany, 1956-59; staff asst. bioastronautics and med. scis. Office Sec. Def., 1959-62; spl. asst. to surgeon gen. for med. research, 1963-67; asst. surgeon gen. for med. staffing and edn., 1967-69; command surgeon Hdqrs. Strategic Air Command, Offutt AFB, Neb., 1969-71, Hdqrs. USAFE, Germany, 1971-73; ret., 1973; cons. in space medicine NASA, 1973-76; cons. EPA, 1974-75; sr. med. cons. Life Scis. Research Office, Fedn. Am. Socs. Exptl. Biology, Bethesda, Md., 1974—. Decorated Soldier's medal, Air medal, Bronze Star, Legion of Merit with 2 oak leaf clusters. Fellow Aerospace Med. Assn., Am. Coll. Preventive Medicine; mem. Air Force Assn., Internat. Acad. Astronautics, Pan Am. Med. Assn. Home: 2509 Carrollton Rd Annapolis MD 21403

TALBOT, MATTHEW JOSEPH, oil co. exec.; b. Mt. Vernon, N.Y., Sept. 4, 1937; s. Matthew J. and Margaret A. (Green) T.; B.B.A., Iona Coll., 1963; m. Maureen Donlan, June 3, 1958; children—Maureen, Kathleen, Matthew. Accountant, S.D. Leidesdorf & Co., N.Y.C., 1961-67; sr. analyst Gen. Foods Corp., White Plains, N.Y., 1967-68; with Tosco (formerly Oil Shale Corp.), Los Angeles, 1968—, comptroller, 1970—, v.p., 1971-76, sr. v.p., 1976-78, exec. v.p., 1978—, also dir. Trustee Craft and Folk Art Mus. Los Angeles County, 1976. C.P.A., N.Y. Mem. Am. Inst. C.P.A.'s, N.Y. State Soc. C.P.A.'s, Nat. Assn. Accountants. Home: 19241 Bernetta Pl Tarzana CA 91356 Office: 10100 Santa Monica Blvd Los Angeles CA 90067

TALBOT, PHILLIPS, orgn. exec.; b. Pitts., June 7, 1915; s. Kenneth Hammet and Gertrude (Phillips) T.; B.A., B.S. in Journalism, U. Ill., 1936; student London Sch. Oriental Studies, 1938-39, Aligarh Muslim U., India, 1939-40; Ph.D., U. Chgo., 1954; LL.D. (hon.), Mills Coll., 1963; m. Mildred Aleen Fisher, Aug. 18, 1943; children—Susan Talbot Jacox, Nancy, Bruce Kenneth. Reporter, Chgo. Daily News, 1936-38, corr., India and Pakistan, 1946-48, 49-50; asso. Inst. Current World Affairs, Eng. and India, 1938-41, part-time, 1946-51; instr. U. Chgo., 1948-50, Columbia, 1951, U. Hawaii, 1953; exec. dir. Am. Univs. Field Staff, 1951-61; asst. sec. state Near Eastern and S. Asian affairs, 1961-65; U.S. ambassador to Greece, 1965-69; pres. Asia Soc., N.Y.C., 1970—; mem. Indo-U.S. Subcommn. on Edn. and Culture. Phi Beta Kappa vis. scholar, 1973-74. Trustee Aspen Inst. Humanistic Studies, China Med. Bd., Inst. Current World Affairs, JDR 3d Fund, Middle East Inst., Served as 2d lt. cav. O.R.C., 1936; as 1st lt. 33d div. Ill. N.G., 1937-38; from lt. (j.g.) to lt. comdr. USNR, 1941-46. Mem. Assn. Asian Studies, Council Fgn. Relations, Pilgrims of U.S., Royal Soc. for Asian Affairs. Presbyterian (elder). Clubs: Century Assn. (N.Y.C.); Cosmos (Washington). Author: (with S.L. Poplai) India and America, 1958. Editor: South Asia in the World Today, 1950. Address: 112 E 64th St New York NY 10021

TALBOT, RICHARD BURRITT, coll. dean; b. Waterville, Kans., Jan. 4, 1933; s. Roy B. and Aleta (Stone) T.; B.S., Kans. State U., 1954, D.V.M., 1958; Ph.D., Iowa State U., 1963; m. Mary Jane Hensley, May 24, 1953; children—Richard Lee, Andrea Jean. From instr. to asso. prof. dept. physiology and pharmacology Coll. Vet. Medicine, Iowa State U., Ames, 1958-65; prof., chmn. dept. physiology and pharmacology U. Ga. Coll. Vet. Medicine, Athens, 1965-68, dean coll., 1968-75; prof., dean vet. medicine Va. Poly. Inst. and State U., Blacksburg, 1975—. Cons. NIH. Dist. commr. Boy Scouts Am. Nat. Heart Inst. postdoctoral fellow, 1959. Mem. Am. Vet. Med. Assn., Assn. (council on edn. 1972—), Am. Physiol. Soc., Conf. Research Workers Animal Diseases, Nat. Bd. Vet. Med. Examiners, Am. Assn. Lab. Animal Sci., Sigma Xi, Phi Zeta, Phi Kappa Phi. Presbyn. (elder). Rotarian. Home: Route 2 Box 561 Newport VA 24128

TALBOT, RICHARD JOSEPH, library adminstr.; b. Lynn, Mass., Dec. 18, 1932; s. Joseph Anthony and Mary Kathleen (Connolly) T.; A.B., Manhattan Coll., 1954; M.S. in L.S., Simmons Coll., 1961; m. Joanne Frances Hines, Sept. 2, 1961; children—Mary Frances, Jean Ann. Reference librarian N.Y. Pub. Library, N.Y.C., 1961-62; cataloger, acquisitions librarian, library systems analyst NASA, Cambridge, Mass., Dept. Air Force, Bedford, Mass., 1962-70; asso. dir. U. Mass. Library, Amherst, 1970-73, dir. libraries, 1973—. Mem. Amherst Democratic Town Com., 1973—. Served to 1st lt. USAF, 1954-57. Mem. A.L.A. Roman Catholic. Home: 40 High Point Dr Amherst MA 01002

TALBOT, TIMOTHY RALPH, physician, cancer center adminstr., educator; b. Berkeley, Calif., July 14, 1916; s. Timothy R. and Caroline E. (Lowe) T.; A.B., U. Pa., 1937, M.D., 1941; m. Mary Robinson, Oct. 16, 1943; children—Timothy R., Mary Talbot Havens, William R., Lucy L., David C. Nat. Cancer Inst. fellow Chester Beatty Research Inst., London, 1954-66; dir. Inst. Cancer Research, Phila., 1957-76; asso. prof. medicine U. Pa., Phila., 1966—; pres. Fox Chase Cancer Center, Phila., 1974—; mem. Pa. Gov.'s Sci. Adv. Com., 1966-75, Pa. Gov.'s Task Force Cancer Control, 1974—; chmn. cancer control grant rev. com. Nat. Cancer Inst., 1974-78. Mem. Assn. Am. Cancer Insts. (pres. 1968, dir. 1972-76, 78—), Am. Assn. Cancer Research. Office: 7701 Burholme Ave Philadelphia PA 19111

TALBOT, WILLIAM HOWE MCELWAIN, sculptor; b. Boston, Jan. 10, 1918; s. John Cleveland and Dorothy Howe (McElwain) T.; student Pa. Acad. Fine Arts, Phila., 1936-41, Academie des Beaux Arts, Paris, France, 1945-46; m. Joan Sangree, Aug. 1, 1946; children—Constance, Augusta, John, Peter. Exhibited in one man shows at Carroll-Knight Gallery, St. Louis, 1948, Andrew-Morris Gallery, N.Y.C., 1963, Martin Schweig Gallery, St. Louis, 1965, 69, Frank Rehn Gallery, N.Y.C., 1968, 71, Arts Club, Chgo., 1972; exhibited in group shows at Whitney Mus. Am. Art, 1950, 61, 63, Pa. Acad. Fine Arts Ann., 1942, 49, Phila. Mus. Internat., 1949, DeCordova & Dana, Lincoln, Mass., 1949, New York World Fair, 1964; commns. include Meml. Sculpture, Rehab. Center, Barnes Hosp., Washington U., St. Louis, 1964, Fountain, Nat. Hdqrs., Nat. Council State Garden Clubs of Am., St. Louis, 1959, Fountain, Fitchburg (Mass.) Youth Library, 1950; artist-in-residence U. Mich., Ann Arbor, 1949; vis. lectr. Earlham Coll., Ind., 1964, St. Lawrence U., Canton, N.Y., 1965; pres. Sculptors Guild, 1965-68, v.p. publs., 1968-72; founder, trustee Washington (Conn.) Art Assn., 1952-58. Served with AUS, 1941-46. Recipient Prix de Rome, Am. Acad. in Rome, 1941, Sculpture award St. Louis Artists Guild, 1950, Penrose prize for sculpture Conn. Acad. Fine Arts, 1953, Am. Acad. and Nat. Inst. Arts and Letters award, 1975. Cresson traveling fellow Pa. Acad. Fine Arts, 1941. Mem. Sculptors Guild, Century Assn. Home: Bell Hill Washington CT 06793 Office: Frank Rehn Gallery 14 E 60 St New York NY 10022

TALBOTT, FRANCIS LEO, physicist, educator; b. Lancaster, Ohio, July 17, 1903; s. Ernest Edgar and Mary A. (Light) T.; A.B., St. John's U., Toledo, 1924; M.A., Cath. U., 1926, Ph.D., 1928; m. Gertrude Louise Ferguson, June 4, 1963. Mem. faculty Catholic U., 1926—, prof., 1953-69, reactor supr., summers 1947-69, chmn. physics, 1947-69., prof. emeritus, 1969—; prof., research coordinator, chmn. physics dept. Allentown Coll. of St. Francis de Sales, Center Valley, Pa., 1970—. Physicist proximity fuze project Johns Hopkins, 1943-46; participant Oak Ridge Nat. Lab., 1947—; mem. council Oak Ridge Inst. Nuclear Studies, 1964—; cons. Naval Research Lab., 1954-56. Recipient De Sales medal Allentown Coll., 1973; award for scholarship and research Alumni Cath. U., 1973. Mem. Am. Phys. Soc., Optical Soc. (recipient Bene Merenti medal, 1960). Am. Assn. U. Profs., Sigma Xi. Research on nuclear physics. Home: Rural Delivery 4 Bethlehem PA 18015 Office: Allentown Coll of St Francis de Sales Center Valley PA 18034

TALBOTT, FRANK, III, lawyer; b. Danville, Va., Mar. 26, 1929; s. Frank and Margaret (Jordan) T.; B.A., U. Va., 1951, LL.B., 1953; m. Mary Beverley Chewning, July 11, 1952; children—Beverley, Frank IV. Admitted to Va. bar, 1952; gen. practice law, Danville, 1956-66; with Dan River Inc., 1966-76, v.p., gen. counsel, 1968-76; partner firm Clement, Wheatley, Winston, Talbott & Majors, Danville, 1976-78; individual practice law, Danville, 1979—; dir. First & Mchts. Nat. Bank, Danville region. Vice chmn. Danville Sch. Bd., 1964-70. Sec. Danville Democratic Com., 1962-63. Trustee Va. Student Aid Found., 1963-68; bd. dirs. United Fund Danville, 1959-63, Meml. Hosp., Danville, 1977—. Served with AUS, 1953-56. Decorated Commendation medal. Mem. Am., Va. (v.p. 1965-66, exec. com. 1967-70), Danville (pres. 1965-66) bar assns., Am. Judicature Soc., Newcomen Soc., U. Va. Alumni Assn. (bd. mgrs.), Delta Psi, Phi Alpha Delta. Methodist. Clubs: Golf, German (Danville). Home: 420 Maple Ln Danville VA 24541 Office: 621 Masonic Bldg Danville VA 24541

TALBOTT, JOHN HAROLD, phsyician, editor; b. Grinnell, Iowa, July 10, 1902; s. Arthur D. and Caroline (Flook) T.; A.B., Grinnell Coll., 1924; D.Sc., 1946; M.D., Harvard, 1929; m. Mildred Cherry, Sept. 3, 1932; children—John A., Cherry (Mrs. John C. Towbridge). Intern, Presbyn Hosp., N.Y.C., 1929-31; faculty Harvard Med. Sch., 1931-46; med. staff Mass. Gen. Hosp., Boston, 1931-46; prof. medicine U. Buffalo, 1946-59; physician-in-chief Buffalo Gen. Hosp., 1946-59; dir. div. sci. publs. AMA, 1959-69, editor Jour. AMA, 1959-69, editor emeritus, 1970-72; clin. prof. medicine U. Miami (Fla.), 1971—. Dir. U.S., Army Frostbite Commn. to Korea, 1951; chmn. Josiah Macy, Jr. Conf. on Cold Injury, 1952-58; mem. sci. adv. panel Dept. Army, 1958-60; mem. sci. com. Nat. Arthritis and Rheumatism Found.; dir. Niagara Share Investment Co., 1956-70. Served to col. AUS, 1941-46; comdg. officer Climatic Research Lab. Decorated Legion of Merit. Mem. A.C.P. (gov. Western N.Y. 1955-59), AMA, Assn. Am. Physicians, Am. Soc. Clin. Investigation. Author: Gout, 3d edit., 1967; (with R. Ferrandis) Collagen Diseases, 1956; (with L.M. Lockie) Progress in Arthritis, 1958; A Biographical History of Medicine, 1970; Collagen-Vascular Diseases, 1974; (with T.F. Yü) Gout and Uric Acid Metabolism, 1976; Clinical Rheumatology, 1978; editor: Medicine, 1947-59, Seminars in Arthritis and Rheumatism, 1971—, Surg. Forum of ACS, 1971; editorial bd. M.D., Magazine, 1973—, Merck Manual, 1971—. Home: 177 Ocean Lane Dr Key Biscayne Miami FL 33149

TALBOTT, MALCOLM DAILY, lawyer, educator; b. London, Ohio, Mar. 25, 1920; s. William Gaston and Mabel (Daily) T.; A.B., Ohio Wesleyan U., 1942; J.D., Western Res. U., 1948; LL.D. (hon.), Bloomfield Coll., 1970. Admitted to Ohio bar, 1948; asst. prof. Rutgers U. Law Sch., Newark, N.J., 1948-50, prof., 1960—, asst. to dean, 1950-59, asst. dean, 1960-63, asso. dean, 1963-65, v.p. Newark Coll., 1965-72, acting dean Newark Coll. Arts and Scis., 1968-69, v.p. univ. relations Rutgers U., 1972-74, pres. Univ. Found., 1975—; vis. prof. U. Ark., U. So. Calif., Northwestern U., Ohio State U., U. N.C., U. Tokyo, U. Sofa, La. State U. Sch. Banking of South, 1950-62. Cons., Carnegie Found. Evaluation, Nat. Def. Edn. Act, Fgn. Lang. Program. Co-chmn. Com. of Concern, 1967-69; mem. Gov.'s Commn. on Capital Punishment, 1961-62; adviser N.Y. Law Revision Commn., 1950-52; adviser, reporter N.J. Commn. Law Revision, 1948-50. Chmn. bd. Law Sch. Admission Test Council, Greater Newark Urban Coalition, Council Higher Edn. in Newark; pres. N.J. Commn. Against Discrimination in Housing; pres. emeritus, trustee Newark Boys Chorus Sch., St. Timothys Home for Boys; v.p., trustee Garden State Ballet Found.; v.p. Robert Treat council Boy Scouts Am., World Federalists of N.J., N.J. chpt. UN Assn., Youth Consultative Service; trustee Newark Mus., N.J. Symphony, Symphony Hall, Inc., United Community Services of Middlesex County, United Way of Essex County and West Hudson County, Opera Theatre of N.J., Fund for N.J., Episcopal Del. Properties, Gen. Theol. Sem., Center for Applied Linguistics, Newark Community Center of Arts; mem. adv. bd. ASPIRA; mem. vis. com. Case Western Res. U., bd. govs. Sch. of Law; bd. overseers Rutgers Univ. Found. Served to capt. USAAF, 1942-46. Recipient Silver Beaver award Boy Scouts Am., 1973; Justice Brandeis Humanitarian award, 1972; Outstanding Citizen of Newark award Prudential Ins. Co., 1966; Red Shield award Salvation Army, 1970. Hon. citizen, P.R., Guyana. Mem. Religious Heritage of Am., Inc. (Outstanding Service award), Am. Law Inst., Am., Ohio bar assns., N.A.A.C.P., N.J. Hist. Soc., Rutgers Law Alumni Assn. (Meritorious Service medal 1958), Am. Legion, Southeastern Assn. (law librarian), Phi Gamma Delta, Phi Delta Phi (Outstanding Service award 1963), Omicron Delta Kappa, Pi Delta Epsilon, Theta Alpha Phi, Beta Gamma Sigma (hon.). Episcopalian. Rotarian. Clubs: Essex, Downtown (Newark); Nassau (Princeton); Rutgers U. Alumni Faculty. Author: (with Toepfer, Shane and Winterbottom) Law School Admission Test Handbook, 1965. Editor: Ann. Survey of New Jersey Law, 1950-51; editor-in-chief Western Res. Law Rev., 1947-48. Contbr. articles profl. jours. Home: 375 Mt Prospect Ave Newark NJ 07104 Office: Rutgers U Found 191 College Ave New Brunswick NJ 08903

TALBOTT, NELSON STROBRIDGE, fin. and mgmt. cons.; b. Dayton, Ohio, Apr. 1, 1920; s. Nelson Strobridge and Elizabeth (Green) T.; B.S., Yale U., 1943; m. Helen J. Large, Oct. 30, 1946;

children—Nelson Strobridge, Elizabeth Page, Mary Josephine, Kirk Large. Asst. to pres. Talbott Corp., Dayton, 1946-51; dir. indsl. devel. Harris Intertype Corp., Cleve., 1951-59; pres. Prescott Ball Turben & Co. (mem. N.Y. Stock Exchange), Cleve., 1959-78; chmn. Strategic Planning Assos., 1979—. Chmn. N.E. Ohio Heart Assn., 1962; mem. Gov.'s Citizen Task Force on Environ. Protection, 1971; v.p. Ohio Conservation Found., 1976—; mem. fin. com. Cleve. Welfare Fedn.; trustee Cleve. Council on World Affairs, 1972-76, Cleve. Ballet Guild, 1964-69, Ducks Unltd., 1970-76, Cleve. Inst. Art, 1970—; trustee, mem. investment com. World Wildlife Fund, 1973—; trustee Inst. Environ. Edn., 1970-77, Cleve. Natural Sci. Mus.; bd. dirs. U.S. Assn. for Club of Rome, 1976—, Cleve. Growth Assn.; mem. fin. com. Case Western Res. U., 1975—. Served to lt. (s.g.) USNR, 1943-46. Mem. Delta Psi. Republican. Episcopalian (vestryman). Clubs: Union; Tavern; River (N.Y.); Chagrin Valley Hunt. Home: Shaker Blvd Chagrin Falls OH 44022

TALBOTT, ORWIN CLARK, hist. preservationist, former army officer; b. San Jose, Calif., June 18, 1918; s. Earnest Orwin and Violet (Smith) T.; student U. Calif. at Berkeley, 1936-39; grad. U.S. Army Infantry Sch., 1943, 49, Command and Gen. Staff Coll., 1954, Nat. War Coll., 1959; m. Nell Coughran, Sept. 6, 1942; children—Marinel (Mrs. Ronendra K. Mukherjee), Stephen Clark. Commd. 2d lt. U.S. Army, 1941, advanced through grades to lt. gen., 1973; exec. officer to army chief staff, chmn. Joint Chiefs Staff, supreme allied comdr., Europe, 1959-63; comdr. 2d Brigade, 24th Div., 1963-64; G-3 Central Army Group NATO, 1964-66; asst. div. comdr. 5th Mechanized Div., 1966-67; dep. chief staff individual tng. CONARC, 1967-68; asst. div. comdr. 1st Inf. Div., 1968, comdr., 1968-69; comdt. U.S. Army Inf. Sch., Ft. Benning, Ga., 1969-73; dep. comdg. gen. Tng. and Doctrine Command, Ft. Monroe, Va., 1973-75; dir. Md. Hist. Trust, 1975—. Decorated D.S.M. with 2 oak leaf clusters, Silver Star with 2 oak leaf clusters, D.F.C. with 3 oak leaf clusters, Bronze Star with oak leaf cluster; Air medal with 5 silver and 4 bronze oak leaf clusters, Purple Heart with 2 oak leaf clusters. Home: 234 Anchorage Dr Annapolis MD 21401 Office: John Shaw House 21 State Circle Annapolis MD 21401

TALBOTT, STROBE, journalist; b. Dayton, Ohio, Apr. 25, 1946; s. Nelson S. and Helen Josephine (Large) T.; B.A., Yale U., 1968, M.A. (hon.), 1976; B.Litt. (Rhodes scholar), Oxford (Eng.) U., 1971; m. Brooke Lloyd Shearer, Nov. 14, 1971; 1 son, Devin Lloyd. Eastern Europe corr. Time Mag., 1971-73, State Dept. corr., Washington, 1973-75, White House corr., 1975-77, diplomatic corr., Washington, 1977—; fellow Yale Corp., 1976—. Mem. Council Fgn. Relations, Am. Assn. Rhodes Scholars (bd. direction). Translator, editor: Khrushchev Remembers, 1970; Khrushchev Remembers: The Last Testament, 1974; author: Endgame: The Inside Story of SALT II, 1979. Home: 2842 28th St NW Washington DC 20008 Office: Time Mag 888 16th St NW Washington DC 20006

TALESE, GAY, writer; b. Ocean City, N.J., Feb. 7, 1932; s. Joseph Francis and Catherine (DePaulo) T.; B.A. in Journalism, U. Ala., 1953; m. Nan Ahearn, June 10, 1959; children—Pamela, Catherine. Staff writer N.Y. Times, N.Y.C., 1953-65; writer Esquire mag., N.Y.C., 1960. Served to 1st lt. AUS, 1954-56. Mem. P.E.N., Phi Sigma Kappa. Author: New York—A Serendipiter's Journey, 1961; The Bridge, 1964; The Overreachers, 1965; The Kingdom and the Power, 1969; Fame and Obscurity, 1970; Honor Thy Father, 1971; Thy Neighbor's Wife, 1980. Contbr. articles to Esquire mag., Harpers mag., others. Address: 109 E 61st St New York NY 10021

TALIAFERRO, FRANCIS TOURNIER, architect; b. Toulon, France, Jan. 20, 1922; s. Edward H. III and Marguerite (Tournier) T.; student Columbia, 1939-40, U. Ala., 1941-42; B.A., U. N.C., 1944; m. Nancy Barrett Clark, June 14, 1947; children—Christie T., Michael Clark, Jeffery Francis, Victoria. Co-founder partnership Rogers & Taliaferro, 1949; partner Rogers, Taliaferro, Kostritsky & Lamb, until 1969; chmn. bd. RTKL Assos., Inc., Balt., 1969—. Served to maj. USMCR, 1942-48. Prin. works include (with Pietro Belluschi, Charles Lamb) Ch. of the Redeemer, Balt. (award of merit A.I.A. 1958), (with Charles Lamb) Girl Scout Lodge, Annapolis, Md. (award of merit A.I.A.), Parole Elementary Sch., Annapolis (A.I.A. Travelling Exhbn.), Harundale Mall Shopping Center (award of merit Nat. Inst. Home Builders 1958), Park Sch. (certificate of merit Balt. Assn. Commerce 1960), (prin.-in-charge) Charles Plaza in Charles Center, Balt. (honor award Middle Atlantic Region A.I.A. 1969, urban design award HUD 1970), Calvert County Vocat. Tech. Tng. Center, Prince Frederick, Md. (archl. award of excellence Am. Inst. Steel Constrn. 1972), South County Library, Deale, Md. (award of merit A.I.A.-A.L.A. 1972), Performing Arts Center for St. Timothy Sch., Balt. (honor award A.I.A. 1973), (prin.-in-charge) IBM facility, Manassas, Va., Paramus Park Shopping Center (N.J.) (archl. award of excellence Am. Inst. Steel Constrn.). Home: Thanksgiving Farm Harwood MD 20776 Office: Village Sq Crosskeys Baltimore MD 21210

TALKINGTON, PERRY CLEMENT, psychiatrist; b. Waco, Tex., Aug. 28, 1909; s. Thomas Walton and Dora Geneva (Clement) T.; student Howard Coll., 1927; student Baylor U., 1927-29, M.D., 1934; m. Ruth Elizabeth Torian, June 25, 1934 (dec.); children—Paul, Robert, Ruth Lynn Talkington Rogers; m. 2d, Grace Louise DeTar, Nov. 11, 1972. Intern, Hamot Hosp., Erie, Pa., 1934-35; resident Taunton (Mass.) State Hosp., 1935-37, Phila. Ortho. Hosp. and Infirmary for Nervous Diseases, 1937-38, Timberlawn Sanatarium, Dallas, 1938-39; practice psychiatry, 1938—; psychiatrist Timberlawn Psychiat. Hosp., 1938-41, 46—, pres., 1949-65, psychiatrist-in-chief, 1949-68, chmn. bd., 1949-68, sr. cons. in psychiatry, 1968—; attending staff Baylor Hosp., Dallas, 1938—, chief psychiatrist, 1955-69; faculty Baylor Med. Sch., Dallas, 1938-42; clin. faculty S.W. Med. Sch., 1942-69; clin. prof. psychiatry S.W. Med. Sch., U. Tex., 1969—; mem. adv. commn. Tex. Dept. Pub. Health, 1962-65, Gov.'s Commn. for Study Sociopathic Personality Problems, 1964. Served with AUS, 1941-46. Decorated Bronze Star. Diplomate Am. Bd. Psychiatrists. Fellow Am. Psychiat. Assn. (life, pres. 1972-73), Am. Coll. Psychiatrists (founding), Royal Coll. Psychiatrists (London) (founding). Editorial bd. History of Psychiatry in World War II; co-editor: Evolving Concepts in Psychiatry, 1969. Home: 5807 Redwood Ln Dallas TX 75209 4645 Samuell Blvd Dallas TX 75228

TALKINGTON, ROBERT VAN, state senator; b. near Patrick, Tex., Aug. 23, 1929; s. William Henry and Nannie J. (Patrick) T.; A.A., Tyler Jr. Coll., 1949; B.S., U. Kans., 1951, LL.B., 1954, J.D., 1971; m. Donna Jill Schmaus, Mar. 25, 1951; children—Jill Talkington McCaskill, Jacki, James, Thomas, Lisa. Admitted to Kans. bar, 1954; county atty. Allen County (Kans.), 1957-63; city atty., Moran, Kans., 1968—; mem. Kans. Ho. of Reps. from 10th Dist., 1969-73; mem. Kans. Senate from 12th Dist., 1973—, v.p., 1977—. Chmn. Republican Party, Allen County, 1964-68, state treas., 1964-66; trustee Iola Pub. Library, 1962-70; mem. advisory bd. Greater U. Fund, U. Kans., 1967-72. Served with CIC, AUS, 1954-56. Mem. Sigma Alpha Epsilon, Phi Delta Phi. Clubs: Masons, Shriners, Elks. Home: 20 W Buchanan St Iola KS 66749 Office: 20 N Washington St Iola KS 66749

TALKOV, LEO, prosthodontist; b. Boston, May 31, 1917; s. Barney and Bessie (Brown) T.; B.A., Tufts U., 1939; D.M.D., Harvard, 1943; m. Celia Rubin, June 8, 1972; children by previous marriage—Roger Charles, Nancy Jane. Intern, Pilgrim State Hosp., L.I., N.Y., 1943-44; head restorative dentistry Beth Israel Hosp., Boston, 1960—; instr. Tufts Dental Sch., Boston, 1950-60; prof., chmn. dept. postdoctoral fixed prosthesis Sch. Grad. Dentistry, Boston U., 1958—. Cons., USPHS, Brighton, Mass., 1955-65. Recipient citation Trustees Boston U. and Faculty Sch. Grad. Dentistry, 1974. Fellow Am. Coll. Dentists, Internat. Coll. Dentists; mem. ADA, Mass., Greater Boston, Met. Dist. dental socs., Am. Acad. Dental Sci., Harvard Odontological Soc., N.E. Prosthodontic Soc., Mass. Soc. Prosthodontists, Alpha Omega. Contbr. articles to profl. jours. Home: 21 Seaborn Pl Lexington MA 02173 Office: 1134 Beacon St Brookline MA 02146

TALLARICO, THOMAS MICHAEL, newspaper exec.; b. Chgo., July 1, 1944; s. Thomas Frank and Edith M. T.; B.S., Miami U., Oxford, Ohio, 1966; m. Mary J. Carsman, Feb. 7, 1967; children—John, Polly. Mem. staff Arthur Anderson & Co., Chgo., 1966-70, mgr., 1971-75; controller newspaper div. Field Enterprises, Chgo., 1975, v.p. fin., 1975-78; v.p. fin., asst. gen. mgr. Chgo. Sun-Times, 1978—; dir. Catching Fluidpower, Inc. C.P.A., Ill. Mem. Fin. Execs. Inst., Inst. Newspaper Controllers and Fin. Officers, Am. Mgmt. Assn., Am. Inst. C.P.A.'s, Ill. Soc. C.P.A.'s. Presbyterian. Clubs: Econ., Univ. (Chgo.). Home: 1110 Western Ave Northbrook IL 60062 Office: 401 N Wabash St Chicago IL 60611

TALLCHIEF, MARIA, ballerina; b. Fairfax, Okla., Jan. 24, 1925; d. Alexander Joseph and Ruth Mary (Porter) T.; student pub. schs., Calif.; A.F.D. (hon.), Lake Forest Coll. (Ill.), Colby Coll., Maine, 1968, Ripon Coll., 1973, Boston Coll.; m. Henry Paschen, Jr., June 3, 1957; 1 dau, Elise. Joined Ballet Russe de Monte Carlo, 1942; prima ballerina N.Y.C. Ballet, 1947-60; guest star Paris Opera, 1947; prima ballerina Am. Ballet Theater, 1960; with N.Y.C. Ballet Co. until 1965; now artistic dir. Lyric Opera Ballet Chgo. Recipient Achievement award Women's Nat. Press Club, 1953; Dance mag. award, 1960; Capezio award, 1965; named Hon. Princess-Osage Indian Tribe, 1953; Distinguished Service award U. Okla., 1972; Jane Addams Humanitarian award Rockford Coll., 1973; award Dance Educators Am., 1956. Mem. Nat. Soc. Arts and Letters. Office: care Lyric Opera 20 N Wacker Dr Chicago IL 60606

TALLEUR, JOHN JOSEPH, printmaker; b. Chgo., May 29, 1925; s. Leo Joseph and Dorothy (Conn) T.; student (Colbaugh scholar, Vandergrift scholar), Sch. Chgo. Art Inst., 1943-47, B.F.A., U. Chgo., 1947; M.F.A., State U. Iowa, 1951; m. Linda Samson, Apr. 19, 1975; 1 dau., Ann Beatrix. Instr., Carleton Coll., 1947-49, St. Paul Gallery and Sch. Art, 1948-49; research asst. State U. Iowa, 1951-52; asst. prof. art U. Kans., 1953, asso. prof., to 1967, prof., 1967—; one-man shows: Walker Art Center, Mpls., Esquire Gallery, Chgo. (Prize award), Mulvane Art Center, Topeka, Little Gallery, Kansas City, Mo., Unitarian Gallery, Kansas City, Mo., Sheldon Mus., U. Nebr., U. Colo., Boulder, Mus. Art U. Kans.; group shows include: Seligmann Gallery, N.Y.C. (Prize award), U. Chgo. (Exhbn. prize), Magnificent Mile Exhbt., Chgo. (award), Foundation des Etats-Unis, Paris, Museo de Art Moderno, Barcelona, Spain, Mus. Modern Art, France, 1955, Tate Gallery, London; represented in permanent collections, including: Smithsonian Inst., Washington, Brit. Mus., London, Art Inst. Chgo., Met. Mus. Art, N.Y.C., Mus. Modern Art, N.Y.C., Whitney Mus. Am. Art, N.Y.C., Phila. Mus. Art; Fulbright fellow, France, 1952-53; owner, operator Holiseventh Press, Lawrence, Kans., 1971—. Rockefeller grantee, 1955. Author and artist: Seven Odd Rhymes, 1978. Home: 242 Concord Rd Lawrence KS 66044 Office: Dept Art U Kans Lawrence KS 66045

TALLEY, CAROL LEE, editor; b. Bklyn., Sept. 10, 1937; d. George Joseph and Viola (Kovash) Talley; student U. Ky., 1955-57, Ohio U., 1957-58; children—Sherry, Jill, Scott. Reporter, Easton (Pa.) Daily Express, 1958-60; reporter N.J. Herald, 1962-64, edn. editor, 1964-66; reporter Daily Advance, Dover, N.J., 1966-68, polit. editor, investigative reporter, 1969—. Mem. A.P. Task Force N.J., 1970. Bd. dirs. Dover Day Care Center. Recipient pub. service awards Nat. Headliners, 1971, Sigma Delta Chi, 1971; George Polk Meml. award for local reporting, 1974. Mem. Nat., N.J. press woman's assns., Sigma Delta Chi. Home: 3 Trenton Pl Newton NJ 07860 Office: 87 E Blackwell St Dover NJ 07801

TALLEY, CHARLES RICHMOND, comml. banking exec.; b. Richmond, Va., Dec. 23, 1925; s. Charles Edward and Marie (Throckmorton) T.; B.A. in Econs., U. Richmond, 1949; postgrad. Sch. Banking Rutgers U., 1959-61, Sch. Fin. Pub. Relations, Northwestern U., 1954-55; grad. exec. program U. Va., 1974; m. Anne Marie Smith, June 4, 1948; children—Laurie Anne, Charles Richmond. With 1st & Mchts. Nat. Bank, Richmond, 1955-75, asst. v.p., 1959-63, v.p., 1963-69, sr. v.p., 1969-73, exec. v.p., 1973-80; v.p., dir. Capital Printing Co., Richmond, 1962—; dir. Security Atlantic Life Ins. Co., Richmond; v.p., dir. Security Atlantic Ins. Co., Richmond. Pres. Richmond Jr. C. of C., 1960-61; pres. Bapt. Extension Bd. Va., 1973-75. Treas. Richmond chpt. The Nat. Found., 1956—; bd. dirs. Richmond Symphony Orch., Richmond Better Bus. Bur. Served with USNR, 1944-46. Mem. Richmond Met. C. of C. (dir. 1979—). Home: 4301 Stratford Rd Richmond VA 23225 Office: 12th and Main Sts Richmond VA 23217

TALLEY, TRUMAN MACDONALD, publisher; b. N.Y.C., Feb. 3, 1925; s. Truman Hughes and Helen Nicholson Macdonald T.; student Buckley Sch., Deerfield Acad., Sorbonne, 1945-46; grad. cum laude, Princeton U., 1949; m. Madelon DeVoe, Oct. 17, 1953; children—Melanie, Macdonald, Marina. Asso. editor New Am. Library of World Lit., N.Y.C., 1949-56, editorial v.p., 1956-64; pres., editorial dir. Weybright & Talley, N.Y.C., 1966-78; pub. Truman Talley Books with Times Books, 1979—. Served with AUS, 1943-46; ETO. Decorated Purple Heart, Combat Inf. badge. Mem. P.E.N. (chmn. admissions com. 1961-63), Am. Book Pubs. Council (freedom to read com. 1964). Clubs: Racquet and Tennis, Anglers. Grad. bd. Princeton Tiger, 1950—. Home: 876 Park Ave New York NY 10021 Office: Times Books 3 Park Ave New York NY 10016

TALLEY, WARREN DENNIS RICK, writer; b. Pinckneyville, Ill., Aug. 12, 1934; s. Virgil and Hannah (Maxwell) T.; B.S. in Journalism, So. Ill. U., 1958; m. Frances Jane Herr, Aug. 9, 1958; children—Wendy Warren, Scott Ryan, Jennifer Jane. Sports writer Decatur (Ill.) Herald, 1958; sports editor Menlo Park (Calif.) Recorder, 1958-59; reporter UPI, San Francisco, 1959-60; sports editor Rockford (Ill.) Morning Star, also Rockford Star & Register Republic, 1960-69; sports editor, columnist Chgo. Today, 1969-74; daily columnist Chgo. Tribune; TV host, interviewer, WLS-TV, Chgo.; commentator WLS Radio, Chgo. Served with AUS, 1953-55; Korea. Recipient Outstanding Journalism Alumni award So. Ill. U., 1967; Bronze medal Olympic Journalism Assn., 1970. Mem. Football Writers Assn., Baseball Writers Assn., Nat. Sportswriters Assn., Pro Football Writers Assn. Contbr. articles to sports mags. Home: 494 Wiltshire Ln Crystal Lake IL 60014 Office: 441 N Michigan Ave Chicago IL 60611

TALLEY-MORRIS, NEVA BENNETT, lawyer; b. Judsonia, Ark., Aug. 12, 1909; d. John W. and Erma (Rhew) Bennett; B.A. magna cum laude, Ouachita Coll., 1930; M.Ed., U. Tex., 1938, postgrad., 1939-41; m. Cecil C. Talley, Jan. 1, 1946 (dec. Oct. 1948); m. 2d, Joseph H. Morris, Mar. 22, 1952 (dec. Dec. 1974). Tchr. high sch., prin., White County, Ark., 1930-42; student asst. U. Tex., summers 1937-41; ordnance insp. war service appointment U.S. Army Service Forces, 1942-45; law office apprentice, pvt. tutor, North Little Rock, Ark., 1945-47; admitted to Ark. bar., 1947, U.S. Supreme Ct. bar, 1950; practiced in Little Rock; del., mem. program coordinating com. World Peace through Law Conf., Manila, 1977, mem. pre-biennial goals and planning com., Madrid, 1978, program participant Jerusalem conf., 1979; mem. Ark. Supreme Ct. com. on Client Security Fund, 1978—; mem. Ark. Lawyers Com. for Appellate Cts., 1978. Chmn., Ark. Council on Children and Youth, 1952-54. Fellow Ark. Bar Found. (bd. fellows), Internat. Biog. Assn., Am. Acad. Matrimonial Lawyers (gov. 1974-79); mem. Nat. (life, council del., pres. 1956-57, Achievement award 1962, hon. chmn. family law com. 1970-71), Ark. (Outstanding Achievement award 1971, program chmn. 1977), Little Rock (pres. 1950-51), assns. women lawyers, North Little Rock Bus. and Profl. Women's Club (pres. 1951-52), AAUW (life), Am. Bar Assn. (mem. family law council 1958—, chmn. family law sect. 1969-70, ho. of dels., com. on late reports 1972-73, com. on hearings 1973-74, standing com. on memberships 1974—, cert. of merit ann. conv. 1979), Ark. Bar Assn. (Distinguished Service to Legal Profession award 1970, chmn. family law reform com. 1960-61, ho. of dels. 1974-78, Outstanding Lawyer-Citizen award 1978), Pulaski County Bar Assn. (chmn. com. on continuing legal edn. and programs 1978), World Assn. Lawyers (founding), Am. Judicature Soc. (cert. of appreciation 1979), Nat. Conf. Lawyers and Social Workers (nat. exec. bd. 1962-66), Phi Alpha Delta (1st woman hon.). Author: Family Law Practice and Procedure Handbook, 1973; Appellate Civil Practice and Procedure, 1975; contbr. articles to profl. publs. Home: 101 N State Little Rock AR 72201 Office: 722 W Markham St Little Rock AR 72201

TALLMAN, JOHANNA ELEONORE, library adminstr.; b. Luebeck, Germany, Aug. 18, 1914; d. Friedrich Franz and Johanna Cornelia (Voget) Allerding; came to U.S., 1923, naturalized, 1930; A.A., Los Angeles Jr. Coll., 1934; A.B., U. Calif. at Berkeley, 1936, certificate in Librarianship, 1937; m. Lloyd Anthony Tallman, May 8, 1954 (dec.). Asst. librarian San Marino (Calif.) Pub. Library, 1937-38; various positions Los Angeles County Pub. Library, 1938-40, tech. reference librarian, 1940-42; asst. librarian Pacific Aero. Library, Hollywood, Calif., 1942-43, head librarian, 1943-44; librarian Engring. and Math. Scis. Library, U. Calif., Los Angeles, 1945-73, coordinator phys. scis. libraries, 1962-73, faculty Sch. Library Service, 1961-73; dir. libraries Calif. Inst. Tech., Pasadena, 1973—. Dir. re-cataloging project U.S. Naval Ordnance Test Sta. Library., China Lake, Calif., 1951; cons. to indsl., research, ednl. instns., 1950-73; mem. trade adv. com. for library assts. Los Angeles Trade Tech. Coll., 1958-73. Fulbright lectr., Brazil, 1966-67. Mem. Am. (chmn. engring. sch. libraries sect. 1949-50), Calif. (chmn. coll., univ. and research libraries sect. So. dist. 1954) library assns., Spl. Libraries Assn. (pres. So. Calif. chpt. 1965-66, chmn. sci.-tech. div. 1969-70), Librarians Assn. U. Calif. (pres. 1971). Club: Zonta. Contbr. articles to profl. jours. Home: 4731 Daleridge Rd La Canada CA 91011 Office: 1201 E California Blvd Pasadena CA 91125

TALLMAN, KENNETH LEE, air force officer; b. Omaha, Mar. 22, 1925; s. Glenn Howard and Bertie Gary (Hawes) T.; student U. Wyo., 1942-43; B.S., U.S. Mil. Acad., 1946; M.S., George Washington U., 1967; LL.D. (hon.), U. Wyo., 1978; m. Jeanne Cay Phillips, June 17, 1951; children—Carol L., Leslie J., Richard L. Commd. 2d U.S. Air Force, 1946, advanced through grades to lt. gen., 1975; comdr. 836th Air Div., 1970-71; dep. comdr. Air Force Mil. Personnel Center, Randolph AFB, Tex., 1971-72, comdr., 1972-73; dir. personnel plans and dep. chief of staff personnel, 1973-77; supt. U.S. Air Force Acad. (Colo.), 1977—. Decorated D.S.M. with oak leaf cluster, Legion of Merit with oak leaf cluster, Air Medal, others. Mem. Air Force Assn. Address: USAF Acad USAF Academy CO 80840

TALLMAN, WILLIAM CHESTER, utility exec.; b. Newton, Mass., May 25, 1920; s. Vernon F. and Phyllis E. (Thayer) T.; A.B., Williams Coll., 1941; B.S. in Elec. Engring., M.I.T., 1942, M.S., 1943; LL.D., U. N.H., 1970; m. Jean O. Gysan, Dec. 19, 1943; 1 dau., Elizabeth Ann. Research asst. M.I.T., 1942-46; with Public Service Co. N.H., 1946—, v.p., 1964-65, pres., 1965—, also dir.; dir. Amoskeag Nat. Bank and Trust Co., Manchester. Trustee Manchester YMCA, Derryfield Sch., Manchester. Mem. IEEE (sr.), Phi Beta Kappa, Eta Kappa Nu, Sigma Xi. Club: Exchange (past pres.) (Manchester). Office: 1000 Elm St Manchester NH 03105

TALLMAN, WILLIAM CHESTER, utility exec.; b. Newton, Mass., May 25, 1920; s. Vernon F. and Phyllis E. (Thayer) T.; A.B., Williams Coll., 1941; B.S. in Elec. Engring., Mass. Inst. Tech., 1942, M.S., 1943; LL.D. (hon.), U.N.H., 1970; m. Jean O. Gysan, Dec. 19, 1943; 1 dau., Elizabeth Ann. Research asst. Mass. Inst. Tech., 1942-46; with Pub. Service Co. N.H., 1946—, v.p., 1964-65, pres., 1965—, also dir.; dir. Amoskeag Nat. Bank and Trust Co., Manchester. Trustee Manchester YMCA; trustee Derryfield Sch., Manchester. Sr. mem. IEEE; mem. Phi Beta Kappa, Eta Kappa Nu, Sigma Zi. Club: Manchester Exchange (past pres.) Office: PO Box 330 Manchester NH 03105*

TALLY, JOHN BENTON, judge; b. Scottsboro, Ala., Mar. 2, 1914; s. John Benton and Irene (Blackmon) T.; m. Lena Blanche McCutchen, Nov. 24, 1937; children—Nancy (Mrs. Gary L. Loper), John B., William Walker. Admitted to Ala. bar, 1937, practiced in Scottsboro, 1937-42, 1955-68; asst. U.S. atty. No. Dist. Ala., 1942-43; investigator OPA, Birmingham, Ala., 1946-47; circuit solicitor 9th Jud. Circuit Ala., 1947-55; circuit judge 9th. Jud. Circuit, Scottsboro, 1968—. Bd. dirs. Jackson County Hosp., pres., 1961; trustee Cumberland Presbyn. Theol. Seminary, 1957-58, Bethel Coll., McKenzie, Tenn., 1975—. Served with USNR, 1943-46. Mem. Jackson County (pres. 1964-68), Ala., Am. bar assns., Am. Judicature Soc. Democrat. Presbyn. (elder 1949—, asst. stated clk. gen. assembly, 1952). Home: 401 Martin St Scottsboro AL 35768 Office: PO Box 236 Scottsboro AL 35768

TALMA, LOUISE J., composer, educator; b. Arcachon, France, Oct. 31, 1906; student Inst. Mus. Art, N.Y.C., 1922-30; pupil Isidore Philipp and Nadia Boulanger, Fontainebleau Sch. Music, 1926-39; B.Mus., N.Y. U., 1931; M.A. in Music, Columbia, 1933. Tchr. Manhattan Sch. Music, 1926-28; Fontainebleau Sch. Music, summers 1936-39, 78—; mem. faculty Hunter Coll., 1928—, prof. music, 1952-76, prof. emeritus, 1976—. Clark fellow Scripps Coll., 1975; Sanford fellow Yale, 1976; mem. Pres.'s Circle, Hunter Coll., 1977. Bd. dirs. League-ISCM. Recipient Koussevitzky Music Found. commn., 1959, Nat. Fedn. Music Clubs award, 1963, Nat. Assn. Am. Composers and Condrs. award, 1963, Sibelius medal 1963, numerous others. Guggenheim fellow, 1946, 47; sr. Fulbright research grantee, 1955-56; Nat. Endowment of the Arts grantee, 1966, 75. Fellow Am. Guild Organists; mem. League of Composers (dir. 1950—), Fontainebleau Fine Arts and Music Assn. (trustee 1950—), Edward MacDowell Assn. (corporate mem.), A.S.C.A.P., Nat. Inst. Arts and Letters, Phi Beta Kappa, Sigma Alpha Iota (hon.). Compositions include opera (with Thornton Wilder as librettist) The Alcestiad, premiered West Germany (Marjorie Peabody Waite award Nat. Inst. Arts and Letters 1960), 2 piano sonatas, 6 études for piano, 1 string quartet, 1 sonata for violin and piano, Toccata for orch., Dialogues for piano and orch., Clarinet Quintet; chamber opera Have You Heard? Do You Know?; also A Time to Remember, The Tolling Bell, Voices of Peace, All the Days of My Life, La Corona, Celebration, Diadem.

TALMADGE, HERMAN EUGENE, U.S. senator; b. McRae, Ga., Aug. 9, 1913; s. Eugene and Mattie Thurmond (Peterson) T.; LL.B., U. Ga., 1936; student Midshipman's Sch., Northwestern U., 1942; m. Leila Elizabeth Shingler, Dec. 24, 1941 (div. 1977); children—Herman Eugene, Robert Shingler (dec.). Admitted to Ga. bar, 1936, practiced with father in Atlanta, 1936-41, 1945-48; gov. of Ga., 1948-55; gen. law practice, Atlanta, 1955-57; U.S. senator from Ga., 1957—. Served with U.S. Navy, 1941-45; commd. ensign and advanced through grades to lt. comdr.; participated in invasion of Guadalcanal aboard U.S.S. Tryon; served as flag sec. to comdt. of Naval Forces at N.Z., June 1943-Apr. 1944; exec. officer U.S.S. Dauphin, and participated in various engagements with Japanese Fleet and in Battle of Okinawa; entered Tokyo Bay, V-J Day. Mem. Am. Legion, VFW, SCV, Am., Ga., Atlanta bar assns., Farm Bur., Sigma Nu, Sigma Delta Kappa. Democrat. Baptist. Clubs: Masons, Shriners, Eagles, Touchdown (Athens, Ga.). Author: You and Segregation, 1955. *

TALMADGE, MARION LYMAN, lumber, plywood, paper and chems. mfg. co. exec.; b. Athens, Ga., Feb. 19, 1923; s. Coke Gerdine and Lucy Marion (Wells) T.; B.B.A., U. Ga., 1943; m. Frances Louise Wooddall, Apr. 4, 1956; 1 son, Wooddall Wells. With Ga.-Pacific Corp., 1946—, asst. treas., 1955-59, treas., 1959—; v.p., treas. Ga.-Pacific Investment Co., 1959—; v.p. Ga.-Pacific Internat. Corp., 1966—; officer subsidiaries Ga.-Pacific Corp.; treas. Ashley, Drew & No. Ry. Co.; dir., treas. Nat. Mgmt. Inc., 1966—. Past bd. dirs. Planned Parenthood, Portland Jr. Symphony; trustee Georgia-Pacific Stock Bonus Trust, Georgia-Pacific Found.; bd. dirs., chmn. Blue Cross, Oreg., N.W. Hosp. Assn., bd. dirs. Oreg. Symphony. Mem. Financial Execs. Inst. (past nat. dir., v.p. Western area), Phi Kappa Phi, Chi Phi. Episcopalian. Clubs: Arlington, Waverley Country, Multnomah Athletic (Portland). Home: 01333 SW Mary Failing Dr Portland OR 97219 Office: 900 SW Fifth Ave Portland OR 97204

TALMADGE, ROBERT LOUIS, librarian; b. Seattle, May 22, 1920; s. Abram John and Ethel (MacKinnon) T.; A.B., U. Kans., 1941; B.S. in L.S., U. Ill., 1946, M.S. in L.S., 1951; student advanced seminar for library adminstrs. Rutgers U., 1956; m. Phyllis M. Wherry, May 8, 1942; children—Patricia (Mrs. Richard A. Gordon), Richard, Barbara (Mrs. Craig H. Werner). Cataloger, U. Ill. Library, 1946-50, bibliographer, 1950-51, adminstrv. asst., 1951-53; asso. dir. U. Kans. Library, 1953-59, acting dir., 1959-60; dir. Tulane U. Library, 1960-66; prof. library adminstrn., dir. tech. depts. U. Ill. Library, 1966-77, prof. emeritus, 1977—; dir. Forest Press, Inc., 1969-78; asst. dir. Farmington Plan survey Assn. Research Libraries, 1957-58; mem. La. Bd. Library Examiners, 1964-66. Served to lt. (s.g.), aviator USNR, 1941-45. Mem. ALA (chmn. membership com. 1960-62, council 1962-70, exec. bd. 1966-70), Kans. Library Assn. (chmn. coll. and univs. sect. 1957-58), Phi Kappa Phi, Beta Phi Mu (pres. 1949-50). Presbyterian. Contbr. articles to profl. jours. Home: 1620 W 20 St Lawrence KS 66044

TALMAGE, DAVID WILSON, physician; b. Kwangju, Korea, Sept. 15, 1919 (parents Am. citizens); s. John Van Neste and Eliza (Emerson) T.; student Maryville (Tenn.) Coll., 1937-38; B.S., Davidson (N.C.) Coll., 1941; M.D., Washington U., St. Louis, 1944; m. LaVeryn Marie Hunicke, June 23, 1944; children—Janet, Marilyn, David, Mark, Carol. Intern, Ga. Baptist Hosp., 1944-45; resident medicine Barnes Hosp., St. Louis, 1948-50, fellow medicine, 1950-51; asst. prof. pathology U. Pitts., 1951-52; asst. prof., then asso. prof. medicine U. Chgo., 1952-59; prof. medicine U. Colo., 1959—, prof. microbiology, 1960—, chmn. dept., 1963-65, asso. dean, 1966-68, dean, 1969-71, dir. Webb-Waring Lung Inst., 1973—; mem. nat. council Nat. Inst. Allergy and Infectious Diseases, NIH, 1963-66, 73-77. Served with M.C., AUS, 1945-48. Markle scholar, 1955-60. Mem. Am. Acad. Allergy (pres.), Am. Acad. Arts and Scis., Nat. Acad. Scis., Inst. Medicine, Phi Beta Kappa. Author: (with John Cann) Chemistry of Immunity in Health and Disease; editor: (with M. Samter) Textbook of Immunological Disease; Jour. Allergy, 1963-67. Office: U Colo Sch Medicine Denver CO 80220

TALMAN, JAMES DAVIS, educator; b. Toronto, Ont., Can., July 24, 1931; s. James John and Ruth (Davis) T.; B.A., U. Western Ont. (London, Can.), 1953, M.Sc., 1954; Ph.D., Princeton, 1959; m. Ragnhild Bruun Nilssen, Feb. 2, 1957; children—Liv Elizabeth, Stephen, Marianne, Eric. Instr. physics Princeton U., 1957-59; asst. prof. Am. Univ. of Beirut (Lebanon), 1959-60; mem. faculty dept. applied math. U. Western Ont., 1960—, asso. prof., 1962-65, prof., 1965—; research asst. U. Calif. at Davis, 1963-64; vis. prof. U. Fla., 1978-79. Mem. Am. Phys. Soc., Canadian Assn. Physicists. Author: Special Functions: A Group Theoretic Approach, 1968. Home: 29 Lonsdale Dr London ON Canada

TALSO, PETER J., physician; b. Ishpeming, Mich., Sept. 22, 1921; s. Jacob and Jennie Olga (Mattson) T.; student No. Mich. U., 1939-41; B.A., Wayne U., 1943, M.D. with high honors, 1945; m. Evelyn M. Lucynski, Dec. 18, 1943; children—Jennifer Talso Alexis, Cassandra, Kathryn, Peter. Intern, U. Chgo., 1945-46, resident, 1946-50, instr., 1950-51, asst. prof., 1951-53, clin. asso. prof., 1976—; asst. prof. Loyola U., Chgo., 1953-55, asso. prof., 1955-58, prof., 1958—, chmn. dept. medicine, 1964-69; med. dir. Little Company of Mary Hosp., 1971. Mem. Gov.'s Adv. Council on Mental Retardation, 1964-67. Bd. govs. Chgo. Heart Assn., 1955-67, Ill. Psychiat. Tng. and Research Authority, 1957-69; bd. dirs. St. Joseph's Child Center, Little Company of Mary Hosp., St. Joseph's Carondelet Child Center, Cath. Charities Chgo., Taxtician Found., Chgo. Served to capt. M.C., AUS, 1946-48. Diplomate Am. Bd. Internal Medicine. Fellow A.C.P.; mem. Am. Coll. Cardiology, Central Soc. Clin. Research, AMA, Ill. State, Chgo. med. socs., Am. Acad. Med. Dirs., Royal Soc. Health, Royal Soc. Medicine, Am. Med. Soc. of Alcoholism, Am. Soc. Internal Medicine (trustee 1964-67), Sigma Xi, Alpha Omega Alpha. Clubs: Beverly Country, Exec. (Chgo.). Editor textbook; contbr. articles to profl. jours. Home: 10359 Longwood Dr Chicago IL 60643 Office: 2800 W 95th St Evergreen Park IL 60642

TAM, REUBEN, painter; b. Kapaa, Kauai, Hawaii, Jan. 17, 1916; s. Kee Tam and Loo-See Tam; Ed.B., U. Hawaii, 1937; postgrad. Calif. Sch. Fine Arts, 1940, Columbia, 1942-45; m. Geraldine King, May 20, 1948. One man shows Calif. Palace Legion Honor, 1940, Honolulu Acad. Arts, 1941, 67, Downtown Gallery, 1945, 46, 49, 52, Phila. Art Alliance, 1954, Alan Gallery, 1954, 57, 59, 61, 64, 67, Portland (Oreg.) Art Mus., 1966, Oreg. State U., 1966, Wichita Art Assn., 1971, Coe Kerr Gallery, 1971, 75, 79, Sheldon Meml. Art Gallery, Lincoln, Nebr., 1976, El Paso Mus., 1978, others; group exhbns. Am. painting surveys, 1943—, including Carnegie Inst., Whitney Mus. Am. Art, Met. Mus. Art, San Francisco Mus. Art, Walker Art Center, Chgo. Art Inst., also S.Am., Australia, Europe; instr. painting Bklyn. Mus. Art Sch., 1948-74; works in permanent collections Mus. Modern Art, Met. Mus. Art, Wichita Art Mus., N.Y. Pub. library, Albright Art Gallery, Whitney Mus. Am. Art, Bklyn Mus., Smithsonian Instn. Nat. Collection Fine Art, Hawaii State Found., others; instr. Bklyn. Mus. Art Sch., 1946-74; prof. Oreg. State U., 1966; adj. asso. prof. Queens Coll., 1973. Recipient 1st prize Honolulu Acad. Arts, 1939, 41, Golden Gate Exposition, 1940, Bklyn. Mus., 1952, NAD, 1974, 77; award Am. Acad. and Inst. Arts and Letters, 1978; Guggenheim fellow, 1948. Address: 549 W 123d St New York NY 10027

TAMARKIN, ROBERT ALLEN, journalist; b. St. Louis, Nov. 5, 1937; s. Marshall Herbert and Dorothy Sylvia (Levy) T.; B.S., Washington U., St. Louis, 1961; B.J., U. Mo., 1963; m. Feb. 17, 1963 (div. 1974); children—Michael, Michele, Meridith, Elisa; m. 2d, Civia Levin Cohen, Jan. 1976. Bus. reporter Fairchild Publs., Chgo., 1963-66; financial writer, stock market columnist Chgo. Daily News, 1966-68, investigative reporter, 1973-74, Saigon (South Vietnam) Bur. Chief, 1975, Southeast Asia corr., bur. chief, Bangkok, Thailand, 1975-76, African corr., bur. chief, Nairobi, Kenya, 1976-77; editor, founder Generation Mag., Chgo., 1968-71; Midwest bur. chief Forbes Mag., 1978—. Contbg. editor Chgo. Ind. Mag., 1975-77; spl. cons. Oyez Lit. Rev., Chgo. Recipient A.T. Kearney Found. award and 1st prize for excellence in bus. reporting, 1968, 1st place award for best investigative series Chgo. Newspaper Guild, 1975; AP awards for public service reporting, 1975, 77. Mem. Chgo. Newspaper Guild, Chgo. Council Fgn. Relations, Chgo. Press Club, Fgn. Corrs. Club of Thailand (Bangkok), Sigma Delta Chi. Jewish. Author: Young Executive Today, 1972; ghost author: Hefner's Gonna Kill Me When He Reads This, 1972. Home: 503 W Briar Pl Chicago IL 60657 Office: Forbes Magazine 410 N Michigan Ave Chicago IL 60611

TAMAYO, RUFINO, painter; b. Oaxaca, Mexico, Aug. 26, 1899; s. Manuel Arellanes and Florentina Tamayo; ed. Sch. Fine Arts, Mexico City; Doctor honoris causa Nat. U. Mex., U. Philippines; m. Olga Flores Rivas, Jan. 24, 1934. Head dept. ethnographic drawing Nat. Mus. Archaeology; head dept. plastic arts Mexican Secretariat Edn., 1932; art instr. Dalton Sch., N.Y.C., 1938—, Bklyn. Mus. Art Sch., 1946; painter, one man shows Weyhe Gallery, N.Y.C., 1926, Art Center, N.Y.C., 1927, Nat. Theater, Mexico City, 1929, John Levy Galleries, N.Y.C., 1931, Carolina Amor Gallery, Mexico City, 1935, Valentine Gallery, N.Y.C., 1939-47, Arts Club Chgo., 1945, Pierre Matisse Gallery, N.Y.C., 1948, Knoedler Gallery, N.Y.C., 1951—, Mus. Fine Arts, Houston, 1956, Palais des Beaux Arts, Brussels, 1950, Galerie des Beaux Arts, Paris, 1950, Guggenheim Mus., 1979, many others U.S., Europe, S.Am., Mexico; represented permanent collections maj. museums U.S. and Europe, including Mus. Modern Art, N.Y.C., Phillips Meml. Gallery, Washington, Art Inst. Chgo., N.Y. Pub. Library, Musee Nat. d'Art Moderne, Paris, Mus. Art Modern, Rome, Mus. Royale, Brussels. Recipient 3d prize Carnegie Internat., Pitts., 1952, 2d prize, 1955; 1st prize Sao Paulo (Brazil) Biennal, 1954; Premio Nac. Mex.; decorated chevalier Legion of Honor, officer Legion of Honor, comdr. Legion of Honor (France); comdr. de la Repubica Italiana. Decorated chevalier de la Legion d'Honneur (France). Hon. mem. Am. Acad. Arts and Letters. Address: Callejon del Santisimo 12 San Angel Mexico City DF Mexico*

TAMBIAH, STANLEY JEYARAJAH, anthropologist; b. Sri Lanka, Jan. 16, 1929; came to U.S., 1973; s. Charles Rajakone and Eliza Chellamma (Moothathamby) T.; B.A., U. Ceylon, Peradeniya, 1951; Ph.D. Cornell U., 1954; m. Mary Wynne Huber, Mar. 15, 1969; children—Jonathan Anand, Matthew Arjun. Lectr., U. Ceylon, 1955-60; UNESCO tech. assistance expert, Thailand, 1960-63; Smuts fellow U. Cambridge (Eng.) and Commonwealth fellow St. John's Coll., U. Cambridge, 1963-64, lectr. U. Cambridge, 1964-72, fellow Clare Hall, 1965-70, fellow, tutor grad. students, dir. studies in social anthropology King's Coll., 1970-72; fellow Center for Advanced Study in Behavioral Scis., Palo Alto, Calif., 1968-69; prof. anthropology U. Chgo., 1973-76; prof., curator South Asian ethnology Peabody Museum, Harvard U., 1976—; Malinowski meml. lectr. London Sch. Econs., 1968; Radcliffe-Brown meml. lectr. Brit. Acad., 1979. Social Sci. Research Council Gt. Brit. grantee, 1971; NSF grantee, 1978. Mem. Royal Anthrop. Inst. (Curl Bequest prize 1964, Rivers Meml. medal 1973), Am. Anthrop. Assn., Assn. Asian Studies, Internat. Assn. Buddhist Studies, Am. Acad. Study Religion. Author: Buddhism and the Spirit Cults in Northeast Thailand, 1970; (with Jack Goody) Brideswealth and Dowry, 1973; World Conqueror and World Renouncer, A Study of Religion and Polity in Thailand against a Historical Background, 1976. Office: Harvard U Dept Anthropology Cambridge MA 02138

TAMBONE, JOSEPH ANTHONY, fgn. service officer; b. N.Y.C., Sept. 9, 1921; s. Anthony Joseph and Mary Agnes (Gallo) T.; B.S., Ind. U., 1941; children—Priscilla Mary, Robert Joseph. Spl. asst. Office War Information, N.Y.C., 1941-42; chief control and distbn. sect. U.S. Mission to UN, N.Y.C., 1946-51, spl. asst. to exec. dir., 1951-55; 2d sec. and sec. U.S. del. to NATO and OEEC, Paris, 1955-61; supervisory adminstrv. officer Dept. State, Washington, 1961-64; 1st sec. The Hague, Netherlands, 1964-66; counselor of embassy, Canberra, Australia, 1966-72; exec. dir. Bureau of Public Affairs, Dept. of State, Washington, 1972-74; counselor of embassy, Santiago, Chile, 1974-77, Bangkok, Thailand, 1977—. Mem. U.S. del. to UN Gen. Assembly, Paris, 1948, 51; mem. U.S. Delegations to NATO Ministerial Meetings, Paris, 1955-61. Served with U.S. Army, 1943-46. Mem. Am. Fgn. Service Assn., Phi Kappa Theta. Clubs: Amphyctions (The Hague); First Tuesday, Refugees (Canberra); Refugees (Washington); Saints and Sinners (Sydney); Royal Bangkok Sports. Home: McLean VA 22101 Office: Am Embassy Bangkok Thailand

TAMIMI, HAMDI A., educator; b. Hebron, Palestine, Aug. 20, 1924; s. Ahmad M. and Libqua (Takrouri) T.; came to U.S., 1947, naturalized, 1958; B.S., Sterling Coll., 1950; M.S., U. Colo., 1954, Ph.D., 1957; m. Anna M. Bishop, Sept. 19, 1953; children—Wally, Suhaila, Amal, Nawal, Jawad. Fellow microbiology, instr. Sch. Nursing, U. Colo. Sch. Medicine, 1955-57; research asso. Sch. Dentistry, Washington U., St. Louis, 1957-59; prof. microbiology, chmn. dept. Sch. Dentistry, U. Pacific, 1960—; cons. Mary's Help Hosp., Daly City, Calif., 1968-73, VA Hosp., San Francisco, 1976-78; mem. staff U. Calif. Extension, Berkeley. Pres., Islamic Center San Francisco, 1968, 73. Mem. N.Y. Acad. Scis., AAUP, Am. Soc. Microbiology. Author papers in field. Home: 113 Yolo St Corte Madera CA 94925 Office: 2155 Webster St San Francisco CA 94115

TAMIR, THEODOR, physicist, educator; b. Bucharest, Roumania, Sept. 17, 1927; s. Martin and Helena (Hart) Berman; B.S., Technion, Israel Inst. Tech., 1953, Dipl. Ingenieur, 1954, M.S., 1958; Ph.D., Poly. Inst. Bklyn., 1962; m. Hadassah Cohen, Oct. 5, 1949; children—Jonathan, Yael. Came to U.S., 1958, naturalized, 1968. Instr. Technion, Israel Inst. Tech., Haifa, 1956-58; research fellow Poly. Inst. N.Y., 1958-62, mem. faculty, 1962—, prof. electrophysics, 1969—, head dept. elec. engring., 1974—; sci. and engring. cons. to indsl. and govtl. labs. Served with Israeli Army, 1947-49. Awarded Instn. Premium, 1964, Electronics Premium, 1967, Instn. Elec. Engrs., London; citation for disting. research Polytechnic chpt. Sigma Xi, 1978. Fellow Instn. Elec. Engrs. (London); Optical Soc. Am., IEEE; mem. Internat. Union Radio Sci., Sigma Xi, Eta Kappa Nu. Editor, author: Integrated Optics, 1975 (Russian transl. 1978); co-editor: Applied Physics; adv. editor Optics Communications; contbr. articles to profl. jours., chpts. to books. Home: 981 E Lawn Dr Teaneck NJ 07666 Office: 333 Jay St Brooklyn NY 11201

TAMKIN, S. JEROME, business exec., cons.; b. Los Angeles, Apr. 19, 1926; s. William W. and Thelma (Brandel) T.; B.S., U. So. Calif., 1950; M.A., Fremont Coll., 1951, Ph.D., 1952; LL.D., St. Andrews U., London, 1954; divorced; 1 dau., Sherry Dawn; m. 2d, Judith Deborah, Mar. 23, 1963; children—Wendy Lynn, Gary William. Mem. research staff chemistry dept. U. Calif. at Los Angeles, 1943; research chemist, analyst supr. synthetic rubber div. U.S. Rubber Co., 1943-44; pres., gen. mgr. Majicolor, Inc., Los Angeles, 1947-49; research engr. Coll. Engring., U. So. Calif., 1946-48; gen. mgr. Pan Pacific Oil Co., Long Beach, Calif., 1948-55; plant mgr. indsl. sales and mfg., 1953-55; v.p., sales mgr. Wilco Co., Los Angeles, 1948-53, v.p. charge indsl. sales and mfg., 1953-55; v.p., sales mgr. Unit Chem. Corp., Los Angeles, 1955-56; pres. Phillips Mfg. Co. (merger Instl. Food Equipment Corp.), Los Angeles, 1957-62; pres. Waste King Corp. subs. Instl. Food Equipment Corp., 1962-67 also dir.; v.p., dir. Dyna Mfg. Co., Los Angeles, 1962-68; pres., dir. Profl. Research, Inc., Los Angeles, 1965-73; exec. v.p. Am. Med. Internat., Inc., Beverly Hills, Calif., 1966-71, dir., 1966—; sec., dir. Rodger Young, Inc., Los Angeles, 1971-77; pres., chmn. bd. TGT Petroleum Corp., Wichita, 1972—; pres., dir. Tamkin Cons. Corp., 1978—; owner, operator Tamkin Securities Co., 1979—; tech. cons. Daylin Inc., Beverly Hills, 1973-75. Bd. dirs. Baldwin Hills Village Gardens Home Owner's Assn., 1950-52; community warden W. Adams-Baldwin Hills Community CD, 1950-52; dep. sheriff Los Angeles County, 1949; bd. dirs. Sunair Home Asthmatic Children; city commr. Los Angeles Bd. Environ. Quality, 1972-73; bd. dirs. Recovery Found., Palm Springs Biltmore Condominium Assn. Served as officer USNR, 1944-46. Mem. AIM, Am. Mgmt. Assn., Inst. Aero. Scis., Am. Soc. Naval Engrs., Soc. Am. Mil. Engrs., Am. Chem. Soc., IEEE, Soc. Motion Picture and TV Engrs., Am. Inst. Chem. Engrs., Soc. Advancement Mgmt., U.S. Naval Inst., Calif. Scholarship Fedn. (life), Alpha Eta Rho. Clubs: Malibu Riding and Tennis, Sunrise Country. Contbr. articles to profl. jours. Patentee electronic gas detector, circuits for automatic control hazardous vapors. Home: Pacific Palisades CA Office: 10889 Wilshire Blvd Suite 1166 Los Angeles CA 90024

TAMM, EDWARD ALLEN, U.S. circuit judge; b. St. Paul, Apr. 21, 1906; s. Edward Allen and Lucille Catherine (Buckley) T.; student Mt. St. Charles Coll., Helena, Mont., 1923-25, U. Mont., 1926-28; LL.B., Georgetown U., 1928-30, LL.D., 1965; J.S.D., Suffolk U., 1971; LL.D., Carroll Coll., 1974; m. Grace Monica Sullivan, Jan. 30, 1934; children—Edward Allen, Grace Escudero. Ofcl., FBI, 1930-48; judge U.S. Dist. Court for D.C., 1948-65, U.S. Ct. Appeals for D.C., Circuit, 1965—; chief judge, U.S. Temporary Emergency Court of Appeals, 1972—; admitted to bar Minn. and U.S. Supreme Ct. Spl. adviser to U.S. delegation UN Conf. on Internat. Orgn., 1945; mem. com. on jud. adminstrn. Jud. Conf. U.S., 1969—, chmn. rev. com., 1969-78, chmn. jud. ethics com., 1978—. Trustee Saint Joseph Coll.; bd. dirs. Police Boys Club, Washington. Formerly lt. comdr., USNR. Decorated comdr. Legion of Merit, Ecuador, 1942; Order of Balboa, Panama, 1945; recipient Judiciary award, 1970, Distinguished Alumnus award Georgetown U., 1964. Mem. Met. Bd. Trade, USCG Aux., Am. (mem. adv. com. on judges function 1969—, spl. com. on prevention and control crime 1969—. Fed., D.C. (hon.) bar assns., Am. Law Inst., Gourmet Soc., Am. Judicature Soc., Friendly Sons St. Patrick, U.S. Power Squadron, Sons Union Vets, John Carroll Soc., President's Cup Regatta Assn., La Confrerie des Chevaliers du Tasterin, Confrerie de la Chaine des Rotisseurs, Newcomen Soc., Sigma Nu. Roman Catholic. Clubs: Columbia Country; Ocean City Light Tackle; Nat. Lawyers; Seaview Country. Home: 3353 Runnymede Pl NW Washington DC 20015 Office: US Ct Appeals DC Circuit Washington DC 20001

TAMMEUS, WILLIAM DAVID, journalist; b. Woodstock, Ill., Jan. 18, 1945; s. W. H. and Bertha H. (Helander) T.; B.J., U. Mo., Columbia, 1967; postgrad. U. Rochester, 1967-69; m. Marcia A. Bloom, Sept. 21, 1968; children—Lisen, Kate. Reporter, Rochester (N.Y.) Times-Union, 1967-70; reporter Kansas City (Mo.) Star, 1970-77, Starbeams columnist, 1977—. Mem. Sigma Delta Chi. Presbyterian. Home: 409 E 65th Terr Kansas City MO 64131 Office: 1729 Grand Ave Kansas City MO 64108

TAMPAS, JOHN PETER, radiologist; b. Burlington, Vt., May 18, 1929; s. Peter John and Virginia (Kokinakos) T.; B.S., U. Vt., 1951, M.D., 1954; m. Kathryn Adams, Dec. 29, 1962; children—Jessica Elaine, Peter John, Andrea Chris, Christiana Jamison. Intern, Bryn Mawr (Pa.) Hosp., 1954-55; resident U. Vt., Burlington, 1957-60; practice medicine specializing in radiology, Burlington, 1962—; mem. staff Med. Center Hosp. Vt., Burlington; asst. prof. radiology U. Vt., Burlington, 1962-65, asso. prof., 1965-70, prof., chmn. dept. radiology, 1970—, teaching fellow in pediatric radiology, 1960—, research fellow in cardiac radiology, 1961; Picker scholar in radiol. research, 1962-65; trustee Assos. in Radiology Found. Served with USAF, 1955-57. Mem. AMA, Assn. Univ. Radiologists, Soc. Pediatric Radiology, Am. Coll. Radiology, Radiol. Soc. N. Am., Am. Roentgen Ray Soc., Alpha Omega Alpha. Greek Orthodox. Home: 84 Ridgewood Dr Burlington VT 05401 Office: Med Center Hosp Vt Burlington VT 05401

TAN, CHOR WENG, sch. dean, educator; b. Canton, China, Apr. 20, 1936; s. Ee Hock and Tung Hong (Khor) T.; came to U.S., 1957, naturalized, 1972; B.S., U. Evansville, 1959; M.S., U. Ill., Urbana, 1961, Ph.D., 1963; m. Yulin Liu, June 8, 1963; children—Stephen, Reynold. Research asst. U. Ill., 1959-63, teaching asst., 1959-61; asst. prof. mech. engring. Cooper Union for Advancement Sci. and Art, N.Y.C., 1963-67, asso. prof., 1967-72, acting chmn. dept. mech. engring., 1971-73, prof., 1972—, head div. engring., 1973-75, dean Sch. Engring., 1975—, trustee, exec. v.p. Cooper Union Research Found.; cons. Grumman Aerospace Corp., N.Y.C. Dept. Air Resources, AEC, Nat. Inst. Mental Health. NSF grantee, 1967-71. Registered profl. engr., N.Y. Mem. Am. Soc. Engring. Edn. (sec., treas.), Assn. Engring. Colls. N.Y. State. Contbr. articles to profl. publs. Home: 85 Columbia Ave Berkeley Heights NJ 07922 Office: 51 Astor Pl New York NY 10003

TANAGHO, EMIL ABDELSAYED, urologist, educator; b. Tahta, Egypt, Aug. 12, 1929; s. Abdel Sayed and Lola (Mankarious) T.; came to U.S., 1963, naturalized, 1972; M.B., Ch.B., U. Alexandria, 1952; m. Mona Armanious Nov. 21, 1957; children—Radgia, Nancy, Rafik. Resident in urology U. Alexandria (Egypt), 1953-55, clin. demonstrator urology, 1957-59, lectr. urology, 1959-62, 64-65, asst. prof., 1965-66; resident in surgery Al-Moossat Hosp., Alexandria, 1955-57; research urologist Inst. Urology, U. London, 1962-63; research urologist U. Calif., San Francisco, 1963-64, asst. prof. in residence, 1966-69, asso. prof. in residence, 1969-72, prof. urology, 1972—, chmn. dept., 1977—; mem. staffs Letterman Army Hosp., San Francisco, Marin Gen. Hosp., San Rafael, Calif., Ross (Calif.) Gen. Hosp., Children's Hosp., San Francisco, VA Hosp., San Francisco, San Francisco Gen. Hosp. and Med. Center, VA Hosp., Palo Alto, Calif. Mem. Egyptian, Calif. med. assns., Am. Urology Assn., Am. Acad. Pediatrics, A.C.S., AMA, Internat. Soc. Urology, Mexican Urologic Assn., Internat. Urodynamic Soc., Soc. Univ. Urologists, Internat. Continence Soc., Calif. Acad. Medicine, Am. Assn. Genito-Urinary Surgeons, Western Urologic Forum. Home: 43 San

Marino Dr San Rafael CA 94901 Office: U Calif Sch Medicine Dept Urology San Francisco CA 94143

TANAKA, KOUICHI ROBERT, physician, educator; b. Fresno, Calif., Dec. 15, 1926; s. Kenjiro and Teru (Arai) T.; B.S., Wayne State U., 1949, M.D., 1952; m. Grace Mutsuko Sakaguchi, Oct. 23, 1965; children—Anne M., Nancy K., David K. Intern Los Angeles County Gen. Hosp., 1952-53; resident, fellow Detroit Receiving Hosp., 1953-57; mem. faculty Sch. Medicine, U. Calif. at Los Angeles, 1957—, asso. prof. medicine, 1961-68, prof., 1968—; asso. chmn., chief hematology, dept. medicine Harbor-UCLA Med. Center, Torrance, Calif., 1961—. Served with AUS, 1946-48. Fellow A.C.P.; mem. Am. Fedn. Clin. Research, Western Soc. Clin. Research, Los Angeles Soc. Internal Medicine (pres. 1971), Am. Soc. Hematology, Western Assn. Physicians, Am. Soc. Clin. Investigation, Assn. Am. Physicians, Sigma Xi, Alpha Omega Alpha. Research red cell metabolism. Home: 4 Cayuse Ln Palos Verdes CA 90274 Office: 1000 W Carson St Torrance CA 90509

TANAKA, TOMOYASU, educator, physicist; b. Toyama, Japan, May 16, 1919; s. Yasutaro Nagasawa and Suzu T.; M.S., Kyushu U., 1943, D.Sc., 1953; m. Sumiko Suzuki, Nov. 18, 1947; children—Minoru, Hiroko, Jiro, Tomoharu, Noriko. Came to U.S., 1960. Asst. prof. Kyushu U., Fukuoka, Japan, 1948-54, prof., 1956-60; Fulbright-Smith-Mundt fellow Enrico Fermi Inst. Nuclear Studies, U. Chgo., 1954-55; vis. physicist Inst. Fluid Dyanamics, and Applied Math, U. Md., 1955-56; prof. Kyushu U., 1956-60, Cath. U. Am., 1960-73, Ohio U., Athens, 1973—. Mem. Phys. Soc. Japan, Am. Phys. Soc., A.A.A.S., Am. Assn. U. Profs., Sigma Xi. Research statis. mechanics coop. phenomena. Home: 141 Morris Ave Athens OH 45701

TANDLER, BERNARD, educator; b. Bklyn., Feb. 18, 1933; s. Arthur and Pauline (Solomon) T.; B.S., Bklyn. Coll., 1955; A.M., Columbia U., 1957; Ph.D., Cornell U., 1961; m. Helen Weisman, Dec. 25, 1955; children—Janice Dena, Evan Charles. Instr. anatomy N.Y. U., 1962-63; asso. Sloan Kettering Inst., 1963-67; asst. prof. cell biology Cornell U., 1965-67; asso. prof. Case Western Res. U., 1967-72, prof. oral biology, 1972—; vis. prof. U. Copenhagen, 1973; cons. NIH, NSF, VA. USPHS fellow, 1957-61, 61-62. Mem. Am. Assn. Anatomists, Am. Soc. Cell Biology, Electron Microscopy Soc. Am., Internat. Assn. Dental Research, Italian Soc. Anatomy (hon.), Sigma Xi. Author: (with C.L. Hoppel) Mitochondria, 1972. Asso. editor: Anatomical Record, 1974—. Contbr. chpts. to books, articles to profl. jours. Office: 2123 Abington Rd Cleveland OH 44106

TANDY, JESSICA, actress; b. London, Eng., June 7, 1909; d. Harry and Jessie Helen (Horspool) Tandy; student Dame Alice Owens Girls Sch., also Ben Greet Acad. Acting, 1924-27; LL.D., U. Western Ont., 1974; m. Jack Hawkins, 1932 (div. 1940); 1 dau., Susan (Mrs. John Tettemer); m. 2d, Hume Cronyn, 1942; children—Christopher Hume, Tandy. First profl. acting role in Manderson Girls, later appeared in Comedy of Good and Evil, Alice Sit-by-the-Fire, Yellow Sands; London debut in The Rumor, 1929, other theatre appearances in Twelfth Night, 1930, Man Who Pays the Piper, Autumn Crocus, Port Said, 1931; various engagements Old Vic, London, including Midsummer Night's Dream, Hamlet, King Lear, 1933-40; first stage appearance U.S., 1930, on Broadway in Time and Conways, 1938, White Steed, 1939, Yesterday's Magic, 1942, Streetcar Named Desire, 1947, Four Poster, 1951-53, Madame Will You Walk, 1953, The Honeys, 1955, A Day by the Sea, 1955, The Man in the Dog Suit, 1958, Five Finger Exercise, 1959, The Physicists, 1964, Noel Coward in Two Keys, 1974; played in Mpls. in Hamlet, Three Sisters, Death of a Salesman, 1963, in Way of the World, The Cherry Orchard, The Caucasian Chalk Circle, 1965; summer theatre prodns., 1950-55; appeared Triple Play, 1958-59, Big Fish, Little Fish, London, 1962; reading tour U.S. (with husband), Face to Face, 1954, A Delicate Balance, 1966-67, The Miser, 1968, Heartbreak House, Shaw Festival, 1968; Tchin-Tchin, Chgo., 1969, Camino Real, Lincoln Center, N.Y.C., 1970, Home, Morosco, N.Y., 1971, All Over, N.Y.C., 1971; appeared (with husband) in Samuel Beckett festival, Lincoln Center, N.Y.C., 1972; tour of Promenade All, 1972-73, Tour Not I, 1973; limited concert recital tour Many Faces of Love, 1974, 75, 76, also Seattle Repertory theatre; tour (with Noel Coward) Two Keys, 1975; appeared in The Way of the World, A Midsummer Night's Dream, Eve, Stratford (Ont.) Festival, 1976; played Mary Tyrone in Long Day's Journey into Night, Theater London (Ont., Can.), 1977; star The Gin Game at Long Wharf Theatre, New Haven, 1977, Golden Theatre, N.Y.C., 1978, on tour in U.S., Toronto, London, USSR, 1978-80; motion pictures include Valley of Decision, Green Years, Desert Fox, A Light in the Forest, 1958, The Birds, 1962, Butley, 1973; TV prodns., Portrait of a Madonna, 1948, Christmas 'Till Closing, 1955, Marriage, series, 1954, The Fallen Idol, 1959, The Moon and Sixpence, 1959. Dramatic adviser Goddard Neighborhood Center, N.Y.C., 1948. Recipient annual Antoinette Perry award for performance Streetcar Named Desire, 1948, also Twelfth Night Club award; Delia Austria Medal from the Drama League N.Y.; bronze medallion (with husband) for performance The Four Poster, Comedia Matinee Club, 1952; Obie award for Not I, 1973; Drama Desk award for Happy Days and Not I; Creative Arts award Brandeis U., 1978; Antoinette Perry award for The Gin Game, 1978; Tony award for The Gin Game, 1978, also Drama Desk award, 1978, Los Angeles Critics award, 1979, Tony award 1979, Sarah Siddons award, 1979. Office: 63-23 Carlton St Rego Park NY 11374

TANEN, NED STONE, motion picture co. exec.; b. Los Angeles, 1931; grad. UCLA, 1954; married. With MCA Inc. and subsidiaries, v.p. MCATTV, 1964-67, exec. v.p. Universal City Records (Calif.), 1967-69, v.p. MCA Inc., Universal City, 1967—, pres. Universal Theatrical Motion Pictures div., 1976, pres. Universal Picture div., 1979—, also dir. Served with USAF, 1950-52. Office: MCA Inc Universal Pictures 100 Universal City Plaza Universal City CA 91608*

TANENBAUM, BERNARD JEROME, JR., retail chain store exec.; b. Little Rock, Nov. 26, 1934; s. Bernard Jerome and Naomi (Dante) T.; B.B.A., Tulane U., 1956; D.Pub. Service, Ark. Bapt. Coll., 1974; m. Patricia Wise, June 9, 1955; children—Bernard Jerome III, Albert Wise. Salesman, Dantan Co., Duams, Ark., 1955; buyer Dantes Stores, Dumas, 1956-61; exec. v.p. Dantes Tanenbaum, Dumas, 1961; pres. UDS Inc. (formerly United Dollar Stores, Inc.), Dumas, 1967—; pres. Pudata Inc.; vice chmn. Ark. Tax Revision Commn. County chmn. A.R.C., 1957-60; v.p., dir. Desota council Boy Scouts Am.; pres. Henry S. Jacobs Camp; v.p. S.W. region Union Am. Hebrew Congregations, also mem. exec. com., mem. nat. com. camps and insts., rep. S.W. region to long-range planning com. Bd. dirs. Dante & Tanenbaum Found., Leon Levi Hosp., Ark. dept. Nat. Conf. Christian and Jews, Ark. chpt. Arthritis Found.; pres., dir. Camp Assn. So. Temples; trustee adv. bd. Tulane U. Recipient Ark. Ten Outstanding Young Men award, 1971, Outstanding Service award Sickle Cell Anemia Found., 1973, Distinguished Arkansan award, 1974. Mem. Ark. Retail Mchts. Assn. (dir.), Dumas Mchts. Assn. (past chmn.), Dumas Jr. C. of C. (past pres.), Ark. Jr. C. of C. (past internat. dir.), Dumas C. of C., Zeta Beta Tau. Jewish religion (past pres., trustee temple). Mason (32); mem. B'nai B'rith (past dir.). Home: 130 N Rankin St Dumas AR 71639 Office: Hwy 54 W Dumas AR 71639

TANENBAUM, ELIAS, composer; b. Bklyn., Aug. 20, 1924; s. Harry and Fannie (Israel) T.; B.S., Juilliard Sch. Music, N.Y.C., 1949; M.A., Columbia U., 1950; m. Mary Weir, Sept. 12, 1952; children—David, Jacob. Dir. electronic music studio, mem. composition faculty Manhattan Sch. Music, N.Y.C., 1971—; compositions and recs. include: Variations for Orchestra, 1958; Patterns and Improvisations for Brass Quintet and Tape, 1970; Arp Art, 1972; Fantasie for 4 Harps and Tape, 1974; Rituals and Reactions, 1974; Images II, 1975. Served with U.S. Army, 1943-45. Recipient Rec. award Am. Composers Alliance, 1975; decorated Purple Heart. Nat. Endowment for Arts grantee, 1974; Ford Found. rec. grantee, 1975; Macdowell fellow, 1958. Mem. Am. Composers Alliance. Home: 30 Irving Pl New Rochelle NY 10801 Studio: 120 Claremont Ave New York City NY 10027

TANENBAUM, MARC HERMAN, clergyman; b. Balt., Oct. 13, 1925; s. Abraham and Sadie (Siger) T.; B.A., Yeshiva U., 1945; M.H.L. in Hebrew Lit., Jewish Theol. Sem. Am., 1950; postgrad. Johns Hopkins, 1951, New Sch. Social Research, 1952; m. Helga Weiss, May 22, 1955; children—Adena Michael, Susan. Rabbi, 1950; rabbi Northeast Hebrew Congregation, Washington, 1951-52, Jewish Center of Mahopacs, 1952-54; exec. dir. Synagogue Council Am., nat. coordinating agy. Orthodox, Conservative and Reform rabbinic and congl. bodies of Judaism U.S., 1954-60; dir. dept. interreligious affairs Am. Jewish Com., 1961—. Editor, pub. relations counselor Abelard Schuman, pub., 1956, Henry Schuman, Farrar, Straus & Cudahy, Chas. Scribner's & Sons; pres. Galtan Assos., pubs., pub. relations cons.; staffs Eternal Light radio program; corr., columnist Overseas News Agy., Seven Arts Feature Syndicate, Jewish Telegraphic Agy.; TV writer and panelist WMAR-TV, Balt.; writer, narrator, dir. religious films; columnist London Jewish Chronicle; editor Interreligious Newsletter; editor Trend of Events, news weekly. Mem. exec. com. White House Conf. on Children and Youth, 1960; nat. adv. council White House Conf. on Aging, 1961; mem. nat. religious policy com. Girl Scouts U.S.A., Camp Fire Girls Am.; nat. vice chmn. ARC; v.p., dir., chmn. copy com. Religion in Am. Life; dir. Clergymen's Econ. Inst.; mem. council trustees United Seamen's Service; mem. religious adv. com. U.S. Com. for UN; mem. U.S. nat. commn. for UNESCO; mem. Com. Internat. Econ. Growth. Recipient Coronet award St Edwards U. Mem. Nat. Conf. Christians and Jews, Rabbinical Assembly Am. Editor: Judaism: Orthodox, Conservative and Reform. Author, co-author various books; contbr. articles to religious publs. Office: 165 E 56th St New York NY 10022*

TANENBAUM, MORRIS, telephone co. exec.; b. Huntington, W.Va., Nov. 10, 1928; s. Reuben S. and Mollie (Kadensky) T.; B.A. in Chemistry, Johns Hopkins U., 1949; M.A. in Chemistry, Princeton U., 1950, Ph.D. in Phys. Chemistry, 1952; m. Charlotte Silver, June 4, 1950; children—Robin Sue, Michael Alan. Mem. tech. staff Bell Telephone Labs., Murray Hill, N.J., 1952-55, dir. solid state device lab., 1962-64, exec. v.p., 1975-76, also dir.; with Western Electric Co., N.Y.C., 1964-74, v.p. engring., 1971-72, v.p. transmission equipment, 1972-75; v.p. engring. and network services AT&T, Basking Ridge, N.J., 1976-78; pres. N.J. Bell Telephone Co., Newark, 1978—; dir. Am. Express Co., Kennecott Copper Corp., 1st Nat. State Bank. Trustee Battelle Meml. Inst., Tufts U., Worcester Poly. Inst.; bd. govs. Rutgers U. Fellow IEEE, Am. Phys. Soc.; mem. Nat. Acad. Engring., Am. Chem. Soc., Am. Inst. Metall., Mining and Petroleum Engrs. Contbr. numerous articles to profl. jours.; patentee in field. Office: 540 Broad St Newark NJ 07101

TANFORD, CHARLES, educator; b. Halle, Germany, Dec. 29, 1921; s. Max and Charlotte (Eisenbruch) T.; came to U.S., 1939, naturalized, 1947; B.A., N.Y. U., 1943; M.A., Princeton, 1944, Ph.D., 1947; m. Lucia Lander Brown, Apr. 3, 1948 (div. Feb. 1969); children—Victoria, James Alexander, Sarah Lander. Postdoctoral fellow Harvard, 1947-49, vis. prof. chemistry, 1966; asst. prof. chemistry U. Iowa, 1949-54, asso. prof., 1954-59, prof., 1956-60; prof. biochemistry Duke, 1960-70, James B. Duke Prof., 1970—; George Eastman vis. prof. Oxford U., 1977-78; Walker-Ames prof. U. Wash., 1979; Reilly lectr. U. Notre Dame, 1979. Guggenheim fellow, 1956. Mem. Am. Acad. Arts, Scis., Nat. Acad. Scis. Unitarian (pres. Unitarian-Universalist Fellowship 1968). Author: Physical Chemistry of Macromolecules, 1961; The Hydrophobic Effect, 1973. Contbr. numerous articles to profl. jour. Home: 1430 N Mangum St Durham NC 27701 Office: Dept Physiology Box 3709 Duke Univ Med Center Durham NC 27710

TANG, ANTHONY MATTHEW, economist; b. Shanghai, China, May 6, 1924; s. Shu-ping and Yueh-pao (Hsu) T.; came to U.S., 1945, naturalized, 1953; B.B.A., Loyola U., New Orleans, 1949; Ph.D., Vanderbilt U., 1955; m. Jane Pentecost, Nov. 27, 1946; children—Matthew, Jeremiah, John, Lyda Anne, Arthur, Patricia. Faculty, Vanderbilt U., Nashville, 1955—, prof. econs. and bus. adminstrn., 1963—, chmn. dept., 1968-71, dir., grad. program in econ. devel., 1961-63; dir. East Asian studies program, 1973-76; vis. lectr. Osaka (Japan) U., 1959-60; vis. prof. U. Calif. at Berkeley, 1963-64, U. Sao Paulo (Brazil), 1973; vis. prof. econs., chmn. dept., dean faculty commerce and social scis. Chinese U., Hong Kong, 1966-68, cons., 1979-80; vis. prof. Nat. Taiwan U., 1974-75, U. Hawaii, summer 1979; vis. prof. econs. Center for Chinese Studies, U. Mich., 1976-77; cons. FOA, 1954, Ford Found., 1973, Internat. Food Policy Research Inst., 1978, Midwest China Study Resource Center, 1979. Mem. Am. Econ. Assn. (adv. com. U.S. Census 1960-63, mem. policy bd. for Econs. Insts. 1963-66), Assn. Comparative Econ. Studies, Am. (editorial council jour. 1968-71), Internat. agrl. econs. assns., Soc. Asian Studies, So. Econ. Assn. (editor jour. 1963-66), Midwest Regional Seminar on China. Author: Economic Development of the Southern Piedmont, 1958; Longterm Economic Projections for Hong Kong, 1969; editor: Evolution, Welfare, and Time in Economics, 1976; Food and Agriculture in China: Trends and Projections, 1979; contbr. to: Theory and Design of Economic Development, 1966, China in Crisis, 1968, Economic Trends in Communist China, 1968, Subsistence Agriculture and Economic Development, 1969, Agrarian Policies and Problems in Communist and Non-communist Countries, 1971, Trade, Agriculture and Development, 1975, Agricultural Growth in Japan, Korea, Taiwan, and the Philippines, 1979; Modern Chinese Economic History, 1979. Home: 6728 Currywood Dr Nashville TN 37205

TANG, THOMAS, judge; b. Phoenix, Jan. 11, 1922; B.S., U. Santa Clara, 1947, postgrad. Law Sch., 1948-50; LL.B. with distinction, U. Ariz., 1950. Admitted to Ariz. bar, 1950, Calif. bar, 1951; dep. county atty. Maricopa County, Ariz., 1953-57; asst. atty. gen. State of Ariz., 1957-58; judge Ariz. Superior Ct., 1963-70; mem. firm Sullivan, Mahoney & Tang, Phoenix, 1971-77; councilman City of Phoenix, 1960-62, vice mayor, 1962; judge U.S. Ct. of Appeals 9th Circuit, Phoenix, 1977—. Mem. State Bar Ariz. (bd. govs. 1971-77, pres. 1977—), State Bar Calif. Office: care US Court of Appeals Federal Bldg 230 N 1st Ave Phoenix AZ 85025

TANGNEY, EUGENE MICHAEL, banker; b. Boston, Apr. 8, 1928; s. Michael Robert and Ann (Donoghue) T.; B.S., Georgetown U., 1951; postgrad. Stonier Grad. Sch. Banking Rutgers U., 1962; m. Mary K. Gormley, Apr. 11, 1959; children—Susan, Elizabeth, Nancy, Maurya. Mem. Fed. Res. System Bd. Govs., Washington, 1953-65; asst. v.p. First Nat. Bank Boston, 1966, v.p., 1967, sr. v.p., 1969-78, exec. v.p., 1978—; dir., pres., First Nat. Boston Clearance Corp., 1971—; pres., dir. New Eng. Automated Clearing House Assn., 1973—; instr. Williams Coll., 1967—, chmn. operations faculty, 1969—. Chmn. Spl. Com. Paperless Entries, Boston, 1971—; mem. operations com. Boston Clearing House Assn. Chmn. finance com., Millis, Mass., 1963, United Fund, Millis, 1967-68. Trustee, treas. Boston Univ. Hosp., 1973—. Served to capt. USMC, 1951-53. Mem. Am. (chmn. exec. com. operations/automation div., also chmn. div.), Mass. (treas., dir. 1977—) bankers assns., Grad. Sodality Boston. Democrat. Roman Catholic. Clubs: Federal, Algonquin (Boston); Internat. (Washington); Brae Burn Country (Newton, Mass.). Home: 34 Chatham Circle Wellesley Hills MA 02181 Office: 100 Federal St Boston MA 02110

TANGUY, CHARLES REED, fgn. service officer; b. Phila., Dec. 24, 1921; s. Edward Earley and Dorothy (Reed) T.; student Swarthmore Coll., 1939-41; A.B., Pa. State Coll., 1947; postgrad. George Washington U., summer 1946, Johns Hopkins, 1947; m. Irene Jane McDaniel, Sept. 4, 1943; children—Charles Reed, Sarah Beauchamp, Peter Sackville. Joined U.S. Fgn. Service, 1947; 3d sec., Athens, Greece, 1947-49; vice consul, Rabat, Morocco, 1949-52; assigned State Dept., 1952; 2d sec., Rome, Italy, 1953-54, Bern, Switzerland, 1954-55; consul, prin. officer, Penang, Malaya, 1955-56; assigned State Dept., 1957, internat. relations officer, 1957-59, officer charge Malayan affairs, 1959-61; 2d sec., later 1st sec., dep. chief polit. sect., Ankara, Turkey, 1961-65, 1st sec. dep. chief polit. sect., Paris, France, 1965-68; country dir. France and Benelux, Dept. State, 1968-72; minister-counselor U.S. embassy, The Hague, Netherlands, 1972-75; mem., pres. 18th sr. seminar in fgn. policy Dept. State, Washington, 1975-76; sr. fgn. service insp., 1976-78, dep. dir. Office of Equal Employment Opportunity, 1978—. Mem. original bldg. comwarden St. Nicolas Anglican Episcopalian Ch., Ankara, 1962. Served to 1st lt. AUS, 1942-46; PTO. Recipient Meritorious Honor award Dept. State. Mem. Sigma Alpha Epsilon. Address: M/EEO Room 3214 Dept State Washington DC 20520

TANGUY, ROBERT BRINGHURST, air force officer; b. Logansport, Ind., Jan. 24, 1927; s. Russell Ralston and Beatrice (Seybold) T.; B.S., U.S. Mil. Acad., 1952; M.S. in Internat. Affairs, George Washington U., 1970; m. Mary Virginia Vallee, June 5, 1952; children—Mark, Robert, Marianna. Commd. 2d lt. U.S. Air Force, 1952, advanced through grades to maj. gen., 1977; comdr. fighter squadron, Viet Nam, 1966; insp. gen. Air Tng. Command, 1974; congressional liaison for Air Force, 1975; vice comdr.-in-chief U.S. So. Command, Panama Canal, 1979—. Pres., Little League, Tampa, Fla., 1964; trustee C.Z. Coll., 1977-79; pres. C.Z. council Boy Scouts Am., 1978. Decorated D.F.C., Legion of Merit, Air medal, Bronze Star. Mem. West Point Assn. Grads., Air Force Assn., Res. Officers Assn., Am. Legion, VFW. Christian Scientist. Office: Comdr USAF Southern Div TAC APO NY 09825

TANIGUCHI, ALAN YAMATO, architect; b. Stockton, Calif., Sept. 13, 1922; s. Isamu and Sadayo (Miyagi) T.; B.Arch., U. Calif. at Berkeley, 1949; m. Leslie E. Honnami, Apr. 29. 1949; children—Evan Key, Keith. Draftsman, Jack Hillmer, San Francisco, 1949, Anshen & Allen, San Francisco, 1950-51; pvt. practce, Harlingen, Tex., 1951-63, Austin, Tex., 1963-69; partner firm Taniguchi, Shefelman, Vacker & Minter, Austin, 1969-76, Alan Y. Taniguchi & Assos., Houston and Austin, 1976—; faculty U. Tex. at Austin, 1961-72, prof. architecture, 1965-72, dean Sch. Architecture, 1967-72; Smith prof. architecture Rice U., Houston, 1974-78, dir. Sch. Architecture, 1972-74, asso. Lovett Coll., 1974; Thomas Jefferson vis. fellow architecture U. Va., 1970; mem. Austin Planning Commn., 1967-72, also chmn. zoning com.; mem. Bd. Nat. Archtl. Accrediting Bd., 1968-72. Bd. dirs. Tex. Archtl. Found., S.W. Inter-Group Relations Council, Corpus Christi (Tex.) Redevel. Assistance Center, Rice Design Alliance, Houston Urban Bunch, Houston Housing Devel. Corp.; chmn. Tex. Com. on Humanities. Named One of Sixteen Young Men with Designs on the Future, Fortune mag., 1966; recipient Teaching Excellence award U. Tex., 1961-62. Fellow AIA; mem. Tex. Soc. Architects (v.p. 1969), Assn. Collegiate Schs. Architecture (v.p. 1969-70, pres. 1971-72, chmn. task force to study prof. orgns. in architecture), Phi Kappa Phi, Tau Sigam Delta. Home: 2818 Wooldridge Austin TX Office: Sch Architecture Rice U Houston TX 77001 also 800 Perry Brooks Bldg Austin TX

TANIMOTO, TAFFEE TADASHI, mathematician, educator; b. Kobe, Japan, Dec. 15, 1917; s. Frank Ryozo and Yoshi (Nakashima) T.; A.B., U. Calif. at Los Angeles, 1942; S.M., U. Chgo., 1946; Ph.D., U. Pitts., 1950; m. Mary Mae Whistler, June 22, 1946; children—Steven Larry, Dana Keith, Erica Jean, Philip Douglas. Instr. math. Ill. Inst. Tech., 1946-49; asst. prof. Allegheny Coll., Meadville, Pa., 1949-54; mathematician IBM, N.Y.C., 1954-61, Melpar, Inc., Watertown, Mass., 1961-62, Honeywell, Inc., Boston, 1963-65; prof. math. U. Mass. at Boston, 1965—, chmn. dept., 1965—, dir. grad. programs, 1975-76; cons. U.S. Office Edn., 1967—, NASA, 1965-67, Model Cities Higher Edn. Program, Boston, 1969—. Mem. tech. adv. com. Gov.'s Com. Law Enforcement of Criminal Justice Mass., 1969—; adv. bd. Roxbury Community Coll., 1970-77. Mem. Am. Math. Soc., Math. Assn. Am. Home: 156 Bellevue St Newton MA 02158 Office: Dept Math U Mass Boston MA 02125

TANIS, JAMES ROBERT, educator, clergyman; b. Phillipsburg N.J., June 26, 1928; s. John Christian and Bertha Marie (Tobiasson) T.; B.A., Yale, 1951; B.D., Union Theol. Sem., N.Y.C., 1954; Dr. Theol., U. Utrecht (Netherlands), 1967; m. Florence Borgmann, June 26, 1963; children—Marjorie Martha, James Tobiasson. Ordained to ministry Presbyn. Ch., 1954; co-pastor Greystone Presbyn. Ch., Elizabeth, N.J., 1954-56; librarian, mem. faculty Harvard Div. Sch., 1957-65; univ. librarian Yale, 1965-68; mem. faculty Yale Div. Sch., 1968-69; dir. libraries, prof. history Bryn Mawr (Pa.) Coll., 1969—. Author: Calvinistic Pietism in the Middle Colonies, 1967. Home: 111 Deep Dene Rd Villanova PA 19085

TANIS, NORMAN EARL, univ. adminstr., librarian; b. Grand Rapids, Mich., Aug. 15, 1929; s. Aaron Orrie and Gertrude (Medendorp) T.; A.B., Calvin Coll., 1951; A.M.L.S., U. Mich., 1952, M.A., 1956, 61; LL.H.D. (hon.), U. San Fernando, 1973; LL.D. (hon.), Mid-Valley Coll. Law, 1976; m. Marion L. Anderson, Aug. 20, 1955; children—Kathryne, Laura. Cataloger, Strauss Meml. Library, U. Mich., 1951-52; librarian Henry Ford Community Coll., 1956-63, head librarian, 1963-66; dir. libraries Kans. State U., Pittsburg, 1966-69; dir. univ. libraries Calif. State U., Northridge, 1969—; trustee San Fernando Valley Coll. Law; mem. adv. council UCLA Library Sch.; mem. adv. com. U. So. Calif. Library Sch. Served with U.S. Army, 1952-54. Mem. ALA, Calif. Library Assn., Nat. Librarians' Assn. (v.p., pres.-elect), Manuscript Soc., Printing Assn. So. Calif., Phi Kappa Phi, Phi Beta Mu. Club: Marine Meml. of San Francisco. Co-author: Problems in Developing Academic Library Collections, 1974; Cost Analysis of Library Functions: A Total System Approach, 1978; China in Books, 1979; contbr. articles to profl. publs.; editor Northridge Facsimilie Series, 1974—; editor Santa Susana Press, 1975—. Home: 18900 Olympia St Northridge CA 91324 Office: Calif State U 18111 Nordhoff St Northridge CA 91330

TANK, MARTIN MARCUS, former govt. ofcl.; b. Winnipeg, Man., Can., Aug. 29, 1916 (parents Am. citizens); s. Leopold Ferdinand and Louise Amanda (Just) T.; B.A., U. Wis., 1939, M.A., 1940; m. Mary

L'Hommedieu, Feb. 22, 1941; children—Holly Louise, Jeffry L'H. Econ. officer Office U.S. Mil. Govt., Berlin, 1947-48; rep., head del. for W. Ger., OEEC, Paris, 1948-49; chief program div. U.S. regional orgn., Marshall Plan and NATO, Paris, 1949-55; econ. counsellor embassy, dep. dir. USOM, London, 1955-58; dep. dir. U.S. AID Ops. Mission, Libya, 1958-60; dir. mil. assistance div. AID, Washington, 1960-63; dep. dir. USOM, Bangkok, Thailand, 1964-68; coordinator Free World Assistance U.S. AID, Saigon, Vietnam, 1968-70, asso. dir. econ. planning and policy, 1970-72; chief policy, planning and rev. div. internat. orgn. Dept. State, 1973-75; econs. cons. developing countries, 1976—. Served with AUS, 1941-43. Home: 500 23d St NW Washington DC 20037

TANKERSLEY, GEORGE JACKSON, natural gas utility exec.; b. Ruston, La., Apr. 21, 1921; s. Homer (Kendall) and Gladys (Nash) T.; B.S. in Engring., Auburn U., 1943; m. Mary Louise Armstrong, July 31, 1943; children—Betty Carol Harvey, George Jackson. Instr., Auburn U., 1946-48; engr. Gas Light Co. of Columbus (Ga.), 1949-54, exec. v.p., 1954-57; pres., dir. Western Ky. Gas Co., Owensboro, Ky., 1957-66, dir., 1957-70; pres. Wesken Corp., Owensboro, 1957-66, dir., 1957-70; pres., dir. E. Ohio Gas Co., Cleve., 1966-73, chmn. bd., dir., 1973-74; chmn. W. Ohio Gas Co., 1969-72, dir., 1969-74; pres., dir. Consol. Natural Gas Co., Consol. Natural Gas Service Co., Inc., Pitts., 1974-79, chmn., dir., 1979—; dir. Midland-Ross Corp., Copperweld Corp., Pitts., B.F. Goodrich, Akron, Ohio; past chmn. bd., dir. Pitts. br. Fed. Res. Bank Cleve. Past chmn. bd. trustees Inst. Gas Tech., Chgo.; mem. Ohio Bd. Regents; mem. distbn. com. Cleve. Found.; vice chmn. bd. dirs. Nat. Jr. Achievement; trustee U. Pitts., Mercy Hosp., Pitts. Served to lt. USNR, 1943-45. Mem. Am. (chmn. 1970-71) Gas Assn., Ky. C. of C. (past pres., dir.), Nat. Alliance Businessmen (Cleve. met. chmn.). Clubs: Rolling Rock (Ligonier, Pa.); Duquesne (Pitts.); Union (Cleve.); Econ. (N.Y.C.). Office: 4 Gateway Center Pittsburgh PA 15222

TANKERSLEY, JAMES ODELL, food processing co. exec.; b. Lewisburg, Tenn., Oct. 11, 1912; s. Nat Baxter and Bertha (Crigger) T.; B.S. in Mech. Engring., U. Tenn., 1934; m. Nancy Ella Ingram, July 7, 1934; children—Nancy (Mrs. Finis Eubanks), Julia (Mrs. Jerry Wells), James. I., Daniel B. Mech. engr. TVA, Dept. Commerce, Knoxville, 1935-45; founder Winter Garden, Inc., Bells, Tenn., 1945; pres. United Foods, Inc., 1972—. Mem. devel. council U. Tenn., Knoxville, 1963-66; trustee devel. council Lambuth Coll., Jackson, Tenn., 1969-75; mem. devel. com. U. Tenn., Martin, 1969-75. Mem. Am. Frozen Food Inst. (dir.), Tenn. Strawberry Packers Assn. (past chmn.), Nat. Frozen Food Packers Assn. (dir. research and tech. com. 1962), U.S. C. of C. Methodist. Club: Lions Internat. Home: N High St Extended Bells TN 38006 Office: PO Box 119 Bells TN 38006

TANKIN, RICHARD SAMUEL, mech. engr.; b. Balt., July 14, 1924; s. Harry Jacob and Bertha (Haberer) T.; B.A., Johns Hopkins U., 1948, B.S., 1950; M.S., Mass. Inst. Tech., 1954; Ph.D., Harvard U., 1960; m. Anne Raudelunas, Dec. 2, 1956; children—Roberta, David, John. Asst. prof. U. Del., 1960-61; mem. faculty Northwestern U., 1961—, prof. fluid dynamics, 1968—, chmn. dept. mech. engring. and astronautical scis., 1973-78. Served with AUS, 1943-44, USNR, 1944-45. Mem. ASME, Am. Inst. Aeros. and Astronautics, Am. Geophys. Union, Tau Beta Pi. Home: 820 Ridge Terr Evanston IL 60201

TANKUS, HARRY, engr., mfg. co. exec.; b. Bialystok, Poland, Aug. 23, 1921; s. Isador and Sima (Siegel) T.; came to U.S., 1929, naturalized, 1929; m. Lilia Beverly Lee, Sept. 9, 1947; children—Rolana, Ilyce. Inspection dept. head Buick div. Gen. Motors Co., Melrose Park, Ill., 1942-44; specification engr. Crane Packing Co., Chgo., 1946-53, chief engr., 1953-62, asst. v.p. engring., Morton Grove, 1962-64, asst. v.p. sales, 1964-71, v.p. product sales, 1971-76, pres., 1976—, also dir. Bd. dirs. Ednl. Found., Oakton Community Coll., 1977—, pres., 1979-82. Served with U.S. Army, 1944-46. Decorated Purple Heart. Mem. Soc. Automotive Engrs. (chmn. seal program aerospace conf. 1965), ASME, Am. Soc. Metals, Western Soc. Engrs., Am. Soc. Lubrication Engrs. (pres. 1975-76), Am. Soc. Tool and Mfg. Engrs., AAAS, Am. Ordnance Assn., Nat. Conf. on Fluid Poer (bd. govs. 1970), Am. Soc. Testing and Materials (chmn. subcom. on carbongraphite 1965), Chgo. Nat. History Mus. (asso.). Club: Mason, Shriner, Moose. Contbr. articles to profl. jours. Patentee in field. Home: 415 Sunset Dr Wilmette IL 60091 Office: 6400 Oakton St Morton Grove IL 60053. *The most dangerous attitude we have is the expectation that every citizen of the United States understands the principles behind this country's birth. The need to communicate these principles is vital; the need to exercise them is critical.*

TANNENBAUM, ALBERT, physician; b. Chgo.; B.S., U. Ill., 1922; M.D., Rush Med. Coll., 1930. Sr. chemist, toxicologist Cook County (Ill.) Coroner's Toxicology Lab., 1923-27; Logan research fellow, 1927-29; intern Michael Reese Med. Center, Chgo., 1930-31, asst. dir. hosp.'s dept. biochemistry, 1932-35, dir. dept. cancer research, 1935-71; cons. cancer research, La Jolla, Calif., 1971—. Sect. chief metall. lab. Manhattan Project, 1942-46. Mem. Am. Assn. Cancer Research (pres. 1956-57), Soc. Exptl. Biology and Medicine, Am. Assn. Pathologists. Contbr. articles to profl. jours. Address: 5680 Chelsea Ave La Jolla CA 92037

TANNENBAUM, PERCY H., educator; b. Montreal, Que., Can., May 31, 1927; s. Charles and Ronya (Tannenbaum) T.; B.Sc., McGill U., 1948; M.S., U. Ill., 1951, Ph.D., 1953; m. Brocha Kaplan, Sept. 16, 1948; children—Brian Dov, Nili. Reporter, staff writer Montreal Herald, 1947-50; asst. prof. Mich. State U., 1953-54; research asst. prof. U. Ill., 1954-59; prof. psychology and journalism, dir. Mass Communication Research Center, U. Wis., 1959-67; prof. communication and psychology U. Pa., 1967-70; prof. public policy, dir. survey research center, research psychologist U. Calif. at Berkeley, 1970—. Cons. panel social psychology NSF, NIMH, Nat. Acad. Scis., govt. and industry. Fellow Center Advanced Study Behavioral Scis., 1965-66. Fellow Am. Psychol. Assn., AAAS; mem. AAUP, Am. Assn. Public Opinion Research, Internat. Assn. Mass. Communications Research. Author: (with others) The Measurement of Meaning, 1957. Co-editor: Theories of Cognitive Consistency: A Sourcebook; editor: Psychological Functions of Television. Home: 962 Cragmont Ave Berkeley CA 94708

TANNENBAUM, SAMUEL WILLIAM, lawyer; b. N.Y.C., Mar. 3, 1890; s. Max and Lena (Falk) T.; A.B., Columbia U., 1910, M.A., 1912, LL.B., 1912; m. Frieda M. Stone, June 4, 1922; children—Claire F. Ollstein, Ellen Shadick. Admitted to N.Y. bar, 1912, also U.S. Supreme Ct.; surviving partner Johnson & Tannenbaum, copyright counsel and cons. Metro-Goldwyn-Mayer, 20th Century Fox, Warner Pictures, Paramount, Universal, United Artists, Fuji Telecasting Co. Japan, CBS, NBC, ABC, other prin. motion picture, TV and radio broadcasting cos., radio and TV agys., Tams-Witmark Music Library; arbitrator under motion picture Fed. consent decree; panel expert UNESCO, Revision U.S. Copyright Law; lectr. on copyrights and unfair competition Yale U., Columbia U., N.Y. U., N.Y. Law Sch., Practising Law Inst. Recipient Columbia Alumni medal, Dean's award of Merit, Columbia Coll.; Certificate of Merit, Practising Law Inst.; Harlan Fiske fellow Columbia Law Sch. Mem. Am. Bar Assn. (chmn. copyright div. 1961-62), Assn. Bar City N.Y. (com. on copyrights, com. on round table confs., municipal cts., legal edn.), N.Y. County Lawyers Assn., N.Y. Patent Law Assn., Fed. Bar Assn. (trustee N. Y. N.J. and Conn., award of Merit 1959, copyright com.), Copyright Soc. U.S.A. (founder, pres., trustee), Copyright Luncheon Circle (founder). Served as ensign U.S.N.R.F. World War I. Club: Masons. Author: Practical Problems in Copyright; Current Problems in Copyright; Oddities and Fatal Errors in Copyright; Legal Protection of Titles and Literary Properties; Principle of National Treatment and Works Protected under U.C.C.; Protection of Fictional Characters in the Entertainment and Literary Fields. Home: 430 E 86th St New York NY 10028 Office: 250 W 57th St New York NY 10019

TANNENBAUM, STANLEY IRVING, advt. exec.; b. Phila., Apr. 14, 1928; s. Morris David and Ida (Levin) T.; B.S., Temple U., 1950; m. Audrey Mae Freedman, Feb. 7, 1953; children—Fredric, George, Nancy. With Weightman, Inc., Phila., 1948-53; with advt. dept. RCA, Camden, N.J., 1953-54; chmn. bd. Kenyon & Eckhardt Advt., Inc., N.Y.C., 1954—. Guest lectr. Hofstra U., U. Tenn., U. Wis.; adj. prof. mktg. C.W. Post Coll. Recipient Man of Year award Am. Jewish Com., 1972. Mem. Am. Assn. Advt. Agys. (dir., chmn. com. for improving advt.), Nat. Advt. Rev. Bd. (dir., mem. steering com., chmn. pub. relations com.), Advt. Council (dir.). Club: Old Oaks Country. Home: 1555 Astor St Chicago IL 60610 Office: 10 S Riverside Chicago IL 60606

TANNENWALD, THEODORE, JR., judge; b. Valatie, N.Y., July 28, 1916; s. Theodore and Myra (Barnet) T.; A.B. summa cum laude, Brown U., 1936; LL.B. magna cum laude, Harvard U., 1939; m. Selma Peterfreund, Aug. 3, 1940; children—Peter, Robert. Admitted to N.Y. bar, 1939, D.C. bar, 1946; asso. firm Weil, Gotshal & Manges, N.Y.C., 1939-42, partner, 1947-65; judge U.S. Tax Ct., Washington, 1965—; prin. legal cons. Lend Lease Adminstrn., 1942; acting asst. chief, fgn. funds control div. Dept. State, 1942-43; spl. cons. sec. war, 1943-45; cons. sec. def., 1947-49; counsel to spl. asst. to pres., 1950-51; asst. dir., chief of staff to dir. for mut. security Exec. Office Pres. 1951-53; spl. counsel to Moreland Commn., 1955-58; N.Y. mem. Tri-State Tax Commn., 1958-59; mem. Pres.'s Task Force on Fgn. Aid, spl. asst. to sec. state, 1961; professorial lectr. George Washington U. Sch. Law, 1968-76. Bd. govs., hon. chmn. Hebrew Union Coll., Jewish Inst. Religion; bd. govs., chmn. nat. adv. panel Am. Jewish Com. Mem. Am., Fed., D.C. bar assns., Council Fgn. Relations, Assn. Bar City N.Y., Phi Beta Kappa, Sigma Xi, Delta Sigma Rho. Club: Nat. Lawyers (D.C.). Office: US Tax Ct 400 2d St NW Washington DC 20217

TANNER, CHARLES WILLIAM, profl. baseball team mgr.; b. New Castle, Pa., July 4, 1929. Player Milw. Braves, 1955-57, Chgo. Cubs, 1957-58, Cleve. Indians, 1959-60, Calif. Angels, 1961-62; mgr. Chgo. White Sox, 1970-75, Oakland A's, 1976, Pitts. Pirates, 1977—. Recipient Major League Mgr. of Year award The Sporting News, 1972, Am. League Mgr. of Year award AP, 1972. Address: Three Rivers Stadium 600 Stadium Circle Pittsburgh PA 15212*

TANNER, DANIEL, educator; b. N.Y.C., Sept. 22, 1926; s. John and Lillian (Jupiter) T.; B.S. with honors, Mich. State U., 1949, M.S., 1952; Ph.D. (Univ. Scholar), Ohio State U., 1955; m. Laurel Nan Jacobson, July 11, 1948. Asst. prof. edn. San Francisco State Coll., 1955-60; asso. prof. edn., coordinator Midwest program on airborne TV instrn. Purdue U., 1960-62; asso. prof. edn., asso. dir. internat. program for edn. leaders Northwestern U., 1962-64; asso. prof. research div. tchr. edn. City U. N.Y., 1964-66; prof. edn., dir. Center for Urban Edn., U. Wis.-Milw. Sch. Edn., 1966-67; prof. edn., dir. grad. programs in curriculum theory and devel. Grad. Sch. Edn., Rutgers U., New Brunswick, N.J., 1967—, chmn. dept. curriculum and instrn., 1969-71, faculty research fellow, 1974-75; vis. lectr. Tchrs. Coll. Columbia, summer 1966; vis. prof. Emory U., summer 1968, SUNY, Binghamton, winter 1968; vis. scholar U. London Inst. Edn., 1974-75. Mem. rev. bd. coll. work-study program U.S. Office Edn., 1965; cons. Chgo. Sch. Survey, 1964-65, Center Urban Edn., N.Y.C., 1964-65, West Chicago (Ill.) Sch. Survey, 1963-64, Nat. Ednl. TV Center, N.Y.C., 1963, Campbell County (Va.) Sch. Survey, 1970, Memphis Schs., 1977-78, others. Fellow AAAS, John Dewey Soc.; mem. Am. Ednl. Research Assn., N.Y. Acad. Sci., AAUP, Am. Polit. Sci. Assn., Am. Ednl. Studies Assn., Phi Kappa Phi, Phi Delta Kappa (Service award 1957). Author: Schools for Youth: Change and Challenge in Secondary Education, 1965; Secondary Curriculum: Theory and Development, 1971; Secondary Education: Perspectives and Prospects, 1972; Using Behavioral Objectives in the Classroom, 1972; Curriculum Development: Theory into Practice, 2d edit., 1980; contbr. author: Readings in Educational Psychology, 1965; Yearbook of the Associations for Student Teaching, 1962; The Great Debate, Our Schools in Crisis, 1959; Educational Issues in a Changing Society, 1964; Programs, Teachers and Machines, 1964; Views on American Schooling, 1964; The Training of America's Teachers, 1975; co-author: Teen Talk: Curriculum Materials in Communications, 1971; contbg. editor Ednl. Leadership, 1969-74; contbr. articles to nat. mags., ednl. jours. Home: Highwood Rd Somerset NJ 08873 Office: Grad Sch Edn Rutgers U New Brunswick NJ 08903. *The essential quality of education and life is growth. Hence problems must be seen as opportunities and not as limitations if solutions are to be found and progress is to be made. The glass half full is more than the glass half empty.*

TANNER, E(LEANOR) J(ANE), mfg. co. exec.; b. Grinnell, Iowa, Nov. 8, 194[illegible] d. Robert Raymond and Dorothy Jeanne (Wood) T.; B.S., U. Iowa, 1964, J.D., 1967; M.B.A., De Paul U., Chgo., 1974. Admitted to Iowa bar, 1967, Ill. bar, 1968; asso. in trust U.S. Comptroller of Currency, Chgo., 1967-69; asso. counsel Chgo. Title Ins. Co., 1969-74; officer Continental Ill. Nat. Bank, Chgo., 1974-78; treas. Wylain, Inc., Dallas, 1978—. Mem. Ill. Bar Assn., Iowa Bar Assn., Fin. Execs. Inst., Delta Mu Delta. Club: Bent Tree Country (Dallas). Home: 7038 Mason Dells Dallas TX 75230 Office: 17250 Dallas Pkwy Dallas TX 75248

TANNER, HAROLD, investment banker; b. N.Y.C., May 7, 1932; s. Irving and Pauline (Steinlauf) T.; B.S., Cornell U., 1952; M.B.A., Harvard U., 1956; m. Estelle Newman, July 6, 1957; children—David, James, Karen. Vice pres., dir. Blyth & Co. Inc., N.Y.C., 1956-69; exec. v.p. New Court Securities Corp., N.Y.C., 1969-76, Blyth Eastman Dillon & Co., Inc., N.Y.C., 1977—; dir. Mark Controls Corp. Co-founder Vol. Urban Cons. Group. Served to lt. (j.g.) USNR, 1952-54. Clubs: Century, Wall St., Bond. Home: 18 Kensington Rd Scarsdale NY 10583 Office: 1221 Ave of Americas New York NY 10020

TANNER, HENRY, newspaperman; b. Berne, Switzerland, July 7, 1918; s. Victor and Anne (Muhleman) T.; student U. Zurich (Switzerland), 1937-38, 41-43, Sorbonne, Paris, France, 1939; 1 son, Victor. Wire editor United Press, 1941-42, corr. in Yugoslavia and Greece, 1945-48; fgn. news analyst, Washington corr. Houston Post, 1948- 58; N.Y. Times corr., Algeria, 1958-60, 62, The Congo, 1960-61, chief corr., Moscow, 1963-65, Paris, 1965-69, UN, 1969-72, Cairo, 1972-77, Rome, 1977—. Nieman fellow Harvard, 1954-55. Office: care NY Times 229 W 43d St New York NY 10036 also NY Times Via Della Dataria 94 Rome Italy

TANNER, LEONARD ROSCOE, III, profl. tennis player; b. Lookout Mountain, Tenn., Oct. 15, 1951; s. Leonard Roscoe and Anne (Brueggeman) T.; B.A., Stanford U.; m. Nancy Cook, May 26, 1973. Ranked #1 Tennis player in U.S. for Males, 18 years old and under, 1969; mem. All-Am. Tennis Player, Stanford U., 1971-72; U.S. Amateur Champion, 1970; U.S. Amateur Indoor Singles and Doubles Champion, 1971; U.S. Clay Court Doubles Champion, 1971; NCAA Doubles Champion, 1972; now profl.; Ranked #5 player in America, 1972, #3, 1975; semi-finalist, Wimbledon, England, 1974, 75, finalist, 1979; semi-finalist Forest Hills, 1975, U.S. Open, 1979; tennis dir. Kiawah Island (S.C.) Resort. Recipient Johnston Sportsmanship Trophy, Forest Hills, N.Y. Mem. Internat. Club Tennis, Assn. Tennis Profl., U.S. Tennis Assn., Zeta Psi. Republican. Presbyterian. Mem. U.S. Davis Cup Team, 1975-78. Home: Kiawah Island SC also 1109 Gnome Tr Lookout Mountain TN 37350 also Eucalyptus Hill Dr Santa Barbara CA

TANNER, NATHAN ELDON, ch. ofcl.; b. Salt Lake City, May 9, 1898; s. Nathan William and Sarah Edna (Brown) T.; spl. courses U. Alta., 1925, U. Utah, 1932-34; m. Sara Isabelle Merrill, Dec. 20, 1919; children—Ruth M. (Mrs. C.R. Walker), Sara Isabelle (Mrs. W.S. Jensen), Zola (Mrs. H.S. Rhodes), Beth (Mrs. Grant Spackman), Helen (Mrs. Jack Beaton). Sch. prin. Hill Spring, Alta., Can., 1919-27, Cardston, Alta., 1928-35; bishop Ch. of Jesus Christ Latter-day Saints Cardston Ward, 1932-35, now 1st pres.; elected to Alta. Legislature, 1935; speaker Legislative Assembly, 1936; minister land and mines Govt. Province Alta., 1937-52; pres., Trans-Canada Pipe Lines, 1951-55; pres., gen. mgr. Merill Petroleum Ltd., Provincial commr. Boy Scout Assn. Alta., 1946. Mem. Town Council Cardston, 1933-34. Mem. Canadian Inst. Mining and Metallurgy, Research Council Alta. (past chmn.). Mem. Social Credit party. Club: Mayfair Golf and Country. Address: 47 East South Temple St Salt Lake City UT 84111

TANNER, RAYMOND LEWIS, educator; b. Memphis, Dec. 11, 1931; s. Arthur Thomas and Josephine (Pearce) T.; B.S. in Phys. Sci., Memphis State U., 1953; M.S. in Physics, Vanderbilt U., 1955; Ph.D. in Med. Physics, U. Calif. at Los Angeles, 1967; m. Margaret Ann Foster, Sept. 4, 1958; children—John William, Paul Russell, Rebecca Lee. Instr. physics Memphis State U., 1955-57, asst. prof., 1958-62; guest instr. radiology Harbor Gen. Hosp., Torrance, Calif., 1963-64; mem. faculty dept. radiology Coll. Medicine, U. Tenn., Memphis, 1967—, asso. prof., 1967-70, prof., 1970—. Cons., VA Hosp., Memphis, Radiation Protection Cons., Memphis; examiner physics Am. Bd. Radiology, 1971—. Recipient radiobiology award So. Calif. Health Physics Soc., 1966; AEC fellow, 1953-55, USPHS fellow, 1957-58, USPHS trainee, 1962-66, NASA research asst., 1966-67. Diplomate Am. Bd. Radiology. Mem. Am. Coll. Radiology, Am. Assn. Physicists in Medicine (pres. 1973-74), Tenn. Acad. Sci. (pres. 1977), Health Physics Soc. (com. ins. 1970—), Radiol. Soc. N.Am. (chmn. asso. sci. com. 1974-77), Tenn. Radiol. Soc., Am. Assn. Physics Tchrs. (pres. Tenn. 1973), Sigma Xi. Contbr. to profl. jours. Home: 450 Avon Rd Memphis TN 38117

TANSELLE, DONALD WILLIAM, banker; b. Pittsboro, Ind., Aug. 4, 1924; s. William Lynn and Edna Gertrude (Gentry) T.; grad. Canterbury Coll.; grad. U. Wis. Grad. Sch. Banking; m. Juanita Eckler, June 30, 1946; children—Tim, John. With Mchts. Nat. Bank & Trust Co., Indpls., 1948—, sr. v.p., 1969-70, exec. v.p., 1970-72, pres., 1972—, also dir.; dir. Resenor Machine & Tool Co., L. C. Cassidy & Son, Inc., Graham's Furniture, Inc., Mchts. Nat. Corp., Circle Leasing Corp., Mchts. Investment Counseling, Inc., Heid Econ. Research, M.N.B. Fin. Corp., Pacific Am. Leasing. Bd. dirs. St. Francis Hosp., Indpls., Ind. Central U., Greater Indpls. Housing Devel., Inc., 500 Festival Assos., Indpls., Jr. Achievement, Indpls., Better Bus. Bur. and Community Devel. Task Force; trustee Ind. Central U.; treas. West Dist. Methodist Ch. Served with U.S. Army, 1943-46. Mem. Ind., Am. bankers assns., Indpls. Clearing House Assn., Assn. Res. City Bankers, Indpls. C. of C. (dir.), Am. Legion, VFW. Clubs: Indpls. Athletic, Indpls. Country, Masons (Pittsboro). Office: Mchts Nat Bank & Trust Co One Merchants Plaza Indianapolis IN 46204

TANSELLE, GEORGE THOMAS, educator, found. exec.; b. Lebanon, Ind., Jan. 29, 1934; s. K. Edwin and Madge R. (Miller) T.; B.A. magna cum laude, Yale U., 1955; M.A., Northwestern U., 1956, Ph.D., 1959. Instr., Chgo. City Jr. Coll., 1958-60; instr. U. Wis., Madison, 1960-61, asst. prof., 1961-63, asso. prof., 1963-68, prof. English, 1968-78; v.p. John Simon Guggenheim Meml. Found., 1978—. Mem. Planning Inst. Commn. on English, 1961; mem. exec. com. Center for Edits. Am. Authors, 1970-73; mem. advisory com. for drama for bicentennial Kennedy Center, 1974-75; mem. exec. com. Center for Scholarly Edits., 1976—; mem. N.Am. Com. for 18th-Century Short Title Catalog, 1978—; mem. nat. adv. bd. Center for Book, Library of Congress, 1978—. Recipient Kiekhofer Teaching award U. Wis., 1963, Jenkins award for bibliography, 1973. Guggenheim fellow, 1969-70; Am. Council Learned Socs. fellow, 1973-74; Nat. Endowment for the Humanities fellow, 1977-78. Mem. Modern Lang. Assn. Am. (mem. exec. com. bibliog. evidence group, 1974-75, methods of lit. research div. 1979—, mem. Hubbell award Com. Am. lit. sect. 1978—), Modern Humanities Research Assn., Bibliog. Soc. London, Bibliog. Soc. Australia, Bibliog. Soc. Am. (mem. council, 1970—, vice chmn. publs. com. 1974-76, 2d v.p. 1978—), Bibliog. Soc. U. Va., Oxford, Cambridge, Edinburgh, Birmingham, Can. bibliog. socs., Soc. for Bibliography of Natural History, Printing Hist. Soc. (Am. corr. 1970—), Am. Printing Hist. Assn., Pvt. Libraries Assn., Fellows Morgan Library, Manuscript Soc. (dir., 1974—), Am. Antiquarian Soc. (mem. publs. com., 1972—, chmn. com. 1978—, mem. council, 1974—, del. to Am. Council Learned Socs. 1978—), Nat. Council Tchrs. English, Book Club Calif., Typophiles, Guild Book Workers, Wis. Acad. Scis., Arts and Letters, Renaissance Soc. Am., Phi Beta Kappa. Clubs: Century, Yale, Caxton, Grolier. Author: Royall Tyler, 1967; Guide to the Study of United States Imprints, 1971; A Checklist of Editions of Moby Dick, 1976; Selected Studies in Bibliography, 1979. Bibliog. editor: The Writings of Herman Melville, 1968—. Mem. editorial bd. Contemporary Literature, 1962—, Abstracts of English Studies, 1964-78, Papers of Bibliog. Soc. Am., 1968—, Resources for American Literary Study, 1971—, Analytical and Enumerative Bibliography, 1977—, Review, 1978—, Am. Literature, 1979—. Contbr. articles to profl. jours. Office: John Simon Guggenheim Memorial Foundation 90 Park Ave New York NY 10016

TANSILL, FREDERICK RIKER, lawyer; b. Washington, July 12, 1914; s. Frederick Guida and Elizabeth Estele (Riker) T.; B.S.S., Georgetown U., 1936, J.D., 1941; postgrad. Benjamin Franklin U., 1951-53; m. Mary Eileen Loftus, Dec. 31, 1940; children—Claire Tansill Hermann, Constance Tansill Gelfuso, Fred, Celine Tansill Kramer, Eileen. Credit reporter Dun & Bradstreet, Washington, 1938; instr. R.O.T.C., Georgetown U., 1940-42; admitted to D.C. bar, 1940; spl. atty. IRS, N.Y.C., 1945-48; partner firm Goodwin, Rosenbaum & Meacham, Washington, 1948-68, firm Cox, Langford & Brown, Washington, 1968-69, firm McInnis, Wilson, Munson & Woods, Washington, 1969-72, firm Bird & Tansill, Washington, 1972-79, firm Ober, Grimes & Shriver, Balt. and Washington, 1979—; instr. tax Ben Franklin U., 1956-57, econs., 1967; acting gen. counsel Children to Children, Inc., Washington, 1975-79. Bd. dirs. Woodley Park Community Assn., Washington, 1968-76, v.p., 1975-76. Served with AUS, 1942-45. Mem. Am., Fed., D.C. bar assns., Delta Theta Phi.

Republican. Roman Catholic (pres. parish council 1973-76, 78). Clubs: Army and Navy, Nat. Lawyers. Home: 2740 Cortland Pl NW Washington DC 20008 Office: 1140 Connecticut Ave NW Washington DC 20036

TANZER, LESTER, editor; b. N.Y.C., Aug. 3, 1929; s. Charles and Clara (Ente) T.; A.B., Columbia U., 1951, M.S., Sch. Journalism, 1952; m. Marlene June Luckton, June 29, 1949; children—Stephen Drew, Jeffrey Marc, Andrew Wayne, M. David. Reporter, Washington bur. Wall St. Jour., 1952-59; asso. editor Changing Times mag., Washington, 1959-64; asso. editor U.S. News & World Report, Washington, 1964-76, mng. editor, 1976—; dir. U.S. News & World Report Corp., Washington. Mem. Nat. Symphony Assn., White House Corrs. Assn. Club: Cosmos. Author: (with Stefan Ilok) Brotherhood of Silence, 1962; editor: The Kennedy Circle, 1961. Home: 4859 N 30th St Arlington VA 22207 Office: 2300 N St NW Washington DC 20037

TAPE, GERALD FREDERICK, assn. adminstr.; b. Ann Arbor, Mich., May 29, 1915; s. Henry A. and Flora (Simmons) T.; A.B., Eastern Mich. U., 1935, Sc.D. (hon.), 1964; M.S., U. Mich., 1936, Ph.D., 1940; m. Josephine Waffen, June 18, 1939; children—Walter Richard, James William, Thomas Gerald. Asst. physics Eastern Mich. U., 1933-35, U. Mich., 1936-39; instr. physics Cornell U., 1939-42; staff mem. radiation lab. Mass. Inst. Tech., 1942-46; asst., then asso. prof. physics U. Ill., 1946-50; asst. to dir., then dep. dir. Brookhaven Nat. Lab., 1950-62; v.p., then pres. Asso. Univs., Inc., 1962-63, pres., 1969—; commr. AEC, 1963-69; U.S. rep. to IAEA with rank of ambassador, 1973-77; mem. Pres.'s Sci. Adv. Com., 1969-73; mem. Def. Sci. Bd., 1970-73, chmn., 1970-72; mem. sci. adv. com. IAEA, 1972-73; mem. gen. adv. com. ERDA, 1975-77. Recipient Army-Navy Certificate of Appreciation, 1947, Meritorious Civilian Service medal Sec. Def., 1969, Dept. State Tribute Appreciation, 1969, Dept. Def. medal for public service, 1973; Henry DeWolf Smyth Nuclear Statesman award Atomic Indsl. Forum/Am. Nuclear Soc., 1978. Fellow Am. Phys. Soc., Am. Nuclear Soc., AAAS; mem. Am. Astron. Soc., Phi Beta Kappa, Sigma Xi, Phi Kappa Phi, Kappa Delta Pi. Author: (with L.J. Haworth) Relay Radar Chapter of MIT Radiation Laboratory Technical Series, 1947; also papers, reports. Home: 6717 Tulip Hill Terr Washington DC 20016 Office: 1717 Massachusetts Ave Suite 603 Washington DC 20036

TAPLEY, BYRON DEAN, aerospace engr.; b. Charleston, Miss., Jan. 16, 1933; s. Ebbie Byron and Myrtle (Myers) T.; B.S., U. Tex., 1956, M.S., 1958, Ph.D., 1960; m. Sophia Philen, Aug. 28, 1959; children—Mark Byron, Craig Philen. Research engr. Structural Mechanics Research Lab., U. Tex., Austin, 1954-58, instr. dept. mech. engring., 1958, prof. dept. aerospace engring. and engring. mechanics, 1960—, chmn. dept. 1966—, adv. scientist Lockheed Missile and Space Vehicle div., Sunnyvale, Calif., 1961, W.R. Woolrich prof. engring., 1974—; cons. NASA Manned Spacecraft Center, 1965—, mem. adv. com. on guidance control and nav., 1966-67, com. on space research, panel I, 1974—, chmn. region IV, engring. council on profl. devel., 1974—. Mem. ASME, Am. Acad. Mechanics, Am. Astronautics Soc., Soc. Engring. Sci., Am. Inst. Aeros. and Astronautics (chmn. com. on astrodynamics 1976—), IEEE, Am. Geophys. Union, Am. Astron. Soc., AAAS, Internat. Astron. Union, Sigma Xi, Pi Tau Sigma, Sigma Gamma Tau, Phi Kappa Phi, Tau Beta Pi. Editor Celestial Mech. Jour., 1976—. Home: 3100 Perry Ln Austin TX 78731

TAPLEY, JAMES LEROY, lawyer, railway co. exec.; b. Greenville, Miss., July 10, 1923; s. Lester Leroy and Lillian (Clark) T.; A.B., U. N.C., 1947, J.D., 1950; m. Priscilla Moore, Sept. 9, 1950; children—Lane, Taylor, Cameron, James Clark, Meredith. Admitted to N.C. bar, 1951, D.C. bar, 1962; with So. Ry. Co., Washington, 1953—, gen. solicitor, 1967-74, asst. v.p.-law, 1974-75, v.p.-law, 1975—. Mem. Kappa Sigma. Clubs: Chevy Chase (Md.), Univ. Home: 7007 Beechwood Dr Chevy Chase MD 20015 Office: PO Box 1808 Washington DC 20013

TAPLIN, FRANK E., trustee edn. and arts instns.; b. Cleve., June 22, 1915; s. Frank Elijah and Edith R. (Smith) T.; B.A. in History, Princeton U., 1937; M.A. in Jurisprudence (Rhodes scholar), Oxford U., 1939; LL.B., Yale U., 1941; m. Ngaio I. Thornton, Sept. 3, 1943 (div. Mar. 1951); children—Caroline I. Taplin Ruschell, Jennifer E. Taplin Jerome, David F.; m. 2d, Margaret A. Eaton, Apr. 27, 1953; stepchildren—Jennifer A. Eaton Dickerman, Martha D. Eaton Kelly, Susan. Admitted to Ohio bar, 1946; with firm Jones, Day Cockley & Reavis, Cleve., 1946-50; asst. to Sen. Taft in Ohio senatorial campaign, 1950; pvt. bus. investments, Cleve., 1951-57; asst. to pres. Princeton U., 1957-59; chmn. bd. Scurry-Rainbow Oil, Ltd., 1954-74; dir. N.Am. Coal Corp.; pres. Cleve. Inst. Music, 1952-56; trustee Cleve. Orch., 1946-57, pres., 1955-57; pres. Nat. Council Met. Opera, 1961-64; dir. Met. Opera Assn., 1961—, 65—, pres., chief exec. officer, 1977—; mem. council for univ. resources Princeton. Hon. trustee Bradford (Mass.) Coll.; trustee Princeton (N.J.) Day Sch., 1966-72, Princeton Area United Community Fund, 1963-76; mem. Princeton U. Music Dept. Adv. Council, 1960—, chmn., 1965-71; trustee Sarah Lawrence Coll., 1969-77, chmn., 1973-77; trustee, mem. exec. com. Lincoln Center for Performing Arts; trustee, v.p. Lincoln Center Chamber Music Soc., 1969—, pres., 1969-73; fellow Morgan Library; mem. council Friends Princeton Library; chmn. bd. Marlboro Sch. Music, 1964-70, now trustee; trustee Woodrow Wilson Nat. Fellowship Found., Inst. for Advanced Study, Princeton, 1971—, Am. Schs. Oriental Research, 1970-75, Western Res. Hist. Soc., Cleve.; internat. bd. dirs. United World Colls., London, 1973-76, also chmn. U.S. commn., 1973-75; bd. dirs. Am. Friends of Covent Garden and Royal Ballet, Friends of Aldeburgh Festival. Served from ensign to lt. comdr., USNR, 1941-46. Decorated hon. mem. (mil. div.) Order Brit. Empire. Mem. Am. Bar Assn., Assn. Am. Rhodes Scholars, Oliver Wendell Holmes Assn. (chmn. bd. 1964-67), World Assn. of World Federalists (asst. to pres. 1967-69, adv. bd. 1970—,), Princeton U. Alumni Council, Phi Beta Kappa. Episcopalian. Clubs: Union, Tavern (Cleve.); Nassau, Pretty Brook (Princeton); Univ., Century (N.Y.C.). Home: 55 Armour Rd Princeton NJ 08540 Office: One Palmer Sq Princeton NJ 08540

TAPLINGER, TERRY LENT, publisher; b. N.Y.C., June 11, 1943; d. Milton and Clara (Green) Lent; student Sorbonne, 1963-64; m. Richard Taplinger, Aug. 28, 1970. Promotion dir. Taplinger Pub. Co., Inc., N.Y.C., 1966-73, pres., 1973-78. Home: 2 Horatio St New York NY 10014

TAPPAN, DAVID S., JR., mfg. co. exec.; b. China, 1922; B.A., Swarthmore Coll., 1943; M.B.A., Stanford, 1948; married. With Fluor Corp., Los Angeles, 1952—, v.p. domestic sales, 1959-68, sr. v.p., gen. mgr. engring. and constrn. div., 1968-72, mem. exec. com., dir.; pres. Fluor Engrs. & Construction, Inc., 1972-76, vice chmn. bd., 1976—. Served to lt. (j.g.) USNR, 1943-46. Office: 3333 Michelson Dr Irvine CA 92730

TAPPAN, JOHN RUDOLPH, ins. co. exec., investment cons.; b. Altoona, Pa., Sept. 29, 1903; s. Arthur Butler and May Agnes (Snyder) T.; B.S., U. Pa. Wharton Sch., 1926; M.B.A., Harvard, 1928; m. Pauline Marguerite Masterson, July 13, 1929; children—Michael Arthur, Deborah Christine. Mem. staff fin. dept. Harvard Bus. Sch., 1929; investment analyst Goldman, Sachs & Co., 1929-31; with Am. Re-Ins. Co., N.Y.C., 1932-70, financial v.p., 1940-65, sr. v.p., 1965-70, also dir., mem. exec. com.; cons. Wyndham Securities Corp. Trustee Packer Collegiate Inst.; bd. dirs., mem. fin. com. Bklyn. Home Children. Mem. Ins. Soc. N.Y., Ins. Investment Officers, Alpha Chi Rho. Clubs: University (N.Y.C.), Rembrant, Ihpetonga (Bklyn.). Home: 200 Hicks St Brooklyn NY 11201 Office 91 Liberty St New York NY 10006

TAPPAN, WILLIAM RICHARD, appliance mfr.; b. Mansfield, Ohio, Nov. 7, 1914; s. Paul R. and Heloise (Hedges) T.; A.B., Denison U., 1936; M.B.A., Harvard, 1938; m. Virginia Starkey, Nov. 11, 1938 (dec. Oct. 1974); children—Margaret, Thomas. With Tappan Co., Mansfield, 1938—, salesman, asst. to sales mgr., mgr. war product devel., mgr. new product devel., exec. v.p., 1938-58, pres., 1958-75, chmn. bd., 1975-79, also dir.; ret., 1979; dir. Ohio Edison Co., Akron, Ohio. Office: Tappan Co Tappan Park Mansfield OH 44901

TAPPÉ, ALBERT ANTHONY, architect; b. Pitts., Aug. 12, 1928; s. Albert Anthony and Martha Ann (McKee) T.; student William and Mary Coll., 1947-48, Fontainebleau Fine Art and Music Sch., 1951; B.S., U. Va., 1952; M.Arch., Mass. Inst. Tech., 1958, M. City Planning; m. Jean Bates, June 27, 1963; children—Eliza Bruce, Albert Anthony III. Designer, McLeod & Ferrara, Architects, Washington, 1954-55; planner Boston City Planning Bd., 1957-58; architect and planner Architects Collaborative, Cambridge, Mass., 1958-61; partner Huygens & Tappé, Inc., architects and planners, Boston, 1962—; instr. dept. city planning Mass. Inst. Tech., 1959-60; cons. architect Mass. Bur. Library Extension, 1965-76; chmn. bldg. commn., Brookline, Mass., 1977, mem. bd. examiners, Brookline; v.p. Guild for Religious Architecture; mem. Back Bay Archtl. Commn. Served with AUS, 1946-47, 52-54. Recipient Progressive Architecture Design award, 1966, 1st place single family category Plywood Design Awards Program, 1973, Award of Merit, 1974. Mem. AIA (mem. nat. urban planning and design com. 1975, citation, hon. mentions 1969, 1st honor award 1970, honor award New Eng. Regional Council 1976), Mass. Assn. Atchitects (exec. com.), Boston Soc. Architects (dir.), Am. Inst. Planners, Am. Soc. Planning Ofcls., Am. Soc. Ch. Architects, Soc. Archtl. Historians. Clubs: Union Boat, Rotary (Boston); Eastern Point Yacht (Gloucester, Mass.). Author: Guide to Planning a Library Building, 1967. Important works include Longy Concert Hall, Cambridge, Mass., Campus N.H. Coll., Franklin Park Zoo, Boston, Lynn Inst. for Savs., Interfaith Religious Center, Columbia, Md., Hotel, Costa Smeralda, Sardinia, also residences in U.S., France, Switzerland and Holland, housing projects in New Eng. Home: 58 Euston St Brookline MA 02146 Office: 462 Boylston St Boston MA 02116

TAPPEN, NEIL CAMPBELL, educator, anthropologist; b. Jacksonville, Fla., Feb. 26, 1920; s. Edgar Leroy and Helen (Jacks) T.; A.B., U. Fla., 1941; M.A., U. Chgo., 1949, Ph.D., 1952; student U. Wis., 1947-48; m. Ardith Donna Bennett, June 29, 1952; children—Helen Louise, Martha Joan. Research asso. U. Mich., 1951-52; instr. U. Pa., 1952-54; instr., then asst. prof. Emory U., 1954-59; asso. prof. Tulane U., 1959-65; prof. anthropology U. Wis.-Milw., 1965—, E.A. Hooton prof., 1969—; Fulbright research scholar, Uganda, 1956-57; field study, Sierra Leone and Liberia, 1963, Amazon River, 1964. Served with USAAF, 1941-42; to lt. USNR, 1942-46. Mem. Am. Anthrop. Assn., Am. Assn. Phys. Anthropologists, A.A.A.S., Soc. Study Evolution, Soc. Cranio-facial Biology, Internat. Primatological Soc., Am. Assn. U. Profs., Phi Beta Kappa, Sigma Xi, Phi Kappa Phi, Kappa Sigma. Research on fossil man, Europe, 1971-72, South Africa, 1975. Home: 2709 E Shorewood Blvd Milwaukee WI 53211

TAQUEY, CHARLES HENRI, writer, cons.; b. Paris, France, Feb. 1912; s. Henri and Marguerite (Normand) T.; B.S., Paris U., 1929; Laureat, Ecole Libre des Sciences Politiques, 1933; Licencié and Lauréat, D.E.S., Paris Law Sch., 1934; m. Ruth McVitty, Feb. 1, 1947; children—Antony, Chantal. French Treasury rep., Paris, London, Berlin, N.Y.C., 1934-47; local currencies mgr. ECA, 1948-51; staff officer Exec. Office of Pres., 1952-57; fgn. service econ. officer Am. embassies, Phnom-Penh, Cambodia, Tunis, Tunisia, Kingston, Jamaica, also detailed to Dept. Commerce as dep. dir. fgn. activities mgmt., 1957-70; mgmt. cons., ecol. economist (internat. trade and resources recovery), 1970—; expert witness Tariff Commn. and ways and means com. U.S. Ho. of Reps., GAO, fgn. govts. Served as lt., arty. French Army, 1940; lt., arty. AUS, 1942-46, capt., 1952. Mem. Chemurgic Council, Soc. Internat. Devel., Acad. Polit. Sci., Am. Acad. Polit. and Social Sci., Council for Competitive Economy, Nat. Planning Assn. Author: German Financial Crisis, 1931; Richard Cobden, 1938; Trusts and Patents, 1946; Obstacles to Development in Indonesia, 1952; Fisheries in Cambodia, 1959; Against Full Employment, 1973; Democracy and Socialism, 1976; Transnational Corporations and the State, 1979. Address: 1681 31st St NW Washington DC 20007 also les Quatre Vents 84580 Oppède France

TARAN, LEONARDO, classicist; b. Galarza, Argentina, Feb. 22, 1933; s. Miguel and Liuba (Etlis) T.; came to U.S., 1958, naturalized, 1976; legal degree U. Buenos Aires, 1958; Ph.D. in Classics, Princeton U., 1962; m. Judit Sofia Lida, Dec. 10, 1971; 1 son, Gabriel Andrew. Jr. fellow Inst. Research in Humanities, U. Wis., 1962-63, Center Hellenic Studies, Washington, 1963-64; asst. prof. classics U. Calif., Los Angeles, 1964-67; mem. faculty Columbia U., 1967—, prof. Greek and Latin, 1971—, chmn. dept., 1976-79; mem. Inst. Advanced Study, Princeton, N.J., 1966-67, 78-79; trustee Assn. Mems. Inst. Advanced Study, 1974-79; mem. mng. com. Am. Sch. Classical Studies, 1976—. Fellow Am. Council Learned Socs., 1966-67, 71-72, Guggenheim Found., 1975; grantee Am. Philos. Soc., 1963, 71, 75, Am. Council Learned Socs., 1968, 72. Mem. Am. Philol. Assn., Classical Assn. Atlantic States, Soc. Ancient Greek Philosophy, Assn. Guillaume Budé. Author: Parmenides, 1965; Asclepius of Tralles, Commentary to Nicomachus' Introduction to Arithmetic, 1969; Plato, Philip of Opus and the Pseudo-Platonic Epinomis, 1975; Anonymous Commentary on Aristotle's De Interpretatione, 1978; co-author: Eraclito: Testimonianze e imitazioni, 1972. Editorial bd. Columbia Studies in the Classical Tradition, 1976—. Home: 39 Claremont Ave New York NY 10027 Office: 615 Hamilton Hall Columbia U New York NY 10027

TARANIK, JAMES VLADIMIR, geologist; b. Los Angeles, Apr. 23, 1940; s. Vladimir James and Jeanette Downing (Smith) T.; B.Sc. in Geology, Stanford U., 1964; Ph.D., Colo. Sch. Mines, 1974; m. Colleen Sue Glessner, Dec. 4, 1971; children—Debra Lynn, Danny Lee. Chief remote sensing Iowa Geol. Survey, Iowa City, 1971-74; prin. remote sensing scientist Earth Resources Observation Systems Data Center, U.S. Geol. Survey, Sioux Falls, S.D., 1975-79; chief non-renewable resources br., resource observation div. Office of Space and Terrestrial Applications, NASA Hdqrs., Washington, 1979—; adj. prof. geology U. Iowa, 1971-79; vis. prof. civil engring. Iowa State U., 1972-74; adj. prof. earth sci. U. S.D., 1976-79. Served with C.E., U.S. Army, 1965-67. Decorated Bronze Star medal. NASA prin. investigator, 1973; NDEA fellow, 1968-71. Fellow Geol. Soc. Am.; mem. Am. Assn. Petroleum Geologists, Soc. Mining Engrs., Am. Inst. Profl. Geologists (certified), AIAA, Soc. Exploration Geophysicists, Am. Soc. Photogrammetry (certified), Internat. Soc. Photogrammetry (pres. Working Group II/4), AAAS, Sigma Xi. Developer remote sensing program and remote sensing lab. for State of Iowa, ednl. program in remote sensing for Iowa univs.; Office Space and Terrestrial Applications program scientist for space shuttle; contbr. to profl. jours. Home: 10608 Margate Rd 107 Silver Spring MD 20901 Office: Resource Observation Div Office of Space and Terrestrial Applications NASA Hdqrs CODE ERS-2 Washington DC 20546. *I have always been in awe of the universe in which we live and the little time we have on earth to perceive and understand it.*

TARANOVSKY, KIRIL, educator; b. Tartu, Estonia, Mar. 19, 1911; s. Theodore and Maria (Stefani) T.; came to U.S., 1958, naturalized, 1968; LL.B., Belgrade U., 1933, M.A., 1936, Ph.D., 1941; M.A. (hon.), Harvard U., 1963; m. Radmila Petrovich, Feb. 4, 1940 (dec. June 1957); children—Theodore, Vidosava; m. 2d, Vera Arandjelovich, June 28, 1958. Asst., Belgrade (Yugoslavia) U., 1937-46, docent, 1946-51, asso. prof. Slavic langs and lits., 1951-56, prof., 1956-59; prof. Slavic langs. and lits. UCLA, 1959-62; vis. lectr. Slavic langs. and lits. Harvard U., Cambridge, Mass., 1958-59, prof., 1963—. Author: Russian Binary Meters, 1953; Essays on Mandel'stam, 1976. Office: Harvard U Boylston Hall 303 Cambridge MA 02138*

TARANTA, ANGELO, physician, educator; b. Rome, 1927; came to U.S., 1952, naturalized, 1956; M.D., U. Rome, 1949. Intern dept. internal medicine and pediatrics Univ. Hosp., Rome, 1949-50, resident, 1950-52; resident in medicine St. Mary's Hosp., Rochester, N.Y., 1952-53; resident in cardiology Irvington (N.Y.) House, 1953-54, research asso., 1955-59, research dir., 1959-62, asso. dir. Irvington House Inst., N.Y.C., 1965-71; research fellow in microbiology N.Y. U. Sch. Medicine, 1955-56, instr. in microbiology, 1955-58, adj. asst. prof. microbiology, 1958-60, asst. prof. medicine, 1960-65, asso. prof., 1965-75, on leave of absence, 1975-79; dir. medicine Cabrini Health Care Center, N.Y.C., 1975—; prof. medicine, chief rheumatology and immunology div. N.Y. Med. Coll., 1979—; co-chmn. study group on heart disease in the young Inter-Soc. Commn. on Heart Disease Resources, 1972—; v.p. Comite Panamericano de Estudio y Prevencion de la Fiebre Reumatica, 1974—; bd. dirs. Am. Heart Assn., 1975-77; chmn. Council on Cardiovascular Disease in the Young, 1975-77; cons. in field. Fulbright travel grantee, 1952. Diplomate Am. Bd. Internal Medicine. Mem. Soc. Clin. Investigation, Am. Assn. Immunologists, N.Y. Acad. Medicine, Italian Rheumatology Assn. (hon.), Argentine Rheumatology Soc. (hon.). Contbr. numerous articles to profl. publs., and textbooks. Office: Cabrini Med Center 227 E Nineteenth St New York NY 10003

TARAS, ANTHONY F., educator; b. Dickson City, Pa., Nov. 13, 1927; s. Stanley and Mary (Zalewska) T.; B.A., U. Scranton, 1948; M.A., Kent State U., 1950; Ph.D., Fordham U., 1961; m. Eleanor M. Sostowski, Aug. 4, 1956; children—Robert, Raymond, Linda. Instr. modern langs. Ida. State U., 1950-52, asst. prof., chmn. dept. modern langs., 1952-58, asso. prof., chmn. dept., 1958-63, designer, dir. lang. labs., 1952-73; asso. prof., chmn. dept. modern langs. Ithaca (N.Y.) Coll., 1963-65, designer, dir. lang. lab., 1963-73, prof. modern langs., 1965—, chmn. dept. modern langs., 1965-73, dir. Peace Corps Tng. session, 1966, designer lang lab. Eisenhower Coll., 1968. Recipient Fulbright Summer Seminar grant Sorbonne, Paris, 1955. Mem. Modern Lang. Assn., Am. Assn. Tchrs. French (chpt. pres. 1972-74), Am. Council on Teaching Fgn. Langs., N.Y. State Fgn. Lang. Tchrs. Assn. Editorial cons. in French and Spanish for Ency. Brit. World Lang. Dictionary, 1955-56. Home: 130 Simbury Dr Ithaca NY 14850. *In most cases where important matters or issues require action, I believe in following a systematic approach. Once an objective has been determined and clarified, much reflection is given to the means for achieving the objective, as well as to the consequences which achieving the objective and the actual achievement of the objective might involve. Subsequently, if in my judgment it is worthwhile to proceed, action is taken as promptly as the matter at hand suggests.*

TARAS, JOHN, ballet master, choreographer; b. N.Y.C., Apr. 18, 1919; s. Vassil and Varvara (Dohunyk) T.; attended N.Y. U., Sch. Am. Ballet. Choreographer, repetiteur, dancer Ballet Theater, 1942-46; asst. regisseur Col. De Basil's Ballet Russes, 1947; ballet master, choreographer Grand Ballets De Marquis De Cuevas, 1948-59, N.Y.C. Ballet, 1959—; ballet master Theatre National de L'Opera, Paris, France, 1969-70; dir. ballet Deutsche's Opera, Berlin, Germany, 1971-73. Home: 123 W 69th St New York NY 10023 Office: NY State Theatre Lincoln Center New York NY 10023

TARAS, PAUL, physicist, educator; b. Tunis, Tunisia, May 12, 1941; s. Wladimir and Benita (Koort) T.; came to Can., 1957, naturalized, 1962; B.A.Sc., U. Toronto, 1962, M.A., 1963, Ph.D., 1965; m. Marja-Leena Malinen, Aug. 3, 1963; children—Lisa Helene, Michele Anne. Asst. prof. physics U. Montreal (Que., Can.), 1965-70, asso. prof., 1970-76, prof., 1976—. U. Toronto, Province of Ont., U.K. Atomic Energy Authority fellowships; France-Que., NRC, Natural Scis. and Engring. Research Council Can. grantee. Mem. Am. Phys. Soc., Can. Assn. Physicists. Contbr. articles, research on nuclear physics. Home: 6 Vercheres St Dollard Des Ormeaux PQ H9A 2K8 Canada Office: Lab Physique Nucleaire Universite De Montreal Montreal PQ H3C 3J7 Canada

TARBELL, DEAN STANLEY, educator; b. Hancock, N.H., Oct. 19, 1913; s. Sanford and Ethel (Millikan) T.; A.B., Harvard, 1934, M.A., 1935, Ph.D., 1937; m. Ann Hoar Tracy, Aug. 15, 1942; children—William Sanford, Linda Tracy, Theodore Dean. Post-doctoral fellow U. Ill., 1937; mem. faculty U. Rochester, 1938—, successively instr., asst. prof., asso. prof., 1938-48, prof. chemistry, 1948-62, Charles Frederick Houghton prof. chemistry, 1960—, chmn. dept., 1964—; Distinguished prof. chemistry Vanderbilt U., 1967—, Branscom Distinguished prof., 1975-76; Guggenheim fellow and vis. lectr. chemistry Stanford, 1961-62; Fuson lectr., 1972; cons. USPHS, Army Q.M.C.; mem. various sci. adv. bds. to govt. agencies. Recipient Herty medal, 1973. Guggenheim fellow, 1946-47. Mem. Nat. Acad. Sci., Am. Chem. Soc., Chem. Soc. London, Am. Acad. Arts and Scis., History of Sci. Soc. Author research papers in field, history of chemistry. Home: 6033 Sherwood Dr Nashville TN 37215

TARBOX, FRANK KOLBE, ins. co. exec.; b. Mineola, N.Y., Feb. 27, 1923; s. John Preston and Mary (Kolbe) T.; student Swarthmore Coll., 1940-42; A.B., U. Pa., 1947, LL.B., 1950; m. Eleanor Borden, May 1, 1948; children—John Borden, Kathryn Ann. Pvt. practice law, 1950-53, 55-60; asst. U.S. atty. Eastern Dist. Pa., 1953-55; v.p. adminstrn. Penn Mut. Life Ins. Co., Phila., 1960-71, pres., 1971-78, chmn., chief exec. officer, 1979—; dir. Phila. Nat. Bank, PNB Corp., ARA Services, Inc. United Fund Phila., Dickinson Coll., Carlisle, Pa. Trustee, chmn. bd. S.S. Huebner Found.; mem. bd. overseers Law Sch., trustee U. Pa.; bd. dirs. Phila. Food Distbn. Center, Phila. Urban Coalition, Old Phila. Devel. Corp. Served with USNR, 1942-46. Mem. Am. Council Life Ins. (bd. dirs.), Ins. Fedn. Pa. Methodist. Office: Independence Sq Philadelphia PA 19172

TARBUTTON, LLOYD TILGHMAN, motel chain exec.; b. Easton, Md., Jan. 3, 1932; s. William Lloyd and Ethel Ford Tarbutton; grad. Realtor's Inst., 1960; m. Virginia Rachael Johnson, Nov. 1, 1952 (div. 1978); children—Gregory Alan, Kenton Lyle. Div. sales mgr. Reuben H. Donnelley Corp., advt., Norfolk, Va., 1953-58; owner, operator Tie

Centre Stores, Norfolk, 1958-60; gen. mgr. Hembress Realty Co., Norfolk, 1960-62; pres., chmn. bd., dir. Lloyd Tarbutton Assos., Inc., real estate, Norfolk, 1962—; co-founder Econo-Travel Motor Hotel Corp., Norfolk, 1967, dir., pres., chmn. bd., 1969—; co-founder, v.p., dir. Consol. Companies Inc., Norfolk, 1972—; co-founder, partner BAL Assos., Norfolk, 1973—; co-founder, pres., dir. Amalgamated Cos., Ltd., 1979—, Am. Nat. Investors Corp., 1979—; dir. Norfolk bd. Bank of Va. Trustee Old Dominion U. Edn. Found., 1979—; del. Democratic State Conv., 1976. Served with USN, 1950-51. Hon. editor Hotel and Motel Mgmt. mag., 1974; hon. mem. motel day's com. Internat. Hotel and Motel Ednl. Exposition, 1974—; recipient Hon. Tchr. award Maury High Sch., Norfolk, 1959. Mem. Internat. Franchising Assn. (dir., pres., vice chmn. bd.), Am., Va. (dir.) hotel and motel assns., Realtor's Inst. Norfolk (chmn. 1965), Nat. Assn. Realtors, Nat. Assn. Real Estate Brokers, Norfolk Bd. Realtors (dir., v.p.), Internat. Sales Execs. Club (dir., v.p., Distinguished Sales award 1957), Norfolk C. of C., Airplane Owners and Pilots Assn. Presbyterian. Clubs: Masons, Shriners. Office: 20 Koger Exec Center Norfolk VA 23502. *I believe the greatest assist to my progress in business and personal life came when I was able to truly understand the "value of self" and thus others.*

TAREN, JAMES ARTHUR, physician; b. Toledo, Nov. 10, 1924; s. Joseph Clarence and Mary Frances (Walker) T.; B.S., U. Toledo, 1948; M.D., U. Mich., 1952. Intern, Mich. Univ. Hosp., Ann Arbor, 1952-53, resident surgery, 1953-54, resident neurosurgery, 1955-57; research fellow neurosurgery Boston Children's Hosp., also Peter Bent Brigham Hosp., Boston, 1954-55; mem. faculty U. Mich. Med. Sch. and Hosp., Ann Arbor, 1957—, asso. prof., 1963-67, prof. neurosurgery, 1967—, dir. neurobehavioral sci. program, 1975-78, asso. dean for edn., student affairs and admissions, 1978—; neurosurgeon Wayne County Gen. Hosp., Eloise, Mich., 1957-71, VA Hosp., Ann Arbor, 1957-73, U.S.S. Hope (Project Hope), Peru, 1962, Ecuador, 1963, Guinea, 1965. Served with USNR, 1943-46; PTO. Fellow neurosurgery Coll. Medicine, U. Paris Hospital Foch, Suresnes, France, 1966-67, 73-74. Diplomate Am. Bd. Neuro. Surgery. Fellow A.C.S.; mem. Royal Soc. Medicine (affiliate), Congress Neurol. Surgeons, N.Y. Acad. Sci., AAAS, Am. Ordnance Assn., Internat. Soc. Research Stereotaxic Surgery, Instrument Soc. Am., Am. Assn. Med. Colls., Am. Assn. Neurol. Surgery, Ferrari Club Am. Author: (with others) Correlative Neurosurgery, 1969. Office: Univ Hosp Ann Arbor MI 48104

TARG, WILLIAM, editor; b. Chgo., Mar. 4, 1907; s. Max and Esther (Solomon) Torgownik; student pub. schs.; m. Anne Jesselson, May 1, 1933 (dec. Feb. 1965); 1 son, Russell; m. 2d, Roslyn Siegel, July 30, 1965. Editor-in-chief, v.p. World Pub. Co., 1942-64; editor-in-chief G.P. Putnam's Sons, N.Y.C., 1965-78, sr. editor, 1974—, also v.p.; pres. Targ Editions. Clubs: P.E.N., Grolier. Author: Indecent Pleasures, 1975; author, editor: Modern English First Editions, 1932; Lafcadio Hearn, 1936; 10,000 Rare Books and Their Prices, 1936; Adventures in Good Reading, 1940; Rare American Books, 1941; The American West, 1946; Carrousel For Bibliophiles, 1947; The Making of the Bruce Rogers Bible, 1949; A Reader for Writers, 1951; Bouillaibaisse For Bibliophiles, 1955; Bibliophile in the Nursery, 1957; editor: Bookman's Progress (L.C. Powell), 1968. Home: 101 W 12th St New York NY 10011 Office: 501 Fifth Ave New York NY 10017. *Work, not pleasure is the only means of making life endurable. Pleasure is merely the punctuation mark in the text of life-not its purpose.*

TARIKA, ELIO E., indsl. mfg. exec.; b. Cairo, Egypt, July 20, 1926; s. Albert and Sara (Galante) T.; B.S., U. Ill., 1949; M.S. in Chem. Engring., Newark Coll. Engring., 1951; M.S. in Bus. Adminstrn., U. Chgo., 1960; m. Virginia Tarika, June 19, 1949; children—Janet, Linda, Roger. With Visking Corp., 1951-57; with Union Carbide Corp., 1957—, asst. to pres., 1971-72, corp. v.p., 1972-77, sr. v.p., 1977—. Office: Union Carbide Corp 270 Park Ave New York NY 10017

TARJAN, GEORGE, educator, psychiatrist; b. Zsolna, Hungary, June 18, 1912; s. Odon and Margaret (Kohn) T.; student Tisza Istvan U., Debrecen, Hungary, 1920-32; M.D., Peter Pazmany U., Budapest, Hungary, 1935; m. Helen E. Blome, June 11, 1941; children—Robert E., James E. Came to U.S., 1939, naturalized, 1943. Intern gen. hosps., Budapest, 1934-35, Menorah Hosp., Kansas City, Mo., 1939-40; resident internal medicine, Budapest, 1935-39, Mercy Hosp., Janesville, Wis., 1940-41; resident psychiatry State Hosp., Provo, Utah, 1941-43; clin. dir. Peoria (Ill.) State Hosp., 1946-47; dir. clin. service Pacific State Hosp., Pomona, Calif., 1947-49, supt., med. dir., 1949-65; asst. prof. psychiatry U. Calif. at Los Angeles Sch. Medicine, 1953-57, asso. prof., 1957-60, clin. prof., 1960-65, prof., 1965—, program dir. mental retardation and child psychiatry Neuropsychiat. Inst., 1965—. Vice chmn. Pres.'s Panel on Mental Retardation, 1961-62; mem. Pres.'s Com. on Mental Retardation 1966-71; cons. Pres.'s Com. on Mental Retardation, 1971—(merit award 1972). Served to capt. M.C., AUS, 1943-46; col. Res. (ret.). Recipient Kennedy Found. Internat. award for distinguished leadership in mental retardation, 1971; Andres Bello award for acad. achievements Venezuela, 1976. Diplomate Am. Bd. Neurology and Psychiatry, Am. Bd. Child Psychiatry, Nat. Bd. Med. Examiners. Fellow Am. Psychiat. Assn. (v.p. 1967-68, sec. 1969-72, Distinguished Service award 1973), Am. Assn. Mental Deficiency (Leadership award 1970); mem. A.M.A., Los Angeles County Med. Soc., Am. Acad. Child Psychiatry (pres. 1977-79), Group for Advancement Psychiatry (pres. 1971-73), So. Calif. Psychiat. Soc., Am. Psychopath. Assn., Am. Coll. Psychiatrists. Home: 3373 Scadlock Ln Sherman Oaks CA 91403 Office: Neuropsychiat Inst 760 Westwood Plaza Los Angeles CA 90024

TARKENTON, FRANCIS ASBURY, former profl. football player, sports commentator, mgmt. cons.; b. Richmond, Va., Feb. 3, 1940; grad. U. Ga., 1961; m. Elaine Tarkenton; 3 children. Quarterback Minn. Vikings Nat. Football League team, 1961-67, 72-79, N.Y. Giants, 1967-72; football commentator ABC Sports, 1979—, also appears on Sta. WXIA affiliate, Atlanta; founder, chmn. bd. Behavioral Systems, Inc., 1969—; writer monthly mgmt. article for Sky mag.; mem. Nat. Football Conf. championship team, 1973. Named Most Valuable Player in NFL, 1975. Mem. Fellowship Christian Athletes. Methodist. Author: Broken Patterns: The Education of a Quarterback, 1971; co-author: Tarkenton, 1976. Address: care ABC Sports 1330 Ave of Americas New York NY 10019. *I've come to really believe that the people who make it in the world aren't the most talented ones or the smartest or the luckiest or necessarily the bravest. The ones who make it are the dogged ones. Just plain tenacity.**

TARLEAU, THOMAS NICHOLAS, lawyer; b. Hamburg, Germany, Sept. 22, 1904; s. Jacob Joseph and Lisa (Ysaye) T.; LL.B., Columbia, 1929; m. Anne Lesenger, Sept. 10, 1939; children—Jennifer (Mrs. Walter G. Shifrin), Alison Thomasina. Admitted to N.Y. bar, 1931; atty. Robert H. Montgomery, 1929-37; legal asst. to undersec. Treasury Dept., Washington, 1937-38, tax legislative counsel, 1938-42; asso. Willkie Owen Farr & Gallagher & Walton, N.Y.C., 1942-43; partner Willkie Farr & Gallagher, and predecessors, 1943-69, counsel, 1969—. Lectr., taxes N.Y. U., Columbia, Practising Law Inst. Mem. adv. group to commr. Internal Revenue Service. Fellow Am. Bar Found.; mem. Am. Bar Assn. (ho. dels. 1955-58), Tax Inst. (pres. 1947), Am. Law Inst., Am. Judicature Soc., Inter-Am., N.Y. bar assns., Assn. Bar City N.Y., Internat. Fiscal Assn., Nat Tax Assn., Commerce and Industry Assn. N.Y. Home: 7400 Manasota Key Rd Englewood FL 33533 Office: 1 Citicorp Center 153 E 53d St New York NY 10022

TARLOV, ALVIN RICHARD, educator; b. Norwalk, Conn. July 11, 1929; s. Charles and Mae (Shelinsky) T.; B.A., Dartmouth, 1951; M.D., U. Chgo., 1956; m. Joan Hylton, June 12, 1956; children—Richard, Elizabeth, Jane, Suzanne, David. Intern medicine Phila. Gen. Hosp., 1956-57; resident U. Chgo. Hosp., 1957-59; research asso. U. Chgo., 1959-61; research asso. dept. biol. chemistry Harvard Med. Sch., 1962-64; asst. prof. medicine U. Chgo. Sch. Medicine, 1964-68, asso. prof., 1968-70, prof., chmn. dept., 1970—; chmn. Federated Council for Internal Medicine, 1978-79; chmn. Grad. Med. Edn. Nat. Adv. Com., 1978—. Served to capt. M.C., AUS, 1959-61. John and Mary R. Markle scholar acad. medicine, 1966-71. Recipient Research Career Devel. award USPHS, 1962-69. Fellow ACP; mem. Am. Fedn. Clin. Research, Central Soc. Clin. Research, Am. Soc. Hematology, Assn. Am. Physicians, Assn. Profs. Medicine (pres. 1979-80), Sigma Xi, Alpha Omega Alpha. Spl. research bio-med. research metabolism red blood cells, congenital disorders red cells asso. with hemolytic anemia, biochemistry cellular membranes, health manpower needs. Home: 1700 E 56th St Chicago IL 60637 Office: 950 E 59th St Chicago IL 60637

TARN, NATHANIEL, poet, translator, educator; b. Paris, France, June 30, 1928; s. Marcel and Yvonne (Suchar) T.; B.A. with honors, Cambridge (Eng.) U., 1948, M.A., 1952; postgrad. Sorbonne, U. Paris, 1949-51; M.A., U. Chgo., 1952, Ph.D., 1957; postgrad. London (Eng.) Sch. Econs., 1953-58; children—Andrea, Marc. Anthropologist, Guatemala, Burma, Alaska, and others, 1952-67; editor Cape Edits. and founder-dir. Cape Goliard Press, J. Cape Ltd., 1967-69; vis. prof. State U. N.Y. at Buffalo, and Princeton, 1969-70; prof. comparative lit. Rutgers U., 1970—. Recipient Guinness prize for poetry, 1963. Author: Old Savage/Young City, 1964; (with Richard Murphy and Jon Silkin) Penguin Modern Poets No. Seven: Richard Murphy, Jon Silkin, Nathaniel Tarn, 1965; Where Babylon Ends, 1968; The Beautiful Contradictions, 1969; October, 1969; A Nowhere for Vallejo, 1971; Lyrics for the Bride of God: Section: The Artemision, 1972; The Persephones, 1974; Lyrics for the Bride of God, 1975; The House of Leaves, 1976; (with Janet Rodney) Alashka, 1979, The Forest, 1978, The Ground of Our Great Admiration of Nature, 1978; Birdscapes, with Seaside, 1978; contbg. author to several anthologies, including: A.P.E.N. Anthology of Contemporary Poetry, 1966; The Penguin Book of Modern Verse Translation, 1966; Poems Addressed to Hugh MacDiarmid, 1967; Music and Sweet Poetry: A Verse Anthology, 1968; Frontier of Going: Anthology of Space Poetry, 1969; British Poetry Today, 1971; Shaking the Pumpkin, 1972; America: A Prophecy, 1973; Open Poetry, 1973; Active Anthology, 1974; translator: The Heights of Macchu Picchu (Pablo Neruda), 1966; Stelae (Victor Segalen), 1969. Editor, co-translator: Con Cuba: An Anthology of Cuban Poetry of the Last Sixty Years, 1969; editor: Selected Poems (Pablo Neruda), 1970. Home: 96 New St New Hope PA 18938 Office: Rutgers U New Brunswick NJ

TARNOPOLSKY, WALTER SURMA, lawyer; b. Gronlid, Sask., Can., Aug. 1, 1932; s. Harry and Mary (Surma) T.; B.A. with honors, U. Sask., Saskatoon, 1953, LL.B., 1958; A.M. in History, Columbia U., 1955; LL.M. (Newton W. Rowell fellow), U. London, 1962; children by previous marriage—Mark Andrew, Christina Helen, Alexandra Justine; m. 2d, Joanne G. Kramer, Aug. 25, 1973; children—Michelle Raissa, Gregory Jan. Lectr. in law U. Ottawa (Ont., Can.), 1962-63; asst. prof. law U. Sask., 1963-67; asso. prof. Osgoode Hall Law Sch., Yorke U., Downsview, Ont., 1967-68, v.p. acad. York U., 1972, prof. law, 1972—; prof., dean of law U. Windsor (Ont.), 1968-72; vice-chmn. Fed. Electoral Boundaries Commn. for Ont., 1972, 75; mem. UN Human Rights Com., 1977-81; mem. Can. Human Rights Commn., 1978—. Mem. Can. Consultative Council on Multiculturalism, 1973-77; pres. Can. Civil Liberties Assn., 1977-79. UN Human Rights fellow, India, Malaysia, 1970. Fellow Royal Soc. Can.; mem. Sask. Bar, Law Soc. Upper Can., Can. Bar Assn. Liberal. Ukrainian Greek Orthodox. Author: The Canadian Bill of Rights, 1966, 2d rev. edit., 1975; editor: Some Civil Rights Liberties Issues of the 70's, 1975. Office: Room 434 Osgoode Hall Law Sch York U 4700 Keele St Downsview ON M3J 2R5 Canada*

TARR, CURTIS W., machinery mfg. co. exec.; b. Stockton, Calif., Sept. 18, 1924; s. F.W. and Esther (Reed) T.; B.A., Stanford U., 1948, Ph.D., 1962; M.B.A., Harvard U., 1950; L.H.D., Ripon Coll., 1965, Grinnell Coll., 1969; LL.D., Lawrence U., 1974; m. Elizabeth May Myers, Feb. 5, 1955 (div. 1978); children—Pamela Elizabeth, Cynthia Leigh. Research asst., instr. Harvard U., 1950-52; v.p. Sierra Tractor & Equipment Co., Chico, Calif., 1952-58; staff mem. 2d Hoover Commn., 1954-55; asst. dir. summer session Stanford U., 1961-62, dir., 1962-63, asst. dean humanities and scis., 1962-63, lectr. bus. sch., 1962-63; pres. Lawrence U., Appleton, Wis., 1963-69; asst. sec. for manpower and res. affairs Air Force, 1969-70; dir. SSS, Washington, 1970-72; under sec. state for security assistance, 1972-73, acting dep. under sec. state for mgmt., 1973; v.p. overseas devel. Deere & Co., Moline, Ill., 1973, v.p. parts distbn. and materials mgmt., 1973—; trustee Inst. Paper Chemistry, 1963-69; dir. Banta Corp., Menasha, Wis. Chmn. Task Force on Govt. Orgn., Fin. and Tax Distbn. for State Wis., 1967-69; chmn. Def. Manpower Commn., 1974-76, Ill. State Scholarship Commn., 1978—; Republican candidate for Congress 2d Dist. Calif., 1958. Served with AUS, 1943-46; ETO. Recipient Exceptional Civilian Service medal Air Force Dept., 1970; Distinguished Service award SSS, 1975. Republican. Mem. United Ch. Christ. Author: Private Soldier, 1976. Home: 3701 39th St Moline IL 61265 Office: Deere & Co John Deere Rd Moline IL 61265

TARR, DAVID WILLIAM, educator, polit. scientist; b. Melrose, Mass., July 25, 1931; s. Charles Howard and Pauline (Bryant) T.; B.A., U. Mass., 1953; M.A., U. Chgo., 1956, Ph.D., 1961; m. Carol M. Huntress, June 13, 1953; children—Susan, Bryant. Instr., Amherst and Mt. Holyoke colls., 1958-59; nat. def. analyst Legis. Reference Service, Library of Congress, 1959-62; research asso. Washington Center Fgn. Policy, 1962-63; mem. faculty U. Wis.-Madison, 1963—, prof. polit. sci., 1969—, dir. nat. security studies group, 1966-69, chmn. dept., 1972-75. Fellow, Inter-Univ. Seminar on Armed Forces and Soc., 1975—. Chmn. U. Wis. Athletic Bd., 1979—. Served to 1st lt. AUS, 1953-55. Rockefeller grantee, 1962-63, fellow, 1977. Mem. Am. Polit. Sci. Assn., AAUP, Internat. Studies Assn., Arms Control Assn. Unitarian. Author: American Strategy in the Nuclear Age, 1966. Co-editor: Modules in Security Studies, 1974. Contbr. articles to profl. jours. Home: 10 Shepard Terr Madison WI 53705

TARRANT, JOHN EDWARD, lawyer; b. Dyersburg, Tenn., Nov. 25, 1898; s. John Morgan and Penelope A. (Fumbanks) T.; B.S., U. Va., 1921; LL.B., Harvard U., 1923; m. Mary Park Kaye, May 26, 1928; children—Mary Kaye Tarrant Durham, Eleanor Tarrant Newman, Penelope Tarrant Morton. Admitted to Ky. bar, 1923; asso. firm Simpson, Thacher & Bartlett, N.Y.C., 1922, Bruce, Bullitt & Gordon, Louisville, 1923-26; partner firm Bruce & Bullitt, 1926-40, Ogden, Tarrant, Galphin & Street, 1940-48, Bullitt, Dawson & Tarrant 1948-70, Tarrant, Combs & Bullitt, and predecessor, 1970—; gen. counsel Fed. Land Bank, Fed. Intermediate Credit Bank, Louisville, 1930; spl. judge Ky. Ct. Appeals, 1948; chmn. bd. dirs. Louisville Investment Co., 1958—; dir. Churchill Downs Inc., 1969—; dir. Citizens Fidelity Bank & Trust Co., 1957-69, adviser, 1969-71. Mem. Louisville Bridge Commn., 1954-57; mem. personnel bd. Ky. State Police, 1957-60; bd. dirs. Louisville Central Area Assn., 1966-68, Norton-Children's Hosps., Inc., 1969—; trustee YWCA, 1939-63, U. Louisville, 1966-70, Norton Meml. Infirmary, 1939-69. Served O.T.C., Camp Fortress Monroe, Va., 1918. Fellow Am. Bar Found. (life); mem. N.C. Soc. Cin., Ky. Soc. Colonial Wars, SAR, Am., Ky., Louisville bar assns., Am. Law Inst. (life), Jud. Conf. Sixth Circuit U.S. (life), Am. Judicature Soc. (life), Phi Beta Kappa, Kappa Sigma. Republican. Episcopalian. Clubs: Pendennis, River Valley, Wynn Stay, Filson, Louisville Country, Jefferson (Louisville); Union, Broad St. (N.Y.C.); Met. (Washington). Home: Beech Grove 3740 Upper River Rd Louisville KY 40207 Office: 2600 Citizens Plaza Louisville KY 40202

TARRANT, STUART STANLEY, food distbn. co. fin. exec.; b. Sussex, Eng., Oct. 14, 1940; came to U.S., 1976; degree in chartered accountancy St. Lawrence Coll.; m. Jennifer Turner, Sept., 1970; children—Jacqueline, Stephen. With internat. corp. fin. dept. Imperial Chem. Industries, 1967-73; asst. group fin. controller Cavenham Ltd. (U.K.), London, Eng., 1974-75, group fin. controller, 1975-76; fin. v.p. Grand Union, Elmwood Park, N.J., 1976-78, exec. v.p. fin. and adminstrn., 1978—. Fellow Inst. Chartered Accts. in Eng. and Wales. Office: 100 Broadway Elmwood Park NJ 07407

TARRANTS, WILLIAM EUGENE, govt. ofcl.; b. Liberty, Mo., Dec. 9, 1927; s. Joseph Eugene and Mildred Jane (Wright) T.; B.Indsl. Engring., Ohio State U., 1951; M.S. in Indsl. Engring., 1959; Ph.D., N.Y. U., 1963; m. Mary Jo Edman, Jan. 19, 1952; children—James Timothy, Jennifer Lynn. Instr. indsl. engring. Ohio State U., Columbus, 1958-59; asst. prof., research asso. N.Y. U., 1959-64; chief accident research div. Bur. Labor Stats., Dept. Labor, Washington, 1964-67; dir. manpower devel. div. Nat. Hwy. Traffic Safety Adminstrn., Dept. Transp., 1967—, also chmn. sci. and tech. info. advisory bd.; mem. planning and adminstrn. transp. safety Transp. Research Bd., Nat. Acad. Scis. Cons. safety program eval. Indsl. Commn. Ohio, 1959. Served to capt. USAF, 1951-57. Recipient Founder's Day award N.Y. U., 1963; 1st place Nat. Tech. Paper awards, 1961, 63, 67; cert. for outstanding performance Nat. Hwy. Traffic Safety Adminstrn., 1973; registered profl. engr., Calif., Ohio, N.Mex. Fellow Am. Soc. Safety Engrs. (dir., v.p. research and tech. devel., pres. 1977-78); mem. Am. Soc. Safety Research (trustee), Am. Inst. Indsl. Engrs., Human Factors Soc., System Safety Soc., Evaluation Research Soc., Vets. of Safety, Am. Nat. Standards Inst. (standards com.), AAAS, Nat. Safety Council (chmn. research projects com. 1973—), Alpha Pi Mu, Kappa Delta Pi. Mem. Evangelical Covent Ch. (trustee, ch. chmn. 1976-80). Contbr. chpt. to Selected Readings in Safety, 1973. Author: A Selected Bibliography of Reference Materials in Safety Engineering and Related Fields, 1967; Dictionary of Terms Used in the Safety Profession, 1971; Measurement of Safety Performance, 1980, also articles. Mem. editorial bd. Accident Analysis and Prevention, Jour. Safety Research. Home: 12134 Long Ridge Ln Bowie MD 20715 Office: 400 7th St SW Washington DC 20590. *We often look with awe at the successful person, much as we admire a well designed structure or a beautiful painting. Behind the finished product usually lies exhaustive effort, frustration, disappointment, and even failure which is obscured by the glow of accomplishment. Success is achieved by some ability, lots of hard work, perserverance, courage of convictions, help and support from others, a desire to reach a goal, self-discipline, and considerable personal sacrifice as we make choices concerning the use of our limited resources. The ability to bounce back from adversity is crucial. Most important of all is the strength and insight gained through prayer and the willingness to permit your life to be guided by Christian faith.*

TARSON, HERBERT HARVEY, ednl. adminstr.; b. N.Y.C., Aug. 28, 1910; s. Harry and Elizabeth (Miller) T.; grad. Army Command Gen. Staff Coll., 1942, Armed Forces Staff Coll., 1951, Adavnced Mgmt. Sch. Sr. Air Force Comdrs., George Washington U., 1954; B.A., U. Calif., Los Angeles, 1949; Ph.D., U.S. Internat. U., 1972; m. Lynne Barnett, June 27, 1941; 1 son, Stephen. Entered U.S. Army as pvt., 1933, advanced through grades to maj., 1942, transfered to U.S. Air Force, 1947, advanced through grades to lt. col., 1949; adj. exec. officer, Ft. Snelling, Minn., 1940-42, asst. adj. gen. 91st Inf. Div., 1942-43; chief of personnel, advisory sec. Comd. Zone, ETO, 1944-45; dir. personnel services 8th Air Force, 1946-47; dep. dir. dept. info. and edn. Armed Forces Info. Sch., 1949-51; dir. personnel services Japan Air Def. Force, 1951-53, Continental Air Command, 1953-62; dir. adminstrv. services, spl. asst. to Comdr. 6th Air Force Res. Region, 1962-64; ret., 1964; asst. to chancellor L.I. U., Brookville, 1964-69; dean admissions Tex. State Tech. Inst., San Diego Indsl. Center, 1970-72; v.p. acad. affairs Nat. U., San Diego, 1972-75, sr. v.p., 1975—. Decorated Bronze Star medal with oak leaf cluster, Air Force Commendation medal with 2 oak leaf clusters. Fellow Bio-Med Research Inst.; mem. Doctoral Soc. U.S. Internat. U., Am. Soc. Tng., Devel., World Affairs Council, Air Force Assn., Navy League U.S., Pres.'s Assos. of Nat. U. (presidential life). Club: Cuyamaca. Home: 4611 Denwood Rd La Mesa CA 92041 Office: 4141 Camino del Rio S San Diego CA 92108. *The greatest motivating force in my life is to explore the challenging frontiers of the future. Nothing can be compared to it.*

TART, STEPHEN M., JR., advt. exec.; b. Superior, Wis., Jan. 6, 1932; s. Stephen M. and Eugenia (Hill) T.; B.A. magna cum laude, Vanderbilt U., 1954; m. Winifred Watson, Jan. 16, 1959; children—Stephen M. III, Lucy Hill, Cynthia Brook. Mktg. analyst Inland Steel Co., Chgo., 1954-58; asst. to pres. EverSweet Corp., Lyons, Ill., 1958-59; account exec. Tatham-Laird & Kudner Advt., Chgo., also N.Y.C., 1959-63, v.p., account supr., 1964-66, v.p., mgr. mktg. services, 1967-70, v.p.. mgmt. rep., 1971-72, also mem. exec. com., dir., trustee profit sharing fund; pres. Target Pub., N.Y.C., 1971-72; sr. v.p., mgmt. rep. McCann-Erickson, Inc., N.Y.C., 1972-73, exec. v.p., 1974, dir. N.Y. accounts, 1975—, mem. exec. com., 1975—, dep. regional dir. McCann-Erickson Europe, 1976, regional dir., 1977—; dir. McCann-Erickson Internat., Interpublic Ltd. U.K. Mem. Phi Beta Kappa. Clubs: Univ., Economic (N.Y.C.); Skating, Belle Haven (Greenwich, Conn.). Home: 14 Broad Rd Greenwich CT 06830

TARTER, FRED BARRY, advt. co. exec.; b. Bklyn., Aug. 16, 1943; s. Irving and Edna (Kupferberg) T.; B.S., Coll. City N.Y., 1966; m. Barbara Jane Smith, Apr. 12, 1969; children—Scott Andrew, Heather, Megan. Pres., Jamie Publs. Hootenanny Enterprises, Inc., mags., 1962-65; mdse. dir. Longines Symphonette Soc., 1965-67; with Universal Communications, Inc., N.Y.C., 1967—, pres., chief exec. officer, 1969-74; exec. v.p. Deerfield Communications, Inc., 1974-77, pres., chief exec. officer, 1977—; pres. Deerfield Books, Inc.; pub. S.E.W. Mag., 1977—; dir. Harvest Group, Inc.; exec. producer Joanne Carson's VIP's, Miss American Teenager Pagent, 1972-73. Clubs: Friars (N.Y.C.); Los Angeles Athletic. Home: 250 Barnard Rd Larchmont NY 10538 Office: 444 Madison Ave New York NY 10022. *An integral part of success is the capacity for failure.*

Persistence, combined with responsibility, has proven to be the winning combination time and again.

TARVER, ERVIN, stockbroker; b. Somerville, Tex., Oct. 8, 1933; s. Leon H. and Ruby L. (Taylor) T.; grad. high sch.; m. Johnie Mae Wilson, July 1, 1956; children—Marcus Neil, Teresa Leah, Byron Vincent. Broker, Eastman Dillon Union Securities, San Diego (became Blyth Eastman Dillon), 1958—. Served with USNR, 1955-57. Home: 5223 Countryside Dr San Diego CA 92115 Office: 7979 Ivanhoe St La Jolla CA 92037

TARVER, JACKSON WILLIAMS, newspaper exec.; b. Savannah, Ga., Mar. 2, 1917; s. Otis Merritt and DeLuth (Williams) T.; student U. Ga., 1936; A.B., Mercer U., 1938, LL.D., 1965; m. Margaret Birch Taylor, Mar. 24, 1940; children—Jack Williams, Margaret (Mrs. Peter Jason). Reporter, Vidalia (Ga.) Advance, 1938; editor Toombs County (Ga.) Democrat, 1939-40, Macon (Ga.) News, 1940-43; asso. editor Atlanta Constn., 1943-49, asst. to pres. Atlanta Newspapers, Inc. (pub. Atlanta Jour., Atlanta Constn.), 1950-53, gen. mgr., 1953-58, v.p., 1956-58, pub., 1958—, also dir.; chmn. Fed. Res. Bank of Atlanta, 1962-68; chmn., dir. Theaters Service Co.; vice chmn. Cox Enterprises, Inc.; dir. So. Bell Telephone Co., Am. Motors Corp., Maccabees Mut. Ins. Co.; chmn. A.P., 1977—. Mem. Ga. Bd. Edn., 1942-43; trustee Mercer U. Reid Found. fellow to S.A., 1949; recipient Humanitarian of Yr. award Inst. Human Relations, 1979. Mem. Am. (chmn. bur. advt. 1962-64), So. (pres. 1976-77) newspaper pubs. assns., Am. Soc. Newspaper Editors, Sigma Delta Chi, Sigma Alpha Epsilon. Clubs: Capital City, Piedmont Driving, Commerce, Stadium (Atlanta). Office: 72 Marietta St Atlanta GA 30303

TARVIN, ROBERT EDWARD, community coll. pres.; b. Covington, Ky., Apr. 16, 1946; s. Fred Irvin and Opal Aliene (McCormick) T.; B.A., Eastern Ky. U., Richmond, 1968, M.A. (President's fellow 1968-69), 1969; D.Ed., Ind. U., 1972; m. Patty Lynn Anderson, Aug. 7, 1969; children—Tonya Lynn, Shanna Rene. Dir. student activities Eastern Ky. U., 1969-72; asso. dean, then v.p. John A. Logan Coll., Carterville, Ill., 1972-74, pres., 1974—; chmn. Ill. Council Community Coll. Presidents, 1979-80, So. Ill. Collegiate Common Market, 1974-79. Named Disting. Alumni, Eastern Ky. U., 1976. Methodist. Contbr. articles to profl. publs. Home: 318 Lakeview St Marion IL 62959 Office: John A Logan Coll Carterville IL 62918

TARZIAN, MARY (MRS. SARKES TARZIAN), corp. exec.; b. Phila.; d. Peter and Natalie (Kassabian) Mangigian; B.S., U. Pa., 1927, M.A., 1928, Ph.D., 1935; postgrad. Inst. Higher Internat. Studies, Geneva, 1930-32, U. Geneva, 1932-33, Bryn Mawr Coll., 1934-35; LL.D. (hon.), Tri-State U., 1971; m. Sarkes Tarzian, July 23, 1930; children—Thomas, Joyce Patricia. Pres., Nat. Student Council, 1927-29; Am. rep. Internat. Student Council, 1930-33; partner Sarkes Tarzian, Inc., Bloomington, Ind., 1944-48, sec.-treas., 1948-52, v.p., sec.-treas., 1952—; v.p. WTTV-TV, WTTV-FM, WTTS radio, 1952, WPTH-FM, 1957—, also v.p. radio sta. WATI; v.p., dir. Bynum Supply Co., 1944—; co-owner LuMar Newspapers, local Ind. publs., 1952—. Auditions chmn. Tri-State area nat. council Met. Opera; chmn. ann. giving U. Pa., 1965, spl. gifts chmn., 1965, also mem. exec. com. gen. alumni bd.; mem. adv. com. J.F. Kennedy Center for Performing Arts; Great Lakes chmn. Friends Kennedy Center; mem. devel. bd. Wabash Coll. Midwest chmn. nat. council Women's Nat. Republican Club; mem. Indpls. Symphony Soc., Indpls. Mus. Art, Civic Ballet Soc., Friends of Music of Ind. U., Orchard Sch., Tudor Hall Sch., Aspen Scholarship Bd., The Twirlers; mem. bd., founder mem. Eisenhower Scholarship Found.; bd. govs. Asso. Colls. Ind.; mem. women's com. Clowes Hall; mem. bd. Soldiers', Sailors' and Airmen's Club, N.Y.C. Named Distinguished Woman of Northwood Inst., 1973; Merit Mother of Ind., 1975, Ind. Mother of Year, 1976. Mem. Ind. Acad., AAUW, Mortar Bd., Traders Point Hunt, Midwest Hunt Assn., Benjamin Franklin Assos., Nat. Inst. Social Sci., Phi Beta Kappa, Kappa Kappa Gamma, Kappa Kappa Kappa. Episcopalian. Clubs: Colony; Woodstock; Faculty Tea (U. Pa.); City Tavern (Washington). Home: 515 W Kessler Blvd Indianapolis IN 46208 Office: E Hillside Dr Bloomington IN 47401

TARZWELL, CLARENCE MATTHEW, aquatic biologist; b. Deckerville, Mich., Sept. 29, 1907; s. Matthew and Jessie J. (Wilson) T.; student Eastern Mich. U., 1925-29; A.B., U. Mich., 1930, M.S., 1932, Ph.D., 1936; Sc. D. (hon.), Baldwin Wallace Coll., 1967; m. Vera V. Paiter, Sept. 3, 1938; children—Diane Kay Tarzwell Siegmund, Barbara Ann Tarzwell Fahey, Thomas Neil. Inst. Fisheries research fellow Mich. Dept. Conservation, Ann Arbor, 1930-33; state stream improvement supr. Mich. Emergency Conservation Work, Lansing, 1933-34; asst. aquatic biologist U.S. Fish and Wildlife Service, Salt Lake City, 1934; asst. range examiner U.S. Forest Service, Region 3, Albuquerque, 1935-38; asso. biologist, chief field sta. TVA, Decatur, Ala., 1938-43; chief biology sect. USPHS, Savannah, Ga., 1944-48, sci. dir., chief aquatic biology R.A. Taft San. Engring. Center, Cin., 1948-65; dir. Nat. Marine Water Quality Lab., West Kingston, R.I., 1965-72; sr. research adviser EPA, Nat. Environ. Research Center, Corvallis, Oreg., 1972-75; acting dir. Nat. Water Quality Lab., Duluth, Minn., 1965-67; adj. prof. Coll. Resource Devel., U. R.I., Kingston, 1966-75, vis. prof., 1976-77; mem. aquatic life adv. com. Ohio River Valley San. Commn., 1952-68, Nat. Acad. Sci.-NRC Com. on Pest Control-Wildlife Relationships, subcom. on research, 1960-63, mem. expert adv. panel environ. health WHO, 1962-64; mem. pesticide com. Internat. Assn. Game, Fish and Conservation Commrs., 1960-61; Am. del. 1st and 2d internat. meetings sci. research into water pollution Orgn. Econ. Coop. and Devel., Paris, 1961, 62, chmn. internat. com. on long-term effects toxicants on aquatic life, 1962-67; mem. adv. com. control stream temperatures Pa. San Water Bd., 1959-62; adv. com. water quality criteria project Calif. Water Pollution Control Bd., 1961-63; chmn. sec. interior's Nat. Tech. Adv. Com. on Water Quality Requirements for Fish, Other Aquatic Life and Wildlife, 1967-68; chmn., mem. Water Pollution Control Fedn. com. for devel. standard methods for bioassays, 1958-75, com. for methods of sampling and analysis, 1965-74; mem. N.Am. Game policy com., 1971-73; mem. com. on power plant siting Nat. Acad. Engring.-Nat. Acad. Scis., 1971-72; pollution abatement com. Am. Fisheries Soc., 1952-73; mem. regional task force, southeastern New Eng. water and related land resources study New Eng. River Basins Com., 1972-75; cons. Kuwait Inst. Sci. Research, 1975; mem. R.I. State Wide Planning Council, Ecology Action for R.I., Save the Bay Battle Bill Coalition. Recipient Conservationist Year award State of Ohio, 1961; Am. Motors Profl. Conservationist award, 1962; Aldo Leopold medal Wildlife Soc., 1963; Meritorious Service medal USPHS, 1964; Distinguished Career award EPA, 1973, Bronze medal, 1974. Mem. Am. Fisheries Soc. (hon. life. mem., chmn. pollution com. 1950-51, 54-61, mem. 1962-73, award of excellence 1974), Am. Soc. Limnology and Oceanography (nat. adv. com. 1950-51, mem.-at-large 1959, bd. dirs. 1960-62), Societas Internationalis Limnologiae, Wildlife Soc. (hon. life), Am. Soc. Ichthyologists and Herpetologists (life), Am. Inst. Biol. Scis., USPHS Commd. Officers Assn. (pres. Cin. br. 1955-56), Stoic (pres. 1928), Phi Beta Kappa, Sigma Xi, Kappa Delta Pi, Phi Kappa Phi, Phi Sigma, Pi Kappa Delta. Author numerous publs. aquatic biology, water pollution, water quality criteria. Home: Route 5 Box 159 Old Post Rd Wakefield RI 02879

TASCHEREAU, PIERRE, airline exec.; b. Quebec City, Que., Can., Jan. 13, 1920; s. Edouard and Juliette (Carroll) T.; B.A., Garnier Co., 1938; LL.L., Laval U., 1941; postgrad. U. Western Ont., 1952; m. Yseult Beaudry, Aug. 13, 1945; children—Paule Taschereau Bernier, Laurent, François. Admitted to Que. bar, 1941, created Queen's counsel, 1955; atty. Canadian Nat. R.R. Co., Montreal, 1946-63, v.p. law, 1971-72, exec. v.p. corporate affairs, 1972-74, chmn. bd., 1974-76; chmn. bd. Air Can., 1977—; sr. mem. firm Geoffrion & Prud'homme, Barr & Solicitors, Montreal, 1963-67; v.p. Canadian Transp. Commn., 1967-71. Bd. govs. Hosp. Marie Enfant, Montreal. Served to capt. Canadian Army, 1942-46. Mem. Canadian, Que. bar assns. Roman Catholic. Club: Mt. Royal (Montreal). Office: Air Canada Pl Ville Marie Montreal PQ H3B 3P7 Canada

TASCONA, ANTONIO, artist; b. St. Boniface, Man., Can., Mar. 16, 1926; s. Sebastiano and Nunziata (Sanfillipo) T.; student Winnipeg Sch. Art, 1947-50; U. Man., 1950-52; m. May Gilchrist, June 1, 1951; children—Lorenzo, Martin, Christopher, Catherine. Technician electro-plating Canadian Aviation Electronics, 1952-56, Air Can., 1956-72; instr. art U. Man., 1976-77; one man shows: Gallerie Soixante, Montreal, 1964, Fathers of Confedn. Art Center, Charlottetown, P.E.I., Can., 1965, Carman Lamanna Gallery, Toronto, 1968, Atlantic Art Circuit, Maritimes, 1972-73, Windsor (Ont.) Pub. Art Gallery, 1976, Winnipeg (Man.) Art Gallery, 1974, La Gallerie Internat., Ribe, Denmark, 1976; group shows include: Walker Art Center, Mpls., 1958, Montreal Beaux Arts, 1963, Que. Mus., 1964, Cardiff Commonwealth Arts Festival, Wales, 1965, Nat. Gallery Can. Traveling Exhbn., Australia, 1967, Nat. Gallery Can. Biennial, Ottawa, 1968; represented permanent collections Winnipeg Art Gallery, Confedn. Art Gallery and Mus., Charlottetown, P.E.I., Art Gallery Ont., Toronto, Nat. Gallery Can., Ottawa, Can. Council Art Collection, Ottawa, Marjory and Sam Drche collection at U. Man. Faculty Law. Recipient Royal Arch. Inst. Can., Ottawa, 1970, Can. Council Arts award 1972, Canadian Silver Jubilee medal, 1977. Served with Canadian Army, 1944-46. Mem. Royal Canadian Acad. Art, Can. Conf. Arts, Canadian Artist Rep. Roman Catholic. Mural Man. Centennial Art Centre, 1967; hanging mobile Fresh Water Inst., U. Man., 1971-72. Address: 151 Tache Winnipeg MB R2H 1Z4 Canada. *I would like to think of myself as an innovative assimilator, who welds minimal concepts into a visual reality. These minimal concepts deal with structural linear/colour vibrations as found in nature and technology.*

TASH, MARTIN ELIAS, publishing co. exec.; b. N.Y.C., Jan. 24, 1941; s. David and Esther (Milch) T.; B.B.A., Baruch Sch. City Coll. N.Y., 1962; m. Arlene Sue Klein, June 23, 1962; children—Nat, Faye, Jill. Staff accountant S.D. Leidesdorf & Co., C.P.A.'s, N.Y.C., 1962-66; v.p. fin., dir. LMC Data Inc., N.Y.C., 1966-71; with Plenum Pub. Corp., N.Y.C., 1971—, chmn. bd., pres., 1977—. C.P.A. Mem. Am. Inst. C.P.A.'s, Beta Alpha Psi. Office: 227 W 17th St New York NY 10011

TASMAN, WILLIAM SAMUEL, ophthalmologist; b. Phila., Aug. 9, 1929; s. Isaac Samuel and Selma (Stern) T.; B.A., Haverford Coll., 1951; M.D., Temple U., 1955; postgrad. U. Pa., 1956-57; m. Alice Lea Mast, Mar. 31, 1962; children—Jim, Alice and Graham (twins). Intern, Phila. Gen. Hosp., 1955-56; resident Wills Eye Hosp., Phila., 1959-61; asso. prof. Temple U. Health Scis. Center, Phila., 1966-71; asso. surgeon Retina service Wills Eye Hosp., Phila., 1962-74, attending surgeons, 1974—; prof. ophthalmology Thomas Jefferson U., Phila., 1974—; prof., chief ophthalmology Med. Coll. Pa., 1979—; practice medicine specializing in ophthalmology, Phila., 1962—; mem. staff Chestnut Hill Hosp., Children's Hosp. of Phila.; co-dir. retina service Wills Eye Hosp., 1976—. Fund raiser Retina Research and Devel. Found., 1968-75. Served with USAF, 1957-59. Recipient Zentmayer award A.C.P., 1970; Honor award Am. Acad. Ophthalmologists and Otolaryngologists, 1976; Billings Gold medal award AMA, 1976; NIH grantee, 1972—. Fellow A.C.S.; mem. AMA, Retina Soc., Jules Gonin Retina Soc., Am. Acad. Ophthalmology and Otolaryngology, Pan Am. Assn. Ophthalmology, Pa. Acad. Ophthalmology and Otolaryngology, Am. Ophthal. Soc., Phila. Mus. Art. Presbyterian. Clubs: Phila. Cricket, Haverford. Contbr. articles to profl. jours.; author: Retinal Diseases in Children, 1971; Diseases of the Peripheral Fundus, 1980; editorial bd. Jour. Survey of Ophthalmology, 1971—, AMA Archives of Ophthalmology, 1972-76. Address: 187 E Evergreen Ave Philadelphia PA 19118

TASSELL, PAUL NORMAN, clergyman, religious orgn. exec.; b. Toledo, July 20, 1934; s. Albert Burton and Bessie Ruth (Gibson) T.; B.A., Bob Jones U., 1955, M.A., 1956, Ph.D., 1958; m. Doris May Jaeger, Aug. 4, 1956; children—Jann Patricia, Jill Priscilla, Joseph Paul. Ordained to ministry Gen. Assn. Regular Baptist Chs., 1958; pastor 2d Bapt. Ch., Elberton, Ga., 1954-58, Bethany Bapt. Ch., Galesburg, Ill., 1958-65, Campus Bapt. Ch., Ames, Iowa, 1965-70; nat. youth rep. Gen. Assn. Regular Bapt. Chs., Des Plaines, Ill., 1970-73; pastor Grandview Park Bapt. Ch., Des Moines, 1973-79; chmn. Gen. Assn. Regular Bapt. Chs., Schaumberg, Ill., 1979—. Trustee Cedarville (Ohio) Coll. Mem. Assn. Baptists for World Evangelism (mem. adv. council). Author: Secrets of the Blessed Man, 1965, Outline Studies of Isaish, 1966, Outline Studies of Jeremiah, 1968, Gospel Views from Grandview, 1976, also author Wise Active Youth quars., 1968—. Office: Gen Assn Regular Bapt Chs 1300 N Meacham Rd Schaumberg IL 60195

TATARIAN, HRACH ROGER, journalist; b. Fresno, Calif., Dec. 25, 1916; s. Edward Y. and Rose (Yegishian) T.; B.A., Fresno State Coll., 1938; Litt.D., Windham Coll., 1967; m. Eunice E. Krauchi, Aug. 1, 1939; 1 son, Allan Roger. With UPI, 1938-72; assigned Fresno, San Francisco and Phoenix, 1938-43, overnight news editor, Washington, 1943-48, mgr., London, 1949-51, mgr. for Italy, 1951-53, gen. European news mgr., London, 1953-59; mng. editor, N.Y.C., 1959-62, exec. editor, 1963-65, v.p. 1963, editor, 1965-72; prof. journalism Calif. State U., Fresno, 1972—. Cons., UNESCO, Paris, 1978, U.S. Nat. Commn. for UNESCO, 1978—. Recipient Distinguished Journalism award Ohio U., 1968; named Outstanding Journalism Prof., Calif. Newspaper Pubs. Assn., 1979; mem. 20th Century Fund Task Force on Internat. News Flow, 1978. Fellow Sigma Delta Chi (Hall of Fame N.Y. chpt. 1975). Clubs: Press (London); Dutch Treat (N.Y.C.). Home: 3625 N Van Ness Blvd Fresno CA 93704 Office: Calif State U Fresno CA 93740

TATE, ALBERT, JR., fed. judge; b. Opelousas, La., Sept. 23, 1920; s. Albert and Adelaide (Therry) T.; student Yale, 1937-38, La. State U., 1938-39; B.A., George Washington U., 1941; LL.B., Yale, 1947; certificate La. State U., 1948; m. Claire Jeanmard, Apr. 23, 1949; children—Albert III, Emma Adelaide, George J., Michael F., Charles E. Admitted to La. bar, 1948; practice law, Ville Platte, La., 1948-54; judge Ct. Appeals, 1st Circuit La., Baton Rouge, 1954-60, presiding judge 3d Circuit, Lakes Charles, La., 1960-70; asso. justice La. Supreme Ct., 1958, 70-79; judge 5th circuit U.S. Ct. Appeals, 1979—; prof. law La. State U., 1967-68; mem. faculty Inst. Jud. Adminstrn., N.Y. U., 1965-76, appellate judges seminar U. Ala., 1966, 68, 69, U. Nev., 1967. Vice chmn. study adminstrn. appelate cts. Am. Bar Found., 1970-76; mem. Appellate Judges Conf., 1970-76; Am. Bar Assn. rep. adv. council Nat. Center for State Cts., Washington, 1971-72; mem. adv. Council for Appellate Justice, 1971-75; mem. com. and council La. State Law Inst., 1954-59; chmn. Jud. Com. La., 1968-70; mem. jud. council Supreme Ct. La., 1960-70; chmn. La. Jud. Planning Council, 1976-79; del. Constl. Conv. La., 1973-74. Chmn. La. Commn. on Aging, 1956-59; pres. La. Cotton Festival, 1955-57; mem. Evangeline Area council Boy Scouts Am., 1948—, dist. chmn., 1949-50; mem. La. Gov.'s Commn. on Rehab. and Corrections, 1970-75. Bd. dirs. La. State U. Found. Served with CIC, AUS, 1942-45; PTO. Recipient Nat. Jud. award of merit Am. Trial Lawyers Assn., 1972. Mem. Am. (chmn. exec. com. appellate judges conf. 1966-76, chmn. com. appellate advocacy 1974-78; mem. com. tech. in courts 1973-78, chmn. 1974-76), La. bar assns., Am. Judicature Soc. (dir. 1969-73), La. Conf. Ct. Appeal Judges (pres. 1967-70), Am. Legion, V.F.W., Woodmen of World, Delta Kappa Epsilon. K.C., Rotarian. Author: Cases and Materials, Louisiana Civil Procedure, 1968, 2d edit., 1975; Treatises for Judges: A Selected Bibliography, 1971, 2d edit., 1972, 3d edit., 1976. Contbr. articles to profl. jours. Home: 410 W Wilson St Ville Platte LA 70586 Office: Room 324 600 Camp St New Orleans LA 70130

TATE, BARBARA LOUISE, coll. dean, nurse; b. Warwick, N.Y., Aug. 6, 1921; d. James Pronk and Caroline (Still) T.; Editor, Nursing Research mag. Am. Jour. of Nursing Co., N.Y.C., 1957-59; asso. dir. research and devel. Nat. League for Nursing, N.Y.C., 1959-66, dir. research and devel., 1966-69; prof., dean Coll. of Nursing, U. R.I., Kingston, 1969—. Trustee South County Hosp., Wakefield, R.I.; pres. Nurse's Ednl. Funds, Inc.; bd. dirs. R.I. Assn. for Prevention of Blindness; trustee R.I. Health Ser. Research, Inc. Mem. Am. Nurses Assn., Nat. League for Nursing, Am. Psychol. Assn. Contbr. articles to nursing jours. Office: White Hall U RI Kingston RI 02881

TATE, GRAYSON D., JR., army officer; b. Mickey, Tex., Jan. 15, 1929; s. Grayson Darnell and Viola Janette (Hope) T.; B.S., U.S. Mil. Acad., 1950; B.S. and M.S. in Aero Engring., Ga. Inst. Tech., 1958; ed. Army Command and Gen. Staff Coll., 1962, Indsl. Coll. Armed Forces, 1968; m. Anne Kyle Hashagen, June 17, 1950; children—Debra, Randall, Lauren, Lisa. Commd. 2d lt. U.S. Army, 1950, advanced through grades to maj. gen., 1979; comdr. 4th Missile Command, Korea, 1971-72; project mgr. Lance Missile System, Redstone Arsenal, Ala., 1974-75, comdg. gen. U.S. Army Missile Research and Devel. Command, Redstone Arsenal, 1977; comdr. Field Command, Def. Nuclear Agy., Kirtland AFB, N.Mex., 1977-79; program mgr. U.S. Army Ballistic Missile Def. Program, comdg. gen. Ballistic Missile Def. Systems Command, Huntsville, Ala., 1979—. Decorated Purple Heart, Bronze Star. Mem. Assn. U.S. Army, Field Arty. Assn., Officers Christian Fellowship. Methodist. Clubs: Kiwanis, Rotary. Office: PO Box 1500 Huntsville AL 35811

TATE, HAROLD SIMMONS, JR., lawyer; b. Taylors, S.C., Sept. 19, 1930; s. Harold Simmons and Cleone (Clayton) T.; A.B. cum laude, Harvard U., 1951, J.D., 1956, postgrad., 1954; m. Elizabeth Anne Coker, Dec. 22, 1952; children—Mary Elizabeth Anne, Martha Coker, Virginia Clayton. Admitted to S.C. bar, 1956; partner firm Boyd, Knowlton, Tate & Finlay, Columbia, S.C., 1962—; lectr. Am. Law Inst.-Am. Bar Assn. seminars. Chmn. Richland County Mental Health Center, 1965-66; co-chmn. Columbia Hearing and Speech Center, 1962-64; mem. admission and scholarship com. Harvard U., 1961—; chmn. subcom. on legislation, legislation and fin. study commn. Gov.'s Adv. Group on Mental Health Planning, 1963-65; chmn. Columbia Bd. Supervisory of Registration, 1961-70; pres. Columbia Philharmonic Orch., 1966-67; pres. Town Theatre, 1967-70; trustee Richland County Pub. Library, 1973-78, Hist. Columbia Found., 1971-75, Caroliniana Soc., 1978—, Bostick Charitable Trust, 1968—. Served to capt. U.S. Army, 1951-53. Mem. Am. Bar Assn., S.C. Bar Assn., Richland County Bar Assn., Am. Law Inst., Am. Judicature Soc., Harvard Law Sch. Assn. S.C. (sec. treas. 1968-70). Episcopalian. Clubs: Tarantella, Forest Lake Country, Columbia Drama (pres. 1963-64), Palmetto (sec. 1963-70, pres. 1973-76), The Forum, Harvard (N.Y.C.); Harvard of S.C. Contbr. articles and book revs. to profl. jours. Home: 15 Gibbes Ct Columbia SC 29201 Office: 1250 SCN Center Columbia SC 29201

TATE, JAMES HUGH JOSEPH, former mayor of Phila.; b. 1910; ed. Strayer's Bus. Coll., Tucker Inst., St. Joseph's Coll., Labor Sch.; LL.B., Temple U., 1938; hon. degrees Villanova U., La Salle Coll., Drexel Inst., St. Joseph Coll.; m. Anne M. Daly; children—Frank X., Anne M. Mem. Pa. Legislature, 1940-46; mem. Phila. City Council, 1951-62, pres., 1955-62; mayor Phila., 1962-72; mem. Delaware River Port Authority, 1956-63, chmn., 1962-63; pres. Nat. League Cities, 1967-68, U.S. Conf. Mayors, 1970-71; exec. and steering com. Nat. Urban Coalition, 1967-74; chmn. Pa. State Tax Equalization Bd., 1975-79; ret. Past vice chmn. Phila. Democratic City Com.; past mem. Pa. Dem. State Com.; chmn. Atlantic County Dem. Fin. Com.; mem. Southeastern Pa. Transp. Authority, 1972-75; del. Dem. Nat. Convs., 1960, 64, 68, 72, 74. Bd. govs., chmn. transp. com. Internat. Eucharistic Congress for 1975-76; trustee, chmn. fin. com. Immaculata Coll.; mem. Villanova Econ. Devel. Council; bd. dirs., exec. com. Old Phila. Devel. Corp.; trustee Einstein Med. Center, Daroff div. Einstein Med. Center, WHYY-TV Public TV Sta.; adv. bd. St. Joseph's Hosp.; bd. dirs., exec. com., investments com. Temple U. Alumni. Mem. Phila. and Atlantic City chpts. Serra Internat. (pres. Phila. 1974-75, chmn. internat. conv. 1975), Temple U. Law Alumni Assn., World Affairs Council Phila., Am. Acad. Polit. and Social Sci., Fed. Bar Assn. Club: Temple U., Atlantic City Country, Seaview Country, Downtown. Home: 2909 Longport Dr Longport NJ 08403

TATE, JOE TOM, clergyman; b. Pulaski, Tenn., Oct. 7 1914; s. Tom T. and Hester (King) T.; A.B. in English, B.Th., Aurora (Ill.) Coll., 1942; m. Velma Evelyn Bowden, July 12, 1942; children—Margaret Lucille, Roxanna, Barry Joe. Ordained to ministry Advent Christian Ch., 1942; pres. Advent Christian Gen. Conf., 1964—. Home: 138 W 17th St Jacksonville FL 32206 Office: 113 W 17th St Jacksonville FL 32206

TATE, RALPH BRYANT, lawyer; b. Cuba, Ala., Jan. 1, 1912; s. William Bryant and Anie (McElroy) T.; A.B., U. Ala., 1932, LL.B., 1936; m. Louise Weakley Cross, Apr. 9, 1949; children—Ellen Anglin (Mrs. Burton R. Patterson), Mary Fern, Louise Bryant. Admitted to Ala. bar, 1936; practice in Birmingham, 1936-42, 46—; mem. firm Spain, Gillon, Riley, Tate & Etheredge and predecessor firms, 1952—. Served to capt. AUS, 1942-46; PTO. Mem. Am., Ala., Birmingham bar assns., Assn. Life Ins. Counsel, Alpha Tau Omega, Phi Delta Phi. Methodist. Club: Mountain Brook (Birmingham). Home: 3200 Pine Ridge Rd Birmingham AL 35213 Office: John A Hand Bldg Birmingham AL 35203

TATE, ROBERT FLEMMING, mathematical statistician, educator; b. Oakland, Calif., Dec. 15, 1921; s. Frank Flemming and Harriet Elizabeth (Hunt) T.; A.B. in Math., U. Calif., at Berkeley, 1944, Ph.D. in Statistics, 1952; M.A. in Math. Statistics, U. N.C., 1949. Statistician, U.S. Naval Ordnance Test Sta., China Lake, Calif., 1946-47; lectr. U. Calif. at Berkeley, 1950-53; faculty U. Wash., 1953-65, asso. prof., 1961-65; asso. prof. U. Oreg., Eugene, 1965-67, prof., 1967—; cons. 1953—. Mem. Matematisches Institut, Institut für Statistik U. Wien, summer, 1964. Fellow Inst. Math. Statistics (asso. sec. 1963-73); mem. Am. Statis. Assn., Sierra Club, Phi Beta Kappa, Sigma Xi. Contbr. articles to profl. jours. Home: 3370 Potter St Eugene OR 97405

TATE, S. SHEPHERD, lawyer; b. Memphis, Dec. 19, 1917; B.A., Southwestern at Memphis, 1939; J.D., U. Va., 1942; LL.D. (hon.), Samford U., 1979; m. Janet Graf; children—Adele Shepherd, Shepherd Davis, Janet Reid. Admitted to Va. bar, 1941, Tenn. bar, 1942; mem. firm Martin, Tate, Morrow & Marston and predecessor firms, Memphis, 1947—. Sec. bd. trustees Southwestern at Memphis, 1968-77; pres. Episcopal Churchmen of Tenn., 1961-62; sec. standing com. Episcopal Diocese of Tenn., 1969-71; pres. Chickasaw council Boy Scouts Am., 1967-78. Served with USNR, 1942-46; comdr. USNR ret. Fellow Am. Bar Found., Am. Coll. Probate Counsel; mem. Am. Judicature Soc. (past bd. dirs.) Am. (past chmn. task force on lawyer advt. 1977, past chmn. standing com. on scope and correlations of work, pres. 1978-79), Tenn. (pres. 1963-64), Memphis and Shelby County (pres. 1959-60) bar assns., Nat. Conf. Bar Pres. (pres. 1972-73), U. Va. Law Sch. Alumni Assn. (mem. exec. council 1974-77), Phi Beta Kappa (hon.). Club: Rotary. Office: 705 Union Planters Nat Bank Bldg Memphis TN 38103

TATE, WILLIS MCDONALD, univ. adminstr.; b. Denver, May 18, 1911; s. Robert Spence and Grace (Brown) T.; A.B., So. Meth. U., 1932, A.M., 1935; grad. student U. Chgo., 1945, U. Tex., 1946-55; LL.D., Tex. Wesleyan Coll., 1951, Centenary Coll., 1954, U. Denver, 1957; L.H.D., Oklahoma City U., 1954, Baker U., 1976, So. Meth. U., 1979; Sc.D., U. Tulsa, 1959; Pd.D., Albright Coll., 1974; m. Joel Estes, Dec. 24, 1932; children—Willis McDonald, Joel Tate Withers. Tchr. elementary sch. and prin. jr. high sch., Alamo Heights, San Antonio, 1932-43; exec. asst. to pastor First Meth. Ch., Houston, 1943-45; with So. Meth. U., Dallas, 1945—, successively asst. dean students, dean, v.p., 1954-71, chancellor, 1971-76, pres., 1974-76, pres. emeritus, 1976—. Pres., Univ. Senate of Meth. Ch.; pres. Tex. Council Chs., 1959-60; chmn. Council Protestant Colls. and Univs., 1966-67; past mem. exec. com. Meth. World Council; mem. Gov.'s Com. on Edn. Beyond High Sch., 1963-64; chmn. Gov. Tex. Adv. Com. on Edn., 1979—; pres. So. Univ. Conf., 1962-63; pres. Dallas Met. YMCA, 1958-59; mem. Goals for Dallas Planning Com. Recipient Alexander Meiklejohn award AAUP, 1965; Distinguished Am. award N. Tex. Nat. Football Found. and Hall of Fame, 1965. Fellow Am. Sociol. Soc.; mem. Nat. Assn. Schs. and Colls. Meth. Ch., Tex. Hist. Assn., Dallas Council World Affairs (pres. 1963-64), Am. Assn. Colls. (chmn. bd. dirs. 1971), Am. Council on Edn. (dir.), Tex. (pres. 1964-65), So. assns. colls., Philos. Soc. Tex. (pres. 1972), Blue Key, Lambda Chi Alpha (Order of Achievement, Grand High Beta), Alpha Kappa Delta, Alpha Phi Omega. Clubs: Dallas Rotary (past pres.); Salesmanship, Town and Gown, Dallas Country, Petroleum, Cosmos (Washington). Author: Human Behavior in Industry (with A.Q. Sartain and W.W. Finlay), 1954. Home: 3600 Marquette St Dallas TX 75225

TATEL, DAVID STEPHEN, former govt. ofcl., lawyer; b. Washington, Mar. 16, 1942; s. Howard E. and Molly (Abramowitz) T.; B.A., U. Mich., 1963; J.D., U. Chgo., 1966; m. Edith S. Bassichis, Aug. 29, 1965; children—Rebecca, Stephanie, Joshua, Emily. Admitted to Ill. bar, 1966, D.C. bar, 1970; instr. in law U. Mich., 1966-67; asso. firm Sidley & Austin, Chgo. and Washington, 1967-69, 70-71; dir. Chgo. Lawyers' Com. for Civil Rights Under Law, 1969-70; dir. Nat. Lawyers' Com. for Civil Rights Under Law, Washington, 1972-74; partner firm Hogan & Hartson, Washington, 1974-77; dir. U.S. Office for Civil Rights, HEW, Washington, 1977-79; partner firm Hogan & Hartson. Home: 24 Grafton St Chevy Chase MD 20015 Office: 815 Connecticut Ave NW Washington DC 20000

TATGENHORST, (CHARLES) ROBERT, lawyer; b. Cin., Apr. 21, 1918; s. Charles and Clara (Strebel) T.; A.B., Dartmouth Coll., 1940; LL.B., U. Cin., 1947; m. Louise Thompson, Sept. 6, 1951; children—David, John, James, Richard. Admitted to Ohio bar, 1947; asst. atty. gen. State of Ohio, 1947-49; asso. firm Taft, Stettinius & Hollister, Cin., 1951-58; partner firm Tatgenhorst & Tatgenhorst, Cin., 1958-61; prin. firm Robert Tatgenhorst & Assos., Cin., 1961—; adj. prof. law Chase Coll. Law, No. Ky. U. Pres. Westwood Civic Assn., Cin., 1959, Methodist Union, Cin., 1960; chmn. dist. Boy Scouts Am., 1970. Served with CIC, U.S. Army, 1942-46. Recipient award of merit Ohio Legal Center Inst., 1975. Mem. Cin. Bar Assn. (sec. 1973-75), Ohio State Bar Assn., Am. Bar Assn., Am. Trial Lawyers Assn. Republican. Clubs: Cin., Ryland Lakes Country, Optimists (pres. Cin. club 1962), Dartmouth of Cin. (pres. 1965), Masons (33 deg.). Home: 2921 Urwiler Ave Cincinnati OH 45211 Office: 600 Atlas Bank Bldg Cincinnati OH 45202

TATHWELL, JAMES LEROY, former engring. and constrn. co. exec.; b. Kansas City, Mo., July 26, 1913; s. James D. and Nellie G. (Robinson) T.; A.B.S., Kansas City Jr. Coll., 1932; B.S., Kans. U., 1935; m. Helen Louise Moore, Jan. 20, 1940; children—Jean Louise, Joy Lynn. Engr., Mobil Oil Co., 1935-37, Phillips Petroleum Co., 1937-41; with Fluor Corp., 1941-78, v.p. internat. ops., 1962-68, sr. v.p., 1968-77, group v.p., Irvine, Calif., 1977-78, also dir.; dir. Fluor PAC. Registered profl. engr., Calif., Wash., Mich., Miss. Mem. ASME, Nat. Soc. Profl. Engrs., Emerald Bay Community Assn. Republican. Baptist. Clubs: Balboa Bay, Masons. Home: 840 Emerald Bay Laguna Beach CA 92651

TATLOW, RICHARD HENRY, III, civil engr.; b. Denver, May 27, 1906; s. Richard Henry, and Viletta (Crow) T.; B.S., U. Colo., 1927, C.E., 1933; m. Annette Hart, June 18, 1932; children—Annette Beedy (Mrs. C. Jackson Ritchie, Jr.), Richard Henry IV. Engr., partner Harrington & Cortelyou, 1929-40; chmn., dir. Abbott, Merkt & Co., Inc., N.Y.C., 1946—; dir. NUS Corp., Washington; chmn., dir. Abbott Merkt Architects, Inc., 1972—. Chmn. bldg. research adv. bd. Nat. Acad. Sci., 1962-64, mem. com. SST-Sonic Boom, 1964-71; v.p. Engrs. Joint Council, 1963-67; trustee United Engring. Trustees, pres., 1975-76. Bd. dirs., v.p. Animal Med. Center, N.Y.C., until 1972. Served to col., C.E., AUS, 1941-46. Decorated Legion of Merit. Fellow ASME, ASCE (pres. 1968, dir.); mem. Nat. Acad. Engring., Am. Inst. Cons. Engrs. (mem. council, past pres.), Newcomen Soc. N.Am. Clubs: Cosmos, Chevy Chase (Washington); Union League (N.Y.C.); Shenorock (Rye). Home: 11 Rutland Rd Scarsdale NY 10583 Office: 10 E 40th St Suite 3400 New York NY 10016

TATUM, DONALD EDWARDS, ins. co. exec.; b. Clover, S.C., Jan. 1, 1924; s. William Otis, Jr. and Eleanor Elizabeth (Mayo) T.; student La. State U., 1940-42; C.L.U., Am. Coll., 1955, C.L.U.M., 1956; m. Sally J. Marsteller, Mar. 13, 1964; children—William Otis, IV, Timothy B., Elizabeth E., Donald Edwards. Life ins. salesman, N.Y.C., 1946-51; home office and field sales mgr. Conn. Gen. Life Ins. Co., Hartford, Cleve., Pitts., 1951-62; v.p. Nat. Union Ins. Cos., Pitts., 1962-67; sr. v.p. U.S. Life Corp., pres. South Coast Life Ins. Co., Gt. Nat. Life, Grenat Corp., Tex. and N.Y., 1967-70; pres. Peninsular Life Ins. Co., George Washington Life Ins. Co., Jacksonville, Fla., 1970-74; pres., dir. Lincoln Am. Life Ins. Co., Memphis, 1974—; dir. United Am. Life Ins. Co., Lincoln Am. Corp., Lincoln Am. Securities, Jacksonville Nat. Bank. Active, United Fund, City of Hope; bd. dirs. Metro YMCA, Jacksonville, 1972-75; mem. Forum for Greater Memphis, 1974, Com. of 100, 1977. Served to lt. USNR, 1942-46. Mem. Am. Soc. Life Underwriters (dir. chpt. 1956-66), Nat. and Local Assn. Life Underwriters (past chpt. dir.), Am. Newcomen Soc., Am. Mgmt. Assn., Tenn. Assn. Life Ins. Cos. (dir. 1975—), Memphis C. of C. Republican. Presbyterian. Clubs: Meadow Brook Country; Petroleum; Tennessee; Delta; Summit. Contbr. articles to ins. and industry publs. Home: Box 95 Route 2 Hughes AR 72348 Office: 60 N Main St Memphis TN 38103. *I always try to be aware of God's Presence within me and in my life. That Presence gives me true confidence and peace of mind.*

TATUM, DONN BENJAMIN, corp. exec., lawyer; b. Los Angeles, Jan. 9, 1913; s. Frank D. and Terese (Murphy) T.; A.B., Stanford U., 1934; postgrad. Loyola U., 1936-38; B.A., Oxford (Eng.) U., 1936, M.A., 1959; D.B.A., Woodbury Coll., 1963; LL.D. (hon.), Pepperdine U., 1978; m. Vernette Ripley, Mar. 20, 1937; children—Frederic, Donn, Vernette, Forbes, Melantha. Admitted to Calif. bar, 1938; practice in Los Angeles, 1938-48; partner Lillick, Geary, McHose & Adams, 1945-48; Pacific coast counsel RCA and subs.'s, 1942-48; v.p., dir. Don Lee Cos., 1948-51; dir. TV Western div. ABC, 1951-54; v.p., dir., mem. exec. com. Walt Disney Prodns., Burbank, Calif., 1956-67, vice-chmn., exec. v.p., 1967-68, pres., 1968-72, chief exec. officer, 1971-76, chmn. bd., 1972—; chmn. bd. Walt Disney World Co. Chmn. bd. trustees Calif. Inst. Arts; pres. John Tracy Clinic. Mem. Acad. TV Arts and Scis., So. Calif. Hist. Soc., Broadcast Pioneers. Office: Walt Disney Prodns 500 S Buena Vista St Burbank CA 91521

TATUM, EDWARD HOWLAND, JR., former banker; b. Glendale, Calif., Oct. 7, 1908; s. Edward Howland and Mary Nina (Martin) T.; A.B., Yale U., 1929; Ph.D., U. Calif. at Berkeley, 1934; m. Eldora Rickey Lyford, Dec. 2, 1944; 1 stepson, John Rickey. Instr., U. Calif. at Los Angeles, 1935-36; asst. to dir. Huntington Library, San Marino, Calif., 1936-39; lectr. U. Calif. at Berkeley, 1939-41; clk. First Nat. Bank, Santa Fe, 1945-49, asst. cashier, 1949-54, v.p., 1954-60, exec. v.p., 1960-62, pres., 1962-68, 71-73, vice-chmn. 1967-79. Chmn. bd. dirs. Opera Assn. N.Mex., 1969—, pres. 1968-69. Served with AUS, 1942-45. Mem. N.Mex. Bankers Assn. (pres. 1969-70), Phi Beta Kappa. Democrat. Episcopalian. Mason. Editor, Jour. of Ambrose Serle, 1775-1778, 1940. also PO Box 1963 Santa Fe NM 87501

TATUM, GEORGE BISHOP, educator; b. Cleve., Aug. 1, 1917; s. Alfred Marion and Myra (Williams) T.; A.B., Princeton U., 1940, M.F.A., 1947, Ph.D., 1949; m. Alma Standish Merry, May 1, 1942; children—Susan, John Richard, Daniel. Instr., Princeton U., 1947; asst. prof. history of art, vice dean Sch. Fine Arts, U. Pa., 1948-53, asso. prof., chmn. dept. history of art, 1954-58, prof. history of art, 1962-67; H. Rodney Sharp prof. history of art U. Del., Newark, 1967-78, prof. emeritus, 1978—; research asso. Henry Francis duPont Winterthur Mus., 1965-78; sr. fellow history of landscape architecture Dumbarton Oaks, Washington, 1967-68; adj. prof. Grad. Sch. Architecture and Planning, Columbia U., spring 1979; adv. bd. Historic Am. Bldgs. Survey, Nat. Park Service, 1966-72, chmn., 1969-71; mem. Nat. Collection of Fine Arts Commn., 1971—, chmn., 1975—; mem. New Castle County (Del.) Beautification Bd., 1970-76; vice chmn. Historic Dist. Commn., Old Lyme, Conn., 1978—; dir. Phila. Soc. for Preservation of Landmarks, 1965-76; trustee Conn. River Found., 1978—, Lyme Acad. Fine Arts, 1978—. Served to capt. USAAF, 1942-46. Fellow Royal Soc. Arts; mem. Coll. Art Assn., Soc. Archtl. Historians (pres. 1966-68), Am. Studies Assn., AIA (hon.), Victorian Soc. Am. (dir. 1968, v.p. 1972-74), Old Lyme Hist. Soc. (trustee 1970-76, pres. 1978—), Phi Beta Kappa, Tau Sigma Delta (hon.), Phi Kappa Phi (hon.). Author: (with others) Philadelphia Architecture in the Nineteenth Century, 1953; Penn's Great Town: Two Hundred Fifty Years of Philadelphia Architecture in Prints and Drawings, 1961; (with others) The Arts in America: The Colonial Period, 1966; Philadelphia Georgian: The City House of Samuel Powel and Some of its Eighteenth-Century Neighbors, 1976; also articles in field. Home: PO Box 763 Academy Ln Old Lyme CT 06371

TATUM, JOHN DAVID (JACK), football player; b. Cherryville, Nov. 18, 1948; student Ohio State U. Defense back Oakland Raiders, 1971—; played in Pro Bowl, 1973, 74, 77. Named to Sporting News Coll. All-Am. Team, 1969, 70, to AFL All-Star Team, 1975, 76, 77. Office: care Oakland Raiders 7811 Oakport St Oakland CA 94621*

TATUM, NANCY COLTHARD, dramatic soprano; b. Memphis, Aug. 25, 1937; studied with Zelma Lee Thomas, Samule Margolis and Wiley E. Tatum; m. Wiley E. Tatum. Opera debut in Aida with Oper Saarbrucker, 1963; appearances with maj. cos. in Europe and North and South Am., including: Cin. Opera, Dallas Civic Opera, Houston Grand Opera, N.Y.C. Opera, Pitts. Opera, San Francisco Opera; also appearances with symphony orchs.; recitalist. Recipient Gold medallion Internat. Opera Competition, Sofia, Bulgaria, 1963. Office: care Hurok Concerts Inc 540 Madison Ave New York NY 10022*

TATUM, SAMUEL CAMERON, ret. ins. co. exec.; b. Salisbury, N.C., Oct. 30, 1904; s. Ezar Walter and Edna (Low) T.; student N.C. State Coll., 1922; Wake Forest Coll., 1922- 26, U. N.C., 1955-56; m. Johnsie Wright, Nov. 6, 1928 (dec. 1961). With Jefferson Standard Life Ins. Co., asst. v.p. 1953, 2d v.p., 1953-56, actuary, 1956-67, chief actuary, 1967-69, v.p., 1956-62, sr. v.p., 1962-69, also past dir. const. actuary, 1970—. Trustee Wake Forest U. 1968-71; hon. lifetime trustee, 1976—. Asso. Soc. Actuaries; mem. Am. Acad. Actuaries, S.A.R., Greensboro C. of C. Clubs: Middle Atlantic Actuarial (past pres.), Greensboro Country. Democrat. Baptist. Clubs: Masons, Shriners. Co-author: The Booke Seminar in Life Ins. Co. Fed. Income Taxation. Home: 606 Elmwood Dr Greensboro NC 27408

TATZ, PAUL HENRY, lawyer; b. Des Moines, June 24, 1935; s. Simon and Esther (Ofstein) T.; student State U. Iowa, 1953, 56; LL.B., Drake U., 1962; m. Judith Catherine Rossiter, June 20, 1964; children—John, Jennifer, Stephen, Suzanne. Admitted to Iowa bar, 1962, Ill. bar, 1968, Mich. bar, 1970, Calif. bar, 1973; practiced in Des Moines, 1962-68, 76—; asst. atty. gen. Iowa, 1968; atty. Inland Steel Co., Chgo., 1968-70; gen. atty. Wickes Corp., Saginaw, Mich., 1970, sec., dir. law dept., 1971-72, sr. v.p., gen. counsel, sec., San Diego, 1972-73, sr. v.p., asst. to pres., chief personnel officer, 1973-74, sr. v.p., gen. mgr. furniture div., Wheeling, Ill., 1974-75. Served with AUS, 1954-56. Mem. Am. Soc. Corporate Secs., Am., Iowa, Chgo. bar assns., Phi Alpha Delta (pres. 1961). Republican. Clubs: Des Moines, Des Moines Golf and Country. Home: 9831 Clark St Des Moines IA 50322 Office: 8350 Hickman Rd Suite 12 Des Moines IA 50322

TAUB, ABRAHAM HASKEL, mathematician; b. Chgo., Feb. 1, 1911; s. Joseph Haskell and Mary (Sherman) T.; B.S., U. Chgo., 1931; Ph.D., Princeton U., 1935; m. Cecilia Vaslow, Dec. 26, 1933; children—Mara, Nadine, Haskell Joseph. Asst., Inst. Advanced Study, Princeton, 1935-36; from instr. to prof. U. Wash., 1936-48; research prof. applied math. U. Ill. at Urbana, 1948-64, head digital computer lab., 1961-64; prof. math. U. Calif. at Berkeley, 1964-78, prof. emeritus, 1978—, dir. computer center, 1964-68; mem. Inst. Advanced Study, 1940-41, 47-48, 62-63; vis. prof. Coll. de France (Paris), 1967, 75, 76; mem. theoretical physicist div. 2 Nat. Def. Research Com., 1942-45; mem. adv. panel applied math. Nat. Bur. Standards, 1951-60. Recipient Pres.'s Certificate of Merit, 1946; medal City of Lille (France), 1969; Guggenheim fellow, 1947-48, 58. Fellow Am. Acad. Arts and Scis., AAAS (v.p. sect. A, 1968-69), Am. Phys. Soc.; mem. Soc. Indsl. and Applied Math. (past trustee), Am. Math. Soc. (past trustee), Math. Assn. Am. Editor: Collected Works of John von Neumann, 1961-63; (with S. Fernbach) Computers and Their Role in the Physical Sciences, 1971; Studies in Applied Mathematics, 1972; editorial bd. Communications in Mathematical Physics, 1965-74. Home: 1526 Arch St Berkeley CA 94708

TAUB, HARALD J., assn. exec.; b. N.Y.C., Feb. 13, 1918; s. Edward and Rose (Gottlieb) T.; A.B., U. Pa., 1938; m. Beverley Ann Matlin, Oct. 25, 1959; children—Alison, Hilary. Personnel cons. Labor Relations Assos., Inc., Chgo., 1938-43; film publicist, 1948-58; staff writer consumer fin. Coronet mag., N.Y.C., 1958-61; editor Prevention mag., Emmaus, Pa., 1962-74; former v.p. Rodale Press; editor, asso. publisher Let's Live mag., 1975-76; pres. Vigor In Maturity Assn., 1976—. Served with AUS, 1943-46. Mem. Am. Soc. Journalists and Authors. Club: Overseas Press (N.Y.C.). Author: Waldorf-in-the-Catskills, 1953; The Takers, 1969; (with Wilfrid Shute) Vitamin E for Ailing and Healthy Hearts, 1970; Keeping Health in a Polluted World, 1974. Home: 22369 Liberty Bell Rd Woodland Hills CA 91364

TAUB, HENRY, computer services co. exec.; b. Paterson, N.J., Sept. 20, 1927; s. Morris and Sylvia (Sievitz) T.; B.S., N.Y. U., 1947; m. Marilyn Adler, Sept. 13, 1958; children—Judith, Steven, Ira. Pres., Automatic Data Processing, Inc., Clifton, N.J., 1949-69, chmn. bd., 1970-77, chmn. exec. com., 1977—; dir. Leumi Bank & Trust Co., N.Y.C.; mem. exec. com. Joint Distbn. Com. Chmn., N.Y. chpt. Hemophilia Found., 1970-76; vice-chmn. Nat. Hemophilia Found.; bd. dirs. Am. Friends Hebrew U.; trustee N.Y. U. Mem. Young Pres. Orgn., Am. Technion Soc. (vice chmn., internat. bd. govs.). Office: 405 Route 3 Clifton NJ 07015

TAUBE, HENRY, chemist; b. Sask., Can., Nov. 30, 1915; s. Samuel and Albertina (Tiledetski) T.; B.S., U. Sask., 1935, M.S., 1937, LL.D., 1973; Ph.D., U. Calif., 1940; Ph.D. (hon.), Hebrew U. of Jerusalem, 1979; m. Mary Alice Wesche, Nov. 27, 1952; children—Linda, Marianna, Heinrich, Karl. Came to U.S., 1937, naturalized, 1942. Instr., U. Calif., 1940-41; instr., asst. prof. Cornell U., 1941-46; faculty U. Chgo., 1946-62, prof., 1952-62, chmn. dept. chemistry, 1955-59; prof. chemistry Stanford U., 1962—, chmn. dept., 1971-74; Baker lectr. Cornell U., 1965. Recipient Harrison Howe award, 1961; Chandler medal Columbia U., 1964; F.P. Dwyer medal U. N.S.W. (Australia), 1973; Nat. medal of Sci., 1976, 77; Allied Chem. award for Excellence in Grad. Teaching and Innovative Sci., 1979; Guggenheim fellow, 1949, 55. Mem. Am. Acad. Arts and Scis., Nat. Acad. Scis., Am. Chem. Soc. (Kirkwood award New Haven sect. 1965, award for nuclear application in chemistry 1955, Nichols medal N.Y. sect. 1971, Willard Gibbs medal Chgo. sect. 1971, Distinguished Service in Advancement Inorganic Chemistry award 1967), Phi Beta Kappa, Sigma Xi, Phi Lambda Upsilon (hon.). Home: 441 Gerona Rd Stanford CA 94305

TAUBE, THADDEUS NORMAN, bus. exec.; b. Cracow, Poland, Apr. 1, 1931; s. Zyg and Lola (Popper) T.; came to U.S., 1939; B.S. in Indsl. Engring., Stanford U., 1954, M.S. in Indsl. Mgmt., 1957; m. Gretchen Foote, June 11, 1956 (div.); children—Mark, Paula; m. 2d, Michele Gadd, July 31, 1977. Indsl. engr. Ampex Corp., electronics mfg., Redwood City, Calif., 1957-58; asst. chief engr. Wesix Co., mfg. elec. systems, San Francisco, 1958-59; v.p. E-H Research Labs., electronics, Oakland, Calif., 1959-63; founder, chmn. bd. Taube Assos. Inc., real estate investment, Belmont, Calif., 1963—; chmn. bd., chief exec. officer Koracorp Industries Inc., mfg. apparel, San Francisco, 1973—, also dir.; dir. Siltec Corp., Menlo Park, Calif., United Pacific Devel. Corp., San Francisco; lectr. real estate investments U. Calif., Coll. San Mateo. Vice chmn. San Mateo County (Calif.) Bus. and Profl. Democrats, 1966-67; bd. dirs. Skylark Homes Inc., foster homes, 1970-73, Technion Soc., 1972-74, Am. Friends of Hebrew U., 1975, NCCJ, 1977, Calif. Housing Council, 1978. Served to 1st lt. USAF, 1954-56. Mem. Calif. Assn. Real Estate Tchrs., San Francisco Bd. Realtors, Nat. Apt. House Assn., Nat. Assn. Apparel Mfrs., ASME, Am. Soc. Indsl. Engrs., Sigma Nu. Jewish. Clubs: Stanford Buck, San Francisco Tennis, San Mateo (Cal.), Commonwealth of San Francisco. Contbr. articles to profl. jours. Home: 1050 Ralston Ave Belmont CA 94002 Office: 617 Mission St San Francisco CA 94105

TAUBES, FREDERICK, artist; b. Austria, Apr. 15, 1900; s. Louis and Fanny (Taëni) T.; ed. Acad. of Art, Munich, 1918-20, Bauhaus, Weimar, 1920-21; student Vienna, France, Italy, 1920-23; m. Lili Jacobsen, May 25, 1923; 1 son, Frank Alex. Came to U.S., 1930. Exhibited in most European art centers, also Palestine, included in all important art exhibits in U.S., 1930—; over 100 one-man exhbns. in museums in U.S., 30 one-man exhbns. N.Y.C.; rep. Met. Mus., San Francisco Mus., Santa Barbara Mus. Art, San Diego Fine Arts Gallery, Bloomington (Ill.) Art Assn, collection of Mills Coll., (Calif.), U. Ill., M.H. De Young Mus, San Francisco, High Mus. Atlanta, William Rockhill Mus., Kansas City, Mo., Ency. Brit., IBM Corp. collections. Former Carnegie vis. prof. art, resident painter U. Ill.; vis. rof. U Hawaii, Mills Coll., U. Wis., Colo State U.; instr. Cooper Unon, N.Y.; head painting div. Corpus Christi (Tex.) Fine Arts Colony, Ruidoso (N.Mex.) Art Colony; art seminars, Palm Springs, Calif., San Antionio; lectr. Art Students League; guest lectr. various schs. art in Eng. Named hon. col. State of N.Mex., hon. adm. Leche State of La., hon. citizen of San Antonio, New Iberia, La., Charlotte, N.C. Fellow Royal Soc. Arts. Author: Technique of Oil Painting, 1941; You Don't Know What You Like, 1942; Studio Secrets, 1943; Oil Painting for the Beginner, 1944; The Amateur Painter's Handbook; The Painters Question and Answer Book; Anatomy of Genius; The Art and Technique of Oil Painting, 1948; Pictorial Composition and the Art of Drawing, 1949; Painting and Essays on Art, The Mastery of Oil Painting, The Quickest Way to Paint Well; Pictorial Anatomy of the Human Body; Dictionary of Artists Materials and Techniques; The Art and Technique of Portrait Painting; Pen and Ink Drawing; Restoration of Antiques; Technique Still Life Painting; others. Contbr. articles to The Illustrator, Mag. of Art, Pacific Art Rev., Groiler Ency; contbg. editor Ency. Brit., Am. Artist mag., 1943-62; columnist Am. editor Artist mag.; lectr., orginator Taubes Painting Media, Taubes Varnishes. Home: The Studio Haverstraw NY 10927

TAUBMAN, MARTIN ARNOLD, immunologist; b. N.Y.C., July 10, 1940; s. Herman and Betty (Berger) T.; B.S., Bklyn. Coll., 1961; D.D.S., Columbia U., 1965; Ph.D., State U. N.Y., Buffalo, 1970; m. Joan Petra Mikelbank, May 30, 1965; children—Benjamin Abbey, Joel David. Asst. mem. staff Forsyth Dental Center, Boston, 1970—, head immunology dept., 1972—, asso. staff mem., 1974—; asst. clin. prof. oral biology and pathophysiology Harvard U. Sch. Dental Medicine, 1976-79, asso. clin. prof., 1979—. Fellow USPHS, 1962-63, postdoctoral fellow, 1966-70, recipient Research Career Devel. award, 1971-76. Mem. AAAS, Internat. Assn. Dental Research, Am. Assn. Immunologists. Author articles, chpts. in books. Office: Forsyth Dental Center 140 Fenway Boston MA 02115

TAUBMAN, PAUL JAMES, economist; b. Fall River, Mass., Dec. 24, 1939; s. Abraham and Lena (Rubin) T.; B.S., U. Pa., 1961, Ph.D., 1964; m. Joan Greenburg, Aug. 19, 1962; children—Geoffry, Rena. Asst. prof. Harvard U., 1964-65; mem. staff Council Econ. Advisers, 1965-66; asso. prof. dept. econs. U. Pa., 1966-72, prof., 1972—; research asso. Nat. Bur. Econ. Research, 1977—. Fellow Econometric Soc., Internat. Soc. for Twin Studies; mem. Am. Econ. Assn., Am. Statis. Assn. Author: Sources of Inequality of Earnings, 1975; Kinometrics: Determinants of Socioeconomic Success Within and Between Families, 1977. Office: Dept Econs U Pa Philadelphia PA 19174

TAUC, JAN, educator, physicist; b. Pardubice, Czechoslovakia, Apr. 15, 1922; s. Jan and Josefa (Semonska) T.; came to U.S., 1969, naturalized, 1978; Ing.Dr. in Elec. Engring., Czech Inst. Tech., Praque, 1949; RNDr., Charles U., Prague, 1956; Dr.Sc. in Physics, Czechoslovak Acad. Scis., 1956; m. Vera Koubelova, Oct. 18, 1947; children—Elena (Mrs. Milan Kokta), Jan. Scientist microwave research Sci. and Tech. Research Inst., Tanvald and Prague, 1949-52; head semiconductor dept. Inst. Solid State Physics, Czechoslovak Acad. Scis., 1953-69; prof. exptl. physics Inst. Physics, Charles U., 1964-69, dir. 1968-69; mem. tech. staff Bell Telephone Labs., Murray Hill, N.J., 1969-70; cons., 1970-78; prof. engring. and physics Brown U., 1970—; dir. E. Fermi Summer Sch., Varenna, Italy, 1965; vis. prof. U. Paris, 1969, Stanford U., 1977. UNESCO fellow, Harvard, 1961-62; recipient Nat. prize Czechoslovak Govt., 1955, 69. Fellow Am. Phys. Soc.; founding mem. European Phys. Soc.; corr. mem. Czechoslovak Acad. Scis., 1963-71. Author: Photo and Thermoelectric Effects in Semiconductors, 1962; also numerous articles. Editor: The Optical Properties of Solids, 1966; Amorphous and Liquid Semiconductors, 1974; co-editor: Solid State Communications, 1963—. Office: Div Engring Brown Univ Providence RI 02912

TAUKE, THOMAS J(OSEPH), Congressman; b. Dubuque, Iowa, Oct. 11, 1950; s. Joseph A. and Esther M. (Reicher) T.; B.A. magna cum laude, Loras Coll., 1972; J.D., U. Iowa, 1974. Admitted to Iowa bar, 1974; mem. firm Curnan, Fitzsimmons, Schilling and Tauke, Dubuque, 1976-79; mem. Iowa Gen. Assembly, 1975-79; mem. 96th Congress from Iowa 2d Dist.; del. Republican Nat. Conv., 1976; chmn. 2d Congl. Dist. of Iowa Rep. Party, 1974-77; mem. Iowa Rep. Central Com., 1974-77; chmn. Dubuque County Rep. Party, 1972-74. Mem. pastoral council Roman Catholic Archdiocese of Dubuque, 1971-73. Mem. Am. Bar Assn., Iowa Bar Assn., Dubuque County Bar Assn., Sierra Club. Club: Rotary. Home: 1715 Glen Oak Dubuque IA 52001 Office: 319 Cannon House Office Bldg Washington DC 20515

TAULBEE, JOHN EARL, utility exec.; b. Moline, Ill., July 9, 1934; s. Marion A. and Mabel (Fowler) T.; B.A., St. Ambrose Coll., Davenport, Ia., 1958; J.D. with honors, George Washington U., 1962; m. Sylvia I. Beer, Aug. 2, 1959; children—Amy L., J. Eric, Joshua J. Accountant, Price Waterhouse & Co., Chgo., 1958-60; admitted to D.C. bar, 1962, Md. bar, 1966; atty. div. corp. finance SEC, 1962-65; atty. Balt. Gas & Electric Co., 1965-68, treas., 1968-72, sec., treas., 1972-74, v.p. finance and acctg., sec., 1974-78; exec. v.p., chief fin. officer Central & South West Corp., Dallas, 1978—. Served with AUS, 1953-55. C.P.A., D.C. Mem. Am. Bar Association, Phi Delta Phi, Delta Epsilon Sigma. Address: 4220 Stanhope Ave Dallas TX 75230

TAULBEE, ORRIN EDISON, univ. adminstr.; b. Taulbee, Ky., Oct. 18, 1927; s. William Perry and Virgie (Carpenter) B.A., Berea Coll., 1950; M.A., Mich. State U., 1951, Ph.D., 1957; m. Margaret Janet MacDougall, Sept. 3, 1955; children—Gregor, Edison, George, Scott. Research mathematician Remington Rand Univac, St. Paul, 1955-58, Lockheed Aircraft Corp., Marietta, Ga., 1958-59; asso. prof. math. Mich. State U., 1959-61; mgr. information sci. Goodyear Aerospace Corp., Akron, Ohio, 1961-66; dir. mgmt. information systems, dir. Computer Center, U. Pitts., 1966-70, prof. computer sci., math., info. sci., chmn. dept. computer sci., 1966—; vis. scientist Nat. Bur. Standards, 1971; cons. in field; Served with AUS, 1946-48. Mem. Am. Soc. Info. Sci., Am. Math. Soc., Math. Assn. Am., Data Processing Mgmt. Assn., N.Y. Acad. Scis., Assn. Computing Machinery (nat. lectr. 1967-68, internat. lectr. 1970, chmn. Pitts. chpt. 1971-74, chmn. computer sci. conf. com. 1973—, dir. computer sci. employment register 1973—, mem. conf. and symposia com. 1973—, vice chmn. computer sci. bd. 1977, chmn. 1978). Editorial bd. Ency. Library and Info. Sci., 1965—, Jour. Info. Systems, 1973—. Contbr. articles to profl. jours. Home: 302 Inglewood Dr Pittsburgh PA 15228 Office: Dept Computer Sci Univ Pitts Pittsburgh PA 15260

TAURO, G. JOSEPH, ret. judge, banker; b. Lynn, Mass., Jan. 10, 1906; s. Orazio and Emma (Amicangelo) T.; student Coll. Bus. Adminstrn., Boston U., 1923-24, J.D., 1927, LL.D., 1964; Dr. Juridical Sci., Suffolk U., 1965; LL.D., U. Mass., 1969, Merrimack Coll., 1970; m. Helen M. Petrossi, Jan. 30, 1929; 1 son, Joseph L. Admitted to Mass. bar, 1927; practice law, Lynn, 1927-61; asso. justice Mass. Superior Ct., 1961-62, chief justice, 1962-70; chief justice Supreme Jud. Ct. Mass., Boston, 1970-76; chief legal counsel to gov. John A. Volpe, 1961; prof. law Boston U., 1976-77; chmn. bd. Security Nat. Bank, Lynn, 1977-78; mem. adv. council Judges Nat. Council Crime and Delinquency, from 1963, nat. trustee, 1963-72; mem. vis. com. judges Inst. Ct. Mgmt., U. Denver, from 1971. Mem. bd. mgrs., exec. com. Lynn Hosp., 1945-61. Mem. Nat. Conf. Met. Ct. Judges (chmn. 1966-67), Boston U. Law Sch. Alumni (nat. pres. 1955-56), Mass. Trial Lawyers Assn. (pres. 1960), Am. Law Inst., Inst. Jud. Adminstrn., Am. Bar Assn., Nat. Conf. State Trial Judges (com. on continuing legal edn. 1971—). Club: Union (Boston). Home: 1 Cliff Rd Swampscott MA 01907*

TAUROG, NORMAN, motion picture dir.; b. Chgo., Feb. 23, 1899; s. Arthur and Anita (Goldsmith) T.; student pub. schs.; m. Julie Leonard, May 23, 1925 (div. 1943); 1 dau., Patricia Anne; m. 2d, Susan Ream, Sept. 16, 1944; children—Jonathan Ream, Priscilla Ream. Actor legitimate stage, 1912-16; engaged in motion picture industry, 1916—, dir., 1919—; films include Skippy, Adventures of Tom Sawyer, Mad About Music, Boys Town, Young Tom Edison, Yank at Eton, Presenting Lily Mars, Girl Crazy, The Beginning of the End, Words and Music, That Midnight Kiss, The Toast of New Orleans, Ricy, Young and Pretty, The Stooge, Room for One More, Jumping Jacks, The Stars Are Singing, The Caddy, Living it Up, You're Never Too Young, Birds and the Bees, Pardners, The Fuzzy Pink Nightgown, Onionhead, Don't Give up the Ship, Visit to A Small Planet, G.I. Blues, Huckleberry Finn, Adventures of Tom Sawyer, others. Prof. cinema dept. So. Calif. Recipient Acad. award for direction Skippy, 1931. Mason. Office: care Annabelle Lewis Brown & Assos 9465 Wilshire Blvd Beverly Hills CA 90212

TAUSSIG, JAMES THOMAS, railroad ofcl.; b. Ft. Leavenworth, Kan., Mar. 18, 1914; s. John O'Keefe and Meredith (Thomas) T.; B.A., Lake Forest (Ill.) Coll., 1937; m. Jane Gregg Cummings, June 28, 1941; children—Meredith J., Jane Ellis, Annie (Mrs. McAdoo). With Chgo. Bd. Edn., 1937-42; mem. sales dept. Am. Car & Foundry Co., 1946-47; asst. to v.p. Shippers Car Line Co., 1947-49; with C. M., St.P. & P. R.R., 1949—, asst. sec., 1951-65, sec., 1965—. Served to capt. AUS, 1942-46. Club: Saddle and Cycle (Chgo.). Home: 1130 Lake Shore Dr Chicago IL 60611 Office: 516 W Jackson Blvd Chicago IL 60606

TAVARD, GEORGE HENRY, educator, clergyman; b. Nancy, France, Feb. 6, 1922; s. Henri Ernest and Marguerite (Wasser) T.; S.T.D., Facultés Catholiques de Lyon, 1949; S.T.D., Kenyon Coll., 1965. Came to U.S., 1953, naturalized, 1960. Ordained priest Roman Cath. Ch., 1947; lectr. theology Capenor House (Eng.), 1948-50; asst. editor Documentation Catholique, Paris, 1950-51; lectr. theology Assumption Coll., Worcester, Mass., 1953-58; prof. theology, chmn. dept. Mt. Mercy Coll., Pitts., 1959-66; fellow Center Advanced Studies, Wesleyan U., Conn., 1966; prof. religious studies Pa. State U., 1967-69; prof. theology Meth. Theol. Sch. Delaware, Ohio, 1970—. Peritus at II Vatican Council, 1962-65; cons. Pontifical Secretariate for Christian Unity; vis. prof. Princeton Theol. Sem., 1970. Author: The Catholic Approach to Protestantism, 1955; Holy Writ or Holy Church, 1959; Paul Tillich and the Christian Message, 1962; The Quest for Catholicity, 1964; Woman in Christian Tradition, 1973; The Seventeenth-Century Tradition, 1978. Office: Meth Theol Sch Delaware OH 43015

TAVE, STUART MALCOLM, educator; b. Bklyn., Apr. 10, 1923; s. Max and Gertrude (Goldinger) T.; B.A., Columbia, 1943; M.A., Harvard, 1947; D.Phil., Oxford (Eng.) U., 1950; m. Edel Petersen, Dec. 28, 1948; children—Douglas, Niels, Karen, Janice. Lectr. English, Columbia, 1950-51; faculty U. Chgo., 1951—, prof. English, 1964—, asso. dean coll., 1966-70, William Rainey Harper prof. humanities, 1971—, chmn. English dept., 1972-78. Vis. prof. U. Wis., 1962, Stanford, 1963, U. Wash., 1966. Served with USNR, 1943-46. Recipient Quantrell award for teaching U. Chgo., 1958. Guggenheim fellow, 1959-60; Am. Council Learned Socs. fellow, 1970-71; Nat. Endowment for Humanities fellow, 1978-79. Author: The Amiable Humorist, 1960; New Essays by De Quincey, 1966; Some Words of Jane Austen (Laing prize 1974), 1973. Home: 1461 E 55th Pl Chicago IL 60637

TAVEL, RONALD, author; b. N.Y.C., May 17, 1941; s. George and Florence (Sterns) T.; M.A., U. Wyo., 1961. Scenarist, Andy Warhol Films, Inc., N.Y.C., 1964-66; founder Theatre Ridiculous movement, N.Y.C., 1965; playwright in residence Play-House of the Ridiculous, N.Y.C., 1965-67, Actors Studio, 1972, Theatre of the Lost Continent, 1971-73; 1st playwright in residence Yale Div. Sch., 1975, 77; author: Street of Stairs (novel), 1968; Bigfoot and Other Plays by Ronald Tavel, 1976; Elephantitis, 1973; Gorilla Queen (play), 1966; lit. adviser Scripts mag., 1971-72; lectr. N.Y. State Council Arts, 1969—; adviser, contbr. Subplot Theatre, Am. Place Complex, N.Y.C., 1969—; playwright-in-residence Williamstown (Mass.) Theatre Summer Festival 2d Co., summer 1977, New Playwrights' Theatre Washington, 1978-79. Recipient Obie award for Boy on the Straight Back Chair, 1969, for Bigfoot, 1973; Rockefeller stipend, 1972, 78; CAPS Program grantee, 1972-73, 74; Guggenheim fellow, 1973-74; Am. Place Theatre grantee, 1970; N.Y. State Council on Arts grantee, 1975— (all for playwrighting); Nat. Endowment for Arts fellow for creative writing, 1974-75; ZBS Found. grantee, 1976. Mem. N.Y. Theatre Strategy (founding). Address: 438 W Broadway New York NY 10012

TAVERAS, JUAN MANUEL, physician, educator; b. Dominican Republic, Sept. 27, 1919; s. Marcos M. and Ana L. (Rodriguez) T.; B.S., Normal Sch. Santiago (Dominican Republic), 1937; M.D., U. Santo Domingo, Domican Republic, 1943, U. Pa., 1949; m. Bernice Helen McGonigle, June 12, 1947; children—Angela Taveras Summers, Louisa Helen Taveras Haug, Jeffrey Lawrence. Came to U.S., 1944, naturalized, 1950. Instr. anatomy U. Santo Domingo, 1943-44; fellow radiology Grad. Hosp. U. Pa., 1945-48; rotating intern Misericordia Hosp., Phila., 1949-50; asst. radiologist Presbyn. Hosp., N.Y.C., 1950-52, asst. attending radiologist, 1953-56, asso. attending radiologist, 1956-60, attending radiologist, 1960-65; dir. radiology Neurol. Inst., N.Y.C., 1952-65; cons. USPHS Hosp., S.I., N.Y., 1952-65, Morristown (N.J.) Meml. Hosp., 1957-65, St. Barnabas Hosp., N.Y.C., 1959-65, VA Hosp., Bronx, N.Y., 1960-65; asst. instr. radiology U. Pa. Sch. Medicine, 1947-48; faculty Columbia Coll. Phys. and Surg., 1950-65, prof. radiology, 1959-65; prof. radiology, chmn. dept., dir. Mallinckrodt Inst. Radiology, Washington U. Sch. Medicine, St. Louis, 1965-71; radiologist-in-chief Barnes and Allied Hosps., St. Louis, 1965-71; cons. neuroradiology service Unit 1, St. Louis City Hosp., 1966-71; cons. radiology Jewish Hosp., St. Louis, 1966-71; prof. radiology Harvard Med. Sch., 1971—; radiologist-in-chief Mass. Gen. Hosp., Boston, 1971—. Pres., VII Symposium Neuroradiologieum, 1964. Decorated Knight Order of Duarte Sanchez y Mella (Dominican Republic), 1972. Diplomate Am. Bd. Radiology, Pan-Am. Med. Assn. Fellow Am. Coll. Radiology; mem. AMA, Am. Neurol. Assn., Am. Roentgen Ray Soc., Radiol. Soc. N.Am., Mass. Med. Soc., Inter-Am. Coll. Radiology, World Fedn. Neurology, Am. Soc. Neuroradiology (pres. 1962-64), N.Y. Acad. Scis., Harvey Cushing Soc. (asso.), Assn. U. Radiologists, Mass. Radiol. Soc., New Eng. Roentgen Ray Soc.; hon. mem. Phila. Roentgen Ray Soc., Radiol. Soc. Venezuela, Rocky Mountain, Tex. radiol. socs., Radiol. Assn. Central Am. and Panama, Alpha Omega Alpha. Republican. Author: (with Ross Golden) Roentgenology of the Abdomen, 1961; (with Ernest H. Wood) Diagnostic Neuroradiology, 1964, 2d edit., 1976; (with Norman Leeds) Dynamic Factors in Diagnosis of Supratentorial Brain Tumors by Cerebral Angiography, 1969. Editor: (with others) Recent Advances in the Study of Cerebral Circulation, 1970; (with Francesco Morello) Normal Neuroradiology; contbr. numerous articles to profl. jours. Home: Lancaster County Rd Harvard MA 01451 Office: Mass Gen Hosp Boston MA 02114

TAVERNER, SONIA, ballerina; b. Byfleet, Eng., May 18, 1936; d. Herbert Frank and Evelyn Norah (Powell) Taverner; scholarship student Elmhurst Ballet Sch., 1952-54, Royal Ballet Sch., 1954-56. Mem. Royal Ballet, 1956-66; mem. Royal Winnipeg Ballet, 1962-66, ballerina, 1966-74; prin. artist Les Grands Ballers Canadiens, 1971-72; guest artist Pa. Ballet, 1975—; tchr. Grant MacEwan Coll., Edmonton, Alta., Can., now head ballet div.; producer, performer own concert Variations, 1977. Recipient Adelines Genee Silver medal Royal Ballet Sch., 1954; Can. Council grantee, 1962-70, Explorations grantee, 1977—, Alta. Culture grantee, 1977. Mem. Royal Acad. Dancing, Actors Equity Assn., Am. Guild Mus. Artists. Home: 9939 115th St Apt 1503 Edmonton AB T5K 1S6 Canada Office: Grant MacEwan Coll Edmonton AB Canada

TAVITIAN, HENRY OHANES, psychiatrist; b. Sofia, Bulgaria, Mar. 13, 1934; M.D. with highest honors, Inst. Medicine, 1960. Intern, Flushing Med. Center, N.Y.C., 1963-64; resident in psychiatry Columbia U., 1964-65, Northwestern U., 1965-67, VA Hosp., Downey, Ill., 1965-67; staff psychiatrist VA Hosp., Bronx, N.Y., 1968-70, chief sect. dept. psychiatry, 1970-74, chief in-patient unit substance abuse program, 1974—, psychiatry out-patient dept. and consultation service, 1978; pvt. tutoring, consultation for Am. Bd. Psychiatry and Neurology Exams., Elmhurst, N.Y.; asst. prof. clin. psychiatry Mt. Sinai Sch. Medicine, N.Y.C.; sr. lectr. Am. Specialty Bd. Examinations in Psychiatry, Neurology. Recipient plaque for outstanding and distinguished serves as pres. Am. Psychiat. Assn. Bronx Dist. Br. and Bronx Soc. Neurology and Psychiatry, 1977, for distinguished and extraordinary service Greater N.Y. Conf. Soviet Jewry, 1977; diplomate Am. Bd. Psychiatry and Neurology. Fellow Am. Psychiat. Assn. (pres. Bronx Dist. br. 1975-77); mem. AMA (Physician's Recognition award 1969-78), Bronx Soc. Neurology and Psychiatry (pres. 1975-77), Am. Ontoanalytic Assn. Home: 90-45 56th Ave Elmhurst NY 11373 Office: 130 W Kingsbridge Rd Bronx NY 10468

TAVOULAREAS, WILLIAM PETER, oil co. exec.; b. Bklyn., Nov. 9, 1919; s. Peter William and Mary (Palisi) T.; B.B.A., St. John's U., 1941, J.D., 1948; m. Adele Maciejewska, Aug. 13, 1941; children—Peter, Patrice, William. Admitted to N.Y. bar, 1948; with Mobil Oil Corp. 1947—, v.p. plans and programs Mobil Internat. Oil Co., 1961-63, v.p. charge supply and distbn. and internat. sales parent co., 1963-65, sr. v.p., dir., mem. exec. com., 1965-67, v.p. charge supply, transport and Middle East and Indonesian affairs, pres. N.Am. div., 1967-69, corp. pres., vice chmn. exec. com., dir., 1976—; dir. Gen. Foods Corp., Bankers Trust Co., Bankers Trust N.Y. Corp. Trustee St. John's U., Athens Coll., St. Paul's Sch.; bd. govs. N.Y. Hosp.; bd. dirs. Near East Coll. Assn. Served with U.S. Army, World War II. Mem. Harbor Acres Assn., Beta Gamma Sigma. Knights of Malta. Clubs: Pinnacle, North Hempstead Country. Home: 171 Harbor Rd Sands Point NY 11050 Office: 150 E 42d St New York NY 10017

TAW, DUDLEY JOSEPH, pub. utility co. exec.; b. Cleve., Mar. 11, 1916; s. William C. and Ella (Gedeon) T.; grad. Hiram Coll., 1938; m. Louise E. Forshey, Sept. 10, 1938; children—Judith (Mrs. William W. Beck, Jr.), Dudley J., Jr. With McKesson & Robbins, Inc., pharm. co., after 1937, sales mgr., Boston, 1947, v.p. sales, N.Y.C., 1953-60; v.p. Revlon, Inc., N.Y.C., 1960-64; v.p. mktg. East Ohio Gas Co., Cleve., 1964-74, pres., dir., 1975—; chmn. bd., dir. West Ohio Gas Co., River Gas Co. dir. Burdox, Inc., Nat. City Bank, Consol. Natural Gas Co. Mem. exec. com. Cleve. Growth Assn.; trustee Cleve. Zool. Soc.; trustee Lakewood Hosp. Served with USNR, 1946-47. Named Sales Exec. of Year, Sales and Mktg. Execs. Cleve., 1966, Man of Year, 1977. Mem. Am. Gas Assn, Better Bus. Bur. (chmn. 1973), Sales and Mktg. Execs. Cleve. (pres. 1969-70). Methodist. Clubs: Clevelander, Mid Day, Westwood Country, Rotary (pres. 1972-73), Pepper Pike, Union. Home: 2 Hidden Valley Rocky River OH 44116 Office: PO Box 5759 Cleveland OH 44101

TAWIL, JOSEPH, archbishop; b. Damascus, Syria, Dec. 25, 1913; student St. Anne's Sem., Jerusalem, 1923-26; D.D.; LL.D.; s. Elias and Malaki (Salman) T. Ordained priest Melkite Catholic Ch., 1936; pres. Patriarchal Coll., Cairo, 1949-59; made archimandrite, 1952; elected patriarchal vicar for Alexandria, 1954, bishop by Melkite Holy Synod, 1959; consecrated bishop, 1960; patriarchal vicar for Damascus, 1960-70; archbishop of Newton, exarch for Melekites in U.S., 1970—; apptd. eparch of Newton for U.S.A., 1976—. Address: 19 Dartmouth St West Newton MA 02165

TAX, SOL, anthropologist; b. Chgo., Oct. 30, 1907; s. Morris Paul and Kate (Hanwit) T.; Ph.B., U. Wis., 1931, D.H.L. (hon.), 1969; Ph.D., U. Chgo., 1935; LL.D., Wilmington Coll., 1974; D.Sci., U. Guatemala, 1974, Beloit Coll., 1975; m. Gertrude Jospe Katz, July 4, 1933; children—Susan Tax Freeman, Marianna Tax Choldin. Mem. Logan Mus. N. Africa Expdn., 1930; mem. field party Lab. Anthropology Mescalero Apache, 1931; research among Fox Indians, 1932-34; ethnologist Carnegie Instn., Washington, 1934-48; field research Indians, Guatemala, 1934-41, Chiapas, Mexico, 1942-46; vis. prof. Nat. Inst. Anthropology and History, Mexico, 1942-43; research asso. U. Chgo., 1940-44, asso. prof., 1944-48, chmn. dept. anthropology, 1955-58, prof., 1948—, asso. dean div. social scis., 1948-53, dean univ. extension, 1963-68; dir. Fox Indian Project, 1948-62; research asso. Wenner-Gren Found. Anthrop. Research, 1957—; chmn. Darwin Centennial Internat. Celebration, 1959; co-ordinator Am. Indian Chgo. Conf., U. Chgo., 1961, Carnegie Cross-Cultural Edn. Program, 1962-67; organizer World Anthrop. Congress, 1973; mem. exec. com. U.S. Nat. Commn. UNESCO, 1963-65; mem. com. internat. relations anthropology NRC, 1956-66, com. internat. relations behavioral scis., 1966-70; spl. adviser anthropology to sec. Smithsonian Instn., 1965—, dir. Center Study of Man, 1968-76; mem. adv. council Nat. Anthrop. Film Center, 1976—; cons. U.S. Office Edn., 1965-70; mem. Community Activities and Continuing Edn. Council Ill., 1965-67; sec. Ill. Mus. Bd., 1958-70; bd. dirs. Council Study of Mankind, 1963-78, mem. exec. com. 1965-78, chmn., 1969-73, bd. advisers Council Internat. Communications, 1966—; bd. dirs. Am. Indian Devel., Native Am. Ednl. Services, 1977—; mem. adv. com. Center for Am. Indian History, Newberry Library, 1979—. Pres., Hyde Park Community Council, 1952-53. Viking medalist, 1961-65; fellow Center Advanced Study Behavioral Scis, 1969-70; decorated Govt. Czechoslovakia, 1969. Fellow Am. Anthrop. Assn. (pres. 1958-59, Distinguished Service award 1977), AAAS, Am. Folklore Soc., Soc. Applied Anthropology (Bronislaw Malinowski award 1977); hon. fellow Royal Anthropol. Inst. Gt. Britain; hon. mem. Zlovakian Anthrop. Soc., Ziovak Acad. Scis., Ethnol. Soc. Hungary, Chilean Anthrop. Soc., Internat. Union Anthrop. and Ethnol. Scis. (pres. 1968-73), Sigma Xi. Club: Quadrangle. Author: Heritage of Conquest: The Ethnology of Middle America, 1952; Penny Capitalism: A Guatemalan Indian Economy, 1953; editor: Civilization of Ancient America, 1951; Acculturation in the Americas, 1952; Indian Tribes of Aboriginal America, 1952; An Appraisal of Anthropology Today, 1953; 29th Internat. Congress Americanists, 1949-52; Current Anthropology, A World Journal of the Sciences of Man, 1958-74 (founder); Evolution after Darwin, 3 vols., 1960; Anthropology Today—Selections, 1962; Horizons of Anthropology, 1964; Viking Fund Publs. in Anthropology, 1960-68; The People vs The System: A Dialogue in Urban Conflict; asso. editor Am. Anthropologist, 1948-53, editor, 1953-56; contbg. editor Handbook Latin Am. Studies, 1947-52; gen. editor World Anthropology. Home: 1700 E 56th St Chicago IL 60637

TAYBACK, VIC (VICTOR TABBACK), actor; b. Bklyn., Jan. 6; s. (Najeeb) James and Helen (Hanood) Tabback; student Glendale Community Coll., Frederick A. Speare Sch. of Radio and TV Broadcasting; m. Sheila McKay Barnard, 1962; 1 son, Christopher. Former bank teller and cab driver; appeared in more than 25 stage prodns., including: The Diary of Anne Frank, Death of A Salesman, Of Mice and Men, Stalag 17; films include: Bullitt, Papillon, The Gambler, Report to the Commissioner, The Big Bus, The Shaggy D.A., The Choirboys, The Cheap Detective, Alice Doesn't Live Here Anymore; TV debut, 1958; regular on TV series Alice, 1976—; other TV appearanges include: Mission: Impossible, Star Trek, The Man from U.N.C.L.E., The Mary Tyler Moore Show, The Streets of San Francisco, Switch, The Blue Knight, Whodunnit, Time Express, Supertrain, Fantasy Island; TV films include: Honor Thy Father, Getting Married, Tut and Tuttle, The Mysterious Two, Portrait of a Stripper; co-founder Company of Angels theater group, Los Angeles. Served with USN. Office: care Public Relations CBS Entertainment 51 W 52d St New York NY 10019*

TAYBI, HOOSHANG, radiologist; b. Malayer, Iran, Oct. 22, 1919; s. Abdol Ali and Jalil T.; came to U.S., 1948; M.D., Teheran U., 1944; M.S. in Pediatrics, N.Y. U., 1954; m. Alice G. Baum, Nov. 25, 1955; children—Paul Siamak, Claude Hooshmand. Intern, St. Vincent's Hosp., S.I., N.Y., 1949-50; resident Children's Hosp., Akron, Ohio, 1952-54, Children's Hosp., Cin., 1954-56, King's County Hosp., Bklyn., 1958-60; asst. prof. radiology Okla. U., 1960-61, asso. prof., 1961-62; asso. prof. Ind. U., 1962-64, prof., 1964; asso. clin. prof. radiology U. Calif., San Francisco, 1964-70, clin. prof., 1970—; invited prof. U. Geneva, 1970; chief dept. radiology Children's Hosp. Med. Center No. Calif., Oakland, Calif., 1967—. Fellow Am. Coll. Radiology; mem. AMA, Calif. Med. Assn., Alameda-Contra Costa Med. Assn., Calif. Radiol. Soc., East Bay Radiol. Soc., Silverman Soc., Soc. Pediatric Radiology (pres. 1973-74), John Caffey Soc., Am. Roentgen Ray Soc., Pacific Coast Pediatric Radiol. Assn. (pres. 1969-70, Rocky Mountain Radiol. Soc. (hon.), Tex. Radiology Soc. (hon.). Author: Radiology of Syndromes. Described (Oto-palato-digital syndrome Taybi Syndrome), 1962, Rubinstein-Taybi Syndrome, 1963, Cephaloskeletal dysplasia (Taybi-Linder Syndrome), 1967. Office: Children's Hosp Med Center Oakland CA 94609. *Thank you, America and Americans, for giving* *me the opportunity to reach my goals. Inspiring teachers and challenging students have contributed to a very rewarding professional life for me. I am most grateful.*

TAYLOR, ALAN ROBERT, librarian; b. London, Sept. 14, 1932; s. Robert Harold and Violet Clara (Wood) T.; came to U.S., 1963; student Ealing Sch. Librarianship, 1949-51, Northwestern Poly. U., 1951-52, U. South Africa, 1955-56, 58-60, Ind. U., 1964-66; m. Diana Thyrza Margaret Vere Clutton, Aug. 2, 1956; children—Robin Elizabeth Susan, Penelope Gillian Vere. Library asst. Ealing Public Library, Middlesex, Eng., 1949-51, London Sch. Hygiene and Tropical Medicine, 1951-53, Central African Archives, Salisbury, Rhodesia, 1953-56; head librarian Nat. Archives of Rhodesia and Nyasaland, Salisbury, 1956-63; African studies librarian Ind. U., Bloomington, 1963-73; asst. dir. libraries U. Md., College Park, 1973-74; asso. librarian Johns Hopkins U., Balt., 1974-77; dir. univ. librarians U. Rochester (N.Y.), 1977—; cons. African Bibliog. Center, 1969-74; vis. lectr. Ind. U. Grad. Library Sch., 1968-72. Fulbright-Hays NDEA Faculty fellow, 1967. Mem. ALA, Library Assn. (U.K.). Contbr. articles to profl. jours. Home: 51 Landsdowne Ln Rochester NY 14618 Office: U Rochester Libraries River Station Rochester NY 14627

TAYLOR, ALLAN RICHARD, banker; b. Prince Albert, Sask., Can., Sept. 14, 1932; s. Norman and Anna Lydia (Norbeck) T.; m. Shirley Irene Ruston, Oct. 5, 1957; children—Rodney Allan, Leslie Ann. With Royal Bank of Can., 1949—, mgr. main br., Toronto, 1971-74, dep. gen. mgr. internat., Montreal, 1974-77, exec. v.p., gen. mgr., 1977—; dir. Libra Bank Ltd., London. Mem. adv. bd. Northeastern U., Boston, Carlton U., Ottawa, Can. Anglican. Clubs: St. James, Royal Montreal; National, Missisaugua Golf and Country (Toronto). Home: 411 Lakeshore Rd Beaconsfield PQ H9W 4J2 Canada Office: 1 Place Ville Marie Montreal PQ H3C 3A9 Canada

TAYLOR, ALLAN ROSS, linguist; b. Palisade, Colo., Dec. 24, 1931; s. Athel Ross and Marjorie Verle (Walters) T.; A.B., U. Colo., Boulder, 1953; Ph.D. (Woodrow Wilson fellow, Fulbright fellow, NDEA fellow), U. Calif., Berkeley, 1969; m. Mary Callas, Sept. 8, 1958; children—Artemisia, Anthony, Peter, Anne, Yoana. Teaching asst., lectr. U. Calif., Berkeley, 1958-63; instr. U. Colo., 1964-65, asst. prof., 1965-70, asso. prof., 1970-77, prof., 1977—, also chmn. dept. linguistics; cons. bilingual edn. for Native Ams. Active Democratic Party, in environ. issues. Served with U.S. Army, 1954-57. Nat. Endowment Humanities grantee (twice). Mem. Linguistic Soc. Am., Am. Anthrop. Assn. Home: 787 17 Boulder CO 80302 Office: Dept Linguistics Box 295 U Colo Boulder CO 80309

TAYLOR, ARTHUR CANNING, JR., educator; b. Bridgeport, Conn., Aug. 8, 1923; s. Arthur Canning and Carolyn (Lord) T.; B.S., Va. Mil. Inst., 1947; M.S., Ohio State U., 1952, Ph.D., 1963; m. Mary Holt Hill, May 1, 1948; children—Arthur Canning III, Mary Ann. Foreman, E.I. duPont de Nemours & Co., Martinsville, Va., 1947-49; instr., asst. prof., asso. prof., prof., head dept. mech. engring. Va. Mil. Inst., Lexington, 1949—. Cons. Harry Diamond Labs., Washington, also contract research; contract research NESC Weather Satellite, Washington. Pres., P.T.A., 1961-62; councilman local troop Stonewall Jackson council Boy Scouts Am., 1965—. Served with USAAF, 1943-46; PTO. Decorated Air medal with two oak leaf clusters. Mem. ASME, ASCE, Am. Soc. Engring. Edn., Sigma Xi. Editor: (with David Lipscomb) Noise Control, Handbook of Principles and Practices, 1978. Home: 405 Overlook Circle Lexington VA 24450

TAYLOR, ARTHUR ROBERT, bus. exec.; b. Elizabeth, N.J., July 6, 1935; s. Arthur Earl and Marion Hilda (Scott) T.; B.A. magna cum laude, Brown U., 1957, M.A. in Am. Econ. History, 1961; H.H.D., Bucknell U., 1975; L.H.D., Rensselaer Poly. Inst., 1975, Simmons Coll., 1975. Asst. dir. admissions Brown U., Providence, 1957-61; with First Boston Corp., N.Y.C., 1961-70, asst. v.p., 1964-66, v.p., 1966-70, also dir.; v.p. fin. Internat. Paper Co., N.Y.C., 1970-71, exec. v.p., dir., 1971-72; pres. CBS Inc., N.Y.C., 1972-76, also dir.; dir. Rockefeller Center Inc., First Boston, Inc., Alleghany Corp., Dillingham Corp., DCL, Inc., Partners Fund, Inc., Frances Denney, Inc. Chmn. Am. Assembly at Columbia U., Vols. in Tech. Assistance; vice chmn. Center for Inter-Am. Relations; pres. Invest-In-Am. Nat. Council, Inc.; bd. dirs. Nat. Com. on Am. Fgn. Policy, Inc.; mem. steering com. Am. Friends of Bilderberg; trustee Brown U., William H. Donner Found., Inc., Franklin Savs. Bank; bd. govs. N.Y. Hosp. Mem. Council Fgn. Relations, Trilateral Commn., Japan Soc., Phi Beta Kappa. Episcopalian. Clubs: Brook, Century (N.Y.C.); California (Los Angeles). Office: 30 Rockefeller Plaza Suite 4345 New York City NY 10020

TAYLOR, BENJAMIN FRANKLIN, corp. exec., former army officer; b. Washington, Pa., Apr. 3, 1912; Oliver Kirk and Roxanna (Whitsett) T.; student Ohio State U., 1930-32, Washington and Jefferson Coll., 1932-33; B.S., U.S. Mil. Acad., 1937; m. Sarah Louise Kirkman, Sept. 30, 1961; 1 dau., Ellen Karena; children by previous marriage—Linda (Mrs. Michael Drustrup), Joan (Mrs. Thomas Moore). Commd. 2d lt. U.S. Army, 1937, advanced through grades to maj. gen., 1962; sec. gen. staff. Hdqrs. China Theatre, 1944-45; strategic planner Army Gen. Staff, 1945-46; liaison officer State Dept., 1947, White House, 1956; with Exec. Office Sec. Def., 1952; exec. officer to sec. army, 1957-59; div. comdr. 24th Inf. Div., 1962-63; dir. army programs, 1963, army budget, 1964-66; chief staff Central Army Group, NATO, 1966-68; chief staff U.S. Army Europe and 7th Army, 1968-70; sr. v.p.-indsl. Internat. Bank, Washington; v.p. Internat. Gen. Industries, Washington, 1970-72, pres., 1972—; dir. IGI, Avis Co., Blasius Industries, Globe, Kliklok. Mem. Phi Kappa Psi. Home: 1226 Perry William Dr McLean VA 22101 Office: Internat Bank 1701 Pennsylvania Ave NW Washington DC 20006

TAYLOR, BERNARD J., II, banker; b. Phila., Nov. 10, 1925; s. Bernard and Marie (Pearce) T.; B.S., U. Pa., 1949; m. Barbara Silverstein; children (by previous marriage)—Dorothy Ann, Lawrence Dean, David Stewart. Asst. mgr. McCrory Stores Corp. Phila., 1949-51; with Fidelity Bank, Phila., 1951-79, fin. analyst, 1951-57, asst. to v.p. investments, 1957-59, asst. to pres., 1959-60, corp. sec., 1960-63, v.p., sec., 1963-66, sr. v.p. in charge adminstrn. dept., 1966-72, exec. v.p., 1972-74; v.p. Fidelcor, Inc., 1969-72, exec. v.p., 1973-76; sr. exec. pres., dir. Fidelity Bldg. Corp., 1970-79, Trefoil Capital Corp., 1972-79, Fidelity Credit Corp., 1969-79; pres., chief exec. officer, dir. Wilmington (Del.) Trust Co., 1979—, chmn., 1980—; dir. Metlab Co., Phila. Prodn. mgr., bd. dirs. Savoy Opera Co. Phila.; pres., bd. dirs. Pa. Opera Theater; mem. adv. bd. mgrs. Inglis House Phila. Served with AUS, 1944-46. Club: Orpheus Club of Phila. Home: 1129 Hillcrest Rd Penn Valley PA 19072 Office: Wilmington Trust Co 10th and Market Sts Wilmington DE 19899

TAYLOR, BILLY (WILLIAM EDWARD), musician; b. Greenville, N.C., July 24, 1921; s. William Edward and Antoinette (Bacon) T.; B.S. in Music., Va., State Coll., 1942; D. Mus. Edn., U. Mass.; L.H.D., Fairfield U.; D. Mus., Va. State Coll.; Ph.D., Clark Coll.; m. Theodora Castion, June 22, 1946; children—Duane, Kim, Jazz pianist, 1937—; lectr. Music Educators Nat. Conf., 1957, New Eng. Music Tchrs. Assn., 1958, New Jazz Soc., Phila., 1967; producer, staff Billy Taylor Show, weekly jazz TV program, 1965; performer, narrator TV prodns. The Pop Explosion, 1966, Dial M for Music, 1965, Jazz Mobile, 1967; host, narrator, performer Black, White and Blue, 1966; music coordinator, leader orch. The Subject was Jazz, 1957; program dir. sta. WLIB-FM, 1965-69; musical dir. David Frost Show, N.Y.C., from 1969; mus. cons. 1964—; owner Sta. WSOK, Savannah, Ga., Sta. WLIB, also WBLS-FM, N.Y.C.; pres. Billy Taylor Productions, Duane Music Co., both N.Y.C.; host Jazz Alive, Nat. Public Radio; guest soloist numerous symphonies; spl. cons. to chmn. Nat. Endowment Arts; chmn. bd. Creative Arts Public Service. Bd. dirs. Harlem Cultural Council; trustee Rockefeller Found., 1978—; mem. Nat. Council Arts, 1972-78; founder, pres. Jazzmobile. Mem. Arts and Bus. Council N.Y. (pres.), Nat. Acad. Rec. Arts and Scis. (v.p. 1964—), ASCAP (dir. 1976-78), Acad. TV Arts and Scis. Composer music ballet Your Arm's Too Short to Box with God; mus. dir. Black Jour. Tonight, PBS variety show. Office: 119 W 57th St New York City NY 10019

TAYLOR, C. BRUCE, physician, surgeon; b. Hecla, S.D., Feb. 6, 1915; s. Robert S. and Sylvia F. (Dewey) T.; B.S., U. Minn., 1938, M.B., M.D., 1941; children—Charles Bruce, Betsy B. Pathologist, Presbyn. Hosp., Chgo., 1946-51, 54-59, U. N.C., 1951-54, Evanston (Ill.) Hosp., 1959-70; prof. pathology U. Ill. Med. Sch., also Northwestern U. Med. Sch.; prof. pathology U. Ala. Med. Sch. in Birmingham; now asso. chief of staff for research VA Hosp., Albany, N.Y.; prof. pathology Albany Med. Coll.; mem. cardiovascular study sect. Nat. Heart Inst., NIH. Mem. Am. (past mem. research com. council arteriosclerosis), Chgo. (past gov.) heart assns., Chgo. Path. Soc. (past pres.), Am. Soc. Exptl. Pathology. Research on arteriosclerosis, metabolism of cholesteral. Home: 23 Sunset Dr Delmar NY 12054

TAYLOR, C. JAMES, railroad exec.; b. Toledo, Aug. 23, 1931; s. Clark James and Marjorie Ellen (Baxter) T.; B.S. in Econs., Wharton Sch. of U. Pa., 1953; certificate transp., Yale, 1954; m. Matilda S. Taft, Sept. 17, 1955; children—Thomas, David, William. Transp. engr. Nickel Plate R.R., 1956-58; cost analyst Union R.R. Co., 1958-61, trainmaster, 1963-65; supr. costs and statistics Bessemer & Lake Erie R.R. Co., 1961-62; with C., R.I. & P. R.R., 1965-75, comptroller, 1971-75, v.p., 1974-75; regional v.p. Amtrak, 1975-78, asst. to pres. Trailer Train, 1978—. Served to 1st lt. AUS, 1954-56. Mem. Am. Assn. R.R. Supts., Western Ry. Club. Club: Union League. Home: 6 S 260 New Hope Rd Naperville IL 60540 Office: 300 S Wacker Dr Chicago IL 60606

TAYLOR, CARL ERNEST, physician, educator; b. Landour, Mussoorie, India, July 26, 1916; (parents Am. citizens); s. John C. and Elizabeth (Siehl) T.; B.S., Muskingum Coll., 1937, D.Sc., 1962; M.D. Harvard, 1941, M.P.H., 1951, D.P.H., 1953; m. Mary Daniels, Feb. 14, 1943; children—Daniel, Elizabeth, Henry. Intern, resident pathology, surg. staff, tropical disease research Gorgas Hosp., Panama C.Z., 1941-44; charge med. service Marine Hosp., Pitts., 1944-46; supt. Meml. Hosp., Fategarh, India, 1947-50; research asso. Harvard Sch. Pub. Health, Boston, 1950-52, asst. prof. epidemiology, 1957-59, asso. prof., 1959-61; prof. preventive and social medicine Christian Med. Coll., Ludhiana, Punjab, India, 1953-56; prof. internat. health Johns Hopkins Sch. Hygiene and Pub. Health, Balt., 1961—, chmn. dept. internat. health, 1961—. Cons. AID, 1959—; mem. expert com. WHO, 1963, 66, 67, 70, 71, 72, 73, 75; mem. Nat. Adv. Commn. Health Manpower; chmn. Nat. Council for Internat. Health. Diplomate Am. Bd. Preventive Medicine. Fellow Royal Coll. Physicians (Can.), Royal Soc. Tropical Medicine and Hygiene, Am. Pub. Health Assn.; mem. Assn. Tchrs. Preventive Medicine, Am. Soc. Tropical Medicine and Hygiene, Indian Assn. for Advancement Med. Edn. Research on rural health, population dynamics, nutrition, epidemiology of leprosy. Contbr. numerous articles to profl. jours. Home: 1106 Bellemore Rd Baltimore MD 21210

TAYLOR, CECIL PERCIVAL, pianist, composer; b. N.Y.C., Mar. 15, 1933; studied music privately, then at N.Y. Coll. Music, New Eng. Conservatory. Played with Hot Lips Page, later with Lawrence Brown; formed own quartet in late 1950's; records and performs as solo pianist and with quartet; instr. U. Wis., 1970-71, Antioch Coll., Glassboro State Coll.; compositions include: Conquistador, Unit Structure, With (Exit), Tales (8 Whisps), Indent; albums include: Silent Tongues, Spring of Two Blue-J's, Cafe Montmartre, Unit Structures, Conquistador, Indent. Recipient Record of Year award Downbeat Critics Poll, 1975, Piano Player of Year award, 1972, 79; elected to Downbeat Hall of Fame, 1975. Office: care Arista Records 6 W 57th St New York NY 10016*

TAYLOR, CHARLES, educator; b. Montreal, Que., Can., Nov. 5, 1931; s. Walter M. and Simone (Bea Bien) T.; B.A. in History, McGill U., Montreal, 1952; B.A., Oxford (Eng.) U., Ph.D., 1961; m. Alba Romer, Apr. 2, 1956; children—Karen, Miriam, Wanda, Gabriela, Gretta. Fellow, All Souls Coll. Oxford U., 1956-61, 76—, Chichele prof. social and polit. thought Oxford U., 1976—; asst. prof. to prof. philosophy and polit. sci. McGill U.; prof. philosophy Universite de Montreal, 1962-71. Vis. prof. philosophy Princeton, 1965, U. Calif., Berkeley, 1974. Vice pres. New Democratic Party of Can., 1966-73. Author: Explanation of Behavior, 1964; Hegel, 1975. Home: 344 Metcalfe Ave Montreal PQ H3Z 2J3 Canada Office: Oxford Univ Wellington Sq Oxford OX1 25D England

TAYLOR, CHARLES, artist; b. Phila., Dec. 15, 1910; s. Andrew and Kathryn (Lohmiller) T.; student pub. schs.; m. Annette Skinner, Feb. 11, 1950; m. 2d, Patricia Cayo, May 5, 1972. Works exhibited Carnegie Inst., 1943, Phila. regional exhbn. Phila. Art Alliance, 1954-55, exhbns. Am. Water Color Soc., Audubon Artist, Nat. Acad., 1954-55, Phila. Sketch Club Show, 1975, 76; one-man show Fine Arts Co., Phila., 1975, retrospective show Hazleton (Pa.) Art League, 1978; represented collections Phila. Art Mus., Woodmere Gallery, Phila. Recipient regular oil exhbn. prize Phila. Art Alliance, 1954, regular water color exhbn. prize, 1955; B. Altman prize Nat. Acad., 1955, Ranger Fund purchase prize, 1955; Bronze medal C. Wolf prize Da Vinci Alliance, Phila., 1958; Grumbacker prize Allied Artists N.Y.; Seeley purchase prize Salmagundi Club, 1961, Mem. Audubon Artists, Phila. Art Alliance, Artists Equity, Phila., Water Color Club, Am. Watercolor Soc., Allied Artists Am. Club: Salmagundi (N.Y.C.) Address: 3406 Higel Ave Sarasota FL 33581

TAYLOR, CHARLES EDWIN, mech. engr.; b. West Lafayette, Ind., Mar. 24, 1924; s. Alvin Lee and Ruby (Hamilton) T.; B.M.E., Purdue U., 1946, M.S. in Engring. Mechanics, 1948; Ph.D., U. Ill., 1953; m. Lucile Mae Nitsche, Aug. 28, 1946; children—Gary Arthur, Glenn Charles. Instr., Purdue U., 1946-48; asst. prof. U. Ill., Urbana, 1951-52, 54-55, asso. prof., 1955-57, prof. theoretical and applied mechanics, 1957—, asst. dean engring., 1976—; research engr. David Taylor Model Basin, Washington, 1952-54; vis. summer prof., India, 1966, 69, U. Colo., 1967; Russell Springer prof. U. Calif. at Berkeley, 1968—; vis. prof. Technische Hogeschool, Delft, Netherlands, 1972. Served to 2d lt., inf., AUS, 1943-45; PTO. Fellow Soc. Exptl. Stress Analysis (pres. 1966-67, M.M. Frocht award 1969, M. Hetenyi award 1970, 73, Murray Lectureship 1974), Am. Acad. Mechanics; mem. Nat. Acad. Engring., ASME (asso. editor Jour. Applied Mechanics 1971-74), Am. Soc. Engring. Edn., Soc. Engring. Sci. (dir. 1974— v.p. 1975, pres. 1978). Research in methods for experimentally determining stresses in structures, especially by optical methods using polarized light, lasers, holography. Home: 3302 Lakeshore Dr Champaign IL 61820 Office: Talbot Lab Urbana IL 61801

TAYLOR, CHARLES FORBES, evangelist; b. Burton-on-Trent, Eng., Aug. 19, 1899; s. Charles and Mary Ada (Forbes) T.; ed. pub. and pvt. schs. Eng.; D.D., Simmons U., 1929; LL.D., Baylor U., 1946; m. Olive May Simmons, Jan. 13, 1922 (dec. 1966); children—Charles Forbes, Jewell Anne. Came to U.S., 1913, naturalized, 1926. Gospel singer since age of 5, preacher since 9; illus. lectr. producing color movie travelogues for colls., chs., TV and lecture series; minister at large First Baptist Ch., Glendale, Calif., 1965. Recipient Gold medal of honor award Religious Heritage Am., 1972. Clubs: University, Rotary (Pasadena, Calif.). Author: The Riveters Gang, 1921; Everlasting Salvation, 1924; The Gospel Wagon, 1928; Christ's Challenge, 1931; Christ for Me!, 1933; Life in a Look, 1936; Up to Now, 1938; Streamlined Idols, 1940; The Story of Jesus, rev. edit., 1961; Why Be Good, 1944; also articles. Address: 4701 Willard Ave Chevy Chase MD 20015 also 209 N Louise St Glendale CA 91206

TAYLOR, CHARLES HENRY JR., psychoanalyst, educator; b. Boston, Oct. 2, 1928; s. Charles Henry and Rosamond (Stewardson) T.; B.A., Yale U., 1950, M.A., 1952, Ph.D., 1955; student Trinity Coll., Cambridge (Eng.) U., 1950-51; children—Stephen, Diana Beth, Charles S., Eleanor. Instr., then asst. prof. English, Ind. U., 1955-61; asst. dean, then asso. dean, also asso. prof. English, Yale U., 1961-63, acting provost, 1963-64, provost, 1964-72; grad. C.G. Jung Tng. Center, 1979; dir. Boston Globe Affiliated Publs. Bd. dirs. Yale-New Haven Med. Center, C.G. Jung Found. Mem. Internat. Assn. Analytical Psychology, N.Y. Assn. Analytical Psychology, Phi Beta Kappa. Author: The Early Collected Editions of Shelley's Poems, 1958; editor: Essays on the Odyssey, 1963. Home: 40 Rogers Ave Milford CT 06460

TAYLOR, CHARLES PERRY, health orgn. exec.; b. Wilson, N.C., Apr. 14, 1913; s. Charles James and Asia Frances (Finch) T.; student Transylvania Coll., 1939; m. Mary Ann Fristoe, Jan. 29, 1943; children—Charles Perry and Ann Fristoe (twins), John Barclay, Frances Finch. Spl. asst. to dir. NYA in Ky., 1939-41; with Am. Cancer Soc., 1947—, dir. field staff, 1960-65, v.p. field services, 1965-71, sr. area v.p., 1971—. Commr. dist. I Am. Legion Baseball, 1946-47; bd. curators Transylvania Coll., 1950-55; pres.-elect alumni exec. bd. Transylvania U., 1978-79. Served to capt. AUS, 1941-46. Mem. Pi Kappa Alpha. Home: 810 Mt Vernon Hwy NW Atlanta GA 30327 Office: 2531 Briarcliff Rd NE Atlanta GA 30329

TAYLOR, CHARLES RICHARD, educator; b. Phoenix, Sept. 8, 1939; s. Norman Worsnop and Rosalind Emily (Gregory) T.; B.A., Occidental Coll., 1960; A.M., Harvard, 1962, Ph.D., 1963; m. Ann Boyd, June 6, 1969; 1 son, Gregory Boyd. Research asso. Harvard, research officer E.Africa Vet. Research Orgn., hon. lectr. U. East Africa, 1964-68; research asso. Duke U., 1968-70; asso. prof. biology Harvard, 1970-73, prof., 1973—, Alexander Agassiz prof. zoology, 1973—, dir. Concord Field Sta., 1973—. Guggenheim fellow, 1977—. Mem. Am. Physiol. Soc., Am. Soc. Zoologists, Am. Soc. Mammalogists. Contbr. articles to profl. jours. Home: 329 Silver Hill Rd Concord MA 01742 Office: Concord Field Sta Harvard U Old Causeway Rd Bedford MA 01730

TAYLOR, CLAUDE I., airlines exec.; b. Salisbury, N.B., Can., May 20, 1925; s. Martin Luther and Essie (Troope) T.; student Robinson Bus. Coll., 1942; R.I.A., McGill U. Extension, 1953; m. Frances Bernice Watters, Nov. 4, 1947; children—Karen, Peter. With Air Can., 1949—, gen. mgr. comml. planning, 1962-64, gen. mgr. marketing services, 1964-70, v.p. strategic devel., 1970-71, v.p. govt. and industry affairs, 1971-73, v.p. pub. affairs, 1973-76, pres., chief exec. officer, 1976—; mem. exec. com. Internat. Air Transport Assn. Hon. dir. Aviation Hall of Fame, Council for Can. Unity, Can. Nat. Exhbn. Assn., Boy Scouts Can. Mem. Can. C. of C. (exec. council). Baptist. Clubs: Mt. Stephen, Mt. Royal, Field and Stream (Montreal); Rideau (Ottawa).

TAYLOR, CLYDE CALVIN, JR., literary agt.; b. Anderson, S.C., July 27, 1936; s. Clyde Calvin and Ellen Letitia (Hamilton) T.; A.B., Wofford Coll., 1958; children—Catherine Ellen, Emily Brenda, Andrew Hamilton. Tchr., Westminster Schs., Atlanta, 1958; advt. copywriter Harper and Row, 1960; advt. copywriter Macmillan & Co., 1961, advt. mgr. Collier-Macmillan Library Div., 1962; asst. bus. mgr. book div. Am. Heritage Pub. Co., 1963-65; dir. subs. rights G.P. Putnam's Sons, 1965-69; v.p. World Pub. Co., 1970; v.p., gen. mgr. G.P. Putnam's Sons, N.Y.C., 1972-74, v.p., pub., 1974-77, exec. v.p.. pub., 1977; pres. Clyde Taylor Lit. Agy., Inc., 1978—. Home: 34 Perry St New York NY 10014

TAYLOR, D(ARL) CODER, architect, engr., planner; b. Ft. Wayne, Ind., July 18, 1913; s. Frank A. and Edith (Zook) T.; B.Arch., Carnegie Inst. Tech., 1935; spl. student U. Wash., 1933; m. Audrey Helen Larkin, June 5, 1944; children—Barbara Helen Taylor Reddy, Thomas Coder, Julie Marie Taylor Hitchins. Draftsman, Chgo., 1935; partner Zook & Taylor, architects, Chgo., 1939-42, Holsman, Holsman, Klekamp & Taylor, architects, Chgo., 1948-52, Yost & Taylor, architects and engrs., Kenilworth, Ill., 1952-60; chmn. bd. Coder Taylor Assos., Inc., architects-engrs.-planners, Kenilworth, 1960—; cons. in field, 1935—; prin. works include Municipal Bldg., St. Charles, Ill., 1940, Prize Home No. 1 (Chgo. Tribune prize home competition), 1946, Sherman Garden Apts. (Chgo. chpt. AIA honor award), 1951, Kincheloe AFB, Mich. (Best Family Housing Project No. Area), 1962, Chanute AFB, Ill. (Best Family Housing Project Central Area), 1959, U.S. Naval Tng. Center, Great Lakes, Ill. (Merit award FHA), 1964, Swimming Pool House, Northfield, Ill. (Chgo. chpt. AIA-Chgo. Assn. Commerce and Industry distinguished bldg. award), 1967, 510 Green Bay Rd. Bldg., Kenilworth, also Roberts Residence, Lake Forest, Ill. (AIA-Chgo. Assn. Commerce and Industry dist. bldg. award), 1968, Glenview Pub. Library (Chgo. chpt. AIA-Chgo. Assn. Commerce and Industry distinguished bldg. award), 1970, Kroch's & Brentano's stores, Chgo., 1961-77, Des Plaines Pub. Library (Des Plaines C. of C. outstanding achievement award), 1974, Wilmette (Ill.) Park Dist. Recreation Center, 1974, Wilmette Village Adminstrn. Bldg., 1975, Glenview Central Fire Sta. (Glenview Appearance Commn. Outstanding Bldg. and Landscape award), 1976, Internat. Hdqrs. Alpha Phi Frat., Evanston, Ill., 1975, Barrington Area Pub. Library, 1977. Mem. Glenview (Ill.) Planning Commn., 1962-65; chmn. Glenview Appearance Commn., 1968-72, Picasso Day Com., Chgo., 1967; mem. fine arts com. Ill. Sesquicentennial Commn., 1967-68; exec. com., treas. Fedn. Open Lakefront, 1966-68; mem. tech. studies adv. com. Nat. Acad. Sci.-NRC, 1962—; mem. tech. panel, adv. com. HUD, Nat. Acad. Scis., Nat. Acad. Engring., 1969; nat. panel arbitrators Am. Arbitration Assn., 1952—. Served to lt. comdr. C.E., USNR, 1942-45. Fellow AIA (dir. Chgo. chpt. 1965-66, pres. 1967, v.p. Ill. council 1968); mem. Ill. Assn. Professions (dir. 1968), Mich. Soc. Architects, Nat. Assn. Redevel. Ofcls., Tau Sigma Delta (pres. 1934- 35), Sigma Phi Epsilon (pres. 1934-35), Scarab (1934-35). Methodist. Club: North Shore Country (Glenview, Ill.) Contbr. articles to profl. jours. Home: 727 Redwood Ln Glenview IL 60025 Office: 500 Green Bay Rd Kenilworth IL 60043 also 1200 Central Ave Wilmette IL 60091

TAYLOR, DANIEL JOHN, corp. exec.; b. Detroit, Feb. 15, 1944; s. Robert Elmer and Mary Esther (Coyne) T.; student Emporia (Kans.) State Tchrs. Coll., 1962-63; B.B.A., Wichita State U., 1967; m. Carol Louise Dugan, June 26, 1965; children—Daniel, Steven. With Ernst & Ernst, 1967-69; treas. Pizza Hut, Inc., Wichita, Kans., 1969-75, sr. v.p. finance, dir., 1975-77; pres., chmn. bd. M.F.Y. Industries, Inc., Wichita, 1977—. Mem. Nat. Restaurant Assn., Nat. Assn. Accountants. Home: 7015 E Zimmerly St Wichita KS 67207 Office: 260 N Rock Rd Suite 100 Wichita KS 67206

TAYLOR, DAVID GEORGE, banker; b. Charlevoix, Mich., July 29, 1929; s. Frank Flagg and Bessie (Strayer) T.; B.S., Denison U., 1951; M.B.A., Northwestern U., 1953; m. Helen N. Alexander, Dec. 28, 1977: children—David, Amy, Jeanine. With 1st Nat. Bank, Chgo., 1953; with Continental Ill. Nat. Bank & Trust Co., Chgo., 1957—, sr. v.p. charge bond dept., 1972-74, exec. v.p. charge bond dept., 1974—; dir. Continental Ill. Ltd.; sect. leader Grad. Sch. Banking, U. Wis., 1971-74, lectr., 1978—. Treas., Mid-Am. chpt. ARC. 1968-71, bd. dirs., 1968-75; trustee Chgo. Ednl. TV Assn., WTTW-TV, Chgo., 1974—; bd. dirs. Sta. WFMT, Inc. Served to lt. USNR, 1953-56. Mem. Dealer Bank Assn. (pres., chmn. 1972-73, dir. 1972-74, mem. legis. com. 1979, taxable securities com. 1979), Assn. Primary Dealers in U.S. Govt. Securities (exec. com. 1969-70, chmn. ednl. seminar com. 1971-73), Pub. Securities Assn. (mem. govt. and fed. agencies securities com. 1975—, chmn. 1977, treas. 1978, mcpl. securities rulemaking bd. 1975—), Kappa Beta Phi, Phi Delta Theta. Clubs: Sequanota (past pres.) (Charlevoix); Chicago, Bond., Bankers, Economic (Chgo.); Skokie Country (Glencoe, Ill.); World Trade Center (N.Y.C.); Internat. (Washington). Home: 908 Wildwood Ln Northbrook IL 60062 Office: 231 S LaSalle St Chicago IL 60693

TAYLOR, DAVID PETER, mgmt. cons.; b. Chgo., Apr. 7, 1934; s. Harry Wilden and Corinne (VanderKloot) T.; B.S., Cornell U., 1956; M.B.A., U. Chgo., 1960, Ph.D., 1966; m. Renata Marion Wittmann, Mar. 19, 1960; children—Steven H., Mark D., Andrea C., Thomas A. Research asso. U. Chgo., 1962-64; asst. prof. indsl. relations Mass. Inst. Tech., Cambridge, 1964-66, asso. prof., 1966-68; exec. asst. to Sec. Labor, Washington, 1969-70; exec. asst. to dir. Office Mgmt. and Budget, Washington, 1970-71, asst. dir., 1971-74; asst. sec. for manpower and res. affairs USAF, 1974-76; asst. sec. for manpower and res. affairs Dept. Def., 1976-77; gen. mgr. Hay Assos., Boston, 1979—. Served with AUS, 1956-58. Contbr. articles to profl. jours. Home: 59 Woodland Newton MA 02166 Office: Hay Assos 5 Fanevil Hall Market Pl Boston MA 02109

TAYLOR, DAVID WYATT AIKEN, clergyman; b. Tsingkiangpu, Kiangsu, China, Dec. 13, 1925; (parents Am. citizens); s. Hugh Kerr and Fanny Bland (Graham) T.; B.A., Vanderbilt U., 1949; B.D. cum laude, Union Theol. Sem. Va., 1952; Th.M., Princeton Theol. Sem., 1953; D.D. (hon.) , King Coll., Bristol, Tenn., 1959; m. Lillian Ross McCulloch, Aug. 25, 1951; children—Frances Bland, David Wyatt. Ordained to ministry Presbyn. Ch. U.S., 1952; pastor in Elkton, Va., 1953-55, Bristol, Va., 1955-62; ednl. sec. bd. world missions Presbyn. Ch. U.S., 1962-68, program div. dir., 1968-73; ecumenical officer gen. assembly mission bd. Presbyn. Ch. U.S., Atlanta, 1973—; instr. Bible Presbyn. Jr. Coll., Maxton, N.C., 1951; mem. program bd., div. Christian edn. Nat. Council Chs., 1965-69, bd. mgrs., dept. edn. for mission, 1962-68, mem. program bd., div. overseas ministries, 1968-78, mem. governing bd., 1976—, chmn. governing bd. credentials com., 1978; chmn. Church World Service, Inc., 1973-75; mem. adminstrn. and fin. com. Nat. Council Chs., 1973-75, mem. commn. on faith and order, 1978—; mem. commn. on interchurch aid World Council Chs., 1973-75, mem. 5th Assembly, 1975; rep. Presbyn. Ch. U.S. to World Alliance Ref. Chs., 1976—; bd. dirs. Presbyn. Survey mag., 1963-68; mem. Consultation on Ch. Union, 1974—. Bd. dirs. Abingdon Presbytery's Children's Home, Wytheville, Va., 1958- 62. Served with AUS, 1944-46; PTO. Mem. Sigma Chi. Home: 2669 Rangewood Ct Atlanta GA 30345 Office: 341 Ponce de Leon Ave Atlanta GA 30308

TAYLOR, DERMOT BROWNRIGG, educator; b. Ireland, Mar. 30, 1915; s. Roland L. and Sarah J. (White) T.; B.A., Trinity Coll., Dublin, 1937, M.B., B.Ch., 1938, M.A., M.D.; m. Charlotte C. Taylor, 1965; 1 dau., Tina. Came to U.S., 1950, naturalized, 1955. Asst. to prof. physiology Trinity Coll., 1938-39; lectr. physiology King's Coll., U. London, 1939-45, lectr. pharmacology, 1945-50; asso. prof. pharmacology U. Calif. at San Francisco, 1950-53; prof. pharmacology U. Calif. at Los Angeles, 1953—, chmn. dept., 1953-68. Travelling fellow U. London, 1948; fellow Yale, 1948. Mem. Faraday Soc., Biochem. Soc., Physiol. Soc., Brit. Pharmacological Soc., Soc. Pharmacology and Exptl. Therapeutics, Soc. Exptl. Biology and Medicine. Contbr. to Essentials of Pharmacology, 1968; A Guide to Molecular Pharmacology-Toxicology, 1973. Home: 196 Colt Ln Thousand Oaks CA 91360

TAYLOR, (WILLIAM) DESMOND, librarian; b. Detroit, May 27, 1930; s. William B. and Elinor B. (Brown) T.; A.B., Emory and Henry Coll., 1953; M.S., U. Ill., 1960; m. Ingeborg Gertroud Krug, Oct. 26, 1957; children—Onica Ingeborg Marta, Erica Ingrid Elinor. Reference asst. Warder Pub. Library, Springfield, Ohio, 1956-59; reference librarian U. Puget Sound, Tacoma, 1960-63, library dir., 1963—, instr. honors program, 1965-67, asst. dir. overseas programs, 1971-73. Faculty mem. Semester Abroad Program, Vienna, 1968, 71. Trustee Comprehensive Mental Health Clinic, 1968-71. Served with AUS, 1953-56. Mem. A.L.A., Am. Assn. U. Profs., Am. Civil Liberties Union, Beta Phi Mu, Mu Sigma Delta. Club: Old Tacoma Improvement (sec. 1966-67, v.p. 1967-68, trustee 1968—). Co-author: Adopting the Library of Congress Classification System, 1971. Contbr. articles to library jours. Home: 2225 N Tacoma Ave Tacoma WA 98403

TAYLOR, DIANA CARTIER, ballet mistress; b. Phila., July 23, 1939; d. Rocco G. and Emma Saulli; student public schs., Phila.; m. Burton Taylor, Mar. 3, 1972. Leading dramatic dancer Joffrey Ballet, N.Y.C., 1964-76, ballet mistress, 1976—. Office: 130 W 56th St New York NY 10019

TAYLOR, DON, film dir.; b. Pitts., Dec. 13, 1920; s. David Edwin and Jessie (Dixon) T.; B.A., Pa. State U., 1942; m. Hazel Court, Mar., 1964; children—Avery Taylor Moore, Anne Taylor Fleming, Jonathan. Actor on Broadway and in film: Winged Victory, 1944; numerous films, including: Naked City, 1947, Father of the Bride, 1950, Flying Leathernecks, 1951, Girls of Pleasure Island, 1951, Japanese War Bride, 1952, Stalag 17, 1952, The Bold and the Brave, 1954, I'll Cry Tomorrow, 1955; dir. films: Jack of Diamonds, 1967, Five Man Army, 1969, Escape from the Planet of the Apes, 1970, Tom Sawyer (Christopher award), 1972, Echoes of a Summer, 1974, Island of Dr. Moreau, 1977, Damien, Omen II, 1978, The Final Countdown, 1979; also author and dir. numerous TV scripts. Served to staff sgt. USAAF, 1943-46. Office: 20th Century Fox 10201 Pico Blvd Los Angeles CA 90064

TAYLOR, DONALD, mfg. co. exec.; b. Worcester, Mass., June 2, 1927; s. John A. B. and Alice M. (Weaver) T.; B.S.M.E., Worcester Polytechnic Inst., 1949; grad. Northeastern U. Mgmt. Devel. Program, 1962, Harvard Bus. Sch. Advanced Mgmt. Program, 1979; m. Ruth L. Partridge, June 2, 1950; children—Linda Taylor Robertson, Donald, Mark, John. With George J. Meyer Mfg. Co., Milw., 1954-69; pres. mfg. div. A-T-O, Inc., 1969; exec. v.p. Nordberg div. Rex Chainbelt, Inc., Milw., 1969-73; v.p. ops. Rexnord, Inc., pres. Nordberg Machinery Group, Milw., 1973-78, pres., chief operating officer Rexnord, Inc., 1978—; dir. Anatar Industries, Inc., Harnischfeger Corp., Johnson Controls, Inc., Marine Corp., Marine Nat. Exchange Bank. Trustee St. Francis Hosp.; bd. dirs., vice chmn. Met. Milw. YMCA; bd. dirs. Milw. Symphony Orch.; mem. Nat. Council of YMCA's. Served with USNR, 1951-54. Registered profl. engr., Mass. Mem. ASME. Clubs: Milw. Country, Milw. Athletic, Town, Univ., Masons. Office: 3500 First Wisconsin Center 777 E Wisconsin Ave Milwaukee WI 53202

TAYLOR, DONALD ARTHUR, educator; b. Windsor, Ont., Can., Sept. 27, 1923; s. David Cameron and Eva (Perry) T.; B.A., U. Western Ont., 1947; M.B.A., U. Mich., 1949, Ph.D. (Horace H. Rackham fellow), 1955; m. Shirley Marion Jenner, 1949; children—John Cameron, Stephen Bruce, Michael James. Came to U.S., 1947, naturalized, 1955. Asst. prof. marketing Mich. State U. at East Lansing, 1955-58, asso. prof., 1958-62, prof., 1962—, chmn. dept. marketing and transportation adminstrn., 1969—; adviser, chief of party to mission at various univs., Brazil, 1956-58, 62-64; dir. Latin Am. Studies Center, 1968-69, also co-dir. Latin-Am. Market Planning Center, sr. cons. food distbrn. studies, N.E. Brazil, Colombia; sr. research asso. Systems Research, Inc., 1969—; cons. Geigy Agrl. Chems., Johnson & Johnson Domestic Operating Co., Ford Motor Co., Westinghouse Electric Corp., Whirlpool Corp. Dir. Clarke-Gravely Corp., 1972-77. Mem. bd. edn. Holt Sch. Dist., 1960-62. Adv. com. Govtl. Affairs Inst., Recipient Homenagen Especial award, 1st graduating class Escola de Administracao de Empresas, Sao Paulo, Brazil, 1958, named hon. prof., 1964. Mem. Am. Marketing Assn. (bd. dirs. 1969). Author: (with D.J. Luck, D.A. Taylor, H. Wales, R. Rubin) Marketing Research, 5th edit., 1978; (with T.A. Staudt, D.A. Taylor and D.J. Bowersox) A Managerial Introduction to Marketing, 3d edit., 1976; Institution Building in Business Administration: The Brazilian Experience, 1968. Home: 4353 Lynn St Holt MI 48842 Office: Eppley Center Michigan State Univ East Lansing MI 48823

TAYLOR, DOUGLAS ROY, lawyer; b. Los Angeles, Sept. 12, 1938; s. Roy and Thelma (Greenross) T.; B.S., U. So. Calif., 1960, J.D., 1963; m. Judith Leah Anderson, Nov. 17, 1962; children—Troy Steven, Tracy Susan. Admitted to Calif. bar, 1964, since practiced in Los Angeles; trial atty. Harney, Ford & Schlottman, Los Angeles, 1963-67; formerly partner Dunbar & Taylor, also dir., sec.-treas. Dunbar & Taylor, Inc., Los Angeles; now prin. firm Douglas Roy Taylor, Inc., Los Angeles. Active Beverly Hills Youth Football Program, YMCA. Football grantee U. So. Calif., 1956-60. Mem. Am. Judicature Soc., Am., Calif., Los Angeles trial lawyers assns., Internat. Acad. Law and Sci., Am., Los Angeles County, Century City bar assns., Legion Lex, Phi Delta Phi, Sigma Chi, Town Hall. Clubs: Trojan (Los Angeles); Hesperia (Calif.) Country (gov. 1970—); Bel Air Bay. Home: 217 17th St Santa Monica CA 90402 Office: Suite 275 10100 Santa Monica Blvd Los Angeles CA 90067

TAYLOR, DWIGHT DAVIDSON, paper co. exec.; b. Mpls., Nov. 25, 1920; s. Dwight Davidson and Ethelyn Maude (Bigglestone) T.; A.B., Harvard U., 1941, LL.B., 1949, Advanced Mgmt. Program, Bus. Sch., 1971. Admitted to Minn., D.C., Fla. bars; practiced in Mpls., 1949-50; asst. to pres. State U. N.Y., 1950-51, Carnegie Found., N.Y.C., 1951-52; v.p. govt. affairs Am. Airlines, Washington, 1953-64; sr. v.p. planning and pub. affairs Eastern Airlines, N.Y.C., 1964-74; sr. v.p. pub. affairs and corporate communications Crown Zellerbach Corp., San Francisco, 1974—. Mem. Am. Bar Assn. Clubs: Met., Univ. (Washington); Harvard, Univ. (N.Y.C.); Harvard (San Francisco). Home: 1854 Vallejo St San Francisco CA 94123 Office: 1 Bush St San Francisco CA 94119

TAYLOR, EDWARD CURTIS, chemist; b. Springfield, Mass., Aug. 3, 1923; s. Edward Curtis and Margaret Louise (Anderson) T.: student Hamilton Coll., 1942-44, D.Sc. (hon.), 1969; A.B., Cornell U., 1946, Ph.D., 1949; m. Virginia Dion Crouse, June 29, 1946; children—Edward Newton, Susan Raines. Postdoctoral fellow Nat. Acad. Scis., Zurich, Switzerland, 1949-50; DuPont postdoctoral fellow chemistry U. Ill., 1950-51, faculty, 1951-54, asst. prof. organic chemistry, 1952-54; faculty Princeton U., 1954—, prof. chemistry, 1964—, A. Barton Hepburn prof. organic chemistry, 1966—, chmn. dept. chemistry, 1974-79; vis. prof. Technische Hochschule, Stuttgart, Germany, 1960, U. East Anglia, 1969, 71; Distinguished vis. prof. U. Buffalo, 1968, U. Wyo., 1977; Backer lectr. U. Groningen (Holland), 1969; mem. chemistry adv. com. Office Sci. Research, USAF, 1962-73, Cancer Chemotherapy Nat. Service Center, 1958-62; cons. research divs. Procter & Gamble, 1953—, Eastman Kodak Co., 1965—, Tenn. Eastman Co., 1968—, Eli Lilly & Co., 1970. Recipient research awards Smith Kline & French Found., 1955, Hoffmann-LaRoche Found., 1964, 65, Ciba Found., 1971; sr. faculty fellow Harvard U., 1959. Recipient Disting. Hamilton award, 1977; Guggenheim fellow, 1979-80. Fellow N.Y. Acad. Scis., Am. Inst. Chemists; mem. Am. (award for creative work in synthetic organic chemistry 1974, chmn. organic chemistry div. 1976-77), German chem. socs., Chem. Soc. London, Phi Beta Kappa, Sigma Xi, Phi Kappa Phi. Author: (with McKillop) Chemistry of Cyclic Enaminonitriles and o-Aminonitriles, 1970; Principles of Heterocyclic Chemistry (film course), 1974; editor: (with Raphael, Wynberg) Advances in Organic Chemistry, vols. I-V, 1960-65, (with Wynberg) vol. VI, 1969, vols. VII-IX, 1970-79; (with W. Pfleiderer) Pteridine Chemistry, 1964; (with A. Weissberger) The Chemistry of Heterocyclic Compounds, 1968—; General Heterocyclic Chemistry, 1968—; organic chemistry editorial adviser John Wiley & Sons, Inc., Intersci. Pubs., 1968—; mem. editorial adv. bd. Jour. Medicinal Chemistry, 1962-66, Jour. Organic Chemistry, 1971-75, Synthetic Communications, 1971—, Heterocycles, 1973—, Chem. Substructure Index, 1971—. Home: 288 Western Way Princeton NJ 08540

TAYLOR, EDWARD STEWART, physician; b. Hecla, S.D., Aug. 20, 1911; s. Robert Stewart and Sylvia Frances (Dewey) T.; B.A., U. Iowa, 1933, M.D., 1936; m. Ruth Fatherson, June 15, 1940; children—Edward Stewart, Elizabeth Dewey Taylor Bryant, Catherine Wells Taylor Lynn. Intern, Hurley Hosp., Flint, Mich., 1936-37; splty. tng. obstetrics and gynecology L.I. Coll. Hosp., 1937-41; prof. obstetrics and gynecology, chmn. dept. Sch. Medicine, U. Colo., 1947-76, clin. prof., 1976—; cons. obstetrics and gynecology Fitzsimons Gen. Hosp.; attending obstetrician and gynecologist St. Joseph's Hosp., Denver; nat. cons. obstetrics, gynecology to surg. gen. USAF, 1958-62. Served to lt. col., AUS, 1943-45; surgeon 107th Evacuation Hosp., ETO. Diplomate Am. Bd. Obstetrics and Gynecology (dir. 1962-69). Fellow A.C.S., Am. Coll. Obstetricians and Gynecologists; mem. AMA, Am. Gynecol. Soc. (v.p. 1974-75), Am. (pres. 1970-71), Central assns. obstetricians and gynecologists, S.W. Obstet. and Gynecol. Soc., Assn. Profs. Gynecology and Obstetrics (pres. 1974-75), Western Surg. Soc., Alpha Omega Alpha. Congregationalist. Club: Univ. (Denver). Author: Manual of Gynecology, 1952; Essentials of Gynecology, 4th edit.; editor: Beck's Obstetrical Practice, 10th edit.; editor-in-chief for obstetrics Obstet. and Gynecol. Survey. Home: 80 S Dexter St Denver CO 80222 Office: 4545 E 9th Ave Denver CO 80220

TAYLOR, EDWIN WILLIAM, educator; b. Toronto, Ont., Can., June 8, 1929; s. William and Jean (Christie) T.; B.A., U. Toronto, 1952; M.Sc., McMaster U., 1955; Ph.D., U. Chgo., 1957; m. Jean Heather Logan, Feb. 29, 1956; children—Michael Charles, Jane Rebecca, Stephen William. Came to U.S., 1957. Asst. prof. dept. biophysics U. Chgo., 1959-63, asso. prof., 1963-67, prof., 1967-72, prof., chmn. dept. physiology, 1971-72; prof. dept. biology and med. research council King's Coll., London, Eng., 1972-74; prof. dept. biophysics U. Chgo., 1975—, asso. dean div. biol. sci. and medicine, 1977-79, prof., chmn. dept. biology, 1979—; cons. NIH, 1970-72, 77-80. Rockefeller Found. fellow, 1957-58; NIH fellow, 1958-59. Fellow Royal Soc.; mem. Am. Biochem. Soc. Editorial bd. Jour. of Theoretical Biology, 1973-75, Jour. Mechanochemistry and Cell Motility, 1972-75, Jour. of Supermolecular Structure, Biophys. Jour., 1977—. Office: Dept Biophysics U Chgo 920 E 58th St Chicago IL 60637

TAYLOR, ELDON DONIVAN, govt. ofcl.; b. Holdenville, Okla., July 29, 1929; s. Rome B. and Alma (Collins) T.; student Murry State A. and M. Coll., 1948-49, George Washington U., 1949-50; B.S. cum laude, Am. U., 1959, M.A., 1966, postgrad., 1966-68; m. Hypatia Ethel Roberts, Feb. 7, 1953; 1 dau., Teresa Lynn. Research budget analyst, budgetary adminstrn. Office Naval Research, Navy Dept., Washington, 1949-51, 55-56, chief research and devel. budget sect., research and devel. planning adminstrn. Bur. Ordnance, 1956-60; dir. program rev. and resources, mgmt. div. research, devel. planning and adminstrn. Office Space Scis., NASA, Washington, 1960-70, insp. gen., 1979—; dep. asst. adminstr. for resources mgmt. EPA, 1970-73; asst. dir. adminstrn. NSF, 1973-79. Served with USAF, 1951-55. Recipient Commendation award for outstanding performance Dept. Navy, 1958; William A. Jump Meritorious award for achievement in pub. adminstrn., 1964; Exceptional Service award NASA, 1969; Disting. Service award NSF, 1978. Mem. Am. Soc. Pub. Adminstrn. (past sec. com. research pub. adminstrn.), Pi Sigma Alpha, Phi Theta Kappa. Home: 4633 Denpat Ct Annandale VA 22003 Office: 1800 G St Washington DC 20003

TAYLOR, ELIZABETH, actress; b. London, Feb. 27, 1932; d. Francis and Sara (Sothern) T.; ed. Byron House, Hawthorne Sch., Metro-Goldwyn-Mayer Sch.; m. Conrad Nicholas Hilton, Jr., May 6, 1950 (div.); m. 2d, Michael Wilding (div.); 2 sons; m. 3d, Mike Todd, Feb. 2, 1957 (dec. Mar. 1958); 1 dau., Liza; m. 4th, Eddie Fisher, May 1959 (div.); m. 5th, Richard Burton, Mar. 15, 1964 (div. June 1974), remarried, Oct. 10, 1975 (div. 1976); 1 dau., Maria; m. 6th, John William Warner, Dec. 1976. Motion pictures include: Lassie Come Home, 1942; The White Cliffs of Dover, 1943; Jane Eyre, 1943; National Velvet, 1944; Life With Father, 1946; Courage of Lassie, 1946; Cynthia, 1947; A Date With Judy, 1948; Julia Misbehaves, 1948; Little Women, 1948; Conspirator, 1949; The Big Hangover, 1949; Father of the Bride, 1950; Father's Little Dividend, 1950; A Place in the Sun, 1950; Love is Better Than Ever, 1951; Ivanhoe, 1951; Elephant Walk, 1954; Rhapsody, 1954; Beau Brummel, 1954; The Last Time I Saw Paris, 1955; Giant, 1956; Raintree County, 1957; Cat on a Hot Tin Roof, 1958; Butterfield 8 (Acad. award best actress), 1960; Cleopatra, 1962; The V.I.P.'s, 1963; The Sandpiper, 1965; Who's Afraid of Virginia Wolfe (Acad. award 1966); Taming of the Shrew, 1967; The Comedians, 1967; Reflections in a Golden Eye, 1967; Dr. Faustus, 1968; Boom, 1968; Secret Ceremony, 1968; The Only Game in Town, 1969; X, Y and Zee, 1971; Under Milk Wood, 1971; Hammersmith is Out, 1972; Night Watch, 1973; Ash Wednesday, 1974; The Driver's Seat, 1975; The Blue Bird, 1976; A Little Night Music, 1977; Victory at Entebbe, 1977; Return Engagement (TV), 1979. Author: Nibbles and Me; (with Richard Burton) World Enough and Time (poetry reading), 1964; Elizabeth Taylor, 1965. Office: care John Springer Assos Inc 667 Madison Ave New York NY 10021

TAYLOR, ESTELLE WORMLEY, educator; b. Washington, Jan. 12, 1924; d. Luther Charles and Wilhelmina Wormley; B.S. magna cum laude, Miner Tchrs. Coll., 1946; M.A., Howard U., 1947; Ph.D., Cath. U. Am., 1969; m. Ivan Earle Taylor, Dec. 26, 1953; Instr. English, Howard U., 1947-52; tchr. Langley Jr. High Sch., Washington, 1952-55, Eastern Sr. High Sch., Washington, 1955-63; instr. D.C. Tchrs. Coll., 1963-66, asst. prof., 1966-69, asso. prof., 1969-71, prof., 1971—, acad. dean, 1975-76; asso. provost Fed. City Coll., Washington, 1974-75; prof., chmn. dept. English, Howard U., 1976—. Trustee, U. D.C., 1979. So. fellow, 1968-69; Rockefeller/Aspen Inst. fellow, 1978-79. Mem. Coll. Lang. Assn., Nat. Council Tchrs. Am., Modern Lang. Assn., Shakespeare Assn. Am. Democrat. Club: Links (pres. Capital City chpt.). Contbr. articles to profl. jours. Home: 3221 20th St NE Washington DC 20018. *Throughout my career I have been climbing a giant ladder, invisible to all but me. The challenging but humbling feature of this ladder is that whenever I get the feeling that I have almost reached the top, several additional rungs attach themselves to my Jacob's Ladder. Thus, that thing called success is for me forever a goal to be reached. As long as I continue to feel a restlessness and a yearning to climb another rung, I shall know that I am alive.*

TAYLOR, EUGENE CHARLES, found. exec.; b. Rochester, N.Y., Aug. 25, 1914; s. Raymond W. and Alice P. (Gleichauf) T.; grad. Advanced Mgmt. Program, Harvard, 1954; m. Priscilla J. Aspinall, Dec. 18, 1954, 1 son Michael. With Am. Airlines Inc., 1935-65, dir. mil. contracts, World War II, asst. v.p., 1955-57, v.p., 1957-65; sr. vice pres. operations Allegheny Airlines, Inc., Washington, 1966-69, exec. v.p. operations, 1969-79; pres. Flight Safety Found., 1979—. Mem. Harvard Advanced Mgmt. Assn., Soc. Automotive Engrs., Air Force Assn. Clubs: Wings (N.Y.C.); Harvard (Boston); Manhasset Bay Yacht (Port Washington, N.Y.). Home: 500 Duke St Alexandria VA 22314

TAYLOR, FOSTER JAY, univ. pres.; b. Gibsland, La., Aug. 9, 1923; s. Lawrence Foster and Marcia Aline (Jay) T.; student La. Poly. Inst., 1940-42; B.A., U. Calif. at Santa Barbara, 1948; M.A., Claremont (Calif.) Grad. Sch., 1949; Ph.D., Tulane U., 1952; m. Evelyn Marie Bast, Apr. 18, 1946; 1 son, Terry Jay. Asso. prof. history, dean men. La. Coll., Pineville, 1952-56, prof., 1956-62, dean coll., 1960-62; pres. La. Tech. U., Ruston, 1962—; past chmn. La. Labor Mediation Bd.; arbitrator Am. Arbitration Assn., Fed. Mediation and Conciliation Service; mem. La. Adv. Council on Vocat.-Tech. Edn. Bd. dirs. Ruston Civic Symphony; chmn. Air Force ROTC Adv. Council. Served to lt. comdr., aviator, USNR, 1942-46. Mem. Ruston C. of C. (dir.), Am., Miss. Valley, So. hist. assns., Nat. Acad. Arbitrators. Phi Alpha Theta. Club: Rotary. Author: The United States and the Spanish Civil War, 1936-39, 1956; Reluctant Rebel, The Secret Diary of Robert Patrick, 1861-1865, 1959. Home: Louisiana Tech Campus Ruston LA 71272

TAYLOR, FRANK EUGENE, publisher; b. Malone, N.Y., Mar. 16, 1916; s. Frank Eugene and Winifred (Mullin) T.; A.B., Hamilton Coll., 1938; postgrad. U. Minn., 1939-40; m. Nan Scallon, Mar. 18, 1941 (div.); children—Michael, Mark, Curtice, Adams. Advt. mgr. Harper & Bros., pubs., N.Y.C., 1940-41; v.p., editor-in-chief Reynal & Hitchcock, Inc., pubs., N.Y.C., 1941-48; film producer MGM, Culver City, Calif., 1948-50, 20th Century Fox, Beverly Hills, Calif., 1950-52; editor-in-chief Dell Books, Western Pub. Co., N.Y.C., 1952-61; producer United Artists film The Misfits, 1961-63, pub. Avon Books div. Hearst Corp., N.Y.C., 1963-65; gen. mgr., editor-in-chief Trade div. McGraw Hill Book Co., N.Y.C., 1965-70; pres., pub. Patent Trader, Mount Kisco, N.Y., 1970-73; pres. Frank E. Taylor Books, N.Y.C., 1974—; dir. George Nelson & Co. Trustee, chmn. bd. dirs. William Alanson White Inst. Psychoanalysis, Psychiatry and Psychology, 1962-72; bd. dirs., sec. S.I.E.C.U.S., N.Y.C. Mem. P.E.N., Chi Psi. Unitarian. Home and Office: 247 E 57th St New York NY 10022

TAYLOR, FRED MONROE, U.S. dist. judge; b. Nampa, Idaho, Feb. 25, 1901; s. Robert F. and Pearl (Christine) T.; LL.B., U. Idaho, 1926; m. Gwen E. McLeod, Mar. 17, 1929; children—Jacquelyn Rae, Marta Kaye. Admitted to Idaho bar, 1926; practiced in Boise, 1938-54; pros. atty. Valley County, Idaho, 1927-33, 35-38; city atty. Boise, 1944-45; U.S. dist. judge, Boise, 1954—. Mem. U.S. Jud. Conf., 1969-72. Mem. Idaho Senate, 1943-51. Mem. Idaho Bar Assn., Am. Judicature Soc., Phi Alpha Delta, Sigma Nu. Republican. Episcopalian. Mason (Shriner). Office: Fed Bldg Boise ID 83702

TAYLOR, GENE, congressman; b. Sarcoxie, Mo., Feb. 10, 1928; ed. S.W. Mo. State Coll.; m. Dorothy Wooldridge, July 26, 1947; children—Linda, Larry. Automobile dealer, Sarcoxie; mayor Sarcoxie, 1954-60; mem. Rep. Nat. Com., 1966-72; mem. 93d-96th Congresses from 7th Dist. Mo. Former trustee Mo. So. Coll., Joplin; trustee Harry S. Truman Scholarship Found.; past bd. dirs. Mo. Automobile Dealers Assn. Served with Mo. N.G., 1948-49. Mem. Mo., Sarcoxie chambers commerce. Methodist. Clubs: Masons (Shriner), Lions. Address: 2430 Rayburn House Office Bldg Washington DC 20515

TAYLOR, GEORGE ALBERT, educator; b. N.Y.C., Mar. 17, 1908; s. George Henry and Elizabeth Pauline (Strout) T.; B.S. summa cum laude, N.Y. U., 1929, M.S., 1940; student Coll. Engring., Columbia, 1936-38; A.M. (hon.), Dartmouth, 1951; m. Winifred Marshall Duffield, Aug. 17, 1946; children—Susan M., Robin S., Loren W., Colden C., Diane E. Trainee Gen. Electric Co., 1929-30, engr. indsl. dept., Schenectady, 1930-32, application engr., N.Y.C., 1932-35; product dept. Ingersoll Rand Co., 1935-40, exec. mgmt., N.Y.C., 1940-49; prof. engring. and mgmt. Dartmouth, 1949—, dir. exec. tng. courses, 1956—, also dir. decision-making and creative improvement programs, mgmt. system revs. Lectr. in numerous fgn. countries. Mem. Am. Inst. Indsl. Engrs., Am. Assn. U. Profs., Industry Devel. Assos., Perstar et Praestare Soc., Tau Beta Pi. Iota Alpha. Clubs: Ski, Dartmouth Golf, Variety Courts Tennis (Hanover). Author: Managerial and Engineering Economy: Economic Decision-Making, 2d edit., 1975; The Development of Creativity in Europe, 1967; Foundations of Decision-Making, 1969; co-author Management Decision Making, 1969. Home: 18 Kingsford Rd Hanover NH 03755. *I sum it up as follows: What we do defines the present consequences. But it is what we think that will produce better consequences in the future.*

TAYLOR, GEORGE ALLEN, advt. exec.; b. Lake City, Iowa, Oct. 26, 1906; s. Bertrand Franklin and Mabel (Minard) T.; Ph.B., Northwestern U., 1947, M.A. in Edn., 1951, postgrad., 1951-54. Art supr. pub. schs., Indianola, Iowa, 1926-29; instr. art Simpson Coll., Indianola, 1926-29; designer Modern Art Studios, Chgo., 1929-30; display designer W.J. Rankin Corp., Chgo., 1930-35; with Arthur Meyerhoff Assos., Inc., 1935—, creative dir., 1935-38, br. mgr., 1938-42, account exec., Chgo., 1942-59, account supr., 1959-61, v.p. adminstrn., 1961-65, vice chmn., 1965—; pres. Taylor-Meyerhoff Co., Ltd. Lectr. semantics Ill. Inst. Tech., Chgo., 1947-50, Northwestern U. Sch. Commerce, 1948. Reader, Recs. for Blind, Inc., 1956—. Recipient First awards in copy and layout Los Angeles Advt. Club, 1940. Mem. AAAS, Ill. C. of C., Chgo. Federated Advt. Club, ANTA, Chgo. Council Fgn. Relations. Lyricist popular songs. Home: 1212 N Lake Shore Dr Apt 29A-S Chicago IL 60610 Office: 410 N Michigan Ave Chicago IL 60611

TAYLOR, GEORGE E., historian and political scientist; b. Coventry, Eng., Dec. 13, 1905; s. Thomas and Sarah (Chapman) T.; A.B., U. Birmingham (Eng.), A.M., 1928, Litt.D., 1957; student Johns Hopkins, Harvard U., 1928-30; m. Roberta Stevens White, June 17, 1933 (dec. 1967); children—Edith C., Gordon T., Jean, Robin. m. 2d, Florence Rockwood Kluckhohn, May 1, 1968; came to U.S., 1928, naturalized, 1943. Commonwealth fund fellow, Johns Hopkins and Harvard, 1928; Harvard-Yenching fellow, China, 1930-32; with Central Polit. Inst., Nanking, China, 1933-36; London U. extension lectr., Leverhulme fellowship, 1936-37; tutor in history Yenching U., Peiping, China, 1937-39; Rockefeller fellow, 1941-42; with OWI 1942-45, State Dept., 1946; dir. Far East and Russian Inst., U. Wash., 1946-69, prof. Asian studies, 1969-76; pres. Washington Council Internat. Trade, 1976—. Mem. joint com. contemporary China, Am. Council Learned Socs.-Social Sci. Research Council. Mem. Enological Soc. Pacific N.W. (pres. 1975—). Club: Cosmos. Author: The Struggle for North China, 1941; Atlas of Far Eastern politics (with others), 1942; America in the New Pacific, 1942; Changing China, 1942; The Phoenix and the Dwarfs (with George Savage), 1944; The Far East in the Modern World (with Franz Michael), 1956; The Philippines and the United States; Problems of Partnership, 1964; Home: The Highlands Seattle WA 98177

TAYLOR, GEORGE FREDERICK, editor; b. Portland, Oreg., Feb. 28, 1928; s. George Noble and Ida Louise (Dixon) T.; B.S., U. Oreg., 1950; m. Georga Bray, Oct. 6, 1951; children—Amelia Ruth, Ross Noble. Reporter, Astoria (Oreg.) Budget, 1950-52, Portland Oregonian, 1952-54; copyreader Wall St. Jour., 1955-57, reporter, 1957-59, Detroit br. chief, 1959-64, Washington corr., 1964-68, asst. mng. editor, San Francisco, 1968-69, mng. editor, N.Y.C., 1970-77, exec. editor, 1977—. Served to lt. USAF, 1955-57. Home: 154 Unadilla Rd Ridgewood NJ 07450 Office: 22 Cortlandt St New York City NY 10007

TAYLOR, GEORGE SIMPSON, business exec.; b. Windsor, Ont., Can., July 23, 1940; s. George and Elta (Simpson) T.; student Can. schs.; m. Nancy Caroline Tremblay, Oct. 31, 1959; children—George William, April Elizabeth, Barbara Gail, Cindy Laura. Treas., controller Mannings Inc, San Francisco, 1970-72; v.p., controller Parnel Goods Ltd., London, Ont., Can., 1972-75; v.p. fin. Laura Secord Candy Shops Ltd., Toronto, 1975-77; v.p. fin., treas. John Labatt Ltd., London, 1977—. Past pres. Catholic PTA, Middlesex, London; past bd. dirs. Boys Scouts Middlesex. Registered indsl. accountant, Ont. Mem. Fin. Execs. Inst. Home: 43 Harrison Crescent London ON Canada Office: 451 Pidout St N London ON Canada

TAYLOR, GEORGE VANDERBECK, educator; b. Trenton, N.J., Dec. 5, 1919; s. Harry Barton and Laura Elma (Atkinson) T.; B.A., Rutgers U., 1941; M.A., U. Wis., 1949, Ph.D., 1950; m. Margaret Priscilla Ewing, Aug. 28, 1948; children—Bruce Jonathan, Elizabeth Hope, Margaret Susan. Instr. Mich. State U., East Lansing, 1950-52; asst. prof. U. N.C., Chapel Hill, 1952-57, asso. prof., 1957-66, prof., 1966—, chmn. div. social scis., 1970-73, chmn. dept. history, 1973-78, chmn. faculty, 1973-76. Served to capt., field arty. AUS, 1942-46; PTO. Decorated Bronze Star; recipient Tanner award U. N.C., 1958, Salgo award, 1967; Koren prize for publs. in French history, 1965, 67, 73. Fulbright research fellow, France, 1953-54; Am. Council Learned Socs. fellow, 1963-64. Mem. Am. Hist. Assn. (com. on rights of historians 1972-74), So. Hist. Assn., Soc. for French Hist. Studies (pres. 1972-73), Societe d'Histoire Moderne, AAUP. Club: Drones (Chapel Hill). Editorial bds. various hist. jours. Contbr. articles to profl. jours. Home: 903 Kings Mill Rd Chapel Hill NC 27514

TAYLOR, GEORGE WINSTON, JR., naval med. officer; b. Mooresville, N.C., Mar. 10, 1920; s. George Winston and Carey (Wilson) T.; B.S., Davidson Coll., 1941; M.D., U. Pa., 1944; m. Ann Louise Winckler, May 31, 1957; children—George Winston III, Stephen William, Carey Louise. Intern U. Pa. Grad. Hosp., 1941-45; resident U. Pa. Hosp., 1947-50; faculty med. Sch., Grad. Sch. U. Pa., 1950-53; commd. lt. USN, 1953, advanced through grades to capt., 1959; chief otolaryngology Nat. Naval Med. Center, Bethesda, Md., 1956-70; comdg. officer Naval Hosp., Orlando, Fla., 1970—. Contbr. articles profl. jours. Address: 1760 Pine Tree Rd Winter Park FL 32789

TAYLOR, GERALD L., publishing exec.; b. Los Angeles, June 29, 1935; s. Zoltan and Esther Jean (Golden) Tronstein; student Calif. Poly. Inst., 1953-54; B.A. magna cum laude, Woodbury Coll., 1958; m. Mary Allin Travers, June 1, 1969 (div. 1975); children—Scott Martin, Julie Dawn. Account exec. Young & Rubicam, Los Angeles, 1958-61; salesman R.J. Friedman, Asso. Pubs. Rep., Los Angeles, 1961-62; partner Taylor/Friedman, Pub. Reps., Chgo., 1962-67; owner Taylor & Son, Pub. Reps., Chgo., N.Y.C., 1962-69; advt. and mktg. dir. Instl. Investor mag., N.Y.C., 1969-70; pres. Commodities Communications, N.Y.C., 1970-71; pub. Nat. Lampoon mag., N.Y.C., 1971-76; sr. v.p. sales 21st Century Communications, 1971-76; exec. producer Nat. Lampoon Phonograph Records; pub. Harpers Bazaar mag., 1976-77; pres. Gerald Taylor Mktg., Inc., N.Y.C., 1977-79; exec. v.p., pub. Nat. Lampoon Inc., N.Y.C., 1979—, also dir.; youth market cons. Gen. Motors Corp., 1965-66; pub. Big Ten mag., 1965-67. Bd. dirs. Coty Inst. Fashion, Phoenix House Drug Rehab. Center, N.Y.C. Served with USNR, 1954-56. Mem. Nat. Rec. Arts and Scis., Am. Acad. Humor, Phi Gamma Kappa. Jewish. Home: 50 Sutton Pl S New York NY 10022 Office: 635 Madison Ave New York NY 10022

TAYLOR, GRAY, architect; b. N.Y.C., Apr. 15, 1916; s. Henry A. and Margherita (Gray) T.; A.B., Harvard U., 1939, M.Arch., Columbia U., 1947, M.S. in Arch., 1971; m. Patsy Raymond, June 8, 1946; children—Dicey, Austin Gray, Mildred Raymond. With Petroff & Clarkson, 1947-48, archtl. dept. N.Y.C. R.R., 1948-50, Roger Halle, 1950-51, Ketchum, Gina & Sharp, 1951-52, William F. Schorn, 1952-54; partner SMS Architects, New Canaan, Conn., 1958-78; works include Briarcliff Coll., Greenwich Acad., Greenwich Acad. Upper Sch., Ramapo Regional High Sch. (Franklin Lakes, N.J.), Indian Hills Regional High Sch., Oakland, N.J., Greenwich Library Addition, Greenwich Acad. Lower Sch., 2d Congl. Ch. restoration, Greenwich, Dayton Ave. Med. Bldg., Greenwich, Bard Coll. Library addition, biol. sci. bldg., Vassar Coll., primary bldg. Greenwich Country Day Sch. Served to capt. C.E., AUS, World War II. Registered architect, Conn., N.Y., Fla. Fellow AIA, mem. N.Y. State Assn. Architects. Episcopalian. Clubs: Harvard (N.Y.C.); Indian Harbor Yacht, Burning Tree Country (Greenwich). Home and Office: Dingletown Rd Greenwich CT 06830

TAYLOR, GUY WATSON, symphonic condr.; b. Anniston, Ala., Dec. 25, 1919; s. Stokely Brackston and Ola Mae (Shaw) T.; diploma Birmingham Conservatory of Music, 1941, Juilliard Sch. Music, 1948; pvt. studies and workshops with Dimitri Mitropoulos, 1941-42, L'Ecole Monteux, 1949, Eugene Ormandy, 1953, George Szell, 1956; m. Renee Lifton, Oct. 19, 1947; children—Eric Anthony, Ellen Jane. Conductor Springfield (Ohio) Symphony Orch., 1948-51, Nashville Symphony Orch., 1951-59, Phoenix Symphony Orch., 1959-69, Fresno Philharmonic Orch., 1969—; guest conductor U.S., Philippines, P.R., Canada and Mexico City; has appeared on BBC Radio, CBS-TV; musical commentator Springfield News & Sun, 1948, Ariz. Republic, 1959-61, Fresno Bee, 1970-76. Served with AUS, 1942-45. Recipient Conductor Recognition award Am. Symphony Orch. League, 1960, Alice M. Ditson Orch. award, 1961, citation for adventuresome programming of contemporary music ASCAP, 1977. Mem. Am. Symphony Orch. League, Phi Mu Alpha Sinfonia. Office: Fresno Philharmonic Orch 1362 N Fresno St Fresno CA 93703

TAYLOR, HAROLD, educator; b. Toronto, Ont., Can., Sept. 28, 1914; s. Charles W. and Elizabeth (Wilson) T.; A.B., U. Toronto, 1935, M.A. in Philosophy and Lit., 1936; Ph.D. in Philosophy, U. London, 1938; m. Grace Muriel Thorne, 1941; children—Mary Elizabeth, Jennifer Thorne. Came to U.S., 1939, naturalized, 1947. Instr., research fellow philosophy U. Wis., 1939-42, asst. prof., 1942-45, armed forces rep., 1943; research asso. psychology, war project OSRD, 1944; pres. Sarah Lawrence Coll., Bronxville, N.Y., 1945-59; faculty New Sch. Social Research, 1947-48, 48-49; vis. lectr. univs. in Australia, Denmark, Finland, Greece, India, Indonesia, Iran, Italy, Japan, Malaysia, Norway, USSR, Sweden, Thailand, Turkey, U.S., 1959-75; dir. tchr. edn. study U.S. Office of Edn., 1967-68; disting. prof. City U. N.Y., 1975-76; dir. Center for Internat. Service, Coll. of S.I., 1976—. Chmn., NRC on Peace Strategy; chmn. U.S. com. for UN Univ. Trustee Inst. for World Order, N.Y. Studio Sch., Coll. for Human Services, Agnes deMille Dance Theatre; pres. Am. Ballet Theatre, 1965-67; vice chmn. Martha Graham Sch. Contemporary Dance, 1965-73. Club: Century Assn. (N.Y.C.). Author: On Education and Freedom, 1954; Art and the Intellect, 1960; Students without Teachers, 1969; The World As Teacher, 1969; How To Change Colleges, 1971; Art and the Future, 1971. Editor, co-author: Essays in Teaching, 1950; Humanities in the Schools, 1968. Editor: The Idea of a World University, 1967. Contbr. articles to Saturday Rev., N.Y. Times Book Rev., N.Y. Times Mag., also ednl. jours. Address: 241 W 12th St New York NY 10014

TAYLOR, HAROLD RALPH, constrn. exec.; b. Somerville, Mass., Nov. 2, 1918; s. Louis and Freda (Pearlson) T.; A.B., Harvard, 1939, M.P.A., 1947; M.A., La. State U., 1946; m. Henrietta Irene Medalia, Nov. 18, 1945; children—Allan, Robert, David. Exec. dir. New Haven Redevel. Agy., 1955-59; exec. v.p. Renewal and Devel. Co., N.Y.C., 1959-62; pres. H.R. Taylor Mgmt., Corp., N.Y.C. 1962-66; asst. sec. Dept. Housing and Urban Devel., 1966-69; exec. v.p. Mid-City Developers, Inc., 1969-72; pres. Building Systems Internat., Inc., 1972-73; cons. in housing and devel., 1973-74; exec. v.p. Ft. Lincoln New Town Corp., 1975—. Spl. asst. to dir. Mass. Housing Bd., 1949-51; asst. dir. Somerville Housing Authority, 1951-55. Served with AUS, 1941-45. Mem. Nat. Assn. Housing and Redevel. Ofcls., Nat. Housing Conf. Home: 608 7th St SW Washington DC 20024

TAYLOR, HAROLD WAYNE, co. fin. exec.; b. St. Elmo, Ill., May 20, 1924; s. Thomas Boyd and Martha Alice (Hill) T.; B.S. in Bus. Adminstrn., So. Ill. U.; M.A. in Bus. Mgmt., Ball State U.; m. Earnestine Cox, Aug. 10, 1946; children—Donald Lynn, Diane Lynnette. Acct. bus. office So. Ill. U., Carbondale, 1943-45; acctg. clk. Tenn. Eastman Corp. Oak Ridge, 1944-46; acctg. clk. and asst. controller Kroger Co., Carbondale, 1946-60; gen. acctg. supr. Marsh Supermarkets, Inc., Muncie, Ind., 1960-65; sr. v.p. fin. Scotty's, Inc., Winter Haven, Fla., 1965—, also dir. Past pres., past bd., now treas. Polk County Assn. Retarded Citizens. Mem. Am. Inst. C.P.A.'s, Ind. C.P.A. Assn., Fla. Inst. C.P.A.'s. Baptist. Home: Two Twin Ln Winter Haven FL 33880 Office: Scotty's Inc PO Box 939 Winter Haven FL 33880

TAYLOR, HARRY WILLIAM, educator; b. nr. Sturgeon Valley, Sask., Can., Sept. 28, 1925; s. William and Gladys (Evans) T.; B.Sc., U. Man., 1951, M.Sc., 1952, Ph.D., 1954; m. Wanda Jason, June 18, 1949; children—Allison Leslie, Karen Elizabeth. Lectr. U. Man. (Can.), Winnipeg, 1952-53; fellow NRC, Ottawa, Ont., Can., 1954-55; mem. faculty Queen's U., Kingston, Ont., 1955-61, asst. prof., 1957-61; asso. prof. U. Alta. (Can.), Edmonton, 1961-65; prof. physics U. Toronto, 1965—. Mem. Am. Phys. Soc., Inst. Physics, Inst. Nuclear Engrs., AAAS Research and publs. in nuclear structure through gamma-ray spectroscopy; observation of angular correlations of cascade gamma rays. Home: 3525 Grand Forks Rd Mississauga ON Canada Office: Physics Dept U Toronto Toronto 5 ON Canada

TAYLOR, HENRY HAMILTON, JR., lawyer; b. Key West, Fla., Dec. 12, 1912; s. Henry Hamilton and Natalie M. (Hayman) T.; LL.B., U. Fla., 1935; m. Ernestina Frade, Dec. 28, 1976; children—Sharon Candice, Henry Hamilton III. Admitted to Fla. bar, 1935, since practiced in Miami; sr. partner firm Taylor, Brion, Buker & Greene; city atty., Key West, 1939-40; municipal judge, Miami Springs, 1946; gen. counsel, sec., chmn. bd., dir. Oolite Industries, Inc., Miami; gen. counsel, sec., dir. Allied Marine Corp.; gen. counsel, dir. Pan Am. Bank Coral Gables N.A. (Fla.). Bd. dirs. Dade County unit Am. Cancer Soc., 1961, pres., 1964-66, chmn. exec. com., 1966-67. Chmn. bd. Walter Hagen Found.; mem. exec. com. Doral/Eastern Open. Lt. col., arty. Fla. N.G., 1933-52. Mem. Am., Dade County bar assns., Fla. Bar, N.G. Assn. Fla. (pres. 1950), Am. Legion, Phi Kappa Tau, Phi Alpha Delta. Elk, Mason. Clubs: LaGorce Country, Country of Coral Gables, Two Hundred (Miami). Home: 145 SE 25 Rd Apt 1202 Miami FL 33129 Office: 1451 Brickell Ave Miami FL 33131

TAYLOR, HENRY JUNIOR, ambassador, journalist, economist, author; b. Chgo., Sept. 2, 1902; s. Henry Noble and Eileen Louise (O'Hare) T.; grad. U. Va., 1924; Litt.D., Marietta Coll., Troy State U.; L.H.D., U. Geneva, U. Lausanne, U. Zurich (Switzerland); m. Olivia Fay Kimbro, Mar. 2, 1928; 1 son, Henry Noble; m. Marion J.E. Richardson, July 3, 1970. Adv. bd. Chem. Bank, N.Y.,; dir. Waldorf-Astoria Hotel, N.Y.C., The Pittston Co.; chmn. bd. Silicone Paper Co. Am., Inc.; fgn. corr. for Scipps-Howard Newspaper Syndicate in Finland, Germany, Eng., Sweden, Switzerland, France, Belgium, Spain, Portugal, Italy, Greece, Egypt, Palestine, Syria, Turkey, West, Central and North Africa, India, China and the Philippines, and on assignment around the world through all theatres of war in 1945; ambassador to Switzerland, 1957-61; del. Disarmament and Nuclear Control Conf., Geneva, 1958-60, Fgn. Minister's Conf., Geneva, 1959; attended Internat. Conf. Dumbarton Oaks, Quebec (2), Cairo, San Francisco, Berlin, Paris, London, also Summit Conf. Geneva. Lifetime trustee U. Va. Endowment Fund; trustee emeritus Thomas Jefferson Meml. Assn. (Monticello); bd. dirs., exec. com. Am.-Scottish Found., Gen. Douglas MacArthur Meml. Found.; trustee Carnegie Lifesaving Fund; bd. dirs. John Paul Jones Found., Herbert Hoover Presdl. Library, Com. to Unite Am.; mem. nat. alumni council Lawrenceville Sch. Recipient Alfred I. Dupont Radio award; war dept. citation for conspicuous service in a theatre of combat; gold medals (9) Freedom Found., Valley Forge; gold medal for pub. service ASME; Paul Revere Bowl for good citizenship SAR; Gen. Douglas MacArthur medal Mil. Order Fgn. Wars; Wallace award Am.-Scottish Found.; French Order of LaFayette; Finland Order of the Rose; Papal Medal Pope Pius XII; Hungarian Freedom medal UN Assn. for Oppressed Nations; Benjamin Franklin medal Poor Richard Club. Mem. Raven Scholastic Soc. (Edgar Allan Poe award (2) Soc., Cin., SAR, Mil. Order Fgn. Wars, Delta Kappa Epsilon (nat. council), Sigma Delta Chi, Colonial Lords of Manor, Loyal Legion. Republican. Clubs: River (N.Y.C.); Farmington Country (Charlottesville, Va.); Corviglia Ski (St. Moritz, Switzerland). Author: It Must Be a Long War, 1939; Germany's Economy of Coercion, 1940; Time Runs Out. 1942; Men in Motion, 1943; Men and Power, 1946; An American Speaks His Mind, 1957; The Big Man (novel), 1964; Men and Moments, 1966; contbr. book Deadline Delayed, 1947; author chpt. on Africa in Book of Knowledge. Broadcast Gen. Motors radio network program Your Land and Mine, 1945-56; columnist United Features Syndicate, 1961—; contbr. to Reader's Digest, Sat. Eve. Post, Sat. Rev. of Lit., N.Y. Times Sunday mag., and econ. jours in U.S., Eng., Switzerland, Sweden. Address: 150 E 69th St New York NY 10021

TAYLOR, HENRY LONGSTREET, physiologist, educator; b. St. Paul, Feb. 2, 1912; s. Henry Longstreet and Ethelberta (Geer) T.; B.S., Harvard, 1935, postgrad. Med. Sch., 1935-37; Ph.D. in Physiology, U. Minn., 1942; m. Catherine Morton Elliott, Mar. 21, 1941; children—David H., James F., Geoffrey E. Staff, Lab. Physiol. Hygiene, U. Minn. Sch. Pub. Health, 1942-44, asst. prof., 1944-49, asso. prof., 1949-56, prof. 1956—, acting dir., 1951-52, 63-64; field work in nutrition, phys. activity, coronary heart disease, Italy, 1955-70; cons. research com. Internat. Cardiol. Soc., 1963-65; chmn. steering com. Nat. Coop. Study Feasibility of Exercise in Trials of Prevention of Coronary Heart Disease, 1965-70; co-prin. investigator Mpls. unit Multiple Risk Factor Intervention Trial, 1972-77; mem. epidemiology com. Lipid Research Clinics. Mem. Am. Heart Assn. (exec. com. council epidemiology 1964-65), Am. Physiol. Soc., Soc. Exptl. Biology and Medicine, Gerontol. Soc., Am. Statis. Soc., Am. Coll. Sports Medicine, Internat. Cardiol. Soc., Am. Pub. Health Assn. Author: (with others) The Biology of Human Starvation, 1950; (monograph) Coronary Heart Disease in Seven Countries, 1970; also numerous articles, sect. in handbook. Home: 665 S Lexington Pkwy St Paul MN 55116 Office: Stadium Gate 27 Lab of Physiological Hygiene Minneapolis MN 55455

TAYLOR, HERBERT CECIL, JR., anthropologist; b. Houston, Nov. 29, 1924; s. Herbert Cecil and Pearl (Alexander) T.; student U. N.Mex., 1942, N.M. A. and M. Coll., 1942; B.A., U. Tex. at Austin, 1949, M.A., 1949; Ph.D., U. Chgo., 1951; m. Ruby Emma Oncken, Oct. 7, 1948 (div.); children—Laura Helen, Herbert Cecil III; m. 2d, Carol Jean Diers, Aug. 17, 1973. Teaching asst. anthropology U. Chgo., 1949-51; mem. faculty Western Wash. U., Bellingham, 1951—, prof. anthropology, 1962—, chmn. dept. sociology-anthropology, 1960-65, dean research and grants, 1965-75; vis. asst. prof. U. B.C., 1954; vis. prof. U. Calgary, 1966, 73. Chmn. steering com. Pacific N.W. Conf. Higher Edn.; chmn. social studies div. N.W. Sci. Assn.; anthrop. cons. Indian Lands Claims Cases. Served with AUS, 1943-46; ETO; lt. col. USAF Res.; dir. personnel Wash. Air N.G., 1973-76. Fellow Am. Anthrop. Assn.; mem. Soc. Am. Archaeology, Am. Sociol. Soc. (asso.), N.W. Anthrop. Assn., Pacific Sociol. Soc., Sigma Xi, Delta Sigma Rho. Author books on Northwest Indians; editor collections sci. papers. Contbr. articles, chpts. on Mexican, Am. and Canadian archaeology and ethno-history to books, profl. publs. Home: 3004 Cherrywood Ave Bellingham WA 98225

TAYLOR, HERMAN, JR., farmer, rancher, banker; b. Natchitoches, La., Oct. 31, 1932; s. Herman and Sadie (Cook) T.; student Northwestern State U., 1951; B.S., La. State U., 1954; m. Evelyne Campbell, June 26, 1954; children—Herman III, Mary Evelyne, Elizabeth Lynn. Farmer, rancher, Natchitoches, 1954—; v.p. Broadmoor Shopping Centers, Inc., 1959-68, Peoples Bank & Trust

Co., 1957—, People's Realty Corp., 1969—, Delta South Oil & Gas Co., 1970—; pres. Taylor & Co., farming, ranching enterprises, Natchitoches, 1954—, Cook-Taylor Land Corp., 1955—, C-T-C Land Corp., 1955—, HT-Stock Farms, Inc., 1954—, Delta Land Corp., 1972—, Lynn-Del Ranches, Inc., 1974—, Hickory Ridge Devel. Co., 1968—; Hickory Ridge Shopping Centers, 1971—; dir. Fed. Land Bank. Chmn., Agrl. Stablzn. and Conservation Service, 1965; mem. state com. La. Farmers Home Adminstrn., 1971—; mem. Nat. Cotton Council; mem. livestock adv. bd. La. State U., 1967—; vice chmn. La. Beef Promotion Commn., 1968. Vice chmn. Natchitoches Water Bd. Dist. 1; mem. Red River Navigation Compact Commn., La. Sovereignty Commn., 1960-64; v.p. Red River Valley Improvement Assn.; Mem. Culver Ednl. Found., La. State U., Found., Northwestern State U. Found.; chmn. Natchitoches Cancer Soc. Bd. dirs. Natchitoches Parish Fair; chmn. bd. dirs. Ducks Unlimited, Inc., 1975-76, nat. pres., 1973-74, nat. trustee, mem. exec. com., 1962—, chmn. exec. com., 1977, sr. v.p. charge internat. ops., 1978; bd. dirs., v.p., mem. exec. com. Ducks Unlimited of Can.; bd. dirs., mem. exec. com. Ducks Unlimited of Mexico. Recipient award for livestock prodn. Gov. of La., 1949, award for outstanding state farmer, 1950; named state farmer Future Farmers Am., 1949; Human Resource award Am. Bicentennial Research Inst., 1974, Albert Gallatin award, 1974. Mem. Am. Brahman Breeders Assn. (past dir.), La. Brahman Assn. (pres. pres.), Am. Nat. (finance com. 1962-63), La. (past v.p.) cattlemen's assns., La. Cotton Producers Assn., Natchitoches Farm Bur. (past pres.), Natchitoches Wildlife Assn. (past pres.), La. Farmer Elected Com. Assn. (v.p.), La. Bankers Assn., La. State U. Alumni Assn., Culver Fathers Assn., Delta Zeta, Sigma Alpha Epsilon. Democrat. Methodist (finance com.). Mason (32 deg., Shriner), Elk, Rotarian. Clubs: Natchotoches Country; Shreveport (La.). Home: Hickory Hill Natchitoches LA 71457 Office: PO Box 947 Natchitoches LA 71457

TAYLOR, HOBART, JR., lawyer; b. Texarkana, Tex., Dec. 17, 1920; s. Hobart and Charlotte (Wallace) T.; A.B., Prairie View (Tex.) State Coll., 1939; A.M., Howard U., 1941; J.D., U. Mich., 1943; L.H.D., Agrl. and Tech. Coll. N.C.; LL.D., Pacific U., Shaw U., Knoxville Coll.; m. Lynnette Dobbins, Jan. 21, 1951 (div. 1978); children—Albert, Hobart. Admitted to Mich. bar, 1944, D.C. bar, 1968; research asst. Mich. Supreme Ct., 1944-45; jr. partner firm Bledsoe & Taylor, Detroit, 1945-48; asst. pros. atty. Wayne County (Mich.), 1949-50, corp. counsel, 1951-61; sr. mem. firm Taylor, Patrick, Bailer & Lee, Detroit, 1958-61; spl. counsel Pres.'s Com. Equal Employment Opportunity, 1961-62, exec. vice chmn., 1962-65; spl. asst. to Vice Pres. U.S., 1963; asso. counsel to Pres. Johnson, 1964-65; dir. Export-Import Bank U.S., 1965-68; partner firm Dawson, Riddell, Taylor, Davis & Holroyd, and predecessor, 1968-79; of counsel firm Jones, Day, Reavis & Pogue, 1980—; dir. Eastern Airlines, Aetna Life and Casualty Co., Gt. Atlantic & Pacific Tea Co., Westinghouse Electric Corp., Burroughs Corp., Standard Oil Co. (Ohio). Vice chmn. bd. trustees Wolf Trap Found. for Performing Arts; mem. Pres.'s Commn. on Exec. Exchange, 1979—; trustee Howard U. Mem. Fed., Inter-Am., Am., Mich., D.C. bar assns. Clubs: Univ. (N.Y.C.); George Town; Nat. Lawyers, Internat., Federal City (Washington); Lyford Cay (Bahamas). Home: 2315 S St NW Washington DC 20008 Office: 1735 Eye St NW Washington DC 20006

TAYLOR, HOWARD DONE, lawyer; b. Payson, Utah, June 27, 1909; s. Lee R. and Ada (Done) T.; B.S., Brigham Young U., 1931; J.D., George Washington U., 1937; m. Jeanne Morris, Sept. 18, 1936; children—Dennis H., Sharon Lee. With IRS, 1939-65, regional commr., N.Y.C., 1961-65; partner firm Wikler, Gottlieb, Taylor & Howard, N.Y.C., 1965—; lectr. taxation, 1955—; chmn. Fed. Exec. Bd., 1964-65. Served as lt. USNR, 1942-46. Club: Wall Street. Contbr. numerous articles to profl. jours. Home: 2756 Edgewood Provo UT 84601 Office: 40 Wall St New York City NY 10005

TAYLOR, HOWARD M., JR., co. exec.; b. Balt., Dec. 12, 1905; s. Howard M. and Susan Roberta (Rynehart) T.; grad. Balt. Poly. Inst., 1926; E.E., Cornell U., 1929; postgrad. study bus. adminstrn., Harvard, 1930; m. Dorothy Ann Wannenwetsch, Sept. 19, 1933; children—Barbara Ann, Howard M. 3d; m. 2d, Verice Hoffman Diver, Oct. 26, 1962 (div. Feb. 1971). Trainee, Western Electric Co., 1929, later planning and devel. engr. at Balt.; with Internat. Bedding Co., Balt., 1933—, dir., 1936—, v.p., 1936-53, pres. 1953-61; regional mgr. Black & Decker Mfg. Co., 1962-65; v.p., dir. Threaded Products Inc. Md., 1966-70; sales adminstr. Sta-put Fastener Mfg. Co. div. Vincent Brass & Aluminum, Mpls., from 1971, now fastener pricing adminstr.; dir. Balt. br. Fed. Res. Bank of Richmond, chmn. bd., 1954. Mem. Am. Mgmt. Assn., N.A.M., Balt. Assn. Commerce, Jr. Assn. Commerce Balt., Sigma Alpha Epsilon. Clubs: Kiwanis, Saints and Sinners, Baltimore Country (Balt.); Cornell of Md.; Statler (Cornell U.); Annapolis Yacht. Home: 10332 H Malcolm Circle Cockeysville MD 21030 Office: 3900 Vero Rd Baltimore MD 21227. *I believe the greatest experience in my youth which has influenced me to follow the path I have chosen in life has been my membership in the Boy Scouts of America. In Scouting there is ample room and reward for individual achievement but the real benefits come from group efforts.*

TAYLOR, HOWARD ROY, hosp. adminstr.; b. Grand Ledge, Mich., July 28, 1918; s. Roy Myron and Mabel (DePue) T.; B.A., Mich. State U., 1939; M.S., Columbia U., 1947; m. Mary Freeman Dodge, July 28, 1943; children—James H., Douglas S. Adminstrv. asst. Johns Hopkins Hosp., 1947-50; asst. dir., then dir. Niagara Falls (N.Y.) Meml. Hosp., 1950-63; dir. Aultman Hosp., Canton, Ohio, 1963-69, exec. v.p., 1969-72, pres., 1972—; trustee Hosp. Assn. N.Y. State, 1958-63, pres., 1963; bd. dirs. Hosp. Bur., Inc., 1959-61. Trustee Family and Children's Service Niagara Falls, 1957-63, United Health Fund Canton, 1964-67, Commn. on Profl. and Hosp. Activities, Ann Arbor, 1977—; trustee, chmn. Ohio Hosp. Assn., 1970-71. Served to capt., Med. Adminstrv. Corps, AUS, 1940-45. Fellow Am. Coll. Hosp. Adminstrs.; mem. Am. Hosp. Assn., Phi Kappa Tau. Republican. Presbyterian. Contbr. articles to profl. jours. Home: 744 Knoll St SE North Canton OH 44709 Office: 2600 6th St Canton OH 44710

TAYLOR, J(AMES) HERBERT, cell biologist; b. Corsicana, Tex., Jan. 14, 1916; s. Charles Aaron and Delia May (McCain) T.; B.S., So. Okla. State U., 1939; M.S., U. Okla., 1941; Ph.D., U. Va., 1944; m. Shirley Catherine Hoover, May 1, 1946; children—Lynne Sue, Lucy Delia, Michael Wesley. Asst. prof. bacteriology and botany U. Okla., Norman, 1946-47; asso. prof. botany U. Tenn., Knoxville, 1948-51; asst. prof. botany Columbia U., N.Y.C., 1951-54, asso. prof., 1954-58, prof. cell biology, 1958-64; prof. biol. sci. Fla. State U., Tallahassee, 1964—, asso. dir. Inst. Molecular Biophysics, 1970—; cons. Oak Ridge Nat. Lab., 1949-51; research collaborator Brookhaven Nat. Lab., 1951-58; nat. lectr. Sigma Xi Research Soc. Pres., Unitarian Ch. Tallahassee, 1968-70. Served with M.C., U.S. Army, 1944-46; PTO. Recipient Meritorious Research award Mich. State U., 1960; Guggenheim fellow Calif. Inst. Tech., 1958-59. Mem. Nat. Acad. Scis., AAAS, Am. Inst. Biol. Sci., Am. Soc. Cell Biologists (pres. 1969-70), Biophysics Soc., Genetics Soc. Am. Democrat. Author: Molecular Genetics, Vol. 1, 1963, Vol. 2, 1964, Vol. 3, 1979; contbr. over 100 articles in field to profl. jours. Office: Inst Molecular Biophysics Fla State U Tallahassee FL 32306

TAYLOR, JAMES STEWART, lawyer, electronics mfg. exec.; b. Corunna, Ind., Feb. 13, 1931; s. Russell and Melissa (Ober) T.; J.D., U. Notre Dame, 1960; A.B., Manchester Coll., 1957; m. Joyce Elaine Rodewald, Feb. 2, 1952; children—Leslie Jo, Jan Marie, Todd Blair. Admitted to Ind. bar, 1960, since practiced in Elkhart; counsel CTS Corp., Elkhart, 1960—, sec., 1962—, v.p. and gen. counsel, 1969—, dir., 1979—; dir. CTS of Elkhart, Inc., CTS of Brownsville, Inc. Bd. dirs. Elkhart Better Bus. Bur., 1965-67, Elkart County Symphony Assn., Elkhart Legal Aid Service; trustee Chgo. Telephone Supply Found., Manchester Coll., 1973—. Served with USNR, 1951-55. Mem. Am., Ind., Elkhart City bar assns., Elkhart C. of C. (dir. 1968-70). Home: 23441 Forest Ln Elkhart IN 46514 Office: 905 N West Blvd Elkhart IN 46514

TAYLOR, JAMES VERNON, musician; b. Boston, Mar. 12, 1948; s. Isaac M. and Gertrude (Woodard) T.; student Milton (Mass.) Acad., 1962-66, Arlington Sch., Belmont, Mass., 1966-67; m. Carly Simon; children—Sarah Maria, Benjamin Simon. Recorded for Apple Records, 1968, Warner Bros. Records, 1970—; numerous concert appearances. Recipient 8 Gold Albums, 4 Platinum Albums, 3 Gold Singles, Grammy award for best male pop vocal performance, 1978. Composer, performer albums Sweet Baby James, 1970, Mud Slide Slim and The Blue Horizon, 1971, One Man Dog, 1972; Walking Man, 1974; Gorilla, 1975; In the Pocket, 1976; James Taylor's Greatest Hits, 1977; J.T., 1977; Flag, 1979. Address: care Peter Asher Mgmt 644 N Doheny Dr Los Angeles CA 90069

TAYLOR, JAMES WATSON, business exec.; b. Bismarck, N.D., June 1918; s. Theodore Ray and Anna (Logan) T.; B.S., Carnegie Inst. Tech., 1940; m. Mary Lou Crago, June 5, 1940; children—Stephen, Dianne, Patricia, David. Prodn. engr. Allison div. Gen. Motors Co., 1940-45; supr. prodn. control Westinghouse Electric Corp., Jersey City, 1945-51; pres., dir. Booz, Allen & Hamilton, Inc., N.Y.C., 1951-73; pres., dir. Bradford Computer & Systems, Inc., N.Y.C., 1973-76; pres., dir. Golightly & Co. Internat. Inc., 1976-77, Taylor Consultants, Inc., 1977—, Aquascooter, Inc., 1976—; dir. Inslico Inc., Producers Chem. Co., R. Hoe & Co. Inc. Life trustee Carnegie Mellon U. Mem. Tau Beta Pi, Sigma Alpha Epsilon. Republican. Presbyterian. Clubs: Echo Lake (Westfield); Sky (N.Y.C.); Chicago; Seaview (Absecon, N.J.). Home: 719 Lenape Trail Westfield NJ 07090 Office: 43 Commerce St Springfield NJ 07081

TAYLOR, JAY EUGENE, educator; b. Stayton, Oreg., Feb. 2, 1918; s. Charles Edward and Elisa (Roy) T.; B.A., Oreg. State U., 1940; M.S., U. Wis., 1943; Ph.D., Purdue U., 1947; m. Carol Ione Cartier, July 24, 1948; children—Barbara Elise, Janet Liana, Pamela Fay, Leann Kay. Indsl. chemist, 1940-44; instr. U. Wis., 1946-48; asst. prof. Miami U., 1948-52; asst. prof. U. Neb., 1954-60; asso. prof. Kent State U., 1960-63, prof., 1964—, dir. grad. studies in chemistry, 1967-70; cons. Goodyear Tire & Rubber Co., 1961—. Mem. Am. Chem. Soc., Sigma Xi, Phi Lambda Upsilon, Pi Mu Epsilon, Tau Kappa Epsilon. Inventor precision stirred flow reactor, wall-less gase phase reactor. Home: 5671 Caranor Dr Kent OH 44240

TAYLOR, JOE CLINTON, judge; b. Durant, Okla., Mar. 28, 1942; s. Luther Clinton and Virena (Parker) T.; student Southeastern State Coll., 1960-62; B.A., Okla. State U., 1965; J.D., U. Okla., 1968; m. Margaret Pearl Byers, June 8, 1963; children—Marna Joanne, Leah Alison, Jocelyn Camille. Admitted to Okla. bar, 1968; practice law, Norman, Okla., 1968-69; apptd. spl. dist. judge, Durant, 1969-72, asso. dist. judge Bryan County, Okla., 1972-76; dist. judge, chief judge 19th Dist. Ct., 1976—; presiding judge Choctaw Tribal Ct., 1979—. Chmn. bd. dirs Durant Youth Services. Served to capt. U.S. Army; capt. Res. Mem. Phi Sigma Epsilon, Delta Theta Phi. Mem. Ch. of Christ. Lion. Home: 424 W Olive St Durant OK 74701 Office: Bryan County Courthouse Durant OK 74701

TAYLOR, JOHN CLYDE, JR., osteo. physician; b. Rising Star, Tex., Mar. 27, 1922; s. John Clyde and Ora (Fleming) T.; student William Jewell Coll., 1940-41, Rockhurst Coll., 1946-47; D.O., Kansas City Coll. Osteopathy and Surgery, 1950; m. Phyllis Jean Arnold, Aug. 1, 1942; children—Kent Arnold, Kimberly Anne. Intern, Hosps. Kansas City Coll. Osteopathy and Surgery, 1950-51; practice osteo. medicine and surgery, Kansas City, Mo., 1951—; chief staff Lakeside Hosp., Kansas City, Mo., 1951—; mem. staffs Lakeside Osteo. Hosp. Vice pres. Nat. Osteo. Found., 1974, A.T. Still Found., 1973-75. Served with Hosp. Corps, USN, 1942-46. Mem. Am. (trustee 1967-76, pres. 1973-74 chmn. council on fed. health programs 1974), Jackson County (pres. 1956-57) osteo. assns., Mo. Assn. Osteo. Physicians and Surgeons (pres. 1966-67), Am. Profl. Practice Assn. (adv. bd. 1972—), Phi Sigma Gamma (grand archon 1964-66), Sigma Sigma Phi, Psi Sigma Alpha. Republican. Mem. Christian Ch. Clubs: Masons, Shriners. Home: 12317 Wenonga Ln Leawood KS 66209 Office: 4321 Main St Kansas City MO 64111

TAYLOR, JOHN FRANK, utility exec.; b. Gillespie, Ill., Jan. 24, 1923; s. John Henry and Dorothy (Green) T.; m. Lois Lucille Fenton, Feb. 22, 1947; children—John Dean, Charles Warren, Kenneth Robert. With Pacific Gas & Electric Co., 1946—, corp. sec., 1969—; sec. Pacific Gas Transmission Co., Pacific Transmission Supply Co., Standard Pacific Gas Line Inc., Natural Gas Corp. Calif., Gas Lines, Inc., Alaska Calif. LNG Co., Pacific Gas LNG Terminal Co., Pacific Gas Marine Co., Calaska Energy Co., Eureka Energy Co. Bd. govs. San Francisco Heart Assn., 1973-77. Served with USCGR, 1942-46. Mem. Am. Soc. Corp. Secs. (pres. San Francisco regional group 1968-69, nat. dir., v.p. 1971-73), Pacific Coast Gas Assn., Pacific Coast Electric Assn., San Francisco C. of C. Office: 77 Beale St San Francisco CA 94106

TAYLOR, JOHN FRANK ADAMS, educator; b. Dallas, Oct. 8, 1915; s. Charles Bachman and Mary (Adams) T.; A.B., Princeton, 1936, Ph.D. in Philosophy, 1940; L.H.D., Lewis and Clark Coll., 1968; m. Elizabeth Frost, Aug. 12, 1939; children—Mary Elizabeth, Deborah Frost. Chancellor Greene fellow philosophy Princeton, 1936-38, asst. instr., 1938-39, fellow dept. art and archaeology, 1941-42; instr. philosophy U. Pa., 1939-40; research in philos., art history Columbia, 1940-41; prof., head dept. lit., fine arts Mich. State U., 1946-52, prof. philosophy, 1952—, Centennial Rev. lectr., 1961, dir. Humanities Research Center, 1966—. Trustee Aquinas Coll., Grand Rapids, Mich. Served as lt. USNR, 1942-46. Guggenheim fellow, 1963-64. Recipient Distinguished Faculty award Mich. State U., 1961. Mem. Am. Philos. Assn., AAUP, John Dewey Soc., Phi Beta Kappa, Phi Kappa Phi. Author: Design and Expression in the Visual Arts, 1964; The Masks of Society, 1966. Editor, contbr.: An Introduction to Literature and the Fine Arts, 1950. Home: 4539 Nakoma Dr Okemos MI 48864

TAYLOR, JOHN FREDERICK REEH, lawyer; b. Forest, Ont., Can., Jan. 24, 1924; s. Frederick Reeh and Enid Margharuita (Bowden) T.; student U. South Wales and Monmouth, 1940-41; student Law Socs. Sch. Law, London, 1941-42; LL.B., U. Man. (Can.), 1951; m. Pamela M. Williams, Aug. 2, 1947; children—Paul, Gail, Judith, Timothy, Mark. Called to Man. bar, 1951; created Queen's counsel, 1971; partner law firm Taylor, McCaffrey, Winnipeg, Man., Can., 1965—. Sec. Codville Distbrs. Ltd., Winnipeg; dir. Spiroll Corp. Ltd., Mcdiarmid Lumber Ltd., McKeag Realty Ltd. Chmn. vol. bur. Welfare Planning Council, Winnipeg, 1961—; chmn. Legal Aid Com., 1968-71; pres. Man. Chamber Orch., 1973-75; chmn. bd. Eckhardt-Gramatté Music Competition, 1974-76. Served with Royal Navy, 1942-46. Mem. Canadian, Man. bar assns., Law Soc. Man. (bencher), Winnipeg Exec. Assn. Anglican (chmn. diocesan council social service 1965-67). Club: Manitoba. Home: Suite 504 200 Tuxedo Blvd Winnipeg MB Canada Office: 274 Garry St Winnipeg MB R3C 1H5 Canada

TAYLOR, JOHN HAMMOND, clergyman, educator; Victoria, B.C., Can., Apr. 14, 1908; s. William and Fanny (O'Keefe) T.; came to U.S., 1913; A.B., Gonzaga U., 1933, M.A., 1934; S.T.L., Alma Coll., 1941; Ph.D., St. Louis U., 1948; postgrad. Am. Sch. Classical Studies, Athens, 1952. Joined S.J., 1927; instr. classics Gonzaga Prep. Sch., Spokane, 1934-37; ordained priest Roman Catholic Ch., 1940; instr. classics Gonzaga U., Sheridan, Oreg. br., 1945-48, asst. prof., 1948-51, prof., 1951—, dean Coll. Arts and Scis., Spokane, 1961-74, academic v.p., 1961-64, chmn. dept. Classical langs., 1961-65, trustee, 1961-69, sec. corp., 1968—, dir. Summer Session Gonzaga-in-Florence, 1965; research scholar Pontifical Bibl. Inst., Rome, 1952-53; mem. Fulbright selection com. Western region, 1970-72, 74-75. Mem. Classical Assn. Pacific N.W. (past pres.), Archaeol. Inst. Am. (past pres. Spokane), Am. Philol. Assn. Contbr. to The Essential Augustine, 1964, Introduction to the Philosophy of Saint Augustine, 1964, Brugger-Baker Philosophical Dictionary, 1972; also articles in philol. jours. Address: Gonzaga U Spokane WA 99258

TAYLOR, JOHN HOWARD, ins. co. exec.; b. Gananoque, Ont., Can., Oct. 8, 1913; s. Howard William and Clara (Reid) T.; B.Engring., McGill U., 1935; m. Marian Isabel Webster, June 5, 1937; children—Howard W., Anthony J., Ann (Mrs. Beverly Collombin), Sherrill (Mrs. John Craig Eaton), Jane (Mrs. James Irwin). Coal salesman F.P. Weaver Coal Co., Toronto, 1935-49, v.p., 1949; v.p. Liquifuels, Toronto, 1950-59, exec. v.p., 1959-60, pres., chief exec. officer, 1960-65; pres., chief exec. officer Weaver Coal Co., Toronto, 1965-67; exec. v.p. Canadian Fuel Marketers Group, Toronto, 1967-70, pres., chief exec. officer, 1970-73; chmn. bd. dirs. North Am. Life Assurance Co., Toronto, 1968—, also Slough Estates Canada Ltd., Cadbury Schweppes Powell Ltd.; chmn. exec. com. Bramalea Ltd.; dir. Canadian Fuel Marketers Ltd., Motor Coach Industries Ltd., Greyhound Lines Can. Ltd., Norin Corp., Mercantile Bank Can., Morton-Norwich Products Inc., Paul Pogue Cos. Ltd., Ultramar Can. Ltd., Procor Ltd., Roy Fund Ltd. Pres. Bd. Trade Met. Toronto, 1964-65. Served with Royal Can. Arty., World War II. Clubs: Toronto, York (Toronto); Naples Yacht, Moorings Country, Royal Poinciana Golf, (Naples, Fla.); Boca Grande (Gasparilla Island, Fla.). Office: 2815 Thames Gate Dr Malton ON L4T 1G5 Canada

TAYLOR, JOHN INGALLS, newspaper exec.; b. Dedham, Mass., July 26, 1911; s. John I. and Cornelia (Van Ness) T.; A.B., Harvard U., 1933; m. Margaret Blake, Apr. 16, 1939; children—John, Timothy, David, Benjamin. With Boston Globe, 1933—, treas., 1952-60, pres., 1961—, also dir.; dir. Million Markets Newspapers, Inc., from 1959; pres. Globe Newspaper Co.; pres., dir. Affiliated Publs., Inc.; chmn. bd. Affiliated Broadcasting; bd. dirs. Bur. Advt., Am. Newspapers Pubs. Assn. Trustee Milton Acad.; bd. dirs. Advt. Research Found., Gesell Inst. Child Behavior. Served with USN, 1943-45. Office: Globe Newspaper Co 135 William T Morrissey Blvd Boston MA 02107

TAYLOR, JOHN JOSEPH, electric co. exec.; b. Hackensack, N.J., Feb. 27, 1922; s. John Daniel and Johanna Frances (Thomas) T.; A.B. (N.Y. Regents scholar, Univ. scholar), St. Johns U., Bklyn., 1942, D.Sc. (hon.), 1974; M.S. (tchg. fellow), Notre Dame U., 1946; m. Lorraine Antoinette Crowley, Feb. 5, 1943; children—John Brian, Nancy Mary, Susan Mary. Mathematician, Bendix Aviation Corp., Teterboro, N.J., 1946-47; scientist Kellex Corp., N.Y.C., 1947-50; mgr. devel. Westinghouse Bettis Atomic Power Lab., Pitts., 1950-67; engring. mgr. Westinghouse Nuclear Energy Systems, Pitts., 1967-70; v.p., gen. mgr. Westinghouse Advanced Nuclear Divs., Pitts., 1970-76, Westinghouse Water Reactor Divs., Pitts., 1976—. Served with USNR, 1942-45; PTO. Recipient Westinghouse Order of Merit, 1955. Fellow A.A.A.S. (mem. council), Am. Nuclear Soc. (dir.); mem. Am. Phys. Soc., Nat. Acad. Engring., Internat. Platform Assn. Co-author: (with T. Rockwell) Reactor Shielding Manual, 1956. Editor: (with A. Radkowsky) Naval Reactor Physics Manual, 1964. Contbr. articles to profl. jours. Home: 98 Hickory Hill Rd Pittsburgh PA 15238 Office: PO Box 355 Pittsburgh PA 15230

TAYLOR, JOHN LOCKHART, city ofcl.; b. N.Y.C., Nov. 4, 1927; s. Floyd and Marian (Lockhart) T.; A.B., Middlebury Coll., 1952; M.Govtl. Adminstrn., U. Pa., 1956; m. Barbara Becker, July 19, 1952; children—Catherine, Robert, William, Patricia. Reporter, Providence Jour.-Bull., 1952-54; adminstrv. intern City of Xenia (Ohio), 1955-56; municipal mgr. Borough of Narberth (Pa.), 1956-60, Twp. of Lakewood (N.J.), 1960-64; asst. city mgr. Fresno (Calif.), 1964-65, city mgr., 1965-68; city mgr. Kansas City (Mo.), 1968-74, Berkeley (Calif.), 1974-76; lectr. U. Pa., 1957-58, Golden Gate U., 1977; sr. urban mgmt. specialist Stanford Research Inst., 1977—. Served with USN, 1945-48. Mem. Internat. City Mgrs. Assn., Nat. Municipal League, Am. Soc. Pub. Adminstrn. Home: 1005 Creston Rd Berkeley CA 94708 Office: Box 782 Berkeley CA 94701

TAYLOR, JOHN LOWE, advt. agy. exec.; b. Washington, Feb. 1, 1934; s. John Barrett and Katharine (Lowe) T.; B.A. in English, U. Rochester, 1955; children—Laura, John Warren. Ter. salesman Procter & Gamble Distbn. Co., 1955-57; with Benton & Bowles, N.Y.C., 1957-64, 65—, v.p., acct. supr., 1965-69, sr. v.p., 1969-75, group exec., 1975—, also dir.; account supr. Ogilvy & Mather, N.Y.C., 1964-65; dir. Benton & Bowles subs. Bd. dirs. Epilepsy Found. Am. Mem. Am. Assn. Advt. Agys. (chmn. com. equal employment opportunity 1975-76). Club: Gipsy Trail (chmn. 1977-78). Home: 1 Nevada Plaza New York NY 10022 Office: 909 Third Ave New York NY 10022

TAYLOR, JOHN MCGUIRE, oil co. exec.; b. Sandgate, Kent, Eng., Nov. 6, 1917; s. John McWilliam and Winifred (McGuire) T.; student U. Birmingham, Eng., 1935-36, U. Western Ont., 1937-39; B.S. in Petroleum Engring., U. Okla., 1947; m. Mary Elizabeth Shaw, Apr. 3, 1948; children—Michael, Mark, Geoffry, Karen. Petroleum engr., cons. various oil cos., Alta., 1947-55; petroleum engr. Canadian Pacific Oil & Gas Ltd., 1955-57, asst. to mgr., 1957-58, mgr., 1958-64, gen. mgr., 1964-68, v.p., gen. mgr., 1968-69; pres., dir. PanCanadian Petroleum Ltd. and predecessors, Calgary, Alta., Can., 1969—; chmn. bd. Panarctic Oils, Ltd., 1967—; dir. Syncrude Can. Ltd.; mem. fuel scis. adv. com. Alta. Research Council; adv. com. Barnfield Marine Sta. Bd. dirs. Calgary Philharm. Orch., SEEDS (Soc., Environ. and Energy Devel. Studies). Served to flight lt. RCAF, 1940-45. Mem. Ind. Petroleum Assn. Can. (dir., past pres.), Coal Assn. Can. (dir.), Am. Inst. Mining Engrs., Assn. Profl. Engrs., Geologists and Geophysicists Alta., Calgary C. of C. (resource com.). Clubs: Glencoe, Calgary Petroleum. Office: 2000 One Palliser Sq PO Box 2850 Calgary AB T2P 2S5 Canada

TAYLOR, JOHN WHITFIELD, former publisher; b. Paterson, N.J., Apr. 20, 1914; s. Frank W. and Ida Dorothy (Westcott) T.; A.B., Princeton, 1935; m. Norma L. Crandall, July 31, 1937;

children—Wendy, Patricia, Joan W., David W. Salesman Shell Oil Co., 1936-41; sales, editorial rep. coll. dept. Prentice-Hall, 1943-45; sales, editorial rep. coll. dept. McGraw-Hill Book Co., 1945-46, editor coll. dept., 1946-51, editor-in-chief, 1951-53, mgr. coll. div., 1953-60, v.p., 1955-59, sr. v.p., 1959-74, also dir., ret., 1974; charge coll. div. tech. edn., div. Blakiston div., 1955-69, profl. reference book div. and Shepard's Citations, a subsidary, 1969-74, chmn. bd., 1971-74; mem. adv. bd. Midlantic Bank, Glen Ridge, N.J., Mcht. Bank, Northfield, Vt. Sec., Glen Ridge Pub. Library, 1958-61; mem. Bd. Edn. Glen Ridge, 1962-65; pres. Glen Ridge Bn. Forum, 1971-72. Chmn. bd. govs. Wesleyan U. Press, 1972—; mem. exec. com. of bd. fellows Norwich U., Northfield, Vt., 1977—; mem. Northfield Charter Rev. Commn., Northfield Planning Bd., 1978—. Mem. Am. Assn. Book Pubs., Nat. Assn. Coll. Stores (dir.), Vt., Northfield hist. socs., Phi Beta Kappa, Alpha Kappa Psi. Congregationalist. Club: Rotary (Northfield). Home: Winch Hill RD 1 Northfield VT 05663

TAYLOR, JOHN WILKINSON, educator; b. Covington, Ky., Sept. 26, 1906; s. John Wesley and Ethel (Wilkinson) T.; A.B., Columbia, 1929, A.M., 1930, Ph.D., 1936; H.D., St. Joseph Coll., 1970; m. Katherine Willis Wright; 1 son, Walter Bradford; m. 2d, Helen Hutchinson Greene (dec. Jan. 1966); stepdau., Patricia (Mrs. H.E. Thornber, Jr.); m. 3d, June Cornell Fairbank; step-children—Margaret, (Mrs. Terrill K. Jory), Laura (Mrs. Louis C. Sudler, Jr.), Kellogg III, Susan (Mrs. Walter B. Taylor), Elizabeth (Mrs. John W. Cameron), David. Asst. curriculum research Tchrs. Coll., Columbia, 1927, asst. elementary edn., 1928, asst. curriculum, 1929, asst. secondary edn., 1929-30, instr. comparative edn., 1930; tchr. English, Kaiser Friederich Realgymnasium, Berlin-Neukoeln, Germany, 1930-31; ednl. adviser to pres. John Day Co., 1932-33; asso. in edn., dir. fgn. study, Columbia, 1934-35, also asst. to chmn. New Coll., 1935-37; chmn. admissions, scholarship, loan, curriculum and personnel guidance coms., 1937-38; asso. prof. comparative edn. and sec. instnl. survey com., adminstrv. asst. to pres. La. State U., 1938-40, dir. bur. ednl. research, 1941-43; pres. U. Louisville, 1947-50; dep. dir.-gen. UNESCO 1951-54, acting dir.-gen., 1952-53; exec. dir. Chgo. Ednl. TV Assn., 1954-71, bd. mem. 1969-73; acting pres. Learning Resources Inst., N.Y.C., 1960-63, pres., Chgo., 1963-70; dir. Midwestern Ednl. Television Network, Inc., 1966-70; spl. cons. on ednl. TV, N.Y. U., 1958. Dir. Adult Edn. Council Greater Chgo., 1956-62, vice chmn., 1959-60; mem. Chgo. Council on Fgn. Relations, 1954—, bd. mem. 1970-72; citizens bd. U. Chgo., 1956—; adv. com. Midwest Office Inst. Internat. Edn., 1954-58; S.E. Chgo. Commn., 1955-63; mem. Midwest Council on Airborne TV Instrn., 1959-62. Exec. sec. to Am. Council on Edn. Commn., survey U. Ill., 1942 (on leave from La. State U.); mem. Round Table Meeting on Peace UNESCO, 1966. Bd. dirs. Chgo. Area Sch. TV, 1964-70, Sight Systems Inst., 1974—; mem. Mass. Edn. Study, 1963-64. Mem. bus. adv. council Chgo. City Jr. 1964-66; chmn. bd. Chgo. City Coll., 1966—; bd. dirs. North River Commn., 1967-70. Commd. capt. O.R.C., AUS, div. mil. govt. occupied countries, 1943, maj. 1944, lt. col. 1945; NATOUSA, N. Africa asst. dir., then dir. studies Mil. Govt. Sch. and Holding Center, 1943-44; chief edn. and religious affairs br. U.S. Mil. Govt. for Germany (planning unit in Eng., 1944-45, operational unit in Berlin, 1945-47); U.S. rep. on Quadripartite Edn. Com. for Germany, Berlin, 1945-47. Bd. dirs. Internat. Inst. Adminstrv. Scis. 1951-55; council advisors U.S. Commr. Edn., 1950-52; adv. panel Comptroller Army, 1950-53. Decorated Legion of Merit; chevalier French Legion of Honor; officer French Legion of Honor; named Man of Year, Louisville, 1950; Chicagoan of Yr. in Edn., Jr. C. of C., 1962, recipient Chgo. Medal for Merit, 1972. Mem. Supts. Roundtable No. Ill., 1954-71, Tri-county Ednl. TV Council, 1955- 63, Citizens Com. U. Ill., 1959-73, Chgo, Civic Com. World Refugees, 1960- 69. Mem. Am. Acad. Polit. and Social Sci., N.E.A., Am. Legion, Chgo. Assn. Commerce and Industry (chmn. edn. com. 1959-69), Internat. Platform Assn., Acad. TV Arts and Scis. (gov. Chgo. 1958-71), Omicron Delta Kappa, Phi Delta Kappa, Kappa Delta Pi, Phi Kappa Phi. Presbyn. Clubs: Executives, Filson, Arts, Rotary, Salmagundi, Pendennis (Louisville); Allied Circle (London); Union League, Wayfarers, Casino, Commercial. (Chgo.). Author: Youth Welfare in Germany, 1936; also survey reports. Contbr. articles to edn. profl. jours. Home: 1244 N State St Chicago IL 60610 Office: 180 N Michigan Ave Chicago IL 60601

TAYLOR, JOHN WILLIAMS, artist; b. Balt., Oct. 12, 1897; s. John Williams and Maude (Butner) T.; studied with S. McDonald Wright, J. Francis Smith, Los Angeles, 1920-23, Boardman Robinson, Art Student's League, N.Y.C., 1927-28; studies abroad, principally France, 1929-31; m. Andree Ruellan, May 28, 1929. Instr. Art Students League N.Y. summer sch., Woodstock, N.Y., 1948, 50, 51, 54, Pa. State U., 1957. Mich State U., 1958; guest instr. John Herron Mus. Sch., Indpls., 1950, 54, 57, 60, U. Tulane, 1956, 58-59, U. Fla., 1960-62, U. Wash., 1963; executed mural decoration Richfield Springs (N.Y.) Post office, 1942; works exhbtd. Macbeth Galleries, 1938, 44, 50, Am. Acad. Arts and Letters, 1948, Milch Galleries, 1955, 63; exhbns. include annuals of Carnegie Inst., Whitney Mus., Pa. Acad., U. Ill., Va. Mus. biennials, Nat. Acad. Design, Art Inst. Chgo., Am. Watercolor Soc., Bklyn. Mus. Internat., John Herron, Met., Balt., Montclair, Worcester and Toledo museums, others; rep. permanent collections Met. Mus., Am. Acad. Arts and Letters, Currier Gallery Am. Art, John Herron Mus., Art Students League N.Y., N.A.D., Whitney Mus. Am. Art, Va. Mus., other museums, galleries, pvt. collections. Guggenheim fellow 1954; recipient 1st prize 42d Watercolor annual Balt. Mus., 1939; John Barton Payne medal and purchase award Va. Mus. Biennial, 1946; hon. mention Carnegie Inst.'s, Painting in the U.S., 1947; $1000 award, Paintings of the Year, Nat. Acad. Galleries, 1948; citation and $1000 grant in arts Am. Acad. Arts and Letters, 1948; gold medal honor Am. Watercolor Soc., 1949; prize for watercolor 33d Ann. Exhbn. Albany Mus., 1968. N.A. Mem. Woodstock Artists Assn. Address: Shady Ulster County NY 12479

TAYLOR, JOSEPH HENRY, educator; b. Burkesville, Ky.; s. Richard Anderson and Mary Tabitha (Bowles) T.; A.B., Eastern Michigan U., 1927; A.M., U. Mich., 1930; Ph.D., U. Calif., 1936; postdoctoral study, U. Chgo., Columbia; m. Lu Sybil Ward, Sept. 3, 1930; (dec. Apr. 1970); 1 son, Richard. Prin. high sch. div. Ala. State Normal Sch., 1927-29; dean. Ala. State Tchrs. Coll., Montgomery, 1930-39; prof. history and chmn. div. social scis. N.C. Coll., Durham, 1939-63, dir. summer sch., 1946-63; prof. history, chmn. div. social scis., dir. summer sch. Bethune-Cookman Coll., 1963-64, acad. dean, 1964-70, dir. projects, 1970-76, acting v.p. for devel., 1978-79. Mem. NEA, Am. Tchrs. Assn. (chmn. bd. trustee 1959-63), Am. Hist. Assn., Assn. Study Afro-Am. Life and History (exec. council), Assn. Social Sci. Tchrs. (pres. 1948), Am. Acad. Polit. and Social Scis., Omega Psi Phi, Sigma Pi Phi, Phi Alpha Theta, Pi Gamma Mu. Democrat. Baptist. Mason (32 deg.). Contbr. articles to learned hist. publs. Home: 404 Margie Ln Daytona Beach FL 32014

TAYLOR, JOSEPH THOMAS, univ. dean; b. Rolling Fork, Miss., Feb. 11, 1913; s. Joseph T. and Willie Ann (Price) T.; A.B., U. Ill., 1936, A.M., 1937; Ph.D., Ind. U., 1952; LL.D., Berea Coll., 1969; Litt.D., Marian Coll., 1979; m. Hertha Mae Ward, Feb. 16, 1944; children—Bruce T., Judith F., Joel H. Instr., Fla. A. and M. Coll., 1939-42, asst. to pres., 1946-48, acting dean grad. div., summer 1949; dir. arts and scis., prof. sociology Albany (Ga.) State Coll., 1950-51; chmn. div. social scis., prof. sociology Dillard U., New Orleans, 1951-54, acting dean, 1954-57; dir. program devel. Flanner House, Indpls., 1957-62; lectr., then asso. prof. sociology Ind. U., 1962-66, dean regional campus, Indpls., 1967-70; prof. sociology, dean Sch. Liberal Arts, Ind. U.-Purdue U., Indpls., 1970—. Bd. dirs. Family Service Assn. Indpls., Greater Indpls. Progress Com., Indpls. YMCA, NCCJ, New Hope Found. Ind., United Way Greater Indpls., Urban League Greater Indpls.; trustee Indpls. YWCA, Berea (Ky.) Coll.; mem. nat. council YMCA; adv. council Christian Theol. Sem., (Indpls.), Ind. Developmental Disabilities, 1973—; mem. Comprehensive Health Planning Council Marion County (Ind.); adv. com. Fedn. Asso. Clubs, Bd. Sch. Commnrs.; mem. Negro colls. advance United Methodist Ch.; mem. Mid-Am. regional council YMCA; vice chmn. human relations task force Greater Indpls. Progress Com.; chmn. admissions com. Indpls. United Way. 1977. Served with U.S. Army, 1942-46. Teaching fellow Fisk U.. Nashville, 1937-38, Rosenwald fellow, 1938-39; named Man of Year, Indpls. B'nai B'rith Lodge 58, 1977. Club: Rotary. Author articles. Home: 300 W Fall Creek Pkwy North Drive Indianapolis IN 46208 Office: 1219 W Michigan St Indianapolis IN 46202

TAYLOR, KEITH BREDEN, physician; b. Wimbledon, Eng., Apr. 16, 1924; s. Francis Henry and Florence (Latham) T.; came to U.S., 1963; B.A., Magdalen Coll., Oxford U., 1946, M.A., 1949, D.M., 1955; m. Kym Williams, Nov. 24, 1972; children—Matthew, Sebastian, Nicholas, Daniel, Kate. Intern, Oxford U. Hosps.; resident Nat. Hosp. Nervous Diseases, London; lectr. in medicine Oxford U. Faculty Medicine, 1954-63; head div. gastroenterology Stanford U. Med. Center, 1963-71, vice chmn. dept. medicine, 1968—, Barnett prof. medicine, 1966—; chief med. service Palo Alto (Calif.) VA Hosp.; cons. Letterman Army Hosp., San Francisco. Served to maj. M.C., Brit. Army, 1951-53. Fellow Rockefeller Found., 1959, Guggenheim Found., 1971; Fogarty sr. internat. fellow NIH, 1979; NIH grantee, 1963-75. Fellow Royal Soc. Medicine, Royal Coll. Physicians (London); mem. Am. Fedn. Clin. Research, Am. Gastroenterol. Assn., Am. Soc. Clin. Investigation, Am. Soc. Clin. Nutrition, Assn. Physicians Gt. Britain, Brit. Soc. Gastroenterology, Brit. Soc. Immunology, Western Assn. Physicians. Author numerous articles in field. Editorial bd. Frontiers Gastrointestinal Research. Home: 20 Oakhill Dr Woodside CA 94062 Office: Stanford Univ Medical Sch Stanford CA 94305

TAYLOR, KENNETH NATHANIEL, publishing co. exec.; b. Portland, Oreg., May 8, 1917; s. George Nathaniel and Charlotte Bodwell (Huff) T.; B.A., Wheaton Coll., 1938, D.Litt. (hon.), 1965; student Dallas Theol. Sem., 1940-43; Th.M., No. Bapt. Theol. Sem., 1944; D.Litt. (hon.), Trinity Evang. Div. Sch., 1972; L.H.D. (hon.), Huntington Coll., 1974; m. Margaret Louise West, Sept. 13, 1940; children—Becky, John, Martha, Peter, Janet, Mark, Cynthia, Gretchen, Mary Lee, Alison. With Moody Press, pub. protestant religious lit., Chgo., 1947-63, dir., 1948-63; dir. Moody Lit. Mission, prodn. and distbn. lit., 1948-62; pres. Tyndale House Publishers, 1963—; chmn. bd. Coverdale House Pubs., London, Eng., 1969—; dir. Short Terms Abroad. Pres. Tyndale House Found.; dir. Inter-Varsity Christian Fellowship, 1956-59, Evang. Lit. Overseas, 1951-70; pres. Living Bibles Internat., Wheaton, Ill., 1968—; chmn. Unilit., Inc., Portland, 1972-73. Bd. dirs. Christian Library Service, 1972-75, InterSkrift forlage Aktiebolag, Sweden; trustee Living Bible Found., Fuller Theol. Sem. Recipient citation Layman's Nat. Bible Com., 1971; award Religious Heritage Am., 1972; distinguished service citation Internat. Soc. Christian Endeavor, 1973; Nelson Bible award, 1973; Better World award VFW Aux., 1974; disting. pub. service award, 1974; Recognition award Urban Ministries, Inc., 1977, Service award Wheaton Coll. Alumni Assn., 1977. Author: Is Christianity Credible, 1946; Living Letters: The Paraphrased Epistles, 1962; (juveniles) Stories for the Children's Hour, 1953, Devotions for the Children's Hour, 1954, I See, 1958, Bible in Pictures for Little Eyes, 1956, Lost on the Trail, 1959, Romans for the Children's Hour, 1959; Living Prophecies-The Minor Prophets Paraphrased, 1965; Living Gospels, 1966; Living Psalms and Proverbs With the Major Prophets Paraphrased, 1967; The Living New Testament, 1967; Living Lessons of Life and Love, 1968; Living Books of Moses, 1969; Living History of Isreal, 1970; The Living Bible, 1971, Taylor's Bible Story Book, 1970. Pub. The Christian Reader, 1964—, Have a Good Day, 1968, The Church Around the World, 1970—, Bookshorts, 1976. Home: 1515 E Forest Ave Wheaton IL 60187 Office: 336 Gundersen St Wheaton IL 60187

TAYLOR, LANE, former banker; b. Phila., June 11, 1911; s. Howard W. and Alice Underhill (Lane) T.; A.B., Princeton U., 1933; m. Elizabeth P. Townsend, Oct. 5, 1940; children—Lane, Elizabeth, Jonathan, Priscilla. With Hamilton Paper Co. (formerly W.C. Hamilton & Sons), Miquon, Pa., 1935-63; v.p. paper div. Weyerhaeuser Co., 1965; exec. v.p., dir. Germantown Savs. Bank, Phila., 1965-66, pres., dir., 1966-71, chmn. bd. dirs., 1971-77; dir. Phila., Germantown & Norristown R.R. Co., Penn Mut. Life Ins. Com., Phila. Trustee Chestnut Hill Hosp., Phila.; trustee Acad. Natural Scis. Phila., chmn. bd., 1967-73. Home: Miquon PA 19452

TAYLOR, LAURISTON SALE, physicist; b. Bklyn., June 1, 1902; s. Charles and Nancy Bell (Sale) T.; student Stevens Inst. Tech., 1920-22; A.B., Cornell, 1926; D.Sc., U. Pa., 1960, St. Procopius Coll. 1965; postgrad. Columbia, 1930, Cornell U., 1927, 30, 31; m. Azulah Frances Walker, Dec. 28, 1925 (dec. 1972); children—Lauriston Sale, Nelson Walker; m. 2d, Robena Harper, Nov. 24, 1973. With Bell Telephone Labs., N.Y.C., 1922; joined Nat. Bur. Standards, 1927, chief X-ray sect., 1940-49, chief proving grounds sect., 1941-42, asst. chief ordnance devel. div., 1942-43, asst. chief optics div., later atomic physics div., 1948-51, chief Radiation Phys. Lab., 1949-51, chief atomic and radiation physics div., 1951-60, chief radiation physics div., 1960-62, asso. dir., 1962-65; spl. asst. to pres. Nat. Acad. Scis., Washington, 1965-69, exec. dir. adv. com. emergency planning, 1965-71. With Internat. Commn. Radiol. Units, 1928-69, sec., 1934-50, chmn., 1953-69, hon. chmn., 1969—; mem. Internat. Commn. Radiol. Protection, 1928-69, sec., 1937-50, mem. emeritus, 1969—; chmn. Nat. Com. Radiation Protection, 1929-64; pres. Nat. Council on Radiation Protection and Measurements, Washington, 1964-77, hon. pres., 1977—; chief biophysics br., div. biology and medicine AEC, 1949. Served as chief operational research activities 8th Fighter Command, 9th USAAF, Europe, 1943-45. Decorated Bronze Star medal, Medal of Freedom. Recipient Exceptional Service medal Dept. Commerce; Sylvanus Thompson medal Brit. Inst. Radiology; gold medal Am. Coll. Radiology, 1965; citation AEC, 1970; citation Exec. Office of Pres., 1973; gold medal Royal Swedish Acad. Scis., 1973; gold medal 13th Internat. Congress Radiology, 1973. Fellow Am. Phys. Soc., Am. Coll. Dentists (hon.); mem. Washington Acad. Sci., Radiation Research Soc., Am. Roentgen Ray Soc. (Janeway medal 1954), Radiol. Soc. N.Am. (gold medal 1954), Washington Acad. Medicine, Deutsche Rontgen-Gesellschaft (hon.), Health Physics Soc. (pres. 1959), Societas Nippon Radiologica (hon., citation 1969). Author sects. 18 sci. books; also 162 sci. articles. Home: 7407 Denton Rd Bethesda MD 20014 Office: 7910 Woodmont Ave Washington DC 20014

TAYLOR, LISA SUTER, museum dir.; b. N.Y.C., Jan. 8, 1933; d. Theo and Martina (Weincerl) von Bergen-Maier; student Corcoran Sch. Art, 1958-65, Georgetown U., 1958-62, Johns Hopkins U., 1956-58; D.F.A. (hon.), Parsons Sch. Design, 1977; m. Bertrand L. Taylor III, Oct. 30, 1968; children—Lauren, Lindsay. Adminstrv. asst. President's Fine Arts Com., 1958-62; membership dir. Corcoran Gallery Art, 1962-66; program dir. Smithsonian Instn., 1966-69; dir. Cooper-Hewitt Mus. Decorative Arts and Design, Smithsonian Instn., 1969—. Mem. adv. bd. N.Y. State Assn. Museums, Fashion Inst. Tech., N.Y., Center for Holographic Art; mem. vis. com. Bank St. Coll. Recipient Exceptional Service award Smithsonian Instn., 1969, also Gold medal, 1972, Thomas Jefferson award, 1976; Bronze plaque Johns Hopkins YMCA, 1958; medal of honor Am. Legion, 1951; Bronze Apple award Am. Soc. Indsl. Designers, 1977. Mem. Am., N.Y. State, N.Y.C. museum assns., Am. Craftsmans Council, Archtl. League, Ceramics Circle, Needle and Bobbin Club, Am. Soc. Interior Designers (hon.). Co-dir. (film) A Living Museum, 1968; editor: Urban Open Spaces, 1979. Office: 2 E 91st St New York NY 10028

TAYLOR, LLOYD F., business exec.; b. 1916; student Brown U., St. John's Coll., Yale; m. Doris A. Taylor. Research asst. Yale, 1939-40; with indsl. relations div. Bridgeport Brass Co., 1940-47; with Casco Products Corp. Subsidiary Standard Kollsman Industries, Inc., 1948—, pres., dir.; with Standard Kollsman Industries, Inc. (now Sun Chem. Corp.), 1961—, v.p., 1963-69, pres., dir., 1969-73, chief exec. officer, 1970-73; group v.p., Sun Chem.; pres. Casco Products div. Sun Chem., 1973—; dir. Tom Wat, Inc., Bridgeport, dir. Union Bank & Trust, Bridgeport. Served to capt. USAAC, World War II. Decorated D.F.C., Air medal with six oak leaf clusters, presdl. citation. Address: 255 Algonquin Rd Bridgeport CT 06604

TAYLOR, LOUISE HARNEY, univ. adminstr., accountant; b. Canton, Ohio, May 31, 1931; d. Ross and Leola Esther (Jenkins) Harney; B.S., Roosevelt U., 1952; M.A., U. Chgo., 1958; Ed.D., Ind. U., 1974; M.B.A., Govs. State U., 1978. Accountant, Mich. Blvd. Apts., Chgo., 1952-55; tchr., chairperson Chgo. Public Schs., 1955-67; state supr. State of Ill., Chgo., 1967-68; asst. prof. acctg. and bus. adminstrn. Chgo. State U., 1969-74, asso. prof., 1974-78, chairperson dept. student affairs, 1975-76, asst. dean Coll. Bus. and Adminstrn., 1976, acting dean, 1976-78; dean Coll. Bus., prof. acctg. Eastern N.Mex. U., 1978—; cons. in field; grad. research asst. Ind. U., 1973-74; mem. profl. adv. council Portales (N.Mex.) Community Services, 1979. Recipient Pub. award Ill. Bus. Edn. Assn., 1970, 76, citation Fed. Exec. Bd., 1977; Am. Assembly Collegiate Schs. of Bus. faculty fellow, 1978. Mem. Am. Acctg. Assn., Nat. Assn. Accts. (Pub. award 1977), AAUP, Am. Assn. Higher Edn., Altrusa Internat., Nat. Bus. Edn. Assn., AAUP, Delta Kappa Gamma, Phi Lambda Theta. Presbyterian. Author: Your Career in Marketing, with workbook, 1976. Home: 1317 W 17th Ln Portales NM 88130 Office: Sta 19 Eastern NMex U Portales NM 88130. *My life is guided by the belief that determination, initiative, integrity, persistence, and aspiration are more than admirable traits. They are essential to success. Success to me is achieved when one demonstrates a willingness to do that which others deem insignificant as well as a desire to do that which others deem illustrious.*

TAYLOR, LYNNETTE DOBBINS, govt. ofcl.; b. Birmingham, Ala.; d. Albert Greene and Louise (Brown) Dobbins; B.S., Ala. State U., 1938; M.Ed., Wayne State U., 1948; m. Hobart Taylor, Jr., Jan. 26, 1950; children—Albert, Hobart III. Tchr. Detroit Pub. Schs., 1945-49; adminstr. elementary schs., 1949-63; exec. dir. Delta Sigma Theta; program analyst, field rep. Midwest region OEO, Washington, 1965—; dir. Jefferson Fed. Savs.; woman's editor N.Y. edit. Chgo. Defender, Detroit Tribune; edn. editor children's page feature and columnist Mich. Chronicle. Adv. com. Truth in Lending, Fed. Res. Bd. Mem. exec. bd. United Found., 1960—. Bd. dirs. Child Health Center Bd. Mem. Edn. Research Council Arts, Nat. Council Vol. Action, Met. YMCA, Nat. Friends Pub. TV. Mem. Internat. Soc. Women Educators, NAACP, Nat. Urban League, Internat. Washington (bd. dirs.), Am. Newspaper Women's Club; Delta Kappa Gamma, Phi Delta Kappa, Delta Sigma Theta. Democrat. Episcopalian. Clubs: Nat. Women's Democratic (Washington), Old Acquaintance (Detroit); LaSerre. Office: 1707 New Hampshire Ave NW Washington DC 20008

TAYLOR, MARSHALL BENNETT, transp. services co. exec.; b. Portland, Maine, May 16, 1946; s. Clifford Brenton and Anne (Marshall) T.; B.S.M.E., Worcester Poly. Inst., 1968; M.B.A., Babson Coll., 1972; m. Nancy Hamilton Smith, June 7, 1969; children—Prescott Bennett, Cameron Clark. Supr. inventory and prodn. control Allis Chalmers Corp., Boston, 1968-71; supr. systems and fin. analysis Mobil Oil Corp., Scarsdale, N.Y., 1972-74; mgr. capital planning Ryder System, Inc., Miami, Fla., 1974, dir. corp. planning, 1974-75, asst. treas., 1975-78, treas., 1978—, v.p., 1979—. Clubs: Coconut Grove Sailing, Royal Palm Tennis. Office: 3600 NW 82d Ave Miami FL 33152

TAYLOR, MAXWELL DAVENPORT, former army officer, govt. ofcl.; b. Keystesville, Mo., Aug. 26, 1901; s. John Earle Maxwell and Pearle (Davenport) T.; B.S., U.S. Mil. Acad., 1922; student Engr. Sch., 1922-23, F.A. Sch., 1932-33, Command and Gen. Staff Sch., 1933-35; Army War Coll., 1939-40; D.Eng., (hon.) N.Y. U., 1946; LL.D., Bowdoin Coll., 1948, U. Mo., 1951, Williams Coll., 1952, Pa. Mil. Coll., 1956, Trinity Coll., Yale, 1956, The Citadel, 1959, Phillips; hon. degrees Lafayette Coll., 1956, Seoul U., 1958, U. Pitts., 1962, U. Akron, 1966, Tarkio Coll., 1966, Norwich U., 1967, Worcester Poly. Inst., 1968, Parsons Coll., 1970, William Jewell Coll., 1970; m. Lydia Gardner Happer, Jan. 26, 1925; children—John Maxwell, Thomas Happer. Commd. 2d lt. C.E. 1922, advanced through grades to gen., 1953; transferred from C.E. to F.A., 1926; instr. French and Spanish, U.S. Mil. Acad., 1927-32; studied Japanese lang. in Tokyo, 1935-39; asst. mil. attache, Peking, China, 1937; spl. mission to Latin Am. countries, 1940; chief of staff, arty. comdr. 82d Airborne Div., 1942; served overseas in Sicilian and Italian campaigns, 1943-44; div. comdr. 101st Airborne Div., Western Front, 1944-45; supt. U.S. Mil. Acad., 1945-49; chief of staff Am. Army Forces in Europe, 1949; comdr. Am. Mil. Govt. and Army Forces in Berlin, 1949-51; dep. chief of staff for operations and adminstrn. U.S. Army, 1951-53, comdr. 8th Army, Korea, 1953; U.S. Army Forces, Far East, 1954; U.S. and UN comdr. in Far East, 1955; chief staff U.S. Army, 1955-59; chmn. bd., chief exec. officer, dir. Mexican Light & Power Co., 1959-60; pres. Lincoln Center for the Performing Arts, 1961; mil. rep. of Pres. U.S., 1961-62; chmn. Joint Chiefs of Staff, 1962-64; U.S. ambassador to Viet Nam, 1964-65; spl. cons. to Pres., 1965-69. Pres., Inst. Def. Analyses, 1966-69; mem., chmn. Pres.'s Fgn. Intelligence Adv. Bd., 1965-69. Decorated Silver Star with oak leaf cluster D.S.C., D.S.M. with 3 oak leaf clusters, Legion of Merit, Bronze Star, Purple Heart (U.S.); hon. knight comdr. Order Brit. Empire, hon. companion Order of Bath (mil. div.), D.S.O. (Eng.); comdr. Legion of Honor, Croix de Guerre with palm (France); cross of grand officer Order of Leopold, Order of Crown with palm, grand officer Croix de Guerre 1940 with palm (Belgium); Order Mil. Merit, 1st class (Mexico); chief comdr. Legion of Honor (P.I.); grand officer Order of Boyaca (Colombia); Taeguk Distinguished Mil. Service medal, 1st and 2d awards (Republic of Korea); grand officer Order of Mil. Merit (Brazil); comdr. Mil. Order of Ayacucho (Peru); Cloud and Banner medal with grand cordon (China); comdr. Mil. Order of Italy, grand ofcl. Order of Mil. Merit (Italy); Militaire Willems-Orde, 4th class (Netherlands); Thai Most Noble Order of the Crown of Thailand, 1st class (Thailand); Cordon of Trinity medal with plaque (Ethiopia); higher comdr.'s cross Order of George the First (Greece); Gt. Cross of Nat.

Order (South Viet Nam); Order Rising Sun (Japan); grand cross Order Mil. Merit (Spain). Clubs: University, Lotus (N.Y.C.); Chevy Chase, Army and Navy, Alibi, Internat. (Washington). Author: The Uncertain Trumpet, 1960; Responsibility and Response, 1967; Swords and Plowshares, 1972; Precarious Security, 1976. Home: 2500 Massachusetts Ave NW Washington DC 20008*

TAYLOR, MILLARD BENJAMIN, concertmaster, educator; b. Crete, Nebr., Aug. 9, 1913; s. Joseph Elbert and Anna Blodgett (Bennett) T.; Mus.B., Eastman Sch. Music, 1935; Mus.D., Doane Coll., 1967; D.Litt., Neb. Wesleyan U., 1975; m. Marie Jeanne Capasso, Jan. 2, 1939; children—Virginia Ann (Mrs. James Edward Smith), Jeanne Marie (Mrs. John Hernandez). Concertmaster, Nat. Symphony Orch., 1938-44, Rochester Philharmonic Orch., 1944-67; prof. violin Eastman Sch. Music, Rochester, N.Y., 1944-79, prof. emeritus, 1979—, chmn. string dept., 1950-76; Edward F. Arnold vis. prof. music Whitman Coll., 1979-80; concertmaster Chautauqua Symphony Orch., 1965—; guest concertmaster Dallas Symphony Orch., N.J. Symphony Orch.; mem. Eastman Quartet; violinist Eastman String Trio; 1st violinist, leader Chautauqua String Quartet; head string dept. Chautauqua Summer Music Schs. Bd. dirs. Rochester Civic Music Assn., 1969-72. Named Musician of Year, Rochester chpt. Mu Phi Epsilon, 1966. Mem. Pi Kappa Lambda, Phi Mu Alpha Sinfonia. Contbr. articles to Instrumentalist mag. Office: 26 Gibbs St Rochester NY 14604

TAYLOR, NELSON FEREBEE, legal educator; b. Oxford, N.C., Jan. 24, 1921; s. Leonidas C. and Martha (Ferebee) T.; A.B. (Herbert Worth Jackson scholar), U. N.C., 1942; LL.B. cum laude, Harvard, 1949; A.B. (Rhodes scholar), Balliol Coll., Oxford (Eng.) U., 1951, M.A., 1955; grad. Advanced Mgmt. Program, Harvard, 1956; m. Louise C. Ellington, Oct. 12, 1946; children—Louise Ferebee, Sarah Ellington, Martha Gregory. Admitted to N.C. bar, 1949, N.Y. bar, 1953; asso. firm Arthur, Dry, Kalish, Taylor & Wood, and predecessor, N.Y.C., 1951-57, partner, 1958-70; asso. gen. counsel Uniroyal, Inc., N.Y.C., 1961-70; v.p. adminstrn. U. N.C., 1970-72; chancellor U. N.C. at Chapel Hill, 1972-80, prof. law, 1980—. Served to lt. USNR, 1942-46. Decorated Bronze Star. Mem. N.C. State Bar, Phi Beta Kappa. Mem. P.E. Ch. Home: 3 The Glen Chapel Hill NC 27514

TAYLOR, NETTIE BARCROFT, librarian; b. Brownsville, Tenn., Aug. 6, 1914; d. Charles W. and Nettie (Barcroft) Taylor; A.B., Fla. State U., 1936; B.S. in Library Sci., U. N.C., 1942; postgrad. U. Md., 1950-60; M.S., Johns Hopkins, 1967. Librarian, Taylor County High Sch., Perry, Fla., 1936-40, Leon County High Sch., Tallahassee, Fla., 1940-42; library dir. various U.S. Army libraries, U.S. and Germany, 1942-47; dir. Pamunkey Regional Library System, Ashland, Va., 1947-48; supr. pub. libraries Md. Dept. Edn., 1948-60, asst. state supt. for libraries, div. library devel. and services, Balt., 1960—; pres. Continuing Library Edn. Network Exchange, 1976. Mem. ALA, Am. Library Trustees Assn. (2d v.p. 1965), Assn. State Libraries (pres. 1969-70), Md. Library Assn. (pres. 1960), ACLU, Common Cause, League Women Voters. Contbr. to publs. in field. Home: 4105 Bedford Rd Baltimore MD 21207

TAYLOR, NORMAN WILLIAM, educator; b. Wigan, Eng., Jan. 9, 1923; s. Albert and Jessie (Slonker) T.; B.Sc., U. London, 1950; M.A., Yale, 1954, Ph.D., 1958; m. Eleanor Dorothy Harper, July 18, 1953; children—David Gordon, Laurie Elizabeth. Clk., London, Midland & Scottish Ry. Co., Preston, Eng., 1939-40; clk. City Treas. Office, Wigan, 1940-42, 47-48; exec. officer War Office, U.K., 1948-49; asst. instr. econs. Yale, 1955-57, instr. econs., 1957-59; asst. prof. econs. Lawrence U., 1959-62; vis. asst. prof. econs. U. Wis., 1961-62; asso. prof. econs. Franklin and Marshall Coll., Lancaster, Pa., 1962-69, prof. econs., 1969—, chmn. dept., 1964-79; vis. prof. Tunghai U., Taiwan, 1967-68. Served to capt. Brit. Army, 1942-47. Mem. Am. Econ. Assn., Econ. History Assn., Econ. History Soc., Am. Anthrop. Assn., Am. Assn. Chinese Studies, AAUP. Contbr. articles profl. jours. Home: 1716 Linwood Ave Lancaster PA 17604

TAYLOR, PAUL, choreographer; b. Allegheny County, Pa., July 29, 1930; s. Paul B. and Elizabeth (Rust) T.; student Syracuse U., 1949-52, Juilliard Sch. Music, 1952-53. Dancer with Martha Graham Co., N.Y.C., 1955-61; guest artist N.Y.C. Ballet, 1959-61; dir., choreographer Paul Taylor Dance Co., N.Y.C., 1955—; appeared at Spoleto (Italy) Festival, 1960, 64, Festival Nations, Paris, 1962, Mexico City, Acapulco, 1963, 65, CBS-TV Repertoire Workshop, Am. Dance Festival, 1961-65, Philharmonic Hall at Lincoln Center, L.I. Festival Arts, Dance Festival Shakespeare Theatre Central Park, 1963, Little Theatre, N.Y.C., 1963, Tyron Guthrie Theatre, Mpls., 1964, Ambassador Theatre, N.Y.C., 1965; State Dept. tours S.Am., C.Am., Holland Festival, Germany, Belgium, 1965, Holland, Hammamet, Israel, Edinburgh Festivals, 1966, also round the world tour, 1967, 14th fgn. tour (Europe) Paris Festival Nations, 1967, Royal Danish Ballet Festival, 1967, Yugoslavia Arts Festival, 1967, 16th Fgn. tour, 1969; dance seasons at ANTA Theater, N.Y.C., 1966, Billy Rose Theater, N.Y.C., 1967, Am. Dance Festival, Newport, R.I., 1976, City Center Theatre, 1977; summer choreographer in residence Lake Placid (N.Y.) Center for Music, Drama and Art, 1974-77; adviser, Rockefeller Report on Arts in U.S. Recipient Internat. Circle of Criticism for Artistic Research and Cultural Exchange award Festival Nations, Paris, 1962, Gold Star award for choreography 2d Internat. Festival, Paris, 1964; named Dancer of Year, London's Dance and Dancers, 1965; decorated chevalier des Arts et Lettres (France); prize for best fgn. attraction by Critics of Chile, 1966; Guggenheim fellow, 1961, 66; Capezio Dance award, 1967; Creative Arts award gold medal Brandeis U., 1978. Address: care Yesselman 550 Broadway New York NY 10012

TAYLOR, PAUL PEAK, educator, dentist; b. Childress, Tex., May 11, 1921; s. Noah Peak and Lois (Vinson) T.; student W. Tex. State Coll., 1938-40; D.D.S., Baylor U., 1944; M.S., U. Mich., 1951; m. LaVerne Countryman, Aug. 11, 1945; children—Scott, Peri Ann. Lectr. anatomy, physiology Flint (Mich.) Jr. Coll., 1950-51; mem. faculty Coll. Dentistry Baylor U., Dallas, 1958—, prof., chmn. grad. pedodontics, 1960-69, prof., chmn. dept. pedodontics, 1969—; dir. dental tng., dental sect. of med. staff Children's Med. Center, Dallas, 1960—, mem. exec. com., 1965—; mem. staff Tex. Scottish Rite Hosp., Dallas; mem. med.-dental com. health adv. bd. Dallas Ind. Sch. Dist., 1974—; mem. adv. com. dental asst. program El Centro Jr. Coll., 1972—; mem. med.-dental adv. bd. Tex. unit Cerebral Palsy Inc., 1973—; mem. tech. adv. com. crippled children's service Tex. Dept. Health, 1977—. Served to capt. AUS, 1951-53. Mott Found. fellow, 1949-51. Diplomate Am. Bd. Pedodontics (examining mem. 1977—). Fellow Am. Coll. Dentists; mem. Am. Dental Assn., Tex., Dallas County dental socs., Am. Soc. Dentistry Children, Southwestern Soc. Pedodontics, Dallas Execs. Assn. (pres. 1970), Xi Psi Phi, Omicron Kappa Upsilon. Episcopalian. Mason (Shriner, 32 deg.). Editorial and publ. commn. Jour. Dentistry for Children, 1968—. Home: 2615 Briarcove St Plano TX 75074 Office: 1935 Amelia St Dallas TX 75235

TAYLOR, PETER HILLSMAN, educator, author; b. Trenton, Tenn., Jan. 8, 1917; s. Matthew Hillsman and Katherine (Taylor) T.; student Vanderbilt U., 1936-37, Southwestern Coll., 1937-38; B.A., Kenyon Coll., 1940; m. Eleanor Lilly Ross, June 4, 1943; children—Katherine Baird, Peter Ross. Mem. vis. com. dept. English, Harvard, 1966—, lectr. in creative writing, 1974—; prof. English, U. Va., 1967—. Served with AUS, 1941-45. Recipient Nat. Acad. award fiction, 1950; Fulbright award. 1955; Guggenheim fellow, 1950; Ford fellow study theatre in Eng., 1961; Rockefeller grantee, 1964. Mem. Nat. Inst. Arts and Letters, Am. Acad. Arts and Scis. Author: A Long Fourth and Other Stories, 1948; A Woman of Means, 1950; The Widows of Thornton, 1954; (play) Tennessee Day in St. Louis, 1957; Happy Families Are All Alike, 1959; Miss Leonora When Last Seen, 1964; The Collected Stories of Peter Taylor, 1969; (play) A Stand in the Mountains, 1968; (one act plays) Presences, 1973; In the Miro District and Other Stories, 1976. Home: 1841 Wayside Pl Charlottesville VA 22903

TAYLOR, PHILLIP SEYFANG, museum dir.; b. Mpls., Dec. 16, 1921; s. Guy Seyfang and Hulda (Renstrom) T.; B.S. with distinction, U. Minn., 1949, M.S., 1952; m. Desiree A. Hill, Oct. 17, 1942. Dir. edn. Sci. Mus., St. Paul, 1952-59, dir. mus., 1959—; instr. microbiology, bacteriology St. Catherines Coll., St. Paul, 1957; mem. adv. com. Title III Projects, Minn. Dept. Edn., 1966-67; mem. tech. rev. panel Minn. Higher Edn Coordinating Commn. on Title I grants, 1977-78. Mem. Lakeland Village Council (Minn.), 1958-72; mem. adv. bd. Thomas Irvine Dodge Found.; trustee Natural Sci. for Youth Found., 1972—; mem. adv. bd. intensive edn. program Breck Sch., Mpls., 1977-78. Served with USNR, 1942-45. Mem. Am., Midwest (v.p. Minn. chpt. 1971—) assns. museums, Am. Assn. Biology Tchrs., Entomol. Soc. Am., Minn. Acad. Sci., Internat. Council Museums, Sigma Xi, Gamma Sigma Delta. Club: Rotary. Author: Science Enrichment Teaching Unit, 1963. Home: 641 Quixote St Lakeland MN 55043 Office: 30 E 10th St Saint Paul MN 55101

TAYLOR, PRENTISS HOTTEL, artist; b. Washington, Dec. 13, 1907; s. John Eastlack and Beatrice (Hottel) T.; student Art Students League; pupil Charles W. Hawthorne. Scenic artist, 1926; lithograph, watercolor artist, 1931—; painter in oils, 1943—; art therapist, psychotherapy dept. St. Elizabeths Hosp., 1943-54, Washington; professorial lectr. Am. U.; art therapist Chestnut Lodge, Rockville, Md. Represented Library of Congress, Phillips Collection, N.Y. Mus. Modern Art, Wadsworth Atheneum (Hartord, Conn.), Addison Gallery (Andover, Mass.), Whitney Mus. Am. Art, Balt. Mus. Art, Seattle Art Mus., N.Y. Pub. Library, Boston Mus. Fine Arts, Phila. Mus., Valentine Mus. (Richmond), Va. Mus. Fine Arts, Yale U. Gallery, Gibbes Gallery, Charleston, S.C., Smithsonian Instn., Washington, Boston Pub. Library, several univs. Exhibited painting in U.S., 1946-49, Carnegie Inst., Corcoran Biennial, 1949-51; A.N.A. lectr. Established, illustrator Winter Wheat Press; established Golden Stair Press with Langston Hughes. Recipient Am. Artists Group lithograph prize, 1953; Cannon graphic prize NAD, 1954; purchase award lithography, nat. exhbn. DePauw U., 1959. Mem. Artists Guild Washington, Soc. Am. Graphic Artists, Soc. Washington Printmakers, Print Club of Albany, Boston Printmakers. Home: J-718 Arlington Towers Arlington VA 22209 Office: 4520 Yuma St NW Washington DC 20016*

TAYLOR, RAYMOND MASON, lawyer, librarian; b. Washington, N.C., Jan. 1, 1933; s. Thaddeus Raymond and Mary Ada (Mason) T.; A.B. in Polit. Sci., U. N.C. at Chapel Hill, 1955, J.D., 1960; m. Rachel High, Apr. 3, 1965; 1 dau., Elizabeth Lee. Staff reporter Wash. Daily News, summers 1952, 54; adminstrv. asst. CD Orgn., Winston-Salem and Forsyth County, N.C., 1955; adminstrv. intern City Winston-Salem, summer 1958; admitted to N.C. bar, 1960, U.S. Supreme Ct. bar, 1970; research asst. to justice Supreme Ct. N.C., 1960-61; asso. firm Gardner, Connor & Lee, Wilson, N.C., 1961-64; adj. instr., then adj. prof. bus. law Atlantic Christian Coll., Wilson, 1962-64; marshal, librarian Supreme Ct. N.C., 1964-77; project dir. Fed. Jud. Center Study of Fed. Ct. Libraries, 1976-77; spl. lectr. econs. and bus. N.C. State U., 1967—; cons., 1977—; pvt. practice law, 1977—; dir. N.C. Law Research Facilities Study, 1970; chmn. State and Ct. Law Libraries U.S.-Can., 1973-74; mem. Wake County Library Commn., 1979—; lectr. in field. Sec. Southeastern Area council Am. Jr. Red Cross, 1949-50, study visitor to Europe, 1950; Democratic chmn. Pineville Precinct, Beaufort County, N.C., 1954-57; parliamentarian Wilson County Dem. Exec. Com., 1962-64; mem. Beaufort County Dem. Exec. Com., 1954-57, N.C. 2d Solicitorial Dist. Dem. Exec. Com., 1962-64. Served with AUS, 1955-57. Recipient awards editorial, news and feature writing U. N.C. Press Club, 1955, award hist. feature writing N.C. Soc. County and Local Historians, 1955; award of excellence Soc. for Tech. Communication, 1976; named Tar Heel of Week, 1971. Mem. Am., N.C., bar assns., Am. Bar Found. (library services com. 1969-73), N.C. State Bar, Am. Assn. Law Libraries (certified), Internat. Assn. Law Libraries (chmn. ct. libraries com. 1977—), Order Golden Fleece (pres. 1958-59), Am. Bus. Law Assn., Associated Clubs (Topeka, Kans.) (nat. speaker 1974—), Pi Sigma Alpha, Phi Delta Phi. Presbyterian. Clubs: Capital City, Exec. (Raleigh). Author articles; asst. editor Tar Heel Barrister, 1958-59; mem. student bd. editors N.C. Law Rev., 1960. Home: 3073 Granville Dr Raleigh NC 27609 Office: PO Box 1590 Insurance Bldg Suite 200 336 Fayetteville St Mall Raleigh NC 27602

TAYLOR, RAYNOR DUNHAM, ret. clergyman; b. Pasadena, Calif., Dec. 7, 1908; s. John Raynor Chadwick and Edna (Lewis) T.; student Occidental Coll., Los Angeles, 1927-30; A.B., Redlands (Calif.) U., 1935; L.Th., Northwestern and Seabury-Western Theol. Sem., 1934, D.D., 1964; m. Martha Virgina Bebee, June 28, 1936. Ordained to diaconate of Episcopal Ch., 1934, to priesthood, 1935; vicar St. Stephen's Ch., Beaumont-Banning, Calif., 1934-37; rector St. Mathew's Ch., National City, Calif., 1937-42, St. Mary's Ch., Laguna Beach, Calif., 1942-43; asst. rector St. Mark's Ch., San Antonio, 1943-45; dean Saint Mark's Cathedral, Salt Lake City, 1945-51; rector Meml. Ch. of the Good Shepherd, Phila., 1951-73, St. Cuthberts Chapel, MacMahan Island, Maine, summer 1958, St. Augustine's Coll., Canterbury, Kent, Eng., summer 1959, St. Mary's Ch., Anchorage, St. Peter's Ch., Sitka, Alaska, summer 1962; now ret.; hon. asso. St. George's Ch., Laguna Hills, 1973—; exam. chaplain to Bishop of Utah, also sec. Corp. of Missionary Dist. Utah; chmn. dept. Christian Edn., mem. Bishop and exec. council, 1945-51. Mem. Newcomen Soc., Ch. Soc. Coll. Work, Ch. Hist. Soc., Alpha Tau Omega. Republican. Clubs: Masons (32 deg.), K.T., Shrine (pres. Leisure World 1979), Rotary (pres. 1950), Univ., Salt Lake Country, Canterbury; Union League, Franklin Inst., Cricket, Racquet (Phila.). Author articles in field. Address: 3298 N Via Carrizo Laguna Hills CA 92653

TAYLOR, RICHARD, educator, philosopher; b. Charlotte, Mich., Nov. 5, 1919; s. Floyd Clyde and Marie Louise (Milbourn) T.; A.B., U. Ill., 1941; A.M., Oberlin Coll., 1947; Ph.D., Brown U., 1951; m. Thelma Maxine Elworthy, Jan. 14, 1944 (div. 1961); children—Christopher, Randall; m. 2d, Hylda Carpenter Higginson, Dec. 26, 1961; 1 step dau., Molly. Faculty, Brown U., 1951-52, 53-63, prof. philosophy, 1958-63, chmn. dept., 1959-60, William Herbert Perry Faunce prof. philosophy, 1959-63; prof. philosophy grad. faculty Columbia 1963-66; prof. philosophy U. Rochester (N.Y.), 1966—, chmn. dept., 1966-69. Faculty Swarthmore Coll., 1953, Ohio State U., summer 1959, Cornell U., summer 1961; vis. prof. philosophy Columbia, 1962, Ohio State U., 1963; vis. Robert D. Campbell prof. philosophy Wells Coll., 1967-68; vis. Robert H. Truax prof. philosophy Hamilton Coll., 1971; vis. Melvin Hill prof. humanities Hobart-William Smith Colls., 1974. Served to lt. USNR, 1943-47. Mem. Am. Philos. Assn., Phi Beta Kappa. Author: Metaphysics (Spanish, Dutch, Japanese, Portugese translations), 1963, rev., 1974; Action and Purpose, 1965; Good and Evil, 1970; Freedom, Anarchy and the Law, 1973; With Heart and Mind, 1973. Editor: Theism (J.S. Mill), 1957; Selected Essays (Schopenhauer), 1963; asso. editor Am. Philos. Quar., 1972—. Contbr. articles to publs. U.S., Eng., Australia. Home: Rural Delivery 3 Savercool Rd Trumansburg NY 14886

TAYLOR, RICHARD WILLIAM, securities broker, investment banker; b. Toledo, Sept. 16, 1926; s. Everett Ellsworth and Hazel (Broer) T.; B.S., U.S. Naval Acad., 1949; postgrad. U. Calif., 1952; m. Lyn Westerlund, Sept. 11, 1954; children—Julie Everett, Richard William, Alison Nichols, Jennifer Broer, Liane Westerlund. Mem. Ohio Ho. of Reps., 100th gen. assembly from 9th Dist.; asst. mgr. Navy sales Martin Aircraft, Balt., 1953-56; with McKinsey & Co., mgmt. cons., N.Y.C., 1956-60; asst. to v.p. Cerro Corp., N.Y.C., 1960-62, spl. asst. to pres., 1965; pres. Cerro Aluminum Co., N.Y.C., 1962-65; successively v.p., exec. v.p., pres. and chief exec. officer Carter, Walker & Co., Inc., 1967-69; pres., chief exec. officer Burton, Dana, Westerlund, Inc., N.Y.C., 1969—; v.p. Sterling, Grace & Co., Inc., 1971-74; v.p. Moseley, Hallgarten, Estabrook & Weeden, Inc., 1975—. Bd. govs., treas. Am. Econ. Found., Inc.; v.p., trustee, chmn. investment com. James Monroe Meml. Found.; bd. regents James Monroe Law Office and Mus.; bd. dirs. Tolstoy Found.; trustee YWCA pension trusts. Served with USN, 1944-52. Decorated Air medal, Navy Commendation medal. Mem. U.S. Naval Acad. Alumni Assn. Clubs: Union League; Rombout Hunt. Home: Route 3 Box 261 Orange VA 22960 Office: 1 New York Plaza New York NY 10004

TAYLOR, RIP, entertainer; b. Washington, Jan. 13, 1931; s. Elmer and Bette T.; B.S. in Polit. Sci., George Washington U. Page, U.S. Senate; entertainer in hosps. and prisons; with USO goodwill tour of mil. bases, U.S.; appeared in leading nightclubs, Tokyo; appeared at Dunes Hotel, Las Vegas, Nev.; on tour with Judy Garland, with Debbie Reynolds; appeared at Copacabana, N.Y.C., Latin Quarter, N.Y.C.; motion picture debut in I'd Rather Be Rich; starred in Funny Farm, Aladdin Hotel, Las Vegas; headliner Sahara's Casbar Theatre, Las Vegas; appeared at Stardust and Tropicana, Las Vegas and Harrah's, Reno, Nev., Tahoe, Nev., $1.98 Beauty Show; appears on TV talk shows, including Tonight Show, Mike Douglas Show, Merv Griffin Show. Served with spl. services br. U.S. Army; Korea. Recipient numerous awards. Office: care Internat Creative Mgmt 8899 Beverly Blvd Los Angeles CA 90048

TAYLOR, ROBERT BERKELEY, bus. exec.; b. St. Thomas, Ont., Can., Sept. 22, 1914; s. Charles Berkeley and Christine Elliott (Coyne) T.; B.A., U. Western Ont., 1941; LL.D., McMaster U., 1976; m. Marian Elizabeth Ingram, Feb. 13, 1943; children—Patricia, Margaret, Paul. Clk., Dominion Bank, London, Ont., 1934-37; faculty U. Western Ont., 1941-42, 45-49, asso. prof. bus. adminstrn., 1948-49; with William Benson & Co., chartered accountants, London, 1941-42, 45-49; with Steel Co. Can., Ltd., Hamilton, Ont., 1949-74, v.p., treas., 1959-74; with Ont. Hydro, Toronto, 1974—, vice chmn., 1974-75, chmn., 1975—. Mem. Canadian-Am. Com.; past chmn. bd. govs. McMaster U.; adv. com. Sch. Bus. Adminstrn. U. Western Ont. Served to lt. Royal Canadian Navy, 1942-45. Fellow Ont. Inst. Chartered Accountants; mem. Delta Upsilon. Mem. United Ch. Clubs: University, Toronto, Lambton Golf and Country. Home: 11 Country Club Dr Islington ON Canada M9A 3J3 Office: Ontario Hydro 700 University Ave Toronto ON M5G 1X6 Canada

TAYLOR, ROBERT CLARK, air force officer; b. Danforth, Ill., July 2, 1932; s. Roy Irving and Margret Louise (Walsh) T.; B.S., U. Md., 1963; M.S., George Washington U., 1965; ed. Indsl. Coll. Armed Forces, 1970, Air Command Staff Coll., 1965; m. Betty J. Densmore, Feb. 26, 1954; children—Dawn Marie, Beverely Ann, Nancy Jean. Served as enlisted man U.S. Air Force, 1951-53, commd. 2d lt., 1953, advanced through grades to maj. gen., 1977; assigned to Nellis AFB, Nev., 1953; pilot Presque Isle AFB, Maine, 1954, Thule Air Base, Greenland, 1954-55, Paine AFB, Wash., 1955-57; aide-de-camp to comdr. 25th Air Div., McChord AFB, Wash., 1957, Hamilton AFB, Calif., 1960; served with 526th Fighter-Interceptor Squadron, Ramstein Air Base, Germany, 1960-62, chief standardization evaluation br., 86th Air Div., 1962-64; dir. Flying tng. Fighter-Interceptor Weapons Sch., Tyndall AFB, Fla., 1965-66, comdr., 1966-67; comdr. F-102 air def. detachment Naval Air Sta., Key West, Fla., 1967-68; aircrew trainee George AFB, Calif., 1968; comdr. 555th Tactical Fighter Squadron and asst. dep. comdr. for ops. of 432d Tactical Reconnaissance Wing, Udorn Royal Thai AFB, Thailand, 1968-69; mil. assigned plans Hdqrs. USAF, 1970-72; asst. to Sec. Def., 1972-74; asst. dep. chief of staff, plans and ops. for plans Pacific Air Forces, Hickam AFB, Hawaii, 1974-75, dep. chief of staff for plans, 1975-77; comdr. 314th Air Div., Pacific Air Forces and comdr. U.S. Air Forces, Korea, at Osan Air Base, Korea, 1977-78; dir. ops. and readiness Hdqrs USAF, Pentagon, 1978—. Decorated D.S.M. with oak leaf cluster, Legion of Merit, D.F.C., Bronze Star, Air medal with 8 oak leaf clusters, Air Force Commendation medal with 3 oak leaf clusters, Presdl. Unit citation. Mem. Air Force Assn. Club: Masons. Home: Quarters 83 Bolling AFB Washington DC 20332 Office: Directorate of Ops and Readiness Pentagon Washington DC 20330

TAYLOR, ROBERT CLEVELAND, lawyer; b. Tulsa, July 31, 1930; s. Eben L. and Jane (Hartshorne) T.; B.A., U. Tulsa, 1952, J.D., 1956; postgrad. So. Meth. U., 1964; m. Barbara B. Kelly, July 25, 1953; children-David Phelps, Kelly Marie, Adrienne Elizabeth, Robert Duff. Admitted to Okla. bar, 1956, Ark. bar, 1965; clk. Tulsa Municipal Ct., 1953-56; asst. v.p. First Nat. Bank & Trust Co., Tulsa, 1956-64; v.p., trust officer City Nat. Bank of Ft. Smith, Ark., 1964-66; partner firm Warner & Smith, and predecessors Ft. Smith, 1966-77, Pryor, Robinson, Taylor & Barry, 1977—. Chmn. membership drive Ft. Smith Symphony Assn., 1964, Ft. Smith Community Concert Assn., 1966. Sebastian County Republican chmn., 1969-70; chmn. Sebastian County Election Commn., 1969-70; bd. dirs. Rosalie Tilles Found., Old Fort Mus. Fellow Am. Coll. Probate Counsel; mem. Am., Ark., Okla. bar assns., Ft. Smith Hist. Soc. (founding dir. 1979), Lambda Chi Alpha, Delta Theta Phi. Clubs: Town, Noon Civics (pres. 1975-76). Home: Bosky Dell Farm Cedarville AR 72932 Office: 315 N 7th St Fort Smith AR 72901

TAYLOR, ROBERT COOPER, educator, phys. chemist; b. Colorado Springs, Colo., May 5, 1917; s. Clarence Egbert and Marjorie C. (Cooper) T.; A.B., Kalamazoo Coll., 1941; Ph.D., Brown U., 1947; m. Evelyn Letitia Seeley, Dec. 27, 1942; children—David Robert, Donald Cooper. Research chemist Manhattan Project, 1942-45; mem. faculty Brown U., 1947-49; mem. faculty U. Mich., Ann Arbor, 1949—, prof. chemistry, 1963—, asso. chmn. dept., 1968—. Vis scientist Los Alamos Sci. Labs., 1974. Mem. Am. Chem. Soc., Am. Phys. Soc., AAAS, Sigma Xi. Asso. editor Inorganic Chemistry, 1964. Home: 850 Heatherway Ann Arbor MI 48104

TAYLOR, ROBERT E. LEE, JR., newspaper exec.; b. Norfolk, Va., June 8, 1913; s. Robert E. Lee and Lelia Symington (Goode) T.; A.B., Princeton U., 1935; m. Leonore McAlpin Shiland, May 23, 1941;

children—Wendy Taylor Foulke, Robert, Lelia. With Phila. Evening and Sunday Bull., 1935—, gen. mgr., 1956-58, pres., 1958-64, publisher, 1964-75, chmn. bd., 1975-78; dir. AP, 1973—; dir., mem. exec. com. Penjerdel Corp. Mem. corporate com. Art Mus.; mem. adv. com. Acad. Music; bd. dirs., mem. exec. com. SE Pa. United Way, Bd. Trade and Convs., Better Bus. Bur. Phila., Childrens Aid Soc., Main Line council Boy Scouts Am.; asso. Nieman Found. Served with USNR, 1942-46. Mem. Am. Newspaper Pubs. Assn. (dir. 1963-72, treas. 1970-71), Am. Newspaper Pubs. Assn. Found. (pres. 1966-68), Am. Newspaper Pubs. Assn. Research Inst. (dir. 1963-72, treas. 1971-72), Bur. of Advt. (dir. 1968-73, 75-79), Greater Phila. C. of C. (past dir.), Ind. Pubs. (chmn. 1975—). Episcopalian. Clubs: Philadelphia; Princeton; Gulph Mills. Office: Evening and Sunday Bull 30th and Market Sts Philadelphia PA 19101

TAYLOR, ROBERT EDWARD, lawyer; b. Ashland, Va., Dec. 21, 1906; s. George William Martin and Florence Ethel (Watson) T.; grad. Randolph-Macon Acad., Bedford, Va., 1923; B.A., U. Va., 1927, LL.B., 1931; m. Margaret Farwell Wayland, Oct. 10, 1936; children—Robert Edward, George W., Helen W. Admitted to Va. bar, 1931, since practiced in Charlottesville; mem. law firm Taylor, Brooks, Zunka & Murray, 1975—. Lectr., U. Va. Law Sch., 1951-68. Mem. Internat. Assn. Ins. Counsel, Am., Va. (pres. 1957-58) bar assns., Delta Upsilon. Methodist. Home: 1602 Grove Rd Charlottesville VA 22901 Office: 433 Park St Charlottesville VA 22901

TAYLOR, ROBERT L., judge; b. Embreeville, Tenn., Dec. 20, 1899; s. Alfred Alexander and Florence Jane (Anderson) T.; Ph.B., Milligan Coll., 1921; student Vanderbilt Law Sch., 1922-23; LL.B., Yale, 1924; m. Florence Fairfax McCain, May 27, 1933; children—Ann, Robert, Admitted to Tenn. bar, 1923; practice law, Johnson City, 1924-49; U.S. judge Eastern Dist. Tenn., 1949—. Trustee Milligan Coll. Mem. Am., Fed., Tenn. bar assns., Jud. Conf. U.S., Am. Judicature Soc., Sigma Alpha Epsilon, Phi Delta Phi, Corby Court. Mem. Christian Ch. Home: 3567 Talahi Dr Knoxville TN 37919 Office: Federal Bldg Knoxville TN 37901

TAYLOR, ROBERT LEE, banker; b. Balt., Jan. 11, 1919; s. Herbert Lee and Ann Marie (O'Keefe) T.; B.A. in Bus. and Indsl. Mgmt., Johns Hopkins, 1948-53; m. Allene Elizabeth Turner, Sept. 29, 1962. With Md. Nat. Bank, Balt., 1953—, asst. cashier, 1960-62, asst. v.p., 1962-64, v.p., 1964-70, vice chmn. finance com., 1967—, sr. v.p. investment mgmt., 1970—; mem. faculty Sch. Bank Adminstrn. Chmn. investments com. Girl Scout council Central Md., 1970-73. Served with USAAF, 1942-45. Mem. Phi Beta Kappa, Phi Beta Kappa Assos. Clubs: Municipal Bond (pres. 1969-70), Homeland Racquet (Balt.); Johns Hopkins, Maryland. Home: 13 Acorn Circle Baltimore MD 21204 Office: PO Box 2218 Baltimore MD 21203

TAYLOR, ROBERT LEWIS, author, journalist; b. So. Ill., Sept. 24, 1912; s. Roscoe Aaron and Mabel (Bowyer) T.; student Southern Ill. U., 1929; A.B., U. Ill., 1930-33; m. Judith Martin, Feb. 3, 1945; children—Martin Lewis, Elizabeth Ann Taylor Peek. Corr., Am. Boy mag., 1935; reporter St. Louis Post Dispatch, 1936-39; profile writer New Yorker mag., 1939-63. Served as lt. comdr. USNR, 1942-46. Recipient Pulitzer prize for The Travels of Jaimie McPheeters, 1959. Mem. Delta Tau Delta. Clubs: Down East Yacht (Boothbay Harbor, Maine); Monte Carlo (Chapala, Mexico); Nautico (Ajijic, Mexico); Oceans Racquet (Daytona Beach, Fla.). Author: Adrift in a Boneyard, 1947; Doctor, Lawyer, Merchant, Chief (collection of mag. articles and stories), 1948; W. C. Fields: His Follies and Fortunes, 1949 (Signet classic edits. 1968; musical W.C. based on book 1971); The Running Pianist, 1950; Professor Fodorski, 1950 (musical All American based on book 1961); Winston Churchill: An Informal Study of Greatness, 1952; The Bright Sands, 1954; Center Ring, The People of the Circus, 1956; The Travels of Jaimie McPheeters 1958 (TV series based on book, 1960; Signet classic edits. 1969); A Journey to Matecumbe, 1961 (film Treasure of Matecumbe 1976); Two Roads to Guadalupe, 1964; Vessel of Wrath: The Life and Times of Carry Nation, 1966; A Roaring in the Wind, 1978; Niagara, 1980; contbr. to New Yorker, Sat. Eve. Post, Life, Collier's, Esquire, Redbook, Reader's Digest. Home: Bulls Bridge Rd South Kent CT 06785 also Ajijic Jalisco Mexico

TAYLOR, ROBERT SAXTON, univ. dean; b. Ithaca, N.Y., June 15, 1918; s. James Barnaby and Flora Estelle (Brown) T.; A.B., Cornell U., 1940; M.S., Columbia, 1950; M.A., Lehigh U., 1954; m. Leni Reichenberger, Aug. 17, 1947. Asso. librarian, dir. Center for Info. Scis., Lehigh U., 1950-67; dir. Library Center, prof. info. sci. Hampshire Coll., 1967-72; dean Sch. Info. Studies, Syracuse (N.Y.) U., 1972—. Cons., NSF, NIH, U.S. Office Edn. Served with CIC, AUS, 1942-46. Decorated Bronze Star medal. Fulbright lectr., Netherlands, 1956-57. Mem. Am. Soc. Info. Sci. (pres. 1968), AAAS (council 1975—), Sigma Xi. Author: Making of a Library, 1972. Editor: Economics of Information Dissemination, 1974. Home: 5085 Skyline Dr Syracuse NY 13215

TAYLOR, ROBERT STEVENS, banker; b. Pitts., July 30, 1929; s. Edward T. and Ruth Virginia (Stevens) T.; B.S., U.S. Naval Acad., 1952; m. Kathryn Nagel, June 14, 1952; children—Kathryn Anne, Robert Stevens, Steven John. With Pitts. Nat. Bank, 1956—, sr. v.p., 1968—. Served to lt. USNR, 1952-56. Mem. Bank Adminstrn. Inst., U.S. Naval Acad. Alumni Assn., U.S. Naval Acad. Athletic Assn., Kappa Sigma. Clubs: Duquesne, St. Clair Country (Pitts.). Home: 732 Brafferton Dr Pittsburgh PA 15228 Office: PO Box 34077 P Pittsburgh PA 15230

TAYLOR, ROBERT WILLIAM, assn. exec.; b. Brownsville, Tenn., July 28, 1929; s. Charles William and Annie Laura (Taliaferro) T.; B.S. in Chemistry, Murray (Ky.) State U., 1949; M.S. in Journalism, Ohio U., 1950; m. Jeanette Henshaw, Jan. 4, 1953; children—Robert William, Teresa, Mark Thomas. Asst. editor Jour. Petroleum Tech., 1953, editor, 1954-63; exec. dir., sec. Am. Inst. Mining, Metall. and Petroleum Engrs., 1963-68; exec. v.p., gen. mgr. Soc. Mfg. Engrs., 1968—; publishing dir. Mfg. Engring., 1968—. Served to 2d lt. USAF, 1951-53. Fellow AAAS; mem. Soc. Mfg. Engrs., Am. Soc. Assn. Execs. (past pres.), Am. Inst. Mining, Metall. and Petroleum Engrs., Jr. Engring. Tech. Soc. (past dir.), Am. Soc. Engring. Edn. (past dir.), Council Engring. and Sci. Soc. Execs. (past pres.), Engrs. Joint Council (dir.). Asso. editor Petroleum Prodn. Handbook, 1961. Home: 3792 Lincoln Rd Birmingham MI 48010 Office: 20501 Ford Rd Dearborn MI 48128

TAYLOR, ROD, actor-producer; b. Sydney, Australia, Jan. 11, 1930; s. William Sturt and Mona (Stewart) T.; student E. Sydney Art Coll., 1944-48; m. Mary Hilem, June 1, 1962 (div. 1969); 1 dau., Felicia Roderica. Came to U.S., 1954, naturalized, 1956. Films include Time Machine, 1960, The Birds, 1964, V.I.P.'s, 1964, Young Cassidy, 1965, Sunday in New York, 1966, Liquidator, 1966, Glass Bottom Boat, 1966, Hotel, 1967, Chuka, 1967, Dark of the Sun, 1968, High Commissioner, 1968, Zabriskie Point, 1969, Man Who Had Power Over Women, 1969, Darker Than Amber, 1970, The Train Robbers, 1973, Trader Horn, 1973, The Deadly Trackers, 1973, Hell River, 1978; TV series Hong Kong, 1960-63, Bearcats, 1971-72, The Oregon Trail, 1977; pres. Rodlor Pictures Inc., 1960—. Recipient Golden Globe award, 1960; Motion Picture Exhibitors Golden Laurel award, 1968. Mem. Producers Guild, Motion Picture Acad. Arts and Scis. Club: Bel Air (Calif.) Country. Office: 315 S Beverly Dr Beverly Hills CA 90212*

TAYLOR, ROGER CONANT, publisher; b. Newport, R.I., Nov. 18, 1931; s. Conant and Marjorie Perry (Buffum) T.; A.B., Harvard, 1953; M.S., Boston U., 1966; m. Priscilla Greene, June 12, 1953; children—Roger Conant, John Dean, Rebecca, Stephen Greene. Commd. ensign U.S. Navy, 1953, advanced through grades to comdr. Res., 1967, ret., 1975; served in destroyers and submarines; editorial dir. U.S. Naval Inst., Annapolis, Md., 1960-69; pres. Internat. Marine Pub. Co., Camden, Maine, 1969—. Mem. U.S. Naval Inst. (life). Author: Good Boats, 1977. Home: 34 High St Camden ME 04843 Office: Internat Marine Pub Co Camden ME 04843

TAYLOR, ROY LEWIS, botanist; b. Olds, Alta., Can., Apr. 12, 1932; s. Martin Gilbert and Crystal (Thomas) T.; B.Sc., Sir George Williams U., Montreal, Que., Can., 1957; Ph.D., U. Cal. at Berkeley, 1962. Pub. sch. tchr. Olds Sch. Div., 1949-52; jr. high sch. tchr. Calgary Sch. Bd., Alta., 1953-55; chief taxonomy sect., research br. Can. Agrl. Dept., Ottawa, Ont., 1962-68; dir. Bot. Garden, prof. botany, prof. plant scis. U. B.C., Vancouver, 1968—. Pres. Western Bot. Services Ltd. Mem. Canadian Bot. Assn. (pres. 1967-68), Biol. Council Can. (pres. 1973—), Am. Inst. Biol. Scis. (dir.), Am. Assn. Bot. Gardens and Arboreta (pres. 1976, 77), Ottawa Valley Curling Assn. (pres. 1968-69). Club: Governor-General's Curling of Canada (life). Author: The Evolution of Canada's Flora, 1966; Flora of the Queen Charlotte Islands, Vols. I and II, 1968; Vascular Plants of British Columbia: A Descriptive Resource Inventory, 1977.

TAYLOR, RYLAND ARTHUR (RILEY), photographer; b. Mpls., Oct. 2, 1912; s. Arthur William and Caroline Marie (Cahlander) T.; ed. high sch.; m. June Audrey Mick, Nov. 23, 1938; children—Ryland Arthur, Linda Marie (Mrs. Jonathan Yoder), William, Mary Louise. Various positions Sears Roebuck & Co., Chgo., 1935-74; pres. Capco., West Chicago, Ill., 1974—; faculty Winona Sch. Profl. Photography, 1962-73, trustee, 1978—. Recipient Photog. Craftsman degree Profl. Photographers Am., 1966, nat. award, 1971, Hon. M.Photography, 1975. Mem. Profl. Photographers Am. (dir. 1967-73, pres. 1975, chmn. bd. 1976). Home: 15 Valewood Rd West Chicago IL 60185

TAYLOR, SAMUEL, lawyer; b. Boston, Nov. 5, 1906; s. Louis and Freda Dora (Pearlson) T.; A.B. magna cum laude, Harvard U., 1927, LL.B., 1930; m. Anna Rose Asher, Dec. 6, 1934; children—Margaret Rose Taylor Gunton, Elizabeth Ann Taylor Meltzer, Jane Deborah Taylor McCoy. Admitted to Mass. bar, 1930, Calif. bar, 1932; law clk. to Supreme Jud. Ct. Mass., Boston, 1930-31; asso. firm Brobeck, Phleger & Harrison, San Francisco, 1931-33; atty. Fed. Emergency Adminstrn. Pub. Works, Washington, 1933-35, regional counsel, 1935-39; atty. IRS, Washington and Los Angeles, 1939-43; pvt. practice, San Francisco, 1943—; partner firm Taylor & Faust, 1975—; prof. taxation Loyola U. Law Sch., Los Angeles, 1941-43; lectr. U. Calif. Law Sch., Berkeley, 1954-70, Stanford U. Law Sch., 1958-60. Bd. dirs., trustee U. Calif. Santa Cruz Found. Mem. Am. Bar Assn., Am. Law Inst., State Bar Calif., Bar Assn. San Francisco, Phi Beta Kappa. Democrat. Jewish. Clubs: World Trade, Concordia-Argonaut (San Francisco). Home: 312 Coleridge Ave Palo Alto CA 94301 Office: 1 California St Suite 2550 San Francisco CA 94111

TAYLOR, SAMUEL ALBERT, playwright; b. Chgo., June 13, 1912; grad. U. Cal. at Berkeley, 1933; m. Suzanne Combes, June 4, 1940; children—Michael W., David C. Pres., Dramatists Play Service, Inc. Club: Century Assn. (N.Y.C.). Author: (plays) The Happy Time, 1950; Sabrina Fair, 1953; (with Cornelia Otis Skinner) The Pleasure of His Company, 1958; First Love, 1961; (with Richard Rodgers) No Strings, 1962; Beekman Place, 1964; Avanti!, 1968; A Touch of Spring, 1975; Legend, 1976; Perfect Pitch, 1976; Gracious Living, 1977. Address: East Blue Hill ME 04629

TAYLOR, SHERRIL WIGHTMAN, broadcasting co. exec.; b. Salt Lake City, Jan. 4, 1924; s. Kenneth E. and Florence May (Wightman) T.; student U. Utah, 1943-46; B.S., U. Mo., 1947; children—Kevin, Sarah; m. 2d, Josephine Vermillion, May 2, 1970. Promotion mgr. KSL Radio, Salt Lake City, 1947-51; sales promotion mgr. CBS, Hollywood, Calif., 1951-53, N.Y.C., 1953-56; v.p. Radio Advt. Bur., N.Y.C., 1956-58; sr. group head J. Walter Thompson, Chgo., 1958-61; ind. TV producer Kukla, Fran, and Ollie Show, N.Y.C., 1961-64; v.p. Nat. Assn. Broadcasters, Washington, 1964-67, dir., 1969-78; v.p. affiliate relations CBS, 1967-79; v.p. Torbet Radio, 1979; cons. Bonneville Internat. Corp., 1979—. Mem. Carnegie Hall Com. for Utah Symphony, Park Ave. Preservation Com.; chmn. Freedom of Info. Fund, U. Mo. Mem. Internat. Radio and TV Soc. (v.p., bd. dirs., pres. bd. dirs. found.), Broadcast Pioneers (dir.), Sigma Chi. Episcopalian. Clubs: Lake Shore (Chgo.); Lochinvar. Author: Radio Programming in Action, 1967. Office: 1 Hammarskold Plaza New York NY 10017

TAYLOR, TELFORD, lawyer, writer; b. Schenectady, Feb. 24, 1908; s. John Bellamy and Marcia Estabrook (Jones) T.; A.B., Williams Coll., 1928, A.M., 1932, LL.D., 1949; LL.B., Harvard, 1932; m. Mary Eleanor Walker, July 2, 1937 (div.); children—Joan, Ellen, John Bellamy II; m. Toby Barbara Golick, Aug. 9, 1974; children—Benjamin Waite, Samuel Bourne. Instr. history and polit. sci. Williams Coll., 1928-29; law clk. to U.S. circuit judge, N.Y.C., 1932-33; asst. solicitor U.S. Dept. Interior, Washington, 1933-34; sr. atty. A.A.A., 1934-35; asso. counsel U.S. Senate com. on inter-state commerce, 1935-39; spl. asst. to atty. gen. U.S., 1939-40; gen. counsel FCC, 1940-42; practiced with Taylor, Scoll, Ferencz & Simon; vis. lectr. Yale Law Sch., 1957-76; vis. lectr. Columbia Law Sch., 1958-63, prof. law, 1963-74, Nash prof., 1974-76, emeritus, 1976—; prof. Cardozo Law Sch., 1976-77, 78—; v.p. prof. Harvard Law Sch., 1977-78. Adminstr., Small Def. Plants Adminstrn., 1951-52; counsel Joint Council for Edn. TV, 1951-61; chmn. N.Y.C. Adv. Bd. Pub. Welfare, 1960-63, mem., 1963-66. Commd. maj. M.I. service U.S. Army, 1942; lt. col. Gen. Staff Corps, 1943, col. (assigned as mil. intelligence officer ETO, 1943-45); asso. counsel, U.S. rep. for prosecution of war criminals, brig. gen., 1946; U.S. chief of counsel for war crimes Office Mil. Govt. (U.S.), 1946-49. Decorated D.S.M. (U.S.); Order Brit. Empire; French Legion of Honor; Polonia Restituta (Poland); comdr. Order of Orange-Nassau (Netherlands), 1950; Lateran Cross, 3d class (Vatican). Overseas fellow Churchill Coll., Cambridge, 1969. Fellow Am. Acad. Arts and Scis.; mem. Am. Law Inst., Am. Mil. Inst., Assn. Bar City N.Y., ASCAP, Res. Officer's Assn., Author's Guild, Mil. Order World Wars, Theta Delta Chi. Democrat. Club: Harvard. Author: Sword and Swastika, 1952; Grand Inquest, 1954; The March of Conquest, 1958; The Breaking Wave, 1967; Two Studies in Constitutional Interpretation, 1969; Nuremberg and Vietnam, 1970; Courts of Terror, 1976; Munich: The Price of Peace, 1979; also articles on polit., legal, mil. subjects. Office: 60 E 42d St New York NY 10017

TAYLOR, THEODORE BREWSTER, physicist; b. Mexico City, Mexico, July 11, 1925 (parents Am. citizens); s. Walter Clyde and Barbara (Howland) T.; grad. Phillips Exeter Acad., 1942; B.S., Calif. Inst. Tech., 1945; Ph.D., Cornell U., 1954; m. Caro Dwight Arnim, June 13, 1948; children—Clare E., Katherine W., Christopher H., Robert P., Jeffrey J. Theoretical physicist U. Calif. Radiation Lab., Berkeley, 1946-49, Los Alamos Sci. Lab., 1949-56; sr. research adviser Gen. Atomic div. Gen. Dynamics Corp., San Diego, 1956-64; dep. dir. (sci.) Def. Atomic Support Agy., Dept. Def., 1964-67; chmn. bd. Internat. Research & Tech. Corp., 1967-76; vis. lectr. Princeton U., 1976—; mem. Pres.'s Commn. on Accident at Three-Mile Island, 1979; cons. Los Alamos Sci. Lab., 1956-64, Aerospace Corp., 1960-61, Air Force Sci. Adv. Bd., 1955-58, AEC, 1966-70, Def. Atomic Support Agy., 1966-69, U.S. Army Sci. Adv. Panel, 1967-71, Office of Tech. Assessment, 1976—, Rockefeller Found., 1977—; chmn. Los Alamos Study Group, Air Force Space Study Com., 1961; mem. panel outer space ACDA, 1961. Served to ensign USNR, 1942-46. Recipient Ernest Orlando Lawrence award, 1965. Mem. AAAS, Am. Phys. Soc., Internat. Solar Energy Soc. Home: 10325 Bethesda Church Rd Damascus MD 20750 Office: Dept Mech and Aerospace Engring Engring Quadrangle Princeton U Princeton NJ 08540

TAYLOR, THEODORE LANGHANS, author; b. Statesville, N.C., June 23, 1921; s. Edward Riley and Elnora Alma (Langhans) T.; student Fork Union Mil. Acad., 1939-40, U.S. Mcht. Marine Acad., 1942-44; m. Gweneth Ann Goodwin, Oct. 25, 1946; children—Mark, Wendy, Michael. Reporter, Portsmouth (Va.) Star, 1941-42, Bluefield (W.Va.) News, 1946-47; sportswriter NBC-Radio, N.Y.C., 1942; asst. dir. pub. relations N.Y. U., 1947-48; dir. pub. relations YMCA Schs. and Colls., N.Y.C., 1948-50; publicist Paramount Pictures, Hollywood, Calif., 1955-56; asso. producer Perlberg-Seaton Prodns., Hollywood, 1956-61; free-lance writer, 1961—; author: The Magnificent Mitscher, 1954; Fire on the Beaches, 1957; People Who Make Movies, 1968; The Cay, 1969; The Children's War, 1971; Air Raid: Pearl Harbor, 1971; The Maldonado Miracle, 1973; Rebellion Town, 1973; (screenplay) Showdown, 1973; Teetoncey, 1974; Teetoncey and Ben O'Neal, 1975; Battle in the Arctic Seas, 1976; The Odyssey of Ben O'Neal, 1977; A Shepherd Watches, A Shepherd Sings, 1977; Jule, 1979. Served with USNR, 1945-46, 50-55. Recipient Jane Addams Children's Book Award for The Cay, 1970; Lewis Carroll Shelf award, 1970. Commonwealth Club Silver medal, 1970; Best Book award, So. Cal. Council on Children's Lit., 1970; Best Book award U. Calif. at Irvine, 1970, 74. Mem. Calif. Writers Guild, Acad. Motion Picture Arts and Scis., Screen Writers Guild. Republican. Lutheran. Address: 730 Griffith Way Laguna Beach CA 92651

TAYLOR, THEOPHILUS MILLS, clergyman, educator; b. Cedarville, Ohio, June 22, 1909; s. Mills J. and Martha Slater (Dill) T.; student Muskingum Coll., 1927-30, D.D. (hon.), 1944; B.Arch., U. Pa., 1935; M.Div., Pitts.-Xenia Theol. Sem., 1941; postgrad. U. Chgo., 1946; Ph.D. in Religion, Yale, 1956; m. Lois Dean McLaughlin, Mar. 12, 1936; children—Martha Renwick, Theophilus Mills III, Jessica Anne, Frances Caroline. Tchr. gen. sci., indsl. arts Woodstock Sch., India, 1935-38; ordained to ministry U.P. Ch., 1941; asst. pastor First Presbyn. Ch., Crafton, Pa., 1940-41; pastor U.P. Ch., Barnet Center, Vt., 1941-43; John McNaugher prof. N.T. lit. and exegesis Pitts.-Xenia Theol. Sem., 1943-59, dean dept. grad. studies, 1946-59; prof. Pitts. Theol. Sem., 1960-62; sec. gen. council Gen. Assembly U.P. Ch. U.S.A., 1962-72, also chmn. Ch. Exec. Devel. Bd., 1968-74; pres. Religion in Am. Life, 1970-73. Asst. dir. archeol. excavations, Beitin, Jordan, 1957, 60; U.P. rep. Am. com. World Council Chs., 1946-48, del. constituting assembly, 1948, rep. to Conf. U.S.A. Mem. Chs., 1948-61; del. 16th Gen. Council of Alliance Ref. Chs., Geneva, 1948, 18th Gen. Council, Sao Paolo, 1959; del. 3d World Conf. on Faith and Order, Lund, Sweden, 1952, 4th conf., Montreal, 1963; del. 2d assembly World Council Chs., Evanston, Ill., 1954, adviser 3d assembly, New Delhi, 1961, mem. com. religion and pub. edn. Pa. Council Christian Edn., 1950-54; sec. joint drafting com. Conf. Ch. Union of Presbyn. U.S.A. and U.P. Chs., 1955-57; moderator gen. assembly U.P. Ch. U.S.A., 1958-59, chmn. commn. ecumenical mission and relations, 1959-62; mem. working com. Commn. Faith and Order, World Council Chs., 1952-71, mem. Commn., 1952-75, chmn. theol. commn. Holy Eucharist, faith and order, 1965-71; mem. exec. com., gen. bd., chmn. gen. constituent membership com. Nat. Council Chs., U.S.A. 1960-72; sec. Am. Council for Boys' Indsl. Home and Tech. Sch., Gujranwala, India, 1944-62. Bd. dirs. Center for Interfaith Research on Religious Architecture; mem. corp. Nyack (N.Y.) Hosp., 1965-72; trustee Muskingum Coll., 1965-78. Mem. Archaeol. Inst. Am., Soc. Bibl. Lit. and Exegesis, Guild for Religious Architecture, Presbyn. Hist. Soc. (pres. 1964-71), Studiorum Novi Testamenti Societos, Internat. Assn. Fed. Union (mem. council, 1972—, pres. 1973—), Am. Oriental Soc. Author: Uncleanness and Purification in Paul, 1956. Asso. editor The United Presbyn., 1947-56; editorial council Theology Today, Princeton, N.J., 1951-73. Contbr. editorials, articles, book revs. to religious jours.; chpts. to Stewardship in Contemporary Life, 1965, Assignment: Overseas, 1966; For Me to Live, 1972. Home: Old Tabor House Topsham VT 05076

TAYLOR, THOMAS NORWOOD, educator, botanist; b. Lakewood, Ohio, June 14, 1937; s. Allyne Charles and Velma Rosemary T.; A.B., Miami U., 1960; Ph.D., U. Ill., Urbana, 1964; postdoctoral fellow Yale, 1964-65; m. Judith C. Taylor, Jan. 30, 1960; children—Tamara, Traci, Trisha, Todd, Trevor. Mem. faculty U. Ill., Ohio U., Athens; mem. faculty Ohio State U., Columbus, now prof. botany, chmn. dept. Mem. sch. bd., Downers Grove, Ill., 1966-67. NSF grantee, 1964—. Mem. Bot. Soc. Am., Paleontol. Assn., Internat. Assn. Plant Morphology, Sigma Xi. Research with fossil plants, electron microscopy of pollen and spores. Home: 2077 Westover St Columbus OH 43221

TAYLOR, WALLACE GINGELL, chem. co. exec.; b. LaPorte, Ind., Sept. 25, 1919; s. Henry and Adele Mae (Wallace) T.; B.C.S., Benjamin Franklin U., 1941; m. Dorothy Eastburn, Apr. 17, 1943 (div. 1966); children—Marlena, Robert, Dorothy; m. 2d, Diane Millian, May 5, 1973. Auditor, Kingsbury Ordnance Plant, LaPorte, 1941-42, Green River Ordnance Plant, Dixon, Ill., 1942-43; treas., controller H.P. Smith Paper Co., Chgo., 1945-53; with Am. Cyanamid Co., Wayne, N.J., 1953-67, treas., 1961-67, dir. investor relations, 1973—; treas. Ariz. Chem. Co., 1961-67; treas., dir. Formica Corp., 1961-67, pres., 1967-73, also dir. Mayor, Mountain Lakes, N.J., 1961-64. Address: 1530 Palisade Ave Fort Lee NJ 07024

TAYLOR, WILLIAM CLARENCE, civil engr.; b. Clyde, Ohio, Feb. 19, 1937; s. Irvin William and Blanche (Wright) T.; B.S.C.E., Case Inst. Tech., 1959, M.S.C.E., 1963; Ph.D., Ohio State U., 1967; m. Norma Nuti, June 13, 1960; children—Andrea, William, Colette, Brent, Matthew. Asst. traffic engr. City of Cleve., 1960; instr. Fenn Coll. Engring., 1961-62; research asso. Ohio State U., 1963-64; dir. traffic research Ohio Dept. Hwys., Columbus, 1965-67; asst. prof. civil engring. Wayne State U., 1967-70, asso. prof., 1970-72; prof. civil and san. engring., chmn. dept. civil and san. engring. Mich. State U., 1972—; dir. Interagy. Transp. Council, Exec. Office of Gov. Mich., Lansing, 1969-72; sci. adv. to gov., 1972—; cons. in field. Chmn., Mich. Gov.'s Land Use Commn., 1970-72, Mich. Gov.'s Task Force on SEAFARER, 1974, on High Level Radioactive Waste Disposal, 1976-77, on Low Level Radioactive Waste, 1978, on Cancer, 1978, on Fluoride, 1979. NSF grantee, 1968-70; Dept. Transp. grantee, 1974-76; Mich. Dept. Transp. grantee, 1970—. Mem. ASCE, Inst. Transp. Engrs. (Past Pres.'s award 1964), Am. Soc. Engring. Educators, Transp. Research Bd. Republican. Roman Catholic. Office: Coll Engring Mich State U East Lansing MI 48824

TAYLOR, WILLIAM DAVIS, newspaperman; b. Boston, Apr. 2, 1908; s. William Osgood and Mary (Moseley) T.; student Harvard, 1927-31; LL.D., Colby Coll., 1968; D.Journalism, Suffolk U., 1974; D.Humane Services, Mass. Maritime Acad., 1975; m. Mary Hammond, 1931 (dec. 1947); children—William Osgood, Anna (Mrs. Ann Taylor Freeman); m. 2d, Ann C. Macy, Nov. 1947; children—Thomas Macy, Margaret Moseley, Wendy Elizabeth, James Morgan. With Globe Newspaper Co., 1931—, treas., 1937-40, gen. mgr., 1940, pub. Boston Globe, 1955—, also chmn. bd., 1963—; chmn. bd., dir. Affiliated Publs., Inc.; dir. Met-Sunday Newspapers, Inc., N.Y.C., Million Market Neswpapers, Inc. Past chmn. bd. Am. Comml. Fish Expn., Inc.; mem. exec. bd. Boston council Boy Scouts Am.; bd. dirs. Am. Cancer Soc., Hurricane Island Outward Bound Sch.; bd. overseers Harvard, Vineyard Open Land Found.; past pres. bd. trustees Noble and Greenough Sch., Dedham, Mass., Woods Hole Oceanographic Instn. Recipient Elijah Lovejoy award Colby Coll., 1975. Mem. Am. Newspaper Pubs. Assn. (past pres. and dir.). Office: Boston Globe 135 Morrissey Blvd Boston MA 02107

TAYLOR, WILLIAM EWART, JR., archaeologist; b. Toronto, Ont., Can., Nov. 21, 1927; s. William Ewart and Margaret (Patrick) T.; B.A., U. Toronto, 1951; A.M., U. Ill., 1952; Ph.D., U. Mich., 1965; D.U.C. (hons.), U. Calgary, 1975; m. Joan Elliott, Sept. 12, 1952; children—Alison, Beth, William. Arctic archaeologist Nat. Museums of Can., 1956-60, chief archaeology div., 1960-67; prof. U. Alaska, 1966; dir. human history br. Nat. Museums of Can., 1967-68; dir. Nat. Mus. of Man, Ottawa, Ont., 1968—. Fellow Am. Anthrop. Assn., Arctic Inst. N.Am.; AAAS, Royal Geog. Soc., Royal Anthrop. Inst.; mem. Internat. Union Anthrop. and Ethnol. Scis., Internat. Union Prehistoric and protohistoric Scis., Sigma Xi. Clubs: National Press, Ottawa Ski. Contbr. articles in field of arctic archaeology to profl. jours. Home: 509 Piccadilly Ave Ottawa ON K1Y 0H7 Canada Office: Nat Mus of Man Metcalfe and McLeod Sts Ottawa ON K1A 0M8 Canada

TAYLOR, WILLIAM JAMES, transp. co. exec.; b. Eddystone, Pa., July 29, 1926; s. William J. and Clara Ella (Harris) T.; A.B., Dickinson Coll., 1949; J.D., U. Pa., 1952; m. Jane Currie, Oct. 18, 1958; children—Deborah Ann, Timothy J., Jeffrey Harris. Admitted to Pa. bar, 1953, N.Y. bar, 1961, also U.S. Supreme Ct.; law clk. to chief justice Supreme Ct. Pa., 1952- 53; mem. legal dept. Pa. R.R., 1953-61; mem. law dept. REA Express, 1961-62, gen. counsel, 1962-65, v.p., gen. counsel, 1965-66, exec. v.p., gen. counsel, 1966, pres., chief exec. officer, 1966-68, chmn., 1968-69; v.p. Ill. Central Gulf R.R., 1969-74; v.p. govtl. affairs I.C. Industries, 1969-74, v.p. legal affairs, 1974-76; pres., chief exec. officer Ill. Central Gulf R.R., 1976—, also dir.; legis. counsel to trustees Penn Central R.R., 1971-74. Trustee Dickinson Coll. Served with USNR, 1944-46. Mem. Am. Bar Assn., Assn. ICC Practitioners, C. of C., Newcomen Soc. N.Am., Sigma Chi, Omicron Delta Kappa. Clubs: Congressional Country, Internat. (Washington); Chgo.; Barrington Hills (Ill.). Office: 233 N Michigan Ave Chicago IL 60601

TAYLOR, WILLIAM O., newspaper exec.; b. Boston, July 19, 1932; s. William Davis and Mary (Hammond) T.; B.A., Harvard U., 1954; m. Sally Coxe, June 20, 1959; children—William Davis II, Edmund C., Augustus R. With Globe Newspaper Co., Boston, 1956—, treas., 1963—, bus. mgr., 1965-69, gen. mgr., 1969—, now pres., pub.; dir. Met. Sunday Newspapers, Million Market Newspapers, Inc. Bd. dirs. Am. Press Inst., United Way of Mass. Bay, United South End Settlement. pres. Cotting Sch. for Handicapped Children, 1973—; bd. overseers Boys' Clubs Boston; trustee New Eng. Aquarium. Served with AUS, 1954-56. Office: 135 William T Morrissey Blvd Boston MA 02107*

TCHERKASSKY, MARIANNA ALEXSAVENA, ballerina; b. Glen Cove, N.Y., Oct. 28, 1952; d. Alexis and Lillian (Oka) Tcherkassky; student Washington Sch. Ballet (scholar), 1965-67, Sch. Am. Ballet and Profl. Children's Sch., 1967-70; pupil of Edward Caton. Appeared with Bolshoi Ballet in Ballet Sch., 1961, 62, N.Y.C. Ballet in A Midsummer Night's Dream, 1963; profl. debut with Andre Eglevsky Ballet Co., 1968; mem. Am. Ballet Theatre, 1970—, soloist, 1972—, prin. dancer, 1976—; guest appearances throughout U.S. and in Europe, also on TV. Winner Nat. Soc. Arts and Letters competition, 1967; Ford Found. scholar, 1967-70. Address: care Am Ballet Theatre 888 7th Ave New York NY 10019*

TEAFF, GRANT GARLAND, football coach; b. Snyder, Tex., Nov. 12, 1933; s. Bill and Inez (Grant) T.; student San Angelo Coll., 1951-53, McMurry Coll., 1953-56; m. Donell Phillips, Nov. 1, 1956; children—Tammy, Tracy, Layne. Asst. coach Tom S. Lubbock High Sch., 1956-57; head football coach, head track coach McMurry U., 1960-66; head coach, recruiting coordinator Tex. Technol. Coll., 1966-69; coach Angelo State U., 1969-72; football coach Baylor U., Waco, Tex., 1972—; head coach South squad Blue-Gray All-Star Game, Montgomery, Ala., 1973, All Am. Game, 1975, East-West Shrine Game, 1977; coach Tex. Sr. Coll., 1973-74. Named Coach of Year UPI-AP, Nat. Football Writers Assn. Author: I Believe. Home: 8265 Forest Ridge Waco TX 76710

TEAGUE, BARRY ELVIN, U.S. atty.; b. Dayton, Ohio, Mar. 10, 1944; s. Arthur Leo and Mary Catherine (Pendley) T.; B.A., Asbury Coll., 1966; J.D., Jones Law Sch., 1971; m. Dianne Duke, Dec. 30, 1966; 1 son, Matthew Patrick. Tchr., coach Montgomery County (Ala.) Sch. System, 1966-68, tchr., 1968-71; admitted to Ala. bar, 1972; dep. clk. U.S. Dist. Ct., Middle Dist. Ala., 1971-73; asst. atty. gen. Ala., 1973-74; chief dep. dist. atty. 15th Jud. Circuit Ala., 1974-77; U.S. atty. for Middle Dist. Ala., 1977—. Mem. Fed., Ala., Montgomery County (dir. young lawyers sect.) bar assns., Ala. (state govt. affairs chmn.), Montgomery (dir., legal counsel) jr. chambers commerce. Democrat. Methodist. Home: 5351 Surrey Rd Montgomery AL 36109 Office: PO Box 197 Montgomery AL 36101

TEAGUE, DONALD, artist; b. Bklyn., Nov. 27, 1897; s. Edwin Dawes and Frances (Ireland) T.; student Art Students League N.Y., 1916-17, 19-20; also studied in London, Eng.; m. Verna Timmins, July 19, 1938; children—Linda, Hilary. Began as illustrator, 1921; illus. for Sat. Eve. Post, McCall's, Collier's, Woman's Home Companion, Am., other mags.; illustrated under pseudonym of Edwin Dawes; paintings exhibited Met. Mus. Art, Nat. Acad. Design Bklyn. Mus., Art Inst. Chgo., Toledo Mus., Royal Watercolor Soc., London, Eng., Conn. Acad., Tokyo Mus., Kyoto Mus., Mus. Watercolor, Mexico City, others, represented in Va. Mus. Fine Arts, Richmond, Frye Mus. Seattle, Collection of State of Calif., Sacramento, Collection of USAF, Colorado Springs, Colo., Mills Coll. Art Gallery, Oakland, Calif., U. Oreg., Eugene, U. Kans., Lawrence, Nat. Cowboy Hall of Fame, Phoenix Mus. Art, several pvt. collections. Recipient J. Francis Murphy Meml. prize Nat. Acad., 1932; Grant prize New Rochelle Art Assn., 1935; Thumb Box prize Salmagundi Club, 1936; Isador watercolor prize, 1939; Zabriskie prize Am. Watercolor Soc., 1944; Winsor & Newton prize, 1954; 1st watercolor prize Nat. Acad., 1947, 49, 52, 59, 65; 1st watercolor prize Soc. Western Artists, 1952, 53, 54; 1st watercolor prize Calif. State Fair, 1952; Gold medal Am. Watercolor Soc., 1953; 1st watercolor prize Santa Cruz Art Assn., 1954; Newcastle Meml. award, 1955, Am. Artist Mag. medal of honor, 1957, Silver medal of Honor Am. Watercolor Soc., 1961, Grand award and Gold medal of Honor, 1964; S.F.B. Morse Gold medal for Watercolor, Nat. Acad., 1962, certificate of Merit Royal Acad. London, 1963; Resolution Commendation Senate State Cal., 1964; Butler prize American Watercolor Soc., 1966, Saportas award, 1967, Oehler award, 1968; Jurors Spl. mention 1st Internat. Exhbn. Marietta Coll., 1968; Obrig prize Nat. Acad., 1969; Lehmann award Am. Watercolor Soc., 1969; Best in Show award Soc. Western Artists, 1969.; Today's Art medal of merit Am. Watercolor Soc., 1971; silver medal for watercolor Cowboy Artists of Am., 1971; William A. Paton award Nat. Acad., 1972; award for excellence Marietta Coll., 1972; gold medal for watercolor Cowboy Artists of Am., 1972, Nat. Cowboy Hall of Fame, 1973, 75; gold medal for Western art Franklin Mint, 1973, 74, for watercolor, 1974. Mem. N.A.D., Nat. Acad. Western Art (Bronze medal 1976, Silver medal for watercolor 1977), Cowboy Artists Am. (Gold medal for watercolor 1977, Silver medal for mixed media 1978), Am. Watercolor Soc. (hon.) Republican. Club: Bohemian (San Francisco), Salmagundi (hon.). Address: PO Box 745 Carmel CA 93921

TEAGUE, JOSEPH GRANT, med. equipment mfg. co. exec.; b. Providence, Ky., Sept. 27, 1933; s. Carroll Hoyt and Ruth (Thompson) T.; B.S. in Mech. Engring., U. Ky., 1956, M.S., 1958; postgrad. Case Western Res. U.; m. Suzanne Wallace, June 4, 1955; 1 son, Mark Wallace. Test engr. Pratt & Whitney Aircraft Co., 1956; devel. engr. Sandia Corp., Albuquerque, 1958-63; program mgr. TRW Inc., Los Angeles and Cleve., 1962-68; mgmt. cons. McKinsey & Co., Cleve., 1968-70; pres. Ohio-Nuclear Inc., 1970-78, Technicare Corp., Cleve., 1978—. Mem. Nat. Elec. Mfrs. Assn. (dir. diagnostic imaging sect., chmn. med. instruments sect.), Phi Delta Theta. Republican. Methodist.

TEAGUE, ROBERT STERLING, educator, pharmacologist; b. Montgomery, Ala., July 13, 1913; s. Robert S. and Sara (Clark) T.; A.B., U. Ala., 1933; M.S., Northwestern U., 1936; M.D., U. Chgo., 1937, Ph.D., 1939; m. Bobby Elgin, Dec. 28, 1935; 1 dau., Katherine E. (Mrs. J.H. Young); m. 2d, Beulah Pittman Shea, Aug. 5, 1961; stepchildren—Michael Bradford, Richard John, Mary Catherine (Mrs. W.C. Hare III), Jane Elizabeth (Mrs. S.Y. Bashinsky, Jr.). Asst., Inst. Neurology, Northwestern U., 1935-36; asst. pharmacology U. Chgo., 1937-39; instr. Tulane U. Sch. Medicine, 1939-43, asst. prof., 1943; asso. prof. Med. Coll. Ala., 1943-48; prof., chmn. dept. pharmacology Sch. Medicine and Sch. Dentistry, U. Ala., Birmingham, 1948-78, prof. emeritus, 1978—; Lewis Cass Ledyard, Jr. fellow N.Y. Hosp. and Cornell U. Sch. Medicine, 1941-42. Fellow AAAS; mem. Am. Soc. Zoology, N.Y. Acad. Scis., Am. Soc. Pharmacology and Exptl. Therapeutics, Endocrine Soc., Soc. Exptl. Biology and Medicine, Soc. Toxicology, Phi Beta Kappa, Sigma Xi, Phi Delta Theta, Phi Chi. Home: 3644 Montevallo Rd Birmingham AL 35213

TEAGUE, SAM FULLER, chem. co. exec.; b. Birmingham, Ala., Aug. 2, 1918; s. Sam Fuller and Virginia (White) T.; B.S., Auburn U., 1939; m. Frances Middleton, July 2, 1939; children—John Russell, Melanie Olivia. Chemist, Sloss-Sheffield Steel & Iron Co., Birmingham, 1939-40; asst. dir. sales Monsanto Chem. Co., St. Louis, 1945-60; gen. mgr. sales ITT Rayonier, Inc., N.Y.C., 1960-67, v.p. planning and devel., 1967-68, sr. v.p., 1968-72, v.p., product mgr., paper and splty. pulp sales, 1972-78, v.p., dir. pulp sales, 1978—, also dir.; dir., mem. exec. com. Rayonier Can. Served to lt. col. AUS, 1940-45. Decorated Bronze Star with oak leaf cluster. Mem. Am. Chem. Soc., Salesmen's Assn. Am. Chem. Industry (past dir.). Congregationalist (deacon). Clubs: Town (past sec., dir.) (Newcastle); Whippoorwill (pres. 1968-69, gov.) (Armonk, N.Y.); Chemists (trustee 1970, pres. 1976-77) (N.Y.C.). Home: 1 Strawberry Hill Ct Stamford CT 06902 Office: 1177 Summer St Stamford CT 06904

TEAGUE, WAYNE, state edn. ofcl.; b. Cullman, Ala., Nov. 19, 1927; s. Levi Wade and Floy Irene (McKelvey) T.; B.S., Auburn U., 1950, M.S., 1953, Ed.D., 1962; LL.D., Troy State U., 1978; m. Eleanor Josephine Jones, June 5, 1949; children—Karen Jo, Dewey Wayne. Tchr., coach, asst. prin. Heard High Sch., Franklin, Ga., 1950-55; prin. Marion County Elem. and High Sch., Buena, Vista, Ga. 1955-56, Jonesboro (Ga.) Sr. High Sch., 1956-58, S.W. DeKalb High Sch., Decatur, Ga., 1958-63; coordinator field services Sch. Edn., dir. correspondence study, asso. prof. ednl. adminstrn. Auburn (Ala.) U., 1963-69; supt. Auburn City Schs., 1969-75; state supt. edn. Ala. Dept. Edn., 1975—. Served with USAAC, 1946. Methodist. Club: Masons. Office: 501 Dexter Ave Montgomery AL 36130

TEAL, GORDON KIDD, phys. scis. cons.; b. Dallas, Jan. 10, 1907; s. Olin Allison and Azelia Clyde (Kidd) T.; A.B. with spl. honors in Math., (Silberstein, Boggess scholar), Baylor U., 1927, LL.D., 1969; Sc.M. (Marston scholar), Brown U., 1928, Ph.D. (U. fellow, Metcalfe fellow), 1931, Sc.D., 1969; m. Lyda Louise Smith, Mar. 7, 1931; children—Robert Carroll, Donald Fraser, Stephen O'Banion Teal. Mem. research staff Bell Telephone Labs., N.Y.C., Murray Hill, N.J., 1930-53; research asso. Columbia U., 1932-35; asst. v.p., dir. materials and components research Tex. Instruments, Dallas, 1953-55, asst. v.p., dir. research, dir. Central Research Labs., 1955-61, asst. v.p. research, engring., 1961-62, asst. v.p., internat. tech. dir., 1962-65, asst. v.p. charge tech. devel. equipment group, 1967-68, v.p., chief scientist corp. devel., 1968-72, cons. to industry and govt., 1972— dir. Inst. for Materials Research Nat. Bur. Standards, Washington, 1964-67; cons. Dept. Def., 1956-64, 70-72, NASA, 1970-72, Nat. Bur. Standards, 1972-73. Chmn. exec. tech. devel. bd. Poly. Inst. Bklyn., 1963-72. Mem. materials adv. bd. Nat. Acad. Scis.-NRC, 1960-64, ad hoc com. on materials and processes for electron devices, 1970-72, adv. panel Inst. Applied Tech., Nat. Bur. Standards, 1969-75, chmn. Nat. Acad. Scis.-NRC adv. panel electronic tech. div., 1972-75, panel for study research facilities and sci. opportunities in use of low and medium energy neutrons, 1977-78, del., Republic of China, 1975. Mem. pres.'s council Calif. Inst. Tech., 1969-71; trustee Brown U., 1969-74, trustee emeritus, 1974—; trustee Baylor U., Baylor U. Med. Center, Dallas, 1970-79; vis. com. elec. engring. dept. U. Tex., 1969-73; mem. U. Tex. at Austin Sch. Arts and Scis. Found. Adv. Council, 1972—. Recipient Distinguished Alumni award Baylor U., 1965; Inventor of Yr. award Patent, Trademark and Copyright Research Inst., George Washington U., 1966; Am. Acad. Achievement award, 1967; Medal of Honor, IEEE, 1968; Creative Invention award Am. Chem. Soc., 1970, Doherty award Dallas-Ft. Worth chpt., 1974; 50th Anniversary Grad. Sch. citation Brown U., 1978; Omicron Delta Kappa outstanding alumnus award Baylor U., 1978. Fellow IEEE (past dir.; editorial bd., awards bd.), Am. Inst. Chemists (50th ann. meeting honor scroll, fellows lectr. 1973), AAAS (v.p., chmn. indsl. sci. sect. 1969, mem. council 1968-71, mem. com. council affairs 1969-71, chmn. com. on industry, tech. and soc. 1972-74), Tex. Acad. Sci. (past pres.), Washington Acad. Sci., Instn. Elec. Engrs. U.K. (chartered elec. engr.); mem. Nat. Acad. Engring. (aeros. and space bd., 1970-73), Council Sci. Socs. Dallas-Ft. Worth (dir., past chmn. bd., chmn. exec. com.), Am. Phys. Soc., Am. Chem. Soc., Electrochemical Soc., Sigma Xi, Sigma Pi Sigma (hon.), Kappa Epsilon Alpha. Clubs: Athenaeum (London); Cosmos (Washington). Contbr.: Transistor Technology, 1952, 58, Microelectronics, 1965, Washington Colloquium on Science and Society, 1967; co-editor Technology Forecast for 1980, 1971; Materials and Processes for Electron Devices, 1972; Bicentennial issue IEEE Transactions on Electron Devices, 1976. Editorial adv. bd. Internat. Jour. Solid State Electronics, 1960-68; contbr. articles to profl. jours. Co-developer junction transistor; inventor, grown junction method making junction transistor structures. Holder 64 patents in U.S. and abroad. Address: 5222 Park Ln Dallas TX 75220

TEAL, JOHN JEROME, JR., educator, ecologist; b. N.Y.C., Feb. 7, 1921; s. John Jerome and Isabelle (O'Sullivan) T.; B.S., Harvard U., 1944; M.A., Yale U., 1946; m. Penelope Holden, May 6, 1950 (div. 1971); children—Pamela N., Ptarmigan P., John A., Lansing H. First sr. fellow McGill U. Arctic Inst. N. Am., 1951-52; traveling fellow Carnegie Corp., 1950-51; research asso. McGill U., 1951-52; fellow Ford Found., 1958; asso. prof. anthropology and geography U. Vt., 1958-59; prof. human ecology U. Alaska, 1964-77; numerous arctic expdns., 1946—; spl. research domestication of musk ox; pres. Inst. No. Agrl. Research, 1954—. Chmn., Fairbanks Sister City Com., 1965-66, Fairbanks PTA, 1966-67, Interior Alaska chpt. Am. Scandinavian Found., 1966-67. Served as pilot USAAF, World War II. Decorated D.F.C., Air medal (6). Lithow Osborne Travelling fellow, 1966-67. Mem. AAAS, Am. Anthrop. Soc., Fedn. Am. Scientists, Am. Soc. Mammalogists, Norwegian Polar Soc., N.Y. Acad. Scis., Conn. Acad. Arts and Scis., Sigma Xi. Author: Gift of Dominion. Contbr. articles to profl. jours., spl. TV programs on human ecology. Home: Tunturi Huntington Center VT 05462 also Box 447 Bainbridge Island WA 98110

TEALE, EDWIN WAY, author, naturalist; b. Joliet, Ill., June 2, 1899; s. Oliver Cromwell and Clara Louise (Way) T.; grad. Joliet Township High Sch.; student U. Ill., 1918; A.B., Earlham Coll., 1922, Litt.D., 1957; A.M., Columbia U., 1926; L.H.D., Ind. U., 1970; Sc.D., U. New Haven, 1978: m. Nellie Imogene Donovan, Aug. 1, 1923; 1 son, David Allen (dec.). Instr. pub. speaking Friends U., Wichita, Kans., 1922-24; editorial asst. to Dr. Frank Crane, 1925-27; staff feature writer, Popular Sci. Monthly, 1928-41; free lance writer, 1941—. Revised insect-study program Boy Scouts Am., 1944. Recipient John Burroughs medal, 1943, Christopher award, 1957; Ind. U. Writers Conf. award, 1960; Secondary Edn. Bd.'s Ann. Book award, 1961; Eva L. Gordon award Am. Nature Study Soc., 1965; Sarah Chapman Francis medal, 1965; Sarah Josepha Hale award, 1975; Ecology award Mass. Hort. Soc., 1975; Conservation Medal New Eng. Wildflower Soc., 1975. Fellow AAAS, N.Y. Acad. Scis. (council 1942-49); mem. Royal Photog. Soc. (asso.), N.Y. (v.p. 1943, pres. 1944), Bklyn. (pres. 1949, 50, 53) entomol. socs., Am. Nature Study Soc. (pres. 1947), Baldwin Bird Club (pres. 1942-43), Nat. Audubon Soc. Thoreau Soc. (pres. 1958), Am. Ornithologists' Union, Linnaean Soc. N.Y., Conn. Entomol. Soc. (hon.). Methodist. Club: Explorers; Appalachian Mountain (corr.). Author: The Book of Gliders, 1930, rev. edit., 1939; Grassroot Jungles, 1937, rev. edit., 1944; Boys Book of Insects, 1939; Boys' Book of Photography, 1939; The Golden Throng, 1940; Byways to Adventure, 1942; Near Horizons; The Story of an Insect Garden, 1942; Dune Boy, The Early Years of a Naturalist, 1943; Armed Services Ed., 1944; Insect Life, 1944; The Lost Woods, 1945; Days Without Time, 1948; W. H. Hudson's Green Mansions, 1949 (intro.); North With The Spring, 1951; Insect Friends, 1955; Autumn Across America, 1956; Adventures in Nature, 1959; Journey Into Summer, 1960; The Lost Dog, 1961; The Bees, 1961; The Strange Lives of Familiar Insects, 1962; Wandering Through Winter, 1965 (Pulitzer prize 1966); Springtime in Britain, 1970; Photographs of American Nature, 1972; A Naturalist Buys an Old Farm, 1974; books also pub. in Brit. Swedish, Spanish, French, Finnish, Arabian and Braille edits. Editor, illustrator Walden, by Henry Thoreau, 1946; editor The Insect World of J. Henri Fabre, 1949; Green Treasury (Nature anthology) 1952; Circle of the Seasons, 1953; (Intro.) M. Maeterlinck's The Life of the Bee, 1954; The Wilderness World of John Muir, 1954; The Long Island Naturalist; The Thoughts of Thoreau, 1962; Audubon's Wildlife, 1964; The American Seasons, 1976; A Walk Through the Year, 1978; contbg. editor Audubon Mag., 1942—. Home: Trail Wood Hampton CT 06247

TEAR, ROBERT, tenor; b. Barry, South Wales, Mar. 8, 1939; s. Thomas and Edith Marion (Dods) T.; B.A., King's Coll., Cambridge (Eng.) U., 1960, M.A., 1967; m. Hilary Thomas, Jan. 10, 1961; children—Rebecca, Elizabeth. Mem. King's Coll. Choir, 1957-60, St. Paul's Cathedral Choir, 1960-62; appeared with: English Opera Group, Welsh Nat. Opera, Scottish Opera, Convent Garden, Dutch Opera, Paris Opera; appeared throughout world as concert singer; rec. artist; prof. singing Royal Coll. Music. London. Club: Garrick. Home: 11 Ravenscourt Sq London W6 England*

TEARE, WALLACE GLEED, architect; b. Cleve., June 5, 1907; s. George Wallace and Florence Elizabeth (Gleed) T.; B.Arch., Western Res. U., 1929, M.A., 1933; diploma Fontainebleau (France) Sch. Fine Arts, 1930; m. Dorothy Gabriel Schaefer, June 24, 1933; children—Richard W., Virginia Gabriel (Mrs. Albert M. Katz). Partner, Conrad & Teare, architects, Cleve., 1931-38, Joseph L. Weinberg and Conrad & Teare, asso. architects, Cleve., 1932-36; housing planner U.S. Housing Authority, Washington, 1938-39; chief planning and research Cleve. Met. Housing Authority, 1939-44; partner Teare & Herman, and predecessor firms, Cleve., 1946—; instr. Western Res. U., 1931-38, 45-47, trustee, 1948-56; housing cons. to gov. Panama Canal, 1945; archtl. cons. Cleve. City Planning Commn., 1959, vice chmn., 1971-74, chmn., 1975—; mem. Lakewood (Ohio) City Planning Commn., 1944-60, chmn., 1952-53; mem. exec. com. Regional Planning Commn. Cuyahoga County, 1951-60, 75—. Trustee Regional Assn. Cleve., treas., 1969—; trustee W. Shore Concerts, Lakewood, Ohio, pres., 1954-56; trustee Koch Sch. Music, Rocky River, Ohio, chmn., 1970-71. Recipient Cleve. Arts prize, 1977. Fellow AIA (sec. Cleve. chpt. 1944, v.p. 1948, pres. 1949, profl. adv. 1978—, mem. nat. housing com. 1972-77, chmn. 1975, HUD/AIA liaison task force 1977—), Royal Soc. Health (London); mem. Architects Soc. Ohio (sec. Cleve. sect. 1937, v.p. 1938), Am. Soc. Planning Ofcls. (hon. life), Am. Inst. Planners (affiliate), Am. Planning Assn., Soc. Archtl. Historians, Western Res. Archtl. Historians, Nat. Assn. Housing and Redevel. Ofcls., Internat. Assn. Housing Sci. Unitarian. Most important works include Lakeview Terrace, Cleve., 1937, O'Neil-Sheffield Shopping Center, Sheffield Twp., O., 1954 (A.I.A. award of merit 1955), West Shore Unitarian Ch., Rocky River, 1962, Jewish Community Fedn. Office Bldg., Cleve. (asso. architects with Edward D. Stone), 1965, Chesterfield Apts., Cleve. (Chas. Luckman Assos. cons.), 1968, Lakeview Tower, Cleve., 1973, other housing for elderly in Ohio, Pa., Conn., 1954—. Author articles on housing for elderly. Home: 16500 Edgewater Dr Lakewood OH 44107 Office Terminal Tower Cleveland OH 44113

TEASDALE, JOSEPH PATRICK, gov. of Mo.; b. Kansas City, Mo., Mar. 29, 1936; s. William B. and Adah (Downey) T.; student St. Benedict's Coll., 1954-55; B.S. in Lit., Rockhurst Coll., 1957; LL.B., St. Louis U., 1960; m. Theresa Ferkenhoff, Oct. 13, 1973; children—William Daniel, John Patrick. Admitted to Mo. bar, 1960; asst. U.S. atty., chief organized crime sect., 1962-66; prof. atty. Jackson County, Mo., 1966-72; gov. State of Mo., Jefferson City, 1976—; adviser Kansas City Drug Program for Youth Offenders. Named outstanding man of year Kansas City C. of C., 1969. Mem. Nat. Govs. Assn., Midwestern Govs. Assn. (chmn. 1979-80). Home: Executive Mansion 100 Madison St Jefferson City MO 65101 Office: State Capitol Bldg Room 216 Jefferson City MO 65101

TEASE, JAMES EDWARD, circuit judge; b. Sheffield, Ala., Dec. 28, 1939; s. James Albert and Hattie Wayne (Counts) T.; B.S., Florence State U., 1961; LL.B., U. Ala., 1964; grad. Nat. Coll. State Judiciary, 1971; m. Anne Elizbeth Gilley, Sept. 2, 1972. Admitted to Ala. bar, 1964; gen. practice law, Florence, 1965-67; city prosecutor, Florence, 1966-67; dep. dist. atty. Lauderdale County, Ala., 1967-71; circuit judge 11th Jud. Circuit Ala., Florence, 1971—. Mem. Ala. Constl. Commn.; chmn. Ala. Citizens Adv. Com. on Election Reform; bd. dirs. Regional Library System. Served with AUS, 1964-65. Named Florence Outstanding Young Man Jaycees, 1974, Alumnus of Year U. Ala., 1975. Mem. Am. Judicature Soc., Nat. Conf. State Trial Judges, Ala. Assn. Circuit Judges (sec.-treas. 1976-77), Lauderdale County Bar Assn. (pres.), Am. Legion, Sigma Delta Kappa. Baptist. Home: 303 Grove St Florence AL 35630 Office: Lauderdale County Courthouse Florence AL 35630

TEBALDI, RENATA, opera singer; b. Pesaro, Italy, Jan. 2, 1922; d. Teobaldo and Giuseppina (Barbieri) T.; student Arrigo Boito Conservatory, Pesaro Gioacchino Rossini Conservatory, Parma, Italy; pupil of Carmen Melis, Giuseppe Pais. Lyric soprano; profl. debut in Mefistofele, Rovigo, 1944; debut at LaScala, 1946; singer opera houses of Naples, Rome, Venice, Bologna, Florence, Modena, Cesana, Turin, Venice, Pompeii; Am. debut in Aida, San Francisco Opera Co., 1950; debut in Otello, Met. Opera House, N.Y.C., 1955; singer operatic roles in La Boheme, Madame Butterfly, Tosca. Roman Catholic. Home: 1 Plazza Guastalla Milan Italy Office: care Herbert H Breslin 119 W 57th St New York NY 10019

TEBBEL, JOHN, educator, writer; b. Boyne City, Mich., Nov. 16, 1912; s. William and Edna (Johnston) T.; A.B., Central Mich Coll. Edn., 1935; M.S., Columbia, 1937; m. Kathryn Carl, Apr. 29, 1939; 1 dau., Judith. City editor Isabella Co. Times-News, Mt. Pleasant, Mich., 1935-36; writer Newsweek mag., 1937; reporter Detroit Free Press, 1937-39; feature writer, roto news editor Providence Jour., 1939-41; mng. editor Am. Mercury, 1941-43; Sunday staff writer N.Y. Times, 1943; asso. editor E.P. Dutton & Co., 1943-47; asst. in journalism Sch. Journalism Columbia, 1943-45; chmn. dept. journalism N.Y. U., 1954-65, prof. journalism, 1965—. Cons. Ford Found., 1966—. Mem. Sigma Delta Chi. Club: The Players. Author: An American Dynasty, 1947; The Marshall Fields, 1947; George Horace Lorimer and the Saturday Evening Post, 1948; Battle for North America, 1948; Your Body, 1951; The Conqueror, 1951; Touched With Fire, 1952; The Life and Good Times of William Randolph Hearst, 1952; George Washington's America, 1954; A Voice in the Street, 1954; The Magic of Balanced Living, 1956; The American Indian Wars, 1960; The Inheritors, 1962; The Epicure's Companion, 1962; David Sarnoff, 1963; Compact History of the American Newspaper, 1964; From Rags to Riches, 1964; Open Letter to Newspaper Readers, 1968; Compact History of American Magazines, 1969; A History of Book Publishing in the United States, 3 vols., 1972, 75, 78; The Battle of Fallen Timbers, 1972; The Media in America, 1975. Contbr. to Sat. Rev., other mags. Home: 876-A Heritage Village Southbury CT 06488. *From the time my writing career began, at 14, I have tried to write as well and clearly and accurately as I can, so that I could best inform the people who read my books and articles about the world they live in. To me it is the obligation of every writer to recognize the responsibility his talent imposes on him, and understand that he is one of the transmitters of knowledge upon whom the world depends for advancement and the betterment of human society.*

TEBET, DAVID WILLIAM, TV exec.; b. Phila., Dec. 27, 1920; student Temple U., 1941. Publicity staff legitimate theatre prodns. for John C. Wilson, Theatre Guild, others; plays include Blithe Spirit, Bloomer Girl, Quadrille, 1943-55; pub. relations Max Leibman Prodns., 1950—; sr. v.p. NBC-TV, N.Y.C.; v.p. talent NBC, Inc. 1959-75, sr. v.p., 1975-79; v.p. talent Marble Arch Prodns., Studio City, Calif., 1979—. Mem. TV-radio and film adv. bd. Stevens Coll., Columbia, Mo. Named Man of Year, Conf. Personnel Mgrs. W. Club: Friars (bd. govs.), chmn. spl. events com., exec. chmn. ann. testimonial dinners). Office: Studio Center 2024 Radford Ave Studio City CA 90964

TECKLENBURG, HARRY, consumer products co. exec.; b. Seattle, Nov. 3, 1927; s. Harry and Frieda (Rasche) T.; B.S. in Chem. Engring., Mass. Inst. Tech., Cambridge, 1950; M.S. in Chem. Engring., U. Wash., 1952; m. Mary Louise Beaty, Sept. 1, 1951; children—Don, Bruce. With Procter & Gamble Co., Cin., 1952—, chem. engr., group leader, sect. leader. dir., mgr. research and devel. dept., v.p. research and devel., 1952-76. sr. v.p., 1976—, rep. to Indsl. Research Inst., 1973-76. Mem. leadership campaign Mass. Inst. Tech., 1975—, corp. devel. com., 1977—; trustee Ohio Valley Goodwill Industries Rehab. Center, 1969—, pres., 1974—; bd. dirs. Goodwill Industries Am., 1978—. Served with AUS, 1946-48. Mem. Engring. Soc. Cin., Am. Inst. Chem. Engrs., Am. Chem. Soc., TAPPI, AAAS. Office: Procter & Gamble Co Ivorydale Technical Center Cincinnati OH 45217

TEDESCHI, HENRY, biologist; b. Novara, Italy, Feb. 3, 1930; s. Edoardo Vittorio and Paola (Minerbi) T.; came to U.S., 1947, naturalized, 1960; B.S., U. Pitts., 1950; Ph.D., U. Chgo., 1955; m. Terry Kershner, Nov. 29, 1957; children—Alexander, Devorah, David. Research asso. U. Chgo., 1955-57, asst. prof., 1957-60, U. Ill. Med. Sch., Chgo., 1960-64, asso. prof., 1964-65; prof. biology State U. N.Y., Albany, 1965—. Author: Cell Physiology, Molecular Dynamics, 1974; Mitochondria: Structure, Biogenesis and Transducing Functions, 1976. Home: 143 Orchard St Delmar NY 12054 Office: State U NY 1400 Washington Ave Albany NY 12222

TEDESCO, TED, univ. adminstr.; b. Providence, July 13, 1931; s. Michael and Minnie (Ruggieri) T.; B.A. in Polit. Sci., U. R.I., 1956; M. Pub. Adminstrn., U. Mich., 1958; m. Rosemary LeVasseur, Aug. 27, 1955; children—Jeffrey, Lisa. David. City mgr. Enfield (Conn.), 1963-67, Boulder (Colo.), 1967-73, San Jose (Calif.), 1973-78; vice chancellor for adminstrn. U. Colo., Boulder, 1978—. Mem. intergovtl. sci., engring. and tech. adv. panel Office Sci. and Tech. Policy, Washington, 1977-78; mem. effective govt. steering com. Nat. League Cities, 1976-77; Distinguished speaker Sloan program Stanford U., 1974-77. Served to 1st lt. AUS, 1957-58. Named Outstanding Young Man Conn., 1965, New Eng., 1966; recipient award for distinguished contbn. to lit. Pub. Mgmt. Mag., 1970, Outstanding Mentor award; Nat. Urban fellow, 1974. Mem. Internat. City Mgmt. Assn. (v.p. 1970-72, Mgmt. Innovation award 1970, Career Devel. award 1974), Pi Sigma Alpha. Office: Regent Hall U Colo Boulder CO 80309

TEDESKO, ANTON, cons. engr.; b. Gruenberg, Germany, May 25, 1903; s. Victor and Alice (Weiss) T.; C.E., Inst. Tech., Vienna, Austria, 1926, D.Sc., 1951; diploma engr. Berlin 1930; D.Eng. (hon.), Lehigh U., 1966; D.Sc. (hon.), Technol. U., Vienna, 1978; m. Sally Murray, June 16, 1938; children—Peter Alden, Suzanne Tedesko Affolter. Came to U.S., 1927, naturalized, 1938. Constrn. engr., Vienna, 1926; with Fairbanks-Morse Co., Chgo., 1927, Miss. Valley Structural Steel Co., Melrose Park, Ill., 1927-28; asst. prof. Inst. Tech., Vienna, 1929; designer dams, bridges, shells, indsl. structures Dyckerhoff & Widmann, Wiesbaden, Germany, 1930-32; with Roberts & Schaefer Co., engrs., Chgo., 1932-67, engring. mgr., Washington, 1943-44, structural mgr., Chgo., 1944-54, mgr., N.Y.C., 1955, v.p., 1956-67; pvt. cons. engring., 1967—; designer, supr. constrn. arenas, air terminals, bridges, toll roads, indsl. structures, ballistic missile and space rocket launching facilities, wide-span hangars, shell structures, evaluator structural failures, rehab. damaged structures; dir. Thompson-Starrett Co., 1960-61; structural engr. responsible for design rocket assembly and launch facilities for manned lunar landing program Kennedy Space Center, 1962-66; lectr. structural engring. numerous univs.; spl. work shell concrete structures of long span, prestressed concrete; cons. Hdqrs. USAF, 1955-70, to Chief Engr., C.E., U.S. Army, 1970-74, other govt. agys.; mem. various commns. and bds.; moderator engring. confs. Recipient Alfred Lindau award in field long-span reinforced concrete structures, 1961, Engring. News Record citation, 1966. Fellow ASCE (hon. mem.); mem. Research Council Performance of Structures, Reinforced Concrete Research Council (exec. com. 1971—, Arthur J. Boase award 1978), Engrs. Joint Council (metric commn.), Am. Concrete Inst. (dir. 1961-64, hon. mem., internat. award of merit in structural engring. 1978), Soc. Am. Mil. Engrs., Am. R.R. Engring. Assn., Internat. Assn. Bridge and Structural Engring. (U.S. del. permanent commn. 1965—), Internat. Assn. Shell and Spatial Structures (Hon. Mem. award 1979), Nat. Acad. Engring. Contbr. articles to profl jours. Address: 26 Brookside Circle Bronxville NY 10708

TEDROW, JOHN CHARLES FREMONT, educator; b. Rockwood, Pa., Apr. 21, 1917; s. John Wesley and Emma Grace (Younkin) T.; B.S., Pa. State U., 1939; M.S., Mich. State U., 1940; Ph.D., Rutgers U., 1950; m. Mary Jane Lough, Mar. 20, 1943; children—John Charles Fremont, Thomas Lough. Jr. soil technologist Dept. Agr., 1941-42, soil scientist, 1946-47; instr. Rutgers U., New Brunswick, N.J., 1947-50, asst. prof., 1950-53, asso. prof., 1953-57, prof. soils, 1957—; cons. N.S. Research Found., 1949—; sr. pedologist Boston U., 1953—; cons. to govt. and industry. Investigator polar soils in Alaska, Can., Greenland, Scandinavia, Siberia and Antarctica. Served to lt. USNR, 1942-46. Recipient Lindback Research award Rutgers U., 1978. Fellow Am. Soc. Agronomy, Soil Sci. Soc. Am., Arctic Inst. N.Am.; mem. N.J. Acad. Sci., Internat. Soc. Soil Sci., Am. Geophys. Union, N.Z. Antarctic Soc., Am. Arbitration Assn., Ghana Jour. Agrl. Sci. (adv. mem.), Sigma Xi. Author: (with R.C. Murray): Forensic Geology: Earth Sciences and Criminal Investigation, 1974; Soils of the Polar Landscapes, 1977. Editor-in-chief Soil Science, 1968-79. Editor: Antarctic Soils and Soil Forming Processes, 1966. Home: 5 Bluebird Ct Edison NJ 08817 Office: Rutgers U Soils and Crops Dept Box 231 Lipman Dr New Brunswick NJ 08903

TEECE, ROBERT DAYTON, SR., heavy equipment mfg. co. exec.; b. Kewanee, Ill., Aug. 22, 1920; s. Robert D. and Vera M. (Peterson) T.; B.S. in Mech. Engring., U. Ill., 1942; D.Engring. (hon.), Milw. Sch. Engring., 1975; m. Florence A. Anderson, Sept. 22, 1943; children—Robert Dayton, Dennis F., Douglas J. Exec. engr. Harnischfeger Corp., Milw., 1954-59, asst. to pres., 1959-61, v.p. engring., 1961-65, exec. v.p., 1975—, also dir.; dir. Control Logic, Inc., Natick, Mass., Gentili Brighi SpA, Milan, Italy. Served in USNR, 1944-46. Named Distinguished Alumnus in Mech. and Indsl. Engring., U. Ill., 1972. Registered profl. engr., Wis. Mem. ASME, Am. Soc. Metals, Engrs. and Scientists of Milw., Am. Mgmt. Assn., Am. Gear Mfrs. Assn., Am. Soc. Testing Materials, Material Handling Inst. Republican. Clubs: Rotary, University (Milw.); Westmoor Country. Contbr. articles in field to profl. jours. Home: 1138 Pilgrim Pkwy Elm Grove WI 53122 Office: PO Box 554 Milwaukee WI 53201

TEED, JOHN EDSON, lawyer; b. Pampa, Tex., Sept. 13, 1936; s. Arthur Milton and Dorothy (Stark) T.; B.A., U. Tex., 1958, LL.B., 1960; m. Cynthia Cason, May 30, 1979; 1 son, Arthur. Admitted to Tex. bar, 1960; asso. firm Royston, Rayzor & Cook, Houston, 1961-66, partner, 1966-68. Served to capt. AUS, 1960-61. Mem. Houston, Am. bar assns., State Bar of Tex., Beta Theta Pi, Phi Alpha Delta. Home: 812 Friar Tuck St Houston TX 77024 Office: 2000 S Post Oak Rd Houston TX 77027

TEEGARDEN, KENNETH LEROY, clergyman; b. Cushing, Okla., Dec. 22, 1921; s. Roy Albert and Eva B. (Swiggart) T.; student Okla. State U., 1938-40; A.B., Phillips U., 1942, M.A., 1945, D.D., 1963; B.D., Tex. Christian U., 1949, D.D., 1976; D.D., Bethany Coll., 1974; LL.D., Lynchburg Coll., 1975; L.H.D., Culver-Stockton Coll., 1975; m. Wanda Jean Strong, May 28, 1944; children—David Kent, Marshall Kirk. Ordained to ministry Christian Ch. (Disciples of Christ), 1940; pastor in Chandler, Okla., 1944-47, Texas City, Tex., 1947-48, Healdton, Okla., 1948-49, Vernon, Tex., 1949-55, Ft. Smith, Ark., 1955-58; exec. minister Christian Ch. in Ark., 1958-65, asst. to pres., Indpls., 1965-69, exec. minister in Tex., 1969-73, gen. minister, pres., Indpls., 1973—. Mem. governing bd. Nat. Council Chs., 1973—; del. 5th Assembly of World Council Chs., Nairobi, Kenya, 1975; rep. Nat. Council Chs. in Exchange of Ch. Leadership with Soviet Union, 1974. Named Distinguished Alumnus, Tex. Christian U., 1973, Phillips U., 1975; Outstanding Citizen, Vernon, Tex., 1954. Author: We Call Ourselves Disciples, 1975. Home: 7232 Highburry Dr Indianapolis IN 46256 Office: 222 S Downey Ave Indianapolis IN 46219

TEELE, ARTHUR EARLE, former educator; b. Vaughan, N.C., Nov. 11, 1910; s. George Washington and Cora (Williams) T.; A.B., N.C. Coll., 1934; A.M., Cornell U., 1941, Ph.D., 1953; m. Florazelle Swayze, Dec. 11, 1937; children—Synthia Florabeale, Arthur Earle. Instr., chmn. dept. social studies Warren County Tng. Sch., Wise, N.C., 1934-39; ednl. therapist VA Hosp., Roanoke, Va., 1946-50; prof. edn., history, head dept. edn. St. Augustine's Coll., 1953-54; prof., chmn. dept. edn. Prairie View (Tex.) A. and M. Coll., 1954-57; prof., head dept. secondary edn. Fla. A. and M. U., Tallahassee, 1957-70, dir. prins., suprs. workshop, 1964-66, prof., dean grad. studies, 1970-76, prof. edn., 1976-78; cons. grad. programs U.S. Office Edn., 1978—; dir. Hardee County Curriculum Workshop, 1960; dir. Hampton Jr. Coll. Workshop, 1962; mem. research council Coop. Coll. Projects (Land Grant TVA), 1963-64. Mem. United Fund steering com. Fla. A. and M. U., 1961-67. Bd. dirs. Leon County United Fund, 1962-69, N.E. Fla. Summer Camp, Jacksonville, 1966-69; pres. Coll. Terrace Community, 1963-68. Served with USAAF, 1943-45. Recipient Grant-in-Aid for research Cornell U., 1952; named Distinguished Alumnus, N.C. Coll., 1960. Mem. N.E.A., Fla. Edn. Assn., Nat. Assn. Secondary Sch. Prins. (nat. adv. bd. 1971-75), Tallahassee Frontiers Internat. (pres. 1972), Nat. Black Alliance for Grad. Edn. (exec. bd., steering com. 1971—), Conf. So. Grad. Deans, Kappa Alpha Psi (dir.), Phi Delta Kappa, Kappa Delta Pi, Sigma Pi Phi. Contbr. to various publs. in field. Home: 620 Howard Ave Tallahassee FL 32304

TEER, NELLO LEGUY, JR., constrn. co. exec.; b. Durham, N.C., Mar. 8, 1914; s. Nello Leguy and Gertrude (Adcock) T.; D.Sc., U. N.C., 1968; m. Dorothy Foster, Nov. 10, 1934 (dec. May 1976); children—Sondra (Mrs. Reece A. Robertson), Nello Leguy III, Dorothy (Mrs. M.B. Liptzin), Michael Page; m. 2d, Ethel Vredevoogd Wyngaarden, Nov. 4, 1978. Pres., Nello L. Teer Co., Durham, 1954—; pres. Nello L. Teer Internat., Inc., Central Engring. & Contracting Corp. Founding dir. Better Hwys. Info. Found.; pres. N.C. Engring. Found., 1963-65; chmn. world council Internat. Rd. Fedn., 1976. Pres. Occoneechee council Boy Scouts Am., 1964, Friends of Watts Hosp., 1965-68. Recipient Civilian Meritorious Service award U.S. Bur. Yards & Docks, USN; Silver Beaver award, 1963, Silver Antelope award, 1969 both Boy Scouts Am.; Ann. Civic award Durham C. of C., 1972, Distinguished Achievement award, 1974; Nat. Brotherhood award NCCJ, 1975. Mem. Asso. Gen. Contractors Am. (pres. 1973), Am. Rd. Builders Assn. (pres. 1959-60; award 1962), Internat. Rd. Fedn. (dir., mem. exec. com., world council), Carolina Rd. BUilders Assn. (pres. 1944-45). Episcopalian. Home: 3200 Rugby Rd Durham NC 27707 Office: PO Box 1131 Durham NC 27702

TEES, MIRIAM HADLEY, librarian; b. Montreal, Que., Can., Feb. 24, 1923; d. Frederick James and Beatrice Mary (Armstrong) T.; B.A., McGill U., 1944, B.L.S., 1951, M.L.S., 1975. Asst. librarian Internat. Civil Aviation Orgn., Montreal, 1951-53; with Royal Bank Can., Montreal, 1953-79, chief librarian, 1953-79; dir. Corp. Profl. Librarian Que., 1969-71, pres., 1971-72; sessional lectr. McGill U., 1971-79, asso. prof. Grad. Sch. Library Sci., 1979—. Commr., Girl Guides Can., 1960-66. Mem. Spl. Libraries Assn. (chpt. pres. 1957-58, dir. 1970-73, asso. pres. 1975-76), Que. Library Assn. (treas. 1964-65; pres. 1965-66). Home: 24 Holton Ave Montreal PQ H3Y 2E8 Canada Office: 3459 McTavish St Montreal PQ H3A 1Y1 Canada

TEETER, KARL VAN DUYN, linguistic scientist, educator; b. Berkeley, Calif., Mar. 2, 1929; s. Charles Edwin and Lura May (Shaffner) T.; A.B., U. Calif., Berkeley, 1959, Ph.D., 1962; A.M. (hon.), Harvard U., 1966; m. Anita Maria Bonacorsi, Aug. 25, 1951; children—Katharine Emilie, Judith Ann, Teresa Maria, Martha Elisabeth. From instr. to prof. linguistics Harvard U., 1962—, chmn. dept. linguistics, 1966-69, 70-71, 77-78; guest research fellow Research Inst. Logopedics and Phoniatrics, Faculty of Medicine, Tokyo U., 1969-70; mem. summer faculty U. Mich., 1962, UCLA, 1966, U. N.C., 1972. Served with AUS, 1946, 51-54. Fulbright research fellow, Japan, 1969-70. Mem. Linguistic Soc. Am. (long range planning com., 1969-73, Lang. rev. com. 1980—), Assn. Tchrs. Japanese, Linguistic Soc. Japan, Phi Beta Kappa, Sigma Xi. Author: The Wiyot Language, 1964; contbr. articles to profl. jours. Home: 16 1/2 Woodbridge St Cambridge MA 02140 Office: Sci Center 223 Cambridge MA 02138

TEETERS, NANCY HAYS, economist, govt. ofcl.; b. Marion, Ind., July 29, 1930; d. S. Edgar and Mabel (Drake) Hays; A.B. in Econs., Oberlin Coll., 1952, LL.D. (hon.), 1979; M.A. in Econs., U. Mich., 1954, postgrad., 1956-57; m. Robert Duane Teeters, June 7, 1952; children—Ann, James, John. Teaching fellow U. Mich., 1954-55, instr., 1956-57; instr. U. Md. Overseas, Germany, 1955-56; staff economist sect. govt. fin. Bd. Govs. of FRS, Washington, 1957-66, mem. bd., 1978—; economist (on loan) Council Econ. Advs., 1962-63; economist Bur. Budget, 1966-70; sr. fellow Brookings Instn., 1970-73; sr. specialist Congl. Research Service, Library of Congress, Washington, 1973-74; asst. dir., chief economist Ho. of Reps. Com. on the Budget, 1974-78; mem. adv. Bd. Inst. for Study Ednl. Policy, Howard U. Recipient Comfort Starr award in econs. Oberlin Coll., 1952. Mem. Nat. Economists Club (v.p. 1973-74, pres. 1974-75, chmn. bd. 1975-76, gov. 1976-79), Am. Econ. Assn. (com. on status of women 1975-78), Am. Fin. Assn. (dir. 1961-71). Democrat. Author: (with others) Setting National Priorities: The 1972 Budget, 1971, Setting National Priorities: The 1973 Budget, 1972, Setting National Priorities: The 1974 Budget, 1973; contbr. articles to profl. publs. Home: 3058 Porter St NW Washington DC 20008 Office: Fed Res Bd 20th and Constitution Ave NW Washington DC 20551

TEEVAN, RICHARD COLLIER, educator; b. Shelton, Conn., June 12, 1919; s. Daniel Joseph and Elizabeth (Hallowell) T.; B.A., Wesleyan U., Middletown, Conn., 1951; M.A., U. Mich., 1952, Ph.D., 1955; m. Virginia Agnes Stehle, July 25, 1945; children—Jan Elizabeth, Kim Ellen, Clay Collier, Allison Tracy. Rubber buffer Sponge Rubber Product Co., Derby, Conn., 1939-41; with U. Mich., 1951-57, teaching fellow, 1951-53, instr., 1953-57; asst. prof. Smith Coll., 1957-60; asso. prof. Bucknell U., 1960-64, prof. 1964-69; chmn. psychology, prof. SUNY, Albany, 1969—. Served to capt. AUS, 1941-47; prisoner of war, Ger., 1943-45. Mem. Am., Eastern psychol. assns., AAUP, AAAS, Phi Beta Kappa, Sigma Xi. Author: Reinforcement, 1961; Instinct, 1961; Color Vision, 1961; Measuring Human Motivation, 1962; Theories of Motivation in Learning, 1964; Theories of Motivation in Personality and Social Psychology, 1964; Motivation, 1967; Fear of Failure, 1969; Readings in Elementary Psychology, 1973. Contbr. articles to sci. jours. Address: 45 Pine St Delmar NY 12054

TEICHER, LOUIS, pianist; b. Wilkes Barre, Pa., Aug. 24, 1924; s. Harry and Dora (Bernhardt) T.; diploma Julliard Sch. Music, 1940, grad. diploma, 1943; m. Elaine Sutin, Oct. 10, 1948 (div. Aug. 1973); children—Richard, Susan Carol, David; m. 2d, Betty Gates, Aug. 21, 1973. Tchr., Juilliard Sch. Music, Manhattan Sch. Music, N.Y.C., 1942-46; mem. team Ferrante & Teicher, 1947—; appeared in numerous concerts, TV, radio stas. throughout U.S., Can., Europe; rec. artist for United Artists records; composer scores for motion pictures. Mem. A.S.C.A.P., Am. Fedn. Musicians, A.F.T.R.A., Tau Kappa Epsilon. Mem. B'nai B'rith. Address: care Glissando Enterprises 1180 Ave of Americas New York NY 10036. *The two characteristics I find lacking in most people are humility and gratitude. In pursuing my career and in living my life, I endeavor to keep both these qualities in the forefront.*

TEICHER, MORTON IRVING, univ. dean; b. N.Y.C., Mar. 10, 1920; s. Sam and Celia (Roth) T.; B.S. in Social Sci., Coll. City N.Y., 1940; M.S.W., U. Pa., 1942; Ph.D., U. Toronto, 1956; m. Mildred Adler, Oct. 4, 1941; children—Phyllis Margaret, Oren Jonathan. Chief social work in New Eng. for VA, 1946-48; asst. prof., clin. tchr. U. Toronto, 1948-56; cons. Oppenheimer Coll., No. Rhodesia, 1962-63; dean Sch. Social Work, Yeshiva U., 1956-72, prof., 1956-72; prof. Sch. Social Work, U. N.C., Chapel Hill, 1972—, dean, 1972—. Seminar asso. creativity in sci. N.Y. U., 1959-73; cons. Bar Ilan U., Israel, 1965-69; cons. VA, 1965-69; cons., vis. prof. Henrietta Szold Inst., Jerusalem, 1975; preceptor Central Inst. Mgmt., Sr. Civil Service, Israel, 1975; external examiner U. Zambia, 1968-69; cons. in field, 1950—; chmn. U.S. com. Internat. Council Social Welfare. Research chmn. Westchester Democratic Com., 1958-62. Bd. dirs. Lake Success Capital Corp., 1967-71; trustee Wurzweiler Found. 1966—, Coler Found., 1970-72; exec. sec. Nat. Conf. Jewish Communal Service, 1968-70; bd. dirs. N.Y. Social Work Recruiting Center, 1969-70; mem. policy bd. Carolina Population Center, 1973-77; bd. dirs. Internat. Conf. Jewish Communal Service, 1965—. Served to 1st lt. AUS, 1942-46; CBI. Certified social worker, N.Y. State. Fellow Soc. Applied Anthropology, Am. Anthrop. Assn.; mem. Acad. Certified Social Workers, Nat. Assn. Social Workers (chmn. Westchester chpt. 1960-62, mem. commn. ethics 1964-67, mem. exec. com. Eastern N.C. chpt. 1972-74), Am. Ethnol. Soc., Otto Rank Soc., Gerontol. Soc. Author: Windigo Psychosis, 1960, also contbr. books, profl. jours. Book rev. editor Jour. Jewish Communal Service, 1961-68; editorial bd. Human Orgn., 1963-66, Jour. Am. Soc. Cybernetics, 1970-72, Ednl. Gerontology, 1978—. Anthrop. field work among the Eskimo and Iroquis. Home: 809-D E Franklin St Chapel Hill NC 27514 Office: Sch Social Work U NC Chapel Hill NC 27514

TEICHERT, CURT, geologist, educator; b. Koenigsberg, Germany, May 8, 1905; s. Richard and Louise (Zander) T.; student U. Munich (Germany), 1923-25, U. Freiburg (Germany), 1925, U. Koenigsberg, 1925-28; Ph.D., Albertus U., 1928; D.Sc., U. Western Australia, Perth, 1944; m. Gertrud Margarete Kaufmann, Dec. 28, 1928. Came to U.S., 1952, naturalized, 1959. Rockefeller fellow, U.S., 1930; privatdozent Tech. U., Berlin, 1931-35; research paleontologist U. Copenhagen (Denmark), 1933-37; research lectr. U. Western Australia, 1937-46; asst. chief govt. geologist Dept. Mines, Melbourne, Australia, 1946-47; sr. lectr. U. Melbourne, 1947-53; Fulbright scholar, U. Kans., Lawrence, 1951-52; prof. geology N.Mex. Sch. Mines, 1953; geologist U.S. Geol. Survey, 1954-64, chief Petroleum Geology Lab., 1954-58, research geologist, 1958-61; AID adviser Geol. Survey, Pakistan, 1961-64; Regents Distinguished prof. geology, dir. Paleontol. Inst., U. Kans., Lawrence, 1964-75, prof. emeritus, 1975—; adj. prof. geol. scis. U. Rochester (N.Y.), 1977—; geologist Danish N.E. Greenland Expdn., 1931-32; guest prof. U. Bonn (Germany), U. Goettingen, U. Freiburg, 1958, U. Tex., 1960; U.S. coordinator AID-CENTO Stratigraphic Working Group, 1965-76. Cons. to oil cos., 1940-53, Australian Bur. Mineral Resources, 1948-52. Recipient David Syme Prize sci. research U. Melbourne, 1950. Mem. Internat. Geol. Congress (past sec. internat. com. Gondwana system). Soc. Geol. France (fgn. asso.), Paleontol. Soc. (past corr., pres. 1971-72), Palaeont. Gesellschaft (hon.), Soc. Geol. Belgique (hon.), Royal Soc. Western Australia (hon.), Palaeontol. Soc. India (fgn. corr.), Geol. Soc. Australia (hon.), Senckenberg. Naturforsch. Gesellschaft (corr. mem.), Internat. Palaeontol. Union (1st v.p., 1968-72), Internat. Palaeontol. Assn. (pres. 1976-80), Royal Danish Acad. Sci. (fgn. mem.), Explorers Club (N.Y.C.). Author: Ordovician and Silurian Faunas from Arctic Canada, 1937; (with Clarke, Prider) Elements of Geology, 1944, 4th ed., 1967; Elementary Practical Geology, 1946, 4th edit., 1968; (with others) Treatise on Invertebrate Paleontology, Part K, 1964; several book size monographs. Editor: Treatise on Invertebrate Paleontology, 1964-77. Contbr. articles to profl. jours. Address: Dept Geological Sciences Univ Rochester Rochester NY 14627

TEICHMANN, HOWARD MILES, author, educator; b. Chgo., Jan. 22, 1916; s. Jack and Rose (Berliner) T.; B.A., U. Wis., 1938; m. Evelyn Jane Goldstein, Apr. 2, 1939; 1 dau., Judith Robin Teichmann Steckler. Stage mgr., script writer Mercury Theatre, N.Y.C., 1938; writer, dir., producer radio and television plays, 1939-53; prof. English, Barnard Coll., Columbia U., 1946—. Mem. mayor's adv. bd. WNYC-AM-FM-TV, 1979. Recipient Peabody award, 1953, Emmy award, 1954, Disting. Service award Sch. Journalism, U. Wis., 1959. Mem. Dramatists Guild (council 1953-73), Dramatists Play Service (dir.), Dramatists Guild Fund (treas.), Writers Guild East. Author: (plays) (with George S. Kaufman) The Solid Gold Cadillac, 1953; Miss Lonelyhearts, 1955; The Girls in 509, 1958; Julia, Jake and Uncle Joe, 1960; A Rainy Day in Newark, 1962; Smart Aleck-Alexander Woollcott at 8:40, 1979; (biographies) George S. Kaufman: An Intimate Portrait, 1972; Smart Aleck, The Wit, World and Life of Alexander Woollcott, 1976; Alice: The Life and Times of Alice Roosevelt Longworth, 1979.

TEIGE, PETER N., airline exec.; b. Chgo., July 9, 1919; s. Melvin H. and Claudine (Johnson) T.; B.A., U. Wis., 1941; J.D., Harvard U., 1947; m. Barbara Kessenich, Jan. 23, 1943; children—Susan, Peter, Ellen, Mary, Ann, Nancy. Admitted to Calif. bar. 1948; with McCutchen, Doyle, Brown & Enersen, San Francisco, 1947-53; legal counsel Am. Pres. Lines, San Francisco, 1953-60, v.p., gen. counsel, dir., 1961-69; v.p. legal affairs, dir. World Airways, Inc., Oakland, Calif., 1969—, sec., 1970—. Served to capt. U.S. Army, 1942-46. Mem. World Affairs Council No. Calif. (trustee), Calif. State Bar, Sierra Club. Clubs: Propeller U.S., Harvard. Home: 2368 Branner Dr Menlo Park CA 94025 Office: World Airways Inc Oakland International Airport Oakland CA 94614

TEIGER, DAVID ALAN, mgmt. cons.; b. Newark, June 13, 1929; s. Samuel and Fannie (Ginsburg) T.; B.S., Cornell U., 1951; m. Florence Haupt, June 19, 1955; children—Lauren, Douglas. Partner firm Samuel Teiger & Co., Newark, 1953-60, Ira Haupt & Co., N.Y.C., 1960-64, Bache & Co., N.Y.C., 1964-65; exec. v.p. Shearson, Hammill & Co., Inc., N.Y.C., 1965-73; pres. United Research Co., South Orange, N.J., 1973—; dir. CHC Corp., Towson, Md. Served to lt. U.S. Army, 1951-53. Mem. N. Am. Soc. Corp. Planning. Clubs: Stock Exchange Luncheon (N.Y.C.); Mountain Ridge Country. Home: 310 Redmond Rd South Orange NJ 07079

TEITELBAUM, DAVID, lawyer; b. N.Y.C., Nov. 20, 1906; s. Raphael and Tessie (Schlanger) T.; B.S., N.Y. U., 1926; J.D., Harvard, 1929; m. Sylvia Lowenthal, Nov. 11, 1937; children—Richard, Ray. Admitted to N.Y. bar, 1930; spl. asst. to atty. gen. U.S., 1930-31; sr. partner Donovan, Leisure, Newton & Irvine, N.Y.C., Washington, London and Paris, 1936—; trustee Practising Law Inst., 1962—; dir. Marcor, Inc. Mem. Mayor N.Y.C. Temporary Commn. N.Y.C. Finances, 1975-77; chmn. bd. Bklyn. Philharmonia, 1960-72. Fellow Am. Bar Found.; mem. Am., N.Y. State, N.Y.C. bar assns., Am. Judicature Soc. Republican. Clubs: Harvard, University, Rockefeller Center, Nat. Lawyers. Office: 30 Rockefeller Plaza New York NY 10020

TEITELBAUM, HUBERT, judge; b. Pitts., July 2, 1915; s. Jack and Anna (Wolk) T.; A.B., U. Pitts., 1937, LL.B., 1940; m. Maja Wahrheit, Dec. 2, 1949; children—Hugh, Bruce. Admitted to Pa. bar, 1940; spl. agt. FBI, 1940-43; atty. U.S. Mil. Govt., Ger., 1945-49; practiced in Pitts., 1949-55; 1st asst. U.S. atty., 1955-58; U.S. dist. atty. Western Dist. Pa., 1958-61; judge U.S. Dist. Ct. for Western Dist. Pa., 1970—; mem. ct. adminstrn. com. Jud. Conf. U.S., 1978—. Trustee Montefiore Hosp., Pitts., 1972, Woodville State Mental Hosp., 1973. Served to capt. AUS, 1944-47; lt. col. Res. Mem. Am., Fed., Pa., Allegheny County bar assns., Am. Law Inst., Am. Judicature Soc., Am. Trial Lawyers Assn., Allegheny County Acad. Trial Lawyers, Am. Legion, Order of Coif. Clubs: Wildwood Golf, Fellows, Amen Corner (pres. 1979), Variety, Nat. Lawyers, Pitts. Athletic Assn., Pitts. Press. Office: US Courthouse Pittsburgh PA 15219

TEITELBAUM, PHILIP, psychologist; b. Bklyn., Oct. 9, 1928; s. Bernard and Betty (Schechter) T.; B.S., Coll. City N.Y., 1950; M.A., Johns Hopkins U., 1952, Ph.D., 1954; m. Evelyn Satinoff, Dec. 26, 1963; children—Benjamin, Daniel, David. Instr., asst. prof. physiol. psychology Harvard U., 1956-59; asso. prof. psychology U. Pa., Phila., 1959-63, prof., 1963-73; prof. psychology U. Ill., Urbana-Champaign, 1973—; fellow Center for Advanced Study in Behavioral Scis., Stanford U., Palo Alto, Calif., 1975-76. Fulbright fellow Tel Aviv U., 1978-79. Fellow Am. Psychol. Assn. (pres. div. physiol. psychology, disting. sci. contbn. award 1978); mem. Nat. Acad. Scis., AAAS, Am. Physiol. Soc., Soc. Neuroscis. Author: Fundamental Principles of Physiological Psychology, 1967. Contbr. chpts. to books, articles to profl. jours. Home: 1410 Waverly St Champaign IL 61820 Office: Dept Psychology U Ill Urbana Champaign IL 61820

TEITELL, CONRAD LAURENCE, lawyer; b. N.Y.C., Nov. 8, 1932; s. Benson and Belle (Altman) T.; A.B., U. Mich., 1954; LL.B., Columbia U., 1957; LL.M., N.Y. U., 1968; m. Adele Mary Crummins, May 26, 1957; children—Beth Mary, Mark Lewis. Admitted to N.Y. bar, 1958, D.C., bar, 1968; mem. firm Prerau & Teitell, N.Y.C., 1964—; dir. Philanthropy Tax Inst., Old Greenwich, Conn., 1964—. Trustee, Am. Arthritis Found., N.Y. Lung Assn., Hendrix Coll., Old Greenwich-Riverside Community Center. Served with U.S. Army, 1957. Recipient Distinguished Service to Higher Edn. award Am. Coll. Pub. Relations Assn., 1970. Mem. Nat. Assn. Coll. Univ. Attys., Am. Soc. Hosp. Attys., Am. Bar Assn. (co-chmn. com. charitable giving, trusts, founds.), N.Y. County Lawyers Assn., Assn. Bar City N.Y. Author: Deferred Giving, 1977; contbr. articles to legal jours.; editor pub. Taxwise Giving, 1964—. Home: 44 Binney Ln Old Greenwich CT 06870 Office: 375 Park Ave New York City NY 10022 also 13 Arcadia Rd Old Greenwich CT 06870

TEITLER, SAMUEL L., lawyer, electronics co. exec.; b. N.Y.C., Apr. 26, 1906; s. Julius and Sarah Teitler; LL.B., St. Lawrence U., 1927; m. Beatrice Ostroleng, Mar. 29, 1931; children—Michael, Robert, Ann T. (Mrs. Ozer). Admitted to N.Y. State bar, 1929; mem. firm Teitler & Teitler, N.Y.C., 1964—; pres. Lepel Corp., Maspeth, N.Y., 1942-46, chmn. bd., 1946—; dir., gen. counsel World Airways, Inc., Oakland, Calif., vice chmn., 1971—; vice chmn., sec., dir. Worldamerica Investors Corp., Oakland, 1971—. Pres. Kew Gardens Community Council, 1954-57. Mem. Am. Bar Assn., Am. Soc. Tool and Mfg. Engrs., Am. Soc. Metals, Soc. Plastics Industry, N.Y. County Lawyers Assn. Jewish religion (pres. temple 1955-56). Club: World Trade Center (N.Y.C.). Home: 82-04 141st St Briarwood New York NY 11435 Office: 59-21 Queens Midtown Expressway Maspeth NY 11378

TEITSWORTH, ROBERT ALLAN, petroleum co. exec.; b. Los Angeles, Apr. 23, 1930; s. Clark S. and Abba (Flint) T.; B.S., Stanford, 1952, M.S. in Engring., 1953; m. Shirley Strode, Sept. 26, 1953 (div. Jan. 1973); children—Stephen Winthrop, James Flint; m. 2d, Sandra Lee Ezell Carlson, Jan. 19, 1973; 1 dau., Susan Lee. Geologist, Amerada Petroleum Co., Los Angeles, 1953-59; with Occidental Petroleum Corp., Bakersfield, Calif., 1959—, exec. v.p., 1971-73, dir., 1979—; pres. Occidental Exploration and Prodn. Co., 1973-75, chmn., chief exec. officer, 1975—; chmn., chief exec. officer Occidental Oil & Gas Corp., 1975—. Dir. Can. Occidental Petroleum Ltd., Calgary, Can., 1964—, chmn., 1970-78. Mem. Am. Assn. Petroleum Geologists, Am. Inst. Profl. Geologists, Am. Inst. Mining, Metall. and Petroleum Engrs. Home: 1 Hidden Ln Bakersfield CA 93309 Office: 5000 Stockdale Hwy Bakersfield CA 93309

TEITZ, RICHARD STUART, museum dir.; b. Fall River, Mass., July 18, 1942; s. Alexander George and Lucille Teitz; A.B., Yale, 1963; M.A., Harvard, 1965; m. Elaine Tallmadge Osborn, 1962; children—Rebecca Eve, Jessica Ann, Alexander Osborn. Asst. curator Fogg Art Mus., Harvard, 1964-65; curatorial asst. Worcester (Mass.) Art Mus., 1965-67, asst. dir., 1969-70, dir., 1970—; dir. Wichita Art Mus., 1967-69; lectr. Boston Archtl. Center, 1964-65; instr. Clark U., 1966-67; asso. dir. Etruscan Found., Siena, 1965, 66—. Mem. Mass. Council on Arts and Humanities. Trustee John Woodman Higgins Armory Mus.; bd. dirs. Worcester Children's Theatre, Worcester County Music Assn., Worcester Heritage Soc. Mem. Assn. Art Mus. Dirs., Archaeol. Inst. Am., Internat. Council Mus., Coll. Art Assn. Clubs: Worcester, Tatnuck Country, Yale (Worcester). Author: Masterpieces of Etruscan Art, 1967; Art of the Victorian Era, 1969; also articles. Home: 7 Massachusetts Ave Worcester MA 01609 Office: 55 Salisbury St Worcester MA 01608

TE KANAWA, KIRI, opera and concert singer; b. Gisborne, N.Z.; d. Thomas and Elanor Te K.; student St. Mary's Coll., Auckland, N.Z., 1957-60, London Opera Centre, 1966-69; m. Desmond Park, Aug. 30, 1967; 1 dau., Antonia Aroha. Joined Royal Opera House, London, 1971, appeared in role of Countess in Le Nozze di Figaro, 1973; U.S. debut in Le Nozze di Figaro, Sante Fe Festival, 1971; Met. Opera debut as Desdemona in Otello, 1974; appears regularly with all major European and Am. opera houses, also Australian opera companies; appeared in film Don Giovanni as Elvira. Decorated comdr. Order Brit. Empire, 1973. Office: care AIM A/G 3 and 4 Albert Terr London NW1 England

TEKOLSTE, DALE, gas utility exec.; b. Hickman, Nebr., June 7, 1920; s. Gerrit and Gladys (TeSelle) TeK.; student Luther Jr. Coll., 1937-39; B.S., U. Nebr., 1941, LL.B., 1948; postgrad. Northwestern U., 1960, Harvard, 1965; m. Patricia J. Purdham, Dec. 15, 1945; children—Sara, Nancy, Robert. Admitted to Nebr. bar, 1948; atty. No. Natural Gas Co., 1948-55, sr. atty., 1955-58, asst. gen. mgr. Peoples Natural Gas div., 1958-60, v.p., gen. mgr., 1960-64, group v.p., 1964-71, exec. v.p., dir., 1971-76, vice-chmn., 1976—; dir. U.S. Nat. Bank, Omaha, Guarantee Mut. Life Ins. Co., Omaha. Trustee Nebr. Ind. Coll. Found., Nebr. Meth. Hosp. U. Served to 1st lt. AUS, 1942-45. Decorated Bronze Star medal. Mem. Am. Gas Assn., Nebr. Bar Assn. Home: 9902 Harney Pkwy N Omaha NE 68114 Office: 2223 Dodge St Omaha NE 68102

TELESCA, FRANCIS EUGENE, architect; b. Dunmore, Pa., Oct. 22, 1921; s. Joseph J. and Bernetta (Bocchiccio) T.; B.Arch. summa cum laude, Catholic U. Am., 1953; m. G. Dianne Willis, July 31, 1968; children—Celeste Telesca Doody, Anthony, Cheryl, Glenn, Francis Eugene II (Gino), Tina Lee. Designer-draftsman, architect various archtl. and engring. firms, Washington and Miami, Fla., 1951-59; individual practice architecture, Miami, 1959-63; pres., dir. Greenleaf/Telesca, engrs., planners and architects, Miami, 1964—; dir. Greenleaf Enterprises, Inc., Bonefish Towers, Inc., Cherry Ridge Campgrounds, Inc. Mem. Nat. Com. Architecture for Commerce and Industry, 1965-66, Fla. Planning and Zoning Assn., 1960—, Met. Dade County Uniform Code Enforcement Com., 1963-64; bd. dirs. South Fla. Inter-Profl. Council, 1965; planning com. U. Miami Inst. Urban Affairs, 1965; adv. com. City Miami Coconut Grove Zoning, 1965; adv. com. dept. architecture and bldg. constrn. Miami Dade Jr. Coll., 1966. Past pres., dir. Coconut Grove Assn. (arts festival), Grove House (sch. and marketplace for Fla. craftsmen). Served with AUS, 1940-45, 50-51. Decorated Bronze Star; recipient Grand Nat. award Nat. Community Fallout Shelter competition (shopping center), 1964; award of merit Fla. chpt. AIA for Miami Lakes Sr. High Sch. Archtl. award of excellence for Hangar 2, Miami Internat. Airport, Am. Inst. Steel Constrn., 1974, also Grand Conceptor award Am. Cons. Engrs. Council, 1974; award of excellence for Primera Casa, Fla. Internat. U., Fla. Concrete and Products Assn., 1973. Mem. A.I.A. (pres. Fla. South chpt. 1965, bd. dirs. Fla. 1966-69), Coconut Grove (past pres., dir.), Greater Miami (mem. aviation com.) chambers commerce, Phi Eta Sigma. Roman Catholic. Home: 7299 SW 79th Ct Miami FL 33143 Office: 1451 Brickell Av Miami FL 33131

TELFER, JAMES GAVIN, physician; b. San Jose, Calif., Sept. 25, 1907; s. Gavin James and Agnes Cecelia (Griffith) T.; student U. Calif. at Los Angeles, 1930; M.P.H., U. Calif. at Berkeley, 1958; M.D., Washington U., St. Louis, 1934; m. Margaret Adele Baldwin, Mar. 22, 1938 (dec. July 1971); children—Margaret Clare, Robert Baldwin, Patricia Adele, Katherine Agnes, James Gavin, Nancy Alice, William Alan, Jacqueline Ann, Thomas Bruce; m. 2d, Betty Jane Hamilton, Sept. 1, 1973; stepchildren—Garin Biester, Susan Reindl, Stephen Mason. Intern, Gorgas Hosp., C.Z., 1934-35, U. Calif. Hosp., 1935-36; resident internal medicine USPHS hosps.; commd. USPHS, 1936, med. dir., 1952; asso. prof. medicine U. Tex., 1953-54; asst. clin. prof. medicine U. Wash., also chief med. services USPHS Hosp., Seattle, 1954-57; Tb cons. European area div. fgn. quarantine USPHS, 1958-60, asst. chief, 1960-61, chief, 1961-64; asst. dir. dept. environmental health AMA, 1964-65, dir., 1965-68; health officer San Benito County, Calif., 1968-74; practice medicine specializing in internal medicine; cons. internal medicine and pub. health, chief staff Hazel Hawkins Meml. Hosp., Hollister, Calif., 1973, v.p., 1979—; mem. expert adv. bd. internat. quarantine WHO, 1963-78; chmn. for USPHS, United Health Fund Washington, 1961; vice chmn. Calif. Central Coast area PSRO, 1977—. Served with USCGR, 1942-43, AUS, 1943-45. Diplomate Am. Bd. Internal Medicine. Fellow A.C.P., Am. Pub. Health Assn., Royal Soc. Health (Eng.); mem. AMA (past sec. council environmental health and pub. health), Calif. med. Assn. (del. 1970—), San Benito County Med. Soc. (pres. 1976), Am. Thoracic Soc., Commd. Officers Assn. USPHS (pres. Seattle 1956, nat. del. 1956), Mission Trail Heart Assn. (pres. 1976, v.p. 1978—). Home: 1833 Araby Dr Palm Springs CA 92262 Office: 891 Sunset Dr Hollister CA 95023

TELFORD, IRA ROCKWOOD, educator, anatomist; b. Lincoln, Idaho, May 6, 1907; s. John Witt and Martha Starr (Rockwood) T.; student Ricks Coll., 1924-26; A.B., U. Utah, 1931, A.M., 1933; student U. Calif. at Berkeley, 1937-40; Ph.D., George Washington U., 1942; m. Thelma Challis Shrives, June 13, 1933; children—Ira Ralph, John Larry, Kent Matthews, Martha Ann. High sch. adminstr., 1933-37; instr., asst. prof. anatomy George Washington U., 1940-47, prof., exec. officer dept. anatomy, 1953-72; prof., chmn. dept. anatomy U. Tex. Dental Br., 1947-53; cons. anatomy Univ. Hosp., 1953-72; prof. anatomy Georgetown U., Washington, 1972-78; vis. prof. anatomy Uniformed Services U., Bethesda, Md., 1978—. Fulbright scholar, Gt. Britain, 1960. Fellow AAAS (council 1958—); mem. Am. Assn. Anatomists, Soc. Exptl. Biology and Medicine, Am. Acad. Neurology, Washington, Tex. acads. sci., Internat. Soc. Dental Research, AMA (asso.), Sigma Xi (chpt. pres. 1958-59), Phi Sigma (chpt. pres. 1932-33). Mem. Ch. of Jesus Christ of Latter-day Saints. Contbr. articles to biol., med. jours. Home: 3424 Garrison St NW Washington DC 20008

TELKES, MARIA, scientist, engr., educator; b. Budapest, Hungary, Dec. 12, 1900; d. Aladar and Maria (Laban) Telkes; Ph.D., U. Budapest, 1924. Came to U.S., 1925, naturalized, 1937. Research asst. U. Budapest, 1923-24; biophysicist Cleve. Clinic, 1925-37; research engr. Westinghouse Research Labs., 1937-39; research asso. Mass. Inst. Tech., 1939-53; project dir. Coll. Engring., N.Y.U., 1953-58; research dir. solar energy lab. Princeton, div. Curtiss-Wright Co., 1958-60; dir. research and devel. Cryo-Therm Co., 1961-64; head solar energy applications lab. MELPAR, Inc., subsidiary Westinghouse Air-Brake Co., 1965-69; chief scientist Inst. Direct Energy Conversion, U. Pa., Phila., 1970-72; adj. prof., cons. energy conversion, Inst. of Energy Conversion, U. Del., 1972-77; dir. solarthermal storage devel. Am. Technol. U., Killeen, Tex., 1977—; specializes in solar energy research; developed solar stills for life rafts, thermoelectric materials and solar thermoelectric generators, designed solar heating equipment for bldgs.; developed heat storage materials used in accessory equipment in spacecraft and solar heated buildings. Mem. Solar Energy Soc. (dir. C.G. Abbott award), Am. Chem. Soc., Soc. Women Engrs. (hon. life; recipient 1st award 1952), Hellenic Soc. Solar Energy (hon.); Quarter Century award Nat. Acad. Sci./NRC. Contbr. numerous articles to profl. jours., chpts. in books. Office: Am Technol U Killeen TX 76541

TELL, WILLIAM KIRN, JR., petroleum co. exec.; b. Evanston, Ill., Feb. 27, 1934; s. William Kirn and Virginia (Snook) T.; A.B., Dartmouth Coll., 1956; J.D., U. Mich., 1959; m. Karen Nelson Tell, July 16, 1960; children—Catherine, Caroline, William. Admitted to Ohio bar, 1959, D.C. bar, 1979; mem. firm McAfee, Hanning, Newcomer & Hazlett, Cleve., 1959-63; atty. Texaco, Inc., 1963-70, asso. gen. counsel, 1970-72, asst. to chmn. bd., 1973-74, v.p., 1974-78, sr. v.p., 1978—; dir. Texaco Can., Inc. Mem. Am. Bar Assn. (mem. bus.-govt. relation council sect. natural resources law 1968-75). Clubs: Bronxville (N.Y.); Field; Congl. Country, Internat., Carlton, Georgetown (Washington). Office: 1050 17th St NW Washington DC 20036

TELLEEN, JOHN MARTIN, lawyer; b. Cambridge, Ill., Dec. 16, 1922; s. Leonard E. and Vina (Elm) T.; A.B., Augustana Coll., 1947; LL.B., U. Ill., 1950; m. Nell Joanne Larson, June 17, 1950; children—Jane, Mary, John D., Thomas. Admitted to Ill. bar, 1950; practice in Moline, 1950-53, Rock Island, 1953—; partner firm Katz, McAndrews, Durkee & Telleen, Rock Island, 1953—; counsel Luth. Hosp., Moline. Bd. dirs. Augustana Coll., Rock Island, 1968-76, sec., 1968-70, vice chmn., 1970, chmn., 1971-76; bd. dirs. Luth. Hosp., 1957-68. Served with USNR, 1943-46. Mem. Am., Ill., Rock Island County (pres. 1970) bar assns. Home: 4344 18th Ave Moline IL 61265 Office: Suite 200 Cleaveland Bldg PO Box 66 Rock Island IL 61201

TELLEP, DANIEL MICHAEL, aero. engr., aerospace co. exec.; b. Forest City, Pa., Nov. 20, 1931; s. John M. and Mary J. (Yusko) T.; B.S. with highest honors, U. Calif., Berkeley, 1954, M.S., 1955; m. Patricia Godfrey Taylor, Sept. 5, 1970; children—Teresa, Mary, Susan, Patricia. With Lockheed Missiles and Space Co., Sunnyvale, Calif., 1955—, mgr. launch and entry thermodynamics, 1962-66, chief poseidon reentry systems, mgr. reentry systems engring., 1966-69, chief engr. missile systems div., 1969-75, v.p., asst. gen. mgr. advanced systems div., 1975—. Bd. regents Inst. Med. Research. Fellow AIAA; mem. Nat. Acad. Engring., Sigma Xi, Pi Tau Sigma, Tau Beta Pi. Contbr. articles to profl. jours. Home: 14680 Fieldstone Dr Saratoga CA 95070 Office: PO Box 504 Sunnyvale CA 94086

TELLEPSEN, HOWARD TELLEF, engr., contractor; b. Houston, Apr. 16, 1913; s. Tom and Ingeborg (Larsen) T.; B.S. in Civil Engring., Ga. Inst. Tech., 1934; m. June Learned, Nov. 29, 1940; children—Karen, Howard Tellef, Tom II. Mgr., Huntsville Stone Co., 1934-35; v.p. Tellepsen Constrn. Co., Houston, Texas, 1935-41, pres., 1941-69, 1973—, chmn. bd., 1969—; vice chmn. First Pasadena State Bank, Pasadena, Tex.; dir. Southwestern Life Corp., Freeport Nat. Bank, Houston First Savs. Assn., Southwestern Bell Telephone Co. Trustee Tex. A. and M. Research Found., Tellepsen Found., Harris County Girl Scout Found. Mem. C. of C. (past pres.), Nat. Soc. Profl. Engrs., ASCE. Episcopalian. Home: 5425 Tupper Lake Dr Houston TX 77056 Office: 1710 Telephone Rd PO Box 2536 Houston TX 77001

TELLER, AARON JOSEPH, chem. engr.; b. Bklyn., June 30, 1921; s. David and Mollie (Tascher) T.; B. Chem. Engring., Cooper Union, 1943; M. Chem. Engring., Bklyn. Poly. Inst., 1949; Ph.D., Case Inst. Tech., 1951; m. Sherry R. April, June 30, 1946; 1 son, Richard Eric. Research engr. Manhattan Project, 1942-44; devel. engr. Publicker Comml. Alcohol Co., 1944-45; prodn. mgr. Martin Labs., 1945-47; chief devel. engr. City Chem. Corp., 1946-47; chmn. chem. engring. and chem. depts. Fenn Coll., 1947-56; research prof., chmn. chem. engring. U. Fla., 1956-60; tech. dir. Mass Transfer, Inc., 1960-62; tech. dir. Colonial Iron Works, Inc., 1960-62, cons. tech. dir., 1962-64; ind. indsl. cons., 1947—; dean Sch. Engring. and Sci., Cooper Union, 1962-70; pres. Teller Environmental Systems, Inc., 1970—. Mem. Nat. Adv. Council on Air Pollution. Recipient Bus. Week environ. award, 1972, Vaaeur award, 1978. Mem. Nat. Engrs. Commn. on Air Resources (chmn. commn. on resource economy, 1972—), Am. Inst.

Chem. Engrs. (chmn. Cleve. and Peninsular Fla. sects. 1953, 58, chmn. pollution control program 1958-61, chmn. air com. 1963-66, 22d ann. inst. lectr., 1972), Am. Inst. Chem. Engring. Editor: Liquid-Gas Operations (Perry's Chem. Engring. Handbook), 4th edit., 1963. Contbr. articles to profl. jours. Patentee in mass transfer and air pollution control systems. Home: 293 Turnpike Rd Apt 802E Westboro MA 01581 Office: 10 Faraday St Worcester MA 01605

TELLER, EDWARD, physicist; b. Budapest, Hungary, Jan. 15, 1908; s. Max and Ilona (Deutch) T.; student Inst. Tech., Karlsruhe, Germany, 1926-28, U. Munich, 1928-29; Ph.D., U. Leipzig (Germany), 1930; D.Sc., Yale, 1954, U. Alaska, 1959, Fordham U., 1960, George Washington U., 1960, U. So. Calif., 1960, St. Louis U., 1960, Rochester Inst. Tech., 1962, PMC Colls., 1963, U. Detroit, 1964, Clemson U., 1966, Clarkson Coll., 1969, U. Md. at Heidelberg, 1977; LL.D., Boston Coll., 1961, Seattle U., U. Cin., 1962, U. Pitts., 1963, Pepperdine Coll., 1973; D.Sc., L.H.D., Mt. Mary Coll., 1964; Ph.D., Tel Aviv U., 1972; m. Augusta Harkanyi, Feb. 26, 1934; children—Paul, Susan Wendy. Naturalized Am. citizen, 1941. Research asso. Leipzig, 1929-31, Gottingen, Germany, 1931-33; Rockefeller fellow, Copenhagen, Denmark, 1934; lectr. U. London, 1934-35; prof. physics George Washington U., Washington, 1935-41, Columbia, 1941-42, physicist Manhattan Engr. Dist., U. Chgo., 1942-43, Los Alamos Sci. Lab., 1943-46, Chgo., 1946-52; prof. physics U. Calif., 1953-60, prof. physics-at-large, 1960-70, Univ. prof., 1970-75, prof. emeritus, chmn. dept. applied sci., Davis and Livermore, 1963-66; asst. dir. Los Alamos Sci. Lab., 1949-52; cons. Livermore br. U. Calif. Radiation Lab., 1952-53; asso. dir. Lawrence Livermore Radiation Lab., U. Calif., 1954-58, 60-75, dir., 1958-60, now dir. emeritus, cons.; concerned with planning and prediction function atomic bomb and hydrogen bomb Manhattan Dist. of Columbia, also Metall. and Lab. of Argonne Nat. Lab., U. Chgo., and Los Alamos, N.Mex., 1941-51, Radiation Lab., Livermore, Calif., 1952-75; sr. research fellow Hoover Instn. War, Revolution and Peace, Stanford, 1975—. Dir., Thermo Electron Corp. Mem. sci. adv. bd. USAF. Mem. bd. Fed. Union; bd. govs. Tel Aviv U.; sponsor Atlantic Union, Atlantic Council of U.S., Univ. Centers for Rational Alternatives; past mem. gen. adv. com. AEC; mem. Com. to Unite Am., Inc.; former mem. President's Fgn. Intelligence Adv. Bd. Bd. visitors, past bd. dirs. Def. Intelligence Sch., Naval War Coll. Recipient Joseph Priestley Meml. award Dickinson Coll., 1957; Albert Einstein award, 1958; Gen. Donovan Meml. award, 1959, Midwest Research Inst. award, 1960, Research Inst. Am. Living History award, 1960, Golden Plate award, 1961, Thomas E. White and Enrico Fermi awards, 1962, Robins award of Am., 1963, Harvey prize in sci. and tech. Technion-Israel Inst., 1975; Semmelweiss medal, 1977; Albert Einstein award Technion Inst., 1977; Henry T. Heald award Ill. Inst. Tech., 1978. Fellow Am. Nuclear Soc., Am. Phys. Soc.; mem. Am. Acad. Arts and Scis., Am. Ordnance Assn., Nat. Acad. Scis., Am. Geophys. Union, Soc. Engring. Scis. Author: (with Francis Owen Rice) The Structure of Matter, 1948; (with A. L. Latter) Our Nuclear Future, 1958; (with Allen Brown) The Legacy of Hiroshima, 1962; The Reluctant Revolutionary, 1964; (with G.W. Johnson, W.K. Talley, G.H. Higgins) The Constructive Uses of Nuclear Explosives; Great Men of Physics, 1969; The Miracle of Freedom, 1972; Energy: A Plan for Action, 1975; Nuclear Energy in the Developing World, 1977; Energy from Heaven and Earth, 1979. Research on chem., molecular and nuclear physics, quantum theory, thermonuclear reactions, applications of nuclear energy, astrophysics, spectroscopy of polyatomic molecules, theory of atomic nuclei. Office: Hoover Instn Stanford CA 94305

TELLEZ, THERESA PINO, author, social anthropologist; b. Mentmore, N.Mex., Oct. 8, 1929; d. Manuel and Julia (Pino) Tellez; B.A. (Marsden Found. grantee, Am. U. Alumni Assn. scholar), Am. U., 1970, M.A. in Anthropology (Univ. fellow), 1974; m. Harrison Brown, Mar. 27, 1975. Sec., com. sci. UNESCO, Nat. Acad. Scis., Washington, 1954-62, mem. profl. staff Latin Am. Sci. Bd., 1963-67, head Latin Am. affairs, 1967-70, profl. asso. Bd. Sci. and Tech. for Internat. Devel., 1971-74; cons. adminstrn. and mgmt., internat. devel., edn., women's programs, 1975—, Sci. and Public Policy Jour., 1973. Mem. A.A.A.S. (chmn. panel Spanish sur-named scientists 1973-75), Am. Anthrop. Assn., Anthrop. Soc. Washington, Center Inter-Am. Relations, Soc. Advancement Chicano and Native Am. Scientists, Women's Equity Action League. Author: (with Harrison Brown) International Development Programs of the Office of the Foreign Secretary, 1973. Contbr. articles to profl. jours. Home and office: 965 Prospect St Apt 611 Honolulu HI 96822

TELLIER, HENRI, ret. Canadian mil. officer, assn. exec.; b. Montreal, Que., Can., Sept. 1, 1918; s. Henri Joseph and Jeanne (St. Cyr) T.; student U. Montreal, 1935-40, U. Ottawa, 1946-47, Canadian Army Staff Coll., 1942-43, Imperial Def. Coll., London, Eng., 1966, Dept. Def. Computer Inst., Washington, 1968; m. Virginia Wright, July 23, 1945; children—Pierre, Michele, Suzanne, Jean, Nicole. With Robert Howard & Co., ins. brokers, Montreal, 1937-40; commd. 2d lt. Canadian Army, 1940, advanced through grades to lt. gen., 1973; asst. sec. to minister Nat. Def., 1945-48; comdg. officer Royal 22d Regt., 1948-51; instr. Canadian Army Staff Coll., 1951-54; army mem. Joint Intelligence Staff, 1954-57; mil. adviser Vietnam, 1957-58; chief of staff Que. Mil. Dist., 1958-60; mil attache, Rome, Italy, 1960- 63; dir. mil. operations and plans Army, 1963-64; dir. internat. plans Integrated Armed Forces, 1964-65; comdr. Canadian Contingent, Cyprus, 1965-66; dir. gen. plans Forces Hdqrs., Ottawa, Ont., 1967-70, dep. chief plans, 1970-71; Canadian mil. rep. to mil. com. NATO Hdqrs., Brussels, Belgium, 1971-73; ret., 1973; asso. nat. commr. Canadian Red Cross Soc., Toronto, Ont., 1973-75, nat. commr., 1975—. Chmn., Canadian sect. Mil. Coop. Com. Can.-U.S., Joint Permanent Bd. Def. Can.-U.S.; commr. Commn. for Strategic and Internat. Studies. Decorated Distinguished Service Order, Canadian Decoration; Inhuldigingsmedaille (Netherlands). Mem. Canadian Inst. Internat. Affairs. Office: Canadian Red Cross Soc 95 Wellesley St E Toronto ON M4Y 1H6 Canada

TELLING, EDWARD RIGGS, corp. exec.; b. Danville, Ill., Apr. 1, 1919; s. Edward Riggs and Margaret Katherine (Matthews) T.; Ph.B., Ill. Wesleyan U., 1942, LL.D., 1978; m. Nancy Hawkins, Dec. 29, 1942; children—Edward R. III, Pamela Telling Grimes, Kathryn Telling Bentley, Nancy Telling O'Shaughnessy, Thomas Cole. With Sears, Roebuck & Co., 1946—, store mgr., 1954-59, zone mgr., 1960-64, mgr. met. N.Y.C. area ops., 1965-67, adminstrv. asst. to v.p. Eastern ter., Phila., 1968, v.p. Eastern ter., 1969-74, exec. v.p. Midwestern ter., Chgo., 1974-75, sr. exec. v.p. field, Chgo., 1976-77, chmn., chief exec. officer, 1978—, also dir.; dir. Allstate Ins. Co., Homart Devel. Co., Kraft, Inc., Sears Roebuck Acceptance Corp., Sears Internat. Fin. Co., Simpsons-Sears Ltd. Bd. dirs. Sears-Roebuck Found.; trustee Savs. and Profit Sharing Fund of Sears Employees, Field Mus. Natural History; mem. Bus. Council, policy com. Bus. Roundtable. Served to lt. USN, 1941-45. Clubs: Chicago, Shoreacres, Old Elm, Commercial. Office: Sears Tower Chicago IL 60684

TELSER, LESTER GREENSPAN, educator, economist; b. Chgo., Jan. 3, 1931; s. Asher and Edith (Greenspan) T.; A.B., Roosevelt U., 1951; student Harvard, 1951-52; A.M., U. Chgo., 1953, Ph.D. in Econs., 1956; m. Sylvia R. Trossman, June 24, 1956; children—Joshua, Tamar. Asst. prof. econs. Iowa State U., 1956; mem. faculty Grad. Sch. Bus., U. Chgo., 1958-64; prof. econs. U. Chgo., 1965—; cons. to industry, 1964—. Served with AUS, 1956-58. Fellow Am. Statis. Assn. (asso. editor jour. 1966-69), Econometric Soc.; mem. Am. Econs. Assn. Author: Competition, Collusion and Game Theory, 1972; Functional Analysis in Mathematical Economics, 1972; Economic Theory and the Core, 1978. Home: 1456 E 56th St Chicago IL 60637

TEMERLIN, LIENER, advt. exec.; b. Ardmore, Okla., Mar. 27, 1928; s. Pincus and Julie (Kahn) T.; B.A., U. Okla., 1950; m. Karla Samuelsohn, July 23, 1950; children—Dana Michelle, Lisa Babette, Sandy Gottesman. Editor Sponsor Mag., N.Y.C., 1950-51; with Glenn Advt. Inc., Dallas, 1952—, creative dir., chief operating officer, 1970-74; pres. Glenn, Bozell & Jacobs, Inc., 1974-79, chmn. bd. Bozell & Jacobs Internat., 1979—. Bd. dirs. Golden Acres Home for Jewish Aged; adv. council, planning com. St. Paul Hosp.; adv. com. U. Tex., Dallas, U. Tex., Arlington; trustee Timberlawn Psychiat. Research Found.; exec. com., bd. dirs. Temple Emanu-El. Served to 1st lt., arty. AUS, 1951-52; Korea. Decorated Bronze Star. Mem. Am. Assn. Advt. Agys. (chmn. S.W. council 1969-70), Dallas Advt. League. Home: 9301 Sunny Brook Ln Dallas TX 75220 Office: PO Box 61200 Dallas/Fort Worth Airport TX 75261

TEMES, GABOR CHARLES, educator; b. Budapest, Hungary, Oct. 14, 1929; s. Erno and Rozsa (Angyal) Wohl-Temes; Dipl.Ing., Tech. U. Budapest, 1952; Dipl.Phys., Eotvos U., Budapest, 1954; Ph.D., U. Ottawa (Ont., Can.), 1961; m. Ibi Kutasi-Temes, Feb. 6, 1954; children—Roy Thomas, Carla Andrea. Asst. prof. Tech. U. Budapest, 1952-56; project engr. Measurement Engring. Ltd., 1956-59; dept. head No. Electric Co. Ltd., 1959-64; group leader Stanford Linear Accelerator Center, 1964-66; corporate cons. Ampex Corp., 1966-69; prof. elec. engring. U. Calif. at Los Angeles, 1969—, chmn. dept., 1975—. Cons. Ampex Corp., Collins Radio Co. Recipient Best Paper award IEEE, 1969. NSF grantee, 1970—. Fellow IEEE (editor Transactions on Circuit Theory, 1969-71). Author: (with others) Introduction to Circuit Synthesis and Design, 1977. Asso. editor Jour. Franklin Inst., 1971—. Co-editor, contbg. author: Modern Filter Theory and Design, 1973. Home: 2015 Stradella Rd Los Angeles CA 90024

TEMIANKA, HENRI, violinist, condr.; b. Greenock, Scotland; s. Israel and Fanny (Hildebrand) T.; ed. Rotterdam, Berlin, Paris; grad. Curtis Inst., 1930; m. Emmy Cowden, Jan. 28, 1943; children—Daniel, David. Came to U.S., 1940. Debut, N.Y.C., 1928, Europe, 1930; soloist with John Barbirolli, George Szell, Vaughan Williams, Sir Adrian Boult, Fritz Reiner, Otto Klemperer; also with Amsterdam Concertgebouw Orch., philharm. orchs. of Warsaw, The Hague, Rotterdam, London, Brussels, Monte-Carlo, Geneva, Stockholm, Copenhagen, Helsinki; toured Russia at govt. invitation, 1935, 36; founded Temianka Chamber Orch., London, 1936; toured U.S., 1942—; leader Paganini String Quartet, 1946-66; head violin dept., summer master classes Santa Barbara Music Acad. of West, 1952; produced, wrote, narrated series ednl. motion pictures commd. by Ednl. TV Center, 1956; artistic adviser Nat. Fedn. Music Clubs; artistic dir. Reno Tahoe Music Festival, 1979; guest condr. Los Angeles Philharmonic Orch., 1958-59, 59-60; U.S. tour of 40 concerts with Temianka Little Symphony, 1960, 61, 64; concert tours Europe, Orient, S.Am., Can., 1960—; vis. prof. U. Calif. at Santa Barbara, 1960-65; lectr. univs.; prof., music dir. Calif. State U. at Long Beach, 1964-74, prof. emeritus, 1974—; lectr. UCLA; founder, condr. Calif. Chamber Symphony: cons. Ford Found. Adviser Young Musicians Found. Served with overseas br. OWI, 1942-44. Decorated officier des Arts et Lettres (France). Author: Facing the Music, 1973; contbr. to magazines. Office: 6380 Wilshire Blvd Los Angeles CA 90048. *I have tried not to dwell on my failures, and to recover as quickly as possible from the wounds inflicted by destructive critics or other antagonists. One's emotional and physical reserves are limited and precious. In order to succeed, one must use them wisely, which means constructively and creatively.*

TEMIN, HOWARD MARTIN, educator, scientist; b. Phila., Dec. 10, 1934; s. Henry and Annette (Lehman) T.; B.A., Swarthmore Coll., 1955, D.Sc. (hon.), 1972; Ph.D., Calif. Inst. Tech., 1959; D.Sc. (hon.), N.Y. Med. Coll., 1972, U. Pa., 1976, Hahnemann Med. Coll., 1976, Lawrence U., 1976, Temple U., 1979; m. Rayla Greenberg, May 27, 1962; children—Sarah Beth, Miriam Judith. Postdoctoral fellow Calif. Inst. Tech., 1959-60; asst. prof. oncology U. Wis., 1960-64, asso. prof., 1964-69, prof., 1969—, Wis. Alumni Research Found. prof. cancer research, 1971—, Am. Cancer Soc. prof. viral oncology and cell biology, 1974—; mem. NIH virology study sect., 1971-75, mem. dir.'s adv. com., 1979—; mem. Nat. Cancer Inst. spl. virus cancer program tumor virus detection segment working group, 1972-73; Charlton lectr. Tufts U., 1976; sponsor Fedn. Am. Scientists, 1976—. Co-recipient Warren Triennial prize Mass. Gen. Hosp., 1971, Gairdner Found. Internat. award, 1974, Nobel Prize in medicine, 1975; recipient Med. Soc. Wis. Spl. commendation, 1971; Papanicolaou Inst. PAP award, 1972; M.D. Anderson Hosp. and Tumor Inst. Bertner award, 1972; U.S. Steel Found. award in Molecular Biology, 1972; Theobald Smith Soc. Waksman award, 1972; Am. Chem. Soc. award in Enzyme Chemistry, 1973; Modern Medicine award for Distinguished Achievement, 1973; Harry Shay Meml. lectr. Fels Research Inst., 1973; Griffuel prize Assn. Devel. Recherche Cancer, Villejuif, 1972; NIH Dyer lectr. award, 1974; Harvey lectr., 1974; Albert Lasker award in basic med. sci., 1974; Lucy Wortham James award Soc. Surg. Oncologists, 1976, Alumni Distinguished Service award Calif. Inst. Tech., 1976; mem. Central High Sch. Hall of Fame, 1976; Pub. Health Service Research Career Devel. awardee Nat. Cancer Inst., 1964-74. Fellow Am. Acad. Arts and Scis.; mem. Nat. Acad. Scis., Am. Philos. Soc., Wis. Acad. Sci., Arts and Letters (hon.). Asso. editor Jour. Cellular physiology, 1966-78, Cancer Research, 1971-74; mem. editorial bd. Jour. Virology, 1971—, Intervirology, 1972-75, Proc. Nat. Acad. Scis., 1975—, Archives of Virology, 1975-77. Office: McArdle Lab 450 N Randall St U Wis Madison WI 53706

TEMIN, PETER, economist; b. Phila., Dec. 17, 1937; s. Henry and Annette Temin; B.A., Swarthmore (Pa.) Coll., 1959; Ph.D., Mass. Inst. Tech., 1964; m. Charlotte Brucar Fox, Aug. 21, 1966; children—Elizabeth Sara, Melanie Wynn. Mem. faculty Mass. Inst. Tech., 1965—, prof. econs., 1970—. Mem. Am. Econ. Assn., Econ. History Assn., Econ. History Soc., Phi Beta Kappa. Author: The Jacksonian Economy, 1969; Casual Factors in American Economic Growth in the 19th Century, 1975; Did Monetary Forces Cause the Great Depression?, 1976. Home: 15 Channing St Cambridge MA 02138 Office: Econs Dept Mass Inst Tech Cambridge MA 02139

TEMKIN, VICTOR, publishing co. exec.; b. Milwaukee, Wis., Aug. 25, 1934; s. Henry and Mae (Balkansky) T.; B.S., U. Wis., 1958, LL.B., 1960; m. Susan Lamm, Apr. 6, 1969; children—Cindy, Jeremy H., Andrew C., Peter M. Admitted to N.Y. bar, 1961, U.S. Supreme Ct. bar, 1964; asst. U.S. atty. So. Dist. N.Y., Dept. Justice, 1961-64; partner firm Temkin & Ginsberg, N.Y.C., 1964-67; v.p., sec., gen. counsel Bantam Books Inc., N.Y.C., 1967-77; pres. chief exec. officer Berkley Pub. Corp., N.Y.C., 1977—, Jove Publs. Inc., N.Y.C., 1979—. Active Police Athletic League, N.Y.C.; Robert F. Kennedy Meml. Found. Democrat. Jewish. Club: Golf at Aspetuck (sec.) (Easton, Conn.). Home: 25 Central Park W New York NY 10023 Office: 200 Madison Ave New York NY 10016

TEMKO, STANLEY LEONARD, lawyer; b. N.Y.C., Jan. 4, 1920; s. Emanuel and Betty (Alderman) T.; A.B., Columbia U., 1940, LL.B., 1943; m. Francine Marie Salzman, Mar. 4, 1944; children—Richard J., Edward J., William D. Admitted to N.Y. bar, 1943, D.C. bar, 1951; practice in N.Y.C., 1943, 46-47; law clk. Mr. Justice Wiley Rutledge, U.S. Supreme Ct., Washington, 1947-48; asso. firm Covington & Burling, Washington, 1949-55, partner, 1955—. Trustee Beauvoir Sch., 1963-69; bd. govs. St. Albans Sch., 1967-73, chmn., 1971-73; bd. visitors Columbia U. Sch. Law, 1961—, mem. exec. com., 1977—. Served to 2d lt. U.S. Army, 1943-46. Decorated Bronze Star; recipient Columbia U. medal for conspicuous alumni service, 1979. Fellow Am. Bar Found. (chmn. research com. 1970-72), mem. Am. Bar Assn., D.C. Bar Assn., Am. Law Inst., Phi Beta Kappa. Clubs: Met., City Tavern. Editor-in-chief Columbia Law Rev., 1942-43. Home: 4811 Dexter Terr NW Washington DC 20007 Office: 888 16th St NW Washington DC 20006

TEMPEST, HARRISON FRANKLAND, banker; b. Evanston, Ill., June 19, 1937; s. William and Gertrude Ada (Noyes) T.; B.A., Miami U., Oxford, Ohio, 1959; LL.B., Ohio State U., 1961; m. Marilyn Fuchs, July 19, 1966; children—Michael, Nicole. Admitted to Ohio bar, 1961; agt. FBI, 1961-65; with First Nat. Bank of Chgo., after 1965, established subs. First Chgo. Australia Ltd., Sydney, 1973, v.p., gen. mgr. London br., 1973-75, area head for British Isles and Scandinavia, after 1975; now exec. v.p. Bank of Calif., San Francisco, also pres., chief exec. officer Bank of California Internat., N.Y.C. Mem. Bankers Assn. for Fgn. Trade (dir. 1979). Clubs: World Trade (San Francisco); Les Ambassadeurs (London). Home: 2325 Forest View Ave Hillsborough CA 94010 Office: Bank of Calif 400 California St San Francisco CA 94104

TEMPLAR, GEORGE, judge; b. Cowley County, Kans., Oct. 18, 1904; s. John and Carlotta E. (Linn) T.; LL.B. cum laude, Washburn Coll., 1927, J.D., 1970, LL.D., 1971; m. Helen Marie Bishop, Mar. 29, 1924; children—Joana (Mrs. Jerry Smith), Ted. Admitted to Kans. bar, 1927; practiced in Arkansas City, 1927; dep. oil insp. State of Kans., 1930-32; mem. Kans. Ho. Reps., 1933-41, Kans. Jud. Council, 1941-45, Kans. Senate, 1945-53; U.S. dist. atty., 1953-54; judge U.S. Dist. Ct., Topeka, 1962—. Trustee Southwestern Coll., 1947—, pres. bd. trustees, 1959-70. Recipient award of merit Assn. Trial Lawyers of Am., 1972, medal honor D.A.R., 1973. Fellow Internat. Acad. Trial Lawyers; mem. Kans., Fed. bar assns., Kans. Hist. Soc. (trustee 1938—, v.p. 1968, pres. 1970). Methodist. Mason (DeMolay Legion of Honor). Club: Nat. Lawyers. Contbr. articles to law jours. Home: PO Box 32 Arkansas City KS 67005 Office: Federal Bldg Topeka KS 66683

TEMPLE, GRAY, bishop; b. Lewiston, Maine, Mar. 13, 1914; s. Charles Hosea and Eleanor (Gray) T.; A.B., Brown U., 1935; M.Div., Va. Theol. Sem., 1938, D.D., 1961; D.D., U. of South, 1961; m. Maria Drane, Jan. 29, 1940; children—Gray, Robert Brent, Charles Adams. Ordained priest P.E. Ch., 1939; rector in Rocky Mt., N.C., 1942-53, Charlotte, N.C., 1953-56, Columbia, S.C., 1956-61; bishop of S.C., 1961—. Successively mem. standing com., exec. council and bd. exam. chaplains P.E. Diocese N.C., 1942-56; successively mem. standing com., exec. com. and bd. exam. chaplains P.E. Diocese S.C., 1956-61; del. gen. Conv. P.E. Ch., 1949-52, 55, 58; exec. council PECUSA, 1970-76. Vice pres. East Carolina council Boy Scouts Am., 1950-53. Trustee Porter Acad., Voorhees Coll., York Orphanage, Church Home Ladies, Kanuga Conf. Center, Canterbury House. Home: King St Charleston SC 29401 Office: 1020 King St Drawer 2127 Charleston SC 29403•

TEMPLE, JEROME BALAAM POUND, JR., hotel exec.; b. Ft. McClellan, Ala., Jan. 10, 1942; s. Jerome Balaam Pound and Ann (Glascock) T.; B.S., Cornell U. Sch. Hotel Adminstrn., 1965; m. Betty Bardin, Aug. 18, 1964; children—Sarah Lynn, Kathleen Page. Trainee, Western Internat. Hotels, Inc., Seattle, 1965-66; gen. mgr. Holiday Inn, Acapulco, Mex., 1972-74, Hollywood, Calif., 1974-75, Chgo., 1975-77; gen. mgr. Marriott Inn, W.B. Johnson Properties, Inc., Orlando, Fla., 1977—. Served to capt. USAF, 1966-71. Decorated Air Force Commendation medal. Mem. Cornell Soc. Hotelmen, Orlando Area Tourist and Trade Assn. Office: 6700 Sandlake Rd Orlando FL 32809

TEMPLE, JOSEPH GEORGE, JR., chem. co. exec.; b. Bklyn., Aug. 29, 1929; s. Joseph George and Helen Frances (Beney) T.; B.S. in Chem. Engring., Purdue U., 1951; m. Ann Elizabeth McFerran, June 21, 1952; children—Linda Jo, James, John. With Dow Chem. Co., 1951—, v.p. mktg., Midland, Mich., 1976-78, dir., 1979—, pres. Dow Chem. Latin Am., Coral Gables, Fla., 1978—; dir. Flagship Banks, Inc., Solar Energy Research Corp. Mem. pres.'s council Purdue U., 1978—; bd. dirs. Citizens Research Council of Mich. Recipient Disting. Engr. Alumni award Purdue U., 1978. Mem. Am. Inst. Chem. Engrs., Nat. Mgmt. Assn. (Silver Knight award 1976). Episcopalian. Office: 2801 Ponce de Leon Blvd Coral Gables FL 33134

TEMPLE, SHIRLEY. see Black, Shirley Temple

TEMPLE, WAYNE CALHOUN, historian; b. nr. Richwood, Ohio, Feb. 5, 1924; s. Howard M. and Ruby March (Calhoun) T.; A.B. cum laude, U. Ill., 1949, A.M., 1951, Ph.D., 1956; Lincoln Diploma Honor, Lincoln Meml. U., Harrogate, Tenn., 1963; m. Lois Marjorie Bridges, Sept. 22, 1956 (dec. Apr. 1978); m. 2d, Sunderine Wilson, Apr. 9, 1979; 1 stepson, Randy Mohn. Research asst. history U. Ill., 1949-53, teaching asst., 1953-54; curator ethnohistory Ill. State Mus., 1954-58; editor-in-chief Lincoln Herald, Lincoln Meml. U., 1958-73, asso. editor, 1973—, also dir. dept. Lincolniana, dir. univ. press, John Wingate Weeks prof. history, 1958-64; with Ill. State Archives, 1964—; lectr. U.S. Mil. Acad., 1975. Sec.-treas. Nat. Lincoln-Civil War Council, 1958-64; mem. bibliography com. Lincoln Lore, 1958—; hon. mem. Lincoln Sesquicentennial Commn., 1959-60, advisory council U.S. Civil War Centennial Commn. 1960-66; maj. Civil War Press Corps, 1962—; sponsor Abraham Lincoln Bay, Washington Nat. Cathedral; mem. Ill. State Flag Commn., 1969—; active Boy Scouts Am., 1956—, asst. dist. commr. Cumberland council, 1958-60, mem. exec. bd., v.p. Abraham Lincoln council, also advisory com. Ill. Lincoln Trail Hike com. Bd. dirs. Vachel Lindsay House; trustee, regent Lincoln Acad. Ill., 1970—; bd. govs. St. Louis unit Shriners Hosps. for Crippled Children, 1975—. Served with U.S. Army, 1943-46; lt. gen. Res. Recipient Order of Arrow, Boy Scouts Am., 1957, Scouters award, 1960, Scouter's Key, also medallion, 1967, Lincoln medallion Lincoln Sesquicentennial Commn., 1960, award of Achievement, U.S. Civil War Centennial Commn., 1965, Algernon Sydney Sullivan medallion, 1969, Distinguished Service award Ill. State Hist. Library, 1969, 77, I.H. Duval Distinguished Service award, 1971, legion of honor, Internat. Supreme Council, Order of De Molay, 1972. Life fellow Royal Soc. Arts; hon. mem. Lincoln Group D.C., U. Ill. Alumni Assn., Ill. State Hist. Soc., Ill. Registered Land Surveyors Assn., Ill. State Dental Soc. (citation plague 1966), Lincoln Fellowship of Wis.; mem. Soc. Am. Archivists, Sons Union Vets. Civil War, Nat. Rifle Assn. (life), Kappa Delta Pi, Phi Alpha Theta (scholarship award Key), Chi Gamma Iota, Tau Kappa Alpha, Alpha Psi Omega, Sigma Pi Beta (Headmaster), Sigma Tau Delta (gold honor key editorial writing). Mason (33 deg., Shriner, Knight Templar, Meritorious Service award), Mil. Order Loyal Legion U.S. (hon. companion). Presbyterian (elder). Author: Indian

Villages of the Illinois Country: Historic Tribes, 1958, rev. edit., 1966, 77; Lincoln the Railsplitter, 1961; Abraham Lincoln and Others at the St. Nicholas, 1968; Alexander Williamson-Tutor to the Lincoln Boys, 1971; (with others) First Steps to Victory: Grant's March to Naples, 1977. Editor: Campaigning with Grant, 1961, 72; The Civil War Letters of Henry C. Bear, 1961; 71 radio scripts, A. Lincoln 1809-1959; Indian Villages of the Illinois Country: Atlas Supplement, 1975. Editorial advisory bd. Am. Biog. Inst., 1971—, Ency. Indians of Ams., 1973—; advisory com. Loyal Legion Hist. Jour., 1972—. Contbr. to profl. jours., encys. Home: 1121 S 4th St Ct Springfield IL 62703 Office: Ill State Archives Springfield IL 62756

TEMPLE, WICK, journalist; b. Little Rock, Oct. 24, 1937; s. Robert Wickliffe and Lorene (Bullard) T.; A.A., Texarkana Coll., 1957; postgrad. U. Tex., 1958-59; m. Lorrie Boring, Oct. 23, 1971; children—Wick, Ellen, Carol, Shawn. Reporter, sports editor Texarkana (Tex.) Gazette-News, 1954-58; reporter Austin (Tex.) American-Statesman, 1958-59; reporter, news editor AP, Little Rock, 1959-65, corr., St. Louis, 1965-66, bur. chief, Helena, Mont., 1966-68, Seattle, 1968-73, gen. sports editor, N.Y.C., 1973—. Home: 18 Edgemont Rd West Orange NJ 07052 Office: 50 Rockefeller Plaza New York NY 10020

TEMPLEMAN, WILFRED, marine biologist; b. Bonavista, Nfdl., Can., Feb. 22, 1908; s. Charles and Sarah (Fisher) T.; student Meml. U. Coll., St. John's, Nfld., 1927-28, D.Sc. (hon.), Meml. U., 1976; B.Sc., Dalhousie U., Halifax, N.S., Can., 1930; M.A., U. Toronto (Ont., Can.), 1931, Ph.D., 1933; m. Eileen Eliza McGrath, Sept. 7, 1937; children—Margaret Elizabeth Templeman Nowe, Barbara Eileen Templeman Hartling, Sheila Joan Templeman Craig, Sandra Louise Templeman Moores. Lectr. dept. biology McGill U., 1933-36; asso. prof. Meml. U. Coll., 1936-43, prof., 1943-44, head dept. biology, 1936-44, J. L. Paton prof. marine biology and fisheries Meml. U., 1972—; dir. Nfld. Govt. Lab., 1944-49; dir. Fisheries Research Bd. of Can. Biol. Sta., St. John's, 1949-72; chmn. standing com. on research and stats. Internat. Commn. for N.W. Atlantic Fisheries, 1964-67. Decorated officer Order Brit. Empire; recipient Merit award Public Service Commn. Can., 1972. Fellow Royal Soc. Can.; mem. Marine Biol. Assn. (U.K.), Am. Fisheries Soc., Am. Soc. Ichthyologists and Herpetologists, Can. Soc. Zoologists. Contbr. numerous articles on marine biology, fish. and fisheries to profl. jours. Office: Meml U Nfld Saint John's NF A1C 5S7 Canada

TEMPLEMAN, WILLIAM DARBY, educator, author; b. Princeton, Ky., Apr. 2, 1903; s. John Dudley and Mary Phelps (Darby) T.; A.B., Adelbert Coll. of Western Res. U., 1924; M.A., Harvard, 1925, Ph.D. (Shattuck scholar 1928-29, Townsend scholar 1929-30, Charles Dexter scholar for study abroad summer 1930), 1930; m. Marion Helen Gillespie, Aug. 14, 1937; children—Katherine Dudley, Constance Mary, John Alden, William Phelps. Instr. English, Adelbert Coll., 1925-28, asst. dean coll., 1927-28; instr. English, Cleve. Coll., 1925-27; vis. asst. prof. English, Western Res. U., Cleve., 1932; asst. prof. English, U. Ill., 1930-45; asso. prof. English, U. So. Calif., 1945-47, prof., 1947—, prof. emeritus, 1972—, head English dept. 1957-64; vis. prof. U. Colo., summer 1954, N.Y.U., summer 1955; Fulbright lectr., Ankara, Turkey, 1966-67; cons. Salem Press, 1972. Mem. Modern Lang. Assn. Am. (sec. Victorian lit. group 1931-38, exec. com. 1938-49, chmn. 1942-46), Philol. Assn. Pacific Coast, Nat. Council Tchrs. English (dir. coll. sect. 1955-58), AAUP, Coll. English Assn. (pres. So. Calif. region), Phi Beta Kappa (pres. U. So. Calif. chpt. 1954-55), Phi Kappa Phi, Beta Theta Pi, Sigma Delta Chi, Epsilon Phi. Congregationalist. Author: Life and Work of William Gilpin (1724-1804), Master of the Picturesque and Vicar of Boldre, 1939; Analysis of Prose, 1964; co-Author: A Freshman Guide to Writing, 1935; Book of Information for Verbal Expression, 1940; Manual and Notebook for Verbal Expression, 1940; Booker Memorial Studies; Eight Essays on Victorian Literature, 1950; Bibliographies of Studies in Victorian Literature for the Ten Years, 1945-54, 1956. Editor: Bibliographies of Studies in Victorian Literature for the Thirteen Years 1932-44, 1945; On Writing Well: Selected Readings from Two Centuries, 1965; co-editor: English Prose of the Victorian Era, 1938; Models and Motivations for Writing, 1941. Contbr. Cambridge Bibliography of English Literature, 1940, and supplement, 1957, Collier's Ency., 1950, Ency. Americana, 1952, 54, 56; articles to profl. jours., mags. Home: 5772 Garden Grove Blvd Westminster CA 92683 Office: Univ Southern California Los Angeles CA 90007

TEMPLETON, ARLEIGH BRANTLEY, univ. pres.; b. New Waverly, Tex., Apr. 18, 1916; s. Claude E. and Jennie (Berter) T.; B.S., Sam Houston State Tchrs. Coll., 1936; M.Ed., U. Houston, 1949, Ed.D., 1961; m. Maxie Groce, June 11, 1938; 1 son, Earl Wayne. Prin., League City (Tex.) High Sch., 1937-40; operator Pan Am. Refining Corp., Texas City, Tex., 1940-42, indsl. relations, coordinator tng. program, supr. personnel, 1945-47; supt. schs., League City, 1947-48; asst. supt. schs., Clear Creek Ind. Sch. Dist., League City, 1948-51; supt. schs. El Campo (Tex.) Ind. Sch. Dist., 1951-54; pres. Alvin (Tex.) Jr. Coll., 1954-63; exec. dir. Gov. Tex. Com. Edn. Beyond High Sch., 1963-64; pres. Sam Houston State U., 1964-70, U. Tex., San Antonio, 1970-73, U. Tex., El Paso, 1973—; dir. Mountain Bell Telephone Co., Farah Mfg. Co. Chmn., Nat. Adv. Com. Dyslexia and Related Reading Disorders; chmn. Adv. Council Lang.-Handicapped Children Tex.; mem. Criminal Justice Council; mem. regional adv. council SBA. Trustee Tex. Ednl. Found., 1965—, chmn., 1968; chmn. bd. Tex. Ednl. Services, 1967—. Served to lt. USNR, 1942-45. Named Distinguished Alumnus, U. Houston, 1969, Distinguished Alumnus, Sam Houston State U., 1977. Mem. So. Assn. Schs. and Colls. (pres. 1966). Democrat. Methodist. Home: 711 Cincinnati Ave El Paso TX 79968

TEMPLETON, DAVID HENRY, educator; b. Houston, Mar. 2, 1920; s. David Henry and Miriam (Clark) T.; B.S., La. Poly. Inst., 1941; M.A., U. Tex., Austin, 1943, postgrad., 1943-44; Ph.D., U. Calif. at Berkeley, 1947; Ph.D. (hon.), U. Uppsala (Sweden), 1977; m. Lieselotte Kamm, June 12, 1948; children—Diana Li, Alan David. Chemist metall. lab., U. Chgo., 1944-46; chemist Radiation Lab., U. Calif. at Berkeley, 1946—, instr., asst. prof., 1947-54, asso. prof., 1954-58, prof. chemistry, 1958—, dean Coll. Chemistry, 1970-75. Guggenheim fellow, 1954, 69. Mem. Am. Chem. Soc., Am. Phys. Soc., Am. Crystallographic Assn. Home: 1244 Brewster Dr El Cerrito CA 94530 Office: U Calif Dept Chemistry Berkeley CA 94720

TEMPLETON, DAVID L., banker; b. Paterson, N.J., Jan. 13, 1925; s. David R. and Florence Marie (Jehlen) T.; student Bucknell U., Stonier Grad. Sch. Banking Rutgers U., N.J. Bankers Assn. Pub. Relations Sch. Princeton, Columbia; m. Margaret More, May 29, 1948; children—Kathy, Jill, Patti. Joined Franklin Soc. Fed. Savs. and Loan Assn.; joined 2d Nat. Bank (merged First Nat. Bank Passaic County), 1947, asst. cashier, 1958, asst. v.p., 1962, v.p., 1965, exec. v.p., 1970—, also dir.; chmn., pres., chief exec. officer, dir. Prospect Park Nat. Bank; dir. Bancshares of N.J. Bd. dirs. Lenni-Lenape council Girl Scouts U.S.A., No. N.J. Planning Assn., Hawthorne Borough Planning Bd.; past bd. dirs. Better Bus. Bur. Bergen, Passaic and Rockland Counties, dir., budget and fin. Served with AUS. Mem. N.E. Jersey Bankers Assn. (trustee). Methodist (trustee; fin. chmn.). Mason. Clubs: N. Jersey Country (Wayne); Upper Montclair Country (Clifton, N.J.); Passaic (N.J.) City. Home: 200 4th Ave Hawthorne NJ 07506 Office: 400 Hamburg Turnpike Wayne NJ 07476

TEMPLETON, IAN MALCOLM, physicist; b. Rugby, Eng., July 31, 1929; s. William and Eleanor Clayton (Butcher) T.; came to Can., 1957, citizen, 1967; M.A., Univ. Coll., Oxford, Eng., 1950, D.Phil., 1953; m. Elsa Wood, Aug. 11, 1956; children—Nicola Jean, Jennifer Jane. Fellow, NRC Can., Ottawa, Ont., 1953-54, asst. research officer physics div., 1957-60, asso. research officer, 1960-64, sr. research officer, 1964-71, prin. research officer, 1971—, joint head metal physics group, 1969-76, head electronic structure and calorimetry group, 1976—; mem. staff research lab. Associated Elec. Industries, Rugby, Eng., 1955-57. Fellow Inst. Physics, Royal Soc. Can.; mem. Can. Assn. Physicists, Am. Phys. Soc. Contbr. articles to profl. jours. Home: 17 Dunvegan Rd Ottawa ON K1K 3E8 Canada Office: National Research Council Ottawa ON K1A 0R6 Canada

TEMPLETON, JOHN MARKS, investment counsel, financial analyst; b. Winchester, Tenn., Nov. 29, 1912; s. Harvey Maxwell and Vella (Handly) T.; A.B., Yale, 1934; M.A. (law) (Rhodes scholar), Balliol Coll., Oxford, Eng., 1936; LL.D., Beaver Coll., 1968; D.Litt., Wilson Coll., 1974; m. Judith Dudley Folk, Apr. 17, 1937 (dec. Feb. 1951); children—John Marks, Anne Dudley, Christopher Winston; m. 2d, Irene Reynolds Butler, Dec. 31, 1958. Sec.-treas., v.p., dir. Nat. Geophys. Co., Dallas and N.Y.C., 1937-41; pres., treas., dir. Templeton, Dobbrow & Vance, Inc., N.Y.C., 1941-65, Growth Companies, Inc., mut. investment fund, 1951-53; pres., dir. Securities Fund Inc., 1952-65; pres., dir. Templeton Growth Fund Can., Ltd., Toronto, 1954—, Templeton World Fund, Inc., 1978—, Research Investing Co., Indpls., 1955-65, Neucleonics Chemistry & Electronics Shares, Inc., N.Y.C., 1956-63; chmn. Templeton Damroth Corp., 1959-62; pres. Corporate Leaders Am., Inc., 1959-62; dir. Standard Security Life Ins. Co. of N.Y., 1957- 62, asst. treas., 1959-62; pres., dir. First Trust Bank Ltd., Bahamas; dir. Magic Chef, Inc., Cleveland, Tenn., Chase Manhattan Trust Co., Ltd. Nassau, Bahamas. Past pres. Lyford Cay (Bahamas) Property Owners Assn. Past dir., vice chmn. No. Valley chpt. A.R.C.; chmn. YMCA Bergen County, 1952-54; dir. Englewood Community Chest, 1953-54; trustee Englewood Hosp., 1953-56; chmn. bd. trustees Princeton Theol. Sem., 1967-73; trustee Olivia Found., Wilson Coll., 1941-73, Chambersburg, Pa., Templeton Found., Inc.; council on theol. sems. United Presbyn. Ch. U.S.A., mem. Commn. on Ecumenical Mission, 1961-70; bd. corporators Presbyn. Ministers Fund, Inc.; mem. council Bahamas Nat. Trust. Mem. Investment Counsel Assn. Am. (past gov.), Soc. Security Analysts, Chief Execs. Forum (pres. 1968-69), Bahamas C. of C. (bd. dirs.), Phi Beta Kappa., Zeta Psi. Clubs: Elihu, Elizabethan (New Haven); Yale, University (N.Y.C.); Rotary, Lyford Cay (gov.) (Bahamas); Lansdowne, Royal Overseas League (Eng.). Contbr. to financial publs. Home: Lyford Cay Club Nassau Bahamas Office: Box N7776 Nassau Bahamas also 155 University Ave Toronto ON M5H 3B7 Canada

TEMPLETON, ROBERT EARL, engring. and constrn. co. exec.; b. Pitts., June 21, 1931; s. Robert James and Alice Wilma (Scheppele) T.; B.S. in Civil Engring., Carnegie Mellon U., 1953; M.S. in Civil Engring., 1954; M.B.A. in Mgmt., N.Y. U., 1960; m. Barbara Ann McDonald, June 9, 1956; children—Shirley Anne (dec.), Susan Elaine, Sally Irene. With Pullman Kellogg Co., Houston, 1954—, project engr., 1963-66, mgr. contract status, 1966-68, mgr. sales forecasting, 1968-72, mgr. market forecasting, 1972-73, mgr. Venture Analysis, 1973-74, mgr. analysis and methods div., 1974-76, mgr. Project Cost Services div., 1976—. Area chmn. United Campaign, Summit, N.J., 1969-70; pres. Jefferson Sch. PTA, Summit, N.J., 1967-69, v.p., 1965-67; security chmn. Fonn Villas Civic Assn., Houston, 1973, chmn. archtl. standards com., 1974, v.p., 1975, pres., 1976—. J. Waldo Smith Hydraulic fellow ASCE, 1953-54. Registered profl. engr., N.Y. Fellow Am. Assn. Cost Engrs. (award of merit 1977, certified, nat. pres. 1971-72, nat. adminstrv. v.p. 1970-71, nat. adv. staff 1973—, spl. projects chmn. 1974-75, certification bd. chmn. 1976-79); mem. N.Am. Soc. Corporate Planners (program dir. 1974), Engrs. Joint Council (exec. com. engring. manpower commn. 1969—), Sigma Xi (sec. Pullman Kellogg br. 1973-74, 2d v.p. 1976-77), Houston Comml. Bridge League (v.p. 1973-75), Sigma Xi, Tau Beta Pi, Beta Theta Pi. Republican. Presbyterian (deacon 1956-59). Editorial bd. Engring. and Process Econs., 1976—. Home: 12718 Old Oaks Dr Houston TX 77024 Office: 1300 Three Greenway Plaza E Houston TX 77046

TEMPLETON, ROBERT JAMES, landscape architect; b. Boston, Mar. 27, 1905; s. James and Isabella Anderson (Rust) T.; B.S. in Landscape Architecture, Mass. Agrl. Coll., 1925; postgrad. in ecology and environment U. Pitts., 1939-42; m. Alice Wilma Scheppele, Mar. 5, 1930 (dec. 1961); 1 son, Robert Earl; m. Helen Mae Barr, Aug. 8, 1964. Pvt. practice landscape architecture, Pitts., 1925-33; park recreation planner Pitts. Dept. City Planning, 1933-34, park supr., 1934-48, supt. of parks, 1948-55, dir. dept. parks recreation, 1955-69; cons., landscape architecture, Pitts., 1969—; bd. dirs. Pitts. Zool. Soc., 1955-69. Registered landscape architect, Pa. Fellow Am. Soc. Landscape Architects; mem. Bot. Soc. Western Pa., Western Pa. Conservancy. Methodist. Home and office: 2453 N Meadowcroft Ave Pittsburgh PA 15216

TEMPLIN, KENNETH ELWOOD, paper co. exec.; b. Mason City, Nebr., Jan. 26, 1927; s. Otto Rudolph and Marianna (Graf) T.; B.S. in Bus. Adminstrn., U. Nebr., 1950; M.B.A., Wayne State U., 1961; m. Harriet Elaine Ressel, Aug. 24, 1951; children—Steven, David, Daniel, Benjamin, Elizabeth. Fin. analyst Ford Motor Co., 1950-54; fin. analyst, corp. staff Chrysler Corp., 1955-60, div. controller marine engine div., 1961-63, gen. sales mgr., 1964-65; v.p. Marsh and Templin, N.Y.C., 1966-69; v.p., gen. mgr. operating group Saxon Industries, N.Y.C., 1970-79, group v.p., 1979—; mem. exec. com. Single Service Inst., 1971-79. Regional chmn. Minn. devel. com. Nat. Multiple Sclerosis Soc., 1970-71; co-pres. Home and Sch. Assn., Bernardsville, N.J., 1975-76. Served with U.S. Army, 1945-47, 50-51. Presbyterian. Home: 34 Harvey Dr Bernardsville NJ 07924 Office: 1220 Ave of Americas New York NY 10020

TEMPLIN, ROBERT EARL, ins. co. exec.; B. Bluffton, Ind., Aug. 20, 1919; s. Lawrence E. Templin; B.S., Ind. U., 1941; m. Dorcas C. Hoagland, Aug. 20, 1942. With Northwestern Mut. Life Ins. Co., Milw., 1946—, supt. agys., 1954-58; dir. agys., 1958-67, v.p., 1963-67, sr. v.p., 1967-77, exec. v.p., 1977—, trustee, 1971—. Bd. dirs. Greater Milw. Open; bd. dirs., pres. Greater Milw. Charities; mem. Greater Milw. Com. Served to maj. USMCR, 1941-45. Mem. Life Ins. Assn. Am., Life Ins. Mktg. and Research Assn., Life Advertisers Assn., Milw. Life Underwriters Assn., Sales Exec. Club, Gen. Agt. and Mgrs. Assn., Met. Milw. Assn. Commerce (dir.), Beta Theta Pi. Methodist. Clubs: Tripoli Golf, Wisconsin, Milwaukee. Home: 500 W Bradley Rd Milwaukee WI 53217 Office: 720 E Wisconsin Ave Milwaukee WI 53202

TENDAM, DONALD JAN, educator; b. Hamilton, Ohio, May 28, 1916; s. William and Bertha (Getz) T.; student U. Cin., 1935-38; A.B., Miami U., 1940; Ph.D., Purdue U., 1949; m. Ruth Eleanor Richardson, June 19, 1939; children—Judith A. (Mrs. James C. Jones), Donald Jan, Barbara E. (Mrs. Ardith Huff). Lab. asst. Miami U., 1939-40; grad. asst. physics Purdue U., 1940-42, instr. physics, 1942-49, asst. prof., 1949-52, asso. prof., 1952-60, prof. physics, 1960—, asso. head dept., 1966—. Mem. Am. Assn. Physics Tchrs., Am. Phys. Soc., AAUP, AAAS, Phi Beta Kappa, Sigma Xi, Sigma Pi Sigma (nat. council 1959-72, nat. v.p. 1967-68, pres. 1970-72). Research, articles radioactivity and nuclear structure. Home: 332 Meridian St West Lafayette IN 47906

TENENBAUM, LOUIS, educator; b. Chelsea, Mass., Aug. 23, 1922; s. Julius and Ida (Dain) T.; student Boston Coll., 1939-42; B.A., U. Wis., 1947, M.A., 1948, Ph.D., 1953; m. Elizabeth Huppler, June 8, 1944; children—Lisa, Thea, Louise, Tobias, Kezia. Instr. romance langs. U. Wis., 1951-53, U. Mich., 1954-57; asst. prof. romance langs. U. Colo., Boulder, 1957-61, asso. prof., 1961-65, prof., chmn. dept. Italian, 1965-77, chmn. arts and scis. study abroad com., 1961-72. Served with AUS, 1942-46. Decorated cavaliere Order of Merit Italian Republic. Mem. Am. Assn. Tchrs. Italian (exec. com., regional rep.), Modern Lang. Assn. Am., Dante Soc. Am., Wilderness Soc. Am., Phi Beta Kappa. Editor: Rocky Mountain Italian Newsletter, 1968-72; contbr. chpt. to Contemporary European Novelists, 1968, articles to profl. jours. Home: 430 Mapleton Ave Boulder CO 80302

TENNANT, DONALD GEORGE, advt. exec.; b. Sterling, Ill. Nov. 23, 1922; s. Charles W. and Grace (Santee) T.; B.A., Knox Coll., Galesburg, Ill., 1943; m. Barbara Jean Fuller, Sept. 13, 1948; children—Timothy, Andrew, Tracy. Producer, NBC, Chgo., 1947-49; writer-actor-producer ABC-TV, 1949-50; with Leo Burnett Co., Chgo., 1950-70, exec. v.p. creative services div., 1962-67, chmn. creative rev. com., chief creative officer, 1967-70; chmn. bd. Clinton E. Frank, Inc., Chgo., 1971-73; chmn. Don Tennant Co., Inc., Chgo., 1973—. Served to lt. (j.g.) USNR, 1943-46; PTO. Mem. ASCAP, Tau Kappa Epsilon. Club: Mid-America (Chgo.). Address: 500 N Michigan Ave Chicago IL 60611

TENNANT, VERONICA, ballerina; b. London, Jan. 15, 1947; immigrated to Can., 1955, naturalized, 1967; s. Harry and Doris (Bassous) T.; student Nat. Ballet Sch., Toronto; m. John Robert Wright, June 11, 1969; 1 dau., Jessica Robin. Prin. dancer Nat. Ballet Can., Toronto, 1965—; guest artist Jacob's Pillow Internat. Dance Festival, 1971, Newport (R.I.) Music Festival, 1973, Dance Detroit, 1975, also in New Orleans, Kansas City, Mo., Toledo, Chgo., Memphis, Stratford Shakespearean Festival, 1978; lectr. on dance Waterloo U., York U.; dancer CBC-TV prodns., including Cinderella (Emmy award), 1967, Sleeping Beauty (Emmy award), 1972; artistic cons. TV prodn. A Party, 1977. Named officer Order Can., 1975. Mem. Ont. Arts Council, Can. Conf. Arts. Author: (juvenile novel) On Stage, Please, 1977. Address: Nat Ballet Canada 157 King St E Toronto ON M5C 1G9 Canada*

TENNENBAUM, ROBERT, architect, planner; b. Vienna, Austria, June 12, 1936; s. Mark and Ernestine (Chayes) T.; B.Arch., Pratt Inst. Sch. Architecture, 1959; M. City Planning, Yale U., 1961; m. Marcelle S. Aiss, June 18, 1961; children—Ann, Eve. Urban designer Nat. Capital Planning Commn., Washington, 1961-62, Doxiadis Assos., planners, Washington, 1962-63; chief architect and planner Rouse Co., Columbia, Md., 1963-69; v.p. planning and urban design R.B.A. Engrs., Planners and Architects, Columbia, 1969-72; prin. Tennenbaum Assos., Columbia, 1972-79; prof., dir. grad. community planning program Sch. Social Work and Community Planning, U. Md., Balt., 1976-78; v.p. Market Center Devel. Corp., Balt., 1979—; past tchr. urban devel. assistance program Balt. Community Colls., New Communities Seminars Program, U. No. Colo.; lectr. urban designs and new towns. Democrat. Jewish. Home: 5422 Wild Turkey Ln Columbia MD 21044

TENNENT, CHARLES GAILLARD, orgn. ofcl.; b. Asheville, N.C., Apr. 5, 1894; s. James E. and Annie L. (Raby) T.; A.B., U. N.C., 1918; m. Jessie L. Mercer, Apr. 5, 1923; children—M. Gail, Charles M., William G., David L. Owner, mgr. Tennent Nurseries, Asheville, 1923—; landscape cons. U. N.C., Asheville. Mem. Rotary Internat., 1939—, 1st v.p., dir., 1948-49, dir., 1958-59, pres., 1957-58. Chmn. Asheville Sch. Bd., 1958-60. Chmn. finance com. Rotary, 1951-52, 54-55, chmn. program planning com., 1950-57, trustee found., 1958-63, chmn., 1958-59, chmn. devel. com., 1962-63. Decorated Order of So. Cross (Brazil); Order of Merit (Chile); Order of Merit for Distinguished Service (Peru); Order of Merit (Ecuador); recipient Distinguished Service award U. N.C. at Asheville, 1977. Served as 2d lt., inf., U.S. Army, 1918; capt. cav., N.C. N.G., 1925. Mem. N.C. Sch. Bd. Assn. (dist. pres. 1956), Thomas Wolfe Meml. Assn. (dir. 1958-64, pres. 1963-64, vice-chmn. advisory com. 1977—), Western N.C. Nurserymen's Assn. (pres. 1962, chmn. bd. 1963), Sigma Upsilon, Phi Delta Theta, Order Golden Fleece. Author: Little Lessons in Rotary. Address: 217 Westover Dr Asheville NC 28801 Died Feb. 22, 1979. *To me good will toward one's fellow man is an essential to success. Good will is like a melody that moves from person to person, a whistled tune that finds its way from vale to vale, over hills and mountains and far away. It is like a pebble tossed into a tranquil pool. The ripples move on and on in ever widening circles.*

TENNEY, CHARLES HENRY, dist. judge; b. N.Y.C., Jan. 28, 1911; s. Daniel Gleason and Marguerite Sedgwick (Smith) T.; grad. Choate Sch., 1929; A.B., Yale, 1933, LL.B., 1936; m. Joan Penfold Lusk, May 14, 1938; children—Patricia Lusk (Mrs. Bernard J. Ruggieri), Charles Henry, Joan Lusk (Mrs. Edgar B. Howard, III), Marguerite Sedgwick (Mrs. Talton R. Embry), Anne Gleason. Admitted to N.Y. bar, 1937; with firm Breed, Abbott & Morgan, N.Y.C., 1936-51, mem. firm, 1951-55; commr. investigation N.Y.C., 1955-58, corp. counsel, 1958-61, dep. mayor, city adminstr., 1961-64; U.S. dist. judge So. Dist. N.Y., 1964—, now sr. judge. Mem. N.Y.C. Bd. Ethics, 1960-61. Served to lt. comdr. USNR, 1942-45. Mem. Am., Fed., N.Y. County, N.Y. State bar assns., Assn. Bar City N.Y., Am. Judicature Soc., Nat. Legal Aid Soc., Phi Beta Kappa. Home: 770 Park Ave New York NY 10021 Office: US Court House Foley Sq New York NY 10007

TENNEY, DANIEL GLEASON, JR., lawyer; b. N.Y. C., Nov. 5, 1913; s. Daniel Gleason and Marguerite Sedgwick (Smith) T.; grad. Choate Sch., 1931; B.A., Yale, 1935, LL.B., 1938; m. Constance Lippincott Franchot, Sept. 16, 1939; children—Constance Franchot (Mrs. Peter Allan Rafle), Pamela Marguerite (Mrs. Keith E. Simpson), Alexandra Diane (Mrs. Arthur G. Potts, Jr.), Daniel Gleason III. Admitted to N.Y. bar, 1938; asso. Milbank, Tweed & Hope, N.Y.C., 1938-42; now partner Milbank, Tweed, Hadley & McCloy; staff, alien control State Dept., 1946. Pres. bd. trustees Green Vale Sch., 1958-62; trustee Choate Sch. Found., 1951-76, pres. bd. trustees, 1967-73; trustee, v.p., sec. ICD Rehab. and Research Center N.Y.C.; trustee Trudeau Inst. Inc., Saranac Lake, N.Y., St. Timothy's Sch., 1960-70; trustee Russell Sage Found., 1949-67, vice-chmn., 1955-67; v.p. Boys' Club. N.Y. Served to lt. comdr. USNR, 1942-45. Mem. N.Y. State Bar Assn., Assn. Bar City N.Y. Home: Piping Rock Rd Locust Valley NY 11560 Office: Chase Manhattan Plaza New York City NY 10005

TENNEY, MERRILL CHAPIN, clergyman, educator; b. Chelsea, Mass., Apr.16, 1904; s. Wallace Fay and Lydia Smith (Goodwin) T.; Diploma, Missionary Tng. Sch. Nyack, N.Y., 1924; Th.B., Gordon Coll. Theology and Missions, Boston, 1927, Litt.D., 1974; A.M., Boston U., 1930; Ph.D., Harvard, 1944; m. Helen Margaret Jaderquist, Sept. 5, 1930; children—Robert Wallace, Philip Chapin. Ordained to ministry Baptist Ch., 1928; pastor Storrs Av. Ch., Braintree, Mass., 1926-28; mem. faculty Gordon Coll., 1930-43, prof. N.T. and Greek, 1938-43; mem. faculty Wheaton (Ill) Coll., 1943—, prof. Bible and theology, 1945—, dean Grad. Sch. 1946-71; spring lectr. Goshen (Ind.) Coll., 1950; Mid. Winter lectures Western Conservative Bapt. Theol. Sem., 1951; Griffith Thomas lectr. Dallas Theol. Sem., 1962; lectr. Denver Bapt. Sem., 1964, Grace Theol. Sem., 1974. Past chmn. ednl. commn. Nat. Soc. Evangs. Mem. Am. Schs. Oriental Research, Soc. Bibl. Research, Soc. Bibl. Lits. and Exegesis, Evang. Theol. Soc. (pres. 1950-51), Phi Alpha Chi. Author: Resurrection Realities, 1945; John: The Gospel of Belief, 1948; Galatians; The Charter of Christian Liberty, 1950; The Genius of the Gospels, 1951; The New Testament: A Survey, 1953; Philippians, 1956; Interpreting Revelation, 1957; Proclaiming the New Testament; The Reality of the Resurrection, 1963; New Testament Times, 1965. Editor: The Word for this Century, 1960; Pictorial Bible Dictionary; The Bible: The Living Word of Revelation, 1967; Pictorial Bible Ency., 1975. Home: 1403 N Washington St Wheaton IL 60187. *Begin each day's work as if it were your first; finish it as if it were your last.*

TENNEY, STEPHEN MARSH, physiologist, educator; b. Bloomington, Ill., Oct. 22, 1922; s. Harry Houser and Caroline (Marsh) T.; A.B., Dartmouth; M.D., Cornell U.; m. Carolyn Cartwright, Oct. 18, 1947; children—Joyce B., Karen M., Stephen M. Instr. medicine U. Rochester Sch. Medicine, 1951-54, instr. physiology, 1953-54, asst. prof. physiology and medicine, 1954-56, asso. prof., 1956; prof. physiology Dartmouth Med. Sch., Hanover, N.H., 1956—, dean, 1960-62, acting dean, 1966, 73—, dir. med. scis., 1957-59, chmn. dept. physiology, 1956-77, Nathan Smith prof. physiology, 1974—; med. dir. Parker B. Francis Found., 1975—. Chmn. physiology study sect. NIH, 1962-65, tng. com. Nat. Heart Inst., 1968-71; mem. exec. com. NRC; mem. physiology panel NIH study Office Sci. and Tech.; mem. regulatory biology panel NSF, 1971-75; chmn. bd. sci. counselors Nat. Heart and Lung Inst., 1974-78; chmn. Commn. Respiratory Physiology Internat. Union Physiol. Scis. Served with USNR, 1947-49; sr. med. officer, Shanghai. Markle scholar in med. sci., 1954-59. Fellow Am. Acad. Arts and Scis.; mem. Inst. Medicine of Nat. Acad. Scis., Am. Physiol. Soc., Am. Soc. Clin. Investigation, N.Y. Acad. Scis., Gerontol. Soc., Am. Heart Assn., Assn. Am. Med. Colls., Sigma Xi. Asso. editor Jour. Applied Physiology, 1976—; editorial bd. Circulation Research, Am. Jour. Physiology, Respiration Physiology, Excerpta Medica, Physiol. Revs. Contbr. articles to sci. jours. Home: 18 Rope Ferry Rd Hanover NH 03755

TENNISON, CHARLES WILLIAMS, plastic surgeon; b. Dallas, Aug. 13, 1908; s. Harrison B. and Addie (Nix) T.; B.S., So. Meth. U., 1931; M.D., Baylor U., 1933; m. Kathleen Buchanan, Aug. 17, 1935 (div. 1967); children—Charles Buchanan, William Thomas; m. 2d, Carmen Klonek, 1967. Intern Baylor U. Hosp., 1933-34; tng. plastic surgery under Dr. J.T. Mills, Dallas, 1934-38; pvt. practice medicine, San Antonio, 1938-44, 46—; asso. prof. clin. surgery Baylor U. Postgrad. Sch., 1947-60; asso. prof. plastic surgery Tex. U. Postgrad. Sch. 1954-67; asso. prof. clin. surgery, div. plastic surgery U. Calif. at San Diego, 1975—; chief plastic surgery service Santa Rosa Med. Center, Robert B. Green Meml. Hosp. Cons. Brooke Army Hosp., 1947-67, Lackland Air Force Hosp., 1950-67; surgeon gen. USAF, 1959-65. Served to lt. comdr., M.C., USNR, 1944-46. Named Adm. of Tex. Navy. Diplomate Am. Bd. Plastic Surgery. Mem. Am. Soc. Plastic and Reconstructive Surgery (pres. 1962), Am. Assn. Plastic Surgeons, Japanese Soc. Plastic Surgeons, San Antonio (past pres.), Southwestern, Tex. surg. socs., Bexar County Med. Soc. (past pres.), Assn. Cleft Palate Rehab., A.C.S., Soc. Air Force Clin. Surgeons (hon.), Phi Chi Club: San Antonio Country. Address: 5350 Baltimore Dr Apt 4 La Mesa CA 92041

TENNSTEDT, KLAUS, conductor; b. Merseburg, Germany, June 6, 1926. Formerly gen. music dir. Dresden Opera and dir. State Orch. and Theatre in Schwerin, German Democratic Republic; gen. music dir. and resident condr. Buehnen der Landeshauptstadt Kiel, Fed. Republic Germany; N.Am. debut Toronto (Ont., Can.) Symphony; U.S. debut Boston Symphony, 1974; named prin. guest condr. Minn. Orch., 1978; conducted opera cos. and orchs. in Europe and N.Am., including: Swedish Radio Symphony, London Symphony Orch., Hamburg Philharm., Mozarteum Orch., N.Y. Philharm., San Francisco Symphony, Berlin Deutsche Oper, Munich State Opera, Hamburg State Opera, Phila. Orch. Office: care Minn Orch 1111 Nicollet Mall Minneapolis MN 55403*

TENNY, FRANCIS BRIGGS, govt. ofcl.; b. Rochester, N.Y., Dec. 22, 1920; s. Charles Buckley and Elizabeth Wilson (Pettee) T.; A.B. magna cum laude, U. Rochester, 1942; postgrad. Columbia, summer 1942; M.A. in Chinese and Japanese Langs. and Lit., Harvard, 1950; m. Nancy Robbins Naramore, June 26, 1948; children—Carol Lee, Charles Wilson, Laura Loveland. News reporter, copy editor, asst. state editor Watertown (N.Y.) Daily Times, 1946-48; with State Dept./USIA, 1951—; assigned Surabaya, Indonesia, 1951-53, Kobe, Japan, 1953-54, Washington, 1954-58; cultural affairs officer, attache ednl. exchange, Tokyo, Japan, 1958-65; cultural attache embassy, Bangkok, Thailand, 1965-68; mem. 11th Sr. Seminar Fgn. Policy, 1968-69; dir. Office E. Asia/Pacific Programs, Bur. Ednl. and Cultural Affairs, State Dept., 1969-74; counselor for pub. affairs Am. embassy, Tokyo, Japan, 1974-76; exec. dir. Japan-U.S. Friendship Commn., 1976—. Mem. U.S. Ednl. Commn. Japan, 1961-65, U.S. Ednl. Found., Thailand, 1963-68. Served to 1st lt. AUS, 1942-46; CBI. Harvard-Yenching Inst. fellow, 1948-50. Mem. Phi Beta Kappa, Theta Delta Chi. Home: 2203 Paul Spring Rd Alexandria VA 22307 Office: Japan-US Friendship Commn 1875 Connecticut Ave NW Suite 709 Washington DC 20009

TENPAS, GARIT HENRY, agronomist; b. Vesper, Wis., Mar. 29, 1923; s. William John and Anna (Nordstrum) T.; B.S., U. Wis., 1948, M.S., 1953; m. Harriet Ann Johnson, Dec. 30, 1950; children—Howard Roy, Paula Jean, Tammie Lynn, Margaret Ann. Grain buyer Ladish Malting, 1948-50; supt. U. Wis. Exptl. Farm, Ashland, 1950-75, Marshfield, Wis., 1975—. Served with USAAF, 1943-45. Decorated Air medal. Mem. Am. Soc. Agronomy, Crop Sci. Soc. Lutheran. Clubs: Rotary, Jaycees. Contbr. articles to profl. jours. Address: Rt 2 Marshfield WI 54449

TEN PAS, HENRY ARNOLD, educator; b. Lima County, Wis., Mar. 31, 1918; s. John Henry and Minnie (Wisselink) Ten P.; B.S., U. Wis., 1940; student U. Ill., summer 1949; M.S., Oreg. State U., 1949; Ed.D., Wash. State U., 1954; m. Lorraine A. Anderson, June 1, 1942; children—John Henry, William Scott, Lyn Anderson, Sue Anderson, Tom Nelson, Libby Anderson. Tchr., Waldo (Wis.) High Sch., 1940-41, Amity (Oreg.) High Sch., 1945-48; mem. faculty Oreg. State U., 1948—, prof. agrl. edn., head dept., 1954—, chmn. council curriculum and acad. policy, 1960-65, dir. div. vocat., adult and community coll. edn., 1968-73, dir. undergrad. edn., 1973—; exchange cons. Maui Community Coll., Hawaii, 1974-75. Mem. faculty Wash. State U., summers 1954, 55, div. continuing edn., Portland, summers and night, 1949—, dir. div. vocat., adult and community coll. edn. adv. council Edn. Profession Devel. Act, 1970; staff devel. facilitator Maui Community Coll., Kahalui, Maui, Hawaii, 1974. Served with AUS, 1941-45; ETO. Decorated Presdl. citation, recipient Outstanding Educator of America award, 1971. Mem. Oreg. Secondary Sch. Prins. Assn. (exec. com. 1956—), Western Regional Tchrs. Edn. Assn. (pres. 1955), A.A.U.P., Am., Oreg. vocat. assns., Phi Kappa Phi (pres. Oreg. State U. 1962), Phi Delta Kappa, Alpha Zeta (rep. for Western States to Washington), Alpha Gamma Rho, Mason. Club: Century (Corvallis). Contbr. to profl. jours., books. Bus. mgr. Agrl. Edn. mag., 1957-62. Home: 5815 SW West Hills Rd Corvallis OR 97330

TENZEL, RICHARD RUVIN, ophthalmologist; b. Phila., Jan. 19, 1929; s. Jack and Pauline (Korenblat) T.; B.A., Vanderbilt U., 1950; M.D., U. Tenn., 1954; m. Shirley Ruth Baum, May 19, 1956; children—Jack, David, Vicki Gail. Intern, Jackson Meml. Hosp., Miami, Fla., 1955; resident Manhattan Eye, Ear, Nose and Throat Hosp., N.Y.C., 1956-60; practice medicine specializing in ophthalmology, Miami Beach, Fla., 1960—; clin. prof. ophthalmology U. Miami, 1975—; chief ophthalmic plastic surgery service Bascom Palmer Eye Inst., Miami. Served with USNR, 1956-58. Fellow A.C.S.; mem. Am. Acad. Ophthalmology and Otolaryngology, Am. Soc. Ocularists (med. adviser 1971—), AMA. Club: Masons (32 deg.). Contbr. articles to profl. jours. Office: 1100 N E 163d St North Miami Beach FL 33162

TENZER, MICHAEL LEONARD, housing devel. exec.; b. N.Y.C., May 7, 1930; s. Sigmund and Rose (Weiss) T.; grad. Art Center Coll. Design, 1949; m. Jacqueline Newmark, Aug. 7, 1952; children—Gary, Marc. Photo-Journalist Look mag., 1949-50; free-lance photography, pub. relations UN, 1950-51; mgr. brand marketing Modern Globe, Inc., 1953-57; gen. sales mgr. Berkshire Knitting Mills, Reading, Pa., 1957-60; gen. sales and marketing mgr. intimate apparel div. Kayser-Roth Corp., N.Y.C., 1960-63; sr. v.p., dir. mktg. The Larwin Group, Inc., Beverly Hills, Calif., 1963-75, pres. housing div., also pres. Larwin Home Center, also corp. dir.; pres. Larwin Realty, Alliance Escrow Corp., Westwood Advt.; pres. Tenzer & Co. Inc., Beverly Hills, 1975-76; pres., chief exec. officer, dir. Leisure Technology Corp., Lakewood, N.J., 1976—; mem. Pres. Carter's Housing Task Force, 1975-76. Regional chmn. Crescent Bay council Boy Scouts Am., 1966-68. Chmn., trustee Young Musicians Found.; bd. dirs. Am. Youth Symphony; trustee Friends of Music, U. So. Calif. Served with Signal Corps, AUS, 1951-52. Recipient Top Performer award House and Home mag., 1968. Mem. Nat. Assn. Home Builders (mem. conventional housing and mortgage banking coms. 1965—). Office: One Airport Rd Lakewood NJ 08701

TEPER, LAZARE, economist; b. Odessa, Russia, Jan. 16, 1908; s. Gedeon and Esther (Bogatirsky) T.; student Université Populaire Russe, 1924-26, Université de Paris, 1926-27; A.M., Johns Hopkins, 1930, Ph.D., 1931. Came to U.S., 1927, naturalized 1938. Student asst. Johns Hopkins, 1929-31; research asst. Walter Hines Page Sch. Internat. Relations, 1931-34; instr. econs. Brookwood, Inc., 1934-36; dir. research Joint Bd. Dressmakers Union, 1935-37, Internat. Ladies Garment Workers Union, 1937—. Cons. to research div. Social Security Bd., 1938-43; mem. com. seasonalty in industry N.Y. Dept. Labor, 1939-40; del. White House Conf. Nutrition for Def., 1941; del. for U.S. to World Statis. Congress, 1947; A.F. of L. and Internat. Conf. of Trade Unions rep. to UN Statis Commn., 1947—; del. Nat. Health Assembly, 1948; cons. N.Y. State Legislative Com. Nutrition, 1942-43, miscellaneous rationing div. OPA, 1942-43, div. statis and standards U.S. Budget Bar., 1950-51; mem. intensive rev. com. Bur. of Census, 1953; mem. Spl. Com. Employment Statistics, 1954; com. statis Program for City N.Y., 1954; mem. com. on work in industry Nat. Acad. Sci. NCR; mem. joint labor adv. council Bur. Labor Statistics; mem. com. nat. policy Nat. Planning Assn.; mem. com. employment 20th Century Fund; mem. exec. com. Productivity Conf.; dir., mem. exec. com. Fedn. Employment and Guidance Service; trustee Fed. Statistics Users Conf., chmn., 1979-80; mem. Nat. Pub. Adv. Com. on Area Redevel., 1963—; mem. Mgmt.-Labor Textile Adv. Com., 1962—; dir.-at-large Nat. Bur. Econ. Research, 1970—; seminar asso. Columbia U., 1961. Served with AUS, World War II. Fellow Am. Statis. Assn., A.A.A.S.; mem. Am. Econ. Assn., Nat. Assn. Bus. Economists, Am. Marketing Assn., Acad. Polit. Sci., Indsl. Relations Research Assn., Econometric Soc., Met. Econ. Assn. (pres. 1975). Author: Hours of Labor, 1932; Women's Garment Industry, 1937. Contr. profl. jours. Home: 650 West End Ave New York NY 10025 Office: 1710 Broadway New York NY 10019

TERAI, KIYOHIDE KIYOSHI, engr., educator; b. Ashiya, Hyogoken, Japan, Jan. 6, 1927; s. Shinobu and Moto (Iwasaki) T.; degree in Naval Architecture, Osaka U., 1951, D.Eng., 1962; m. Hiroko Mary Futami, Apr. 17, 1961; children—Yasuo Henry and Yoshiko Terai, Takako Sophia. Mgr. shipbldg. dept. Kobe Shipyard, Kawasaki Heavy Industries, Inc., Kobe, Japan, 1966-69, mgr. welding research lab. Tech. Inst., 1969-77; vis. prof. dept. ocean engring. M.I.T., Cambridge, Mass., 1977—; vis. lectr. Nagoya U., Tohoku U., Osaka U., U. Tokyo. Recipient numerous awards Soc. Naval Architects Japan, Japan Welding Soc. Mem. Japan Welding Soc. (past dir.), Japan Welding Engring. Soc. (past dir.), Am. Welding Soc., Soc. Naval Architects and Mech. Engrs., ASME, Am. Soc. Naval Engrs., Welding Inst. (U.K.). Buddhist. Author books in field; contbr. articles to profl. jours. Home: 20 Hamilton Rd Arlington MA 02174 Office: Dept Ocean Engring Mass Inst Tech Cambridge MA 02139

TER-ARUTUNIAN, ROUBEN, scenery, costume designer; b. Tiflis, Russia, July 24, 1920; s. Guegam Ter-Arutunian and Anaida Seylanian; student Reimann Art Sch., Berlin, Germany, 1939-41, Friedrich-Wilhelm U., Berlin, 1941-43, U. Vienna, 1943-44, Acad. Music, Berlin, 1943, Ecole des Beaux Arts, Paris, 1947-50. Came to U.S., 1951, naturalized 1957. Created costumes for Salome, Operahouse, Vienna, 1944; scenery and costumes for Ballet at Opera-Comique, 1950—, Festival of Two Worlds, Spoleto, Italy, 1958; TV scenery and costumes for Anouilh's Antigone, Shakespeare's Taming of the Shrew, Twelfth Night, The Tempest, Mozart's Magic Flute; Memotti's Maria Golovin for Brussels World's Fair, 1958, then La Scala, Milan; scenery and costumes La Cenerentola, N.Y.C. Opera, Souvenirs and The Seven Deadly Sins, also scenery for The Nutcracker, N.Y.C. Ballet; permanent dramatic set for festival stage Am. Shakespeare Festival, Stratford, Conn., 1956-61, scenery and costumes for prodns., 1956, 57, Broadway show New Girl in Town Redhead; scenery Who was That Lady I Saw You With?; Arturo Ui; designer The Deputy, 1964; The Flood (Stravinsky), CBS-TV, 1962; Pelleas and Melisande (Debussy), Spoleto, Italy, 1966; The Bassarids (Henze), Santa Fe, 1968; Goodtime Charlie, 1975; designer sets and costumes for play Days in the Trees, 1976. Recipient Emmy award for best art direction Twelfth Night, 1957; Tony award for best costume design, Redhead, 1958-59. Home: 360 E 55th St New York NY 10022*

TERENZIO, JOSEPH VINCENT, hosp. adminstr.; b. New Haven, Feb. 4, 1918; s. Vincent and Marianna (Piantino) T.; B.A., Yale U., 1939; J.D., Fordham U., 1947; M.S., Columbia U., 1954; m. Marie Louise Cozzolino, Feb. 3, 1945; children—Mary Louise (Mrs. Jeffrey Shafer), Joanne (Mrs. Walter R. Brewster, Jr.), John Joseph. Admitted to Conn. bar, 1947; mem. firm Curran, DiSesa and Vining, New Haven, 1947-50; asst. adminstr. Knickerbocker Hosp., N.Y.C., 1951-52; asst. adminstr. Western Pa. Hosp., Pitts., 1952-56; exec. dir. Knickerbocker Hosp., N.Y.C., 1956-60; dir. Brooklyn Hosp., 1960-64, exec. v.p., 1964-66; commnr. hosps. City N.Y., 1966-70; pres. Evanston (Ill.) Hosp., 1970-72; exec. v.p. United Hosp. Fund of N.Y., 1972-74, pres., 1974—; lectr. hosp. law U. Pitts., 1952-56, U. Mich. Sch. Bus. Adminstrn., 1955—, Cornell U., 1958—; lectr. hosp. adminstrn. Columbia, 1958-72, spl. adviser to pres., 1972—, adj. prof. pub. health, 1972—; mem. N.Y. State Hosp. Rev. and Planning Council, 1976-78; chmn. N.Y.C. Adv. Com. on Office of Chief Med. Examiner, 1976-77; asst. prof. Bklyn. Coll. Pharmacy, 1963-66; trustee Emigrant Savs. Bank N.Y.C. Nat. Health Council, 1979-80; mem. tech. adv. bd. Nat. Exec. Service Corps. Sec., Yale U. Class of 1939, 1975—; bd. mgrs. New Haven Boys Club, 1948-50; bd. dirs. Tb Inst. Chgo., 1970-72, Harlem Neighborhoods Assn., Health Manpower Devel. Corp., Washington, 1970-77; dir. Med. and Health Research Assn., N.Y.C., 1972-77; treas. Health and Hosp. Planning Council So. N.Y., 1972-78; trustee Coll. Mt. St. Vincent, Riverdale, N.Y. Served to lt. comdr. USNR, 1941-46. Fellow Am. Coll. Hosp. Adminstrs., Am. Pub. Health Assn.; mem. Hosp. Assn. N.Y. State, Am., N.Y.C. pub. health assns., Am. (chmn. com. on health care for disadvantaged 1971-74, mem. nat. adv. com. on health 1970-72), Greater N.Y. hosp. assns., Hosp. Assn. Pa., Am. Bar Assn. Clubs: University (N.Y.C.); Rembrandt, N.Y. Athletic, Yale (N.Y.C.); Faculty House (Columbia); Pequot Yacht Club (Southport, Conn.). Home: 66E 79th St New York NY 10021 Office: 3E 54th St New York NY 10022

TERENZIO, PETER BERNARD, hosp. adminstr.; b. N.Y.C., Mar. 6, 1916; s. Vincent and Marianna (Piantino) T.; student Yale, 1934-37; J.D., U. Conn., 1940; M. Hosp. Adminstrn., Northwestern U., 1950; m. Eileen Alma Mosher, May 29, 1941; children—Mary Ellen Alecci, Vincent, Nancy Britton, Peter Bernard. Admitted to Conn. bar, 1941; practice in New Haven, 1945-48; with standardization div. A.C.S., Chgo., 1948-49; adminstrv. resident Evanston (Ill.) Hosp., 1949-50; asst. dir. Roosevelt Hosp., N.Y.C., 1950-52, exec. v.p., dir., 1953-76, cons., 1976—; pres. Hosp. Bur. Inc., Pleasantville, N.Y., 1977—; dir. Greenville (S.C.) Gen. Hosp., 1952-53; cons. to surgeon gen. USPHS, 1960-65, 66-69; to commr. Dept. Hosps., N.Y.C. 1961-68; prof. clin. dentistry Sch. Dental and Oral Surgery, Columbia, 1963—, univ. lectr. pub. health and adminstrv. medicine; adj. prof. Pace U., 1978—, New Sch. Social Research, 1977—. Mem. facilities planning com. Hosp. Rev. and Planning Council of So. N.Y., 1963-69; mem. vol. adv. staff N.Y. State Health and Mental Retardation, 1966-69. Bd. dirs., exec. com. Asso. Hosp. Service N.Y., 1970-74, N.Y. Coll. Podiatry 1971-73; bd. dirs. Blue Cross-Blue Shield Greater N.Y., 1974-78, Abacus, 1965—, Dominican Sisters Mental Health Agy., 1977—, Health Services Improvement Fund, 1978—. Served to capt., Med. Adminstrn. Corps, AUS, 1941-45. Fellow Am. Coll. Hosp. Adminstrs. (gov. 1964-65, regent 2d dist. 1960-64, pres. 1966-67), Am. Pub. Health Assn.; mem. Am. Hosp. Assn. (ho. of dels. 1969-76, rep. Am. Blood Commn., trustee liaison com. podiatry), Hosp. Research and Devel. Inst., N.Y. Acad. Medicine, Pub. Health Assn. N.Y.C. (dir., v.p. 1973-74, pres. 1976-77), Roosevelt Hosp. Alumni Assn. (asso.), Hosp. Assn. N.Y. (pres. 1970-71), Middle Atlantic Hosp. Assembly (bd. govs.), Hosp. Adminstrs. Study Soc., Am. Bar Assn., Greater N.Y. Hosp. Assn. (pres. 1960), Hosp. Adminstrs. Club (pres. 1959), Hosp. Soc. (pres. 1965). Roman Catholic. Adv. editorial bd. Hosp. and Health Services Adminstrn. Home: 160 Tuttle Rd Briarcliff Manor NY 10510 Office: 80 Wheeler Ave Pleasantville NY 10570

TERESHKO, DANIEL WILLIAM, artist, educator; b. Cleve., June 19, 1935; s. William and Mary Helen (Dubovec) T.; diploma Cleve. Art Inst., 1962; B.F.A., San Francisco Art Inst., 1963; M.F.A., Mills Coll., 1965. Prof. art Clarke Coll., Dubuque, Iowa, 1965-66, Elmira (N.Y.) Coll., 1966-69, Moravian Coll., Bethlehem, Pa., 1969—; one-man shows Lerner-Heller Gallery, 1973, 76, Allentown (Pa.) Art Mus., 1974; 10-yr. retrospective exhbn. paintings and drawings Lehigh U., 1979. Home: Box 373 RD #1 Slatington PA 18080 Office: care Lerner-Heller Gallery 956 Madison Ave New York NY 10021

TERFERA, RAYMOND ANTHONY, ins., fin. and real estate co. exec.; b. Springfield, Mass., July 21, 1929; s. Peter Joseph and Angela (Guidi) Tergliafera; J.D., Boston Coll., 1953; B.S., Am. Internat. Coll., 1957; m. Grace Doris Ayers, Sept. 1, 1952; children—Catherine, Lynn, Lisa, David. Admitted to Mass. bar, 1954; supt. claims Comml. Union Group, Manchester, Conn., 1956-61; asso. Charles H. Blackall, Esq., Manchester, 1961-63, Bulkley, Richardson and Gelinas, Springfield, 1963; with Monarch Life Ins. Co. and Springfield Life Ins. Co. Inc., 1963—; now v.p., gen. counsel Monarch Life Ins. Co., Springfield Life Ins. Co., Inc., Monarch Capital Corp.; dir. Monarch Life Ins. Co., Monarch Securities, Inc., Forge, Middlesex and Stockbridge Devel. Corp., Monarch Investment Mgmt. Corp. Served with USMCR, 1946-48. Mem. Am. Bar Assn., Assn. Life Ins. Counsel, Mass. Bar Assn., Conn. Bar Assn. Address: Monarch Capital Corp 1250 State St Springfield MA 01133

TERHAAR, ALBERT JOSEPH, bank exec.; b. Rochester, N.Y., Apr. 9, 1916; s. John Albert and Anna Mary (Schnorr) T.; m. Edna Mary Scheible, Sept. 17, 1938; children—Ronald G., Kenneth J., Judith M., Ellen M., Mary L. Teller, Monroe County Savs. Bank, Rochester, 1934-44; with Eastman Savs. and Loan Assn., Rochester, 1944—, v.p. for ops, 1965-67, exec. v.p., 1967-77, pres., 1977—; bd. dirs. Rochester Credit and Fin. Mgmt. Assn., Rochester Credit Center, Inc. Mem. Rochester C. of C. Roman Catholic. Clubs: St. Margaret Mary's Men's, Ridgemont Country (dir., treas.). Home: 637 Oakridge Dr Rochester NY 14617 Office: 377 State St Rochester NY 14650. *The man who succeeds is the man who gives something extra of his talent and service. He may not be recognized for a time-but the day of his glory always happens.*

TER HAAR, OTTO, publisher; b. Amsterdam, Netherlands, June 14, 1929; s. Otto and Martha Amalia (Craandijk) ter H.; grad. Kennemer Lyceum, Haarlem, 1948; m. Almina Cremers, Oct. 29, 1960; children—Otto, Floris, Iskjen, Almina. With nv Deli Maatschappij, Indonesia and Netherlands, 1951-60; with Elsevier Publishing House, Amsterdam, 1960—; mng. dir. Elsevier Sci. Pubs., Amsterdam; chmn. bd. dirs. Elsevier North-Holland Inc., N.Y.C. Mem. Internat. Pubs. Assn., Internat. Group Sci., Tech. and Med. Pubs., Royal Netherlands Pubs. Assn. Club: Amsterdam-Halfweg Rotary. Home: 21 Crayenesterlaan Haarlem 2012 TH Netherlands Office: 52 Vanderbilt Ave New York NY 10017

TER HORST, JERALD FRANKLIN, newspaperman; b. Grand Rapids, Mich., July 11, 1922; s. John Henry and Maude (Van Strien) ter H.; student Mich. State U., 1941-42; A.B., U. Mich., 1947; m. Louise Jeffers Roth, Jan. 20, 1945; children—Karen Bayens, Margaret Fulton Robinson, Peter Roth, Martha Morgan. Reporter, Grand Rapids Press, 1946-51; mem. staff Detroit News, 1953-74, city and state polit. writer, 1953-57, Washington corr., 1958-60, chief Washington bur., 1961-74; White House press sec. to Pres., 1974; columnist Universal Press Syndicate, 1974—; fgn. assignments include Berlin crisis, Geneva Fgn. Ministers Conf., Yugoslavia, 1959, 70, Israel, 1960, Eng., Ireland, Germany, Italy and France, 1963, 69, Vietnam, India and Pakistan, 1966, 70, China, 1972, Moscow, 1974, Africa, 1978; writer N.Am. Newspaper Alliance, 1958-74. Served as capt. USMCR, 1943-46, 51-52. Mem. White House Corr. Assn., Sigma Delta Chi, Psi Upsilon. Presbyterian (elder). Clubs: Gridiron, Nat. Press, Overseas Writers, Washington Press, Internat. (Washington). Author: Gerald Ford and Future of the Presidency, 1974; The Flying White House: The Story of Air Force One, 1979; contbr. to mags. Home: 7815 Evening Ln Alexandria VA 22306 Office: 525 Nat Press Bldg Washington DC 20045

TERHORST, PAUL BYRNE, mfg. co. exec.; b. Terre Haute, Ind., Nov. 30, 1914; s. Frank John and Delia Ann (Byrne) T.; B.S. in Mech. Engring., Rose Poly. Inst., 1931-35; m. Mary E. Baier, Apr. 20, 1940; children—Richard B., John C., Mary Teresa. Indsl. sales engr. Ind. Gas Utilities Co., Terre Haute, 1935-36, Citizens Gas & Coke Utility Co., Indpls., 1936-41; plant engr. propeller div. Curtiss-Wright Corp., Indpls., 1941-45; chief plant and indsl. engr. Philco Corp., Phila., 1945-49; works mgr. comml. div. York Corp. (Pa.), 1949-56; v.p. ops. Power Products Corp., Grafton, Wis., 1956-57; v.p., asst. to pres. Briggs & Stratton Corp., Milw., 1957-59; v.p., gen. mgr. Scott div. McCulloch Corp., Mpls., 1959-62; pres., dir. Sterling Precision Corp., N.Y.C., 1962-65; v.p., gen. mgr. Phila. divs. SKF Industries, Inc., Phila., 1965-73; pres., chief exec. Delbar Products, Inc., Perkasie, Pa., 1974—. Registered profl. engr., Ind. Address: 1125 Clubhouse Rd Gladwyne PA 19035

TERHUNE, CHARLES HOUSTON, JR., univ. research adminstr.; b. Dayton, Ohio, May 7, 1916; s. Charles Houston and Linnie Lee (Wigham) T.; B.S.M.E., Purdue U., 1938, Ph.D. in Engring. (hon.), 1966; Aero. Engr., Calif. Inst. Tech., 1941; student Air Corps Flying Sch., 1939; m. Beatrice Holcombe, Sept. 9, 1939; children—Donna, Terry Lea, Charles Houston, III. Commd. flying cadet U.S. Army Air Force, 1938, advanced through grades to lt. gen., U.S. Air Force, 1967; comdr. electronic systems div. Hanscom Field, Bedford, Mass., 1962-64; comdr. aero. systems div. Wright-Patterson AFB (Ohio), 1964-67; vice comdr. Air Force Systems Command, Washington, 1967-69; ret., 1969; dep. dir. Jet Propulsion Lab., Calif. Inst. Tech., La Canada, 1971—. Decorated Army D.S.M., Air Force D.S.M. Office: 4800 Oak Grove Dr La Canada CA 91011

TERKEL, STUDS LOUIS, interviewer, author; b. N.Y.C., May 16, 1912; s. Samuel and Anna (Finkel) T.; Ph.B., U. Chgo., 1932, J.D., 1934; m. Ida Goldberg, July 2, 1939; 1 son, Paul. Stage appearances include Detective Story, 1950, A View From the Bridge, 1958, Light Up the Sky, 1959, The Cave Dwellers, 1960; star TV program, Studs Place, 1950-53, radio program Wax Mus., 1945—, Studs Terkel Almanac, 1952—, Studs Terkel Show, Sta. WFMT-FM, Chgo.; master of ceremonies Newport Folk Festival, 1959, 60, Ravinia Music Festival, 1959, U. Chgo. Folk Festival, 1961, others; panel moderator, lectr., narrator films. Program, Wax Museum, winner 1st award as best cultural program in regional radio category Inst. Edn. by Radio-TV, Ohio State U., 1959; recipient Prix Italia, UNESCO award for best radio program East-West Values, 1962; Communicator of Year award U. Chgo. Alumni Assn., 1969. Author: (book) Giants of Jazz, 1956; Division Street America, 1966; (play) Amazing Grace, 1959; Hard Times, 1970; Working, 1974; Talking to Myself, 1977; also short stories. Home: 850 W Castlewood Terr Chicago IL 60640 Office: 500 N Michigan Chicago IL 60611

TERKHORN, HENRY K., food co. exec.; b. Brownstown, Ind., July 10, 1930; s. Henry K. and Louise M. (Wolka) T.; B.S., Ind. U., 1957; m. Imogene Grant, May 23, 1952; children—Deborah, Pamela. Div. controller, internat. controller Cummins Engine Co., Dallas, London, Eng., 1966-69; v.p. finance Streater Industries div. Litton Industries, Albert Lea, Minn., 1969-70; asst. controller Oscar Mayer & Co., Madison, Wis., 1970-74, corporate controller, 1974—, v.p., 1976—. Bd. dirs. Family Service, 1972—, treas., 1973-74. Served with USN, 1950-54. C.P.A., Tex. Mem. Am. Inst. C.P.A.'s, Nat. Assn. Accountants, Financial Execs. Inst. Elk. Home: 5601 Comanche Way Madison WI 53704 Office: 910 Mayer Ave Madison WI 53704

TERKLA, LOUIS GABRIEL, univ. dean; b. Anaconda, Mont., Mar. 24, 1925; s. George G. and Blanche (Wareham) T.; student U. Mont., 1946-48; D.M.D., U. Oreg., 1952; m. Phyllis Jean Cohn, Aug. 21, 1949; children—David G., Linda J. Mem. faculty U. Oreg. Dental Sch., 1952—, prof., asst. to dean acad. affairs, 1961-67, dean, 1967—. Served with inf. AUS, World War II. Fellow Am. Coll. Dentists (pres. 1973-74), Acad. Gen. Dentistry (hon.); mem. Am., Oreg. dental assns., Am. Assn. Dental Schs. pres. 1975-76), Western Conf. Dental Examiners and Dental Sch. Deans (pres. 1975-76), Internat. Assn. Dental Research, Sigma Xi, Omicron Kappa Upsilon. Author: (with others) Partial Dentures, 3d edit., 1963; also articles, chpts. in books. Home: 1215 SW Lancaster St Portland OR 97219

TERMAN, FREDERICK EMMONS, educator, electronics engr.; b. English, Ind., June 7, 1900; s. Lewis Madison and Anna Belle (Minton) T.; A.B. in Chem. Engring., Stanford U., 1920, E.E., 1922; Sc.D. in Elec. Engring., M.I.T., 1924; Sc.D. (hon.), Harvard U., 1945, U. B.C., 1950, Syracuse U., 1955, So. Meth. U., 1977; D.H.L. (hon.), J.F. Kennedy U., 1978; m. Sibyl Walcutt, Mar. 22, 1928 (dec. 1975); children—Frederick Walcutt, Terence Christopher, Lewis Madison. Instr. to prof. elec. engring. Stanford U., 1925-37, exec. head elec. engring. dept., 1937-45, dean engring., 1945-58, provost, 1955-65, v.p., 1959-65, emeritus, 1965—; pres. SMU Found. Sci. and Engring., 1965-74; cons. ednl. surveys, Calif., Colo., N.Y., Fla., Mass., Utah, others, 1965—; dir. Harvard Radio Research Lab., 1942-45. Mem. divs. 14 and 15 Nat. Def. Research Com., 1942-45; mem. spl. tech. adv. group and TAPEC com. Dept. of Def., 1953-56, research and devel. adv. com. Signal Corps, 1954-62; mem. Bd. Fgn. Scholarships, Dept. State, 1960-65; adv. council Army Electronics Proving Ground, 1954-57; mem. Naval Res. Adv. Com., 1956-64, chmn., 1957-58; mem. Def. Sci. Bd., 1957-58; dir. emeritus Hewlett-Packard Co.; dir. Watkins-Johnson Co., Granger Assos. Trustee Inst. Def. Analyses, 1956-73. Decorated by Brit. govt., 1946, U.S. Medal for Merit, 1948, Herbert Hoover medal Stanford Alumni Assn., 1969, U.S. Medal Sci., 1975, Uncommon Man award Stanford U., 1978, Order Civil Merit (South Korea). Fellow IEEE (pres. predecessor assn. 1941, medal of honor 1950, edn. medal 1956, founders award 1962), Nat. Acad. Sci. (chmn. engring. sect. 1953-55, mem. council 1956-59), Am. Soc. Engring. Edn. (hon. mem., v.p. 1949-51, Lamme medal 1964, named to Hall of Fame 1968), Audio Engring. Soc. (hon. mem.), Am. Philos. Soc., Nat. Acad. Engring. (founding mem.), Phi Beta Kappa, Sigma Xi (exec. bd. 1956-58, 67-70, 74-76, pres. 1975), Theta Xi, Tau Beta Pi, Eta Kappa Nu. Author several books 1927—; latest being Electronic Measurements (with J.M. Pettit), 1952; Electronic and Radio Engineering, 4th ed. 1955. Contbr. to tech. mags. Cons. editor Elec. and Electronic Engring. Series of McGraw-Hill Book Co., Inc. Home: 445 El Escarpado Stanford CA 94305

TERNER, EMANUEL M., container mfr.; b. N.Y.C., May 2, 1909; s. Louis and Ida (Katz) T.; student N.Y.U. Sch. Commerce, 1930; H.H.D. (hon.), L.I. U.; m. Mathilda Weisenfeld, June 14, 1931; children—Nancy, Elaine, Carol. Various positions glass container industry, 1929—; with Metro Glass Bottle Co., 1935-66, sec.-treas., 1935-49, pres., 1949-66, now Metro Glass div. Nat. Diary Products Corp.; founder Midland Glass Co., 1968, pres., chmn., chief exec. officer, dir.; dir. Nat. Dairy Products Corp., 1955-66. Trustee Village of South Orange, 1958, Rutgers U., 1979-84; mem. dean's adv. council N.Y. U.; mem. pres.'s council Coll. of Holy Cross, Marquette U. Recipient Madden Meml. award N.Y. U., 1979. Mem. U.S. Brewers Assn. (former trustee), Beta Gamma Sigma (hon.). Club: Tower of Cornell U. Home: Oakhurst NJ 07755 Office: 277 Park Ave New York NY 10017 also Cliffwood Ave Cliffwood NJ 07721

TERNES, ALAN PAUL, editor; b. Detroit, Apr. 28, 1931; s. Peter and Vera Regina (Boush) T.; student U. Mich., 1953-54, 56; B.S., Columbia U., 1963, M.Ph., 1972; children—Kate, Marie. Reporter Detroit News, 1953-54, 56-57; reporter Pacific Stars and Stripes, Tokyo, Japan, 1954-55, bur. chief, 1955-56; city editor Middletown (N.Y.) Record, 1964-66; asso. dir. univ. relations Columbia, N.Y.C., 1967-68; sr. editor Nat. History Mag., N.Y.C., 1969-72, editor, 1972—. Trustee Piermont (N.Y.) Pub. Library, 1962-63. Served with AUS, 1954-56. Columbia U. fellow, 1962-63; Ford Found. fellow, 1969-70. Mem. AAAS, N.Y. Acad. Sci., Assn. Am. Geographers. Editor: Ants, Indians and Little Dinosaurs, 1975. Editorial bd. Curator mag., 1973—. Contbr. articles to mags. Home: 333 Central Park West New York NY 10025 Office: Natural History 79th St and Central Park West New York NY 10024

TER-POGOSSIAN, MICHEL MATHIEU, educator; b. Berlin, Germany, Apr. 21, 1925; s. Michel and Anna (Sovratoff) Ter-P.; came to U.S., 1947, naturalized, 1954; B.A., U. Paris, 1943; postgrad. Inst. of Radium, Paris, 1945-46; M.S., Washington U., St. Louis, 1948, Ph.D., 1950; m. Ann Scott Dodson, Mar. 3, 1966. Instr. radiation physics Washington U. Sch. Medicine, St. Louis, 1950-51, asst. prof., 1951-56, asso. prof., 1956-61, prof., 1961-73, prof. biophysics in physiology, 1964—, prof. radiation scis. Mallinkrodt Inst. Radiology, 1973—. Recipient Paul C. Aebersold award Soc. Nuclear Medicine, 1976. Fellow Am. Physics Soc.; mem. Am. Nuclear Soc., Am. Radium Soc., Radiation Research Soc., Radiol. Soc. N. Am., Societe Belge de Medecine Nucleaire (hon.). Club: Univ. Author: The Physical Aspects of Diagnostic Radiology, 1971; editor: Reconstruction Tomography in Diagnostic Radiology and Nuclear Medicine, 1976; patentee in field of x-ray intensifying screens and positron emission tomography. Office: Mallinckrodt Inst of Radiology Washington U Sch Medicine 510 S Kingshighway Saint Louis MO 63110*

TERPSTRA, WILLIAM CORNELIUS, utilities exec.; b. Hammond, Ind., Nov. 27, 1939; s. William W. and Hermine J. (DeLeeuw) T.; B.S., U. Ill., 1961; m. Judith Lee Hartman, May 16, 1964; children—Michele, William. With Price Waterhouse & Co., C.P.A.'s, Chgo., 1961-68, sr., 1964-66, mgr., 1966-68; asst. controller Miehle-Goss-Dexter, Inc., Cicero, Ill., 1968-71, controller Goss Co., 1969; dir. audit Peoples Gas Co., Chgo., 1971-73, controller, 1973-74, now v.p., controller; v.p., controller Peoples Gas, Light & Coke Co., Chgo., 1974-75, Peoples Gas Co., 1977—. Mem. adv. council Coll. Commerce, U. Ill., 1972—. Bd. dirs. Civic Fedn., Better Bus. Bur. Chgo., 1976-77; mem. allocations com. United Way of Met. Chgo., 1975—; trustee Village of Lansing (Ill.), 1977-79, Taxpayers Fedn. Ill. Served with USMCR, 1962-63. C.P.A., Ill. Mem. Am. Inst. C.P.A.'s, Ill. Soc. C.P.A.'s, Alpha Chi Rho, Beta Alpha Psi, Sigma Iota Epsilon. Mem. Christian Reformed Ch. Club: University (Chgo.). Office: 122 S Michigan Ave Chicago IL 60603

TERRA, DANIEL JAMES, chem. co. exec.; b. Phila., June 9, 1911; s. Louis J. and Mary (DeLuca) T.; B.S., Pa. State U., 1931; m. Adeline Evans Richards, Aug. 7, 1937; children—Penny Jane (dec.), James D. Founder, Lawter Chems., Inc., Chgo., 1940, chmn. bd., chief exec. officer, 1964—, also dir.; dir. McLouth Steel Corp., Stewart-Warner Corp., 1st Nat. Bank & Trust Co., Evanston. Mem. Chgo. Crime Commn. Past v.p., mem. exec. com. United Republican Fund Ill., now pres.; past chmn. Everett Dirksen 500 Club. Bd. dirs. Easter Seal Soc., Chgo. Lyric Opera, Evanston Hosp., Assn.; trustee Ravinia Festival Assn., Chgo. Orchestral Assn., Ill. Inst. Tech., Dickinson Coll., Roycemore Sch.; mem. adv. council Grad. Sch. Mgmt., Northwestern U.; mem. pres.'s council Nat. Coll. Edn.; mem. council Pa. State U.; mem. exec. com. Ill. Inst. Tech. Research Inst.; mem. grand council Am. Indian Center; mem. com. on Am. arts Art Inst. Chgo.; mem. citizen's bd. U. Chgo. Recipient Winthrop Sears medal Chem. Industry Assn., 1972; Distinguished Alumni medal Pa. State U., 1976. Mem. Ill. Mfrs. Assn. (dir.), Pres.'s Club of Loyola U. Chgo., Chgo. Com., Assos. Northwestern U. Clubs: Westmoreland Country (Wilmette, Ill.); Kenilworth; Capitol Hill (Washington); Chicago, Commercial, Metropolitan, Chicago Mid-America, Casino (Chgo.); Lauderdale Yacht (Fort Lauderdale, Fla.); Nat. Arts, Links (N.Y.C.). Home: 528 Roslyn Rd Kenilworth IL 60043 also 19 Isla Bahia Dr Fort Lauderdale FL 33361 Office: 990 Skokie Blvd Northbrook IL 60062

TERRACE, HERBERT S(YDNEY), psychologist; b. Bklyn., Nov. 29, 1936; s. Morris Abraham and Esther (Marsh) T.; A.B., Cornell U., 1957, M.A., 1958; Ph.D., Harvard U., 1961. Instr. psychology Columbia U., 1961-63, asst. prof. psychology, 1963-66, asso. prof., 1966-68, prof., 1968—; vis. prof. Harvard U., 1972-73. John Simon Guggenheim fellow, 1969-70; NIMH grantee, 1962—; NSF grantee, 1963-76; W.T. Grant Found. grantee, 1975-76; Harry Frank Guggenheim Found. grantee, 1976-78. Fellow Am. Psychol. Assn.; mem. AAAS, Eastern Psychol. Assn., Soc. Exptl. Analysis Behavior. Author: Introduction to Statistics, 1971; (with Scott Parker) Individual Learning Systems, 1971; editor: (with T. G. Bever) Human Behavior: Prediction and Control in Modern Society, 1973; Nim, 1979; asso. editor Jour. Exptl. Analysis Behavior, 1966-74, Animal Learning and Behavior, 1971-75, Learning and Motivation, 1970-72, Behaviorism, 1972—. Home: 460 Riverside Dr Apt 91 New York NY 10027 Office: 418 Schermerhorn Hall Columbia U New York NY 10027

TERREL, CHARLES LYNN, cons.; b. DeGraff, Ohio, Apr. 19, 1904; s. Charles and Rose B. (Pence) T.; B.A., Ohio State U., 1928; M.B.A. cum laude, Harvard Bus. Sch., 1932; m. Lela Fern Heaston, June 15, 1935; children—Sondra Lee, Mark Heaston; m. 2d, Mary Emily Masterson, Sept. 3, 1956. Engr., Western Electric Co., 1926-32; credit dept. Continental Ill. Nat. Bank & Trust Co., Chgo., 1932-36; pres. Jones Abstract Co., 1936-43; treas. Albra Castings Co., 1938-43; asst. adminstr. Lend Lease Adminstrn., 1941-42; program dir. Allied Combined Chiefs of Staff, 1942; chmn. North African Econ. Bd., Algiers, 1943; pres. mgmt. Service Co., 1943-48; v.p. Terrel Estate, Inc., 1943-48; fgn. trade cons. Dept. State, 1948; fgn. trade adminstr. Greek Govt., Athens, 1948-51; dep. chief U.S. spl. mission to China, Formosa, 1951-53; pres. Internat. Consultants, Inc., 1953-60; chief indsl. devel. div. Dept. of State, Nigeria, 1960-63; dir. Devel. Service Inst., Nat. Investment Bank, Accra, Ghana, 1963-66, fin. adviser, 1966-68; fin. adviser Korea Devel. Finance Corp., 1968-73, Korea Investment and Finance Corp., 1971-73, Korea Capital Corp., Seoul, 1973-74, Indsl. Devel. Bank, Saigon, 1973-75, Kuwait Indsl. Devel. Bank, 1974, Banco Unido de Fomento, Santiago, Chile, 1974; mission chief Internat. Finance Corp. (World Bank), Washington, 1974; financial adviser Compagnie Financiere et Touristique, Tunis, 1975-78; program evaluator AID, Abidjan, Ivory Coast, 1978; adv. Saudi Indsl. Devel. Fund, Riyadh, Saudi Arabia, 1979—; pres. Internat. Devel. Consultants, Inc., 1965—; asst. prof. bus. adminstrn. San Diego State Coll., 1957-60. Decorated Order of Bn. of George I (Greece). Mem. Ops. Research Soc. Home: PO Box 266 Vigie Castries Saint Lucia West Indies Office: 6301 Stevenson Ave Alexandria VA 22304. *Accomplishment is a product of the passage of time, the effectivenss of its utilization, innate intelligence, and the factor of chance. The first three can maximize or ameliorate the fourth. Targets for accomplishment, set early in one's career, serve to separate the useful from the aimless utilization of time. Satisfaction with accomplishment is a product of accomplishment and character. The longer one lives, the more one appreciates the validity of the tenet: "Do unto others as you would have others do unto you." In this validity lies the reward of good character.*

TERREL, RONALD LEE, civil engr.; b. Klamath Falls, Oreg., Sept. 2, 1936; s. Theodore Thomas and Ruth Margaret (Fausset) T.; B.S. in C.E., Purdue U., 1960, M.S., 1961; Ph.D., U. Calif., Berkeley, 1967; m. Susan Laura Harrower, Feb. 28, 1959 (div. Jan. 1980); children—Douglas Scott, Nancy Dawn, Janet Lynn. Estimator, J. H. Pomeroy & Co., San Francisco, 1955; lab. asst. Purdue U., 1956-60; asst. field geologist Bear Creek Mining Co., Mpls., 1957-58; materials engr. U.S. Bur. Reclamation, Denver, 1960-64; project engr. J. H. Pomeroy & Co., Antigua, B.W.I., 1964-65; research asst. U. Calif., Berkeley, 1965-66; asst. prof. U. Wash., Seattle, 1967-70, asso. prof., 1970-75, prof., 1975—, head Transp. Constrn. and Geometrics div., 1976; pres. Pavement Systems, Inc., Seattle, 1970—; exec. v.p. Seattle Engring. Internat., Inc., 1979—; cons. to pvt. industry, U.S. Govt., UN. Nominated Constrn. Man of Year, Engring. News-Record, 1972; Ford fellow, 1965-67; Purdue Alumni scholar, 1959-60. Mem. ASCE, Transp. Research Bd., Assn. Asphalt Paving Technologists, Am. Concrete Inst., ASTM, Triaxial Inst. (chmn. 1971-73), Am. Roadbuilders Assn., Can. Tech. Asphalt Assn., Assn. Engring. Geologists, Sigma Xi, Tau Beta Pi, Chi Epsilon, Sigma Gamma Epsilon. Office: Dept of Civil Engineering FX 10 University of Washington Seattle WA 98195

TERRELL, ALLEN TOWNSEND, sculptor; b. Riverhead, N.Y., Nov. 2, 1897; s. John Robinson and Jennie Luville (Hawkins) T.; cert. Columbia U. Sch. Architecture, 1921; student Art Students League, N.Y.C., 1920-24, Fontainebleau (France) Schs., 1924-26, 28-30, Acad. Scaninave, Paris, 1928-31; pupil of George Bridgman, Andrew Dasburg, Paul Baudoin, Jean Despulols, Charles Despiau, Marcel Gimond. Archtl. draftsman, N.Y.C., 1921-24; tchr. water color Parsons Sch. Design, N.Y.C., 1933-34; freelance artist, portrait sculptor, also work in ceramics, decorative accessories, 1930—; one-man exhbns. include: E. Hampton (N.Y.) Guild Hall, 1936, 38, Decorators Club, N.Y.C., 1940, Village Art Center, N.Y.C., 1943, Mildred Irby Gallery, N.Y.C., 1954, Benefit for Central Suffolk Hosp., Riverhead, N.Y., 1962; group exhbns. include Salon d'Automne, Paris, 1926, NAD, N.Y.C., 1932, Pa. Acad., 1933; represented in permanent collections: Smithsonian Instn., Met. Mus. Art, N.Y.C., Mus. City N.Y., Bklyn. Mus.; executed murals for S.S. America, 1940, 45, decorative accessories, ceramics and murals for Aluminum Co. Am., 1936, murals (with Henry Hennoch) for dirs. room Williamsburg Savs. Bank, Bklyn., 1950; trustee Fontainbleau Schs., 1950—. Fellow Nat. Sculpture Soc.; life mem. Art Students League; mem. Watercolor Soc. Am. (hon.), Pastel Soc. Am. (hon.), Allied Artists Am., Hort. Soc. N.Y., Nat. Arts Club (Paul Manship award 1972), Nat. Trust Historic Preservation. Republican. Methodist.

TERRELL, ARTHUR P., lawyer; b. Navasota, Tex., 1910; B.S., Princeton, 1933; LL.B., U. Tex., 1936. Admitted to Tex. bar, 1936; now partner firm Butler, Binion, Rice, Cook & Knapp, Houston. Mem. Am., Houston (past pres.) bar assns., State Bar Tex., Phi Delta Phi. Address: Esperson Bldg Houston TX 77002

TERRELL, CHARLES WILLIAM, engr., educator; b. Louisville, May 10, 1927; s. John Upton and Adelaide (Crush) T.; B.S. in Elec. Engring., Purdue U., 1952, Ph.D. in Nuclear Engring., 1970; B.S. in Nuclear Engring., N.C. State U., 1955, M.S., 1956; m. Emily Jane Thomas, Nov. 10, 1952; children—Kathryn, Bennett. Lectr. nuclear sci. N.C. State U., 1955-57; with Ill. Inst. Tech. Research Inst. and predecessor, Chgo., 1957-67, dir. physics div., 1965-67; fast reactor research Purdue U., 1967-70, asso. prof. and supr. Computer Center staff, 1969-70; mgr. applied sci. div. Computer Sci. Corp., Oak Brook, Ill., 1970-72; pres. Ind. Inst. Tech., Ft. Wayne, 1972-77; prof. nuclear engring. and dir. nuclear reactor U. Okla., Norman, 1977—. Served with AUS, 1945-47. Mem. Am. Soc. Engring. Edn., Am. Nuclear Soc. Home: 2504 Linden Ave Norman OK 73069 Office: 865 Asp Ave Norman OK 73019

TERRELL, FREDERICK REYNOLDS, ret. air force officer; b. Boonville, Mo., Nov. 13, 1913; s. Frederick Brahan and Jessie (Reynolds) T.; B.S., U.S. Mil. Acad., 1936; grad. Air Command and Staff Coll., 1947, Air War Coll., 1950, Nat. War Coll., 1953; m. Annie Lee Lancaster, Feb. 26, 1938; children—Priscilla Anne (Mrs. Ellsworth), Frederick Kenyon. Commd. 2d lt. U.S. Army, 1936, advanced through grades to maj. gen. USAF, 1962; rated pilot, 1937; comdr. 20th Squadron, 1941, 97th Squadron, 1941, 47th Bombardment Group, 1942-44; assigned gen. staff War Dept., 1944-46; mem. faculty Air U., 1946-49; chief new devel. div., asst. comdt. Air Tactical Sch., 20th Air Force, Korea, 1950-52; assigned Joint Chiefs Staff, 1953-56; comdr. 34th CONAD Div., 1956-58, 64th NORAD Div., 1958-60, 73d Air Div., 1960-62, 30th Air Div., 30th NORAD Region, 1962-66; mem. staff N. Am. Air Def. Command, 1966-67, ret., 1967. Decorated Silver Star, Legion of Merit with oak leaf cluster, Bronze Star with oak leaf cluster, Air medal, Commendation medal with oak leaf cluster. Mem. Air Force Assn. (charter), Air Force Aid Soc. (life), Assn. Grads. U.S. Mil. Acad. (life), Combat Pilots Assn. U.S.A. (charter), Order Daedalians. Episcopalian. Home: 1341 San Julian Ln Lake San Marcos CA 92069

TERRELL, GLENN, univ. pres.; b. Tallahassee, May 24, 1920; s. William Glenn and Esther (Collins) T.; B.A., Davidson (N.C.) Coll., 1942; M.S., Fla. State U., 1948; Ph.D., State U. Iowa, 1952; children—Francine Elizabeth, William Glenn III. Instr., then asst. prof. Fla. State U., 1948-55; asst. prof., then asso. prof., chmn. dept. psychology U. Colo., 1955-59, asso., acting dean Coll. Arts and Scis., 1959-63; prof. psychology, dean Coll. Liberal Arts and Scis., U. Ill. at Chgo. Circle, 1963-65, dean faculties, 1965-67; pres. Wash. State U., Pullman, 1967—. Pres., Nat. Assn. State Univs. and Land-Grant Colls., 1977-78. Served with AUS, 1942-46. Mem. Am. Psychol. Assn., AAAS, Sigma Xi. Home: 755 Campus Ave NE Pullman WA 99163 Office: Wash State U Pullman WA 99164

TERRELL, HUNTINGTON, educator; b. Syracuse, N.Y., Oct. 7, 1925; s. William Sale and Marjorie (Smith) T.; A.B., Colgate U., 1944; A.M., Harvard, 1948, Ph.D., 1956; children—Bruce, Nathan, Nancy, Cynthia. Instr. Colgate U., Hamilton, N.Y., 1951-56; asst. prof., 1956-62, asso. prof., 1962-67, prof., 1967—, dir. gen. edn. in philosophy and religion, 1958-63. Vis. scholar Inst. in Indian Civilization, Hyderabad, India, 1961; vis. fellow Princeton, 1962, 76-77; spl. auditor Harvard, 1968. Served with USNR, 1944-46. Fulbright fellow, 1961. Mem. Am. Philos. Assn., Soc. for Philosophy and Pub. Affairs, Am. Soc. for Polit. and Legal Philosophy, AAUP, ACLU. Contbr. articles to profl. jours. Home: 106 Rural Route 2 Preston Hill Hamilton NY 13346

TERRELL, NORMAN EDWARDS, govt. ofcl.; b. Fort Worth, Tex., Apr. 12, 1933; s. John Cecil and Devie Dell (Edwards) T.; B.A., U. Wash., 1958; M.A., Oxford U., 1961; m. Thalia Barzacos, Sept. 22, 1960; children—John, Audrey, Vanessa. Commd. fgn. service officer Dept. State, 1963; spl. asst. to counselor, 1973-75; asst. dir. for policy rev. Nuclear Regulatory Commn., 1975-77; dir. internat. affairs NASA, 1977-78; dep. asst. sec. for sci. and tech. Dept. State, 1978—. Served with USAF, 1951-55. Rhodes scholar, 1958-61. Home: 5623 Lamar Rd Washington DC 20016 Office: Dept State Washington DC 20520

TERRELL, TOL, hosp. adminstr.; b. Merit, Tex., Jan. 25, 1916; s. Burl Toliver and Mary Julia (Swift) T.; A.B., Austin Coll., Sherman, Tex., 1937; m. Grace Hopson Moody, Aug. 28, 1937; children—Charles, Mary Nelle (Mrs. Don Cummins), Hal and Suzanne (Mrs. James Mitchell) (twins). Adminstr., Wilson N. Jones Hosp., Sherman, 1937-39, Harris Hosp., Ft. Worth, 1939-48, Shannon West Tex. Meml. Hosp., San Angelo, Tex., 1948—. Bd. dirs. Blue Cross-Blue Shield of Tex., 1943—. Recipient Service award N.W. Tex. Hosp. Assn., 1957, Meritorious Service award Austin Coll., 1959, Gold Medal award Am. Coll. Hosp. Aminstrs., 1964. Fellow. Am. Coll. Hosp. Adminstrs. (regent 1952-58, pres. 1961-62); mem. Am. (chmn. council 1946-47, trustee 1952-58, pres. 1957-58), Tex. (treas. 1942-44, trustee 1945-48, pres. 1946-47, Earl M. Collier award distinguished hosp. adminstrn. 1966) hosp. assns. Episcopalian. Home: 220 W Twohig Apt D San Angelo TX 76901 Office: 9 S Magdalen St San Angelo TX 76901

TERRES, JOHN KENNETH, naturalist, author, editor; b. Phila., Dec. 17, 1905; s. John Brown and Edna Katherine (Gaskill) T.; student State Tchrs. Coll., Indiana, Pa., 1935-36, Cornell U. and State Coll. Agr., Ithaca, N.Y., 1938-40, Sch. Adult Edn., N.Y. U., 1945-50; m. Mabel Ridenour, 1926 (div. 1938); m. 2d, Marion Coles, July 29, 1950. Engaged in civil engring. and constrn., 1922-34; field biologist Dept. Agr., 1935-42; free-lance writer, 1945-49; news editor Am. Chem. Soc., 1948; acting editor Audubon mag., 1948-49, mng. editor, 1949-55, editor, 1955-60; gen. editor nature books J.B. Lippincott Co., Phila. and N.Y.C., 1959-76; editor-in-chief Audubon Nature Ency., 1964-65; contbg. editor The Chat, 1964-70; free-lance writer, 1960—; reviewer N.Y. Times Sunday Book Rev. sect., 1951—; cons. editor Doubleday & Co., Inc., 1966-68; contbg. editor Audubon mag., 1966—; cons. editor Wonders of Trees Books. Mem. Lab. Ornithology, Cornell U., 1956—. Served with AUS, 1942-45. Mem. Wildlife Soc., Am. Ornithologists Union, Am. Soc. Mammalogists, Am. Soc. Ichthyologists and Herpetologists, Wilderness Soc., Cooper Ornithol. Soc., Wilson Ornithol. Soc., Bklyn. Entomol. Soc., Nat. Audubon Soc., Avicultural Soc. (London), Wildlife Disease Assn., N.E. Bird Banding Assn., Raptor Research Found., Authors Guild, John Burroughs Meml. Assn. (dir.). Author: Songbirds in Your Garden, 1953, rev. edit., 1968, 77; The Wonders I See, 1960; How To Attract Birds the Year Round, 1964; Flashing Wings: The Drama of Bird Flight, 1968; From Laurel Hill to Siler's Bog: The Walking Adventures of a Naturalist, 1969 (John Burroughs medal 1971); How Birds Fly, Under the Water and Through the Air, 1975. Editor: The Audubon Book of True Nature Stories, 1958; Discovery, 1961; The World of the White-tailed Deer, 1962; The World of the Bobcat, 1963; The World of the Beaver, 1964; The World of the Raccoon, 1964; The World of the Coyote, 1964; The World of the Red-Tailed Hawk, 1964; The World of the Great Horned Owl, 1966; The World of the Black Bear, 1966; The World of the Porcupine, 1966; The World of the Woodchuck, 1966; The World of the Opossum, 1967; The World of the Frog and the Toad, 1967; The World of the Wolf, 1967; The World of the Ant, 1968; The World of the Grizzly Bear, 1968; The World of the Canada Goose, 1968; The World of the Pronghorn, 1968; The World of the Red Fox, 1969; The World of the Bison, 1969; The World of the American Elk, 1969; The World of the Prairie Dog, 1970; The World of the Snake, 1971; The World of the Otter, 1971; The World of the Gull, 1971; The World of the Bottle-nosed Dolphin, 1972; The World of the Swan, 1972; The World of the Moose, 1972; The World of the Ruffed Grouse, 1973; The World of the Wild Turkey, 1973; The World of the Wood Duck, 1973; The World of the Gray Squirrel, 1973; The World of the Bat, 1976. Contbr. numerous articles to mags., jours. in field. Address: 51 W 81 St New York NY 10024

TERRIE, HENRY LARKIN, JR., educator; b. Charleston, W.Va., Jan. 10, 1921; s. Henry Larkin and Mary Gibson (Hunley) T.; grad. Phillips Andover Acad., 1939; B.A., Yale, 1943; M.A., Princeton, 1952, Ph.D., 1955; m. Jeanne Margaret Cox, June 12, 1948; children—Henry Larkin III, David Leslie. Instr. English, Phillips Andover Acad., 1948, U. Minn., 1948-49; instr. English, Dartmouth, Hanover, N.H., 1952-59, prof., 1959—, chmn. humanities, 1959-63, chmn. dept. English, 1967-72, asso. dean of faculty for humanities, 1972-76. Prof. Bread Loaf Sch. English, 1958. Mem. alumni bd. Yale, 1964-71. Served to lt. USNR, 1943-46. Mem. AAUP, Modern Lang. Assn. Am., Zeta Psi. Club: Century Assn. Editor: (with A.J. Porter) American Literature, 1964. Contbr. articles to profl. jours. Home: 4 Parkway Hanover NH 03755

TERRILL, CLAIR ELMAN, geneticist; b. Rippey, Iowa, Oct. 27, 1910; s. Otis Wallace and Mary Irene (Grow) T.; B.S., Iowa State U., 1932; Ph.D., U. Mo., 1936; m. Zola Mae Alexander, June 9, 1932; children—Ronald L. (dec.), Richard E. Research asst. U. Mo., 1932-36; asst. animal husbandman Ga. Agr. Expt. Sta., 1936; animal husbandman Agrl. Research Service, Dept. Agr., Dubois, Idaho, 1936-53, dir. U.S. Sheep Expt. Sta. and Western Sheep Breeding Lab., Dubois, 1953-55, chief sheep and fur animal research br., animal sci. research dir. Agrl. Research Service, Beltsville, Md., 1955-72, nat. program staff scientist, 1972—. Mem. sub-panel President's Sci. Adv. Com. World Food Supply, 1966. Fellow Am. Soc. Animal Sci. (hon., pres. Western section 1951, chmn. com. research 1950-52, com. monographs, 1955-60, editorial bd. 1954-57, v.p., 1963, pres. 1964, dir.); mem. World Assn. Animal Prodn. (council 1965-68), Am. Grasslands Council (dir. 1963-65), Genetic Soc. Am., Am. Genetic Assn. (council 1965-68, v.p., pres. 1970), Am. Meat Sci. Assn., Am. Assn. Anatomists, Am. Inst. Biol. Scis., Soc. Study Reprodn., AAAS, Sigma Xi, Alpha Zeta, Gamma Sigma Delta. Home: 318 Apple Grove Rd Silver Spring MD 20904 Office: Nat Program Staff Agrl Research Service Dept of Agr Beltsville MD 20705

TERRILL, ROBERT CARL, hosp. adminstr.; b. Oklahoma City, Dec. 10, 1927; s. D. Willard and Velma (Mitchell) T.; B.A., U. Okla., 1948, M.A. in History, 1961; M.A. in Hosp. Adminstrn., State U. Iowa, 1954; Ed.D. in Ednl. Adminstrn., Ind. U., 1978; m. Jessica Doe, Dec. 14, 1957; children—Thane Bennett, Sarah Haven. Adminstrv. resident Mary Fletcher Hosp., Burlington, Vt., 1953-55, asst. adminstr., personnel dir., 1955-61, asso. adminstr., 1961-65; adminstr. Hosps. of U. Okla., Oklahoma City, 1965-72; dir. Ind. Univ. Hosps., Indpls., 1973-76; instr. health adminstrn. Ind. U., 1976-77; asso. prof. Coll. Mgmt. and Profl. Studies, U. Mass., Boston; preceptor in hosp. adminstrn. Washington U., St. Louis, Trinity U., San Antonio; asst. prof. U. Okla. Health Scis. Center. Fellow Am. Coll. Hosp. Adminstrs.; mem. Mass. Hosp. Assn., Am. Hosp. Assn., Assn. Programs in Hosp. Adminstrn., Pub. Health Assn., New Eng. Hosp. Assembly, Nat. League for Nursing, State U. Iowa. Alumni Assn., Ind. U. Alumni Assn. Rotarian. Home: 20 Ripley St Wilbraham MA 01095 Office: Coll Mgmt and Profl Studies U Mass Boston MA 02125

TERRILL, ROSS GLADWIN, author, educator; b. Melbourne, Australia, Aug. 22, 1938; s. Frank and Miriel (Lloyd) T.; B.A. with honors, U. Melbourne, 1962; Ph.D., Harvard, 1970. Came to U.S., 1965, naturalized, 1979. Tutor in polit. sci. U. Melbourne, 1962-63; staff sec. Australian Student Christian Movement, 1962, 1964-65; teaching fellow Harvard, 1968-70, lectr. govt., 1970-73, asso. prof., 1974-78, research fellow East Asian studies, 1970—, dir. programs Center Internat. Affairs, 1974-78; contbg. editor Atlantic Monthly, 1970—; research fellow Asia Soc., 1977—. Recipient Nat. Mag. award, 1972; George Polk Meml. award outstanding mag. reporting, 1972; Sumner prize, 1970; Queen's Coll. exhbn. U. Melbourne, 1957. Mem. Authors Guild, Am. Polit. Sci. Assn. Author: China Profile, 1969; China and Ourselves, 1971; 800,000,000: The Real China, 1972; R.H. Tawney and His Times, 1973; Flowers on an Iron Tree, 1975; The Future of China, 1978; The China Difference, 1979; Mao: A Biography, 1980; contbr. numerous articles to Atlantic Monthly, New Republic, N.Y. Review, N.Y. Times, Foreign Affairs. Home: 395 Broadway Cambridge MA 02139

TERRIS, MILTON, physician, educator; b. N.Y.C., Apr. 22, 1915; s. Harry and Gussie (Dokshitski) T.; A.B., Columbia, 1935; M.D., N.Y.U., 1939; M.P.H., Johns Hopkins, 1944; m. Rema Lapouse, Nov. 23, 1941 (dec. Aug. 1970); children—Andrew David, Eugene Charles; m. 2d, Lillian Long, Feb. 6, 1971. Intern, Harlem Hosp., N.Y.C., 1939-41; resident Bellevue Hosp., N.Y.C. 1941-42; practice medicine specializing in preventive medicine, Buffalo, 1951-58, N.Y.C., 1960—; asst. dean post-grad. edn. Sch. Medicine, U. Buffalo, 1951-58, asso., 1952-54, asst. prof., 1954-55, asso. prof. preventive medicine, 1955-58; prof. epidemiology Sch. Medicine, Tulane U., 1958-60; head chronic disease unit dept. epidemiology Pub. Health Research Inst., N.Y.C., 1960-64; prof. preventive medicine N.Y. Med. Coll., 1964—, chmn. dept. community and preventive medicine, 1968—. Fellow N.Y. Acad. Medicine, Am. Pub. Health Assn. (past pres.); mem. Assn. Tchrs. Preventive Medicine (past pres.), Phi Beta Kappa, Alpha Omega Alpha, Delta Omega. Author: Goldberger on Pellagra, 1964. Home: 1120 Fifth Ave New York City NY 10028 Office: NY Medical College Fifth Ave and 106th St New York City NY 10029

TERRY, CLARK, musician; b. St. Louis, Dec. 14, 1920; privately educated; m. Pauline Reddon; 2 children. Pres., Etoile Music Prodns., 1955—, Pastel Music, 1958—; v.p. Creative Jazz Composers, Inc., 1972—; leader Clark Terry Big Bad Band, 1966—; itinerate jazz clinician and educator; exec. dir. Internat. of Jazz. Served with USN, 1942-45. Recipient numerous awards, including Grammy nominations. Author: Let's Talk Trumpet, 1973; Interpretation of the Jazz Language, 1976; Circular Breathing, 1977. Office: Creative Jazz Composers PO Box T Bowie MD 20715*

TERRY, CLIFFORD LEWIS, journalist; b. Highland Park, Ill., Jan. 19, 1937; s. Clifford Lewis and Isabelle (Marlow) T.; student Carleton Coll., Northfield, Minn., 1954-55; B.A., Trinity Coll., Hartford, Conn., 1958; postgrad. Columbia, 1962-63; m. Patricia West Dickelman, Sept. 1, 1966; children—Christopher West, Scott Marlow. Tchr., English and history Mt. Hermon (Mass.) Sch., 1958-59; police reporter City News Bur. Chgo., 1959-60; mem. staff Chgo. Tribune, 1960—, movie critic, 1965-70, asso. editor Sunday mag., 1970—. Served with AUS, 1960. Nieman fellow Harvard, 1969-70. Mem. Phi Beta Kappa. Office: 435 N Michigan Ave Chicago IL 60611

TERRY, FRANK REILLY, banker; b. Newton, Kans., Mar. 8, 1928; s. Brooks and Audrey (Winger) T.; B.S. in Bus. Adminstrn., Northwestern U., 1951; student Nat. Trust Sch., Evanston, Ill., 1961; J.D., U. Mo. at Kansas City, 1966; m. Susan Smart; children—Brian, Michael, Robert, Thomas. Ins. analyst Gen. Motors Corp.; with City Nat. Bank and Trust Co. (name changed to United Mo. Bank of Kansas City 1973), 1960—, now vice-chmn. bd. and sr. trust officer; dir. Howard Constrn. Co., Bowen Constrn. Co., Elko Photo Products Co. Mem. Estate Planning Council Kansas City (Mo.). Served to 1st lt. arty. AUS. Mem. Mo. Bankers Assn. (trust com.), Kansas City (Mo.) Bar Assn., Lawyers Assn. Kansas City (Mo.). Club: University (Kansas City, Mo.). Home: 5226 Pawnee Dr Roeland Park KS 66205 Office: United Mo Bank Kansas City PO Box 226 10th St and Grand Av Kansas City MO 64141

TERRY, JAMES ANDERSON, ins. co. exec.; b. Augusta, Ga., Sept. 4, 1924; s. Walter Anderson and Marion (Wills) T.; student Tex. A. and M. U., 1941-43; student Tex. U., 1945-46; m. Jane Abalene Atkins, Nov. 21, 1968. Spl. agt. Nat. of Hartford Group, Houston, 1947-50; office mgr. Hassell & Kellogg Ins. Agy., Houston, 1950-53; br. mgr. Am. Internat. Group, Houston, 1953-57; with Highlands Ins. Co., Houston, 1957—, v.p., mgr., until 1971, pres., chief exec. officer, 1971—, also dir.; dir. Life of S.W. Ins. Co. Served with A.C., U.S. Army, 1943-45; ETO. Decorated D.F.C., Air medal. Mem. Am. Inst. Property and Liability Underwriters (certified property and casualty underwriter). Republican. Baptist. Clubs: Houston, Lakeside Country (Houston). Home: 3802 Essex Green Houston TX 77027 Office: 600 Jefferson St Houston TX 77002

TERRY, JOHN HART, lawyer, utility co. exec.; former congressman; b. Syracuse, N.Y., Nov. 14, 1924; s. Frank and Saydee (Hart) T.; B.A., U. Notre Dame, 1945; J.D. Syracuse U., 1948; m. Catherine Jean Taylor Phelan, Apr. 15, 1950; children—Catherine Jean (Mrs. Richard Thompson), Lynn Marie, Susan Louise, Mary Carole. Admitted to N.Y. bar, 1950, D.C. bar, 1972; asso. to partner Smith & Sovik, 1948-59; asst. sec. to Gov. State of N.Y., 1959-61; sr. partner firm Smith, Sovik, Terry, Kendrick, McAuliffe & Schwarzer, 1961-73; sr. v.p., gen. counsel, sec. Niagara Mohawk Power Corp., Syracuse, 1973—. mem. N.Y. State Assembly, 1962-70; mem. 92d Congress from 34th Dist. N.Y., 1971-73; del. N.Y. Republican State Conv., 1962, 66. State chmn. United Services Orgn., 1964-73; past pres. John Timothy Smith Found. Founder, dir. Bishop Foery Found., Inc.; dir. Cath. Youth Orgn. of Diocese of Syracuse; pres. Lourdes Camp; bd. dirs. N.Y. State Traffic Council, Onondaga Com. Alcoholism, Children's Ct. Citizen Com.; chmn. bd. dirs. Am. Cancer Soc.; trustee Maria Regina Coll. Served to 1st lt. AUS, 1943-46. Decorated Purple Heart, Bronze Star; named Young Man of Year, Syracuse Jr. C. of C., 1958, N.Y. State Jr. C. of C., 1959, U. Notre Dame Club Central N.Y., 1959. Mem. Am. (utility law, municipal law and ins. law sect.), N.Y. State, Onondaga County, D.C., bar assns., County Officers Assn., Citizens Found., U. Notre Dame, Syracuse U. law assns., Old Boys Assn., Syracuse Boy's Club, Am. Legion, VFW, DAV, 40 and 8, Mil. Order of Purple Heart. Roman Catholic (pres. Cath. Youth Orgn.). Clubs: Century, Bellevue Country; Syracuse Liederkranz; University; Fort Orange (Albany, N.Y.); Capitol Hill (Washington); University of Notre Dame Central N.Y. Home: 25 Erregger Terr Syracuse NY 13224 Office: 300 Erie Blvd W Syracuse NY 13202

TERRY, LUTHER LEONIDAS, physician, heart specialist, educator; b. Red Level, Ala., Sept. 15, 1911; s. James Edward and Lula M. (Durham) T.; B.S., Birmingham-So. Coll., 1931, D.Sc., 1961; M.D., Tulane U., 1935; D.Sc., Jefferson Med. Coll., 1962, Union Coll., 1964, Rose Poly. Inst., 1965, McGill U., 1966, U. Ala., 1966, St. Joseph's Coll., 1966; LL.D., U. Alaska, 1964, Calif. Coll. of Med., 1965; M.D. (hon.), Women's Med. Coll., Phila., 1964; D.Sc., U. R.I., 1964, Tulane U. Sch. Medicine, 1964; LL.D., Marquette U., 1968, Phila. Coll. Pharmacy and Sci., 1970; m. Beryl Janet Reynolds, June 29, 1940; children—Janet Reynolds Kollock, Luther Leonidas, Michael D. Intern Hillman Hosp., Birmingham, Ala., 1935-36; asst. resident medicine Univ. Hosps., Cleve., 1936-37; resident medicine City Hosps., Cleve., 1937-38, asst. admitting officer, intern pathology, 1938-39; instr., research fellow medicine Washington U., St. Louis, 1939-40; instr. medicine and preventive medicine and pub. health U. Tex., Galveston, 1940-41, asst. prof., 1941-42, asso. prof. 1942-46; instr. medicine Johns Hopkins Med. Sch., 1944-53, asst. prof., 1953-61; mem. staff USPHS Hosp., Balt., 1942-43, chief med. service, 1943-53; chief clinic, gen. medicine and exptl. therapeutics Nat. Heart Inst., Bethesda, Md., 1950-58, asst. dir., 1958-61; surgeon gen., USPHS, 1961-65; v.p. med. affairs U. Pa., Phila., 1965-71, prof. medicine, 1965-75, prof. community medicine, 1965-75, adj. prof., 1975—. Mem. cardiovascular study sect. NIH, 1950-55, chmn. med. bd. Clin. Center, 1953-55, mem., 1953-58; dir. residency tng. program Nat. Heart Inst., 1953-61, chmn. cardiovascular research tng. com., 1957-61; mem. med. div. Strategic Bombing Survey, Japan, 1945-46; com civilian health requirements USPHS, 1955-58, mem. adv. com. nutrition div. Indian health, 1957-61; chief U.S. del. WHO, 1961-65; mem. adv. bd. Leonard Wood Meml. Inst. Nutrition Scis., Columbia U.; Herman E. Hilleboe prize lectr. in pub. health N.Y. State Ann. Health Conf., 1965; mem. chmn. Nat. Interagy. Council on Smoking and Health, 1967-70; mem. facilities and resources com. Nat. Library Medicine; mem. adv. bd. Nat. Resuscitation Soc.; mem. adv. council Am. Mus. Health; mem. expert com. WHO, 1974. Mem.-at-large Nat. council Boy Scouts Am. Trustee, Inst. for Advancement Med. Communication, Inst. Med. Research; pub. trustee Nutrition Found; vis. com. Sch. Hygiene and Pub. Health, Johns Hopkins; bd. dirs., trustee, bd. govs. many insts., orgns. Diplomate Am. Bd. Internal Medicine, Nat. Bd. Med. Examiners. Recipient George B. Glendening Meml. award washington Dental Soc., 1965, Distinguished Service medal USPHS, 1965. Fellow A.C.P. (past gov., hon. master 1973), Am. Coll. Cardiology (Robert D. Bruce award 1965), Am. Coll. Chest Physicians, Am. Coll. Hosp. Adminstrs., Am. Coll. Dentists, Phila. Coll. Physicians; mem. A.M.A. (past mem. ho. dels), Am. Heart Assn. (com. ethics), Am. Pub. Health Assn., Am. Found. Tropical Medicine (hon. dir.; also hon. dir. Liberian Inst.), Assn. Am. Physicians, Am. Social Health Assn. (dir.), Nat. Tb Assn. (hon. v.p.), Am. Hosp. Assn. (hon.), Heart Assn. Southeastern Pa. (gov.), N.Y. Acad. Medicine, Nat. Soc. for Med. Research (dir.), Nat. Wildlife Fedn. (asso.), Royal Soc. Health (Gt. Britain), Pub. Health Service Clin. Soc. (past pres.), Pan Am. Med. Assn., Med. and Chirurgical Faculty Md. (hon.), Montgomery County (Md.) Med. Soc. (hon.), Ala. Acad. Honor, Omicron Delta Kappa, Pi Kappa Alpha (Distinguished Alumnus award Delta chpt. 1961, Distinguished Achievement award 1962). Office: 2035 Delancey Pl Philadelphia PA 19103 also Univ Assos Inc 475 L'Enfant Plaza West Suite 2100 Washington DC 20024

TERRY, MEGAN, playwright; b. Seattle, July 22, 1932; student Banff Sch. Fine Arts, summers, 1950-52, 56, U. Alta., Edmondon, Can., 1952-53; B.Ed., U. Wash., 1956. Dir. Cornish players Cornish Sch. Allied Arts, Seattle, 1954-56; founding mem., dir. playwrights workshop Open Theatre, N.Y.C., 1963-68; ABC fellow Yale U., 1966-67; founding mem., v.p. N.Y. Theatre Strategy, 1971; adj. prof. theatre U. Nebr., Omaha; playwright-in-residence Omaha Magic Theatre, 1977; author plays including: Beach Grass; Seascape; Go Out and Move the Car; New York Comedy: Two; Ex-Miss Copper Queen on a Set of Pills; When My Girlhood Was Still All Flowers; Eat at Joe's; Calm Down Mother; Keep Tightly Closed in a Cool Dry Place; The Magic Realists; Comings and Goings; The Gloaming, Oh My Darling; Viet Rock: A Folk War Movie; The Key Is on the Bottom; The People vs Ranchman; Home; Jack-Jack; Massachusetts Trust; Sanibel and Captiva; One More Little Drinkie; Approaching Simone; The Tommy Allen Show; Grooving: Choose a Spot on the Floor; Couplings and Groupings; Hothouse; Babes in the Bighouse; Pro Game; The Pioneer; Brazil Fado; Lady Rose's Brazil Hideout; editor, writer 100,001 Horror Stories of the Plains; American King's English for Queens. Mem. theatre panel Nat. Endowment Arts; mem. theatre panel Rockefeller Found., 1977—; mem. performing arts panel Nebr. State Council for Arts, 1977. Recipient Stanley Drama award, 1965, Office of Advanced Drama Research award, 1965, Obie award, 1970, Silver medal for distinguished contribution to and service in Am. Theatre Amoco Oil Co., 1977; Rockefeller grantee, 1968; NEA Lit. fellow, 1973; Guggenheim fellow, 1978. Mem. Women's Theatre Council (founding 1971), Am. Theatre Assn. (co-chmn. playwriting program 1977, chmn. playwrights project com. 1978-79). Contbr. articles in field to profl. jours. Address: care E Marton 96 Fifth Ave New York NY 10011*

TERRY, NATHAN MAXSON, lawyer; b. Camden, Del., Feb. 15, 1904; s. Charles L. and Elizabeth B. (Maxson) T.; certificate Sch. Bus. Adminstrn., Washington and Lee U., 1926, LL.B., 1927; J.D., 1971; m. Rebecca Dashiell Wolcott, Oct. 3, 1939; children—Nathan Maxson (dec.), Harry Kendall Fooks, Mary Elizabeth. Admitted to Del. bar, 1929; mem. firm Hughes, Terry & Terry, Dover, Del., 1933-39; practiced in Dover, 1939—; atty. levy ct. Kent County, 1936-40, 49-67; chief atty. Del. Pub. Service Commn., 1951-55; mem. Del. Bd. Bar Examiners, 1955-74; atty. for Kent County, Del. Hwy. Dept., 1957-61, chmn. dept., 1961-64. Dir. Farmers Mut. Ins. Co. Del; mem. adv. bd. Wilmington Trust Co. Pres. Del. Bd. Edn., 1951-53; mem. Gov. Del. Goals Com., 1961-65. Del., Democratic Nat. Conv., 1954. Bd. dirs. U. Del., 1964—, Del. Steeplechase and Race Assn. Mem. Am. Law Inst. (ex-officio), Am. Judicature Soc., Del. Bar Assn. (pres. 1961-62), Soc. Colonial Wars, Phi Kappa Sigma, Phi Delta Phi. Episcopalian. Clubs: Wilmington (Del.). Home: 36 The Green Dover DE 19901 Office: 48 The Green Dover DE 19901

TERRY, RICHARD ALLAN, coll. pres.; b. Lincoln, Nebr., June 4, 1920; s. Lester C. and Dorothy (Weeden) T.; A.B., U. Notre Dame, 1944; M.S., Catholic U. Am., 1950, Ph.D., 1954; m. Z. Inci Incikaya, June 3, 1959; 1 son, Deniz. Instr., asst. prof., chmn. psychol. dept. U. Portland (Oreg.), 1953-59; prin. scientist, chief advanced research, life scis. North Am. Aviation, Downey, Calif., 1959-63; asso. prof. indsl. engring., dir. systems research center U. Okla., Norman, 1963-69; prof., head dept. psychology U. Tulsa, 1970-73; prof. psychology State U. N.Y. Coll. at Oswego, 1973-75, dean grad. studies and research, 1973-75, acting v.p. acad. affairs, 1973-74; v.p. for instrn. and curriculum State U. N.Y. Coll. at Brockport, 1975-78; pres. Quinnipiac Coll., Hamden, Conn., 1978—; vis. prof. Hacettepe U., Ankara, Turkey, 1969-70; v.p. Found. for Study of Behavioral Scis., Downey, 1965-68. Mem. Am. Psychol. Assn., AAAS. Democrat. Roman Catholic.

TERRY, ROBERT DAVIS, educator, neuropathologist; b. Hartford, Conn., Jan. 13, 1924; s. Barney and Minnie (Davis) Toretsky; A.B., Williams Coll., 1946; M.D., Albany (N.Y.) Med. Coll., 1950; m. Patricia Ann Blech, June 27, 1952; 1 son, Nicolas Saul. Postdoctoral tng. St. Francis Hosp., Hartford, 1950, Bellevue Hosp., N.Y.C., 1951, Montefiore Hosp., N.Y.C., 1952-53, 54-55, Inst. Recherches sur le Cancer, Paris, Franc, 1953-54, sr. postdoctoral fellow, 1965-66; asst. pathologist Montefiore Hosp., 1955-59; asso. prof. dept. pathology Einstein Coll. Medicine, Bronx, N.Y., 1959-64, prof., 1964—, acting chmn. dept., 1969-70, chmn., 1970—; cons. A study sect. Nat. Insts. Health Pathology, 1964-68, study sects. Nat. Multiple Sclerosis Soc., 1964-68, 72-78; mem. bd. sci. counselors Nat. Inst. Neurol. and Communicative Disorders and Stroke, NIH, 1977—, chmn., 1978-80; mem. nat. sci. council Huntington's Disease Assn.; mem. med. and sci. adv. bd. Alzheimer's Disease Soc., Inc. Served with AUS, 1943-46. Diplomate Am. Bd. Pathology. Mem. Am. Assn. Neuropathologists (pres. 1969-70), N.Y. Path. Soc. (v.p. 1969-71, pres. 1971-73), Am. Soc. Exptl. Pathology. Editorial adv. bd. Jour. Neuropathology and Exptl. Neurology, 1963—, Lab. Investigation, 1967-77, Revue Neurologique, 1977—, Annals of Neurology, 1978—, Ultrastructural Pathology, 1978—. Home: Long Ridge Rd Bedford NY 10506 Office: Einstein Coll Medicine 1300 Morris Park Ave Bronx NY 10461

TERRY, RONALD ANDERSON, bank holding co. exec.; b. Memphis, Dec. 5, 1930; s. John Burnett and Vernon (Lucas) T.; B.S., Memphis State U., 1952; postgrad. So. Meth. U., 1961, Harvard U., 1970; m. Beth Howard, Feb. 1, 1953; children—Natalie Carol, Cynthia Leigh. Mgmt. trainee First Tenn. Bank, Memphis, 1957-71; pres. First Tenn. Nat. Corp., Memphis, 1971-73, chmn., chief exec. officer, 1973—. Past pres., bd. dirs. Boys Clubs Memphis, Arts Appreciation Found.; bd. dirs. Future Memphis; trustee Memphis State U. Found. Served to lt. USN, 1953-57. Mem. Am. Bankers Assn., Assn. Res. City Bankers (dir., vice chmn. govt. relations com.), Assn. Bank Holding Cos. (legis. policy com.), Tenn. Bankers Assn. (dir., chmn. corr. bank com.), Econ. Club of Memphis (past pres.). Office: PO Box 84 Memphis TN 38101

TERRY, THOMAS DUTTON, clergyman, educator; b. Pitts., May 20, 1922; s. Charles Dutton and Catherine (McQuade) T.; student U. Santa Clara, 1941-43; A.B., St. Louis U., 1945, B.S., 1947, Ph.L., 1947, S.T.L., 1953; postgrad. Alma (Calif.) Coll., 1949-51; Ph.D., U. Calif. at Davis, 1959. Joined Soc. Jesus, 1939, ordained priest Roman Cath. Ch., 1952; instr. chemistry, math. Loyola High Sch., Los Angeles, 1947-49; enologist, viticulturist Novitiate Los Gatos (Calif.), 1959-61; dean Coll. Arts and Scis. U. Santa Clara (Calif.), 1961-66, dir. grad. div., 1961-63, dir. summer session, 1962, pres., 1968-76; acad. v.p. Loyola U., Los Angeles, 1966-68; dir. planning Calif. Province, Soc. of Jesus, 1977—; pres. Novitiate Wines, 1978—. Mem. Am. Soc. Enologists, Sigma Xi. Contbr. articles to profl. jours. Address: PO Box 519 Los Gatos CA 95030

TERRY, WALTER, dance critic; b. Bklyn., May 14, 1913; s. Walter Matthews and Frances Lindsay (Gray) T.; A.B., U. N.C., 1935; A.F.D. (hon.), Ricker Coll., 1968. Dance critic Boston Herald, 1936-39; dance critic, editor N.Y. Herald Tribune, 1939-42, 45-66; editor World Jour. Tribune, 1966-67; editor Saturday Rev., 1967-72; with World Magazine, 1972-73, Saturday Rev./World mag., 1973-75, Saturday Rev., 1975—; lectr., condr. radio program on subject of dance, 1940; tchr. dance Adelphi Coll., 1942, Yale, 1975, So. Conn. State Coll., 1974-75; dancer mus. comedy Rose Marie, Royal Opera House, Cairo, 1943; selected dances and dancers for Ford TV Workshop's Excursion, 1953, Frontiers of Faith, 1955, Eye on New York, 1958; several appearances and selection of dances and dancers for Camera 3, CBS-TV, 1953, 54. Served with USAAF, 1942-45. Decorated knight Order of Dannebrog (Denmark); Egyptian-Am. U. fellowship. Mem. Newspaper Guild N.Y. Author: Invitation to Dance, 1942; Star Performance, 1954; (with Paul Himmel) Ballet in Action, 1954; The Dance in America, 1956, rev., 1971; Ballet: A New Guide to the Liveliet Art, 1959; On Pointe, 1962; Isadora Duncan, 1964; The Ballet Companion, 1968; Miss Ruth: The More Living Life of Ruth St. Denis, 1969; Ballet: A Pictorial History, 1970; Careers for the '70's: Dance, 1971; Ballet Guide, 1976; Ted Shawn: Father of American Dance, 1976; I Was There, 1978; Great Male Dancers of the Ballet, 1978; The King's Ballet Master: A Biography of Denmark's August Bournonville, 1979. Contbr. chpt. to Dance: A Basic Educational Technique, 1941; also articles dance publs. Dance editor Ency. Brit. Office: Saturday Review Magazine 1290 Ave of Americas New York NY 10019

TERRY, WALTER ENGLISH, advt. exec.; b. Long Beach, Calif., Aug. 1, 1921; s. Walter and Mary (English) T.; B.S., Northwestern U., 1945; M.B.A., Harvard, 1948; m. Judith Ann Mikesell, Nov. 28, 1959; children—Brian Douglas, Kevin Bradford. Financial analyst Dun & Bradstreet, Los Angeles, 1946-47; asst. prof. marketing, asst. dean Sch. Commerce, U. So. Calif., 1948-51; marketing research, advt. mgr. Fluor Corp., Los Angeles, 1952-57; v.p., gen. mgr. D'Arcy Advt. Co. (now D'Arcy-MacManus & Masius) San Francisco, 1957-68, exec. v.p., head West Coast operations, also dir., 1968-75, pres., 1975—. Asso., Golden Gate U.; mem. adv. com. world bus. div. San Francisco State U. Bd. dirs. Multiple Sclerosis Soc. Served to lt. (j.g.) USNR, 1942-46. Mem. Advt. Assn. West (chmn. bd. 1963-64), Internat. Advt. Assn., San Francisco C. of C., San Francisco Advt. Club (dir. 1961-63), Am. Advt. Fedn. (chmn. bd. 1968-69), Alpha Delta Sigma. Clubs: Bohemian (San Francisco); Meadow Golf (Marin County, Cal.). Home: 60 Fairway Dr San Rafael CA 94901 Office: 433 California St San Francisco CA 94104

TERWILLIGER, HERBERT LEE, lawyer; b. Madison, Wis., June 22, 1914; s. Walter E. and Laura (Stone) T.; Ph.B., U. Wis., 1936, J.D., 1938; m. Catharine O'Connor, Oct. 19, 1940; children—Sara (Mrs. Mancer J. Cyr), Walter Thomas, Martha (Mrs. Craig Coburn), Mary (Mrs. Stuart Campbell). Admitted to Wis. bar, 1938, since practiced in Wausau; asso. firm Genrich & Genrich, 1938-42, 45-46; pres. Terwilliger, Wakeen, Piehler, Conway & Klingberg, S.C., and predecessor, 1946—; spl. agt. FBI, 1943-44. Dir. Citizens State Bank & Trust Co., Wausau. Mem. Gov.'s Commn. on Constl. Revision, 1960-61, 63-65, Gov.'s Com. on Eminent Domain, 1965-66, 68-69. Trustee, Meml. Union, U. Wis. Mem. Am., Marathon County, 7th Circuit Ct. Appeals bar assns., State Bar Wis. (pres. 1959-60, treas. 1953-55, chmn. ins. sect. 1954-55, dir. corp. and bus law sect. 1956-58, 62-65), Am. Coll. Trial Layers, Internat. Assn. Ins. Counsel, Wausau Area C. of C. (pres. 1973), Order of Coif, Phi Kappa Phi, Delta Upsilon. Presbyn. (elder). Elk, Mason (Shriner). Clubs: Wausau, Wausau Country. Bd. editors Wis. Law. Rev., 1936-38. Home: 1 North Hill Rd Wausau WI 54401 Office: Security Bldg 401 4th St Wausau WI 54401

TERZICK, PETER EDWARD, labor union exec.; b. Rossland, B.C., Can., July 12, 1904; s. Edward and Martha (Radovich) T.; came to U.S., 1922, naturalized, 1929; student U. Wash., 1923-25, Ind. U. extension, 1954; m. Hazel Hawkins, July 2, 1935; 1 dau., Jane Ellen. Journalist-editor Union Register, Seattle, 1936-43; editor The Carpenter, ofcl. publ. United Brotherhood Carpenters and Joiners of Am., 1943—, gen. treas. union, 1961—. Adv. com. N. Central region U.S. Forest Service, 1955-60; mem. Marion County (Ind.) Health and Welfare Council, 1955-61; pres. Ind. Assn. Adult Edn., 1957-58. Recipient Freedom Found. award, 1950, Industry Coop. award Forest Products Industry Assn., Eugene V. Debs Journalism award, 1973. Mem. Internat. Labour Press Assn. (pres. 1958-59), Am. Forestry Assn. (regional v.p.), Pi Kappa Phi, Lutheran. Clubs: Nat. Press, Nat. Capitol Democratic (Washington). Author: What is Brotherhood?, 1957; I am a Building Tradesman, 1963. Home: 417 Northwest Dr Silver Spring MD 20901 Office: 101 Constitution Av NW Washington DC 20001. *From the vantage point of three score ten, nothing seems more important in life than giving your honest best-be the objective love, understanding, fame, or financial success. Therefore, I hope my epitaph can be: When Death creeps up some distant day To launch me on the Timeless Tide Let there be some at least to say "Before he died he tried."*

TESARIK, DAVID BREESE, diversified industry exec.; b. Spokane, Wash., July 18, 1922; s. Otto E. and Lillian May (Allison) T.; student Willamette U., 1940-41; B.A., Whitworth Coll., 1947; m. Nancy Teixeira, May 12, 1945; 1 dau., Deborah Ann. With Internat. Gen. Electric Co., Caracas, Venezuela, Bombay, India, Montevideo, Uruguay, N.Y.C., 1947-61, Internat. Tel. & Tel. Co., Rio de Janeiro, Brazil, N.Y.C., 1961-67; v.p., controller Shulton, Inc., N.Y.C. and Clifton, N.J., 1968-73; controller Schering-Plough Corp., Kenilworth, N.J., 1973-75, v.p. internat. div., 1975-76, sr. v.p., 1976—. Served with USNR, 1941-45. Home: 251 Oak Ridge Ave Summit NJ 07901 Office: Galloping Hill Rd Kenilworth NJ 07033

TESAURO, DOMINIC ALOYSIUS, lawyer; b. Washington, Pa., Jan. 25, 1910; s. John B. and Sylvia (Longo) T.; B.A., Washington and Jefferson Coll., 1930; J.D., U. Chgo., 1933; m. Zoe DeFina, June 5, 1946; children—George, Joan Mary (Mrs. Berch Parker), John, Anthony. Admitted to Ill. bar, 1934; practice in Chgo., 1933-35, 75—; atty., sr. title examiner, title officer Chgo. Title & Trust Co., 1935-61; regional adminstr. Region 5, Gen. Services Adminstrn., Chgo., 1961-67; asst. chief title officer Chgo. Title and Trust Co., 1967-73, office counsel, 1974-75. Chmn. fed. employee award com., equal employment opportunity com., fiscal and mgmt. improvement com. Fed. Exec. Bd., Chgo. Chmn. fund raising drives A.R.C., 1961-62, Cook council Boy Scouts Am., 1957-60, Community Chest, 1957-58, Crusade of Mercy, 1962—; chmn. lawyers com. Villa Scalabrini Devel. Fund, 1960-63; mem. staff Ill. Civil Def., 1957-63. Trustee Chgo. chpt. Am. Com. Italian Migration, Columbus-Cuneo-Cabrini Med. Found., Washington and Jane Smith Home; bd. dirs. S.W. Beverly Improvement Assn., 1959-77. Served to lt. col., C.E., AUS, 1941-46. Decorated Bronze Star; Order Brit. Empire; Carpathian medal (Poland); knight Order Merit (Italy). Mem. Justinian Soc. Lawyers (past pres.), Fed., Ill., Chgo. bar assns., Mil. Govt. Assn., Ret. Officers Assn., Assn. U.S. Army, Joint Civic Com. Italian Ams., Beverly Art Center, Field Mus. Natural History, Smithsonian Instn., Art Inst. Chgo., Lyric Opera Chgo. Home: 4 Oak Brook Club Dr Oak Brook IL 60521 Office: 3252 S Halsted St Chicago IL 60608

TESCHNER, RICHARD REWA, lawyer; b. Milw., Feb. 5, 1908; s. Bruno A. and Thekla (Rewa) T.; B.A., U. Wis., 1931, LL.B., 1934; L.H.D. (hon.), Carroll Coll., 1976; m. D. Joy Griesbach, Sept. 24, 1932; 1 son, Richard Vincent. Admitted to Wis. bar, 1934, U.S. Supreme Ct. bar, 1944; tax counsel Wis. Dept. Taxation, 1938-45; partner Quarles & Brady. Dir. Oshkosh B'Gosh, Inc., Young Radiator Co. Mem. Milwaukee County War Meml. Devel. Com., chmn., 1960-70; mem. Greater Milw. Com., Wis. Arts Bd.; bd. dirs. U. Wis. Found.; mem. Milw. Performing Arts Center, chmn., 1969-74; co-chmn. United Performing Arts Fund drive, 1977; sec. Will Ross Meml. Found.; bd. dirs. Milw. Found., chmn., 1978-79; bd. dirs. Carroll Coll. Fellow Am. Coll. Probate Counsel; mem. Am., Wis., Milw. (pres. 1964-65) bar assns., Wis. Lung Assn., Pi Kappa Alpha, Phi Delta Phi. Republican. Presbyterian. Rotarian. Home: 929 N Astor St Milwaukee WI 53202 Office: 780 N Water St Milwaukee WI 53202

TESH, CHARLES PINKNEY, naval officer; b. Winston-Salem, N.C., Mar. 22, 1926; s. Charles Petree and Mattie Rachael (Tucker) T.; B.S., U. Md.; M.S., George Washington U.; m. Mary Louise Schoenfeldt, Nov. 16, 1946; children—Charles Pinkney, Mary Jayne, Robert Michael, Susan Cecelia. Commd. officer U.S. Navy, 1945, advanced through grades to rear adm.; successively comdg. officer, USS Forster, USS Orlect, USS King; head systems and plans policy sect. info. systems div., Office Chief of Naval Ops.; military fellow to Council of Fgn. Relations; dep. dir. security assistance plans, policy and programs; comdr. Cruiser-Destroyer Group 5; now dep. comdr. in chief U.S. Naval Forces Europe, London. Decorated Legion of Merit, Bronze star, others. Mem. U.S. Naval Inst. Home: 25 Orchard Ct Portman Sq London WI England Office: 7 N Audley St London WI England

TESSENEER, RALPH ATHEN, JR., coll. adminstr.; b. Russellville, Ala., Apr. 23, 1924; s. Ralph Athen and Geneva (Kirkland) T.; A.B., Tufts U., 1947; A.M., Geroge Peabody Coll., 1948; Ph.D., La. State U., 1956; m. Laura Mae Fisher, May 5, 1946; children—Susan Wyman, Ralph Athen III, Herbert Hoffman. Asst. prof. psychology Western Ky. U., Bowling Green, Ky., 1948-52; asso. prof. psychology McNeese State U., Lake Charles, La., 1952-59; prof. psychology Murray (Ky.) State U., 1959-70, dean Grad. Sch., 1963-70; v.p. acad. affairs No. Ky. U., Highland Heights, 1970-76, pres. univ. found., 1977—; cons. Ky. Dept. Mental Health, 1960—. Mem. Am., Ky. psychol. assns., Phi Delta Kappa, Kappa Delta Pi, Pi Kappa Alpha. Baptist. Rotarian. Home: 18 Linden Hill Crescent Springs KY 41011

TESSIERI, JOHN EDWARD, petroleum co. exec.; b. Vineland, N.J., Sept. 3, 1920; B.S., Pa. State U., 1942, M.S., 1947; Ph.D., Stanford, 1949. With Texaco, Inc., 1949—, staff coordinator strategic planning group, 1969-70, gen. mgr. strategic planning group, 1970-71, v.p. charge research, environ. and safety dept., 1971—. Home: 27 Lincoln Dr Poughkeepsie NY 12601 Office: Texaco Inc PO Box 509 Beacon NY 12508

TESSMAN, IRWIN, molecular biologist; b. Bklyn., Nov. 24, 1929; s. Morris and Anna T.; A.B., Cornell U., 1950; Ph.D., Yale U. 1954; m. Ethel Stolzenberg, June 19, 1949; 1 son, Adam. Research fellow Cornell U., 1954-57; research asso. M.I.T., 1957-59; asso. prof. biology Purdue U., West Lafayette, Ind., 1959-62, prof., 1962—; vis. prof. Harvard U. Med. Sch., Boston, 1967-68; prof. U. Calif., Irvine, 1970-72. Recipient prize Gravity Research Found., 1953, Research award Sigma Xi, 1966; NSF sr. postdoctoral fellow, 1967. Mem. Am. Soc. Biol. Chemists, Genetics Soc. Am., Phi Beta Kappa. Contbr. numerous articles on molecular genetics and biophysics to profl. jours.; asso. editor Virology, 1959-63, 66-77, editor, 1963-65. Home: 512 Hillcrest Rd West Lafayette IN 47906 Office: Purdue U West Lafayette IN 47907

TEST, CHARLES EDWARD, physician; b. Indpls., Jan. 10, 1916; s. Donald Newby and Marion (Porter) T.; A.B., Princeton, 1937; M.D., U. Chgo., 1941; m. Nora Judith Chambers, 1938 (dec. 1954); children—Deborah, Samuel; m. 2d, Sarah Chase Davol, Feb. 2, 1955; children—Charles, Abigail. Individual practice medicine, Indpls., 1951—; prof. medicine Ind. U. Sch. Medicine. Served with M.C., AUS, 1942-46. Mem. Phi Beta Kappa, Alpha Omega Alpha. Episcopalian. Clubs: Nassau, Acoaxet. Home: 4430 N Meridian St Indianapolis IN 46208 Office: 115 N Pennsylvania St Indianapolis IN 46204

TESTER, JOHN ROBERT, biologist, educator; b. New Ulm, Minn., Nov. 18, 1929; s. Roland Otto and Evelyn Anna (Monson) T.; B.S., U. Minn., 1951, Ph.D., 1960; M.S., Colo. State U., 1953; m. Joyce Jeanette Lund, Sept. 12, 1959; children—Hans, Peter. Research biologist Minn. Dept. Natural Resources, St. Paul, 1954-56; ecologist Minn. Mus. Natural History, Mpls., 1956-61; lectr. to prof., head dept. ecology and behavioral biology U. Minn., St. Paul, 1961—; v.p. State Bank Gibbon (Minn.), 1966—, also dir.; cons. in field. Fellow AAAS, Aberdeen U. (Scotland) (hon.); mem. Ecol. Soc. Am., Am. Inst. Biol. Sci., Wildlife Soc., Am. Soc. Mammalogists, N.Y., Minn. acads. sci., Sigma Xi. Contbr. articles sci. publs. Mem. behavioral scis. tng. com. NIH, 1968-73. Republican. Lutheran. Home: 10 Eagle Ridge Rd St Paul MN 55110

TESTOLIN, RENO JOSEPH, mfg. co. exec.; b. Quarry, Wis., Sept. 19, 1922; s. Nicholas and Mary (Canale) T.; B.S.M.E., U. Wis., 1948; M.B.A., U. Chgo., 1966; m. Beverley Elizabeth O'Connor, Sept. 22, 1943; children—Elizabeth Stanage, April Rinder, Reno Bruce, Audrey, Katy King. With Richardson Co., 1948—, became engr., 1948, plant mgr., 1950, v.p., 1963, dir. operations, 1968, exec. v.p., dir., 1973, pres., 1974—, chief exec. officer, 1975—. Served with USNR, 1942-45. Decorated Navy Cross, D.F.C., Air medal. Mem. Pi Tau Sigma, Beta Gamma Sigma. Republican. Methodist. Club: Chicago Golf. Home: 1150 Oakview Dr Wheaton IL 60187 Office: 2400 E Devon Ave Des Plaines IL 60018

TETLEY, GLEN, choreographer; b. Cleve., Feb. 3, 1926; s. Glenford and Eleanor (Byrne) T.; student Franklin and Marshall Coll., 1944-46; B.Sc., N.Y. U., 1948; student contemporary dance with Hanya Holm, Martha Graham, 1946, classical ballet with Margaret Craske, Anthony Tudor at Met. Opera Ballet Sch., 1949. Featured dancer in Broadway musical Kiss Me Kate, 1949, Out of This World 1950, Juno, 1958; premiered in Menotti's Amahl and the Night Visitors, NBC Opera, 1951; soloist with N.Y.C. Opera, 1951-54, John Butler's Am. Dance Theatre, 1951-55, Robert Joffrey Ballet, 1955-56, Martha Graham Dance Co., 1957-59, Am. Ballet Theatre, 1959-61, Jerome Robbins: Ballets USA, 1961-62, Netherlands Dance Theater, 1962-65; own co., 1962-69 (made govt.-sponsored tour of Europe, 1969); appearances at Spoleto Festival, all maj. Am. dance festivals; guest choreographer Netherlands Dance Theatre, artistic dir., 1969; guest choreographer Am. Ballet Theatre, Ballet Rambert, Batsheva Co. Israel, Robert Joffrey Ballet, Alvin Alley Co., U. Utah Repertory Dance Theatre, Vancouver Festival, Royal Danish Ballet, 1969, Royal Ballet Covent Garden, Royal Swedish Ballet, Den Norske Opera, Hamberg State Opera; guest instr. Yale Dramatic Workshop, 1947-48, Colo. Coll., 1946-49, Hanya Holm Sch. Contemporary Dance, 1946-52, Ballet Rambert, 1966-68, Netherlands Dance Theatre, 1962-65, B. De Rothschild Found., Israel, 1965-67; artistic dir. Stuttgart Ballet Co. Served with USNR, 1944-46. Recipient German critics award for Die Feder, 1969. Ballets include: Pierrot Lunaire, 1962; Birds of Sorrow, 1962; The Anatomy Lesson, 1964; Sargasso, 1964; Field Mass, 1965; Mythical Hunters, 1965; Recercare, 1966; Chronochromie, 1966; Tehilim, 1966; Freefall, 1967; The Seven Deadly Sins, 1967; Dithyramb, 1967; Ziggurat, 1967; Circles, 1968; Embrace Tiger and Return to Mountain, 1968; Arena, 1968; Imaginary Film, 1970; Mutations, 1970; Field Figures, 1971; Rag Dances, 1971; Small Parades, 1972; Threshold, 1972; Laborintus, 1972; Strope-Antistrophe, 1972; The Moveable Garden, 1973; Gemini, 1973; Voluntaries, 1973; Sacre du Printemps, 1974; Tristan, 1974; Strender, 1974; Daphnis and Chloe, 1975; Greening, 1975; Alegrias, 1975; Poeme Nocturne, 1977; off-Broadway choreographer-dir.; Fortuna, 1961; Ballet Ballads, 1961. Address: 4 Goodwin's Ct St Martin's Ln London WCZN 4LL England

TETLOW, EDWIN, author; b. Altrinoham, Eng., May 19, 1905; s. William Chadwick and Mary (Entwhistle) T.; student Manchester (Eng.) U., 1924; m. Kathleen Whitworth Brown, Sept. 14, 1932; children—Susan Edwina (Mrs. Ray F. Bentley), Timothy Chadwick. Student journalist Daily Dispatch, Manchester, 1924-30; mem. staff Eve. News. London, 1930-33; mem. staff Daily Mail, London, 1933-45, naval war corr., 1940-42, army War corr., 1942-45, Berlin corr. Daily Telegraph, 1945-50, N.Y. corr., 1950-65; free-lance author 1965—. Life mem. Fgn. Press Assn. (pres. 1964-65, mem. exec. bd. 1965—). Author: Eye on Cuba, 1966; The United Nations, 1971; The Enigma of Hastings, 1974. Home: Peterskill House Alligerville High Falls NY 12440

TETRICK, ELBERT LAIN, physician, corp. med. dir.; b. Greensburg, Ind., May 16, 1923; s. Paul Rodney and Nora Eleanor (Jones) T.; student DePauw U., 1941-44; A.B., Ind. U., 1945, M.D., 1949; m. Elva Ann Dalenberg, Sept. 23, 1950; children—Susan Lee, Jonathan Lain, Timothy Judd, David Woodward. Intern St. Luke's Hosp., Chgo., 1949-50; resident in internal medicine Indpls. Gen. Hosp., 1950-51, Northwestern U., Chgo., 1951-53; pvt. practice internal medicine, Northbrook, Ill., 1955-61; med. dir. Midwest Steel div. Nat. Steel Corp., Portage, 1961-75, corp. med. dir., 1975—; asso. medicine Northwestern Med. Sch., Porter County Hosp.; electrocardiographer, cons. in field, 1961—. Pres. Portage Twp. Sch. Bd., 1967-71. Served to 1st. lt. M.C., AUS, 1953-55. Fellow Am. Occupational Med. Assn. (pres. Central States chpt. 1973-74); mem. Am. Diabetes Assn. (chmn. com. employment and ops. Greater Chgo.-No. Ill. affiliate 1968—, sec. 1975), Am. Heart Assn., Am. Iron and Steel Inst. (chmn. com. indsl. health 1971-73), A.M.A., Ind. Med. Assn., Porter County Med. Soc., Acad. Occupational Medicine, Phi Gamma Delta, Nu Sigma Nu. Republican. Presbyn. (elder). Contbr. articles to profl. jours. Home: 728 N Old Suman Rd Valparaiso IN 46383 Office: Nat Steel Corp Portage IN 46368

TEUBNER, FERDINAND CARY, JR., pub. co. exec.; b. Phila., Sept. 22, 1921; s. Ferdinand Cary and Esther Roslyn (Test) E.; student U. Pa., 1940-41; grad. Charles Morris Price Sch. Advt. and Journalism, 1949; m. Ruth May Hazen, Nov. 1, 1953; 1 dau., Janell Caron. Rep., W.H. Hoedt Studios, Inc., Phila., 1945-53; account exec. Patterson Prodns., Inc., Phila., 1955-56, v.p., 1956-57; staff exec. Am. Assn. Advt. Agys., N.Y.C., 1957-59; rep. W.H. Martin & Co., Inc., N.Y.C., 1959-62; advt. salesman Editor & Pub. Co., Inc., N.Y.C., 1962-65, advt. mgr., 1965-76, gen. mgr., treas., 1976-78, treas., pub., 1978—, dir., 1969—. Served with USAAF, 1942-45, ETO; served to capt. U.S. Army, 1953-55, Korea. Decorated Purple Heart. Mem. Sales Execs. Club N.Y.C., Res. Officer Assn. Episcopalian. Clubs: Union League, Lake Valhalla Country. Home: 18 Lenape Dr Montville NJ 07045 Office: Editor and Publisher Co Inc 575 Lexington Ave New York NY 10022

TEUSCHER, GEORGE WILLIAM, educator; b. Chgo., Jan. 11, 1908; s. Albert Christian and Elizabeth (Klesch) T.; D.D.S., Northwestern U., 1929, M.S.D., 1936, A.M., 1940, Ph.D., 1942; Sc.D. (hon.), N.Y. U., 1965; m. Eleanor C. Oeler, Sept. 29, 1934 (div.); children—Carol Ann, John William; m. 2d, Eleanor E. Wilson, May, 1968. Engaged in gen. practice of dentistry, 1929-34, in pedodontics, 1934-69; instr. pedodontics Northwestern U., 1933-38, asst. prof., 1938-41, asso. prof., 1941, lectr. surgery Northwestern U. Med. Sch., 1945—, prof. pedodontics, 1946—, dean Dental Sch., 1953-71; mem. staff Wesley Meml. Hosp., 1946-69, chief dental sect. dept. otolaryngology, 1961-69; mem. adv. com. dentistry Smithsonian Instn., 1967—; lectr. on pedodontics and edn. in U.S. and Can.; cons. Naval Dental Research Inst., Gt. Lakes. Bd. dirs. Tb Inst. Chgo. and Cook County, 1964-70; regent Nat. Library Medicine, 1968-72; bd. govs. Chgo. Heart Assn., 1967-74. Pres. Gen. Alumni Assn., Northwestern U., 1948-51. Served with Res. Officers Corps, 1929-42. Charter mem. Am. Acad. Pedodontics (pres. 1960-61), Am. Bd. Pedodontics. Fellow Am. Coll. Dentists, Inst. Medicine Chgo.; mem. Internat. Assn. Dental Research, Am. Assn. Dental Schs. (pres. 1962-63), Am. Dental Assn. (council dental edn. 1964-70), Ill., Chgo. (pres. 1958-59) dental socs., Odontographic Soc. (pres. 1952-53), Am. Soc. Dentistry for Children (pres. 1952-53), Am. Dental Soc. Europe (hon.), Xi Psi Phi, Omicron Kappa Upsilon. Clubs: Tavern, Chicago Literary (Chgo.). Editor: Dental Progress 1959-63, Jour. Dentistry for Children, 1967—, Jour. Dental Edn., 1970-73; contbr. articles to dental jours. Home: 730 Blaney Dr Dixon IL 46311

TEVERBAUGH, HAROLD GARLAND, chem. co. exec.; b. Oklahoma City, July 21, 1920; s. Lon Eugene and Olive (Townsend) T.; B.S. in Chem. Engring., Okla. State U., 1948; m. Betty Lou Neil, July 24, 1942; children—Harold Neil, Jack Lon, Monte Jay. Chem. engr. Pan Am. Oil Co., 1948; chief engr. Sunray DX Oil Co., 1948-53; v.p., dir. Tex. Natural Gas Corp., 1953-61; exec. v.p. Union Tex. Petroleum div. Allied Chem. Corp., Houston, 1961-68, pres., 1968-75, group v.p., Morristown, N.J., 1974-75, sr. v.p., 1975—; pres., dir. Allied Chem. (North Sea) Ltd., Tex. Gas Pipe Line Corp.; dir. Uno-Tex. Petroleum Corp., Unola de Argentina, Ltd., Union Tex. Indonesia Ltd., Union Tex. Far East Corp. Served with USAAF, 1942-45. Registered profl engr., Okla. Mem. Nat. Assn. Profl. Engrs., Am. Petroleum Inst., Nat. Petroleum Refiners Inst., Ind. Petroleum Assn. Am., Mfg. Chemists Assn., Phi Gamma Delta. Presbyn. Home: 12523 Overcup Dr Houston TX 77024 Office: 3000 Richmond Ave Houston TX 77006 also Box 3000R Morristown NJ 07960

TEWELL, JOSEPH ROBERT, JR., elec. engr.; b. Albany, N.Y., May 19, 1934; s. Joseph Robert and Florence Edna (MacKinnon) T.; B.E.E., Rensselaer Poly. Inst., 1955, M.E.E., 1958; m. Barbara Ann Johnson, Nov. 20, 1960; children—Patricia Ann, Donna Lynn, Joseph Robert, III. Research engr. N.Am. Aviation, Inc., Downey, Calif., 1955; asso. research engr. Lockheed Aircraft Corp., Burbank, Calif., 1956; instr. Rensselaer Poly. Inst., 1957-64; sr. research scientist Martin Marietta Corp., Denver, 1964-79, mgr. advanced programs, Michoud, La., 1979—; cons. Redford Corp., Scotia, N.Y., 1961. Served with Army Security Agy., 1957. Recipient NASA Manned Awareness citation, 1970, NASA Skylab Achievement award, 1974, NASA New Tech. award, 1976, Tech. Achievement award Martin Marietta Corp., 1977, NASA cert. of recognition, 1977, also 21 publ. awards, 1965—. Fellow Explorers Club; mem. Smithsonian Instn. (asso.), Sigma Xi, Eta Kappa Nu, Tau Beta Pi, Theta Chi. Contbr. articles to profl. jours. Inventor dual action single drive actuator, spacecraft docking and retrieval mechanism. Home: 619 Legendre Dr Slidell LA 70458 Office: Mail No 3011 PO Box 29304 New Orleans LA 70189

TEXTER, E(LMER) CLINTON, JR., physician; b. Detroit, June 12, 1923; s. Elmer Clinton and Helen (Rotchford) T.; B.A., Mich. State U., 1943; M.D., Wayne State U., 1946; postgrad. U. Detroit, 1946-47, N.Y. U. Postgrad. Med. Sch., 1948-49, Northwestern U., 1959-60, Williams Coll., 1975; m. Jane Starke Curtis, Feb. 19, 1949; children—Phyllis Cardew, Patricia Ann, Catherine Jane. Intern, Providence Hosp., Detroit, 1946-47; Heart Assn. research fellow in medicine Cornell U. Med. Coll., N.Y.C., 1949-50; asst. physician to outpatients N.Y. Hosp., N.Y.C., 1949-50; asst. resident medicine 3d div. N.Y. U., Goldwater Meml. Hosp., N.Y.C., 1950-51; instr. medicine Duke U. Sch. Medicine, Durham, N.C., asst. physician Duke U. Hosp., 1951-53; asso. medicine Northwestern U. Med. Sch., Chgo., 1953-56, asst. prof. medicine, 1956-61, asso. prof., 1961-68, dir. tng. program in gastroenterology, 1954-65; attending physician Northwestern Meml. Hosp., VA Lakeside Hosp., Chgo., 1953-68; asso. med. dir. Profl. Life & Casualty Co., Chgo., 1965-68; mem. adv. bd. Skokie Valley Community Hosp., 1959-68; chmn. dept. clin. physiology, cons. gastroenterology, publs. sects. Scott and White Clinic, Temple Tex., 1968-72; cons. gastroenterology U.S. Naval Hosp., Great Lakes, 1963-68; cons. William Beaumont Army Med. Center, El Paso, Tex., 1968—; surgeon gen. U.S. Army, 1970—; prof. physiology adj. U. Tex. S.W. Med. Sch. Dallas, 1969-72; coordinator allied health programs Temple (Tex.) Jr. Coll., 1969-72; prof. medicine, physiology, biophysics, dir. div. gastroenterology Coll. Medicine, 1972—, asst. dean Coll. Health Related Professions, U. Ark., Little Rock, 1972-73, asso. dean, 1973-75; mem. active staff Univ. Hosp., Little Rock, 1972—, asso. chief staff for edn., 1972-75; chief gastroenterology VA Hosp., Little Rock, 1972-79; cons. St. Vincent Infirmary, Little Rock, 1973—, Doctors Hosp., Little Rock, Jefferson Hosp., Pine Bluff, Ark., 1975—; dir. Ark. Digestive Disease Center, 1975—; cons. Ark. regional med. program Ark. Health Systems Found., 1972—, Council on Drugs, 1958—. Active Ark. Art Center, Ark. Symphony Soc.; bd. dirs. Wayne State Fund, Detroit, 1975—. Served with USNR, 1947-49. Recipient Disting. Service awards Wayne State U., 1969-74; Clarence F.G. Brown fellow Inst. Medicine, Chgo., 1953-56; diplomate Am. Bd. Internal Medicine. Fellow A.C.P.; mem. AMA (com. on med. rating phys. impairment 1960-64), Am. Gastroent. Assn., Am. Fedn. Clin. Research (chmn. gastroenterology 1956, 63), Am. Med. Writers Assn. (pres. 1973-74), Am. Assn. Study Liver Disease, Am. Soc. Gastrointestinal Edoscopy, Am. Physiol. Soc., Am. Soc. Clin. Pharmacology and Therapeutics (dir. 1971-76), Am. Coll. Gastroenterology (gov. So. region A 1978-79), So. Soc. Clin. Investigation, Central Soc. Clin. Research, Sigma Xi, Theta Alpha Phi, Delta Chi, Nu Sigma Nu. Episcopalian (lay reader 1968—, chalicer 1979—). Clubs: Literary (Chgo.); John Evans of Northwestern U.; Country of Va. Author: Peptic Ulcer - Diagnosis and Treatment, 1955, Physiology of the Gastrointestinal Tract, 1968. Contbr. articles to profl. jours. Home: 11519 Tahoe Ln Little Rock AR 72212 Office: U Ark 4301 W Markham St Little Rock AR 72201

THACHER, HENRY CLARKE, JR., educator; b. N.Y.C., Aug. 8, 1918; s. Henry Clarke and Ethel (Anderson) T.; B.A., Yale, 1940, Ph.D., 1949; A.M., Harvard, 1942; m. Ann Babcock Peters, Aug. 29, 1942; children—Mary Babcock (Mrs. Michael J. Kelly), Ann Kelsey (Mrs. Clifford Thacher-Renshaw), Harriet Foster (Mrs. Kenneth G. Holbrook), Alida McKay, Henry Clarke III. Instr. Yale, 1947-48; asst. prof. chemistry Ind. U., 1949-54; task scientist Aero. Research Lab., Wright Patterson AFB, Ohio, 1954-58; asso. chemist Argonne (Ill.) Nat. Lab., 1958-66; prof. computing sci. U. Notre Dame, 1966-71; prof. computer sci. U. Ky., Lexington, 1971—. Mem. com. revision math. tables NRC, 1958-64; cons. in field. Served with AUS, 1942-46. Fellow AAAS; mem. N.Y. Acad. Sci. Author: (with others) Computer Approximations, 1968. Contbr. articles to profl. jours. Home: 1601 Ashwood Rd Lexington KY 40502

THACKRAY, ARNOLD WILFRID, historian, educator; b. Eng., July 30, 1939; s. Wilfrid Cecil and Mary (Clarke) T.; B.Sc., Bristol (Eng.) U., 1960; M.A., Cambridge (Eng.) U., 1965, Ph.D., 1966; m. Barbara Mary Hughes, July 25, 1964; children—Helen Mary, Gillian Winifrid. Came to U.S., 1967. Research chemist Robert Dempster and Co., Yorkshire, Eng., 1960-63; research fellow Churchill Coll., Cambridge U., 1965-68; vis. lectr. Harvard, 1967-68; prof. history and sociology of sci. U. Pa., Phila., 1968—, chmn. dept., 1970-77; editor Isis, An Internat. Rev. of History of Sci. and its Cultural Influences, 1978—. Cons. Nat. Endowment for Humanities, NSF, Josiah Macy Jr. Found., others. Recipient Gladstone Essay prize, also pub. speaking prize Churchill Coll., Cambridge U. Guggenheim fellow, 1971-72; Center for Advanced Study in Behavioral Scis. fellow, 1974; vis. fellow All Souls Coll., Oxford, Eng., 1977-78. Fellow AAAS; mem. Royal Inst. Chemistry, Am. Hist. Assn., AAAS, Manchester Lit. and Philos. Soc. (corr.), History of Sci. Soc. (exec. com.), Soc. for History Tech., Soc. for Social Studies of Sci. (council). Author: Atoms and Powers, 1970; John Dalton, 1972. Editor (with others) Science and Values, 1974, Toward A Metric of Science, 1978; mem. editorial bd. Minerva, History of Sci., Victorian Studies, Humanities in Soc., Jour. Research Communication Studies, Social Studies of Sci. Contbr. articles to profl. jours. Home: 2 Chestnut Ln Wayne PA 19087 Office: History and Sociology of Sci Dept EF Smith Hall D6 U Pa 215 S 34th St Philadelphia PA 19104

THACKRAY, JAMES CARDEN, telecommunications co. exec.; b. Granby, Que., Can., Feb. 25, 1924; s. Carden Cousens and Maud Stewart Barclay (Macpherson) T.; B.Sc., McGill U., Montreal, 1946; m. Marie Theresa Stephenson, Mar. 6, 1948; children—David, James, Anne, Elizabeth. With Bell Can., 1940-42, 45—, v.p., 1965-70, exec. v.p., Montreal, 1970-76, pres., 1976—; dir. Bank of Montreal, Union Carbide Can. Ltd., Le Conseil du Patronat, Kimberly-Clark Co. USA, N. Am. Telegraph Co., No. Telecom Ltd., No. Telecom Inc., USA, No. Telecom Systems Corp. (U.S.A.). Bd. govs. Montreal Gen. Hosp. Found.; bd. dirs. Can. Safety Council; past campaign chmn. Met. Toronto United Way. Served to lt. Canadian Navy, 1942-45. Anglican. Clubs: Forest and Stream, Mt. Royal; Toronto; Rideau (Ottawa). Home: 481 Roslyn Ave Westmount PQ H3Y 2T6 Canada Office: 1050 Beaver Hall Hill Montreal PQ H3C 3G4 Canada

THADDEUS, PATRICK, physicist; b. Wilmington, Del., June 6, 1932; s. Victor and Elizabeth (Ross) T.; B.Sc., U. Del., 1953; M.A., Oxford (Eng.) U., 1955; Ph.D., Columbia, 1960; m. Janice Petherbridge Farrar, Apr. 6, 1963; children—Eva, Michael. Research asso. Columbia Radiation Lab., 1960-61; research asso. Goddard Inst. Space Studies, N.Y.C., 1961-63, mem. sci. staff, 1963—; mem. faculty Columbia U., 1965—, adj. prof. physics, 1971—; vis. com. Nat. Radio Astronomy Obs., 1973-76. Fulbright fellow, 1953-55; recipient Exceptional Sci. Achievement medal NASA, 1970; John C. Lindsay Meml. award Goddard Space Flight Center, 1976. Fellow Am. Phys. Soc.; mem. Am. Astron. Soc., Sigma Xi. Author papers on microwave spectroscopy, optical and radio astronomy. Address: 606 W 116th St New York NY 10027

THADEN, EDWARD CARL, educator; b. Seattle, Apr. 24, 1922; s. Edward Carl and Astrid (Engvik) T.; B.A., U. Wash., 1944; student U. Zurich (Switzerland), 1948; Ph.D., U. Paris, 1950; m. Marianna Theresia Forster, Aug. 7, 1952. Instr. Russian history Pa. State U., 1952-55, asst. prof., 1955-58, asso. prof., 1958-64, prof., 1964-68; vis. asst. prof. Ind. U., 1957; vis. prof. U. Marburg, 1965; prof. U. Ill. at Chgo., 1968—, chmn. dept. history, 1971-73; editorial cons. Can. Rev. Studies in Nationalism, 1973—; vis. research scholar USSR Acad. Scis., 1975; Ford Found. project prin. researcher, 1975—. Served to lt. (j.g.) USNR, 1943-46. Carnegie Inter-Univ. Com. travel grantee to USSR, 1956; Fulbright research grantee, Finland, 1957-58, Germany, 1965, Poland and Finland, 1968; Soc. Sci. Research Council grantee, 1957; Am. Council Learned Socs. grantee 1963, 65-66. Mem. Am. Assn. for Advancement Slavic Studies (pres. Midwest Slavic conf. 1975-77). Author: Conservative Nationalism in Nineteenth-Century Russia, 1964; Russia and the Balkan Alliance of 1912, 1965; Russia Since 1801: The Making of a New Society, 1971. Office: Dept History U Ill Chicago IL 60680

THAGARD, WARREN THOMAS, III, former pipeline co. exec.; b. Greenville, Ala., Aug. 7, 1912; s. Warren Thomas and Berta (Canady) T.; B.S., Rice U., 1934; m. Alice W. Epke, May 26, 1956; 1 dau. by previous marriage, Rebecca (Mrs. David Gelert Hughes). Indsl. gas sales engr. Atlanta Gas Light Co., 1935-38, mgr. Newnan (Ga.) div., 1938-41; v.p. N.C. Gas Corp., 1946; rate cons. Ebasco Services, Inc., N.Y.C., 1946-47; adminstrv. engr. Tex. Eastern Transmission Corp., Shreveport, La. and Houston, 1947-55, dir. plans and econ. research, 1955-58, mgr. coordinating and planning dept., 1958-60, v.p., 1960-71, sr. v.p., 1971-74, exec. v.p., 1974-75, vice chmn. bd. dirs., 1975-78, also dir., ret., 1978. Served to lt. col. AUS, World War II; ETO. Decorated Medaille de La Reconnaissance (France). Registered profl. engr., Ga. Mem. Am., Ind. natural gas assns. Republican. Episcopalian. Clubs: Lakeside Country, Ramada, Houston. Home: 2014 Stonewalk Dr Houston TX 77056 Office: PO Box 2521 Houston TX 77001

THALBERG, IRVING, JR., educator, philosopher; b. Los Angeles, Aug. 24, 1930; s. Irving Grant and Norma (Shearer) T.; B.A., Stanford, 1953, Ph.D., 1960; children by previous marriage—Shoshana, Deborah, Elana. Instr. Oberlin Coll., 1960-63; asst. prof. U. Wash., Wash., 1963-64; prof. philosophy U. Ill. Chgo. Circle, 1965—. Served with AUS, 1953-56. Mem. Am. Civil Liberties Union, N.A.A.C.P. Author: Enigmas of Agency, 1972; Perception, Emotion and Action, 1977. Contbr. philos. essays to profl. jours. and anthologies. Office: U Ill Chgo Circle Box 4348 Chicago IL 60680

THALER, ALAN MAURICE, cons. actuary, former ins. co. exec.; b. Toronto, Ont., Can., Mar. 15, 1917; s. Maurice J. and Diana (Oberlander) T.; B.A., U. Toronto, 1938; m. Roslyn Melnikoff, Aug. 9, 1941; children—Richard, Donald, Maurice. With Prudential Ins. Co. Am., 1938-76, sr. v.p. charge financial security program office, Phoenix; pres., dir. Prudential's Gibraltar Fund, 1968-74; sr. v.p. health ins. activities Prudential Ins. Co., 1974-76; cons. v.p., prin. Phoenix office Milliman & Robertson, Inc., 1976—; pres. Alan M. Thaler & Assos., Inc., 1977—. Fellow Soc. Actuaries; mem. Nat. Assn. Securities Dealers, Investment Co. Inst., Ariz. Acad. Clubs: Phoenix Country; Continental Country (Flagstaff, Ariz.). Home: 8306 N Merion Way Paradise Valley AZ 85253 Office: 6900 E Camelback Rd Scottsdale AZ 85251

THALER, WILLIAM JOHN, physicist; b. Balt., Dec. 4, 1925; s. Thomas Joseph and Catherine Loretta (Russanowski) T.; B.S., Loyola Coll., Balt., 1947; M.S., Cath. U. Am., 1949, Ph.D., 1952; m. Barbara Jane Jarnagin, June 16, 1951; children—Mark, Paul Alice, Gregory, Geoffrey, Peter. Physicist., Baird Assos., Inc., Cambridge, 1947; research asst. Cath. U. Am., 1947-51; physicist acoustics br. Office Naval Research, 1951-52, field projects br. 1952-55, acting head field projects br., 1955, physicist, head field projects br., 1955-62; prof. physics Georgetown U., 1960—; acting dir., chief scientist, office telecommunications policy Exec. Office U.S. Pres., 1976—. Mem. Am. Physics Soc., Acoustical Soc. Am., Optical Soc. Am., Am. Geophys. Union, Sigma Xi. Contbr. articles profl. publs. Office: Dept Physics Georgetown U Washington DC 20007

THALHIMER, WILLIAM B., JR., retail exec.; b. Richmond, Va., June 12, 1914; s. William B. and Annette (Goldsmith) T.; D.C.S. (hon.), U. Richmond, 1973; m. Barbara Jacobs, Dec. 28, 1939; children—Barbara, William B., III, Robert L. With Thalhimer Bros., Inc., Richmond, 1934—, pres., 1950-73, chmn. bd., 1973—, also dir.; dir. Central Nat. Bank, C.&P. Telephone Co., Fidelity Bankers Life Ins. Co., Asso. Merchandising Corp. Past pres. Temple Beth Ahabah, Richmond, Richmond Area Community Chest, Richmond Jewish Community Center; trustee U. Richmond, St. Mary's Hosp., Crippled Children's Hosp. Recipient Distinguished Service award Richmond Jewish Community Council, 1964; Citizenship and Human Relationship award 5th St. Baptist Ch., Richmond, 1966; Brotherhood citation NCCJ, 1971. Mem. Nat. (dir.), Richmond (past pres.; Outstanding Retailer of Year award 1966) retail mchts. assns. Clubs: Bull and Bear, Commonwealth, Jefferson Lakeside. Home: 402 Old Locke Ln Richmond VA 23226 Office: Thalhimer Bros Inc PO Box 26724 Richmond VA 23261

THALKEN, MARGARET MARY, fashion editor; b. Ogallala, Nebr., Nov. 8, 1926; d. William G. and Frances (Flynn) Thalken; B.A., Mt. St. Marys Coll., 1948; m. James H. Kahn, July 3, 1957 (div. July 1966). Divisional advt. mgr. Bullock's Downtown Los Angeles, 1951-54; West Coast editor Glamour mag., Los Angeles, 1954-65, exec. editor, 1965-68; fashion coordinator Grey Advt. Co., N.Y.C., 1968-69; fashion cons. Eastern Airlines, 1968-72; mdse. editor, Vogue mag., N.Y.C., 1972-75, travel mgr., 1975—. Mem. Jrs. Social Service Aux., Fashion Group. Club: Quoque (L.I.) Field. Home: 360 E 55th St New York City NY 10022 Office: 350 Madison Ave New York City NY 10017

THALKEN, THOMAS THEODORE, librarian; b. Kansas City, Mo., Jan. 19, 1919; s. William G. and Jane Frances (Flynn) T.; B.S., Loyola U., Los Angeles, 1949; M.A., Loyola U., Chgo., 1950; postgrad. Georgetown U., 1950-54; M.S. in L.S., E. Tex. State U., 1963; m. Rita Ann Hall, Aug. 13, 1949; children—Stephen, Lawrence, Frances, Margaret, Patricia, Richard, James, Jane, Janet, Regina, Sally, Andrew. Manuscripts specialist Library of Congress, Washington, D.C., 1951-55; archivist Herbert Hoover Archives, Stanford (Calif.) U., 1955-61; asst. prof. history U. Dallas, 1961-63; library dir. Center for Am. Studies, Burlingame, Calif., 1963-64, Buena Park (Calif.) Library Dist., 1964-69; dir. Herbert Hoover Presdl. Library, West Branch, Iowa, 1969—; research cons. to Herbert Hoover, 1955-61; mem. adv. bd. Iowa Hist. Records, Center for the Study of Recent Am. History, U. Iowa. Served with USN, 1938-45. Decorated Purple Heart. Roman Catholic. Editor: Herbert Hoover: The UnCommon Man, 1974. Home: Route 5 Box 47 Iowa City IA 52240 Office: Hoover Library West Branch IA 52358

THARP, TWYLA, dancer, choreographer; b. Portland, Ind., July 1, 1941; student Pomona Coll., Am. Ballet Theatre Sch.; grad. Barnard Coll.; D. Performing Arts (hon.), Calif. Inst. Arts, 1978; student Richard Thomas, Merce Cunningham, Igor Schwezoff, Louis Mattox, Paul Taylor, Margaet Craske, Erick Hawkins; m. Robert Huot (div.); 1 son, Jesse. With Paul Taylor Dance Co., 1963-65; freelance choreographer with own modern dance troupe and various other cos. including Joffrey Ballet and Am. Ballet Theatre, 1965—; teaching residencies various colls. and univs. including U. Mass., Oberlin Coll., Walker Art Center; major works choreographed: Tank Dive, 1965; Re-Moves, 1966; Forevermore, 1967; Generation, 1968; Medley, 1969; Fugue, 1970; Eight Jelly Rolls, 1971; The Raggedy Dances, 1972; As Time Goes By, 1974; Sue's Leg, 1975; Push Comes to Shove, 1976; Once More Frank, 1976; Mud, 1977; Baker's Dozen, 1979; film Hair, 1979; videotape Making Television Dance, 1977. Recipient Creative Arts award Brandeis U., 1972. Office: care Twyla Tharp Dance Found 38 Walker St New York NY 10013

THARPE, FRAZIER EUGENE, journalist; b. Panama City, Fla., Jan. 10, 1941; s. Henry Clayton and Margaret Jane (Jenkins) T.; B.A. in Polit. Sci. and History, Vanderbilt U., Nashville, 1963; m. Barbara Ann Hembree, Oct. 30, 1971. Reporter, Miami (Fla.) News, 1963; reporter U.P.I., Atlanta and Columbia, S.C., 1964; pub. relations exec., Atlanta, 1965-69; financial editor Atlanta Constn., 1969-73, editorial asso., columnist, 1974—. Free-lance writer. Office: 72 Marietta St NW Atlanta GA 30303

THARRINGTON, ROBERT WILLIAM, aerospace co. exec.; b. Girard, Kans., Feb. 28, 1919; s. Robert C. and Anne M. (Hamilton) T.; B.S. in Bus. Adminstrn., Kans. State Coll., 1940; grad. exec. devel. program Cornell U., 1956; m. Shirley L. McFarland, Sept. 28, 1941; 1 son, William S. With Boeing Co., 1941-44, 48—, asst. gen. mgr. aerospace div., 1961-62, v.p. co., 1962—; v.p., gen. mgr. Vertol div., Morton, Pa., 1962-71; v.p., dir. Boeing Can. Ltd., 1962-71; pres., chief exec. officer Boeing Computer Services Co., Morristown, N.J., 1971—. Clubs: Seattle Golf, Rainier Golf and Country (Seattle); Orange Lawn Tennis (South Orange, N.J.). Home: 8 Arlene Ct Short Hills NJ 07078 Office: Boeing Computer Services Co 177 Madison Ave Morristown NJ 07960

THATCHER, CHARLES MANSON, educator; b. Milw., Apr. 4, 1922; s. Oliver Victor and Carrie Mae (Shaw) T.; B.S. in Chem. Engring., U. Mich., 1943, M.S., 1950, Ph.D., 1955; m. Florence Margarete Reilly, Aug. 10, 1946; children—Carol Margaret, Charles Marshall. Adminstrv. asst. to dean students U. Mich., Ann Arbor, 1946-47, instr. chem. engring., 1947-54, asst. prof., 1955-58; tech. service engr. Standard Oil Co. Ind., Whiting, 1954-55; mem. faculty Pratt Inst., N.Y.C., 1958-70, dean engring. and sci., 1963-70; distinguished prof. chem. engring. U. Ark., Fayetteville, 1970—, head dept., 1979-80; cons. chem. engring., 1949—, data processing, 1961—; adviser Arctic Environmental Engring. Lab., 1966-72. Past bd. mem. N.Y. State Edn. Dept. Served to capt., ordnance dept., AUS, 1943-46. Recipient Distinguished Teaching award U. Ark. Alumni Assn., 1977. Mem. Am. Inst. Chem. Engrs., Am. Chem. Soc., Am. Soc. Engring. Edn. (dir. chem. engring. div. 1973-74, Western Electric award excellence teaching 1967), AAAS, Nat. Soc. Profl. Engrs., N.Y. Acad. Scis., AAUP, Sigma Xi, Tau Beta Pi, Phi Kappa Phi, Sigma Chi (nat. exec. com. 1964-79, internat. pres. 1975-77, leadership tng. bd. 1958-75, chmn. 1970-73). Author: Fundamentals of Chemical Engineering, 1962; (with A.J. Capato) Digital Computer Programming: Logic and Language, 1967. Home: 1935 Applebury Dr Fayetteville AR 72701

THATCHER, GEORGE ALFRED, banker; b. Los Angeles, June 9, 1915; s. George Benjamin and Lillian (Blanc) T.; student Santa Monica Jr. Coll., 1933-34; m. Georgia R. Borrmann, Oct. 20, 1939; children—Suzanne, Nancy, Diane, George A., Thomas. Gen. contractor Thatcher Constrn. Co., Los Angeles, 1936-48; pres. Occidental Savs. & Loan Assn., Los Angeles, 1948-52; founder, pres. Occidental Bank, North Hollywood, Calif., 1954-57; regional v.p. Union Bank, Los Angeles, 1957-59, dir., 1957—, pres., 1969-75; pres. Union Bancorp., Los Angeles, 1974-79; pres., chmn. bd. United Fin. Corp., Los Angeles, 1960-64, First Surety Corp., Burbank, Calif., 1960-69; pres. Occidental Properties Inc.; dir. Union Bank, Union Internat. Bank. Past pres. San Fernando Valley council Boy Scouts Am., now mem. at large Los Angeles Area council. Club: Los Angeles. Office: 1901 Ave of Stars Los Angeles CA 90067

THATCHER, JOHN SHERMAN, ins. co. exec.; b. Buffalo, July 31, 1917; s. Romeyn Y. and Gertrude K. T.; A.B., Cornell U., 1940, M.A., U. Md., 1941; m. Doris J. Van Natta, Feb. 15, 1947; children—Carolyn, Stephen. With Equitable Life Assurance Soc., N.Y.C., 1947-57, Am. Life of N.Y., 1957-59; pres., chief exec. officer Colonial Life Ins. Co. of Am., East Orange, N.J., 1959-75, vice chmn. bd., 1975-76; v.p. Equitable Life of Iowa, 1976—; pres. Equitable Am. Life, 1977—, also dir. Home: 1712 Casady Dr Des Moines IA 50315 Office: 604 E Locust St Des Moines IA 50306

THATCHER, RICHARD CASSIN, JR., textile mill exec.; b. Atlanta, Feb. 23, 1916; s. Richard Cassin and Mary (Adamson) T.; B.S., Swarthmore Coll., 1937; m. Martha Carter, Nov. 23, 1940; children—Richard C. III, William C., Albert G. With Standard-Coosa-Thatcher Co., Chattanooga, 1937—, thread salesman, Chgo., 1941, thread sales mgr., Cattanooga, 1946-56, v.p., 1956-62, pres., 1962—. Bd. dirs. ARC, Chattanooga; trustee McCallie Sch., Chattanooga; mem. bd. visitors Berry Coll., Mt. Berry, Ga. Served to lt. USN, 1942-46; PTO. Mem. Am. Textile Mfrs. Inst. (dir.), Nat. Cotton Council (dir.), Am. Yarn Spinners Assn. (past pres.), Thread Inst. Am. (past pres.). Presbyterian. Clubs: Rotary (pres. 1972), Mountain City, Lookout Mountain Golf, Lookout Mountain Fairyland. Home: 7 Bartram Rd Lookout Mountain TN 37350 Office: PO Box 791 Chattanooga TN 37401

THAXTON, CARLTON JAMES, librarian; b. Tucson, May 23, 1935; s. Carl Newton and Daisy (Conard) T.; A.B., U. Ga., 1957; M.S., Fla. State U., 1958; m. Donna Jean Bradley, Aug. 25, 1957; children—James Bradley, Carl Stanton. Dir., Coastal Plain Regional Library, Tifton, Ga., 1958-60, 61-68, Kingsport (Tenn.) Pub. Library, 1960-61; dir. div. pub. library services Ga. Dept. Edn., Atlanta,

1968—; instr. library sci. U. Ga., Albany, 1960—, Tifton, 1960—. Mem. Am.. Ga., Southeastern library assns. Democrat. Methodist. Home: 3207 Oxbridge Way Lithonia GA 30058 Office: 156 Trinity Ave SW Atlanta GA 30303

THAXTON, MARVIN DELL, lawyer; b. Electra, Tex., June 1, 1925; s. Montgomery Dell and Ida (Scheurer) T.; J.D., U. Ark., 1949; m. Carolyn Moore Alexander, Aug. 30, 1949; children—Rebecca Annette, Martha Gail, Marvin Dell. Engaged in furniture bus., 1949; admitted to Ark. bar, 1949; practiced in Newport, Ark., 1950—; mem. firm Thaxton & Hout, 1950—; spl. asso. justice Ark. Supreme Ct., 1978; mem. Ark. Gov.'s Study Commn. on Uniform Probate Code, 1977-78; mem. Bd. Ark. Law Examiners, 1968-73, chmn., 1972-73. Pres., Newport Young Businessmen's Club, 1951, Eastern Ark. Young Men's Club, 1954, Bd. Edn. Newport Spl. Sch. Dist., 1962-64. Served with U.S. Mcht. Marine, 1945-46. Mem. Am., Ark. (chmn. real estate law com. 1972-75, chmn. probate law com. 1976-77), Jackson County (past pres.) bar assns., Newport C. of C. (pres. 1957), Sigma Chi. Methodist (past chmn. ofcl. bd., trustee and lay leader). Rotarian (past pres. Newport). Home: 12 Lakeside Ln Newport AR 72112 Office: 600 3d St Newport AR 72112

THAYER, EDWIN CABOT, musician; b. Weymouth, Mass., May 16, 1935; s. Elliot Pierce and Barbara (Senior) T.; B.Mus. cum laude, U. Ill., 1957, M.Mus. with performing honors, 1958; m. Joan Peregoy, June 24, 1961; children—Bruce, Laura, Richard William. Instr. horn Brevard (N.C.) Music Center, summers 1957-58, 62; grad. asst. U. Ill., 1957-58; prin. horn Washington Brass Choir, 1958-61, Norfolk (Va.) Symphony, 1961-65, Richmond (Va.) Symphony, 1960-72; asst. prof. music Va. Commonwealth U. (formerly Richmond Profl. Inst.), Richmond, 1963-72. head piano dept., 1965-69, head brass and winds dept.. 1969-72, music librarian, 1965-72; prin. horn Washington Nat. Symphony, 1972—; hornist Nat. Symphony Wind Soloists, 1978—, Tanglewood (Mass.) Berkshire Music Festival Orch., summers 1955-56; solo recitalist, chamber ensemble recitalist, horn soloist; guest artist Internat. Horn Workshop, Hartford, 1977. Served with AUS, 1958-61. Mem. Internat. Horn Soc., Musicians Union, Pi Kappa Lambda, Phi Mu Alpha Sinfonia. Home: 11902 Triple Crown Rd Reston VA 22091 Office: Nat Symphony Orch Kennedy Center Performing Arts Washington DC 20566

THAYER, H. STANDISH, educator; b. N.Y.C., May 6, 1923; s. Vivian Trow and Florence (Adams) T.; A.B., Bard Coll., 1945; M.A., Columbia, 1947, Ph.D., 1949; m. Elisabeth B. Hewitt, Feb. 28, 1958; children—Hewitt Standish, Alexandrea Adams, Jonathan Trow. Instr. philosophy Bard Coll., 1947; asst. prof. Columbia, 1949-61; prof. philosophy City Coll., City U. N.Y., 1961—. Vis. prof. N.Y. Sch. Psychiatry, 1959-67; mem. Inst. Advanced Study, Princeton, N.J., 1974-75. W.T. Bush fellow philosophy Columbia, 1947-48; Guggenheim fellow, 1970 Nat. Endowment for Humanities fellow, 1974-75. Mem. Am. Philos. Assn., Assn. Symbolic Logic, Mind. Assn. Author: The Logic of Pragmatism, 1952; Newton's Philosophy of Nature, 1953; Meaning and Action, 1968, rev., 1973; Pragmatism; The Classic Writings, 1970. Home: Oak Tree Rd Palisades NY 10964 Office: Dept Philosophy City Coll City U NY Convent Ave and 138th St New York City NY 10031

THAYER, HAROLD EUGENE, pharm. and chem. co. exec.,; b. Rochester, N.Y., Mar. 3, 1912; s. Herbert Aldrich and Helen (Hazels) T.; B.S., Mass. Inst. Tech., 1934; D.Sc. (hon.), St. Louis Coll. Pharmacy, 1963; m. Elinor Constantinides, May 14, 1939 (dec.); 1 son, Lawrence Aldrich; m. 2d, Bess Agnew, Jan. 24, 1974. Engr. tech. sales Calco div. Am. Cynamid Co., 1934-39; sales research and devel. Mallinckrodt, Inc., St. Louis, 1939-41, coordinator WPB, 1941-43, project mgr. Mallinckrodt-operated Manhattan Dist.-AEC plants, 1943-52, v.p., 1950-59, dir. devel., 1952-55, project mgr. Mallinckrodt-operated AEC plant, 1955-58, exec. v.p., 1959-60, pres. 1960-71, 76, chmn. bd., chief exec. officer, 1965—, also dir.; dir. Seven-Up Co., Alvey Inc., Am. Air Filter Co., Inc., Automobile Club Mo., Carboline Co., First Nat. Bank St. Louis, First Union Inc., S.W. Bell Telephone Co., Gen. Am. Life Ins. Co., Laclede Gas Co., M.P. R.R., St. Louis Union Trust. Met. area vice chmn. Nat. Alliance Businessmen, 1968-70; tech. adviser State Dept. for 2d Internat Conf. Peaceful Uses Atomic Energy, 1958; mem. corp. Mass. Inst. Tech., 1969-74, chmn. vis. com. dept. nutrition and food sci., 1973-74; mem. pres.'s council St. Louis U., 1970—; mem. med. scis. vis. com. Harvard, 1973—. Pres. Backstoppers, 1968-69; bd. dirs. St. Louis area council Boy Scouts Am., 1961—, v.p., 1965-69, 73—, pres., 1970-72; bd. dirs. United Way Greater St. Louis, 1961—, campaign chmn., 1967-68, pres., 1969-70, mem. exec. com., 1963—; bd. dirs. St. Louis area Girl Scouts U.S.A., 1962—, v.p., 1965; bd. dirs. Jr. Achievement of Miss. Valley, 1958—, v.p., 1965—; bd. dirs. Civic Progress, Inc., 1966—, v.p., 1972-73, pres., 1975-77, chmn. bd., 1977—; bd. dirs. Washington U., 1967—, mem. exec. com., 1968-72; bd. dirs. David Ranken, Jr. Tech. Inst., 1970—, v.p. bd., 1972—; bd. dirs. St. Louis Arts and Edn. Council, 1972—, campaign chmn., 1972; bd. dirs. Barnes Hosp., 1973—, Washington U. Med. Center Bd., 1973—; trustee St. Luke's Hosp., 1966-72, Nat. Jewish Hosp. and Research Center, Denver, 1972-75. Recipient Silver Beaver award Boy Scouts Am., 1969, Silver Antelope award, 1974; Distinguished Exec. of Year award Sales and Mktg. Execs. of Met.. St. Louis, 1970; St. Louis award Nat. Jewish Hosp. and Research Center, 1971; St. Louis award Nat. Conf. Christians and Jews, 1971; Right Arm St. Louis award, 1974 St. Louis Regional Commerce and Growth Assn., 1974; Lamplighter award St. Louis chpt. Pub. Relations Soc. Am., 1974; Honor award for distinguished service in engring. U. Missouri, 1974; Chem. Industry medal Am. sect. Soc. Chem. Industry, 1976; named Man of Yr. St. Louis Globe-Democrat, 1972; elected Missouri Squires, 1975. Mem. Mfg. Chemist's Assn. (dir. 1963-66, 68-71, 72-75, v.p. 1970-71, chmn. exec. com., 1972-73, vice chmn. bd. 1973-74), N.A.M. (regional dir. 1966, dir. at large 1967-70), St. Louis Regional Commerce and Growth Assn. (dir. 1972—, exec. com. 1972—, pres. 1972-74), U.S. (pub. affairs com. 1974—), St. Louis (dir. 1962-70, exec. com. 1965-67, 69-70), Mo. State (dir. 1968-74) chambers of commerce, Am. Chem. Soc., Am. Inst. Chem. Engrs., Alpha Chi Sigma. Clubs: Bogey, Mo. Athletic, Noonday, Old Warson, Racquet, St. Louis, Media, Washington U. (St. Louis); Wings (St. Albans, Mo.); Metropolitan (Washington); University, Metropolitan (N.Y.C.); Ocean, Country of Fla. (Delray Beach); Highland Country (Highland, N.C.). Home: 48 Portland Dr Saint Louis MO 63131 Office: 675 Brown Rd PO Box 5840 Saint Louis MO 63134

THAYER, HARVEL HILL, camera co. exec.; b. Providence, July 29, 1927; s. Robert F. and Katherine (Harvey) T.; A.B., Harvard U., 1950; m. Pollie Straw, Mar. 23, 1957; children—Jennifer, Harvey, David, Tracy. Asst. plant mgr., asst. to v.p. mfg. Ludlow Mfg. & Sales Co., Needham, Mass., 1950-56; v.p., treas. Polaroid Corp., Cambridge, Mass., 1956—; dir. Newton Waltham Bank & Trust Co. Bd. dirs. Cambridge YMCA. Served with USNR, 1945-46. Mem. Fin. Execs. Inst., AIM (taxation com.), Treasurers Club, Friends of Harvard Track (exec. com. 1959-71). Clubs: Harvard Varsity (Cambridge); Dedham Country; Sakonnet Golf (Little Compton, R.I.). Office: 549 Technology Sq Cambridge MA 02139

THAYER, JACK GLOVER, broadcasting exec.; b. Chgo., Nov. 22, 1922; s. Harley George and Martha Louise (Pasque) T.; ed. Neb. State Coll.; divorced; children—Tracie Nan, Todd Neal, Timm Nelson. Announcer radio sta. KOBH, Rapid City, N.D., 1942-43; announcer, music librarian, traffic mgr. radio sta. WLOL, Mpls.-St. Paul, 1943-52; radio personality, TV producer, sales promotion work sta. WTCN, Mpls.-St. Paul, 1952-55; personality sta. WDGY, Mpls.-St. Paul, 1955-57, gen. mgr., 1957-59; v.p., gen. mgr. radio sta. KFRC, San Francisco, 1957-59, radio sta. WHK, Cleve., 1959-65, radio sta. KLAC, Los Angeles, 1965-70, radio sta. KXOA, Sacramento, 1970, radio sta. WGAR, Cleve., 1970-73; exec. v.p. Nationwide Communications Co., Columbus, Ohio, 1972-74; with NBC, N.Y.C., 1974—; pres. NBC Radio, from 1974, now exec. v.p. spl. projects. Office: NBC 30 Rockefeller Plaza New York NY 10020*

THAYER, JAMES NORRIS, mfg. co. exec.; b. Janesville, Wis., July 9, 1926; s. James Norris and Hazel (VanWormer) T.; B.S., U. Calif. at Los Angeles, 1948; m. Sylvia Lucille Kittell, June 26, 1948; children—Scott Norris, Diane Marie, Bradley Raymond. With Prudential Ins. Co. Am., 1948-55; with William R. Staats & Co., 1955-65, partner, 1960-65; sr. v.p. Glore Forgan-Wm. R. Staats Inc., 1965-67; treas. Lear Siegler, Inc., 1967—, v.p., 1969—, sec., 1972—, sr. v.p. fin., 1977—; dir. Gibraltar Fin. Corp., 1976—. Bd. dirs., treas. Hathaway Home Children, Highland Park, Calif., 1956-62. Served with USAAF, 1944-47. Mem. Delta Sigma Phi, Beta Gamma Sigma. Clubs: Bel Air Country, Jonathan (Los Angeles). Home: 305 S Camden Dr Beverly Hills CA 90212 Office: 3171 S Bundy Dr Santa Monica CA 90406

THAYER, LEE, educator, author; b. Grenola, Kans., Dec. 18, 1927; s. Garrett Osborne and Ruth (Ray) T.; B.A. cum laude, U. Wichita, 1953, M.A., 1956; Ph.D., U. Okla., 1963; m. Nancy Lee Wright, Aug. 14, 1964 (d. Feb. 1980); children—Cassandra Lee, Stephanie Lynn, Joshua Lee, Jessica Sam. Instr., U. Okla., 1956-58; with Pratt & Whitney Co., Inc., 1958-59; asso. prof. adminstrn. and psychology U. Wichita, 1959-64; prof., dir. Center Advanced Study Communication, U. Mo. at Kansas City, 1964-68; George H. Gallup prof. communication research U. Iowa, Iowa City, 1968-73; prof. communication studies Simon Fraser U., Burnaby, B.C., Can., 1973-76; vis. prof. U. Mass., 1976—; Fulbright prof. U. Helsinki (Finland), 1977; Disting. vis. prof. U. Houston, 1978; prof. communication U. Wis.-Parkside, Racine, 1978—; cons. to govt. and industry, 1956—. Served to lt. USNR, 1953-55. Danforth Found. tchr., 1961-63; Found. Econ. Edn. fellow 1963-64. Mem. Nat. Soc. Study Communication (pres. 1968). Author: Administrative Communication, 1961; Communication and Communication Systems, 1968. Editor: Communication: Theory and Research, 1967; Communication: Concepts and Perspectives, 1967; Communication: General Semantics Perspectives, 1969; Communication: Ethical and Moral Issues, 1974; Ethics, Morality, and the Media, 1980; Communication. Home: 1600 S Main St Racine WI 53403

THAYER, PAUL, diversified co. exec.; b. Henryetta, Okla., Nov. 23, 1919; s. Paul Ernest and Opal Marie (Ashenhurst) T.; student U. Wichita, 1937-38, U. Kans., 1939-41; m. Margery Schwartz, Feb. 14, 1947; 1 dau., Brynn. Pilot, Trans World Airlines, 1945-47; chief exptl. test pilot Chance Vought Corp., 1948-50, sales mgr., 1951, sales and service mgr., 1952-54, v.p. sales and service, 1954-58, v.p. Washington operations, 1958-59, v.p., gen. mgr. Vought Aeros. div., 1959-63, pres., 1963; chief flight test Northrop Aircraft Co., 1950-51; sr. v.p. Ling-Temco-Vought, Inc. (name now LTV Corp.), Dallas, 1963, exec. v.p., 1964, chmn. bd., chief exec. officer, 1970—; chmn. bd., chief exec. officer LTV Aerospace Corp., Dallas, 1965-70. Served from ensign to lt. comdr. USNR, 1941-45. Decorated D.F.C., Air medal with nine oak leaf clusters. Recipient Distinguished Service award sec. navy, 1962. Mem. Soc. Exptl. Test Pilots, Phi Gamma Delta. Home: 10200 Hollow Way Dallas TX 75229 Office: PO Box 225003 Dallas TX 75265

THAYER, ROBERT HELYER, diplomat: b. Southboro, Mass., Sept. 22, 1901; s. William Greenough and Violet (Otis) T.; student Amherst Coll., 1918-19; A.B., Harvard, 1922, LL.B., 1926; m. Virginia Pratt, Dec. 30, 1926; children—Robert Helyer, Sally Sears, Stephen Badger. Admitted to N.Y. bar, 1926; with Cadwalader, Wickersham & Taft, 1926-29, 47-49; asso. counsel pub. service law investigation N.Y. State, 1929; asso. counsel fed. bankruptcy laws investigation So. Dist. N.Y., 1929; with Donovan, Leisure, Newton & Lumbard, 1929-32, mem. firm. 1932-37; asst. dist. atty. N.Y. County, 1937-41, chief indictment br., 1938-41; asst. N.Y. State commr. housing, 1946; commr. against discrimination N.Y. State, 1949-51; asst. U.S. ambassador to France, 1951-54; officer charge Western European affairs Ops. Coordination Bd., 1954-55; U.S. minister to Rumania, 1955-58; asst. sec. of state Dept. of State, 1958-61; asso. dir. gen. Am. Field Service Internat. Scholarships, 1961-65, dir. govt. relations, 1965-71; cons. to sec. of state, 1961—. Asst. to John Foster Dulles, UN Charter Conf., San Francisco, 1945. Candidate for Congress from Bklyn., 1946. Bd. dirs. N.Y. Philharmonic Soc., 1935-55; bd. mgrs. N.Y.C. Mission Soc., 1939-55; bd. dirs. Fgn. student Service Council, 1964-78, Washington Performing Arts Soc., 1967-72, Kennedy Center Prodns. Inc., Alliance Française, AFS Internat. Scholarships, 1967-78; trustee St. Mark's Sch., 1940-78, Nat. Trust Hist. Preservation, 1966-77; life trustee AFS Internat./Intercultural Programs. Served from lt. comdr. to comdr., USNR, 1941-45. Decorated French Legion of Honor. Mem. N.Y. Bar Assn., Audubon Soc., Fgn. Policy Assn., Washington Inst. Fgn. Affairs, Council on Fgn. Relations, English Speaking Union. Clubs: Somerset (Boston); Racquet and Tennis, Coffee House, Harvard (N.Y.C.); Porcellian (Cambridge, Mass.); Met. (Washington); Travellers (Paris). Home: 3010 O St NW Washington DC 20007 Office: 1616 H St NW Washington DC 20006

THAYER, RUSSELL, III, airlines exec.; b. Phila., Dec. 5, 1922; s. Russell and Shelby Wentworth (Johnson) T.; student St. George's Sch., 1937-42; A.B., Princeton, 1949; m. Elizabeth Wright Mifflin, June 12, 1947; children—Elizabeth, Dixon, Shelby, Samuel, David. Mgmt. trainee Eastern Air Lines, 1949-52; mgr. cargo sales and service Am. Airlines, Los Angeles, 1952-63; v.p. marketing Seaboard World Airlines, N.Y.C., 1963-70; sr. v.p. Braniff Airways, Inc., Dallas, 1970-72, exec. v.p., 1972-77, pres., chief operating officer, 1977—, dir., 1971—; dir. Ft. Worth Nat. Bank. Mem. Trinity Ch. Ushers Guild, Princeton, N.J., 1968—. Served with USAAF, 1942-45; ETO. Decorated D.F.C., Air medal with 11 oak leaf clusters. Mem. Am. Aviation Hist. Soc., Air Force Assn., Delta Psi. Clubs: Ivy, Pretty Brook Tennis (Princeton); Princeton (N.Y.C.); Philadelphia. Home: 21 Lilac Ln Princeton NJ 08540 Office: Braniff Airways Inc Exchange Park Dallas TX 75235

THAYER, WALTER NELSON, lawyer, investment and communications co. exec.; b. Dannemora, N.Y., Apr. 24, 1910; s. Walter Nelson and Adelaide (McDonell) T.; A.B., Colgate U., 1931; LL.B., Yale, 1935; m. Jeanne Cooley Greeley, Dec. 27, 1945; children—Ann, Susan, Gail, Thomas. Admitted to N.Y. bar, 1935; spl. asst. atty. gen. N.Y. State, 1935-36; with firm Donovan, Leisure, Newton & Lumbard, N.Y.C., 1936-37, 38-40; asst. U.S. atty. So. Dist. N.Y., 1937-38; atty. Lend-Lease Adminstrn., 1941-42; mem. Harriman Mission, London, Eng., 1942-45; gen. counsel Fgn. Econ. Adminstrn., 1945; partner Thayer & Gilbert, N.Y.C., 1946-55, J. H. Whitney & Co., 1955-59; pres. Whitney Communications Corp., 1960—, pres. N.Y. Herald Tribune, 1961-66; partner Whitcom Investment Co., 1967—; pres., dir. Internat. Herald Tribune, 1973—; dir. Dun & Bradstreet Cos., Inc., Kraft, Inc., Bankers Trust Co. Mem. President's Commn. on Campaign Costs, 1961-62, President's Adv. Council Exec. Orgn., 1969-71; spl. cons. to Pres. Nixon, 1969-71. Chmn., trustee Vocat. Found., Inc.; trustee Columbia, 1965-69, Mus. Modern Art. Mem. Com. Econ. Devel. (trustee). Episcopalian. Clubs: Links (N.Y.C.); Augusta (Ga.) Nat. Golf; Racquet and Tennis; Lyford Cay (Nassau, Bahamas). Home: 450 E 52d St New York NY 10022 Office: Time and Life Bldg Rockefeller Center New York NY 10020

THEALL, DONALD FRANCIS, educator; b. Mt. Vernon, N.Y., Oct. 13, 1928; s. Harold A. and Helen (Donaldson) T.; B.A., Yale, 1950; M.A., U. Toronto, 1951, Ph.D., 1954; m. Joan Ada Benedict, June 14, 1950; children—Thomas, Margaret, John, Harold, Lawrence, Michael. From lectr. to prof. U. Toronto, 1950-65, chmn. joint depts. English, 1964-65; prof., chmn. dept. English, dir. communications York U., Toronto, 1965-66; prof., chmn. dept. English, McGill U., 1966-74, Molson prof. English, 1972—, dir. grad. programme in communications, 1976-79; pres., vice chancellor Trent U., Peterborough, Ont., Can., 1980—; cons. in field. Can.-People's Republic China Cultural Exchange prof., 1974-75; Can. Council sr. leave fellow, 1975. Mem. Can. Communications Assn. (pres. 1979—), Can. Assn. U. Tchrs., Can. Assn. Chmn. English (chmn. 1971-74), Cinemateque Canadienne, Arts Can., Modern Lang. Assn., Linguistic Soc. Am., Internat. Communications Assn. (mem. bd. 1978—), Ont. Council Tchrs. (past dir.), Internat. Inst. Communications (dir. 1978-81), Philol. Soc.; corr. fellow Acad. Medicine Toronto. Author: Let's Speak English, 4 vols., 21 translations (ednl. TV hon. mention Ohio State U. 1962), 1960-62; Report on the Creation of a Visual Arts Information Service for Canada, 1968; The Medium Is the Rear View Mirror: Understanding Marshall McLuhan, 1970. Editor: Studies in Canadian Communications, 1975. Editorial bd. Sci. Fiction Studies, 1976—, Jour. Can. Communications, 1979—, Culture and Context, 1979—. Home: 1604 Champlain Dr Peterborough ON K9L 1N6 Canada Office: Office of Pres Trent U Peterborough ON Canada

THEBERGE, JAMES DANIEL, U.S. ambassador; b. Oceanside, N.Y., Dec. 28, 1930; s. Lionel J. and Antoinette Marie Theberge; B.A., Columbia U., 1952; B.A. with honors, Oxford (Eng.) U., 1956, M.A., 1960; M.P.A. (Littauer fellow), Harvard U., 1965; postgrad. (Fed. German Republic fellow), Heidelberg (Ger.) U., 1957-59; m. Giselle Fages, Mar. 4, 1964; children—James Christopher, John Paul, Alexander Leonard. Econ. adv. Am. embassy, Argentina, 1961-64; spl. adv. U.S. sec. Treasury, 1966; adv., sr. economist Inter-Am. Devel. Bank, Washington, 1966-69; research asso. St. Antony's Coll., Oxford U., 1969-70, joint tutor St. Peter's Coll., 1960, vis. lectr., 1968; dir. Latin Am. and Hispanic studies Center Strategic and Internat. Studies, Georgetown U., 1970-75; dir. Latin Am. project Rockefeller Commn. on Critical Choices for Ams., 1974-75; ambassador to Nicaragua, 1975-77; vis. prof. econs. Catholic U., Buenos Aires, U. Ceara (Brazil), U. Calif., Los Angeles; cons. internat. orgns. Bd. dirs. St. Peter's Coll. Found.; mem. bd. fgn. scholarships Fulbright-Hays Act. Served to 1st lt. USMCR, 1952-54. Mem. Inst. Strategic Studies, Caribbean Studies Assn., New Coll. Soc., English Speaking Union. Clubs: Cosmos, Metropolitan, Kenwood Golf and Country (Washington); Harvard (N.Y.C.); Najapa Country (Managua, Nicaragua). Author, editor: Economics of Trade and Development, 1968; The Western Mediterranean, 1972; Soviet Sea Power in The Caribbean, 1972; Russia in The Caribbean, 1973; Soviet Presence in Latin America, 1975; Latin America in The World System, 1975; Spain in the Seventies, 1976; Latin America: Struggle for Progress, 1977; also numerous articles. Home: 4426 Cathedral Ave Washington DC 20016 Office: Suite 201 1627 K St NW Washington DC 20006

THEDENS, EDGAR OTTO, drug and chem. co. exec.; b. Michigan City, Ind., June 6, 1924; s. Eugene Otto and Elizabeth Edgar (Patton) T.; A.B. magna cum laude, Harvard, 1949, LL.B., 1955. With CIA, 1949-52; admitted to N.Y. State bar, 1956, Calif. bar, 1960; asso. firm Davies, Hardy & Schenck, N.Y.C., 1955-59; with Dart Industries Inc., 1959—, sec. 1967—. Served to 1st lt. USAAF, 1942-45. Decorated D.F.C., Air medal with clusters, cross Order St. Stanislas (Poland). Mem. Am., N.Y., Calif. bar assns. Home: 123 Groverton Pl Los Angeles CA 90024 Office: 8480 Beverly Blvd Los Angeles CA 90048

THEIL, HENRI, economist, educator; b. Amsterdam, Netherlands, Oct. 31, 1924; s. Hendrik and Hermina (Siegmann) T.; Ph.D. in Econs., U. Amsterdam, 1951; LL.D. (hon.), U. Chgo., 1964; D. honoris causa, Free U. Brussels, 1974; m. Eleonore A.I. Goldschmidt, June 15, 1951. Mem. staff Central Planning Bur., The Hague, 1952-55; prof. econometrics Netherlands Sch. Econs., Rotterdam, 1953-66; vis. prof. econs. U. Chgo., 1955-56, 64, Harvard, 1960, U. So. Calif., 1979; dir. Econometric Inst., Netherlands Sch. Econs., 1956-66; prof. U. Chgo., 1965—, dir. Center Math. Studies in Bus. and Econs., 1965—. Fellow Am. Acad. Arts and Scis., Am. Statis. Assn.; mem. Internat. Statis. Inst., Am. Econ. Assn., Ops. Research Soc. Am., Econometric Soc. (pres. 1961), Inst. Mgmt. Scis. (council 1961-64). Author: Linear Aggregation of Economic Relations, 1954; Economic Forecasts and Policy, 2d edit., 1961; Optimal Decision Rules for Government and Industry, 1964; Operations Research and Quantitative Economics, 1965; Applied Economic Forecasting, 1966; Economics and Information Theory, 1967; Principles of Econometrics, 1971; Statistical Decomposition Analysis with Applications in the Social and Administrative Sciences, 1972; Theory and Measurement of Consumer Demand, Vol. 1, 1975, Vol. 2, 1976; Introduction to Econometrics, 1978; The System-Wide Approach to Microeconomics, 1979. Editor: Studies in Mathematical and Managerial Economics, 1964—. Home: 1345 East Park Pl Chicago IL 60637

THEIS, FRANCIS WILLIAM, business exec.; b. Joliet, Ill., July 10, 1920; s. Frank G. and Hilda F. (Lloyd) T.; student Joliet Jr. Coll., 1937-39; B.S., Purdue U., 1941; m. Helen Jean Wickizer, Oct. 12, 1941; children—Margaret D., Steven W., Philip C., Elizabeth, Catherine. Dir. devel. PPG Industries, Barberton, Ohio, 1951-56, mgr. planning chem. div., Pitts., 1956-60, pres., chief exec. officer PPG Internat., Pitts., 1960-63, v.p. internat., Pitts., 1963-65; pres., chief exec. officer Devoe & Raynaolds Co., Louisville, 1965-67; pres. Celanese Chem. Co., N.Y.C., 1967-71; group v.p. Celanese Corp., N.Y.C., 1971-72; exec. v.p. Internat. Paper Corp., N.Y.C., 1972-73; pres., chief exec. officer Hooker Chem. Corp., Stamford, Conn., 1973; dir. Occidental Petroleum Corp., Stamford, 1973; pres., chief exec. officer, dir. Am. Ship Bldg. Co., Cleve., 1975-79; pres., chief operating officer GATX Corp., Chgo., 1979—. Named Disting. Alumnus, Purdue U., 1965. Mem. Shipbuilders Council Am. (dir.), Nat. Maritime Council (bd. govs.). Clubs: Cleve. Athletic; Shaker Heights (Ohio) Country; Clifton (Lakewood, Ohio); Landmark (Stamford); Sky (N.Y.C.). Office: GATX Corp 120 S Riverside Plaza Chicago IL 60606*

THEIS, FRANK GORDON, judge, past mem. Democratic Nat. Com.; b. Yale, Kans., June 26, 1911; s. Peter F. and Maude (Cook) T.; A.B. cum laude, U. Kans., 1933; LL.B., U. Mich., 1936; m. Marjorie Riddle, Feb. 1, 1939 (dec. 1970); children—Franklin, Roger. Admitted to Kans. bar, 1937, since practiced in Arkansas City; sr. mem. firm Frank G. Theis, 1957—; atty. Kans. Tax Commn., 1937-39; chief counsel OPS for Kans., 1951-52; U.S. dist. judge Dist. Kans., 1967—, chief judge, 1977—. Pres., Young Democrats Kan., 1942-46, Kans. Dem. Club, 1944-46; chmn. Kans. Dem. Com., 1955-60; mem.

nat. adv. com. polit. orgn. Dem. Nat. Com., 1956-58, nat. committeeman from Kans., 1957-67; chmn. Dem. Midwest Conf., 1959-60; Dem. nominee for Kans., Supreme Ct. 1950, U.S. Senate, 1960. Mem. Kans. Jr. Bar Conf. (pres. 1942), Am., Kans. bar assns., Phi Beta Kappa. Phi Delta Phi, Sachem. Presbyn. Mason. Home: 1034 N C St Arkansas City KS 67005 Office: US Fed Bldg Wichita KS 67202

THEIS, JOHN WILLIAM, newspaperman; b. Pitts., Aug. 21, 1911; s. John and Lillian V. (Lindsay) T.; B.A., U. Pitts., 1933; m. Jane B. McAlister, 1937; children—Suzanne McAlister, John William, Jane. With Internat. News Service, 1933-58, bur. mgr., Harrisburg, Pa., 1935-39, mgr., Pa., 1939-42, Washington corr., 1942-58, chief Senate staff, 1945-58; Internat. News Service merged with United Press, 1958; chief Senate staff U.P.I., 1958-68; bur. chief Hearst Newspapers, Washington, 1968-76; sr. communications advisor Am. Petroleum Inst., Washington, 1976—. Chmn. Standing Com. Corr. in Washington, 1948. Mem. Sigma Delta Chi. Lutheran. Clubs: Nat. Press, Federal City, International (Washington). Author: (with Raymond M. Lahr) Congress: Power and Purpose on Capitol Hill, 1967. Home: 705 Winhall Way Silver Spring MD 20904

THEIS, ROBERT J., business exec.; b. Indpls., Mar. 30, 1924; s. Edward J. and Edna T.; student Notre Dame U.; m. Margaret Jones; 4 children. Sr. exec. Philco/Ford Co., GTE/Sylvania Co.; corp. v.p., group gen. mgr. ITT; now chmn. bd. Syracuse China Corp. (N.Y.), now pres. Canellus Inc.; mem. exec. com. Lincoln First Bank. Mem. adv. bd. Grad. Sch. Mgmt., Syracuse U. Served with USAAF. Mem. Internat. Foodservice Mfrs. Assn., Am. Restaurant China Council (past pres.). Home: Fayetteville NY 13066 Office: 2900 Court St Syracuse NY 13221

THEISMANN, JOSEPH ROBERT, profl. football player; b. New Brunswick, N.J., Sept. 9, 1949; s. Joseph James and Olga (Tobias) T.; B.A. in Sociology, U. Notre Dame, 1971; m. Chery Lynn Brown, Dec. 5, 1970; children—Joseph Winton, Amy Lynn, Patrick James. Played in Can., 1971-74; with Washington Redskins, 1974—, punt returner, 1974-79, starting quarterback, 1979—; tchr. Offense-Def. Football Camp; Superstar participant, 1979-80; mem. Pres.'s Athletic Adv. Com., 1975. Mem. Corp. bd. Children's Hosp. Nat. Med. Center, Washington; participant benefits for Multiple Sclerosis, children's hosps., Armed Forces Christmas benefits. High sch. All-Am. Football, 1967; All-Am. Coll., 1971; Acad.-All-Am.; All-Pro, UPI; recipient Brian Picollo award. Mem. Nat. Football Players Assn. Republican. Methodist. Author: Quarter Backing. Office: 5912 Leesburg Pike Bailey's Crossroads VA 22041

THELEN, HERBERT ARNOLD, ednl. psychologist; b. Berkeley, Calif., May 8, 1913; s. Paul and Alice (Arnold) T.; B.S. in Chemistry, U. Calif. at Berkeley, 1934, M.S., 1938; Ph.D. in Edn., U. Chgo., 1944; m. Leonora Elizabeth Knox, Oct. 15, 1937; children—David Paul, Janet Alice, Marian Elizabeth; m. 2d, Sophia Kaplan Lazarus, Oct. 6, 1978. With Shell Chem. Co., Pittsburg, Calif., 1934-36; high sch. tchr., Oakland (Calif.) pub. schs., 1937-41; instr. chemistry Okla. A. and M. Coll., 1941-42; dir. research U. Chgo. Lab. Sch., 1944-46; mem. faculty U. Chgo., 1945—, prof. edn., 1955—; human relations trainer European Productivity Agy., Paris, France, 1956; fellow Center Advanced Study Behavioral Scis., Palo Alto, Calif., 1960-61. Developed block orgn. Hyde-Park-Kenwood Community Conf., 1949-55. Bd. dirs. Nat. Tng. Lab., Washington, 1948-52. Recipient award human relations Mayors Commn. Human Relations, Chgo., 1951. Author: Dynamics of Groups at Work, 1954; (with Dorothy S. Whitaker) Emotional Dynamics and Group Culture, 1959; Education and the Human Quest, 1960; Classroom Grouping for Teachability, 1967. Home: 4840 S Kimbark Ave Chicago IL 60615

THELEN, MAX, JR., found. exec., lawyer; b. Berkeley, Calif., Aug. 18, 1919; s. Max and Ora Emily (Muir) T.; A.B. with highest honors, U. Calif., Berkeley, 1940; J.D. cum laude, Harvard U., 1946; m. Phyllis J. Barnhill, Mar. 8, 1952; children—Nancy B., Jane M., Max, III, William B. Admitted to Calif. bar, 1946, since practiced in San Francisco; partner firm Thelen, Marrin, Johnson & Bridges, 1957—; pres., trustee S.H. Cowell Found., 1970—; pres., dir. Oramax Fund; dir. Ind. Bankshares Corp., Kaiser Steel Corp. Trustee, v.p. World Affairs Council. Served to lt. USNR, 1942-46. Mem. Am. Coll. Trial Lawyers, Am. Bar Assn., State Bar Calif., Bar Assn. San Francisco, Com. Fgn. Relations. Republican. Presbyterian. Clubs: Commonwealth (past gov.), World Trade, Marin Tennis, Marines Meml. Home: 199 Mountain View Ave San Rafael CA 94901 Office: 2 Embarcadero Center Suite 2200 San Francisco CA 94111

THELIN, CALVIN BLAINE, lawyer; b. Oak Park, Ill., Sept. 8, 1929; s. Erick Blaine and Hilda (Schmidt) T.; B.A., Colgate U., 1951; postgrad. Stanford, 1956-57; J.D., Northwestern U., 1957; m. Helen Roderick Lewis, June 8, 1957; children-Louise Roderick, Elizabeth Ann, Eleanor Winifred. Admitted to Ill. bar, 1958; since practiced in Aurora; partner firm Goldsmith, Thelin, Schiller & Dickson, asst. atty. gen. Ill., 1960-61, 70—; city atty., Aurora, 1961-65, spl. counsel, 1974—; counsel Aurora Redevel. and Civic Center Authority, 1975—. Pres. Project 330 Aurora Devel., 1963—, Aurora United Way, 1966-67; state sec. Ill. Republican Vets. League, 1966—; pres. John Ericsson Rep. League Kane County, Ill., 1966; pres. Foxhill Home, 1973-76. Served to lt. (j.g.) USNR, 1951-55. Mem. Am., Ill., Kane County bar assns., Am. Legion, Greater Aurora C. of C. (pres. 1970-71), Navy League. Congregationalist. Clubs: Masons, Lions. Home: 38W128 Horseshoe Dr Batavia IL 60510 Office: Mchts Nat Bank Aurora IL 60504

THEOBALD, GEORGE JOHN, JR., vol. health agy. exec.; b. Bronx, N.Y., June 1, 1926; s. George John and Marguerite Rose (Susser) T.; B.S., Fordham U., 1950, postgrad., 1950-51; m. Barbara Ammann, June 1, 1960. Dir. bus. div. Salvation Army Greater N.Y. Command, 1962-67; devel. dir. N.Y. chpt. Arthritis Found., 1967-69; account exec. Holland Estill & Co., N.Y.C., 1969-71; nat. field dir. Nat. Multiple Sclerosis Soc., 1971-73; nat. exec. dir. Nat. Hemophilia Found., N.Y.C., 1973-79; cons. various vol. health and social welfare orgns.; lectr. various financial devel. confs. Served with AUS, 1944-46; PTO. Mem. Am. Blood Commn. (chmn. legis. action com.), 1975-79, World Fedn. Hemophilia (ofcl. del. U.S.A., gen. sec. XII Congress 1977), Council World Orgns. Interested in Handicapped, 1977-79, Nat. Soc. Fund Raising Execs. Roman Catholic. Club: Fordham (N.Y.C.). Home: 145 E 15th St New York NY 10003

THEOBALD, ROBERT, socioeconomist; married. Author: Economizing Abundance; (with J.M. Scott) Teg's 1994; Habit and Habitat; Beyond Despair; An Alternative Future for America's Third Century; also other books. Editor: Futures Conditional; The Guaranteed Income; also other books. Home and Office: Box 2240 Wickenburg AZ 85358. *I am convinced that it is necessary to move from a society based on force and competition to one based on process and cooperation. I have tried to build my activities on this belief and thus to facilitate the present transition from the industrial era to the communications era. The immediately coming years will determine whether we are successful in moving toward the more human and humane society we so urgently need.*

THEODORESCU, RADU AMZA SERBAN, mathematician, educator; b. Bucharest, Romania, Apr. 12, 1933; s. Dan and Ortensia Maria (Butoianu) T.; B.Sc., U. Bucharest, 1954, D.Sc., 1967; Ph.D., Acad. Romania, 1958; m. Ana Elena Florescu, Apr. 28, 1955 (div.); 1 son, Dan; came to Can., 1968, naturalized, 1975. Asst. prof. Inst. Math. of Acad. Romania, Bucharest, 1954-57, sr. asst. prof., 1957-60, asso. prof., sci. sec., 1960-64, prof., head dept. Center Math. Statistics, 1964-68; prof. U. Bucharest, 1968-69, Laval U., Quebec, Que., Can. 1969—; guest prof., lectr. univs. in Europe, N.Am. Mem. bd. European Orgn. Quality Control, 1966-69. Recipient prize Acad. Romania, 1960. Mem. Can. Math. Congress, Can. Statis. Assn., Statis. Scis. Assn. Can., German, Am. math. socs., Internat. Statis. Inst., Inst. Math. Statistics, Am. Soc. Quality Control. Author: (with G. Ciucu) Processes with Complete Connections, 1960; (with S. Guiasu) Mathematical Information Theory, 1968, Uncertainty and Information, 1971; (with M. Iosifescu) Random Processes and Learning, 1969; (with W. Hengartner) Concentration Functions, 1973, 2d edit., 1980; Monte-Carlo Methods, 1978. Editorial bd. Mathematische Operationsforschung und Statistik; Annales des Sciences Mathématiques du Québec. Contbr. articles to profl. jours. Home: 2276 Chemin Ste-Foy Apt 300 Ste-Foy PQ G1V 1S7 Canada Office: Dept Math Laval Univ Laval Quebec PQ G1K 7P4 Canada

THEODOROFF, B. JAMES, banker; b. Pontiac, Mich., Sept. 4, 1921; s. James D. and Anna (Pancheff) T.; B.B.A., U. Mich., 1943, M.B.A., 1949, J.D., 1949; grad. Stonier Grad. Sch. Banking, Rutgers U., 1960, Command and Gen. Staff Coll., 1964; m. Gloria F. Brugaletta, Aug. 30, 1947; children—Nancy Diane (Mrs. Charles S. Townsend), Debra Sue (Mrs. Walter J. Oben, Jr.), Bradford James. Admitted to Mich. bar, 1950; asst. v.p. Detroit Trust Co., 1949-56; with Detroit Bank and Trust Co., 1956—, exec. v.p., chief trust officer, 1964—; dir. U.S. Truck Co., W.H. Edgar & Sons, Inc. (all Detroit), Detroit Bank-Livonia (Mich.), Detroit Bank-Southfield (Mich.). Exec. bd. Detroit Area Council Boy Scouts Am., 1965. Trustee, Merrill Palmer Inst., 1964—, Birmingham Community House, 1962—, Baldwin Pub. Library, Birmingham, 1964-66, Mich. Found. Med. and Health Edn., 1967—; YWCA Met. Detroit, 1973—. Served to lt. col. AUS, 1944-46. Mem. Econ. Club Detroit, Greater Detroit C. of C., Am. (chmn. personnel com. trust div. 1960-65; exec. com. trust div. 1968-71, chmn. 38th Mid-Continent Trust Conf. 1968), Mich. (chmn. trust com. 1963, 72) bankers assns., Am., Mich., Detroit bar assns., Alpha Kappa Psi. Conglist. (chmn. ch. bldg. fund capital gifts 1965, trustee ch. 1972-76). Mason. Clubs: Detroit; Orchard Lake (Mich.). Home: 240 Warrington Rd Bloomfield Hills MI 48013 Office: 211 W Fort St Detroit MI 48231

THEODOSIUS, (THEODORE LAZOR), clergyman; b. Canonsburg, Pa., Oct. 27, 1933; s. John and Mary (Kirr) L.; A.B., Washington and Jefferson Coll., 1957, D.D. (hon.), 1973; B.D., St. Vladimir's Orthodox Theol. Sem., 1960; postgrad. Ecumenical Inst., Bossey, Switzerland, 1961. Tonsured monk Orthodox Ch. in Am., 1961, ordained priest, 1961; priest Nativity of Holy Virgin Mary Ch., Madison, Ill., 1961-66; elected bishop of Washington, 1967, elected bishop of Sitka and Alaska, 1967; elected bishop of Pitts. and W.Va., 1972; elected archbishop of N.Y., 1977; Metropolitan of All Am. and Can., 1977—. Address: PO Box 675 Rt 25A Syosset NY 11791

THEON, JOHN SPERIDON, meteorologist; b. Washington, Dec. 12, 1934; s. Lewis and Merope (Xydias) T.; B.S. in Aero. Engring., U. Md., 1957; B.S. in Meteorology, Pa. State U., 1959, M.S., 1962; m. Joanne Edens, July 31, 1965; children—Christopher James, Catherine. Aero. engr. Douglas Aircraft Co., Santa Monica, Calif., 1957-58; engr. U.S. Naval Ordnance Lab., White Oak, Md., 1962; research meteorologist NASA Goddard Space Flight Center, Greenbelt, Md., 1962-74, head meteorology br., 1974-77, asst. chief Lab. for Atmospheric Scis., 1977-78, Nimbus project scientist, 1972-78, Landsat discipline leader meteorol. investigations, 1974-78; mgr. global weather research program NASA Hdqrs., Washington, 1978—. Served with USAF, 1958-60. Recipient Nimbus F Instrument Team award NASA-Goddard, 1976, Exceptional Performance award, 1978. Mem. Am. Meteorol. Soc., Am. Geophys. Union, AAAS. Presbyterian. Contbr. articles to profl. jours. Home: 6801 Lupine Ln McLean VA 22101 Office: 600 Independence Ave Washington DC 20546

THÉRIO, ADRIEN, writer, educator; b. St.-Modeste, Que., Can., Aug. 15, 1925; s. Charles-Eugène and Eva (Bouchard) Thériault; B.A., U. Ottawa (Ont., Can.), 1950; Ph.D. in Lit., Laval U., Québec, Que., Can., 1952; M.A. in Polit. Sci., U. Notre Dame, 1959. Faculty, Bellarmine Coll., Louisville, 1954-56, U. Notre Dame, 1956-59, U. Toronto, 1959-60; prof. Royal Mil. Coll. Can., Kingston, Ont., 1960-69, head French dept., 1962-69; prof. dept. lettres françaises U. Ottawa, 1969—; author: (fiction) Les Brèves années, 1953; Ceux du Chemin Taché (short stories), 1963; Mes Beaux meurtres, 1961; Soliloque en hommage à une femme, 1968; La Colère du père, 1974; La tête en fête, 1975; C'est ici que le monde à commencé, 1978; (anthologies) Conteurs canadiens-francais, 1967; L'Humour au Canada francais, 1967; (studies) Jules Fournier, journaliste de combat, 1955; editor: Mon Encrier (Jules Fournier), 1960. Fellow Royal Soc. Can.; mem. Union des Ecrivains québécois. Founder, dir. Livres et auteurs québécois, ann., 1961-72; founder, editor Lettres québécoises, quar., 1976—. Office: U Ottawa Ottawa ON K1N 6N5 Canada

THERNSTROM, STEPHAN ALBERT, historian, educator; b. Port Huron, Mich., Nov. 5, 1934; s. Albert George and Bernadene (Robbins) T.; B.S., Northwestern U., 1956; A.M., Harvard, 1958, Ph.D., 1962; m. Abigail Mann, Jan. 3, 1959; children—Melanie Rachel, Samuel Altgeld. Instr. history Harvard, 1962-66, asst. prof., 1966-67, prof., 1973—; prof. Brandeis U., 1967-69, U. Calif. at Los Angeles, 1969-73; Pitt. prof. Am. history and instns. Cambridge U., 1978-79. Bd. dirs. Social Sci. Research Council. Recipient Bancroft prize, Faculty prize Harvard U. Press; Guggenheim fellow, Am. Council Learned Socs. fellow. Author: Poverty and Progress, 1964; Poverty, Planning and Politics in the New Boston, 1969; The Other Bostonians, 1973; editor Harvard Ency. Am. Ethnic Groups; co-editor: 19th-Century Cities: Interdisciplinary Perspectives on Modern History; Harvard Studies in Urban History. Home: 1445 Massachusetts Ave Lexington MA 02173 Office: 215 Robinson Hall Harvard U Cambridge MA 02138

THEROUX, PAUL EDWARD, author; b. Medford, Mass., Apr. 10, 1941; s. Albert Eugene and Anne (Dittami) T.; B.A., U. Mass., Amherst; m. Anne Castle, Dec. 4, 1967; children—Marcel, Louis. Lectr., U. Urbino (Italy), 1963, Soche Hill Coll., Malawi, 1963-65; mem. faculty English dept. Makerere (Uganda) U., 1965-68, U. Singapore, 1968-71; vis. lectr. U. Va., 1972-73; author: (fiction) Waldo, 1967; Fong and The Indians, 1968; Girls at Play, 1969; Murder in Mt. Holly, 1969; Jungle Lovers, 1971; Sinning With Annie, 1972; Saint Jack, 1973; The Black House, 1974; The Family Arsenal, 1976; The Consul's File, 1977; Picture Palace, 1978 (Whitbread prize for fiction); A Christmas Card, 1978; London Snow, 1980; (non-fiction) V.S. Naipaul, 1973; The Great Railway Bazaar, 1975; The Old Patagonian Express, 1979; Saint Jack (filmstrip), 1979. Recipient Editorial award Playboy mag., 1972, 76, 77, 79; Lit. award AAAL, 1977. Address: 35 Elsynge Rd London SW18 England

THESING, ROBERT HENRY, hardware co. exec.; b. Salem, Mass., June 7, 1928; m. Claudia Lynn Islieb, June 7, 1975. With Stanley Works, v.p., gen. mgr., 1968-69, v.p. Europe, 1969-72, group v.p. internat., 1972-77, exec. v.p. New Britain, Conn., 1977—. Home: 65 Elbridge Rd New Britain CT 06052 Office: 195 Lake St New Britain CT 06050*

THEUER, FRED GEORGE, savs. and loan exec.; b. Cleve., June 8, 1927; s. Fred G. and Agnes F. (Glesher) T.; B.A., Yale, 1949; LL.B., Harvard, 1952; grad. Grad. Sch. Savs. and Loan of U. Ind., 1961; m. Patricia A. Rupert, June 2, 1956; children—Kathryn, John. With Broadview Savs. & Loan Co., Cleve., 1954-64, v.p. mortgage loan div., 1964-65; exec. v.p., dir. Family Fed. Savs. & Loan Assn., Saginaw, Mich., 1965-70, pres., dir., chmn. bd., 1971—; dir. Fed. Home Loan Bank Indpls., 1977—. Active Saginaw United Fund; mem. adv. bd. St. Mary's Hosp. Served as 1st lt., J.A.G.D., USAF, 1952-53. Mem. Mich. Savs. and Loan League (pres., dir.), Am., Internat., Mich. bar assns., Saginaw County Bar Assn., Internat. Union Bldg. Socs. Clubs: Saginaw, Saginaw Country; Otsego (Mich.) Ski. Home: 1465 Hawthorne St Saginaw MI 48603 Office: Saginaw MI

THEUS, LUCIUS, air force officer; b. nr. Bells, Tenn., Oct. 11, 1922; s. William O. and Flora Ann (Walker) T.; grad. Armed Forces Staff Coll., 1960; hon. grad. Indsl. Coll. Armed Forces, 1964; Distinguished grad. Air War Coll., 1966; B.S., U. Md., 1956; M.B.A., George Washington U., 1957; postgrad. Advanced Mgmt. Program, Harvard, 1969; m. Gladys Marie Davis, Feb. 28, 1942. Joined USAAF, 1942, commd. 2d lt., 1946, advanced through grades to maj. gen., 1975; assigned chief clk., 1st sgt. Keesler Field, Miss., 1942-45; squadron adj. Tuskegee AFB, Ala.; with statis. services Lockbourne AFB, Ohio, Erding Air Depot, Germany, Hdqrs. U.S. Air Force, Washington, Chateauroux Air Base, France, 1946-57; mgmt. analyst Eastern Air Logistics Office, Athens, Greece, Larson AFB, Washington, 1958-62; comptroller Kingsley Field, Oreg., 1962-65; comptroller, dep. base comdr., Cam Ranh Bay, Vietnam, 1966-67; data automation staff officer, dir. mgmt. analysis, spl. asst. for social actions Hdqrs USAF, Pentagon, Washington, 1967-74; comdr. Air Force Accounting and Finance Center, also dir. accounting and finance Hdqrs. U.S. Air Force, Denver, also asst. dir. def. security Agy. for Fgn. Mil. Sales Acctg., 1974—; extension instr. bus. adminstrn. Central Washington State Coll., 1961-62; guest lectr. colls., univs., TV and radio; speaker profl. service schs.; mem. policy com. Denver Fed. Exec. Bd.; mem. Colo. Gov.'s Mil. Adv. Council. Co-chmn. Mile High United Way, 1975, chmn., 1976, now bd. dirs.; bd. dirs. Denver Area council Boy Scouts Am., 1975, regional chmn. Explorer Scouts, 1975. Decorated D.S.M. with oak leaf cluster, Legion of Merit, Bronze Star, Air Force Commendation medal with oak leaf cluster; recipient Disting. Fed. Service award Denver Fed. Exec. Bd., 1978, Alumni Achievement award Harvard Bus. Sch., 1979. Mem. Am. Soc. Mil. Comptrollers (pres. Washington chpt. 1972-73, Denver chpt. 1975), Assn. Computing Machinery, Denver C. of C., Am. Radio Relay League, Nat. Rifle Assn., Harvard Bus. Sch. Assn. (exec. council 1976—). Rotarian. Clubs: Harvard, Harvard Business School (service v.p. 1973, advanced mgmt. program v.p. 1975, dir. 1976—), Tuskegee Airmen (nat. v.p. 1978—), George Washington University (Washington). Contbr. articles to profl. publs. Home: 3965 S Niagara Way Denver CO 80237 also 13718 Central Park Robbins IL 60472 Office: Gilchrist Bldg Lowry AFB Denver CO 80279. *I have always believed, and still firmly believe that to be successful as you move through life you must never miss an opportunity to grasp a challenge to learn, to perform, and to demonstrate that you can excel in your chosen profession or career.*

THIBAULT, CLAUDE JOSEPH, assn. exec.; b. Quebec City, Can., May 10, 1931; s. Charles Ferdinand and Blanche (Bedard) T.; B.A., Laval U., 1950, M.A., 1960; M.A., Bishop's U., 1963; Ph.D., U. Rochester, 1965; m. Geneva White, May 23, 1953; children—Bruce, Marc, Linda. Asst. prof. history U. Sherbrooke, 1960-66; prof., asst. to prin. Bishop's U., Lennoxville, Que., 1966-74; exec. dir. Assn. of Univs. and Colls. of Can., Ottawa, Ont., 1974—. Served with Royal Can. Army, 1951-60. Mem. Inst. Assn. Execs. Can. Roman Catholic. Compiler: Bibliographia Canadiana, 1973. Office: 151 Slater St Ottawa ON K1P 5N1 Canada

THIBAULT, CONRAD, singer; b. Northbridge, Mass., Nov. 13, 1908; s. Louis and Paula (De Levecque) T.; student Curtis Inst. Music, 1928-33; 1 son, William A. Baritone soloist 1st Am. performance Faurés' Requiem, Phila., Eugene D'Alberts Tiefland; mem. faculty Manhattan Sch. Music, Palm Beach Atlantic Coll.; theatrical producer; rec. artist RCA Victor, Decca Records. Trustee Ithaca Coll., Guild Hall, Inc. Home: 210 El Dorado Ln Palm Beach FL 33480 Studio: 225 Southern Blvd West Palm Beach FL 33405

THIBAULT, JOHN CROWELL, educator; b. Spalding, Mich., Apr. 26, 1922; s. John Craske and Lillian Cleopatra (Crowell) T.; Litt.B., Xavier U., 1944; M.A. in Philosophy, Loyola U., Chgo., 1947; A.B. in Theology, Alma Coll., 1954; M.A. in Classical Philology, U. Ill. at Urbana, 1956, Ph.D. in Classical Philology, 1960; m. Barbara Orilla Story, May 10, 1960; 1 dau., Nicole Story. Instr. St. Xavier High Sch., 1947-50; asst. prof. U. Calif. at Santa Barbara, 1960-64; asso. prof. U. Mo., Columbia, 1965-70, prof., 1970—, chmn. dept. classical studies, 1966—. Mem. Am. Philol. Assn., Classical Assn. Midwest and South, Archaeol. Inst. Am. Author: The Mystery of Ovid's Exile, 1964. Home: RD 1 Harrisburg MO 65256

THIBAUT, CHAREST DELAUZON, JR., lawyer; b. Donaldsonville, La., Jan. 6, 1922; s. Charest deLauzon and Mildred (Winship) T.; B.A., La. State U., 1943, LL.B., J.D., 1946; m. Lillie M. Major, May 15, 1943; children—Natalie Major (Mrs. Clifford C. Comeaux, Jr.), Charest deLauzon III, Joseph Major, Cherie Adele. Admitted to La. bar, 1946, since practiced in Baton Rouge; mem. firm Thibaut & Thibaut and predecessor firms, 1951—. Chmn. bd., gen. counsel Republic Securities Corp. Mem. La. State U. Found. Served with AUS, 1943. Mem. Am., La., Baton Rouge bar assns., Omicron Delta Kappa, Delta Kappa Epsilon, Phi Delta Phi. Clubs: Baton Rouge Country (past pres.), Kiwanis. Home: Pleasant View Plantation Oscar LA 70762 Office: 209 St Ferdinand St Baton Rouge LA 70821

THIE, WILLIAM ARCHIBALD, lawyer; b. St. Louis, Oct. 1, 1915; s. Otto William and Mary (Wasson) T.; A.B., Washington U., LL.B., 1938; m. Alma C. Smith, Nov. 18, 1942; 1 dau., Deborah M. Gannon. Admitted to Mo. bar, Tex. bar.; atty. Terminal R.R. Assn. of St. Louis, 1938-41, 45-50; gen. atty. Mo.-Kans.-Tex. R.R. Co., Dallas, 1950-58, gen. counsel, 1958—. Served with U.S. Army, 1941-45. Mem. Dallas Bar Assn., Tex. Bar Assn., Assn. ICC Practitioners. Republican. Lutheran. Home: 6630 Stefani St Dallas TX 75225 Office: 701 Commerce St Dallas TX 75202

THIEBAUD, WAYNE, artist; b. Mesa, Ariz., Nov. 15, 1920; s. Morton J. and Alice Eugenia (LeBaron) T.; B.A., Sacramento State Coll., 1951, M.A., 1952; D.F.A. (hon.), Calif. Coll. Arts and Crafts, 1975; m. Betty Jean Carr, Dec. 11, 1959; children—Twinka, Mallary Ann, Paul LeBaron. Art dir., N.Y.C., also Hollywood, 1946-49; chmn. art dept. Sacramento City Coll., 1951; design cons. Calif. State Fair and Expn.; guest instr. San Francisco Art Inst., 1958; asso. prof. art U. Calif. at Davis, now prof., Faculty Research lectr., 1973—; vis. artist Cornell U., U. Hawaii, U. Wis., U. Utah, U. Ill., Yale, U. Va.,

Bradley U.; one man shows include Crocker Art Gallery, Sacramento, 1952, Artists Coop. Gallery, Sacramento, 1954, DeYoung Mus., San Francisco, 1962, Allan Stone Gallery, N.Y.C., 1962-70, Stanford, 1965, Galleria Schwarz, Milan, Italy, 1963, San Francisco Mus., 1967, Whitney Mus., 1972; exhibited museums U.S., Toronto, Can., Hague, Holland, Vienna, Berlin, Hong Kong, S.Am.; traveling exhibit Pasadena Mus. Art, 1967-68; one-man traveling exhibit Survey of Works, Oakland Mus., Phoenix Mus., U. So. Calif., Des Moines Mus., Boston Inst. Contemporary Art, 1976. U.S. rep. Sao Paulo Biennale, 1966, Indocumenta, 1972; represented permanent collections museums and galleries Europe, U.S. including Mus. Modern Art, Whitney Mus., Albright Knox Mus., Wadsworth Athenaeum, Library Congress, Woodward Found., Rose Art Mus., Brandeis U., Stanford, also numerous pvt. collections; commd. fountain mobile sculpture Calif. State Fair, 1952, Sacramento Municipal Utility Dist. Bldg., 1959; producer, dir. 12 ednl. motion pictures. Recipient 1st prize Art Film Festival, 1956; Golden Reel Film Festival award for Space, Calif. State Fair, 1956. Author: (etchings) Delights, 1965; Prints, 1970-71; Seven Still Lifes and a Rabbit. Home: 1617 7th Ave Sacramento CA 95818 Office: U Calif Davis CA 95616

THIEBLOT, ROBERT JEAN, lawyer; b. Teaneck, N.J., Apr. 7, 1933; s. Armand Jean and Eva P. (Mancini) T.; A.B., Princeton, 1955; LL.B., Harvard, 1960; m. Suzanna Lee Cohoes, Aug. 8, 1958; 1 dau., Aline. Admitted to Md. bar, 1960; asso. firm Rollins, Smalkin, Weston & Andrew, Balt., 1960-64; partner firm Allen, Thieblot & Hughes (name now changed to Allen, Thieblot & Alexander), Balt., 1964—; mem. Appellate Jud. Nominating Selection Commn., 1979—; lectr. law Eastern Coll., Balt., 1964-70, U. Balt., 1970-76. Commr., Hist. and Archtl. Preservation Balt., 1969-73; mem. Commr. to Revise Annotated Code Md., 1975-79; mem. Bd. Sch. Commrs., Balt., 1971-72. Dir., Peale Mus., 1976—. Served to lt. j.g. USNR, 1955-57. Mem. Am., Md. bar assns., Md. Hist. Trust (chmn. Balt. City Com. 1975), Md. Club, Mchts. Club (dir. 1975—, pres. 1976), Library Co. Balt. Bar (pres. 1974-75, dir. 1976). Home: 1508 Park Ave Baltimore MD 21217 Office: 4th Floor World Trade Center Baltimore MD 21202

THIEDE, WILSON BICKFORD, educator; b. Blue Earth, Minn., Mar. 20, 1916; s. Adolph R. and Mandie (Wilson) T.; B.S., U. Wis., 1939, M.S., 1941, Ph.D., 1950; m. Grace V. Loeffler, June 17, 1940; children—Susan, Eric, Kirsten. Sr. high sch. tchr., Fond du Lac, Wis., 1940-41; mem. faculty U. Wis., Madison, 1946-49, 51-74, prof. adult edn., 1961—, chmn. dept., 1962-63, asso. dean Sch. Edn., 1963-66, provost for Univ. Outreach, U. Wis. System, 1974-79; registrar La. State U., 1949-51; exec. editor, pub. Jour. Ednl. Research, 1962-74, Pub. Jour. Exptl. Edn., 1962-74, Jour. Environ. Edn., 1970-74. Served with USNR, 1942-46. Mem. Adult Edn. Assn. (bd. dir. 1964, pres. 1966), Nat. Assn. Pub. Sch. Adult Edn., (dir. 1965-66), Phi Kappa Phi. Home: 4825 Bayfield Terr Madison WI 53705

THIELE, ALBERT E., foundation exec.; b. Bklyn., Oct. 1, 1892; s. Albert E. and Matilda (Foster) T.; B.C.S., N.Y. U.; m. Alice Irene Kelly, Sept. 26, 1918; 1 son, Roger Harvey. With Guggenheim Bros., 1909—, now partner; pres., dir. Elgerbar Corp.; dir., mem. audit com. Anglo Co. Ltd. Bd. dirs. Corlette Glorney Found., Inc.; trustee Estate Solomon R. Guggenheim; life trustee N.Y. U.; trustee, chmn. exec. and finance coms. Solomon R. Guggenheim Found. Clubs: Maidstone, Bankers, Blind Brook, N.Y. Univ. Finance, N.Y. Univ. (N.Y.C.); (N.Y.C.); Scarsdale Golf, Devon Yacht; Everglades (Palm Beach). Home: Sherbrooke Park Scarsdale NY 10583 (summer) East Hampton Long Island NY 11937 Office: 120 Broadway New York NY 10005

THIELENS, ALEXIS OLLIER, banker; b. Tuscaloosa, Ala., Oct. 19, 1933; s. Wagner Perrin and Geraldine (Ollier) T.; grad. Phillips Acad., Andover, Mass., 1952; B.A., Harvard, 1956; m. Kathleen Brown, Nov. 14, 1959; children—Elizabeth, John, David. Trust trainee State St. Bank and Trust Co., Boston, 1960-64; asst. trust officer First Nat. Bank, Birmingham, Ala., 1964-67; sr. trust officer First Nat. Bank South Jersey, Atlantic City, 1967-73; v.p. Provident Nat. Bank, Phila., 1973—. Bd. dirs. Cathedral Village, Phila. Served with AUS, 1956-59. Toastmaster. Home: 79 Conestoga Rd Devon PA 19333 Office: Provident Nat Bank 17th and Chestnut Sts Philadelphia PA 19103

THIELSCH, HELMUT JOHN, pipe materials co. exec.; b. Berlin, Nov. 16, 1922; came to U.S., 1939, naturalized, 1954; s. Kurt and Anna-Sibylle T.; B.S., Auburn U., 1953; postgrad. U. Mich., 1943-45, Lehigh U., 1948; m. Margaret E. McKenna, Aug. 15, 1952; children—Barbara Anne, Donald Kurt, Deborah Lee, Helmut John. Research engr. Allis Chalmers Co., Milw., 1945-46; metall. engr. Black, Sivalls & Bryson, Inc., Kansas City, Mo., 1946-47; research engr. Lukens Steel Co., Coatsville, Pa., 1948-49; engr. Welding Research Council, N.Y.C., 1949-52; dir. research Eutectic Welding Alloys Co., N.Y.C., 1952-53; v.p., dir. research, devel. and engring. ITT Grinnell Corp., Providence, 1954—; cons. on failure analysis to industry, public utilities, equipment builders, 1954—; lectr. at confs. on failures and failure prevention; mem. component tech. com. Argonne (Ill.) Nat. Lab. Registered profl. engr., R.I., Mass., Maine, N.J., Ga., Calif. Fellow Am. Soc. Metals, Am. Soc. Nondestructive Testing, ASME; mem. Am. Welding Soc., Am. Soc. Quality Control, Am. Nuclear Soc., Nat. Assn. Corrosion Engrs., Am. Chem. Soc., Am. Mgmt. Assn. Author: Defects and Failures in Pressure Vessels and Piping, 1965; contbr. numerous articles to profl. publs.; patentee in field. Office: 260 W Exchange St Providence RI 02901

THIEMANN, CHARLES LEE, banker; b. Louisville, Nov. 21, 1937; s. Paul and Helen (Kern) T.; B.A. in Chemistry, Bellarmine Coll., Louisville, 1959; M.B.A., Ind. U., 1961, D.B.A., 1963; m. Donna Timperman, June 18, 1960; children— Laura Gerette, Charles Lee, Rodney Gerard, Jeffrey Michael, Matthew Joseph. Mem. faculty Grad. Sch. Bus., also Grad. Sch. Savs. and Loan, Ind. U., 1959-61; mgmt. cons., 1961-63; mem. research dept. Fed. Res. Bank St. Louis, 1963-64; with Fed. Home Loan Bank Cin., 1964—, sr. v.p., then exec. v.p., 1974, pres., 1975—; adj. prof. Grad. Sch. Bus., Xavier U., Cin.; mem. faculty Sch. Mortgage Banking, Northwestern U.; exec. com. Savs. Instns. Thrift Plan; trustee Savs. Assns. Retirement Fund. Past mem. Mayor Cin. Housing Com. Mem. Am. Mgmt. Assn., Am. Fin. Assn., Am. Econ. Assn., Presidents' Assn., Urban Land Inst., Nat. Assn. Bus. Economists, Cin. C. of C. Roman Catholic. Clubs: Rotary, Bankers, Queen City (Cin.). Home: 6010 Gaines Rd Cincinnati OH 45239 Office: 2500 Dubois Tower Cincinnati OH 45202

THIEME, THEODORE LOUIS, consumer products co. exec.; b. Newark, Feb. 6, 1920; s. Theodore A. and Rose (Muller) T.; B.S., Rutgers U., 1949; m. Helen Emily Miller, Feb. 5, 1944; children—Judith Louise, Donald Theodore. Chief accountant, budget dir. Rubberset Brush Co. div. Bristol Myers, 1940-49; asst. budget dir. Lever Bros. Co., 1949-51; asst. treas. E.R. Squibb & Sons, 1951-54; treas. Unette Corp., 1954-58; asst. to treas. Am. Home Products Corp., 1958-64, asst. treas., 1964-76, treas., 1976—. Served to capt. U.S. Army, 1941-46. Republican. Club: Mendham Golf and Tennis. Home: 17 Starlight Dr Morristown NJ 07960 Office: 685 3d Ave New York NY 10017

THIEME, WALTER IRVING, constrn. materials co. exec.; b. Missoula, Mont., Sept. 11, 1920; s. Fred E. and Ella (Hopkins) T.; B.S. in Mech. Engring., Mont. State Coll., 1942; M.B.A., Harvard, 1949; m. Jean Louise Hole, June 18, 1948; children—Michael Alan, Rebecca Louise, Susan Kathleen. Indsl. engr. Crown Zellerbach Corp., 1949-51; with Am. Aggregates Corp., 1953—, exec. v.p., 1963-64, pres., 1964-69, chmn. bd. dirs., 1969—; dir. Grant Contracting Co., Am. Materials Corp. Served to capt. USAAF and USAF, 1942-46, 51-52. Home: 3565 Hollansburg-Sampson Rd Greenville OH 45331 Office: Am Aggregates Corp Garst Ave Greenville OH 45331

THIER, HERBERT DAVID, univ. adminstr.; b. N.Y.C., Feb. 27, 1932; s. Benjamin and Hannah (Greenberg) T.; B.A., State U. N.Y., 1952, M.A., 1954; Ed.D., N.Y. U., 1962; m. Marlene Bach, Dec. 19, 1954; children—Maura, Lynne, Holli. Sci. coordinator and tchr. gen. sci. and physics pub. high schs., N.Y., 1954-59; dir. secondary edn. New Brunswick (N.J.) pub. schs., 1959-62; asst. supt. pub. schs., Falls Church, Va., 1962-63; mem. research faculty, research educator, asst. dir. sci. curriculum improvement study Lawrence Hall of Sci. U. Calif. at Berkeley, 1963—, dir. research and devel. work for the blind, 1969—, co-dir. instructional strategies for outdoor biology project, asso. dir., 1974—; dir. U.S.-Philippine spl. sci. tng. program, 1975; head team authors Rand McNally sci. curriculum improvement study elementary sch. sci. program, 1978; dir. Asian Bilingual Sci. Activities Project (Sci. Component), 1978, Sci. Enrichment for Learners with Phys. Handicaps Project, 1978—; cons. various sch. systems, univs.; UNESCO cons. Israel Elementary Sci. Project, Tel Aviv U., summer, 1970; cons. Orgn. Am. States, Trinidad, 1975, Jamaica, 1976; vis. prof. Simon Fraser U., Vancouver, B.C., Can., summer, 1972, Tel Aviv U., Israel summer, 1974, Ben-Gurion U., Israel, summer, 1977, 78. Mem. Nat. Assn. Research in Sci. Teaching, Nat. Sci. Tchrs. Assn. Democrat. Jewish religion. Author: A New Look at Elementary Science, 1967; Teaching Elementary Science, A Laboratory Approach, 1970; contbg. author: New Trends in Integrated Science Teaching, Vol. II, 1973, Vol. III, 1974. Contbr. numerous articles to profl. jours. Home: 142 Hodges Dr Moraga CA 94556 Office: Lawrence Hall of Sci U Calif Berkeley CA 94720

THIER, SAMUEL OSIAH, physician, educator; b. Bklyn., June 23, 1937; s. Sidney and May Henrietta (Kanner) T.; student Cornell U., 1953-56; M.D., State U. N.Y., Syracuse, 1960; m. Paula Dell Finkelstein, June 28, 1958; children—Audrey Lauren, Stephanie Ellen, Sara Leslie. Intern, Mass. Gen. Hosp., Boston, 1960-61, asst. resident, 1961-62, sr. resident, 1964-65, clin. and research fellow, 1965, chief resident, 1966; clin. asso. Nat. Inst. Arthritis and Metabolic Diseases, 1962-64; from instr. to asst. prof. medicine Harvard U. Med. Sch., 1967-69; asst. in medicine, chief renal unit Mass. Gen. Hosp., Boston, 1967-69; asso. prof., then prof. medicine U. Pa. Med. Sch., 1969-72, vice chmn. dept., 1971-74; asso. dir. med. services Hosp. U. Pa., 1969-74; David Paige Smith prof. internal medicine, chmn. dept. Yale U. Sch. Medicine, 1975—; chief medicine Yale-New Haven Hosp., 1975—, bd. dirs., 1978—; dir. Hospice, Inc. Served with USPHS, 1962-64. Recipient Christian R. and Mary F. Lindback Found. Distinguished Teaching award, 1971. Diplomate Am. Bd. Internal Medicine (dir. 1977—). Fellow A.C.P.; mem. Assn. Am. Med. Colls. (adminstrv. bd. council acad. socs.), John Morgan Soc., Am. Fedn. Clin. Research (pres. 1976-77), Am. Soc. Nephrology, Am. Physiol. Soc., Inst. Medicine, Nat. Acad. Scis., Internat. Soc. Nephrology, Assn. Profs. Medicine, Assn. Am. Physicians, Interurban Clin. Club, Alpha Omega Alpha. Editorial bd. New Eng. Jour. Medicine, 1978—. Contbr. articles to med. jours. Home: 8 Spector Rd Woodbridge CT 06525 Office: 333 Cedar St New Haven CT 06510

THIERIOT, RICHARD TOBIN, publisher; b. San Francisco, Jan. 18, 1942; s. Charles de Young and Barbara Mary (Tobin) T.; B.A., Yale U., 1963; M.B.A., Stanford U., 1969; m. Angelica Maria Reynal, Sept. 30, 1972; children—Charles de Young, II, Richard Reynal; stepchildren—Juan P. Withers, Simon Withers. Reporter, Camden (N.J.) Courier-Post, 1963-64; asso. editor San Francisco Chronicle, 1969-77, editor, pub., 1977—; treas. Chronicle Pub. Co., 1969-77, pres., 1977—. Served with USMCR, 1964-67. Mem. Am. Newspaper Pubs. Assn., A.P., Am. Soc. Newspaper Editors, Am. Press Inst., Calif. Press Assn., Calif. Newspaper Pubs. Assn., Sigma Delta Chi. Address: 901 Mission St San Francisco CA 94103

THIERRY, JOHN ADAMS, heavy machinery mfg. co. exec., lawyer; b. Watertown, Mass., May 8, 1913; s. Louis Sidney and Adelaide (Hamlin) T.; A.B., Harvard, 1935, A.M., 1936, J.D., 1940; postgrad. (Sheldon traveling fellow Harvard), U. Cambridge (Eng.), 1936-37; m. Mary Mills Hatch, June 6, 1953 (div. 1977); 1 son, Charles Adams; m. 2d, Silvie Marie Frère, Dec. 1977. Admitted to Wis. bar, 1941; with Bucyrus-Erie Co., South Milwaukee, Wis., 1940—, sec., 1958-77, gen. atty., 1958-76, v.p., 1960-77, sr. v.p., 1977-78, dir., 1961-79, mem. exec. com., 1967-78; v.p., dir. Bucyrus Erie Co. Can., Ltd., 1959-78; dir. Ruston-Bucyrus, Ltd., Lincoln, Eng., 1964-79, Komatsu-Bucyrus K.K., Japan, 1971—. Dir. Wis. Pub. Expenditure Survey, 1954-78; v.p., bd. dirs. Bucyrus-Erie Found., 1963-78; bd. dirs. Pub. Expenditure Research Found., 1964-78, YMCA, Milw., 1973-78, Milw. Symphony Orch., 1974-78; trustee Wis. Conservatory Music, 1969-78, S.E. Asia Art Found. Served to capt., C.E., AUS, 1942-46. Mem. Mass., Wis. patent office bars, Phi Beta Kappa. Episcopalian. Clubs: Milwaukee; Harvard (Boston and N.Y.C.). Home: Murray Hill Rd Hill NH 03243 Office: care Bucyrus-Erie Co South Milwaukee WI 53172

THIES, AUSTIN COLE, utility co. exec.; b. Charlotte, N.C., July 18, 1921; s. Oscar Julius and Blanche (Austin) T.; B.S. in Mech. Engring., Ga. Inst. Tech., 1943; m. Marilyn Joy Walker, June 26, 1945; children—Austin Cole, Robert Melvin, Marilyn Leone. With Duke Power Co., Charlotte, 1946—, mgr. steam prodn., 1963-65, asst. v.p., 1965-67, v.p. prodn. and operation, 1967-71, sr. v.p., 1971—, also dir.; past chmn. prodn. com., engring. and operating div. Southeastern Electric Exchange; chmn. tech. advisory com. Carolinas Va. Nuclear Power Assos.; chmn. N.C. Air Control Advisory Council. Mem. nat. adv. council Ga. Inst. Tech.; pres. Arts and Scis. Council; bd. dirs. Mercy Hosp. Served with USNR, 1943-46. Decorated Purple Heart. Mem. Edison Electric Inst., Charlotte C. of C., ASME (past chmn. Piedmont Carolina sect.), Am. Nuclear Soc., Air Pollution Control Assn., N.C. Soc. Engrs. (past pres.), Charlotte Engrs. Club, Nat. Rifle Assn. (life), Charlotte C. of C., Kappa Sigma. Presbyterian. Clubs: Rotary (past pres., dir. N. Charlotte), Cowans Ford Country, Quail Hollow Country, Charlotte City, Charlotte Ga. Inst. Tech. (past pres.), Charlotte Rifle and Pistol (past pres.). Home: 2429 Red Fox Trail Charlotte NC 28211 Office: 422 S Church St Charlotte NC 28242

THIESENHUSEN, WILLIAM CHARLES, agrl. economist; b. Waukesha, Wis., Feb. 12, 1936; s. Arthur Henry and Myrtle O. (Honeyager) T.; B.S., U. Wis., 1958, M.S., 1960, Ph.D., 1965; M.P.A. (Danforth Found. fellow), Harvard U., 1962, postgrad., 1968-69; children—James Waring, Kathryn Hague, Gail Ann. Instr. agrl. extension U. Wis., Madison, 1959-61, exec. asst. Land Tenure Center and Instituto de Economia Universidad de Chile research team in Santiago, 1963-65, asst. prof. agrl. econs., 1965-68, asso. prof. agrl. econs., 1971-72, asso. prof. agrl. journalism, 1968-72, prof. agrl. journalism and agrl. econs., 1972—, dir. Land Tenure Center, 1971-75; asst. prof. econs. U. Wis., Milw., 1966-67; prof. agrl. econs. Escuela Nacional de Agricultura, Chapingo, Mexico, under AID contract, summer 1965; vis. prof. Universidad Autonoma de Madrid, Fulbright Program, 1977; cons., condr. seminars in field; Fulbright-Hays lectr., 1965, 72. Bd. dirs. Center for Adult Detoxification and Referral, Dane County, Wis. Served with USAR, 1960. Recipient award for best article Am. Jour. Agrl. Econs., 1969; Alpha Zeta nat. fellow, 1957; U. Wis. fellow, 1956; Harvard U. Adminstrn. fellow, 1962. Mem. Am. Agrl. Econs. Assn., Am. Econ. Assn., Latin Am. Studies Assn., Council Internat. Exchange Scholars (chmn. com. econs. selection 1979-80), Inter-Am. Found. (selection bd.), Phi Kappa Phi, Alpha Zeta, Sigma Delta Chi. Unitarian. Author: Chile's Experiments in Agrarian Reform, 1966; Reforma agraria en Chile: experimentos en cuatro fundos de la iglesia, 1968; contbr. articles to profl. publs. Office: Land Tenure Center U Wis 310 King Hall Madison WI 53706

THIESSEN, CORNIE R., state senator; b. Mountain Lake, Minn., July 7, 1910; s. David and Aganetha (Holzrichter) T.; A.B., N.W. Nazarene Coll., Nampa, Idaho, 1936; M.A., So. Bapt. Coll., Louisville, and Pasadena (Calif.) Coll., 1940; m. Ailee Elizabeth Buck, Nov. 25, 1938; children—Corlea (dec.), Anita Sue Thiessen Toavs, James E. Owner, operator Thiessen Angus Ranch, Lambert, Mont., 1944—; pres. Mid Rivers Telephone Coop., 1952-57, Basin Electric Power Coop., Bismarck, N.D., 1976—; mem. Mont. Senate form 27th Dist., 1959—, sec. legis. audit, 1969, chmn. fin. and claims com., 1961, pres., 1977-79; pres. Lower Yellowstone REA, 1945; mem. Richland County Soil and Water Conservation Dist., 1946-56, Upper Mo. Generation and Transmission Bd., 1957—, Com. on Western Regional Energy Policy, 1976—; adv. com. Rural Telephone Adminstrn., 1954-56; pres. Mont. Telephone Assn., 1954-57, Nat. Telephone Assn., 1954-57. Bd. dirs. Community Meml. Hosp., 1948-66, St. Paul Bible Coll., 1952-66, Richland Home, 1958-68, Christian Missionary Alliance, 1961-67, 69-75; v.p. Alliance Men Internat., 1967-69. Mem. Western Fuels Assn. (v.p., dir. 1978—). Democrat. Club: Toastmasters. Address: Box 195 Lambert MT 59243. *Early in Life established these priorities: First among persons the LORD JESUS CHRIST, First among books the BIBLE, First among institutions the CHRISTIAN CHURCH, First among days the LORD'S DAY, First among dollars the LORD'S TITHE.*

THIESSEN, DELBERT DUANE, psychologist; b. Julesberg, Colo., Aug. 13, 1932; s. David and Eva Peters (Wetherby) T.; B.A. in Psychology with great distinction, San Jose (Calif.) State Coll., 1958; Ph.D., U. Calif., Berkeley, 1963; children—Trevor, Theron, Kendell Courtney. Extension instr. U. Calif., La Jolla, fall 1964; asst. sect. med. psychology, div. psychiatry and neurology Scripps Clinic and Research Found., La Jolla, 1962-65; mem. faculty U. Tex., Austin, 1965—, prof. psychology, 1971—; research cons. NIMH. Served with AUS, 1952-54; Korea. Fellow USPHS, 1960-61; recipient Career Devel. award NIMH, 1967-72, grantee, 1967-78; grantee Russel Sage Found., NSF, U. Tex. Research Inst. Mem. AAAS, Alumni Assn. Roscoe B. Jackson Meml. Lab., Am. Psychol. Assn., Am. Genetic Assn., Psychonomic Soc., Animal Behavior Soc., Southwestern Psychol. Assn., Behavior Genetics Assn., Sigma Xi, Phi Kappa Phi, Psi Chi. Author: Gene Organization and Behavior, 1972, The Evolution and Biochemistry of Aggression, 1976; also articles, chpts. in books. Home: 7300 Barcelona Dr Austin TX 78752 Office: Mezes 330 Dept Psychology Univ Tex Austin TX 78712

THIGPEN, ALTON HILL, motor transp. co. exec.; b. Kinston, N.C., Feb. 3, 1927; s. Kirby Alton and Alice (Hill) T.; B.S. in Indsl. Engring., N.C. State U., 1950; m. Rebecca Ann Braswell, May 16, 1953; children-David Alton, Jennifer Ann, Steven Roy. With Asso. Transport, Inc., Burlington N.C., 1950-71, engr., 1950-57, asst. terminal mgr., Phila., 1957-58, terminal mgr., Knoxville, Tenn., 1959, regional mgr. Valley region, 1960-62, regional mgr. South region, 1962-68, v.p.-dir. So. div., 1968-71; v.p. R.S. Braswell Co. Inc., Kannapolis, 1971—; dir. First Union Nat. Bank. Bd. regents Berkshire Christian Coll., Lenox, Mass., 1975—. Served with USNR, 1945-46. Mem. Motor Carriers Va. (pres. 1967-68), N.C. Motor Carriers Assn. (dir. 1968—), Sigma Chi, Tau Beta Pi. Mem. Advent Christian Ch. Mason (32 deg.). Home: Route 4 Box 518-B Kannapolis NC 28081 Office: PO Drawer EE Kannapolis NC 28081

THIGPEN, JOSEPH JACKSON, engring. educator; b. Ruston, La., Feb. 4, 1917; s. Andrew Jackson and Myrtle (Goyne) T.; B.S. in Mech. Engring., La. Poly. Inst., 1936; B.S., U.S. Mil. Acad., 1941; M.S., U. Tex., 1951, Ph.D., 1959; m. Ruth Elizabeth Ensley, June 11, 1941; children—Joseph Jackson, Sally Elizabeth. With Seismic Explorations, Inc., 1936-37; commd. 2d lt. U.S. Army, 1941, advanced through grades to col., 1971; assigned S.W. Pacific Theatre, 1942-44, U.S. Mil. Acad., 1944-47, 51-53; resigned, 1947; mem. faculty La. Poly. Inst., Ruston, 1947-51, 53—, prof. mech. engring., head dept., 1953-75, dean Coll. Engring., 1976—; cons. Operations Research Office, Johns Hopkins, 1948-50. Alderman, Ruston, 1962-66. Fellow ASME; mem. Nat. Soc. Profl. Engrs., Am. Soc. Engring. Edn., La. Engring. Soc. (pres. 1973-74), Ruston C. of C., Am. Legion, Sigma Xi, Tau Beta Pi, Pi Tau Sigma. Baptist (chmn. deacons 1966-67). Home: 1116 Carey Ave Ruston LA 71270

THIGPEN, RICHARD ELTON, ret. lawyer; b. Wilmington, N.C., May 9, 1900; s. William W. and Katherine (Canaday) T.; A.B., Duke, 1922, postgrad. in law, 1922-23; m. Dorathy F. Dotger, June 28, 1923; children—Dorathy T. Elliot (dec.), Harriet (Mrs. Ivey W. Stewart, Jr.), Richard Elton. Alumni sec. Trinity Coll. and Duke U., 1923-29; treas. Am. Alumni Council, 1929; admitted to N.C. bar, 1925; sr. atty. U.S. Bd. Tax Appeals (now Tax Ct.), Washington, 1929-33; pvt. practice, specializing in matters of taxation, Charlotte, 1933-76; ret. founder firm Thigpen & Hines, P.A. School commr. City of Charlotte, 1939-45; rationing adminstr. Mecklenburg County, 1942. Bd. dirs., trustee Charlotte YMCA, pres., 1953-54, mem. interstate com., 1945-64, mem. nat. bd. and nat. council, 1962-68; trustee Duke, 1953-73, vice chmn., 1958-63, exec. com., 1958-63, 68-72; chmn. Duke Nat. Council, 1948-49; trustee Western N.C. Conf. Meth. Ch., 1956-66, rep. Meth. Ch. to gen. bd. Nat. Council Chs., 1960-63, mem. commn. higher edn., mem. Council on World Service and Finance, Meth. Ch., 1966-70; bd. mgrs. Meth. Home for Aged, 1958-63; chmn. Com. to Study Conf. Orgn., 1965-66. Mem. Am., N.C. (pres. 1948-49, exec. com. 1949-50), Mecklenburg bar assns., N.C. State Bar, Inc., Duke U. Alumni Assn. (pres. 1952-53), Charlotte C. of C. (dir. 1957-59), Newcomen Soc., Omicron Delta Kappa, Delta Sigma Phi, Tombs. Meth. (mem. bd. stewards, chmn. 1948, dist. lay leader 1953). Clubs: Charlotte Country (bd. govs., sec. 1950-53), Charlotte City (bd. govs., sec. 1959), Execs. (pres. 1947, dir.), Kiwanis (lt. gov. Carolinas dist. 1937, gov. 1939). Home: 735 Colville Rd Charlotte NC 28207

THIMANN, KENNETH VIVIAN, educator, biologist; b. Ashford, Eng., Aug. 5, 1904; s. Israel Phoebus and Muriel Kate (Harding) T.; student Caterham Sch., Eng., 1915-21; B.Sc., Imperial Coll. Sci. and Tech., London (Royal Coll. Sci.), 1924, A.R.C.S., 1924, Ph.D., 1928; A.M. (hon.), Harvard, 1938; Ph.D. (hon.), U. Basel (Switzerland), 1960, Clermont-Ferrand, France, 1961; m. Ann Mary Bateman, Mar. 20, 1929; children—Vivianne (Mrs. J. Nachmias), Karen (Mrs. James Romer), Linda Thimann Dewing. Came to U.S., 1930, naturalized Am. citizen. Demonstrator bacteriology King's Coll., London,

1927-29; instr. biochemistry and bacteriology Calif. Inst. Tech., Pasadena, 1930-35; lectr. botany Harvard, 1935-36, asst. prof. plant physiology, 1936-39, asso., 1939-46, prof., 1946-62, Higgins prof. biology, 1962-65, emeritus, 1965—; prof. biology U. Calif. at Santa Cruz, 1965—, provost Crown Coll., 1965-72; dir. Biol. Labs., Harvard, 1946-50, tutor in biology Eliot House, 1936-52, asso., 1952-65; master East House, Radcliffe Coll., 1962-65; exchange prof. U. Paris, 1954-55; vis. prof. U. Mass., 1974, U. Tex., 1976; pres. XI Internat. Bot. Congress, 1969, 2d Nat. Biol. Congress, 1971, Internat. Plant Growth Substance Assn. Congress, Tokyo, 1973. Bd. dirs. Found. Microbiology, Biol. Scis. Info. Services. Served as civilian scientist, USN, 1942-45. Recipient Stephen Hales prize research Am. Soc. Plant Physiologists, 1936; Guggenheim fellow, Eng., 1950-51, Italy, 1958; medallist Internat. Plant Growth Substance Assn., 1976. Fgn. mem. Royal Soc. (London), Soc. Nazionale dei Lincei (Rome), Akad. Leopoldina (Halle), Acad. Nat. de Roumanie (Bucharest), Acad. des Sci. (Paris), Bot. Soc. Netherlands, Bot. Soc. Japan; mem. Am. Soc. Biol. Chemists, Am. Philos. Soc. (council 1973-76), Am. Acad. Arts and Scis., Nat. Acad. Scis. (chmn. botany sect. 1962-65, mem. council 1967-71, exec. com. assembly life scis. 1972-76), Bot. Soc. Am. (pres. 1960), AAAS (dir. 1968-72), Am. Soc. Plant Physiologists (pres. 1950-51), Soc. Gen. Physiologists (pres. 1949-50), Biochem. Soc., Am. Soc. Naturalists (pres. 1954-55), Am. Inst. Biol. Scis. (pres. 1965), Soc. Study Devel. and Growth (pres. 1955-56). Author: (with F. W. Went) Phytohormones, 1937; The Life of Bacteria, 2d edit., 1963; The Natural Plant Hormones, 1972; Hormones in the Whole Life of Plants, 1977. Editor: (with R. S. Harris) Vitamins and Hormones (annual) Vol. 1, 1943, to Vol. 20, 1962; (with G. Pincus) The Hormones, 5 vols., 1948, 55, 63. Editorial bd. Archives of Biochemistry and Biophysics, 1949-70; Canadian Jour. Botany, 1966-73, Plant Physiology, 1974—. Contbr. numerous articles to tech. jours. Home: 36 Pasatiempo Dr Santa Cruz CA 95060 Office: Thimann Labs Univ Calif Santa Cruz CA 95064

THIMMESCH, NICHOLAS PALEN, columnist; b. Dubuque, Iowa, Nov. 13, 1927; s. Leo Nicholas and Victoria Maria (Glatzmaier) T.; B.A., Iowa State U., 1950, postgrad., 1955; m. Wynora Susan Plum, Apr. 17, 1953 (div. 1975); children—Nicholas Palen, Elizabeth, Martha, Peter, Michael. Reporter, Davenport (Iowa) Times, 1950-52, Des Moines Register, 1953-55; corr. Time Mag., 1955-67; Washington Bur. chief Newsday, 1967-69; syndicated columnist, Washington, 1969—; contbg. editor New York mag., 1976-78. Mem. Nat. Commn. for Observance of World Population Year, 1974-75; nat. adv. council St. John's U., Minn. Served with U.S. Mcht. Marines, 1945-47. Mem. H.L. Mencken Soc. Roman Catholic. Author: (with William Johnson) Robert Kennedy at 40, 1965; The Bobby Kennedy Nobody Knows, 1966; Condition of Republicanism, 1968. Home: 6301 Broad Branch Rd Chevy Chase MD 20015 Office: 1750 Pennsylvania Ave NW Washington DC 20006

THINNES, ROY, actor; b. Chgo., Apr. 6; student public schs., Chgo.; m. Lynn Loring; children—Leslie Neila, Christopher Dylan. Formerly worked as cab driver, copy boy for Chgo. Sun-Times, hotel clk., salesman; appeared off-Broadway; regular on daytime TV serial General Hospital, 1963; starred in TV series The Long, Hot Summer, 1965-66, The Invaders, 1966-68, The Psychiatrist, 1971; appeared in mini-series From Here to Eternity, 1979, numerous other TV shows; TV films include: The Other Man, 1970, Black Noon, 1971, The Horror at 37,000 Feet, 1973, Satan's School for Girls, 1973, Death Race, 1973, The Manhunter, 1976, Secrets, 1977, Code Name: Diamond Head, 1977; films include: Airport '75, The Hindenburg, Journey to the Far Side of the Sun. Served with U.S. Army. Office: care Press Dept NBC 30 Rockefeller Plaza New York NY 10020*

THIRY, PAUL, architect; b. Nome, Alaska, Sept. 11, 1904; s. Hippolyte A. and Louise Marie (Schwaebele) T.; Diploma, Ecole des Beaux Arts, Fontainebleau, France, 1927; A.B., U. Wash., 1928; D.F.A. (hon.), St. Martins Coll., 1970; D.Arts (hon.), Lewis & Clark Coll., 1979; m. Mary Thomas, Oct. 26, 1940; children—Paul Albert, Pierre, Pvt. practice architecture, 1929—; mem. Thiry & Shay, 1935-39; co-architect war work U.S. Navy Advance Base Depot, Tacoma, Fed. Pub. Housing Adminstrn. projects, community centers and appurtenances, Port Orchard, Wash., 1940-44; practice in Salt Lake City, Alaska, Seattle, 1945—; pres. Thiry Architects, Inc., 1971—; architect in residence Am. Acad. in Rome, 1969; works include coll. bldgs., chs., museums, and govt. projects; also designer fabrics, carpets, furniture. Commnr., City of Seattle Planning Commn., 1952-61, chmn. 1953-54, rep. on exec. bd. Puget Sound Regional Planning Council, 1954-57, chmn. Central Bus. Dist. Study, 1957-60; mem. exec. com. Wash. State Hosp. Adv. Council, 1953-57; architect in charge Century 21 Expn., Seattle, 1957-62; mem. Dept. Interior Historic Am. Bldg. Survey Bd., 1956-61, vice chmn., 1958-61; mem. Joint Com. Nat. Capital, 1961, exec. bd., 1962-72; mem. President's Council Redevel. Pennsylvania Av., Washington, 1962-65; cons. FHA, 1963-67; cons. architect Nat. Capitol, 1964—; mem. Nat. Capital Planning Commn., 1963-75, vice chmn., 1972-75; mem. arts and archtl. com. J. F. Kennedy Meml. Library, 1964; mem. Postmaster Gen.'s Council Research and Engring., 1968-70. Decorated officier d'Academie with palms (France); recipient Paul Bunyan award Seattle C. of C., 1949, Outstanding Architect-Engr. award Am. Mil. Engrs., 1977; named Distinguished Citizen in the Arts, Seattle, 1962; named Constrn. Man of Year, 1963. Academician N.A.D. Fellow A.I.A. (pres. Wash. chpt. 1951-53, preservation officer 1952-62, chancellor coll. fellows 1962-64, chmn. com. nat. capital 1960-64, chmn. com. hon. fellowships 1962-64); mem. Nat. Sculpture Soc. (hon., Herbert Adams Meml. medal 1974, Henry Hering medal 1976) Am. Inst. Planners (exec. bd. Pacific N.W. chpt. 1949-52, hon. life), Am. Planning Assn. (hon. life), Soc. Archtl. Historians (life mem., dir. 1967-70), Nat. Trust Historic Preservation, Am. Inst. Interior Designers (hon.), Liturgical Conf. (life), Seattle Art Mus. (life), Seattle Hist. Soc. (hon. life), Oreg. Cavemen (hon.), Delta Upsilon, Tau Sigma Delta, Scarab (hon.). Clubs: Cosmos (Washington); Century (N.Y.C.); Architectural League N.Y. Author: Churches and Temples (with Richard Bennett and Henry Kamphoefner, 1953; (with Mary Thiry) Eskimo Artifacts Designed for Use, 1978. Contbr. articles to profl. jours. Projects exhibited and illustrated in books and periodicals. Prin. works include: Am. Embassy residence, Santiago, Chile (awarded Diploma Clegio de Arquitectos de Chile 1965); comprehensive plan Seattle Center (awarded A.I.A. citation for excellence in community architecture 1966); Seattle Coliseum (A.I.S.I. awards for design and engring. 1965, A.I.S.C. award of excellence 1965); Washington State Library (AIA-ALA award, 1964); U.S. 4th Inf. (Ivy) Div. Monument, Utah Beach, France, 1969); cons. Libby Dam Project, Mont.; architect for Powerhouse, Visitors Center (C.E. distinguished design award 1970, certificate of appreciation 1974); cons. New Melones Dam/Reservoir Project, Calif., 1972, Reregulating dam and powerhouse, Libby, Mass., 1977—, others. Home: 1017 E Blaine St Seattle WA 98102 Office: 800 Columbia St Seattle WA 98104

THOBURN, DAVID MILLS, ship building co. exec.; b. Cleve., Jan. 31, 1930; s. Theodore and Frances (Goff) T.; B.A., Allegheny Coll., Meadville, Pa., 1951; children—David Mills, Mark Vines. With Cleve. Trust Co., 1954—, asst. v.p., 1965-67, v.p., 1967-69, sr. v.p., 1969-78; exec. v.p. Am. Ship Building Co., 1978—, also dir.; dir. AAV Cos., Gray Drug Stores, Inc., Bowden Mfg. Co. Mem. civic adv. bd. Cystic Fibrosis Found., Greater Cleve. Growth Corp., Soc. Crippled Children. Served with U.S. Army, 1951-54. Mem. S.A.R., Phi Gamma Delta. Clubs: Kirtland Country (Willoughby, Ohio); Mid-Day, Cleve. Athletic, Union (Cleve.). Home: 21210 Colby Rd Shaker Heights OH 44122 Office: 911 Bond Ct Bldg Cleveland OH 44114

THODE, HENRY GEORGE, scientist, educator; b. Dundurn, Sask., Can., Sept. 10, 1910; s. Charles Herman and Zelma Ann (Jacoby) T.; B.Sc., U. Sask., 1930, M.Sc., 1932, LL.D., 1958; Ph.D., U. Chgo., 1934; D.Sc. (hon.), U. Toronto, 1955, U. B.C., 1960, Acadia U., 1960, Laval U., 1963, Royal Mil. Coll. Can., 1964, McGill U., 1966, Queen's U., 1967, York U., 1972, McMaster U., 1973; m. Sadie Alicia Patrick, Feb. 1, 1935; children—John Charles, Henry Patrick, Richard Lee. Research asst. chemistry Columbia, 1936-38; research chemist U.S. Rubber Co., Passaic, N.J., 1938-39; asst. prof. chemistry McMaster U., 1939-42, asso. prof. chemistry, 1942-44, prof. chemistry, 1944-79, prof. emeritus, 1979—, head dept. chemistry, 1948-52, dir. research, 1947-61, prin. Hamilton Coll., 1949-63, v.p., 1957-61, pres. and vice chancellor, 1961-72. Research asso. atomic energy project NRC, 1943-46; Sr. Fgn. Scientist fellow NSF, 1970; mem. commn. on atomic weights Internat. Union Pure and Applied Chemistry, 1963-79, mem. Can. nat. com. to internat. union, 1975-79; dir. Atomic Energy Can. Ltd., Steel Co. Can. Ltd. Bd. govs. Ont. Research Found., 1956—; bd. dirs. Western N.Y. Nuclear Research Centre, 1965-72, Royal Bot. Gardens, 1961-72. Decorated mem. Order Brit. Empire, companion Order Can.; recipient medal Chem. Inst. Can., 1957. Shell Can. merit fellow, 1974. Fellow Royal Soc. Can. (pres. 1959-60, Tory medal 1959), Chem. Inst. Can. (hon.; pres. 1951-52), Royal Soc. (London). Mem. editorial adv. bd. Jour. Inorganic and Nuclear Chemistry, 1954—, Earth and Planetary Sci. Letters, 1965—. Contbr. numerous articles in field. Office: Nuclear Research Bldg McMaster Univ 1280 Main St W Hamilton ON L8S 4K1 Canada

THODOS, GEORGE, educator; b. Chgo., Sept. 15, 1915; s. John and Florence (Karavites) T.; B.S. in Chem. Engring., Armour Inst. Tech., 1938, M.S., 1939; Ph.D., U. Wis., 1943; m. Lena K. Natsis, Dec. 29, 1957; children—Jason, Diane and Melissa (twins), Anna-Maria, Christina. With Standard Oil Co. (Ind.), 1939-40, Phillips Petroleum Co., 1940-41, 43-46, Pure Oil Co., 1946-47; faculty Northwestern U., Evanston, Ill., 1947—, chmn. dept. chem. engring., 1960-64, Walter P. Murphy prof. chem. engring., 1963—; cons. U.S. Navy, Office Naval Research, Pure Oil Co., Chgo. Bridge and Iron Co. Mem. distinguished appointment bd. Argonne Univs. Assn., 1975; mem. Ill. Exam. Com. Profl. Engring. Registration, 1955-60; spl. research heat, mass and momentum transfer, transport properties, pressure volume temperature relations, vapor pressures, critical constants pure components and mixtures, vapor-liquid equilibrium constants, hydrodesulphurization of coal, utilization of solar energy for thermal energy generation, removal of particulates from atmospheric air, regeneration of sulphated dolomite. Fellow Am. Inst. Chem. Engrs.; mem. Am. Chem. Soc. (adv. bd. applied publs. and news service 1959-62), Sigma Xi, Tau Beta Pi, Phi Lambda Upsilon, Pi Mu Epsilon. Home: 2668 Orrington Ave Evanston IL 60201 Office: Chem Engring Dept Northwestern U Evanston IL 60201

THOM, JOSEPH M., librarian; b. Bronx, N.Y., Oct. 22, 1919; s. Harry and Jennie Thom; B.A., N.Y.U., 1948, M.A., 1949; M.S. in L.S., Columbia, 1950; postgrad. Washington U., St. Louis, 1951-53, Ohio U., 1958-59; m. Lillian Rosenstein, Sept. 1, 1945; children—Janice Eleanor, Eric Frederick. Library asst. N.Y.U., 1940-42, 46-49; library fellow Bklyn. Coll., 1949-50; chief reference dept. Washington U., 1950-53, instr. librarianship, 1950-54; dir. Research Information Service of St. Louis, 1954-55; supr. records and library Goodyear Atomic Corp., 1955-60; dir. libraries Yeshiva U., 1960; now librarian Port Jefferson (N.Y.) Schs.; library and multi-media cons. on design and services. Served with AUS, 1942-45. Mem. A.L.A., Spl. Libraries Assn., Suffolk Sch. Library Media Assn., N.Y. Library Assn. Editor: Reference Sources in Education, 1953; Personnel Notes and News. Compiler: Reference Sources in Politcal Science, 1953. Contbr. articles to profl. jours. Home: Setauket NY 11733 Office: Port Jefferson Schs Port Jefferson NY 11777

THOMAS, ADEEB ELIAS, dentist, educator; b. Lawrence, Mass., Sept. 16, 1923; s. Elias Ayoub and Edna (Abraham) T.; grad. Boston Latin Sch., 1940; D.M.D., Tufts Coll., 1945; M.S., U. Ala., 1964; m. Frances Anne Pharo, Dec. 29, 1952; 1 son, Adeeb Elias Jr. Externship oral surgery Capt. John Andrews Hosp., Boston, 1943-45; pvt. practice dentistry, Scituate, Mass., 1947-52; instr. clin. dentistry Tufts Coll. Dental Sch., 1947-52; prof. dentistry, chmn. dept. operative dentistry and endodontics U. Ala. Sch. Dentistry, 1952-68; cons. endodontics VA Hosp., Tuskegee and Birmingham, Ala., Am. Dental Assn. Jour. Chmn., Teenagers March, Birmingham, 1970—. Bd. govs. St. Jude Children's Research Hosp., also mem. exec. mgmt. bd. Served with USNR, 1945-47. Diplomate Am. Bd. Endodontics; Fellow Am. Assn. Endodontists; mem. Am., Ala. dental assns., Am. Assn. Endodontists, Internat. Assn. for Dental Research, Sigma Xi, Omicron Kappa Upsilon. Roman Catholic. Contbr. articles to dental jours., also chpts. to dental textbooks. Research on efficacy of therapeutic dentifrices in preventing dental decay in children, cavity preparation design. Home: 1316 Wickford Rd Birmingham AL 35216. *Honesty in all endeavors may be distasteful, distressing and at times somewhat tactless. However, every achievement throughout life remains untarnished by hypocrisy or deceit.*

THOMAS, ALEXANDER, psychiatrist; b. N.Y.C., Jan. 11, 1914; s. Herman and Rose Thomas; B.S. magna cum laude, Coll. City N.Y., 1932; M.D., N.Y. U., 1936; m. Stella Chess, June 28, 1938; children—Joan, Richard, Leonard, Kenneth. Intern, Mt. Sinai Hosp., N.Y.C., 1936-39; resident Bellevue Hosp., N.Y.C., 1946-48; dir. psychiat. div. Bellevue Hosp., 1968-78; attending psychiatrist U. Hosp., 1966—; prof. psychiatry N.Y. U. Med. Center, 1966—; prin. investigator longitudinal study child devel., 1960—. Served to capt. USAAF, 1942-46,. Diplomate Am. Bd. Psychiatry, 1948. Fellow Am. Psychiat. Assn. (pres. N.Y. dist. br. 1973); mem. Phi Beta Kappa, Sigma Xi, Alpha Omega Alpha. Author: (with others) Behavioral Individuality in Early Childhood, 1963; (with others) Your Child is a Person, 1965; Temperament and Behavior Disorders in Children; Racism and Psychiatry, 1972; Temperament and Development, 1977; contbr. articles to profl. jours. Home: 10 Mitchell Pl New York NY 10017 Office: 333 E 49th St New York NY 10017

THOMAS, ANDREW JOHNSTON, lawyer; b. Birmingham, Ala., Sept. 1, 1897; s. John Marion and Lola (Johnston) T.; A.B., U. Richmond, 1918; LL.B., U. Ala., 1920, Columbia, 1922. Admitted to Ala. bar, 1920; practiced in Birmingham, 1922—; mem. Thomas, Taliaferro, Forman, Burr & Murray. Mem. adv. bd. Cumberland Sch. Law, Samford U. Pres. Birmingham YMCA, 1957-61. Served from capt. to maj., USAAF, 1942-45. Mem. Am., Ala., Birmingham (pres. 1934-35) bar assns., Am. Coll. Trial Lawyers, Am. Judicature Soc., Am. Legion, Phi Delta Phi, Phi Gamma Delta. Democrat. Baptist. Clubs: Exchange (pres. Birmingham 1937-38, pres. Ala. 1940-41, nat. regional v.p. 1941-42), Redstone (pres. 1932-33), Birmingham Country (Birmingham). Home: 3112 Pine Ridge Rd Mountain Brook Birmingham AL 35213 Office: Bank for Savs Bldg Birmingham AL 35203

THOMAS, ANN VAN WYNEN, lawyer; b. The Netherlands, May 27, 1919; d. Cornelius and Cora Jacoba (Daansen) Van Wynen; brought to U.S., 1921, naturalized, 1926; A.B. with distinction, U. Rochester, 1940; J.D., U. Tex., 1943; LL.M., So. Meth. U., 1952; m. A. J. Thomas, Jr., Sept. 20, 1948. U.S. fgn. service officer, Johannesburg, London, The Hague, 1943-47; research atty., Southwestern Legal Found., So. Meth. U. Sch. Law, Dallas, 1952-67, asst. prof. polit. sci., 1968-73, asso. prof., 1973-76, prof., 1976—. Mem. Tex. Bar Assn., Am. Soc. Internat. Law, London Inst. World Affairs. Author: Communist versus International Law, 1953; (with husband) International Treaties, 1950; Non-Intervention—The Law and its Import in the Americas, 1956; OAS: The Organization of American States, 1962; (with husband) International Legal Aspects of Civil War in Spain, 1936-1939, 1967; (with husband) Legal Limitations on Chemical and Biological Weapons, 1970; (with husband) The Concept of Aggression, 1972; An International Rule of Law—Problems and Prospects, 1974. Home: Spaniel Hall Pottsboro TX 75076

THOMAS, ARTHUR LAWRENCE, educator; b. Ithaca, N.Y., Sept. 11, 1931; s. Charles Kenneth and Carolyn Newcomb (Pomeroy) T.; B.A., Cornell U., 1952, M.B.A., 1956; Ph.D., U. Mich., 1963; m. Mary Eliza Taylor, Aug. 16, 1958; children—Robin Catherine, Susan Margaret, Stephen James. Prof. acctg. U. Oreg., Eugene, 1968-69, McMaster U., Hamilton, Ont., Can., 1969-76; Harmon Whittington prof. Rice U., Houston, 1977—. Served with USAF, 1952-54. Grantee, Am. Acctg. Assn., 1973, Clarkson, Gordon Found., 1976, Internat. Centre for Research in Acctg./Arthur Andersen & Co., 1977, Peat, Marwick, Mitchell Found., 1978; C.P.A., N.Y. Mem. Am. Inst. C.P.A.'s, Acctg. Researchers Internat. Assn., Am. Acctg. Assn. Author 5 books on acctg.; contbr. articles to profl. jours. Home: 2324 McClendon Houston TX 77030 Office: Grad Sch Adminstrn Rice U Houston TX 77001

THOMAS, B(ILLY) J(OE), singer; b. Houston, Aug. 7, 1942. Played with group The Triumphs, later B.J. Thomas and the Triumphs; solo rec. artist for Scepter Records, from 1966; concert artist; singles recorded: I'm So Lonesome I Could Cry, Mama, Billy & Sue, Bring Back the Time, Tomorrow Never Comes, I Can't Believe It, The Eyes of a New York Woman, Hooked on a Feeling, It's Only Love, Pass the Apple, Eve, Raindrops Keep Fallin' On My Head, I Just Can't Help Believing, Everybody's Out of Town, Most of All, No Love At All, Mighty Clouds of Joy, Long Ago Tomorrow, Rock & Roll Lullabye, That's What Friends Are For, Happier Than the Morning, Another Somebody Done Something Wrong Song, Help Me Make It, Don't Worry Baby, Still the Lovin' Is Fun, Everybody Loves a Rain Song; album: Raindrops Keep Fallin' On My Head. Named Top Male Vocalist of Year, Record World, 1970; awarded Gold Record, Rec. Industry Assn. Am., 1971; recipient Grammy award, 1978. Office: care Don Perry Prodns PO Box 1569 Fayetteville NC 28302*

THOMAS, BERT LESTER, supermarket chain exec.; b. Malad, Idaho, Feb. 27, 1918; s. Henry E. and Pearl (Ward) T.; B.S. in Bus. Adminstrn., Utah State U., 1939, D. Bus. (hon.), 1977; m. Barbara Palmer, Apr. 30, 1941; children—Bert L., Val, Scott. Auditor, Standard Stas., Los Angeles, 1939-41; with Winn-Dixie Stores, Inc., Jacksonville, Fla., 1946—, v.p., 1952-65, pres., 1965—, chmn. exec. com., 1976—, also dir.; dir. Barnett Banks of Fla. Trustee Jacksonville U. Served to maj. Q.M.C., U.S. Army, 1941-46. Mem. Food Mktg. Inst. (vice chmn. pub. and legis. affairs). Mormon. Clubs: River, San Jose Country (Jacksonville); Masons, Shriners, Jesters. Office: Winn-Dixie Stores Inc 5050 Edgewood Ct Jacksonville FL 32203*

THOMAS, BETH EILEEN WOOD (MRS. RAYMOND O. THOMAS), editor; b. North Vernon, Ind., May 12, 1916; d. Fayette J. and Emma J. (Ream) Wood; grad. Bedford High Sch., 1934; comml. diploma Lockyear Bus. Coll., 1936; m. Raymond O. Thomas, Feb. 28, 1941; 1 son, Stephen W. Sec., WPA, Vincennes, Ind., 1935-36, Evansville, Ind., 1937-38, Indpls., 1939-41; sec. to adj. AAF Storage Depot, Indpls., 1941-44; sec. Coll. Life Ins., Indpls., 1957-58, Indpls. Sch. Bd., 1958-59; classified office mgr., North Side Topics Newspaper, Indpls., 1960-67; editor Child Life Mag., Indpls., 1967-71, Brownie Reader, 1971-73, Children's Playmate mag., Indpls., 1968—; editorial asso. Saturday Evening Post, Indpls., 1971; exec. editorial dir. Jack and Jill mag., 1971—, Young World mag., 1971-79, Child Life mag., 1971—, Design mag., 1977—, Turle Mag. for Presch. Kids, 1979—. Mem. Women in Communications, Indpls. Press Club. Club: Thetis. Home: 6172 Compton B Indianapolis IN 46220 Office: 1100 Waterway Blvd Indianapolis IN 46202

THOMAS, BLAKEMORE EWING, educator, geologist; b. Okmulgee, Okla., Nov. 6, 1917; s. Frederick Trent and Louisa (Ewing) T.; A.B., U. Cal. at Berkeley, 1940; M.S., Calif. Inst. Tech., 1943, Ph.D., 1949; m. Carolyn Taufenbach, Mar. 2, 1945 (div. 1968); children—Leslie, Blakemore Thomas II, Kathryn; m. 2d, Lorraine Furrer, Dec. 21, 1968. Instr. meteorology Calif. Inst. Tech., Pasadena, 1943-44; asst. prof. geology U. Kans., Lawrence, 1949-51; with firm William Ross Cabeen & Assos., Cons. Geologists and Engrs., North Hollywood, Calif., 1951-56; asst. prof. geology San Diego State U., 1956-59, asso. prof, 1959-62, prof., 1962—, chmn. dept. geology, 1961-67. Dir. New Camp Minerals, Inc., Wichita, Kans. Geol. cons. to industry, Dept. Navy, Dept. Justice, Dept. Army-C.E.; mem. nat. potential gas com. Colo. Sch. Mines Found., 1967-76; mem. Calif. Exam. Com. for Profl. Registration in Geology, 1971; Served to capt. USAAF, 1942-46. Fellow Geol. Soc. Am.; mem. Am. Inst. Mining, Metall. and Petroleum Engrs., Am. Assn. Petroleum Geologists, Phi Beta Kappa, Sigma Xi, Theta Tau. Contbr. vols. on geology. Address: 2316 Calle Colibri Santa Fe NM 87501

THOMAS, BROOKS, pub. co. exec.; b. Phila., Nov. 28, 1931; s. Walter Horstman and Ruth Sterling (Boomer) T.; B.A., Yale, 1953, LL.B., 1956; grad. Advanced Mgmt. Program, Harvard, 1973; m. Galen Pinckard Clark, Apr. 15, 1969 (div. 1973). Admitted to Pa. bar, 1957, N.Y. bar, 1960; with law firm Winthrop, Stimson, Putnam & Roberts, N.Y.C., 1960-68; sec., gen. counsel Harper & Row, Pubs., Inc., N.Y.C., 1968-69, v.p., gen. counsel, 1969-73, exec. v.p., 1973-79, chief operating officer, 1977—, pres., 1979—, also dir.; chmn. bd. Harper & Row, Ltd., London, 1973—; dir. Harper & Row, Pty. Ltd., Australia, Harla S.A. de C.V., Mex., Harper & Row do Brasil Ltda., Sao Paulo, PM Life Ins. Co. (N.Y.). Pres., bd. dirs. Butterfield House, 1968-72; bd. dirs. Young Audiences, Inc., 1977—. Served to lt. (j.g.) USNR, 1956-59. Mem. Am. Bar Assn., Assn. Bar City of N.Y., Assn. Am. Pubs. Clubs: Merion Cricket (Phila.); Yale, University, N.Y. Yacht (N.Y.C.). Home: 37 W 12th St New York NY 10011 also Essex CT 06426 Office: 10 E 53d St New York NY 10022

THOMAS, BRUCE WALLACE, librarian; b. Ravenna, Ohio, Nov. 25, 1918; s. William Jones and Jessie Martha (Wilson) T.; B.A., Hiram Coll., 1944; M.A., Western Res. U., 1945, M.L.S., 1949; Ph.D., Ohio State U., 1970; m. Janet Lee Sheldon, Feb. 4, 1945; children—Dirk Sheldon, Stefany, Ethan Wilson. Editor, World Pub. Co., Cleve., 1944-47; reference librarian Antioch Coll., Yellow Springs, Ohio, 1949-56, asst. librarian, 1956-61, asso. librarian, 1961-65, librarian, 1965—; mem. Ohio adv. bd. Library Services Constrn. Act, 1966-67. Mem. Ohio Coll. Assn. (pres. library div. 1967-68). Democrat. Asst. editor Websters New World Dictionary of the American Language, 1951; contbr. articles to profl. jours. Home: 106 Tower Ct Yellow

Springs OH 45387 Office: Antioch Coll Library Yellow Springs OH 45387

THOMAS, BYRON, painter; b. Balt., 1902; ed. Md. Inst. Art, Martinet Sch. Art (both Balt.), Art Students League, N.Y.C.; Tiffany Found. fellow; later studied in Europe; m. Ivy Bacon, 1950; children—Murray, Richard, Mary Elizabeth. Tchr. painting Cooper Union, N.Y.C., 1931-50; war artist Life mag., Europe, 1943-44; later life artist in Germany, Poland, France, Spain; exhibited numerous one-man shows, group shows U.S. and abroad; represented in permanent collections Mus. Modern Art (Pastime Bowling Alley 1939), Pa. Acad. Fine Arts (Pine Trees 1946), Springfield (Mo.) Art Mus. (Maples 1929), U.S. Dept. Army, Washington, also numerous pvt. collections. Recipient many prizes and awards. Clubs: Century (N.Y.C.); Woodstock (Vt.) Country. Address: 48 Elm St Woodstock VT 05091. *To seek style and originality in my painting, I have looked to discover in nature what has not been seen by anyone else. Time is the only criterion that may determine if I have succeeded in my task.*

THOMAS, C. DEAN, mfg. co. exec.; b. Golden, Ill., Apr. 19, 1920; s. Arch and Anna Mae (Sharrow) T.; B.S., Carthage Coll., 1948; postgrad. in labor and indsl. relations U. Ill.; m. Dorothy Adams, Mar. 10, 1944; children—Carlton Dean, Patricia Ann, Suellen Jane. With Moorman Mfg. Co., Quincy, Ill., 1949—, v.p. sales, to 1975, exec. v.p. mktg. and distbn., 1975—; dir. Quincy Soybean Co. Indsl. chmn. United Way, 1970, gen. chmn., 1971, also bd. dirs.; trustee Blessing Hosp., 1973—, also pres. bd. trustees. Mem. Sales and Mktg. Execs. (past pres. chpt.). Republican. Clubs: Circle K, Masons, Shriners, Spring Lake Country (past pres., dir. 1978—). Home: 18 Springlake Country Club Quincy IL 62301 Office: 1000 N 30th Quincy IL 62301

THOMAS, CALVERT, lawyer; b. Balt., Nov. 1, 1916; s. William Douglas Nelson and Elizabeth Steuart (Calvert) T.; B.S., Washington and Lee U., 1938; LL.B., U. Md., 1940; m. Margaret Somervell Berry, Sept. 1, 1943; children—Calvert Bowie, Carolyn Brooke Dold. Douglas Mackubin. Admitted to Md. bar, 1940, D.C. bar, 1972, Mich. bar, 1947, N.Y. State bar, 1974; asso. atty. Legal Aid Bur., Balt., 1940-41; atty. Lehmeyer & Moser, Balt., 1941-42; atty. Solicitor's Office, Dept. Labor, Washington, 1942-43; atty. Tax Ct. of U.S., Washington, 1943-44; atty. Chief Counsel's Office, Bur. Internal Revenue, Washington, 1944-46; atty. legal staff Gen. Motors Corp., Detroit, 1946-72, asst. gen. counsel, 1972-78, sec., asst. gen. counsel in charge N.Y. legal staff, N.Y.C., 1973-78; pres. Thomas Cadillac, Inc., 1978—. Councilman, Franklin Village, Mich., 1958-60, pres., 1960-64. Bd. dirs. Franklin Community Assn., 1956-58; vice chmn. Kingswood Sch., Cranbrook, 1968-69, chmn., 1969-71; trustee Cranbrook Schs., 1971-73, Washington and Lee U., 1975—. Mem. Am., Fed., Detroit, Md., N.Y. bar assns., State Bar Mich. (chmn. tax sect. 1971-72), Am. Soc. Corp. Secs., So. Md. Soc., Beta Theta Pi, Phi Delta Phi, Omicron Delta Kappa. Republican. Episcopalian. Clubs: Orchard Lake (Mich.) Country; Recess (Detroit); Princeton (N.Y.C.). Home: 138 Stoner Dr West Hartford CT 06107 Office: 1530 Albany Ave Hartford CT 06101

THOMAS, CARL HENRY, educator; b. Holly Hill, S.C., Apr. 4, 1925; s. Eugene David and Maybelle Marian (Myers) T.; B.S., Clemson U., 1950; M.S., La. State U., 1957; Ph.D., Mich. State U., 1969; m. Christine Isabel Flint, Feb. 28, 1952; children—Michael Dale, Daniel Lanair, Steven Bryan, Jill Patricia. Salesman, Internat. Harvester dealer, Camden, S.C., 1950; research asso., asst. agrl. engr., asst. prof., asso. prof., prof. and head agrl. engring. dept. La. State U., Baton Rouge, 1950—; mem. staff Dept. Agr., Washington, 1976-77. Scoutmaster, Istrouma council Boy Scouts Am., 1970-71. Served with USMCR, 1944-46. NSF fellow, 1965. Mem. Am. Soc. Agrl. Engrs., La. Engring. Soc. (sec.-treas., v.p., pres.), Am. Soc. Engring. Edn., Nat. Soc. Profl. Engrs., Alpha Zeta, Gamma Sigma Delta, Phi Kappa Phi, Omicron Delta Kappa. Home: 5845 Hyacinth St Baton Rouge LA 70808

THOMAS, CHARLES ALLEN, ret. chem. co. exec.; b. Scott County, Ky., Feb. 15, 1900; s. Charles Allen and Frances (Carrick) T.; A.B., Transylvania Coll., 1920, D.Sc., 1933; M.S., Mass. Inst. Tech., 1924; LL.D., Hobart Coll., 1950; D.Sc., Washington U., St. Louis, 1947, Kenyon Coll., 1952, Princeton, 1953, Ohio Wesleyan U., 1953, Brown U., 1956, Bklyn. Poly. Inst., 1957, U. Ala., 1958, St. Louis U., 1965, Simpson Coll., 1967; Engring., U. Mo., 1965; LL.D., Lehigh U., 1960, Westminster Coll., 1968; m. Margaret Stoddard Talbott, Sept. 25, 1926; children—Charles, Margaret (Mrs. James A. Walsh), Frances (Mrs. T.R. Martin), Katharine (Mrs. Stephen E. O'Neil). Research chemist Gen. Motors Research Corp., 1923-24, Ethyl Gasoline Corp., 1924-25; pres. Thomas & Hochwalt Labs., 1926-36; v.p., tech. dir., mem. exec. com. Monsanto Co., 1945, exec. v.p., 1947-51, pres., 1951-60, chmn. bd., 1960-65; dir. St. Louis Union Trust Co. Dep. chief NDRC, 1942-43, sect. mem., 1943—; mem. Manhattan project, in charge Clinton Labs., Oak Ridge; mem. sci. panel U.S. Rep. to UN AEC; apptd. chmn. sci. manpower adv. com. NSRB, 1950, mem. sci. adv. com. ODM, 1951; cons. Nat. Security Council, 1953. Formerly chmn. bd. trustees Washington U.; mem. corp. Mass. Inst. Tech.; curator Transylvania U.; mem. adv. bd. St. Louis council Boy Scouts Am. Recipient Medal for Merit by Pres. Truman, 1946, Gold medal Am. Inst. Chemists, 1948, Mo. Honor award for Distinguished Service in Engring., 1952, Perkin medal Am. sect. Soc. Chem. Industry, 1953, Order of Leopold, 1962, Palladium medal Am. sect. Soc. de Chimie Industrielle, 1963; named Globe Democrat Man of Year award, 1966. Fellow A.A.A.S., Am. Acad. Arts and Scis.; mem. Nat. Acad. Engring., Am. Chem. Soc. (dir., mem. bd. editors 1937-38, pres. 1948, chmn. bd. dirs., 1950-53, recipient Priestley Medal 1955), Nat. Acad. Sci., Am. Philos. Soc., Am. Inst. Chem. Engrs., Am. Inst. Chemists, Chem. Soc. London, Soc. Chem. Industries, Phi Beta Kappa, Sigma Xi, Alpha Chi Sigma. Clubs: Chemists, Links (N.Y.C., D.C.); Cosmos (Washington); Log Cabin, St. Louis Country (St. Louis). Patentee in field. Home: 609 South Warson Road St Louis MO 63124 Office: 7701 Forsyth Blvd St Louis MO 63105

THOMAS, CHARLES ALLEN, JR., molecular biologist, educator; b. Dayton, Ohio, July 7, 1927; s. Charles Allen and Margaret (Talbott) T.; A.B., Princeton, 1950; Ph.D., Harvard, 1954; m. Margaret M. Gay, July 7, 1951; children—Linda Carrick, Stephen Gay. Rsearch scientist Eli Lilly Co., Indpls., 1954-55; NRC fellow U. Mich., 1955-56, instr. physics, 1956-57; prof. biophysics Johns Hopkins, 1957-67; prof. biol. chemistry Harvard Med. Sch., 1967-77; chmn. dept. cellular biology Research Found., Scripps Clinic, La Jolla, Calif., 1977—; mem. genetics study sect. NIH, 1968-72; mem. research grants com. Am. Cancer Soc., 1972-76, 79—. Served with USNR, 1945-46. Mem. Am. Acad. Arts and Scis., Am. Fedn. Biol. Chemists, Genetics Soc. Am., Am. Chem. Soc. Mem. editorial bd. Virology, 1967-73, Jour. Molecular Biology, 1968-72, Biophys. Jour., 1965-68, Chromosoma, 1969-79, Analytic Biochemistry, 1970-79, Biochim Biophys Acta, 1973-79. Research on genetic and structural orgn. of chromosomes. Home: 1640 El Paso Real La Jolla CA 92037 Office: 10666 N Torrey Pines Rd La Jolla CA 92037

THOMAS, CHARLES COLUMBUS, educator; b. McAlester, Okla., Sept. 10, 1940; s. Claude Morris and Wilhelmina Rebecca (Threat) T.; B.A. in Music, Langston (Okla.) U., 1962; teaching credentials San Francisco State Coll., 1964; M.F.A. in Theatre, Bklyn. Coll., 1972; postgrad. Coll. City N.Y., 1973. Asst. prof. ethnic studies Richmond Coll., City U. N.Y., S.I., 1970—, dir. African Am. Inst., 1972-73. Vis. prof. U. Ghana, Accra, 1972; adj. asst. prof. N.Y.C. Community Coll., 1972-74; artistic dir. Afro-Am. Folkloric Troupe, San Francisco and N.Y.C., 1963-70; artistic dir. Egbe Omo Nago Folkloric Ensemble, N.Y.C., 1967-69; dancer Chuck Davis Dance Co., N.Y.C., 1970-72; cons. N.Y. State Council on the Arts, 1968-70. Cons. Mayor N.Y. Council Youth, Phys. Fitness, 1969; performing artist Harlem Cultural Council, 1969; dir. Big Bros.-OEO project Pub. Sch. 138, Bklyn., summer 1968; tchr.-in-charge Black-Puerto Rican cultural project Intermedite Sch. 201, Harlem, N.Y., summer 1966. Recipient Faculty Research award City U. N.Y., 1972. Mem. Screen Actors Guild, Nat. Acad. Rec. Arts and Scis., Nat. Acad. TV Arts and Scis., African Heritage Studies Assn., Omega Psi Phi, Kappa Delta Pi, Alpha Kappa Mu, Kappa Kappa Psi. Contbg. author: We Speak as Liberators-Young Black Poets, 1971; An Introduction to Poetry, 1973. Home: 1245 Park Ave Apt 11K New York City NY 10028 Office: 130 Stuyvesant Pl Staten Island NY 10301. *The fruits of true success may still be measured by one's dedication to high ideals and the principles of love and respect for fellow beings.*

THOMAS, CHARLES DAVIS, editor; b. Detroit, Dec. 20, 1928; s. Charles Richard and Nellie Clare (Davis) T.; B.A., U. Mich., 1950; m. Karin Ronnefeldt, Apr. 21, 1956; 1 son, Cord Alexander. Reporter Detroit News, 1950; reporter Life Mag., N.Y.C., 1954-57, staff corr., Los Angeles, 1957-60; photography editor Saturday Evening Post, Phila., 1961, asst. mng. editor, 1962, mng. editor, 1962-63; editor in chief Ladies' Home Jour., N.Y.C., 1964-65; pub. cons., N.Y.C., Toronto, Geneva, Switzerland, 1965-70; exec. editor Holiday Mag., N.Y.C., 1970; exec. editor Travel & Leisure Mag., N.Y.C., 1971-75; editor in chief Down East Mag., Camden, Maine, 1976—. Served with AUS, 1951-54. Editor: Moon, Man's Greatest Adventure, 1970 (Annual award Aviation Space Writers' Assn. 1971); (with Karin Ronnefeldt) People of the First Man: Life Among the Plains Indians in their Final Days of Glory, 1976. Home: 57 Megunticook Camden ME 04843

THOMAS, CHRISTOPHER YANCEY, business exec.; b. Roanoke, Va., Jan. 5, 1900; s. Frank Watkins and Elizabeth (Carson) T.; B.S., Purdue U., 1921, M.E., 1926; LL.B. (hon.), Baker U., 1966; m. Dorothea Louise Engel, June 12, 1922 (dec. Apr. 1977); children—Christopher Yancey, Dorothea Louise (Mrs. Joe B. Dickey, Jr.), Cora Elizabeth (Mrs. Paul R. Dring); m. 2d, Georgia Wilhelm Hall, Aug. 18, 1978. Apprentice instr. A.T. & S.F. Ry., 1921-24; supr. apprentices K.C.S. Ry., 1925-29; mech. engr. Pittsburg & Midway Coal Mining Co. (Kans.), 1930-41, chmn. bd., 1964-65; gen. mgr. Mil. Chem. Works, Pittsburg, Kans., 1941-46, Spencer Chem. Co. Kansas City, Mo., 1946-63, chmn., 1960-63; chmn. Thomas Mfg. Corp., Parkton, Md. Mayor, City of Mission Hills, 1959-63; mem. Kans. Senate from Johnson County, 1969-73. Del. Republican Nat. Conv., 1964; presdl. elector, 1972. Trustee So. Meth. U., 1956-68; chmn. bd. trustees Baker U., Baldwin, Kans., 1956-64, 66—; v.p. K.A. & H.F. Spencer Found., Kansas City, Mo. Mem. Kans. C. of C. (pres. 1965-66), Nat. Soc. Profl. Engrs., Am. Inst. Mining and Metall. Engrs., ASME, Kans. Engring. Soc., Sigma Delta Chi, Tau Beta Pi, Beta Theta Pi. Methodist. Mason (Shriner). Clubs: Univ., River, Mission Hills Country, Rotary (pres. 1963-64) (Kansas City, Mo.). Home: 5519 E Mission Dr Shawnee Mission KS 66208

THOMAS, CLAUDEWELL SIDNEY, phychiatrist; b. Bronx, N.Y., Oct. 5, 1932; s. Humphrey Sidney and Frances Elizabeth (Collins) T., A.B., Columbia U., 1952; M.D., SUNY, Downstate Med. Center, 1956; M.P.H., Yale U., 1964; m. Carolyn Pauline M. Rozansky, Sept. 6, 1958; children—Jeffrey Evan, Julie Anne Elizabeth, Jessica Edith. Intern, Flushing Hosp., Queens, N.Y., 1956-57; resident in psychiatry Bklyn. VA Hosp., 1957-59, Yale-West Haven Program 1961-62; instr. to asst. prof. Yale U., 1963-68, asso. prof., 1968-73, dir. Yale Tng. Program in Social Community Psychiatry, 1967-70; dir. div. mental health service programs NIMH, 1970-73; prof., chmn. dept. psychiatry and mental health sci. Coll. Medicine and Dentistry N.J., Newark, 1973—; prof. sociology Rutgers U., 1976—; cons. Washington Sch. Psychiatry; fellow A.K. Rice Inst., 1978—. Mem. Conn. Gov.'s Council on Children and Youth, 1968-70; mem. public policy com. N.J. Mental Health Assn., 1976—. Served with M.C., USAF, 1959-61. Fellow Am. Psychiat. Assn., Am. Public Health Assn., N.Y. Acad. Medicine, Royal Soc. Health, N.Y. Acad. Sci.; mem. Am. Sociol. Assn., Assembly of Behavioral Social Scis. of Nat. Acad. Scis., Am. Assn. Chmn. Depts. Psychiatry. Editor: (with R. Bryce LaPorte) Alienation in Contemporary Society, 1976; (with B. Bergen) Issues and Problems in Social Psychiatry, 1966; editorial bd. Adminstrn. in Mental Health, Social Psychiatry, Internat. Jour. Mental Health, Group Relations, World Jour. Psychosynthesis. Home: 346 Upper Mountain Ave Upper Montclair NJ 07043 Office: 100 Bergen St Newark NJ 07103. *The balancing of creativity and lassitude, professional and personal identities, public self and private self with an ongoing sense of integrity has been and will be the work of a lifetime. The ability to retreat to home, to music and to sports has been helpful; for while competence is my personal watchword, it is also a hard and elusive taskmaster.*

THOMAS, COLIN GORDON, JR., medical educator; b. Iowa City, July 25, 1918; s. Colin Gordon and Eloise Kinzer (Brainerd) T.; B.S., U. Chgo., 1940, M.D., 1943; m. Shirley Forbes, Sept. 12, 1946; children—Karen, Barbara, James G., John F. Intern U. Iowa Hosp., 1943-44, resident surgery, 1944-45, 47-50; asso. in surgery U. Iowa Med. Sch., 1950-51, asst. prof., 1951-52; mem. faculty U. N.C. Med. Sch., Chapel Hill, 1952—, prof. surgery, 1961—, chmn. dept., 1966—; chmn. dept. surgery N.C. Meml. Hosp. Mem. surgery test com. Nat. Bd. Med. Examiners. Served to capt., M.C., AUS, 1945-47. Recipient Prof. award U. N.C. Sch. Medicine, 1964. Diplomate Am. Bd. Surgery. Mem. A.M.A., A.C.S., Am. Thyroid Assn., Am. Assn. Cancer Research, Soc. Univ. Surgeons, So. Soc. Clin. Research, So. Surg. Assn., N.Y. Acad. Scis., Am. Assn. U. Profs., Halsted Soc., Ga. Surg. Soc., Soc. Exptl. Biology and Medicine, Am. Surg. Assn., Allen Whipple Surg. Soc., Womack Surg. Soc., Soc. Surg. Chmn., Soc. Internationale de Chirurgie, Soc. Surgery Alimentary Tract, N.C. Surg. Assn., Alpha Omega Alpha. Episcopalian (warden 1961-62). Editorial bd. Review of Surgery. Contbr. numerous articles to med. jours. Home: 408 Morgan Creek Rd Chapel Hill NC 27514

THOMAS, DAN ANDERSON, univ. dean; b. Ooltewah, Tenn., Oct. 1, 1922; s. Daniel Bryson and Blanche (Sylar) T.; B.S., U. Chattanooga, 1945; Ph.D., Vanderbilt U., 1952; m. Margaret Elizabeth Glaze, Mar. 19, 1944; children—Roger Nelson, Rebecca Lynn. Asst. prof. physics U. South, 1949-51; research physicist U.S. Naval Ordnance Lab., White Oak, Md., 1951-52; asso. prof. physics Rollins Coll., 1952-57, prof., 1957-63, chmn. div. sci. and math., 1956-59, dir. grad. program physics, 1959-63; dean faculty, prof. physics Jacksonville (Fla.) U., 1963-67, prof. physics, v.p., dean faculties, 1967—; cons. U.S. Navy Underwater Sound Reference Lab., Orlando, Fla., 1953-63. Mem. adv. com. student sects. Am. Inst. Physics, 1963-68, del. to Am. Council on Edn., 1968-72; mem. Fla. Fulbright Com., 1963-68. Mem. exec. com. North Fla. Council Boy Scouts Am. Trustee Jacksonville Childrens' Mus., 1970—, 1st v.p., 1977—; trustee Jacksonville Mus. Arts and Scis., 1978—, pres., 1978-79; trustee Meninak Found., 1974—. AEC fellow, 1947-48; Danforth Asso., 1958-62. Served with USNR, World War II. Fellow A.A.A.S. (mem. council 1961-63); mem. Am. Assn. U. Profs. (exec. com. Fla. 1961-63), Am. Assn. Physics Tchrs., Acoustical Soc. Am., Am. Phys. Soc., Am. Conf. Acad. Deans, Conf. Acad. Deans of So. States, So. Conf. Deans Faculties and Acad. Vice Pres.'s, Fla. Acad. Sci. (pres. 1958), Fla. Audubon Soc. (dir. 1957-60), Sigma Xi, Alpha Soc., Blue Key, Omicron Delta Kappa, Sigma Pi Sigma, Kappa Sigma. Club: Meninak (pres. 1973). Contbr. articles to profl. jours. Home: 3272 University Blvd N Jacksonville FL 32211

THOMAS, DANIEL HOLCOMBE, judge; b. Prattville, Ala., Aug. 25, 1906; s. Columbus Eugene and Augusta (Pratt) T.; LL.B., U. Ala., 1928; m. Dorothy Quina, Sept. 26, 1936 (dec. 1977); children—Daniel H., Jr., Merrill Pratt; m. 2d, Catharine J. Miller, Oct. 25, 1979. Admitted to bar; practice law, Mobile, Ala., 1929; asst. solicitor Mobile County; mem. firm Lyons, Chamberlain & Courtney, 1932-37; judge U.S. Dist. Ct., Mobile, 1951—. Mem. exec. bd. Mobile Area council Boy Scouts Am., 1963—, v.p., 1967-69, pres., 1973—, mem. nat. council, 1973—. Trustee dept. archieves and history State of Ala. Served with USNR, 1943-45. Recipient Silver Beaver award Boy Scouts Am., 1970, Silver Antelope award, 1975. Methodist. Club: Mobile Country. Home: 13 Dogwood Circle Mobile AL 36608 Office: US Fed Bldg Mobile AL 36602

THOMAS, DANNY (AMOS JACOBS), entertainer, TV producer; b. Deerfield, Mich., Jan. 6, 1914; s. Charles and Margaret Christen (Simon) Jacobs; ed. high sch.; L.H.D., Belmont Abbey, Internat. Coll., Springfield, Mass., 1970, Christian Bros. Coll., Memphis; LL.D., Loyola U., Chgo.; D.Performing Arts (hon.), Toledo U., Loyola-Marymount U. at Los Angeles; m. Rose Marie Cassaniti, Jan. 15, 1936; children—Margaret Julia, Theresa Cecelia, Charles Anthony. Radio work, 1934; appeared as master ceremonies night club, 1938-40; radio, Chgo. 1940; master ceremonies 5100 Club, Chgo. night club, 1940-43; developed own radio, TV program; appeared Oriental Theatre, Chgo., 1943, La Martinique (night club), N.Y., 1943-44, Roxy Theatre, N.Y., 1948, Ciro's, Hollywood, Calif., 1949, London Palladium (Eng.), Chgo. Theatre; overseas entertainer, ETO with Marlene Dietrich & Co.; with Fanny Brice on radio, season 1944; overseas entertainer with own troupe, Pacific Area; returned to Chgo. as entertainer Chez Paree (night club), 1945-46; appeared in first motion picture The Unfinished Dance, 1946; The Big City, 1947; Call Me Mister, 1948; I'll See You in My Dreams, 1951; Jazz Singer, 1952; TV shows Make Room for Daddy (Emmy awards 1953-64), Danny Thomas Spls., 1964-68, Thomas-Leonard Prodns., Danny Thomas Hours, 1967-68, Thomas-Spelling Prodns., TV shows Make Room for Granddaddy, 1970, The Practice, 1976-77; numerous engagements night clubs and theatres. Recipient awards NCCJ, 1957; Layman's award AMA; Better World award Ladies Aux., VFW, 1972; Michelango award Boys Town of Italy, 1973; award Gov. of Ohio, 1975; Entertainment award White House Corrs., 1975; Humanitarian award Lions Internat., 1975; decorated Knight Malta; knight comdr. with star Knights of Holy Sepulchre, Pope Paul VI. Roman Catholic. Founder, St. Jude Children's Research Hosp., Memphis, honoree testimonial dinner, 1975. Address: 1801 Ave of the Stars Los Angeles CA 90067

THOMAS, DAVID ANSELL, univ. dean; b. Holliday, Tex., July 5, 1917; s. John Calvin Mitchell and Alice (Willet) T.; B.A., Tex. Tech. Coll., 1937; M.B.A., Tex. Christian U., 1948; Ph.D., U. Mich., 1956; m. Mary Elizabeth Smith, May 18, 1946; 1 dau., Ann Elizabeth. Accountant, Texaco, Inc., 1937-42; asso. prof. Tex. Christian U., 1946-49; lectr. U. Mich., 1949-53; prof. accounting Cornell U., Ithaca, N.Y., 1953—, asso. dean Grad. Sch. Bus. and Pub. Adminstrn., 1962—. Pres., Exec. Investors, Inc.; exec. dir. Charles E. Merrill Family Found., 1954-57, Robert A. Magowan Found., 1957-60; adminstr. Charles E. Merrill Trust, 1957—, Ithaca Growth Fund. Bd. dirs. Ithaca Opera Assn., Cornell Student Agys. Served to capt. USAAF, 1942-46; PTO. C.P.A., Tex. Mem. Tex. Soc. C.P.A.'s, Nat. Assn. Accountants, Am. Accounting Assn., Phi Beta Kappa, Beta Alpha Psi. Clubs: Cornell of N.Y., Statler (pres., dir.). Author: Accelerated Amortization of Defense Facilities, 1958; (with R. Lee Brummet) Accounting for Home Builders, 1952. Contbr. numerous articles to publs. Editor: Fed. Accountant, 1956-58. Home: 150 N Sunset Dr Ithaca NY 14850

THOMAS, DAVID DIPLOCK, resource co. exec.; b. Winnipeg, Man., Can., July 23, 1924; s. Edgar James and Blanche Elizabeth (Stevens) T.; Chartered Accountant, U. Man., Winnipeg, 1947; m. 2d, Eva Josephine Johnston, Nov. 16, 1968; children—Nancy Elizabeth, John Edgar, Gordon James, Patricia Ann. Chartered accountant trainee Millar Macdonald & Co., Winnipeg, 1941-47; with Sherritt Gordon Mines Ltd., Toronto, 1947—, treas., 1964-67, pres., chief exec. officer, 1967—, also dir., and dir. subs. cos.; dir. Marinduque Mining & Indsl. Corp., Cassiar Asbestos Corp. Ltd. Bd. dirs. Centre for Precambrian Studies, U. Man. Fellow, Chartered Accountants, Man. Inst., 1975. Mem. Canadian Inst. Mining and Metallurgy, Mining Assn. Can. (dir.), Canadian Bus. Council on Nat. Issues. Clubs: Donalda, Bd. of Trade (Toronto). Home: 52 Lawrence Crescent Toronto ON M4N 1N2 Canada Office: PO Box 28 Commerce Ct W Toronto ON M5L 1B1 Canada

THOMAS, DAVID LLOYD, diversified corp. exec.; b. Ames, Iowa, July 19, 1927; s. E. Anson and Mary F. (Weeks) T.; B.S. in Bus. Adminstrn. with distinction, U. Nebr., 1949; m. Mary Lou Artman, Sept. 1, 1946; children—David L., Carol. Various financial positions Gen. Electric Co., Syracuse and Schenectady, 1949-59; controller McCall Corp., N.Y.C., 1959-61; with Gen. Dynamics Corp., N.Y.C., 1961—, comptroller, 1967-71; v.p. fin. Dun & Bradstreet Cos., Inc., 1971-76, sr. v.p. fin., 1976—. Served with USNR, 1945-46. C.P.A. Mem. Fin. Execs. Inst., Treasurers Club. Home: 121 Brite Ave Scarsdale NY 10583 Office: 299 Park Ave New York City NY 10017

THOMAS, DAVID ST JOHN, publisher; b. Romford, Eng., Aug. 30, 1929; s. Gilbert Oliver and Dorothy Kathleen Thomas; student pub. schs., Devon, Eng.; m. Pamela Mary Shepherd, Feb. 16, 1954; children—Alison Clare, Gareth St John. Founder, chmn. David & Charles Publishing Group, Readers Union Bookclubs, Devon, Eng., and David & Charles Inc., North Pomfret, Vt., 1960—. Author: The Rural Transport Problem, 1971; Getting Published, 1971, 74; Great Way West, 1975; The Country Railway, 1976; editor: Regional History of the Railways of Great Britain, 1960-78; author children's books; contbr. articles to mags. Home: Hylton 26 Keyberry Park Newton Abbot Devon England Office: Brunel House Newton Abbot Devon England also David and Charles Inc North Pomfret VT 05053

THOMAS, DEROY C., lawyer, ins. co. exec.; b. Utica, N.Y., Feb. 16, 1926; B.A., Iona Coll., 1949; LL.B., Fordham U., 1952; m. Emily Clark, Feb. 7, 1953. Admitted to N.Y. State bar, 1952; asst. prof. law Fordham U., N.Y.C., 1953-58; asst. counsel Assn. Casualty and Surety Cos., N.Y.C., 1959-64; with firm Watters & Donovan, 1964; with Hartford Fire Ins. Co. (Conn.), 1964—, gen. counsel, 1966-69, v.p., 1968-69, sr. v.p., 1969-73, exec. v.p., 1973-76, pres., 1976—, chief exec. officer, 1978—, chmn., 1979—, also dir.; exec. v.p. Hartford Accident & Indemnity Co., 1973-76, pres., 1976—, chief exec. officer, 1978—, chmn., 1979—, also dir.; dir. Hartford Casualty Co., N.Y. Underwriters, Twin City Fire Ins. Co., Hartford Life Ins. Co. Mem. Am. Bar Assn. Home: 88 Van Buren Ave West Hartford CT 06107 Office: Hartford Plaza Hartford CT 06115

THOMAS, DONALD LLEWELLYN, banker; b. Niagara Falls, N.Y., Mar. 5, 1917; s. Philip Charles and Dora (Redpath) T.; grad. magna cum laude in bus. adminstrn. Niagara U., 1949; grad. Stonier Sch. Banking, Rutgers U.; m. Barbara Mae Williams, May 20, 1942; children—Donald Llewellyn, Rhys E. Treas., Niagara County Savs. Bank, Niagara Falls, 1946-58; v.p. No. Trust Co., Chgo., 1958-66; chmn., chief exec. officer Anchor Savs. Bank, Bklyn., 1966—, Anchor Property Corp.; chmn. Thriftpac, Inc.; dir. Thrift Publishers, Inc., Drayton Co. Ltd., Savs. Banks Trust Co. N.Y.; mem. adv. bd. Mfrs. Hanover Trust Co.; faculty Grad. Sch. Savs. Banking Brown U., 1966—. Mem. N.Y. adv. com. Revolving Fund Home Mortgage Requirements; chmn. Savs. Bank Fund for New Homes, 1969—. Vice chmn. bd. Luth. Med. Center; bd. dirs. Community Preservation Program, Central Industry Fund, Inc., Bklyn. Philharmonia, Mut. Instns. Nat. Transfer Systems, Inc.; mem. adv. bd. Niagara U. Served to capt. AUS. World War II. Mem. Bklyn. C. of C. (dir.), Savs. Bank Assn. N.Y. State (co-ins. com., com. urban affairs), Nat. Assn. Mut. Savs. Banks (dir.). Author: (with others) Commercial Bankers Handbook; Am. Inst. Banking textbook Saving and Time Deposit Banking. Home: 90 Whitehall Blvd Garden City NY 11530 Office: 5323 Fifth Ave Brooklyn NY 11220

THOMAS, EDMOND GEORGE, advt. exec.; b. St. Louis, May 4, 1912; s. Edmond Austin and Rosalind Sailer (Lodge) T.; B.A., Yale, 1933, postgrad. in medicine, 1934-37; m. Virginia McBlair Garesché, Nov. 6, 1940 (div. Sept. 1969); children—Michael, Elizabeth, Juliet Thomas Beckett; m. 2d, Sarah Tracy Sigler, Aug. 18, 1978. Copy writer Burroughs-Wellcome (U.S.A.), Inc., N.Y.C., 1937-40; asst. advt. mgr. Sharp & Dohme, Phila., 1940-43; advt. mgr. William R. Warner, N.Y.C., 1943-45; partner Gray & Rogers, advt., Phila., 1945-53; founder, partner Chew, Harvey & Thomas Advt., Phila., 1953-58; partner Harvey & Thomas, Phila., 1958-64; pres. Ted Thomas Assos., Inc., advt., Phila., 1964-76, chmn., chief exec. officer, 1976—; pres. Extar Co., distbr. dental products, 1974—. Clubs: Phila. Racquet, Peale, Pohoqualine Fish Assn. Home: 10 Norman Ln Philadelphia PA 19118 Office: 255 S 17th St Philidelphia PA 19103

THOMAS, EDWARD DONNALL, physician, educator; b. Mart, Tex., Mar. 15, 1920; s. Edward E. and Angie (Hill) T.; B.A., U. Tex., 1941, M.A., 1943; M.D., Harvard, 1946; m. Dorothy Martin, Dec. 20, 1942; children—Edward Donnall, Jeffery A., Elaine. NRC fellow medicine dept. biology Mass. Inst. Tech., 1950-51; instr. medicine dept. biology Mass. Inst. Tech., 1950-51; instr. medicine Harvard Med. Sch., Boston, also hematologist Peter Bent Brigham Hosp., 1953-55; research asso. Cancer Research Found., Children Med. Center, Boston, 1953-55; physician in chief Mary Imogene Bassett Hosp., also asso. clin. prof. medicine Coll. Phys. and Surg., Columbia, 1955-63; prof. U. Wash. Sch. Medicine, Seattle, 1963—. Diplomate Am. Bd. Internal Medicine. Mem. Am. Soc. Clin. Investigation, Assn. Am. Physicians, Am. Soc. Hematology, Am. Fedn. Clin. Research, Internat. Soc. Hematology, Am. Assn. for Cancer Research, Western Assn. Physicians. Research and numerous publs. on hematology, marrow transplantation, biochemistry and irradiation biology. Home: 1920 92d Ave NE Bellevue WA 98004 Office: Fred Hutchinson Cancer Research Center 1124 Columbia St Seattle WA 98104

THOMAS, EDWARD FRANCIS, pub. relations counsel; b. N.Y.C., Oct. 15, 1910; s. Faber and Helen (Hall) T.; student Columbia, 1933-35, N.Y. U., 1937-38; m. Alyce Sawyer, Sept. 3, 1929 (div.); children—Barbara, Mark; m. 2d, Helen Baker, May 29, 1936; children—Edward Francis, Stuart Ronald. Editor, Collier Advt. Service, 1933-35; dir. pub. relations Young Republican Nat. Fedn., 1935-37; press relations dir. Thomas E. Dewey Citizens Com., 1937; dir. research and planning, account exec. Carl Byoir & Assos., 1938-43; v.p., dir. pub. relations Geyer Advt., Inc., 1943-54; v.p., pub. relations account supr. J. Walter Thompson Co., 1954-59; v.p. pub. relations NAM, 1955-56; pres. Edward Thomas Assos., Inc., N.Y.C., 1959-70; vice chmn. Booke & Co., Inc., N.Y.C., 1970-74; pres. Edward Thomas & Co., Phoenix, 1974-76. Pub. relations cons. U.S. Army, 1951, Office Sec. Def., 1951-53. Mem. Nat. council Boy Scouts Am., recipient Silver Beaver award Greater N.Y. councils, 1952; chmn. nat. pub. affairs adv. com. ARC, 1977-79, mem. Mid-Atlantic div. council, mem. nat. centennial roll call com., 1977-79. Mem. Pub. Relations Soc. Am. (accredited, founding mem., past nat. dir.), Dramatists Guild, Nat. Pub. Relations Council for Health and Welfare Services (nat. chmn. 1964-66). Republican. Episcopalian. Club: Scranton. Address: A5 Parkland Village Rte 6 Blakely PA 18447. *Seek excellence in all things.*

THOMAS, EDWIN JOHN, psychologist, social worker, educator; b. Flint, Mich., Nov. 14, 1927; s. Charles Jess and Florence Cynthia (Gass) T.; A.B. with high distinction, Wayne State U., Detroit, 1951, M.S.W., 1953; Ph.D., U. Mich., 1956; m. Vivian A. Walz, June 24, 1950; children—Melinda Sue, Lisa Kay. Research asso. Research Center Group Dynamics, U. Mich., Ann Arbor, 1955-56, mem. faculty U. Mich., 1956—, prof. Sch. Social Work and dept. psychology, 1963—, head doctoral program in social work and social sci., 1965-66, 68-69, chmn. supervising com., 1969-76; pvt. practice behavior therapy, also cons. Served with AUS, 1946-48. Fulbright vis. prof. U. Bradford (Eng.), 1967-68. Fellow Am. Psychol. Assn.; mem. Nat. Assn. Social Workers, Assn. Advancement Behavioral Therapies, Acad. Certified Social Workers, Behavior Therapy and Research Soc. (charter clin. fellow). Author: Marital Communication and Decision Making, 1976; also articles. Editor: Behavioral Science for Social Workers, 1967; Behavior Modification Procedure, 1974; co-editor: Role Theory: Concepts and Research, 1966. Home: 5555 Dexter Ann Arbor Rd Dexter MI 48130

THOMAS, ELMER MARSHALL, lawyer; b. Ft. Madison, Iowa, Mar. 17, 1907; s. Elmer Martin and Hilda Rosette (Anderssen) T.; B.A., State U. Iowa, 1930, J.D. magna cum laude, 1932, m. Marjorie J. Bolon, Oct. 31, 1932 (dec. Nov. 1967); children—Marsha Ann, Marjo May (Mrs. Erickson); m. 2d, Merceles Benedict, May 27, 1969. Admitted to Iowa bar, 1932; law practice with O. H. Allbee, Marshalltown, Iowa, 1932-33; mem. legal dept. Fed. Land Bank, Omaha, 1933-34; asso. mem. firm O'Connor, Thomas, Wright, Hammer, Bertsch & Norby, and predecessors, Dubuque, Iowa, 1934—, partner, 1946-72, of counsel, 1973—. Mem. Iowa Bd. Bar Examiners, 1953-61; chmn. Nat. Conf. Bar Examiners, 1964-65. Mem. Commn. on World Service and Fin. of North Iowa Meth. Conf., 1958-64; pres. Dubuque Community Chest, 1941; mem. Dubuque Planning and Zoning Commn., 1946-49; trustee Finley Hosp., 1954-65, pres. bd. trustees, 1963-64; bd. dirs. U. Dubuque, 1968-73, YMCA. Served with USAF, 1944-45. Fellow Am. Bar Found.; mem. Fedn. Ins. Counsel (v.p. 1953-54), Am. Coll. Probate Counsel, Am. Bar Assn. (mem. council sect. of legal edn. and admissions to bar 1966-70, sec. 1970-72, vice chmn., 1972-73), Iowa State Bar Assn. (chmn. com. uniform jury instructions 1963-79, award of merit 1976), Dubuque County Bar Assn., Assn. Ins. Counsel, Am. Legion, Order of Coif, C. of C., Am. Coll. Trial Lawyers, Acacia. Republican. Methodist. Clubs: Masons, Rotary (pres. Dubuque, 1949), High Twelve, Dubuque Golf (Dubuque). Home: 3156 Hillcrest St Dubuque IA 52001 Office: 200 Dubuque Bldg Dubuque IA 52001

THOMAS, EVAN WELLING, II, publishing co. exec.; b. N.Y.C., July 14, 1920; s. Norman Mattoon and Frances Violet (Stewart) T.; grad. Kent Sch., 1938; student Princeton, 1938-41; m. Anne Robins, Aug. 22, 1943; children—Wendy, Louisa, Evan Welling III. With Harper & Brothers (then Harper & Row, Publishers, Inc.), N.Y.C., 1945-68, beginning as mem. trade editorial staff, successively asst. editor, mng. editor, 1945-57, dir. gen. books dept., 1957-61, v.p., bd. dirs., 1958-61, exec. v.p., mem. exec. com., 1961-68; editor, v.p., dir. W. W. Norton & Co., Inc., N.Y.C., 1968—. With Am. Field Service Vol. Ambulance Corps, 1941-43; served to lt. (j.g.) USNR, 1943-45. Mem. Am. Arbitration Assn. (arbitrator), Council Fgn. Relations. Clubs: Ivy (Princeton), Century Assn., University. Author: Ambulance in Africa, 1943. Home: 350 E 57th St New York City NY 10022 Office: 500 Fifth Ave New York City NY 10036

THOMAS, FRANK ALMERINE, JR., mech engr., educator; b. Atlanta, Jan. 14, 1924; s. Frank Almerine and Lois Opal (Hall) T.; student Auburn U., 1942-43, Duke, 1943-44; B.S. in Mech. Engring., Purdue U., 1947; M.S. in Mech. Engring., Ga. Inst. Tech., 1949, Ph.D., 1958; m. Dorothy Mary Havens, June 9, 1947; children—Sarah Lou, Nancy Ann, Frank Almerine III. With Calif. Cotton Mills, 1942, Buckeye Cotton Oil Co., 1942, Hollingsworth Whitney Co., 1942-43; engr. W.A. Roger Industries, 1947; indsl. hygienist Ga. Dept. Pub. Health, 1947-49, AEC, 1949-51; successively instr., asst. prof., research asso. Ga. Inst. Tech., 1951-58; prof. mech. engring., head dept. Lamar U., Beaumont, Tex., 1958-62, head dept. indsl. engring., 1962-64, prof. mech. engring., 1958-72, dean engring., 1961-67, v.p. acad. affairs, 1967-69, pres., 1969-72, regents prof., 1972-74; v.p. prodn., dir. Neo-Sum Systems, Inc., Long Beach, Cal., 1973-74; dean Community and Tech. Coll., U. Toledo, 1974—. Mem., adviser Concerned Citizens for Spanish Speaking Ams., 1974-76. Bd. dirs. Beaumont chpt. A.R.C., 1967-72, St. Elizabeth Hosp., 1969-72, No. Jefferson County United Appeals, 1970-72; campaign chmn., bd. dirs. No. Jefferson County chpt. Am. Heart Assn., 1968-72; trustee Baptist Hosp. S.E. Tex., 1967-73, SOL Regional Health Services, 1974-77. Served to 2d lt. USMCR, 1943-46. Registered profl. engr., Ga., Tex. Mem. ASME (sec. region X 1969-71, mem. council, v.p. 1971-73, com. on planning and orgn. 1974—), Am. Soc. for Engring. Edn., Gulf Coast Engring. and Sci. Soc. (dir.), Lamar Honor Soc., Toledo C. of C. (legis. com. 1974—), Tech. Soc. Toledo, Sigma Xi, Pi Tau Sigma, Kappa Sigma, Alpha Phi Omega, Phi Kappa Phi, Tau Beta Pi, Phi Eta Sigma. Baptist (deacon). Contbr. tech. papers to profl. jours. Home: 2644 Sherbrooke Rd Toledo OH 43606 Office: Scott Park Campus U Toledo Toledo OH 43606

THOMAS, FRANKLIN AUGUSTINE, found. exec.; b. Bklyn., May 27, 1934; s. James and Viola (Atherley) T.; B.A., Columbia Coll., 1956; LL.B., Columbia, 1963; LL.D. (hon.), Yale, 1970, Fordham U., 1972, Pratt Inst., 1974, Columbia U., 1979; div.; children—Keith, Hillary, Kerrie, Kyle. Admitted to N.Y. State bar, 1964; atty. Fed. Housing and Home Finance Agy., N.Y.C., 1963-64; asst. U.S. atty. for So. Dist. N.Y., 1964-65; dep. police commr. charge legal matters, N.Y.C., 1965-67; pres., chief exec. officer Bedford Stuyvesant Restoration Corp., Bklyn., 1967-77; pres. The Ford Found., 1979—; dir. Citicorp./Citibank, CBS, Inc., Aluminum Co. Am., Allied Stores Corp., Cummins Engine Co. Trustee, J.H. Whitney Found., Columbia U., 1969-75. Served with USAF, 1956-60. Recipient LBJ Found. award for contbn. to betterment of urban life, 1974, medal of excellence Columbia U., 1976. Home: 308 Lafayette Ave Brooklyn NY 11238

THOMAS, FREDERICK W., lawyer;l b. Mpls., 1911; B.A., U. Minn., 1936; LL.B., Harvard, 1939. Admitted to Minn. bar, 1940, D.C. bar, 1964; mem. firm O'Connor & Hannan, Mpls. Mem. Hennepin County, Minn., Am. bar assns., Phi Beta Kappa. Office: IDS Tower 80 S 8th St Minneapolis MN 55402

THOMAS, GARETH, educator; b. Maesteg, U.K., Aug. 9, 1932; s. David Bassett and Edith May (Gregory) T.; came to U.S., 1960, naturalized, 1977; B.Sc., U. Wales, 1952; Ph.D., Cambridge U., 1955, Sc.D., 1969; m. Elizabeth Virginia Cawdry, Jan. 5, 1960; 1 son, Julian Guy David. I.C.I. fellow Cambridge U., 1956-59; asst. prof. U. Calif., Berkeley, 1960-63, asso. prof., 1963-67, prof. metallurgy, 1967—, asso. dean grad. div., 1968-69, asst. chancellor, acting vice chancellor for acad. affairs, 1969-72; cons. to industry. Recipient Curtis McGraw Research award Am. Soc. Engring. Edn., 1966; E.O. Lawrence award Dept. Energy, 1978. Guggenheim fellow, 1972. Fellow Am. Soc. Metals (Bradley Stoughton Young Tchrs. award 1965, Grossman Publ. award 1966), Am. Inst. Mining, Metall. and Petroleum Engrs.; mem. Electron Microscopy Soc. Am. (prize 1965, pres. 1976), Am. Phys. Soc., Brit. Inst. Metals (Rosenheim medal 1977), Internat. Fedn. Electron Microscopy Socs. (sec. gen. 1974-82), Brit. Iron and Steel Inst. Club: Marylebone Cricket (Eng.). Author: Transmission Electron Microscopy of Metals, 1962; Electron Microscopy and Strength of Crystals, 1963; (with O. Johari) Stereographic Projection and Applications, 1969; Electron Microscopy and Structure of Materials, 1972; contbr. articles in field to profl. jours.; patentee in field. Home: 1372 Summit Rd Berkeley CA 94708 Office: U Calif Dept Materials Sci and Mineral Engring Berkeley CA 94720

THOMAS, GARTH JOHNSON, educator; b. Pittsburg, Kans., Sept. 8, 1916; s. Leslie Homer and Lou Opal (Johnson) T.; A.B., Kans. State Tchrs. Coll. at Pittsburg, 1938; M.A., U. Kans., 1941; M.A., Harvard, 1943, Ph.D., 1948; m. Mary Mona Gee, Sept. 21, 1945; children—Gregory Allen, Barbara Elizabeth. Instr., asst. prof. U. Chgo., 1948-54; asso. prof. U. Ill. Med. Sch., 1954-57, research prof. physiology and elec. engring., Urbana, 1957-66; prof. Center for Brain Research, U. Rochester (N.Y.), 1966—, dir., 1970-77. Mem. rev. com. Exptl. Psychology Fellowship panel NIMH, 1965-70, chmn., 1970; mem. psychobiology panel NSF; cons. editor McGraw-Hill Ency. of Sci. and Tech., Sinauer Press, Inc. Served to 1st lt. AUS, 1944-47. Recipient research grants NSF, NIMH, U.S. Army, 1951—; Alumni Meritorious Achievement award Kans. State Coll. at Pittsburg, 1976. Mem. Am. Psychol. Assn., Animal Behavior Soc., AAAS, Psychonomic Soc., Soc. Exptl. Psychology, Soc. for Neurosci. Editor: Jour. Comparative and Physiol. Psychology, 1975—. Contbr. articles to profl. jours. Home: 186 Buckland Ave Rochester NY 14618

THOMAS, GARY LYNN, banking exec.; b. Port Vue, Pa., May 15, 1942; s. Willis L. and Luella M. (Rorabaugh) T.; B.S. in Bus. Adminstrn., Pa. State U., 1964; grad. Sch. Bank Adminstrn., U. Wis., 1973; m. Sharen A. Gibbons, May 13, 1967; children—Gregory Scott, Tara Elizabeth. Sr. auditor Arthur Andersen & Co., Los Angeles and Pitts., 1964-69; v.p. and dep. comptroller Pitts. Nat. Bank, 1969-77; v.p. and treas. Md. Nat. Corp., Balt., 1977—; v.p., mgr. corp. fin. div. Md. Nat. Bank, Balt.; adj. instr. Sch. Bank Adminstrn., U. Wis.; speaker 14th ann. Bank Tax Inst., 1978. Served with USAR, 1968. C.P.A., Pa. Mem. Am. Inst. C.P.A.'s, Pa. Inst. C.P.A.'s, Md. Assn. C.P.A.'s. Republican. Methodist. Home: 2211 Springlake Dr Timonium MD 21093 Office: 10 Light St Rm 640 Baltimore MD 21203

THOMAS, GEORGE EDWARD, museum adminstr.; b. Sao Paulo, Brazil, June 3, 1943; B.A., U. Calif., Santa Barbara, 1966, M.F.A., 1968; m. Anara C. German, Apr. 28, 1962; children—George Clifford, Daniel Leigh. Teaching fellow art dept. U. Calif., Santa Barbara, 1967-68; prodn. designer Ben Mayer Design, Inc., Los Angeles, 1968-70; mem. vis. faculty, dept. art Western Wash. U., 1969; curator Whatcom Mus. History and Art, Bellingham, Wash., 1970-77, dir., 1977—. Mem. Whatcom County Adv. Council Hist. Preservation. Mem. Am. Assn. Museums, Allied Arts of Whatcom County (steering com. 1979). Club: Lions. Author intro. to exhibit catalog: Margaret Tomkin paintings and sculpture 1969-1978, 1978; editor: Beyond The Veil: The Etchings of Helen Loggie, 1979. Office: 121 Prospect St Bellingham WA 98225

THOMAS, GEORGE EDWARD, pharm. co. exec.; b. Bayonne, N.J., Nov. 28, 1914; s. George Henry and Mae Franklin T.; student U. Va., 1932-35, Fordham U. Law Sch., 1935-37; m. Muriel Hennessy, Apr. 21, 1948; children—George Edward, Jeffrey Burke. With Johnson & Johnson, U.S.A., 1938-42; with Sterling Drug Internat., Latin Am., 1942-56, gen. mgr. Uruguay, 1953-56; asst. area mgr. So. Europe, Pfizer Internat., Spain, 1956-57, pres., gen. mgr. Pfizer Argentina, 1958-60, area mgr. S. Am., 1961-64; dir. internat. devel. A.H. Robins, Richmond, Va., 1965-67, v.p., 1967-75, exec. v.p., 1975—, also dir. Office: AH Robins Co Inc 1407 Cummings Dr Richmond VA 23220

THOMAS, GEORGE RIXSE, educator, architect; b. Portsmouth, Va., Dec. 8, 1906; s. George John and Ida May (Rixse) T.; student U. N.C., 1924-25; B.Arch., Carnegie Inst. Tech., 1930; student Columbia, 1938; European study; m. Naomi Williams, Sept. 11, 1931; 1 dau., Ann Lee. With archtl. offices in Norfolk, Va., and Washington, 1930; pvt. practice architecture, Portsmouth, Va., 1930, Durham, N.H., 1931—; instr. Mary Washington Coll., U. Va., 1935; mem. faculty, U. of N.H., 1931—, prof. architecture and the arts, 1947—, chmn. dept. arts, 1940—, dir. Art Gallery, 1937—. Registered architect. Mem. AIA, AAUP, N.H. Art Assn., League of N.H. Arts and Crafts (council), Pi Kappa Alpha, Scarab. Contbr. articles on archtl. design and edn. to various publs. Home: 17 Bagdad Rd Durham NH 03824

THOMAS, GEORGE SLOAN, lawyer; b. St. Louis, July 29, 1942; s. Lewis Proctor and Katherine May (Sloan) T.; B.S. in Bus. Adminstrn., U. N.C., 1964; LL.B., U. Va., 1967; m. Joan Ellen Pyshny, Jan. 9, 1964; children—Clark, Katherine. Admitted to Mo. bar, 1967; asso. firm Armstrong, Teasdale, Kramer & Vaughan, St. Louis, 1967-71; sec., gen. counsel Gen. Grocer Co., St. Louis, 1971-78; asso. gen. counsel Anheuser-Busch, Inc., St. Louis, 1978—; vice chmn. Mo. Product Liability Task Force. Mem. Am. Bar Assn., Bar Assn. Met. St. Louis. Republican. Episcopalian. Club: Old Warson Country. Home: 1618 Copper Hill Rd Saint Louis MO 63124 Office: 721 Pestalozzi St Saint Louis MO 63118

THOMAS, GERALD WAYLETT, univ. pres.; b. Small, Idaho, July 3, 1919; s. Daniel Waylett and Mary (Evans) T.; student Pasadena Jr. Coll., 1936-38; B.S., U. Idaho, 1941; M.S., Tex. A. and M. Coll., 1951, Ph.D., 1954; m. Jean Ellis, June 2, 1945; children—David Gerald, Peggy Jeane, Marianne. With U.S. Forest Service in Idaho, 1938-40; range conservationist, work unit conservationist Soil Conservation Service, St. Anthony and Rexburg, Idaho, 1946-50; asst. and asso. prof. dept. range and forestry Tex. A. and M. Coll., College Station, 1951-56; research coordinator Tex. Agrl. Expt. Sta., 1956-58; dean agr. Tex. Technol. U., 1958, exec. v.p., 1968; now pres. N.Mex. State U., Las Cruces; mem. Bd. for Internat. Food and Agrl. Devel.; mem. exec. bd. Assn. State Univs. and Land-Grant Colls., Asso. Western Univs. Served to lt. USNR, 1942-45. Decorated D.F.C. (3), Air medal (2). Mem. Am. Soc. Range Mgmt. (bd. dirs.), Soil Conservation Soc., AAAS, Sigma Xi, Phi Kappa Phi. Rotarian. Author: Progress and Change in the Agricultural Industry; Food and Fiber for a Changing World; also numerous publs. on ecology and agrl. subjects. Home: University Park Las Cruces NM 88001

THOMAS, GORDON ALEXANDER, baking co. exec.; b. Newton Center, Mass., Jan. 19, 1928; s. Earle Lewis and Helen Westmoreland (Browder) T.; A.B., Dartmouth Coll., 1950; LL.B., Columbia U., 1953; m. Doris Anita Aakervik, June 17, 1955; children—Krista Lynn, Alix Elizabeth. Admitted to N.Y. bar, 1954, Calif. bar, 1956; with firm Sage, Gray, Todd & Sims, N.Y.C., 1953-54; with Travelers Ins. Co., Los Angeles, 1954-58; with ITT Continental Baking Co., Rye, N.Y., 1958—, v.p., gen. counsel, 1969—; dir. Nat. Continental Corp., Kingston, Jamaica, Continental de Alimentos, S.A., Mexico City; adj. prof. Marymount Coll., Tarrytown, N.Y. Dist. chmn. Lewisboro (N.Y.) Town Republican Com., 1974—. Served with AUS, 1945-47. Mem. Am., Calif. bar assns., Am. Frozen Food Inst., Grocery Mfrs. Am. Republican. Clubs: Wilson Cove Yacht, Lake. Home: RD 2 Box 234 New Canaan CT 06840 Office: PO Box 731 Rye NY 10580

THOMAS, GORDON WALTER, ins. co. exec.; b. Providence, Jan. 26, 1928; s. Clarence Walter and Ethel May (Aldrich) T.; B.S. in Econs., Wharton Sch., U. Pa., 1949; m. Alice Marie Daley, Apr. 25, 1953; children—Kathryn Ann, Alison Aldrich, Douglas Walter. With John Hancock Life Ins. Co., Boston, 1949—, sales exec., 1961-67, 2d v.p., 1968-71, v.p., 1972-79, sr. v.p., 1979—. Mem. Master Plan Com., Medfield, Mass., 1962-63, co-chmn. Sch. Land Needs Com., 1964, mem. Sch. Com., 1963-74, chmn., 1969, 73. C.L.U. Mem. Health Ins. Assn. Am. (council on profl. and consumer relations), Internat. Claim Assn. Contbr. chpt. on Group Ins. Underwriting to life and health ins. handbook. Home: 314 Hemlock Circle Lincoln MA 01773 Office: 1 Hancock Pl Boston MA 02116

THOMAS, HAROLD ALLEN, JR., civil engr., educator; b. Terre Haute, Ind., Aug. 14, 1913; s. Harold A. and Katherine (Sass) T.; B.S. in Civil Engring., Carnegie Inst. Tech., 1935; S.D., Harvard, 1938; m. Gertrude A. Grim, July 2, 1935; children—Harold Allen III, Stephen C., Calvin R. Faculty mem. Harvard, 1939—, successively instr., asst. prof., asso. prof., 1939-56, Gordon McKay prof. civil and san. engring., 1956—; profl. cons. HEW, 1949—, div. med. scis. NRC-Nat. Acad. Scis., 1943-63, also Dept. Def., AEC; cons. Exec. Office Pres., also Dept. Interior, 1961—. Mem. sci. bd. for Middle East and Southeast Asia, Nat. Acad. Scis., 1964-66, exec. com. social consequences of population changes, 1968—. Fellow Am. Acad. of Arts and Scis.; mem. Am. Geophys. Union (RE Horton medal 1978), ASCE, Nat. Acad. Engring., Boston Soc. C.E. Co-author: Design Water Resource Systems, 1961; Models for Managing Regional Water Quality, 1973. Home: 61 Cotuit Rd Sandwich MA 02563 Office: Harvard U Cambridge MA 02138

THOMAS, HAROLD B., ret. drug bus. exec.; b. Hoboken, N.J., Jan. 9, 1897; s. Will N. and Caroline A. (Brightman) T.; ed. Phillips Acad. Andover, Yale U.; m. Marion E. Lane, Oct. 9, 1926; children—Nancy (Mrs. E. Q. Adams), Peter, Stephen. Formerly sr. v.p. Sterling Drugs, Inc. Former chmn. Advertising Research Found., Assn. Natl. Advertisers; former trustee Columbia Coll. Pharmacy; mem. alumni council Philips Acad., Andover, Mass. Served as capt. U.S. subchaser with Brit., World War I; spl. asst. to Sec. Treasury in World War II. Mem. N.Y. Acad. Sci., Advt. Council (co-founder; organizer, mgr. internat. econ. confs. India, 1965, Brazil, 1966), Aurelian Honor Soc. (Yale). Clubs: New Canaan Country; Peddie Golf; Hillsboro (Fla.); Univ. (N.Y.). Home: Meadow Lakes Apt 43-01 Hightstown NJ 08520

THOMAS, HELEN A. (MRS. DOUGLAS B. CORNELL), journalist; b. Winchester, Ky., Aug. 4, 1920; d. George and Mary (Thomas) Thomas; B.A., Wayne U., 1942; LL.D., Eastern Mich. State U., 1972, Ferris State Coll., 1978; L.H.D., Wayne State U., 1974, U. Detroit, 1979; m. Douglas B. Cornell. With UPI, 1943—, wire service reporter, Washington, 1943-74, White House bur. chief, 1974—.

Recipient Woman of Year in Communications award Ladies Home Jour., 1975. Mem. Women's Nat. Press Club (pres., 1959-60), Am. Newspaper Women's Club (past v.p.), White House Corrs. Assn. (pres. 1976), Sigma Delta Chi (Hall of Fame), Delta Sigma Phi (hon.). Author: Dateline White House. Home: 2501 Calvert St NW Washington DC 20008 Office: Nat Press Bldg Washington DC 20004

THOMAS, HERBERT LEON, JR., life ins. co. exec.; b. Little Rock, Jan. 8, 1921; s. Herbert Leon and Ruby (Collier) T.; B.S. in Econs., Wharton Sch. of U. Pa., 1942; postgrad. Harvard U.; m. Rayma Jean Pickens, June 7, 1947; children—Gray Rodriques-Barbera, Clare Williams, Herbert Leon. With First Pyramid Life Ins. Co., Little Rock, 1946—, exec. v.p., agy. dir., 1958-59, exec. v.p., 1959-60, pres., 1968—; chmn. bd. City Nat. Bank, Ft. Smith, Ark.; chmn. bd. Citizens Bank, Booneville, Ark.; dir. First Nat. Bank, Little Rock. Past pres., bd. dirs. Little Rock Boys' Club; bd. dirs. Little Rock United Way, YMCA. Served with USNR, World War II. C.L.U. Mem. Am. Assn. C.L.U.'s, Nat. Assn. Life Cos., Am. Mgmt. Assn. (president's assn.), U. Ark. Wild Hogs, Ark. Tennis Patrons Found. Clubs: Little Rock Country, Eden Isle Country. Home: 1709 N Spruce St Little Rock AR 72207 Office: 221 W 2d St Little Rock AR 72201

THOMAS, HOWARD BERKELEY, lawyer; b. Berkeley, Calif., Apr. 26, 1912; s. Samuel D. and Jessie Belle (Gartner) T.; B.A., U. Calif. at Berkeley, 1933, J.D., 1936; m. Betty Macaulay, June 11, 1938; children—Elizabeth (Mrs. Peter Burton), Jeanne (Mrs. Harold Dickerson), Barbara (Mrs. Nicholas Brereton). Admitted to Calif. bar, 1936, U.S. Supreme Ct. bar, 1968; practiced in Fresno, Calif., 1940—; partner firm Thomas, Snell, Jamison, Russell, Williamson & Asperger, 1940—; vis. lectr. U Calif. at Berkeley Law Sch., 1956-58. Certified taxation law specialist, Calif. Mem. Am., Fresno County (dir. 1958) bar assns., State Bar Calif. (vice chmn. com. taxation 1959-62), Alumni Assn. U. Calif. at Berkeley (trustee 1969-71), Phi Beta Kappa, Order of Coif, Delta Theta Phi, Pi Sigma Alpha. Co-author booklet Estate Planning For Farmers, 1957, rev. 1968. Asso. editor Cal. Law Rev., 1935-36. Home: 4821 N Wishon St Fresno CA 93704 Office: 10th Floor Del Webb Center Fresno CA 93721

THOMAS, JAMES GLADWYN, lawyer; b. Akron, N.Y., Oct. 5, 1901; s. James Robinson and Fannie (Wilder) T.; A.B., U. Ill., 1923, J.D., 1928; m. Helen H. Herrick, Aug. 19, 1925; children—Carol (Mrs. William Brigham), (dec.), Lott H. Asst. dean men U. Ill., 1923-28; admitted to Ill. bar, 1928, since practiced in Champaign; partner firm Thomas, Mamer, Haughey & Miller, and predecessor firms, 1946—; part-time prof. law U. Ill. Coll. Law, 1947-65. Past dir., v.p. Champaign Asphalt Co., Reliable Plumbing and Heating Co., Sandwells, Inc.; dir. First Nat. Bank of Champaign. Past pres. YMCA, Community Chest, War Chest. Past bd. dirs. Ill. Bar Found.; past dir., pres. U. Ill. Found.; past pres., dir. Carle Hosp. Found. Fellow Am. Bar Found.; mem. Am. (ho. dels. 1956), Ill. (bd. govs. 1941-58, v.p. 1953-56, pres. 1956-57) bar assns., Am. Law Inst., Am. Judicature Soc., Am. Coll. Probate Counsel, Sigma Chi. Republican. Episcopalian. Home: 2015 Duncan Rd Champaign IL 61820 Office: 30 Main St Champaign IL 61820

THOMAS, JAMES SAMUEL, bishop; b. Orangeburg, S.C., Apr. 8, 1919; s. James and Dessie Veronica (Mark) T.; A.B., Clafin Coll., Orangeburg, 1939, D.D., 1953; B.D., Gammon Theol. Sem., Atlanta, 1943; M.A., Drew U., 1944; Ph.D., Cornell U., 1953; LL.D., Bethune Cookman Coll., 1963, Simpson Coll., 1965, Morningside Coll., 1966, Iowa Wesleyan Coll., Coe Coll., 1968, Westmar Coll., 1970; L.H.D., Cornell Coll., 1965, Ohio Weslyan U., 1967, DePauw U., 1969; H.H.D., St. Ambrose Coll., 1970; S.T.D., Baldwin-Wallace Coll., 1977; D.H., Rust Coll., 1975; m. Ruth Naomi Wilson, July 7, 1945; children—Claudie (Mrs. Williamson), Gloria Jean, Margaret Yvonne, Patricia Elaine. Ordained to ministry Meth. Ch., 1944; pastor Orangeburg Circuit, 1942-43, York, S.C., 1946-48; chaplain S.C. State Coll., 1944-46; prof. Gammon Theol. Sem., 1948-53; asso. sec. Meth. Bd. Edn., 1953-64; bishop Iowa area Meth. Ch., 1964-76; bishop Ohio East area United Meth. Ch., 1976—; mem. Gen. Council on Fin. and Adminstrn.; dir. Equitable of Iowa; vis. prof. Perkins Sch. Theology, So. Meth. U., summer 1958, Duke U. Div. Sch., fall 1978. Trustee Baldwin-Wallace Coll., Meth. Theol. Sch. in Ohio, Mt. Union Coll., Ohio Wesleyan U., Otterbein Coll., Copeland Oaks, Elyria Home, Berea Children's Home, St. Luke's Hosp. Address: 1226 Market Ave N Canton OH 44714

THOMAS, JEROME FRANCIS, chemist; b. Chgo., Jan. 8, 1922; s. John L. and Martha E. T.; B.S. in Chemistry, De Paul U., 1942; Ph.D. in Chemistry, U. Calif., 1950; m. Rosemary L., Mar. 3, 1944; children—Jerrie Ann, Nicki, Peter, Kathy, Patrick, Michelle, Michael, Sean, Jeff. Mem. faculty U. Calif., Berkeley, 1945—, prof., chmn. div. hydraulic and san. engring.; cons. to fed. and state govt., industry. Served with USNR, 1941-45. Named Disting. Alumni, DePaul U.; registered profl. engr., Calif. Mem. Am. Chem. Soc., Am. Water Works Assn. Roman Catholic. Contbr. numerous articles to profl. jours. Home: 1104 Woodside Rd Berkeley CA 94708 Office: Davis Hall U Calif Berkeley CA 94720*

THOMAS, JESS, tenor; b. Hot Springs, S.D., Aug. 4, 1927; s. Charles A. and H. Ellen (Yocam) T.; A.B., U. Nebr., 1949; M.A., Stanford, 1953; student Otto Schulmann, San Francisco, 1953-57; m. Violeta Maria de Los Angeles Rios Andino Figueroa, 1974; children—Victor Justin, Lisa Jess David. Guidance counselor pub. schs., Hermiston, Oreg., 1949-52, Alameda, Cal., 1953-56; winner San Francisco Opera audition, 1957; profl. debut Baden State Theatre, Karlsruhe, Germany, 1958; appeared in Stuttgart, Germany, 1959-64, Bavarian State Opera, Munich, 1959—, Munich Festival, 1960—, Bayreuth Festival, 1961—, Berlin Philharmonic, 1962, Met. Opera Co., 1962—, Venice, Italy Wagner Festival, 1963, Deutsche Oper, Berlin, 1961-64, Frankfurt Opera, 1963, Salzburg Summer Festival, 1964—, Vienna State Opera, 1964—, La Scala Opera, 1965, Opening Night New Met. Opera, 1966, Osaka Japan Festival, 1967, Convent Garden Opera, 1969—, Salzburg Easter Festival, 1969—, Paris Grand Opera, 1967—, San Francisco Opera, 1965—; sang Tristan in Covent Garden, Met. Opera, Vienna State Opera, Palacio de Bellas Artes, Mexico City, 1971—, Casals Festival, 1976—, Teatro Colon Opera, Buenos Aires, 1976—; Bolshoi Theatre, Moscow, 1971; recording artist for Angel Records, Deutsche Grammophon, Phillips, RCA, Columbia; N.Y. Philharmonic debut, 1967; Boston Symphony debut, 1967. Named Kammersänger, Bavarian State Govt., 1963; recipient San Francisco Opera medallion, 1972; named Kammersänger, Austrian Govt., 1976. Mem. Beta Theta Pi, Phi Delta Kappa. Home: PO Box 662 Tiburon CA 94920 Office: care Colbert Artists Mgmt 111 W 57th St New York NY 10019

THOMAS, JIMMY LYNN, fin. exec.; b. Mayfield, Ky., Aug. 3, 1941; s. Alben Stanley and Emma Laura (Alexander) T.; B.S. (Ashland Oil Co. scholar 1959-63), U. Ky., 1963; M.B.A. (Samuel Bronfman fellow 1963-64; McKinsey scholar 1964), Columbia U., 1964; m. Nancy Nelson Danforth, June 5, 1964; children—James Nelson, Carter Danforth. Financial analyst Ford Motor Co., Detroit, 1964-66; asst. treas. Joel Dean Assos., N.Y.C., 1966-67; asst. controller Trans World Airlines, N.Y.C., 1967-73; treas. Gannett Co., Inc., Rochester, N.Y., 1973—; dir. Marine Midland Bank, Rochester, Charlevoix Paper Co. Treas. Frank E. Gannett Found.; bd. overseers Strong Meml. Hosp., Rochester; co-chmn. United Negro Coll. Fund, Rochester, Rochester Community Chest. Served with AUS, 1967-68. Mem. Rochester C. of C., U. Ky., Columbia U. alumni assns., Beta Gamma Sigma, Omicron Delta Kappa, Sigma Alpha Epsilon. Democrat. Mem. Christian Ch. (Disciples of Christ). Club: Genessee Valley (Rochester). Home: 13 New England Dr Rochester NY 14618 Office: Gannett Co Inc Lincoln Tower Rochester NY 14604

THOMAS, JOAB LANGSTON, univ. chancellor; b. Holt, Ala., Feb. 14, 1933; s. Ralph Cage and Chamintney Elizabeth (Stovall) T.; A.B., Harvard, 1955, M.A., 1957, Ph.D., 1959; m. Marly A. Dukes, Dec. 22, 1954; children—Catherine, David, Jennifer, Frances. Cytotaxonomist, Arnold Aboretum, Harvard, 1959-61; faculty U. Ala., University, 1961-76, prof. biology, 1966-76, asst. dean Coll. Arts and Scis., 1964-65, 69, dean for student devel., 1969-74, v.p., 1974-76, dir. Herbarium, 1961-76, dir. Arboretum, 1964-65, 66-69; chancellor N.C. State U., Raleigh, 1976—. Intern acad. adminstrn., Am. Council on Edn., 1971. Named Outstanding Prof., U. Ala., 1964-65. Mem. Phi Beta Kappa (hon.), Sigma Xi, Omicron Delta Kappa (hon.), Phi Kappa Phi. Author: A Monographic Study of the Cyrillaceae, 1960; Wildflowers of Alabama and Adjoining States, 1973; The Rising South, 1976. Home: 1903 Hillsborough St Raleigh NC 27607

THOMAS, JOHN BOWMAN, educator, elec. engr.; b. New Kensington, Pa., July 14, 1925; s. John Bowman and Lenna Iva (Sturms) T.; A.B., Gettysburg Coll., 1944; B.S., Johns Hopkins, 1952; M.S., Stanford, 1953, Ph.D., 1955; m. Eleanor W. Graefe, June 3, 1944; children—Sharon Lenore (Mrs. Guy G. Miller), Bronwyn Lee (Mrs. Robert Knight), John Andrew, Gwendolyn Elizabeth (Mrs. John L. Harer), Randall Stuart, Gailyn Brooke. Elec. engr., then asst. chief engr. Koppers Co., Inc., 1946-52; faculty Princeton, 1955—, prof. elec. engring., 1962—. Indsl. cons., 1955—. NSF sr. postdoctoral fellow Berkeley, Stanford, 1967-68. Served with AUS, 1944-46. Fellow I.E.E.E. (exec. com. Princeton sect. 1955-63, officer 1960-63); mem. Sigma Xi, Tau Beta Pi. Author tech. papers, books. Home: 900 Kingston Rd Princeton NJ 08540

THOMAS, JOHN EDWIN, univ. adminstr.; b. Fort Worth, Tex., Apr. 23, 1931; s. John L. and Dorothy F. T.; B.S.E.E., U. Kans., 1953; J.D., U. Mo., Kansas City, 1961; M.S., Fla. State U., 1965, D.B.A., 1970; m. Janice Paula Winzenik, Jan. 29, 1967; children—John L., Christa T., Scott A., Brandon F. With Wagner Electric Corp., St. Louis, 1955-63, mgr. elec. apparatus div., Atlanta, 1961-63; with NASA, Cape Kennedy, Fla., 1963-70, chief requirements and resources office, dir. tech. support, 1966-70; prof., head gen. bus. dept. East Tex. State U., 1970-72; dean Coll. Scis. and Tech., 1972-74; vice chancellor for acad. affairs Appalachian State U., Boone, N.C., 1974-79, chancellor, 1979—. Served with USMC, 1953-55. NDEA fellow, 1968. Mem. Fed. Bar Assn., Soc. Advancement Mgmt., So. Mgmt. Assn., Phi Delta Kappa, Delta Gamma Sigma. Methodist. Club: Kiwanis. Home: Appalachian State Univ Chancellor's Home Boone NC 28608 Office: Office of Chancellor Appalachian State U Boone NC 28608

THOMAS, JOHN EUGENE, educator; b. Youngstown, Ohio, July 5, 1914; s. Homer J. and Cassell M. (Phillips) T.; B.Sc., Ohio State U., 1941; Ph.D., U. Wis., 1947; m. Della P. Farmer, Feb. 1, 1942; children—Susan J. (Mrs. Joel Lynd), Thomas R., Peter M. Research asst. Ohio Agrl. Expt. Sta., Wooster, 1940; research asst. plant pathology U. Wis., Madison, 1941-45, instr., 1945-47, asst. prof., 1947-50; asso. prof. plant pathology and botany Okla. State U., Stillwater, 1950-57, prof., 1957—, head dept., 1966—. Mem. Am. Phytopath. Soc., Mycological. Soc. Am., Am. Inst. Biol. Sci., Okla. Acad. Sci., Sigma Xi, Phi Sigma. Home: 217 N Stallard St Stillwater OK 74074

THOMAS, JOHN JOSEPH, metal products co. exec.; b. Pine Grove, Pa., Dec. 10, 1932; s. John Wesley and Mary Grace (Angst) T.; B.A. with distinction, U. Nebr., 1954; J.D., U. Wash., 1959; m. Elsie Marie Koubsky, Sept. 23, 1958. Admitted to Wash. bar, 1960, Ind. bar, 1967; with Guttormsen, Scholfield, Willits and Ager, Seattle, 1959-61; atty. Sweden Freezer Mfg. Co., Seattle, 1961-66; with Arvin Industries, Inc., Columbus, Ind., 1966—, v.p., sec., 1971—, gen. counsel, 1976—. Served with USNR, 1954-57, 61-62. Mem. Am., Wash., Ind. bar assns., Phi Beta Kappa, Delta Theta Phi. Home: 4216 N Riverside Dr Columbus IN 47201 Office: 1531 E 13th St Columbus IN 47201

THOMAS, JOHN KELLINGER, ret. assn. exec.; b. Greenwich, Conn., Dec. 31, 1915; s. Samuel Kellinger and Helen Emily (Serre) T.; B.A., Colgate U., 1938; m. Madelaine White, Sept. 28, 1940; children—Lesley, John, Elaine. Salesman, Gen. Foods Corp., Conn. and N.J., 1939-41; ops. agt. Am. Airlines, N.Y.C., Boston, New Haven, 1941-44; trader Thomas, Haab & Botts, Stock Option Brokers, N.Y.C., 1950-70; exec. dir. St. Croix C. of C., Christiansted, V.I., 1972-79. Served with USNR, 1944-46. Mem. Beta Theta Pi. Clubs: Ha' Penny Bay Beach, St. Croix Country. Address: 117 Van Dyke Dr Nokomis FL 33555

THOMAS, JOHN M., corp. exec.; b. Iowa, Oct. 12, 1926; m. Evalyn Bates. Clk. typist Dept. State, Washington, 1951-52, adminstrv. asst., 1952-56, adminstrv. officer, 1956-65, supervisory adminstrv. officer, 1965, supervisory adminstrv. officer, Manila, 1965-67, dir. Office Ops., Washington, 1967-69, dep. asst. sec. ops., 1969-73, asst. sec. adminstrn., 1973-79; v.p. Norton Simon Co., N.Y.C., 1979—. Office: Norton Simon Inc 277 Park Ave New York NY 10017*

THOMAS, JOHN MELVIN, physician; b. Carmarthen, Gt. Brit., Apr. 26, 1933; s. Morgan and Margaret (Morgan) T.; M.B., Ch.B., Univ. Coll. Wales, U. Edinburgh, 1958; m. Betty Ann Mayo, Nov. 3, 1958; children—James, Hugh, Pamela. Intern, Robert Packer Hosp., Sayre, Pa., 1958-59, chief surg. resident, 1963; asso. surgeon Guthrie Clinic Ltd., Sayre, Pa., 1963-69, chmn. dept. surgery, 1969—; pres. med. staff Robert Packer Hosp., 1968; guest examiner Am. Bd. Surgery, 1979. Chmn. licensure and accountability Gov.'s Conf., 1974; bd. dirs. Donald Guthrie Found. for Research; trustee Robert Packer Hosp.; pres. bd. dirs. Guthire Clinic Ltd., 1972—. Mem. A.C.S., AMA, Am. Group Practice Assn., Pa. Med. Soc., Bradford County Med. Soc., Central N.Y. Surg. Soc., Soc. Surgery Alimentary Tract, Am. Soc. Parenteral and Enteral Nutrition. Presbyterian. Clubs: Shepard Hills Country, Moselem Springs Golf. Home: Box 113 Walker Hill Waverly NY 14892 Office: Guthrie Clinic Ltd Sayre PA 18840

THOMAS, JOHN RICHARD, chemist; b. Anchorage, Ky., Aug. 26, 1921; s. John R. and Mildred (Woods) T.; B.S., U. Calif., Berkeley, 1943, Ph.D., 1947; m. Beatrice Ann Davidson, Dec. 7, 1944; children—Jonnie Sue Jacobs, Richard G. With U.S. AEC, 1949-51; research chemist Chevron Research Co., Richmond, Calif., 1948-49, sr. research asso., 1951-60, sr. research scientist, 1961-67; mgr. research and devel. Ortho div. Chevron Chem. Co., Richmond, 1967-68; asst. sec. Standard Oil Co. Calif., 1968-70; pres. Chevron Research Co., 1970—, also dir.; dir. Cetus Corp., Vectra Corp. Bd. dirs. Intellectual Property Owners Assn., Inc. Mem. Am. Chem. Soc., AAAS, Indsl. Research Inst., Soc. Automotive Engrs. Republican. Patentee in field; contbr. articles to profl. jours. Home: 847 McEllen Way Lafayette CA 94549 Office: Chevron Research Co 576 Standard Ave Richmond CA 94802

THOMAS, JOSEPH ALLAN, lawyer; b. Los Angeles, Aug. 12, 1929; s. Joseph Smith and Blanche Aileen (Henry) T.; B.S., U. So. Calif., 1954, J.D., 1957; m. Jacquelynne B. Jones, June 13, 1954; children—Douglas, Scott, Kevin, Matthew. Admitted to Calif. bar, 1958; individual practice law, Downey, Calif., 1958-60; mem. legal staff Pacific Mut. Life Ins. Co., Newport Beach, Calif., 1960—, now also v.p., gen. counsel. Bd. dirs. Orange County YMCA, 1977—, chmn. bd., 1979—; bd. dirs. South Coast YMCA, 1974—, chmn. bd., 1977-79; mem. Orange County Citizens Direction Finding Commn., 1979—; bd. dirs. Laguna Niguel Community Assn., 1974-77. Fellow Life Office Mgmt. Assn.; mem. Calif. State Bar Assn., Orange County Bar Assn., Los Angeles County Bar Assn. Republican. Home: Laguna Niguel CA 92677 Office: 700 Newport Center Dr Newport Beach CA 92660

THOMAS, JOSEPH FLESHMAN, architect; b. Oak Hill, W.Va., Mar. 23, 1915; s. Robert Russel and Effie (Fleshman) T.; student Duke, 1931-32; B.Arch., Carnegie-Mellon U., 1938; m. Margaret Ruth Lively, Feb. 28, 1939 (dec.); m. 2d., Dorothy Francene Root, Apr. 29, 1967; children—Anita Carol, Joseph Stephan. Practice architecture various firms, W. Va., Va., Tenn., Calif., 1938-49; staff architect Calif. Div. Architecture, Los Angeles, 1949-52; prin. Joseph F. Thomas, architect, Pasadena, Calif., 1952-53; pres. Neptune & Thomas, architects-engrs., Pasadena and San Diego, 1953—. Mem. Pasadena Planning Commn., 1956-64, chmn., 1963-64; pres. Citizens Council for Planning, Pasadena, 1966-67; mem. steering com. Pasadena NOW, 1970—; mem. Pasadena Design Com., 1979—; mem. adv. bd. Calif. Office Architecture and Constrn., 1970-72. Served to lt. (j.g.) USNR, 1943-46. Recipient Service award City of Pasadena, 1964, Distinguished Service award Calif. Dept. Gen. Services, 1972. Fellow AIA (4 awards honor, 13 awards merit 1957-78; dir. Calif. council 1966-68, exec. com. 1974-77, pres. Pasadena chpt. 1967, chmn. Calif. sch. facilities com. 1970-72, mem. nat. jud. bd. 1973-74, nat. dir. 1974-77, treas. 1977-79, exec. com., planning com., chmn. finance com.); mem. Breakfast Forum, Pi Kappa Alpha. Republican. Methodist. Kiwanian. Clubs: Univ., Annandale Golf (Pasadena). Prin. works include Meth. Hosp., Arcadia, Calif., Foothill Presbyn. Hosp., Glendora, Calif., master plans and bldgs. Citrus Coll., Azusa, Calif., Riverside (Calif.) Coll., Westmont Coll., Monticeto, Calif., Northrop Inst. Tech., Inglewood, Calif., Indian Valley Coll., Marin County, Calif., other coll. bldgs.; Pacific Telephone Co., Pasadena, Los Angeles County Superior Ct. Bldg., U.S. Naval Hosp., San Diego. Home: 330 San Miguel Rd Pasadena CA 91105 Office: 1560 W Colorado Blvd Pasadena CA 91105

THOMAS, JOSEPH HARRUFF, securities broker; b. Marion, Ohio, Jan. 11, 1934; s. Marvin C. and Irene E. (Harruff) T.; B.A. with honors in Econs., Denison U., 1956; M.B.A., U. Cin., 1964; m. Ellen T. Blemker, Feb. 16, 1963; children—Virginia, Elizabeth. With McDonald & Co., Cleve., 1959—, underwriting syndicate mgr., 1966-69, sales mgr., 1969-71, mng. partner, 1971-79, sr. partner, 1979—; dir. Fabri Centers Am., Cleve., N.Y. Stock Exchange. Bd. dirs., mem. exec. com. Cleve. Growth Assn.; trustee Denison U., St. Luke's Hosp. Served to 1st lt. USAAF, 1956-59. Republican. Episcopalian. Clubs: Union (Cleve.); Pepper Pike, The Country (Pepper Pike, Ohio). Home: 2692 Wadsworth Rd Shaker Heights OH 44122 Office: McDonald & Co 2100 Central Nat Bank Bldg Cleveland OH 44114

THOMAS, JOSEPH HENRY, former profl. football exec.; b. Warren, O., Mar. 18, 1921; s. Henry and Mary (Mitrovich) T.; B.S. in Edn., Ohio No. U., 1943; M.S. in Health and Phys. Edn., 1950, dir.'s degree in health and phys. edn., 1952; m. Judith A. Demian, June 12, 1969; 1 dau., Paige Judith. Football coach, New Albany, Ind., 1946-47, Renselaer, Ind., 1947-48; asst. coach De Pauw U., 1948-51, Ind. U., 1952-54, Balt. Colts Profl. Football Team, 1954-55, Los Angeles Rams Profl. Football Team, 1955-57, Toronto Argonauts Profl. Football Team, 1957-59; dir. player personnel Minn. Vikings Profl. Football Team, 1960-65; exec. asst., dir. player personnel Miami Dolphins Profl. Football Team (Fla.), 1965-72; v.p., gen. mgr. Balt. Colts Football, Inc., 1972-77, head coach, 1974-77; exec. v.p., gen. mgr. San Francisco 49ers Football Club, 1977-78. Served with USNR, 1943-46. Recipient citation Ohio No. U., 1969. Roman Catholic. Home: 499 Walsh Rd Atherton CA 94025

THOMAS, JOYCE KILMER, clergyman; b. Paxton, W.Va., Jan. 20, 1923; s. Edward Elliot and Dahlia (Procious) T.; A.B., Morris Harvey Coll., 1948; B.Th., Aurora Coll., 1950; m. Evelyn Lee Shell, Jan. 10, 1945; children—Glenda Joan (Mrs. David R. O'Coin), Mark Elliott, Paul Frederick, Karen Anne, David Edward. Ordained to ministry Advent Christian Ch., 1946; pastor in Galesburg, Ill., 1951-53, Miami, Fla., 1953-61, Jacksonville, Fla., 1961-65, Mendota, Ill., 1965-66, Durham, N.C., 1966-67, Panama City, Fla., 1969-73, Clendenin, W.Va., 1973-77, Miramar, Fla., 1977—; exec. sec. So. Ga. and Fla. Conf. Advent Christian Chs., 1967-72. Sec., Ill. Advent Christian Conf., 1951-53; v.p. So. Advent Christian Assn., 1959-64; pres. So. Ga. and Fla. Conf. Advent Christian Chs., 1959-64; mem. bd. Am. Advent Mission Soc., 1960-65; v.p. Central Advent Mission Soc., 1965-66; rec. sec. Advent Christian Gen. Conf. Am., 1965—. Sec., Dowling Park Campmeeting Assn., 1958-61, treas., 1961-62. Served with AUS, 1943-46. Home: 7820 Biltmore Blvd Miramar FL 33023

THOMAS, JULIAN JOHNSON, JR., dentist, naval officer; b. Nashville, Oct. 10, 1927; s. Julian Johnson and Martha Warner T.; student Vanderbilt U., 1946-49; D.D.S., U. Tenn., 1953; M.S., Ind. U., 1966; m. Joan White, Aug. 18, 1956; children—Martha R., Julian Johnson. Commd. lt. (j.g.) U.S. Navy, 1953, advanced through grades to lt., 1956; dental intern Naval Hosp., Phila., 1953-54; asst. dental officer USS Albany, 1954-56; discharged, 1956; gen. practice dentistry, Nashville, 1956-58; recommd. lt. U.S. Navy, 1958, advanced through grades to rear adm., 1977; asst. dental officer, instr. Naval Dental Sch., Bethesda, Md., 1958-60, instr., clinic supr., 1966-70; head dental dept. U.S.S. Little Rock (CLG-4), 1961-63; asst. dental officer Navy Dept., Washington, 1963; White House dentist, Washington, 1967-70; head dental dept. U.S. Naval Support Activity, Naples, Italy, 1970-74; comdg. officer Naval Regional Dental Center, Parris Island, S.C., 1974-77; dep. chief dental div., insp. gen., dental Bur. Medicine and Surgery, Navy Dept., Washington, 1977-79; comdg. officer Naval Regional Dental Center, San Diego, 1979—. Mem. ADA, Am. Coll. Dentists, Internat. Assn. for Dental Research, Acad. Operative Dentistry, Internat. Coll. Dentists. Episcopalian. Club: Hilton Head Racquet (Hilton Head Island, S.C.). Home: 303 Silvergate Ct San Diego CA 92106 Office: Comdg Officer Naval Regional Dental Center San Diego CA 92136

THOMAS, LARRY LEE, trade assn. exec.; b. Norfolk, Va., Mar. 13, 1941; s. St. Clair Ellison and Dorothy Lee (Poplin) T.; B.A. in Philosophy, Coll. William and Mary, 1965; J.D., George Washington U., 1968; m. Jane Ann Cox, Oct. 18, 1969; 1 son, Brett Ellison. Admitted to D.C. bar, 1969; atty. advisor FTC, 1968-70; counsel Nat. Paint and Coatings Assn., 1970-74, asso. gen. counsel, 1974-77, gen. counsel, 1977-78, exec. dir., chief operating officer, 1978—; dir. Verlan Ltd. Mem. Am. Bar Assn., Am. Soc. Assn. Execs., Washington Soc. Assn. Execs. Club: Nat. Democratic, Univ. Office: 1500 Rhode Island Ave NW Washington DC 20005

THOMAS, LAWRENCE BRUCE, food co. exec.; b. St. Joseph, Mo., Mar. 3, 1936; s. Bruce Henry and Mary Elizabeth (Birch) T.; B.S.B.A., Kans. U., 1958; M.B.A. in Fin., Ind. U., 1959; m. Jann Eola Walker, Aug. 22, 1958; children—Bruce Henry II, Evelyn B., E. Birch. With ConAgra, Omaha, 1960—, asst. treas., 1967-69, v.p. fin., 1969-74, v.p. fin., treas., 1974—; dir. Exchange Bank, Mound City. Bd. dirs. Mo. Activities YMCA, PTA, Boys Clubs of Omaha; pres., bd. dirs. Big Bros. Assn., Omaha; bd. dirs. United Community Services of Midlands, also mem. exec. com., sec., mem. com. program planning and budget, fin. com. nominating com. fund raising com.; bd. dirs., pres. Jr. Achievement, Omaha, also mem. exec. com., pres., treas., sec., v.p.; trustee D. Cary Found.; v.p., bd. dirs. Clarkson Hosp.; bd. dirs. Boys Club Omaha, Omaha Symphony, Mid-Am. council Boy Scouts Am.; adv. council U. Nebr. at Omaha Sch. Bus. and Sch. Fine Arts. Served to capt. Q.M.C., U.S. Army. Mem. Fin. Execs. Inst., Conf. Bd. (panel sr. fin. execs.), Sister City Assn., Phi Delta Theta, Alpha Kappa Psi. Republican. Presbyterian. Club: Omaha (pres.). Home: 7813 Pierce St Omaha NE 68124 Office: 200 Kiewit Plaza Omaha NE 68131

THOMAS, LEE BALDWIN, mfg. co. exec.; b. Alma, Nebr., Sept. 17, 1900; s. Rees and Fannie (Baldwin) T.; B.B.A., U. Wash., 1923; m. Margaret Thomas, 1924 (dec.); children—Lee Baldwin, Margaret Ellen (Mrs. Wallace H. Dunbar), Susan Jane (Mrs. A. Scott Hamilton, Jr.); m. 2d, Elizabeth C. Bromley. Advt. mgr. Ernst Hardware Co., Seattle, 1923-24, sales mgr., 1926-29; buyer R.H. Macy Co., N.Y.C., 1924-25; dir. home goods merchandising Butler Bros., Chgo., 1929-41; pres. Ekco Products Co., Chgo., 1941-47; with Am. Elevator & Machine Co., Louisville, 1947-48; chmn. Thomas Industries, Louisville; chmn. Vt. Am. Corp., Louisville; owner Honey Locust Valley Farms, Cloverport, Ky. Bd. dirs. Honey Locust Found., Louisville. Episcopalian. Clubs: Owl Creek Country (Anchorage, Ky.); Harmony Landing Country (Prospect, Ky.); Jefferson, Pendennis (Louisville); Union League, Mid-Day (Chgo.); Lake Region Yacht and Country (Winter Haven, Fla.); Mountain Lake (Lake Wales, Fla.); Delray (Fla.) Dunes Country. Home: Evergreen Rd Anchorage KY 40223 Office: 100 E Liberty St Louisville KY 40202

THOMAS, LEWIS, physician, educator, med. adminstr.; b. Flushing, N.Y., Nov. 25, 1913; s. Joseph S. and Grace Emma (Peck) T.; B.S., Princeton, 1933, Sc.D., 1976; M.D., Harvard, 1937; M.A., Yale, 1969; Sc.D. (hon.), U. Rochester, 1974, U. Ohio at Toledo, 1976, Columbia U., 1978, Meml. U. of Nfld., 1978, U. N.C., 1979; LL.D., Johns Hopkins U., 1976; L.H.D. (hon.), Duke U., 1976, Reed Coll., 1978; m. Beryl Dawson, Jan. 1, 1941; children—Abigail Luttinger, Judith, Eliza. Intern, Boston City Hosp., 1937-39, Neurol. Inst., N.Y.C., 1939-41; Tilney Meml. fellow Thorndike Lab., Boston City Hosp., 1941-42; vis. investigator Rockefeller Inst. 1942-46; asst. prof. pediatrics Med. Sch. Johns Hopkins, 1946-48; asso. prof. medicine Med. Sch. Tulane, 1948-50, prof. medicine, 1950; prof. pediatrics and medicine, dir. pediatric research labs. Heart Hosp., U. Minn., 1950-54; prof., chmn. dept. pathology N.Y. U. Sch. Medicine, 1954-58, prof., chmn. dept. medicine, 1958-66, dean, 1966-69; prof., chmn. dept. pathology Yale, 1969-72, dean Sch. Medicine, 1972-73; prof. medicine, pathology Med. Sch. Cornell U., N.Y.C., 1973—, prof. biology (SKI) div. Grad. Sch. Med. Sci., 1973—, co-dir., 1974—; adj. prof. Rockefeller U., 1975—; pres., chief exec. officer Meml. Sloan-Kettering Cancer Center, N.Y.C., 1973—; dir. 3d and 4th med. divs. Bellevue Hosp., 1958-66, pres. med. bd., 1963-66; cons. Manhattan VA Hosp., 1954-69; cons. to surgeon gen. Dept. Army, surgeon gen. USPHS; mem. pathology study sect. NIH, 1954-58, nat. adv. health council, 1958-62, nat. adv. child health and human devel. council, 1963-67; mem. commn. on streptococcal disease Armed Forces Epidemiological Bd., 1950-62; mem. Pres.'s Sci. Adv. Com., 1967-70; mem. Inst. Medicine, Nat. Acad. Scis., 1971—, mem. council and governing bd., 1979—; chmn. overview cluster subcom. Pres.'s Biomed. Research Panel, 1975—. Dir., Squibb Corp.; mem. adv. council Internat. Exec. Services Corp., 1978—. Mem. Bd. Health, N.Y.C., 1956-69; mem. bd. sci. consultants Sloan-Kettering Inst. Cancer Research, 1966-72; mem. Sloan-Kettering Inst., 1973—; mem. med. adv. com. Center for Biomed. Edn. City U. N.Y., 1972—; mem. div. biology and med. sci. com. on edn. Brown U., 1974-76; mem. scientific adv. com. The Inst. for Cancer Research, 1974—; mem. com. on health professions of the bd. trustees Sch. Med. U. Pitts., 1974-76; mem. med. adv. com. Irvington House Inst., N.Y.C., 1974—; bd. dirs. Josiah Macy Jr. Found., 1975—, Found. Advancement Internat. Research in Microbiology, 1979—; bd. sci. advisers Mass. Gen. Hosp., 1970-73, Scripps Clinic and Research Found., 1969—; bd. dirs., research council Public Health Research Inst. of City N.Y., 1974—; bd. overseers Harvard Coll., 1976—; mem. sci. adv. com. Sidney Farker Cancer Inst., 1978—; mem. council Grad. Sch. Bus. and Public Adminstrn., Cornell U., 1978—; mem. awards assembly Gen. Motors Cancer Research Found., 1978—. Trustee, N.Y.C.-Rand Inst., 1967-71, The Rockefeller U., 1975—, Draper Lab., 1975—, John Simon Guggenheim Meml. Found., 1975—, Mt. Sinai Sch. Medicine, 1979—. Asso. fellow Ezra Stiles Coll. Yale U. Served as lt. comdr. M.C., USNR, 1941-46. Recipient Distinguished Achievement award Modern Medicine, 1975; Nat. Book award for arts and letters, 1975; Honor award Am. Med. Writers Assn., 1978; Med. Edn. award AMA, 1979; Bard award in medicine and sci. Bard Coll., 1979; Harrington Lectr. award SUNY, Buffalo, 1979. Fellow Am. Acad. Arts and Scis., Am. Rheumatism Assn.; mem. Nat. Acad. Scis., Am. Philos. Assn., Am. Pub. Health Assn., Am. Acad. Neurology, Internat. Acad. Pathology, Am. Soc. Exptl. Pathology, Practitioners Soc., Am. Acad. Microbiology, Peripatetic Clin. Soc., Am. Cancer Soc. (dir. at large 1974—), Am. Heart Assn., Am. Soc. Clin. Investigation, Am. Assn. Immunologists, Soc. Am. Bacteriologist, Assn. Am. Physicians, Am. Pediatric Soc., Soc. Pediatric Research, N.Y. Acad. Scis., Harvey Soc. (councillor), A.A.U.P., Soc. Exptl. Biology and Medicine, Soc. Health and Human Values (council), Am. Soc. Clin. Oncology, Interurban Clin. Club, Phi Beta Kappa, Alpha Omega Alpha. Clubs: Harvard (N.Y.C.); Union; Century Assn. Author: Lives of a Cell, 1974; Medusa and the Snail, 1979. Editorial bd. Cellular Immunology, Am. Jour. Pathology, Jour. of Medicine and Philosophy, Inflammation. Office: Memorial-Sloan Kettering Cancer Center 1275 York Ave New York NY 10021

THOMAS, LIONEL ARTHUR JOHN, artist; b. Toronto, Ont., Can., Apr. 3, 1915; s. Arthur Edward and Ida Mae (Mooney) T.; student John Russel Sch. Fine Arts, Toronto, 1933-35, Ont. Coll. Art, Toronto, 1936-37, Karl Godwin Sch. Illustration, Toronto, 1937; Diploma, Canadian Coll. Music, 1930; grad. Hans Hofman Sch. Fine Arts, Provincetown, Mass., 1947, Calif. Sch. Fine Arts, San Francisco, 1949; m. Sept. 10, 1940; children—Elyse Thomas Stewart, Michau Tristan. One-man shows Vancouver Art Gallery, 1942, 48, Fine Arts Gallery, U. B.C., 1947, 48, 51, Toronto, 1976, Expn. Galleries, Vancouver, 1976, Honolulu, 1976, Captain's Gallery, Maui, Hawaii, 1976, Students Union Bldg. Art Gallery, U. B.C., 1977, Harrison Galleries, Vancouver, 1978, The Ommiplex Mus. Oklahoma City, 1978; exhibited in group shows Ont. Soc. Artists, 1941, Canadian Soc. Graphic Arts, 1947, Montreal Mus. Fine Arts, 1949, Hart House, U. Toronto, 1950, Grand Central Galleries, N.Y.C., 1952, Canadian Abstract Painters Exhbn., 1952, Nat. Gallery Can., Ottawa, 1953, Toronto Art Gallery, 1953, Sao Paulo Biennial, 1954, Seattle Art Mus., 1954, U. Calif. at San Francisco, 1960, U. Calgary, Edwards U. Gallery, Alta., 1960, Corvallis (Oreg.) State U., 1963, Zan Art Gallery, Victoria, B.C., 1973, U. B.C., 1976, Yorkville Gallery, Toronto, 1976, Ala Mona Center, Honolulu, 1976, U. Nev., Reno, 1978, Hansen Planetarium, Salt Lake City, 1978, Hasenburgh Planetarium, Rochester, N.Y., 1978, Reading (Pa.) Coll., 1978; works represented in permanent collections Nat. Gallery Can., Art Gallery Ont., Vancouver Arts Gallery, U. Victoria, Fla. So. Coll., also numerous pvt. collections; commns. Vancouver Pub., Library, U. Sask., U. Man., St. John's Cathedral, Winnipeg, Man., Merc. Bank Can., Vancouver, U. B.C., Phillips Barrett Engring. Bldg., Vancouver, Royal Bank Can., Vancouver, York U., Toronto, Our Lady of Perpetual Help, Calgary, St. Mary's Ch., Saskatoon, Great West Life Bldg., Winnipeg, Block Bros. Bldg., Vancouver, Beach Towers Apt., Vancouver, B.C. Provincial Mus., Victoria; instr. Sch. Architecture, U. B.C., Vancouver, 1950-59, asst. prof., 1959-64, asso. prof. dept. fine arts, 1964—; engaged in interpretation universe through enameled copper plates, 1973—. Chmn. com. applied design B.C. Archives and Mus. Centennial Project, 1967. Served as pvt. Seaforth Highlanders Regt., 1941-44. Recipient award Internat. div. Fla. Internat. Art Exhbn.; Allied Arts medal Royal Archtl. Inst. Can., 1956; award Pacific Northwest Artists Exhbn., Seattle, 1952. Mem. Royal Can. Acad. Arts, Royal Astron. Soc., Canadian Group Painters, B.C. Soc. Artists, Pacific Artists Assn., Northwest Inst. Sculptors, Soc. Am. Archaeologists, Am. Craftsmen Council. Home: 3351 Craigend Rd West Vancouver BC Canada Office: Dept Fine Arts University Brit Columbia Vancouver BC Canada

THOMAS, LOUIS GODFREY LEE, ret. metals mfr.; b. Chgo., Jan. 26, 1896; s. Richard H. and Lucille A. (Rousseau) T.; B.S., Lewis Inst., 1918; S.B. in Mech. Engring., Mass. Inst. Tech., 1920; L.H.D., Hahnemann Med. Coll., 1972; m. Florence Louise Sammons, Sept. 19, 1952. With DeLaval Steam Turbine Co., 1920-21; engr. Economy Pumps, Inc., 1921-40, exec. v.p., 1941-48; chmn. Sci. & Mechanics Pub. Co., 1940-51; v.p. Liberty Planers, Inc., 1940-48, pres., 1948-51; pres. Smith & Mills Shapers, 1940-51; pres. Hamilton-Thomas Corp., 1948-62, C.H. Wheeler Mfg. Co., 1950-62, Klipfel Valves, Inc., 1950-62, Griscom-Russell Co., 1959-62; chmn. Smart-Turner Machine Co., Ltd., 1949-62; dir. Fibre Formations, Inc., Fischer and Porter Co. Trustee Hahnemann Medical Coll. and Hosp., 1957-70; exec. devel. com. Villanova U., 1955-63; mem. adv. com. to dean Coll. Engring., U. Cin., 1958-63; bd. dirs. Magee Meml. Hosp. for Convalescents, 1965-70, Ursinus Coll., 1976—. Served with USA, 1917-19. Mem. Inst. Mech. Engrs. London, Soc. Naval Architects and Marine Engrs., Am. Legion, ASME, Am. Soc. Naval Engrs., Hydraulic Inst. (pres. 1955), Metal Mfrs. Assn. (v.p. 1959). Republican. Clubs: Engineers, Overbrook Golf, Peale, Merion Golf, Union League (Phila.); Moorings Country (Naples, Fla.). Home: 908 Tedwyn Apts 840 Montgomery Ave Bryn Mawr PA 19010 also 207 Kings Port Club Naples FL Office: Thomas & Co 1102 Western Savings Fund Bldg Broad and Chestnut Sts Philadelphia PA 19107

THOMAS, LOWELL, author, cinerama and TV producer, radio and TV commentator; b. Woodington, Ohio, Apr. 6, 1892; s. Harry George and Harriet (Wagner) T.; B.S., U. No. Ind., 1911; B.A., M.A., U. Denver, 1912; M.A., Princeton, 1916; Litt.D., Grove City Coll., 1933, St. Bonaventure, 1938, Franklin and Marshall Coll., 1942, Rider Coll., 1948, Ohio Wesleyan, 1949; LL.D., Albright Coll., 1934, Lafayette Coll., 1937, Washington and Jefferson Coll., 1942, Olivet Coll., 1950; L.H.D., Clark U., 1941, Boston U., 1943, Union Coll., 1944, U. Tampa, 1949; H.H.D., Temple U., 1942; D.L., Olivet Coll., 1950; m. Frances Ryan, Aug. 4, 1917; 1 son, Lowell. Reporter, editor various newspapers, Cripple Creek, reporter Chgo. Jour. until 1914; prof. oratory Chgo. Kent Coll. Law, 1912-14; instr. dept. English, Princeton, 1914-16; lectr. on Alaska, 1914-16; chief civilian mission sent to Europe by Pres. Wilson to prepare hist. record of World War I; news commentator, radio 1930—, movie news reels, 1935, television 1940—, producer-host High Adventure TV series, 1957-59; asso. editor Asia Mag., 1919-23. Recipient Chauncey M. Depew medal SAR, 1964; Nat. Assn. Broadcasters Distinguished Service award, 1968; named Personality of Year, Internat. Radio and TV Soc.; George Washington award Freedoms Found., 1978. Fellow Am. Geog. Soc., Royal Geog. Soc.; mem. Assn. Radio News Analysts, English Speaking Union (hon. life), Explorers Club, Kappa Sigma, Tau Kappa Alpha, Phi Delta Phi, Sigma Delta Chi, Alpha Epsilon. Mason. Clubs: Princeton, Dutch Treat, Overseas Press (N.Y.C.); St. Andrew's Golf, Bohemian (San Francisco). Author books latest being; These Men Shall Never Die, 1943; The Seven Wonders of the World, 1956; History As You Heard It, 1957; The Vital Spark; A Hundred and One Outstanding Lives, 1959; The Silent War in Tibet, 1959; Sir Hubert Wilkins, His World of Adventure, 1961; More Great True Adventures, 1963; Book of the High Mountains, 1964; Raiders of the Deep, 1964; Story of the St. Lawrence Seaway; With Lawrence in Arabia, 1971; (with Lowell Thomas, Jr.) Famous First Flights That Changed, 1969; (with Edward Jablonski) Doolittle: a Biography, 1976; (autobiography) Good Evening, Everybody: From Cripple Creek to Samarkand, 1976; (with Joy L. Sanderson) First Aid for Backpackers and Campers; So Long until Tomorrow, 1977; contbr. to periodicals. Home: Hammersley Hill Pawling NY 12564 Office: care William Morrow & Co 105 Madison Ave New York NY 10016*

THOMAS, LOWELL, JR., former lt. gov. Alaska, former state senator, author, lectr.; b. London, Eng., Oct. 6, 1923; s. Lowell Jackson and Frances (Ryan) T.; student Taft Sch., 1942; B.A., Dartmouth, 1948; postgrad. Princeton Sch. Pub. and Internat. Affairs, 1952; m. Mary Taylor Pryor, May 20, 1950; children—Anne Frazier, David Lowell. Asst. cameraman Fox Movietone News, S.Am., 1939, Bradford Washburn Alaskan mountaineering expdn., 1940; illustrated lecturer, 1946—; asst. economist, photographer with Max Weston Thornburg, Turkey, 1947, Iran, 1948; film prodn., Iran, 1949; Tibet expdn. with Lowell Thomas, Sr., 1949; field work Cinerama, S.Am., Africa, Asia, 1951-52; travels by small airplane with wife, writing and filming, Europe, Africa, Middle East, 1954-55; mem. Rockwell polar flight (1st flight around world over both Poles), 1965; prod. series of films, Flight to Adventure, NBC-TV, 1956; producer, writer TV series High Adventure, 1957-59, prod. documentary film Adaq, King of Alaskan Seas, 1960, two films on Alaska, 1962, 63, film on U. Alaska 1964, travel documentary, 1965, film on Arctic oil exploration for Atlantic-Richfield Co., 1969. Mem. Alaska State Senate, 1967-75, lt. gov. State of Alaska, 1975-79. Past pres. Western Alaska council Boy Scouts Am. Bd. dirs. Anchorage unit Salvation Army. Served 1st lt. USAAF, 1943-45. Mem. Screen Actors Guild, Alaska C. of C., Aircraft Owners and Pilots Assn. Clubs: Explorers, Marco Polo, Dutch Treat (N.Y.C.); Bohemian (San Francisco); Rotary, Press (Anchorage); Dartmouth Outing. Author: Out of this World, A Journey to Tibet, 1950; (with Mrs. Lowell Thomas, Jr.) Our Flight to Adventure, 1956; The Silent War in Tibet, 1959; The Dalai Lama, 1961; The Trail of Ninety-Eight, 1962; (with Lowell Thomas Sr.) Famous First Flights that Changed History, 1968. Address: 7022 Tanaina Dr Anchorage AK 99502

THOMAS, M. DONALD, supt. schs.; b. Bugnara, Italy, Apr. 21, 1926; s. Louis and Rose (Manna) T. (parents Am. citizens); B.A., U. Dubuque, Iowa, 1948; M.A., U. Ill., 1951, Ed.D., 1956; D.Litt., Westminster Coll., 1974; m. Frances Gaylord, Dec. 21, 1948; children—Marc, Marcia, David. Tchr. English, speech Mason City (Iowa) Pub. Schs., 1950-54; dir. speech activities Bloom Twp. High Sch., Chicago Heights, Ill., 1954-59; counselor high sch., Mt. Prospect, Ill., 1959-65; supt. Elk Grove (Ill.) Elementary Dist., 1966-69, Amsterdam (N.Y.) Unified Sch. Dist., 1969-71, Newark (Calif.) Unified Sch. Dist., 1971-73, Salt Lake City Sch. Dist., 1973—; lectr. Grad. Sch. Edn., Denver, 1970, U. Utah, 1974; cons. to N.Y. Dept. Edn., 1969-70, Calif. Dept. Edn., 1971—; adv. com. Cook County Supt. Schs., 1966-67; cons. U.S. Dept. Edn., 1969-70, Alameda County (Calif.) Schs. Dept., 1972-73; mem. Aspen Conf. on Edn. and the Human Potential, 1967, 68; mem. Supt.'s Workshop, Tchrs. Coll., Columbia U., N.Y.C., 1974. Mem. Youth Commn., Salt Lake City, 1974-75; chmn. steering com. N. Cook County (Ill.) Office of Econ. Opportunity, 1966-67; exec. com. Cook County Council of Govts., 1966-68. Recipient Best Mag. Article award Council Advancement of Edn. Writing, 1972-73. Mem. NEA (bd. dirs. 1968-71). Clubs: Rotary. Contbr. articles in edn. to popular mags. and profl. jours.; research in learning theories, personnel evaluation and child devel. Home: 860 18th Ave Salt Lake City UT 84103 Office: 440 E 1st St S Salt Lake City UT 84111. *Our nation provides opportunities to succeed far beyond those provided by any other country. Central to these opportunities is a system of free public education. It is our schools that give reality to the American Dream.*

THOMAS, MARK STANTON, flutist; b. Lakeland, Fla., Apr. 24, 1931; s. Gwillym Llewelyn Glendare and Marian Lorene (Peck) T.; diploma Peabody Conservatory of Music, 1949; student Am. U., 1960-61, Internat. Graphonanalysis Soc., 1966-68; m. Judith Ann Clapp, Sept. 12, 1964; children—Scott, Jeffrey, David, Elizabeth, Eric. Dir. Foxes Sch. Music, Falls Church, Va., 1958-60; prof. flute, chmn. woodwind dept. Am. U., 1960-68; v.p. W.T. Armstrong Co., Inc., mfrs. flutes and piccolos, Elkhart, Ind., 1968—, flute artist in residence, 1969—, also dir.; v.p. Armstrong Edu-Tainment Pub. Co., music pubs., Elkhart, 1974—; head Armstrong Pub. Co., 1976—; lectr. in flute Notre Dame U., 1975—. Mem. Elkhart County Humanities Council, 1972-75. Bd. dirs. Am. Youth Symphony Orch. and Chorus; Elkhart Symphony Orch.; pres. Elkhart Symphony Soc., 1978—. Served with AUS, 1949-58. Mem. Nat. Flute Assn. (founder, hon. life pres.), Am. Fedn. Musicians, A.S.C.A.P.; asso. Am. Bandmasters Assn. Episcopalian (lay reader, past vestryman). Elk. Author: Learning the Flute, 6 vols., 1974; My First Book of Christmas Flute Solos, 1976; My First Book of Sacred Flute Solos, 1976; also articles, brochures; (film) The Flute, A Study with Mark Thomas, 1971. Rec. artist flute solo albums Crest, Armstrong records, 1969-75. Flute designer, 1968—. Office: 1000 Industrial Pkwy Elkhart IN 46514. *Before I leave this world, I wish to give back to others, using the talents I have, more than I used. We are all here for a purpose and should work together, in honesty, for the betterment of our fellow man.*

THOMAS, MARLO, actress; b. Detroit, Nov. 21, 1943; d. Danny Thomas; ed. U. So. Calif. Theatrical appearances in Broadway prodn. Thieves, 1974, London prodn. Barefoot in the Park; star TV series That Girl, 1966; conceived book and record, starred in TV spl. Free to Be. . . You and Me (Emmy for best children's show), 1974; films include Jenny, Thieves, 1977. Recipient George Foster Peabody award; Tom Paine award Nat. Emergency Civil Liberties Com.; named Most Promising Newcomer, Fame, also Photoplay. Address: care ABC TV Studio 4151 Prospect St Los Angeles CA 90027

THOMAS, MICHAEL TILSON, symphony condr.; s. Ted and Roberta Thomas; b. Hollywood, Calif., 1944; pupil Ingolf Dahl, others; student conducting Berkshire Music Festival, Tanglewood, Mass. (Koussevitsky prize 1968); LL.D., Hamilton Coll.; L.H.D. (hon.), D'Youville Coll., 1976. Asst. condr. Boston Symphony Orch., 1969, asso. condr., 1970-72, prin. guest condr., 1972-74, also Berkshire Music Festival, summer 1970, 74; music dir., condr. Buffalo Philharmonic Orch., 1971-79; condr., dir. N.Y. Philharmonic Young People's Concerts, CBS-TV, 1971-77; vis. condr. numerous orchs. U.S., Europe, Japan; dir. Ojai Festival, 1972-77; opera debut, Cin., 1975; condr. Am. premiere Lulu (Alban Berg), Santa Fe Opera, summer 1979. Named Musician of Year, Musical Am., 1970; recipient Grammy award, 1976. Address: care Carson Office 119 W 57th St New York NY 10019. *First I am a human being alive in the late twentieth century. Next I am a musician. Then someplace under all that I am a symphony conductor, a pianist, a composer, who does this or that kind of music. I am interested in figuring out how I can use music to express and to testify to the feelings, the realities, the problems, the states of being that I go through or discover as a human being of this time.*

THOMAS, MINOR WINE, JR., mus. dir.; b. Hamburg, Va., Aug. 20, 1917; s. Minor Wine and Grace Lee (Nesselrodt) T.; B.S., Coll. William and Mary, 1939; m. Annabel Brubaker, Aug. 30, 1940; children—Minor Wine III, Phyllis Ann. Archaeologist Colonial Williamsburg, Inc., 1938-42, 46-50, dir. dept. craft shops, 1950-56; chemist Solvay Process Co., Hopewell, Va., 1942-46; dir. craft shops and reprodns. program Henry Ford Mus. and Greenfield Village, Dearborn, Mich., 1956-57, chief curator, 1957-64; asst. dir. N.Y. State Hist. Assn., Cooperstown, N.Y., 1964-72, chief curator, 1964—, asso. dir., 1972-75, sec., 1969-75, dir., 1975—; prof. history of tech. Cooperstown Grad. Programs. Participant study group on English country houses of Eng. Nat. Trust. Mem. Am. Assn. Museums, Early Am. Industries Assn. (v.p.), Am. Assn. State and Local History, Lambda Chi Alpha. Club: Rotary (Cooperstown). Contbr. articles profl. jours. Home: Fernleigh Cooperstown NY 13326 Office: New York State Historical Assn Cooperstown NY 13326

THOMAS, MORGAN DAVID, educator; b. South Wales, Jan. 5, 1925; s. Edward and Jane (Owens) T.; came to U.S., 1954, naturalized, 1962; B.A. with honors, Queen's U., Belfast, No. Ireland, 1951, Ph.D., 1954; m. Muriel M. McCahon, July 27, 1949; children—Siobhan, Moira Myfanwy, Michael, Sine. Instr. geography and Conservation U. Mich., 1955-56, lectr., research asso. conservation, 1956-57; asso. prof. U. Mont., Missoula, 1957-59, chmn. geography dept., 1958-59; vis. asso. prof. econ. geography U. Wash., Seattle, 1959-60, asso. prof. geography, 1960-66, prof. geography, 1966—, asso. dean grad. sch., 1969-75, 76—, acting dean grad. sch., 1975-76. Mem. Assn. Am. Geographers, Am. Econ. Assn., Regional Sci. Assn. (internat. pres. 1975-76). Contbr. numerous articles to profl. jours. Home: 20139 106th St NE Bothell WA 98011 Office: U Wash Dept Geography Seattle WA 98195

THOMAS, MORGAN IRWYN, educator; b. Hartley, Iowa, Apr. 1, 1917; s. Morgan Irwyn and Amanda (Flick) T.; B.A., Westmar Coll., 1940; M.A., State U. Iowa, 1947, Ph.D., 1955; m. Marjorie Mae James, June 2, 1947; children—James Morgan, Richard Morgan. Tchr. business Aurelia (Iowa) High Sch., 1940-42, Boone (Iowa) High Sch. and Jr. Coll., 1943-48, Wis. State Coll., Whitewater, 1948-52; mem. faculty Mankato (Minn.) State U., 1952—, chmn. div. bus., 1960—, prof. bus., 1960—, dean Sch. Bus., 1964-77, dean Coll. Bus., 1977—; faculty rep. No. Intercollegiate Conf., 1977—. Mem. Mankato (Minn.) City Council, 1965-66. Mem. bd. United Fund. Served USAAF, 1942-43. Mem. Am., Midwest econ. assns., United (Minn. rep. to central region 1959-61), Minn. (pres. 1959-61) bus. edn. assns., Mankato C. of C. (dir., pub. relations council), Pi Kappa Delta, Pi Omega Pi, Delta Pi Epsilon, Phi Delta Kappa. Presbyn. Lion (treas. Mankato 1955-57), Mason (Shriner). Home: 115 Ellis Ave Mankato MN 56001

THOMAS, NATHANIEL CHARLES, clergyman; b. Jonesboro, Ark., June 24, 1929; s. Willie James and Linnie (Elias) T.; B.A., Miss. Indsl. Coll., Holly Springs, 1951; B.D., Lincoln U., 1954; student Lancaster (Pa.) Theol. Sem., 1952-53; m. Juanita Fanny Jefferson, May 20, 1961 (dec. 1970); children—Gina Charlise, Nathaniel Charles, Keith Antony; m. 2d, Mary Elizabeth Partee, June 8, 1971. Ordained to ministry Christian Meth. Episcopal Ch., 1954; dir. Christian edn. 8th dist. Christian Meth. Episc. Ch., 1954-58; pastor in Waterford, Miss., 1949-51, Wrightville, Ark., 1955-57, Hot Springs, Ark., 1957-60, Little Rock, 1960-62, Memphis, 1966-67; dir. Christian edn., adminstrv. asst. to Bishop B. Julian Smith, Christian Meth. Episc. Ch., Memphis, 1954-74, sec. gen. conf. of ch., 1970-82, gen. sec. gen. bd. personnel services, 1978—, also mem. gen. bd. Christian edn. and gen. connectional bd., program adminstr. ministerial salary supplement program, 1974—, asst. to sec. gen. Gen. Bd. Pensions. Sec. Ministerial Assn. Little Rock, 1960-62; v.p. youth work sect., div. Christian edn. Nat. Council Chs., del. World Council Chs. Conf., Upsalla Sweden, 1968. Dir. Haygood-Neal Garden Apts., Inc., Eldorado, Ark., 1969—, Smith-Keys Village Apts., Inc., Texarkana, Ark., 1968—, East Gate Village Apts., Inc., Union City, Tenn., 1971—. Trustee, Collins Chapel Health Care Center, Memphis, 1974—; bd. dirs. Family Service Memphis, 1972-73; chmn. bd. dirs. Memphis Opportunities Indsl. Center, 1976—. Mem. NAACP, Urban League, Community on Move for Equality, Memphis Interdenomminational Ministers Alliance, Memphis Ministers Assn., Tenn. Assn. Chs., Ark. Council Chs., Ark. Council Human Relations, Tenn. Council Human Relations, Family Service Memphis, A.B. Hill P.T.A. Author: Christian Youth Fellow Guide, 8th Episcopal District, 1959; Living Up To My Obligations of the Christian Methodist Episcopal Church, 1956; Steps Toward Developing an Effective Program of Christian Education, 1972; co-author: Worship in the Local Church, 1966; co-author, editor: Coming to Grips with the Teaching Work of the Church, 1966. Co-editor: Developing Black Families, 1975; compiling editor: Dedicated . . . Committed-Autobiography of Bishop B. Julian Smith, 1978—. Home: PO Box 9 Memphis TN 38101 Office: PO Box 74 Memphis TN 38101. *My life has been guided by the faith and admonitions of my mother, a dedicated and devoted Christian. She said to me almost daily, "If you want to be successful, keep God in front and always believe that you can do all things through Christ who strengthens you." I have been as faithful as I could to these principles, however, often failing.*

THOMAS, NORMAN CARL, educator; b. Sioux Falls, S.D., Feb. 16, 1932; s. Russell and Helen Victoria (Matson) T.; B.A., U. Mich., 1953; M.A., Princeton, 1958, Ph.D., 1959; m. Marilyn Lou Murphy, Jan. 31, 1953; children—Robert, Margaret, Elizabeth, Anne. Instr. polit. sci. U. Mich., Ann Arbor, 1959-62, asst. prof., 1962-65, asso. prof., 1965-69; prof. Duke, 1969-71; prof. polit. sci. U. Cin., 1971—, head dept., 1971-76; cons. Adminstrv. Conf. U.S., 1971-75. Served to lt. (j.g.) USNR, 1953-56. Woodrow Wilson fellow, 1956-57; recipient Distinguished Service award U. Mich. Devel. Council, 1964. Mem. Am. Polit. Sci. Assn., Am. Soc. Pub. Adminstrn., Kappa Sigma. Democrat. Presbyn. Author: Rule 9: Politics, Administration and Civil Rights, 1966; (with Karl A. Lamb) Congress: Politics and Practice, 1964; Education in National Politics, 1975. Editor, contbr.: The Presidency in Contemporary Context, 1975; (with A.A. Altshuler) The Politics of the Federal Bureaucracy, 1977. Contbr. articles to profl. jours. Home: 510 Oliver Ct Cincinnati OH 45215

THOMAS, NORMAN EDWIN, clergyman, sem. ofcl.; b. Bklyn., Sept. 24, 1919; s. William Humphrey and Hazel Romer (Croft) T.; B.A. with honors, Rutgers U., 1941; B.D. cum laude, New Brunswick Theol. Sem., 1944; S.T.M., Union Theol. Sem., 1966; D.D., Central Coll., 1962; m. Myrtle Marie Johnson, Aug. 13, 1944; children—Noela (Mrs. David B. Hooper), Norman D., Holly. Ordained to ministry Ref. Ch. in Am., 1944; pastor St. John's Ref. Ch., St. Johnsville, N.Y., 1944-47, Bellevue Ref. Ch., Schenectady, 1947-57; First Ch., Albany, Ref. Ch. in Am., 1957-59; dean New Brunswick (N.J.) Theol. Sem., 1969-73, provost, 1973—. Mem. bd. supts. New Brunswick Sem., 1950-51, 55-61, pres. 1960-61; chmn. Chaplain's Commn. Ref. Ch. Am., rep. Gen. Commn. on Chaplain's and Armed Forced Personnel, 1956-59; mem. bd. World Mission Ref. Ch. Am., 1957-63, pres., 1962-63; v.p. Gen. Synod Ref. Ch. Am., 1960-61, pres., 1961-62; co-chmn. joint com. twenty-four Ref. Ch. in Am.-Presbyn. Ch. in U.S., 1962-69. Mem. Schenectady Planning Commn., 1953-57; pres. Capitol Area Council Chs. Devel. Corp., 1967-69. Served from 1st lt. to capt. Chaplains Corps, AUS, 1951-52. Decorated Bronze Star. Mem. Schenectady (pres. 1957), Capitol Area (pres. 1965-66) councils chs., Phi Beta Kappa, Tau Kappa Alpha. Author: History of St. John Reformed Church, 1947. Editor: Horses for Humanity, 1947. Editor, Armed Forces Messenger, Reformed Ch. Am., 1958- 66. Home: 31 Agate Rd East Brunswick NJ 08816 Office: New Brunswick Theol Sem New Brunswick NJ 08901

THOMAS, OWEN CLARK, educator, clergyman; b. N.Y.C., Oct. 11, 1922; s. Harrison Cook and Frances (Arnold) T.; A.B., Hamilton Coll., 1944, D.D., 1970; grad. student physics Cornell U., 1943-44; B.D., Episcopal Theol. Sch., Cambridge, Mass., 1949; Ph.D., Columbia, 1956; m. Bernice Louise Lippitt, May 26, 1951; children—Aaron Beecher, Addison Lippitt, Owen Clark. Ordained to ministry Episcopal Ch., 1949; dir. coll. work Episcopal Diocese N.Y., 1951-52; chaplain to Episcopal students Sarah Lawrence Coll., 1950-52; mem. faculty Episcopal Theol. Sch., Cambridge, Mass., 1952—, prof. theology, 1965—; chmn. dept. coll. work Episcopal Diocese Mass., 1956-59. Vis. prof. Pontifical Gregorian U., 1973-74. Mem. Cambridge Democratic City Com., 1966—. Served to ensign USNR, 1944-45. Elihu Root fellow Hamilton Coll., 1943; Univ. fellow Columbia, 1949-50. Fellow Soc. Values in Higher Edn., Assn. Theol. Schs.; mem. Am. Theol. Soc., Phi Beta Kappa. Author: William Temple's Philosophy of Religion, 1961; Science Challenges Faith, 1967; Attitudes Toward Other Religions, 1969; Introduction To Theology, 1973. Contbr. chpts. to books. Home: 10 St John's Rd Cambridge MA 02138

THOMAS, PAUL EMERY, educator; b. Phoenix, Feb. 15, 1927; B.A., Oberlin Coll., 1950; B.A. (Rhodes scholar), Oxford U. (Eng.), 1952; Ph.D. in Math. (NSF fellow), Princeton, 1955; m. Chi-Yuen Chan, 1958; children—Jenny, Valerie. Research instr. Columbia, 1955-56; asst. prof. math. U. Calif. at Berkeley, 1956-60, asso. prof., 1960-63, prof., 1963—. Prof., Miller Inst., 1966-67. Served with USNR, 1945-46. NSF fellow, 1958-59; Guggenheim Meml. Found. fellow, 1961. Mem. Am. Math. Soc. Office: Evans Hall Mathematics Dept U Calif Berkeley CA 94720

THOMAS, PAYNE EDWARD LLOYD, publisher; b. Balt., May 11, 1919; s. Charles C. and Nanette (Payne) T.; m. Joan Duncan; children—John Fuller, Michael Payne, Peter Charles, LeAnne Marie, Jennifer Nanette. Founder, dir. Thomas Found. and its memorials: Edward Waldron Payne Library, Harvey Cushing Hall, Chapel of Margaret and Charles Crankshaw; exec. v.p. Charles C. Thomas, Pub., Springfield, Ill., 1942-48, editor- in-chief sci., tech., med. depts., 1948-55, pres., 1955—. Presbyterian. Clubs: Tavern (Chgo.); Coral Reef Yacht, Riviera Country (Miami, Fla.). Home: 6915 Granada Blvd Coral Gables FL 33146 Office: 301-327 E Lawrence Ave Springfield IL 62717

THOMAS, PHILIP STANLEY, educator; b. Hinsdale, Ill., Oct. 23, 1928; s. Roy Kehl and Pauline (Grafton) T.; B.A., Oberlin Coll., 1950; M.A., U. Mich., 1951, Ph.D., 1961; postgrad. Delhi U., 1953-54; m. Carol Morris, Dec. 27, 1950; children—Lindsey Carol, Daniel Kyle, Lauren Louise, Gay Richardson. Instr. U. Mich., 1956-57; asst. prof. Grinnell (Ia.) Coll., 1957-63, asso. prof., 1963-65; asso. prof. econs. Kalamazoo Coll., 1965-68, prof., 1968—. Research adviser Pakistan Inst. Devel. Econs., 1963-64; econ. cons. USAID, 1965-68, 71; econ. advisor Planning Commn., Govt. of Pakistan, 1969-70; research mgr. Monetary Authority of Swaziland, 1974-75. Mem. alumni bd. Oberlin Coll., 1961-63, 74-76. Served with AUS, 1954-56. Fulbright scholar, Ford Found. overseas fellow, India, 1953-54. Mem. Am., Midwest econs. assns., Assn. Asian Studies, AAUP, ACLU, Phi Beta Kappa. Contbr. articles to profl. jours. Home: 1416 Academy St Kalamazoo MI 49007

THOMAS, R. DAVID, food services co. exec.; b. Atlantic City, July 2, 1932; s. R. and Olivia (Sinclair) T.; student pub. schs., m. I. Lorraine Buskirk, May 21, 1954; children— Pam, Kenny, Molly, Wendy, Lori. Past owner, mgr. Ky. Fried Chicken Franchise; founder, chmn. bd. Wendy's Internat., Inc., Columbus, Ohio, 1969—, also Dublin, Ohio. Hon. chmn. Central Ohio Easter Seal Soc.; bd. dirs. Children's Hosp., Columbus, Ohio Dominican Coll., Columbus Cancer Found., St. Jude Children's Research Hosp., Memphis. Served with U.S. Army, also with USAFR. Recipient Horatio Alger award, 1979. Mem. Ohio, Nat. (dir.) restaurant assns. Club: Ohio Commodores. Office: 4288 W Dublin-Granville Rd PO Box 256 Dublin OH 43017

THOMAS, RALPH STEPHENS, mfg. co. exec.; b. East St. Louis, Ill., July 30, 1923; s. Joe N. and Florence (Stephens) T.; student Washington U., St. Louis, 1942; m. Bertha M. Farenzena, Dec. 14, 1944; children—Judith A. Thomas Ghaffari, Barbara J. Thomas Harris. Works mgr. Walworth Co., Greensburg, Pa., 1941-65; with Robertshaw Controls Co., Richmond, Va., 1965—, pres., chief exec. officer, 1972—; dir. Reynolds Metals Co., Gen. Med. Corp., Bank of Va. Trust Co., Bank of Va. Co. Bd. dirs. YMCA, 1970—, Jr. Achievement, 1970—, So. States Indsl. Council, United Givers Fund, 1970—; trustee Inst. Gas Tech., Richmond Meml. Hosp. Served with USNR, 1943-46. Mem. Am. Gas Assn., Nat. Elec. Mfrs. Assn., Gas Appliance Mfrs. Assn. (chmn.-elect 1979), Richmond C. of C. (dir.). Clubs: Commonwealth, Country of Va. (Richmond). Home: 104 Sleepy Hollow Rd Richmond VA 23229 Office: 1701 Byrd Ave Richmond VA 23261

THOMAS, RICHARD, actor; b. N.Y.C., June 13, 1951; s. Richard and Barbara (Fallis) T.; student Columbia U.; m. Alma Gonzalez, Feb. 14, 1975. Made Broadway debut at age 7 in Sunrise at Campobello; other stage appearances include: Strange Interlude, Richard III, The Playroom, Everything in the Garden, Saint Joan; numerous guest appearances on TV; regular children's series One, Two, Three — Go!, 1961-62; regular TV series The Waltons (Emmy award Outstanding Continued Performance by an Actor in Leading Role), 1972-77; films include: Winning, 1969, Last Summer, 1969, Red Sky at Morning, 1971, The Todd Killings, 1971, Cactus in the Snow, 1971, You'll Like My Mother, 9/30/55, 1977, All Quiet on the Western Front, 1979; author: Poems by Richard Thomas, 1974; TV dramatic spl. The Homecoming—A Christmas Story, 1971, The Red Badge of Courage, 1974; TV movie The Silence, 1975; host children's spl. H.M.S. Pinafore, 1973. Office: care Internat Creative Mgmt 40 W 57 St New York NY 10019*

THOMAS, RICHARD EDWARD, architect; b. Schenectady, Aug. 26, 1942; s. Frank E. and Jean (Bakowski) T.; B.S., Rensselaer Poly. Inst., 1964, B.Arch., 1965; m. Shirley Jean Hebert, June 26, 1965; children—Lisa Marie, David Scott, Kevin Richard. Project capt. Cadman & Droste, Troy, N.Y., 1965-69, project architect, 1969, prin., 1970-79; sr. bldg. constrn. project mgr. N.Y. State Office Gen. Services, 1979—; partner Cadman, Droste & Thomas, 1974—. Mem, Vols. for Internat. Tech. Assistance, 1970—. Mem. AIA (sec. Eastern N.Y. chpt. 1971-72, v.p. 1973), N.Y. State Assn. Architects, Jaycees (charter Rotterdam, N.Y., pres. 1973) Asso. editor Am. Architects Directory, 1970, newsletter editor ency., 1970. Home: 31 Crestwood Dr Schenectady NY 12306 Office: Tower Bldg Empire State Plaza Albany NY

THOMAS, RICHARD L., banker; b. Marion, Ohio, Jan. 11, 1931; s. Marvin C. and Irene (Harruff) T.; B.A., Kenyon Coll., 1953; postgrad. (Fulbright scholar) U. Copenhagen (Denmark), 1954; M.B.A. (George F. Baker scholar), Harvard, 1958; m. Helen Moore, June 17, 1953; children—Richard L., David Paul, Laura Sue. With First Nat. Bank Chgo., 1958—, asst. v.p., 1962-63, v.p., 1963-65, v.p., gen. mgr. London (Eng.) br., 1965-66, v.p. term loan div., 1968, vice-chmn. bd., 1973-75, pres., dir., 1975—; sr. v.p., gen. mgr. First Chgo. Corp., 1969-72, exec. v.p., 1972-73, vice chmn. bd., 1973-74, pres., 1974—, also dir.; dir. CNA Fin. Corp., Consol. Foods Corp., Chgo. Bd. Options Exchange. Vice chmn. bd. trustees Kenyon Coll.; trustee Rush-Presbyn.-St. Luke's Med. Center, Glenwood Sch. Boys, Northwestern U., Orchestral Assn. Served with AUS, 1954-56. Mem. Chgo. Council Fgn. Relations (chmn.), Phi Beta Kappa, Beta Theta Pi. Clubs: Sunningdale Golf (London); Econ., Comml., Chgo., Casino, Mid-Am. (Chgo.); Indian Hill (Winnetka, Ill.); Old Elm (Ft. Sheridan, Ill.). Office: 1st Nat Bank of Chgo 1 First Nat Plaza Chicago IL 60670

THOMAS, RICHARD VAN, state justice; b. Superior, Wyo., Oct. 11, 1932; s. John W. and Gertrude (McCloskey) T.; B.S. in Bus. Adminstrn., U. Wyo., 1954, LL.B., 1956; LL.M., N.Y. U., 1961; m. Lesley Arlene Ekman, June 23, 1956; children—Tara Lynn, Richard Ross, Laura Lee, Sidney Marie. Admitted to Wyo. bar, 1956; law clk. to judge U.S. Ct. Appeals for 10th Circuit, Cheyenne, 1960-63; asso. firm Hirst & Applegate, Cheyenne, 1963-64; partner firm Hirst, Applegate & Thomas, Cheyenne, 1964-69; U.S. atty. Dist. Wyo., Cheyenne, 1969-74; justice Wyo. Supreme Ct., Cheyenne, 1974—. Chmn. bd. trustees Laramie County United Way, 1973, pres., 1972, chmn. admissions and allocations com., 1968-69, chmn. combined fed. campaign, 1974; bd. dirs. Goodwill Industries Wyo., Inc., 1974-77; exec. com. Cheyenne Crusade for Christ, 1974; chancellor Episcopal Diocese of Wyo., 1972—, chmn. search evaluation nomination com., 1976-77, lay reader, 1965—; bd. dirs. Community Action of Laramie County, 1977—; chmn. Cheyenne dist. Boy Scouts Am., 1977-79, mem. Longs Peak council, 1977—. Served with JAGC, USAF, 1957-60. Named Boss of Year, Indian Paintbrush chpt. Nat. Secs. Assn., 1974; Civil Servant of Year, Cheyenne Assn. Govt. Employees, 1973. Mem. Am., Laramie County bar assns., Wyo. State Bar, Phi Kappa Phi, Omicron Delta Kappa, Sigma Nu. Clubs: Kiwanis (pres. elect program com. 1969-70, dir. 1970-72, chmn. key club com. 1973-76), Masons (33 deg., past master), Nat. Sojourners (Cheyenne). Home: 212 W Pershing Blvd Cheyenne WY 82001 Office: Supreme Ct Bldg Cheyenne WY 82001

THOMAS, ROBERT, co. exec.; b. Seffner, Fla., July 13, 1924; s. Wayne and Dorothy (Durand) T.; student Coll. Holy Cross, 1942-45; m. Susan Anna Bidwell, Aug. 26, 1950; children—Susan D., Anne L., Robert M., Christina M. Pres., Port Sutton, Inc., Tampa, Fla., 1955—, Two Rivers Ranch, Inc., Zephyrhills, Fla., 1969—, Fla. State Fair Horse Show Assn., Tampa, 1976—; dir. Freedom Fed. Savs & Loan Assn. Tampa, Trend Publs., Inc. Vice chmn. bd. trustees Dorothy Thomas Found., Inc.; trustee U. Tampa, St. Leo Coll.; trustee emeritus Rensselaer Newman Found. Served with USNR, 1943-46, 52-53. Mem. Fla. Council of 100 (chmn. 1972-73). Clubs: Univ., Tampa Yacht and Country, Palma Ceia Golf and Country (Tampa); Two Rivers Hunt (master 1970), Zephyrhills, Masters of Foxhounds Assn. Am. Home: 3416 Almeria Ave Tampa FL 33609 Office: PO Box E Tampa FL 33675

THOMAS, ROBERT DAVID, banker; b. Pueblo, Colo., Aug. 4, 1927; s. David and Anna (Lee) T.; B.A., U. Colo., 1955; postgrad. (Exec. award 1965) Stanford Grad. Sch. Bus. and Fin Mgmt., 1963-65; m. Susan Sherwood, July 30, 1955; children—Kathleen Diana, David Richard. With Wells Fargo bank, 1960—, v.p., Torrance, Calif., 1968-72, v.p. So. Calif. div., El Monte, 1972-73, v.p. Santa Ana, Calif., 1973-74, v.p., dist. mgr. Orange County dist., 1974-75, v.p., regional mgr. Orange County region, 1975—. Area gen. chmn. United Bay Area Crusade, 1963; vice chmn. commerce and industry div. United Crusade, 1970. Bd. dirs. Jr. Achievement, 1961. Served with AUS, 1952-54. Mem. Credit Mgrs. Assn. (bd. govs. bankers chpt. 1965-68), Robert Morris Assos., Town Hall Calif., World Affairs Council, Orange County Fin. Soc., Kappa Sigma. Episcopalian. Clubs: Santa Ana (Calif.) Country; Balboa Bay, Racquet (Newport Beach, Calif.); Racquet (Irvine, Calif.). Home: 2657 Vista Ornada Newport Beach CA 92660 Office: Wells Fargo Bank 401 Civic Center Dr W Suite 400 Santa Ana CA 92706

THOMAS, ROBERT DEAN, publisher; b. Elkhart, Ind., Mar. 28, 1933; s. Floyd D. and Ottie (Silvers) T.; B.F.A., Bradley U., 1956; m. Beverly I. Neuhaus, Apr. 21, 1956; children—Mary Beth, Matthew, Susanna. Staff asst. to gen. mgr. Ruben H. Donnelley Co., dist. mgr.; Western mgr. Conde Nast, account mgr. Mademoiselle mag.; Western mgr. Ladies Home Jour., N.Y.C., account mgr., now pub. Served with U.S. Army, 1956-58. Mem. Mag. Publishers Assn. Clubs: Silver Spring Country (Ridgefield, Conn.); Mid-Am. (Chgo.). Office: 641 Lexington Ave New York NY 10022*

THOMAS, ROBERT EGGLESTON, corp. ofcl.; b. Cuyahoga Falls, Ohio, July 28, 1914; s. Talbott E. and Jane S. (Eggleston) T.; B.S. in Econs., U. Pa., 1936; children—Robert Eggleston, Barbara Ann. Asst. to gen. mgr., sec., mgr. r.r. investments Keystone Custodian Funds, Boston, 1936-53; v.p. Pennroad Corp., N.Y.C., 1953-59; chmn. exec. com., dir. M.-K.- T. R.R., 1956-65; dir., chief exec. officer, mem. exec. com. MAPCO Inc., 1960—, pres., 1960-76, chmn. bd., 1973—; dir., mem. exec. com. Perkin-Elmer Corp.; dir. Bank of Okla. Mem. Am. Petroleum Inst. (dir.), Nat. Coal Assn. (dir.), Transp. Assn. Am. (dir.), Newcomen Soc., Nat. Petroleum Council. Episcopalian. Clubs: Links, Metropolitan, N.Y. Yacht (N.Y.C.); Kansas City (Mo.); Southern Hills Country, Tulsa, Summit (Tulsa); Ocean Reef Yacht (North Key Largo, Fla.); Cat Cay, Chub Cay (Bahamas). Office: 1800 S Baltimore Ave Tulsa OK 74119

THOMAS, ROBERT JAY, educator; b. Harvey, Ill., Mar. 30, 1930; s. Jay Clyde and Mildred (Robinson) T.; A.B. in Physics, Oberlin Coll., 1952; M.S. in Recreation, Ind. U., 1954; M.S. in Physics, U. Ill., 1958, Ph.D. in Computer Math., 1964, certificate in data processing, 1977; m. Doris Ruth Kline, Sept. 13, 1953; children—Sharon Kay, Andrew Jay. Dir. recreational therapy Central State Hosp., Indpls., 1954-55; faculty DePauw U., 1958—, prof. math., computers, human sexuality, sr. colloquium, folklore, 1962—, dir. Computer Center, 1962-66, dir. NSF computer conf., summer 1966, adviser 3-2 engring. coop. programs, 1963-72. Vis. prof. Ill. State U., summer 1964; research asst., research participant Argonne Nat. Lab., 1967, cons., 1967-71. Served with AUS, 1955-56. Danforth Found. teaching fellow, 1961-62, 63. Mem. Assn. Computing Machinery, A.A.A.S., Math. Assn. Am., Country Dance Soc. Am., Am. Assn. U. Profs., MENSA, Am. Civil Liberties Union (organizer, 1st pres. bd. dirs. region 7 Ind. soc. 1972—, dir. state bd.), Nat. Council Tchrs. Math., Ind. Acad. Sci., Am., Hoosier folklore socs., Sex Info. and Edn. Council U.S., Sex Info. and Edn. Council Ind. (organizer, dir., sec., mem. exec. com. edn. com., regional rep.), Am. Assn. Sex Educators, Counselors and Therapists, Sigma Xi, Pi Mu Epsilon, Chi Gamma Iota. Presbyn. Home: 809 E Franklin St Greencastle IN 46135

THOMAS, ROBERT JOSEPH, columnist, author; b. San Diego, Jan. 26, 1922; s. George H. and Marguerite (Creelman) T.; student U. Calif. at Los Angeles, 1943; m. Patricia Thompson, Sept. 6, 1947; children—Nancy Katherine, Janet Elizabeth, Caroline Brooke. With A.P., 1943—, Hollywood columnist, 1944—; radio, TV, lecture appearances; editor Action Mag., 1968—. Mem. Beta Theta Pi. Author: The Art of Animation, 1958; (novel) Flesh Merchants, 1959; The Massie Case, 1966; King Cohn, 1967; Walt Disney: Magician of the Movies, 1967; Will Penny, Star, 1968; Thalberg, 1969; Selznick, 1970; The Heart of Hollywood, The Secret Boss of California, Winchell, 1971; Weekend '33, 1972; Marlon, 1974; Walt Disney, An American Original, 1976; Bud and Lou, The Abbott and Costello Story, 1977; The Road to Hollywood (with Bob Hope), 1977; The One and Only Bing, 1977; Joan Crawford, 1978; also numerous mag. articles. Home: 16509 Adlon Rd Encino CA 91316 Office: 1111 S Hill St Los Angeles CA 90054

THOMAS, ROBERT MURRAY, educator; b. Cheyenne, Wyo., July 28, 1921; s. Robert MacDonald and Elizabeth (Carson) T.; A.B., Colo. State Coll., 1943, M.A., 1944; Ph.D., Stanford, 1950; m. Shirley Louise Moore, July 3, 1948; children—Robert Gilmour, Kathryn Elizabeth. Tchr., Kamehameha Schs., Honolulu, 1944-45, Mid-Pacific Inst., Honolulu, 1945-47; instr. San Francisco State Coll., 1949-50; prof. State U. Coll., Brockport, N.Y., 1950-58, Padjadjaran (Indonesia) U., 1958-61, 64-65; prof. ednl. psychology U. Calif. at Santa Barbara, 1961-64, 69—, dean Grad. Sch., 1965-69. Author: Judging Student Progress, 2d edit., 1960; Ways of Teaching, 1955; Integrated Teaching Materials, 2d edit., 1963; Individual Differences in the Classroom, 1965; Social Differences in the Classroom, 1965; Aiding the Maladjusted Pupil, 1967; A Chronicle of Indonesian Higher Education, 1973; Comparing Theories of Child Development, 1979. Editor: Strategies for Curriculum Change; Cases from 13 Nations, 1968. Co-author: Decisions in Teaching Elementary Social Studies 1971; Curriculum Patterns in Elementary Social Studies, 1971; Penggunaan Statistik Dalam Ilmu Pengetahuan Sosial, 1971; Teaching Elementary Social Studies: Readings, 1972; Indonesian Education—An Annotated Bibliography, 1973; Social Strata in Indonesia, 1975. Home: 728 Calle De Los Amigos Santa Barbara CA 93105

THOMAS, ROBERT WILBURN, broadcasting exec.; b. Athens, Ga., Nov. 20, 1937; s. Ernest Wilburn and Bobbie (Morton) T.; B.S. in Speech, Northwestern U., 1960, M.A., 1961; m. Betsey Ruth Thorne, Sept. 6, 1958; children—Richard Gregory, Coleen Suzanne. Producer radio, TV broadcasts Northwestern U., Evanston, Ill., 1961-68, instr., 1967-68; exec. producer Sta. WCNY-TV, Syracuse, N.Y., 1968-70; gen. mgr., v.p Sta. WEKT-FM, Hammondsport, N.Y., 1970-71; gen. mgr. Sta. KWMU-FM, St. Louis, 1971-76; dir. broadcasting Sta. KWIT, Sioux City, Iowa, 1976-79; radio projects mgr. Corp. for Public Broadcasting, Washington, 1979—; mem. Emmy awards com. Chgo. chpt. Nat. Acad. TV Arts and Scis., 1962-65; mem. radio advisory com. Ill. Telecommunications Commn., 1968; chmn. radio div. Midwest Telecommunications Conf., Nat. Assn. Ednl. Broadcasters, 1972. Mem. pack com. Cub Scouts Am., Florissant, Mo., 1971-72; chmn. Mo. Jr. Miss Pagent, 1971-72, co-chmn., 1972-73, exec. dir., 1973-76; past bd. dirs. Sioux City Youth Orch. Assn., Siouxland Arts Council, Sioux City Chamber Music Assn.; founding mem. Pub. Radio in Mid. Am., program chmn., 1976-77. Recipient award Freedoms Found., 1963, 65. Outstanding Program award Ill. Med. Soc., 1965; named Outstanding State chmn. in Nation, America's Jr. Miss Pageant, 1974. Mem. Mo. Jaycees (pub. relations officer 1971-72), Mo. Pub. Radio Assn. (pres. 1975-76). Hone: 3139 Woodland Ln Alexandria VA 22309 Office: 1111 16th St NW Washington DC 20036. *Without belief in and enthusiasm for the undertakings of life, achievement is slowed, if not actually blocked.*

THOMAS, ROLAND EVERETT, ret. air force officer, scientist; b. Austin, Tex., Apr. 12, 1930; s. Melvin Aubrey and Myrtle (Nelson) T.; B.S. in Agrl. Engring., N.Mex. State U., 1951, B.S. in Elec. Engring., 1952; M.S., Stanford U., 1953; Ph.D., U. Ill., 1959; m. Juanita Rhodes, June 15, 1951; children—Lynnette, Christine, Lee Everett. Commd. 2d lt. USAF, 1952, advanced through grades to brig. gen.; cons. engr. Wright-Patterson AFB, Ohio, 1953-57; asso. prof. USAF Acad., 1959-63, permanent prof., 1963-79, prof., head dept. astronautics, 1965-66, prof., head dept. elec. engring., 1966-79; research scientist Kaman Scis. Corp., Colorado Springs, 1979—. Mem. Am. Soc. Engring. Edn., IEEE, Research Soc. Am., Sigma Xi, Sigma Tau, Tau Beta Pi. Home: 160 Dolomite Dr Colorado Springs CO 80919

THOMAS, ROSS ELMORE, author; b. Oklahoma City, Feb. 19, 1926; s. J. Edwin and Laura (Dean) T.; B.A., U. Okla., 1949. Reporter, Daily Oklahoman, Oklahoma City, 1943-44; pub. relations dir. Nat. Farmers Union, 1952-56; pres. Stapp, Thomas & Wade, Inc., Denver, 1956-57; reporter, Bonn, Germany, 1958-59; rep. Patrick Dolan & Assos., Ltd., Ibadan, Nigeria, 1959-61; cons. U.S. Govt., 1964-66. Served with inf. AUS, 1944-46. Recipient Mystery Writers Am. award for best 1st mystery, 1966, Edgar award, 1967. Author: The Cold War Swap, 1966; The Seersucker Whipsaw, 1967; Cast a Yellow Shadow, 1967; The Singapore Wink, 1969; (pseudoname Oliver Bleeck) The Brass Go-Between, 1969; The Fools in Town are on Our Side, 1971; The Back-Up Men, 1971; Protocol For Kidnapping, 1971; The Procane Chronicle, 1972; The Porkchoppers, 1972; If You Can't Be Good, 1973; The Highbinders, 1974; The Money Harvest, 1975; Yellow-Dog Contract, 1977; Chinaman's Chance, 1978; The Eighth Dwarf, 1979.

THOMAS, RUSSELL, profl. football team exec.; b. Griffithsville, W.Va., July 24, 1924; student Ohio State U., 1943-46; m. Dorothy Thomas, Aug. 3, 1945; children—John, Jim. Formerly asst. coach St. Bonaventure Coll.; player Detroit Lions, then mem. coaching staff, scout, mem. radio broadcasting team, dir. player personnel, 1964, v.p., gen. mgr., 1966—. Dir. Nat. Football League Properties. Address: Detroit Lions 1200 Featherstone Rd Box 4200 Pontiac MI 48057

THOMAS, RUTH HARRELL, retail food chain exec.; b. Bessemer, Ala., Aug. 3, 1924; d. John Henry and Lela Marian (Thaxton) Harrell; B.Bus. Edn., U. Tex., 1944; certified shorthand reporter Bryan (Tex.) Coll., 1955; m. Gerald G. Thomas, Aug. 23, 1947; 1 dau., Edith Geraldene. Various secretarial positions, 1944-57; sec. to pres./chmn. bd. Alpha Beta Co., La Habra, Calif., 1957-73, corporate sec., 1973—, also sec. subs.'s; asst. sec. Am. Stores Realty Co. Mem. Women in Mgmt., Nat. Sec.'s Assn. Baptist. Club: Order Eastern Star. Home: 15949 Rushford St Whittier CA 90603 Office: 777 S Harbor Blvd La Habra CA 90631

THOMAS, THOMAS A., lawyer; b. Geneva, N.Y., May 16, 1919; s. Abraham and Mary (Norman) T.; B.A., Syracuse (N.Y.) U., 1942; LL.B., Vanderbilt U., 1948; LL.M., Harvard U., 1948; m. Margaret Jane Ajay, Mar. 30, 1947; children—Frank Thomas, II, Thomas A., Mary Frances, Julie Ann. Admitted to Fla. bar, 1953; pvt. practice. Hollywood, 1953—; partner firm Thomas & Thomas, 1973—; prof. law U. Miami Law Sch., 1949-74, asso. dean, 1969-72; chmn. bd. Am. Bank, Hollywood, 1972-75, Am. Bank, Hallandale, Fla., 1973-75; city atty., Hollywood, 1965-69. Served with U.S. Army, 1942-46. Van Allen scholar, 1940. Mem. Fla., S. Broward County bar assns., Hollywood C. of C., Order of Coif, Iron Arrow, Omega Delta Kappa. Episcopalian. Club: Jockey. Author: Florida Estates Practice Guide, 2 vols., 1964. Home: 2519 Madison St Hollywood FL 33020 Office: 1911 Harrison St Hollywood FL 33020

THOMAS, W. BRUCE, steel co. exec.; b. Ripley, Mich., Oct. 25, 1926; s. William and Ethel (Collins) T.; B.A. magna cum laude, Western Mich. U., 1950; J.D. with distinction, U. Mich., 1952; postgrad. Law Sch., N.Y. U., 1953; m. Phyllis Jeanne Smith, June 25, 1950; 1 son, Robert William. Admitted to Mich. bar, 1952; with U.S. Steel Corp. and subsidiaries, 1952—, tax atty., Duluth, Minn., 1952-53, tax atty., tax supr., controller Orinoco Mining Co., N.Y.C., Venezuela, 1953-64, dir. taxes, N.Y.C., 1964-67, v.p. taxes, N.Y.C., 1967-70, v.p., asst. treas., 1970-71, treas., v.p., 1971-75, exec. v.p., dir., 1975—; dir. Mfrs. Hanover Corp., Mfrs. Hanover Trust Co., Discount Corp. N.Y., Adela Investment Co., S.A. Bd. dirs. Duquesne U.; trustee Allegheny Gen. Hosp., Com. Econ. Devel. Served with USAAF, 1943-45. Mem. Mich., Am. bar assns., N.Y., N.J. chambers commerce, Fin. Execs. Inst., Order of Coif, Phi Alpha Delta. Methodist. Clubs: Duquesne (Pitts.); Laurel Valley Golf, Rolling Rock (Ligonier, Pa.); Allegheny Country (Sewickley, Pa.); Edgeworth (Pa.); Sky (N.Y.C.); Pine Valley Golf. Home: Blackburn Rd Sewickley PA 15143 Office: 767 Fifth Ave New York City NY 10022 also 600 Grant St Pittsburgh PA 15230

THOMAS, WALTER IVAN, govt. ofcl., educator, agronomist; b. Elwood, Nebr., Mar. 27, 1919; s. Percy E. and Ethel (Major) T.; B.S., Iowa State U., 1949, M.S., 1953, Ph.D., 1955; m. Margaret Ann Thompson, Feb. 15, 1941; 1 dau., Linda Margaret. Clk., Soil Conservation Service, Civilian Conservation Corps, Broken Bow, Nebr., 1937-39, U.S. Civil Service, Washington, 1940-41; grad. asst. Iowa State U., Ames, 1949-50, instr., then asst. prof., 1953-59; mem. faculty Pa. State U., University Park, 1959-79, prof. agronomy, 1963-79, head dept., 1964-69, chmn. div. plant scis., 1967-69, asso. dean for research Coll. Agr., 1969-79, asso. dir. Agrl. Exptl. Sta., 1969-79; dep. dir. coop. research Sci. and Edn. Adminstrn., U.S. Dept. Agr., 1979—. Pres. Pinchot Consortium for Environ. Forestry Studies, 1976-78. Served with the USMCR, 1942-45, 50-52; col. Res. (ret.), 1966. Decorated Bronze Star with combat V, Navy Commendation medal. Fellow AAAS, Am. Soc. Agronomy, Soil Sci. Soc. Am.; mem. Am. Soc. Agronomy, Am. Inst. Biol. Sci., Sigma Xi, Alpha Zeta, Gamma Sigma Delta, Alpha Gamma Rho, Phi Mu Alpha. Presbyn. (elder). Home: 1340 19th Rd S Arlington VA 22202 Office: US Dept Agr Washington DC 20250

THOMAS, WARREN DEANE, zoo adminstr.; b. Columbus, Ohio, Nov. 27, 1930; s. Oval Charles and Mary Ernestine (Wardlow) T.; B.S., Ohio State U., 1952, D.V.M., 1959; m. Maria Luisa Tamayo, May 13, 1953; children—Mary Christine, Cherry Teresa, Eric Warren. Dir., Oklahoma City Zoo, 1959-64, Henry Doorly Zoo, Omaha, 1965-70, Gladys Porter Zoo, Brownsville, Tex., 1970-74, Los Angeles Zoo, 1974—; asst. clin. prof. pathology U. So. Calif. Sch. Medicine, 1974—; asso. research veterinarian UCLA Sch. Medicine, 1975—; cons. in field. Served with U.S. Army, 1952-55; Korea. Decorated Bronze star. Mem. Am. Mus. Assn. (councilor-at-large), Am. Assn. Zool. Parks and Aquariums, Explorers Club. Club: Rotary. Contbr. articles in field of gen. animal medicine and animal behavior to profl. jours. Home: 3035 Paulcrest Dr Los Angeles CA 90046 Office: Los Angeles Zoo 5333 Zoo Dr Los Angeles CA 90027

THOMAS, WILLIAM, JR., mfg. co. exec.; b. Edgar, Nebr., Jan. 19, 1923; s. William L. and Marie I. (Culver) T.; student U. Nebr., 1940-41; m. Marjorie E. Harman, June 14, 1947; children—Randy L., Ronald, Deborah, Bruce, Patricia. Various mgmt. positions Montgomery Ward Co., 1946-48, Greeley Gas Co., 1948-52, Norge Sales Corp., Chgo., 1952-56, Chambers Corp., 1956-60; pres., chief exec. officer Preway, Inc., Wisconsin Rapids, Wis., 1975—; dir. Wood County Nat. Bank. Bd. dirs. Riverview Hosp., 1977-78. Served with U.S. Army, 1941-46. Mem. Gas Appliance Mfg. Assn., Fireplace Inst. (past pres.). Republican. Clubs: Bulls Eye Country, Up River Gun, Rotary, Masons. Home: 730 3d St S Wisconsin Rapids WI 54494 Office: 1430 2d St N Wisconsin Rapids WI 54494

THOMAS, WILLIAM F., newspaper editor; b. Bay City, Mich., June 11, 1924; s. William F. and Irene Marie (Billette) T.; B.S., Northwestern U., 1950, M.S. magna cum laude, 1951; L.H.D. (hon.), Pepperdine U., Los Angeles; m. Patricia Ann Wendland, Dec. 28, 1948; children—Michael William, Peter Matthew, Scott Anthony. Asst. chief copy editor Buffalo Eve. News, 1950-55; editor Sierra Madre (Calif.) News, 1955-56; city editor Los Angeles Mirror, 1957-62; asst. city editor, then met. editor, Los Angeles Times, 1968-71, exec. editor, then editor, 1971-72, exec. v.p., editor, 1972—. Served with U.S. Army, 1943-46. Recipient Harrington award Medill Grad. Sch. Journalism, Northwestern U., 1951. Home: 16025 Valley Wood Rd Sherman Oaks CA 91403 Office: Times Mirror Sq Los Angeles CA 90053

THOMAS, WILLIAM GORDON, coll. adminstr.; b. Los Angeles, June 5, 1931; s. Ernest Leslie and Marian (Bowers) T.; student Occidental Coll., 1949-50, U. Calif. at Berkeley, 1952-54; B.A., U. Calif. at Los Angeles, 1956, M.A., 1957, Ed.D., 1965; m. Diane R. McCulloch, Sept. 8, 1951; children—Gregory, Mark, Scott, Christopher. Instr. speech and drama Immaculate Heart and Mt. St. Marys Colls., 1956-57; dir. cultural programs U.S. Forces in Europe, 1957-59; dir. pub. relations Immaculate Heart Coll., Los Angeles, 1959-61; coll. and univ. placement adviser U. Calif., Los Angeles, 1961-62, asso. dean students, mgr. Student and Alumni Placement Center, 1962-67, also instr. U. Calif. Extension; dean students Calif. State U., Northridge, 1967-69; dean ednl. career services U. Calif., Los Angeles, 1969-75, also dean exptl. ednl. programs; chancellor Johnston Coll. U. Redlands, 1975-76; dir. New Dimensions, Los Angeles Community Colls., 1976—. Pres., Northridge Western Boys Baseball Assn.; bd. mgrs. YMCA. Served with USN, 1950-54. Mem. Am. Assn. Higher Edn., Am. Personnel and Guidance Assn., Nat. Assn. Student Personnel Adminstrs., Phi Delta Kappa, Alpha Tau Omega. Club: Rotary. Co-author, editor books. Contbr. articles to profl. jours. Home: 17187 Marilla St Northridge CA 91325

THOMAS, WILLIAM KERNAHAN, lawyer, judge; b. Columbus, Ohio, Feb. 15, 1911; B.A., Ohio State U., 1932, LL.B., 1935; m. Dorothy Good, 1936; children—John R., Richard G., Stephen G., Cynthia G. Admitted to Ohio Bar, 1935, practiced in Cleve. until 1950; judge Ct. of Common Pleas, Geauga County, Ohio, 1950-53, Cuyahoga County, Cleve., 1953-66; now judge U.S. Dist. Ct., No. Dist. Ohio, Eastern div., Cleve. Served with USNR, 1944-46. Mem. Common Pleas Judges Assn. (pres. 1959-60), Nat. Conf. State Trial Judges (chmn. sociopathic offender com. 1963-66), Jud. Conf. U.S. (com. on adminstrn. bankruptcy system 1968-71, com. on ops. of jury system in U.S. 1971-77, com. on fair trial free press 1977—). Office: US Dist Ct No Dist Cleveland OH 44114

THOMAS, WILLIAM LEROY, educator; b. Long Beach, Calif., Mar. 18, 1920; s. William LeRoy and Margaret Lucile (Young) T.; A.B., U. Calif. at Los Angeles, 1941, M.A., 1948; Ph.D., Yale, 1955; m. Mildred Phyllis Smith, Apr. 10, 1942 (div.); children—Barbara Jean, Lawrence Charles, Virginia Jane, Margaret Joan, Pamela June; m. 2d, Loida Ayson Aquino, Aug. 29, 1964; children—William John Aquino, Lloyd Aquino. Instr. geography Rutgers U., 1947-50; research asst. S.E. Asia studies Yale, 1949-50; asst. dir. research Wenner-Gren Found. Anthrop. Research, N.Y.C., 1950-57; asst. to asso. prof. geography U. Calif. at Riverside, 1957-63; prof. anthropology and geography Calif. State U., Hayward, 1963-71, chmn. dept. anthropology and geography, 1963-66, prof. geography and Southeast Asian studies, 1971—, chmn. dept. geography, 1971-74; vis. prof. La. State U., spring 1966, U. Hawaii, summer 1966, U. Wis., fall 1966, U. Toronto (Canada), fall 1968, 69; vis. research asso. Inst. Philippine Culture, Ateneo de Manila U., Quezon City, 1970, 76-77; Fulbright lectr. Centre for Asian Studies, U. Western Australia, Nedlands, 1974. Organizer, internat. symposium Man's Role in Changing the Face of the Earth, Princeton, N.J., 1955; cons. Nat. Acad. Scis.-NRC, in orgn. of sect. 6th Nat. Conf. UNESCO, 1957; mem. tech. cons. group Calif. Pub. Outdoor Recreation Plan Com., 1958-60; geog. cons. Pacific Missile Range Pt. Mugu, Calif., 1958-60; organizer geography sect. 10th Pacific Sci. Congress, 1961; foreign field research, Philippines, 1961-62, Philippines, Thailand, Burma, 1970, Australia, Indonesia, 1974, Philippines, 1976-77; mem. ad hoc com. on geography Nat. Acad. Scis.-NRC, 1963-65, cons. effects of herbicides in Vietnam, 1972-74; chmn. Asian studies council Cal. State Colls., 1971-72. Served to first lt. C.E., AUS, 1942-45. Fulbright sr. scholar, Australia, 1974. Mem. Assn. Asian Studies, Asia Soc., Asian Studies on Pacific Coast (chmn. standing com. 1979-80, conf. chmn. 1980), Explorers Club, Pacific Sci. Assn. (U.S. mem. sci. com. on geography), Assn. Am. Geographers (Pacific Coast regional councilor 1971-74, citation for meritorious contbn. to geography 1961), Assn. Pacific Coast Geographers (v.p. 1976-77, pres. 1977-78), Calif. Council Geog. Edn. (pres. 1967-68); realtor-asso. So. Alameda County Bd. Realtors. Democrat. Author: (with J. F. Embree) Ethnic Groups of Northern Southeast Asia, 1950; Land, Man and Culture in Mainland Southeast Asia, 1957; (with J.E. Spencer) Cultural Geography, 1969, Asia, East by South, 2d edit., 1971; Introducing Cultural Geography, 1973, 2d edit., 1978. Editor: (with Anna M. Pikells) International Directory of Anthropological Institutions, 1953; Yearbook of Anthropology, 1955; Current Anthropology, 1956; Man's Role in Changing the Face of the Earth, 1956; Am. Anthrop. Assn. Bull., 1958-60; Man, Time, and Space in Southern California, 1959; (paperback series) Man-Environment System in The Late 20th Century, 1969-75. Address: Geography Dept Calif State Univ Hayward CA 94542

THOMAS, WILLIAM MARSHALL, congressman; b. Wallace, Idaho, Dec. 6, 1941; s. Virgil and Gertrude T.; B.A., San Francisco State U., 1963, M.A., 1965; m. Sharon Lynn Hamilton, Jan., 1967; children—Christopher, Amelia. Mem. faculty dept. Am. govt. Bakersfield (Calif.) Coll., 1965-74, prof., 1965-74; mem. Calif. State Assembly, 1974-78; mem. 96th Congress from 18th Calif. Dist. Mem. delegation to Soviet Union by Am. Council Young Polit. Leaders, 1977; chmn. Kern County Republican Central Com., 1972-74; mem. Calif. Republican Com., 1972-80. Home: 1830 Truxtun Ave Bakersfield CA Office: 324 Cannon Bldg Washington DC 20515

THOMAS, WILLIAM RICHARD, financial exec.; b. Sacramento, Apr. 13, 1920; s. Raymond Joseph and Annie (Clemence) T.; B.S., U. Calif. at Berkeley, 1941; m. Jane Dunning Lasher, Nov. 3, 1964; children—Paul Kenneth, Susan Jane; children by previous marriage—William Richard, Robert Charles, Alan James. Accountant, Gen. Mills, Inc., 1941-42; with Cutter Labs., Inc., Berkeley, Calif., 1945-67, v.p. finance, 1957-67, also dir.; pres., dir. Optical Coating Lab., Inc., Santa Rosa, 1967-68; v.p. Pacific Lighting Corp., 1968-73, sr. fin. v.p., 1973-77; sr. v.p. fin. and adminstrn. Global Marine Inc., 1977—, also dir.; dir. R&D Assos., Marina del Rey, Calif., French Bank of Calif. Served to lt. USNR, 1942-45; PTO. Mem. Fin. Execs. Inst. (nat. pres. 1966), U. Calif. Bus. Adminstrn. Alumni Assn. (past pres.). Lutheran. Clubs: Calif., Los Companeros de Palos Verdes. Home: 2701 Paseo del Mar Palos Verdes Estates CA 90274 Office: 811 W 7th St Los Angeles CA 90017

THOMAS, WILLIAM STEPHEN, museum cons.; b. N.Y.C., Sept. 5, 1909; s. William Sturgis and Emma (Rheinfrank) T.; A.B. cum laude, Harvard U., 1932; postgrad. N.Y. U., U. Hawaii; m. Katharine Cornish, Aug. 1, 1942; children—William Cornish, Stephen Livingston. Museum apprentice Newark Mus., 1933-34; asst. registrar Met. Mus. Art, N.Y.C., 1934-36; dir. edn. Phila. Acad. Natural Scis., 1936-39; exec. sec. com. edn. in sci. Am. Philos. Soc., Phila., 1939-42; co-founder, sec. adult sch. The Junto, Phila., 1941-42; dir. Rochester (N.Y.) Mus. Arts and Scis. (now Rochester Mus. and Sci. Center), 1946-68, dir. devel., 1969-71, exec. sec. bd., 1972-73, dir. emeritus, 1974—; lectr. museum studies U. Rochester, 1976-77; accrediation cons. Am. Assn. Museums, 1976—; Dept. State lectr., Havana, Cuba, 1949; mus. planner UNESCO, Montevideo, Uruguay and Paris, 1949; sec. com. sci. tech. museums Internat. Council Museums, 1953-67, sec. U.S. nat. com., 1957-65, chmn., 1966-70; sec. N.Y. State Mus. Assn., 1961-63, v.p., 1963-65; cons. museums, Hawaii and Japan, 1951-52; lectr., France, 1953, 64, Israel, 1962, Cairo, 1967. Served as lt. USNR, 1942-45; also Korea; comdr. Res. ret. Grantee NSF, Sweden, 1959, NRC, Hawaii, 1961; Katherine Coffey award N.E. Mus. Conf., 1975. Fellow Rochester Acad. Sci., Rochester Mus. and Sci. Center; mem. Am. Assn. Museums, N.Am. Mycological Soc., Thoreau Soc. (pres. 1977). Clubs: Explorers, Century (N.Y.C.); Harvard Travellers (Boston). Author: The Amateur Scientist, 1942; El Museo y El Mundo Moderno, 1954; Fort Davis and the Texas Frontier: Paintings by Captain Arthur L. Lee, Eighth U.S. Infantry, 1976; also articles. Mem. expdns. to Costa Rica, Guatemala, Peru, Chile for sci. museums. Home: 988 Park Ave Rochester NY 14610 Office: 657 East Ave Rochester NY 14603

THOMASON, IVAN JAMES, educator; b. Burney, Calif., June 27, 1925; s. Boris John and Ellen (Greer) T.; B.S., U. Calif. at Davis, 1950; Ph.D., U. Wis., 1954; m. Harriet Braum, Dec. 21, 1950; children—David, Eric, Alan, Martha, Will. Research asst. plant pathology U. Wis., 1950-54; mem. faculty U. Calif. at Riverside, 1954—, prof. nematology, 1967—, chmn. dept., 1963-69; asst. dir. So. Calif. region Coop. Extension Service, program leader pest and disease mgmt. statewide, prof. plant pathology, 1976—. Active Box Spring dist. Boy Scouts Am. Served with AUS, 1943-46. Fellow AAAS; mem. Am. Phytopathol. Soc., Soc. Nematologists (v.p. 1974-75, pres. 1975-76), Sigma Xi, Alpha Zeta. Research on control of plant parasitic nematodes. Home: 4686 Holyoke Pl Riverside CA 92507

THOMASON, JAMES R., mgmt. cons.; b. Sullivan, Ill. Aug. 27, 1913; s. Carl and Frances (Stiarwalt) T.; B.S., Bradley U., 1937; grad. student Am. U., 1938-40, Georgetown U., 1940-41; m. Mary A. Banks, May 7, 1946; 1 dau., Carol. With Wyo. Nat. Bank, Casper, 1937-38, Office of Architect of Capitol and Sec. U.S. Senate, 1938-40; investigator U.S. Civil Service Commn., Phila., 1941-49; prin. budget examiner Bur. Budget, 1949-60; asst. dep. postmaster gen. Post Office Dept., 1961-66, dep. asst. postmaster gen., controller, 1966-71; expert cons. finance and mgmt. UN, Brazil, 1972-73; mgmt. cons. Arthur D. Little, Washington, 1973—, Exec. Mgmt. Services, Arlington, Va., 1973—, Commn. on Postal Service, 1973—. Served with AUS, 1943-46; ETO. Mem. Am. Soc. Pub. Adminstrn., Soc. Advancement Mgmt. Baptist. Club: Cosmos (Washington). Home: 2709 Dawson Ave Wheaton MD 20902 Office: Exec Mgmt Services Inc 2201 Wilson Blvd Arlington VA 22201

THOMFORD, NEIL ROGER, surgeon; b. Red Wing, Minn., July 22, 1931; s. Orie H. and Beatrice Elvira (Anderson) T.; B.S., U. Minn., 1952, M.D., 1955; M.S., Mayo Clinic, 1965; m. Pamela Morris, Nov., 1968; children—Kimberly Anderson, Matthew Orie, Todd Andrew, Mark Joseph. Intern, Highland-Alameda County Hosp., Oakland, Calif., 1955-56; resident Mayo Grad. Sch., Mayo Clinic, Rochester, Minn., 1958-59, 60-63; asst. prof. surgery Ohio State U., Columbus, 1966-70, asso. prof., 1970-73, prof., 1973-75; prof., chmn. dept. surgery U. N.D. Sch. Medicine, Grand Forks, 1975—, acting dean, 1976-77; chief surgery United Hosp., Grand Forks, 1978—. Served to lt. USN, 1956-58. Recipient Bronze Teaching award Ohio State Med. Assn., 1969. Mem. A.C.S., Assn. for Acad. Surgery, Central Surg. Assn., Western Surg. Assn., Soc. Surgery Alimentary Tract, Am. Gastroenterol. Assn., AMA, N.D. Med. Assn., 3d Dist. Med. Soc., Am. Fedn. Clin. Research, Sigma Xi. Contbr. numerous articles on gastroenterology and surgery to sci. jours. Home: 2114 Belmont Rd Grand Forks ND 58201 Office: 501 Columbia Rd Grand Forks ND 58201*

THOMFORDE, CLIFFORD JOHN, educator; b. Crookston, Minn., Dec. 15, 1917; s. John J. and Sophia (Karver) T.; B.S. in Elec. Engring., U. N.D., 1941; M.S., Iowa State U., 1951; m. Evelyn G. Ramstad, June 11, 1941; children—Jacqueline (Mrs. Bruce Spillum), Kathleen (Mrs. Gordon Longmuir), Dale. Radio engr. FCC, 1941-42, Collins Radio Co., Cedar Rapids, Iowa, 1942-47; asst. prof. elec. engring. U. N.D., Grand Forks, 1947-54, prof., 1954—, chmn. dept., 1954-75, acting dean engring., 1963-64. Alderman, Grand Forks, N.D., 1968-76, pres. city council, 1973-76; chmn. Grand Forks Planning and Zoning Commn., 1973—. Trustee, Wesley Meth. Ch., Grand Forks. Registered profl. engr., N.D. Mem. IEEE, Soc. Profl. Engrs., Am. Soc. Engring. Edn., Phi Eta Sigma, Sigma Tau, Phi Kappa Phi, Eta Kappa Nu. Elk. Home: 2615 4th Ave N Grand Forks ND 58201

THOMLINSON, RALPH, demographer, educator; b. St. Louis, Feb. 12, 1925; s. Ralph and Ora Lee (Barr) T.; B.A., Oberlin Coll., 1948; postgrad. U. Pitts., 1943-44, Harvard, 1948; M.A., Yale, 1949; Ph.D., Columbia, 1960; m. Margaret Mary Willits, Dec. 21, 1946; children—Elizabeth Barr (Mrs. John Alston Householder), William Lockwood. Asst. town planner Montclair, N.J., 1949-50; asst. city planner Paterson, N.J., 1950; research asst. Bur. Applied Social Research, N.Y.C., 1952; med. statistics asst. actuarial dept. Met. Life Ins. Co., N.Y.C., 1952-53; instr. statistics and population U. Wis., 1953-56; instr. sociology and anthropology Denison U., Granville, Ohio, 1956-59; asst. prof. sociology Calif. State U., Los Angeles, 1959-62, asso. prof., 1962-65, prof., 1965—, chmn. dept. sociology, 1967-69; vis. prof. sociology U. Alta., Can., 1966; vis. prof. biostatistics U. N.C., Chapel Hill, 1972-73. Demographic adviser Inst. Population Studies, Chulalongkorn U., Bangkok, Thailand, 1969-71; cons. Nat. Family Planning Program, Thailand, also Census of Thailand, 1970-71, Population/Food Fund, 1977—, also various research centers abroad, 1969-73; field asso. Population Council, N.Y.C., 1969-71; research adviser Center for Research and Demographic Studies, Rabat, Morocco, 1972-73; acad. visitor Population Investigation Com., London Sch. Econs., 1973; vis.

scholar Nat. Inst. Demographic Studies, Paris, 1973-74. Served with AUS, 1943-45; ETO. Mem. Population Assn. Am., Internat. Union for Sci. Study Population, Am. Sociol. Assn., Internat. Assn. Survey Statisticians, Assn. Asian Studies. Author: A Mathematical Model for Migration, 1960; Population Dynamics, 2d edit., 1976; Sociological Concepts and Research, 1965; Demographic Problems, 2d edit., 1975; Urban Structure, 1969; Thailand's Population, 1971; (with others) The Methodology of the Longitudinal Study of Social, Economic and Demographic Change, 1971. Editor: (with Visid Prachuabmoh) The Potharam Study, 1971; adv. editor Sociol. Abstracts, 1963-67, Sociology Quar., 1978—; cons. editor As-Soukan, 1972-73; asso. editor Pacific Sociol. Rev., 1976—; cons. Dictionary of Modern Sociology, 1969. Contbr. to books, profl. jours. Home: 762 Enchanted Way Pacific Palisades CA 90272 Office: Dept Sociology Calif State Univ Los Angeles CA 90032

THOMOPOULOS, ANTHONY D., broadcasting exec.; B.S. in Fgn. Service, Georgetown U.; m. Pipina Linakis; 3 children. With NBC, 1959-64; dir. fgn. sales, then v.p., exec. v.p. Four Star Entertainment Corp., 1964-70; dir. programming selectavision div. RCA, 1970-71; v.p. TV mktg. Tomorrow Entertainment, 1971-73; with ABC, 1973—, v.p. prime time programs entertainment div., N.Y.C., 1973-74, v.p. prime time TV creative ops., 1974-75, v.p. spl. programs, 1975-76, v.p. TV div., 1976-78, pres. entertainment div., 1978—. Address: care ABC 1330 Ave Americas New York NY 10019

THOMPSON, ALLEN PAUL, bank exec.; b. Wagoner, Okla., Nov. 29, 1909; s. A. Roy and Grace (Rule) T.; A.B. cum laude, Ohio Wesleyan U., 1931; LL.B. cum laude, Cleve. Law Sch., 1935; grad. Rutgers U. Grad. Sch. Banking, 1945; LL.D., Simpson Coll., 1957; m. Phyllis Clark, June 23, 1934; children—Susan (Mrs. David W. Packer), Allen Paul, Peter. With Central Nat. Bank of Cleve., 1931-50, auditor, 1941-43, asst. v.p., 1943-45, cashier charge operations, 1945-50; admitted to Ohio bar, 1935; panel examiner Rutgers U. Grad. Sch. Banking, 1948-49, lectr. 1949; with Iowa Power & Light Co., Des Moines, 1950-69, exec. v.p., 1959, pres., 1959-65, chmn., 1965-69, also dir.; pres. Hawkeye Bank Investment Mgmt., Inc., Des Moines, 1970-74, chmn., 1974—; dir. Hawkeye Bancorp., Dial Corp., Des Moines. Bd. dirs. Iowa Methodist Med. Center; trustee Simpson Coll., St. John's Coll. C.P.A., Ohio. Mem. Ohio Soc. C.P.A.'s, Am. Gas Assn., Midwest Gas Assn. (pres.), Greater Des Moines C. of C. (past pres., dir.), Phi Beta Kappa, Omicron Delta Kappa, Phi Gamma Delta, Beta Gamma Sigma. Methodist (trustee). Mason (32 deg.). Clubs: Des Moines, Wakonda (Des Moines). Home: 3500 Southern Hills Dr Des Moines IA 50321 Office: Stephens Bldg Des Moines IA 50309

THOMPSON, ALLISON GARNETT, lawyer; b. Lawson, Mo., Aug. 11, 1892; s. Ernest and Jimmie (Graves) T.; A.B., Hampden-Sydney Coll., 1912; LL.B., Harvard, 1915; m. Elizabeth Louise Brown Barber, Nov. 6, 1924; 1 dau., Ruth Elizabeth. Admitted to W. Va. State bar, 1915; since practiced in Charleston; mem. firm Conley, Thompson, Lambert & Legg; 1st asst. U.S. atty. So. Dist. W. Va., 1943-50, U.S. atty., 1950-53; vice chmn., dir. Bank of Dunbar, 1934—; pres., dir. 1st Fed. Savs. and Loan Assn.; dir. Sta. WTIP, Glade Creek Land Co., Laurel Creek Land Co., United Farm Tools, Inc., J.L. Beury Estate, Inc. Mem. chmn. W. Va. Turnpike Commn., 1954-57; chmn. Democratic county exec. com., 1968-72. Trustee, Morris-Harvey Coll.; bd. dirs. Charleston YMCA, 1925-75. Mem. Am., W. Va., Charleston bar assns., Kappa Sigma. Democrat. Presbyterian. (elder). Clubs: Edgewood Country, Boat, Tennis, Masons, Shriners. Home: 61 Abney Circle Charleston WV 25314 Office: Union Bldg Charleston WV 25301

THOMPSON, BARBARA STORCK, state ofcl.; b. McFarland, Wis., Oct. 15, 1924; d. John Casper and Marie Ann (Kassabaum) Storck; B.S., Wis. State U., 1956; M.S., U. Wis., 1959, Ph.D., 1969; L.H.D. (hon.), Carroll Coll., 1974; m. Glenn T. Thompson, July 1, 1944; children—David C., James T. Tchr. pub. schs. West Dane County, Mt. Horeb, Wis., 1944-56; instr. Green County Tchrs. Coll., Monroe, Wis., 1956-57; coordinator curriculum Monroe Pub. Schs., 1957-60; instr. U. Wis., Platteville, 1960; supr. schs. Waukesha (Wis.) County Schs., 1960-63, supt. schs., 1963-65; prin. Fairview Elementary Schs., Brookfield, Wis., 1962-64; adminstrv. cons. Wis. Dept. Pub. Instrn., Madison, 1964-72, state coordinator, 1971-72; instr. U. Wis., Madison and Green Bay, 1972; supt. pub. instrn. State of Wis., Madison, 1973—. Mem. White House Conf. Children, 1970, Gov.'s Com. State Conf. Children and Youth, 1969-70, Manpower Council, 1973—. Bd. dirs. Vocational, Tech. and Adult Edn., 1973—, Ednl. Communications, 1973—, Higher Edn. Aids, 1973—, Agy. Instructional TV, 1975—; mem. nat. panel on SAT score decline. Recipient State Conservation award Madison Lions CLub, 1956; Waukesha Freeman award, 1961. Mem. Nat. Council Adminstrv. Women in Edn. (named Woman of Year 1974), Nat. Council State Cons. in Elementary Edn. (pres. 1974-75), Wis. Assn. Sch. Dist. Adminstrs., Assn. Supervision and Curriculum Devel., Wis. Assn. Supervision and Curriculum Devel., Southwestern Wis., Southeastern Wis. (mem. exec. council 1972-73) assns. supervision and curriculum devel., Dept. Elementary Sch. Prins., Wis. Elementary Sch. Prins. Assn., Nat., Wis. (pres. local chpt. 1970-71, life mem.), So. Wis. edn. assns., Wis. Ednl. Research Assn., Dept. Elementary-Kindergarten-Nursery Edn., Assn. Childhood Edn. Internat., Assn. Childhood Edn., Council Chief State Sch. Officers, Edn. Commn. of States, Nat. Council State Cons. in Elementary Edn. (pres. 1974-75), Delta Kappa Gamma. Author: A Candid Discussion of Critical Issues, 1975. Mem. editorial bd. The Education Digest, 1975—. Contbr. articles to profl. jours. Home: 3591 Sabaka Trail Rt 7 Verona WI 53593 Office: 126 Langdon St Madison WI 53702

THOMPSON, BARD, univ. dean; b. Waynesboro, Pa., June 18, 1925; s. Charles Herbert and Frances (Beard) T.; grad. Mercersburg Acad., 1944; A.B. Haverford Coll., 1947; B.D., Union Theol. Sem., N.Y.C., 1949; Ph.D., Columbia, 1953; m. Bertha Denning, Sept. 1, 1951; children—Andrew Bard, Frances Rutledge. Instr., then asst. prof. ch. history Emory U., Atlanta, 1951-55; asso. prof. ch. history Vanderbilt U., Nashville, 1955-59, Buffington prof. ch. history, 1959-62; Heilman prof. ch. history Lancaster Theol. Sem., 1962-65; prof. ch. history Drew U., Madison, N.J., 1965—, dean Grad. Sch., 1969—; research in history ch. 16th, 17th centuries. Ofcl. observer Vatican II, 1964. Mem. Am. Soc. Ch. History, S.A.R., Phi Beta Kappa. Author: Liturgies of the Western Church, 1961; (with others) Essays on the Heidelberg Catechism, 1963. Co- editor: Principle of Protestantism, 1964; Mystical Presence and Other Writings on the Eucharist, 1966. Home: Spring Valley Rd Morristown NJ 07960 Office: Drew U Madison NJ 07940

THOMPSON, BASIL FREDERICK, ballet exec.; b. Newcastle-Tyne, Eng., June 29, 1937; s. William Basil and Penelope Lilian (Robertson) T.; student Sadlers Wells Ballet Sch., London, 1951-55. Dancer, Royal Ballet Co. (U.K.), 1955-58; soloist dancer Am. Ballet Theatre, N.Y.C., 1960-67; ballet master City Center Joffrey Ballet Co., N.Y.C., 1967-76, asso. dir. ballet Joffrey Ballet Sch., 1976—. Mem. N.J. Arts Council, 1975. Office: 434 6th Ave New York NY

THOMPSON, BENJAMIN, architect; b. St. Paul, July 3, 1918; s. Benjamin Casper and Lynne (Mudge) T.; B.F.A., Yale, 1941; m. Mary Okes, Dec. 4, 1942 (div. 1967); children—Deborah, Anthony, Marina, Nicholas, Benjamin; m. 2d, Jane Fiske McCullough, Sept. 13, 1969. Founding partner Architects Collaborative, Inc., Cambridge, Mass., 1946-65; pres., chmn. bd. Design Research Internat., Inc., Cambridge, 1953-70; chmn. dept. architecture Harvard, 1963-68; pres. Benjamin Thompson & Assos., Inc., Cambridge, 1966—; prin. works include faculty office, classroom Harvard Law Sch., edn. library Harvard Grad. Sch., Kirkland (N.Y.) Coll., indsl. and fine arts bldg. Mass. State Coll., St. Paul Acad., Phillips Acad., Andover, Mass., sci. bldg. dormitories Williams Coll., Mt. Anthony Union High Sch., Bennington Vt., music bldg. Amherst Coll., State U. N.Y. at Buffalo, other acad. structures; important commns. include Intercontinental hotels, Abu Dhabi, Al Ain, Abu Dhabi, Cairo, Cambridge elderly housing, Worcester family housing, Harvard married student housing, restoration of Faneuil Hall Markets, Boston (Progressive Architecture award 1975, Design and Environment Mag. award 1976, Harleston Parker medal 1978, Nat. Honor award, Bartlett award 1978, Internat. Design award 1978), New River Center, Ft. Lauderdale, Fla. Mem. com. arts and architecture John F. Kennedy Meml. Library, 1964, Blue Ribbon Panel for Parcel 8, Boston Govt. Center, 1964; mem. vis. com. R.I. Sch. Design, 1964; juror Boston Archtl. Center Competition, 1964; bd. overseers for fine arts Brandeis U., 1964; vis. com. Boston Mus. Fine Arts, 1964; chmn. design adv. panel city of Cambridge NASA project, 1967-68; design adv. com. Boston Redevel. Authority, 1972—. Served as lt. USNR, 1942-45. Recipient New Eng. Architecture and Landscape award Boston Arts Festival for Acad. Quadrangle Brandeis U., 1963, Maine Arts award Colby Coll, dormitories, 1967, Pres.'s Medal of Honor Kirkland Coll., 1972; Spl. award for Alaska Capital Competition entry Am. Soc. Landscape Architects, 1978. Registered architect, Mass., Minn., Ohio, R.I., Vt., N.Y., Maine. Mem. Boston Soc. Architects (Harleston Parker medal 1961, 71, 73, Neighborhood Housing award 1974), Archtl. League N.Y. (Nat. Gold medal 1962), AIA (honor award merit 1963, 1st honor award 1964, Nat. firm award 1964, New Eng. honor award 1966, 1970-72, 74, Library award 1968, 74, nat. honor award 1968, 70, 71), Am. Assn. Sch. Adminstrs. (sch. design citation 1965). Home: 27 Willard St Cambridge MA 02138 Office: Benjamin Thompson and Assos 1 Story St Cambridge MA 02138

THOMPSON, BERT ALLEN, librarian; b. Bloomington, Ind., Dec. 13, 1930; s. James Albert and Dorothy Fern (Myers) T.; B.S., Ball State Tchrs. Coll., 1953; A.M., Ind. U., 1960; certificate in archival adm. U. Denver, 1967; m. Martha Ellen Palmer; children—John Carter II, Anne Palmer, Paul Julian. Tchr., librarian Ind. pub. schs., 1953-55; reference asst. Indpls. Pub. Library, 1956-59; head reference service Mankato (Minn.) State Coll., 1959-61; instr. Grad. Library Sch., No. Ill. U., Dekalb, 1961-63; dir. libraries, asst. prof. ednl. media Kearney (Nebr.) State Coll., 1963-69; dir. library service Ill. Benedictine Coll., Lisle, Ill., 1969—; mem. exec. bd. Ill. regional Library Council, 1976—. Mem. Ill. (de Lafayette Reid Research scholar 1976), Catholic (treas. Ill. chpt. 1973—), Nebr. (chmn. coll. and univ. sect. 1963-64) library assns. Episcopalian. Home: 1011 N Cross St Wheaton IL 60187 Office: Theodore Lownik Library Ill Benedictine Coll Lisle IL 60532

THOMPSON, BEVERLEY VENABLE, JR., steel co. exec.; b. Ft. Worth, Dec. 2, 1919; s. Beverley Venable and Anna Mae (Armstrong) T.; grad. Woodberry Forest Sch., 1937; student U. Va., 1937-38, Tex. Christian U., 1938-40; LL.D., Northwood Inst., 1972, LL.D., Okla. Christian Coll., 1974; m. Betty Jo Copeland, Dec. 29, 1959; children—Beverley Venable III, Melissa Margaret. With Tex. Steel Co., Ft. Worth, 1940—, v.p., 1952-65, pres., 1965-75, chmn. bd., 1972—, dir., 1952—; dir. Liberty Mfg. Co., Lauritzen & Makin Mfg. Co., Bus. Communications, Inc., Continental Nat. Bank, Ft. Worth; breeder French Charolais cattle, miniature horses. Pres., gen. mgr. Tex. Ednl. Assn., 1965—. Bd. dirs. Tex. Bur. for Econ. Understanding. Served to capt. USAAF, 1941-46. Decorated Air medal. Mem. Steel Founders Soc. Am. (dir. 1958-60), NAM (dir. 1967-73, 76—, regional v.p. 1968-71), Newcomen Soc., Tex. Mfrs. Assn. (dir. 1974-76), Sigma Alpha Epsilon. Republican. Episcopalian. Clubs: Rivercrest Country, Ft. Worth, Shady Oaks Country, (Ft. Worth). Home: 4041 Shadow Dr Fort Worth TX 76116 Office: 3901 Hemphill St Fort Worth TX 76110

THOMPSON, BLAIR HARRIS, elec. machinery co. exec.; b. Scotts, Mich., Apr. 2, 1925; s. Bradley Harris and Bonnie Frances (Blair) T.; M.B.A., U. Mich., 1949; m. Marleah Romola McCarty, Apr. 13, 1944; children—Linda (Mrs. Willard Teare), Paula (Mrs. Steven Reiley), Lowell Bradley. Auditor, U.S. Gen. Accounting Office, Washington, 1949-52; auditor Ford div. Ford Motor Co., Detroit, 1952-53; adminstrv. asst. to v.p. finance Grace Lines, Inc., N.Y.C., 1953-54; plant accountant, then gen. mgr. Hytron div. CBS, Kalamazoo, 1954-58; controller Sparton Corp., Jackson, Mich., 1958—, v.p., treas., 1963—, also dir.; dir. 8 subsidiaries. Served to 2d lt. USAAF, 1943-45. Republican. Methodist. Mason. Home: 1701 Shoemaker St Jackson MI 49203 Office: 2400 E Ganson St Jackson MI 49202

THOMPSON, BRIAN JOHN, coll. dean; b. Glossop, Derbyshire, Eng., June 10, 1932; s. Alexander William and Edna May (Gould) T.; came to U.S., 1962; B.Sc.Tech., U. Manchester, Eng., 1955, Ph.D., 1959; m. Joyce Emily Cheshire, Mar. 31, 1956; children—Karen Joyce, Andrew Derrick. Demonstrator in physics Faculty of Tech., U. Manchester, 1955-56, asst. lectr., 1957-59; lectr. physics U. Leeds, Eng., 1959-62; sr. physicist Tech. Ops., Inc., Burlington, Mass., 1963-65, dir. optics dept., 1965-67, mgr. West, tech. dir. Beckman & Whitley div., 1967-68; prof. Inst. Optics, U. Rochester, N.Y., 1968—, dir., 1968-75, dean Coll. Engring. and Applied Sci., 1974—. Served with Brit. Army, 1950-52. Fellow Optical Soc. Am. (dir. 1969-72, exec. com. 1970-73, asso. editor Jour. 1966-77), Inst. Physics and Phys. Soc. (Gt. Britain), Soc. Photo-Optical Instrumentation Engrs. (pres. 1974, 75-76, Pres.'s award 1967, Pezzuto award 1978, Kingslake medal 1978); mem. Am. Phys. Soc., AAAS, N.Y. Acad. Scis. Mem. Christ Ch. Am. editor: Optica Acta, 1974—. Asso. editor: Optics Communications, 1974—, Optical Engring., 1973—. Mem. editorial adv. bd. Laser Focus, 1967—, internat. editor Optics and Laser Tech., 1970—. Contbr. articles to profl. jours. Home: 9 Esternay Ln Pittsford NY 14534 Office: U Rochester Coll Engring and Applied Sci Rochester NY 14627

THOMPSON, BRUCE RUTHERFORD, judge; b. Reno, July 31, 1911; s. Reuben Cyril and Mabel (McLeran) T.; A.B., U. Nev., 1932; LL.B., Stanford, 1936; m. Frances Ellen Creek, Sept. 11, 1938; children—Jeffrey, Judith, Harold. Admitted to Nev. bar, 1936; since practiced in Reno; asst. U.S. atty. Dist. Nev., 1942-52; spl. master U.S. Dist. Ct., Reno, 1952-53; U.S. dist. judge Dist. Nev., Reno, 1963—. Mem. Nev. State Planning Bd., 1959—, chmn., 1960-61. Regent, U. Nev. Mem. Am. Judicature Soc. (dir.), Am. Bar Assn., Bar of Nev., Am. Coll. Trial Lawyers, Am. Law Inst., Alpha Tau Omega. Democrat. Baptist. Elk. Home: 1550 Plumb Ln Reno NV 89502 Office: Fed Bldg 300 Booth St Reno NV 89109

THOMPSON, CAROL LEWIS, editor; b. N.Y.C., Dec. 26, 1918; d. Jasper Robert and Freda (Rafalsky) Lewis; A.B., Wellesley Coll., 1940; M.A., Mt. Holyoke Coll., 1942; m. Elbert Paul Thompson, July 4, 1942; children—Timothy Lewis, Ellen, John, Abigail. Asst. editor Current History 1943, asso. editor, 1943-55, editor, 1955—; editor Ency. of Developing Nations; asso. editor Forum mag., 1945-49. Mem. Am. Hist. Assn., Nat. Council Social Studies, AAUW, Phi Beta Kappa. Editor: Ency. of Developing Nations. Contbr. to World Book Ency. and Annual, Ency. Brit. Home and Office: Rural Rt 1 Box 132 Furlong PA 18925

THOMPSON, CLARK WALLACE, former congressman; b. La Crosse, Wis., Aug. 6, 1896; s. Clark Wallace and Jessie Marilla (Hyde) T.; student U. Oreg., 1915-17; m. Libbie Moody, Nov. 16, 1918; children—Libbie (Mrs. James Stansell) (dec.), Clark Wallace. Treas. Am. Nat. Ins. Co., Galveston, Tex., 1919-20; pres. Clark W. Thompson Co., 1920-32; sec.-treas. Cedar Lawn Co., 1927-34; pub. relations counsel Am. Nat. Ins. Co., allied Moody interests, 1936-47; dir. Washington operations Tenneco, Inc. Mem. 73d, 80th to 89th U.S. Congresses, 9th Tex. Dist.; now public affairs cons. Served with USMC, 1917-18; lt. col. Res.; organized and commanded 15th Bn. Marine Corps Res., on active duty, 1940-46; served with 2d Marine Div., and various units in Southwest Pacific area; grad. Naval War Coll.; dir. Marine Corps Res., ret. as col., 1946. Mem. Galveston C. of C. (past pres.), Am. Legion, VFW, Phi Delta Theta. Democrat. Episcopalian. Mason (32 deg., KCCH), Eagle, Red Man. Clubs: Georgetown, 1925 F St., Army and Navy (Washington); Arty. (Galveston). Home: 1616 Driftwood Ln Galveston TX 77551 also 3301 Massachusetts Ave NW Washington DC 20008 Office: Suite 500 1629 K St NW Washington DC 20006

THOMPSON, CLIVE DUNAVON, dancer, choreographer; b. Jamaica, W.I., Oct. 20; s. Herman James and Caseta Isolyn (Golding) T.; came to U.S., 1960, naturalized, 1963; ed. Kitson Coll., Jamaica, Martha Graham Sch., N.Y.C.; m. Elizabeth Jane Lauter, Mar. 21, 1963; children—Christopher Eric, Jason Matthew. Prin. dancer Martha Graham Dance Co., 1961-70, Alvin Alley Am. Dance Theatre, 1970—; guest artist Toronto Dance Theatre, 1979: toured with Talley Beatty and Co., Yuriko and Co., Pearl Lang and Co., Clive Thompson and Co., Clive Thompson and Tina Yuan in Concert; featured dancer (Broadway musicals) The King and I, 1963, Baker Street, 1965, Where's Charley?, 1966, LaStrada, 1970, (Off Broadway musicals) Black Nativity, 1961, African Carnival, 1962, Plain and Fancy, 1963, Around the World in 80 Days, 1964; creator ballet for Ballet Co. of Sao Paolo, Brazil, 1979; choreographer Norwegian Royal Opera Co. production Othello, 1967, ABC-TV's Pueblo, 1975, Sesame Street, Clive Thompson and Co., 1968-69, Kansas City Philharmonic Soc. production Bernstein's Mass, 1977, Phoenix Players (S.Africa) production Emperor Jones, 1977, prodn. for Takarazuka Reviue Co., Japan, 1978; artist in residence Princeton U., Harvard U., Sarah Lawrence Coll., Jamaica Sch. Dance, others; faculty Martha Graham Sch. Dance, London Sch. Contemporary Dance, Julliard Sch. Mus., Trinity Coll., S.I. Community Coll., others. Creator Community Action Arts program Conn. Commn. on Arts, Waterbury, Hartford and New Britain; creator, chmn. dance dept. Trinity Coll., Hartford, 1968; bd. dirs. Alvin Alley Am. Dance Theatre, 1976, Snug Harbour Cultural Center, S.I., 1977. Recipient Medal Honour, Govt. Jamaica, 1975; certificate of recognition in dance Harvard U., 1977; named hon. citizen Atlanta, 1977; USIA grantee, 1977. Office: care Ailey and Co 1515 Broadway New York NY 10022. *The accomplishments of man cannot be measured by his talents alone; it is the talent plus the discipline, dedication, self-sacrifice and hard work that makes for success.*

THOMPSON, CRAIG RINGWALT, educator; b. Carlisle, Pa., June 25, 1911; s. Allan Douglas and Varie Rachel (Shetron) T.; A.B., Dickinson Coll. 1933, Litt.D., 1966; A.M., Princeton, 1935, Ph.D., 1937; m. Isabella Thoburn McMaster, Aug. 20, 1938; children—Allan, James. Instr. English, Cornell U., 1937-42, vis. asso. prof. English, summer 1947; instr. English, Yale, 1943-45; asso. prof. English, Elmira Coll., 1945-46; asso. prof. English, Lawrence Coll., Appleton, Wis., 1946-50, prof., 1950-60; spl. cons. Folger Shakespeare Library, 1957-58; librarian, prof. English and history Haverford (Pa.) Coll., 1960-68; prof. English, U. Pa., Phila., 1968-78. Guggenheim fellow, 1942-43, 54-55, 68-69; Am. Council Learned Socs. fellow, 1953; Folger Shakespeare Library fellow, summers 1953, 56, 57, 59, 65, 74. Mem. Modern Lang. Assn., Am. Soc. Reformation Research, Am. Soc. Church History, Phi Beta Kappa, Kappa Sigma. Presbyn. Clubs: Cosmos (Washington); Nassau (Princeton); Franklin Inn (Phila.). Editor: Erasmus' Inquisitio de Fide, 1950; Thomas More's Translations of Lucian, 1974; Erasmus, Literary and Educational Works, 1978. Co-editor: Thought and Experience in Prose, 1951. Translator: Ten Colloquies of Erasmus, 1957, The Colloquies of Erasmus, 1965; editor: Erasmus: Literary and Educational Writings, vols. 1-2, 1978; also articles and monographs on Renaissance lit. and history. Home: 830 Montgomery Ave Bryn Mawr PA 19010

THOMPSON, CRAIG SNOVER, truck co. exec.; b. Bklyn., May 24, 1932; s. Craig F. and Edith (Williams) T.; grad. Valley Forge Mil. Acad., 1951; B.A., Johns Hopkins, 1954; m. Masae Sugizaki, Feb. 21, 1957; children—Lee Anne, Jane Laura. Newspaper and radio reporter Easton (Pa.) Express, 1954-55, 57-59, Wall St. Jour., 1959-60; account exec. Moore, Meldrum & Assos., 1960; mgr. pub. relations Central Nat. Bank of Cleve., 1961-62; account exec. Edward Howard & Co., Cleve., 1962-67, v.p., 1967-69, sr. v.p., 1969-71; dir. pub. relations White Motor Corp., Cleve., 1971-76; v.p. pub. relations No. Telecom Inc., Nashville, 1976-77; v.p. pub. relations White Motor Corp., Farmington Hills, Mich., 1977—. Bd. dirs. Shaker Lakes Regional Nature Center, 1970-73. Served from 2d lt. to 1st lt., inf., AUS, 1955-57. Mem. Pub. Relations Soc. Am. (accredited). Office: 34500 Grand River Ave Farmington Hills MI 48024

THOMPSON, CYRUS WELTER, security services co. exec.; b. Detroit, Jan. 14, 1927; s. Cyrus O. and Genevieve (Welter) T.; B.B.A., U. Miami (Fla.), 1950, postgrad., 1957; postgrad. U. Fla., 1965, U. Tampa, 1956, Purdue U., 1960; m. Joyce McEaddy, Dec. 27, 1950; children—Michael Henry, Kenneth Edward, Mary Ann, Geneva. Unit mgr. Comml. Credit Corp., Miami, Fla., 1950-51; spl. agt. FBI, Washington, 1951, Detroit, 1951-53; spl. investigator to chief of staff services Dade County (Fla.) Sheriff's Dept. and Dept. Pub. Safety, 1953-59; spl. investigator Fla. Atty. Gen.'s Office, 1959; dir. tng. and inspection Wackenhut Corp., Coral Gables, Fla., 1959-65, dir. spl. services div., 1965-67, v.p. adminstrv. services, 1967-68, v.p. ops., 1968-72, sr. v.p., 1972-74, exec. v.p., 1975—; pres., dir. Wackenhut Protective Systems, Inc., 1974—; instr. Fla. Police Acad., Miami, 1953-60, Miami Dade Jr. Coll., 1958-60. Chmn. Coral Gables Citizens Advisory Com. on Law Enforcement, 1968—; mem. pvt. security advisory council Law Enforcement Assistance Adminstrn. Dept. Justice, 1973-77. Served with M.C., U.S. Army, 1945-46. Recipient Silver medal of Bolivarian Merit Order, Internat. League Bolivarian Action, 1958. Mem. Am. Soc. Indsl. Security, Am. Soc. Tng. and Devel. (past v.p. Fla., past sec.-treas. Fla.), Soc. Former Agents FBI (past chmn. local chpt.), Fla. Chiefs Police Assn., Am. Police Communications Officers, Pi Kappa Alpha. Roman Catholic. Home: 5918 The Mall Coral Gables FL 33146 Office: 3280 Ponce de Leon Blvd Coral Gables FL 33134

THOMPSON, DALE MOORE, mortgage banker; b. Kansas City, Kans., Nov. 19, 1897; s. George Curl and Ruth Anna (Moore) T.; A.B. cum laude, U. Mich., 1920; m. Dorothy Allen Brown, July 2, 1921; 1 son, William Brown. With City Nat. Bank and Trust Co., and predecessor, Kansas City Mo., 1920-34, v.p., 1930-34; with City Bond & Mortgage Co., Kansas City, Mo., 1934—, exec. v.p., 1943-48, pres., 1948-68, chmn. bd., 1968-74, hon. chmn., 1974—; chmn. emeritus Central Mortgage & Realty Trust, Kansas City, 1975—; dir. Regency Bldg. Co., Kansas City. Lectr. schs. mortgage banking Northwestern U., Stanford. Mem. Mo. Bd. Edn., 1966—, pres., 1968-69; pres. Kansas City Philharmonic Assn., 1944-54, bd. dirs., 1943—; bd. dirs., exec. com. Truman Med. Center (formerly Kansas City Gen. Hosp. and Med. Center) 1962—, treas., 1962-78; chmn. Kansas City campaign United Negro Coll. Fund, 1958-59. Trustee Childrens Mercy Hosp., U. Kansas City, Kansas City Art Inst., Conservatory Music Kansas City. Recipient Distinguished Service citation Mayor Kansas City, 1955, Community Service citation Archbishop Kansas City, 1954, citation Kansas City C. of C. 1954; Protestant honoree Nat. Conf. Christians and Jews, 1966. Mem. Mortgage Bankers Assn. Am. (nat. pres. 1962-63, gov. 1956—, distinguished service award 1968), U. Mich. Alumni Assn. (past dir.), English-Speaking Union (pres. Kansas City br. 1966-67), Phi Beta Kappa (pres. Kansas City 1946-49), Phi Kappa Psi, Trigon. Mem. Christian Ch. Clubs: Monterey Peninsula Country (Pebble Beach, Calif.); River, University, Indian Hills Country (Kansas City, Mo.). Home: 221 W 48th St Kansas City MO 64112 Office: United Missouri Bank Bldg Kansas City MO 64142

THOMPSON, DAVID DUVALL, physician; b. N.Y.C., June 1, 1922; s. Homer C. and Clara (Smith) T.; B.A., Cornell U., 1943, M.D., 1946; m. Lynn Poucher, Dec. 22, 1945; children—David D., Richard M., Catherine R., Peter L. Intern, resident N.Y. Hosp., N.Y.C., 1946-50; head div. metabolism N.Y. Hosp., 1957-65; acting physician in chief, 1965-66, dir., 1967—; vis. prof. hosp. adminstrn. Cornell U., 1974—. Trustee Mut. Life Ins. of N.Y. Mem. med. adv. bd. Kidney Found. N.Y., 1963—; trustee Mary Imogene Bassett Hosp., Cooperstown, N.Y. Recipient Lederle Med. Faculty award, 1955-57. Fellow A.C.P.; mem AMA, Am. Physiol. Soc., Harvey Soc., Am. Soc. Clin. Investigation, Assn. Am. Med. Colls., Am. Fedn. Clin. Research, Soc. Med. Adminstrs., Sigma Xi. Club: University. Home: 11 Creston Ave Tenafly NJ 07670 Office: 525 E 68th St New York City NY 10021

THOMPSON, DONALD ALEXANDER, lawyer; b. Winnipeg, Man., Can., Feb. 12, 1904; s. Frank W. and Mabel (Summerhayes) T.; student St. John's Coll., Winnipeg, 1920-21, D.C.L., 1973; student Man. Law Sch., 1921-24; LL.D., U. Man., 1969; m. Lillian Ruby Loud, Aug. 23, 1930; children—Bruce, David, Margaret (Mrs. Owen William Steele), Donald. Called to bar, Man., 1925, created queen's counsel, 1951; practice in Winnipeg, 1925—; solicitor Aikins, Loftus & Co., 1925-43; mem. firm Aikins, MacAulay, Thompson, Tritschler & Hinch, 1943-53; mem. firm Thompson, Dorfman, Sweatman and predecessor firm, 1953—. Dir. Gordon Hotels (1971) Ltd., Supercrete Inc., Can. Cement Lafarge, Ltd. Vice pres. Community Welfare Planning Council, Winnipeg, 1965-70; pres. Nat. council Boy Scouts Can., 1967-69; past chmn. adv. bd. Misericordia Gen. Hosp., Winnipeg; vice chmn. bd. govs., chmn. fin. com. U. Man. Mem. Man. Law Soc. (past pres.). Anglican (chancellor Diocese Rupert's Land). Club: Manitoba (Winnipeg). Home: 3 Oakdale Dr N Charleswood MB R3R 0Z3 Canada Office: Bank Can Bldg 3 Lombard Pl Winnipeg MB R3B 1N4 Canada

THOMPSON, DRURY BLAIR, lawyer, communications co. exec.; b. Pittsylvania County, Va., Apr. 25, 1919; s. James Samuel and Ethel Blair (Reynolds) T.; A.B., Davidson Coll., 1941; LL.B., J.D., Duke U., 1948; m. Virginia Creel Jones, Oct. 14, 1941; children—Terry Elizabeth, Drury Blair, James Reynolds. Admitted to N.C. bar, 1948, Ga. bar, 1953; individual practice law, Raleigh, 1948-53; atty. So. Bell Tel. & Tel. Co., Atlanta, 1953-58, gen. atty., 1958-73, asso. gen. counsel, 1973-74, v.p., gen. counsel, 1974—. Served with inf., AUS, 1941-46, U.S. Army, 1951-52; lt. col. Res. ret. Decorated Silver Star medal, Bronze Star medal, Purple Heart. Mem. Am., Ga., Atlanta, N.C. bar assns., Atlanta Lawyers Club, Atlanta Corporate Counsel Assn. Methodist. Clubs: Commerce, Cherokee Town and Country (Atlanta). Office: 1245 Hurt Bldg Atlanta GA 30303

THOMPSON, EARLE CROSLAND, librarian; b. Louisville, Jan. 2, 1917; s. Jefferson Davis and Lisabel (Crosland) T.; B.A., Union U., 1938; M.A., Duke, 1951; M.L.S., Emory, 1951; m. Emma Franceschi, Nov. 14, 1945; children—Carl Franceschi, Jane Christine, Marie Frances, Henry Waddy, John William. Order librarian Emory U. Library, Atlanta, 1951-53, serials librarian, 1953-54; acquisition librarian La. State U. Library, Baton Rouge, 1954-56, asst. dir., 1956-62, asso. dir., 1962-64; dean library service U. Mont., Missoula, 1964—. Served with CIC, USAAF, 1941-46. Decorated Bronze Star. Mem. A.L.A., Pacific N.W., Mont. library assns., Alpha Tau Omega, Tau Kappa Alpha, Phi Kappa Phi. Democrat. Roman Catholic. Club: Rotary. Home: 426 McLeod Ave Missoula MT 59801

THOMPSON, EDWARD CHARLES, JR., banker; b. Hancock, Iowa, July 12, 1922; s. Edward Charles and Grethel (Griffith) T.; student Parsons Coll., 1939, Peru State Tchrs. Coll., 1940-41; grad. Sch. Banking, U. Wis., 1952; student financial pub. relations, Northwestern U., 1955; m. Harriett Jean Dickson, Jan. 14, 1943; children—Charles Michael, Ann. With Security Nat. Bank, Sioux City, Iowa, 1941—, exec. v.p., 1963-65, pres., 1965—; dir. Security Nat. Corp., Payless Cashways, Inc. Treas. St. Lukes Hosp., Sioux City. Bd. dirs., vice chmn. bd. Morningside Coll. Served with USAAF, 1942-46. Mem. Sioux City C. of C. (pres. 1971-72). Republican. Methodist (trustee, chmn. bd. dirs.). Mason. Clubs: Sioux City Country, Sioux City Racquet. Home: 3640 Cheyenne St Sioux City IA 51104 Office: Security Nat Bank 6th and Pierce St Sioux City IA 51102

THOMPSON, EDWARD FRANCIS, computer mfg. co. exec.; b. Waukegan, Ill., June 23, 1938; s. Francis Edward and Elsie (Birtic) T.; B.S. in Aero. Engring., U. Ill., 1961; M.B.A. in Ops. Research, U. Santa Clara, 1968; m. Gail Jean Walulis, Dec. 26, 1964; children—Michele Lisa, Melinda Joy, Holly Beth. Asso. engr. Lockheed Missile & Space Co., Sunnyvale, Calif., 1963-65; mktg. rep. IBM Service Bur Corp., Palo Alto, Calif., 1965-68; mgr. program devel. Computer Scis. Corp., Los Altos, Calif., 1968-72; v.p. U.S. Leasing Internat., Inc., San Francisco, 1972-76; treas. Amdahl Corp., Sunnyvale, Calif., 1976—. Bd. dirs. Jr. Achievement, Santa Clara County. Served to 1st lt. C.E., U.S. Army, 1961-63. Mem. Beta Gamma Sigma. Home: 1517 Edgewood Dr Palo Alto CA 94303 Office: 1250 E Arques Ave Sunnyvale CA 94086

THOMPSON, EDWARD KRAMER, editor, publisher; b. Mpls., Sept. 17, 1907; s. Edward T. and Bertha E. (Kramer) T.; A.B., U. N.D., 1927, H.H.D., 1958; m. Marguerite M. Maxam, May 14, 1927 (div.); children—Edward T. Colin R.; m. 2d, Lee Eitingon, Apr. 1, 1962. Editor, Foster County Independent, Carrington N.D., 1927; city editor Fargo (N.D.) Morning Forum, 1927; picture editor, asst. news editor Milw. Jour., 1927-37; asso. editor Life, 1937-42, asst. mng. editor, 1945-49, mng. editor, 1961, editor, 1961-68; spl. asst. to sec. state, 1968; editor, pub. Smithsonian mag., 1969—. Served to lt. col. USAAF, 1942-45. Decorated Legion of Merit; Order Brit. Empire; named to N.D. Hall of Fame, 1968; named Editor of Year, Nat. Press Photographers Assn., 1968; recipient Joseph Henry medal Smithsonian Instn., 1973. Mem. Phi Beta Kappa, Sigma Delta Chi, Phi Delta Theta. Home: Rock Ledge Farm Union Valley Rd Mahopac NY 10541 Office: Smithsonian Instn Washington DC 20560

THOMPSON, EDWARD THORWALD, magazine editor; b. Milw., Feb. 13, 1928; s. Edward Kramer and Marguerite Minerva (Maxam) T.; grad. Lawrenceville Sch., 1945; S.B., Mass. Inst. Tech., 1949; m. Margaret Kessler, 1949; children—Edward Thorwald, Anne B., Evan K., David S.; m. 2d, Nancy Cale, May 28, 1966; 1 dau., Julie. Engr., Mobil Oil Co., Beaumont, Tex., 1949-52; asso. editor Chem. Engr. mag., N.Y.C., 1952-55; mng. editor Chem. Week mag., N.Y.C., 1955-56; asso. editor Fortune mag., 1956-60; with Reader's Digest, Pleasantville, N.Y., 1960—, asst. mng. editor, then mng. editor, 1973-76, editor-in-chief, mem. exec. com., 1976—; dir. Reader's Digest Assn. Trustee Reader's Digest Found. Recipient Golden Plate award Am. Acad. Achievement, 1977. Mem. Am. Soc. Mag. Editors. Clubs: Dutch Treat, River (N.Y.C.); Bedford Golf & Tennis, Jupiter Hills Country. Home: Guard Hill Rd Bedford NY 10506 Office: Reader's Digest Pleasantville NY 10570

THOMPSON, ELISABETH KENDALL, archtl. journalist; b. New Orleans; d. John S. and Isoline (Rodd) Kendall; B.A., Tulane U., 1929, postgrad. in Arch., 1930-32; M.A., U. Wis., 1930; postgrad. in Arch., U. Calif., 1932-34; m. Frank Hofmann Thompson, May 29, 1941; children—Susan Elizabeth Thompson Bailey, Lawrence Kendall (dec.). Reporter, feature writer New Orleans Times Picayune, 1927-29; draftsman, designer, New Orleans, 1935; instr. Holmquist Sch., New Hope, Pa.. 1935-36; asst. news editor, then asso. editor Archtl. Record, N.Y.C., 1937-41, Western editor, Berkeley, Calif., 1947-58, sr. asso. editor, 1953-58, sr. editor, San Francisco, 1958-75; free-lance writer, Berkeley, 1975—; asst. prof. architecture Calif. Coll. Arts and Crafts, Oakland, 1955-56. Mem. Civic Art Commn., Berkeley, 1962-68, pres., 1963-64; mem. Civic Art Found., Berkeley, pres., 1966-69; mem. archtl. adv. bd. San Francisco Heritage, 1975—; mem. council on architecture Oakland Mus. Assn., 1972—. Recipient Jesse Neal award for editorial excellence, 1972. Fellow AIA (Pub. Info. award Calif. Council 1967); mem. Women's Archtl. League Oreg. (hon.), Nat. Trust Historic Preservation. Club: Town and Gown (Berkeley). Editor: Apartments, Townhouses and Condominiums, 1975; Recycling Buildings, 1977; Houses of the West, 1979; author articles in field. Home: 2877 Shasta Rd Berkeley CA 94708

THOMPSON, ELMER ANDREW, paper and packaging co. exec.; b. New Westminster, B.C., Can., June 11, 1920; s. Andrew Johnson and Ellen (Thompson) T.; B.A. Sc., U. B.C., 1942; m. Gwynneth Catherine Jones, Dec. 20, 1945; children—James E., Donald A., Robert G. With Domtar Ltd., Montreal, Que., Can., 1945-67, sr. v.p., 1964-67; exec. v.p. Domglas, Montreal, 1967, pres., chief exec. officer, 1967-75; chmn. bd., exec. v.p. Consol.-Bathurst Ltd., 1975—, also dir.; pres. Consol. Bathurst Packaging Ltd., Mississauga, Ont., Can., 1975—; vice-chmn., mem. supervisory bd. Europa Carton A.G. (W.Ger.); dir. Maritime Paper Products Ltd., DGHC Inc., Royersford, Pa., Twinpak Ltd. Served with RCAF, 1942-45. Mem. Glass Container Mfrs. Inst. (past trustee). Clubs: St. James's, Mt. Royal (Montreal); National (Toronto). Home: 116 Chartwell Rd Oakville ON L6J 3Z6 Canada Office: 2070 Hadwen Rd Mississauga ON L5K 2C9 Canada

THOMPSON, ERA BELL, mag. editor; b. Des Moines; d. Stewart C. and Mary (Logan) T.; student (Wesleyan Service Guild scholar 1931) U. N.D., 1929-31, L.H.D., 1969; B.A., Morningside Coll., 1933, LL.D., 1965; postgrad. Northwesten U. Sch. Journalism, 1938, 40. Sr. interviewer U.S. and Ill. Employment Service, 1942-47; asso. editor Johnson Pub. Co., Chgo., 1947-51; co-mng. editor Ebony mag., 1951-64; internat. editor, 1964—; mem. N. Central Region Manpower Adv. Com., 1965-67; pub. mem. USIA Fgn. Service Selection Bds., Washington, 1976—. Mem. Community Art Center, Chgo., 1942-44; mem. Chgo. met. bd. YWCA, 1944-47; trustee Hull House, Chgo., 1960-64. Recipient Newberry Library fellowship to write autobiography, 1945; Soc. Midland Authors Patron Saints award, 1968; Theodore Roosevelt Roughrider award, 1976; fellow Bread Loaf Writers Conf., 1949. Mem. Soc. Midland Authors (dir. 1961-75), Urban League (Chgo. edn. com. 1953-56), Friends Chgo. Pub. Library (bd. 1959-60), NAACP, Assn. Study of Afro-Am. Life and History, Iota Phi Lambda (Woman of Year 1965), Sigma Gamma Rho (hon.). Author: American Daughter, 1946; Africa, Land of My Fathers, 1954; co-editor: White on Black, 1963. Home: 2851 Martin Luther King Dr Apt 1910 Chicago IL 60616 Office: 820 S Michigan Ave Chicago IL 60605. *I have always believed that I could do anything I wanted to do, if willing to make the necessary effort and sacrifices.*

THOMPSON, ERIC DOUGLAS, elec. engr., physicist; b. Buffalo, Mar. 24, 1934; s. Milton Leslie and Nellie Evelyn (Throop) T.; B.S.E.E., M.I.T., 1956, M.S.E.E., 1956, Ph.D. in Physics, 1960; m. Gail Michelle O'Brien, July 2, 1960; children—Aileen Jo, Eric Douglas, Ronald Brien. Mem. tech. staff Bell Telephone Labs., Murray Hill, N.J., 1953-55; staff asso. Lincoln Labs., Lexington, Mass., 1957-60; instr. elec. engring. and applied physics Case Western Res. U., 1963-66, asst. prof., 1966-70, asso. prof., 1970—. Served with USAF, 1960-62. NSF postdoctoral fellow, 1962-63; NRC sr. resident research asso., 1972-73. Mem. IEEE, Am. Phys. Soc., Sigma Xi, Eta Kappa Nu, Tau Beta Pi. Home: 2165 N Saint James Pkwy Cleveland OH 44106 Office: Elec Engring and Applied Physics Dept Univ Circle Case Western Res U Cleveland OH 44106

THOMPSON, EVERETT STEVEN, civil engr.; b. Detroit, May 19, 1924; s. Everett Steven and Virginia Leigh (Hale) T.; B.A. in Pub. Adminstrn., Mich. State U., 1950, B.S. in Civil Engring., 1951; m. Janet Lucille Williams, Mar. 25, 1950; children—Daniel Steven, Douglas Everett, Virginia Leigh, Bruce Williams. Asst. city mgr. City of Mt. Pleasant (Mich.), 1951-53, city mgr., 1953-56; treas. Williams & Works, Inc., cons. engrs., Grand Rapids, Mich., 1956-71, pres., 1971—. Chmn. Cascade Twp. (Mich.) Planning Commn., 1957-68; mem. planning subcom. United Community Fund. Served with U.S. Army, 1943-46. Mem. Mich. (Engr. of Yr. 1970, Western chpt.), Nat. socs. profl. engrs., Mich. Soc. Registered Land Surveyors, Cons. Engrs. Council Mich., Mich., Am. socs. planning ofcls., Mich. Assn. Professions, Am. Cons. Engrs. Council (v.p. 1977-79, pres.-elect 1979-80), Am. Congress Surveying, Mapping. Congregationlist. Clubs: Rotary (Grand Rapids); Shriners. Home: 1501 Briarcliff Dr SE Grand Rapids MI 49506 Office: 611 Cascade W Pkwy SE Grand Rapids MI 49506

THOMPSON, FRANK, JR., congressman; b. Trenton, N.J., July 26, 1918; s. Frank and Beatrice (Jamieson) T.; ed. Wake Forest Coll., 1941, H.H.D., 1977; LL.D., Rider Coll., 1962, Princeton U., 1969; m. Evelina Gleaves Van Metre, Jan. 10, 1942; children—Anne Thompson Henderson, Evelina Thompson Lyons. Admitted to N.J. bar, 1948, practiced in Trenton; mem. 84th-96th congresses from 4th N.J. Dist.; mem. N.J. Gen. Assembly, 1949-54, asst. minority leader, 1950, minority leader, 1954; mem. com. on edn. and labor, chmn. com. House Adminstrn.; chmn. labor-mgmt. relations sub-com. Chmn., Nat. Voters Registration Com., 1960, 72, Erisa Task Force; trustee John F. Kennedy Center for Performing Arts; bd. regents Smithsonian Instn. Served as comdr. USNR, 1953. Decorated Bronze Star, Gold Star, Sec. Navy Commendation medal. Mem. N.J., Mercer County bar assns. Club: Players (N.Y.). Home: 455 W State St Trenton NJ 08618 Office: Rayburn Office Bldg Washington DC 20515

THOMPSON, FRED PRIESTLY, JR., religious sch. adminstr.; b. Lawton, Kans., Nov. 15, 1917; s. Fred Priestly and Mattie (Leonard) T.; B.A., Pacific Christian Coll., 1939; B.A., George Pepperdine Coll., 1948, M.A., 1950; B.D., Butler U., 1956; student Garrett Theol. Sem., 1957-64, U. Chgo., 1966-67; S.T.D., Milligan Coll., 1970; m. Dorothy Louise Williams, Sept. 30, 1940; children—Janet (Mrs. Dan Richard McClain), David, Donald, Dennis. Ordained to ministry Ch. of Christ, 1938; pastor Central Ch. of Christ, Medford, Oreg., 1939-40, Christian Ch., Elsinore, Calif., 1940-42, Shorb Av. Christian Ch., Los Angeles, 1942-43, Alvarado Christian Ch., Los Angeles, 1943-50, First Christian Ch., Greenwood, Ind., 1950-52, First Christian Ch., Chgo., 1952-68, First Christian Ch., Kingsport, Tenn., 1968-70; prof. Christian doctrine, pres. Emmanuel Sch. Religion, Johnson City, Tenn., 1969—. Mem. bd. adminstrn. Nat. Assn. Evangelicals; mem. Interfaith com. World Conv. of Chs. of Christ. Bd. dirs. Chgo. Bible Soc., European Evangelistic Soc., Christian Missionary Fellowship. Mem. Johnson City C. of C., Am. Acad. Religion, Karl Barth Soc. N.Am., Theta Phi, Eta Beta Rho. Author: Biblical Prophecies, 1967; The Holy Spirit: Comforter, Teacher, Guide, 1978; columnist Action mag.; contbg. editor Christianity Today. Home: 1906 Eastwood Dr Johnson City TN 37601 Office: Emmanuel Sch Religion Johnson City TN 37601

THOMPSON, GEORGE ALBERT, educator, geophysicist; b. Swissvale, Pa., June 5, 1919; s. George A. and Maude A. (Harkness) T.; B.S., Pa. State U., 1941; M.S., Mass. Inst. Tech., 1942; Ph.D., Stanford, 1949; m. Anita Kimmell, July 20, 1944; children—Albert J., Dan A., David C. Geologist, geophysicist U.S. Geol. Survey, 1942-76; asst. prof. Stanford, 1949-55, asso. prof., 1955-60, prof. geophysics, 1960—, chmn. geophysics dept., 1967—, geology dept., 1979-80. NSF postdoctoral fellow, 1956-57; Guggenheim fellow, 1963-64. Recipient G.K. Gilbert award in seismic geology, 1964. Served from ensign to lt. (j.g.), USNR, 1944-46. Fellow AAAS, Geol. Soc. Am., Geophys. Union; mem. Seismol. Soc. Am., Soc. Exploration Geophysicists, Soc. Econ. Geologists. Home: 421 Adobe Pl Palo Alto CA 94306 Office: Geophysics Dept Stanford U Stanford CA 94305

THOMPSON, GEORGE CLIFFORD, educator, author; b. N.Y.C., May 3, 1920; s. W. Stuart and M. Gladys (Slade) T.; B.A., Columbia, 1942, M.S., 1943, J.D., 1949; m. Barbara F. Churchill, 1962; children—Elizabeth, Stuart, Anne. Admitted to N.Y. bar, 1949; asso. Arthur Andersen, C.P.A., 1943-47; with financial survey Western Europe, 1946-47; asso. Columbia, 1947-49, asst. prof., 1949-54, asso. prof., 1954-58, prof., 1958—, James L. Dohr prof. accounting and bus. law, 1960—; dir. several corps. and founds. Mem. N.Y. State Bar Assn., Phi Beta Kappa, Beta Gamma Sigma, Phi Delta Phi, Alpha Kappa Psi. Clubs: Rocky Point, Indian Harbor Yacht (Greenwich, Conn.). Author: (with others) Accounting and the Law; Shortened C.P.A. Review: Law in an Economic Environment, 2 vols.; Antitrust Fundamentals. Contbr. articles to profl. publs. Home: 164 Shore Rd Old Greenwich CT 06830. *My primary goal is education of graduate business and law students. Such education must not be sterile or taught in a vacuum; thus I have sought varied professional and business experience and seek to enrich my teaching through this experience. Likewise I have sought to bring the high standards of academic life to the business world. The spheres of education and practical business or professional life must intermesh, as each can vitalize the other.*

THOMPSON, GEORGE GREENE, psychologist, educator; b. Bucklin, Kans., Mar. 17, 1914; s. Otis Kenrick and Georgia (Beach) T.; B.A., Ft. Hays (Kans.) State Coll., 1937, M.S., 1938; Ph.D., State U. Iowa, 1941; m. Evelyn Schuller, Oct. 25, 1940; 1 son, Kenrick Steven. Asst. prof. psychology So. Ill. U., Carbondale, 1941-42; asst. prof. psychology Syracuse U., 1942-46, asso. prof., 1946-49, prof., 1949-59; prof. psychology Ohio State U., Columbus, 1959—; spl. research asso. psycho-acoustic lab. Harvard U., 1943-45; mem. rev. com. research grants div. NIMH, 1964-67. Fellow Am. Psychol. Assn., Am. Sociol. Assn.; mem. Soc. Research in Child Devel., Am. Ednl. Research Assn., AAAS, Sigma Xi. Author: Child Psychology, 2d edit., 1962; (with F.J. Di Vesta) Educational Psychology, 1971; (with R.G. Kuhlen) Psychological Studies of Human Devel., 3d edit., 1971; (with E.F. Gardner) Social Relations and Morale in Small Groups, 1957. Editor: Social Development and Personality, 1971. Cons. editor Jour. Genetic Psychology, 1959—, Genetic Psychology Monographs, 1959—, Jour. Ednl. Psychology, 1958—. Home: 203 W Southington Ave Worthington OH 43085

THOMPSON, GEORGE LEE, mfg. co. exec.; b. Denver, June 12, 1933; s. George H. and Frances M. (Murphy) T.; B.S. in Bus., U. Colo., 1957; postgrad. in advanced mgmt. N.Y. U., 1969; m. Jean G. Meier, Aug. 25, 1957; children—Shannon, Tracy, Bradley. With GTE Sylvania, Denvers, Mass., 1957-65, nat. sales mgr., 1965-67, mktg. mgr., 1967-68, v.p. sales entertainment products, Batavia, N.Y., 1968-73, dir. mktg., Stamford, Conn., 1973-74; v.p. mktg. Servomation Corp., N.Y.C., 1974-76, exec. v.p., 1976-78; exec. v.p. Singer Co., Elizabeth, N.J., 1978—. Mem. Republican Town Com., Wilton, Conn., 1976. Served to lt. USN, 1951-54. Decorated Air medal, UN medal; recipient Most Valuable Promotion award Nat. Restaurant Assn., 1976. Mem. Illuminating Engring. Soc., Am. Mgmt. Assn., Am. Home Sewing Assn., Chi Psi. Episcopalian. Clubs: Wilton Riding (bd. govs.), Navesink Country, Newcomen, Seabright Beach. Home: 6 Northover Pl Middletown NJ 07748 Office: 321 First St Elizabeth NJ 07207

THOMPSON, GEORGE LOUIS, glass designer; b. Winnetoon, Nebr., Oct. 14, 1913; s. George Littleton and Jessie (Lindsay) T.; B.S.A., U. Minn., 1935; M.A., Mass. Inst. Tech., 1936. Mem. design dept. Steuben Glass Co., 1936—, sr. staff designer, 1948—; rep. permanent collections Met. Mus. Art, William Rockhill Nelson Gallery, Kansas City, Mo., Louvre, Paris, France, others. Recipient Class medal Mass. Inst. Tech., 1936, prize Boston Inst. Architects, 1936. Mem. Mass. Inst. Tech. Alumni Assn. Home: Silver Springs Shores 611-A Midway Dr Ocala FL 32670 Office: care Steuben Glass Co 717 Fifth Ave New York NY 10022*

THOMPSON, GEORGE ROBERT, life ins. co. exec.; b. Brunswick, Maine, Mar. 29, 1917; s. Albert E. and Mabel (Burditt) T.; B.A., Brown U., 1940; m. Ruth Eleanor Blake, May 3, 1941; children—William, Mary Louise, Robert, James. With Am. Mut. Liability Ins. Co., Boston 1940-41, Devonshire Financial Service, Portland, Maine, 1941-56; with Nat. Life Ins. Co., Montpelier, Vt., 1956—, treas. 1967-74, v.p. policyholder services, 1974—; dir. Vt. Fed. Savs. & Loan Assn. Pres., Montpelier Home for Aged, 1971—. Served with USAAF, 1943-46. Mason. Home: Towne Hill Rd Montpelier VT 05602 Office: Nat Life Ins Co Nat Life Dr Montpelier VT 05602

THOMPSON, GEORGE WESLEY, mfg. co. exec.; b. Syracuse, Kans., Mar. 15, 1915; s. Talmadge Dewitt and Ruth Anell (Calkin) T.; student pub. schs., Syracuse; m. Margaret Doyle, May 7, 1934; 1 dau., Sue Thompson Guenther. Laborer, Kans. Hwy. Dept., Syracuse,

1934-35, Am. Sisters Mining Co., Lawson, Colo., 1935-36, in rd. constrn. Hamilton Gleason Co., Littletown, Colo., 1936-37; with shipping and receiving dept. Montgomery Ward, Denver, 1937-41; worker transp. and purchasing Swift & Co., Denver, 1941-45, with purchasing dept. Chgo. gen. offices, 1945-47; with Indpls. Wire Bound Box Co., 1947-61, subsequently gen. mgr.; v.p., gen. mgr. box div. Altamil Corp. (merger Indpls. Wire Bound Box Co. and Altamil Corp.), Indpls., 1961-70, pres., chief exec. officer, 1970-77, chmn. bd., New Orleans, 1977—, also dir., dir. subsidiaries Fontaine Truck Equipment Co., Aluminum Forge Co.; chmn. bd. Am. Box Co., also dir. Republican. Presbyterian. Clubs: Metairie (La.) Country, Fernwood (Miss.) Country; Plimsoll (New Orleans); Mispah (Chgo.). Home: 109 E William David Pkwy Metairie LA 70005 Office: Altamil Corp PO Box 51600 New Orleans LA 70151

THOMPSON, GERALD LUTHER, educator; b. Rolfe, Iowa, Nov. 25, 1923; s. Luther and Sylva Carlotta (Larson) T.; B.S. in Elec. Engring., Iowa State U., 1944; M.S. in Math., Mass. Inst. Tech., 1948; Ph.D., U. Mich., 1953; m. Dorothea Vivian Mosley, Aug. 25, 1954; children—Allison M., Emily A., Abigail E. Instr. math. Princeton, 1951-53; asst. prof. math. Dartmouth, 1953-58; prof. math. Ohio Wesleyan U., Delaware, 1958-59; asso. prof. applied math. and indsl. adminstrn. Carnegie-Mellon U., Pitts., 1959-63, prof., 1963—; cons. Econometric Research Program, Princeton, IBM, Bethlehem Steel Co., Port Authority of Allegheny County, McKinsey & Co., Applied Devices Corp., PPG Industries, Westinghouse Electric Corp., Timken Co., J & L Steel; prin. investigator Mgmt. Scis. Research Group, Carnegie-Mellon U. Served with USNR, 1943-46. Ford Found. research fellow, 1963-64. Rep. of Inst. Mgmt. Scis. to NRC. Mem. Am. Math. Soc., Math. Assn. Am., Soc. for Indsl. and Applied Math., Econometric Soc., Inst. Mgmt. Scis., Operations Research Soc. Am., Phi Beta Kappa, Phi Kappa Phi, Tau Beta Phi, Eta Kappa Nu, Phi Mu Alpha. Club: Fox Chapel Racquet (Pitts.). Author: (with J.G. Kemeny and J.L. Snell) Introduction to Finite Mathematics, 1957; Finite Mathematical Structures, 1959; Finite Mathematics with Business Applications, 1962; Industrial Scheduling, 1963; Programming and Probability Models in Operations Research, 1973; Mathematical Theory of Expanding and Contracting Economies, 1976. Asso. editor Inst. Mgmt. Scis. Jour., 1966-69. Contbr. articles to profl. jours. Home: 15 Wedgewood Ln Pittsburgh PA 15215

THOMPSON, GLENN, ret. newspaperman; b. Ripley, Tenn., Nov. 7, 1904; s. William Chapman and Rylla (Glenn) T.; A.B., Princeton, 1927; m. Margaret Dennison Lee, Nov. 19, 1932. Became copy reader Cin. Enquirer, 1929, gen. assignments reporter, 1936, Washington corr., 1946-56, exec. editor, 1956-59; editor Dayton Jour. Herald, 1959-68. Bd. dirs. Little Miami, Inc., pres., 1978-79. Served to capt. inf. U.S. Army, 1942-46. Mem. Am. Soc. Newspaper Editors. Clubs: Nat. Press, Gridiron; Moraine Country, Buz Fuz. Home: 4716 Fawnwood Rd Dayton OH 45429

THOMPSON, GORDON, JR., judge; b. San Diego, Dec. 28, 1929; s. Gordon and Garnet (Meese) T.; grad. U. So. Calif., 1951, Southwestern U. Sch. Law, Los Angeles, 1956; m. Jean Peters, Mar. 17, 1951; children—John M., Peter Renwick, Gordon III. Admitted to Calif. bar, 1956; with Dist. Atty.'s Office, County of San Diego, 1957-60; partner firm Thompson & Thompson, San Diego, 1960-70; U.S. dist. judge So. Dist. Calif., San Diego, 1970—. Bd. visitors U. San Diego. Mem. Am. Bd. Trial Advocates (treas.), Am., San Diego County (v.p. 1970) bar assns., Delta Chi. Clubs: Lomas Santa Fe Country; San Diego Yacht. Office: 940 Front St San Diego CA 92189

THOMPSON, GORDON WILLIAM, dentist; b. Vancouver, B.C., Can., Dec. 22, 1940; s. Clarence and Emma Jean T.; student U. B.C., Vancouver, 1958-61; D.D.S., U. Alta. (Can.), Edmondton, 1965; M.Sc.D., U. Toronto (Ont., Can.), 1969, Ph.D., 1971; m. Marilyn Jean Lust, May 23, 1964; children—Janice Lynne, Phillip Glen. Practice dentistry, Wetaskiwin, Alta., 1965; asst. prof. dentistry U. Toronto, 1969-72, asso. prof., 1972-77, prof., 1977-78; prof., dean Faculty of Dentistry, U. Alta., 1978—. Fellow Royal Coll. Dentists (Can.); mem. Alta. Dental Assn., Can. Dental Assn., Internat. Assn. Dental Research. Conservative. Mem. United Ch. Canada. Contbr. numerous articles on craniofacial growth to profl. jours.; editor Ont. Dental Assn. Jour., 1977-78. Home: 12429 28th Ave Edmonton AB T6J 4G4 Canada Office: 3036 Dentistry Centre U Alta Edmonton AB T6J 2N8 Canada

THOMPSON, HALE GEORGE, lawyer; b. Williams, Iowa, Sept. 26, 1913; s. George W. and Vera M. (Shaffer) T.; LL.B., U. Oreg., 1937; m. Ruth May Chilcote, Sept. 26, 1939; children—Julie Ann, John Edmund, Emilie Ruth. Admitted to Oreg. bar, 1937, since practiced in Eugene; mem. firm Thompson, Mumford, Woodrich & Anderson. Pres., Frances Willard P.T.A., 1947-48; chmn. A.R.C. Rollcall, 1941-42; chmn. Spl. Mayor's Com. on City Ct. Study, 1965; mem. U. Oreg. Devel. Fund, Eugene Jr. C. of C. Trust Fund; mem. lay adv. com. Sacred Heart Gen. Hosp., Eugene. Bd. dirs. Cascade Manor, Eugene; dir. bd. govs. Friends of Mus. U. Oreg. Served to lt. (j.g.) USNR, 1943-46. Recipient Hilton prize essay, 1937; named Boss of Year, Amanuenses chpt. Nat. Secs. Assn., 1959. Mem. Am., Oreg. (pres., bd. govs.), Lane County (pres., chmn. med.-legal relations) bar assns., Nat. Assn. Bar Presidents, Eugene C. of C. (pres. 1966, chmn. Fern Ridge Water Recreational Study), Willamette Ski Patrol (charter pres.). Methodist (pres. bd. trustees). Lion. Clubs: Eugene Country (pres.), Assembly (pres.) (Eugene); Tri-Pass Ski (v.p.). Home: 1600 Skyline Blvd Eugene OR 97403 Office: 777 High St Eugene OR 97401

THOMPSON, HANNIS WOODSON, JR., elec. engr.; b. Salisbury, N.C., Sept. 3, 1928; s. Hannis Woodson and Lillian Eicie (Boger) T.; B.E.E., N.C. State Coll., 1953, M.S. in Elec. Engring., 1959; Ph.D. (Ford Found. fellow), Purdue U., 1963; m. Frances Elizabeth Almond, Aug. 12, 1951; children—Hannis, Cheryl. Engr., Western Electric Co., Burlington, N.C., 1953-57; with dept. elec. engring. Purdue U., West Lafayette, 1960—, prof., 1972—; research scientist Navy Electronics Lab., San Diego, Calif., summers 1963, 64; instr. N.C. State Coll., 1957-60; cons. in field. Advisor Explorer Scout Post 99, Boy Scouts Am., 1964-71; city coordinator Here's Life Lafayette, 1976-77. Served with USN, 1947-51. Recipient key Boy Scouts Am. Mem. Am. Soc. Engring. Edn., IEEE, Am. Phys. Soc., Sigma Xi, Sigma Pi Sigma, Tau Beta Pi, Eta Kappa Nu. Republican. Presbyterian. Clubs: Tecumseh Kiwanis, Lafayette Sailing. Contbr. articles to profl. jours. Home: 601 Robinson West Lafayette IN 47906 Office: Sch Electrical Engring Purdue U West Lafayette IN 47907

THOMPSON, HAROLD, ins. co. exec.; b. Winnipeg, Man., Can., Aug. 18, 1922; s. Harry and Hrodny (Finnson) T.; B. Commerce with honors, U. Man., Winnipeg, 1944; m. Beatrice May Shipman, Sept. 21, 1946; children—Patricia Lynn, Gordon Douglas. With Monarch Life Assurance Co., Winnipeg, 1946—, v.p. adminstrn., 1968-70, exec. v.p., 1970, pres., chief exec. officer, 1971—. Home: 53 Aldershot Blvd Winnipeg MB R3P 0C9 Canada Office: 333 Broadway Winnipeg MB Canada

THOMPSON, HARRY CHARLES, publishing exec.; b. Yonkers, N.Y., Jan. 16, 1921; s. Charles Henry and Adele (Gross) T.; B.A., Colgate U., 1942; grad. Advanced Mgmt. Program, Harvard U.; m. Eleanor Louise Balcke, May 25, 1946; children—Charles, Katharine. Pub. relations exec. Newell Emmett Co., 1946; free-lance mag. writer, 1946; promotion mgr. Popular Publs., 1947-49; merchandising mgr. Time mag., 1949-51; promotion dir. Newsweek mag., 1951-58, exec. dir. Newsweek Internat., 1958-62, v.p., exec. dir., 1962-64, v.p., advt. dir., 1964-69; pub. Newsweek mag., 1969-72; exec. v.p., dir. Newsweek, Inc., 1969-72; pres. Mag. Networks Inc., N.Y.C., 1972-74, The Washingtonian Mag., 1972-74; v.p., asso. pub. U.S. News & World Report, 1975—; partner Bourne-Thompson & Assos.; chmn. 13th World Congress, Internat. Advt. Assn., 1961. Bd. dirs. Colgate U. Alumni Corp. Served to lt. USNR, 1942-45. Mem. Mag. Mktg. Com. (chmn. 1968-70), Mag. Pub. Assn. (vice chmn. 1970-72, chmn. 1972-74), Phi Beta Kappa, Sigma Chi. Club: Univ. (N.Y.C.). Home: 45 Owenoke Park Westport CT 06880

THOMPSON, HARTWELL GREENE, physician, educator; b. Hartford, Conn., Aug. 30, 1924; s. Hartwell Greene and Sigrid (Johnson) T.; B.A., Yale, 1946; M.D., Cornell U., 1950; m. Frances May Salter, May 21, 1955; children—Sarah, Elisabeth, Mary, Benjamin. Intern Bellevue Hosp., N.Y.C., 1950-51, resident, 1952-54; intern Hartford Hosp., 1951-52; resident Neurol. Inst. N.Y., Columbia Presbyn. Med. Center, 1954-59; asst. prof., then asso. prof. U. Wis., 1959-64; prof., chmn. dept. neurology W.Va. U. Med. Center, Morgantown, 1964-69, dean Med. Center, Charleston; resident, fellowship tng. in neurology, Phila.; asso. dean, prof. neurology U. Pa. Sch. Medicine; now prof. neurology U. Conn. Med. Center, Farmington. Mem. Neurol. Sci. Research Tng. Com., 1967-70, chmn., 1970-71. Fellow Am. Acad. Neurology; mem. Am. Assn. U. Profs., A.A.A.S., N.Y. Acad. Medicine, Sigma Xi. Home: 55 Hunter Dr West Hartford CT 06107 Office: U Conn Med Center Farmington CT 06032

THOMPSON, HARVEY WESLEY, petroleum co. exec.; b. Pocatello, Idaho, May 22, 1922; s. Milton Woodruff and Mary Ann (Wardle) T.; student Wash. State Coll., 1943; grad. in accounting Internat. Accountants Soc., 1956; m. Helen Middleton, Oct. 10, 1942; children—Diane, Laurie Hayden, Brian Wesley, Alan Middleton. Sales clk. Western Auto Supply Co., Pocatello, 1939-40; office mgr. Idaho Gas & Oil Co., Pocatello, 1940-47; accountant Wasatch Oil Co., Salt Lake City and Bartlesville, Okla., 1947-49; with Phillips Petroleum Co., Bartlesville, 1947—, asst. to asst. sec., 1962-63, asst. sec., 1963-71, sec., 1971—. Served with USAAF, 1943-46. Mem. Am. Soc. Corporate Secs. Republican. Mem. Ch. of Jesus Christ of Latter-day Saints (2d counselor Tulsa Okla. stake presidency 1962-77). Club: Frank Phillips Men's (Bartlesville). Home: 2604 SE Quail Pl Bartlesville OK 74003 Office: Phillips Bldg Bartlesville OK 74004

THOMPSON, HOWARD ELLIOTT, educator; b. West Allis, Wis., July 30, 1934; s. Leonard Adolph and Hulda Axelina (Granstrom) T.; B.S., U. Wis., 1956, M.S., 1958, Ph.D., 1964; m. Judith M. Gram, June 30, 1956; children—Linda Kay, Karen Marie, James Howard, John Leonard, Ann Elizabeth. Mathematician, ops. research analyst A.O. Smith Corp., Milw., 1957-61; asst. prof. Sch. Bus., U. Wis., Madison, 1964-67, asso. prof., 1967-69, prof., 1969—, Mary Rennebohm prof., 1975—; vis. prof. Ohio State U., 1970-71; cons. various utilities and utility commns., 1968—. Wis. atty. gen., 1973-74. Mem. Am. Fin. Assn., Am. Econs. Assn., Ops. Research Soc., Am. Inst. Mgmt. Scis., Am. Inst. Decision Scis., Math. Assn. Am., Pi Mu Epsilon, Beta Gamma Sigma, Alpha Iota Delta. Author: Applications of Calculus in Business and Economics, 1973; A Brief Calculus with Applications to Business and Economics, 1976. Contbr. articles to profl. jours. Home: 6302 Bradley Pl Madison WI 53711 Office: Commerce Bldg U Wis Madison WI 53706

THOMPSON, HUGH CURRIE, physician; b. New Rochelle, N.Y., Jan. 3, 1906; s. Hugh Currie and Alice (Snyder) T.; B.A., Yale, 1926; M.D., Columbia, 1930; m. Victoria Buel, Sept. 20, 1933; children—Hugh Currie III, Richard M., Betsy C. (Mrs. Denney E. Miller). Intern St. Luke's Hosp., N.Y.C., 1930-32, Babies Hosp., N.Y.C., 1932-33; practice medicine, specializing in pediatrics, Albany, N.Y., 1933-38, Tucson, 1938—; instr. pediatrics Albany Med. Coll., 1933-38; now prof. pediatrics U. Ariz. Coll. Medicine; cons. Pima County Hosp., Tucson; attending pediatrician Tucson Med. Center. Pres., Big Bros. of Tucson, Tucson Child Guidance Clinic. Served to maj. AUS, 1943-45; ETO. Mem. Am. Acad. Pediatrics (past pres., mem. exec. bd.), Pima County Med. Soc. (past pres.). Clubs: Yale (past pres.), Tucson Country (Tucson). Author: (with Joseph B. Seagle) The Management of Pediatric Practice—A Philosophy and Guide, 1961. Editor, co-author Standards of Child Health Care, 1967, 76. Home: 5015 N Camino Arenosa Tucson AZ 85718 Office: Dept Pediatrics Arizona Med Center 1501 N Campbell St Tucson AZ 85724

THOMPSON, HUGH LEE, ednl. adminstr.; b. Martinsburg, W.Va., Mar. 25, 1934; s. Frank Leslie and Althea Thompson; B.S., B.A. in English and Secondary Edn., Shepherd Coll., Shepherdstown, W.Va., 1956; M.A., Pa. State U., 1958; Ph.D. in Higher Edn. Adminstrn., Case Western Res. U., 1969; m. Patricia Smith; children—Cheri, Linda, Tempe, Vicki. Mem. faculty Pa. State U., 1957-60, Akron (Ohio) U., 1960-62; mem. faculty Baldwin-Wallace Coll., Berea, Ohio, 1966-70, asso. prof. edn., 1969-70, asst. to pres., 1966-69, dir. instl. planning, asst. to pres., 1969-70; coordinator Associated Colls. Cleve., 1970-71; pres. Siena Heights Coll., Adrian, Mich., 1971-77; pres. Detroit Inst. Tech., 1977—. Mem. com. continuing edn. Lutheran Ch. Mich. Synod, 1974. Clubs: Detroit Athletic, Detroit, Shriners. Home: 871 Balfour St Grosse Pointe Park MI 48230 Office: 2727 2d Ave Detroit MI 48201. *I have found that to be successful in any field of endeavor an individual must work very diligently at finding solutions to problems, should be highly goal oriented, honest and forthright, and adhere to the teachings of Christ.*

THOMPSON, HUNTER STOCKTON, author, editor, journalist; b. Louisville, July 18, 1939; s. Jack R. and Virginia (Ray) T.; 1 son, Juan. Carribean corr. Time mag., 1959, N.Y. Herald Tribune, 1959-60; South Am. corr. Nat. Observer, 1961-63; West Coast corr. The Nation, 1964-66; columnist Ramparts, 1967-68, Scanlan's, 1969-70; nat. affairs editor Rolling Stone, San Francisco, 1970-75; global affairs corr. High Times, 1977—. Mem. Sheriff's Adv. Com., Pitkin County, Colo., 1976—; a judge Nat. Book Awards, 1975; mem. nat. adv. bd. NORML, 1976—; exec. dir. Woody Creek Rod and Gun Club. Served with USAF, 1956-58. Author: Hell's Angels, 1966; Fear and Loathing in Las Vegas, 1972; Fear and Loathing On the Campaign Trail '72, 1973; The Great Shark Hunt, 1977. Creator Gonzo journalism. Home: Woody Creek CO 81656 Office: 625 3d St San Francisco CA 94107

THOMPSON, JACK EDWARD, mining co. exec.; b. Central City, Nebr., Nov. 17, 1924; s. Ray Elbert and Bessie Fay (Davis) T.; student Northwestern U., 1942-43, Colo. Sch. Mines, 1944-45; m. Maria del Carmen Larrea, May 8, 1948; children—Jack Edward, Ray Anthony, Robert Davis. Vice pres. Cia. Quimica Comercial de Cuba S.A., 1946-60; v.p. Cia. de Fomento Quimico S.A., 1946-60; with Newmont Mining Corp., N.Y.C., 1960—, asst. to pres., 1964-67, v.p., 1967-71, dir., 1969—, exec. v.p., 1971-74, pres., 1974—; dir. Sherritt Gordon Mines Ltd., Peabody Coal Co., Atlantic Cement Co., O'Okiep Copper Co. Ltd., Idarado Mining Co., Tsumeb Corp. Ltd., Foote Mineral Co., Bethlehem Copper Corp. Ltd., Cassiar Asbestos Corp. Ltd.; mem. East Side adv. bd. Chem. Bank. Chmn. bd. trustees Minerals Industry Ednl. Found. Recipient Distinguished Achievement medal Colo. Sch. Mines, 1974. Mem. Mining Club N.Y. (chmn. bd. govs.), Am. Inst. Mining and Metall. Engrs. Clubs: Mount Kisco Country; Canadian (N.Y.C.). Home: Old Road Ln Mount Kisco NY 10549 Office: 300 Park Ave New York NY 10022

THOMPSON, JAMES BERNARD, civil engr.; b. Fullerton, Calif., Apr. 22, 1922; s. James Bernard and Bertha (Marolf) T.; B.S., U. Calif., 1943; M.S., Harvard U., 1947; m. Annabelle Dougherty, June 18, 1944; children—James Bernard, III, Richard B., Joanne. With Dames & Moore, Los Angeles, 1953—, partner, 1954—, charge soil mechanics and founds., 1953—; mem. faculty 8th ann. conf. soil mechanics and found. engring. U. Minn., 1959; vis. prof. U. Ill., 1972-75. Served with AUS, 1943-46. Fellow ASCE, Am. Cons. Engring. Council; mem. Nat. Soc. Profl. Engrs., Am. Rd. and Transp. Assn., Am. Assn. Port Authorities. Contbr. profl. jours. Address: 445 S Figueroa St Room 3500 Los Angeles CA 90071

THOMPSON, JAMES BURLEIGH, JR., geologist, educator; b. Calais, Maine, Nov. 20, 1921; s. James Burleigh and Edith (Peabody) T.; A.B., Dartmouth, 1942, D.Sc. (hon.), 1975; Ph.D., Mass. Inst. Tech., 1950; m. Eleanora Mairs, Aug. 3, 1957; 1 son, Michael A. Instr. geology Dartmouth, 1942; research asst. Mass. Inst. Tech., 1946-47, instr., 1947-49; instr. petrology Harvard, 1949-50, asst. prof., 1950-55, asso. prof. mineralogy, 1955-60, prof., 1960—. Served to 1st lt. USAAF, 1942-46. Guggenheim fellow 1963; Sherman Fairchild distinguished scholar Calif. Inst. Tech., 1976. Fellow Mineral. Soc. Am. (pres. 1967-68, recipient Roebling medal 1978), Geol. Soc. Am. (A.L. Day medal, 1964), Am. Acad. Arts and Scis.; mem. AAAS, Am. Geophys. Union, Nat. Acad. Scis., Geochem. Soc. (pres. 1968-69), Sigma Xi. Home: 20 Richmond Rd Belmont MA 02178 Office: Harvard U Cambridge MA 02138

THOMPSON, JAMES C., bus. cons.; b. Chgo., Feb. 15, 1894; s. William James and Delphia (Cotton) T.; student pub. schs., Chgo. and Toledo; m. Ruth Elsie Mirick, Mar. 22, 1919; 1 dau., Phyllis Ruth. With Willys Overland Co., Toledo, 1910-12, Gen. Electric Co., 1912-13, Am. Tobacco Co., 1913-17, U.S. Treasury Dept., Washington, 1917-19; sales mgr. Wertheimer Bros., Balt., 1919-29; pres. Metropolitan Co., Toledo, 1928-29; asso. Fred B. Prophet Co., Detroit, 1929-30; sr. exec. Walgreen Co., Chgo., 1930-36; pres. Twenty North Wacker Corp., 1936-52; pres. Wacker Drive Safe Deposit Co. since 1937; dir. LaSalle Indsl. Finance Co., Chgo. Nat. Bank; pres., dir. Continental Indsl. Engrs.; mgr. 201 North Wells Bldg., 1942-46; bus. cons., 1952—; dir. Gen. Finance Corp.; a founder Chgo. Nat. Bank; trustee, executor Howard Young Estate; pres., treas. Howard Young Gallery; chmn. bd., chief exec. officer Howard Young Med. Center. Chmn. exec. com. Lakeland Meml. Hosp.; bd. dirs. Research Found., Goodwill Industries, Town and Country Equestrian Assn. Clubs: Variety, Execs., Minocqua Country (dir., chmn. house com.; chmn.); Everglades, Bath and Tennis (Palm Beach, Fla.); Pickwick, New Orleans Athletic (New Orleans); Metropolitan (N.Y.C.). Home: PO Box 2016 Palm Beach FL 33480 also Woodruff WI 54568 Office: 2100 St Charles Ave New Orleans LA 70140

THOMPSON, JAMES CHARLES, surgeon; b. San Antonio, Aug. 16, 1928; s. Oscar Augustus and Vera Marie (Powell) T.; B.S., A&M Coll. Tex., 1948; M.D., U. Tex. Med. Br., Galveston, 1951, M.A. in Anatomy and Endocrinology, 1952; m. Marilyn Anderson Fargas, Apr. 14, 1967; children—Patricia A. Thompson Frnka, Jan L. Thompson Ellwood, Gayle A., James Charles, John W.; 1 stepdau., Laura V. Fargas. Intern, U. Tex. Med. Br. Hosps., 1951-52, chief of surgery, 1970—, prof., chmn. dept. surgery, 1970—, prof. physiology and biophysics, 1975—; resident in surgery Hosp. U. Pa., 1952-54, 56-59; surgeon Pa. Hosp., Phila., 1959-63; asso. in surgery U. Pa. Sch. Medicine, 1959-61, asst. prof. surgery, 1961-63; surgeon Harbor Gen. Hosp., Torrance, Calif., 1963-67, chief of surgery, 1967-70; asso. prof. UCLA, 1963-67, prof., 1967-70; U.S.-USSR health exchange prof., 1973; examiner Am. Bd. Surgery, 1978—. Served with M.C., U.S. Army, 1954-56. Recipient Career Devel. award NIH, 1961-62; Outstanding Clin. Prof. award U. Tex. Med. Br., 1973, Herman Barnett award, 1975, Ashbel Smith Disting. Alumnus award, 1979; NIH grantee, 1960—; John A. Hartford Found. grantee, 1963-73, 77—. Diplomate Am. Bd. Surgery. Fellow A.C.S. (chmn. surg. forum com. 1977-78); mem. AAAS, Am. Assn. Surgery of Trauma, Am. Fedn. Clin. Research, Am. Gastroenterol. Assn., Am. Physiol. Soc., Am. Surg. Assn., Endocrine Soc., Pacific Coast Surg. Assn., Soc. for Surgery Alimentary Tract, Soc. Univ. Surgeons (chmn. com. on edn. 1970-72, mem. exec. council 1967-69), So. Surg. Assn., Surg. Biology Club, Transplantation Soc., Alpha Omega Alpha. Democrat. Contbr. numerous articles on gastrointestinal physiology and clin. surgery to profl. publs.; editor: Gastrointestinal Hormones, 1975. Office: Dept Surgery U Tex Med Br Galveston TX 77550

THOMPSON, JAMES CHILTON, educator, physicist; b. Ft. Worth, June 14, 1930; s. Frederick Moon and Anna (Chilton) T.; B.A., Tex. Christian U., 1952; M.A., Rice U., 1954, Ph.D., 1956; m. Carol May O'Connor, June 11, 1955; children—K. Kelvin, Denis B., Alan K. Asst. prof. physics U. Tex., Austin, 1956-61, asso. prof., 1961-67, prof., 1967—; mgr. physics Energy Conversion Devices, Inc., Troy, Mich., 1969-70; cons. Boeing Sci. Research Labs., 1966-67; vis. scientist NSF, 1963-68. Fellow Am. Phys. Soc.; mem. Am. Phys. Soc., A.A.A.S., Sigma Xi. Home: 6103 Rickey Dr Austin TX 78731

THOMPSON, JAMES ELLIOTT, lawyer; b. Pilot Grove, Mo., Aug. 2, 1915; s. James and Charlotte (Vaughn) T.; student U. Okla., 1933-35; LL.B., U. Tex., 1938; m. Frances Sawyer Peck, June 1, 1935; children—Herbert Peck, James Page, Stephen Elliott. Admitted to Tex. bar, 1938, Okla. bar, 1939; law clk. to U.S. dist. judge, 1940-41; probate atty. Office Solicitor, Dept. Interior, Office Indian Affairs, 1942-43; gen. counsel Noble Drilling Corp., Tulsa, 1943-45; counsel, exec. v.p. Samedan Oil Corp., Ardmore, Okla., 1946-62, dir., 1950-69; gen. counsel, 1969-76, dir. Noble Affiliates, Inc., 1969—. Trustee Ardmore Devel. Authority, 1970-77, chmn., 1974; trustee Samuel Roberts Noble Found., Inc., Ardmore, 1952-72, pres. 1952-65; trustee Community Activities of Ardmore, 1970—. Mem. Okla. Bar Assn., Ardmore C. of C. (pres. 1965, Outstanding Citizen's award 1974). Presbyn. Home: 2211 Cloverleaf Pl Ardmore OK 73401 Office: 302 Exchange Plaza Ardmore OK 73401

THOMPSON, JAMES HARRY, food co. exec.; b. Sioux Falls, S.D., Nov. 30, 1925; s. Harry Peter and Mary Francis (Wright) T.; B.S. in Bus. Adminstrn., U. S.D., 1950; m. Margaret Gretchen Menke, June 29, 1957; children—James Harry, William, Timothy. Audit principal Haskins & Sells, C.P.A.'s, Denver, 1952-67; asst. controller Great Western United Co., Denver, 1967-72; sec., treas. Federal Co., Memphis, 1972—; instr. auditing U. Denver, 1959-61. Served with AUS, 1946-47, 50-52. C.P.A., Colo. Mem. Am. Inst. C.P.A.'s. Home: 7260 Pittsfield Cove Germantown TN 38138 Office: 1755-D Lynnfield Rd Memphis TN 38117

THOMPSON, JAMES HOWARD, historian, library adminstr.; b. Memphis, Aug. 20, 1934; s. Curtis Barnabas and Clara (Terry) T.; B.A. in History, Southwestern U., Memphis, 1955; M.A., U. N.C., Chapel Hill, 1957, Ph.D. in History, 1961; M.S. in Library Sci., U. Ill., 1963; m. Margareta Ortenblad, Nov. 24, 1961; children—Ralph, Anna, Howard. Teaching fellow U. N.C., Chapel Hill, 1955-56, departmental asst., 1956-57, reference asst., 1959-61, dir. undergrad. library, lectr. in history, 1968-70; circulation asst. U. Ill., 1961-63, asst. Center for Russian Area and Lang. Studies, 1962-63; cataloger Duke U., 1963-65; asst. prof. history U. S.W. La., 1965-66; asst. prof. U. Colo., 1966-68; dir. libraries, prof. history U. N.C., Greensboro, 1970—; bd. dirs. Southeastern Library Network, 1979—. Ford Found. research fellow, 1957-58; U. Colo. grantee, 1967; U. N.C. at Greensboro grantee, 1977-78. Mem. Phi Beta Kappa, Beta Phi Mu, Phi Alpha Theta, Chi Beta Phi. Episcopalian. Contbr. articles, revs. to profl. jours. Home: 3006 New Hanover Dr Greensboro NC 27408 Office: Jackson Library U NC Greensboro NC 27412

THOMPSON, JAMES MASON, army officer; b. Boise, Idaho, Nov. 6, 1927; s. Roy Glenn and Mary Elaine (Rinehart) T.; B.S., U.S. Mil. Acad., 1950; M.A. (Rhodes scholar 1951-54), Oxford (Eng.) U., 1954; grad. Army War Coll., 1968; m. Karin Renate Kopelke, Oct. 28, 1972; children—Celia, Christopher, Constance, Matthew. Commd. 2d lt. U.S. Army, 1950, advanced through grades to maj. gen.; dir. policy, planning and nat. security affairs Office Sec. Def., 1976-79; chief U.S. mil. mission for AID, Ankara, Turkey, 1979—. Trustee German Sch., Potomac, Md., 1966-68; mem. Ft. Benning (Ga.) Sch. Bd., 1972-74; dist. commr. Boy Scouts Am., 1973-74. Decorated Legion of Merit, Meritorious Service medal, Joint Services Commendation medal, Army Commendation medal; fellow Council Fgn. Relations, 1971-72. Mem. Assn. Grads. U.S. Mil. Acad., Assn. Am. Scholars, Assn. U.S. Army. Episcopalian. Home: 115 Pine Hill Rd McLean VA 22101 Office: Chief JUSMMAT APO New York NY 09254

THOMPSON, JAMES ROBERT, gov. Ill.; b. Chgo., May 8, 1936; s. James Robert and Agnes Josephine (Swanson) T.; student U. Ill., Chgo., 1953-55, Washington U., St. Louis, 1955-56; J.D., Northwestern U., 1959; m. Jayne Carr, 1976; 1 dau., Samantha Jayne. Admitted to Ill. bar, 1959, U.S. Supreme Ct. bar, 1964; asst. state's atty., Cook County, Ill., 1959-64; asso. prof. law Northwestern U. Law Sch., 1964-69; asst. atty. gen., State Ill., 1969-70, chief criminal div., 1969, chief dept. law enforcement and pub. protection, 1969-70; 1st atty. U.S. atty. No. Dist. Ill., 1970-71, U.S. atty., 1971-7S; counsel firm Winston & Strong, Chgo., 1975-77; gov. Ill., 1977—. Mem. joint com. to revise Ill. criminal code, mem. drafting subcom. Chgo.-Ill. bar assns., 1959-63, chmn. joint com. to draft indigent def. legis., 1966-68; mem. com. to draft handbooks for petit jurors in civil and criminal cases and for grand jurors Jud. Conf. Ill., 1959; mem. com. to draft uniform instrn. in criminal cases Ill. Supreme Ct.; co-dir. criminal law course for Chgo. Police and Indsl. Security Personnel, 1962-64; mem. Chgo. Mayor's Com. to Draft Legis. to Combat Organized Crime, 1964-67; adviser Pres.'s Commn. Law Enforcement and Adminstrn. Justice, 1966; mem. Pres.'s Task Force on Crime, 1967; lectr. Northwestern U. Law Sch., U. Cal. at Davis, Mich. State U., Nat., Ill., Ohio, N.D., Va., N.J., Ala., Md. and Ga. prosecutors' assns.; former bd. dirs. Chgo. Crime Commn.; v.p. Americans for Effective Law Enforcement, 1967-69. Mem. Am., Ill. (past chmn. criminal law sect.) bar assns. Republican. Co-author: Cases and Comments on Criminal Justice, 2 vols., 1968, 74; Criminal Law and Its Adminstration, 1970, 74. Asst. editor-in-chief Jour. Criminal Law, Criminology and Police Sci., 1965-69; bd. editors Criminal Law Bull., Address: Office of Governor State House Springfield IL 62706

THOMPSON, JAMES SCOTT, educator; b. Saskatoon, Sask., Can., July 31, 1919; s. Walter Palmer and Marjorie (Gordon) T.; B.A., U. Sask., Saskatoon, 1940, M.A., 1941; M.D., U. Toronto (Ont., Can.), 1945; m. Margaret Anne Wilson, Aug. 19, 1944; children—Gordon Moore, David Bruce. Lectr. anatomy U. Western Ont., London, 1948-50, asst. prof., 1950; asso. prof. anatomy U. Alta., Edmonton, Can., 1950-55, prof., 1955-63, also asst. dean faculty medicine, 1959-62; prof. anatomy U. Toronto, 1963—, chmn. dept. anatomy, 1966-76. Served with Royal Canadian Army M.C., 1943-46. Mem. AAAS, Am., Can. (pres. 1975-77) assns. anatomists, genetics socs. Can., Am., Am. Soc. Human Genetics, Alpha Omega Alpha. Author: (with M.W. Thompson) Genetics in Medicine, 1966, 73; Core Textbook of Anatomy, 1977. Home: 7 Danville Dr Willowdale ON Canada Office: Dept Anatomy Univ Toronto Toronto 2 ON Canada

THOMPSON, JB, artist; b. Vernon, Tex., Jan. 30, 1932; s. Farris Lee and Salena Ladelle (Bowers) T.; student U. Okla., 1950-54, 56-57, Mexico City Coll., 1957-58; m. Mary Sue Goff, May 3, 1957; 1 son, Kristopher Scott. One-man exhibitions include: Maxwell Gallery, San Francisco, 1972, Roten Galleries, Balt., 1974, U. So. Calif. Mus. Art, 1975, Honolulu Acad. Art, 1979, Bowles-Hopkins Gallery, San Francisco, 1979; group exhibitions include: Seattle Art Mus., Long Beach Mus. Art, Nat. Exhbn. Contemporary Am. Art, Okla. Art Center, So. Calif. Expn., Tucson Mus. Art; represented in permanent collections: Seattle Mus. Art, Mint Mus. Art, Charlotte, N.C., U. So. Calif., Okla. Art Center, La. State U., and numerous corporate collections; guest artist Calif. Inst. Arts, Art Center Coll. Design. Served with U.S. Army, 1954-56. Huntington Hartford fellow, 1964, 66. Mem. Los Angeles Art Assn., World Print Council, Am. Graphics Soc. Address: 665 Oleander Dr Los Angeles CA 90042

THOMPSON, JOHN ALBERT, profl. football exec.; b. South Bend, Wash., May 19, 1927; s. Hans Albert and Marjorie Aurelia (Heath) T.; B.A., U. Wash., 1951; m. Marilyn Mitchell, Apr. 7. 1951; children—Richard, Michael, Kathi. Athletic news dir., then dir. pub. relations U. Wash., 1955-60; dir. pub. relations, then asst. gen. mgr. Minn. Vikings Profl. Football Club, 1961-69; asst. to pres. Nat. Football Conf., N.Y.C., 1970-71; exec. dir. NFL Mgmt. Council, 1971-75; gen. mgr. Seattle Seahawks Profl. Football Club, 1975—. Bd. dirs. Bloomington (Minn.) C. of C., 1966-69; mem. Bloomington SSS, 1967-68; bd. dirs. King County Conv. and Tourist Bur., 1976—. Mem. U. Wash. Alumni Assn. Presbyn. Clubs: Broadmoor Golf and Country, Overlake Golf and Country, Wash. Athletic, Elks. Home: 8210 SE 33d Pl Mercer Island WA 98040 Office: Seattle Seahawks 5305 Lake Washington Blvd Kirkland WA 98033

THOMPSON, JOHN BROWN, physician; b. Eugene, Oreg., Mar. 18, 1929; s. Kenneth Guy and Alta Mae (Brown) T.; A.B. in Chemistry, Willamette U., 1951; M.D., U. Oreg., 1956; children—Sheri, Mark. Intern, Salt Lake Gen. Hosp., Salt Lake City, 1956-57; resident Denver VA Hosp., 1957-60; practice medicine, specializing in gastroenterology, Oklahoma City, 1962-75, Fargo, N.D., 1975-78, Fresno, Calif., 1978—; instr. medicine U. Okla. Sch. Medicine, Oklahoma City, 1962-67, asst. prof., 1967-72, asso. prof., 1972-75, co-dir. NIH Gastroenterology Traineeship Program, 1967-71, co-dir. VA Research and Edn., 1968-72; prof. medicine U. N.D. Dept. Medicine, Fargo, 1975-78, chief div. gastroenterology, 1975-78; chief gastroenterology sect. VA Hosp., Oklahoma City, 1966-74, Fargo, 1975-78; chief of staff VA Med. Center, Fresno, 1978—. Served with USAF, 1960-62. Diplomate Am. Bd. Internal Medicine. Fellow A.C.P.; mem. Am. Gastroenterol. Assn., N.Y. Acad. Scis., Am. Fedn. Clin. Research. Contbr. articles to profl. jours. Home: 1585 W Keats Fresno CA 93711 Office: VA Med Center 2615 E Clinton Fresno CA 93703

THOMPSON, JOHN BURTON, mfg. co. exec.; b. Greensboro, N.C., 1917; B.S. in Commerce, U. N.C., 1938. Sec., treas. Dixie Yarns, Inc., Chattanooga, Dixie Yarns Found., Inc. Bd. dirs. Better Bus. Bur Greater Chattanooga; mem. Citizens Taxpayers Assn. Office: 1100 Watkins St Chattanooga TN 37401

THOMPSON, JOHN DANIEL, med. educator; b. Plains, Ga., 1927; M.D., Emory U., 1951. Intern, Johns Hopkins Hosp., 1951-52, resident obstetrics and gynecology, 1952-56, instr. gynecology, 1954-56; instr. obstetrics and gynecology La. State U., 1956-57, asst. prof., 1957-59; asso. prof. Emory U. Sch. Medicine, Atlanta, 1959-61, prof., chmn. dept. obstetrics and gynecology, 1961—. Served with USNR, 1945-46. Diplomate Am. Bd. Obstetrics and Gynecology. Fellow Am. Coll. Obstetrics and Gynecology; mem. AMA. Office: Sch Medicine Emory U Atlanta GA 30303

THOMPSON, JOHN DOUGLAS, business exec.; b. Montreal, Que., Can., Sept. 28, 1934; s. William Douglas and Anne F. (Whebby) T.; B.Eng., McGill U., 1957; M.B.A., U. Western Ont., 1960; m. Ursula McColeman, May 28, 1960; children—Jacqueline, Catherine, Peter. Pres., chief exec. officer, dir. RoyNat Ltd., Montreal; dir. Can. Pacific Hotels Ltd. Bd. dirs. Montreal Children's Hosp. Found., St. Mary's Hosp. Corp., Montreal Met. YMCA. Mem. Assn. Profl. Engrs. Que., Assn. Profl. Engrs. Ont., Montreal Bd. Trade. Roman Catholic. Clubs: Royal Montreal Golf, Montreal Amateur Athletic Assn., St. James's. Office: 620 Dorchester Blvd W Montreal PQ H3B 1P2 Canada

THOMPSON, JOHN DOUGLAS, real estate broker, state assemblyman; b. Cleve., Aug. 23, 1927; s. John Douglas and Bertha Bohles T.; student Feen Coll., Franklin U.; m. Doris V. Walker, Mar. 28, 1953; children—Joni Denise, Janet Renee. Real estate broker John D. Thompson Real Estate Co., Cleve., 1961—; mem. Ohio Ho. of Reps., 1970—, chmn. health and retirement com., vice-chmn. ins., financial insts. and pub. utilities com. Served with AUS; PTO. Named man of year Mt. Pleasant Community Assn. Mem. Lee Harvard Community Area, Mt. Pleasant Community, Lee Seville Area council assns. Mason (Shriner, 32 deg.). Asst. dir. Dept. Minority Affairs, Ohio State Democratic Exec. Com., also chmn. 15th Dist. Orgn. Home: 15611 Stockbridge Ave Cleveland OH 44128 Office: 17017 Miles Ave Cleveland OH 44128

THOMPSON, JOHN IRVIN, engring and marketing cons.; b. Bellefonte, Pa., Jan. 12, 1907; s. George B. and Magdalene (Callaway) T.; B.S. in Civil Engring., Pa. State U., 1925; m. Gwenyth Bruyere, Jan. 12, 1927; children—John I., Owen B., Daniel B. Engr. and exec. Campbell Soup Co., 1939-43, Sharp & Dohme, Inc., 1937-39, Bristol-Myers Co., 1930-37, Central R.R. Co. of N.J., 1925-30; indsl. adviser and spl. lectr. on prodn. mgmt. Wharton Sch., U. Pa., 1940-42; cons. to Bur. Ordnance, Navy Dept., 1942-47; partner John I. Thompson & Co. (now Tracor Jitco, Inc.), Bay Head, N.J., 1943—, pres., dir., 1945—, chief engr., 1951—, chmn. bd., 1968—. Asst. adminstr. for marketing prodn. and marketing adminstrn., v.p., dir. Commodity Credit Corp., U.S. Dept. Agr., Washington, 1948-51; exec. com. Nat. Conf. on Adminstrn. of Research, 1959-70 chmn., 1964; U.S., rep. OECD Conf. on Research Mgmt., Monte Carlo, 1965. Trustee Oglethorpe U. Recipient medal for Merit Bur. Ordnance U.S. Navy, 1946. Mem. ASME, Inst. Food Technologists, Nat. Soc. Profl. Engrs. Republican. Presbyterian. Clubs: Congressional Country, Admirals, Dacor House, Metropolitan (Washington); Bay Head (N.J.) Yacht; Manasquan (N.J.) River Golf. Contbr. articles to profl. jours. Patentee in field. Address: 463 Main Ave Bay Head NJ 08742. *"Getting up early" is important. Then show stability by several years with the same employer while gaining at least "normal" promotion. Then, with this record, advancement during your thirties by changing employment can be advantageous. But by your early forties, find your final employment.*

THOMPSON, JOHN LESLIE, educator; b. New Castle, Pa., July 11, 1917; s. Ralph McClain and Edith (Wilkins) T.; B.S., State Tchrs. Coll., Slippery Rock, Pa., 1940; M.S., U. Wis., 1948, Ph.D., 1956; m. Bertha Marie Boya, Mar. 27, 1942; children—Kay Lynn (Mrs. William W. Koolage), Scott McClain. High sch. tchr., Sharpsville, Pa., 1940-41; mem. faculty Miami U., Oxford, Ohio, 1949—, prof. geography, 1961—, chmn. dept., 1965-73. Chmn. spl. task force Ohio Water Commn.; adv. council S.W. Ohio Water Plan. Served with USAAF, 1941-45. Recipient Meritorious award Ohio Dept. Natural Resources, 1970; Regional Environ. Quality award EPA, 1974. Fellow Ohio Acad. Sci. (v.p. 1960); mem. Assn. Am. Geographers, Am. Geog. Soc. Co-author: Ohio Population, 1960; Ohio Manufacturing, 1962; Student Guide and Laboratory Manual, 1963. Home: 6073 Contreras Rd Oxford OH 45056

THOMPSON, JOHN LESTER, bishop; b. Youngstown, Ohio, May 11, 1926; s. John Lester and Irene (Brown) T.; B.A., Youngstown Coll., 1948; S.T.B., Episcopal Theol. Sch., Cambridge, Mass., 1951; m. Shirley Amanda Scott, Aug. 1, 1951; children—Amanda, Ian. Ordained priest Episcopal Ch., 1951; curate, then rector chs. in Ohio, Oreg. and Calif., 1951-78; bishop Episcopal Diocese No. Calif., Sacramento, 1978—. Pres. Oreg. Shakespeare Festival, 1955-56, chmn. bldg. com. for outdoor theatre, 1957-58. Served with USNR, 1943-46. Home: 3210 Clairidge Way Sacramento CA 95821 Office: PO Box 161268 Sacramento CA 95816

THOMPSON, JOHN MUNRO, beverage co. exec.; b. Montreal, Que., Can., Sept. 4, 1915; s. John Munro and Muriel Mary (Brodie) T.; student Lower Can. Coll., 1928-34; m. Joyce Townsend Horsey, May 20, 1941; children—John Munro, Joyce (Mrs. Maris Andersons), Jennifer (Mrs. Ian Christopher Carter). With John Hyde Audit Corp., Montreal, 1934-35, Standard Brands, Montreal, 1936-38, Dominion Stores, Toronto, Ont., Can., 1938-40; traffic mgr. Apte Horsey Foods, Tampa, Fla., 1945-48; with Orange Crush Ltd., Toronto, 1948-54, pres., 1954, with Crush Internat. Ltd., Toronto and Chgo., 1959—, pres., 1964-65, chmn., 1965—. Served to capt. RCAF, 1940-45. Mem. United Ch. Clubs: Tavern (Chgo.); Board of Trade Golf, National, Badminton and Racquet (Toronto). Home: 2626 Bayview Ave Willowdale ON M2L 1B3 Canada Office: 48 Saint Clair Ave W Toronto ON M4V 2Z2 Canada

THOMPSON, JOHN MURRAY, ret. economist; b. Kokomo, Ind., Dec. 22, 1902; s. Owen J. and Daisie (Dronberger) T.; A.B., De Pauw U., 1925; M.S., Lehigh U., 1929; Ph.D., U. Calif., 1935; m. Dorothy Doggette, Jan. 23, 1926 (dec. 1956); children—Duane (Mrs. F.T. Holt, Jr.), Janis (Mrs. J.W. Ferguson), Miriam (Mrs. M.W. Blake), Patricia (Mrs. Don Sutton), Karen (Mrs. James R. Achen); m. 2d, Helen Tarko, May 15, 1965. Tchr., Melbourne (Fla.) High Sch., 1925-27, Lehigh U., 1927-29, Purdue U., 1929-32, Rice Inst., 1932-34, U. Calif., 1934-37; joined USDA, 1937, former econ. adviser CCC and dir. policy and program appraisal div. Agrl. Stblzn. and Conservation Service; head USDA group in devel. agrl. phases Marshall Plan, 1947; U.S. rep. FAO meetings, 1958; now ret. Pres., Camp Appalachia, Hot Springs, Va. Recipient Superior Service award USDA, 1962. Mem. Am. Farm Econs. Assn., Internat. Agrl. Econs. Assn., Econometric Soc., Phi Beta Kappa, Sigma Xi, Phi Delta Theta. Home: 2 Midhurst Rd Silver Spring MD 20910

THOMPSON, JOHN P., retail food co. exec.; b. Dallas, Nov. 2, 1925; s. Joe E. and Margaret (Philip) T.; B.B.A., U. Tex., 1948; m. Mary Carol Thomson, June 5, 1948; children—Mary Margaret, Henry Douglas, John P. With Southland Corp., 1948—, pres., 1961-69, chmn., chief exec. officer, 1969—. Office: Southland Corp 2828 N Haskell Ave Dallas TX 75221*

THOMPSON, JOHN S., physician, educator; b. Lincoln, Nebr., Oct. 29, 1928; s. John Clark and Florence (Second) T.; student Hamilton Coll., 1945-47; B.A., U. Calif. at Berkeley, 1949; M.D., U. Chgo., 1953; m. Vera B. Hainsey, Dec. 11, 1954 (dec. Aug. 1969); children—John Hainsey, Frankie Lee; m. 2d, Helen Lester Thompson, 1972. Intern, U. Chgo. Hosps., 1953-54, resident medicine, 1957-58; jr. asst. resident medicine Columbia-Presbyn. Hosp., N.Y.C., 1954-55; postgrad. fellow Nat. Cancer Inst., 1958-60; physician, dir. med. edn. Bryan Meml. Hosp., also instr. Coll. Dentistry, U. Nebr., 1960-63; mem. faculty U. Chgo. Med. Sch., 1963-69, asso. prof. medicine, chmn. clin. curriculum, div. biol. scis., 1966-69; prof. medicine, vice chmn. dept. medicine U. Iowa, 1969—, chmn. med. edn. com., 1971-72, chmn. transplantation com., 1972—; chief med. service VA Hosp., Iowa City. Served to capt. M.C., AUS, 1955-57. Recipient Lederle Med. Faculty award 1966-68; Distinguished Service award U. Chgo., 1976. Mem. Am. Assn. Clin. Histocompatibility Testing (pres. 1978-78), A.C.P. (mem. internal medicine residency rev. com.). Asso. editor Jour. Lab. and Clin. Medicine; editorial bd. Journal Allergy and Clin. Immunology, 1971—. Contbr. articles on hematology and immunology to profl. jours. Home: 435 Lexington St Iowa City IA 52240

THOMPSON, JOHN SILVEY, JR., banker; b. Upland, Pa., Feb. 20, 1935; s. John Silvey and Ruth Anna (Dutton) T.; B.S. in Engring., Princeton U., 1957; postgrad. Claremont U., 1961-62; children—John Silvey, III, Robin John Christopher, Michael John Stuart. Mgmt. trainee Union Carbide Corp., 1957-59; region mgr. Avisun Corp., Phila., Can., Europe and Los Angeles, 1959-63; asso. McKinsey & Co., Los Angeles, N.Y.C., London and Amsterdam, 1963-67; v.p., gen. mgr. Sealed Air Corp., Los Angeles and N.Y.C., 1969-74; asst. to chmn., dir. adminstrn. Transam. Corp., San Francisco, 1969-74; pres. Transam. Research Corp., San Francisco, 1971-74; pres. Pyramid Investment Corp., San Francisco, 1971-74; sr. v.p., planning officer Crocker Nat. Bank, San Francisco, 1974—; cons. in field. Served with U.S. Army, 1957-58. Bd. assos. Golden Gate U., 1974-76; trustee West Coast Cancer Found., 1975—. Republican. Episcopalian. Clubs: Princeton. Ivy, 1st Phila., City Troop Cavalry; Union League. Office: 1 Montgomery St San Francisco CA 94104

THOMPSON, JOHN THEODORE, ret. communications co. exec.; b. Decorah, Iowa, Mar. 5, 1917; s. Theodore Elmer and Bertha (Rod) T.; A.B., U. Mich., 1939; m. Dorothea Mae Green, Oct. 3, 1942; children—Jennifer Lynn, Melinda McLean. With Gen. Electric Co., 1939-58, mgr. distbn. sales electronics div., Schenectady, 1948-58; v.p. Raytheon Co., 1958-62; v.p. IT&T, 1962-67, sr. v.p., 1967-69; pres., chmn. bd., chief exec. officer Advance Ross Corp., 1969-70; v.p. Gen Telephone & Electronics Internat. Co., 1970-72; now cons.; dir. Emery Air Freight Corp., First Bancorp. Served to lt. (s.g.) USNR, 1943-46. Mem. Delta Upsilon. Clubs: Canadian (N.Y.C.); Greenwich Country; Indian Harbor Yacht. Home: Lake Ave Greenwich CT 06830 Office: 375 Park Ave New York NY 10022

THOMPSON, JON F., mag. editor; b. Culver City, Calif., June 8, 1943; s. John Ronald and Dorothy Ann (Dunnington) T.; B.A. Journalism, U. Calif., Northridge, 1970; m. Carolyn Lee Noe, June 10, 1967; children—Jonathan Joseph, Matthew Ronald. Staff writer South Bay Daily Breeze, Torrance, Calif., 1971-73; auto editor Copley News Service, San Diego, 1972-73; editor Am. Boating mag., Reno, Nev., 1973-75; mng. editor Autoweek, Reno, 1975-76, Pickup Van and 4 Wheeldrive, Newport Beach, Calif., 1978—; editor Road Test mag., Los Angeles, 1977-78. Mem. Soc. Profl. Journalists, Sigma Delta Chi. Home: 26875 Calle Alcala Mission Viejo CA 92675 Office: 7499 Monrovia St Newport Beach CA

THOMPSON, JOSEPH EARL, ret. pipeline co. exec.; b. Glasco, Kans., Aug. 7, 1914; s. Claude Lewellen and Harriet Frances (Bullock) T.; B.S. in Civil Engring., Kans. State U., 1939; m. Crystle Marie Gabhart, Oct. 14, 1941 (dec. Mar. 1978); 1 son, Steven Michael. With Natural Gas Pipe Line Co. Am., Chgo., 1940-42, 47-64, chief engr., 1964-66, v.p. engring., 1966-78, v.p. spl. engring. projects, 1978-79; civilian engr. C.E., Tulsa, 1942-47. Registered profl. engr., Ill. Mem. ASCE (Stephen D. Bechtel Pipeline Engring. award 1975), Nat. Soc. Profl. Engrs., Western Soc. Engrs. Republican. Presbyterian. Author tech. papers. Home: RD 3 Box 369 Felton DE 19943

THOMPSON, KARL FREDERICK, educator; b. York, Pa., Dec. 31, 1917; s. Charles William and Virginia Grace (Pfeiffer) T.; B.A., Yale U., 1941, M.A., 1942, Ph.D., 1950; m. Jean Cooper Adie, May 2, 1942; children—Virginia Ann, David Charles, Elizabeth Adie. Instr. English, Oberlin (Ohio) Coll., 1948-53; instr. humanities Mich. State U., East Lansing, 1953-55, asst. prof., 1955-59, asso. prof., 1959-64, prof., 1964—, chmn. dept., 1968-78. Served with USAAF, 1942-46. Folger Library fellow, 1958; Guggenheim fellow, 1959-60. Mem. Modern Lang. Assn. Am., Mich. Acad. Sci., Arts and Letters, Renaissance Soc. Am., Phi Beta Kappa, Phi Kappa Phi. Episcopalian. Author: Modesty and Cunning: Shakespeare's Use of Literary Tradition, 1971. Editor: Classics of Western Thought: Middle Ages, Renaissance and Reformation, 1973, 3d edit., 1980. Home: 550 Collingwood Dr East Lansing MI 48823 Office: Dept Humanities Michigan State University East Lansing MI 48824

THOMPSON, KENNETH FREDERICK, mfg. co. exec.; b. Mpls., Jan. 24, 1926; s. Fred Edwin and Minnie Bertha (Klaus) T.; B.S., U. Minn., 1948; m. Carol Ann Stewart, June 3, 1949; children—Richard S., David F. Sales rep. Sperry New Holland div. Sperry Rand Corp., New Holland, Pa., 1953, advanced through mgmt. positions to pres., 1971-77; v.p. Sperry Rand Corp., 1975, exec. v.p., 1976-79, group exec. v.p., 1979—. Chmn. Lancaster County United Way campaign, 1970; pres. bd. dirs. Lancaster County Community Chest, 1971. Served with USNR, 1944-45. Episcopalian. Home: 34 Island Dr Rye NY 10580 Office: Sperry Rand Bldg 1290 Ave of Americas New York NY 10019

THOMPSON, KENNETH W(INFRED), ednl. assn. exec., educator; b. Des Moines, Aug. 29, 1921; s. Thor Carlyle and Agnes (Rorbeck) T.; A.B., Augustana Coll., 1943; M.A., U. Chgo., 1948, Ph.D., 1950; LL.D., U. Notre Dame, 1964, Bowdoin Coll., 1972, St. Michael's Coll., 1973, St. Olaf Coll., 1974; L.H.D., W.Va. Wesleyan U., 1970, Nebr. Wesleyan Coll., 1971; m. Beverly B. Thompson; children—Kenneth Carlyle, Paul Andrew, James David, Carolyn A. Lectr. social scis. U. Chgo., 1948, asst. prof. polit. sci., 1951-53; instr., then asst. prof. polit. sci. Northwestern U., 1948-51, asso. prof. polit. sci., chmn. internat. relations com., 1953-55; cons. internat. relations Rockefeller Found., 1953-55, asst. dir. social scis., 1955-57, asso. dir. social scis., 1957-60, dir. social scis., 1960-61, v.p., 1961-73; dir. higher edn. for devel. Internat. Council for Ednl. Devel., 1974-76; Commonwealth prof. govt. and fgn. affairs U. Va., 1975-78, White Burkett Miller prof. govt. and fgn. affairs, 1979—, dir. White Burkett Miller Center of Public Affairs, 1978—; Riverside Meml. lectr. Riverside Ch., N.Y.C., 1958; Lilly lectr. Duke, 1959; James Stokes lectr. N.Y.U., 1962; Rockwell lectr. Rice U., 1965; univ. seminar asso. Columbia, 1957—; pres. Consortium for World Order Studies, 1974-76; bd. dirs. Inst. Study World Politics, N.Y.C., 1975—; mem. Am. Com. East-West Accords, Stanton Panel on Internat. Info., Edn. and Cultural Relations; v.p. Latin Am. Scholarship Program in Am. Univs., 1975—. Pres., Dist. of Scarsdale and Mamaroneck (N.Y.) Bd. Edn., 1965-68. Trustee Union Theol. Sem., 1967-71, Grinnell Coll.,

1974-78; trustee Dillard U., 1975—, chmn. editorial policy com.; trustee Social Sci. Found., U. Denver, 1974—; dir. ethics and fgn. policy project Council Religion and Internat. Affairs; dir. Scarsdale Found., 1964-74; bd. advisers Patterson Sch., U. Ky., 1974—; com. advisers Sumitomo Fund, 1974—; vice chmn. Feris Found., 1973—; bd. dirs. Music for Westchester. Served to 1st lt. AUS, 1943-46. Fellow Soc. Religion Higher Edn., Am. Acad. Arts and Scis.; mem. Am. Polit. Sci. Assn., Council Fgn. Relations, Internat. Studies Assn., UN Assn. U.S.A., Am. Univs. Field Staff (bd.), Phi Beta Kappa, Sigma Nu (hon.). Clubs: Century, Scarsdale Town. Author: (with Ivo Duchacek) Conflict and Cooperation Among Nations, 1960; (with Karl de Schweinitz) Man and Modern Society, 1953; (with Hans J. Morgenthau) Principles and Problems of International Politics, 1951; Christian Ethics and the Dilemmas of Foreign Policy, 1959; Political Realism and the Crisis of World Politics, 1960; American Diplomacy and Emergent Patterns, 1962; (with Joseph E. Black) Foreign Policies in a World of Change, 1964; The Moral Issue in Statecraft, 1966; Reconstituting the Human Community, 1972; Foreign Assistance: A View From A Private Sector, 1972; Higher Education for National Development, 1972; Understanding World Politics, 1975; Higher Edn. and Social Change, 1976; (with Rosenau and Boyd) World Politics, 1976; Truth and Tragedy, 1977; Ethics and Foreign Policy, 1978; Interpreters and Critics of the Cold War, 1978; Foreign Policy and the Democratic Process, 1978; Ethics, Functionalism and Power, 1979; Morality and Foreign Policy, 1980; Masters of International Thought, 1980; bd. editors Internat. Orgn., 1956-76, Monograph Series in Internat. Affairs, 1974—, Interpretation, Worldview; asso. editor The Rev. of Politics. Contbr. articles to profl. jours. Office: Cabell 206 and Miller Center Univ Va Charlottesville VA 22904

THOMPSON, LAROY BERNARD, univ. adminstr.; b. Laconia, N.H., Oct. 16, 1920; s. John Fawdrey and Anna (Hildebrand) T.; B.Chem. Engring., Cornell U., 1943; m. Edwina Brown Graf, June 12, 1948; children—Virginia K. Graf, Steven M. Thompson. Engring. lab. adminstr. U. Chgo., 1943-44; engring. research asst. U. Calif., Los Alamos, N.Mex., 1944-46; adminstrv. aide U. Rochester (N.Y.), Cyclotron Lab., engring., research asst. Cornell U., 1947-49; dir. research U. Rochester, 1949-57, asso. treas., 1957-59, v.p., treas., 1959-70, sr. v.p., treas., 1970—; dir. Voplex Corp., Lincoln 1st Bank of Rochester, Info. Assos., Inc., Star Supermarkets, Inc. Bd. dirs. Rochester Area Hosps. Corp., Rochester Hosp. Service, United Community Chest, Rochester; bd. overseers Center Naval Analyses; trustee Tilton (N.H.) Sch., Asso. Univs., Inc.; bd. mgrs. Meml. Art Gallery. Mem. Rochester C. of C. Home: 216 Danbury Circle N Rochester NY 14618

THOMPSON, LARRY CLARK, educator; b. Hoquiam, Wash., June 13, 1935; s. Lester Clark and Elizabeth (Young) T.; B.S., Willamette U., 1957; M.S., U. Ill., 1959, Ph.D., 1960; m. Frances Eula Dressel, Sept. 11, 1955; children—Martha Elaine, Whitney Kathryn. Asst. prof. U. Minn., Duluth, 1960-63, asso. prof., 1963-68, prof. chemistry, 1968—, chmn. dept., 1972—. Vis. prof. Universidade de Sao Paulo (Brazil), 1969, Fed. U. Ceará (Brazil), 1973, 74, Fed. U. Pernambuco (Brazil), 1977. NSF grantee 1961-67; NIH grantee 1961-67; Research Corp. grantee 1964. Mem. Am. Chem. Soc., Sigma Xi, Phi Lambda Upsilon. Contbr. articles to profl. jours. Home: 301 W Oxford St Duluth MN 55803

THOMPSON, LAWRENCE SIDNEY, educator; b. Raleigh, N.C., Dec. 21, 1916; s. Lawrence Sidney and Elizabeth Luraa (Jones) T.; A.B., U. N.C., 1934, Ph.D., 1938; A.M., U. Chgo., 1935; A.B. in L.S., U. Mich., 1940; m. Algernon Smith Dickson, Sept. 23, 1950 (dec. July 1962); children—Sarah E., Mary L., Richard; m. 2d, Ellen Marshall Dunlap, May 18, 1968 (dec. Feb. 1975); m. 3d, Anna Murashko O'Brien, Aug. 16, 1975 (div. Mar. 1979). Fellow Am.-Scandinavian Found. for study in Uppsala and Lund, Sweden, 1938-39; asst. to librarian Iowa State Coll., 1940-42; spl. agt. FBI, Washington, 1942-45; bibliographer U.S. Dept. Agr. Library, 1945-46; head librarian Western Mich. Coll., 1946-48; dir. libraries U. Ky., Lexington, 1948-65, prof. classics. 1948—. Cons. Erasmus Press, Inc., Lexington. Advisor on library problems Turkish ministry of edn., Ankara, 1951-52; conducted survey of library of Caribbean Commn. Port-of-Spain, Trinidad, B.W.I., 1953. Mem ALA, Bibliog. Soc. Am., Saellskapet Bokvaennerna (Stockholm), Ky. Library Assn., Ky. Folklore Soc. (pres. 1963-64), Mediaeval Acad. Am., Ky. Hist. Soc., Sociedad de Bibliófilos de Argentina, Buenos Aires, Sociedad de Bibliófilos de Barcelona, Soc. Cincinnati, Beta Theta Pi, Phi Beta Kappa, Beta Phi Mu (founder). Democrat. Presbyn. Clubs: Caxton (Chgo.); Rowfant (Cleve.); Grolier (N.Y.C.); Rounce and Coffin (Los Angeles); Filson (Louisville); Gutenberg-Gesellschaft (Mainz). Rotarian. Author: Folklore of the Chapel, 1950; The Kentucky Novel, 1953; Wilhelm Waiblinger in Italy, 1953; Foreign Travellers in the South, 1900-1950; The Club Bindery, 1955; Kentucky Tradition, 1956; Kurze Geschichte des Handeinbandes in den Vereinigten Staaten von Amerika, 1955; Boktryckarkonstens uppkomst Förenta staterna, 1956; History of Printing in Colonial Spanish America, 1962, 2d edit. (with Woodbridge), 1976; Bibliologia Comica, 1968; A Bibliography of Spanish Plays on Microcard, 1967; Essays in Hispanic Bibliography, 1970; The Southern Black: A Bibliography of Books in Microform, 1970; Books In Our Time, 1972; The New Sabin, Vol. I-V, 1974—. Publisher: American Notes and Queries, 1962—, Germanic Notes, 1969—, Appalachian Notes, 1972—. Contbr. on lit., hist. subjects to learned jours. Am. and Scandinavia. Home: 225 Culpepper Dr Lexington KY 40502

THOMPSON, LEE BENNETT, lawyer; b. Miami, Indian Ter., Mar. 2, 1902; s. P.C. and Margerie Constance (Jackson) T.; B.A., U. Okla., 1925, LL.B., 1927; m. Elaine Bizzell, Nov. 27, 1928; children—Lee Bennett, Ralph Gordon, Carolyn Elaine (Mrs. Don T. Zachritz). Admitted to Okla. bar, 1927, since practiced in Oklahoma City; spl. justice Okla. Supreme Ct., 1967-68; sec., gen. counsel, dir. Mustang Fuel Corp. Past sec. Masonic Charity Found. Okla.; past chmn. Okla. County chpt. A.R.C., past chmn. resolutions com. nat. conv. Served from capt. to col. AUS, 1940-46. Decorated Legion. of Merit; recipient Distinguished Service citation U. Okla., 1971. Fellow Am. Bar Found., Okla. Bar Found., Am. Coll. Trial Lawyers; mem. Oklahoma City C. of C. (past bd. dirs.), Oklahoma City Jr. (past pres.), U.S. Jr. (past dir., v.p.) chambers commerce, Oklahoma City Symphony Orch. (past dir.), Oklahoma City Community Fund (past dir.), Am. (del. 1972, mem. com. law and nat. security, mem. spl. com. on fed. ct. procedure), Okla. (past mem. ho. dels., pres. 1972), Oklahoma County (past pres.) bar assns., Okla. Bar Found. (trustee), U. Okla. Alumni Assn. (past mem. exec. com.), U. Okla. Meml. Student Union (pres.), Oklahoma City Zool. Soc. (past bd. dirs.), Am. Judicature Soc., Mil. Order World Wars, Mil. Order Carabao, Am. Legion, Phi Beta Kappa, Beta Theta Pi (past v.p., trustee). Democrat. Mem. Christian Ch. (past elder). Mason (Shriner, Jester, 33 deg.), Rotarian (past pres.). Clubs: Okla. U. Faculty, Seventy Five, Men's Dinner, (past mem. exec. com.), Oklahoma City Golf and Country, Beacon. Home: 539 NW 38th St Oklahoma City OK 73118 Office: 2120 First Nat Bldg Oklahoma City OK 73102

THOMPSON, LORING MOORE, coll. adminstr.; b. Newton, Mass., Feb. 17, 1918; s. Henry E. and Ella (Gould) T.; B.S. in Indsl. Engring., Northeastern U., 1940; M.S., U. R.I., 1947; Ph.D., U. Chgo., 1956; m. Pearl E. Judiesch, Dec. 30, 1949; children—Bruce C., Douglas P. (dec.). Instr., U. R.I., 1946; asst. to pres. Assn. Colls. Upper N.Y., 1947-49; asso. prof. U. Toledo, 1952-59, asst. dean acad. adminstrn., 1958-59; dir. univ. planning Northeastern U., Boston, 1959-63, dean adult programs, 1964-66, v.p. planning, 1967—; cons. in field. Bd. dirs. Back Bay Assn., Boston, 1961-63, v.p., 1963; trustee Huntington Gen. Hosp., Boston, 1970—; mem. Fenway Project Area Com., Boston, 1973-76; mem. Mass. conf. ch. and edn. com. United Ch. of Christ, 1972-78, chairperson, 1973-74, mem. task force on ch. growth, 1978—. Served to lt. USNR, 1942-45. Mem. Soc. Coll. and Univ. Planning, World Future Soc., Spiritual Frontiers Fellowship, Nat. Planning Assn., Tau Beta Pi. Author: (with others) Business Communication, 1949. Contbr. articles to profl. publs. Home: 5 Middle St Lexington MA 02173 Office: Northeastern Univ Boston MA 02115

THOMPSON, LOUIS MILTON, educator; b. Throckmorton, Tex., May 15, 1914; s. Aubrey Lafayette and Lola Terry (Frazier) T.; B.S., Tex. A. and M. Coll., 1935; M.S., Iowa State U., 1947, Ph.D., 1950; m. Margaret Stromberg, July 10, 1937 (dec. Nov. 1972); children—Louis Milton, Margaret Ann, Glenda Ray, Carolyn Terry, Jerome Lafayette. Soil surveyor, Tex., 1935-36, 39-40; instr. Tex. A. and M. Coll., 1936-39, 40-42; asst. prof. soils Iowa State U., Ames, 1947-50, prof. soils, head farm operation curriculum, 1950-58, asso. dean agr. charge resident instrn., 1958—. Served with AUS, 1942-46; col. Res. (ret.). Fellow AAAS, Am. Soc. Agronomy, soil Sci. Soc. Am.; mem. Sigma Xi, Alpha Zeta (Tall Corn award 1957), Gamma Sigma Delta (nat. pres. 1956-58), Phi Kappa Phi (chpt. pres. 1961), Farm House (hon.). Presbyn. (elder). Rotarian (past local pres.). Author: Soils and Soil Fertility, rev. edit., 1957, co-author rev. edit., 1978. Contbr. articles on weather-crop yield models and climate change to profl. jours. Home: 414 Lynn Ave Ames IA 50010

THOMPSON, LOVELL, publisher; b. Nahant, Mass., Sept. 8, 1902; s. Charles Miner and Isabella (Carr) T.; A.B., Harvard, 1925; m. Katharine Simonds, Sept. 2, 1929 (dec. 1966); children—Daniel Pierce, Judith (Mrs. Carl M. Sapers), Nicholas Simonds; m. 2d, Constance Purtell Coyle, 1969 (dec. 1978); m. 3d, Mary Hopkinson Gibbon. With Houghton Mifflin Co., Boston, 1925—, clk., prodn. mgr., advt. mgr., 1925-42, v.p., 1942-63, exec. v.p., 1963-67, mng. dir. Gambit, Ipswich, 1968—. Trustee, Ipswich Heritage Trust, 1965—. Home: Argilia Rd Ipswich MA 01938 Office: 27 N Main St Meeting House Green Ipswich MA 01938

THOMPSON, MANLEY HAWN, JR., educator; b. Zanesville, Ohio, Apr. 12, 1917; s. Manley Hawn and May (Ross) T.; A.B., A.M., U. Chgo., 1938; Ph.D., 1942; m. Margaret Phyllis MacKenzie, July 8, 1947; children—Katherine Anne, Roderick Manley, Clark MacKenzie. Lectr. philosophy U. Toronto, 1946-49; mem. faculty U. Chgo., 1949—, prof. philosophy, 1961—, chmn. dept., 1960-69; vis. lectr. Harvard, 1954-55. Asso., Council of Humanities, Princeton, 1959-64; vis. com. dept. philosophy, bd. Overseers Harvard Coll., 1963-69, 78—, chmn., 1978—; cons. Nat. Endowment for Humanities, 1968-69, N.Y. State Regents Doctoral Evaluation Project, 1976-77. Served to lt. USNR, 1942-46. Rockefeller fellow, 1948-49. Mem. Am. Philos. Assn. (nat. bd. officers 1967-70), Mind Assn., Aristotelian Soc., AAAS, Am. Council Learned Socs. (mem. fellowship selection com. 1969), Phi Beta Kappa. Author: The Pragmatic Philosophy of C.S. Peirce, 1953. Home: 5337 University Ave Chicago IL 60615

THOMPSON, MARGARET M., educator; b. nr. Falls Church, Va., Aug. 1, 1921; d. Lesley L. and Madeline (Shawen) T.; B.S., Mary Washington Coll., U. Va., 1941; M.A., George Washington U., 1947; Ph.D., U. Iowa, 1961. Tchr., supr. phys. edn. Staunton (Va.) City Schs., 1941-44; tchr. jr. high sch. phys. edn., Arlington County, Va., 1944-47; instr. women's phys. edn. Fla. State U., Tallahassee, 1947-51; instr., asst. prof., asso. prof. phys. edn. Purdue U., Lafayette, Ind., 1951-65, dir. gross motor therapy lab., 1963-65; asso. prof. phys. edn. U. Mo., Columbia, 1965-68, prof., 1968-71, dir. Cinematography and Motor Learning Lab. Dept. Health and Phys. Edn., 1965-71; prof. phys. edn. U. Ill., Champaign-Urbana, 1971—. Mem. Am., Ill. assns. health, phys. edn. and recreation, Nat., Midwest assns. phys. edn. for coll. women, Nat. Found. Health, Phys. Edn. and Recreation, Nat. Assn. Higher Edn., AAUP, Internat. Assn. Phys. Edn. and Sports for Coll. Women, Pi Lambda Theta. Author: (with Barbara B. Godfrey) Movement Pattern Checklists, 1966; (with Chappelle Arnett) Perceptual Motor and Motor Test Battery for Children, 1968; (with Barbara Mann) An Holistic Approach to Physical Education Curriculum: Objectives Classification System for Elementary Schools, 1977, Gross Motor Inventory, 1976; also film strips. Contbr. articles to profl. jours. Home: 3 Wildwood Ln Mahomet IL 61853 Office: 211 Freer Gymnasium Dept Phys Edn U Ill Urbana IL 61801

THOMPSON, MARGARET MYRTLE, ret. museum curator; b. Trenton, N.J., Feb. 22, 1911; d. Albert Gillingham and Hannah (Booth) Thompson; B.A., Radcliffe Coll., 1931. Mem. staff Agora Excavations, Athens, Greece, 1937-40, 48; field dir., publicity dir. Greek War Relief Assn., 1942-46; curator Greek coins Am. Numis. Soc., N.Y.C., 1949-76, chief curator, 1969-79, emeritus, 1979—. Adj. prof. art history and archaeology Columbia, 1965—; mem. Inst. Advanced Study, Princeton, 1969; Regents' prof. U. Calif., Berkeley, 1974; mem. bur. Internat. Numis. Commn., 1970-79; chmn. Internat. Numis. Congress, 1973. Medallist, Am. Numis. Soc., 1961, Royal Numis. Soc., 1967. Fellow Royal Numis. Soc. (hon.); hon. mem. French Numis. Soc., Belgian Numis. Soc., Rumanian Numis. Soc.; mem. Archeol. Inst. Am. (hon. pres., trustee), German Archaeol. Inst., Am. Philos. Soc., Phi Beta Kappa. Author: The Athenian Agora, vol. 2, Coins, 1954; The New Style Silver Coinage of Athens, 1961; Sylloge Nummorum Graecorum, The Burton Y. Berry Collection, 1961-62; The Agrinion Hoard, 1968; (with others) An Inventory of Greek Coin Hoards, 1973. Asso. editor Archaeology, 1954-58, mem. editorial adv. bd., 1958-67. Home: 140 Cabrini Blvd New York NY 10033 Office: American Numismatic Soc Broadway at 156th St New York NY 10032

THOMPSON, MAYNARD, educator; b. Michigan City, Ind., Sept. 8, 1936; s. Almer Dail and Gladys Fern (Whitmer) T.; A.B., DePauw U., 1958; M.S., U. Wis.-Madison, 1959, Ph.D., 1962; m. Judith Ann Bryan; children—Bryan, Rebecca. Lectr. math. Ind. U., Bloomington, 1962-64, asst. prof., 1964-68, asso. prof., 1968-73, prof., 1973—, chmn. dept. math., 1974-77; research asso. U. Md., College Park, 1970-71; sr. research scientist Gen. Motors Research Labs., 1978. Mem. Math. Assn. Am., Am. Math. Soc., Soc. Indsl. and Applied Math. Author: (with D. Maki) Mathematical Models and Applications, 1973. Contbr. articles to profl. jours. Home: 2303 Montclair Ave Bloomington IN 47401 Office: Dept of Mathematics Ind U Bloomington IN 47401

THOMPSON, MICHAEL DAVID, lawyer; b. Toronto, Ont., Can., Mar. 15, 1929; s. Thomas Clive and Isabel Catherine (Cope) T.; B.A., Trinity Coll. U. Toronto, 1951; Barrister and Solicitor, Osgoode Hall Law Sch., 1956; m. Mary Lou Emmerson, Dec. 21, 1953; children—Suzanne, Judith, Jennifer. Called to Supreme Ct. of Ont. bar, 1956; partner firm Reycraft, MacDonald & Thompson, Toronto, 1956-58, MacDonald & Thompson, Toronto, 1958-61; solicitor Abitibi Paper Co. Ltd., Toronto, 1961-75, sec., gen. counsel, 1975—. Mem. Canadian Bar Assn., Assn. Canadian Gen. Counsel. Anglican. Home: 36 Ridge Dr Toronto ON M4T 1B7 Canada Office: Box 21 Toronto-Dominion Centre Toronto ON M5K 1B3 Canada

THOMPSON, MILTON DOUHAN, mus. dir.; b. Haxtun, Colo., Aug. 25, 1909; s. Roy C. and Elvera (Douhan) T.; B.S., U. Minn., 1935; H.H.D., Lincoln Coll., 1970; m. Patricia Ellen Holman, Apr. 11, 1938. Dir., Mpls. Sci. Mus., 1936-51; asst. dir. Ill. State Mus., Springfield, 1951-62, dir., 1963-77, dir. emeritus, 1977—; dir. Dickson Mounds, Lewistown, Ill., 1965-77; mus. cons., 1977—. Mem. Ill. Spl. Events Commn., 1969-77, Ill. Bicentennial Commn., 1972-77; bd. dirs. Ill. Presbyterian Home, Springfield, pres., 1972-76. Served to lt. comdr. USNR, 1942-45. Mem. Midwest Mus. Conf. (pres. 1950), Ill. Acad. Sci. (pres. 1967), Am. Assn. Sci. Mus. Dirs. (sec.-treas. 1969-73). Club: Rotary (dir. 1962-63, v.p. 1965-66, pres. 1966). Author: Illinois Man and Resources; co-author: Birds in Your Backyard; editor Midwest Museums Quar., 1951-54. Home: 1433 S Belcher Rd Clearwater FL 33516

THOMPSON, MILTON ORVILLE, aero. engr.; b. Crookston, Minn., May 4, 1926; s. Peter and Alma Teresa (Evenson) T.; B.S. in Engring., U. Wash., 1953; postgrad. U. So. Calif., 1956-59; m. Therese Mary Beytebiere, June 25, 1949; children—Eric P., Milton Orville, Brett, Peter K., Kye C. Asso. engr. Boeing Co., Seattle, 1953-55; research pilot NASA (formerly NACA), Edwards, Calif., 1956-66, asst. dir. research, 1967-72, dir. research projects, 1972-74, chief engr., 1974-78, asso. dir. NASA Dryden Flight Research Center, 1978—. Served with USNR, 1944-49. Recipient Octave Chanute award Am. Inst. Aeros. and Astronautics, 1967; Disting. Service medal NASA, 1978. Fellow Explorers Club; mem. Soc. Exptl. Test Pilots (Ivan C. Kinchloe award 1966). Contbr. articles to tech. jours. X-15 rocket air plane pilot; First to fly lifting body entry vehicle. Home: 1640 W Ave L-12 Lancaster CA 93534 Office: NASA-Dryden Flight Research Center PO Box 273 Edwards CA 93523

THOMPSON, MORLEY PUNSHON, mfg. co. exec.; b. San Francisco, Jan. 2, 1927; s. Morley Punshon and Ruth (Wetmore) T.; A.B., Stanford, 1948; M.B.A., Harvard, 1950; J.D., Chase Law Sch., 1969; m. Patricia Ann Smith, Jan. 31, 1953; children—Page Elizabeth, Morley Punshon. With Baldwin-United Corp., Cin., 1950—, dir., 1962—, v.p., 1967-70, pres., 1970—; dir. Midland Co., Xomox Corp., Kroger Co., Cin. Bell, Stearns & Foster, Inc., Anchor Hocking Corp., FMC Corp. Bd. dirs. Cin. Inst. Fine Arts. Served to lt. Supply Corps, USNR, 1952-54. C.P.A., Ohio. Mem. Beta Theta Pi. Office: 1801 Gilbert Ave Cincinnati OH 45202

THOMPSON, MORRIS MILHOLLAND, coll. pres.; b. nr. Cameron, Mo., Jan. 5, 1916; s. Samuel Floyd and Chelsea E. (Milholland) T.; A.B., U. Kans., 1937; D.Sc., Des Moines Still Coll. of Osteopathy and Surgery; Litt.D., Coll. Osteo. Physicians and Surgeons; L.H.D., Chgo. Coll. Osteopathy, 1961; Ed.D., Kansas City Coll. Osteo. Medicine, 1969; m. Ella Mayse Reed, June 5, 1938 (dec. Jan. 1951); 1 dau., Martha Mildred; m. 2d, Charlotte Hanson Whitman, Aug. 7, 1953 (dec. Nov. 1962); children—Sydney, Samuel, Chelsea, Timothy; m. 3d, Martha J. Smith Herboth, July 27, 1963; 1 dau., Helen. Mem. bus. and editorial staff Trenton (Mo.) Daily Republican-Times, 1933-36; mgr. C. of C., Trenton, 1938-39, Kirksville, Mo., 1939-40; supr. distributive vocational edn. Mo. Dept. Edn., 1940-41; dir. small stores bur. Nat. Retail Dry Goods Assn., N.Y.C., 1941-43; mem. adminstrv. staff Kirksville Coll. Osteo. Medicine, 1943, pres. 1945-73, cons., pres. emeritus, 1973—; pres. Nat. Osteo. Found., 1973-77. Cons. Found. Research N.Y. Acad. Osteopathy, Surgeon Gen. Group Med. Edn., 1958-59, Council on Fed. Health Programs. Mem. Am. Assn. Osteo. Colls. (past pres.), Am. Osteo. Assn. Episcopalian, Mason. Contbr. articles to jours. Home: Spring Lake Box 1066 Kirksville MO 63501. *I have been blessed with the privilege of serving a high cause, that of human health, through service to the profession of osteopathic medicine. Such a cause challenges me to generate my maximum energies, ingenuity, and talent.*

THOMPSON, N. DAVID, ins. co. exec.; b. Rockville Centre, N.Y., July 30, 1934; s. Norman J. and Laurel H. (Johnson) T.; B.A. with distinction, Wesleyan U., 1956; LL.B., Columbia U., 1959; postgrad. Harvard U., 1973; m. Joyce L. Angeletti, June 7, 1958; children—John L., Jennifer L., Sarah S. Admitted to N.Y. bar; individual practice law, N.Y.C., 1961-62; corp. sec. Gen. Reins. Corp., N.Y.C., 1964-69, v.p., Greenwich, Conn., 1969, v.p., gen. counsel, sec., 1976-77; exec. v.p. N.Am. Reins. Corp., N.Y.C., 1977-78, pres., 1978—. Served with U.S. Army, 1959-60. Club: Univ. (N.Y.C.). Home: 47 Kettle Creek Rd Weston CT 06883 Office: 245 Park Ave New York NY 10017

THOMPSON, NATHANIEL ROSS, JR., army officer; b. Phila., Sept. 5, 1927; s. Nathaniel Ross and Dorothy Marie (Bardon) T.; B.S., Temple U., 1951; M.B.A., Syracuse U., 1957; m. Dolores Casey, Sept. 29, 1951; children—Nathaniel R., Kathleen, Barbara, James, Patrick. Commd. 2d lt. U.S. Army, 1951, advanced through grades to maj. gen., 1979; comdr. 11th Transp. Bn., Vietnam, 1968-69; dep. and asst. comdt. U.S. Army Transp. Sch., 1973-75; dir. logistics U.S. Readiness Command, 1975-77; dir. transp. energy, troop support Dept. Army, 1977-79; comdr. Hdqrs. 21st Support Command, Kaiserslautern, W. Ger., 1979—. Decorated Legion of Merit, Bronze Star. Mem. Assn. U.S. Army, Nat. Def. Transp. Assn. Presbyterian. Club: Masons. Home: 2408 S 24th St Philadelphia PA 19145 Office: Comdr Hdqrs 21st Support Command APO NY 09325

THOMPSON, PAGE, fin. exec.; b. Boston, June 28, 1932; s. Page Hamilton and Gladys Evelyn (Alcock) T.; A.B., Dartmouth Coll., 1953; M.B.A., Harvard U., 1965; m. Jane Duniway Ryan, May 11, 1957; children—Page Hamilton, Benjamin Scott, Andrew Ryan. Pres., dir. Cia Atlantic de Petroleo, Brazil, 1972-75; treas. Atlantic Richfield Co., Los Angeles, 1975-77; pres. Arco Med. Products Co., Phila., 1977-79; chief fin. officer Rouse & Assos., Malvern, Pa., 1979—; bus. cons., 1978—. Bd. dirs. Los Angeles Symphony, 1975-77; adviser Grad. Sch. Bus., Calif. State U., Los Angeles. Served with USMCR, 1953-55. Recipient medal State of Guanahara, Brazil. Mem. Am. Petroleum Inst., Internat. Bus. Forum. Democrat. Episcopalian. Clubs: Harvard (N.Y.C.); Cape Arundel Golf; Racquet (Phila.); Cynwyd. Home: 501 Lynmere Rd Bryn Mawr PA 19010

THOMPSON, PHILIP ANTHONY, assn. exec.; b. Ottawa, Kans., Aug. 10, 1937; s. John R. and Eleanor (Griggs) T.; B.S. in Bus. Adminstrn., U.S. Mil. Acad.; postgrad. Seton Hall U.; m. Suzanne Sisson, Oct. 8, 1960; children—Brenda, Bruce, Kathleen. With Trans World Airlines, N.Y.C., 1960-67, Mo. C. of C., Jefferson City, 1967-70, C. of C. of the U.S., Mpls., 1970-71; pres. Ky. C. of C., Frankfort, 1971—. Served with U.S. Army. Republican. Office: Box 817 Versailles Rd Frankfort KY 40601

THOMPSON, PORTER, lawyer; b. Berlin, N.H., Aug. 1, 1904; s. Frederick William and Grace (Porter) T.; grad. Phillips Exeter Acad., 1922; B.S., Bowdoin Coll., 1926; LL.B., Harvard, 1929; m. Fanny Lois Mapel, July 31, 1928. Admitted to Mass. and Maine bars, 1929; asso. firm Warner, Stackpole, Bradlee & Cabot, Boston, 1929-31; partner firm Linnell, Perkins, Thompson, Hinckley & Keddy, Portland, Maine, 1931-73, of counsel, 1973—; dir. Canal Nat. Bank, Portland, 1953—, Am. Hoist & Derick Co., 1959-66, United Bancorp Maine,

1969-71. Trustee Maine Eye and Ear Infirmary, 1950—, pres., 1972—; trustee Maine Med. Center, 1971-78; bd. incorporators Maine Med. Center, 1951—. Served to maj. USAAF, 1942-45; PTO. Decorated Legion of Merit. Mem. Am., Maine, Cumberland County bar assns. Home: 65 Waites Landing Rd Falmouth ME 04105 Office: 1 Canal Plaza PO Box 426 Portland ME 04112

THOMPSON, R. E., lawyer; b. Lubbock, Tex., Aug. 15, 1943; s. Glenn Wesley and Naomi Elvina T.; B.B.A., U. Tex., Austin, 1965, J.D., 1968; m. Sandra Jean Lemons, Aug. 8, 1965; children—Michael Glenn, Mark Gregory, Matthew Wesley. Admitted to Tex. bar, 1968, N.Mex. bar, 1969; asso. firm Atwood & Malone, Roswell, N.Mex., 1968-71; partner firm Atwood, Malone, Mann & Cooter, Roswell, 1971-78; U.S. Atty., Dist. N.Mex., Albuquerque, 1978—; commr. Nat. Conf. of Commrs. on Uniform State Laws, 1975-79; chmn. N.Mex. Supreme Ct. Com. on Uniform Rules of Evidence, 1972—; mem. U.S. Atty. Gen.'s Adv. Com., 1980—. Mem. N.Mex. Democratic Party Central Com., 1972-78; mem. N.Mex. State Senate, 1973-78. Mem. Am. Bar Assn. (exec. council young lawyers sect. 1972), N.Mex. Bar Assn. (chmn. young lawyers sect. 1970). Baptist. Office: PO Box 607 Albuquerque NM 87103

THOMPSON, RALPH GORDON, judge; b. Oklahoma City, Dec. 15, 1934; s. Lee Bennett and Elaine (Bizzell) T.; B.B.A., U. Okla., 1956, J.D., 1961; m. Barbara Irene Hencke, Sept. 5, 1964; children—Lisa, Elaine, Maria. Admitted to Okla. bar, 1961; spl. agt. Office Spl. Investigations, U.S. Air Force, 1957-60; partner firm Thompson, Thompson, Harbour & Selph and predecessors, Oklahoma City, 1961-75; judge U.S. Dist. Ct., Western Dist., Okla., 1975—; mem. Okla. Ho. of Reps., 1966-70, asst. minority floor leader, 1969-70; spl. justice Supreme Ct. Okla., 1970-71. Republican nominee for lt. gov. Okla., 1970; chmn. bd. ARC, Oklahoma City, 1970-72, chmn. Midwestern area advisory council, 1973-74; pres. Okla. Young Lawyers Conf., 1965; mem. bd. visitors U. Okla., 1975-78. Served as lt. USAF, 1957-60, lt. col. USAFR. Named Outstanding Young Man, Oklahoma City Jaycees, 1967; Outstanding Young Oklahoman, Okla. Jaycees, 1968. Fellow Am. Bar. Found.; Mem. Nat. Conf. Fed. Trial Judges, Am. Bar Assn., Fed. Bar Assn., Okla. Bar Assn. (chmn. sect. internat. law and gen. practice 1974-75), Oklahoma County Bar Assn. (dir.), Phi Beta Kappa, Beta Theta Pi, Phi Alpha Delta. Episcopalian. Club: Rotary (hon.). Home: 1109 Huntington St Oklahoma City OK 73116 Office: US Courthouse Oklahoma OK 73102

THOMPSON, RALPH NEWELL, chem. corp. exec.; b. Boston, Mar. 4, 1918; s. Ralph and Lillian May (Davenport) T.; B.S., MIT, 1940; m. Virginia Kenniston, Jan. 31, 1942; children—Pamela, Nicholas, Diana. Research engr. Middlesex Products Co., Cambridge, Mass., 1940-42; tech. dir. Falulah Paper Co., Fitchburg, Mass., 1945-48; staff engr. to v.p., div. gen. mgr. Calgon Corp., Pitts., 1948-70; v.p. mktg., corp. devel. Pa. Indsl. Chem. Corp., Clairton, 1970-74; gen. mgr. chem. div. Thiokol Corp., Trenton, N.J., 1974-76, group v.p.-chem., Newtown, Pa., 1976—; dir. Mulford Co. Inc. (Mass.), 1956—, Thiokol Can. Ltd., 1975—, Thiokol Chems., Ltd. (Eng.), 1976—, Toray Thiokol Co. Ltd. (Japan), 1976—, Nisso-Ventron K.K. (Japan), 1977—, S.W. Chem. Services Inc. (Tex.), 1978—, S.W. Plastics Europe S.A. (Belgium), 1978—, Dynachem. Corp. (Calif.), 1979—. Mem. Mt. Lebanon (Pa.) Civic League, 1950-74. Served with USNR, 1942-45. Recipient Goodreau Meml. Fund medal in chemistry, 1936. Fellow Am. Inst. Chemists; mem. TAPPI (contributor monograph series 1950-65), N.Y. Acad. Scis., Soc. Chem. Industry, Soc. Rheology, Am. Inst. Mgmt., Mil. Order World Wars, Pa. Soc., Soc. Descs. Colonial Clergy. Republican. Presbyterian. Patentee in field. Home: 1006 Lehigh Dr Yardley PA 19067 Office: Thiokol Corp Yardley-Newton Rd PO Box 1000 Newtown PA 18940

THOMPSON, RANDALL, musician, composer; b. N.Y.C., Apr. 21, 1899; s. Daniel Varney and Grace Brightman (Randall) T.; A.B., Harvard, 1920, M.A., 1922; postgrad. (Walter Damrosch fellow in music composition) Am. Acad. in Rome, 1922-25; Mus.D., U. Rochester, 1933, U. Pa., 1969; studied composition under Ernest Bloch, N.Y.C., 1920-21; m. Margaret Quayle Whitney, Feb. 26, 1927; children—Varney, Edward Samuel Whitney, Rosemary, Randall. Wrote music for The Straw Hat, 1926, Grand Street Follies, 1926; asst. prof. music, organist, choir dir. Wellesley Coll., 1927-29, apptd. lectr. music, 1936; lectr. music Harvard, 1929; Guggenheim fellow, 1929-31; guest condr. Dessoff Choirs, N.Y.C., 1931-32; condr. Madrigal Choir and Suprs. Chorus, Juilliard Sch. Music, 1931-32; dir. coll. music study, investigation Assn. Am. Colls., 1932-35; prof. music, dir. chorus U. Calif., Berkeley, 1937-39; dir. Curtis Inst. Music, 1939-41; prof. music, head dept. U. Va., 1941-45; prof. music Princeton, 1945-48; prof. music Harvard, 1948-65, now Walter Bigelow Rosen prof. music emeritus, chmn. dept., 1952-57. Dir. U.S. sect. Internat. Soc. for Contemporary Music, 1934-35; mem. exec. bd. League Composers, 1939-41, dir., 1945-48. Decorated Cavaliere Ufficiale al Merito della Repubblica (Italy); recipient Elizabeth Sprague Coolidge medal, 1941; Ditson award, 1944. Mem. Nat. Inst. Arts and Letters, Am. Acad. Arts and Scis., ASCAP, Phi Beta Kappa. Clubs: Century (N.Y.C.); Somerset, Tavern (Boston). Composer symphonies, choral works, string quartets, opera and other forms of mus. works; composition include: The Last Words of David (commd. by Boston Symphony Orch. for Voice of America film, Tanglewood), 1949; A Trip to Nahant, Fantasy-Rondo for Orch. (commd. by Koussevitzky Found.), 1954; Mass of the Holy Spirit, 1955; Ode to the Virginian Voyage, 1956; Requiem (commd. by U. Calif.), 1958; Frostiana (commd. by 200th Anniversary of Amherst, Mass.), 1959; The Nativity according to Saint Luke (commd. by Christ Ch., Cambridge, Mass.), 1961; cantata, A Feast of Praise (commd. by Stanford U. music dept.), 1963; oratorio, The Passion According to St. Luke (commd. by Handel and Haydn Soc.), 1965; String Quartet No. 2 (commd. by Harvard Mus. Assn.); 1967; The Place of the Blest (commd. by St. Thomas Ch., N.Y.C.), 1969. Author: College Music, 1935. Contbr. articles to mus. revs. Home: 22 Larch Rd Cambridge MA 02138

THOMPSON, RAYMOND HARRIS, educator, anthropologist; b. Portland, Me., May 10, 1924; s. Raymond and Eloise (MacIntyre) T.; B.S., Tufts U., 1947; A.M., Harvard, 1950, Ph.D., 1955; m. Molly Kendall, Sept. 9, 1948; children—Margaret Kelsey, Mary Frances. Fellow div. hist. research Carnegie Instn., Washington, 1950-52; asst. prof. anthropology, curator Mus. Anthropology, U. Ky., 1952-56; faculty U. Ariz., 1956—, prof. anthropology, head dept., 1964—; dir. Ariz. State Mus., 1964—. Mem. advisory panel program in anthropology NSF, 1963-64; mem. NSF grad. fellowship panel Nat. Acad. Scis.-NRC, 1964-66; mem. research in nursing in patient care rev. com. USPHS, 1967-69, com. on social sci. commn. edn. in agr. and natural resources Nat. Acad. Scis., 1968-69. Mem. anthropology com. examiners Grad. Record Exam., 1967-70, chmn., 1969-70; mem. com. recovery archaeol. remains, 1972-77, chmn., 1973-77; collaborator Nat. Park Service, 1972-76. Mem. Ariz. Hist. Advisory Commn., 1966-76, chmn., 1971-74; chmn. Ariz. Council Humanities and Pub. Policy, 1973-77, mem., 1979—; mem. Ariz. Hist. Records Advisory Bd., 1976-77; mem. research review panel for archaelogy Nat. Endowment for Humanities, 1976-77, mem. rev. panel for museums, 1978; cons. task force on archaeology Adv. Council on Historic Preservation, 1978. Trustee Mus. No. Ariz., 1969-77; bd. dirs. Tucson Mus. Art, 1974-77. Served with USNR, 1944-45; PTO. Fellow AAAS (chmn. sect. H, 1977-78, editorial bd. Sci. 1972-77), Am. Anthrop. Assn.; mem. Soc. Am. Archaeology (editor 1958-62, mem. exec. com. 1963-64, pres. 1976-77, Am. Ethnol. Soc., Am. Soc. Ethnohistory, Seminario de Cultura Maya, Am. Assn. Museums, Internat. Council Museums (asso.), Assn. Sci. Mus. Dirs. (sec.-treas. 1978—), Ariz. Acad. Sci., Ariz. Archaeol. and Hist. Soc., Phi Beta Kappa, Sigma Xi. Author: Modern Yucatecan Maya Pottery Making, 1958. Editor: Migrations in New World Culture History, 1958; editorial bd. Science 1972—. Home: 6130 Cerrada el Ocote Tucson AZ 85718

THOMPSON, RENOLD DURANT, mining and shipping co. exec.; b. Cleve., July 28, 1926; s. James Renold and Gertrude Goldie (Meyers) T.; B.A., Dartmouth Coll., 1946; B.S., Case Inst. Tech., 1948; m. Shirley Ann Sprague, June 24, 1949; children—Renold Durant, Bradley Sprague, Patricia Sprague. Metallurgist, U.S. Steel Corp., Duluth, Minn., 1948-49, Cleve., 1949-52; with Oglebay Norton Co., Cleve., 1952—, sr. v.p., 1972-73, exec. v.p. ops., 1973—, also dir.; dir. Central Nat. Bank, Cleve., Eveleth Taconite Co., Licking River Terminal Co., Lubrizol Corp., Saginaw Mining Co., Tex. Mining Co.; vice chmn. mgmt. com. Eveleth Expansion Co. Mem. Am. Iron and Steel Inst., AIME, Am. Iron Ore Assn., Eastern States Blast Furnace and Coke Oven Assn., Lake Carriers' Assn. Clubs: Duquesne, Hillbrook, Mayfield Country, Pepper Pike, Tavern, Union. Home: 14883 Hillbrook Dr Hunting Valley Chagrin Falls OH 44022 Office: 1200 Hanna Bldg Cleveland OH 44115

THOMPSON, RICHARD FREDERICK, psychologist; b. Portland, Oreg., Setp. 6, 1930; s. Frederick Albert and Margaret St. Clair (Marr) T.; B.A., Reed Coll., 1952; M.S., U. Wis., 1953, Ph.D., 1956; m. Judith K. Pedersen, May 22, 1960; children—Kathryn M., Elizabeth K., Virginia St. C. Asst. prof. med. psychology Med. Sch. U. Oreg., Portland, 1959-63, asso. prof., 1963-65, prof., 1965-67; prof. psychobiology U. Calif., Irvine, 1967-73; prof. psychology Harvard U., 1973-74, Lashley chair, 1973; prof. psychobiology U. Calif., Irvine, 1975—. Fellow AAAS, Am. Psychol. Assn. (Disting. Sci. Contbn. award 1974, governing council 1974—), Soc. Neunosci. (councilor 1972-76); mem. Internat. Brain Research Orgn., Psychonomic Soc. (gov. 1972-77, chmn. 1976), Nat. Acad. Scis., Soc. Exptl. Psychology. Author: Foundations of Physiological Psychology, 1967; (with others) Psychology, 1971; Introduction to Physiological Psychology, 1975. Editor Physiol. Psychology, 1971—; psychology editor W.H. Freeman & Co. publs.; rev. editor Jour. Comparative and Physiol. Psychology; regional editor Physiology and Behavior. Contbr. articles to profl. jours. Home: 28 Skysail Corona del Mar CA 92625 Office: Dept of Psychobiology U Calif Irvine CA 92717

THOMPSON, RICHARD HORNER, army officer; b. N.Y.C., Sept. 24, 1926; s. John West and Erna (Muller) T.; B.A. in Social Sci., Coll. of the Ozarks, 1959; M.P.A., George Washington U., 1964; m. Patricia E. Palm, May 8, 1949; children—Christine, Claudia, Richard Horner. Commd. 2d lt. U.S. Army, 1950, advanced through grades to maj. gen., 1975; chief tactical support systems group, Office of Asst. Vice Chief of Staff, Washington, 1969-70; comdg. officer U.S. Army Inventory Control Center, Vietnam, 1970-71; comdr. Def. Logistics Services Center, comdr. Def. Property Disposal Service, Battle Creek, Mich., 1971-73; dir. logistics, plans, ops. and systems Dept. of Army, Washington, 1973-75; dir. supply and maintenance ODCSLOG, Washington, 1975-77; comdr. U.S. Army Troop Support and Aviation Materiel Readiness Command, St. Louis, 1977—. Decorated Army Commendation medal with 2 oak leaf clusters, Legion of Merit with 2 clusters, Joint Service Commendation medal with oak leaf cluster. Office: 4300 Goodfellow Blvd Saint Louis MO 63120

THOMPSON, RICHARD NEIL, lawyer; b. Newman Grove, Nebr., Nov. 20, 1933; s. Oscar T. and Gladys M. (Olson) T.; student Wayne (Nebr.) State Coll., 1951-52; B.S. in Law, U. Nebr., 1955, J.D., 1957; m. Dorothy M. Bilson, Aug. 15, 1957; children—Pamela Sue, Richard Neil II, Beth Ann. Admitted to Nebr. bar, 1957, asso. firm Cline, Williams, Wright, Johnson & Oldfather, Lincoln, Nebr., 1957-60, mem. firm, 1960-70; mem. firm Thompson & Sweet, Lincoln, 1970-75; practiced in Lincoln, 1975—. Bd. dirs. Lincoln Symphony Assn., 1975-78; trustee Westminster Ch. Found., 1975—, chmn. investment com., 1975—. Served with AUS, 1950-58. Mem. Lincoln, Nebr., Am. (com. fed. regulation securities 1969—) bar assns., Lincoln C. of C., Phi Delta Phi, Pi Delta Kappa, Phi Gamma Delta. Presbyn. Clubs: Lincoln U., Lincoln Country; Palmas del Mar. Home: 2909 Bonacum Dr Lincoln NE 68502 also Lake Okoboji IA also Palmas del Mar Humacao PR Office: 968 NBC Center Lincoln NE 68508

THOMPSON, ROBERT B(ODEN), savs. and loan assn. exec.; b. Salt Lake City, Apr. 21, 1935; s. Edgar and Dorothy T.; B.S., U. So. Calif., 1957, M.B.A. in Real Estate and Fin., 1963; m. Bonnie L.; children—Becky, Theresa, Michael, Elizabeth. Market analyst and appraiser Real Estate Research Corp., Los Angeles, 1961-64; with Western Fed. Savs. & Loan Assn., Los Angeles, 1964—, dir. research, 1964-75, exec. v.p., chief loan officer, 1975—. Served with U.S. Army, 1958-60. Mem. Calif. Savs. and Loan League (chmn. com. lending procedures 1975), Central City Assn. (exec. com.), Town Hall, World Affairs Council, Commerce Assos., Nat. Assn. Bus. Economists. Office: 600 S Hill St Los Angeles CA 90014

THOMPSON, ROBERT CARLYSLE, motion picture, TV producer; b. Palmyra, N.Y., May 31, 1937; s. Roger and Gladys (Smith) T.; B.S. in Radio-Television, Ithaca Coll., 1960; M.F.A., U. Calif. at Los Angeles, 1961; m. Helen Marie Miller, Aug. 31, 1957; children—Mark, Peter, Patrick. Head of talent, signing of contract players Universal Studios, Universal City, Calif., 1961-68; head of talent, creative affairs Cinema Center Films, CBS, Los Angeles, 1968-72; pres. Thompson-Paul Prodns. Inc., Sherman Oaks, Calif., 1972—, Thompson-Paul-Poe Mgmt. Inc., Sherman Oaks, 1974—; producer motion picture The Paper Chase, 1974, also TV pilots Lanigan's Rabbi, 1977, The Paper Chase, Mark of Zorro; exec. producer CBS-TV series The Paper Chase, 1978; producer, div. NBC-TV movie Bud and Lou, 1978; supervising producer and dir. TV series California Fever, 1979. Home: 4536 Mary Ellen Ave Sherman Oaks CA 91423 Office: 4000 Warner Blvd Burbank CA 91522

THOMPSON, ROBERT CHARLES, oil co. fin. exec.; b. Minooka, Ill., Oct. 28, 1923; s. Charles and Sadie B. (Petersen) T.; B.S. in Commerce and Law, U. Ill., 1950; LL.B., U. Tulsa, 1954; m. Helen Emily Hartt, July 25, 1946; children—Carol Sue, David Hartt, Jane Ann, Sara Elizabeth Brooks, Suanna Beth. Admitted to Okla bar, 1954; with Shell Oil Co., 1953-63, 66—, treas., N.Y.C., 1970-77, controller, Houston, 1977, v.p. fin., 1977—; treas. Shell Pipe Line Corp., Houston, 1963-65; pres. Resonant Pile Corp. subs. Shell Oil Co., East Providence, R.I., 1965-66; dir. and officer numerous Shell Oil Co. subs.'s and affiliates. Mem. acctg. council Rice U.; mem. adv. council Fin. Acctg. Standards Bd, Stamford, Conn.; mem. profl. adv. bd. dept. accountancy U. Ill. Served with USAAF, 1943-46, to capt. USAF, 1951-53. Mem. Okla. Bar Assn., Fin. Execs. Inst. (pres. Houston chpt. 1979-80, nat. dir. 1978—, trustee Fin. Execs. Research Found. 1978—), Am. Petroleum Inst. Republican. Presbyterian. Office: One Shell Plaza PO Box 2463 Houston TX 77001

THOMPSON, ROBERT DAN, oil co. exec.; b. Hubbard, Tex., Sept. 21, 1920; s. Oscar Scott and Mary Katurah (Foster) T.; B.S., Tex. Tech. Coll., Lubbock, 1941; LL.B., U. Tulsa, 1955; m. Rose Ann Knowland, Mar. 16, 1949; children—Danna Lee, Linda Kay, Mary Ann. With Standard Oil Co. (Ind.), 1941—, asst. sec., Chgo., 1964-69, corp. sec., 1969—. Served with USAAF, 1943-46. Decorated D.F.C., Air medal with 10 oak leaf clusters. Mem. Am. Soc. Corp. Secs. Home: 1342 Cambridge St Flossmoor IL 60422 Office: 200 E Randolph Dr Chicago IL 60601

THOMPSON, ROBERT FRANKLIN, univ. chancellor; b. Primrose, Nebr., May 30, 1908; s. John Franklin and Sophia Agnes (Maxwell) Thompson; A.B., Nebr. Wesleyan U., 1930, LL.D., 1947; B.D., Drew U., 1933, M.A., 1934, Ph.D., 1940; postgrad. (Delaplaine-McDaniel fellow) Oxford (Eng.) U., 1936-37, U. Zürich, 1937; hon. fellow Union Scandinavian Sch. Theology, 1952; LL.D., Nebr. Wesleyan U., 1947; L.H.D., Am. U., 1959, Alaska Meth. U., 1974, U. Puget Sound, 1978; D.H., Willamette U., 1967; Dr. Pub. Service, U. Pacific, 1967; m. Lucille Burtner, June 30, 1931; children—Martha (Mrs. Walter Dragelevich), Mary (Mrs. George Turnbull). Began as Methodist minister, 1927; mem. N.Y. East Ann. Conf., 1932; asst. prof. social sci. Willamette U., Salem, Oreg., 1937; asso. prof., 1938, prof., dean of freshmen, 1939, v.p., 1941; pres. U. Puget Sound, Tacoma, 1942-73, chancellor, 1973—. Dir. Pacific First Fed. Savs. & Loan Assn. Trustee U. Puget Sound, Tacoma Gen. Hosp. Mem. audit com. Council on Fin. and Adminstrn. of Meth. Ch., 1972-76; mem. exec. and fin. coms. World Methodist Council; bd. curators Wash. State Hist. Soc.; mem. State Ofcls. Salary Rev. Bd.; mem. Pacific N.W. Meth. Conf. Rotarian. Clubs: Tacoma, Tacoma Country, Rainier; Fircrest Golf. Home: 1742 S Fairview Dr Tacoma WA 98465 Office: Collins Library Univ Puget Sound Tacoma WA 98416

THOMPSON, ROBERT MARION, assn. exec.; b. Portland, Oreg., June 9, 1917; s. William Jasper and Anna (Beckman) T.; student Multnomah Coll., 1946-48; m. Helen Patricia Reiner, June 8, 1941; 1 dau., Sharon Kay. Clk., L.H. Butcher Co., Portland, 1935-40; accountant Crown-Zellerbach Corp., Camas, Wash., 1940-42; accountant, budget mgr., controller Montgomery Ward & Co., Portland and Chgo., 1946-66; treas., controller United Grocers, Inc., Portland, 1966-72; treas., adminstrn. mgr. Diamond Fruit Growers Inc., Hood River, Oreg., 1972-76, pres., gen. mgr., 1977—. Treas., controller N.W. Grocery Co.; treas., asst. sec. United Supermarket Investment Co.; dir. United Grocers Ins., Inc., Shears Corp. Pres. United Cerebral Palsy Assns. N.W. Oreg. and Oreg., 1966-70, Gutman Rehab. Programs, 1977; asst. regional v.p. United Cerebral Palsy Assns., 1970—. Bd. dirs. Gutman Rehab. Programs, Inc.; trustee United N.W. Pension Trust. Served to capt., Signal Corps, USAAC, 1942-46. Mem. Financial Execs. Inst. (pres. Portland chpt. 1973). Home: 7812 SE Carlton St Portland OR 97206 Office: PO Box 180 Hood River OR 97031

THOMPSON, ROBERT MCBROOM, publishing co. exec.; b. Evanston, Ill., Nov. 15, 1928; s. William M. and Ethel (McBroom) T.; B.S., U. Ill., 1950; m. Barbara J. Roepke, June 8, 1957; children—Janet, Sandra, Steven, Michael, Linda. Sr. accountant Walton, Joplin, Langer & Co., Chgo., 1952-57; controller Modern Hosp. Pub. Co., Chgo., 1957-64; controller McGraw-Hill, Inc., N.Y.C., 1964—, v.p., controller, 1969—. Served with AUS, 1950-52. C.P.A., Ill. Mem. Am. Inst. C.P.A.'s, Financial Execs. Inst. Home: 21 Gulf Rd East Brunswick NJ 08816 Office: 1221 Ave of Americas New York City NY 10020

THOMPSON, ROBERT RUSSELL, JR., retail store chain exec.; b. Pitts., Oct. 11, 1922; s. Robert Russell and Lillian M. T.; M.S., Springfield Coll., 1943; M.Ed., U. Pitts., 1948; m. Judy Hance, June 25, 1949; children—Perry, David. Asst. prof., basketball coach Elmhurst (Ill.) Coll., 1946-51; with Sears, Roebuck & Co., 1951—, v.p. home appliance group, Chgo., 1978—. Trustee Springfield Coll., Chgo. Jr. Achievement; chmn. bd. trustees Sears YMCA, 1970—; chmn. bd. DuPage chpt. Am. Cancer Soc., 1969-75; elder, chmn. St. Peter's United Ch. of Christ, Elmhurst, 1968—. Served with USNR, 1943-46. Club: Masons. Office: Sears Tower Dept 700-1 Chicago IL 60684

THOMPSON, ROBERT SIDNEY, lawyer, educator; b. Los Angeles, June 2, 1918; s. George M. and Anne (Center) T.; B.S. in Bus. Adminstrn. magna cum laude, U. So. Calif., 1940, LL.B., 1942; m. Elizabeth Arrol Baker, Apr. 10, 1942; children—William Baker, Ann Elizabeth. Admitted to Calif. bar, 1946; mem. firm Thompson, Royston & Moss, Los Angeles, 1946-53; chief asst. U.S. atty. So. Dist. Calif., 1953; mem. firm Nossaman, Thompson, Waters & Moss, Los Angeles, 1954-65; judge Los Angeles Jud. Dist., 1965-66; judge Superior Ct. County of Los Angeles, 1966-68; justice Calif. Ct. Appeals, 1968-79; prof. U. So. Calif. Law Center, Los Angeles, 1979—; lectr. in field, 1950—. Pres. Jewish Vocat. Service, Los Angeles, 1963-64; chmn. Calif. Republican Speakers Bur., 1952; bd. dirs. Jewish Fedn. Council Los Angeles, 1964-66. Served to capt. USAAF, 1942-46. Fellow Am. Bar Found.; mem. Am., Fed., Los Angeles bar assns., Am. Law Inst., Conf. Calif. Judges (mem. exec. bd., pres. 1973-74), Order of Coif. Contbr. to profl. jours. and books. Home: 463 S Spalding Dr Beverly Hills CA 90210 Office: U So Calif Law Center University Park Los Angeles CA 90007

THOMPSON, SADA CAROLYN, actress; b. Des Moines, Sept. 27, 1929; d. Hugh Woodruff and Corlyss Elizabeth (Gibson) Thompson; B.F.A., Carnegie Inst. Tech., 1949; m. Donald E. Stewart, 1949; 1 dau., Liza. Stage debut in The Time of Your Life at Carnegie Inst. Tech. Drama Sch., 1945; co-founder Univ. Playhouse, Mashpee, Mass., 1947; appeared at Pitts. Playhouse, The Playhouse, Erie, Pa., summer stock prodns. at Henrietta Hayloft Theatre, Rochester, N.Y., Brattle Theatre Co., Cambridge, Mass.; speech tchr. 92d St YMHA, N.Y.C.; New York debut at YMHA in Under Milk Wood, 1953; appeared in Off-Broadway revival at Circle in the Sq. Theatre, 1961 and Nat. Edn. Television presentation, 1966; appeared in plays The Clandestine Marriage, Provincetown Playhouse, N.Y.C., 1954, The White Devil and The Carefree Tree at Phoenix Theatre, N.Y.C., 1955, The Misanthrope, Off Broadways Theatre East, 1956, The River Line, Carnegie Hall Playhouse, 1957; joined Am. Shakespeare Festival, Stratford, Conn., 1957, appearing in Othello, Much Ado About Nothing, 1957-58, The Merry Wives of Windsor, Alls Well That Ends Well, 1959, Twelfth Night, The Tempest and Antony and Cleopatra, 1960; appeared in Off Broadway prodn. of Chekhov's Ivanov, 1958, Broadway prodn. of Juno and the Paycock, 1959; appeared in Tartuffe at Lincoln Center Repertory Theatre, 1965, Johnny No-Trump, 1967, The American Dream, 1968, The Effect of Gamma Rays on Man-in-the-Moon Marigolds, 1970, Twigs, 1971, Mourning Becomes Electra, 1971; appeared in motion picture Desperate Characters, 1971; star TV series Sandburg's Lincoln, 1974-76, Family, 1976—; TV spl. The Entertainer, 1976. Recipient Tony award, 1972, New York Drama Critics award for best actress of year Variety, 1971-72, also 2 Obie awards; Atlanta Drama Critics Mask award as best actress for performance in The Vinegar Tree, 1978. Address: care Arcara Bauman & Hiller 9220 Sunset Blvd Suite 322 Los Angeles CA 90069*

THOMPSON, SAMUEL DEAN, JR., food corp. exec.; b. Milw., June 12, 1929; s. Samuel Dean and Edna G. (Eimon) T.; B.A., Colgate U., 1952; M.A., Mich. State U., 1957; m. Tommie Jean Davis, Apr. 29, 1961; children—Samuel Dean III, Brett, Mark. With Grand Union Co., 1954-59; with Li'l Gen. Stores, Inc., 1959-72, pres., 1970-72; pres. Happy Stores, Inc. subs. Kroger Co., Cin., 1972-76; div. ops. mgr. Southland Corp., Chgo., 1976-77; pres. The Lawson Co. subs. Consol. Foods Corp., Chgo., 1977—, sr. v.p. parent co., 1979—. Bd. dirs. ARC, Tampa, Fla., 1969-72, Jr. Achievement, Akron, Ohio, 1977—. Served to 1st lt. USAF, 1952-54. Mem. Nat. Assn. Convenience Stores (pres. 1972-73), Ohio Assn. Convenience Stores (dir. 1978—). Republican. Episcopalian. Home: 3354 Stanley Rd Akron OH 44313 Office: Lawson Co 210 Broadway E Cuyahoga Falls OH 44222

THOMPSON, THOMAS EDWARD, educator; b. Cin., Mar. 15, 1926; s. Theron S. and Florence (Barth) T.; B.A., Kalamazoo Coll., 1949; Ph.D., Harvard, 1955; m. Maria Michaela Smits, Dec. 18, 1953; children—Peter J., Stephen M., Christopher M., David M. Fellow biol. chemistry Harvard, 1955-57; Swedish-Am. exchange fellow Am. Cancer Soc., Stockholm, 1957-58; research fellow exptl. pathology U. Birmingham (Eng.), 1958; asst. prof., then asso. prof. physiol. chemistry Johns Hopkins Sch. Medicine, 1958-66; prof. biochemistry U. Va. Sch. Medicine, Charlottesville, 1966—, chmn. dept. biochemistry, 1966-76, mem. Center for Advanced Studies, U. Va. Mem. Am. Soc. Biol. Chemists, Am. Chem. Soc., Biophys. Soc. (pres. 1976). Mem. editorial staff Biochem. et Biophys. Acta, Biomembrane Rev., Jour. Membrane Biology, Biochemistry. Home: Route 1 Box 319 Afton VA 22920 Office: Dept Biochemistry Univ Virginia Charlottesville VA 22901

THOMPSON, THOMAS FRANKLIN, JR., utilities exec.; b. St. Petersburg, Fla., Sept. 18, 1924; s. Thomas Franklin and Mabel (Staley) T.; B.E.E., U. Fla., 1948; m. Helen Venetia Tarapani, May 19, 1946; children—Thomas L., Jerry Mizell. Engr., Westinghouse Electric Corp., Pitts., 1948-49; with Fla. Power Corp., St. Petersburg, 1949—, exec. asst., 1962-64, dir. adminstrv. services, 1964-67, v.p., 1967—. Chmn. Community Alliance, 1970-71; state fund raising chmn. Fla. Soc. Prevention Blindness, 1977-78. Bd. dirs. Suncoast Health Council, Inc.; chmn. bd. Bayfront Med. Center, Inc.; vice chmn. Pinellas County Mental Health Dist. Bd. Served to 1st lt. USAAF, 1943-46. Recipient Distinguished Service award Coll. Engring., U. Fla., 1967. Registered profl. engr., Fla. Fellow Fla. Engring. Soc.; mem. Nat. Soc. Profl. Engrs., Edison Electric Inst., Southeastern Electric Exchange, St. Petersburg Area C. of C. (chmn. health com. 1968-69, v.p. community devel. div. 1971-72), Sigma Tau, Tau Beta Pi. Democrat. Home: 135 59th Ave S St Petersburg FL 33705 Office: 3201 34th St S St Petersburg FL 33711

THOMPSON, THOMAS HENRY, educator; b. Sioux City, Iowa, Jan. 10, 1924; s. Elmer Edwin and Ruth Alma (Baker) T.; B.A., U. Iowa, 1948, M.A., 1950, Ph.D., 1952; m. Diane Sargent, Nov. 23, 1955; children—Brenda, Alicia, Mark, Rosemary. Asst., instr. U. Iowa, Iowa City, 1948-52; mem. faculty U. No. Iowa, Cedar Falls, 1952—, prof. philosophy, 1965—, head dept., 1969—. Mem. AAAS, AAUP, Sigmund Freud Gesellschaft (Vienna), Am. Philosophy Assn. Home: 2122 California St Cedar Falls IA 50613

THOMPSON, THOMAS KIRKLAND, clergyman, religious adminstr.; b. Little Rock, Nov. 10, 1914; s. Earl Dare and Madeline (Dace) T.; A.B., Baylor U., 1934; Th.M., So. Bapt. Theol. Sem., 1937; S.T.M., Union Theol. Sem., N.Y.C., 1939; D.D., Hillsdale Coll., 1960; m. Elsie Lydia Press, Sept. 3, 1939; children—Judith Irma, Cynthia Louise, Rosemary Margaret. Ordained to ministry Bapt. Ch., 1935; asst. pastor Tompkins Ave. Congl. Ch., Bklyn., 1940-42; pastor First Congl. Ch., Angola, N.Y., 1942-44, Essex Community Ch., Chgo., 1944-45, United Ch. Christ (Congl.), Cranston, R.I., 1950-51; sec. Christian stewardship Missions Council Congl. Christian Chs., 1945-50; exec. dir. dept. stewardship and benevolence Nat. Council Chs. Christ in U.S. Am., N.Y.C., 1951—; v.p. Wagner Coll., 1965-67; dir. devel. Am. Bible Soc., N.Y.C., 1967-70; v.p. for devel. Eden Theol. Sem., Webster Groves, Mo., 1970-72; area counsellor 17/76 Achievement Fund United Ch. Christ, Montclair, N.J., 1972-74; exec. dir. Spiritual Frontiers Fellowship, 1974-75; minister United Ch. of Christ, Paris, N.Y., 1975-79, United Ch. of New Marlborough, Southfield, Mass., 1979—. Christian Chs., 1945-50. Mem. Am. Soc. Ch. History. Author: Handbook of Stewardship Procedures, 1964. Editor: Stewardship in Contemporary Theology, 1960; Stewardship in Contemporary Life, 1965; Stewardship Illustrations, 1965. Home: Southfield MA 01259

THOMPSON, THOMAS MILLER, former transp. co. exec.; b. 1917; ed. Case-Western Res. U.; m.; three children. With East Chicago office GATX Corp., 1939-41, Union Refrigerator Transit div., 1941, office mgr., Cleve., 1945-52, asst. v.p., Chgo., 1952-58, dir., v.p., 1958-60, pres., 1960-61, chmn. bd., chief exec. officer, 1961-78; dir. U.S. Gypsum Co., Internat. Harvester Co., Chgo. Chmn. Lyric Opera of Chgo. Trustee Rush-Presbyn.-St. Luke's Hosp., Nat. Council on Crime and Delinquency. Served with USMCR, 1942-45. Mem. Delta Sigma, Beta Gamma Sigma (hon.). Home: 1621 Palmgren Dr Glenview IL 60025 also 2898 Date Palm Rd Boca Raton FL 33432

THOMPSON, THOMAS SANFORD, former coll. pres.; b. Lewistown, Mont., Apr. 9, 1916; s. Thomas Swing and Sadie (Mixer) T.; B.S., Pacific U., 1938, L.H.D., 1966; postgrad. U. Wash., 1939, U. Oreg., 1941; M.Ed., Oreg. State U., 1949; m. Margaret Ann Wiese, June 1, 1941; children—Roger John, Thomas Warren, Pamela Ann, Mary Ann. Tchr.-coach Siuslaw Union High Sch., Florence, Oreg., 1938, prin., 1939-42; coordinator tng. within industry War Manpower Commn., Portland, Oreg., 1942-43; employee utilization dir. North Pacific div. U.S. Army C.E., 1946-47; acting prin. Portland Apprentice Sch., 1947-48; partner Davis Sales Cons., Portland, 1948-51; dir. devel. Lewis and Clark Coll., Portland, 1952-57; dir. sustaining assos. program Washington U., St. Louis, 1957-60; dir. devel. Knox Coll., Galesburg, Ill., 1960-63; v.p. for devel. U. Pacific, Stockton, Calif., 1963-69; pres. Morningside Coll., Sioux City, Iowa, 1969-78. Cons. Council on Christian Philanthropy, 1970, Council for Financial Aid to Edn., 1963. Bd. dirs. United Fund, Sioux City, 1969-78. Bd. dirs. Pacific Med. Center, San Francisco, 1966-68, Marian Health Center, Sioux City, 1977-78, St. Joseph's Hosp., Stockton, 1979—. Served to lt. col USAAF, 1943-46, USAF, 1951-52. Mem. Greater Stockton (dir. 1967-69), Galesburg (dir. 1961-63) Sioux City (dir. 1971—) chambers commerce, Oreg. Mental Health Assn. (pres. 1956-57), Assn. Am. Colls., Am. Colls. Pub. Relations Assn., Royal Rosarians, Phi Delta Kappa. Republican. Roman Catholic. Club: Rotary. Lectr. coll.-univ. devel., adminstrn. Home: 6879 Atlanta Circle Stockton CA 95209

THOMPSON, THOMAS WILLIAM, zoo exec.; b. Toronto, Ont., Can., Oct. 15, 1913; s. Robert George and Cecelia Emily (House) T.; B.S.A., U. Toronto Ont. Agrl. Coll., 1936; m. Lois Beryl Noble, Oct. 23, 1937; children—Barry Noble, Thomas Bryce, Randolph Kent. Horticulturist, landscape designer Toronto Gen. Burying Grounds, 1936-44; dir. parks and recreation City of Port Arthur (Ont.), 1945-50; adv. parks and recreation facilities, community programs br. Ont. Dept. Edn., 1950-55; met. parks commr. Municipality of Met. Toronto, 1955-78; interim dir. Met. Toronto Zoo, 1976-78, gen. dir., 1978—; bd. dirs. Royal Agrl. Winter Fair, 1962-78; mem. Provincial Parks Adv. Council; bd. dirs. Civic Garden Centre, 1970-78. Mem. senate U. Guelph (Ont.), 1974-77; bd. dirs. Sports Hall of Fame, Toronto, Hockey Hall of Fame, Toronto. Served with RCAF, 1941-42. Decorated Queen's Silver medal; recipient Centennial medal Ont. Agrl. Soc., 1977; Gold medal Garden Club Toronto, 1978. Mem. Can. Parks and Recreation Assn. (pres. 1965-66, award of merit 1968), Gardeners and Florists Assn. (pres. 1940-41), Toronto Soc. Architects, Ont. Landscape Architects Assn., Bruce Tr. Assn. (hon. pres.), Am. Assn. Zool. Parks and Aquariums. Anglican. Contbr. numerous articles to profl. jours., poetry to lit. jours. Home: 4 Fairmar Ave Toronto ON M8Y 2C8 Canada Office: Box 280 West Hill ON M1E 4R5 Canada

THOMPSON, TYLER, clergyman, educator; b. Corona, Calif., Oct. 18, 1915; s. Francis Forbes and Sadie Cassandra (Tyler) T.; B.S., Calif. Inst. Tech., 1936; S.T.B., Boston U., 1939, Ph.D., 1950; m. Phyllis Elizabeth Oechsli, June 19, 1937; children—Francia, Wendy, Heidi, Becky, Peter. Exec. sec. Calif. Inst. Tech. YMCA, 1935-36; ordained to ministry Methodist Ch.; asst. pastor Epworth Meth. Ch., Cambridge, Mass., 1936-37; pastor Barre (Mass.) Meth. Ch., 1937-39; Meth. missionary, Singapore, 1939-46; pastor Weston (Mass.) Meth. Ch., 1946-49; asst. prof. religion and philosophy Allegheny Coll., 1949-51, chaplain, 1950-51; asso. prof. philosophy of religion Garrett-Evangelical Theol. Sem., 1951-56, prof., 1956-78, dir. summer sessions, 1959-72. Vis. prof. philosophy Northwestern U., 1952-58; vis. prof. philosophy of religion McCormick Theol. Sem., 1963-65. Pres. Evanston (Ill.) Human Relations Council, 1952-54. Pres. Evanston Democratic Club, 1956-58; Dem. nominee for Congress 13th Dist. in Ill., 1960; mem. Cook County (Ill.) Central Com. Dem. Party, 1966-68; pres. Dem. Party Evanston, 1970-72. Bd. dirs. Ill. div. A.C.L.U., 1953-68, pres., 1959-64. Am. Assn. Theol. Schs. Faculty fellow, 1965. Mem. Am. Theol. Soc. (pres. div. 1965-66), Am. Philos. Assn., A.A.U.P., Am. Acad. Religion, Tau Beta Pi. Home: 1811 Wesley Ave Evanston IL 60201 Office: Garrett-Evangelical Theol Sem Evanston IL 60201

THOMPSON, VICTOR ALEXANDER, educator; b. Hannah, N.D., Sept. 23, 1912; s. Alexander Wood and Amelia (Gagstad) T.; B.A., U. Wash., 1939, postgrad., 1939-41; Ph.D., Columbia, 1949; m. Elnora Haynie, June 18, 1947; children—Victoria Wood, Alexander Wood. Prof., chmn. dept. polit. and social sci. Ill. Inst. Tech., Chgo., 1950-62; prof. Syracuse U., 1962-66; prof. U. Ill., Urbana, 1966-71, head dept. polit. sci., 1966-68; grad. research prof. polit. sci. U. Fla., Gainesville, 1971—, chmn., 1975-77; vis. prof. Makerere Coll., Uganda, 1960-61. Asst. dir. fuel and automotive rationing OPA, 1944-45; cons. NSRB, 1948-51, Econ. Stblzn. Agy., 1951; spl. asst. to dir. econ. stablzn., 1952-53; tng. contractor Internal Revenue Service, 1956, 64. Mem. Nat. Adv. Health Manpower Council, 1967-69. Mem. Am. Sociol. Soc., Am. Polit. Sci. Assn., Am. Soc. Pub. Adminstrn., Phi Beta Kappa, Sigma Iota Epsilon. Author: The Regulatory Process in OPA Rationing, 1950; (with Herbert A. Simon and Donald W. Smithburg) Public Administration, 1950; Modern Organization, 1961; Bureaucracy and Innovation, 1969; Without Sympathy or Enthusiasm: The Problem of Administrative Compassion, 1975; Bureaucracy and the Modern World, 1976. Home: 2255 NW 4th Pl Gainesville FL 32603

THOMPSON, VICTOR KING, architect; b. Columbus, Ohio, June 18, 1913; s. King Gibson and Ethel (Herrick) T.; B.F.A., Ohio State U., 1934, B.Arch., 1941; postgrad. Cranbrook Acad. Art, 1939-40; m. Marianne Grainger Randall, June 18, 1940; children—Sara (Mrs. John T. Donnelly), Victor Scott, Douglas Randall, Andrew King. Instr. architecture Ohio State U., 1946-47; faculty Stanford, 1947—, prof. architecture, 1947-72, emeritus prof., 1972—; asso. Saratoga Hort. Found., 1975; treas. Friends of Filoli, 1976-77. Architect, Ladera Community Ch., Menlo Park, Calif., 1960. Served to maj. C.E., AUS, 1941-46. Mem. AIA, Tau Sigma Delta, Sigma Alpha Epsilon. Clubs: Menlo Polo; Los Altos Hunt. Home: 207 Westridge Dr Portola Valley CA 94025

THOMPSON, W. BLAKE, airline co. exec.; b. Washington, Sept. 11, 1919; s. Irving G. and Josephine (Gibson) T.; A.B., George Washington U., 1947, postgrad., 1948-49; m. Eileen Kendrick, Apr. 24, 1948; children—Blake K., Blair W., Clark G. With Capital Airlines, Washington, 1945-61, comptroller, 1959-61; controller Allegheny Airlines, Washington, 1961—, v.p., 1963-72, sr. v.p., 1972—. Served with AUS, 1942-45; PTO. Mem. Financial Execs. Inst. (pres. D.C. 1967-68), Sigma Alpha Epsilon. Home: 302 High St Alexandria VA 22302 Office: National Airport Washington DC 20001

THOMPSON, WARREN, govt. ofcl.; b. Clarkston, Utah, Dec. 28, 1920; s. George and Esther K. (Godfrey) T.; B.S., U. Utah, 1943, grad. certificate in Social Work, 1947; postgrad. N.Y. U., 1951; m. Ivagene Olson, Dec. 21, 1943; children—Marilyn, Paul, Janice, Julie, Mark, Charlene, Bradley. Rehab. counselor Utah Dept. Edn., 1947-50, asst. state dir. div. Vocational Rehab., 1950-55; rehab. specialist Dept. Health, Edn. and Welfare, Washington, 1955; asst. regional rep. Office Vocational Rehab., Denver, 1955-59; dir. Colo. Dept. Rehab., Denver, 1959-63, Calif. Dept. Rehab., Sacramento, 1963-69; asst. regional dir. Dept. Health, Education and Welfare, Denver, 1967—; instr. sociology U. Utah, 1946-47. Chmn. Western region workshop, spl. edn. and rehab. Ho. of Reps., 1959. Served to 1st lt. AUS, 1943-45. Mem. Nat. Rehab. Assn. (nat. pres. 1966-67) Phi Kappa Phi, Phi Delta Kappa. Mem. Ch. of Jesus Christ of Latter-day Saints. Home: 2480 S Zephyr St Denver CO 80227 Office: Fed Bldg 19th and Stout St Denver CO 80202

THOMPSON, WAYNE EDWARD, retailing exec.; b. St. Paul, July 22, 1916; s. Edward and Elma (Aamodt) T.; B.A. in Polit. Sci. and Pub. Adminstrn., U. Calif. at Berkeley, 1937, postgrad., 1938; m. Ann Braun, Aug. 6, 1941; children—Wayne Charles, Christine A. Mgr. City of Richmond (Calif.), 1944-54, City of Oakland (Calif.), 1954-65; sr. v.p. environmental devel. Dayton-Hudson Corp., Mpls., 1965—. Former mem. exec. com. San Francisco Bay Area Council; former cons. Nat. Urban Coalition; former chmn. Minn. Gov.'s Council on Exec. Reorgn., Minn. Planning Commn.; mem. President's Adv. Council on Mgmt. Improvement; mem. council Stanford Research Inst.; mem. steering com. Minn. Exptl. City; mem. commn. on nat. inst. justice Am. Bar Assn. Bd. dirs. Minn. Orchestral Assn., Am. Retail Fedn.; former mem. Harvard vis. com. John F. Kennedy Sch. Govt.; former trustee Golden Gate Coll. Served with USNR, 1940-42. Mem. Com. for Econ. Devel. (trustee), Nat. Acad. Pub. Adminstrn., Nat. Municipal League (v.p.), Pub. Affairs Council (dir.). Office: Dayton-Hudson Corp 777 Nicollet Mall IDS Tower 15th Floor Minneapolis MN 55402

THOMPSON, WAYNE EDWIN, educator, sociologist; b. Hunter, Kans., Mar. 3, 1927; s. Carlin T. and Zella (Van Leewen) T.; B.A. cum laude in Econs. and Polit. Sci., U. Colo., 1949, M.A., 1951; Ph.D. in Sociology, Cornell U., 1956; m. Ruth C. Cortis-Stanford, Sept. 27, 1953; 1 son, David C. Field dir. study occupational retirement dept. sociology and anthropology Cornell U., Ithaca, N.Y., 1952-53, research asso., 1956-58, faculty, 1957-68, prof. sociology, 1964-68, sr. researcher studies of community issues, 1958-68, asst. dir. Social Sci. Research Center, 1958-61, dir., 1961-66; prof., head dept. sociology and anthropology U. N.C., Greensboro, 1968-71; prof. head dept. sociology and anthropology Calif. State Coll., Bakersfield, 1971-74; prof., head dept. sociology Brock U., St. Catharines, Ont., Can., 1974-78; prof., head dept. sociology and anthropology Guelph (Ont.) U., 1978—; Fulbright lectr. Sch. Social Scis., Tampere, Finland, 1964-65. Mem. Am. Sociol. Assn., So. Sociol. Soc., Phi Beta Kappa, Phi Kappa Phi. Research, publs. on social gerontology especially on relationship of retirement to health, relationship of pre-retirement factors to adjustment in retirement, family in later years; also studies in community politics especially the negativist role of the politically alienated in local referenda. Address: U Guelph Guelph ON N1G 2W1 Canada

THOMPSON, WILLARD LINN, educator; b. LaSalle, Ill., Nov. 14, 1914; s. William Sherman and Millie (Schinz) T.; A.A., LaSalle-Peru-Oglesby Jr. Coll., 1934; B.S., U. Ill., 1937, M.S., 1949, Ph.D., 1958; m. Mabel Louise Lohnes, Sept. 22, 1942; children—Julia Linn (Mrs. Bruce Erickson), Susan Louise. Reporter, Peoria (Ill.) Jour.-Transcript, 1937-39; with advt. dept. Pekin (Ill.) Daily Times, 1939-41, mng. editor, 1946-47; pres. Effingham (Ill.) Broadcasting Co., gen. mgr. radio sta. WCRA, 1947-48; asst. prof. U. Okla., 1949-51; asst. prof., asso. prof. U. Oreg., 1952-60, dir. pub. services and devel., 1956-60; prof., asst. to pres. U. Minn., Mpls., 1960-63, dean gen. extension div. and summer session, 1963-71, dir. summer session, prof. journalism, 1971—. Cons., examiner Commn. on Instns. Higher Edn., North Central Assn. Colls. and Secondary Schs.; mem. Upper Midwest Research and Devel. Council, 1963—; mem. St. Paul-Mpls. Com. on Fgn. Relations, 1960-74. Mem. exec. com. Office for Advanced Drama Research. Bd. govs. Univ. YMCA, Mpls. YMCA. Served to capt. AUS, 1941-45. Decorated Bronze Star medal, Order Oranje-Nassau (Netherlands); recipient Golden Fifty award for contbns. to teaching advt. Alpha Delta Sigma, 1963. Mem. Assn. for Edn. in Journalism, Am. Acad. Advt. (treas. 1976-78), Minn. Hist. Soc., AAUP, Assn. Univ. Summer Sessions (pres. 1973), North Central Conf. Summer Schs. (pres. 1975), Alpha Delta Sigma. Rotarian. Editor: The NUEA Spectator, 1963-71. Co-editor: Expanding Horizons, Continuing Education, 1965. Home: 1569 Northrop St Saint Paul MN 55108 Office: Johnston Hall U Minn Minneapolis MN 55455

THOMPSON, WILLARD SPENCER, former bus. adminstr.; b. Butte, Mont., June 20, 1913; s. Willard and Daisy (Spencer) T.; A.B. cum laude, Stanford, 1935; grad. pub. service fellow Harvard, 1937-39; m. Evelyn Keegan, Dec. 28, 1978. Adminstrv. asst. Nat. Emergency Council, Washington, 1935-36, pres. com. on adminstrative mgmt., 1936-37; asst. and dep. commr. Bur. Pub. Debt, Treasury Dept., Washington, 1939-43; dir. in adminstrn., UN, 1946-49; dir. indsl. relations internat. div. Ford Motor Co., 1949-55; dir. indsl. relations Atlas Chem. Industries, Inc., 1956-61, v.p. indsl. relations ICI U.S. (formerly Atlas Chem. Industries, Inc.), 1961-74, dir., 1974—; v.p. employee and pub. relations ICI Americas, 1974-78. Chmn., Sec. Air Forces Com. on Personnel Utilization and Tng., 1951-52; mem. exec. com. G.W.D.C. Chmn. econ. devel. com. Del. Tomorrow Commn., 1974—; past chmn. Del. Bd. Pension Trustees. Served as lt. USNR, 1943-45. Home: 111 Thissell Ln Centerville Wilmington DE 19807

THOMPSON, WILLIAM BELL, educator, physicist; b. Belfast, No. Ireland, Feb. 27, 1922; s. Herbert Ginnif and Mary (Bell) T.; B.A., U. B.C., 1945, M.A., 1947; Ph.D., U. Toronto, 1950; M.A., (hon.), Oxford (Eng.) U., 1962; m. Gertrude Helene Goldschmidt, Mar. 24, 1954 (div. 1971); children—Kathleen Susan, Graham Jonathan; m. 2d, Johanna Elzelina Ladestein Korevaar, Jan. 29, 1972. With U.K. AEC, Harwell, Eng., 1950-60, sr. prin. sci. officer, head plasma theory group, 1959-60; head plasma theory div. Culham Lab. Plasma Physics and Controlled Fusion Research, Culham, Eng., 1960-62; prof. plasma physics U. Oxford, 1962-65; prof. physics U. Calif. at San Diego, 1965—, chmn. dept., 1969-72; cons. in field. Recipient Hulton award achievement Brit. sci., 1958; fellow St. Peters Coll., U. Oxford, 1962-65. Fellow Am. Phys. Soc., Royal Astron. Soc.; mem. Canadian Assn. Physics. Contbr. papers in field. Joint editor: Advances in Plasma Physics, 1967—; asso. editor Jour. Plasma Physics, 1966—. Address: Box 109 La Jolla CA 92093

THOMPSON, WILLIAM CANNON, JR., advt. agy. exec.; b. Phila., Aug. 21, 1938; s. William Cannon and Mary Bertha (Harris) T.; A.B., U. N.C., 1959; m. Linda Krutchkoff, Nov. 6, 1965; children—William Cannon III, James Stuart, Kevin Harris. Media planner Doyle Dane Bernbach Advt., N.Y.C., 1960-63; media supr. Batten Barton Durstine & Osborn, N.Y.C., 1963-65; account mgmt. J. Walter Thompson Co., N.Y.C., 1965—, sr. v.p. in charge account mgmt., 1974-75, sr. v.p., group account dir., 1976-79, exec. v.p., 1979—. Republican. Presbyn. Club: Wykagyl Country. Home: 112 Bon Air New Rochelle NY 10804 Office: 420 Lexington Ave New York NY 10021

THOMPSON, WILLIAM DAVID, advt. exec.; b. Pitts.; s. Ross Ephraim and Blanche (Watson) T.; B.S., Yale U.; m. Margaret Elizabeth Anderson; children—Elizabeth Thompson Post, Margaret Thompson Weekley, Susan Thompson McNamee. With Thompson Furniture Co., Braddock, Pa.; mem. sales dept. Scovill Mfg. Co., Waterbury, Conn., 1945-48; account exec. James Thomas Chirurg Co., N.Y.C., 1948-50, McCann-Erickson, Inc., N.Y.C., 1951-52; with Young & Rubicam, Inc., N.Y.C., 1952-, sr. v.p., 1961-79, exec. v.p., 1979—. Adv. bd. Norwalk (Conn.) Hosp. Clubs: Wee Burn Country (Darien, Conn.); Union League (N.Y.C.). Home: Nolen Ln Darien CT 06820 Office: 285 Madison Ave New York NY 10017

THOMPSON, WILLIAM DONALD, educator; b. Kansas City, Mo., June 27, 1921; B.A., U. Kans., 1947, M.A., 1948, Ph.D., 1954; married; 4 children. Instr. in psychology U. Kans., 1949-54; research asso. psychophysiology Fels Research Inst., Antioch Coll., 1954-57, asst. prof. psychology, 1955-57; asso. prof. Baylor U., Waco, Tex., 1957-62, prof., dir. grad. studies, 1962-69, chmn. dept. psychology, 1969-79. Served to capt. AUS, 1942-46. Mem. Am. Psychol. Assn., Soc. Psychophysiol. Research. Office: Dept Psychology Baylor U Waco TX 76703

THOMPSON, WILLIAM FRANKLIN, r.r. exec.; b. Ft. Worth, Feb. 27, 1926; s. Robert Pink and Reva (Wilson) T.; student Northwestern U., 1959, Harvard, 1967; m. Betty Jo Thorn, Oct. 11, 1946; children—William Edward, Melissa Ann, Beckie Jo. With Tex. and Pacific R.R., 1942-44, Chgo., Rock Island and Pacific R.R., 1947-53, Terminal R.R. Assn. of St. Louis, 1970-73; officer St. Louis-San Francisco Ry. Co., Springfield, Mo., 1974—, also dir.; dir. Boatmen's Union Nat. Bank, Springfield, Railbox, Kansas City Terminal R.R. Served with USNR, 1944-46. Mem. Assn. Am. Railroads (gen. com.), C. of C. Springfield (dir.). Mason. Club: Hickory Hills Country (Springfield, Mo.). Home: 3565 E Linwood St Springfield MO 65804 Office: 3253 E Trafficway Springfield MO 65802

THOMPSON, WILLIAM HAYTON, educator; b. Scranton, Pa., Oct. 13, 1909; s. Garfield and Mae (Price) T.; B.S., Pa. State U., 1934; M.S., Syracuse U., 1939; Ph.D., Iowa State U., 1948; m. Evelyn Covault, June 22, 1938; children—Louise Thompson Stefanowicz, Lawrence, Neil, Mary Thompson Hampton. Tchr., Matamoras (Pa.)

High Sch., 1935-38; instr. Colby Jr. Coll., 1938-42, Miami U., 1942-44; mem. faculty Iowa State U., Ames, 1944—, prof., 1952—, chmn. indsl. adminstrn. dept. 1968-75; cons. Rock Island R.R., U.S. Dept. Agr., Iowa State Mktg. Bd. Trustee Center for Indsl. Research and Service, Iowa Ins. Found. Mem. Am. Soc. Traffic and Transp., Transp. Research Council, Midwest Econs. Assn. Kiwanian. Home: 1105 Kennedy St Ames IA 50010

THOMPSON, WILLIAM IRWIN, educator, instl. dir.; b. Chgo., July 16, 1938; s. Chester Andrew and Lillian Margaret (Fahey) T.; B.A. with honors in Philosophy, Pomona Coll., 1962; M.A. (Woodrow Wilson fellow), Cornell U., 1964, Ph.D. (Woodrow Wilson dissertation fellow), 1966; m. Gail Joan Gordon, Feb. 3, 1960 (div. Jan. 1979); children—Evan Timothy, Hilary Joan, Andrew Rhys; m. 2d, Beatrice Madeleine Rudin, Mar. 1, 1979. Instr. Humanities Mass. Inst. Tech., Cambridge, 1965-66, asst. prof., 1966-67, Old Dominion fellow, 1967, asso. prof. humanities, 1968; asso. prof. humanities York U., Toronto, Ont., Can., 1968-72, prof., 1973; vis. prof. religion Syracuse (N.Y.) U., 1973; founder, dir. Lindisfarne Assn., N.Y.C., 1973—. Hon. colleague Ch. St. John Divine, N.Y.C. Author: Imagination of an Insurrection: Dublin, Easter 1916, 1967; At the Edge of History, 1971; Passages about Earth, 1974; Evil and World Order, 1976; Darkness and Scattered Light, 1978; The Time Falling Bodies Take to Light, 1980. Address: RFD 2 West Stockbridge MA 01266 81131

THOMPSON, WILLIAM IVES, office equipment mfg. co. exec.; b. Glenrock, N.J., Feb. 28, 1922; s. Elmer Ives and Evelyn (Renton) T.; student St. John's U., Jamaica, N.Y. 1940-41, CCNY, 1947-48; m. Rhoda Simpson, Oct. 11, 1975; children—Dana, Eleanor, Laurance, Woodman. Regional mgr. Diebold Inc., 1949-51, N.Y. met. mgr., 1951-55; sales mgr. Oxford Pendaflex Co., Garden City, N.Y., 1955-61, v.p. mktg., 1961-69, pres., chief exec. officer, 1969-75; chmn., chief exec. officer Esselte Pendaflex, Garden City, 1975—. Chmn., Center for Econ. Research, C.W. Post Coll., L.I. U. Served with A.C., USNR, 1942-46. Decorated Air medal, D.F.C. Mem. Nat. Office Products Assn. (chmn. mfrs. div. 1969-70), Bus. Records Mfrs. Assn. (pres. 1975-76, dir. 1975—). Clubs: Huntington Country, Seabrook Island. Patentee office furniture system. Home: 19 Heckscher Dr Huntington NY 11743 Office: Esselte Pendaflex Corp Clinton Rd Garden City NY 11530

THOMPSON, WILLIAM NEIL, educator; b. Atlanta, Ill., Dec. 6, 1920; s. Ray Eugene and Ida Florence (Crihfield) T.; B.S., U. Ill., 1941, M.S., 1942, Ph.D., 1952; postgrad. (Farm Found. fellow), U. Chgo., 1947-48; m. Geraldine Alice Pech, Jan. 31, 1942; children—William Ray, John David, Julia (Mrs. Paul Z. Han). Instr., asst. prof. U. Ill., 1946-53; agriculturist TVA, Knoxville, Tenn., 1954-55; mem. faculty U. Ill. at Urbana-Champaign, 1955—, prof. agrl. econs., 1959—, asso. dir. internat. agrl. programs, 1973-78, asso. dean, dir. internat. agr., 1978—; chief party, adviser adminstrn. Njala Univ. Coll., Sierra Leone, 1964-66; cons. TVA, AID; spl. internat. agr. assignments in Sierra Leone, India, Pakistan, Nepal, Thailand, Saudi Arabia. Served with AUS, 1943-46; ETO, PTO. Recipient Outstanding Service award U. Ill. Coll. Agrl. Alumni Assn., 1959. Mem. Am. Econ. Assn., Am. Agrl. Econs. Assn., Am. Soc. Farm Mgrs. and Rural Appraisers (v.p. 1964), Soc. Internat. Devel., African Assn. Advancement Agr. Mem. Ch. Disciples of Christ. Author: Building Institutions to Serve Agriculture, 1968; Mission Overseas, A Handbook for U.S. Families in Developing Countries, 1969; A Method of Assessing Progress of Agricultural Universities in India, 1970; The Punjab Agricultural University An Assessment of Progress to 1970, 1970; NIDA: A Case Study in Institution Development, 1974. Home: 2118 Bristol Rd Champaign IL 61820 Office: Internat Agr U Ill 113 Mumford Hall Urbana IL 61801

THOMPSON, WILLIAM PHELPS, lawyer, ch. ofcl.; b. Beloit, Kans., Sept. 14, 1918; s. William Frederick and Vera (Phelps) T.; student Bethel Coll., North Newton, Kans., 1935-36; A.B., McPherson (Kans.) Coll., 1939, J.C.D., 1956; J.D., U. Chgo., 1942; LL.D., Coll. Emporia, 1965, U. Dubuque, 1966, Missouri Valley Coll., 1967, LaSalle Coll., Phila., 1974; L.H.D., Tusculum Coll., 1977; m. Mary Alice Wood, Jan. 23, 1949; children—Judith (Mrs. Dwight A. Koop), William Wood, Margaret. Admitted to Kans. bar, 1942; practiced in Wichita, 1946-66; partner firm Hershberger, Patterson, Jones & Thompson, 1951-66. Mem. gen. Council Synod Kans., United Presbyn. Ch. U.S.A., 1958-64, chmn. budget and finance com., 1959-62; mem. gen. council Gen. Assembly, United Presbyn. Ch. U.S.A., 1958-64, vice chmn., 1960-64, mem. budget and finance com., 1958-64, chmn., 1960-64, moderator 177th Gen. Assembly, 1965, stated clk., 1966—; dir. Wichita Council Chs., 1954-59, v.p., 1954, pres. 1955, chmn. trustees, 1957-59; dir. Westminster Found., Synod Kans., 1955-62; mem. central com. World Council Chs., 1966—, exec. com. commn. on internat. affairs, 1973-75; exec. com., mem. gov. bd. Nat. Council Chs. Christ in U.S.A., 1966—, chmn. gen. planning and program com., 1969-72, pres., 1976-78; exec. com. World Alliance Reformed Chs., 1966—, pres., 1970-77. Pres., Civic Progress, Wichita, 1961; mem. Mayor of Wichita's Adv. Com. on Water, 1955, Adv. Com. Civic Center, 1962. Bd. dirs. Wichita Community Planning Council, 1952-60, pres., 1959; bd. dirs. Wichita Community Chest, 1955-57, Wichita Civic Music Assn., 1953-63, Wichita Council Campfire Girls, 1960-65, Wichita Symphony Soc., 1960-64, 65-66; bd. dirs. United Fund Wichita and Sedgwick County, 1957-66, chmn. fund raising campaign, 1964, v.p., 1965; trustee Midwest Med. Research Found., 1965-66; trustee Nat. Council for Children and TV, 1977—, chmn., 1979—. Served to capt. USAAF, 1942-46. Mem. Am., Kans., Wichita bar assns., Order of Coif, Pi Kappa Delta, Phi Delta Phi. Home: 60 Ross Stevenson Circle Princeton NJ 08540 Office: Room 1201 475 Riverside Dr New York NY 10027

THOMPSON, WILLIAM REID, public utility exec.; b. Durham, N.C., Aug. 13, 1924; s. William Reid and Myrtle (Siler) T.; B.S., U. N.C., 1945; LL.B., Harvard, 1949; m. Mary Louise Milliken, Aug. 16, 1952; children—Mary Elizabeth, William Reid III, John Milliken, Susan Siler. Admitted to N.C. bar, 1949; mem. firm Barber and Thompson, Pittsboro, N.C., 1949-58; judge Superior Cts. N.C., 1958-60; asso. gen. counsel Carolina Power & Light Co., 1960-63, v.p., gen. counsel, 1963-67, exec. v.p., 1967-71; chmn. bd., pres., chief exec. officer Potomac Electric Power Co., Washington, 1971—; dir. Riggs Nat. Bank of Washington, Garfinckel, Brooks Bros., Miller & Rhoads, Inc., Acacia Mut. Life Ins. Co. Dir. Washington Bd. Trade. Bd. dirs. Nat. Symphony Orch. Assn.; trustee Fed. City Council. Mem. N.C. Gen. Assembly from Chatham County, 1955-57. Served to lt. (j.g.) USNR, 1943-45; PTO. Mem. Am. Bar Assn., Edison Electric Inst. (past chmn.), Southeastern Electric Exchange (dir.), Assn. Edison Illuminating Cos. (pres.), NAM (dir.), Bus. Council, Bus. Roundtable, Phi Beta Kappa, Delta Kappa Epsilon. Democrat. Methodist. Clubs: Metropolitan, Burning Tree, Chevy Chase, 1925 F St (Washington); Gibson Island (Md.), Rotary. Home: 2441 Tracy Pl NW Washington DC 20008 Office: 1900 Pennsylvania Ave NW Washington DC 20068

THOMPSON, WILLIAM TALIAFERRO, JR., educator, physician; b. Petersburg, Va., May 26, 1913; s. William Taliaferro and Ann C. (McIlwaine) T.; A.B., Davidson Coll., 1934, Sc.D. (hon.), 1975; M.D., Med. Coll. Va., 1938; m. Jessie G. Baker, June 21, 1941; children—William Taliaferro III, Addison Baker, Jessie Ball. Intern 4th med. service Boston City Hosp., 1938-40; asst. resident Mass. Gen. Hosp., 1940-41; resident Med. Coll. Va., Richmond, 1941, mem. faculty, 1946—, prof., 1959-75, emeritus prof., 1975—, chmn. dept. medicine, also chief med. services hosps., 1959-73; mem. staff McGuire Clinic-St. Luke's Hosp., 1946-54; chief medicine service McGuire VA Hosp., 1954-59; med. dir. Westminister-Canterbury House, Richmond, 1975—. Chmn. bd. mgrs., mem. med. adv. bd. Alfred I. DuPont Inst. and Nemours Found., 1962-78; med. adv. bd., Greenbrier Clinic. Pres., Va. Assn. Mental Health, 1955-57, Richmond Bd. Housing and Hygiene, 1952-59. Bd. dirs. Meml. Guidance Clinic, 1950-59, Maymont Found., Richmond, 1975-78; trustee Collegiate Sch., 1952-69, pres., 1965-67; trustee Davidson Coll., 1965-73, 78-80, Mary Baldwin Coll., 1959-64; Union Theol. Sem., Richmond, 1960-70, 78—, Crippled Childrens' Hosp., Richmond, 1975—. Served to maj. M.C., AUS, 1941-46. Diplomate Am. Bd. Internal Medicine. Master A.C.P. (chmn. Va. sect. 1961, gov. for Va. 1971-75); mem. Am. Clin. and Climatological Assn., N.Y. Acad. Scis., Am. Fedn. Clin. Research, So. Soc. Clin. Investigation, Richmond Acad. Medicine (pres. 1972), Davidson Coll. Nat. Alumni Assn. (pres. 1979-80), Phi Beta Kappa, Alpha Omega Alpha, Omicron Delta Kappa, Kappa Sigma. Presbyn. Clubs: Country of Va., Commonwealth (Richmond). Editor Va. Med. Monthly, 1976—. Contbr. to med. jours. Home: 4602 Sulgrave Rd Richmond VA 23221

THOMPSON, WILLIAM YOUNG, educator, author; b. Baton Rouge, Oct. 15, 1922; s. Henry Howard and Frances (Ellzey) T.; B.A., U. Ala., 1946; M.A., Emory U., 1948; Ph.D., U. N.C., 1953; m. Helen Sherard McCarley, Dec. 27, 1947; children—Sherard Ellen, Richard Howard. Prof. history Presbyn. Coll., Clinton, S.C., 1950-55; prof. history La. Tech. U., Ruston, 1955—, head dept., 1965—. Served to 1st lt. USAAF, 1943-45; ETO; lt. col. Res. Decorated D.F.C., Air medal with 3 oak leaf clusters. Mem. So., La. hist. assns. Author: Robert Toombs of Georgia, 1966. Home: 1504 Elizabeth St Ruston LA 71270

THOMPSON, WILLIS HERBERT, JR., oil co. exec.; b. Mpls., Apr. 19, 1934; s. Willis Herbert and Wilma (Brookshire) T.; B.A. in Geology, U. Minn., 1956, M.S., 1959; m. Byrdie A. Herring, Feb. 23, 1968; children—Barbara, Nancy, Kim, Roger, Michael. Exploration geologist, geophysicist Standard Oil Co. Tex., Midland, Houston, 1959-64; with Signal Oil and Gas Co., 1964-73, mgr. internat. exploration, 1970-71, sr. v.p., 1970-71, exec. v.p., chief operating officer, 1971-72, pres., 1972-74, chief exec. officer, 1973-74, dir., 1970-74, dir. subs., 1972-74, pres., chief exec. officer Burmah Oil and Gas Co., 1974-76; v.p., dir. Burmah Oil, Inc., N.Y.C., 1974-76; pres., chief exec. officer Aminoil U.S.A., Inc., 1976; pres., chief operating officer MAPCO, Inc., Tulsa, Okla., 1976—; dir. 1st Nat. Bank of Tulsa, 1st Nat. Bancorp. Bd. dirs. Tulsa YMCA, Tulsa Philharmonic, Salvation Army, St. Johns Med. Center. Served with C.E., U.S. Army, 1956-57. Mem. Am. Petroleum Inst. (dir.), Ind. Petroleum Assn. Am. (dir.), Okla. Petroleum Council (dir.), Am. Assn. Petroleum Geologists, Tex. Mid-Continent Oil and Gas Assn., Tulsa Geol. Soc., Young Pres.' Orgn. Republican. Presbyterian. Clubs: Tulsa, Southern Hills Country (Tulsa). Home: 6770 S Timberlane Rd Tulsa OK 74136 Office: 1800 S Baltimore Ave Tulsa OK 74119

THOMPSON, YEWELL REYNOLDS, ret. educator; b. Hazlehurst, Miss., Nov. 26, 1912; s. Francis G. and Lula (Donahue) T.; B.A., Millsaps Coll., 1948; M.A., George Peabody Coll. Tchrs., 1949; Ed.D., U. Fla., 1954; m. Alice E. Jenkins, June 29, 1936; 1 son, Yewell Reynolds. Elementary classroom tchr., Copiah and Yazoo Counties, Miss., 1934-42, 46-47; prin. Ga. Tchrs. Coll. Lab. Sch., 1949-51; elementary sch. supr. Brevard County, Fla., 1953-55; chmn. programs in elementary and early childhood edn. Coll. Edn., U. Ala., University, 1955-75, head area curriculum and instrn., 1975-79. Served with AUS, 1942-46; CBI. Mem. Ala., Nat. edn. assns., Assn. Supervision and Curriculum Devel., Dept. Elementary Sch. Prins., Phi Delta Kappa, Kappa Phi Kappa. Mem. Christian Ch. Rotarian. Contbr. articles to bulls., chpts. in books. Home: 2 Twin Lakes Northport AL 35476 Office: Box 5196 University AL 35486

THOMSEN, CHARLES BURTON, construction mgmt. firm exec.; b. Springfield, Mo., Sept. 25, 1932; s. Fred Charles and Sunbeam (Burton) T.; B.Arch., U. Okla., 1957; M.Arch., M.I.T., 1963; m. Lois Ann Leivestad, June 8, 1956; children—Melissa Ann, Charles Jeffrey. Mem. faculty Rice U. Sch. Architecture, Houston, 1962-65; asso. Caudill Rowlett Scott, Inc., Houston, 1965-67, asso. partner, 1967-69, asso. partner, office mgr., N.Y.C., 1969-71; chmn. bd., pres. CM, Inc., Houston, 1971-79, chmn. bd., chief exec. officer, 1979—; bd. dirs. CRS Group, Inc., Houston, 1974—; vis. critic Boston U. Sch. Architecture, 1961-62, Columbia U. Sch. Architecture, 1969; adj. prof. Rice U., 1971—. Served with USMCR, 1951-52. Fellow AIA. Episcopalian. Contbr. articles to profl. jours., books. Office: 2700 S Post Oak Dr Houston TX 77056

THOMSEN, DONALD LAURENCE, JR., assn. exec., mathematician; b. Stamford, Conn., Apr. 21, 1921; s. Donald Laurence and Linda (Comstock) T.; grad. Phillips Exeter Acad., 1938; B.A. magna cum laude in Math., Amherst Coll., 1942; Ph.D., Mass. Inst. Tech., 1947; m. Linda Rollins Leach, June 14, 1958; children—Melinda Rollins, Katherine Long, Donald Laurence III. Teaching fellow Mass. Inst. Tech., 1942, instr., 1943-47; instr., then asst. prof. Haverford (Pa.) Coll., 1947-50; research fellow, then research engr. Jet Propulsion Lab., Calif. Inst. Tech., 1950-52; asst. prof. Pa. State U., 1952-54; with IBM Corp., 1954-72, spl. asst. to dir. edn., 1961-62, dir. profl. activities, 1963-66, corp. dir. engring. edn., 1967-72; pres. SIAM Inst. for Math. and Soc., New Canaan, Conn., 1972—, also bd. dirs.; mem. vis. com. Coll. Sci., Drexel Inst. Tech., 1969—; mem. adv. com. for individualized sci. instructional system Coll. Edn., Fla. State U., 1973—. Recipient spl. certificate Milw. Sch. Engring., 1969. Mem. AAAS, Am. Math. Soc., Am. Statis. Assn., Math. Assn. Am. (chmn. com insts.), Soc. Indsl. and Applied Math. (pres. 1959, chmn. trustees 1960-72), Am. Fedn. Information Processing Socs. (chmn. edn. com. 1965-66, chmn. U.S. com. IFIP Congress 1968, 66-69, dir. 1969—, mem. exec. com. 1975-77), Assn. Computing Machinery, Am. Ordnance Assn. (chmn. research div.), Internat. Fedn. Info. Processing (chmn. exhibits com. N.Y.C. Congress 1965), Conf. Bd. Math. Scis. (chmn. budget and finance com.), Phi Beta Kappa, Sigma Xi, Delta Tau Delta. Republican. Presbyn. Clubs: The Princeton (N.Y.C.); Woodway Country (Darien, Conn.); New Canaan (Conn.) Winter. Author: Tables of Integral Transforms, 2 vols.; Higher Transcendental Functions, 3 vols. Contbr. articles to profl. jours. Home: 97 Parish Rd S New Canaan CT 06840 Office: SIMS 97 Parish Rd S New Canaan CT 06840

THOMSEN, IB, rubber products co. exec.; b. Denmark, Oct. 8, 1925; s. Thomas and Magda (Thyboe) T.; came to U.S., 1950; M.B.A., Harvard, 1952; m. Lisa Edith Voss, Aug. 19, 1947; children—Sandra Lee, Kenneth Alan, Stephen Eric. With Goodyear Internat. Corp., 1952—, asst. to finance dir. Goodyear-Sweden, 1952-57, finance dir. India, 1957-58, treas. U.K., 1958-61, finance dir., 1961-66, mng. dir., chmn. U.K., 1966-71, v.p., 1971, pres., 1972—; exec. v.p., dir. Goodyear Tire & Rubber Co., Akron, Ohio, 1971—. Mem. Nat. Fgn. Trade Council (dir.), Internat. Rd. Fedn. (dir.), Council of Ams. (trustee). Office: Goodyear Tire & Rubber Co 1144 E Market St Akron OH 44316*

THOMSEN, JOHN G., physician; b. Estherville, Iowa, June 2, 1921; s. John and Kirstine (Thisgaard) T.; B.A., St. Olaf Coll., 1943; M.D., U. Iowa, 1945; m. Pearle J. Maxwell, Sept. 14, 1945; children—Jane, Robert, Margaret. Intern Swedish Hosp., Seattle, 1945-46; asst. resident dermatology and syphilogy Univ. Hosps., Cleve., 1948-50; spl. resident dermatology and syphilology, City Hosp., Cleve., also preceptee office Dr. John E. Rauschkolb, 1950-51; practice medicine specializing in dermatology, Des Moines, 1953—; mem. staff Iowa Methodist Hosp., Iowa Lutheran Hosp., Broadlawns Hosp. (all Des Moines); cons. VA Hosp., Des Moines. Served with M.C., AUS, 1946-48. Diplomate Am. Bd. Dermatology and Syphilology. Fellow Am. Acad. Dermatology; mem. AMA (chmn. com. quackery 1964-66), Iowa Med. Soc., Chgo., Iowa, Minn. dermatol. socs. Home: 207 Glenview Dr Des Moines IA 50312 Office: 1212 Pleasant St Des Moines IA 50309

THOMSEN, ROSZEL C., judge; b. Balt., Aug. 17, 1900; s. William Edward and George A. (Cathcart) T.; ed. Boys Latin Sch., Balt., 1908-15; A.B., Johns Hopkins, 1919; LL.B., U. Md., 1922; LL.D., Goucher Coll., 1967; m. Carol Griffing Wolf, June 1, 1929; children—George, Grace (Mrs. Richard M. Babcock), Margaret Thomsen Moler. Asso. law firm Soper, Bowie & Clark, attys., 1922-27; partner Clark, Thomsen & Smith, 1927-54; U.S. dist. judge Dist. Md., 1954—, chief judge, 1955-70, now sr. judge; judge spl. ct. Regional Rail Reorgn. Act of 1973, 1973—. Instr. comml. law Johns Hopkins, 1933-43; sec. State Bd. Law Examiners, 1943-44; instr. law sch. U. Md., 1952-55. Mem. Jud. Conf. U.S., 1958-64, mem. adv. com. on civil rules, 1960-73, mem. com. to implement Criminal Justice Act, 1964-74, mem. interim adv. com. on jud. activities, 1969-74, mem. com. on adminstrn. criminial law, 1970-73, chmn. standing com. on rules of practice and procedure, 1973—. Pres., Bd. School Commrs. Balt., 1944-54, Alumni Assn. Johns Hopkins, 1947-48; Trustee emeritus, past chmn. bd. Goucher Coll.; v.p. Balt. Council Social Agys., 1943-46. Served with S.A.T.C., 1918. Mem. Am., Md. (pres. 1971), Balt. bar assns., Delta Upsilon, Delta Theta Phi, Phi Beta Kappa, Omicron Delta Kappa. Club: Hamilton Street (Balt.). Home: 118 Enfield Rd Baltimore MD 21212 Office: US Court House Bldg Baltimore MD 21201

THOMSON, ANDREW FRANCIS, film producer; b. Montreal, Que., Can., May 30, 1946; s. Arthur Hugh and Ida Jean (Sears) T.; B.A., Acadia U., 1967; m. Lynn Kristine Walter, Dec. 3, 1971. Film dir. Nat. Film Bd. Can., Montreal, 1968-77, film producer, 1977—. Recipient Acad. Award nomination for documentary short subject, 1976; Yorkton Internat. Film Festival award for best arts film, 1976; Festival of Tourist and Folklore Films award, Brussels, Belgium, 1977 (all for film Blackwood); award Ergofest Film Festival for best safety film, 1975; Diploma of Honour, Poznan Film Festival, Poland, 1978 (both for film The Unplanned). Club: Hudson Yacht. Home: PO Box 76 Como PQ J0P 1A0 Canada Office: PO Box 6100 Montreal PQ H3C 3H5 Canada

THOMSON, BRUCE RANDOLPH, clergyman, coll. adminstr.; b. Harlan, Iowa, Feb. 13, 1922; s. Howard Peter and Myrtle (Knudsen) T.; A.B., William Jewell Coll., 1949; B.D., So. Bapt. Theol. Sem., 1952, Th.M., 1953; M.A., U. Louisville, 1955; Ph.D., Fla. State U., 1959; m. Margaret Ellen Beasley, June 1, 1948; children—Susan Kay, Bruce Randolph. Ordained to ministry Baptist Ch., 1951; prin. San Jacinto Pub. Sch., Vernon, Ind.; instr. U. Louisville, 1954-55; instr. Fla. State U., 1955-57; asso. prof. Queens Coll., Charlotte, N.C., 1957-59; prof., head dept. sociology William Jewell Coll., Liberty, Mo., 1959-64, coll. dean, prof. sociology, 1964—, v.p. academic affairs, dean of coll., 1973-76, v.p. adminstrn., 1976-78, exec. v.p., 1978—; vis. prof. sociology Tex. Tech. U. at Lubbock, 1962 (summer). Mem. Family Life Council, Charlotte, 1957-59; adv. bd. Clay County Welfare Assn., Mo., 1960-63. Served with USNR, 1943-46; capt. Res. Mem. Am. Sociol. Soc., Nat. Council Family Relations, Pi Gamma Mu. Home: 1114 Ridgeway Dr Liberty MO 64068

THOMSON, CLIFTON SAMUEL, lawyer; b. Johannesburg, South Africa, Jan. 3, 1903 (parents Am. citizens); s. Samuel C. and Victoria (Stanton) T.; grad. Hotchkiss Sch., 1920; A.B., Yale, 1924; LL.B., Columbia, 1929; m. Charlotte Calhoun Deyer, June 4, 1927; children—Victoria (Mrs. David W. Romig), Charlotte (Mrs. Johan Iserbyt). Admitted to N.Y. bar, 1929; partner firm Appleton, Rice & Perrin, N.Y.C., 1934-70; gen. counsel, dir. United Dyewood Corp., 1942-50, CIBA Corp., 1946-63. Mayor, Sands Point, N.Y., 1940-47; mem. township com., chmn. police and finance, Mendham Twp., N.J., 1962-68. Mem. Am., N.Y.C. bar assns. Republican. Home: Mosle Rd Far Hills NJ 07931

THOMSON, FREDERICK BURTON, JR., advt. agy. exec.; b. Kingston, N.Y., Mar. 25, 1925; s. Frederick Burton and Nellie Mitchell (Monel) T.; B.A. in Econs., Yale U., 1948; M.B.A., Columbia U., 1950; m. Jean Ruth Lindstrom, June 25, 1949; children—Cynthia Jean, Diane Carol. Account supr. J. Walter Thompson Co., N.Y.C., 1965; account dir. Ted Bates Co., N.Y.C., 1965-73; v.p. mktg. Norton Simon Inc., N.Y.C., 1973-76; mgmt. rep., exec. v.p. Norman Craig & Kummel, N.Y.C., 1976—, also dir. Chmn. Weston (Conn.) Sch. Bd., 1969-72; vice chmn. Youth Fund, Weston; bd. dirs. YMCA, Weston. Served to 1st lt. USMCR, 1943-46, 51-53. Mem. Yale U. Alumni Assn., Columbia Bus. Sch. Assn. Republican. Presbyterian. Club: Duck Island Yacht. Office: 919 3d Ave New York NY 10022

THOMSON, GERALD EDMUND, physician, educator; b. N.Y.C., 1932; s. Lloyd and Sybil (Gilbourne) T.; M.D., Howard U., 1959; m. Carolyn Webber; children—Gregory, Karen. Intern, SUNY-Kings County Hosp. Center, Bklyn., 1959-60, resident in medicine, 1960-62, chief resident, 1962-63, N.Y. Heart Assn. fellow in nephrology, 1964-65, asst. vis. physician, 1963-70, clin. dir. dialysis unit, 1965-67; practice medicine specializing in internal medicine, N.Y.C., 1963—; attending physician SUNY Med. Bklyn. Hosp., 1966-70; instr. in medicine SUNY, Bklyn., 1963-68, clin. asst. prof. medicine, 1968-70; asso. chief med. services Coney Island Hosp., Bklyn., 1967-70; attending physician Presbyn. Hosp., 1970—; dir. nephrology Harlem Hosp. Center, N.Y.C., 1970-71, dir. med. services, 1971—, pres. med. bd., 1976-78; asso. prof. medicine Columbia Coll. Physicians and Surgeons, 1970-72, prof., 1972—. Mem. Health Research Council City N.Y., 1972-75; mem. Hypertension adv. bd. N.Y. Kidney Found., 1971—; mem. Health Research Council, State N.Y., 1975—; mem. hypertension info. and edn. adv. com. NIH, 1973-74, N.Y. State Adv. Com. on Hypertension, 1977—; mem. med. adv. bd. Nat. Assn. Patients on Hemodialysis and Transplantation, 1973—; mem. adv. bd. Sch. Biomed. Edn., City U. N.Y., 1979—; mem. com. on mild hypertension Nat. Heart and Lung Inst., 1976; bd. dirs. N.Y. Heart Assn., 1973—, chmn. com. high blood pressure, 1976—; chmn. com. hypertension N.Y. Met. Regional Med. Program, 1974-76. Diplomate Am. Bd. Internal Medicine. Fellow A.C.P., N.Y. Acad. Medicine (mem. com. medicine in soc. 1974-76); mem. AAAS, N.Y. Soc. Nephrology (pres. 1973-74), Am. Fedn. Clin. Research, Soc. Urban Physicians (pres. 1972-73), Am. Soc. Artificial Internal Organs, Assn. Program Dirs. in Internal Medicine, Alpha Omega Alpha. Mem. adv. bd. Jour. Urban Health, 1974—. Home: 118 Whitman Dr Brooklyn NY 11234 Office: Harlem Hosp Center 506 Lenox Ave New York NY 10037

THOMSON, HARRY PLEASANT, JR., lawyer; b. Kansas City, Mo., May 9, 1917; s. Harry Pleasant and Alice F. (DeWolff) T.; A.B., U. Mo., 1937, J.D., 1939; m. Martha Jean Martin, May 3, 1941; children—Jane Anne (Mrs. Edward G. McCarthy), Carol Lee, (Mrs. George Hodgkin), Lisa Clair. Admitted to Mo. bar, 1939, also U.S. Supreme Ct. bar; practiced in Kansas City, 1939—; chmn. bd. firm Shughart, Thomson & Kilroy, P.C.; lectr. Mo. Continuing Legal Edn. Programs, 1961-78. Mem. Mo. Supreme Ct. Com. on Jury Instrns., 1962—, chmn., 1977—; mem. Commn. on Retirement, Removal & Discipline of Judges, 1972—. Trustee U. Mo. Law Sch. Found., 1975—. Served to lt. USNR, 1942-46. Recipient certificate of appreciation for distinguished service Mo. Bar, 1964. Fellow Am. Coll. Trial Lawyers (regent 1967-68); mem. Lawyers Assn. Kanss City (past pres.), Kansas City Claims Assn. (past pres.), Internat. Assn. Ins. Counsel, Mo. Bar Assn. (bd. govs. 1967-71, exec. com. 1970-71), Am. Bar Assn., Am. Judicature Soc., Internat. Soc. Barristers, Order DeMolay Legion of Honor, Phi Beta Kappa, Order of Coif, Psi Chi, Sigma Chi, Delta Theta Phi. Clubs: University (pres. 1977), Carriage (Kansas City); Rotary. Author: (with others) Missouri Approved Jury Instructions, 1964. Mem. bd. editors Mo. Law Rev., 1938-39; contbr. articles to profl. jours. Home: 1216 W 69th St Kansas City MO 64113 Office: Commerce Bldg Kansas City MO 64106

THOMSON, JAMES CAMPBELL, editor; b. Hamilton, Scotland, Dec. 19, 1912 (came to U.S. 1924, naturalized 1930); s. John Dick and Isabelle (Casement) T.; B.S., U. Ill. at Urbana, 1935, postgrad., 1937; postgrad. Northwestern U., 1946; m. Ruth Varner, July 10, 1958; children—Gael Thomson Romoser, Shelley Thomson Reichle, James M., Scot D., Alison. With Ill. Newspapers, 1935-41, Chgo. Bur. A.P., 1941-46; editor Record, Ill. Agrl. Assn., Chgo., 1946-50; mng. editor Prairie Farmer, Chgo., 1950-64, editor, 1964-78; info. dir. Assn. Am. Physicians and Surgeons, Burke, Va. Adv. com. U. Ill. Coll. Agr., 1968-74; mem. Gov.'s Agrl. Export Adv. Com. Bd. dirs. Country Life Assn. (4-H citation 1969), Scottish Home, Riverside, Ill.; bd. dirs. Chgo. Farmers Club, pres., 1978-79. Recipient Editor's award DeKalb Agr. Assn., 1960, 67, Service medal Fed. Land Bank, St. Louis, 1967, editor's award Pfizer & Co., 1967; Ill. Hon. Star Farmer, Future Farmers Am., 1964; Service to Agr. award U. Ill. Coll. Agr. Alumni Assn., 1977; Ill. Agr. Extension award, 1975. Mem. Am. Agrl. Editors Assn. (pres. 1966), Chgo. Fin. Writers Assn. (pres. 1970-71), Ill. St. Andrew Soc. (pres. 1979-80), Sigma Delta Chi, Gamma Sigma Delta. Presbyn. Mason. Clubs: Press, Headline, Agribusiness (pres. 1970) (Chgo.). Home: 2 Atrium Way Elmhurst IL 60126

THOMSON, JAMES CLAUDE, JR., educator; b. Princeton, N.J., Sept. 14, 1931; s. James Claude and Margaret Seabury (Cook) T.; grad. Lawrenceville Sch., 1948; student U. Nanking (China), 1948-49; B.A., Yale, 1953; B.A. (Yale-Clare fellow), U. Cambridge (Eng.), 1955, M.A., 1959; Ph.D., Harvard, 1961; m. Diana Dodge Duffy Butler, Dec. 19, 1959; stepchildren—Anne Butler, Lawrence D. Butler. Teaching fellow, tutor Harvard, 1956-59; spl. asst. to U.S. congressman, 1960-61; spl. asst. to under sec. state Dept. State, 1961; spl. asst. to Pres.'s Spl. Rep. and Adviser on African, Asian, Latin Am. affairs, 1961-63; spl. asst. to asst. Sec. State for Far Eastern Affairs, 1963-64; staff mem. Nat. Security Council, 1964-66; asst. prof. history, research fellow Inst. Politics, Harvard 1966-70; curator Nieman Found. for Journalism, 1972—; lectr. history, gen. edn., 1970—. Trustee Lawrenceville Sch., Yale China Assn. Mem. Nat. Com. on U.S.-China Relations, Assn. Asian Studies, Council on Fgn. Relations, Am. Hist. Assn., Phi Beta Kappa, Zeta Psi, Scroll and Key. Democrat. Presbyn. Clubs: Signet (Cambridge); Elizabethan (New Haven); Harvard, St. Botolph (Boston). Author: While China Faced West-American Reformers in Nationalist China, 1928-37, 1969; (with E.R. May) American-East Asian Relations-A Survey, 1972. Pub. Nieman Reports. Editorial bd. Fgn. Policy Mag. Contbr. to mags., newspapers, TV, profl. jours. Home: 21 Sibley Ct Cambridge MA 02138 Office: Nieman Found for Journalism 1 Francis Ave Cambridge MA 02138

THOMSON, JAMES ROBERT, JR., educator; b. Tuscaloosa, Ala., Aug. 9, 1926; s. James Robert and Ruth (Dorman) T.; A.B., U. Ala., 1949, M.A., 1954, Ed.D., 1960; m. Rebecca Ramsey, Mar. 18, 1948; children—James Robert III, Ollie Ramsey. Tchr., Tuscaloosa County High Sch., Northport, Ala., 1949-56; prin. Hope Elementary Sch., Tuscaloosa County, Ala., 1956-58; asst. prof. gen. edn. Miss. State U., 1960-63, head dept. elementary and secondary edn., 1963-72, dir. student teaching, 1963-69, 72—. Dir. recreation, Northport, 1953-58. Served with AUS, 1945-46. Mem. Assn. Student Teaching, Miss. Assn. Student Teaching (pres. 1968), Nat., Miss. edn. assns., Phi Delta Kappa, Kappa Delta Pi. Methodist (chmn. ofcl. bd. 1951-52, chmn. com. edn. 1958-60, supt. ch. sch. 1963-67). Home: 109 Margaretta Dr Starkville MS 39759 Office: PO Drawer LM Mississippi State MS 39762

THOMSON, KEITH STEWART, biologist, univ. dean; b. Heanor, Eng., July 29, 1938; s. Ronald William and Marian Adelaide (Coster) T.; B.Sc. with honors, U. Birmingham (Eng.), 1960; A.M., Harvard U., 1961, Ph.D. (NATO fellow), 1963; m. Linda Gailbreath Price, Sept. 27, 1963; children—Jessica Adelaide, Elizabeth Rose. NATO postdoctoral fellow Univ. Coll., London U., 1963-65; asst. prof. to prof. biology Yale U., 1965—, dean Grad. Sch., 1979—, dir. Peabody Mus. Natural History, 1977-79; dir. Sears Found. Marine Research and Oceanographic History; hon. research fellow Australian Nat. U., 1967. Fellow Linaean Soc. London, Zool. Soc. London; mem. Am. Soc. Naturalists, Am. Soc. Zoologists, Soc. Nautical Research, Soc. Vertebrate Palaeontology, Sigma Xi. Club: Yale (N.Y.C.). Contbr. numerous articles to profl. jours.; research in vertebrate evolution. Office: Hall of Grad Studies Yale U New Haven CT 06520

THOMSON, KENNETH ROY, newspaper exec.; b. Toronto, Ont., Can., Sept. 1, 1923; s. Roy Herbert and Edna (Irvine) T.; student Upper Can. Coll.; B.A., U. Cambridge (Eng.), 1945, M.A., 1947; m. Nora Marilyn Lavis, June 13, 1956; children—David Kenneth Roy, Lesley Lynne, Peter John. With Thomson Newspapers, Ltd., 1947—, with editorial dept. Timmins (Ont.) Daily Press, 1947; with advt. dept. Galt (Ont.) Reporter, 1948-50, gen. mgr., 1950-53, dir. Can. and Am. ops., 1953-67, now chmn. bd., chief exec. officer, dir.; chmn. bd., dir. Thomson Corp. Ltd., Thomson Orgn. Ltd., Woodbridge Co. Ltd., Thomson Equitable Corp. Ltd., Thomson Newspapers Inc. (U.S.), Thomson Brit. Holdings Ltd., Eng., Internat. Thomson Orgn., Ltd., Toronto; co-pres. Times Newspapers, Ltd., London; pres., dir. Dominion-Consol. Holdings Ltd., Fleet St. Pubs. Ltd., Kenthom Holdings Ltd., 96015 Ont. Ltd., Ont. Newspapers Ltd., Standard St. Lawrence Co. Ltd., Thomson Internat. Corp. Ltd., Thomson Mississauga Properties Ltd., Thomson Works of Art Ltd., Thomwood Holdings Ltd.; dir. Abitibi-Price Inc., Toronto Dominion Bank, others; v.p., dir. Cablevue (Quinte) Ltd., Veribest Products Ltd. Served with RCAF, World War II. Baptist. Clubs: National, Toronto, Granite, York Downs, Toronto Hunt, York (Toronto). Home: 8 Castle Frank Rd Toronto ON M4W 2Z4 Canada also 8 Kensington Palace Gardens London W8 England Office: Thomson Orgn Ltd 4 Stratford Pl London W1 England also Thomson Newspapers Ltd 65 Queen St W Toronto ON M5H 2M8 Canada also Times Newspapers Ltd Printing House Sq Gray's Inn Rd London EC4 England

THOMSON, LEWIS CLARK, co. exec., lawyer; b. Cin., Nov. 25, 1917; s. Alexander and Mary Moore (Dabney) T.; A.B., Yale, 1940; law student U. Va., 1940-41; LL.B., U. Cin., 1946; m. Betty Orr Bullock, July 5, 1947; children—Margaret McCreadie, Christie Dabney, Carol Orr. Admitted to Ohio bar, 1947; asso. Frost & Jacobs, Cin., 1947-48; asso. counsel legal dept. Champion Paper & Fibre Co., 1948, dir. gen. legal dept., 1949-55, dir., 1944-62, asst. sec., 1950-55, v.p. and sec., 1955-60; v.p., sec., dir. Thomson Bros., Inc., Cin., 1945-62; v.p., sec. Silverlith Corp., Washington, 1962—. Trustee Western Coll. Women, Oxford, Ohio, 1955-67, Cin. Art Mus., 1961-63. Served as lt. USNR, 1942-46. Decorated Navy unit commendation medal. Mem. Ohio Mfrs. Assn. (pres. 1958-60), Ohio C. of C. (dir. 1959-61, exec. com. 1959-61), Ohio Bar Assn., Chi Psi, Phi Delta Phi. Episcopalian. Clubs: Chevy Chase (Md.). Address: 201 W Chew Ave Humboldt Pravada 70A Cuernevaca Morales Mexico

THOMSON, PAUL RICE, JR., U.S. atty.; b. Syracuse, N.Y., Dec. 28, 1941; B.A. in History, Va. Mil. Inst., 1963; J.D., Washington and Lee U., 1966. Admitted to Va. bar, 1966, Ct. Mil. Appeals bar, 1967; judge adv. USMC, 1966-69; asso. firm Clement, Wheatley, Winston & Ingram, Danville, Va., 1969-71; asst. U.S. atty. Western Dist. Va., Roanoke, 1971-75, U.S. atty., 1975—; pres. Roanoke Valley Law Enforcement Council, 1975-76; mem. Bd. Conciliation and Arbitration Panel, Richmond (Va.) Diocese; mem. Fed.-State Law Enforcement Council, 1975—. Vice pres. Danville Jr. C. of C., 1971. Recipient Spl. Achievement award Dept. Justice, 1974. Mem. Va. Bar Assn., Assn. Trial Lawyers Am. Office: Poff Fed Bldg Franklin and 2d St PO Box 1709 Roanoke VA 24008

THOMSON, PETER NESBITT, corp. exec.; b. Westmount, Que., Can., Mar. 22, 1926; s. Peter Alfred and Charlotte (Corey) T.; student Lower Can. Coll., Sir George Williams Coll.; LL.D. (hon.), St. Thomas U., Fredericton, N.B., Can., 1968; children—Peter Alfred W., Frances Patricia. With Investment Secretariat Ltd., Montreal, Ont., 1944; chmn. TWI Industries Ltd., Ottawa, Ont., Can.; chmn., chief exec. officer Thomcor Holdings Ltd., P. Lawson Travel Ltd.; dir. Bathurst Paper Ltd., Caribbean Utilities Co. Ltd., Canbro U.K. Ltd., Commonwealth Indsl. Bank Ltd., Nassau, Consol. Bathurst Inc., Domglas Ltd., Garibaldi Lifts Ltd., Petrofina Can. Ltd., Power Corp. Can., Ltd., Power Corp. Internat. Ltd., Radisson Furniture Ltd., Roy West Banking Corp., Shawiningan Industries Ltd., Sterling Tankers Ltd., The Point Farm Inc., Trans Can. Corp. Funds, Royal Bank of Can., W.I. Power Corp. Ltd. Clubs: Mt. Bruno Golf (Montreal); Saint James, Royal Canadian Yacht; Royal St. Lawrence Yacht; Annabel's; Palm Bay (Miami); Lyford Cay (Nassau); Eastern Ionosphere. Office: 150 Albert St Ottawa ON K1P 5G2 Canada

THOMSON, RICHARD JAMES, petroleum co. exec.; b. Pomona, Calif., Oct. 4, 1932; s. James Frederick and Ruth Elizabeth (Howell) T.; B.A., Pomona Coll., 1954; postgrad. Calif. State U. at Los Angeles, 1956-59; m. Annette B. Heath, Aug. 8, 1965; children—Gary, Linda, Mark, Gary, Lee, Alan. Staff accountant Price Waterhouse, Los Angeles, 1956-60; mgr. corp. accounting Aerojet Gen. Corp., El Monte, Calif., 1960-67; controller Santa Fe Internat. Corp., Orange, Calif., 1967—. Served with AUS, 1954-56. Mem. Town Hall Los Angeles, Am. Inst. C.P.A.'s, Calif. Soc. C.P.A.'s, Fin. Execs. Inst. Republican. Home: 15439 Los Altos Dr Hacienda Heights CA 91745 Office: PO Box 1401 Orange CA 92668

THOMSON, RICHARD MURRAY, banker; b. Winnipeg, Can., Aug. 14, 1933; s. H.W. and Mary T.; B.A.Sc. in Engring., U. Toronto, 1955; M.B.A., Harvard, 1957; fellow course banking, Queen's U., 1958; m. Heather Lorimer; children—Robin, Elizabeth, Mary Dawn, Richard. With Toronto Dominion Bank, 1957—, chief gen. mgr., 1968-72, v.p., dir., 1971-72, pres., 1972-77, chmn., chief exec. officer, 1977—, chmn., 1978—; dir. Canadian Gypsum Co. Ltd., Eaton's of Can., S.C. Johnson & Co. Ltd., Texasgulf, Inc., Union Carbide Can., Cadillac Fairview Corp. Ltd., Prudential Ins. Co. Am., Midland & Internat. Banks Ltd. Trustee Hosp. for Sick Children. Office: Toronto Dominion Bank PO Box 1 Toronto Dominion Centre Toronto ON M5K 1A2 Canada

THOMSON, ROBERT WILLIAM, educator; b. Cheam, Eng., Mar. 24, 1934 (came to U.S., 1963); s. David William and Lilian (Cramphorn) T.; B.A., Cambridge (Eng.) U., 1955, M.A., 1958, Ph.D., 1962; licence, Louvain (Belgium) U.; 1962; M.A. (hon.), Harvard, 1969; m. Judith Ailsa Cawdry, Apr. 20, 1963; children—Jasper Rupert, Crispin Simon. Jr. fellow Dumbarton Oaks, 1960-61; research fellow Harvard, 1961-63, mem. faculty, 1963—, prof. Armenian studies, 1969—. Mem. Am. Oriental Soc., Brit. Sch. Archaeology in Ankara, Brit. Inst. Persian Studies in Teheran, Mediaeval Acad. Am. Author: Athanasiana Syriaca, Part I, 1965, Part II, 1967, Part III, 1972, Part IV, 1977; The Teaching of Saint Gregory, 1970; Athanasius: Contra Gentes and De Incarnatione, 1970; An Introduction to Classical Armenian, 1975; Agathangelos: History of the Armenians, 1976; (with K.B. Bardakjian) Textbook of Modern Western Armenian, 1977; Moses Khorenatsi: History of the Armenians, 1978; editor: (with J.N. Birdsall) Biblical and Patristic Studies in Memory of Robert Pierce Casey, 1963; Recent Studies in Modern Armenian History, 1972. Home: 77 Kensington Park Arlington MA 02174

THOMSON, THYRA GODFREY, state ofcl.; b. Florence, Colo., July 30, 1916; d. John and Rosalie (Altman) Godfrey; B.A. cum laude, U. Wyo., 1939; m. Keith Thomson, Aug. 6, 1939 (dec. Dec. 1960); children—William John, Bruce Godfrey, Keith Coffey. With dept. agronomy and agrl. econs. U. Wyo., 1938-39; writer weekly column Watching Washington pub. in 14 papers, Wyo., 1955-60; planning chmn. Nat. Fedn. Republican Women, Washington, 1961; sec. state Wyo., Cheyenne, 1962—. Mem. Marshall Scholarships Com. for Pacific region, 1964-68; del. 72d Wilton Park Conf., Eng., 1965; mem. youth commn. UNESCO, 1970-71, Allied Health Professions Council HEW, 1971-72. Recipient Distinguished Alumni award U. Wyo., 1969; named Internat. Woman of Distinction, Alpha Delta Kappa; recipient citation Omicron Delta Epsilon, 1965, Beta Gamma Sigma, 1968, Delta Kappa Gamma, 1973. Mem. N.Am. Securities Adminstrs. (pres. 1973-74), Nat. Assn. Secs. of State, Council State Govts. (chmn. natural resources com. Western states 1966-68), Nat. Conf. Lt. Govs. (exec. com. 1976-79). Home: 3102 Sunrise Rd Cheyenne WY 82001 Office: Capitol Bldg Cheyenne WY 82002

THOMSON, VERNON WALLACE, former congressman, govt. ofcl.; b. Richland Center, Wis., Nov. 5, 1905; s. Alva A. and Ella M. (Wallace) T.; student Carroll Coll., 1923-25, LL.D., 1956; B.A., U. Wis., 1927, LL.B., 1932; m. Helen Davis, June 6, 1936 (dec.); children—Patricia, Susan, Vernon Wallace. Tchr., Viroqua (Wis.) High Sch., 1927-29, Madison (Wis.) Vocational Sch.; admitted to Wis. bar, 1932; practiced law, Richland Center, until 1951; enrolling officer Civilian Conservation Corps, 1933-35; asst. dist. atty. Richland County, 1933-35; city atty. Richland Center, 1933-37, 42-44; mem. Wis. Assembly, 1935-51, speaker, 1939, 41, 43, Republican floor leader, 1945, 47, 49; mayor Richland Center, 1944-51; atty. gen. Wis., 1951-57; gov. Wis., 1956-58; practice law, Madison, 1959-60; mem. 87th-93d congresses 3d Dist. Wis.; mem. house com. on fgn. affairs, house select com. on small bus.; mem. Fed. Election Commn., 1975—, chmn., 1976-77. Mem. advisory com. on rules, pleadings, practice, procedure Wis. Supreme Ct., 1945-51; mem., sec. Wis. Legis. Council, 1949-51; mem. Wis. Jud. Council, 1951—. Pres., Richland Center Library Bd., 1939-51. Del. to Rep. nat. convs., 1936, 40, 52, 56; presdl. elector, 1952, 56. Mem. Order of Coif, Chi Phi, Phi Delta Phi. Mason (33 deg.). Home: 6213 Kellogg Dr McLean VA 22101 Office: 1325 K St NW Washington DC 20463

THOMSON, VIRGIL, composer, music critic; b. Kansas City, Mo., Nov. 25, 1896; s. Quincy A. and May (Gaines) T.; A.B., Harvard, 1922; studied in Paris under Nadia Boulanger; A.F.D., Syracuse U., 1949; Lit.D., Rutgers U., 1956; L.H.D., Park Coll., 1966, Johns Hopkins U., 1978; A.F.D., (hon.), Roosevelt U., 1968, U. Mo., 1971; Mus.D., Fairfield U., 1968, N.Y. U., 1971, Columbia U., 1978. U. Mo., 1972. Began as choirmaster and organist, King's Chapel, Boston; lived in Paris 10 years; has been writer on music for Vanity Fair, Boston Transcript, Modern Music, N.Y. Rev. of Books; music critic N.Y. Herald Tribune, 1940-54. Composer: (opera) Four Saints in Three Acts, The Mother of Us All, Lord Byron; (ballet) Filling Station, The Harvest According, Bayou, Hurrah!, Parson Weems and the Cherry Tree; (for orch.) Symphony on a Hymn Tune, Second Symphony, Third Symphony, Five Suites, Five Songs from William Blake, Concerto for Cello and Orchestra, Concerto for Flute, Strings and Percussion, Autumn Concertino for Harp, Strings and Percussion, The Feast of Love for baritone and orch., The Seine at Night, Wheat Field at Noon, Sea Piece with Birds, Fugues and Cantilenas, Fantasy in Homage to an Earlier England, A Solemn Music and A Joyful Fugue, Ode to the Wonders of Nature, Ship Wreck and Love Scene from Byron's Don Juan for tenor and orch.; Eleven Organ Chorales by Brahms; (choral works) Capital Capitals, Masses, Medea, Scenes from the Holy Infancy, Missa Pro Defunctis (with orch.), The Nativity for Choir, Orchestra and Organ, Cantata on Poems of Edward Lear with soprano and baritone, Dance in Praise; (chamber music) Sonata da Chiesa, Sonata for Violin and Piano, Four Piano Sonatas, 100 Portraits, Family Portrait for brass quintet, Three String Quartets; (music for motion pictures) The Plow that Broke the Plains, The River, Louisiana Story, The Goddess, Power Among Men, Tuesday in November, Journey to America; also many songs and selections for piano and organ. Decorated Officer Legion d'Honneur; recipient gold medal National Inst. Arts and Letters, 1966; Creative Arts award medal Brandeis U., 1968; Pulitzer prize, 1949; Macdowell award, 1977; Guggenheim fellow, 1960. Fellow Am. Acad. Arts and Scis.; mem. Am. Acad. Arts and Letters. Author: State of Music, 1939; The Musical Scene, 1945; The Art of Judging Music, 1948; Music Right and Left, 1951; Virgil Thomson by Virgil Thomson, 1966; Music Reviewed, 1940-54, 1967; American Music Since 1910, 1971. Address: 222 W 23d St New York City NY 10011

THON, J. GEORGE, cons. engr.; b. Lwow, Austria, Dec. 6, 1908; s. Osias and Claire S. (Rittel) T.; came to U.S., 1949, naturalized, 1952; B.S. in Civil Engring., U. Lwow, 1932; Diplomate Imperial Coll. Sci. and Tech., London, 1939; M.S. in Structural Engring., U. London, 1941; postgrad. exec. program Stanford U., 1967; m. Dawn C. Newberger, Oct. 23, 1949; 1 dau., Carolyn Alice. Design engr. Sir William Halcrow & Partners, London, 1941-48; hydraulic engr. Pioneer Service and Engring. Co., Chgo., 1949-51; chief civil engr. Bechtel Corp., San Francisco, 1951-58; div. mgr. engring., 1958-74, exec. cons., 1974-76; v.p. Overseas Bechtel Inc., San Francisco, 1958-74; cons. engr., San Mateo, Calif., 1977—; cons. NSF, NRC. Served with Brit. Armed Forces, 1942. Recipient Tercer Lugar prize Pan-Am. Congress Engrs., 1964. Fellow ASCE (chmn. power div. exec. com. 1963-65, 72-73, Thomas Fitch Rowland prize 1959, Rickey medal 1971, mem. nat. energy policy com.), Instn. Civil Engrs.; mem. Nat. Acad. Engring., U.S. Commn. on Large Dams, Engrs. Club San Francisco (dir. 1965-68). Clubs: Commonwealth, Old Centralians, London. Patentee in field. Contbr. articles to profl. jours. Home: 465 Barbara Way Hillsborough CA 94010 Office: Suite 310 100 S Ellsworth Ave San Mateo CA 94401

THON, ROBERT WILLIAM, JR., banker; b. Richmond, Va., Dec. 23, 1908; s. Robert William and Amanda (Kosslow) T.; Ph.D., Johns Hopkins, 1933; m. Evelyn Ellen Singleton, Apr. 1, 1936; children—Robert William III, Susan Cecelia, Richard McMichael. Asst. to pres. Savs. Bank of Balt., 1933-45, v.p., dir., 1945-59, pres., dir., 1959-75, chmn. bd., 1975—. Mem. Banking Bd. of Md., Bank Relations Bd. of Md. Commr., Balt. Urban Renewal and Housing Agy., 1962-64. Chmn., Balt. Community Chest-Red Cross United Appeal, 1958. Mem. C. of C. of Met. Balt., Nat. Assn. Mut. Savs. Banks (exec. com. 1956-57), Asso. Mut. Savs. Banks Md. (pres. 1956-57). Clubs: Johns Hopkins, Bond, Municipal Bond (Balt.); Country of Md.; Merchants; Virginians of Md. Home: 109 Ridgewood Rd Baltimore MD 21210 Office: 1 E Baltimore St Baltimore MD 21203

THON, WILLIAM, artist; b. N.Y.C., Aug. 8, 1906; s. Felix Leo and Jane (Upham) T.; student Art Students League, 1924-25; A.F.D., Bates Coll., 1957; m. Helen Elizabeth Walters, June 3, 1929. Represented in nat. art exhibits at Corcoran, Art Inst. Chgo., Pa. Acad., Va. Mus., Toldeo Mus., Met. Mus., Nat. Acad., Carnegie Inst.; represented in permanent collections of Swope Art Gallery, Terre Haute, Ind.; Farnsworth Mus., Rockland, Maine; Bloomington Art Assn., Encyclopedia Brit., Toledo Mus., Am. Acad. Arts and Letters; Mus. of Ann Arbor, Mich., Met. Mus., N.Y.C., U. Hawaii, Honolulu, Johnson's Wax Collection, and others. Artist in residence Am. Acad., Rome, 1956. Recipient prize Salmagundi Club, 1941, Bklyn. Mus., 1942, Dana Watercolor medal Pa. Acad., 1950; recipient 2d Altman prize for landscape, Nat. Acad., N.Y.C., 1951, 1st Altman prize, 1954, 67; Nat. Inst. Arts and Letters grant, 1951, Palmer Meml. prize, Nat. Acad., 1944, Bklyn. Mus. prize, 1945, Prix de Rome, 1947, Samuel F.B. Morse medal Nat. Acad., 1956, silver medal Am. Watercolor Soc., 1957, 67, gold medal of honor, 1970; recipient Altman prize, landscape, Nat. Acad., 1961, Gordon Grant Meml. Award, Am. Watercolcor Soc., 1963, Adolph and Clara Obrig prize Nat. Acad., 1965, Maine State award, 1970, Lena Newcastle Meml. award Am. Watercolor Soc., 1976, Ranger Fund Purchase award Nat. Acad., 1976. Served with USNR, 1942-46. Mem. Nat. Inst. Arts and Letters, N.A.D., Am. Watercolor Soc. (Gold Medal of Honor 1979), Audubon Artists, Friendship Sloop Soc. Home: Port Clyde ME 04855

THONE, CHARLES, gov. Nebr.; b. Hartington, Nebr., Jan. 4, 1924; J.D., U. Nebr., 1950; m. Ruth Raymond, 1953; children—Ann, Mary, Amy. Admitted to Nebr. bar, 1950, U.S. Supreme Ct. bar, 1956; individual practice law, 1959—; dep. sec. state Nebr., 1950-51, Republican presdl. elector, 1952, 56, 60, 68; asst. U.S. dist. atty., Lincoln, Nebr., 1952-54; adminstrv. asst. Senator Roman Hruska, 1954-59; mem. 92d-95th Congresses from 1st dist. Nebr.; gov. State of Nebr., Lincoln, 1979—. Chmn., Lincoln Human Rights Commn., 1967-68; bd. govs. John G. Neihardt Found., 1968—. Mem. Lincoln, Nebr., Am. bar assns. Office: Governor's Office State Capitol Lincoln NE 68509

THOR, DANIEL EINAR, immunologist; b. Davenport, Iowa, Sept. 4, 1938; s. Harry Raymond and Florence Elvira (Berglund) T.; student Monmouth Coll., 1956-59; M.D., U. Ill., 1963, Ph.D., 1968; m. Lois Anita Vistain, Jan. 9, 1971; children—Emaly Alida, Carlton George James Vistain. Intern, Presbyn.-St. Luke's Hosp., Chgo., 1963-64, resident, 1964-66; instr. surgery, medicine, microbiology U. Ill. Hosps., Chgo., 1966-68; research investigator NIH, Bethesda, Md., 1968-71; asso. prof. microbiology, pathology U. Tex. Health Sci.

Center, San Antonio, 1971-76, prof., 1976—; mem. com. immunodiagnosis Nat. Cancer Inst., NIH, 1973-78. Bd. dirs. Cancer Therapy and Research Found. S. Tex., Asthma and Immunology Found., San Antonio. Served to sr. surgeon USPHS, 1968-71. Recipient Landsteiner Centennial award, 1969. Fellow Am. Soc. Clin. Oncology, Am. Soc. Exptl. Biology; mem. Am. Assn. Immunologists, Am. Assn. Cancer Research, AAAS, Reticuloendothelial Soc., AAUP, Gideons Internat. (pres. San Antonio North Camp 1974-76), Am. Soc. Internal Medicine, Sigma Xi. Contbr. articles to profl. jours. Home: 2743 Whisper Path San Antonio TX 78230 Office: U Tex Health Sci Center 7703 Floyd Curl Dr San Antonio TX 78284

THORBECKE, ERIK, economist; b. Berlin, Feb. 17, 1929; s. William and Madelaine (Salisbury) T.; student Netherlands Sch. Econs., Rotterdam, 1948-51; Ph.D., U. Calif., 1957; m. Charla J. Westerberg, Oct. 17, 1954; children—Erik Charles, Willem, Jon. Asst. prof. econs. Iowa State U., 1957-60, asso. prof., 1960-63, prof., 1963-73; prof. Cornell U., 1974—, chmn. dept. econs., 1975-78, H.E. Babcock prof. econs. and food econs., 1978—; econ. adviser Nat. Planning Inst., Lima, Peru, 1963-64; asso. asst. adminstr. for program policy AID, Washington, 1966-68, mem. research advisory com., 1976—; sr. economist world employment program Internat. Labor Office, Geneva, 1972-73; cons. in field. Mem. Am. Econ. Assn., Am. Assn. Agrl. Econs. (Nat. award for best pub. research 1970). Author: The Tendency Towards Regionalization in International Trade, 1960; (with Irma Adelman) Theory and Design of Economic Development, 1966; (with K. Fox, J. Sengupta) Theory of Quantitative Economic Policy, 1968; Role of Agriculture in Economic Development, 1968; (with G. Pyatt) Planning Techniques for a Better Future, 1976. Home: 108 N Sunset Dr Ithaca NY 14850 Office: Dept Econs Cornell U Ithaca NY 14853

THORELLI, HANS B., economist, educator; Ph.D., LL.B., U. Stockholm; m.; 2 children. E.W. Kelley prof. bus. adminstrn., former chmn. mktg. Grad. Sch. Bus., Ind. U., Bloomington; former mem. faculty U. Chgo.; indsl. cons.; staff cons. UN, Gen. Electric; vis. prof. U. Chile, U. Argentina, U. S. Africa, London Grad. Sch. Bus. Studies, U. Lausanne. Mem. Pres.'s Consumer Adv. Council, 1975-77; mem. nat. adv. council SBA, 1976-78. Mem. Am. Mktg. Assn. (v.p. 1972-73), other profl. orgns. Author: The Federal Anti-Trust Policy of the United States; International Operations Simulation; International Marketing Strategy; Consumer Information Handbook; The Information Seekers; Consumer Information Systems and Public Policy; Strategy Plus Structure Equals Performance; numerous other publs. Address: Ind University Graduate School of Business Bloomington IN 47401

THORESEN, ASA CLIFFORD, educator; b. Blenheim, New Zealand, Sept. 9, 1930 (came to U.S. 1949, naturalized 1958); s. Francis Olaf and Helen (Hagan) T.; B.A., Andrews U., 1954; M.A., Walla Walla Coll., 1958; Ph.D., Ore. State U., 1960; m. Shirley Avona Scarr, Aug. 31, 1952; children—Davona Gae, Meylan Craig. Asst. prof. biology Andrews U., Berrien Springs, Mich., 1960-63, asso. prof., 1963-67, prof., 1967—, chmn. dept. biology, 1963—; vis. prof. biology Walla Walla Coll. Marine Biol. Sta., summers, 1960, 63, 70, 76. Served with AUS, 1954-56. Mem. Ornithol. Union Am., Cooper, New Zealand ornithol. socs., Sigma Xi. Mem. Seventh-day Adventist Ch. Home: Rt 1 Box 379D Berrien Springs MI 49103

THORFINNSON, ARTHUR RODNEY, hosp. adminstr.; b. Sask., Can., Nov. 30, 1934; s. Arthur Sigurjon and Wilhelmine Bernice (Krause) T.; B.A., U. Sask., 1958; D.H.A., U. Toronto, 1960; m. Kathleen Elizabeth Fennell, Sept. 10, 1957; children—LeAnne Elizabeth, Rodney Michael, John Douglas. Hosp. adminstrv. cons. Govt. Sask., 1960-61; asst. exec. dir., then exec. dir. Sask. Hosp. Assn., 1961-64; asst. dir. Univ. Hosp., Saskatoon, 1964-65; asst. dir.-adminstr. Victoria Hosp., London, Ont., Can., 1965-69, exec. dir., 1970—; pres. Victoria Hosp. Corp., London, 1977—; v.p. Com-Tron Systems Ltd., London, Ont., 1969-70. Fellow Am. Coll. Hosp. Adminstrs.; mem. Canadian Coll. Health Service Execs., London C. of C. Home: 10 Friars Way London ON N6G 2A8 Canada Office: 375 South St London ON N6A 4G5 Canada

THORINGTON, ROBERT DINNING, lawyer; b. Montgomery, Ala., Sept. 30, 1932; s. Jack and Anne Paul (Thompson) T.; B.S., U. Ala., 1953, LL.B., 1957; LL.M. in Taxation, N.Y.U., 1958; m. Winifred Ann Pilcher, Aug. 1, 1953; children—Winifred Goldthwaite, Elisabeth Gindrat, Robert Dinning. Admitted to Ala. bar, 1957; since practiced in Montgomery; partner firm Johnson & Thorington, 1973—. Mem. spl. liaison tax com. Southeastern Region, 1966-69; chmn. bd. So. Fed. Tax Inst., 1968-69, trustee, 1965—. Bd. dirs., co-founder, pres. Montgomery Community Concerts Assn.; bd. dirs. Landmarks Found. Served to 1st lt. AUS, 1953-55. Fellow Am. Coll. Probate Counsel; mem. Ala. State Bar (chmn. sect. taxation 1965-66), Men of Montgomery, Soc. Pioneers Montgomery (trustee), Farrah Law Soc., Phi Eta Sigma, Phi Gamma Delta. Episcopalian (vestryman 1974-77). Kiwanian. Home: 2425 Midfield Dr Montgomery AL 36111 Office: 504 S Perry St Montgomery AL 36104

THORKELSON, WILLMAR, journalist; b. Trail, Minn., June 15, 1918; s. William and Lena (Langseth) T.; B.A., Concordia Coll., Moorhead, Minn., 1936-40, Litt. D. (hon.), 1962; M.A., U. Minn., 1948; m. Maxine B. Mohn, June 22, 1945; children—Susan, Peter. Reporter, Bismarck (N.D.) Tribune, 1940-41; asst. editor Detroit Lakes (Minn.) Tribune, 1941; teaching asst. U. Minn., 1941-42; mem. staff Mpls. Star, 1942—, religion editor, 1946—; press officer World Council Chs., Geneva, Switzerland, 1948-49; corr. Religious News Service; past sec., dir. Augsburg Pub. House. Past sec., dir. Greater Mpls. Council Chs. Recipient Faith and Freedom award Religious Heritage Am., 1959, 76; citation NCCJ, 1963; William E. Leidt award Exec. Council Episcopal Ch., 1977. Mem. Religion Newswriters Assn. (pres. 1962-64, Supple award, 1955), Nordmanns-Forbundet, Sons of Norway, Sigma Delta Chi. Lutheran. Author: Fifty Fraternal Years, History of Lutheran Brotherhood, 1968; Lutherans in the U.S.A., 1969, rev., 1978; Report on Conference on Relevancy and Future of Organized Religion, 1970. Home: 4851 Dawnview Terr Minneapolis MN 55422 Office: 425 Portland Ave Minneapolis MN 55415

THORN, FRANK JOSEF, hotel exec.; b. Munich, W. Ger., Apr. 21, 1938; s. Josef and Rosa (Welker) T.; B.A., Hotel Sch. Munich; postgrad. Cornell U.; m. Ingrid Huber, Feb. 25, 1961; children—Frank Josef, Heico, Sabina. Regional food and beverage dir. Loew's Hotel Corp., N.Y.C.; gen. mgr. various Sheraton Corp. hotels, including Sheraton Ft. Worth, Sheraton Schroeder, Milw.; gen. mgr., v.p. Whitehall Hotel, Chgo., 1976; gen. mgr. Omni Internat. Hotel, Norfolk, Va., 1976-77, Miami, Fla., 1977—; dir. Central Nat. Bank, Miami. Honored for many contbns. City of Norfolk. Mem. Chaine des Rotisseurs, Greater Miami Hotel and Motel Assn. (treas., v.p.). Roman Catholic. Club: Masons. Home and Office: Omni Internat Hotel 16th St at Biscayne Blvd Miami FL 33132•

THORN, ROBERT NICOL, physicist; b. Coeur d'Alene, Idaho, Aug. 31, 1924; s. Harry Grover and Grace (Nicol) T.; A.B., Harvard, 1948, A.M., 1949, Ph.D. in Theoretical Physics, 1953; m. Betty Vogel, June 15, 1948; children—Karen, Kyle, Gretchen, Robert Nicol; m. 2d, Lorraine Patten, Oct. 10, 1962; 1 dau., Andrea Kay. Mem. staff Los Alamos Sci. Lab., 1953—, div. leader theoretical design div., 1971-76, asso. dir. for weapons, lasers, computers and reactor safety, 1976-79, acting dir., 1979, dep. dir., 1979—; cons. to bus. and govt., 1959—; mem. USAF Sci. Adv. Bd., 1962; mem. sci. adv. group Def. Atomic Support Agy., 1966-72; mem. sci. adv. com. Def. Intelligency Agy., 1971—. Chmn. Los Alamos County Commn., 1958-60. Served with AUS, 1943-46; ETO. Recipient Ernest Orlando Lawrence award AEC, 1967. Mem. Am. Phys. Soc., AAAS, Los Alamos Ski Club (pres. 1957-58), Los Alamos Ski Racing Club (pres. 1974-76), U.S. Ski Assn. (chmn. Alpine competition com.), Phi Beta Kappa, Sigma Xi. Home: 981 Barranca Rd Los Alamos NM 87544 Office: Los Alamos Sci Lab Los Alamos NM 87544

THORNBERRY, WILLIAM HOMER, circuit judge, lawyer; b. Austin, Tex., Jan. 9, 1909; s. William Moore and Mary Lillian (Jones) T.; B.B.A., U. Tex., 1932, LL.B., 1936; LL.D., Gallaudet Coll.; m. Eloise Engle, Feb. 24, 1945; children—Molly, David, Kate. Admitted to Tex. bar, 1936, since practiced in Austin; dist. atty. 53d Jud. Dist., Travis County, Tex., 1941-42. Mem. city council, Austin, 1946-48; mayor pro tem, 1947-48; mem. Tex. Ho. of Reps., 1937-40; mem. 81st-88th congresses, 10th Tex. Dist.; U.S. dist. judge Western Dist. Tex., 1963-65, U.S. judge Ct. Appeals, 5th Jud. Circuit, 1965—, sr. judge, 1979—. Served to lt. comdr. USNR, 1942-46. Recipient Silver Beaver Boy Scouts Am.; Distinguished Alumnus award U. Tex., 1965. Mem. Tex. State Bar, Am., Travis County bar assns., Order Coif (hon.). Democrat. Methodist. Mason (32 deg., Shriner), Kiwanian. Office: 108 US Courthouse 200 W 8th St Austin TX 78701

THORNBROUGH, ALBERT A., mfg. co. exec.; b. Lakin, Kans., 1912; grad. Kans. State Coll., 1935; student Harvard U., 1937. Dep. chmn. bd., chief exec. officer Massey-Ferguson Ltd., Toronto, Ont., Can., pres., 1956-78. Mem. Farm Equipment Inst. (pres. 1962-63). Office: 200 University Ave Toronto ON M5H 3E4 Canada

THORNBURGH, RICHARD LEWIS, gov. Pa.; b. Pitts., July 16, 1932; s. Charles Garland and Alice (Sanborn) T.; B.Engring., Yale, 1954; LL.B. with high honors, U. Pitts., 1957; LL.D., Washington and Jefferson Coll., 1976, Bucknell U., 1979, LaSalle Coll., 1979, Temple U., 1979, Lincoln U., 1979; m. Virginia Walton Judson, Oct. 12, 1963; children—John, David, Peter, William. Admitted to Pa. bar, 1958, U.S. Supreme Ct. bar, 1965; atty. firm Kirkpatrick, Lockhart, Johnson & Hutchison, Pitts., 1959-69, 77-79; U.S. atty. for Western Pa., Pitts., 1969-75; asst. atty. gen., head criminal div. Dept. Justice, Washington, 1975-77; gov. State of Pa., Harrisburg, 1979—; del. Pa. Constl. Conv., 1967-68. Bd. dirs. Urban League Pitts., 1967-72. Fellow Am. Bar Found.; mem. Am. Judicature Soc. Republican. Contbr. articles to profl. jours. Home: 2035 N Front St Harrisburg PA 17102 Office: Office of Gov 225 Main Capitol Bldg Harrisburg PA 17120

THORNBURY, JOHN ROUSSEAU, physician; b. Cleve., Mar. 16, 1929; s. Purla Lee and Gertrude (Glidden) T.; A.B. cum laude, Miami U., Oxford, Ohio, 1950; M.D., Ohio State U., 1955; m. Julia Lee McGregor, Mar. 20, 1955; children—Lee Allison, John McGregor. Intern, Hurley Hosp., Flint, Mich., 1955-56; resident U. Iowa Hosps., Iowa City, 1958-61; instr., asst. prof. radiology U. Colo. Med. Center, Denver, 1962-63; practice medicine specializing in radiology, Denver, 1962-63, Iowa City, 1963-66, Seattle, 1966-68, Ann Arbor, Mich., 1968—; mem. staff U. Hosp., Ann Arbor; asst. prof. radiology U. Iowa Hosps., 1963-66, U. Wash. Hosp., Seattle, 1966-68; asso. prof. radiology U. Mich. Med. Center, 1968-71, prof. radiology, 1971-79; prof. radiology, chief div. diagnostic radiology dept. radiology Sch. Medicine, U. N.Mex., 1979—. Served to capt., M.C., USAF, 1956-58. Diplomate Am. Bd. Radiology. Fellow Am. Coll. Radiology; mem. Soc. Uroradiology (pres. 1976-77, dir. 1977-79), Assn. U. Radiologists (pres. elect 1979—), Radiol. Soc. N.Am., Am. Roentgen Ray Soc., Rocky Mountain Radiol. Soc., Phi Beta Kappa, Delta Tau Delta, Omicron Delta Kappa, Phi Chi. Republican. Presbyterian. Asso. editor Yearbook of Radiology, 1971—; editorial bd. Contemporary Diagnostic Radiology, 1977—, Urologic Radiology. Home: 1035 Red Oaks NE Albuquerque NM 87122

THORNDAL, HERBERT LOUIS, banker; b. Minot, N.D., Jan. 21, 1929; s. Herbert L. and Lucille (LaFleur) T.; B.S., N.D. State U., 1951; m. Nancy Wright Herbison, June 30, 1951; children—Herbert Louis III, Ann, Matthew, Earl, Helen, Christine, Joseph, Pearl, Janet. Adjuster, First Nat. Bank, Mankato, Minn., 1953-54; from asst. cashier to pres. Columbus State Bank (N.D.), 1954-66; commnr. banking N.D., 1966-69; pres. Bank of N.D., Bismarck, 1969—. Served to 1st lt. USAF, 1951-53. Decorated Bronze Star. Mem. Am., N.D. Bankers assns., Nat. Assn. Suprs. State Banks, Am. Inst. Banking, Bank Adminstrv. Inst., N.D. State U. Alumni Assn., Am. Legion, VFW, 40 and 8, Sigma Alpha Epsilon. Elk. Home: 221 Ave B W Bismarck ND 58501 Office: 700 E Main St Bismarck ND 58501

THORNDIKE, CHARLES JESSE (CHUCK), cartoonist; b. Seattle, Jan. 20, 1897; s. Charles Adelbert and Hortense Victoria T.; student U. Wash., 1919-20, U. Calif., 1920-22; m. Anne Lee; 1 dau., Barbara Ann. Began as cartoonist 1916; successively with San Francisco Bulletin, Animated Cartoon Film Corp., N.Y. Herald-Tribune Syndicate, Van Tine Syndicate; art dir. for Gen. Motors Corp., Forbes Mag., A.M. Walzer Co., Dover, N.J.; artist for Fox Films, United Artists, Universal and Ednl. Films; has conducted cartoon classes in N.Y.C. for 3 yrs.; on radio programs "Cartoon Club of the Air", "Behind the Cartoon"; mem. advisory board Washington Sch. Art; sr. visual information specialist USN, 1941—; art dir. OAS; did articles and cartoons for Carter. Served in USMC, 1918-19. Mem. Pi Kappa Alpha. Club: Jockey. Democrat. Episcopalian. Author several books relating to field of interest, 1937—; latest being: Susie and Sam in Silver Springs, 1949; Susie and Sam at Rock City, 1950; New Secrets of Cartooning, 1957; How to Enjoy Good Health, 1966. Originator of newspaper syndicate feature: Oddities of Nature; writer syndicated newspaper feature, World of Tomorrow. Contbr. cartoons to Coll. Humor, Sat. Eve. Post, New Yorker, others; contbr. Community Reporter, 1969-71; cartoonist for Jockey Clubs Internat. mag. Winner's Circle. Lectr. schs. and clubs. Home: 11660 Canal Dr North Miami FL 33161. *Emerson said: "Happiness is a high degree of contentment." Tolstoi said: "Happiness is a high degree of accomplishment." To me success means a combination of these two principles, plus a steady application of the Golden Rule. Huge accumulations of money, often through inheritance or exploitation of others, does not automatically bring happiness. What you do for your country and other people, plus love of your work, is the true measure of success in life!*

THORNDIKE, JOSEPH JACOBS, JR., editor; b. Peabody, Mass., July 29, 1913; s. Joseph Jacobs and Susan Ellison (Farnham) T.; A.B., Harvard, 1934; m. Virginia Lemont, Sept. 7, 1940; children—John, Alan; m. 2d, Margery Darrell, Oct. 3, 1963; 1 son, Joseph Jacobs III. Asst. editor Time Mag., 1934-36; asso. editor Life Mag., 1936-46, mng. editor Life, 1946-49; pres. Thorndike, Jensen & Parton, Inc.; co-founder, sr. editor Am. Heritage Pub. Co., also v.p. Unitarian. Clubs: Harvard (N.Y.C.); Century. Author: The Very Rich, 1976; The Magnificent Builders, 1978; editor: Seafaring America, 1974; Mysteries of the Past, 1977; Discovery of Lost Worlds, 1979. Home: 20 Cedar St Chatham MA 02633 Office: 10 Rockefeller Plaza New York NY 10020

THORNDIKE, RICHARD KING, brokerage co. exec.; b. Millis, Mass., 1913; s. Richard King and Florence A. (Macy) T.; grad. Harvard, 1935; m. Lucy Saltonstall Rantoul, Sept. 21, 1935 (dec. May 1958); children—Richard III, Rose, Sylvia; m. 2d, Mercy Bours Archibald, Oct. 1, 1960. With F.S. Moseley & Co., Boston, 1935—, asst. analyst, 1937-46, partner, 1947-73; v.p. Moseley, Hallgarten, Estabrook & Weeden Inc., 1973—; dir. Daniel Green Co. Republican. Episcopalian. Clubs: Myopia (Hamilton, Mass.); Eastern Yacht (Marblehead, Mass.); Somerset (Boston); Phoenix-SK (Harvard). Home: 18 Perky Rd Key Largo FL 33037 Office: 60 State St Boston MA 02101

THORNE, FRANCIS, composer; b. Bay Shore, N.Y., June 23, 1922; s. Francis Burritt and Hildegarde (Kobbé) T.; B.A. in Music Theory, Yale, 1942; m. Ann Cobb, Dec. 9, 1942; children—Ann Boughton (Mrs. William F. Niles), Wendy Oakleigh (Mrs. William H. Forsyth, Jr.), Candace Kobbé (Mrs. Anthony M. Canton). Founder, pres. Thorne Music Fund, Inc., 1965—; pub. Edward B. Marks Music Corp., 1963—, Gen. Music Pub. Co., 1971—; exec. dir. Lenox Arts Center, 1972-76, Am. Composers Alliance, 1975—; recs. on Composers' Recs., Inc., Serenus, Owl Louisville and Opus One; founder, pres. Am. Composers Orch., 1976. Trustee, Manhattan Sch. Music, Am. Music Center, MacDowell Colony, Walter W. Naumburg Found., Contemporary Music Soc., Theater Devel. Fund. Served to lt. USNR, 1942-45. Nat. Endowment Arts grantee, 1966, 73, fellow, 1976, 79; Nat. Inst. Arts and Letters grantee, 1968; N.Y. State Arts Council ballet commn., 1973. Mem. Contemporary Music Soc. (dir.), Broadcast Music, Inc., Am. Composers Alliance. Composer: Elegy for Orch., 1964: Burlesque Overture, 1966; Lyric Variations for Orch., 1967; Symphony No. 1, 1963, No. II, 1966, No. III, 1970, No. IV, 1977; Fortuna, 1961-62; Liebesrock, 1969; Sonar Plexus, 1969; Six Set-Pieces, 1969; Contra Band Music, 1970; Antiphonies, 1970; Simultaneities, 1971; Quartessence, 1971; Fanfare, Fugue and Funk, 1972; Lyric Variations II, 1972; Piano Sonata, 1972; Lyric Variations III, 1973; Cantata Sauce, 1973; Evensongs, 1973; Cello Concerto, 1974; Piano Concerto, 1974; Violin Concerto, 1975; String Quartet #3, 1976; Spoon River Overture, 1976; Grand Duo, 1976; Five Set Pieces, 1976; Love's Variations, 1976; Pop Partita, 1978; The Eternal Light for Soprano and Orchestra, 1979; Divertimento for Flute, Strings and Percussion, 1979. Club: Century Assn. (N.Y.C.). Home: 116 E 66th St New York NY 10021

THORNE, KIP STEPHEN, physicist, educator; b. Logan, Utah, June 1, 1940; s. David Wynne and Alison (Comish) T.; B.S. in Physics, Calif. Inst. Tech., 1962; A.M. in Physics (Woodrow Wilson fellow 1962-63, Danforth Found. fellow 1962-63), Princeton, 1963, Ph.D. in Physics (Danforth Found. fellow 1963-65, NSF fellow 1964-65), 1965, postgrad. (NSF Postdoctoral fellow), 1965-66; m. Linda Jeanne Peterson, Sept. 12, 1960 (div. 1977); children—Kares Anne, Bret Carter. Research fellow Calif. Inst. Tech., 1966-67, asso. prof. theoretical physics, 1967-70, prof., 1970—. Fulbright lectr., France, 1966; vis. asso. prof. U. Chgo., 1968; vis. prof. Moscow U., 1969, 75, 78; vis. sr. research asso. Cornell U., 1977; adj. prof. U. Utah, 1971—. Alfred P. Sloan Found. Research fellow, 1966-68; John Simon Guggenheim fellow, 1967; recipient Sci. Writing award in physics and astronomy Am. Inst. Physics-U.S. Steel Found., 1969. Mem. Nat. Acad. Scis., Am. Acad. Arts and Scis., Am. Astron. Soc., Am. Phys. Soc., Internat. Astron. Union, AAAS, Internat. Com. on Gen. Relativity and Gravitation, Com. on U.S.-USSR Coop. in Physics, Sigma Xi, Tau Beta Pi. Co-author: Gravitation Theory and Gravitational Collapse, 1965; Gravitation, 1973. Research in gravitation physics and astrophysics. Office: 130-33 Calif Inst Tech Pasadena CA 91125

THORNE, MARLOWE DRIGGS, agronomist, educator; b. Perry, Utah, Nov. 4, 1918; s. Milton Jefferson and Ida (Young) T.; B.S., Utah State U., 1940; M.S., Iowa State U., 1941; Ph.D., Cornell U., 1948; m. Merle Carter, June 24, 1941; children—Terry Carter, Judy, Melvin Jay, Elaine. Soil scientist, head soil dept. Pineapple Research Inst. Hawaii, 1947-52, soil physicist, head dept. agronomy, 1952-54; irrigation work project leader Eastern soil and water mgmt. sect. Agrl. Research Service, Dept. Agr., 1954-56; prof. agronomy, head dept. Okla. State U., 1956-63; head dept. agronomy U. Ill., Urbana, 1963-70, prof. agronomy, 1970—. Prof. agronomy U.P. Agrl. U., Pant Nagar, India, 1970-72. Served as pilot USAAF, 1943-45. Mem. Am. Soc. Agronomy (nat. pres. 1977), Soil Sci. Soc. Am. (chmn. budget and fin. com. 1962), Soil Conservation Soc. Am., Sigma Xi. Mem. Ch. of Jesus Christ of Latter-day Saints. Home: 2205 S Cottage Grove Urbana IL 61801

THORNE, OAKLEIGH BLAKEMAN, bus. exec.; b. Santa Barbara, Calif., Aug. 11, 1932; s. Oakleigh Lewis and Bertha (Palmer) T.; B.A., Harvard Coll., 1954; m. Felicitas Selter, Oct. 26, 1969; children—Oakleigh, Henry, Jonathan, Eliza. Officer trainee 1st Nat. City Bank, 1956-61; asst. v.p. CT Corp. System, N.Y.C., 1961-65, exec. v.p., 1965-68, pres., 1968—, chmn. bd., 1977—; dir. Bank of Millbrook. Served with U.S. Army, 1953-55. Home: Thorndale Millbrook NY 12545 Office: 277 Park Ave New York City NY 10017

THORNE, RICHARD MANSERGH, physicist; b. Birmingham, Eng., July 25, 1942; s. Robert George and Dorothy Lena (Goodchild) T.; B.Sc., Birmingham U., 1963; Ph.D., M.I.T., 1968; m. Jutta Mangler, July 13, 1963; children—Peter Baring, Michael Thomas. Grad. asst. M.I.T., 1963-68; asst. prof. dept. atmospheric scis. UCLA, 1968-71, asso. prof., 1971-75, prof., 1975—, chmn. dept., 1976-79; cons. Jet Propulsion Lab. Recipient numerous grants NSF, NASA, Jet Propulsion Lab. Mem. Am. Geophys. Union. Contbr. articles to profl. jours. Home: 10390 Caribou Ln Los Angeles CA 90024 Office: Dept Atmospheric Scis UCLA Los Angeles CA 90024

THORNE, ROBERT DOUGLAS, govt. ofcl.; b. Boulder, Colo., July 22, 1928; s. Harold Monroe and Ruth (Plew) T.; B.A. in Chemistry, U. Colo., 1951; m. Helen Emily Sill, Dec. 22, 1949. With Dow Chem. Co., 1952-55; with AEC, 1955-75, dep. mgr., then mgr. ops. office, San Francisco, 1970-74, dep. gen. mgr., then gen. mgr. hdqrs., Washington, 1974-75; acting dep. asst. adminstr. ERDA, 1975-77; asst. sec. energy tech. Dept. Energy, 1975-78, cons., 1979—. Recipient certificate appreciation AEC, 1973, EEO award, 1974, Disting. Service award, 1974, Meritorious Service award, 1976. Home: 3338 Doral Ct Walnut Creek CA 94598

THORNE, SAMUEL EDMUND, educator; b. N.Y.C., Oct. 14, 1907; s. Bernard and Julia (Powell) T.; A.B., Coll. City N.Y., 1927; LL.B., Harvard, 1930; M.A. Yale, 1948; Litt.D., Wesleyan U., 1957; LL.D. (hon.) U. Cambridge, 1969; m. Margaret Ewen MacVeagh, Mar. 19, 1945; children—Samuel Lincoln, Stuart Ewen. Asst., asso. prof. law Northwestern U., 1933-41; asso. prof. law Yale, 1945-48, prof. law, 1948-55, Simeon E. Baldwin prof. legal history, 1955-56; prof. legal history Harvard, 1956-73, Charles Stebbins Fairchild prof. legal history, 1973—. Vis. prof. legal history Cambridge U., 1951-52, Maitland lectr., 1959. Served from lt. to lt. comdr. USNR, 1941-45. Henry E. Huntington Library fellow, 1937-39; Guggenheim fellow, 1948, 51, 57. Fellow Am. Acad. Arts and Scis., Mediaeval Acad. Am. (pres.), Brit. Acad., Soc. Antiquaries (London), Societa Italiana di storia del diritto; mem. Mass., Royal hist. socs., Am. Philos. Soc., Bibliog. Soc. London, Selden Soc., Am. Soc. Legal History (pres.), Pipe Roll Soc., Soc. Pub. Tchrs. Law. Clubs: Athenaeum (London);

Chgo. Literary. Editor: A Discourse Upon Statutes, 1942; Prerogativa Regis, 1949; Readings and Moots at the Inns of Court in the Fifteenth Century, 1954. Editor, translator Bracton, On the Laws and Customs of England, 1968-77. Home: 3 Berkeley Pl Cambridge MA 02138

THORNELL, JACK RANDOLPH, photographer; b. Vicksburg, Miss., Aug. 29, 1939; s. Benjamin O. and Myrtice (Jones) T.; ed. pub. schs.; m. Carolyn Wilson, June 12, 1964; children—Candice, Jay Randolph. Photographer, Jackson (Miss.) Daily News, 1960-64; with A.P., 1964—, assigned Dominican Republic, 1965, Selma, Ala., 1965, Democratic Nat. Conv., 1968. Served with AUS, 1958-60. Recipient Pulitzer prize for news photography of shooting of James Meredith, 1967; Headliners Photography award, 1967. Home: 5236 Utica St Metairie LA 70002 Office: 3800 Howard St New Orleans LA 70160

THORNHILL, ARTHUR HORACE, JR., book publisher; b. Boston, Jan. 1, 1924; s. Arthur Horace and Mary Josephine (Peterson) T.; A.B. magna cum laude, Princeton U., 1948; m. Dorothy M. Matheis, Oct. 28, 1944; children—Sandra Susanne Thornhill Brushart, Arthur Horace. With Little, Brown & Co., Inc., Boston, 1948—, v.p., 1955-58, exec. v.p., 1958-62, pres., 1962—, chmn. bd., 1970—, gen. mgr., 1960—; pres., dir. Little, Brown & Co. (Can.), Ltd.; v.p. Time, Inc., 1968—; dir. Conrac Corp. Mem. adv. council history dept. Princeton U., 1964—; trustee, treas. Princeton U. Press; dir. Am. Textbook Pubs. Inst., 1965-68; trustee Bennington Coll., 1969-76; bd. dirs. Am. Book Pubs. Council, 1964-67. Served to 1st lt. USAAF, World War II. Decorated Air medal. Mem. Assn. Am. Pubs. (dir. 1978—). Clubs: Union, Princeton, Century, Publs., Lunch (N.Y.C.); P.E.N.; Union, St. Botolph (Boston). Home: 200 Cliff Rd Wellesley Hills MA 02181 Office: 34 Beacon St Boston MA 02106

THORNSJO, DOUGLAS FREDRIC, fin. services co. exec.; b. Mpls., July 10, 1927; s. Adolph Fredric and Agnes Emily (Gryniewski) T.; B.S. in Law, U. Minn., 1948, J.D., 1951; children—Claudia, Douglas Fredric. Admitted to Minn. bar, 1951, N.Y. bar, 1954, Me. bar, 1966, also U.S. Supreme Ct. bar, with firm Dewey, Ballantine, Bushby, Palmer & Wood, N.Y.C., 1951-54; with Investors Diversified Services, 1956-57; gen. counsel Investors Syndicate Life Co., 1957-59; pres., gen. counsel Investment Policies, Inc., also Consumers Investment Fund, 1959-61; chief operating officer Midwest Tech. Devel. Co., 1962-64; partner firm Thornsjo, Smith & Johnson, Mpls., 1961-66; with Union Mut. Life Ins. Co., Portland, Maine, 1966-76, sr. v.p., 1970-76; sr. v.p. law and adminstrn. Bradford Nat. Corp., N.Y.C., 1976—; chmn. First Internat. Realty/Securities Fund, Ltd. (Nassau), 1966-69; instr. corp. fin. U. Maine, 1969; dir. Union Mut. Stock Life Ins. Co. N.Y. Vice chmn. legis. commns. to revise ins. laws Maine Legislature, 1970-73; mem. Maine Health Facilities Authority, 1972-76; bd. dirs. Nat. Multiple Sclerosis Soc. Served with U.S. Mcht. Marine, 1945-47, to lt. USNR, 1952-54. Recipient Eagle Scout award Boy Scouts Am. Mem. Am. Bar Assn., Maine C. of C. (dir.). Author: The Mutual Company, 1973. Contbr. articles to profl. jours. Home: Albion ME 04910 Office: care Bradford 2 Broadway New York NY 10019

THORNTON, ARCHIBALD PATON, educator; b. Glasgow, Scotland, Oct. 21, 1921; s. John Joseph and Margaret (Paton) T.; M.A., U. Glasgow, 1947; D.Phil., Oxford (Eng.) U., 1952; m. Janet Joan Mowat, July 30, 1948; children—Roderick, Andrew. Came to Can., 1960. Lectr. modern history Trinity Coll., Oxford (Eng.) U., 1948-50; lectr. British Imperial and Commonwealth history U. Aberdeen (Scotland), 1950-57; prof., chmn. dept. history, dean faculty arts U. West Indies, 1957-60; prof. history U. Toronto (Ont., Can.), 1960—, also chmn. dept., 1967-72. With H.M. Colonial Service, 1952-57. Served to capt. tank regt. Brit. Army, 1941-45. Smuts fellow Cambridge U. (Eng.), 1965-66, also Commonwealth fellow St. John's Coll., Cambridge U., 1965-66. Fellow Royal Hist. Soc., Royal Soc. Can. Club: Reform (London). Author: West-India Policy under the Restoration, 1956; The Imperial Idea and Its Enemies, 1959; Doctrines of Imperialism, 1965; The Habit of Authority, 1966; For the File on Empire, 1968; Imperialism in the Twentieth Century, 1978. Home: 282 Spadina Rd Toronto ON M5R 2V4 Canada

THORNTON, CHARLES BATES, industrialist; b. Knox County, Tex., July 22, 1913; s. W.A. and Sara Alice (Bates) T.; B.C.S., Columbus U., 1937; LL.D., Tex. Tech U., 1957, U. So. Calif., Pepperdine U., 1971; D.C.S., George Washington U., 1964; m. Flora Laney, Apr. 19, 1937; children—Charles Bates, William Laney. Dir. planning Ford Motor Co., 1946-48; v.p., asst. gen. mgr. Hughes Aircraft Co., Culver City, Calif., v.p. Hughes Tool Co., 1948-53; pres. Litton Industries, Inc., 1953-61, chmn. bd., chief exec. officer, 1953—; dir., mem. exec. com. Cyprus Mines Corp.; dir. Trans World Airlines, Inc., United Calif. Bank, Western Bancorp., MCA, Inc. Mem. Bus. Council; nat. execs. com. Nat. Council on Crime and Delinquency; mem. Emergency Com. for Am. Trade; co-vice chmn. U.S. Internat. Transp. Exposition Com., 1971-72; mem. internat. bus. advisory com. Sec. Commerce, 1971-73; chmn. Pres.'s Commn. on White House Fellows, 1971-73; vice chmn. United Crusade campaign, 1972-75, gen. chmn., 1976; mem. Stanford Bus. Sch. Adv. Council; mem. headmasters council Harvard Sch.; life trustee U. So. Calif.; bd. dirs. Greater Los Angeles Visitors and Conv. Bur., So. Calif. Visitors Council, Los Angeles World Affairs Council; nat. dir. Jr. Achievement. Served to col. USAAF, World War II; cons. to comdg. gen. AAF, 1946, to undersec. Dept. State, 1947. Decorated D.S.M., Legion of Merit, Commendation ribbon with two oak leaf clusters; recipient numerous awards including Merit award Albert Einstein Coll. Medicine, Yeshiva U., 1963; Horatio Alger award Am. Schs. and Colls. Assn.,, 1964; Western Electronic medal achievement Western Electronic Mfrs. Assn., 1965; Golden Plate award Am. Acad. Achievement, 1966; Nat. Industry Leader award B'nai B'rith, 1967; Outstanding Achievement in Bus. Mgmt. award U. So. Calif., 1967; Bus. Leadership award U. Mich., 1968; Big Bro. Community Service award Jewish Big Bros. Assn. Los Angeles County, 1975; Community Leadership award United Way, 1976; named Man of Year, Beverly Hills C. of C., 1964, Calif. Industrialist of Year, Calif. Mus. Sci. and Industry, 1964, Industrialist of Year, Soc. Indsl. Realtors, 1966, Exec. of Yr., UCLA, Exec. Program Assn., 1978. Mem. Calif. Inst. Assos., U. So. Calif. Assos., Music Center Opera Assn. (dir., exec. com. 1966-68), Beta Gamma Sigma (hon.), Sigma Alpha Epsilon (life). Clubs: Army and Navy (Washington); Beach (Santa Monica); Los Angeles Country, California, One Hundred (Los Angeles); Hollywood Turf (dir.); Tex. Tech U. Century. Office: 360 N Crescent Dr Beverly Hills CA 90213

THORNTON, CHARLES VICTOR, metals co. exec.; b. Salt Lake City, Feb. 8, 1915; s. Charles Victor and Winnie May (Fitts) T.; B.S. in Civil Engring., U. Utah, 1935; H.H.D., Ind. Inst. Tech., 1972; m. Margaret Louise Wiggins, Apr. 17, 1937; children—Charles Victor III, Carolyn Louise (Mrs. John J. Moorhouse), David Frank. Engr., Truscon Steel Co., Youngstown, Ohio, 1935-37, dist. engr., Washington, 1937-40; chief engr. So. Iron Works, Inc., Alexandria, Va., 1940-45; pres. Thornton Industries, Inc., Ft. Worth, 1945-75, chmn. bd., 1975—; chmn. bd. Western Steel Co., Corpus Christi, Tex., 1971—; dir. Bank of Commerce, Ft. Worth. Mem. Tarrant County Water Bd.; pres., chmn. bd. trustees Shriners Hosp. for Crippled Children. Mem. Ft. Worth C. of C. (pres. 1960), Am. Assn. Pvt. R.R. Car Owners, Tau Beta Pi. Clubs: Masons, Shriners, Kiwanis. Clubs: Colonial Country (past pres.), Shady Oaks Country, Fort Worth (Ft. Worth). Office: Suite 919 Ridglea Bank Bldg Fort Worth TX 76116

THORNTON, EDWARD RALPH, educator; b. Syracuse, N.Y., July 19, 1935; s. Ralph Olin and Edna Rosamund (Hettinger) T.; B.A., Syracuse U., 1957; Ph.D. (NIH Predoctoral fellow), Mass. Inst. Tech., 1959; m. Elizabeth Dee Kaplan, Feb. 18, 1969; 1 dau., Cara Emily. NIH Postdoctoral fellow Mass. Inst. Tech., 1959-60, Harvard, 1960-61; asst. prof. chemistry U. Pa., Phila., 1961-65, asso. prof., 1965-69, prof., 1969—. NIH, NSF grantee. Mem. Am. Chem. Soc. (9th Phila. sect. award 1970), Fedn. Am. Scientists, Chem. Soc. (London), ACLU, Common Cause, Friends of Earth, Sierra Club, Phi Beta Kappa, Sigma Xi, Phi Kappa Phi, Phi Lambda Upsilon, Sigma Pi Sigma, Pi Mu Epsilon. Democrat. Author: Solvolysis Mechanisms, 1964. Home: 7 Swarthmore Pl Swarthmore PA 19081

THORNTON, FRANK EBERLE, orthopaedic surgeon; b. Valley Junction, Iowa, Nov. 21, 1912; s. Frank E. and Eva (Tussing) T.; M.D., State U. Iowa, 1937; m. Carol Edgington, Sept. 2, 1936; children—Richard, Thomas, Jerry. Rotating intern Meth. Hosp., Indpls., 1937-38; staff Meth. Hosp., Des Moines, 1945—, chief orthopedics, 1950-72, pres. elect staff, 1966, chief of staff, 1968-70; resident orthopedics State U. Iowa Hosp., 1938-41, asst. prof. orthopedic surgery, 1941-46; pvt. practice, Des Moines, 1945-52, Spencer, Iowa, 1972-76; chief orthopedic sect. surgery VA Hosp., Des Moines, 1976—; chief surgery Broadlawn Polk County Hosp., 1970-72. Served to lt. comdr. M.C., USNR, 1952-54. Mem. Am. Acad. Orthopaedic Surgery, A.C.S., Clin. Orthopaedic Soc., Central Iowa, Mid Central States (pres. 1968-69), Iowa orthopaedic socs., AMA, Iowa Med. Soc. Address: VA Hospital 30th and Euclid Des Moines IA 50310

THORNTON, GERALD DEWAYNE, publishing co. exec.; b. Sioux City, Iowa, Aug. 16, 1924; s. Edward Joseph and Louise (Robertson) T.; B.A., U. Iowa, 1949, J.D., 1951; m. Anne Elizabeth Irwin, June 22, 1951; children—Lawrence, Elizabeth, Daniel, Margaret, Christopher, Katherine, Patrick, Michael. Admitted to Iowa bar, 1951; corp. counsel Meredith Corp., Des Moines, 1951-65, gen. counsel, 1965-76, asst. sec., 1965-66, sec., 1966—, v.p. adminstrv. services, 1968—, also dir.; sec., dir. Meredith-Burda, Inc.; sec. Siegwerk, Inc., Edwin T. Meredith Found. Sec. Central Iowa Regional Airport Com., 1969-70. Bd. dirs., vice chmn. Central Iowa Airport Authority; bd. dirs. Dowling Club, Dowling High Sch., Des Moines. Served with USAAF, 1943-45. Mem. Mag. Pubs. Assn. (ad hoc com. on P.O. activities, mem. legis. com.), U.S. (communications com., chmn. subcom. communication policy and legislation 1971, mem. subcom. on privacy legislation 1975-78, postal adv. panel 1967), Des Moines (dir., v.p., mem. legis. com., chmn. aviation com. 1969, chmn. financing local govt. com. 1974-75, pres. 1976, mem. econ. devel. bur. 1979), chambers commerce. Am., Iowa, Polk County bar assns., Phi Delta Theta, Phi Delta Phi. Republican. Roman Catholic (past chmn. ch. council and fin. com., dir.; pres. Holy Trinity Found. 1974—). Home: 3908 Adams St Des Moines IA 50310 Office: 1716 Locust St Des Moines IA 50336

THORNTON, HENRY MOSER, dental and optical supplies co. exec.; b. Mechanicsburg, Pa., Sept. 12, 1915; s. William Foster and Ruth (Moser) T.; student Princeton, 1933-35; L.H.D. (hon.), Loyola U., Chgo., 1970; LL.D. (hon.), Northwestern U., 1975, Dalhousie U., 1978; m. Virginia Whiteley, Dec. 7, 1935; children—Henry Moser, George, Virginia Thornton Parker, Michael, John. Chief examiner personal property tax div. Dept. of Revenue, Harrisburg, Pa., 1935-38; asst. prodn. mgr. Dentsply Internat., Inc., York, Pa., 1938-42, v.p., 1942-49, exec. v.p., 1949-55, pres., 1955-72, chmn. bd., chief exec. officer, 1972—, also dir.; dir. Commonwealth Nat. Bank. Past pres. York Country Day Sch.; trustee Am. Fund for Dental Health. Recipient spl. awards and citations St. Louis Dental Soc., 1958, Am. Coll. Dentists, 1970, Am. Student Dental Assn., 1974, Odontographic Soc. Chgo., 1974, Am. Fund for Dental Health, 1977, Pa. Dental Assn., 1978. Hon. mem. ADA, Internat. Coll. Dentists, Am. Assn. Dental Schs., Fifth Dist. Pa. dental socs., Mfrs. Assn. York (dir., past pres.), Delta Sigma Delta. Clubs: Merion Cricket; Lafayette; Country of York. Home: Boxhill York PA 17403 Office: 570 W College Ave York PA 17405

THORNTON, J. EDWARD, lawyer; b. Starkville, Miss., Nov. 25, 1907; s. Marmaduke Kimbrough and Annie (Knox) T.; A.B., Miss. Coll., 1928; LL.B., Harvard, 1933; m. Mary Belle Quinn. Admitted to Ala. bar, 1934, Mass. bar, 1936; asst. prosecutor Jefferson County, 1936-39; asst. gen. counsel Ala. Dept. Revenue, 1939-42; mem. firm Thornton & McGowin, Mobile. Mem. Spl. Supreme Ct. Ala., 1967-68; mem. adv. com. on proposed new appellate rules Ala. Supreme Ct., 1972-74, mem. standing com. on appellate rules, 1974—; chmn. sect. on practice and procedure Ala. State Bar, 1969-72, 73-75. Pres., Mobile Chamber Mus. Soc., 1972-73; adv. council home health services Mobile County Bd. Health, 1969-74. Mem. Ala. Democratic Com., 1950-54. Served to lt. comdr. USNR, 1942-45. Fellow Am. Bar Found.; mem. Am. (ho. dels., state del. for Ala. 1958-59), Ala. (chmn. com. on jurisprudence and law reform 1951-63; pres. 1963-64), Mobile (pres. 1955, founder, editor Mobile Bar Bull. 1966—) bar assns., Jud. Conf. 5th Circuit U.S., Selden Soc., Am. Law Inst., Ala. Law Inst., Mobile Arts Council (pres. 1956), English Speaking Union (pres. Mobile 1960-61), Mobile Opera Guild (pres. 1963-65), Mobile C. of C., Scribes. Baptist. Clubs: Athelstan, Bienville (dir.), International Trade. Contbr. articles to prof. publs. Address: PO Box 23 Mobile AL 36601

THORNTON, JACK NELSON, publishing co. exec.; b. Columbia, Mo., Nov. 9, 1932; s. Samuel Calvin and Mary Elizabeth (Nelson) T.; B.A., U. Mo., 1954; m. Patricia Helmke, Sept. 15, 1973; children—Gray Nelson, Elizabeth Susan. Group v.p., officer Wadsworth Inc., Belmont, Calif., 1957—; pres. Brooks/Cole Pub. Co., Monterey, Calif., 1966—. Bd. dirs. Monterey County Mental Health Assn., 1975-76. Served to 1st lt. USAF, 1954-57. Mem. Am. Math. Assn., Am. Soc. Engring. Edn., Am. Rocket Soc., Nat. Council Tchrs. Math., Greater El Paso Area Council Tchrs. Math., Kappa Alpha Order.

THORNTON, JAMES FRANCIS, engr.; b. Hartford, Conn., Apr. 20, 1912; s. James H. and Terese Agnes (King) T.; B.S., Yale, 1933; m. Annette Kent, July 4, 1956. Former chmn., dir. Lummus Co., design engrs. and constructors for chem. and petroleum industries; dir. Combustion Engring., Inc.; mem. adv. council Hercules, Inc., 1979—. Chmn. adv. com. on emergency planning Nat. Acad. Sci., 1972-75. Bd. dirs. Am. Grad. Sch. Internat. Mgmt. Decorated knight comdr. Order White Rose Finland; recipient Distinguished Profl. Engr. in Industry award N.Y. State Soc. Profl. Engrs., 1964. Mem. Am. Inst. Chem. Engrs., Yale Sci. and Engring. Assn. (past pres.). Clubs: Yale, Pinnacle (past pres.) (N.Y.C.). Home: 3500 E Lincoln Dr Phoenix AZ 85018 Office: 277 Park Ave New York NY 10017

THORNTON, JOHN VINCENT, utilities exec.; b. N.Y.C., Jan. 13, 1924; s. Thomas Francis and Elizabeth Rose (McCullough) T.; B.S., St. Johns U., 1944; J.D., Yale, 1948; LL.D. (hon.), N.Y. Law Sch., 1969; m. Edna Grace Lawson, June 28, 1952; children—John, Nancy, Sarah, Amy, Laura. Admitted to N.Y. bar, 1948; asso. in law Columbia Sch. Law, 1948-49; law clk. to asso. judge N.Y. Ct. of Appeals, 1950-52; asso., partner Whitman & Ransom, N.Y.C., 1952-69; asst. gen. counsel Consol. Edison Co. of New York, Inc., 1969, v.p., 1970-73, v.p., treas., 1973-76, sr. v.p. fin., 1976-79, exec. v.p. fin., 1979—; treas. Empire State Electric Energy Research Corp., 1975-78; dir. Empire Savs. Bank, Pub. Utilities Reports, Inc. Adj. prof. law N.Y. U. Sch. Law, 1949-66, N.Y. Law Sch., 1973—; asst. in econs. Yale, 1946-48; asso. dir. USPHS Study on Heart Disease and the Law, 1958-61. Counsel judiciary com. N.Y. State Constl. Conv., 1967; mem. Bd. Edn., Bronxville, N.Y., 1970-76, pres. bd., 1972-74. Bd. dirs. Hall of Sci. N.Y.C., 1968-76; chmn. bd. trustees N.Y. Law Sch.; trustee Pace U.; bd. visitors City Coll. of City U. N.Y.; trustee, mem. bd. advisers Dickinson Coll., chmn., 1979—; mem. pres.'s adv. council N.Y. U. Sch. Social Work, 1969-75; trustee N.Y.C. Citizens' Budget Commn. Served to lt. (j.g.) USNR, 1944-46; PTO. Mem. Am. Bar Assn., Edison Electric Inst. (exec. com. fin. div.), Am. Gas Assn. (fin. com.), Order of Coif, Phi Delta Phi. Clubs: Downtown Assn., Bronxville Field. Contbg. editor Ann. Survey of Am. Law, 1950-60, Ann. Survey of N.Y. Law, 1950-60, Jour. of Occupational Medicine, 1964-67, Pub. Utilities Fortnightly, 1969—. Home: 55 Prescott Ave Bronxville NY 10708 Office: 4 Irving Pl New York City NY 10003. *Although integrity is not invariably a mark of the successful person, "honesty is the best policy" is generally a counsel of practicality as well as morality. The intellectually dishonest person can seldom inspire the confidence of superiors, associates and subordinates upon which promotion to high office in business and law most often depends.*

THORNTON, JOHN WILLIAM, mgmt. cons.; b. LaCrosse, Wis., May 29, 1921; s. John W. and Blanche F. (O'Donnell) T.; A.B., Loras Coll., 1942; LL.B., Boston Coll., 1953; m. Mary A. Wilshear, Apr. 23, 1946; children—John, Elizabeth, Catherine, Thomas, Barbara. Admitted to Mass. bar, 1953; with Brown Bros., Harriman & Co., 1946-54, McKinsey & Co., 1954-57; v.p. marketing Joy Mfg. Co., 1957-61, v.p., gen. mgr. indsl. div., 1961-62; with Blaw-Knox Co., 1962-68, v.p., 1966-68; pres., chief exec., dir., mem. exec. com. Seaport Corp., 1968-75; chmn. Seaport Auto Warehouse, 1968-75; dir., mem. exec. com. Brown Co., 1964-68; dir. First Bancorp., Interphoto Corp., 1969-75; mgmt. cons. Denney & Co., Pitts., 1975—. Mem. bd. adminstrn. Diocese of Pitts. Trustee Robert Morris Coll. Served with USNR, 1942-46. Clubs: Duquesne, St. Clair Country (Pitts.); Union League (Chgo.). Home: 410 Olympia Rd Pittsburgh PA 15211 Office: Denney & Co 3 Gateway Center Pittsburgh PA 15222

THORNTON, O. FRANK, state ofcl.; b. Mullins, S.C., July 26, 1905; s. O. F. and Lucendia (Cooper) T.; LL.B., U. S.C., 1928; m. Rosa Waring, Aug. 19, 1933; children—Rosa Thornton Cherry, Frances C. Thornton Shelton. Admitted to S.C. bar, 1928; practiced in Clover, S.C., 1930-50; editor Clover Herald, 1931-50; city atty. Clover, 1940-50; mem. S.C. Ho. of Reps., 1935-36, reading clk. of house, 1936-50; sec. of state S.C., Columbia, 1950-79. Chmn. S.C. fund dr. Crippled Children's Soc., 1960-61; mem. county election bd., 1940-50, county Democratic exec. com., 1935-50; bd. dirs. United Fund Richland-Lexington Counties, Travelers Aid Soc. Mem. Nat. Assn. Secs. of State (pres. 1959-60). Methodist. Clubs: Elks, Masons, Lions (dir. 1961-62, 66-68). Home: 712 Arbutus Dr Columbia SC 29205 Office: Wade Hampton Office Bldg Columbia SC 29211

THORNTON, RAY HUDSON, clergyman; b. Raleigh, Miss., Apr. 8, 1925; s. Thomas Benjamin and Minnie Lee (Ishee) T.; student Jacksonville (Tex.) Baptist Coll., 1952, Millsaps Coll., Jackson, Miss., 1957; m. Shirley Magdeline Musgrove, Aug. 9, 1947; children—Linda Rachel Thornton Blanchard, Sherrell Ray. Ordained to ministry Bapt. Ch., 1950; pastor chs. in Tex., Miss. and Fla., 1950-67; pastor Norwood Valley Bapt. Ch., Jackson, 1952-64, 67—76, Inwood Forest Bapt. Ch., Houston, 1977-78, Parkview Bapt. Ch., Laurel, Miss., 1978—; pres. Capitol Bapt. Assn., 1958-60, Bapt. Missionary Assn. Fla., 1964-66, Bapt. Missionary Assn. Miss., 1971-73; dir. youth dept. Bapt. Missionary Assn. Miss., 1972-76; chmn. publns. com. Bapt. Missionary Assn. Am., 1968-70, chmn. missionary com., 1974-76, pres. assn., 1976-78; mission tours in Mex., 1957, Cyprus, Lebanon, Israel and Turkey, 1974, Brazil and Bolivia, 1975. Served with USNR, 1943. Club: Masons. Home: 920 10th Ave Laurel MS 39440 Office: 930 10th Ave Laurel MS 39440

THORNTON, RAYMOND HOYT, JR., ednl. adminstr.; b. Conway, Ark., July 16, 1928; s. R.H. and Wilma (Stephens) T.; B.A., Yale, 1950; J.D., U. Ark., 1956; m. Betty Jo Mann, Jan. 27, 1956; children—Nancy, Mary, Stephanie. Admitted to Ark. bar, 1956, also U.S. Supreme Ct.; pvt. practice in Sheridan; atty. gen. Ark., 1971-73; mem. 93d-95th congresses 4th Ark. Dist.; exec. dir. Joint Ednl. Consortium, Arkadelphia, Ark.; chmn. Ark. Bd. Law Examiners, 1967-70. Del. 7th Ark. Constl. Conv., 1969-70. Chmn. pres.'s devel. council Harding Coll., Searcy, Ark., 1971-73. Served with USN, 1951-54; Korea. Home: 301 N Rose St Sheridan AR 72150 Office: PO Box 499 14th and Pine Sts Arkadelphia AR

THORNTON, RICHARD STANLEY, banker; b. Phila., Dec. 31, 1930; s. Stanley Linham and Bernice (Fooks) T.; B.A., Wesleyan U., Middletown, Conn., 1952; m. Sandra Hendren Rex, May 4, 1957; children—Sandra Hendren, Cynthia Campbell, Richard Rex. With First Pa. Bank N.A., Phila., 1955—, exec. v.p., chief fin. officer, 1976—; exec. v.p., chief fin. officer, dir. First Pa. Corp., 1976—; dir. First Pa. Bank N.A., First Pennco Securities, Inc., Pennamco, Inc. Bd. dirs. N. Pa. Vis. Nurses Assn., 1966-70, Wissachickon br. ARC, 1967-74, Wissahickon Sch. Dist., 1977—. Served to lt. (j.g.) USNR, 1952-55. Mem. Fin. Analysts Phila. (treas. 1964-65), Phila. Clearing House Assn. (sec., treas., mgr. 1966-68). Clubs: Phila. Aviation Country, Union League (Phila.). Contbr. articles to profl. jours. Home: Gypsy Hill Rd Penllyn PA 19422 Office: Centre Sq Philadelphia PA 19101

THORNTON, ROBERT AMBROSE, educator; b. Houston, Mar. 6, 1902; s. Frank and Mary Jane (Sullivan) T.; B.S., Howard U., 1922; M.S., Ohio State U., 1925; postgrad. (Rockefeller fellow) U. Chgo., 1928-29; Ph.D., U. Minn., 1946; postgrad. Harvard U., summers 1949, 51; D.Sc. (hon.), U. San Francisco, 1979; m. Jessie Lea Bullock, June 4, 1925. Instr. physics, math. Shaw U., 1922-25; faculty physics, math. Talladega Coll., 1929-44; dir. basic studies, prof. physics U. P.R., 1944-47; asso. prof. phys. scis. U. Chgo., 1947-50; asso. prof. physics Brandeis U., 1950-53; dean Dillard U., 1953-55; dean basic coll. Fisk U., 1955-56; prof. physics San Francisco State Coll., 1956-63, dean Sch. Natural Scis., 1963-67, prof. physics, 1967—; prof. physics U. San Francisco, 1967-77; Disting. vis. prof. U. D.C., 1980—; participant Einstein Project 1977. Mem. Gov. Calif. TV Adv. Com., 1964-74; mem. accrediation com. Calif. Bd. Edn., 1965-74; mem. Statewide Liaison Com. for Natural Scis., 1965-69; mem. planning com. for program, leadership, structure, theme issues and total activities ann. meeting Assn. Higher Edn., 1954-56; mem. adv. panel for natural and phys. scis. Calif. Commn. Tchr. Preparation and Licensing, 1972-76; mem. sr. commn. Western Assn. Schs. and Colls. for Accrediting Sr. Colls. and Univs., 1972-75; mem. adv. com. Consortium Colls. and Univs. San Francisco, 1977-80; sr. commn. rep. on accrediting commn. Western Assn. Schs. and Colls. for Secondary Schs., 1973-75; mem. panels NSF. Regent, St. Ignatius Coll. Prep., 1972-78; mem. adv. bd. Schs. of Sacred Heart, 1972-79; lectr. Fromm Inst. Continuing Edn., 1976—; mem. Sr. Citizens Com. San Francisco, 1978-80; mem. engring. adv. bd. Calif. State U., San Francisco,

1969-78. Recipient Disting. Teaching award Calif. State Coll., 1968; Asso. Students Faculty award San Francisco State Coll., 1959; commendation Calif. Senate, 1978. Rockefeller fellow, 1935-36. Mem. Am. Physics Soc., N.A.A.C.P., Phi Delta Kappa, Phi Beta Sigma, Alpha Sigma Nu. Episcopalian. Co-author: Introduction to the Physical Sciences, 1937; Course in The Physical Sciences, 3 vols., 1949; Problems in Physics, 1949. Home: 3422 Barkley Dr Fairfax VA 22031

THORNTON, ROBERT DONALD, educator; b. West Somerville, Mass., Aug. 10, 1917; s. John William and Winifred (Harrington) T.; B.A. with high distinction (Denison fellow, Caleb Winchester fellow), Wesleyan U., Middletown, Conn., 1939; M.A. in English, Western Res. U., 1940; M.A. in English (Univ. fellow), Harvard, 1942, Ph.D. (Dexter fellow), 1949; m. Grace Ellen Baker, May 22, 1943; children—Robert, David. Instr. English, Fenn Coll., Cleve., 1939-40, Worcester (Mass.) Acad., 1940-41; teaching fellow English, Harvard, 1941-42, 46-49; asst. prof. English, U. Colo. at Boulder, 1949-56; chmn. English, St. Stephen's Episcopal Sch., Austin, Tex., 1956-57; asso. prof. English, U. S.C., Columbia, 1957-60; prof. English, Kans. State U., Manhattan, 1960-68; prof. English, world lit., chmn. dept. State U. N.Y. Coll. at New Paltz, 1968-71, faculty research fellow, 1973, univ. exchange scholar, 1974—. Served with USNR, 1942-46; PTO. Am. Philos. Soc. grantee, 1955-56, Am. Council Learned Socs., 1963; Guggenheim fellow, 1958-59. Mem. Modern Lang. Assn., Modern Humanities Research Assn., AAUP, Am., Internat. socs. eighteenth-century studies, Am. Center Students and Artists, Chi Psi. Republican. Episcopalian. Clubs: Folio, Mid-Hudson Harvard. Author: A Manual for Reading Improvement, 1953; The Tuneful Flame, 1957; James Currie: The Entire Stranger and Robert Burns, 1963; Selected Poetry and Prose of Robert Burns, 1966; William Maxwell to Robert Burns, 1979. Contbr. to Ency. Ednl. Research, World Poetry and Poetics, Ency. World Lit. in Twentieth Century. Home: 190 Rt 208 New Paltz NY 12561

THORNTON, SPENCER P., ophthalmologist; b. West Palm Beach, Fla., Sept. 16, 1929; s. Ray Spencer and Mae (Phillips) T.; B.S., Wake Forest Coll., 1951; M.D., Bowman Gray Sch. Medicine, 1954; postgrad. So. Bapt. Theol. Sem., Louisville, 1959-60, Colby Coll., summer 1961, Tulane U., summer 1962; m. Annie Glenn Cooper, Oct. 6, 1956; children—Steven Pitts, David Spencer, Ray Cooper, Beth Ellen. Intern, Ga. Bapt. Hosp., Atlanta, 1954-55; resident gen. surgery U. Ala. Med. Center, 1955-56; resident ophthalmology Vanderbilt U. Sch. Medicine, 1960-63, clin. instr. eye surgery, 1963—; practice medicine specializing in ophthalmic surgery, Nashville, 1960—; mem. staff Mid State Bapt. (chief ophthalmology service 1972—), Vanderbilt, Nashville Meml., St. Thomas, Parkview hosps.; instr. surgery U. Ala. Sch. Medicine, 1955-56; med. adviser Nashville Regional Eye Bank, 1966—; King Features syndicated newspaper columnist, 1959-60; feature writer NBC radio and TV, 1958-60. Dir. Webster's Internat. Tutoring Systems, Memoread Systems, Inc., Am. Health Profiles Corp. (med. adv. bd. 1971—); chmn. bd. Ednl. Services Inc., 1970-72; devel. cons. Aurora Pubs., Inc., Nashville, London, 1969-72, pres., chmn. bd. Spencer Thornton Profl. Assn., 1972—. Mem. Gov. Tenn. Com. Employment Handicapped, 1964-66. Pres. Eye Found. Tenn., 1974—; vice pres. Outlook Nashville, 1965-66, bd. dirs., 1964; mem. med. adv. bd. Cumberland Mus. and Sci. Center, Nashville, 1977—; bd. dirs. Found. Human Betterment. Served to capt. M.C., AUS, 1956-58. Named among Outstanding Young Men of Year, U.S. Jr. C. of C., 1965. Diplomate Am. Bd. Ophthalmology. Fellow Royal Soc. Health London, Am. Acad. Ophthalmology, A.C.S.; mem. Nashville Acad. Ophthalmology and Otolaryngology (pres. 1974-75), Soc. for Cryosurgery, Am. Assn. Ophthalmology, Pan Am. Ophthalmology Assn., Contact Lens Soc. Ophthalmologists, Am. Intra-Ocular Implant Soc. (founding mem.), AMA, Tenn. Soc. Medicine, Nashville Acad. Medicine, Nat. Geog. Soc. (life), Tenn. Acad. Ophthalmology (dir. 1976—, public relations chmn. 1979—), Phi Rho Sigma, Delta Kappa Alpha. Baptist. Author: Ophthalmic Eponyms, An Encyclopedia of Named Signs, Syndromes and Diseases in Ophthalmology, 1967; editor Insights, 1979—; contbr. articles to profl. jours. Home: 4014 Sunnybrook Dr Nashville TN 37205 Office: 2000 Church St Nashville TN 37203

THORNTON, SUE BONNER, former librarian; b. nr. Fairfield, Tex.; d. John Carder and Mary (Bonner) Thornton; A.B., U. Okla., 1920, A.B. in L.S. 1938, Mus.B. in Piano, 1921; M.A. Columbia, 1932; postgrad. U. Hawaii, summer 1936. Music supr. Okla. pub. schs., 1921-25; head music dept. Northeastern State Coll., Tahlequah, Okla., 1925-32, librarian, 1932-64. Mem. Central Area, Freestone County, B-RI museums; chmn. bd. dirs. Freestone County (Tex.) Mus. Mem. NEA, ALA, Daus. Am. Colonists, Colonial Dames of 17th Century, Tahlequah C. of C., League Women Voters, United Ch. Women Tahlequah (chmn. 1960), D.A.R. (chmn. good citizens com. for Okla. 1958-60), Magna Charta Dames, Ams. Royal Descent, Plantagenet Soc., Soc. Descs. Knights Garter, Nat. Soc. U.S. Daus. 1812, Huguenot Soc. S.C., P.E.O., Order Washington Daus. Colonial Wars, Colonial Order of Crown, Tex. and Southwestern Cattle Raisers Assn., Pan Am. Round Table, Alpha Gamma Delta. Democrat. Presbyn. Clubs: History (Fairfield, Tex.); Harvey Woman's (Palestine, Tex.); Soroptimist; Freestone County Country. Author: The Bonner Family History. Home: Fairfield TX 75840

THORNTON, WILLIAM E., astronaut; b. Faison, N.C., Apr. 29, 1929; B.S., U. N.C., 1952, M.D., 1963; m. Elizabeth Jennifer Fowler; 2 sons. Dir. electronics div. Del Mar Engring. Labs., Los Angeles, 1956-62; intern U. N.C. Med. Sch., 1963-64; intern Wilford Hall, USAF Hosp., Lackland AFB, San Antonio, 1964-65; with aerospace med. div. Brooks AFB, San Antonio, 1965-67; scientist-astronaut NASA, 1967—; instr. dept. medicine U. Tex. Med. Br., 1977—. Decorated Legion of Merit. Recipient Exceptional Service, Exceptional Sci. Achievement awards NASA Address: Manned Spacecraft Center NASA Houston TX 77058

THORNTON, WILLIAM JAMES, JR., educator; b. Birmingham, July 31, 1919; s. William James and Ada Blanche (Gray) T.; B.Mus., La. State U., 1941, Mus.M., 1948; B.A., Birmingham-So. Coll., 1949; Ph.D., U. So. Calif., 1953; m. Vivian Quine Dyer, Nov. 11, 1939. Instr. music U. Minn., 1955-56; prof., chmn. div. fine arts Parsons Coll., Fairfield, Iowa, 1956-60; prof., chmn. music dept. Trinity U., San Antonio, 1960—. Performer double bass, 1939-54; tchr. music, Pointe Coupee Parish, La., 1939-40, St. James Parish, La., 1942, San Juan Capistrano, Calif., 1952-54, Pleasanton, Cal., 1954-55. Served with USAAF, 1942-46; PTO. Elected to Archives Tex. Composers, Composers of La.; composition commns. from San Antonio Symphony, Parsons Coll., La. State U., Trinity U. Mem. Phi Mu Alpha Sinfonia, Phi Kappa Phi, Phi Sigma Iota, Sigma Nu. Composer major mus. works including String Quartet 1, 1949, Sonata for Cello and Piano, 1950, Serenade for Winds, 1950, Symphony 1, 1953, Sonata for Piano, 1955, Festive Music for Orchestra, 1962, Ceremony of Psalms for Soloists, Choir, Percussion, Organ, 1969, Sinfonía Bejar, Bicentennial commn. San Antonio Symphony, 1976, others. Home: 347 Sharon Dr San Antonio TX 78216

THORNTON, WILLIAM NORMAN, JR., physician, educator; b. Courtland, Va., July 26, 1912; s. William Norman and Evie Rebecca (Williams) T.; B.S., U. Va., 1933, M.D., 1936; m. Kate Sharp Robinson, Jan. 2, 1946; children—William Norman, Linda Evelyn, Frank Curtis. Intern, U. Rochester, 1936-37; intern surgery U. Va., 1937-38, asst. resident, 1938-40, resident obstetrics and gynecology, 1940-42, asst. prof., 1946-48, asso. prof., 1948-50, prof., chmn. dept. obstetrics and gynecology, 1950-67, Robert C. Taylor prof. obstetrics and gynecology, 1967-79, emeritus, 1979—, chmn. dept., 1967-79; obstetrician, gynecologist-in-chief U. Va. Hosp., 1950—. Served as maj. M.C., U.S. Army, 1942-46. Diplomate Am. Bd. Obstetrics and Gynecology. Fellow A.C.S., Am. Assn. Obstetricians and Gynecologists, Am. Coll. Obstetricians and Gynecologists, Am. Gynecol. Soc.; mem. AMA, So. Med. Assn., South-Atlantic Assn. Obstetricians and Gynecologists, Soc. Gynecol. Oncologists, Am. Gynecol. Club. Home: 134 Indian Spring Rd Charlottesville VA 22901 Box 387 University Hospital Charlottesville VA 22901

THORON, GRAY, lawyer, educator; b. Danvers, Mass., July 14, 1916; s. Ward and Louisa Chapin (Hooper) T.; grad. St. Paul's Sch., 1934; A.B., Harvard, 1938, LL.B., 1941; m. Pattie Porter Holmes, Dec. 30, 1971; children (by previous marriage)—Claire, Louisa, Grenville C., Molly D., Thomas G. Admitted to N.Y. bar, 1942; practice law Sullivan & Cromwell, N.Y.C., 1942, 45-48; asso. prof. law U. Tex., 1948-50, prof., 1950-56; dean Law Sch. Cornell U., Ithaca, N.Y., 1956-63, prof. law, 1956—. Vis. prof. law summers U. Mich., 1951, U. Tex., 1970; faculty Salzburg Seminar in Am. Studies, summer 1959; asst. to solicitor gen. Dept. Justice, Washington, 1954-56; mem. N.Y. State Laporte Legislative Ethics Com., 1964; spl. asst. atty. gen. N.Y. State, 1965. Del. Republican Nat. Conv., 1952. Trustee Concord Acad., 1958-61. Served with inf. AUS, 1942-45. Decorated Silver Star, Bronze Star, Purple Heart with oak leaf cluster. Fellow Am. Bar Found.; mem. Am. Law Inst., Am. Judicature Soc., Am., N.Y. State (chmn. spl. com. to rev. code of profl. responsibility 1974—, mem. com. profl. ethics 1965—, vice chmn. 1974—) bar assns., Assn. Bar City N.Y., Phi Alpha Delta, Phi Kappa Phi. Clubs: Century Assn., Harvard (N.Y.C.). Office: Myron Taylor Hall Cornell U Law Sch Ithaca NY 14853

THORP, KENNETH EDWARD, mfg. co. exec.; b. Howard City, Mich., May 16, 1926; s. Vern and Ella Clare (McCloskey) T.; B.S.M.E., U. Mich., 1949; m. Mary Lou Prieskorn, Sept. 16, 1949; children—Ken, Jim, John, Joe, Mary, Amy. Sales engr., zone mgr. Gen. Motors Corp., Detroit, 1952-58; resident mgr., export mgr. Hoover Ball and Bearing Co., Tokyo, 1958-62; gen. sales mgr., gen. mgr. Am. Koyo Corp., Cleve., 1964-70; gen. mgr., pres. Tractech, Inc. Dyneer Corp., Warren, Mich., 1970-79, v.p. Mobile Equipment Products Group Dyneer Corp., Westport, Conn., 1979—. Mem. Am. Mgmt. Assn., Soc. Automotive Engrs. Home: 5141 Forest Way Bloomfield Hills MI 48013 Office: Riverside Bldg Westport CT 06880

THORPE, JAMES, instn. exec.; b. Aiken, S.C., Aug. 17, 1915; s. J. Ernest and Ruby (Holloway) T.; A.B., The Citadel, 1936, LL.D., 1971; M.A., U. N.C., 1937; Ph.D., Harvard, 1941; Litt.D., Occidental Coll., 1968; L.H.D., Claremont Grad. Sch., 1968; H.H.D., U. Toledo, 1977; m. Elizabeth McLean Daniells, July 19, 1941; children—James III, John D., Sally Thorpe Smith. Instr. to prof. English, Princeton, 1946-66; dir. Huntington Library, Art Gallery and Bot. Gardens, San Marino, Calif., 1966—. Bd. fellows Claremont U. Center. Served to col. USAAF, 1941-46. Decorated Bronze Star medal. Guggenheim fellow, 1949-50, 65-66. Fellow Am. Acad. Arts and Scis.; mem. Modern Lang. Assn., Am. Antiquarian Soc. Democrat. Episcopalian. Clubs: Grolier, Zamorano, Twilight. Author: Bibliography of the Writings of George Lyman Kittredge, 1948; Milton Criticism, 1950; Rochester's Poems on Several Occasions, 1950; Poems of Sir George Etherege, 1963; Aims and Methods of Scholarship, 1963, 70; Literary Scholarship, 1964; Relations of Literary Study, 1967; Bunyan's Grace Abounding and Pilgrim's Progress, 1969; Principles of Textual Criticism, 2d edit., 1979; Use of Manuscripts in Literary Research, 2d edit., 1979. Home: 1650 Orlando Rd San Marino CA 91108 Office: Huntington Library Art Gallery and Bot Gardens San Marino CA 91108

THORPE, JAMES ALFRED, utilities exec.; b. Fall River, Mass., Apr. 19, 1929; s. James and Charlotte Ann (Brearley) T.; B.S., Northeastern U., 1951; m. Maxine Elva Thompson, Mar. 4, 1950; children—James Alfred, Peter R., David T., Carol L., Mark W. Asst. supt. prodn. Fall River Gas Co., 1951-55; chief engr. Lake Shore Gas Co., Ashtabula, Ohio, 1955-57; cons. Stone & Webster Mgmt. Corp., 1958-67; pres. Wash. Natural Gas Co., Seattle, 1967, also chief exec. officer; dir. Puget Sound Mut. Savs. Bank, Sea First Corp., Unigard Ins. Group, Seattle 1st Nat. Bank. Bd. dirs. Salvation Army. Mem. Am. (dir., pres. 1977-78), Pacific Coast gas assns., Nat. Alliance Businessmen (dir. Seattle 1972—). Methodist. Clubs: Rainier, Wash. Athletic, Masons, Rotary (Seattle). Home: 11160 SE 59th St Bellevue WA 98006 Office: 815 Mercer St Seattle WA 98111

THORPE, JAMES FRANKLIN, educator; b. Sandusky, Ohio, Oct. 2, 1926; s. Wayne and Adeline (Nuhn) T.; M.E., U. Cin., 1952; M.S., U. Ky., 1955; Ph.D. (Westinghouse reactor fellow), U. Pitts., 1960; m. Sarah Mae Dwenger, Aug. 20, 1959; children—Robert Michael, Thomas Edward, Janet Susan. Project engr. E.W. Buschman Co., Cin., 1947-53; sr. engr. Westinghouse Electric Corp., Pitts., 1955-61; asso. prof., then prof. U. Ky., 1961-67; prof., head mech. engring. dept. U. Cin., 1967—. Pres., Field-Forest-Stream, Inc., Frankfort, Ky., 1964—, Ky. Corp., 1952—. Mem. ASME, Am. Soc. Engring. Edn., Sigma Xi, Tau Beta Pi, Pi Tau Sigma. Served with AUS, 1945-46. Clubs: Western Hills Country; Cincinnati. Contbr. articles to profl. jours. Home: 1478 Beechgrove Dr Cincinnati OH 45238

THORPE, MERLE, JR., lawyer; b. Washington, Apr. 25, 1917; s. Merle and Lilian I. (Day) T.; grad. cum laude, Phillips Exeter Acad., 1934; B.A., Yale, 1938, LL.B., 1941. Admitted to D.C. bar, 1941; with Hogan & Hartson, Washington, 1941—, partner, 1956—. Chmn., Atomics, Physics and Sci. Fund, Washington, 1953-65, Columbian Financial Corp., 1955-65, Shares in Am. Industry, Inc., Washington, 1959-65; dir. Greater Washington Investors, Inc. Asst., asso. gen. counsel Petroleum Adminstrn. Def., 1950-52. Trustee Louise Home, Greater Washington Ednl. Telecommunications Assn.; trustee, gen. counsel Fed. City Council; pres. Merle Thorpe Jr. Found. Served as officer with Intelligence Service, USNR, 1942-46. Mem. Am., D.C. bar assns., Phi Delta Phi. Episcopalian. Clubs: Lawyers, Chevy Chase (pres. 1969), Metropolitan, Alfalfa, Barristers (Washington); Pine Valley Golf (Clementon, N.J.); Yale (N.Y.C.). Home: 3507 Thornapple St Chevy Chase MD 20015 Office: 815 Connecticut Ave Washington DC 20006

THORSEN, ROBERT MITCHEL, advt. exec.; b. Chgo., Aug. 25, 1914; s. George S. and Lorene (Mitten) T.; B.A., Denison U., 1937; m. Barbara Gertrude Kaumanns, June 14, 1947; children—Wendy Josephine (Mrs. Russell J. MacMullan, Jr.), Robert Mitten. Publisher, Bride's Mag., N.Y.C., 1966-75; gen. mgr. book div. Conde Nast Publs., Inc., 1971-75; v.p., dir. advt. 1,001 Communications Co., N.Y.C., 1975-76; sr. v.p. Family Media, Inc., N.Y.C., 1976—; pub. 1,000 Decorating Ideas, 1978—. Trustee Bronxville Pub. Library, 1973-78. Served as lt. USNR, 1942-45. Decorated Purple Heart. Mem. Phi Beta Kappa, Beta Theta Pi. Republican. Episcopalian. Club: Siwanoy Country (Bronxville, N.Y.). Home: 13 Hawthorne Rd Bronxville NY 10708 Office: 149 Fifth Ave New York City NY 10010

THORSHOV, ROY NORMAN, architect; b. Hudson, Wis., Mar. 13, 1905; s. Olaf and Helen (Hansen) T.; B.Arch., U. Minn., 1928; diploma Fontainbleau Sch. Fine Arts, 1929; m. Sylvia Serum, Aug. 22, 1931; children—Sonja Louise, Jon Roland (dec.). Mem. Thorshov & Cerny, Inc., architects, Mpls., 1927-60, pres., 1935-60; mem. Thorsen & Thorshov Assos., Inc., 1960—, v.p., treas.; mem. Minn. State Bd. Registration for Architects, Engrs. and Land Surveyors, 1966-72, sec.-treas., 1967-72; chmn. Mpls. Heritage Preservation Commn., 1972-76, sec., 1976—. Bd. dirs., treas. Sons of Norway Found.; bd. dirs. Pillsbury Waite Neighborhood Services, 1949—, Hennepin County Bicentennial Commn., 1973-76. Registered architect, Minn. Mem. AIA (past sec., pres. Mpls. chpt.), Am. Philatelic Soc., Minn. Soc. Architects (pres. 1964), Constrn. Specifications Inst., Inc. (dir. Minn. chpt. 1958-59), Minn. Hist. Soc., Walker Art Center, Torske-Klubben (pres. 1946—), Hennepin County Hist. Soc. (dir., life mem., pres. 1971—), Norwegian-Am. C. of C. (dir. upper Midwest chpt.), Norwegian-Am. Hist. Soc. (v.p., dir.), Norwegian-Am. Mus. (dir., v.p. 1971), Nordmanns Forbundet (v.p. 1968, pres. 1971-75, dir. internat. bd. 1973—), Tau Sigma Delta, Tau Beta Pi. Architect: St. Francis Cabrini Ch., Mpls. (1st prize 1951); Richfield (Minn.) Central Elementary Sch. (honorable mention 1951); Clearwater County Meml. Hosp., Bagley, Minn. (top award AIA 1951); 1st Unitarian Soc Ch., Mpls. (2d prize Religious Arts Guild); Trinity Luth. Ch., La Crosse, Wis. (honor awards Progressive Architecture 1952); Minn. State Assn. Architecture awards for Elk River Steam Generating Plant, A.S. Aloe Bldg. St. Louis Park Med. Center, 1952; honor awards for Am. Hardware Mut. Bldg., Mpls., 1st Christian Ch., Mpls., 1957; honor awards AIA for Fairmount Fed. Savs. and Loan Assn. (Minn.), St. Mary's Greek Orthodox Ch., Mpls., 1958, Dunwiddie Elementary Sch., Port Washington, Wis., 1959, Lyndale Homes, Mpls., Pearson Candy Co., St. Paul, Grandview Jr. High Sch., Mound, Minn., 1960; 1st honor award for Elliot-Twins Apts., U.S. Pub. Housing Authority, 1964; 1st honor award AIA for Ebenezer Tower housing for elderly, 1972. Decorated Knight's Cross 1st Class Royal Order St. Olav, comdr. Order St. Olav (Norway). Clubs: Athletic (dir. 1958-60), Six O'Clock (pres. 1964), Ten Men's, Shriners. Home: 124 Ottawa Ave S Minneapolis MN 55416 Office: Title Insurance Bldg Minneapolis MN 55401. *Growth in any endeavor can only occur with delegation of responsibility and trust under experienced guidance. Accomplishment by fellow associates must be recognized and credited to them.*

THORSLEV, PETER LARSEN, JR., educator; b. Harlan, Iowa, Oct. 17, 1929; s. Peter Larsen and Marie Christine (Andersen) T.; B.A., Dana Coll., Blair, Neb., 1950; M.A., U. Minn., 1957, Ph.D., 1959. Instr. English, Northwestern U., 1959-60; asst. prof. English, U. Calif., Los Angeles, 1960-66, asso. prof., 1966-71, prof., 1971—. Served with AUS, 1950-53. Guggenheim fellow, 1967-68. Mem. Modern Lang. Assn. Author: The Byronic Hero, 1962. Office: Dept English U Calif Los Angeles CA 90024

THORSON, OSWALD HAGEN, architect; b. Forest City, Iowa, Dec. 19, 1912; s. Thorwald and Josephine (Hagen) T.; B.Arch., U. Minn., 1937; m. Maxine Rustad, Dec. 27, 1941; children—Sigrin, Thorwald. Practicing architect, Forest City, 1937-42, Waterloo, Iowa, 1945—. Developer, Key Condo Condominiums, Dillon, Colo., 1972. Mem. Waterloo Zoning Appeal Bd., 1946—. Served with AUS, 1943. Mem. Iowa Bd. Archtl. Examiners, 1957—, pres., 1962-64. Fellow AIA (pres. Iowa 1953-54, regional dir. central states 1960-63, nat. sec. 1964-66). Home: 919 N Barfield St Marco Island FL 33937

THORSON, PHILLIP THORWALD, govt. ofcl.; b. Forest City, Iowa, Feb. 23, 1915; s. Thorwald and Josephine (Hagen) T.; student Waldorf Coll., 1932-34; B.A., U. Minn., 1937; M.A., Am. U., 1938; postgrad. N.Y. U., 1938-40 m. Marit Woods Beckman, June 10, 1941; children—Ingrid Thorson Mongini, Erik, Louise Thorson Gregory. Instr. govt. N.Y. U., 1940-41; with budget and finance office Dept. Agr., 1941; exec. officer Fgn. Funds Control, Treasury Dept., 1942-44, 46; asst. sec. IMF, Washington, 1946-54, dir. adminstrn., 1954-76, cons., 1977—. Dir. Md. Com. for Fair Representation, 1960-65. Served with AUS, 1944-45. Mem. Am. Soc. Public Adminstrn. (past pres. Nat. Capital Area chpt.), Nat. Acad. Public Adminstrn., Phi Beta Kappa. Democrat. Home: 7001 MacArthur Blvd Washington DC 20016 Office: 700 19th St NW Washington DC 20431

THORSON, RALPH EDWARD, educator, biologist; b. Chatfield, Minn., June 25, 1923; s. Edne Odin and Grace Margaret (Tuohy) T.; B.S., U. Notre Dame, 1948, M.S. in Zoology, 1949; Sc.D. in Hygiene, Johns Hopkins, 1952; m. Margaret Elizabeth Voith, Oct. 4, 1952; children—Margaret Jane, Kristin Inger, Julianne. Instr. parasitology Johns Hopkins, 1952-53; asso. prof. parasitology Auburn U., 1953-57, prof., 1958-59; group leader parasitic chemotherapy Am. Cyanamid Co., 1957-58; prof. biology, head dept. U. Notre Dame (Ind.), 1959-64, prof., 1966—, acting chmn. dept., 1967-68, mem. Grad. Council, 1959-64, 67-71, Research Council, 1961-63, 71-73; prof., chmn. dept. tropical health Am. U. Beirut, 1964-66; Served as 1st lt., navigator USAAF, 1942-45. Decorated D.F.C., Air medal with four oak leaf clusters. Fellow AAAS, Am. Acad. Microbiology; mem. Am. Soc. Parasitologists (editorial bd.), Am. Soc. Tropical Medicine and Hygiene, Sigma Xi (grants-in-aid research com.). Home: 217 Peashway South Bend IN 46617 Office: Dept Biology U Notre Dame Notre Dame IN 46556

THORSON, REUBEN, stock broker, investment banker; b. Madison, Minn., Nov. 20, 1901; s. H.O. and Pauline (Satre) T.; B.S., U. Minn., 1924; m. Dorothy DeVry Whalen, 1930; children—Dorothy Jean (Mrs. Frederick A. Foord), Robert Douglas (dec.), Virginia Luise (Mrs. John C. Goodall, Jr.), Donald Richard. Stock broker Paul H. Davis & Co., Chgo., 1924-31; mgr. Jackson & Curtis, 1931-36, gen. partner, 1936-42, gen. partner Paine, Webber, Jackson & Curtis, Chgo., 1942-68, ltd. partner, 1969—, chmn. policy com., 1955-68; dir. Anchor Coupling Co., 1961-73, Tech. Fund, Inc., Sullair Corp., 1972—, Kemper Preservation Income and Capital Fund, 1971—, Balanced Income Fund, Inc., 1971—, Supervised Investors Growth Fund, Inc., Supervised Investors Summit Fund, Inc. Mem. Chgo. Stock Exchange 1936-49, former gov. and chmn. exec. com.; mem. Midwest Stock Exchange, 1949-69, gov., 1949-55, chmn. bd. govs. 1953-55; mem. Chgo. Bd. Trade, 1942-69, Chgo. Merc. Exchange, 1942-69, Winnipeg Grain Exchange, 1942-67. Pres., Thorson Found., 1954—; mem. adv. bd. Jr. Achievement, Chgo., 1955-70; mem. Auditorium Theater Council, 1960-68. Bd. dirs. Am. Scandinavian Found., 1955-67, U. Chgo. Cancer Research Found., 1961—; bd. dirs. Cook County Sch. Nursing, 1952-65, pres., 1956-58; mem. citizens bd. U. Chgo., 1959—; bd. lay trustees Loyola U., 1959—. Mem. Investment Bankers Assn., Art Inst. Chgo. (life), Lincoln Park Zool. Soc., Kappa Beta Phi, Sigma Nu. Republican. Clubs: Saddle and Cycle, Attic, Edgewater Golf, Chicago Athletic Assn., Chicago, Tavern, Bond (Chgo.); Brook (N.Y.C.); Everglades, Beach, Bath and Tennis (Palm Beach, Fla.). Home: 399 Fullerton Pkwy Chicago IL 60614 also 1 Royal Palm Way Palm Beach FL 33480 Office: 208 S LaSalle St Chicago IL 60604. *If young Americans will pursue their interests and vocations diligently and with genuine consideration for others, any reasonable objective can be attained. The added ingredients of integrity, credibility, and intelligent application are also qualities necessary to achieve one's goal. The opportunities* *for self-improvement and success were never greater than they are today.*

THORSON, THOMAS BERTEL, educator, zoologist; b. Rowe, Ill., Jan. 12, 1917; s. Thomas B. and Hertha (Fylpaa) T.; student Waldorf Coll., 1934-36; B.A., St. Olaf Coll., 1938; M.S., U. Wash., 1941, Ph.D., 1952; m. Margaret L. Overgaard, Dec. 31, 1941; children—Sharon M., Joel T. Faculty, Yakima (Wash.) Jr. Coll., 1946-48, San Francisco State U., 1952-54, S.D. State U., 1954-56; faculty U. Nebr., Lincoln, 1948-50, 56—, prof. zoology, 1961—, chmn. dept., 1967-71, vice dir. Sch. Life Scis., 1975-77. Served to capt. USAAF, 1942-46. Fellow AAAS, Explorers Club; mem. Am. Inst. Biol. Scis., Ecol. Soc. Am., Am. Soc. Zoologists, Am. Soc. Ichthyologists and Herpetologists, Am. Fisheries Soc., Sigma Xi (pres. Nebr. chpt. 1972-74), Phi Sigma. Editor: Investigations of the Ichthyofauna of Nicaraguan Lakes, 1976. Research, publs. on water economy of amphibians, patterns of body water partitioning in cold-blooded vertebrates, osmoregulation freshwater sharks and sawfish of Lake Nicaragua, Amazon River freshwater stingrays S. Am., Africa. Home: 1545 W Manor Dr Lincoln NE 68506

THORUP, OSCAR ANDREAS, educator, physician; b. Washington, Mar. 12, 1922; s. Oscar Andreas and Pattie (Creecy) T.; B.A., U. Va., 1944, M.D., 1946; m. Barbara Turnbull, Sept. 17, 1944; children—Cathryn Lynn, Lisbeth Todd, Matthew Schuyler. Intern, Queen's Hosp., Honolulu, 1946-47; asst. resident U. Va. Hosp., 1949-50, fellow internal medicine, 1950, asst. resident medicine, 1950-51, resident internal medicine, 1951-52; research fellow U. N.C., 1952-53; from. instr. to asso. prof. medicine U. Va. Sch. Medicine, 1953-66; vis. research asso. Radcliffe Infirmary, Oxford (Eng.) U., 1958-59, 72; prof., head dept. internal medicine U. Ariz. Med. Sch., Tucson, 1966-74; prof. medicine, asso. dean, dir. continuing edn. U. Va. Med. Sch., Charlottesville, 1974—. Cons. in field. Pres., Tucson Health Planning Council, 1970-74, also dir.; mem. planning and allocation com. United Way Tucson, 1973. Bd. dirs. Tucson chpt. ARC, 1968-71, Va. Heart Assn., 1975-77. Served with M.C., AUS, 1947-49. Markle scholar med. scis., 1954-59. Fellow A.C.P.; mem. Am. Clin. and Climatol. Assn., Am. Fedn. Clin. Research, Am., Va. med. assns., Va., Albemarle County (pres. 1977) med. socs., Am., Internat. socs. hematology, So. Soc. Clin. Research, Raven Soc., Sigma Xi, Alpha Omega Alpha. Co-author: Fundamentals of Hematology, 4th edit., 1976. Address: Dean's Office Sch Medicine U Va Charlottesville VA 22901

THRALL, ARTHUR ALVIN, artist; b. Milw., Mar. 18, 1926; s. Irving and Helen (Fabich) T.; B.S., Milw. State Tchrs. Coll., 1950; M.S., Wis. State Coll., Milw., 1954; postgrad. (fellow) U. Ill., 1954-55; m. Winifred Rogers, 1960; children—Grant, Wade, Sara, Jay. One man shows: Smithsonian Instn., 1960, Silvermine Artists, New Canaan, Conn., 1964, Ohio State U., Columbus, 1967, Bergstrom Art Center, Neenah, Wis., 1973; group shows include: Corcoran bienials, Washington, 1951, 53, 55, 57, 62, Bklyn. Mus. annuals, Mus. Modern Art, N.Y.C., N.A.D., N.Y.C.; represented in permanent collections: Tate Gallery, Victoria and Albert Mus., Brit. Mus. (all London), Phila. Mus., Seattle Mus., Art Inst. Chgo., Bklyn. Mus., U. Calif., Los Angeles, Smithsonian Instn., USIA, Washington, others; tchr. art Lincoln Jr. High Sch., Kenosha, Wis., 1951-54; asst. prof. State U. N.Y., Geneseo, 1955-56; asso. prof. Milw.-Downer Coll., 1956-64; prof. Lawrence U., Appleton, Wis., 1964—. Served with U.S. Army, 1944-46; ETO. Recipient Bklyn. Mus. print awards, 1952, 64, Pa. Acad. Arts award, 1960, NAD awards, 1956, 68; Louis Comfort Tiffany fellow, 1963. Mem. AAUP, Boston Printmakers (awards 1963, 65), Soc. Am. Graphic Artists (awards 1951, 52, 60, 78), Audubon Artists Inc. (award 1977). Home: 59 Bellaire Ct Appleton WI 54911 Office: Lawrence Univ Appleton WI 54911

THRALL, DONALD STUART, painter; b. Detroit, Mar. 29, 1918; s. Ernest Lawrence and Gertrude Marie (Aikenhead) T.; B.A., Mich. State U., 1940; M.A., Columbia U. Tchrs. Coll., 1946; summer student Skowhegan (Maine) Sch. Painting and Sculpture, 1947, Black Mountain (N.C.) Coll., 1948. Instr. painting and design Cass Tech. Sch., Detroit, 1949-55; ednl. coordinator Guggenheim Mus., N.Y.C., 1961-73; one-man exhbn. Contemporary Arts Gallery, N.Y.C., 1961; group exhbns. include Met. Mus. Art, 1950, Detroit Inst. Arts, 1947-55 (award 1950, 53, 55), Mich. Artists invited survey show, 1951, Butler Inst. Am. Art, Youngstown, Ohio (1st prize 1951), 1950-52, Whitney Mus., N.Y.C., 1953, Bklyn. Mus., 1961, others; group exhbns. include Wildenstein Galleries, N.Y.C. (Hallmark Art prize), 1952, Downtown Gallery, N.Y.C., 1950-53, Detroit Artists Market, 1948-54, Scarab Gallery, Detroit (award 1948, 51, 53, 54), 1949-53, Mich. Watercolor Soc. (award 1950, 52, 53, 55), 1949-55, Mich. State Fair (1st prize 1952), 1952, Detroit Art Instr. Exhbn. (1st award 1946, 48, 50, 51, 53), 1946-53, 16th Serigraph Internat., N.Y.C., 1955, others; represented in permanent collections Detroit Inst. Arts, Butler Inst. Am. Art, U. Mich. Mus. Art, Mus. Wayne State U., Cranbrook Acad. Art Mus., Bloomfield Hills, Mich., numerous pvt. collections. Bd. dirs. Mich. Watercolor Soc., 1950-55, Detroit Met. Art Assn., 1948-54; exhibiting mem. Detroit Inst. Arts, 1947-53. Served with AUS, 1941-45. Guggenheim fellow, 1955. Mem. Mich. Acad. Sci., Arts and Letters, Beta Alpha Sigma (pres. 1940). Address: 945 West End Ave New York City NY 10025

THRALL, ROBERT MCDOWELL, mathematician, educator; b. Toledo, Ill., Sept. 23, 1914; s. Charles Haven and Gertrude (Gerking) T.; B.A., Ill. Coll., 1935, Sc.D., 1966; M.A., U. Ill., 1935, Ph.D., 1937; m. Natalie Hunter, Sept. 3, 1936; children—Charles A., James H., Mary Emily. Teaching fellow U. Ill., 1935-37; instr. math. U. Mich., 1937-42, asst. prof., 1942-48, asso. prof., 1948-55, prof., 1955-69, prof. operation analysis, 1956-69, head ops. research dept. U. Mich. Research Inst., 1957-60; prof., chmn. dept. math. scis. Rice U., Houston, 1969-78, Noah Harding prof. math. scis., 1978—; adj. prof. biomath. dept. rehab. Baylor Sch. Medicine, 1969—, adj. prof. Computer Sci. Inst., 1971—; adj. prof. U. Tex. Sch. Pub. Health, 1971—. Faculty, Stanford Summer Inst., 1957, Dartmouth Summer Inst., 1953, Inst. Advanced Study, Princeton, 1940-42; cons. RAND Corp., 1951—, U.S. Army OCRD, 1958—, Holt, Rinehart & Winston, Inc., 1961—, Gen. Electric Co., 1963-69, Dow Chem. Co., 1965-69, Comshare Co., 1967-69, Gen. Motors Corp., 1967-69, Nat. Water Commn., 1970-71; pres. R.M. Thrall & Assos., Inc., 1970—; regional lectr. Math. Assn. Am., 1961; Sigma Xi nat. lectr., 1968-69; SIAM lectr., 1970-72; TIMS-ORSA lectr., 1972-75. Mem. NRC div. math. scis., 1967-70. Recipient Henry Russell award U. Mich., 1947, Distinguished Faculty award U. Mich., 1965. Mem. AAAS, AAUP, Am. Math. Soc., Am. Statis. Assn., Assn. Computing Machinery, Can. Math. Congress, Econometric Soc., Math. Assn. Am., Nat. Council Tchrs. Math., Inst. Mgmt. Scis., Operations Research Soc. Am., Operational Research Soc. (Gt. Britain), Psychometric Soc., Soc. Gen. Systems Research, Soc. for Indsl. and Applied Math., Phi Beta Kappa, Sigma Xi, Phi Kappa Phi. Author: (with E.B. Miller) College Algebra, 1950; (with L. Tornheim) Vector Spaces and Matrices, 1957; (with A. Spivey) Linear Optimization, 1970. Editor-in-chief Mgmt. Sci., 1960-69; mem. editorial bd. SIAM Rev., 1959-76, Operational Research Quar., 1960-69, Jour. of Conflict Resolution, 1961-71, Behavioral Sci., 1964—, Operations Research, 1965-69, Zeitschrift fur Wahrscheinlichkeitstheorie und verwandte Gebiete, 1962-71. Contbr. articles to profl. jours. Home: 12003 Pebble Hill Houston TX 77024

THRASH, EDSEL E., ednl. adminstr.; b. Lake, Miss., Aug. 28, 1925; B.S. in Bus. Adminstrn., La. State U., 1950, M.B.A., 1951, Ph.D., 1963; m. Jessie McLendon, Apr. 16, 1949; children—Jane, Catherine, George. Acct., Esso Standard Oil Co., 1951-55; dir. alumni affairs La. State U., 1957-68, mem. dept. econs., 1966-68; exec. sec., dir. bd. trustees State Instns. Higher Learning in Miss., Jackson, 1968—. Bd. dirs. Miss. Heart Assn., 1970-76; mem. exec. council Andrew Jackson council Boy Scouts Am.; mem. council on ministries United Meth. Ch., Raymond, Miss., 1973—. Recipient Silver Beaver award Boy Scouts Am., 1977; Gold Heart award Miss. Heart Assn., 1976. Mem. Omicron Delta Kappa, Alpha Kappa Psi. Club: Rotary. Office: PO Box 2336 Jackson MS 39205

THRASH, PATRICIA ANN, assn. exec.; b. Grenada, Miss., May 4, 1929; d. Lewis Edgar and Weaver (Betts) Thrash; B.S., Delta State Coll., 1950; M.A., Northwestern U., 1953, Ph.D., 1959. Tchr. high sch. English, Clarksdale, Miss., 1950-52; head resident Northwestern U., 1953-55, asst. to dean of women, 1955-58, asst. dean women, 1958-60, lectr. edn., 1959-65, dean women, 1960-69, asso. prof. edn., 1965-72, asso. dean students, 1969-71; asst. exec. sec. Commn. on Instns. Higher Edn., North Central Assn. Colls. and Secondary Schs., 1972-73, asso. exec. dir., 1973—. Mem. Nat. (v.p. 1967-69, pres. 1972-73), Ill. (sec. 1961-63, pres. 1964-66) assns. women deans and counselors, Am. Coll. Personnel Assn. (editorial bd. jour. 1971-74), Council Student Personel Assns. in Higher Edn. (sec.-treas. 1969-71), Am. Assn. Higher Edn. (program, nominations com. 1974-75, adv. panel Am. Coll. Testing Coll. Outcome Measures project 1977-78, staff COPA project for evaluation nontraditional edn. 1977-78, mem. editorial bd. Jour. Higher Edn. 1975—, guest editor Mar.-Apr. 1979), Mortar Bd. (hon.), Phi Delta Theta, Pi Lambda Theta, Alpha Psi Omega, Alpha Lambda Delta, Chi Omega, Zonta. Methodist. Contbr. chpt. to Handbook of College and University Administration, 1970; articles to ednl. jours. Home: 2337 Hartrey Ave Evanston IL 60201

THRASHER, JAMES PARKER, container and trailer leasing co. exec.; b. Waltham, Mass., Jan. 15, 1932; s. Linus James and Doris Melissa (Parker) T.; B.S. in Indsl. Adminstrn., Yale U., 1953; m. Mary Patricia Mayer, Dec. 31, 1965; children—Deborah Anne, Linda Carol, Anne Elizabeth. With U.S. Steel Corp., Cleve., 1953-60; cons. Booz, Allen & Hamilton, London, 1960-65; with McKinsey & Co., Inc., mgmt. cons., London, 1965-67; with Integrated Container Service, Inc., 1967—, exec. v.p., 1969-70, pres., chief exec. officer, N.Y.C., 1970—; v.p. Interway Corp. (now TransAm. Interway Inc.), N.Y.C., 1969-75, pres., chief exec. officer, 1975—; Registered profl. engr., Ohio. Clubs: Yale; American (London). Home: 2 Langdon Terr Bronxville NY 10708 Office: 522 Fifth Ave New York NY 10036

THREEFOOT, SAM ABRAHAM, physician, educator; b. Meridian, Miss., Apr. 10, 1921; s. Sam Abraham and Ruth Frances (Lilienthal) T.; B.S., Tulane U., 1943, M.D., 1945; m. Virginia Rush, Feb. 6, 1954; children—Barbara Jane Denman, Ginny Ruth, Tracyann, Shelley Ann. Intern, Michael Reese Hosp., Chgo., 1945-47; asst. vis. physician Charity Hosp. New Orleans, 1947-50, vis. physician, 1950-57, sr. vis. physician, 1957-69, cons., 1969-70, 76—; clin. asst. dept. medicine Touro Infirmary, New Orleans, 1953-56, jr. asst., 1956-60, sr. asst., 1960-63, dir. med. edn., 1953-63, dir. research, 1953-70, sr. dept. medicine, 1963-70; fellow dept. medicine Tulane U., 1947-49, instr., 1948-53, asst. prof., 1953-59, asso. prof., 1959-63, prof., 1963-70, 76—; chief of staff VA Hosp., Forest Hills div., Augusta, Ga., 1970-76; asso. chief staff VA Hosp., New Orleans, 1976-79, chief of staff, 1979—; asst. dean Med. Coll. Ga., 1970-76, prof. medicine, 1970-76. Cons. physician Lallie Kemp Charity Hosp., Independence, La., 1951-53. Served with AUS, 1943-45. La. Heart Assn. grantee, 1953-55; John A. Hartford Found. grantee, 1956-74; Am. Heart Assn. grantee, 1959-61; USPHS grantee, 1953-66. Diplomate Am. Bd. Internal Medicine. Fellow A.C.P., Am. Coll. Cardiology, N.Y. Acad. Sci.; mem. Am. Heart Assn. (v.p. 1970, fellow council on circulation), Central Soc. Clin. Research, So. Soc. Clin. Investigation (pres. 1967), AAAS, Internat. Soc. Lymphology, Soc. Exptl. Biology and Medicine, Soc. Nuclear Medicine, Microcirculatory Conf., Inc., Am. Fedn. Clin. Research, La. Heart Assn. (pres. 1967), La., Orleans Parish med. socs., AMA, Richmond County Med. Soc., Phi Beta Kappa, Sigma Xi. Jewish. Editor Lymphology, 1967-70. Contbr. articles profl. jours. Home: 347 Millaudon St New Orleans LA 70118 Office: VA Med Center 1601 Perdido St New Orleans LA 70146. *I am one of those fortunate individuals who has been able to approach goals set early in life. Although my achievements are far short of my aspirations, at least I have had the opportunity. In dealing with both people and things, I have always felt that no detail was too small to receive attention.*

THRELKELD, WILLIAM BERRY, gas transmission co. exec.; b. Memphis, Aug. 13, 1919; s. Earl R. and Marguerite (Berry) T.; LL.B., Memphis State U., 1950; m. Laura Ledbetter, Aug. 14, 1943; children—Kathleen, Kendall. Vice pres., corp. sec. Texas Gas Transmission Corp, Owensboro, Ky., 1970—. Served with USAAF, 1941-45. Office: Texas Gas Transmission Corp 3800 Frederica St Owensboro KY 42301

THRIFT, CHARLES TINSLEY, JR., coll. pres.; b. Kenbridge, Va., Apr. 11, 1911; s. Charles Tinsley and Nell (Webb) T.; A.B., Duke, 1930, A.M., 1932, R.D., 1933; Ph.D., U. Chgo. (fellow in ch. history), 1936; D.D., Southwestern U., 1965; L.H.D., Bethune-Cookman Coll., 1976; m. Ruth King, June 30, 1934; children—Ruth Nell, Helen Sue, Mary King. Prof. religion, dir. religious life Southwestern U., Georgetown, Tex., 1936-39; prof. religion Fla. So. Coll., Lakeland, 1940—, v.p. of coll., 1946-57, acting pres., 1957, pres., 1957—. Vis. prof. Northwestern U. Garrett Bibl. Inst., summer 1946, Emory U., summer 1949, 52, Perkins Sch. Theology, So. Meth. U., 1952. Mem. Meth. Gen. Conf., 1960, 64, Bd. Edn., 1960—. Certification com. So. Regional Edn. (Fla.), 1949—. Mem. Fla. Conf. Meth. Ch.; dean Fla. Pastors' (Meth.) Sch., 1945-60. Mem. Am. Soc. Church History, Southeastern Hist. Soc. (Meth.) (sec. 1944-48), Fla. Assn. Colls. and Univs. (exec. com., 1945-53, v.p., 1949-50, pres., 1950-51), Ind. Colls. and Univs. Fla. (chmn. 1974-76), Fla. Hist. Soc. (dir. 1944-46, v.p. 1952-54, pres. 1954-56), Fla. Acad. Scis., Phi Beta Kappa, Omicron Delta Kappa, Kappa Delta Pi, Pi Gamma Mu. Author: The Trail of the Florida Circuit Rider, 1944; Through Three Decades at Florida Southern College, 1955; A Study of Theological Education in The Methodist Church, 1956. Contbr. to The Florida Story, Fla. papers. Editor: Marshaling Florida's Resources, 1945. Contbr. articles to religious, ednl., hist. publs. Home: 969 Hollingsworth Dr Lakeland FL 33801

THRIFT, ERIC WILLIAM, educator, cons.; b. Winnipeg, Man., Can., Aug. 23, 1912; s. William David and Amy Eveline (Daw) T.; B.Arch., U. Man., 1935; M.Arch., Mass. Inst. Tech., 1938; m. Melba Maude Belyea, Aug. 22, 1940; children—Kristin Elizabeth, Murray Eric, William David, Dennis Gordon. Archtl. asst. H.H.G. Moody, architect, 1935-36, supt. bldgs. office Hudson's Bay Co., 1938-42; lectr. architecture U. Man., 1942-43, spl. lectr. housing and planning, 1943-50; tech. adv. planning, postwar reconstrn. com. Province Man., also archtl. designer Green, Blankstein, Russell & Assos., architects, 1943-44; dir. planning Met. Planning Com., Winnipeg Town Planning Commn., 1945-49; dir. Met. Planning Commn. Greater Winnipeg, 1949-60; gen. mgr. Nat. Capital Commn., Ottawa, 1960-70, planning adviser, 1970-71; prof. urban and regional planning Queen's U., Kingston, Ont., Can., 1971—. Cons., adviser in field to govt., industry. Chmn., Greater Winnipeg Transp. Study, 1955-56; vice chmn. Winnipeg Renewal Bd., 1958-60; mem. Ottawa Planning Bd., 1960-71, Canadian Council Urban and Regional Research, 1963-66; mem. exec. com. Comml. and Indsl. Corp. Ottawa, 1964-71. Recipient gold medal U. Man., 1935, travelling fellow engring. and architecture, 1936, Centennial medal of Can., 1967, Queen's Silver Jubilee medal Can., 1977. Fellow Royal Archtl. Inst. Can. (council 1948-49, Gold medal 1935), Can. Inst. Planners (pres. 1953-54, 61-62, mem. council 1952-55, 57-63); mem. Man. Assn. Architects (pres. 1949, mem. council 1948-50, 52-54, 56-58, 60), Am. Inst. Planners, Am. Soc. Planning Ofcls. (mem. bd. 1959-63, pres. 1964-65), Community Planning Assn. Can. (council 1950-59), U. Man. Alumni Assn. (pres. 1950), Nat. Gallery Assn. (v.p. 1961-62, pres. 1968-71). Mem. United Ch. Can. Kiwanian (bd. Winnipeg 1958-60). Home: 1088 Johnson St Kingston ON K7M 2N5 Canada

THROCKMORTON, LYNN HIRAM, biologist, educator; b. Loup City, Nebr., Dec. 20, 1927; s. Alonzo Joseph and Lyal Geneveive (Cramer) T.; B.Sc., U. Nebr., 1949, M.Sc., 1956; Ph.D., U. Tex., 1959. Mem. faculty U. Chgo., 1962—, prof. biology, 1971—. Served with AUS, 1951-54. Mem. AAAS, Soc. Study Evolution, Am. Soc. Naturalists, Soc. Systematic Zoologists, Genetics Soc. Am., Entomol. Soc. Am., Am. Genetics Soc., Am. Soc. Zoology, Am. Inst. Biol. Scis. Home: 1451 E 55th St Chicago IL 60615 Office: 1103 E 57th St Chicago IL 60637

THROCKMORTON, ROBERT BENTLEY, lawyer; b. Des Moines, June 25, 1915; s. Tom Bentley and Edna J. (Dudley) T.; B.A., Drake U., 1936, J.D. with honors, 1938; LL.M., Harvard, 1939; m. Frances Louise Turman, Oct. 19, 1940; children—Gail (Mrs. Tony L. Lowenberg), Tom Dudley. Admitted to Ia. bar, 1938, Ill. bar, 1965; with Solicitor's Office, Dept. Agr., 1939-42; project atty. War Relocation Authority, 1942-43; partner firm Dickinson, Throckmorton, Parker, Mannheimer & Raife, Des Moines, 1949-63, 65—. Dir. BLC Growth Fund, Inc., BLC Income Fund, Inc., BLC Fund, Inc. Gen. counsel AMA, 1963-65; lectr. Drake U. Law Sch., 1946-51, 68, chmn. law faculty, 1946. Bd. dirs. Iowa Council Chs., 1967-69, Scottish Rite Charitable and Ednl. Found. Iowa, 1963—, S. Iowa Meth. Homes, 1955-72. Served to lt. (j.g.) USNR, 1943-46. Recipient Sanford award Iowa Med. Soc., 1967; Drake Class of 1915 medal, 1936. Mem. Am. Law Inst., Am., Iowa (pres. jr. bar sect. 1949), Polk County bar assns., Drake Nat. Alumni Assn. (dir., award 1961), Phi Beta Kappa, Order of Coif, Phi Alpha Delta, Alpha Tau Omega (Thomas Arkle Clark award 1936), Omicron Delta Kappa. Republican. Methodist. Mason (33 deg.). Home: 1121 Americana Ct Des Moines IA 50314

THROCKMORTON, TOM D., surgeon; b. Des Moines, Sept. 19, 1913; s. Tom Bentley and Edna J.J. (Dudley) T.; B.A. magna cum laude, Drake U., 1934; B.S. in Medicine, Northwestern U., 1936, M.D. with honors, 1937; M.S. in Surgery, U. Minn., 1942; m. Grace Elizabeth Cleland, June 28, 1938 (dec. Oct. 1968); children—Toni Joanne (Mrs. James W. Walling), Terri Jean (Mrs. O. Johnson), Hance C.; m. 2d, Jean Bolman, July 31, 1969. Dean's intern U. Pa. Hosps., 1937-39; fellow surgery Mayo Clinic, 1939-42, asst. to surg. staff, 1943; gen. practice surgery, Des Moines, 1943—; chief surgery Iowa Meth. Hosp., 1949-56, 66-68; mem. hon. staff Mercy, Broadlawns; staff Polk County hosps. Bd. dirs. Iowa Med. Service, 1955-59, exec. v.p., 1958-59; bd. dirs. Hosp. Service Inc., 1958-63. Mem. Iowa Wine Commn.; bd. dirs. Des Moines Symphony Orch., 1956-60; mem. dean's com. com. State U. Iowa Med. Sch., 1965—; pres. Pleasantwood Found.; past trustee Mayo Alumni Bd., chmn. alumni bd. Mayo Devel.; trustee Mayo Found. Named chevalier du Tastevin; recipient Peter Borr Meml. Cup., Royal Hort. Soc. London, 1977; Nat. Hort. award Men's Garden Clubs Am., 1978; Spl. award Women's Garden Clubs Am., 1978. Fellow A.C.S.; mem. AMA, Iowa Med. Soc. (award of merit 1956), Iowa Acad. Surgery (pres. 1973), Western Surg. Assn. (pres. 1973), AAAS, Priestley Surg. Soc. (pres. 1967), Am. Daffodil Soc. (pres. 1968-70, dir., Silver medal 1977), Am. Hort. Soc., Commanderie de Bordeaux, Phi Beta Kappa, Alpha Omega Alpha, Alpha Tau Omega, Phi Beta Phi, Helmut and Spurs Hon. Soc. Methodist. Mason (32 deg.). Spl. work repair complicated hernias with tantalum mesh, amateur application electronic data processing methods to horticulture. Home: 2909 Gilmore Ave Des Moines IA 50309 Office: 1407 Woodland Ave Des Moines IA 50312

THRODAHL, MONTE CORDEN, chem. co. exec.; b. Mpls., Mar. 25, 1919; s. Monte Conrad and Hilda (Larson) T.; B.S., Iowa State U., 1941; m. Josephine Crandall, Nov. 6, 1948; children—Mark Crandall, Peter Douglas. With Monsanto Co., St. Louis, 1941—, gen. mgr. internat. div., 1964-66, v.p., 1965—, dir., 1966—, group v.p. tech., 1974—, sr. v.p., 1979—; v.p., dir. Monsanto Research Corp. Bd. dirs. Salzburg Seminar in Am. Studies; chmn. bd. dirs., mem. exec. com. Webster Coll., Chem. Industry Inst. Toxicology. Fellow Am. Inst. Chemists; mem. Am. Chem. Soc., Am. Inst. Chem. Engrs., Comml. Devel. Assn., AAAS, Soc. Chem. Industry, Alpha Chi Sigma. Clubs: Old Warson Country, St. Louis (St. Louis). Home: No 36 Briarcliff Ladue MO 63124 Office: 800 N Lindbergh Blvd St Louis MO 63166

THROOP, ALLEN EATON, lawyer; b. Niagara Falls, N.Y., Jan. 2, 1900; s. Augustus Thompson and Helen Maria (Eaton) T.; A.B., Hamilton Coll., 1921; A.M., Harvard, 1922, LL.B., 1925, S.J.D., 1926; m. E. Wilhelmina Westbrook, Jan. 19, 1929; children—Thomas Augustus, Adrian Westbrook. Admitted to N.Y. bar, 1928, D.C. bar, 1966; practiced with Cotton & Franklin (later Cotton, Franklin, Wright & Gordon), N.Y.C., 1926-34; counsel RFC, Washington, 1932; sec. Fgn. Bondholders Protective Council, N.Y.C., 1934; asst. gen. counsel SEC, Washington, 1934-37, gen. counsel, 1937-38; asso. prof. law Yale, 1938-40; gen. counsel Trustees of Assos. Gas & Electric Corp., N.Y.C., 1940-46, trustee corp., 1946-55; mem. firm Shearman & Sterling, N.Y.C., 1945-63; v.p., gen. counsel Communications Satellite Corp., Washington, 1963-66; asso. firm Corcoran, Youngman & Rowe, 1967—. Edwin A. Mooers lectr. Washington Coll. Law, Am. U., Washington, 1967; adviser fed. securities code project Am. Law Inst., 1969—; mem. adv. bd. Securities Regulation and Law Report, 1969—. Pres., Friends Scarsdale Library, 1959-60. Mem. D.C. Bar, Bar Assn. D.C., Am. (chmn. com. fed. regulation securities 1960-62), Fed. bar assns., Fed. Communications Bar Assn., Am. Law Inst., Am. Bar Found., Phi Beta Kappa. Presbyterian. Clubs: University, Kenwood Golf and Country (Washington). Contbg. author: A Lawyer's Guide to International Business Transactions. Contbr. articles to law jours. Home: 4301 Massachusetts Ave NW Washington DC 20016 Office: Suite 1100 1511 K St NW Washington DC 20005

THROWER, RANDOLPH WILLIAM, lawyer; b. Tampa, Fla., Sept. 5, 1913; s. Benjamin Key and Ora (Hammond) T.; grad. Ga. Mil. Acad., 1930; Ph.B., Emory U., 1934, J.D., 1936; m. Margaret Munroe, Feb. 2, 1939; children—Margaret (Mrs. W. Thomas MacCary), Patricia (Mrs. John R. Barmeyer), Laura (Mrs. David T. Harris, Jr.), Randolph William, Mary. Admitted to Ga. bar, 1935, D.C. bar, 1953; partner Sutherland, Asbill & Brennan, Atlanta, Washington, 1947-69, 71—; commr. internal revenue, 1969-71. Lectr. bar, legal meetings; spl. agt. FBI, 1942-43; mem. Arthur Andersen & Co. Bd. of Rev., 1974—; mem. Nat. Council on Organized Crime, mem. exec. com., 1970-71. Past pres. Ga., Met. Atlanta mental health assns.; trustee Emory U.; chmn. Wesleyan Coll.; bd. govs. Woodward Acad.; past chmn. bd. visitors Emory U. Served as capt. USMCR, 1944-45. Mem. Atlanta Legal Aid Soc. (past pres.), Emory U. Alumni Assn. (past pres.), Am. (chmn. spl. com. on survey local needs 1971—, past chmn. sect. taxation; mem. ho. of dels. 1964-66, 74—), Ga., Atlanta (past pres.) bar assns., Am. Law Inst., Atlanta Lawyers Club (past pres.), Phi Delta Phi. Republican. Methodist. Clubs: Commerce, Capital City, Piedmont Driving (Atlanta); Metropolitan, Chevy Chase (Washington). Home: 2240 Woodward Way NW Atlanta GA 30305 Office: First Nat Bank Tower Atlanta GA 30303

THRUN, ROBERT, lawyer; b. Eagle River, Wis., July 1, 1913; s. Ferdinand Julius and Florence (Zwicker) T.; B.A., U. Wis., 1936; J.D., Harvard, 1939; m. Roberta Read Lewis, June 22, 1937; children—Sally Grosvenor, Roberta Read, Robert Read. Sec., Wis. R.R. Assn., 1934-36; admitted to N.Y. bar, 1940, since practiced in N.Y.C.; mem. firm Reavis & McGrath, 1946—; atty. Village of Croton-on-Hudson, N.Y., 1959-60, 61-67; gen. counsel, v.p., mem. bd., exec. com. U.S. com. for UNICEF, 1954—. Counsel, sec. Ringling Bros.-Barnum & Bailey Combined Shows, Inc., 1952-67, dir., gen. counsel, 1971—; gen. counsel Pulitzer Pub. Co., 1971—, dir., 1977—; v.p., gen. counsel, dir. Sells-Floto, Inc., 1974—; dir., mem. exec. com. Nat. City Lines, Inc., 1978—. Trustee, sec. Sotterley Mansion Found., Hollywood, Md., 1962—. Served with AUS, 1943-44; to lt. (j.G.) USNR, 1944-46. Decorated commendations from sec. navy, sec. war. Mem. Am. Bar Assn., Assn. Bar City N.Y., Phi Beta Kappa, Phi Gamma Delta. Home: Finney Farm Rd Croton-on-Hudson NY 10520 Office: 345 Park Ave New York NY 10022

THUERING, GEORGE LEWIS, engr., adminstr.; b. Milw., Sept. 2, 1919; s. Louis Charles and Elsie (Luetzow) T.; B.S., U. Wis., 1941, M.E., 1954; M.S., Pa. State U., 1949; m. Lillian May Cline, Dec. 7, 1945 (dec.); 1 dau., Jean Carol Thuering Ameringer; m. 2d, Betty L. McBride, Aug. 9, 1975. Mfg. engr. Lockheed Aircraft Corp., Burbank, Calif., 1941-47, supr. plant layout, Marietta, Ga., 1951-52; mem. faculty Pa. State U., University Park, 1947—, asso. prof. indsl. engring., 1952-56, prof., 1956—, dir. mgmt. engring., 1961—; cons. engring. Registered profl. engr., Pa. Fellow Soc. Advancement Mgmt.; mem. ASME (chmn. mgmt. div. 1976-77, mem. exec. com. mgmt. div. 1973-77, chmn. papers rev. com. 1969-73), Am. Inst. Indsl. Engrs. (dir. students affairs 1972-74), Am. Soc. Engring. Edn. (chmn. indsl. engring. div. 1956-57), Sigma Xi, Tau Beta Pi, Pi Tau Sigma, Alpha Pi Mu. Contbr. articles to profl. jours. Home: 436 Homan Ave State College PA 16801 Office: 207 Hammond Bldg University Park PA 16802

THUESEN, GERALD JORGEN, indsl. engr.; b. Oklahoma City, July 20, 1938; s. Holger G. and Helen S. T.; B.S., Stanford U., 1960, M.S., 1961, Ph.D., 1968; children—Karen E., Dyan L. Engr., Pacific Telephone Co., San Francisco, 1961-62, Atlantic Richfield Co., Dallas, 1962-63; asst. prof. indsl. engring. U. Tex., Arlington, 1963, 67-68; asso. prof. indsl. and systems engring. Ga. Inst. Tech., 1968-76, prof., 1976—. Recipient Eugene L. Grant award Am. Soc. Engring. Edn., 1977; NASA/Am. Soc. Engring. Edn. summer faculty fellow, 1970. Mem. Am. Inst. Indsl. Engring. (deptl. editor Trans. 1976—, v.p. publs. 1979—, div. dir. 1978—), Am. Soc. Engring. Edn. (dir.), Ops. Research Soc. Am., Inst. Mgmt. Sci., Sigma Xi. Author: Engineering Economy, 4th edit., 1971, 5th edit., 1977; Economic Decision Analysis, 1974, 2d edit., 1980; asso. editor The Engring. Economist, 1974—. Office: Sch Indsl and Systems Engring Ga Inst Tech Atlanta GA 30332

THULEAN, DONALD MYRON, symphony condr.; b. Wenatchee, Wash., June 24, 1929; s. Elmer Edward and Mary (Myron) T.; B.A., U. Wash., 1950, M.A. in Music, 1952; Mus.D. (hon.), Whitworth Coll., 1967; m. Meryl Mary Parnell, Mar. 17, 1951; children—Dorcas Marie, Mark Myron, William Norton. Faculty, Pacific U., 1955-62, dean Sch. Music, 1957-62; asso. condr. Portland (Oreg.) Symphony, 1961-62; condr., music dir. Spokane Symphony, 1962—; asst. condr. Seattle Symphony, 1966-69; chorus master Aspen Music Festival, 1957-61; artistic cons. Title III project in performing arts Wash. State, 1966-68; music dir. Tamarack Music Festival, 1971. Served with AUS, 1953-55. Unitarian (trustee). Office: West 621 Mallon St Spokane WA 99201

THULEEN, ROLAND HOWARD, banker; b. Mpls., July 21, 1917; s. Albert Axel and Ruth Blanche (Hanson) T.; certificate Am. Inst. Banking, 1950; grad. Stonier Grad. Sch. Banking, Rutgers U., 1955; m. Eileen Lora Walvatne, Sept. 12, 1942; children—Pamela (Mrs. G. Scott Giebink), Randall Howard, Scott Alan. With First Nat. Bank Mpls., 1936—, sr. v.p., 1971-75, vice chmn., 1975—. Treas., mem. bd. Crop Quality Council, 1971; mem. Internat. Monetary Conf., 1972. Bd. dirs. United Cerebral Palsy Greater Mpls., 1955—, pres., 1962-73. Served to 1st lt. USAAF, 1942-45. Recipient Good Neighbor award radio sta. WCCO, 1957. Mem. Robert Morris Assos. (past pres. Minn., past nat. chmn. com. cooperation with constrn. industry), Mpls. Citizens League, Assn. Res. City Bankers, Am. Inst. Banking. Lutheran (past trustee). Clubs: Minneapolis, Minikahda. Home: 9700 Am Ln Hopkins MN 55343 Office: 120 S 6th St Minneapolis MN 55402

THUMANN, ALBERT, assn. exec., engr.; b. Bronx, N.Y., Mar. 12, 1942; s. Albert and Ella (Josephy) T.; B.S., City U. N.Y., 1964; M.S. in Elec. Engring., N.Y. U., 1967, M.S. in Indsl. Engring., 1970; m. Susan Stock, Jan. 23, 1966; 1 son, Brian. Project engring. mgr. Bechtel Corp., N.Y.C., Louisville, 1964-77; exec. dir. Assn. Energy Engrs., 1977—. Adj. prof. environmental engring. U. Louisville, 1974-75. Registered profl. engr., N.Y., Ky. Named Young Engr. of Year, Ky. Soc. Profl. Engrs., 1974-75, Ky. col. Mem. IEEE, Nat. Soc. Profl. Engrs., Acoustical Soc. Am., City Coll. Alumni Assn. Author: Electrical Consulting-Engineering and Design, 1973; (with R.K. Miller) Secrets of Noise Control, 1976; Plant Engineers and Managers Guide to Energy Conservation, 1977; Biorhythms and Industrial Safety, 1977; How to Patent Without a Lawyer, 1978; Electrical Design, Safety and Energy Conservation, 1978; Handbook of Energy Audits, 1979. Contbr. articles to profl. jours.; lectr. on energy conservation. Creater retng. course for unemployed aerospace engrs. Home: 931 Smoketree Dr Tucker GA 30084 Office: 4025 Pleasantdale Rd Suite 340 Atlanta GA 30340. *Where am I going and what am I doing, is a phrase which I have repeated many times. Constant appraisal of what one is doing and evaluation of this action with the goal are necessary for achieving ones objective. Salesmanship is the guiding tool which helps to obtain the objective once the course is chosen.*

THUMM, GAROLD WESLEY, educator; b. Pinch, W.Va., Sept. 22, 1915; s. George Wesley and Myrtle (Jarrett) T.; A.B., Morris Harvey Coll., 1940; M.A., U. Pa., 1947, Ph.D., 1954. With dept. polit. sci. U. Pa., 1947-49, 50, 53-61; prof., chmn. social sci. div. Bates Coll., Lewiston, Maine, 1961—; vis. prof. Nat. War Coll., 1966-68. Served to 1st lt. AUS, 1941-46, capt., 1951-53. Mem. AAUP, Am. Polit. Sci. Assn., Internat. Polit. Sci. Assn., Internat. Studies Assn. Republican. Methodist. Co-editor: The Challenge of Politics, 2d edit., 1964, 3d edit., 1970. Parties and the Governmental System, 1967. Contbr. articles to profl. jours. Home: 15 Ware St Lewiston ME 04240

THUNMAN, NILS RONALD, naval officer; b. Cleve., Feb. 26, 1932; s. Carl Erik and Julia (Lindblum) T.; student U. Ill., 1950-51; B.S. in Naval Sci., U.S. Naval Acad., 1954; student U.S. Naval Submarine Sch., 1959, U.S. Naval Nuclear Power Sch., Vallejo, Calif., 1961, U.S. Nuclear Power Tng. Unit, Windsor, Conn., 1961; m. Elizabeth Chase Caldwell, Sept. 6, 1954; children—Nils Ronald, Michael Erik. Commd. ensign U.S. Navy, 1954, advanced through grades to rear adm., 1977; Engr. officer U.S.S. Shelton, 1954-57; comdg. officer U.S.S. Marysville, 1957-58; engr. officer U.S.S. Volador, 1959-60; instr. U.S. Naval Submarine Sch., New London, Conn., U.S. Naval Nuclear Power Sch., Bainbridge, Md., 1962-63; engr. officer U.S.S. Robert E. Lee, 1963; exec. officer U.S.S. Snook, 1964-66; asst. program mgr. for nuclear power personnel Bur. Naval Personnel, Washington, 1966-68; comdg. officer U.S.S. Plunger, 1968-71; asst. chief of staff for tng. and readiness, on staff Comdr. Submarine Force, U.S. Pacific Fleet, Pearl Harbor, Hawaii, 1971-72, sr. mem. nuclear propulsion examining bd., 1972-74; comdr. Submarine Squadron 15, Apra Harbor, Guam, Marianas Islands, 1974-76; asst. chief naval personnel for officer devel. and distbn. Bur. Naval Personnel, 1976-78; dir. mil. personnel and tng. div. Office Chief Naval Ops., Washington, 1978-79; comdr. submarine force U.S. Pacific Fleet, Pearl Harbor, 1979—. Decorated Legion of Merit with 2 gold stars, Sec. of Navy Commendation medal with gold star, Navy Expeditionary medal (U.S.), Navy Unit Commendation with Bronze Star, Meritorious Unit Commendation. Mem. Phi Kappa Sigma. Home: 30 Makalapa Honolulu HI 96818 Office: Comdr Submarine Force US Pacific Fleet Pearl Harbor HI 96860

THURBER, CLEVELAND, JR., trust banker; b. Detroit, Aug. 2, 1925; s. Cleveland and Marie Louise (Palms) T.; student Purdue U.; B.A., Williams Coll., 1948; m. Elizabeth-Mary Hamilton, June 22, 1946; children—Cleveland III, Elizabeth King (Mrs. David C. Wells), David. Asst. trust officer Detroit Bank & Trust Co., 1958-61, trust officer, 1961-63, v.p., 1963-69, sr. v.p., 1969—. Pres., Friends of Grosse Pointe Pub. Library, 1971-72, Mich. Heart Assn., 1969-74; sec. United Community Services, 1968-70. Bd. dirs. Cottage Hosp., United Found., Mich. Humane Soc., Elmwood Cemetery, Center for Creative Studies. Served with USMCR, 1943-46. Clubs: Detroit (past pres.), Yondotega, Country (Detroit). Home: 34 Edgemere Rd Grosse Pointe Farms MI 48236 Office: 211 W Fort St Detroit MI 48226

THURBER, DAVID LAWERENCE, educator; b. Oneonta, N.Y., Dec. 29, 1934; s. Walter Arthur and Alice Laura (Herald) T.; B.S., Union Coll., Schenectady, 1956; M.A., Columbia, 1959, Ph.D., 1963; m. Doris Estelle Long, Aug. 22, 1964; 1 son, Alistair Clark. Research scientist Lamont-Doherty Geol. Obs., Palisades, N.Y., 1963-65, research asso., 1965-66, vis. sr. research asso., 1966-74; lectr. Queen's Coll., City U. N.Y., 1965—66, asso. prof., 1966-70, prof. earth and environ. sci., 1970—; vis. prof. Universidade Federal, Bahia, Brazil, 1974—. Am. Geophys. Union vis. lectr., 1965; participant Nobel Symposium, 1969, Wenner-Gren Symposium, 1971. Research grantee AEC, 1963—, NSF, 1963—, City U. N.Y. Research Found., 1970-71; Research fellow ESSO Research Found., 1956-57. Fellow Am. Inst. Chemists; mem. AAAS, Am. Geophys. Union, Geochem. Soc., Am. Mus. Natural History, Sigma Xi, Alpha Delta Phi. Contbr. articles to profl. jours. Home: 59 W Forest Ave Teaneck NJ 07666 Office: Dept Earth and Environmental Sci Queens Coll Flushing NY 11367

THURBER, DAVIS PEABODY, banker; b. Nashua, N.H., May 20, 1925; s. George Freeman and Muriel (Davis) T.; grad. Phillips Acad., Andover, Mass., 1943; B.Naval Sci., Coll. Holy Cross, 1945; M.S., Mass. Inst. Tech., 1948; m. Shirley Ann Amos, July 14, 1946 (dec. Jan. 1970); children—Shelley Davis, Steven Anderson, George Frederick, Matthew Thomas; m. 2d, Patricia Martin Skillas, Apr. 25, 1971. Sales engr. Amos Thompson Corp., Edinburg, Ind., 1950-55; asst. to pres. White Mountain Freezer Co., Inc., Nashua, 1955-56; with Second Nat. Bank Nashua (merged to form Bank of N.H., N.A.), 1956—, pres., 1962-72, chmn., 1972—; dir. Gas Service, Inc., Whitney Screw Corp., Wonalancet Co. (all Nashua); underwriting mem. Lloyd's of London. Bd. dirs. Tee Squam Lakes Sci. Center, Tee Currier Gallery Art, Manchester, Nutt Hosp.; mem. adv. bd. St. Joseph's Hosp. Served to lt. (j.g.) USNR, 1943-46. Mem. Squam Lakes Assn. (pres. 1966-67). Republican. Episcopalian. Mason (33 deg.), Rotarian. Club: Nashua Country. Home: 25 Swart Terr Nashua NH 03060 Office: Franklin St Manchester NH 03105

THURBER, JAMES PERRY, JR., govt. ofcl.; b. Westfield, N.J., June 3, 1928; s. James Perry and Ruth (Burnett) T.; A.B. in Journalism, Stanford, 1950; M.S. in Internat. Relations, George Washington U., 1974; m. Emily Maulsby Forrest, Aug. 8, 1950; children—James Perry III, Harriette C., Alexander F., Mary M. Reporter, editor Wall St. Jour., N.Y.C., 1952-56; asst. to provost Stanford, 1956-67; fgn. service officer USIA, Dar es Salaam, Tanzania, Blantyre, Malawi, Lagos, Nigeria, 1967—, dep. pub. affairs officer, Lagos, until 1973; detailed to Nat. War Coll., 1973-74; chief policy guidance USIA, Washington, 1974-78; counselor for public affairs Am. embassy, Islamabad, Pakistan, 1978—. Councilman, Los Altos, Calif., 1960-67, mayor, 1962-66; commr. San Francisco Bay Conservation and Devel. Commn., 1966-67; mem. Calif. Democratic Central Com., 1962-66. Served with AUS, 1950-52. Named outstanding young man of year, Calif., 1963. Mem. Internat. House Japan, Sigma Delta Chi. Clubs: Nat. Press; Ikoyi (Lagos). Office: Am Embassy Islamabad Dept State Washington DC 20520

THURLBECK, WILLIAM MICHAEL, pathologist; b. Johannesburg, South Africa, Sept. 7, 1929; s. William and Enid Muriel (Mears) T.; B.Sc., U. Cape Town, 1951, M.B., Ch.B., 1953; m. Elizabeth Anne Tippett, Oct. 28, 1955; children—Sarah Margaret, David William, Alison Mary. Intern, Groote Schuur Hosp., Cape Town, 1955; research fellow resident in pathology Mass. Gen. Hosp. and Harvard U., 1955-61; asst. prof. to prof. pathology McGill U., 1961-73; sr. investigator Midhurst Med. Research Inst. and Royal Postgrad. Med. Sch., Eng., 1973-75; prof. pathology, head U. Man. and Health Scis. Centre, Winnipeg, 1975—; examiner in pathology Royal Coll. Physicians and Surgeons of Can., 1964-70; mem. McGill Interdisciplinary Com. on Air Pollution, 1967-73; cons. Cardiovascular Research Inst., San Francisco; pulmonary diseases adv. com. Nat. Heart and Lung Inst., 1971-74; task force research planning in environ. health scis. NIH; adv. fellow Indsl. Hygiene Found., Pitts., 1967-71, Paul Dudley White fellow in cardiology, 1960-61; Med. Research Council vis. scientist Oxford (Eng.) U., 1970-71; Schering travelling fellow Canadian Soc. Clin. Investigation, 1971. Fellow Royal Coll. Physicians, Royal Coll. Pathologists, Am. Coll. Chest Physicians (medalist), Royal Coll. Pathology; mem. Am. Assn. Pathologists, Internat. Acad. Pathology, Path. Soc. Gt. Britain and Ireland, Canadian Soc. Clin. Investigation, Am. Thoracic Soc., Fleischner Soc. Clubs: Rondebosch Old Boys, Pluto. Author: Chronic Airflow Obstruction in Lung Disease, 1976; The Lung: Structure, Function and Disease, 1978. Contbr. articles to med. jours. Home: 201 2A Emily St Winnipeg MB R3E 1Y7 Canada Office: Dept of Pathology 700 William Ave Winnipeg MB R3E 0Z3 Canada

THURLOW, ARTHUR LOUIS, justice Fed. Ct. Can.; b. Lunenburg, N.S., Can., May 5, 1913; s. Charles William and Emily Maud (Kinley) T.; B.A., Dalhousie U., 1933, LL.B., 1935; m. Mabel Rosina Maxwell, July 5, 1941; 1 son, James Maxwell. Called to N.S. bar, 1935, created queen's counsel, 1954; mem. Legis. As Assembly of N.S., 1949-53; apptd. puisne judge of Exchequer Ct. Can., 1956-71, Ct. Martial Appeal Ct. Can., 1959—; chmn. Copyright Appeal Bd., 1964-72; judge Fed. Ct. Appeal, Ottawa, Ont., 1971-75; asso. chief justice Fed. Ct. Can., Ottawa, 1975—. Served in Can. Army, 1943-46. Office: Fed Ct Can Supreme Ct Bldg Wellington St Ottawa ON K1A 0H9 Canada*

THURLOW, ELWIN WILBUR, power co. exec.; b. Auburn, Maine, Jan. 2, 1924; s. Wilbur Frederick and Helen Maud (Hunt) T.; B.S. in Elec. Engring., U. Maine, 1950, M.B.A., 1970; m. Jacqueline Thompson, June 18, 1947; children—Diane Thurlow Wood, Cynthia Thurlow Sayles, Donna. With Central Maine Power Co., 1950—, distbn. engr., 1952-66, system planning engr., Augusta, 1968-70, v.p., 1970-72, pres., dir., 1972—, chief exec. officer, 1975—; pres. dir. Central Securities Corp., Cumberland Securities Corp. (both Augusta), Maine Yankee Atomic Power Co., 1975—; dir. Depositors Trust Co., Gt. No. Nekoosa. Chmn., Sch. Dist., 1960-65. Served with USAAF, 1942-45. Decorated Air medal, D.F.C. Sr. mem. IEEE (chmn. Me. sect. 1964-65). Office: Edison Dr Augusta ME 04330

THURLOW, WILLARD ROWAND, educator; b. N.Y.C., Sept. 5, 1918; s. Harry H. and Ethel I. (Rowand) T.; B.A., Brown U., 1939; M.A., Princeton, 1941, Ph.D., 1942; m. Constance E. Farwell, June 30, 1945; children—Thomas F., Peter M., Stephen Y. With div. war research Columbia, 1944-45; instr., asst. prof. psychology U. Mo., 1945-46; asst. prof. U. Va., 1946-52; mem. psychology dept. U. Wis.-Madison, 1952—, prof. psychology, 1958—. Served with USAAF, 1942-43. Fellow Am. Psychol. Assn., AAAS; mem. Acoustical Soc. Am., Psychonomic Soc., Soc. Neurosci., Midwestern Psychol. Assn., Phi Beta Kappa, Sigma Xi. Research, publs. in auditory perception. Home: 1819 Van Hise Ave Madison WI 53705

THURMAN, HENRY LOUIS, JR., educator; b. Lawrenceville, Va., Jan. 14, 1927; s. Henry Louis and Helen Francis (Frey) T.; B.S. in Archtl. Engring., Hampton Inst., 1947; M.S. in Archtl. Engring., U. Ill., 1949; m. Alena E. Johnson, Aug. 13, 1952; children—Dart Steven, Henry Louis III. Faculty, So. U., 1948—, dean Coll. Engring., 1953-72, prof. archtl. engring., 1972—. Mem. Am. Soc. Engring. Edn., AIA, Omega Psi Phi. Episcopalian. Mason. Home: 2845 79th Ave Baton Rouge LA 70807

THURMAN, JOHN ROYSTER, III, ret. army officer; b. Lexington, Ky., Apr. 11, 1924; s. John Royster, Jr. and Rose Feeney (Moran) T.; B.S., U.S. Mil. Acad., 1946; M.S., George Washington U., 1965. Commd. 2d lt. U.S. Army, 1946, advanced through grades to lt. gen., 1977; service in Vietnam, Korea and Ger.; dir. program analysis and evaluation Office Chief Staff, U.S. Army, 1972-75; comdr. 2d Inf. Div., Korea, 1975-76; comdr. Combined Arms Center, also comdt. Command and Gen. Staff Coll., Ft. Leavenworth, Kans., 1976-79; ret., 1979. Decorated Legion of Merit (6), D.F.C. (2), Bronze Star, Air medal (35), Purple Heart, Combat Inf. badge, Master Parachutist badge; knight Order St. Sylvester (Vatican). Mem. Assn. U.S. Army, Mil. Order World Wars. Roman Catholic. Club: Army-Navy (Washington). Home: 4013 Ellicott St Alexandria VA 22304

THURMAN, SAMUEL DAVID, educator, lawyer; b. Washington, Dec. 7, 1913; s. Sam D. and Henrietta (Young) T.; A.B., U. Utah, 1935; J.D., Stanford U., 1939; m. Emeline Nebeker, June 16, 1939; children—David, Sally (Mrs. Ware), Susan, Walter. Admitted to Utah bar, 1939; practiced law with Irvine, Skeen, Thurman, Salt Lake City, 1939-42; asso. prof. law Stanford, 1942-47, prof. law, 1947-62, Marion Rice Kirkwood prof. law, 1961-62, asso. dean Law Sch., 1947-49, acting dean, 1952-53; dean Coll. Law, U. Utah, Salt Lake City, 1962-75, Distinguished prof. law, 1975—; advisory bd. Found. Press U. Casebook Series, 1962—; vis. prof. law U. Mich., summer 1949, N.Y. U., 1955-56, U. Tex., 1976, La. State U., 1977. Commr., Calif. Law Revision Commn., 1954-59; chmn. Utah appeals bd. SSS. mem. Council Legal Edn. for Profl. Responsibility, 1968-73. Sec.-treas. Assn. Am. Law Schs., 1959-61, pres., 1962. Bd. dirs. Nat. Legal Services Corp., 1975-78. Fellow Am. Bar Found.; mem. Am. (sec. council legal edn. and admission to bar 1965-70, 74—, chmn. 1978-79), Utah, San Francisco bar assns., State Bar Calif., AAUP, Am. Law Inst. (life), Order of Coif (nat. exec. com. 1964-67, nat. pres. 1977—), Phi Beta Kappa, Phi Kappa Phi, Sigma Chi, Delta Theta Phi. Mem. Ch. of Jesus Christ of Latter-day Saints. Clubs: Commonwealth (quar. chmn. San Francisco 1955), Timpanogos, Ft. Douglas, Hidden Valley. Co-author: Coursebook on The Legal Profession; The Study of Federal Tax Law; adviser Restatement of Torts, Second, Am. Law Inst. Contbr. articles to law revs., bar assn. jours. Home: 875 Donner Way #405 Salt Lake City UT 84108 Office: Coll Law U Utah Salt Lake City UT 84112

THURMOND, STROM, U.S. senator; b. Edgefield, S.C., Dec. 5, 1902; s. John William and Eleanor Gertrude (Strom) T.; B.S., Clemson Coll., 1923; 14 hon. degrees; m. Jean Crouch, Nov. 7, 1947 (dec. Jan. 1960); m. 2d, Nancy Moore, Dec. 22, 1968; children—Nancy Moore, J. Strom, Jr., Juliana Gertrude, Paul Reynolds. Tchr., S.C. schs., 1923-29; admitted to bar, 1930; city atty.; county atty.; supt. edn. Edgefield County, 1929-33; state senator, 1933-38; circuit judge, 1938-46; gov. of S.C., 1947-51, chmn. So. Govs. Conf., 1950; practiced in Aiken, S.C., 1951-55; U.S. senator from S.C., 1955—. Del., Nat. Democratic Conv., 1932, 36, 48, 52, 56, 60; chmn. S.C. dels., mem. Dem. Nat. Com., 1948; States Rights candidate for Pres. U.S., 1948; del. Nat. Republican Conv., 1968, 72, 76. Bd. dirs. Ga.-Carolina council Boy Scouts Am. Served with AUS, attached to 82d Airborne Div. for invasion Europe, 1942-46; maj. gen. Res. Decorated Legion of Merit with oak leaf cluster, Bronze Star with V, Purple Heart, Croix de Guerre (France); Cross of Order of Crown (Belgium), others; recipient Congl. Medal Honor, Soc. Nat. Patriots award, 1974. Mem. S.C. (past v.p.), Am. bar assns., Clemson Coll. Alumni Assn. (past pres.), also numerous def., vets., civic, fraternal and farm orgns. Baptist. Home: Aiken SC 29801 Office: Aiken SC also Columbia SC also Charleston SC also Florence SC also Senate Office Bldg Washington DC 20510

THURSTON, ALICE JANET, coll. pres.; b. Milw., Mar. 20, 1916; d. Karl J. and Nellie Ann (Smith) Stouffer; B.A., Denison U., 1937; M.A., Northwestern U., 1938; Ph.D., George Washington U., 1960; children—Anne, Robert. Mem. faculty dept. psychology, counselor, dean students Montgomery Coll., Takoma Park, Md., 1950-65; dir. counseling Met. Campus, Cuyahoga Community Coll., Cleve., 1965-66, dean of students, Western campus, 1966-67; vis. lectr. U. Ill., 1968-69; dir. Inst. Research and Student Services Met. Jr. Coll. Dist., Kansas City, Mo., 1969-71; pres. Garland Jr. Coll., Boston, 1971-75; pres. Los Angeles Valley Coll., Van Nuys, Calif., 1975—; lectr. Pepperdine U., Los Angeles, 1978—. Mem. monitoring com. Los Angeles Sch. Desegregation Plan; mem. State Community Coll. Chancellor's Adv. and Rev. Council for Institutional Improvement. Mem. Los Angeles Community Coll. Dist. Adminstrs., Calif. Community and Jr. Coll. Assn. (mem. commn. on women), Assn. Calif. Community Coll. Adminstrs. Democrat. Unitarian. Author works in field. Home: 13156 Crewe North Hollywood CA 91605 Office: 5800 Fulton Van Nuys CA 91401

THURSTON, CARL GIVENS, hotel exec.; b. Glen Wilton, Va., Dec. 28, 1917; s. Arthur Lynwood and Merle (Hill) T.; grad. Roanoke (Va.) Bus. Coll., 1938; student bus. courses U. Buffalo, 1947, Cornell U.,

1949, U. Minn., 1950; m. Dorothy Louise Deppensmith, Feb. 16, 1945; children—John Kent, Carole Anne, Robert Gordon. With Appalachian Elec. Co., 1938-41; dir. personnel Hotel Statler, Buffalo, 1947-48, Hotel Statler, N.Y.C., 1948-51, personnel asst. Hotels Statler Co., 1951-54, resident mgr. Hotel Statler, Buffalo, 1955-58, gen. mgr. Statler-Hilton Hotel, Buffalo, 1958-61; mgr. Waldorf-Astoria Hotel, N.Y.C., 1961-62, Hilton Hawaiian Village, Honolulu, 1962-64; gen. mgr. Hotel Roanoke (Va.), 1964-69; hotel cons., 1969-70; v.p., mng. dir. Hunt Valley Inn, Inc., Hunt Valley, Md., 1970-71; hotel cons., 1971-73; exec. v.p. Leisure Mgmt. Corp. (hotel mgmt., devel.), Lansing, Mich., 1973-74, Carl G. Thurston Assos., Hotel Mgmt. and Devel., Plymouth, Mich., 1974-76, Carl G. Thurston & Assos., Roanoke, Va., 1976—; dir. Bank of Va., Internat. Exec. Service Corp., N.Y.C. Chmn. design and constrn. com. Roanoke Civic Center; mem. Statler Found. Scholarship Com.; mem. adv. council U.S. Job Corps. Bd. dirs. Roanoke Conv. Bur. Served to capt. AUS, 1941-46; PTO. Mem. Va., Roanoke chambers commerce, Internat. Exec. Ser. Corp., Newcomen Soc. N.Am., Internat., Am. (dir.), So. (dir.), Va. (dir.), Md. (dir.), Mich. hotel assns., Hotels Greeters Am. (past pres.), Va. Travel Council, Nat., Va. restaurant assns., Assn. U.S. Army (cons. directory 1977). Republican. Methodist. Rotarian. Clubs: Pickwick, Roanoke Country. Home and Office: 3541 Valley View Ave NW Roanoke VA 24012

THURSTON, DONALD ALLEN, broadcasting co. exec.; b. Gloucester, Mass., Apr. 2, 1930; s. Joseph Allen and Helen Ruth (Leach) T.; grad. Mass. Radio and Telegraph, 1949; H.H.D. (hon.) North Adams (Mass.) State Coll., 1977; m. Oralie Alice Lane, Sept. 9, 1951; children—Corydon Leach, Carolie Lane. Announcer, engr. Sta. WTWN, St. Johnsbury, Vt., 1949-52; v.p., gen. mgr. Sta. WIKE, Newport, Vt., 1952-60; v.p., treas., gen. mgr. Sta. WMNB, North Adams, 1960-66; pres., treas. Berkshire Broadcasting Co., Inc., North Adams, 1966—; pres. North Adams Futures Inc.; dir. Berkshire Bank and Trust Co. Commr. Vt. State Devel. Commn., 1959-60; pres. No. Berkshire Indsl. Devel. Corp., 1965-67; commr. Mass. Community Antenna TV Commn., 1972-74. Recipient Laymen's award Vt. Tchrs. Assn., 1958; Laymen's award Mass. Tchrs. Assn., 1962; Abe Lincoln Merit award So. Baptist Radio and TV Commn., 1975; named Man of Yr., Vt. Assn. Broadcasters, 1978. Mem. North Adams C. of C. (recipient Hayden award 1967, pres. 1964-67), Nat. Assn. Broadcasters (dir. 1965-69, 73-77, chmn. radio 1976-77, chmn. bd., chmn. exec. com. 1977-79), Mass. Broadcasters Assn. (pres. 1964, recipient Disting. Service award 1964, 71, 78). Republican. Methodist. Club: Taconic Golf (dir. 1975—) (Williamston, Mass.). Office: 466 Curran Hwy North Adams MA 01247. *My goals have been to make my community, profession and life in general better because I was a positive participant, not poorer by being a simple recipient; and to provide independence, a sense of responsibility and a love of humanity for my family.*

THURSTON, FRANK RUSSEL, aero. research adminstr.; b. Chgo., Dec. 5, 1914; s. Charles William and Emma Louise (Connor) T.; B.Sc., U. London, 1940; m. Olive Cullingworth, Nov. 23, 1940; 1 son, Peter Russel. Research engr. Nat. Phys. Lab., Eng., 1940-47; with NRC Can., Ottawa, 1947—, dir. Nat. Aero. Establishment, 1959—. Mem. Can. Aero. and Space Inst., Inst. Physics. Contbr. articles to profl. jours. Home: 793 Hemlock Rd Ottawa ON K1K 0K6 Canada Office: Nat Research Council Montreal Rd Ottawa ON Canada

THURSTON, GEORGE BUTTE, educator; b. Austin, Tex., Oct. 8, 1924; s. Rudolph D. and Olivia Ruth (Lester) T.; B.S., U. Tex., Austin, 1944, M.A., 1948, Ph.D., 1952; m. Carol A. McWharter, Apr. 5, 1947; children—John Douglas, Mary Elizabeth. Supr. hydroacoustics sect. Def. Research Lab., U. Tex., Austin, 1949-52; asst. prof. physics U. Wyo., Laramie, 1952-53; asst. prof. physics U. Ark., Fayetteville, 1953-54; physicist Naval Ordnance Test Sta., Inyokern, Calif., 1954, 55; asso. prof. Okla. State U., Stillwater, 1954-59; research physicist U. Mich., Ann Arbor, 1958-59; prof. Okla. State U., 1959-68; vis. scientist Centre de Recherche sur les Macromolecules, Strasbourg, France, 1963-64; prof. mech. engring. and biomed. engring. U. Tex., Austin, 1968—; vis. prof. Helmholtz Inst. fur Biomedizinische Technik, Aachen, West Germany, 1975-76; cons. for govt., industry. Recipient Brown U. Calculus prize, 1942. Alexander von Humboldt Found. Sr. U.S. Scientist award, 1975; NSF faculty fellow, 1963-64; numerous grants. Registered profl. engr., Tex. Fellow Am. Phys. Soc., Acoustical Soc. Am.; mem. ASME, Soc. Rheology, Internat. Soc. Biorheology, Brit. Soc. Rheology, Sigma Xi, Sigma Pi Sigma. Contbr. articles to profl. jours. Home: 1000 Madrone Rd Austin TX 78746 Office: Dept Mech Engring Univ Tex Austin TX 78712

THURSTON, GEORGE RILEY, JR., lumber co. exec.; b. Rushville, Ind., Dec. 18, 1942; s. George Riley and Etta Margaret (Berry) T.; B.S., Northwestern U., 1965, M.B.A., 1966; m. Lunda Jo Stanley, Oct. 13, 1962; children—Deborah Kay, Diane Kathleen, Marcy Jo. With Cummins Engine Co., Inc., Columbus, Ind., 1966-78, treas., 1971-72, v.p. fin., treas., 1972-75, v.p. internat. adminstrn., 1975-78; v.p. fin. N.Pacific Lumber Co., Portland, Oreg., 1978—. Bd. dirs. Bartholomew County March of Dimes, 1967. Troop chmn. Hoosier Trails council Boy Scouts Am., 1969-71. Mem. Phi Delta Theta, Beta Alpha Psi, Beta Gamma Sigma. Lutheran. Home: 585 NW Torreyview Dr Portland OR 97229 Office: 1515 SE Gideon Portland OR 97208

THURSTON, JAMES NORTON, educator; b. Murphysboro, Ill., May 6, 1915; s. Ariel Norton and Beatrice (Muster) T.; B.S., Ohio State U., 1936; M.S., Mass. Inst. Tech., 1943, Sc.D., 1950; m. Agnes Wallner, Sept. 21, 1940; children—Anita, Paul, Eric, Peter. Test engr. Gen. Electric Co., Schenectady, also Pittsfield, Erie, Bridgeport, 1936-38; geophysicist Mott-Smith Corp., Houston, 1938-40; teaching asst Mass. Inst. Tech., 1940-43, instr., 1943-47, asst. prof. elec. engring., 1947-49; asso. prof. elec. engring. U. Fla., 1949-52, Calif. Inst. Tech., 1952-54; prof., head dept. elec. engring. Clemson (S.C.) U., 1954-66, Alumni prof. elec. engring., 1966—. Cons. Firestone Tire & Rubber Co., Los Angeles, 1953-54, Nat. Council Engring. Examiners. Registered profl. engr., S.C. Mem. IEEE, Am. Soc. Engring. Edn. (chmn. elec. div. 1954-55), Sigma Xi, Tau Beta Pi. Home: 322 Woodland Way Clemson SC 29631

THURSTON, MARLIN OAKES, educator; b. Denver, Sept. 20, 1918; s. Harold M. and Sylva (Howard) T.; B.A., U. Colo., 1940, M.S., 1946; Ph.D., Ohio State U., 1955; m. Helen Marie Dunton, Mar. 15, 1942; children—Richard Ben, Kenneth Paul, Charles Marlin. Acting head dept. physics USAF Inst. Tech., 1946-49, acting head dept. elec. engring., 1946-52; faculty Ohio State U., 1955—, prof. elec. engring., 1959—, chmn. dept., 1965-77; cons. to govt. agys., industry; chmn. bd. dirs. Nat. Engring. Consortium, Inc., 1977-79. Served with AUS, 1942-46. Fellow IEEE; mem. Am. Phys. Soc., Sigma Xi, Tau Beta Pi, Eta Kappa Nu. Elec. engring. series editor Marcel Dekker, Inc., 1976—. Spl. research microwave tubes, semiconductor devices. Home: 3751 Kioka Ave Columbus OH 43220

THURSTON, PHILIP HALE, educator; b. Ocean Park, Maine, Aug. 20, 1918; s. Frank Hale and Alice Lee (Wilson) T.; B.A., Columbia Coll., 1940; M.S., Columbia U., 1951; D.B.A., Harvard U., 1959; m. Jean Willis McIntosh, June 19, 1965; 1 son, Bruce. Supr. Sperry Gyroscope Co., 1941-42; self-employed, 1946-48; supr. Gen. Electric Co., 1949-57; successively lectr., asso. prof., prof. Harvard U. Grad. Sch. Bus. Adminstrn., Cambridge, Mass., 1958—; dir. United Life & Accident Ins. Co. Served to 1st lt. USAAF, 1942-46. Ford Found. fellow, 1957-58. Mem. Inst. Mgmt. Scis. Author: Systems and Procedures Responsibility, 1959; Casebooks in Production Management, 1964. Contbr. articles to Harvard Bus. Rev. Home: 10 Fiske Ln Weston MA 02193 Office: Morgan Hall 223 Harvard Bus Sch Boston MA 02163

THURSTON, RAYMOND LEROY, ambassador, educator; b. St. Louis, Feb. 4, 1913; s. Charles LeRoy and Hazel May (Ruth) T.; student Washington U., St. Louis, 1930-31; B.A. with highest honors, U. Tex., 1931-34, M.A., 1935; Ph.D., U. Wis., 1937; postgrad. Russian, Fgn. Service Inst., 1948; grad. Nat. War Coll., 1951-52; m. Elizabeth Sherman, Nov. 30, 1934; 1 dau., Ruth; m. 2d, Gabriella Mariani, Jan. 29, 1970. Joined U.S. Fgn. Service, 1937; vice consul in Can., Italy, India, 1937-45; asst. chief div. Middle Eastern, later S. Asian affairs State Dept., 1945-49; 1st sec., later counselor embassy, Moscow, USSR, 1949-51; dep. dir., later dir. Office Eastern European affairs State Dept., 1952-55; counselor embassy, dep. chief mission, Athens, Greece, 1955-57; counselor embassy, Paris, France, also polit. adviser to SHAPE, 1957-61; alternate rep. U.S. delegation to NATO, 1961; dep. dir. operations center State Dept., 1961; U.S. ambassador to Haiti, 1961-63; State Dept. adviser to Air U., 1963-65; ambassador to Somali Republic, Mogadiscio, 1965-69; vis. asso. prof. polit. sci. U. Nev., 1969-70, lectr. polit. sci., 1970-71; vis. prof. govt. Chapman Coll. World Campus Afloat, Orange, Calif., 1971—, dir. program devel., 1971-76, asso. prof. internat. studies, dean, 1972-74, East Coast rep., 1975-76; Fla. rep. Lifelong Learning, Inc., 1975-77; acad. adv. bd. Inst. Shipboard Edn., 1976—. Adviser U.S. del. to UN Security Council and Gen. Assembly, 1947-50, U.S. dels. internat. confs. Bermuda, Berlin, Geneva, 1953-54; attached to ICA, 1956-57. Founder, Anglo-Am. Childrens Sch., Moscow, 1949. Mem. Am. Fgn. Service Assn., Am. Polit. Sci. Assn., DACOR House, Phi Beta Kappa. Editor: Fgn. Service Jour., 1952-55. Contbr. articles to profl. jours. Home and office: 5400 Ocean Blvd 3-1 Sarasota FL 33581

THURSTONE, FREDRICK LOUIS, educator; b. Chgo., Feb. 12, 1932; s. Louis Leon and Thelma (Gwinn) T.; student Calif. Inst. Tech., 1949-51; B.S., U. N.C., 1953; M.S., N.C. State U., 1957, Ph.D., 1961; m. Arlene Morgan, Nov. 11, 1954; children—Conrad Leon, Eric Morgan, Elizabeth Gwinn. Instr., asst. prof. elec. engring. N.C. State U., Raleigh, 1956-62; asst. prof., asso. prof., dir. dept. biomed. engring. Bowman Gray Sch. Medicine, Wake Forest U., Winston-Salem, N.C., 1962-67; asso. prof., prof. biomed. and elec. engring. Duke, Durham, N.C., 1967—. Recipient Research Career Devel. award Nat. Heart and Lung Inst., 1968-73. Mem. Am. Inst. Ultrasound in Medicine (treas. 1972-74), Acoustical Soc. Am., Optical Soc. Am., Biomed. Engring. Soc. (dir.), IEEE (adminstrv. com. group on sonics and ultrasonics). Club: Antique Automobile of Am. Contbr. articles to profl. jours. Home: 2532 Sevier St Durham NC 27705

THURSZ, DANIEL, orgn. exec.; b. Casablanca, Morocco, Jan. 25, 1929; s. Jonathan and Franka (Gutlas) T.; came to U.S., 1941; B.A., Queens Coll., 1949; M.S.W., Catholic U. Am., 1955, D.S.W., 1960; L.H.D., U. Md., 1977; m. Hadassah Neulander, Feb. 8, 1953; children—Deborah Thursz Bleiweis, David, Deena, Tamar. Asso. prof. social welfare Sch. Social Service, Cath. U. Am., 1961-63, Sch. Social Work, U. Md., 1963-65; nat. asso. dir. VISTA, OEO, Washington, 1965-67; dean, prof. U. Md. Sch. Social Work and Community Planning, 1967-77; exec. v.p. B'nai B'rith Internat., Washington, 1977—; cons. social welfare agencies, mem. nat. and state commns. social welfare. Served with AUS, 1951-53. Alvin Johnson scholar. Mem. Acad. Certified Social Workers, Md. Welfare Conf. (pres. 1969-71), Nat. Assn. Social Workers (1st v.p. 1973-75), Assn. Jewish Communal Service (exec. com.). Jewish. Club: B'nai B'rith. Author books, monographs, articles in field. Co-editor: Meeting Human Needs, Vol. 1, 1975, Vol. 11, 1977, Vol. III, Reaching People, 1978. Home: 8605 Carlynn Dr Bethesda MD 20034 Office: 1640 Rhode Island Ave NW Washington DC 20036

THWAITS, JAMES ARTHUR, mfg. co. exec.; b. London, Apr. 3, 1923; s. Arthur Roper and Iris Maud (Mason) T.; grad. East-Ham Coll. Tech., London, 1939, Thames Poly., London, 1942; came to U.S., 1958, naturalized, 1973; grad. East-Ham Coll. Tech., London, 1939, Thames Poly., London, 1942; Higher Nat. Cert. in Elec. Engring., Cert. Higher Math., Poly. of South Bank, London, 1944; m. Joyce Holmes, July 26, 1947; children—Joanna, Philip, David, Steven. Project engr. Standard Telephones and Cables Ltd., Eng., 1945-46; plant engr. Kelvinator Ltd., Eng., 1946-49; with 3M, St. Paul, 1949—, v.p. Afro-Asian and Can. areas, 1968-71, v.p. Tape and Allied Products Group, 1972-74, v.p. Internat. Group, 1974-75, pres. Internat. Ops., 1975—, also dir. 3M; dir. First Trust Co., St. Paul. Mem. Inst. Elec. Engrs. (London). Clubs: St. Paul Athletic; White Bear (Minn.) Yacht; North Oaks (Minn.) Golf; King Solomon's Lodge (London, Ont., Can.).

TIANO, ANTHONY S., public television exec.; b. Albuquerque, Mar. 27, 1941; s. Joseph A. and Marian T.; B.S., U. N.Mex., 1969, M.A., 1971; m. Kathleen Tiano, Dec. 29, 1972; children—Mark, Steven. Program mgr., dir. spl. projects Sta. KNME-TV, U. N.Mex., 1968-72; dir. programming, asst. prof. Sta. WHA-TV, Madison, Wis., 1972-73, sta. mgr., asso. prof., 1973-76; exec. dir., gen. mgr. Sta. KETC-TV, St. Louis, 1976-78; pres., gen. mgr. Sta. KQED, Inc., San Francisco, 1978—. Contbr. articles to profl. jours. Home: 562 Morecroft Lafayette CA 94549 Office: 500 8th St San Francisco CA 94103

TIANT, LUIS CLEMENTE (VEGA), baseball player; b. Havana, Cuba, Nov. 23, 1940; s. Luis Clemente and Isabel (Vega) Tiant; m. Maria del Refugio Navarro, 1961; children—Luis, Isabel, Danny. With Cleve. Indians, 1964-69, Minn. Twins, 1969-71, Boston Red Sox, 1971—; Am. League player in All-Star Game, 1968, 74, 76. *

TIBBETTS, HUBERT M., food products co. exec.; b. 1924; grad. Harvard. With Lever Bros. Co., 1950-57, Salada Foods Co., 1957-60, Lennen & Newell, 1960-62; pres. Borden Foods div. Borden Inc., 1962-69; exec. v.p. Thomas J. Lipton, Inc., 1969, now pres., chief exec. officer, also dir. Office: 800 Sylvan Ave Englewood Cliffs NJ 07632

TIBBITTS, SAMUEL JOHN, hosp. admistr.; b. Chgo., Oct. 7, 1924; s. Samuel and Marion (Swanson) T.; B.S. U. Calif., Los Angeles, 1949, M.S., Berkeley, 1950; m. Audrey Slottelid, Aug. 28, 1949; children—Scott, Brett. Adminstrv. resident Calif. Hosp., Los Angeles, 1950-51, adminstrv. asst., 1951-52, asst. supt., 1954-59, admistr., 1959-66; chmn. mgmt. com., asst. sec. Luth. Hosp. Soc. So. Calif., 1962-66, pres., 1966—; asst. supt. Santa Monica (Calif.) Hosp., 1952-54. Pres., Commn. for Adminstrv. Services in Hosps., 1963, 64, 67, Calif. Health Data Corp., 1968-71; mem. Calif. Health Planning Council and Steering Com., 1968—, Los Angeles City Adv. Med. Council, 1971, 73, Pres.'s Com. Health Services Industry, Adv. Health Council, Calif., 1973; mem. adv. panel Pres.'s Cost of Living Council, Price Commn. and Pay Bd., Phase II; mem. Calif. Hosp. Commn., State of Calif., 1974—. Bd. dirs. Calif. Hosp. Med. Center, Martin Luther Hosp., Henry Mayo Newhall Meml. Hosp.; trustee, exec. com. Blue Cross So. Calif., 1966-75. Served with M.C., U.S. Army, 1946-47. Recipient Service to Humanity award Luth. Mut. Life Ins. Co., Outstanding Achievement award Hosp. Council So. Calif., 1972; named asso. officer most Venerable Order of St. John, 1972. Fellow Am. Coll. Hosp. Adminstrs.; mem. Am. (chmn. council research and planning 1964-67, trustee 1968-70, chmn. bd. trustees 1978, Meritorious Service citation 1973), San Diego (dir.), Calif. (pres. 1968-69, trustee 1966-70, recipient Ritz E. Heerman award 1960) hosp. assns., Hosp. Council So. Calif. (pres. 1961-62), Delta Omega. Home: 1224 Adair St San Marino CA 91108 Office: 1423 S Grand Ave Los Angeles CA 90015

TIBBS, DELLOYD ORVILLE, assn. exec.; b. Silver Lake, Kans., Aug. 27, 1917; s. Harry Pence and Dora Beatrice (Howell) T.; B.A., U. Kans., 1947; M.A., Columbia U., 1948, profl. diploma, 1949; m. Marcelle Fotheringhame, Mar. 9, 1946. Singer with N.Y.C. Opera Co., Cin. Opera Co., Chautauqua Opera Co., P.R. Opera Co., 1950-56; asst. exec. sec. Am. Guild Mus. Artists, N.Y.C., 1956-66, asso. exec. sec., 1967-70, nat. exec. sec., 1970—. Mem. dance adv. panel N.Y. State Council on Arts, 1971-72; treas. Theater Authority, 1971—; mem. Artists in Sch. adv. panel Nat. Endowment for Arts, 1976-78; trustee Relief Fund and Welfare Fund, Am. Guild Mus. Artists. Served to capt. Transp. Corps AUS, 1942-46. Mem. Asso. Actors and Artists Am. (5th v.p. 1971—), Phi Mu Alpha Sinfonia. Home: 340 W 57th St New York NY 10019 Office: 1841 Broadway New York NY 10023

TIBBY, JOHN KNOX MILLIGAN, JR., editor; b. Pitts., Jan. 23, 1913; s. John Knox Milligan and Margaret (McAteer) T.; A.B. magna cum laude, U. Pitts., 1935; m. Emily Virginia Foresman, Aug. 6, 1938; children—Joanna, Ellen, William Oliver. Reporter, Pitts. Post-Gazette, 1935; co-editor Am. Inst. Pub. Opinion (Gallup Poll), 1935-41; intelligence officer Bd. Econ. Warfare, 1942-43; mem. mil. secretariat U.S. Joint Chiefs of Staff, 1943-46; asst. sec. Nat. Intelligence Authority, 1946; editorial staff Time Mag., 1946, became sr. editor, 1948; a founding editor Sports Illustrated, 1954-78. Decorated Legion of Merit. Mem. Phi Beta Kappa, Omicron Delta Kappa. Address: Harbor Rd Port Washington NY 11050

TICE, GEORGE ANDREW, photographer; b. Newark, Oct. 13, 1938; s. William S. and Margaret T. (Robertson) T.; m. Joanna Blaylock, 1958; m. 2d, Marie Tremmel, 1960; children—Christopher, Loretta, Lisa, Lynn, Jennifer. One-man shows: Witkin Gallery, 1970, Met. Mus. Art, 1972; group shows include: Whitney Mus. Am. Art, 1974, Mus. Modern Art, 1978; represented in permanent collections: Mus. Modern Art, Met. Mus. Art, Art Inst. Chgo., Bibliotheque Nationale, Victoria and Albert Mus.; instr. photography New Sch. Social Research, 1970—. Served with USNR, 1956-59. Guggenheim Found. fellow, 1973-74; Nat. Endowment Arts fellow, 1973—. Recipient Grand prix for best photography book of Year, Arles, France, 1973. Books include: Fields of Peace, 1970; Goodbye River, Goodbye, 1971; Paterson, 1972; Seacoast Maine, 1973; George A. Ticel Photographs, 1953-73, 1975; Urban Landscapes, 1975; Artie Van Blarcum, 1977. Address: 323 Gill Ln Iselin NJ 08830

TICE, LINWOOD FRANKLIN, educator, cons.; b. Salem, N. J., Feb. 17, 1909; s. Walter C. and Bessie (Waddington) T.; Ph.G., Phila. Coll. Pharmacy and Sci., 1929, B.Sc., 1933, M.Sc., 1935; D.Sc., St. Louis Coll. Pharmacy and Allied Scis., 1954; m. Marjorie Purnell, Aug. 4, 1929 (dec. Apr. 1976); children—Gregory, David P. Research fellow Iodine Ednl. Bur., Phila. Coll. Pharmacy and Sci., 1929-30; research fellow Wm. R. Warner & Co., 1931-35, research fellow Edible Gelatin Mfrs. Research Soc. Am., 1935-38; prof. pharmacy Baylor U., 1930-31; asst. prof. pharmacy Phila. Coll. Pharmacy and Sci., 1938-40, prof., 1940-75, dir. dept. pharmacy, 1941-71, asst. dean, 1941-56, asso. dean, 1956-59, dean pharmacy, 1959-63, dean, 1963-75, dean and prof. emeritus, 1975—; cons. Gelatin Mfg. Inst. Am., 1936-58, Merck Sharp & Dohme, 1958-71; mem. Greater Phila. Com. for Med. Pharm. Scis. Coll. Physicians, 1963-75. Mem. Commonwealth of Pa. Disaster Med. Council, 1961-63. Trustee U.S. Pharmacopeia, 1960-75, mem. revision com., 1940-60; bd. dirs. Blue Cross Greater Phila., 1971—; trustee Am. Pharm. Assn. Found., 1974—. Recipient Remington medal, 1971, Distinguished Civilian Ser., medal U.S. Army, 1976; J. Leon Lascoff award Am. Coll. Apothecaries, 1976. Fellow Am. Inst. Chemists, AAAS (v.p. 1971-72), Am. Coll. Apothecaries, Coll. Physicians of Phila., Am. Pharm. Assn. (pres. 1966-67, trustee 1960-68); mem. N.J., Del., Pa. pharm. assns., Am. Chem. Soc., N.Y. Acad. Sci., Am. Soc. Hosp. Pharmacists, Am. Inst. History of Pharmacy, Am. Assn. Colls. Pharmacy (pres. 1955-56), Am. Found. Pharm. Edn. (bd. dirs. 1954-59), Am. Council Pharm. Edn. (dir. 1960-66, v.p. 1964-66), Kappa Psi, Rho Pi Phi, Phi Delta Chi, Alpha Zeta Omega, Upsilon Sigma Phi. Editor: Am. Jour. Pharmacy, 1941-77; asso. editor Remington's Practice of Pharmacy, 1948-63; tech. editor El Farmaceutico, 1941-59, Pharmacy Internat., 1946-59; editorial bd. Remington's Pharm. Scis., 1965—. Contbr. numerous articles to sci., profl. jours. Home: 322 Morrison Ave Salem NJ 08079 Office: Phila Coll Pharmacy and Sci 43d St and Kingsessing Ave Philadelphia PA 19104

TICE, RAPHAEL DEAN, army officer; b. Topeka, Kans., Dec. 4, 1927; s. Arthur Taylor and Mamie (McDonald) T.; B.S. in Mil. Sci., U. Md., 1963; M.S. in Bus. Adminstrn., George Washington U., 1970; m. Eunice Miriam Suddarth, Dec. 23, 1946; children—Karen Ann Tice Claterbos, William Dean. Served as enlisted man U.S. Army, 1946-47; commd. 2d lt., 1947, advanced through grades to maj. gen., 1976; platoon leader and co. comdr. 1st Infantry div., W.Ger., 1949-52; co. comdr., regimental adj. 8th Infantry div., 1955-56; tng. advisor, Vietnam, 1956-57; mem. staff Office of Dep. Chief of Staff for Personnel, Dept. Army, 1960-63; chief personnel mgmt. div. Office of Under Sec. of Army, 1963-64; plans Officer So. Command, Panama, 1965-67; dep. brigade comdr. 3d Brigade, 45th Infantry div., 1967; comdr. 2d Bn., 12th Infantry of 25th Infantry div., Vietnam, 1968; exec. for personnel procurement Office of Sec. of Def. for Manpower and Res. Affairs, 1968-69; comdr. 1st Brigade, 1st Infantry div., 1970, chief of staff, 1971; dep. dir. mil. personnel mgmt. Dept. Army, 1972-73; comdg. gen. Berlin Brigade, 1974-76; dep. chief of staff personnel U.S. Army Europe, 1976-77; comdg. gen. 3d. inf. div., 1977—. Decorated Silver Star, Legion of Merit with 2 oak leaf clusters, Air Medal with V and 7 Oak leaf clusters, Bronze Star with V., Vietnam Cross of Gallantry with Palm, Purple Heart. Mem. Assn. U.S. Army, Transatlantic Council, Boy Scouts Am. Home: 8655 Gateshead Rd Alexandria VA 22309

TICE, WILLIAM RUSSELL, designer; b. Tipton, Ind.; s. Earl O. Tice and Mary Elizabeth Schergens; D.A.A., U. Cin. Designer, pres. Bill Tice Design Co., N.Y.C.; licenses include Swirl Inc., McCalls Pattern Co., Oomphies, Inc.; costume designer for theatre and TV, including Merv Griffin, Mike Douglas, Dinah Shore shows, TV spl. Royal Celebrity Tennis-Monte Carlo, TV movie S.H.E. Recipient Tommy Print award (2); Spl. Coty award, 1974.

TICHENOR, DONALD KEITH, assn. exec.; b. Battle Creek, Mich., Apr. 14, 1937; s. Don Leighton and Sarah Sophia (Parry) T.; B.A., Hillsdale Coll., 1961; M.B.A., Loyola U., Chgo., 1974; m. Mary Gay Shields, Nov. 23, 1963; children—Don Kenneth, Andrew Scott, Thomas Dwight. Service analyst Mich. Med. Service, Detroit, 1965-66; adminstrv. asst. Port Huron (Mich.) Hosp., 1966-70; coordinator affiliated socs. Am. Hosp. Assn., Chgo., 1970-71, dir. div.

membership, 1971-72, dir. div. registration and membership, 1972-73, asst. dir. Bur. of Mgmt. and Planning, 1973-75, acting dir., 1975; exec. dir. Internat. Personnel Mgmt. Assn., Washington, 1975—. Served with U.S. Army, 1958-60. Mem. Am. Soc. Assn. Execs., Washington Soc. Assn. Execs. Office: 1850 K St NW Washington DC 20006

TICHO, HAROLD KLEIN, educator, physicist; b. Brno, Czechoslovakia, Dec. 21, 1921; s. Nathan and Frances (Klein) T.; came to U.S., 1939, naturalized, 1944; B.S., U. Chgo., 1942, M.S., 1944, Ph.D., 1949; m. Suzy L. Pansing, 1972. Faculty, U. Calif. at Los Angeles, 1949—, prof. physics, 1959—, chmn. dept., 1967-71, dean div. phys. scis., 1974—; trustee Univ. Research Assn., Inc., 1976—; vis. prof. Stanford, 1973-74. Guggenheim fellow, 1966-67, 73-74. Research exptl. elementary particle and cosmic ray physics. Home: 306 S Westgate Ave Los Angeles CA 90049 Office: 405 Hilgard Ave Los Angeles CA 90024

TICKLE, ROBERT SIMPSON, physicist; b. Norfolk, Va., July 31, 1930; s. William Bryant and Lillian (Lowe) T.; B.S., U.S. Mil. Acad., 1952; M.S., U. Va., 1958, Ph.D., 1960; m. Mildred Louise Magurk, May 21, 1955; 1 son, Robert Simpson. Faculty, U. Mich., Ann Arbor, 1960—, prof. physics, 1968—. Served as lt. U.S. Army, 1952-56. Decorated Bronze Star medal. Mem. Am. Phys. Soc., Am. Assn. Physics Tchrs., Phi Beta Kappa, Sigma Xi. Club: Exchange of Ann Arbor (pres. 1974-75). Contbr. articles to profl. jours. Home: 1408 Beechwood Dr Ann Arbor MI 48103 Office: Physics Dept U Mich Ann Arbor MI 48109

TICKTIN, RICHARD MAYER, lawyer; b. N.Y.C., Oct. 26, 1928; s. David Alvin and Gertrude (Cohen) T.; B.A., Syracuse U., 1949; LL.B., N.Y. U., 1951; m. Nancy Sherwood, Aug. 23, 1952; children—Diane, Karen. Admitted to N.Y. bar, 1952; with Met. Distbrs., N.Y.C., 1951-55; with Hertz Corp., 1955-67, v.p., sec., 1962-67; partner firm Ticktin, Malkin & Rosenberg, N.Y.C., 1968-75, Gottlieb Schiff Ticktin Fabricant Sternklar & Singer, P.C., N.Y.C., 1975—. Chmn., N.Y.C. corp. adv. council Syracuse U., 1964—; founding mem. Center Study Democratic Instns., Santa Barbara, Calif., 1964—; mem. N.Y.C. Youth Bd., 1966-75; pres. Manhattan Theatre Club, N.Y.C., 1976—. Mem. N.Y. State Bar Assn. Clubs: Atrium, City Athletic (N.Y.C.). Home: 40 E 88th St New York NY 10028 Office: 555 Fifth Ave New York NY 10017

TIDBALL, M(ARY) ELIZABETH PETERS (MRS. CHARLES S. TIDBALL), educator; b. Anderson, Ind., Oct. 15, 1929; d. John Winton and Beatrice (Ryan) Peters; B.A., Mt. Holyoke Coll., 1951, L.H.D., 1976; M.S., U. Wis., 1955, Ph.D., 1959; Sc.D., Wilson Coll., 1973, Trinity Coll., 1974, Cedar Crest Coll., 1977, U. of South, 1978; H.H.D., St. Mary's Coll., 1977; D.Sc., Goucher Coll., 1979; m. Charles S. Tidball, Oct. 25, 1952. Teaching asst. physiology dept. U. Wis., 1952-55, 58-59; research asst. anatomy dept. U. Chgo., 1955-56, research asst. physiology dept., 1956-58; USPHS postdoctoral fellow NIH, Bethesda, Md., 1959-61; staff pharmacologist Hazleton Labs., Falls Church, Va., 1961, cons. 1962; asst. research prof. dept. pharmacology George Washington U. Med. Center, 1962-64, asso. research prof. dept. physiology, 1964-70, research prof., 1970-71, prof., 1971—. Cons. FDA, 1966-67, asso. sci. coordinator sci. assos. tng. program, 1966-67; mem. com. on NIH tng. programs and fellowships Nat. Acad. Scis., 1972-75; lectr. on edn. of women, dual career marriage; faculty summer confs. Am. Youth Found., 1967—; cons. for instl. research Wellesley Coll., 1974-75; exec. sec. com. on edn. and employment women in sci. and engring. Commn. on Human Resources, NRC/Nat. Acad. Scis., 1974-75, vice chmn., 1977—; cons., staff officer NRC/Nat. Acad. Scis., 1974-75; cons. Woodrow Wilson Nat. Fellowship Found., 1975—, NSF, 1974—. Rep. to D.C. Commn. on Status of Women, 1972-75. Trustee Mt. Holyoke Coll., 1968-73, vice chmn., 1972-73; trustee Hood Coll., 1972—, exec. com., 1974—; overseer Sweet Briar Coll., 1978—; councillor Coll. of Preachers, Washington Cathedral Found., 1979—. Shattuck fellow, 1955-56; Mary E. Woolley fellow Mt. Holyoke Coll., 1958-59; USPHS postdoctoral fellow, 1959-61; recipient Alumnae Medal of Honor, Mt. Holyoke Coll., 1971. Mem. AAAS, Am. Physiol. Soc. (chmn. task force on women in physiology, com. coms. 1977—), Mt. Holyoke Alumnae Assn. (dir. 1966-70, 76-77), Histamine Club, Sigma Delta Epsilon, Sigma Xi. Episcopalian. Contbr. sci. articles and research on edn. of women to profl. jours. Home: 4100 Cathedral Ave NW Washington DC 20016 Office: George Washington U 2300 I St NW Washington DC 20037

TIDMARSH, GEORGE FRANCIS, retail chain exec.; b. Milw., Feb. 12, 1923; s. Harvey John and Janet Elizabeth (Young) T.; B.S. in Chem. Engring., Marquette U., 1946; m. Marion McNeany, June 24, 1944; children—Marianne, Catherine, Patricia, David, Carol, Susan, Margaret, Elizabeth, George Francis. With Sears, Roebuck and Co., 1946—, nat. mgr. field operating, Chgo., 1966-75, nat. mgr. phys. distbn., 1975, v.p. phys. distbn. and transp., 1975—; pres. Terminal Freight Handling Co.; dir. Signal Delivery Service. Served with USN, 1944-46. Mem. Chgo. Assn. Commerce and Industry (v.p. transp.), Transp. Assn. Am. (dir.). Office: Sears Tower BSC 49/33 Chicago IL 60684

TIDYMAN, ERNEST, screenwriter, author, film producer; b. Cleve., Jan. 1, 1928; s. Benjamin and Catherine (Kascsak) T.; ed. pub. schs.; m. Susan Gould, Dec. 25, 1970; children—Adam, Nicholas; children by previous marriage—Benjamin, Nathaniel. Newspaper writer, editor Cleve. News, 1954-57, N.Y. Post, 1957-60; editor N.Y. Times, N.Y.C., 1960-66; mag. editor, writer Signature Mag., also others, N.Y.C., 1966; freelance screenwriter, author, 1969—; lectr. in field. Served with AUS, 1945-46. Recipient Acad. award, 1971, Writers Guild award, 1971, Mystery Writers Am. award, 1971, for best screenplay The French Connection; N.A.A.C.P. Image award for motion picture Shaft, 1971. Mem. Acad. Motion Picture Arts and Scis., Writers Guild Am. West. Author: series Shaft, 1970-75; Absolute Zero, 1971; High Plains Drifter, 1973; Dummy, 1974; Line of Duty, 1974; writer screenplay The French Connection, 1971; Shaft, 1971; Shaft's Big Score, 1972; High Plains Drifter, 1973; Report to the Commissioner, 1975; The Sicilian Cross, 1975. Address: care Paul Marshall 130 W 57th St New York NY 10019

TIECKE, RICHARD WILLIAM, assn. exec., oral pathologist; b. Muscatine, Iowa, Apr. 5, 1917; s. Harry Frederick and Nell Eola (McKibben) T.; B.S., U. Iowa, 1940, D.D.S., 1942, M.S., 1947; postgrad. U. Chgo., 1947-49. Jr. pathologist, asst. pathologist, dep. chief oral pathology div. Armed Forces Inst. Pathology, 1949-54; asso. prof. pathology Georgetown 1949-54; prof. pathology Northwestern U. Sch. Dentistry, Chgo., 1954—, head oral pathology, asso. cancer coordinator, 1954-62; prof. dept. oral pathology U. Ill., 1962—; research fellow Hektoen Inst. Med. Research, Cook County Hosp., Chgo.; dir. research inst. Am. Dental Assn., Chgo., 1968-71, asst. exec. dir., 1971—; cons. U.S. Naval Hosp., Great Lakes, Ill., VA Research Hosp., VA West Side Hosp., Pub. Health Hosp., Chgo., City Chgo. Bd. Health, surgeon gen. USPHS, head and neck cancer detection Nat. Center Chronic Disease Control-USPHS, Nat. Cancer Inst. NIH; cons. to surgeon gen. Army, 1969—. Served from 1st lt. to col., AUS, 1942-54; now col. Res. (ret.). Diplomate Am. Bd. Oral Pathology (dir., past pres.). Fellow Am. Acad. Oral Pathology (past pres.), Am. Coll. Dentists; mem. ADA (asst. sec. Council Dental Therapeutics 1962-68), Ill., Chgo. dental socs., Internat. Assn. Dental Research, Psi Omega, Omicron Kappa Upsilon. Author: Physiologic Pathology of Oral Disease, 1959; Oral Pathology, 1964; Atlas on Oral Cytology, 1969; also research articles. Home: 179 E Lake Shore Dr Chicago IL 60611

TIECKELMANN, HOWARD, educator; b. Chgo., Oct. 29, 1916; s. Hugo A.M. and Thora (Behrends) T.; B.A., Carthage Coll., 1942; Ph.D., U. Buffalo, 1948; m. L. Elizabeth Cook, Sept., 1942; children—H. William, Bonnie, Robert, Barbara, Betty. Chemist Armor Research Found., 1946; instr. organic chemistry U. Buffalo, 1946-49; asst. prof., 1949-56, asso. prof., 1956-61; prof. chemistry State U. N.Y. at Buffalo, 1961-75, chmn. dept., 1970-75, Distinguished Teaching prof., 1975—. Served with USNR, 1945-46. Mem. Am. Chem. Soc., Chem. Soc. London, AAUP, AAAS. Contbr. to Methods in Enzymology, Vol. 18, 1971; Pyridine and Its Derivatives, 1973; also articles in profl. jours. Home: 59 Chaumont Dr Williamsville NY 14221 Office: Dept Chemistry State U NY at Buffalo Buffalo NY 14214

TIEDE, TOM ROBERT, journalist; b. Huron, S.D., Feb. 24, 1937; s. Leslie Albert and Rose (Allen) T.; B.A. in Journalism, Wash. State U., 1959; m. Patricia Lee Chisholm, Apr. 4, 1959; children—Kristina Anne, Thomas Patrick. Mem. staff Kalispell (Mont.) Daily Interlake, 1960-61, Daytona Beach (Fla.) News Jour., 1961-63; war corr. Newspaper Enterprise Assn., N.Y.C., 1964—; lectr. in field., 1965—. Served as lt., inf., AUS, 1960. Recipient Ernie Pyle Meml. award, 1965; Freedoms Found. award, 1966; George Washington medal, 1972. Mem. Internat. Platform Assn., Sigma Delta Chi, Lambda Chi Alpha. Roman Catholic. Clubs: Overseas Press, Nat. Headliners (award 1966 Atlantic City). Author: Your Men at War, 1965; Coward, 1968; Calley: Soldier or Killer?, 1971; Welcome to Washington, Mr. Witherspoon, 1979. Work collected by Boston U. Library. Home: 14809 Carrollton Rd Rockville MD 20853 Office: 777 14th St NW Washington DC 20005

TIEDEMAN, DAVID VALENTINE, educator; b. Americus, Ga., Aug. 12, 1919; s. Walter Dohlen and Edna M(arie) (Komfort) T.; A.B., Union Coll., Schenectady, 1941; A.M., U. Rochester, 1943; Ed.M., Harvard, 1948, Ed.D., 1949; m. Marjorie I(da) Denman, Sept. 26, 1942 (div. Jan. 2, 1973); children—David Michael, Jeffrey Denman; m. 2d, Anna Louise Miller, Jan. 6, 1973. Staff mem. NRC com. selection and tng. aircraft pilots U. Rochester, 1941-43, staff mem. test constrn. dept. Coll. Entrance Exam. Bd., 1943-44, asso. head statistics div. Manhattan Project, 1944-46; Milton teaching fellow, instr. edn. Harvard Grad. Sch. Edn., 1946-48, Sheldon travelling fellow, 1948-49, instr. edn., 1949-51, asst. prof. edn., 1951-52, lectr. edn., 1952-55, asso. prof., 1955-59, prof., 1959-71, asso. dir. Center for Research in Careers, 1963-66, research asso. Center for Research in Careers, also chmn. exec. com., information system for vocational decisions, 1966-69; prin. research scientist Palo Alto office Am. Insts. for Research, 1971-73; prof. edn. No. Ill. U., DeKalb, 1973—, dir. ERIC Clearinghouse in Career Edn., 1973-76, coordinator Office Vocat., Tech., and Career Edn., 1978—. Editorial asso. Jour. Counseling Psychology, 1957-63, Personnel and Guidance Jour., 1960-63, Jour. Career Edn., 1979—; mem. Adv. Council on Guidance Dept. Edn. Commonwealth Mass., 1957-63; chmn. commn. on tests Coll. Entrance Exam. Bd., 1967-70; mem. advisory screening com. in edn. Council Internat. Exchange of Scholars, 1975-79, chmn., 1978-79. Bd. dirs. Mass. Com. Children and Youth, 1961-63. Fellow Center for Advanced Study in Behavioral Scis., spl. fellow NIMH, 1963-64. Mem. Am. Ednl. Research Assn., Am. Personnel and Guidance Assn., Nat. Vocat. Guidance Assn. (pres. 1965-66, Eminent Career award 1979), Am. Psychol. Assn. (pres. div. counseling psychology 1965-66), Nat. Council on Measurement in Edn. (pres. 1962-63), NEA, Phi Beta Kappa, Sigma Xi, Phi Delta Kappa, Phi Kappa Phi. Contbr. articles to profl. jours., chpts. to books. Office: No Ill U Office Vocat Tech and Career Edn 305 Swen Parson DeKalb IL 60115

TIEDEMANN, ARTHUR EVERETT, coll. dean, historian; b. Bklyn., Mar. 22, 1921; s. William Frederick and Mary Agnes (Hailey) T.; B.S.S., Coll. City N.Y., 1943; M.A., Columbia, 1949, Ph.D., 1959; m. Margaret Nicholson, Jan. 22, 1949; children—Karl Christopher, Eric Scott. Faculty, Coll. City N.Y., 1949—, prof. history, 1968—, chmn. dept., 1965-69, 75-77, dean social sci., 1977—. Served with AUS, 1942-46. Mem. Am. Hist. Assn., Assn. Asian Studies, Japan Soc. N.Y., Phi Beta Kappa. Author: Modern Japan: A Brief History, rev. edit., 1962. Editor: An Introduction to Japanese Civilization, 1974. Address: 90 LaSalle St New York City NY 10027

TIEDEMANN, CARL HANS, securities co. exec.; b. Cleve., June 3, 1926; s. Carl Hans and Mary Owen (Glenn) T.; grad. Philips Exeter Acad., 1944; B.A., Trinity Coll., Hartford, Conn., 1950; M.S., Columbia; m. Mary B. Cumming, Oct. 24, 1959; children—Carl H., Mark B., Leigh C., Michael G. Salesman, Am. Cyanamid Co., 1950-57; with Stone & Webster Securities Co., 1957-62; with Donaldson, Lufkin & Jenrette, Inc., N.Y.C., 1962—, chmn. bd., until 1974, vice chmn. bd., 1974-75, pres., 1975—; dir. Curtice-Burns, Inc., Rochester, N.Y. Bd. govs. Am. Stock Exchange. Served with USNR, 1944-46. Mem. Nat. Assn. Security Dealers. Clubs: University (N.Y.C.); Maidstone (Easthampton, N.Y.). Home: 1030 Fifth Ave New York City NY 10028 Office: 140 Broadway New York City NY 10005

TIEGS, CHERYL, model; b. Calif.; d. Theodore and Phyllis Tiegs; student Calif. State U., Los Angeles; m. Stan Dragoti, 1970. Profl. model, appearing in nat. mags. weekly appearances on ABC's Good Morning America; also appearing in television commls. Address: care Eileen Ford 344 E 59th St New York NY 10022

TIEGS, FAY ADAMS, educator; b. Dinuba, Calif.; d. Samuel K. and Lulu J. (Harper) Greene; A.B., U. So. Calif., 1926, A.M., 1929; Ph.D., Columbia, 1934; m. William Douglas Adams, Nov. 1, 1924; 1 dau., Marilinda; m. 2d, Ernest W. Tiegs, Sept. 1, 1949. Elementary tchr. pub. schs., Los Angeles, 1924-26, secondary tchr., 1926-29; tng. tchr. U. Calif., Los Angeles, 1929; instr. edn. U. So. Calif., 1929-34, asst. prof. edn., also dir. elementary tchr. tng., 1934-40, asso. prof. edn., 1940-46, prof. edn., 1946—. Mem. Phi Beta Kappa, Kappa Delta, Pi Lambda Theta, Delta Kappa Gamma (Calif. treas. 1937-38). Author: Initiating an Activity Program into a Public School, 1934; Educating America's Children: Elementary School Curriculum and Method, 1954; Co-author: Teaching the Bright Pupil, 1928; Man-The Nature Tamer, 1941; Teaching Children to Read, 1949; Story of Nations, 1952; The Problems of Education, 1938. Editor: (with Ernest W. Tiegs) Tiegs-Adams Social Studies Series (Books 1-9), 1949, 54, 56, 58, 60, 65, 68, 75-79; Teaching the Social Studies, 1959, 65. Home: 5825 Green Oak Dr Los Angeles CA 90028

TIEKEN, THEODORE DAVID, lawyer; b. Chgo., Mar. 30, 1909; s. Theodore and Elizabeth (Chapman) T.; B.S., U. Chgo., 1929, J.D., 1933; m. Elizabeth S. Babson, Dec. 3, 1936; children—Nancy Babson, Theodore David, Elizabeth Chapman. Admitted to Ill. bar, 1933; with firm Winston, Strawn & Shaw, Chgo., 1933-46; gen. atty. C.,I. &L. Ry., 1946-47; v.p., gen. counsel Babson Bros. Co., Chgo., 1958-64, pres., 1964-76, chmn., 1976—; dir. Rand McNally & Co. Trustee, pres. Chgo. Hist. Soc.; trustee Infant Welfare Soc. Chgo.; bd. dirs. Arabian Horse Registry Am. Served as lt. comdr. USNR, 1942-45. Mem. Am., Chgo. bar assns. Republican. Episcopalian. Clubs: Chicago, Racquet, Yacht (Chgo.); Shoreacres (Lake Bluff, Ill.). Home: 1500 Lake Shore Dr Chicago IL 60610 Office: 2100 S York Rd Oak Brook IL 60521

TIEMANN, NORBERT THEODORE, govt. ofcl., former gov. Nebr.; b. Minden, Nebr., July 18, 1924; s. Martin William and Alvina (Rathert) T.; student U. Nebr., 1942-43, 46-49; D.Agr., Midland Luth. Coll., Fremont, Nebr., 1967, Ph.D. (hon.); m. Lorna Lou Bornholdt, July 19, 1950; children—Mary Catherine, Norbert Theodore, Lorna Christine, Amy Eileen. Asst. county agt., Lexington, 1949-50; asst. mgr. Nebr. Hereford Assn., Central City, 1950; exec. sec. Nat. Livestock Feeders Assn., Omaha, 1952; dir. industry relations Nat. Livestock and Meat Bd., Chgo., 1952-54; pres. Comml. State Bank, Wausa, 1957-70; gov. Nebr., 1967-71; fed. hwy. adminstr. Dept. Transp., Washington, 1973—; v.p. firm Henningson, Durham and Richardson. Washington. Leader, 4-H Club, 1949-50; mem. Cover Wagon council Boy Scouts Am., 1954-62; state chmn. Heart Fund drive, 1964; exec. bd. Nat. Gov.'s Conf. Mayor, Wausa, 1956-62. Mem. exec. com. Neb. Synod. Bd. dirs. Luth. Ch. Am. Served with AUS, 1943-46; to 2d lt., 1950-52. Mem. Am. Legion, V.F.W., Beta Sigma Psi. Republican. Home: 8440 Brook Rd McLean VA 22101 Office: Dept Transp Washington DC 20590

TIEMEYER, CHRISTIAN, symphony condr., cellist; b. Balt., Sept. 21, 1940; s. Henry Christian and Bertha Hegler (Kappler) T.; B.M., Peabody Conservatory, 1962, M.M., 1963; postgrad. Juilliard Sch. Music, 1963-64; D.M.A., Catholic U. Am., 1977; m. Patti Jeanine Farris, June 22, 1968; children—Jeanine Elizabeth, Henry Christian IV. Cellist, Balt. Symphony, 1959-60; mem. faculty Peabody Inst., 1961-63; asst. and acting prin. cellist Am. Symphony, N.Y.C., 1962-64; mem. U.S. Army Band-Strolling Strings, 1964-67; prin. cellist Utah Symphony, 1968-75; asso. condr. Dallas Symphony, 1978—; chmn. conducting and string faculties U. Utah, 1968-77; adj. faculty mem. Brigham Young U., 1968-75; founding condr. Salt Lake Civic Orch., 1974, Utah Chamber Orch., 1975, Snowbird/U. Utah Summer Arts Inst., 1975—, Dallas Chamber Orch., 1978-79; music dir. Young Audiences, Inc., Salt Lake City, 1974-76. Served with U.S. Army, 1964-67. Office: Dallas Symphony Music Hall PO Box 26207 Dallas TX 75226

TIEN, CHANG LIN, engring. educator; b. Wuhan, China, July 24, 1935; s. Yun Chien and Yun Di (Lee) T.; came to U.S., 1956, naturalized, 1969; B.S., Nat. Taiwan U., 1955; M.M.E., U. Louisville, 1957; M.A., Ph.D., Princeton U., 1959; m. Di Hwa Liu, July 25, 1959; children—Norman Chihnan, Phyllis Chihping, Christine Chihyih. Acting asst. prof. dept. mech. engring. U. Calif., Berkeley, 1959-60, asst. prof., 1960-64, asso. prof., 1964-68, prof., 1968—, dept. chmn., 1974—; tech. cons. Lockheed Missiles & Space Co., Gen. Electric Co. Guggenheim fellow, 1965. Fellow ASME (Heat Transfer Meml. award 1974, Larson Meml. award 1975), AIAA (asso.; Thermophysics award 1977); mem. Nat. Acad. Engring. Contbr. articles to profl jours. Home: 1425 Grizzly Peak Blvd Berkeley CA 94708 Office: Dept Mech Engring U Calif Berkeley CA 94720

TIEN, PING KING, electronic engr.; b. Chekieng, China, Aug. 2, 1919; s. N.S. and Y.S. (Chao) T.; came to U.S., 1947; M.S., Stanford U., 1948, Ph.D., 1951; m. Nancy N.Y. Chen, Apr. 19, 1952; children—Emily Ju-Psia, Julia Ju-Wen. Head dept. electron physics Bell Telephone Labs., Holmdel, N.J., 1952—. Recipient Achievement award Chinese Inst. Engrs., 1966. Fellow IEEE, Optical Soc. Am.; mem. Nat. Acad. Sci., Nat. Acad. Engring. Contbr. sci. and tech. articles to profl. jours. Patentee in field. Home: 19 Lisa Dr Chatham NJ 07928 Office: Bell Labs Holmdel NJ 07733

TIENKEN, ARTHUR T., ambassador; b. Yonkers, N.Y., Aug. 5, 1922; B.A., Princeton U., 1947, M.A., 1949. With U.S. Fgn. Service, 1949—, dep. chief mission, Tunis, Tunisia, 1973-75, Addis Ababa, Ethiopia, 1975-77, ambassador to Gabonese Republic and Democratic Republic of Sao Tome and Principe with residence at Libreville, Gabon, 1978—; diplomat-in-residence Marquette U., 1972-73. Served with U.S. Army, 1943-46. Office: American Embassy Blvd de la Mer Boite Postale 4000 Libreville Gabon

TIERNAN, ROBERT OWENS, lawyer; b. Providence, R.I., Feb. 24, 1929; s. Joseph John and Mary Elizabeth (McConnell) T.; grad. Providence Coll., 1953; J.D., Cath. U. Am., 1956; H.L.D., U. R.I.; m. July 13, 1953; children—Michael Moss, Robert Ownes, Christopher Paul. Admitted to R.I. bar, 1957; practiced law, R.I., 1957—; mem. R.I. State Senate, 1961-68; mem. U.S. Congress from R.I., 1968-75; vice chmn. Fed. Election Commn., Washington, 1975—. Mem. R.I. Bar Assn., Am. Bar Assn., R.I. Mental Health Assn. Democrat. Roman Catholic. Clubs: Point Judith Country, Pawtucket Country. Home: 1922 Warwick Ave Warwick RI 02889 Office: Fed Election Commn 1325 K St NW Washington DC 20463*

TIERNEY, BRIAN, educator, historian; b. Scunthorpe, Eng., May 7, 1922; s. John Patrick and Helena (McGuire) T.; B.A., Pembroke Coll., Cambridge U., 1948, M.A., 1951, Ph.D., 1951; Dr.Theol. (hon.), Uppsala (Sweden) U., 1964; m. Theresa O'Dowd, Aug. 24, 1949; children—John, Helen, Christopher, Ann Jane. Came to U. S., 1951, naturalized, 1966. From instr. to asso. prof. history Cath. U. Am., 1951-59; prof. medieval history Cornell U., Ithaca, N.Y., 1959-77, Bowmar prof. humanistic studies, 1977—. Served with RAF, 1941-46. Decorated D.F.C. and bar. Guggenheim fellow, 1955, 56; Am. Council Learned Socs. fellow, 1961, 66. fellow Inst. Advanced Study, Princeton, 1961; fellow Nat. Endowment Humanities, 1977. Fellow Mediaeval Acad. Am.; mem. Am., Am. Cath. (pres. 1965) hist. assns. Author: Foundations of the Conciliar Theory, 1955; Medieval Poor Law, 1959; The Crisis of Church and State, 1050-1300, 1964; Origins of Papal Infallibility, 1150-1350, 1971. Home: 201 Willard Way Ithaca NY 14850

TIERNEY, DONALD FRANK, physician; b. Butte, Mont., May 24, 1931; s. Frank J. and Violet (MacDonald) T.; student Calif. Inst. Tech., 1949-52; B.A., U. Calif., Berkeley, 1953; M.D., U. Calif., San Francisco, 1956; m. Claire Nelson, June 22, 1954; children—Laura, Bruce. Postdoctoral fellow Cardiovascular Research Inst., U. Calif., San Francisco, 1962-65, asst. prof. physiology univ., 1965-68; asso. prof. medicine UCLA-Harbor Gen. Hosp., 1968-75; prof. medicine UCLA Center Health Sci., 1975—; established investigator Am. Heart Assn., 1965-70; mem. pulmonary disease adv. com. Nat. Heart, Lung and Blood Inst., 1973-76. Served with U.S. Army, 1960-62. Recipient Career Devel. award Lung div. Nat. Heart, Lung and Blood Inst., 1970-75; Nat. Heart, Lung and Blood Inst. grantee. Mem. Am. Thoracic Soc. (v.p. and pres. 1978-79), Am. Soc. Clin. Investigation, Assn. Am. Physicians, Am. Physiol. Soc. Western Soc. Clin. Medicine, Am. Fedn. Clin. Research. Research, numerous publs. on lung physiology, metabolism, biochemistry. Home: 17144 Ave de Santa Ynez Pacific Palisades CA 90272 Office: Dept Medicine UCLA Los Angeles CA 90024

TIERNEY, HOWARD SHERWOOD, pharm. co. exec.; b. N.Y.C., Apr. 27, 1918; s. Howard Sherwood and Belle Lavinia (Taylor) T.; B.A., Yale, 1940; student Harvard Grad. Sch. Bus. Adminstrn., 1941; m. Jane Meldrin Hewitt, Sept. 22, 1941; children—Michele T. Eklund, Patricia (Mrs. Robert Falkenhagen), Alison, George. With

Bridgeport Brass Co. (Conn.), 1941-42; with E.R. Squibb & Sons, 1945-55, v.p. overseas ops., to 1955; pres., chief exec. officer, chmn. exec. com. Denver Chem. Mfg. Co., 1955-72; exec. v.p., mem. exec. com., dir. Carter-Wallace, Inc., N.Y.C., 1973-78; pres. Culbro Corp., 1978—; dir. Lafayette Bank and Trust Co., Bridgeport, Harold B. Scott, Inc., Stamford, Conn., Syracuse Supply Co. (N.Y.). Served to lt. (s.g.), pilot USNR, 1943-45. Mem. Phi Beta Kappa. Republican. Episcopalian. Clubs: Country of Fairfield (Conn.), Aubichwi Gun (Fairfield); Fairfield County Hunt (Westport, Conn.); Jupiter Island (Hobe Sound, Fla.); Ekwanok Country (Manchester, Vt.); University (N.Y.C.). Home: 1130 Mine Hill Rd Fairfield CT 06430 Office: Culbro Corp 605 3d Ave New York NY 10016

TIERNEY, RICHARD HOAG, investment banking co. exec.; b. N.Y.C., Aug. 1, 1932; s. Raymond Moran and Alice Mary (Hoag) T.; B.A., U. Notre Dame, 1954; postgrad. Grad. Sch. Bus., N.Y. U., 1956-58; m. Virginia Ann Byrne, Oct. 1, 1955; children—Barbara Ann Tierney Messmer, Joanne Marie, Maria Gerard, Richard Hoag. With Blyth & Co. Inc., 1956-72, trader, mgr. trading, N.Y.C.; 1st v.p., mgr. block trading Blyth Eastman Dillon & Co., Inc., N.Y.C., 1972-73, exec. v.p. equity trading div., 1974—; gen. partner charge equity trading Loeb Rhoades & Co., 1973-74. Served to 1st lt. USMC, 1954-56. Mem. Bond Club N.Y., Securities Traders Assn. N.Y., Corp. Bond Traders Club N.Y. Clubs: Navesink Country, Seaview Country, Madison Sq. Garden. Home: 2 Vista Pl Red Bank NJ 07701 Office: 1221 Ave of Americas New York NY 10020*

TIETJEN, JOHN HENRY, sem. pres.; b. N.Y.C., June 18, 1928; s. John N. and Anna (Harders) T.; diploma Concordia Coll., Bronxville, N.Y., 1948; B.A., Concordia Sem., St. Louis, 1950, B.D., 1953; S.T.M., Union Theol. Sem., N.Y.C., 1954, Th.D., 1959; m. Ernestine C. Damits, June 13, 1953; children—Catherine Anne, Laurence John, Mary Angela, Sarah Elizabeth. Ordained to ministry Luth. Ch., 1953; asst. pastor in Teaneck, N.J., 1953-56; pastor in Leonia, N.J., 1956-66; exec. sec. div. pub. relations Luth. Council U.S.A., 1966-69; pres. Concordia Sem., 1969-74, Christ Seminex, 1975—. Mem. Youth Guidance Council, Leonia, 1961-66. Bd. dirs. St. Louis Bach Soc., Evangelical Lutherans in Mission. Mem. Am. Soc. Ch. History. Author: Which Way to Lutheran Unity?, 1966; also chpts in books, articles. Mng. editor Am. Luth., 1960-61, editor, 1962-66; editorial asso. Luth. Forum, 1967-71, Currents in Theology and Mission, 1974—; editor Profiles in Belief: The Religious Bodies of the United States and Canada, 7 vols. Home: 6229 Pershing St Louis MO 63130

TIETJENS, NORMAN ORWIG, judge; b. Napoleon, Ohio, July 8, 1903; s. Otto Peter and Corinne Hannah (Orwig) T.; Ph.B., magna cum laude, Brown U., 1925, M.A., 1927; J.D., magna cum laude, U. Mich., 1930; m. Lucretia Norvell Larkin, Apr. 18, 1936; children—Corinne N. (Mrs. Sommer), Anne (Mrs. Guandolo). Instr., Napoleon High Sch., 1925-26; admitted to Ohio bar, 1930; asso. Williams, Eversman & Morgan, Toledo, 1930-32; pvt. practice, Napoleon, 1932-33; spl. counsel Fed. Emergency Adminstrn. of Pub. Works, 1933-37; counsel U.S. Maritime Commn., 1937-38; atty. Office Gen. Counsel, U.S. Treasury Dept., 1938-39, asst. gen. counsel, 1939-50; apptd. judge Tax Ct. U.S., 1950, chief judge, 1961-67, ret. 1971, now recalled. Recipient Achievement award Tax Soc. N.Y. U. for outstanding service in field taxation, 1964; Bic medallion Brown U., 1965; Sesquicentennial award U. Mich., 1967. Mem. Order of Coif, Phi Beta Kappa, Sigma Nu, Phi Delta Phi. Democrat. Clubs: Congressional Country, Asso. editor Mich. Law Rev., 1929-30. Home: 3509 Overlook Ln Washington DC 20016

TIETZ, WILLIAM JOHN, JR., univ. pres.; b. Chgo., Mar. 6, 1927; s. William John and Irma (Neuman) T.; B.A., Swarthmore Coll., 1950; M.S., U. Wis., 1952; D.V.M., Colo. State U., 1957; Ph.D., Purdue U., 1961; m. Patricia Lane Wells, Apr. 25, 1953; children—Karen Elizabeth, William John, Julia Wells. Research asso. Baxter Labs., Morton Grove, Ill., 1952-53; instr., then asso. prof. Purdue U., 1957-64; faculty Colo. State U., 1964-77, prof., chmn. physiology and biophysics, 1967-70, v.p. student and univ. relations, 1970-71, dean Coll. Vet. Medicine and Biomed. Scis., 1971-77, asso. dir. Agr. Expt. Sta., 1975-77; pres. Mont. State U., Bozeman, 1977—. Bd. dirs. Children's House, Montessori Sch., 1966-70, chmn., 1968-70; bd. dirs. Colo. State U. Found., 1970-71; bd. dirs. Colo. chpt. Am. Cancer Soc., 1976-79; mem. research bd. Denver Zool. Soc., 1975-77; treas. Mont. Energy Research and Devel. Inst., 1977-78, v.p., 1978-80; bd. dirs. Greater Mont. Found., 1979-80; mem. Mont. Com. for Humanities, 1980; mem. div. resources adv. council NIH, 1979-80. Served with USNR, 1945-46. Recipient Service award Colo. Vet. Med. Assn., 1976. Mem. Larimer County Vet. Med. Assn. (pres. 1968-69), Am. Assn. Vet. Physiologists and Pharmacologists (pres. 1971-72), Am. Physiol. Soc., Sigma Xi, Phi Zeta (sec.-treas. 1970-71), Assn. Am. Colls. Vet. Medicine (chmn. council of deans 1975-76), Phi Kappa Phi, Phi Sigma Kappa, Omicron Delta Kappa, Beta Beta Beta. Address: Office of Pres Mont State U Bozeman MT 59715

TIFFANY, LAWRENCE PAUL, lawyer; b. Houston, Oct. 7, 1936; s. Murray L. and Vera Tiffany (Armstrong) T.; A.B., Washington U., St. Louis, 1961, LL.B., 1963; S.J.D. (Univ. fellow), U. Wis., 1967; m. Mary Ryan, Dec. 27, 1965; children—Eric, Julie. Admitted to Mo. bar, 1963; asst. prof. law U. Denver, 1964-67, asso. prof., 1967-69, prof., 1970—, acting dean Coll. Law, 1977-78; mem. Am. Bar Found. Scholar in Residence Program, 1969-70; co-dir. Denver Plea Bargaining Reduction Project, 1978-79; bd. advs. Nat. Center for State Cts. Study of Guideline Sentencing, 1979; dir. Am. Samoa Criminal Code Revision Project, 1979. Served with USN, 1954-57; China, Korea. Am. Bar Found. affiliated scholar, 1972-77. Mem. Mo. Bar, Law and Soc. Assn., Am. Bar Assn., Order Coif. Author: (with McIntyre and Rotenberg) Detection of Crime, 1967; (with Reese, Beaney and Blumenthal) The Drinking Driver, 1973; contbr. articles to law revs.; research on plea bargaining and sentencing practices. Office: 200 W 14th Ave Denver CO 80204

TIFFEAU, JACQUES EMILE, fashion designer; b. Poitou, France, Oct. 11, 1927; s. Auguste and Celine (Meunier) T. Came to U.S., 1931. Fashion designer Monte-Sano & Pruzan, Ltd., N.Y.C., 1951—; v.p., treas. Tiffeau & Busch, Ltd., N.Y.C., 1958-70; now designer Originala, N.Y.C.; fashion critic Parsons Sch. Design. Served with French Army Air Force, World War II. Recipient Coty Design award, 1960, 64; Nat. Cotton award, 1961; Internat. Fashion award London (Eng.) Sunday Times, 1964; Tobe-CoBurn Fashion award. Office: 512 7th Ave New York NY 10018 also 25 rue Faubourg St Honoré F-75008 Paris France*

TIFT, MARY LOUISE, artist; b. Seattle, Jan. 2, 1913; d. John Howard and Wilhelmina (Pressler) Dreher; B.F.A. cum laude, U. Wash., 1933; postgrad. Art Center Coll., Los Angeles, 1945-48, U. Calif., San Francisco, 1962-63; m. William Raymond Tift, Dec. 4, 1948. Art dir. Vaughn Shedd Advt., Los Angeles, 1948; asst. prof. design Calif. Coll. Arts and Crafts, Oakland, Calif., 1949-59; coordinator design dept. San Francisco Art Inst., 1959-62; one woman shows: Gumps Gallery, San Francisco, 1977, Diane Gilson Gallery, Seattle, 1978; group shows include: Brit. Biennale, Yorkshire, Eng., 1970, Grenchen Triennale, Switzerland, 1970, Polish Biennale, Crakow, 1972, Nat. Gallery, Washington, 1973; represented in permanent collections: Phila. Mus. Art, Bklyn. Mus., Seattle Art Mus., Library Congress, Achenbach Print Collection, San Francisco Palace Legion of Honor. Served to lt. USNR, 1943-45. Mem. Print Club Phila., Calif. Soc. Printmakers, Phi Beta Kappa, Lambda Rho. Christian Scientist. Home: 607 Chapman Dr Corte Madera CA 94925 Office: 112 Industrial Center Bldg Sausalito CA 94965

TIGER, LIONEL, social scientist, found. cons.; b. Montreal, Que., Can., Feb. 5, 1937; s. Martin and Lillian (Schneider) T.; B.A., M.A., McGill U., 1953-59; Ph.D., U. London, 1962; m. Virginia Conner, Aug. 19, 1964; 1 son, Sebastian Benjamin. Asst. Prof. sociology U. B.C., Vancouver, 1963-68; asso. prof. anthropology Livingston Coll., Rutgers U., New Brunswick, N.J., 1968-72, prof. Grad. Sch., 1972—; cons., research dir. Harry F. Guggenheim Found., N.Y.C., 1972—. Recipient McNaughton prize for creative writing; Can. Council Research fellow; Ford Found. Fgn. Area Tng. fellow; Can. Council-Killam fellow for interdisciplinary research; Guggenheim fellow; Rockefeller fellow Aspen Inst., 1979. Fellow Royal Anthrop. Inst., Gt. Britain; mem. Am., Canadian Anthrop. Assn., Am. Sociol. Assn., Soc. for Study Evolution. Author: Men in Groups, 1969; (with Robin Fox) The Imperial Animal, 1971; (with Joseph Shepher) Women in the Kibbutz, 1975; Optimism: The Biology of Hope, 1979. Editor: Female Hierarchies, 1978. Editorial bd. Social Science Information; Ethology and Sociobiology. Address: 17 W 9th St New York NY 10011

TIGERMAN, STANLEY, architect; b. Chgo., Sept. 20, 1930; s. Samuel Bernard and Emma Louise (Stern) T.; student Mass. Inst. Tech., 1948-49; B.Arch., Yale, 1960, M.Arch., 1961; m. Margaret I. McCurry; children—Judson Joel, Tracy Leigh. Archtl. draftsman firm George Fred Keck, Chgo., 1949-50, Skidmore, Owings and Merrill, Chgo., 1957-59, Paul Rudolph, New Haven, 1959-61, Harry Weese, Chgo., 1961-62; partner firm Tigerman & Koglin, Chgo., 1962-64; prin. firm Stanley Tigerman & Assos., Chgo., 1964—. Prof. architecture U. Ill., Chgo. Circle, 1967-71; vis. lectr. Yale, 1974, Cornell U., Ithaca, N.Y., 1963, Cooper Union, 1970, U. Calif. at Berkeley, 1968, Cardiff (Wales) Coll., 1965, Engring. U. Bangladesh, 1967. Pres. Yale Arts Assn., 1969-70; mem. advisory com. Yale Archtl. Sch., 1976—; bd. dirs. Bangladesh Found. Served with USN, 1950-54. Recipient Alpha Rho Chi medal Yale, 1961; Archtl. Record award, 1970; Chgo. Masonry award, 1974, Masonry Gold Medal award, 1974; Graham Fedn. for Advanced Studies in Fine Arts grantee, 1965. Fellow AIA (chmn. com. design 1976-77, recipient Chgo. Honor awards 1971, 73, 75, 77, 78, 79, Nat. Modern Income Housing award, 1970, Nat. Homes for Better Living award 1974, 75, Ill. awards 1976). Clubs: Arts of Chgo.; Yale of N.Y.C. Contbg. author: Design of the Housing Site, 1966; Chicago on Foot, 1969; Art Today, 1969; New Directions in American Architecture, 1969; Contemporary Jewelry, 1970; Urban Structures for the Future, 1972; Spaces for Living, 1973; Chicago 1930-70, 1974; Interior Spaces Designed by Architects, 1974; Housing, 1976; Chicago Architects, 1976; 100 Years of Architecture in Chicago, 1976; Architectural Graphics Primer, 1976; others; also numerous articles in newspapers and profl. jours.; exhibited Venice Biennale, 1976. Office: 920 N Michigan Ave Chicago IL 60611

TIGGES, KENNETH EDWIN, glass co. exec.; b. Sandusky, Ohio, Sept. 4, 1927; s. Edwin Ernest and Ruth Dorothea (Krapp) T.; B.S. in Bus. Adminstrn., Bowling Green State U., 1950; m. Mary Anne Richardson, June 11, 1955. With Konopak & Dalton, C.P.A.'s, Toledo, 1950-57; with Owens-Illinois, Inc., 1957—, comptroller, 1963-71, v.p., comptroller, 1971—. C.P.A., Ohio. Mem. Am. Inst. C.P.A.'s, Ohio Soc. C.P.A.'s, Fin. Execs. Inst., Sigma Chi. Home: 6655 Mill Ridge Rd Maumee OH 43537 Office: Toledo OH 43666

TIGHE, MARY ANN SCARANGELLO (MARY ANN HIDALGO), govt. ofcl.; b. Bronx, N.Y., Aug. 24, 1948; d. Francis Peter and Edith (Zarro) Scarangello; B.A. magna cum laude, Cath. U. Am., 1970; M.A. in Art History, U. Md., 1976; m. David A. Hidalgo, Oct. 27, 1979; 1 son, Aaron Mathieson Tighe. Museum asst. Smithsonian Instn., 1970-72; mem. faculty art dept. Georgetown U., Washington, 1973-74; mem. staff Hirshhorn Museum and Sculpture Garden, Washington, 1974-77; arts adviser Office of Vice Pres., Washington, 1977-78; dep. chmn. for programs Nat. Endowment for Arts, Washington, 1978—; lectr., cons. Coll. scholar, 1967-70; Timken scholar, 1966-70; U. Md. fellow, 1971-72. Mem. Phi Beta Kappa. Author: (with E. Lang) Art America, 1977; producer, writer Art America TV series, 1974-75; contbr. articles to various publs. Office: Nat Endowment for Arts 2401 E St NW Washington DC 20506

TIGNOR, ROBERT LEE, historian; b. Phila., Nov. 20, 1933; s. Robert Max and Martha Arvilla (Stalter) T.; B.A., Coll. Wooster, 1955; M.A., Yale U., 1956, Ph.D., 1960; m. Marian Ann Shaw, June 16, 1956; children—Laura, Jeffrey, Sandra. Mem. faculty dept. history Princeton U., 1960—, prof., 1976—, chmn. dept. history, 1976—; mem. faculty U. Ibadan, Nigeria, U. Nairobi, Kenya, 1965-66. Ford Found. fellow, 1959-60; Rockefeller Found. fellow, 1965-66; Am. Council Learned Socs.-Social Sci. Research Council fellow, 1969-70. Mem. Am. Hist. Assn., Middle East Studies Assn. Democrat. Unitarian. Author: Modernization and British Colonial Rule in Egypt, 1882-1914, 1966; The Colonial Transformation of Kenya, 1976. Home: 69 Maclean Circle Princeton NJ 08540 Office: Dept History Princeton Univ Princeton NJ 08540

TIGRAK, MEHMET FAUT, structural engr.; b. Istanbul, Turkey, Aug. 26, 1911; s. M. Suleyman and Hediye (Harputlu) T.; Diploma, Mil. Coll., Habiye-Istanbul, 1932; Diploma Mil. Engring., 1934; Certificate, U. Berlin (Germany), 1938; student Technische Hochschule, Berlin, 1938-39; B.S., U. Ill., 1942, M.S., 1943, Ph.D., 1945; m. Mary Louise Evans; children—William M. U., James A.F., Hediye L. Came to U.S., 1958, naturalized. With Turkish Army Corps Engrs., 1934-51, resigned sr. maj., 1951; tech. dir. Turk Yapi Ltd. Co., Ankara, Turkey, 1951; dept. head Metcalf, Hamilton, Grove, Kansas City, Mo., 1951-53; prin. engr. project coordinator Hamilton Co., Kansas City, Mo., 1953-54; owner, operator Tigrak Cons. Engring. Co., Tigrak Constrn. Co., Ankara, 1954-58; prin. partner, mgr. Tigrak & Kolbasi, Engrs.-Contractors, Ankara, 1956-58; asso. in charge structure Clark, Daily, Dietz & Assos., Urbana, Ill., 1958-62; v.p. in charge structure and hwy. div. Clark, Dietz & Assos., Engrs. Inc., Urbana, Ill., 1962-66, v.p. in charge fed. and railroad projects, 1966—. Recipient Honorable Mention award for Findlay Bridge (Shelbyville, Ill.), U.S. Army C.E., 1969. Registered profl. engr., Ill., Ind., Mo., Ky., Tenn., Wis., Turkey; Registered structural engr., Ill., Ky., Turkey. Life mem. ASCE; mem. Ill. Assn. Professions, Nat., Ill. socs. profl. engrs., Am. Concrete Inst., Am. Ry. Engring. Assn. Soc. Am. Mil. Engrs., AAAS, Chamber Architects and Engrs. Turkey, Sigma Xi, Chi Epsilon, Phi Kappa Epsilon. Mason (32 deg., Shriner). Home: 23 Briarcliff Rural Route 1 Mahomet IL 61853 Office: 211 N Race St Urbana IL 61801

TIHANY, LESLIE CHARLES, ret. fgn. ser. officer; b. Hungary, Dec. 28, 1911; s. Béla and Katalin (Báródy) T.; B.S., Franklin and Marshall Coll., 1931; M.A., Northwestern U., 1933, Ph.D., 1936; A.M., Harvard, 1938, Ph.D., U. Chgo., 1943; postgrad. U. Helsinki; m. Elizabeth Derricott, 1936; m. 2d, Maria Dekom, 1959; children—Elizabeth, Richard, Peter. Came to U.S., 1930, naturalized, 1940. Research fellow Am. Council Learned Socs., 1938-40; asst. history U. Chgo., 1941; teaching fellow Harvard U., 1942-43; prof. U. Denver, 1943; vis. prof. Northwestern U., summer 1947; professorial lectr. Am. U., 1955-57, George Washington U, 1968—; fgn. affairs specialist Dept. State, 1943-56, fgn. service officer, 1956; consul, Salzburg, Austria, 1956-57; consul, Bombay, India, 1957-59, first sec. Am. embassy, Beirut, Lebanon, 1960-61; 1st sec., chief econ. officer, 1961-65; 1st sec. chief econ. officer Am. embassy, Saigon, Vietnam, 1965-66; pub. affairs officer Bur. Far Eastern affairs Dept. State, 1966; counselor of embassy, assigned Dept. State, 1966; internat. relations officer Bur. European Affairs, Dept. State, 1966-69; Am. consul gen., Antwerp, Belgium, 1969-72; ordained minister Conglist. Ch., 1979. Disting. prof. humanities and social sci. Commonwealth of Ky. Univ. System, 1972-76; prof. emeritus Commonwealth Ky. U. System, 1976—; adj. prof. history U. Cin., 1978—. Bd. dirs. Inst. Mediterranean Art and Archaeology. Lt. col. USAF Res. ret. Decorated comdr. Order Concordia, Rome, 1949; recipient Meritorious Honor award Dept. State. 1965; Frederick Sheldon prize fellow Harvard, 1938-39, 39-40; Professorial certificate of ch. history Gen. Synod Reformed Ch. in Am., 1975. Mem. Société Finno-Ougrienne (Helsinki). Clubs: Cosmos (Washington); Cin. Author: History of Middle Europe, 1976; The Baranya Dispute, 1978. Contbr. articles, revs. to profl. jours. Home: 218 Scenic View Dr Fort Thomas KY 41075 Office: Suite 909 18 E 4th St Cincinnati OH 45202. *I feel that, on the whole, my life has been shaped more by being acted upon than by my own acting. Plans I had made often led to disappointment; good things usually came providentially, sometimes recognizable only in retrospect.*

TILBURY, ROGER GRAYDON, lawyer; b. Guthrie, Okla., July 30, 1925; s. Graydon and Minnie (Lee) T.; B.S., U. So. Calif., 1945; J.D., U. Kan., 1949; LL.M., Columbia, 1950; postgrad. Oxford (Eng.) U., 1949; m. Margaret Dear, June 24, 1952; 1 dau., Elizabeth Ann. Admitted to Mo. bar, 1950, Oreg. bar, 1953; practiced in Kansas City, Mo., 1950-53, Portland, Oreg., 1953—; asso. firm Rogers, Field, Gentry, Kansas City, Mo., 1950-53, Stern, Reiter & Day, Portland, 1953-56; partner firm Roth & Tilbury, Portland, 1956-58, Tilbury & Kane, 1970-72, Haessler, Stamer & Tilbury, 1978—; circuit judge pro tem., Oreg., 1972—, arbitrator and fact finder, 1973—; sec. Barrington Properties; mem. nat. panel arbitrators U.S. Mediation Conciliation Service; atty., Animal Defender League, 1969-73. Dep. election commr., Kansas City, Mo., 1952-53. Bd. dirs. Multnomah Bar Found. Served to lt. (j.g.) USNR, 1943-45. Battenfeld scholar, 1943. Mem. Oreg. State Bar, Soc. Barristers, Am. Arbitration Assn., Save the Redwoods League, East African Wildlife League, Nat. Wildlife Found., Am. Trial Lawyers Assn., Delta Tau Delta, Phi Delta Phi. Club: White Elephant (London). Home: 9310 NW Cornell Rd Portland OR 97229 Office: 2626 1st Nat Bank Tower Portland OR 97201. *To paraphrase Winston Churchill, live in such way that this hour (this God-given hour) might someday be regarded as your finest hour.*

TILDEN, ELWYN EARLE, educator, clergyman; b. Everett, Mass., Mar. 24, 1914; s. Elwyn Earle and Louise (Tilden) T.; A.B., Harvard U., 1936; Th.B., Princeton Theol. Sem., 1939, Th.M., 1940, Th.D., 1945; m. Marguerite Elizabeth Hodgman, June 28, 1939; children—Elwyn Earle, Harold Harvey. Ordained to ministry Conglist. Ch., 1940; teaching fellow Princeton Theol. Sem., 1941-43; interim minister Ashbourne Presbyn. Ch., Elkins Park, Pa., 1943-45; prof. N.T., Lincoln Sem., 1945-49; prof. religion Lafayette Coll., 1949-78, head dept., 1949-77, Helen H. P. Manson prof. Bible, 1951-78, prof. emeritus, 1978—. Mem. Alumni Assn. Princeton Theol. Sem. (pres. 1963-64). Author: Toward Understanding Jesus, 1956. Contbr. Oxford Annotated Bible. Rev. Standard Version Holy Bible, 1962, 73. Home: 4 Pine Circle Green Ridge Village Newville PA 17241

TILL, JAMES EDGAR, biophysicist; b. Lloydminster, Sask., Can., Aug. 25, 1931; s. William and Gertrude Ruth (Isaac) T.; B.A., U. Sask., 1952, M.A., 1954; Ph.D., Yale U., 1957; m. Marion Joyce Sinclair, June 6, 1959; children—David William, Karen Sinclair, Susan Elizabeth. Postdoctoral fellow Connaught Med. Research Labs., Toronto, Ont., Can., 1956-57; mem. physics div. Ont. Cancer Inst., Toronto, 1957-67, div. biol. research, 1967-69, div. head, 1969—; prof. dept. med. biophysics U. Toronto. Recipient Gairdner Found. Internat. award, 1969. Fellow Royal Soc. Can.; mem. Biophys. Soc., Can Soc. Cell Biology, Internat. Soc. Exptl. Hematology, Am. Assn. Immunologists, Am. Assn. Cancer Research. Contbr. articles on biophysics, cell biology, cancer research to sci. jours. Home: 45 Doonaree Dr Don Mills ON M3A 1M5 Canada Office: 500 Sherbourne St Toronto ON M4X 1K9 Canada. *Albert Einstein said: "The most beautiful thing we can experience is the mysterious. It is the source of all true art and science." And, "Concern for man himself and his fate must always form the chief interest of all technical endeavors—in order that the creations of our mind shall be a blessing and not a curse to mankind." Is there a more eloquent summary of standards for the scientist than this? I don't think so.*

TILLACK, THOMAS WARNER, pathologist; b. Jacksonville, Fla., Nov. 16, 1937; s. Warner S. and Charlotte G. T.; B.A., U. Rochester, 1959; M.D., Yale U., 1963; m. Lynne Anne Beam, Oct. 30, 1970; children—Jonathan Allan, Allison Anne. Intern, Barnes Hosp., St. Louis, 1963-64, resident, 1964-66; staff asso. NIH, Bethesda, Md., 1966-69, sr. staff fellow, 1969-71; asst. prof. pathology Washington U., St. Louis, 1971-73, asso. prof., 1973-76; Walter Reed prof., chmn. dept. pathology U. Va. Med. Center, 1976—. Served with USPHS, 1966-69. Diploma Am. Bd. Pathology. Mem. Am. Assn. Pathologists, Internat. Acad. Pathology, Am. Soc. Cell Biology, Assn. Pathology Chairmen, Phi Beta Kappa. Research, publs. in cell biology and pathology. Home: Route 10 Box 36 Charlottesville VA 22901 Office: Dept Pathology Box 214 U Va Med Center Charlottesville VA 22908

TILLER, CARL WILLIAM, church ofcl.; b. Battle Lake, Minn., Sept. 25, 1915; s. Carl J(ohn) and Edith (Wells) T.; B.A., Concordia Coll., Moorhead, Minn., 1935, LL.D., 1966; M.A. in Pub. Adminstrn., U. Minn., 1940; m. Olive M. Foerster, June 21, 1940; children—Robert W., Jeanne L. (Mrs. John E. Peterson). Budget sec., examiner Minn., 1936-41; exec. asst. to dir. Municipal Finance Officers Assn., 1941-42; with U.S. Office of Mgmt. and Budget, 1942-72, spl. adviser budgetary devel., 1967-72; adj. prof. Am. U., 1952-70; asso. sec. Baptist World Alliance, Washington, 1972-78; dir. Interchurch Center, N.Y.C., 1978—. Mem. gen. bd. Nat. Council Chs., 1963-75, treas., 1970-75; mem. gen. council Am. Baptist Conv., 1946-53, 54-60, 63-68, pres., 1966-67; Western treas. Bapt. World Alliance, 1956-72; sec. N.Am. Bapt. Fellowship, 1972-78. Active Am. Cancer Soc. Bd. dirs. Luther Rice Coll., 1971-77, chmn., 1973-76; bd. dirs. Japan Internat. Christian U. Found. Mem. Am. Polit. Sci. Assn., Am. Soc. Pub. Adminstrn., Am. Accounting Assn., Fed. Govt. Accountants Assn., Assn. Statisticians of Am. Religious Bodies. Contbr. articles to profl. jours. Home: 528 Cumberland Ave Teaneck NJ 07666 Office: 475 Riverside Dr New York NY 10027

TILLER, FRANK MONTERAY, educator; b. Louisville, Feb. 26, 1917; s. Frank M. and Nellie (Lawson) T.; B. Chem. Engring., U. Louisville, 1937; M.S., U. Cin., 1939, Ph.D., 1946; Doutor Honoris Causa, U. Brazil, 1962, U. Guanabara, 1967; m. Ann W. Quiggins, Dec. 20, 1941; children—Faith Lee, Richard Bertrand. Chem. engr. C.M. Hall Lamp Co., Detroit, 1940; instr. chem. engring. U. Cin., 1940-42; asst., then asso. prof. chem. engring. Vanderbilt U., 1942-51;

dean engring. Lamar State Coll. Tech., 1951-55; dean engring. U. Houston, 1955-63, M.D. Anderson prof. chem. engring., 1963—, dir. internat. affairs, 1963-67, dir. Center Study Higher Edn. in Latin Am., 1967-73; lectr. Instituto de Oleos, Rio de Janeiro, 1952, Universidade do Brasil, 1962-63; hon. prof. Universidad Central, Quito, Ecuador, Universidad Guayaquil, 1964, Pontificia Universidade Catolica Rio de Janeiro, 1962, Universidade Federal da Santa Maria Brasil, 1969, Universidad Autonoma de Guadalajara, 1971, Universidade Federal do Espirito Santo, 1971; vis. research asso. Univ. Coll., London, Eng., 1970; vis. prof. Rice U., 1973-74, Loughborough U., 1976; Phillips lectr. Okla. State U., 1977; Fulbright grantee in Ecuador, 1958. hon. pres. 1st World Filtration Congress, 1973; dir. Gupton-Jones Coll. Mortuary Sci., 1945-51, Unitarian Service Com., 1960-63; pres. Internat. Consortium Filtration Research Groups, 1971-77; bd. dirs. Alliance for Devel. of Higher Edn. in Latin Am., 1973—. Recipient Streng award U. Louisville, 1937; Allan Colburn award 1950, presentation award, 1952, 62, publ. award S. Tex. sect. 1959, Am. Inst. Chem. Engrs.; NATO sr. engring. grantee, 1969; Distinguished Alumnus award U. Cin., 1969; Brit. Sci. Research Council grantee, 1976. Mem. Am. Inst. Chem. Engrs., Am. Soc. Engring. Edn., Filtration Soc., Tex. Filtration Soc. (pres. 1966-67, 72-74, Gold medal 1978), Fine Particle Soc., Sigma Xi, Sigma Tau, Phi Lambda Upsilon, Theta Chi Delta. Author: Vector Algebra, 1958; Introduction to Vector Analysis, 1963; also tech. articles. Editor: Theory and Practice of Solid-Liquid Separation, 2d edit., 1978. Home: 7901 Montglen Dr Houston TX 77061 Office: Office Chem Engring U Houston Houston TX 77004

TILLEY, BRUCE JOHN, Can. city ofcl.; b. Bell Island, Nfld., Can., Apr. 29, 1941; s. John Franklyn and Nina Emma (Dawe) T.; diploma in orgn. mgmt. Sishopfield Coll., St. John's, Nfld., Meml. U. of Nfld. and Can. Inst. Orgn. Mgmt.; m. Ruth Hussey, Aug. 28, 1964; children—John, David. Asst. acct. Eastern Trust Co. Ltd., 1960-63; cost acct. Brookfield Ice Cream Ltd., 1964-65; purchasing agt., dir. adminstrn., J.J. Hussey Ltd., 1965-71; gen. mgr. St. John's Bd. Trade, 1972—. Mem. St. John's Jaycees (past. pres., internat. senator), Can. Chamber Execs. of Can. (v.p.). Anglican. Club: Rotary. Home: 97 Ferryland St Saint John's NF Canada Office: 155 Water St Saint John's NF Canada

TILLEY, ROBERT JAMES, editor; b. Terre Haute, Ind., July 16, 1925; s. Robert Light and Ethel Emeline (Hadden) T.; B.A., DePauw U., 1948; postgrad. Russian Inst., Columbia, 1948-49; m. Mary Frances Torbert, Dec. 21, 1957. Project officer U.S. Civil Service, 1949-53; with John Wiley & Sons, Inc., N.Y.C., 1953-59, asso. editor, 1957-59; with Columbia U. Press, N.Y.C., 1959—, exec. editor, 1960-62, asst. dir., 1962-71, editor-in-chief, 1971—; editor Oxford U. Press, 1974—. Mem. Govt. Adv. Com. on Internat. Book and Library Programs, 1972-76. Vice pres. Madison Sq. Church House, 1966-68, pres., 1968-70. Served with USNR, 1943-45. Mem. Am. Inst. Biol. Scis. Presbyn. (elder 1960—). Clubs: Princeton (N.Y.C.); Washington (Conn.). Home: Baldwin Hill New Preston CT 06777 Office: 200 Madison Ave New York City NY 10016

TILLINGHAST, CHARLES CARPENTER, JR., brokerage co. exec.; b. Saxton's River, Vt., June 30, 1911; s. Charles C. and Adelaide Barrows (Shaw) T.; Ph.B., Brown U., 1932; J.D., Columbia U., 1935; L.H.D., S.D. Sch. Mines and Tech., 1959; LL.D., Franklin Coll., 1963, U. Redlands, 1964, Brown U., 1967, Drury Coll., 1967, William Jewell Coll., 1973; m. Lisette Micoleau, Nov. 16, 1935; children—Charles Carpenter III, Elizabeth, Jane, Anne Shaw. Admitted to N.Y. State bar, 1935, Mich. bar, 1943; asso. firm Hughes, Schurman & Dwight, 1935-37; dep. asst. dist. atty. N.Y. County, 1938-40; asso. firm Hughes, Richards Hubbard & Ewing, 1940-42, partner Hughes, Hubbard, Blair & Reed and predecessor, N.Y.C., 1942-57; v.p., dir. Bendix Corp., Detroit, 1957-61; pres., chief exec. officer TWA, Inc., 1961-69, chmn. bd., chief exec. officer, 1969-76, dir., 1961—; vice chmn. bd., dir. White Weld & Co., Inc., 1977-78; mng. dir. Merrill Lynch White Weld Capital Markets Group, N.Y.C., 1978—; trustee Met. Life Ins. Co., N.Y.; dir. Amstar Corp., Merck & Co. Bd. dirs. Community Welfare Fund, Bronxville, 1951-53, pres. 1953; bd. govs. Lawrence Hosp., Bronxville, 1955-59; trustee Brown U., 1954-61, 65-79, chancellor, 1968-79, fellow, 1979—; trustee M.W. Research Inst., 1963-76, Conf. Bd., 1965-76, People to People Program, 1961-70, Com. for Econ. Devel., 1967—, Luce Found.; bd. visitors Sch. Law, Columbia U., 1962—. Mem. Am. Bar Assn., Bar Assn. City N.Y. Clubs: Brown U.; Sky (N.Y.C.); Blind Brook; Conquistadores del Cielo; Econ. of N.Y.; Hope (R.I.); Sakonnet Golf; Siwanoy Country. Office: Merrill Lynch White Weld Capital Markets Group One Liberty Plaza 165 Broadway New York NY 10080

TILLINGHAST, CHARLES CARPENTER, JR., investment banker; b. Saxton's River, Vt., Jan. 30, 1911; s. Charles C. and Adelaide Barrows (Shaw) T.; Ph.B., Brown U., 1932; J.D., Columbia, 1935; L.H.D., S.D. Sch. Mines and Tech., 1959; LL.D., Franklin Coll., 1963, U. Redlands, 1964, Brown U., 1967, Drury Coll., 1967, William Jewell Coll., 1973; m. Lisette Micoleau, Nov. 16, 1935; children—Charles Carpenter III, Elizabeth, Jane, Anne Shaw. Admitted to N.Y. bar, 1935, Mich. bar, 1943; asso. Hughes, Schurman & Dwight, 1935-37; dep. asst. dist. atty. N.Y. County, 1938-40; asso. Hughes, Richards, Hubbard & Ewing, 1940-42, partner Hughes, Hubbard, Blair & Reed and predecessor firm, N.Y.C., 1942-57; v.p., dir. The Bendix Corp., Detroit, 1957-61; pres., chief exec. officer Trans World Airlines, Inc., 1961-69, chmn. bd., chief exec. officer, 1969-76, dir., 1961—; dir., vice chmn. bd. White Weld & Co., Inc., 1976-78; mng. dir. Merrill Lynch White Weld Capital Markets Group, 1978—; trustee Mut. Life Ins. Co. of N.Y., Luce Found.; dir. Amstar Corp., Merck & Co. Dir. Air Transport Assn., 1961-72, 74-75; mem. exec. com. Internat. Air Transport Assn., 1969-75; dir. Internat. Exec. Service Corp. Bd. dirs. Community Welfare Fund, Bronxville, 1951-53; pres., 1953; gov. Lawrence Hosp., Bronxville, 1955-59; trustee Brown U., 1954-61, 65-79, chancellor, 1968-79, fellow, 1979—. Midwest Research Inst., 1963-76, The Conference Bd., 1965-76, People to People Program, 1961-70, Com. for Econ. Devel., 1967—; bd. visitors Sch. Law, Columbia, 1962—. Mem. Am. Bar Assn., Bar Assn. City N.Y. Clubs: Brown University; Sky (N.Y.C.); Blind Brook; Conquistadores del Cielo; Economic of N.Y., Hope (R.I.); Sakonnet Golf; Siwanoy Country. Home: 56 Oakledge Rd Bronxville NY 10708 Office: 91 Liberty St New York NY 10006

TILLINGHAST, CHARLES CARPENTER, III, publishing co. exec.; b. N.Y.C., Nov. 16, 1936; s. Charles Carpenter, Jr. and Lisette (Micoleau) T.; B.S., Lehigh U., 1958; M.B.A., Harvard U., 1963; m. Cynthia Branch, Sept. 28, 1974; children by previous marriage—Avery D., Charles W., David C. Asst. to dir. devel. Lehigh U., 1958-61; adminstrv. asst. Boise Cascade Corp., 1961-63, asst. to v.p., 1964-65, gen. mgr. office supply div., 1965-67, v.p. bus. products, 1967-69, sr. v.p. housing group, 1969-71; pres. CRM div. Ziff-Davis Pub. Co., Inc., Del Mar, Calif., 1971-75; pres., treas. Value Communications, Inc., La Jolla, Calif., 1975-76; pres. Oak Tree Publs., Inc., San Diego, 1976—; dir. Leisure Dynamics Corp., A.S. Barnes and Co. Served with AUS, 1959. Home: 1762 Nautilus St La Jolla CA 92037 Office: Oak Tree Publs Inc 11175 Flintkote Ave San Diego CA 92121

TILLINGHAST, JOHN AVERY, utilities exec.; b. N.Y.C., Apr. 30, 1927; s. Charles C. and Dorothy J. (Rollhaus) T.; B.S. in Mech. Engring., Columbia U., 1948, M.S., 1949; m. Mabel Healy, Sept. 11, 1948; children—Katherine Brickley, Susan Trainor, Abigail Ryan. With Am. Elec. Power Service Corp., N.Y.C., 1949—, exec. v.p. engring. and constrn., 1967-72, sr. exec. v.p., 1972-75, vice chmn. engring. and constrn., 1975—, also dir.; dir. Am. Electric Power Co., Appalachian Power Co., Ohio Power Co., Ind. & Mich. Electric Co., Ky. Power Co., Kingsport Power Co., Wheeling Electric Co. Elder, Reformed Ch., 1976—. Served with USN, 1944-46. Registered profl. engr., Ky., Ind., Mich., N.Y., Ohio, Va., W.Va. Fellow ASME; mem. Edison Electric Inst. (dir.), Atomic Indsl. Forum, Nat. Acad. Engring., IEEE. Club: Shenorock Shore (pres., gov., Rye, N.Y.). Patentee generating unit control system. Office: 2 Broadway New York NY 10004

TILLINGHAST, PARDON ELISHA, historian, educator; B. Providence, Apr. 19, 1920; s. Frederick W. and Helen (Darling) T.; student Williams Coll., 1938-41; A.B., Brown U., 1942; postgrad. U. Okla., 1944-45; M.A., Harvard, 1947, Ph.D., 1952; children—Margaret, Anne, Elizabeth. Instr., Middlebury (Vt.) Coll., 1947-65, prof., 1965—. Served with USNR, 1942- 46. Fulbright fellow, 1956-57. Mem. Am. Hist. Assn., Medieval Acad. Renaissance Soc. Am., Phi Beta Kappa. Episcopalian. Author: Approaches to History, 1963; The Specious Past, 1972. Home: 6 Adirondack View Middlebury VT 05753

TILLINGHAST, WILLIAM CLOYD, stapling and nailing equipment mfg. co. exec.; b. Indpls., Mar. 4, 1922; s. Carl Frank and Violet May (Wolfelt) T.; student U. Cin., 1941-42; m. Helga M. Rebing, Aug. 27, 1963; children—Donna Jean Tillinghast Casey, William Bruce. With Senco Products, Inc., and predecessor, Cin., 1948—, chmn. bd., 1966—, also dir.; mem. Cin. Bus. Com., 1978—. Trustee Cin. Museum Natural History, Wilmington (Ohio) Coll.; mem. Cin. Adv. Com. Airports. Served with USAAF, 1945-46. Mem. Greater Cin. C. of C. (chmn. aviation devel. com. 1977), Am. Mgmt. Assn. (council), Indsl. Stapling and Nailing Tech. Assn., Cin. Council World Affairs. Clubs: Queen City, Comml., Hyde Park Country (Cin.); Ocean Reef (Key Largo, Fla.). Office: 8485 Broadwell Rd Cincinnati OH 45244

TILLIS, MEL(VIN), musician, songwriter; b. Tampa, Fla., Aug. 8, 1932; student U. Fla.; m. Judy Edwards, 1979; children—Pam, Connie, Cindy, Melvin, Carrie. Songwriter, Cedarwood Music, Nashville, 10 years; founder Sawgrass Music, Nashville; numerous personal and TV appearances; composer over 450 songs recorded by Webb Pierce, Ray Price, Carl Smith, Brenda Lee, Kenny Rogers, Charlie Pride, Burl Ives, others; albums include: Detroit City, Best of Mel Tillis, Big 'n' Country, Heart over Mind, Live at the Sam Houston Coliseum, Love Revival, M-M-Mel, Walking on New Grass, Welcome to Country; (with The Statesiders) Best Way, Mel Tillis and the Statesiders on Stage, many others. Served in USAF. Named Entertainer of Year, Country Music Assn., 1976. Office: care Jim Halsey Co Inc 3225 S Norwood Tulsa OK 74135

TILLMAN, FRANK AUBREY, govt. ofcl.; b. Linn, Mo., July 22, 1937; s. Clarence and Josephine (Balkenbusch) T.; B.S., U. Mo., 1960, M.S., 1961; Ph.D./(Ford Found. grantee), U. Iowa, 1965; m. Barbara L. Langendoerfer, Jan. 31, 1959; children—Michelle, Deandra, Lisa. Instr. indsl. engring. U. Mo., 1960-61; operations research analyst Standard Oil of Ohio, 1961-63; instr. indsl. engring. U. Iowa, 1963-65; asst. prof. indsl. engring. Kans. State U., 1965-66, asso. prof., head, dept., 1966-69, prof., head, dept., 1969—; dir. program control Price Commn., 1972—. Cons., U.S. Dept. Agr., other cos.; asso. dir. Inst. for Systems Design and Optimization, 1967—; pres. Systems Research Corp., Manhattan, 1968—; chmn. Council Acad. Indsl. Engring. Dept. Heads, 1973-74; mem. joint com. Council Indsl. Engring. and Council Indsl. Engring. Acad. Dept. Heads; in insp. indsl. engring. Engrs. Council for Profl. Devel., 1972-76. NSF grantee, 1966-68; NASA grantee, 1964-69; U.S. Post Office Dept. grantee, 1970-71; Dept. Health, Edn. and Welfare Urban and Indsl. Health grantee, 1970-71; Office of Naval Research grantee, 1976-79; Nuclear Regulatory Commn. grantee, 1976-79. Registered profl. engr., Calif. Mem. Am. Inst. Indsl. Engrs. (dir. student chpt. affairs 1969-72, v.p. edn. and profl. devel. 1975-77, trustee nat. orgn. 1975-77, Inst. Mgmt. Sci., Operations Research Soc. Am., Sigma Xi, Tau Beta Phi, Alpha Pi Mu. Contbr. numerous articles to tech. jours. Home: 1919 Indiana Ln Manhattan KS 66502

TILLMAN, RODNEY, educator; b. Okolona, Ark., Aug. 6, 1922; s. Joseph Edmon and Blanche (Stewart) T.; B.A., Henderson State Tchrs. Coll., 1943; M.A., Columbia, 1949, Ed.D., 1955; m. Ann Davis Nickle, June 9, 1951; children—Davis Edmon, Mark Stephen, Rodney Nickle. Tchr., Hughes (Ark.) Pub. Schs., 1946-48; prin. Pine Bluff (Ark.) Pub. Schs., 1948-50; asst. prof. U. Ark., 1953-54; asso. sec. Assn. Supervision and Curriculum Devel., 1954-56, exec. sec., 1956-59, mem. exec. com., 1966-69; dir. Montgomery County (Md.) Pub. Schs., 1959-60; prof. George Peabody Coll. for Tchrs., 1960-63; asst. supt. Mpls. Pub. Schs., 1963-67; prof., dept. chmn. Memphis State U., 1967-68; dean Sch. Edn., George Washington U., Washington, 1968-79, prof. edn., 1968—. Pres. Am. Assn. Elementary-Kindergarten-Nursery Educators, 1964-66; adv. com. Model Secondary Sch. Deaf; trustee Joint Council on Econ. Edn. Served with AUS, 1942-46, U.S. Army, 1950-52. Recipient Ethel Thompson Distinguished Service award, 1973. Mem. Am. Assn. Sch. Adminstrs., NEA, Nat. Assn. Elementary Sch. Prins., Assn. Childhood Edn. Internat., Nat. Soc. Study Edn. Home: 13 Over Ridge Ct Potomac MD 20854 Office: Sch Edn George Washington U Washington DC 20052

TILLMANN, GEORGE LLOYD, metals co. exec.; b. Canton, Mo., Feb. 22, 1931; s. George Frederick and Margaret Frances (Lloyd) T.; B.S., U. Ill., 1958; m. Winifred Oswald, June 16, 1956; children—Susan, Mary, David. With Whirlpool Corp., Benton Harbor, Mich., 1958-64, St. Paul, 1964-66, Niles, Ill., 1966-68; controller, sec. Buckbee-Mears Co., St. Paul, 1969-75, v.p., treas., 1975-79, v.p. adminstrn., 1979—. Served with USAF, 1951-55. Office: 1150 Am Nat Bank Bldg Saint Paul MN 55101

TILLSTROM, BURR, television performer; b. Chgo., Oct. 13, 1917; s. Dr. Bert F. and Alice (Burr) T.; student U. Chgo.; D.Litt., Hope Coll., Holland, Mich., 1972. With WPA-Chicago Park Dist. Theatre, 1936; traveled with puppet, marionette and stock shows; mgr. puppet exhibits and Marionette Theatre, Marshall Field & Co., Chgo. (performed on exptl. television for RCA), 1939; sent to Bermuda by RCA to do ship to shore TV broadcasts, 1940; creator and impressario puppet show Kukla, Fran and Ollie with Fran Allison, 1947—; pioneer in television when he presented puppets on Balaban and Katz first telecast, sta. WBKB, Chgo., 1941; show developed by and for television. Recipient George Peabody award, 1949, 64, Nat. Acad. Television Arts and Scis., Emmy award, 1953 also Emmy award for individual achievement, 1965, 71. Address: care Wm B Boulter & Co 20 N Wacker Dr Chicago IL 60606

TILMAN, ROBERT OLIVER, polit. scientist, ednl. adminstr.; b. Caruthersville, Mo., July 21, 1929; s. Alfred Owen and Jeanette (Powell) T.; B.S., Memphis State U., 1957; M.A. (James B. Duke fellow), Duke U., 1959, Ph.D. (Social Sci. Research Council fellow), 1961; m. Jo Carolyn Huddleston, Dec. 19, 1954. Asst. prof. polit. sci. Tulane U., New Orleans, 1962-65; asst. prof. Yale U., New Haven, 1965-67, asso. prof., 1967-70; sr. scholar Columbia U., N.Y.C., 1970-71; prof. polit. sci., dean sch. humanities and social sci. N.C. State U., Raleigh, 1971—; cons. Research Analysis Corp., 1967-70; lectr. Nat. War Coll., 1967-74. Served with U.S. Army, 1951-54. Am. Soc. Internat. Law fellow, 1962; Am. Council Learned Socs. grantee, 1963, NDEA, 1966, NSF, 1969-70, Am. Philos. Soc., 1974. Mem. So. Polit. Sci. Assn., Southeastern Regional Conf. on Asia (pres. 1972-73), Assn. Asian Studies (chmn. S.E. Asia com. 1964-68, chmn. program com. 1978), Asia Soc. (chmn. Malaysia-Singapore council 1968-69), Phi Beta Kappa, Phi Kappa Phi. Author: Bureaucratic Transition in Malaya, 1964; Directory of Southeast Asia Scholars, 1969; The Centralization Theme in Malaysian Federal-State Relations, 1957-75, 1976; editor (with Taylor Cole) The Nigerian Political Scene, 1962; Man, State and Society in Contemporary Southeast Asia, 1969; S.E. Asia editor Jour. Asian Studies, 1965-68; contbr. articles in field to profl. jours. Home: 2800 Wycliff Rd Raleigh NC 27607 Office: Sch Humanities and Social Sci NC State U Raleigh NC 27650

TILSON, HUGH HANNA, state health officer; b. New Kensington, Pa., Jan. 6, 1940; s. Donald Heath and Ann Coe T.; B.A., Reed Coll., 1963; M.D., Washington U., 1964; M.P.H., Harvard U., 1969, Dr.P.H., 1972; m. Judith Scullin, June 10, 1961; children—Hugh, Richard S., Ann C., Alice H. Intern, Yale-New Haven Med. Center, 1964-65; resident in preventive medicine Harvard Sch. Public Health, 1968-72; research mem. John F. Kennedy Inst. Politics, 1969-70; research asso. Health Services Research Center, U. N.C., Chapel Hill, 1970—; asst. prof. preventive medicine and public health U. Oreg. Med. Sch., 1971-74, asso. prof., 1974-76, clin. prof., 1976-78; asst. health officer Multnomah County, Oreg., 1971-75, health officer, dir. div. health services, 1975-76, health officer, dir. dept. human services, 1976-78; dir. div. health services State of N.C., Raleigh, 1979—; adj. prof. health adminstrn. U. N.C. Sch. Public Health and U. N.C. Med. Sch., 1979—; cons. in field; examiner Am. Bd. Preventive Medicine, 1974-75; cons. Nat. Center for Health Services Research, HEW, 1975—; mem. external adv. bd. Health Services Research Center, U. Wash. Sch. Public Health, 1977—; mem. public health standards work group USPHS, 1977—; mem. external adv. bd. Health Services Research Center, U. N.C., 1979—. Mem. med. adv. bd. Planned Parenthood of Portland, 1973-79; bd. dirs. N.W. Oreg. Health Systems Agy., 1976-79; bd. dirs. United Way of Columbia-Willamette (Oreg.), 1977-78; bd. dirs. Portland Opera Assn., 1977-79. Served with M.C., U.S. Army, 1963-68. Diplomate Am. Bd. Preventive Medicine. Mem. Nat. Assn. County Health Officers (pres. 1977-79), N.C. Med. Soc. (mem. exec. council), N.C. Public Health Assn., Am. Public Health Assn., Assn. Tchrs. Preventive Medicine, Wake County Med. Soc., Assn. State and Territorial Health Ofcls., Harvard Sch. Public Health Alumni Assn. (past v.p.). Democrat. Episcopalian. Mem. editorial bd. Jour. Community Health, 1977—, Am. Jour. Public Health, 1976—, Jour. Public Health Policy, 1979—. Home: 1116 Cowper Dr Raleigh NC 27608 Office: PO Box 2091 Raleigh NC 27602

TILSON, JOHN QUILLIN, lawyer; b. New Haven, Aug. 27, 1911; s. John Quillin and Marguerite (North) T.; grad. Hotchkiss Sch., 1929; B.A., Yale, 1933, LL.B., 1936; m. Catherine E. Jackson, Sept. 14, 1934; children—John Quillin III, Thomas D., Rebecca E. Admitted to Conn. bar, 1936, since practiced in New Haven; asso. Wiggin & Dana, 1936-48, partner, 1948—; lectr. hosp. law Yale Sch. Medicine, 1959—. Chmn. plan and zoning commn., Hamden, Conn., 1949-51; pres. Conn. Conf. Social Work, 1949-50. Bd. aldermen, New Haven, 1935-37; rep. Conn. Gen. Assembly, 1953; alternate Republican Nat. Conv., 1956, del., 1964; chmn. Hamden Rep. Town Com., 1964-68. Corporator Inst. Living, Hartford, 1959—; bd. dirs. New Haven Vis. Nurse Assn., New Haven United Fund; trustee Yale in China, 1936-62; bd. dirs. Yale New Haven Hosp., Yale Psychiat. Inst.; bd. dels. Am. Hosp. Assn. Served to lt. comdr. USNR, 1943-46, 51-53. Mem. Am. (del.), Conn. (pres.), New Haven County bar assns. Clubs: Quinnipiack, Graduate (New Haven). Home: 4 Marshall Rd Hamden CT 06517 Office: 195 Church St New Haven CT 06510

TILTON, DAVID LLOYD, savs. and loan assn. exec.; b. Santa Barbara, Calif., Sept. 21, 1926; s. Lloyd Irving and Grace (Hart) T.; A.B., Stanford, 1949, M.B.A., 1951; m. Mary Caroline Knudtson, June 6, 1953; children—Peter, Jennifer, Michael, Catharine. With Santa Barbara Savs. & Loan Assn., 1951—, exec. v.p., 1959-65, pres., 1965—, also dir.; pres., dir. Fin. Corp. Santa Barbara; dir. Collins Ford Internat., Savs. Assn. Clearing Corp. Trustee, Cancer Found. Santa Barbara, 1965-80, pres., 1976-80; mem., trustee, v.p. Santa Barbara Found., 1960—. Served with USNR, World War II. Mem. Calif. Savs. and Loan League (dir. 1980), Delta Chi. Home: 630 Oak Grove Dr Santa Barbara CA 93108 Office: 7 W Figueroa St Santa Barbara CA 93101

TILTON, GEORGE ROBERT, educator; b. Danville, Ill., June 3, 1923; s. Edgar Josiah and Caroline Lenore (Burkmeyer) T.; student Blackburn Coll., 1940-42; B.S., U. Ill., 1947; Ph.D., U. Chgo., 1951; m. Elizabeth Jane Foster, Feb. 7, 1948; children—Linda Ruth, Helen Elizabeth, Elaine Lee, David Foster, John Robert. Phys. chemist Carnegie Instn. Washington, 1951-65; prof. geochemistry U. Calif., Santa Barbara, 1965—, chmn. dept. geol. scis., 1973-77. Guest prof. Swiss Fed. Inst., Zurich, Switzerland, 1971-72; prin. investigator NSF research grants, 1965—, mem. earth scis. panel NSF, 1966-69. Served with AUS, 1942-45. Decorated Purple Heart. Fellow Am. Geophys. Union, Geol. Soc. Am.; mem. Nat. Acad. Scis., Geochem. Soc., AAAS, Sigma Xi. Episcopalian. Asso. editor Jour. Geophys. Research, 1962-65, Geochimica et Cosmochimica Acta, 1973—; contbr. articles to sci. jours. Home: 3425 Madrona Dr Santa Barbara CA 93105

TILTON, LAWRENCE MARION, real estate co. exec.; b. Fullerton, Calif., Feb. 23, 1927; s. Arthur Lawrence and Marion (Koltz) T.; B.A., Whittier Coll., 1949; M.B.A., Stanford, 1951; m. Betty Ruth Cleavinger, June 9, 1948; children—Lynda Carol, David Lawrence, Laurie Fern, John Richard. Salesman, North Am. Securities Corp., San Francisco, 1951-52, Axe Securities Corp., Los Angeles, 1952-54; v.p. Vance, Sanders & Co., Los Angeles, 1954-64, v.p. nat. sales, Boston, 1964-67; pres., dir. Chase Investment Services Boston, 1967-73; pres. Bray, Clotfelter, Jessup & Tilton, Inc., Rancho Santa Fe, Calif., 1975—. Mem. adv. com. investment mgmt. service SEC, 1972-73. Trustee Rivers Country Day Sch., Weston, Mass. Served with USCGR, 1945-46. Mem. Whittier Coll. Assos. Republican. Mem. Ch. Christ Scientist (dir., exec. bd. 1976—). Rotarian. Home: Rancho Santa Fe CA 92067

TIMASHEFF, SERGE NICHOLAS, educator; b. Paris, France, Apr. 7, 1926; s. Nicholas S. and Tatiana (Rouzsky) T.; came to U.S., 1939, naturalized, 1944; B.S. magna cum laude, Fordham U., 1946, M.S., 1947, Ph.D., 1951; m. Marina Gorbunoff; 1 dau., Marina. Instr., Fordham U., 1949-50; postdoctoral fellow Calif. Inst. Tech., 1951, Yale, 1951-55; head phys. chemistry unit Eastern Regional Lab., Dept. Agr., 1955-66; prof. biochemistry Brandeis U., 1966—; head Pioneering Research Lab., Dept. Agr., 1966-73; adj. prof. Drexel Inst. Tech., 1962-63; vis. prof. U. Ariz., 1966; vis. prof. U. Paris, 1972-73, Duke U., 1977; Disting. lectr. U. Maine, 1979; Guggenheim fellow

Institut de Biologie Moléculaire, Faculté des Scis., Paris, 1972-73; sr. research postdoctoral fellow NSF, Centre de Recherches sur les Macromolecules, Strasbourg, France, 1959-61; mem. biophysics and biophys. chemistry A study sect. NIH, 1968-72. Charter mem. Fordham U. Council, 1967. Recipient Arthur H. Fleming award Washington Jr. C. of C., 1964; Distinguished Service award Dept. Agr., 1965; Fordham U. Achievement award, 1967; Frances Stone Burns award Mass. div. Am. Cancer Soc., 1974. Mem. Am. Chem. Soc. (Nat. award chemistry milk 1963; award imaginative research Phila. sect. 1966), Am. Soc. Biol. Chemists, Biophys. Soc., AAAS, Sigma Xi, Alpha Chi Sigma. Contbr. profl. jours. Co-editor: Biological Macromolecules; vol. editor Methods in Enzymology; bd. editors Jour. Biol. Chemistry, Biochemistry, Biochimica et Biophysica Acta. Exec. editor Archives of Biochemistry and Biophysics. Office: Grad Dept Biochemistry Brandeis Univ Waltham MA 02154

TIMBERG, SIGMUND, lawyer; b. Antwerp, Belgium, Mar. 5, 1911; s. Arnold and Rose (Mahler) T.; came to U.S., 1916, naturalized, 1921; A.B., Columbia, 1930, A.M., 1930, LL.B., 1933; m. Eleanor Ernst, Sept. 22, 1940; children—Thomas Arnold, Bernard Mahler, Rosamund and Richard Ernst (twins). Admitted to N.Y. bar, 1935, D.C. bar, 1954, U.S. Supreme Ct. bar, 1940; sr. atty., solicitors' office Dept. Agr., 1933-35, chief, soil conservation sect., 1935-38; staff mem. Temporary Nat. Econ. Com., 1938-39; sr. atty. SEC, 1938-42; chief, property relations and indsl. orgn. div., reoccupation br. Bd. Econ. Warfare and Fgn. Econ. Adminstrn., 1942-44; spl. asst. to atty. gen., antitrust div. Dept. Justice, 1944-45, chief judgment, judgment enforcement sect., 1946-52; sec. UN Com. on Restrictive Bus. Practices, 1952-53; cons. UN 1953-55, 62-64; pvt. law practice, 1954—. Prof. law Georgetown U. Law School, 1952-54; faculty Parker Sch. Comparative Law, Columbia, 1967—. Spl. counsel Senate Mil. Affairs Subcom. on Surplus Property Legislation, 1944; mem. Mission for Econ. Affairs, Am. embassy, London, 1945; del. Anglo-Am. Telecommunications Conf. (Bermuda), 1945, Geneva Copyright Conf., 1952; cons. Senate Patents Subcom., 1961, UN Patents Study, 1962-64, OAS, 1970. Mem. Am., Internat., D.C. bar assns., Am. Patent Law Assn., Internat. Law Assn., Am. Soc. Internat. Law, Am. Econ. Assn., Am. Fgn. Law Assn., Am. Law Inst., Assn. Bar City N.Y. Clubs: Nat. Lawyers, Cosmos, Torch, Philosophy (Washington). Contbr. articles on antitrust, indsl. property and internat. law to legal periodicals. Home: 3519 Porter St Washington DC 20016 Office: 1700 K St NW Washington DC 20006

TIMBERS, WILLIAM HOMER, judge; b. Yonkers, N.Y., Sept. 5, 1915; s. Harley Homer and Florence (Birmingham) T.; A.B. magna cum laude, Dartmouth Coll., 1937; LL.B., Yale U., 1940; LL.D. (hon.), Fairfield U., 1977; m. Charlotte MacLachlan Tanner, June 21, 1941; children—John William, Nancy Joan, Dwight Edward, William Homer. Admitted to N.Y. bar, 1940, Conn. bar, 1948, D.C. bar, 1954; U.S. Supreme Ct., 1946, also other fed. cts.; asso. firm Davis, Polk, Wardwell, Sunderland & Kiendl, N.Y.C., 1940-48; mem. firm Cummings & Lockwood, Stamford, Conn., 1948-53; gen. counsel SEC, Washington, 1953-56; mem. firm Skadden, Arps, Slate & Timbers, N.Y.C., 1956-60; judge U.S. Dist. Ct., Dist. Conn., 1960-71, chief judge, 1964-71; judge U.S. Ct. Appeals, 2d Circuit, 1971—. Mem. alumni council Dartmouth Coll., 1967-71, pres., 1969-71. Mem. Phi Beta Kappa, Phi Kappa Psi. Presbyterian (elder, trustee). Clubs: Am. Kennel (dir. 1968—); Norwegian Elkhound Assn. Am. (pres. 1963-66, dir. 1969-71); Ox Ridge Kennel (pres. 1958-68, dir. 1958—); Westminster Kennel. Home: 256 Brookside Rd Darien CT 06820 also 109 Newbury Neck Rd Surry ME 04684 Office: US Courthouse Foley Sq New York NY 10007 also US Courthouse Bridgeport CT 06604*

TIME, FRED, lawyer; b. St. Lo, France, May 30, 1933; s. Sol and Berta T.; B.B.A., So. Meth. U., 1958, J.D., 1963; m. Judith Richman, Aug. 27, 1958; children—Robin, Brenda, Ralph. Admitted to Tex. bar, 1962; since practiced in Dallas. Mem. faculty Nat. Coll. Criminal Def. Lawyers and Pub. Defenders, U. Houston. Served with AUS, 1954-56. Mem. Am., Dallas bar assns., State Bar Tex., Tex. Criminal Def. Lawyers Assn., Nat. Assn. Def. Lawyers in Criminal Cases. Contbr. articles to profl. jours. Home: 10746 St Michaels Dr Dallas TX 75230 Office: 600 Jackson St Dallas TX 75202

TIMKO, STEPHEN, textile co. exec.; b. Carteret, N.J., June 28, 1928; s. John and Mary (Breschak) T.; B.S., Temple U., 1951; M.B.A., N.Y. U., 1960, postgrad., 1961—; m. Dolores J. Varallo, May 31, 1952; children—Andrea A., Stephanie J., Patricia A. Staff acct. Peat, Marwick, Mitchell, C.P.A.'s, Phila., 1951-57; faculty Temple U., Phila., 1957-71, asst. prof. acctg., 1961-71, asst. v.p., 1966-69, asso. v.p. fin. affairs, 1969-71; chief fin. officer, exec. v.p. finance and adminstrn. Beaunit Corp., Raleigh, N.C., 1972-79, pres., chief exec. officer, 1979—, also dir.; partner Wheeler, Crosbie, Seiler, C.P.A.'s, Phila., 1959-66; dir. N.Am. Rayon Corp. Mem. Republican Policy Com. Phila., 1962-65, Rep. Platform Com. Phila., 1964. Served with USNR, 1952-54. C.P.A., Pa. Mem. Am., Pa. insts. C.P.A.'s, Am. Acctg. Assn. Roman Catholic. Home: 719 Staley Dr Raleigh NC 27609 Office: 1000 Wade Ave PO Box 12400 Raleigh NC 27605

TIMLEN, THOMAS MICHAEL, banker; b. Jersey City, Oct. 27, 1928; s. Thomas M. and Catherine (Murphy) T.; A.B. cum laude, St. Peter's Coll., 1950; LL.B., Harvard U., 1953; cert. Stonier Sch. Banking, Rutgers U., 1967; m. Elizabeth Egli, June 1, 1957 (div. 1975); children—Thomas John, Daniel Karl. Admitted to D.C. bar, 1953, N.Y. State bar, 1957; with Fed. Res. Bank N.Y., N.Y.C., 1955—, sr. v.p., 1973-75, exec. v.p., 1975-76, 1st v.p., chief adminstrv. officer, 1976—; alt. mem. Fed. Open Market Com., 1976—; chmn. com. on fiscal agy. ops. Fed. Res. System, 1976—. Formerly trustee Manhattanville Coll., Purchase, N.Y. Served with U.S. Army, 1953-55. Mem. Downtown-Lower Manhattan Assn., N.Y. Chamber Commerce and Industry, Harvard Law Sch. Alumni Assn., Am. Judicature Soc., Econ. Club N.Y., Assn. Bar City N.Y., Robert Morris Assos. Contbg. author: Financial Crisis, 1977. Home: 1619-22 3d Ave New York NY 10028 Office: 33 Liberty St New York NY 10045

TIMLIN, JAMES CLIFFORD, clergyman; b. Scranton, Pa., Aug. 5, 1927; s. James C. and Helen E. (Norton) T.; A.B., St. Mary's Sem., Balt., 1948; S.T.B., Gregorian U., Rome, Italy, 1950. Ordained priest Roman Catholic Ch., 1951; asst. pastor St. John the Evangelist Ch., Pittston, Pa., 1952-53, St. Peter's Cathedral, Scranton, Pa., 1953-66; asst. chancellor, sec. Diocese of Scranton, 1966-71, chancellor, 1971-77, aux. bishop, vicar gen., Scranton, 1976—; pastor Ch. of Nativity, Scranton, 1979—. Address: 300 Wyoming Ave Scranton PA 18503

TIMM, EVERETT LEROY, univ. dean; b. Highmore, S.D., Jan. 8, 1914; s. Henry R. and Bertha (Hoffman) T.; student Juilliard Sch. Music, 1935; Mus.B., Morningside Coll., 1936, Mus.D., 1967; Mus.M., Eastman Sch. Music, U. Rochester, 1943, Ph.D., 1948; m. Margaret Jeanne Anderson, Aug. 5, 1940; children-Gary Everett, Laurance Milo. 1st flutist Sioux City (Ia.) Symphony and Monahan Post Band, 1930-42; mem. staff orch. Orpheum Theater, Sioux City, Ia., 1931-33; tchr. woodwinds, dir. band Morningside Coll., Sioux City, 1933-42; tchr. instrumental music, Westfield, Ia., 1932-38; staff conductor KSCJ, Sioux City, 1939-42; asst. prof. woodwinds La. State U., Baton Rouge, 1942-43, conductor Symphony, 1948-55, dean Sch. Music, 1955-79; mem. 455 Army Service Forces Band, 1943-46; tchr. flute Eastman Rochester Music, U. Rochester, 1946-48; adjudicator Music Festivals; guest conductor throughout U.S. Bd. dirs. La. Council for Music and Performing Arts; bd. dirs. Baton Rouge Symphony; v.p. Community Concerts Baton Rouge. Mem. La. Music Educators Assn. (past sec.), Nat. Assn. Schs. of Music (past pres., past treas., past chmn. grad. commn., cons. grad. commn.), Music Tchrs. Nat. Assn., Music Educators Nat. Conf. (past div. pres.), La. Music Tchrs. Assn., Phi Mu Alpha Sinfonia, Phi Kappa Phi, Omicron Delta Kappa, Tau Kappa Epsilon, Pi Kappa Lambda. Rotarian. Author: A Treatise on Flute Playing, 1943; Training Requirements for Careers in Music, 1948: Woodwinds: Performance and Teaching Techniques, 1964, rev., 1970. Home: 465 Magnolia Woods Dr Baton Rouge LA 70808

TIMMER, CHARLES PETER, economist; b. Troy, Ohio, July 29, 1941; s. Thomas Gerhart and Rose Marie (Hoffman) T.; A.B. in Econs. magna cum laude, Harvard U., 1963, Ph.D. in Econs., 1969; m. Carol Falb, Aug. 31, 1963; children—Anne Carol, Ashley Susan. Commodity analyst W.R. Grace and Co., N.Y.C., 1964-66; asst. prof. econs. Food Research Inst., Stanford U., 1968-74, asso. prof., 1974-75; econ. adv. Indonesian Nat. Planning Agy., Harvard Adv. Group, Jakarta, 1970-71; H.E. Babcock prof. food econs. Cornell U., 1975-77; prof. econs. of food and agr. Harvard U. Sch. Public Health, Boston, 1977—; cons. in field. John Harvard scholar, 1960-63; Fulbright fellow, 1963-64; NSF fellow, 1966-68. Mem. Am. Econ. Assn., Am. Agrl. Econs. Assn., AAAS, Phi Beta Kappa. Author: (with others) Choice of Technology in Developing Countries, 1975; (with Perkins et al) Rural Small Scale Industry in the People's Republic of China, 1977; editor, contbg. author: Rice in Indonesia, 1974; The Political Economy of Rice in Asia, 1976. Home: 15 Winnetaska Rd Waban MA 02168 Office: 1737 Cambridge St Cambridge MA 02138

TIMMERBERG, PAUL MILLER, army officer; b. Montgomery City, Mo., Aug. 17, 1927; s. Paul Edward and Martha Margaret (Tate) T.; B.S., U. Md., 1966, postgrad., 1968; grad. Army Command and Gen. Staff Coll., 1961, Army War Coll., 1970; m. Dorothy children—Paul D., Debra A. Blanton, John E., James M. Commd. 2d lt. U.S. Army, 1949, advanced through grades to maj. gen., 1974; service in Vietnam, 1970-72; dep. chief staff ops. and res. forces continental Army Command, Fort Monroe, Va., 1972-73; comdr. 15th MP Brigade, Mannheim, Germany, 1973-75; comdg. gen. U.S. Army Criminal Investigation Command, Falls Church, Va., 1975—. Mem. nat. law enforcement exploring com. Boy Scouts Am. Explorer Program. Decorated D.S.M., Bronze Star with 3 oak leaf clusters, Air medal, Meritorious Service medal. Mem. Internat. Assn. Chiefs Police (exec. com.), Assn. U.S. Army, Soc. 1st Inf. Div. Baptist. Home: 60 Fairfax Dr Fort Belvoir VA 22060 Office: 5611 Columbia Pike Falls Church VA 22041

TIMMERHAUS, KLAUS DIETER, coll. dean; b. Mpls., Sept. 10, 1924; s. Paul P. and Elsa L. (Bever) T.; B.S. in Chem. Engring., U. Ill., 1948, M.S., 1949, Ph.D., 1951; m. Jean L. Mevis, Aug. 3, 1952; 1 dau., Carol Jane. Process design engr. Calif. Research Corp., Richmond, 1952-53; extension lectr. U. Calif. at Berkeley, 1952; mem. faculty U. Colo., 1953—, prof. chem. engring., 1961—, asso. dean engring., 1963—, dir. engring. research center Coll. Engring., 1963—, chmn. aeorspace dept., 1979—; chem. engr. cryogenics lab. Nat. Bur. Standards, Boulder, summers 1955,57,59,61; lectr. U. Calif. at Los Angeles, 1961-62; sect. head Engring. div. NSF, 1972-73; cons. in field. Bd. dirs. Colo. Engring. Expt. Sta., Inc., Engring. Measurements Co (both Boulder). Served with USNR, 1944-46. Recipient Distinguished Service award Dept. Commerce, 1957; Samuel C. Collins award outstanding contbns. to cryogenic tech., 1967; George Westinghouse award, 1968; Alpha Chi Sigma award chem. engring. research, 1968; Meritorious Service award Cryogenic Engring. Conf., 1967. Registered profl. engr., Colo. Mem. Nat. Acad. Engring., AAAS, Am. Astronautical Soc., Am. Inst. Chem. Engrs. (pres. 1976, Founders award 1978), Am. Soc. for Engring. Edn., Internat. Inst. Refrigeration (v.p. 1979—), Cryogenic Engring. Conf. (chmn. 1956-67), Sigma Xi, Sigma Tau, Tau Beta Pi, Phi Lambda Upsilon. Editor: Advances in Cryogenic Engineering, vols. 1-24, 1954—; co-editor: Internat. Cryogenic Monograph Series, 1965—. Home: 905 Brooklawn Dr Boulder CO 80303

TIMMERMAN, GEORGE BELL, JR., judge; b. Anderson, S.C., Aug. 11, 1912; s. George Bell and Mary Vandiver (Sullivan) T.; student The Citadel, 1930-34, LL.D. (hon.), 1950; LL.B., U. S.C., 1937, J.D., 1970; m. Helen Miller DuPre, Feb. 16, 1936. Admitted to S.C. bar, 1937; practicing atty., Lexington, S.C., 1937-41, 46-55, 59-67; asst. chief trial atty. S.C. Pub. Service Authority, Charleston, 1941; judge 11th Jud. Circuit of S.C., 1967—. Lt. gov. State of S.C., 1947-55, gov., 1955-59; pres. S.C. Dem. Conv., 1948, Lexington County Dem. Conv., 1950; S.C. Dem. committeeman, 1952-53; chmn. S.C. Delegation Dem. Nat. Conv., 1956; Dem. presdl. elector, 1964. Served with USNR, 1942-46. Mem. Am., S.C. bar assns., Am. Judicature Soc., Lexington C. of C., Am. Legion, Wig and Robe, Phi Delta Phi, Pi Kappa Phi, Blue Key. Baptist (deacon). Lion; mem. Woodmen of the World. Club: Ponderosa Country (Batesburg, S.C.). Home: Line St Batesburg SC 29006 Office: Main St Lexington SC 29072

TIMMERMAN, ROBERT MCFEE, environ. air control mfg. co. exec.; b. Mayville, Wis., Sept. 14, 1923; s. McFee and Geneva Grace (White) T.; B.B.A. in Commerce, U. Wis., Madison, 1948; m. Cornelia Caroline Oakey, Oct. 27, 1945; children—Erica J., William A. Div. mgr. A.O. Smith Corp., Milw. and Kankakee, Ill., 1948-64; with Am. Air Filter Co., Inc., Louisville, 1964—, dir., 1970—, treas., 1967—, v.p., 1972—. Pres. Kankakee Bd. Edn., 1963-64; mem. budget com. Louisville United Way, 1971-73, bd. dirs., 1974-77, treas., 1977-78. Served to ensign USNR, 1943-45; PTO. Decorated Navy Cross, D.F.C. Mem. Fin. Execs. Inst., Machinery and Allied Products Inst. Home: 2009 Camargo Rd Louisville KY 40207 Office: 215 Central Ave Louisville KY 40277

TIMMERMAN, ROBERT PHINIZY, textile co. exec.; b. Warrenville, S.C., Nov. 9, 1920; s. Clarence Simpson and Addie (Arthur) T.; B.S. in Textile Chemistry, Clemson U., 1941; m. Maxine Watts, June 6, 1946; children—Deborah, Susan. With Graniteville Co. (S.C.), 1945—, v.p., 1962-68, pres., chief exec. officer, 1968—; also dir.; chmn. bd., dir. C.H. Patrick & Co.; chmn. bd. Olde Towne Fabrics, Inc., Saluda, S.C.; dir. Citizens and So. Nat. Bank Ga., McCampbell Co., Ltd., Tokyo, Japan. Chmn. bd. dirs. Community Services, Graniteville; bd. dirs., pres. Gregg-Graniteville Found.; chmn. bd. trustees Gregg Found., Graniteville; trustee J.E. Sirrine Found., Clemson, S.C. Served to maj. USAAF. World War II. Mem. Am. Textile Mfrs. Inst. (pres. 1977-78, dir.), S.C. Textile Mfrs. Assn. (pres. 1974-75), C. of C. (dir. Greater Augusta chpt.), Am. Legion. Methodist. Mason. Clubs: Exchange (Graniteville); Augusta Nat. Golf. Augusta Country, Goshen Plantation Country Pinnacle (Augusta, Ga.); Midland Valley Country, Houndslake Country (Aiken, S.C.); Ponte Vedra (Ponte Vedra Beach, Fla.). Home: 607 Laurel Dr Aiken SC 29801 Office: Graniteville Co Graniteville SC 29829

TIMMONS, BASCOM N., newspaper writer; b. Collin County, Tex., Mar. 31, 1890; s. Commodore Amplias and Martha Ann (Crenshaw) T.; ed. pub. schs. and mil. acad.; m. Ethel Boardman, Aug. 8, 1925 (dec. Oct. 1970). Began as reporter Ft. Worth Record, 1906; with Dallas Times Herald, 1907; mng. editor Amarillo News, 1910; with Milw. Sentinel, 1911, Washington Post, 1912-13; editor and owner Daily Panhandle, Amarillo, Tex., 1914-16; Washington corr. for Houston Chronicle, 1917-73 (except for leave military service World War I). Recipient award Biography, Tex. Heritage Found., 1958. Mem. Philos. Soc. of Tex. Methodist. Elk. Clubs: Nat. Press (pres. 1932), Gridiron. Author: Garner of Texas; Portrait of An American, a Biography of Charles Gates Dawes; Jesse H. Jones, The Man and The Statesman. Home: 1316 30th St NW Washington DC 20007

TIMMONS, EARL, marketing exec.; b. Hanford, Calif., Dec. 5, 1923; s. Earl and Mildred (Judkins) T.; student Santa Monica City Coll., 1941-43, U. Ark., 1943-44; B.S., U. Calif., Los Angeles, 1948; m. Margaret Ann Fox, Nov. 27, 1957; children—Lisa Ann, Linda Christine. Dir. research Eberle Econ. Service, Los Angeles, 1948-50; adminstrv. asst. Gen. Telephone Co. of Calif., Santa Monica, 1950-53; prin. Market Research Assos., Los Angeles, 1953-54; research mgr. Erwin Wasey & Co., advt., Los Angeles, 1954-57; dir. research Fuller & Smith & Ross, advt., Los Angeles, 1957-65; dir. research Pacific Coast, J. Walter Thompson Co., Los Angeles, 1965-71; dir. mktg. services Irvine Co., Newport Beach, Calif., 1971—. Served with AUS, 1943-46. Mem. Am. Mktg. Assn. (pres. So. Calif. chpt. 1966-67, dir. Western region 1970-72), Los Angeles C. of C. (research exec. com). Editor: SCAMA Marketing Digest, 1962. Asst. editor: What Makes Southern California Different?, 1969. Home: 400 Vista Trucha Newport Beach CA 92660 Office: 550 Newport Center Dr Newport Beach CA 92663

TIMMONS, EDWIN O'NEAL, psychologist; b. West Point, Ga., May 12, 1928; s. Robert A. and Lois O. T.; B.S., Auburn U., 1951; M.A., U. Tenn., 1956, Ph.D., 1959; m. Mary Birmingham, June 21, 1952; children—Robert A., Laura W., Jenny O., William B. Staff psychologist Tuscaloosa (Ala.) VA Hosp., 1958-59; clin. psychologist Gulfport (Miss.) VA Hosp., 1960-61; asso. prof., then Alumni prof. psychology La. State U., 1961-78, prof. bus. adminstrn. and Alumni prof. psychology, 1978—, mem. faculty Sch. Banking of South, 1975—; prin. Timmons & Assos., Psychol. Cons., Baton Rouge; mem. faculty So. Meth. U. Grad. Sch. Banking, 1976—. Served with U.S. Army, 1946-48, 51-53. Mem. Am. Psychol. Assn., La. Psychol. Assn., Southeastern Psychol. Assn., AAAS, AAUP, Sigma Xi. Author TV-based tng. series on sales, mgmt. human relations, 1979. Office: Coll Bus CEBA La State U Baton Rouge LA 70803. *Assume we have a given amount of elan vital. If we overinvest it in the past, we reap guilt over what we should or shouldn't have done. If we overinvest it in the future, we gain anxiety over what may happen. How better to invest it mainly in the here-and-now, to live the most fully human life possible for each of us.*

TIMMONS, WILLIAM EVAN, bus. exec.; b. Chattanooga, Dec. 27, 1930; s. Owen Walter and Doris (Eckenrod) T.; grad. Baylor Mil. Acad., Chattanooga, 1949; B.S. in Fgn. Service, Georgetown U., 1959; postgrad. George Washington U., 1959-61; m. Mimi Bakshian, Sept. 28, 1966; children—Karen Leigh, Kimberly Anne, William Evan. Aide to U.S. Senator Alexander Wiley, 1955-62; adminstrv. asst. to U.S. Rep. William Brock, 1963-69; dep. asst. to Pres. Richard M. Nixon, 1969-70, asst., 1970-74; asst. to Pres. Gerald R. Ford, 1974; pres. Timmons & Co. Inc., 1975—. Mem. Fed. Property Rev. Bd., 1972-75, Pres.'s Trade Adv. Com., 1975—. U.S. del. to Internat. Conf. on Viet Nam, Paris, France, 1973. Exec. dir. Tenn. Republican Com., 1962; mgr. Brock campaigns, 1962, 64, 66, 68; dir. congl. relations Nixon-Agnew campaign, 1968; co-ordinator Nixon for Pres., Rep. Nat. Conv., Miami, Fla., 1968, 72; dir. Pres. Ford com. Rep. Nat. Conv., Kansas City, 1976; mem. exec. com. Nat. Young Reps., 1965-67; mem. faculty Nat. Rep. campaign workshops, 1963-69. Bd. dirs. Radio Free Europe/Liberty, 1975—. Served with USAF, 1951-55. Named Outstanding Young Rep. of Year Nat. Rep. Com., 1965; recipient 1970 Ann. Achievement award Georgetown Alumni Club; citation for Distinguished Service Baylor Mil. Acad. Alumni Assn., 1970. Mem. C. of C. of U.S., Am. Legion. Mason (33 deg.). Clubs: Columbia Country, George Towne, F. Street, Capitol Hill. Home: 9501 Newbold Pl Bethesda MD 20034 Office: 1776 F St NW Washington DC 20006

TIMMS, PETER ROWLAND, art mus. adminstr.; b. Phila., Aug. 26, 1942; s. H. Rowland and Nancy Virginia (Shaub) T.; B.A., Brown U., 1964; M.A., Harvard U., 1970, Ph.D., 1976; m. Romayne Julian Dawnay, Jan. 8, 1972; children—Matthew, Zöe, Christopher. Instr. Internat. Coll., Beirut, Lebanon, 1967-68; dir. Fitchburg (Mass.) Art Mus., 1973—; dir. Spofford Garrison Excavations, 1978. Teaching fellow Harvard U., 1969-71, M.I.T., 1973. Mem. Fitchburg Bicentennial Com., 1974; mem. art selection com. Fitchburg Pub. Library, 1975. Bd. dirs. Central Mass. Tourist Council, 1974, Fitchburg chpt. ARC, 1975-79, Nashua River Watershed Assn., 1979—, Spofford Garrison Excavations, 1978, 79; pres. Fitchburg Cultural Alliance, 1979—. Served to capt. USMCR, 1964-67; Vietnam. Mem. Am. Assn. Museums, Prehistoric Soc. (Gt. Britain), Fitchburg Hist. Soc., Société Préhistorique Française. Episcopalian. Republican. Author: Flint Implements of the Old Stone Age, 1974. Home: 70 Prichard St Fitchburg MA 01420 Office: Fitchburg Art Mus 25 Merriam Pkwy Fitchburg MA 01420

TIMNICK, ANDREW, chemist; b. Kremianka, Russia, Dec. 29, 1918; came to U.S., 1947, naturalized, 1952; s. Gustav Adolf and Ottilie (Schroeter) T.; B.A., Wartburg Coll., 1940; M.S., State U. Iowa, 1942, Ph.D., 1947; m. Margaret K. Barton, Dec. 26, 1943; children—Sandra Ann, Paul Andrew. Chemist, Imperial Oil Co., subs. Polymer Corp., Sarnia, Ont., Can., 1943-46; asst. prof. chemistry W.Va. U., 1947-49; prof. Mich. State U., 1949—; cons. Oak Ridge Nat. Lab., 1952-62. Mem. Am. Chem. Soc., AAAS, Sigma Xi, Alpha Chi Sigma. Lutheran. Club: Univ. Faculty. Research, publs. in analytical chemistry.

TIMON, WILLIAM EDWARD, JR., educator; b. Natchitoches, La., Jan. 13, 1924; s. William Edward and Arvy (Butcher) T.; B.S., Northwestern State U., Natchitoches, 1950; M.S., Tulane U., 1951; Ph.D. (NSF Sci. faculty fellow, NSF coop. grad. fellow), Okla. State U., 1962; m. Elsie Katherine Muse, Nov. 22, 1956; children—Camille Elizabeth, William Edward III, Robert Paul, Cynthia Katherine. Mathematician, Esso Standard Oil Co., Baton Rouge, 1951-53; instr. math. La. State U. at Baton Rouge, 1951-54; asst. prof. Northwestern State U., Natchitoches, 1954-56, 1957-62, asso. prof., 1962-64, prof., 1964-65, chmn. dept. math., 1962-65, vis. prof. summer 1966, 73; prof. Parsons Coll., Fairfield, Iowa, 1965-73, also chmn. math. dept.; chmn. dept. math. Fairfield High Sch., 1973-74; prof. math. Glassboro (N.J.) State Coll., 1974—; vis. prof. Northeast Mo. State U. 1967, Wis. State U. at Superior, 1969, Austin Peay State U., 1970, 71. Jacobs prof. math. Wis. State U. at Stevens Point, 1970. Chmn. La. Adv. Com. on Math., 1964-65. Served with AUS, 1943-45. Mem. Nat. Council Tchrs. Math., Math. Assn. Am., La. Assn. Tchrs. of Math. (pres. 1964-65), Sigma Xi, Phi Kappa Phi. Home: 129 Alfred Ave Glassboro NJ 08028

TIMOTHY, ROBERT KELLER, telephone co. exec.; b. Gilcrest, Colo., June 27, 1918; s. Virge and Alice (Patterson) T.; A.B., U. No. Colo., 1941; m. Elaine Hurd, Oct. 23, 1941; children—Mrs. Kristen Connor, Robert Alan. High sch. sci. tchr., Ft. Lupton, Colo., 1941-42;

with Mountain States Tel. & Tel. Co., 1946—, v.p. operations, 1968-69, pres., 1970—, also dir.; dir. United Bank Denver, United Banks Colo. Pres., campaign chmn. United Fund Boise, Idaho, 1962-64. Bd. dirs. Air Force Acad. Found., Bus.-Industry Polit. Action Com., Luth. Med. Center, Nat. Safety Council; trustee Colo. Womens Coll.; pres. Telephone Pioneers Am., 1977-78. Served to capt., Signal Corps, U.S. Army, 1943-46. Mem. Newcomen Soc. (chmn. Colo. 1978-79), Civilian/Mil. Inst. (founding bd.), Denver C. of C. Republican. Clubs: Denver, Denver Country, Rotary, University (Denver). Home: 2155 E Alameda Ave Denver CO 80209 Office: 931 14th St Denver CO 80202

TIMS, EUGENE FRANCIS, elec. engr., educator; b. Madison, Wis., Oct. 31, 1921; s. Eugene Chapel and Maud Virginia (Bingham) T.; B.S., La. State U., 1943, M.S., 1949; D.Sc. (Century Electric Co. fellow), Washington U., St. Louis, 1955; m. Jeanne Patricia Mehler, Jan. 25, 1949; children—William, Patricia, Mary, Julia. Asst. prof. elec. engring. La. State U., Baton Rouge, 1946-50, prof. elec. engring., 1964—; lectr. Washington U., 1950-55; sr. engr. applied physics lab. Johns Hopkins U., 1955-58; engr. Martin Co., Orlando, Fla., 1958-59; prin. staff engr. Honeywell Corp., St. Petersburg, Fla., 1959-64; exec. v.p. Nemist Inc., 1970-77, NOCON Corp., 1977—. Bd. dirs. Catholic Presbyn. Apts., Inc., Baton Rouge, 1970—. Served with AUS, 1943-46. Mem. AAAS, IEEE, Acoustical Soc. Am., Inst. Noise Control Engrs., La. Engring. Soc., Archtl. Acoustical Soc., Midwest Noise Council, Sigma Xi, Theta Xi. Presbyterian (elder). Home: 4840 Newcomb Dr Baton Rouge LA 70808 Office: Dept Elec Engring La State U Baton Rouge LA 70803

TINCHER, WILLIAM R., corp. exec.; b. Wichita, Kans., 1926; B.S., Wichita U., 1950; J.D., Washburn U., 1953. Admitted to Kans. bar; individual practice law, Topeka; with FTC, Washington; with Purex Corp. Lakewood, Calif., 1961—, corp. v.p., 1963, chmn. corp. study group, 1962, sr. v.p., 1963-65, chmn. corp. devel. com., 1965, pres., chief exec. officer, 1965—, chmn. bd., chmn. exec. com., 1968—; dir. 1st Western Bank & Trust Co., C.H.B. Foods, Inc. Bd. dirs. Martin Luther Hosp.; bd. councilors Sch. Bus. Adminstrn., U. So. Calif. Mem. NAM (dir., mem. exec. com.), Soap and Detergent Assn. (dir.). Office: 5101 Clark Ave Lakewood CA 90712*

TINDALL, CHARLES WILLIAM, JR., electronics co. exec.; b. Kirksville, Mo., Feb. 7, 1926; s. Charles W. and Lottie Bell (Rowe) T.; student N.E. Mo. State U., 1946-48; B.S. in Accounting, U. Mo., 1950; m. Bettie Susan Myers, Aug. 27, 1948; children—Jerry Ann Tindall Taylor, John Scott. With Price Waterhouse & Co., Houston, 1951-56, Dallas, 1956-66; sr. v.p., treas. Tandy Corp., Ft. Worth, 1966—; dir. Tex. Commerce Bank of Ft. Worth, Wolfe Pecanlands, Inc., Tex. Greenhouse, Tri-Chick, Inc., Ft. Worth Texans, Inc. Served with USMC, 1944-46. Decorated Purple Heart; C.P.A., Tex. Mem. Am. Inst. C.P.A.'s, Tex. Soc. C.P.A.'s, Fin. Execs. Inst. Presbyterian. Clubs: Shady Oaks Country, Colonial Country, Century II. Home: 3952 Thistle Ln Fort Worth TX 76109 Office: 1800 One Tandy Center Fort Worth TX 76102

TINDALL, GEORGE BROWN, educator, historian; b. Greenville, S.C., Feb. 26, 1921; s. Goin Roscoe and Nellie Evelyn (Brown) T.; A.B., Furman U., 1942, LL.D., 1971; M.A., U. N.C., 1948, Ph.D., 1951; m. Carliss Blossom McGarrity, June 29, 1946; children—Bruce McGarrity, Blair Alston Mercer. Asst. prof. history Eastern Ky. State Coll., 1950-51, U. Miss., 1951-52, Woman's Coll. of U. N.C., 1952-53, La. State U., 1953-58; asso. prof. history U. N.C., Chapel Hill, 1958-64, prof., 1964-69, Kenan prof., 1969—; mem. Inst. for Advanced Study, Princeton, 1963-64; Fulbright lectr. U. Vienna, 1967-68, Kyoto Am. Studies Summer Seminar, 1977. Served to 2d lt. USAAF, 1942-46. Guggenheim fellow, 1957-58; Faculty Research fellow Social Sci. Research Council, 1959-60; Nat. Endowment for Humanities, Center for Advanced Studies in Behavioral Scis. fellow, 1979-80. Mem. Am., So. (pres. 1973) hist. assns., Orgn. Am. Historians, Soc. Am. Historians. Author: South Carolina Negroes, 1877-1900, 1952; The Emergence of the New South, 1913-1945, 1967; The Disruption of the Solid South, 1972; The Persistent Tradition in New South Politics, 1975; The Ethnic Southerners, 1976; also articles, revs., chpts. in books. Editor: The Pursuit of Southern History, 1964; A Populist Reader, 1966. Editorial bd. Am. Hist. Rev., 1970-74. Home: 305 Burlage Circle Chapel Hill NC 27514

TING, SAMUEL CHAO CHUNG, physicist; b. Ann Arbor, Mich., Jan. 27, 1936; s. Kuan H. and Jeanne (Wong) T.; B.S. in Engring., U. Mich., 1959, M.S., 1960, Ph.D., 1962, Sc.D. (hon.), 1978; m. Kay Louise Kuhne, Nov. 23, 1960; children—Jeanne Min, Amy Min. Ford Found. fellow CERN (European Orgn. Nuclear Research), Geneva, 1963; instr. physics Columbia U., 1964, asst. prof., 1965-67; group leader Deutsches Elektronen-Synchrotron, Hamburg, W.Ger., 1966; asso. prof. physics M.I.T., Cambridge, 1967-68, prof., 1969—, Thomas Dudley Cabot Inst. prof., 1977—; program cons. Div. Particles and Fields, Am. Phys. Soc., 1970. Recipient Nobel prize in Physics, 1976; Am. Acad. Sci. and Arts fellow, 1975; Ernest Orlando Lawrence award U.S. Govt., 1976; Eringen medal Soc. Engring. Sci., 1977. Mem. Nat. Acad. Sci. (com. for scholarly communications with China 1978—). Asso. editor Nuclear Physics B., 1970; contbr. articles in field to profl. jours.; editorial bd. Nuclear Instruments and Methods. Home: 15 Moon Hill Rd Lexington MA 02173 Office: Dept Physics Mass Inst Tech 51 Vassar St Cambridge MA 02139

TING, TSUAN WU, educator; b. Anking, China, Oct. 10, 1922; s. Che Kao and Lu Bee (Liu) T.; B.S., China Nat. Central U., 1947; M.S., U. R.I., 1956; M.A., Ind. U., 1959, Ph.D., 1960; m. Eutrice Liu, Oct. 12, 1957; children—Pauline Carol, Thomas Leo. Came to U.S., 1954, naturalized, 1969. Technician, asst., asso. engr. China 60th Arsenal, 1947-53; sr. mathematician G.M. Research Labs., Warren, Mich., 1960-61; asst. prof. U. Tex., Austin, 1961-63; vis. mem. Courant Inst., N.Y. U., N.Y.C., 1963-64; asso. prof. N.C. State U., Raleigh, 1964-66; prof. U. Ill., Urbana, 1966—. Mem. Am. Math. Soc., Soc. Indsl. and Applied Math., Soc. Natural Philosophy, Phi Kappa Phi, Sigma Xi. Contbr. articles to sci. jours. Home: 403 E Sherwin Dr Urbana IL 61801

TING, WALASSE, artist, poet; b. Shanghai, China, Oct. 13, 1929; s. Ho Chang and Ping (Sen) T.; self ed.; m. Natalie R. Lipton, June 4, 1962; 1 dau., Mia. Came to U.S., 1957. Exhibited one man shows Martha Jackson Gallery, N.Y.C., 1959-60, Gallerie Rive Gauche, Paris, 1961, Lefebre Gallery, N.Y.C., 1963, 65, 66, 71; represented permanent collections Chgo. Art Inst., Detroit Inst. Art, Chrysler Mus., Rockefeller Inst., Mus. Modern Art, Balt. Mus. Stedelejk Mus., Amsterdam, Silkebork Kunstmuseum, Denmark, Israel Mus., Jerusalem. Guggenheim fellow, 1970. Author: (poems) One Cent Life, 1964; Chinese Moonlight, 1967; Hot and Sour Soup, 1967; Green Banana, 1971. Studio: 100 W 25th St New York NY 10001*

TINGHITELLA, STEPHEN, editor, publishing co. exec.; b. Bklyn., May 21, 1915; s. Michael and Carmela (Cestaro) T.; student Acad. Advanced Traffic, 1946-50; m. Inez Barbara Albertelli, May 20, 1945; children—Vilma, Stephen, John. Traffic mgr. John Sexton & Co., wholesale grocery distbn., Long Island City, N.Y., 1947-53; v.p. Rupp Trucking Co., N.Y.C., 1953-56; dir. transp. Commerce and Industry Assn. N.Y., N.Y.C., 1956-62; editor-in-chief Traffic Mgmt. mag. Cahners Pub. Co., N.Y.C., 1962—, pub., 1970—, v.p., 1975—. Served to master sgt. AUS, 1942-46. Recipient Spl. citation Pres's. Com. Employment of Handicapped, 1967, Editor's award Cahners Pub. Co., 1968, Editorial Achievement award Am. Bus. Press, 1974, 78. Mem. Delta Nu Alpha (Transp. Man of Year award 1964). Author: (with Jack W. Farrell) Physical Distribution Forum, 1973. Sponsoring editor: Distribution & Transportation Handbook, 1970, Red Book on Transportation of Hazardous Materials, 1977. Office: 205 E 42d St New York NY 10017

TINGLEY, HENRY FRANCIS, JR., banker; b. Providence, July 28, 1920; s. Henry F. and Madeleine (Reynolds) T.; A.B., Brown U., 1942; m. Virginia Perkins, Apr. 3, 1953 (div. 1970); children-William, Catherine. With Indsl. Nat. Bank R.I., Providence, 1946—, vice chmn., dir., 1969—; dir. Westminster Properties, Inc., Ambassador Factors Corp., Inleasing Corp., So. Discount Corp., Indsl. Mortgage Co., Indsl. Capital Corp., Providence; sr. v.p. Indsl. Nat. Corp.; dir. Bus. Devel. Co. R.I. Served to lt. USNR, 1942-46. Clubs: Hope, Art (Providence). Home: 6 Cooke St Providence RI 02906 Office: 111 Westminster St Providence RI 02903

TINKER, GRANT A., TV prodn. co. exec.; b. Stamford, Conn., Jan. 11, 1926; student Dartmouth Coll.; m. Mary Tyler Moore. With radio program dept. NBC, 1949-54; TV dept. McCann-Erickson Advt. Agy., 1954-58, Benton & Bowles Advt. Agy., 1958-61; v.p.-programs West Coast, NBC, 1961-66, v.p. in charge programming, N.Y.C., 1966-67; v.p. Universal TV, 1968-69, 20th-Fox, 1969-70; pres. Mary Tyler Moore (MTM) Enterprises, Inc., Studio City, Calif., 1970—. Office: MTM Enterprises 4024 Radford Ave Studio City CA

TINKHAM, MICHAEL, educator, physicist; b. Green Lake County, Wis., Feb. 23, 1928; s. Clayton Harold and LaVerna (Krause) T.; A.B., Ripon (Wis.) Coll., 1951, Sc.D. (hon.), 1976; M.S., M.I.T., 1951; Ph.D., 1954; M.A. (hon.), Harvard, 1966; m. Mary Stephanie Merin, June 24, 1961; children—Jeffrey Michael, Christopher Gillespie. NSF postdoctoral fellow at Clarendon Lab., Oxford (Eng.) U., 1954-55; successively research physicist, lectr., asst. prof., asso. prof., prof. physics U. Calif. at Berkeley, 1955-66; Gordon McKay prof. applied physics, also prof. physics Harvard U., 1966—, chmn. physics dept., 1975-78; cons. to industry, 1958—; participant internat. seminars and confs. Mem. commn. on very low temperatures Internat. Union Pure and Applied Physics, 1972-78. Guggenheim fellow, 1963-64. Served USNR, 1945-46. Recipient award Alexander von Humboldt Found. U. Karlsruhe (W. Ger.), 1978-79. NSF sr. postdoctoral fellow Cavendish lab., vis. fellow Clare Hall, Cambridge (Eng.) U., 1971-72. Fellow Am. Phys. Soc. (chmn. div. solid state physics 1966-67, Buckley prize 1974, Richtmyer lectr. 1977), AAAS; mem. Am. Acad. Arts and Scis., Nat. Acad. Scis. Author: Group Theory and Quantum Mechanics, 1964: Superconductivity, 1965; Introduction to Superconductivity, 1975; also numerous articles. Home: 98 Rutledge Rd Belmont MA 02178 Office: Physics Dept Harvard Univ Cambridge MA 02138

TINKLE, DONALD WARD, zoologist; b. Dallas, Dec. 3, 1930; s. Maurice Ward and Rubye Lucille (Still) T.; B.S., So. Meth. U., 1952; M.S., Tulane U., 1955, Ph.D., 1956; m. Marjorie Anne White, Feb. 24, 1951; children—Donna Lynn, Randall Troy, Steven Lance, Melanie Anne. Asst. prof. biology West Tex. State U., 1956-57; asst. prof. zoology Tex. Tech. U., 1957-60, asso. prof. zoology, 1960-63, prof. zoology, 1963-65; prof. zoology, curator amphibeans and reptiles U. Mich., 1965—, dir. Mus. Zoology, 1975-80; Maytag prof. vertebrate ecology Ariz. State U., 1972. NSF fellow, 1955-56; Carnegie Found. fellow, 1954-55; Guggenheim fellow, 1979-80; Fellow AAAS, Herpetologists League; mem. Am. Soc. Naturalists, Ecol. Soc. Am., Am. Soc. Ichthyologists and Herpetologists, Soc. for Study Evolution, Southwestern Assn. Naturalists, Sigma Xi. Author: The Life and Demography of the Side-blotched Lizard, 1967; editor: (with Carl Gans) Biology of the Reptilia on Ecology and Behavior, 1978; editor Southwestern Naturalist, 1958-63; asso. editor Evolution, 1966-71, Biology of Reptilia, 1969—. Home: 3527 Weber Rd Saline MI 48176 Office: Museum of Zoology U Mich Ann Arbor MI 48109. *I've had the opportunity to spend my life doing the things that interest me most, and particularly research on natural populations and teaching. The rewards of personal satisfaction from these endeavors have never left me with any doubts about my chosen profession.*

TINLIN, RONALD GLENN, mfg. co. exec.; b. Canton, Ohio, Jan. 9, 1928; s. Samuel Louis and Georgia Jenette Georgia (King) T.; student Kenyon Coll., 1946-48; B.B.A., U. Miami, 1954; m. Rena Bruce, June 15, 1952; children—Crystal, Charles, Robert. Vice pres. lighting fixture div. IT&T, gen. mgr. Am. Electric Co., Southaven, Miss., 1960-72; pres. lamp div. IT&T, Lynn, Mass., 1972-74, pres. Huffman Mfg. Co. outdoor power equipment div. parent co., 1974-75; pres. Lawn and Garden div. AMF, Des Moines, 1975-77; pres. Moldcast div. Wylain Inc., Pine Brook, N.J., 1978; chmn. Hi-Mark Industries, Richardson, Tex., 1978—. Served as officer USNR, 1946-53. Home: 60 Crown Pl Richardson TX 75080 Office: 307 Hilltop Ave Richardson TX 75080

TINOCO, IGNACIO, JR., educator, chemist; b. El Paso, Tex., Nov. 22, 1930; s. Ignacio and Laurencia (Aizpuru) T.; B.S., U. N.Mex., 1951, D.Sc., 1972; Ph.D., U. Wis., 1954; postgrad. Yale, 1954-56; 1 dau. Mem. faculty U. Calif. at Berkeley, 1956—, prof. chemistry, 1966—. Guggenheim fellow, 1964. Mem. Am. Chem. Soc. (Calif. award 1965), Am. Biophysics Soc., Am. Phys. Soc. Office: Dept Chemistry Univ Calif Berkeley CA 94720

TINSLEY, SAMUEL WEAVER, research exec.; b. Hopkinsville, Ky., July 15, 1923; s. Samuel Weaver and Willie (Harned) T.; B.A. in Chemistry, Western Ky. State U., 1944; Ph.D. in Organic Chemistry, Northwestern U., 1950; m. Jeane Payne, Sept. 1, 1945; children—Samuel Weaver III, Kathryn Tinsley Clark, Kristen Tinsley Jackson. Research chemist Carbide and Carbon Chems. Co., South Charleston, W.Va., 1950-55; with Union Carbide Corp., 1955—, beginning as group leader chems. div., South Charleston, 1955-60, successively asst. dir. research and devel., asso. dir. research and devel., market area mgr. chems. and plastics, N.Y.C., ops. mgr., 1955-72, dir. corp. research, Tarrytown, N.Y., 1972-77, dir. corporate tech., N.Y.C., 1977—; asst. prof. Tex. Tech. Coll., Lubbock, 1949-50. Served with USNR, 1944-46. Mem. Am. Chem. Soc., Comml. Devel. Assn. Republican. Episcopalian. Club: Darien Country. Contbr. articles tech. jours. Holder 50 patents in field. Home: 18 Holly Ln Darien CT 06820 Office: 270 Park Ave New York NY 10017

TINSLEY, THOMAS A., cons., former govt. ofcl.; b. Scranton, Pa., Apr. 29, 1924; s. David William and Ida (McGuigan) T.; B.S., U. Scranton, 1948; M.A. in Pub. Adminstrn., Am. U., 1955; m. Mary Harrington, Dec. 31, 1949; children—Mary Ellen, Thomas, David, Margaret Mary, William, Mary Elizabeth. With Dept. Labor, Washington, 1948—, mgmt. analyst, 1952-56, program mgr., 1956-60, dep. dir. Bur. Employees Compensation, 1963-65, dir., 1965-69; dep. dir. Bur. Retirement, Ins. and Occupational Health, Civil Service Commn., Washington, 1969-73, dir. Bur. Retirement, Ins. and Occupational Health, 1973-79; ret., 1979; cons. Burda Assos. Served with USNR, 1943-46. Mem. Soc. Advancement Mgmt., Am. Soc. Pub. Adminstrn., Am. Legion. Home: 8112 Smithfield Ave Springfield VA 22152

TINSLEY, WALTON EUGENE, lawyer; b. Vanceburg, Ky., Jan. 22, 1921; s. Wilbur Walton and Sarah Edith (Frizzell) T.; E.E., U. Cin., 1943; M.S. in Aero. Engring., N.Y. U., 1947; J.D., U. So. Calif., 1953; m. Joy Mae Matthews, Aug. 31, 1952; children—Merry Walton, Troy Eugene, Paul Richard. Admitted to Calif. bar, 1954, U.S. Supreme Ct. bar, 1971; practiced in Los Angeles, 1954—; mem. firm Harris, Kern, Wallen & Tinsley, patent attys., 1958—. Fellow Royal Philatelic Soc. London; mem. IEEE (asso.), Am. Inst. Aeros. and Astronautics, Am., Los Angeles County bar assns., Am. Philatelic Soc. (v.p. 1965-69), S.A.R., English Speaking Union (dir. Los Angeles br.). Presbyterian (elder, trustee, chmn. trustees 1972). Home: 2210 Moreno Dr Los Angeles CA 90039 Office: 650 S Grand Ave Los Angeles CA 90017

TINSTMAN, DALE CLINTON, beef processing co. exec.; b. Chester, Nebr., May 19, 1919; s. Clinton Lewis and Elizabeth Golashin (Gretzinger) T.; B.S., U. Nebr., 1941, D.J., 1947; m. Jean Sundell, Oct. 1, 1942; children—Thomas C., Nancy (Mrs. Rockey White), Jane C. (Mrs. Stephen Kramer). Asst. sec., asst. mgr. investment dept. First Trust Co., Lincoln, Nebr., 1947-58; v.p., asst. treas. Securities Acceptance Corp., Omaha, financial v.p., treas. Central Nat. Ins. Group, Omaha, 1958-60; pres., treas. Tinstman & Co., Inc., Lincoln, 1960-61; exec. v.p. First Mid Am., Inc., Lincoln, 1961-68, pres., 1968-74, fin. cons., 1974—; pres., dir. Iowa Beef Processors, Inc., 1976-77, vice chmn., 1977—; dir. Intermountain Bancorp., Nebr. Boiler Co.; trustee Lievestock Merchandising Inst. Past chmn. Nebr. Investment Council. Trustee U. Nebr. Found., Lincoln Found., Nebr. Council Econ. Edn., Midwest Research Inst. Served with USAAF, World War II, Korea; to col. Nebr. Air NG. Mem. Nebr. Bar Assn., Neb. Diplomats, Newcomen Soc. N.Am., Am. Legion, Nebr. Assn. Commerce and Industry, Alpha Sigma Phi, Phi Delta Phi. Republican. Presbyterian (elder). Clubs: Lincoln Country, Lincoln U., Nebraska. Home: 40 Bishop Sq Lincoln NE 68502 Office: 1712 First Nat Bank Bldg Lincoln NE 68508

TINSTMAN, ROBERT MECHLING, utility exec.; b. Johnstown, Pa., Apr. 4, 1928; s. Carl C. and Irene (Mechling) T.; B.S. in Archtl. Engring, Pa. State U., 1950; M.A. in Govtl. Adminstrn., U. Pa., 1955; m. Lela Jane Akin, Jan. 8, 1977; children by previous marriage—Robert O., Torre R., Tracy D. Asst. city mgr., Kansas City, Mo., 1954-59; mgr. Downtown Com., Kansas City, Mo., 1959-60; city mgr., Abilene, Tex., 1960-63, Oklahoma City, 1963-67, Austin, Tex., 1967-69; v.p., gen. mgr. E.E. Stuessy Co., Inc., Austin, 1969-73, pres., 1973-75; asst. gen. mgr. Lower Colo. River Authority, 1975—. Trustee Oklahoma City Airport Trust, 1963-67; bd. dirs. Tex. Mcpl. League, 1962-63; bd. dirs. Capitol Area United Way, 1968-76, pres., 1975, chmn. bd. trustees, 1976—; bd. govs. Austin Community Found., 1977-78; pres. Community Council, 1977-78. Served with AUS, 1951-54. Mem. Internat. City Mgrs. Assn., Austin C. of C. (dir. 1975-77, v.p. 1977), Am. Pub. Works Assn., Tau Beta Pi, Sigma Tau, Alpha Rho Chi, Scarab. Mason. Home: 2406 Pemberton Pl Austin TX 78703 Office: PO Box 220 Austin TX 78767

TINTERA, GLENN JOEL, advt. agy. exec.; b. St. Louis, Sept. 26, 1931; s. Joseph P. and Mildred R. (Fendler) T.; B.S., Washington U., St. Louis, 1956, M.B.A., 1961; m. Arline Kriemelman, May 17, 1958; children—Lora, Linda, Lisa. Market analyst Longstreet Abbot & Co., 1956-60, Metal Goods Corp., 1960-63; dir. research Am. Investment Co., 1964-67; v.p., dir. research D'Arcy Advt. Co., St. Louis, 1967-72; mgmt. supr. D'Arcy MacManus & Masius, St. Louis, 1972-77, exec. v.p., gen. mgr., 1977—; mem. faculty Washington U., 1962-72. Served with AUS, 1952-54. Mem. Am. Mktg. Assn. (pres. St. Louis chpt. 1970-71), Am. Psychol. Assn. Home: 1940 Tricorn St Des Peres MO 63131 Office: d Arcy MacManus & Masius Gateway Tower 1 Memorial Dr Saint Louis MO 63102

TIPLER, FRANK JENNINGS, lawyer; b. Stevenson, Ala., Mar. 28, 1917; s. Frank J. and Grace (Peacock) T.; LL.B., U. Ala., 1939; m. Anne Kearley, Jan. 1, 1942; children—Frank Jennings III, James Harvey. Admitted to Ala. bar, 1939, since practiced in Andalusia; mem. firm Tipler & Fuller & Sikes, 1958—; lectr. trial cases for plaintiff, 1954—. Dir. Andalusia Savs. & Loan Assn., Delta Electric Co. Trustee U. Ala. Law Sch. Found. Served to lt. comdr. USNR, 1942-45; PTO. Fellow Internat. Acad. Trial Lawyers, Am. Coll. Trial Lawyers; mem. Ala. (pres. 1964-65), Covington County (pres. 1960) bar assns., Ala. Plaintiff's Lawyers Assn. (pres. 1959), Ala. Law Inst. Home: 1205 Youpon Dr Andalusia AL 36420 Office: Tipler Bldg Andalusia AL 36420

TIPPER, DONALD JOHN, microbiologist, educator; b. Birmingham, Eng., July 21, 1935; s. Arnold and Doris Vera (Wiseman) T.; came to U.S., 1959; B.Sc., U. Birmingham, 1956, Ph.D. in Chemistry, 1959; m. Karen Sasha Anthony, June 5, 1965; children—Geoffrey Adrian, Christopher Hilary, Megan Frances Susan. Postdoctoral fellow St. Luke's Hosp., Cleve., 1959-60; chemist Arthur Guiness Son & Co., Ltd., Dublin, Ireland, 1960-62; project asso. dept. pharmacology Washington U. Med. Sch., St. Louis, 1962-64; from instr. to asso. prof. dept. pharmacology U. Wis. Med. Sch., Madison, 1964-71; prof. microbiology U. Mass. Med. Sch., Worcester, 1971—, chmn. dept., 1971-79; mem. microbial chemistry study sect. NIH, 1977—. Recipient Frankland prize, 1956; USPHS Career Devel. award, 1968-71, numerous grants. Mem. Am. Soc. Microbiology, Soc. Gen. Microbiology, Am. Soc. Biol. Chemists. Contbr. articles to profl. jours., chpts. to books; editor: Ency. Pharm. Therapeutics. Home: 216 Newton St Northborough MA 01532 Office: Dept Microbiology U Mass Med Sch Worcester MA 01605

TIPPET, ALGERNON CLARK, dancer; b. Parsons, Kans., Oct. 5, 1954; s. David Charles and Virginia Lee (Rose) T.; student Nat. Acad. Ballet, N.Y.C., 1966-72. Joined Am. Ballet Theatre, N.Y.C., 1972, soloist, 1975, prin. dancer, 1976-79; with Cleve. Ballet, 1979—. Mem. Am. Guild Musical Artists. Office: Cleve Ballet 1375 Euclid Ave Cleveland OH 44115*

TIPPETT, DONALD HARVEY, bishop; b. Central City, Colo., Mar. 15, 1896; s. William and Louise Eugenia (Magor) T.; A.B., U. Colo., 1920, D.D., 1930; M.Div., Iliff Grad. Sch. Theology, 1924; M.A., N.Y.U., 1932; L.H.D., U. So. Calif., 1943; LL.D., Coll. Surgeons and Physicians, 1944, Coll. of Pacific, 1949; Litt.D., Samuel Houston Coll., 1944; S.T.D., Westminster Theol. Sem. of Meth. Ch., 1956; Dr. Sacred Lit., Ill. Wesleyan U., 1959; D.D., Pacific Sch. Religion, 1962; D. Arts, Willamette U., 1963; D.Canon Law, Morningside Coll., 1970; m. Ruth Underwood, June 16, 1922; children—Donald Mead, Philip Auman. Ordained to ministry Meth. Ch., 1919; minister, Longmont, Colo., 1919, Johnstown, Colo., 1920-21; pastor Christ Ch., Denver, 1922-25, Gunnison, Colo., 1926-27, Ch. of All Nations, N.Y.C., 1928-31, Bexley Ch., Columbus, Ohio, 1931-40; First Meth. Ch., Los Angeles, 1940-48; bishop Meth. Ch., San Francisco Area, 1948-68, pres. Council of Bishops, 1967-68; instr. U. Colo., 1918-20, Western State Coll. of Colo., 1926-27; instr. extension div. Tchrs. Coll., Columbia, 1929-31; lectr. in homiletics U. So. Calif., 1944-48; Glide Found. lectr., 1956; Fondren lectr. So. Meth. U., 1960; Willson lectr. Vanderbilt U. and Scarritt Coll., 1961; Jarrell lectr. Emory U., 1962; Danforth Assos. lectr., 1962; spl. lectr. U.S. Armed Forces at Retreat, Berchtesgaden, Germany, 1961, 62, 63; ofcl. rep. of Chief Air Force Chaplains, 1962; ofcl. visitation and preaching mission U.S. Armed Forces in Europe and Asia, 1963; Air Force preaching mission Alaska, 1968; Fondren lectr. Scaritt Coll., 1968. Del., Meth. Gen. Conf.,

1944-48, Jurisdictional Conf., 1940, 44, 48. Trustee Iliff Sch. Theology, Pacific Sch. of Religion, U. of Pacific, pres. commn. on promotion and cultivation. Pres. Radio and Film Commn. Chmn. bd. Ministerial Edn., chmn. Chaplains Commn., Meth. Ch.; chmn. bd. mgrs. broadcasting and film Commn. Nat. Council Chs.; pres. No. Calif.-Nev. Council of Chs., 1966-67. Recipient Norlin medal U. Colo., 1949; Distinguished Citizenship award County and City of Denver, work in field, 1958; certificate of Honor City and County San Francisco, 1968; named Iliff Alumnus of Year, 1962, award of Honor, 1967; named hon. canon Grace Cathedral (Episcopal), 1968; Rock award Youth for Service, 1965. Mem. Kappa Delta Pi, Phi Delta Kappa, Theta Phi. Mason (K.T., 33; grand chaplain R.A.M. Calif., 1945-51, 57-58, 61-62; Grand Prelate Grand Commandery Cal. 1951-52). Clubs: Variety, Optimist, Commonwealth. Author: Voices of Yesterday Speak to Today, 1940; The Desires of a Godly Man, 1941; The Desires of a Religious Man, 1942; Towards A Responsible Ministry, 1961; contbg. author Strength for Service to God and County, 1942, Minister's Annual, 1942; World's Missions Textbook, 1960. Contbr. to Childhood Edn., Christian Century, Christian Adv., Epworth Herald, Ch. Sch. Jour., Adult Bible Class Monthly, Home Quar. Home: 45 Southampton Ave Berkeley CA 94707

TIPPETT, JAMES RUSSELL, publishing exec.; b. Grass Valley, Calif., June 25, 1911; s. George Henry and Corinda Lee (Morrish) T.; B.S., Stanford, 1935; m. Glenda Alice Speakman, Sept. 21, 1940; children—Merrill Lee, Susan Linda, James Russell. Circulation mgr. Dell Pub. Co., 1938-42, circulation dir., 1945-53; dir. advt. and exhibitors Disneyland, Inc., 1953-55; newsstand sales mgr. McCall Corp., N.Y.C., 1955-57, circulation dir., 1957-64, v.p., 1958-64; dir. Select Mags., Inc., 1957-64, sec., 1958-64; dir. Nat. Mag. Service, 1958-64, v.p., 1959; v.p., gen. mgr. Internat. Circulation Distbrs. Hearst mags., N.Y.C., 1964-66; pres. J. Russell Tippett, Inc., 1964-77, Franconia Pub. Co., Inc., 1964—; v.p. Zenith Pub. Co. Inc., 1969-73, Fairhaven Press, Inc., 1971-76. Served as lt. USNR, 1942-45; staff Chief Naval Operations for Air. Mem. Mag. Pubs. Assn. (dir. central registry bur. 1958-60, 65—). Club: Bronxville (N.Y.) Field. Home: 17 Course View Rd Bronxville NY 10708 Office: PO Box 116 Bronxville NY 10708

TIPPETT, WILLIS PAUL, JR., automobile co. exec.; b. Cin., Dec. 27, 1932; s. Willis Paul and Edna Marie (Conn) T.; A.B., Wabash Coll., 1953; m. Carlotta Prichard, Jan. 24, 1959; children—Willis Paul III, Holly. Brand mgr., advt. supr. Procter & Gamble Co., Cin., 1958-64; advt. and sales promotion mgr. Ford Motor Co., Dearborn, Mich., 1964-65, gen. mktg. mgr., 1965-69, advt. mgr. Ford div., 1969-70, advt. and sales promotion mgr., 1970-72; v.p. product and mktg. Philco-Ford Corp., Phila., 1972-73; dir. sales and mktg. Ford of Europe, Inc., Brentwood, Essex, Eng., 1973-75; pres., dir. STP Corp., Ft. Lauderdale, Fla., 1975-76; exec. v.p., dir. Singer Co., N.Y.C., 1976-78; pres., chief operating officer, dir. Am. Motors Corp., Southfield, Mich., 1978—. Bd. dirs. Nat. Minority Purchasing Council; trustee Wabash Coll., Greenhills Sch. Served with USN, 1953-58. Mem. Motor Vehicles Mfrs. Assn. (dir.). Club: Econs. of Detroit. Office: Am Motors Corp 27777 Franklin Rd Southfield MI 48034

TIPPIT, CLIFFORD CARLISLE, business exec., baseball team exec.; b. Cleve., Jan. 18, 1920; s. Hassel and Kittye (Tucker) T.; B.A., Williams Coll., 1942; postgrad. M.I.T., 1942-43; m. Margaret Mayo, Dec. 29, 1951; children—Susan, Christine, Nancy, Virginia, Carl. With Reliance Electric Co., 1946-56, head purchasing agt., to 1956; with Mogul Corp., Chagrin Falls, Ohio, 1956—, now pres.; now chmn. bd. Cleve. Indians; dir. Midland Ross Corp., White Motor, Midwest Bancorp. Trustee, Cleve. Clinic, 1970—; bd. dirs. Univ. Sch., Salvation Army, 1975-78. Served with USAAC, 1942-45. Republican. Presbyterian. Clubs: Union, Pepper Pike, Mayfield Country, Hillbrook (Cleve.); Bay Hill (Orlando, Fla.); Country of N.C.

TIPPLE, JOHN ORD, educator; b. Pueblo, Colo., July 20, 1916; s. Albert Benjamin and Frances Bell (Karrick) T.; B.A., U. Colo., 1938; M.A., Stanford U., 1952, Ph.D., 1958; m. Catherine Owens, June 12, 1947 (div. Nov. 1958); children—Jonathan, Nicole, Clare; m. 2d, Edith Harrison Dickinson, Oct. 27, 1961; 1 dau., Jocelyn. Instr. history Stanford (Calif.) U., 1954-56; prof. Calif. State U., Los Angeles, 1957—. Author: Crisis of the American Dream, 1968; The Capitalist Revolution, 1970; Practical Christianity, 1978. Home: 2810 E Valley Rd Santa Barbara CA 93108

TIPPO, OSWALD, educator; b. Milo, Maine, Nov. 27, 1911; s. John and Anna (Kimen) T.; B.S., U. Mass., 1932, D.Sc., 1954; M.A., Harvard, 1933, Ph.D., 1937; m. Emmie Fernas, Sept. 21, 1934; children—Ray Ethan, Denis Robert. Austin teaching fellow Harvard, 1932-35, Harvard fellow Atkins Instn., Arnold Arboretum, Cuba, 1937; teaching asst. Radcliffe Coll., 1935-37; instr. botany U. Ill., 1937-39, asso. botany, 1939-41, asst. prof., 1941-47, asso. prof., 1947-49, acting head dept., 1947-48, chmn. dept., 1948-55, prof. botany, 1949-55, chmn. div. biol. scis., 1949-51, dean grad. coll., 1953-55; Eaton prof. botany, chmn. dept. Yale, 1955-60, dir. Marsh Bot. Garden, 1955-60; provost U. Colo., 1960-63; exec. dean Arts and Scis., N.Y. U., 1963-64; provost U. Mass., 1964-70, chancellor, 1970-71, Commonwealth prof. botany and higher edn., 1971—; mem. com. on instns. of higher edn. New Eng. Assn. Schs. and Colls., 1977-81; chmn. editorial com. in biol. scis. Rinehart & Co., 1958-60. Mem. Harvard U. bd. overseers com. to visit Arnold Arboretum, 1957-62; mem. Mass. bd. Found. for Sci. and Tech., 1970-71. Trustee Hampshire Coll., 1970-71. Biologist wood sect., test lab. USN Yard, Phila., 1943-45. Fellow Am. Acad. Arts and Scis. (council 1968—); mem. Bot. Soc. Am. (pres. 1955), AAUP (pres. Ill. chpt. 1952-53), A.A.A.S. (v.p., chmn. sect. G 1958), Am. Inst. Biol. Scis. (chmn. ednl. commn. 1956-60, chmn. steering com. on secondary sch. biology film series 1958-60), Conn. Bot. Soc. (dir. 1955-60), New Eng. Bot. Club, Internat. Assn. Wood Anatomists, Sigma Xi (pres. Ill. chpt. 1951-52, Yale chpt. 1958). Author: (with H.J. Fuller) College Botany, 1949, rev. edit. 1954; (with W.L. Stern) Humanistic Botany, 1977. Editor-in-chief: Am. Jour. Botany, 1951-53; mem. com. on Handbook of Biol. Data, 1953-60; trustee Biol. Abstracts, 1957-63, pres., 1963-64. Editor, Econ. Botany, 1979—; contbr. profl. publs. Home: 95 Aubinwood Rd Amherst MA 01002 Office: Botany Dept Univ Mass Amherst MA 01003

TIPTON, CLYDE RAYMOND, JR., research inst. exec.; b. Cin., Nov. 13, 1921; s. Clyde Raymond and Ida Marie (Molitor) T.; B.S., U. Ky., 1946, M.S. (Haggin fellow), 1947; m. Marian Gertrude Beushausen, Aug. 6, 1942; children—Marian Page Cuddy, Robert Bruce. Research engr. Battelle Meml. Inst., Columbus, Ohio, 1947-49, sr. tech. adviser, 1951-62, coordinator corporate communications, 1969-73, v.p. communications, 1973-75, asst. to pres., 1978-79, v.p., corp. dir. communications and public affairs, 1979—; staff mem. Los Alamos Sci. Lab., 1949-51; dir. research Basic, Inc., Bettsville, Ohio, 1962-64; asst. dir. Battelle Pacific N.W. Labs., Richland, Wash., 1964-69; pres., trustee Battelle Commons Co. for Community Urban Redevel., Columbus, 1975-78. Secretariat, U.S. Del., 2d Internat. Conf. on Peaceful Uses Atomic Energy, Geneva, Switzerland, 1958; cons. U.S. AEC in Atoms for Peace Program, Tokyo, Japan, 1959, New Delhi, India, 1959-60, Rio de Janeiro, Brazil, 1961. Bd. dirs., pres. Pilot Dogs; bd. dirs. Central Ohio United Negro Coll. Fund, Columbus Jr. Theatre of Arts, Columbus Assn. for Performing Arts, Central Ohio resource bd. CARE, Pilot Guide Dog Found., 1979—, Architects Soc. Ohio Found., 1978—, Greater Columbus Arts Council (past pres.). Served with USAAF, 1943. Sr. fellow Otterbein Coll., 1978. Mem. AAAS, Am. Mgmt. Assn., Am. Soc. Metals, Nat., Ohio socs. profl. engrs., Ohio Acad. Sci., Sigma Xi, Alpha Chi Sigma. Episcopalian. Lion. Clubs: Athletic (Columbus, Washington). Editor: Jour. Soc. for Nondestructive Testing, 1953-57; The Reactor Handbook, Reactor Materials, vol. 3, 1955, vol. 1, 1960; Learning to Live on a Small Planet, 1974. Patentee in field. Home: 2354 Dorset Rd Columbus OH 43221 Office: 505 King Ave Columbus OH 43201

TIPTON, ISABEL HANSON, educator, physicist; b. Monroe, Ga., June 17, 1909; d. Wesley Turnell and Ruth (Gardner) Hanson; B.S., U. Ga., 1929, M.S., 1930; Ph.D., Duke U., 1934; m. Samuel Ridley Tipton, Dec. 18, 1934; children—Jennifer, Samuel Ridley, Hiram Gardner, Joseph Mangham. Tutor math. Ohio State U., 1935-37; spectroscopist Chrysler Corp., Detroit, 1942; instr. physics U. Ala., 1943-44; instr. physics U. Tenn., 1948-49, asst. prof., 1949-54, asso. prof., 1954-64, prof., 1964-72, emeritus prof., 1972—; cons. Oak Ridge Nat. Lab., 1949-72; chmn. bd. dirs. Stewart Labs., Inc., 1968-72. Trustee Webb Sch., Knoxville, 1963-69, 70-72. Recipient Alumni Outstanding Tchr. award U. Tenn., 1966. Mem. Optical Soc. Am., Am. Assn. Physics Tchrs., Health Physics Soc., Soc. Applied Spectroscopy (treas. 1962-64), Tenn. Acad. Sci. (pres. 1957), Eastern Bird-Banding Assn. (councillor 1979-81), Phi Beta Kappa, Sigma Xi, Phi Kappa Phi, Sigma Pi Sigma, Phi Mu. Research, publs. on raman spectroscopy, optical spectroscopy, trace elements in humans, ornithology.

TIPTON, JENNIFER, lighting designer; b. Columbus, Ohio, Sept. 11, 1937; d. Samuel Ridley and Isabel (Hanson) Tipton; B.A., Cornell U., 1958; m. William F. Beaton. Aug. 29, 1976. Lighting designer Paul Taylor Dance Co., Twyla Tharp and Dancers, 1965, Pa. Ballet Co., 1966, Macbeth, Am. Shakespeare Festival, Stratford, Conn.. Harkness Ballet Co., 1967, Dan Wagoner Dancers, Richard II, Love's Labour's Lost, Am. Shakespeare Festival, HB Studios N.Y., 1968, Horseman Pass By, Fortune Theatre, Les Grands Ballet Canadiens, Yvonne Rainer Co., City Center Joffrey Ballet, Our Town Anta Theatre, 1969, Anta Theatre Dance Series, 1971, 72, Eliot Feld Ballet Co., Am. Ballet Theatre, 1971, Kazuko Hirabayashi Dance Co., A Ballet Behind the Bridge, Negro Ensemble Co., Delacorte Dance Festival, Houston Ballet Co., 1972, Nat. Ballet Co., Hartford Ballet Co., Celebration: The Art of Pas de Deux, Jerome Robbins, Jose Limon Dance Co., 1973, Tempest, Macbeth, Midsummer Night's Dream, N.Y. Shakespeare Festival-Newhouse Theatre, The Killdeer, Newman Theatre, Jerome Robbins' The Dybbuk, N.Y.C. Ballet, Dreyfus in Rehearsal, Barrymore Theatre, 1974, San Francisco Ballet Co., Anthony Tudor's The Leaves Are Fading, Am. Ballet Theatre, Habeas Corpus, Martin Beck Theatre, Murder Among Friends, Biltmore Theatre, 1975, Rex, Lunt-Fontanne Theatre, For Colored Girls Who Consider Suicide When the Rainbow is Enuf, Booth Theatre, Cleve. Ballet Co., Mikhail Baryshuikov's The Nutcracker, Am. Ballet Theatre, 1976, The Landscape of the Body, Newman Theatre, The Cherry Orchard, Agamemnon, Beaumont Theatre, Happy End, Martin Beck Theatre, Agamemnon, Delacorte Theatre, 1977, Museum, Public Theatre; Runaways, Public Theatre and Plymouth Theatre, All's Well That Ends Well, Taming of the Shrew, Delacorte Theatre, After the Season, Academy Festival Theatre, A Month in the Country, Williamstown Theatre Festival, Mikhail Baryshnikov's Don Quixote, Am. Ballet Theatre, The Goodbye People, Westport Playhouse, Funny Face, Buffalo Studio Arena, Drinks Before Dinner, Public Theatre, Alice in Wonderland, Public Theatre, 1978. Recipient Drama Desk award for For Colored Girls, The Cherry Orchard, 1977; Tony award for The Cherry Orchard, 1977; Joseph Jefferson award for the Landscape of the Body, 1977. Home: 35 E 10th St New York NY 10003 Office: 25 E 10th St New York NY 10003

TIPTON, JOHN HOWARD, JR., ins. co. exec.; b. Chattanooga, Nov. 9, 1926; s. John Howard and Blanche Gertrude (Viall) T.; B.S. in Engring., Vanderbilt U., 1950; m. Frances Jarrell Adams, Feb. 16, 1952; children—Frances Adams Tipton Smith, Ann Blanche, Virginia Howard. With Nat. Life & Accident Ins. Co., Nashville, 1950—, v.p., mgr. investments, 1967-74, dir., 1970—, exec. v.p. fin., 1974-77, pres., 1977—; dir. NLT Corp., Gt. So. Life Ins. Co., Guardsman Life Ins. Co., Intereal Co., WSM, Inc., Nat. Property Owners Ins. Co. Served with USN, 1944-46. Mem. Am. Inst. Real Estate Appraisers, Omicron Delta Kappa, Tau Beta Pi. Presbyterian. Club: Belle Meade Country. Home: 503 Huckleberry Rd Nashville TN 37205 Office: Nat Life Center Nashville TN 37250

TIPTON, RUSSELL D., acct.; b. Zanesville, Ohio, Sept. 25, 1914; s. Leroy Dewitt and Clara (Nider) T.; B.S., Ohio State U., 1936; m. Elizabeth Sharick, Feb. 11, 1939; children—Nancy Jeanne Myers, Andrew Russell. With Deloitte, Haskins & Sells, C.P.A.'s, N.Y.C., 1936-77, mem. firm, 1952-77, exec. office partner, 1973-74, partner in charge N.Y. office, 1974-77; v.p. fin. Nat. Exec. Service Corp., 1977—. Pres. Morris Sussex council Boy Scouts Am., 1966-70, 77-79, fin. chmn. N.E. region, 1975—. Methodist. Clubs: Panther Valley Golf (N.J.); Eastpointe Country (Fla.). Home: PO Box 218 Allamuchy NJ 07820

TIPTON, SAMUEL RIDLEY, educator; b. Sylvester, Ga., Oct. 6, 1907; s. James Harrison and Rosalie (Mangham) T.; A.B., Mercer U., 1928; Ph.D., Duke U., 1933; m. Isabel Hanson, Dec. 18, 1934; children—Jennifer, Samuel, Hiram, Joseph. Instr. physiology U. Rochester Med. Sch., 1933-35; instr. Ohio State U. Med. Sch., 1935-41; asst. prof. Wayne U. Med. Sch., 1941-43; asso. prof. U. Ala. Med. Sch., 1943-47; prof. U. Tenn., 1947-72, head dept. zoology and entomology, 1967-71, emeritus prof., 1972—. Fellow AAAS; mem. Am. Physiol. Soc., Am. Soc. Zoologists, Soc. Gen. Physiologists, Am. Ornithol. Union, Eastern Bird Banding Assn. (councillor 1976-78), Inland Bird Banding Assn., Manomet Bird Obs., Sigma Alpha Epsilon, Sigma Xi. Research, publs. in cell and thyroid physiology, bird populations and migration.

TIRADO PEDRAZA, JOSE DE JESUS, archbishop; b. Santa Ana Maya, Michoacan, Mex., Mar. 31, 1908; s. Pipino Orduna Tirado and Maria del Refugio Ortiz Pedraza; ed. Seminari o de Morelia (Mex.), 1919-31. Ordained priest, Roman Catholic Ch., 1931; tchr., sem. adminstr., 1932-36, vice rector, 1938-49, rector, 1949-65; aux. bishop State of Morelia, 1963-65; bishop City of Victoria (Mex.), 1965-73; aux. bishop City of Monterrey (Mex.), 1973-76, apostolic adminstr., 1976, archbishop, 1976—; pres. Comision Nacional Evangelizacion y Catequesis; coordinator Grupo Episcopal Region Noreste; nat. del. Movimiento Familiar Cristiano. Mem. Conferencia del Episcopado Nacional, Comision Nacional de Arte Sacro, Comision Episcopal para el Apostolado de los Laicos. Clubs: Caballeros de Colon, Serra. Office: 453 Juarez Sur Monterrey Nuevo Leon Mexico

TIRANA, BARDYL RIFAT, lawyer, mfg. co. exec.; b. Geneva, Dec. 16, 1937 (parents Am. citizens); S. Rifat and Rosamond English (Walling) T.; A.B., Princeton U., 1959; LL.B., Columbia U., 1962; children by previous marriage—Kyra, Amina. Admitted to D.C. bar, 1962; trial atty. Dept. Justice, 1962-64; asso. firm Amram, Hahn & Sundlun, Washington, 1965-68, partner, 1969-72; dir., sec. Exec. Jet Aviation, Inc., Columbus, Ohio, 1970-77; Technics, Inc., Alexandria, Va., 1971-77; partner firm Sundlun, Tirana & Scher, Washington, 1972-77; dir. def. civil preparedness agy. Dept. Def., Washington, 1977-79; chmn. bd. Technics, Inc., Springfield, Va., 1979—. Trustee Washington Ballet, Nat. Repertory Theatre Found., Washington; mem.-at-large D.C. Bd. Edn., 1970-74; trustee Jimmy Carter Inaugural Trust, Washington, 1977—; co-chmn. 1977 Presdl. Inaugural Com., Washington, 1976—. Mem. D.C. Bar Assn. Clubs: Univ.; Racquet & Tennis. Home: 3550 Tilden St NW Washington DC 20008 Office: 7950 Cluny Ct Springfield VA 22153

TIRYAKIAN, EDWARD ASHOD, educator; b. Bronxville, N.Y., Aug. 6, 1929; s. Ashod Haroutioun and Keghinee (Agathon) T.; B.A. summa cum laude, Princeton U., 1952; M.A., Harvard U., 1954, Ph.D., 1956; m. Josefina Cintron, Sept. 5, 1953; children—Edmund Carlos, Edwyn Ashod. Instr., Princeton U., 1956-57, asst. prof., 1957-62; lectr. Harvard, 1962-65; asso. prof. Duke U., Durham, N.C., 1965-67, prof., 1967—, chmn. dept. sociology and anthropology, 1969-72; vis. lectr. U. Philippines, 1954-55, Bryn Mawr Coll., 1957-59; vis. scientist program Am. Socl. Assn., 1967-70; vis. prof. Laval U., Quebec, Que., Can., 1978. Recipient Fulbright Research award, 1954-55. Ford Faculty Research fellow, 1971-72. Mem. Am. Sociol. Assn., African Studies Assn., Am. Soc. for Study Religion (council 1975—), Assn. Internationale des Sociologues de Langue Francaise (mem. council 1971—), Soc. for Phenomenology and Existential Philosophy, Phi Beta Kappa. Club: Princeton (N.Y.C.). Author: Sociologism and Existentialism, 1962. Editor: Sociological Theory, Values and Sociocultural Change: Essays in Honor of P.A. Sorokin, 1963; The Phenomenon of Sociology, 1971; On the Margin of the Visible: Sociology, the Esoteric, and the Occult, 1974. Co-editor: Theoretical Sociology: Perspectives and Developments, 1970. Home: 1523 Hermitage Ct Durham NC 27707. *I have had four great teachers as a student (Jacques Maritain, Joseph Lehrl, Talcott Parsons, and Pitirim Sorokin). They have motivated me to be worthy of them. In doing so, I seek to develop bridges between different currents of thought pertaining to deepen our understanding of how the person's basic reality both reflects and contributes to society's unfolding in the historical process. To further a creative, responsible sociology in the vanguard of knowledge is my basic life-long project.*

TISCH, LAURENCE ALAN, hotel, tobacco, ins. and theatre exec.; b. N.Y.C., Mar. 15, 1923; s. Al and Sadye (Brenner) T.; B.Sc. cum laude, N.Y.U., 1942; M.A. in Indsl. Engring., U. Pa., 1943; student Harvard Law Sch., 1946; m. Wilma Stein, Oct. 31, 1948; children—Andrew, Daniel, James, Thomas. Pres. Tisch Hotels, Inc., N.Y.C., 1946—; chmn. exec. com. Loew's Theaters, Inc (co. name changed to Loew's Corp.), N.Y.C., 1959-65, chmn. bd., 1960—, pres., 1965-69, chief exec. officer, 1969—; chmn. bd. CNA; dir. Automatic Data Processing Corp., Inexco Oil. Trustee, chmn. bd. N.Y. U., Whitney Mus., N.Y.C.; trustee Legal Aid Soc.; trustee-at-large Fedn. Jewish Philanthropies N.Y. Home: Island Dr North Manursing Island Rye NY 10580 Office: Loew's 666 Fifth Ave New York NY 10019

TISCH, PRESTON ROBERT, business exec.; b. Bklyn., Apr. 29, 1926; s. Abraham Solomon and Sayde (Brenner) T.; student Bucknell U., 1943-44; B.A., U. Mich., 1948; m. Joan Hyman, Mar. 14, 1948; children—Steven E., Laurie M., Jonathan M. Pres., chief operating officer chmn. exec. com., dir. Loews Corp., N.Y.C.; chmn. Lorillard Corp., Loews Hotels, Inc.; chmn. bd., chmn. exec. com. CNA Fin.; chmn. exec. com. Bulova Watch Co. Chmn. N.Y. Conv. and Visitors Bur. Served with AUS, 1943-44. Mem. Am. Hotel Assn., Theatre Owners Am., Chief Execs. Forum, Sigma Alpha Mu. Clubs: Harrison (N.Y.); Rye Racquet; Century Country (Purchase, N.Y.). Office: 666 Fifth Ave New York NY 10019

TISCHLER, HERBERT, geologist; b. Detroit, Apr. 28, 1924; s. Louis and Hermina (Leb) T.; B.S., Wayne U., 1950; M.A., U. Calif., Berkeley, 1955; Ph.D., U. Mich., 1961; m. Annette Zeidman, Aug. 10, 1954; children—Michael A., Robert D. Instr., Wayne State U., 1956-58; asso. prof. No. Ill. U., 1958-65; prof., chmn. dept. earth scis. U. N.H., 1965—. Served with USCG, 1943-46. Fellow Geol. Soc. Am.; mem. Am. Assn. Petroleum Geologists, Paleontological Soc., Soc. Econ. Paleontologists and Mineralogists, Nat. Assn. Geology Tchrs. Home: 36 Oyster Rd Durham NH 03824 Office: Dept Earth Scis U NH James Hall Durham NH 03824

TISCORNIA, LESTER CLINTON, mfg. co. exec.; b. Oakland, Calif., Oct. 24, 1910; s. Chester Joseph and Grace (Gnecco) T.; A.B. in Econs. and Accounting, Coll. of Pacific, 1932; LL.D., Andrews U., 1971; m. Bernice Gilmore, June 12, 1934; children—Laurianne (Mrs. Barry Davis), James Waldo, Edward Chester. With Civil Works Adminstrn., Stockton, Calif., 1933-34; auditor Calif. Bd. Equalization, 1934-47; with Auto Spltys. Mfg. Co., St. Joseph, Mich., 1947—, pres., 1964—; pres., dir. Lambert Brake Corp.; dir. Peoples State Bank, St. Joseph. Past pres., past budget chmn. St. Joseph Community Chest; adv. bd. Twin Cities Salvation Army. Bd. dirs. St. Joseph Improvement Assn.; pres., trustee Southwestern Mich. Health Care Assn., St. Joseph; trustee Mich. Colls. Found., 1960-66, v.p., 1966-73, pres., 1973-74, chmn. bd., 1975-76, trustee on exec. com., 1977-78; pres., trustee Tiscornia Found., 1964—; trustee adv. com. Mich. Hosp. Assn., 1970—; bd. dirs. Area Resources Improvement Council, pres., 1972-75; bd. dirs. Mich. State U. Found., 1973—. Recipient McCrea award Malleable Founders Soc., 1974; Distinguished Alumnus award U. Pacific, 1971; hon. alumnus award Mich. State U., 1974. Mem. Metals Research and Devel. Found. (trustee, past chmn.), Am. Foundrymen's Soc., Iron Castings Soc., Soc. Automotive Engrs. Congregationalist. Clubs: Rotary, Masons (32 deg.), Shriners, Elks. Home: 2008 Sunset Dr St Joseph MI 49085 Office: 643 Graves St St Joseph MI 49085

TISDALE, STUART WILLIAMS, mfg. co. exec.; b. Leominster, Mass., Aug. 15, 1928; s. Malcolm and Ruth (Williams) T.; B.A., Yale U., 1951; m. Ann Howard, Dec. 7, 1967; children—Stuart, Walter, Malcolm, Andrew, Ward; stepchildren—Peter, Scott, Bruce. Pres., Southworth Machine Co., Portland, Maine, 1954-65; pres. climate control div. Singer Co., N.Y.C., 1965-74; exec. v.p. Dover Corp., N.Y.C., 1974-76; pres., chief exec. officer, dir. Sta-Rite Industries, Inc., Milw., 1976—, also chmn.; dir. Marshall and Isley Bank, Am. Appraisal Assos., Inc. Bd. dirs. Greater Milw. Com., 1977—, Milw. Symphony, 1977—, Milw. Florentine Opera, 1977—, U. Wis.-Milw. Found., 1978—, Jr. Achievement S.E. Wis., 1978—; trustee Milw. Boys Club, 1977—; bd. regents Milw. Sch. Engring., 1977—; mem. adv. council Bus. Sch., U. Wis., Milw., 1979—; mem. president's exec. senate Marquette U., 1977—; dir., mem. exec. com. Public Expenditure Survey of Wis., 1977—. Served with USN, 1952-54. Home: 2535 E Lake Bluff Blvd Milwaukee WI 53211 Office: 777 E Wisconsin Ave Milwaukee WI 53202

TISHLER, MAX, chemist; b. Boston, Oct. 30, 1906; s. Samuel and Anna (Gray) T.; B.S., Tufts Coll., 1928; M.A., Harvard U., 1933, Ph.D., 1934; D.Sc., Tufts U., 1956, Bucknell U., 1962, Phila. Coll. Pharmacy, 1966, U. Strathlyde, Glasgow, 1969, Rider Coll., 1970, Upsala Coll., 1972, Fairfield U., 1972; D.Eng., Stevens Inst. Tech., 1966; m. Elizabeth M. Verveer, June 17, 1934; children—Peter Verveer, Carl Lewis. Teaching asst. Tufts Coll., 1924; Austin teaching fellow Harvard, 1930-34, research asso., 1934-36, instr. chemistry, 1936-37; research chemist Merck & Co., Inc., 1937-41, head sect. process devel., 1941-44, dir. devel. research, 1944-51, asso. dir.

research and devel., 1951-54, v.p. sci. activities, chem. div., 1954-56, pres. Merck, Sharp & Dohme Research Lab. div., pres. Merck Inst. Therapeutic Research, 1956-69, sr. v.p. research and devel., 1969-70; Rennebohm lectr. sch. pharmacy U. Wis., 1963; prof. chemistry Wesleyan U., Middletown, Conn., 1970-72, Univ. prof. scis., 1972-75, Univ. prof. scis. emeritus, 1975—, chmn. dept. chemistry, 1973-75. Mem. vis. com. dept. chemistry Harvard U., 1965-71, Sch. Pub. Health, 1963-69; mem. vis. com. dept. chem. engring. M.I.T.; trustee, chmn. vis. com. dept. chemistry Tufts U.; trustee Union (N.J.) Coll., 1965-70; asso. trustee sci. U. Pa., 1960-65, 70; adv. council Newark Coll. Engring., 1956-59; adminstrv. bd. Tufts New Eng. Med. Center, adv. bd. Coll., 1964-68; adv. com. biol. scis. Princeton U., 1972-75. Bd. dirs. Merck & Co. Found.; bd. govs. Weizmann Inst.; mem. nat. adv. council Hampshire Coll., 1964-68; bd. visitors Faculty Health Scis., SUNY, Buffalo, 1965-68; trustee Royal Soc. Medicine Found., 1965-69; bd. sci. advisers Sloan Kettering Inst., 1974—. Recipient Merck & Co., Inc. Bd. Dirs. Sci. award (resulting in establishment Max Tishler Vis. Lectureship at Harvard, and Max Tishler Scholarship (ann.) at Tufts Coll.), 1951; medalist Indsl. Research Inst., 1961, Soc. Chem. Industry, 1963; Julius W. Sturmer Meml. Lecture award Phila. Coll. Pharmacy, 1964; Chemistry lectr. Royal Swedish Acad. Engring. Scis., 1964; Kauffman Meml. lectr. Ohio State U., 1967; Chem. Pioneer award Am. Inst. Chemists, 1968, Gold medal, 1977; DuPont lectr. Dartmouth; Priestley medalist Am. Chem. Soc., 1970; Found. Patent award, 1970; Eli Whitney award Conn. Patent Law Assn., 1974; New Brunswick lectr. Am. Soc. Microbiology, 1974. Fellow N.Y. Acad. Sci., Chem. Soc. London, Am. Inst. Chemists, Soc. Chem. Industry (chmn. Am. sect. 1966, hon. v.p. 1968), AAAS, Acad. Pharm. Scis. of Am. Pharm. Assn. (hon. mem.), Conn. Acad. Sci. and Engring.; mem. Am. Acad. Arts and Scis., Indsl. Research Inst., Nat. Acad. Scis., Am. Chem. Soc. (chmn. dir. organic chemistry 1951, pres. 1972, bd. dirs. 1973), Swiss Chem. Soc., Conn. Acad. Scis. and Engring., Harvard Assn. Chemists, Société Chimique de France (hon.), Phi Beta Kappa, Sigma Xi, Pi Lambda Phi (Big Pi award 1951). Club: Chemists (hon.) (N.Y.C.). Author: Chemistry of Organic Compounds (with J.B. Conant), 1937; Streptomycin (with S. A. Waksman), 1949; co-chmn. study group, author Chemistry in the Economy, 1973. Editorial bd. Organic Syntheses, 1953-61, Separation Science, Clin. Pharmacology and Therapeutics, editor Organic Syntheses, 1960-61. Patentee in field. Home: 6 Red-Orange Rd Middletown CT 06457

TISHLER, WILLIAM HENRY, landscape architect, educator; b. Baileys Harbor, Wis., June 22, 1936; s. William John and Mary Viola (Sarter) T.; B.S. in Landscape Architecture, U. Wis.. 1960; M.L.A., Harvard U., 1964; m. Betsy Lehner, Sept. 23, 1961; children—William Phillip, Robin Elizabeth. Urban planner City of Milw., 1961-62; mem. faculty dept. landscape architecture U. Wis.-Madison, 1964—; asso. Hugh A Dega & Assos., Landscape Architects, 1964-66; prin. Land Plans Inc., Land and Historic Preservation Planning Cons., Madison, 1966—; bd. advs. Nat. Trust Historic Preservation. Served with C.E., U.S. Army, 1960. Recipient Nat. merit award Am. Soc. Landscape Archtiects, 1971. Mem. Assn. Preservation Tech., Wis. Acad. Arts, Letters and Scis., Pioneer Am. Soc., Am. Soc. Landscape Architects, Soc. Archtl. Historians, Phi Kappa Phi, Sigma Nu. Lutheran. Contbr. articles to profl. jours. Home: 3925 Regent St Madison WI 53705 Office: Dept Landscape Architecture Univ of Wis Madison WI 53706

TISHMAN, ROBERT V., realtor; b. N.Y.C., Apr. 7, 1916; s. David and Ann (Valentine) T.; B.A., Cornell U., 1937; m. Phyllis Gordon, June 12, 1941; children—Lynne Tishman Speyer, Nancy Tishman Gonchar. With Tishman Realty & Constrn. Co., Inc., N.Y.C., 1938—, pres., 1962-78; mng. partner Tishman Speyer Properties; bd. govs. Real Estate Bd. N.Y.; mem. N.Y. State Econ. Devel. Bd.; bd. dirs. Citizens Housing and Planning Council; trustee Citizens Budget Commn. Chmn. Montefiore Hosp. and Med. Center, 1973—; trustee, v.p. Jewish Assn. Services to Aged; bd. dirs. United Hosp. Fund, Fifth Ave. Assn. Served to lt. comdr. USNR, World War II. Home: 1095 Park Ave New York City NY 10028 Office: 666 Fifth Ave New York City NY 10019

TISSEYRE, PIERRE, publisher; b. Paris, May 5, 1909; s. Charles and Marguerite (Jabre) T.; Lic. en Droit, U. Paris, 1930; m. Michelle Ahern, Jan. 17, 1947; children—Peter, Michelle, Charles, Francois, Philippe. Admitted to bar, 1931; copyright atty., Paris, 1932-35; newspaperman, 1935-40; pres., pub. Le Cercle du Livre de France Ltee., Montreal, Que., Can., 1947—; v.p. Edit. du Renouveau Pedago-gique, Inc., Montreal, 1965—. Served to 1st lt. French Army, World War II; prisoner-of-war. Decorated Croix de Guerre, chevalier Legion of Honor (France); officer Order Can. Mem. Assn. Conseil Superieur du Livre French-Can. Books (pres. 1961-76), Société des Editeurs de Manuel Scolaire du Quebec (pres. 1977-78), Assn. Exportation Can. Books (pres. 1974-80), Soc. Can.-Francais Protection Droit d'Auteur (pres. 1977-80). Liberal. Roman Catholic. Author: Cinquante Cinq Heures de Guerre, 1943; Tu M'Aimeras Deux Fois, 1958. Office: 8955 St Laurent Ave Montreal PQ H2N 1M6 Canada

TISSOT, ERNEST EUGENE, JR., naval officer; b. Upland, Calif., Dec. 16, 1927; s. Ernest Eugene and Beulah Louise (Rehkopf) T.; B.S. in Engring., Stanford U., 1958; M.S. in Aero. Engring., U.S. Naval Postgrad. Sch., 1960; m. Mildred Ellen Patton, June 23, 1951; children—Ernest Craig, Brian Nelson. Commd. U.S. Navy, 1945, advanced through grades to rear adm.; comdg. officer Carrier Attack Squadron, Lemoore, Calif., 1964-65; comdr. Carrier Air Wing; Miramar, Calif., 1967-68; comdg. officer Dock Landing Ship, San Diego, 1970-71, U.S.S. Enterprise, nuclear powered aircraft carrier, Alameda, Calif., 1971-74; comdr. Carrier Group 5, Subic Bay, 1977—. Decorated Silver Star with gold star, Dept. Def. Superior Service medal with gold star, Legion of Merit with gold star, D.F.C. with 4 gold stars, Air medal with 26 gold stars, Navy Commendation medal with 4 gold stars. Mem. Phi Beta Kappa. Roman Catholic. Home: 12681 Central Ave Chino CA 91710 Office: COMGARGRU Five FPO San Francisco CA 96601

TITKEMEYER, CHARLES WILLIAM, educator, veterinarian; b. Rising Sun, Ind., Jan. 14, 1919; s. Andrew Henry and Mary Catherine (Detmer) T.; student Purdue U., 1939-42; D.V.M., Ohio State U., 1949; M.S., Mich. State U., 1951, Ph.D., 1956; m. Mary Agnes Hoeferkamp, June 14, 1947; children—James Charles, Robert William. With Mich. State U., 1949-60, 62-66, 68-69, U. Indonesia, 1960-62, U. Nigeria, 1966-68; prof., head vet. anatomy dept. La. State U., 1969—; cons. Served with AUS, 1942-45; ETO. Decorated D.F.C. (2), Air medal (3); recipient Distinguished Alumnus award Coll. Vet. Medicine Ohio State U., 1978. Mem. Am. Vet. Med. Assn., Am., World assns. Vet. Anatomists Sigma Xi, Phi Zeta, Omega Tau Sigma. Methodist. Contbr. articles to sci. publs. Home: 1148 Aurora Pl Baton Rouge LA 70806

TITLEY, RICHARD MARTIN, photojournalist; b. St. Catharines, Ont., Can., Dec. 9, 1940; s. Albert Richard and Helen Marie (Wolf) T.; came to U.S., 1965; children by previous marriage—Sean David, Steven Richard. Photographer, Titley Studios, St. Catharines, 1961-62, St. Catharines Standard, 1962-64, Kingsport (Tenn.) Times-News, 1964-65, Delaware County Daily Times, Chester, Pa., 1966-68, Phila., Inquirer, 1968—; mem. faculty Glassboro State Coll., 1975. Recipient several Pa. Press Photo awards, 1969-78; Gold medal World Press Photo Contest, Amsterdam, Netherlands, 1978; Headliner award Nat. Headliners Assn., 1978; nominated for Pulitzer Prize, 1973; Keystone Press award, 1969; AP awards, 1969, 73. Mem. Nat. Press Photographers Assn. (award 1973, 76, 78), Pa. Press Photographers Assn., Nat. Headliners Club, Newspaper Guild, Sigma Delta Chi. Episcopalian. Office: Phila Inquirer 400 N Broad St Philadelphia PA 19101. *To preserve with integrity and impartiality the daily events around me through photographs. To be where others cannot and see what they would if they could.*

TITSWORTH, JOHN VALENTINE, computer co. exec.; b. Hutsonville, Ill., Aug. 15, 1925; s. Walter Valentine and Mabel E. (Poorman) T.; B.S. in Mech. Engring., Rose Hulman Inst., 1949; m. Jeannette Marie Crossman, Mar. 31, 1946; children—John, Steven, Susan, Sandra. Engr., Navy Dept., Indpls., 1949-53; engr., then chief engr. Lear, Inc. and Lear Siegler, 1953-65; v.p. Lear Jet Industries, 1965-68; exec. v.p. Control Data Corp., Mpls., 1968-79; group v.p. Xerox Corp., Stamford, Conn., 1979—; pres. Xerox Info. Products Group, Stamford, 1979—. Served with USAAF, 1943-45. Mem. Community Ch. (trustee). Patentee fore aft accelerometer, 4-gimbal gyro platform. Home: 95 Hemlock Hill Rd New Canaan CT 06840 Office: Xerox Corp Long Ridge Rd Stamford CT 06904

TITUS, ALAN WITKOWSKI, lyric baritone; b. N.Y.C., Oct. 28, 1945; studied with Hans Heinz and Daniel Ferro. Opera debut as Marcello in La Bohème, Washington Opera Soc., 1969; sang with maj. cos. in U.S. and Europe, including: Opera Co. Boston, N.Y.C. Opera, Santa Fe Opera, Phila. Lyric Opera, Dallas Civic Opera; appearances with symphony orchs.; recitalist. Juilliard Sch. Sergius Kagen Meml. scholar. Office: care Columbia Artists Mgmt Inc 165 W 57th St New York NY 10019*

TITUS, ROBERT FARREN, land developer, ret. air force officer; b. Orange, N.J., Dec. 6, 1926; s. Allen Van Why and Helen Marian (Farren) T.; student Va. Poly. Inst., 1948; M.B.A., U. Chgo., 1961; ed. Advanced Mgmt. Program, Harvard U., 1968; grad. Nat. War Coll., 1970; m. Marjorie Jeanette Winkler, Dec. 19, 1953; children—Cynthia, Robert, Melinda, Andrea. Commd. 2d lt. USAF, 1949, advanced through grades to brig. gen., 1972; various pilot assignments, including combat and test, 1949-53; exptl. test pilot Edwards AFB, 1954-59; operations officer 53d Tactical Fighter Squadron, Germany, 1961-63; staff officer Hdqrs. USAFE, Europe, 1964; staff officer Hdqrs. Tactical Air Command, 1964-66; comdr. 10th Fighter Commando Squadron, Vietnam, 1966-67; comdr. 389 Tac Fighter Squadron, Vietnam, 1967; research and devel. staff officer Hdqrs. USAF, 1967-69; vice comdr. 15th TAC Fighter Wing, MacDill AFB, Fla., 1970, comdr. 1st TAC Fighter Wing, 1971; comdr. 18th TAC Fighter Wing, Kadena, Japan, 1971-73; comdr. 313th Air Div., Kadena, 1973; dep. chief staff operations Air Force Systems Command, 1973-74; dep. chief staff, Live Oak, SHAPE, Belgium, 1974-76; insp. gen. NORAD-ADCOM, Colorado Springs, Colo., 1977; ret., 1977; pres. Titus Enterprises, real estate, land devel., Colorado Springs, 1978—; mng. partner Titus & Wilbourn Devel. Co., Colorado Springs, 1979—. Decorated Air Force cross, Silver Star, Legion of Merit, D.F.C. with 3 oak leaf clusters, Meritorious Service medal with oak leaf cluster, Air medal with 4 silver, 3 bronze oak leaf clusters, Bronze Star, Air Force Commendation medal. Fellow Soc. Exptl. Test Pilots; mem. Fighter Aces Assn. (hon.). Clubs: Explorers; Serra. Flew 1st jet fighter over North Pole from Eng. to Alaska (with Charles F. Blair). Address: 1110 Garlock Ln Colorado Springs CO 80907

TJOFLAT, GERALD BARD, judge; b. Pitts., Dec. 6, 1929; s. Gerald Benjamin and Sarita (Romero-Hermoso) T.; student U. Va., 1947-50, U. Cin., 1950-52; LL.B., Duke U., 1957; D.C.L., Jacksonville U., 1978; m. Sarah Marie Pfohl, July 27, 1957; children—Gerald Bard, Marie Elizabeth. Admitted to Fla. bar, 1957; individual practice law, Jacksonville, Fla., 1957-68; judge 4th Jud. Circuit Ct. Fla., 1968-70, U.S. Dist. Ct. for Middle Dist. Fla., Jacksonville, 1970-75, U.S. Ct. Appeals, 5th Circuit, Jacksonville, 1975—; mem. Advisory Corrections Council U.S., 1975—; mem. com. adminstrn. probation system Jud. Conf. U.S., 1972—, chmn., 1978—; mem. bd. visitors Duke U. Law Sch. Trustee, Jacksonville Episcopal High Sch. Served with AUS, 1953-55. Mem. Am. Law Inst., Am. Bar Assn., Am. Judicature Soc., Fla. Bar. Episcopalian. Clubs: Masons, Shriners. Home: 2970 St Johns Ave Apt 6-D Jacksonville FL 32205 Office: US Ct Appeals 5th Circuit PO Box 960 Jacksonville FL 32201

TKACH, WALTER ROBERT, physician, ret. air force officer; b. LaBelle, Pa., Feb. 9, 1917; s. Joseph and Irene (Leschak) T.; B.S., Pa. State U., 1941; M.D., U. Pitts., 1945; 1 son, John R.; m. 2d, Cheryle Ann Gaillard, Dec. 28, 1973; 1 son, Marc G. Commd. 1st lt. U.S. Army, advanced through grades to maj. gen., USAF, 1970; ret., 1979; assigned Hdqrs. Japan, 1946-48; Pentagon staff duty, then asst. physician to Pres. Eisenhower, 1953-61; surgeon SAC, 1961-65, PACAF, 1965-68; comdg. surgeon 7th Air Force, Vietnam, 1968; physician to Pres. Richard Nixon, 1968-74. Decorated D.S.M., Legion of Merit, Bronze Star, Air medal, USAF Commendation medal. Mem. A.M.A., Aerospace Med. Assn., Assn. Mil. Surgeons U.S., Soc. USAF Flight Surgeons, Fed. Hosp. Inst. Alumni Assn., Air Force Assn., alumni assns. U. Pitts., Pa. State U. Clubs: Nat. Press, Circus Saints and Sinners. Address: care Gaillard 7946 Ivanhoe Suite 222 La Jolla CA 92037

TOALSON, NATHAN AUGUSTUS, mfr. elec. equipment; b. Centralia, Mo., Jan. 25, 1911; s. Alex R. and Alice Lee (Hardin) T.; student U. Mo., 1929-30; m. Gara C. Williams, Oct. 5, 1941; children—Gara Ann, William Nathan, Alice Bowman. With A.B. Chance Co., Centralia, Mo., 1930—, exec. v.p., 1956-60, pres., 1960-72, chmn. bd., 1972—; dir. A. B. Chance Co., Can. Dir. Asso. Industries Mo., Mo. Pub. Expenditures Survey, So. States Indsl. Council; pres., exec. com. Gt. Rivers council Boy Scouts Am. Pres. bd. trustees William Jewell Coll.; bd. mgrs. Mo. Bapt. Hosp., St. Louis; bd. dirs. Chance Found. Mem. Am. Inst. E.E. Home: S Jefferson St Centralia MO 65240 Office: 210 N Allen St Centralia MO 65240

TOBEN, MARVIN, publisher; b. N.Y.C., Sept. 9, 1932; s. Israel and Pauline (Zazula) T.; B.A. in Journalism, N.Y. U., 1954; m. Harriet J. Toben, Nov. 26, 1957; children—Pamela C., Nancy G. Gen. news reporter Bryan (Ohio) Daily Times, 1954-55; news editor Food Topics, reporter Food Field, Topics Pub. Co., N.Y.C., 1955-57; mem. public relations dept. Continental Can Co., N.Y.C., 1957-60; editor Food and Drug Packaging, 1960-67; editorial dir., v.p. Mags. for Industry, 1967-70; pub. Paperboard Packaging, 1969-73, Legal Aspects of Med. Practice mag., 1972—; pres. Mags. for Industry, N.Y.C., 1970—. Mem. Am. Bus. Press. Office: Magazines for Industry 777 3d Ave New York NY 10017

TOBER, BARBARA D. (MRS. DONALD GIBBS TOBER), editor; b. Summit, N.J., Aug. 19, 1934; d. Rodney Fielding and Maude (Grebbin) Starkey; student Traphagen Sch. Fashion, 1954-56, Fashion Inst. Tech., 1956-58, N.Y. Sch. Interior Design, 1964; m. Donald Gibbs Tober, Apr. 5, 1973. Copy editor Vogue Pattern Book, 1958-60; beauty editor Vogue mag., 1961; dir. womens services Bartell Media Corp., 1961-66; editor-in-chief Bride's mag., N.Y.C., 1966—; dir. Sugar Foods Corp. Cons. Traphagen Sch. Fashion Bd. Dirs. Mem. Nat. Council on Family Relations, 1966, nat. council Am. Ballet Theatre, 1973, Lincoln Center Performing Arts, 1974, Met. Opera Guild. Recipient Alma award, 1968, Penney-Mo. award, 1972. Mem. Fashion Group, Cosmetic Career Women, Nat. Home Fashions League (v.p., program chmn.), Am. Soc. Mag. Editors, Am. Soc. Interior Designers (press mem.), Intercorporate Group, Viviane Woodard Council Fine Arts, Pan Pacific and S.E. Asia Women's Assn., Asia Soc., Internat. Side Saddle Orgn., Golden's Bridge Hounds, North Salem Bridle Trail Assn., Wine and Food Soc., Chaines des Rotisseurs (membership com.). Club: Town Tennis. Author: The ABC's of Beauty, 1963. Home: 215 E 68th St New York NY 10021 Office: 350 Madison Ave New York NY 10017

TOBER, LESTER VICTOR, shoe co. exec.; b. St. Louis, Dec. 29, 1916; s. Abraham E.M. and Anna (Saifer) T.; B.S., U. Wis., 1935; postgrad. Washington U., 1936, U. Mo., 1936-39; m. Sylvia Isenburg, Aug. 4, 1940; children—Neil Steven, Robert Boyd, Cristie Elizabeth. Sec. Tober-Saifer Shoe Mfg. Co., St. Louis, 1955-65, v.p., 1966-68, exec. v.p., 1969-71, pres., 1974—; pres., chief exec. officer Tober Industries, Inc., 1977—; chmn. bd. dirs., chief exec. officer Wilkerson Shoe Co.; dir. Stevens Shoe Co., Robinson Shoe Racks. Active St. Louis Ambassadors, United Fund. Trustee A.E. Tober Charitable Trust. Served to lt. (j.g.), USNR, 1944-46. Mem. St. Louis Shoe Mfrs. Assn. (pres. 1955), Zeta Beta Tau. Republican. Jewish (pres. temple brotherhood 1957). Elk. Clubs: St. Louis Missouri Athletic (St. Louis). Home: 19 Maryhill St St Louis MO 63124 Office: 1520 Washington Ave St Louis MO 63103

TOBEY, ALTON, painter; b. Middletown, Conn., Nov. 5, 1914; B.F.A., M.F.A. , Yale. Executed numerous murals, including 2 for Smithsonian Mus. Natural History, 6 for McArthur Meml., 3 for Am. Bur. Shipping; portraits of many notable persons; exhibited numerous mus., univs., pub. collections, including Smithsonian Instn., Wadsworth Antheneum, Nat. Acad., ABC-TV; exhibited one-man shows, Copenhagen, Stockholm; represented in permanent collections, Sweden, Denmark, France, Israel, Peru, Guatemala and U.S.A. Mem. Artists Equity N.Y. (pres.). Address: 296 Murray Ave Larchmont NY 10538. *Art is a voyage of self discovery. It is ever before us and the fulfillment is in the search. Work, in this manner, is prayer.*

TOBEY, CARL WADSWORTH, publisher; b. Meriden, Conn., Nov. 18, 1923; s. Carl W. and Prudence (Wadsworth) T.; ed. U.S. Mcht. Marine Acad.; m. Charlotte Butterworth, Aug. 19, 1944; children—Peter Wadsworth, Carl Eric, Cheryl L. Regional sales mgr. Northeastern div. Dell Pub. Co., Inc., 1953-58, sales mgr. Dell Books, 1958-64, v.p. co., 1964-68, sr. v.p., 1968, exec. v.p., dir., 1968-76; pres. Dell Pub. Co. Inc., 1976—. Served with U.S. Mcht. Marine, 1943-46. Republican. Conglist. Club: Woodway Country. Home: Deacons Way New Canaan CT 06840 Office: 1 Dag Hammarskjold New York City NY 10017

TOBIAS, ABRAHAM JOEL, artist; b. Rochester, N.Y., Nov. 21, 1913; s. Israel and Jennie (Warnick) T.; student Cooper Union Art Sch., 1930-31, Art Students League, 1931-33; m. Carolyn Patt, Oct. 29, 1949; 1 dau., Maya. Exhibited works in one-man shows at Delphic Studios, 1935, 37, 39, New Sch. for Social Research, 1937, Gallery of Art, Howard U., 1938, Everhart Mus., Scranton, Pa., 1939; exhibited in group shows at Mus. Modern Art, N.Y.C., Bklyn. Mus., Adelphi Coll., Archtl. League of N.Y., N.Y.C. Municipal Art Commn., San Francisco Mus., Howard U.; works represented in permanent collections at Bklyn. Mus., N.Y. Pub. Library, Rochester Pub. Library, Los Angeles Mus.; created The Freedom Monument for Bklyn. Bicentennial Commn., 1976; artist-in-residence Adelphi U., 1947-52; inst. artist Poly. Inst. N.Y., 1970. Served with U.S. Army, 1942-43. Finalist in Nat. Fine Arts Commn. Mural Competition, 1940; recipient Archtl. League award for mural painting, 1952. Home and office: 98-51 65th Ave Rego Park Queens NY 11374. *In 1946, after giving a lecture and a show of slides which depicted my work as a muralist, I was asked by a student what my purpose was in being a muralist. My answer, as recorded in the University bulletin, was, "My purpose is to paint on the walls of public buildings, with fresh and readily understood symbolism, the idea and the hope of America." Today, my answer would be basically the same, although I would enlarge the word paint to include mosaic, stained glass and sculpture.*

TOBIAS, CHARLES HARRISON, JR., lawyer; b. Cin., Apr. 16, 1921; s. Charles Harrison and Charlotte (Westheimer) T.; B.A. cum laude, Harvard U., 1943, LL.B., 1949; m. Mary J. Kaufman, June 15, 1946; children—Jean M., Thomas Charles, Robert Charles. Admitted to Ohio Bar, 1949; asso. firm Steer, Strauss and Adair, Cin., 1949-56; partner firm Steer, Strauss, White and Tobias, Cin., 1956—. Bd. dirs. Cin. City Charter Com., 1955-75; mem. Wyoming (Ohio) City Council, 1972-77, vice mayor, 1974-77; bd. govs. Hebrew Union Coll., Jewish Inst. Religion; pres. Met. Area Religious Coalition of Cin., 1977—; pres. Jewish Fedn. Cin., 1972-74; mem. nat. exec. bd. Am. Jewish Com., 1975—. Served with USN, 1943-46. Mem. Ohio State Bar Assn., Cin. Bar Assn. Club: Losantiville Country (Cin.). Home: 21 Reily Rd Cincinnati OH 45215 Office: 2208 Central Trust Tower Cincinnati OH 45202

TOBIAS, CHARLES WILLIAM, educator, chem. engr.; b. Budapest, Hungary, Nov. 2, 1920; s. Karoly and Elizabeth (Milko) T.; dipl. chem. engring. U. Tech. Scis. Budapest, 1942, Ph.D., 1946; m. Marcia Rous, Sept. 10, 1950; children—Carla, Eric, Anthony. Came to U.S., 1947; naturalized, 1952. Research, devel. engr. United Incandescent & Elec. Co., Ltd., Ujpest, Hungary, 1942-47; instr. phys. chemistry U. Tech. Scis., 1945-46; mem. faculty U. Calif. at Berkeley, 1947—, prof. chem. engring., 1960—, chmn. dept., 1967-72, faculty sr. scientist Lawrence Berkeley Lab., 1954—; asso. research prof. Miller Inst. Basic Sci., 1958-59. Registered profl. engr., Calif. Fellow AAAS; mem. Am. Chem. Soc., Am. Inst. Chem. Engrs., Am. Soc. Engring. Edn., Electrochem. Soc. (asso. editor Jour. 1955—, v.p. 1967-70, pres. 1970-71; Acheson award 1972, hon. mem. 1977—), Internat. Soc. Electrochemistry (v.p. 1975-76, pres. 1977-78), Deutsche Bunsen-Gesellschaft, Sigma Xi. Editor: (with Paul Delahay and Heinz Gerischer) Advances in Electrochemistry and Electrochemical Engineering, 1961—; editorial bd. Jour. Applied Electrochemistry, Chem. Engring. Communications; researcher numerous publs. on mass and charge transport in electrochem. systems, design of electrolytic processes, batteries and fuel cells, electrolysis in non-aqueous solvents. Home: 524 Morage Way Orinda CA 94563 Office: Dept Chem Engring U Calif Berkeley CA 94720

TOBIAS, JULIUS, artist, sculptor; b. N.Y.C., Aug. 27, 1915; s. Louis and Anna (Tabachnick) T.; student Atelier Fernand Leger, Paris, 1949-52; m. Suzanne Tobias. Pvt. tchr., 1950-63; tchr. Morris Davidson Sch. Modern Painting, 1947-48; instr. N.Y. Inst. Tech., 1966-70; lectr. Rutgers U., Queens Coll., N.Y.C., 1966-67, Ind. U., Bloomington, 1974; one-man shows include Esther Stuttman Gallery, 1959, Bleecker Gallery, 1961, Easthampton Gallery, 1962, 10 Downtown, 1968, Max Hutchinson Gallery, 1970, 71, 72, Alessandra Gallery, 1976, 55 Mercer St. Gallery, 1976, 77, 78 (all N.Y.C.), Zriny-Hayes Gallery, Chgo., 1979; group shows include Provincetown (Mass.) Art Assn., 1946, Roko Gallery, N.Y.C., 1946, Camino Gallery, N.Y.C., 1957, Polari Gallery, Woodstock, N.Y., 1957, Art USA, Coliseum, N.Y.C., 1957, Brata Gallery, N.Y.C., 1957- 59, Pa. Acad. Fine Arts, 1958, Gallery Creuze, Paris, 1958,

Knoedler Gallery, N.Y.C., 1959, Mus. Modern Art traveling exhbn. to Tokyo, 1959, New Eng. Exhbn., Silvermine, Conn., 1960, De Aenlle Gallery, N.Y.C., 1961, Bleecker Gallery, N.Y.C., 1962, Staten Island Mus., N.Y.C., 1962, Allan Stone Gallery, N.Y.C., 1962, Easthampton Gallery, N.Y.C., 1962-66, Windham Coll., Putney, Vt., 1963, Rutgers U., 1966, Park Pl. Gallery, N.Y.C., 1967, Tibor Dinagy Gallery, N.Y.C., 1968, Whitney Mus. Annual, N.Y.C., 1968, Parker St. 470, Boston, 1969, Everson Mus., Syracuse, N.Y., 1972; represented in numerous collections Europe, N. and S.Am., also pvt. collections. Served to 1st lt. USAAF, 1942-45. Decorated D.F.C., Air medal with 3 oak leaf clusters; Guggenheim fellow, 1972-73, 78-79; Nat. Endowment for Arts grantee, 1975-76. Address: 9 Great Jones St New York NY 10012

TOBIAS, PAUL HENRY, lawyer; b. Cin., Jan. 5, 1930; s. Charles H. and Charlotte (Westheimer) T.; A.B., Harvard U., 1951, LL.B., 1958; 1 dau., Eliza L. Admitted to Mass. bar, 1958, Ohio bar, 1962; mem. firm Stoneman & Chandler, Boston, 1958-61, Goldman & Putnick, Cin., 1962-75; partner firm Tobias & Kraus, Cin., 1976—; instr. U. Cin. Law Sch., 1975-77. Mem. Cin. Bd. of Park Commrs., 1973—, Cin. Human Relations Commn., 1980—. Served with U.S. Army, 1952-54. Mem. Cin. Bar Assn., Ohio Bar Assn., Am. Bar Assn. Contbr. articles to profl. jours. Home: 15 Hill and Hollow Ln Cincinnati OH 45208 Office: 911 First National Bank Bldg Cincinnati OH 45202

TOBIAS, RUSSELL STUART, educator, chemist; b. Columbus, Ohio, Sept. 11, 1930; s. Russell Stewart and Mary (Bigger) T.; B.Sc. in Chemistry, Ohio State U., 1952, Ph.D., 1956; m. Nancy Ann Westbrook, Apr. 14, 1956; children—Janet Lenore, Douglas Andrew, Ellen Elizabeth. NSF postdoctoral fellow Royal Inst. Tech., Stockholm, Sweden, 1956-57; research asso. U. N.C., 1958-59; mem. faculty U. Minn., 1959-69, prof. chemistry, 1966-69; prof. chemistry Purdue U., Lafayette, Ind., 1969—; NSF sr. postdoctoral fellow Technische Hochschule, Munich, Germany, also Imperial Coll., London, Eng., 1967-68; cons. Mobil Oil Corp., 1964-67. NATO sr. postdoctoral fellow Ludwig Maximilian U., Munich, Germany, 1977. Fellow Am. Soc. Biol. Chemists; mem. Am. Chem. Soc., Chem. Soc. (London), Phi Beta Kappa, Sigma Xi, Phi Lambda Upsilon. Author: (with L.E. Conroy and R.C. Brasted) General Chemistry Laboratory Operations, 1977. Editorial bd. Jour. Coordination Chemistry, 1970—. Contbr. articles to profl. jours. Home: 706 Bexley Rd West Lafayette IN 47906 Office: Dept of Chemistry Purdue U Lafayette IN 47907

TOBIASON, ORVILLE L., army officer; b. Alexandria, Minn., Nov. 2, 1920; s. Walter and Pearl L. (Bundy) T.; student U.S. Army Command and Gen. Staff Coll., Cameron Coll., 1954-56, U. Md., Armed Forces Staff Coll., 1961, Nat. War Coll., 1964-65; m. Patricia A. Lindsey, May 23, 1942; children—Thomas L., Jo Ann (Mrs. Steve L. Crawford), Christine L. Served as enlisted man U.S. Army, 1940-42, to capt. 2d F.A. Bn., 1942-45; commd. capt. U.S. Army, 1950, advanced through grades to maj. gen., 1973; assigned to Korea and Japan, 1951-53, to Ft. Sill, Okla., Ft. Hood, Germany, 1956-61, to Pentagon, 1961-64, to Ft. Sill, Vietnam, Aberdeen Proving Ground, Md., Ft. Hood, 1965-71, Korea and Turkey, 1971-75; comdr. White Sands Missile Range, N.M., 1975—. Decorated Legion of Merit with three oak leaf clusters, Bronze Star, also numerous other Am. and fgn. decorations and awards. Mem. Am. Def. Preparedness Assn. Mason. Home: 214 Goddard Ave White Sands Missile Range NM 88002 Office: Commander White Sands Missile Range NM 88002

TOBIN, CALVIN JAY, architect; b. Boston, Feb. 15, 1927; s. David and Bertha (Tanfield) T.; B.Arch., U. Mich., 1949; m. Joan Hope Fink, July 15, 1951; children—Michael Alan, Nancy Ann. Designer, draftsman Arlen & Lowenfish, architects, N.Y.C., 1949-51; with Samuel Arlen, N.Y.C., 1951-53, Skidmore, Owings & Merrill, N.Y.C., 1953; architect Loebl, Schlossman & Bennett, architects, Chgo., 1953-57; v.p. Loebl, Schlossman & Bennett, architects, Chgo., 1953-57; v.p. Loebl, Schlossman & Hackl, 1957—. Chmn., Jewish United Fund Bldg. Trades Div., 1969; chmn. AIA and Chgo. Hosp. Council Com. of Hosp. Architecture, 1968-76. Chmn. Highland Park (Ill.) Appearance Rev. Commn., 1972-73; mem. Highland Park Plan Commn., 1972-78; mem. Highland Park City Council, 1974-81, mayor pro-tem, 1979-81; bd. dirs. Young Men's Jewish Council, 1953-67, pres., 1967; bd. dirs. Jewish Community Centers Chgo., 1973-78. Served with USNR, 1945-46. Mem. AIA (2d v.p. Chgo. chpt.), Pi Lambda Phi. Jewish. Archtl. works include Michael Reese Hosp. and Med. Center, 1954—, Prairie Shores Apt. Urban Redevel., 1957-62, Louis A. Weiss Meml. Hosp., Chgo., Chgo. State Hosp., Central Community Hosp., Chgo., Gottlieb Meml. Hosp., Melrose Park, Ill., Water Tower Pl., Chgo., also numerous apt., comml. and community bldgs. Home: 814 Dean Ave Highland Park IL 60035 Office: 845 N Michigan Ave Chicago IL 60611

TOBIN, JAMES, educator; b. Champaign, Ill., Mar. 5, 1918; s. Louis Michael and Margaret (Edgerton) T.; A.B. summa cum laude, Harvard, 1939, M.A., 1940, Ph.D., 1947; LL.D., Syracuse U., 1967, U. Ill., 1969, Dartmouth, 1970; m. Elizabeth Fay Ringo, Sept. 14, 1946; children—Margaret Ringo, Louis Michael, Hugh Ringo, Roger Gill. Asso. economist OPA, WPB, Washington, 1941-42; teaching fellow econs. Harvard, 1946-47; Soc. Fellows, Harvard, 1947-50; asso. prof. econs. Yale, 1950-55, prof., 1955—, Sterling prof. econs., 1957—. Mem. Council Econ. Advisers, 1961-62, Nat. Acad. Scis. Served to lt. USNR, 1942-46. Social Sci. Research Council faculty fellow, 1951-54. Fellow Am. Acad. Arts and Scis., Econometric Soc. (pres. 1958), Am. Statis. Assn.; mem. Am. Philos. Soc., Am. Econ. Assn. (John Bates Clark medal 1955, v.p. 1964, pres. 1971), Phi Beta Kappa. Author: National Economic Policy, 1966; Essays in Economics-Macroeconomics, vol. 1, 1972, Consumption and Econometrics, vol. 2, 1975; The New Economics One Deade Older, 1974. Home: 117 Alden Ave New Haven CT 06515

TOBIN, MICHAEL E., banker; B.S. in Econs., U. Pa., 1948; m. Judith Tobin; children—Michael E., Allegra, Corey. Cons. RCA, Ebasco Service, Inc., 1954-56; sr. cons. Arthur Young & Co., N.Y.C., 1956-59, Midwest dir. cons. services, Chgo., 1959-68; pres. Midwest Stock Exchange, Chgo., 1968-78; chmn. bd. Am. Nat. Bank & Trust, Chgo., 1979—. Active in Community Fund Chgo., Welfare Council Met. Chgo. Office: Am Nat Bank & Trust 33 N LaSalle St Chicago IL 60690

TOBIN, ROBERT LYNN BATTS, opera exec.; b. San Antonio, Mar. 12, 1934; s. Edgar Gardner and Margaret Lynn (Batts) T.; student U. Tex., 1951-52. Prodn. coordinator San Antonio Grand Opera Festival, 1951-57, 60-63; mem. bd. mng. dirs. Met. Opera Co., N.Y.C.; producer, curator numerous exhbns. stage and costume design, including Three Centuries of Design for the Stage for Spoleto, Thespis Adorned for various colls. and Univs.; v.p. cultural participation San Antonio Fair, Inc., 1966-68; v.p., dir. Am. Nat. Opera Co., 1967-68; pres. Festival Found., Festivale dei Due Monde, Spoleto, 1970-71; nat. chmn. Central Opera Service of Met. Opera Nat. Council, N.Y.C., 1961—. Mem. internat. council, trustee Mus. Modern Art; chief exec. officer, sec.-treas. Tobin Surveys, Inc.; chmn. bd. Tobin Research, Inc.; past pres. Childrens Service Bur., Allied Childrens Services; mem. bus. com. for arts N.Y. Quadriennale for Stage and Designs, Prague, Czechoslovakia, 1979; bd. dirs. Worden Sch. Social Work, Our Lady of the Lake Coll., Childrens Hosp. Found., Fine Arts Found. U. Tex., Edgar G. Tobin Found.; pres. bd. trustees Nat. Opera Inst., Washington; past chmn. bd. mgrs. Bexar County Hosp. Dist. Decorated cavaliere ufficiale Ordine Merito della Republica Italiana, corrispondenti Academia Spoletina. Mem. Order of Alamo (past pres.), Kappa Alpha. Clubs: German, San Antonio, San Antonio Country, Argyle (past pres. bd. govs.) (San Antonio); Grolier, Metropolitan Opera (N.Y.C.). Address: PO Box 2101 San Antonio TX 78297 also Met Opera Lincoln Center New York NY 10023

TOBIN, RONALD WILLIAM, educator; b. N.Y.C., June 19, 1936; s. William P. and Mary (Jadoff) T.; A.B., St. Peters Coll., 1957; M.A. (Woodrow Wilson fellow), Princeton, 1959, Ph.D., 1962; Fulbright fellow, U. Lille (France), 1959-60; m. Ann L. Pollmann, Feb. 20, 1960; 1 son, Roger. Instr. French, Williams Coll., Williamstown, Mass., 1961-63; asst. prof. U. Kans., 1963-65, asso. prof., chmn. dept. French and Italian, 1965-69; prof. French, U. Calif. at Santa Barbara, 1969—, chmn. dept. French and Italian, 1969-71, 75—. Vis. prof. Claremont (Calif.) Grad. Div., 1972, U. Ariz., 1972, U. Calif. at Los Angeles, 1973. Mem. univ. adv. council to Inst. Life Ins., 1969—. Am. Philos. Soc. grantee, 1963, 67. Fellow Nat. Endowment for Humanities, 1967; decorated Acad. Palms, 1972. Mem. Modern Lang. Assn., Modern Humanities Research Assn., Societe d'Etude du 17e siecle, Alliance Francaise. Democrat. Roman Catholic. Author: Racine and Seneca, 1971. Editor: L'Esprit Createur: Seventeenth-Century Studies in Honor of E.B.O. Borgerhoff, 1971; L'Esprit Createur: Myth and Mythology in the Seventeenth Century, 1976; Papers on French Seventeenth Century Literature: Esthétique et Société au XVII e Siècle, 1977. Home: 26 La Cumbre Circle Santa Barbara CA 93105

TOBIN, WILLIAM THOMAS, retail co. exec.; b. Cleve., May 31, 1931; s. Paul William and Ellen Louise (Fenlon) T.; B.A., Yale U., 1949-53; m. Mary Ellen Fawcett, May 22, 1976; children—William Thomas, Bradford Fenlon. With M. O'Neil Co., Akron, Ohio, 1953-73, exec. v.p., 1973-75, pres., 1975-79; pres., chief exec. officer Kaufmann's, Pitts., 1979—. Episcopalian. Clubs: Portage Country, Rolling Rock, Duquesne. Office: 400 5th Ave Pittsburgh PA 15219

TOBIS, JEROME SANFORD, physician; b. Syracuse, N.Y., July 23, 1915; s. David George and Anna (Feinberg) T.; B.S., Coll. City N.Y., 1936; M.D., Chgo. Med. Sch., 1943; m. Hazel Weisbard, Sept. 18, 1938; children—David, Heather, Jonathan. Intern Knickerbocker Hosp., 1943-44; resident Bronx VA Hosp., 1946-48; med. dir. state fever therapy unit USPHS, Brookhaven, Miss., 1944-46; practice medicine, N.Y.C., 1948-70; prof. dir. dept. phys. medicine and rehab. N.Y. Med. Coll., Flower and Fifth Av. Hosps., 1948-61; prof. rehab. medicine Albert Einstein Coll. of Medicine, 1963-70; chief div. rehab. medicine Montefiore Hosp., 1961-70; dir. vis. physician Met., Bird S. Coler hosps., 1952-61; prof., chmn. dept. phys. medicine and rehab. Calif. Coll. Medicine, U. Calif. at Irvine, 1970—; cons. Dept. Health, N.Y.C.; mem. expert med. com. Am. Rehab. Found., 1961—; mem. adv. council council phys. medicine and rehab. for appeals com. Calif. Med. Assn., 1971—. Named physician of the year, 1957; recipient Distinguished Alumnus award Chgo. Med. Sch., 1972. Diplomate Am. Bd. Phys. Medicine and Rehab. Fellow A.C.P., Am. Coll. Cardiology; mem. Orange County Med. Soc., A.M.A. (mem. residency rev. com. Council Med. Edn. 1973), A.A.A.S., N.Y. Acad. Medicine, N.Y. Acad. Sci., Am. Acad. Cerebral Palsy, Am. Acad. Phys. Medicine and Rehab., Am. Congress Rehab. Medicine (pres. 1962). Mem. editorial bd. Heart and Lung, 1973-76, Geriatrics, 1975—, Archives of Phys. Medicine and Rehab., 1958-73. Home: 1115 Goldenrod St Corona del Mar CA 92625 Office: Dept Phys Medicine and Rehab U Calif Irvine CA 92664

TOBRINER, MATHEW OSCAR, state justice; b. San Francisco, Apr. 2, 1904; s. Oscar and Maude (Lezinsky) T.; A.B., Stanford U., 1924, M.A., 1925; LL.B., Harvard U., 1927; S.J.D., U. Calif., 1932; LL.D., U. Santa Clara; m. Rosabelle Rose, May 19, 1939; children—Michael Charles, Stephen Oscar. Admitted to Calif. bar, 1928; sr. partner Tobriner, Lazarus, Brundage & Neyhart, San Francisco and Los Angeles, 1928-59; justice Dist. Ct. Appeal, 1st Dist. Calif., 1959-62; asso. justice Supreme Ct. of Calif., 1962—. Chief atty. solicitor's office Dept. Agr., 1932-36; atty. various unions AFL, counsel before Calif. Supreme Ct. on major labor issues; asso. prof. Hastings Law Sch., 1958-59; mem. Jud. Council Calif., 1965-67, 78-79. Del. Democratic Nat. Conv., 1956; exec. com. gubernatorial campaign, 1958. Mem. San Francisco Legal Aid Soc. (pres. 1961), Jewish Community Relations Council (chmn. 1962-64), Order of Coif (hon.), Phi Beta Kappa, Delta Sigma Rho. Author: (with E. G. Mears) Principles and Practices of Cooperative Marketing. Advisory com. Hastings Law Jour., 1959—. Contbr. articles to legal jours. Home: 3494 Jackson St San Francisco CA 94118 Office: State Bldg San Francisco CA 94102

TOBUREN, LAWRENCE RICHTER, transp. co. exec.; b. Cleburne, Kans., July 11, 1915; s. Edward Franklin and Anna Fredericka (Richter) T.; student U. Denver, 1937-41; m. Ella Joyner Brame, Dec. 16, 1942; children—Lawrence Richter, William Brame, Luanne Brame, Gwendolyn Brame. Dispatch clk. Continental Airlines, Denver, 1943-48; dispatcher Pacific Intermountain Express, Denver, 1948-52, dir. dispatch, Oakland, Calif., 1952-57, western region ops. mgr., 1957-58; with Pilot Freight Carriers, Inc., 1958—, exec. v.p., Winston-Salem, N.C., 1972-76, pres., 1976—, also dir. Served with USAAC, 1941-43. Republican. Methodist. Home: 4116 Wedge Dr Pfafftown NC 27040 Office: Pilot Freight Carriers Inc N Cherry St and Polo Rd Winston-Salem NC 27102

TOBY, JACKSON, educator, sociologist; b. N.Y.C., Sept. 10, 1925; S. Phineas and Anna (Weissman) T.; B.A., Bklyn. Coll., 1946; M.A. in Econs., Harvard, 1947, M.A. in Sociology, 1949, Ph.D. in Sociology, 1950; m. Marcia Lifshitz, Aug. 1, 1952; children—Alan Steven, Gail Afriat. Research asso. Lab. Social Relations, Harvard, 1950-51; mem. faculty Rutgers U., 1951—, prof. sociology, chmn. dept., 1961-68, dir. Inst. for Criminological Research, 1969—; cons. Youth Devel. Program, Ford Found., 1959-63; spl. research adolescent delinquency in U.S., Sweden, Japan, other countries. Cons. Pres.'s Commn. Law Enforcement and Adminstrn. Justice, 1967; mem. Univ. Centers for Rational Alternatives. Mem. Am. Sociol. Assn., Eastern Sociol. Soc., AAUP, Coalition for a Democratic Majority. Author: (with H. C. Bredemeier) Social Problems in America, 1960, 2d edit., 1972; Contemporary Society, 1964, 2d edit., 1971. Contbr. numerous articles to profl. jours. Home: 17 Harrison Ave Highland Park NJ 08904 Office: Dept Sociology Murray Hall Rutgers Univ New Brunswick NJ 08903

TOCCO, JAMES, pianist; b. Detroit, Sept. 21, 1943; s. Vincenzo and Rose (Tabbita) T.; pupil Boris Maximovich, Magda Tagliaferro, Claudio Arrau; m. Gilan Akbar, Sept. 27, 1969. Debut with orch., Detroit, 1956, since performed with symphony orchs. including Chgo. Symphony, Detroit Symphony, Nat. Symphony, Balt. Symphony, Atlanta Symphony, Denver Symphony, Montreal Symphony, Berlin Philharm., Moscow Radio-TV Orch., Amsterdam Philharmonic, Munich Philharmonic, Bavarian Radio Orch., also recitals, U.S. and abroad, and performances CBS and NBC networks; guest performer, White House; prof. music Ind. U., Bloomington, 1977—. Guest lectr., instr. master classes, various univs. and music schs., U.S. and abroad. Recipient Bronze medal Tchaikovsky Competition, Moscow, 1970, Bronze medal Queen Elisabeth of Belgium Competition, Brussels, 1972, 1st prize Piano Competition of Americas, Rio de Janeiro, 1973, 1st prize Munich Internat. Competition, 1973. U. Wis. sr. fellow, 1968-70. Recs. include The Complete Preludes of Chopin. Home: 800 Sheridan Rd Bloomington IN 47401 Office: Sch Music Indiana U Bloomington IN 47401

TOCKER, PHILLIP, lawyer, advt. exec.; b. Cleve., Sept. 15, 1910; s. Joe and Pearl (Lerman) T.; B.A., J.D., U. Tex., 1933; m. Olive Farbstein, Aug. 3, 1950; children—Donald, Madeline. Admitted to Tex. bar, 1933, also U.S. Supreme Ct.; sr. mem. firm Tocker, Todd, Donoho, Dillon & Sellers, Wash.; pres. Outdoor Advt. Assn. Am., Inc.; dir. Am. Income Life Ins. Co. Mem. Tex. Commn. Interstate Coop., 1938-40; dir. trade barrier sect. So. Govs.' Conf., 1939. Mem. Waco Planning Commn., 1956-59. Served to lt. USNR, World War II. Mem. Tex. Bar Assn., Order of Coif. Mason (32 deg., Shriner). Contbr. articles to legal publs. Home and Office: 49 Woodstone Sq Austin TX 78703

TODARO, GEORGE JOSEPH, physician; b. N.Y.C., July 1, 1937; s. George J. and Antoinette (Piccinni) T.; B.S., Swarthmore Coll., 1958; M.D., N.Y. U., 1963; m. Jane Lehv, Aug. 12, 1962; children—Wendy C., Thomas M., Anthony A. Intern, N.Y. U. Sch. Medicine, N.Y.C., 1963-64, fellow in pathology, 1964-65, asst. prof. pathology, 1965-67; staff asso. Viral Carcinogenesis br. Nat. Cancer Inst., Bethesda, Md., 1967-70, head molecular biology sect., 1969-70, chief Lab. Viral Carcinogenesis, 1970—; faculty mem. Genetics Program, George Washington U. Served as med. officer USPHS, 1967-69. Recipient Borden Undergrad. Research award, 1963, USPHS Career Devel. award, 1967, HEW Superior Service award, 1971, Gustav Stern award for virology, 1972, Parke-Davis award in exptl. pathology, 1975; Walter Hubert lectr. Brit. Cancer Soc., 1977. Mem. Am. Soc. Microbiology, Am. Assn. Cancer Research, Soc. Exptl. Biology and Medicine, Am. Soc. Biol. Chemists, Am. Soc. Clin. Investigation. Editor Cancer Research, 1973—; Archives of Virology, 1976—; contbr. articles to profl. jours. Home: 5311 Locust Ave Bethesda MD 20014 Office: Bldg 37 Room 1B-22 Nat Cancer Inst 9000 Rockville Pike Bethesda MD 20205

TODD, ALEXANDER CALHOUN, JR., mining co. exec.; b. Sandersville, Ga., Sept. 8, 1912; s. Alexander Calhoun and Sarah (Cason) T.; student Ga. Mil. Coll., 1930-31; B.S., Ga. Inst. Tech., 1935; m. Louise Quenel, Dec. 15, 1947; 1 dau., Sarah Martha. With Edgar Bros. Co., McIntyre, Ga., 1935-54, with corp. after merger into Minerals & Chems. Corp. Am., then into Minerals & Chems. Philipp Corp., Menlo Park, N.J., 1954-67, prodn. mgr., 1954-61, dir. prodn. Minerals and Chems. div., 1961-65, v.p. prodn., 1965-67, corp. merged with Engelhard Industries to become Engelhard Minerals & Chems. Corp., 1967, sr. v.p. prodn. minerals and chems. div., corporate v.p., 1967-70, v.p. spl. assignments, minerals and chems. div., 1970-74, cons. engr., 1974—; v.p., asst. sec., dir. Chemstone Corp., Porocel Corp., Cuyahoga Lime Corp., 1967-70. Bd. dirs. Ga. Dept. Natural Resources, North Ga. Mountains Authority. Served to maj. C.E., AUS, 1941-46. Mem. Am. Inst. Mining Engrs., Delta Sigma Phi. Club: Idle Hour Golf and Country (Macon, Ga.). Home: 4909-H Rivoli Dr Macon GA 31210 Office: Engelhard Minerals & Chems Corp Menlo Park Edison NJ 08817

TODD, ALVA CRESS, educator, engr.; b. Ligonier, Ind., July 30, 1917; s. Frederick White and Bessie Pearl (Cress) T.; B.S. in Elec. Engring., Purdue U., 1947, M.S., 1949, Ph.D., 1957; m. Mary Elizabeth Schelle, Apr. 17, 1941; children—Richard Schelle, Carol Jean (Mrs. Everett A. Biegalski), Joanne Frances (Mrs. Louis E. Horton), Elizabeth Ann (Mrs. Scott R. Lowry). Broadcast engr. radio sta. WSBT, South Bend, Ind., 1936-40, radio sta. WBAA, Lafayette, Ind., 1940-42; elec. engr. U.S. Signal Corps., Washington, 1942; instr., research engr. Sch. Elec. Engring., Purdue U., 1947-53, asst. prof., 1953; dir. engring. Fournier Inst. Tech., Lemont, Ill., 1953-55; sr. engr. Farnsworth Electronics Co., Ft. Wayne, Ind., 1955-56; individual practice engring., Lafayette, 1956-57; research engr. Ill. Inst. Tech. Research Inst., 1957-60; mgr. active electronic warfare div. Hallicrafters Co., 1960-61; mem. faculty Ill. Inst. Tech., 1961-62, prof. elec. engring., 1962-67; founder, pres. Midwest Coll. Engring., 1967—; sr. partner Todd Assos., Villa Park, Ill., 1961—. Served to lt. USCGR, 1942-46. Registered profl. engr., Ind., Ill. Mem. IEEE (sr.), Armed Forces Communications and Electronics Assn., AAAS, Nat. Fire Protection Assn., Nat., Ill. socs. profl. engrs., Am. Soc. Engring. Edn., Soc. Broadcast Engrs., Sigma Xi, Tau Beta Pi, Eta Kappa Nu. Patentee in field. Home: 827 S Summit Ave Villa Park IL 60181 Office: Midwest Coll of Engineering 440 S Finley Rd Lombard IL 60148

TODD, ANDERSON, architect; b. Washington, Oct. 22, 1921; s. Forde Anderson and Sylvia Leland (Barnes) T.; B.A. in Architecture with honors, Princeton U., 1943, M.F.A. in Architecture, 1949; m. Lucie Halm Wray, May 26, 1953; children—Emily Leland, David Anderson. Draftsman, Wilson, Morris and Crain, Architects, Houston, 1951-55; prin. Anderson Todd, Architect, Houston, 1956-63; partner Todd Tackett Lacy, Architects and Planning Cons., Houston, 1963-70, Anderson Todd and William T. Cannady Architects, Houston, 1970—; instr. architecture Rice U., 1949-52, asst. prof. 1952-56, asso. prof., 1956-66, prof., 1966—, Wortham prof. architecture, 1978—, dir. Sch. Architecture, 1969-72; bd. dirs., chmn. bldg. com. Houston Mus. Fine Arts, Contemporary Arts Mus. Bd. dirs. Planned Parenthood Houston. Served with USNR, 1942-47. Recipient George R. Brown award Rice U., 1968; Nat. award Am. Inst. Steel Constrn., 1968; Honor award Tex. Soc. Architects, 1975-79, award of Merit, 1976. Fellow AIA (Houston chpt. Honor awards 1966, 68, 69). Episcopalian. Clubs: Bayou, Tejas (Houston); Princeton (N.Y.C.). Prin. works: Todd Residence, Houston, 1961; Meml. Lutheran Ch., Houston, 1965; Superior Oil Co. Geophys. Lab., Houston, 1967; Fire Station 59, Houston, 1968; Brochstein House, Houston, 1975; Children's Mental Health Services Bldg., Houston, 1976. Home: 9 Shadowlawn Circle Houston TX 77005 Office: 2403 Sunset Blvd Houston TX 77005

TODD, CHARLES GILLETT, food co. exec.; b. Indpls., Feb. 28, 1914; s. John Picken and Laura (Gillett) T.; A.B., Ind. U., 1935; LL.B., Chgo. Kent Coll. Law, 1940; student Wabash Coll., 1931-33, DePaul U., 1940, Northwestern U., 1941-42; m. Genevieve Steiner, Dec. 11, 1939; children—John P., Suzanne (Mrs. Milton R. Dodge). Admitted to Ill. bar, 1940, Calif. bar, 1951; atty., tax mgr. First Nat. Bank Chgo., 1936-41; tax mgr. Allen R. Smart Co., Chgo., 1941-44; with Carnation Co., 1944-50, 56—, sec., asst. v.p., 1962-63, treas., 1963-69, v.p., 1965-67, mem. exec. com., chmn. finance com., dir., 1965—, sr. v.p., 1967-73, exec. v.p., 1973—; v.p. Gen. Milk Co., 1951-56. Bd. dirs. Carnation Found. Mem. State Bar Calif., Phi Delta Phi, Phi Delta Theta. Clubs: Wilshire Country (Los Angeles), Lomas Santa Fe Country (Solana Beach). Home: 5243 Yarmouth Ave No 28 Encino CA 91316 Office: 5045 Wilshire Blvd Los Angeles CA 90036

TODD, DAVID ARNOLD, II, savs. and loan exec.; b. Kansas City, Mo., Mar. 24, 1932; s. David Arnold and Inez Marie (Porta) T.; B.A., U. Mo., 1957; m. Yvon Forderer, Aug. 22, 1957; children—Elizabeth Ellen, David Arnold, Judith Claire. With Farm and Home Savs. Assn., 1958—, v.p., Dallas, 1968-75, exec. v.p., Nevada, Mo., 1975—.

Served with U.S. Army, 1952-54. Mem. Mo. Savs. and Loan League (dir.), Nevada C. of C. (dir.), U.S. League Savs. Assns., Nat. Assn. Home Builders, Mortgage Bankers Assn. Republican. Episcopalian. Office: 221 W Cherry Nevada MO 64772

TODD, DAVID FENTON MICHIE, architect; b. Middletown, Ohio, Feb. 22, 1915; s. Robert Chalmers and Frances Fenton (Michie) T.; A.B., Dartmouth, 1937; B.Arch., U. Mich., 1940; m. Suzanne Williams, Sept. 1, 1942; 1 son, Gregory F.W. Draftsman, J.R.F. Swanson, Birmingham, Mich., 1940-41; archtl. designer W. Ray Yount, Dayton, Ohio, 1941-42; architect Harrison, Ballard & Allen, N.Y.C., 1942-53; architect, prin. Ballard, Todd & Snibbe, N.Y.C., 1957-62, Ballard Todd Assos., 1962-66, David Todd & Assos., 1966—. Mem. vestry Trinity Ch., N.Y.C. Served to 1st lt. AUS, 1942-46. Fellow AIA (pres. N.Y.C., 1969-70, chmn. jury of fellows 1971, chmn. task force on housing policy 1974), Constrn. Specifications Inst. (pres. N.Y.C. 1960-61). Works include Grad. Sch. Dorms, Faculty Housing and Tennis Pavillion at Princeton U.; Lehman Coll. of City U. N.Y.; Manhattan Plaza, N.Y.C.; Collegiate Sch., N.Y.C.; Rye (N.Y.) Country Day Sch. Clubs: Century Assn., Amateur Comedy. Home and office: 134 E 95th St New York NY 10028

TODD, DAVID KEITH, hydrologist, educator; b. Lafayette, Ind., Dec. 30, 1923; s. Marion W. and Evangeline (Klinkel) T.; B.S. in Civil Engring., Purdue U., 1948; M.S. in Meteorology, N.Y. U., 1949; Ph.D. in Civil Engring., U. Calif. at Berkeley, 1953; m. Caroline Lark, June 15, 1948; children—Stuart K., Brian W. Hydraulic engr. U.S. Bur. Reclamation, Denver, 1948-50; mem. faculty dept. civil engring. U. Calif. at Berkeley, 1950—, prof. civil engring., 1953—, chmn. div. hydraulic and san. engring., 1970-74. Cons. to UN, govt. and state agys. NSF fellow, 1957- 58, 64-65. Mem. Am. Geophys. Union (pres. sect. hydrology 1964-68), Univs. Council on Hydrology (chmn. 1962-64), ASCE (Research prize 1960), Am. Meteorol. Soc., AAAS, Am. Water Works Assn. Author: Ground Water Hydrology, 1959; Polluted Groundwater, 1976; also numerous articles. Editor: The Water Ency., 1970; Water Publications of State Agencies, 1972. Research on frequency rainfall and floods, ground water flow theory, ground water pollution, sea water intrusion of ground water zones, recharge of ground water artificially, mgmt. of ground water resources, application of nuclear energy to water resources, underground storage of energy. Home: 2938 Avalon Ave Berkeley CA 94705

TODD, JOHN, educator, mathematician; b. Carnacally, Ireland, May 16, 1911; s. William Robert and Catherine (Stewart) T.; B.S., Queen's U., Belfast, Ireland, 1931; student St. John's Coll., Cambridge (Eng.) U., 1931-33; m. Olga Taussky, Sept. 29, 1938. Came to U.S., 1947, naturalized, 1953. Lectr., Queen's U., 1933-37, King's Coll., London, Eng., 1937-49; chief computation lab., then chief numerical analysis Nat. Bur. Standards, 1947-57; prof. math. Calif. Inst. Tech., 1957—; Fulbright prof., Vienna, Austria, 1965. Mem. Am. Math. Soc., Soc. Indsl. and Applied Math., Math. Assn. Am. Author, editor books on numerical analysis and tables, also numerous articles. Editor in chief Numerische Mathematik, 1959—; asso. editor Aequationes Mathematicae, 1967—, Jour. Approximation Theory, 1967—. Office: Mathematics 253-37 Calif Inst Technology Pasadena CA 91125

TODD, JOHN DICKERSON, JR., lawyer; b. Macon, Ga., June 30, 1912; s. J.D. and Hazel (McManus) T.; student Va. Mil. Inst., 1930-32; LL.B., U. Ga., 1935; m. Mellicent McWhorter, Mar. 7, 1943; children—Rosalind (Mrs. Jack Harding Tedards, Jr.), John D. Admitted to S.C. bar, 1935; with firm Hingson & Todd, 1935-51; partner firm Leatherwood, Walker, Todd & Mann, Greenville, S.C., 1952—, now sr. partner. Judge Greenville City Ct., 1939; atty. County of Greenville, 1948-56. Served to maj. AUS, 1941-45. Mem. Greenville Jr. C. of C. (pres.), Greenville County (past pres.), S.C. (bd. govs., pres. 1978—), Am. bar assns., Am. Coll. Trial Lawyers, Phi Delta Phi, Sigma Nu. Baptist (chmn., deacon). Kiwanian (past pres.). Clubs: Greenville Country (past pres.), Tarentella (Greenville). Home: 200 Riverside Dr Greenville SC 29605 Office: 217 E Coffee St Greenville SC 29602

TODD, JOHN JOSEPH, judge; b. St. Paul, Mar. 16, 1927; s. John Alfred and Martha Agnes (Jagoe) T.; student St. Thomas Coll., 1944, 46-47; B.Sci. and Law, U. Minn., 1949, LL.B., 1950; m. Dolores Jean Shanahan, Sept. 9, 1950; children—Richard M., Jane E., John P. Admitted to Minn. bar, 1951; practice in South St. Paul, Minn., 1951-72; partner Thuet and Todd, 1953-72; asso. justice Minn. Supreme Ct., St. Paul, 1972—. Served with USNR, 1945-46. Mem. Am., Minn. (bd. govs. 1972—) bar assns., Am. Legion, VFW. Home: 6659 Argenta Trail W Inver Grove Heights MN 55075 Office: 225 State Capitol St Paul MN 55155

TODD, LEE JOHN, chemist. educator; b. Denver, Nov. 8, 1936; s. Norman Hagen and Lillian (Filbin) T.; B.S., Notre Dame U., 1958; M.S. in Chemistry, Fla. State U., 1960; Ph.D. in Chemistry, Ind. U., 1963; children—Jacqueline, John Christopher, Gregory Lee. Research asso. Mass. Inst. Tech., Cambridge, 1963-64; asst. prof. chemistry U. Ill., Urbana, 1964-68; asso. prof. Ind. U., Bloomington, 1968-74, prof., 1974—. Mem. Am. Chem. Soc. Research in boron hydride and organometallic chemistry. Contbr. articles to profl. jours. Home: 3740 N Russell Rd Bloomington IN 47401 Office: Dept Chemistry Indiana U Bloomington IN 47401

TODD, MALCOLM CLIFFORD, surgeon; b. Carlyle, Ill., Apr. 10, 1913; s. Malcolm N. and Grace (Heitmeier) T.; A.B., U. Ill., 1934; M.B., Northwestern U., 1934, M.D., 1938; D.Sc. (hon.), Brown U., 1975; m. Ruth Holle Schlake, June 12, 1945; 1 son, Malcolm Douglas. Intern, St. Lukes Hosp., Chgo., 1937-38; resident Cook County Hosp., Chgo., 1938-41; instr. surgery Northwestern U., 1939-46; practice medicine, specializing in surgery, Long Beach, Calif., 1946—; clin. prof. surgery U. Calif. at Irvine, 1964—; chief of staff Long Beach Meml. Hosp., 1955-60; attending surgeon Long Beach VA Hosp., 1954—, Los Angeles County Gen. Hosp., 1964—; dir. Harbor Bank Long Beach. Mem. Nat. Adv. Com. Health Manpower; U.S. del. WHO, 1970-72; dir. Calif. Health Planning Council, 1966-74; mem. Calif. Regional Med. Programs Council, 1968-74, Presdl. Commn. on Refugees, 1975; Chmn. Long Beach br. ARC, 1957-58; mem. Long Beach Ednl. TV Bd., 1956—; trustee Long Beach Meml. Hosp.; bd. dirs. Medic Alert Found., Georgetown U. Health Policy Bd.; regent Uniformed Services Health Scis. U., 1973—. Served to maj. AUS, 1942-46. Diplomate Am. Bd. Surgery. Fellow A.C.S., Internat. Coll. Surgeons (pres. 1977), Royal Soc. Medicine, Am. Coll. Gastroenterology, Societe Internationale de Chirurgie; mem. AMA (trustee 1973-76, pres. 1974-75; chmn. council health manpower, Calif. Med. Assn. (pres. 1968-69), Los Angeles County, Long Beach (pres. 1953-54) med. socs., Karl A. Meyer Surg. Soc. (pres.). Clubs: Kiwanis, Virginia Country, Internat. City (Long Beach); Torch Internat. Contbr. sci. and socio-econ. articles to med. jours. Home: 5330 El Parque Long Beach CA 90815 Office: 2840 Long Beach Blvd Long Beach CA 90806

TODD, MICHAEL CULLEN, sculptor, painter; b. Omaha, June 20, 1935; s. Patrick Cullen and Helen Lorraine (Round) T.; B.F.A. magna cum laude, U. Notre Dame, 1957; M.A., UCLA, 1959; m. Kathryn Asako Doi, June 16, 1974; 1 dau., Mia Doi. Exhbns. in Paris, London, N.Y.C., Boston, Detroit, Los Angeles, Washington and San Diego, 1960—; represented in permanent collections Whitney Mus., Los Angeles County Mus. Art, La Jolla Mus., San Diego, Oakland (Calif.) Mus., Norton Simon Mus., Pasadena, Calif., Hirshhorn Mus., Washington. Woodrow Wilson fellow, 1957-59; Fulbright fellow, 1961-63; recipient award Nat. Endowment Arts, 1974-75. Address: 816 E 4th Pl Los Angeles CA 90013

TODD, PAUL HAROLD, JR., chem. co. exec.; b. Kalamazoo, Sept. 22, 1921; s. Paul Harold and Adeline Herr (Allais) T.; B.Sc., Cornell U., 1943; m. Ruth Newell, Apr. 16, 1946; children—George, Charles, Elizabeth, Paul. Founder, pres. Kalamazoo Spice Extraction Co., 1958-64, chmn. bd., 1964; v.p. Farmers' Chem. Co., Kalamazoo, 1946-70, pres., 1970—; mem. 89th Congress 3d Mich. Dist. Mem. State Mich. Bd. Ethics, 1973-74. Chief exec. officer Planned Parenthood-World Population, N.Y.C., 1967-70. Trustee Kalamazoo Coll., Deep Springs Coll. Mem. Am. Econ. Soc., Am. Chem. Soc., Econometric Soc., Am. Farm Econ. Assn., Inst. Food Tech., Inst. Brewing Chemists. Democrat. Home: 3713 W Main St Kalamazoo MI 49007 Office: Box 511 Kalamazoo MI 49005

TODD, SAMUEL RICHARD, JR., editor; b. Newburgh, N.Y., Aug. 29, 1940; s. Samuel Richard and Miriam Agnes (Walsh) T.; B.A., Amherst Coll., 1962; student Stanford U., 1963-65; m. Susan Burgess Bagg, Nov. 9, 1964; children—Emily, Margaret, Elinor. Advt. copywriter Batten, Barton, Durstine & Osborn, N.Y.C., 1962-63; free-lance writer, Los Altos Hills, Calif., 1965-67; editor Houghton Mifflin Co., Boston, 1967-69; with Atlantic Monthly Co., Boston, 1969—, asso. editor, 1970-77, exec. editor, 1977—. Club: St. Botolph (Boston). Home: 294 Marlborough St Boston MA 02116 Office: 8 Arlington St Boston MA 02116

TODD, THOMAS CARMEL, state ofcl.; b. Dothan, Ala., Jan. 9, 1929; s. Alda Thomas and Ada Estelle (Tharp) T.; B.S., Troy (Ala.) State Tchrs. Coll., 1955; M.S., Fla. State U., 1957; m. Barbara Irene Sheen, May 15, 1973; children—Tom, Teri, Kimberly, Tamara, Tiffany. Teaching prin. Liberty County, Fla., 1955; elementary sch. prin., Clearwater, Fla., 1957-63; supt. schs., Bay County, Fla., 1966-72; exec. asst. to commnr. edn. State of Fla., 1972-75; state supt. div. elementary and secondary edn. State of S.D., Pierre, 1975—; owner, operator retail furniture store, 1963-73. Mem. Am. Assn. Sch. Adminstrs., Council Chief State Sch. Officers, Phi Delta Kappa. Kappa Delta Phi. Clubs: Elks, Rotary. Home: 218 Neltom Dr Pierre SD 57501 Office: Div Elementary and Secondary Edn Richard F Kneip Bldg Pierre SD 57501

TODD, WEBSTER BRAY, bus. exec.; b. Yonkers, N.Y., Aug. 27, 1899; s. John R. and Alice Peck (Bray) T.; B.A., Princeton, 1922; LL.B., Fordham U., 1927, Jesus Coll. Cambridge (Eng.) U., 1922-23; m. Eleanor Prentice Schley, Oct. 12, 1933; children—Kate (Mrs. Samuel Beach), John, Webster Bray, Christine Temple (Mrs. John R. Whitman). With Todd, Robertson, Todd Engring. Corp., 1923-28; pres. Todd & Brown, Inc., 1928-40; chmn. bd. dirs., mem. exec. com., treas. Todd & Brown, Inc., 1940-50; dir. chmn. exec. com. Equity Corp., 1947-53, dir., 1954-55; dir. Office Econ. Affairs, U.S. Mission to NATO, European Regional Orgns., Paris, 1953-54. Chmn. N.J. Republican Finance Com., 1948-53, 73-74, state com., 1961-69, 74-77. Trustee emeritus Stevens Inst. Tech. Presbyn. Clubs: River, Essex, Nassau, Princeton, Maidstone, Somerset Hills Country. Home: Oldwick NJ 08858

TODD, WILLIAM BURTON, scholar, educator; b. Chester, Pa., Apr. 11, 1919; s. William Booth and Edith Hawkins (Burton) T.; B.A., Lehigh U., 1940, M.A., 1947, L.H.D. (hon.), 1975; Ph.D., U. Chgo., 1949; m. Mary Chestnut, Dec. 6, 1942; children—Marilyn Chestnut Todd Guinn, Susan Linda Todd Kramer, Deborah Burton, Terence Kingsley; m. 2d, Ann Bowden, 1969. Prof., head dept. English, Salem (N.C.) Coll., 1949-54; asst. librarian Houghton Library, Harvard, 1955-58; asso. prof. English, U. Tex., Austin, 1958, prof., dir. bibliog. research, 1959—; J.P.R. Lyell reader in bibliography Oxford (Eng.) U., 1969-70, vis. fellow All Souls Coll., 1970; Andrew D. Osborn lectr. U. Western Ont., 1978; cons. Nat. Library Australia, 1973, Nat. Endowment Humanities Research Tools Program, 1977-78; D. Nichol Smith lectr. Australian Nat. U., Canberra, 1973; Cecil Oldman Meml. lectr. Leeds (Eng.) U., 1975. Nat. advisory bd. Center for the Book, 1978—. Recipient Oldman Meml. award and Marc Fitch bibliography prize, 1975. Fulbright fellow, U.K., 1952-53; Am. Council Learned Socs. fellow, 1961-62; Guggenheim fellow, 1965-66. Author: New Adventures among Old Books, 1958; Prize Books: Awards Granted to Scholars, 1961; Bibliography of Edmund Burke, 1964; The White House Transcripts: An Enquiry, 1974. Editor: Goldsmith's Prospect of Society, 1954; Burke's Reflections on the Revolution in France, 1959; Thomas J. Wise Centenary Studies, 1959; (with E. Stenbock-Fermor) The Kilgour Collection of Russian Literature, 1959; Suppressed Commentaries on the Wiseian Forgeries, 1969; Hume and the Enlightenment, 1974; (with R.H. Campbell and A.S. Skinner) Smith's Wealth of Nations, 1976; editor Papers Bibliog. Soc. Am., 1967—. Contbr. articles to profl. jours. Home: 2109B Exposition Blvd Austin TX 78703

TODD, WILLIAM KENNETH, newspaper exec.; b. South Bend, Ind., July 3, 1916; s. Elmer Kenneth and Dorothy Hoagland (Pepple) T.; student Knox Coll., 1935-36, Loyola U., Chgo., 1936-37; m. Dorothy Marion Davies, Jan. 18, 1942; children—Nancy Lynn Catherman, Dana Joan Long, William K., Dorothy, Mary Jane, Laury-Lee Toungate. Reporter Rockford (Ill.) Register-Republic, 1934-35, Chgo. Herald Examiner, 1936; circulation dist. mgr. News Telegram, Portland, Oreg., 1937; circulation mgr. Wheaton (Ill.) Daily Jour., 1938; circulation mgr. Gary (Ind.) Post-Tribune, 1939-40; circulation mgr. Rockford Consol. Newspapers, 1947-52; bus. mgr., asst. treas. Winnebago Newspapers, Inc., 1952-58; sec.-treas. Rockford Broadcasters, Inc., WROK, 1952-63; pres. Ill. Daily Newspaper Markets, 1955-56; dir. Inland Daily Press Assn., 1962-64; treas. Rockford Newspapers, Inc. 1958-62, asso. pub., gen. mgr. 1958-67, pres., 1962-71, pub., 1967-71; pres. Todd Publs., Inc., Austin, Tex., 1972—. Adviser St. Anthony Hosp., 1958-68. Served from 2d lt. to lt. col., AUS, 1941-46; maj. Ill. N.G., 1946. Mem. Central Assn. Amateur Athletic Union (v.p. 1949-52), Sigma Delta Chi. Republican. Elk, Mason (32 deg., Shriner). Clubs: Balcones Country, Austin Country, Headliner (Austin). Home: 4620 Lake View Austin TX 78731 Office: 2304 Hancock Austin TX 78756

TODD, WILLIAM MILLER, paper co. exec.; b. Cin., Sept. 22, 1943; s. Francis West and Grace Charlotte (Miller) T.; B.A., Duke U., 1965; M.B.A., Emory U., 1967, J.D., 1970; m. Lynn Oberlin Craig, Sept. 3, 1966; children—Sarah Craig, Virginia Miller. Admitted to Ohio bar, 1970; tax atty. U.S. Steel Corp., N.Y.C., 1970-72; fin. cons. Morgan Guaranty Trust Co., N.Y.C., 1972-74; sr. tax atty. Kimberly-Clark Corp., Neenah, Wis., 1974, treas., 1974—. Mem. Am., Ohio State bar assns. Home: 240 N Park Ave Neenah WI 54956 Office: Kimberly-Clark Corp N Lake St Neenah WI 54956

TODD, WILLIAM RUSSELL, army officer; b. Seattle, May 1, 1928; s. William Thomas and Miriam (Westland) T.; B.A., Norwich U., 1950; Ph.D. (hon.), 1975; M.B.A., U. Ala., 1963; Caroline Wyeth, June 19, 1952; children—William Thomas, Sarah Lee, Ellen Wyeth. Commd. officer, U.S. Army, 1950, advanced through grades to maj. gen., 1975; comdr. 1st Cavalry div., Fort Hood, Tex., 1976-78, comdg. gen. TRADOC Combined Arms Test Activity, 1978—; dep. chief of staff for ops. Hdqrs. U.S. Army Forces Command, 1975-76. Decorated Bronze Star, Silver Star, others. Bd. fellow Norwich U. Mem. Assn. U.S. Army, Armor Assn., Beta Tau Sigma. Home: 6796 Patton Dr Fort Hood TX 76544 Office: Office of Comdr TRADOC Combined Arms Test Activity Fort Hood TX 76544

TODD, ZANE GREY, utility exec.; b. Hanson, Ky., Feb. 3, 1924; s. Marshall Elvin and Kate (McCormick) T.; student Evansville Coll., 1947-49; B.S. summa cum laude, Purdue U., 1951, D.Engring., 1979; postgrad. U. Mich., 1965; m. Marysnow Stone, Feb. 8, 1950. Fingerprint classifier FBI, 1942-43; electric system planning engr. Indpls. Power & Light Co., 1951-56, spl. assignments supr., 1956-60, head elec. system planning, 1960-64, head substation design div., 1964-68, head distbn. engring. dept., 1968-70, asst. to v.p., 1970-72, v.p., 1972-74, exec. v.p., 1974-75, pres., dir., 1975—, chmn., 1976—; gen. mgr. Mooreville Pub. Service Co., Inc. (Ind.), 1956-60; dir. Mchts. Nat. Bank, Am. States Ins. Co., Environ. Quality Control, Inc., "500" Festival Assos., Inc., Edison Electric Inst. Mem. advisory bd. St. Vincent Hosp.; bd. dirs. United Hosp. Services, United Way Greater Indpls., Greater Indpls. Progress Com., Consumer Credit Counseling Service, Jr. Achievement Central Ind., Commn. for Downtown, YMCA Found.; advisory council, trustee Christian Theol. Sem.; advisory bd. Salvation Army, Clowes Hall. Served as sgt. AUS, 1943-47. Named Distinguished Alumnus, Purdue U., 1976. Fellow IEEE (past chmn. power system engring. com.; mem. Ind. (dir.), Indpls. (dir.), Mooreville (past pres.) chambers commerce, Am. Mgmt. Assn. (gen. mgmt. council), Power Engring. Soc., Ind. Electric Assn. (dir., past chmn.), NAM (dir.). Eta Kappa Nu, Tau Beta Pi. Clubs: Rotary, Lions (past pres.), Columbia, Indpls. Athletic, Meridian Hills Country; La Coquille (Palm Beach, Fla.). Contbr. articles to tech. jours. and mags.; originator probability analysis of power system reliability. Home: 1941 Remington Dr Indianapolis IN 46227 Office: 25 Monument Circle Indianapolis IN 46206

TODMAN, TERENCE A., ambassador; b. St. Thomas, V.I., Mar. 13, 1926; s. Alphonso and Rachel (Callwood) T.; B.A., Poly. Inst. P.R., 1951; M.P.A., Syracuse U., 1953; postgrad. Am. U. 1953-54; m. Doris T. Weston, July 26, 1952; children—Terence A., Patricia, Kathryn, Michael. Asst. personnel officer Govt. V.I., 1951; internat. relations officer State Dept., 1952-54; fgn. affairs officer, 1955; U.S. nominee UN intern program, 1955; adviser U.S. delegation UN Gen. Assembly, 1956-57; U.S. rep. UN trusteeship council petitions com. and com. rural econ. devel., 1956-57; 2d sec., polit. officer Am. embassy, Beirut, Lebanon, 1960-61; 2d sec., polit. officer Am. embassy, Tunis, 1961-63; counselor, dep. chief mission Am. embassy, Lome, 1965-68; dir. Office E. African Affairs, State Dept., 1968-69; U.S. ambassador to Chad, 1969-72, Republic Guinea, 1972-74, Costa Rica, San Jose, 1975-77: asst. sec. state, 1977-78; ambassador to Spain, 1978—. Served to 1st lt. AUS, 1945-49. Recipient Superior Honor award State Dept., 1966. Mem. Am. Fgn. Service Assn. Office: Am Embassy Spain APO New York NY 09285

TODOROVIC, PETAR, educator; b. Belgrade, Yugoslavia, Nov. 10, 1932; s. Nikola D. and Milica (Savic) T.; came to Can., 1973; B.S., Belgrade U., 1958, Ph.D., 1964; m. Zivadinka Babic, Dec. 31, 1964; children—Natasha, Michal, Stevan. Docent, Belgrade U., 1958-66; asso. prof. Colo. State U., 1966-73; research prof. probability and engring. U. Montreal (Que., Can.), 1973—; cons. AEA in Vienna, Inst. Devel. Water Resources, Belgrade, U.S. Dept. Agr., U.S. Geol. Survey, UNESCO. NSF grantee, 1971-73; Nat. Research Council Can. grantee, 1974—. Mem. Inst. Math. Stats., Am. Geophys. Union, N.Y. Acad. Sci., Math. Assn. Am. Contbr. articles to sci. jours. Home: 5 Vincent D Indy Ave Outremont PQ N2V 2S7 Canada Office: 2500 Ave Marie Guyard Montreal PQ H3C 3A7 Canada

TODRANK, GUSTAVE HERMAN, educator; b. Huntingburg, Ind., Apr. 9, 1924; s. Christian William and Lillian Catherine (Ahrens) T.; B.A., DePauw U., 1948; S.T.B., Boston U., 1951, Ph.D. (Boston U. Alumni fellow), 1956; m. Elizabeth Chalmers, June 25, 1949; children—Stephen Knight, Josephine. Ordained to ministry United Ch. Christ, 1951; minister North Congl. Ch., Newton, Mass., 1951-56; mem. faculty Colby Coll., Waterville, Maine, 1956—, prof. philosophy and religion, 1970—. Served with USAAF, 1943-46. Mem. Am. Acad. Religion, Am. Soc. Christian Ethics, Am. Philos. Assn., Phi Beta Kappa. Author: The Secular Search for a New Christ, 1969; also articles, book revs. Home: 38 Pleasant St Waterville ME 04901

TOEPFER, LOUIS ADELBERT, univ. pres.; b. Sheboygan, Wis., Aug. 31, 1919; s. Albert and Laura (Reed) T.; B.A., Beloit Coll., 1940; LL.B., Harvard U., 1947; m. Alice Mary Willy, Aug. 7, 1942; children—Thomas Michael, Anthony, Daniel, Andrew, John. Asst. dean Law Sch. Harvard U., 1947-56, sec., 1956-59, vice dean, 1959-66, dir. admissions, 1947-66, mem. faculty, 1959-66, dean, prof. law Case Western Res. U., Cleve., 1966-71, pres., 1971—. Mem. Ct. Nisi Prius. Cleve. Bar Assn., Phi Beta Kappa. Home: Route 3 Chagrin Falls OH 44022 Office: Presidents Office Case Western Reserve U Cleveland OH 44106

TOFANY, VINCENT LEON, safety council exec.; b. Rochester, N.Y., Dec. 16, 1926; s. Ezra B. and Mary I. (Roberts) T.; student St. Bonaventure U., 1947-49; LL.B., Albany Law Sch., 1952; m. Jane Truax, June 30, 1951; children—Pamela, Mary Ann, John, Edward, Cynthia. Admitted to N.Y. State bar, 1952, practiced in Rochester; asst. dist. atty. Monroe County (N.Y.), 1954-57; town atty. Greece, N.Y., 1957-60, town supr., 1960-65; mem., majority leader Monroe County Bd. Suprs., Rochester, 1963-65; N.Y. State Commr. Motor Vehicles, 1967-73; dir. pres. Nat. Safety Council Chgo-, 1973—. Mem. adv. council Nat. Motor Vehicle Safety, 1971-74. Vice-pres. bd. dirs. Muscular Dystrophy Assn.; trustee Daytop Village Found., Inc., 1971—. Served with USMCR, 1944-47; PTO. Mem. ASTM (dir. 1974—), Am. Trauma Soc. (dir. 1974—), Nat. Acad. Scis. (mem. hwy. research bd. com. on motor vehicles and traffic safety), Internat. Assn. Chiefs Police, NCCJ (dir.), Am. Legion, VFW, Knights of Equity. K.C., Elk. Office: 444 N Michigan Ave Chicago IL 60611*

TOFFLER, ALVIN, author; b. N.Y.C., Oct. 4, 1928; s. Sam and Rose (Albaum) T.; A.B., N.Y. U., 1949; LL.D. (hon.), U. Western Ont.; Litt.D. (hon.), U. Cin., Miami U.; D.Sc. (hon.), Rensselaer Poly. Inst.; Litt.D. (hon.), Ripon Coll.; m. Adelaide Elizabeth Farrell, Apr. 29, 1950; 1 dau., Karen. Washington corr. various newspapers, mags., 1957-58; asso. editor Fortune, 1959-61; mem. faculty New Sch. for Social Research, 1965-67; vis. scholar Russell Sage Found., 1969-70; vis. prof. Cornell U., Ithaca, N.Y., 1969. Cons. Rockefeller Bros. Fund., Inst. for Future, Am. Tel. & Tel. Co., Ednl. Facilities Labs., Inc., others. Trustee Antioch U.; bd. govs. Internat. Inst. Stress; advisory bd. Center Govt. Responsibility, Inst. Alternative Futures, Nat. Alliance for Optional Parenthood, Nat. Self-Help Clearinghouse, Internat. Commn. Futuribles, Nevis Inst. Recipient Nat. Council for Advancement Ednl. Writing award, 1969; McKinsey Found. Book award, 1970; Prix du Meilleur Livre Etranger, 1972. Author: The Culture Consumers, 1964; Future Shock, 1970; The Eco-Spasm Report, 1975. Editor: Schoolhouse in the City, 1968; The Futurists, 1972; Learning for Tomorrow, 1974. Contbg. editor Art News. Contbr. articles to nat. mags., profl. jours. Address: Washington CT 06793

TOGNONI, HALE CHRISTOPHER, mineral devel. cons., lawyer, engr.; b. Preston, Nev., Apr. 16, 1921; s. Joseph Russell and Ina B. (Cates) T.; student Va. Mil. Inst., 1943-44, Colo. Sch. Mines, summer 1947; B.S. in Geol. Engring., U. Nev., 1948; law student Am. U., 1950-52; J.D., U. Idaho, 1953; m. George-Ann Neudeck, Mar. 13, 1947; children—Becky Lou, Brian Hale, David Quentin, Sandra-Ann, Jeffrey R. Foreman, Molina sect. New Idria Quicksilver Mining Co. (Calif.), 1940-41; geol. asst. U.S. Geol. Survey, Steamboat Springs, Nev., 1946-48; engr., geologist Anaconda Copper Mining Co., Butte, Mont., also Darwin, Calif., 1948-50; staff asst. Carnegie Inst. Tech., Dept. Terrestrial Magnetism, Washington, 1950; hwy. testing engr. Corps Engrs., Ft. Belvoir, 1951; geologist Magna Mine, Superior, Ariz., 1953; asst. dir. research Ariz. Legislative Council, 1953-54; state mineral examiner Ariz. Land Dept., 1954-55; in pvt. practice as lawyer, also cons. engr., Phoenix, 1954—; partner law firm Tognoni & Pugh and predecessor firms, 1956-71; lectr. engring. law Ariz. State U., 1962—. Pres. Multiple Use Inc., Mineral Econs. Corp., Minerals Trust Corp., v.p., dir. Gunsight Mining Co., Mineral Services Corp., Tognoni Fine Arts Inc., Wollastonite Copper Corp., Tonto Basin Uranium Corp. Chmn. Ariz. State Land Law Study Com., 1954-56; sec. Ariz. Council for Edn., 1957-58; mem. Flood Protection Improvement Com. representing Maricopa County, 1957-59; chmn. Gov.'s Com. on Arid Lands, 1959-60. Served to 1st lt., C.E., AUS, 1942-46. Mem. Nat. Soc. Profl. Engrs., Ariz. Soc. Profl. Engrs. (sec. Central chpt. 1958-60, pres., 1961, chmn. legislative com. 1959-68, state pres. 1968-69, nat. dir. 1970-71), Am., Ariz., Maricopa County bar assns., Oil and Gas Assn. (pres. 1969), Am. Inst. Mining and Metall. Engrs. (chmn. Maricopa subsect. 1975). Club: Kiva. Home: 1525 W Northern Ave Phoenix AZ 85021 Office: 100 W Clarendon Ave Phoenix AZ 85013

TOKSÖZ, MEHMET NAFI, geophysicist; b. Antakya, Turkey, Apr. 18, 1934; s. Mahmut and Nazime (Taylan) T.; came to U.S., 1954, naturalized, 1973; B.S., Colo. Sch. Mines, 1958; M.S., Calif. Inst. Tech., 1960, Ph.D., 1963; m. Helena Terzian, Aug. 9, 1969. Postdoctoral research fellow Calif. Inst. Tech., 1963-65; mem. faculty Mass. Inst. Tech., 1965—, prof. geophysics, 1971—, dir. Wallace Geophys. Obs., 1975—; cons. NASA, also indsl. research labs. Recipient Exceptional Sci. Achievement medal NASA, 1976. Mem. Am. Geophys. Union, Seismological Soc. Am., Am. Soc. Exploration Geophysicists, AAAS, Sigma Xi. Contbr. profl. jours. Home: 362 Memorial Dr Cambridge MA 02139 Office: Mass Inst Tech 54-518 Cambridge MA 02139

TOKUHATA, GEORGE KAZUNARI, educator, health scientist; b. Matsue, Japan, Aug. 25, 1924; s. Yujiro and Hama (Watanabe) T.; B.A., Keio U., Tokyo, 1950; M.A., Miami U., Oxford, Ohio, 1953; Ph.D., State U. Iowa, 1956; D.P.H., Johns Hopkins U., 1962; m. Sumiko Matsui, June 10, 1949; came to U.S., 1950, naturalized, 1959. Research asst. Scripps Found. for Population Research, Miami U., 1951-53; instr. State U. Iowa, 1954-56; research scientist Mich. Dept. Mental Health, Lansing, 1956-59; postdoctoral fellow Johns Hopkins U. Med. Center, Balt., 1959-61; spl. asst. div. dir. div. chronic diseases USPHS, Washington, 1961-62, prin. epidemiologist, 1962-63; asso. prof. preventive medicine U. Tenn., Memphis, 1963-67; dir. div. research and biostats. Pa. Dept. Health, Harrisburg, 1967—; asso. prof. community medicine Temple U., 1967—; prof. epidemiology and biostats. U. Pitts., 1967—; cons. public health research. Fellow Am. Public Health Assn., Am. Sociol. Assn.; mem. Soc. Epidemiologic Research, N.Y. Acad. Scis. Contbr. numerous articles to profl. jours. Home: 410 Rupley Rd Camp Hill PA 17011 Office: PO Box 90 Harrisburg PA 17120

TOLAND, JAMES ALFRED LEWIS, ret. hosp. adminstr.; b. Rayland, O., Apr. 29, 1908; s. Rufus Addison and Olive Lydia (Hutton) T.; A.B., Marietta Coll., 1929; M.D., U. Cin., 1934; m. Anna Louise Bell, June 5, 1935; children—Martha (Mrs. Frederic W. Oakhill), Sally (Mrs. Samuel A. Moore). Intern, Ohio Valley Gen. Hosp., Wheeling, W.Va., 1933-34; practice medicine, Jewett, Ohio, 1934-45, Cambridge, Ohio, 1945-67; staff physician Cambridge State Hosp., 1967-72, supt., 1972—. Mem. Am., Ohio med. assns., Guernsey County Med. Soc. Mason, Rotarian. Club: Cambridge Country. Home: 731 N 8th St Cambridge OH 43725

TOLAND, JOHN WILLARD, author, historian; b. La Crosse, Wis., June 29, 1912; s. Ralph and Helen Chandler (Snow) T.; B.A., Williams Coll., 1936, L.H.D., 1968; student Yale Drama Sch., 1936-37; L.H.D., U. Alaska, 1977; m. Toshiko Matsumura, Mar. 12, 1960; 1 dau., Tamiko; children by previous marriage—Diana, Marcia. Author: Ships in the Sky, 1957; Battle: the Story of the Bulge, 1959; But Not in Shame (Best Book Fgn. Affairs award Overseas Press Club), 1961; The Dillinger Days, 1963; The Flying Tigers, 1963; The Last 100 Days (Best Book Fgn. Affairs citation Overseas Press Club, 1966; The Battle of the Bulge, 1966; The Rising Sun (Van Wyck Brooks award for non-fiction, Best Book Fgn. Affairs award Overseas Press Club, Pulitzer prize for non-fiction), 1970: Adolf Hitler (Best Book Fgn. Affairs award Overseas Press Club, Gold medal Nat. Soc. Arts and Letters), 1976; Hitler, The Pictorial Documentary of His Life, 1978; also short stories. Mem. adv. council Nat. Archives. Mem. Authors Guild, Accademia del Mediterraneo. Home: 1 Long Ridge Rd Danbury CT 06810

TOLAND, WILLIAM GIPSY, univ. adminstr.; b. D'Lo, Miss., Nov. 12, 1922; s. William Otis and Quinnie (Grubbs) T.; B.A., Millsaps Coll., 1947; M.A., U. Miss., 1949; Ph.D., U. N.C., 1967; certificate mgmt. devel. Harvard, 1973; m. Eveline Bush, Oct. 31, 1942; children—Carole (Mrs. Charles Tatum), Judith Eveline (Mrs. Harry Houchens). Athletic dir., coach, social studies instr. Anding Central High Sch., Bentonia, Miss., 1947-48; asst. prof. polit. sci. Baylor U., 1953-55, prof. philosophy, 1957—, dean Grad. Sch., 1969—, asso. dean univ., grad. dean, 1973-77; grad. dean, asst. v.p., 1977-79, asst. v.p., dean Coll. Arts and Scis., 1979—; asst. prof. philosophy U. Md., 1955-56. Vice pres. Conf. So. Grad. Schs., 1971-72, pres., 1972-73; pres. Assn. Tex. Grad. Schs., 1974-75. Tng. officer cons. Peace Corps, 1962-64, 66; mem. exec. bd. Southwest Alliance for Latin Am., 1966-70; Air Force Res. Officer Tng. Corps, asst. prof. air sci. in polit. geography Baylor U., 1951-55; mem. Waco Model Cities Commn., 1968-69; mem. adv. bd. Intercultural Edn. Found., 1966-67; bd. dirs. Econ. Opportunities Advancement Corp., 1968-70; mem. exec. bd. Inner City Ministry, 1975-77; mem. Tex. Rangers Commemorative Commn., 1971-76; mem. Tex. Com. on Humanities and Pub. Policy. Served with USAAF, 1943-46, USAF, 1951-57. Decorated Commendation medal, Air medal with 2 oak leaf clusters; recipient decoration for Disting. Civilian Service, U.S. Army, 1979. Danforth Found. grantee, 1959-60; Kenan fellow philosophy, 1949-51. Mem. Am., Southwestern philos. assns., So. Soc. Philosophy and Psychology, AAUP (pres. Baylor U. chpt. 1963-64), Omicron Delta Kappa, Phi Sigma Tau, Kappa Alpha, Pi Sigma Alpha. Baptist (deacon 1961—). Editorial bd. Jour. Ch. and State, 1961—, book rev. editor, 1972-75. Contbr. articles to profl. jours. Home: 2631 Glendale St Waco TX 76710

TOLBERT, BERT MILLS, educator, biochemist; b. Twin Falls, Idaho, Jan. 15, 1921; s. Ed. and Helen (Mills) T.; student Idaho State U., 1938-40; B.S., U. Calif. at Berkeley, 1942, Ph.D., 1945; postgrad. Fed. Inst. Tech., Zurich, Switzerland, 1952-53; m. Anne Grace Zweifler, July 20, 1959; children—Elizabeth Dawn, Margaret Anne, Caroline Joan, Sarah Helen. Chemist, Lawrence Radiation Lab., Berkeley, 1944-57; faculty U. Colo., Boulder, 1957—, prof., 1961—; vis. prof. IAEA, Buenos Aires, Argentina, 1961-62. Biophysicist, U.S. AEC, Washington, 1967-68; cons. pvt. cos, govt. agys. Fellow AAAS; mem. Am. Chem. Soc., Am. Soc. Biol. Chemists, Radiation Research Soc., Soc. for Exptl. Biology and Medicine. Author: (with others) Isotopic Carbon, 1948; contbr. articles to profl. jours. Research on phys. organic chemistry, including use of isotopes in chemistry and biology, radiation chemistry, radiation effects in protein, intermediary metabolism, metabolism of ascorbic acid, nutritional role, instrumentation in radioactivity. Home: 444 Kalmia Ave Boulder CO 80302

TOLBERT, CHARLES MADDEN, educator; b. Union, Miss., Sept. 14, 1922; s. Burton Ethel and Eula (Madden) T.; B.A., Miss. Coll., 1948; M.A., U. N.C., 1954; Ph.D., La. State U., 1958; m. Rosa Jean Furr, June 2, 1949; 1 son, Charles Madden II. Instr. sociology Miss. Coll., 1949-54; research asst. Inst. Population Research, La. State U., 1956-57; mem. faculty Baylor U., 1957—, prof. sociology, 1960—, chmn. dept., 1960—; vis. prof. La. State U., summer 1963. Bd. dirs. Heart of Tex. chpt. Am. Nat. Red Cross, 1974—. Served with AUS, 1943-46. Fellow Tex. Acad. Sci. (v.p. social scis. sect. 1972); mem. Am., Southwestern (sec.-treas. 1972-74, membership v.p. 1975-76, 1st v.p.-program chairperson 1976-77, pres. 1977-78) sociol. assns., So. Sociol. Soc., Southwestern Social Sci. Assn. (program chmn. 1978-79), AAUP (pres. Baylor U. chpt. 1962-63), Waco Heritage Soc. (bd. dirs. Fort House 1975—). Asso. editor Jour. Ch. and State, 1974-78. Home: 5206 Lake Arrowhead Dr Waco TX 76710

TOLBERT, JAMES R., III, diversified mfg. and service co. exec.; b. Amarillo, Tex., Apr. 29, 1935; s. James R. and Mary (Noble) T.; student Stanford U., 1953-55; B.A., Okla. U., 1957; M.B.A., Stanford U., 1959; m. Elizabeth McMahan, Dec. 26, 1956; children—James R. IV, Cannon Miles, Elizabeth Nelson, Lee Mitchener. Vice pres. acquisitions Mid-Am. Corp., 1959-64; pres. James R. Tolbert & Assos., Inc., 1964-69; chmn. bd., treas., co-founder Holden Tolbert & Co., 1967—; sr. partner, co-founder Resource Analysis and Mgmt. Group, 1969—; trustee in bankruptcy Four Seasons Nursing Centers of Am., Inc., 1971-72; pres., treas., chmn. bd. Anta Corp., Oklahoma City, 1972—; dir. Pepsi-Cola Bottling Co., TIERCO; trustee Kerr Consol., Inc., Capitol Steel Corp. Bd. dirs. McGee Eye Inst.; chmn. adv. bd. Sch. Bus. Okla. U.; trustee Westminster Day Sch., Westminster Presbyn. Ch.; pres. Coalition for Transp. Choices, 1976—; vice chmn. Central Okla. Transp. and Parking Authority, 1966-75. Recipient Exec. Leadership of Year award Oklahoma City U., 1975. Mem. Young Pres.'s Orgn. Democrat. Home: 2321 Belleview Terr Oklahoma City OK 73112 Office: 2400 First National Center Oklahoma City OK 73102

TOLEDANO, RALPH DE, columnist, author, photographer; b. Internat. Zone of Tangier, Aug. 17, 1916; student Fieldston Sch., N.Y.C., 1928-34; B.A., Columbia Coll., 1938; m. Nora Romaine, July 6, 1938 (div. 1968); children—James, Paul. Founder, co-editor Jazz Info., 1938-39; asso. editor The New Leader, 1941-43; editor The Standard, 1946; mng. editor Plain Talk, 1946-47; pub. dir. Dress Joint Bd., Internat. Ladies Garment Workers Union, 1947-48; asst. editor Newsweek, 1948, nat. reports editor, 1950-60; Washington corr., 1956-60; syndicated columnist King Features, 1960-71, Nat. News Research Syndicate, 1971-74, Copley News Service, 1974—; chief Washington Bur., Taft Broadcasting Co., 1960-61; contbg. editor Nat. Rev., 1960—; pres. Nat. News-Research, 1960—, Anthem Books, 1970; editor-in-chief Washington World, 1961-62; mem. 20th Century Fund Task Force on Freedom Press, 1971-72. Served in OSS and as info. specialist, AUS, 1943-46. Recipient Freedoms Found. award, 1950, 61, 74; Americanism award VFW, 1953. Mem. Internat. Mark Twain Soc. (chevalier), Sigma Delta Chi. Clubs: Dutch Treat, Nat. Press. Author: Seeds of Treason, 1950; Spies, Dupes and Diplomats, 1952; Day of Reckoning, 1955; Nixon, 1956; Lament for a Generation, 1960; The Greatest Plot in History, 1963; The Winning Side, 1963; The Goldwater Story, 1964; RFK: The Man Who Would be President, 1967; America, I-Love-You, 1968; One Man Alone: Richard M. Nixon, 1969; Claude Kirk: Man and Myth, 1970; Little Cesar, 1971; J. Edgar Hoover: The Man in His Time, 1973; Hit and Run: The Ralph Nader Story, 1975; Let Our Cities Burn, 1975; Poems: You & I, 1978; Devil Take Him, 1979; editor: Frontiers of Jazz, 1947; co-editor: The Conservative Papers, 1964; editor-in-chief Political Success, 1968-69; contbr. to nat. mags. Office: Nat Press Bldg Washington DC 20045. *Words have been my legacy, and I have mined that precious metal since I was a boy. Writing--fashioning a good sentence, a good poem, a few lines that clarify or strike fire--that has been my life. This sounds pretentious in a day when writing is a business, not a vocation. But this is how I was brought up by a father who believed that the best was hardly enough. Most writers, myself included, leave a mark on water. But if that mark is made with honesty, if it is an expression of man's dignity, then that is a beginning. If for however briefly it communicates, that is success.*

TOLEDO, JOSE VICTOR, lawyer, judge; b. Arecibo, P.R., Aug. 14, 1931; s. Jose M. and Isabel M. (Toledo) T.; B.A., U. Fla., 1950; B.L., U. P.R., 1955; m. Clara J. Buscaglia, July 9, 1955; children—Jose Rafael, Carlos Jose, Clara Isabel, Sonia Mercedes, Maria Isabel. Admitted to P.R. bar, Fed. bar, 1956; judge U.S. Dist. Ct., Dist. P.R., 1970—, now chief judge; asst. U.S. atty., Dist. P.R., 1960-61; partner firm Rivera Zayas, Rivera Cestero & Rua, San Juan, P.R., 1961-63, Segurola, Romero & Toledo, 1963-67, Toledo & Cordova, 1967-70; Mem., sec. P.R. Civil Rights Commn., 1969-70; chmn. mcpl. grievances com., San Juan, 1969-70; mem. com. adminstrn. criminal law Judicial Conf. U.S. Served with JAG Corps, AUS, 1956-60. Mem. Exchange Club (pres. 1964-65). Home: 1917 Platanillo St Santa Maria San Juan PR 00927 Office: care US Courthouse Old San Juan PR 00904

TOLENTINO, SHIRLEY ANN, judge, lawyer; b. Jersey City, Feb. 2, 1944; d. Jack and Mattie Theresa (Kelly) Hayes; A.B., Coll. of St. Elizabeth, Convent, N.J., 1965; J.D., Seton Hall U., 1971; postgrad. N.Y. U., 1972—; m. Ernesto Tolentino, Aug. 31, 1967; children—Ana-Ramona, Candida. Tchr. Latin, English, Coll. of St. Elizabeth, 1965-67, 68-69; asst. project dir. Upward Bound, 1967-68, 69-71; admitted to N.J. bar, 1972; with legal dept. VA, Newark, 1972; dep. atty. gen. N.J., Trenton, 1972-76; judge Municipal Ct., Jersey City, N.J., 1976—. Counsel div. youth and family services Jersey City br. N.A.A.C.P., 1974-75. Mem. Am., Fed., N.J., Garden State bar assns., Delta Sigma Theta. Home: 41 Gifford Ave Jersey City NJ 07304 Office: Municipal Ct Jersey City NJ 07306

TOLER, GEORGE HERBERT, utility exec.; b. Richmond, Ind., Mar. 14, 1938; s. George Herbert and Madelaine (Lahr) T.; B.A., Miami U., Oxford, Ohio, 1959; M.B.A., Bowling Green (Ohio) State U., 1964; m. Constance L. McFann, Jan. 9, 1977; children by previous marriage—Eric, Leanne. With Marathon Oil Co., Findlay, Ohio, 1959-77, asst. treas., 1973-77; treas. Ariz. Public Service Co., Phoenix, 1977—; part-time instr. econs. Bowling Green State U., 1968-72. Served with AUS, 1962. Mem. Assn. Corp. Growth, Edison Electric Inst. Republican. Club: University. Office: PO Box 21666 Phoenix AZ 85036

TOLER, JAMES LARKIN, real estate co. exec.; b. Plano, Tex., Feb. 21, 1935; s. Allen Berryman and Ruth Olivia (Back) T.; B.A., Baylor U., 1957; M.A., East Tex. State U., 1962; m. Sarah Ruth Baker, June 25, 1955; children—Amy Ruth, James Larkin, Tobin Daniel, Nancy Jane. Tchr., Dallas Pub. Schs., 1957-59, Highland Park Schs., Dallas, 1959-62, Garland (Tex.) Pub. Schs., 1962-64; pres. Jim Toler & Co., Garland, 1964—; chmn. bd. Century Bank & Trust Co. of Garland; dir. Lakewood Bank & Trust Co., Dallas. Pres., Garland Homebuilders. Mayor, Garland, 1966-70; del. Nat. Democratic Conv., 1968. Recipient Hugh Prather award for outstanding homebuilder in Dallas County, 1973; named Garland Realtor of Year, 1965. Mem. Garland C. of C. (pres. 1972). Club: Garland Civitan. Home: 1800 Country Club Circle Garland TX 75041 Office: 200 Century Bank Bldg Garland TX 75040

TOLER, LOOMIS HARVEY, educator; b. nr. Smithfield, N.C., Sept. 25, 1933; s. Jimmie Harvey and Viola (Hartley) T.; B.S., Atlantic Christian Coll., 1960; M.B.A., La. State U., 1961, Ph.D., 1963; m. Emma Lucille Griswold, Oct. 16, 1954; 1 dau., Sandra Elaine. Driver license examiner N.C. Dept. Motor Vehicles, 1955-59; prof. acctg. Miss. State U., 1963—, head dept., 1967-79. Served with USN, 1951-54. NDEA fellow, 1960-63. Mem. Am. Acctg. Assn., Nat. Assn. Accts. (pres. chpt. 1974-75, nat. dir. 1979-81), Beta Alpha Psi, Alpha Kappa Psi. Home: 706 Cypress Rd Starkville MS 39759 Office: PO Box 724 Mississippi State MS 39762

TOLES, EDWARD BERNARD, judge; b. Columbus, Ga., Sept. 17, 1909; s. Alex and Virginia Frances (Luke) T.; A.B., U. Ill., 1932, postgrad. Law Sch., 1932-34; J.D., Loyola U., Chgo., 1936; m. Susan Evelyn Echols, Jan. 24, 1944; 1 son, Edward Bernard. Admitted to Ill. bar, 1936; practiced in Chgo., 1936-69; asst. atty. U.S. Housing Authority, 1939-40; asst. gen. counsel, war corr. ETO, Chgo. Defender, 1943-45; U.S. bankruptcy judge No. Dist. Ill., Chgo., 1969—. Recipient U.S. War Dept. award for services as war corr., 1947. Mem. Am., Fed., Nat. (Barrister of Year award 1960, C.F. Stradford award, columnist Bench and Bar Bull.), Chgo. (bd. mgrs. 1969-70), Cook County (Edward H. Wright award 1962, pres. 1960-62), 7th Circuit, World Peace Through Law bar assns., Am. Judicature Soc., Nat. Conf. Bankruptcy Judges, Alpha Phi Alpha, Omega Psi Phi (Ode to Excellence award 1963). Democrat. Author: Chicago Negro Judges, 1959; Negro Federal Judges, 1960; Negro Lawyer in Crisis, 1966; Black Lawyers and Judges in the U.S., 1971; also articles. Editor: Cook County Bar News, 1961-63. Columnist, Bench and Bar, Nat. Bar Assn. Bull., 1968-75. Home: 4800 Chicago Beach Dr Chicago IL 60615 Office: US Courthouse 219 S Dearborn St Chicago IL 60604

TOLK, ROY, utilities exec.; b. Gage, Okla., Apr. 9, 1916; s. Nicholas and Marie (Molenaar) T.; B.S., U. Tex., 1938; m. Mary Ester Hodges, Nov. 25, 1937 (dec. Mar. 1979); children—Alice Jean Tolk Cheatham, Kenneth Cornelius, Keith Michael; m. 2d, Anna Mary Murphy, Nov. 9, 1979; 1 stepdau., Mary Gail Murphy. Draftsman, Marsh Electric Supply Co., Amarillo, Tex., 1938; with Southwestern Pub. Service Co., Amarillo, 1938—, exec. v.p., 1960-67, pres., 1967-76, chmn. bd., chief exec. officer, 1972—; dir. First Nat. Bank Amarillo, Am. Smelting and Refining Co., Fort Worth & Denver Ry. Co., Southwestern Pub. Service Co. Mem. Study Com. for Engring. Edn. in Tex. Chmn. bd. trustees St. Anthony's Hosp.; bd. dirs. Tex. Research League, Tex. Atomic Energy Research Found. Named Distinguished Grad., U. Tex. at Austin, 1972; Man of Year, Amarillo Globe-News, 1974. Registered profl. engr., Tex. Clubs: Amarillo, One Hundred (charter mem., dir.), Amarillo Country (Amarillo), Masons. Home: 1607 Austin St Amarillo TX 79102 Office: PO Box 1261 Amarillo TX 79170

TOLL, DANIEL ROGER, fin. services co. exec.; b. Denver, Dec. 3, 1927; s. Oliver W. and Merle D'Aubigne (Sampson) T.; A.B. magna cum laude, Princeton U., 1949; M.B.A. with distinction (Baker scholar), Harvard U., 1955; m. Sue Andersen, June 15, 1963; children—Daniel Andersen, Matthew Mitchell. Asst. mgr. product supply and distbn. Deep Rock Oil Corp., 1949-51; with Helmerich & Payne, Tulsa, 1955-64, fin. v.p., 1961-64; treas., dir. corp. planning Sunray DX Oil Co., Tulsa, 1964-66, v.p. corp. planning and devel., 1966-68; v.p. Sun Oil Co., 1969; sr. v.p. fin., dir., mem. exec. com. Walter E. Heller Internat. Corp., Chgo., 1970—; exec. v.p. Walter E. Heller & Co., Chgo., 1976—. Vice chmn., mem. budget com. Tulsa Community Chest, 1964-66; v.p., dir. Tulsa Opera, 1960-69; dir., chmn. play choosing and casting coms. Tulsa Little Theatre, 1963-69; chief crusader Chgo. Crusade Mercy, 1972—; chmn. fin. and profl. fund raising Chgo. area council Boy Scouts Am., 1974-76, bd. dirs., 1976—, pack master Kenilworth Cub Scouts, 1972-75; mem. Sch. Bd. Dist. 38, Kenilworth, Ill., 1975—, pres., 1978—, also chmn. fin. com. Served to lt. (j.g.) USNR, 1951-52. Mem. Phi Beta Kappa. Clubs: Union League, Economic, Harvard Bus. Sch. (past pres. local chpt., dir. 1971—) (Chgo.); Indian Hill (Winnetka). Home: 125 Abingdon Ave Kenilworth IL 60043 Office: 105 W Adams St Chicago IL 60690

TOLL, JACK BENJAMIN, govt. ofcl.; b. Denver, Nov. 25, 1925; s. John B. and Vera (Calabrese) T.; J.D., U. Denver, 1947; postgrad. Westminster Law Sch., Denver, 1950; m. Jean Small, Dec. 31, 1946; children—Robert John, Barbara, Susan Jean, Jack Edward, Carol. Admitted to Colo. bar, 1950; inland marine mgr. Gen. Adjustment Bur., Denver, 1949-53; dir. legal dept. Denver Chgo. Trucking Co., 1953-65, sec., 1965-69; dir. D.C. Internat., Inc., Denver, 1966-69, v.p., 1967-69, sec., 1965-69; gen. counsel Denver Urban Renewal Authority, 1969-71; regional counsel Dept. Housing and Urban Devel., 1971—; judge Jefferson County, Colo., 1955-59. Mem. Am., Colo., Denver bar assns. Republican. Home: 14020n Elderberry Rd Golden CO 80401 Office: 2700 Executive Tower 1405 Curtis St Denver CO 80202

TOLL, JOHN SAMPSON, univ. pres.; b. Denver, Oct. 25, 1923; s. Oliver Wolcott and Merle d'Aubigne (Sampson) T.; B.S. with highest honors, Yale, 1944, A.M., Princeton, 1948, Ph.D., 1952; D. Sc., U. Md., 1973, U. Wroclaw (Poland), 1975; LL.D., Adelphi U., 1978; m. Deborah Ann Taintor, Oct. 24, 1970; children—Dacia Merle Sampson, Caroline Taintor. Mng. editor, acting chmn. Yale Sci. mag., 1943-44; with Princeton, 1946-49, Proctor fellow, 1948-49; Friends of Elementary Particle Theory Research grantee for study in France 1950; theoretical physicist Los Alamos Sci. Lab. 1950-51; staff mem., asso. dir. Project Matterhorn Forrestal Research Center, Princeton, 1951-53; prof. chmn. physics and astronomy U. Md., 1953-65; pres., prof. physics State U. N.Y. at Stony Brook, 1965-78; pres., prof. physics U. Md., College Park, 1978—; 1st dir. State U. N.Y. Chancellor's Panel on Univ. Purposes, 1970. Physics cons. to editorial staff Nat. Sci. Tchrs. Assn., 1957-61; U.S. del., head sci. secretariat Internat. Conf. on High Energy Physics, 1960; mem-at-large U.S. Nat. Com. for Internat. Union of Pure and Applied Physics, 1960-63; chmn. research adv. com. on electrophysics to NASA, 1961-65; mem. gov. Md. Sci. Resources Adv. bd. 1963-65; mem., also chmn. NSF adv. panel for physics, 1964-67; mem. N.Y. Gov.'s Adv. Com. Atomic Energy, 1966-68; mem. commn. plans and objectives higher edn. Am. Council Edn., 1966-69; mem. N.Y. Adv. Council for Advancement Indsl. Research and Devel., 1970—; mem. Hall of Records Commn., 1979; bd. dirs. Dairy Council, 1979—. Recipient Benjamin Barge prize in math. Yale, 1943, also George Beckwith medal for Proficiency in Astronomy, 1944; Outstanding citizen award City of Denver, 1958,

Outstanding Tchr. award U. Md. Men's League, 1965, Nat. Golden Plate award Am. Acad. Achievement, 1968. John Simon Guggenheim Meml. Found. fellow Inst. Theoretical Physics U. Copenhagen, U. Lund (Sweden). Fellow Am. Phys. Soc.; mem. Am. Assn. Physics Tchrs., AAUP, Fedn. Am. Scientists (chmn. 1954), Washington Acad. Scis., Philos. Soc. Washington, Assn. Higher Edn., Nat. Sci. Tchrs. Assn., Yale Engring. Assn., Phi Beta Kappa, Sigma Xi (sci. achievement award U. Md. chpt. 1965), Phi Kappa Phi, Sigma Pi Sigma. Contbr. articles to sci. jours. Research on elementary particle theory; scattering. Address: U Md Adelphi MD 20783. *Throughout my life I have tried mainly to do whatever seemed most important and useful to others.*

TOLL, MAYNARD JOY, lawyer; b. Los Angeles, Sept. 11, 1906; s. Charles Hulbert and Eleanor Margaret (Joy) T.; A.B., U. Calif. at Berkeley, 1927; LL.B. magna cum laude, Harvard U., 1930; LL.D., Occidental Coll., 1963, Northrop U., 1975; m. Ethel B. Coleman, Aug. 16, 1929; children—Arline T. (Mrs. Milburne E. Kensinger), Deborah (Mrs. Russell S. Reynolds, Jr.), Janet (Mrs. Garrison H. Davidson, Jr.), Maynard Joy, Roger Coleman. Admitted to Calif. bar, 1930, since practiced in Los Angeles; partner firm O'Melveny & Myers, 1940—. Dir. Western Fed. Savs. & Loan Assn., Earle M. Jorgensen Co., Russell Reynolds Assos. Inc. Chmn. Los Angeles Community Chest campaign, 1953; trustee Los Angeles City Bd. Edn., 1944-49, pres., 1947-48. Trustee Los Angeles County Bar Found., 1965-77, Los Angeles County Mus. Art, 1962-78, Hollywood Turf Club Asso. Charities, John R. and Dora Haynes Found., Hosp. Good Samaritan, Voluntary Action Center; bd. dirs. Automobile Club So. Calif., 1970—, v.p., 1971-73, chmn. bd., 1973-75; bd. dirs. Am. Automobile Assn., 1972-74; mem. exec. council Nat. Conf. Bar Presidents, 1968-70; bd. dirs. Council Legal Edn. Profl. Responsibility, 1973—, Council on Founds., 1976-78. Fellow Am. Coll. Probate Counsel, Am. Bar Found. (dir., pres. 1974-76); mem. Am., Los Angeles County (pres. 1963) bar assns., Inst. Jud. Adminstrn., Nat. Legal Aid and Defender Assn. (pres. 1966-70), State Bar Calif., Am. Judicature Soc. (chmn. bd. dirs. 1972-74), Calif. Alumni Assn. (past pres.). Clubs: Los Angeles, California, Town Hall (past pres.) (Los Angeles); Salt Air (Santa Monica, Calif.). Home: 414 S Irving Blvd Los Angeles CA 90020 Office: 611 W 6th St Los Angeles CA 90017

TOLLE, DONALD JAMES, educator; b. Roxbury, Kans., May 29, 1918; s. Edgar Earl and Sadie M. (Lott) T.; A.B., Fla. So. Coll.,, 1940; M.A., U. Fla., 1947; Ed.D., Fla. State U., 1957; m. Mary Alice McNeill, July 24, 1945; children—Donald MacDavid, Louise Margaret, Theresa Love. Tchr., Palmetto (Fla.) Jr.-Sr. High Sch., 1940-42, Winter Haven (Fla.) High Sch., 1946-47, Monticello (Fla.) Jr. High Sch. 1947-48; prin. Jefferson County High Sch., Monticello, also supervising prin. Monticello public schs. 1949-51; instr. St. Petersburg (Fla.) Jr. Coll., 1951-55, dean of men, 1953-58, dean instrn., 1958-66; dean acad. studies Fla. Jr. Coll., Jacksonville, 1966-67; asso. prof. higher edn., asso. dir. community coll. coop. internship program So. Ill. U., Carbondale, 1967-71, prof. higher edn., 1971—; vis. prof. Appalachian State U., summer 1964; acting prof. U. South Fla., 1965-66. Mem. Fla. Gov's Advisory Com. Law Enforcement Edn., 1964-66; mem. exec. com. Fla. Center for Edn. in Politics, 1958-66; cons. to several jr. colls. Served with USAAF, 1942-45. Mem. Am. Assn. Higher Edn., North Central Council Jr. Colls., Am. Assn. Community and Jr. Colls. (council univs. and colls.), Kappa Delta Pi, Phi Delta Kappa. Democrat. Methodist (mem. bd., chmn. edn. commn. 1959-61, trustee). Author books; contbr. articles to profl. jours. Home: 907 Skyline Dr Carbondale IL 62901

TOLLENAERE, LAWRENCE ROBERT, indsl. products co. exec.; b. Berwyn, Ill., Nov. 19, 1922; s. Cyrille and Modesta (Van Damme) T.; B.S. in Engring., Iowa State U., 1944, M.S. in Engring., 1949; M.B.A., U. So. Calif., 1969; LL.D., Claremont U. Center, 1977; m. Mary Hansen, Aug. 14, 1948; children—Elizabeth, Homer, Stephanie, Caswell Ann, Jennifer Mary. Time and motion engr. Aluminum Co. Am., Huntington Park, Calif., 1946-47; asst. prof. engring. Iowa State U., 1947-50; sales rep. Ameron (formerly Am. Pipe & Constrn. Co.), South Gate, Calif., 1950-53, spl. rep., Santiago, Chile, 1953-54, 2d v.p., div. mgr., Bogota, Colombia, 1955- 57, v.p., mgr., South Gate, Calif., 1958-63, v.p. corp. offices, Monterey Park, Calif., 1963-64, pres. 1965—, chief exec. officer, 1967—, also dir.; dir. Gifford-Hill-Am., Inc., Dallas, Avery Internat., Norris Industries, Los Angeles, Pacific Mut. Life Ins. Co., Los Angeles, Newhall Land & Farming Co., Valencia, Calif., Ralph M. Parsons Co., Pasadena, Calif. Bd. fellows Claremont U. Center; bd. govs. Iowa State U., Ames; bd. dirs. Beavers, pres., 1979; chmn. bd. overseers Henry E. Huntington Library, Art Galleries and Bot. Gardens. Served from ensign to lt. (j.g.) USNR, 1944-46. Mem. Soc. for Advancement Mgmt., Am. Water Works Assn., Mchts. and Mfrs. Assn. (chmn. bd. 1975), NAM (dir.), Newcomen Soc., Alpha Tau Omega. Clubs: California; San Gabriel (Calif.) Country; Jonathan (Los Angeles); Pauma Valley Country (Calif.); Confrerie des Chevaliers du Tastevin. Office: 4700 Ramona Blvd PO Box 3000 Monterey Park CA 91754

TOLLES, E. LEROY, lawyer; b. Winchester, Conn., Aug. 13, 1922; B.A. cum laude, Williams Coll., 1943; LL.B. cum laude, Harvard U., 1948; m. Martha Gregory, June 21, 1944; children—Stephen, Henry, Cynthia, Roy, James, Thomas. Admitted to Calif. bar, 1949; now mem. firm Munger, Tolles & Rickershauser, Los Angeles. Chmn. bd. student advisers Harvard U. Law Sch., 1947-48. Mem. Am., Los Angeles County bar assns., State Bar Calif. Home: 860 Oxford Rd San Marino CA 91108 Office: 616 S Flower St Los Angeles CA 90017

TOLLES, WALTER EDWIN, physicist; b. Moline, Ill., Feb. 1, 1916; s. Walter Edwin and Aileen (Sessions) T.; B.S., Antioch Coll., 1939; M.S., U. Minn., 1941; Ph.D., State U. N.Y., Bklyn., 1969; m. Gudrun Kercher, June 11, 1939; 1 dau., Mary Wesley. Asst., Kettering Found., Antioch Coll., 1937- 39; teaching asst. U. Minn., 1939-42; physicist div. war research Airborne Instruments Lab., Columbia, 1942-45; supr. Airborne Instruments Lab., Inc., 1945-54, head dept. med. and biol. physics, 1954-68; asso. prof. obstetrics and gynecology Coll. Medicine, State U. N.Y., Bklyn., 1969—; research magnetic techniques undersea warfare, spl. purpose radio receiving and transmitting systems, electronic countermeasures, high speed scanning systems measurement morphological and chem. properties microscopic objects, date handling systems, physiol. monitoring systems, clin. instrumentation, diagnostic computer methods. Bd. dirs. Inst. Oceanography and Marine Biology, 1959. Fellow N.Y. Acad. Scis. (sci. council 1965—), IEEE (chmn. profl. group bio-med. electronics 1959), AAAS; mem. Biophys. Soc., Am. Phys. Soc., Am. Soc. Limnology and Oceanography, Am. Soc. Cytology. Home: Lee Hwy Fairfield VA 24435

TOLLESON, JOHN CARTER, banker; b. Ennis, Tex., Aug. 16, 1948; s. Cecil H. and Frances Louise (Carter) T.; B.B.A., So. Meth. U., 1970; m. Debra June Stewart, Jan. 8, 1977; 1 son, John Carter. With Nat. Bank of Commerce, Dallas, 1969-75; sr. v.p. Mercantile Nat. Bank, Dallas, 1975-77; pres., chief exec. officer Am. Nat. Bank, Austin, Tex., 1977—; dir. Am. Bank, Affiliated Computer Services, Citizens Bank of Austin; sr. v.p. Mercantile Tex. Corp. Chmn. comml. div. United Way, 1977; bd. dirs. Capital Area United Way; mem. adv. bd. Brackenridge Hosp.; mem. exec. bd. Boy Scouts Am. Mem. Tex. Bankers Assn., Am. Inst. Bankers, Am. Bankers Assn., Austin C. of C. (dir., treas. 1978). Methodist. Clubs: Admirals, Headliners (exec. bd.). Office: PO Box 2266 Austin TX 78780

TOLLEY, AUBREY GRANVILLE, hosp. adminstr.; b. Lynchburg, Va., Nov. 15, 1924; student Duke, 1942-43; M.D., U. Va., Hosp., 1952; married. Intern, St. Elizabeths Hosp., Washington, 1952-53; asst. resident psychiatry U. Va. Hosp., Charlottesville, 1953-54; resident psychiatry VA Hosp., Roanoke, Va., 1954-56; instr. U. N.C. Sch. Medicine, 1956-61, asst. prof., 1961-66, clin. asst. prof. psychiatry, 1966-72, clin. asso. prof., 1972-76, clin. prof., 1976—; dir. psychotherapy Dorothea Dix Hosp., Raleigh, 1962-67, dir. hosp., 1973—; dir. resident tng. John Umstead Hosp., Butner, N.C., 1966-67; dir. profl. tng. and edn. N.C. Dept. Mental Health, Raleigh, 1967-72, asst. dir., 1972-73. Prin. investigator USPHS grant, 1957-59; cons. VA Hosp., Fayetteville, N.C., 1957-78; sr. cons., supervising faculty, community psychiatry sect. dept. psychiatry U. N.C. Sch. Medicine, 1971—; exec. sec. Multiversity Group, 1968-73. Served with USNR, 1943-46. Diplomate Am. Bd. Psychiatry and Neurology. Fellow Am. Psychiat. Assn. (rep. N.C. Dist. br.); mem. N.C., Durham-Orange County med. socs., N.C. Neuropsychiat. Assn., Am. Assn. Dirs. Psychiat. Residency Tng. Home: 110 Laurel Hill Rd Chapel Hill NC 27514 Office: Dorothea Dix Hosp Sta B Box 7527 Raleigh NC 27611

TOLLEY, WILLIAM PEARSON, former univ. chancellor, airline exec.; b. Honesdale, Pa., Sept. 13, 1900; s. Adolphus Charles and Emma Grace (Sumner) T.; A.B., Syracuse U., 1922, A.M., 1924; B.D., Drew Theol. Sem., 1925; A.M., Columbia, 1927, Ph.D., 1930; D.D., Mt. Union Coll., Alliance, Ohio, 1931; LL.D., Dickinson Coll., Carlisle, Pa., 1933, Bucknell U., 1943, Rensselaer Poly. Inst., 1954, Marshall Coll., Huntington, W.Va., 1957, Pratt Inst., Bklyn., 1959, Northeastern U., 1943, Allegheny Coll., 1943, Villanova Coll., 1943, Temple U., 1944, Juniata coll., Colgate U., 1944, Boston U., 1950, U. Chattanooga, 1951, Oklahoma City U., Columbia U., 1955, St. Lawrence U., 1956, Lycoming Coll., 1962, Drew U., 1966, Concord Coll., 1967; Litt.D., Grove City (Pa.) Coll., 1938; L.H.D., Hamilton Coll., 1943, Albion Coll., 1945, Hobart Coll., 1946, Union Coll., 1946, Alfred U., 1951, Pace Coll., 1963, Japan Internat. Christian U., 1966, Elmira Coll., 1970; Ed.D., Fla. So. U., 1948; D.P.A., U. Puget Sound, 1963; H.H.D., Bowling Green State U., 1964; L.H.D., Rosary Hill Coll., 1967; Ped.D., Baldwin-Wallace Coll., 1967; LL.D., Syracuse U., 1969; m. Ruth Marian Canfield, July 3, 1925; children—Nelda Ruth (Mrs. Richard Preston Price), William Pearson, Katryn (Mrs. Arthur Fritz, Jr.). Ordained to ministry Meth. Episcopal Ch., 1923; alumni sec. Drew Theol. Sem., 1925-27; instr. systematic theology Drew Theol. Sem., 1926-28, asst. to pres., 1927-28, acting dean Brothers Coll., instr. in philosophy, 1928-29, dean Brothers Coll., 1929-31, prof. philosophy, 1930-31; pres. Allegheny Coll., 1931-42; chancellor, Syracuse (N.Y.) U., 1942-69, chancellor emeritus, 1969—; chmn. bd. Mohawk Airlines Inc., 1970-71, chmn., pres., 1971-72; dir. First Trust & Deposit Co. Vice pres. Japan Internat. Christian U. Found., Inc.; dir. Air U., 1961-63. Pres. Assn. Colls. and Univs. State N.Y.; mem. U. Senate of Meth. Ch., 1932-36, 38—, pres., 1960-70; pres., dir. Assn. Am. Colls., 1942-43; chmn. exec. com. Coop. Study in Gen. Edn., Am. Council of Edn., 1940-46; pres. Nat. Meth. Found. for Christian Higher Edn., 1969-73; pres. Pi Kappa Alpha Meml. Found., 1975-76. Served with U.S. Army, 1918. Decorated chavalier Legion of Honor (France); recipient George Arents Alumni medal, Salzberg medal in transp. Syracuse U. Mem. Newcomen Soc. Eng., Phi Beta Kappa, Beta Gamma Sigma, Delta Sigma Rho, Phi Kappa Phi, Pi Delta Epsilon, Pi Kappa Alpha, Omicron Delta Kappa, Phi Delta Kappa. Republican. Clubs: Cosmos (Washington); Iron City Fishing (Pittsburgh); Century (Syracuse); Grolier, Univ., Century Assn. (N.Y.C.); Oswelewgois, Drumlins Racquet, First String Tennis, Sedgwick Farm Tennis. Author: The Idea of God in the Philosophy of St. Augustine, 1930; The Transcendent Aim, 1967; The Meaning of Freedom, 1969; The Adventure of Learning, 1977. Editor: Alumni Record of Drew Theological Seminary (1867-1925), 1926. Editor: Preface to Philosophy, 1945. Home: 107 Windsor Pl Syracuse NY 13210

TOLMIE, KENNETH DONALD, artist, author; b. Halifax, N.S., Can., Sept. 18, 1941; s. Archibald and Mary Evelyn (Murray) T.; B.F.A., Mt. Allison U., 1962; m. Ruth Mackenzie, Aug. 11, 1962; children—Sarah Katherine, Jane Marianna. One-man shows: Dorothy Cameron Gallery, Toronto, 1963, Lofthouse Gallery, Ottawa, 1969, Wells Gallery, Ottawa, 1974, 75; group shows include: Banfer Gallery, N.Y.C., 1963, Nat. Gallery Can. Watercolors Prints and Drawing, 1964, 66, London Art Mus. (Ont.), 1966, Atlantic award exhibition Dalhousie U. Gallery, 1967, Can. Soc. Graphic Art, 1973; represented in permanent collections: Nat. Gallery Can., Ottawa, Montreal Mus. Fine Arts, Confedn. Centre for Arts, Hirshhorn Collection, Washington, Calif. Coll. Arts and Crafts, Oakland, U. Western Ont., Carleton U.; owner Tolmie Gallery Social Realism, Bridgetown; Chmn., Visual Arts Ottawa, 1975-76. Founding mem. Bridgetown and Area Hist. Soc., James House Mus. Author: (children's book) Tale of an Egg, 1974. Address: 115 South St Bridgetown NS B0S 1C0 Canada

TOLOR, ALEXANDER, educator, psychologist; b. Vienna, Austria, Oct. 21, 1928; s. Stanley and Josephine (Kellner) T.; B.A., N.Y. U., 1949, M.A., 1950, Ph.D., 1954; m. Belle Simon, Sept. 2, 1951; children—Karen Beth, Lori Ann, Diana Susan. Grad. asst. N.Y.U., 1950-52; intern Neurol. Inst., N.Y.C., 1952-53, clin. psychologist, 1953-55; sr. clin. psychologist Inst. of Living, Hartford, Conn., 1957-59; dir. psychol. services Fairfield Hills Hosp., Newtown, Conn., 1959-64; clinic dir. Kennedy Center, Bridgeport, Conn., 1964-65; dir. Inst. for Human Devel., Fairfield U., 1965-77, asso. prof. psychology, 1965-68, research prof. psychology, 1968-75, prof. psychology, 1975—, dir. school psychology div., 1975-77; practice psychology, Danbury, Conn., 1960—; clin. instr. psychology Yale, 1963-67. Cons., West Haven VA Hosp., 1962-66, Bridgeport Bd. Edn., Silver Hill Found., 1972-75, Fairfield Hills Hosp., 1973—, Hallbrooke Hosp., 1975—. Served to 1st lt. USAF, 1955-57. Diplomate Am. Bd. Examiners in Profl. Psychology. Fellow Am. Psychol. Assn., Soc. for Personality Assessment; mem. Conn. State (mem. council 1964), N.Y. State, Eastern psychol. assns., Psi Chi, Delta Phi Alpha, Beta Lambda Sigma. Author: (with H. C. Schulberg) An Evaluation of the Bender-Gestalt Test, 1963. Adv. editor Jour. Cons. and Clin. Psychology; cons. editor Personality: An Internat. Jour. Contbr. articles to profl. jours. Home: Route 3 Saw Mill Ridge Rd Newtown CT 06470 Office: Fairfield U Fairfield CT 06430

TOLSON, HILLORY ALFRED, conservationist, lawyer; b. nr. Laredo, Mo., Oct. 24, 1897; s. James William and Joaquin Miller (Anderson) T.; grad. Cedar Rapids (Iowa) Bus. Coll., 1918; A.B., George Washington U., 1924, A.M., 1927; J.D., Nat. U., 1930, LL.M., M.P.L., 1931; m. Catharine Ann Hough, May 31, 1926 (div.); children—Walter J., Robert H.; m. 2d, Charlotte May Nell, Aug. 2, 1941; 1 dau., Pamela Lynn. With war plans div. War Dept., Washington, 1919-21, Panama Canal, Washington, 1921-31; spl. agt. FBI and atty. Nat. Park Service, Dept. Interior, 1932, asst. dir., 1933-39, regional dir. region 3, Santa Fe, 1939-40, chief of ops., 1940-43, asst. dir., 1943-63, cons., 1964-66; exec. dir. White House Hist. Assn., 1966-78. Served with USMC, World War I; lt. comdr. USNR, 1935-41. Chmn. Coronado Internat. Meml. Commn. to Mex., 1942. Mem. Internat. Park Commn., Mex.-U.S., and conservation com. Micronesia, Pacific Sci. Bd. Admitted to D.C. bar, 1930, U.S. Supreme Ct. bar, 1935. Awarded Delta Tau Delta Activity medal George Washington U., 1924; Cornelius Pugsley Conservation medal Am. Scenic and Historic Preservation Soc., 1949; named to Hall of Fame, 1959, recipient Alumni Achievement award George Washington U., 1962; Distinguished Service award Interior Dept., 1963. Mem. Am., Fed., D.C. bar assns., Westerners, Am. Legion, Save-the-Redwoods League, Thornton Soc., Interior Dept. Recreation Assn. (founder), George Washington U. Alumni Assn. (life), U.S. Supreme Ct. Hist. Assn., Sigma Nu, Pi Delta Epsilon. Mason. Clubs: Cosmos, Nat. Lawyers (Washington); Kenwood Country. Compiler: Laws Relating to the National Park Service, 1933, 63. Home: 5200 Sangamore Rd Bethesda MD 20016

TOLSON, JAY HENRY, lawyer, elec. equipment co. exec.; b. Phila., May 15, 1935; s. Julius Henry and Lois Carolyn Ruth (Leidich) T.; B.S., Pa. State U., 1957; LL.B., Temple U., 1960, J.D., 1968; m. Elizabeth J. Fischer, Aug. 22, 1962 (dec. June 1972); children—Jon H., Carrie L., Lori D., Julie I., Karen L.; m. 2d, Inger L. Uhrenholt, Dec. 2, 1973. Admitted to Pa. bar, 1961; partner Solomon, Tolson & Resnick, Phila., 1961-70; partner firm Malis, Tolson & Malis, Phila., 1970-74, chmn. exec. com., 1972—. Chmn. bd. Fischer & Porter Co., pres., 1974—; chmn. bd., Mantua Indsl. Devel. Corp., 1967-68, dir. 1967-74; mem. listed co. advisory com. Am. Stock Exchange. Pres., trustee mem. exec. com. Delaware Valley Com. to Combat Huntington's Disease; bd. dirs. Washington Sq. West Civic Assn., 1965-68; trustee, treas. Community Legal Services, Inc., Baldwin Sch., 1973-76; trustee, mem. fin. com., chmn. audit com. Hahnemann Med. Coll. and Hosp., Phila.; v.p., trustee, mem. exec. com. Com. to Combat Huntington's Disease. Served with AUS, 1960-61. Mem. Am., Pa., Phila. (chmn. subcom. on community legal services 1968-70, chmn. subcom. on juvenile services 1965-68) bar assns., Instrument Soc. Am., Young Presidents Orgn., S.R. Soc. War 1812, S.A.R. Clubs: Explorers, Locust (Phila.). Home: 265 Highview Dr Radnor PA 19087 Office: 1 Gibraltar Plaza Horsham PA 19044

TOLSON, JOHN JARVIS, III, former state ofcl., ret. army officer; b. New Bern, N.C., Oct. 22, 1915; s. John Jarvis and Lillian (Bartling) T.; student U. N.C., 1932-33; B.S., U.S. Mil. Acad., 1937; grad. Chem. Warfare Sch., 1937, Army Parachute Sch., 1941, Air and Command Staff Sch., 1947, Brit. Staff Coll., 1951, Army War Coll., 1953, Army Aviation Sch., 1956, mgmt. course U. Pitts., 1960; m. Margaret Jordan Young, May 19, 1947; children—David Chillingsworth, John Jarvis IV, Harriet Boykin. Commd. 2d lt. U.S. Army, 1937, advanced through grades to lt. gen., 1968; various assignments, U.S., Hawaii, S.W. Pacific, 1937-46; served with 503d Parachute Regiment, 6th Army, World War II; mem. staff and faculty Air U., 1946-49; assigned 325th Airborne Inf. Regt., 1949-50; G-3, 82d Airborne Div., 1950: U.S. Army airborne-inf. rep. to U.K., 1952; assigned Office Asst. Chief Staff G-3, Dept. Army, 1953-55; dir. airborne-army aviation dept., Inf. Sch., 1955-56; asst. comdt. U.S. Army Aviation Sch., 1957-59; dep. dir. army aviation Office Dept. Chief Staff Ops., Dept. Army, 1959-61; chief MAAG, Ethiopia, 1961-63; dir. army aviation Office Asst. Chief Staff Force Devel., Dept. Army, 1963-65; comdg. gen. U.S. Army Aviation Center, also comdt. U.S. Army Aviation Sch., 1965-67; comdg. gen. 1st Cav. Div. (air mobile), 1967-68; comdg. gen. XVIII Airborne Corps and Ft. Bragg, 1968-71; dep. comdg. gen. Continental Army Command, 1971-73; ret., 1973; sec. mil. and vet. affairs State N.C., Raleigh, 1973-77. Pres. Army Aviation Mus. Found., 1977—. Decorated D.S.C., D.S.M. with 2 oak leaf clusters, Silver Star, Legion of Merit with 2 oak leaf clusters, D.F.C., Bronze Star, Bronze Star, Air medal with 44 oak leaf clusters, Army Commendation medal, Purple Heart, Combat Inf. badge, numerous unit and area ribbons; named to Army Aviation Hall of Fame, 1975. Mem. Assn. U.S. Army (pres. 1976-77, v.p. 1974-78), Army Aviation Assn. Am., Am. Helicopter Soc., Airborne Assn. (pres. 1975-76), Order Daedalians, Legion of Valor, Zeta Psi. Home: 1610 Canterbury Rd Raleigh NC 27608

TOLSON, JULIUS HENRY, lawyer; b. Phila., Apr. 11, 1904; s. Henry F. and Lena (Segal) T.; B.S. in Edn., U. Pa., 1925, M.A., 1932, Ph.D., 1951; postgrad. Exeter Coll., Oxford U., Eng., 1925-26, Temple U. Law Sch., 1926-30; m. Lois C. Leidich, June 29, 1934; children—Jay H., Jayne E. (Mrs. Michael J. Berman), Ann R. (Mrs. Richard D. Lippe). Admitted to Pa. bar, 1931; atty. firm Jenkins & Bennett, Phila., 1926-30; head English dept. La Salle Coll., Phila., 1931-32; chief claims settlement, spl. dep. atty. gen. Dept. Pub. Assistance, Commonwealth of Pa., 1932-45; practice law, Phila., 1931—; mem. firm Solomon, Tolson & Resnick, 1953-69; partner firm Malis, Tolson & Malis, 1969—. Dir., gen. counsel Fischer & Porter Co., Earl P.L. Apfelbaum, Inc., Jonnez Corp. Served to lt. comdr. USNR, 1942-45. Mem. Pa., Phila. bar assns., Lawyers Club Phila., Am. Vets. World War II (past county comdr. Phila.), China Stamp Soc. (v.p.). Mason. Club: Explorers. Asso. editor: Temple U. Law Quarterly, 1928-30. Home: 6376 Overbrook Ave Philadelphia PA 19151 Office: 305 Six Penn Center Plaza Philadelphia PA 19103

TOLSTED, ELMER BEAUMONT, educator; b. Phila., Apr. 28, 1920; s. Elmer Beaumont and Ella Margaret (Robertson) T.; B.S., U. Chgo., 1940, M.S., 1941; Ph.D., Brown U., 1946. Instr., Brown U., 1942-47; asst. prof. math. Pomona Coll., Claremont, Calif., 1947-54, asso. prof., 1954-62, prof., 1962—, chmn. math. dept., 1972-79; Fulbright exchange prof. Exeter, Eng., 1949-50; instr. cello Claremont Coll., summers 1951-52, Chapman Coll., 1971-73; violon cellist Okla. Symphony, 1940, R.I. Symphony, 1942, Chapman Coll. Chamber Players, 1971-73. Mem. Am. Math. Soc., Math. Assn. Am. (Lester Ford award 1965), Valley Chamber Music Soc. (pres. 1962-66), Phi Beta Kappa, Sigma Xi. Home: 337 W Harrison St Claremont CA 91711

TOLSTOY, PAUL, archeologist, anthropologist; b. Versailles, France, Sept. 20, 1929; s. Andre and Mary (Shuvalov) T.; came to U.S., 1946; B.A., Columbia U., 1951, Ph.D., 1959; 1 dau., Irina. Asst. prof. anthropology U. Montreal (Que., Can.), 1961-64, prof. agrégé, 1964-66, prof. anthropology, dir. dept. anthropology, 1977—; asso. prof. anthropology Queens Coll., City U. N.Y., 1966-73, prof., 1974-77; Fulbright grantee, Peru, 1958-59, Uruguay, 1962; leader archeol. research projects, Mexico, 1963, 65-68, 71-78. Can. Council grantee, 1963, 65; NSF grantee, 1965, 71, 72, 73, 75, 77. Mem. Soc. Am. Archaeology, Am. Anthrop. Assn., AAAS, Sigma Xi. Contbr. articles to profl. publs. Office: Dept Anthropology U Montreal Montreal PQ H3C 1J7 Canada

TOMANEK, GERALD WAYNE, educator; b. Collyer, Kans., Sept. 16, 1921; s. John James and Hazel Marie (Orten) T.; B.A., Ft. Hays (Kans.) State U., 1942, M.S., 1947; Ph.D., U. Nebr., 1951; m. Ruth Ardis Morell, Apr. 30, 1943; children—Walta, Sheila, Lisa. Mem. faculty Ft. Hays State U., 1947—, prof. biology, chmn. div. natural scis. and math., 1970-72, v.p. acad. affairs, 1972-75, acting pres., 1975-76, pres., 1976—; exec. dir. Hadley Regional Med. Center. Served to capt. USMCR, 1942-46. Named Conservationist Educator of Year; recipient Alumni Achievement award Ft. Hays State U.; Kansan of Yr. award, 1979. Mem. Soc. Range Mgmt., Ecol. Soc. Am., Am. Inst. Biol. Scis., Southwestern Assn. Naturalists, Kans. Wildlife Assn., Kans. Acad. Sci., Nature Conservancy, Sigma Xi, Phi Kappa Phi, Phi Delta Kappa. Methodist. Author, editor in field. Office: Fort Hays State UniV Hays KS 67601

TOMAS, JEROLD FREDERIC, bus. exec., mgmt. cons.; b. N.Y.C., July 25, 1945; s. Samuel and Jean (Brodsky) T.; B.S. (football scholar), U. Bridgeport, 1968; M.S., U. Mass., 1971, Doctorate in Applied Behavioral Sci., 1973. Research asst. Evaluation Service Center, U. Mass., Amherst, 1969-70, asst. dir. completely modular curriculum, 1970-71, project mgr. Marathon Forum, 1971-72, fellow Center for Leadership, 1971-73; asst. dean, asst. prof. behavioral sci. Met. Learning Center, Empire State Coll., SUNY, N.Y.C., 1973-75; dir. edn. Young Pres.'s Orgn., Inc., N.Y.C., 1975-77; chief research scientist mgmt. decision lab. Grad. Sch. Bus. Adminstrn., N.Y. U., 1977-78; officer, sr. cons., mgmt. and orgn. devel. Morgan Guaranty Trust Co. of N.Y., N.Y.C., 1979—; guest lectr. at univs. including Worcester Poly. Inst., 1977-78; cons. in field. Mem. N.Y. Vol. Urban Cons. Group, N.Y.C.; mem. bd. overseers Northampton (Mass.) Jail and House of Corrections Tutorial Program, 1971-73; mem. Career Opportunities Tng. Team, Bedford-Stuyvesant, N.Y.C., 1972. Mem. Human Resources Planning Soc., Mgmt. Devel. Forum, Met. Assn. Applied Psychology, Société Internationale Pour Le Développement Des Organisations, Am. Soc. Personnel Adminstrn. Author: (monograph) Specifications for Advanced Continuing Education - The Young Presidents Organization, 1976; contbr. articles to profl. publs. Office: 23 Wall St New York NY 10015

TOMASEK, HENRY JOHN, educator; b. Berwyn, Ill., July 21, 1920; s. Joseph and Christine (Frycek) T.; B.A., U. Chgo., 1942, M.A., 1946, Ph.D., 1959; m. Ann Elisabeth Howell, Sept. 4, 1948; children—Paul, Susan. Faculty, U. N.D., 1946—, prof. polit. sci., 1961—, chmn. dept., 1963-74, dean Coll. Human Resources Devel., 1974—. Mem. Grand Forks Civil Service Commn., 1963-73, N.D. Constl. Revision Commn., 1962—, N.D. Merit System Council 1968-75; sci. adviser N.D. gov. Served with inf. AUS, 1942-45; PTO. Decorated Purple Heart. Mem. AAUP, Am. Polit. Sci. Assn. Home: 724 S 3d St Grand Forks ND 58201

TOMASELLI, JULIUS LOUIS, bldg. materials co. exec.; b. Teaneck, N.J., Nov. 2, 1928; s. Vincent and Beatrice (De Paoli) T.; B.A., Lehigh U., 1951; LL.B., Columbia U., 1955; m. Jacqueline Morino, July 26, 1952; children—Raymond, Robert. Admitted to D.C. bar, 1956, N.Y. State bar, 1957; asso. firm Pollard, Johnson, Smythe & Robertson, N.Y.C., 1956-60; patent atty. Gen. Foods Corp., White Plains, N.Y., 1960-62; with The Flintkote Co., Irving, Tex., 1962—, patent counsel, 1962-66, asst. sec., 1966-67, dir. adminstrv. services bldg. products group, 1967-69, asst. sec., asst. gen. counsel, 1969-73, sec., gen. counsel, 1973, v.p. adminstrn., 1973-75, v.p. employee relations, 1975—. Vice pres. Seabrook (Md.) Civic Assn., 1956-57; bd. dirs. Citizens for Schs., Greenburgh, N.Y., 1959-60; bd. dirs. White Plains YMCA, 1971-72. Mem. Am. Bar Assn., Am., N.Y. patent law assns., U.S. Trademark Assn., Theta Chi, Pi Gamma Mu, Phi Alpha Theta. Club: Whippoorwill Country (Armonk, N.Y.). Home: 724 Sam Hill St Irving TX 75062 Office: Flintkote Co PO Box 800 Dallas TX 75221

TOMASH, ERWIN, computer equipment co. exec.; b. St. Paul, Nov. 17, 1921; s. Noah and Milka (Ehrlich) T.; B.S., U. Minn., 1943; M.S., U. Md., 1950; m. Adelle Ruben, July 31, 1943; children—Judith Freya Tomash Diffenbaugh, Barbara Ann. Instr. elec. engring. U. Minn., 1946; asso. dir. computer devel. Univac div. Remington Rand Corp., St. Paul, 1947-51; dir. West Coast ops. Univac div. Sperry Rand Corp., Los Angeles, 1953-55; pres. Telemeter Magnetics, Inc., Los Angeles, 1956-60; v.p. Ampex Corp., Los Angeles, 1961; founder, pres. Dataproducts Corp., Los Angeles, 1962-71, chmn. bd., 1971—; dir. Data Card Corp., Mpls., Teleproducts Corp., Thousand Oaks, Calif., Micropolis Corp., Canoga Park, Calif.; mem. listed cos. advisory com. Am. Stock Exchange; hon. chmn. U.S.-Hungarian Econ. Council. Founder, chmn. bd. trustees Charles Babbage Inst.; trustee Coro Found., Los Angeles. Served to capt. Signal Corps, AUS, 1943-46. Decorated Bronze Star. Mem. IEEE, Assn. Computing Machinery. Home: 110 S Rockingham Ave Los Angeles CA 90049 Office: 6219 DeSoto Ave Woodland Hills CA 91365

TOMASINI, WALLACE J(OHN), art historian, univ. adminstr.; b. Bklyn., Oct. 19, 1926; s. Giacinto Giorgio and Clothilde Mathilde (Radaelli-Visconti) T.; A.B., U. Mich., 1949, A.M., 1950, Ph.D., 1953; m. Kossia Orloff, Feb. 1, 1953; children—David, Seth. Instr. in history of art Finch Coll., 1954-57; asst. prof. history of art U. Iowa, 1957-61, asso. prof., 1961-64, prof., 1964—, dir. Sch. Art and Art History, 1973—. Fulbright scholar, 1951-52; Am. Numismatic Soc. fellow, 1957-58; Am. Philos. Soc. grantee, 1958-59. Mem. Coll. Art Assn., Mid Am. Coll. Art Assn. (dir.), Midwest Art History Soc. (dir.), Nat. Assn. Art Adminstrs. (dir.), Renaissance Soc. Am. Author: The Barbaric Tremissis in Spain and Southern France: Anastasius to Leovigild, 1964; Early Visigothic Numismatics, 1964. Office: Sch Art and Art History U Iowa Room E100 Art Bldg Iowa City IA 52242

TOMASSON, HELGI, dancer, choreographer; b. Reykjavik, Iceland, 1942; student Sigridur Arman, Erik Bidsted, Vera Volkova; student Sch. Am. Ballet, Tivoli Pantomime Theatre, Copenhagen; m. Marlene Rizzo, 1965; children—Kristin, Eric. Debut with Tivoli Pantomime Theatre, 1958; with Joffrey Ballet, 1961-64; soloist Harkness Ballet, 1964-70; prin. dancer N.Y.C. Ballet, 1970—. Office: care NYC Ballet Lincoln Center Plaza New York NY 10023*

TOMB, PAUL DAVID, naval officer; b. Syracuse, N.Y., Aug. 8, 1929; s. Glenni David and Hazel (Milback) T.; student Syracuse U., 1946-47; B.S., U.S. Naval Acad., 1951; m. Mary Elizabeth Taylor, Mar. 22, 1952; children—Laura Cynthia Tomb Ryan, Kimberly Anne, Mark Christopher. Commd. ensign U.S. Navy, 1951, advanced through grades to rear adm., 1976; comdg. officer USS Skipjack, 1964-67, U.S.S. George Washington Carver, 1967-69; spl. asst. to dir. navy program planning, 1970-71; exec. asst., sr. aide to Asst. Sec. Navy, 1971-72; comdg. officer submarine base, Pearl Harbor, 1972-75; dep. dir. attack submarine programs, 1975-76; chief Navy sect. Joint U.S. Mil. Mission for Aid to Turkey. 1976-78; comdr. Submarine Group 8, also comdr. submarines, Mediterranean, 1978—. Decorated Legion of Merit, Meritorious Service medal. Mem. U.S. Naval Inst., U.S. Naval Acad. Alumni Assn. Republican. Baptist. Club: Rotary Internat. Home: 106 Via Stazio Posillipo Naples Italy Office: COM SUB GRU 8 Box 16 FPO New York NY 09521. *The earlier your lifetime goals are established, the more optimistic you can be about attaining these goals. The goals must be reasonable, demanding, and not in conflict with your own morals and beliefs. The establishment of these goals enables you to project your path toward these goals and then pursue that path with a minimum of wasted effort and a maximum of attention to the learning process required of you.*

TOMBRELLO, THOMAS ANTHONY, JR., physicist, educator; b. Austin, Tex., Sept. 20, 1936; s. Thomas Anthony and Jeanette Lillian (Marcuse) T.; B.A., Rice U., 1958, M.A., 1960, Ph.D., 1961; m. Stephanie Merton Russell, Jan. 15, 1977; children—Christopher, Susan, Karen, Kerstin Russell. Research fellow Cal. Inst. Tech., Pasadena, 1961-62, 64-65, asst. prof., 1965-67, asso. prof., 1967-71, prof. physics, 1971—; asst. prof. Yale U., 1962-63. Cons., Los Alamos Sci. Lab., NSF; chmn. vis. com. physics dept. Tex. A. and M. U. NSF postdoctoral fellow, 1961-62, Alfred P. Sloan fellow, 1971-73. Fellow Am. Phys. Soc.; mem. Phi Beta Kappa, Sigma Xi, Delta Phi Alpha. Asso. editor Nuclear Physics, 1972—; Applied Nuclear Sci., 1978—. Office: 106-38 Calif Inst Tech Pasadena CA 91125

TOMCHIN, JULIAN, designer; b. N.Y.C., Apr. 28, 1932; s. Samuel and Rose (Thompson) T.; B.F.A., Syracuse U., 1953. Designer, Couture Fabrics, Ltd., N.Y.C., 1956-59; v.p. Maxwell Textiles, N.Y.C., 1959-66, Chardon-Marche div. Maxwell Industries, N.Y.C., 1966-71; dir. design Wamsutta Mills div. M. Lowenstein & Sons, N.Y.C., 1976-78; dir. home furnishings fashion office Bloomingdale's, N.Y.C., 1978—; instr. Parsons Sch. Design; dir. textile design dept. Shenkar Coll., Ramat Gan, Israel. Recipient Coty award Am. Fashion Critics, 1969, Vogue Am. Fabrics award, 1968; named Outstanding Alumnus Syracuse U., 1973. Home: 400 E 59th St New York NY 10022 Office: 1000 3d Ave New York NY 10022

TOMES, MARK LOUIS, geneticist; b. Ft. Wayne, Ind., Nov. 15, 1917; s. Orlando Essex and Edna Idonia (Knause) T.; A.B., Ind. U., 1939; M.S., Tex. A. and M. U., 1941; Ph.D., Purdue U., 1952; m. Charlotte Perrine, Apr. 15, 1944; children—Charles Mark, Carol Ellen. Agrl. research Stokely-Van Camp, Inc., 1946-48; asst. geneticist Purdue U. Agrl. Expt. Sta., 1948-53; mem. faculty Purdue U., 1952—, prof. genetics, head dept. botany and plant pathology, 1969-77, asso. dir. Agrl. Expt. Sta., 1977—; vis. prof. Pa. State U., 1966-67. Served with AUS, 1943-46. Mem. Genetics Soc. Am., Am. Genetics Assn., Am. Phytopathol. Soc., Am. Soc. Hort. Sci., AAAS, Sigma Xi. Rotarian. Author numerous papers in field. Home: 1129 Glenway St West Lafayette IN 47906

TOMJANOVICH, RUDY, basketball player; b. Hamtramck, Mich., Nov. 24, 1948; grad. U. Mich., 1970. Basketball player San Diego Rockets, 1970-71, Houston Rockets, 1971—. Office: care Houston Rockets The Summit Ten Greenway Plaza E Houston TX 77046*

TOMKINS, FRANK SARGENT, physicist; b. Petoskey, Mich., June 24, 1915; s. Charles Frederick and Irene Eugenie (Gouin) T.; B.S., Kalamazoo Coll., 1937; Ph.D. (Parke-Davis fellow), Mich. State U., 1941; m. Mary Ann Lynch, Jan. 6, 1964; 1 son, Frank Sargent. Physicist, Buick Aviation Engine Div., Melrose Park, Ill., 1941-42; scientist Manhattan Project U. Chgo., 1943-45; sr. scientist Argonne (Ill.) Nat. Lab., 1945—, group leader, 1944—; cons. Bendix Corp., Cin., 1963-69. John Simon Guggenheim fellow Laboratoire Aime-Cotton, Bellevue, France, 1960-61; Sci. Research Council fellow Imperial Coll., London, 1975; recipient Argonne Univs. Assn. Disting. Appointment, 1975-76. Fellow Optical Soc. Am. (William F. Meggers award 1977); mem. Am. Phys. Soc., Societe Francaise de Physique, AAAS, N.Y. Acad. Scis., Sigma Xi. Contbr. articles to sci. jours. Home: 11714 S 83d Ave Palos Park IL 60464 Office: 9700 S Cass Ave Argonne IL 60439

TOMKOWIT, THADDEUS WALTER, chem. co. exec.; b. Maspeth, N.Y., Sept. 10, 1918; s. Walter and Theodora (Dulska) T.; B.S. in Chem. Engring., Columbia, 1941, postgrad. in chem. engring., 1941-42; m. Ann D. Czyzewski, June 20, 1943; children—Barbara Ann (Mrs. William Anderson), Judith Lynn (Mrs. John Feeney), Richard T. With Du Pont de Nemours, 1942—, mgr. logistics organic chems. dept., Wilmington, Del., 1972-78, mgr. logistics and works supplies, chems., dyes and pigments dept., 1978—. Mem. dean's adv. bd. Sch. Engring., Catholic U., 1970—, also Lehigh U., U. Tex., Worcester Poly. Tech. Pres. Civic Assn., 1966. Bd. dirs. Catholic Social Services Del. Recipient Achievement award Ams. of Polish Descent Del. Registered profl. engr., Del. Mem. Am. Inst. Chem. Engrs. (dir., pres. 1972, founders award 1975), Sigma Xi. Republican. Roman Catholic. Home: 511 Clearview Ave Woodside Hills Wilmington DE 19809 Office: 13366 Brandywine Bldg Wilmington DE 19898

TOMLIN, DANIEL OTIS, real estate broker, developer, investor; b. Duster, Tex., Feb. 14, 1915; s. Daniel and Marie (Echols) T.; B.S., So. Methodist U., 1935; postgrad. Harvard Grad. Sch. Bus. Adminstrn., 1935-37, Washington U., St. Louis, 1937-38; m. Erline Schuessler, June 4, 1938; children—Daniel Otis, Carolyn Orene (Mrs. Tomlin Hurst). Accounting clk. Am. Zinc Co., St. Louis, 1937-40, chief accountant, Dumas, Tex., 1940-42, asst. mgr., 1942-46; treas., asst. gen. mgr. Briggs-Weaver Machinery Co., Dallas, 1946-53, dir., 1959-61; pres. Dearborn Stove Co., Dallas, 1953-56; pres. Lone Star Boat Co. (now Chrysler Boat div.), Plano, Tex., 1956-61; pres., dir. 1st Worth Corp. (now Justin Industries), Ft. Worth, 1961-69; v.p., dir. Good & Assos., Inc., Dallas, 1970-72; now real estate broker, investor Tomlin Properties, Dallas. Mem. adv. bd. U. Dallas, 1961-72, Pvt. Jr. Coll. Found., 1961-69; mem. adv. council U. Tex. at Arlington, 1967-72; mem. com. of 125, Southwestern U., 1966-74; mem. Tex. Air Control Bd., 1968-69, Tex. Advisory Commn. on Tech. Services, 1966-69, Nat. Indsl. Conf. Bd., 1957-69. Trustee Tarrant County United Fund, 1964-69, v.p., 1968; trustee Harris Hosp., Ft. Worth, 1968-71, So. Meth. U., 1969-72, Tex. Christian U. Research Found., 1969-72; bd. dirs. Casa Manana Theatre, 1964-69, Ft. Worth Chamber Devel. Corp., 1965-69. Mem. NAM (dir. 1967-69), Clay Products Assn. S.W. (pres. 1965-66), Tex. Assn. Bus. (pres. 1958, dir. 1955—), Soc. for Advancement Mgmt. (pres. Dallas chpt. 1955), Am. Mgmt. Assn. (gen. mgmt. council 1968-71), Structural Clay Products Inst. (dir. 1967-69, mem. exec. com. 1967-69), Boat Mfrs. Assn. Am. (pres. 1959-60), West Tex. (v.p. 1965-66), Ft. Worth (dir. 1962-69) chambers commerce, Lambda Chi Alpha. Clubs: Northwood Country, Lancers, Chaparral, Salesmanship (Dallas). Home: 4009 Windsor Ave Dallas TX 75205 Office: 2 Turtle Creek Village Suite 520 Dallas TX 75219

TOMLIN, EUGENE BERNARD, retail co. exec.; b. Belvidere, Ill., Aug. 27, 1933; s. Buford Ernest and Lela Mae (Miller) T.; B.S., U. Ill., 1956; m. Joan Rueckert, June 18, 1956; children—Michael, Mark, Bruce. Traffic mgr. Swift & Co., Frankfort, Ind., 1956-58, sales mgr., Champaign, Ill., 1959-64; v.p. I.H. French & Co., Champaign, 1965-75, pres., 1976—. Bd. dirs. 1st United Meth. Ch. Served with U.S. Army, 1956-57. Club: Champaign Country. Home: 102 Greencroft St Champaign IL 61820 Office: 502 W Clark St Champaign IL 61820

TOMLIN, LILY, actress; b. Detroit, 1939; student Wayne State U.; studied mime with Paul Curtis. Appearances in concerts and colls. throughout U.S.; TV appearances include Lily Tomlin CBS Spls., 1972—; formerly mem. cast The Music Scene, Laugh In; motion picture debut in Nashville, 1975, also appeared in The Late Show, Moment by Moment; records for Polydor Records. Recipient Grammy award, 1971; 2 Emmy awards for CBS Spl., 1972. Records: This Is A Recording; And That's The Truth; Modern Scream; On Stage, 1977. Address: PO Box 69330 Los Angeles CA 90069*

TOMLINSON, ALEXANDER COOPER, investment banker; b. Haddonfield, N.J., May 13, 1922; s. Alexander Cooper and Mary Cooper (Buzby) T.; B.S., Haverford Coll., 1943; postgrad. London Sch. Econs. and Polit. Sci., 1947-48; M.B.A., Harvard U., 1950; m. Elizabeth Anne Brierley, Jan. 10, 1953; children—William Brierley, Deborah Kay, Alexander Cooper III. With Morgan Stanley & Co., N.Y.C., 1950-76, partner, 1958—, mng. dir. Morgan Stanley & Co. Inc., 1970—, dir., pres. Morgan Stanley Can. Ltd., Montreal, Que., 1972-76; chmn. exec. com., dir. First Boston Corp., N.Y.C., 1976—; dir. First Boston (Can.) Ltd., Financière Credit Swisse-First Boston; dir. Churchill Falls Corp., 1974-76. Trustee, Village of Cove Neck, N.Y.; trustee Salisbury (Conn.) Sch.; bd. dirs. Beekman-Downtown Hosp., N.Y.C., Cold Spring Harbor Lab.; trustee East Woods Sch., Oyster Bay, N.Y., 1959-66. Served to lt. USNR, 1943-46. Mem. Fedn. Security Analysts, Econs. Club N.Y., Council on Fgn. Relations N.Y., N.Y., Am. stock exchanges, Nature Conservancy (dir.). Clubs: Links, Recess, Bond (N.Y.C.); Mt. Royal, St. James (Montreal). Home: Cove Neck Rd Oyster Bay NY 11771 Office: 20 Exchange Pl New York NY 10005

TOMLINSON, ALLAN JOHN, JR., chem. co. exec.; b. Houston, Aug. 30, 1932; s. Allan John and Edyna Mae (Kuehn) T.; B.S.Chem.E., Tex. Tech. U., 1954; M.B.A., Harvard U., 1960; m. Helen E. Nebeker, July 7, 1960; children—Allan John, III, Laura Ellen, William Marc. Engr., Shell Oil Co., 1954-58; mktg. mgr. Dow Chem. Co., Midland, Mich., 1960-66; cons. McKinsey & Co., Cleve., 1966-68; exec. v.p. Diamond Shamrock Corp., Cleve., 1968—. Vice pres. Shaker Heights (Ohio) Bd. Edn.; trustee Cleve. Ballet, St. Lukes Hosp., Cleve. Served with USAF, 1955-58. Office: 1100 Superior Ave Cleveland OH 44114

TOMLINSON, GEORGE HERBERT, indsl. research co. exec.; b. Fullerton, La., May 2, 1912; s. George Herbert and Irene Loretta (Nourse) T.; came to Can., 1914; B.A., Bishop's U., 1931; Ph.D., McGill U., 1935; m. Frances Fowler, July 17, 1937; children—Peter George, David Lester, Susan Margaret Tomlinson Goff. Chief chemist Howard Smith Chem. Ltd., Cornwall, Ont., Can., 1936-39; research dir. Howard Smith Paper Mills Ltd., Cornwall, 1939-61; research dir. Domtar Ltd., Montreal, Que., 1961-70, v.p. research and environ. tech., 1970-77, sr. sci. adv., 1977—. Recipient Gov. Gen.'s Gold medal, 1931. Fellow Royal Soc. Can., Internat. Acad. Wood Sci., Chem. Inst. Can.; mem. Am. Chem. Soc., TAPPI (dir. 1976-79), Can. Pulp and Paper Assn. Anglican. Clubs: Univ. (Montreal); Chemists (N.Y.). Contbr. articles to profl. jours. Patentee in field. Home: 920 Perrot Blvd N Ile Perrot PQ J7V 3K1 Canada Office: 395 de Maisonneuve Blvd W Montreal PQ H3C 2R3 Canada

TOMLINSON, GUS, educator; b. Bon Aqua, Tenn., Apr. 30, 1933; s. Clarence Doyle and Ina Mae (Hutcheson) T.; B.S.in Math., George Peabody Coll., 1958; M.A. in Molecular Biology, Vanderbilt U., 1961, Ph.D., 1962; postgrad. (Nat. Cancer Inst. fellow) Swiss Fed. Inst., Zurich, Switzerland, 1963-64; m. Opal Aline Bowman, May 10, 1952; children—Jeffrey Lynn, Jenifer Lynne, Tracey Eileen. Asst. prof. biology George Peabody Coll., Nashville, 1962-63, asso. prof. biology, 1964-67, prof., 1968—, chmn. dept. biology, 1966—, chmn. div. natural scis., 1967—, dir. NSF summer insts., 1966—, dir. sci. leadership devel. program, 1973-74, dir. instrnl. improvement implementation program, 1974—. Cons. project Reach High (Tenn.) and Project MAMOS (Mo.); cons. cardiovascular edn. Bapt. Hosp., Nashville, 1971—. Served with AUS, 1953-55. Nat. Med. Scis. research grantee, 1965-70. Fellow Tenn. Acad. Sci. (exec. com. 1970—, editor jour. 1970—); mem. Southeastern Electron Microscopic Soc., Sigma Xi. Contbr. articles to sci. jours. Office: Box 153 George Peabody Coll Tchrs Nashville TN 37203. *I have never met anyone from whom I could not learn something.*

TOMLINSON, J. RICHARD, business exec.; b. Newton, Pa., Mar. 26, 1930; s. Robert K. and Margaret (Wright) T.; B.A., Swarthmore Coll., 1952; postgrad. George Washington U., 1952-53, U. Mich., 1955-57, Drexel Inst. Tech., 1954-57, Am. U., 1965; m. Barbara Elizabeth Brazill, Apr. 30, 1955; children—Karin Kathleen, Kimberly Ann. Mgmt. analyst Dept. State, Washington, 1952-53; with Old Republic Life Ins. Co., Washington, 1953-54; supr. financial analysis Ford Motor Co., Detroit, 1954-61; cons. McKinsey & Co., Washington, 1961-65; v.p. finance, dir. passenger services Reading Co., Phila., 1965-69, v.p. finance Rollins Internat., Inc., 1969-71; exec. v.p. Amtrak, Washington, 1972-74; partner L.T. Klander and Asso., 1974-75, 79—; exec. v.p. Penn Central Transp. Co., 1975-78. Named Man of Month, Phila. C. of C., 1967. Mem. Transp. Research Forum, Soc. Investment Analysts. Clubs: Union League (Phila.); Stone Harbor (N.J.) Yacht. Home: 1656 Susquehanna Rd Rydal PA 19046 Office: PNB Bldg Philadelphia PA 19107

TOMLINSON, JAMES FRANCIS, news agy. exec.; b. Long Beach, Calif., Oct. 18, 1925; s. L. J. and Margaret (Roemer) T.; B.A., U. Va., 1950; student Harvard U., Grad. Sch. Arts and Scis., 1950-51; grad. Advanced Mgmt. Program, Harvard U., 1977; m. Sally JoAnne Ryan, Aug. 12, 1967; children— Elizabeth Anne, Victoria Alexandra. With A.P., 1951—, chief bur., Newark, 1957-63, bus. news editor, N.Y.C., 1963-67, dep. treas., 1967-68, treas., 1968—, v.p., 1972—, sec., 1978—. Served with AUS, 1943-46; ETO. Mem. Phi Beta Kappa, Phi Eta Sigma. Clubs: N.Y. Athletic, Harvard (N.Y.C.). Home: 1165 Park Ave New York NY 10028 Office: 50 Rockefeller Plaza New York NY 10020

TOMLINSON, JOHN DOREN, ret. fgn. service officer; b. Wheaton, Ill., Mar. 7, 1903; s. George Horace and Marian (Doren) T.; B.S., Northwestern U., 1925; A.M., Columbia, 1927; Docteur es Sciences Politiques, Grad. Inst. Internat. Studies, U. Geneva, 1938; m. Jean Duncan-Clark, June 10, 1936; 1 dau., Elizabeth Murray (Mrs. Russel V. Theiss). Asst. prof., then prof. polit. sci. Wabash Coll., 1927-41; dir. Am. Com. in Geneva and Geneva Inst. Internat. Relations, summers 1931-38; staff div. export controls State Dept., 1941, div. Am. Republics, 1942, div. polit. studies, 1943-44, div. internat. orgn. affairs, 1945-46, asst. chief, 1946, adviser Office UN Econ. and Social Affairs, 1948-54; U.S. mem. adv. commn. UNRWA, Beirut, 1954-56; Am. consul, Port Elizabeth, South Africa, 1956-58; Am. consul gen., Leopoldville, Belgian Congo, 1958-60, Casablanca, Morocco, 1960-63; exec. Church Center for UN, 1963-66; Moroccan rep. Am. Friends of Middle East, 1966-73. Adviser, U.S. delegations Gen. Council UNRRA, Atlantic City, 1943, Dumbarton Oaks Conversations, 1944, San Francisco Conf., Internat. Orgn., 1945, UN Prep. Commn., London, 1945, Prep. Commn. WHO, Geneva, 1947-48, UN Gen. Assembly, 1946, 1958, others. Mem. Delta Upsilon, Sigma Delta Chi. Methodist. Home: 3938 Morrison St NW Washington DC 20015

TOMLINSON, JOSEPH ROBERT, mfg. co. exec.; b. Phila., Nov. 29, 1916; s. Joseph L. and Louise (Gillingham) T.; B.S. in Mech. Engring., Syracuse U., 1941; m. Marilyn Huber, June 27, 1942; children—J. Bradley, Marilyn, William Charles, Barbara. With Barden Corp., Danbury, Conn., 1946-77, exec. v.p., 1949-56, pres., 1956-77, also dir.; v.p. ops. Insilco Corp., Meriden, Conn., 1977—. Bd. dirs., vice chmn. Conn. Blue Cross/Blue Shield; trustee Syracuse U. 1966-78. Served to lt. comdr. USNR, 1942-46. Home: Brookfield Center CT 06805 Office: Insilco Corp 1000 Research Pkwy Meriden CT 06450

TOMLINSON, MEL ALEXANDER, dancer; b. Raleigh, N.C., Jan. 3, 1954; s. Tommy Willie Amos and Marjorieline (Henry) T.; B.F.A. (Jessica T. Fogle award scholar), N.C. Sch. of Arts, 1974. Prin., Agnes DeMille's Heritage Dance Theatre, N.Y.C., 1973-74; soloist Dance Theatre of Harlem, N.Y.C., 1974-77, prin., 1978—; prin. with Alvin Ailey Am. Dance Theatre, 1977-78; guest artist Joffrey Ballet for tribute to Agnes De Mille, 1978; appearance Brit. royal family; toured S. Am. Recipient letter of commendation Mayor of Raleigh, 1976. Mem. Am. Guild Musical Artists, Brit. Equity. Democrat. Baptist. Home: 1216 Bunche Dr Raleigh NC 27610 Office: 466 W 152d St New York NY 10031. *Everything has a rhythm of its own which is unique unto itself. Creativity is a toy for reality. The simplicity of a* *dream can be destroyed so easily by the dreamer who awakens to the reality that he's fallen asleep. Sincerity is an emotion whereas honesty is a virtue. The only honesty to be found is in truth.*

TOMLINSON, MILTON AMBROSE, clergyman; b. Cleveland, Tenn., Oct. 19, 1906; s. Ambrose Jessup and Mary Jane (Taylor) T.; ed. Tenn. pub. schs.; m. Ina Mae Turner, Sept. 18, 1928; children—Wanda Jeanne (Mrs. Hugh Ralph Edwards), Carolyn Joy (Mrs. Verlin Dean Thornton). Printer, Herald Printing Co., Cleveland, ten years; pastor church Henderson, Ky., 1 yr.; gen. overseer Church of God of Prophecy, Cleveland, 1943—, editor and publisher The White Wing Messengers, pres. Bible Tng. Inst., chmn. trustees. Pres. Tomlinson Home for Children. Author: The Glorious Church of God; Basic Bible Beliefs. Office: Bible Pl Cleveland TN 37311*

TOMLINSON, WILLIAM D. (FRANK), pub. relations exec., broadcaster, writer; b. Bellevue, Ky., Sept. 19, 1928; s. Frank Rufner and Mary Ethel (Tipps) T.; student U. Wash., 1952-53, U. Minn., Duluth, 1954-55; m. Eleanor Joyce Smith, June 5, 1952; children—Scott W., Keith P. Newscaster, Sta. WEBC, Duluth, Minn., 1954-57, Sta. WOWO, Ft. Wayne, Ind., 1957-59; news editor WJR, Detroit, 1959-62, news dir., 1962-66; news dir. Sta. WXYZ, Detroit, 1966-69; network corr. ABC News, Washington, 1969—, Pentagon corr., 1973-76, White House corr., 1976. Lectr. journalism U. Mich., 1965-66. Served with USAF, 1946-49, 50-57; Korea. Recipient best regularly scheduled newscast award AP, 1965-68; Spl. AP awards coverage Vietnam, 1965, Detroit riots, 1967. Mem. White House Corrs. Assn., State Dept. Corrs. Assn., Capitol Hill Radio-TV Corrs. Assn. Sigma Delta Chi. Clubs: Nat. Press, Nat. Aviation. Home: 6800 Melrose Dr McLean VA 22101 Office: McDonnell Douglas Corp 1150 17th St NW Washington DC 20036

TOMLINSON, WILLIAM WEST, univ. adminstr.; b. Salem, Ohio, Nov. 28, 1893; s. Lindley and Miriam Belle (Lease) T.; A.B., Swarthmore Coll., 1917; L.H.D., Susquehanna U., 1954; LL.D., Gettysburg Coll., 1954, Phila. Coll. Osteopathy, 1954, Phila. Textile Inst., 1959; m. Rebecca Kirkpatrick Scott, Mar. 6, 1923; children—Jane (Mrs. Jane Myhre), William, Rebecca (Mrs. William L. Lindblom). Exec., Scott Paper Co., Chester, Pa., 1922-37, dir., 1934-37; adminstrv. dir. William W. Tomlinson & Assos., ednl. pub. relations, Phila., 1937-42; sec. Temple U., 1942-44, v.p., 1944—. Chmn. projects com., mem. exec. and edn. coms. Pres.' People-to-People program; spl. ednl. mission to Germany, 1955-56, 58. Chmn. Christmas Seal campaign, 1956-58; bd. mgrs. Armed Services YMCA, Phila., 1940—, chmn. bd., 1953-58; pres. YMCA Met. Phila., 1964-65; armed services com. nat. council YMCA, now mem. internat. com.; mem. nat. council USO, 1971-72; pres. Phila. Tb and Health Assn., 1959-64; mem. Mayor's Adv. Council on Tb; adv. bd. Am. Coll. Admissions Adv. Center; trustee Eastern Pa. Psychiat. Inst.; hon. trustee Phila. Coll. Textiles and Sci.; vice chmn. Phila. United Charities campaign, 1939; bd. mgrs. Swarthmore Coll., 1944-48; trustee Penn Center Acad., chmn. bd., 1969-73; hon. life trustee Temple U. Served as ensign USNRF, World War I. Recipient Freedoms Found. award, 1951, 65; Russell H. Conwell award Temple U., 1966; Layman of Year award Met. Phila. YMCA, 1968; Outstanding Career citation George Sch. Pa., 1970; Distinguished Service medal Huguenot Soc. Pa., 1974. Mem. Am. Acad. Polit. and Social Sci., Am. Scandinavian Found., Pa. Hist. Soc., World Affairs Council Phila., English Speaking Union, Acad. Polit. Sci., Franklin Inst., Newcomen Soc., Swarthmore Coll. Alumni Assn. (pres. 1935-37), Phi Beta Kappa, Delta Sigma Rho, Delta Upsilon, Pi Gamma Mu, Alpha Phi Omega. Presbyterian. Clubs: Rotary, Merion Cricket. Author: Time Out to Live, 1939; The Flickering Torch, 1942; There is No End, 1952. CBS Script This I Believe, 1952 on Voice of America to 97 countries. Contbr. to radio series, Search For Peace, 1958; nat. award winning series, Anatomy of Freedom, 1961-62. Home: Cheswold and Elbow Lanes Haverford PA 19041 Office: Temple Univ Philadelphia PA 19122. *"Walk together, talk together, all ye people of the earth-then you shall have peace." Sanskrit (The inperative of our nuclear age).*

TOMPA, ROBERT JAMES, educator; b. Newark, July 12, 1921; s. Karl and Elizabeth (Barna) T.; A.B., Dartmouth, 1940; A.M., Montclair State Coll., 1950; Ph.D., Rutgers U., 1964; m. Rita Galdiero, June 16, 1957; children—Peter, Carol Beth. Prof. econs. Monmouth Coll., West Long Branch, N.J., 1954—; participant Computer Workshop U. Colo., 1974; ednl. cons., Ft. Monmouth and Ft. Dix, N.J. Served with USAAF, 1943-46. Leonard P. Ayres fellow Stonier Grad. Sch. Banking, Rutgers U., 1967; Mut. Savs. Bank fellow Brown U., 1967; Gen. Electric fellow U. Calif., Los Angeles, 1969. Mem. Am. Econs. Assn. Home: 401 Ocean Ave Spring Lake NJ 07762 Office: Dept Bus Adminstrn Monmouth Coll West Long Branch NJ 07764

TOMPKINS, HARVEY JOHN, physician; b. Chgo., June 14, 1906; s. Harvey John and Josephine (Burke) T.; B.S., Loyola U., 1927, M.D., 1931; m. Margaret Catherine Ruddy, Feb. 13, 1934; children—Harvey John, Patricia Marie. Intern Mercy Hosp., 1931-32; resident in pediatrics and obstetrics Lewis Meml. Hosp., 1933; resident in contagious diseases Municipal Contagious Disease Hosp. (all Chgo.), 1934; camp surgeon Three Lakes, Wis., Civilian Conservation Corps, 1934-35; resident physician VA Hosp., North Little Rock, Ark., 1935, asso. med. officer VA Hosp., Danville, Ill., 1935-37, med. officer VA Hosp., Mendota, Wis., 1937-39, sr. med. officer VA Hosp. St. Cloud, Minn., 1939-42, chief med. officer VA Hosp., Knoxville, Ia., 1942-43, chief profl. service VA Neuropsychiat. Diagnostic Center, Mendota, Wis., 1943-45, chief inpatient sect., asst. chief psychiatry and neurology div. VA Central Office, Washington, 1945-48, dir. psychiatry and neurology service, Dept. Medicine and Surgery, 1948-55; clin. prof. psychiatry N.Y. U. Med. Sch., 1955-73, now emeritus; clin. prof. Georgetown U. Med. Sch., 1947-55; dir. Jacob L. Reiss Mental Health Pavilion, St. Vincent's Hosp. and Med. Center N.Y., 1955-72, dir. emeritus, 1973—; pres. N.Y. Sch. Psychiatry, N.Y.C., 1972—, chmn. bd. trustees, 1959—; coordinator psychiat. activities Roman Cath. Archdiocese N.Y., 1955-71. Pres. Mental Health Film Bd., 1962-69; bd. dirs., mem. exec. com. Group Health Inc., N.Y.C.; Mem. com. on Standards Am. Bd. Med. Specialties, 1972—; mem. panel profl. consultants Nat. Assn. Mental Health; chmn. N.Y.C. Community Mental Health Bd., 1958-69; mem. N.Y. City Health Research Council, 1958—, chmn. study panel on psychiatry and neurology, 1961-73, mem. exec. com., 1972-74; corporate mem. Nat. Assembly for Social Policy and Devel.; mem. Gov.'s Mental Hygiene Council N.Y., 1956-73. Trustee St. Vincent's Hosp. and Med. Center, Manhattan Bowery Project, St. Vincent's Med. Center, Richmond, S.I., N.Y.; mem. adv. com. St Vincent's Hosp. and Med. Center, Harrison, N.Y. Commd. 1st lt. M.C., U.S. Army, 1934, advanced through grades to col. AUS, ret., 1966. Certified mental hosp. adminstr. Diplomate Am. Bd. Psychiatry and Neurology (dir. 1967, v.p. 1972-73, pres. 1974-75). Fellow Am. (life; past pres.), So. (hon.), World (asso. sec.-gen. 1966-72) psychiat. assns., Am. Coll. Psychiatrists, A.C.P., N.Y. Acad. Medicine (v.p. 1972—); mem. AMA (residency review com. Council Med. Edn.), Acad. Religion and Mental Health (past pres.), Nat. Guild Catholic Psychiatrists (past pres.), Catholic Physicians Guild, N.Y. Psychiat. Soc. (pres. 1978), N.Y. Soc. Clin. Psychiatry (past pres.), N.Y. Celtic Med. Soc., Group for Advancement Psychiatry, Soc. Med. Cons. to Armed Forces, Am. Acad. Neurology, Royal Medico-Psychol. Assn. (Gt. Britain) (corr.), Royal Soc. Medicine (Gt. Britain) (affiliate), Catholic Commn. on Intellectual and Cultural Affairs, Alpha Omega Alpha. Roman Catholic. Knight of Malta. Clubs: Cosmos (Washington); Strathmore-Vanderbilt Country (Manhasset, N.Y.); Vidonian of New York (N.Y.C.). Contbr. articles to med. jours. Home: 157 Chapel Rd Manhasset NY 11030 Office: 130 W 12th St New York NY 10011

TOMPKINS, JAMES MCLANE, ins. co. exec., govt. adviser; b. Balt., Jan. 1, 1913; s. John Almy and Frederica (McLane) T.; grad Phillips Acad., 1931; B.A., Yale, 1935, M.A. (Pierson Coll. fellow 1940-43), 1943; certificate grad. study labor relations, N.Y. U.; m. Barbara Miller, Nov. 22, 1965. Research fellow Yale, 1937-40; dir. Bur. Mil. Service and Information, Yale and Dept. Def., 1940-43; dir. exec. placement, asst. chmn. bd. Vick Chem. Co., N.Y.C., 1943-48; with C.V. Starr & Co., Inc., N.Y.C., 1948—, v.p. pub. affairs, 1968—, also dir.; dir. Am. Internat. Underwriters Overseas, TAM Sigorta, Turkey; chmn. AIU Pakistan, Vt. Accident Ins. Co. Int., Uganda Am. Ins. Co., AIU Mediterranean, Inc.; vice chmn. bd. Am. Life Ins. Co., Wilmington, Del. Mem. U.S. delegation UN Conf. Trade and Devel., 1968—; adviser U.S. delegation OECD, 1969—; mem. U.S. Maritime Transport Com.; mem. U.S. del. London Diplomatic Conf. Maritime Claims, 1976, Geneva Conf. Multi Modal Transport, 1975, 77, 78. Trustee Asia Soc., Samuel Goodyear Scholarship Fund (Yale); chmn. Eisenhower Fellowship Com., Pakistan, 1955-60; mem. Yale Alumni Bd. Mem. Yale Alumni Assn. (pres. New Canaan chpt.), Alpha Sigma Phi (past nat. trustee). Clubs: Yale, India House, Sky (N.Y.C.); American (London); Sind (Karachi, Pakistan). Home: Inshallah Dunrovin Wilton Creek Rd PO Box 6 Hartfield VA 23071 Office: 102 Maiden Ln New York NY 10005. *After living around the world many years I'm convinced that the greatest factor for building a stable, progressive and free community in which citizens can develop personal satisfaction and well-being is the American worth ethic, no matter where or by whom practiced.*

TOMPKINS, ROBERT GEORGE, physician; b. Portland, Oreg., May 29, 1923; s. George Henry and Minnie (Davies) T.; B.S., U. Wash., 1943; M.B., Northwestern U., 1947; M.D., 1949; M.S., U. Minn., 1954; m. Rosemarie Nowicki, June 6, 1948 (dec. 1960); children—Timothy Michael, Mary Eileen, George Henry, Robert George. Intern, King County Hosp., Seattle, 1948-49, resident, 1949-50; fellow, 1st asst. Mayo Found., Rochester, Minn., 1950-54; practice medicine specializing in cardiology and internal medicine, Tulsa, 1954—; mem. staff St. Francis Hosp., chief staff, 1964, med. dir., 1968—; asso. clin. prof. medicine Tulsa Med. Coll.-U. Okla.; v.p. William K. Warren Med. Research Center; med. chmn. Guatemala Mission Hosp., Diocese Oklahoma City and Tulsa; coordinator planning program Okla. Regional Med. Program; mem. Tulsa Health and Hsp. Planning Council; bd. dirs. St. Francis Hosp. Diplomate Am. Bd. Internal Medicine; decorated Knight of Equestrian Order Holy Sepulchre of Jerusalem (Vatican). Fellow A.C.P., Royal Coll. Medicine, Am. Coll. Cardiology; mem. AAAS, AMA, Am. Diabetic Assn., Am., Tulsa County (pres. 1959) heart assns., Am. rheumatism Assn., Mayo Alumni Assn., Alpha Kappa Kappa. Club: K.C. Contbr. articles to profl. jours; editor Jour. Okla. State Med. Assn., 1974—. Home: 2221 22d Pl E Tulsa OK 74114 Office: 6161 Yale St S Tulsa OK 74177

TOMPKINS, WILLIAM F., lawyer; b. 1913; A.B., Wesleyan U., Middletown, Conn.; LL.B., U. Newark; m. Jane Davis Bryant; 1 son, William F. Admitted to N.J. bar, 1942; former U.S. dist. atty. for N.J., former asst. atty. gen. U.S.; partner firm Lum, Biunno and Tompkins. Mem. N.J. Assembly, 1951-53. Pres. bd. trustees Newark Acad., Livingston, N.J., 1964-69, chmn. bd. trustees, 1969-75. Fellow Am. Coll. Trial Lawyers, Am. Bar Found.; mem. Am. (spl. com. on minimum standards adminstrn. criminal justice 1964), Fed., N.J., Essex County bar assns. Clubs: Baltusrol, Essex, Mid-Ocean. Author: (with Harry J. Anslinger) Traffic in Narcotics, 1953. Home: 589 Ridgewood Rd Maplewood NJ 07040 Office: 550 Broad St Newark NJ 07102

TOMPSETT, RALPH, physician, educator; b. Tidioute, Pa., Oct. 8, 1913; s. William C. and Madora (Foster) T.; A.B., Cornell U., 1934; M.D., Cornell U., 1939; m. Jean Mac Ewen, June 30, 1942; children—Joan, William, Polly, Selene. Intern, resident N.Y. Hosp., 1939-42; from instr. to asso. prof. medicine and clin. medicine Cornell Med. Coll., 1946-57; dir. med. edn., chief internal medicine Baylor U. Med. Center, 1957—; prof. internal medicine U. Tex. Southwestern Med. Sch., 1957—. Diplomate Am. Bd. Internal Medicine. Master A.C.P.; mem. Am. Fedn. Clin. Research, Am. Soc. Clin. Investigation, Assn. Am. Physicians. Home: 6338 Stefani Dr Dallas TX 75225

TOMPSON, CARROLL GRAY, tobacco co. exec.; b. Mexico, Mo., Mar. 24, 1928; s. Willard Dudley and Nellie Gray (Vaughn) T.; A.A., Moberly Jr. Coll., 1948; B.A., William Jewel Coll., 1950; M.S., M.I.T., 1969; m. Marsha Anne Carroll, May 16, 1951; children—Randolph Carroll, Catherine Gray. With R.J. Reynolds Tobacco Co., Winston-Salem, N.C., 1953—, mfg. mgr., 1973-74, v.p., dir. mfg., 1974-75, v.p., 1975-76, exec. v.p., 1979—; pres., chief exec. officer RJR Archer, Inc., Winston-Salem, 1976-79. Bd. trustees Forsyth Tech. Inst., Winston-Salem, 1975-79, chmn., 1977—; pres. Old Hickory council Boy Scouts Am., 1980—; vice chmn. Forsyth County United Way, 1979; mem. Winston-Salem Arts Council, 1967-78; v.p. Consumer Credit Counseling Service of Forsyth County, 1978-79; mem. Winston-Salem-Forsyth County Bd. Edn., 1970-74. Served with U.S. Army, 1951-53. Recipient Achievement award William Jewell Coll., 1978; mem. Sloan Fellows Soc., 1969-79. Mem. Am. Chem. Soc., Aluminum Assn. Am., Nat. Minority Purchasing Council (dir.). Republican. Baptist. Clubs: Rotary, Forsyth Country. Office: 401 N Main St Winston-Salem NC 27102

TOMPSON, MARIAN LEONARD, assn. exec.; b. Chgo., Dec. 5, 1929; d. Charles Clark and Marie Christine (Bernardini) Leonard; student public and parochial schs., Chgo. and Franklin Park, Ill.; m. Clement R. Tompson, May 7, 1949; children—Melanie Tompson Kandler, Deborah Tompson Mikolajczak, Allison Tompson Fagerholm, Laurel Tompson Davies, Sheila, Brian, Philip. Co-founder La Leche League, Internat., Franklin Park, Ill., 1956, pres., dir., 1956—; cons. WHO; bd. dirs. North Am. Soc. Psychosomatic Ob-Gyn; mem. adv. bd. Nat. Assn. Parents and Profls. for Safe Alternatives in Childbirth; mem. profl. adv. bd. Home Oriented Maternity Experience; guest lectr. Harvard U. Med. Sch., UCLA Sch. Public Health, U. Antioquia Med. Sch., Medellin, Columbia, U. Ill. Sch. Medicine, Chgo., U. W.I., Jamaica, U. N.C.; mem. family com. Ill. Commn. on Status of Women, 1976—. Recipient Gold medal of honor Centro de Rehabilitacao Nossa Senhora da Gloria, 1975. Author: (with others) The Womanly Art of Breastfeeding, 1958, 2d, revised edit., 1963; columnist La Leche League News, 1958—, People's Doctor Newsletter, 1977—; contbr. articles to profl. jours.; asso. editor Child and Family Quar., 1967—. Office: 9616 Minneapolis Ave Franklin Park IL 60131

TOMSICK, FRANK, architect; b. Cleve., Feb. 6, 1934; s. Frank and Matilda (Kalcic) T.; B.A. with honors, U. Calif., Berkeley, 1956, M.Arch., 1958; m. Chrie Tomsick, June 28, 1958. Vice-pres. Gerald M. McCue & Assos., San Francisco, 1964-70; v.p. McCue Boone Tomsick, San Francisco, 1970-72, exec. v.p., 1973-79; pres. MBT Assos., San Francisco, 1976—; lectr. dept. architecture U. Calif., Berkeley, 1970. Served with C.E., U.S. Army, 1958-60. Fellow AIA. Democrat. Office: 631 Clay St San Francisco CA 94111

TOMSKEY, GILBERT CHARLES, urologist; b. Wisconsin Rapids, Wis., Mar. 10, 1911; s. George G. and Laura L. Tomskey; B.S., U. Wis., 1932, M.D., 1935; m. Kitty M. Logan, Dec. 19, 1939; children—W. H. Tomskey Wilkerson, M.D. Tomskey Charbonnet. Intern, Touro Infirmary, New Orleans, 1935-36, resident inurology, 1936-37, mem. staff, 1939-77, sr. in urology, 1955—; resident in urology Charity Hosp., New Orleans, 1937-39, sr. vis. surgeon, 1955—, chmn. med. com. 1960-70, bd. adminstrs., 1960-72; practice medicine specializing in urology, New Orleans, 1939-79; asso. prof. urology Tulane U., 1956-61; prof., chmn. dept. urology La. State U., New Orleans, 1961-79; mem. vis. staff Touro Infirmary, cons. to hosps.; pres. Cancer Assn. Greater New Orleans, 1970-72; mem. adv. com. Regional Heart, Stroke and Cancer Program La. Mem. com. on agy. relations United Fund, New Orleans. Served to maj. M.C., U.S. Army, 1942-46; ETO. Diplomate Am. Bd. Urology. Fellow A.C.S.; mem. Am. Urol. Assn., La. State Urol. Assn. (pres. 1969-70), AMA, So. Med. Assn., La. State Med. Soc., Indsl. Med. Assn., Soc. Univ. Urologists, Am. Assn. Clin. Urologists, Orleans Parish Med. Soc. (dir. 1955-57), New Orleans Grad. Med. Assembly (dir. 1957-58), La. State U. Urology Alumni Assn. (Gilbert C. Tomskey Lectures 1973-79). Democrat. Episcopalian. Clubs: Boston, La. Contbr. articles to profl. jours. Office: 3439 Prytania St New Orleans LA 70115

TONDEUR, PHILIPPE MAURICE, mathematician, educator; b. Zurich, Switzerland, Dec. 7, 1932; s. Jean and Simone (Lapaire) T.; came to U.S., 1964, naturalized, 1974; Ph.D., U. Zurich, 1961; m. Claire-Lise Ballansat, Dec. 20, 1965. Research fellow U. Paris, 1961-63; lectr. math. U. Zurich, 1963-64, U. Buenos Aires (Argentina), 1964, Harvard U., Cambridge, Mass., 1964-65, U. Calif., Berkeley, 1965-66; asso. prof. Wesleyan U., Middletown, Conn., 1966-68; asso. prof. U. Ill., Urbana, 1968-70, prof., 1970—; vis. prof. Auckland U., 1968, Eidg. Techn. Hochschule, U. Heidelberg, 1973. Recipient fellowships Swiss Nat. Sci. Found., Harvard U., U. Ill. Mem. Am. Math. Soc., Schweiz Math. Gesellschaft, Société Math. de France. Contbr. articles to profl. jours. Office: Math Dept U Ill Urbana IL 61801

TONE, KENNETH EDWARD, lawyer; b. Tiffin, Ohio, July 15, 1930; s. Harry Frederick and Lucille (Wahl) T.; B.S., Miami U., Oxford, Ohio, 1950; LL.B., J.D., Ohio No. U., 1953; m. Mary Zeitzheim, July 19, 1954; children—Mary Robin, Tygh Mathew. Admitted to Ohio bar, 1953, Fed. dist. bar, 1955, U.S. Supreme Ct. bar, 1962; practice in Sandusky, Ohio, 1953—; partner firm Tone, Maddrell, Eastman & Grubbe, 1960—; solicitor Village of Bay View, Ohio, also Village of Milan, Ohio, 1955-60; spl. legal counsel to atty. gen. Ohio, 1971—; acting judge Sandusky Mcpl. Ct. Sec. Sandusky Planning and Zoning Commn., 1956-65, Sandusky Zoning Code Bd. Appeals, 1956-65, Sandusky Bldg. Code Bd. Appeals, 1956-65, Sandusky Civil Service Commn., 1953-72; mem. Sandusky City Charter Revision Com., 1954-55, 64; chmn. Erie County Bd. Visitors to Public Instns., 1976—; mem. Erie County Democratic Exec. Com. and Central Com., 1962—: bd. dirs. Goodwill Industries, 1969-79; bd. dirs. Vols. of Am., 1955-63, v.p., 1959-60, pres., 1960-62; bd. dirs., drive chmn., legal counsel Erie County chpt. Am. Heart Assn., 1956-58, chmn. Heart Ball, 1969; bd. dirs., v.p. Sandusky Area council Girl Scouts U.S.A., 1956-59; trustee Sandusky chpt. Am. Cancer Soc., 1958-60, pres., 1960. Served with USNR, 1950-52. Mem. Am., Ohio (probate and trust com. 1964-74), Erie County (pres. 1978), Fed. bar assns., Am. Judicature Soc., Sandusky Area C. of C. (steering, legis. coms.), Sandusky Jaycees (past treas., v.p., dir., parliamentarian), N. Central Ohio Arts Council, Internat. Platform Assn., AMVETS (life), Ohio Fire Chiefs Assn. (hon.), Ohio Protective Assn. (hon.), Nat. Eagle Scout Assn., Sandusky Power Squadron (lt. comdr. 1978), Ohio Geneal. Soc., Phi Kappa Tau, Delta Theta Phi. Mem. United Ch. Christ (past mem. consistory). Clubs: Plum Brook Country, Southwood Racquet, Ski (founder), Torch (founder), Sandusky Yacht (past commodore), Interlake Yachting Assn., (Sandusky), Elks, Masons, Shriners. Author: Sandusky Civil Service Rules, 1955-56; Your Budget and You, 1966. Home: Whitehall 566 Bimini Dr Sandusky OH 44870 Office: Suite 300 Feick Bldg Sandusky OH 44870

TONE, PHILIP WILLIS, fed. judge; b. Chgo., Apr. 9, 1923; s. Elmer James and Frances (Willis) T.; B.A., U. Iowa, 1943, J.D., 1948; grad. fellow Yale Law Sch., 1948; m. Gretchen Altfillisch, Mar. 10, 1945; children—Michael P., Jeffrey R., Susan A. Admitted to Iowa bar, 1948, Ill. bar, 1950, D.C. bar, 1950; law clk. Justice Wiley B. Rutledge, Supreme Ct. U.S., Washington, 1948-49; asso. firm Covington & Burling, Washington, 1949-50; asso., partner firm Jenner & Block, Chgo., 1950-72; judge U.S. Dist. Ct., Chgo., 1972-74, U.S. Ct. Appeals, Chgo., 1974—; spl. counsel Nat. Commn. on Causes and Prevention of Violence, 1968-69. Chmn. Ill. Supreme Ct. Rules Com., 1968-71, sec., 1963-68. Served with AUS, 1943-46. Jud. fellow Am. Coll. Trial Lawyers; mem. Am. Law Inst., Am., Ill. (bd. govs. 1960-64), Chgo. (bd. mgrs. 1966-69) bar assns., Ill. Soc. Trial Lawyers, Am. Judicature Soc., Law Club Chgo., Legal Club Chgo. Author (with A.E. Jenner, Jr.): Historical and Practice Notes, Ill. Civil Practice Act and Supreme Court Rules, 1956, 68. Contbr. articles to legal periodicals. Office: 219 S Dearborn St # 2774 Chicago IL 60604

TONER, RICHARD KENNETH, chem. engr.; b. Terre Haute, Ind., Jan. 9, 1913; s. James Madison and Anna Eva (Deeter) T.; B.S.Ch.E., Rose-Hulman Inst. Tech., 1934, D.Eng. (hon.), 1972; M.S.E., Purdue U., 1936, Ph.D., 1939; m. Virginia Martin, Sept. 1, 1937; 1 dau., Virginia Kay Toner Silverthorne. Instr. chem. engring. Purdue U., 1937-39, Lehigh U., 1939-40, N.Y. U., 1940-42; asst. prof. chem. engring. Princeton U., 1942-48, asso. prof., 1948-71, prof., 1971—, asso. chmn. dept. chem. engring., clk. Univ. Faculty; dir. publs., editor Textile Research Jour., Textile Research Inst. Priest asso. Trinity Episcopal Ch., Princeton, N.J., 1955—. Recipient Best Tchr. award Mfg. Chemists Assn., 1975. Mem. Am. Inst. Chem. Engrs., Am. Chem. Soc., AAUP, Fiber Soc., Am. Soc. Engring. Edn., Episcopal Guild Scholars, Sigma Xi, Tau Beta Pi, Alpha Chi Sigma. Republican. Author: (with John C. Whitwell) Conservation of Mass and Energy, 1969. Home: 50 McCosh Circle Princeton NJ 08540 Office: A321 Engring Quadrangle Princeton U Princeton NJ 08544

TONEY, ANTHONY, artist; b. Gloversville, N.Y., June 28, 1913; s. Michael and Susan (Betor) T.; B.F.A., Syracuse U., 1930; M.A., Columbia Tchrs. Coll., 1952, Ed.D., 1955; m. Edna Amadon Greenfield, Apr. 8, 1947; children—Anita Karen, Adele Susan. Executed mural Gloversville (N.Y.) High Schs., 1937, Bowne Hall, 1967, Brockway Cafeteria Syracuse U., 1971; one-man shows Wakefield Gallery, 1941, Artists Gallery, 1948, A.C.A. Gallery, 1949, 51, 54, 55, 57, 59, 62, 64, 68, 70, 72, 75, 77, Syracuse Mus., Roswell Mus., Kansas City Art Inst., U. N.Mex., 1956, Berkshire Mus., 1957, 60, S.I. Mus., Rochester Inst. Tech., 1958, U. So. Ill., Tyringham (Mass.) Gallery, 1960, 61, 66, Katonah Gallery, Albany Inst. History and Art, Lenox (Mass.) Art Gallery, Cayuga Mus., Auburn, N.Y., 1959, Harbor Gallery, L.I., N.Y., 1965, Dutchess Community Coll., Fordham Coll., 1967, Pace Coll., 1968, New Sch. for Social Research, 1970, 77, St. Mary's Coll. Md., 1974, Bridge Gallery, White Plains,

N.Y., 1975, Virginia Barrett Gallery, 1978, others; also exhibited many group shows including Syracuse Mus., Whitney Mus., U. Ill., U. Nebr., Carnegie Biennial, Pa. Acad., Nat. Acad., Walker Art Center, Nat. Inst. Arts and Letters, Am. Acad. Arts and Letters, Katonah Gallery, Corcoran Biennial; works in permanent collections U. Ill., Ind. Fine Arts Center, Ohio Wesleyan U., Wichita State U. Mus., U. Wyo. Mus. Art, Norton Gallery (Fla.), New Britain (Conn.) Mus., Whitney Mus., Tchrs. Coll. Columbia U., Nat. Acad., Chrysler Mus. at Norfolk, Montgomery Community Coll., S.I. Mus., Berkshire Mus., also pvt. collections; free-lance comml. artist, 1945—; instr. art Stevenson Sch., N.Y.C., 1948-52, Hofstra Coll., Hempstead, N.Y., 1953-55, New Sch. Social Research, others, 1953—; vis. artist Brandeis U., spring 1973, 74. Served as sgt. AUS, 1942-45. Decorated D.F.C. with clusters, Air medal with clusters; recipient purchase prize U. Ill., 1950; 1st prize Artists Equity Assn., 1952; Grumbacher award Audubon Artists, 1954; Emily Lowe award, 1955; Mickewiecz Art Competition 1st prize, 1956; Purchase prize S.I. Mus., 1957; Ranger purchase Nat. Acad., 1966, 76; Childe Hassam purchase prize Nat. Inst. Arts and Letters, 1967, 76; medal Honor, Audubon Artists Nat. Show, 1967, 75; Mintz Meml. award, 1974; Benjamin Altman Figure prize Nat. Acad., 1975. Mem. Nat. Soc. Mural Painters (treas. 1973-74), Artists Equity Assn. (nat. dir. 1952-56, 71-72, sec. nat. bd. 1956-57, exec. bd. N.Y. chpt. 1960-62, 71-72), Audubon Artists (mem. bd. 1959, 75-78), Coll. Art Assn., NEA, Kappa Delta Pi. Author: Creative Painting and Drawing, 1966; Painting and Drawing, 1978; Leonardo; also articles. Editor: 150 Masterpieces of Drawing, 1963. Contbr. to The Tune of the Calliope, 1958, Family Creative Workshop, 1975. Home: 16 Hampton Pl Katonah NY 10536 Office: care A C A Gallery 21 E 67 St New York City NY 10021. *I consider persistent struggle in the context of as much awareness of all possible factors of key importance. It is necessary to be as whole as possible in one's understanding of self, life, society and one's individual endeavor. One's goal must be the survival of life, the earth and solar system that makes it possible, and the solution of the problems that threaten human survival and perhaps all existence as we know it.*

TONG, HING, educator, mathematician; b. Canton, China, Feb. 16, 1922; s. Shen-Beu and Fung-Kam (Cheng) T.; A.B., U. Pa., 1943; Ph.D., Columbia, 1947; M.A. (hon.), Wesleyan U., Middletown, Conn., 1961; m. Mary Josephine Powderly, Aug. 19, 1956; children—Christopher Hing, Mary Elizabeth, William Joseph, Jane Frances, James John. NRC postdoctoral fellow Inst. Advanced Study, Princeton, 1947-48; lectr. Canton (China) U., 1949; Cutting travelling fellow Inst. Henri Poincare, Paris, France, 1950-51; asst. prof. Reed Coll., 1952-53; vis. asst. prof. Barnard Coll., 1953-54; mem. faculty Wesleyan U., 1954-67, prof. math., 1960-67, chmn. dept., 1962-64; prof. math. Fordham U., Bronx, N.Y., 1966—, chmn. dept. 1967-74; mem. U.S. subcom. World Orgn. Gen. Systems and Cybernetics. Mem. Phi Beta Kappa, Sigma Xi. Contbr. profl. jours. Home: 725 Cooper Ave Oradell NJ 07649 Office: Fordham Univ Bronx NY 10458

TONGUE, THOMAS H., state justice; b. Hillsboro, Oreg., Feb. 4, 1912; s. Thomas H. and Irene (Cadwell) T.; B.S., U. Oreg., 1934, J.D., 1937; J.S.D., Yale, 1939; m. Bernice M. Healy, Nov. 30, 1939; children—Thomas Healy, James Cadwell, John Richard. Admitted to Oreg. bar, 1937; atty. Bur. Municipal Research, U. Oreg., 1938-39, wage and hour div. U.S. Dept. Labor, 1939-42; exec. sec. West coast labor com. Nat. War Labor Bd., 1942-44; practice in Portland, 1944-69; partner firm Hicks, Davis, Tongue & Dale, 1948-67; of counsel firm Mautz, Souther, Spaulding, Kinsey & Williamson, 1967-69; asso. justice Oreg. Supreme Ct., 1969—. Chmn. jud. fitness commn. State of Oreg., 1969, chmn. labor mgmt. relations bd., 1962-63. Mem. Oreg. State Bar (v.p., bd. govs. 1952-55, chmn. com. jud. adminstrn. 1960-62). Episcopalian. Club: Illhee Hills Country (Salem). Contbr. to legal jours. Home: 3421 Country Club Dr S Salem OR 97302 Office: Oregon Supreme Ct Salem OR 97310

TONGUE, WILLIAM WALTER, educator, business cons.; b. Worcester, Mass., May 24, 1915; s. Walter Ernest and Lena (Brown) T.; A.B., Dartmouth, 1937, M.C.S., 1938; Ph.D., U. Chgo., 1947; m. Beverly Harriet Cohan, Dec. 26, 1936; children—Barbara Tongue Duggan, Kathleen Tongue Alligood. Jr. acct. Price, Waterhouse & Co., C.P.A.'s, N.Y.C., 1938; instr. Coe Coll., Cedar Rapids, Iowa, 1941-42; spl. cons. OSS, 1942; financial economist Fed. Res. Bank Chgo., 1942-44; economist Jewel Companies, Inc., Chgo., 1944-64; prof. econs. and finance U. Ill. at Chgo. Circle, also bus. cons., 1965—; econ. cons. LaSalle Nat. Bank, Chgo., 1968—, Alliance Savs. & Loan Assn., Chgo., 1977—; dir. St. Joseph Light & Power Co. (Mo.). Bd. dirs., v.p. research and statistics Chgo. Assn. Commerce and Industry, 1968-69. Mem. Nat. Assn. Bus. Economists (pres. 1962-63), Conf. Bus. Economists, Am. Statis. Assn. (pres. Chgo. chpt. 1951-52), Am. Econ. Assn., Am. Finance Assn., Econ. Club Chgo., Investment Analysts Assn. Chgo., Inst. Chartered Financial Analysts (chartered financial analyst 1963). Author articles; contbr. to books including How We Can Halt Inflation and Still Keep Our Jobs, 1974. Home: 212 Shoreline Dr Park Ridge IL 60068 Office: Box 4348 Chicago IL 60680

TONKIN, LEO SAMPSON, ednl. adminstr.; b. Suffern, N.Y., Apr. 2, 1937; s. Leo S. and Ann (Petrone) T.; A.B., Johns Hopkins, 1959, postgrad. Sch. Advanced Internat. Studies, 1962-63; J.D., Harvard, 1962; Dr. Pedagogy, St. Thomas Aquinas Coll., 1973. Legis.-adminstrv. asst. to U.S. Congressman, now Sen. Charles McC. Mathias, Jr., of Md., 1962-63; asso. counsel U.S. Ho. of Reps. Select Com. on Govt. Research, 1964, spl. cons. Ho. Spl. Subcom. on Edn., 1965-66; exec. dir. D.C. Commrs. Council on Higher Edn., 1965-66; pres. Leo S. Tonkin Assos., Inc., 1966—; founder, dir., chmn. bd. Washington Workshops Found., 1967—. Mem. White House Conf. on Edn., 1965, White House Conf. on Youth, 1971; spl. asst. to chmn. U.S. Ho. of Reps. Select Com. on Crime, 1972; mem. bd. plebe sponsors U.S. Naval Acad., 1977—; mem. adv. panel Nat. Commn. for Protection of Human Subjects of Biomed. and Behavioral Research, HEW, 1976-77. Bd. dirs. Washington Choral Arts Soc., 1971-73, Nat. Coordinating Council on Drug Edn., 1973, Nat. Student Ednl. Fund, 1974—, Wall St. Workshops Found., 1978—; chmn. bd. trustees St. Thomas Aquinas Coll., City of Phila. Govt. Honors Program; trustee Southeastern U., 1966-73; asso. bd. trustees Immaculata Coll., 1966-73; mem. advisory bd. Pub. Affairs and Govt. Degree Program, Mt. Vernon Coll., 1971-74; bd. dirs. YMCA, Washington, 1969-71. Recipient Americanism award Valley Forge Freedoms Found., 1973. Mem. Johns Hopkins Alumni Assn. of Washington (pres. 1969-72). Clubs: Georgetown, City Tavern, Nat. Press, Capitol Hill, Capitol Yacht (Washington); Harvard (N.Y.C.). Contbr. articles to mags. Home: Watergate South 700 New Hampshire Ave NW Washington DC 20037 Office: 3222 N St NW Washington DC 20007

TONKS, ROBERT STANLEY, pharmacologist; b. Aberystwyth, Wales, Aug. 13, 1928; s. Robert Patrick Dennis and Prudence Violet (Williams) T.; came to Can., 1973; student U. Coll. of South Wales, 1948-49, Welsh Coll. Pharmacy, 1949-51; B.Pharm., Welsh Nat. Sch. Medicine, Cardiff, 1951, Ph.D., 1954; m. Diana Mary Cownie, July 29, 1953; children—Pamela Mary, Julia Rosalind, Robert Michael, Sara Katharine. Organon postdoctoral fellow Med. Sch., Cardiff, 1954-55, Nat. Health Service postdoctoral fellow, 1955-56; Nat. Health Service sr. fellow Cardiff and Nevill Hall Hosp., Abergavenny, 1957-58; clin. lectr. pharmacology U. Wales, Cardiff, 1958-72; vis. fellow Claude Bernard Research Assn., Faculté de Medicine, Paris, 1959; sr. lectr. pharmacology and therapeutics Med. Sch. and U. Wales Hosp., Cardiff, 1972-73; dir., prof. Coll. Pharmacy, Dalhousie U., Halifax, N.S., Can., 1973-77, dean Faculty Health Professions, 1977—; cons. Pharm. Industry in U.K., Govt. of N.B., Can., Health and Welfare Can.; coordinator N.E. Can./Am. Health Conf., 1977—: chmn. pharm. scis. grants com. Med. Research Council Can.; mem. rev. com. Fed. Govt. Research Program on Drugs, Can.; chmn. advisory com. N.B. Minister of Health, 1974-78. Served with Royal Navy, 1946-48; PTO. Fellow Pharm. Soc. Gt. Britain, Inst. Biology; mem. Brit. Pharmacol. Soc., Biochemical Soc., Physiol. Soc., Internat. Soc. Thrombosis and Haemostasis, Pharmacology Soc. Can., Canadian Soc. Clin. Investigation, Assn. Acad. Health Centres, Canadian Soc. Hosp. Pharmacy (hon.), N.B. (hon.), N.S. (certificate of merit 1977) pharm. socs. Anglican. Club: Waegwoltic. Contbr. articles on pharmacology and pathology to profl. jours. Home: 6061 Fraser St Halifax NS B3H 1RS Canada Office: Dalhousie U Coburg Rd Halifax NS Canada

TONNDORF, JUERGEN, educator, otolaryngologist; b. Goettingen, Germany, Feb. 1, 1914; s. Woldemar and Lilli (Schneidewin) T.; B.S., U. Kiel (Germany), 1934, M.D., 1938; Ph.D., U. Heidelberg (Germany), 1945; m. Mechtild Brandts, Mar. 27, 1940. Came to U.S., 1947, naturalized, 1957. Dozent, U. Heidelberg, 1945-47; mem. research staff USAF Sch. Aviation Medicine, Randolph Field, Tex., 1947-52; from asst. prof. to prof. U. Ia., 1953-62; prof. otolaryngology Columbia Coll. Phys. and Surgeons, 1962—. Served with German Navy, 1939-45. Recipient von Eicken award German Otolaryng. Soc., 1942, L. Haymann award, 1970; Research Career award NIH, 1964, award merit Am. Otol. Soc. Fellow Acoustical Soc. Am.; mem. Am. Acad. Otolaryngology (hon.), Assn. Research in Otolaryngology, Am., German (hon.) otol. socs., Royal Soc. Medicine, Leopoldina Acad., Collegium Oto-Rhino-Laryngologicum. Editor Beltone Translation Series, 1961—. Editorial bd. Annals of Otology, Rhinology and Laryngology, 1957—; German Archives HNO Heilk., 1968—; Practica Otolaryngologica, 1970—. Contbr. articles to profl. jours. and handbooks. Home: 4425 Tibbett Ave New York NY 10471 Office: 630 W 168th St New York NY 10032

TONSMEIRE, ARTHUR C., JR., savs. and loan assn. exec.; b. Mobile, Aug. 26, 1913; s. Arthur C. and Eha Lee (McGowin) T.; B.S. in Commerce, Washington and Lee U., Lexington, Va., 1934; m. Elaine Henderson, June 18, 1966; children—Arthur C., III, Joseph L., Daniel L., Edward C., Robert C., Thomas H., Lee McGowin, William T. Propr. Tonsmeire Real Estate and Ins. Agy., Mobile, 1934-39; with First So. Fed. Savs. & Loan Assn., Mobile, 1940—, now pres., chmn. bd.; former vice chmn. bd. dirs. Fed. Home Loan Bank Atlanta; pub. South mag., Tampa, Fla.; dir. First Miss. Nat. Bank, Biloxi, Inter-Am. Savs. and Loan Union; vice chmn. internat. com. Internat. Housing Adv. Com., Dept. State. Chmn. bd., pres. Mobile United Way; trustee, bd. dirs. Mobile Area council Boy Scouts Am.; former chmn. Ala.-Guatemala Partners of Alliance; bd. dirs. Ala. Assn. Ind. Colls. Served to capt. U.S. Army, 1942-46. Mem. Nat. Savs. and Loan League (past pres.), U.S. League Savs. Assn. (vice chmn. internat. com., dir.), Ala. (dir.), Mobile (dir.) chambers commerce, Ala. (past pres., dir.), Mobile County (past pres., dir.) cattlemen's assns. Episcopalian. Clubs: Rotary, Kiwanis. Home: 3000 Tonsmeire Rd Theodore AL 36582 Office: PO Box 16267 Mobile AL 36616

TONSOR, STEPHEN JOHN, historian; b. Jerseyville, Ill., Nov. 26, 1923; s. Stephen John and Rose Mary (Schmidt) T.; student Blackburn Coll., 1941-43, D. Litt. (hon.), 1972; student U. Zurich (Switzerland), 1948-49, U. Munich (W.Ger.), 1953-54; Ph.D., U. Ill., 1954; m. Caroline Maddox, Sept. 6, 1949; children—Ann Tonsor Zeddies, Stephen John, IV, Claire Alice Pruss, Margaret Grace. From asst. prof. to prof. history U. Mich., 1954—; adj. scholar Am. Enterprise Inst., Washington; vis.-insp. North Central Assn.; sr. vis. research fellow Hoover Instn., 1972-73. Cons., Pres.'s Council Econ. Advisers, Washington, 1970-73; bd. dirs. Ann Arbor (Mich.) YM-YWCA, 1974-77. Served as sgt. Signal Corps, U.S. Army, 1943-46. Recipient Distinguished Teaching award U. Mich., 1962; Horace H. Rackham grantee, 1957, 62, 72; Relm Found. grantee, 1962-63; Earhart Found. summer grantee, 1971; Am. Council Learned Socs. travel grantee, 1972. Mem. Am. Catholic Hist. Assn. (exec. council), Am. Hist. Assn., Phila. Soc. (pres.), Mt. Pelerin Soc. Republican. Roman Catholic. Author: Tradition and Reform in Education, 1974; asso. editor Modern Age, 1969. Home: 1505 Morton St Ann Arbor MI 48104 Office: History Dept U of Mich Ann Arbor MI 48109

TONTZ, ROBERT L., govt. ofcl.; b. Guthrie, Okla., May 18, 1917; s. John and Mabel (Johnson) T.; B.S., Okla. State U., 1940, Ph.D., 1952; M.S. (fellow), Ia. State U., 1941; m. Hazel D. Crothers, June 10, 1944; children—John W., Brenda Kay. Asst. agrl. economist U. Tenn., 1942; asso. agrl. economist U.S. Dept. Agr., 1942-45; agrl. statistician Bur. Census U.S. Dept. Commerce, 1946; asst. prof. Okla. State U., 1947-55; agrl. economist U.S. Dept. Agr., Washington, 1956-68, supervisory agrl. economist, 1971—; internat. economist Dept. State, Paris, 1968-71. Recipient Superior Service award U.S. Dept. Agr., 1965, 75, Blue Ribbon award, 1972. Mem. Am. Agrl. Econ. Assn., Orgn. Profl. Employees U.S. Dept. Agr., Nat. Orgn. Fed.-State Employees (v.p.), Agr. History Soc., Sigma Xi, Phi Kappa Phi, Alpha Phi Sigma, Alpha Zeta, Phi Eta Sigma. Mem. Christian Ch. (chmn. bd., elder). Editor: Foreign Agricultural Trade: Selected Readings, 1966. Contbr. numerous econ. studies to profl. jours. Home: 8712 Braeburn Dr Annandale VA 22003 Office: US Dept Agr Washington DC

TOOKER, GEORGE, painter; b. Bklyn., Aug. 5, 1920; s. George Clair and Angela Montejo (Roura) T.; B.A., Harvard, 1942; student Art Students League, N.Y.C., 1943-44. One man exhbns. Edwin Hewitt Gallery, 1951, 55, Robert Isaacson Gallery, 1960, 62, Durlacher Bros., 1964, 67, Hopkins Center at Dartmouth Coll., 1967, Fine Arts Mus. San Francisco, 1974, Mus. Contemporary Art, Chgo., 1974, Whitney Mus., N.Y.C., 1975, Indpls. Mus. Art, 1975; group exhbns. Whitney Mus., 1947-50, 53, 55-58, 61, 64, 65, 67, 75, Venice Biennale, 1956, Art Inst. Chgo., 1951, 52, 54, 59, Inst. Contemporary Arts, London, 1950, Va. Mus., 1954, 62, Pa. Acad., 1966; represented permanent collections: Whitney Mus., Dartmouth Coll., Met. Mus., Walker Art Center, Mus. Modern Art, S.C. Johnson & Sons, Inc., Art: U.S.A., Sara Roby Found. Collection Am. Art; instr. Art Students League N.Y. Grantee Nat. Inst. Arts and Letters, 1960. Mem. NAD. Address: care Frank K Rehn Inc 14 E 60 St New York City NY 10022

TOOLAN, JOHN PETER, investment banker; b. N.Y.C., Sept. 26, 1930; s. John Joseph and Marcella S. (Scheid) T.; B.S., Fordham U., 1952; M.B.A., N.Y. U., 1954; m. Kathleen Murphy, Sept. 15, 1961; children—John, Peter, David, Kiley. With Loeb Rhoades, Hornblower & Co., N.Y.C., 1954—, pres., 1975—, chief exec. officer, 1976—. Served with USNR, 1952-54. Mem. Chgo. Bd. Trade, Bond Club N.Y.C. Roman Catholic. Clubs: Canoe Brook Country, Downtown Assn. Address: 14 Wall St New York NY 10005

TOOLE, ALBERT JULIUS, III, life ins. co. exec.; b. Dallas, Dec. 1, 1937; s. Albert Julius, Jr. and Louise (Foster) T.; B.B.A. in Fin., U. Tex., 1959; M.B.A. in Fin. and Accounting, So. Methodist U., 1962; chartered fin. analyst, 1969; m. Carolyn Hendrie, June 13, 1959; children—Albert Julius, IV, James Hendrie. With Southwestern Life Ins. Co., Dallas, 1962-68, Lionel D. Edie & Co., Inc., Dallas, 1968-71; sr. v.p., treas. Gulf Life Ins. Co., Jacksonville, Fla., 1971—; sr. v.p. Gulf United Corp., 1973—; chmn. bd. GMR Properties, 1972—, GULFCO Capital Mgmt., Inc., 1971—; officer, dir. numerous subs. and affiliated cos. Exec. com. Jacksonville United Way; bd. dirs. Jacksonville Conv. and Visitors Bur., Jacksonville Children's Mus., Jacksonville Downtown Council, Riverside Hosp., 1979-80. Served as officer USNR, 1959-61. Mem. Fin. Analysts Soc. Jacksonville, Inst. Chartered Fin. Analysts, Mortgage Bankers Assn. Am. Home: 3824 Bettes Circle Jacksonville FL 32210 Office: 1301 Gulf Life Dr Jacksonville FL 32207

TOOLE, ALLAN H., lawyer; b. Spokane, Wash., Nov. 4, 1920; LL.B., Gonzaga U., 1948. Admitted to Wash. bar, 1948; partner firm Witherspoon, Kelly, Davenport & Toole, Spokane. Dir. Old Nat. Bancorp., Old Nat. Bank Washington. Mem. Wash. Commn. for Expo '74. Trustee Spokane Symphony Soc., Greater Spokane Community Found., Leuthold Found. Fellow Am. Coll. Probate Counsel; mem. Spokane County, Wash. State, Am. bar assns. Office: 1114 Old Nat Bank Bldg Spokane WA 99201

TOOLE, BRUCE RYAN, lawyer; b. Missoula, Mont., June 21, 1924; J.D., U. Mont., 1949. Admitted to Mont. bar, 1950, U.S. Supreme Ct. bar, 1978; individual practice law, Missoula, 1950; dep. county atty. Missoula County (Mont.), 1952; asso. firm Crowley, Haughey, Hanson, Toole & Dietrich and predecessors, Billings, Mont., 1951-59, partner, 1959—. Mem. Gov.'s Adv. Council on Workmen's Compensation Mont., 1972-74; bd. visitors Law Sch., U. Mont., 1971—. Fellow Am. Coll. Trial Lawyers; mem. Internat. Assn. Ins. Counsel, Assn. Ins. Attys., Am., Yellowstone County (pres. 1973) bar assns., State Bar Mont. (trustee 1974-75, 78-79, pres. 1977-78). Home: 3019 Glacier Dr Billings MT 59102 Office: 500 Electric Bldg Billings MT 59101

TOOLE, JAMES FRANCIS, med. educator; b. Atlanta, Mar. 22, 1925; s. Walter O. Brien and Helen (Whitehurst) T.; B.A., Princeton U., 1947; M.D., Cornell U., 1949; LL.B., LaSalle Extension U., 1962; m. Patricia Anne Woolridge, Oct. 25, 1952; children—William, Anne, James, Sean. Intern, then resident internal medicine and neurology U. Pa. Hosp., Nat. Hosp., London, Eng., 1953-58; mem. faculty U. Pa. Sch. Medicine, 1958-62; prof. neurology, chmn. dept. Bowman Gray Sch. Medicine, 1962—; vis. prof. neuroscis. U. Calif. at San Diego, 1969-70. Mem. Nat. Bd. Med. Examiners, 1970—; mem. task force arteriosclerosis Nat. Heart Lung & Blood Inst., 1970-78; chmn. 6th and 7th Princeton confs. cerebrovascular diseases; cons. epidemiology WHO, 1968, 74, Japan, 1971, USSR, 1968, Ivory Coast, 1977; mem. Lasker Awards Com., 1976-77; chmn. neuropharmocologic drugs com. FDA, 1979—. Pres., N.C. Heart Assn., 1976-77. Served with AUS, 1950-51, USNR, 1951-53. Decorated Bronze Star with V, Combat Med. badge. Fellow A.C.P.; mem. Am. Clin. and Climatol. Assn., AMA, Am. Heart Assn. (chmn. com ethics 1970-75), Am. Physiol. Soc., Am. Neurol. Assn. (sec.-treas. 1978—), Am. Acad. Neurology. Author: (with A.N. Patel) Cerebrovascular Diseases, 1967, 2d edit., 1974. Editor: Current Concepts in Cerebrovascular Disease, 1969-73. Editorial bd. Annals Internal Medicine, 1968-75, Stroke, 1972—, Jour. AMA, 1975-77. Home: 1836 Virginia Rd Winston Salem NC 27104

TOOLEY, JAMES FRANCIS, airline exec.; b. Winnipeg, Man., Can., Sept. 9, 1915; s. Herbert and Hannah (MacBeath) T.; Chartered Accountant, U. Man., 1939; m. Dorothy B. Yates, Sept. 16, 1939; children—Heather Jane, James Arthur, George. With Canadair Ltd., 1947-57, v.p., 1954-57; pres. CAE Industries Ltd., 1957-67; chmn. bd. Nordair Ltd., Dorval, Que., Can., 1967-77, chmn. exec. com., 1977-79; chmn. bd. Jaytowl Inc., 1979—; chmn. bd. Mitchell-Holland Ltd., Montreal; dir. Marine Transport, Winnipeg. Mem. Inst. Chartered Accountants. Address: Suite 2425 1 Place Ville Marie Montreal PQ H3B 3M9 Canada

TOOMAN, H. KENNETH, truck co. exec.; b. Carnegie, Okla., Feb. 4, 1921; s. Ernest and Alcy Mabel (Barnes) T.; B.S., Okla. State U., 1948; G.S.S.M., Syracuse U., 1964-65; m. Virginia Elizabeth Newland; children—Paula K., Sidney L. With Internat. Harvester Co., 1954-68, regional mgr., Chgo., until 1968; asst. to sr. v.p. Mack Trucks, Inc., Allentown, Pa., 1968, mgr. nat. accounts and fleet sales, 1968-69, v.p. br. ops., 1969-73, exec. v.p. mktg., 1973—, also dir.; dir. Mack Fin. Corp. Served as 1st lt. USAF. Decorated D.F.C., Air medal with 5 clusters. Mem. Allentown-Lehigh C. of C. (dir.), Heavy Duty Truck Mfrs. Assn. (dir.). Republican. Lutheran. Club: Lehigh Country. Home: Box 108 Tumblebrook Rd Coopersburg PA 18036 Office: Box M 2100 Mack Blvd Allentown PA 18105

TOOMAY, JOHN CRAWFORD, air force officer; b. Ontario, Calif., Aug. 9, 1922; s. John Barron and Inez Lillian (Crawford) T.; B.A., U. Pacific, 1947; B.S. in Elec. Engring., U. So. Calif., 1947; M.S., George Washington U., 1970; m. Virginia Sadler, Oct. 11, 1944; children—Patrick J., Timothy L., Michele L., Leslie A. Enlisted U.S. Army, 1943, commd. 2d lt. USAAC, 1944, advanced through grades to maj. gen. U.S. Air Force, 1976; detachment comdr. ETO, 1945-46; communications security officer PTO, 1950-53; communications security staff officer, Washington, 1953-57; radar engr., program mgr. research and devel., Rome, N.Y., 1959-62; program dir. radar systems Advanced Research Project Agy., Washington, 1962-66; research and devel. mgr. advanced reentry systems, Norton AFB, Calif., 1966-69; comdr. Rome Air Devel. Center, 1971-72; mil. asst. dir. def. research and engring. Office Sec. Def., Washington, 1972-75; dir. devel. and acquisition USAF Hdqrs., 1975-76; dep. chief staff plans and programs Air Force Systems Command, Andrews AFB, Md., 1976—; profl. basketball player Nat. Basketball Assn., 1947-50. Decorated D.S.M., Legion of Merit with oak leaf cluster. Mem. Air Force Assn., Tau Beta Pi, Sigma Delta Psi. Home: 7103 Primrose Way Carlsbad CA 92008 Office: Hdqrs Air Force Systems Command Andrews Air Force Base MD 20335. *I follow Spinoza, Hobbes, and recently, Bronowski in believing the essential condition for man is rationality (i.e., the scientific method) applied in a free society. Other attributes we crave—dignity, brotherhood, happiness—follow only if the first condition is realized.*

TOOMBS, KENNETH ELDRIDGE, librarian; b. Colonial Heights, Va., Aug. 25, 1928; s. Garnett Edlridge and Susie W. (Bryant) T.; A.A., Tenn. Wesleyan Coll., 1950; B.S., Tenn. Poly. Inst., 1951; M.A., U. Va., 1955; M.L.S., Rutgers U., 1956; student La. State U., 1961-63; m. Ada Teresa Hornsby, Aug. 29, 1949; children—Susan Elizabeth, Cheri Lynn, Teresa Ann. Reference asst. Alderman Library, U. Va., 1954-55; research asst. Grad. Sch . Library Sci., Rutgers U., 1955-56; mem. staff and faculty La. State U., 1956-63, asst. dir. charge pub. services, 1962-63; dir. libraries, prof. library sci. U. Southwestern La., 1963-67; dir. libraries U. S.C. Columbia, 1967—; vice-chmn. Southeastern Library Network, 1973-74, chmn., 1974-75, mem. exec. bd., 1973-76. Cons. library bldgs. Chmn. librarians sect. La. Coll. Conf., 1965-67; mem. Bd. La. Library Examiners, 1966-67; participant Library Mgmt. Inst., U. Wash., Seattle, 1969, Library Bldg. Problems Inst., U. Calif. at Los Angeles, 1970. Treas. Wesley Found.; v.p. Am. Field Services Internat. Scholarships; bd. dirs. U. S.C. Ednl. Found., 1975—. Danforth asso., 1967—. Served to 1st lt.

AUS, 1946-47, 51-53. Mem. Am. (life), La. (parliamentarian 1962-63, 66-67), Southeastern (Rothrock award 1978), Southwestern, S.C. (pres. 1976) library assns., Assn. Southeastern Research Libraries (chmn. 1973-75), AAUP (sec.), La. Hist. Assn., La. Tchrs. Assn., Soc. Tympanuchus Cupido Pinnatus, South Caroliniana Soc. Mason (Shriner), Kiwanian. Methodist. Contbr. articles to profl. jours. Editor Bull. La. Library Assn., 1959-62; mng. editor Southwest La. Jour., 1963-67; adv. bd. Linguistic Atlas Am. Home: 16 Garden Springs Rd Columbia SC 29209

TOOMEY, ROBERT E., hosp. adminstr.; b. Cambridge, Mass., Mar. 18, 1916; s. Daniel J. and Catherine (Shanley) T.; B.S., Harvard, 1940; M. Ed., Boston U., 1941; M.S., Columbia, 1951; LL.D. (hon.), Clemson U., 1968; m. Laurette Creighton, Oct. 9, 1943; children—Robert Creighton, Carole Laurette, Richard Kirk, Jeanette Elizabeth. Tchr., coach Browne & Nichols Sch., Cambridge, 1940-42; psychologist VA, Detroit, 1946-49; adminstrv. asst. Roosevelt Hosp., N.Y.C., 1951-52; dir. North Country Hosps., Gouverneur, N.Y., 1952-53; asst. dir. Greenville (S.C.) Gen. Hosp., 1953; gen. dir., asst. sec., trustee Greenville Hosp. System, including Greenville Gen. Hosp., Allen Bennett Meml. Hosp., Greer, S.C., Hillcrest Hosp., Simpsonville, S.C., Roger Huntington Nursing Center, Greer, Sirrine Family Practice Center, M. Pickens Hosp., Greenville Meml. Hosp., Roger C. Peace Inst., North Greenville Hosp., Travelers Rest, S.C., 1954-77, cons./adviser, asst. sec. bd. trustees, 1977—; cons. dir. Center for Multi-Institutional systems Am. Hosp. Assn.; dir. Blue Cross/Blue Shield S.C., 1977. Vis. lectr. Clemson U., 1969—. Pres. Carolinas-Va. Hosp. Conf., 1957-58; mem. Gov. S.C. Com. Nursing, 1963, S.C. Study Com. on Alcohol and Drug Addiction, 1963—, S.C. Bd. Health Hosp. Adv. Council, 1964, Gov.'s Spl. Health Service Study Com. 1972; sec. Com. for Med. Sch. in Greenville, 1962—; mem. com. planning and implementation Nat. League Nursing, 1966—; adviser on health care programs Gov. S.C., 1973. Trustee United Fund Greenville County, 1963-66; chmn. trustees Episcopal Day Sch., Greenville, 1959; bd. dirs. Greenville Community Council, 1966—; trustee Carolina Hosp. and Health Services, 1977—. Served as lt. AUS, 1942-46. Fellow Am. Coll. Hosp. Adminstrs. (council regents 1964-71, chmn. ednl. planning com. dist. III, 1966); mem. Am. (ho. of dels. 1959-63, trustee; mem. spl. com. provision health care 1970, adv. panel on multi-nat. systems 1977), S.C. (pres. 1957-58, 70, trustee 1955-59, 61, 70, chmn. long range planning com. 1977, also past or present chmn. numerous coms. and divs.) hosp. assns., Greenville C. of C. Contbr. articles to profl. jours. Home: 702 Crescent Ave Greenville SC 29601 Office: 701 Grove Rd Greenville SC 29605

TOOMEY, THOMAS MURRAY, lawyer; b. Washington, Dec. 9, 1923; s. Vincent L. and Catherine V. (McCann) T.; student Duke U., 1943-44; student Catholic U. Am., 1942-43, 45-47, J.D., 1949; m. Grace Donohoe, June 22, 1948; children—Isabelle Marie Toomey Hessick, Helen Marie, Mary Louise, Thomas Murray. Admitted to D.C. bar, 1949, Md. bar, 1952; individual practice law, Washington, 1949—; sec., gen. counsel, dir. Allied Capital Corp., Washington and Ft. Lauderdale, Fla.; founder, organizer, dir. Pepsi-Cola Bottling Co. of Hartford-Springfield, Inc.; dir. Pepsi-Cola Bottling Co. of New Haven, Inc., M.S. Ginn Co., Inc., Washington, Donohoe Constrn. Co., Inc.; past dir. Pepsi-Cola Bottling Co. of Hawaii, Pepsi-Cola Bottling Co. of Houston, Park Shore Hotel, Honolulu, Libby Welding Co., Inc., Kansas City, Mo. Chmn. aviation and transp. coms. Met. Washington Bd. Trade, 1954-76, chmn. zoning com., 1955-57, chmn. ann. spring outing, 1961, bd. dirs., 1962-77; chmn. dedication Dulles Internat. Airport, 1962; asso. trustee Cath. U. Am.; founding trustee Heights Sch. Served to 1st lt. USMC, 1942-46, 50-52. Recipient Ann. Alumni Achievement award Cath. U., 1977. Mem. Am., D.C., Md. bar assns., Bar Assn. D.C., Am. Judicature Soc., Comml. Law League Am., Nat. Assn. Small Bus. Investment Cos. (chmn. legal com. 1968-72), Friendly Sons St. Patrick, Sovereign Mil. Order of Malta (So. Assn. U.S.A.). Clubs: Congressional Golf and Country; Kenwood Golf and Country; Univ., Army and Navy (Washington); Tower, Lago Mar Beach and Country (Ft. Lauderdale); Rehoboth Beach (Del.) Country. Home: 6204 Garnett Dr Chevy Chase MD 20015 also 2000 S Ocean Dr Apt 1410 Fort Lauderdale FL 33315 Apt 1106-S Edgewater House Bethany Beach DE 19930 Office: 1625 Eye St NW Washington DC 20006

TOOMRE, ALAR, educator; b. Rakvere, Estonia, Feb. 5, 1937; s. Elmar and Linda (Aghen) T.; came to U.S., 1949, naturalized, 1955; B.S. in Physics, M.I.T., 1957, B.S. in Aero Engring., 1957; Ph.D. (Marshall scholar), Manchester U. (Eng.), 1960; m. Joyce Stetson, June 14, 1958; children—Lars, Erik, Anya. Instr., M.I.T., 1960-62, asst. prof., 1963-65, asso. prof., 1965-70, prof. applied math., 1970—; fellow Inst. for Advanced Study, Princeton, N.J., 1962-63; vis. asso. Calif. Inst. Tech., 1969-70. Guggenheim fellow, 1969-70; Fairchild scholar Calif. Inst. Tech., 1975. Mem. Am. Astron. Soc., Internat. Astron. Union, Am. Acad. Arts and Scis. Research in fluid dynamics and theoretical astronomy. Office: Room 2-371 MIT Cambridge MA 02139

TOON, M. SPALDING, r.r. exec.; b. Troy, N.Y., Jan. 28, 1918; s. George and Margaret Harcomb (Broadfoot) T.; B.S., Mass. Inst. Tech., 1940; m. Ann Pause, Aug. 1, 1942; children—Patricia (Mrs. Stewart Early), Susan (Mrs. Richard B. Wright). With Isthmian Steamship Co., N.Y.C., 1940-51, U.S. Steel Corp., Pitts., 1952-53, 55-59; with Bessemer & Lake Erie RR, Pitts., 1954—, pres., 1972—; pres. Ohio Barge Line Inc., Dravosburg, Pa., 1960-72, Warrior & Gulf Navigation Co., Chickasaw, Ala., 1960-72, Carbon County Rwy. Co., East Carbon, Utah, 1969—, Duluth, Missabe & Iron Range Rwy., Duluth, Minn., 1972—, Elgin, Joliet and Eastern Rwy., Joliet, Ill., 1972—, Union RR Co., Pitts., 1972—, Pitts. & Conneaut Dock Co., Conneaut, Ohio, 1972—, Birmingham So. R.R. Co., Fairfield, Ala., 1976—; dir. Cartier Rwy. Co. Trustee Thiel Coll., Greenville, Pa., 1975—. Mem. Assn. Am. Railroads (dir. 1973—), Western R.R. Assn. (dir. 1973—), Eastern R.R. Assn. (dir. 1972—), Nat. Freight Traffic Assn., Am. Bur. Shipping, Soc. Naval Architects and Marine Engrs. Republican. Presbyn. Clubs: Traffic, Duquesne, Chartiers Country (Pitts.); Rolling Rock (Ligonier, Pa.); Union League (Chgo.); Kitchi Gammi (Duluth, Minn.); Capitol Hill (Washington). Home: 1413 Terrace Dr Pittsburgh PA 15228 Office: 600 Grant St PO Box 536 Pittsburgh PA 15230

TOON, MALCOLM, former U.S. ambassador; b. Troy, N.Y., July 4, 1916; s. George and Margaret Harcomb (Broadfoot) T.; A.B., Tufts U., 1937, LL.D. (hon.), 1977; M.A., Fletcher Sch. Law and Diplomacy, 1939; student Middlebury Coll., 1950, Harvard U., 1950-51; LL.D. (hon.), Middlebury Coll., 1978; m. Elizabeth Jane Taylor, Aug. 28, 1943; children—Barbara, Alan, Nancy. Fgn. service officer, 1946-79, assigned successively Warsaw, Budapest, Moscow, Rome, Berlin, Washington, 1946-60; assigned Am. embassy, London, 1960-63, counselor political affairs, Moscow, 1963-67; with Dept. of State, Washington, 1967-69; ambassador to Czechoslovakia, 1969-71, to Yugoslavia, 1971-75, to Israel, 1975-76, to USSR, 1976-79; mem. U.S. del. Nuclear Test Conf., Geneva, 1958-59, Four Power Working Group, Washington, London, Paris, 1959, Fgn. Ministers Conf., Geneva, 1969, Ten Nation Disarmament Com., Geneva, 1960. Served from ensign to lt. comdr., USNR, 1942-46.

TOONE, ELAM COOKSEY, JR., educator, physician; b. Richmond, Va., Nov. 4, 1908; s. Elam C. and Elizabeth (Ryland) T.; B.A. magna cum laude, Hampden Sydney Coll., 1929, LL.D., 1973; M.D., Med. Coll. Va., 1934; m. Marion Van Nostrand, July 20, 1964; 1 son, Elam Cooksey III. House officer Hillman Hosp., Birmingham, Ala., also Med. Coll. Va. Hosp., Richmond, 1934-38; from asst. to prof. medicine Med. Coll. Va., 1936-60, chmn. div. connective tissue diseases, 1966-74; dir. sect. rheumatology McGuire VA Hosp., 1975—; cons. two area hosps. Pres., chmn. bd. trustees Richmond Acad. Med., 1957-58; bd. advisers Family Service Soc., 1950, Dept. Pub. Welfare, Richmond, 1961-63. Bd. govs., dir. Nat. Arthritis Found., 1958-60, chpts., 1955—, chmn. inter-chpt. advisory com., 1957; bd. dirs. Charles W. Thomas Arthritis Research Fund, 1965-74; trustee MCV Found., 1970. Served to lt. col. AUS, 1942-46: MTO. Decorated Bronze Star medal; recipient Distinguished Service award Nat. Arthritis Found., 1966. Diplomate Am. Bd. Internal Medicine. Fellow A.C.P.; mem. Am. Rheumatism Assn. (v.p. 1963), AAAS, Richmond Soc. Internal Medicine (pres. 1963), Va. Med. Soc. (program chmn. 1957), AMA, Clin. and Climatol. Assn., Am. Fedn. Clin. Research, Phi Beta Kappa, Alpha Omega Alpha, Kappa Sigma. Democrat. Episcopalian. Club: Commonwealth (Richmond). Contbr. papers dealing with arthritis and related subjects to profl. jours. Home: 4402 W Franklin St Richmond VA 23221 Office: McGuire VA Hosp Richmond VA 23249

TOONG, TAU-YI, educator; b. Shanghai, China, Aug. 15, 1918; s. Zen-Liang and Su (Hsu) T.; B.S., Chiao-Tung U., 1940; M.S., Mass. Inst. Tech., 1948, Sc.D., 1952; m. Shan-Ching Cheng, Jan. 17, 1943; children—Mei-Gi, Mei-Lyn. Came to U.S., 1947, naturalized, 1957. Pres. Nanyang Engring. Corp., China, 1942-45; plant supt. Shanghai Transit Co., China, 1945-47; instr. Mass. Inst. Tech., 1951-52, asst. prof., 1952-55, asso. prof., 1955-63, prof., 1963—; cons. Joseph Kaye & Co., Stewart-Warner Corp., USAF, Churchill Lighting Corp., Thermo Electron Engring. Corp., Foster-Miller Assos., Dynatech Corp., Avco-Everett Research Lab., Kenics Corp., Steam Engine Systems Corp. Recipient Alfred P. Sloan award for outstanding performance, 1957; Chinese Ministry Edn. fellow, 1947-49; Guggenheim fellow, 1959. Mem. Am. Soc. Mech. Engrs., Combustion Inst., Am. Soc. Engring. Edn., N.Y. Acad. Scis., Am. Inst. Aeros. and Astronautics, Sigma Xi, Phi Tau Phi (v.p. 1969-70). Contbr. articles profl. jours. Home: 30 Bradford Rd Weston MA 02193 Office: Mass Inst Tech Cambridge MA 02139

TOOR, HERBERT LAWRENCE, ednl. dean, chem. engr.; b. Phila., June 22, 1927; s. Matthew and Jean (Mogul) T.; B.S., Drexel Inst. Tech., 1948; M.S., Northwestern U., 1950, Ph.D., 1952; m. Elizabeth Weir, Dec. 9, 1950; children—Helen Mary, John Weir, William Ramsay. Research chemist Monsanto Chems., Ltd., London, 1952-53; mem. faculty Carnegie-Mellon U., 1953—, prof. chem. engring., 1961—, head dept., 1965—, dean Carnegie Inst. Tech., 1970—; UNESCO expert, vis. prof. A.C. Coll. Tech., U. Madras (India), 1962-63. Mem. bd. overseers Thayer Sch. Engring., Dartmouth Coll.; chmn. com. on evaluation of sulfur oxides control tech. NRC. Mem. Am. Inst. Chem. Engrs. (Alan P. Colburn award 1964), Am. Chem. Soc., Am. Soc. Engring. Edn., AAAS, AAUP, Sigma Xi, Tau Beta Pi. Mem. adv. bd. Chem. and Engring. News. Home: 5369 Northumberland St Pittsburgh PA 15217

TOOTE, GLORIA E.A., lawyer, former govt. ofcl.; b. N.Y.C., Nov. 8, 1931; d. Fredrick A. and Lillie M. (Tooks) Toote; B.A., Howard U., 1952, J.D., 1954; LL.M., Columbia, 1956. Admitted to N.Y. State bar, 1955; practiced in N.Y.C., 1957, 75—; with law firm Greenbaum, Wolff & Ernst, N.Y.C., 1957; pres. Toote Town Pub. Co., also Town Sound Rec. Studios, Inc., 1966-70; aide to gov. N.Y., 1958; asst. dir. ACTION Agy., Washington, 1971-73; asst. sec. for equal opportunity HUD, 1973-75; pres. TREA Estates and Enterprises, Inc.; syndicated columnist. Founding mem. bd. govs. Nat. Black United Fund, Inc.; mem. steering com. Citizens for Republic, adv. council Consumer Alert; mem. council econ. affairs Republican Nat. Com.; pres. N.Y.C. Black Rep. Council. Recipient Newsmaker award for distinguished pub. service Nat. Newspaper Pubs. Assn., 1974; citation Nat. Bus. League, C. of C. U.S., 1970; spl. achievement awards Nat. Assn. Black Women Attys., 1974, N.Y. Fedn. Civil Service Orgns., 1975; also citations Alpha Kappa Alpha, C. of C. U.S., Navajo Tribe, Nat. Assn. Real Estate Brokers, Nat. Citizens Participation Council, Nat. Bar Assn., YMCA, Delta Sigma Theta. Mem. Am. Arbitration Assn. (dir.). Address: 282 W 137th St New York NY 10030

TOPAZIO, VIRGIL WILLIAM, univ. ofcl.; b. Middletown, Conn., Mar. 27, 1915; s. Concetto and Corradina (Rizzo) T.; B.A., Wesleyan U., Middletown; m. Juwil E. Child, July 28, 1941; 1 dau., Jula Diane. Lectr., Columbia, 1947-48; from instr. to prof. French lit. U. Rochester, 1948-65; prof. French, chmn. dept. Rice U., 1965-67, dean humanities and social scis., 1967—, also acad. v.p. Fulbright vis. lectr. U. Rennes (France), 1964-65. Served with AUS, 1945-46. Decorated Palmes Academiques (France), 1966, 76. Mem. Alliance Francaise (pres. 1963-65), Modern Lang. Assn. (pres. 18th century sect. 1965), Council Fgn. Langs. (v.p. 1967-68). Author: D'Holbach's Moral Philosophy, 1956; Voltaire: A Critical Study of His Major Works, 1967. Home: 717 Creekside Ln Houston TX 77024

TOPEL, BERNARD JOSEPH, bishop, educator; b. Bozeman, Mont., May 31, 1903; s. Henry and Pauline (Hagen) T.; A.B., Carroll Coll., 1923; S.T.B., Cath. U. Am., 1927, M.A. in Edn., 1927; M.A. in Math., Harvard U., 1933; Ph.D., Notre Dame U., 1937; LL.D., Portland U., 1956. Ordained priest Roman Catholic Ch., 1927, consecrated bishop, 1955; instr. Carroll Coll., 1927-32, prof., 1932-36, 38-55, dir. vocations, 1946-55; lectr. U. Notre Dame. 1937-38; bishop of Spokane, 1955-78. Home: E 1908 14th Spokane WA 99202 Office: PO Box 1453 1023 W Riverside St Spokane WA 92210

TOPKINS, KATHARINE, author; b. Seattle, July 22, 1927; d. Paul Joseph and Katharine (Crane) Theda; student Maryville (Tenn.) Coll.; B.S., Columbia, 1949; M.A., Claremont Grad. Sch., 1951; m. Richard Marvin Topkins, July 18, 1952; children—Richard, Joan, Deborah. Author: (novels) All the Tea in China, 1962, Kotch, 1965; (with Richard Topkins) Passing Go, 1968, IL Boom, 1974. also short stories. Home and Office: PO Box 198 Ross CA 94957

TOPOL, SIDNEY, electronics co. exec.; b. Boston, Dec. 28, 1924; s. Morris and Dora (Kalinsky) T.; B.S., U. Mass., 1947; postgrad. U. Calif., 1948-49; m. Lillian Friedman, Dec. 15, 1951; children—Deborah Jane, Joanne, Martha Grace. Physicist, Naval Research Lab., 1947-48; engr. Raytheon Co., Boston, 1949-57, asst. mgr. engring., comml. equipment div., 1957-59, dir. planning and mktg. Raytheon-Europe, Rome, Italy, 1959-65, gen. mgr. communications ops., 1965-71; pres., dir. Sci.-Atlanta, Inc., 1971—, chief exec. officer, 1975—, chmn. bd., 1978—; dir. 1st Atlanta Corp., 1st Nat. Bank of Atlanta. Mem. adv. council Coll. Indsl. Mgmt., Ga. Inst. Tech.; mem. exec. com. mgmt. conf. bd. Emory U.; bd. advisors Morris Brown Coll.; chmn. Ga. com. CARE. Served with USAAF, 1943-46. Mem. IEEE, Electronic Industries Assn. (bd. govs.). Club: Rotary. Office: 3845 Pleasantdale Rd Atlanta GA 30340

TOPP, LEE JAY, pump mfg. co. exec.; b. Bayonne, N.J., Dec. 26, 1928; s. Karl T. and Anne T.; B.C.E., Syracuse (N.Y.) U., 1951; m. Joan Shepperd, May 18, 1956; children—Catherine, Michael. Mktg. mgr. Goulds Pumps Inc., Seneca Falls, N.Y., 1957-65; gen. mgr. pump div. Ingersoll-Rand Co., 1965-74; pres. Worthington Pumps Inc., Mountainside, N.J., 1974—. Served with USAF, 1952-56. Recipient C. Arents award Syracuse U., 1976. Mem. Sales Execs. Club N.Y.C. Republican. Episcopalian. Club: Echo Lake Country (Westfield). Address: Worthington Pump Inc 270 Sheffield St Mountainside NJ 07092*

TOPP, ROBERT FRANSEN, educator; b. DeKalb, Ill., Oct. 30, 1915; s. John George and Ellen Victoria (Fransen) T.; B.E., No. Ill. U., 1938; M.A., U. Colo., 1941, Ph.D., 1949; m. Rowena May Baker, Aug. 17, 1952; children—Ellen, Bruce, Laurie. Asst. supt. schs., Boulder, Colo., 1947-49; asst. dir. tchr. edn. U. Ill., 1949-50; dir. lab. sch. No. Ariz. U., Flagstaff, 1950-52, prof. edn. and psychology, 1972—; dean Grad. Sch., Nat. Coll. Edn., Evanston, Ill., 1952-54, dean coll., 1954-58; asst. prof. edn. U. Calif. at Santa Barbara, 1958-60; dean Coll. Edn., No. Ill. U., 1960-69; provost Elliott campus U.S. Internat. U., San Diego, 1969-71, dean tchr. edn., 1971-72. Bd. dirs., mem. exec. com. Am. Assn. Colls. for Tchr. Edn.; steering com. dept. baccalaureate and higher degree programs in nursing Nat. League Nursing, 1961—. Served to 2d lt. AUS, 1942-46. Mem. Am. Psychol. Assn., Am. Assn. Sch. Adminstrs., Nat. Soc. Study Edn., NEA, Phi Delta Kappa, Kappa Delta Pi. Contbr. articles to profl. jours. Home: 2961 W Wilson Dr Flagstaff AZ 86001

TOPPER, JOSEPH RAY, glass mfg. co. exec.; b. Waynesboro, Pa., May 8, 1928; s. Clarence E. and Sarah Frances (Stahley) T.; B.S. in Elec. Engring., Brown U., 1952; m. Mary Helen Bromage, July 25, 1953; children—Mary Kathleen, Sarah Helen, Joseph Ray, James Michael. With Gen. Electric Co., 1952-71, gen. mgr. personal appliances dept., Fairfield, Conn., 1968-71; v.p. Anchor Hocking Corp., Lancaster, Ohio, 1972-76, exec. v.p., 1977-78, pres., chief operating officer, 1978—, also dir. Chmn. bd. trustees Lancaster-Fairfield County Hosp. Served with USN, 1946-48. Mem. IEEE, Nat. C. of C., Am. Mgmt. Assn., Am. Glass Assn. (past chmn.), Glass Packaging Inst. Republican. Roman Catholic. Club: Lancaster Country. Home: 2800 Marietta Rd Lancaster OH 43130 Office: 109 N Broad St Lancaster OH 43130

TOPPIN, CLARE THOMAS, lawyer; b. Detroit, Oct. 16, 1937; s. Clare I. and Margaret M. (Markey) T.; B.A., U. Detroit, 1959, LL.B., 1963; m. Bernice A. Grabowski, Nov. 1963; children—Laura Ann, Cathleen Mary. Tech. writer Chrysler Corp., 1959-61; admitted to Mich. bar, 1964; asso. firm Keller, Thoma, Toppin & Schwarze, Detroit, 1964-68, partner, 1968-78, v.p., 1972-78; of counsel firm Monaghan, Campbell, LoPrete, McDonald & Norris, Detroit, 1978—; dir. Mills Products, Inc. Trustee McNamara Hosp., Detroit. Mem. Am., Mich., Detroit bar assns. Republican. Roman Catholic. Club: Detroit Athletic. Home: 3345 Newgate St Troy MI 48084 Office: 1732 Buhl Bldg Detroit MI 48226 also 1700 N Woodward Bloomfield Hills MI 48013

TOPPING, NORMAN HAWKINS, univ. chancellor; b. Flat River, Mo., Jan. 12, 1908; s. Moses H. and Charlotte Amanda (Blue) T.; A.B., U. So. Calif., 1933, M.D., 1936; m. Helen Rummens, Sept. 2, 1930; children—Brian, Linda. Intern, USPHS marine hosps., San Francisco, Seattle; mem. staff NIH, Bethesda, Md., 1937-52, asst. chief div. infectious diseases, 1946-48, asst. surgeon gen. USPHS, asso. dir. NIH, 1948-52; v.p. for med. affairs U. Pa., 1952-58; pres. U. So. Calif., 1958-70, chancellor, 1970—. Engaged in med. research, viral and rickettsial diseases, 1937-48; mem. com. on virus research and epidemiology Nat. Found. Infantile Paralysis, 1950-56, chmn., 1956-58; mem. research com. Nat. Found., chmn., 1958-77; pres. Am. Soc. Tropical Medicine, 1949. Pres. So. Calif. Rapid Transit Dist., 1971-73. Recipient Bailey K. Ashford award, 1943; Wash. Acad. Sci. award, 1944; U.S.A. Typhus Commn. medal, 1945. Diplomate Am. Bd. Preventive Medicine and Pub. Health. Mem. A.A.A.S., Assn. Am. Physicians, Am. Epidemiological Soc., Soc. Exptl. Biology and Medicine. Author articles on typhus, Rocky Mountain spotted fever, Q fever, pub. health. Home: 100 S Plymouth Blvd Los Angeles CA 90004 Office: U So Cal 3810 Wilshire Blvd Los Angeles CA 90010

TOPPING, PETER (WILLIAM), educator, historian; b. Milw., May 13, 1916; s. William P. and Anastasia (Makri) Topitzes; B.A., U. Wis., 1937, M.A., 1938; postgrad. U. Cin., 1939-40; Ph.D., U. Pa., 1942; m. Eva V. Catafygiotu, June 20, 1951; 1 son, John Themis. Instr. history U. Wis., 1943-44, Northwestern U., 1944-45; asst. prof. history U. Calif. at Santa Barbara, 1948-53; librarian Gennadeion Am. Sch. Classical Studies, Athens, Greece, 1953-60, mem. mng. com., 1961—; vis. asso. prof. history, library cons. U. Pa., 1960-61; asso. prof. history, later Greek studies U. Cin., 1961-64, prof., 1964-67, Charles Phelps Taft prof., 1967—, fellow Grad. Sch., 1972—; sr. research asso. Dumbarton Oaks Center for Byzantine Studies, Washington, 1978—, mem. bd. scholars, 1972-74; interpreting officer U.S. staff Allied Mission to Observe Greek Elections, 1946; mem. exec. com. Frank L. Weil Inst. in Religion and Humanities, 1964—. Advanced fellow Belgian Am. Edn. Found., 1947-48; Fulbright sr. research awardee Greece, 1950-51; sr. fellow Nat. Endowment for the Humanities, 1974-75. Mem. Am. Hist. Assn., Mediaeval Acad. Am., Modern Greek Studies Assn., Phi Beta Kappa. Mem. Greek Orthodox Ch. Author: Feudal Institutions as Revealed in the Assizes of Romania, 1949; (with Jean Longnon) Documents sur le régime des terres dans la principauté de Moreé au XIVme siècle, 1969; Studies on Latin Greece A.D. 1205-1715, 1977; contbr. articles, revs. to hist. jours. Home: 1823 Rupert St McLean VA 22101

TOPPING, SEYMOUR, newspaperman; b. N.Y.C., Dec. 11, 1921; s. Joseph and Anna (Seidman) Topolsky; B.J., U. Mo., 1943; m. Audrey Elaine Ronning, Nov. 10, 1949; children—Susan, Karen, Lesley, Rebecca, Joanna. With I.N.S., China civil war, 1946-47; with A.P., 1948-59, corr., Berlin, Germany, 1957-59; mem. staff N.Y. Times, 1959—, chief corr., Moscow, USSR, 1960-63, Southeast Asia, 1963-66, fgn. editor, 1966-69, asst. mng. editor, 1969-76, dep. mng. editor, 1976-77, mng. editor, 1977—; lectr. in field. Mem. Nat. Com. U.S.-China Relations. Served with inf. AUS, 1943-46; PTO. Mem. Council Fgn. Relations, Asia Soc., The Pilgrims, Century Assn. Author: Journey Between Two Chinas, 1972. Home: 5 Heathcote Rd Scarsdale NY 10583 Office: care NY Times New York NY 10036

TORBERT, CLEMENT CLAY, JR., state chief justice; b. Opelika, Ala., Aug. 31, 1929; s. Clement Clay and Lynda (Meadows) T.; student U.S. Naval Acad., 1948-49; B.S., Auburn U., 1951; postgrad. U. Md., 1952; LL.B., U. Ala., 1954; m. Gene Hurt, May 2, 1952; children—Mary Dixon, Gene Shealy, Clement Clay. Admitted to Ala. bar, 1954; practiced in Opelika, 1954-77; city judge, Opelika, 1954-58; partner firm Samford, Torbert, Denson & Horsley, 1959-74; chief justice Ala. Supreme Ct., 1977—. Dir. First Nat. Bank Opelika, Opelika-Auburn Broadcasting Co. Mem. Ala. Ho. of Reps., 1958-62, Ala. Senate, 1966-70, 74-77. Served to capt. USAF, 1952-53. Mem. Phi Beta Kappa, Phi Delta Phi, Phi Kappa Phi, Alpha Tau Omega. Methodist (trustee). Kiwanian. Home: 611 Terracewood Dr Opelika AL 36801 Office: Judicial Bldg PO Box 218 Montgomery AL 36101

TORBET, ROBERT GEORGE, clergyman; b. Spokane, Dec. 25, 1912; s. A.M. and Alberta (Harpel) T.; A.B., Wheaton (Ill.) Coll., 1934; B.D., Eastern Baptist Theol. Sem., Phila., 1937; M.A., U. Pa., 1937, Ph.D., 1944. Ordained to ministry Bapt. Ch., 1936; prof.

Eastern Bapt. Theol. Sem., 1937-51; editor, dir. dept. edn. and publs. Am. Bapt. Bd., 1951-58; dean, prof. ch. history Central Bapt. Theol. Sem., Kansas City, Kans., 1958-66; ecumenical officer Am. Bapt. Churches in U.S.A., Valley Forge, Pa., 1967-77; bd. mgrs. Am. Bapt. Hist. Soc., 1950-59, Am. Bapt. Bd. Edn. and Publs., 1959-65; pres. Am. Bapt. Conv., 1965-66. Mem. Am. Soc. Ch. History. Author: History of the Baptists, 1950, 3d edit., 1973; The Baptist Ministry; Then and Now, 1953; Venture of Faith: A History of American Baptist Foreign Missions, 1955; The Baptist Story, 1957; The Protest Reformation, 1961; Reuben E. Nelson: Free Churchman, 1961: (with S.E. Hill) Baptists North and South, 1964; Ecumenism: Free Church Dilemma, 1968. Home: Montgomery Ct (E-31) N Narberth and Price Aves Narberth PA 19072

TORCHIANA, DONALD THORNHILL, educator; b. Swarthmore, Pa., Oct. 22, 1923; s. Paul John and Martha (FitzGerald) T.; B.A., DePauw U., 1947; M.A., U. Iowa, 1949, Ph.D., 1953; m. Rena Margarida LeSueur, May 17, 1952 (div. July 1972); children—Katherine Leslie, David FitzGerald, William DeGroot. Instr. English, Northwestern U., Evanston, Ill., 1953-59, asst. prof., 1959-63, asso. prof., 1963-68, prof. English, 1968—; cons. Royal Irish Acad., Dublin, 1970—; Fulbright lectr., Ireland, 1960-62, 69-70; lectr. W.B. Yeats Internat. Summer Sch., 1961, 62, 65, 72, 76. Served with USAAF, 1943-45. Decorated Air medal with 3 oak leaf clusters. Newberry Library fellow, 1959; Am. Council Learned Socs. grantee, 1963. Mem. Modern Lang. Assn. (chmn. Celtic sect. 1970-71), 18th Century Studies Soc. Am., Irish Georgian Soc., Phi Beta Kappa. Club: United Arts (Dublin). Author: W.B. Yeats and Georgian Ireland, 1966. Home: 1220 Hinman Ave Evanston IL 60202

TORCHINSKY, ABE, musician; b. Phila., Mar. 30, 1920; s. Benjamin and Celia (Targan) T.; ed. Curtis Inst. Music; m. Berta Brenner, Aug. 17, 1941; children—Barbara (Mrs. Adriann Volger), Ann Penny (Mrs. Kenneth Clark), Beth Ellen. With Nat. Symphony Orch., 1941, NBC Symphony, 1946-49; musician Phila. Orch., 1949-72; prof. music U. Mich., Ann Arbor, 1973—. Formerly mem. faculties Temple U., Curtis Inst. Music, Phila. Mus. Acad., Catholic U., Washington. Author: 20th Century Orchestra Studies, 1969; Dance Suites for Tuba, 1975; Orchestral Repertoire for the Tuba, Vols. I, II, III, IV. Home: 654 Greenhills Dr Ann Arbor MI 48105

TORDOFF, HARRISON BRUCE, zoologist; b. Mechanicville, N.Y., Feb. 8, 1923; s. Harry F. and Ethel M. (Dormandy) T.; B.S., Cornell U., 1946; M.A., U. Mich., 1949, Ph.D., 1952; m. Jean Van Nostrand, July 3, 1946; children—Jeffrey, James. Curator Inst. of Jamaica, Kingston, 1946-47; instr. U. Kans., 1950-52, asst. prof., 1952-57, asso. prof., 1957; asst. prof. U. Mich., 1957-59, asso. prof., 1959-62, prof., 1962-70; dir. Bell Mus. Natural History, prof. ecology U. Minn., Mpls., 1970—. Served with USAF, 1942-45. Decorated D.F.C., 17 Air medals. Fellow Am. Ornithologists Union (pres. 1978-80); mem. Nature Conservancy (chmn. bd. Minn. chpt. 1975-77), Wilson (editor 1952-54), Cooper ornithol. socs., Brit. Ornithologists Union. Contbr. articles in ornithology to profl. jours. Home: 6 Chickadee Ln North Oaks Saint Paul MN 55110 Office: 10 Church St SE Minneapolis MN 55455

TORELL, BRUCE NORRIS, mgmt. cons.; b. Winnipeg, Man., Can., Mar. 1, 1920; s. Levi Harris and Jessie Gladys (Norris) T.; came to U.S., 1946, naturalized, 1952; B.S. in Mech. Engring., U. Minn., 1942; postgrad. U. Conn., 1951-52; m. Mary Elizabeth Lynott, May 16, 1944; children—Paul B., Mary Ann Torell Juliano, Mark J., Craig S. Chief engr. Fla. Research and Devel. Center, Pratt & Whitney Aircraft, West Palm Beach, 1963-67, engring. mgr. prodn. programs Pratt & Whitney Aircraft, East Hartford, Conn., 1967-68, exec. v.p., 1968-71, pres., 1971—; group v.p. propulsion United Technologies and pres. Pratt & Whitney Aircraft Group, 1974-79; pres. B.N. Torell, Inc., mgmt. cons., West Hartford, 1979—; dir. Phoenix Mut. Life Ins. Co., Hartford, Conn. Natural Gas Corp., Mechanics Savs. Bank, Hartford. Trustee Hartford Grad. Center; corporator Inst. of Living, St. Francis Hosp., Hartford. Recipient U. Minn. Outstanding Achievement award, 1973. Mem. Navy League, Air Force Assn. Clubs: Wings; Hartford Golf, Hartford, Univ.; Conquistadores del Cielo. Patentee gas turbine components. Home: 245 Westmont West Hartford CT 06117 Office: 245 Westmont West Hartford CT 06117

TORELL, JOHN RAYMOND, III, banker; b. Hartford, Conn., July 10, 1939; s. Raymond John and Gertrude May (Bent) T.; B.A., Princeton U., 1961; m. Anne A. Keller, Feb. 17, 1962; children—John Raymond, Anne Elizabeth, Susan Allgood. With Mfrs. Hanover Trust Co., N.Y.C., 1961—, asst. sec., 1964-67, asst. v.p., 1967-70, v.p. nat. div., 1970, v.p. credit dept., 1970-71, v.p. corporate planning, 1971-72, sr. v.p. planning, mktg., spl. products, 1973-75, sr. v.p., dep. gen., mgr. retail banking, 1975-76, exec. v.p. met. div., 1976-78, vice chmn. dir., 1978—; vice chmn., dir. Mfrs. Hanover Corp.; dir. Mfrs. Hanover Comml. Corp., Ritter Fin. Corp., Nat. Reins. Corp., Econ. Capital Corp. of N.Y.C. Mem. Bus./Labor Working Group; mem. fin. com. Juilliard Mus. Found.; mem. consistory Ref. Ch. of Bronxville; trustee Hackley Sch. Served with USNR, 1962. Republican. Clubs: Blind Brook, Siwanoy Country, Bronxville Field, Union League. Home: 16 Birchbrook Rd Bronxville NY 10708 Office: 350 Park Ave New York NY 10022

TORG, JOSEPH STEVEN, orthopaedic surgeon, educator; b. Phila., Oct. 25, 1934; s. Jay and Elva Dorothy (May) T.; A.B., Haverford Coll., 1957; M.D., Temple U., 1961; m. Barbara Jane Groenendaal, May 23, 1959; children—Joseph Steven, Elisabeth Jay Michael. Intern, San Francisco Gen. Hosp., 1961-62; resident in orthopaedic surgery Temple U. Hosp., Phila., 1964-68, Shriners Hosp. for Crippled Children, Phila., 1966-67; asst. surgeon Episcopal Hosp., Phila., 1968-70; surgeon Shriners Hosp. Crippled Children, 1970-78; mem. staff Temple U. Hosp., 1970-78, instr. orthopaedic surgery, 1968-70, asst. prof., 1970-75, asso. prof., 1976-78, dir. Center for Sports Medicine and Sci., 1974-78; chief orthopaedic sect. St. Christopher's Hosp. for Children, Phila., 1971-74, mem. staff, 1974—; active staff St. Joseph's Hosp., Phila., 1977—; prof. U. Pa., 1978—, active staff hosp., 1978—, dir. Sports Medicine Center, 1978—; mem. active staff Children's Hosp., Phila., 1978; mem. subcom. on sports medicine Pa. Dept. Health, 1975; team physician Phila. Fury's, Phila. Flyers; cons. in field. Served with M.C., U.S. Army, 1962-64. Recipient Layman Honor award Pa. State Assn. Health, Phys. Edn. and Recreation, 1970, Grad. Honor award, 1975; Commendation of Merit, Phila. Public High Sch. Football Coaches, 1974; diplomate Am. Bd. Orthopaedic Surgeons. Fellow Am. Acad. Orthopaedic Surgeons, Am. Coll. Sports Medicine (trustee 1975-78), ACS, Phila. Coll. Physicians; mem. AMA, Eastern Orthopaedic Soc., ASTM, Am. Orthopaedic Soc., Sports Medicine, Phila. County Med. Soc., Phila. Orthopaedic Soc., Pa. State Med. Soc., Pa. State Orthopaedic Soc. Contbr. articles to profl. jours. Home: 401 Conestoga Rd Saint Davids PA 19087 Office: Sports Medicine Center Hosp of U Pa 3400 Spruce St Philadelphia PA 19104

TORGERSEN, PAUL ERNEST, univ. adminstr.; b. N.Y.C., Oct. 13, 1931; s. Einar and Francis (Hansen) T.; B.S., Lehigh U., 1953; M.S., Ohio State U., 1956, Ph.D., 1959; m. Dorothea Zuschlag, Sept. 11, 1954; children—Karen Elizabeth, Janis Elaine, James Einar. instr. Ohio State U., 1956-59; asst., then asso. prof. Okla. State U., 1959-67; prof., head dept. indsl. engring. Va. Poly. Inst., 1967-70, dean Coll. Engring., 1970—. Served to 1st lt. USAF, 1953-55. Recipient Outstanding Tchr. award Okla. State U., 1963; Distinguished Alumnus award Ohio State U., 1971. Mem. Am. Inst. Indsl. Engring. (editorial bd. 1967-70, publs. policy bd. 1970-72, v.p. publs. 1972—), Am. Soc. Engring. Edn. (chmn. I.E. div. 1966-67, exec. bd. engring. coll. council 1974—), Soc. Logistics Engrs. (advisory bd. 1975—), Alpha Pi Mu (nat. regional dir. 1962-70). Author: (with W.J. Fabrycky) Operations Economy, 1966; A Concept of Organization, 1968; (with I. T. Weinstock) Management: An Integrated Approach, 1972; (with W.J. Fabrycky and P.M. Ghare) Industrial Operations Research (H.B. Maynard Book of the Year award 1972), 1972; (with M.H. Agee and R.E. Taylor) Quantitative Analysis for Management Decisions, 1975. Home: 1510 Palmer Dr Blacksburg VA 24060

TORGERSEN, TORWALD HAROLD, architect, designer; b. Chgo., Sept. 2, 1929; s. Peder and Hansine Malene (Hansen) T.; B.S. in Archtl. Engring. with honors, U. Ill., 1951; m. Dorothy Darlene Peterson, June 22, 1963. Partner, Coyle & Torgersen Architects-Engrs., Washington, Chgo. and Joliet, Ill., 1955-56; project coordinator Skidmore, Owings & Merrill, Chgo., 1956-60; corp. architect, dir. architecture, constrn. and interiors Container Corp. Am., Chgo., 1960—; guest lectr. U. Wis. Served to capt. USNR, 1951-55. Recipient Top Ten Design award Factory mag., 1964. Registered architect Nat. Council Archtl. Registration Bds. Fellow Am. Soc. Interior Designers; mem. AIA, Naval Res. Assn., Ill. Naval Militia, Am. Arbitration Assn., Am. Soc. Mil. Engrs., Paper Industry Mgmt. Assn. (hon.), Sports Car Club Am., Nat. Eagle Scout Assn. Club: 20 Fathoms. Home: 3750 N Lake Shore Dr Chicago IL 60613 Office: 500 E North Ave Carol Stream IL 60187

TORGERSON, FERNANDO GORDON, univ. dean; b. Plaza, N.D., Mar. 5, 1918; s. Nels and Marie (Hafthorn) T.; B.A., State Tchrs. Coll., Minot, N.D., 1939; M.S., Columbia, 1949; Ph.D., U. Minn., 1956; m. Gertrude Irene Hall, Aug. 14, 1949. Asso. dir. spl. services Montefiore Hosp., N.Y.C., 1962-66; asst. prof. Columbia Sch. Pub. Health and Adminstrv. Medicine, 1962-66; dir. Cal. Office Health and Welfare Agy., 1966-67; dean Grad. Sch. Social Work, U. Tex. at Arlington, 1967—; cons. in field. Mem. social work professional advisory bd. Emory U.; mem. criminal justice policy, devel. com. N. Tex. Council Govts.; mem. Tex. Urban Devel. Commn., 1970—. Served with U.S. Army, 1941-62. Rotarian. Author articles. Home: 555 Franklin Dr Arlington TX 76011

TORGERSON, TRUMAN, coop. exec.; b. Meridean, Wis., Dec. 28, 1915; s. Ole and Anna T.; B.S., U. Wis., 1939; m. Ruth Torgerson, Sept. 17, 1939; children—Randall, Patricia (Mrs. Joel Peterson), Oliver, Ted, Nan. Formerly tchr. vocational agr., county agrl. agt. Rusk and Manitowoc counties, Wis., gen. mgr. Lake to Lake Dairy Coop., Manitowoc; now sec., dir. Land O'Lakes Creameries, Mpls. Served with USNR, World War II. Recipient Distinguished Service award U. Wis. Coll. Agr., 1972; named food industry man of the year, World Food and Agrl. Found., 1969; Service award Wis. 4-H, 1974; Hon. State Farmer award Future Farmers Am., 1976. Mem. Wis. Fedn. Coops. (dir.), Am. Dry Milk Inst., Nat. Milk Producers Fedn., Am. Dry Milk Inst. (trustee), Nat. Dairy Council (dir.), U. Wis. Alumni Assn. (past chmn. bd.), Am. Inst. Cooperation (past trustee, mem. exec. com.). Lutheran. Clubs: Masons, Elks. Home: 618 N 9th St Manitowoc WI 54220 Office: 2000 S 10th St Manitowoc WI 54220

TORIBARA, TAFT YUTAKA, radiation biologist, biophysicist; b. Seattle, Apr. 10, 1917; s. Minekichi and Hisano (Miyata) T.; B.S. in Chem. Engring., U. Wash., 1938, M.S. in Chem. Engring, 1939; Ph.D., U. Mich., 1942; m. Masako Ono. Aug. 28, 1948; children—Lynne Suzanne, Neil Willard. Research chemist dept. engring. research U. Mich., 1942-48; from asst. prof. to prof. radiation biology and biophysics Sch. Medicine and Dentistry, U. Rochester (N.Y.), 1948—; cons. in field. Chmn. advancement com. Boy Scouts Am., 1964-67; pres. Jr. High Family Faculty Forum, 1964-66; mem. Gates Library Bd., 1965-75, pres., 1972-74. NIH Spl. Research fellow, 1961-62; AAAS fellow, 1966. Mem. Am. Chem. Soc., AAAS. Inventor ultrafiltration apparatus, 1953. Editor: Modern Techniques for the Detection and Measurement of Environmental Pollutants, 1978. Contbr. articles to profl. jours. Home: 54 Timpat Dr Rochester NY 14624 Office: RBB University of Rochester Medical Center Rochester NY 14642. *My life might be summarized by the Statement, "Adversity is not always bad."*

TORLEY, JOHN FREDERIC, iron and steel co. exec.; b. Pitts., June 5, 1911; s. Walter Anderson and Emma Katherine (Hacker) T.; B.S. in Mech. Engring., Carnegie-Mellon U., 1940; Indsl. Engr., Youngstown U., 1948; m. Leona Helen Depp, Oct. 5, 1940; children—Lois Leona, Jane Mildred. With Nat. Castings div. Midland Ross Co., Sharon, Pa., Phoenix and Chgo., 1946-61, v.p., 1958-61; pres., chmn. Dayton Malleable Inc. (Ohio), 1961—, also dir.; pres. Morris Bean & Co.; dir. Monarch Machine Tool Co., Dayton Power & Light Co., Citizens Fed. Savs. & Loan, Huffman Mfg. Co., Winters Nat. Bank & Trust Co., Dayton, Ponderosa Systems Inc., Tait Mfg. Inc., MAPI Inc. Pres., Dayton Mus. Natural History, Malleable Research and Devel. Found., Air Force Mus. Found., Kettering Meml. Hosp.; trustee, chmn. bd. U. Dayton, Wright State U. Served with USNR, World War II; comdr. Res. Registered profl. engr., Pa. Mem. ASME. Home: 236 Glenridge Rd Dayton OH 45429 Office: 3931 S Dixie Hwy Dayton OH 45439

TORME, MELVIN HOWARD, musician; b. Chgo., Sept. 13, 1925. Studied drums at age seven, acted in radio soap operas, sang with Buddy Rogers, other name bands during early sch. years; toured with Chico Marx band, 1942-43; motion picture debut in Higher and Higher, 1943; leader vocal group Mel-Tones, Calif.; solo singer, 1947—; numerous compositions including Lament to Love, Stranger in Town, Christmas Song, Born to be Blue, County Fair; vaudeville tour, Eng., 1956, 57; recs. include California Suite, Torme Sings Astaire, At the Crescendo, It's a Blue World, Prelude to a Kiss, Mel Torme Back in Town, Live at the Maisonette; appeared in motion picture Snowman. Author: The Other Side of the Rainbow. Address: care Dale Sheets & Assos 3518 Cahuenga Blvd W Suite 206 Los Angeles CA 90068*

TORMEY, JOHN L., corp. exec.; b. 1913; grad. U. Wis., 1940; married. Partner Charter Harrison Assos., bus. cons., 1945-50; with Roadway Express, Inc., 1950-77, exec. v.p. finance and adminstrn., 1966-73, vice-chmn., 1973-74, chmn., chief exec. officer, 1974-77, also dir.; dir. Firestone Bank. Trustee Akron City Hosp., Akron YMCA. Served with AUS, 1942-45. Address: 1077 Gorge Blvd Akron OH 44309

TORN, RIP (ELMORE TORN, JR.), actor, dir.; b. Temple, Tex., Feb. 6, 1931; s. Elmore and Thelma (Spacek) T.; student Tex. A. & M. Coll., 1948-50; B.S., U. Tex.; m. Ann Wedgeworth, Jan. 15, 1955 (div.); 1 dau., Danae; m. 2d, Geraldine Page; children—Angelica, Anthony, Jonathan. Stage performances include: Cat on a Hot Tin Roof, 1955, Orpheus Descending, 1958, Chaparral (Theatre World award), 1958, Sweet Bird of Youth, 1959 (on tour 1960), Daughter of Silence, 1961, Macbeth, 1962, Desire Under the Elms, 1963, Strange Interlude, 1963, Blues for Mr. Charlie, 1964, The Kitchen, 1966, The Country Girl, 1966, The Deer Park (Obie award), 1967, The Cuban Thing, 1968, The Honest-to-God Schnozzola, 1969, Dream of a Blacklisted Actor, 1969, The Dance of Death, 1970-71, The Marriage Proposal, 1971, Marriage and Money, 1971, Barbary Shore, The Little Foxes, 1974, The Father, 1975, The Glass Menagerie, 1975, Fever for Life, 1975, Creditors, 1977, Night Shift, 1977, Seduced; dir. plays: The Beard (Obie award), 1968, Look Away, 1973; motion picture performances include: Baby Doll, 1956, Time Limit, 1957, Pork Chop Hill, 1959, King of Kings, 1961, Hero's Island, 1962, Sweet Bird of Youth, 1962, Critic's Choice, 1963, The Cincinnati Kid, 1965, One Spy Too Many, 1966, Beach Red, 1967, You're a Big Boy Now, 1967, Beyond the Law, 1968, Sol Madrid, 1968, Coming Apart, 1969, Tropic of Cancer, 1970, Slaughter, 1972, Payday, 1973, Crazy Joe, 1974, Birch Interval, 1976, Maidstone, The Man Who Fell to Earth, 1976, Nasty Habits, 1977, Coma, 1978, The Seduction of Joe Tynan, 1979; TV appearances include: Two Plays, 1971, The President's Plane Is Missing, 1973, The FBI Versus the Ku Klux Klan, 1975, Song of Myself, 1976, also series U.S. Steel Hour, Alcoa Hour, Playhouse 90, Hallmark Hall of Fame, The Untouchables, Combat, The Man from U.N.C.L.E., Bonanza, Mannix. Mem. Actors Equity, AFTRA, Screen Actors Guild, Actors' Studio (bd. dirs., prodn. bd., 1st chmn. founding com.), Dirs. Guild Am. *

TORNEY, JUDITH VOLLMAR, psychologist; b. Oakland, Calif., Oct. 2, 1937; d. Ralph C. and Anne F. Vollmar; A.B. with gt. distinction in Psychology, Stanford U., 1959; M.A., U. Chgo., 1962, Ph.D., 1965; m. E. Keith Torney, Sept. 10, 1960 (div.); children—Susan, Elizabeth, Katherine. Asst. prof. psychology Ill. Inst. Tech., 1965-67; asso. prof. psychology and edn. U. Ill., Chgo. Circle, 1969-77, prof. psychology, head developmental psychology, 1977—; mem. U.S. Nat. Commn. for UNESCO, 1976—, chmn. human rights com., 1979—; MacKenzie traveling lectr. New Zealand Council for Ednl. Research, 1977. Recipient citation for exemplary research Nat. Council for Social Studies, 1977. Mem. Am. Psychol. Assn., Soc. for Research in Child Devel., Am. Ednl. Research Assn. Author: (with others) Civic Education in Ten Countries, 1975; asso. editor Internat. Studies Quar., 1975-79. Office: Dept Psychology U Ill Box 4348 Chicago IL 60680

TORNO, NOAH, bus. exec.; b. Toronto, Ont., Can., Nov. 27, 1910; s. Fred and Sophie T.; m. Rose Rein Laine, Apr. 10, 1950; 1 stepson, Michael Laine. Chmn. bd. Cygnus Corp. Ltd.; dir. Can. Trust, Carling O'Keefe Breweries Ltd., Consumers' Gas Co. Ltd., Cygnus Corp. Ltd. Bd. dirs. Mt. Sinai Inst., Toronto; past chmn. bd. trustees Royal Ont. Mus.; bd. mgmt. O'Keefe Centre for Performing Arts; bd. govs. Toronto Arts Found. Served as lt. Royal Can. Navy, 1942-45. Home: 155 Cumberland St Toronto ON M5R 1A2 Canada Office: PO Box 3 Toronto-Dominion Centre Toronto ON M5K 1A1 Canada

TORNQUIST, HAROLD EVERETT, ins. co. exec.; b. St. Joseph, Mich., Nov. 6, 1918; s. Milton Leonard and Lillian Harriet (Pope) T.; B.A. in Polit. Sci., U. Calif., Berkeley, 1940; postgrad. UCLA, 1942; m. Mary Elizabeth Gordon, 1958; children—John, Susan, Carolyn, Julie. With Johnson & Higgins Calif., 1940-48; ins. agt. and broker, 1948-55; v.p. Holland-Am. Ins. Co., 1955-56; exec. v.p. Corp. Insurers Services, 1957-58; pres. New Providence Corp., 1958-78; exec. v.p., then pres. Appalachian Ins. Co., 1966-78; pres. Affiliated FM Ins. Co., 1971-78; sr. v.p., then exec. v.p. Allendale Mut. Ins. Co., 1972-78; pres., treas. Indian Mountain Mgmt. Corp., Providence, 1978—; pres., chief exec. officer, dir. Am. Bristol Ins. Co., Providence, 1978—. Served as officer USNR, 1943-46. Mem. Delta Phi Epsilon, Pi Sigma Alpha. Clubs: University (Providence); Highlands (N.C.) Country; Sharon (Conn.) Country. Home: Indian Mountain Rd Lakeville CT 06039 Office: 251 George St Providence RI 02906

TORRANCE, ELLIS PAUL, ednl. psychologist; b. Milledgeville, Ga., Oct. 8, 1915; s. Ellis Watson and Jimmie Pearl (Ennis) T.; B.A., Mercer U., 1940; M.A., U. Minn., 1944; Ph.D., U. Mich., 1951; m. Jessie Pansy Nigh, Nov. 25, 1959. Tchr., Midway Vocational High Sch., Milledgeville, 1936-37; tchr., counselor Ga. Mil. Coll., 1937-40, prin., 1941-44; counselor student counseling bur. U. Minn., 1945; counselor counseling bur. Kans. State Coll., 1946-48, dir., 1949-51; dir. survival research field unit Stead AFB, Nev., 1951-57; dir. Bur. Ednl. Research, 1958-64, prof. ednl. psychology U. Minn., 1958-66; chmn., prof. dept. ednl. psychology U. Ga., 1966-78, Alumni Found. Disting. prof., 1974—. Trustee, Creative Edn. Found. Fellow Am. Psychol. Assn.; mem. Am. Ednl. Research Assn., Am. Soc. Group Psychotherapy and Psychodrama, NEA, Creative Education Leadership Council, Ga. Psychol. Assn., Nat. Assn. Gifted Children, Phi Delta Kappa. Baptist. Author: Torrance Tests of Creative Thinking; also books, articles; contbr. jours., mags., books. Home: 185 Riverhill Dr Athens GA 30606

TORRAS, JOSEPH HILL, pulp and paper co. exec.; b. Americus, Ga., Nov. 14, 1924; s. Fernando Joseph and Nell Wilson (Hill) T.; S.B., Yale, 1948; M.B.A., Harvard, 1950; m. Mary Ravenel Robertson, Sept. 20, 1952; children—Mary Martin, Fernanda Maria, Joseph Hill. Asst. to financial v.p. Seatrian Lines, Inc., 1950-51; with St. Regis Paper Co., 1951-60, sales mgr. printing papers div., 1956-60; exec. v.p. Brown Co., Boston, 1960-64; pres., chmn. bd. Premoid Corp., West Springfield, Mass., 1964—; pres. Precon, Inc., Ludlow, 1967—, Lincoln Pulp & Paper Co., Lincoln, Maine, 1968—, Astro Tissue Co., Battleboro, Vt., 1968—; chmn. bd. Whitman Products, Ltd., 1976—; pres., chief exec. officer Preco Corp., 1976—. Mem. Nat. UN Day Com., 1977; bd. dirs. Mass. Taxpayers Assn., 1976—. Served to lt. (j.g.), as aviator USNR, 1943-46. Mem. Tissue Paper Mfrs. Assn. (dir. 1963-64), Am. Pulp and Paper Mill Supts. Assn., Salesmans Assn. Paper Industry, NAM (dir. 1974—). Home: Bardwell's Ferry Rd Shelburne Falls MA 01370 Office: Front St West Springfield MA 01089

TORRE, DOUGLAS PAUL, dermatologist; b. New Orleans, Feb. 6, 1919; s. Peter and Jeanne Renee (Mottram) T.; B.S., Tulane U., 1940, M.D., 1943; postgrad. Cornell U., 1946-50; m. Sylvia Elizabeth Stenmark, Apr. 22, 1954 (div. May 1977); children—Eric, Jeanne; m. 2d, Catherine Babcock, May 28, 1977. Intern, Phila. Gen. Hosp., 1943-44; fellow Cornell U. Med. Coll.-N.Y. Hosp., 1946-50; practice medicine, specializing in dermatology, N.Y.C., 1946—; instr. Cornell U. Med. Coll., N.Y.C., 1950-55, asst. prof., 1956-59, asso. prof., 1960-65, clin. prof. medicine and dermatology, 1966—; attending physician N.Y. Hosp., Meml. Hosp. Served to lt., M.C., USNR, 1944-46; PTO. Mem. AMA, Am. Acad. Dermatology, Soc. Investigative Dermatology, Atlantic (pres. 1969), N.Y. (pres. 1969, 79) dermatology socs., Am. Soc. Dermatol. Surgery (v.p. 1979), N.Y. Acad. Medicine, Phi Beta Kappa, Delta Tau Delta. Club: University (N.Y.C.). Contbr. articles to profl. jours. and chpts. to textbooks. Home: 7 Parkview Rd Rowayton CT 06853 Office: 22 E 36 St New York NY 10016

TORRE, JOSEPH PAUL (JOE), profl. baseball mgr.; b. Bklyn., July 18, 1940; s. Joseph Paul and Margaret Torre; m. Jacqueline Ann Reed; m. 2d, Diane Romaine, Jan. 1968. First baseman Milw. Braves (name changed to Atlanta Braves), 1961-68; first baseman St. Louis Cardinals, Nat. League baseball team, 1969-70, 73-75, third baseman, 1971-72, team capt., player rep.; player N.Y. Mets, Nat. League, 1975-76, mgr., 1977—. Mem. Nat. League All-Star Team, 1963-67, 70-73; named Most Valuable Player, Nat. League, 1971, Maj. League Player of Year, Sporting News, 1971. Address: care NY Mets Shea Stadium Flushing NY 11368*

TORRENCE, ANDREW PUMPHREY, univ. pres.; b. Little Rock, Nov. 20, 1920; s. Boston Lafayette and Nancy (Pumphrey) T.; B.S., Tenn. A. and I. U., 1948; M.S., U. Wis., 1951, Ph.D., 1954, m. Marian Salters, June 26, 1948; children—Kenneth, Andrea. Tchr. vocat. agr. Immanuel High Sch., Almyra, Ark., 1948-50; asso. prof. agrl. edn., head dept. Tuskegee Inst., 1954-62, prof., dean acad. affairs, 1962-67, prof., v.p., 1967-68; pres. Tenn. State U., Nashville, 1968-74; provost, exec. v.p. Tuskegee Inst., 1974—. Research asso. Center Study Edn. Adults, Chgo., 1959-60; vis. prof. U. Wis., summer 1962; participant ednl. travel groups AID, 1960, 71; cons. Negro Coll. Com. Adult Edn., 1960-64. Mem. numerous ednl. coms. and councils including Gov.'s Sci. Adv. Com., 1969—, nat. adv. council Human Resources Devel. Center, Tuskegee Inst., 1969-74, com. on indsl. extension State Land-Grant Assn., 1969—, joint com. Negro Coll. Fund, 1969—, inst. policy comm. So. Regional Edn. Bd., 1970-74, Jud. Council Tenn., 1971-74; vice chmn. Coop. Coll. Devel. Program, 1970-73. Bd. dirs. Nashville Urban League, Nat. Alliance Businessmen, Heifer Project Internat.; mem. United Bd. for Homeland Ministries, 1969-74. Served with AUS, 1943-46. Recipient Alumni citation Tenn. A. and I. U., 1962. Mem. Adult Edn. Assn. Am. (sec. 1968), NEA, Rural Edn. Dept., Tenn. Edn. Assn., Tenn. Coll. Assn. (exec. com. 1969-70), Tenn. Adult Edn. Assn. (2d v.p. 1969), So. Assn. Coll. Deans, Tuskegee Civic Assn., Arnold Air Soc., Phi Delta Kappa, Alpha Phi Alpha, Sigma Pi Phi Boule, Phi Kappa Delta. Baptist (deacon, trustee). Clubs: Tuskegee Optimist, Masons. Author: (with B.W. Kreitlow and E.W. Aiton) Leadership for Action in Rural Communities, 1960; also numerous articles. Co-author: Teacher Education in Agriculture, 1967; Careers and Curriculum Change, 1968. Address: 516 Montgomery Rd Tuskegee Institute AL 36088

TORRENCE, (JOHN) RICHARD, mktg. co. exec.; b. Ottumwa, Iowa, Oct. 12, 1936; s. John W. and Louise Lucy (Willey) T.; B.S., U. Wis., Madison, 1958. Pres., Richard Torrence Mgmt., N.Y.C., 1962-72, WTM Inc., Englewood, N.J., 1966-71, Torrence/Perrotta Mgmt. Inc., N.Y.C., 1972-76, Torrence Assos., N.Y.C., 1976-78; pres. PMC Mgmt., 1978—, v.p. Performance Mktg. Corp., 1978—; dir. pub. relations Rodgers Organ Co., Hillsboro, Oreg., 1971-75, v.p. mktg., 1975; cons. in field; mem. advisory bd. Van Cliburn Internat. Piano Competition. Recipient Consumer Products award Oreg. chpt. Am. Mktg. Assn., 1974, 75, Promotions award Nat. Entertainment Conf., 1977. Mem. Carnegie Hall Nat. Endowment Fund (founding), Nat. Entertainment and Campus Activities Assn., Internat. Soc. Performing Arts Adminstrs. (Graphics award 1976, 77), Am. Symphony Orch. League, Assn. Coll., Univ. Campus Arts Adminstrs. Democrat. Home: One Lincoln Plaza New York NY 10023 Office: 1860 Broadway New York NY 10023

TORRES, ESTEBAN EDWARD, govt. ofcl.; b. Miami, Ariz., Jan. 27, 1930; s. Esteban Torres and Rena Baron (Gomez) T.; A.A., E. Los Angeles Coll., 1960; B.A., Calif. State U. at Los Angeles, 1963; postgrad., U. Md., 1965, Am. U., 1966; m. Arcy Sanchez, Jan. 22, 1955; children—Carmen D'Arcy, Rena Denise, Camilla Bianca, Selina Andre, Esteban Adrian. Chief steward United Auto Workers, local 230, 1954-63, dir. polit. com., editor, 1963, organizer, internat. rep., Washingtdn, 1964, asst. dir. Internat. Affairs Dept., 1975-77; dir. Inter-Am. Bureau for Latin Am., Caribbean, 1965-67; exec. dir. E. Los Angeles Community Union (TELACU), 1967-74; U.S. ambassador to UNESCO, Paris, 1977-79, chmn. Geneva Grp., 1977-78, chmn. U.S. del. Gen. Conf., 1978, spl. asst. to Pres. U.S., 1979—. Campaign coordinator Jerry Brown for Gov., 1974; Hispanic coordinator Los Angeles County campaign Jimmy Carter for Pres., 1976; v.p. Nat. Congress Community Econ. Devel., 1973-74; pres. Congress Mex.-Am. Unity, 1970-71; pres. Los Angeles Plaza de la Raza Cultural Center, 1974; dir. Nat. Com. on Citizens Broadcasting, 1977. Cons. U.S. Congress office of tech. assessment, 1976-77. Bd. visitors Sch. Architecture U. Calif. at Los Angeles, 1971-73; bd. dirs. Los Angeles County Econ. Devel. Com., 1972-75, Internat. Devel. Conf., 1976-78. Served in AUS, ETO, Korea, 1949-53. Recipient various awards for public service. Mem. Americans for Dem. Action (exec. bd. 1975—). Contbr. numerous articles to profl. jours. Office: White House 1600 Pennsylvania Ave Washington DC 20500*

TORRES, FERNANDO, physician, educator; b. Paris, France, Nov. 29, 1924; s. Calixto and Dona Isabel (Restrepo) Torres-Umana; B.A., German Coll., Bogota, Colombia, 1941; M.D., Nat. U., Bogota, 1948; m. Komtesse Edeltraud Maria Schradin, Nov. 15, 1955. Resident physician medicine and surgery Hosp. San Jose, Bogota, 1948-49; asst. in neurosurgery Instituto de Medicine Experimental, Buenos Aires, 1949-50; research fellow Johns Hopkins, Balt., 1950-52; postdoctoral research fellow NIH, Bethesda, Md., 1952-53; asst. resident in neurology Montefiore Hosp., N.Y.C., 1953-54; resident, 1954-55; asst. neurology Columbia, 1954-55; practice medicine specializing in neurology and electroencephalography, Bogota, 1955-56; dir. EEG Lab., Hosp San Juan de Dios, Bogota, 1955-56; faculty U. Minn., Mpls., 1956—, prof. neurology, 1964—, dir. electroencephalography lab., 1956—; cons. prof. neurology U. P.R. Med. Sch., 1961; spl. fellow Nat. Inst. Neural Diseases and Blindness, NIH, USPHS, Lab. EEG and Applied Neurophysiology, LaSalpetriere Hosp., Paris, 1963-64. Consul of Colombia in Mpls., 1960—; staff neurologist S.S. Hope, Cartagena, Colombia, 1967; mem. exec. com. profl. adv. bd. Epilepsy Found. Am., 1970-77, sec. profl. adv. bd., 1975-77; mem. Am. Bd. Qualification in Electroencephalography, 1972—, sec.-treas., 1974—. Diplomate Am. Bd. Qualification in Electroencephalography, Am. Bi. Psyciatry and Neurology. Mem. Am. Acad. Neurology, Am. Neurol. Assn., Am. Electroencephalographic Soc. (pres. 1976-77), Central Assn. Electroencephalographers (pres. 1971-72), AAAS, Soc. Neuroscis., Acad. Medicine Colombia, Nat. Acad. Medicine Buenos Aires. Research and publs. in neurology. Home: 2218 West Lake of the Isles Pkwy Minneapolis MN 55405 Office: 412 Union St SE Minneapolis MN 55455

TORRES-RIGUAL, HIRAM, asso. justice Supreme Ct. of P.R.; b. Mayaguez, P.R., July 15, 1922; s. Jose Torres Santiago and Julia America Rigual; B.A. cum laude, U. P.R., 1946, LL.B. cum laude, 1949; LL.M., Harvard U., 1962; m. Lillian Bayouth, Aug. 17, 1977; children—Lilliana Torres, Janina Torres, Ilya Torres. Admitted to P.R. bar; law clk. to P.R. Supreme Ct. Justice, 1949-50; atty. legal div. Land Authority P.R., 1950-51; legal and legis. asst. to Govs. P.R., 1951-65; judge Superior Ct. of Commonwealth P.R., 1965-68; asso. justice Supreme Ct. P.R., San Juan, 1968—. Served with U.S. N.G., 1965. Mem. PTA Vedruna Coll. (v.p.), PTA Providencia Coll., P.R. Bar Assn., Phi Eta Mu. Roman Catholic. Author: Social Interest and Legal Sanction for Price Fixing by Producers, 1957; Control of Land Values Through Taxation, 1964. Office: Supreme Ct of PR Box 2392 San Juan PR

TORREY, HENRY CUTLER, physicist, educator; b. Yonkers, N.Y., Apr. 4, 1911; s. John Cutler and Mabel (Kelso) T.; B.Sc., U. Vt., 1932, D.Sc., 1965; M.A., Columbia, 1933, Ph.D. (G.W. Ellis fellow 1933-34, Univ. fellow 1935-36), 1937; m. Helen Post Hubert, Sept. 11, 1937; children—John Cutler, Meriel Hubert. Instr. physics Princeton, 1937; instr. physics Pa. State U., 1937-41, asst. prof., 1941-42; mem. staff radiation lab. Mass. Inst. Tech., 1942-46; asso. prof. physics Rutgers U., 1946-50, prof., 1950-77, prof. emeritus, 1976—, chmn. dept., 1959-64, dean Grad. Sch., 1965-74, dir. research council, 1965-74; Guggenheim fellow Faculte des Scis. de Paris, 1964-65; cons. Cal. Research Corp., Standard Oil Co. Cal., 1952-64. Past trustee William Alexander Proctor Found.; mem. organizing com. Univs. Space Research Assn., 1968-69, trustee, 1969-70; bd. govs. Lunar Sci. Inst., Houston, 1969-70. Fellow Am. Phys. Soc.; mem. Am. Assn. Physics Thcrs., AAAS, Sigma Xi, Sigma Phi. Co-author: Crystal Rectifiers, 1948. Collaborator 1st observation nuclear magnetic resonance in bulk matter, 1945. Editorial bd. Rev. Sci. Instruments, 1962-64. Home: 32 Harrison Ave Highland Park NJ 08904 also 9 Leisurely Ln Bellport NY 11713 Office: Rutgers University New Brunswick NJ 08903

TORREY, JOHN GORDON, educator; b. Phila., Feb. 22, 1921; s. William Edward and Elsie Davis (Gordon) T.; B.A., Williams Coll., 1942; M.A., Harvard, 1947, Ph.D., 1950; research student Emmanuel Coll., Cambridge (Eng.) U., 1948-49; m. Norah Jamison Lea-Wilson, June 25, 1949; children—Jennifer, Joanna, Susan, Sarah, Carolyn. From instr. to asso. prof. botany U. Calif. at Berkeley, 1949-60; prof. botany Harvard, 1960—, dir. Maria Moors Cabot Found. Bot. Research, 1966-76; vis. asso. mem. Inst. Cancer Research, Phila., 1959-60; Merck sr. post-doctoral fellow Strangeways Research lab., Cambridge, Eng., 1956-57. Served to capt., Med. Adminstrv. Corps, AUS, 1942-46. Guggenheim fellow, 1965-66; hon. sr. research fellow U. Glasgow (Scotland), 1973. Mem. Bot. Soc. Am., Am. Soc. Plant Physiologists, Scandinavian Soc. Plant Physiology, Soc. Devel. Biology (pres. 1963), AAAS, Am. Acad. Arts and Sci., Phi Beta Kappa, Sigma Xi. Congregationalist. Home: 75 Arnold Rd Pelham MA 01002 Office: Harvard Forest Petersham MA 01366

TORREY, WILLIAM ARTHUR, profl. hockey team exec.; b. Montreal, Que., Can., June 23, 1934; B.S., St. Lawrence U., 1957. Dir. pub. relations to bus. mgr. Pitts. Hornets Am. Hockey League team, 1960-68; exec. v.p. Calif. Golden Seals, 1968-72; pres., gen. mgr. N.Y. Islanders (both Nat. Hockey League teams), 1972—. Address: care New York Islanders Nassau Coliseum Hempstead Turnpike Uniondale NY 11553

TORRINGTON, WILLIAM PAUL, pharm. co. cons.; b. N.Y.C., Feb. 29, 1908; s. Paul and Margarit (Weiss) T.; m. Mildred Barth, Dec. 18, 1932; 1 dau., Rosemarie Albers. Engr., Intercontinent Gas Corp., Gas Fuel Corp., 1929-37; chief engr. Process Corp., 1937-42; asst. to pres. Mead Johnson & Co., Evansville, Ind., 1942-48, v.p. mfg., 1949-59, exec. v.p., 1959-73, vice chmn. bd., 1968-73, cons., 1973—, dir., 1957-74; Dir. Evansville-Vanderburgh County Bldg. Authority, 1960-70, Mead Johnson Found. Mem. Ind. Mfrs. Assn. (dir. 1958-64), S.A.R. Clubs: Evansville Country, Evansville Petroleum, Columbia, Key Biscayne Yacht. Home: 2317 E Gum St Evansville IN 47714 Office: 2404 Pennsylvania St Evansville IN 47721

TORRISON, MANDT, lawyer; b. Manitowoc, Wis., Mar. 29, 1900; s. Gustav and Tilla (Mandt) T.; student Beloit Coll., 1917-19; B.A., U. Wis., 1921; student Harvard Law Sch., 1921-22, U. Wis. Law Sch., 1923-24; m. Sallie Carol Johnson, Aug. 9, 1926; 1 dau., Sara Jane (Mrs. Frederick C. Ewald). Admitted to Wis., Minn. bars, 1924; mem. editorial staff West Pub. Co., 1925-26; editorial work U.S. Bd. Tax Appeals, 1927; practice in St. Paul, 1927-38, 46—; asst. atty. gen. Minn., 1939-45; partner firm Kelley Torrison & O'Neill and predecessor firms, St. Paul, 1955—. Recodified Minn. laws on railroads, motor vehicle and truck transp., 1955, on game, fish, forestry and conservation, 1945. Sec. Minn. Game Protective League, 1953-57, pres., 1957-61; dir. Minn. Conservation Fedn.; nat. trustee Ducks Unlimited; trustee Ducks Unlimited of Canada, Inc., 1960-65. Mem. Am., Minn., Ramsey County bar assns., Beta Theta Pi, Phi Delta Phi. Mason (Shriner). Home: 824 Lincoln Ave St Paul MN 55105 Office: Hamm Bldg St Paul MN 55102

TORS, IVAN, producer, dir.; b. Budapest, Hungary, June 12, 1916; ed. U. Budapest, Fordham U. Author plays in Europe: Mimi, Keep Your Distance, Wind Without Rain; now in U.S.; author original story Below the Deadlines; collaborator screen plays Song of Love, Watch the Birdie; author screen plays That Forsyth Woman, In The Good Old Summertime; co-producer, collaborator screen play Storm Over Tibet; producer, collaborator screen plays The Glass Wall, The Magnetic Monster; pres. Ivan Tors Films, producers TV program A-Men; charge prodn. Ziv Sci. Fiction Theatre, Sea Hunt, Man and the Challenge, The Aquanauts, Ripcord; motion pictures include Story, 49th Man; producer Riders To The Stars, Underwater Warrior, Flipper, Flipper's New Adventure, Clarence The Cross-Eyed Lion, Around the World Under the Sea, Birds Do It, Namu-The Killer Whale, Africa, Texas Style, 1967, Gentle Giant, 1967, Daring Game, 1968, Hello Down There, 1969, Island of the Lost, The Aquarians; producer story G.O.G.; co-producer Battle Taxi; producer, dir. Rhino, Zebra in the Kitchen; exec. producer TV shows Flipper, Daktari, Gentle Ben, Cowboy in Africa, Primus, Elephant Country; creator Lorne Greene's Last of The Wild; 3 spls. animal mysteries, Where the Lions Rule; producer, dir. March of the Desert; exec. producer Escape from Angola, theatrical feature; dir. Galyon and the Abductors; lectr. U. Calif. at Irvine. Bd. dirs. Vista Hill Found. Mem. Acad. Motion Picture Arts and Scis., Writers Guild, Dirs. Guild, Explorers Club. Author: My Life in the Wild. Address: Universal Studios Los Angeles CA 91608

TOSDEVIN, CLIFFORD WILLIAM, museum adminstr.; b. Isle of Wight, Eng., Apr. 7, 1932; s. Harold William and Rosetta T.; N.D.D., M.S.I.A., Portsmouth Coll Art, Eng.; m. Marjorie May Biggar, Apr. 1, 1961; 1 dau., Sarah. Indsl. designer, Eng., 1955-65; with Brit. Govt. Info. Services, 1965-74; curator/chief exhbns. officer Commonwealth Inst., London, 1974-76; dir. Vancouver (B.C., Can.) Museums and Planetarium, 1976—. Bd. dirs. Vancouver Opera Assn., 1978-79. Mem. Can. Asso. Mus.'s Dirs. Council, Can. Mus.'s Assn., Internat. Council Mus.'s. Office: Centennial Mus 1100 Chestnut St Vancouver BC V6J 3J9 Canada

TOSE, LEONARD H., profl. football team exec.; b. Bridgeport, Pa.; s. Mike Tose; grad. U. Notre Dame, 1937. With Tose Trucking Co., Bridgeport, 1946—, now pres.; pres. K & S Canning Co., Bridgeport; pres., owner Phila. Eagles Nat. Football League team, 1969—. Donor Phila. Sch. System Varsity Football Program, 1971. Address: Philadelphia Eagles Veterans Stadium Broad St and Patterson Ave Philadelphia PA 19148*

TOSI, OSCAR I., educator; b. Trento, Italy, June 17, 1929; s. Mario and Ethel (Manescu) T.; came to U.S., 1962, naturalized, 1973; D.Sc. cum laude, Nat. U. Buenos Aires, 1951; Ph.D., Ohio State U., 1965. Asso. prof. physics Nat. U. Buenos Aires, 1952-62; asst. prof. acoustics Mich. State U., East Lansing, 1966-68, asso. prof., 1968-71, prof., 1971—, dir. Speech and Hearing Lab., 1970—, asst. dean (research) Coll. Communication Arts and Scis., 1972-76; expert witness voice identification in fed., state cts., U.S. and Can.; founder, dir. Internat. Assn. Voice Identification, Inc., Lansing, 1971—; mem. com. on evaluation sound spectrograms Nat. Acad. Scis., 1976—. Recipient Certificate of Appreciation, Mich. State Police, 1971, award Spanish Assn. Phoniatrics and Logopedics, 1973. Mem. Internat. Collegium Phonology, Internat. Assn. Phoniatrics and Logopedics, Acoustical Soc. Am. (staff mem. tech. com. speech communication 1974-77), Am. Speech and Hearing Assn., Am. Assn. Tchrs. Physics, Internat. Assn. Phonetics, Opera Guild Greater Lansing (founder 1973), Italian Am. Club of Lansing. Author: Physics for Medical Students, 1962; Voice Identification, 1971; contbr. chpts. to Theory of Speech Production and Acoustic Phonetics, 1972, The Problem of Voice Identification and Elimination, 1974, Pausometry, 1974; Voice Identification: Theory and Legal Applications, 1979. Contbr. articles to profl. jours. Research dir. voice identification project U.S. Dept. Justice, 1968-71; expert witness for Italian Govt. to analyze tape recs. related to assassination of Premier Aldo Moro, 1979. Home: 221 Bessemaur East Lansing MI 48823 Office: 247 Auditorium Mich State U East Lansing MI 48824

TOSTENRUD, DONALD BOYD, banker; b. Estherville, Iowa, Mar. 24, 1925; s. O.M. and Irene (Connell) T.; B.B.A., U. Minn., 1948; grad. Rutgers U. Grad. Sch. Banking, 1957; m. Arlene Girg, Jan. 12, 1950; children—Eric, Amy. Nat. bank examiner, Mpls., 1948-57; v.p. First Nat. Bank Black Hills, Rapid City, S.D., 1958-59; with Ariz. Bank, Phoenix, 1959—, exec. v.p., 1967-69, sr. exec. v.p., 1969-71, pres., 1971-78, chmn. bd., chief exec. officer, 1978—, also dir.; pres. COMPAS 6; dir. Southwest Gas Corp. Bd. dirs. Western Art Assos., Phoenix Art Museum, Mus. No. Ariz., Samaritan Health Service; trustee Grand Central Art Galleries, Inc., N.Y.C., Am. Grad. Sch. Internat. Mgmt. Served with AUS, 1943-45. Mem. Tucson C. of C. (past pres.), Ariz. (dir., past pres.), Am. (governing council) bankers assns. 5301 E Royal View Dr Phoenix AZ 85018

TOSTESON, DANIEL CHARLES, physiologist, univ. dean; b. Milw. Feb. 5, 1925; s. Alexis H. and Dilys (Bodycombe) T.; student Harvard, 1942-44, M.D., 1949; m. Penelope Kinsley, Dec. 17, 1949 (div. 1969); children—Carrie Marias, Heather Reich, Tor, Zoe Losada; m. 2d, Magdalena Tieffenberg, July 8, 1969; children—Joshua, Ingrid. Fellow physiology Harvard Med. Sch., 1947-48; intern, then asst. resident medicine Presbyn. Hosp., N.Y.C., 1949-51; research fellow medicine Brookhaven Nat. Lab., 1951-53, lab. kidney and electrolyte metabolism Nat. Heart Inst., 1953-55, 57, research fellow biol. isotope research lab., Copenhagen, 1955-56, Physiol. Lab., Cambridge Eng., 1956-57; asso. prof. physiology Washington U. Sch. Medicine, St. Louis, 1958-61; prof., chmn. dept. physiology and pharmacology Duke U. Sch. Medicine, 1961-75, James B. Duke Distinguished prof., 1971-75; dean div. biol. scis., dean Pritzker Sch. Medicine, v.p. for Med. Center, U. Chgo., 1975-77; dean and Caroline Shields Walker prof. physiology Harvard Med. Sch., Boston, 1977—, pres. Med. Center, 1977; cons. sci. rev. com. NIH, 1964-67; sci. advisory bd. Nat. Kidney Disease Found., 1963-65; com. blood NRC, 1962—, mem. governing bd., 1977; bd. govs. Imperial Med. Center of Iran, 1977; bd. dirs. Keystone Center for Continuing Edn. Mem. N.C. Council Human Relations, 1961—; nat. com. coll. work, exec. council Episcopal Ch., 1966-69. Mem. Am. Physiol. Soc. (council 1967—, pres. 1973-74), Soc. Gen. Physiologists (pres. 1968-69), Biophys. Soc. (council 1970-73), AAAS, Assn. Am. Med. Colls. (chmn. council acad. socs. 1969-70, chmn. assembly 1973-74), Assn. Am. Physicians, Inst. Medicine, Nat. Acad. Sci. (council 1975-78), Nat. Insts. Health (ethics advisory bd. 1977—), Danish Royal Soc. (fellow), Alpha Omega Alpha. Spl. research cellular transport processes, red cell membranes. Office: Office of Dean Harvard Medical School 25 Shattuck St Boston MA 02115

TOTENBERG, ROMAN, violinist; b. Lodz, Poland, Jan. 1, 1912; s. Adam and Stanislawa (Winawer) T.; grad. Acad. Music, Berlin, 1932, Paris Inst. Instrumental Music, 1937; m. Melanie Shroder, 1941; children—Nina, Jill, Amy. Came to U.S., 1936, naturalized, 1943. Concerts prin. cities Europe, N.Am., S.Am. toured Europe with Karol Szymanoski; permanent soloist, dir. chamber music Interstate Broadcasting Co., N.Y.C., 1937-42; head violin dept. Peabody Conservatory, 1943-44, Mannes Coll. Music, N.Y.C., 1951-57; dir. Totenberg Instrumental Ensemble, 1953-60; chmn. string dept. Boston U., 1962-78, prof., 1978—; dir. Longy Sch. Music, Cambridge, Mass., 1978—. Prin. soloist, head string dept. Music Acad. West, Santa Barbara, Calif., summers 1948-51; with Music Assos., Aspen, Colo., summers 1951-62, Salzburg Mozarteum, summer 1962; George Miller vis. prof. U. Ill., 1960-61; head string dept. Boston U. Tanglewood Inst., summers 1966-74; performer, tchr. Kneisel Hall Festival, Blue Hill, Maine, 1975—; rec. artist Vanguard, DGG, Mus. Heritage Soc. records. Held scholarships coll., acads.; won Polish competition for presenting Polish music in fgn. countries; awarded Mendelsohn prize, Berlin, 1932; Wieniawski Soc. medal, 1965, Eugene Ysaye Soc. medal, 1971. Mem. Phi Kappa Lambda. Home: 329 Waverley Ave Newton MA 02158 Office: Longy Sch Music 1 Follen St Cambridge MA 02138

TOTH, CARL WAYNE, photographer; b. Cleve., Dec. 7, 1947; s. Carl and Elizabeth (Varga) T.; A.A.S., Rochester Inst. Tech., 1968; B.A., SUNY, Buffalo, 1970, M.F.A., 1972; m. Judith Lynn Stricker, Aug. 27, 1972; 1 son, Matthew Simon. Exhibited in one-man shows: Internat. Mus. Photography, Rochester, N.Y., 1972; Light Gallery, N.Y.C., 1974, 77, 79; Temple U., Phila., 1976; Phila. Coll. Art, 1979; group shows include: travelling exhbn. Visual Studies Workshop, Santa Barbara (Calif.) Mus. Art, 1979; New Mus., N.Y.C., 1979; San Francisco Mus. Art, 1979; Photography Workshop, Berlin, Ger., 1978; represented in permanent collections: Internat. Mus. Photography, Rochester, N.Y., Visual Studies Workshop, Rochester, Mus. Modern Art, N.Y.C., Australian Nat. Gallery Canberra, Detroit Inst. Art, San Francisco Mus. Art; head dept. photography Cranbrook Acad. Art, 1972—. Nat. Endowment for Arts grantee, 1975. Mem. Soc. Photog. Edn. Office: Cranbrook Acad Art PO Box 801 Bloomfield Hills MI 48013

TOTH, LOUIS EDMUND, materials scientist; b. N.Y.C.; s. Louis and Anna Helen Toth; B.S., Calif. Inst. Tech., 1960; Ph.D., U. Calif., Berkeley, 1963; divorced; 1 dau., Jennifer. Mem. faculty U. Minn., Mpls., 1964—, prof. materials sci., 1971—. Author: Transition Metal Carbides and Mitrides, 1971. Home: 17 S Long Lake Trail St Paul MN 55110 Office: Chem Engring Dept Univ Minn Minneapolis MN 55455

TOTH, ROBERT CHARLES, journalist; b. Blakely, Pa., Dec. 24, 1928; s. John and Tillie (Szuch) T.; B.S. in Chem. Engring., Washington U., St. Louis, 1952; M.S. in Journalism, Columbia U., 1955; postgrad. Harvard U., 1960-61; m. Paula Goldberg, Apr. 12, 1954; children—Jessica, Jennifer, John. Started as engr. in Army Ordnance Dept., 1952-54; reporter Providence Jour., 1955-57; sci. reporter N.Y. Herald Tribune, 1957-62, N.Y. Times, 1962-63; mem. staff Los Angeles Times, 1963—, bur. chief, London, 1965-70, diplomatic corr., 1970-71, White House corr., 1972-74, bur. chief, Moscow, 1974-77, now staff writer Washington bur. Served with USMC, 1946-48. Recipient Overseas Press Club award, 1977, Sigma Delta Chi award, 1977, George Polk award in Journalism for fgn. reporting L.I. U., 1978, Columbia U. Alumni award, 1978. Pulitzer Travelling scholar, 1955; Nieman fellow Harvard U., 1960-61. Home: 21 Primrose St Chevy Chase MD 20015 Office: Los Angeles Times 1700 Pennsylvania Ave NW Washington DC 20006

TOTMAN, CONRAD DAVIS, educator; b. Conway, Mass., Jan. 5, 1934; s. Raymond Smith and Mildred Edna (Kingsbury) T.; B.A., U. Mass., 1958; M.A., Harvard U., 1960, Ph.D., 1964; m. Michiko Ikegami, Jan. 21, 1958; children—Kathleen Junko, Christopher Ken. Asst. prof. U. Calif., Santa Barbara, 1964-66; asst. prof. Northwestern U., Evanston, Ill., 1966-68, asso. prof., 1968-72, prof. Japanese history, 1972—, chmn. dept. history, 1977—. Served with U.S. Army,

1953-56. Woodrow Wilson nat. fellow, 1958-59, Social Sci. Research Council-Am. Council Learned Socs. fellow, 1968-69, Nat. Endowment Humanities sr. fellow, 1972-73; Fulbright-Hays research grantee, 1968-69. Mem. Assn. Asian Studies (N.E. Asia council 1977—, chmn. 1978—; exec. com. 1978—), Am. Hist. Assn. Author: Politics in the Tokugawa Bakufu, 1600-1843, 1968; The Collapse of the Tokugawa Bakufu, 1862-1868, 1979. Office: Dept History Northwestern Univ Evanston IL 60201

TOTTER, JOHN RANDOLPH, biochemist; b. Saragosa, Tex., Jan. 7, 1914; s.Mathias and Agnes (Smith) T.; B.A., U. Wyo., 1934, M.A., 1935; Ph.D., State U. Iowa, 1938; m. Elizabeth Margaret Van Sant, Aug. 6, 1938; children—Lorena E. (Mrs. Dewey R. Henderson), Anita Ruth, John Alan. Instr. biochemistry U. W.Va., 1938-39; instr. biochemistry Ark. Sch. Medicine, 1939-42, asst. prof., 1942-45, asso. prof., 1945-52; chemist Oak Ridge Nat. Lab., 1952-56; biochemist AEC, Washington, 1956-58; vis. staff mem. U. of Republic, Montevideo, Uruguay, 1958-60; prof. biochemistry, chmn. div. biol. scis. U. Ga., 1960-62; asst. dir. for biol. scis. div. biology and medicine U.S. AEC, 1962-63, dir., 1967-72, asso. dir. for research, 1963-67; asso. dir. biomed. and environ. scis. Oak Ridge Nat. Lab., 1972-74; vis. staff mem. Inst. for Energy Analysis, Oak Ridge Asso. Univs., 1976-79, staff mem., 1979—. Participant nutritional survey, Alaska 1947. Mem. Am. Chem Soc., Am. Soc. Biol. Chemists, Soc. for Exptl. Biology and Medicine (chmn. S.W. sect. 1950), Soc. Nuclear Medicine, Sigma Xi. Home: 109 Wedgewood Dr Oak Ridge TN 37830 Office: Inst Energy Analysis Oak Ridge Asso Univs Oak Ridge TN 37830

TOULMIN, PRIESTLEY, III, geologist; b. Birmingham, Ala., June 5, 1930; s. Priestley and Catharine Augusta (Carey) T.; A.B., Harvard U., 1951, Ph.D., 1959; M.S., U. Colo., 1953; m. Martha Jane Slason, Aug. 30, 1952; children—Catharine Bosier, Priestley Chewning. With U.S. Geol. Survey, Washington, 1953-56, 57—, staff geologist for exptl. geology, 1966, chief Exptl. Geochemistry and Mineralogy Br., 1966-71, geologist Geologic div., 1971—, Reston, Va., 1974—, also leader inorganic chemistry team Viking Project; adj. prof. Columbia U., 1966; research asso. in geochemistry Calif. Inst. Tech., 1976-77; vis. lectr. Am. Geol. Inst. Mem. advisory com. spl. edn., Alexandria, Va., 1977—. Recipient Exceptional Service medal NASA, 1977; Meritorious Service award U.S. Dept. Interior, 1978. Fellow Geol. Soc. Am., Mineral. Soc. Am. (bd. asso. editors 1974-76); mem. Geochem. Soc. (jour. transls. editor 1965-68, councillor 1975-77), Soc. Econ. Geologists, Mineral. Soc. Gt. Britain, Mineral. Assn. Can., Geol. Soc. Washington (2d v.p. 1976-77, councillor 1973-75), AAAS, Explorers Club, Sigma Xi, Sigma Gamma Epsilon. Club: Cosmos (Washington). Asso. editor Am. Mineralogist, 1974-76; contbr. articles to profl. jours. Home: 418 Summers Dr Alexandria VA 22301 Office: US Geol Survey 959 Nat Center Reston VA 22092

TOULMIN, STEPHEN EDELSTON, educator; b. London, Eng., Mar. 25, 1922; s. Geoffrey Edelston and Doris (Holman) T.; B.A., King's Coll., Cambridge (Eng.) U., 1942, M.A., 1948, Ph.D., 1948. Fellow King's Coll., 1947-51; lectr. philosophy sci. Oxford (Eng.) U., 1949-55; prof. philosophy, head dept. Leeds (Eng.) U., 1955-59; dir. unit history ideas Nuffield Found., London, 1960-65; prof. history ideas and philosophy Brandeis U., 1965-69; prof. philosophy Mich. State U., 1969-72; prof. humanities, provost Crown Coll., U. Calif. at Santa Cruz, 1972-73; prof. social thought and philosophy U. Chgo., 1973—; vis. prof. Melbourne U. (Australia), 1954-55, N.Y. U., 1959, Columbia, 1959-60, Hebrew U., Jerusalem, 1964, Dartmouth Coll., 1979; Tate-Wilson lectr. So. Meth. U., 1979; Sigma Xi nat. lectr., 1966; counsellor Smithsonian Instn., 1966-75; Mary Flexner lectr. Bryn Mawr Coll., 1977; Phi Beta Kappa nat. lectr., 1978-79. Guggenheim fellow, 1977. Author: Reason in Ethics, 1949; Philosophy of Science, 1953; The Uses of Argument, 1958; Foresight and Understanding, 1961; Human Understanding, 1972; Knowing and Acting, 1976; (all with June Goodfield) The Fabric of the Heavens, 1961; The Architecture of Matter, 1963; The Discovery of Time, 1965; (with Allen Janik) Wittgenstein's Vienna, 1973; (with Richard Rieke and Allen Janik) Introduction to Reasoning, 1979. Office: Com Social Thought U Chgo Chicago IL 60637

TOULOUKIAN, YERAM SARKIS, educator; b. Istanbul, Turkey, Dec. 28, 1920; s. Sarkis Hagop and Zaruhi (Feradian) T.; B.S., Robert Coll., 1939; M.S., M.I.T., 1941; Ph.D., Purdue U., 1946; m. Arsilya Istanbulian, Aug. 8, 1948; children—James Sarkis, Eileen Zabell. Came to U.S., 1939, naturalized, 1952. Dir., Center for Info. and Numerical Data Analysis and Synthesis. Distinguished Atkins prof. engrng. Purdue U., 1944—; vis. prof. thermodynamics Auburn U., 1963—; cons. to maj. indsl. cos. and U.S. Govt. Dir. OEA, Inc., Denver. Recipient Gold medal Associatione Termotecnica Italiana, Bologne, Italy, 1968. Registered profl. engr., Ind. Fellow ASME (meml. award heat transfer div.), Am. Inst. Aeros. and Astronautics (asso.). Co-author, editor Thermophysical Properties of Matter-TPRC Data Series, 13 vols., 1970—. Mem. editorial advisory bd. jours. in field. Home: 233 Pawnee Dr West Lafayette IN 47906

TOULOUSE, ROBERT BARTELL, coll. dean; b. Wellsville, Mo., May 8, 1918; s. Walter Eaton and Emma (Schmidt) T.; student Central Coll., 1935-37; B.S., U. Mo., 1939, M.Ed., 1947, Ed.D., 1948; m. Virginia Lee Danford, Aug. 7, 1948; children—Samuel Phillip, Robert Bartell. Tchr. sci. and social studies, high sch., Mountain View, Mo., 1939-41; asst. prof. to prof. N. Tex. State U., 1949-54, dean Grad. Sch., 1954—. State sponsor Future Tchrs. Am. Served from pvt. to lt. col. AUS, World War II. Mem. Assn. Tex. Grad. Schs. (pres.), Assn. Coll. Tchr. Edn. (v.p.), Tex. Assn. Audio-Visual Edn. Dirs. (v.p.), AAUP, NEA, Phi Delta Kappa. Democrat. Presbyterian. Club: Kiwanis (pres.). Contbr. articles profl. jours. Home: 1218 Emerson Ln Denton TX 76201

TOUMEY, HUBERT (HUGH) JOHN, textile mfg. co. exec.; b. N.Y.C.; s. William Joseph and Mary Veronica (Drury) T.; A.B., Fordham U., 1936; M.B.A., Harvard, 1938; m. Dorothy A. Henry, Oct. 16,1954; children—Donald Joseph, Kenneth Drury. With Cannon Mills, Inc., 1938—, v.p., mgr. towel sales, 1959-60, v.p., gen. sales mgr., 1960-62, exec. v.p., 1962-67, pres., chief adminstrv. and mktg. officer, 1967—, chmn., chief exec. officer, 1978—, also dir.; dir. Cannon Mills Co. Mem. mktg. com. Am. Textile Mfrs. Inst., 1967—, chmn., 1977—. Trustee Coll. Mt. St. Vincent, Riverdale, N.Y., 1977—, chmn., 1979—. Club: Windham (N.Y.) Mountain (gov. 1975—). Home: 388 Middlesex Rd Darien CT 06820 Office: 1271 Ave of Americas New York NY 10020

TOUPIN, ARTHUR VERNON, banker; b. Oklee, Minn., Oct. 14, 1921; s. Irvin D. and Inger (Sorenson) T.; A.B., Gustavus Adolphus Coll., 1943; J.D., Stanford U., 1949; postgrad. Advanced Mgmt. Program, Harvard U., 1971; m. Lillian J. Blass, Dec. 19, 1945; 1 son, James Arthur. Counsel legal dept., trust officer, v.p. bus. relationships Bank Am. subs. Bank Am. Corp., San Francisco, 1949-60, exec. v.p., exec. officer trust activities, 1969-74, exec. officer bank investment securities div., 1974-76, exec. v.p. and sr. adminstrv. officer, 1976-78, vice chmn. and sr. adminstrv. officer, 1978—, also dir.; dir. BA Investment Mgmt. Corp. subs., Montreal Trust Co. (Que., Can.); pres., dir. Montgomery St. Income Securities, Inc., San Francisco, 1972—; gen. counsel ISI Corp., San Francisco, 1960-69. Past bd. dirs. Calif. Assn. Mental Health; pres. San Francisco Assn. Mental Health, Hinckley Fund. Served with USNR, 1943-46. Recipient Disting. Alumni citation in field bus. Gustavus Adolphus Coll., 1970. Mem. San Francisco C. of C. (dir.), Order of Coif. Clubs: Olympic, Bankers (dir.), Commonwealth, Villa Taverna (San Francisco). Editor: Stanford Law Rev., 1947-49. Office: PO Box 37000 San Francisco CA 94137

TOUPS, JOHN MELBURN, sci. and tech. co. exec.; b. Wichita Falls, Tex., Jan. 10, 1926; s. Sidney P. and Alice (Bryant) T.; B.S. in Civil Engrng., U. Calif., Berkeley, 1949; m. Mary Pat Powers, Jan. 30, 1950; children—Paul, Charles, Dana, Ellen. Engr., Calif. Div. Hwys., Los Angeles, 1949, Asso. Oil Co., Ventura, Calif., 1949-52, United Water Conservation Dist., Santa Paula, Calif., 1952-53; city engr. City of Seal Beach (Calif.), 1953-55, City of Fullerton (Calif.), 1955-56; dist. engr. Orange County Water Dist., Orange, Calif., 1956-58; founder, pres. Toups Corp., Santa Ana, Calif., 1958-74; sr. v.p. Planning Research Corp., Los Angeles, 1974-77, pres., chief exec. officer, Washington, 1977—, also dir. Served with U.S. Army, 1944-45. Decorated Silver Star, Purple Heart. Mem. Nat. Soc. Profl. Engrs., Cons. Engrs. Assn. Calif., Am. Cons. Engrs. Council, Am. Water Works Assn. Home: 700 New Hampshire Ave NW Washington DC 20037 Office: Planning Research Corp 1850 K St NW Suite 1100 Washington DC 20006

TOURLENTES, THOMAS THEODORE, psychiatrist; b. Chgo., Dec. 7, 1922; s. Theodore A. and Mary (Xenosathy) T.; B.S., U. Chgo., 1945, M.D., 1947; m. Mona Belle Land, Sept. 9, 1956; children—Theodore W., Stephen C., Elizabeth A. Intern Cook County Hosp., Chgo., 1947-48; resident psychiatry Downey (Ill.) VA Hosp., 1948-51; practice Medicine specializing in psychiatry, Chgo., 1952, Camp Atterbury, Ind., 1953, Ft. Carson, Colo., 1954, Galesburg, Ill., 1955-71; staff psychiatrist Chgo. VA Clinic, 1952; clin. instr. psychiatry Med. Sch., Northwestern U., 1952; dir. mental hygiene consultation service Camp Atterbury, 1953-54, Ft. Carson, 1953-54; asst. supt. Galesburg State Research Hosp., 1954-58, supt., 1958-71; dir. Comprehensive Community Mental Health Center Rock Island and Mercer Counties; dir. psychiat. services Franciscan Hosp., 1971—; asso. clin. prof. psychiatry U. Ill., Chgo., 1955—; preceptor in hosp. adminstrn. State U. Iowa, Iowa City, 1958-64. Councilor, del. Ill. Psychiat. Soc.; chmn. liaison com. Am. hosp. and psychiat. assns., 1978-79. Mem. Gov. Ill. Com. Employment Handicapped, 1962-64; zone dir. Ill. Dept. Mental Health, 1964-71; mem. Spl. Survey Joint Commn. Accreditation Hosps., Commn. Certification Psychiat. Adminstrs. Pres., Knox-Galesburg Symphony Soc., 1966-68. Bd. dirs. Galesburg Civic Music Assn., pres., 1968-70. Served to capt. M.C., AUS, 1943-46, 52-54. Diplomate Am. Bd. Psychiatry and Neurology, asst. examiner, 1964-78. Fellow AMA, Am. Psychiat. Assn., AAAS, Am. Coll. Psychiatrists; mem. Ill. Med. Soc. (chmn. aging com. 1968-71), Ill. Psychiat. Soc. (pres. 1969-70), Am. Pub. Health Assn., Soc. Biol. Psychiatry, Ill. Hosp. Assn. (trustee 1968-70), Am. Coll. Hosp. Adminstrs., Assn. for Research Nervous and Mental Diseases, Am. Assn. Psychiat. Adminstrs. (pres. 1978-79), Knox County Mental Health Assn. (dir.). Rotarian. Contbr. articles profl. jours. Home: Rural Rt 2 Valley View Rd Galesburg IL 61401. *Feeling useful and needed is the greatest recognition and reward of all!*

TOUSEY, RICHARD, physicist; b. Somerville, Mass., May 18, 1908; s. Coleman and Adella Richards (Hill) T.; A.B., Tufts U., 1928, Sc.D. (hon.), 1961; A.M., Harvard, 1929; Ph.D., 1933; m. Ruth Lowe, June 29, 1932; 1 dau., Joanna. Instr. physics Harvard, 1933-36, tutor div. phys. scis., 1934-36; research instr. Tufts U., 1936-41; physicist U.S. Naval Research Lab. optics div., 1941-58, head instrument sect., 1942-45, head micron waves br., 1945-58, head rocket spectroscopy br., atmosphere and astrophysics div., 1958-67, space sci. div., 1967—. Mem. com. vision Armed Forces-NRC, 1944—; line spectra of elements com. NRC, 1960-72; mem. Rocket and Satellite Research Panel, 1958—; mem. astronomy subcom. space sci. steering com. NASA, 1960-62, mem. solar physics subcom., 1969-71, prin. investigator expts. including Skylab; mem. com. aeronomy Internat. Union Geodesy and Geophysics, 1958—; U.S. nat. com. Internat. Commn. Optics, 1960-66; mem. sci. steering com. Project Vanguard, 1956-58; mem. adv. com. to office sci. personnel Nat. Acad. Scis.-NRC, 1969-72. Bayard Cutting fellow Harvard, 1931-33, 35-36; recipient Meritorious Civilian Service award U.S. Navy, 1945; E.O. Hulburt award Naval Research Labs., 1958; Progress medal photog. Soc. Am. 1959; Prix Ancel Soc. Francaise de Photographie, 1962; Henry Draper medal Nat. Acad. Scis., 1963; Navy award for distinguished achievement in sci, 1963; Eddington medal 1964; NASA medal for exceptional sci. achievement, 1974; George Darwin lectr. Royal Astron. Soc. 1963. Fellow Am. Acad. Arts and Scis., Am. Phys. Soc., Optical Soc. Am. (dir. 1953-57; Frederic Ives medal 1960), Am. Geophys. Union; mem. Internat. Acad. Astronautics, Nat., Washington acads. scis., Am. Astron. Soc. (v.p. 1964-66 Henry Norris Russell lectr. 1966), Soc. Applied Spectroscopy, AAAS, Am. Geophys. Union, Philos. Soc. Washington, Internat. Astron. Union, Nuttall Ornithol. Club, Audubon Naturalists Soc., Phi Beta Kappa, Sigma Xi, Theta Delta Chi. Contbr. articles in field to sci. jours. and books. Home: 7725 Oxon Hill Rd SE Washington DC 20021 Office: US Naval Research Lab Washington DC 20375

TOUSSAINT, ALLEN RICHARD, record producer, composer, pianist; b. New Orleans, Jan. 14, 1938; s. Clarence Matthew and Naomi (Neville) T.; student public and pvt. schs., New Orleans; children—Naomi, Clarence, Alison. Pianist for Shirley & Lee, 1957, U.S. Army Soldiers Choir, 1963-65; recorded albums: Tousan-Wild Sounds of New Orleans, 1958, Life, Love & Faith, 1972, Southern Nights, 1975, Motion, 1978; a founder, v.p. Sansu Enterprises, Inc., from 1965; pres. Sea-Saint Rec. Studio, Inc., New Orleans, Marsaint Music, Inc.; composer songs: Can I Hear It Again, Declaration Of Love, Draining, Dreamer Of Dreams, Everything I Do Gonna Be Funky, Get Out Of my Life Woman, God Must Have Blessed America, Holy Cow, I Like It Like That, Java, Mother-In-Law, Motion, Night People, Occapella, Performance, Play Something Sweet (Brickyard Blues), Ride Your Pony, Shoo-Rah, Shoo-Rah, Southern Nights, (Country Music Assn. Song of Yr., Broadcast Music, Inc. citation of achievement), The Greatest Love, The Optimism Blues, Viva La Money, Whipped Cream, With You In Mind, Working In A Coal Mine, Yes We Can, Can, All These Things (Broadcast Music, Inc. citation of achievement; performer New Orleans Jazz Festival, annually; lectr. in field. Served with U.S. Army, 1963-65. Mem. Broadcast Music, Inc., Am. Fedn. Musicians, Contemporary Arts Center. Office: 3809 Clematis Ave New Orleans LA 70122

TOUSSAINT, WAYNE E., mfg. co. exec.; b. Princeton, Minn., Jan. 22, 1918; s. Jacob and Lettie (Nichols) T.; B.S., Northwestern U., 1939; m. Frances Cooper, Aug. 14, 1939; children—Jacqueline Carol (Mrs. William Rapp), Laurel Patrice (Mrs. John Brandon). With Barrow, Wade, Guthrie & Co., Chgo., 1939-42; pres., chief exec. officer Frederick Post Co. (now Teledyne Post), Chgo., 1942-71, 73-75; chmn., chief exec. officer Vance Industries, Inc., Chgo., 1971—. Served with USNR, 1945-46. C.P.A., Ill. Mem. Ill. Soc. C.P.A.'s, Delta Sigma Pi, Beta Gamma Sigma Mason (32 deg.). Clubs: North Shore Country (Glenview, Ill.), Minocqua. Home: 1012 S Hamlin Ave Park Ridge IL 60068 Office: 7401 W Wilson Ave Chicago IL 60656

TOUSTER, BEN, ret. bus. exec.; b. N.Y.C., Apr. 8, 1893; s. Oscar and Betty (Ehrhlich) T.; student N.Y. pub. schs.; m. Bertha Landau, Feb. 22, 1920 (dec.); children—Irwin, Saul. Founder, pres., dir. Cinderella Hat Co., Inc., 1922-63; v.p. CARE (Coop. for Am. Relief Everywhere), N.Y.C., 1953-57, treas., 1957-67, chmn. bd., 1967-79. Pres., United Hias Service, 1954-56, asso. chmn. bd., Hias Inc., 1960-79, exec. com., 1954-79; pres. YM & YWHA Boro Park, Bklyn., 1949-55, hon. pres., 1955; hon. chmn. Bklyn. div. Fedn. Jewish Philanthropics N.Y., 1952-79, trustee, 1945-79, chmn. functional com. on community centers, 1950-53, mem. religious affairs com., 1960-79, trustee Maimonides Med. Center, Bklyn., also hon. v.p., 1958-79; trustee Jewish Home and Hosp. for Aged of N.Y., 1952-79; pres. Hebrew Sheltering and Immigrant Aid Soc., 1952-54; dir., mem. exec. com. Council Jewish Fedns. and Welfare Fund, 1953-59; dir., mem. exec. bd., fgn. affairs com. Am. Jewish Com., 1950-79; mem. nat. council Am. Joint Distbn. Com.; mem. Nat. Conf. for Jewish Communal Service; bd. dirs. Touro Synagogue Nat. Historic Shrine, 1950-79, Alliance Israelite Universelle, 1953-79; bd. govs. N.Y. Bd. Rabbis Advisory Council; lay mem. Brith Milah Bd. N.Y. Served with U.S. Army, 1918. Mem. publ. com. Commentary, 1950-79. Home: 41 Park Ave New York NY 10016 Died Sept. 25, 1979.

TOUSTER, OSCAR, educator; b. N.Y.C., July 3, 1921; s. Mayer Herman and Henrietta Esther (Silberstein) T.; B.S., Coll. City N.Y., 1941; M.A., Oberlin Coll., 1942; Ph.D., U. Ill., 1947; m. Eva Katherine Beach, Aug. 24, 1944; 1 dau., Alison Blair. Chemist Atlas Powder Co., 1942-43; research biochemist Abbott Labs, 1943-45; mem. faculty Vanderbilt U., 1947—, instr. biochemistry, 1947-50, asst. prof., 1950-54, asso. prof., 1954-58, prof. biochemistry, 1958—, prof. molecular biology, 1973—, chmn. dept. molecular biology, 1963—; Hughes investigator, 1957-60; vis. specialist USIA, Germany, summer 1958; vis. lectr. chemistry U. Ill., 1959; vis. prof. biochemistry Cornell U., 1963; councillor Oak Ridge Asso. Univs., 1963-73, chmn. council, 1970-73, bd. dirs., 1970—, v.p., 1973-76, pres., 1976—; mem. USPHS Biochemistry Tng. Com. 1961-66; mem. med. scientist tng. com. USPHS, 1966-70; mem. orgn. com. VI Internat. Congress Biochemistry, N.Y.C., 1964; mem. subcom. metabolic intermediates NRC, 1966—; mem. sci. adv. bd. Eunice Kennedy Shriver Center for Mental Retardation, Waltham, Mass., 1974—. Guggenheim fellow, 1957-58; recipient Theobald Smith award in med. sci. AAAS, 1956, NSF Travel awards to Internat. Congresses of Biochemistry, Paris, 1952, Moscow, 1961. Mem. Am. Chem. Soc. (chmn. Nashville sect.), Biochem. Soc., AAAS (council), Am. Soc. Biol. Chemists (asso. editor), Fed. Am. Soc. Exptl. Biology (mem. pub. info. com.), AAUP, Soc. for Complex Carbohydrates (exec. com.), Phi Beta Kappa, Sigma Xi, Phi Kappa Phi, Phi Lambda Upsilon. Translator, reviser Hollmann's Non-Glycolytic Pathways of Metabolism of Glucose, 1964; asso. ed. Organic Reactions, Vol. 7, 1952. Editorial bd. Jour. Biol. Chemistry, 1964-69, 76—, Archives of Biochemistry and Biophysics, 1969—, Soundings, Interdisciplinary Jour., 1971-74. Contbr. articles to med., chem., biochem. jours., The Chemistry of Penicillin, 1948. Home: 114 Vaughn Rd Nashville TN 37221

TOUSTER, SAUL, educator; b. Bklyn., Oct. 12, 1925; s. Ben and Bertha (Landau) T.; A.B. magna cum laude, Harvard, 1944, J.D., 1948; m. Helen Davidson, Nov. 23, 1954 (div. 1967); children—Natasha Ann, Jonathan Bach; m. 2d, Irene Tayler, Jan. 14, 1978. Admitted to N.Y. State bar, 1949; practiced in N.Y.C., 1949-55; prof. law State U. N.Y. at Buffalo, 1955-69, asst. to pres., 1966-68, mem. adj. faculty in medicine, edn., psychology, 1964-69; prof. law and social scis. State Coll. at Old Westbury, 1969-71; prof., provost, acad. v.p. City Coll. N.Y., 1971-73; acting pres. Richmond Coll. City U. N.Y., 1973-74; prof. law City U. N.Y. Grad. Sch. also John Jay Coll. of Criminal Justice, 1974—; legis. cons. N.Y. State Law Review Commn., 1956-61; vis. prof. U. Brussels, summer 1968. Mem. nat. bd. cons. Nat. Endowment for Humanities. Served to lt. (j.g.) USNR, 1944-46. Nat. Endowment for Humanities fellow, 1978; Am. Bar Found. Legal History fellow, 1977-78. Mem. Am. Acad. Arts and Scis. (dir. studies, policy council on learning, teaching and evaluation, assembly on univ. goals 1969-70), ACLU, Phi Beta Kappa. Club: Harvard. Author: Still Lives and Other Lives, 1966 (Devins Meml. prize 1966). Contbr. articles to legal periodicals. Home: 96 Monadnock Rd Chestnut Hill MA 02167 Office: City U N Y 33 W 42d St New York City NY 10036

TOVISH, HAROLD, sculptor; b. N.Y.C., July 31, 1921; s. Louis Goodman and Anna (Treffman) T.; student WPA Art Project, 1938-40, Columbia, 1940-43, Ossip Zadkine Sch. Drawing and Sculpture, Paris, France, 1949-50, Acad. De La Grande Chaumiere, Paris, 1950-51; m. Marianna Pineda Packard, Jan. 14, 1946; children—Margo, Aaron, Nina. Tchr. sculpture N.Y. State Coll. Ceramics, 1947-49, U. Minn., 1951-54, Sch. of Boston Mus., 1957-66; sculptor in residence Am. Acad. in Rome, 1966; group exhbns. include Met. Mus. of Art, 1943, Toledo Mus. Art, 1948, Galerie 8, 1949, Walker Art Center, 1951, Mpls. Inst. Art, 1953, San Francisco Art Assn., 1953, Whitney Mus. Am. Art, 1954, 58, 60, 64, Mus. Modern Art, 1960, Chgo. Art Inst., 1960, Carnegie Internat, 1960, Am. Fedn. Art, 1964, Decordova Mus., 1964, 23d Venice Biennial, 1956, Boston Visual Artists Union Gallery, 1975, Boston U., 1975, 78, Colby Coll., 1975, Inst. Contemporary Art, Boston, 1975, 76, Skowhegan Sch., 1975, N.Y. U., 1976, Boston Mus. Fine Arts, 1977; one man shows include Walker Art Center, 1953, Swetzoff Gallery, Boston, 1957, 60, 65, Dintenfass Gallery, N.Y.C., 1965, 72, Addison Gallery Am. Art, Andover, Mass., 1965, Alpha Gallery, Boston, 1968, 73, Terry Dintenfass, Inc., N.Y.C., 1980; retrospective exhibit Wheaton Coll., 1967; survey exhibit Solomon Guggenheim Meml. Mus., 1968; represented in permanent collections Phila. Mus. Art, Whitney Mus. Am. Art, Walker Art Center, Mpls. Inst. Art, Addison Gallery Am. Art, Chgo. Art Inst., Mus. Modern Art, Boston Mus. Fine Art, Guggenheim Mus., Worcester Mus. Art, Hirshhorn Collection, Sara Roby Found., Colby Coll., Sara Roby Found.; prof. art Boston U., 1971—; vis. prof. U. Hawaii, 1969. Recipient 1st prize sculpture Boston Arts Festival, 1957, 1st prize drawing, 1958; award Am. Inst. Arts and Letters, 1971; sculpture grantee Am. Inst. Arts and Letters, 1960; Guggenheim fellow, 1967; research fellow Center for Advanced Visual Studies, M.I.T., 1967-68. Mem. Boston Visual Artists Union. Address: 380 Marlborough St Boston MA 02115

TOW, CLARENCE WESLEY, economist, banker; b. Gilman, Iowa, Oct. 14, 1907; s. Andrew A. and Minnie (Berntson) T.; B.A., State U. Iowa, 1928, M.A., 1929; postgrad. Harvard, 1934; Ph.D., U. Minn., 1949; m. Mary Campbell, July 26, 1942 (dec. 1970). Tchr. social studies U. Iowa High Sch., 1928-29, Burlington (Iowa) Jr. Coll., 1929-37; instr. econs. U. Minn., Mpls., 1937-42; economist OPA, Washington, 1942-44; financial economist Fed. Res. Bank of Kansas City (Mo.), 1944-50, dir. research, 1950-52, v.p., 1952-62, sr. v.p., 1963-72. Asso. economist Fed. Open Market Com., 1951-72; cons. bd. govs. Fed. Res. System, 1973-75. Mem. Am., Midwest econ. assns., Am. Finance Assn. Contbr. articles to profl. jours. Home: 221 W 48th St Kansas City MO 64112

TOWBIN, ABRAHAM ROBERT, investment banker; b. N.Y.C., May 26, 1935; s. Harold Clay and Minna (Berlin) T.; B.A., Dartmouth Coll., 1957; m. Irene K. Lyons, Sept. 15, 1957; children—Minna Joyce, Abraham Robert, Zachary Harold. With Asiel & Co., N.Y.C., 1958-59; with L.F. Rothschild, Unterberg, Towbin (merged with C.E. Unterberg, Towbin Co. 1977), N.Y.C., 1959—, partner, 1961—; dir.

Presidents-First Lady Spa. Inc., Houston, AVX Corp., Community Foods, Inc., Unity Broadcasting Corp.; adv. bd. N.Y. Mag. Vice chmn. N.Y. State Council Arts; bd. dirs., vice chmn., treas. Film Soc. Lincoln Center; mem. adv. bd. Nat. Com. Arts for Handicapped; bd. dirs. Ind. Sch. Orch., Grand St. Settlement, Maimonides Med. Center, St. David's Sch., Marymount Sch. Mem. Securities Industry Assn., Bond Club N.Y. Clubs: Stock Exchange Luncheon, Harmonie (N.Y.C.); Nat. Golf Links Am. Home: 1010 Fifth Ave New York NY 10028 Office: LF Rothschild Unterberg Towbin 55 Water St New York NY 10041

TOWE, GEORGE COFFIN, educator, physicist; b. Passaic, N.J., Nov. 28, 1921; s. Walter Allan and Frances (Coffin) T.; B.S., Hamilton Coll., 1943; M.S., U. Mich., 1947, Ph.D., 1954; m. Dorothy May Etris; 1 son, Robert David. Physicist, Naval Ordnance Lab., Washington, 1943-45; engr. Ford Motor Co., Dearborn, Mich., 1953-55; asst. prof. to asso. prof. physics Mont. State Coll., 1955-61; prof., head dept. physics, chmn. div. natural sci. Findlay Coll., 1961-62; asso. prof. to prof. physics Alfred U., 1962—, chmn. dept., 1962-72, chmn. div. spl. programs, 1974-77; vis. sci. UKAEA (Harwell, Eng.), 1967-68; cons., lectr. Oak Ridge Asso. U.; cons. edn. Australian univs., 1977-78. Served from ensign to lt. (j.g.), USNR, 1944-45. Mem. Am. Assn. Physics Tchrs., Nat. Sci. Tchrs. Assn., Am. Radio Relay League, Sigma Xi. Home: 5573 Jericho Hill Rd Alfred Station NY 14803 Office: Alfred University Alfred NY 14802

TOWE, PETER M., Canadian govt. ofcl.; b. London, Ont., Can., Nov. 1, 1922; s. Allen M. and Clare (Durdle) T.; B.A., U. Western Ont., 1943; M.A., Queens U., 1947; m. Carol Krumm, Aug. 2, 1953; children—Christopher, Fredericka, Jennifer. Joined Dept. External Affairs Can., Ottawa, 1947; assigned Washington, Ottawa, Bonn and Paris, 1949-60; permanent rep. OECD, Paris, 1960-62, econ. minister, Washington, 1967-72; ambassador, permanent rep. OECD, 1972-75; asst. under-sec. of state for external affairs, Ottawa, 1975-77; Canadian ambassador to U.S., 1977—; dep. head Can. Internat. Devel. Agy. (formerly External Aid Office), Ottawa, 1962-67. Served with RCAF, 1942-45. Home: 2825 Rock Creek Dr Washington DC 20008 Office: Canadian Embassy 1746 Massachusetts Ave NW Washington DC 20036

TOWELL, WILLIAM EARNEST, forestry cons., former assn. exec.; b. St. James, Mo., June 11, 1916; s. Esco Joel and Margaret (Pinto) T.; B.S. in Forestry, U. Mich., 1938, M.S. in Silviculture, 1938; m. Virginia Ruth Dotter, Aug. 31, 1940; children—Jane Towell Darrough, Linda Towell Hatfield. With Mo. Dept. Conservation, 1938-67, dir., 1957-67; exec. v.p. Am. Forestry Assn., Washington, 1967-78; forestry cons., N.C., 1978—. Mem. Pres.'s Water Pollution Control Adv. Bd., 1963-66, Sec. Agr. Wildlife Advisory Bd., 1965-69, Lewis and Clark Trail Commn., 1965-67; Mo. liaison officer Bur. Outdoor Recreation, 1963-65; mem. conservation com. Boy Scouts Am., 1968—, nat. chmn., 1975-78, nat. chmn. project SOAR, 1970-74; advisory mem. com. interrelations wildlife and agr. Nat. Acad. Scis., 1965-70, mem. advisory team to Indonesia, 1972; mem. Cradle of Forestry Advisory Commn., Dept. Agr., 1971-76; mem. tech. advisory com. transmission Nat. Gas Survey, 1971-73; exec. advisory com. Nat. Gas Survey, 1975-78; conservation cons. Walt Disney Prodns., 1969-78; chmn. endangered species com., chmn. fed. aid com., chmn. legis. com., chmn. exec. com. Internat. Assn. Fish and Wildlife Agys., 1964-65, pres., 1965-66; mem. exec. com. Fontana Conservation Roundup, 1969—; mem. exec. com. Nat. Resources Council Am., 1968-78, treas., 1971-73, vice chm., 1973-75, chmn., 1975-77; bd. dirs. Americans for Energy Independence, 1975-78, Keep Am. Beautiful, 1977-78; mem. conservation awards com. Am. Rifle Assn., 1974-77. Served to lt. USNR, 1943-46. Recipient Merit de Agrico medal (France), 1970; Conservationist of Year award Nat. Wildlife Fedn., 1976; Disting. Service award U. Mich. Sch. Natural Resources Alumni Soc., 1978; Lifetime Achievement award Nat. Assn. State Foresters, 1978. Fellow Soc. Am. Foresters (chmn. Ozark sect. 1950, Sir William Schlich Meml. medal 1978); mem. Wildlife Soc., Am. Fisheries Soc. Democrat. Episcopalian (past sr. warden, mem. diocesan council). Clubs: Kiwanis; Cosmos (chmn. house com. 1975-77, bd. mgmt. 1977-78) (Washington). Contbr. articles to profl. jours. Home: 165 Country Club Hills Southern Pines NC 28387

TOWER, BERTRAM B., communications exec.; b. West Bridgewater, Mass., Aug. 10, 1914; s. Harry L. and Olive H. (Churchill) T.; B.S., U. N.H., 1935; postgrad. Columbia; m. Jean Newport, June 3, 1939; children—Jean C. (Mrs.. Keplinger), Bertram B. With Arthur Andersen & Co., accountants and auditors, 1935-43; asst. controller Am. Cable & Radio Corp., 1943-47, dir., v.p., comptroller, 1948-58, v.p. finance, 1958, pres., dir., 1958-64; chmn., dir. ITT World Communications, Inc., 1964—; vice chmn., dir. All Am. Cables and Radio, Inc.; chmn. bd., dir. Comml. Cable Co.; vice chmn., dir, Globe-Mackay Cable & Radio (Philippines); dir. ITT-Communications Inc. Virgin Islands, ITT Central Am. Cables & Radio. C.P.A., N.Y. Mem. Far East-Am. Council, Am. Inst. Accountants, Controllers Inst. Mason. Clubs: Downtown Athletic, Canadian (N.Y.C.). Office: ITT World Communications Inc 67 Broad St New York NY 10004*

TOWER, DONALD BAYLEY, biomed. research adminstr.; b. Orange, N.J., Dec. 11, 1919; s. Walter Sheldon and Edith Florence (Jones) T.; A.B., Harvard U., 1941, M.D., 1944; M.Sc., McGill U., Montreal, 1948, Ph.D., 1951; m. Arline Belle Croft, Aug. 5, 1947; 1 dau., Deborah Alden Tower Fretwell. Intern in surgery U. Minn. Hosp., Mpls., 1944-45; research fellow neurochemistry Montreal Neurol. Inst., 1947-48, 49-51, asst. resident in neurosurgery, 1948-49, asso. neurochemist, 1951-53; instr., then asst. prof. exptl. neurology McGill U. Med. Sch., 1951-53; joined USPHS, 1953, asst. surgeon gen., 1975; chief sect. clin. neurochemistry Nat. Inst. Neurol. Diseases and Stroke, NIH, Bethesda, Md., 1953-61, chief lab. neurochemistry, 1961-74; dir. Nat. Inst. Neurol. and Communicative Disorders and Stroke, NIH, 1974—; clin. asso. prof. neurology Georgetown U. Med. Sch., 1953—; chmn. U.S. neurochemistry del. to USSR, 1969; temporary adviser neuroscis. WHO, 1976—. John and Mary R. Markle scholar acad. medicine, 1951-53; recipient Distinguished Service medal USPHS, 1977. Mem. Am. Acad. Neurology, AAAS, Am. Neurol. Assn., Am., Internat. socs. neurochemistry, Am. Soc. Biol. Chemists, Canadian Neurol. Soc., Canadian Physiol. Soc., Internat. Brain Research Orgn., Soc. Neuroscis., Washington Acad. Medicine. Author: Neurochemistry of Epilepsy, 1960; also numerous research papers. Editor: The Nervous System, 3 vols., 1975; chief editor Jour. Neurochemistry, 1968-73. Address: Room 8A52 Bldg 31 Nat Insts Health Bethesda MD 20014

TOWER, HORACE LINWOOD, III, consumer products co. exec.; b. New Haven, July 16, 1932; s. Horace Linwood, Jr. and Madeline Elizabeth (Davin) T.; B.A., Cornell U., 1955, M.B.A., 1960; m. Elizabeth Wright, Dec. 29, 1956; children—Cynthia, William, John. Br. mgr. Procter & Gamble Corp., Cin., 1960-62; mgmt. cons. Booz, Allen & Hamilton, N.Y.C., 1962-63; product mgr. Gen. Foods Corp., White Plains, N.Y., 1963-67, advt. and merchandising mgr., 1967-69, dir. corporate devel., 1969-71, exec. v.p. Maxwell House div., 1971-73, pres. div., 1973-78, v.p. parent corp., 1973-78; pres., chief exec. officer Stanley Home Products, Inc., Westfield, Mass., 1978—. Mem. Cornell Fund, Mass. Bus. Devel. Council, Mass. Bus. Roundtable. Served to capt. USAF, 1956-59. Mem. Am. Mktg. Assn., Cornell Alumni Assn., Direct Selling Assn., Pi Kappa Phi, Sigma Gamma Epsilon. Clubs: Tokeneke (Darien, Conn.); Suffield (Conn.) Country; Thimble Island Sailing and Lit. Soc.; Stoney Creek Boating. Home: 118 Five Mile River Rd Darien CT 06820 also Governors Island Stoney Creek CT Office: 333 Western Ave Westfield MA 01085

TOWER, JOHN GOODWIN, U.S. senator; b. Houston, Sept. 29, 1925; s. Joe Z. and Beryl (Goodwin) T.; B.A., Southwestern U., Tex., 1948, also LL.D. (hon.); M.A. in Polit. Sci., So. Meth. U., 1953; postgrad. London Sch. Econs. and Polit. Sci., U. London, 1952-53; LL.D. (hon.), Howard Payne Coll., Alfred U.; m. Lilla Burt Cummings, May 29, 1977; children by previous marriage—Penelope, Marian, Jeanne. Radio announcer sta. KFDM, Beaumont, Tex., 1948, sta. KTAE, Taylor, Tex., 1948-49; ins. agt., Dallas, 1950-51; asst. prof. polit. sci. Midwestern U., Wichita Falls, Tex., 1951-61; U.S. senator from Tex., 1961—, mem. Ethics Com., Com. on Banking, Housing and Urban Affairs, Com. on Armed Services, chmn. Senate Rep. Policy Com. Del. Rep. Nat. Conv., 1956, 60, 64, 68, 72, leader Tex. delegation, 1972, mem. platform com., 1960, 64, 68, chmn. platform subcom. nat. security and fgn. policy, 1972; chmn. Rep. Senatorial Campaign Com. Bd. dirs. Wichita Falls Symphony Orch., Inc.; trustee So. Meth. U., Southwestern U. Served with USN, World War II. Mem. Am. Assn. U. Profs., Am., Internat. polit. sci. assns., Tex. Hist. Soc., Am. Legion, Kappa Sigma (former nat. pres.). Methodist. Kiwanian, Mason (32 deg., Shriner). Author: A Program for Conservatives. Home: Official Residence Wichita Falls TX Office: Russell Senate Office Bldg Washington DC 20510

TOWERS, BERNARD, med. educator; b. Preston, Eng., Aug. 20, 1922; s. Thomas Francis and Isabella Ellen (Dobson) T.; M.B., Ch.B., U. Liverpool, 1947; M.A., U. Cambridge, 1954; m. Beryl Helen Davies, Dec. 14, 1951; children—Marianne, Celia, Julie; m. 2d, Nancy Vinetz-Arnold, Dec. 30, 1971. House surgeon Royal Infirmary, Liverpool, 1947; lectr. U. Bristol, 1949-50, U. Wales, 1950-51; lectr. Cambridge U., 1954-70; fellow Jesus Coll., 1957-70, steward, 1961-64, tutor, 1964-69; dir. med. studies, 1964-70; prof. pediatrics and anatomy UCLA, 1971—, convenor, moderator medicine and soc. forum, 1974—, co-dir. Program in Medicine, Law and Human Values, 1977—; cons. Inst. Human Values in Medicine, 1971—; adv. bd. Am. Teilhard Assn. for Future of Man, 1971—; v.p. Teilhard Centre for Future Man, London, 1974—. Served to capt. RAMC, 1947-49. NIH grantee, 1974-78; Nat. Endowment Humanities grantee, 1977-79. Fellow Cambridge Philos. Soc., Royal Soc. Medicine; mem. Brit. Soc. History of Medicine, Soc. Health and Human Values (pres. 1977-78), Anat. Soc. Gt. Britain, Worshipful Soc. Apothecaries London, Am. Assn. Anatomists, Western Soc. Pediatric Research, Western Assn. Physicians, Sigma Xi. Author: Teilhard de Chardin, 1966; Naked Ape or Homo Sapiens?, 1969; Concerning Teilhard, 1969, also articles, chpts. on sci. and philosophy. Editor anat. sect. Brit. Abstracts Med. Scis., 1954-56, Teilhard Study Library, 1966-70; adv. bd. Jour. Medicine and Philosophy, 1974—. Office: Dept of Pediatrics University of California Los Angeles CA 90024

TOWERS, CHARLES DAUGHTRY, JR., lawyer; b. Jacksonville, Fla., Nov. 9, 1923; s. Charles Daughtry and Elizabeth (Morley) T.; B.A., Princeton U., 1944; student Harvard Law Sch., 1946-47; LL.B., Stetson U., 1949; m. Louise DeVore, June 2, 1950; children—Louise Cathcart, Elizabeth Morley, Susan Sheffield, Sarah Sherwood, Margaret DeVore. Admitted to Fla. bar, 1949, since practiced in Jacksonville; partner firm Rogers, Towers, Bailey, Jones & Gay, 1957—. Dir. Fla. First Nat. Bank, 1st Fed. Savs. & Loan Assn. (both Jacksonville); pres., and/or chmn. bd., dir. Fla. Title Group, Inc., Fla. Title & Mortgage Co., Lakeshore Shopping Center, Gainesville Shopping Center. Bd. dirs. Jacksonville United Way, chmn., 1964, pres., 1968; bd. dirs. Greater Jacksonville Safety Council, v.p., 1955, pres., 1970-71; bd. dirs. Riverside Hosp. Assn., v.p., 1975-76, pres., 1976-78; bd. dirs., mem. exec. com. Jacksonville Salvation Army, Presbyn. Homes Fla. Synod. Served to lt. (j.g.) USNR, World War II. Decorated Silver Star. Mem. Am., Fla., Jacksonville bar assns., Am. Trial Lawyers Assn., Internat. Assn. Ins. Counsel, Jacksonville Area C. of C. (v.p. econ. devel. 1978-79, chmn. com. of 100, 1978-79). Presbyterian (sec.-treas. bd. trustees, elder). Home: 4589 Ortega Blvd Jacksonville FL 32210 Office: Florida Title Bldg Jacksonville FL 32202

TOWERS, CONSTANCE MARY, actress, singer; b. Whitefish, Mont., May 20; d. Harry Joseph and Ardath Lucille (Reynolds) Towers; student Juillard Sch. Music, Am. Acad. Dramatic Arts; m. John Anthony Gavin, Sept. 8, 1974; children—Michael Ford McGrath, Maureen McGrath, Cristina Gavin, Maria Gavin. Night club appearances in N.Y.C., Las Vegas and Miami, Fla.; film appearances include Horse Soldiers, 1960, Sgt. Rutledge, 1961, Shock Corridor, 1962, Naked Kiss, 1963, Fate Is The Hunter, 1963; Broadway appearances include Anya, 1965, Engagement Baby, 1969, Ari, 1970, The King and I, 1977, 78; TV appearances include Love is a Many Splendored Thing, 1972-73, Hawaii Five-O, also Carson Show, Merv Griffith Show, Mike Douglas Show, Fantasy Island, Rockford Files, Miss Universe; co-host AM New York, 1978. Recipient Achievement award Am. Acad., 1973; Best Actress award N.J. Critics Circle, 1973; Outstanding Contbn. to Mus. Theatre award N.Y. Critics Outercircle.

TOWERS, GEORGE HUGH NEIL, botanist; b. Bombay, India, Sept. 28, 1923; B.Sc., McGill U., 1950, M.Sc., 1951; Ph.D., Cornell U., 1954. Mem. faculty dept. botany McGill U., 1953-62, asso. prof., to 1962; sr. research officer Nat. Research Council Can., 1962-64, head dept., 1964-70; prof. botany U. B.C., Vancouver, 1970—. Recipient Gold medal Can. Soc. Plant Physiologists, 1973. Fellow Royal Soc. Can.; mem. Bot. Soc. Am., Can. Soc. Plant Physiologists (past pres.), Linnean Soc. London. Home: 3874 W 13th Ave Vancouver BC V6R 2S8 Canada Office: Botany Dept Univ BC Vancouver BC V6T 1W5 Canada

TOWERS, JOHN, bus. exec.; b. Scotland, Aug. 11, 1921; s. John and Agnes (McPhee) T.; came to U.S., 1921, naturalized, 1935; B.S. in Metall. Engring., Mich. Coll. Mining and Tech., 1943; M.S. in Metallurgy, U. Notre Dame, 1949; m. Virginia R. Spayd, 1947; children—Lois Jean Klein, John David. With Am. Metal Climax, Inc. (now Amax, Inc.), N.Y.C., 1946—, v.p. parent co., 1966-75, group v.p. base metals div., 1967-75, dir., 1969—; exec. v.p. Amax Inc., Greenwich, Conn., 1975-77, pres., 1977—; dir. O'okiep Copper Co., Ltd., Tsumeb Corp., Ltd. Trustee Mich. Tech. Fund, Minerals Industry Ednl. Found. Served to capt. U.S. Army, 1943-46. Mem. AIME, Mining and Metall. Soc. Am. Clubs: Mining (former gov.); Belle Haven (Conn.); Blind Brook (N.Y.); Saugatuck Harbor Yacht (Conn.). Office: AMAX Center Greenwich CT 06830

TOWERY, HOSIA MALCOLM, JR., hosp. adminstr.; b. San Diego, lMar. 21, 1934; s. Hosia Malcolm and Mary Catherine (Emmanuel) T.; A.A., R.N., Fullerton Jr. Coll., 1970; student Chapman Coll., 1979—; m. Margaret Ann Scouten, Nov. 29, 1969; children—David, Midge, Malcolm, Scott. Various positions in industry, 1952-60; with Dept. Mental Hygiene, State of Calif., 1960—, cons. Office of Program Rev., 1971-75, program dir., 1975-76, exec. dir. Met. State Hosp., Norwalk, 1976—. Served with USN, 1952. Mem. Am. Mgmt. Assn., Am. Hosp. Assn., Nat. League for Nursing, Calif. Assn. Mgmt., Striped Bass Assn. Calif. Home: 11400 S Norwalk Blvd Residence 20 Norwalk CA 90650 Office: 1140 S Norwalk Blvd Norwalk CA 90650. *The words of Peter Drucker coupled with Skinner's writings, and something told to me years ago by a supervisor, "professional is as professional does," have had the most profound impact on my career. I strive to be a humanistic manager; my goal is to make the world a better place for my having been here, specifically, the world of the mentally ill and the mentally retarded.*

TOWEY, JAMES FISCHER, chem. co. exec.; b. Wood River, Ill., Mar. 1, 1916; s. James Keener and Anna (Fischer) T.; B.S., U. Ill., 1939; LL.D. (hon.), Morehouse Coll., 1973; m. Virginia Elnor Anderson, Mar. 30, 1940; children—James Mayo, Susan Kay. With Western Cartridge Co., East Alton, Ill., 1939-47; chief acct. Olin Industries, Inc., East Alton, 1947-51, plant controller, 1951-55; asst. controller Olin Mathieson Chem. Co., N.Y.C., 1955-58, fin. officer aluminum div., 1958-64, v.p. brass operation, 1964-70; v.p., chief fin. officer Olin Corp., Stamford, Conn., 1970-71, sr. v.p., 1971-72, pres., 1972-73, chmn. bd., chief exec. officer, 1972-78, chmn. bd., 1978—; dir. Olin-American, Inc. Trustee Atlanta U. Served with Signal Corps, AUS, 1945-46. Mem. Fin. Execs. Inst., Conf. Bd., Ill. State C. of C. (past v.p.), Bus. Roundtable. Clubs: Country of Darien (Conn.); Lockhaven Country (Alton, Ill.). Home: 40 Charter Oak Ln New Canaan CT 06840 Office: 120 Long Ridge Rd Stamford CT 06904

TOWI, THEA, sculptor; b. Berlin, Germany; d. Jules and Claire (Kochmann) Wittner; came to U.S., 1938, naturalized, 1943; grad. Nat. Acad. Fine Arts, Berlin; student New Sch., N.Y.C., 1953-55, Art Students League, 1956-57; m. Charles K. Schlachet; 1 son, Peter. Exhibited in one-man shows at Village Art Center, N.Y.C., 1961, La Boetie Gallery, N.Y.C., 1966, 68, 70, Sala Michelangelo, Carrara, Italy, 1969, Lehigh U., Bethelhem, Pa., 1970, U. Notre Dame, 1970, Hallway Gallery, Washington, 1976, Randall Gallery, N.Y.C., 1977, others, exhibited to numerous group shows; represented in permanent collections at Smithsonian Instn., Washington, Cin. Art Mus., Norfolk (Va.) Mus. Arts and Scis., U. Notre Dame, Norton Simon Collection, Citicorp, N.Y., Fort Worth Nat. Bank, also pvt. collections in U.S., France, Italy, Spain, Switzerland. Pres., League of Present Day Artists, 1964-70; pres. Sculptors League, 1970—. Recipient numerous awards and purchase awards, including 1st prize Am. Soc. Contemporary Artists, 1971, 75, 76, 78, medal of merit Nat. Arts Club, 1974, Nawa Peabody award Nat. Acad., 1975, medal of merit Knickerbocker Artists, 1975. Mem. Nat. Assn. Women Artists, Knickerbocker Artists. Home: 100-30 67th Dr Forest Hills NY 11375

TOWILL, JOHN BELL, lawyer; b. Batesburg, S.C., Apr. 5, 1907; s. John Bell and Daisy (Pearce) T.; LL.B., Washington and Lee U., 1929, LL.D., 1972; m. Harriet Sommerville Dunlap, Oct. 8, 1930 (dec.); children—Virginia Dunlap (Mrs. George M. Maxwell), Rebecca Hobbs (Mrs. William H. McNair); m. 2d, Marilyn B. Pilcher. Admitted to Ga. bar, 1929, U.S. Supreme Ct., also trial and appellate cts.; practiced in Augusta, 1929—; asso., then partner Hull, Towill, Norman, Barrett & Johnson, 1929—. Organizer, past pres. Home Fed. Savs. & Loan of Augusta, now chmn., dir.; dir. emeritus Verex Assurance, Inc., Cullum's Inc., Ga. Fed. Savs. & Loan Assn. Mem. Ga. Ho. of Reps., 1947-48. Bd. dirs. Ga. Savs. and Loan League, also past pres.; bd. dirs. Boys Club Augusta; pres. Richmond County Tb Assn.; trustee Merry Found. Served to comdr. USNR, 1942-46. Fellow Am. Bar Found., Am. Coll. Probate Counsel (regent, pres.); mem. Am. Law Inst., Am. Judicature Soc., Fedn. Ins. Counsel, Am., Ga., Augusta (pres.) bar assns., Am. Legion, Soc. Colonial Wars Ga., Jamestowne Soc., Pi Kappa Phi, Phi Delta Phi, Omicron Delta Kappa, Alpha Kappa Psi. Episcopalian (past mem. diocesan exec. council, jr. warden, vestryman). Clubs: Elks, Augusta Country, Rotary (dist. gov.) (Augusta); Commerce, Capital City (Atlanta); Army and Navy (Washington); Pinnacle. Home: 2223 Overton Rd Augusta GA 30904 Office: First National Bank Bldg Augusta GA 30902

TOWLE, SIDNEY NORWOOD, headmaster; b. Brookline, Mass., Feb. 16, 1913; s. Sidney Norwood and Hazel W.M. (Safford) T.; B.A., Yale, 1935, J.D., 1938; m. Nancy Lois Roberts, Apr. 25, 1943; children—Sidney Norwood, Alexis Charles, Diana, Christopher Philip. Admitted to Mass. bar, 1939; asso. firm Withington, Cross, Park & McCann, Boston, 1938-47, partner, 1947-59; asso. headmaster Kent (Conn.) Sch., 1959-62, headmaster, 1962—, trustee, 1963—. Mem. sch. com., Newburyport, Mass., 1950-52. Mem. Newburyport City Council, 1940-41. Trustee Conn. Jr. Republic, Litchfield, Conn., 1961-63, Harvey Sch., Katonah, N.Y., 1963-71, Indian Mountain Sch., Lakeville, Conn., 1965-67; v.p., trustee Ipswich Hist. Soc., 1958-59. Served to lt. col. AUS, 1941-46. Decorated Legion of Merit; recipient All Am. award Sports Illus. Silver Anniversary, 1959; Martin W. Souders award New Eng. Prep. Schs. Athletic Council, 1977. Mem. Boston Bar Assn., Conn. Assn. Ind. Schs. (v.p. 1968-69), Headmasters Assn. (v.p. 1978-79), Scroll and Key Soc. Republican. Episcopalian (vestry 1959). Clubs: Fence (Yale); Leander (Henley-on-Thames). Home: Skiff Mountain Kent CT 06757

TOWN, HAROLD BARLING, artist; b. Toronto, Ont., Can., June 13, 1924; s. William Harry and Ellen (Watson) T.; grad. Ont. Coll. Art, 1944; Litt.D. (hon.), York U., Toronto, 1966; m. Trudella Carol Tredwell, Sept. 7, 1957; children—Heather Allison, Shelley Catherine. Exhibited Venice Biennale, 1956, 64, 72, Sao Paulo Biennale, 1957, 61, 2d to 6th expn. Gravure, Ljubljana, Yugoslavia, Documenta, Kassel, Germany, 1964, Carnegie Internat., 1964, Arte of Am. and Spain, 1964-65, 1st Brit. Internat. Print Biennale, Bradford, 1968, Can. 101 Edinburgh (Scotland) Internat. Festival, 1968, 7th Biennial Canadian Painting, Ottawa, 1968; Ont. Pavillion, Expo 70, Japan; one-man show Robert McLaughlin Gallery Civic Centre, Oshawa, 1973; retrospective 1944-1975 at Windsor Art Gallery, 1975; represented in permanent collections including those of Mus. Modern Art, N.Y.C., Guggenheim Mus., Tate Gallery, London, Stedelijk Mus., Amsterdam, Nat. Gallery of Can., Bklyn. Mus., Detroit Art Inst., Met. Mus. Art, Toronto Pub. Library, York U., others; murals for St. Lawrence Seaway, Power Dam, Cornwall, Ont., 1958, mural and sculpture Malton Internat. Airport, Ont., 1962-63, mural Telegram Bldg., Toronto, 1963; mural Queen's Park Project, Toronto, 1967; initial opening poster Ontario Place, Provincial Govt. Can., 1971. Decorated Order Can.; recipient Arno prize Sao Paulo Biennale, 1957; internat. prize exhbn. drawings and prints, Lugano, Switzerland, 1958; Centennial medal, 1967; officer Order Can., 1968; award of merit for disting. public service City of Toronto, 1979; fellow Instituto de Cultura Hispanica-Arte de America y Espana, Madrid, 1963; hon. fellow Founders Coll., York U., Toronto. Bd. govs. Ont. Coll. Art. Mem. Toronto Art Dirs. Club, Royal Canadian Acad. Author: Albert Franck, 1974. Author, illustrator: Enigmas, 1964; Banner and Symbol, 1965; Silent Stars, Sound Stars, Film Stars, 1971 (with David Silcox) Tom Thomson (The Silence and the Storm), 1977 (Can. Booksellers Assn. award); The Ice Rage of Inugrump, 1979. Decor and costumes House of Atreus, Nat. Ballet Co. of Can., 1964; The Drawings of Harold Town, 1969. Columnist Toronto Life Mag. Home: 9 Castle Frank Crescent Toronto ON M4W 3A2 Canada Office: 25 Severn St Toronto ON M4W 3A2 Canada. *I paint to defy death.*

TOWNE, FRANK MCCONNELL, ret. educator; b. Fullerton, Calif., Jan. 8, 1913; s. Dwight Fox and Amy Anna (McConnell) T.; A.B., U. Calif. at Berkeley, 1935; M.A., UCLA, 1941, Ph.D., 1949; m. Sophia Iacovides, July 17, 1939; children—Helen Frances, Kathryn Anne. Instr. English, Athens (Greece) Coll., 1936-40; mem. faculty Wash. State U., 1947-79, prof. English, 1959-79, chmn. dept., 1968-70, chmn. comparative lit., 1973-75; vis. asso. prof. Columbia, 1953-54; Fulbright lectr. U. Thessaloniki (Greece), 1957-58, U. Athens, 1958-59. Served with AUS, 1943-45. Mem. Modern Lang. Assn., Nat. Council Tchrs. English, Phi Beta Kappa. Author articles in field. Home: 14625 NE 34 St Bellevue WA 98007

TOWNEND, FRANK, lawyer; b. Wilkes-Barre, Pa., July 1, 1911; s. Richard Henry Mitchell and Mae E. Townend; grad. Phillips Andover Acad., 1929; A.B., Princeton, 1934; LL.B., Harvard, 1937; postgrad. Command and Gen. Staff Coll., 1961; m. Lenchen Coughlin, Nov. 28, 1942; children—Cynthia Barring (Mrs. Gordon A. Donaldson, Jr.), David Stark (dec.), Stephen. Practiced in Wilkes-Barre; mem. firm Silverblatt & Townend, and predecessor, 1938—; solicitor Dallas Twp., 1952—; commd. 2d lt. Pa. Army N.G., 1933, advanced through grades to maj. gen., 1971; a.d.c. 28th Div., 1966-68, 42d Div., 1968-71; ret., 1971; dir. First Eastern Bank, N.A. Civil Def. dir. Luzerne County, 1956—; chmn. United Fund Campaign, 1959; pres. Wyoming Valley United Way, 1976-78; sec.-treas., bd. dirs. Nesbitt Meml. Hosp.; treas., bd. dirs. Blue Cross N.E. Pa. Decorated Bronze Star medal, 1944, Legion of Merit, 1971; recipient Distinguished Service award Wyoming Sem., 1976. Mem. Am., Pa., Wilkes-Barre bar assns., Am. Legion (Americanism award Wilkes-Barre post 1970), VFW. Republican. Methodist. Mason. Kiwanian. Home: 428 N Pioneer Ave RD 2 Dallas PA 18612 Office: 1400 United Penn Bank Bldg Wilkes-Barre PA 18701

TOWNER, LAWRENCE WILLIAM, historian; b. St. Paul, Sept. 10, 1921; s. Earl Chadwick and Cornelia Josephine (Mallum) T.; B.A., Cornell Coll., Mt. Vernon, Iowa, 1942, L.H.D.; M.A., Northwestern U., 1950, Ph.D., 1955, L.H.D.; Litt.D., Lake Forest Coll.; m. Rachel E. Bauman, Nov. 28, 1943; children—Wendy Kay Towner Yanikoski, Kristin Anne Towner Moses, Lawrence Baumann, Elizabeth Gail, Peter Mallum, Michael Chadwick. History master Chgo. Latin Sch., 1946-47; instr., then asst. prof. history Mass. Inst. Tech., 1950-55; asso. prof. history Coll. William and Mary, 1955-62; editor William and Mary Quar., 1956-62, mem. bd. editors, 1970-71; fellow Center Study History of Liberty, Harvard U., 1961-62; librarian Newberry Library, Chgo., 1962—, dir. library, 1964—, pres., 1975—; vis. prof. English, Northwestern U., 1968-70; professorial lectr. U. Chgo., 1968. Mem. council Eleutherian Mills, Hagley Found., 1965-69, 77-78, Inst. Early Am. History, Williamsburg, Va., 1970-73, 79—; trustee Grinnell Coll., 1966-72, Latin Sch. Chgo., 1970-72, Mus. Contemporary Art, 1972-75; bd. dirs. Ill. Humanities Council, 1974-78, chmn., 1976-78; mem. exec. com. Fedn. Public Programs in the Humanities, 1977-78. Served to lst lt. pilot USAAF, World War II. Mem. Am. Hist. Assn. (mem. council 1973-75), Orgn. Am. Historians, Bibliog. Soc. Am., Ind. Research Libraries Assn. (chmn. 1976-78), Colonial Soc. Mass., Va., Mass. hist. socs., Modern Poetry Assn. (pres. 1967-69, trustee 1962-75), Am. Antiquarian Soc., Phi Beta Kappa. Clubs: Cosmos (Washington); Grolier (N.Y.C.); Caxton, Econ., Tavern, Arts (dir. 1964), Columbia Yacht, Wayfarers (Chgo.). Contbr. numerous articles to mags., jours.; bd. editors. Jour. Am. History, Am., History and Life. Home: 65 E Bellevue Pl Chicago IL 60611 Office: 60 W Walton St Chicago IL 60610

TOWNER, LEONARD WIMBERLEY, JR., educator; b. Long Beach, Calif., Dec. 3, 1918; s. Leonard Wimberley and K. Ione (Tiernan) T.; student Pasadena Jr. Coll., 1936-38; B.A., U. Calif. at Berkeley, 1940, postgrad., 1941-42, M.A., 1947, Ph.D., 1948; postgrad. U. Calif. at Los Angeles, 1943; m. Caroline Warren Frost, Jan. 24, 1942 (div. 1974); children—Howard Frost, Joseph Francis, Barbara Jane, Robert Leonard, Margaret Ann; m. 2d, Patricia Jean Balestra Vogel, Sept. 28, 1974; children—Geoffrey Morris, Christine Frances, Michael Anthony, Deborah Jean. Asst. prof., asso. prof. psychology Drake U., Des Moines, 1948-51; research asso., asst. research oncologist U. Calif. Med. Sch., San Francisco, 1951-55; from asst. prof. to prof. psychology Calif. State U., Long Beach, 1955—, asso. dean instrn., 1967-69, dean acad. planning, 1969-71; vis. prof. edn. U. Calif. at Berkeley, 1953-55, 67. Served with USNR, 1943-46. Mem. Am. Psychol. Assn. Am. Statis. Assn., AAAS, Calif. Ednl. Research Assn. (pres. 1961), Phi Kappa Phi, Phi Delta Kappa. Office: Calif State University Long Beach CA 90840

TOWNES, CHARLES HARD, physicist; b. Greenville, S.C., July 28, 1915; s. Henry Keith and Ellen Sumter (Hard) T.; B.A., B.S., Furman U., 1935; M.A., Duke U., 1937; Ph.D., Calif. Inst. Tech., 1939; m. Frances H. Brown, May 4, 1941; children—Linda Lewis, Ellen Screven, Carla Keith, Holly Robinson. Mem. tech. staff Bell Telephone Lab., 1939-47; asso. prof. physics Columbia U., 1948-50, prof. physics, 1950-61, exec. dir. Columbia Radiation Lab., 1950-52, chmn. physics dept., 1952-55; provost and prof. physics Mass. Inst. Tech., 1961-66, Inst. prof., 1966-67, v.p., dir. research Inst. Def. Analyses, Washington, 1959-61; Univ. prof. U. Calif. at Berkeley, 1967—; Guggenheim fellow, 1955-56; Fulbright lectr. U. Paris, 1955-56, U. Tokyo, 1956; lectr., 1955, 60, dir. Enrico Fermi Internat. Sch. Physics, 1963; Scott lectr. U. Cambridge, 1963; Centennial lectr. U. Toronto, 1967; Lincoln lectr., 1972-73; Halley lectr., 1976; dir. Perkin-Elmer Corp., Gen. Motors Corp.; mem. Pres.'s Sci. Adv. Com., 1966-69, vice chmn., 1967-69; chmn. sci. and tech. adv. com. for manned space flight NASA, 1964-69; mem. Pres.'s Com. on Sci. and Tech., 1976. Trustee, Calif. Inst. Tech., Carnegie Instn. of Washington; mem. corp. Woods Hole Oceanographic Instn. Recipient numerous hon. degrees and awards, including Nobel prize for physics, 1964; Stuart Ballantine medal Franklin Inst., 1959, 62, Thomas Young medal and prize Inst. Physics and Phys. Soc. (Eng.), 1963, Disting. Public Service medal NASA, 1969; Wilhelm Exner award, Austria, 1970; Niels Bohr Internat. Gold medal, 1979; named to Nat. Inventors Hall of Fame, 1976. Fellow Am. Phys. Soc. (council 1959-62, 65-71, pres. 1967; Plyler prize 1977), Optical Soc. Am. (hon.; Mees medal 1968), IEEE (medal honor 1967); mem. Am. Philos. Soc., Am. Astron. Soc., Am. Acad. Arts and Scis., Nat. Acad. Scis. (council 1969-72, 78—, chmn. space sci. bd. 1970-73; Comstock award 1959), Société Française de Physique (council 1956-58), Royal Soc. (fgn.). Author: (with A.L. Schawlow) Microwave Spectroscopy, 1955; author, co-editor: Quantum Electronics, 1960; Quantum Electronics and Coherent Light, 1964; editorial bd. Rev. Sci. Instrument, 1950-52, Phys. Rev., 1951-53, bd. Rev. Sci. Instrument, 1950-52, Phys., Rev., 1951-53, Jour. Molecular Spectroscopy, 1957-60; Procs. Nat. Acad. Scis., 1978-81; contbr. articles to sci. publs. Patentee masers and lasers; research nuclear and molecular structure, quantum electronics, interstellar molecules, radio and infrared astrophysics. Office: Dept Physics U Calif at Berkeley Berkeley CA 94720

TOWNES, PHILIP LEONARD, physician, educator; b. Salem, Mass., Feb. 18, 1927; s. Saul and Lillian (Kravetsky) T.; A.B., Harvard, 1948; Ph.D., U. Rochester, 1952, M.D., 1959; m. Marjorie Joan Greenstone, Aug. 27, 1956; children—Elizabeth Ann, Susan Jane, David Andrew. Intern, Strong Meml. Hosp., Rochester, 1959-60, asst. resident, 1963, chief resident pediatrics, 1965; mem. faculty U. Rochester Sch. Medicine, 1952-79, prof. pediatrics, 1969-79, prof. anatomy (genetics), chmn. div. genetics, dir. Genetic Clinic, 1966-79; prof. pediatrics U. Mass. Sch. Medicine, 1979—; pediatrician Strong Meml. Hosp.; cons. attending Newark State Hosp., Genesee Hosp.; hon. research asst. Univ. Coll., London, Eng., 1965-66. Mem. com. qualifications cytogenetics N.Y. State Dept. Health, 1968-74; bd. dirs. Monroe County chpt. Nat. Found., 1965-79, chmn. med. adv. com., 1967-79, hon. bd. dirs., 1979—, also cons. Served with USNR, 1945-46. USPHS predoctoral fellow, 1951-52, sr. research fellow, 1960-61, research career devel. award, 1961-66. Mem. Am. Assn. Anatomists, Soc. Pediatric Research, Am. Soc. Human Genetics, Am. Pediatric Soc., Teratology Soc., Sigma Xi, Alpha Omega Alpha. Contbr. articles to med. jours. Home: 14 Spring Valley Rd Worcester MA 01609

TOWNLEY, HUGH, sculptor, educator; b. West Lafayette, Ind., Feb. 6, 1923; s. Hubert Claude and Marguerite (Ozburn) T.; student U. Wis., 1946-48, London County Council Sch. Arts and Crafts, 1949-50; studied with Ossip Zadkine, Paris, 1948-49; m. Mary Ross, Oct. 3, 1961; 1 son, Hugh Merlyn Zadkine. One man shows at Gallerie Appollnaire, London, 1951, Meml. Union Gallery U. Wis., 1955, Milw. Art Inst., 1957, Swetzoff Gallery, Boston, 1958, 59, Pace Gallery, Boston, 1962, 64, 65, Pace Gallery, N.Y.C., 1964, Tyler Sch. Art, Phila., 1966, Rigelhaupt Gallery, Boston, 1966, Yale, 1966, DeCordova Dana Mus., Lincoln, Mass., 1969 Bradley Galleries, Milw., 1970, Bell Gallery, Brown U., 1972, Tyler Sch. Arts, Phila., 1972, U. Oreg., 1976, Schochet Garden, Newport, 1977, Western Carolina U., 1978, Worcester (Mass.) Art Mus., 1980; others; 2 man show Brockton Mus., 1971, U. Oreg., 1975, Dartmouth Coll., 1975, Keene State U., 1976, Wingspread Gallery, Northeast Harbor, Maine, 1977, Inst. Contemporary Art, Boston, 1977; exhibited in group shows at Chgo. Art Inst., 1953, 54, 64, Mus. Modern Art, 1955, 63, Carnegie Inst. Biennial, 1958, Inst. Contemporary Art, Boston, 1960, 61, 62, 65, 66, U. Ill., 1961-63, New Sch. for Social Research, 1962, Wadsworth Atheneum, Hartford, 1963, Decordova Mus., 1964, 65, Flint Inst. Art, 1966, Nat. Inst. Arts and Letters, 1967, Munson-Williams Proctor Mus., 1970, Monumenta, Newport, R.I., 1974, Portland (Oreg.) Mus. Art, 1976, Keene (N.H.) State U., 1976, others; represented in permanent collections at San Francisco Art Mus., Whitney Mus., Milw. Art Inst., Munson-Williams- Proctor Inst., Ithaca, N.Y., Addison Gallery, Andover, Mass., Boston Mus. Fine Arts, De Cordova Mus., Fogg Mus., Williams Coll. Mus., Brown U., Wrexham Found., Mead Corp., First Nat. Bank Boston, others; tchr. Layton Sch. Art, Milw., 1951-56, Beloit (Wis.) Coll., 1956-57, Boston U., 1957-61; prof. art Brown U., Providence, 1961—; vis. prof. U. Calif., Berkeley, 1961, U. Calif. at Santa Barbara, 1968; vis. lectr. Harvard, summer 1967, Ft. Wright Coll., Spokane, 1971; participant symposium on 20th century sculpture Mus. N. Ariz., 1978. Served with USAAF, 1942- 46. Recipient awards Kalamazoo Art Center Lithographic Workshop, 1964, Nat. Inst. Arts and Letters, 1967; Award for Arts, Gov. R.I., 1972. Yaddo Found. fellow, 1964; Tamarind Lithography Workshop fellow, 1969. Mem. Soaring Soc. Am. Home: 1 Resolute Ln Bristol RI 02809 Office: Dept Art Brown U Providence RI 02912*

TOWNSEND, BURT ALLISON, ret. soybean co. exec.; b. Kokomo, Ind., July 8, 1916; s. Burt Allison and Ruth Cowles (Parsons) T.; m. Marjorie May DeVoss, June 6, 1942; children—Burt Allison III, Michael Scott. With Central Soya Co., Inc., Ft. Wayne, Ind., 1937-79, v.p., 1966-70, exec. v.p., 1970-74, vice chmn. bd., 1974-79, also dir., mem. exec. com. Mem. Chgo. Bd. Trade, also dir., mem. exec. com. Served with U.S. Army, 1942-45. Mem. Nat. Soybean Processors Assn., Am. Soybean Assn., Soybean Council Am. Clubs: Ft. Wayne Country, Ft. Wayne Summit, Coldwater (Mich.) Country. Home: 8564 N Arnold Palmer Dr Tucson AZ 85704

TOWNSEND, CHARLES COE, advt. co. exec.; b. N.Y.C., Mar. 5, 1917; s. Charles Coe and Edythe Y.C. (Hewitt) T.; A.B., Harvard U., 1939; M.S., Columbia U., 1941; m. Anita van L. Higgins, Mar. 29, 1947 (div. 1971); children—Charles Coe III, Frederic, James B., Claire; m. 2d, Jocelyne F. Bertal, Aug. 21, 1971. Mgr., Peat, Marwick, Mitchell & Co., N.Y.C., 1946-55; controller Chesapeake Industries, Inc., N.Y.C., 1955-57; analyst Lambert & Co., N.Y.C., 1957-58; treas. IBM World Trade Corp., N.Y.C., 1958-74; exec. v.p., dir. Interpublic Group Cos., N.Y.C., 1974—. Bd. dirs. N.Y. Sch. Deaf. Served to capt. AUS, 1942-46; ETO. Mason. Club: Union (N.Y.C.). Co-author: International Money Management. Home: 167 E 67th St New York NY 10021 Office: 1271 Ave of Americas New York NY 10020

TOWNSEND, CHARLES EDWARD, educator; b. New Rochelle, N.Y., Sept. 29, 1932; s. Charles Edward and Lois (Fukushima) T.; B.A., Yale, 1954; M.A., Harvard, 1960, Ph.D., 1962; m. Janet Linner, Sept. 18, 1957; children—Erica, Sylvia, Louise. Instr., then asst. prof. Harvard, 1962-66; mem. faculty Princeton, 1966—, dir. critical langs. program, 1968-70, prof. Slavic langs., 1971—, chmn. dept., 1970—. Served with U.S. Army, 1955-58. IREX grantee, 1968; Fulbright grantee, 1954-55, 71; Ford Found. fellow, 1958-60; NDEA fellow, 1960-62. Mem. Am. Council Tchrs. Russian (dir.), Am. Assn. Tchrs. Slavic and East European Langs., Am. Assn. Advancement Slavic Studies, Linguistic Soc. Am., Phi Beta Kappa. Author: Russian Word Formation, 1968; Continuing with Russian, 1970; Memoirs of Princess Natalja Borisovna Dolgorukaja, 1977. Home: 145 Hickory Ct Princeton NJ 08540

TOWNSEND, EARL CUNNINGHAM, JR., lawyer, author, composer; b. Indpls., Nov. 9, 1914; s. Earl Cunningham and Besse (Kuhn) T.; student De Pauw U., 1932-34; A.B., U. Mich., 1936, J.D., 1939; m. Emily Macnab, Apr. 3, 1947; children—Starr (Mrs. John R. Laughlin), Vicki M. (Mrs. Christopher Ketterjohn), Julia E. (Mrs. Edward Goodrich Dunn, Jr.), Earl Cunningham III, Clyde G. Admitted to Ind. bar, 1939, Mich. bar, 1973, also U.S. Supreme Ct. bar; sr. partner firm Townsend & Townsend, Indpls., 1940-69; sr. partner Townsend, Hovde & Townsend, Indpls., 1970—; individual practice, Roscommon, Mich., 1973—; dep. prosecutor, Marion County, Ind., 1942-44; radio-TV announcer WIRE, WFBM, WFBM-TV, Indpls., 1940-49, 1st TV announcer 500 mile race, 1949, 50; Big Ten basketball referee, 1940-47; lectr. trial tactics U. Notre Dame, Ind. U., U. Mich., 1968-79; owner Tropical Isle Palm Tree Farms, Key Biscayne, Fla., Terney-Townsend Historic House, Roscommon, Mich.; founder, v.p., treas. Am. Underwriters, Inc., Am. Interinsurance Exchange, 1965-70; mem. Com. to Revise Ind. Supreme Ct. Pattern Jury Instructions, 1975—. Founder, life fellow Roscoe Pound Trial Lawyers Found., Cambridge, Mass.; co-founder, dir. Meridian St. Found.; mem. fin. and bldg. coms., bd. dirs., later life trustee Indpls. Mus. Art; trustee Cathedral High Sch., Indpls., Ind. State Mus., Starlight Musicals; fellow Meth. Hosp. Found. Recipient Ind. Univ. Writers Conf. award, 1960; Hanson H. Anderson medal of honor Arsenal Tech. Schs., Indpls., 1971; named to Council Sagamores of Wabash, 1969, Ind. Basketball Hall of Fame; hon. chief Black River-Swan Creek Saginaw-Chippewa Indian tribe, 1971. Fellow Ind. Coll. Trial Lawyers, Internat. Acad. Trial Lawyers, Internat. Soc. Barristers; mem. Ind. Trial Lawyers Assn. (pres. 1963-64), Am. (com. trial techniques 1964-76, com. aviation and space 1977—), Ind. State (del. 1977-79), Indpls., 34th Dist. (Mich.) bar assns., State Bar Mich., Assn. Am. Trial Lawyers (v.p. Ind. 1959-60, bd. govs. 7th jud. circuit 1966-68, asso. editor Jour. 1964—), Bar Assn. 7th Fed. Circuit, Lawyers Assn. Indpls., Ind. Archaeol. Soc. (founder, pres.), Genuine Indian Relic Soc. (co-founder, chmn. frauds com.), Ind. Hist. Soc., Trowel and Brush Soc. (hon.), U. Mich. Pres.'s Club, U. Mich. Victors Club (charter), Soc. Mayflower Descs. (gov. 1947-49), Key Biscayne C. of C., Delta Kappa Epsilon, Phi Kappa Phi. Republican. Methodist. Mason (32 deg., Shriner). Clubs: Players; U. Mich. (local pres. 1950); Columbia; Key Biscayne Yacht. Author: Birdstones of the North American Indian, 1959; also articles in legal and archeol. fields; composer Moon of Halloween. Home: 5008 N Meridian St Indianapolis IN 46208 Office: 150 E Market St Indianapolis IN 46204 also 603 Lake St Roscommon MI 48653

TOWNSEND, EDWARD THOMAS, journalist; b. Charleston, S.C., Feb. 8, 1910; s. Edward Thomas and Mathilde (Riecke) T.; A.B. in Econs., Birmingham-So. Coll., 1931, grad. student, 1931-32; m. Thelma Maye Blezard, Sept. 17, 1933; children—Thomas Edward, James Courtland, Charles Lewis, Peggy Joy (Mrs. Greydon Cruse, Jr.), John David, Richard Blezard. Asst. econs. Birmingham-So. Coll., 1930-31; reporter, then city editor Daytona Beach (Fla.) Sun Record, 1932-35, mng. editor, then editor, 1936-41; with U.P., 1935; copy desk chief Birmingham Age-Herald, 1941-44; asst. labor editor Business Week mag., 1944-58, labor editor, 1958-68, asso. editor, 1969-75, bd. editors, 1966-75; nat. labor corr. Christian Sci. Monitor, 1950—; speaker in field, 1958—; labor cons. Recipient Loeb award bus. and financial journalism, 1960; Louis Stark award Inst. Collective Bargaining, 1971. Republican. Lutheran. Contbr. articles to Compton Yearbook, profl. jours. Home: 84 Woodland Ave Summit NJ 07901

TOWNSEND, ELIAS CARTER, bus. cons., ret. army officer; b. Cartersville, Ga., Aug. 10, 1912; s. William Thomas and Elizabeth B. (Conyers) T.; student Ga. Mil. Coll., 1929-30; B.S., U. Ga., 1934; postgrad. Command and Gen. Staff Coll., 1942, Armed Forces Staff Coll., 1948-49, Brit. Land/Air Warfare Sch., 1950, U.S. Nat. War Coll., 1955-56; m. Zelle Wade, July 21, 1943. Entered U.S. Army as pvt., 1935, advanced through grades to maj. gen., 1967; faculty Armed Forces Staff Coll., 1952-55; faculty U.S. Army Command and gen. Staff Coll., 1946-48, asst. comdt., 1963-65; asst. chief staff operations J-3, Hdqrs. Mil. Assistance Command, Vietnam, 1968-69, chief staff U.S. Mil. Assistance Command, Vietnam, 1969-70; bus. cons., lectr., 1970—. Bd. govs. Thomas Aquinas Coll., Santa Paula, Calif. Decorated D.S.M. with two oak leaf clusters, Legion of Merit, Bronze star medal with oak leaf cluster, Combat Inf. Badge. Mem. San Francisco Com. Fgn. Relations, Assn. U.S. Army, Sigma Alpha Epsilon. Club: Commonwealth. Author: Risks: The Key to Combat Intelligence, 1955. Home: 1880 Jackson St San Francisco CA 94109. *It was my good fortune to learn early in life that true education consists of knowing, understanding, and living by, i.e. in harmony with, God's universal laws, physical, spiritual, and moral.*

TOWNSEND, FRANK MARION, physician; b. Stamford, Tex., Oct. 29, 1914; s. Frank M. and Beatrice (House) T.; student San Antonio Coll., 1931-32, U. Tex., 1932-34; M.D., Tulane U., 1938; m. Gerda Eberlein, 1940 (div. 1944); 1 son, Frank M.; m. 2d, Ann Graf, Aug. 25, 1951; 1 son, Robert N. Intern, Polyclinic Hosp., N.Y.C., 1939-40; commd. 1st lt. M.C., U.S. Army, 1940, advanced through grades to lt. col., 1946; resident instr. pathology Washington U., 1945-47; trans. to USAF, 1949, advanced through grades to col., 1956; instr. pathology Coll. Medicine, U. Neb., 1947-48; asso. pathologist Scott and White Clinic, Temple, Tex., 1948-49; asso. prof. pathology Med. Br. U. Tex., Galveston, 1949-59; dir. labs. USAF Hosp., Lackland AFB, 1950-54; cons. pathology, chief cons. group Office Surgeon Gen. Hdqrs. SAF, Washington, 1954-55, cons., 1955-63; dep. dir. Armed Forces Inst. Pathology, Washington, 1955-59, dir., 1959-63, now cons. vice comdr. aerospace med. div. Air Forces Systems Command, 1963-65; ret., 1965; practice medicine specializing in pathology, San Antonio, 1965—; dir. labs. San Antonio State Chest Hosp., 1965-72; clin. prof. pathology U. Tex. Med. Sch., San Antonio, 1969-72, prof., chmn. dept. pathology, 1972—; cons. U. Tex. Cancer Center-M.D. Anderson Hosp., 1966—, NASA, 1967-75; mem. advisory bd. cancer WHO, 1958-75. Mem. advisory council Civil War Centennial Commn., 1960-65; bd. dirs. Alamo Area Sci. Fair, 1967-73. Decorated D.S.M., Legion of Merit; recipient Founders medal Assn. Mil. Surgeons, 1961. Diplomate Am. Bd. Pathology. Fellow A.C.P., Coll. Am. Pathologists (regional commr. lab. inspection and accreditation 1971—), Am. Soc. Clin. Pathologists, Aerospace Med. Assn. (H.G. Moseley award 1962); mem. AMA, Internat. Acad. Aviation and Space Medicine, Am. Assn. Pathologists, Am. Soc. Exptl. Pathologists. Club: Torch. Contbr. med. articles to profl. jours. Home: 10406 Mt Marcy Dr San Antonio TX 78213 Office: Dept Pathology U Tex Health Sci Center 7703 Floyd Curl Dr San Antonio TX 78284

TOWNSEND, G(EORGE) MARSHALL, univ. press dir.; b. Murdo, S.D., Aug. 2, 1916; s. George Marshall and Freda E. (Gilkinson) T.; B.S., Iowa State U., 1941; m. Ruth Helen Killam, July 29, 1951; children—Gregg Marshall, Jane Elizabeth. Sales mgr., prodn. mgr. Iowa State U. Press, Ames, 1945-48, dir. book pub., 1948-63; asst. dir., bus. mgr. U. Chgo. Press, 1963-65; dir. U. Ariz. Press, Tucson, 1965—, mem. faculty Senate, 1976—, univ. long-range planning com., 1978—. Mem. Govt. Industry Adv. Bd., 1952. Pres. Iowa TB and Health Assn., 1956, mem. exec. com., 1950-56; hon. chmn. Iowa Christmas Seal, 1962; pres. Ames PTA Council, 1962-63; sec. Mary Greeley Hosp. Assn., 1953-56. Recipient Ames Community Service award, 1952; Service to Univ. and Community award Tucson Trade Bur., 1972. Mem. Assn. Am. Univ. Presses (exec. bd. 1951-52, nat. v.p. 1960-61, treas. 1963-64), Phi Kappa Phi, Sigma Delta Chi. Methodist. Kiwanian (pres. Ames 1954, Tucson 1972). Office: Box 3398 Tucson AZ 85722

TOWNSEND, IRVING JOSEPH, producer phonograph records, writer; b. Springfield, Mass., Nov. 27, 1920; s. Irving Joseph and Marguerite (Noble) T.; A.B., Princeton U., 1943; children—Nicole L., Jeremy N. Profl. musician to 1950; v.p., producer Columbia Records, Hollywood, Calif., 1950—. Columnist, Santa Barbara (Calif.) News-Press, 1972-74. Served to lt. USNR, 1943-46. Mem. Nat. Acad. Recording Arts and Scis. (past pres.). Author: The Less Expensive Spread, 1971; John Hammond on Records, 1977; The Tavern, 1978; contbr. articles to mags. Home: 2146 Refugio Rd Santa Ynez CA 93460

TOWNSEND, JAMES BENJAMIN, educator; b. Stillwater, N.Y., Feb. 17, 1918; s. Jackson and Lula May (Townsend) T.; grad. Phillips Acad., Andover, 1936; A.B., Princeton, 1940; M.A., Harvard, 1942; Ph.D., Yale, 1951; m. Jeanette Thankful Rice, Sept. 15, 1945; children—Josephine Rice (Mrs. Benjamin Henry Kaestner, III), Jackson II, Rhys Frederick, Clarissa Rowe. Instr. English, Yale, 1947-50, 51-53; asst. prof. English, U. N.C. at Greensboro, 1953-57; asst. prof. to prof. English, State U. N.Y. at Buffalo, 1957—, dir. Master of Arts in Humanities program, 1960-66, vice chmn. dept. English, 1966-67, chmn. dept. art, 1969-71, co-founder, master Modern Coll., 1969-71; asst. dir. Nat. Portrait Gallery of Smithsonian Instn., 1967-68, bibliog. asso. Archives Am. Art, 1974—; editor Jours. of Charles Burchfield, 1909-65, 1976—. Mem. exec. com., mem. adv. council Albright-Knox Art Gallery, 1958-70; mem. adv. com. Charles Burchfield Center, Buffalo, 1970—; trustee Park Sch., Buffalo, 1969-72; v.p. Co. Man, Buffalo, 1970-73. Served with AUS, 1942-45; ETO. Mem. Phi Beta Kappa. Club: Princeton (N.Y.C.). Author: John Davidson, Poet of Armageddon, 1961; 100, 1962; Martha Visser't Hooft: Paintings and Drawings 1950-1973, 1973; Harvey Breverman:

Paintings and Drawings, 1965-76, 1976. Editor: Presidential Portraits, 1968; This New Man: a Discourse in Portraits, 1968. Home: 879 W Ferry St Buffalo NY 14209. *I was thirty-five before I found the interest and activity that have given me the greatest satisfaction and self-realization. Keep everything open; eyes, ears, mind, doors, and - you will know what. Hang loose and learn when to let go. Keep the faith, but keep it ready to exchange for a better. Before leading the assault, take your enemy around the corner to see if he isn't open to reason and arbitration. Remember Robert Herrick's wish in a moment of deepest pessimism: And once more yet (ere I am laid out dead) Knock at a Starre with my exalted Head.*

TOWNSEND, JOHN ROBERT, educator; b. Brooten, Minn., Oct. 26, 1925; s. Dewayne and Corinna Jeanette (Jansen) T.; B.S. in Physics, Cornell U., 1945, Ph.D., 1951; m. Rita Mary Walker, Sept. 11, 1948; children—Mary C., Margaret A. With Hanford (Wash.) Atomic Power Works, Gen. Electric Co., 1951-54; mem. faculty U. Pitts., 1954—, prof. physics, 1965—; vis. scientist Brookhaven Nat. Lab., 1964, AERE, Harwell, Eng., 1976. Served with USMCR, 1943-45. Mem. Fedn. Am. Scientists (chmn. Pitts. 1965), Am. Phys. Soc. Editor: Effects of Nuclear War on Pittsburgh Area, 1962. Home: 203 Carnegie Pl Pittsburgh PA 15208. *The tension between personal commitment and balanced overviews can never be eliminated; in my life this tension has played an important and useful role.*

TOWNSEND, JOHN WILLIAM, JR., physicist, electronics co. exec.; b. Washington, Mar. 19, 1924; s. John William and Elenore (Eby) T.; B.A., Williams Coll., 1947, M.A., 1949, Sc.D., 1961; m. Mary Irene Lewis, Feb. 7, 1948; children—Bruce Alan, Nancy Dewitt, John William III, Megan Lewis. With Naval Research Lab., 1949-55, br. head, 1955-58; with NASA, 1958—, dep. dir. Goddard Space Flight Center, 1965-68, dep. adminstrn. Environmental Scis. Services Adminstrn., 1968-70, asso. adminstr. Nat. Oceanic and Atmospheric Adminstrn., 1970-77; pres. Fairchild Space and Electronics Co., 1977—. Mem. U.S. Rocket, Satellite Research Panel, 1950—. Pres. town council, Forest Heights, Md., 1951-55. Served with USAAF, 1943-46. Recipient Profl. Achievement award Engrs. and Architects Day, 1957; Meritorious Civilian Service award Navy Dept., 1957; Outstanding Leadership medal NASA, 1962, Distinguished Service medal, 1971; recipient Arthur S. Fleming award Fed. Govt., 1963. Fellow Am. Meteorol. Soc., Am. Inst. Aero. and Astronautics, Sci. Research Soc. Am.; mem. Am. Phys. Soc., Nat. Acad. Engring., Am. Geophys. Union. Internat. Astronautical Fedn. (mem. internat., acad. astronautics). Author numerous papers, reports in field. Home: 15810 Comus Rd Clarksburg MD 20734

TOWNSEND, LEE HILL, educator; b. Leland, Miss., Jan. 20, 1903; s. Newitt Lee and Mabel Lyle (McNeill) T.; B.S., U. Va., 1925; M.S., U. Ill., 1932, Ph.D., 1935; m. Anna Louise Talbott, Aug. 31, 1940; 1 son, Lee Hill. Sci. instr. Greenwood (Miss.) High Sch., 1925-27; grad. asst. entomology U. Ill., 1927-30; asst. entomologist Ill. Natural History Surveys, Urbana, 1932-36; faculty agrl. entomology U. Ky., 1936—, prof., 1948-73, emeritus, 1973—, acting asst. dean in resident teaching Coll. Agr. and Home Econs., 1947, acting head dept. entomology and botany, 1957, head dept., 1957-73. State entomologist, adminstr. Ky. Seed Law and Plant Pest Control Law, 1957—. Mem. Entomol. Soc. Am., Entomol. Soc. Washington, Ky. Beekeepers Assn. (v.p.), Ky. Acad. Sci., Sigma Xi (pres. 1951-52), Phi Sigma, Gamma Alpha, Phi Eta Sigma, Alpha Gamma Rho (scholarship chmn. 1946-50, province counselor 1950-58). Methodist. Home: 1348 Sequoia Dr Lexington KY 40502

TOWNSEND, LYNN ALFRED, ret. car mfg. exec.; b. Flint, Mich., May 12, 1919; s. Lynn A. and Georgia E. (Crandall) T.; A.B., U. Mich., 1940, M.B.A., 1941, LL.D., 1965; LL.D., Bucknell U., 1965, Alma Coll., 1966, U. Del., 1967; D.Bus. Adminstrn., U. Evansville (Ind.), 1968, Rider Coll., 1973; m. Ruth M. Laing, Sept. 14, 1940; children—James L., Charles S., Richard J. Accountant Briggs & Icerman, 1939-41, Ernst & Ernst, 1941-44, 46-47; supervising accountant George Bailey & Co., 1947; supervising accountant, partner Touche, Niven, Bailey & Smart, 1947-57; comptroller Chrysler Corp., Detroit, 1957-58, group v.p. internat. operations, 1958-60, dir., 1959-75, adminstrv. v.p., 1960-61, pres., chief operating and adminstrv. officer, 1961-66, chmn. bd., chief exec. officer, 1967-75. Bd. dirs. New Detroit, chmn., 1972; mem. U.S. Indsl. Payroll Savs. Com., chmn., 1966. Co-chmn. Econ. Growth Council Detroit. Recipient Man of Year award Nat. Mgmt. Assn., 1968; Presdl. commendation, 1967; Builders of Detroit award, 1975; decorated chevalier Legion of Honor (France). Mem. Bus. Council, Am. Accounting Assn., Am. Inst. C.P.A.'s, Mich. Assn. C.P.A.'s, Nat. Alliance Businessmen (chmn. 1970, Presdl. citation 1971), Puamana Community Assn. (dir., pres.), Beta Gamma Sigma, Phi Kappa Phi, Beta Alpha Psi, Beta Theta Pi. Clubs: Economic (dir.), Detroit Athletic (past pres., dir.), University of Mich. Detroit, Bloomfield Hills (Mich.) Country. Home and office: Bloomfield Hills MI 48013

TOWNSEND, M. WILBUR, bus. exec.; b. Oyster Bay, N.Y., Jan. 17, 1912; s. Maurice West and Alberta (Say) T.; A.B., Wesleyan U., Middletown, Conn., 1934; m. Barbara White Hayden, Oct. 1, 1938; children—Barrett Say, Philip Hayden. With Handy & Harman, N.Y.C., 1946—, exec. v.p., 1961-64, pres., 1964—, chmn. bd., 1967—; past pres. 24 Karat Club, N.Y.C.; 1st v.p. Jewelers Vigilance Com.; mem. Midtown adv. com. Chase Manhattan Bank; dir. Home Life Equity Fund, Inc., Lazare Kaplan Internat. Inc. Mem. Community Ch. Clubs: Union League, Manhattan (N.Y.C.); Westchester Country. Office: Handy & Harman 850 3d Ave New York NY 10022

TOWNSEND, MAURICE KARLEN, coll. pres.; b. Yakima, Wash., Feb. 9, 1926; s. Marion J. and Marie (Karlen) T.; A.B. cum laude, Boston U., 1949; A.M., U. Chgo., 1950, Ph.D., 1954; m. Lucille Schoolcraft, Sept. 8, 1956; children—Leslie, Leah, Steven, Bradley. Lectr. U. Chgo., 1953-56; instr. Ill. Inst. Tech., 1954-56; asst. to dir. Pub. Adminstrn. Clearing House, Chgo., 1954-56; asst. prof. and research asst. U. Va., Charlottesville, 1956-57; mem. field staff Pub. Adminstrn. Service, Chgo., 1957-59; adminstr. Sperry Gyroscope Co., Lake Success, N.Y., 1959-63; acad. dean Moorhead (Minn.) State Coll., 1963-66; dean Stanislaus State Coll., Turlock, Calif., 1966-68; v.p. Ind. State U., Terre Haute, 1969-75; pres. W. Ga. Coll., Carrollton, 1975—. Chmn. bd. dirs. S. Atlantic Conf., 1978-79; trustee Ga. Council Econ. Edn., 1976—; mem. dist. com. Carroll County council Boy Scouts Am., 1979-80. Served with USAAF, 1944-45. Mem. Am. Polit. Sci. Assn., Am. Soc. Pub. Adminstrn., Inst. for Mgmt. Scis., Inst. Coll. and Univ. Adminstrs. of Am. Council Edn., Am. Assn. Higher Edn., Am. Assn. Univ. Adminstrs., Phi Beta Kappa, Omicron Delta Kappa, Phi Beta Lambda (hon.). Club: Rotary. Home: 1903 Maple St Carrollton GA 30117 Office: West Georgia College Carrollton GA 30118

TOWNSEND, PAUL HENSON, ret. bus. exec.; b. Clermont, N.J., Dec. 19, 1889; s. Eli and Frances (Dryburgh) T.; grad. Hotchkiss Sch., 1913; B.A. honoris causa, Yale, 1918; m. Clarissa Marie Davis, Sept. 3, 1920; children—Ann (Mrs. Rodney F. Wood), Paul H. Tchr. grade schs., Cape May County, N.J., 1908-10, 13-14; clk. Huron Portland Cement Co., 1919, supt. plants, ships, 1920-39, gen. mgr., 1938-53, v.p., 1942- 53, dir., 1944-69, pres., 1953-59, chmn. bd., 1959-66; v.p., dir. Detroit Chem. Works, 1937-63; dir. Fed. Motor Truck Co., 1942-49, Nat. Gypsum Co., 1957-64. Dir. adv. com. Great Lakes Protective Assn., 1940-58, mem. exec. com., 1940-57. Served as capt. 315th F.A., U.S. Army, World War 1. Recipient Purple Heart. Mem. Lake Carriers Assn. (dir.), Detroit Bd. Commerce, Detroit Engring. Soc., N.J. Hist. Soc., Detroit Soc. Geneal. Research, Newcomen Soc., Alpha Delta Phi. Mem. Grosse Pointe Meml. Ch. Clubs: Propeller, Detroit, Univ. (Detroit); Hunters Creek. Home: 866 Lincoln Rd Grosse Pointe MI 48230

TOWNSEND, RICHARD MARVIN, city mgr.; b. White Plains, N.Y., Dec. 28, 1933; s. B. Richter and Frances (Mills) T.; B.A., Cornell U., 1955, M.P.A., 1956; m. Joanne Schwartz, Apr. 25, 1959; children—Drue, Brent, Merric. With City Corpus Christi, Tex., 1956—, city mgr., 1968—. Mem. Tex. Mobile Home Performance Bd., 1971-75; mem. workmen's compensation bd. Tex. Municipal League, 1974—. Pres. Corpus Christi dist. mission bd. United Methodist Ch., 1965-68; trustee St. Luke's United Meth. Ch., 1966-69. Mem. Internat. City Mgrs. Assn., Am. Soc. Pub. Adminstrn., Tex. City Mgmt. Assn. (v.p. 1978). Contbr. articles to profl. jours. Home: 4425 Bluefield Dr Corpus Christi TX 78413 Office: P O Box 9277 Corpus Christi TX 78408

TOWNSEND, ROBERT (CHASE), author; b. Washington, July 30, 1920; s. Clinton Paul and Kathryn Spiller (Moses) T.; B.A., Princeton, 1942; postgrad. Columbia, 1945-46; m. Joan Tours, May 1943; children—Jill (Mrs. Nicol Williamson), Joan, Robert, Claire, Jeff. With Hertz Am. Express Co., 1948-62, sr. v.p. charge investment and internat. banking operations, dir. Hertz Am. Express Internat., Ltd., 1952-62; pres., chmn. bd. Avis Rent A Car, Garden City, N.Y., 1962-65, dir., 1965-67; dir. Dun and Bradstreet, N.Y.C., 1959-69; pub. Congl. Monitor, from 1969. Founder Rosewater Found. Author: Up the Organization, 1970. Address: care Alfred A Knopf Inc 201 E 50th St New York NY 10022*

TOWNSEND, RONALD DEE, ednl. adminstr.; b. nr. Ossian, Ind., Feb. 2, 1932; s. Robert Francis and Ruth (Kirkwood) T.; B.S., Taylor U., 1954; M.A., Ball State U., 1959; postgrad. Washington U., St. Louis, 1958-59, Vanderbilt U., 1959-60; Ed.D., Fla. State U., 1968; m. Marilyn Ruth Lehman, May 29, 1955; children—Donald, Randall, Twannette. Tchr. pub. schs., Geneva, Ind., 1956-58, Highland Park, Ill., 1960-62, Park Ridge, Ill., 1962-64; physics cons. Nat. Sci. Lise project, Ford Found., Ankara, Turkey, 1964-66; instr. Fla. State U., Tallahassee, 1966-68; asst. prof. sci. edn. U. Iowa, Iowa City, 1969-72; supr. sci. pub. schs., Evanston, Ill., 1972-75, coordinator research, evaluation and devel. Dist. 202, Evanston Twp. High Schs., 1975—; mem. com. for sci. performance Ill. Inventory of Ednl. Progress, 1973-78; center leader Individualized Sci. Instrn. System curriculum project NSF, 1973-78, leader resource person tng. program, 1974-75; coordinator writing conf. Leadership Instructional Material for Individual Material for Individual Sci. Instructional System project, 1975; instr. ETS Workshop Program Eval., 1978; cons. ednl. films. Served with AUS, 1954-56. AEC fellow, 1958-59; recipient improvement of instrn. award U. Iowa, 1972. Fellow AAAS (mem. nominating com. 1973-76, committeeman-at-large 1972-75); mem. Assn. Edn. Tchrs. in Sci. (mem. adv. com. guidelines doctorate programs sci. edn.), Internat. Conf. Edn. Tchrs. Integrated Sci., Sch. Sci. and Math. Assn. (dir. 1973-76), Nat. Assn. Research Sci. Teaching (nominating com. 1971), Ill. Sci. Tchrs. Assn., Am. Ednl. Research Assn. Baptist (instr. Gen. Conf. Iowa Learning Labs. 1971-72). Author: Contemporary Practices in Teaching Science, 1968; Energy, Matter and Change, 1973; Marvels of Science, 1976. Home: 1522 S Kennicott Dr Arlington Heights IL 60005 Office: Evanston Twp High Schs Evanston IL 60204

TOWNSEND, STUART ROSS, educator, physician; b. Montreal, Que., Can., June 2, 1907; s. James Edward and Helen (Robertson) T.; B.A., McGill U., 1929, M.D., C.M., 1933; m. Catherine L. Anderson, Mar. 27, 1943. Research fellow medicine Harvard, 1936-37; asst. medicine Johns Hopkins, 1937-38; former sr. physician Montreal Gen. Hosp., also dir. div. hematology, now cons.; prof. medicine and clin. medicine McGill U. Served with RCAF. Fellow Royal Coll. Physicians, A.C.P. (Que. gov.), Internat. Soc. Haematology. Contbr. articles to profl. jours. Home: 570 Chester Ave Town of Mt Royal Montreal PQ 305 Canada

TOWNSEND, THOMAS PERKINS, mining co. exec.; b. Bryn Mawr, Pa., Mar. 28, 1917; s. John and Mildred (Perkins T.; B.S. in Econs., Wharton Sch. U. Pa., 1939; postgrad. Harvard, 1944; m. Laura M. Trench, Sept. 14, 1940; children—Joanne (Mrs. Richard T. Taber), Hunter, Elizabeth (Mrs. David Ballinger). Sr. acct. Price Waterhouse & Co., 1945-48; treas., dir. Fox Products Co., 1948-53, Wilcolator Co., 1953-55; staff acct. Tex. Gulf Sulphur Co., N.Y.C., 1955-57, asst. treas., 1958-61, v.p. controller, 1961-62, v.p., treas., 1962-64, v.p. internat. ops., 1964-68; exec. v.p. Bosco Middle East Oil Corp., Greenwich, Conn., 1968-69; pres. Conn. Real Estate Corp., Greenwich, 1969-70, dir., 1969—; treas., chief fin. officer N.Y. and Rosaria Resources Corp., N.Y.C., v.p. fin., 1971—. Chmn. nat. com. for employment youth Nat. Child Labor Com., 1968-70. Trustee South Kent Sch., Soc. to Advance Retarded, Norwalk, Conn. Served to lt. (s.g.) Supply Corps, USNR, World War II. C.P.A., Pa. Mem. Am. Inst. Accountants, N.Y. State Soc. C.P.A.'s, Financial Execs. Inst. Episcopalian (treas., vestryman 1960-72). Clubs: Country (New Canaan); Mason's Island Yacht (Mystic, Conn.); Sky (N.Y.C.). Home: 609 Weed St New Canaan CT 06840 Office: 375 Park Ave New York NY 10022. *The principal goal in my life has been to be a straight dealer, to be honest in thought, word and deed. It has paid off for me. Crooked dealing may make more money, but it does not lead to a happier life. One must live by his God.*

TOWNSHEND, PETER, musician, composer, singer; b. London, May 19, 1945. Co-founder, guitarist, composer music and lyrics for musical group The Who (originally called The High Numbers), 1964—; composer rock operas: Tommy, 1969, Quadrophenia, 1973; composer rock songs, including: My Generation, I Can See for Miles, Magic Bus, Won't Get Fooled Again, Who Are You; producer films: The Kids Are All Right, 1979, Quadrophenia, 1979. Office: MCA Records Inc 445 Park Ave New York NY 10022*

TOY, HENRY, JR., cons.; b. Easton, Pa., Feb. 1, 1915; s. Henry and Pauline (Pfenning) T.; certificate sch. accounts and finance U. Pa., 1939; B.S., George Peabody Coll. Tchrs., 1961, M.A., 1962; m. Elizabeth Voelker, Aug. 31, 1935; children—Tod Jeffrey, Charles Henry. File clk., accountant Atlantic Refining Co., 1933-41; expediter, priorities mgr. E.I. duPont de Nemours & Co., 1941-45, purchasing agt., 1945-49; exec. dir. Nat. Citizens Commn. Pub. Schs., 1949-56; pres. Nat. Citizens Council for Better Schs., 1956-59; exec. dir. The Robert A. Taft Inst. Govt., 1962-63; founder Henry Toy, Jr. and Assos., cons. in edn. and community relations, N.Y.C. and Washington, 1963—; pres. Nu-Toy, Inc., 1970—. Instr., Community Coll. Denver. Bd. mem. citizens Scholarship Found. Am., 1963-73; mem. planning com. Nat. Conf. Citizenship. Adviser to com. White House Conf. on Edn., 1954-55; trustee Center for Information on Am., Inc. Recipient U.S. Jr. C. of C. distinguished service award, Del., 1948; Nat. assn. Purchasing Agts. award, 1949; Classroom Tchrs. Assn. N.Y. State Award, 1957; Distinguished Merit award U. Pa. Alumni Soc., 1957. Mem. Phi Delta Kappa (Lay Citizens award 1960), Kappa Delta Pi, Sigma Kappa Phi. Author: Federal Dollars for Scholars. Home: 13100 W 31st Ave Golden CO 80401

TOYODA, EIJI, automobile mfg. co. exec.; b. Kinjo, Nishikasugai, Japan, Sept. 12, 1913; s. Heikichi and Nao Toyoda; B.Mech.Engring., Tokyo U., 1936; m. Kazuko Takahashi, Dec. 19, 1939; children—Kanshiro, Tetsuro, Shuhei, Sonoko. Pres., Toyota Motor Ltd., Aichi, Japan; dir. Towa Real Estate Co., Toyota Central Research and Devel. Lab., Aichi Steel Works, Toyoda Machine Works, Toyoda Automatic Loom Works, Aishin Seiki Co., Toyota Motor Sales Co.; dir., auditor Toyoda Tsusho Kaisha. Mem. Japan Automobile Mfrs. Assn. (chmn. 1972—), Japan Motor Indsl. Fedn. (chmn. 1972—). Office: Toyota Motor Co Ltd 1 Toyota-cho Toyota-shi Aichi Japan*

TOZER, W. JAMES, JR., banker; b. Salt Lake City, Feb. 9, 1941; s. W. James and Virginia (Somerville) T.; B.A. cum laude, Trinity Coll., 1963; M.B.A., Harvard U., 1965; m. Elizabeth Farran, July 30, 1965; children—Farran Virginia, Katharine Coppins. Investment officer First Nat. City Overseas Investment Corp., N.Y.C., 1965-70; v.p. corp. devel. Citicorp, N.A., N.Y.C., 1970-71, sr. v.p. and head Citicorp Subsidiaries Group, 1971-74, sr. v.p., gen. mgr., head Merchant Banking Group, 1974-75, head N.Y. Banking Div., 1975-77; sr. exec. v.p., head investment banking div. Shearson Hayden Stone, Inc., N.Y.C., 1978-79, also dir.; exec. v.p. Marine Midland Bank and Marine Midland Banks, Inc., N.Y.C., 1979—; trustee Mktg. Sci. Inst., 1975-78. Chmn. bd. Fellows Trinity Coll., 1972-78; trustee, chmn. fin. com. Community Service Soc., 1974—. Mem. Securities Industry Assn., 1977-78. Clubs: Univ. of N.Y., Bond of N.Y., River (N.Y.C.). Home: 1112 Park Ave New York NY 10028 Office: 140 Broadway New York NY 10015

TOZZI, GIORGIO, bass-baritone; b. Chgo., Jan. 8, 1923; s. Enrico and Anna (Bontempi) T.; grad. DePaul Acad., Chgo., 1940; student DePaul U., 1940-43. Conservatorio G. Verdi, Milan, also Scuola Musicale de Milano, 1951; m. Monte Amundsen, Mar. 15, 1967; children—Eric John, Jennifer. Appeared Ziegfeld Theatre, N.Y.C., 1948, Adelphi Theatre, London, Eng., 1949; Italian operatic debut, Teatro Nuovo, Milan, 1950; debut La Scala, Milan, 1953, Met. Opera, N.Y.C., 1955; leading bass-baritone Met. Opera Assn., San Francisco Opera Co., Salzburg Music Festival; soloist with orchs. including N.Y. Philharmonic, Boston Symphony, Phila. Philharmonic, Mpls. Symphony, Chgo. Symphony; appeared as Hans Sachs in film Die Meistersinger, also in film Shamus, 1973; also actor TV series; former mem. faculty Juilliard Sch. Music, N.Y.C.; rec. artist RCA Victor, also London, Cestra; played Emile de Becque, opposite Mary Martin in South Pacific, also made sound-track for film, 1957. Mem. Am. Guild Musical Artists, AFTRA, Actors Equity Am., The Bohemians, YMCA. Office: care Curtis Roberts ILRD Prodns Ltd 9056 Santa Monica Blvd Los Angeles CA 90069*

TRABANT, EDWARD ARTHUR, univ. pres.; b. Los Angeles, Feb. 28, 1920; s. Edward Arthur and Nellie (Thompson) T.; A.B., Occidental Coll., Los Angeles, 1940; Ph.D., Calif. Inst. Tech., 1947; m. Jeraldine Shanessy, Oct. 24, 1943; children—Jeraldine, Arta, Amanda Merle. Instr. physics and math. Calif. Inst. Tech., 1945-47; prof. engring. scis. Purdue U., 1955-60, head div. engring. scis., 1957-60, dir. nuclear engring. lab., 1957-59, dir. off-campus grad. programs engring., 1956-59, asst. dean Grad. Sch., 1956-60; dean Sch. Engring., State U. N.Y. at Buffalo, 1960-66; v.p. acad. affairs Ga. Inst. Tech., Atlanta, 1966-68; pres. U. Del., Newark, 1968—; cons. editor Wadsworth Pub. Co. San Francisco; dir. Aegis Corp., Miami, Fla., Delmarva Power & Light Co., Wilmington, Del. Trust Co., Wilmington. Bd. dirs. Henry Francis du Pont Winterbur Mus., Wilmington Med. Center, Del. Art Mus., WHYY-TV; trustee Wilkes Coll., Wilkes-Barre, Pa. Mem. Am. Soc. Engring. Edn., ASME, Am. Math. Soc., Phi Beta Kappa, Sigma Xi. Home: 47 Kent Way Newark DE 19711

TRACEY, EDWARD LORNE, assn. exec.; b. Montreal, Can., Mar. 19, 1916; s. Edward Noble and Jennie Brown (Murison) T.; student Sir George Williams U., Montreal, McGill U., Northwestern U., Ill.; m. Ruth Gittus, Apr. 21, 1945; children—Janet Ruth Tracey Compton, Elizabeth Lorna Tracey Ing. Mem. staff Montreal Bd. Trade, gen. mgr., 1967—. Served to capt. Canadian Army, 1942-45. Mem. C. of C. Execs. Can., Inst. Assn. Execs., Montreal Amateur Athletic Assn. Mem. United Ch. Can. Clubs: Canadian, Rotary, Masons (Montreal). Address: 98 Brentwood Rd Beaconsfield PQ H9W 4L6 Canada

TRACHTA, STANLEY WILLARD, lawyer; b. Meeker, Colo., Aug. 16, 1911; s. Joseph E. and Glenn (Jones) T.; student U. Wyo., 1929-31; B.A., U. Mont., 1933, J.D., 1935; postgrad. George Washington U., 1956-57; m. Margaret Barner, Jan. 6, 1939; children—Mary Glenn, Stanley Jon. Admitted to Mont. bar, 1935, Ariz. bar, 1958; practice in Tucson, 1958—; partner firm Molloy Jones Donahue Trachta Childers & Mallamo, P.C., 1963—. Bd. dirs. Met. YMCA, Pima County Sheriffs Posse. Served from 2d lt. to col. USMC, 1935-58; PTO, Korea. Decorated Legion of Merit with oak leaf cluster, Bronze Star with oak leaf cluster. Mem. Phi Delta Phi, Kappa Sigma. Kiwanian (past pres.). Club: Skyline Country. Home: 1550 W Moore Rd Tucson AZ 85704 Office: Ariz Bank Plaza Tucson AZ 85702

TRACHTENBERG, ALAN, educator; b. Phila., Mar. 22, 1932; s. Isadore and Norma T.; A.B. in English, Temple U., 1954; M.A., U. Conn., 1956; Ph.D. in Am. Studies, U. Minn., 1962; m. Betty Glassman, Dec. 21, 1952; children—Zev, Elissa, Julia. Instr., U. Minn., 1956-61; mem. faculty Pa. State U., 1961-69, prof. English, 1969; vis. prof. English and Am. studies Yale U., 1969-70, mem. faculty, 1970—, prof., 1972—, dir. grad. studies Am. studies, 1970-72, 74-75, chmn. Am. studies, 1971-73. Fellow Am. Council Learned Socs., 1968-69, Center Advanced Study Behavioral Scis., 1968-69. Mem. Am. Studies Assn., MLA. Author: Brooklyn Bridge: Fact and Symbol, 1965; Democratic Vistas, 1986-1880, 1970; The City: American Experience, 1972; Memoirs of Waldo Frank, 1973; Critics of Culture, 1976. Home: 972 Prospect St Hamden CT 06511 Office: Am Studies Program Yale U New Haven CT 06520

TRACHTENBERG, MARVIN LAWRENCE, educator, art historian; b. Tulsa, June 6, 1939; s. William and Leona (Fox) T.; B.A., Yale U., 1961; M.A., N.Y. U., 1963, Ph.D., 1967; m. Heidi Feldmeier, Nov. 10, 1961; children—Malcolm Blake, Gordon Charles. Asst. prof. fine arts Inst. Fine Arts, N.Y. U., 1967-69, asso. prof., 1969-76, prof., 1976—, mem. humanities council, 1976-78; mem. vis. com. dept. fine arts Harvard U., 1976—. Fulbright fellow U. Florence (Italy), 1964-66; Bernard Berenson fellow N.Y. U., 1966-67; Kress Found. postdoctoral fellow, Italy, France and Germany, 1970; Nat. Endowment for Humanities fellow, Florence, 1974-75; I. Tatti fellow Harvard U. Center for Renaissance Studies in Florence, 1974-76. Mem. Coll. Art Assn., Soc. Archtl. Historians. Club: Bellport Yacht. Author: The Campanile of Florence Cathedral - Giotto's Tower (Hitchcock prize Soc. Archtl. Historians 1973), 1971; The Statue of Liberty, 1976. Office: Inst Fine Arts 1 E 78th St New York NY 10021

TRACHTENBERG, STEPHEN JOEL, univ. pres.; b. Bklyn., Dec. 14, 1937; s. Oscar M. and Shoshana G. (Weinstock) T.; B.A., Columbia U., 1959; J.D., Yale U., 1962; M.Pub.Adminstrn., Harvard U., 1966; m. Francine Zorn, June 24, 1971; children—Adam Maccabee, Ben-Lev. Admitted to N.Y. State bar, 1964, U.S. Supreme

Ct. bar, 1967; atty. AEC, 1962-65; legis. asst. to Congressman John Brademas of Ind., Washington, 1965; tutor law Harvard Coll., also teaching fellow edn. and pub. policy J.F. Kennedy Grad. Sch. Govt., Harvard U., 1965-66; spl. asst. to U.S. edn. commr. Office of Edn., HEW, Washington, 1966-68; asso. prof. polit. sci. Boston U., 1969-77, asso. dean, 1969-70, dean, 1970-74, asso. v.p., co-counsel 1974-76, v.p. acad. services, 1976-77; pres., prof. law U. Hartford (Conn.), 1977—; faculty asso. Grad. Sch. Edn., Harvard U., 1973—; dir. Mass. Ednl. Seminar, 1974-77. Trustee Tougaloo Coll.; elector Hartford Hosp.; corporator Mt. Sinai Hosp.; bd. dirs. Urban League, Am. Jewish Com., Hartford; elector Wadsworth Atheneum, Inst. Living; bd. dirs. Hartford Process; commr. B'nai B'rith Nat. Hillel Commn., 1975—. Winston Churchill fellow, Eng., 1969; named Outstanding Young Man, Boston Jr. C. of C., 1970, One of 100 Young Leaders Acad. Council Learning, 1978. Recipient numerous certificates, commendations, citations; asso fellow Morse Coll. Yale U. Mem. Am. Bar Assn., Am. Polit. Sci. Assn., English Speaking Union, AAUP, Assn. Higher Edn., Am. Soc. Pub. Adminstrn., Newcomen Soc. N.Am., Phi Beta Kappa. Clubs: Univ. (Hartford); Harvard (N.Y.C.); Yale (Boston); Tumblebrook Country (Bloomfield, Conn.); Cosmos (Washington). Editorial bd. Jour. Edn. Home: 85 Bloomfield Ave Hartford CT 06105 Office: U Hartford West Hartford CT 06117

TRACHTMAN, ARNOLD SHELDON, artist; b. Lynn, Mass., Oct. 5, 1930; s. Hyman and Dorothy (Levine) T.; B.F.A., Mass. Sch. Art, 1953; B.F.A., Sch. Art Inst. Chgo., 1955, M.F.A., 1959; m. Joan Haas, May 26, 1956; 1 dau., Maxima. Instr. adult edn. art Chgo. Park Dist., 1955-58; instr. art Boston Center for Adult Edn., 1960-63, Cambridge (Mass.) Center for Adult Edn., 1961-62; instr. art history Chamberlayne Jr. Coll., Boston, 1964-71; tchr. art Lynnfield (Mass.) High Sch., 1971—; one-man shows: South Side Community Art Gallery, Chgo., 1955, Loft Gallery, Chgo., 1957-58, Lighting Group Gallery, N.Y.C., 1957, 60-63, Nexus Gallery, Boston, 1961-65, Community Ch. Art Center, 1965, 73, Inst. Contemporary Art, Boston, 1970, Nasrudin Gallery, Boston, 1974, Addison Gallery Am. Art, 1976; group shows include: Boston Arts Festival, 1953, 66, Art Inst. Chgo., 1958, Harvard Grad. Sch. Design, 1973, Boston Public Library, 1977, Brockton (Mass.) Art Center, 1973, 78, 79; Gallerie Borjeson, Malmo, Sweden, 1974; represented in permanent collections: Fogg Art Mus., Harvard U., Addison Gallery Am. Art, Andover, Mass., Wiggin Collection Boston Public Library, Boston Mus. Fine Arts. Served with U.S. Army, 1953-55. Mem. Boston Visual Artists Union (founding mem., chmn. 1971, exec. com. 1978-79, sec., 1978-79).

TRACHTMAN, PAUL, mag. editor, writer; b. Bklyn., Jan. 7, 1938; s. Benjamin and Fae (Feldman) T.; B.A. in Biology, Swarthmore Coll., 1959; M.A. in English, Columbia U., 1961; m. Marcia Haines, Aug. 12, 1961; children—Sean, Dylan. Editorial asst. New Leader, 1961; staff writer Time-Life Books, 1962-65; sr. editor LIFE Internat. Editions, 1966-67; asso. editor LIFE Mag., 1968-70; freelance writer, 1970-74; editor Horticulture Mag., Boston, 1975-78; bd. editors Smithsonian Mag., 1978—. Recipient Nat. Mag. award, 1976. Mem. AAAS. Author: The Gunfighters, 1975. Address: 3723 S St NW Washington DC 20007

TRACY, BERRY BRYSON, art museum curator; b. Hampton, Iowa, Sept. 4, 1933; s. James Bendel and Muriel (Bryson) T.; B.A., U. Iowa, 1955; student Attingham Park (Eng.) Adult Coll., 1955. Hist. technician Ill. Dept. Conservation, Springfield, 1957-60; curator decorative arts Newark Mus., 1960-64; asst. curator Am. wing Met. Mus. Art, N.Y.C., 1964-65, asso. curator, 1965-68, curator, 1968-72, curator-in-charge, 1973—, charge New Am. Wing, 1980; cons. restoration and furnishing Old Merchants House, N.Y.C., Bull Jackson House, Orange County, N.Y., re-restoration Boscobel Restoration Inc., 1976-77; mem. spl. fine arts com. Dept. State, Washington, 1971-77, 77—. Bd. dirs. Am. Friends of Attingham Inc. Served with USN, 1955-57. Mem. Mus. City N.Y., Nat. Trust Historic Preservation, Newark Mus. Assn. Episcopalian. Exhbns. and catalogues include Classical America, 1815-1845, Newark Mus., 1963; 19th Century America, Met. Mus. Art, 1970; Boscobel Restoration, Inc., 1980. Home: RD 1 Farmingdale Rd Goshen NY 10924 Office: Metropolitan Museum of Art Fifth Ave and 82d St New York NY 10028

TRACY, EUGENE ARTHUR, utility exec.; b. Oak Park, Ill., Dec. 14, 1927; s. Arthur Huntington and Emily Margaret (Groff) T.; B.S. in Bus. Adminstrn., Northwestern U., 1951; M.B.A., DePaul U., Chgo., 1958; m. Irene Walburga Kacin, June 30, 1951; children—Glen Eugene, Diane Emily, Janet Freda. With Peoples Gas Light & Coke Co., Chgo., 1951-69, 77—, pres., 1977—; with Peoples Gas Co., Chgo., 1969-77, v.p., 1973-77, controller, 1974-77, also dir.; pres., dir. N. Shore Gas Co., Waukegan, Ill., 1977—; dir. First Fed. Savs. & Loan Assn. Chgo., Natural Gas Pipeline Co. Am. Trustee Taxpayers Fedn. Ill., 1973-77; bd. dirs. Civic Fedn. Chgo., 1976-77; bd. dirs. Central YMCA Community Coll., Chgo., 1971—, treas., 1972-77, chmn. bd., 1977—; treas. St. David's Episcopal Ch., Glenview, Ill., 1970—; bd. dirs. Jr. Achievement, Chgo., 1978—; trustee Inst. Gas Tech., Chgo., 1978—. Served with U.S. Army, 1946-47. Mem. Am., Midwest gas assns., Chgo. Assn. Commerce and Industry (dir. 1979—). Clubs: Econ., Univ., Chicago (Chgo.). Home: 1424 Sequoia Trail Glenview IL 60025 Office: 122 S Michigan Ave Chicago IL 60603

TRACY, JAMES DONALD, historian; b. St. Louis, Feb. 14, 1938; s. Leo W. and Marguerite M. (Meehan) T.; B.A., St. Louis U., 1959; M.A.S., Johns Hopkins U., 1960; postgrad. Notre Dame U., 1961; Ph.D., Princeton U., 1967; m. Nancy Ann McBride, Sept. 6, 1968; children—Patrick, Samuel, Mary Ann. Instr., U. Mich., 1964-66; instr. to prof. history U. Minn., Mpls., 1966—. Guggenheim fellow, 1972-73; Nat. Endowment for Humanities summer grantee, 1977; Fulbright research grantee, 1979. Mem. Am. Catholic Hist. Soc. (council 1978—). Democrat. Roman Catholic. Author: Erasmus: The Growth of a Mind, 1972; The Politics of Erasmus: A Pacifist Intellectual and His Political Milieu, 1979; editorial bd. Sixteenth Century Jour., 1979—. Home: 934 Portland St Saint Paul MN 55104 Office: 614 Social Sci Tower U Minn Minneapolis MN 55455

TRACY, JAMES JARED, JR., mfg. co. exec.; b. Cleve., Jan. 17, 1929; s. James Jared and Florence (Comey) T.; A.B., Harvard, 1950, M.B.A., 1953; m. Elizabeth Jane Bourne, June 30, 1953; children—Jane Mackintosh, Elizabeth Boyd, James Jared IV, Margaret Gardiner. With Price Waterhouse & Co., Cleve., 1953-65; with Clevite Corp., Cleve., 1965-69, treas., chief fin. officer, 1968-69; with Republic Steel Corp., Cleve., 1969-75, treas., 1970-75; v.p., treas. Johns-Manville Corp., Denver, 1976—. Trustee Denver YMCA. C.P.A., Ohio. Mem. Am. Inst. C.P.A.'s, Ohio, Colo. socs. C.P.A.'s, Fin. Execs. Inst. (dir. chpt.). Clubs: Harvard, Union (Cleve.); Columbine Country (Denver). Home: 35 Wedge Way Littleton CO 80123 Office: Ken-Caryl Ranch Denver CO 80217

TRACY, OSGOOD VOSE, chem. co. exec.; b. Syracuse, N.Y., Oct. 27, 1902; s. James G. and Florida (Seay) T.; B.S., U.S. Naval Acad., 1924; Sc.D., Clarkson Coll. Tech., 1958; m. Pauline Crawford, Oct. 2, 1926; children—Sally (Mrs. Edmond G. Thomas), Mary M., Susan C. (Mrs. Timothy Mellon). Ensign, USN, 1924-25; with Solvay Process Co., 1926-30, Standard Oil Co. La., 1930-39; with Esso Standard Oil Co., N.Y.C., 1939-60, v.p., 1956-59, pres., 1959-60, dir., 1954-60; dir. Enjay Co., Inc., 1948-60, pres., 1953-58; exec. v.p., dir. W.R. Grace & Co., N.Y.C., 1960-67, dir. emeritus, cons., 1968—; chmn., dir. RAC Corp., 1963-79; dir. Inexco Oil Co. Dir. chem. div. NPA, 1951-52. Trustee Clarkson Coll. Tech., 1958-67. Mem. Am. Chem. Soc., Mfg. Chemists Assn., Soc. Chem. Industry. Clubs: N.Y. Yacht (N.Y.C.); Metropolitan, Army and Navy (Washington); Morris County (N.J.) Golf. Home: Kahdena Rd Morristown NJ 07960 Office: 1114 Ave of Americas New York NY 10036

TRACY, ROBERT ALLEN, research and devel. exec.; b. Detroit, Dec. 22, 1923; s. Guy Allen and Florence May (Butterfield) T.; B.S.E. in Physics, U. Mich., Ann Arbor, 1950, M.S. in Physics, 1951; m. Margaret Jean Carraher, Aug. 22, 1945; children—James Allen, Christine Ann, Karin Ilene. Dep. dir. research Burroughs Corp., Paoli, Pa., until 1964; dir. applied scis. div. Friden div. Singer Co., San Leandro, Calif., 1964-68, sr. staff scientist Office Products div., Albuquerque, 1968-71; dir. electronics and mech. lab. Research Center, Addressograph-Multigraph Corp., Cleve., 1971-74, dir. Multigraphics Devel. Center, Multigraph div., 1974-77; dir. devel. engring. Copier Systems div. Pitney-Bowes Corp., Danbury, Conn., 1977—. Served with USAAF, 1943-47. Decorated D.F.C. (2), Air Medal (2). Mem. Am. Phys. Soc., IEEE, Sigma Xi, Tau Beta Pi. Contbr. articles in computer field to profl. jours. Patentee in field. Home: 11 Allan Way Bethel CT 06801

TRACY, ROBERT M., ret. ins. co. exec.; b. Burlington, Vt., May 16, 1907; s. James E. and Mary R. (Long) T.; B.S., U. Vt., 1930; m. Helen Prouty, Oct. 9, 1937. Staff accountant Lybrand, Ross Bros. & Montgomery, N.Y.C., 1930-40; asst. to treas. Nat. Life Ins. Co., 1940-43, asst. treas., 1943, treas., 1944, treas., controller, 1958-59, v.p., controller, 1959-61, sr. v.p., controller, 1961-72; past dir. Nat. Life Ins. Investment Mgmt. Corp. Past mem. finance com., treas., dir., mem. exec. com. Asso. Industries Vt. Mem. budget com. United Fund, 1956-57. Trustee U. Vt.; past pres. trustees Aldrich Pub. Library; chmn. bd. trustees, past chmn. exec. com. Central Vt. Med. Center; treas. Vt. Ednl. and Health Bldgs. Finance Agy.; past treas. Vt. Library Trustees' Assn.; bd. dirs. Vt. YMCA, Barre City Hosp.; bd. dirs., chmn., past v.p., sec.-treas. Vt. sect. New Eng. Council. Mem. A.I.M. (asso.), Controllers Inst. Am., Barre Brotherhood Assn. (past pres.), Am. Inst. Accountants, N.Y., Vt. socs. C.P.A.'s, Inst. Internal Auditors, Am. Accounting Assn., A.L.A., S.A.R. Baptist. Mason (Shriner). Club: Lake Mansfield Trout. Home: 112 Washington St Barre VT 05641 also 55 Maushop's Path West Yarmouth MA 02673

TRACY, WARREN FRANCIS, librarian; b. Richmond, Ind., Nov. 26, 1914; s. Timothy Leo and Eleanor (Moore) T.; B.A., Earlham Coll., Richmond, 1938; B.L.S., Western Res. U., 1940; M.A., U. Chgo., 1953, Ph.D., 1958; m. Georgia Garber, May 24, 1941; 1 son, Warren Francis. Dir. Henry County (Ind.) Library Demonstration, 1940-41; asst. librarian Knox Coll., 1946-47, Northwestern State Coll. La., Natchitoches, 1947-51; librarian Coe Coll., 1954-62; librarian U. So. Miss., Hattiesburg, 1962-76, chmn. dept. library sci., 1962-68, prof. library sci., 1976—; chmn. coll. sect. Iowa Library Assn., 1958, chmn. com. grad. library sch., 1962. Served to 1st lt. AUS, 1941-46. Mem. Am., Miss. (pres. 1974) library assns., Phi Delta Kappa, Phi Kappa Phi (charter). Presbyterian. Club: Rotary (pres. 1972). Contbr. articles to profl. jours. Home: Lake Serene Route 4 Hattiesburg MS 39401

TRAEGER, CHARLES HENRY, III, bank holding co. exec.; b. Bethlehem, Pa., Sept. 30, 1942; s. Charles Henry, Jr. and Dorothy Shelley (Weinberger) T.; A.B., Coll. William and Mary, 1964; J.D., Stanford U., 1967; m. Carole Lynn DeGraff, Feb. 20, 1972; children—Charles Henry, IV, Erin Elizabeth, Seth David. Admitted to N.Y. bar, Mass. bar; asso. firm Milbank, Tweed, Hadley & McCloy, N.Y.C., 1971-76; v.p., gen. counsel Shawmut Corp., Boston, 1976—, Shawmut Bank Boston, N.A., 1976—; dir. New Eng. Bankcard Assn. Served to lt. USNR, 1968-71. Mem. Am. Bar Assn., Assn. Bank Holding Cos., Mass. Bar Assn., Assn. Bar City N.Y., Phi Beta Kappa. Mormon. Editor Stanford Law Rev., 1965-67. Home: 64 Frost Rd Belmont MA 02178 Office: 1 Federal St Boston MA 02110

TRAENDLY, WALLACE FRANCIS, ret. publishing co. exec.; b. Bklyn., June 5, 1910; s. George Henry and Ada (Dalton) T.; student Colgate U., 1931-32; B. Chem. Engring., Pratt Inst., 1934; m. Mary Elizabeth Comes, June 13, 1942; children—Joy, W. Blake. Tech. salesman Internat. Nickel Co., 1935-36, Victor Chem. Works, 1937-38; advt. sales rep. Am. Chem. Soc. publs. Reinhold Pub. Corp., 1939-47, advt. sales mgr., 1947-49, v.p., dir. Reinhold Pub. Corp., 1947-49; with McGraw Hill Pub. Co., N.Y.C., 1949—, pub. Food Industries, 1949-50, Chem. Industries, 1950-51, Chem. Engring., 1949-60, Chem. Week, 1951-60, sr. v.p. McGraw-Hill Publs. Co., 1960-63, dir. McGraw-Hill, Inc., 1964-75, chmn. exec. com., 1974-75; pres., chief exec. officer McGraw-Hill Info. Systems Co., 1963-72, group pres. McGraw Hill Publs. Co./McGraw Hill Info. Systems Co. (formerly F.W. Dodge Co.), N.Y.C., 1972-75; chmn. bd. Photronix Inc., Clayton, Mo., 1966-68, N.Y.C., 1968; dir. Annin Co., Verona, N.J. Bd. govs. N.Y. Bldg. Congress; chmn. adv. council Engring. Sch., Pratt Inst., 1958-59, chmn. alumni fund com., 1962-63; trustee U.S. Naval Acad. Found. Recipient Pratt Inst. Alumni award, 1964. Mem. Am. Chem. Soc., Constrn. Specifications Inst., ABP, AIA (hon.), Mexican Inst. Architects (hon.), Beta Theta Pi. Episcopalian. Clubs: Union League (N.Y.C.); Essex Fells (N.J.) Country; Overseas Press. Home: Norcroft Rd Essex Fells NJ 07021

TRAFFORD, WILLIAM BRADFORD, lawyer; b. N.Y.C., Mar. 22, 1910; s. Perry D. and Elizabeth (Meeker) T.; grad. St. Paul's Sch., 1927; student U. Freiburg (Germany), 1927-28; A.B., Harvard U., 1932, LL.B., 1936; m. Abigail Sard, Jan 26, 1937 (div. 1965); children—Abigail (Mrs. P. Robin Brett), Elizabeth, William Bradford; m. 2d, Stella M. Champollion, Sept. 3, 1965. Admitted to Mass. bar, 1936, N.Y. bar, 1937; law clk. to circuit ct. appeals judge William Clark, 1937-39; asst. corp. counsel, N.Y.C., 1939-42; mem. firm Peabody, Brown, Rowley & Storey, Boston, 1946—; town counsel, Wenham, Mass., 1948-65. Bd. dirs. Mass. Soc. Prevention Cruelty to Children. Served to 1st lt., inf., AUS, 1942-45; ETO. Decorated Bronze Star, Purple Heart. Mem. Am. Law Inst., Boston Bar Assn., Mass. Hist. Soc. Clubs: City, Tavern (Boston). Home: 380 Marlborough St Boston MA 02115 Office: 1 Boston Pl Boston MA 12110

TRAFTON, ROLAND MILTON, corp. exec.; b. Los Angeles, Jan. 1, 1920; s. Roland Brunswick and Lola Montana (Mills) T.; B.Sc. in Law, U. Wash., 1947, J.D., 1949; m. Rose Marie Ray, Apr. 25, 1942; children—Roger Milton, Stephen John, David Roland, Byron Gardner, Dwight Elliott. Admitted to Wash. bar, 1950; pvt. practice accounting, 1946-49; sr. tax accountant Arthur Andersen & Co., Seattle, 1950-51; controller, counsel Jam Handy Orgn., Detroit, 1951-52; with SAFECO Corp., Seattle, 1952—, pres., dir., 1970—; dir. affiliated cos. Trustee CAPRI Found., 1972—. Served with Q.M.C., U.S. Army, 1942-46. C.P.A., Wash. Mem. Wash. Bar Assn. Office: SAFECO Corp SAFECO Plaza Seattle WA 98185*

TRAGER, FRANK NEWTON, educator; b. N.Y.C., Oct. 9, 1905; s. Benjamin and Eda (Schapiro) T.; B.S., N.Y. U., 1927, A.M. (Butler fellow philosophy), 1928, Ph.D., 1951; grad. scholar philosophy Johns Hopkins, 1928-31; m. Helen Gilbson, Oct. 9, 1936. Instr. philosophy Johns Hopkins, 1928-34; with Resettlement Adminstrn., 1935-36; nat. labor sec. Socialist Party of U.S., 1936-37; program dir. Am. Jewish Com., 1938-43; asst. to pres. NCCJ, 1945-46; program dir. Anti-Defamation League, 1946-51; dir. AID mission, Rangoon, Burma, 1951-53; adminstr., research prof. N.Y. U., 1953-58, prof. internat. affairs, 1958—; prof. Nat. War Coll., 1961-63; vis. prof. Yale, 1960-61; dir. studies Nat. Strategy Info. Center, 1966—. Cons. RAND Corp., Hudson Inst., govt., industry and founds. Mem. adv. panel East Asian and Pacific Affairs, Dept. State, 1966-69; sec.-treas. Bur. Intercultural Edn., 1938-53; chmn. Am. Asian Ednl. Exchange. Bd. dirs., mem. editorial bd. Fgn. Policy Research Inst. Served with USAAF, 1943-45. Fellow Center Internat. Studies, Mass. Inst. Tech., 1953-54; Carnegie Research fellow Council Fgn. Relations, 1957-58. Mem. Am. Polit. Sci. Assn., Assn. Asian Studies (dir., acting treas.), Fgn. Policy Research Inst. (dir.), Asia Soc. (exec. com. Burma council), Council Fgn. Relations, Royal Siam Soc., Burma Research Soc. Editor, author: (with others) Burma, 3 vols., 1956; Burma: Japanese Military, Selected Documents, 1941-45, 1971; (with William Henderson) Communist China, 1949-69, A Twenty Year Appraisal, 1970; author: Building a Welfare State in Burma, rev. edit., 1958; (with others) Marxism in Southeast Asia, A Study of Four Countries, 1959; Furnivall of Burma: An Annotated Bibliography, 1963; Why Viet Nam?, 1968; Burma, From Kingdom to Republic, a Historical and Political Analysis, 1966; (with others) National Security and American Society: Theory, Process and Policy, 1973; (with William J. Koenig) Burmese Sit-tans 1764-1826, Records of Rural Life and Administration, 1979. Editor: Annotated Bibliography of Burma, 1971; Japanese and Chinese Language Sources on Burma: An Annotated Bibliography, 1957 (with Klaus Knorr) Economics Issues and National Security, 1977; Oil, Divestiture and National Security, 1976. Contbr. articles and revs. to publs., chpts. to books. Mem. editorial bd. Orbis, Asian Affairs; chmn. editorial bd. Nat. Security Studies, Strategy Reports Series. Home: 785 Park Ave New York NY 10021 Office: Nat Strategy Info Center 111 E 58th St New York NY 10022 also New York U 4 Washington Sq N New York NY 10003

TRAGER, WILLIAM, biologist, educator; b. Newark, Mar. 20, 1910; s. Leon and Anna (Emilfork) T.; B.S., Rutgers U., 1930, Sc.D. (hon.), 1965; M.A., Harvard, 1931, Ph.D., 1933; m. Ida Sosnow, June 16, 1935; children—Leslie, Carolyn, Lillian. Fellow Rockefeller U., N.Y.C., 1934-35, mem. faculty, 1935—, asso. prof., 1950-64, prof. biology, 1964—; guest investigator West African Inst. Trypanosomiasis Research, 1958-59; vis. prof. Fla. State U., 1962, U. P.R. Med. Sch., 1963, U. Mexico Med. Sch., 1965; guest investigator Nigerian Inst. Trypanosomiasis Research, 1973-74. Mem. study sect. parasitology and tropical medicine Nat. Inst. Allergy and Infectious Diseases, 1954-58, 67-70, tng. grant com., 1961-64, microbiology and infectious diseases adv. com., 1978-79; mem. malaria commn. Armed Forces Epidemiol. Bd., 1965-73; mem. study group parasitic diseases Walter Reed Army Inst. Research, 1977-79; chmn. sci. adv. council Liberian Inst. Tropical Medicine, 1965-66; rapporteur 6th, 7th Congresses Tropical Medicine; pres. Am. Found. for Tropical Medicine, 1966-69; mem. steering com. Malaria Immunology Group, WHO, 1977—; cons. WHO, Bangkok, 1978, Panama, 1979, Shanghai, 1979. Served to capt. AUS, 1943-45. NRC fellow, 1933-34; Guggenheim Found. fellow, 1973-74. Fellow AAAS, N.Y. Acad. Scis.; mem. Nat. Acad. Sci., Am. Soc. Parasitologists (council 1956-57, v.p. 1973, pres. 1974), Soc. Protozoologists (pres. 1960-61), Am. Soc. Tropical Medicine and Hygiene (pres. 1978-79). Author: Symbiosis, 1970. Editor Jour. Protozoology, 1954-65. Contbr. articles on insect physiology and exptl. parasitology to profl. jours. Home: 89 Lee Rd Scarsdale NY 10583 Office: Rockefeller Univ York Ave at 66th St New York NY 10021

TRAHER, WILLIAM HENRY, artist, mural painter; b. Rock Springs, Wyo., Apr. 6, 1908; s. Stephen John and Catherine Laura (Utzinger) T.; student Nat. Acad. Design, N.Y.C., 1930-33, Sch. Fine Arts, Yale, 1938-39; m. Frances Manette White, June 14, 1942; children—Anita, Elissa, Steven. Exhibited woodcuts State Hist. Mus., Denver, 1934-35; art dir. Philip H. Gray, Inc., advt., 1945-47; 1952; sr. staff artist Denver Mus. Natural History, completing over 26,000 square feet of super-real life size diarama backgrounds, 1954-76; other major works include Traher Wilderness murals Columbia Savs. & Loan Assn., Pueblo, Colo., 1967, Four Faces of the West paintings (7 X 10 feet each) Jefferson Nat. Expansion Meml., under the Arch, St. Louis, 1970. Bd. dirs. Floyd Wilson Wilderness Edn. Found., Denver Art Mus., 1960-62. Served with USAAF, 1942-46; PTO. Mem. Denver Artists Guild (hon. life, past pres.). Clubs: Jackson Color Camera, Denver Figure Skating (a founder, soloist). Home: 2331 Niagara St Denver CO 80207

TRAHMAN, CARL RICHARD, educator; b. Irvington, N.J., Mar. 10, 1917; s. Charles and Anna (Moeller) T.; A.B., Union Coll. (N.Y.), 1938; Ph.D., U. Cin., 1942. Instr. Classics Yale, 1946-48; asst. prof. classics U. Cin., 1948-53, asso. prof., 1953-64, Burnam prof. Latin and Romance palaeography, 1964—. Served with Signal Corps, AUS, 1944-46. Mem. Alumni Am. Acad. Rome, Am. Philol. Assn., Archeol. Inst. Am., Renaissance Soc. Am., Phi Beta Kappa. Home: 2930 Scioto St Cincinnati OH 45219

TRAICOFF, GEORGE, coll. pres.; b. Elyria, Ohio, May 16, 1932; s. George and Lena T.; B.S., Miami U., Oxford, Ohio, 1954; M.Ed., Kent State U., 1959; Ed.D., Ind. U., 1967; m. Diane C. Schneider, Dec. 28, 1965; children—George Scott, Paula Jane, Amy Jo. Tchr. bus. Elyria (Ohio) High Sch., La Grante (Ohio) High Sch., 1956-59; instr., coordinator Ind. U., 1959-60, Ohio State U., 1960-63; prof., head dept. No. Mich. U., Marquette, 1963-66, dir. program gen. studies, 1966-67; dean community services Cuyahoga Community Coll., Cleve., 1967-73; pres. North Shore Community Coll., Beverly, Mass., 1973—. Served with U.S. Army, 1954-56. Mem. Am. Assn. Community and Jr. Colls., Nat. Council Community Services (past pres.), Mass. Adminstrs. Community Colls. Episcopalian. Office: 3 Essex St Beverly MA 01915

TRAIN, HARRY DEPUE, II, naval officer; b. Washington, Nov. 5, 1927; s. Harold Cecil and May (Philipps) T.; B.S., U.S. Naval Acad., 1949; m. Catharine Peck Kinnear, July 8, 1950; children—Louise Lucas, Catharine Philipps, Elizabeth Langdon, Cecilia Spencer. Commd. ensign U.S. Navy, 1949, advanced through grades to adm., 1978; comdr. Cruiser-Destroyer Flotilla 8, 1971-72; dir. internat. security affairs East Asia and Pacific Region, Office Asst. Sec. Def., 1972-73; dir. Systems Analysis Div., Office Chief Naval Ops., 1973-74; dir. joint staff Orgn. Joint Chiefs of Staff, 1974-76; comdr. U.S. 6th Fleet, 1976-78; comdr.-in-chief U.S. Atlantic Fleet and supreme allied comdr. Atlantic, 1978—. Decorated D.S.M. with two gold stars, Legion of Merit with 3 gold stars, Meritorious Service medal, Joint Services Commendation medal, Navy Commendation medal; comdr. Order Republic of Tunisia. Mem. U.S. Naval Inst. Roman Catholic. Club: Columbia Country (Chevy Chase, Md.). Home: 465 Dillingham Blvd Norfolk VA 23511 Office: Comdr-in-chief US Atlantic Fleet Norfolk VA 23511

TRAIN, JACK DURKEE, architect; b. Cairo, Ill., Apr. 8, 1922; s. Cyril C. and Yuba (Whitaker) T.; B.S. in Archtl. Engring., U. Ill., 1944; student advanced structures, U. Tenn., 1949-51; m. Virginia Lee Gher, June 1, 1944; children—Jack Douglas, Barbara Train

Hammond, Pamela Train Leutz. Structural engr. Skidmore, Owings & Merrill, Chgo., 1946-50, archtl. job capt., project mgr., 1950-54, asso. partner, 1954-60, 62-66; partner Perkins & Will, Chgo., 1960-62; exec. v.p. Metz Train & Youngren, Inc. Chgo., 1966-69, pres., 1969—, also dir.; chmn. Prodn. Systems For Architects And Engrs., Inc., 1969-72; dir., 1969-73. Mem. Nat. Archtl. Accrediting Bd., 1973—, pres., 1978-79. Principal works include Inland Steel Bldg., Chgo., 1957, U.S. Air Force Acad., Colorado Springs, Colo., 1961, Acad. Facility of Rush U., Rush-Presbyn.-St. Luke's Med. Center, Chgo., 1976, Osco Drug Inc. Hdqrs. Office Bldg., Oak Brook, Ill., 1975, Marjorie B. Kovler Viral Oncology Labs., U. Chgo., 1977. Mem. Mayor Chgo. Adv. Com. Community Renewal Program, 1964-68; dir. Barrington (Ill.) Area Devel. Council, 1965-66; mem. Barrington Hills Plan Commn., 1964-74, 76—, chmn., 1972-74; mem. adv. bd. U.S. Gen Services Adminstrn., 1968-71; mem. Md. Gov.'s Commn. to Review State Procedures for Awarding Non-Competitive Architect/Engr. State Contracts, 1973; bd. dirs. Chgo. Bldg. Congress, 1975-77. Mem. dept. new ch. devel. Presbytery Chgo., 1961-67. Served to lt. USNR, 1944-46; PTO. Recipient 17 awards for archtl. works. Fellow AIA (pres. Chgo. 1962-64, nat. bd. dirs. 1966-69, pres. Ill. council 1966-68, mem. nat. exec. com. 1968-69; Edward C. Kemper award 1974); mem. U. Ill. Archtl. Alumni Assn. (pres. 1971-79), Am. Arbitration Assn. (mem. nat. panel arbitrators 1966—), Newcomen Soc. N.Am., Alpha Kappa Lambda, Scarab. Rotarian. Clubs: Union League, Executives, Economic (Chgo.); Barrington Hills Country. Office: 1 E Wacker Dr Chicago IL 60601

TRAINOR, BERNARD EDMUND, marine corps officer; b. N.Y.C., Sept. 2, 1928; s. Joseph Patrick and Ann Veronica (Whalen) T.; B.S., Coll. of Holy Cross, 1951; M.A., U. Colo., 1963, postgrad., 1970—; m. Margaret Ann Hamilton, June 13, 1959; children—Kathleen Marie, Theresa Ann, Eileen Cecile, Claire Hamilton. Commd. 2d lt. USMC, 1951, advanced through grades to maj. gen., 1978; inf. comdr. Korea, 1952; assigned USS Columbus, 1953-55; staff Marine Corps Hdqrs., 1955-58; exchange office Royal Marine Commandos, 1958-59; inf. comdr. First Marine Div., 1959-61; asst. prof. naval sci. U. Colo., Boulder, 1961-64; assigned to Marine Corps Command and Staff Coll., 1964-65; adv. Republic of Vietnam, 1965-66; instr. Marine Corps Command and Staff Coll., 1966-69; student Air War Coll., Montgomery, Ala., 1969-70; bn. comdr., Vietnam, 1970-71; staff officer Hdqrs. Marine Corps, Washington, 1970-71; dir. First Marine Corps Dist., N.Y.C., 1974-76; asst. depot comdr. Marine Corps Recruit Depot, Parris Island, S.C., 1976-78; dir. Edn. Center, Quantico, Va., 1978—. Decorated Legion of Merit (2), Bronze Star, Navy Commendation medal (2), others; recipient Anderson Meml. award Air War Coll., 1970. Mem. Marine Corps Assn., Naval Inst., Am. Hist. Assn. Roman Catholic. Club: Edns of the Eartn. Author: History of the U.S. Marine Corps, 1968. Home: Quarters 12 MCDEC Quantico VA 22134 Office: Edn Center MCDEC Quantico VA 22134. *The man who succeeds in a highly competitive profession is the one who seeks the toughest jobs with the highest risk. If he fails he is respected for trying: if he wins he makes to the top. His motto: high risk-high pay-off.*

TRALINS, S(ANDOR) ROBERT, author; b. Balt., Apr. 28, 1926; s. Emanuel and Rose (Miller) T.; student John Hopkins, 1949, Eastern Coll., 1950-51; m. Sonya Lee Mandel, Sept. 2, 1945; children—Myles Jay, Alan Harvey. Freelance writer of short stories, essays, studies, articles, screenplays and numerous books, including: Pleasure Was my Business, 1961; Dynamic Selling, 1962; Squaresville Jag, 1965; Beyond Human Understanding, 1966; The Cosmozoids, 1966; Clairvoyant Strangers, 1968; Cairo Madam, 1969; Black Brute, Runaway Slave and Slave's Revenge, 1969; ESP Forewarnings, 1969; Song of Africa, 1969; Panther John, 1970; Clairvoyant Women, 1970; The Mind Code, 1972; Supernatural Warnings, 1972; Black Pirate, 1973; Android Armageddon, 1974; The Arthur Godfrey Radio Show, 1976; pres. Alpha Group/Pubs., Inc., 1976—; editor-pub. Nat. Crime Reporter, 1977—. Address: care S Safran Assos Ltd Lit Agents 866 UN Plaza New York NY 10017 also 21 Ladbroke Gardens London W11 England

TRANQUADA, ROBERT ERNEST, ednl. adminstrn., physician; b. Los Angeles, Aug. 27, 1930; s. Ernest Alvro and Katharine (Jacobus) T.; B.A., Pomona Coll., 1951; M.D., Stanford U., 1955; m. Janet Martin, Aug. 31, 1951; children—John Martin, James Robert, Katherine Anne. Intern, in medicine UCLA Med. Center, 1955-56, resident in medicine, 1956-57; resident Los Angeles VA Hosp., 1957-58; fellow in diabetes and metabolic diseases UCLA, 1958-59; fellow in diabetes U. So. Calif., 1959-60; asst. prof. medicine U. So. Calif., 1959-63, asso. prof., 1963-67, prof., chmn. dept. community medicine, 1967-75, med. dir. Los Angeles County/U. So. Calif. Med. Center, 1969-74; regional dir. Central Region, Los Angeles County Dept. Health Services, 1975-76; asso. dean UCLA, 1976-79; chancellor/dean U. Mass. Med. Sch., 1979—; trustee Pomona Coll., 1969—; mem. bd. fellows Claremont U. Center, 1971-79; bd. dirs. Nat. Med. Fellowships, Inc., 1973—. Milbank faculty fellow, 1967-72; diplomate Am. Bd. Internal Medicine. Mem. Am. Diabetes Assn., Am. Public Health Assn., Western Soc. Clin. Investigation, Los Angeles Soc. Internal Medicine, Los Angeles Acad. Medicine, Calif. Med. Assn., Mass. Med. Soc., Phi Beta Kappa, Sigma Xi, Alpha Omega Alpha. Clubs: Worcester, Tatnuck Country. Contbr. numerous articles to profl. publs. Office: U Mass Med Center 55 Lake Ave N Worcester MA 01605. *It is a reasonable conclusion that there is, in this world, no surplus of people who are both competent and willing to work hard, and that for those who share these attributes, there will always be a demand, sometimes in the most surprising places.*

TRANSUE, WILLIAM REAGLE, educator, mathematician; b. Pen Argyl, Pa., Nov. 30, 1914; s. Ray Frank and Emily (Reagle) T.; B.S., Lafayette Coll., 1935; postgrad. U. Bordeaux (France), 1935-36, Yale, 1936-37; M.S., Lehigh U., 1939, Ph.D., 1941; m. Monique Serpette, May 27, 1936; children—William Raoul Reagle, Jacques Henry, John Ray. Chief ballistic research sect. Office Chief Ordnance, Washington, 1943-45; asso prof. math. Kenyon Coll., Gambier, Ohio, 1945-48, prof. 1948-66; prof. math. State U. N.Y. at Binghamton, 1966—. Mem. Am. Math. Soc., Math. Assn. Am., Phi Beta Kappa. Sigma Xi. Author research papers. Home: 2093 E Hamton Rd Binghamton NY 13903

TRANTHAM, WILLIAM EUGENE, coll. dean; b. Elkland, Mo., Aug. 6, 1929; s. Harvey Wilson and Lola (Minor) T.; B.S., B.S. in Edn., Southwest Mo. State Coll., 1951; M.M., Northwestern U., 1955, Ph.D., 1966; m. Patsy Ann Starr, June 7, 1959; children—Rachel Ann, Gene Starr. Chmn. music dept. Southwest Baptist Coll., 1955-60; chmn. applied music dept. Ouachita Baptist U., Arkadelphia, Ark., 1960—, dean Sch. Music, 1968—; piano recitalist, ch. organist, dir.; organist, dir. Westminster-Presbyn. Ch., Hot Springs, Ark., 1975—. Sec. Bolivar (Mo.) Community Concert Assn., 1957-60. Served with AUS, 1953-55. Mem. Ark. State Music Teachers Assn. (pres. 1977), Am. Musicol. Soc., Music Tchrs. Nat. Assn., Music Educators Nat. Conf., Phi Mu Alpha, Sinfonia. Baptist (deacon 1971—, chmn. 1973). Contbr. articles to profl. jours. Home: 688 Carter Rd Arkadelphia AR 71923

TRAPP, FRANK ANDERSON, educator; b. Pitts., June 13, 1922; s. Frank Louis and Mary (Anderson) T.; B.A., Carnegie Inst. Tech., 1943; A.M., Harvard, 1947, Ph.D., 1952. Teaching fellow Harvard, also resident tutor Adams House, 1948-51; mem. faculty Williams Coll., 1951-56; mem. faculty Amherst (Mass.) Coll., 1956—, prof. art, 1963—, William R. Mead prof., 1976—, chmn. dept. fine arts, 1965-75, 76-78, dir. Mead Art Bldg., 1969—; vis. Mellon prof. dept. fine arts U. Pitts., 1979-80; lectr., writer, painter. Served with AUS, 1943-46; PTO. Fulbright grantee, 1949-50; Belgium-Am. Ednl. Found. fellow, 1954; Nat. Endowment for the Humanities sr. fellow, 1971-72. Mem. Coll. Art Assn. Am. Club: Century Assn. (N.Y.C.). Author: The Attainment of Delacroix, 1970. Contbr. articles to art publs. Home: 71 Spring St Amherst MA 01002

TRAPP, GERALD BERNARD, journalist; b. St. Paul, May 7, 1932; s. Bernard Edward and Lauretta (Mueller) T.; B.A., Macalester Coll., St. Paul, 1954; m. Bente Joan Moe, Jan. 24, 1954; children—Eric Gerald, Lise Joan, Alex Harold. Editor, Mankato (Minn.) Free Press, 1954-57; with AP, 1957—, nat. broadcast exec. charge sales East of Miss., 1966-68, gen. broadcast news editor, N.Y.C., 1968-79, dep. dir. broadcast services, 1979—, liaison broadcast networks, 1968—; sec. AP Broadcasters, Inc. Mem. Radio TV News Dirs. Assn., Sigma Delta Chi. Presbyterian. Home: 15 Reynal Rd White Plains NY 10605 Office: 50 Rockefeller Plaza New York NY 10020

TRAPP, MARIA AUGUSTA VON, musician, author; b. Vienna, Austria, Jan. 26, 1905 (came to U.S. 1939, naturalized 1948); d. Karl and Augusta (Rainer) Kutschera; student State Tchrs. Coll. Progressive Edn., Vienna; LL.D., St. Mary's Coll., Notre Dame, Ind., 1957; Mus. D., St. Anselms Coll., Manchester, N.H., 1966, St. Michael's Coll., Winooski, Vt., 1971; m. Baron Georg von Trapp, Nov. 26, 1927 (dec. May 30, 1947); children—Rupert, Agathe, Maria, Werner, Hedwig, Johanna Trapp Winter, Martina, Rosemarie, Eleanor Trapp Campbell, Johannes. Concert tours with family, Trapp Family Singers, Europe, S.Am., Central Am., Can., Hawaii, U.S., Australia, New Zealand, 1938-56; organizer Trapp Family Austrian Relief, Inc., pres., 1947; mgr. Trapp Family Lodge, Stowe, Vt., until 1967; dir. Trapp Family Music Camp, 1940-56. Decorated Papal decoration, Bene Merenti medal, 1949, Gold Cross for Meritorious Service (Austria), Austrian Cross of Honor; recipient St. Francis de Sales award, Cath. Writers Guild, Gold Medal award, Nat. Cath. Family Life Conf., named Cath. Mother of the Year, 1957, Lady of Holy Sepulchre, 1951. Club: Cath. Women's of Stowe. Author: The Story of the Trapp Family Singers, 1948; Yesterday, Today and Forever, 1952; Around the Year with the Trapp Family, 1955; A Family on Wheels, 1959; Maria, 1972; When the King Was Carpenter, 1976. Home: Stowe VT 05672

TRASCHEN, ISADORE, educator; b. Newark, Dec. 24, 1915; s. Hyman and Jennie (Abramowitz) T.; B.S., N.Y. U., 1939; M.A., Columbia, 1949; Ph.D., 1952; m. Doris Gibbs, Dec. 21, 1944; children—Julia, Jennie, Ida, Jesse, Frances. Mem. faculty Rensselaer Poly. Inst., Troy, N.Y., 1952—, prof. lit., 1964—; Fulbright lectr. Am. lit. U. Poitiers (France), 1963-64. Organizer peace vigils. Served with USAAF, 1942-45. Decorated Air medals, Bronze Star, Purple Heart; recipient Distinguished Faculty award Rensselaer Poly. Inst., 1976. Editor: Short Fiction: A Critical Collection, 2d edit., 1968; The Drama: Traditional and Modern, 1968. Contbr. articles to profl. jours. Home: RD 5 Box 211 Troy NY 12180 Office: Rensselaer Poly Inst Troy NY 12180

TRASK, DAVID FREDERIC, historian; b. Erie, Pa., May 15, 1929; s. Hugh Archie and Martha (Miller) T.; B.A., Wesleyan U., 1951; A.M., Harvard, 1952, Ph.D., 1958; m. Roberta Kirsch (div. July 1964); children—Noel Hugh, Amanda Ruth; m. 2d, Elizabeth Marie Brooks, Feb. 6, 1965. Instr. polit. economy Boston U., 1955-58; asst. prof. Wesleyan U., Middletown, Conn., 1958-62, U. Nebr., Lincoln, 1962-66; prof. history State U. N.Y. at Stony Brook, 1966-79, chmn. dept., 1969-74; vis. prof. Naval War Coll., 1974-75; dir. Office of Historian, Dept. State, Washington, 1976—; mem. Nat. Hist. Publs. and Records Commn., 1976—. Pres. Portland-Middletown br. NAACP, 1960-61, Lincoln chpt. UN Assn., 1965. Vice chmn. bd. dirs. United Campus Ministries L.I., 1971-72. Served to lt. AUS, 1952-54. Wesleyan U. faculty fellow, 1959, U. Nebr. faculty fellow, 1963, State U. N.Y. faculty fellow, 1967, 73. Mem. Am. Hist. Assn. (chmn. com. undergrad. teaching 1971), Soc. History Am. Fgn. Relations (bd. dirs. 1973-75), Orgn. Am. Historians, Social Sci. History Assn., Phi Beta Kappa, Phi Alpha Theta. Unitarian. Clubs: Cosmos, Fgn. Service. Author: The United States in the Supreme War Council, 1961; General Tasker Howard Bliss and the "Sessions of the World", 1919, 1966; Victory without Peace, 1968; Captains and Cabinets, 1972; (with Samuel Wells, Jr. and Robert H. Ferrell) Ordeal of World Power, 1975. Editor: (with Michael C. Meyer and Roger R. Trask) A Bibliography of United States-Latin American Relations Since 1810, 1968; World War I at Home, 1970. Editorial bd. Jour. Am. History, 1973-76. Home: 3100 Connecticut Ave NW Apt 307 Washington DC 20008

TRASK, FREDERICK KINGSBURY, JR., former banker; b. Short Hills, N.J., Oct. 8, 1907; s. Frederick K. and Katharine Stagg (Jacquelin) T.; A.B., Harvard U., 1930; postgrad. Am. Inst. Banking, 1931-32, N.Y. U. Bus. Extension Coll., 1932-33; m. Margaret Moulton Pope, June 14, 1930; children—Jacquelin (Mrs. A.A. Duffek), Jane (Mrs. Jane T. Freund), Frederick K. III, Frances Pope (Mrs. John M. Wozencraft). With N.Y. Trust Co., N.Y.C., 1930-35; with Farmers Deposit Nat. Bank, Pitts., 1935-46, asst. cashier, 1940-43, asst. v.p., 1943-44, v.p., 1944-46; organized Payson & Trask, 1947, gen. partner, 1947-78; dir. N.Y. Met. Baseball Club, Inc.: cons. dir. Gt. No. Nekoosa Corp., Stamford, Conn., dir. emeritus Gen. Reins. Corp.; trustee U.S. Trust Co. N.Y., 1949-79; asst. dir. Contract Settlement, Washington, 1944-45. Pres., Soc. N.Y. Hosp., 1961-65, bd. govs., 1954—; councilman Borough of Sewickley, 1941-45; del. Pitts. Community Fund Bd., 1940-46; bd. dirs. Family Service Assn., Pitts., 1941-44, 46; bd. dirs. Helen Hay Whitney Found., 1947-78; trustee China Med. Bd. N.Y., 1956-76. Served as maj. Army Service Forces and Finance Dept., AUS, 1942-43, lt. col., 1943-44. Republican. Episcopalian. Clubs: Round Hill (Greenwich, Conn.); Links, Harvard, Union (N.Y.C.); Sea Pines Golf, Plantation (Hilton Head, S.C.). Home: 1 Marsh Dr Hilton Head Island SC 29928

TRASK, HARRY ALBERT, educator; b. Boston, Apr. 15, 1928; s. Harry S. and Bertha (Muise) T.; grad. Eastern Sch. Photography, Boston, 1951; B.A., U. Mass., 1969; M.Ed., Bridgewater State Coll., 1973; m. Joan Mueller, Sept. 24, 1955; children—Mark, Matthew, Peter, Claire, Andrew, Philip, Sarah. Staff photographer Boston Herald Traveler, 1955-73; tchr. history Jeremiah E. Burke High Sch., Boston, 1973—. Recipient Pulitzer prize for photography, 1957; Graflex Diamond award Graflex Camera Co., 1957. Mem. Nat. (winner photo competition 1957), Boston (winner photo competition 1957), press photographers assns. Home: 55 Bancroft Rd Cohasset MA 02025 Office: Jeremiah E Burke High Sch 60 Washington St Boston MA 02121

TRASK, OZELL MILLER, judge; b. Wakita, Okla., July 4, 1909; s. Ozell and Nina (Miller) T.; A.B., magna cum laude, Washburn Coll., 1931; LL.B., Harvard, 1934; m. Barbara Draper, Oct. 2, 1939; children—Deborah, Melinda. Admitted to Kan., Mo. bars, 1934, Ariz. bar, 1940; mem. firm Jennings, Strouss, Salmon & Trask, Phoenix; now judge U.S. Ct. Appeals, 9th Circuit, Phoenix. Bd. dirs. Am. Cancer Soc., dir., past pres. Ariz. div.; pres. bd. dirs. Phoenix YMCA; trustee Phoenix Art Mus. Mem Am., Ariz., Maricopa County bar assns., State Bar Ariz. (past chmn. com. examinations and admissions), Phoenix C. of C. (past pres., dir.), Phi Delta Theta Conglist, (chmn. cabinet). Clubs: Arizona (past pres., dir.), Paradise Valley Country. Home: 6125 N Central Ave Phoenix AZ 85012 Office: Federal Bldg Phoenix AZ 85025

TRAUB, CHARLES, gallery adminstr., photographer; b. Louisville, Apr. 6, 1945; s. David and Jean T.; B.A., U. Ill., 1967; M.A., U. Louisville, 1969, Ill. Inst. Tech., 1971; m. Mary; 1 son, Aaron. Prof. photography Columbia Coll., Chgo., 1971-78, chmn. dept. photography, 1975-78; dir. Light Gallery, N.Y.C., 1978—; one-man shows: Art Inst. Chgo., 1975, Speed Mus., Louisville, 1978; group shows: Addison Gallery, 1979, Bard Coll., 1980, Vision Gallery, Boston; vis. lectr. Internat. Center Photography, N.Y.C., 1979-80; photographer Seagram's Bicentennial Project to document Architecturally Disting. Courthouses in Am., spring and summer, 1975; with Peace corps., Ethiopia, 1968. Served with U.S. Army, 1969. Recipient Hendricks award Ill. Arts Council, 1977. Mem. Soc. Photog. Edn. Contbr. to Modern Photography, Picture Magazine, Cajun Documents (Southern Voices), Beach; documented Cajun people and culture in La., spring 1974. Address: 907 Aislie St Chicago IL 60640

TRAUB, J(OSEPH) F(REDERICK), educator; b. Karlsruhe, West Germany, June 24, 1932; s. Leo H. and Mina (Nussbaum) T.; came to U.S., 1939, naturalized, 1944; B.S., Coll. City N.Y., 1954; Ph.D., Columbia U., 1959; m. Pamela Ann McCorduck, Dec. 6, 1969; children—Claudia Renee, Hillary Anne. Mem. tech. staff Bell Labs., Murray Hill, N.J., 1959-70; prof. computer sci. and math., head dept. computer sci. Carnegie-Mellon U., Pitts., 1971-79; Edwin Howard Armstrong prof. computer sci., chmn. dept. Columbia U., 1979—; Distinguished lectr. M.I.T., 1977; vis. Mackay prof. U. Calif., Berkeley, 1978-79; cons. Lawrence Livermore (Calif.) Lab., 1970-75, Internat. Math. and Statistics Libraries, Houston, 1970—, Math. Software Alliance planning project NSF, 1974-76. Mem. pres.'s advisory com. computer sci. Stanford U., 1972-75, chmn., 1975-76, mem. advisory com. Fed. Judicial Center; mem. sci. council I.R.I.A., Paris, 1976—; mem. central steering com., computing sci. and engring. research study NSF, also liaison to panel on theoretical computer sci. and panel on numerical comp., 1974—; mem. advisory com. Carnegie-Mellon Inst. Research, 1978-79; mem. advisory com. Inst. Def. Analysis, 1976-79; mem. applied math. div. rev. com. Argonne Nat. Lab., 1973-75; mem. adv. com. math. and computer sci. NSF, 1978—. Fellow AAAS (mem. council 1971-74); mem. Conf. Bd. Math. Scis. (council 1971-74), Spl. Interest Group Numerical Math. (chmn. 1966-73), Assn. Computing Machinery (chmn. awards com. 1974-76, chmn. com. on relations between ACM and research computing 1974-75, mem. com. on fellows), Am. Math Soc. Author: Iterative Methods for the Solution of Equations, 1964; (with H. Wozniakowski) A General Theory of Optimal Algorithms, 1980. Editor: Complexity of Sequential and Parallel Numerical Algorithms, 1973; Analytical Computational Complexity, 1976; Algorithms and Complexity: New Directions and Recent Results, 1976. Editor Jour. Assn. Computing Machinery, 1970-76, Jour. Numerical Analysis (Soc. Indsl. and Applied Math.), 1970-76, Transactions on Math. Software, 1974-76, Jour. Computer and System Scis., 1973—, Internat. Jour. on Computers and Math. with Applications, 1974—. Home: 450 Riverside Dr New York NY 10027

TRAUB, MARVIN STUART, dept. store exec.; b. N.Y.C., Apr. 14, 1925; s. Sam D. and Bea (Bruckman) T.; B.A. magna cum laude Harvard U., 1947, M.B.A., 1949; m. Lee Laufer, Sept. 2, 1948; children—Andrew D., James S., Peggy Ann. Trainee Macy's, N.Y.C., 1947-49; asso. buyer Alexander's, N.Y.C., 1949; with Bloomingdale Bros., N.Y.C., 1950—, asst. to v.p., 1950-51, mgr. hosier dept., 1951-52, asst. to chmn., 1952-53, mgr. rug dept., 1953-57, mgr. div. merchandise, 1956-60, v.p. merchandise, 1960-62, exec. v.p., gen. merchandise mgr., 1962-69, pres., from 1969, now chmn., chief exec. officer. Mem. Mayor's Com. in the Pub. Interest, 1975; trustee, mem. bd. Hosp. Joint Diseases and Med. Center; mem. vis. com. Tobe-Coburn Sch. for Fashion Careers; bd. dirs. Am. Health Found., Ednl. Found. of Fashion Inst. Tech.; trustee Nat. Jewish Hosp., Denver; mem. exec. com. Phoenix Theatre; mem. vis. com. Costume Inst., Met. Mus. Art; mem. adv. council vol. Urban Consulting Program, Harvard Bus. Sch. Club of N.Y. Served with AUS, 1942-46. Decorated Purple Heart. Clubs: Sunningdale Country; Harvard (N.Y.C.). Office: Bloomingdale Bros 59th St and Lexington Ave New York NY 10022

TRAUBE, SHEPARD, theatrical producer and dir.; b. Malden, Mass., Feb. 27, 1907; s. William and Helen (Newhouse) T.; student U. Pa., 1925-26; B.S., N.Y. U., 1929; m. Mildred Gilbert, June 29, 1935; children—Victoria, Elizabeth. Producer, dir. Precedent, 1931; No More Frontier, 1932; A Thousand Summers, 1933; Angel Street, 1941, revival, 1976; The Patriots, 1942; The Gioconda Smile, 1950; Time Out for Ginger, 1952; The Girl in Pink Tights, 1952; Holiday for Lovers, 1957; Monique, 1957; Children of the Wind, 1973. Served to maj. U.S. Army, 1943-46. Voted Best Dir., N.Y. Drama Critics, 1942; recipient Sidney Howard prize for Winter Soldiers, Playwrights Co., 1942. Mem. Soc. Stage Dirs. and Choreographers (past pres.), League N.Y. Theatres (gov. 1954—), Dirs. Guild Am. Democrat. Club: Beverly Hills Tennis. Author: Glory Road, 1935; So You Want To Go into the Theatre, 1936. Contbr. articles to profl. jours. Home: 168 W 86th St New York NY 10024 Office: 711 Fifth Ave New York NY 10022

TRAUM, JEROME S., lawyer, lit. agt.; b. Newark, Sept. 26, 1935; s. Max and Evelyn (Fein) T.; A.B., U. Mich., 1956, J.D. with distinction, 1959; m. Lynda Sturner, Apr. 16, 1972; children—David, Norman, Daniel, Edward. Admitted to N.Y. bar, 1960, U.S. Supreme Ct. bar, 1976; asso. firm Chadbourne, Parke, Whiteside & Wolff, N.Y.C., 1959-62; asso. to partner firm Spear and Hill, N.Y.C., 1962-67; partner firm Janklow and Traum, N.Y.C., 1967—; adj. prof. fed. securities regulation Syracuse U. Coll. Law, 1975. Bd. dirs. Open Channel, 1971-77, Call for Action, 1978—; trustee Jose Limon Dance Found., 1968. Mem. Assn. Bar City N.Y., Am. (com. on fed. regulation securities), FCC bar assns., Order of Coif. Club: Marco Polo (N.Y.C.). Home: 935 Park Ave New York NY 10028 Office: 375 Park Ave New York NY 10022

TRAUTLEIN, DONALD HENRY, steel mfg. co. exec.; b. Sandusky, Ohio, Aug. 19, 1926; s. Henry Francis and Lillian Amelia (Russell) T.; student Bowling Green State U., 1946-47; B.S. in Bus. Adminstrn. cum laude, Miami U., Oxford, Ohio, 1950; m. Mary Rankin, Apr. 28, 1956; children—John Russell, James Rankin, Katherine. Bus. trainee Gen. Electric Corp., 1950-51; partner Price Waterhouse & Co., N.Y.C., 1951-76; comptroller Bethlehem Steel Corp. (Pa.), 1977-78, exec. v.p., dir., 1979—. Bd. dirs. Historic Bethlehem, Inc. Served with USN, 1945-46. Mem. Am. Inst. C.P.A.'s, N.Y. State Soc. C.P.A.'s. Episcopalian. Clubs: Univ. (N.Y.C.); Bethlehem, Saucon Valley Country. Home: RFD 1 Coopersburg PA 18036 Office: Bethlehem Steel Corp 8th & Eaton Aves Bethlehem PA 18016

TRAUTMAN, DONALD THEODORE, educator, lawyer; b. Cleve., June 6, 1924; s. William Daniel and Florence Elizabeth (Zimmermann) T.; grad. Western Res. Acad., Hudson, Ohio, 1942;

A.B., Harvard, 1951, LL.B., 1951; m. Susanah Conklin Bailie, Aug. 28, 1954; children—William, Ann, Benjamin. Admitted to D.C. bar, 1953; law clk. to Justice Frankfurter, Supreme Ct. of the U.S., 1952-53; asst. prof. law Harvard, Cambridge, Mass., 1953-56, prof., 1956—, co-chmn. div. grad. studies, 1969-75. Served with AUS, 1943-46. Guggenheim fellow, 1969. Mem. Phi Beta Kappa. Author: (with David R. Herwitz) Amory and Hardee, Materials on Accounting, 3d edit., 1959; (with Arthur T. von Mehren) von Mehren and Trautman, Law of Multistate Problems, 1965. Home: 20 Craigie St Cambridge MA 02138

TRAUTMAN, GERALD HOUGH, transp. co. exec., lawyer; b. Petoskey, Mich., Aug. 27, 1912; s. Newton Ellsworth and Madeline (Hough) T.; B.A., Stanford, 1934; LL.B., Harvard, 1937. Admitted to Calif. bar, 1937, since practiced in San Francisco; partner firm McCutchen, Doyle, Brown, Trautman & Enersen, 1937-65; pres., chief exec. officer Greyhound Corp., 1966-70, chmn. exec. com., 1968—, chmn. bd., chief exec. officer, 1970—, pres., 1977-79, also dir.; pres., dir. Greyhound de Mexico, S.A. de C.V.; dir. Armour & Co., 1969—; dir., mem. exec. com. Armour-Dial, Inc., 1970—; chmn. bd., dir. Greyhound Leasing & Financial Corp., Greyhound Financial & Leasing Corp., A G, Greyhound Computer Corp., Greyhound Computer Can., Ltd., Pinetop Ins. Co.; dir. Air Service Internat., Inc., Border Brokers, Ltd., Brewster Transport Co. Ltd., Carey Transp., Inc., Coachways System, Ltd., Consultants & Designers, Inc., Dispatch Services, Inc., Fla. Export Tobacco Co., Inc., Fla. Parlor Car Tours, Gray Line, Inc., Gray Line N.Y. Tours Corp., Greyhound Airport Service, Inc., Greyhound Food Mgmt., Inc., Greyhound World Tours, Inc., Greyhound Lines, Inc., Greyhound Lines Can. Ltd., Greyhound Rent-A-Car, Inc., Manncraft Exhibitors Service, Inc., Motor Coach Industries, Inc., Motor Coach Industries, Ltd., Post Houses, Inc., Prophet Foods Co., Red Top Sedan Service, Inc., Restaura, S.A., Trade Wind Service, Ltd., Verex Corp., Travelers Express Co., Inc., Lehman Corp., 20th Century Fox Film Corp., Herdez-Mex. Bd. dirs. Salk Inst. Served to lt. USNR, 1944-46. Mem. Am. Bar Assn., U.S. C. of C. (dir.), Delta Kappa Epsilon. Clubs: Golf (Camelback, Phoenix); Links (N.Y.C.); Arizona (Phoenix). Office: Greyhound Tower Phoenix AZ 85077

TRAUTMAN, RAY L., ret. educator, librarian; b. Mowrystown, Ohio, July 22, 1907; s. George H. and Bertha (Parrot) T.; B.S., U. Ky., 1931, M.S., 1932; B.S. in L.S., Columbia, 1940; m. Jane MacDonald, Aug. 20, 1937; children—Eric Ray, Roger Scot. Mgr. bookstore, Lexington, Ky., 1932, San Antonio, Tex. 1933-34; dist. ednl. adviser CCC, Fort Thomas, Ky., 1935-39; with Enoch Pratt Free Library, Balt., 1940; v.p., gen. mgr. Omnibook, Inc., N.Y.C., 1945-48; prof. library service Columbia U., 1948-76; cons. MBA Communications, Inc., N.Y.C., 1978-79; cons. instn. libraries, N.Y. State; cons. Job Corps, Office Econ. Opportunity, Nat. Accreditation Council for Agys. Serving Blind, Corning Glass Works Found. on Libraries, St. Thomas Aquinas Coll.; dir. Swinburne Press. Trustee Yonkers Pub. Library, 1947-58, pres., 1953-54; adviser spl. services div. War Dept. Bd. dirs. Wilderness Resources Center. Served as flying cadet, U.S. Air Corps, 1933, 1st lt. to col., U.S. Army, 1940-46; war dept. observer ETO, 1944-45; comdg. officer Spl. Services Unit Tng. Center, N.Y.C., 1949-62. Awarded Legion of Merit, Conspicuous Service Cross. Author: History of School Library Service Columbia University, 1954; co-author Tech. Dict. of Librarianship (Spanish-English) (Mexico), 1965; A Plan To Provide Library Services to People in N.Y. State Institutions, 1965; Standards for Reading Materials for Blind and Physically Handicapped, 1970. Cons. editor 20 books Individualized Reading series McGraw-Hill, 1966. Home: RFD Rensselaerville NY 12147. *Have a high opinion of yourself. Be prepared and ready for promotion. Be alert to the needs of subordinates and all those less fortunate than yourself and spare no effort to further their aims and aspirations. Never trust a lawyer, banker or politician, in or out of office-in fact, take action in reverse to such advice. Spend some time each week to help correct abuses-write letters of complaint. Take time to help others in trouble with business and government.*

TRAUTMANN, LES RAYMOND, editor; b. S.I., N.Y., July 18, 1918; s. Henry E. and Bertha (Strofield) T.; B.A., Wagner Coll., 1940; M.S., Columbia, 1941; L.H.D., St. Johns U., 1973; m. Virginia Mackoy, Aug. 21, 1943; 1 dau., Julie. Reporter, S.I. Advance, 1940-41, editorial writer, 1946-53, editorial page editor, 1955-60, city editor, 1961-64, mng. editor, 1965—; editor editorial page St. Petersburg (Fla.) Times, 1954-55. Interview show host WNYC-TV, 1970-72. Alumni pres. Wagner Coll., 1953-54. Trustee S.I. Bot. Soc., St. Vincents Med. Center; bd. govs. Daytop Village. Served to capt. AUS, 1942-46. Recipient Distinguished Journalism award Columbia, 1971; Distinguished Citizen award Wagner Coll., 1971. Mem. Am. Soc. Newspaper Editors, Sigma Delta Chi. Democrat. Home: 101 Highland Ave Staten Island NY 10301 Office: 950 Fingerboard Rd Staten Island NY 10305

TRAUTMANN, ROBERT DALE, educator; b. Cleveland, N.D., June 1, 1930; B.A., Jamestown Coll., 1952; M.A., U. No. Colo., 1957, Ed.D., 1964; m. Patricia Ann Doling, Aug. 11, 1954; children—Kurt, Elaine, Sarah, Cynthia, Gretchen. Instr. Central Mich. U., 1960-63; asst. prof. Mich. State U., 1963-67; prof., chmn. dept. curriculum Kan. State Coll., Pittsburg, 1967-70; chmn. div. edn. Baldwin-Wallace Coll., Berea, Ohio, 1970-73, prof., after 1968; chmn. dept. edn. George Peabody Coll. Tchrs., 1973-78; dean Sch. Edn. Valdosta (Ga.) Coll., 1978—. Served with AUS, 1952-54. Mem. Assn. Supervision and Curriculum Devel., Phi Delta Kappa, Kappa Delta Pi. Presbyterian. Home: 2209 Briarcliff Dr Valdosta GA 31601

TRAUTWEIN, GEORGE, orch. condr.; b. Chgo.; s. William Jacob and Hilda (Martin) T.; B.Mus., Oberlin (Ohio) Conservatory, 1951; M.Mus., Cleve. Inst. Music, 1955; Fulbright grantee Mozarteum, Salzburg, 1958; D.Mus., Ind. U., 1961; m. Barbara Wilson; children—Paul, Matthew. Violinist, Indspls. Symphony Orch., 1947-48, Balt. Symphony Orch., 1951-52, Nat. Symphony Orch., Washington, 1952-53, Cleve. Orch., 1953-57, Chautauqua (N.Y.) Symphony Orch., 1953-59, Camerata Acad., Salzburg, 1957-58, Mozarteum Orch., Salzburg, 1958; asso. condr. Dallas Symphony Orch., 1962-66, Mpls. Symphony, 1966-73; music dir. S.D. Symphony, 1971-75, Internat. Congress Strings, Ohio, 1973-75; music dir., condr. Savannah (Ga.) Symphony Orch., 1974-77; music adv., prin. guest condr. Evansville (Ind.) Philharm., 1979-80; music dir., condr. Tuscon Symphony Orch., 1977—; guest appearances with orchs. in U.S., Europe, P.R. and Philippines; mem. faculty U. Minn., U. Tex., Austin, Armstrong (Ga.) State Coll.; arts cons. Nat. Endowment Arts; adv. bd. Avery Fisher Found., N.Y.C. Recipient ASCAP award, 1979. Address: care Tucson Symphony Orch 443 S Stone Ave Tucson AZ 85701

TRAVELSTEAD, CHESTER COLEMAN, former ednl. adminstr.; b. Franklin, Ky., Sept. 25, 1911; s. Conley and Nelle (Gooch) T.; A.B., Western Ky. State Coll., Bowling Green, 1933; M.Music, Northwestern U., 1947; Ph.D., U. Ky., 1950; D.Hum., Morehead State U., 1975; Ph.D., John F. Kennedy U., Buenos Aires, 1975; m. Marita Hawley, Aug. 1, 1936; children—Coleman, Jimmie. Tchr., prin. rural and consol. schs., Mecklenberg County, Va., 1931-32, 33-35; tchr. gen. sci., math., music Picadome High Sch., Lexington, Ky., 1935-37; dir. music Henry Clay High Sch., Lexington, 1937-42; personnel supr. Lexington Signal Dept., Dept. War, 1942-43; supr. music Lexington pub. schs., 1945-47; rep. Investors Diversified Services, Inc., 1947-48; coordinator in-service tchr. edn. Ky. Dept. Edn., 1950-51; asst. prof. edn., asst. dean Coll. Edn., U. Ga., Athens, 1951-53; dean Sch. Edn., U. S.C., Columbia, 1953-56; dean Coll. Edn., U. N.Mex., Albuquerque, 1956-68, acad. v.p., 1968-76, provost, 1976-77. Mem. Nat. Council Accreditation Tchr. Edn., 1960-66, chmn., 1963-65. Served with USNR, 1943-45; PTO. Mem. NEA, Nat. Soc. Study Edn., Soc. Advancement Edn., AAUP, Phi Kappa Phi, Phi Delta Kappa. Author books; contbr. articles in field to profl. jours. Home: 320 Fontana Pl NE Albuquerque NM 87108

TRAVERS, ROBERT MORRIS WILLIAM, educator, psychologist; b. Bangalore, India, Oct. 16, 1913 (came to U.S. 1938, naturalized 1942); s. Morris William and Dorothy (Gray) T.; B.Sc., Univ. Coll. U. London (Eng.), 1935; Ph.D., Columbia, 1942; m. Norma Colcaire, Oct. 19, 1940; children—Michael, David, Deborah. Asso. prof. edn. and psychology U. Mich., 1947-49; asso. prof. edn. Bd. Higher Edn. N.Y.C., 1949-52; research psychologist USAF, 1952-57; prof. ednl. psychology U. Utah, Salt Lake City, 1957-62, head dept. ednl. psychology, 1957-62, dir. Bur. Ednl. Research, 1962-65; Distinguished Univ. prof. Western Mich. U., Kalamazoo, 1965—. Chmn., Kalamazoo Peace Council, 1968-69. Fellow Am. Psychol. Assn. (pres. div. ednl. psychology 1964), Am. Ednl. Research Assn. Author: Educational Measurement, 1954; Introduction to Educational Research, 1958; Essentials of Learning, 1963; The Making of a Teacher, 1975. Address: Coll of Edn Western Mich U Kalamazoo MI 49008

TRAVERS, THOMAS JOSEPH, metal products co. exec.; b. Boston, Jan. 13, 1918; s. Daniel A. and Mary H. (McGarry) T.; A.B. cum laude, Boston Coll., 1939, M.S., 1941; m. Katherine O'Leary, June 29, 1946; children—Thomas Joseph, Stephen, Maureen, Daniel, Richard, Robert. Mgmt. services rep. Ernst & Ernst, Boston, 1946-49; labor relations dir. Comml. Shearing, Inc., Youngstown, Ohio, 1949-61, v.p., 1961—, also vice chmn., sec., dir.; chmn. bd. Comml. Shearing, Inc., Youngstown, 1975; mgr. European ops. Diekirch, Luxembourg, 1963-65; dir. Comml. Hydraulics S.A., Diekirch, Luxembourg, Comml. Hydraulics Ltd., Bedford, Eng., Eurocast S.A., Grevenmacher, Luxembourg, Comml. Hydraulics A.G., Lucerne, Switzerland, Am. Welding & Mfg. Co., Warren, Ohio, Dollar Savs. & Trust Co., Youngstown. Trustee, Youngstown Ednl. Found., Youngstown Hosp. Assn.; pres. Youngstown Community Corp., 1978-79, Indsl. Info. Inst. Mem. Nat. Fluid Power Assn. (dir., chmn. 1978-79). Clubs: Youngstown, Youngstown Country. Home: 230 N Cadillac Dr Youngstown OH 44512 Office: 1775 Logan Ave Youngstown OH 44505

TRAVERSE, ALFRED, clergyman, educator; b. Port Hill, P.E.I., Can., Sept. 7, 1925; s. Alfred Freeman and Pearle (Akerley) T.; S.B., Harvard U., 1946, A.M., 1948, Ph.D., 1951; cert. in Botany, Kings Coll., Cambridge, Eng., 1947; M.Div., Episcopal Theol. Sem. S.W., 1965; m. Elizabeth Jane Insley, June 30, 1951; children—Paul, Martha, John, Celia. Teaching fellow Harvard U., 1947-51; coal technologist U.S. Bur. Mines, Grand Forks, N.D., 1951-55; head Fuels Microscopy Lab., Denver, 1955; palynologist Shell Devel. Co., Houston, 1955-62; cons. palynologist, Austin, Tex., 1962-65; asst. prof. geology U. Tex., Austin, 1965-66; asso. prof. geology and biology Pa. State U., University Park, 1966-70, prof., 1970—; ordained to ministry Episcopal Ch., 1965; asst. priest St. Matthew's Ch., Austin, 1965-66, St. Paul's Ch., Philipsburg, Pa., 1966-75; vicar St. John's Ch., Huntingdon, Pa., 1975—; adj. prof. geobiology Juniata Coll., 1977—; councillor Internat. Commn. Palynology, 1973-77, pres., 1977—; on-bd. scientist Glomar Challenger, 1975. Recipient research grants, NSF, 1966-79, Best Paper award Am. Assn. Stratigraphic Palynologists, 1973. Fellow Geol. Soc. Am., AAAS; mem. Bot. Soc. Am. (sec.-treas. paleobot. sect. 1957-60, chmn. sect. 1960-61), Paleontol. Soc., Internat. Assn. Plant Taxonomists (sec. com. fossil plants 1969—), Am. Assn. Stratigraphic Palynologists (sec.-treas. 1967-70, pres. 1970-71). Club: Harvard of Central Pa. (mem. schs. com. 1966-77). Editorial bd. Catalog Fossil Spores and Pollen, 1957-66; editor-in-chief 1966-76. Home: RD 2 Box 390 Huntingdon PA 16652 Office: 435 Deike Bldg University Park PA 16802. *Characterized from an early age by a love of natural history and born in an Anglican rectory, I have always lived in oscillation between worship of God and helping my fellow humans on the one hand, and research and teaching in the biological-geological science on the other. I have never seen this as paradoxical but rather as natural and personally fulfilling.*

TRAVERSI, DEREK ANTONA, educator; b. Caersws, Wales, Nov. 7, 1912; s. Hugh Antona and Marjorie (Snow) T.; B.A., Merton Coll., Oxford (Eng.), U., 1934, M.A., 1938, B.Litt., 1937; m. Concepcion Vazquez de Castro, Dec. 28, 1944; children—Elizabeth, Margaret, John, Susan, Helen. Dir., Brit. Inst., Barcelona, Spain, 1945-48; rep. Brit. Council for Cultural Relations, Montevideo, Uruguay, 1948-50, Santiago, Chile, 1950-55, Teheran, Iran, 1955-59, Madrid, Spain, 1959-65, Rome, Italy, 1965-70; prof. English lit. Swarthmore (Pa.) Coll., 1970—. Named comdr., Order Brit. Empire, 1970. Author: Shakespeare: the Last Phase, 1954; Approach to Shakespeare, 3d. rev. edit., 1968; Shakespeare: From Richard II to Henry V, 1957; The Roman Plays, 1963; T.S. Eliot: The Longer Poems, 1976. Home: 401 Walnut Ln Swarthmore PA 19081

TRAVIESAS, HERMINIO, TV exec.; b. Sagua La Grande, Cuba, Oct. 1, 1914; s. Juan and Isabel (Negrete) T.; came to U.S., 1917, naturalized, 1939; B.A. in Econs., Princeton, 1935; m. Florence V. Whittemore, Oct. 5, 1946. Classified advt. solicitor N.Y. Am., 1935-36; securities salesman Bristol & Willett, 1936-37; traffic mgr. internat. div. NBC, 1937-47; network sales service mgr. CBS-TV, Inc., 1947-50; v.p., mgr. radio TV dept. Batten, Barton, Durstine & Osborn, Inc., 1950-64, v.p., mgr. Hollywood office, 1964-67; dir. standards practices West Coast, NBC-TV, 1967-69; v.p. broadcast standards NBC, N.Y.C., 1969-77, v.p. broadcast standards policy, 1977—. Served with USAAF, 1943-45; charge radio network broadcast studios SHAEF, Paris. Mem. Acad. TV Arts and Scis., Internat. Radio-TV Exec. Soc., Hollywood Radio and TV Soc. Presbyn. (elder). Clubs: Atlantis Country, Winged Foot Golf, Larchmont Univ., Princeton. Home: 525 S Country Club Dr Atlantis FL 33462 Office: NBC New York NY 10020

TRAVIS, ALBERT HARTMAN, educator; b. Los Angeles, Dec. 22, 1913; s. Hartman Porter and Adelaide (Ball) T.; B.A., U. So. Calif., 1936; M.A., Harvard U., 1938, Ph.D., 1940; m. Lucile A. Diehl, May 8, 1938; 1 dau., Isabel Adelaide Travis Pulvers; m. 2d, Barbara Brown Bettingen, Jan. 25, 1957. Instr. Greek and Latin, Harvard and Radcliffe Coll., 1940-42; asst. prof. U. So. Calif., 1946-47; mem. faculty UCLA, 1947—, prof. classics, 1959-76, prof. emeritus, 1976—, chmn. dept., 1954-62, 65-68, acting chmn., 1975-76. Served to lt. comdr. USNR, 1942-46. Decorated Bronze Star with combat V. Mem. Am. Philol. Assn., Archaeol. Inst. Am. (pres. So. Calif. Soc. 1951-53), Philol. Assn. Pacific Coast (pres. 1960), Calif. Classical Assn. (pres. So. sect. 1946-47), Mediaeval Acad. Am., Mediaeval Assn. Pacific, Renaissance Conf. So. Calif., Wine and Food Socs. So. Calif. and Pasadena (bd. govs. 1958—), Calif. Vintage Wine Soc., Phi Beta Kappa, Phi Kappa Phi, Kappa Alpha. Clubs: Valley Hunt (Pasadena); La Grulla Gun (Baja Calif.). Co-editor: Servianorum in Vergilii Carmina Commentariorum, Vol. III, 1965, prin. editor Vol IV; co-editor U. Calif. Studies in Classical Antiquity, Vols. IV, 1971 and V, 1972. Contbr. articles to profl. jours. Home: 1166 Mill Ln San Marino CA 91108 Office: Dept Classics UCLA Los Angeles CA 90024

TRAVIS, DEMPSEY JEROME, real estate counselor, mortgage banker; b. Chgo., Feb. 25, 1920; s. Louis and Mittie (Strickland) T.; B.A., Roosevelt U., 1949; grad. Sch. Mortgage Banking, Northwestern U., 1969; D.Econs., Olive Harvey Coll., 1974; D.Bus.Adminstrn. (hon.), Daniel Hale Williams U., Chgo., 1976; m. Moselynne Hardwick, Sept. 17, 1949. Pres. Travis Realty Co., Chgo., 1953—, Sivart Mortgage Corp., Chgo., 1949—, Freeway Mortgage & Investment Co., Chgo., 1961—, Dempsey J. Travis Security & Investment Co., Chgo., 1961—, Urban Research Inst., 1969—; dir. Sears Bank & Trust Co., Chgo. Mem. Presdl. Task Force on Urban Renewal, Washington, 1970—; mem. adv. com. Fed. Nat. Mortgage Assn., Washington, 1971—; mem. Fed. Energy Commn.; dir. Nat. Housing Conf. Inc., Washington; mem. Ill. Ins. Consumers Adv. Panel, 1970, Mayor's Adv. Com. Bldg. Code Amendments, 1970, Mayor's Commn. for Preservation Chgo.'s Historic Bldgs. Trustee Northwestern Meml. Hosp., Chgo.; bd. dirs. Chgo. Econ. Devel. Corp. Served with AUS, 1942-46. Certified property mgr., certified real estate counselor. Mem. United Mortgage Bankers Assn. Am. (pres. 1961-74), Dearborn Real Estate Bd. (pres. 1957-59, 70—), Nat. Assn. Real Estate Brokers (1st v.p. 1959-60), Am. Soc. Real Estate Counselors, Chgo. Mortgage Bankers Assn., Inst. Real Estate Mgmt., NAACP (pres. Chgo. 1959-60), Chgo. Art Inst. (life), Field Mus. Nat. Sci. (life), Cosmopolitan C. of C. (dir., vice chmn. ins. com.), Internat. Platform Assn., Beta Gamma Sigma, Lambda Alpha. Clubs: Economics, Executives, Forty of Chgo., Assembly (Chgo.). Author: Don't Stop Me Now, 1970; A 100-Year Odyssey on Black Housing: Chicago 1900-2000, 1977; How Whites Take Back Black Neighborhoods, 1978; Black Chicago: Three Score Plus One, 1979. Office: 840 E 87th St Chicago IL 60619

TRAVIS, IRVEN, mgmt. cons.; b. McConnelsville, Ohio, Mar. 30, 1904; s. Frank Leslie Hattie (Masterson) T.; S.B., E.E., Drexel Inst. Tech., 1926, E.D. (hon.), 1962; S.M., U. Pa., 1928, Sc.D., 1938; m. Helen B. Hartzell, 1932; 1 dau. Leslie Jane (Mrs. Richard Wendel); m. 2d, Anita Schwalbe, Nov. 30, 1935 (dec. Apr. 1969); children—Lane Schofield, William Whipple; m. 3d, Elizabeth Frazer Sauer, Jan. 4, 1972. From instr. to prof. elec. engring. U. Pa., Phila., 1928-49; cons. engr. Gen. Electric Co., 1939-40, Reeves Instrument Corp., 1946-48, Burroughs Corp., 1948-49, dir. research, 1949-52, research v.p., 1952-56, became v.p. research and engring., 1956, v.p. and group exec. def. and space group, dir., 1960-65, v.p. tech. devel., 1965-69, dir. 1950-71; mgmt. cons., Paoli, Pa., 1969—; pres. Burroughs Labs., 1963-65. Trustee Detroit Inst. Tech., Upper Main Line YMCA; chmn. bd. engring. edn. U. Pa. Served from lt. to comdr. USNR, 1941-46. Decorated Naval Commendation. Fellow IEEE; mem. AAAS, Soc. Engring. Edn., Franklin Inst., Soc. Naval Engrs. Insl. Research Inst., Am. Ordnance Assn, Engring. Soc. Detroit, Sigma Xi, Tau Beta Pi, Eta Kappa Nu. Contbr. articles to profl. jours. Clubs: Engineers (Phila.); Detroit Athletic, Economic (Detroit); Waynesboro Country, Ocean Reef. Home: 121 S Valley Rd Paoli PA 19301

TRAVIS, JANET L., coll. pres.; b. Boston, Mar. 6, 1935; d. Francis Ernest and Dorothy May (Sharkey) Evans; A.B. in Geology, Boston U., 1959, M.A. in Philosophy, 1967, Ph.D., 1969; m. Robert U. Travis, Apr. 26, 1962. Instr., U. Nevada, Las Vegas, 1968-69, asst. prof., 1969-72, asso. prof., 1972-74, chmn. dept., 1969-74, acad. counselor, 1973-74; dean humanities and fine arts, asso. prof. philosophy U. No. Iowa, 1974-75, dean humanities, prof., 1976-77; provost, prof. philosophy No. Ky. U., 1977-79; pres. Mansfield (Pa.) State Coll., 1979—. Mem. Am. Assn. Higher Edn., Am. Philos. Assn., Philosophy Sci. Assn., Soc. Study of Evolution, Personalist Discussion Group, Paleontological Soc., Am. Assn. Univ. Adminstrs., Egypt Exploration Soc., Phi Delta Kappa. Home: 75 Academy St Mansfield PA 16933 Office: Mansfield State Coll Mansfield PA 16933

TRAVIS, LEOLA ELIZABETH MADISON, educator; b. Phila., May 22, 1927; d. Alexander and Pauline (Kemp) Madison; B.S., Hampton Inst., 1949; M.A., Marshall U., 1957; Ed.D., Ind. U., 1969; postgrad. W.Va. U., 1955-56, U. Wis., 1960; m. Oneth Morview Travis (dec.). Adminstrv. sec. to dean of instrn. W.Va. State Coll., Inst., 1952-58; mem. faculty dept. bus. and econs. Ky. State U., Frankfort, 1958—, prof., 1969—, acting chmn. dept. bus. and econs., 1973—; cons. IBM, N.Y.C., 1969, Kingston, N.Y., 1970; personnel specialist dept. personnel Ky. State Govt., Frankfort, 1972; liaison officer Danforth Fellowship program, 1975—. Mem. Ky. adv. commn. Study of Electric Rates and Regulations, 1975-76, Ky. Minority Bus. Adv. Council, 1974—, Computer Services Policy commn. Ky. Council on Pub. Higher Edn., 1974-77; mem. Gov.'s Sub-com. on Study of Edn. in Ky., 1977—. Urban League fellow NOAA div. Dept. Commerce, 1977. Mem. Nat., So. bus. edn. assns., Am. Vocat. Assn., AAUP, LWV (treas. bd. dirs. Frankfort-Franklin County Ky. chpt. 1973-77), Nat. Assn. for Tchrs. of Bus. Edn. (sec. bd. dirs. 1975-77), Delta Pi Epsilon, Kappa Delta Pi, Pi Lambda Theta, Alpha Kappa Alpha (chairperson nat. standards com. 1975—). Clubs: Democratic Womens' of Ky., Frankfort-Lexington Links. Office: Box 60 Bradford Hall Ky State Univ Frankfort KY 40601

TRAVIS, MARTIN BICE, educator, polit. scientist; b. Iron Mountain, Mich., Sept. 22, 1917; s. Martin Bice and Helen (Carrett) T.; A.B., Amherst Coll., 1939; student Heidelberg (Germany) U., 1937; M.A., Fletcher Sch. Law and Diplomacy, 1940; Ph.D., U. Chgo., 1948; m. Olivia Brewster Taylor, Nov. 29, 1942; children—Elizabeth Nichols (Mrs. Mugharbil), Helen Willard. Asst. prof. internat. relations Syracuse U., 1948-49; asst. prof. polit. sci. Duke U., 1949-52; asst. prof., then asso. prof. polit. sci. Stanford U., 1953-61; prof. polit. sci. SUNY at Stony Brook, 1961—, coordinator State U. N.Y. at Am. U. Beirut (Lebanon), 1972-73; chmn. dept., 1961-68, dir. Inst. Am. History and Govt., 1964—; vis. prof. Sch. Internat. Affairs, Columbia, 1956-57; vis. summer prof. U. Guadalajara (Mex.), 1959, 62, U. Wash., 1961. Bd. dirs. State U N.Y. Inst. Am. Studies in France, 1976-77; cons. to industry. Mem. sch. bd. Cold Spring Harbor, N.Y., 1965-71, v.p., 1967-68, pres., 1968-69. Served with USAAF, 1942-45. Ford Found. grantee 1960-61. Mem. Acad. Polit. Sci., Am. Soc. Internat. Law, Council Fgn. Relations, Phi Delta Theta, Phi Delta Kappa. Author: (with E.E. Robinson) Powers of the President in Foreign Affairs, 1966. Co-editor, contbr. Control of Foreign Relations in Modern Nations, 1957; bd. editors Western Polit. Quar., 1956-58; adv. bd. Almanac of Current World Leaders, 1957—; editoral critic for book pubs. Home: 533 Cold Spring Harbor Rd Syosset NY 11791 Office: Dept Polit Science SUNY Stony Brook NY 11794

TRAVIS, MERLE ROBERT, country music singer, songwriter; b. Rosewood, Ky., Nov. 29, 1917; s. William Robert and Laura Etta (Latham) T.; student public sch., Muhlenburg County, Ky.; children—Patricia, Chelene, Rebecka. Debut with Knox County Knockabouts, Sta. WGBF, Evansville, Ind., 1937-38; appeared with Tennessee Tomcats, Sta. WGBF, 1938; appeared in road shows with Clayton McMichen's Georgia Wildcats, 1939, Drifting Pioneers, 1939-42; appeared on program Hometown Jamboree, Hollywood, Calif., 1944-50, Town Hall Party, Hollywood, 1953-59, Hollywood

Barndance, CBS, 1945-47, Renfro Valley (Ky.) Barndance, 1938-39, Gene Autry's Melody Ranch, CBS Radio, Hollywood, 1954-58, Grand Ole Opry, Nashville, 1960's, also numerous other TV and radio appearances; master of ceremonies, various shows; rec. artist; songs written include: Sixteen Tons, 1945, Smoke, Smoke, Smoke, 1947, Bayou Baby, 1948, Sweet Temptation, 1949, others. Served with USMC, 1942-43. Named to Songwriters Hall of Fame, 1970, Country Music Hall of Fame, Nashville, 1977, Gibson Guitar Hall of Fame, 1979; recipient 7 Gold Records, Capitol Records, 1945-68, 12 Broadcast Music, Inc. awards, 1947-69, Country Music Pioneer award, 1979. Mem. AFTRA, Screen Actors Guild, Musicians Union, Nashville Assn. Musicians, Nat. Acad. Rec. Arts and Scis. (Grammy award 1976), Country Music Assn., Writers Guild Am., Acad. Country Music. Designer solid body guitar, built first by Paul A. Bigsby. Office: care Buddy Lee Attractions Inc 38 Music Sq E Suite 300 Nashville TN 37203

TRAVIS, STEPHEN MICHAEL, govt. research ofcl.; b. Charlotte, N.C., July 1, 1942; s. Milton B. and Rosa (Kingloff) T.; B.A. in History, U. Ga., 1964, postgrad., 1964-66. Reporter, Atlanta Constn., 1966, Washington Post, 1966-67; community action specialist OEO, Washington, 1968-70; dir. publs. U.S. Conf. Mayors, Washington, 1971; cons. govt., politics, Washington, 1972-74; press dir. Mineta for Congress, San Jose, Calif., 1974; asso. Kingloff-Travis Realty, Atlanta, 1975; researcher Carter Campaign and Transition, Atlanta and Washington, 1976-77; dir. Research Office, The White House, Washington, 1977-78, dir. research domestic policy staff, 1978—. Served with U.S. Army, 1960. Democrat. Jewish. Office: Domestic Policy Staff The White House Washington DC 20500

TRAVOLTA, JOHN, actor; b. Englewood, N.J., Feb. 18, 1954; s. Salvatore and Helen (Burke) T. Appeared TV series Welcome Back Kotter, 1975—; films include: Carrie, 1976; Saturday Night Fever, 1977; Grease, 1978; Moment-By-Moment, 1978; Urban Cowboy, 1980; Boy in the Plastic Bubble (TV), 1976; rec. artist album, 1976, 77. Recipient Billboard award for Best New Male Vocalist, 1976, also Record World and Music Retail Mag.; Best Actor award Nat. Bd. of Rev.; named one of best actors Nat. Soc. Film Critics, N.Y. Film Critics Circle; named best actor, recipient Golden Apple award Cue Mag. nominated for Best New Male Star, Women's Press Club, 1976; nominated as best actor Nat. Acad. Motion Picture Arts and Scis. Office: care Lemond/Zetter Inc 5160 Genesta Ave Encino CA 91316

TRAXLER, BOB, congressman; b. Kawkawlin, Mich., July 21, 1931; B.A. in Polit. Sci., Mich. State U., 1953; LL.B., Detroit Coll. Law, 1959; children—Tamara, Bradley. Admitted to Mich. bar; asst. prosecutor Bay County, 1960-62; individual practice; mem. Mich. Ho. of Reps., 1963-74, majority floor leader, 1965-66, chmn. judiciary com., 1969-74; mem. 93d-96th Congresses from 8th Dist. Mich. Served with U.S. Army, 1954-56. Mem. Am., Mich., Bay County bar assns. Democrat. Episcopalian. Office: 2448 Rayburn House Office Bldg Washington DC 20515

TRAYLOR, ORBA FOREST, economist, lawyer, educator; b. Providence, Ky., June 16, 1910; s. Eddie Ewing and Dillie (Stuart) T.; B.A., Western Ky. U., 1930; M.A., U. Ky., 1932, Ph.D., 1948; J.D., Northwestern U., 1936; m. Josephine Zananiri, Nov. 17, 1945; children—Joseph Marion, Robert Forest, John Christopher. Head dept. econs. Ashland Coll., 1935-36; legal asst. trust dept. 1st Nat. Bank, Chgo., 1936-37; asso. prof. econs., sociology Western Ky. U., 1938-40; research asst. Bur. Bus. Research, U. Ky., 1939; research dir. Ky. Legislative Council, 1939-41; admitted to Ky. bar, 1941; dir. research and statistics Ky. Dept. Welfare, 1941; asso. econ. analyst div. tax research U.S. Treasury Dept., 1942; acting chief accounting UNRRA, Balkan Mission, 1944-45; asst. prof. econs. and bus. U. Denver, 1946-47, U. Mo., 1947-50; tax specialist, asst. econ. commr. ECA, Greece, 1950-53; coordinator exec. devel. programs Ordnance Corps, Dept. Army, 1954; pub. finance expert UN, lectr. financial adminstrn. Inst. Pub. Adminstrn., Egypt, 1954-56; exec. asst. to lt. gov. Ky. Legislative Research Commn., Frankfort, 1956-58; commr. finance State of Ky., Frankfort, 1958-59; dir. finance Office High Commr. Ryukyu Islands, 1960-64, dir. econ. affairs, 1964-65; prof. econs. and pub. adminstrn. U. Ala., Huntsville, 1965-75, chmn. dept. bus. and pub. adminstrn., 1966-68, chmn. econs., 1968-70; vis. prof. pub. adminstrn. San Diego State U., 1975-76, Western Ky. U., 1976-77; fin. economist AID, U.S. State Dept., 1977-78; adj. prof. Ala. A&M U., 1978—; cons. ops. research Johns Hopkins, 1957-61; fiscal cons. various orgns.; vis. lectr. econs. various univs. and colls.; lectr. U. Md. Far East Div., 1960-65, Ala. A&M U., 1976-77, Fla. Inst. Tech., 1977; sr. adv. Bank of Ryukyus, 1960-65, Joint Fgn. Investment Bd., 1964-65; chmn. bd. Ryukyuan Devel. Loan Corp., 1960-65, Joint Petroleum Bd., 1960-65; counsellor Oak Ridge Asso. Univs., 1966-67. Mem. Ala. Edn. Study Commn. Fin. Task Force, 1968-69; chmn. fin. com. Top of Ala. Health Planning Agy., 1974-75. Served with AUS, 1942-46; lt. col. Res. (ret.). Mem. Am., So. econs. assns., Am. Soc. for Pub. Adminstrn. (council 1973-75), Am., Ky. bar assns., Nat. Tax Assn. (dir. 1971-74), Res. Officers Assn., Beta Gamma Sigma, Delta Sigma Pi. Democrat. Baptist. Rotarian. Mem. editorial bd. Public Adminstrn. Rev., 1973-79; contbr. articles to profl. publs. Address: 216 Westmoreland Huntsville AL 35801

TRAYNOR, HARRY SHEEHY, consultant; b. Lexington, Ky., Sept. 4, 1911; s. John Hanrahan and Augusta (Sheehy) T.; B.S. in Mech. Engring., U. Ky., 1935; m. Helen Mae Ingalls, June 28, 1941; children—Martha Ingalls (Mrs. Paul J. Sweeney), Harry Sheehy. Test engr. Aerofin Corp., Newark, 1935; air conditioning, refrigeration engr. Carrier Corp., Newark, also Syracuse, N.Y., 1935-42; pres., gen mgr. Regent Knitting Co., Inc., Syracuse, 1946-50; contract sales mgr. Remington Corp., Auburn, N.Y., 1950-54; spl. asst. to gen. mgr., asst. gen. mgr. adminstrn. AEC, 1954-64, asst. to gen. mgr., 1964-71; asst. to dean Grad. Sch., coordinator research U. Ky., Lexington, 1972-73, cons. Inst. Mining and Minerals Research, 1974—, Ky. Center for Energy Research, 1976—; exec. officer U.S. del. Internat. Conf. on Peaceful Uses of Atomic Energy, Geneva, 1955. Chmn., Met. Environ. Improvement Commn., Lexington, 1975. Mem. U. Ky. Research Found. Served from 2d lt. to lt. col. C.E., AUS, 1942-46. Decorated Legion of Merit; recipient Distinguished Alumni award U. Ky., 1965. Mem. Am. Soc. Heating and Air Conditioning Engrs. (asso.), AAAS, Pi Kappa Alpha, Pi Tau Sigma. Roman Catholic. Clubs: Lafayette, Kiwanis, Spindletop (Lexington). Home: 1336 Prather Rd Lexington KY 40502

TRAYNOR, J. MICHAEL, lawyer; b. Oakland, Calif., Oct. 25, 1934; B.A., U. Calif., Berkeley, 1955; J.D., Harvard U., 1960; m. Shirley Williams, Feb. 11, 1956; children—Kathleen, Elizabeth, Thomas. Admitted to Calif. bar, 1961, U.S. Supreme Ct. bar, 1966; dep. atty. gen. State of Calif., San Francisco, 1961-63; spl. counsel Calif. Senate Com. on Local Govt., Sacramento, 1963; asso. firm Cooley, Godward, Castro, Huddleson & Tatum, San Francisco, 1963-69, partner, 1969—; vice chmn. San Francisco Spl. Cts. Com., 1971-75; mem. Joint Commn. on Fair Jud. Election Practices, 1976—, Calif. Chief Justice's Com. on Appellate Practices and Procedures, 1977—; acting and vice chmn. San Francisco Neighborhood Legal Assistance Found., 1967. Trustee Head-Royce Sch., Oakland, 1974—, Lawyers Com. for Civil Rights Under Law, 1976—; trustee Sierra Club Legal Def. Fund, 1974—, treas., 1979—. Fellow Am. Bar Found.; mem. Am. Law Inst., Am. Bar Assn., Am. Judicature Soc., Calif. State Bar, Bar Assn. San Francisco (pres. 1973), Lawyers Club San Francisco. Contbr. articles to legal jours. Home: 3131 Eton Ave Berkeley CA 94705 Office: 20th Floor Alcoa Bldg One Maritime Plaza San Francisco CA 94111

TRAYNOR, ROGER JOHN, educator, former judge; b. Park City, Utah, Feb. 12, 1900; s. Felix and Elizabeth (O'Hagan) T.; A.B., U. Calif., 1923, J.D., 1927, Ph.D., 1927, LL.D., 1958; LL.D., U. Chgo., 1960, U. Utah, 1963, Boston Coll., 1968; m. Madeleine Lackmann, August 23, 1933; children—Michael, Joseph, Stephen (dec.). Instr. polit. sci. U. Calif. at Berkeley, 1926-29, prof. law, 1929-40; acting dean, 1939; dep. atty. gen. Calif., 1940; asso. justice Supreme Ct. Calif., 1940-64, chief justice, 1964-70; prof. law U. Va., U. Colo., U. Utah, Hastings Coll. Law, San Francisco, 1970—; Goodhart prof. legal sci. Cambridge (Eng.) U., 1974-75. Chmn. Nat. News Council, 1973-74. Cons. expert U.S. Treasury Dept., 1937-40; cons. tax counsel State Bd. Equalization Calif., 1932-40; lectr. Inst. Am. Studies, Salzburg, summer, 1956. Mem. Am. Law Inst. (mem. council), Am. Acad. Arts and Scis., Phi Beta Kappa, Order of Coif. Home: 2643 Piedmont Ave Berkeley CA 94704 Address: Hastings Coll Law 198 McAllister St San Francisco CA 94102

TREADGOLD, DONALD WARREN, educator, historian; b. Silverton, Oreg., Nov. 24, 1922; s. Frederic Vere and Mina Belle (Hubbs) T.; B.A., U. Oreg., 1943; M.A., Harvard U., 1947; D.Phil. (Rhodes scholar 1947), U. Oxford (Eng.), 1950; m. Alva Adele Granquist, Aug. 24, 1947; children—Warren Templeton, Laura Margaret, Catherine Mina. Mem. faculty U. Wash., Seattle, 1949—, prof. history, 1959—, chmn. dept., 1972—; vis. prof. Nat. Taiwan (Taipei) U., 1959; vis. research prof. USSR Acad. Scis., Moscow, 1965, Toyo Bunko, Tokyo, 1968. Chmn. Far Western Slavic Conf., 1961-62, Conf. on Slavic and East European History of Am. Hist. Assn., 1965, mem. council, 1960-63; chmn. joint com. Slavic studies Social Sci. Research Council and Am. Council Learned Socs., 1962-64; chmn. organizing com. XIV Internat. Congress Hist. Scis., San Francisco, 1975; mem. acad. council Kennan Inst. for Advanced Russian Studies, 1977—; trustee Nat. Council Soviet and E. European Research, 1977—. Trustee Bush Sch., 1973-76. Served to capt. AUS, 1943-46. Decorated Bronze Star; recipient E. Harris Harbison award, 1968. Ford fellow, 1954-55; Rockefeller grantee, 1959, 61; Guggenheim fellow, 1964-65; Phi Beta Kappa vis. scholar, 1974-75. Mem. Am. Hist. Assn. (mem. council 1970-73, v.p. Pacific Coast br. 1977-78, pres. 1978-79), Am. Assn. Advancement Slavic Studies (dir. 1968-75, Distinguished Service award 1975, pres. 1977-78), Am. Assn. Rhodes Scholars, Phi Beta Kappa (council nominating com. 1973—, chmn. 1977—), Sigma Delta Pi. Author: Lenin and His Rivals, 1955; The Great Siberian Migration, 1957; Twentieth Century Russia, 4th edit., 1976; The West in Russia and China, 2 vols., 1973; A History of Christianity, 1979; also articles; editor: The Development of the USSR, 1964; Soviet and Chinese Communism, 1967; Slavic Review, 1961-65, 68-75; (with P.F. Sugar) A History of East Central Europe, Vols. V-IX, 1974-77. Home: 4507 52d Ave NE Seattle WA 98105

TREADWAY, LYMAN HAMBRIGHT, III, banker; b. Cleve., Dec. 29, 1929; s. Lyman H. and Martha (Sawyer) T.; B.A., Yale, 1952; LL.B., Case Western Res U., 1959; m. Nancy B. Kadow, Aug. 15, 1959; children—Katherine, Jennifer, John. Admitted to Ohio bar, 1959; exec. v.p., chmn. exec. com. Western Res. Life Assurance Co. Ohio, Cleve., 1959-68; chief exec., chmn. bd. 1st Nat. Bank Ashland (Ohio) and 1st Citizens Bank Greencastle (Ind.), 1969-73; pres., dir., chief exec. officer, chmn. bd. Union Commerce Bank, Cleve., 1974—; pres., chief exec. officer, dir. Union Commerce Corp., Cleve., 1979—; dir. Merriman Constrn. Co., Cleve., Forest City Enterprises, Inc., Cleve. Treas., trustee United Torch, 1974—; mem. vis. com. Sch. Mgmt., Case Western Res. U., 1974—, bd. overseers, 1975—; trustee Cleve. Inst. Music, 1970—, Greater Cleve. Growth Assn., 1974—, Ohio Bur. Drug Abuse, 1971—, Cleve. Mus. Health, 1973—, Ednl. Research Council, 1974—; bd. overseers Cleve. Scholarship Program, 1975—, Hathaway Brown Sch., 1978—, Downtown Cleve. Corp., 1975—, No. Ohio Opera Assn., 1976—, Playhouse Sq. Assn., 1974—, Univ. Sch. Alumni Council, 1976—; mem. nat. adv. council SBA, 1978. Mem. Ohio Bar Assn., Young Pres. Orgn. Office: Union Commerce Bank 917 Euclid Ave Cleveland OH 44115

TREADWELL, HUGH WILSON, publishing exec.; b. Waurika, Okla., Nov. 21, 1921; s. Hugh and Jessie Ellen (Cogdell) T.; B.A., U. Okla., 1949, M.A., 1952; diploma in French Studies (Rotary Found. fellow), Institut de Touraine, U. Poitiers (France), 1950; m. Edith Albena Doolittle, June 20, 1959; children—Pamela, Hugh, Cynthia. Asst. editor internat. lit. quar. Books Abroad, U. Okla., 1952-53; field rep. coll. dept. The Macmillan Co., 1953-60; field rep. coll. dept. Holt, Rinehart & Winston, Inc., Okla. and Tex., 1960-62, mgr. coll. programs in fgn. lang. dept., N.Y.C., 1962-67; sr. editor coll. dept. Random House-Knopf, N.Y.C., 1967-72; dir. U. N.Mex. Press, Albuquerque, 1973—; instr. French, U. Okla., 1952-53. Industry rep. Nat. Com. Support of Fgn. Langs., 1971. Served with USAAF, 1943-46. Decorated Air medal. Mem. Phi Beta Kappa. Democrat. Club: Sierra-Vista Tennis (Albuquerque). Home: 4321 Cobblestone Pl NE Albuquerque NM 87109 Office: U New Mexico Press Albuquerque NM 87131. *In my mind, the pursuit of happiness has always been bound up with the pursuit of knowledge—knowledge not in a purely abstract sense, but purposeful knowledge humanely applied. The professions of teaching and publishing, if practiced in the light of the highest ethical standards associated with each, make this pursuit possible and offer the greatest satisfaction to those who view life as I do. I consider myself fortunate to have served in both of these professions.*

TREADWELL, MARY, bus. exec.; b. Lexington, Ky., Apr. 8, 1941; d. James William and Ollie B. (Davis) Miller; student Fisk U., 1959-60, Ohio State U., 1960-64, Franklin Sch. Bus., 1962-63, Antioch Sch. of Law, 1975—. Buyer, mdse. coordinator E.L. Schottensteins, Inc., Columbus, Ohio, 1961-65; founder, co-exec. dir. Youth Pride, Inc., Washington, 1967-72, exec. dir., 1971—; pres. Pride Environ. Sers. Inc., Sticks & Stones, Inc., P.I. Properties, Inc., Washington. Mem. Center for Study of Presidency, Nat. Bicentennial Ethnic Racial Council, D.C. Citizens for Better Pub. Edn.; mem. steering com. Nat. Peoples Coalition for Justice; chairwoman Nat. Capital Head Start, 1970-71. Bd. dirs. Urban Law Inst., 1977-78, Nat. Citizens Com. on Population and Am. Future, 1972-73. Mem. Internat. Platform Assn., Am. Mgmt. Assn., Nat. Council of Negro Women (life), D.C. C. of C. Home: 411 7th St SE Washington DC 20001 Office: 1536 U St NW Washington DC 20009

TREANOR, WALTER GLADSTONE, lawyer; b. N.Y.C., Feb. 19, 1922; s. Frank Eugene and Jane Brice (Arthur) T.; B.A., Principia Coll., 1943; J.D., Washington U., St. Louis, 1949; m. Betty Bartlett, June 29, 1946; children—Steven B., Susan Jane. Admitted to Mo. bar, 1949, Cal. bar, 1959; atty. Fanchon & Marco Enterprises, St. Louis, 1949-51; commerce atty. Mo. Pacific R.R., St. Louis, 1951-58; gen. atty. Western Pacific R.R., San Francisco, 1958-69, gen. counsel, 1970-73, v.p. law, 1973—. Instr., Golden Gate Coll., San Francisco, 1959-62; instr. Chabot Jr. Coll., Hayward, Calif., 1964-68; city atty. St. Ann, Mo., 1951-56, Breckenridge Hills, Mo., 1956-58. Commr., Contra Costa County Civil Service Commn., 1965—, pres., 1969-73. Served to lt. USNR, 1943-46; ETO, PTO. Named Man of Yr., Orinda, Calif., 1966. Mem. Nat. Assn. R.R. Trial Counsel, Calif. Bar Assn., Delta Theta Phi. Republican. Clubs: Contra Costa Country (Pleasant Hill, Calif.); World Trade (San Francisco). Home: 5 Keith Dr Orinda CA 94563 Office: 526 Mission St San Francisco CA 94105

TREASH, LEONARD WILSON, opera producer and dir., educator; b. Akron, Ohio, Jan. 1, 1909; s. Harvey Beaumont and Bernice (Pugsley) T.; B.Music, Cin. Conservatory Music, 1931; grad. degree in music, Curtis Inst. Music, 1938; m. Martha Fenton, Dec. 28, 1932; children—Leonard, Dorothy Jane Treash Flanagan. Concert and opera singer, 1931-47; head voice and opera depts. Baldwin Wallace Conservatory, Berea, Ohio, 1943-47; head opera dept. Eastman Sch. Music, 1947-76, chmn. voice dept., 1966-76; dir. Buffalo Opera Workshop, 1949-62; co-dir. Oglebay Opera Workshop, Wheeling, W.Va., 1954-61; founder, dir. Opera Under the Stars, Rochester, N.Y., 1953-68; dir. Chatham Opera Workshop, Pitts., 1963-66; prof. opera Toronto U., 1976-79; prof., head opera dept. U. Tex., Austin, 1977-78; gen. dir. Chautauqua (N.Y.) Opera Assn., 1966—; mem., chmn. Fulbright screening com., 1962-66. Recipient nat. award Nat. Fedn. Music Clubs Best Opera Voice award, 1935; award for service to music in Rochester, Sigma Alpha Iota, 1970. Mem. Nat. Opera Assn. (founder, 1st pres.), Central Opera Service (dir.), Am. Guild Musical Artists, Opera Am., Phi Mu Alpha. Republican. Methodist. Producer 7 world premieres of operas; producer more than 100 operas. Home: 18 Tuxford Rd Pittsford NY 14534

TREASURE, JOHN ALBERT PENBERTHY, coll. dean; b. Usk, Monmouthsire, Eng., June 20, 1924; s. Harold Paul and Constance (Shapland) T.; Ph.D., Cambridge U., 1956; m. Valerie Bell, Apr. 1954; children—Julian, Simon. Research officer Brit. Market Research Bur., Ltd., London, 1952-56, mng. dir., 1957-60; dir. research and mktg. J. Walter Thompson Co., Ltd., London, 1960-66, chmn., 1967-73, vice chmn., 1973-76; dean City University Bus. Sch., London, 1978—; dir. J. Walter Thompson Co., N.Y.C. Mem. Ashridge Mgmt. Coll. Mktg. Com.; friend Royal Coll. Physicians; trustee Found. for Bus. Responsibilities; vis. fellow U. Lancaster. Fellow Inst. Practitioners in Advt. (past pres.); mem. Royal Econ. Soc. (council), Market Research Soc. (past pres.). Contbr. articles to profl. jours. Home: Cholmondeley Lodge Friars Ln Richmond Surrey England Office: City U Bus Sch Lionel Denny House 23 Goswell Rd London EC1M 7BB England

TREAT, WILLIAM WARDWELL, judge; b. Boston, May 23, 1918; A.B., U. Maine, 1940; M.B.A., Harvard U., 1947. Admitted to Maine bar, 1945, N.H. bar, 1949, U.S. Supreme Ct. bar, 1955; judge N.H. Probate Ct., Exeter, 1958—; pres., chmn. bd. Hampton Nat. Bank, 1958—; faculty Nat. Center for State Judiciary, Reno, 1975—; chmn. N.H. Jud. Council, 1976; adv. bd. Nat. Center for State Cts., 1973—; pres. Nat. Coll. Probate Judges, 1968—. Bd. dirs., v.p. Hundred Club of N.H. Mem. Am. Law Inst., Am., N.H. bar assns. Author: Treat on Probate, 3 vols., 1968; Local Justice in the Granite State, 1961; contbr. articles to profl. jours. Home: PO Box 498 Hampton NH 03842 Office: 100 Winnacunnet Rd Hampton NH 03842

TREBILCOCK, PAUL, portrait painter; b. Chgo., Feb. 13, 1902; s. William Paul and Adele Christine (Christensen) T.; grad. Oak Park and River Forest High Sch., 1920; student U. Ill., 1920-22, Art Inst. Chgo., 1922-24; m. Amaylia Chiarina Castaldo, Apr. 8, 1929; children—William Anthony, Adrienne Claire. Principal works: portraits of notable persons, including: President Franklin D. Roosevelt, Governor Albert A. Ritchie, Mrs. Reginald Vanderbilt, Viscountess Furness, Harold W. Dodds, Stephen Francis Voorhees, Charles H. Warren, Edward Shelton, Willard C. Rappleye, Charles Proctor Cooper, Dr. William G. MacCallum, Dr. Edwards A. Park, Dr. George E. Bennett, Dr. E.V. McCollum, David Kinley, George Eastman, Rush Rhees, Harvie Branscomb, Walter Dill Scott, Irving S. Cutter, George I. Haight, Oliver C. Carmichael, Francis Henry Taylor, Bishop Horace W. B. Donegan, Benjamin F. Fairless, Mrs. Benjamin F. Fairless, Wilfred S. Sykes, Cleo F. Craig, Walter S. Franklin, William B. Storey, Carle C. Conway, K. S. Adams, Harrison Jones, Charles Hayden, Lucius M. Boomer, George O. May, Harold H. Helm, Clarence C. Michalis, James E. Gowan, J. Hamilton Cheston, Edwin S.S. Sutherland, Alfred H. Cosden, C. Brewster Rhoads, others. Recipient Martin B. Cahn prize, 1925, William Randolph Hearst prize, 1926, Frank G. Logan medal and prize, 1928, William H. French gold medal, 1929, Municipal Art League Portrait prize, 1937 (all recieved at Chicago Art Inst.), first prize $1,000 Chicago Galleries Assn., 1926, 1st Hallgarten prize NAD, N.Y., 1931; Newport (R.I.) Art Assn. prize. Mem. NAD. Clubs: Arts, Tavern, Cliff Dwellers (Chgo.); Chelsea Arts (London); Century Assn. (N.Y.C.). Studio: 44 W 77th St New York City NY 10024

TREBILCOTT, JAMES JOSEPH, utility co. exec.; b. Kansas City, Mo., June 20, 1917; s. William Henry and Catherine (Curran) T.; B.S., U. Mo., 1938; postgrad. Harvard, 1942, Mass. Inst. Tech., 1942, U. Mich., 1952; m. Maureen E. Ball, Dec. 16, 1944; children—Katherine, Michael. With Pub. Service Co. Okla., 1946-48; with Mich. Wis. Pipe Line Co., Detroit, 1948—, v.p., chief ops. officer, dir., 1960-72, exec. v.p., dir., 1973—; v.p., chief ops. officer, dir. Am. La. Pipe Line Co., Detroit, 1960-66; v.p., dir. Am. Natural Gas Prodn. Co., 1962—; exec. v.p., dir. Am. Nat. Alaskan Co., 1979—, Am. Natural Offshore Co., 1975—; pres., dir. Am. Nat. LNG Corp., ANR LaSalle LNG Transmission Corp., ANR Elba LNG Transmission Corp. (all 1979—); dir. Gt. Lakes Gas Transmission Co., Alaska N.W. Transmission Corp. Served to capt. USAAF, 1942-46. Mem. Engring. Soc. Detroit, Greater Detroit Bd. Commerce, Detroit Econ. Club, Newcomen Soc., Am., Midwest (chmn.), So. gas assns., Ind. Natural Gas Assn., Internat. Gas. Union (com. mem.). Clubs: Detroit Athletic, Detroit, Detroit Golf, Circumnavigators (pres., dir.) (Detroit), Rotary, K.C. Home: 3 Alger Pl Grosse Pointe MI 48230 Office: 1 Woodward Ave Detroit MI 48226

TREBUS, ROBERT STANLEY, advt. exec.; b. E. Orange, N.J., Feb. 8, 1933; s. Stanley Walter and Sophie (Berman) T.; B.A., Duke U., 1954; postgrad. Seton Hall U., 1954-55; m. Dorothy J. Ilgunas, Jan. 3, 1963; children—Christopher, Tami. Tech. rep., promotion mgr. Union Carbide Chems., N.Y.C., 1955-62; account exec. Marsteller, Inc., N.Y.C., 1962-65, account supr., Brussels, 1965-67, gen. mgr. Brussels office, 1967-70, exec. Y.p., N.Y.C., 1970—; dir. Chipark Services, N.Y.C. Served with U.S. Army, 1956-58. Mem. Internat. Advt. Assn. (v.p.), Bus./Profl. Advt. Assn. Roman Catholic. Clubs: Beacon Hill; Baltusrol Golf. Home: 16 Upper Warren Way Warren NJ 07060 Office: 866 3d Ave New York NY 10022

TRECKELO, RICHARD M., lawyer; b. Elkhart, Ind., Oct. 22, 1926; s. Frank J. and Mary (Ferro) T.; A.B., U. Mich., 1951, J.D., 1953; m. Anne C. Kosick, June 25, 1955; children—Marla, Mary. Admitted to Ind. bar, 1953; since practiced in Elkhart; partner firm Thornburg McGill, Deahl, Harman, Carey & Murray, Elkhart, South Bend, Ind., also Washington, 1971—. Sec. Skyline Corp., Elkhart, 1959—, dir., 1961—; dir. Valley Fin. Sers., Inc., Stoutco, Inc., Bristol, Ind. Pres., bd. dirs. Elkhart Legal Aid Soc. Elkhart; 1973. Served with USAAF, 1945-46. Mem. Elkhart City (pres. 1975), Ind., Am., Elkhart County, bar assns., Ind. Soc. Chgo., Elkhart C. of C. Republican. Clubs: Summit (bd. govs. 1971-73) (South Bend); Elcona Country. Office: First Nat Bank Bldg Elkhart IN 46514

TRECKER, FRANCIS JULIUS, machinery mfg. co. exec.; b. Milw., Dec. 17, 1909; s. Theodore and Emma (Pufahl) T.; student Marquette U. Sch. Bus. Adminstrn., 1928-32; B.S. in Mech. and Adminstrv. Engring., Cornell U., 1935; m. Dorothy G. Knowles, 1968. With Pratt & Whitney Aircraft Corp., Hartford, Conn., Pratt & Whitney Machine Tool Corp., 3 years; cons. engr. Stevenson, Jordan & Harrison, Inc., N.Y.C., 3 years; various mfg. and sales dept. positions Kearney & Trecker Corp., Milw., asst. chief engr., 1938-43, sec., 1943-47, pres., dir., 1947, chmn., 1968—, chief exec. officer, 1968-73; chmn., dir. Trecker Aircraft Corp., 1954-59; vice-chmn. Cross & Trecker Corp., Bloomfield Hills, Mich., 1979—; v.p., dir. Milw. Community Devel. Corp.; dir. Kearney & Trecker, Ltd., Eng., KTTK, Tokyo, 1968-73. Trustee, Ripon Coll., 1952-71, Council Tech. Advancement, 1952—, Am. Heritage Found., Ducks Unlimited. Expert cons. to Sec. War for subcontracting and facilities procurement, 2 years; cons. to sec. air force, 1964-68, chmn. air force ad hoc com. vice chmn. Tools for Freedom; chief of engring. and subcontracting OPM and WPB, 1 year, also dep. dir. def. contract service WPB; mem. tool advisory com. Munitions Bd., 1948. Chmn. legislative com. Wis. Aero. Advisory Bd., 1944, Milw. Citizens Com. on Aviation, 1944; dir. Greater Milw. Com., 1946-57. Fellow in perpetuity Met. Mus. Art, N.Y.C. Mem. Nat. Machine Tool Builders Assn. (dir. 1950-53, 59-62, pres. 1961-62), ASME, Am. Soc. Tool Engrs., Wis. C. of C. (chmn. aviation com.), Am. Arbitration Assn., Young Presidents Orgn. (dir. 1952-58), Chief Execs. Forum (pres. 1962-63), Shikar Safari, Air Power League (charter), Nat. Aero. Assn. (life). Office: 11000 Theodore Trecker Way Milwaukee WI 53214

TRECKER, HARLEIGH BRADLEY, educator; b. Cabery, Ill., Feb. 11, 1911; s. William Henry and Henrietta (Goodberlet) T.; B.S., George Williams Coll., Chgo., 1934; A.M., U. Chgo., 1938; m. Audrey Ricker, Nov. 10, 1932; children—Jerrold Bradley, James Ernest. Field supr., exec. dir. Chgo. Leisure Time Service, 1934-38; instr., dir. field work George Williams Coll., 1938-41; asso. prof. Sch. Social Work, U. So. Calif., Los Angeles, 1941-49, prof., 1949-51; prof. Sch. Social Work, U. Conn., Storrs, 1951-68, Univ. prof., 1968-77, Univ. prof. emeritus, 1977—, scholar in residence Sch. Social Work, 1979, dean Sch. Social Work, 1951-68, mem. dean's adv. com. Fed. Welfare Agys., 1965-68; vis. lectr. Ohio State U. Sch. Social Adminstrn., 1950; inst. leader N.Y. Sch. Social Work, summer 1950, also state confs. social work in various states, Boston U. Sch. Social Work, 1953; cons. community recreation surveys, 1956—; chmn. nat. recruitment com. Council of Social Work Edn., 1953, dir., 1955-57; mem. dean's adv. com. to sec. HEW, 1956; chmn. Gov.'s Com. Mentally Retarded Children, 1956; chmn. edn. recreation div. Chgo. Council Social Agys., 1939-41; chmn. Gov.'s Commn. on Human Services, 1960; mem. exec. bd. Welfare Council Met. Los Angeles, 1945-47, chmn. research dept. com., 1949-51; chmn. Conn. Commn. on Youth Services, 1963-65 mem. citizen's adv. com. welfare Conn. Welfare Dept., 1963-70. Library of U. Conn. Sch. Social Work named in his honor, 1977. Mem. Am. Assn. Social Workers, Nat. Conf. Social Work (sec. 1953-54), Am. Assn. Group Workers (mem. exec. bd. 1945-50, pres. 1954-55), Conf. Nat. Agencies and Profl. Schs. of Group Work and Recreation (chmn. 1952-53), Conn. Conf. Social Work (mem. exec. bd. 1951-54), Nat. Assn. Social Workers (chmn. nat. nominating com. 1956, chmn. council social work adminstrn. 1964-66), AAUP, Alpha Kappa Delta, Kappa Delta Pi. Author: Group Process in Administration, 1946; Social Group Work-Principles and Practices, 2d rev. edit., 1955; Supervision of Group Work and Recreation (with Hedley S. Dimock), 1949; Group Process in Administration, rev., 1950; (with Audrey Trecker) How to Work with Groups, 1952; Social Agency Board Member Institutes-An Analysis of the Experience of Eighteen Cities, 1952; (with Frank Z. Glick and John C. Kidneigh) Education for Social Work Administration, 1953; (with Audrey Trecker) Committee Common Sense, 1954; Building the Board, 1954; (with Audrey R. Trecker) Handbook of Community Service Projects, 1960, Working with Groups, Committees, and Communities, 1979; editor: Group Work-Foundations and Frontiers, 1955; Group Work in Psychiatric Setting, 1956; New Understandings of Administration, 1961; Group Services in Public Welfare, 1964; Citizen Boards, at Work-New Challenges to Effective Action, 1970; Social Work Administration: Principles and Practices, 1971, 2d edit., 1977; Social Group Work: Principles and Practices, 1972; Goals for Social Welfare 1973-1993: An Overview of the Next 20 Years, 1973. Contbr. articles to profl. jours. Home: 2404 Adams Ct Sanford FL 32771

TREDINNICK, GEORGE DONALD, banker; b. Wilkes Barre, Pa., June 8, 1926; s. Dell Roy and Magdalene (Smith) T.; ed. U. Pa. Evening Sch. Accounts and Finance, 1953, U. Wis. Sch. for Bank Adminstrn., 1961; m. Myrtal Dodd Hartman, Mar. 4, 1949; children—Donna Lee Tredinnick McWilliams, Donald Glenn, Dale Jayne Tredinnick Morgan. Fiscal accounts clk. VA, Phila., 1946-47; with Fidelity Bank, Phila., 1948-78, auditor, 1965-78, v.p., 1966-78; v.p. Flagship Banks Inc., Miami, Fla., 1978-79, Southeast First Nat. Bank Miami, 1980—; instr., U. Wis. Sch. for Bank Adminstrn., 1970-71; lectr. Pa. Sch. Banking, Bucknell U., 1970, mem. adv. com., 1972-75, asso. dir., 1975-76, dir., 1976-77. Ordained deacon, elder United Presbyterian Ch. Served with AUS, 1944-46. Chartered bank auditor; cert. internal auditor. Mem. Bank Adminstrn. Inst. (dir. Phila. 1967-75, pres. 1973-74, mem. audit commn. 1972-74), Inst. Internal Auditors (gov. Phila. 1972-78, pres. 1975-76). Home: 7520 SW 174th St Miami FL 33157 Office: 1111 Lincoln Road Mall Miami Beach FL 33139

TREDWAY, JOHN THOMAS, coll. pres.; b. North Tonawanda, N.Y., Sept. 4, 1935; s. Harold and Melanya (Scorby) T.; B.A., Augustana Coll., 1957; M.A., U. Ill., 1958; B.D., Garrett Theol. Sem., 1961; Ph.D., Northwestern U., 1964; m. Carol Christine Andersen, Sept. 10, 1960; children—Daniel John, Rebecca Elizabeth. Instr. history Augustana Coll., Rock Island, Ill., 1964-65, asst. prof., 1965-69, asso. prof., 1969-71, prof., 1971—, v.p. acad. affairs, 1970-75, pres., 1975—; vis. prof. ch. history Waterloo Lutheran Sem., 1967-68. Trustee St. Katherine's Sch., Davenport, Ia. Mem. Am. Hist. Assn., Am. Soc. Ch. History, Phi Beta Kappa, Omicron Delta Kappa. Lutheran. Club: Rock Island Arsenal. Editor: Immigration of Ideas, 1968. Home: 3601 11th Ave Rock Island IL 61201

TREE, MARIETTA PEABODY, city planner; b. Lawrence, Mass.; d. Malcolm Endicott and Mary Elizabeth (Parkman) Peabody; student La Petite Ecole Florentine, Florence, Italy, 1934-35; student U. Pa., 1936-39, LL.D., 1964; L.H.D., Russell Sage Coll., 1962, Bard Coll., 1964, Hobart and William Coll., 1967; LL.D., Drexel Inst. Tech., 1965; hon. degrees Franklin Pierce Coll., Coll. New Rochelle, Skidmore Coll.; m. Desmond FitzGerald, Sept. 2, 1939; 1 dau., Frances; m. 2d, Ronald Tree, July 28, 1947; 1 dau., Penelope. With hospitality div. Office Coordinator Inter-Am. Affairs, 1942-43; researcher Life mag., 1943-45; mem. Fair Housing Practices Panel, N.Y.C., 1958; mem. bd. commrs. N.Y.C. Commn. on Human Rights, 1959-61; U.S. rep. to Human Rights Commn. of UN, 1961-64, mem. U.S. delegation to UN, 1961; U.S. rep. Trusteeship Council of UN with rank of ambassador, 1964-65; mem. staff U Thant, UN Secretariat, 1966-67; partner Llewelyn-Davies Assos., city planners, 1968—; dir. CBS, Pan Am. Airways, U.S. Trust Co., N.Y.C., Lend-Lease Corp. (Australia), Internat. Income Properties, Salomon Bros. Internat. Ltd. Del. N.Y. State Constl. Conv., 1967; mem. N.Y. State Democratic Com., 1954-60; mem. civil rights com. Dem. Adv. Council, 1959-60. A founder Sydenham Hosp., interracial hosp., N.Y.C., 1943; past bd. dirs. UN Assn., Citizens Housing and Planning Council, Center Internat. Studies-N.Y. U., African-Am. Inst.; bd. dirs. Asia Soc.; trustee U. Pa., chmn. bd. overseers Sch. Fine Arts. Mem. Pilgrim Soc., Council Fgn. Relations. Episcopalian. Home: One Sutton Pl South New York NY 10022

TREE, MICHAEL, violinist, violist; b. Newark, Feb. 19, 1934; s. Samuel and Sada (Rothman) Applebaum; diploma, Curtis Inst. Music, 1955; D.F.A. (hon.), U. South Fla., 1976; m. Johanna Kreck, Sept. 8, 1966; children—Konred Efrem, Anna Louise. Violin recital debut at Carnegie Hall, 1954; soloist with maj. orchs. and at maj. internat. festivals, 1958—; founding mem. Guarneri String Quartet, 1964—; rec. artist for RCA, Columbia, Vanguard records. Faculty, Harper Coll., Binghamton, N.Y., 1964-68, Curtis Inst. Music, 1968—. Home: 45 E 89th St New York NY 10028 Office: care Harry Beall Mgmt Inc 119 W 57th St New York NY 10019

TREEN, DAVID CONNER, gov. La.; b. Baton Rouge, July 16, 1928; s. Joseph Paul and Elizabeth (Speir) T.; B.A., Tulane U., 1948, LL.B., 1950; m. Dolores Yvonne Brisbi, May 26, 1951; children—Jennifer Anne Treen Neville, David Conner and Cynthia Treen Lunceford (twins). Admitted to La. bar, 1950; with firm Deutsch, Kerrigan & Stiles, New Orleans, 1950-51; v.p. Simplex Mfg. Corp., New Orleans, 1952-57; mem. firm Beard, Blue, Schmitt & Treen, New Orleans, 1957-74; mem. 93d-96th Congresses from 3d Dist. La., chmn. Ho. Republican Study Com., 1978; gov. State of La., 1980—; Rep. candidate for Congress, 1962, 64, 68, for gov. of La., 1972, 79; del. Rep. Nat. Conv., 1964, 68, 72, 76, chmn. La. del., 1968, 72, mem. Rep. Platform Com., 1976, La. Rep. Central Com., 1962—; Rep. nat. committeeman, 1972-74. Chmn. exec. com. Jefferson Parish, 1962-67. Served as 1st lt. USAF, 1951-52. Mem. La. Bar Assn., Order of Coif, Phi Delta Phi, Kappa Sigma. Methodist. Club: Metairie (La.) Country. Office: Office of Gov State Capitol Baton Rouge LA 70804

TREFETHEN, LLOYD MACGREGOR, educator; b. Boston, Mar. 5, 1919; s. Francis Lord and Harriet (Nichols) T.; B.S., Webb Inst. Naval Architecture, 1940; M.S., Mass. Inst. Tech., 1942; Ph.D., Cambridge U., Eng., 1950; m. Florence Marion Newman, May 17, 1944; children—Gwyned, Lloyd. Engr. Gen. Electric Co., Schenectady, 1940, 42-44; sci cons. Office Naval Research, Am. Embassy, London, 1947-50; tech. aide to chief scientist Office Naval Research, exec. sec. Naval Research Adv. Com., Washington, 1951; exec. sec. Nat. Sci. Bd., tech. aide to dir. NSF, Washington, 1951-54; asst. prof. of mech. engr. Harvard U., 1954-58; prof. of mech. engring. Tufts U., Medford, Mass., 1958—, chmn. dept. mech. engring., 1958-70; cons. to Gen. Electric Co., 1955—; NSF fellow Cambridge (Eng.) U., 1956; vis. prof. U. Sydney, Australia, 1964-65, 72, 79; vis. fellow Battelle Seattle Research Center, 1971; sr. vis. scientist Commonwealth Sci. and Indsl. Research Orgn., Melbourne, Australia, 1972; hon. research asso. Harvard U., 1978; vis. prof. Stanford U., 1979. Served with USN, 1944-46. Recipient Golden Eagle award CINE Soc., 1967, honors Am. Film Festival, 1965, 66, Le Prix de Physique, 5th Internat. Sci. Film Festival, Lyon, 1968 (for films on surface tension phenomena). Mem. Soc. Naval Architects and Marine Engrs., ASME, Sigma Xi, Tau Beta Pi. Home: 23 Barberry Rd Lexington MA 02173

TREFFERT, DAROLD ALLEN, psychiatrist, hosp. supt.; b. Fond du Lac, Wis., Mar. 12, 1933; s. Walter O. and Emma (Leu) T.; B.S., U. Wis., 1955, M.D., 1958; m. Dorothy Marie Sorgatz, June 11, 1955; children—Jon, Joni, Jill, Jay. Resident in psychiatry U. Wis. Med. Sch., 1959-62, asso. clin. prof. psychiatry, 1965—; chief children's unit Winnebago (Wis.) Mental Health Inst., 1962-64, supt., 1964—; supt. Central State Hosp., Waupun, Wis., 1977—; dir. Dodge County Mental Health Center, Juneau, Wis., 1964—; mem. staff St. Agnes Hosp., Fond du Lac, 1963—. Chmn. Controlled Substances Bd. Wis.; mem. critical health problems com. Wis. Dept. Pub. Instrn. Diplomate Am. Bd. Psychiatry and Neurology. Fellow Am. Coll. Psychiatrists; mem. AMA, Wis. Med. Soc. (pres. 1979-80), Wis. Psychiat. Assn. (pres.), Assn. Med. Supts. Mental Hosps., Alpha Omega Alpha. Contbr. articles to profl. jours. Home: 2334 Maplewood Ln Fond du Lac WI 54935 Office: Winnebago Mental Health Inst Winnebago WI 54985. *People often spend too much time regretting what they are not and far too little time savoring that which they are.*

TREFFINGER, KARL EDWARD, architect; b. Columbus, Ohio, Oct. 21, 1927; s. Raymond Hartman and Eldred (Ruffner) T.; B.A., Yale U., 1948, M.Arch., 1951; m. Beverly Jean Beck, Mar. 29, 1957; children—Kathy Anne, Julia Frances, Karl Raymond, Frederick Charles. Various archtl. positions, Colo. and Ohio, 1954-57; draftsman Edward Durell Stone, Palo Alto, Calif., 1957-58; designer Wurster, Bernard & Emmons, San Francisco, 1958-60; pvt. practice architecture, San Francisco, 1960-78; prin. Treffinger, Walz & Macleod, Architects and Planners, San Francisco, 1978—. Served to lt. USN, 1951-54; Korea. Fellow AIA. Republican. Club: San Geronimo Nat. Country. Archtl. projects include: Harbor Point Apts., Strawberry Peninsula, Calif., Hyde/Lombard homes, San Francisco, Park Newport, Newport Beach, Calif., Telegraph Hill apts., San Francisco, Walden, Schaumburg, Ill. Home: 24 Tamarack St San Geronimo CA 94963 Office: 50 Green St San Francisco CA 94111

TREFFTZS, KENNETH LEWIS, educator; b. Sparta, Ill., Dec. 28, 1911; s. John Sidney and Dorothy Nora (Wright) T.; B.S., U. Ill., 1936, M.S., 1937, Ph.D., 1939; m. Ellen Lois Ryniker, Aug. 7, 1937; children—Jeffrey Lewis, Ellen Sterling. Asst. economist, com. on bank research Ill. Bankers Assn., 1937-39; instr. Carnegie Inst. Tech., 1939-41; asst. prof. finance U. So. Calif., Los Angeles, 1941-45, asso. prof., 1945-50, prof., 1951—, head dept. finance, 1945-57, head dept. finance and real estate, 1959-66, chmn. dept. finance and bus. econs., 1966-71; vis. asso. prof. U. Calif. at Los Angeles, 1948; vis. asso. prof. sch. bus. adminstrn. U. Wash., 1949-50; instr. Pacific Coast Banking Sch., Seattle, summer, 1949; dir., chmn. bd. Comstock Fund, Inc., Am. Gen. Enterprise Fund, Inc., Total Return Fund, Inc., Harbor Fund, Inc., Pace Fund, Inc.; dir. Source Capitol Inc., Colwell Co., Fremont Gen. Corp. Conf. dir. Ann. Inst. Finance, So. Calif., 1962, 63, 64; cons. (under AID) U. Karachi (Pakistan), 1962. Recipient Dean's award Grad. Sch. Bus., U. So. Calif., 1963; Teaching Excellence award U. So. Calif., 1974-75, Assos. award for excellence in teaching, 1977. Mem. Am., Western (pres. 1955-56) econ. assns., Western (pres. 1965-66), Am. (v.p. 1946-48), fin. assns., Beta Gamma Sigma, Phi Kappa Phi, Rho Epsilon, Omicron Delta Epsilon, Lambda Alpha, Beta Alpha Psi, Alpha Kappa Psi. Author: Mathematics of Banking and Finance, 1944; (with E.J. Hills) Mathematics of Business and Accounting, 1947; (with E.J. Hills) Mathematics of Business, Accounting and Finance, 1956; (with Harold Dilbeck) Some Current Practices in Capital Budgeting, also What Put the Stock Market Where It Is. Contbr. articles to profl. jours. Home: 5402 Weatherford Dr Los Angeles CA 90008

TREFONAS, LOUIS MARCO, educator; b. Chgo., June 21, 1931; s. Peter and Eugenia (Xidis) T.; B.A., U. Chgo., 1951, M.S., 1954; Ph.D., U. Minn., 1959; m. Gail Haley Thames, Nov. 10, 1957; children—Peter, Stephanie, Jennifer, Mark, Paul, Jason. Asst. prof. U. New Orleans, 1959-62, asso. prof., 1962-66, asso. prof., chmn. chemistry dept., 1963-66, prof., chmn., 1966—. Named hon. research asso. Harvard, 1972-73. NIH Spl. fellow, 1972-73. Mem. Am. Chem. Soc., Am. Crystallographic Assn., Am. Phys. Soc., AAUP, Sigma Xi. Author: Integrated Laboratory Sequence Vols. 1 and 2, 1967. Contbr. articles to profl. jours. Home: 22 Bluebird Dr New Orleans LA 70124

TREFRY, RICHARD GREENLEAF, army officer; b. Newburyport, Mass., Aug. 6, 1924; s. Raymond Hale and Elizabeth (Johnson) T.; B.S., U.S. Mil. Acad., 1950; m. Jacquelyn Lou Dahlkoetter, Nov. 10, 1969. Commd. 2d lt. U.S. Army, 1950, advanced through grades to lt. gen.; dir. human resources devel. Office Dep. Chief of Staff for Personnel, Dept. Army, Washington, 1975, asst. dep. chief of staff for personnel, 1975-76, dir. mgmt. Office of Chief of Staff, Dept. Army, 1976-77; insp. gen. Hdqrs. Dept. Army, Washington, 1977—. Decorated Legion of Merit, others. Mem. Assn. U.S. Army, Armor Assn. Episcopalian. Club: Appalachian Mountain. Home: 12750 Wycklow Dr Clifton VA 22024 Office: Dept of Army Office of Insp Gen Washington DC 20310*

TREIMAN, EDWARD, elec. engr.; b. Toledo, Iowa, July 29, 1910; s. Samuel E. and Dorothy (Walker) T.; B.S. in Elec. Engring., Iowa State Coll., 1933, E.E., 1943; m. Selma White, June 24, 1942; children—Sue, Terri, Larry. With Western Electric Co., Chicago and New York, engring., research and transcontinental line experimentations, 1933-37; asst. purchasing agent Allied Machinery Corp., Feb.-Sept. 1937; with Internat. Western Electric Co., 1938-39; mng. dir. Nat. Electric Light Assn., 1946-52; cons. engr., Chgo., 1952—; sec. St. Lawrence Commn. of U.S., 1944-46, Second Nat. Radio Conf., 1945. Commd. 1st lt., Signal Corps, U.S. Army, 1937, later capt.; served in U.S. and France. Mem. Am. Inst. E.E., Edison Electric Inst., NAM, Tau Beta Pi, Delta Upsilon. Republican. Clubs: Union League, Univ., Recess (N.Y.C.); Univ. (Chgo.). Address: 2918 W Fargo St Chicago IL 60645

TREIMAN, JOYCE WAHL, artist; b. Evanston, Ill., May 29, 1922; d. Rene and Rose (Doppelt) Wahl; A.A., Stephens Coll., 1941; B.F.A. (grad. fellow 1943), State U. Iowa, 1943; m. Kenneth Treiman, Apr. 25, 1945; 1 son, Donald. One man shows include Paul Theobald Gallery, Chgo., 1942, John Snowden Gallery, Chgo., 1945, Art Inst. Chgo., 1947, North Shore Country Day Sch., Winnetka, Ill., 1947, Fairweather-Garnett Gallery, Evanston, 1950, Edwin Hewitt Gallery, N.Y.C., 1950, Palmer House Galleries, Chgo., 1952, Glencoe (Ill.) Library, 1953, Elizabeth Nelson Gallery, Chgo., 1953, Charles Feingarten Gallery, Chgo., 1955, Cliff Dwellers Club, Chgo., 1955, Fairweather-Hardin Gallery, Chgo., 1955, 58, 73, Marian Willard Gallery, N.Y.C., 1960, Felix Landau Gallery, Los Angeles, 1961, 64, Adele Bednarz Gallery, Los Angeles, 1969-71, 74, La Jolla (Calif.) Mus. 1962-72, Palos Verdes (Calif.) Art Mus., 1976, Forum Gallery, N.Y., 1963, 66, 75; numerous exhbns. including Carnegie Internat., 1955, 57, Met. Mus., 1950, Whitney Mus., 1951, 52, 53, 58, Art Inst. Chgo., 1945-59, John Herron Art Inst., 1953, Library of Congress, 1954, Cocoran Gallery, 1957, Pa. Acad. Fine Arts, 1958, Mus. Modern Art, 1962, Am. Acad. Arts and Letters, N.Y.C., 1974, 75, 76, Retrospective Exhbn., Municipal Art Gallery, Los Angeles, 1978; represented in permanent collections Denver Mus. Art, State U. Iowa, Ill. State Mus., Long Beach (Calif.) Mus., Whitney Mus. Am. Art, N.Y.C., Tupperware Art Mus., Orlando, Fla., Art Inst. Chgo., Utah State U., Abbott Labs., Oberlin Allen Art Mus., Internat. Mineral Corp., Pasadena Art Mus., U. Calif. at Santa Cruz, Grunwald Found., U. Calif. at Los Angeles; vis. prof. San Fernando Valley State Coll., 1968; lectr. U. Calif. at Los Angeles, 1969-70; vis. prof. State U. Calif., Long Beach, 1977. Recipient numerous awards including Logan purchase prize Art Inst. Chgo., 1951, Martin B. Cahn prize, 1959, 60, Pauline Palmer prize, 1953, Saratosa Am. Painting Exhbn. award, 1959, Ford Found. purchase prize, 1960, Purchase prize Ball State Coll., 1961, prize La Jolla Art Mus., 1961, Purchase prize Pasadena Art Mus., 1961. Tiffany fellow, 1947; Tupperware Art Fund fellow, 1955; Tamerind Lithography fellow, 1961. Address: 712 Amalfi Dr Pacific Palisades CA 90272. *I paint what I see, feel, and think about my own reality. I hope to leave an "after image" that is meaningful to others, as well as to myself.*

TREIMAN, SAM BARD, educator; b. Chgo., May 27, 1925; s. Abraham and Sarah (Bard) T.; student Northwestern U., 1942-44; S.B., U. Chgo., 1948, S.M., 1949, Ph.D., 1952; m. Joan Little, Dec. 27, 1952; children—Rebecca, Katherine, Thomas. Mem. faculty Princeton, 1952—, instr., 1952-54, asst. prof., 1954-58, asso. prof., 1958-63, prof. physics, 1963—. Served with USNR, 1944-46. Mem. Am. Phys. Soc., Nat. Acad. Sci., Am. Acad. Arts and Scis. Author: (with M. Grossjean) Formal Scattering Theory, 1960; (with R. Jackiw and D.J. Gross) Current Algebra and Its Applications, 1972. Contbr. articles to profl. jours. Home: 60 McCosh Circle Princeton NJ 08540

TREINEN, SYLVESTER WILLIAM, bishop; b. Donnelly, Minn., Nov. 19, 1917; s. William John and Kathryn (Krausert) T.; student Crosier Sem., Onamia, Minn., 1935-41; B.A., St. Paul's Sem., 1943. Ordained priest Roman Cath. Ch., 1946; asst. pastor in Dickinson, N.D., 1946-50; sec. to bishops Ryan and Hoch, 1950-53; asst. pastor Cathedral Holy Spirit, Bismarck, N.D., 1950-57; chancellor Diocese Bismark, 1953-59; asst. pastor St. Anne's Ch., Bismarck, 1957-59; pastor St. Joseph's Ch., Mandan, N.D., 1959-62; bishop Boise, Idaho, 1962—. Address: PO Box 769 Boise ID 83701*

TREISTER, GEORGE MARVIN, lawyer; b. Oxnard, Calif., Sept. 5, 1923; s. Isadore Harry and Augusta Lee (Bloom) T.; B.S., UCLA, 1943; LL.B., Yale U., 1949; m. Jane Goldberg, Jan. 24, 1946; children—Laura, Neil, Adam, Dana. Admitted to Calif. bar, 1950; law clk. to chief justice Cal. Supreme Ct., 1949-50, to Hugo L. Black, asso. justice U.S. Supreme Ct., 1950-51; asst. U.S. atty. So. Dist. Calif., 1951-53; dep. atty. gen. Calif., 1953; practiced in Los Angeles, 1953—; mem. firm Stutman, Treister and Glatt, 1953—; instr. U. So. Calif. Law Sch., 1954—, Stanford U. Law Sch., 1977—; vice chmn. Nat. Bankruptcy Conf.; mem. advisory com. on bankruptcy rules Jud. Conf. U.S. Served with USNR, 1943-46. Mem. Am. Law Inst., Am. Judicature Soc. Contbr. articles to profl. jours. Home: 282 S San Rafael Ave Pasadena CA 91105 Office: 3701 Wilshire Blvd Los Angeles CA 90010

TREIT, ELROY MALCOLM, clergyman; b. Wilkie, Sask., Can., Mar. 6, 1933; s. Henry and Hilda (Rosnau) T.; A.A., Concordia Coll., 1953, B.A., 1954; B.D., Concordia Sem., 1959; M.S. in Sociology, Simon Fraser U.; m. Carol Jean Schneider, Jan. 29, 1960; children—Jonathan, Matthew, Marla Jean. Ordained to ministry Luth. Ch., 1959; pastor Parish Killarney Park Luth. Ch., Vancouver (B.C., Can.), 1959—; 2d v.p. Alta.-B.C. Dist. Lutheran Ch. of Can., 1970—, dir. fund raising, 1971—, family life dir. Western Region, 1972-76; pres. Luth. Ch. of Can., 1977—; mem. Fed. Family Life Bd.; counsellor ABC Dist. for women's orgns.; lectr. in seminars on human sexuality. Bd. dirs Vancouver YMCA, 1961-76; adv. B.C. Human Resources Dept., 1976-79. Mem. Profl. Counsellors Assn. of Province B.C., Luth. Laymen's League, Luth. Women's Missionary League (counsellor). Conservative. Research, publs. in philately, early 1960's. Home: 3871 Hurst St Burnaby BC V5J 1M4 Canada Office: 3022 E 49th St Vancouver BC V5J 1K9 Canada

TRELEASE, ALLEN WILLIAM, educator, historian; b. Boulder, Colo., Jan. 31, 1928; s. William, Jr. and Helen (Waldo) T.; A.B., U. Ill., 1950, M.A., 1951; Ph.D., Harvard U., 1955; children—William C., Mary E., John A. Mem. faculty Wells Coll., Aurora, N.Y.,

1955-67, prof. history, 1965-67, chmn. dept. history and govt., 1963-67; prof. history U. N.C. at Greensboro, 1967—. Mem. Am., So. hist. assns., Orgn. Am. Historians, AAUP, Phi Beta Kappa, Phi Kappa Phi, Phi Eta Sigma, Phi Kappa Psi. Author: Indian Affairs in Colonial New York: The Seventeenth Century, 1960; White Terror: The Ku Klux Klan Conspiracy and Southern Reconstruction, 1971; Reconstruction: The Great Experiment, 1971. Home: 307 Kirk Rd Greensboro NC 27408

TRELEASE, RICHARD MITCHELL, JR., bishop; b. Berkeley, Calif., Apr. 16, 1921; s. Richard Mitchell and Ruth (Walker) T.; B.A., U. Mo., 1943; B.D., Ch. Div. Sch. Pacific, 1945, D.D., 1966; D.S., U. of South, 1972; m. Jean Ronayne, July 2, 1943; children—Richard Mitchell III, Christopher, Phyllis Hope. Ordained priest Episcopal Ch., 1945; curate St. Andrew's Cathedral, Honolulu, 1945; vicar, rector St. Christopher's Ch., Kailua, St. John's-by-the-Sea, Keneohe, 1947-50; rector St. Andrew's Cathedral, Honolulu, 1950-54, dean, 1954, St. Andrew's, Wilmington, Del., 1954-61, St. Paul's Episcopal Ch., Akron, Ohio, 1962-71; bishop Diocese of Rio Grande (New Mexico and S.W. Tex.), 1971—. Pres. Akron Ministerial Alliance, pres. Inpost, Akron, 1966-68, Goodwill Industries Akron, 1965-68; chmn. Kent State Chaplaincy Com., 1963; adv. com. United Community Council Akron, 1968-70, Poverty Program Akron, 1968-70, Eye Bank Akron, 1965-71; pres. N.Mex. Inter-Ch. Agy., 1974—; mem. Nat. Coalition for Ordination Women, Episcopal Ch., 1975—; mem. Nat. Commn. Regional and Local Ecumenism Nat. Council Chs., 1975—; mem. N.M. Humanities Council, 1974—. Bd. dirs. Tb Soc., Multiple Sclerosis Soc., Planned Parenthood Soc., Youth Service Advisory; v.p. Newcastle County Council Chs.; pres. People's Settlement; trustee Ch. Div. Sch. Chs.; pres. People's Settlement; trustee Ch. Div. Sch. Pacific, 1969-75, Episcopal Radio TV Found.; mem. adv. bd. Bataan Hosp. and Lovelace Clinic; bd. dirs. Santa Fe Opera Guild, 1973-74; adv. bd. Episcopal Theol. Sem. of Southwest. Mem. Aloha Tau Omega, Psi Chi. Rotarian (asso. mem.; trustee 1961-71). Office: PO Box 4130 Albuquerque NM 87196

TRELEAVEN, PHILLIPS ALBERT, pub. co. exec.; b. Oak Park, Ill., July 20, 1928; s. Harry William and Mary Elizabeth (Gregory) T.; B.A., Duke U., 1950; A.M., Boston U., 1959. With G. K. Hall & Co., Boston, 1956-60, 61-67, 69-79, pres., 1969-78, chmn. bd., 1970-78; underwriter mcpl. bonds Scharff & Jones, New Orleans, 1959-61; instr. in polit. economy Boston U., 1967-69; vis. lectr. econs. Unity Coll., 1979—; owner Odyssey Hill Farms, Thorndike, Maine, 1971-75; owner and pub. The Thorndike Press, 1977—. Selectman, Thorndike, 1979—. Served with AUS, 1950-53. Mem. Phi Beta Kappa. Home: Thorndike ME 04986 Office: 70 Lincoln St Boston MA 02111. *The biggest blunders I have made in my life have usually resulted from taking myself or my circumstances too seriously.*

TRELFA, RICHARD THOMAS, paper co. exec.; b. Alpena, Mich., July 5, 1918; s. Fred R. and Mable (Hagen) T.; B.S., U. Mich., 1940; m. Heidi Brigitte Ruckstuhl, Dec. 3, 1965; children—Thomas W., Barbara E., Jeffrey C., Michael F. With Hercules Powder Co., 1941-52; with Watervliet (Mich.) Paper Co., 1952-58; exec. v.p., treas., dir. Perkins-Goodwin Co., Inc., N.Y.C., 1958-70, v.p., treas., chief fin. officer, 1970, sr. v.p., 1974—; treas., dir. Kennebec River Pulp & Paper Co., Madison, Me., 1967-69, chmn. bd., treas., 1969-72, chmn. bd., mem. exec. com., 1972-73, dir., mem. exec. com., 1973-75; pres. Castle & Overton (Can.) Ltd., 1971—; chmn. bd. EHV Weidmann Industries, Ltd., St. Johnsbury, Vt., 1974—, Franconia Paper Co. Inc., Lincoln, N.H., 1978—. Fellow Am. Soc. Quality Control, TAPPI (former div. chmn., dir.); mem. Paper Industry Mgmt. Assn. (former div. chmn.), Am. Inst. Chem. Engrs., Am. Chem. Soc., Soc. Rheology. Republican. Mason. Clubs: Rockefeller Center Luncheon, U. Mich. (N.Y.C.). Home: Fox Run Rd 5E Box 125 Lincoln NH 03251 Office: 8 Main St Lincoln NH 03251

TRELOGAN, HARRY CHESTER, cons. agrl. economist and statistician; b. Versailles, Pa., Dec. 29, 1908; s. Charles Henry and Annie May (Dowie) T.; B.S., W.Va. U., 1931; M.S., U. Minn., 1933, Ph.D., 1938; m. Ruth Grytbak, June 21, 1937; children—Robert Martin, Peter Dowie, Susan Lynn (dec.), Jeanne Karen (Ms. J.K. Trelogan-Nutter). Mgr. Kanawha Valley Milk Producers Assn., 1931; instr. agrl. mktg. U. Minn., 1936-38; economist FCA, 1939-41; economist Dept. Agr., 1942; chief order adminstrn. div. dairy and poultry br. War Food Adminstrn., 1943-44; chief research and analysis div. dairy br. Dept. Agr., 1945-46, asst. adminstr. Research and Mktg. Act, 1947-49, asst. adminstr. Agrl. Research Adminstrn., 1950-53; dir. mktg. research Agrl. Mktg. Service, 1954-59, asst. adminstr. agrl. mktg. service, 1960-61, adminstr. statis. reporting service, 1961-75; mem. faculty U.S. Dept. Agr. Grad. Sch., 1948—, mem. gen. adminstrv. bd., 1965-72, mem. soc. sci. com., 1956-76, chmn., 1972-76; cons. Nat. Agrl. Mktg. Workshop, 1949-56. U.S. del. 13th Internat. Dairy Congress, The Hague, 1952. Recipient Outstanding Achievement award U. Minn., 1964; superior service award Dept. Agr., 1952, Distinguished Service award, 1960; Fed. Land Banks' 50th Anniversary Commemorative medal, 1967; Soc. Am. Florists Research/Edn. award, 1971, Distinguished Service plaque Nat. Assn. State Depts. Agr., 1975, others. Fellow Am. Agrl. Econs. Assn., Am. Statis. Assn., AAAS; mem. Am. Agrl. Econ. Assn. (pres. 1957-58), Am. Econ. Assn., Am. Dairy Sci. Assn., Agrl. Research Inst. (gov. bd. 1957-58). Internat. Assn. Agrl. Economists (hon. life), Internat. Statis. Inst., Alpha Zeta, Gamma Sigma Delta, Gamma Alpha, Alpha Gamma Rho (Outstanding Alumni award 1967). Clubs: Cosmos; Nat. Economists (Washington). Author: (with Warren C. Waite) Agricultural Market Prices, 1951. Contbr. to textbooks, standard and year books. Home: 3625 N Piedmont St Arlington VA 22207

TREMAIN, ALAN, hotel exec.; b. Kent, Eng., Aug. 18, 1935; s. Archibald and Elizabeth (Morris) T.; grad. Westminster Hotel Sch., 1952, Canterbury Sch. Econs., 1962; LL.B., La Salle Sch., Chgo., 1971; m. Anita P. DeVienne, July 31, 1961; children—Warren, Nathlie, Hugo, Philippe. Came to U.S., 1966. Chef de Pertie Grosvenor House, London, 1954-55; food and beverage mgr. Peninsula, Hong Kong, 1956-57; gen. mgr. Warners Hotel, also The Russley, Christchurch, New Zealand, 1958-64, Menzies, Sydney, Australia, 1964-65, Empress Hotel, Vancouver, B.C., Can. 1966-69; with Planned Food Facilities (Internat.) Ltd., Toronto, 1970-72; resident mgr. Sheraton Boston, 1972; mng. dir. Copley Plaza Hotel, Boston, 1972—; pres. Hotels of Distinction, Inc., Boston. Recipient Culinary Merit award from Cerde Epicurien Mondel, Paris, 1956. Fellow Hotel and Catering Inst. (U.K.); founding mem. Internat. Soc. Chefs de Cuisine (chmn. 1954). Mason. Clubs: Montreal Badminton and Squash; Brae Burn Country; Rolls Royce Owners. Author: A Guide to the Fine Art of Living, 1963; A Meal for To-Night, 1965. Address: Copley Plaza Copley Sq Boston MA 02116

TREMAINE, FRANK, news exec., b. Detroit, May 30, 1914; s. Gage Canfield and Kate Amelia (Rutter) T.; B.A., Stanford, 1936; m. Katherine McCoy Newland, Sept. 2, 1939; children—Nancy McCoy, Frank Gage. With United Press Assns. (became United Press Internat., Inc. 1958), successively assigned Salt Lake City, San Diego, San Francisco, N.Y.C., mgr., Honolulu, war corr. in charge coverage Central and South Pacific, World War II, including Pearl Harbor attack, Japanese surrender, Japanese peace conf. in San Francisco, mgr. Tokyo, Mexico and Central Am., Los Angeles, 1936-51, asst. gen. mgr. Newspictures, Dept., 1952-55, gen. mgr., 1955-58, v.p., dir., gen. mgr. newspictures and film UPI, 1958-65, v.p., gen. bus. mgr., 1965-69, v.p., gen. mgr. N.Am., 1969-72, sr. v.p., 1972—, dir. UPITN, 1969—. Mem. Sigma Delta Chi, Phi Kappa Psi. Presbyn. Clubs: Shenorock Shore; Fox Meadow Tennis, Dutch Treat. Home: 42 Woodland Dr Port Chester NY 10573 Office: 220 E 42d St New York City NY 10017

TREMAN, ARTHUR BOTT, JR., investment banking firm exec.; b. Ithaca, N.Y., May 21, 1929; s. Arthur Bott and Louise (Warren) T.; A.B., Williams Coll., 1951; M.B.A., Harvard U., 1954. With Dillon, Read & Co. Inc., N.Y.C., 1954—, now mng. dir.; dir. U.S. Finance Co. (now Unicapital, Inc.), 1961-65; dir. Rouse Co. Active Big Bros., 1955-61. Bd. mgrs. Meml. Hosp. for Cancer and Allied Diseases, N.Y.C.; trustee Outward Bound, Inc., Deerfield Acad. Mem. Securities Industry Assn. (governing council), Bond Club of N.Y. (gov.), Delta Kappa Epsilon. Republican. Presbyterian (deacon 1955-60). Clubs: University, Madison Sq. Garden, Links, River, Recess (N.Y.C.). Home: 167 E 80th St New York City NY 10021 Office: 46 William St New York NY 10005

TREMAYNE, BERTRAM WILLIAM, JR., lawyer; b. St. Louis, Feb. 23, 1914; s. Bertram William and Pearl Inez (Flory) T.; A.B., Washington U., St. Louis, 1935, J.D., 1938; m. Frances Lewis, July 6, 1940 (dec. Jan. 1964); children—Pamela L., Eric F.; m. 2d, Clara Tarling, Jan. 2, 1966. Admitted to Mo. bar, 1938; with firm Neuhoff & Millar, St. Louis, 1938-41; dist. rationing atty. OPA, 1941-43; partner firm Neuhoff, Millar, Tremayne & Schaefer, St. Louis, 1946-54, Tremayne, Lay, Carr & Bauer, and predecessor, St. Louis, 1954—. Mem. St. Louis County Parks and Recreation Adv. Bd., 1956-63, chmn., 1959-63. Mem. met. bd. dirs. St. Louis and St. Louis County YMCA, 1960—, pres., 1970-73; mem. nat. council YMCAs, 1970-77; bd. dirs. Washington U., 1961-65; trustee Deaconess Hosp., St. Louis, 1973—. Served to capt. AUS, 1943-46. Recipient Distinguished Eagle Scout award Boy Scouts Am., 1973. Mem. Am., St. Louis County bar assns., Mo. Bar (bd. govs. 1973—, pres. 1978-79), Bar Assn. Met. St. Louis, Am. Judicature Soc., Judge Advs. Assn., Phi Delta Phi, Omicron Delta Kappa. Conglist. (pres. 1960-63). Club: Algonquin Golf. Home: 58 Frederick Ln Glendale MO 63122 Office: 222 S Central Ave Clayton MO 63105

TREMAYNE, LES, actor; b. London, Eng., Apr. 16, 1913; s. Walter Carl Christian and Dorothy Alice Tremayne (Gwilliam) Henning; student Greek drama Northwestern U., 1937-39, anthropology Columbia, 1949-50, anthropology U. Calif. at Los Angeles, 1951-52; m. Alice Joan Reinheart, Dec. 11, 1945 (div. 1962). Actor in films in Eng., 1917, in Hollywood, 1951—, on radio, 1931—, on TV, 1939—; radio programs include The First Nighter, 1933-43, Grand Hotel, 1934-40, The Thin Man, 1945-50, The Falcon, 1946-49, Betty and Bob, 1935-39, also original leading man on Helen Trent, 1934; Broadway appearance in Detective Story, 1948-49; TV appearances in One Man's Family, Perry Mason, Matinee Theatre, Thin Man, Bonanza, The Man and The City; now Mr. Mentor, children's TV series SHAZAM!; films include The Racket, 1951, The Blue Veil, 1951, Francis Goes to West Point, 1951, It Grows on Trees, 1952, Dream Wife, 1953, I Love Melvin, 1952, North by Northwest, 1958, War of the Worlds, 1954, A Man Called Peter, 1955, Susan Slept Here, 1954, The Lieutenant Wore Skirts, 1958, Perfect Furlough, 1958, Say One for Me, 1958, Gallant Hours, 1958, Story of Ruth, 1959, Fortune Cookie, 1966, Goldfinger, 1966, Holy Wednesday, 1974. Narrator, portrayer voices ednl., indsl., documentary films. Pres. Hollywood Actors Council, 1952-56. Bd. dirs. Los Angeles chpt. Air Force Assn., 1966—. Recipient Blue Ribbon award for Best Actor of Month, Box Office mag., 1955; named Best Radio Actor in U.S., 1938; recipient Indsl. Film award, 1968, Blue Ribbon award Am. Film Festival, 1964; certificate merit Info. Film Producers Am., 1967, Cindy award, 1967, 71, finalist award, 1970; Andy award Advt. Club N.Y., 1968; Cine Golden Eagle award, 1978; award of merit Braille Inst. Am., 1977; named one of three most distinctive voices in U.S., 1940; numerous others. Mem. Am. Fedn. Radio Artists (charter; del. 1st conv. 1938), AFTRA (del., bd. dirs. 1965—; chmn. local, nat., internat. coms.), Acad. TV Arts and Scis. (past chmn. actors div. workshop com.), Screen Actors Guild, Actors Equity, Actors Fund Am. (life), Pacific Pioneer Broadcasters (founder, incorporator, charter, life; past bd. dirs.; now chmn. audio history com. and speakers' bur.), Archaeol. Inst. Am. Club: Lambs (Silver Tankard award 1949) (N.Y.C.). Author archaeol. paper. Address: 1435 N Ogden Dr Los Angeles CA 90046. *How I was able to attain whatever status I enjoy with meager education and no powerful or influential friends to assist me, remains a mystery to me. Stubborn perseverance, I guess. However, I must state that the climate has changed so in "show-business" that even this no longer seems to apply - at least for me. The Public remembers - the Powers that Be, whoever they are, do not. It is comforting, confusing and sad to be "a legend in one's own time"! I am grateful for the good things I have been given in my lifetime. Were it possible to live it over I would change very little. I've had a good time in my work. I have simply not attained what I felt I should have. There are few "redeeming features" to growing old in our society.*

TREMBLAY, JEAN-LOUIS, biologist; b. Les Eboulements, Charlevaoix, Que., Can., Nov. 22, 1906; s. Joseph and Georgianna T.; grad. in Chemistry, Laval U., 1931; grad. in Biology U. Strasbourg (France), 1934; Ph.D., Laval U., 1935; m. Therese Dulac, Sept. 5, 1931; children—Adrienne, Jacques. Prof. chemistry Med. Sch., Lava U., 1934-35, prof. biology faculty of sci., 1938—, founder dept. biology, prof. emeritus, 1974—. Recipient medal P.Q., 1967, Centennary medal, 1967, Silver Jubilee medal, 1978. Fellow Royal Soc. Can.; mem. AAAS, Can. Inst. Chemistry, Am. Fisheries Soc., Nature Can., Linnean Soc. Quebec, Quebec Zool. Soc. Contbr. articles on marine biology to profl. jours. Home: 1601 Blvd de l'Entente Quebec PQ G1S 2V3 Canada Office: Dept Biology Faculty of Sci Laval Univ Quebec PQ G1K 7P4 Canada

TREMBLAY, LUCIEN, lawyer, former Can. provincial judge; b. Montreal, Que., Can., Mar. 25, 1912; s. Joseph and Marie (Bois) T.; B.A., Sem. Philosophy, Montreal, 1933; LL.M., U. Montreal, 1936, LL.D., 1944, hon. LL.D., 1965; LL.D., Laval U., 1963; m. Jeannine Martin, May 30, 1939; children—Monique, Pierre, Jean, Francois. Admitted to Que. bar, 1936; practice in Montreal, 1936-61; prof. civil procedure U. Montreal, 1949-59; chief justice Province Que., 1961-77; counsel firm Gilbert, Magnan, Marcotte, Trembley and Forget, Montreal, 1977—. Chancellor, U. Montreal, 1967-70. Clubs: Cercle de la Place d'armies (Montreal); Garrison (Quebec). Home: 209 Habitat 67 Cite Du Havre Montreal PQ H3C 3R6 Canada Office: Suite 1935 Place Villoc Marie Montreal PQ H3B 2C3 Canada

TREMBLAY, MARC ADÉLARD, univ. dean; b. Les Eboulements, Que., Can., Apr. 24, 1922; s. Willie and Laurette (Tremblay) T.; A.B., U. Montreal, 1944, L.S.A., 1948; M.A., Laval U., 1950; Ph.D., Cornell U., 1954; m. Jacqueline Cyr, Dec. 27, 1949; children—Geneviève, Lorraine, Marc, Colette, Dominique, Suzanne. Research asso. Cornell U., 1953-56; mem. faculty Laval U., 1956—, prof. anthropology, 1963-68, vice dean social scis., 1968-71, dean Grad. Sch., 1971-79, also mem. univ. council. Chmn. acad. panel Can. Council; spl. councillor Can. Dept. Social Scis.; mem. Regional Council Health and Social Services. Recipient Literary prize, 1965. Mem. Royal Soc. Can., Acad. des Scis. Morales et Politiques, Research Inst. Pub. Policy, Am. Anthrop. Assn., Soc. Applied Anthropology, Can. Soc. Sociology and Anthropology (founding pres.). Author 10 books in social scis., numerous articles. Home: 835 N Orleáns St Ste Foy 10 PQ Canada Office: Grad Sch Laval Univ Quebec 10 PQ Canada

TREMBLY, DENNIS MICHAEL, musician; b. Long Beach, Calif., Apr. 16, 1947; s. Fred Leland and Jewel Fern (Bouldin) T.; student Juilliard Sch. Music, 1965-68. Bass player, 1959—; bass player Los Angeles Philharmonic Orch., 1970—, co-prin. bass, 1973—. Recipient 2d pl. Internat. Solo Bass competition, Isle of Man, 1978. Mem. Internat. Soc. Bassists. Home: 222 S Figueroa St Los Angeles CA 90012 Office: 135 N Grand Ave Los Angeles CA 90012

TREML, VLADIMIR GUY, economist; b. Kharkov, USSR, Mar. 27, 1929; s. Guy Alexey and Lydia Vladimir (Timofeev) T.; came to U.S., 1950, naturalized, 1953; B.A. in Econs., Bklyn. Coll., 1955; M.A. in Econs., Columbia U., 1956; Ph.D. in Econs., U. N.C., 1963; m. Emma Miro, July 12, 1952; children—Irene, Tatiana, Alexey. Dept. supr. Bache & Co., N.Y.C., 1953-58; research asso. Inst. for Social Scis., U. N.C., Chapel Hill, 1958-61; asso. prof. econs. Franklin and Marshall Coll., 1961-66; research asso. Inst. Study USSR, Munich, Germany, 1966-67; prof. econs. Duke U., 1967—; cons. in field; expert Dept. Commerce, 1971—. Trustee Nat. Council for Soviet and East European Research, Inc., Washington, 1978—. Served with USMC, 1951-53. Ford Found. grantee, 1972-75; Dept. Def.-Advanced Research Project Agy. grantee, 1975-76; Dept. State grantee, 1976-77. Mem. So. Econ. Assn., Am. Econ. Assn., Assn. Comparative Econ. Studies (exec. com. 1972-74), Am. Assn. Advancement Slavic Studies, So. Conf. on Slavic Studies (pres. 1977-78), Phi Beta Kappa. Democrat. Eastern Orthodox. Author: (with others) Structure of the Soviet Economy, 1972; Input-Output Analysis and the Soviet Economy, 1975; contbr. reports to publs. of Joint Econ. Com., U.S. Congress, articles to profl. publs.; editor: Soviet Economic Statistics, 1972; editor, contbg. author: Studies in Soviet Input-Output Analysis, 1977. Home: 603 Long Leaf Dr Chapel Hill NC 27514 Office: Dept Econs Duke U Durham NC 27706

TREMPER, DONALD NEWTON, mining co. exec.; b. Streator, Ill., Feb. 3, 1919; s. Jacob and Louise Fern (Jones) T.; student U. Ill., 1937-38, DePauw U., 1938-41; B.S. in Accounting, Tri-State Coll., Ind., 1943; m. Elinor J. Kirkpatrick, Feb. 15, 1941. Jr. acct. various acctg. firms, Tucson, Los Angeles, 1946-48; prodn. and transp. acct. Union Oil Co., Los Angeles, 1948-51; acctg. and fin. adminstrn. Cyprus Pima Mining Co. and Cyprus Bruce Copper & Zinc Co., Cyprus Johnson Copper Co., Tucson, 1951—, treas., Rental Properties, 1951-73. Served with AUS, 1943-46. Mem. Ariz. Mining Assn. (sec.-treas. 1970-71, 74-75), Ariz. Self-Insurers Assn. (dir., treas. 1970-71), Nat. Assn. Accts., Alpha Beta Alpha. Home: 7940 W Linda Vista Tucson AZ 85704 Office: PO Box 7187 Tucson AZ 85725

TRENCH, WILLIAM FREDERICK, educator; b. Trenton, N.J., July 31, 1931; s. George Daniel and Anna Elizabeth (Taylor) T.; B.A. in Math., Lehigh U., 1953; A.M., U. Pa., 1955; Ph.D., 1958; m. Lucille Ann Marasco, Dec. 26, 1954 (div. Dec. 1978); children—Joseph William, Randolph Clifford, John Frederick, Gina Margaret. Applied mathematician Moore Sch. Elec. Engring., U. Pa., 1953-56; with Gen. Electric Corp., Phila., 1956-57, Philco Corp., Phila., 1957-59; with RCA, Moorestown, N.J., 1957-64; asso. prof. math. Drexel U., Phila., 1964-67, prof., 1967—. Mem. Math. Assn. Am., Am. Math. Soc., Soc. Indsl. and Applied Math., Phi Beta Kappa, Sigma Xi, Eta Kappa Nu, Pi Mu Epsilon. Contbr. research articles in numerical analysis, ordinary differential equations, smoothing, prediction and spl. functions to profl. jours. Author: (with Bernard Kolman) Elementary Multivariable Calculus, 1971, Multivariable Calculus with Linear Algebra and Series, 1972; Advanced Calculus, 1978. Home: 32 Rockwood Rd Levittown PA 19056 Office: Math Dept Drexel U Philadelphia PA 19104

TRENKMANN, RICHARD J., finance co. exec.; b. Chgo., Mar. 6, 1916; s. R.A. and Pearl Edith (Thompson) T.; B.S. in Commerce, Northwestern U., 1938; m. Elizabeth Williams, Nov. 9, 1940; children—Richard S., Stephen, Pamela. Owner community newspaper, 1938-40; advt. and sales mgr. Frederick Post & Co., 1940-44; with Gen. Finance Corp., Evanston, Ill., 1946—, exec. v.p., 1962-63, pres., 1963-71, chmn. bd., pres., chief exec. officer, 1971—, also dir. Bd. dirs. North Shore Jr. Achievement. Served with USNR, 1944-45. Mem. Nat. Consumer Fin. Assn. (mem. exec. com.), Phi Kappa Sigma. Episcopalian. Clubs: John Evans, Bench Warmers (Northwestern U.); Executive (Chgo.); Westmoreland Country (Wilmette, Ill.). Home: 3008 Iroquois Rd Wilmette IL 60091 Office: 1301 Central St Evanston IL 60201

TRENT, BUCK, banjoist; b. Spartanburg, S.C., Feb. 17, 1938; s. Charles Hugh and Eva Viola (Johnson) T.; student pub. schs.; m. Patsy Sneed, Apr. 22, 1957 (div. Nov. 1978); children—Charlie, Melissa. Banjoist, Grand Ole Opry, 1960-74, Porter Wagoner show, 1962-74, Roy Clark show, 1974—; regular performer TV show Hee Haw, 1974—; rec. artist Smash, Boone, RCA, ABC Dot records. Named Number One Instrumentalist, Internat. Fan Club, 1975, 76. Mem. AFTRA, Broadcast Music Inc. Clubs: Tulsa Country; Las Vegas Country; Masons (32 deg.). Composer own songs. Office: 5800 E Skelly Dr Penthouse Tulsa OK 74135

TRENT, PETER CARSON, investment co. exec.; b. West Hollywood, Calif., Mar. 1, 1933; s. Philip and Isabel (Carson) T.; B.A. magna cum laude, Princeton U., 1954; m. May Wong, Apr. 15, 1971. With James A. Andrews & Co., Inc., 1955-64, v.p., 1958-64, mgr. mcpl. trading, 1962-64; pres. Peter C. Trent & Co., Inc., 1964-66; joint mgr. mcpl. bond dept. Gregory & Sons, N.Y.C., 1966-69; v.p., mgr. mcpl. bond dept. Cogan Berlind Weill & Levitt, Inc., N.Y.C., 1970-72; exec. v.p., mgr. mcpls. bond dept. Shearson Hayden Stone Inc. (merger Cogan Berlind Weill & Levitt, Inc., Hayden, Stone Inc. and Shearson, Hammill & Co., Inc. 1972), dir., 1973—; mem. Mcpls. Securities Rulemaking Bd., 1977-79. Mem. Public Securities Assn. (dir. 1977-79, vice chmn. 1979), Securities Industry Assn. (public fin. council 1976), Mcpls. Fin. Officers Assn. (asso.). Office: 14 Wall St New York NY 10005

TRENTHAM, DAVID R., biochemist; b. Solihull, Warwickshire, Eng., Sept. 22, 1938; came to U.S., 1977; s. John A. and Julia A. M. (Kemble) T.; B.A. (Maj. Open Entrance scholar), Cambridge (Eng.) U., 1961, Ph.D., 1964; m. Kamalini Bhargava, 1966; children—Ian, Neil. Postdoctoral fellow Salk Inst. Biol. Studies, La Jolla, Calif., 1964-65; postdoctoral fellow M.I.T., 1966; jr. research fellow Bristol (Eng.) U., 1966-69, research asso. dept. biochemistry, 1969-72, lectr. in biochemistry, 1972-75, reader, 1975-77; Edwin M. Chance prof. biochemistry and biophysics, chmn. dept. biochemistry and biophysics U. Pa. Sch. Medicine, 1977—. Recipient Colworth medal Biochem. Soc. U.K., 1974. Contbr. articles to profl. pubs. Office: 358 Anatomy-Chemistry Bldg/G3 Dept Biochemistry and Biophysics U Pa Sch Medicine Philadelphia PA 19104

TRENTIN, JOHN JOSEPH, med. scientist, educator; b. Newark, Dec. 15, 1918; s. Joseph and Angelina (Lavaggi) T.; B.S. (Allan Nutt Meml. scholar), Pa. State Coll., 1940; A.M. (John W. White fellow),

U. Mo., 1941; Ph.D., 1947; m. Charline Jenkins, Aug. 29, 1946; children—Jane Louise, Ann Marie. Postdoctoral fellow Yale Med. Sch., 1948-51, instr. dept. anatomy, 1951-52, asst. prof., 1952-54; asso. prof. dept. anatomy Baylor Coll. Medicine, Houston, 1954-58, prof., acting chmn. dept. anatomy, 1958-60, prof., head div. exptl. biology, 1960—; asso. prof. U. Tex. Dental Br., part-time 1954-60; cons. biology U. Tex. M.D. Anderson Hosp. and Tumor Inst., 1958-62; mem. com. for med. research VA Hosp., Houston, 1960-65. Mem. adv. com. on pathogenesis of cancer Am. Cancer Soc., 1958-60; mem. com. on tissue transplantation NRC, 1960-70; mem. bd. sci. counsellors Nat. Cancer Inst., 1963-67, chmn., 1965-67; mem. spl. animal leukemia ecology studies com. NIH, 1964-67; rep. Am. Assn. Cancer Research to nat. organizing com. 10th Internat. Cancer Congress, 1967-70. Served with AUS, 1942-46. Recipient Esther Langer-Bertha Teplitz award for cancer research Ann Langer Cancer Research Found., 1963; Golden Plate award Am. Acad. Achievement, 1965; Ad Fontes medal of Erasmus, U. Rotterdam, 1979. Mem. Am. Assn. of Immunologists, Am. Assn. Cancer Research (editorial com. 1970-73, publs. com. 1979—), N.Y. Acad. Scis., Reticulo-Endothelial Soc., Soc. for Exptl. Biology and Medicine, Am. Soc. for Exptl. Pathology, AAAS, Am. Assn. Lab. Animal Sci., Am. Soc. for Microbiology, Transplantation Soc., Assn. for Gnotobiotics, Internat. Soc. Exptl. Hematology (pres. 1978-79). Roman Catholic. Mem. editorial bd. Transplantation Jour., 1962-71, Proc. of Transplantation Soc., 1968—; editor 2 books: contbr. numerous articles to med. lit. Home: 4609 Waycross Dr Houston TX 77035 Office: Div Exptl Biology Baylor Coll Medicine Houston TX 77030

TRENTMAN, JOHN ALLEN, educator; b. Willmar, Minn., Feb. 17, 1935; s. John Libory and Hannah (Johnson) T.; B.A., U. Minn., 1956, M.A., 1958, Ph.D., 1964; postgrad. Lund (Sweden) U., 1958-59; m. Florine Opal Tweeten, July 16, 1955; children—Anne Elisabeth, Karna Marie, John Stefan Per, Denise Erika. Came to Can., 1963, naturalized, 1972. Lectr. philosophy Huron Coll., U. Western Ont., London, Can., 1963-64, asst. prof., 1964-67; asso. prof. McGill U., Montreal, Que., 1967-70, prof., 1971—, chmn. dept., 1967-72, vice dean humanities Faculty Arts and Scis., 1968-71; dir. McGill-Queen's Univ. Press; corr. mem. Humanities Research Council Can., 1970—. Bd. govs. Montreal Diocesan Theol. Coll., 1978—. Am.-Scandinavian fellow, 1958-59; Kent fellow Nat. Soc. Religion in Higher Edn., 1957; Canada Council leave fellow, 1974-75. Mem. Internat. Soc. Study Mediaeval Philosophy, Canadian Philos. Assn., Canadian Soc. Study History and Philosophy of Sci., Assn. Symbolic Logic, Phi Beta Kappa. Anglican. Club: Faculty (McGill Univ.). Author: Vincent Ferrer's Tractatus de Suppositionibus, 1977. Editorial cons. Grammatica Specilativa; editorial adviser Jour. History Philosophy, 1970—. Contbr. articles to profl. jours. Chmn. editorial adv. com., bd. dirs. McGill-Queen's U. Press, 1976-77. Home: 212 Kindersley Ave Montreal PQ H3R 1R7 Canada

TRESCHER, ROBERT LINCOLN, lawyer; b. Jeannette, Pa., May 20, 1912; s. John Henry and Maud Mellon (Byers) T.; grad. Kiski Springs Sch., 1930; B.S., Wharton Sch. of U. Pa., 1934; LL.B., U. Pa., 1937; m. Glendora Ellen Rollins, Jan. 2, 1943; children—Victoria (Mrs. R.J. Aqnich), Ellen Rollins. Admitted to Pa. bar, 1938, since practiced in Phila.; partner firm Montgomery, McCracken, Walker & Rhoads, 1951—. Dir. Heublein, Inc., Lucker Mfg. Co. Permanent del. Jud. Conf. U.S. Ct. Appeals 3d Circuit, 1957—. Trustee (life) U. Pa. 64. Served to lt. comdr. USNR, 1942-46. Fellow Am. Bar Found., Am. Coll. Trial Lawyers; mem. Am., Pa. (chancellor 1966), Phila. bar assns., Am. Law Inst., Order of Coif, Phi Delta Theta. Republican. Episcopalian. Club: Union League (past dir.). Home: 191 Presidential Blvd Apt 220 Bala Cynwyd PA 19004 Office: 20th Floor/3 Parkway St Philadelphia PA

TRESSLER, JOSEF SNYDER, banker; b. Meyersdale, Pa., Sept. 11, 1918; s. Joseph Leroy and Jennie Lanah (Snyder) T.; B.A., Gettysburg Coll., 1940; m. Jane Elizabeth Livengood, Sept. 19, 1943; children—Barbara, Ernest. With Hawkeye Security Ins. Co., Northeastern Ins. Co., United Security Ins. Co., 1946-69, pres., dir., 1965—; pres. Internat. Bank, Washington, 1979; dir. Fin. Security Group, Inc., Des Moines. Served in AUS, 1941-46; CBI; lt. col. Res. ret. Decorated Bronze Star. Mem. Iowa Ins. Inst. (past pres.), Phi Sigma Kappa. Republican. Mem. United Ch. of Christ. Mason (Shriner). Clubs: Washington Golf and Country (Arlington, Va.); Farmington Country (Charlottesville, Va.); Army-Navy (Washington). Contbr. articles to profl. jours. Home: 4110 N River St Arlington VA 22207

TRETICK, STANLEY, photo-journalist; b. Balt., July 21, 1921; s. William and Sophia (Rosenberg) T.; grad. high sch.; m. Maureen Hesselroth, Mar. 30, 1963. With editorial dept. Washington Post, 1940-42; photographer U.P.I. News Pictures, 1945-61; staff photographer Look mag., Washington, 1961-71; ofcl. photographer McGovern presdl. campaign, 1972, Carter presdl. campaign, 1976-77. Served with USMCR, 1942-45; PTO. Recipient Nat. Headliners award for Korean War pictures, 1951, Graflex Achievement award, 1955, Grand award White House News Photographers Assn., 1956, First prize color class for portrait Pres. Kennedy, 62, 63, First prize picture story, 1965, First prize color class and grand award White House Photographers competition, 1966. Mem. White House Photographers Assn., U.S. Senate Photographers Gallery. Contbr. all photographs Pres. Kennedy to A Very Special President, 1965; co-author, contbr. all photographs They Could Not Trust the King, 1974; A Portrait of All the President's Men, 1976. Address: 2953 Arizona Ave NW Washington DC 20016

TREUMANN, WILLIAM BORGEN, univ. dean; b. Grafton, N.D., Feb. 26, 1916; s. William King and Dagny Helen (Borgen) T.; B.S., U. N.D., 1942; M.A., U. Ill., 1944, Ph.D., 1947; m. Mildred Elizabeth Jenkins, Aug. 14, 1948; children—Richard Roy, Robert Evan, Beverly Kay. Teaching asst. chemistry U. Ill., 1942-45, teaching asst. math., 1945-46, vis. prof., summers 1948-50; from asst. prof. to prof. chemistry N.D. State U., 1946-55; mem. faculty Moorhead (Minn.) State U., 1960—, prof. chemistry, 1962—, asso. dean acad. affairs, 1968-70, dean faculty math. and sci., 1970—. Research Corp. Am. grantee, 1954, Minn. U. Bd. grantee, 1967. Fellow Am. Inst. Chemists; mem. Am. Chem. Soc., Am. Assn. U. Profs., Minn. Acad. Sci., Fedn. Am. Scientists, Phi Beta Kappa, Sigma Xi. Contbr. to profl. jours. Home: 433 8th Ave S Fargo ND 58102 Office: Moorhead State U Moorhead MN 56560

TREVAS, SIMON HARRISON, lawyer; b. Bklyn., Aug. 16, 1910; s. Julius Alexander and Dora (Silverman) T.; student Columbia, 1927-28; LL.B., Bklyn. Law Sch., 1932; m. Jean Goldstein, Dec. 29, 1934; children—Robert J., Suzanne (Mrs. Marvin Rosenblatt). Admitted to bar; atty., later chief trial counsel Home Owners Loan Corp., 1934-51; legis. atty. Housing and Home Finance Agy., 1951-56; with Office Gen. Counsel, Fed. Home Loan Bank Bd., 1956-62, exec. asst. to chmn., 1963-69; spl. counsel govt. ops. U.S. Savs. and Loan League, 1969-75; counsel firm Gailor Elias & Matz, 1975—; spl. assignments in Latin Am. for Inter-Am. Devel. Bank and AID, 1961-65. Tchr. law for fed. mgrs. Agr. Dept. Grad. Sch., 1968-69; lectr. internat. banking and housing groups. Mem. Fed. (pres. 1973), Am. (ho. of dels.), Inter-Am., Internat. bar assns. Clubs: Nat. Lawyers, Indian Spring Country. Contbr. chpt. to West's Federal Practice Manual, articles on housing law to trade jours. Home: 204 E Indian Spring Dr Silver Spring MD 20901 Office: 700 E St SE NW Washington DC 20003

TREVES, SAMUEL BLAIN, educator, geologist; b. Detroit, Sept. 11, 1925; s. Samuel and Stella (Stork) T.; B.S., Mich. Technol. U., 1951; postgrad. (Fulbright scholar), U. Otago (New Zealand), 1953-54; M.S., U. Idaho, 1953; Ph.D., Ohio State U., 1959; m. Jane Patricia Mitoray, Nov. 24, 1960; children—John Samuel, David Samuel. Geologist, Ford Motor Co., 1951, Idaho Bur. Mines and Geology, 1952, Otago Catchment Bd., N.Z., 1953-54; mem. faculty U. Nebr., Lincoln, 1958—, prof. geology, 1966—, chmn. dept., 1964-70, 74—; curator geology Nebr. State Mus., 1964—; expdns. to Antarctica and Greenland, 1960, 61, 63, 65, 70, 72, 73, 74, 75, 76. Fellow Geol. Soc. Am.; mem. Am. Mineral. Soc., Royal Soc. New Zealand, Nat. Assn. Geology Tchrs., Am. Polar Soc., AAAS, Sigma Xi, Tau Beta Pi, Sigma Gamma Epsilon. Research and publs. on geology of igneous and metamorphic rocks of Idaho, N.Z., Mich., Antarctica, Greenland, emphasis on origin of Precambrian granite complexes and volcanology. Home: 1710 B St Lincoln NE 68502

TREVILLIAN, WALLACE DABNEY, coll. dean; b. Charlottesville, Va., May 1, 1918; s. Robert Carr and Mary Anna (Perry) T.; B.S., U. Va., 1940, M.A., 1947, Ph.D., 1954; postgrad. U. Calif., 1950-51; m. Mary Lou McEachern Moody, Nov. 28, 1963; children—Malcolm McEachern, Edward Dabney. Mem. faculty Clemson (S.C.) U., 1947—, successively instr. econs., asst. prof., asso. prof., 1947-55, prof. econs., head dept. indsl. mgmt., 1955-63, dean coll. indsl. mgmt. and textile sci., 1963—. Dir. Clemson Nat. Bank. Mem. Regional Export Expansion Council, 1965-77; sec. commn. on edn. for bus. professions Nat. Assn. State Univs. and Land-Grant Colls., 1975-77; pres. Nat. Council for Textile Edn., 1978—. Served as master sgt. AUS, 1941-45. Mem. Am., So. econ. assns., Acad. Mgmt. Episcopalian. Address: Clemson U Clemson SC 29631

TREVINO, ALBERTO FAUSTINO, telecommunications, devel. co. exec.; b. Inglewood, Calif., Dec. 28, 1931; s. Alberto F. and Adelina (Escajeda) T.; B.S., U. Calif., Berkeley, 1957; M.L.A., Harvard, 1958; m. Dolores M. DuPont, Apr. 16, 1955; children—Paul A., Anita M., Teresa R., Leo A., Vincent A., Dominic X, Mary Maguerita, Clara C., J. Antonio, John A., Laurence N. Sr. planner Victor Gruen Assos., Beverly Hills, Calif., 1959-60; prof. landscape architecture Calif. Poly. U., Pomona, 1960-61; chief planner Irvine Co., Newport Beach, Calif., 1961-66; mgr. community research and planning Gen. Electric Co., Los Angeles, N.Y.C., 1966-68; pres. Concept Environment, Inc., Laguna Beach, Calif., 1969-70; pres. Urban Interface Group, Laguna Beach, 1970-73, 75—; gen. mgr. Community Devel. Corp., HUD, Washington, 1973-74; v.p. Walt Disney Prodns., Burbank, Calif., 1974-75; founder, dir. Los Angeles Nat. Bank. Vis. lectr. Columbia, 1967, U. N.C., 1970-71, U. Calif., Berkeley, 1968, U. So. Calif., 1968-70, Harvard, 1967; speaker on urban planning and design, 1964—. Mem. adv. com. Laguna Beach Citizens, 1960, Orange County council Girl Scouts Am., 1965; mem. Orange County Regional Open Space Com., 1966; head U.S. del. to USSR, 1974. Served with AUS, 1955-56. Clubs: Harvard of Orange County; University (Los Angeles). Author: The University and the New Community, 1966; Insight into Systems Building, 1970; The Federal New Community Program, 1974. Home: 1015 Madison Pl Laguna Beach CA 92651. *Our concern must be for man in society. The complex composition and interdependence of the world requires a need to solve problems on a scale not previously dealt with, yet the greatest impact will be how we treat all individuals. There is a need to think big and solve problems on a large scale but to also possess humility and help man, especially the disadvantaged.*

TREVINO, ELIZABETH BORTON DE, author; b. Bakersfield, Calif., Sept. 2, 1904; d. Fred Ellsworth and Carrie (Christensen) Borton; B.A., Stanford, 1925; m. Luis Trevino Gomez, Aug. 10, 1935; children—Luis Federico (dec.), Enrique Ricardo. Free-lance writer, journalist; hon. lectr. Am. Inst. Fgn. Trade, 1960. Recipient medal Kansas City (Mo.) Women's Commn., 1961; named hon. Texan, 1963; recipient Opie award for best novel hist. fiction, 1970. Mem. Author's Guild Am., Am. Hispanic Soc., Pan-Am. Round Table, Cath. Guild, Humane Soc., Women in Communications, Phi Beta Kappa. Author: (juveniles) Our Little Ethiopian Cousin, 1935, Our Little Aztec Cousin, 1934, About Bellamy, 1940, A Carpet of Flowers, 1955, Nacar, the White Deer, 1963, I, Juan de Pareja (Newberry medal), 1965, Casilda of the Rising Moon, 1967, Turi's Poppa, 1969, Here is Mexico, 1970; Beyond The Gates of Hercules, 1971; Juarez, Man of Law, 1974; (adult books) My Heart Lies South, 1953, Where the Heart Is, 1962; (novels) Even As You Love, 1957, The Greek of Toledo, 1959, Fourth Gift, 1966; The House on Bitterness Street, 1970; The Music Within, 1973; The Hearthstone of My Heart, 1977; The Heart Possessed, 1978. Home: Ave Pres Lopez Matos 308 Cuernavaca Mexico Office: Apartado 827 Cuernavaca Morelos Mexico

TREVINO, LEE BUCK, profl. golfer; b. Dallas, Dec. 1, 1939; s. Joe and Juanita (Barrett) T.; ed. pub. schs.; m. Claudia Ann Fenley, Aug. 24, 1964; children—Richard Lee, Lesley Ann, Tony Lee, Troy Liana. Head profl. Hardy's Driving Range, Dallas, 1961-65; asst. profl. Horizon Hills Country Club, El Paso, Tex., 1966-67; chmn. bd. Lee Trevino Enterprises, Santa Teresa Country Club; touring profl., 1967—; tournament winner Tex. Open, 1965, 66, N.Mex. Open, 1966, U.S. Open, 1968, 71, Amana Open, 1968, 69, Hawaiian Open, 1968, Tucson Open, 1969, 70, World Cup, 1969, 71, Nat. Airlines Open, 1970, Brit. Open, 1971, 72, Canadian Open 1971, 77, 79, Can. PGA, 1979, Danny Thomas-Memphis Classic, 1971, 72, Tallahassee Open, 1971, Sahara Invitational, 1971, St. Louis Classic, 1972, Hartford Open, 1972, Jackie Gleason Classic, 1973, Doral-Eastern Open, 1973, Mexican Open, 1973, 75; Chrysler Classic, Australia, 1973, PGA Championship, 1974, World Series Golf, 1974, Greater New Orleans Open, 1974, Fla. Citrus Open, 1975, Colonial Nat. Invitational, 1976, 78, Colgate Mixed Team Matches, 1979; King Hassan Moroccan trophy II, 1977; Lancome trophy Benson & Hedges, 1978; 1st golfer to have scored four sub-par rounds in U.S. Open Competition, 1968; co-holder all time low scoring record U.S. Open Competition Ann.; Hickok Belt award, 1971; Leading Money winner, 1970, 2d pl. money winner 1971, 72; Vardon trophy winner, 1970-72, 74; named Golf Rookie of Year, 1967, PGA Player Year, 1971, Tex. Pro Athlete of Year, 1970; Gold Tee award 1971; AP Pro Athlete of Year, 1971; Player of Year, Golf Mag., 1971; Sportsman of Year, Sports Illustrated, 1971; Internat. Sports Personality of Year, Brit. Broadcasting Assn., 1971; mem. Tex. Hall of Fame, Am. Gulf Hall of Fame. Hon. chmn. Christmas Seal campaign, 1969-72, sports ambassador, 1971; mem. Pres.'s Conf. on Phys. Fitness and Sports; grand marshal Sun Carnival Parade, 1969-70, 71-72; mem. sports com. Nat. Multiple Sclerosis Soc. Served with USMCR, 1956-60. Office: 8515 Greenville Ave Suite S-207 Dallas TX 75243

TREVOR, ELLESTON, author; b. Bromley, Eng., Feb. 17, 1920; ed. Sevenoaks Pub. Sch.; m. Jonquil Burgess, Dec. 11, 1946; 1 son, Peregrine Scott. Founder Center d'Art Méditerrannée, Vallauris, France, 1964. Served with RAF, 1939-45. Recipient Edgar award Mystery Writers Am., 1965, Grand Prix de Littérature de Policière, France, 1966. Mem. Authors Guild Am., Roses, Guild Gt. Britain. Author about 40 novels, also many short stories, radio and screenplays; novels under own name include: Chorus of Echoes, 1950; Tiger Street, 1951; Redfern's Miracle, 1951; A Blaze of Roses; 1952; The Passion and the Pity, 1953; The Big Pick-Up, 1955; Squadron Airborne, 1955; The Killing Ground, 1956; Gale Force, 1957; The Pillars of Midnight, 1957; The V.I.P., 1959; The Billboard Madonna, 1961; Flight of the Phoenix, 1964; The Shoot, 1965; The Freebooters, 1967; A Place for the Wicked, 1968; Bury Him Among Kings, 1970; (under pseudonym Warwick Scott) Image in the Dust, 1951; The Domesday Story, 1951; Naked Canvas, 1952; (under Simon Rattray) Knight Sinister, 1951; Queen in Danger, 1951; Bishop in Check, 1953; Dead Silence, 1954; Dead Circuit, 1955 (all republished under Adam Hall, 1972); (under Caesar Smith) Heatwave, 1957; (under Roger Fitzalan) A Blaze of Arms, 1967; (under Adam Hall) Volcanoes of San Domingo, 1964; The Mandarin Cypher, 1975; The Kobra Manifesto, 1976; The Sinkiang Executive, 1978; The Quiller Memorandum, 1964; The Ninth Directive, 1966; The Striker Portfolio, 1969; The Warsaw Document, 1971; The Tango Briefing, 1973; The Scorpion Signal, 1979; (under Howard North) Expressway, 1973; (under own name) The Paragon, 1975; The Theta Syndrome, 1977; Blue Jay Summer, 1977; The Sibling, 1979. Address: Fountain Hills AZ 85268

TREXLER, EDGAR RAY, minister, editor; b. Salisbury, N.C., Sept. 17, 1937; s. Edgar Ray and Eula Belle (Farmer) T.; A.B., Lenoir-Rhyne Coll., 1959, Litt. D., 1978; M.Div., Luth. Theol. So. Sem., 1962; M.A., Syracuse U., 1964; postgrad. Boston U., 1960, Luth. World Fedn. Study Project, Geneva, 1977; m. Emily Louise Kees, Aug. 21, 1960; children—David Ray, Mark Raymond, Karen Emily. Ordained to ministry Luth. Ch. Am., 1962; pastor St. John's Luth. Ch., Lyons, N.Y., 1962-65; articles editor Luth. Mag., Phila., 1965-72, asso. editor, 1972-78, editor, 1978—; sec. Commn. Ch. Papers, Luth. Ch. Am., 1971-72, mem. staff team communications, 1972-78; chmn. Interch. Features, 1971-76. Pres. Lyons Council Chs., 1964; trustee Lenoir Rhyne Coll., 1975—. Mem. Nat. Luth. Editors Assn. (pres. 1975-77). Named for Best Articles in Mission Mags., Assoc. Ch. Press, 1974. Author: Ways to Wake Up Your Church, 1969; Creative Congregations, 1972; The New Face of Missions, 1973; Mission in a New World, 1977; LWF/6, 1978. Home: RD 1 Hickory Hill Dr Norristown PA 19401 Office: Lutheran Mag 2900 Queen Ln Philadelphia PA 19129

TREYZ, JOSEPH HENRY, librarian; b. Binghamton, N.Y., Nov. 23, 1926; s. Joseph Henry and Edna Belle (Leonard) T.; B.A., Oberlin Coll., 1950; postgrad. Harvard U., 1951; M.L.S., Columbia U., 1952. Circulation asst. N.Y. Acad. Medicine Library, 1950-51; cataloger Columbia Libraries, N.Y.C., 1951-53, Stevens Inst. Tech., Hoboken, N.J., 1953-54; adminstrv. asst. Yale Library, 1955, asst. head catalogue dept., 1955-61; head new campuses program U. Calif., La Jolla, 1961-65; asst. dir. U. Mich. Library, Ann Arbor, 1965-71; dir. libraries U. Wis., Madison, 1971—; univ. rep. Consumer Reaction Project for Catalog Card Reprodn. Study, 1961; condr. survey tech. services Fordham U. Libraries, 1967-69, Brandeis U. Libraries, 1970-71; mem. Wis. Gov.'s Com. on Library Devel., 1973—. Bd. dirs. Wis. Center for Theatre Research. Served with AUS, 1945-46. Mem. Universal Serials and Book Exchange (v.p. 1976, pres., chmn. bd. dirs. 1977), ALA (councilor 1970-74, 77—, chmn. various coms. 1967-69, recipient Melvil Dewey medal 1970), Assn. Research Libraries (commn. orgn. materials, bd. dirs. 1975—), Midlnet (v.p. 1978-79), pres. 1979-80 Assn. Coll. and Research Libraries (chmn. editorial bd. Choice 1968-70), Wis. Library Consortium (pres. 1975-76), Wis. Assn. Acad. Libraries (chmn. 1973-74), Council Wis. Librarians (chmn. 1975-76, 79-80), Wis. Library Assn. (bd. dirs. 1973-74, mem. White House Conf. com. 1977—), Madison Area Library Council (v.p. 1973-74), Mich. Library Assn. (chmn. tech. services sect. 1968-69), N.Y. Tech. Services Librarians (pres. 1959-60), Am. Soc. Info. Sci., Bibliog. Soc. Am. Methodist. Clubs: Masons, Shriners, Signature (sec.-treas. 1969-70), University (Madison). Author: Books for College Libraries, 1967; also articles. Home: 843 Farwell Dr Madison WI 53704

TREZEVANT, JOHN GRAY, publishing co. exec.; b. Alameda, Calif., May 21, 1923; s. Gray and Ann (Bevan) T.; A.B., U. Calif. at Berkeley, 1943; m. Dorothy Jean Heath, Mar. 13, 1948; children—Robert, Richard, John. Editorial staff San Francisco Chronicle, 1942-55, asst. news editor, 1951-55; asso. journalism U. Calif., 1946-48; asst. to editor-in-chief Crowell-Collier Pub. Co., N.Y.C., 1955-56; mng. editor Colliers mag., 1956-57; mgr. news and publs. Nat. Assn. Broadcasters, Washington, 1957-58; Sunday editor Chgo. Sun-Times, 1958-61, mng. editor, 1962-64; exec. v.p. Chgo. Sun-Times, Chgo. Daily News, 1964-77; exec. v.p., dir., mem. exec. com. Field Enterprises, Inc.; chmn. Field Newspaper Syndicate; pres. Met. Printing Co., Elk Grove Village, Ill.; dir. World Book-Childcraft Internat., Inc., FSC Forest Products Corp., Alsip, Ill., Manistique Pulp and Paper Co. (Mich.), Gt. Lakes Paper Co., Thunder Bay, Ont., Can. Asso. Northwestern U., United Charities Chgo.; mem. citizens com. U. Ill. Served as lt. USNR, 1943-46. Mem. Sigma Delta Chi. Roman Catholic. Clubs: Nat. Press (Washington); Chgo., Press, Tavern, Chicago (Chgo.); Balboa Bay (Newport Beach, Calif.). Home: 1139 Granville Dr Newport Beach CA 92660 Office: 1703 Kaiser Ave Irvine CA 92714

TREZISE, PHILIP HAROLD, govt. ofcl.; b. Calumet, Mich., May 27, 1912; s. Norman and Emma (Anderson) T.; A.B., U. Mich., 1936, M.A., 1939; student Nat. War Coll., 1949-50; m. Ruth Elenor Dorsey, Nov. 26, 1938; children—John Dorsey, David Philip. Research asso. U. Mich., 1940-41; fellow Social Sci. Research Council, 1941-42; ofcl. Officer Def. Transportation, 1942-43; with Dept. State, 1946-71, advisor U.S. delegation to U.N. Commn. on Indonesian question, 1948, cons. report to Pres. on fgn. econ. policy, 1950, dep. dir. Office Intelligence Research, intelligence activities, 1952-55, mem. policy planning staff, 1956-57, minister econ. affairs Am. embassy, Tokyo, 1957-61; dep. asst. sec. for econ. affairs Dept. State, 1961-65; U.S. ambassador to OECD, Paris, France, 1966-69; asst. sec. state econ. affairs, 1969-71; mem. Washington Policy Council Internat. Mgmt. and Devel. Inst.; commr. Trilateral Commn., 1976—; sr. fellow Brookings Instn., 1971—. Adj. prof. dept. polit. sci. Columbia U., 1978. Dir. Bank of Tokyo Trust Co., 1976, Atlantic Council; mem. Nat. Commn. Supplies and Shortages, 1975-76. Pres., Japan-Am. Soc., 1973-76. Served as lt. OSS, USNR, 1943-46. Recipient Pres.'s award for disting. fed. civilian service, 1965; Disting. Honor award Dept. State, 1971. Mem. Council Fgn. Relations, Phi Beta Kappa. Episcopalian. Clubs: Internat. Nat. Economists (Washington). Home: 6900 Broxburn Dr Bethesda MD 20034 Office: 1775 Massachusetts Ave NW Washington DC 20036

TREZZA, ALPHONSE FIORE, librarian; b. Phila., Dec. 27, 1920; s. Vincent and Amalia (Ferrari) T.; B.S., U. Pa., 1948, M.S., 1950, grad. study; librarian certificate Drexel Inst., 1949; m. Mildred Di Pietro, May 19, 1945; children—Carol Ann Trezza Johnston, Alphonse Fiore. Page, Free Library, Phila., 1940-41, 45-48, library asst., 1948-49; cataloger, asst. reference librarian Villanova U., 1949-50, instr., 1956-60; head circulation dept. U. Pa. Library, 1950-56; lectr. Drexel Inst. Sch. Library Sci., 1951-60; editor Cath. Library world, 1956-60; exec. sec. Cath. Library Assn., 1956-60; asso. exec. dir. ALA, exec. sec. library adminstrn. div., 1960-67, asso. dir. adminstrv. services, 1967-69; dir. Ill. State Library, Springfield, 1969-74; exec. dir. Nat. Commn. on Libraries and Info. Scis., Washington, 1974—. Nat. chmn. Cath. Book Week, 1954-56; pres.

Joliet Diocesan Bd. Edn., 1966-68; mem. Ill. Library LSCA TITLE I-II Adv. Commn., 1963-69; Democratic committeeman, Lombard, Ill., 1961-69; auditor Borough of Norwood (Pa.), 1958-60. Served to 1st lt. USAAF, 1942-45. Decorated Air medal. Mem. ALA (council 1973—, mem. exec. bd. 1974-79, chmn. statistics coordinating com. 1970-74, mem. pub. com. 1975-78), Cath. (adv. council 1960—), Ill. (chmn. legis.-library devel. com. 1964-69, mem. exec. bd.) library assns., Council Nat. Library Assns. (chmn. 1959-61), Assn. Coll. and Research Librarians (pres. Phila. chpt. 1953-55), Drexel Inst. Library Sch. Alumni Assn. (pres. 1955-56, exec. bd. 1956-60, chmn. chief officers State Library Agys. 1973-74), Chgo. Library Club (pres. 1969), Kappa Phi Kappa (chpt. pres. 1948). Club: K.C. Home: 3292 Blue Heron Dr Falls Church VA 22042 Office: Nat Commn on Libraries and Info Scis 1717 K St NW Washington DC 20036

TRIANDIS, HARRY CHARALAMBOS, educator; b. Patras, Greece, Oct. 16, 1926; s. Christos Charalambos and Louise J. (Nikokavouras) T.; B.Engring., McGill U., 1951; M.Commerce, U. Toronto (Ont., Can.), 1954; Ph.D., Cornell U., 1958; m. Pola Fotitch, Dec. 23, 1966; 1 dau., Louise. Asst. prof. U. Ill., Champaign, 1958-61, asso. prof., 1961-66, prof. psychology, 1966—; cons. USIA, 1970-75, NSF, 1968-75. Sr. fellow Ford Found., 1964-65; Guggenheim fellow, 1972-73; grantee USPHS, 1956-60, 62, Office Naval Research, 1960-68, Social and Rehab. Service, HEW, 1968-73, Ford Found., 1973-75. Chmn. fgn. grants com. Am. Psychol. Found., 1968—. Mem. Soc. for Psychol. Study of Social Issues (pres. 1975-76), Internat. Assn. Cross-Cultural Psychology (pres. 1974-76), Interam. Soc. Psychology (v.p. 1974-76), Soc. for Exptl. Social Psychology (chmn. 1972-74), Soc. for Personality and Social Psychology (pres. 1976-77). Author: Attitudes and Attitude Change, 1971; The Analysis of Subjective Culture, 1972; Varieties of Black and White Perceptions of the Social Environment, 1975; Interpersonal Behavior, 1977; editor: Handbook of Cross-Cultural Psychology, Vol. 1-6, 1979. Editorial cons. Jour. Personality and Social Psychology, 1963-71, Jour. Applied Psychology, 1970—, Sociometry, 1971-74, Jour. Cross-Cultural Psychology, 1974—, others. Home: 1 Lake Park Champaign IL 61820

TRIAS-MONGE, JOSE, chief justice P.R.; b. San Juan, P.R., May 5, 1920; s. Jose Trias-Duffrent and Belen Monge; B.A., U. P.R., 1940; M.A., Harvard U., 1943, LL.B., 1944; J.S.D., Yale U., 1947; m. Jane G. Trias, June 3, 1943; children—Jose Enrique, Peter James, Arturo Trias. Admitted to P.R. bar, 1945, U.S. Supreme Ct., 1949; teaching fellow Harvard U., 1943-44; practiced law, San Juan, 1950-52, 57-74; atty. gen. P.R., 1953-57; chief justice Supreme Ct. P.R., San Juan, 1974—; mem. P.R. Constl. Conv., 1951-52; mem. Inter-Am. Juridical Commn., OAS, 1966-67; lectr. U. P.R., 1947-49. Mem. nat. com. ACLU, 1958-74; v.p. Festival Casals, Inc., 1957-69, 73-74; trustee U. P.R., 1962-72. Mem. Bar Assn. P.R., Am. Bar Assn., Royal Acad. Spanish Lang. Roman Catholic. Author: El Sistema Judicial de Puerto Rico, 1978; Historia Constitucional de Puerto Rico, vol. I, 1979. Office: PO Box 2392 San Juan PR 00903

TRIAS-MONGE, JOSE, chief justice P.R.; b. San Juan, P.R., May 5, 1920; s. Jose and Belen (Monge) Trias-Duffrent; B.A., U. P.R., 1940; M.A., Harvard U., 1943, LL.B., 1944; J.S.D., Yale U., 1947; m. Jane Grimes Trias, June 3, 1943; children—Jose Enrique, Peter James, J. Arturo. Admitted to P.R. bar, 1945; mem. faculty U. P.R. Law Sch., 1947—; 1st asst. Atty. Gen., P.R., 1949-53, Atty. Gen., 1953-57; practiced law, San Juan, 1957-74; chief justice Supreme Ct. of P.R., 1974—. Mem. Constl. Conv. of P.R., 1951-52; U.S. rep. to Caribbean Commn., 1954-60; rep. Inter-Am. Juridical Com. of OAS, 1966-67; trustee U. P.R., 1962-72; v.p. Festival Casals, Inc., 1957-69, 73-74; mem. Gov.'s Commn. for Reform of Judicial Systems P.R. Mem. Am., Inter-Am., P.R. bar assns., World Assn. Judges, Royal Acad. Spanish Lang. (life). Roman Catholic. Author: El Sistema Judicial de Puerto Rico, 1978. Home: Box 4006 San Juan PR 00905 Office: Box 2392 San Juan PR 00903

TRIBBITT, SHERMAN WILLARD, former gov. Del.; b. Easton, Md., Nov. 9, 1922; s. Sherman Lawrence and Minnie (Thawley) T.; A.A., Beacom Coll., 1941; m. Jeanne Cleaver Webb, July 24, 1943; children—James, Carole, Sherman Webb. Teller Security Trust Co., Wilmington, Del., 1941-42; owner Odessa (Del.) Supply Co., 1947-75; dir. Farmer's Mutual Ins. Co.; chmn. adv. bd. Farmers Bank, Del. Savs. & Loan Co.; mem. Del. Gen. Assembly, 1957-65, 70-72, speaker of house, 1958-65, minority leader, 1970-73; lt. gov., 1965-69, gov. Del., 1973-77; U.S. commr. Delaware River Basin Commn., 1978—. Trustee, Beacom Coll. Served with USNR, 1942-45. Recipient Legislative Conservation award, 1965. Mem. VFW, Am. Legion. Democrat. Methodist. Mason, Moose, Rotarian. Home: 39 Hazel Rd Dover DE 19701 Office: Delaware River Basin Commn US Dept Interior Washington DC 20240

TRIBLE, PAUL SEWARD, JR., congressman; b. Balt., Dec. 29, 1946; s. Paul Seward and Katherine (Schilpp) T.; B.A., Hampden-Sydney Coll., 1968; J.D., Washington and Lee U., Lexington, Va., 1971; m. Rosemary Dunaway; 1 dau., Mary Katherine. Admitted to Va. bar, 1971; law clk. to U.S. dist. judge Albert V. Bryan, 1971-72; asst. U.S. atty. Eastern Dist. Va., 1972-74; commonwealth's atty. Essex County, Va., 1974-76; mem. 95th-96th congresses from 1st Dist. Va. Mem. Va. Jaycees (named Outstanding Young Man of Va. 1978). Republican. Episcopalian. Clubs: Ruritans, Lions, Kiwanis. Mem. Washington and Lee Law Rev. Home: Newport News VA 23606 Office: Cannon House Office Bldg Washington DC 20515

TRIBLE, WILLIAM MACLOHON, otolaryngologist; b. Washington, July 3, 1924; s. George Barnett and Letha (MacLohon) T.; A.B., Princeton U., 1943; M.D., George Washington U., 1950; M.S., U. Pa., 1956; m. Elizabeth Stuart Henley, Feb. 3, 1956; children—Letha, George, Elizabeth, Annadelia. Intern, George Washington U. Hosp., 1950-51; resident in otolaryngology Manhattan Eye, Ear and Throat Hosp., 1952-55; practice medicine specializing in otolaryngology, Washington; clin. asst. prof. Howard U. and Freedman's Hosp., Washington, 1959-66; clin. asst. George Washington Sch. Medicine, 1956-58, asso., 1958-60, clin. asst. prof., 1961-68, clin. prof. otolaryngology, 1969—; chief otolaryngology Washington Hosp. Center, 1972-78. Mem. exec. com. D.C. div. Am. Cancer Soc., 1969—. Served with AUS, 1943-46. Diplomate Am. Bd. Otolaryngology. Fellow A.C.S. (gov. 1972-78); mem. Am. Soc. Head and Neck Surgery (pres. 1978-79), Am. Laryngol. Assn. (sec. 1977—), Am. Council Otolaryngology (treas. 1974—), Soc. Surg. Oncology, Am. Laryngol., Rhinol. and Otol. Soc. Republican. Episcopalian. Clubs: Met., Chevy Chase, City Tavern. Contbr. articles to med. jours. Home: 4101 Cathedral Ave Washington DC 20016 Office: 1234 19th St NW Washington DC 20036

TRIBUS, MYRON, engr., educator; b. San Francisco, Oct. 30, 1921; s. Edward and Marie D. (Kramer) T.; B.S. in Chemistry, U. Calif. at Berkeley, 1942; Ph.D. in Engring., U. Calif. at Los Angeles, 1949; D.Sc. (hon.), Rockford (Ill.) Coll., 1965, Oakland (Mich.) U., 1971; m. Sue Davis, Aug. 30, 1945; children—Louanne, Kamala. Instr. to prof. engring. U. Calif. at Los Angeles, 1946-61; dir. aircraft icing research U. Mich., 1951-54; dean engring. Thayer Sch. Engring., Dartmouth, 1961-69; asst. sec. sci. and tech. Dept. Commerce, Washington, 1969-70; sr. v.p. tech. and engring. info. tech. group Xerox Corp., Rochester, N.Y., 1970-74; dir. Center for Advanced Engring. Study, Mass. Inst. Tech., Cambridge, 1974—. Cons. heat transfer Gen. Electric Co., 1950; cons. Fed. Office Saline Water, tech. adv. bd. Dept. Commerce; adviser to NATO, 1953; mem. Nat. Adv. Com. Oceans and Atmosphere, 1971-72. Bd. govs. Technion, Haifa, Israel, 1973—. Served to capt. USAAF, 1942-46. Recipient Thurman H. Bane award Inst. Aero. Scis., 1945; Wright Bros. medal Soc. Automotive Engrs., 1945; Alfred Noble prize Engring. Socs., 1952; named U. Calif. at Los Angeles Alumnus Year, 1972. Registered profl. engr., Mass. Mem. Am. Soc. M.E., I.E.E.E., Am. Soc. for Engring. Edn., Nat. Soc. Profl. Engrs. Author: Thermostatics and Thermodynamics, 1961; Rational Descriptions, Decisions and Designs, 1969. Contbr. articles to profl. jours. Office: 77 Massachusetts Ave Boston MA 02139

TRICE, WILLIAM HENRY, paper co. exec.; b. Geneva, N.Y., Apr. 4, 1933; s. Clyde H. Trice; B.S. in Forestry, State U. N.Y., 1955; M.S., Inst. Paper Chemistry, Appleton, Wis., 1960, Ph.D., 1963; m. Sandra Clayton, July 16, 1955; children—Russell, Amy. With Union Camp Corp., 1963—, tech. dir. bleached div., 1972-74, v.p., corp. tech. dir. research and devel., Wayne, N.J., 1974-79, sr. v.p. tech., 1979—. Trustee, pres. Western Mich. U.-Paper Tech. Found.; advisory com. So. Forest Research Center N.C. State U. Served with USAF, 1955-57. Mem. TAAPI (dir. 1978—), U. Maine Pulp and Paper Found. Indsl. Research Inst. (co. rep.). Home: 6 Hanover Rd Mountain Lakes NJ 07046 Office: Union Camp Corp 1600 Valley Rd Wayne NJ 07470

TRICHEL, GERVAIS WILLIAM, ret. corp. exec.; b. Trichel, La., Sept. 10, 1898; s. Eugene Hippolyte and Nancy Bett (Hughes) T.; B.S., U.S. Mil. Acad., 1918; M.S., M.I.T., 1935; Ph.D., U. Calif., 1938; m. Elaine Margaret Hennig, Sept. 20, 1928; children—Paul Frederick, Gervais William; m. 2d, Elizabeth Oldberg Colmar, Sept. 25, 1954. Commd. 2d lt. Coast Arty. Corps, 1918, advanced through grades to col., 1942; served at Ft. Monroe, Va., 1918-23; aide-de-camp to comdr. gen. Panama Coast Arty. Dist., Panama, 1923-26, Air Forces, Brooks Field, Tex., 1926-27; duty with Sperry Gyroscope Co., Bklyn., 1929-30; instr. elec. engring. Coast Arty. Sch., Ft. Monroe, 1930-34; transferred to Ordnance Dept., 1934; asst. to chief fire control design div. Frankfort Arsenal, Pa., 1938-40; asst. mil. attache, Paris, France, 1940; in charge fire control instrument design Frankfort Arsenal, 1941-43; took part in early devel. anti-aircraft arty., fire control computing devices, 1920-29; chief rocket devel. div. Office Chief of Ordnance, Washington, 1943-45; dep. ordnance officer chief ordnance officer Am. Forces, Western Pacific, 1945; asst. dir. new devel. div. War Dept. Spl. Staff, Washington, 1946; mem. adv. bd. to dir. atomic bomb project, 1946; mem. Nat. Inventor's Council, 1946; dep. dir. research and devel. div. War Dept. Gen. Staff, 1946-47; mem. gen. mgrs. staff Chrysler Corp., 1947-54, v.p., gen. mgr., dir. Amplex div., 1954-56, pres., dir., 1956-59, staff def. and spl. products group, 1959-60, mgr. European office Chrysler Def. Group, 1960-63; v.p., dir. Fargo Motor Corp., 1951-56. Awarded Legion of Merit with oak leaf cluster, Army Commendation ribbon. Mem. Sigma Xi. Republican. Episcopalian. Mason. Club: Orchard Lake Country. Mem. U.S. Internat. Palma Rifle Team, 1923, 24. Home: 616 Puritan Rd Birmingham MI 48009

TRICOMI, VINCENT JAMES, obstetrician, gynecologist; b. N.Y.C., Sept. 16, 1921; s. Frank and Amelia (Pafumi) T.; A.B., Syracuse U., 1942; M.D., SUNY Downstate Med. Center, Bklyn., 1950; m. J. Marie Abair, Dec. 29, 1949; children—Frank, Mary, Nancy, Ellen, Charles, Linda. Intern, Kings County Hosp., Bklyn., 1950-51, resident, 1951-55; practice medicine specializing in ob-gyn. Bklyn., 1955—; instr. ob-gyn SUNY Downstate Med. Center, 1955-57, asst. prof., 1957-63, asso. prof., 1963-69, clin. prof., 1969-73, asst. dean, 1971-73, prof., 1973—, asso. dean, 1973—; obstetrician, gynecologist-in-chief Bklyn.-Cumberland Med. Center, Bklyn., 1965—, dir. med. affairs, 1970; cons. Lutheran Med. Center, Kings County Med. Center. Mem. exec. bd. Bklyn. unit Am. Cancer Soc. Served with U.S. Army, 1942-45. Bowen Brooks scholar, 1954-55; diplomate Am. Bd. Obstetrics and Gynecology. Fellow A.C.S., Am. Coll. Obstetricians and Gynecologists (chmn. dist. 2 1978), N.Y. Obstet. Soc. (pres. 1979—), Bklyn. Gynecol. Soc. (pres. 1974-75); mem. Soc. Gynecol. Investigation, Coordinating Com. for Control Cancer of Uterine Cervix N.Y.C. (chmn. 1966-68), Royal Soc. Medicine (affiliate). Asso. editorial bd. N.Y. State Jour. Medicine. Home: 25-31 West Dr Douglaston NY 11363 Office: 121 DeKalb Ave Brooklyn NY 11201

TRIEM, EVE, poet; b. San Francisco, Nov. 2, 1902; d. Nathaniel and Rose (Etienne) Plashnek; B.A., U. Calif. at Berkeley, 1924; postgrad. in Greek Studies, U. Dubuque and U. Wash., 1954-61; m. Paul Ellsworth Triem, Sept. 20, 1924 (dec.); children—Yvonne (Mrs. Joseph Prete), Peter. Dir. poetry workshops throughout U.S.; lectr. on poetry. Formerly active Woman's Orgn. for Prohibition Reform, N.H. Recipient two Charlotte Arthur awards, League to Support Poetry award, Nat. Inst. Arts and Letters award, Authors' League award, Nat. Endowment for Arts award, Hart Crane & Alice Crane Meml. Fund award; named Woman of Achievement in Poetry, Past Pres. Assembly, State of Wash., 1976. Mem. AAUW, Poetry Soc. Am., Wash. State Herb Soc. (program dir. 1968-72). Episcopalian (chmn. com. visiting the sick and dying). Author: Parade of Doves; Poems; Heliodora: Translations from the Greek Anthology; E. E. Cummings, a monograph for Am. Writers Series; The Process (2d prize Nat. League Am. Penwomen book contest), 1976; Dark to Glow - Winter 1979; contbg. author anthologies, including: Paebar; The Golden Year: Poetry Society of America Anthology; Borestone Mountain Poetry Awards; Iowa Poets Anthology; American Women Poets. Guest editor Acad. Am. Poets: Poetry Pilot, October 1965. Contbr. poetry to lit., popular publs. Recorded for Library of Congress. Address: PO Box 523 Seattle WA 98111 also Poetry Soc Am 15 Gramercy Park New York NY. *In publication my reality is to translate experience into poem: turning a loaf of bread into stardust, a murder into revelation, giving clues to the reader how to read disaster into joy. I have lived in terrible situations; the poems are a consolation prize.*

TRIENENS, HOWARD JOSEPH, lawyer; b. Chgo., Sept. 13, 1923; s. Joseph Herman and Myrtle (Wilsberg) T.; B.S., Northwestern U., 1945; J.D., 1949; m. Paula Miller, Aug. 27, 1946; children—John, Thomas, Nancy. Admitted to Ill. bar, 1949; asso. firm Sidley, Austin, Burgess & Harper, Chgo., 1949-51; law clk. to Chief Justice Vinson, 1950-52; asso. firm Sidley, Austin, Burgess & Smith, Chgo., 1952-56; partner firm Sidley & Austin, Chgo., 1956—; dir. R.R. Donnelley & Sons Co. Trustee Northwestern U. Served with USAAF, 1943-46. Mem. Am., Ill., Chgo. bar assns., Am. Coll. Trial Lawyers, Sigma Chi. Democrat. Clubs: Legal, Law, Chgo., Casino, Mid-Day (Chgo.); Skokie Country; Glen View Country (Golf, Ill.); Metropolitan (Washington); Old Elm Country. Home: 690 Longwood Dr Glencoe IL 60022 Office: 1 First Nat Plaza Chicago IL 60603

TRIER, JERRY STEVEN, gastroenterologist, educator; b. Frankfurt, Ger., Apr. 12, 1933; s. Kurt J. and Alice L. (Cahn) T.; came to U.S., 1938, naturalized, 1943; M.D., U. Wash., 1957; M.A. (hon.), Harvard U., 1973; m. Laurel M. Bryan, June 8, 1957; children—Stanley, Jeryl, Stephen. Intern, U. Rochester (N.Y.), 1957-58, resident in medicine, 1958-59; clin. asso. Nat. Cancer Inst., Bethesda, Md., 1959-61; trainee in gastroenterology U. Wash., Seattle, 1961-63; physician Peter Bent Brigham Hosp.; asst. prof. medicine U. Wis., Madison, 1963-67; asso. prof. U. N.Mex., Albuquerque, 1967-69, Boston U., 1969-73; asso. prof. Harvard U. Med. Sch., Cambridge, Mass., 1973-76, prof., 1976—; cons. Sidney Farber Cancer Center, Boston VA Hosp., W. Roxbury VA Hosp. Served as surgeon USPHS, 1959-61. USPHS-NIH grantee, 1963—. Diplomate Am. Bd. Internal Medicine. Mem. Am. Soc. Clin. Investigation, Assn. Am. Physicians, Am. Gastroent. Assn., Am. Soc. Cell Biology, Am. Fedn. Clin. Research, Australian Gastroent. Assn. (Bushell prof. 1973). Asso. editor Anatomical Record, 1969—, Gastroenterology, 1971-77; mem. editorial bd. Gastroenterology, 1967-71, 78—, Am. Jour. Medicine, 1978—; contbr. articles and chpts. on gastrointestinal histology, pathology, devel. and disease to med. jours. and books. Home: 119 Pine St Weston MA 02193 Office: Peter Bent Brigham Hosp 721 Huntington Ave Boston MA 02115*

TRIER, WILLIAM CRONIN, surgeon, educator; b. N.Y.C., Feb. 11, 1922; s. John and Anne (Cronin) T.; A.B., Dartmouth Coll., 1943; M.D., N.Y. Med. Coll., 1947; m. Kathleen Emily Renz, June 14, 1947; children—William Cronin, Peter Louis. Commd. lt. (j.g.) M.C., U.S. Navy, 1948, advanced through grades to capt., 1964; intern St. Agnes Hosp., White Plains, N.Y., 1947-48; intern Grasslands Hosp., Valhalla, N.Y., 1948-49, surg. resident, 1949-50; surg. resident U.S. Naval Hosp., St. Albans, N.Y., 1952-55; asst. med. officer U.S.S. Midway and U.S.S. Wasp, 1951-52; tng. plastic surgery Barnes Hosp. and Washington U., St. Louis, 1956-58; assigned U.S. Naval Hosps. in Portsmouth, Va., 1950-51, St. Albans, L.I., N.Y., 1958-60, Phila., 1960-63; chief plastic surgery U.S. Naval Hosp., Bethesda, Md., 1963-67, ret., 1967; asst. prof. dept. surgery U. N.C. Sch. Medicine, Chapel Hill, 1967-69; asso. prof. dept. surgery, chief sect. plastic surgery Coll. Medicine, U. Ariz., Tucson, 1969-76; prof. surgery Sch. Medicine, U. N.C., 1976—, prof. dental ecology Sch. Dentistry, also dir. oro-facial and communicative disorders program, 1976—. Diplomate Am. Bd. Surgery, Am. Bd. Plastic Surgery (dir. 1976—). Fellow A.C.S.; mem. AMA, Am. Soc. Plastic and Reconstructive Surgeons, Am. Assn. Plastic Surgeons, Am. Soc. Aesthetic Plastic Surgery (exec. com. 1977-79), Am. Burn Assn., Am. Cleft Palate Assn. (v.p. 1972-73, pres.-elect 1979-80), Southeastern Soc. Plastic and Reconstructive Surgeons, Am. Cleft Palate Ednl. Found. (treas. 1976-79), Am. Cancer Soc. (pres. Ariz. div. 1975-76, dir. N.C. div. 1976—), N.C. Soc. Plastic and Reconstructive Surgeons (founding), Nat. Rifle Assn. (life), Gamma Delta Chi, Alpha Kappa Kappa. Episcopalian (vestryman 1961-67). Contbr. to med. jours. Home: 782 Old Mill Rd Chapel Hill NC 27514 Office: Div Plastic Surgery Dept Surgery Sch Medicine U NC Chapel Hill NC 27514

TRIFA, VALERIAN D., archbishop; b. Campeni, Rumania, June 28, 1914; s. Dionisie and Macinica (Motora) T.; came to U.S., 1950, naturalized, 1957; L.Th., U. Jassy (Rumania), 1935; postgrad. U. Bucharest (Rumania), 1936-38, U. Berlin, 1939-40. Ordained bishop Romanian Orthodox Episcopate of Am., 1952; bishop Romanian Orthodox Episcopate of Am., Jackson, Mich., 1952-70, archbishop, 1970—; mem. governing bd. Nat. Council Chs., 1952-78; mem. Holy Synod, Orthodox Ch. in Am., 1960—; mem. central com. World Council Chs., 1968-75. Address: 2522 Grey Tower Rd Jackson MI 49201

TRIFFIN, ROBERT, educator, economist; b. Flobecq, Belgium, Oct. 5, 1911; s. Francois and Céline (van Hooland) T.; LL.D., Louvain U., 1934, M.A. in Econs., 1935; Ph.D. in Econs., Harvard U., 1938; Dr. Honoris Causa, Louvain U., 1970; LL.D., U. New Haven; m. Lois Brandt, May 30, 1940; children—Nicholas, Marc Kerry, Eric. Came to U.S., 1939, naturalized, 1942. Lectr. econs. U. Louvain, Belgium, 1938-39; instr. econs. Harvard, 1939-42; chief Latin Am. sect. bd. of govs., FRS, 1942-46; dir. exchange control div. Internat. Monetary Fund, 1946-48, head tech. rep. in Europe, 1948-49; observer to intra-European payments com. Orgn. European Econ. Coop., 1948-49, U.S. rep., 1949-51; spl. adviser on policy, trade and finance div., Office Spl. Rep. in Paris, ECA, 1949-51; U.S. alternate rep. mng. bd. European Payments Union, 1950-51; Frederick William Beinecke prof. econs., Yale U., 1951—, master Berkeley Coll., 1969-77; vis. prof. Louvain Laneuve U. (Belgium), 1977—; cons. European Econ. Community, 1959—. Recipient Wells prize in econs. Harvard, 1940; de Laveleye prize and Gouverneur Cornez prize, 1970. Mem. World Acad. Art and Sci., Am. Acad. Arts and Scis., Am. Econ. Assn., Académie Royale de Belgique, Council Fgn. Relations, Société d'Economie Politique. Author: Monopolistic Competition and General Equilibrium Theory, 1940; Monetary and Banking Reform in Paraguay, 1946; Monetary and Banking Legislation of the Dominican Republic (with H.C. Wallich), 1953; Monetary Reconstruction in Europe, 1952; Europe and the Money Muddle, From Bilateralism to Near- Convertibility, 1947-56, 1957; Gold and the Dollar Crisis, the Future of Convertibility, 1960; The Evolution of the International Monetary System; Historical Reappraisal and Future Perspectives, 1964; The World Money Maze: National Currencies in International Payments, 1966; Our International Monetary System: Yesterday, Today and Tomorrow, 1968; Fate of the Pound, 1969; How to Arrest a Threatening Relapse into the 1930's?, 1971. Contbr. numerous articles to profl. jours. Home: 10 Ave Hennebel 1348 Louvain La Neuve Belgium. *I feel that much of my impact on policy has been due to: 1. Systematic concentration on those issues that appeared to me as most relevant and crucial to an orderly evolution; 2. Recognition that such an evolution entails an imaginative view of desirable changes, based on the materials and trends that the present has inherited from the past, rather than a vain attempt to stop, or set back the clock, or to set it ahead far ahead of the times. A realistic appraisal of the steps immediately feasible is as important as a forward-looking vision of long-term goals.*

TRIGERE, PAULINE, dress designer; b. Paris, France, Nov. 4, 1912; d. Alexandre and Cecile (Coriene) Trigère; student Victor Hugo Coll., Paris; children—Jean-Pierre, Philippe Radley. Came to U.S., 1937, naturalized, 1942. Began career at Martial et Armand, Place Vendome, Paris; started own bus. with bro. N.Y.C. 1942. Recipient Am. Fashion Critics' award, 1949; Return award, 1951; Neiman-Marcus award, 1950; Cotton award Nat. Cotton Council of Am., 1959; Filene's award, 1959; Hall of Fame award, 1959. Office: 550 7th Ave New York NY 10018*

TRIGG, D. THOMAS, banker; b. Eureka, Kans., June 30 1915; student U. Kans.; grad. Babson Coll., 1937; m. Marie Forbes, 1938; children—Carol Trigg Friedley, Marie Trigg Puffer, Margery Trigg Duncan, Gayle Trigg Hoshour, Ruth Trigg Barrett. With Shawmut Bank of Boston, 1937—, sr. v.p., 1960-66, exec. v.p., 1966-68, pres., 1968—, chief exec. officer, 1972—, chmn., chief exec. officer, 1974—; chmn., chief exec. officer Shawmut Corp.; dir. Shawmut Internat. Corp., Liberty Mut. Ins. Co., Atlantic Internat. Bank Ltd., Shawmut Credit Corp., Am. AgCredit Corp. Treas., trustee, mem. exec. com. Northeastern U.; overseer Boston Symphony Orch.; corporator Mus. Sci.; bd. dirs. JOBS for Mass., Inc. Served to lt. (j.g.) USNR, 1944-46. Mem. Assn. Res. City Bankers, Am. Bankers Assn. Clubs: Country, Commercial (Boston). Home: 17 Brook St Wellesley Hills MA 02181 also Waquoit MA 02356 Office: 1 Federal St Boston MA 02110

TRIGG, ERIC AUSTIN, aluminum co. exec.; b. Verdun, Que., Can., Dec. 5, 1923; s. Walter A.L. and Winifred (Tupling) T.; B.Commerce, McGill U., 1944; M.B.A., Harvard U., 1947; m. Marjorie Evelyn

Berry, Aug. 20, 1949; children—Linda Joyce, Heather Ann, Eric Bruce, David Michael. With Alcan Aluminum Ltd., 1947—, dir., 1973—, exec. v.p. corp. devel., 1975-77, regional exec. v.p. Asia, Iran and S. Pacific, 1978—; dir. subsidiaries. Served as officer, pilot, RCAF, World War II. Clubs: Wentworth (Virginia Water, Eng.); Canada (London); Univ. (Montreal and N.Y.). Home: 57 De Lavigne Rd Westmount PQ H3Y 2C3 Canada Office: PO Box 6090 Montreal PQ H3C 3H2 Canada

TRIGG, PAUL REGINALD, JR., lawyer; b. Lewistown, Mont., Mar. 25, 1913; s. Paul Reginald and Opal Stella (Fay) T.; B.A., Grinnell Coll., 1935; J.D., U. Mich., 1938; m. Helen Ruth Leake, Dec. 25, 1938; children—Paul Reginald III, Mary Adra. Admitted to Mich. bar, 1938, since practiced in Detroit; partner firm Dykema, Gossett, Spencer, Goodnow & Trigg, and predecessor, 1938—; dir. Excello Corp., Alma Piston Co., Overhead Door Corp., Gross Telecasting Inc., Daedalus Enterprises, Inc., Bundy Corp. Mem. Am., Mich., Detroit bar assns. Clubs: Detroit, Renaissance, Detroit Country; Yondotega. Home: 179 Earl Ct Grosse Pointe Farms MI 48236 Office: 35th Floor 400 Tower Renaissance Center Detroit MI 48243

TRIGGER, BRUCE GRAHAM, educator; b. Cambridge (formerly Preston), Ont., Can., June 18, 1937; s. John Wesley and Gertrude Elizabeth (Graham) T.; B.A., U. Toronto, 1959; Ph.D., Yale, 1964; m. Barbara Marian Welch, Dec. 7, 1968; children—Isabel Marian, Rosalyn Theodora. Asst. prof. Northwestern U., 1963-64; asst. prof. McGill U., 1964-67, asso. prof., 1967-69, prof. anthopology, 1969—, chmn. dept., 1970-75. Woodrow Wilson fellow, 1959-60; Woodrow Wilson dissertation fellow, 1962-63; Can. Council Leave fellow, 1968-69, 76-77; recipient Killam award Can. Council, 1970-71; Can. Silver Jubilee medal, 1977. Fellow Royal Soc. Can., Royal Anthrop. Assn.; mem. Sigma Xi. Author: History and Settlement in Lower Nubia, 1965; Beyond History, 1968; The Huron: Farmers of the North, 1969; Cartier's Hochelaga, 1972; Nubia Under the Pharaohs, 1976; The Children of Aataentsic, 1976; Time and Tradition, 1978; vol. editor: Handbook of North American Indians, Vol. 15, 1978. Home: Apt 603 3495 Mountain St Montreal PQ Canada Office: Dept Anthropology McGill U 855 Sherbrooke St W Montreal PQ H3A 2T7 Canada

TRIGGIANI, LEONARD VINCENT, chem. co. exec.; b. Paterson, N.J., June 24, 1930; s. Mario and Theresa (Tierno) T.; B.A., Drew U., 1952; M.S., Catholic U. Am., 1954, Ph.D., 1958; postgrad. Duke U. Sch. Medicine, 1956; m. Aldona Witko, Apr. 24, 1965: 1 son, Paul. Instr., Cath. U. Am., Washington, 1958-60; with research div. W.R. Grace & Co., Columbia, Md., 1960—, sr. research chemist, research supr., 1960-66, mgr.-dir. nuclear research, 1967-72, dir. inorganic research, 1972-73, dir. indsl. research, 1973-74, pres. research div., 1974—, v.p. co., 1978—; symposium chmn. nuclear fuels, 1967, 70. Bd. dirs. Montgomery Gen. Hosp.; mem. adv. bd. Carnegie-Mellon Inst. Research, Town and Country Day Sch., Silver Spring, Md. Recipient Alumni Achievement award Cath. U. Am., 1978, Drew U., 1978. Mem. Am. Chem. Soc. (chmn. governing com. 1980), Soc. Chem. Industry, Am. Nuclear Soc., Indsl. Research Inst., Am. Inst. Chem. Engrs., Chem. Industry Inst. Toxicology (dir., auditing com.), AAAS, Electrochem. Soc., Licensing Execs. Soc., Comml. Devel. Assn., Sigma Xi. Methodist. Clubs: Princeton, Chemists (N.Y.C.); Manor Country (Rockville, Md.); DeMolay. Author and patentee in fields. Home: 4005 Beverly Rd Rockville MD 20853 Office: 7379 Route 32 Columbia MD 21044

TRIGGLE, DAVID JOHN, educator; b. London, Eng., May 4, 1935; s. William John and Maud Florence (Henderson) T,; B.Sc., U. Southampton (Eng.), 1956; Ph.D., U.Hull (Eng.), 1959; m. Ann Maureen Jones, Sept. 22, 1959. Came to U.S., 1962. Asst. prof. State U. N.Y. at Buffalo, 1962-65, asso. prof. biochem. pharmacology, 1965-69, prof., 1969—, chmn. dept., 1971—. Mem. Am. Chem. Soc., Chem. Soc. Gt. Britian, Am. Soc. Pharmacology Exptl. Therapeutics. Author: Chemical Aspects of the Autonomic Nervous System, 1965; Neurotransmitter-Receptor Interactions, 1971; Chemical Pharmacology of the Synapse, 1976. Home: 11 Hampton Ct Buffalo NY 14221

TRILLING, DIANA, writer; b. N.Y.C., July 21, 1905; d. Joseph and Sadie Helene (Forbert) Rubin; A.B., Radcliffe U., 1925; m. Lionel Trilling, June 12, 1929; 1 son, James Lionel. Fiction critic The Nation, 1941-48; free-lance writer on lit., social and polit. subjects, 1948—; author: Claremont Essays, 1964; We Must March My Darlings, 1977; Reviewing The Forties, 1978; contbr. numerous articles to mags., newspapers, including Partisan Rev., Commentary, Am. Scholar, N.Y. Times Book Rev., Harpers, Atlantic, Esquire, Red Book, McCalls, Encounter, Times Lit. Supplement of London. Chmn. bd. dirs. Am. Com. for Cultural Freedom, 1955-57. Guggenheim fellow, 1950-51; Rockefeller-Nat. Endowment for Humanities grantee, 1977-79. Fellow Am. Acad. Arts and Scis. Editor: Viking Portable D. H. Lawrence, 1947; Selected Letters of D. H. Lawrence, 1958.

TRILLING, GEORGE HENRY, educator, physicist; b. Bialystok, Poland, Sept. 18, 1930; s. Max and Eugenia (Wallis) T.; came to U.S., 1941, naturalized, 1947; B.S., Calif. Inst. Tech., 1951, Ph.D., 1955; m. Madeleine Alice Monic, June 26, 1955; children—Stephen Matthew, Yvonne Katherine, David Michael. Asst. prof., then asso. prof. physics U. Mich., 1956-60; mem. faculty U. Calif. at Berkeley, 1960—, prof. physics, 1964—, chmn. dept., 1968-72; co-group leader Lawrence Radiation Lab., 1963—. Fulbright research fellow, 1956-57; NSF sr. postdoctoral fellow, 1966-67; Guggenheim fellow, 1973-74. Fellow Am. Phys. Soc.; mem. Tau Beta Pi. Home: 770 Wildcat Canyon Rd Berkeley CA 94708

TRILLING, LEON, aero. engr., educator; b. Bialystok, Poland, July 15, 1924; s. Oswald and Regina (Zakhejm) T.; came to U.S., 1940, naturalized, 1946; B.S., Calif. Inst. Tech., 1944, M.S., 1946, Ph.D., 1948; m. Edna Yuval, Feb. 17, 1946; children—Alex R., Roger S. Research fellow Cal. Inst. Tech., 1948- 50; Fulbright scholar U. Paris, 1950-51, vis. prof., 1963-64; mem. faculty Mass. Inst. Tech., Cambridge, 1951—, prof. aeros. and astronautics, 1962—; cons. McGraw-Mill, Raytheon. Mem. adv. com. Air Force Office Sci. Research; mem. Engring. Edn. Mission to Soviet Union, 1958; vis. prof. Delft Tech. U., 1974-75. Pres. Met. Com. Ednl. Opportunity, 1967-70. Guggenheim fellow, 1963-64. Mem. A.A.A.S. Home: 180 Beacon St Boston MA 02116 Office: Mass Inst Tech Cambridge MA 02139

TRIMBLE, GEORGE SIMPSON, indsl. exec.; b. Phila., Oct. 12, 1915; s. George Simpson and Edna Mae (Mytinger) T.; S.B., Mass. Inst. Tech., 1936; m. Janet Anna Bogue, Apr. 15, 1939; children—Robert Bogue, Frank George. With The Martin Co., Balt., 1937-67, successively draftsman, design engr., chief fluid dynamics, mgr. aerodynamics, mgr. advanced design, v.p. advanced design, 1937-55, v.p. engring., 1955-60, v.p. advanced programs, 1960-67, dir. Advanced Manned Missions Program, NASA, Washington, 1967, dep. dir. Manned Spacecraft Center, Houston, 1967-69; pres., dir. Bunker Ramo Corp., Oak Brook, Ill., 1970—; dir. Richardson Co., Des Plaines, Ill.; cons. Sci. Adv. Bd. Aero Vehicle Panel, 1959-61, Office Dir. Def., Research and Engring. Fellow Am. Inst. Aeros. and Astronautics; mem. Tau Beta Pi. Home: 737 Elm St Hinsdale IL 60521 Office: Bunker Ramo Corp Oak Brook IL 60521

TRIMBLE, HENRY WEEKS, JR., lawyer; b. Glen Ridge, N.J., June 6, 1920; s. Henry Weeks and Laura (Lyman) T.; A.B. in Psychology, Princeton U., 1942; LL.B., Yale U., 1947; m. Diana Neill, Nov. 10, 1942 (div. 1970); children—Pamela Van B., Henry W., Neill F. Admitted to N.Y. bar, 1947; asso. Cravath, Swaine & Moore, N.Y.C., 1947-56; sec., gen. counsel IBM Corp., N.Y.C., 1956-70; sr. v.p. Hayden, Stone, Inc., N.Y.C., 1970-73; sr. partner Trimble Assos., N.Y.C., 1973—; dir. Seaboard Surety Co., Internat. Aviation Industries, Inc., Leaseway Transp. Corp., Magnetic Head Corp. Bd. dirs. YMCA Counseling and Testing Service. Served as 1st lt. F.A., AUS, 1942-45. Mem. Am., N.Y. State bar assns., Assn. Gen. Counsel, Am. Soc. Corporate Secs., No. Westchester Bar Assn. Address: 715 Park Ave New York NY 10021

TRIMBLE, LESTER ALBERT, composer; b. Bangor, Wis., Aug. 29, 1923; s. John Lester and Clara Frieda Amanda (Piske) T.; M.F.A., Carnegie Inst. Tech., 1948, student Conservatoire Nat. de Musique, Paris, 1951, Ecole Normale De Musique, Paris, 1951, Berkshire (Mass.) Music Center, summer 1947; student electronic music, Columbia, 1969; m. Mary Constance Wilhelm, July 5, 1947. Mem. faculty Chatham Coll., Pitts., 1949-50; music criticis for N.Y. Herald Tribune, 1952-60, The Nation, 1956-61, Washington Star, 1963-64, Notes mag., the Music Quar., occasionally 1952-62; gen. mgr. Am. Music Center, N.Y.C., 1960-62, bd. dirs., 1959—; prof. music U. Md., 1963-68; composer-in-residence N.Y. Philharmonic Orch., 1967-68; music critic Stereo Rev. mag., 1970-73; mem. faculty Juilliard Sch., 1971—, New Sch. Social Research, 1969-70; performance of music with maj. symphony orchs. and chamber ensembles throughout world; recs. on Columbia, Desto, C.R.I. records, judge numerous composition competitions; mem. rec. com. Walter W. Naumburg Found. Bd. dirs. MacDowell Colony, Am. Composers Alliance, Bennington Composers Conf., Music in Our Time, Concert Artists Guild. Served with USAAF, 1942-44. Guggenheim fellow, 1964; recipient award and citation Nat. Inst. Arts and Letters, 1961; award Soc. Publn. Am. Music, 1964; Thorne Fund award, 1968-69; award Columbia Records Modern Music Series, 1958; Ford Found. Publn.-Rec. award, 1972; Dial Press Creative Writing award, 1947; Alice Ditson award, 1957; Sigma Alpha Iota Publn. award, 1964; Rockefeller grant, 1967; fellow MacDowell Colony, 1958-59, Yaddo Found., 1959, Huntington Hartford Found., 1957. Home: 98 Riverside Dr New York NY 10024 Office: Juilliard Sch Lincoln Center New York NY 10023*

TRIMBLE, MARSH PAUL, publisher; b. Albia, Iowa, Dec. 5, 1921; s. Paul Harry and Truie (Nelson) T.; m. Joy Roud, Sept. 24, 1971; children—Paul, Susan, Mark, Darcy. Bus. mgr. Indsl. Publs., Chgo., 1946-52; gen. sales mgr. Midland Distbg. Co., Chgo., 1952-54; bus. mgr. Profl. Builder mag., Chgo., 1954-61, asso. publisher, 1962-63, publisher, 1964—; dir. M. & J. Bldg. Co., Glenview, Ill.; mem. adv. council Cahners Pub. Co. Served with USNR, 1941-46. Recipient Eugene R. Kurtz Meml. award Nat. Assn. Bldg. Mfrs., 1971; named Bldg. Industry Man of Year, Volume Builders Am., 1974. Clubs: Ill. Athletic, Valley Lo Sports. Home: 3055 Lindenwood Ln Glenview IL 60025 Office: Professional Builder 5 S Wabash Chicago IL 60603

TRIMBLE, PAUL EDWIN, shipping assn. exec.; b. Agenda, Kans., Mar. 24, 1913; s. Harry Leon and Velma Ellen (Long) T.; B.S., U.S. Coast Guard Acad., 1936; M.B.A., Harvard, 1942; m. Marie Schwenk Waring, 1980; children—Sharrol Lee (Mrs. James E. Foels), James Patton. Commd. ensign USCG, 1936, advanced through grades to vice adm., 1966; budget officer U.S. Coast Guard, Washington, 1953-55, dep. comptroller, 1955-57, comptroller, 1957-59, dep. chief staff, 1962-64, chief staff, 1964-66, vice comdt., 1966-70; pres. Lake Carriers' Assn., Cleve., 1970—. Mem. bd. visitors Gt. Lake Maritime Acad. Bd. dirs. United Seamen's Service, Nat. Waterways Conf. Mem. Coast Guard Alumni Assn. (pres. 1964-66), Am. Bur. Shipping, Soc. Naval Architects and Marine Engrs. Clubs: N.Y. Yacht, Meadowood Country, U.S. Propeller, Cleve. Athletic, Cleve. Playhouse. Home: 100 Herring Run Dr Centerville MA 02632 also 1717 Walnut Ln Rocky River OH 44116 Office: 1411 Rockefeller Bldg Cleveland OH 44113

TRIMBLE, PRESTON ALBERT, judge; b. Salina, Okla., Aug. 27, 1930; s. James Albert and Winnie Louella (Walker) T.; B.A., U. Okla., 1956, LL.B., 1960; m. Patricia Ann Beadle; children—Todd, Beth, Amy. Admitted to Okla. bar, 1960; practice law, 1960; asst. county atty. Cleveland County, Okla., 1960-62, county atty., 1962-67, dist. atty., 1967-79; dist. judge, 1979—; spl. instr. S.W. Center Law Enforcement Edn.; cons. prosecution mgmt. Mem. Jud. Council Okla.; chmn. Okla. Corrections Workshop; mem. planning com. Nat. Inst. Crime and Delinquency; mem. com. on multi-agy. problems in criminal justice Appellate Judges Conf. Bd. dirs. Okla. U. Crisis Center, 1970—, ARC; trustee Nat. Assn. Pretrial Service Agys. Resource Center. Served with USNR, 1948-52; lt. col. USAFR. Mem. Okla., Cleveland County bar assns., Nat. (past pres.), Okla. (past pres.) dist attys. assns., Nat. Coll. Dist. Attys. (bd. regents), Am. Legion. Democrat. Methodist. Lion. Home: 1441 Cherry Laurel St Norman OK 73069 Office: Courthouse Norman OK 73069. *An elected public official must remember that the people own his position and he only holds it in trust for them.*

TRIMBLE, VANCE HENRY, ret. newspaper editor; b. Harrison, Ark., July 6, 1913; s. Guy L. and Josephine (Crump) T.; student pub. schs., Wewoka, Okla.; m. Elzene Miller, Jan. 9, 1932; 1 dau., Carol Ann. Cub reporter Okemah (Okla.) Daily Leader, 1928; worked various newspapers in Okmulgee, Muskogee, Tulsa (Okla.); successively reporter, rewrite man, city editor Houston Press, 1939-50, mng. editor, 1950-55; news editor Scripps-Howard Newspaper Alliance, Washington, 1955-63; editor Ky. Post and Times-Star, Covington, 1963-79. Trustee, Scripps-Howard Found., 1974-79. Recipient Pultizer prize for nat. reporting, 1960, Raymond Clapper award, 1960, Sigma Delta Chi award for distinguished Washington correspondence, 1960; named to Okla. Journalism Hall of Fame, 1974. Mem. Am. Soc. Newspaper Editors. Baptist. Clubs: Nat. Press (Washington); Press (Houston); Cincinnati. Author: The Uncertain Miracle, 1974. Home: 1013 Sunset Ave Kenton Hills KY 41011

TRIMBLE, WILLIAM CATTELL, JR., lawyer; b. Buenos Aires, Argentina, Feb. 7, 1935; s. William Cattell and Nancy Gordon (Carroll) T.; A.B., Princeton U., 1958; LL.B., U. Md., 1964; m. Barbara Janney, June 19, 1960; children—William C., Margery M. Admitted to Md. bar, 1965; asso. firm Cross, Shriver, Bright & Washburne, Balt., 1965-69; asso. firm Ober, Grimes & Shriver, Balt., 1969-70, partner, 1970—, mng. partner, 1973-77; mem. Gov.'s Commn. to Revise Annotated Code of Md., 1975—. Pres. bd. trustees Valley Sch., 1968-73; trustee Garrison Forest Sch., 1975—. Served to lt. USNR, 1958-61. Mem. Am., Md., Balt. bar assns. Episcopalian. Clubs: Colonial (Princeton); Md., Greenspring Valley Hunt, Soc. of Cin. Home: 409 Chattolanee Hill Owings Mills MD 21117 Office: 1600 Maryland Nat Bank Bldg Baltimore MD 21202

TRIMBORN, HARRY, journalist. Correspondent, Los Angeles Times, Vietnam, 1969, Moscow, 1970-72, Israel 1972-74, London, 1975-76, Bonn, W. Ger., 1978—, editorial writer, 1976-78. Office: care Times Mirror Co Times Mirror Sq Los Angeles CA 90053

TRIMMER, HAROLD SHARP, JR., lawyer, retail exec.; b. Somerville, N.J., July 27, 1938; s. Harold Sharp and Mary Elizabeth (Knox) T.; B.A., Wesleyan U., 1960; J.D., Harvard, 1963. Instr. law U. Calif. at Los Angeles, 1963-64; Congl. fellow Am. Polit. Sci. Assn., Washington, 1964-65; asso. firm Royall, Koegel & Rogers, Washington and N.Y.C., 1965-66, McCutchen, Doyle, Brown & Enersen, San Francisco, 1966-69; with GSA, Washington, 1969-75, exec. asst. to adminstr., 1969-70, asst. adminstr., 1970-72, commr. automated data and telecommunications, 1972-73, asso. adminstr. fed. mgmt. policy, 1973, gen. counsel, 1974-75; sec., gen. counsel Garfinckel, Brooks Bros., Miller & Rhoads, Inc., Washington, 1976—, v.p., 1979—. Trustee, World Affairs Council No. Calif., 1969-70, Wesleyan U., 1971-74. George F. Baker scholar. Mem. Am. Bar Assn., State Bar Calif., Phi Beta Kappa. Home: 812 A 3d St SW Washington DC 20024 Office: 1629 K St NW Washington DC 20006

TRINKAUS, CHARLES EDWARD, JR., historian, educator; b. Bklyn., Oct. 25, 1911; s. Charles Edward and Frances (Krueger) T.; B.A., Wesleyan U., Middletown, Conn., 1933; Ph.D. (Univ. fellow), Columbia, 1940; m. Pauline Moffitt Watts, Mar. 1, 1975; children—John Aaron (dec.), Peter Mark. Mem. faculty Sarah Lawrence Coll., Bronxville, N.Y., 1936-70, mem. faculty Florence Summer Program, 1958-72, dir., 1966-72, faculty trustee, 1963-66; prof. history U. Mich., Ann Arbor, 1970—, dir. Medieval and Renaissance Collegium, 1974-75. Life mem. Columbia Seminar on Renaissance, 1945—, also former sec., chmn.; vis. prof. Center for Medieval and Renaissance Studies, U. Calif. at Los Angeles, 1976. Recipient citation for distinction in scholarship and teaching Wesleyan U., 1965. Am. Council Learned Socs. humanities fellow, 1965-66; Nat. Endowment for Humanities sr. humanities fellow, 1972-73; John Simon Guggenheim fellow, 1976-77. Fellow Am. Acad. Arts and Scis.; mem. Am. Hist. Assn., Am. Soc. Reformation Research, Medieval Acad. Am., Renaissance Soc. Am. (pres. 1973-76). Author: Adversity's Noblemen: The Italian Humanists on Happiness, 1940, reprinted, 1965; In Our Image and Likeness: Humanity and Divinity in Italian Humanist Thought, 2 vols., 1970; The Poet as Philosopher, Petrarch and the Formation of Renaissance Consciousness, 1979; editor: Graduate Study in an Undergraduate College, 1956; (with H.A. Oberman) The Pursuit of Holiness in Late Medieval and Renaissance Religion, 1974. Home: 1831 Coronada Dr Ann Arbor MI 48103

TRINKAUS, JOHN PHILIP, biologist; b. Rockville Centre, N.Y., May 23, 1918; s. Charles Edward and Fransiska Magdalena (Krueger) T.; B.A., Wesleyan U., Middletown, Conn., 1940; M.A., Columbia U., 1941; Ph.D., Johns Hopkins U., 1948; m. Madeleine Francine Marguerite Bazin, Oct. 6, 1963; children—Gregor, Tanya, Erik. Mem. faculty Yale U., New Haven, 1948—, prof. cell. and developmental biology, 1964—, dir. grad. studies in biology, 1965, master Branford Coll., 1966-73; chmn. Gordon Research Conf. on Cell Contact and Movement, 1979; mem. staff Woods Hole (Mass.) Marine Biol. Lab., 1953-57, 78; mem. space biology adv. panel NASA, 1976-79. Served to capt. USAAF, 1942-46. Guggenheim fellow, 1959-60; NSF grantee, 1952-76; NIH grantee, 1974—. Mem. Am. Soc. Zoologists, Am. Soc. Cell Biology, Am. Soc. Developmental Biology, Internat. Inst. Embryology, ACLU. Clubs: Yale (N.Y.C.); Mory's. Author: Cells into Organs—The Forces that Shape the Embryo, 1969; On the Mechanism of Metazoan Cell Movements, 1976; also articles; asso. editor Jour. Exptl. Zoology, 1964-68. Home: Moose Hill Rd Guilford CT 06437 Office: Dept Biology Yale U New Haven CT 09620

TRIPP, GRANGER, advt. exec.; b. Mt. Kisco, N.Y., Sept. 20, 1922; s. Granger and Helen (Brown) T.; B.A., Union Coll., 1943; m. Kathleen Martin, Aug. 24, 1946; children—Kathleen, Rosemary, Valerie, Suzanne, Granger Edward. Vice-pres. sales Radio Reports, 1946-53; with J. Walter Thompson, N.Y.C., 1953—, now sr. v.p., creative dir. Served with AUS, 1943-45. Office: 420 Lexington Ave New York NY 10017

TRIPP, LOUIS REED, economist; b. Schenectady, Sept. 25, 1913; s. Louis Ledoux and Ella Mae (Butler) T.; A.B., Union Coll., Schenectady, 1934; Ph.D., Yale, 1942; m. Mary M. Frelick, Nov. 23, 1940 (div. Jan. 1970); children—Carolyn (Mrs. Arthur J. Ray), Barbara (Mrs. Strohl), Thomas Reed, Jonathan Reed; m. 2d, Jan W. Crawford, Apr. 14, 1973. Instr. econs. Lehigh U., 1938-42; economist, sect. chief, asso. dir. disputes Phila. Regional Wage Stblzn. Bd., 1943-54; economist, asst. coordinator labor relations Pitts. Plate Glass Co., Libbey-Owens-Ford Glass Co., 1946-49; prof. econs. U. Wis., 1950-63, dir. Indsl. Relations Research Center, 1954-63, field chmn. Indonesia project, Gadjah Mada U., Jogjakarta, 1957-59; dean Lehigh U. Coll. Bus. Adminstrn., 1964-71, prof. econs., 1971—. Arbitrator labor-mgmt. grievances, 1949—; chief economist Wage Stblzn. Bd., 1951-52; cons. Bur. Employment Security, Dept. Labor, 1961-62. Mem. Indsl. Relations Research Assn. (editor 1953-56), Am. Econ. Assn., Nat. Acad. Arbitrators (gov. 1976—), Adminsrv. Mgmt. Soc., Phi Beta Kappa, Delta Phi. Author: (with Sylvester Garrett) Management Problems Implicit in Multi-Employer Bargaining, 1950; Wage Reopening Arbitration, 1952; Labor Problems and Processes, 1960. Contbr. articles to profl. jours. Home: 577 Biery's Bridge Rd Bethlehem PA 18017

TRIPP, RALPH HARRY, aircraft co. exec.; b. Denton, Mont., Mar. 11, 1915; s. Harry W. and Hallie (King) T.; B.A., Drake U., 1937; M.S., Iowa State Coll., 1939, Ph.D., 1942; D.Sc. (hon.), Rocky Mountain Coll., 1970; m. LaVone Semingson, Aug. 21, 1938; children—Virginia, Hallie, Roberta. Group leader charge vibration and flutter in structures dept. Grumman Aircraft Engring. Corp., 1942-48, head research dept., 1948-50, dept. head charge test instrumentation, 1950-57, asst. dir. flight test dept., 1957-62, program dir. orbiting Astron. Obs., 1962-68, dir. lunar module program, 1968-72, v.p., space programs dir., 1970-72, v.p., dir. Grumman Mgmt. Systems, 1972-73, v.p., gen. mgr. Great River Avionics Facility, also v.p., dir. Grumman Tng. Systems div., 1973-75; exec. v.p. Grumman Aerospace Corp., 1975-79, also dir.; vice-chmn. bd. Grumman Allied Industries, Inc., Melville, N.Y., 1979—. Asso. fellow Inst. Aero. Scis.; mem. Instrument Soc. Am. (sr. mem.; past pres.), Am. Astronautical Soc. Home: 9 Apex Rd Melville NY 11746 Office: 445 Broadhollow Rd Melville NY 11747

TRIPP, ROBERT D., educator; b. Oakland, Calif., Jan. 9, 1927; B.S., Mass. Inst. Tech., 1949; Ph.D., U. Calif., 1955; married; 3 children. Physicist, Lawrence Berkeley Lab., U. Calif. at Berkeley, 1955—, prof. physics, 1966—. Physicist, AEC France, 1959-60; NSF sr. fellow European Orgn. Nuclear Research, Geneva, Switzerland, 1964-65, vis. scientist, 1971-72, 79-80. Served with USNR, 1945-46. Office: Le Conte Hall U Calif Berkeley CA 94720

TRIPPE, KENNETH ALVIN BATTERSHILL, bus. exec.; b. Kansas City, Mo., Jan. 3, 1933; s. Alvin C. and Blanche (Battershill) T.; B.S. in Bus. Adminstrn., Kans. U., 1955; LL.B., U. Mo., 1958; m. Jane Muir Mitchell, June 11, 1955; children—Kenneth, Tracy, Robert. Admitted to Mo. bar, 1958; with Miss. River Corp., St. Louis, 1958-68, asst. sec., 1958-64, sec., 1964-65, asst. to pres., 1965-68; asst. treas. Internat. Utilities Corp. (name IU Internat. Corp. 1973), Phila., 1968-69, asst. treas. corporate and internat. fin., 70-72, v.p., treas., 1972-75, exec. v.p., dir. subs. Gotaas-Larsen Shipping Corp., 1975-77, pres., chief exec. officer, dir., 1977—; v.p. fin. Kans. Gas & Electric

Co., Wichita, 1969-70. Bd. dirs. World Affairs Council. Mem. Am., Mo. bar assns., Newcomen Soc., Japan Soc., Phi Delta Phi, Sigma Chi. Republican. Episcopalian. Clubs: Phila. Country; Union League (N.Y.C.). Home: 1431 Beaumont Dr Gladwyne PA 19035 Office: 1114 Ave of Americas New York NY 10036 also Washington Mall Hamilton 5 Bermuda

TRIPPET, BYRON KIGHTLY, former assn. exec.; b. Princeton, Ind., Sept. 21, 1908; s. Sanford and Edith (Kightly) T.; B.A., Wabash Coll., 1930; postgrad. Geneva (Switzerland) Inst. Internat. Studies, 1930-31; B.A., Oxford (Eng.) U., 1934, M.A., 1939; LL.D., Ind. U., 1962; L.H.D., Wabash Coll., 1955, DePauw U., 1957, Valparaiso U., 1958; m. Dorothy Clark O'Neall, June 21, 1936 (div. July, 1967); 1 stepson, David C.; m. 2d, Lorenza Galdeano Turillas, Nov. 8, 1968. Mem. faculty and adminstrn., Wabash Coll., 1935-65, dean coll., prof. history, 1942-55, pres., 1955-65; v.p. U. Americas, Mexico City, 1965-66, cons., 1966-68, pres., 1973-75; pres. Independent Coll. Funds Am., N.Y.C., 1968-73; dir. Lilly Endowment Inc., 1973—; dir. Princeton Telephone Co. Coll. examiner N. Central Assn. Colls. and Secondary Schs., 1948-54; mem. Rhodes Scholar Selection Com., Great Lakes dist., 1946-64; mem. exec. com., trustee United Student Aid Funds, Inc., 1968—; mem. coll. self study com. Ford Found., 1952-54. Chmn. bd. dirs. Independent Coll. Funds Am., Inc., 1963; bd. dirs. Tuition Exchange Inc., 1957-61, Research Corp., N.Y.C., 1959-62. Served to lt. comdr. USNR, 1942-46. Rhodes scholar, 1931-34. Mem. Am. Conf. Acad. Deans (chmn. 1955), Assn. Am. Colls. (chmn. commn. liberal edn. 1958-61), Am. Council Edn. (sec. 1962-63), Ind. Hist. Soc., Phi Beta Kappa (nat. lectr. panel 1955-60), Beta Theta Pi. Club: University (N.Y.C.). Home: 403 W Walnut St Princeton IN 47670 Office: 222 W Broadway Princeton IN 47670

TRIST, ERIC LANSDOWN, educator; b. Dover, Eng., Sept. 11, 1909; s. Frederick James Lansdown and Alexina (Middleton) T.; B.A. in English Lit. with 1st class honors, Cambridge U., 1931, in Psychology with 1st class honors (distinction star), 1933, M.A., 1940; m. Beulah Joyce Varney, June 20, 1959; 1 dau., Carolyn Rachel; 1 son by previous marriage, Alan Caven. Chmn. Tavistock Inst. Human Relations, London, 1958-66; prof. emeritus organizational behavior and ecology Wharton Sch., U. Pa., Phila., chmn. Mgmt. and Behavioral Sci. Center; now prof. faculty environ. studies York U., Toronto; cons. Unilever, Shell, Philips Elec., ICI, Gen. Foods Corp., Gen. Electric, others; cons. various govt. agys. U.S., U.K., UN. Served to lt. col. Brit. Army, 1942-46. Decorated Order Brit. Empire; Foundress scholar; Commonwealth Fund fellow Yale U., 1933-35; Center for Advanced Study in Behavioral Scis. fellow, 1960-61. Mem. Brit. Psychol. Assn., Brit. Sociol. Assn., Internat. Assn. Applied Behavioral Scientists, European Inst. for Trans-nat. Studies in Group and Organizational Devel., Internt. Council for Quality of Working Life. Author: (with B. Semeunott) Diagnostic Performance Tests, 1958; (with C. Sofer) Exploring Group Relations, 1958; (with others) Organizational Choice, 1963; (with Hugh Beaver) Social Research, a National Policy for Science, 1964; Environmental Analysis, 1969; Organization and Support of the Social Sciences, 1970; (with F.E. Emery) Towards a Social Ecology, 1973, others. Coordinating editor: Human Relations, 1966—; contbr. articles to profl. jours. Home: 115 College Ave Swarthmore PA 19081

TRITSCH, ROBERT GRANT, lawyer, mfg. co. exec.; b. N.Y.C., May 9, 1926; s. John Edgar and Irene Wilkenson (Grant) T.; A.B., Princeton U., 1947; LL.B., U. Va., 1950; LL.M., N.Y. U., 1956; m. Susan Colwell, Mar. 31, 1962; children—Constance Louise, Nancy Irene, Caroline Grant. Admitted to N.Y. bar, 1954; atty. Heyden Newport Chem. Corp., N.Y.C., 1953-59, Cerro Corp., N.Y.C., 1959-61; corporate sec. Chem. Fund Inc., N.Y.C., 1961-63; trademark counsel Borden Inc., N.Y.C., 1963-71, asst. sec., 1971-74, corporate sec., 1974—. Mem. Pelham Manor (N.Y.) Zoning Bd., 1976—; elder Huguenot Presbyterian Ch., Pelham Manor, 1977—; trustee Colburn Meml. Home. Served with U.S. Army, 1951-53. Mem. Am. Soc. Corporate Secs. (sec.), U.S. Trademark Assn., Stockholder Relations Soc. N.Y. Republican. Clubs: Princeton (N.Y.C.); Huguenot Yacht (counsel) (New Rochelle, N.Y.). Home: 678 Ely Ave Pelham NY 10803 Office: 277 Park Ave New York NY 10017

TRITTEN, RAY ALBERT, mfg. co. exec.; b. Utica, N.Y., Feb. 21, 1919; s. Charles A. and Hazel (Chapman) T.; B.S. Chem. Engring., U. Mich., 1942; m. Shirley Elaine Johnson, Sept. 19, 1942; children—Craig A., Stephen E. With Carrier Corp., 1955-70, pres. div. Day & Night Mfg. Co., La Puente, Calif., 1965-70, pres. div. Payne Co., La Puente, 1965-70; with AMF Inc., 1970—, group exec., motorcycle products group, Stamford, Conn., 1974-78, v.p. ops., leisure products, White Plains, N.Y., 1978-79, pres., chief operating officer, White Plains, N.Y., 1979—. Served with USNR, 1942-45. Mem. Sigma Xi, Tau Beta Pi. Club: Country of Darien (Conn.). Office: 777 Westchester Ave White Plains NY 10604

TRIVELPIECE, ALVIN WILLIAM, physicist, corp. exec.; b. Stockton, Calif., Mar. 15, 1931; s. Alvin Stevens and Mae (Hughes) T.; B.S., Calif. Poly. Coll., San Luis Obispo, 1953; M.S., Calif. Inst. Tech., 1955, Ph.D., 1958; m. Shirley Ann Ross, Mar. 23, 1953; children—Craig Evan, Steve Edward, Keith Eric. Fulbright scholar Delft (Netherlands) U., 1958-59; asst. prof., then asso. prof. U. Calif. at Berkeley, 1959-66; prof. physics U. Md., 1966-76; on leave as asst. dir. for research div. controlled thermonuclear research AEC, Washington, 1973-75; v.p. Maxwell Labs. Inc., San Diego, 1976-78; corp. v.p. Sci. Applications, Inc., La Jolla, Calif., 1978—; cons. to govt. and industry. Named Distinguished Alumnus Calif. Poly. State U., 1978. Guggenheim fellow, 1966. Fellow Am. Phys. Soc., AAAS; mem. IEEE, Washington Philos. Soc., Am. Nuclear Soc., Ams. for Energy Independence, AAUP, N.Y. Acad. Scis., Am. Assn. Physics Tchrs., Sigma Xi. Author: Slow Wave Propagation in Plasma Wave Guides, 1966; (with N.A. Krall) Principles of Plasma Physics, 1973; also articles. Patentee in field. Home: 7080 Caminito Estrada La Jolla CA 92037 Office: 1200 Prospect St La Jolla CA 92038

TROAN, JOHN, newspaperman; b. Jessup, Pa., Aug. 23, 1918; s. Andrew and Veronica (Troanovitch) Troanovitch; A.B., Pa. State U., 1939; D.H.L., Westminster Coll., 1975; m. Varcey Morrissey, Oct. 23, 1943; children—Lawrence E., Judy A. (Mrs. C.R. Nowe), Mary Lou (Mrs. Douglas A. Satterfield), Geoffrey J. Staff writer Pitts. Press, 1939-47, sci. editor, 1947-58, asso. editor, 1966-67, editor, 1967—; sci. writer Scripps-Howard Newspaper Alliance, 1958-66. Mem. Allegheny Conf. Community Devel. Pa. S.W. Assn. Incorporator Central Blood Bank Pitts., 1953-57; incorporator Pitts. Communications Found., 1968, pres., 1968-70; trustee Sci. Service, 1967—. Served with USNR, 1944-46. Named One of Pitts. 100 Outstanding Young Men, Time mag., 1953; named Man of Year in Communications, Pitts. Jr. C. of C., 1956, 66; recipient Freedoms Found. award, 1968. Fellow A.A.A.S.; mem. Am., Pa. (Keystone award 1968) socs. newspaper editors, Am. Press Inst. (mem. adv. bd. 1969—), Nat. Assn. Sci. Writers (pres. 1958-59), Council Advancement Sci. Writing (incorporator 1960, exec. bd. 1960-72), World Affairs Council Pitts., Carnegie Inst. Soc., Sigma Delta Chi, Pi Gamma Mu, Pi Delta Epsilon. Clubs: Pittsburgh Press; Duquesne, Allegheny, Chartiers Country. Home: 301 Shadowlawn Ave Pittsburgh PA 15216 Office: 34 Blvd of Allies Pittsburgh PA 15230

TROCIN, ROBERT EDWARD, hardware co. exec.; b. Dayton, Ohio, Sept. 30, 1936; s. Jack Rego and Helen (Jordan) T.; B.S. in Bus. Adminstrn., Miami U., Ohio, 1958; m. Martha Elizabeth Longstreth, Aug. 30, 1958; children—Jeffrey, Lauren. Vice pres., gen. mgr., partner Interstate Supply Inc., Huntington, W.Va., 1963-69, dir., 1963-72; pres., gen. mgr. Banks-Miller Supply Co., Huntington, 1969-74, chmn., chief exec. officer, 1974-79; chmn., chief exec. officer Tidewater Supply Co., Norfolk, Va., 1974-79; dir., pres. Buchanan Wholesale Co., Grundy, Va., 1970-76; sec., dir. Mingo Wyo. Coal Land Co., Huntington, 1969-76; pres., owner J. L. Cook Hardware Co., Huntington, 1979—, Wearing Apparel Unltd., Inc., Huntington, 1979—; dir. Leasing Inc., Am. Nat. Rubber Co. (both Huntington). Gen. chmn. fund dr. United Community Services, Cabell and Wayne counties, W.Va., 1971; mem. Huntington Park Commn., 1972-73; bd. dirs. Drs. Meml. Hosp., Huntington, 1971-75; trustee Cammack Children's Center, Huntington, 1970—, Marshall U. Found., 1972-74; trustee Cabell Huntington Hosp., 1975—, v.p., 1976-77; W.Va. rep. to nat. adv. council Am. Hosp. Assn. Mem. Greater Huntington C. of C. (pres. 1972-73). Episcopalian. Home: 103 Whitaker Blvd Huntington WV 25701 Office: 330 3d Ave Huntington WV 25706

TROEN, PHILIP, physician, educator; b. Portland, Maine, Nov. 24, 1925; s. Ben and Gertrude (Cope) T.; A.B., Harvard U., 1944, M.D., 1948; m. Betty Ann Zelig, Mar. 22, 1953; children—Mark Lawrence, Bruce Robert, Gail Sheri. Intern, Boston City Hosp., 1948-49, asst. resident medicine, 1949-50; asst. resident medicine Beth Israel Hosp., Boston, 1950, 52-53, chief resident, 1953-54, asst. in medicine, 1955-56, USPHS research fellow, 1955-56, asso. in med. research, 1956-64, asso. in medicine, 1956-58, asst. vis. physician, 1959-64; teaching fellow Harvard Med. Sch., 1952-53, asst. in medicine, 1953-54, research fellow, 1955-56, instr. medicine, 1956-59, asso. in medicine, 1959-60, asst. prof., 1960-64; prof. medicine U. Pitts. Sch. Medicine, 1964—, asso. chmn. dept. medicine, 1969-79, vice chmn. dept. medicine, 1979—; physician-in-chief Montefiore Hosp., 1964—; sci. counselor NIH; sci. counselor rev. Intramural Reproductive Biology Program Nat. Inst. Child Health and Human Devel., 1977; cons. male fertility and infertility Nat. Inst. Occupational Safety and Health, 1977. Fellow in endocrinology and metabolism Mayo Clinic, Rochester, Minn., 1954-55, Kendall-Hench research fellow, 1955; Ziskind teaching fellow, 1956-59, Med. Found. Greater Boston research fellow, 1959-63; John Simon Guggenheim Found. fellow, Stockholm, Sweden, 1960-61; mem. med. res. service merit rev. bd. in endocrinology VA, 1979-82. Mem. contract rev. com. Nat. Insts. Child Health and Human Devel., 1975-79. Served to capt. M.C., AUS, 1950-52. Diplomate Nat. Bd. Med. Examiners, Am. Bd. Internal Medicine. Mem. Am. Soc. Clin. Investigation, Am. Soc. Biol. Chemists, AAAS, Am. Fedn. Clin. Research, Am. Soc. Andrology (program and publs. com., exec. council 1977— v.p. 1979-80), Endocrine Soc., N.Y. Acad. Scis., Am. Soc. Andrology (exec. council 1977—), Central Soc. Clin. Research, Soc. for Study of Reproduction. Mem. editorial bd. Andrologia, Jour. Clin. Endrocrinology and Metabolism, Internat. Jour. Andrology, Jour. Andrology. Contbr. articles to profl. jours. Office: 3459 Fifth Ave Pittsburgh PA 15213

TROESTER, CARL AUGUSTUS, JR., assn. cons.; b. Kirksville, Mo., May 27, 1916; s. Carl Augustus and Katherine (Magnus) T.; B.S. in Edn., N.E. Mo. State U., Kirksville, 1937; M.A., U. Mo., 1938; Ed.D., Columbia, 1942, also postdoctoral; postgrad. U. Pa., 1945; m. Thelma Schwab, Sept. 3, 1940; children—Carl Augustus III, Thelma Ann. Jeffrey. Instr. phys. edn. N.E. Mo. State Tchrs. Coll., 1937, U. Mo., 1937-39; asst. health and phys. edn. Columbia Tchrs. Coll., 1939-40; dir. health and phys. edn., dean of men, dir. summer session Eastern Conn. State Coll., Willimantic, 1940-46; dual prof. edn. and phys. edn. Syracuse U., 1946-48; exec. sec. AAHPER, 1948-74, cons. pub. affairs and legislation, 1974-76; exec. dir. Am. Council Internat. Sports, Washington, 1976—; vis. instr. Columbia U., summer 1944; vis. instr. health and phys. edn. grad. extension courses health edn. U. Conn., 1945-46; cons. Conn. Dept. Edn., 1945; mem. U.S. del. UNESCO Conf. Phys. Edn. and Sport, 1976, 77, 78, 79; mem. Citizens's Adv. Com., also Exec. Com. Pres. Eisenhower's Council Youth Fitness, 1956—; professorial lectr. George Washington U., 1976—; sec. gen. internat. council health, phys. edn. and recreation World Confedn. Orgns. Teaching Profession, 1958—. Bd. dirs. Internat. Sports Found., 1968—, Hugh O'Brien Found., 1966—. Recipient Honor award World Confedn. Tchrs. Orgns., 1968; achievement award Am. Soc. Assn. Execs., 1976; awards govts. of Indonesia, Ireland, Korea, Mex., Taiwan. Mem. Am. Acad. Phys. Edn., Conn. Assn. Health, Phys. Edn. and Recreation (hon. life), Coll. Phys. Edn. Assn., AAHPER, Soc. State Dirs. Health, Phys. Edn. and Recreation, Am. Sch. Health Assn., Am. Pub. Health Assn., Phi Delta Kappa, Kappa Delta Phi. Author: Everyday Games for Children, 1948; (with John H. Shaw) Individual Sports for Men, 1949; contbr. articles to profl. jours., encys. Home: 10917 Mariner Dr Silesia MD 20022 Office: 817 23d St NW Washington DC 20052

TROFIMENKOFF, FREDERICK NICHOLAS, educator; b. Veregin, Sask., Can., Aug. 10, 1934; s. Nicholas Peter and Mary William (Sherstobitoff) T.; B.E., U. Sask., 1957, M.Sc., 1959; Ph.D., U. London (Eng.), 1962; m. Gayle Louise Isabel Ashworth, Oct. 19, 1957; children—Margo Beverly, Gregory William, Carmen Gay. Jr. research officer Nat. Research Council, Saskatoon, Sask., 1957-59; asst. prof. U. Sask., Saskatoon, 1962-66; asso. prof. elec. engring. U. Calgary (Alta., Can.), 1966-68, prof., 1968—. Vis. prof. No. Electric Co., Ltd., Ottawa, summer, 1965, U. Essex, Colchester, Eng., 1971. Mem. Assn. Profl. Engrs., Geologists and Geophysicists of Alta., Engring. Inst. Can., Canadian Assn. Physicists, I.E.E.E. (sr.). Contbr. profl. jours. Home: 20 Varcourt Pl NW Calgary AB T3A 0G8 Canada

TROGDON, DEWEY LEONARD, JR., textile co. exec.; b. Summerfield, N.C., Feb. 17, 1932; s. Dewey Leonard and Ethel (Miller) T.; A.B. in Econs., Guillford Coll., Greensboro, N.C., 1958; postgrad. U. N.C., 1967-68, U. Va., 1970, Advanced Mgmt. Program, Harvard U., 1978; m. Barbara Jean Ayers, Sept. 10, 1955; children—Mark, Leonard. With Cone Mills Corp., Greensboro, 1958—, staff asst. to chief exec. officer, 1970-74, pres. Otto B. May, subs. co., 1974-78, v.p. Cone Mills Mktg. Co., 1977-78, exec. v.p. Cone Mills Corp., 1978, pres., 1979—. Bd. dirs. Jr. Achievement. Served with USNR, 1949-53. Mem. Am. Textile Mfrs. Inst. Methodist. Office: Cone Mills Corp 120 Maple St Greensboro NC 27405

TROGDON, WILLIAM OREN, univ. pres.; b. Anadarko, Okla., Nov. 1, 1920; s. Otis H. and Anna (Jackson) T.; B.S., Okla. State U., 1942; Ph.D., Ohio State U., 1949; m. Altha Florene Tucker, Aug. 2, 1942; children—Stephen William, Patricia Ann. Asst. agronomist, soil scientist Blackland Expt. Sta., Temple, Tex., 1948-49; chmn. dept. agr., dir. soils lab. Midwestern U., Wichita Falls, Tex., 1949-53; agronomist Olin Mathieson Chem. Corp., Houston, 1953-58; prof., head dept. soil and crop scis. Tex. A. and M. Coll., College Sta., 1958-63; exec. v.p. Best Fertilizers Co., Plainview, Tex., 1963-65; dir. agronomy and Market devel. Occidental Agrl. Chem. Corp., N.Y.C., 1965-66; pres. Tarleton State U., Stephenville, Tex., 1966—; cons. agronomy, 1958-63. Served with AUS, 1942-46. Mem. Am. Soc. Agronomy, Crops Sci. Soc. Am., Soil Sci. Soc. Am., Internat. Soil Sci. Soc. Research on fertilizers, water quality for irrigation, soil fertility, crop mgmt., turf. Home: PO Box 1039 Tarleton Sta Stephenville TX 76402

TROHAN, WALTER, newspaperman; b. Mt. Carmel, Pa., July 4, 1903; s. E. Henry and Bernice (Skindzier) T.; A.B., U. Notre Dame, 1926; D.Litt., Lincoln Coll., 1958; m. Carol Rowland, Mar. 17, 1929; children—Carol (Mrs. Wayne A. Glover), Walter, Nancy (Mrs. Robert W. Dollar). Reporter, Daily Calumet, Chgo., 1922, City News Bur., Chgo., 1927-29; with Chgo. Tribune, 1929-71, became asst. Washington corr., 1934, exec. dir. Washington bur., 1947-49, chief Washington bur., 1949-69, columnist, 1960-71; spl. assignments. South Am., 1936, 41, Europe, 1940, Summit Confs., 1955, 60, 61, Fgn. Ministers Confs., 1957, 59, Paris Peace talks, 1968, Turkey, Iran, Greece, 1971; news commentator W.G.N., M.B.S., 1951-69. Emeritus trustee Lincoln Coll. Decorated comdr. Order of Isabel La Catholica (Spain). Recipient Captive Nations medal; named to Sigma Delta Chi Washington Hall of Fame, 1973. Mem. White House Corr. Assn. (pres. 1937-38), Overseas Writers, Chgo. Hist. Soc., J. Russel Young Sch. of Expression. Roman Catholic. Clubs: Gridiron (pres. 1967); George Town (Washington); Civil War Round Table, Baker Street Irregulars (hon.) (Chgo.); Bohemian (San Francisco). Author: Political Animals, 1975. Editor: Jim Farley's Story; The Roosevelt Years, 1948. Contbr. to various mags. Address: 5711 Phelps Luck Dr Columbia MD 21045 also Carrowmeer House Newmarket-on-Fergus County Clare Ireland. *Give every man the benefit of your doubts of the worst you may think of him and your prayers.*

TROILO, JOSEPH CARMEN, supermarket exec.; b. Phila., Mar. 7, 1934; s. Joseph and Susie (Maiuri) T.; accounting certificate U. Pa., 1960; m. Anita Costanzo, Sept. 15, 1956; children—Lisa, Vicki, Marc. Controller Foodarama Supermarkets, Inc., Freehold, N.J., 1968, v.p. fin., asst. treas., 1974—. Served with AUS, 1954-56. C.P.A., Pa. Mem. Am., Pa. insts. C.P.A.'s. Home: 3542 Windmill Circle Huntingdon Valley PA 19006 Office: PO Box 592 Freehold NJ 07728

TROMBINO, ROGER A., food co. exec.; b. Kenosha, Wis., Sept., 1939; s. Paul and Lena T.; B.S., U. Wis., 1962; m. Joann M. Buchholtz, Nov., 1961; children—Tracey, Suzanne, Steven. Mgr., Arthur Young & Co., Chgo., 1962-72; sr. v.p., chief fin. officer Norin Corp., North Miami, Fla., 1973—; dir. Homosassa Springs Resort. Bd. dirs. Villa Maria Rehab. Inst. Mem. Fin. Execs. Inst., Am. Inst. C.P.A.'s. Clubs: Jockey, Riviera Country. Office: 12100 NE 16th Ave North Miami FL 33161

TROMBLEY, KENNETH EDWARD, pub. co. exec.; b. Aberdeen, S.D., Sept. 27, 1920; s. Edward Abraham and Dorothy Lillian (Lindekugel) T.; student S.D. State Coll., 1938-41, George Washington U., 1948; m. Patricia Dorcas Margaret Batchelor, Feb. 7, 1945; children—Diane Patricia, Robin Wilson. Copywriter Romer Advt. Agy., Washington, 1946; dir. pub. relations Calcium Chloride Assn., Washington, 1947-48; editor ofcl. publ. Nat. Soc. Profl. Engrs., Profl. Engineer, Washington, 1949—, also dir. pub. relations, 1958-72, pres., editor-in-chief Trombley Pub. Co., Adelphi, Md., 1972—. Served as capt. C.E., U.S. Army, 1941-45, with 34th infantry div. S.D.N.G., and Chief of Engrs. Office, E.T.O. Clubs: Nat. Press; Bethesda Country. Author: Life and Times of a Happy Liberal, 1954. Home: 1836 Metzerott Rd Adelphi MD 20783 Office: PO Box 772 Adelphi MD 20783

TROOBOFF, PETER DENNIS, lawyer; b. Balt., June 22, 1942; s. Benjamin M. and Rebecca C. T.; A.B. cum laude, Columbia U., 1964; LL.B. cum laude (Frank Knox Meml. fellow), Harvard U., 1967; LL.M., London Sch. Econs., 1968; diploma cum laude, Hague Acad. Internat. Law, 1968; m. Rhoda Morss, Aug. 10, 1969; children—Hannah Elizabeth, Eden Abigail. Admitted to D.C. bar, 1970, N.Y. bar, 1968; research asso. Harvard Law Sch., 1968-69; asst. to exec. editor The Advocates program Sta. WGBH-TV, Boston, 1969; asso. firm. Covington and Burling, Washington, 1969-75, partner firm, 1975—; dir. seminars Hague Acad. Internat. Law, 1972; lectr. U. Va. Law Sch., 1973-74. Mem. Council Fgn. Relations, Am. Soc. Internat. Law, Am. Bar Assn., Internat. Law Assn. Club: Internat. (Washington). Editor: Law and Responsibility in Warfare: The Vietnam Experience, 1975. Office: 888 16th St NW Washington DC 20006

TROPEA, ORLAND, telephone co. exec.; b. Toronto, Ont., Can., Feb. 15, 1919; s. Joseph and Mary (Irwin) T.; B.Commerce, U. Toronto, 1942; m. Betty June Kaiser, Dec. 11, 1943; children—Ronald, Robert, Richard, Thomas, Peter, Elizabeth. Controller, then v.p. regulatory matters Bell Can., 1966-75, exec. v.p. adminstrn., 1975-79, exec. v.p. corporate, 1979—; chmn. Teledirect, Ltd.; dir. N.B. Telephone Co. Served with RCAF. 1943-4S. Mem. Fin. Execs. Inst., Canadian C. of C. (chmn. exec. council 1973, chmn. Can.-U.S. com. 1978—). Clubs: St. James, Columbus Fishing, Mt. Bruno Country. Home: 139 Bathurst Pointe Claire PQ H9S 4Z8 Canada Office: 1050 Beaver Hall Hill Montreal PQ H3C 3G4 Canada

TROST, CARLISLE ALBERT HERMAN, naval officer; b. Valmeyer, Ill., Apr. 24, 1930; s. Elmer Herman and Luella Caroline (Hoffman) T.; student Washington U., St. Louis, 1948-49; B.S., U.S. Naval Acad., 1953; Olmsted scholar, U. Freiburg, W. Ger., 1960-62; m. Pauline Louise Haley, May 1, 1954; children—Carl, Laura Lee, Steven, Kathleen. Commd. ensign U.S. Navy, 1953, advanced through grades to vice adm., 1978; exec. officer U.S.S. Scorpion, 1962-63, U.S.S. Von Steuben, 1963-65; mil. asst. to Dep. Sec. Def., 1965-68; comdg. officer U.S.S. Sam Rayburn, 1968-69; staff, Comdr. Sub Force Atlantic, 1969-70; exec. asst. to Sec. Navy, 1970-73; comdr. Submarine Group Five, 1973-74; asst. chief Bur. Naval Personnel, 1974-76; dir. systems analysis div. Office Chief Naval Ops., Washington, 1976-78; dep. comdr.-in-chief U.S. Pacific Fleet, 1978—. Trustee, U.S. Naval Acad. Found. Decorated Legion of Merit with oak leaf cluster, Navy Achievement medal; named Outstanding Young Man of Am., Nat. Jr. C. of C., 1964. Mem. U.S. Naval Inst., U.S. Naval Acad. Alumni Assn. Episcopalian. Home: 29 Makalapa Dr Honolulu HI 96818 Office: Dep CINCPACFLT Pearl Harbor HI 96860

TROTTENBERG, ARTHUR DONALD, found. exec.; b. Rochester, N.Y., Dec. 30, 1917; s. Isaac and Anna (Lipsky) T.; A.B., Harvard, 1948; m. Margaret F. Wilson, June 18, 1948; children—Jan, Mark, Polly. Mgr. operating services Harvard, 1948-54, asst. dean faculty arts and scis., 1954-60, asst. dean resources and planning faculty arts and scis., 1965-68; adminstrv. v.p. Radcliffe Coll., 1960-65; v.p. adminstrn. Ford Found., 1968—; dir. Salzburg Seminar Am. Studies, 1964; cons. in field, 1955—. Trustee Cambridge Savs. Bank (Mass.). Bd. dirs. Garland (Mass.) Jr. Coll.; trustee Cold Spring Biol. Lab., L.I. U., Radcliffe Coll. Served to capt. USAAF, 1942-46. Decorated Air medal with 7 oak leaf clusters, D.F.C. with 3 oak leaf clusters. Mem. N.Y.C. C. of C. Clubs: Harvard Faculty (Cambridge); Harvard, Century Assn. (N.Y.C.). Author: A Vision of Paris, 1963; also articles. Home: 219 Pelhamdale Ave Pelham NY 10803 Office: 320 E 43d St New York City NY 10017

TROTTER, DONALD MCLEAN, educator; b. Dawson, Minn., Oct. 22, 1920; s. L.F. and Ruth E. (McLean) T.; M.S., Kans. State U., 1957, D.V.M., 1946; m. Marilyn Button, June, 1946; children—Donald McLean, Steven. Instr., Iowa State U.; asst. prof. U. Mo.; prof., head dept. pathology Okla. State U.; dept. head Pharm. and Biologics Co.; presently prof., dean coll. vet. medicine Kans. State U., Manhattan. Named Distinguished Prof., 1963. Mem. Am., Kans. vet. med. assns.,

Sigma Xi, Phi Kappa Phi, Phi Sigma, Gamma Sigma Delta. Co-author textbooks on bovine and avian anatomy. Home: 1822 Elaine Dr Manhattan KS 66502 Office: Coll Vet Med Kans State U Manhattan KS 66502

TROTTER, FREDERICK THOMAS, ch. ofcl.; b. Los Angeles, Apr. 17, 1926; s. Fred B. and Hazel (Thomas) T.; A.B., Occidental Coll., 1950, D.D., 1968; S.T.B., Boston U., 1953, Ph.D., 1958; L.H.D., Ill. Wesleyan U., 1974; LL.D., U. Pacific, 1978; m. Gania Demaree, June 27, 1953; children—Ruth Elizabeth, Paula Anne (dec.), Tania, Mary. Exec. sec. Boston U. Student Christian Assn., 1951-54; ordained elder Pacific and Southwest Conf., Methodist Ch., 1953; pastor Montclair (Calif.) Meth. Ch., 1956-59; lectr. So. Calif. Sch. Theology at Claremont, 1957-59, instr., 1959-60, asst. prof., 1960-63, asso. prof., 1963-66, prof., 1966, dean, 1961; prof. religion and the arts, dean Sch. Theology, Claremont, 1961-73; mem. Bd. Higher Edn. and Ministry, United Meth. Ch., 1972-73, gen. sec., 1973—; dir. Third Nat. Bank, Nashville, Mack Printing Co., Easton, Pa. Trustee Am. U., Dickinson Coll., Dillard U., Meharry Med. Coll. Served with USAAF, 1944-46. Kent fellow Soc. for Values in Higher Edn., 1954, Dempster fellow Meth. Ch., 1954. Author: Jesus and the Historian, 1968. Editor-at-large Christian Century, 1969—. Club: University. Office: United Meth Ch PO Box 871 Nashville TN 37202

TROTTER, JOHN ELLIS, educator; b. Chgo., May 18, 1921; s. John William and Helen (Ellis) T.; S.M., U. Chgo., 1953, Ph.D., 1962. Faculty, Ill. State U., 1956—, prof. geography, 1965—, head dept. geography and geology, 1967-78. Served with USAAF, 1943-45. Decorated Air medal, D.F.C. Mem. Assn. Am. Geographers, Am. Geog. Soc. Contbr. articles to profl. jours. Home: 16 Knollcrest Ct Normal IL 61761

TROTTER, MILDRED, anatomist; b. Monaca, Pa., Feb. 3, 1899; d. James Robert and Jennie Bruce (Zimmerly) Trotter; A.B., Mt. Holyoke Coll., 1920, D.Sc., 1960; M.S., Washington U., St. Louis, 1921, Ph.D., 1924; postgrad. NRC fellow), Oxford U., 1925-26; D.Sc., Western Coll. for Women, 1956. Mem. faculty Washington U., 1920—, prof. gross anatomy, 1946-58, prof. anatomy, 1958-67, prof. emeritus, lectr. in anatomy, 1967—; vis. prof. anatomy Makerere U. Coll., Kampala, Uganda, 1963; cons. Rockefeller Found., 1963; spl. cons. USPHS, 1943-45; anthropologist Schofield Barracks, Hawaii, U.S. Dept. Army, 1948-49, Fort McKinley, Philippines, 1951. Recipient Viking Fund medal and award in phys. anthropology, 1956. Mem. Am. Assn. Anatomists (exec. com. 1969-73), Am. Assn. Phys. Anthropologists (pres. 1955-57), Anat. Soc. Gt. Britain and Ireland (life), Am. Anthrop. Assn., Mo. State Anat. Bd. (pres. 1957-67), Anat. Bd. St. Louis (pres. 1941-48, 49-67), Phi Beta Kappa, Sigma Xi, Alpha Omega Alpha. Democrat. Presbyterian. Contbr. chpts. to books, articles to med. and biol. jours. Office: 4580 Scott Ave Saint Louis MO 63110

TROTTER, ROBERT MOORE, educator; b. Charlotte, N.C., Jan. 31, 1922; s. John Scott and Lelia (Bias) T.; Mus.B., Northwestern U., 1942; M.A., U. Chgo., 1947; Ph.D., U. So. Calif., 1957; m. Claire Anderson, Feb. 25, 1944; children—Margaret Claire (Mrs. Richard Marcus), Robert Bruce. Instr. music and humanities Eastern Wash. State Coll., Cheney, 1947-49; acting instr. music U. Calif. at Los Angeles, 1955-56, asst. prof., 1956-61, asso. prof., chmn. dept. music, 1962-63; prof. music U. Oreg., Eugene, 1963—, dean Sch. Music, 1963-75. Cons. in humanities U. Calif. at Los Angeles Extension, 1956-63; music dir. Pacifica Found., sta. KPFK-FM, Los Angeles, 1959-62. Bd. dirs. Eugene Jr. Symphony, 1963-74. Served to lt. (j.g.) USNR, 1942-45; PTO. Recipient award cultural program Ohio State U., 1959; Fulbright grantee, Belgium, 1951. Mem. Coll. Music Soc. (past pres., mem. council 1975—), Music Educators Nat. Assn. (life), Am. Musicology Soc. (council 1962-65), Soc. for Ethnomusicology, Internat. Soc. Music Edn. Home: 1975 Potter St Eugene OR 97405

TROTTER, SAMUEL EUGENE, educator; b. Stockton, Ala., Feb. 4, 1917; s. Joseph Bascomb and Janie Rebecca (Athey) T.; B.S., Auburn U., 1939; M.S., 1951; Ph.D., U. Ala., 1956; m. Frances Dixon, Jan. 18, 1942; 1 son, Robert Eugene. With Sears, Roebuck & Co., Mobile, 1939-50; asst. prof. bus. adminstrn. U. Ark., 1954-58; prof. bus. adminstrn. Miss. State U., 1958-60, prof. finance, 1960—, head finance dept., 1960-68, dir. div. bus. services, 1966-70, dir. grad. studies in bus., 1969—. Mem. Am., So. finance assns., So. Econ. Assn., Phi Kappa Phi, Beta Gamma Sigma, Alpha Kappa Psi. Methodist. Home: PO Box 65 Mississippi State MS 39762

TROTTER, THOMAS FALLON, editor; b. Prattville, Ala., Jan. 27, 1920; s. Julius Carroll and Thomas Ella (Fallon) T.; student Howard Coll., 1943-44; m. Freida Marie Cowherd, May 4, 1944; 1 dau., Gayle (Mrs. Charles E. Agee). Reporter Birmingham (Ala.) Age Herald, 1943-44; sports editor Albany (Ga.) Herald, 1944; sports editor Mobile (Ala.) Press, 1945, city editor, 1947-54; asso. exec. editor Mobile Press Register, 1954-67, exec. editor, 1967—, sec. corp., 1968—. Sec. Goodwill Industries, Mobile, 1959-60, pres., 1961. Bd. dirs. Downtown Mobile Unltd. Mem. Am. Press Inst., Mobile Area C. of C., Sigma Delta Chi. Home: 4204 Springview Dr Mobile AL 36609 Office: PO Box 2488 Mobile AL 36630

TROTTER, VIRGINIA YAPP, univ. adminstr.; b. Boise, Idaho, Nov. 29, 1921; d. Rockford Glenn and Lena Idylla (Topliff) Yapp; B.S., Kans. State U., 1943, M.S., 1949; Ph.D., Ohio State U., 1959; m. Robert Talbot Trotter, July 1943 (dec.); 1 son, Robert Talbot. Instr. home mgmt., dir. dept. U. Utah, Salt Lake City, 1948-50; asst. prof., head dept. family econs. U. Nebr., Lincoln, 1950-55, dir. Sch. Home Econs., 1955-63, asso. dean, 1963-70, dean Coll. Home Econs., 1970-72, asso. dir. Agrl. Experiment Sta. also Agrl. Extension Service, 1970-72, vice chancellor acad. affairs, 1972-74; asst. sec. for edn. HEW, Washington, 1974-77; v.p. acad. affairs U. Ga., Athens, 1977—; cons. J.C. Penney Research Co., 1966-74, Nebr. Mission in Colombia, 1966-73, Hacettepe U., Ankara, Turkey, 1967, Pres.'s Com. on Employment of Handicapped, 1967-73; mem. Nat. Advt. Rev. Bd., 1971-72. Mem. adv. council N.Y. State Coll. Home Econs., Cornell U., Ithaca, 1967-71; mem. Gov.'s Com. on Employment of Handicapped, State of Nebr., 1971—. Recipient Melvin McArtor Distinguished Service award, 1971. Mem. Am. (v.p. 1970-72), Nebr. (pres. 1968-70) home econs. assns., Nebr. Heart Assn. (chmn. bd. dirs. 1970-72). Contbr. articles to profl. jours. Home: 215 Hickory Hill Dr Watkinsville GA 30677 Office: U Ga Athens GA 30602

TROTTI, JOHN BOONE, educator, librarian; b. Asheville, N.C., Dec. 11, 1935; s. Clarence and Janice (Lyon) T.; B.A., Davidson Coll., 1957; B.D. cum laude, Union Theol. Sem. Va., 1960; M.A., Yale U., 1961, Ph.D., 1964; M.L.S., U. N.C., 1964; m. Joan Thompson, June 12, 1957; children—Elizabeth, Margaret, Michael. Ordained to ministry, Presbyterian Ch. in the U.S., 1964; instr. O.T., Yale Div. Sch., 1961-62; minister ch., Altavista, Va., 1964-68; asst. prof. religion Randolph Macon Woman's Coll., Lynchburg, Va., 1965-68; asst. librarian, asst. prof. Union Theol. Sem. Va., 1968-70, librarian, 1970—, asso. prof. bibliography, 1972—; mem. library adv. com. Va.; pres. Altavista Area Ministerial Assn., 1967. Trustee, Stillman Coll., 1969-78; bd. dirs. Hist. Found. Presbyn. and Ref. Chs., 1979—. Mem. Am. Theol. Library Assn. (exec. com. 1971-74, pres. 1977—), Va. Library Assn., Presbyterian Library Assn. (pres. 1973), Soc. Bibl. Lit., Beta Phi Mu. Editor: Aids to a Theological Library, 1977; asso. editor Interpretation; editor Scholar's Choice; contbr. articles to religious and profl. jours. Home: 1222 Rennie Ave Richmond VA 23227 Office: 3401 Brook Rd Richmond VA 23227

TROTTIER, BRYAN JOHN, profl. hockey player; b. Val Marie, Sask., Can., July 17, 1956; s. Eldon J. and Mary (Gardner) T.; student public schs., Val Marie; m. Laura Lynn Theis, July 14, 1976; 1 son, Bryan John. Mem. N.Y. Islanders Hockey Club, Farmingdale, 1975—; hockey cons. Right Gard Corp., Phila; spokesman 1980 Winter Olympics, Lake Placid, N.Y. Recipient Calder Meml. trophy as Rookie of Yr., Nat. Hockey League, 1976. Hart Meml. trophy as Most Valuable Player; Art Ross trophy as Leading Scorer. Office: care Internat Sports Mgmt 488 Madison Ave New York NY 10022

TROUGHTON, JOHN DAVID, atty. gen. Wyo.; b. Deadwood, S.D., Mar. 15, 1939; s. John Franklin and Evangeline Angela (Vehar) T.; B.S., U. Wyo., 1962, J.D., 1966; m. Barbara J. Storey, Nov. 27, 1965; children—Angela Ellen, John David. Admitted to Wyo. bar; clk. U.S. 10th Circuit Ct. Appeals, Hon. J.J. Hickey; legal specialist Alaska Supreme Ct.; pros. atty. Lincoln County (Wyo.); partner firm Troughton & Vehar, Kemmerer, Wyo.; now atty. gen. State of Wyo., Cheyenne; chmn. Wyo. Indsl. Siting Council, 1975-79. Mem. Wyo. State Bar Assn. Office: Office Atty Gen State Capitol Cheyenne WY 82002

TROUP, THOMAS JAMES, chem. co. exec.; b. Council Bluffs, Iowa, Sept. 4, 1923; s. Ralph Leslie and Ruth (Beaumont) T.; B.Sc. in Chem. Engring., U. Wis., 1945; M.B.A. with high distinction, Harvard U., 1952; m. Marjory Alice Suelflow, Feb. 2, 1946; children—Robert, Patricia Alice, James Thomas. With Internat. Minerals & Chem. Corp., 1945-53, asst. to gen. mgr., Chgo., 1950-53; sales rep. Foxboro Co., Los Angeles, 1949-50; with W.R. Grace Co., 1954-68, v.p. chem. group, N.Y.C., 1965-68; treas. Burr-Brown Research Co., Tucson, 1968-71, dir., 1967—; v.p., treas. Akzona, Inc., Asheville, N.C., 1971—, also dir. Trustee Warren Wilson Coll., Swannanoa, N.C. Clubs: Biltmore Forest Country (Asheville); Red Fox Country (Tryon, N.C.); University (N.Y.C.); Farmers (London). Home: Red Ridge Farm Route 1 Landrum SC 29356 Office: PO Box 2930 Asheville NC 28802

TROUPE, RALPH ANDERSON, educator; b. Darby, Pa., Apr. 21, 1916; s. Ralph S. and Janet (Anderson) T.; B.S., Drexel Inst. Tech., 1939; M.S., Va. Poly. Inst., 1940; Ph.D., U. Tex., 1949; m. Ada Giunta, Feb. 3, 1951; children—Janet A., Barbara J., Laurel A., Ralph S. Instr. Northeastern U., Boston, 1940-43, asso. prof., 1946-47, prof., 1954—, chmn. chem. engring. dept., 1962—; supr., prodn. engr. synthetic div. Gen. Tire & Rubber Co. Baytown, Tex., 1943-46; asst. prof. U. Tex., 1949; asso. prof. U. Louisville, 1949-50; tech. supt. Goodyear Synthetic Rubber Corp., Akron, O., 1950-54; lectr. in field, participant internat. seminars. Year-in-Industry prof. duPont, 1961-62; Fulbright lectr. Seville, Spain, 1967-68. Named Outstanding Grad., Drexel Inst. Tech., 1961. Fellow Am. Inst. Chem. Engrs. (chmn. research com. 1975, past local chmn., treas.), mem. Am. Chem. Soc., Nat. Assn. Corrosion Engrs., Sigma Xi, Tau Beta Pi, Phi Kappa Phi, Omega Chi Epsilon. Contbr. articles to profl. jours. Home: 4 Parker Rd Wakefield MA 01880 Office: Northeastern U Boston MA 02115

TROUT, ARTHUR ROGER, ins. co. exec.; b. Trenton, N.J., July 10, 1917; s. Arthur B. and Olive (Hockenbury) T.; B.S., Rider Coll., 1943; postgrad. Sch. Bus. Adminstrn., N.Y. U., 1950-58; m. Irene Walker, June 18, 1938; children—Jane Hope (Mrs. Richard Clippinger), Roger Lee, Trudy Ellen (Mrs. Kenneth Dougherty), Holly Jean (Mrs. Edwin Kaniewski). With N.J. Mfrs. Ins. Co., Trenton, 1935—, treas., 1964—, also dir. Bd. dirs. Mercer Med. Center; protestant chaplain Trenton Fire Dept. Methodist (ordained lay minister, pastor Wesley Ch., Trenton). Lion. Home: RFD 1 Box 380 Titusville NJ 08560 Office: Sullivan Way Trenton NJ 08607

TROUT, JOHN FRANCIS, advt. exec.; b. N.Y.C., Jan. 31, 1935; s. John Joseph and Doris (Kroll) T.; B.A. in Econs., Iona Coll., New Rochelle, N.Y., 1956; m. Patricia Daley, Dec. 22, 1956; children—Timothy, Joanne, Nancy, Susan, Christine, Peter. With Gen. Electric Co., 1959-65; divisional advt. mgr. Uniroyal Co., 1965-68; v.p., dir. mktg. services Trout & Ries Advt., N.Y.C., 1968-73, pres., 1973—. Named Advt. Mgr. of Year, N.Y. chpt. Assn. Indsl. Advertisers, 1968; Agy. Man of Year, Indsl. Mktg. mag., 1969. Roman Catholic. Clubs: Union League (N.Y.C.); Innis Arden (Greenwich, Conn.). Home: 10 Wahneta Rd Old Greenwich CT 06870 Office: 1212 Ave of Americas New York NY 10036

TROUT, MAURICE ELMORE, fgn. service officer; b. Clifton Hill, Mo., Sept. 17, 1917; s. David McCamel and Charlotte Temple (Woods) T.; B.A., Hillsdale Coll., 1939; M.A. in Pub. Adminstrn., St. Louis U., 1948, Ph.D. in Polit. Sci., 1950; m. Margie Marie Mueller, Aug. 24, 1943; children—Richard Willis, Babette Yvonne. Joined U.S. Fgn. Service, 1950; assigned Paris, France, 1950-52, Vienna, Austria, 1952-55, London, Eng., 1955-59, Vientiane, Laos, 1959-61; with Office Exec. Dir. Bur. Far Eastern Affairs, Dept. State, Washington, 1961-65; Am. consulate gen., Munich, Germany, 1965-69; 1st sec., consul Am. embassy, Bangkok, Thailand, 1969-72; dep. office dir. Bur. Politico-Mil. Affairs, Dept. State, Washington, 1972-75; Dept. State advisor Armed Forces Staff Coll., Norfolk, Va., 1975-77. Bd. dirs. Internat. Sch., Bangkok, 1970-72. Served with USCG, 1939-45. Recipient Achievement award diplomacy and internat. affairs Hillsdale Coll., 1962. Mem. Am. Fgn. Service Assn., Diplomatic and Consular Officer, Delta Tau Delta, Delta Theta Phi, Pi Gamma Mu. Home: 6203 Hardy Dr McLean VA 22101

TROUT, MONROE EUGENE, pharm. co. exec.; b. Harrisburg, Pa., Apr. 5, 1931; s. David Michael and Florence Margaret (Kashner) T.; A.B., U. Pa., 1953, M.D., 1957; LL.B., Dickinson Sch. of Law, 1964, J.D., 1969; m. Sandra Louise Lemke, June 11, 1960; children—Monroe Eugene, Timothy William. Intern Great Lakes (Ill.) Naval Hosp., 1957-58; resident Portsmouth (Va.) Naval Hosp., 1959-61; chief med. dept. Harrisburg State Hosp., 1961-64; dir. drug regulatory affairs Pfizer, Inc., N.Y.C., 1964-68; v.p., med. dir. Winthrop Labs., N.Y.C., 1968-70; med. dir. Sterling Drug, Inc., N.Y.C., 1970-74, v.p., dir. med. affairs, 1974-78, sr. v.p., 1978—, also dir.; adj. asso. prof. Bklyn. Coll. Pharmacy; spl. lectr. legal medicine Dickinson Sch. of Law. Mem. Sterling Winthrop Research Bd. Sec., Commn. on Med. Malpractice, HEW, 1971-73; cons. HEW, 1974; mem. Joint Commn. Prescription Drug Use, 1976—; mem. profl. advisory bd. Comml. Credit Corp., 1976-78, Control Data Corp., 1978—; mem. Council Sci. and Indsl. Research, 1976—. Republican dist. leader, New Canaan, Conn., 1966-68; bd. dirs. New Canaan Interchurch Service Com., 1965-69; bd. dirs. Athletes Kidney Found.; trustee Dickinson Sch. of Law, Cleve. Clinic, Albany Med. Coll.; mem. Nat. Health Advisory Bd. AAA; mem. N.Y. State Commn. Substance Abuse, 1978—. Served to lt. comdr. USNR, 1956-61. Recipient Alumni award of merit U. Pa., 1953. Named Tenn. Col. Fellow Am. Coll. Legal Medicine (v.p., pres., bd. govs.); mem. Am. (Physicians Recognition awards 1969, 72, 76), Pa. med. assns., Med. Execs. (pres. 1975-76), Delta Tau Delta. Lutheran. Editorial bd. Hosp. Formulary Mgmt., 1969—, Forensic Science, 1971—, Jour. Legal Medicine, 1973—. Contbr. articles to profl. jours. Home: 81 Mariomi Rd New Canaan CT 06840 Office: 90 Park Ave New York NY 10016

TROUTMAN, E. MAC, U.S. judge; b. Greenwood Township, Pa., Jan. 7, 1915; s. Emmett Theodore and Kathryn (Holman) T.; A.B., Dickinson Coll., 1934, LL.B., 1936; m. Margaret Petrick, Nov. 23, 1944; children—Jane A., Jean K. Admitted to Pa. bar, 1937; with Phila. and Reading Coal and Iron Co., 1937-58, gen. counsel, 1954-58; gen. atty. Phila. and Reading Corp., 1958-67; gen. counsel Reading Anthracita Co., 1958-61; gen. counsel Reserve Carbon Corp., 1961-66, So. Carbon Corp., 1966-67; solicitor Blue Mountain Sch. Dist., 1963-67, Blue Mountain Area Sch. Authority, 1963-67, Orwigsburg Municipal Authority, 1966-67, Am. Bank and Trust Co., Reading and Pottsville, Pa., 1957-67; exec. sec., gen. counsel Pa. Self-Insurers Assn., 1962-67; U.S. judge Eastern Dist. Pa., 1967—. Bd. dirs. Greater Pottsville Indsl. Devel. Corp., 1963-67, Pa. C. of C., 1955-65, Greater Pottsville Area C. of C., 1961-64. Bd. dirs. Orwigsburg Community Meml. Assn., 1950-66, Schuylkill County Soc. Crippled Children, 1945-67; v.p., dir. Pottsville Hosp. and Warne Clinic, 1960-67. Served with AUS, World War II. Mem. Am., Pa., Schuylkill County (vice chancellor 1955-57, chmn. jud. vacancies and unauthorized practice coms. 1960, chmn. medico-legal com. 1963-65) bar assns. Lutheran (pres. council 1961—). Lion (bd. dirs. Orwigsburg 1964). Home: Kimmel's Rd Orwigsburg PA 17961 Office: 14613S US Courthouse 601 Market St Philadelphia PA 19106

TROUTMAN, HOLMES RUSSELL, lawyer; b. Beckley, W.Va., July 27, 1933; s. Holmes Fielding and Florence Lillo (Wallett) T.; A.B., Marshall U., 1955; postgrad. Stetson Law Sch., 1955-56; LL.B., U. Miami, 1958; m. Patricia Lee Bullion, Nov. 12, 1954; children—Holmes Russell, Richard Byron, Teresa Lee. Admitted to Fla. bar, 1958; asso., partner firm Akerman, Turnbull, Senterfitt & Eidson, Orlando, Fla., 1958-62; partner firm Fishback, Davis, Dominick & Troutman, Orlando, 1962-69, Troutman, Parrish & Kanar, Winter Park, Fla., 1969—; spl. city prosecutor City of Winter Park, 1965; acting county solicitor, 1967-69; Winter Park city atty., 1968-72; spl. counsel Fla. Turnpike Authority, 1968-70, Fla. Public Service Commn., 1978—; mem. Fla. Supreme Ct. Nominating Commn., 1978—. Pres., Friends of Orlando Public Library, 1971-73; mem. Orange County Charter Study Commn., 1973-74. Recipient Orlando Jr. C. of C. Good Govt. award, 1969, Marshall U. Alumnus Civic Contbrn. award, 1979. Mem. Am. Bar Assn. (ho. of dels. 1978—), Fla. Bar (bd. govs. 1972-78, pres. 1977-78), Orange County Bar Assn. (exec. counsel 1966-68, pres. 1968-69, co-founder Legal Aid Soc., 1969), Am. Acad. Trial Lawyers, Fla. Acad. Trial Lawyers. Contbr. articles to profl. jours. Home: 1600 Barcelona Way Winter Park FL 32789 Office: Troutman Parrish & Kanar 222 W Comstock St Winter Park FL 32789

TROVA, ERNEST TINO, painter, sculptor; b. St. Louis, Feb. 19, 1927. One-man exhbns. include Pace Gallery, Boston and N.Y.C., 1963, 69, 70, 71, 73, 75, Hanover Gallery, London, Eng., 1964, 68, 70, Container Corp. Am., 1965, Harcus/Krakow Gallery, Boston, 1968, Dunkelman Gallery Toronto, Ont., Can., 1969 Hanover-Gimpel, Zurich, Switzerland, 1970, Galerie Der Spiegel, Cologne, Germany, 1970, Block Gallery, St. Louis, 1970, Galerie Brusberg, Hanover, Germany, 1970, Venezuela, 1971, Israel, 1971, Makler Gallery, Phila., 1972, Phoenix Art Mus., 1974, Hokin Gallery, Palm Beach, Fla., 1975, others; numerous group exhbns. including Chgo. Art Inst., 1964, Pasadena (Calif.) Art Mus., 1964, De Cordova Mus., Documenta IV, Kassel, Germany, 1968, Mus. Modern Art, 1968, Internat. Biennale, Warsaw, 1968, Whitney Mus. Modern Art, 1968, Cleve. Inst. Art, 1969, Jewish Mus., N.Y.C., 1969, Contemporary Arts Center, Cin., 1970, 72, Princeton, 1970, U. Wis.-Milw., 1973, Hirshorn Mus. and Sculpture Garden, 1974, others; represented in permanent collections including Mus. Modern Art, Larry Aldrich Mus., Tate Gallery, London, City Art Mus., Guggenheim Mus., Hirshorn Mus., St. Louis, Springfield (Mo.). Art Mus., Phoenix Art Mus., Atkins Mus. Fine Art, Laumeier Sculpture Garden, also pvt. Whitney Mus.; and corporate collections. Address: 6 Layton Terr Saint Louis MO 63124*

TROW, ROBERT CHARLES, mfg. co. exec.; b. Albert Lea, Minn., Feb. 14, 1923; s. Fayville Anthony and Luella (Mickelson) T.; student U. Minn., 1941-42; m. Jean Louise Bublitz, Jan. 28, 1945; children—Shelley Jo, Michael Robert, Jodi Michelle, Robin Lynn. With King-Seeley Thermos Co., Prospect Heights, Ill., and predecessors, 1942—, pres., 1971—, also dir.; dir. Household Fin. Corp. Served with USMCR, 1942-45. Episcopalian. Club: Bob O Link (Highland Park, Ill.). Home: 1457 Calais Circle Highland Park IL 60035 Office: 2700 Sanders Rd Prospect Heights IL 60070

TROWBRIDGE, ALEXANDER BUEL, JR., chem. co. exec.; b. Englewood, N.J., Dec. 12, 1929; s. Alexander Buel and Julie (Chamberlain) T.; A.B. cum laude, Princeton U., 1951; LL.D. (hon.), D'Youville Coll., 1967, Hofstra U., 1968, Hobart & William Smith Colls., 1975; m. Nancey Horst, July 2, 1955; children—Stephen C., Corrin S., Kimberly. With Calif. Tex. Oil Co., 1954-59; operations mgr. Esso Standard Oil S.A. Ltd., Panama C.Z., 1959-61, div. mgr., El Salvador, 1961-63; pres., mgr. div. Esso Standard Oil Co. (P.R.), 1963-65; asst. sec. for domestic and internat. bus. Dept. Commerce, 1965-67, sec. of commerce, 1967-68; pres., chief exec. officer Am. Mgmt. Assn., N.Y.C., 1968-70; pres. The Conf. Bd., Inc., N.Y.C., 1970-76; vice chmn. bd. Allied Chem. Corp., 1976—, dir., 1968—; dir. IBM World Trade Ams.-Far East Corp.; mem. bd. cons.'s to comptroller gen. U.S. Bd. dirs. A.I.E.S.E.C.-U.S., trustee Inst. Internat. Edn., Aspen Inst. Humanistic Studies; mem. vis. com. Harvard Grad. Sch. Bus. Served with USMCR, 1951-53; maj. Res. Decorated Bronze Star with combat V; recipient Arthur Flemming award, 1966, Pres.'s E certificate for export service, 1968. Mem. NAM, Mfg. Chemists Assn., Council Fgn. Relations. Clubs: Univ., Pinnacle, Links (N.Y.C.); Foxmeadow Tennis; Federal City (Washington). Office: PO Box 3000R Morristown NJ 07960

TROWBRIDGE, C. ROBERTSON, publishing co. exec.; b. Salem, Mass., Mar. 31, 1932; s. Cornelius P. and Margaret M. (Laird) T.; A.B., Princeton U., 1954; LL.B., Harvard U., 1957; L.H.D. (hon.), Franklin Pierce Coll., 1976, Keene State Coll., 1979; m. Lorna Sagendorph, July 7, 1956; children—James, Cornelia, Beatrix, Philip. Admitted to Pa. bar, 1958; asso. firm Drinker, Biddle & Reath, Phila., 1957-59; exec. Englehard Industries, Inc., Newark, 1959-64; pres., pub. Yankee mag. Yankee, Inc., Dublin, N.H., 1964—, pub. New Eng. Bus. mag.; mem. N.H. Senate, 1973-78, chmn. fin.; mem. N.H. Ho. of Reps., 1967-72, chmn. public works com.; dir. First Nat. Bank of Peterborough. Distbg. dir. N.H. Charitable Fund; mem. exec. com. N.H. Citizen Task Force, 1969; trustee Phillips Exeter Acad., Franklin Pierce Coll., Soc. for Protection N.H. Forests; moderator Town of Dublin. Clubs: Country (Brookline, Mass.); Princeton (N.Y.C.); Union (Boston). Home: Old Marlborough Rd Dublin NH 03444 Office: Yankee Inc Dublin NH 03444

TROWBRIDGE, C. ROBERTSON, pub. co. exec.; b. Salem, Mass., Mar. 31, 1932; s. Cornelius P. and Margaret M. (Laird) T.; student Princeton U., 1954; LL.B., Harvard U., 1957; m. Lorna Sagendorph, July 7, 1956; children—James, Cornelia, Beatrix, Philip. Admitted to Pa. bar, 1958; asso. Drinker, Biddle & Reath, Phila., 1957-59; exec. Engelhard Industries, Inc., Newark, 1959-64; pres., pub. Yankee mag.

Yankee, Inc., Dublin, N.H., 1964—; pub. New England Bus. mag.; mem. N.H. Senate, finance chmn., 1973—. Mem. N.H. Ho. of Reps., 1967-72, chmn. pub. works com., 1969-72. Bd. dirs. Monadhock Family Health, Dublin Community Found.; mem. exec. com. N.H. Citizen Task Force, 1969. Clubs: Country (Brookline); Princeton (N.Y.C.); Union (Boston). Home: Old Marlborough Rd Dublin NH 03444 Office: Yankee Inc Dublin NH 03444

TROWBRIDGE, CHARLES LAMBERT, actuary, educator; b. Iowa City, Oct. 11, 1916; s. Arthur Carleton and Sue (Bussey) T.; B.A., State U. Iowa, 1937, M.S., 1938; m. Norma Magda Thomsen, Mar. 18, 1944; children—Brett Carleton, Lisa Katherine. With Bankers Life Co., Des Moines, 1938-70, v.p., chief actuary, 1965-70, chief actuary, sr. v.p., 1973-79; chief actuary Social Security Adminstrn., HEW, Washington, 1971-73; prof. actuarial sci. Grad. Sch. Bus. Adminstrn., U. Mich., Ann Arbor, 1979—. Served to capt., C.E., AUS, 1942-45. Fellow Soc. Actuaries (bd. govs.; pres. 1975), Phi Beta Kappa. Contbr. articles to profl. jours. Home: 1611 Anderson St Ann Arbor MI 48104

TROWBRIDGE, EDWARD KENNETH, insurance co. exec.; b. Phila., Nov. 17, 1928; certificate of proficiency in bus. adminstrn. U. Pa., 1956; student Harvard U. Grad. Sch. Bus. Adminstrn., 1976-77; m. Marie; 3 children. With Wm. H. McGee Co., Phila., 1951-52; with Atlantic Cos., 1952—, marine sec., N.Y.C., 1965-67, v.p. marine underwriting, 1967-73, sr. v.p. mktg. adminstrn., 1973-77, sr. exec. v.p., 1977—; trustee Atlantic Mut. Ins. Co.; dir. Centennial Ins. Co., J.A. Blondeau, Ltd., Nat. Cargo Bur., Inc., Security Bur., Inc. Served with U.S. Army, 1948-51. Mem. Am. Hull Ins. Syndicate (dir.), Am. Inst. Marine Underwriters (dir.), Assn. Marine Underwriters U.S. (dir.), Bd. Underwriters N.Y. (dir.), U.S. Salvage Assn. (dir.), Life Saving Benevolent Assn. (dir.), Maritime Law Assn. U.S. Clubs: Met., India House (bd. govs.) (N.Y.C.); Raritan Valley Country (Somerville, N.J.). Address: Atlantic Bldg 45 Wall St New York NY 10005

TROWBRIDGE, FREDERICK NEWELL, lawyer; b. Viroqua, Wis., Feb. 18, 1900; s. William Marshall and Regina L. (Lindeman) T.; B.A., U. Wis., 1923, LL.B., 1925; m. Virginia Bensley, Apr. 28, 1928; children—Frederick Newell, Jane Regina. Admitted to Wis. bar, 1925, since practiced in Green Bay; gen. counsel various corps.; local counsel C. & N.W. Ry. Co., C. M., St. P. & P. R.R., Green Bay & Western R.R.; dir., local counsel Paper Converting Machine Co.; counsel, dir., mem. exec. com. Green Bay Packers, Inc., Krueger Metal Products, Inc.; counsel, dir. F. Hurlbut Co., Tape, Inc.; counsel Elliott Glove Co., Inc., Leicht Transfer & Storage Co., Bark River Culvert & Equipment Corp. Chmn. Com. 25, State of Wis. Mem. Am. Coll. Trial Lawyers, Wis. Bar Assn. (pres. 1955-56). Home: 247 Miramar Dr Green Bay WI 54301 Office: 225 S Monroe St PO Box 189 Green Bay WI 54305

TROWBRIDGE, ROY POST, motor vehicle co. exec.; b. Sacramento, Dec. 16, 1918; s. Frank Hudson and Fawn Retta (Post) T.; B.A. in Mech. Engring., Stanford U., 1940; m. Virginia Mae Mott, Mar. 26, 1940; children—Susan Trowbridge Kukuk, John. With Gen. Motors Corp., Detroit, 1940—, dir. engring. standards, 1956—; vice chmn. Am. Nat. Metric Council, 1976—. Served with AUS, 1945-46. Recipient Leo B. Moore award Standards Engrs. Soc., 1969; Interprofl. Cooperation award Soc. Mfg. Engrs., 1975. Fellow ASME (v.p. 1966-68, 76—), Standards Engrs. Soc., Engring. Soc. Detroit; mem. Am. Nat. Standards Inst. (dir. 1966—, v.p. 1969-70, pres. 1971-74 Howard Coonley medal 1976), Soc. Automotive Engrs., ASTM (dir. 1975-78), Chemists Club N.Y., Am. Def. Preparedness Assn., Tau Beta Pi. Contbr. numerous articles on standards promotion and tech. standards to profl. jours. Home: 17377 Westmoreland St Detroit MI 48219 Office: Engring Staff GM Technical Center Warren MI 48090

TROXEL, BENNIE WYATT, geologist; b. Osawatomie, Kans., Aug. 9, 1920; s. Manfred Raymond and Sybil Josephine (Bussert) T.; B.A., UCLA, 1951, M.A., 1958; m. Betty Lee Patriquin, June 12, 1943; children—Wyatt Lee, Mona Kay (Mrs. Norman Winter). Geologist Calif. Div. Mines and Geology, Sacramento, 1952-71, 75-76; sci. editor Geol. Soc. Am., Boulder, Colo., 1971-75; geologic cons., 1976—. Faculty Pa. State U., 1962, U. So. Calif., 1968, Napa Coll., 1970, U. Calif. at Berkeley, 1972—, U. Colo., 1975, U. Nev. at Las Vegas, 1975—, U. Calif. at Santa Barbara, 1975—, U. Calif. at Davis, 1976—, Calif. State U. at Sacramento, 1976-77. Served with USAAF, 1943-46. Fellow Geol. Soc. Am., AAAS; mem. Soc. Econ. Geology, Assn. Earth Sci. Editors, AIME. Contbr. numerous articles to profl. jours. Home: 2961 Redwood Rd Napa CA 94558

TROY, B. THEODORE, apparel co. exec.; b. Huntington Park, Calif., Jan. 16, 1932; s. Bernard and Florence Ruth (Stillman) T.; B.A. in Econs., U. Calif., Santa Barbara, 1953; B.Fgn. Trade, Am. Grad. Sch. Internat. Mgmt., 1957; m. Pauline Pearson, Feb. 25, 1960; 1 son, Kevin. Brand mgr. Procter & Gamble, Eng., 1957-61; account exec. McCann-Erickson, Los Angeles, 1961-62; with R.J. Reynolds Co., 1962-77, pres. Mexican subs., 1968-75, pres. Brazilian subs., 1976-77; pres. Burlington Export Co. (Inc.), 1977-78; pres. Kayser-Roth Internat., Kayser-Roth Corp., N.Y.C., 1978—. Served with U.S. Army, 1953-55. Recipient Distinguished Achievement award U. Calif., Santa Barbara Alumni Assn., 1979.

TROY, KENNETH DOUGLAS, lawyer; b. Cin., Dec. 13, 1918; s. Orville A. and Rose N. (Reinhardt) T.; A.B., U. Mich., 1942; J.D., U. Cin., 1944; m. Virginia M. Downey, Oct. 6, 1945; children—Gregory S., Jeffrey D., Nancy K. Admitted to Ohio bar, 1944, U.S. Tax Ct., 1945; mem. firm Frost and Jacobs, Cin., 1944-46; mem. firm Strauss, Troy and Ruehlmann Co., L.P.A., Cin., 1947—, chmn. bd., 1975—; instr. estate planning Coll. Law, U. Cin., 1960-68; dir. Cin. Gear Co., Cin. Steel Treating Co. Mem. Am. Bar Assn., Ohio State Bar Assn., Cin. Bar Assn. Clubs: Univ., Punta Gorda Yacht, Masons. Office: 2100 Central Trust Center 201 E 5th St Cincinnati OH 45202

TROYANOS, TATIANA, opera singer; b. N.Y.C., Sept. 12, 1938; d. Nickolas and Hildagod (Langera) Troyanos; diploma Juilliard Sch. Music. Debut N.Y.C. Opera as Jocasta in Oedipus Rex, 1963, at La Scala as Adalgisa in Norma, 1977; singer operas in Hamburg, Berlin, and Munich, Ger., Vienna and Salzburg, Austria, Milan, Rome, Florence and Palermo, Italy, Paris and Strasbourg, France, London, 1965-75; debut Met. Opera, 1976; prin. roles include Carmen, Sextus in Clemenza di Tito, Dido in Dido and Aeneas, Octavian in Der Rosenkavalier, the composer in Ariadne auf Naxos, Santuzza in Cavalleria Rusticana; soloist with symphony orchs. including Boston, Cin., Chgo., Los Angeles, Phila., London, N.Y. Philharmonic; rec. artist with RCA, Victor Red Seal, Deutsche Grammophon Gesellschaft, EMI, London, Columbia. Juilliard Alumnae scholar. Office: care Columbia Artists Mgmt Inc 165 W 57th St New York NY 10019

TROYAT, HENRI (PSEUDONYM TARASOFF), writer; b. 1911; ed. Lycee Pasteur, also Law Faculty, U. Paris. Decorated Legion of Honor (France). Mem. Acad. Francaise. Author: Faux-Jour (prix Populiste), 1935; L'Araigne (prix Goncourt), 1938; La Neige en Deuil (grand prix litteraire de Monaco), 1952; Tant que la terre durera, 3 vols., 1947-50; Les semailles et les moissons, 5 vols., 1953-58; La Lumiere des Justes, 5 vols., 1960—; Les Eygletiere, 3 vols., 1965; Les Hèritieurs de l'Avenir, 3 vols., 1968; Le Moscovite, 3 vols., 1975; also biographies of Dostoievsky, Pouchkine, Tolstoi, Gogol, Catherine la Grande, Pierre le Grand. Address: 23 quai de Conti Paris 6e France

TROZZOLO, ANTHONY MARION, chemist; b. Chgo., Jan. 11, 1930; s. Pasquale and Francesca (Vercillo) T.; B.S., Ill. Inst. Tech., 1950; M.S., U. Chgo., 1957, Ph.D., 1960; m. Doris C. Stoffregen, Oct. 8, 1955; children—Thomas, Susan, Patricia, Michael, Lisa, Laura. Asst. chemist Chgo. Midway Labs., 1952-53; asso. chemist Armour Research Found., Chgo., 1953-56; mem. tech. staff Bell Labs., Murray Hill, N.J., 1959-75; Charles L. Huisking prof. chemistry U. Notre Dame, 1975—; vis. prof. Columbia U., N.Y.C., 1971. AEC fellow, 1951; NSF fellow, 1957-59; Phillips lectr. U. Okla., 1971, P.C. Reilly lectr. U. Notre Dame, 1972, C.L. Brown lectr. Rutgers U., 1975, Sigma Xi lectr. Bowling Green U., 1976, M. Faraday lectr. No. Ill. U., 1976, F.O. Butler lectr. S.D. State U., 1978. Fellow N.Y. Acad. Scis., AAAS, Am. Inst. Chemists; mem. Am. Chem. Soc., AAUP, Sigma Xi. Roman Catholic. Asso. editor Jour. Am. Chem. Soc., 1975-76; editor Chem. Reviews, 1977—; patentee; contbr. articles to profl. jours. Home: 1329 E Washington St South Bend IN 46617 Office: U Notre Dame Notre Dame IN 46556

TRUAX, DONALD ROBERT, educator; b. Mpls., Aug. 29, 1927; s. William Raymond and Hermina Wilhelmina (Sobolik) T.; B.S., U. Wash., 1951, M.S., 1953; Ph.D., Stanford, 1955; m. Barbara June Eckton, Sept. 16, 1950; children—Mary, Catherine, Patricia, Gail. Research fellow Cal. Inst. Tech., 1955-56; asst. prof. math. U. Kans., 1956-59; asst. prof. math. U. Oreg., 1959-62, asso. prof., 1962-69, prof., 1969—. Served with AUS, 1945-47. Mem. Inst. Math. Statistics, Am. Statis. Assn., Am. Math. Soc., Math. Assn. Am., Delta Sigma Phi. Author research articles; mng. editor Annals of Statistics, 1975—, Annals of Probability, 1975—. Home: 2323 University St Eugene OR 97403

TRUBIN, JOHN, lawyer; b. East Orange, N.J., Aug. 1, 1917; s. Albert J. and Fanny (Babetch) T.; student Johns Hopkins U., 1935-36; student Coll. City N.Y., 1936-39; J.D., N.Y.U., 1943; m. Edna Glassman, June 24, 1945; children—Priscilla Jo, Andrew James. Admitted to N.Y. bar, 1943; asso. firm Strauss, Reich & Boyer, N.Y.C., 1943-46; practice law, N.Y.C., 1946-48; asst. atty. gen. N.Y. State, 1948-50; law sec. to Surrogate George Frankenthaler, 1950-53; chief counsel to Moreland Act Commn. on Workmen's Compensation, N.Y.C., 1953-54; first asst. atty. gen. N.Y. State, 1955-57; partner firm Trubin Sillcocks Edelman and Knapp, N.Y.C., 1958—. Trustee-at-large Fedn. Jewish Philanthropies; trustee N.Y.C. Police Found., Inc.; bd. overseers Center for N.Y.C. Affairs, New Sch. for Social Research; bd. dirs. United Jewish Appeal Greater N.Y., Benjamin N. Cardozo Sch. Law. Mem. N.Y. County Lawyers Assn. (dir. 1967-73), Assn. Bar City N.Y., N.Y. State, Am. bar assns., Am. Judicature Soc. Home: 26 E 10th St New York City NY 10003 Office: 375 Park Ave New York City NY 10022

TRUBY, JOHN LOUIS, bus. co. exec.; b. New Kensington, Pa., Nov. 28, 1933; s. George N., Sr., and Bertha (Deyber) T.; B.B.A. cum laude, U. Pitts., 1959; m. Mary Ann Holmes, Dec. 10, 1952; children—Leslie Ann, Jacque Lee, Barbara Holmes. Fin. analyst Union R.R., East Pittsburgh, Pa., 1959-64; adminstrn. mgr. Westvaco, Luke, Md., 1964-70; controller Lehigh Portland Cement Co., Allentown, Pa., 1970-72, v.p. finance, 1972-74; pres. J. Truby Co., Allentown, 1974—, J.T. Coal Co., 1976—, D.M.I. & J.T. Coal Co., 1977—, Irish Ridge Coal Co., 1977—, Irish Ridge Trucking Co., 1977—. Past pres. Keyser Jaycees, Mineral County Sch. Bd. Levy; class of 1959 agt. U. Pitts.; bd. dirs. Willow Lake Assn. Served to 1st lt., AUS, 1953-56. Named Outstanding Personality of the South, 1967. Mem. Nat. Assn. Accts., Fin. Execs. Inst., Ohio Coal and Energy Assn. Presbyterian. Club: Zanesville Country. Home: 225 W Willow Ave Zanesville OH 43701 Office: PO Box 2519 Zanesville OH 43701

TRUCE, WILLIAM EVERETT, educator, chemist; b. Chgo., Sept. 30, 1917; s. Stanley C. and Frances (Novak) T.; B.S., U. Ill., 1939; Ph.D., Northwestern U., 1943; m. Eloise Joyce McBroom, June 16, 1940; children—Nancy Jane, Roger William. Mem. faculty Purdue U., 1946—, prof. chemistry, 1956—, asst. dean Grad. Sch., 1963—. Mem. numerous univ. dept. and profl. coms.; chmn. various profl. meetings. Guggenheim fellow Oxford U., 1957. Mem. Am. Chem. Soc., Phi Beta Kappa, Sigma Xi. Co-author book, contbr. articles to profl. jours., chpts. to books; helped develop rule of transnucleophilic addition; research in new methods of synthesis, devel. new kinds of compounds and reactions. Home: 156 Creighton Rd West Lafayette IN 47906 Office: Purdue U Dept Chemistry Lafayette IN 47907

TRUDEAU, GARRY B., cartoonist; b. N.Y.C., 1948; grad. Yale U. and Yale U. Sch. Art and Architecture. Creator comic strip Doonesbury, syndicated nationwide; contbr. N.Y. Mag.; publs. include: Doonesbury; (with Nicholas von Hoffman) The Fireside Watergate, Trout Fishing in the Reflecting Pool; Don't Ever Change Boopsie; I Have No Son; Speaking of Inalienable Rights, Amy; Wouldn't a Germlin Have Been More Sensible?; Dare to Be Great, Ms. Caucus; As the Kid Goes for Broke; many others. Recipient Pulitzer prize, 1975. Office: care United Press Syndicate 6700 Squibb Rd Mission KS 66202*

TRUDEAU, PIERRE ELLIOTT, Can. prime minister; b. Montreal, Que., Can., Oct. 18, 1919; s. Charles-Emile and Grace (Elliott) T.; B.A., Jean de Brebeuf Coll., Montreal, 1940; LL.L., U. Montreal, 1943; M.A., Harvard U., 1945; student Ecole des Sciences Politiques, Paris, London Sch. Econs.; numerous hon. degrees; m. Margaret Sinclair, Mar. 4, 1971; children—Justin Pierre, Alexandre Emmanuel, Michel Charles Emile. Called to Que. bar, 1943; created Queen's counsel, 1969; practiced in Montreal; jr. economist staff Privy Council, Ottawa, Ont., Can.; asso. prof. law, mem. Inst. Pub. Law U. Montreal, 1961-65; mem. Ho. of Commons, 1965—; parliamentary sec. to prime minister, 1966-67, minister justice, atty. gen. Can., 1967-68; prime minister, 1968-79, 80—; leader ofcl. opposition in Parliament, 1979-80; mem. Privy Council, 1967—; leader Liberal party, 1968—; co-founder Cité Libre, monthly rev.; del. France-Can. Interparliamentary Assn., 1966, UN, 1966. Mem. Canadian Bar Assn., Montreal Civil Liberties Union, Royal Soc. Can. Liberal. Roman Catholic. Author: Federalism and the French Canadians, 1968; Réponses, 1967; co-author: Deux Innocents en Chine, 1961; editor: La Grève del'Amiante, 1956; contbr. articles to profl. jours. Office: Office of Prime Minister Langevin Block Parliamentary Bldgs Ottawa ON K1A 0A2 Canada*

TRUDEL, JEAN, art historian, museum adminstr.; b. Que., Can July 1, 1940; s. Ferdinand and Rita (Lebrun) T.; B.A., College des Jesuites, Quebec, 1961; Licencé es Lettres, U. Laval, Quebec, 1964; m. Louise Saint-Pierre, 1963; children—Pascale, Nicholas. Curator, Musée du Que., Quebec, 1966-70; curator early Can. art Nat. Gallery Can., Ottawa, Ont., 1971-76, gallery interim chief curator, 1975-76; dir. Montreal (Que.) Mus. Fine Arts, 1977—. Mem. Société des musées quebecois (pres. 1979), Internat. Council Mus's., Can. Mus's. Assn., Am. Assn. Mus's., N.E. Mus. Conf. (bd. govs. 1979), Can. Art Mus's. Dirs. Orgn., Assn. Art Mus. Dirs. Author: Silver in New France, 1974; The Calvary at Oka, 1974; The Drawings of James Cockburn, 1976. Office: 3400 Ave du musee Montreal PQ H3G 1K3 Canada

TRUE, EDWARD KEENE, engring. educator; b. Boston, July 12, 1915; s. Edward Payson and Laura Keene (Darling) T.; B.S., Mass. Inst. Tech., 1939; m. Mildred Louise Richenburg, Aug. 31, 1940; children—Edward Bartlett, Robert Payson, Peter Keene, James Duncan. Engr., Concrete Steel Co., Boston, 1939-40; instr. architecture U. Oreg., 1940-42; sr. engr. Raytheon Mfg. Co., Waltham, Mass., 1943-45; mem. faculty Grad. Sch. Design, Harvard, 1945-76, prof. arch., 1958-76; cons. engr. and architect, 1947-59; partner Souza and True, engrs., Cambridge, 1959—, inc., 1970, pres., 1970—; trustee, mem. bd. investment Middlesex Instn. Savs., Concord, Mass. Mem. Concord Planning Bd., 1948-58, chmn., 1954-58; mem. Concord Bd. Appeals, 1959-68, chmn., 1959-61; mem. Concord Bd. Selectmen, 1970-76, chmn., 1972-73; mem. exec. com. Mass. League of Cities and Towns, 1974-76. Trustee Theta Chi Trust. Mem. Boston Soc. Civil Engrs., Boston Assn. Structural Engrs., Am. Concrete Inst., Mass. Selectmans Assn., Unitarian Laymans League. Rotarian. Club: Concord Country. Home: 108 Commerford Rd Concord MA 01742 Office: 8 Story St Cambridge MA 02138

TRUE, HENRY ALFONSO, JR., oil producer, drilling contractor, rancher; b. Cheyenne, Wyo., June 12, 1915; s. Henry A. and Barbara (Diemer) T.; B.S. in Indsl. Engring., Mont. State Coll., 1937; m. Jean Durland, Mar. 20, 1938; children—Tamma Jean (Mrs. Donald G. Hatten), Henry Alfonso III, Diemer D., David L. Roustabout, pumper, foreman The Tex. Co., 1937-45, supt. drilling and prodn. for Wyo., 1945-48; mgr. Res. Drilling Co., 1948-51, pres., 1951-59; partner True Drilling Co. (formerly True & Brown Drilling Contractors), Casper, Wyo., 1951—, True Oil Co. (formerly True & Brown Oil Producers), Casper, 1951—; v.p., sec. Toolpushers Supply Co., 1952-53, pres., 1954—; v.p., sec. True Service Co., 1953, pres., 1954-70, pres. True Bldg. Corp., 1956-67, Little Smokey Oil Co., 1956-68, Belle Fourche Pipeline Co., 1957—; owner True Ranches, 1957—; chmn. bd. Powder River Oil Shippers Service, Inc., 1963-67; pres. Camp Creek Gas Co., 1964—; v.p. George Mancini Feed Lots, Brighton, Colo., 1964-72; dir. Black Hills Oil Marketers, Inc., 1965—, v.p., 1966-72, pres., 1973—; v.p. White Stallion Ranch, Inc., Tucson, 1965—; dir. Res. Oil Purchasing Co., 1965-73, pres., 1972-73; dir. First Nat. Bank Casper; bd. advisers Mountain Bell, 1965—, dir. Rocky Mountain region, 1973—. Mem. exec. com. Wyo. Oil Industry Com., 1958-74, treas., 1958-59, pres., 1960-62; dir. Rocky Mountain Oil Show, 1955; advisory bd. Internat. Oil and Gas Edn. Center, 1964—, vice chmn., 1969-73; mem. natural gas advisory council Fed. Power Commn., 1964-65, mem. exec. advisory com., 1971-74; mem. exec. co com. Gas Supply Com., 1965-69, vice chmn., 1967-69; mem. adv. council Pub. Land Law Rev. Commn., 1965-70; dir. U.S. (formerly So. States) Indsl. Council, 1971—, exec. com., 1974—; mem. Nat. Petroleum Council, 1962—, nat. oil policy com., 1965, vice chmn., 1970-71, chmn., 1972-73; mem. Rocky Mountain Petroleum industry adv. com. Fed. Energy Office, 1973—. Chmn. advance gifts com. United Fund, 1962; nat. asso. Boys Clubs Am., 1964-69, hon. chmn. local chpt., 1971, trustee Casper Air Terminal, 1961-71, pres., 1964-65, 67-68; bd. dirs. Bus.-Industry Polit. Action Com., 1964—, regional vice chmn., 1966-70, 73-74, sec.-treas., 1973-74; mem. research fellows Southwestern Legal Found., 1968—; trustee U. Wyo., 1965—, pres. bd., 1971-73, mem. adult edn. and community service council, 1961-64; bd. govs Western Ind. Colls. Found., 1963-65; nat. trustee Voice of Youth, 1968—; bd. dirs., trustee Nat. Cowboy Hall of Fame, 1975—; Named Oil Man of Year, Wyo. C. of C., 1959; recipient Honored Citizen award, Casper, 1964; chief Roughneck of Yr. award Lone Star Steel, 1965; Ann. Indsl. award Wyo. Assn. Realtors, 1965; named Distinguished Businessman U. Wyo., 1967, Nat. Small Businessman of Year, Nat. Council for Small Bus. Devel., 1967; Distinguished Service award ind. oil operator Tex. Mid-Continent Oil and Gas Assn., 1971; John Rogers award Southwestern Legal Found., 1975; Ky. Col.; named to Wisdom Hall Fame; named to Cowboy Hall Fame, Western Heritage Center. Mem. Internat. Assn. Drilling Contractors (dir. 1950—), Am. Petroleum Inst. (dir. 1960—, exec. com. 1970—), Rocky Mountain Oil and Gas Assn. (treas. 1954-55, v.p. Wyo. 1956-58, dir. 1950—, pres. 1962-63, exec. com. 1954—), Ind. Petroleum Assn. Am. (v.p. Wyo. 1960-61, exec. com. 1962—, pres. 1964-65; Russell B. Brown Meml. award 1975), N.A.M. (Wyo. chmn. membership com. 1965—), Rocky Mountain Petroleum Pioneers, Wyo. Stockgrowers Assn., Casper Petroleum Club (dir. 1954), U.S. (policy com. 1966-72, dir. 1975—), Casper chambers commerce, All-Am. Wildcatters, 25 Year Club Petroleum Industry, Ind. Petroleum Assn. Mountain States, Petroleum Assn. Wyo. (dir. 1974—), Am. Judicature Soc. (mem. com. justice 1976), Sigma Chi, Beta Gamma Sigma (hon. mem. Alpha chpt. Wyo.). Republican. Episcopalian (vestry 1960-62). Mason (32 deg., Shriner), Elk. Home: 6000 S Poplar St Casper WY 82601 also Double Four Ranch Fletcher Park Rt Wheatland WY 82201 Office: 106 River Cross Rd PO Box 2360 Casper WY 82601 also LAK Ranch Newcastle WY 82701

TRUE, ROY JOE, lawyer; b. Shreveport, La., Feb. 20, 1938; s. Collins B. and Lula Mae (Cady) T.; student Centenary Coll., 1957; B.S. (scholar), Tex. Christian U., 1961; LL.B. (scholar), So. Meth. U., 1963, postgrad., 1968-69; m. Patsy Jean Hudsmith, Aug. 29, 1959; children—Andrea Alane, Alyssa Anne, Ashley Alisbeth. Admitted to Tex. bar, 1963; practiced in Dallas, 1963—; pres. Invesco Internat. Corp., 1969-70, True & Zable, P.C., 1975-78, The True Firm, 1979—; bus. adviser, counselor Mickey Mantle, 1969—. Served with AUS, 1956. Mem. Am., Dallas bar assns., Tex. Assn. Bank Counsel, Phi Alpha Delta. Editorial bd. Southwestern Law Jour., 1962-63. Home: 5601 Ursula Ln Dallas TX 75229 Office: 1515 Dallas Fed Savs Tower Dallas TX 75225

TRUEBLOOD, ALAN STUBBS, educator; b. Haverford, Pa., May 3, 1917; s. Howard M. and Louise (Nyitray) T.; A.B., Harvard, 1938, M.A., 1941, Ph.D., 1951; M.A. (hon.), Brown U., 1957. Ednl. dir. Chile-U.S. Cultural Inst., Santiago, 1942-43; mem. faculty Brown U., 1947—, prof. Spanish, 1963—, chmn. dept. Hispanic and Italian studies, 1967-72, chmn. dept. comparative lit., 1973-77; vis. asso. prof. Harvard, 1959-60, vis. lectr., 1963; Fulbright lectr. Am. studies, Colombia, 1972; Sr. Resident scholar Merton Coll., Oxford (Eng.) U., 1973—. Served to lt. USNR, 1943-46. Fulbright research scholar, Chile, 1958; Guggenheim fellow, 1965-66. Author: Experience and Artistic Expression in Lope de Vega, 1974. Home: Willow Ave Little Compton RI 02837 Office: Box E Brown Univ Providence RI 02912

TRUEBLOOD, DAVID ELTON, educator; b. Pleasantville, Iowa, Dec. 12, 1900; s. Samuel and Effie (Crew) T.; A.B., Penn Coll., Oskaloosa, Iowa, 1922; student Brown U., 1922-23, Hartford Theol. Sem., 1923-24; S.T.B., Harvard, 1926; Ph.D., Johns Hopkins, 1934; Litt.D., Washington and Lee U., 1949; Litt.D., U. Vt., 1951, William Penn Coll., 1959; LL.D., Miami U., 1951; S.I.D., Ripon Coll., 1954, McKendree Coll., 1969; L.H.D., Simpson Coll., 1955, Otterbein Coll., 1960; Litt.D., Tarkio Coll., 1963, Friends U., 1973, John Brown U., 1977; D.D., Kenyon Coll., 1964, Pepperdine U., 1971; m. Pauline Goodenew, Aug. 24, 1925 (dec.); children—David M., Arnold, Samuel J. II, Elizabeth; m. 2d, Virginia Zuttermeister, Aug. 5, 1956. Prof. philosophy and dean men Guilford (N.C.) Coll., 1927-30; exec. sec. Balt. Yearly Meeting of Friends, 1930-33; asst. prof. philosophy Haverford (Pa.) Coll., 1933-36; acting chaplian Harvard, summer 1935; prof. philosophy religion and chaplain Stanford U., 1936-45; fellow of Woodbrooke, 1939; Swarthmore lectr. (Eng.), 1939; acting prof. Harvard U., 1944; acting prof. Garrett Bibl. Sem., 1944, 45, 46;

prof. philosophy Earlham Coll., 1946-66, prof.-at large, 1966—; Purington lectr. Mt. Holyoke Coll., 1970; chief religious information USIA, 1954-55; pres. Yokefellows Internat.; clk. Ind. Yearly Meeting Friends, 1955-60. Named Churchman of Year, Am. Heritage, 1960; Doan Distinguished Prof. award Earlham Coll., 1964, Ind. Acad., 1971. Mem. Soc. of Friends. Author books relating to field, latest: Philosophy of Religion; The Yoke of Christ, 1958; The Idea of College, 1959; Confronting Christ, 1960; The Company of the Committed, 1961; General Philosophy, 1963; The Humor of Christ, 1964; The Lord's Prayers, 1965; The People Called Quakers, 1966; The Incendiary Fellowship, 1967; Robert Barclay, 1968; A Place to Stand, 1969; The New Man for our Time, 1970; The Future of the Christian, 1971; The Validity of The Christian Mission, 1972; Abraham Lincoln, Theologian of American Anguish, 1973; While It's Day: An Autobiography. Editor: The Friend, 1935-47. Home: 230 College Ave Richmond IN 47374

TRUEBLOOD, HARRY ALBERT, JR., oil co. exec.; b. Wichita Falls, Tex., Aug. 28, 1925; s. Harry A. and Marguerite (Barnhart) T.; student Tex. A. and M. Coll., 1942-43; B.S. in Petroleum Engring., U. Tex., 1948; m. Lucile Bernard, Jan. 22, 1953; children—Katherine A., John B. Petroleum engr. Cal. Co., 1948-51; chief engr. McDermott & Barnhart Co., Colo., Tex., 1951-52; cons. petroleum and geol. engr., Denver, 1952-55; pres. Colo. Western Exploration Inc., Denver, 1955-58; pres. Consol. Oil and Gas., Inc., 1958—, chmn. bd., 1969—, also chief exec. officer; dir. Holiday Resources, Inc., R.L. Burns Corp. Served to ensign USNR, 1944-46. Mem. Soc. Petroleum Engrs., Am. Petroleum Inst., World Bus. Council and Chief Execs. Forum (dir.), Ind. Petroleum Assn. Am. Róman Catholic. Clubs: Denver Petroleum, Cherry Hills Country, Univ. Home: 29 Sunset Dr Englewood CO 80110 Office: Lincoln Towers Bldg 1860 Lincoln CO 80245

TRUEBLOOD, KENNETH NYITRAY, chemist, educator; b. Dobbs Ferry, N.Y., Apr. 24, 1920; s. Howard Moffit and Louise (Nyitray) T.; A.B., Harvard, 1941; Ph.D., Calif. Inst. Tech., 1947; m. Jean Turner, Mar. 7, 1970. Postdoctoral fellow chemistry dept. Calif. Inst. Tech., Pasadena, 1947-49; faculty U. Calif. at Los Angeles, 1949—, prof. chemistry, 1960—, chmn. dept. chemistry, 1965-70, dean Coll. Letters and Sci., 1971-74; vis. prof. chemistry U. Ibadan (Nigeria), 1964-65. Mem. U.S. Nat. Com. on Crystallography, 1960-65, vice chmn., 1963-65; exchange visitor to USSR, 1965. Recipient Fulbright award Oxford (Eng.) U., 1956-57; U. Calif. at Los Angeles Distinguished Teaching award, 1961; award excellence teaching Mfg. Chemists Assn., 1978; Guggenheim fellow Eidgenössiche Technische Hochschule Zurich (Switzerland), 1976-77. Mem. Am. Chem. Soc., Am. Crystallographic Assn., Phi Beta Kappa, Sigma Xi, Alpha Chi Sigma. Research and publs. on theory of chromatography, chem. crystallography including high speed computer applications; analysis of molecule motion in crystals. Home: 1089 Moraga Dr Los Angeles CA 90049

TRUED, CONSTANTINE, clergyman; b. Kiahsien, China, Feb. 11, 1914; s. Alfred Edward and Hulda Theolina (Erickson) T.; A.B., Augustana Coll., 1936; B.D., Augustana Theol. Sem., 1940; postgrad. U. Chgo., 1943-44; D.D., Carthage Coll., 1968; m. Dorothy Lydia Bergquist, Oct. 23, 1940; children—Kathleen (Mrs. Marvin Peterson), Marcia Louise (Mrs. Stanley Yamada). Ordained to ministry Augustana Lutheran Ch., 1940; pastor in Granville, Utica and Putnam, Ill., 1940-42, Chgo., 1943-49, St. Paul, 1949-53, Immanuel Luth. Ch., Detroit, 1953-79. Mem. bd. world missions Augustana Evang. Luth. Ch., 1951-62, chmn., 1956-61; mem. Augustana Ch. Music Commn., 1955-62; mem. Joint Commn. Luth. Unity, 1960-62; mem. Bd. Luth. Social Services, 1960-62; mem. bd. world missions Luth. Ch. Am., 1962-70, chmn., 1964-70; mem. Bd. Santal Missions, 1964-70; mem. dept. world missions Nat. Luth. Council, 1963-66; mem. div. overseas ministeries Nat. Council Ch. U.S., 1965-72, Luth. Council U.S.A., 1966-70; sec. Mich. Synod, Luth. Ch. Am., 1963-72, chmn. constituting conv., Detroit, 1962, mem. exec. com., 1972-76; pres. Council Christian Communication Met. Detroit, 1977-78; bd. dirs. Met. Detroit Council Chs., 1968-78, Carthage Coll., 1975—; mem. adv. bd. Met. Guidance Center, 1972-74; mem. Detroit Eastside Council Human Services, 1972-75; mem. Citizens Com. Pub. Schs., Detroit, 1958. Bd. dirs. Parkside Day Care Center, Inc., Detroit, 1968-71, pres. bd., 1968-70. Recipient Outstanding Service award Augustana Coll. Alumni Assn., 1977. Club: Detroit Wranglers. Address: 705 Perrien Pl Grosse Pointe Woods MI 48236

TRUEMAN, WILLIAM PETER MAIN, television news anchorman; b. Sackville, N.B., Can., Dec. 25, 1934; s. Albert William and Jean Alberta (Miller) T.; student U. N.B., 1951-54; m. Eleanor Joy Wark, Dec. 22, 1956; children—Anne, Mark, Victoria. UN corr. Montreal Star, 1957-62, Washington corr., 1962-65; Parliamentary corr. Toronto Star, Ottawa, Ont., 1965-67; nat. dir. UN Assn. in Can., 1967-68; nat. news writer CBC, Toronto, 1968-69, exec. producer news, head network news, 1969-72; freelance reporter, 1972-73; anchorman Global TV News, Don Mills, Ont., 1974—. Mem. bd. United Ch. Observer, United Ch. of Can. Recipient Bowater award for journalism, 1962. Club: Arts and Letters (Toronto). Office: 81 Barber Greene Rd Don Mills ON M3C 2A2 Canada

TRUESCHLER, BERNARD CHARLES, utility exec.; b. Balt., Jan. 3, 1923; s. Philip Joseph and Gertrude Cecilia (Carey) T.; B.A. in Chemistry, Johns Hopkins, 1947; LL.B., U. Md., 1952; m. Helen Rita Golley, Nov. 19, 1956; children—John G., Jeanne C., Paul C., Mary K. With Balt. Gas & Electric Co., 1948—, v.p. gas ops., 1971-74, pres., 1974—, chmn. bd., 1980—, also dir.; dir. Union Trust Bancorp., Union Trust Co. Md., Monumental Corp., Monumental Life Ins. Co. Bd. dirs. Bus. and Industry Polit. Action Com.; trustee Coll. Notre Dame of Md., Balt. Opera Co.; mem. adv. bd. Nat. Alliance Businessmen. Served with AUS, 1944-46. Mem. Am. Gas Assn., Engring. Soc. Balt., Md. C. of C. (dir.), Kappa Alpha. Republican. Roman Catholic. Clubs: Balt. Country, Center (gov.) (Balt.). Office: Balt Gas & Electric Co 19th Floor Gas and Electric Bldg Baltimore MD 21203

TRUESDELL, CLIFFORD AMBROSE, III, author, educator, editor; b. Los Angeles, Feb. 18, 1919; s. Clifford Ambrose and Yetta Helen (Walker) T.; B.S. in Math., Calif. Inst. Tech., 1941, B.S. in Physics, 1941, M.S., 1942; certificate in mechanics Brown U., 1942; Ph.D. in Math., Princeton, 1943; D.Sc., Tulane U., 1976; Fil. D. H.C., Uppsala U., 1979; Dr. Rer. Nat. H.C., Basel U., 1979; m. Beverly Poland, Nov. 18, 1939; 1 son, Clifford Ambrose IV; m. 2d, Charlotte Janice Brudno, Sept. 16, 1951. Asst. in history, debating and math. Calif. Inst. Tech., Pasadena, 1940-42; asst. in mechanics Brown U., Providence, 1942; instr. math. Princeton U., 1942-43, U. Mich., Ann Arbor, 1943-44; mem. staff radiation lab. Mass. Inst. Tech., Cambridge, 1944-46; chief theoretical mechanics subdiv. U.S. Naval Ordnance Lab., White Oak, Md., 1946-48; head theoretical mechanics sect. U.S. Naval Research Lab., Washington, 1948-51; prof. math. Ind. U., Bloomington, 1950-61; prof. rational mechanics Johns Hopkins, Balt., 1961—. Recipient Bingham medal Soc. of Rheology, 1963, Dott.ing.h.c. in mech. engring. at Centenary of Politecnico di Milano, 1965, gold medal and internat. prize Modesto Panetti, Accademia di Scienze di Torino, 1967; Birkhoff prize Am. Math. Soc., 1978; Ordine del Cherubino U. Pisa (Italy), 1978; Guggenheim fellow, 1957; NSF Sr. Postdoctoral fellow, 1960-61. Mem. Soc. for Natural Philosophy (dir. 1963—), Socio Onorario dell'Accademia Nazionale di Scienze, Lettere ed Arti (Modena, Italy), Académie Internationale d'Histoire des Sciences (Paris, France), Istituto Lombardo Accademia di Scienze e Lettere (Milano, Italy), Istituto Veneto di Scienze, Lettere ed Arti (Venice, Italy), Accademia delle Scienze dell'Istituto di Bologna (Italy), Accademia Nazionale dei Lincei (Rome, Italy), Académie Internationale de Philosophie des Sciences (Bruxelles, Belgium), Accademia delle Scienze di Torino (Italy). Author 20 books including: Mechanical Foundations, 1952; Classical Field Theories, 1960; Non-linear Field Theories of Mechanics, 1965; Essays in the History of Mechanics, 1968; Rational Thermodynamics, 1969; Introduction to Rational Elasticity, 1973; Rational Continuum Mechanics, 1977; Concepts and Logic of Classical Thermodynamics, 1977; Maxwell's Kinetic Theory, 1979; Co-founder, co-editor Jour. Rational Mechanics and Analysis, 1952-56; editor or co-editor Leonhardi Euleri Opera Omnia Series II, vols. 11-13, 18, 19, 1952-71; co-editor Handbuch der Physik, vols. 6a, 8-9, 1956-74; founder, editor Archive for Rational Mechanics and Analysis, 1957-67, co-editor, 1967—; founder, editor Archive for History of Exact Sciences, 1960—; founder, editor Springer Tracts in Natural Philosophy, 1962-66, co-editor, 1967-78, editor, 1979—; editorial bd. Rendiconti del Circolo Matematico di Palermo, 1971—, Annali della Scuola Normale Superiore, Pisa, 1974—, Meccanica, 1974—, IlNuovo Cimento, 1979—, Miscellanea di Storia della Matematica, 1979—. Home: 4007 Greenway Baltimore MD 21218

TRUESWELL, RICHARD WILLIAM, educator, indsl. engr.; b. Newark, Oct. 12, 1929; s. Richard and Mary (Sudsbear) T.; M.E., Stevens Inst. Tech., 1952; M.S. in Indsl. Mgmt., 1958; Ph.D. in Indsl. Engring., Northwestern U., 1964; m. Wilma Anita Morgan, June 27, 1953; children—Wilma Mary, Richard Douglas, William James, John Charles. Mfg. engr. Westinghouse Electric Corp., Pitts., Bath, N.Y., 1954-56; instr. Stevens Inst. Tech., Hoboken, N.J., 1957-58; instr. U. Mass., Amherst, 1958-59, asst. prof., 1959-63, asso. prof., 1963-65, chmn. indsl. engring. program, 1965-66, prof., head dept. indsl. engring., 1966-75, prof., 1975—; Joseph Lucas vis. prof. U. Birmingham (Eng.), 1971-72; cons. Savage Arms Corp., So. Hadley Electric Light Dept., Pro-Phy-Lac-Tic Brush Co., Asso. Data Processing Co., Nonotuck Mfg. Co. Served to 1st lt. USAF, 1952-54; col. Res. Registered profl. engr., Mass. Mem. Am. Soc. Mech. Engrs., Am. Inst. Indsl. Engrs., Am. Soc. Engring. Edn., Operations Research Soc. Am., ALA, Inst. Mgmt. Scis., Am. Soc. for Information Scis., Sigma Xi, Alpha Pi Mu (nat. pres. 1970-72). Editor: Collection Mgmt. quar. jour. Contbr. articles to profl. jours. Home: 3 Kennedy Dr Hadley MA 01035 Office: Dept Indsl Engring and Operations Research U Mass Amherst MA 01002

TRUETT, BOB, zoo ofcl.; b. Jacksonville, Tex., July 17, 1932; s. Robert E. and Katherine (Sheets) T.; B.S. in Zoology, U. Ark., 1955; m. Lisa Vila Wys, July 14, 1956; children—Marietta, Bob. Animal keeper Cin. Zoo, 1957; zoologist Lincoln Park Zoo, Chgo., 1957-60; dir. Birmingham (Ala.) Zoo, 1960—; appeared on TV and radio shows. Founder, trustee Natural Way Religious and Philos. Soc., 1977-78; actor in community theaters Town and Gown, 1962-78, Center Players, 1963-72, Birmingham Festival Theater, 1972-77. Served with U.S. Army, 1955-57. Fellow Am. Assn. Zool. Parks and Aquariums; mem. Phi Beta Kappa. Club: Am. Sunbathing Assn., Gymno Vita Park (founder, owner). Contbr. articles to mags. Home and Office: 2630 Cahaba Rd Birmingham AL 35223

TRUEX, DOROTHY ADINE, univ. dean, assn. exec.; b. Sedalia, Mo., Oct. 6, 1915; d. Chester Morrison and Madge (Nicholson) T.; A.B., William Jewell Coll., 1936; M.A., U. Mo., 1937; Ed.D., Columbia, 1956. Asst. dean women N.W. Mo. State U., Maryville, 1939-43, dean women, 1943-45; dean women Mercer U., Macon, Ga., 1945-47; dean women U. Okla., Norman, 1947-69, asso. prof. higher edn., 1969-72, dir. research and program devel., 1969-74, prof. edn., 1972-74, dir. grad. program in student personnel services, 1969-74, vice chancellor for student affairs U. Ark., Little Rock, 1974—, adv. bd. quality assurance, experiential learning, 1978—. Nat. adviser, mem. resource personnel bd. Intercollegiate Assn. Women Students; exec. bd. N. Central Assn. Schs. and Colls., 1977—. Mem. Nat. Assn. Women Deans, Adminstrs. and Counselors (pres. 1973-74), So. Coll. Personnel Assn. (pres. 1970), Okla. Coll. Personnel Assn. (pres. 1972-73), William Jewell Coll. Alumni Assn. (pres. 1970-73), Pi Beta Phi, Alpha Lambda Delta, Mortar Bd., Sigma Tau Delta, Cardinal Key, Gamma Alpha Chi, Kappa Delta Pi, Pi Lambda Theta, Alpha Psi Omega, Pi Gamma Mu, Delta Kappa Gamma, Phi Delta Kappa. Editorial bd. Jour. Coll. Student Personnel, 1974—. Home: 1421 N University N203 Little Rock AR 72207 Office: 33d and University Ave U Ark Little Rock AR 72204

TRUEX, GEORGE ROBERT, JR., banker; b. Red Bank, N.J., May 29, 1924; s. George Robert and Elsie D. (White) T.; A.B. in Econs., Rutgers U., 1949; m. Nancy Carroll Burt, May 10, 1947; children—Peter Barclay, Amy Dinsmore. Sr. v.p. Irving Trust Co., N.Y.C., 1949-66; exec. v.p. Bank of Am., San Francisco, 1966-73, vice chmn. Small Bus. Enterprises Co. subsidiary, 1968-72; chmn., chief exec. officer Rainier Bancorp., Seattle, 1973—, chmn. bd., chief exec. Rainier Nat. Bank, 1973—; dir., mem. exec. com. Nat. Airlines, Inc., Miami, Fla., 1962—, INA Life Ins. Co. N.Y., 1965-68; dir. Pvt. Export Funding Corp., N.Y.C. Bd. dirs. Calif. Bankers Assn., 1969-73. Fin. chmn. Calif. Gov.'s Task Force on Flood Relief, 1969-73; mem. fin. advisory com. CAB, 1970-71; mem. orthopaedic council Orthopaedic Hosp., Los Angeles, 1969-72. Trustee, Calif. Inst. Arts, Los Angeles, 1968-72; bd. dirs. Walt Disney Assos. for Calif. Inst. Arts, 1972—, San Francisco Planning and Urban Renewal Assn., 1973; bd. dirs. Jr. Achievement So. Calif., 1967-72, pres., 1968-70, Western Regional bd. dirs., 1968-72; nat. bd. dirs. Jr. Achievement, Inc., 1968-75; bd. dirs. Jr. Achievement Greater Seattle, 1976-77; div. chmn. United Way, Inc., Los Angeles, 1970, 71; asso. gen. campaign chmn. United Way of King County, 1976-78, gen. chmn., 1979; bd. dirs. Virgina Mason Hosp., 1976—; bd. regents Seattle U., 1976—; trustee Bank of Am. Found., 1973; mem. adv. bd. Grad. Sch. Bus. Adminstrn., U. Wash., 1975—. Served to capt., cav. AUS, World War II; ETO. Mem. Assn. Res. City Bankers, Seattle C. of C. (trustee 1975-78). Clubs: California (Los Angeles); Bankers, Bohemian (San Francisco); Seattle Golf, Wash. Athletic, Rainier, Broadmoor Golf (Seattle); Bellevue (Wash.) Athletic. Office: Rainier Nat Bank Box 3966 Seattle WA 98124

TRUFFAUT, FRANCOIS, motion picture dir.; b. Paris, France, Feb. 6, 1932; s. Roland and Janine (de Monferrand) T.; m. Madeleine Morgenstern, Oct. 29, 1957 (div.); children—Laura, Eva. Reporter, motion picture critic Movie Jour. and Arts, 1954-58; dir. motion pictures, 1957—, producer, 1961—; prodns. include Les Mistons, 1958, Les 400 Coups, 1959, Tirez sur le Pianiste, 1960, L'Amour a 20 ans, 1962, Jules and Jim, 1961, La Peau Douce, 1963, Fahrenheit 451, 1966, La Mariée était en Noir, 1967, Baisers Voles, 1968, La Sirène du Mississippi, 1969, L'Enfant Sauvage, 1969, Domicile Conjugal, 1970, Les Deux Anglaises et le Continent, 1971, Une Belle Fille Comme Moi (Such a Gorgeous Kid Like Me), 1972, La Nuit Américaine, (Day for Night) 1972-73, L'Histoire d' Adèle H. (The Story of Adele H.), 1975, L'Argent de Poche (Small Change), 1975-76, L'Homme qui aimait les Femmes, 1976-77; La Chambre Verte, 1977-78, L'Amour en Fuite, 1978-79; appeared in film Close Encounters of the Third Kind, 1977; dir., appeared in The Green Room, 1979. Recipient Cannes Film Festival prize for Les 400 Coups, 1959; best dir. and best film award for Day for Night, N.Y. Film Critics, 1973; Oscar award for best fgn. lang. film Am. Acad. Motion Picture Arts and Scis., 1974. Author: Le Cinema Selon Hitchcock, 1966; Les Aventures d'Antoine Doinel, 1970; La Nuit Americaine et le Journal de Fahrenheit, 1974; Les Films de Ma Vie, 1975; L'Argent de Poche, 1976; L'Homme qui aimait les Femmes, 1977. *

TRUHLAR, DONALD GENE, chemist; b. Chgo., Feb. 27, 1944; s. John Joseph and Lucille Marie (Vancura) T.; B.A. in Chemistry summa cum laude (scholar), St. Mary's Coll., Winona, Minn., 1965; Ph.D. in Chemistry, Calif. Inst. Tech., 1969; m. Jane Teresa Gust, Aug. 28, 1965; children—Sara Elizabeth, Stephanie Marie. Asst. prof. chemistry and chem. physics U. Minn., Mpls, 1969-72, asso. prof., 1972-76, prof., 1976—; cons. Los Alamos Sci. Lab.; vis. fellow Joint Inst. for Lab. Astrophysics, 1975-76. Ruhland Walzer Meml. scholar, 1961-62; John Stauffer fellow, 1965-66; NDEA fellow, 1966-68; Alfred P. Sloan Found. fellow, 1973-77; NSF grantee, 1971—; Dept. Energy contractor, 1979—. Mem. Am. Phys. Soc., Am. Chem. Soc. Research, numerous publs. in field. Home: 5033 Thomas Ave S Minneapolis MN 55410 Office: 207 Pleasant St SE Minneapolis MN 55455

TRUHLSEN, STANLEY MARSHALL, physician; b. Herman, Nebr., Nov. 13, 1920; s. Henry and Lola Mollie (Marshall) T.; A.B., U. Nebr., 1941, M.D., 1944; m. Ruth Haney, June 2, 1943; children—William, Nancy, Stanley M., Barbara. Intern, Albany (N.Y.) Hosp., 1944-45; resident Barnes Hosp., St. Louis, 1948-51; practice medicine specializing in ophthalmology, Omaha, 1951—; mem. staff U. Nebr., Clarkson, Immanuel, Children's, Methodist hosps.; pres. med. staff Immanuel Hosp., 1961, Clarkson Hosp., 1972-73; prof. ophthalmology U. Nebr. Coll. Medicine, 1974—; dir. Nebr. Blue Shield, Health Planning Council Midlands, 1972-75, Clarkson Hosp., 1974-76, Nebr. Soc. Prevention Blindness. Trustee Omaha Home of Boys, Brownell Talbot Sch., 1966-69, Omaha Citizens Assembly, 1972—. Served with AUS, 1946-48. Fellow A.C.S.; mem. Am. Ophthal. Soc. (asst. editor transactions 1973-79, editor 1979—), Am. Acad. Ophthalmology and Otolaryngology (asso. editor transactions 1968-75, editor 1975—), Nebr. Acad. Ophthalmology (pres. 1975), Assn. Research in Vision and Ophthalmology, Omaha Med. Soc. (pres. 1973), Sigma Xi, Alpha Omega Alpha, Sigma Nu, Phi Rho Sigma. Republican. Clubs: Masons, Shriners, Rotary, Omaha, Omaha Country (pres. 1977-78). Home: 10086 Fieldcrest Dr Omaha NE 68114 Office: 710 Doctors Bldg Omaha NE 68131

TRUITT, ANNE DEAN, artist; b. Balt., Mar. 16, 1921; d. Duncan Witt and Louisa Folsom (Williams) Dean; B.A., Bryn Mawr Coll., 1943; postgrad. Inst. Contemporary Art, Washington, 1948-50; m. James McConnell Truitt, Sept. 19, 1947 (div.); children—Alexandra, Mary McConnell, Samuel Rogers. Exhibited in one woman shows at Andre Emmerich Gallery, N.Y.C., 1963, 65, 69, 75, Minami Gallery, Tokyo, 1964, 67, Balt. Mus. Art, 1969, 75, Pyramid Galleries, Washington, 1971, 73, 75, 77, Whitney Mus. Am. Art, N.Y.C., 1973-74, Corcoran Gallery of Art, Washington, 1974; exhibited in group shows at Balt. Mus. Art, 1970, 72-73, Whitney Mus. Am. Art, 1970-71, 72, 77, Phillips Collection, Washington, 1971-72, Pyramid Galleries, 1972, 73, Mus. Contemporary Art, Chgo., 1974, 77, Indpls. Mus. Art, 1974, Nat. Gallery Art, Washington, 1974, Corcoran Gallery Art, Washington, 1975, numerous others. Guggenheim fellow, 1970, Nat. Endowment for Arts fellow, 1971, 77. Translator: (with C.J. Hill) Marcel Proust and Deliverance from Time (Germaine Brée) 1955. Home: 3506 35th St NW Washington DC 20016

TRUITT, RICHARD HUNT, public relations agy. exec.; b. Chgo., June 12, 1932; s. Richard B. and Cleon (Johnson) T.; B.S. in Polit. Sci., Northwestern U., 1953; M.S. in Journalism, 1957; m. Ruth Annette Young, Oct. 4, 1958; children—Susan, Thomas, Stephen. Reporter, editor Chgo. Tribune, 1957-59; account exec., v.p., sr. v.p., group v.p. Carl Byoir & Assos., Inc., N.Y.C., 1959—, now exec. v.p. Pres., Winnebago Day Sch., Menasha, Wis., 1969-70; mem. Neenah (Wis.) Bd. Edn., 1970-71. Served with USMC, 1954-55; maj. Res. (ret.). Mem. Pub. Relations Soc. Am. (accredited, Silver Anvil award 1972, 73, Thoth award 1973, Cee Bee award 1974), Environ. Writers Assn., Beta Theta Pi, Sigma Delta Chi. Clubs: Nat. Press (Washington); Indiana Soc. (v.p.); Norwalk Yacht. Author: A History of the Marine Corps Reserve, 1966. Contbr. numerous articles to profl. jours. and popular mags. Home: 162 Logan Rd New Canaan CT 06840 Office: 380 Madison Ave New York NY 10017

TRUMAN, BESS WALLACE (MRS. HARRY S. TRUMAN), wife of former pres. U.S.: b. Independence, Mo., Feb. 13, 1885; grad. high sch.; student Barstow Sch. for Girls, Kansas City, Mo.; m. Harry S. Truman, June 28, 1919 (dec. Dec. 26, 1972); 1 dau., Mary Margaret (Mrs. E. Clifton Daniel, Jr.). Democrat. Episcopalian.*

TRUMAN, DAVID BICKNELL, former found. pres.; b. Evanston, Ill., June 1, 1913; s. Malcolm George and Jane (Mackintosh) T.; A.B., Amherst Coll., 1935, L.H.D., 1964; M.A., U. Chgo., 1936, Ph.D., 1939; Litt.D., Am. Internat. Coll., 1972; LL.D., Mt. Holyoke Coll., 1978; m. Elinor Jane Griffenhagen, Feb. 4, 1939; 1 son, Edwin Malcolm. Instr. Bennington Coll., 1939-41, Cornell, 1941-44; lectr. govt. Harvard, 1946-47; asso. prof. polit. sci. Williams Coll., 1947-51; on leave as vis. asso. prof. govt. Columbia, N.Y.C., 1950-51, prof. govt., 1951-69, dean Columbia Coll., 1963-67, v.p. and provost Columbia, 1967-69; pres. Mt. Holyoke Coll., 1969-78, Russell Sage Found., N.Y., 1978-79; staff mem. com. pre-election polls and forecasts Social Sci. Research Council, 1948-49, mem. com. polit. behavior, 1950-62; vis. lectr. Yale U., 1956-57. Guggenheim fellow, 1955-56. With F.C.C. and Dept. Agr., 1942-44; staff mem. U.S. Strategic Bombing Survey, Pacific, 1945-46; bd. dirs. Social Sci. Research Council, 1959-71; mem. Pres.'s Commn. on White House Fellowships, 1975-77; trustee Russell Sage Found., 20th Century Fund. Served from ensign to lt. (j.g.), USNR, 1944-45. Fellow Am. Acad. Arts and Sci.; mem. Am. Polit. Sci. Assn. (pres. 1964-65), Am. Philos. Soc., Council Fgn. Relations, Alpha Delta Phi. Club: Century (N.Y.C.). Author: Administrative Decentralization, 1940; The Pre-Election Polls of 1948 (with others), 1949; The Governmental Process, 1951; The Congressional Party, 1959; contbr. to profl. jours. Home: Tory Hill Rd Hillsdale NY 12529

TRUMAN, JOCK CURTIS, dealer in contemporary art; b. Mpls., Sept. 4, 1920; s. Curtis and Athelyn Irene Amundsen T.; student U. Cin., 1938-41, Harvard Grad. Sch. Design, 1946-50. Owner, operator Thirty-five River St. Inc., Boston, archtl. and interior design, 1950-58; asst. to dir. contemporary realism Robert Isaacson Gallery, N.Y.C., 1958-61; with Betty Parsons Gallery, N.Y.C., 1961—, dir., 1974-76; dir. Parsons-Truman Gallery, N.Y.C., 1975-76, Truman Gallery, 1976—. Editor, pub. 57th St. Rev., N.Y.C., 1966-67, 75-76; instr. sr. art students Drew U., Madison, N.J., 1973, adviser to art dept., 1973—, fellow, 1979—. Bd. dirs. Found. Open Eye, 1978—; with Art and the Community Inst. New Sch. Social Research, 1978—. Served with AUS, 1942-46. Home: 310 E 55th St New York NY 10022 Office: Truman Gallery 38 E 57th St New York NY 10022. *To live ones life seriously, trying to contribute to this world, but knowing its only a game.*

TRUMAN, MARGARET (DANIEL), author; b. Independence, Mo., Feb. 17, 1924; d. Harry S. (Pres. U.S.) and Bess (Wallace) T.; A.B., George Washington U., 1946, Litt.D., 1975; L.H.D., Wake Forest U., 1972; H.H.D., Rockhurst Coll., 1976—; m. E. Clifton Daniel, Jr., Apr. 21, 1956; children—Clifton, William, Harrison, Thomas. Concert singer, 1947-54; actress, broadcaster, author, 1954—; dir. Riggs Nat. Bank, Washington. Trustee Harry S. Truman Inst.; sec. Harry S. Truman Scholarship Found. Author: Souvenir, 1956; White House Pets, 1969; Harry S. Truman, 1973; Women of Courage, 1976.

TRUMBULL, RICHARD, psychologist; b. Johnstown, N.Y., Apr. 6, 1916; s. Milton Elmer and Hazel (Busse) T.; A.B., Union Coll., 1937; M.S., Union U., 1939; Ph.D., Syracuse U., 1951; m. Alice Esther McDaniel, June 17, 1939; children—Judith Trumbull Townsend, Joanne Trumbull Titus, Janice Trumbull Smith, Joyce Ellen Trumbull Setzer. Asst. prof. psychology Green Mountain Jr. Coll., Poultney, Vt., 1939-41, chmn. dept. psychology, 46-49; lectr. Syracuse U., 1941-43, chmn. undergrad program psychology, 49-51; mem. research staff Sch. Aviation Medicine, U.S. Navy, 1951-53, asst. head physiol. psychology br., 1953-54, head physiol. psychology br., 1954-61, dir. psychol. scis., 1961-67; dir. research Office Naval Research, Washington, 1970-74; dep. exec. officer AAAS, 1970-74; exec. dir. Am. Inst. Biol. Scis., Arlington, Va., 1974-79; exec. dir. Renewable Natural Resources Found., Bethesda, Md., 1979—; chmn. adv. group on human factors NATO, research advisory com. NASA, surgeon gen. advisory com. FAA. Trustee, Green Mountain Jr. Coll., Biol. Scis. Info. Service. Served with USNR, 1943-46, 51-53. Recipient Navy Distinguished Civilian Service award, 1961, Longacre award in aerospace medicine, 1966; Sustained Super Accomplishment award, 1966. Mem. AAAS, Am. Inst. Biol. Scis., Aerospace Med. Assn., Natural Resources Council Am. (sec. 1977), Sigma Xi. Joint editor: Sensory Deprivation, 1961; Psychological Stress: Issues in Research, 1966. Contbr. articles to profl. jours. Home: 4708 N Chelsea Ln Bethesda MD 20014

TRUMBULL, ROBERT, fgn. corr.; b. Chgo., May 26, 1912; s. Oliver Morton and Sydney (Farmer) T.; student U. Wash., 1930-33; m. Jean Magnier Musson, Sept. 30, 1934; children—Suzanne, Joan, Stephanie. Reporter, city editor Honolulu Advertiser, 1933-43; war corr. Pacific area N.Y. Times, 1941-45, fgn. corr., Japan, Philippines, South and S.E. Asia, 1945-54, chief bur., Tokyo, 1954-61, 64-68, chief corr., China-S.E. Asia, 1961-63, chief S. Pacific bur., corr. Australia-N.Z.-Pacific Islands, 1968-73, chief corr., Can., 1974-78, Pacific corr., Honolulu, 1978—. Former mem. U.S. Ednl. Commn. in Japan; former mem. bd. dirs. U.S. Ednl. Found. in India. Decorated Commendations, Pacific Theatre Ribbon (Navy). Recipient Better Understanding award English Speaking Union, 1951. Mem. Authors Guild, Authors League Am., Phi Sigma Kappa, Sigma Delta Chi. Clubs: Overseas Press Am. (N.Y.C.); Fgn. Corrs. Japan; Am. Nat., Journalists (Sydney, Australia); Gymkhana (New Delhi, India); Rideau, Nat. Press Canada (Ottawa). Author: The Raft (Book-of-the-Month Club selection), 1942; Sol Pluvius' Hawaiian Communiques, 1942; Silversides, 1945; India Since Independence, 1954; As I See India, 1956; Nine Who Survived Hiroshima and Nagasaki, 1957; Paradise in Trust, 1959; The Scrutable East (Overseas Press Club Am. award), 1964; Tin Roofs and Palm Trees, 1977; contbr. on Asian and Pacific affairs various publs. Editor: This Is Communist China, 1968. Address: 431 Nahua St Apt 1107 Honolulu HI 96815

TRUMP, BENJAMIN FRANLIN, pathologist; b. Kansas City, Mo., July 23, 1932; s. Lyle Franklin and Helen Muriel (Smith) T.; B.A., U. Kans., 1953, M.D., 1957; m. Elizabeth Scanlan, Nov. 8, 1976; children—Lisa, Rebecca. Intern, U. Kans. Med. Center, Kansas City, 1957-58, resident-fellow dept. pathology, 1958-59; research asso. dept. anatomy U. Wash. Sch. Medicine, Seattle, 1959-60, trainee in exptl. pathology, 1960-61, asst. prof. dept. pathology, 1963-65; investigator in exptl. pathology Office of Sci. Dir., Armed Forces Inst. Pathology, Washington, 1961-63; asso. prof. pathology Duke U. Med. Center, Durham, N.C., 1965-67, prof., 1967-70; prof., chmn. dept. pathology U. Md. Sch. Medicine, Balt., 1970—, Am. Cancer Soc. prof. oncology, 1977—, v.p., 1978-79, dir. Md. cancer program, 1977—; lab. dir. U. Md. Hosp., 1979—; dir. Univs. Asso. for Research and Edn. in Pathology, Md., 1970—; chmn. Md. Post Mortem Examiner's Commn., Balt., 1970—; mem. research and edn. com. Balt. VA Hosp., 1970—, cons., 1970—; cons. Union Meml. Hosp., Balt., 1976—; cons. FDA, 1971-76, animal strain selection panel Nat. Center Toxicol. Research, Bethesda, Md., 1971-73, biol. models segment Nat. Cancer Inst., 1972-75; adv. com. Atlas of Tumor Pathology, Armed Forces Inst. Pathology, 1971—; cons., dir. research, Md. Inst. Emergency Medicine, 1970—, mem. manuscript com., 1976—; N.Am. sci. program com. biol. sci. Internat. Congress on Electron Miscoscopy/Micros. Soc. Can., 1976—; mem. research council Md. affiliate Am. Heart Assn., 1976—; cons. cancer policy Occupational Safety and Health Adminstrn., 1977—; mem. subcom. on long-range planning council on toxic substances, dept. health and mental hygiene Md. Environ. Health Adminstrn., 1978—; mem. tech. adv. group on cancer health planning com. Central Md. Health Dept. Agy., 1978—; at-large dir. Md. div. Am. Cancer Soc., 1978—; mem. environ. cancer control program com. Md. Dept. Health and Mental Hygiene, 1978—; mem. Balt. City PSRO, Inc., 1979—; chmn. environ. pathology registry com. Internat. Acad. Path./Armed Forces Inst. Path., 1979—. mem. N.Am. sci. program com. biol. sci. Internat. Congress on Electron Miscoscopy/Micros. Soc. Can., 1976—; mem. research council Md. affiliate Am. Heart Assn., 1976—; cons. cancer policy Occupational Safety and Health Adminstrn., 1977—; mem. subcom. on long-range planning council on toxic substances, dept. health and mental hygiene Md. Environ. Health Adminstrn., 1978—; mem. tech. adv. group on cancer health planning com. Central Md. Health Dept. Agy., 1978—; at-large dir. Md. div. Am. Cancer Soc., 1978—; mem. environ. cancer control program com. Md. Dept. Health and Mental Hygiene, 1978—; mem. Balt. City PSRO, Inc., 1979—; chmn. environ. pathology registry com. Internat. Acad. Path. Armed Forces Inst. Path., 1979—. Served with U.S. Army, 1961-64. Mem. Internat. Acad. Pathology (v.p. U.S.-Can. div. 1975-76, mem. council 1972—, div. pres. 1976-77), Acad. Clin. Lab. Physicians and Scientists, Assn. Pathologists and Bacteriologists, AAUP, Am. Soc. Cell Biology, Am. Soc. Exptl. Pathology, Am. Soc. Microbiology, Fedn. Am. Socs. Exptl. Biology, Histochem. Soc. Am. (nominating com. 1979—), N.E. Assn. Pathology Chmn., AAAS, Electronic Microscope Soc., Md. Soc. Histology Technicians, Balt. City Med. Soc. (environ. problems subcom. 1975—), Am. Soc. Clin. Pathology (environ. task force 1977—). Author: (with D. G. Scarpelli) Cell Injury, 1971; (with others) Pathology and Toxicology, 1972; (with A.U. Arstila) Pathobiology of Cell Membranes, Vol. I, 1975, Vol. II; (with R.T. Jones) Diagnostic Electron Microscopy, Vol. I, 1978, Vol. II, 1979; editor Lab. Investigation, 1967—; Pathology Research and Practice (formerly Beitrage zue Pathologie), 1975—; adv. editor Electron Microscopy, Internat. Dictionary of Biology and Medicine, 1979—. Home: 500 Hawthorne Rd Baltimore MD 21210 Office: 10 S Pine St Baltimore MD 21201. *To make significant achievements one must devote virtually 100% effort to his goals. The total enterprise must combine work, recreation, religion, and art.*

TRUMP, GUY WINSTON, assn. exec.; b. Churubusco, Ind., Mar. 30, 1918; s. Lewis Orland and Romalie (Hapner) T.; B.B.A., Tulane U., 1947, M.B.A., 1948; Ph.D., State U. Iowa, 1951; m. Virginia Lucille Stillwaugh, Nov. 22, 1941; children—Kristan, Virginia, Kathryn. Prof., chmn. dept. bus. Stephen F. Austin State Coll., Nacogdoches, Tex., 1950-52; prof., chmn. dept. bus. So. Ill. U., Carbondale, 1952-55; dean U.S. Mcht. Marine Acad., 1955-59; dean Emory U. Sch. Bus. Adminstrn., 1959-65; v.p. edn. Am. Inst. C.P.A.'s, N.Y.C., 1965—. Served with USNR, 1941-46. Mem. La. Soc. C.P.A.'s. Home: 693 Densley Dr Decatur GA 30033

TRUMP, JOHN GEORGE, engr.; b. N.Y.C., Aug. 21, 1907; s. Frederick and Elizabeth (Christ) T.; E.E., Poly. Inst. Bklyn., 1929; M.A., Columbia, 1931; D.Sc., Mass. Inst. Tech., 1933; m. Elora Gordon Sauerbrun, May 25, 1935; children—John Gordon, Christine Elora, Karen Elizabeth. Instr. elec. engring. Poly. Inst. Bklyn., 1929-31; research asso. Mass. Inst. Tech., 1933-36, asst. prof., 1936-41, asso. prof. elec. engring., 1941-52, prof. elec. engring., 1952-73; sec. microwave com. Nat. Def. Research Com., 1940-42; dir. Brit. Br. Radiation Lab., Gt. Malverne, Eng., 1944-45, asst. dir. Radiation Lab., 1945; chmn. bd. Electronized Chems. Corp., 1963-78, High Voltage Power Corp., 1967-72; dir., tech. dir. High Voltage Engring. Corp., 1947—. Chmn. bd. trustees Lahey Clinic Found., 1974—. Decorated King's medal (Eng.), 1946, Presdl. citation, 1946. Fellow Am. Phys. Soc., I.E.E.E. (Lamme medal 1961, Power-Life award 1973), Am. Acad. Arts and Sci., Am. Coll. Radiology (hon.); mem. New Eng. Roentgen Ray Soc., Nat. Acad. Engring., Am. Radium Soc. Contbr. sci. papers to profl. lit. Home: 9 Cambridge St Winchester MA 01890 Office: Mass Inst Tech Cambridge MA 02139

TRUMP, ROBERT M., advt. exec.; b. 1921; A.B., U. Kans.; M.S. in Journalism, Northwestern U.; M.B.A., Harvard. With Foote, Cone & Belding, Inc., 1948—, chmn. finance com., mem. exec. com. Foote, Cone & Belding Communications, Inc., also dir Served with AUS, World War II. Clubs: Economic, Executives, Harvard Business School, Glen View, Mid-America (Chgo.); Sky (N.Y.C.). Address: Foote Cone and Belding Inc 401 N Michigan Ave Chicago IL 60611

TRUMP, ROSS MYRON, educator; b. West Manchester, Ohio, Dec. 25, 1911; s. Lewis O. and Roma L. (Hapner) T.; B.S., Ohio State U., 1937, M.B.A., 1938, Ph.D., 1947, D.Econs. (hon.), 1965; m. Flora Leah Douglass, Feb. 10, 1934; children—Barbara, Cynthia. Asst. prof. marketing Tulane U., 1938-42, asso. prof., 1942-43, asst. dean and asso. prof. marketing Coll. Commerce, 1943-46, dir. Univ. Coll. (adult edn.), prof. Coll. Commerce, 1946-47, exec. asst. to pres., prof. adminstrn., 1947; asst. dean Am. Coll. Life Underwriters, Phila., 1947-49; prof. adminstrn. Washington U., St. Louis, 1949—, dean Sch. Bus. and Pub. Adminstrn., 1954-58, Grad. Sch. Bus. Adminstrn., 1958-67. U.S. del. 5th Internat. Conf. Mgmt. Edn., Germany, 1958, Lisbon, 1959, Paris, 1960, 64; resident cons. European Productivity Agy., Paris, 1960-61; vice chmn. Regional Export Expansion Council, 1965; cons. Asian Productivity Orgn., 1970, United Bd., Taiwan, Philippines, Hong Kong, 1973, AID, Tunisia, 1975, Taiwan and Korea, 1976; mem. Regional P.O. Selection Bd., 1969-76. C.L.U., 1949. Mem. Am. Assn. Collegiate Schs. Bus. (sec. 1957-58, pres. 1959-60, bd. govs. 1965), Am. Mktg. Assn. Author: Developments in Governmental Supervision of Insurance, 1947. Co-author: Essentials of Marketing Management, 1966. Office: Prince Hall Washington U St Louis MO 63130

TRUMPLER, PAUL ROBERT, engring. exec.; b. Rahway, N.J., Nov. 3, 1914; s. William Ernst and Louise (Jelinek) T.; B.S. in Mech. Engring. magna cum laude, Lafayette Coll., 1936; Ph.D., Yale, 1940; m. Edith M. Osterman, June 7, 1938; children—Jean Elizabeth, Allan Paul, Martin Robert. Instr. heat power engring. Ill. Inst. Tech., Chgo., 1939-41, prof. mech. engring., charge machine design, 1949-57; devel. engr. Western Electric Co., Kearny, N.J., 1941-42; heat transfer develop. engr. M.W. Kellogg Co., N.Y., 1942- 47; engr. centrifugal engring. dept. Clark Bros. Co., Olean, N.Y., 1947-49; dir. Sch. Mech. Engring. U. Pa., 1957-60, prof. mech. engring., 1957-69; cons. engr. turbomachinery problems. Founder, pres. Turbo Research, Inc., 1961-74, Trumpler Assos., Inc., 1974—, Turbotherm Corp., 1974—; pres. Turbo Research Found., 1966—. Fellow Am. Soc. M.E. (life; chmn. heat transfer 1953); mem. Am. Soc. Engring. Edn., Phi Beta Kappa, Sigma Xi, Tau Beta Pi, Pi Tau Sigma. Presbyn. Author: Design of Film Bearings, 1966. Contbr. tech. articles to profl. jours. Patentee. Home: 449 Woodcrest Rd Wayne PA 19087

TRURAN, JAMES WELLINGTON, JR., astrophysicist; b. Brewster, N.Y., July 12, 1940; s. James Wellington and Suzanne (Foglesong) T.; B.A. in Physics, Cornell U., 1961; M.S. in Physics, Yale U., 1963, Ph.D. in Physics, 1966; m. Carol Kay Dell'Acy, June 26, 1965; children—Elaina Michelle, Diana Lee, Anastrasia Elizabeth. Nat. Acad. Scis.-NRC postdoctoral resident research asso. Goddard Inst. Space Studies, NASA, N.Y.C., 1965-67; research fellow in physics Calif. Inst. Tech., 1968-69; asst. prof. physics Belfer Grad. Sch. Sci., Yeshiva U. 1967-70, asso. prof., 1970-72, prof., 1972-73; prof. astronomy U. Ill., Urbana, 1973—, acting head dept. astronomy, 1977; sr. vis. fellow, Guggenheim Meml. Found. fellow Inst. Astronomy, U. Cambridge (Eng.), 1979-80; William Pyle Philips lectr. in astronomy Haverford Coll., 1979; lectr. in nuclear astrophysics Internat. Sch. Nuclear Physics, Erice, Sicily, 1980; trustee Aspen Center Physics, 1979—; asso. U. Ill. Center for Advanced Study, 1980. Mem. Am. Astron. Soc., Am. Phys. Soc., Internat. Astron. Union. Contbr. articles to profl. jours.; co-editor: Nucleosynthesis, 1968; editor Contbns. on Nuclear and High-Energy Astrophysics, Physics Letters B, 1974—. *

TRUSSEL, JACQUE, opera singer; b. San Francisco, Apr. 7, 1943; s. Jack B. and Mary Jean (Grantham) T.; B.S., M.M. Ball State U. Appeared throughout U.S. and Europe including: N.Y.C. Opera, Spoleto Featival Italy and U.S., Chgo. Lyric Opera, Dallas Civic Opera, Houston Grand Opera, Boston Opera, Washington Opera, Phila. Opera, Santa Fe Opera Co., Milw. Opera Co., San Francisco Opera Co.; appeared in world premieres: Bibly's Doll, Sea Gull; U.S. premiere: Hugh the Drover, La Navarraise. Home: 240 Town Creek Dr Lexington Park MD 20653

TRUSSELL, ALBERT CLYDE, ins. co. exec.; b. Norwalk, Conn., Aug. 5, 1917; s. Verlyn A. and Mary Elizabeth (Gumaer) T.; B.S. in Bus., Syracuse U., 1939; m. Helen Pilling, Dec. 24, 1942; children—David W., Stephen A., Peter T.B. Copywriter, McCann-Erickson, advt., N.Y.C., 1939-42; cons. Life Ins. Agy. Mgmt. Assn., 1942-44; with Mut. Life Ins. Co. N.Y., 1944-60; chief operating officer Fidelity & Guaranty Life of Balt., 1960-74; pres., chief exec. officer Fed. Life & Casualty Co., also Peoples Home Life Ins. Co. of Ind., Battle Creek, Mich., 1974-77, Fed. Home Life Ins. Co., 1978—, PHF Life Ins. Co., Battle Creek, 1978—. C.L.U. Mem. Am. Soc. C.L.U.'s, Nat. Speakers Assn. Clubs: Battle Creek Country, Athelstan (Battle Creek). Home: 151 S Minges Rd Battle Creek MI 49015 Office: 78 W Michigan Mall Battle Creek MI 49017

TRUSSELL, CHARLES EUGENE, retail clothing chain exec.; b. Jewel County, Kans., Dec. 15, 1933; s. Willis Eugene and Helen Louise (Press) T.; student U. Omaha, 1957-58; m. Carol June Calkins, Apr. 10, 1954; children—Tony, Susan, Robert, Kay. In various acctg. positions, 1956-60; asst. sec.-treas. J. M. McDonald Co., Hastings, Nebr., 1960-69, pres., chief exec. officer, 1976—; v.p., asst. to pres. Gamble Skogmo, Mpls., 1969-76; dir. First Nat. Bank, Hastings. Bd. dirs. YMCA, Hastings, 1978—. C.P.A., Nebr. Mem. Am. Inst. C.P.A.'s. Republican. Lutheran. Home: 1117 N Kansas St Hastings NE 68901 Office: 2635 W 2d St Hastings NE 68901*

TRUSSELL, CHARLES TAIT, journalist; b. Balt., May 9, 1925; s. Charles Prescott and Beatrice (Tait) T.; B.A. in Journalism, Washington and Lee U., 1949; m. Woodley Grizzard, Dec. 27, 1953; children—Galen Tait, Thomas Marshall. Reporter, St. Petersburg (Fla.) Times, also writer Congl. Quar. News Features, 1949-54; reporter Wall St. Jour., 1954-56, Washington Evening Star, 1956; asso. editor Nation's Business mag., 1956-64, mng. editor, 1964-69; sr. editor Congl. Quar., Inc., 1969-70; dir. pub. relations and advt. Investment Co. Inst., Washington, 1970-72; free-lance writer, real estate investor, 1972-74; v.p. Am. Forest Inst., Washington, 1974-79, sr. v.p., 1980—; producer documentary record album The Best of Washington Humor, 1963. Served with USNR, 1944-46. Recipient Loeb Spl. Achievement award for mags. U. Conn., 1961. Mem. Washington Assembly (exec. com. 1961-65, chmn. 1965), White House Corr. Assn., Sigma Delta Chi, Beta Theta Pi. Rotarian. Clubs: Nat. Press (Washington); Kenwood Golf and Country. Editor: (with others) Successful Management, 1964; (with Paul Hencke) Dear NASA Please Send Me a Rocket, 1964. Home: 2828 Wisconsin Ave Washington DC 20007 Office: 1619 Massachusetts Ave Washington DC 20036

TRUSSELL, RAY ELBERT, physician; b. Toledo, Iowa, Feb. 7, 1914; s. Ray E. and Verna (Cannon) T.; student Chaffey Jr. Coll., Ontario, Calif., 1931-32; A.B., U. Iowa, 1935, M.D., 1941; M.P.H., Johns Hopkins U., 1947; m. Elizabeth Davis. Lab. instr. Coll. Medicine U. Iowa, 1935-37, research asst. dept. obstetrics and gynecology, 1936-41, intern U. Hosp., 1941-42, instr., asso. preventive medicine, 1942-43, 1946; epidemiologist N.Y. State Dept. Health, 1947-48; asst. prof. Albany (N.Y.) Med. Coll., 1947-48, prof., 1948-50; clin. prof. preventive medicine N.Y. U. Bellevue Med. Center, 1951-55; epidemiologist Albany, Brady hosps. 1948-50; dir. Hunterdon Med Center, 1950-55; asso. dean, dir., DeLamar prof. adminstrv. medicine Columbia, 1955-68; gen. dir. Beth Israel Med. Center, 1968-79; prof. adminstrv. medicine Mt. Sinai Sch. Medicine, 1968-79, prof. emeritus adminstrv. medicine, 1979—; commr. hosps. City N.Y., 1961-65. Mem. Fed. Health Ins. Benefits Adv. Council, 1964-68. Served as epidemiologist AUS, 1943-46. Decorated Bronze Star. Fellow N.Y. Acad. Medicine; mem. Phi Beta Kappa, Sigma Xi, Alpha Omega Alpha. Author: Trichomonas vaginalis and Trichomoniasis, 1947; Hunterdon Medical Center, 1956; (with Jack Elinson) Chronic Illness in a Rural Area, 1959. Contbr. many articles to med. jours. Home: 353 E 17th St New York NY 10003

TRUST, SAMUEL SMITH, music pub. co. exec.; b. Pitts., July 22, 1933; s. Matthew and Esther Astor (Smith) T.; student Oberlin Coll., 1951-53, Cin. Conservatory Music, 1953-55; Mus. B., Manhattan Sch. Music, 1958; postgrad. Rutgers U., 1962-63; m. Anita Joan Van Genderen, June 28, 1959; children—Jennifer Helen, Benjamin Carl. Trumpeter, Cin. Symphony, 1955; soloist U.S. Naval Bands, 7th Fleet, 1956-57; exec. dir. pub. adminstrn. Broadcast Music Inc., music licensing orgn., N.Y.C., 1958-68; pres. Beechwood Music Corp. music pub. div. Capitol Records, Hollywood, Calif., 1969-71; pres. ATV Music Group, Hollywood, 1973—. Expert cons. in appraisal music pub. catalogues. Served with USNR, 1955-57. Mem. Calif. Copyright Conf., Country Music Assn., Nat. Acad. Rec. Arts, Scis., Nat. Music Pubs. Assn. (dir.). Composer background music for TV programs; created TV logging system currently in operation at Broadcast Music Inc. Home: 23955 Park Belonte Calabasas Park CA 91302 Office: 6255 Sunset Blvd Hollywood CA 90028

TRUSTMAN, BENJAMIN ARTHUR, lawyer; b. June 14, 1902; s. Israel and Pessie (Rubin) T.; A.B. summa cum laude, Harvard U., 1922, J.D., 1925; Sc.D. (hon.), Lowell Coll., 1964; fellow Brandies U. m. Julia Bertha Myerson, July 31, 1927; children—Alan Robert, Phyllis Anne (Mrs. Robert W. Gelfman). Admitted to Mass. bar, 1925, Fla. bar, 1953; asso. Nutter, McClennen & Fish, and predecessor, Boston, 1925-34, mem. firm, 1934-77; past dir. Wm. Filene's Sons Co., Shawmut Bank of Boston N.A.; dir., past pres., chief exec. officer, treas. World Jai-Alai, Inc.; past chmn. bd., treas., dir. Miami Jai-Alai, Inc., Tampa Jai Alai Inc., Hartford Jai-Alai Inc.; past dir. Shawmut Assn., Inc. Former town moderator Brookline, Mass.; past chmn. Brookline Housing Authority; nat. adv. council Am. Assn. Jewish Edn.; mem. advisory council Lincoln Filene Center Law in Social Studies Project, Tufts U.; former treas., sec., dir., now hon. life dir. Lincoln and Therese Filene Found., past v.p. United Community Services Met. Boston; life trustee, past pres. Hebrew Coll., Boston; life trustee, past chmn. bd. mgrs., past pres. Combined Jewish Philanthropies Greater Boston; life trustee, past chmn. bd. mgrs. Beth Israel Hosp. Assn.; past mem. Mass. Council Arts and Humanities; mem. corp. Eye Research Inst. of Retina Found.; trustee John F. Kennedy Center Performing Arts, Washington; bd. visitors dept. prints Boston Mus. Fine Arts; bd. visitors Lowell Coll.; nat. council Am. Jewish Joint Distbn. Com.; mem. com. Harvard U. Center for Jewish Studies. Recipient Nat. Brotherhood award NCCJ, 1964; Benjamin A. Trustman Apts. dedicated by Brookline Housing Authority, 1975. Mem. Mass. Moderators Assn. (past pres., dir., mem. exec. com.), Harvard U. Law Sch. Assn. (life), NCCJ, Am., Mass., Fla. Boston bar assns., Am. Law Inst. (life), Phi Beta Kappa Assos., Phi Beta Kappa. Jewish (trustee temple). Clubs: Belmont Country, Miami Shores Country. Co-author: Town Meeting Time, 1962. Home: 1700 NE 105th St Apt 119 Miami Shores Village FL 33138 also 80 Park St Brookline MA 02146 Office: 1200 NW 87th Ave Miami FL 33131

TRUXAL, JOHN GROFF, educator; b. Lancaster, Pa., Feb. 19, 1924; s.Andrew Gehr and Leah Deldee (Groff) T.; A.B., Dartmouth, 1944; B.S., Mass. Inst. Tech., 1947, Sc.D., 1950; D.Eng. (hon.), Purdue U., 1964, Ind. Inst. Tech., 1971; m. Doris Teresa Mastrangelo, June 11, 1949; children—Brian Andrew, Carol Jean. Asso. prof. elec. engring. Purdue U., 1950-54; asso. prof. elec. engring. Poly. Inst. Bklyn., 1954- 57, prof., head dept., 1957-72, v.p. ednl. devel., 1961-72, dean engring., 1964-66, provost, 1966-68, acad. v.p., 1969-72; dean engring. State U. N.Y., Stony Brook, 1972-76, prof. engring., 1976—. Cons. control engring. Fellow I.E.E.E., A.A.A.S.; mem. Nat. Acad. Engring., Instrument Soc. Am. (pres. 1965—), Am. Soc. Engring. Edn., Phi Beta Kappa, Sigma Xi, Tau Beta Pi, Eta Kappa Nu, Phi Kappa Psi. Author: Automatic Feedback Control System Synthesis, 1955; Introductory System Engineering, 1972; (with W.A. Lynch) Signals and Systems in Electrical Engineering, 1962; co-author: The Man Made World, 1969; Man and His Technology, 1973; Technology: Handle With Care, 1975. Editor: Control Engineers' Handbook, 1958. Home: 8 Avon Ct Dix Hills NY 11746 Office: State U NY Stony Brook NY 11794

TRUXELL, ROBERT W., automobile mfg. co. exec.; b. Lansing, Mich., Sept. 16, 1924; s. Warren E. and Hazel I. (McKinley) T.; B.S., Gen. Motors Inst., 1949; m. Norma J. Menkman, Apr. 24, 1948; 1 dau., Barbara J. With Oldsmobile div. Gen. Motors Corp., 1949-69, 72-73, dir. reliability, 1960-61, asst. chief engr., 1961-64, dir. mfg. engring., 1964-69, mgr. production, purchasing, traffic, 1972-73, dir. mfg. devel. Mfg. Devel. Staff, Warren, Mich., 1969-72, gen. mgr. Delco Moraine div., Dayton, Ohio, 1973-75, gen. mgr. Truck and Coach div., v.p. parent co., Pontiac, Mich., 1975—. Mem. advisory and rev. bd. St. Joseph Mercy Hosp., Pontiac. Served with USAF,

1943-46. Mem. Soc. Automotive Engrs., Engring. Soc. Detroit, Am. Ordnance Assn. Home: 1543 Island Ln Bloomfield Hills MI 48013 Office: 660 South Blvd E Pontiac MI 48053

TRYGSTAD, LAWRENCE BENSON, lawyer; b. Holton, Mich., Mar. 22, 1937; s. Russell and Gussie (Benson) T.; B.A., U. Mich., 1959; J.D., U. So. Calif., 1967; m. Ann J. Quirino, Dec. 21, 1963; children—Michael, Shanon, David. Tchr. Am. history and govt. Los Angeles Unified Sch. Dist., 1959-68, asst. vice prin., 1965-68; pres. faculty assn., 1965-66, 67-68; admitted to Calif. bar, 1968, U.S. Supreme Ct. bar, 1974, U.S. Tax Ct. bar, 1969; legal counsel Calif. Tchrs. Assn., Los Angeles, 1968-71; individual practice law, Los Angeles, 1971—; instr. tchr. negotiations U. Calif. at Northridge; panelist TV show Law and the Teacher. Bd. dirs. George Washington Carver Found. Recipient Am. Jurisprudence award Highest Grade Equity U. So. Calif., 1967. Mem. State Bar Calif., Am., Los Angeles County bar assns., Calif., Los Angeles trial lawyers assns., Nat. Assn. Tchr. Attys., Phi Alpha Delta. Author publs. for tchr. orgns. Home: 4209 Aleman Dr Tarzana CA 91356 Office: 1880 Century Park East Century City CA 90067

TRYON, JOHN GRIGGS, educator; b. Washington, Dec. 18, 1920; s. Frederick Gale and Ruth (Wilson) T.; B.S., U. Minn., 1941; Ph.D., Cornell U., 1952; m. Helen Elsie Muenscher, June 21, 1948; children—Ralph Worthen, Peter Roop. Mem. tech. staff Bell Telephone Labs., 1951-58; prof. elec. engring. U. Alaska, 1958-69, head dept., 1958-68; prof. elec. engring. Tuskegee Inst. Ala., 1969-71, prof. math., 1972-75; prof. engring. U. Nev., Las Vegas, 1975—. Served to capt. Signal Corps, AUS, 1942-46. Mem. IEEE, Am. Phys. Soc., Am. Soc. for Engring. Edn., Internat. Solar Energy Soc., Sigma Xi. Unitarian. Office: Dept Engring U Nev Las Vegas NV 89154

TRYON, LAWRENCE EDWIN, lawyer; b. Channahon, Ill., Nov. 25, 1899; s. Allison and Mary (Alexander) T.; student Northwestern U., Salt City Bus. Coll., Hutchinson, Kans., LaSalle Extension U.; m. Mary A. Bradshaw, Apr. 12, 1925; children-Myrna Jewell (Mrs. Monte L. Thomas), Allison Charles, Mary Kathryn (Mrs. Delbert Carter); m. 2d, Eugenia Shaw. Admitted to Okla. bar, 1929; county judge, Texas County, Okla., 1931-36, county atty., 1937-38; pvt. practice in Guymon, Okla., 1938—, partner firm Tryon Field & Petty; dir. City Nat. Bank & Trust Co., Guymon. Del. Gen. Conf. Meth. Ch., 1936. Republican nominee Supreme Ct. Okla., 1950; del. Rep. Nat. Conv., 1960. Pres. bd. control Meml. Hosp., Guymon, 1948—. Served with U.S. Army, World War I. Fellow Am. Coll. Probate Counsel; mem. Am., Okla. bar assns. Methodist. Clubs: Masons (32 deg.), K.T. (past dep. grand comdr.), Shriners, Lions (past dist. gov.). Home: 6044 Sunset Dr Guymon OK 73942 Office: Professional Bldg Guymon OK 73942

TRYON, ROLLA MILTON, biologist; b. Chgo., Aug. 26, 1916; s. Rolla Milton and Agnes Cary (Polk) T.; Ph.D., Harvard U., 1941; m. Mar. 16, 1945. Prof. biology Harvard U., Cambridge, Mass. Office: Harvard U Dept Biology 22 Divinity Ave Cambridge MA 02138*

TRYON, THOMAS, actor, author; b. Hartford, Conn., Jan. 14, 1926; s. Arthur Lane and Elizabeth (Lester) T.; B.A., Yale, 1949, studied at Art Students League. Formerly with Cape Playhouse, Dennis, Mass.; prodn. asst. CBS-TV; actor plays Wish You Were Here, Cyrano de Bergerac, Richard III; actor films including Scarlet Hours, Screaming Eagles, Three Violent People, Moon Pilot, The Cardinal, The Glory Guys; author The Other, 1971, screenplay, 1971; exec. producer film The Other, 1971. Served with USNR, 1943-46. Recipient Prix Femina de Belgique, 1964; Motion Picture Exhibitors Laurel award, 1964. Author: Harvest Home, 1973; Lady, 1974; Crowned Heads, 1976.

TRYTHALL, HARRY GILBERT, univ. adminstr., composer; b. Knoxville, Tenn., Oct. 28, 1930; s. Harry Gilbert and Clara Hannah (Akre) T.; B.A., U. Tenn., 1951; M.M., Northwestern U., 1952; D.M.A., Cornell U., 1960; m. Jean Marie Slater, Dec. 28, 1951 (div. 1976); children—Linda Marie, Karen Elizabeth. Asst. prof. music Knox Coll., Galesburg, Ill., 1960-64; prof. music theory and composition George Peabody Coll. Tchrs., Nashville, 1964-75; dean Creative Arts Center, prof. music W.Va. U., Morgantown, 1975—. Served with USAF, 1953-57. Mem. Music Educators Nat. Conf., Am. Fedn. Musicians. Author: Principles and Practice of Electronic Music, 1974. Past mem. editorial bd. Music Educators Jour. Composer of orchestral music, chamber and electronic music. Home: 905 W Park Morgantown WV 26505 Office: Creative Arts Center W VA U Morgantown WV 26506

TSAI WEN-YING, sculptor, painter, engr.; b. Amoy, Fukien, China, Oct. 13, 1928; s. Chen-Dak and Ching-Miau (Chen) T.; came to U.S., 1950, naturalized, 1962; student Ta Tung U., 1947-49; B.S. in Mech. Engring., U. Mich., 1953; student Art Students League N.Y., 1953-57, Grad. Faculty Polit. and Social Sci., New Sch., 1956-58; m. Pui-De Chang, Aug. 7, 1968; children—Lun-Yi and Mung Yi (twins). One-man shows include: Ruth Sherman Gallery, N.Y.C., 1961, Amel Gallery, N.Y.C., 1964, 65, Howard Wise Gallery, N.Y.C., 1968, Kaiser Wilhelm Mus. Haus Lange, Krefeld, Germany, 1970, Hayden Gallery of M.I.T., Cambridge, Ont. Sci. Centre, Toronto, Can., 1971, Corcoran Gallery Art, 1972, Denise René Gallery, 1972, 73, Musée d'Art Contemporain, Montreal, 1973, Museo de Arte Contemporaneo, Caracas, 1975, Wildenstein Art Center, Houston, 1978, Museo de Bellas Artes, Caracas, Venezuela, 1978, Hong Kong Mus. Art, 1979; represented maj. internat. exhbns., also numerous groups exhbns.; represented in permanent collections: Centre Georges Pompidou, Paris, Tate Gallery, London, Albright-Knox Gallery, Buffalo, Addison Gallery Am. Art, Andover, Mass., Museo de Arte Contemporaneo, Caracas, Whitney Mus., Chrysler Art Mus., M.I.T., Hayden Gallery, Kaiser Wilhelm Mus., Mus. Modern Art, others; cons. engr., 1953-63; project engr. Cosentini Assos., 1962-63, Guy B. Panero, Engrs., 1956-60. John Hay Whitney fellow, 1963; MacDowell fellow, 1965; fellow Center Advanced Visual Studies, Mass. Inst. Tech., 1969, 70. Creator cybernetic sculpture based on prin. harmonic motion, stroboscopic effects; inventor upward falling fountain, computer mural, utilizing environ. feedback control system.

TSANTES, JOHN FRANK, lock and hardware co. exec.; b. Icaria Island, Greece, Jan. 30, 1926; s. Frank and Despina T.; B.A. in Econs., U. N.C., 1950; M.B.A., George Washington U., 1955; m. Marie Sunas, July 23, 1950; children—Deidre Z., Keith J., Adrienne M. Sr. fin. analyst Chrysler Corp., Detroit, 1954-62; acquisition specialist Schlumberger Corp., Houston, 1962-65; Western planning mgr. Lone Star Industries, San Francisco, 1965-74; pres. hardware div. Emhart Industries, Berlin, Conn., 1974-79; group v.p. Yale Security Products, Scovill, Inc., Charlotte, N.C., 1979—. Bd. dirs. New Britain Meml. Hosp. Served with USAAF, 1944-46. Mem. Nat. Assn. Accts., Am. Mgmt. Assn., New Britain C. of C., Mfrs. Council New Britain (dir.), Phi Beta Kappa. Republican. Greek Orthodox. Home: 4133 Woodfox Dr Matthews NC 28105 Office: PO Box 25288 Charlotte NC 28212

TSANTES, JOHN JAMES, editor; b. Bklyn., Aug. 2, 1946; s. James John and Ann (Antoniades) T.; B.S. in Elec. Engring., Poly. Inst. Bklyn., 1968, M.S., 1972; m. Zoi Polymenakos, Nov. 28, 1971. Elec. engr. Raytheon Co., Sudbury, Mass., 1968-69; sr. engr. Potter Instrument Co., Plainview, N.Y., 1969-72; project engr. Mohawk Data Sci./Bucode, Inc., Hauppage, N.Y., 1972-74; cons. elec. engr., 1974-75; asso. editor Electronic Engring. Times/CMP Publs., Manhasset, N.Y., 1975, editor, 1975-78; editor Circuit News div. Morgan-Grampian Pub. Co., Jericho, N.Y., 1978—; cons. analog/digital electronics. Mem. Poly. Inst. Bklyn. Alumni Assn. Mem. Greek Orthodox Ch. Author articles. Home: 346 Richard Ave Hicksville NY 11801 Office: 125 Jericho Turnpike Jericho NY 11753

TSCHACBASOV, NAHUM, artist; b. Baku, Russia, Aug. 31, 1899; s. Stephen and Sophia (Tibel) T.; student Lewis Inst., Chgo., Armour Inst. Tech., Columbia; m. Esther Liss, 1919; children—David, Corinne; m. 2d, Esther Sorokin, 1929; 1 dau., Sondra; m. 3d, Irene Zevon, Aug. 30, 1966; came to U.S., 1907, derivative citizenship. Exhibited one-man shows: Galerie Zak, Paris, 1933, Gallery Secession, N.Y.C., 1934, A.C.A. Gallery, 1936, 38, 40, 42, Perls Galleries, 1944, 46-48, Arts and Crafts Club, New Orleans, 1945, Colorado Springs Fine Arts Center, 1946, U. Tex., 1946, James Vigeveno Gallery, Los Angeles, Jewish Mus., N.Y.C., 1955, San Francisco Mus., 1946, William Rockhill Nelson Gallery Art, John Heller Gallery, Waker Art Gallery, Delgado Mus., La Jolla (Calif.) Mus. Art, Columbus (Ga.) Mus. Arts and Crafts, Carnegie Pub. Library, Clarksdale, Miss., Pace U., N.Y.C., 1974, also numerous colls., Univ. Mus., 1951, 52, 53, 55; exhibited France, Spain, Whitney Mus. Am. Art, Mus. Modern Art, Met. Mus. Art, Art Inst. Chgo., Carnegie Internat., Phila. Acad., Corcoran Gallery Art, St. Louis, San Francisco, Richmond museums fine arts, Berkshire Mus., Rochester Meml. Gallery, Riverside Mus., Ind. U., U. Ill., U. Iowa, Galerie Bonaparte, Salon de Tuilerie, Paris; represented in permanent collections Met. Mus. Art, Whitney Mus. Am. Art, Dallas Mus., Pa. Acad., Butler Art Inst., Youngstown, Ohio, Jewish Mus., N.Y.C., Bklyn. Mus., Tel Aviv Mus. (Israel), Pensacola (Fla.) Art Center, Wustom Mus. Fine Arts, Racine, Wis., Devereux Found., Phoenix and Devon, Pa., also numerous colls., univs., and pvt. collections; three paintings purchased by State Dept.; former instr. Am. Artists Sch., Art Students League; formerly operated Tschachasov Sch. of Fine Arts; pres. Am. Archives of World Art, N.Y.C. Served as seaman USN on U.S.S. Delaware, Scapa Flow, 1917-18. Awarded Pepsi-Cola prize, 1947. Author: (autobiography) The Moon is My Uncle. Contbr. articles to art mags. Pub. 2 portfolios of etchings, 1947; compiler, author, pub. American Library Compendium and Index of World Art, 1961, An Illustrated Survey of Western Art. Address: 222 W 23 St New York NY 10011

TSCHANTZ, BRUCE ALLEN, civil engr., educator; b. Akron, Ohio, Sept. 15, 1938; s. Miles Emerson and Gladys Marcella (Krichbaum) T.; B.S., Ohio No. U., 1960; M.S., N.Mex. State U., 1962, Sc.D., 1965; m. Penelope Ann Ford, Dec. 20, 1962; children—Peter Allen, Michael Ford. San. engr. Bur. Indian Affairs, Albuquerque, 1962-63; civil engr. White Sands (N.Mex.) Missile Range, 1965; asst. prof. civil engring. U. Tenn., Knoxville, 1965-69, asso. prof., 1969-74, prof., 1974—, M. E. Brooks Disting. prof., 1978; cons. hydrologist U.S. Geol. Survey, Knoxville, 1973-76; cons. Exec. Office of Pres., Office Sci. Tech. Policy, Washington, 1977—, Tenn. Dept. Transp., 1976—; chief fed. dam safety Fed. Emergency Mgmt. Agy., Washington, 1979—; mem. Tenn. Gov.'s Adv. Com. on Dams, 1972, Tenn. Legis. Land Use Planning Task Force, 1973; cons. Tenn. Dept. Conservation, 1978. Recipient Engring. Coll. Faculty Achievement award U. Tenn., 1977; registered profl. engr., Ohio, Tenn., Va. Mem. ASCE (Faculty of Year award Student chpt. 1968), Am. Soc. Engring. Edn. (civil engr. chmn. S.E. sect. 1972, Dow Chem. award 1969), Nat. Soc. Profl. Engrs., Tenn. Soc. Profl. Engrs. (v.p., pres. Knoxville br. 1973-75, Knoxville Young Engr. award 1970), Knoxville Tech. Soc., Sigma Xi, Tau Beta Pi, Chi Epsilon. Contbr. articles on dam safety, flood control, hydrologic impacts of strip mining to profl. jours. Home: 1508 Meeting House Rd Knoxville TN 37921 Office: 63 Perkins Hall U Tenn Knoxville TN 37916

TSCHEBOTARIOFF, GREGORY P., educator, cons. engr.; b. Pavlovsk, Russia, Feb. 15, 1899; s. Porphyry G. and Valentina I. (Doubiagsky) T.; grad. gen. classes Imperial Law Sch., Petrograd, Russia, 1916; C.E., Dept. Technische Hochschule, Berlin-Charlottenburg, Germany, 1925; Dr. Ing., Technische Hochschule Aachen, Germany, 1952; Docteur honoris causa Faculty Applied Scis., Université de Bruxelles, 1959; m. Florence D. Bill, Apr. 2, 1939. Calculator draftsman Pelnard-Considere & A. Caquot, cons. engrs., Paris, 1924; engr. with Dr. Kirchhoff, Berlin, Germany, 1926; engr. Paul Kossel & Co., Bremen, Germany, 1926-27, Austrian Bldg. Co., Cairo, Egypt, 1927-29, Haberman & Guckes-Liebold A.G., Hameln, Germany, 1929, Egyptian Govt., 1929-33; research engr. Egyptian U., 1933-37; ofcl. del. Egyptian U. to 1st Internat. Conf. on soil mechanics and found. engring. Harvard, 1936; lectr. Princeton, 1937, asst. prof. civil engring., 1937-43, asso. prof., 1943-51, prof., 1951-64, emeritus prof., 1964-70. In charge research projects in applied soil mechanics for CAA, 1943-46, for Bur. Yards and Docks, 1943-49, for Office Naval Research, 1951-56; ofcl. del. from Princeton to 2nd Internat. conf. on soil mechanics and foundn. engring., Rotterdam, 1948; former cons. engr. on founds. of bldgs., bridges, tunnels and dams. Mem. ASCE (hon.). Author: Soil Mechanics, Foundations and Earth Structures, McGraw-Hill Civil Engineering Series, 1951; Russia, My Native Land, A U.S. Engineer Reminisces and Looks at the Present, 1964; Foundations, Retaining and Earth Structures, 1973. Contbr. to engring. jours. Home: 26 George St Lawrenceville NJ 08648. *Unyielding adherence to professional duty, common sense, and human and engineering ethics, in spite of exposure to various pressure - politics, brought many temporary tribulations but, in the long run, was responsible for whatever positive achievements I can claim.*

TSCHIRGI, ROBERT DONALD, educator; b. Sheridan, Wyo., Oct. 9, 1924; s. Frank Horace and Kathleen Louise (German) T.; student Purdue U., 1943-44; B.S., U. Chgo., 1945, M.S., 1947, Ph.D., 1949, M.D., 1950. Asst. prof. physiology U. Chgo., 1950-53; asso. prof. physiology and anatomy U. Calif. Los Angeles Sch. Medicine, 1953-59, prof., 1959-66; acad. asst. to pres. U. Calif., 1960-63, univ. dean acad. planning, 1964-66; vice chancellor acad. planning U. Calif., San Diego, 1966-67, acting dean Sch. Medicine, 1966-67, prof. neurosci., 1966—, vice chancellor acad. affairs, 1967-68; project dir. med. edn. study U. Hawaii, 1963-64. Cons. to Greek govt. on planning U. Patras, 1964-67; cons. on med. edn. to states N.Y., Ohio, Mont., Idaho, Wyo., 1965—; cons. med. edn. Brit. Med. Assn., 1973-74. Served with USNR, 1943-47. Mem. Am. Physiol. Soc., Am. Acad. Neurology, Internat. Brain Research Orgn., Sigma Xi. Home: 8737 Caminito Abrazo LaJolla CA 92037 Office: U Calif San Diego CA 92093. *As a scientist, I dedicate my activities to the principle that it is less important to see something new than to think something new about that which everyone can see (Schopenhauer). As an academic administrator, I attempt to be a leader of my institution but a servant of my constituency. As an educator, I try to reveal as much of myself as possible, allowing my students to select the relevant from the rubbish.*

TSCHIRLEY, FRED HAROLD, botanist, plant pathologist; b. S.D., Dec. 19, 1925; s. William and Emma (Struck) T.; B.A., U. Colo., 1955, M.A., 1959; Ph.D., U. Ariz., 1963; m. Mary Joan Brielmaier, Dec. 28, 1948; children—Ann Elizabeth, Jon Dennis, Jeffrey Bernard, David Lawrence, Adele Marie. Instr., U. Ariz., 1952-54; range conservationist Agrl. Research Service, Dept. Agr., Tucson, 1954-63, 67-68, Mayaguez, P.R., 1963-66, adminstrv. trainee, Beltsville, Md., 1966-67, asst. chief crops protection research br., 1968-70; pesticide coordinator Office Sec. Dept. Agr., Washington, 1971-73, environ. quality coordinator, 1973-74; prof. botany and plant pathology Mich. State U., 1974—, chmn. dept. botany and plant pathology, 1974-79. Served with USMC, 1944-46. Mem. Weed Sci. Soc. Am., AAAS, Ecol. Soc. Am., Am. Soc. Phytopathology. Republican. Roman Catholic. Research in woody plant control, ecol. effects of vegetation disturbance. Home: 131 Feldspar St Williamston MI 48895 Office: Mich State U East Lansing MI 48824*

TSCHOEGL, NICHOLAS WILLIAM, educator; b. Zidlochovice, Czechoslovakia, June 4, 1918; s. Paul John and Harriet (Robert) T.; B.S., New South Wales U. Tech., 1954; Ph.D., U. New South Wales, 1958; m. Sophie Marie Glazmak, Apr. 6, 1946; children—Adrian E., Christopher A. Sr. research officer Bread Research Inst. Australia, Sydney, 1958-61; project asso. dept. chemistry U. Wis., 1961-63; sr. phys. chemist Stanford Research Inst., Menlo Park, Calif., 1963-65; asso. prof. Calif. Inst. Tech., Pasadena, 1965-67, prof., 1967—. Cons. Phillips Petroleum Co., Bartlesville, Okla., Avery Internat., Pasadena. Fellow Royal Australian Chem. Inst., Am. Phys. Soc. mem. Am. Chem. Soc., Brit. Soc. Rheology, Soc. Rheology, Deutsche Rheol.-gesellschaft. Contbr. articles to profl. jours. Home: 566 W California Blvd Pasadena CA 91105

TSCHOEPE, THOMAS, clergyman; b. Pilot Point, Tex., Dec. 17, 1915; s. Louis and Catherine (Sloan) T.; student St. Thomas Sch. Pilot Point, 1930, Pontifical Coll. Josephinum, Worthington, Ohio, 1943. Ordained priest Roman Cath. Ch., 1943; asst. pastor in Ft. Worth, 1943-46, Sherman, Tex., 1946-48, Dallas, 1948-53; adminstr. St. Patrick Ch., Dallas, 1953-56; pastor St. Augustine Ch., Dallas, 1956-62, Sacred Heart Cathedral, Dallas, 1962-65; bishop San Angelo, Tex., 1966-69, Dallas, 1969—. Home: 3915 Lemmon Ave Dallas TX 75219 Office: PO Box 19507 Dallas TX 75219

TSE, CHARLES YUNG CHANG, corp. exec.; b. Shanghai, China, Mar. 22, 1926; s. Kung Chao and Say Ying (Chen) T.; B.A. in Econs., St. John's U., Shanghai, 1949; M.S. in Acctg., U. Ill., 1950; m. Vivian Chang, Apr. 25, 1955; 1 dau., Roberta. Asst. to controller Am. Internat. Group, N.Y.C., 1950-54, asst. mgr., Singapore-Malaysia, 1955-57; with Warner-Lambert Co., Morris Plains, N.J., 1957—, area mgr. S.E. Asia, 1966-68, regional dir. S.E. Asia, 1968-69, v.p. Australasia, 1970-71, pres. Western Hemisphere Group, 1971-72, pres. Pan Am. Mgmt. Center, 1972-76, pres. European Mgmt. Center, 1976-78, pres. Warner-Lambert Internat. Group, 1979—; mem. faculty bus. adminstrn. dept. Fairleigh Dickinson U., 1961-64. Bd. visitors CCNY, 1974-78. Office: 201 Tabor Rd Morris Plains NJ 07950

TSIAPERA, MARIA, educator; b. Cyprus, July 26, 1935; d. Anastasis and Aphrodite T.; naturalized, 1964; B.A., U. Tex., Austin, 1957, M.A., 1959, Ph.D., 1963; m. Jeff Beaubier, May 1, 1969; 1 dau., Nike Tsiapera. Asst. prof. linguistics Fresno (Calif.) State U., 1964-66; asst. prof. U. N.C., Chapel Hill, 1966-67, asso. prof., chmn. dept., 1967-72, prof., chmn., 1972-73, prof., 1973—. NSF travel grantee, 1977; U. N.C. research grantee, 1967, 69, 72, 74, 77. Mem. Linguistic Soc. Am. (exec. com.), Southeastern Conf. Linguistics (founder, pres.), Am. Oriental Soc., Modern Greek Studies Assn., Am. Assn. Tchrs. Arabic. Democrat. Greek Orthodox. Author: Maronite Cypriot Arabic, 1969; Generative Studies in Historical Linguistics, 1971; contbr. articles to profl. jours. Research on history and philosophy of linguistics and human scis. since 1660. Home: 1051 Burning Tree Dr Chapel Hill NC 27514 Office: Dept Linguistics U NC Chapel Hill NC 27514

TSO, TIEN CHIOH, ofcl. U.S. Dept. Agr.; b. Hupeh, China, July 25, 1917; s. Ya Fu and Suhwa (Wang) T.; came to U.S., 1947, naturalized, 1961; B.S., Nanking U., China, 1941, M.S., 1944; Ph.D., Pa. State U., 1950; postgrad. Oak Ridge Inst. Nuclear Studies; m. Margaret Lu, Aug. 28, 1949; children—Elizabeth, Paul. Supt. exptl. farm Ministry Social Affairs, China, 1944-46; exec. sec. Tobacco Improvement Bur., 1946-47; research chemist Gen. Cigar Research Lab., 1950-51; with U.S. Dept. Agr., 1952—, prin. plant physiologist crop research div. Agrl. Research Service, Beltsville, Md., 1964-66, leader tobacco quality investigations, tobacco and sugar crops research br., 1966-71, chief tobacco lab., 1972-74, sr. exec. service, 1974—; cons. Nat. Cancer Inst., Ky. Tobacco Health Research Inst. Fellow AAAS, Agronomy Soc., Am. Inst. Chemists; mem. Am. Chem. Soc., Am. Soc. Plant Physiologists, Phytochem. Soc. N.Am. (pres. 1971), Tobacco Chemists Research Conf. (symposium chmn. 1965, 79, chmn. 1975), World Conf. Smoking and Health (sect. chmn. 1967, 71, 75), Tobacco Workers Conf., Sigma Xi. Author: Physiology and Biochemistry of Tobacco Plants, 1972; contbg. author Ann. Rev. Plant Physiology, Vol. 9, 1958; The Chemistry of Tobacco and Tobacco Smoke, 1972; Toward Less Harmful Cigarettes, 1968, 71, 75. Editor: Structural and Functional Aspects of Phytochemistry, 1972; Recent Advances in Tobacco Science, vol. 1, 1975. Research publs. on establishment of loci of alkaloid formation, biosynthetic pathway, interconversion and fate of alkaloids in tobacco plants, chem. composition as affected by macro and micro elements, homogenized leaf curing, health-related factors including mycotoxins and phenolics, established source of radio-elements and their elimination in tobacco, prodn. safer tobacco; developed fatty esters and fatty alcohols as sucker control and plant pruning agts.; tobacco as sources of food and safer smoking material. Patentee in field. Home: 4306 Yates Rd Beltsville MD 20705 Office: Bldg #001 Beltsville Agr Research Center Beltsville MD 20705. *We are thankful to those fools. They are the only ones who dare to dream of something new and seemingly impossible.*

TSONGAS, PAUL EFTHEMIOS, Senator; b. Lowell, Mass., Feb. 14, 1941; s. Efthemios and Katina T.; B.A., Dartmouth Coll., 1962; LL.B., Yale U., 1967; M.P.A., Harvard U., 1973; m. Nicola Sauvage, Dec. 21, 1969; children—Ashley, Katina. Peace Corps vol, Ethiopia, 1962-64, tgn. coordinator, W.I., 1967-68; mem. Gov.'s Com. on Law Enforcement, 1968-69; admitted to Mass. bar; dep. asst. atty. gen. Mass., 1969-71; individual practice law, 1971-74; mem. 94th-95th Congresses from 5th Mass. Dist.; mem. U.S. Senate from Mass., 1979—, mem. energy and natural resources com., banking com., housing and urban affairs com., chmn. consumer affairs subcom., co-chmn. ad-hoc Congl. monitoring group on So. Africa. City councillor, Lowell, 1969-72; county commr., Middlesex County, 1973-74. Democrat. Greek Orthodox. Office: 342 Russell Senate Office Bldg Washington DC 20510

TSOU TANG, educator; b. Canton, China, Dec. 10, 1918; s. Lu and Chien (Hsu) T.; B.A., Nat. S.W. Associated U., Kumming, China, 1940; Ph.D., U. Chgo., 1951; m. Yi-chuang Lu, Jan. 29, 1943. Came to U.S., 1941, naturalized, 1961. Mem. faculty dept. polit. sci. U. Chgo., 1959—, asso. prof., 1962-66, prof., 1966—, also prof. dept. Far Eastern langs. and civilizations, 1966—. Mem. joint com. on contemporary China, Social Sci. Research Council and Am. Council Learned Socs., 1972-74. Bd. dirs. Nat. Com. on U.S.-China Relations, 1971—. Univ. Chgo. fellow, 1946-47; research grantee Social Sci. Research Council, 1968-69, 75-76, Rockefeller Found., 1966-67, Nat. Endowment for Humanities. Mem. Am. Polit. Sci. Assn., Assn. Asian Studies (dir. 1974-77). Author: America's Failure in China (Gordon J. Laing prize U. Chgo. Press), 1963; (with Ping-ti Ho) China in Crisis,

2 vols., 1968; editorial bd. China Quar., Modern China, Asian Survey. Home: 5608 S Harper Ave Chicago IL 60637

TSU, JOHN B., educator; b. China, Dec. 1, 1924; s. Tsu Kwei and Tsu Cheng-shih; LL.B., Imperial U., Tokyo, Japan, 1943; M.A., Georgetown U., 1949; Ph.D., Fordham U., 1953; m. Susan Fu, Jan. 22, 1966. Prof. polit. sci., co-dir. Inst. Far Eastern Studies, Seton Hall U., 1958-60, prof. Asian Studies, dir. inst., 1960-77, dir. Carnegie Chinese and Japanese program, 1961-77, dir. internat. studies, 1974-77, dir. Nat. Def. Lang. Inst., 1963-65, Chinese Dictionary Project, 1965-66; prof. and dir. Multicultural Inst., spl. asst. to pres. U. San Francisco, 1977—; vis. prof. East-West Center, U. Hawaii, 1966; pioneer in introducing Chinese and Japanese in Am. secondary schs.; mem. univ. seminar on China, Columbia; exec. sec. Sino-Am. Amity, 1953-55; cons. Center for 20th Century Studies, U. Wis., 1969—; dir. Chinese/Japanese-English Bilingual Inst., U.S. Office Edn.-Seton Hall U., 1974-77; advisor Asian Am. Assembly, City Coll. N.Y., 1977—. Mem. Pres.'s Nat. Adv. Council on Edn. for Disadvantaged Children, 1971-73; mem. Nat. Adv. Council on Ethnic Heritage Studies, 1975—; trustee Dhara Realm U., 1977—. Mem. Am. Assn. UN (chmn. ednl. com. Newark chpt., 1964-66, chpt. trustee), Chinese Lang. Tchrs. Assn. (chmn. 1967-69), Assn. Japanese Lang. Tchrs. (exec. com.), Am. Polit. Sci. Assn., Assn. Asian Studies, Modern Lang. Assn., Am. Assn. Internat. Law, Am. Acad. Polit. and Social Sci. Author: Sino-Soviet Relations: 1949-1952, 1953; The World of Asia, 1966. Contbr. to Ency. Americana, Funk & Wagnalls Ency.; articles to profl. jours. Home: 2 Denslowe Dr San Francisco CA 94132 Office: U San Francisco San Francisco CA 94117

TSUANG, MING TSO, psychiatrist, educator; b. Tainan, Taiwan, Nov. 16, 1931; s. Ping Tang and Chhun Kuei (Lin) T.; came to U.S., 1971; M.D., Nat. Taiwan U., Taipei, 1957; Ph.D. in Psychiatry (Sino-Brit. Fellowship Trust scholar), certs. in epidemiology and stats., population genetics, psychiat. genetics, U. London, 1965; m. Snow Hue S. Ko, Nov. 24, 1958; children—John, Debby, Grace. Intern, Nat. Taiwan U. Hosp., 1956-57, resident in psychiatry, 1957-61, asso. prof. psychiatry, staff psychiatrist, 1968-71; collaborating investigator Internat. Pilot Study of Schizophrenia, WHO, 1966-71; vis. asso. prof. psychiatry Washington U. Sch. Medicine, St. Louis, 1971-72; asso. prof., staff psychiatrist U. Iowa Coll. Medicine, Iowa City, 1972-75, prof. psychiatry, 1975—, prof. psychiat. epidemiology, 1978—; clin. tchr., lectr. to residents, med. students; cons. psychiatrist VA Hosp., Iowa City, 1972—; mem. epidemiol. studies rev. com. NIMH, 1976—. Bd. dirs. Midwest Formosan Christian Found., 1974, pres., 1975-76; elder Trinity Christian Reformed Ch., Iowa City, 1976-78. Research fellow Chinese Nat. Council Sci. Devel., 1966-70; NIMH grantee, 1973—; Macy Faculty scholar, 1979-80. Mem. Psychiat. Research Soc., Am. Psychopathol. Assn., Behavior Genetics Assn., AMA, Am. Psychiat. Assn., Sigma Xi. Author: A Study of Pairs of Sibs Both Hospitalized for Mental Disorder, 1965; Criteria for Subtyping Schizophrenia, 1974; Schizophrenia and Affective Disorders: One Illness or Many?, 1975; A Study of Atypical Schizophrenia, 1976; A Combined 35-Year Follow-up and Family Study of Schizophrenia and Primary Affective Disorders, 1977; Mortality in Patients with Schizophrenia, Mania, Depression, and Surgical Conditions, 1977; Suicide in Schizophrenics, Manics, Depressives and Surgical Controls, 1978; Genetic Counseling for Psychiatric Patients and Their Families, 1978; contbr. chpts. to books, articles to profl. jours. Home: 350 Hutchinson Ave Iowa City IA 52240 Office: 500 Newton Rd Iowa City IA 52242. *My constant goal is to do the best work I can, to eschew anxiety about the result, to learn from failure, and to build upon success, not for personal honor but for the good of mankind, as God's servant within a serving profession. Helping others is not possible without self-discipline, self-sufficience, and self-sacrifice; at the same time, helping others strengthens the self for its tasks.*

TSUCHIYA, HENRY MITSUMASA, educator, bioengr.; b. Seattle, Dec. 9, 1914; s. Seishiro and Masa (Kanagaki) T.; B.S., U. Wash., 1936, M.S., 1938; Ph.D., U. Minn., 1942; m. Miyo Kitagawa, July 28, 1941; children—Marilyn (Mrs. Jon Lauglo), Arthur Kitagawa. Research asso. U. Minn., 1942-47; bacteriologist No. Regional Lab., U.S. Dept. Agr., 1947-56; asso. prof. U. Minn., Mpls., 1956-63, prof. chem. engring., microbiology, 1963—. NSF vis. scientist, vis. prof. U. Tokyo, 1966; mem. environ. pollutant movement and transformation com., sci. adv. bd. EPA, 1976-79. Recipient Superior Service award U.S. Dept. Agr., 1953, Distinguished Service Team award, 1955. Mem. Am. Soc. Microbiology, Am. Chem. Soc., Am. Inst. Biol. Scis., Soc. Indsl. Microbiology, Ecol. Soc. Am., Am. Soc. Limnology and Oceanography, AAAS, Soc. Gen. Microbiology, Sigma Xi. Author: (with C.E. Skinner, C.W. Emmons) Molds, Yeasts, Actinomycetes, 1947. Contbr. articles to profl. jours. Home: 201 Burntside Dr Minneapolis MN 55422

TSUJI, TAKASHI KENRYU, clergyman; b. Mission City, B.C., Can., Mar. 14, 1919; s. Kamejiro and Suye (Minaguro) T.; student U. B.C., 1937, Ryukoku U., Kyoto, Japan, 1938-41, U. Toronto, 1942; m. Sakaye Kawabata, Jan. 31, 1946; children—Elizabeth Noriko Tsuji Wadleigh, Maya Margaret Tsuji Lawrence. Rosalind Eiko, Eleanor Takako, Carolyn Emiko. Came to U.S., 1959, naturalized, 1964. Ordained to ministry Buddhist Ch., 1941; minister Vancouver (B.C.) Buddhist Temple, 1941-42, Slocan (B.C.) Buddhist Temple, 1942-45, Toronto (Ont.) Buddhist Temple, 1945-58; dir. Buddhist edn. Buddhist Chs. Am., San Francisco, 1959-68, bishop of U.S., 1968—. Pres. Inst. Buddhist Studies, Berkeley, 1968—; chmn. Buddhist Chs. Am. Fraternal Benefit Assn., 1970—; filmed, editor, narrator documentary films In the Footsteps of Shinran Shonin, 1970, Story of Hongwanji, 1972, A Buddhist Pilgrimage, 1975, Sri Lanka, Where the Dhamma Is Preserved, 1976. Mem. Human Resources Commn. San Mateo County, 1967; mem. adv. bd. Calif. Inst. Asian Studies, 1969—. Bd. mem. World Conf. on Religion and Peace, 1979. Office: 1710 Octavia St San Francisco CA 94109

TSUTSUI, MINORU, chemist, educator; b. Wakayama City, Japan, Mar. 31, 1918; s. Juntaro and Tazu (Hirata) T.; came to U.S., 1951, naturalized, 1960; B.A., Gifu (Japan) U., 1938; M.S., Tokyo (Japan) U. Lit. and Sci., 1941; M.S., Yale, 1953, Ph.D., 1954; D.Sc., Nagoya (Japan) U., 1960; m. Ethel Ashworth, Mar. 3, 1956; 1 son, William Minoru. Asst. prof. Tokyo U. Lit. and Sci., 1950-53; vis. research fellow Sloan-Kettering Inst., N.Y.C., 1954-56; research chemist Monsanto Chem. Co., 1957-60; research scientist N.Y. U., 1960-69, project dir., 1962-65, lectr. chemistry, 1964-65, asso. prof. dept. chemistry, 1965-69; prof. Tex. A. and M. U., College Station, 1969—. U.S.-USSR exchange scholar, 1967; Ford Found. cons. U. Delhi (India), 1977; invited scholar Japan Soc. Promotion Sci., 1978; cons. to industry, 1963—. Mem. Am. Chem. Soc. (ad hoc com. on pub. relations 1972), N.Y. Acad. Scis. (v.p. 1965, chmn. chem. scis. sect. 1963, div. organometallic chemistry 1964, A. Cressy Morrison award 1960, pres. 1968), Japan-U.S. Chemists Assn. N.Y. (pres. 1967), chem. socs. Japan, London, West Germany, Am. Inst. Chemists, S.W. Catalysis Soc. (dir. 1972-74), S.W. Sci. Forum (exec. officer, dir. 1976—), Japan Soc., Tex. Acad. Scis., AAAS, Sigma Xi. Editor: (with E.I. Becker) Organometallic Reactions, 1965-76, Organometallic Syntheses and Reactions, 1976—; Characterization of Organometallic Compounds, 1969—; asso. editor Jour. Coordination Chemistry, 1970—, Am. Chem. Soc. Monographs, 1970—. Contbr. articles to profl. jours. Patentee in field. Home: 413 Brookside Dr Bryan TX 77801 Office: Dept Chemistry Tex A and M U College Station TX 77843

TSUYAMA, MASAO, banker; b. Manchuria, China, Mar. 19, 1918; s. Eikichi and Masako (Egi) T.; M.A. in Econs., Keio U., 1940; s. Eiko Chigira, Jan. 1957; children—Maki, Kay. With Yokohoma Specie Bank, Yokohoma office, 1940-46, Tokyo br., 1946-47; with Tokyo office Bank of Tokyo, Ltd., 1947-51, adminstrn. dept., 1951-54, pro-mgr. Marunouchi office, 1954-58, Osaka br., 1958, N.Y. agy., 1958, pro-agt., 1959, sub-agt., 1960, sub-mgr. Marunouchi br., 1962, mgr. Shimbashi br., 1966, mgr. internat. investment dept., Tokyo, 1967, mgr. Marunouchi br., 1970, also dir.; mng. dir. Internat. Bank of Iran and Japan, 1963, vice-chmn., 1964; pres., dir. Bank of Tokyo of Calif., San Francisco, 1972; pres., chief exec. officer, dir. Calif. First Bank, San Francisco, 1975-78, chmn. bd., dir., 1978—; dir. Bank of Tokyo Trust Co. Second v.p., mem. fin. com. Japan Soc. San Francisco, 1976—; trustee, dir. World Affairs Council of No. Calif., San Francisco Area World Trade Assn. Mem. Am., Calif. bankers assns., Overseas Bankers Assn. in Calif. (chmn.), Japanese Am. Assn. of San Francisco, Japanese C. of C. of No. Calif. (pres. 1973-74, dir. 1975—). Club: World Trade, Bankers, Stock Exchange, Calif. Golf (San Francisco); Univ. (Los Angeles); Indsl. of Japan (Tokyo). Home: 2023 Oakland Ave Piedmont CA 94611 Office: 350 California St San Francisco CA 94104

TUAN, SAN FU, educator; b. Tientsin, China, May 14, 1932; s. Mao Lan and Lu-Kung (Tao) T.; B.A. (MacKinnon scholar), Magdalen Coll., Oxford U., 1954, M.A., 1958; Ph.D., U. Calif. at Berkeley, 1958; m. Loretta Kan, Dec. 15, 1963; children—Katherine Tsung Yen, Melinda Tsung Tao, Priscilla Tsung Pei, David Tsung Lien. Came to U.S., 1954, naturalized, 1967. Research asso. Enrico Fermi Inst., U. Chgo., 1958-60; asst. prof. physics Brown U., 1960-62; asso. prof. physics Purdue U., 1962-65, vis. prof., 1973; vis. prof. U. Hawaii, Honolulu, 1965-66, prof. theoretical physics, 1966—, prin. investigator Theoretical High Energy Program sponsored by U.S. AEC, 1967—. Mem. Inst. for Advanced Study, Princeton, N.J., 1966, 72; cons. Argonne Nat. Lab., 1963-70; dir. Hawaii Topical Confs. in Particle Physics, 1967, 69, 73, 75, 77; vis. lectr. Bariloche Summer Sch., Argentina, 1969-70, U.S.-China Sci. Coop. Program sponsored by NSF, 1970-71. Coordinator, State of Hawaii on initial planning for projected Internat. Sci. Found., 1970; Mem. Hawaii Subcom. Alt. Energy, 1974. Participant exploratory mission to China, U. Hawaii-China Sci. Cooperation, 1973. Guggenheim fellow, 1965-66. Fellow Am. Phys. Soc.; mem. Am. Math. Soc. (reviewer Math. Rev. 1962-70, Phys. Rev. 1963—), Phi Beta Kappa. Co-editor: Procs. of Hawaii Topical Confs. in Particle Physics, 1967, 69, 73, 75, 77. Contbr. articles to profl. jours. Home: 3634 Woodlawn Terrace Pl Honolulu HI 96822

TUATAY, HULUSI, psychiatrist, state ofcl.; b. Kirsehir, Turkey, June 10, 1921; s. Osman Necati and Munevver (Ozturk) T.; A.B., U. Istanbul (Turkey), 1941; M.D., Istanbul Med. Sch., 1946; m. Grace Arlene Bethel, Mar. 27, 1956; children—Susan L., Dennis I. Came to U.S., 1950, naturalized, 1959. Intern, Herrick Meml. Hosp., Berkeley, Calif., 1951-52; resident internal medicine Maumee Valley Hosp., Toledo, 1953-56; resident psychiatry Columbus (Ohio) State Hosp., 1957-60, instr. psychiatry, 1960-66, supt., 1965-67; asst. commr. charge bur. research and tng. Div. Mental Hygiene Ohio, 1967-72; dir. Marion (Ohio) Area Counseling Center, 1972-76; sr. psychiatrist div. forensic psychiatry Dept. Mental Health and Retardation, Columbus, 1976; med. dir. Central Ohio Psychiat. Hosp., Columbus, 1976—. Trustee Columbus Area Community Mental Health Center, 1965-67. Diplomate Am. Bd. Psychiatry and Neurology. Fellow Am. Psychiat. Assn.; mem. Am., Ohio med. assns., Neuropsychiat. Soc. Central Ohio (sec. 1965-66), Nat. Assn. Med. Supts. Mental Hosps., Acad. Medicine Franklin County. Contbr. articles to profl. jours. Home: 1418 Zollinger Rd Columbus OH 43221

TUBB, ERNEST DALE, singer, composer; b. nr. Crisp, Tex., Feb. 9, 1914; ed. Tex. pub. schs.; m. Olene Adams, June 3, 1949; children—Elaine Walker, Justin Wayne, Erlene Dale, Olene Gayle, Ernest Dale, Larry Dean, Karen Delene. With radio sta. KONO, San Antonio, 1933-35, radio sta. KGKL, San Angelo, Tex., 1936-40, radio sta. KGKO, Ft. Worth, 1941-42; with Grand Ole Opry radio sta. WSM, Nashville, 1943—, own weekly show Ernest Tubb Midnight Jamboree; owner, operator Ernest Tubb Record Shop, Nashville; rec. artist Decca Records (now MCA Records), 1940—, numerous albums and songs including Rainbow at Midnight, Soldier's Last Letter, Letters Have No Arms, Mr. and Mrs. Used to Be, Sweet Thing, Let's Say Goodbye Like We Said Hello, Blue Christmas, It's Been So Long, Darling; composer songs including Walking the Floor Over You, Try Me One More Time; entertained troops in Korea, 1950, 51; performs in nightclubs. Named to Country Music Hall of Fame Country Music Assn., 1965. Home: PO Box 11308 Nashville TN 37211 Office care Ernest Tubb Record Shop 417 Broad St Nashville TN 37203*

TUBB, JAMES CLARENCE, lawyer; b. Corsicana, Tex., Mar. 13, 1930; s. Cullen L. and Sarah (Chapman) T.; B.A., So. Meth. U., 1951, J.D., 1954; m. Suzanne Smith, Nov. 25, 1954; children—James Richard, Sara Elizabeth, Daniel Chapman. Partner firm Vial, Hamilton, Koch, Tubb, Knox & Stradley, Dallas. Active Boy Scouts Am., 1967; co-chmn. 25th Reunion So. Meth. U. Class of '51; pres. Park Cities Dads Club, 1976-77, mem. Alcohol Awareness Task Force, 1977—; sec. bd. deacons Highland Park Presbyn. Ch., 1976-77, ruling elder, 1978; sec. Dallas County Republican Men's Club, 1974—; bd. dirs. Bible Transls. on Tape, Inc., Christian Concern Found. Served to 1st lt. USAF, 1955-57. Mem. local, nat. bar assns., Kappa Alpha, Phi Alpha Delta. Clubs: Northwood, Dallas Country. Home: 3524 Greenbrier St Dallas TX 75225 Office: 1500 Republic Nat Bank Tower Dallas TX 75201

TUBBY, ROGER WELLINGTON, govt. adminstr.; b. Greenwich, Conn., Dec. 30, 1910; s. George Prentiss and Frances Reynolds (Kidder) T.; student Choate Sch., 1923-29; A.B., Yale, 1933, postgrad. law sch., 1933-34, London Sch. Econs., 1935-36; m. Anne Williams, Mar. 8, 1936; children—Suzanne (Mrs. L. Batra), Jean (Mrs. R. Sherwood), Peter, Brenda. Reporter, Bennington (Vt.) Banner, 1938-40, mng. editor, 1940-42; info. specialist Bd. Econ. Warfare, 1942-44; dir. info. Fgn. Econ. Adminstrn., 1944-45, asst. to adminstr., 1945; dir. info. Office Internat. Trade, Dept. Commerce, 1945-46; press officer Dept. State, 1945-49, exec. asst. press relations, 1950, asst. press sec. White House, 1950-52; acting press sec. to Pres., Oct.-Dec. 1952, press sec., Dec. 1952; personal asst. to Democratic presdl. candidate, 1956; co-pub. Adirondack Daily Enterprise, Saranac Lake, N.Y., 1953-70, Lake Placid News, 1957-70; faculty Paul Smith's (N.Y.) Coll., 1959-61, dir. devel., 1972-75; dep. commr. ops. and planning N.Y. State Dept. Parks and Recreation, 1975-77; asst. sec. for pub. affairs Dept. State, 1961-62; ambassador, U.S. rep. to European office UN, other internat. agys., Geneva, Switzerland, 1962-69; acting dean, dean acad. relations Fgn. Service Inst. Dept. State, 1969-72. Del. numerous internat. confs.; mem. Gov.'s Commn. Sports and Winter Olympics; gov.'s rep. to 1980 Winter Olympics; exec. dir. North Country Econ. Council; chmn. Olympic Accomodations Corp. Dir. Farmers' Nat. Bank, Saranac Lake, N.Y. Champlain Valley Physicians' Hosp., Plattsburgh, N.Y. News dir. Dem. Nat. Com., 1960; Dem. candidate for Congress from 30th N.Y. Dist., 1974. Trustee Trudeau Found.; trustee emeritus Coll. of Atlantic, Bar Harbor, Maine; bd. dirs. Adirondack Conservancy; past pres., dir. Adirondack Park Assn. Mem. Acad. Polit. Sci. Home: Trudeau Rd Saranac Lake NY 12983 Office: PO Box 11980 Lake Placid NY 12946

TUBIS, SEYMOUR, painter, printmaker, sculptor; b. Phila., Sept. 20, 1919; student Temple U., 1937-39, Phila. Mus. Sch. Art, 1941-42, Art Students League of N.Y., 1946-49, Academie Graande-Chaumiere, Paris, 1949-50, Instituto d'Arte, Florence, Italy, 1950; student of Hans Hofmann, N.Y.C., 1951. Pvt. tchr. art, N.Y.C., Rockport, Mass., 1948-60; tchr. art, summer program Bd. Edn., Great Neck, N.Y., 1949; asst. instr. Art Students League of N.Y., 1948, 49, Bklyn. Mus. Sch. Art, 1950-51; instr. N.Y.C. Adult Edn. Program, 1950-52; head dept. fine arts, instr. printmaking, painting and design Inst. of Am. Indian Arts, Santa Fe, 1963—; exhibited in one man shows at Galerie St. Placide, Paris, 1950, Lowe Found. Galleries, N.Y.C., 1953, 55, Taft Sch., Conn., 1953, La Chapelle Gallery, Sante Fe, 1960, Mus. of N.Mex., Santa Fe, 1964, Accents Gallery, Cleve., 1966, U. Calgary (Alta., Can.), 1967, Jamison Galleries, Santa Fe, 1967, N.M. State Library, Santa Fe, 1968, Coll. of Santa Fe, 1969, The New West, Albuquerque, 1969, 71, 72, 73, 75, 77, 78, Gallery Contemporary Art, Taos, N.Mex., 1969, Antioch Coll., Balt., Washington, 1973, numerous others; exhibited in group shows at Library of Congress, Carnegie Inst., Bklyn. Mus., Pa. Acad. Fine Arts, Dallas Mus. Art, Syracuse U., Royal Soc., London, Eng., Hofstra Coll., Asso. Gallery Art, Detroit, Riverside Mus., N.Y.C., Met. Mus. Art, N.Y.C., Seattle Art Mus., Dept. Interior, Dept. State Embassies Program, Mus. Modern Art, N.Y.C., Mus. of N.Mex., St. Johns Coll., Santa Fe, Mus. Internat. Folk Art, Santa Fe, Pa. State Coll., Wichita Art Assn., John F. Kennedy Center for Performing Arts, Washington, also others represented in permanent collections Library of Congress, Soc. Am. Graphic Artists, Met. Mus. Art, Pa. State Coll., U. Ariz., U. Calgary, Joe and Emily Lowe Found., Art Students League N.Y., U.S. Dept. Interior, Dept. State, Antioch Coll., also numerous pvt. collections; artist-cons. N.Y. World-Telegram and Sun, 1955-59, St. Johns Coll., 1960, Mus. of N.Mex., 1960, N.Y. Times, 1961-63; research grantee U. Ariz., U. Calif. at Santa Barbara. Recipient 4th purchase award in painting Joe and Emily Lowe Found., 1st prize in painting Newspaper Guild N.Y. Mem. Soc. Am. Graphic Artists (1st prize in etching), Art Students League N.Y., Coll. Art Assn. Home: 947 Acequia Madre Santa Fe NM 87501 Office: Inst Am Indian Arts Santa Fe NM 87501. *As I now review the naive innocence of my early years, I ask "what is reality and what is illusion?" As each year passes, the continuing search for revelation strips away only layers of innocence, leaving barely visible a world so complex, so ordered, so tentatively beautiful, that I want more than ever to return to a state of innocence. It is only in this condition that I can conceive of discovering a passage from the beginning to the end—to a new beginning.*

TUCH, HANS NATHAN, fgn. service officer; b. Berlin, Germany, Oct. 15, 1924; s. Bruno and Rosa (Oelsner) T.; came to U.S., 1938, naturalized, 1943; B.A., U. Kansas City (Mo.), 1947; M.A., Johns Hopkins, 1948; m. Ruth Marie Lord, Dec. 17, 1949; children—David Lord, Andrea Susan. Fgn. rep. Chase Nat. Bank, Stuttgart, Germany, 1948-49; joined U.S. Fgn. Service, 1949; assigned Frankfurt, Germany, 1949-55, Washington, 1955-57, Munich, Germany, 1957-58, Moscow, 1958-61, Washington, 1961-65, Sofia, Bulgaria, 1965-67, Berlin, 1967-70; counselor Am. embassy, Brasilia, Brazil, 1971-75; apptd. career minister, 1975; Edward R. Murrow fellow Fletcher Sch. Law and Diplomacy, Tufts U., 1975-76; dep. dir. Voice of Am., Washington, 1976—. Co-chmn. bd. John F. Kennedy Sch., Berlin, 1969-70; bd. dirs. Escola Americana, Brasilia, 1971-73; chmn. Fulbright Commn. Brazil, 1974-75. Served with AUS, 1943-45. Decorated Bronze Star. Mem. Am. Fgn. Service Assn. Club: Internat. (Washington). Author: (with Henry A. Dunlap) Atoms at Your Service, 1957. Address: 5209 Massachusetts Ave Bethesda MD 20016

TUCHMAN, BARBARA WERTHEIM, writer; b. N.Y.C., Jan. 30, 1912; d. Maurice and Alma (Morgenthau) Wertheim; B.A., Radcliffe Coll., 1933; D.Litt., Yale, Columbia, others; m. Lester R. Tuchman, 1940; children—Lucy, Jessica, Alma. Research asst. Inst. Pacific Relations, N.Y.C., 1934, Tokyo, 1935; editorial asst. The Nation, N.Y.C., 1936, Spain, 1937; staff writer War in Spain, London, 1937-38; Am. corr. New Statesman and Nation, London, 1939; with Far East news desk, OWI, N.Y.C., 1944-45. Mem. Smithsonian Council, 1971—. Trustee Radcliffe Coll., 1960-72. Decorated Order Leopold 1st class (Belgium.) Fellow Am. Acad. Arts and Scis., AAAL vice chancellor lit. 1976-78, pres. 1979—, Gold medal 1978. mem. Author's Guild (treas.), Authors League (council), Soc. Am. Historians (pres. 1971-73). Club: Cosmopolitan. Author: The Lost British Policy, 1938; Bible and Sword, 1956; The Zimmerman Telegram, 1958; The Guns of August, 1962 (Pulitzer prize 1963); The Proud Tower, 1966; Stilwell and the American Experience in China, 1911-45, (Pulitzer prize 1972), 1971; Notes from China, 1972; A Distant Mirror, 1978. Contbr. to Fgn. Affairs, Atlantic Monthly, Am. Heritage, Harper's, N.Y. Times, others. Home: Cos Cob CT 06807 Office: care Russell & Volkening 551 Fifth Ave New York NY 10017

TUCHMAN, JOSEPH, architect; b. Akron, Ohio, Oct. 20, 1920; s. Samuel and Celia (Magilowitz) T.; B.Arch., Carnegie Inst. Tech., 1942; m. Evelyn R. Siplow, Nov. 3, 1946; 1 dau., Janice Lyn. Partner, Tuchman-Canute, architects, Akron, 1951—. Pres., Internat. Inst., 1964-65. Served with AUS, 1943-45. Fellow A.I.A. (pres. Eastern Ohio chpt. 1957-58, regional dir. 1967-70, mem. finance com. 1972, 73 resolutions com. 1972, treas. 1974-75); mem. Architects Soc. Ohio (pres. 1964-65), Akron C. of C. (chmn. betterment com. 1956). Club: Atwood Yacht. Home: 619 Upper Merriman Akron OH 44303 Office: 1650 W Market St Akron OH 44313. *Soft sell and hard work will bring success.*

TUCK, GRAYSON EDWIN, natural gas transmission exec.; b. Richmond, Va., May 11, 1927; s. Bernard Okly and Erma (Wiltshire) T.; B.S., U. Richmond, 1950; m. Rosalie Scroggs, June 6, 1947; children—Janice Lorrain, Kenneth Edwin, Carol Lynn. Payroll clk., cost clk. Gen. Baking Co., Richmond, 1948-51; jr. accountant Commonwealth Natural Gas Corp., Richmond, 1951-55, sr. accountant, 1956-57, accounting supr., 1957-58, asst. treas., 1959-62, asst. sec., asst. treas., 1963-64, treas., asst. sec., 1965-77; treas. Commonwealth Natural Resources, Inc., 1977—, CNG Transmission Co. subs., 1977-79; sec.-treas. Air Pollution Control Products, Inc., Richmond, 1970-73; asst. treas., asst. sec. Commonwealth Gas Distbn. Corp., Richmond, 1969-79, treas. parent co. Commonwealth Natural Resources, Inc., 1979—. Active Boy Scouts Am., 1965-69. Served with USNR, 1945-46. Mem. Nat. Assn. Accountants (asso. dir. 1963-64). Presbyn. (deacon 1958—, treas. 1968-70). Home: 2923 Oakland Ave Richmond VA 23228 Office: 200 S 3d St Richmond VA 23219

TUCK, JAMES LESLIE, physicist; b. Manchester, Eng., Jan. 9, 1910; s. James Henry and Selina Jane (Reece) T.; B.Sc., Victoria U., Manchester, 1932, M.Sc., 1936; Salter fellow Clarendon Lab., U. Oxford, 1936-39, M.A., 1949; m. Elsie Mary Harper, Aug. 11, 1937; children—Sarah Catherine Mary (Mrs. Donald F. Pasieka), Peter Humphrey James. Came to U.S., 1949, naturalized, 1955. Chief sci. adviser to Lord Cherwell, mem. personal staff Winston Churchill,

1939-44; mem. Brit. mission to Manhattan Project, Los Alamos, 1944-46; supr. Inst. Advanced Studies, Clarendon Lab., Oxford U., 1946-49; mem. staff theoretical div. Los Alamos Sci. Lab., 1950-55, asso. physics div. leader, also head controlled thermonuclear research, 1955-73; Walker-Ames distinguished prof. U. Wash., 1974—; vis. prof. U. Waikeato, New Zealand, 1974; Regents' lectr. U. Calif. at La Jolla, 1975. Guggenheim fellow, Paris, Rome, 1962; decorated Order Brit. Empire. Fellow Am. Phys. Soc. Contbr. numerous papers to profl. lit. Home: 2502 35th St Los Alamos NM 87544

TUCK, LEO DALLAS, chemist, educator; b. San Francisco, Oct. 12, 1916; s. Leo Clyde and Sarah (Black) T.; A.B., U. Calif., Berkeley, 1939, Ph.D., 1948; m. Grace Mildred Gardner, Aug. 15, 1953; children—Richard Dallas, David Michael. Faculty, Sch. Pharmacy U. Calif., San Francisco, 1948—, prof. chemistry, pharm. chemistry, 1963—, also univ. vice chancellor acad. affairs, 1971-73. Fellow AAAS; mem. Am. Chem. Soc., Am. Phys. Soc., Acad. Pharm. Scis., Am. Pharm. Assn., Sigma Xi, Rho Chi. Home: 833 Eucalyptus Ave Novato CA 94947 Office: U Calif Med Center San Francisco CA 94143

TUCK, WILLIAM MUNFORD, lawyer, former gov. and congressman; b. Halifax County, Va., Sept. 28, 1896; LL.B., Washington and Lee U., 1921, LL.D., 1949; LL.D., Hampden Sydney Coll., William and Mary Coll., 1946, Elon Coll., 1948; m. Eva Lovelace Dillard, Feb. 26, 1928 (dec.). Admitted to Va. bar, 1921, since practiced in South Boston, Va.; mem. Ho. of Dels. Va., 1924-32, Va. State Senate 1932-42; gov. Va., 1946-50; now sr. mem. Tuck, Bagwell, Dillard, Mapp & Nelson. Mem. 83d to 90th congresses, 5th Dist. Va. Served with USMC, World War I. Mem. Am., Va. State bar assns., Sigma Phi Epsilon, Phi Delta Phi. Ind.-Democrat. Mason (33 deg., Shriner). Club: Commonwealth (Richmond, Va.). Home: 1352 Jeffress St South Boston VA 24592 Office: 401 Main St South Boston VA 24592

TUCKER, ALAN DAVID, pub. co. exec.; b. Erie, Pa., Mar. 9, 1936; s. Meredith LaDue and Monica (Klocko) T.; A.B., Princeton U., 1957; m. Kiyoko Iizuka, Feb. 8, 1963; 1 dau., Kumi Tucker. Asso. editor Hawthorn Books, N.Y.C., 1964-66; editor John Day Co., Inc., N.Y.C., 1966-72; mng. editor David McKay Co., Inc., N.Y.C., 1972-75, v.p., 1975-78, exec. v.p., 1978—. Trustee Princeton Library in N.Y. Served to USNR, 1957-60. Office: 2 Park Ave New York NY 10016

TUCKER, ALLAN, educator; b. Calgary, Alta., Can., Sept. 29, 1921; s. Frank and Nellie (Chester) T.; B.A., U. Toronto (Ont., Can.), 1943, M.A., 1946; Ph.D., U. Mich., 1952; postgrad. U. London (Eng.), summer 1955; D.Sc. (hon.), Fla. Inst. Tech., 1971; m. Rebecca Cope Kimber; children—Edwin Kimber, David Gregory. Came to U.S., 1946, naturalized, 1952. Instr. biology Mich. State U., 1946-52, asst. prof., 1952-58, asso. prof., 1958-62, prof., 1962-64, asst. dean for advanced grad. studies, 1959-64, asst. to v.p. for research, 1959-64; vice chancellor for acad. affairs State U. System of Fla., Tallahassee, 1964-75, chmn. council acad. vice presidents, 1964-75; prof. higher edn. Fla. State U., 1975—, dir. inst. dept. leadership, 1976—. Chmn. edn. com. Fla.-Colombia Alliance, 1969-75; mem. exec. com. Gov.'s Commn. for Quality Edn. in Fla., 1967; mem. panel to select NATO postdoctoral fellows in sci. Nat. Acad. Scis., 1969-71; mem. steering com. Navy Campus for Achievement, 1972-73; sci. adviser U. Ryukyus on Okinawa, 1953-55, cons. to pres. 1957-59. Recipient certificate of leadership Adult Edn. Assn. U.S.A., 1971. Mem. Council Grad. Schs. U.S. (mem. grad. edn. cost com. 1968-71), Am. Council Edn. (mem. commn. on ednl. credit 1969-76), Adult Edn. Assn. U.S.A. (mem. nat. com. on external degrees 1971-72), Nat. U. Extension Assn. (mem. nat. com. on govtl. relations 1971-74), Council on Edn. for Pub. Health (v.p. 1979), Am. Assn. Higher Edn., Sigma Xi. Author: Pigment Extraction as a Method of Quantitative Analysis of Phytoplankton, 1949; The Relation of Phytoplankton Periodicity to the Nature of the Physico-chemical Environment with special Reference to Phosphorus, 1957; Attrition of Graduate Students at the Ph.D. Level in the Traditional Arts and Sciences 1964; Decentralized Graduate Administration with Centralized Accountability, 1965; Involvement of Statewide Governing Boards in Accreditation, 1978. Contbr. articles to profl. jours. Home: 2072 Trescott Dr Tallahassee FL 32312 Office: Fla State Univ Tallahassee FL 32306

TUCKER, CARLL, editor; b. N.Y.C., Oct. 8, 1951; s. Carll and Emily (O'Connor) T.; B.A. (scholar), Yale U., 1973; m. Diane Straus, Mar. 20, 1976. Columnist, Patent Trader newspaper, Mt. Kisco, N.Y., 1969-73; theater critic, book columnist Village Voice, N.Y.C., 1974-77; chmn., editor Saturday Rev. Mag. Corp., N.Y.C., 1977—. Bd. dirs. Inst. for Future; adviser Center for Research in Bus. and Social Policy; v.p. Marcia Brady Tucker Found. Mem. Phi Beta Kappa. Office: Saturday Rev Mag Corp 1290 Ave of Americas New York NY 10019

TUCKER, CYNTHIA DELORES NOTTAGE (MRS. WILLIAM M. TUCKER), polit. party ofcl., former state ofcl.; b. Phila., Oct. 4, 1927; d. Whitfield and Captilda (Gardiner) Nottage; student Temple U., Pa. State U., U. Pa.; hon. degrees Villa Maria Coll., Erie, Pa., 1972, Morris Coll., Sumter, S.C., 1976; m. William M. Tucker, July 21, 1951. Sec., Commonwealth of Pa., Harrisburg, 1971-77; nat. pres. Fedn. Democratic Women, 1979—; v.p. Pa. chpt. NAACP; mem. nat. adv. bd. Nat. Women's Polit. Caucus; mem., vice chmn. Pa. Black Dem. Com., 1966—; chmn. Women for Dem. Action, 1967—; sec., mem. Phila. Zoning Bd. Adjustment, 1968-70; vice chmn. Pa. Dem. State C Com., 1970-76; mem. exec. com. Dem. Nat. Com., 1972-76; mem. Dem. Nat. Com.; Dem. candidate lt. gov. Pa., 1978; bd. dirs. Phila. YWCA, New Sch. Music, Phila. Tribune Charities, Martin Luther King Center for Social Change; mem. Commonwealth bd. Med. Coll. Pa.; bd. assos. Messiah Coll. Recipient Service and Achievement award NAACP, 1964; Phila. Tribune Charities Ann. award; Community Service award Opportunities Industrialization Center, Emma V. Kelley Achievement award Nat. Elks, 1971; named Best Dressed Woman of Year, Ebony Mag., One of 100 Most Influential Black Ams., 1973-77; Woman of Year Pa. Beauticians Assn., 1971; Community Service award Quaker City chpt. B'nai B'rith. Mem. Nat. Assn. Secs. State (v.p.), Bus. and Profl. Women's Club, Links (dir.), Alpha Kappa Alpha (hon.). Home: 6700 Lincoln Dr Philadelphia PA 19119

TUCKER, DANIEL EUGENE, editorial writer; b. Chgo., Mar. 31, 1925; s. Irwin St. John and Dorothy (O'Reilly) T.; student Loyola U., 1946-49; Mus.B., Am. Conservatory Music, 1961, Mus.M., 1974; m. Margaret Grace Rattenbury, Sept. 29, 1956; children—Ellen Marguerite, Andrew Daniel. With Chgo. Sun, 1942, 46; with Chgo. Today (formerly Chgo. Am.), 1950-74, telegraph editor, spl. writer, asst. music critic, 1950-57, asst. editorial writer, 1957-65, chief editorial writer, 1965-68, editor editorial page, 1968-74; editorial writer Chgo. Tribune, 1974—; also free-lance writer, book reviewer. Served with AUS, 1943-46. Recipient award nat. contest for composition Chamber Symphony, Richmond Profl. Inst., 1963. Mem. Chgo. Editorial Assn., Chgo. Press Club. Roman Catholic. Compositions: Trio for Violin, Cello, Piano, 1959; (ballet) Hopscotch, 1961; Incidental Music for Henry IV, Part I; Chamber Symphony, 1964; A Fragment from Christopher Fry, 1964; Three Irish Songs (on 10th Century texts), 1971; Songs from the Pentagon Papers for a cappella chorus, 1972; Celebration for Orch., 1975; (opera) Many Moons, 1978. Home: 2743 Highland Ave Evanston IL 60201 Office: 435 N Michigan Ave Chicago IL 60611. *Having spent much of my life in writing and composing, I have come to believe that the same fundamental rules apply to these two crafts and to life in general. What makes a good editorial or a good piece of music is also what makes a good life (in the sense of "satisfying"-not necessarily "prosperous"). The purpose of all three is to communicate-that is, to share; to receive gladly what is given and pass it on, freely and with love, knowing that there will always be more.*

TUCKER, DON EUGENE, lawyer; b. Rockbridge, Ohio, Feb. 3, 1928; s. Beryl Hollis and Ruth (Primmer) T.; B.A. Aurora Coll., 1951; LL.B., Yale, 1956; m. Elizabeth Jane Parke, Aug. 2, 1950; children—Janet Elizabeth, Kerry Jane, Richard Parke. Admitted to Ohio bar, 1956, since practiced in Youngstown; asso. Manchester, Bennett, Powers & Ullman, 1956-62, partner, 1962—, of counsel, 1973—; gen. counsel Comml. Shearing, Inc., 1973-75, v.p., gen. counsel, 1975—, also dir.; instr., Am. Inst. Banking, 1964, 66; dir. Union Nat. Bank Youngstown. Solicitor, Village of Poland, Ohio, 1961-63. Former chmn. bd., pres., trustee United Cerebral Palsy Assn. Youngstown and Mahoning County; trustee Mahoning County Tb and Health Assn.; pres., trustee Eastern Ohio Lung Assn.; bd. dirs. Ohio Lung Assn. Served with USMCR, 1946-48, 51-53. Mem. Am., Ohio, Mahoning County (pres. 1972, trustee 1970-73) bar assns., Youngstown Area C. of C. (chmn. bd. dirs. 1979). Methodist. Home: 6838 Tanglewood Dr Boardman OH 44512 Office: 1775 Logan Ave Youngstown OH 44501

TUCKER, FORREST MEREDITH, actor; b. Plainfield, Ind., Feb. 12, 1919; s. Forrest A. and Doris P. (Heringláke) T.; student Mt. Hermon (Mass.) Prep., 1933; 1 dau., Pamela Brooke; m. 2d, Marilyn Johnson, Mar. 28, 1950 (dec. July 1960); m. 3d, Marilyn Fisk, Oct. 23, 1961; children—Cynthia Brooke, Forrest Sean. Motion picture debut in The Westerner, 1939; actor Columbia Pictures, 1940-42, Warner Bros., 1946-48, Republic Pictures, 1948-55; appeared on TV series Crunch and Des, NBC-TV, 1956; star mus. prodn. on tour Music Man, 1958; star TV series F Troop, 1966-69, Dusty's Trail, 1974, Ghost Busters, 1975; asso. producer Drury Lane Theatre, Chgo., 1969; mem. nat. co. That Championship Season, 1972-73, Plaza Suite, 1971-72; appeared in The Confidence Game, Drury Lane Theater, 1975-76; appeared in movies, including: Sands of Iwo Jima, 1950, Auntie Mame, 1958, The Night They Raided Minsky's, 1968, Wild McCullochs, 1975; appeared in TV movie The Incredible Rocky Mountain Race, 1977. Served to 2d lt. Signal Corps, U.S. Army, 1942-45. Clubs: Am., Stage Golfing (London); Masquers (dir.) (Hollywood, Calif.); Players, Lambs, Friar's (N.Y.C.); Variety Internat. (dir.). Office: care Lew Sherrell Agy Ltd 7060 Hollywood Blvd Hollywood CA 90028*

TUCKER, FRANK MAYER, JR., fgn. service officer; b. Sewickley, Pa., July 24, 1928; s. Frank Mayer and Wilhelmina (Wehrum) T.; B.S., U.S. Mcht. Marine Acad., 1950; B.A., Georgetown U., 1955; M.P.A., Harvard, 1959; m. Ingrid Schmidt, Feb. 14, 1958; 1 son, Frank Mayer. Deck officer Am. Export Lines, Inc., 1950-54; with Fgn. Service, Dept. State, 1956—; econ. officer Am. embassy, Bogota, Colombia, 1956-58; 2d sec. Am. embassy, Oslo, Norway, 1959-63; econ. officer Office U.K. Affairs, Washington, 1963-65, officer in charge Norway, Denmark and Iceland affairs, 1965-68, officer in charge Sierra Leone and Liberia affairs, 1968; chief econ. sect., Monrovia, Liberia, 1968-70; dep. chief mission, Valletta, Malta, 1970-74; chief fgn. service counseling and assignments div. Dept. State, Washington, 1974-76; fgn. service insp., 1976-78; dep. chief mission, Managua, Nicaragua, 1978—. Mem. Am. Fgn. Service Assn., Am.-Scandinavian Found. Address: Am Embassy Managua Dept State Washington DC 20520

TUCKER, FRED C., JR., Realtor, developer; b. Indpls., Oct. 25, 1918; s. Fred C. and Bernice (Caldwell) T.; grad. Lawrenceville Sch., 1936; A.B., DePauw U., 1940; student law Harvard U., 1940-41; m. Ermajean MacDonald, Sept. 2, 1944; children—Fred C. III, Lucinda Ann. Pres., F. C. Tucker Co., Inc., Indpls., 1946—; dir. Ind. Nat. Bank, Jefferson Nat. Life Ins. Co., Jefferson Corp.; prin. officer, dir. real estate and devel. cos. Pres., Indpls. Met. YMCA, 1964-65; Ind. chmn. Crusade Freedom, 1954-55; chmn. bd. trustees DePauw U.; trustee Arthur Jordan Found., Indpls., Indpls.-Marion County Bldg. Authority. Served as lt. USNR, World War II. Mem. Nat. Inst. Real Estate Brokers (pres. 1966), Indpls. Real Estate Bd. (pres. 1961), Nat. Assn. Realtors (nat. pres. 1972), Arbitration Assn., Am. Soc. Real Estate Counselors, Rep. Vets. Ind., Central Ind. DePauw Alumni Assn. (past pres.), Indpls. C. of C. (pres. 1973-74), Am. Legion (past comdr.), Ind. Acad., Delta Tau Delta (past nat. pres.). Methodist. Clubs: Rotary, Meridian Hills Country, Crooked Stick, Indpls. Athletic, Columbia; Royal Poinciana (Naples, Fla.). Office: 1 Indiana Sq Indianapolis IN 46204

TUCKER, JOHN ANDREW, III, newspaper exec.; b. Atlanta, July 11, 1929; s. John Andrew and Dorothy Matthew T.; B.S. in Communications, U. Fla., 1955; children—Angel, John, Nancy, Chris, Clay, Lee, Jill. Mgr. telephone operations So. Bell, Orlando, Fla., 1955-65, dist. mgr., Jacksonville, Fla., 1965; dir. bus. devel. Fla. Pub. Co., Jacksonville, 1965-66, v.p., 1966-77, pres., gen. mgr., 1977—; dir. Flagship Banks. Bd. dirs. Mental Health Assn., Jacksonville, Meml. Hosp., Jacksonville. Served with USAF, 1950-53. Recipient Distinguished Service award Jacksonville Jr. C. of C., 1964. Mem. Fla. Press Assn. (past pres., bd. dirs.), Sales and Mktg. Execs., Jacksonville C. of C. Roman Catholic. Home: 6740 Strawberry Ln Jacksonville FL 32211 Office: 1 Riverside Ave Jacksonville FL 32202

TUCKER, JOHN HELLUMS, JR., lawyer; b. Pine Bluff, Ark., Feb. 25, 1891; s. John Hellums and Lucille (LePhiew) T.; A.B., Washington and Lee U., 1910, LL.D., 1958; LL.B., La. State U., 1920, LL.D., 1956; LL.D., Tulane U., 1959, Loyola U., 1966; D.H.L., Centenary Coll., 1972; m. Hortense Rigby, Apr. 23, 1924. Admitted to La. bar, 1920, since practiced in Shreveport; mem. firm Tucker, Martin, Holder, Jeter & Jackson; agt. Consulaire de France at Shreveport. Dir. Home Fed. Bldg. & Loan Assn., Pan Am. Life Ins. Co. New Orleans. Chmn., La. State Law Inst. Mem. Gen. Staff Com. on Res. and N.G. Policy, 1946-49. Served as mem. com. on ethics and disbarment Supreme Ct. La. Served as sgt. U.S. Army, Mexican Border, 1916; 1st lt., World War I; col., inf., World War II; col. inf. res., 1943-51. Decorated French Legion of Honor, 1956. Mem. La. (past gov.), Shreveport bar assns., Phi Beta Kappa, Sigma Nu, Phi Delta Phi, Omicron Delta Kappa, Order of Coif. Clubs: International House, Boston, Pickwick, New Orleans Country (New Orleans): Union (Cleve.); Westbook (Mansfield, Ohio); Shreveport, Shreveport Country; Army and Navy, Chevy Chase (Washington); Confrérie des Chevaliers du Tastevin (grand officier). Author: Source Books of Louisiana Law (vols. VI-IX, Tulane Law Rev.), 1931-35; Bartolus Soc. Juridical Studies 1, Effects on the Civil Law of La. Brought about by the Changes in its Sovereignty; Tradition and Techniques of Codification: The Louisiana Experience; Au-Delà Du Code Civil, Mais Par Le Code Civil. Home: 906 McCormick Blvd Shreveport LA 71104 Office: 1300 Beck Bldg Shreveport LA 71101

TUCKER, LAUREY DAN, lawyer; b. El Dorado, Ark., Oct. 23, 1936; s. Floyd A. and Harriet Kathleen (Graves) T.; B.S. in Chem. Engring., U. Okla., 1959, LL.B., 1962; m. Katherine Ellen Washburn, June 21, 1958; children—Laurie Kathleen, Dana Elizabeth. Admitted to Okla. bar, 1962, Tex. bar, 1973; patent atty. Phillips Petroleum Co., Bartlesville, Okla., 1963-67; patent atty., then patent mgr. Monsanto Co., 1967-74; partner firm Hubbard, Thurman, Turner, Tucker & Glaser, Dallas, 1974—; lectr. environ. sci. U. Tex., Dallas, 1974-76. Trustee, Episcopal Community Service Bd., Diocese of Dallas, 1977—. Served to 1st lt. AUS, 1962-64; capt. Res. ret. Mem. Am., Okla., Dallas bar assns., State Bar Tex., Am. Patent Law Assn., Dallas-Ft. Worth Patent Assn. (pres. 1978-79). Republican. Home: 6612 St Anne St Dallas TX 75248 Office: 1200 North Dallas Bank Tower Dallas TX 75230

TUCKER, LEM (LEMUEL), journalist; b. Saginaw, Mich., May 26, 1938; s. Stewart Edward and Missouri (Ward) T.; B.A. in Polit. Sci., Central Mich. U., 1960; div.; 1 dau., Linn Carol. Copy boy, adminstr. Viet Nam Bur., reporter WNBC-TV, reporter network TV news NBC News, 1965-70; TV news dir. WOR-TV, 1970-71; reporter ABC News, N.Y.C., 1972-77, CBS News, Washington, 1977—; cons. Ford Found., 1970; founding mem. Reporters Com. for Freedom of Press. Asst. to auditor gen. of Mich., 1960. Served to 1st lt. AUS, 1961-62. Recipient Emmy award for series of news stories on hunger in Am., 1968-69. Mem. AFTRA. Office: 2020 M St NW Washington DC 20036

TUCKER, MARCIA, curator; b. N.Y.C., Apr. 11, 1940; d. Emanuel and Dorothy (Wald) Silverman; student École du Louvre, Paris, 1959-60; B.A., Conn. Coll., New London, 1961; M.A., Inst. Fine Arts, N.Y. U., 1969. Curator, William N. Copley Collection, N.Y.C., 1963-66; editorial asso. Art News mag., N.Y.C., 1965-69; collection cataloger Alfred H. Barr, Jr., N.Y.C., 1966-67, Columbus (Ohio) Gallery Fine Arts, 1966-69; catalog raisonée Howald Collection Am. Art, Ford Found., 1966-69; asso. curator Whitney Mus. Am. Art, N.Y.C., 1969-73, curator, 1973-77; dir./founder The New Museum, N.Y.C., 1977—; faculty U. R.I., Kingston, 1966-68, City U. N.Y., 1967-68, Sch. Visual Arts, 1969-73; guest lectr. San Francisco Art Inst., Yale U., New Sch. for Social Research, U. Colo., U. Wis., Princeton U. Mem. Redstockings, 1970, Radical Feminists, 1971. Mem. Coll. Art Assn., Am. Assn. Museums, Phi Beta Kappa. Author: Anti-Illusion: Procedures/Materials, 1969; Catalogue of Ferdinand Howald Collection, 1969; Robert Morris, 1970; The Structure of Color, 1971; James Rosenquist, 1972; Bruce Nauman, 1973; Al Held, 1974; Richard Tuttle, 1975; Early Work by 5 Contemporary Artists, 1977; Bad Painting, 1978; Barry Le Va, 1978; also articles. Home: 140 Sullivan St New York NY 10012 Office: New Museum 65 Fifth Ave New York NY 10003

TUCKER, MORRISON GRAHAM, banker; b. Lincoln, Nebr., May 24, 1911; s. Charles Andrew and Olive Myrtle (Graham) T.; A.B., Dartmouth Coll., 1932; m. Gladys Mae Hartz, Nov. 25, 1944; children—Suzanne, John Graham. Asst. nat. bank examiner U.S. Treasury Dept., 1932-36; fed. bank examiner, 1936-38; asst. chief div. exam. Fed. Deposit Ins. Corp., 1939-42; banking adviser to pres. of Philippines, 1944-47; mgr. Latin Am. interests Rockefeller family, 1947-51; chmn. exec. com. Liberty Nat. Bank & Trust Co., Oklahoma City, 1951-69; owner Morrison G. Tucker & Co., banking and investments; chmn. bd. First Security Bank & Trust Co., United Okla. Bank, Union Bank & Trust Co., Southwestern Bank & Trust Co., Will Rogers Bank & Trust Co.; dir. Am. Gen. Life Ins. Co., Capitol Steel & Iron Co., ANTA Corp., S.W. Title & Trust Co. (all Oklahoma City). Bd. dirs. Frontiers of Sci. Found.; trustee Oklahoma City U.; pres. alumni council Dartmouth Coll., 1965-66. Served as lt. (j.g.) USNR, 1941-44. Mem. Am. Econ. Assn., Okla. Bankers Assn. (pres. 1974-75). Episcopalian. Clubs: Metropolitan (Washington); University (N.Y.C.); Oklahoma City Golf and Country, Petroleum, Men's Dinner (Oklahoma City). Home: 2403 NW Grand Blvd Oklahoma City OK 73116 Office: 2401 Exchange Ave Oklahoma City OK 73108

TUCKER, PRISCILLA ANNE MEYER, journalist; b. Chgo., June 28, 1932; d. Arthur C. and Hester Truslow (Sheldon) M.; grad. Conn. Coll., 1951; m. Benjamin F. Tucker, Apr. 7, 1961; children—Katrina Plum, Mary Mitie. Reporter, Hartford (Conn.) Courant, 1952-55, Women's Wear Daily, 1957-60, N.Y. Herald Tribune, 1961-65; corr. London Daily Mail, 1966-67, London Daily Mirror, 1968-74; contbg. editor New York mag., 1972-78; fashion editor N.Y. Daily News, 1978—; contbr. articles to nat. mags. Democrat. Episcopalian. Home: 1264 Lexington Ave New York NY 10028 Office: NY News 220 E 42d St New York NY 10017

TUCKER, RICHARD CLIVE, banker; b. Cheyenne, Wyo., June 30, 1930; s. Robert Henry and Daisy Urdona (Nidelkoff) T.; student Colo. U., Boulder, 1948-50, Denver U., 1951-53; m. Patricia Anne Tillotson, Oct. 25, 1950; children—Katherine Anne Tucker Thompson, Susan Tucker Luther, Richard Clive. Regional mgr. Seaboard Finance Co., Denver, 1953-63; pres. Tri-State Indsl. Bank, Denver and Boulder, 1963—, also dir.; formerly v.p., dir. Indsl. Bank Guaranty Corp., pres., 1978-80. Co-chmn. bus. and finance United Way Denver, 1962-63. Dir. Colo. Young Republicans, 1968-70; capt. Republican Dist. Com., 1968-70. Bd. dirs. Purdue U. Credit Research Center, 1974-75, Marquette U. Consumer Finance Mgmt., 1972—, Nat. Installment Banking Sch. Colo. U., 1974—; bd. dirs. Nat. Camp Fire Girls, 1970-71, asst. treas., 1971—, pres. Denver Area, 1969-70; bd. dirs. Colo. Philharmonic Orch., 1968. Served to sgt. USAF, 1950-52. Recipient Luther Halsey Gulick award Nat. Camp Fire Girls, 1969. Mem. Pres.'s Roundtable Denver (pres. 1973-74), Nat. (pres. 1974-75, mem. exec. com. 1975—), Colo. (pres. 1968-70, Distinguished Service award 1977) consumer finance assns., Indsl. Bank Assn. (dir. 1974—), Better Bus. Bur. Denver (dir. 1967-69), Retail Credit Assn., Denver Lenders Exchange, Beta Theta Pi. Republican. Presbyn. (elder). Mason (Shriner), Kiwanian (dist. gov. 1973-74). Clubs: Hiwan Country, Mt. Vernon Country, Court. Home: Douglas Park Box 538 Evergreen CO 80439 Office: Tri-State Indsl Bank 616 E Speer Blvd Denver CO 80203 also 1611 Canyon Blvd Boulder CO

TUCKER, RICHARD FRANK, petroleum co. exec.; b. N.Y.C., Dec. 25, 1926; s. Frank W. and Marion (Ohm) T.; B.Chem. Engring., Cornell U., 1950; m. Genevieve P. Martinson, Oct. 13, 1951. Engr., Esso Standard Oil Co., 1950-55; asst. mgr., process eng. Caltex Oil Co., 1955-61; with Mobil Oil Corp., 1961—, exec. v.p., 1969—, pres. N.Am. div., 1969-75, pres. Mobil Chem. Co., 1975—, also dir.; pres., chief exec. officer Container Corp. Am.; dir. Mobil Corp. Chmn. adv. council Cornell U. Sch. Bus. and Pub. Adminstrn.; trustee Cornell U.; dir. Am. Paper Inst., Econ. Devel. Council N.Y.C.; vis. com. M.I.T. Sch. Chem. Engring. Served with USNR, 1945-46. Mem. N.Y. Chamber of Commerce and Industry (dir.), Chem. Mfrs. Assn. (dir.). Clubs: Cornell, Pinnacle (N.Y.C.). Office: 150 E 42d St New York NY 10017

TUCKER, ROBERT CHARLES, polit. scientist, educator; b. Kansas City, Mo., May 29, 1918; s. Charles and Adele (Steinfels) T.; student U. Mich., 1935-37; A.B., Harvard, 1939, M.A., 1941, Ph.D., 1958; m. Eugenia Pestretsova, Aug. 21, 1946; 1 dau., Elizabeth Adele. Attache embassy, Moscow, USSR, editor embassy's joint press reading service,

1944-53; asso. prof., then prof. govt. Ind. U., 1958-62; vis. prof. Soviet studies Johns Hopkins Sch. Advanced Internat. Studies, 1962; prof. politics Princeton, 1962—, dir. program Russian studies, 1963-73, chmn. Council Internat. and Regional Studies, 1977—, McCosh faculty fellow, 1968-69. Served with OSS, 1942-44. Fellow Center Advanced Study Behavioral Scis., 1964-65; Guggenheim fellow, 1968-69; mem. Inst. for Advanced Studies, Sch. Hist. Studies, 1968-69; Nat. Endowment for Humanities fellow, 1975-76. Chmn. planning group on comparative govt. studies Am. Council Learned Socs., 1969-73. Mem. Am. Polit. Sci. Assn. (chmn. conf. Soviet and Communist studies 1963-64), Am. Philos. Assn., Am. Soc. Polit. and Legal Philosophy, Am. Assn. Advancement Slavic Studies (bd. 1963-64). Author: Philosophy and Myth in Karl Marx, 1961; The Soviet Political Mind, 1963; The Marxian Revolutionary Idea, 1969; Stalin as Revolutionary, 1973. Editor: (with S.F. Cohen) The Great Purge Trial, 1965; The Marx-Engels Reader, 1972; The Lenin Anthology, 1975; Stalinism: Essays in Historical Interpretation, 1977. Home: 44 Hartley Ave Princeton NJ 08540

TUCKER, ROBERT L., lawyer, educator; b. Chattanooaga, Feb. 14, 1929; s. Oscar and Isabelle (Lucas) T.; B.S., Tenn. State U., 1951; J.D., Northwestern U., 1955; m. Shirley Cross, Dec. 24, 1964; 1 dau., Teri E. Admitted to Ill. bar, 1955; since practiced in Chgo.; asso. firm McCoy, Ming & Leighton, 1956-65; asst. regional adminstr. HUD, Chgo., 1968-71; partner firm McCarty, Watson & Tucker, 1971-73, Tucker, Watson, Butler & Todd, Chgo., 1973-77, firm Tucker & Watson, 1977—: instr. law Northwestern U., 1972-76. Gen. counsel People United To Save Humanity, Chgo. Bd. dirs. ACLU, Bus. and Profl. People for Pub. Interest. Mem. Am., Ill., Chgo., Cook County (Ill.) (Richard E. Westbrook award for outstanding contbns. to legal profession 1968), Nat. bar assns., Chgo. Urban League. Home: 6901 Oglesby Ave Chicago IL 60649 Office: 1 N LaSalle St Chicago IL 60602

TUCKER, ROBERT WARREN, polit. scientist; b. Inspiration, Ariz., Aug. 25, 1924; s. Louis Herald and Jeannette T.; B.S., U.S. Naval Acad., 1945; M.A., U. Calif., Berkeley, 1947, Ph.D., 1949; m. Joan Jordan, Jan. 18, 1946; children—Peter A., Robert J. Faculty, Wash. State Coll., 1948-49, San Francisco State Coll., 1949-50, Stanford U., 1950-51; faculty Johns Hopkins U., Balt., 1954—, prof. polit. sci., 1960—; trustee, co-dir. studies Lehrman Inst., 1978—. Served to lt. USN, 1942-46, 52-54. Mem. Council on Fgn. Relations, Am. Soc. Internat. Law, Am. Polit. Sci. Assn. Author: Law of War and Neutrality, 1957; The Just War, 1960; (with Robert E. Osgood) Force, Order and Justice, 1967; Nation or Empire, 1968; The Radical Left and American Foreign Policy, 1971; A New Isolationism - Threat or Promise, 1972; The Inequality of Nations, 1977. Home: 220 Stony Run Ln Baltimore MD 21210 Office: Dept Polit Sci Johns Hopkins U Baltimore MD 21218

TUCKER, RONALD DWAIN, advt. exec.; b. Centerburg, Ohio, Aug. 16, 1925; s. Ernest C. and Bessie P. (Huddlestun) T.; B.A., Miami U., Oxford, Ohio, 1949; m. Jane B. Knowlton, June 4, 1949; children—Susan Tucker Sabo, Cindy Tucker Smith. Sales rep. Remington Rand Co., 1949-50; student trainee Westinghouse Electric Corp., 1950-51, asst. to dir. dept. store sales, 1951-53; sales promotion mgr. Westinghouse Electric Supply Co., Cleve., 1953-56; copywriter Hutchins Advt. Agy., Phila., 1956-57; with Maxwell Assos. Inc., 1957-64, v.p., 1961-64; v.p. copy, then sr. v.p. copy and plans Mel Richman Inc., Bala Cynwyd, Pa., 1964-73, exec. v.p., 1973—. Served with USNR, 1943-46. Decorated D.F.C., Air medal with 6 oak leaf clusters. Presbyterian. Club: Roosevelt Racquet (Huntingdon Valley, Pa.). Home: 727 Woodside Rd Jenkintown PA 19046 Office: 15 N Presidential Blvd Bala Cynwyd PA 19004

TUCKER, STEFAN FRANKLIN, lawyer; b. Detroit, Dec. 31, 1938; Asso. Bus., Flint Jr. Community Coll., 1958; B.B.A., U. Mich., 1960, J.D., 1963. Admitted to D.C. bar, 1964, U.S. Ct. Claims bar, 1964, U.S. Tax Ct. bar, 1964; clk. to judge U.S. Tax Ct., Washington, 1963-64; asso. firm Arent, Fox, Kintner, Plotkin & Kahn, Washington, 1964-69, partner, 1970-74; partner firm Tucker, Flyer, Sanger, Reider & Lewis, Washington, 1975—; speaker in field; professional lectr. law George Washington U., 1970—; adj. professional lectr. law U. Miami Law Center, 1975-78, mem. adv. com. ann. inst. estate planning, 1978—. Mem. nat. com. U. Mich. Law Sch. Fund, 1972-78. Mem. Am., Fed., D.C. bar assns., Nat. Trust Hist. Preservation (com. legal services 1978—). Contbr. articles to legal jours; mem. editorial bd. Taxation for Lawyers, 1972—; mem. advisory bd. Bur. Nat. Affairs Housing and Devel. Reporter, 1973-76; mem. editorial advisory bd. Jour. Real Estate Taxation, 1975—. Office: 1730 Massachusetts Ave NW Washington DC 20036

TUCKER, STERLING, govt. ofcl.; b. Akron, Ohio, Dec. 21, 1923; s. John Clifford and Una Mave (Vinson) T.; B.A., U. Akron, 1946, M.A., 1950; m. Edna Alloyce Robinson, Aug. 14, 1948; children—Michele Alloyce, Lauren Alloyce. Exec. dir. Canton (Ohio) Urban League, 1953-56; dir. field services Nat. Urban League, coordinator planning, 1968-71; exec. dir. Washington Urban League, 1956-78; asst. sec. for fair housing and equal opportunity HUD, Washington, 1979—; chmn. Washington Met. Area Transit Authority; chmn. D.C. City Council, 1975-79; vis. lectr. Fgn. Service Inst.; lectr. USIA. Mem. Urban Coalition Washington, Mayor's Com. on Econ. Devel.; co-chmn. Poverty Task Force of White House Conf. on Youth; advisory council Washington Urban Semester Am. U.; mem. Adv. Council on Vocat. Rehab.; pres. Self-Determination for D.C. Cited by Republic of Liberia, 1966. Mem. Nat. Assn. Social Workers, Acad. Certified Social Workers, Polit. Sci. Acad. (bd.). Author: Beyond the Burning, 1968; Black Reflections on White Power, 1969; For Blacks Only, 1970. Home: 6505 16th St NW Washington DC 20012 Office: 451 7th St SW DC 20410. *I believe most problems can be solved given time, inclination and energy.*

TUCKER, TANYA DENISE, singer, rec. artist; b. Seminole, Tex., Oct. 10, 1958; d. Jesse and Juanita T.; Regular on Lew King Show; appeared in film Jeremiah Johnson; with Columbia Records, now MCA Records; albums include: Delta Dawn, What's Your Mama's Name, Greatest Hits, Here's Some Love, Tanya Tucker, Lovin' and Learnin', Ridin' Rainbows. Office: care Far Out Prodns Inc 7417 Sunset Blvd Hollywood CA 90046*

TUCKER, THOMAS ALLEN, advt. exec.; b. Chgo., Sept. 26, 1919; s. Benjamin H. and Agnes (Neumann) T.; B.A., St. Olaf Coll., Northfield, Minn., 1942; m. Marian Beth Ness, Apr. 25, 1943; children—Philip, Brian, Gail, James. Tchr., Internat. Falls (Minn.) High Sch., 1942; editor Ecorse (Mich.) Advertiser (weekly), 1946; asst. research mgr. Campbell Ewald Co., Detroit, 1946-48; supr. nat. advt. Burroughs Corp., Detroit, 1948-52; account exec. Grant Advt., Detroit, 1952-54; sr. account exec. Campbell-Ewald Co., Detroit, 1954-68, v.p., asst. to chmn. bd., 1968-72, v.p. adminstrn., 1972-73, chmn. bd. CECO Pub. Co. subsidiary, 1973-76, pres., 1975-76, exec. v.p. Clinton E. Frank, Inc. div., Chgo., 1977-78; sr. v.p., gen. mgr. Campbell-Ewald Co., Detroit, 1978—. Pres., Mich. Assn. Retarded Children, 1959-61, Nat. Assn. Retarded Children, 1965-66; mem. subcom. mental retardation Detroit Commn. Children and Youth, 1961-68, Pres.'s Com. Mental Retardation, 1966-71, cons., 1971-75; mem. Nat. Budget and Consultation Com., 1965-67; adv. bd. mental retardation U.S. Jr. C. of C., 1965; mem. nat. adv. com. U.S. Office Child Devel., 1973-74. Chmn. bd. trustees Wayne County Referral Center, 1974-76; mem. adv. commn. Mich. Dept. Mental Health, 1975-77. Bd. dirs. Detroit Council Chs., 1974-76. Served to lt. USNR, World War II; PTO. Mem. Adcraft Club Detroit, Chgo. Advt. Club (dir. 1977-78), Direct Mail Advt. Assn. (dir. 1967-70), Am. Assn. Mental Deficiency. Democrat. Lutheran. Home: 1279 Oakwood Ct Rochester MI 48063 Office: Campbell-Ewald Co 30400 Van Dyke Warren MI 48093

TUCKER, WILLIAM EARLE, lawyer; b. Plant City, Fla., Sept. 12, 1921; s. Jasper William and Lillian (Turner) T.; student Fla. So. Coll., 1939-42; J.D., Washington and Lee U., 1948; m. Gloria B. Wright, Dec. 3, 1944; children—Pamela Suzanne Shipp, Karen Lee. Admitted to Fla. bar, 1948; with firm Cooper, Cooper & Tucker, and predecessor, Tampa, Fla., 1948-54; asst. county solicitor Hillsborough County, Fla., 1954-57; partner firm Gibbons, Tucker, McEwen, Smith, Miller & Whatley, P.A., Tampa, 1957—; dir., atty. First Ruskin Bank (Fla.), 1962—; v.p., atty., dir. Sun City Center Bank (Fla.), 1971—. Served with USAAF, 1942-45. Mem. Am., Fla., Tampa, Hillsborough County bar assns., C. of C. Temple Terrace (sec. 1969), Phi Alpha Delta. Democrat. Baptist. Clubs: Exchange, University, Tower (Tampa); Temple Terrace Golf and Country. Home: 502 Fern Cliff Ave Temple Terrace FL 33617 Office: 606 Madison St PO Box 1363 Tampa FL 33601

TUCKER, WILLIAM EDWARD, univ. chancellor, clergyman; b. Charlotte, N.C., June 22, 1932; s. Cecil Edward and Ethel Elizabeth (Godley) T.; B.A., Atlantic Christian Coll., Wilson, N.C., 1953; B.D., Tex. Christian U., 1956; M.A., Yale U., 1958, Ph.D., 1960; LL.D., Atlantic Christian Coll., 1978; m. Ruby Jean Jones, Apr. 8, 1955; children—Janet Sue, William Edward, Gordon Vance. Ordained to ministry Disciples of Christ Ch., 1956; prof. Atlantic Christian Coll., 1959-66, chmn. dept. religion and philosophy, 1961-66; mem. faculty Brite Div. Sch., Tex. Christian U., 1966-76, prof. ch. history, 1969-76, dean, 1971-76, chancellor, 1979—; pres. Bethany (W.Va.) Coll., 1976-79; vis. prof. Christian Theol. Sem., 1965. Mem. gen. bd. (Christian Ch.) Disciples of Christ, 1971-74, 75—, adminstrv. com., 1975—, exec. com., 1970-73, chmn. theol. edn. commn., 1972-73, mem. exec. com., chmn. bd. higher edn., 1975-77; pres. Council Southwestern Theol. Schs., 1975-76. Mem. Am. Hist. Assn., Am. Soc. Ch. History, Am. Acad. Religion, Disciples of Christ Hist. Soc. (trustee 1971—), Phi Beta Kappa, Theta Phi. Clubs: Colonial (Ft. Worth); Rotary; Univ. (N.Y.C.). Author: J.H. Garrison and Disciples of Christ, 1964; (with others) Journey in Faith: A History of the Christian Church (Disciples of Christ), 1975; also articles. Home: 2900 Simondale Dr Fort Worth TX 76109

TUCKER, WILLIAM ELLSWORTH, JR., petroleum co. exec.; b. Chelsea, Mass., July 27, 1918; s. William E. and Edith (Joy) T.; A.B., Dartmouth Coll., 1939; S.M., M.I.T., 1942; m. Beryl Weisman, Oct. 3, 1942; children—Sandra, Pamela. With Standard Oil Co. Cal., 1942-44; with Caltex Petroleum Corp., N.Y.C., 1944—, exec. v.p., 1969-70, pres., 1970—, also dir.; dir. Behrain Petroleum Co. Ltd. Recipient Service certificate OSRD, 1946. Mem. Nat. Fgn. Trade Council (dir. 1967—), Far East-Am. Council (dir. 1974-75, mem. exec. com. 1976—, pres. 1977—), Asian-U.S. Bus. Council (exec. com. 1979—, vice-chmn. 1979—), Am. Petroleum Inst., Am. Inst. Chem. Engrs. Republican. Presbyn. Home: 7 Gracie Sq New York NY 10028 Office: 380 Madison Ave New York NY 10017

TUCKER, WILLIAM GORDON, ret. oil co. exec., barrister, solicitor; b. Weyburn, Sask., Can., Feb. 14, 1918; s. James Miller and Elsie Maude (Shortt) T.; LL.B., U. B.C., Vancouver, 1949; m. Margaret Richardson, Apr. 4, 1944; children—Gary, Diane, James. Called to B.C. bar, 1949; pvt. practice, Vancouver, 1949-50; with Gulf Oil Co., Calgary, Alta., 1950-51, Anglo-Canadian Oil Co., also Canadian Oil Cos., White Rose, Calgary, 1951-56; legal counsel Royalite Oil Co., Calgary, 1956-61; with Total Petroleum (N.Am.) Ltd., and predecessor, Calgary, 1961-78, sec., gen. counsel, 1963-78, v.p., 1972-78; v.p., dir. Total Petroleum, Inc., Detroit and Alma, Mich. and Houston, 1972-78; dir. Eastcan Exploration Ltd., Calgary, Total Petroleum (N. Am.) Ltd., 1978. Served as pilot RCAF, 1940-45. Mem. Canadian, Internat. bar assns., law socs. Alta., B.C., Calgary C. of C. Mem. United Ch. Can. Clubs: Calgary Petroleum, Alta. United Services Inst. Home: 3316 Rideau Pl Calgary AB T2S 1Z4 Canada Office: 115 635 6th Ave SW Calgary AB T2P 0T5 Canada

TUCKER, WILLIAM THOMAS, educator; b. Rushville, Ind., Jan. 26, 1919; s. Glenn Irving and Dorothy Gale (Thomas) T.; A.B., DePauw U., 1941; M.S., U. Ill., 1950, Ph.D., 1955; m. Marjorie Ann Driscoll, June 6, 1942; children—Jeffrey, Nancy, Kathleen, Margaret, Mary, Sarah, Leah. Pub. relations, 1945-48; instr. U. Ill., 1948-54, Ga. State Coll., 1954-59; faculty U. Tex., 1959—, prof. mktg., 1961—, chmn. dept., 1963-67. Served with USMCR, 1941-45. Author: The Social Context of Economic Behavior, 1964; Foundations for a Theory of Consumer Behavior, 1966. Author articles, monographs. Home: 111 San Gabriel Rd Liberty Hill TX 78642

TUCKER, WILLIAM VINCENT, coll. exec.; b. Beatrice, Nebr., May 23, 1934; s. Casimir Augustine and Mary Margaret (Carmichael) T.; B.A., Benedictine Coll., 1955; M.S., Emporia State U., 1963; Ed.D., U. S.D., 1968; m. Marian Elizabeth Cooper, Aug. 9, 1958; children—Catherine, Jean, Rose Marie, Alan. Tchr., Kelly (Kans.) High Sch., 1958-61; grad. asst. Emporia State U., 1960-61, instr., 1961-63; instr. Briar Cliff Coll., 1963-65, asst. prof. ednl. psychology, asso. prof., 1968-70, prof., 1970-71, acad. v.p., 1967-71; pres., prof. St. Mary of the Plains Coll., 1971-75; pres. Mt. Marty Coll., 1975—; cons. Social Security Adminstrn., 1962-79. Trustee, Dodge City (Kans.) Area Hosp. Assn. Served with U.S. Army, 1955-57. Mem. Am. Council Edn., Assn. Am. Colls., Yankton C. of C. (dir.), Phi Delta Kappa. Roman Catholic. Clubs: Elks, Rotary. Contbr. articles on ednl. rehab., placement of physically handicapped to profl. jours. Home: 1116 Walnut St Yankton SD 57078 Office: 1100 W 5th St Yankton SD 57078

TUCKER, WILLIS CARLETON, educator; b. Beckley, W.Va., Mar. 14, 1907; s. Charles Cherrington and Bessie Alma (Willis) T.; B.A., W.Va. Inst. Tech., 1930; M.A., W.Va. U., 1931; postgrad. U. So. Calif., 1940, Ohio State U., summers 1931, 33, 35, 37, 41; m. Julia Belle Infield, Mar. 15, 1941. Reporter daily newspapers, editor and bus. mgr. weekly, press assn. corr., coll. publicity, 1924-33; asst. prof. Marshall Coll., 1934-37, co-editor quar., 1936-37; asst. prof. journalism U. Ky., 1938-42, asso. prof., 1943-47; telegraph, news editor daily newspapers, 1942-47; Nat. Assn. Broadcasters radio news intern WGAR, Cleve., summer 1945; prof., head dept. journalism U. Tenn., 1947-57, dir. Sch. Journalism, 1957-72, prof., 1972-74, dir. emeritus, 1974—; pres. U. Tenn. Pub. Assn., 1955-70, univ. dir. Indsl. Editing Inst., 1948-72. Editorial cons., trade and indsl. publs., 1952—; pres. Precision Editing, 1975—; sec. U. Tenn.-Tenn. Press Assn. Press Inst., 1952-73; cons. Am. Assn. Indsl. Editors, 1963-70; exec. dir. Tenn. High Sch. Press Assn., 1948-74. Recipient Gov.'s Merit award, 1972. Mem. Assn. Edn. in Journalism, Kappa Tau Alpha, Phi Kappa Phi, Kappa Alpha, Sigma Delta Chi, Omicron Delta Kappa. Co-author books; contbr. articles to profl. jours. Home: Route 1 Canyon Rd Hiwasse AR 72739. *I value people whose work is paced not by timepieces but by a high regard for accuracy and quality—professionals who are happy in giving more than they receive.*

TUCKER, WOODIE, educator; b. Gladys, Va., May 25, 1918; s. Ottie W. and Estelle (Hodnette) T.; B.S., U. Va., 1949; M.Ed., U. Pitts., 1952, Ph.D., 1959; m. Neda Betchan Bine, June 22, 1952. Tchr., Woodrow Wilson Rehab. Center, Fisherville, Va., 1949-51, Washington County Tech. Sch., Abingdon, Va., 1952-55; faculty U. Pitts., 1955-57; chmn. bus. edn. dept. Va. Commonwealth U., Richmond, 1957-74, prof. bus. edn., 1974—. Served with AUS, 1941-45. Mem. So., Nat., Va. (past pres., membership chmn.) bus. edn. assns., Adminstrv. Mgmt. Soc. (past dir., treas. Richmond), Delta Pi Epsilon. Home: 2310-A Grove Ave Richmond VA 23220

TUCKEY, JOHN SUTTON, educator; b. Washington, July 27, 1921; s. William Dyson and Nellie (Sutton) T.; A.B., U. Notre Dame, 1943, M.A., 1949, Ph.D., 1953; m. Irene Louise Swinehart, Nov. 18, 1945; children—Alan, Janis. Instr. English Purdue U., Hammond, Ind., 1953-55, asst. prof., 1956-59, asso. prof., 1960-64, prof., 1965—, chmn. dept., 1963—, asst. dean grad. sch., 1974—. Served to lt. (j.g.) USNR, 1944-46. Purdue Research Found. grantee, 1961, 62, 64; Am. Philos. Soc. grantee, 1965; Nat. Endowment for Humanities sr. fellow, 1973. Mem. Modern Lang. Assn., Coll. English Assn., Ind. Coll. English Assn. (pres. 1965), Midwest Modern Lang. Assn., Ind. Com. for Humanities, Am. Studies Assn. Author: Mark Twain and Little Satan-The Writing of the Mysterious Stranger, 1963. Editor: Mark Twain's Which Was the Dream and other Symbolical Writings of the Later Years, 1967; Mark Twain's Mysterious Stranger— and the Critics, 1968; Mark Twain's Fables of Man, 1972. Home: 12412 Kingfisher Rd Crown Point IN 46307 Office: 2233 171st St St Hammond IN 46323. *Not manipulation-minded master-planning but unforcing responsiveness to situations, and movement in accord with their inherent patterns and rhythms: this is the approach I have found most helpful. To be sure, there must be planning, organizing, and evaluating, in education as elsewhere in our society; but I believe we need to safeguard the humanities—and our humanity—against the compelling pseudoefficiencies of imposed systems. In methodology there is madness if it is not moderated to allow room for spontaneity, individuality, and even uniqueness. Our systems are for the sake of people, who come in lots of one.*

TUCKNER, HOWARD MELVIN, television corr.; b. N.Y.C., July 10, 1931; s. Irving and Jeanette Tuckner; B.A., Columbia Coll., 1956; M.S. (Univ. fellow), Columbia U., 1957. Staff and mag. writer New York Times, 1956-63; writer, fgn. corr. NBC-TV, N.Y.C., Vietnam, 1964-68; corr. ABC-TV, Chgo. bur., fgn. corr. London bur., Vietnam, Laos, Cambodia, India, Pakistan, Bangledesh, bur. chief, Hong Kong, 1969-73, bur. chief, television-radio chief corr. So. Africa bur., Johannesburg, 1977—. Served with USN, 1952-54. Recipient Emmy award nomination for reporting while wounded in Vietnam, 1968, award for Bangledesh documentary, 1971. Mem. Fgn. Corrs. Club S. Africa. Contbr. articles to anthologies. Office: So Africa Bur ABC Exec Centre 54 Sauer St Johannesburg South Africa

TUCKSON, COLEMAN REED, dental educator; b. Washington, Sept. 2, 1923; s. Coleman Reed and Estelle (Keeves) T.; D.D.S., Howard U., 1947; M.Sc., U. Pa., 1953; m. Evelyn Burton, Nov. 4, 1949; children—Reed Vaughn, Wayne Bruce. Intern, Freedman's Hosp., Washington, 1947-48; faculty Howard U. Coll. Dentistry, 1948—, prof., 1964—; mem. teaching staff intern and residency program Dental Corps, USAF, 1960—. Active local Boy Scouts Am. Served with USAF, 1960; lt. col. Res. Fellow Am. Acad. Oral Roentgenology; mem. Am. Dental Assn., D.C., Robert T. Freeman dental socs., Omicron Kappa Upsilon (past pres., sec.-treas. Pi Pi chpt.), Alpha Phi Alpha. Democrat. Episcopalian (past mem. vestry). Home: 7827 13th St NW Washington DC 20012 Office: 600 W St NW Washington DC 20001

TUCKWELL, BARRY EMMANUEL, musician; b. Melbourne, Australia, Mar. 5, 1931; s. Charles Robert and Elizabeth (Hill) T.; grad. Sydney (Australia) State Conservatorium; children by previous marriage—David Michael, Jane Madeleine; m. Hilary Jane Warburton; 1 son, Thomas James. With Melbourne, Sydney, Halle, Scottish Nat. and Bournemouth symphony orchs., 1947-55; solo French horn London Symphony Orch., 1955-68; tchr., soloist and chamber music player, 1968—; mem. Chamber Music Soc. of Lincoln Center, N.Y.C., 1974—; dir. London Symphony Orch. Ltd., 1957-68, chmn., 1961-68; prof. French horn Royal Acad. Music, 1962-74; mem. mgmt. com. London Symphony Orch. Trust, 1963-68; mem. Tuckwell Wind Ensemble, Tuckwell Wind Quintet, Tuckwell Horn Quartet; mem. faculty congregation arts Dartmouth Coll., 1968-69, ann. French horn workshop Fla. State U., Claremont Music Festival, 1970-71; guest prof. Harvard U., others; guest condr. Phila. Symphony Chamber Orch., 1979; rec. artist for RCA, CRI, Angel, London, Argo. Decorated Order Brit. Empire, 1965; recipient Harriet Cohen Meml. medal for soloists, 1968. Mem. Internat. Horn Soc. (pres. 1969-77); hon. mem. Royal Acad. Music, Guildhall Sch. Art and Music. Author: Playing the Horn, 1978; editor Horn Lit. for G. Schirmer, Inc. Office: care Columbia Artists Mgmt 165 W 57th St New York NY 10019*

TUDOR, ANTONY, dancer, choreographer; b. London, Eng., Apr. 4, 1908; studied dancing under Marie Rambert. Came to U.S., 1938. Made debut as dancer with Ballet Rambert, London, 1930, dir. and choreographer, 1930-38; with Sadler-Wells Ballet, 1931-36; choreographer to Royal Opera House Covent Garden, 1935-38; formed London Ballet; joined Am. Ballet Theatre 1939, collaborated, 1956, asso. dir., 1974—; ballet dir. Met. Opera House, 1957-63; artistic dir. Royal Swedish Ballet, 1963-64; producer ballets in Japan, Sweden, Greece, Can.; notable choreographic works include Dark Elegies, Pillar of Fire, Lilac Garden, Offenbach in the Underworld, Dim Lustre, Romeo and Juliet, Undertow, Success Story (in Hollywood Pinafore), The Leaves Are Fading, 1975. Recipient Carina Ari gold medal, 1973; Dance Mag. award, 1974. Office: 113 E 30th St New York NY 10016*

TUDOR, DAVID, musician, composer; b. Phila., Jan. 20, 1926; student organ and theory with H. William Hawke, Phila., piano with Josef Martin and Irma Wolpe, Phila. and N.Y.C., composition and analysis with Srefan Wolpe, N.Y.C. Organist, Swarthmore Coll., 1944-48; instr. piano Contemporary Music Sch., N.Y.C., 1948-51; pianist in residence, instr. piano Black Mountain Coll., 1951-53; lectr., instr. piano Internat. Vacation Courses for New Music, Darmstadt, Germany, 1956-61; creative asso. State U. N.Y. at Buffalo, 1965-66; guest lectr. U. Calif. at Davis, 1967, Mills Coll., 1967-68; performer contemporary piano music throughout Europe and U.S., including premieres, also compositions written for him, 1948—; exhbns. include Variations (with Robert Rauschenberg, Jasper Johns, Jean Tinguely, Niki De Saint-Phalle) Am. Center, Paris, 1961, Flourescent Sound (with Robert Rauschenberg, Steve Paxton) Moderna Museet, Stockholm, 1964, 9 Evenings: Theater and Engring., 26th St. Armory, N.Y.C., 1966, Reunion (with David Behrman, John Cage, Lowell Cross, Marcel Duchamp, Gordon Mumma) U. Toronto, 1968, A Project of Experiments in Art and Tech. Inc. (with Robert Breer, Frosty Myers, Fujiko Nakaya, David Tudor, Robert Whitman) Pepsi Pavilion, Expo '70, Osaka, Japan, Video/Laser III (with Lowell Cross, Carson Jeffries) U. Iowa Mus. Art, Iowa City, 1973, Rainforest 4: Ft.

Worth Art Mus., 1975, Los Angeles County Mus., 1975, De Saisset Art Mus., Santa Clara, Calif., 1975, Contemporary Arts Mus., Houston, 1975, Walker Art Center, Mpls., 1976, Espace Pierre Cardin, 1976, Carpenter Center for Visual Arts, Harvard U., 1976, Brazos River: A Television Exhibition (with Viola Farber, Robert Rauschenberg) Ft. Worth Art Mus., 1976-77; rec. artist for Time Records, CBS Records, Odyssey, Disques Vega, Wergo, Cramps Records. Composer: Bandoneon Factorial, 1966; Rainforest, 1968; Video III, 1968; Video/Laser I, 1969; 4 Pepsi Pieces, 1970; Untitled, 1972; Monobird, 1972; Microphone 1-9, 1973; Laser Bird, 1973; Rainforest 4, 1973; Toneburst, 1974; Pulsers, 1975; Forest Speech, 1976; Video Pulsers, 1977; Weatherings, 1978. Address: Gate Hill Rd Stony Point NY 10980

TUELL, JACK MARVIN, clergyman; b. Tacoma, Nov. 14, 1923; s. Frank Harry and Anne Helen (Bertelson) T.; B.S., U. Wash., 1947, LL.B., 1948; S.T.B., Boston U., 1955; M.A., U. Puget Sound, 1961; D.D., Pacific Sch. Religion, 1966; m. Marjorie Ida Beadles, June 17, 1946; children—Jacqueline, Cynthia, James. Admitted to Wash. bar, 1948; practice law with firm Holte & Tuell, Edmonds, Wash., 1948-50; ordained to ministry Methodist Ch., 1953; pastor Grace Meth. Ch., Everett, Wash., 1950-52, South Tewksbury Meth. Ch., Tewksbury, Mass., 1952-55, Lakewood Meth. Ch., Tacoma, 1955-61; dist. supt. Puget Sound dist. Meth. Ch., Everett, 1961-67; pastor 1st United Meth. Ch., Vancouver, Wash., 1967-72; bishop United Meth. Ch., Portland, Oreg., 1972—. Mem. gen. conf. United Meth. Ch., 1964, 66, 68, 70, 72. Pres., Tacoma U.S.O., 1959-61, Vancouver YMCA, 1968; v.p. Ft. Vancouver Seamens Center, 1969-72; vice chmn. Vancouver Human Relations Commn., 1970-72; pres. Oreg. Council Alcohol Problems, 1972-76. Trustee U. Puget Sound, 1961-73, Vancouver Meml. Hosp., 1967-72, Alaska Meth. U., Anchorage, 1972—, Willamette U., Salem, Oreg., 1972—, Willamette View Manor, Portland, 1972—, Rogue Valley Manor, Medford, Oreg., 1972-76; pres. nat. div. bd. global ministries United Meth. Ch., 1972-76, pres. ecumenical and interreligious concerns div., 1976—. Jacob Sleeper fellow, 1955. Rotarian. Author: The Organization of the United Methodist Church, 1970. Home: 15088 SW Trillium Ln Beaverton OR 97005 Office: 1505 SW 18th Ave Portland OR 97201

TUERKHEIMER, FRANK MITCHEL, lawyer, educator; b. N.Y.C., July 27, 1939; s. Max and Elisabeth Regina (Leva) T.; B.A., Columbia, 1960; LL.B., N.Y. U., 1963; m. Barbara Linda Wolfson, Dec. 14, 1968; children—Deborah Beth, Alan Michael. Admitted to N.Y. bar, Wis. bar; asst. U.S. Atty., So. dist. N.Y., 1965-70; prof. law U. Wis. at Madison, 1970—; asso. spl. prosecutor Watergate Spl. Prosecution Force, Washington, 1973-75, cons. to spl. prosecutor, 1975—; atty. Natural Resources Def. Council, 1976-77; U.S. atty. for Western dist. Wis., 1977—. Maxwell Sch. Pub. Service fellow, 1964-65. Jewish. Contbr. articles to legal jours. Home: 122 Quarterdeck Dr Madison WI 53705

TUFTE, VIRGINIA JAMES, educator; b. Nebr.; d. M.D. and Sarah Elizabeth (Bartee) James; A.B., U. Nebr.; M.A., Ph.D., UCLA; m. Edward E. Tufte; 1 son, Edward R. Asst. prof. English, U. So. Calif., Los Angeles, 1964-68, asso. prof., 1969-74, prof., 1974—. Author: Grammar as Style, 1971; Poetry of Marriage: The Epithalamium in Europe and Its Development in England, 1970. Editor: High Wedlock Then Be Honoured, an Anthology of Nuptial Poems, 1970; (with Barbara Myerhoff) Changing Images of the Family, 1979. Office: Dept English U Southern Calif Los Angeles CA 90007

TUFTS, ELEANOR MAY, art historian; b. Exeter, N.H.; d. James Arthur and Hazel (Weinbeck) Tufts; B.S., Simmons Coll., 1949; M.A., Harvard U., 1957; Ph.D., N.Y. U., 1971. Sec., Harvard U., 1949-50; exec. sec. Boston U. travel courses, 1950-56; dir. program devel. Council on Internat. Ednl. Exchange, N.Y.C., 1957-60; asso. sec. World U. Service, N.Y.C., 1960-64; asst. prof. art history U. Bridgeport, 1964-66; asso. prof. So. Conn. State Coll., New Haven, 1966-74; prof. So. Meth. U., Dallas, 1974—, chmn. div. fine arts, 1974-78. Trustee, Dallas Mus. Fine Arts, 1975—. Nat. Endowment Humanities grantee, summer 1974. Mem. AAUP (v.p. 1972-74) 75-76), Coll. Art Assn. (nat. bd. 1979—), Am. Soc. Hispanic Art Hist. Studies, Renaissance Soc. Am. Democrat. Club: Town and Gown. Author: Our Hidden Heritage: Five Centuries of Women Artists, 1974. Office: Dept Art History So Methodist Univ Dallas TX 75275

TUHOLSKI, JAMES M., pharm. co. exec.; b. Henning, Tenn., 1924; M.D., U. Tenn., 1948. Intern, U.S. Naval Hosp., St. Albans, N.Y., 1948; resident in pediatrics U. Tenn., Memphis, 1949-51, St. Louis Children's Hosp., 1953-54; practice medicine specializing in pediatrics, Memphis, 1954-56; mem. staff Le Bonheur Children's Hosp., Memphis, 1954-56; with Mead Johnson & Co., 1956—, v.p. product devel., 1960, pres. Mead Johnson Labs., 1961-66, exec. v.p., 1966-68, pres., chief exec. officer, 1968-77; v.p. Bristol Myers Co., N.Y.C., 1970-77, exec. v.p., 1977—. Home: 22 Stepping Stone Ln Greenwich CT 06830 Office: Bristol Myers Co 345 Park Ave New York City NY 10022

TUITE, JOHN FRANCIS, plant pathologist; b. Bronx, N.Y., Nov. 23, 1927; s. Patrick and Fanny (Donohue) T.; B.A., Hunter Coll., 1951; M.S., U. Minn., 1953, Ph.D., 1956; m. Camille Maloof, July 5, 1952; children—Kathy, Frances, Brian, Ann, Paul, Clare. Asst. prof. plant pathology Purdue U., West Lafayette, Ind., 1956-60, asso. prof., 1961-69, prof., 1970—. Served with U.S. Army, 1946-47. Mem. Am. Phytopath. Soc. (pres. N.Central br.), Mycol. Soc. Am., Soc. Indsl. Microbiology, Sigma Xi. Roman Catholic. Author: Plant Pathological Methods: Fungi and Bacteria, 1969. Home: 212 Quincy St West Lafayette IN 47906 Office: Dept Botany and Plant Pathology Purdue Univ Lafayette IN 47907

TUITE, JOSEPH PATRICK, clergyman, educator; b. Newark, July 31, 1914; s. Patrick J. and Ann (Sheridan) T.; B.A., Seton Hall Coll., 1937; grad. Immaculate Conception Sem., 1941; Ph.D., St. John U., 1954. Ordained priest Roman Cath. Ch., 1941; tchr. classical langs. Seton Hall Prep. Sch., 1941-42, 46-59; comptroller Seton Hall Coll., 1942-43; mem. Archdiocesan Ednl. Commn., Newark, 1954-59; supt. schs. Archdiocese of Newark, 1959-72; episcopal vicar/sec. edn. Archdiocese Newark, 1972-76; prof. Seton Hall U. Sch. Edn., South Orange, N.J., 1972—, dir. budget, 1973—; mem. Archdiocese Newark Bd. Edn., 1972-76. Served to capt. Chaplains Corps, AUS 1943-46. Address: Seton Hall U South Orange NJ 07079

TUKEY, JOHN WILDER, scientist, educator; b. New Bedford, Mass., June 16, 1915; s. Ralph H. and Adah M. (Tasker) T.; Sc.B., Brown U., 1936, Sc.M., 1937, D.Sc., 1965; A.M., Princeton, 1938, Ph.D., 1939; Sc.D. (hon.), Case Inst. Tech., 1962, Yale, 1968, U. Chgo., 1969; m. Elizabeth L. Rapp, July 19, 1950. Faculty math. Princeton, 1939-65, prof., 1950-65, prof. statistics, 1965—, Donner prof. sci., 1976—, chmn. dept. statistics, 1965-70, research asso. fire control research office, Princeton, 1941-45; Hitchcock prof. U. Cal. at Berkeley, 1975. Mem. tech. staff Bell Labs., 1945—, asst. dir. research communication principles, 1958-62, asso. exec. dir. research, 1961—. Mem. NRC, 1951-60, Pres.'s Sci. Adv. Com., 1960-63, Pres.'s Air Quality Adv. Bd., 1968-71, U.S. del. UN Conf. on Human Environment, Stockholm, 1972, Nat. Adv. Com. on Oceans and Atmosphere, 1975—. Bd. fellows, mem. corp. Brown U., 1974—. Guggenheim fellow, 1949-50; Center Advanced Study in Behavioral Scis. fellow, 1957-58. Recipient Nat. medal of sci., 1973. Fellow A.A.A.S., Am. Statis. Assn., Am. Soc. Quality Control, Inst. Math. Statistics, N.Y. Acad. Sci., Ops. Research Soc. Am., Royal Statis. Soc. (hon.); mem. Am. Math. Soc., Assn. Computing Machinery, Biometric Soc., Math. Assn. Am., Nat. Acad. Scis., Am. Philos. Soc., Am. Acad. Arts and Scis., Internat. Statis. Inst., Sigma Xi. Club: Cosmos. Author: Denumerability and Convergence in Topology, 1940; (with Cochran and Mosteller) Statistical Problems of the Kinsey Report, 1954; (with R.B. Blackman) The Measurement of Power Spectra from the Point of View of Communications Engineering, 1958. Contbr. articles to sci. tech. publs. Office: Dept Statistics Princeton U Princeton NJ 08540 also Bell Labs 600 Mountain Ave Murray Hill NJ 07974*

TULL, DAVID ADOLPHUS, physician, hosp. adminstr.; b. Phila., Oct. 15, 1933; s. Dewey H. and Beulah Mae (Lewis) T.; B.A., Lincoln U., Oxford, Pa., 1954; M.D., Howard U., 1961; m. Maxine F. Webb, Sept. 6, 1959 (div. 1974); children—Heidi M., David Adolphus, II, Leilani M. Intern, St. Rita Hosp., Lima, Ohio, 1962; resident in phys. medicine and rehab. VA Hosp., Phila., 1963-66, mem. phys. medicine and rehab. staff, 1966-69, asst. chief phys. medicine and rehab., 1967-69, chief phys. medicine and rehab., 1969-71; chief of staff VA Hosp., Ft. Howard, Md., 1972-73, VA Hosp., Pitts., 1973-76; dir. VA Hosp., Tuskegee, Ala., 1976—; asst. phys. medicine and rehab. dept. U. Pa., 1966-69, asso., 1969-71; prof. clin. medicine dept. phys. therapy Tuskegee Inst., 1977—; adj. asst. prof. hosp. and health adminstrn., public and allied health U. Ala., Birmingham, 1977—, mem. V.A. Deans Com., 1976—; Ala. VA rep. Governing Body of S.E. Ala. Health Systems; mem. mgmt. bd. John A. Andrew Hosp., Tuskegee Inst.; lectr., speaker in field. Chmn. Combined Fed. Campaign, Tuskegee, Ala. area, 1976-78; hon. chmn. United Negro Coll. Fund, 1977. Served with U.S. Army, 1954-56; Korea. Named Hon. Adm., Ala. Navy, 1976, Hon. Lt. Col. Aide-de-Camp, Ala. Militia, 1976, hon. mem. Lt. Gov.'s Staff, State Ala., 1978, Hon. Citizen of New Orleans, 1978; recipient award for loyal and devoted services to disabled vets. DAV of Ga., 1977, cert. appreciation Optimist Club Tuskegee, 1977, proclamation Martin Luther King, Jr. Community Players, New Brunswick, N.J., 1978, cert. appreciation Carver dist. Boy Scouts Am., 1978, Tuskegee Lions Club, 1978. Mem. AMA, Nat. Med. Assn., Am. Acad. Phys. Medicine and Rehab., Am. Congress Rehab. Medicine, Pa. Soc. Phys. Medicine and Rehab., Omega Psi Phi. Republican. Methodist. Home: Cottage 63 VA Med Center Tuskegee AL 36083 Office: VA Med Center Tuskegee AL 36083. *A copy of Kipling's poem "If" is always pasted on my bathroom mirror so that it will be the last thing I see at night and the first thing I see in the morning. It has guided me throughout my adult life.*

TULL, DONALD STANLEY, educator; b. Cross Timbers, Mo., Oct. 28, 1924; s. Raymond Edgar and Ethel (Stanley) T.; S.B., U. Chgo., 1948, M.B.A., 1949, Ph.D., 1956; m. Marjorie Ann Dobbie, May 15, 1948; children—Susan Margaret, David Dobbie, Brooks William. Analyst, U.S. Steel Corp., 1949-50; instr. U. Wash., 1950-52; mgr. adminstrn. N.Am. Aviation, 1954-61; prof. mktg. Calif. State U., Fullerton, 1961-67, dean Sch. Bus. Adminstrn. and Econs., 1966-67; prof. mktg. Coll. Mgmt. and Bus. U. Oreg., 1967—, chmn. dept. mktg., transp. and bus. environment, 1967-69, 73—. Served to lt. (j.g.) USNR, 1943-46. Mem. AAUP (exec. com. 1968-69), Am. Mktg. Assn., Am. Statis. Assn., Am. Econ. Assn., Beta Gamma Sigma. Author: (with P.E. Green) Research for Marketing Decisions, 1978; (with G.S. Albaum) Survey Research, 1973; (with D.I. Hawkins) Marketing Research: Measurement Method, 1979. Contbr. articles to profl. jours. Home: 2580 Highland Oaks Eugene OR 97405

TULL, E. DON, indsl. mfg. exec.; b. Columbus, Ind., Aug. 28, 1906; s. Elmer and Ethel (Rockwell) T.; m. 2d, Joyce Skaggs; children (by previous marriage)—Kenneth Wayne, Frank David. With Cummins Engine Co., Inc., Columbus, 1928—, succesively various positions in shop, factory supt., supt. and asst. works mgr., mgr. mfg., v.p. personnel and plant, v.p., gen. mgr., 1928-55, exec. v.p., 1955-60, pres., 1960-69, vice chmn. exec. com., 1969—, also dir.; dir. Irwin Mgmt. Co., Columbus. Trustee, Asso. Colls. Ind.; bd. dirs. Cummins Engine Found. Mem. Ind. C. of C. Baptist. Kiwanian. Club: Paradise Valley Country (Scottsdale, Ariz.). Home: 3980 Waycross Dr PO Box 841 Columbus IN 47201 Office: 301 Washington St Columbus IN 47201

TULLIO, LOUIS JOSEPH, city ofcl.; b. Erie, Pa., May 17, 1917; s. Anthony and Ersilia (Nardone) T.; B.S., Holy Cross Coll., 1939; M.Ed., Boston U., 1957; m. Mary Cecelia McHale, June 21, 1941; children—Betty Ann (Mrs. Elsworth), June Cecelia (Mrs. Geisler), Marilyn Lou. Former high sch. tchr., asst. to pres. Gannon Coll.; asst. dir. health and phys. edn. Erie City Sch. Dist., 1957-60, sec., bus. mgr., 1960-65; mem. exec. com. Erie County Democratic Com.; mayor Erie, 1966—. Bd. dirs. Harborcreek Sch. for Boys, Little Gridders of Erie, Booker T. Washington Center; trustee Erie Library and Mus. Served to lt. USNR, 1943-45. Recipient Profl. Honor award Pa. Health, Phys. Edn. and Recreation; named All-Am. Coach of Year. Roman Catholic. Office: Office of Mayor City Hall Erie PA 17101*

TULLIS, EDWARD LEWIS, bishop; b. Cin., Mar. 9, 1917; s. Ashar Spence and Priscilla (Daugherty) T.; A.B., Ky. Wesleyan Coll., 1939, L.H.D., 1975; B.D., Louisville Presbyn. Theol. Sem., 1947; D.D., Union Coll., Barbourville, Ky., 1954, Wofford Coll., 1976; D.Hum., Claflin Coll., 1976; m. Mary Jane Talley, Sept. 25, 1937; children—Frank Loyd, Jane Allen (Mrs. William Nelson Offutt IV). Ordained to ministry Methodist Ch., 1941; service in chs., Frenchburg, Ky., 1937-39, Lawrenceburg, Ky., 1939-44; asso. pastor 4th Ave. Meth. Ch., Louisville, 1944-47, Irvine, Ky., 1947-49; asso. sec. ch. extension sect. Bd. Missions, Meth. Ch., Louisville, 1949-52; pastor First Meth. Ch., Frankfort, Ky., 1952-61, First Meth. Ch., Ashland, Ky., 1961-72; resident bishop United Meth. Ch., Columbia, S.C., 1972—; instr. Bible, Ky. Wesleyan Coll., 1947-48; instr. Louisville Presbyn. Theol. Sem., 1949-52. Mem. Meth. Gen. Conf., 1956, 60, 64, 66, 68, 70, 72, Southeastern Jurisdictional Conf., 1952, 56, 60, 64, 68, 72; bd. mgrs. Bd. Missions, 1962-72; mem. bd. discipleship, 1972—. Chaplain, Ky. Gen. Assembly, 1952-61; chmn. Frankfort Com. Human Rights, 1956-61; chmn. Mayor's Advisory Com. Human Relations, Ashland, 1968-72. Pres. bd. dirs. Magee Christian Edn. Found.; trustee Emory U., Alaska Meth. U., Ky. Wesleyan Coll. Recipient Outstanding Citizen award Frankfort VFW, 1961, Mayor's award for outstanding service. Ashland, 1971. Kiwanian. Contbr. articles to religious jours. Home: 741 Albion Rd Columbia SC 29205 Office: 1420 Lady St Columbia SC 29201

TULLIS, RICHARD BARCLAY, communication and info. handling equipment mfg. exec.; b. Western Springs, Ill., July 12, 1913; s. Lauren Barclay and Izelah (Gilmore) T.; A.B., Principia Coll., Elsah, Ill., 1934; m. Chaille Handy, Aug. 17, 1935; children—Sarah (Mrs. Charles de Barcza), Barclay J., Garner H. With Miller Printing Machinery Co., Pitts., 1938-56, pres., 1952-56; with Harris Corp., Cleve., 1956—, exec. v.p., 1957-61, pres., 1961-72, chief exec. officer, 1968-78, chmn., 1972-78, chmn. exec. com., 1978—, also dir.; dir. Gen. Tire & Rubber Co., Cleve. Electric Illuminating Co.; trustee First Union Real Estate Investments, Cleve. Trustee Principia Coll., Elsah, Ill., Musical Arts Assn., Cleve., Civic Music Assn., Melbourne, Fla. Home: 221 Indian Harbor Rd Vero Beach FL 32960 Melbourne FL 32919

TULLOCH, GEORGE SHERLOCK, JR., elec. distbn. co. exec.; b. Bklyn., Aug. 18, 1932; s. George Sherlock and Dorothy (Gooch) T.; B.A. in History, Amherst Coll., 1954; LL.B., U. Mich., 1959; m. Edyth Benson Woodroofe, June 16, 1956; children—Michael, Daniel, Lindsay. Admitted to N.Y. bar, 1960; asso. Breed, Abbott & Morgan, N.Y.C., 1959-66; sec., asst. gen. counsel Westvaco Corp., N.Y.C., 1966-78; sec., gen. counsel, dir. Graybar Electric Co., N.Y.C., 1978—; dir. Blue Cross and Blue Shield Greater N.Y. Mem. North Shore Republican Club, 1966—. Bd. dirs., pres. Stony Wold Found. Served to 1st lt. USMCR, 1954-56. Mem. Am. Bar Assn., Assn. Bar City N.Y., Am. Soc. Corp. Secs., Am. Arbitration Assn. (panelist), Am. Mgmt. Assn., Practicing Law Inst. Home: 58 Prospect Ave Sea Cliff NY 11579 Office: 420 Lexington Ave New York NY 10017

TULLOCK, GORDON, educator; b. Rockford, Ill., Feb. 13, 1922; s. George and Helen T.; J.D., U. Chgo., 1947; postdoctoral fellow U. Va., 1958-59. Fgn. service officer, China, 1947-56; asst. prof. U. S.C., 1959-60, asso. prof., 1960-62; asso. prof. U. Va., Charlottesville, 1962-67; prof. econs. and polit. sci. Rice U., Houston, 1967-68; prof. econs. and pub. choice Va. Poly. Inst. and State U., Blacksburg, 1968-72, Univ. Distinguished prof. econs. and pub. choice, 1972—, editorial dir. Center for Study of Pub. Choice, 1968—; dir. Dodger Products, Eldora, Iowa. Mem. Am. So. (pres. elect), Western econ. assns., Am. Polit. Sci. Assn., Pub. Choice Soc. (sec. 1965—), Assn. for Asian Studies, Brit. Interplanetary Soc. Author: (with J.M. Buchanan) The Calculus of Consent, 1962; The Organization of Inquiry, 1965; Towards a Mathematics of Politics, 1967; Private Wants, Public Means, 1970; The Logic of the Law, 1971; The Social Dilemma, 1974; (with Richard B. McKenzie) The New World of Economics, 1975. Home: 4 West Ridge Dr Blacksburg VA 24060

TULLOS, JOHN BAXTER, banker; b. Morton, Miss., Dec. 3, 1915; s. William Baxter and Mell (Roberts) T.; student Miss. Coll., 1934, Am. Inst. Bank, Jackson, Miss., 1936-40, Sch. Banking South, La. State U., 1955-57; m. Maxine Stone, Sept. 20, 1941. With First Nat. Bank, Jackson, 1935—, now exec. v.p., cashier; sec.-treas. First Capital Corp. Faculty, Sch. Banking South La. State U. First pres. Miss. Young Bankers Assn.; mem. Miss. Valley World Trade Council, 1965—; mem. La.-Miss. Regional Export Expansion Council div. U.S. Dept. Commerce, 1967-74; vice-chmn. Ala.-Miss. Dist. Export Council, 1975—; treas. Col. Money in Miss. Assn., 1965—. Former chmn. budget com. United Givers Fund. Served with AUS, World War II. Mem. Miss. Bankers Assn. (past chmn. operations/automation com.). Methodist. Lion. Clubs: Jackson Country; Capitol City Petroleum. Home: 8 Eastbrooke Jackson MS 39216 Office: PO Box 291 Jackson MS 39205

TULLY, ALBERT JULIAN, lawyer; b. Laurel, Miss., July 10, 1911; s. Albert Jefferson and Julia (Dahmer) T.; J.D., U. Ala., 1935; m. Jane Silverwood Wildman, Dec. 29, 1934; children—Albert Julian, Jane Tully Dunnavant. Admitted to Ala. bar, 1935; practice law, Mobile, Ala., 1935—; U.S. dist. atty. So. Dist. Ala., 1943-48; partner firm Holberg, Tully, Holberg & Danley, and predecessors, 1938—. Pres. Cawthon Real Estate Corp., Mobile, 1970—, also dir. Chancellor, Episcopal Diocese Central Gulf Coast, 1971, 73, 75, 77, 79, vice chancellor, 1972, 74, 76, 78, pres. standing com., 1974; chmn. bd. trustees Wilmer Hall; bd. dirs. So. region Boys Clubs Am., 1975-76, Mobile Mental Health Center, South Ala. chpt. Arthritis Found. Recipient Man and Boy award, Bronze and Silver Keystone awards Boys' Clubs Am. Mem. Am., Ala., Mobile (pres. 1978-79) bar assns., Mobile C. of C. (dir. 1976-78), Navy League, Internat. Trade Club (pres. chpt. 1966-71), Ala. Wildlife Fedn. (past dir., v.p.), Mobile County Wildlife and Conservation Assn. (past pres., chmn. bd.), Mobile Art Assn., Internat. Oceanographic Found. Episcopalian (lay reader, vestryman, treas., past sr. warden; Distinguished Service award Episcopal Diocese Central Gulf Coast 1974). Kiwanian (internat. trustee 1953-61, internat. pres. 1959-60; past trustee, v.p. found.). Club: Isle Dauphine Country (pres. 1964-68). Home: 1809 Spring Hill Ave Mobile AL 36607 Office: Commerce Bldg Mobile AL 36602

TULLY, ANDREW FREDERICK, JR., writer; b. Southbridge, Mass., Oct. 24, 1914; s. Andrew F. and Amelia (Mason) T.; grad. high sch.; m. Mary Dani, Apr. 15, 1939 (div.); children—Martha Hardy, Mary Elizabeth, Sheila, Andrew Frederick III, Mark; m. 2d, Barbara Witchell, Sept. 5, 1960 (div.); m. 3d, Mary Ellen Wood, Dec. 19, 1964; 1 son, John Spaulding. Reporter, Worcester (Mass.) Post, 1936-38, Southbridge Evening News, 1933-36; editor, owner Southbridge Press, weekly, 1939-42; war corr. Boston Traveller, ETO, 1944-45; rewrite, feature N.Y. World Telegram, 1945-47; freelance, 1947-48; Washington bur. Scripps-Howard Newspapers, 1948-61; Washington columnist McNaught Syndicate. Dir., United Dairy Equipment Co., West Chester, Pa. Recipient Ernie Pyle award for series on Soviet Russia, 1955; Headliners award, 1956. Mem. White House Corrs. Assn. Clubs: Overseas Writers, Fed. City, Nat. Press (Washington). Author: Era of Elegance, 1947; Treasury Agent, 1958; A Race of Rebels, 1960; When They Burned the White House, 1961; CIA: The Inside Story, 1962; Capitol Hill, 1962; Berlin: Story of a Battle, 1963; Supreme Court, 1963; (with Milton Britten) Where Did Your Money Go?, 1964; The FBI's Most Famous Cases, 1965; The Time of the Hawk, 1967; White Tie and Dagger, 1967; The Super Spies, 1969; The Secret War Against Dope, 1973; The Brahmin Arrangement, 1974; This is the FBI, 1979; also articles in mags. Address: 2104 48th St NW Washington DC 20007

TULLY, DARROW, publisher; b. Charleston, W.Va., Feb. 27, 1932; s. William Albert and Dora (McCann) T.; student Purdue U., 1951; B.A. in Journalism, St. Joseph's Coll., 1972; Ph.D. in Journalism (hon.), Calumet Coll., 1975; m. Patricia Ann Fellner, Oct. 11, 1974; children—Bonnie Tully Paul, Michael Andrew. Vice pres., gen. mgr. Sta.-WDSM-AM-FM-TV, Duluth, Minn., 1956-59; bus. mgr. Duluth Herald & News Tribune, 1960-62; gen. mgr. St. Paul Dispatch & Pioneer Press, 1962-66; pub. Gary (Ind.) Post-Tribune, 1966-73; v.p., pub. Wichita (Kans.) Eagle & Beacon, 1973-75; pres., San Francisco Newspaper Agy., 1975-78; v.p., pub. Ariz. Republic & Phoenix Gazette, 1978—; trustee Calumet Coll., William Allen White Found. at U. Kans. Bd. dirs. NCCJ, Phoenix, Phoenix Symphony, Valley Shakespeare Theatre, Phoenix. Mem. Am. Newspaper Pubs. Assn. (vice chmn. labor and personnel com.), Ariz. Newspaper Assn., Phoenix C. of C. (dir.), Sigma Delta Chi. Author: Minority Representation in the Media, 1968. Home: 7201 N Redledge Dr Paradise Valley AZ 85253 Office: 120 E Van Buren St Phoenix AZ 85004

TULLY, RICHARD LOWDEN, architect; b. New Orleans, May 24, 1911; s. Thomas James and Elizabeth (Lowden) T.; B.Arch., Ohio State U., 1937, spl. degree safety engring., 1943; m. Frances Louise Gross, Oct. 3, 1942; children—Mary Elizabeth Tully Pratt, Richard Lowden. Architect, Thomas J. Tully, Columbus, 1941-46; plant architect Denison Engring. Co., Columbus, 1941-46; partner F.H. Hobbs, Jr., architects, Columbus, 1966, Tully, Hobbs and partners, Columbus, 1966-72, Tully, Ames, Elzey & Thomas, 1972—. Mem. design adv. panel Gen. Services Adminstrn., 1970—; mem. Columbus Bldg. Com., 1961-63; mem. adv. com. Capitol Dist., 1969—; past chmn. Capitol Sq. Commn.; chmn. Land Use Planning-Devel. Com. Columbus, 1971—; chmn. Devel. Com. for Greater Columbus, 1975; vice chmn. Gov.'s Com. on Nuclear Emergency, 1968—. Vice pres., treas. Planned Parenthood Columbus, Architects Soc. Ohio Found. Recipient Silver Shovel award Am. Subcontractors Assn., 1976. Fellow AIA (past pres. Columbus chpt.), Architects Soc. Ohio (past pres.; Gold medal 1975); mem. Constrn. Specifications Inst. (past pres. Columbus), Newcomen Soc. N.Am., Delta Chi. Episcopalian (sr. warden). Clubs: University (past v.p.), Columbus Country, Golf (Columbus); Gator Creek Golf (Sarasota, Fla.). Prin. archtl. works include: Thurber Village Urban Renewal, Sci. Campus Ohio U., Athens, Federated Dept. Stores (Lazarus and Gold Circle), office bldg. Blue Cross Central Ohio, 7th Ave. Ch. of Christ (P.L.A.N. award; Architects Soc. Ohio award 1966), Ohio State U. married housing (AIA award), City Nat. Bank, Columbus (Man of Year award Columbus Citizen Jour. 1972). Home: 74 S Stanwood Rd Columbus OH 43209 Office: 222 E Town St Columbus OH 43215

TULLY, RICHARD WILLIAM, mgmt. cons.; b. Beaver Dam, Wis., Aug. 11, 1917; s. Williiam M. and Erma (Thiede) T.; B.S.C., Northwestern U., 1940, M.B.A., 1945; m. Helen M. Blidy, Sept. 21, 1940; 1 dau., Carolyn H. With Montgomery Ward & Co., 1941-43, Swift & Co., 1943-46; with Foote, Cone & Belding, 1946-70, sr. v.p., 1958-61, exec. v.p., 1961-66, chmn. bd., 1966-70; mgmt. cons., 1970-77; prin. R.W. Tully Co. Inc., Honolulu, 1977—. Lectr., Northwestern U. Sch. Bus., 1946-50. Served with AUS, 1944-45, 50-51. Club: Oahu Country (Honolulu). Address: 529 Ahina St Honolulu HI 96815

TULSKY, ALEX SOL, physician; b. Chgo., Aug. 10, 1911; s. Solomon and Clara (Tarnipolsky) T.; B.S., U. Ill., 1932, M.D., 1934; m. Klara Glottmann, July 20, 1948; children—Shayne Lee, Steven Henry, Asher Arthur, James Aaron. Intern, Michael Reese Hosp., Chgo., 1934-36, attending obstetrician and gynecologist, 1938—, pres. med. staff, 1962-64; house officer Bklyn. Jewish Hosp., 1937-38; pvt. practice, Chgo., 1938—; clin. asso. prof. obstetrics and gynecology Pritzker Sch. Medicine, U. Chgo., 1974—. Served to lt. col. M.C., AUS, 1941-45. Decorated Bronze Star. Mem. A.M.A., Chgo., Ill. med. socs., Chgo. Gynecol. Soc., Chgo. Inst. Medicine, Chgo. Oriental Inst., Pan Am. Med. Assn., Chgo. Soc. History Medicine. Home: 442 Wellington Ave Chicago IL 60657 Office: 111 N Wabash Ave Chicago IL 60602

TULSKY, FREDRIC NEAL, journalist; b. Chgo., Sept. 30, 1950; s. George and Helen (Mailick) T.; B.J. (Eugene Sharpe scholar), U. Mo., 1972; m. Kim Rennard, June 20, 1971; 1 son, Eric George. Reporter, Saginaw (Mich.) News, 1973-74, Port Huron (Mich.) Times-Herald, 1974-75; investigative reporter Jackson (Miss.) Clarion-Ledger, 1975-78, Los Angeles Herald Examiner, 1978-79, Phila. Inquirer, 1979—. Recipient numerous nat., regional awards, including Robert F. Kennedy Found. award, 1979, Heywood Broun award Newspaper Guild, 1978, Disting. Service medal Sigma Delta Chi, 1978, Public Service award AP Mng. Editors, 1978, Silver Gavel award Am. Bar Assn., 1979. Mem. Investigative Reporters and Editors, Reporters Com. for Freedom of Press, Kappa Tau Alpha. Office: 400 N Broad St Philadelphia PA 19101

TUMIN, DAVID ULLMAN, lawyer; b. Buffalo, Mar. 28, 1927; s. Leon Earl and Edith (Ullman) T.; A.B. cum laude, U. Colo., 1950; J.D., Yale U., 1954. Admitted to Fla. bar; asst. atty. gen. Fla., Tallahassee, 1954-58, 70, Miami, 1958-62; partner firm Rothstein and Tumin, Miami, 1962-66; chief litigation gen. counsel's office City of Jacksonville (Fla.), 1968-72; ct. exec. 4th Jud. Circuit, Jacksonville, 1972-75; partner firm Montgomery, Tumin, Buschman, Elrod & Showalter, Jacksonville, 1975-76; individual practice law, Jacksonville, 1976—; vis. prof. U. Miami Law Sch., Coral Gables, Fla., 1962-66. Served with USN, World War II. Mem. Am., Jacksonville bar assns., Am. Arbitration Assn., Fla. Bar, Am. Judicature Soc., Phi Beta Kappa, Phi Alpha Delta. Democrat. Jewish. Clubs: River, Bay Meadows Country, Masons, Shriners. Author: Authors' Comments, Fla. Rules Civil Procedure, 1967; Authors' Comments, Fla. Rules Appellate Procedure, 1967; Authors' Comments: Fla. Rules Criminal Procedure, 1967, 75; contbr. articles to profl. jours. Home: 3830 University Blvds Jacksonville FL 32216 Office: 1008 Blackstone Bldg Jacksonville FL 32202

TUMIN, MELVIN MARVIN, educator; b. Newark, Feb. 10, 1919; s. Robert M. and Rose (Yawitz) T.; student U. Newark, 1934-38; B.A., U. Wis., 1939, M.A., 1940; Ph.D. (fellow Social Sci. Research Council), Northwestern U., 1944; m. Sylvia Yarost, June 18, 1948; children—Jonathan Robert, Robert Zachary. Asst. prof. sociology and anthropology Wayne U., 1944-47; research dir. Mayor Detroit Com. Race Relations, 1945-47; prof. sociology and anthropology Princeton, 1947—; vis. prof. Columbia Tchrs. Coll., 1960-67. Cons. AID, 1962-69, U.S. Office Edn., 1963—, Ednl. Testing Service, 1970—; cons. ednl. research Anti-Defamation League, 1959—; visitor Inst. for Advanced Study, 1973-74. Adv. com. Pa. Bd. Edn., 1963-65; task force dir. Nat. Commn. on Causes and Prevention Violence, 1968-69; coroner, Mercer County, N.J., 1960-65. Trustee, Newark State Coll., 1970-72; bd. mgrs. N.J. Reformatory, 1961-64. Guggenheim fellow, 1969-70; Nat. Endowment for Humanities Faculty fellow, 1973-74. Mem. Am. Sociol. Assn., Eastern Sociol. Soc. (pres. 1967-68), Soc. for Study Social Problems (pres. 1966-67), Am. Anthrop. Assn., Phi Beta Kappa, Sigma Xi. Author: Social Life: Structure and Function, 1948; Caste in a Peasant Society, 1952; Segregation and Desegregation, 1957; Desegregation: Resistance and Readiness, 1958; An Inventory and Evaluation of Research and Theory in Anti-Semitism, 1960; Social Class and Social Change in Puerto Rico, 1961; Intergroup Attitudes of Youth and Adults in England, France and Germany, 1965; Quality and Equality in Education, 1966; Social Stratification, 1967; Crimes of Violence: Causes and Preventions, 1969; A Model for Evaluation of Effectiveness of Schools, 1969; Patterns of Society, 1973. Editor: Race and Intelligence, 1963; Comparative Race Relations, 1970; Readings on Social Stratification, 1970. Home: 119 Fitzrandolph Rd Princeton NJ 08540

TUMULTY, PHILIP ANTHONY, physician, educator; b. Jersey City, Nov. 4, 1912; s. Joseph Patrick and Mary Alicia (Byrne) T.; A.B. cum laude, Georgetown U., 1935; M.D., Johns Hopkins, 1940; m. Claire Cotter, Jan. 24, 1942; children—Claire, Philip, Cathy, Mary, Alicia. Intern medicine Johns Hopkins Hosp., 1940-41, asst. resident medicine, 1941-42, 45-46, resident physician, 1946-48, instr. medicine, 1946-49, asst. dir. med. clinics, 1948-50, dir. med. clinics, 1950-53, physician charge med.- surg. group clinic, 1948-53, chmn. pvt. med. service, 1955—, physician charge pvt. patient clinic, 1956—; asst. prof. medicine Johns Hopkins Sch. Medicine, 1949-51, asso. prof., 1951-53, 55-63, prof. medicine, 1963—, David J. Carver prof. medicine, 1974—; prof., dir. dept. medicine St. Louis U. Sch. Medicine, 1953-54; lectr. medicine Harvard Med. Sch., 1967; James Howard Means vis. physician Mass. Gen. Hosp.; physician-in-chief pro tem dept. medicine R.I. Hosp., 1957; cons. physician Balt. City Hosp.; spl. cons. medicine NIH; cons. medicine USPHS, VA Hosp., Balt., Walter Reed Gen. Hosp.; lectr. medicine Nat. Naval Med. Center, Bethesda. Served with AUS, 1942-45. Clin. fellow A.C.P., 1947-48. Diplomate Am. Bd. Internal Medicine. Mem. Am. Clin. and Climatol. Assn., Assn. Am. Physicians, Phi Beta Kappa, Alpha Omega Alpha. Home: 5001 St Albans Way Baltimore MD 21212 Office: 601 N Broadway Baltimore MD 21205

TUNE, TOMMY, musical theatre dir.; b. Wichita Falls, Tex., Feb. 28, 1939, s. Jim P. and Eva Mae (Clark) T.; student Lon Morris Jr. Coll., 1958-59; B.F.A., U. Houston, 1962. Dancer, Broadway musicals, 1965-68, including Baker St., A Joyful Noise, How Now Dow Jones; actor in films Hello Dolly, 1968, The Boyfriend, 1971; featured actor in Broadway prodn. Seesaw, 1974; choreographer for stage prodns. The Club, 1977, The Best Little Whorehouse in Texas, 1978. Recipient Antoinette Perry award, 1974, OBIE award, 1976; Drama Desk award, 1978. Mem. Dirs. Guild Am., Stage Soc. Dirs. and Choreographers, Actors Equity Assn. Office: Marvin Shulman Inc 890 Broadway New York NY 10003

TUNG, DAVID HSI HSIN, engr., educator; b. Hong Kong, Sept. 2, 1923; s. Hok Nin and Sheung-Yee (Ho) T.; B.S. in Civil Engring., Chiao Tung U., 1947; M.Civil Engring., Cornell U., 1950; Ph.D., U. Mich., 1953; m. Vera Gien, June 7, 1949; children—Leslie, Ronald Stanley, Elaine, Thomas. Came to U.S., 1948, naturalized, 1958. Designer, Giffels & Vallet, Detroit, 1950-52; sr. designer Hardesty & Hanover, N.Y.C., 1953-56; sr. designer Severud-Elstad-Krueger, N.Y.C., 1956-57; project mgr., project engr. Praeger-Kavanagh-Waterbury, N.Y.C., 1957-65; asso. prof. Cooper Union, N.Y.C., 1965-68, prof. civil engring., 1968—, chmn. curriculum dept. civil engring., 1974-76; cons. engr., 1965—. Fellow ASCE; mem. Sigma Xi, Tau Beta Pi, Chi Epsilon (hon.). Contbr. articles to profl. jours. Home: 461 Park Ave Rye NY 10580 Office: Cooper Union Cooper Sq New York NY 10003. *To guide and not to force; To be strong but not to suppress; To enlighten and not to saturate; To be intellectual but not to become intolerant.*

TUNGATE, MACE, JR., architect; b. Hearne, Tex., Dec. 17, 1916; s. Mace and Fanye (Stewart) T.; B.A., Rice U., 1938, B.S. in Architecture, 1939; m. Annie Laurie Mott, Sept. 14, 1940; 1 dau., Barbara Mott. Partner, Wirtz, Calhoun & Tungate, Architects, 1947-65, Wirtz, Calhoun, Tungate & Jackson, 1965-66, Calhoun, Tungate & Jackson, 1966-75, Calhoun, Tungate, Jackson & Dill, Houston, 1975—; mem. Tex. Bd. Archtl. Examiners, 1969-75. Served with AUS, 1944-46. Fellow AIA; mem. Tex. Soc. Architects (L.W. Pitts award 1973), Nat. Council Archtl. Registration Bds. (treas. 1975-78). Methodist. Club: Rotary of River Oaks (Houston). Home: 6234 Queenswood St Houston TX 77008 Office: Suite 600 7011 SW Freeway Houston TX 77074

TUNICK, STANLEY BLOCH, educator, accountant, lawyer; b. N.Y.C., Mar. 6, 1900; s. Abraham and Mary (Bloch) T.; A.B., Coll. City N.Y., 1919, M.B.A., 1923; J.D., St. Lawrence U., 1928; Ph.D., N.Y. U., 1938; m. Mildred P. Superior, June 26, 1942; children—Andrew Jeffrey, Richard David. Fgn. corr. export Loeb & Schoenfeld Co., 1919-20; chief accountant motion pictures Asso. Exhibitors, Inc., 1920-24; traveling auditor motion pictures Pathe Exchange, Inc., 1924-25; auditor Pathex, Inc., 1925-26; sr. accountant, staff C.P.A. firms, 1926-28; practicing C.P.A., 1928—, partner Tunick & Platkin, C.P.A.'s, 1941-71, cons., 1971-78; cons. firm Buchbinder, Stein, Tunick & Platkin, 1978—; tchr. bookkeeping Haaren High Sch., N.Y.C., 1928-31; admitted to N.Y. bar, 1929, practice law, 1929—; faculty Baruch Sch. Bus. and Public Adminstrn. of CCNY, 1931—, asst. prof., 1942-48, asso. prof., 1948-51, prof., 1951-62, prof. emeritus, 1962—, chmn. accountancy dept., 1956-62; dir., pres., treas., sec. Thirty Third Equities, Inc., Abstan Realty Corp.; v.p. Kamber Mgmt., Inc.; dir. Camp Loyaltown, Inc. Bd. dirs. City Coll. Fund, United Jewish Appeal Greater N.Y.; council of govs. Albert Einstein Coll. Medicine, Yeshiva U., 1979—; trustee Student Aid Assn. City Coll., 1958—; mem. nat. council Joint Distbn. Com., 1967—. Mem. N.Y. State Bd. C.P.A. Examiners, 1962-70, sec., 1964-65, vice chmn., 1965-67, chmn., 1967-69. Served as pvt., inf. U.S. Army, World War I; lt. col. C.E., AUS, World War II; lt. col. O.R.C. Decorated Army Commendation medal. C.P.A., N.Y., Pa., N.J., Fla. Recipient Townsend Harris medal Alumni City Coll., N.Y., 1966; medallion Baruch Sch. Alumni Soc., 1968, 125th Anniversary medal City Coll. N.Y., 1973; honored by Israel Bond Orgn., 1958, United Jewish Appeal, 1964, Fedn. Jewish Philanthropies, 1969, Albert Einstein Coll. Medicine, 1973, Am. Jewish Com., 1974, Town Club N.Y.-Fedn. Jewish Philanthropies, 1972. Mem. N.Y. State Soc. C.P.A.'s (award for contbn. to profession 1965, dir. 1948-51, treas. 1951-53, v.p. 1955-56, trustee disability ins. trust 1956—), Am. Inst. C.P.A.'s (nat. council 1967-70), Am. Accounting Assn., Am. Legion, Res. Officers Assn., A.A.U.P., Am. Arbitration Assn. (nat. panel arbitrators), Assn. Alumni City Coll. N.Y. (dir. 1952-58, hon. dir. 1959—, Alumni Service medal 1940), UN Assn., Internat. Brotherhood Magicians, Phi Beta Kappa, Phi Delta Kappa, Beta Gamma Sigma, Beta Alpha Psi, Delta Pi Epsilon, Iota Theta. Clubs: Accountants of America, Town of City of N.Y., The 100 (pres. 1972-73), N.Y. University. Author: (with E. Saxe) Fundamental Accounting-Theory and Practice, 1950, rev., 1956, 63; author of Accounting I, II, III. Collaborating editor: N.Y. Tax Course, 1939-62; cons. editor Fed. Tax Course Annual, 1952-63. Contbr. articles to profl. jours., mags. Home: 300 Seminole Ave Palm Beach FL 33480 Office: 1 Pennsylvania Plaza New York NY 10001

TUNIS, WILLIAM DAVID, univ. dean; b. Northampton, Mass., Nov. 11, 1924; B.S., U. Mass., 1949, Ph.D. in Entomology, 1959; M.S., U. Minn., 1951; m. 1973; 3 children. Asst. prof. entomology U. Conn., 1952-59; prof. entomology, U. Mass., dean admissions and records, now dir. undergrad. affairs Coll. Food and Natural Resources. Served with AUS, 1942-45. Mem. Nat. Assn. Coll. Admissions Counselors, Am. Assn. Collegiate Registrars and Admissions Officers. Address: care Stockbridge Hall Univ Mass Amherst MA 01003

TUNISON, EILEEN FERETIC, editor; b. N.Y.C., Aug. 31, 1949; d. Joseph Anthony and Eileen Helen (Sohl) Feretic; B.A., Fordham U., 1971; m. James F. Tunison, Sept. 25, 1971. Editor, Manpower Edn. Inst., N.Y.C., 1970-72, United Tech. Publs., L.I., N.Y., 1972—, Corporate Systems mag., 1975—, Office Products News, 1972—, editorial dir., 1978—, also editorial dir. Office Systems Group, 1978—. Recipient N.Y. Daily News award journalism, 1970. Mem. Am. Bus. Press Editors Assn., N.Y. Bus. Press Editors Assn. Co-author textbook secretarial procedures in electronics office, 1979. Home: 149-33 Hollywood Ave Flushing NY 11355 Office: 645 Stewart Ave Garden City NY 11530

TUNKS, FREDERICK EDWARD, public relations counselor; b. Center Point, Iowa, Feb. 2, 1928; s. Frederick Charles and Lovon Ann (Robertson) T.; B.S., Iowa State U., 1953; m. Ruth Ann Beckman, June 14, 1953; children—Brian, Lynne, Karen. News editor Independence (Iowa) Newspapers, 1953-54, Monticello (Iowa) Express, 1954-59; markets editor, news editor, mng. editor Feedstuffs mag., Miller Pub. Co., Mpls., 1959-66, editor, pub. Agri-Vertical unit, 1966-76, sr. editor company, 1976—, also chmn. photography, graphics and editorial coms.; pres. Tunks, Inc., Mpls. Chmn. promotion com. New Hope (Minn.) Indsl. Commn., 1969-70; mem. Hennepin County Overall Econ. Devel. Planning Com. Served with USN, 1946-49. Mem. Nat. Agri-Mktg. Assn., Am. Bus. Press, Minn. Press Club, Livestock Merchandising Inst. (trustee), Cardinal Key, Alpha Zeta, Alpha Gamma Rho, Sigma Delta Chi. Republican. Presbyterian. Clubs: Lions, Kiwanis, Hopewood Internat. Friendship. Home: 8416 39th Ave N New Hope MN 55427 Office: 12800 Olson Meml Hwy Suite 202 Minneapolis MN 55441

TUNLEY, ROUL, author; b. Chgo., May 12, 1912; s. Joseph Hartley and Lillian (Boyd) T.; B.A., Yale, 1934. Reporter, N.Y. Herald Tribune, 1934-37; asst. circulation mgr. Look mag., 1937-39; syndicated columnist pub. opinion poll., 1939-41; mem. English faculty Yale, 1946-47, fellow Jonathan Edwards Coll., 1946—; dir. editorial promotion Look mag., 1948-50; staff writer, asso. editor Am. mag., 1951-56; asst. mng. editor Woman's Home Companion, 1956; asso. editor Sat. Eve. Post, 1961-63. Served to lt. comdr. USNR, 1942-45. Mem. Authors Guild (council). Club: Elizabethan (Yale). Author: Kids, Crime and Chaos, 1962; The American Health Scandal, 1966; (with Anne Wahle) Ordeal by Fire, 1966. Frequent contbr. Reader's Digest, other. nat. mags., 1951—. Address: Strimple Mill Rd Stockton NJ 08559

TUNNELL, DOUGLAS ALAN, broadcast journalist; b. Oregon City, Oreg., Nov. 13, 1949; s. Chester Leonard and Evelyn (Harrington) T.; B.A. cum laude, Lewis and Clark Coll., 1972; M.S. in Journalism, Columbia U., 1975. Free-lance journalist, 1972-74; stringer CBS Radio, Beirut, 1975, reporter, Middle East, 1976, corr., London, 1977—. Co-recipient Disting. Service award Sigma Delta Chi; award for radio reporting Overseas Press Club, 1976, 78; recipient Alumni award Columbia U. Sch. Journalism, 1977; Nat. Endowment for Humanities grantee, 1973-74. Presbyterian. Club: Fgn. Corrs. (Beirut). Home: Apt 4 Pembroke Ct South Edwardes Sq London W8 England Office: CBS News 100 Brompton Rd London SW3 England*

TUNNELL, JAMES MILLER, JR., lawyer; b. Frankford, Del., June 17, 1910; s. James M. and Sarah Ethel (Dukes) T.; B.A., Princeton, 1932; B.A. in Jurisprudence, Oxford U., 1934, B.C.L., 1935 (Rhodes scholar); m. Mildred South, Mar. 28, 1936; children—John Payson, James Scarborough. Admitted to Del. bar, 1936, practiced in Georgetown, 1936-51, 54-58; partner Morris, Nichols, Arsht & Tunnell, Wilmington, 1958—; pres. Sussex Trust Co., 1949-51; asso. justice Del. Supreme Ct., 1951-54. Dir. Wilmington Trust Co., Delmarva Power & Light Co. Trustee Princeton Theol. Sem., U. Del. Fellow Am. Coll. Trial Lawyers; mem. Am. Law Inst., Soc. Colonial Wars. Clubs: Greenville Country; Wilmington. Home: 1301 N Harrison St Wilmington DE 19806 Office: Am Life Bldg Wilmington DE 19801

TUNNEY, JOHN VARICK, lawyer, former senator; b. N.Y.C., June 26, 1934; s. Gene and Mary (Lauder) T.; B.A. in Anthropology, Yale, 1956; J.D., U. Va., 1959; student Acad. Internat. Law, The Hague, Netherlands, 1957; children—Edward Eugene, Mark Andrew, Arianne Sprengers Tunney; m. Kathinka Osborne, April 1977. Admitted to N.Y. bar, 1959, Calif. bar, 1963; with firm Cahill, Gordon, Reindel & Ohl, N.Y.C., 1959-60; tchr. bus. law U. Calif. at Riverside, 1961-62; practice law, Riverside, 1963—; mem. 89th-91st Congresses from 38th Dist. Calif.; U.S. senator from Calif., 1971-77; mem. firm Manatt, Phelps, Rothenberg & Tunney, Los Angeles, 1977—. Legal adviser Riverside area Aiding Leukemic Stricken Am. Children, 1962. Chubb fellow Yale, 1967. Served with USAF, 1961-63. Office: 1888 Century Park East Los Angeles CA 90067

TUNSTALL, EDMUND JOSEPH, newspaper editor; b. Mobile, Oct. 9, 1924; s. George Washington and Virginia Ruth (Oberkirch) T.; B.A., Tulane U., 1952; m. Valerie Elizabeth Gatipon, Sept. 7, 1949; children—Bonnie Lee, Terrie Lee and Kerrie Lee (twins), Sherrie Lee. With AP, 1952-74, bur. chief, W.Va., 1965-69, bur. chief La.-Miss., New Orleans, 1969-74; editor Times-Picayune, New Orleans, 1974—, v.p., 1975—; bd. dirs. Internat. Trade Mart, New Orleans. Served with AUS, 1943-45. Recipient Best Sports Photography award New Orleans Press Club, 1959, Best News Story award, 1962. Mem. Am. Soc. Newspaper Editors, Sigma Delta Chi. Democrat. Roman Cath. Office: Times-Picayune Pub Co 3800 Howard Ave New Orleans LA 70140*

TUOHY, JOHN JOSEPH, banker; b. Indpls., June 27, 1926; s. Joseph K. and Winifred (McMahan) T.; B.S. in Econs., Wharton Sch. U. Pa., 1949; m. Mary Virginia Koschnick, Apr. 16, 1955; children—Philip Gerard, Mary Virginia. In trust dept. Mchts. Nat. Bank & Trust Co., Indpls., 1949-58; investment counselor Scudder, Stevens & Clark, Cin., 1958-61; asst. v.p. investment dept. Am. Fletcher Nat. Bank & Trust Co., Indpls., 1961-62, v.p. investment dept., 1962-66, sr. v.p. trust dept., 1966-68, exec. v.p., 1969-70, pres., 1970-72, vice chmn., 1972-79, also dir.; v.p. Am. Fletcher Corp., 1968-71, pres., 1971, vice chmn., 1976-79, also dir.; pres., chief exec. officer, dir. Landmark Banking Corp., Ft. Lauderdale, Fla., 1979—; dir. Landmark First Nat. Bank, Ft. Lauderdale, Landmark Union Trust Bank of St. Petersburg (Fla.). Served with USNR, 1944-46. Mem. Assn. Bank Holding Cos., Fla. Assn. Bank Holding Cos., Am. Bankers Assn., Fla. Bankers Assn., South Fla. Coordinating Council, Am. Mgmt. Assn., Indpls. Fin. Analysts Soc. (past pres.), Sigma Chi. Clubs: Columbia, Ind. Athletic, Gyro Meridian Hills Country (Indpls.); Tower (Ft. Lauderdale). Home: One Mendota Ln Fort Lauderdale FL 33308 Office: Landmark Banking Corp PO Box 5367 Fort Lauderdale FL 33310

TUOHY, WILLIAM KLAUS, journalist; b. Chgo., Oct. 1, 1926; s. John Marshall and Lolita (Klaus) T.; B.S., Northwestern U., 1951; m. Johanna Iselin, Nov. 24, 1964; 1 son, Cyril Iselin. Copy boy, reporter, night city editor San Francisco Chronicle, 1952-59; asso. editor, nat. polit. corr., fgn. corr. Newsweek mag., 1959-66; Vietnam corr. Los Angeles Times, 1966-68, Middle East corr., Beirut, 1969-71, Rome bur. chief, 1971-77, London bur. chief, 1977—. Served with USNR, 1944-46. Recipient Nat. Headliner award for Vietnam bur. coverage, 1965; Pulitzer prize internat. reporting (Vietnam), 1969; Overseas Press Club award for best internat. reporting (Middle East), 1970. Address: care Fgn Editor Los Angeles Times Los Angeles CA 90053

TUPPER, CHARLES JOHN, physician, univ. dean.; b. Miami, Ariz., Mar. 7, 1920; s. Charles Ralph and Grace (Alexander) T.; B.A. in Zoology, San Diego State Coll., 1943; M.D., U. Nebr., 1948; m. Mary Hewes, Aug. 4, 1942; children—Mary Elizabeth, Charles John. Intern, U. Mich. Hosp., Ann Arbor, 1948-49, asst. resident, 1949-50, resident, 1950-51, jr. clin. instr., 1951-52; practice medicine specializing internal medicine, Ann Arbor, 1954-55, Davis, Calif., 1966—; research asst. Inst. Indsl. Health, U. Mich., 1951-52, research asso., 1954-56, instr. internal medicine, 1954-56 asst. prof., 1956-59, asso. prof., 1959-66, sec. Med. Sch., 1957-59, asst. dean, 1959-61, asso. dean, 1961-66, dir. periodic health appraisal program univ. faculty, 1956-66; prof. internal medicine, dean Sch. Medicine U. Calif., Davis, 1966—. Dir. consultation services U. Mich. Health Service, 1956-66; pres. Calif. Com. Regional Med. Programs. Bd. dirs. Sacramento-Yolo-Sierra Heart Assn. Served from 1st lt. to capt. USAF, 1952-54. Diplomate Am. Bd. Internal Medicine. Fellow A.C.P.; mem. AMA (chmn. council sci. affairs, council sect. med. schs.), Internat., Am., Calif. socs. internal medicine, Am. Coll. Health Assn., Assn. Am. Med. Colls., Am. Assn. Automotive Medicine, Yolo County Med. Soc., Calif. Med. Assn. (pres. 1979-80, chmn. sci. bd., chmn. com. on accreditation, del. to AMA), U. Calif. Council Med. Sch. Deans, Sci. Research Club, Sturgis C. of C., Internists Club, U. Mich. Med. Center Alumni Soc., Alpha Omega Alpha, Nu Sigma Nu.

Club: El Macero Country (dir.). Home: 3408 Lakeview Dr El Macero Davis CA 95618

TUPPER, ELEANOR (MRS. GEORGE O. BIERKOE), coll. pres.; b. Fitchburg, Mass., d. Clarence E. and Ella G. (Webster) Tupper; student Wheaton Coll.; 1922-24; A.B. magna cum laude, Brown U. 1926; A.M., Clark U., 1927, Ph.D. 1929; postgrad. N.Y. U., 1933-34, Columbia, 1938-39; m. George O. Bierkoe, June 21, 1933; children—Priscilla Tupper Schneider, Barbara Tupper Bierkoe-Peer. Prof., head dept. history and govt. Lindenwood Coll., St. Charles, Mo., 1929-30, 32-33, head history dept., 1933; adminstr. Pine Manor Jr. Coll., Dana Hall Schs., Wellesley, Mass.; acad. dean Stoneleigh Coll., Rye, N.H.; acad. head Emma Willard Sch., Troy, N.Y.; adminstr. Lay Council, Tchrs. Coll. Columbia U.; dean, v.p. Endicott Coll., Beverly, Mass., 1939-71, pres., 1971—. Lectr. on current events and European history. Former mem. archives advisory commn. Commonwealth Mass. Mem. div. for adminstrn. and communications N.E. Synod, Lutheran Ch. in Am., also former mem. liaison com. with Upsala Coll.; mem. Beverly Mayor's Revitalization Com.; mem. Republican Nat. Com.; trustee Upsala Coll., East Orange, N.J. Mem. Am. Acad. Polit. and Social Sci. (former del.), AAUW, Am., Beverly hist. assns., Am. Geog. Assn., Salem Hosp. Aid Assn., Beverly C. of C., YMCA, Sandwich Hist. Soc., Beverly Improvement Soc., D.A.R., Marquis Biog. Library Soc., Nat. Council Women of U.S., North Shore Am. Univ. Women, Phi Beta Kappa, Phi Beta Kappa Assos., Pi Gamma Mu, Phi Theta Kappa (nat. dir.). Lutheran. Clubs: Rotary Women (former pres.), Beverly Women's, Zonta (dir.), North Shore Wheaton (past pres.), Women's (N.Y., Mass.). Author: Syllabus on European History, 1931; Japan in American Public Opinion (with George E. McReynolds), 1937; Tupper Family Genealogy, 1972. Home: 375 Hale St Beverly MA 01915 Office: Endicott Coll Beverly MA 01915

TURANO, EMANUEL NICOLAS, architect; b. Bklyn., Mar. 1, 1917; s. Dominick and Ann (Girordi) T.; Certificate Architecture, Cooper Union, 1941, Profl. Achievement citation (hon. Ph.D.), 1964; B.Arch., Harvard, 1947, M.Arch., 1963; m. Sybyl Rosmarin, July 1, 1951; children—Lisa, Laurie, Leslie. Designer, Skidmore, Owings & Merrill, 1947-50; chief design Kelly & Gruzen, N.Y.C., 1950-52; prin. E.N. Turano, architects and planners, N.Y.C., 1952—; dir. T-4 Studios, N.Y.C., 1965; tchr. 3d, 4th, 5th and master studios Pratt Inst., Bklyn., 1959-62; archtl. instr. 4th yr. studio Columbia, N.Y.C., 1959-60. Cons. HUD, 1963-67, Sussex Woodlands, Inc., N.J., 1963-66. Mem. Boca Raton (Fla.) Bd. Adjustments and Appeals, 1979—. Served with USAAF, 1941-45; PTO. Decorated D.F.C., Air medal. Recipient several awards, including Pub. Housing Authority awards, Archtl. award excellence for Pan Am. Passenger Terminal Bldg., Am. Inst. Steel Constrn., 1961; Fulbright fellow, 1950. Fellow AIA (exec. com. N.Y.C. 1962-66); mem. N.Y. State Assn. Architects, Nat. Inst. Archtl. Edn. (past sec. treas.), N.Y. Soc. Architects, Municipal Art Soc., Cooper Union Alumni Assn. (gov. 1964-67), Cooper Union Adv. Council (chmn. edn. com. 1957-59). Home: 1900 Isabel Rd Este Boca Raton FL 33432

TURBAYNE, COLIN MURRAY, philosopher; b. Tanny Morel, Queensland, Australia, Feb. 7, 1916; came to U.S., 1947, naturalized, 1957; s. David Livingston and Alice Rene (Lahey) T.; B.A., U. Queensland, 1940, M.A., 1950; Ph.D., U. Pa., 1950; m. Allsa Margaret Krimmer, June 22, 1940; children—Ronald Murray, John Garvald. Instr. in philosophy U. Pa., Phila., 1947-50; asst. prof. philosophy U. Wash., 1950-55; asst. prof. speech U. Calif., Berkeley, 1955-57; asso. prof. philosophy U. Rochester, 1957-62, prof., 1962—. Served with Australian Mil. Forces Intelligence, 1940-45. Fulbright fellow, 1963; Guggenheim fellow, 1965-66; Nat. Endowment for Humanities sr. fellow, 1974; Am. Council Learned Soc. grantee, 1958-59; Am. Philos. Soc. grantee, 1958-59. Mem. Am. Philos. Assn., AAUP. Author: The Myth of Metaphor, 1962, 2d, rev. edit, 1970; also articles. Home: 185 Highland Pkwy Rochester NY 14620 Office: Dept Philosophy U Rochester Rochester NY 14627. *In trying to understand the philosophy of the present age, I have been helped not so much by looking at what our great thinkers have said as by looking for their hidden assumptions. In this search, I have found it increasingly important to study the writings of the great thinkers of the past, especially the Greeks, because in them many of our assumptions are not taken for granted: they are examined.*

TURBEN, CLAUDE FRANKLIN, investment banker; b. Chesterhill, Ohio, Sept. 29, 1903; s. Isaiah Emery and Ethel (Graham) T.; A.B., Ohio U., 1925; m. Dorothy Schwingel, Dec. 25, 1930; children—John Franklin, Judith Ellen. Partner, Merrill, Hawley & Co., 1926-35; exec. v.p. Merrill, Turben & Co., Inc., 1936-59, pres., 1959-63, chmn. bd., 1963-68; partner Prescott, Merrill, Turben & Co., 1968-72; ltd. partner Prescott Ball & Turben, Cleve., 1972—; pres. Turben Investment Co.; dir. Greylock & Co., Big Drum, Inc. Mem. bd. govs. N. Y. Stock Exchange, 1965-68; mem. Midwest Stock Exchange. Trustee Am. Found., Cleve. Community Fund. Mem. Assn. Stock Exchange Firms (gov.), Nat. Assn. Securities Dealers (gov. 1958-61). Clubs: Union, Bond Pepper Pike, Chagrin Valley Hunt (Cleve.); Rolling Rock (Ligonier, Pa.); Hole-in-the-Wall Golf (Naples, Fla.), Naples Yacht. Home: 20101 Shelburne Rd Shaker Heights OH 44118 Office: Nat City Bank Bldg Cleveland OH 44114

TURBEVILLE, WILLIAM JACKSON, JR., agrl. chem. co. exec.; b. Turbeville, S.C., Apr. 29, 1915; s. William Jackson and Lucille (Morris) T.; B.A., Ky. Wesleyan Coll., 1936; m. Ruth M. Mooar, Nov. 2, 1945; children—Daniel Jackson, Thomas Lawrence. With Am. Agrl. Chem. Co. (merger into Continental Oil Co. 1966), N.Y.C., 1936—, v.p. marketing, 1962-63, exec. v.p., 1963, pres., 1963-66, v.p., gen. mgr. plant foods, 1966-69, v.p., gen. mgr., 1969—; pres., chmn. Agrico Chem. Co., 1966-72; dir. 1st Nat. Bank Fla., Tampa Electric Co.; mem. fertilizer industry adv. com. FAO, Rome. Active local fund raising YMCA, United Fund. Chmn. bd., mem. exec. com. Fertilizer Inst.; bd. dirs., mem. exec. com. Nat. Plant Food Inst.; bd. overseers Old Sturbridge (Mass.) Village. Served to maj., arty. AUS, 1941-46. Mem. Nat. Panel Arbitrators, Internat. Superphosphate Mfrs. Assn. Paris (pres. exec. com.), Phosphate Rock Export Assn. (chmn. bd., chief exec. officer 1972), Tampa C. of C. (exec. com.), Tampa Com. 100 (pres.), Fla. Council 100, Newcomen Soc. Methodist (past mem. ofcl. bd.). Mason, Rotarian. Home: 2407 Ardson Pl Tampa FL 33609 Office: 1311 N Westshore Blvd Tampa FL 33607

TURBIDY, JOHN BERRY, mfg. co. exec.; b. Rome, Ga., Oct. 18, 1928; s. Joseph Leo and Louyse (Berry) T.; grad. Darlington Sch., 1945; B.A., Duke U., 1950; postgrad., N.Y. U., 1952, Emory U., 1954-56; m. Joan Marsales, Dec. 19, 1958; children—John Berry, Trevor Martin. Personnel positions Lockheed Aircraft, Marietta, Ga., 1951-56; gen. mgmt. cons. McKinsey & Co., N.Y.C. and London, 1956-63; v.p. adminstrn. for Europe, Africa and Middle East, ITT Europe, Inc., Brussels, 1963, v.p., group exec. European consumer products, 1964-65, v.p., group exec. for No. Europe, 1965-67; corp. v.p. adminstrn. Celanese Corp., N.Y.C., 1967-68, pres., mng. dir. SIACE, SP.A., subs., Milan, Italy, 1968-69; chmn. bd., pres. The Vecta Group, Dallas, 1970-74; v.p. corp. devel. IU Internat. Corp., Phila., 1974-76, sr. v.p., 1976-77, exec. v.p., 1978—. Served with USNR, 1952. Clubs: Racquet (Phila.); Atrium (N.Y.C.); Windham (N.Y.); Mountain, Merion Golf, Ardmore. Office: IU Internat Corp 1500 Walnut St Philadelphia PA 19102

TURBYFILL, JOHN RAY, ry. exec.; b. Newland, N.C., Sept. 28, 1931; s. Thomas Manuel and Della Isabell (Braswell) T.; B.A., Roanoke Coll., 1953; LL.B., U. Va., 1956; m. Joyce Lorraine Wainwright Bolton, Aug. 14, 1954; children—Karen Denise, John Ray. Admitted to Va., N.Y. bars, 1956; asso. mem. firm Cravath, Swaine & Moore, N.Y.C., 1956-60; mem. law dept. Norfolk & Western Ry. Co., Roanoke, Va., 1960-70; sr. v.p. Erie Lackawanna Ry. Co. and Delaware & Hudson Ry. Co., Cleve., 1970-72; v.p. Dereco, Inc., Cleve., 1970-72, 73—; v.p. adminstrn. Norfolk & Western Ry. Co., Roanoke, 1972-74, v.p. fin., 1974—; v.p. Va. Holding Corp., Roanoke, 1973—; dir. Ill. Terminal R.R. Co., St. Louis, Fairport, Painesville & Eastern Ry. Co., Fairport Harbor, Norfolk, Franklin & Danville Ry. Co., Suffolk, Pocahontas Land Corp., Roanoke; Trailer Train Co., Chgo., Am. Rail Box Car Co., Chgo. Mem. Am. Bar Assn., Roanoke Valley C. of C. (v.p. 1974-76, pres. 1976), Phi Delta Phi. Democrat. Home: 2860 S Jefferson St Roanoke VA 24014 Office: 8 N Jefferson St Roanoke VA 24042

TURCI, GEORGE PRIMO, food co. exec.; b. Portsmouth, N.H., Aug. 3, 1929; s. Primo and Candida (Zavaloni) T.; B.S., Rensselaer Poly. Inst., 1951; M.S., Mass. Inst. Tech., 1956; M.B.A., Harvard, 1959; m. Carol Grace, June 14, 1952; children—Andrea Marie, Paul Matthew. Exptl. test engr. Curtiss Wright Corp., Wood Ridge, N.J., 1955-57; asst. to gen. mgr. Polaroid Corp., Cambridge, Mass., 1959-63; prin. Rath & Strong, Inc., Boston, 1963-69; v.p., then dir. Grant Capital Mgmt. Corp., Providence, 1969—. Pres., dir. Am. Bakeries Co., Chgo., 1969—; dir. Grant Capital Mgmt. Corp., Am. Bakeries Co. Served with USNR, 1951-54. Club: Harvard (Boston). Home: Windsor Rd Dover MA 02030 Office: 10 S Riverside Plaza Chicago IL 60606

TURCOTTE, DONALD LAWSON, educator; b. Bellingham, Wash., Apr. 22, 1932; s. Lawson Phillip and Eva (Pearson) T.; B.S., Calif. Inst. Tech., 1954, Ph.D., 1958; M.Aero.Engring., Cornell U., 1955; m. Joan Meredith Luecke, May 17, 1957; children—Phillip Lawson, Stephen Bradford. Asst. prof. aero. engring. U.S. Naval Postgrad. Sch., Monterey, Calif., 1958-59; asst. prof. aero. engring. Cornell U., Ithaca, N.Y., 1959-63, asso. prof., 1963-67, prof., 1967-73, prof. geol. scis., 1973—, trustee U. Space Research Assn., 1975-79. NSF sr. postdoctoral research fellow, 1965-66; Guggenheim fellow, 1972-73. Mem. Am. Geophys. Union, Am. Phys. Soc., Geol. Soc. Am., Seismol. Soc. Am. Club: Ithaca Country. Author: (with others) Statistical Thermodynamics, 1963; Space Propulsion, 1965. Home: 703 Cayuga Heights Rd Ithaca NY 14850 Office: Kimball Hall Cornell U Ithaca NY 14853

TURCOTTE, JEREMIAH GEORGE, physician; b. Detroit. Jan. 20, 1933; s. Vincent Joseph and Margaret Campau (Meldrum) T.; B.S. with high distinction, U. Mich., 1955, M.D. cum laude, 1957; m. Claire Mary Lenz, July 5, 1958; children—Elizabeth Margaret, John Jeremiah, Sara Lenz, Claire Meldrum. Intern, U. Mich. Med. Center, 1957-58, resident in surgery, 1958-60, 61-63, research asst. USPHS grant U. Mich. surgery dept., 1960-61; mem. faculty U. Mich. Med. Sch., 1963—, prof. surgery, 1971—, chmn. dept., head sect. gen. surgery, 1974—; sci. adv. bd. Mich. Kidney Found. Recipient Henry Russell award U. Mich., 1970. Diplomate Am. Bd. Surgery. Fellow A.C.S.; mem. Transplantation Soc. Mich. (pres. 1973-75), Assn. Academic Surgeons, Am. Surg. Assn., Soc. Univ. Surgeons. Internat. Transplantation Soc., Central Surg. Assn., Western Surg. Assn., Soc. Surgery Alimentary Tract, Am. Soc. Transplant Surgeons (pres. 1979-80), Frederick A. Coller Soc., Am. Trauma Soc. (a founder). Roman Catholic. Contbr. to med. jours. Home: 769 Heatherway St Ann Arbor MI 48104 Office: Univ Hosp B3912 1405 E Ann St Ann Arbor MI 48109

TURECK, ROSALYN, concert artist, educator; b. Chgo., Dec. 14, 1914; d. Samuel and Monya (Lipson) Tureck; studied with Sophia Brilliant-Liven, 1925-29, with Jan Chiapusso, 1929-31, with Gavin Williamson, 1931-32; grad. cum laude (4 yr. fellowship; studied with Olga Samaroff), Juilliard Sch., 1935; studied electronic instruments with theremin; D.Mus. (hon.), Colby Coll., 1964, Roosevelt U., 1968, Wilson Coll., 1968, Oxford U., 1977. Debut 2 solo recitals, Chgo., 1924; soloist Chgo. Symphony Orch., 1926; 2 all-Bach recitals, Chgo., 1930; N.Y.C. debut Carnegie Hall with Phila. Orch., 1936; series 6 all-Bach recitals Town Hall, N.Y.C., 1937; ann. U.S.-Can. tours, 1937—; ann. series 3 all-Bach recitals, N.Y.C., 1944-54, 59—; European debut, Copenhagen, Denmark, 1947; organizer, dir. soc. for performance internat. contemporary music, Composers of Today, Inc., 1951-55; extensive European tours, 1954—; condr.-soloist London Philharmonia, 1958; founder-dir. Tureck Bach Players, London 1957; Bach festivals cities Eng., Ireland, 1959—; TV series Well-Tempered Clavier, Book I, Granada TV, Eng., 1961; BBC series Well-Tempered Clavier, Books 1 and 2, 1976; numerous TV appearances, U.S., 1961—; Bach recitals on piano, harpsichord, clavichord, antique and electronic instruments, 1963—; world tour, Far East, India, Australia, Europe, 1971; N.Y.C. series Met. Mus. Art and Carnegie Hall, 1969—; appeared with leading orchs. U.S., Can., Europe, S. Africa, S.Am., Israel; recordings for HMV, Odeon, Decca, Columbia Masterworks. Mem. faculty Phila. Conservatory Music, 1935-42, Mannes Sch., N.Y.C., 1940-44, Juilliard Sch. Music, 1943-55, Columbia U., 1953-55; vis. prof. Washington U., St. Louis, 1963-64; Regent's lectr. U. Calif., San Diego, 1966, prof. music, 1966-72; vis. fellow St. Hilda's Coll., Oxford (Eng.) U., 1974, hon. life fellow, 1974—, vis. fellow Wolfson Coll., Oxford, 1975—; lectr. numerous ednl. instns., U.S. and Eng., Spain. Hon. mem. adv. council Ams. for Music Library, Hebrew U., Israel. Bd. dirs., founder Internat. Bach Soc., 1966—, Inst. for Bach Studies, 1968—. Recipient 1st prize Greater Chgo. Piano Playing Tournament, 1928; winner Schubert Meml. Contest, 1935, Nat. Fedn. Music Clubs Competition, 1935, Phi Beta award for excellence in music and arts, 1946, 1st Town Hall endowment award for series 6 Bach concerts, 1937; 1st woman invited to conduct N.Y. Philharmonic, 1958, San Antonio Symphony, Okla. Symphony, 1962; condr. soloist Israel Philharmonic, Tel Aviv, Haifa and Kol Israel orchs., 1963, Israel Festival, Internat. Bach Soc. Orchs., 1967, 69, 70, Washington Nat. Symphony, 1970, Madrid Chamber Orch., 1970. Hon. fellow Guildhall Sch. Music and Drama; mem. Royal Mus. Assn. London, Am. Musicological Soc., Inc. Soc. Musicians (London), Royal Philharmonic Soc. London, Sebastian Bach de Belgique (hon.), New Bach Soc., Oxford Soc. Clubs: Cosmopolitan Bohemians (hon.) (N.Y.C.). Author: An Introduction to the Performance of Bach, 3 vols., 1960. Contbr. articles to various mags. Editor: Bach-Sarabande, C minor, 1960, Bach Keyboard works Schirmer Music, Inc., 1977—; Paginini-Tureck—Moto Perpetuo; A. Scarlatti—Air and Gavotte; films: Fantasy and Fugue: Rosalyn Tureck Plays Bach, 1972, Rosalyn Tureck plays on Harpsichord and Organ, 1977, Joy of Bach, 1978; numerous recs. Address: care Columbia Artists Mgmt Inc 165 W 57th St New York NY 10019. *My work in Bach is not a specialization, although concentration on a single composer may seemingly give that impression. It spreads to performance on antique instruments harpsichord, clavichord, Fortepiano, to the contemporary piano and electronic Moog, to the organ, to conducting, writing, editing and research. The years of concertizing in compositions of all periods—pre-Bach, romantic, contemporary and electronic music—have all brought a rich tapestry of understanding to the magisterial requirements for interpreting music of a past era authentically and significantly as a contemporary artist.*

TUREKIAN, KARL KAREKIN, educator; b. N.Y.C., Oct. 25, 1927; s. Vaughan Thomas and Victoria (Guleserian) T.; A.B., Wheaton (Ill.) Coll., 1949; M.A., Columbia, 1951, Ph.D., 1955; m. Arax Roxanne Hagopian, Apr. 22, 1962; children—Karla Ann, Vaughan Charles. Lectr. geology Columbia, 1953-54, research asso., 1954-56; faculty Yale, 1956—, prof. geology and geophysics, 1965-72, Henry Barnard Davis prof. geology and geophysics, 1972—; curator meteorites Peabody Mus., 1964—. Cons. Pres.'s Commn. Marine Sci., Engring. and Resources, 1967-68, oceanography panel NSF, 1968-70, exobiology panel for NASA of Am. Inst. Biol. Scientists, 1966-69; U.S. nat. com. for geochemistry NAS-NRC, 1970-73, mem. climate research bd., 1977—; mem. group experts sci. aspects Marine Pollution UN, 1971-73. Served with USNR, 1945-46. Guggenheim fellow, 1962-63. Fellow Geol. Soc. Am., Meteoritical Soc., Am. Geophys. Union; mem. Am. Chem. Soc., A.A.A.S., Geochem. Soc. (pres. 1975-76), Sigma Xi. Author: Oceans, 1968, 2d edit., 1976; Chemistry of the Earth, 1972; (with B.J. Skinner) Man and the Ocean, 1973; (with C.L. Drake, J. Imbrie and J.A. Knauss) Oceanography, 1978. Editor: Jour. Geophys. Rev., 1969-75; Late Cenozoic Glacial Ages, 1971; asso. editor Geochim. et Cosmochim. Acta, 1967-70; asso. editor Earth and Planetary Sci. Letters, 1973-75, editor, 1975—. Contbr. articles to profl. jours. Home: 555 Skiff St North Haven CT 06473 Office: Dept Geology and Geophysics Yale U New Haven CT 06520

TURIN, GEORGE LEWIS, educator; b. N.Y.C., Jan. 27, 1930; s. Meyer H. and Lillian (Podolsky) T.; B.S., Mass. Inst. Tech., 1952, M.S., 1952, Sc.D., 1957; m. Helen F. Green, Sept. 11, 1964; children—David, Abigail. Engr., Philco Corp., Phila., 1948-51; staff mem. Mass. Inst. Tech. Lincoln Lab., Lexington, 1952-56; cons. Edgerton, Germeshausen & Grier, Boston, 1954-56; mem. staff Hughes Aircraft Co., Culver City, Calif., 1956-60; mem. faculty U. Calif., Berkeley, 1960—, prof. elec. engring., vice chmn. dept. elec. engring. and computer sci., 1975-77; dir. engring. sci. div. Teknekron, Inc., Berkeley, 1970-73; v.p. engring. Ins. Tech. Co., Berkeley, 1973-74, exec. v.p., 1974-76; cons. to corps. and govt. agys. Guggenheim fellow, 1966-67. Fellow IEEE. Author: Notes on Digital Communication, 1969. Contbr. articles to profl. jours. Home: 763 San Diego Rd Berkeley CA 94707 Office: U Calif Dept Elec Engring and Computer Sci Berkeley CA 94720

TURINI, RONALD WALTER, pianist; b. Montreal, Que., Can., Sept. 30, 1933; s. Walter Giovanni and Ellen (Jensen) T.; grad. (prize with distinction), Que. Provincial Conservatory, 1950; pupil of Vladimir Horowitz, 1955-60. Tours U.S., Can., 1961—, USSR, 1962, 63, 65, S. Am., 1963-65, Europe, 1965-67; rec. artist RCA Victor Records. Prize winner, Bolzano, Italy, 1958, Geneva, Switzerland, 1958; recipient Gold medal Queen Elisabeth of Belgium Internat. Competition, Brussels, 1960. Home: 6550 Sherbrooke St W Montreal 28 PQ Canada Office: care David Haber Artists Mgmt Inc 1235 Bay St Suite 500 Toronto ON M5R 3K4 Canada*

TURK, JAMES CLINTON, chief judge; b. Roanoke, Va., May 3, 1923; s. James Alexander and Geneva (Richardson) T.; A.B., Roanoke Coll., 1949; L.L.B., Washington and Lee U., 1952; m. Barbara Duncan, Aug. 21, 1954; children—Ramona Leah, James Clinton, Robert Malcolm Duncan, Mary Elizabeth, David Michael. Admitted to Va. bar, 1952; mem. firm Dalton, Poff & Turk, Radford, Va., from 1959; chief judge U.S. Dist. Ct., Western Dist. Va.; dir. 1st & Mchts. Nat. Bank of Radford; mem. Va. Senate, from 1959, minority leader. Trustee Radford Community Hosp., 1959—. Served with AUS, 1943-46. Mem. Order of Coif, Phi Beta Kappa, Omicron Delta Kappa. Baptist (deacon). Home: 1102 Walker Dr Radford VA 24141 Office: US Courthouse Roanoke VA 24006

TURK, LEONARD GERALD, machinery mfr.; b. Rochester, N.Y., July 10, 1916; s. Benjamin and Pauline (Alder) T.; B.S., Carnegie Inst. Tech., 1939; m. Jayne Kaylor, June 20, 1942; children—James L., Thomas A., William R. With NRM Corp., Akron, Ohio, 1946-48, 55—, asst. v.p. rubber machinery div., 1960-62, v.p., gen. mgr., 1962-65, pres., chief exec. officer, 1965-76, chmn. bd., 1976—; owner home constrn. bus., 1948-55. Mem. exec. council Akron Area Boy Scouts Am.; mem. bus. adv. council Kent State U. Bd. dirs. Akron Jr. Achievement. Registered profl. engr., Ohio. Mem. Soc. Plastics Industry, Akron Rubber Group, Akron Council Engring. and Sci. Socs., Machinery and Allied Products Inst., Akron C. of C. Episcopalian. Clubs: Portage Country, Akron City, Cascade (Akron); Lost Tree (Lost Tree Village, Fla.). Home: 333 N Portage Path Akron OH 44303 Office: 3200 Gilchrist Rd Akron OH 44202

TURKEVICH, ANTHONY LEONID, chemist, educator; b. N.Y.C., July 23, 1916; s. Leonid Jerome and Anna (Chervinsky) T.; B.A., Dartmouth Coll., 1937, D.Sc., 1971; Ph.D., Princeton U., 1940; m. Ireene Podlesak, Sept. 20, 1948; children—Leonid, Darya. Research asso. spectroscopy physics dept. U. Chgo., 1940-41, asst. prof., research on nuclear transformations Enrico Fermi Inst. and chemistry dept., 1946-48, asso. prof., 1948-53, prof., 1953—, James Franck prof. chemistry, 1965-70, Distinguished Ser. prof., 1970—; war research Manhattan Project, Columbia U., 1942-43, U. Chgo., 1943-45, Los Alamos Sci. Lab., 1945-46. Participant test first nuclear bomb, Alamagordo, N.Mex., 1945, in theoretical work on and test of thermonuclear reactions, 1945—, chem. analysis of moon, 1967—; cons. to AEC Labs.; fellow Los Alamos Sci. Lab., 1972—. Del., Geneva Conf. on Nuclear Test Suspension, 1958, 59. Recipient E.O. Lawrence Meml. award AEC, 1962; Atoms for Peace award, 1969. Fellow Am. Phys. Soc.; mem. Am. Chem. Soc. (nuclear applications award 1972), AAAS, Nat. Acad. Scis., Am. Acad. Arts and Scis., Royal Soc. Arts (London), Phi Beta Kappa. Mem. Russian Orthodox Greek Cath. Ch. Club: Quadrangle, Cosmos. Home: 175 Briarwood Loop Briarwood Lakes Oak Brook IL 60521 Office: 5640 S Ellis Ave Chicago IL 60637

TURKIN, MARSHALL W., symphony orch. adminstr.; b. Chgo., Apr. 1, 1926; student U. Kans., 1946-48; Mus. B. in Music Composition, Northwestern U., 19—, Mus. M., 1951; postgrad. Juilliard Sch. Music, Columbia U., U. Ind.; 4 children. Record rev. columnist; classical music commentator; gen. mgr. Honolulu Symphony and Opera Co., 1959-66; orch. festival mgr. Ravinia Festival for Chgo. Symphony, 1966-68; founding mgr. Blossom Festival for Cleve. Orch., 1968-70; gen. mgr. Detroit Symphony, 1970-73, exec. dir., 1973-79; mng. dir. Pitts. Symphony Orch., 1979—; arranger, composer. Served with USN, World War II. Office: care Detroit Symphony Orch Ford Auditorium Detroit MI 48226

TURLEY, JOSEPH FRANCIS, personal care products mfg. co. exec.; b. Boston, June 2, 1925; s. Joseph and Margaret T.; A.B., Harvard U., 1950; M.A., U. Minn., 1950; m. Frances Marie Hurley, Sept. 5, 1948; children—Sharon Ann, Donna Marie, Joseph Francis. Asst. sec. Boston Mcpl. Research Bur., 1951-52; chief economist Mass. Dept. Commerce, 1952-55; dir. bus. research Boston Coll., 1955-60; city planning cons., 1955-60; with Gillette Co., 1960—, pres. Gillette Spain, 1968-69, Gillette Can., 1969-71, Safety Razor Div. U.S., Boston, 1971-76, exec. v.p. Gillette Co., Boston, 1976—; dir. E G & G, Inc.; trustee South Boston Savs. Bank. Bd. dirs. Greater Boston C. of C., Boys' Clubs Boston, United Way Massachusetts Bay, Mass. Gov.'s Mgmt. Task Force; governing councillor Nat. Mcpl. League. Served with USN, 1943-46. Mem. Cosmetics, Toiletries and

Fragrances Assn. (dir.), Nat. Assn. Bus. Economists. Clubs: Corinthian Yacht, Harvard, Algonquin. Home: 24 Coolidge Rd Marblehead MA 01945 Office: Gillette Co Prudential Tower Bldg Boston MA 02199

TURLEY, KEITH L., utilities exec.; b. Mesa, Ariz., June 16, 1923; s. Ora Elmer and Zella Exa (Thurman) T.; B.A., Ariz. State U., 1948; m. Dorothy Rae Welton, Sept. 2, 1950; children—Sue Ann, Cinda Jane, Nancy Lynn, Robert. With Central Ariz. Light & Power Co., Phoenix, 1948-51, Stanolind Oil & Gas Co., Okla., 1951; with Ariz. Pub. Service Co., Phoenix, 1952—, v.p. marketing, 1967-69, exec. v.p. customer services, 1969-72, exec. v.p., gen. mgr., dir., 1972-73, pres., chief exec. officer, 1974—; dir. Ariz. Bank, Del E. Webb Corp., Western Energy Supply & Transmission Assos. Dir., Central Ariz. Project, 1971—; chmn. Phoenix Commn. on Housing, 1972. Trustee Meml. Hosp., Am. Grad. Sch. Internat. Mgmt., Heard Mus.; bd. dirs. Sun Angel Found.; mem. pres.'s adv. council Ariz. State U. Served to lt. (j.g.) USNR, 1943-47. Recipient Alumni Service award Ariz. State U., 1971. Mem. Pacific Coast Electric Assn. (dir.), Pacific Coast Gas Assn., Edison Electric Inst. (dir.), Atomic Indsl. Forum (dir.), Ariz. State U. Alumni Assn. (pres. 1966). Clubs: Arizona Country, Arizona. Office: Ariz Public Service Co PO Box 21666 Phoenix AZ 85036

TURLEY, STEWART, retail co. exec.; b. Mt. Sterling, Ky., July 20, 1934; s. R. Joe and Mavis S. Turley; student Rollins Coll., 1952-53, U. Ky., 1953-55; m. Judy Turley, July 1953; children—Carol, Karen. Plant mgr. Crown Cork & Seal Co., Orlando, Fla., Phila., 1955-66; mgr. non-drug ops., dir. corporate employee relations and spl. services Jack Eckerd Corp., Clearwater, Fla., 1966-68, v.p., 1968-71, sr. v.p., 1971-74, dir. 1971—, pres., chief exec. officer, 1974—, chmn. bd., 1975—. Dir. Gulf Coast Art Center, 1970-74; trustee Eckerd Coll., St. Petersburg. Mem. Young Pres.'s Orgn., Nat. Assn. Chain Drug Stores (dir.), Am. Retail Fedn. (dir.), Fla. C. of C. (dir.), Kappa Alpha. Clubs: Rotary (dir. 1970-74), Carlouel Yacht (Clearwater); Feather Sound Country (St. Petersburg). Home: Belleair FL 33516 Office: PO Box 4689 Clearwater FL 33518

TURLEY, (RONALD) WINDLE, lawyer; b. Cheyenne, Okla., Jan. 25, 1939; s. O. C. and Virginia Lee (Taylor) T.; B.A., Oklahoma City U., 1962; J.D., So. Meth. U., 1965; m. Shirley Ann Lacey, Dec. 8, 1957; children—Linda, Ronald. Admitted to Tex. bar, 1965, since practiced in Dallas; firms Fritz, Vinson & Turley, 1965-68, McKool, Jones, Shoemaker, Turley & Vassallo, 1968-73; lectr. in field. Mem. Dallas, Am. bar assns., State Bar Tex., Dallas (pres. 1972-73), Tex. (dir.), Am. (chmn. com. safety) trials lawyers assns. Contbr. articles on trial of product defect and aviation crash litigation to profl. jours. Home: 7630 Southwestern Blvd Dallas TX 75225 Office: 1 Campbell Centre Dallas TX 75206

TURLINGTON, EDGAR LAWRENCE, JR., lawyer; b. Richmond, Va., Sept. 23, 1932; s. Edgar Lawrence and Mabel J. (Arvin) T.; B.A., U. Richmond, 1954, LL.B., 1959; m. Barbara Helen Kriz, Mar. 14, 1964; children—Carol Lawrence, John Randall. Admitted to Va. bar, 1959, since practiced in Richmond; partner firm White, Cabell, Paris & Lowenstein and predecessor firms, 1959—. Instr. domestic relations J. Sargeant Reynolds Community Coll., 1975. Served to 1st lt. AUS, 1954-56. Mem. Am., Va., Richmond (sec.-treas. family law sect. 1978-79) bar assns., Va. State Bar (mem. 3d dist. com. 1974-77), Va., Richmond assns. trial lawyers. Home: 104 Portland Pl Richmond VA 23221 Office: 523 E Main St Richmond VA 23219

TURMEL, ANTOINE, grocery co. exec.; b. Thetford Mines, Que., Can., Apr. 25, 1918; s. Irene and Claire (Hebert) T.; student comml. studies Sherbrooke (Que., Can.) Sem., 1933-34, Alexander Hamilton Inst., N.Y.C., 1936-37, IBM, 1957, Laval U. (Can.), 1961; hon. degree adminstrn. U. Sherbrooke, 1970; children—Andre, Jean-Francois, Helene, Marie-Josee. Accountant, Genest & Nadeau, wholesale grocers, Sherbrooke, 1935-45; pres. Provigo (Sherbrooke) Inc. (formerly Denault Limitee), wholesale grocers, Sherbrooke, 1945—; chmn. bd., chief exec. officer Provigo Inc., Montreal, Que., 1969—, M. Loeb Ltd., Ottawa, Ont., Can., 1977—, Horne & Pitfield Foods Ltd., Edmonton, Alta., 1978—, Market Wholesale Grocery Co., Calif., 1978—, Nat. Drug & Chem. Co. Can. Ltd., Pointe Claire, Que., 1978—; dir. Provincial Bank Can., La Prevoyance Ins. Co., United Auto Parts, Inc., Que. Telephone, Paquet Inc., Quebec, Que., Nat. Cablevision Ltd., Delmar Investment Co., Sherbrooke, Longchamp Golf Course, Sherbrooke, Syndicat de Que., Can. Gen. Electric Co. Ltd., Western Tire & Auto Supply (Can.) Ltd. Formerly gov. Montreal Stock Exchange. Pres., Operation Universitrie, 1972—; bd. dirs. Pro-Can. Found. Named Man of Month, Commerce Rev., 1963, French Canadian Man of Year, CJMS Radio, Montreal, 1967; Personality of Year, Assn. Détaillants en Alimentation, 1977. Mem. Order St. John (hon. dir. Que. council 1978). Mem. Can. C. of C., Montreal Bd. Trade, Conseil du Patronat du Que., Assn. Montréalaise d'Activités récréatives et culturelles. Home: 32 Surrey Gardens Westmount PQ Canada Office: 800 Dorchester Blvd Suite 500 Montreal PQ Canada

TURNAGE, WILLIAM ALBERT, assn. exec.; b. Tucson, Dec. 9, 1942; s. William Vincent and Erna (Rassow) T.; B.A., Yale U., 1965, postgrad. (Chubb fellow), 1969-71; postgrad. Balliol Coll., Oxford, Eng., 1965-66. Program economist U.S. AID, 1966-67; spl. asst. U.S. Dept. State, Washington, 1967-69; bus. mgr. Ansel Adams, Carmel, Calif., 1971-78; exec. dir. Wilderness Soc., Washington, 1978—; asso. fellow Berkeley Coll., Yale U., 1979—. Democrat. Clubs: Swiss Alpine, Elizabethan of Yale. Home: 1256 Martha Custis Dr Alexandria VA 22302 Office: 1901 Pennsylvania Ave NW Washington DC 20006

TURNBAUGH, DOUGLAS BLAIR, arts founds./assns. exec.; b. Lewiston, Idaho, May 17, 1934; s. Orville Wendel and Geneva Violet (Blair) T.; B.A., U. Wash., 1956; divorced. Exec. dir. Fine Arts Workshop, Inc., 1963-73, Brandon Films, Inc., 1966, Dance Notation Bur., Inc., 1967, Dance Theatre Found., Inc., for Alvin Ailey Dance Theatre, 1970; pres. Am. Inst. Chorelogy, Inc., N.Y.C., 1970—; exec. dir., treas. Ludwig Vogelstein Found., Inc., N.Y.C., 1973—; exec. dir. Poetry Soc. Am., Inc., N.Y.C., 1978—; dir. Inst. Choreology, London, Four Winds Theatre of Cooper Hewitt Mus. of Smithsonian Instn., Dance Theatre Workshop, Inc., Alt. Center for Internat. Arts, Inc., Musica Reservata, Inc.; adj. faculty N.Y. U., N.Y.C., York U., Toronto. Nat. Endowment for Arts grantee, 1968. Mem. Dance Critics Assn. (founder). Club: Nat. Arts (N.Y.C.). Contbr. articles to various publs. including N.Y. mag., Dance mag., Atlantic Monthly, Asia mag., Filmmakers Newsletter, others; editor Poetry Soc. Am. Bull.; contbg. editor Appearances mag. Home: 96 Grand St New York NY 10013 Office: 3325 #30 Rockefeller Plaza New York NY 10020

TURNBULL, AGNES SLIGH (MRS. JAMES LYALL TURNBULL), author; b. New Alexandria, Pa., Oct. 14, 1888; d. Alexander Halliday and Lucinda Hannah (McConnell) Sligh; student Washington (Pa.) Sem.; grad. Indiana (Pa.) State Normal, 1910; hon. Litt.D., Indiana U. of Pa., 1974; studied U. Chgo., 1 year; Litt.D., Westminster Coll., 1945; m. James Turnbull, July 27, 1918; 1 dau., Martha (Mrs. Paul O'Hearn). Mem. Phi Beta Kappa, Pi Kappa Sigma, Kappa Delta Pi. Republican. Presbyterian. Author: The Rolling Years, 1936; Remember the End, 1938; Elijah the Fish-bite, 1940; Dear Me, a Diary, 1941; The Day Must Dawn, 1942; The Bishop's Mantle, 1947; The Gown of Glory, 1952; The Golden Journey, 1955: Out of My Heart, 1958; The Nightingale, 1960; The King's Orchard, 1963; Little Christmas, 1964; George, 1965; The Wedding Bargain, 1966; Many a Green Isle, 1968; The White Lark, 1968, Whistle and I'll Come to You, 1970; The Flowering, 1972; The Richlands, 1974; The Winds of Love, 1977. Home: 46 Claremont Ave Maplewood NJ 07040. *I feel that there are more good people in the world than bad and that it is just as realistic to write of the former as the latter, and much more satisfying. I have tried in each of my books to tell as good a story as I could, since I feel this is the first duty of a novelist. But in each one I have done my best to portray normal people, most of whom through all the joys and sorrow of their lives have had an instinctive reach upward.*

TURNBULL, BENJAMIN WALTON, banker; b. Leesburg, Va., Jan. 7, 1920; s. Charles D. and Pearl (Berger) T.; B.A., Coll. William and Mary, 1949; grad. Rutgers U. Grad. Sch. Banking, 1960; exec. program U. Va. Grad. Sch. Bus. Adminstrn., 1962; m. Ellen Montgomery Phlegar, Sept. 6, 1947; children—Robert Mosby, Benjamin Harrison, Sarah Walton. With United Va. Bank, Richmond, and predecessors, 1949—, exec. v.p., 1967—; past dir. A.T. Massey Coal Co., Inc. Mem. contact banker program Am. Bankers Assn., past mem. trust legislative council trust div. Mem. adv. bd. Fed. Arts Richmond; trustee Historic Richmond Found.; bd. dirs. Children's Home Soc. Va.; past bd. visitors, chmn. acad policy com., mem. exec., finance, com. Va. Commonwealth U.; past mem. exec. bd. Diocese Va., past trustee, chmn. exec. com. ch. schs.; past mem. bd. regents Nat. Trust Sch., Northwestern U.; pres. sponsor trustees Colgate Darden Grad. Sch., U. Va. Served with USAAF, 1941-45; ETO. Decorated Air medal, Bronze Star. Mem. Phi Beta Kappa. Democrat. Episcopalian. Clubs: Country of Va., Downtown (Richmond). Home: 5304 Tuckahoe Ave Richmond VA 23226 Office: PO Box 26665 Richmond VA 23261

TURNBULL, CHARLES VINCENT, hosp. adminstr.; b. Mpls., May 13, 1933; s. Charles Vivien and Lucille Frances (Dallas) T.; B.A., U. Minn., 1960, M.S.W., 1962; m. Gloria Marlene Tilley, July 21, 1956; children—Charlene Kay, Charles Vincent II, Terry Lucille, Mary Marlene. Unit dir. Mental Health Treatment Service, Cambridge (Minn.) State Hosp., 1962-67, dir. rehab. therapies, 1967-68, program dir., 1973-74; program dir. Minn. Valley Social Adaptation Center, St. Peter, Minn., 1968-73; chief exec. officer Faribault (Minn.) State Hosp., 1974—. Program cons. Rochester (Minn.) Social Adaptation Center, 1970-71; cons. St. Louis State Sch. and Hosp., 1973-74. Chmn., United Fund Drive, St. Peter, 1971; scoutmaster Twin Valley council Boy Scouts Am., 1973-75; co-chmn. Faribault Bi-Centennial Horizons Subcom., 1975-76; Mem. Minn. Developmental Disabilities Planning Council, 1975, Chmn. comprehensive plan subcom., 1977-78; mem. Cannon River Adv. Council, 1978—. Mayor, Village of Lexington, Minn., 1962-64; candidate for U.S. rep. 2d Dist. Minn., 1972, 74. Served with USMC, 1953-56. Mem. Assn. for Retarded Children, Am. Assn. Mental Deficiency, Nat. Assn. Developmental Disabilities Mgrs. (bd. dirs. 1977—). Mem. Democratic Farmer Labor party. Lutheran. Home: Box 147 Route 3 Faribault MN 55021 Office: Faribault State Hosp Faribault MN 55021

TURNBULL, DAVID, educator, phys. chemist; b. Elmira, Ill., Feb. 18, 1915; s. David and Luzetta Agnes (Murray) T.; B.S., Monmouth (Ill.) Coll., 1936, Sc.D. (hon.), 1958; Ph.D., U. Ill., 1939; A.M. (hon.), Harvard, 1962; m. Carol May Cornell, Aug. 3, 1946; children—Lowell D., Murray M., Joyce M. Tchr. research Case Sch. Applied Sci., 1939-46; scientist Gen. Electric Co. Research Lab., 1946-62, mgr. chem. metallurgy sect., 1950-58; adj. prof. metallurgy Rennselaer Poly. Inst., 1954-62; Gordon McKay prof. applied physics Harvard, 1962—, Chmn., Gordon Conf. Physics and Chemistry Metals, 1952, internat. confs. Crystal Growth, 1958, Chem. Physics of Non-metallic Crystals, 1961, Office Naval Research panel study growth and morphology crystals, 1959-60. Chmn. citizens curriculum com. Niskayuna (N.Y.) Sr. High Sch., 1954. Fellow Am. Phys. Soc., N.Y. Acad. Scis.; mem. Am. Soc. Metals (chmn. seminar com. 1954), Am. Inst. Mining and Metall. Engrs. (lectr. Inst. Metals div. 1961), Am. Chem. Soc., Nat. Acad. Scis., Am. Acad. Arts and Scis. Editor: (with Seitz, Ehrenreich) Solid State Physics, 35 vols., 1955—; (with Doremus, Roberts) Growth and Perfection of Crystals, 1958. Asso. editor Jour. Chem. Physics, 1961-63; editorial adv. bd. Jour. Physics and Chemistry Solids, 1955—. Home: 77 Summer St Weston MA 02193 Office: Applied Physics Dept Harvard Univ Cambridge MA 02138

TURNBULL, HARRISON FREEMAN, lawyer; b. Hartford, Conn., May 14, 1903; s. James A. and Frances (Freeman) T.; B.S., Yale, 1925, LL.B., 1931; m. Frances Drew, Sept. 22, 1927 (dec. 1959); children—Joan D. (Mrs. Bruce L. Roberts), H. James, David D.; m. 2d, Katharine MacAllister, June 4, 1960. Admitted to Conn. bar, 1931, since practiced in New Haven; partner firm Wiggin & Dana, 1941—. Mem. Bd. Alderman New Haven, 1942-51. Mem. Am., Conn. bar assns., New Haven Hist. Soc. Episcopalian. Clubs: Mory's Assn (gov. emeritus), Lawn, Quinnipiack (New Haven). Home: 82 Blake Rd Hamden CT 06517 Office: 195 Church St New Haven CT 06508

TURNBULL, JOHN CAMERON, assn. exec.; b. Regina, Sask., Can., Sept. 5, 1923; s. Cameron Joseph and Lillian Irene (Pentz) T.; B.S. in Pharmacy, U. Sask., 1949; m. Hazel Evelyn Rockwell, July 31, 1948; children—Lillian Elizabeth, John Rockwell, Jocelyn Hazel. Pharmacist with village and city pharmacies, 1945-50; supr. pharm services Dept. Pub. Health, Province of Sask., Regina, 1950-52; operations mgr. Nat. Drugs, Ltd., Winnipeg, and Saskatoon, 1953; exec. dir. Canadian Pharm. Assn., Toronto, Ont., 1953-78; sec.-treas., mng. dir. Canadian Pharm. Realty Co. Ltd.; mem. provisional bd. Pharmacare Ltd.; registrar-treas., Pharmacy Examining Bd. of Can., 1963-68, mem. bd., 1963-78; pharmacy cons. Ministry of Health, Barbados, 1979—. Chmn. Govt.'s Spl. Com. on Acetylsalicylic Poisonings, 1967; mem. Emergency Health Services Advisory Com. Served with RCAF, 1941-45. Decorated D.F.C., Order of Can.; recipient Canadian Centennial medal, 1967, Queen's Jubilee medal, 1977. Mem. Federation Internationale Pharmaceutique (v.p.), Inst. of Assn. Execs., Conf. on Pharmacy Registrars of Can. (sec.), Commonwealth Pharm. Assn. (council 1969—); hon. mem. Am., Canadian, Sask., B.C., Alta. pharm. assns., N.S. Pharm. Soc., Ont. Pharmacists Assn., Canadian Soc. Hosp. Pharmacists, Rho Pi Phi. Mem. United Ch. of Canada. Club: Bayview Country (past dir.). Home: 40 Banstock Dr Willowdale ON M2K 2H6 Canada

TURNBULL, WILLIAM, JR., architect; b. N.Y.C., Apr. 1, 1935; s. William and Elizabeth (Howe) T.; A.B., Princeton U., 1956, M.F.A. in Architecture, 1959; student Ecole des Beaux Art Fontainebleau, 1956; m. Wendy Wilson Woods, Apr. 1, 1967. With Skidmore, Owings & Merrill, San Francisco, 1960-63; founding partner Moore, Lyndon, Turnbull, Whitaker, 1962, partner charge San Francisco office, 1965-69; lectr. U. Calif. at Berkeley, 1965-69; dir. MLTW-Turnbull Assos., 1970—; lectr. Stanford U., 1973-77; vis. design critic M.I.T., 1975, U. Calif., Berkeley, 1977—; design cons. Formica Corp., 1978—; prin. works include Sea Ranch Condominium I, 1965, Sea Ranch Swim Tennis Club, 1966; asso. architect Lovejoy Fountain Plaza, Portland, Faculty Club at U. Calif. at Santa Barbara, Kresge Coll. at U. Calif. at Santa Cruz, Biloxi (Miss.) Library; vis. prof. U. Oreg., 1966-68. Mem. design group Pres.'s Advisory Council Pa. Ave., 1963; mem. tech. advisory com. Calif. Legislature Joint Com. Open Space Lands, 1968-69; mem. regional honor awards (10) jury AIA, 1968—, nat. honor awards jury, 1969, chmn. jury, 1977; C.E. honor award, 1973, 79; mem. Progressive Architecture Honor Awards Jury, 1975. Served with AUS, 1959-60. Recipient Nat. honor award AIA, 1967, 68, 73, 79; Calif. Gov. award planned communities, 1966; award of merit, bay region honor awards AIA, 1963, 67, 78; citation Progressive Architecture Design awards, 1962-66, 68-70, 1st honor award, 1971. First honor award Homes for Better Living, 1963, Merit award, 1966; Honor award Western Home awards, 1961-62, 62, 63, 66-67, Merit award, 1966-67; House of Year award Archtl. Record, 1961, 67, 69, 70, 72. Fellow AIA. Author: Global Architecture Series: Moore, Lyndon, Turnbull & Whitaker: The Sea Ranch, The Sea Ranch Details. Illustrator: The Place of Houses. Office: Pier 1 1/2 The Embarcadero San Francisco CA 94111

TURNBULL, WILLIAM WATSON, ednl. testing firm exec.; b. St. Thomas, Ont., Can., Dec. 26, 1919; s. William Watson and Elsie (Rodd) T.; came to U.S., 1942, naturalized, 1953; B.A., U. Western Ont., 1942; A.M., Princeton U., 1943, Ph.D., 1944; hon. degrees; m. Mary Elizabeth Sinclair, June 30, 1944; 1 dau., Brenda Jean. Head dept. test constrn. Coll. Entrance Exam. Bd., Princeton, 1944-48, sec., 1946-48; dir. test constrn., analysis and research Ednl. Testing Service, Princeton, 1948-49, v.p. test devel., analysis and research, 1949-53, v.p. for testing ops., 1953-56, exec. v.p., 1956-70, pres., 1970—. chmn. bd. Center for Applied Linguistics, Miss Mason's Sch. trustee Coll. Entrance Exam. Bd., Ednl. Products Info. Exchange. Mem. Internat. Assn. Ednl. Assessment (pres.), AAAS, Am. Ednl. Research Assn., Am. Assn. Higher Edn., Internat. Assn. Applied Psychology, Am. Psychol. Assn., Am. Personnel and Guidance Assn., Internat. Assn. Ednl. and Vocat. Guidance, Internat. Council Psychologists, Nat. Council Measurement in Edn., Psychometric Soc., Psychonomic Soc., Sigma Xi. Clubs: Nassau (Princeton); Century Assn., Princeton of N.Y.C. Home: 4690 Province Line Rd Princeton NJ 08540 Office: Ednl Testing Service Princeton NJ 08541

TURNDORF, HERMAN, anesthesiologist; b. Paterson, N.J., Dec. 22, 1930; s. Charles R. and Ruth (Blumberg) T.; A.B., Oberlin Coll., 1952; M.D., U. Pa., 1956; m. Sietske Huisman, Nov. 24, 1957; children—David, Michael Pieter. Instr. surgery U. Pa. Hosp., 1957-59; asst. anesthetist med. sch. Harvard U., Mass. Gen. Hosp., Boston, 1961-63; asso. attending anesthesiologist, asst. dir. dept. anesthesiology Mt. Sinai Hosp., N.Y.C., 1963-70, clin. prof. anesthesiology, 1966-70; prof., chmn. dept. anesthesiology W.Va. U. Sch. Medicine and Med. Center, Morgantown, 1970-74, N.Y. U. Sch. Medicine, 1974—; dir. anesthesiology N.Y. U. Hosp., 1974—, Bellevue Hosp. Med. Center, 1974—; cons. in anesthesiology U.S. Naval Hosp., Portsmouth, Va., Manhattan VA Hosp., Armed Forces Sch. Medicine, 1974—. Served to lt. M.C., USNR, 1959-61. Diplomate Am. Bd. Anesthesiology. Fellow Am. Coll. Chest Physicians, Am. Coll. Anesthesiologists (bd. govs. 1977—); mem. N.Y. Acad. Medicine, Soc. Critical Care Medicine. Home: 37 Hyatt Rd Briarcliff Manor NY 10510

TURNER, ALICE KENNEDY, editor; b. Mukden, Manchuria; d. William Taylor and Florence Bell (Green) Turner; B.A., Bryn Mawr Coll., 1962. Sr. editor Holiday mag., N.Y.C., 1969-70; asso. editor Publishers Weekly, N.Y.C., 1972-74; sr. editor Ballantine Books, N.Y.C., 1974-76; sr. editor New York mag., N.Y.C., 1976—. Author: Yoga for Beginners, 1973; co-author: The New York Woman's Guide, 1975. Home: 527 E 72d St New York NY 10014

TURNER, ALLEN MARK, lawyer; b. Chgo., June 27, 1937; s. Myer H. and Madeline G. (Gross) T.; B.B.A., U. Wis., 1958; J.D., U. Chgo., 1961; m. Lynn Sharon Bernberg, Mar. 22, 1959; children—Jennifer Ellen, Christopher Marshall Richard. Admitted to Ill. bar, 1961; since practiced in Chgo.; mem. firm Portes & Green, 1961-64, Pritzker & Pritzker, 1965—; dir., chmn. exec. com. Hyatt Internat. Corp., 1965—; dir., sec., gen. counsel Agrow Industries, Inc., 1965—; chmn. bd. McCall's mag.; dir. McCall's Pub. Co.; lectr. philosophy Chgo. Sch. for Gifted, 1960-61; instr. Chgo. Police Acad., 1966-68. Bd. dirs. Jewish Welfare Fund Met. Chgo., Am. Jewish Com., Jewish Student Service Com.; pres. com. on Goodman Theater, Art Inst. Chgo., Chgo. Theater Group; chmn. bd. dirs. Victory Gardens Theater. Recipient Glasser award, 1969; Jewish Fedn. Chgo. travel grantee, 1965. Mem. Am. Bar Assn., Chgo. Bar Assn. Club: Standard (Chgo.). Home: 521 Stratford Pl Chicago IL 60657 Office: 2 First Nat Plaza Chicago IL 60670

TURNER, ALMON RICHARD, educator; b. New Bedford, Mass., July 28, 1932; s. Louis Alexander and Margaret (Mather) T.; A.B., Princeton, 1955, M.F.A., 1958, Ph.D., 1959; m. Jane Wymond Beebe, June 25, 1955; children—Louis Hamilton, David Alexander. Instr. art history U. Mich., 1959-60; from asst. prof. art and archaeology to prof. Princeton, 1960-68; prof. art, chmn. dept. Middlebury (Vt.) Coll., 1968-74, dean faculty, 1970-74; pres. coll., prof. art Grinnell (Iowa) Coll., 1975-79; dir. Inst. Fine Arts, N.Y. U., N.Y.C., 1979—. Chmn., Edward F. Hazen Found. Mem. Coll. Art Assn. Am., Renaissance Soc. Am., Phi Beta Kappa. Unitarian-Universalist. Club: Century Assn. Author: The Vision of Landscape in Renaissance Italy, 1966. Office: Inst Fine Arts 1 E 78 St New York NY 10021

TURNER, (HENRY) ARLIN, educator; b. Abilene, Tex., Nov. 25, 1909; s. John Henry and Verna Lee (Hatchell) T.; B.A., W. Tex. State Coll., 1927; M.A., U. Tex., 1930, Ph.D., 1934; L.H.D., Berea Coll., 1976; m. Thelma Elizabeth Sherrill, Aug. 7, 1937; children—Arline Elizabeth (Mrs. Richard W. Fonda), Jack Sherrill, Richard Arlin. Instr. English, U. Tex., 1933-36; from instr. to prof. La. State U., 1936-53; prof. Duke, 1953-74, James B. Duke prof., 1974-79, James B. Duke prof. emeritus, 1979—, chmn. English dept., 1958-64; Lindsey prof. lit. S.W. Tex. State U., San Marcos, 1979—. Staff summer sch. W. Tex. State Coll., 1934, E. Tex. State Coll., 1935, 36, N. Tex. State Coll., 1939, Duke, 1947-49, 53, U. Colo., 1951, U. Tex., 1957, U. Va., 1958, U. Ill., 1961, U. Iowa, 1963, N.Y. U., 1964, U. Pa., 1968; vis. prof. U. Montreal, 1951, U. Bombay, 1964, State U. N.Y., Albany, 1978; Fulbright lectr. U. Western Australia, 1952, U. Hull, 1966-67. Mem. Fulbright Screening Com., Am. Studies, 1956-60, 62, 67-68, chmn., 1957-60. Served from lt. (j.g.) to lt. comdr. USNR, 1942-46. Guggenheim fellow, 1947-48, 59-60; Nat. Endowment for Humanities sr. fellow, 1973-74, Huntington Library-Nat. Endowment for Humanities fellow, 1977. Mem. Modern Lang. Assn. Am. (sec. Am. lit. group 1949-53, chmn. 1966-67), Soc. for Study So. Lit. (v.p. 1971-73, pres. 1973-74), South Atlantic Modern Lang. Assn. (chmn. Am. lit. sect. 1956-57), Am. Studies Assn. (exec. council 1955-57, 67-69, exec. com. 1958-59, 67-68, v.p. 1969-70), Southeastern Am. Studies Assn. (pres. 1956-57, v.p. 1955-56, 68-70, pres. 1970-72), Coll. English Assn., So. Hist. Assn. (Sydnor award 1956-57); Soc. Am. Historians, Nat. Council Tchrs. English (dir. 1961-66), Am. Council Learned Socs. (asso. mem., former mem. fellowship selection com.), N.C. Lit. and Hist. Soc. (v.p. 1976-77), Nathaniel Hawthorne Soc. (pres. 1979—), Poe Studies Assn. (hon.), Phi Beta Kappa (hon.), Alpha Chi, Phi Delta Kappa. Author: George W. Cable: A Biography, 1956; Nathaniel Hawthorne: An Introduction and Interpretation, 1961. Editor: Hawthorne as Editor, 1941; The Negro Question, 1958; Creoles and Cajuns, 1959; Southern Stories, 1960; Mark Twain and

George W. Cable, 1960; Studies in The Scarlet Letter, 1970. Mng. editor Am. Lit., 1954-63, editor, 1969-78; mem. editorial bd. South Atlantic Quar., 1956—, So. Lit. Jour., 1968—, Arlington Quar., 1967, Resources for Am. Lit. Study, 1970—, Studies in American Humor, 1974—, Ga. Rev., 1975—. Office: Dept English SW Tex State U San Marcos TX 78666

TURNER, ARTHUR CAMPBELL, educator; b. Glasgow, Scotland, May 19, 1918; s. Malcolm and Robina Arthur (Miller) T.; M.A. with 1st class honors, U. Glasgow, 1941; B.A. with 1st class honors in Modern History, Queen's Coll., Oxford U., 1943, M.A., 1947, B.Litt., 1948, M.Litt., 1979; Ph.D., U. Calif., Berkeley, 1951; m. Anne Gordzialkowska, Jan. 21, 1950; 1 dau., Nadine (Mrs. M.J. O'Sullivan). Naturalized Am. citizen, 1958. Lectr. history U. Glasgow, 1945-51; Commonwealth Fund fellow U. Calif., Berkeley, 1948-50, vis. prof. summers 1950, 66, 71, 78; asst. prof. history U. Toronto, 1951-53; asso. prof. polit. sci. U. Calif., Riverside, 1953-58, prof., 1958—, chmn. div. social scis., 1953-61, dean grad. div., 1960-61, chmn. dept. polit. sci., 1961-66; prof. internat. relations, govt. Claremont Grad. Sch., part-time 1962-72; vis. prof. govt. Pomona Coll., 1977. Exec. com. Inst. World Affairs, 1960—, dir., 1965. Recipient Cecil prize, 1939; Blackwell prize U. Aberdeen, 1943, 51. Rockefeller research grantee, Cambridge, 1959-60; NSF travel grantee, 1964; Wilton Park fellow, 1966, 76. Mem. Am. Soc. Internat. Law, Am., Canadian hist. assns., Am. Polit. Sci. Assn., Hist. Assn. (Eng.). Presbyn. Author: The Post-War House of Commons, 1942; Free Speech and Broadcasting, 1944; Mr. Buchan. Writer: A Life of the First Lord Tweedsmuir, 1949; Scottish Home Rule, 1952; Bulwark of the West: Implications and Problems of NATO, 1953; Towards European Integration, 1953; Pakistan: The Impossible Made Real, 1957; (co-author) Control of Foreign Relations, 1957; (with L. Freedman) Tension Areas in World Affairs, 1964; The Unique Partnership: Britain and the United States, 1971. Chmn. editorial com. U. Calif. Press, 1962-65. Home: 1992 Rincon Ave Riverside CA 92506. *It is now popular to say that we are nothing but the playthings of large, impersonal forces. Actually people, and peoples, bring most of their troubles on themselves. Our success and happiness are, to a large extent, in our own hands.*

TURNER, ARTHUR EDWARD, coll. adminstr.; b. Hemlock, Mich., Jan. 31, 1931; s. Alvin S. and Grace E. (Champlain) T.; B.S. (Silliman scholar), Alma (Mich.) Coll., 1952; M.Ed., Wayne State U., 1954; postgrad. Central Mich. U., U. Mich.; LL.D. (hon.), Ashland Coll., 1968; Hu.D. (hon.), Colegio Americano de Quito (Ecuador), 1968; m. Johann May Jordan, May 10, 1953; children—Steven Arthur, Michael Scott, Kathryn Jo. Admissions counselor Alma Coll., 1952-53, dir. admissions, alumni relations, 1953-59; Presbyterian lay minister, 1956-59; organizer Eastminister Presbyn. Ch., Alma, 1956; co-founder, 1st pres., trustee Northwood Inst., Alma, 1959, Midland, Mich., 1962, now with campuses at Midland, Cedar Hill, Tex., West Baden, Ind., Quito, Ecuador (Extension Center), 1966, Bloomfield Hills (Mich.) Acad. (formerly Bloomfield Country Day Sch. for Girls), affiliated 1971, chmn., chief exec. officer, trustee, 1974-78, chmn. bd. trustees, 1978—. Trustee nat. council Boy Scouts Am.; elder Meml. Presbyn. Ch., Midland, 1955—. Recipient People of Peru award, 1966; named One of Ten Outstanding Young Ams., 1965. Mem. Alpha Psi Omega, Phi Phi Alpha. Mason (33 deg., Shriner), Rotarian. Clubs: Detroit; Midland Country; Poinciani (Miami, Fla.); Columbia (Indpls.). Home: 4608 Arbor Dr Midland MI 48640 Office: Northwood Inst Midland MI 48640

TURNER, BASIL SIDNEY, mfg. exec.; b. Paradise, Ky., Dec. 5, 1908; s. Henry Harlan and Dora (Pendley) T.; B.S. in Elec. Engring., Purdue U., 1930, Dr. Indsl. Adminstrn. (hon.), 1965; D.Engring., Tri-State U., 1976; m. Ethel L. Holben, May 14, 1932; 1 dau., Laura C. With CTS Corp. (formerly Chgo. Telephone Supply Corp.), Elkhart, Ind., 1930—, successively engr., asst. chief engr., gen. supt., v.p. and gen. mgr., 1930-50, exec. v.p., gen. mgr., 1950-60, pres., dir., 1960-67, chmn. exec. com., treas., 1968-70, chmn. bd., 1971—; treas., dir. CTS Can. Ltd., CTS Brownsville, Inc., Tex., CTS Paducah (Ky.), Inc., CTS Berne, Inc., CTS Microelectronics, Inc., Lafayette, Ind., CTS Asheville, Inc. (N.C.), CTS Tool, Die & Machine, Inc., Ft. Wayne, Ind.; pres., dir. CTS Components Taiwan, Ltd., Kaohsiung, CTS Knights, Inc., Sandwich, Ill., Owners Discount Corp. Chmn., trustee CTS Found.; bd. dirs. Salvation Army, Elkhart. Registered profl. engr., Ind. Mem. I.R.E., Elkhart C. of C. Methodist. Rotarian. Home: 2705 Greenleaf Blvd Elkhart IN 46514 Office: 905 N West Blvd Elkhart IN 46514

TURNER, BILLIE LEE, botanist, educator; b. Yoakum, Tex., Feb. 22, 1925; s. James Madison and Julia Irene (Harper) T.; B.S., Sul Ross State Coll., 1949; M.S., So. Meth. U., 1950; Ph.D., Wash. State U., 1953; m. Virginia Ruth Mathis, Sept. 27, 1944 (div. Feb. 1968); children—Billie Lee, Matt Warnock; m. 2d, Pauline Henderson, Oct. 22, 1969 (div. Jan. 1975). Teaching asst. botany dept. Wash. State U., 1951-53; instr. botany dept. U. Tex., Austin, 1953, asst. prof., 1954-58, asso. prof., 1958-61, prof., 1961—, chmn., 1967-75, dir. U. Tex. Herbarium, 1957—. Asso. investigator ecol. study vegetation of Africa, U. Ariz., Office Naval Research, 1956-57. Served to 1st lt. USAAF, 1943-47. NSF postdoctoral fellow U. Liverpool, 1965-66; vis. prof. U. Mont., summers 1971, 73, U. Mass., 1974. Mem. Bot. Soc. Am. (sec. 1958-59, 60-64, v.p. 1969), Tex. Acad. Sci., Southwestern Assn. Naturalists (pres. 1967, gov.), Am. Soc. Plant Taxonomists, Internat. Assn. Plant Taxonomists, Soc. Study Evolution, Phi Beta Kappa, Sigma Xi. Author: Vegetational Changes in Africa Over a Third of a Century, 1959; Leguminosae of Texas, 1960; Biochemical Systematics, 1963; Chemotaxonomy of Leguminosae, 1972; Biology and Chemistry of Compositae, 1977. Asso. editor Southwestern Naturalist, 1959—. Address: Dept Botany U Tex Austin TX 78712

TURNER, BURNETT COBURN, architect; b. Los Angeles, Dec. 3, 1902; s. Harry Coburn and Marie Ada (Burnett) T.; student U. Calif., Los Angeles, 1920-21; B.S., Princeton, 1925, C.E., 1926; B.S. in Architecture, Mass. Inst. Tech., 1928; m. Miriam Fechimer, Jan. 23, 1932; 1 son, Peter Coburn. Asso., Horace W. Peaslee, architect, Washington, 1928-30, Alfred Hopkins & Assos., N.Y.C., 1930-35; architect-engr., cons. architect U.S. Housing Authority, Washington, regional tech. adviser, San Francisco, Los Angeles, 1935-41; asst. dir. West Coast office, Housing Div., Fed. Works Adminstrn., 1941-42; pvt. practice architecture and planning cons., Los Angeles, 1946—; v.p. Turner Oil Co., Los Angeles. Mem. Town Hall Los Angeles. Mem. Hist. Soc. So. Calif., v.p., 1966; bd. dirs. Calif. Heritage Council; mem. Mayor's Com. Los Angeles Bicentennial. Served to lt. col. C.E., AUS, 1942-58. Decorated Army medal for mil. merit, 1946. Fellow AIA (dir. So. Calif. chpt. 1957-59); mem. Am. Inst. Planners, Am. Arbitration Assn. (arbitrator), Nat. Trust Historic Preservation, Soc. Archtl. Historians. Clubs: Economic Round Table (pres. 1974-75), Scribes (pres. 1956), University (Los Angeles); Southern Skis (pres. 1953-54). Home: 3730 Amesbury Rd Los Angeles CA 90027 Office: 2410 Beverly Blvd Los Angeles CA 90057

TURNER, DARWIN THEODORE TROY, educator; b. Cin., May 7, 1931; s. Darwin R. and Laura (Knight) T.; B.A., U. Cin., 1947, M.A., 1949; Ph.D., U. Chgo., 1956; m. Maggie Jean Lewis; children—Pamela, Darwin K., Rachon. Asst. prof. English, Clark Coll., Atlanta, 1949-51; asst. prof. English, Morgan State Coll., Balt., 1952-57; prof., chmn. English dept. Fla. A. and M. State U., Tallahassee, 1957-59; prof., chmn. English dept. N.C. A. and T. State U., Greensboro, 1959-66, dean Grad. Sch., 1966-70; vis. prof. English, U. Wis., 1969; prof. English, U. Mich., Ann Arbor, 1970-71; vis. prof. U. Hawaii, summer, 1971; prof. English, U. Iowa, Iowa City, 1971—, dir. Afro-Am. studies, 1972—. Mem. exec. com. Conf. on Coll. Composition and Communication, 1967-69; cons. in English and Afro-Am. studies for high schs., colls., pvt. founds., fed. agys., profl. socs.; mem. grad. record exams. bd., 1970-73; state chmn., mem. regional exec. com. 2d World Festival Black and African Arts and Culture, 1973-77; chmn. Iowa Colls. and Univs. Consortium for Teaching Afro-Am. Culture. Mem. Guilford County Bicentennial Commn., 1969-70. Bd. dirs. Black Caucus Coll. English Tchrs., 1977-78; trustee Nat. Council Tchrs. English Research Found., 1970-73, Nat. Humanities Center, 1978—; mem. Commn. on the Humanities, 1978—. Recipient U. Chgo. Alumni Assn. Profl. Achievement award, 1972. Am. Council Learned Socs. grantee, 1965, 78; fellow Duke-N.C. univs. humanities program, 1965-66; Rockefeller Found. grantee, 1972; del. African Regional Am. Studies Conf., Ivory Coast, 1976; del. 2d World Festival African Arts and Culture, Nigeria, 1977. Mem. Coll. Lang. Assn. (pres. 1963-65), N.C.-Va. Coll. English Assn. (pres. 1964-65), Modern Lang. Assn. (chmn. com. on edn. of minority groups 1970-72, del. assembly 1974-77, chmn. ethnic studies div. 1978—), Nat. Assn. Black Profs., Nat. Humanities Faculty, Nat. Council Tchrs. English (chmn. com. on lit. minority groups 1969—, dir.-at-large 1967-70, chmn. resolutions com. 1972), Nat. Council Black Studies (exec. com. 1976-78), Coll. English Assn. (dir. 1971-74), AAUP (com. A. 1977—), Phi Beta Kappa, Alpha Phi Alpha, Theta Alpha Phi, Lambda Iota Tau. Author: (poems) Katharsis, 1964; Hawthorne's Scarlet Letter, 1967; In a Minor Chord, 1971; Afro-American Literature and Syllabus, 1977; co-author Theory and Practice in the Teaching of Literature by Afro-Americans, 1971. Editor: Black American Literature: Essays, Fiction, Poetry 3 vols., 1969; Black American Literature (combined edit.), 1970; Black Drama in America-an Anthology, 1971; The Wayward and the Seeking: a Miscellany of Writings by Jean Toomer, 1979. Co-editor: Images of the Negro in America, 1965; Voices from the Black Experience: African and Afro-American Literature, 1972; Responding-Five, 1973. Compiler: Afro-American Writers (a bibliography), 1970. Contbg. editor: Black Books Bull., Obsidian, CLA Jour.; advisory editor Am. Lit. Office: 303 English-Philosophy Bldg U Iowa Iowa City IA 52242

TURNER, DAVID REUBEN, publisher, author; b. N.Y.C., Dec. 9, 1915; s. Charles and Eva (Turner) Moskowitz; B.S., Coll. City N.Y., 1936, M.S. in Edn., 1937; m. Ann Louise Perkins, Apr. 29, 1946 (div. 1976); children—Eve (Mrs. William Watters), Ruth. Co-founder Arco Pub. Co., N.Y.C., 1937, pub., dir., 1937—, v.p. parent co. Prentice-Hall, Inc., 1979—; pub. cons. under Ford Found. contract Burma Translation Soc., Rangoon, 1959-60. Adviser bd. publs. Union Am. Hebrew Congregations. Author more than 300 books on tests and testing, including: High School Equivalency Diploma Tests, 1951, 75; How to Win a Scholarship, 1955; Scoring High On College Entrance Tests, 1969, 71; Food Service Supervisor, 1968; Bank Examiner, 1968; Accountant-Auditor, 1960, 77; Officer Candidate Tests, 1978; Professional-Administrative Career Exams, 1979; English Grammar and Usage for Test-Takers, 1976; College Level Examination Program, 1979. Home: 177 Firenze Ave Northvale NJ 07647 Office: Box 256 Scarborough NY 10510

TURNER, DONALD FRANK, lawyer; b. Chippewa Falls, Wis., Mar. 19, 1921; s. Paul and Elizabeth (Catterlin) T.; B.A., Northwestern U., 1941; M.A., Harvard, 1943, Ph.D., 1947; LL.B., Yale, 1950; m. Joan Pearson, Dec. 17, 1955; children—Paul Alfred, Katherine. Admitted to D.C. bar, 1951; law clk. U.S. Supreme Ct., 1950-51; asso. law firm Cox, Langford, Stoddard & Cutler, Washington, 1951-54; asst. prof. Harvard Law Sch., 1954-57, prof., 1957-65, 68-79; of counsel firm Wilmer & Pickering, Washington, 1979—; asst. atty. gen. charge anti-trust div. U.S. Dept. Justice, 1965-68. Served to lt. USNR, 1943-46. Mem. Am. Bar Assn., Phi Beta Kappa. Home: 2101 Connecticut Ave NW Washington DC 20008 Office: 1666 K St NW Washington DC 20008

TURNER, EDWARD CLARK, clergyman; b. Buenos Aires, Argentina, Mar. 26, 1915; s. Edward and Eva Helen (Clark) T.; came to U.S., 1922; A.B., Northwestern U., 1937; B.D., Seabury Western Theol. Sem., Evanston, Ill., 1940, D.D., 1954; m. Virginia Hunter, Nov. 19, 1938; children—John Bowen, Mary, David Hunter, James Clark. Ordained priest Episcopal Ch., 1940; assigned missions St. John, Okanogan, St. Paul, Omak, Trinity, Oroville and Tranfiguration, Twisp, Washington, 1940-44; rector Ch. Ascension, Pueblo, Colo., 1944; bishop coadjutor Diocese Kans., Topeka, 1956, diocesan, 1959. Pres., Pueblo City-County Bd. Health, 1953-56. Chmn. bd. dirs. Parkview Episc. Hosp., Pueblo; bd. dirs. ARC, Pueblo chpt., Pueblo Family Service Soc., Stormant-Vail Hosp., Topeka; trustee Seabury-Western Theol. Sem. Home: Bethany Pl Topeka KS 66612

TURNER, EDWARD MASON, bishop; b. Chgo., Nov. 13, 1918; s. Allen Bowden and Frances Marjory (Miller) T.; B.A., Carroll Coll., 1941; M.Div., Nashotah Ho. Sem., 1944, D.D., 1972; postgrad. Marquette U., 1947; m. May 29, 1944; 2 children; m. 2d, Shirley Louise Dittmer, May 1, 1958. Ordained priest Episcopal Ch., 1944; priest-in-charge St. Peter's Ch., Seward, Alaska, 1944-49; asst. to dir. overseas dept. Episcopal Ch., N.Y.C., 1949-53; canon St. John's Cathedral, Santurce, San Juan, P.R., 1953-57; rector St. Paul's Ch., Frederiksted, V.I., 1958-72; bishop V.I., 1972—; del. Gen. Conv. Episcopal Ch., 1964-70. Served as chaplain USN, 1950-51. Address: PO Box 7488 Saint Thomas VI 00801

TURNER, EVAN HOPKINS, art mus. dir., educator; b. Orono, Me., Nov. 8, 1927; s. Albert Morton and Percie Trowbridge (Hopkins) T.; A.B. cum laude, Harvard, 1949, M.A., 1950, Ph.D., 1954; m. Brenda Winthrop Bowman, May 12, 1956; children—John, Jennifer. Head docent service Fogg Mus., 1950-51; curator Robbins Art Collection of Prints, Arlington, Mass., 1951; teaching fellow fine arts Harvard, 1951-52; lectr., research asst. Frick Collection, N.Y.C., 1953-56; gen. curator, asst. dir. Wadsworth Atheneum, Hartford, Conn., 1956-59; dir. Montreal (Can.) Mus. Fine Arts, 1959-64, Phila. Mus. Art, 1964-77; dir. Ackland Art Mus., adj. prof. U. N.C., Chapel Hill, 1978—. Adj. prof. art history U. Pa.; chmn. mus. panel Nat. Endowment for Arts. Benjamin Franklin fellow Royal Soc. Arts. Mem. Assn. Art Mus. Dirs., Coll. Art Assn. Am., Am. Mus. Assn., Am. Fedn. Arts. Unitarian. Clubs: Harvard, Franklin Inn (Phila.); Century Assn. Home: 103 E Queen St Hillsborough NC 27270 Office: Ackland Art Mus Chapel Hill NC 27504

TURNER, FRANCIS JOHN, ret. educator, geologist; b. Auckland, New Zealand, Apr. 10, 1904; s. Joseph Hurst and Gertrude (Reid) T.; B.S., Auckland U. Coll., 1924, M.S., 1926; D.Sc., U. New Zealand, 1933; fellow Yale, 1938; D.Sc. (hon.), Auckland U., 1965; m. Esme Rena Bentham, Aug. 29, 1930; 1 child, Gillian Bentham McKercher. Came to U.S., 1946, naturalized, 1953. Lectr. geology U. Otago, 1926-46; asso. prof. geology U. Calif., 1946-48, prof., 1948-72, prof. emeritus, 1972—. Guggenheim fellow, 1950, 60; Fulbright fellow, 1956; fgn. corr. Academia delle Scienze, Instituto di Bolongna, Italy, 1953; vis. fellow Brasenose Coll., Oxford, 1972-73. Recipient Berkeley award U. Calif., 1972. Fellow Geol. Soc. Am., Royal Soc. New Zealand (Hector medal 1950), Mineral. Soc. Am. (pres. 1968-69), Geol. Soc. Edinburgh (corr.), Calif. Acad. Sci.; mem. Nat. Acad. Scis., Geol. Soc. London (fgn., Lyell medal 1969). Author: Evolution of Metamorphic Rocks, 1948; (with J. Verhoogen) Igneous and Metamorphic Petrology, 1951; (with H. Williams, C.M. Gilbert) Petrography, 1953; (with L.E. Weiss) Metamorphic Tectonites, 1963; Metamorphic Petrology, 1968; (with J. Verhoogen, others) The Earth, 1970; (with I.S.E. Carmichael and J. Verhoogen) Igneous Petrology, 1974. Co-editor: Contributions to Mineralogy and Petrology, 1965—. Home: 2525 Hill Ct Berkeley CA 94708

TURNER, FRED L., fast food restaurant co. exec.; b. 1933; B.S., De Paul U., 1952; married. With McDonald's Corp., Oak Brook, Ill., 1956—, exec. v.p., 1967-68, pres., chief adminstrv. officer, 1968-77, chmn. bd., chief exec. officer, 1977—, also dir. Served as 1st lt. U.S. Army, 1943-45. Office: McDonald's Corp One McDonald's Plaza Oak Brook IL 60521*

TURNER, GEORGE PEARCE, investment co. exec.; b. Dallas, Aug. 22, 1915; s. Fred Horatio and Florence (Phillips) T.; architecture-engring. student U. Tex., 1932-33, 35-36, 40-41, So. Methodist U., 1934; B.A. cum laude, U. So. Calif., 1962, M.S. summa cum laude in Internat. Pub. Adminstrn., 1966; m. June Lori Haney, Feb. 4, 1943 (div. 1976); children—Bruce Haney, Brian Phillips, Mark Richardson; m. 2d, Kathryn Blank Hauf, June 1976. Archtl. designer, Los Angeles, 1946-48; prin. Lieburg & Turner, cons. engrs., Pasadena, Calif., 1947-48; pres. Radiant Heat Engring., Inc., Pasadena, 1948-53; exec. asst. to dir. fgn. subsidiaries S.Am. Fluor Corp. Ltd., Los Angeles, 1953-54; exec. staff mem. Coast Fed. Savs. & Loan Assn., 1954-55, Holmes & Narver, Inc., 1955-61, Los Angeles; mgr. project devel. S.Am. operations Southwestern Engring. Co., Los Angeles, 1962; pres. Haney Devel. Corp., 1964—, Fomento e Inversiones Quisqueyanos C. por A., Santo Domingo de Guzman, Dominican Republic, 1967—; gen. mgr. for Venezuelan operations Hale Internat. Inc., Caracas, 1970-71; dir.-mgr. Consortium Lomas de La Lagunita, Caracas, 1970, Consortium Desarrollos Urbanos, Valencia, Venezeula, 1970; pres. Haney Investment Corp. (HANCO), 1974—; pres. Caribbean Vagabond Ltd., Grand Cayman Island, B.W.I., Casa Fomig, Newtown Square, Pa.; cons. econ. devel., 1976—, adviser, provisional pres. Dominican Republic, 1965-66, constl. pres. of republic, 1966-68, projects programmer Nat. Planning Inst. Peru Tri-Partite Mission, 1963-65; ofcl. adviser Nat. Office Tourism Dominican Republic, 1966-67, Nat. Office Cultural Patrimony, 1967-68; Liga Municipal Dominicana; OAS cons., dir. projects, programming, tech. matters Mission Recovery and Rehab., Dominican Republic, 1963-67; dep. dir. Tech. Assistance Mission Dominican Republic; cons. assignments for program assistance Inter-Am. Tng. Center, Fed. U. Ceara (Brazil); OAS adviser on tech. assistance to Chile, Argentina, Uruguay, Peru, Brazil, 1962-68; cons. Capital Investment Devel. Corp., Downing Center, Downingtown, Pa., 1971-77; dir. for Project Monitor and owners agt., hosp. tower Hahnemann Med. Coll. and Hosp., Phila., 1975-78; pres. Urban Planning and Devel. Corp., Exton, Pa., 1978—; cons., corp. sec. Integrated Industries Inc., Exton, 1978—. Served with USAAF, 1941-45. Recipient Medal of Honor and citation for valiant service in Dominican Republic OAS, 1965-66, ofcl. commendation program contbns. Peru, Dominican Republic, Brazil, Venezuela, 1969. Mem. Delta Phi Epsilon, Alpha Sigma Lambda. Author: An Analysis of the Economy of El Salvador, 1961; The Alliance for Progress: Concept Versus Structure, 1966. Contbr. articles to profl. publs. Home: 8 Fox Run Ln Newtown Square PA 19073 Office: Haney Investment Corp PO Box 158 Lionville PA 19353

TURNER, GERALD PHILLIP, hosp. adminstr.; b. Winnipeg, Man., Can., May 13, 1930; s. Lorry and Shirley (Litman) Turbovsky; B.Sc. in Pharmacy, U. Man., Winnipeg, 1953; Diploma in Hosp. Adminstrn., U. Toronto (Ont., Can.), 1955; m. Clare Henteleff, June 12, 1955; children—Robin Joy, Neil Lindsay, Darryl Lyon. Asst. adminstr. Mt. Sinai Hosp., Toronto, 1955-62, asso. adminstr., 1962-66, adminstr. 1966-74, exec. dir., chief exec. officer, 1974—; exec. v.p. Mt. Sinai Inst., Toronto, 1976—; asso. prof. health adminstrn. U. Toronto, 1971—; dir. Booth Ave. Hosp. Laundry Inc., Hosp. Purchasing Inc., Toronto Hosps. Steam Corp. Recipient Queen's Silver Jubilee medal. Fellow Am. Coll. Hosp. Adminstrs.; mem. Can. Coll. Health Service Execs. (founder mem.), Ont. Hosp. Assn. (dir.), Hosp. Council Met. Toronto (dir.). Editor: (with Joseph Mapa) Humanizing Hospital Care, 1979. Office: 600 University Ave Toronto ON M5G 1X5 Canada

TURNER, HALCOTT MEBANE, univ. pres.; b. Danville, Va., Dec. 28, 1930; s. Edgar Halcott and Betty Graham (Tarpley) T.; B.S., U. Va., 1954; B.D., Union Theol. Sem., 1957; M.A., Tchrs. Coll., Columbia, 1960; Ed.D., Am. U., 1974. Asst. financial aid officer U. Va., 1963-64, field sec. Alumni Assn., 1964-65, dean students, dir. admissions George Mason U., 1965-68; provost U. Balt., 1968-69, pres., 1969—; dir. Loyola Fed. Savs. and Loan Assn., Balt. Life Ins. Co. Pres., Balt. City Jail Bd., 1972; bd. dirs. Ch. Hosp. Corp. Served with Chaplain Corps, U.S. Army, 1957-59. Mem. Omicron Delta Kappa, Phi Delta Kappa. Rotarian. Clubs: Maryland; Rotary. Home: 700 N Charles St Baltimore MD 21201 Office: Charles at Mt Royal Baltimore MD 21201

TURNER, HAROLD EDWARD, educator; b. Hamilton, Ill., Nov. 22, 1921; s. Edward Jesse and Beulah May (White) T.; A.B., Carthage Coll., 1950; M.S., U. Ill. at Urbana, 1951, Ed.D. (George Peabody fellow), 1956; m. Catherine Skeeters, Apr. 5, 1946; children—Michele (Mrs. William Warren), Thomas, Barbara (Mrs. Pat McMahon), Krista. Tchr., Taylorville (Ill.) Jr. High Sch., 1951-52, Moline (Ill.) Jr. High Sch., 1952-54; dir. elementary edn. Jefferson County, Colo., 1955-57; prin. Jefferson County High Sch., 1957-60; asst. prof. edn. North Tex. State U., Denton, 1960-63; asst. supt. curriculum Sacramento City Schs., 1963-66; asso. prof., chmn. dept. curriculum and instrn. U. Mo. at St. Louis, 1966-69, prof., 1971—, chmn. dept. adminstrn., founds., secondary edn. Vis. prof. Adams State Coll., Alamosa, Colo., 1959; adj. prof. N.Y. U., 1965; cons. in field to various sch. dists., Tex., Mo.; spl. cons. Mo. State Dept. Edn., 1973. Served with USNR, 1942-46. Mem. Nat., Mo. (exec. sec. 1967-77, pres. 1977-78) assns. supervision and curriculum devel., Greater St. Louis Curriculum Dirs., John Dewey Soc. (chmn. meetings 1973—), Profs. Supervision, Nat. Soc. Study Edn., Soc. Profs. Edn., Am. Assn. Sch. Adminstrs., Mo. State Tchrs. Assn., Greater St. Louis White House Conf. Edn., Phi Delta Kappa. Presbyterian (elder). Club: Masons. Author: (with Adolph Unruh) Supervision for Change Innovation, 1970. Contbr. articles in field to profl. jours. Home: 12184 Gladshire St Bridgeton MO 63044 Office: Sch Edn U Mo 8001 Natural Bridge Rd Saint Louis MO 63121

TURNER, HARRY EDWARD, lawyer; b. Mt. Vernon, Ohio, Dec. 25, 1927; s. Paul Hamilton and Harriett (Kraft) T.; B.A., Baldwin Wallace Coll., 1951; J.D., Ohio No. U., 1954; m. Shirley Marilyn Eggert, July 8, 1950; children—Harry Edward, Thomas Frederick. Admitted to Ohio bar, 1954, U.S. Supreme Ct. bar; practice in Mt. Vernon 1954—. Dir. Fairfield Engring. Co.; sec., dir. Curtis Investment Corp. State rep. Ohio Gen. Assembly, 1973—. Prosecutor, Mt. Vernon Municipal Ct., 1955-58; solicitor Mt. Vernon, 1958-62; mem. Mt. Vernon City Sch. Bd., 1964-70, pres., 1965-70; trustee Ohio Sch. Bd. Assn., 1968-70. Served with USN, 1946-47.

Mem. Am., Ohio, Knox County (pres. 1970) bar assns., Alpha Sigma Phi, Sigma Delta Kappa. Republican. Lutheran. Home: 400 E Vine St Mount Vernon OH 43050 Office: 118 E High St Mount Vernon OH 43050

TURNER, HENRY A., JR., educator, author; b. King City, Mo., Jan. 2, 1919; s. Henry A. and Bessie Marie (Claxton) T.; B.S., N.W. Mo. State U., 1939; M.A., Mo. U., 1941; Ph.D., U. Chgo., 1950; m. Mary Margaret Tilton, May 23, 1943; children—John Andrew, Nancy Ellen, Stephen Heald. Jr. coll. instr., 1940-42; instr. Iowa State U., 1945-46; from instr. to asso. prof. U. Calif., Santa Barbara, 1948-62, prof., 1962—, chmn. dept. polit. sci., 1960-65, acad. vice chancellor, 1971-73. Summer faculty U. Mo., 1951, U. Nebr., 1956, U. Calif., Berkeley, 1958; vis. prof. polit. sci. U. Khartoum, Sudan, 1962-63; Fulbright lectr. U. Witwatersrand, South Africa, 1968, U. Teheran (Iran), 1974; cons. Bur. Budget, 1953; mem. staff White House, 1953. Staff mem. Democratic Nat. Com., 1952. Served from ensign to lt. USNR, 1942-45. Mem. Am., Western polit. sci. assns. Author: (with J.A. Vieg) The Government and Politics of California, 4th edit., 1971; American Democracy: State and Local Government, 1968, 2d edit., 1970; co-author: American Democracy in World Perspective, 1967, 4th edit., 1976. Editor: Politics in the United States, 1955. Contbr. articles to profl. jours. Home: 955 Camino Medio Santa Barbara CA 93105

TURNER, HENRY BROWN, govt. ofcl.; b. N.Y.C., Sept. 3, 1936; s. Henry Brown III and Gertrude (Adams) T.; A.B., Duke U., 1958; M.B.A., Harvard, 1962; m. Sarah Jean Thomas, June 7, 1958; children—Laura Eleanor, Steven Bristow, Nancy Carolyn. Controller, Fin. Corp. of Ariz., Phoenix, 1962-64; treas., dir. corporate planning Star-Kist Foods, Terminal Island, Calif., 1964-67; dir., 1st v.p. Mitchum, Jones & Templeton, Los Angeles, 1967-73; asst. sec. commerce, Washington, 1973-74; v.p. fin. N-Ren Corp., Cin., 1975-76; v.p. Oppenheimer & Co., N.Y.C., 1976-78; exec. v.p., mng. dir. corporate fin. Shearson Hayden Stone Inc., N.Y.C., 1978—; dir. Mobex, Cousteau Group, Korn/Ferry Internat., Redken Labs., Exec. Confs., Ltd., Swift-Ships, Inc., Shirley of Atlanta, Inc., Monroc, Inc., MacDonald & Co. Sponsor, Jr. Achievement, 1964-67. Bd. dirs. Harvard Bus. Sch. Club of So. Calif. Served to lt. (j.g.) USNR, 1958-60. Coll. Men's Club scholar, Westfield, N.J., 1954-55. Mem. Fed. Govt. Accountants Assn. (hon.), Omicron Delta Kappa. Home: 1100 Park Ave Apt 8A New York NY 10028 Office: Shearson Hayden Stone Inc 767 Fifth Ave New York NY 10022

TURNER, HERBERT DAVID, mech. engr.; b. N.Y.C., Feb. 24, 1923; s. Leo and Mollie (Dobrikin) T.; student Ohio State U., 1941; B.S. in Mech. Engring., Case Inst. Tech., 1950; postgrad. St. Catherine's Soc., U. Oxford, Eng., 1950-51; m. Edna Pauline Gluck, Sept. 11, 1948; children—Mark Ian, Steven Ives, Perry Adam. Tool and die maker, design draftsman, mech. engr. Perfection Steel Body Co., Monsanto Chem. Co., Internat. Gen. Electric Corp., 1940-51; prodn. assn., then prodn. assistance specialist, productivity and tech. exchange officer FOA, U.S. mission, Copenhagen, Denmark, 1951-56, chief tng. br., dep. dir. tech. coop. div., ICA, U.S. mission to NATO, other European orgns. in Paris, 1956-60, chief program devel. div. Office Participant Tng., Washington, 1960-61; dep. exec. sec. Pres.'s Task Force on Fgn. Aid, 1961; sr. evaluation officer AID, 1961-64, sr. sci. research adminstr., 1964-66, chief policy planning Office Tech. Co-operation and Research, 1966-67, chief tech. assistance policy div., 1967-70, chief evaluation staff, 1970-72, dep. coordinator Office Programs Methods and Evaluation, 1972-74, chief program design and evaluation div., 1974—. Alternate U.S. rep., governing body of European Productivity Agy.; guest lectr. Centre de Formation des Experts de La Cooperation Technique Internationale; indsl. studies in Sweden, Internat. Assn. for Exchange of Scientists, Technicians and Engrs., 1951. Mem. exec. bd. UN Internat. Sch., Paris. Served with USAAF, World War II. Recipient Superior Honor award AID, 1976. Mem. Am. Soc. M.E., Am. Soc. Tool Engrs., Research Inst. Mgmt. Sci. (Delft Tech. U.). Home: 3419 Cummings Ln Chevy Chase MD 20015 Office: Agy Internat Devel/W care Dept of State Washington DC 20525

TURNER, HESTER HILL, assn. exec.; b. San Antonio, Jan. 31, 1917; d. Orvin A. and Edna Lee (Guerguin) Hill; B.S., Our Lady of Lake Coll., 1938; M.A., S.W. Tex. State Coll., 1940; J.D., U. Ariz., 1945; Ed.D., Oreg. State U., 1956; m. William Hoag Turner, Mar. 7, 1939 (div. Aug. 1957); children—William Hoag, John Daniel, Mary Lee Turner Maguire, Jane Livingston (Mrs. S. Thomas Toleno). Faculty, Lewis and Clark Coll., Portland, 1947-66, dean students, 1961-66; nat. exec. dir. Camp Fire Girls, Inc., Kansas City, Mo., 1966-79. Vis. instr. Oreg. State U., Western Wash. Coll., Portland State Coll.; dir. profl. services Oreg. Edn. Assn., Portland, 1959-61; dir. Mohasco Corp., Am. Humanics. Mem. Oreg. Commn. on Status of Women, 1964-66; del. White House Conf. on Status of Women, 1965; mem. Portland met. steering com. OEO, 1965-66, Nat. Citizens Adv. Com. Vocat. Rehab., 1966-68; mem. Def. Adv. Com. Women in Services, 1966-69, chmn., 1968-69; mem. N.Y. State Vocat. Rehab. Planning Council, 1967-68. Recipient Dept. Def. medal for distinguished pub. service, 1970. Mem. NEA, Oreg. Assn. Health and Phys. Edn. (pres. 1959-60), Oreg., Ariz. bar assns., Am. Forestry Assn. (v.p. 1977-79, pres. 1980—), Phi Kappa Phi, Delta Kappa Gamma. Contbr. articles and chpts. to profl. publs. Office: 601 E 20th St New York NY 10010. *One learns to make decisions only by making them. All adults who care about young people are presented with a special challenge: If we want to help them become responsible adults, we must have both the courage to stand for our own beliefs, and the faith to allow them to discover their own.*

TURNER, HOWARD SINCLAIR, corp. ofcl.; b. Jenkintown, Pa., Nov. 27, 1911; s. Joseph Archer and Helen (Carre) T.; A.B., Swarthmore Coll., 1933, LL.D. (hon.), 1977; Ph.D., M.I.T., 1936; m. Katharine Swett, 1936; children—Susan, Helen Christine, Barbara Jean. Research chemist, technologist, supr. E.I. duPont de Nemours & Co., Inc., 1936-47; dir. research and devel. Pitts. Consolidation Coal Co., 1947-54; v.p. research and devel. Jones & Laughlin Steel Corp., 1954-65, dir., 1965-71; pres. Turner Constrn. Co., N.Y.C., 1965-70, chief exec. officer, 1968-76, chmn. bd., 1971-78, chmn. exec. com., 1978—, dir. 1952—); dir. Ingersoll-Rand, Tchrs. Ins. & Annuity Assn., Asarco, Dime Savs. Bank of N.Y. Adviser to Q.M. Gen. on research, 1942-44, Office Indsl. Applications, NASA, 1962-65; mem. vis. com. dept. chem. engring. Carnegie Inst. Tech., 1962-65; mem. tech. adv. bd. Dept. Commerce, 1963-67; mem. Viet Nam task force HEW, 1966; mem. research and engring. adv. council P.O. Dept., 1967-68; exec. com. div.. engring. NRC, 1967-71; mem. Pres.'s Sci. Advisory Com., 1972; mem. adv. com. Center for Bldg. Tech., Nat. Bur. Standards, 1973-75; mem. vis. com. dept. civil engring. Mass. Inst. Tech., 1974; mem. adv. council Sch. Architecture and Urban Planning, Princeton U., 1974. Mem. Swarthmore Borough Council, 1944-47. Bd. mgrs. Swarthmore Coll., 1952-64, 68-72; trustee Am. Acad. Ednl. Devel., C.F. Kettering Found., 1979—; former pres. Indsl. Research Inst.; mem. council Rockefeller U. Mem. Am. Chem. Soc. (emeritus), Dirs. Indsl. Research, Com. for Econ. Devel. (trustee), Nat. Acad. Engring., Econ. Club N.Y. Phi Beta Kappa, Sigma Xi, Phi Kappa Psi. Club: University. Home: 870 UN Plaza New York NY 10017 Office: 150 E 42d St New York NY 10017

TURNER, IKE, musician; b. Clarksdale, Miss., 1934; m. Annie Mae Bullock, 1956. Leader, Ike Turner Kings of Rhythm and Ike and Tina Turner Revue; appeared in films Gimme Shelter, 1970, Soul to Soul, 1971; concert tours in Europe, 1966, in Japan and Africa, 1971. Recipient Grammy award for rec. Proud Mary, 1972. Office: care Internat Recording Studio 1310 N LaBrea Ave Inglewood CA 90302

TURNER, JAMES CASTLE, union ofcl.; b. Beaumont, Tex., Nov. 4, 1916; s. James Castle and Lydia (Carley) T.; A.B., Catholic U. Am., 1940; m. Mary Pauline Curtis, Apr. 14, 1934; children—Vivian, Daniel, Brian, Lisa, Lauran. Bus. mgr., bus. rep. local 77, Internat. Union Operating Engrs., Washington, 1940-71, nat. v.p., 1956-72, gen. sec.-treas., 1972-75, gen. pres., 1975—; U.S. rep. ILO, Geneva, 1952, 64, 74, 75, 77; tchr. adult edn. Am. U. Del. Democratic Nat. Conv., 1952, 56, 60, 64; vice chmn. D.C. Dem. Central Com., 1950-60, 63-67; Dem. nat. commiteeman for D.C., 1960, 76—; mem. D.C. City Council, 1967-68; trustee Nat. Urban League, Nat. Urban Coalition; v.p., bd. govs., chmn. exec. com. United Way Am. Mem. Nat. Planning Assn. (trustee), Blue Key. Episcopalian. Clubs: Nat. Dem., Nat. Press, Touchdown. Editor: Internat. Engr., 1972-75. Home: 6961 32d St NW Washington DC 20015 Office: 1125 17th St NW Washington DC 20036

TURNER, JAMES PHILIP, govt. ofcl., lawyer; b. Pueblo, Colo., Oct. 27, 1930; s. James Charles and Florence Ethel (Sturtevant) T.; B.J., U. Mo., 1952; LL.B., U. Colo., 1957; m. Jean Curtis, June 7, 1952 (dec. 1975); children—James C., Robert Curtis, Barbara Jean, Amy Florence; m. 2d, Anita Jeanne Stephens, Aug. 6, 1977. Admitted to Colo. bar, 1957, U.S. Supreme Ct. bar, 1960, D.C. bar, 1972; mem. staff tax div. Dept. Justice, Washington, 1957-61; asso. firm Calkins, Rodden & Kramer, Denver, 1961-64; individual practice law, Denver, 1964-65; mem. staff civil rights div. Dept. Justice, Washington, 1965—, dep. asst. atty. gen., 1970—. Pres., Northgleen (Colo.) Civic Assn., 1963. Served with USMC, 1952-54. Recipient Disting. Service award Dept. Justice, 1978. Mem. Am. Bar Assn. Office: Dept Justice Washington DC 20530

TURNER, JAMES STEVEN, lawyer; b. Columbus, Ohio, Apr. 21, 1940; s. James and Mary Bryan (Hunter) T.; B.A. in History and Polit. Sci., Ohio State U., 1962, J.D., 1969; m. Mary Dustin, Jan. 4, 1963; children—Christopher Bryan, Victoria Margaret. Asst. in founding Center for Study of Responsive Law (Nader Research Group), Washington, 1968-71; admitted to D.C. bar, 1971; asso. firm Fensterwald & Ohlhausen, 1971-73, Swankin & Turner, Washington, 1973—; adj. faculty mem. George Washington U. Law Center; mem. bd. Nat. Consumers League, Food Safety Council. Served with USN, 1962-66. Mem. Am., D.C. bar assns. Democrat. Congregationalist. Author: The Chemical Feast, 1970; (with Mary Turner) Making Your Own Baby Food, 1972. Home: 532 Cedar St NW Washington DC 20012 Office: 1625 Eye St NW Washington DC 20006

TURNER, JANET E., artist; b. Kansas City, Mo., 1914; d. James Ernest and Hortense (Taylor) Turner; A.B., Stanford, 1936; diploma, postgrad. Kansas City Art Inst. (under Thomas H. Benton, John de Martelly), 5 years; student art Claremont Grad. Sch. (Millard Sheets, Henry McFee), 2 years, M.F.A., 1947; student serigraphy, Edward Landon; Ed.D., Columbia, 1960. Faculty, Girls Collegiate Sch., Claremont, Calif., 1942-47; asst. prof. art Stephen F. Austin State Coll., Nacogdoches, Tex., 1947-56; asst. prof. Chico State U., 1959-63, asso. prof., 1963-68, prof., 1968—. Works have been shown in painting, water colors and prints exhbns. throughout U.S.; exhibited over 140 one-man shows in U.S., Israel, Japan; exhibited in Internat. Biannual of Graphics, Krakow, Poland, Internat. Exchange Exhbn., Seoul, Korea; represented in collections in U.S., fgn. countries. Illustrator The Yazoo, F. Smith. Guggenheim fellow, 1952; Tupperware fellow, 1956—. Recipient prizes including: (painting) 1st prize Tex. Fine Arts Assn., 1948; Dealey purchase prize and Comini popular prize 11th Tex. Gen. Exhbn.; R.D. Straus prize 13th Tex. Gen. Exhbn.; 3 prize oils 50th Anniversary Exhbn. Art Assn. New Orleans; S. Karasick prize 59th Ann. Nat. Assn. Women Artists; (water colors) purchase prize 2d Tex. Water Color Soc.; Sun Carnival prize 3d Ann. Southwestern Sun Carnival Fine Arts Exhbn., El Paso; purchase prize Smith Coll. Mus. Art, 37th Ann. Exhbn. Western Art, Denver; Marcia Tucker prize Nat. Assn. Women Artists; (prints) Nat. Assn. Women Artists 1950; (graphics) 1st prize Painters and Sculptors Soc. N.J., 32d Ann. Springfield (Mass.) Art League, Pen and Brush Black and White Exhbn., N.Y.C.; purchase prize Soc. Am. Graphic Artists 36th Ann. A.N.A., 2d prize, Springfield Art League, Mass., 1955, 1st prize, Pen and Brush, 1956, 8th ann. Boston Printmakers purchase prize; 6th Southwestern Dallas Mus. Fine Arts, 1st prize graphics, Painters Sculptors Soc. of N.J., Tupperware Art Fund Fellowship award for painting, Los Angeles County Nat. purchase prize, purchase prize Calif. State Fair, 1960, Cannon prize N.A.D., 1961; Medal of Honor and Alice S. Buell Meml. prize Nat. Assn. Women Artists, 1963, Katheryn Colton prize, Medal of Honor and Mabel M. Garner award, 1967; A.P. Hankins Meml. prize Print Club Pa., 1972; co-recipient Outstanding Prof. award Calif. State U. and Colls., 1975. Mem. League Am. Pen Women, Los Angeles Printmaking Soc. (Purchase prize 1971), Nat. Assn. Women Artists, Audubon Artists, Am. Color Print Soc., Soc. Am. Graphic Artists, N.A.D. (academician), Nat. Art Edn. Assn., A.A.U.W., Calif. Soc. Printmakers, San Francisco Women Artists, Internat. Arts Guild, Centro Studie Scambi Internazionale, Delta Kappa Gamma, Alpha Omicron Pi, Kappa Delta Pi, Pi Lambda Theta. Home: 567 E Lassen St Sp 701 Chico CA 95926

TURNER, JIM B., profl. football player; b. Martinez, Calif., Mar. 28, 1941; s. Bayard P. and Bethel L. (Ary) T.; B.S., Utah State U., 1963; postgrad. San Francisco State U., Calif. State U., Hayward; m. Mary Katherine Turner, June 5, 1965; children—Lisa, Christine, Alison. Profl. football player, 1964—; field goal kicker Denver Broncos Football Club. First nat. sports chmn. Muscular Dystrophy; chmn. Am. Cancer Soc., Jefferson County, Colo. Mem. Sigma Chi. Office: 5700 Logan St Denver CO 80216

TURNER, JOHN BRISTER, social work adminstr., educator; b. Fort Valley, Ga., Feb. 28, 1922; s. Brister William and Virginia Hulsey (Brown) T.; B.A., Morehouse Coll., 1946; M.Sc., Case Western Res. U., 1948, D. Social Work, 1959; m. Marian Floredia Wilson, Sept. 8, 1947; children—Marian Elizabeth, Charles Brister. Program sec. Butler St. YMCA, Atlanta, 1948-50; instr. Atlanta U., 1950-52; field worker Welfare Fedn., Cleve., 1952-56, dir. field service, 1959-61; chmn. community orgn. sequence Case Western Res. U., Cleve., 1959-67, dean Sch. Applied Social Scis., 1968-73; Kenan prof. social work U. N.C., Chapel Hill, 1974—; cons. Nat. Urban League, 1966-71; chmn. social work tng. com. NIMH; vis. prof. Smith Coll., McGill U., U. Ga., U. Minia (Egypt). Trustee Cleve. Inst. Art, 1970-74, Heidelberg Coll., 1971-73; bd. dirs. Kaiser Community Health Found., Cleve.; city commr. East Cleveland, Ohio. Served to 1st lt. USAF, 1943-45. Fulbright scholar, Egypt, summer 1965. Mem. Internat. Council on Social Welfare (chmn. U.S. com.), Nat. Assn. Social Workers, Nat. Conf. Social Welfare (pres. 1977—), Inst. Medicine Nat. Acad. Sci. Editor: Neighborhood Organization for Community Action, 1968; The Future of Social Service in the U.S., 1977; Ency. Social Work, 17th ed., 1977. Home: 1703 Michaux Rd Chapel Hill NC 27514 Office: Sch Social Work Univ NC Chapel Hill NC 27514

TURNER, JOHN ELLIOT, educator; b. Amble, Eng., Sept. 25, 1917; s. George Murray and Helen Barry (Elliot) T.; came to U.S., 1927, naturalized, 1932; B.A. magna cum laude, Yankton Coll., 1939, LL.D., 1967; M.A., U. Minn., 1949, Ph.D., 1950; m. Elsie Linda Reinschmidt, July 7, 1944; children—Debra Marléne, Noel Sean. High sch. tchr., 1939-42; faculty U. Minn., Mpls., 1950—, prof. polit. sci., 1959-74, Regents' prof., 1974—. Vis. prof. U. Hawaii, summers, 1963, 65. Mem. rev. panel Nat. Endowment for Humanities, 1969-74. Trustee Yankton Coll. Served with AUS, 1942-46. Sr. Fulbright Research scholar, Eng., 1961-62; Social Sci. Research Council fellow, 1968-69; N.W. Area Found. traveling fellow, 1958, 68, 76, 78. Mem. Internat. Studies Assn. (exec. dir. 1970-73), Am. (editorial bd. Rev. 1965-70, mem. program com. 1964, Wilson award com. 1972, chmn. election com. 1975, 76, mem. council 1975-76), Midwest (program chmn. 1965, nominating chmn. 1965, bus. mgr. jours., mem. council 1974-77) polit. sci. assns. Author: Labour's Doorstep Politics in London, 1978; (with R.T. Holt) Political Parties in Action, 1965; (with H.S. Quigley) The New Japan, 1956; (with H. McClosky) Soviet Dictatorship, 1960; (with R. Holt) Political Basis of Economic Development, 1966. Editor: (with Holt) USSR—Paradox and Change, 1962; Methodology of Comparative Research, 1970; (with Holt) Wiley Series, Comparative Studies in the Behavioral Sciences, 1968-76. Home: 1576 Vincent St St Paul MN 55108 Office: 1425 Social Sci Tower U Minn Minneapolis MN 55455

TURNER, JOHN GOSNEY, ins. co. exec.; b. Springfield, Mass., Oct. 3, 1939; s. John William and Clarence Oma (Gosney) T.; B.A., Amherst Coll., 1961; m. Leslie Corrigan, June 23, 1962; children—John Fredric, Mary Leslie, James Gosney, Andrew William. Asso. actuary Monarch Life Ins. Co., Springfield, Mass., 1961-67; group actuary Northwestern Nat. Life Ins. Co., Mpls., 1967-75, sr. v.p. group, 1975-79, sr. v.p., chief actuary, 1979—; pres., chief exec. officer, dir. NWNL Property and Casualty Ins. Co.; dir. N.Atlantic Life Ins. Co. N.Y.; dir., sec. MedCenter Health Plan, Inc. Bd. trustees Abbott-Northwestern Hosps.; chmn. Minn. Trustees of the Evans Scholars Found. Fellow Soc. Actuaries; mem. Am. Acad. Actuaries, Western Golf Assn. (dir.), Minn. Golf Assn. Club: Minikahda (Mpls.). Office: 20 Washington Ave S Minneapolis MN 55440

TURNER, JOHN NAPIER, lawyer, ret. govt. ofcl. Canada; b. Richmond, Eng., June 7, 1929; s. Leonard and Phyllis (Gregory) T.; B.A., U. B.C., 1949; B.A., Oxford U., 1951, B.C.L., 1952, M.A., 1957; postgrad. U. Paris, 1952-53; m. Geills McCrae Kilgour, May 11, 1963; children—Elizabeth, Michael, David, Andrew. Asso. and partner firm Stikeman, Elliott, Montreal, Que., Can., 1953-65; minister of state Canadian Govt., 1965-67, minister consumer and corporate affairs, 1967, solicitor gen., 1968, minister justice and atty. gen., 1968-72, minister finance, 1972-75; partner firm McMillan, Binch, Toronto, 1976—; dir. Canadian Investment Fund, Canadian Pacific Ltd., Credit Foncier Franco-Canadien, Crown Life Ins. Co., MacMillan Bloedel Ltd., Marathon Realty Ltd., Sandoz (Can.) Ltd., Wander Ltd., Bechtel Can. Ltd., Massey-Ferguson Ltd. Lectr., Sir George Williams U., 1956-58. Bd. dirs. Canadian Council Christians and Jews, York U., Salvation Army Met. Toronto; bd. govs. Ashbury Coll., Bishop Strachan Sch., Toronto Sch. Theology. Author: Senate of Canada, 1961; Politics of Purpose, 1968. Home: 435 Russell Hill Rd Toronto ON M5P 2S4 Canada Office: PO Box 38 Royal Bank Plaza Toronto ON M5J 2J7 Canada

TURNER, JOHN SIDNEY, JR., otolaryngologist; b. Bainbridge, Ga., July 25, 1930; s. John Sidney and Rose Lee (Rogers) T.; B.S., Emory U., 1952, M.D., 1955; m. Betty Jane Tigner, June 5, 1955; children—Elizabeth, Rebecca, Jan Marie. Intern, U. Va. Hosp., 1955-56; resident in otolaryngology Duke U. Med. Center, 1958-61; prof., chmn. dept. otolaryngology Emory U., Atlanta, 1961—, ear specialist, chief otolaryngology Univ. Clinic, 1961—; area cons. otolaryngology U.S. 3d Army, 1962-69; asso. dir. heart disease control program Fla. Bd. Health, 1956-58; Ga. state chmn. Deafness Research Found., 1968—. Served with USPHS, 1956-58. Recipient award of appreciation Children of Fulton County/Fulton County Health Dept., 1975; named Outstanding Clin. Tchr., Emory U. students, 1972; diplomate Am. Bd. Otolaryngology. Mem. So. Med. Assn. (certificate of appreciation 1974, chmn. otolaryngology sect sect. 1974), Ga. Soc. Otolaryngology (pres. 1973), AMA, Med. Assn. Ga., Med. Assn. Atlanta, Am. Acad. Otolaryngology, Triological Soc., Am. Council Otolaryngology, Alpha Omega Alpha. Democrat. Methodist. Club: Atlanta Optimist (pres. 1975-76). Contbr. chpts. to books, articles on ear disease to profl. jours. Home: 1388 Council Bluff Dr NE Atlanta GA 30345 Office: 1365 Clifton Rd NE Atlanta GA 30322

TURNER, JOHN WALTER, investor; b. Cleve., June 4, 1923; s. John H. and Dessa (Walter) T.; student N.M. Mil. Inst., 1942-43, U. N.M., 1943-44; m. Marion T. Taylor, Feb. 3, 1945; children—Scott T., Leslie Ann. With Davis, Skaggs & Co., investment bankers, San Francisco, 1946-49; Southwest rep. Axe Securities Corp., 1949-52; a founder Eppler Guerin & Turner, Inc., mems. N.Y. Stock Exchange, Dallas, 1952, pres., 1952-65, chmn. bd., 1965-73; dir. Fleet Truck Equipment Co., Dallas, Mid-Western Nurseries, Inc., Tahlequah, Okla., Slaughter Bros. Inc., Dallas, Varo Inc., Dallas, David Allsopp & Assos. N.V., Williamstad, Curacao, Comml. Metals, Dallas, Mid-Am. Industries, Ft. Smith, Ark., Hunt Internat. Resources Corp., Dallas, Lakewood Bank and Trust Co., Dallas, So. Union Co., Dallas. Past gov. Am. Stock Exchange, Midwest Stock Exchange; mem. Tex. State Securities Bd. Past pres. Dallas Charity Horseshow Assn.; bd. dirs. Baylor U. Med. Center Found. Served as officer USNR, 1943-46; PTO. Mem. Ind. Petroleum Assn. Am., Newcomen Soc. N.Am., Sigma Chi (life). Clubs: Dallas Petroleum, Dallas Country; T-Bar-M. Home: 4340 Versailles St Dallas TX 75205 Office: 2001 Bryan Tower Suite 2875 Dallas TX 75201

TURNER, KEITH STANLEY, aerospace engr., educator; b. Oak Park, Ill., Dec. 24, 1929; s. Joe Clifford and Evanae T. (Pinch) T.; B.B.A., U. Miami, 1959; M.A. in Internat. Relations, U. So. Calif., 1968; Ph.D., Fla. State U., 1973; m. Matha Jean Webb, Apr. 27, 1974; children by previous marriage—Richard, Linda, Tina. Enlisted in U.S. Navy, 1949, commd. ensign, 1951, advanced through grades to comdr., 1965; acad. dir. U.S. Naval Sch., Saufley Field, Fla., 1964-65; cons. to comdg. air officer RAF Coastal Command, 1965-69; exec. officer Naval Air Sta., Ellyson Field, Fla., 1970-71; indsl. relations officer, Pensacola, Fla., 1971; sr. research asso. dept. higher edn. Fla. State U., 1971-72; research asso. div. community colls. Fla. Dept. Edn., 1972-73; dir. spl. projects and adminstrv. services W.Va. Bd. Regents, Charleston, 1973-74; asso. prof. bus. adminstrn. Shepherd Coll., 1974-78, dean community services, 1974-78; prof., chmn. dept. aerospace tech. Ind. State U., 1978—; dir. W.Va. Task Force Continuing Edn. and Community Services, 1973-74; pres. TPT, Inc., Wilmington, Del. Pres., Babe Ruth League, London, 1968-69; chmn. Shepherdstown (W.Va.) chpt. ARC, 1975-76; bd. dirs. Wabash Valley Pilots Assn., Terre Haute, Ind.; FAA accident prevention counselor, 1978-79. Decorated Navy Commendation medal; recipient George Washington Honor medal Freedoms Found., 1965; Kellogg fellow Fla. State U., 1972-73; Disting. Achievement citation Nat. Pilots Assn., 1978. Mem. Am. Assn. Higher Edn., Profs. Higher Edn., AAUP, W.Va. Adult Edn. Assn., Am. Soc. Aerospace Edn., Steamboat Run Assn. (pres. 1977), Sigma Alpha Tau, Phi Delta

Kappa, Lambda Chi Alpha. Clubs: Rotary; Scenic Hills Country (dir. 1970) (Pensacola). Office: Ind State U Terre Haute IN 47809

TURNER, LANA (JULIA JEAN MILDRED FRANCES TURNER), actress; b. Wallace, Idaho, Feb. 8, 1920; d. Virgil and Mildred Turner; ed. pub. schs., Convent of Immaculate Conception, Hollywood, Calif.; m. Artie Shaw, Feb. 8, 1940 (div.); m. 2d, Steven Crane, 1942 (div.); m. 3d, Bob Topping (div.); m. 4th, Lex Barker (div.); m. 5th, Fred May, Nov. 27, 1960 (div.); m. 6th, Robert Eaton; m. 7th, Ronald Dante. Motion picture actress, 1937—; appeared in motion pictures including: Love Finds Andy Hardy, 1938; Dramatic School, 1938; Calling Dr. Kildare, Those Glamour Girls, Dancing Co-ed, 1939; Two Girls on Broadway, We Who Are Young, 1940; Ziegfeld Girl, Dr. Jekyll and Mr. Hyde, Honky Tonk, Johnny Eager, 1941; Red Light, Somewhere I'll Find You, Slightly Dangerous, 1942; Marriage Is a Private Affair, Women's Army, 1944; Keep Your Powder Dry, Week End at the Waldorf; Cass Timberlane, Homecoming, 1947; The Merry Widow, 1951; The Bad and the Beautiful, 1952; Latin Lovers, Flame and the Flesh; Betrayed; The Sea Chase; The Prodigal; Rains of Ranchipur; Another Time, 1958; Imitation of Life, 1959; By Love Possessed, 1961; Bachelor in Paradise; Who's Got the Action; Love Has Many Faces; Madame X; The Big Cube; Persecution, Bittersweet Love, 1976; appeared in TV series The Survivors, 1969; also numerous theatrical appearances.*

TURNER, LARRY EUGENE, ins. co. exec.; b. Colby, Kans., Dec. 5, 1941; s. Earl Everett and Ethel Mae (Smith) T.; B.B.A., Washburn U., 1966; m. Virginia Lee McAlexander, May 28, 1961; children—Elizabeth Ann, Jennifer Lynn, Heather Renee. With 1st Nat. Bank, Topeka, Kans., 1966-73, asst. trust officer, 1966-68, trust investment officer, 1968-70, asst. v.p., mgr. bond dept., 1970-72, asst. v.p., trust investment officer, 1972-73; asst. treas., investment officer Bituminous Casualty Corp., Rock Island, Ill., 1973-74, treas., 1974—. Mem. Rock Island C. of C. Republican. Kiwanian. Home: 1830 22d St Rock Island IL 61201 Office: 320 18th St Rock Island IL 61201

TURNER, LYNNE ALISON (MRS. PAUL H. SINGER), harpist; b. St. Louis, July 31, 1941; d. Sol and Evelyn (Klein) Turner; student Paris Conservatory Music (Premier Prix Hors Concours-Harp), 1959-60; pupil of Pierre Jamet; m. Paul H. Singer, June 2, 1963; children—Bennett Lloyd, Rachel Elise. Harpist, Chgo. Symphony Orch., 1962—; soloist Chgo. Symphony Orch., Israel Philharmonic Orch., other maj. orchs. in U.S. and Europe, also chamber groups; founding mem. L'Ensemble Recamier, Chgo. Chamber Ensemble; instr. harp DePaul U. Sch. Music, Chgo., 1976—; instr. pvt. student. Recipient 1st prize 2d Internat. Harp Competition, Israel, 1962. Mem. Am. Harp Soc., Arts Club Chgo. Home: 1316 Sheridan Rd Highland Park IL 60035 Office: Orchestra Hall 220 S Michigan Ave Chicago IL 60604

TURNER, MALCOLM ELIJAH, JR., educator, biomathematician; b. Atlanta, May 27, 1929; s. Malcolm Elijah and Margaret (Parker) T.; student Emory U., 1947-48; B.A., Duke U., 1952; M.Exptl. Stats., N.C. State U., 1955, Ph.D., 1959; m. Ann Clay Bowers, Sept. 16, 1948; children—Malcolm Elijah IV, Allison Ann, Clay Shumate, Margaret Jean; m. 2d, Rachel Patricia Farmer, Feb. 1, 1968; children—Aleta van Riper, Leila Samantha, Alexis St. John. Analytical statistician Communicable Disease Center, USPHS, Atlanta, 1953; research asso. U. Cin., 1955, asst. prof., 1955-58; asst. statistician N.C. State U., Raleigh, 1957-58; asso. prof. Med. Coll. Va., Richmond, 1958-63, chmn. div. biometry, 1959-63; prof., chmn. dept. statistics and biometry Emory U., Atlanta, 1963-69; prof., chmn. dept. biomath., prof. biostats. and math. U. Ala., Birmingham, 1970—; instr. summers Yale U., 1966, U. Calif. at Berkeley, 1971, Vanderbilt U., 1975; prof. U. Kans., 1968-69; vis. prof. Atlanta U., 1969; cons. to industry. Fellow Ala. Acad. Sci.; hon. fellow Am. Statis. Assn., A.A.A.S.; mem. Biometric Soc. (mng. editor Biometrics 1962-69), N.Y. Acad. Sci., Soc. for Math. Biology, Soc. for Indsl. and Applied Math., AMA (affiliate), Mensa, Sigma Xi, Phi Kappa Phi, Phi Delta Theta. Contbr. articles to profl. jours. Home: 1734 Tecumseh Trail Pelham AL 35124

TURNER, MORRIE NOLTEN, cartoonist; b. Oakland, Calif., Dec. 11, 1923; s. James Edward and Nora C. (Spears) T.; grad. high sch.; m. Letha Mae Harvey, Apr. 6, 1946; 1 son, Morris Arnold. Police clk. Oakland Police Dept., 1950-64; cartoonist Wee Pals cartoon strip, 106 U.S. newspapers, 1964-72; syndicated Des Moines Register & Tribune Syndicate, 1972—, King Features Syndicate, N.Y.C., 1972-74, Oakland, 1974—. Tchr. cartooning Laney Coll., Oakland, 1971-72, San Mateo (Calif.) Coll., 1971-72. Bd. dirs. Vol. Bur., YMCA, Boys Club. Served with USAAF, 1943-46. Recipient Inter-Group Relations award B'nai B'rith Anti-Defamation League, 1966; Brotherhood award NCCJ, 1966. Mem. Nat. Cartoonist Soc., Mag. Cartoonist Guild, No. Calif. Cartoonist and Gagwriters Assn. Author: Nipper, 1970; Nipper's Secret Power, 1971; Black & White Coloring Book, 1971; Willis and Friends, 1972; Freedom Is, 1971; Kid Power, 1972; Getting It All Together, 1972; Wee Pals, 1970; God is Groovy, 1972; Right On, 1971. Creator TV series Kid Power, 1972. Address: care King Features Syndicate 200 Park Ave New York NY 10017

TURNER, OTHEL DEVOICE, state ofcl.; b. Van Buren, Ark., Dec. 11, 1917; s. John W. and Myrtle May (Smith) T.; B.A., U. Tulsa, 1940; LL.B., U. Ark., 1948; M.B.A., U. Tex., 1953, Ph.D., 1958; m. Leize Galloway Leachman, July 18, 1941; 1 dau., Marsha Lee. Propr., Green Valley Poultry Farms, 1946-48; gen. mgr. automobile agy., Okla., 1949-51; lectr. mgmt. U. Tex., 1951-53; head dept. bus. adminstrn. U. Wyo., 1953-61; mgmt. cons., 1953—; dir. mgmt. tng. Nat. Hwy. Users Conf., Inc., hwy. mgmt. devel. project, 1956-67; dir. hwy. mgmt. seminar program Canadian Good Rds. Assn., 1961-71; prin. asso. Roy Jorgensen & Assos., Washington, 1961-67; dir. Nat. Hwy. Mgmt. Inst., U. Miss., 1967-68; dean Sch. Bus. Auburn (Ala.) U., 1968-73; chmn. bd., chief exec. officer Bus. Sci. Corp., Frederick, Md., 1973-75; sec. transp. State of Kans., Topeka, 1975—. Served from flying cadet to lt. col. USAAF, 1940-46. Decorated D.F.C., Air medal, Purple Heart. Mem. Nat., Am. mgmt. assns., Mississippi Valley Conf. State Hwy. and Transp. Ofcls. (pres. 1978-79), Am. Assn. State Hwy. and Transp. Ofcls. (exec. com. 1977-78), Beta Gamma Sigma, Omicron Delta Kappa, Alpha Kappa Psi, Pi Kappa Alpha. Episcopalian (vestryman). Clubs: Masons, Kiwanis. Home: 1626 Withdean Rd Topeka KS 66611

TURNER, PETE, photographer; b. Albany, N.Y., May 30, 1934; s. Donald Edward and Ruth (Murray) T.; B.S., Rochester Inst. Tech., 1956; m. Reine Marie Francoise Angeli, May 20, 1965; 1 son, Alexander Peter. One man shows Am. Soc. Mag. Photographers Group Show, N.Y. Cultural Center, 1970, The Photograph as a Permanent Color Print, N.Y. Cultural Center, 1970, George Eastman House, 1968, PhotoKinaKoln, Germany, 1968, Art Inst. Mpls., 1976, Nikon Gallery, Paris, 1976, Realisierte Impressionen, Zurich, 1977; majors color pub. many mags.; rep. in many permanent collections, 1972-73. Home: 300 E 33d St New York City NY 10016 Studio: Carnegie Hall 154 W 57th St New York City NY 10019

TURNER, PETER MERRICK, mfg. co. exec.; b. Toronto, Ont., Can., July 4, 1931; s. William Ian MacKenzie and Marjorie (Merrick) T.; B.A.Sc., U. Toronto, 1954; M.B.A., Harvard, 1956; m. Beverley Brophey, Sept. 13, 1958; children—Peter Merrick, Christopher Harold, David MacKenzie. Staff asst. controllers dept. Bridgeport Brass Co. (Conn.), 1956-57; sec. treas. Perkins Paper Products Co., Montreal, Can., 1957-58; with Texaco Can. Ltd., Montreal, 1958-68, treas., 1966-68; dir. budgeting and planning, corp. devel., Molson Breweries Ltd., Montreal, 1968—; v.p. planning Molson Breweries Can. Ltd., 1968-70; v.p. corp. devel. Molson Industries Ltd., Toronto, 1970-72; exec. v.p. Bennett Pump Inc., Muskegon, Mich., 1972-73, pres., chief exec. officer, 1973-78; v.p. corp. planning and devel. Sealed Power Corp., Muskegon, 1978—; dir. Grand Trunk Western Ry., Grand Trunk Corp.; lectr. extension dept. Grand Valley State Coll., 1979. Lectr. extension dept. McGill U., 1960-67. Gen. chmn. red shield appeal Montreal Salvation Army, 1969-70; chmn. McGill Assos., Montreal, 1969-70. Bd. dirs. Hackley Hosp., Muskegon; chmn. long-range planning com. Muskegon Community Coll. Mem. Zeta Psi. Mem. Anglican Ch. Clubs: Mount Royal (Montreal); Granite, Canadian (Toronto); Century (pres.) (Muskegon); Lake O'Hara Trail (B.C.). Home: 1001 Moulton Ave North Muskegon MI 49444 Office: 100 Terrace Plaza Muskegon MI 49443

TURNER, RALPH HERBERT, educator, sociologist; b. Effingham, Ill., Dec. 15, 1919; s. Herbert Turner and Hilda Pearl (Bohn) T.; B.A., U So. Calif., 1941, M.A., 1942; postgrad. U. Wis., 1942-43; Ph.D., U. Chgo., 1948; m. Christine Elizabeth Hanks, Nov. 2, 1943; children—Lowell Ralph, Cheryl Christine. Research asso. Am. Council Race Relations, 1947-48; faculty U. Calif. at Los Angeles, 1948—, prof. sociology and anthropology, 1959—, chmn. dept. sociology, 1963-68. Vis. summer prof. U. Wash., 1960, U. Hawaii, 1962; vis. scholar Australian Nat. U., 1972; vis. prof. U. Ga., 1975. Mem. behavioral scis. study sect. NIH, 1961-66, chmn., 1963-64; dir.-at-large Social Sci. Research Council, 1965-66; chmn. panel on pub. policy implications of earthquake prediction Nat. Acad. Scis., 1974-75. Mem. com. social edn. and action Los Angeles Presbytery, 1954-56. Served to lt. (j.g.) USNR, 1943-46. Faculty Research fellow Social Sci. Research Council. 1953-56; Sr. Fulbright scholar, U.K., 1956-57; Guggenheim fellow, 1964-65. Mem. Am. (council 1959-64, chmn. social psychology sect. 1960-61, pres. 1968-69, chmn. sect. theoretical sociology 1973-74), Pacific (pres. 1957), Internat. (council 1974—, v.p. 1978—) sociol. assns., Soc. Study Social Problems (exec. com. 1962-63), Am. Council Family Relations, Soc. for Study Symbolic Interaction (Charles Horton Cooley award 1978), AAUP. Author: (with L. Killian) Collective Behavior, 1957, 2d edit., 1972; The Social Context of Ambition, 1964; Robert Park on Social Control and Collective Behavior, 1967; Family Interaction, 1970; Earthquake Prediction and Public Policy, 1975. Editor: Sociometry, 1962-64, editorial cons., 1959-62; acting editor Ann. Rev. of Sociology, 1977-78, asso. editor, 1978—; adv. editor Am. Jour. Sociology, 1954-56, Sociology and Social Research, 1961-74; editorial staff Am. Sociol Rev., 1955-56; asso. editor Social Problems, 1959-62, 67-69; cons. editor Sociol. Inquiry, 1968-73, Western Sociol. Rev., 1975—; editorial bd. Ann. Rev. Sociology, 1973—, Mass Emergencies, 1975—, Internat. Jour. Critical Sociology, 1974—. Home: 1126 Chautauqua Blvd Pacific Palisades CA 90272 Office: 405 Hilgard Ave Los Angeles CA 90024

TURNER, RICHARD LAZEAR, textile, rubber and plastic products mfg. co. exec.; b. Huntington, W.Va., Feb. 22, 1925; s. Clyde Baker and Jess L. (Lazear) T.; B.A., Yale U., 1948, LL.B., 1951; m. Nancy Elena Riford, June 9, 1951; children—Richard R., Sarah L., James R., Molly L. Admitted to N.Y. bar, 1952; asso., then partner firm Nixon, Hargrave, Devans and Dey, Rochester, N.Y., 1951-62; chmn. bd. Schlegel Corp., and predecessor, Rochester, 1962—, chief exec. officer, 1964—, pres., 1972—; dir. Forbes Products Corp., Genesee Brewing Co., Rochester Marine Midland Bank, Rochester Telephone Corp. (all Rochester), Fasco Industries, Boca Raton, Fla. Trustee Genesee Country Mus., Munford, N.Y., Preservation League N.Y. State; bd. dirs., past chmn. bd. Hochstein Sch. Music, Rochester; trustee U. Rochester; bd. dirs. Vis. Nurse Service Rochester and Monroe County. Served with USMC, 1943-46. Mem. Rochester Indsl. Mgmt. Council (dir., treas.), Rochester Area C. of C. (trustee). Home: 22 Stoney Clover Ln Pittsford NY 14534 Office: 400 East Ave PO Box 23113 Rochester NY 14692

TURNER, RICHARD LEE, ednl. adminstr.; b. Richmond, Ind., May 6, 1929; s. William and Mildred Elizabeth (Klotz) T.; B.S., Northwestern U., 1951, M.A., 1952; Ph.D., Ind. U., 1959; m. Anne Prosser, Nov. 22, 1951; children—Elizabeth, Katherine, Constance, Judith. Instr., Antioch Coll., 1952-54, U. Wis., Whitewater, 1954-56; from asst. prof. to prof. edn. Ind. U., Bloomington, 1960-69, asso. dean Sch. Edn., asso. dean research and devel., 1972-76, acting dean research and devel., 1976-77; dean Sch. Edn., U. Colo., 1977—, prof., 1977—; cons. U.S. Office Edn., 1970—. U.S. Office Edn. grantee, 1958, 60, 64, 70, 73. Mem. Am. Ednl. Research Assn., Rocky Mountain Psychol. Assn., Phi Delta Kappa. Author: General Catalog of Teaching Skills; editor Am. Ednl. Research Jour., 1969-72. Office: PO Box 249 U Colo Boulder CO 80309

TURNER, ROBERT COMRIE, composer; b. Montreal, Que., Can., June 6, 1920; s. William Thomson and Myrtle Wellsteed (Snowdon) T.; B.M., McGill U., 1943, D.M., 1953; student Royal Coll. Music, 1947-48; M.Mus., George Peabody Coll. Tchrs., 1950; m. Sara Nan Scott, June 30, 1949; children—Alden, Martin, Carolyn. Sr. music producer Canadian Broadcasting Corp., Vancouver, B.C., 1952-68; lectr. in music U. B.C., Vancouver, 1955-57; asst. prof. music Acadia U., Wolfville, N.S., Can., 1968-69; prof. composition U. Manitoba, Winnipeg, 1969—; composer: The Third Day (Easter Cantata), 1962, Symphony for Strings, 1960, Capriccio Concertante, 1975, 3d String Quartet, 1975; (opera) The Brideship, 1967; Eidolons, 1972; Johann's Gift to Christmas, 1972; Variations on The Prairie Seattler's Song, 1974; Trio for violin, cello and piano, 1969; The Phoenix and the Turtle, 1964; Concerto for Two Pianos and Orch., 1971; rec. on Can. Broadcasting Corp. Program com. mem. Vancouver Internat. Festival; adjudicator Met. and San Francisco Opera auditions. Served with Royal Can. Air Force, 1943-45. Can. Council fellow, 1966-67. Mem. Broadcast Music Inc. Ltd., Can. League Composers, Can. Assn. Univ. Schs. of Music, Coll. Music Soc., Canadian Assn. Univ. Tchrs. Home: 104 Yale Ave Winnipeg MB R3M 0L6 Canada Office: Sch of Music U Manitoba Winnipeg MB R3T 2N2 Canada

TURNER, ROBERT EDWARD, psychiatrist; b. Hamilton, Ont., Can., June 8, 1926; s. Robert William and Alice May (Johnson) T.; B.A. with honors in Zoology and Chemistry, McMaster U., 1948; M.D., U. Toronto, 1952; m. Gene Anne Stewart, Sept. 27, 1952; children—Margaret, John, Robert, Richard. Intern, Hamilton Gen. Hosp., 1952-53; resident Bristol (Eng.) Mental Hosps. Group, 1953-55; practice medicine specializing in psychiatry, Toronto, Ont.; dir. Forensic Clinic Toronto Psychiat. Hosp., 1958-66; sr. psychiatrist forensic service Clarke Inst. Psychiatry, Toronto, 1966, chief forensic service, 1967-69, med. dir., 1969-76; asst. prof. dept. psychiatry U. Toronto, 1964-68, prof., 1973-77, prof. forensic psychiatry, 1977—, mem. adv. bd. Centre of Criminology, 1977—; cons. in psychiatry Law Reform Commn. Can., 1972—; psychiatrist in charge, dir. Met. Toronto Forensic Service, 1977—. Pres., Kenneth G. Gray Found., 1971—; mem. legal task force Com. on Mental Health Services for Ont., Ont. Council Health, 1978-79; dep. warden Cathedral Ch. of St. James, Toronto; bd. dirs. Clin. Inst. Addiction Research Found. Ont., 1973—. Fellow Royal Coll. Physicians and Surgeons Can., Am. Psychiat. Assn.; mem. Can. (dir. 1974-77), Ont. (pres. 1975-76), psychiat. assns., Can., Ont. med. assns., Med.-Legal Soc. Toronto (council), Royal Coll. Psychiatrists. Author: Pedophilia and Exhibitionism, 1964; contbr. articles on psychiatry and law to profl. jours. Home: 163 Bayview Heights Dr Toronto ON M4G 2Y7 Canada Office: 999 Queen St W Toronto ON M6J 1H4 Canada

TURNER, ROBERT EDWARD, III (TED), broadcasting and sports exec., yachtsman; b. 1938; ed. Brown U.; m. Jane Turner. Chmn. bd., pres. Turner Broadcasting System, Inc.; pres. Atlanta Braves, 1976—; chmn. bd. Atlanta Hawks, 1977—; won America's Cup in his yacht Courageous, 1977.

TURNER, ROBERT KEAN, JR., educator; b. Richmond, Va., Nov. 30, 1926; s. Robert Kean and Eunice (Henderson) T.; B.A., Va. Mil. Inst., 1947; M.A., U. Va., 1949, Ph.D., 1958; m. Janet Gascoyne Bridges, Aug. 21, 1949; children—Robert Kean III, Janet Gascoyne (Mrs. John Crouch), William John Gascoyne. Instr., U. Va. Sch. Engring., 1955-56, U. Va. Coll. Letters and Sci., 1956-57; instr., then asst. prof. Va. Mil. Inst., 1957-62; mem. faculty U. Wis.-Milw., 1962—, prof. English, 1965—, chmn. dept., 1967-70. Served to ensign USNR, 1944-46. Mem. Modern Lang. Assn. (chmn. bibliog. evidence sect. 1968-70, chmn. New Variorum Shakespeare com. 1972—, gen. editor New Variorum Shakespeare 1974—). Episcopalian. Club: Milwaukee Yacht. Contbr. articles to profl. jours.; editor Elizabethan plays. Home: 4068 N Lake Dr Milwaukee WI 53211

TURNER, ROBERT WAYNE, lawyer; b. Omaha, Jan. 22, 1919; s. Ernest Oliver and Anna Victoria (Seaburg) T.; B.A., U. Nebr., Omaha, 1942; J.D., Northwestern U., 1948; m. Maedine Dussolna Foletti, July 9, 1966. Asso. firm Carney, Crowell & Leibman, Chgo., 1948-49; partner firm Swensen, Viren & Turner, Omaha, 1949-50; asso. counsel East Bay Municipal Utility Dist., Oakland, Calif., 1954-55; with Kaiser Aluminum and Chem. Corp., Oakland, Calif., 1955—, v.p., counsel, sec., 1970—. Chmn. Oakland Citizens Com. for Urban Renewal, 1960-62; sec. Oakland Mus. Assn., 1960-62. Served to lt. comdr. USNR, 1942-46, 50-52. Decorated Bronze Star with oak leaf cluster. Mem. Calif., Am., Ill., Alameda County, San Francisco County bar assns., Oakland C. of C. (dir. 1977, chmn. 1979-80), U. Nebr. at Omaha Alumni Assn. (chpt. pres. 1949-50), Order of Coif. Democrat. Lutheran. Mason. Home: 15 Marr Ave Oakland CA 94611 Office: 300 Lakeside Dr Oakland CA 94604

TURNER, RODERICK L., consumer packaged products mfg. co. exec.; b. Mineola, N.Y., June 1, 1931; s. Claude E. and Eulalia (Rodriguez) T.; B.A., Cornell U., 1952; m. Teresa C. Vadetaire, May, 1957; children—R. Bradford, Melissa A. Vice-pres. Benton & Bowles, Inc., N.Y.C., 1958-63; group product mgr. personal products div. Colgate-Palmolive Co., N.Y.C., 1963-67, group product mgr. h.p. div., 1967-68, pres., gen. mgr. Colgate Canadian Co., 1969-72, v.p. mktg. sers. div., 1973, corp. v.p., gen. mgr. Western hemisphere div. Colgate-Palmolive Co., 1974-76, gen. mgr. European div., 1977-78, group v.p., internat. ops., 1979—. Served to 1st lt. AUS, 1952-54; Korea. Club: Cornell (N.Y.C.). Home: 36 Cornwell Beach Rd Sands Point NY 11050 Office: Colgate Palmolive Co 300 Park Ave New York NY 10022

TURNER, ROSS JAMES, business exec.; b. Winnipeg, Man., Can., May 1, 1930; s. James Valentine and Gretta H. (Ross) T.; student U. Man. Extension, 1951, Banff Sch. Advanced Mgmt., 1956; m. Helen Elizabeth Todd, June 9, 1950; children—Ralph, Rick, Tracy Lee. Accountant, Dominion Bridge Co., Winnipeg, 1951-53, controller Alta. div., Edmonton, 1958, mgr. accounting service, Montreal, 1959-61; sec.-treas. Standard Iron & Engring. Works, Ltd., Alta., 1954-57; div. v.p. BACM Industries, Ltd., Winnipeg, 1962-63, treas., dir., 1963-64, exec. v.p., 1965-68; pres., chief operating officer, dir. Neonex Internat., Ltd., 1969-71, Seaspan Internat., Ltd., North Vancouver, B.C., 1971-72; pres., dir. Genstar Western Ltd., Vancouver, 1973-76; pres., chief exec. officer Genstar Ltd., 1976—, also dir.; dir. Rio Algom Ltd., Crown Zellerbach Can. Ltd., New Eng. Fish Co. Mem. Soc. Mgmt. Accountants Can., Young Pres.'s Orgn. Clubs: Mount Royal, St. James's (Montreal); Vancouver, Capilano Golf and Country (Vancouver). Home: 3204 Port Royal Apts 1455 Sherbrooke St W Montreal PQ H3G 1L2 Canada Office: 4105-1 Pl Ville Marie Montreal PQ H3B 3R1 Canada

TURNER, STANSFIELD, govt. ofcl.; b. Chgo., Dec. 1, 1923; s. Oliver Stansfield and Wilhelmina Josephine (Wagner) T.; student Amherst Coll., 1941-43, D.C.L., 1976; B.S., U.S. Naval Acad., 1946; M.A. (Rhodes scholar), Oxford U., 1950; Hum.D., Roger Williams Coll., 1976; D.Sc. in Edn., Bryant Coll., 1977; LL.D., Salve Regina Coll., 1977; m. Patricia Busby Whitney, Dec. 23, 1953; children—Laurel (Mrs. Frank G. Echevarria), Geoffrey. Ensign, USN, 1946, advanced through grades to adm., 1975, ret., 1979; served primarily in destroyers; commd. U.S.S. Horne, guided missile frigate, 1967, comdr. in Vietnam conflict; aide to sec. Navy, 1968-70; comdr. carrier task group 6th Fleet, 1970-71; dir. systems analysis div. Office Chief Naval Ops., Navy Dept., Washington, 1971-72; pres. Naval War Coll., Newport, R.I., 1972-74; comdr. U.S. Second Fleet, 1974-75; comdr.-in-chief Allied Forces, So. Europe (NATO), 1975-77; dir. CIA, Washington, 1977—. Decorated D.S.M., Legion of Merit, Bronze Star. Address: Dir CIA Washington DC 20505

TURNER, TINA (ANNIE MAE), singer; b. Brownsville, Tenn., Nov. 25, 1941; m. Ike Turner, 1956 (div.). Singer with Ike Turner Kings of Rhythm and Ike and Tina Turner Revue; appeared in films Gimme Shelter, 1970, Soul to Soul, 1971, Tommy, 1975; concert tours of Europe, 1966, Japan and Africa, 1971; rec. artist. Recipient Grammy award-Best Rhythm and Blues Vocal for rec. Proud Mary, 1972. Office: care ICM 40 W 57th St New York NY 10019*

TURNER, VERNON MAGRUDER, oil co. exec.; b. Ennis, Tex., Nov. 6, 1922; s. Magruder Hershell and Callie (Turner) T.; student Tyler Jr. Coll., 1940-41; LL.B., Baylor U., 1947; M.Letters, U. Houston, 1955; m. Helen Jauneita Forte, July 18, 1942; children—Linda (Mrs. Robert Lewis Hill), Deborah, Jenny, Robert. Admitted to Tex. bar, 1947; practice in Cisco, 1947-48; atty. Texaco, Inc., Houston, 1948-50; div. atty. Midstates Oil Corp., 1952-55; sr. v.p., gen. counsel Tenneco Oil Co., Houston, 1955—. Mem. sch. bd., Cypress-Fairbanks Ind. Sch. Dist., 1966-75, v.p., 1971-73, pres bd., 1973-75. Served to capt. AUS, 1943-46, 50-52. Mem. Am., Tex. (vice chmn. corporate counsel sect. 1975-76), Houston bar assns. Home: 5807 Bermuda Dunes Houston TX 77069 Office: PO Box 2511 Houston TX 77001

TURNER, VICTOR WITTER, educator; b. Glasgow, Scotland, May 28, 1920; s. Norman and Violet (Witter) T.; B.A. with honours, Univ. Coll., London, Eng., 1949; Ph.D., U. Manchester (Eng.), 1955; m. Edith Lucy Brocklesby Davis, Jan. 30, 1943; children—Frederick, Robert, Irene Helen, Alexander Lewis Charles, Rory Peter Benedict. Came to U.S., 1964. Research officer Rhodes-Livingstone Inst., Lusaka, No. Rhodesia, 1950-54; Simon research fellow U. Manchester, 1955-57, from lectr. to sr. lectr., 1958-64; fellow Center Advanced Study Behavioral Scis., 1961-62; prof. anthropology Cornell U., 1964-68; prof. social thought, anthropology U. Chgo., 1968—. chmn. social thought, 1976-77; William R. Kenan Jr. prof. anthropology U. Va., Charlottesville, 1977—; Lewis Henry Morgan lectr., 1966; Am. lectr. history religions Am. Council Learned Socs.,

1973-74, Inst. for Advanced Study, Princeton, 1975-76. Served with Brit. Army, 1941-46. Fellow Am. Soc. for Study Religions, Am. Acad. Arts and Scis., Royal Anthrop. Inst. (Rivers Meml. medal 1965), Am. Anthrop. Assn., Internat. African Inst., African Studies Assn., Soc. for Humanities. Author: Schism and Continuity in an African Society, 1957; Chihamba The White Spirit, 1962; The Forest of Symbols, 1967; The Drums of Affliction, 1968; The Ritual Process, 1969; Dramas, Fields and Metaphors, 1974; Revelation and Divination in Ndembu Ritual, 1975; Image and Pilgrimage in Christian Culture, 1978. Editor: Profiles of Change: African Society and Colonial Rule, 1970; series Symbol, Myth, Ritual, 1972—. Home: 107 Carrsbrook Dr Charlottesville VA 22901

TURNER, W. B., mgmt. cons.; b. Dayton, O., 1888. Mem. Turner, Granzow, Spayd & Hollenkamp; gen. counsel, dir. emeritus, hon. chmn. Standard Register Co.; hon. dir. Third Nat. Bank & Trust Co. of Dayton. Address: Hulman Bldg Dayton OH 45402

TURNER, WALLACE L., journalist; b. Titusville, Fla., Mar. 15, 1921; s. Clyde H. and Ina B. (Wallace) T.; B.J., U. Mo., 1943; postgrad. (Nieman fellow) Harvard U., 1958-59; m. Pearl Burk, June 12, 1943; children—Kathleen Turner Morris, Elizabeth. Reporter, Springfield (Mo.) Daily News, 1943, Portland Oregonian, 1943-59; news dir. Sta. KPTV, Portland, 1959-61; asst. sec. HEW, Washington, 1961-62; reporter N.Y. Times, San Francisco, 1962—, bur. chief, 1970—. Mem. adv. com. Nieman Found., Harvard U. Recipient Heywood Broun award for reporting, 1952, 56; Pulitzer Prize for reporting, 1957. Mem. San Francisco Press Club. Democrat. Author: Gamblers Money, 1965; The Morman Establishment, 1967. Office: Suite 925 Fox Plaza 1390 Market St San Francisco CA 94102

TURNER, WALTER JAMES, auto parts mfg. co. exec.; b. Vanderbilt, Mich., May 1, 1918; s. Arthur Robert and Lena (Stone) T.; certificate in accounting U. Detroit, 1942; m. Dorothy Jean McKinnon, Nov. 15, 1941 (dec. Aug. 1965); children—Cheryl J. Turner Vogel, Marilyn Turner Clem; m. 2d, Lois Carpenter, Oct. 7, 1967. Accountant, Ernst & Ernst, Detroit, 1942-53; v.p., treas. Ironrite, Inc., Mt. Clemens, Mich., 1953-62; v.p., treas. Hayes-Albion Corp., Jackson, Mich., 1962—. Dir. Employees Unemployment Compensation Commn. Mich., 1962-74; pres. Jackson Goodwill Industries, 1968-71; budget dir. Jackson United Community Services, 1964—. C.P.A., Mich. Mem. Fin. Execs. Inst., Am. Inst. C.P.A.'s, Mich. Assn. C.P.A.'s. Methodist (chmn. fin. 1963-64). Club: Country of Jackson (treas., v.p., dir.). Home: 1340 Badgley Rd Jackson MI 49203 Office: 1999 Wildwood Ave Jackson MI 49202

TURNER, WILLIAM HOMER HEYWARD, engr., atty., exec.; b. Atlanta, Oct. 4, 1904; s. William Heyward and Maud (Dowling) T.; B.S., M.E., U. Ga. Inst. Tech., 1925; B.Litt., Columbia, 1927, Ph.D.; 1958; J.D., J.S.D., N.Y. U., 1936-45; U. Havana Extension Arts and Langs.; LL.D., Pacific U., Westminster Coll., Heidelberg Coll., Occidental Coll., St. Mary's U., San Antonio; D.Eng., Ohio U.; L.H.D., Denison U.; L.H.D., Alfred U.; m. Clara M. Anderson, May 14, 1929; children—Roger J.A., W.H. Heyward; m. 2d, Veda Brock, Feb. 26, 1965. Engr., Found. Co., bldg. constrn. and structural fabrication, 1921; writer So. newspapers, N.Y. Herald-Tribune and McGraw-Hill Publs., 1926-28; asst. to chief editor 14th edit. Ency. Brit. in charge econs., industry and applied sci., 1928-31; exec. John Price Jones Corp., promotion and orgn., 1931-33; economist, dir. pub. relations Nat. Fedn. Textiles, 1933-36; dir. research in charge product devel. and gen. marketing Marshall Field & Co., 1936-38; statis. supr., asst. to comptroller and chmn. finance com. U.S. Steel Corp., 1938-70; v.p., exec. dir. U.S. Steel Found., Inc., 1953-70; v.p., dir. studies in philanthropy and liberal edn. Acad. Edn. Devel., 1970—; exec. v.p. Nat. Council on Philanthropy, 1971-77. Exec. sec. Steel Case Research Com., aiding in War Labor Bd. rev. Little Steel wage formula. Admitted to N.Y. bar 1937; counsel Brown & Turner, specialist in Latin-Am. legal problems; U.S. Dept. State, Urban Mass. Transp. Adminstrn. Registered cons. engr., N.Y.; practice mgmt. field. Co-founder Found. for Human Resources Devel.; mem. bd., officer Council on Founds. Served in USNR; commd. 2d lt. USAAF Res. Mem. Nat. Soc. Profl. Engrs., Assn. Bar City N.Y., Am. Bar Assn., Am. Mktg. Assn., Am. Statis. Assn., Am. Fgn. Law Assn., Royal Soc. Arts (London), Latin-Am. Econ. Inst., Menninger Found., Atomic Industry Forum, Nat. Better Bus. Bur., Newcomen Soc. Democrat. Episcopalian. Rotarian. Clubs: Cosmos (Washington); Century, University; Lansdown (London). Author fiction and non-fiction under pseudonyms; (co-author) Production and Distribution of Textiles; The Fourth Brazilian Constitution; Financing Higher Education, 1960-70; Sponsored Research in American Colleges and Universities; Social Responsibilities of Business; Corporate Philanthropy in a Free Society. Office: 680 Fifth Ave New York City NY 10019 also 811 Riverbank Rd Stamford CT 06903. *Faith in the essential goodness and improvability of mankind and his social mutual help institutions is one major guiding start; to this must be joined dedication to service above self-the self being taken care of by hard work, perserverance, and, if one is very fortunate, a good and loving family and opportunity for education and advancement in a society or culture where the four freedoms operate. Love of truth, curiosity, the Golden Rule and the Ten Commandments take care of the specifics of living out a good life. Only ill health, or accident, can diminish the good life under these guidelines.*

TURNER, WILLIAM IAN MACKENZIE, JR., paper co. exec.; b. Sharon, Pa., Jan. 17, 1929; s. William Ian MacKenzie and Marjorie (Merrick) T.; B.A. in Mech. Engring. with honors, U. Toronto (Ont., Can.), 1951; M.B.A. with distinction, Harvard, 1953; m. Ann McCreery, June 13, 1953; children—William Ian MacKenzie III, Julia McCreery, James Zachry, Carol Merrick. Pres., Power Corp. of Can., Ltd., Montreal, 1966-70, also mem. exec. com., dir.; pres., chief exec. officer, dir., mem. exec. com. Consol.-Bathurst, Ltd., Montreal, 1970—; dir. Domglas Ltd., Celanese Can. Ltd., Norcen Energy Resources Ltd., J. Henry Schroder Banking Corp., Investors Group, Bombardier-MLW Ltd., Can. Ingersoll-Rand Co. Ltd.; mem. internat. bd. Wells Fargo Bank. Chmn., Canadian Econ. Policy Com.; trustee The Conf. Bd.; bd. dirs. Stratford Shakespearean Festival Found. Can.; vice chmn. bd. govs. Royal Victoria Hosp. Clubs: Montreal Amateur Athletic Assn., Montreal Racket, Mount Royal, Saint James, Hillside Tennis (Montreal); Nat., Toronto, York (Toronto); Brook, Knickerbocker (N.Y.C.). Home: 4294 Montrose Ave Westmount PQ H3Y 2A5 Canada Office: Consol-Bathurst Ltd 800 Dorchester Blvd W Montreal PQ H3B 1Y9 Canada

TURNER, WILLIAM WILSON, hosp. exec.; b. Valley Mills, Tex., Apr. 21, 1916; s. Will S. and Nettie A. (Vickrey) T.; B.B.A., Baylor U., 1938; postgrad. Grad. Sch. Bus. Northwestern U., 1939; m. Wilma David, Feb. 22, 1945; 1 dau., Elizabeth Ann. Bus. mgr. Hillcrest Meml. Hosp., Waco, Tex., 1941-47; asst. adminstr. Meml. Bapt. Hosp. (name changed to Meml. Hosp. System), Houston, 1947-50, adminstr., 1955-63, exec. dir. hosp. system, 1963-71, pres. system, 1971—; adminstr. Bapt. Hosp., Alexandria, La., 1950-54, Miss. Bapt. Hosp., Jackson, 1954-55. Dir. Blue Cross-Blue Shield Tex., Group Life and Health Ins. Co. Mem. Council on Manpower and Edn., 1974-77. Trustee Union Bapt. Assn. Served to lt. USNR, 1942-45; PTO, ATO. Recipient Collier award for distinguished hosp. adminstrn., 1974. Fellow Am. Coll. Hosp. Adminstrs.; mem. Am. Prostestant Hosp. Assn. (del. 1970—, council ch.-hosp. relations 1962-66, council on edn. 1972-75; Hosp. Adminstrn. award 1979), Am. (del. 1969—), Tex. (trustee 1961-68, treas. 1969, pres. 1971-72), Bapt. (past pres., trustee), Houston Area (past pres.) hosp. assns., Mental Health Assn. Houston (profl. adv. com.), Tex. Assn. Hosp. Accountants (past pres.), Houston Area Hosp. Council (past pres.), Houston C. of C., Tex. League Nursing (dir. 1961-63), Delta Sigma Pi. Baptist (deacon). Mason. Developer satellite hosp. concept. Home: 9607 Hendon Houston TX 77036 Office: 7600 Beechnut Houston TX 77074

TURNER, WILLIE, microbiologist; b. Suffolk, Va., Feb. 1, 1935; s. Willie and Lena T.; B.S., Md. State Coll., 1957; M.S., Ohio State U., Ph.D., 1961; m. Mar. 27, 1964; children—Vincent, Austin, Nicki, Deana. Asst. prof. microbiology Meharry Med. Coll., Nashville, 1962-66; Staff fellow Nat. Cancer Inst., NIH, Bethesda, Md., 1966-70, sect. head, microbiology, 1970-71; prof., chmn. dept. microbiology Howard U. Coll. Medicine, Washington, 1971—; cons. in field. Mem. Nat. Acad. Microbiology, AAAS, N.Y. Acad. Sci., Am. Assn. Cancer Research, Tissue Culture Assn., Soc. Exptl. Biology and Medi-Cine, Am. Assn. Immunologists, Am. Soc. Microbiology. Home: 14608 Stonewall Dr Silver Spring MD 20904 Office: Dept Microbiology Coll Medicine Howard U 520 W St NW Washington DC 20001

TURNEY, CHARLES, coll. adminstr.; b. Phila., Dec. 1, 1930; s. Charles Albert and Marion (Moitz) T.; B.A., U. Richmond, 1958, M.A., 1959; Ph.D., Rutgers U., 1965; m. Ruth De Figueiredo, Aug. 22, 1959; children—Paul Humberto, Quelly Elizabeth. Teaching asst. Rutgers U., 1959-61; instr., asst. prof. Douglass Coll.; 1961-66; asso. prof., chmn. dept. lit. and langs. U. Richmond, 1966-69; v.p. acad. affairs, dean coll., prof. English, Catawba Coll., Salisbury, N.C., 1969—. Vice pres. Richmond Internat. Council, 1968. Served with U.S. Mcht. Marines, 1950-54, 56-57, AUS, 1954-56. Mem. Modern Lang. Assn., S. Atlantic Modern Lang. Assn., Am. Assn. U. Profs., Am. Conf. Acad. Deans. Democrat. Baptist. Address: Catawba Coll Salisbury NC 28144

TURNEY, DAVID THOMAS, educator; b. Sedro Woolley, Wash., Oct. 8, 1915; s. Jared Scott and Anna (Thomas) T.; B.A., U. Wash., 1939, M.Ed., 1949; Ed.D., George Peabody Coll. Tchrs., 1959, m. Miriam Howell, Aug. 29, 1943; children—Jon Scott, Constance Louise. Music dir. Oakesdale (Wash.) High Sch., 1938-42; curriculum dir. Battle Ground (Wash.) High Sch., 1946-57; coordinator lab. expt. for tchrs. George Peabody Coll. Tchrs., 1959-60, dir. pub. sch. coop. program, 1960-61, dir. exptl. program tchr. edn., 1961-63; dir. Lab. Sch. Kent State U., 1963-65, asst. dean grad. studies, 1965-67; dean Sch. Edn. Ind. State U., Terre Haute, 1967-77; asst. to supt. Seattle pub. schs., 1977-79; prof. edn. Ind. State U., 1979—. Served to 1st lt. AUS, 1942-46. Recipient Algernon Sidney Sullivan award George Peabody Coll. Tchrs., 1959. Mem. Am. Soc. Curriculum and Devel. (chmn. Ohio 1965; chmn. Nat. council tchr. edn. 1969), Assn. Higher Edn. (bd. dirs. Ind. 1966-67). Methodist. Kiwanian (pres. Battle Ground 1952-57), Rotarian. Contbr. articles to profl. jours., chpt. to book. Home: Rural Route 32 Box 317 Terre Haute IN 47803

TURNHEIM, PALMER, banker; b. S.I., N.Y., June 30, 1921; s. Gustav and Helga (Hansen) T.; B.S. magna cum laude, N.Y. U., 1960; 4 year diploma Am. Inst. Banking, 1947; grad. Stonier Grad. Sch. Banking, Rutgers U., 1958, Advanced Mgmt. Program, Harvard, 1962; m. Gloria Freer, June 6, 1948; 1 dau., Joy Karen. Asst. mgr. credit dept. Chase Nat. Bank, 1951-55, asst. treas., 1955; asst. v.p. Chase Manhattan Bank, also Chase Manhattan Corp. parent, N.Y.C., 1956-61, v.p., 1961-71, sr. v.p., 1971—. Nat. pres. United Cerebral Palsy Assns., Inc., 1967-70; exec. v.p. United Cerebral Palsy Research and Ednl. Found. Mem. U.S. govt. com. on cash mgmt. Gen. Services Adminstrn., Washington. Bd. dirs. Fund for Theol. Edn., N.Y. Inst. Credit, 1971-74. Served with USAAF, 1942-46. Mem. N.Y. State Bankers Assn. (dir. 1972-75), Am. Legion, Beta Gamma Sigma, Phi Alpha Kappa. Lutheran. Clubs: Harvard Bus. Sch., Union League, Penn Plaza (N.Y.C.); Ponte Vedra (Fla.); Internat. (Washington). Author: International Finance Corporation, 1958. Home: 23 Oak Ln Mountain Lakes NJ 07046 Office: 1 Chase Manhattan Plaza New York NY 10081

TURNMEYER, GEORGE EARL, ret. army officer; b. Dubuque, Iowa, July 12, 1925; s. George E. and Louise B. (Kovanda) T.; B.S. in Mil. Sci., U. Md., 1954; M.B.A. in Indsl. Mgmt., Babson Coll., 1957; postgrad. Indsl. Coll. Armed Forces, 1967, Army Command and Gen. Staff Coll., 1961; m. Jean Fahey, Nov. 10, 1947; children—Ann, Robert. Served as enlisted man U.S. Army, 1944-45; commd., 1945, advanced through grades to maj. gen., 1975; various logistics assignments, 1948-77; bn. comdr. 7th Inf. Div., Korea, 1964-65; staff logistics specialist in S.E. Asia planning, Joint Chiefs of Staff, 1967-70; dep. comdr., then comdr. U.S. Army Materiel Command, Europe, 1970-73; project mgr. Lance Ballistic Missile, 1973; dep. comdr., then comdr. U.S. Army Missile Command, Huntsville, Ala., 1974-77; comdr. U.S. Army Missile Materiel Readiness Command and Redstone Arsenal, Ala., 1977, ret., 1977; mgmt. cons., 1977—. Decorated D.S.M. Mem. Soc. Logistics Engrs., Assn. U.S. Army. Roman Catholic. Club: Rotary. Home: 7705 Foxfire Dr Huntsville AL 35802

TURNQUIST, NELS ERNEST, banker; b. Three Forks, Mont., Mar. 7, 1925; s. Carl J. and Kathryn (Sandin) T.; B.A., U. Mont., 1947; m. Margaret Garrison; 1 son, R. Lynn. With First Nat. Bank and Trust Co., Helena, Mont., 1951-68, pres., 1959-68; v.p., sr. liaison officer First Bank System, Inc., Mpls., 1968-72; pres. Nat. Bank S.D., Sioux Falls, 1972—; dir. Mpls. Fed. Res. Bank. Trustee, chmn. fin. com. Sioux Valley Hosp., Sioux Falls; campaign chmn. Sioux Empire United Way; treas. Episcopal Diocese S.D.; trustee U. Mont. Found., Sioux Falls Coll. Served as pilot USNR, World War II. Mem. Am. Bankers Assn. Republican. Club: Sioux Falls Rotary. Office: PO Box 1308 Sioux Falls SD 57101

TURNURE, JAMES HARVEY, educator; b. Yonkers, N.Y., July 8, 1924; s. James Harvey and Annie Morton (Walls) T.; A.B., Princeton, 1950, M.F.A., 1953, Ph.D., 1963; m. Elizabeth Florence Sims, June 28, 1955; 1 son, James Harvey. Instr., Cornell U., 1953-58, asst. prof., 1958-64, asso. prof., 1964-68; prof., chmn. dept. art Bucknell U., Lewisburg, Pa., 1968-74, Samuel H. Kress prof. art history, 1974—, Class of 1956 lectr., 1974. Asso. prof. U. Del., summer 1964; cons. editor Bucknell U. Press. Trustee E.H. Fetherston Found. Served with AUS, 1942-46. Recipient Lindback award for distinguished teaching Bucknell U., 1974. Fulbright fellow, 1959-60. Mem. Coll. Art Assn., Am. Inst. Archaeology, Instituto per la Storia dell' Arte Lombarda, Phi Beta Kappa. Contbr. articles to profl. jours. Home: Glendale RD 1 Box 398A Lewisburg PA 17837

TURPIN, JAMES WESLEY, physician; b. Ashland, Ky., Dec. 18, 1927; s. James William and Evelyn Hope (Duke) T.; M.D., Emory U., 1955; L.H.D. (hon.), George Williams Coll., 1967; D.Sc. (hon.), Berea Coll., 1968; degree (hon.), Pa. Coll. Pharmacy and Sci., 1970; m. Donna Wrenn Turner, Sept. 14, 1974; children—Rabbani Hope, Joy Carmel; children by previous marriage—James Keith (dec.), Payton Duke, Scott Alan, Jan Evelyn. Intern, Crawford W. Long Hosp., Atlanta; resident in gen. practice Sonoma County Hosp., Santa Rosa, Calif.; practice medicine, Coronado, Calif., 1957-62; apptd. med. cons. to floating population of Hong Kong, 1971; founder Project Concern, 1962, established hosps. in Vietnam, Hong Kong, Mexico, Ethiopia, Guatemala and Bali, clinics in Appalachia and Navajo lands. City councilman, Coronado, Calif., 1960. Chmn., Sister City Assn.-Coronado/Puerto Montt, Chile. Served with USNR, 1945-46. Recipient Freedom Leadership medal Freedoms Found., Valley Forge, 1965; made hon. mem. Koho Tribe, South Vietnam, 1966; named Outstanding Young Man, U.S. Jr. C. of C., 1962; recipient Silver Bowl for Contbn. toward Peace, State of Mass., 1966; Gold Key award for Outsanding Dedication to Fellow Man, Boston Coll., AMA Humanitarian Service award, 1966; decorated mem. Loyal Order St. John the Divine Jerusalem (Gt. Britain). Mem. Am. Legion, Phi Rho Sigma. Mem. Baha'i Faith. Author: Vietnam Doctor; A Faraway Country. Home: 3808 Ainsley Ct Campbell CA 95008 Office: Palo Alto Med Clinic 300 Homer Ave Palo Alto CA 94301. *As a Bahai I live in the midst of a grand expectancy, anticipating the wonders oa a new society. As the old passes away, taking with it the deformed remnants of prejudice, injustice, illiteracy, war, and poverty, I sense the excitement and grandeur of a world brotherhood, lasting peace, universal education and justice—divine justice. First, the awesome convulsions, then the magnificent joy and Oneness.*

TURRELL, GEORGE CHARLES, chemist, educator; b. Portland, Oreg., June 19, 1931; s. Charles A. and Frances V. (Berry) T.; B.A., Lewis and Clark Coll., 1950; M.S., Ore. State U., 1952, Ph.D., 1954; m. Sylvia Elaine Jones, Sept. 4, 1970; children—Yvonne Nathalie, Marc Daniel. Chemist E.I. DuPont, Wilmington, Del., 1952; mem. tech. staff Bell Telephone Labs., Murray Hill, N.J., 1954-56; research asso. Brown U., Providence, 1956-57, instr., 1957-58; asst. prof. chemistry Howard U., Washington, 1959-62, asso. prof., 1962-66; vis. prof. U. de Bordeaux, France, 1966-70; prof. ordinaire U. Nat. du Zaire, Kisangani, 1970-71, Kinshasa, 1971-72; vis. prof. U. Montreal (Que.), Can., 1972-74, McGill U., Montreal, 1973-75; prof. chercheur Centre de Recherches sur les atoms et les molecules dept. de chimie, U. Laval, Que., Can., 1975—. Guggenheim fellow, 1958-59, Fulbright fellow, 1966-67. Mem. Am. Phys. Soc., Coblentz Soc., Sigma Xi, Phi Lambda Upsilon, Pi Mu Epsilon. Author: Infrared and Raman Spectra of Crystals, 1972. Contbr. articles on molecular spectroscopy to profl. jours. Home: 2777 Rue Le Breton Ste-Foy PQ GIW 2A6 Canada Office: Dept de Chimie Univ Laval Cite Universitaire PQ GIK 7P4 Canada

TURRELL, JAMES ARCHIE, artist; b. Los Angeles, May 6, 1943; s. Archibald Milton and Margaret (Hodges) T.; B.A., Pomona Coll., Claremont, Calif., 1965; M.A., Claremont Grad. Sch., 1974; children—Shana Cequoia, Jennifer Lynn, Anya Dehr. Lectr., UCLA, 1968, U. Calif., Riverside, 1971, U. Calif., Santa Barbara, 1977, 78, Calif. State U., Bakersfield, 1978, Northridge, 1978; vis. artist Pomona Coll., 1971-73, Claremont Grad. Sch., 1972-73; artist-in-residence Mus. No. Ariz., Flagstaff, 1979—; prin. media light and space, 1966—; one-man exhbns. include Psadena (Calif.) Art Mus., 1967, Main and Hill Studio, Santa Monica, Calif., 1968-70, Stedelijk Mus., Amsterdam, Netherlands, 1976, ARCO Center Visual Arts, Los Angeles, 1976, Rice Inst. Arts, Houston, 1979; commns. include Villa Panza, Varese, Italy, 1974, Villa Schiebler, Milan, Italy, 1979, Roden Crater (Ariz.) project, 1975—. Conscientious objector, 1966. Grantee Nat. Endowment Arts, 1968, 75, Dia Art Found., 1975-79; Guggenfellow fellow, 1974. Mem. Soaring Soc. Am., Nat. Rifle Assn.

TURRENTINE, HOWARD BOYD, judge; b. Escondido, Calif., Jan. 22, 1914; s. Howard and Veda Lillian (Maxfield) T.; A.B., San Diego State Coll., 1936; LL.B., U. So. Calif., 1939; m. Virginia Jacobsen, May 13, 1965; children—Howard Robert, Terry Beverly. Admitted to Calif. bar, 1939; practiced in San Diego, 1939-68; judge Superior Ct. County of San Diego, 1968-70; judge U.S. Dist. Ct. for So. Dist. Calif., San Diego, 1970—. Served with USNR, 1941-45. Home: 717 Armada Terr San Diego CA 92106 Office: 940 Front St San Diego CA 92189

TURRENTINE, ROBERT CLEVELAND, boot mfg. co. exec.; b. Steubenville, Ohio, Aug. 15, 1925; s. Chesley Dean and Grace Lillian (Evans) T.; student Austin Peay State U., Clarksville, Tenn., 1946-47; m. Imogene Morgan, May 31, 1951; children—Carol, Richard, Ross, Grace. With Acme Boot Co., Inc., Clarksville, Tenn., 1947—, gen. mgr., then v.p. ops., 1950-62, pres., 1962—, chief exec. officer, 1970—; dir. First Nat. Bank, Clarksville. Trustee Meml. Hosp., Clarksville. Served with USAAF, 1943-46. Mem. Am. Footwear Industries Assn., Tenn. Mfrs. Assn., Tenn. Taxpayers Assn. Methodist. Home: 12 Dogwood Ln Clarksville TN 37040 Office: 1002 Stafford St Clarksville TN 37040

TURRENTINE, STANLEY WILLIAM, musician; b. Pitts., Apr. 5, 1934; m. Shirley Scott (div.). Plays tenor saxophone; played with Ray Charles, 1952, Earl Bostic, 1953, Max Roach, 1959-60; led group with wife, organist Shirley Scott, 1960-71, solo artist thereafter; rec. numerous albums for Blue Note, C.T.I., Fantasy, now with Elektra Records; night club and concert performances; composer song Sugar; albums include: Look for Love, Come on Out, Sugar, What About You?, Betcha. Office: care Associated Booking Corp 1955 Broadway New York NY 10023*

TURRO, NICHOLAS JOHN, educator; b. Middletown, Conn., May 18, 1938; s. Nicholas John and Philomena (Russo) T.; B.A., Wesleyan U., 1960; Ph.D., Calif. Inst. Tech., 1963; m. Sandra Jean Misenti, Aug. 6, 1960; children—Cynthia Suzanne, Claire Melinda. Instr., Columbia, 1964-65, asst. prof., 1965-67, asso. prof., 1967-69, prof. chemistry, 1969—. Cons. E.I. duPont de Nemours and Co., Inc., Bogden & Quigley, Inc. Pubs. NSF fellow; Alfred P. Sloan Found. fellow. Recipient Eastman Kodak award for excellence in grad. research (award for pure chemistry 1973). Mem. Am. Chem. Soc. (Fresenius award 1973, award for pure chemistry 1974), Chem. Soc. (London), N.Y. Acad. Scis. (Freda and Gregory Halpern award in photochemistry 1977), Am. Soc. Photochemistry and Photobiology, Internat. Solar Energy Soc., Phi Beta Kappa, Sigma Xi. Author: Molecular Photochemistry, 1965; (with G.S. Hammond, J.N. Pitts, D.H. Valentine) Survey of Photochemistry, vol. 1, 1968, vol. 2, 1970, vol. 3, 1971; (with A.A. Lamola) Energy Transfer and Organic Photochemistry, 1971; Modern Molecular Photochemistry, 1978. Editorial bd. Jour. Organic Chemistry, 1974—. Home: 125 Downey Dr Tenafly NJ 07670

TURVEY, CHARLES ROBERT, petroleum co. exec.; b. Douglas, Ariz., Feb. 2, 1923; s. Harry E. and Gladys R. (Schindler) T.; U. Notre Dame, 1948; m. Marie Bellville Whitehead, June 6, 1949; children—Harry, Anne, Christine, Sarah, Thomas, Teresa, David. With Conoc Inc., 1951—, mng. dir. Conoco Europe, London, 1970-74, v.p. transp. and supply, Stamford, Conn., 1974-75, exec. v.p. mktg., Houston, 1975—. Served with USN, 1942-46. Decorated Air medal. Home: 371 Tynebridge Piney Point Village Houston TX 77024 Office: PO Box 2197 5 Greenway Plaza E Houston TX 77001

TUSHER, THOMAS WILLIAM, apparel co. exec.; b. Oakland, Calif., Apr. 5, 1941; s. William C. and Betty J. (Brown) T.; B.A., U. Calif., Berkeley, 1963; M.B.A., Stanford U., 1965; m. Pauline B. Kensett, Jan. 1, 1967; children—Gregory Malcolm, Michael Scott. Asst. to v.p. internat. Colgate Palmolive Co., N.Y.C., 1965-67; product mgr., Colgate-Palmolive P.R., 1967-68; supt. corp. planning Levi Strauss & Co., San Francisco, 1969; pres. Levi Strauss Internat.,

1977—, also sr. v.p., dir. parent co.; regional gen. mgr. Australia/N.Z., Levi Strauss Australia, 1970-74; area gen. mgr. Levi Strauss No. Europe, London, 1974-75; pres. European div. Levi Strauss Internat., San Francisco, 1976; dir. various subs's. Levi Strauss Internat.; dir. Gt. Western Garment Co. (Can.). Bd. dirs. Calif. Council Internat. Trade, 1977—, U. Calif. Grad. Bus. Sch. Served with Intelligence Corps., USAR, 1966-67. Mem. San Francisco C. of C. (dir.). Republican. Presbyterian. Clubs: World Trade, Bay. Office: 2 Embarcadero Center San Francisco CA 94106

TUSHINGHAM, (ARLOTTE) DOUGLAS, educator; b. Toronto, Ont., Can., Jan. 19, 1914; s. Arthur Douglas and Lottie Elizabeth (Betts) T.; B.A., U. Toronto, 1936; B.D., U. Chgo., 1941, Ph.D., 1948; m. Margaret McAndrew Thomson, Apr. 9, 1948; children—Margaret Elizabeth (Mrs. J.C. Wylie), Ian Douglas. Instr., U. Chgo., 1948-51; ann. prof. Am. Sch. Oriental Research, Jerusalem, 1951-52, dir., 1952-53; asso. prof. Queen's U., 1953-55; head art and archaeology div. Royal Ont. Mus., Toronto, 1955-64, chief archaeologist, 1964—; prof. dept. Nr. Eastern studies U. Toronto (Ont.), 1955—. Asst. dir. Jericho Excavations, 1952, 53, 56; dir. Dhiban Excavations, 1952-53; asso. dir. Jerusalem Excavations, 1962-67; mem. Toronto Hist. Bd., 1967—, chmn., 1967-73. Served as lt. Royal Canadian Navy, 1942-45. Fellow Soc. Antiquaries of London, Royal Soc. Can., Canadian Museums Assn. (pres. 1964, 65), Archaeol. Inst. Am. Author: (with V.B. Meen) Crown Jewels of Iran, 1968; (with Denis Baly) Atlas of the Biblical World, 1971; The Excavations at Dibon (Dhîbân) in Moab, 1952-53, 1972; Gold for the Gods, 1976. Home: 66 Collier St Apt 8A Toronto ON M4W 1L9 Canada Office: Royal Ontario Museum 100 Queen's Park Toronto ON M5S 2C6 Canada

TUSIANI, JOSEPH, educator, author; b. Foggia, Italy, Jan. 14, 1924; s. Michael and Maria (Pisone) T.; Dottore in Lettere summa cum laude, U. Naples, 1947, Litt.D., 1971. Came to U.S., 1947, naturalized, 1956. Lectr. in Italian lit. Hunter Coll., 1950-62; chmn. Italian dept. Coll. Mt. St. Vincent, 1948-71; vis. asso. prof. N.Y. U., 1956-64; vis. asso. prof. City U. N.Y., 1971—, prof. Herbert H. Lehman Coll., 1971—; NDEA vis. prof. Italian, Conn. State Coll., 1962. Recipient Greenwood Prize for poetry in Eng., 1956; Outstanding Tchr. award, 1969; cavaliere ufficiale Italian Republic, 1973. Mem. Poetry Soc. Am. (v.p.), Cath. Poetry Soc. Am. (dir. 1958, Spirit gold medal 1968). Author: Dante in Licenza, 1952; Two Critical Essays on Emily Dickinson, 1952; Poesia Missionaria in Inghilterra Ed America, 1953; Sonettisti Americani, 1954; Melos Cordis (poems in Latin), 1955; Lo Speco Celeste, 1956; Odi Sacre (poems), 1958; The Complete Poems of Michelangelo, 1960; Rind and All (poems), 1962; Lust and Liberty (The Poems of Machiavelli), 1963; The Fifth Season, 1963; Dante's Inferno (Introduced to Young People), 1964; Envoy from Heaven, 1965; Dante's Purgatorio (Introduced to Young People), 1969; Dante's Paradise (Introduced to Young People), 1970; Tasso's Jerusalem Delivered (verse transl.), 1970; Boccaccio's Nymphs of Fiesole, 1971; Italian Poets of the Renaissance, 1971; From Marino to Marinetti, 1973; The Age of Dante, 1973; America the Free, 1976; Tìreca Tàreca (poems), 1978; Gente Mia and Other Poems, 1978. Home: 2140 Tomlinson Ave Bronx NY 10461. *Strange how this continually re-edited Who's Who forces one to work and achieve!*

TUSKEN, ROGER ANTHONY, assn. exec.; b. Chgo., Sept. 3, 1929; s. Anton Ludwig and Bessie (Nalevac) T.; B.A. in Journalism, Mich. State U., 1951, postgrad., 1956-57; m. Margaret June Barnes, Oct. 30, 1954; children—Mark Anthony, Michael Alan, Matthew Allen. Reporter Central Press Assn., Chgo., 1952; editor Suburban Life, Lowell, Mich., 1955-56; field asst. Am. Acad. Family Physicians, Kansas City, Mo., 1957-61, mgr. membership services dept., 1961-65, dir. communications div., 1965-68, asst. exec. dir., 1968-71, exec. dir., 1971—. Bd. dirs. Rehab. Inst. Served with Mil. Police, U.S. Army, 1952-53. Mem. Am. Assn. Med. Soc. Execs., Am., Mid-Am. (past pres.) socs. assn. execs., Profl. Conv. Mgmt. Assn. (pres. 1978), Jackson County hist. socs., Kansas City C. of C., Sigma Delta Chi. Episcopalian. Home: 9 E 109th St Kansas City MO 64114 Office: 1740 W 92d St Kansas City MO 64114

TUSSING, ROBERT THEODORE, educator; b. San Benito, Tex., Sept. 13, 1925; s. Glen Harold and Gladys (Houghtling) T.; B.B.A. summa cum laude, Tex. A. and I. Coll., 1948, M.S., 1949; postgrad. Trinity U., San Antonio, 1953; Ph.D., U. Tex., 1957; m. Anna Mae Darling, Nov. 19, 1945; children—Robert Theodore (dec.), Donald Glynn, Melody Ann, Dennis Dale. Pub. accounting practice, San Benito, 1949-50; staff accountant George, Thrift & Cochrell, San Antonio, 1952; parttime instr. bus. adminstrn. Trinity U., 1952-53; instr. accounting U. Tex., 1953-57; prof. accounting and bus. adminstrn. N.Mex. Highlands U., 1957-68, head dept. bus. adminstrn., 1957-67; asso. prof. accounting Ill. State U., Normal, 1968-71, prof., 1971—; cons. in field, 1952—. Mem. Gov. N.Mex. Com. Long-Range State Planning, 1960. Served to 1st lt. AUS, 1944-46, 50-52. C.P.A., cert. in data processing, Tex. Mem. Am. Inst. C.P.A.'s, Data Processing Mgmt. Assn., Am. Acctg. Assn. (chmn. membership N.Mex. 1957-59), Phi Theta Kappa, Alpha Chi, Beta Alpha Psi, Beta Gamma Sigma. Mem. Christian Ch. (elder. lay preacher, v.p. 1966-68). Contbr. articles to profl. jours. Editor: The Role of Industry in the American System, 1958. Home: 401 E Lincoln St Normal IL 61761

TUTEN, JOHN COLE, banker; b. Bellefonte, Pa., Oct. 25, 1910; s. Earle C. and Rebecca (Cole) T.; grad. Pa. State U., 1933; grad. Stonier Sch. Banking, Rutgers U., 1961; m. Sarah Boas Gilbert, June 14, 1941; children—John Cole, Henderson Gilbert, Sarah Boas. With Harrisburg Rys. Co. (Pa.), 1945-55; v.p. Central Trust Co., Harrisburg, 1955-58; v.p. Nat. Bank and Trust Co. Central Pa. (successor bank to Central Trust Co.), Harrisburg, 1958-60, exec. v.p., 1960-62, pres., 1962-70; chmn. bd., chief exec. officer Nat. Central Bank (successor bank to Nat. Bank and Trust Co., Central Pa.), Harrisburg, 1970-75, chmn. bd., 1975—, also dir.; dir. Fed. Res. Bank, 1973-74; mem. Pa. Banking Bd., from 1976; mem. adv. com. on banking policies and practices Adminstr. Nat. Banks. Trustee Kline Found., Harrisburg; mem. bd. mgrs., treas. Harrisburg Hosp. Served to maj. U.S. Army, 1941-46; ETO. Decorated Bronze Star (U.S.); Croix de Guerre (Belgium). Mem. Am., Pa. bankers assns., Harrisburg C. of C. Presbyterian. Clubs: Harrisburg Country, Rotary (pres. local club) (Harrisburg); Hamilton (Lancaster, Pa.); Union League of Phila. Home: Bowmansdale PA 17008 Office: 222 Market St Harrisburg PA 17108

TUTHILL, JOHN BEAKES, mfg. co. exec.; b. Michigan City, Ind. Sept. 25, 1915; s. Ralph Wells and Winifred (Maxwell) T.; B.S., Ind. U., 1939; Indsl. Adminstr., Harvard, 1943; m. Barbara Brooke Musgrave, Jan. 26, 1943; children—John Beakes, Paul Arthur, Helen Brooke, David Wells. Asst. v.p. Am. Nat. Bank, Indpls., 1939-40, 46-51; v.p. Collins Radio Co., Cedar Rapids, Iowa and Dallas, 1951-64; treas. Allis-Chalmers Mfg. Co., 1965; v.p. Pioneer Tex. Corp., Dallas, 1965-66, pres., 1966-78, chmn. bd., 1972—; dir. Walraven Book Cover Co., Dallas, Pioneer Tex. Corp., Dallas, Burton Shipyard, Inc., Port Arthur, Tex., Hydrotex Industries, Inc. Instr. corp. finance Ind. U., Indpls. div., 1946-51. Cedar Rapids Community Chest campaign, 1954. Chmn., Linn County (Iowa) Republican Central Com., 1958-60. Served to 1st lt. AUS, 1943-45. Mem. Sigma Alpha Epsilon. Episcopalian. Clubs: City, Las Colinas Country (Dallas). Home: 11745 Valleydale Dallas TX 75230 Office: 1165 Empire Central Pl Dallas TX 75247

TUTHILL, JOHN WILLS, educator; b. Montclair, N.J., Nov. 10, 1910; s. Oliver Bailey and Louise Jerolomen (Wills) B.; S.B., Coll. William and Mary, 1932, LL.D., 1978; M.B.A., N.Y. U., 1936; A.M., Harvard, 1943; LL.D., MacMurray Coll., 1967; m. Erna Lueders, July 3, 1937; children—Carol Anne, David. Teller First Nat. Bank, Paterson, N.J., 1932-34; corporate trust adminstr. Bankers Trust Co. N.Y., 1934-36; investment counsel Fiduciary Counsel, N.Y.C., 1936-37; instr. Northeastern, 1937-39, asst. prof. banking and finance, 1939-40; apptd. fgn. service officer Dept. State, 1940, served as vice counsul, Windsor, Can., 1940-41, Mazatlan, Mexico, 1942; 3d sec. embassy, Ottawa, 1942-44; sec. mission Office U.S. Polit. Adviser SHAEF, 1944-45, and Am. Mil. Govt. for Germany, 1945-47, Am. consul, 1947; asst. chief shipping div. Dept. State, 1948, adviser, 1949; counselor of embassy, Stockholm, 1949-51; spl. asst. ambassador, London, 1952; dep. dir. Office Econ. Affairs, Bonn, Germany, 1952-54, USOM, Bonn, 1954, dir., 1954-56, counselor of embassy for econ. affairs, 1955-56; counselor embassy for econ. affairs with personal rank of minister, Paris, France, 1956-59; dir. Office European Regional Affairs, Dept. State, 1959; minister-counselor econ. affairs U.S. Mission to NATO, European Regional Orgns., U.S. rep. prep. com. for OECD, also dep. U.S. rep. OEEC, 1960; U.S. rep. OECD with personal rank of ambassador, 1960-62; U.S. ambassador to European Communities, 1962-66, Brazil, 1966-69; prof. internat. politics Johns Hopkins Bologna Center, Italy, 1969; pres. Salzburg Seminars in Am. Studies, Cambridge, Mass., 1977—; vis. fellow Woodrow Wilson Nat. Fellowship Found., Princeton, 1978—; dir.-gen., gov. Atlantic Inst. for Internat. Affairs, Paris, France, 1969-76. Mem. Brit.-N.Am. Com.; mem. adv. bd. Internat. Mgmt. and Devel. Inst., Mem. N.Y. Council Fgn. Relations, Omicron Delta Kappa, Theta Delta Chi. Clubs: Century Assn., Harvard (N.Y.C.); Cosmos (Washington); Flat Hat of William and Mary. Office: 17 Dunster St Cambridge MA 02138

TUTT, CHARLES LEAMING, JR., educator, mech. engr.; b. Coronodo, Cal., Jan. 26, 1911; s. Charles Leaming and Eleanor (Armit) T.; B.S.E., Princeton, 1933, M.E., 1934; D.Eng., Norwich U., 1967; m. Pauline Barbara Shaffer, Aug. 16, 1933; children—Charles Leaming IV, William Bullard. Student engr. Buick Motor div. Gen. Motors Corp., Flint, Mich., 1934-36, engr. chassis unit sect., 1936-38, spl. assignment engr., 1938-40; asst. prof. mech. engring. Princeton, 1940-46; staff asst. ASME, N.Y.C., 1940-44; asso. editor Product Engring. mag. McGraw-Hill Pub. Co., N.Y.C., 1944-46; asst. to pres. Gen. Motors Inst., Flint, 1946-50, adminstrv. chmn., 1950-60, dean engring., 1960-69, dean acad. affairs, 1969-74. Mem. adv. com. Sloan Mus., Flint, 1965—. Trustee Norwich U., Northfield, Vt., 1963-76. Mem. Engring. Found. Bd., N.Y.C., 1963-75, chmn., 1967-73. Fellow ASME (v.p. 1964-66, pres. 1975-76); mem. Soc. Mfg. Engrs. (dir. 1972-78), Am. Soc. for Engring. Edn., Soc. Automotive Engrs., Mich. Soc. Profl. Engrs., Engrs. Council for Profl. Devel. (dir. 1975—), Am. Soc. Metals, Soc. of Cin. in State of Va., Sigma Xi, Delta Tau Delta, Tau Beta Pi. Rotarian. Clubs: Flint City, Flint Rainbow, University (Flint); Wigwam (Deckers, Colo.); Princeton (N.Y.C.). Contbr. articles to profl. jours. Home: 3401 Westwood Pkwy Flint MI 48503

TUTT, RUSSELL THAYER, investment co. exec.; b. Coronado, Cal., July 27, 1913; s. Charles Leaming and Eleanor (Armit) T.; grad. Thacher Sch., 1931; B.S. in Engring., Princeton, 1935; m. Margaret Louise Honnen, Aug. 12, 1950 (dec. Nov. 1974); children—Margaret Honnen Tutt Steinegger, Russell Thayer. With buying dept. Halsey, Stuart & Co., Inc., N.Y.C., 1935-40; v.p., gen. mgr. Garden City (Kans.) Co., 1946-56; pres. S.W. Kans. Power, Inc., Garden City, 1946-56; v.p. El Pomar Investment Co., Colorado Springs, Colo., 1956-61, pres., 1961—; chmn. exec. com. Holly Sugar Corp., Affiliated Bank Shares of Colo., Inc., Central Telephone & Utilities Corp.; pres. Garden City Co.; pres. Broadmoor Hotel, Inc.; chmn. bd. First Nat. Bank Colorado Springs. Trustee Cheyenne Mountain Mus. and Zool. Soc., 1956—, pres., 1963-74, chmn. bd., 1974—; pres., trustee El Pomar Found.; trustee Colo. Coll. (chmn. 1966—), Fountain Valley Sch. of Colo., Nat. Park and Recreation Assn., Washington. Served to maj. AUS, 1940-45. Decorated Bronze Star. Republican. Episcopalian. Clubs: Cheyenne Mountain Country, Broadmoor Golf, El Paso, Country of Colo., Cooking (Colorado Springs). Home: 100 Marland Rd Colorado Springs CO 80906 Office: El Pomar Bldg Broadmoor Colorado Springs CO 80906

TUTT, WILLIAM THAYER, hotel and investment exec.; b. Coronado, Calif., Mar. 2, 1912; s. Charles L. and Eleanor (Armit) T.; student Denver U. Bus. Sch., bus. coll.; m. Yvonne S. McGowan, Jan. 6, 1978; 1 dau., Margaret Eleanor (Mrs. McColl.). With Colo. Title & Trust, 1930-32; mgr. Manitou Mineral Water Co., 1932-35, pres., dir.; mgr. Manitou Mineral Water & Sales Co., 1932-35; pres. Gen. Liquors, 1935-38; partner Boettcher & Co., 1938-42; chmn. bd., dir. Broadmoor Hotel, Inc.; chmn. bd., dir. El Pomar Investment Co. and pres. subs. cos.; dir. Golden Cycle Corp., Kennecott Copper Corp., Braden Copper Co., Affiliated Bankshares Colo., Inc., San Juan Tours, Inc., Rio Grande Industries, D. & R.G.W. Ry. Co., First Nat. Bank of Colorado Springs, Mountain States Tel. & Tel. Co. Pres., bd. dirs. Air Force Acad. Found.; chmn. bd., trustee El Pomar Found.; chmn. bd. Sunnyrest Sanatorium; trustee emeritus Lovelace Found.; bd. dirs., exec. com. U.S. Olympic Com. Served to lt. col. AUS, 1942-46. Decorated Legion of Merit, Officer dans l'Ordre du Merite Touristique, French Govt.; Grand Insignia for Merits for Republic, Austria; named to Nat. Cowboy Hall of Fame, Colo. Sports Hall Fame, U.S. Hockey Hall Fame, Can. Hockey Hall of Fame, Colo. Golf Hall of Fame; recipient Am. Acad. Achievement Golden Plate award. Mem. Internat. Ice Hockey Fedn. (1st v.p.), Amateur Hockey Assn. U.S. (pres., dir.). Republican. Clubs: Broadmoor Golf (pres., dir.); Cheyenne Mountain Country, Garden of the Gods, Cooking (pres., trustee), Wigwam. Home: 2621 Spring Grove Terr Colorado Springs CO 80906 Office: Broadmoor Hotel Colorado Springs CO 80906

TUTTLE, ALBERT THEODORE, clergyman; b. Manti, Utah, Mar. 2, 1919; s. Albert Mervin and Clarice (Beal) T.; A.B., Brigham Young U., 1943; M.A., Stanford, 1949; postgrad. U. Utah; M. Marne Whitaker, July 26, 1943; children—David M., Diane, Robert T., Clarissa Marne, Jonathan W., Melissa, Boyd Jeremy. Missionary, No. States Mission, 1939-41; sem. tchr., Menan, Idaho, Brigham City, Kaysville, Utah, Salt Lake City, 1946-52; dir. Inst. of Religion, U. Nev., 1952; supr. sems. and insts. Latter-day Saints Dept. Edn., 1953—; supr. S.Am. missions, 1961; gen. authority Latter-day Saints Ch., First Council of Seventy, 1958—; supr. S. Am. missions, 1975. Served as 1st lt. 5th Div., USMCR, 1943-46. Named Outstanding Student in Religion, Brigham Young U., 1943. Mem. Phi Delta Kappa, Delta Phi (past pres.), Blue Key. Office: 47 E South Temple Salt Lake City UT 84111

TUTTLE, CHARLES EGBERT, publisher, bookseller; b. Rutland, Vt., Apr. 5, 1915; s. Charles Egbert and Helen Sarah (Woolverton) T.; grad. Phillips Exeter Acad., 1933; A.B., Harvard, 1937; m. Reiko Chiba, Feb. 16, 1952. Pres., Charles E. Tuttle Co., Rutland, 1938—; v.p. Tuttle-Mori Agy., Inc., Tokyo, Japan. Mem. selection com. for Japan, Eisenhower Exchange Fellowships, 1960-62. Served to capt. AUS, 1942-46. Recipient commendation Japan Soc. Translators, 1965; Pubs. Assn. for Cultural Exchange (Japan) awards, 1969, 70; Broadcast Preceptor award San Francisco State Coll., 1970; award of merit Vt. Council on the Arts, 1970; John Barnes Pub. of Year award Am. Booksellers Assn., 1970; named Most Successful Grad. Rutland High Sch. 35th reunion, 1967; Internat. Publs. Cultural awards Japan Broadcasting Corp., 1969, 70. Mem. Internat. House Tokyo, Am.-Japan Soc., Vt. Hist. Soc., ALA, Asia Soc., Japan Soc., Asiatic Soc. Japan, Phi Beta Kappa. Clubs: American (Tokyo); Harvard (Boston, N.Y.C.); Army and Navy (Washington). Publisher numerous books on Japan, Asia. Home: 28 S Main St Rutland VT 05701 Office: 26-28 S Main St Rutland VT 05701

TUTTLE, EDWIN ELLSWORTH, chem. co. exec.; b. Syracuse, N.Y., Apr. 24, 1927; s. John Ross and Celia (Boyington) T.; B.S., Haverford Coll., 1949; M.B.A., Harvard U., 1951. Apptd. asst. to pres. Pennwalt Corp., Phila., 1957, v.p., treas., 1965-70, v.p. finance, 1971-72, group v.p. chems., 1972-74, exec. v.p. adminstrn., 1974-76, pres., 1976-77, vice chmn., 1977-78, chmn., chief exec. officer, 1978—; dir. CVI, Inc., 1st Pa. Corp., 1st Pa. Bank N.V., Westmoreland Coal. Bd. dirs. Pa. Economy League, Pa. Ballet; bd. mgrs. Haverford Coll. Mem. Pa. C. of C. (vice chmn., dir.). Home: 514 Pine St Philadelphia PA 19106 Office: Pennwalt Bldg Philadelphia PA 19102

TUTTLE, ELBERT PARR, fed. judge; b. Pasadena, Calif., July 17, 1897; s. Guy Harmon and Margie Etta (Parr) T.; student Punahou Acad., Honolulu, 1909-14; A.B., Cornell, 1918, LL.B., 1923; LL.D., Emory U., 1958, Harvard, 1965, Georgetown U., 1978; m. Sara Sutherland, Oct. 22, 1919; children—Elbert Parr, Jane T. (Mrs. John J. Harmon). News and editorial N.Y. Evening Sun, N.Y.C., also Army and Navy Jour. and Am. Legion Weekly, Washington, 1919; admitted to Ga. bar, 1923; since practiced in Atlanta, and Washington, 1946—; mem. Sutherland, Tuttle & Brennan; gen. counsel, head legal div. Treasury Dept., 1953-54; judge 5th circuit U.S. Ct. Appeals, 1954—, chief judge, 1961-67. Chmn. adv. com. on civil rules Jud. Conf. U.S., 1972-78, chmn. adv. com. on jud. activities, 1969-77. Comdr. 304th F.A., 77th Inf. Div. U.S. Army, 1941-46, disch. as col.; comdg. gen. 108th Airborne Div. (res.), 1947-50, brig. gen. U.S. Army Res. Decorated Legion of Merit, Bronze Star, Purple Heart with oak leaf cluster. Trustee Atlanta Community Chest, 1947-49; v.p. Atlanta Community Planning Council, 1951. Past trustee Interdonominational Theol. Center, Cornell U., Atlanta U., Spelman Coll., Morehouse Coll., Piedmost Hosp. Mem. Am., Atlanta (pres. 1948) bar assns., Atlanta C. of C. (pres. 1949), Sigma Delta Chi, Alpha Kappa Psi, Phi Kappa Phi, Pi Kappa Alpha (nat. pres. 1930-36), Order of Coif. Episcopalian. Home: 101 Peachtree Circle NE Atlanta GA 30309

TUTTLE, GEORGE MILLEDGE, clergyman; b. Medicine Hat, Alta., Can., Oct. 4, 1915; s. Aubrey Stephen and Mary Anna (Johnson) T.; B.A., U. Alta., 1937, B.D., 1941; Th.D., Victoria U., Toronto, 1961; m. Helen Robertson Mitchell, July 1, 1944; children—Julia Margaret Tuttle Devereux, John Robert. Ordained to ministry United Ch. of Can., 1941; nat. youth dir., 1941-44; pastor chs., Sangudo, Alta., 1945-51; prof. Christian theology Union Coll., Vancouver, B.C., 1951-66; prin. St. Stephen's Coll., Edmonton, Alta., 1966-79; moderator United Ch. of Can., Toronto, 1977—. Mem. Can. Assn. Pastoral Edn., Can. Theol. Soc., Delta Kappa Epsilon. Office: United Church House 85 St Clair Ave E Toronto ON M4T 1M8 Canada

TUTTLE, HARRIS BENJAMIN, SR., ret. photog. co. exec.; b. Clarkson, N.Y., Oct. 30, 1902; s. Elmer Ellsworth and Clarie Adelia (Ball) T.; student Rochester Inst. Tech., 1918-22, U. Rochester Ext. Sch., 1922-25; m. Olive J. Klem, Feb. 28, 1922; children—Phyllis Dawn (Mrs. Robert C. Kelley (dec.), Harris (dec.). With Eastman Kodak Co., Rochester, N.Y., 1918-66, research lab. tech., 1918-25, advt. dept. dir. motion picture demonstration reels, 1926-38, sales dept., 1939-53, lectr., cons. on law enforcement photography, 1954-66; cons. med. photography U. Rochester Sch. Medicine, 1928-47; advisor on photography Nat. Football Coaches Assn., 1934-47; cons. Inst. Applied Scis., 1955-74; lectr. in field. Pres. Conesus Lake Assn., 1946-47. Photographic Soc. Am. fellow, 1950. Recipient Medal of Valor, Nat. Police Officers Assn., 1964; Distinguished Service award, Readers Digest Assn., 1964; Progress medal, Photographic Soc. Am., 1974. Fellow Royal Photographic Soc. Gt. Britain, Am. Acad. Forensic Sci., Biol. Photographic Assn., Soc. Motion Picture and Television Engrs.; hon. fellow Soc. Amateur Cinematographers; mem. S.A.R. Clubs: E.K., Camera, Oval Table Soc. Author: Color Movies for Beginners, 1940. Contbr. 156 articles to profl. jours. Address: 2735 Silver King Way Sarasota FL 33581. *Through my lectures and articles I believe I have brought knowledge and pleasure to thousands through photography. I enjoy today by seeing my dreams of yesterday come true.*

TUTTLE, JAY FORRESTER, physician, hosp. adminstr.; b. Seattle, Nov. 17, 1913; s. Jay M. and Stella M. (Forrester) T.; B.S., Walla Walla Coll., 1939; M.D., Coll. Med. Evangelists, 1938; M.S. in Psychiatry, U. Colo., 1952; m. Helen C. Rompel, Aug. 12, 1939; children—Jay, Ronald, David. Intern, Seattle Gen. Hosp., 1938-39; resident Fitzsimmons Army Hosp., Denver, 1950-52; commd. 2d lt. U.S. Army, 1938, advanced through grades to lt. col., 1952; ret., 1964; asst. supt. Fulton (Mo.) State Hosp., 1964-72; supt. Farmington (Mo.) State Hosp., 1972-78; chief outpatient dept. St. Louis State Hosp., 1978—. Mem. Am. Psychiat. Assn. Address: 421 Hickory Glen Ln Creve Coeur MO 63141

TUTTLE, SHERWOOD DODGE, educator, geologist; b. Medford, Mass., June 8, 1918; s. Maurice Samuel and Beulah Sherwood (Skillman) T.; B.S., U. N.H., 1939; M.S., Wash. State U., 1941; M.A., Ph.D., Harvard, 1953; m. Esther Barrett, Sept. 15, 1941; children—Mark Samuel, Beverly Ruth, Owen Sherwood. Instr. Wash. State U., 1941, 46-48; mem. Wash. State Geol. Survey, 1939, U.S. Geol. Survey, 1941, 47, 48, Nat. Park Service, 1946; mem. faculty U. Iowa, 1952—, prof. geology, 1961—, chmn. dept., 1962-68, asso. dean Coll. Liberal Arts, 1970—; mem. Ia. Geol. Survey, 1953-56; research asso. Woods Hole Oceanographic Insts., 1958-67; mem. Ia. Vis. Scientist Program, 1960-67; Fulbright lectr. United Coll., Chinese U. of Hong Kong, 1968-69. Served to major AUS, 1942-46; col. Res. Fellow Geol. Soc. Am.; mem. Am. Inst. Profl. Geologists (charter), Assn. Geology Tchrs., Geol. Soc. Iowa, Iowa Acad. Sci. Sigma Xi. Home: 21 George St Iowa City IA 52240

TUTUNJIAN, JERRY JIRAIR, editor, pub. co. exec.; b. Jerusalem, Nov. 23, 1945; s. Apraham George and Cecile Dyran (Chekgenian) T.; came to Can., 1965, naturalized, 1970; diploma Ryerson Poly. Inst., Toronto, Ont., Can., 1968; B.A. in Journalism, U. Toronto, 1974; m. Mary, Aug. 10, 1975; 1 son, Aram. Reporter, photographer Goderich (Ont.) Signal Star, 1968, Grimsby (Ont.) Ind., 1968; sr. reporter, photographer, wire editor Brampton (Ont.) Times, 1969; asst. editor Canadian Motorist Mag., Toronto, 1970-71, editor, 1971-75, mng. editor, 1975-77, gen. mgr., editor, 1977—; cons. Armenian Community Mag. Recipient State Tourism award State of S.C., 1973. Home: 50 Quebec Ave Apt 903 Toronto ON M6P 4B4 Canada Office: 2 Carlton St Toronto ON M5B 1K4 Canada

TUVE, MERLE ANTONY, research physicist; b. Canton, S.D., June 27, 1901; s. Anthony G. and Ida Marie (Larsen) T.; prep. edn. Augustana Acad., Canton, 1915-18; B.S. in Elec. Engring., U. Minn., 1922, A.M., 1923; Ph.D., Johns Hopkins, 1926; D.Sc., Case, Kenyon, Williams, Johns Hopkins, U. Alaska; LL.D., Augustana Coll., Carleton; m. Winifred Gray Whitman (M.D.), Oct. 27, 1927; children—Trygve Whitman (dec. 1972), Lucy Winifred Tuve Comly. Teaching fellow U. Minn., 1922-23; instr. physics Princeton, 1923-24, Johns Hopkins, 1924-26; mem. staff dept. terrestrial magnetism Carnegie Inst. Washington, 1926-46, dir. 1946-66, distinguished service mem., 1966—; on leave, 1940-46, war work (proximity fuse, etc.); home sec. Nat. Acad. Scis., 1966-72. Chmn. Sect. T. OSRD, 1940-45; dir. Applied Physics Lab., Johns Hopkins (Navy) 1942-46; U.S. exec. com. Nat. Com of IGY, 1954-59; mem. Pres.'s Sci. Adv. Com.-Internat. Sci. Panel. Recipient AAAS prize (with L.R. Hafstad, O. Dahl), 1931— Presdl. Medal of Merit, 1946; Research Corp. Award 1947; comdr. Order of Brit. Empire, 1948; John Scott Award, 1948; Comstock Prize, Nat. Acad. Sci., 1949; Howard N. Potts medal Franklin Inst., 1950; Achievement medal U. Minn., 1950; Barnard medal Columbia, 1955, Medal Condor de Los Andes (Bolivia); Bowie medal Am. Geophys. Union, 1963; Cosmos Club award, 1963. Fellow Am. Phys. Soc., IEEE, AAAS, Am. Acad. Arts and Sci.; mem. Am. Philos. Soc., Nat. Acad. Scis. (chmn. NRC geophysics research bd. 1969-72), Philos. Soc. Washington, Washington Acad. Scis., Phi Beta Kappa, Sigma Xi, Tau Beta Pi, Gamma Alpha. Club: Cosmos. Contbr. to Phys. Rev., other sci. jours. on nuclear physics, geophysics and biophysics. Editor: Jour. Geophys. Research, 1949-58. Home: 135 Hesketh St Chevy Chase MD 20015 Office: 5241 Broad Branch Rd NW Washington DC 20015

TWADDELL, WILLIAM HARTSHORNE, govt. ofcl.; b. Madison, Wis., Jan. 25, 1941; s. William Freeman and Helen (Johnson) T.; B.A., Brown U., 1963; m. Kristie Miller, June 11, 1966; children—William Sanderson, Ellen Johnson. Vol. Peace Corps, Brazil, 1963-65; reporter N.Y. Daily News, 1967-69; fgn. service officer Dept. State, 1969—, spl. asst. to sec. State, Washington, 1979—. Served with U.S. Army, 1965-67. Office: Office of the Sec US Dept State 2201 C St NW Washington DC 20520

TWAITS, WILLIAM OSBORN, oil exec.; b. Galt, Ont., Can.; s. William and Laura (Osborn) T.; B.Commerce, U. Toronto, 1933; D.C.L., Acadia U.; Dr. Bus. Adminstrn., U. Ottawa; LL.D., U. Windsor; m. Frances Begg, May 29, 1937; children—Judith T. Allan, Sheryl T. Young. With Imperial Oil Ltd., Toronto, Ont., 1933-73, served in refining, research, crude oil prodn., supply and transp., petroleum econs. and other phases of petroleum and petrochem. industries, dir., 1950-73, exec. v.p., 1956-60, pres., 1960-70, chmn. bd., chief exec. officer, 1970-73; v.p., dir. Royal Bank Can.; pres. Sarcalto Ltd.; dir. Abitibi Paper Co. Ltd. Alcan Aluminium Ltd., Tri Ltd., Ford Motor Co. Can. Ltd., N.Y. Life Ins. Co., Norcen Energy Resources Ltd. Former chmn. Bus. Council on Nat. Issues; mem. exec. com. Brit.-N.Am. com., mem. Canadian-Am. com. C.D. Howe Research Inst.; bd. govs., hon. treas. Olympic Trust Can.; mem. council of honor Stanford Research Inst.; hon. pres. Canadian Arthritis Soc.; councillor Conf. Bd.; mem. Can. council Conf. Bd. Can.; hon. bd. dirs. Can.'s Aviation Hall Fame. Decorated companion Order of Can. Fellow Royal Soc. Arts; mem. Delta Kappa Epsilon. Clubs: York, Canadian, Rosedale Golf (Toronto); Augusta Nat.; Rideau (Ottawa); Empire of Canada. Home: 17 Old Forest Hill Rd Toronto ON M5P 2P6 Canada Office: 1235 Bay St Suite 300 Toronto ON M5R 3K4 Canada

TWARDOWICZ, STANLEY JAN, artist, photographer; b. Detroit, July 8, 1917; s. Joseph and Anna Ligenski; student Meinzinger Art Sch., Detroit, 1940-44, Skowhegan (Maine) Sch. Painting and Sculpture, summer 1946; m. Lillian Dodson, Mar. 15, 1971. Exhibited paintings Mus. Modern Art, Guggenheim Mus., Whitney Mus., Chgo. Art Inst., Carnegie Internat., Pa. Acad. Fine Arts, Am. Acad. Arts and Letters, Houston Mus., Milw. Art Center, Peridot Gallery, N.Y.C., others; retrospective exhbn. Heckscher Mus., Huntington, N.Y., 1974, Emily Lowe Gallery, Hempstead, N.Y., 1979; exhibited photographs Images Gallery, N.Y.C.; represented in permanent collections including Mus. Modern Art, Los Angeles County Mus., Newark Mus., Milw. Art Center, Ball State Tchrs. Coll., Harvard U., Vassar Coll., Hirshhorn Mus. and Sculpture Garden, others; instr. Ohio State U., 1946-51; asst. prof. Hofstra U., 1965—. Guggenheim fellow, 1956. Home: 133 Crooked Hill Huntington NY 11743 Office: 57 Main St Northport NY 11768

TWEEDIE, EARL ROBERT, investment co. exec.; b. Walton, N.Y., Sept. 30, 1917; s. Robert Andrew and Nellie Mabel (Anderson) T.; A.B., Ohio State U., 1939, J.D., 1941; m. Jane Charlton Harmount, Oct. 12, 1941 (dec. July 1972); children—Robert Timmons, Ann Tweedie Few, Sara Tweedie Losse, Susan Tweedie Sprague; m. 2d, Idah Caroline Lord, Nov. 24, 1973. Admitted to Ohio bar, 1941; adjuster Nationwide Ins. Co., Columbus, Ohio, 1941-42; house counsel Ohio Finance Co., Columbus, 1946-49; with Am. Investment Co., St. Louis, 1949—, dir. advt., 1960-70, v.p., 1970—, treas., 1973—, dir., 1976—; tchr. pub. relations Washington U., St. Louis, 1962-63, Meramec Jr. Coll., St. Louis, 1976. Chmn. St. Louis County Civil Service Commn., 1975; pres. Webster Groves (Mo.) Bd. Edn., 1964. Served with USNR, 1942-46. Mem. Ohio, Mo. bar assns. Episcopalian. Clubs: Westborough Country, Clayton. Office: 8251 Maryland Ave St Louis MO 63105

TWEEDY, GORDON BRADFORD, retired ins. co. exec., lawyer; b. Bridgeport, Conn., Feb. 8, 1907; s. Henry Hallam and Grace Hannah (Landfield) T.; grad. Taft Sch., 1924, Phillips Andover Acad., 1925; A.B., Yale, 1929. LL.B. cum laude, 1932; m. Mary Johnson, June 7, 1944; children—Clare Bradford, Ann Sellett, Margot Martin. Admitted to Conn. bar, 1933, N.Y. State bar, 1934, U.S. Supreme Ct. bar, 1935, Vt. bar, 1973; instr. Yale Law Sch., 1933-34; asso. firm Sullivan & Cromwell, N.Y.C., Paris, France, 1934-38; with SEC, Washington, 1938-39, tax div. Dept. Justice, Washington, 1939-41; v.p., dir. China Nat. Aviation Corp., 1944-48; v.p., gen. counsel C.V. Starr & Co., Inc., N.Y.C., 1948-61, sr. exec. v.p., 1961-68, chmn. bd., 1968-72; dir. Am. Internat. Group, Consol. Securities Corp. Trustee China Inst. Mem. Council Fgn. Relations, Assos. Fgn. Policy Assn., Far East Am. Council, Council for Latin Am., Order of Coif. Clubs: Down Town Assn., River, Yale, Century (N.Y.C.); Metropolitan (Washington); Royal Bermuda Yacht. Home: Federal Hill Rd Brewster NY 10509

TWERSKY, VICTOR, educator, math. physicist; b. Lublin, Poland, Aug. 10, 1923; s. Israel and Gertrude (Levinson) T.; came to U.S., 1928, naturalized, 1940; B.S., Coll. City N.Y., 1947; A.M., Columbia, 1948; Ph.D., N.Y. U., 1950; m. Shirley Fine, Feb. 26, 1950; children—Lori, Mark, Nina. Asso. guidance project, biology dept. Coll. City N.Y., 1946-49; teaching asst. physics N.Y. U., 1949, research asso. electromagnetic theory Courant Inst. Math. Scis., 1950-53; asso. Nuclear Devel. Assos., 1951-53; with Sylvania Electric-Gen. Telephone Electronics 1953-66, head research Electronic Def. Labs., 1958-66, Electronics Systems-West, 1964-66; prof. math. U. Ill., Chgo. Circle, 1966—. Lectr., Stanford, 1956-58; vis. prof. Technion-Israel Inst. Tech., Haifa, 1962-63, Hebrew U., Jerusalem, summer 1972, Tel Aviv U., summer 1972, Stanford, summers 1967-77; summer mem. Courant Inst. Math. Scis., 1963; asso. Center Advanced Study, U. Ill., 1969-70; cons. in field. Mem. tech. research com. Am. Found. for Blind, 1947-49; mem. Sch. Math. Study Group, 1964-66; mem. U.S. com. VI, Internat. Sci. Radio Union; mem.-at-large Conf. Bd. Math. Scis., 1975-77. Served with AUS, 1943-46. NSF grantee, 1967—; Guggenheim fellow, 1972-73. Fellow AAAS, Am. Phys. Soc., Acoustical Soc. Am., Optical Soc. Am., IEEE; mem. Am. Math Soc., N.Y. Acad. Sci., Sci. Research So. Am. (pres. Sequoia br. 1958). Editor jours. in field. Contbr. articles to profl. jours. Home: 317 SEO Box 4348 Chicago IL 60680

TWIGG, BERNARD ALVIN, horticulturist; b. Oldtown, Md., Oct. 15, 1928; s. Michael C.S. and Rosa (Huff) T.; B.S., U. Md., 1952, M.S., 1955, Ph.D., 1959; m. Jean Carr Bryan, June 16, 1951; children—Michael B., Patricia A., Stephen C., Richard B. Mem. faculty U. Md., 1954—, prof. food sci., 1969—, chmn. hort. dept., 1974—; cons. Food Mfg. Co., Europe and U.S. Served with AUS, 1946-48. Mem. Inst. Food Technologists, Am. Soc. Hort. Sci., Sigma Xi, Alpha Zeta, Phi Kappa Phi, Phi Tau Sigma. Democrat. Episcopalian. Co-author: Quality Control for Food Industry, Vols. I, II. Home: 3537 Duke St College Park MD 20740 Office: Dept Hort Univ Md College Park MD 20742

TWIGGS, RUSSELL GOULD, artist; b. Sandusky, Ohio, Apr. 29, 1898; s. William Richard and Fanny (Gould) T.; B.F.A., Carnegie-Mellon U., 1921; m. 1930 (dec. 1952). Mcht. seaman, 1919-24; departmental asst. Coll. Fine Arts, Carnegie-Mellon U., 1924-74; exhibited in group shows: Art Inst. Chgo., 1947, Whitney Museum Am. Art, N.Y.C., 1955, Carnegie Inst. Internat., Pitts., 1955-67, Mus. Modern Art, N.Y.C., 1956, Corcoran Gallery Art, Washington, 1957; represented in permanent collections: Whitney Mus. Am. Art, Wadsworth Atheneum, Hartford, Conn., Mus. Art at Carnegie Inst. Internat., Bklyn. Mus., Westmoreland County Mus. Art, Greensburg, Pa. Served with USNR, 1917-1919. Recipient 2d prize for painting Cin. Art Mus., 1955. Mem. Associated Artists of Pitts. (Mrs. Henry J. Heinz, II award 1962, Carnegie Inst. Group prize 1949), Abstract Group of Pitts., Pitts. Plan for Art. Subject of book: Russell Twiggs (Connie Kienzle), 1971. Home: 652 Maryland Ave Pittsburgh PA 15232 Office: PO Box 10193 Shadyside Pittsburgh PA 15232

TWIGG-SMITH, THURSTON, newspaper pub.; b. Honolulu, Aug. 17, 1921; s. William and Margaret Carter (Thurston) Twigg-S.; B.Engring., Yale U., 1942; m. Bessie Bell, June 9, 1942; children—Elizabeth, Thurston, William, Margaret, Evelyn. With Honolulu Advertiser, 1946—, mng. editor, 1954-60, asst. bus. mgr., 1960-61, pub., 1961—; pres., pub., dir. Honolulu Advertiser, Inc., 1962—; pres., dir. Peris Corp.; chmn. Asa Properties Hawaii, Asa Properties Vt., Asa Properties Mass., Shiny Rock Mining Corp.; dir. First Fed. Savs. & Loan Assn., Hawaiian Electric Co., Ltd., Tongg Pub. Co., Am. Trust Co., Kamehameha Devel. Corp. Trustee Punahou Sch., Old Sturbridge Inc., Honolulu Acad. Arts; chmn. bd. dirs. Honolulu Symphony Orch. Served to maj. AUS, 1942-46. Mem. Honolulu C. of C. Clubs: Waialae, Pacific, Oahu (Honolulu). Home: Holualoa HI 96725 Office: PO Box 3110 Honolulu HI 96802

TWIGGY. see Hornby, Lesley

TWILEGAR, BURT I., editor, pub. co. exec.; b. Los Angeles, May 20, 1917; s. Burt I. and Winnefred (Gardner) T.; ed. Los Angeles City Coll., U. So. Calif.; children—Judy (Mrs. John Hope), Laurel (Mrs. J. Paul Robinson), Robert. Sports columnist Los Angeles Examiner, 1951-59; founder Western Outdoors Publs., Newport Beach, Calif., 1954, pres., editor, pub. Western Outdoor News, Western Outdoors Mag., 1960—. Served with USCGR. Mem. Regional, Western pubs. assns., Outdoor Writers Am., Los Angeles Sports Council. Republican. Club: Balboa Bay. Pub. series of outdoor paperback books. Home: 2009 Vista Caudal Newport Beach CA 92660 Office: PO Box 2027 Newport Beach CA 92663

TWINAM, JOSEPH WRIGHT, govt. ofcl., former ambassador; b. Chattanooga, July 11, 1934; s. John Courtenay and Daisy Agnes (Murphy) T.; B.A., U. Va., 1956; postgrad. Georgetown U., 1960-61; m. Janet Ashby, May 30, 1959; children—Courtenay Jane, Marshall Ashby. Joined U.S. Fgn. Service, 1959; assigned The Netherlands, 1961-64, Kuwait, 1964-66, Lebanon, 1966-68, Saudi Arabia, 1968-70; ambassador to State of Bahrain, 1974-76; dir. Arabian Peninsula affairs Dept. State, 1976-79, dep. asst. sec., 1979—. Served with USNR, 1956-59. Mem. Phi Beta Kappa, Kappa Alpha, Omicron Delta Kappa. Address: 8019 Garlot Dr Annandale VA 22003

TWINAME, JOHN DEAN, business exec.; b. Mt. Kisco, N.Y., Dec. 27, 1931; s. C.G. and Constance Jean (Ulmer) T.; A.B., Cornell U., 1953; M.B.A., Harvard, 1957; m. Carolyn Anderson, Aug. 6, 1955; children—Karen, Jeanne, Julia. Sales rep. Am. Hosp. Supply Corp., Evanston, Ill., 1957-60, dir. product research, 1961, sales mgr., 1962, asst. to div. pres., 1963, product mgr., 1964, mktg. mgr., 1965-67, mktg. v.p., 1968-69; dep. adminstr. Social and Rehab. Service, HEW, Washington, 1969-70, adminstr., 1970-73, adminstr. health Cost of Living Council, 1973-74; pvt. cons. Mott-McDonald Assos., Inc., Washington, 1974-76, pres., 1976-78; mng. dir. Am. Health Found., N.Y.C., 1978—. Chmn. bd. Chgo. Bus.-Indsl. Project, 1967-68; chmn. bd. People to People Com. for Handicapped, 1976-78, Bauman Bible Telecasts, Inc., 1976—; treas. U.S. com. Internat. Council Social Welfare. Served to 1st lt., AUS, 1953-55. Home: 60 East End Ave New York NY 10028 Office: 320 E 43d St New York NY 10017

TWISDALE, HAROLD WINFRED, dentist; b. Roanoke Rapids, N.C., Apr. 28, 1933; s. James Robert and Elma (Smith) T.; B.S. in Dentistry, U. N.C., 1955, D.D.S., 1958; m. Barbara Ann Edmonds, Aug. 2, 1958 (div. Apr. 1974); children—Harold Winfred, Leigh Ann. Individual practice dentistry, Charlotte, N.C., 1961—; head, dept. dental prosthetics Meml. Hosp., 1964-66; lectr. dental subjects.; pres., gen. mgr. WCTU-TV, Charlotte Telecasters, Inc., 1967-69, WATU-TV, Augusta, Ga., Augusta Telecasters, Inc., 1968-69, Television Presentations, Inc., Charlotte, 1967-69; partner Twisdale and Steel Assos., Charlotte, 1965-70; propr. Twisdale Enterprises, Charlotte, 1965-70. Pres., Memphis Telecasters, Inc., 1966-76, Va. Telecasters, Inc., Richmond, 1966—, Durham-Raleigh Telecasters, Inc., Durham, N.C., 1966-70. Transp. chmn. Miss N.C. Pageant, 1965; v.p. N.C. Jaycees, 1963-64. Trustee Boys Home, Lake Waccomaw, N.C., 1966-67. Served to capt. USAF, 1958-60. Recipient various awards Charlotte Jaycees, 1962-66. Mem. ADA, N.C. Dental Found., N.C., Charlotte (chmn. various coms. 1961—) dental socs., Am. Analgesia Soc., Internat. Analgesic Soc. (dir. 1980—), N.C. Dental Soc. Anesthesiology, Charlotte Analgesia Study Club (co-founder 1970), N.C. 2d Dist. Dental Soc., U. N.C. Dental Alumni Assn., Southeastern Analgesia Soc. (founder 1972, pres. 1972-74), Lambda Chi Alpha, Delta Sigma Delta. Democrat. Methodist. Home: 4212 Burning Tree Ln Mathews NC 28105 Office: 4421 Central Ave PO Box 12685 Charlotte NC 28205. *I must give the full credit for any achievement I might have accomplished in life to my mother and father. They not only provided me the means and direction one needs to make even the slightest accomplishment in our mortal life, but most of all, they gave me love, understanding, and a sense of values. These values have never deserted me, nor have they been compromised, even in the darkest hours of depression or during the brightest times of accomplishment. They have been my steady companions!*

TWISS, JOHN RUSSELL, JR., govt. ofcl.; b. N.Y.C., Sept. 16, 1938; s. John Russell and Edith Jordan (Liddell) T.; B.A., Yale U., 1961; m. Mary Hawthorne Sheldon, Jan. 20, 1973; children—John Stewart, Alison McIntosh, Emily Ellsworth. In logistic support of polar research, U.S. Govt., 1961-63; NSF rep. mng. sci. program in Antarctica, 1964-65; with Internat. div. Smith Kline & French Labs., 1966-67; v.p. EPC Labs. 1967-68; dir. So. Ocean shipbd. research project and cons. on oceanographic equipment devel., 1968-69; acting head and spl. asst. to head Internat. Decade of Ocean Exploration, NSF, 1970-74; exec. dir. Marine Mammal Commn., Washington, 1974—; mem. numerous U.S. dels. to negotiate internat. agreements on oceanographic and environ. issues; cons. on wire rope usage in comml. fishing; lectr. on Antarctica and conservation issues; exptl. tree farmer. Bd. on Geog. Names designated Antarctic mountain as Mt. Twiss; recipient award for outstanding support of marine mammal research, 1977, Antarctic medal. Mem. AAAS, Am. Inst. Biol. Scis. Republican. Episcopalian. Club: Racquet of Phila. Research in Antarctic, Arctic, New Guinea, Ethiopia, So. Ocean. Office: 1625 Eye St NW Washington DC 20006

TWISS, PAGE CHARLES, educator; b. Columbus, Ohio, Jan. 2, 1929; s. George Ransom and Blanche (Olin) T.; B.S. in Geology, Kans. State U., 1950, M.S., 1955; Ph.D., U. Tex. at Austin, 1959; m. Nancy Homer Hubbard, Aug. 29, 1954; children—Stephen Ransom, Catherine Grace, Thomas Stuart. Mem. faculty dept. geology Kans. State U., Manhattan, 1959—, asso. prof., 1964-69, prof., 1969—, also head dept., 1968-77. Geologist agrl. research service U.S. Dept. Agr., 1966-68; research scientist U. Tex., Austin, 1966-67. Chmn. Manhattan Council Human Relations, 1960-61. Vice pres. Riley County Democratic Club, 1970-71; mem. Dem. Precinct Com., Manhattan, 1970-72, 74—. Served with USAAF, 1951-53. Fellow Pan Am. Petroleum Found., 1957-58; Shell Found. fellow, 1958-59. Fellow Geol. Soc. Am.; mem. Geol. Soc. Am. (chmn. South-Central sect. 1972-73), Am. Assn. Petroleum Geologists (geologic maps com. 1968-70), Soc. Econ. Paleontologists and Mineralogists, Kans. Acad. Sci. (mem. research awards com. 1966—, asso. editor 1977—), AAAS, Clay Minerals Soc., Kans. Geol. Soc., W. Tex. Geol. Soc., Am. Soc. Agronomy, Soil Sci. Soc. Am., Internat. Soc. Soil Sci., Internat. Assn. Sedimentologists, Assn. Internationale pour l'Etude des Argiles, Am. Quaternary Assn., AAUP (chpt. v.p. 1971-72, chpt. pres. 1972-73), Nat. Assn. Geology Tchrs., Mineral. Soc. Am., Sigma Xi, Sigma Gamma Epsilon, Gamma Sigma Delta. Mason. Contbr. articles to profl. jours. Home: 2327 Bailey Dr Manhattan KS 66502

TWITTY, CONWAY, country and western entertainer; b. Friarspoint, Miss., Sept. 1, 1933; s. Floyd and Velma (McGinnis) Jenkins; student pub. schs.; m. Mickey Jaco, Oct. 22, 1956; children—Mike, Joni, Kathy, Jimmy. Rock and roll entertainer, 1965-69; country and western entertainer, 1969—; composer numerous songs including It's Only Make Believe, 1958, Hello Darlin', 1970. Served with U.S. Army, 1954-57. Recipient several gold records. Baptist. Home: 123 Walnut Dr Hendersonville TN 37075 Office: 394 W Main St C-16 Hendersonville TN 37075

TWITTY, HOWARD ALLEN, lawyer; b. Williams, Ariz., Sept. 6, 1909; s. Edgar Montrue and Emilie Marie (Kaiser) T.; A.B., U. So. Calif., 1931, LL.B., 1934; m. Zoraida Stoddard, July 26, 1947; children—Hudson Barnes (dec.), Howard Allen, Mary Marie. Admitted to Calif. bar, 1934, Ariz. bar, 1935; atty. Indsl. Commn. of Ariz., 1935-42; pvt. practice of law, Phoenix, 1946—; specializing mining law, 1950—; partner firm Twitty, Sievwright & Mills, 1962—. Served to capt. Q.M.C., AUS, 1942-46. Mem. Am. Bar Assn. (chmn. sect. natural resources law 1962-63), state bars Calif., Ariz. Republican. Methodist. Mason, Rotarian. Clubs: Arizona, Phoenix Country (Phoenix). Author papers on mining law. Home: 520 W Lamar Rd Phoenix AZ 85013 Office: 1700 Towne House Tower 100 W Clarendon St Phoenix AZ 85013

TWITTY, JAMES WATSON, artist; b. Mt. Vernon, N.Y., Apr. 13, 1916; s. James Chapman and Amelia Madelon (Lang) T.; student U. Miami, 1958-59, Art Students League, N.Y.C., 1960-61; m. Anne Marsh Butler, May 18, 1952; children—James Watson, Gary Lee. One man exhibitions include: Corcoran Gallery Art, Washington, 1966, Lehigh U., Bethlehem, Pa., 1967, David Findlay Gallery, N.Y.C., 1971, 73, 74, 76, 78, McNay Art Inst., San Antonio, 1972, George Washington U., 1975, Bettina Gallery, Zurich, Switzerland, 1977, numerous others; represented in permanent collections: Nat. Gallery Art, Nat. Collection Fine Arts, Corcoran Gallery Art, Balt. Mus. Art, Bklyn. Mus., San Francisco Mus. Art, Dallas Mus. Fine Arts, Mus. Fine Arts, Houston, Minn. Mus. Art, Oxford U., White House and others; asso. prof. painting Corcoran Sch. Art, Washington, 1964-74; lectr. George Washington U., 1964-74; exchange prof. Leeds Coll. Art (Eng.), 1967-68; vis. prof. painting San Antonio Art Inst. Bd. dirs. No. Va. Art League, 1974-77. Served with USAF, World War II and Korea. Clubs: Pisces (Washington); Coral Reef Yacht (Miami, Fla.). Home: 1600 S Eads St Arlington VA 22202

TWOMEY, DAVID MALONE, marine corps officer; b. Lynn, Mass., July 19, 1928; s. John Joseph and Emeline Frances (Malone) T.; B.S., Coll. of Holy Cross, 1950; M.A., U. Md., 1959; postgrad. Naval War Coll., 1969; m. Helen Joyce Thomas, Mar. 5, 1955; children—Helen Joyce, Mary Teresa, Patricia Marie, Michael Jude, David Thomas, Carol Mary. Commd. 2d lt. USMC, 1950, advanced through grades to maj. gen., 1974; inf. officer, commanded every type inf. unit from rifle platoon to inf. div.; comdr. Amphibious Ready Force, U.S. 7th Fleet, 1973-74; comdr. recruit tng. regt., 1974-75; comdg. gen. 2d Marine Div., Camp Le Jeune, N.C., 1979—. Decorated Legion of Merit, Bronze Star with combat V, Navy Commendation medal, others. Roman Catholic. Compiler, pub. monthly mag. Lessons Learned from Operational Experience in Vietnam, 1966-68. Home: 10408 Hunt Country Ln Vienna VA 22180 Office: Hdqrs 2d Marine Div Camp LeJeune NC 28542

TWOMEY, JEROME DENIS, banker; b. Jersey City, Oct. 27, 1920; s. Jerome D. and Mary C. (Mulligan) T.; Student St. John's U., 1939, Coll. City N.Y., 1940-41, Am. Inst. Banking, 1942-48, Rutgers U., 1956-58; m. Eileen T. O'Shaughnessy, June 1, 1946; children—Robert, Diane, Carol, Brian. Asst. cashier Public Nat. Bank, N.Y.C., 1950-52, asst. v.p., 1952-55; asst. treas. Bankers Trust Co., N.Y.C., 1955-58, asst. v.p., 1958-60; asst. v.p. Franklin Nat. Bank, N.Y.C., 1960-61, v.p., 1961-65, pres. met. div., 1965-70, exec. v.p., 1970-73; sr. exec. v.p., dir., chmn. exec. com. Sterling Nat. Bank, N.Y.C., 1973, pres., chief exec. officer, 1973-78; pres., chief exec. officer, dir. State Bank of N.J., Ft. Lee, 1978—. Recipient achievement awards Anti Defamation League Textile Vets. Assn., 1968, State of Israel, 1974. Mem. N.Y. Credit and Financial Mgmt. Assn., Textile Vets. Assn., Checkmates, Inc (past pres.), Robert Morris Assos., Am. Bankers Assn. (chmn. bankers-accountants com.), N.J. Bankers Assn. (trustee). Clubs: 475 (dir.), Marco Polo (N.Y.C.). Home: 123 Brookview Dr N Woodcliff Lake NJ 07675 Office: 2121 Lemoine Ave Fort Lee NJ 07024

TWOMEY, WILLIAM PETER, hotel exec.; b. N.Y.C., Aug. 30, 1942; s. John and Matilda (McNally) T.; B.B.A. cum laude, Manhattan Coll., 1967; postgrad. St. Johns U., 1973-75; m. Carol Ann Eiring, May 4, 1968. Sr. auditor Arthur Young & Co., N.Y.C., 1967-71; dir. corp. accounting Am. Airlines, Inc., Lake Success, N.Y., 1971-74, asst. controller corp. accounting, 1974-75, v.p., controller, 1975-77; pres., chief exec. officer Americana Hotels, Inc., N.Y.C., 1977—; mem. nat. adv. council Nat. Restaurant Assn., Washington. Bd. dirs. I Love a Clean New York, Inc., New York Conv. and Visitors Bur., Inc. Served with U.S. Army, 1962-64. C.P.A., N.Y. Mem. Am. Inst. C.P.A.'s, N.Y. State Soc. C.P.A.'s. Republican. Roman Catholic. Clubs: Wings, Pinnacle (N.Y.C.). Office: Americana Hotels Exec Offices 405 Lexington Ave New York NY 10017

TWORKOV, JACK, artist; b. Biala, Poland, 1900; s. Hyman and Esther (Singer) T.; came to U.S., 1913, naturalized, 1928; student Columbia, 1920-23, N.A.D., 1923-25, Art Students League, 1925-26; D.F.A., Md. Inst. Art, 1971; L.H.D., Columbia, 1972; children—Hermine, Helen. One man shows Egan Gallery, 1947, 49, 52, 54, Balt. Mus. Art, 1948, Miss. U., 1954, Stable Gallery, 1957, 59, Walker Art Center, 1957, Castelli Gallery, 1961, 63, Whitney Mus., 1971, Toledo Mus. Art, 1971, French & Co., 1971, Gertrude Kasle Gallery, Detroit, 1966, 69, 71, 73, Jaffe-Friede Gallery, Dartmouth Coll., Hanover, N.H., 1973, Harcus, Krakow, Rosen, Sonnabend Gallery, Boston, 1974, Portland Center for Visual Arts, 1974, Denver Mus., 1975; retropective exhbn. Whitney Mus. Am. Art, 1964, others; exhibited N.Y. Soc. Anonyme, 1929, Dudensing Gallery, 1931-35; recent group shows include Whitney Mus., Mus. Modern Art, Am. Vanguard Art of Paris, Pa. Acad. Art Ann., Calif. Palace Legion of Honor, Pitts. Internat. Carnegie Inst., Santa Barbara Mus., Corcoran Gallery, Va. Mus., Chgo. Arts Club, Mus. Modern Art New Am. Painting Show, Amsterdam, Basle, Berlin, Belgrade, London, Madrid, Paris, Rome, 1958-60, many others including Documenta II exhbn. Mus. Fridericianum, Kassel, Germany, 1959; represented in permanent collections Watkins Gallery, Am. U., Balt. Mus. Fine Arts, New Paltz State Tchrs. Coll., U. N.Y., Walker Art Center, Milw., Mus. Modern Art, Met. Mus. Art, Santa Barbara Mus., Cleve. Mus., Hartford Athaeneum, Whitney Mus. Am. Art, Guggenheim Mus., Ciba Geigy collection, others; tchr. Queens Coll. Sch. Gen. Studies, 1948-55, Am. U., summers 1948-51, Black Mountain Coll., summer 1952, U. Ind., summers 1954, 55, U. Miss., fall 1954; formerly with Pratt Inst., Bklyn.; lectr. modern Am. painting; vis. artist Yale, 1962, chmn. dept. art, 1963-69, William Leffingwell prof. painting emeritus Sch. Art and Architecture, Yale; vis. prof. Cooper Union, 1970-71. Recipient 1st William A. Clark award and Corcoran Gold medal Corcoran Gallery Art, 1963; Painter of Year award Skowhegan Sch. Art, 1974. Guggenheim fellow, 1970. Author articles in field. Home: 161 W 22d St New York City NY 10011

TWYMAN, JOSEPH PASCHAL, univ. pres.; b. Prairie Hill, Mo., Nov. 21, 1933; s. William L. and Hazel (Dry) T.; B.A., U. Mo. at Kansas City, 1955, M.A., 1959, Ph.D., 1962; m. Patricia Joanne Harper, July 26, 1953; children—Mark Kevin, Patricia Lynn. Asst. prof., then asso. prof. Okla. State U., 1960-66, asso. dir. Research Found., 1965-66; dir. research U. Mo. at St. Louis, 1966-67; v.p. U. Tulsa, 1967-68, pres., 1968—; cons. in field, 1960—. Dir. Sooner Fed. Savs. & Loan Assn., Atlas Life Ins. Co. Mem. adv. panel Southwestern Coop. Ednl. Lab., 1967-68; adv. council Okla. Lung Research and Devel. Council, 1970—; scholarship com. Skelly Oil Co., 1968—, Marathon Oil Co., 1970-73; pres. Okla. Ind. Coll. Found., 1971-74. Adv. bd. Salvation Army, 1972—, Tulsa Opera, 1968—, St. John's Hosp., Tulsa, 1969-76; acting chmn. Tulsa Area Health Edn. Center, 1977—; bd. dirs. Goodwill Industries, Tulsa, 1975—, Okla Council Econ. Edn., 1968—, Tulsa Area United Way, 1968—, Tulsa Civic Ballet, 1968—, Arts and Humanities Council Tulsa, 1970-77, Thomas Gilcrease Mus. Assn., 1970—; trustee Undercroft Montessori Sch., Tulsa, 1967-72, Children's Med. Center, Tulsa, 1968-73, Hillcrest Med. Center, Tulsa, 1969—; mem. exec. com. Frontiers of Sci. Found. Okla., 1968—; bd. dirs. Tulsa Mental Health Assn., 1967-74, 75-78, Mid-Continent Research and Devel. Council, 1967-69; mem. commn. on instns. of higher edn. North Central Assn. Colls. and Schs., 1975—; trustee Tech. Edn. Research Center, Inc., Cambridge, Mass., 1977—. Grantee Ford Found., 1963-66, U.S. Office Edn., 1958-60, 61-62, 62-63, 64-66. Mem. AAAS, Am. Acad. Polit. and Social Sci., Young Pres.'s Orgn., Okla. Cattlemen's Assn., Phi Delta Kappa, Omicron Delta Kappa. Presbyn. Clubs: Tulsa, Southern Hills, Univ., Summit (Tulsa); Belted Galloway Soc. Author: (with others) The Concept of Role Conflict, 1964; also articles. Home: 1775 E 31st St Tulsa OK 74105

TWYMAN, ROBERT WICKLIFFE, educator; b. Louisville, Jan. 31, 1919; s. Allen Piatt and Agnes (Miekle) T.; A.B., Ind. U., 1940; M.A., U. Chgo., 1942, Ph.D., 1950; m. Betty Jane Williams, Aug. 8, 1944; 1 son, Jeffrey Robert. Instr., Gary (Ind.) Coll., 1945-46; asst. prof. Simpson Coll., 1946-47; instr. U. Minn., 1947-48; mem. faculty Bowling Green State U., 1948—; prof. history, 1963—, chmn. dept., 1960-65. Named faculty Man of Year, Omicron Delta Kappa chpt. Bowling Green State U., 1961; recipient 1st Liberal Arts Teaching award, 1968. Mem. Orgn. Am. Historians, So. Hist. Assn., Ohio Acad. History (pres., 1969-70), Phi Beta Kappa. Author: History of Marshall Field and Company, 1852-1906 (Beveridge award hon. mention Am. Hist. Assn. 1952), 1954; co-editor Ency. of So. History, 1979; also numerous articles. Home: 853 Scott Blvd Bowling Green OH 43402

TYAACK, FRANZ HALS, appliance mfg. co. exec.; b. Elizabeth, N.J., May 24, 1927; s. William and Hedwig Margaret (Kratschmer) T.; B.S. in Elec. Engring., M.I.T., 1950; m. Lois Mae Hoy, Oct. 6, 1951; children—Janet, Patti. With Arma Corp., L.I., N.Y., 1950-53; engr. Westinghouse Electric Corp., Balt., 1953-59, v.p., Pitts., 1960-78; cons. Inst. for Def. Analyses, Washington, 1959-60; pres., chief exec. officer Westinghouse Can., Ltd., Hamilton, Ont., 1978—. Served with USAAF, 1945-46. Office: Westinghouse Can Ltd 286 Sanford Ave N Hamilton ON L8L 6A1 Canada

TYCE, FRANCIS ANTHONY, hosp. adminstr.; b. Swansea, South Wales, U.K., Oct. 31, 1917; s. Peter and Theresa (Troy) T.; M.D., B.S., U. Durham (Eng.), 1952; M.Sc. in Psychiatry, Mayo Grad. Sch., 1959; m. Gertrude Mary Sidebottom, June 21, 1952; 1 son, John Christopher. Came to U.S., 1956. Intern St. Vincent's Hosp., Erie, Pa., 1952-53; gen. practice in U.K., 1953-56; mem. staff Rochester (Minn.) State Hosp., 1959—, med. dir., chief exec. officer, 1960—; asso. prof. psychiatry Mayo Grad. Sch., 1965-73, asso. prof., 1973-79, prof., 1979—; cons. adminstrv. psychiatry WHO; dir. counseling St. Mary's Coll.; field rep. Accreditation Council for Psychiat. Facilities-Joint Commn. on Accreditation Hosps. Sem.; mem. juvenile delinquency task force Nat. Adv. Com. Criminal Justice Standards and Goals, 1975; dir. Northwestern Nat. Bank, Rochester. Mem. Rochester Civic Theatre. Served with Brit. Army, 1939-46. Diplomate Am. Bd. Psychiatry and Neurology. Fellow Am. Psychiat. Assn. (chmn. task force com. psychiat. rehab. correctional systems 1973—); mem. Zumbro Valley Med. Soc. (pres. 1972-73), Minn. Psychiat. Assn. (sec.-treas.), Assn. Med. Supts. Mental Hosps. (pres.). Author articles in field. Chmn. editorial bd. Jour. Hosp. and Community Psychiatry. Home: 1520 E Center St Rochester MN 55901 Office: Rochester State Hosp Rochester MN 55902

TYDINGS, JOSEPH DAVIES, lawyer, former senator; b. Asheville, N.C., May 4, 1928; s. Millard E. and Eleanor (Davies) T.; grad. McDonogh (Md.) Sch., 1946; B.A., U. Md., 1951, LL.B., 1953; m. Terry Lynn Huntingdon, Apr. 20, 1975; children—Mary Campbell, Millard E. II, Emlen, Eleanor Davies, Paige Crowley, Alexandra. Admitted to Md. bar, 1952; asso. firm Tydings, Sauerwein, Benson & Boyd, Balt., 1952-57; partner firm Tydings & Rosenberg, Balt., 1958-61; U.S. atty. Dist. Md., 1961-64; U.S. senator from Md., 1965-71; partner firm Danzansky, Dickey, Tydings, Quint & Gordon, Washington, 1971—; of counsel Tydings & Rosenberg, Balt.; spl. counsel UN Fund for Population Activities, 1971—. Del., Internat. Penal Conf., Bellagio, Italy, 1963, Interpol Conf., Helsinki, 1963, Mexican-U.S. Interparliamentary Conf., Mexico City, 1965, Council Intergovtl. Com. for European Migration, Geneva, 1966, NATO Assembly, Brussels, 1968, Atlantic Conf., P.R., 1970. Mem. Md. Ho. of Dels. from Hartford Country, 1955-61; campaign mgr. for John F. Kennedy in Md. Primary, 1960. Served with AUS, 1946-48; ETO. Cited as outstanding legislator Md. Press Corr., 1961; named One of 10 Outstanding Young Men, Balt. Jr. Assn. Commerce, 1962; recipient August Volmer award Am. Soc. Criminology, 1969; Nat. Brotherhood citation Washington chpt. NCCJ, 1970; Margaret Sanger award for distinguished pub. service Planned Parenthood-World Population. Mem. Am., Fed., D.C., Md., Balt., Harford County, Balt. Jr. (pres. 1960) bar assns. Democrat. Episcopalian. Mason. Home: Oakington Havre de Grace MD 21078 Office: 1120 Connecticut Ave Washington DC 20036

TYE, JOSEPH CLAIRE, lawyer; b. Griswold, Iowa, Jan. 2, 1904; s. Joseph F. and Etta U. (Jameson) T.; student Grinnell Coll.; LL.B., U. S.D., 1926; m. Opal M. Graham, June 24, 1926; children—Joseph N., James S., Thomas W. Admitted to Nebr. and S.D. bars, 1926; city atty., Kearney, Nebr., 1932-38; firm Pratt, Hamer & Tye, Kearney, 1927-58, Tye, Worlock & Knapp, 1958-62, Tye, Worlock, Knapp & Tye, 1962-66, Tye, Worlock, Tye & Jacobsen, 1967-69, Tye, Worlock, Tye, Jacobsen & Orr, 1969-78, Tye, Worlock, Tye & Taylor, 1978—. Mem. Nebr. com. Nat. Endowment for Humanities. County chmn., mem. Nebr. Republican Central Com.; mayor, Kearney, 1941-45. Trustee Nebr. Masonic Home, 1965—. Fellow Am. Coll. Trial Lawyers; mem. Kearney C. of C. (pres.), Am. (judiciary com.), Nebr. (exec. council. pres. 1959-60; chmn. com. world peace through law 1960—), Buffalo County bar assns., Assn. Ins. Attys., Internat. Assn. Ins. Counsel, Kappa Sigma, Phi Delta Phi. Mason (grand master Neb. 1959-60, 33 deg.). Elk (trustee 1959-63). Home: 1026 W 22d St Kearney NE 68847 Office: 1419 Central Ave Kearney NE 68847

TYER, TRAVIS EARL, librarian; b. Lorenzo, Tex., Oct. 23, 1930; s. Charlie Earl and Juanita (Travis) T.; B.S., Abilene Christian U., 1952; B.S. in L.S., N. Tex. State U., 1959; Ad.M. in L.S., Fla. State U., 1969, postgrad., 1969—; m. Alma Lois Davis, Nov. 6, 1951; children—Alan Ross, Juanita Linn. Librarian, tchr. pub. schs., Gail, Lubbock, and Seminole, Tex., 1952-61; with Dallas Pub. Library, 1961-66, coordinator young adult services, 1962-66; library dir. Lubbock Pub. Library, 1966, Lubbock City-County Libraries, 1967-68; grad. library sch. faculty-state personnel coordinator Emporia (Kans.) State U., 1971-72; sr. cons. profl. devel. Ill. State Library, Springfield, 1972—; lectr. summer workshops Tex. Woman's U., U. Okla., U. Utah, Fla. State U., N. Tex. State U.; cons. in field. Mem. ALA (pub. com. 1973-77), Southwestern, Ill. library assns., Adult Edn. Assn., Continuing Library Edn. Network and Exchange, N. Tex. State U. Sch. Library and Info. Sci. (life), Friends Lubbock City-County Libraries (life). Democrat. Mem. Church of Christ. Contbr. articles to library jours. Home: 119 Laconwood Dr Springfield IL 62703 Office: Centennial Bldg Room 526 Springfield IL 62756

TYGRETT, HOWARD VOLNEY, JR., lawyer; b. Lake Charles, La., Jan. 12, 1940; s. Howard Volney and Hazel (Wheeler) T.; B.A., Williams Coll., 1961; LL.B., So. Methodist U., 1964; m. Judy Beene, Dec. 30, 1964; children—Carroll Diane, Howard V. III. Admitted to Tex. bar, 1964; gen. atty. SEC, 1964-65; law clk. to Chief Judge Joe E. Estes, U.S. Dist. Ct., No. Dist. Tex., 1965-67; partner firm Tygrett Walker & Lamb, and predecessors, Dallas, 1968—. Bd. dirs. Routh St. Center, 1976—; dir. Theatre Three, 1974-75, Shakespeare Festival, 1978—. Mem. Am., Tex., Dallas bar assns., Dallas Estate Council, Delta Phi, Delta Theta Phi. Episcopalian. Clubs: Willow Bend; Civitan (lt. gov. Tex. dist. 1976-77; gov. 1979-80). Home: 8530 Jourdan Way Dallas TX 75225 Office: 715 Preston State Bank Bldg 8111 Preston Rd Dallas TX 75225

TYL, NOEL JAN, baritone, astrologer; b. West Chester, Pa., Dec. 31, 1936; B.A., Harvard U., 1958. Bus. mgr. Houston Grand Opera Assn., 1958-60; account exec. Ruder & Finn Public Relations, N.Y.C., 1960-62; specialist in works of Wagner, U.S. and Europe; appearances include Vienna State Opera, Düsseldorf, Rome, Milan, Barcelona; profl. astrologer, Arlington, Va., 1970—; author: Principles and Practice of Astrology, 12 vols., 1973-75; Teaching and Study Guide, 1976; The Horoscope as Identity, 1974; pres. TYL Assos., Inc., mgmt. cons.; astrology library dir. Telecomputing Corp. Am. Winner, Am. Opera Auditions, 1964. Editor Astrology Now mag., 1974—. Home and Office: PO Box 927 McLean VA 22101

TYLER, ANNE (MRS. TAGHI M. MODARRESSI), author; b. Mpls., Oct. 25, 1941; d. Lloyd Parry and Phyllis (Mahon) Tyler; B.A., Duke U., 1961; postgrad. Columbia U., 1962; m. Taghi M. Modarressi, May 3, 1963; children—Tezh, Mitra. Author: (novels) If Morning Ever Comes, 1964; The Tin Can Tree, 1965; A Slipping-Down Life, 1970; The Clock Winder, 1972; Celestial Navigation, 1974; Searching for Caleb, 1976; Earthly Possessions, 1977. Contbr. short stories to nat. mags. Home: 222 Tunbridge Rd Baltimore MD 21212

TYLER, DAVID EARL, educator; b. Carlisle, Iowa, July 12, 1928; s. Guy Earl and Beatrice Virginia (Slack) T.; B.S., Iowa State U., 1953, D.V.M., 1957, Ph.D., 1963; M.S., Purdue U., 1960; m. Alice LaVon Smith, Sept. 6, 1952; children—John William, Anne Elizabeth. Instr. dept. vet. sci. Purdue U., 1957-60; asst. prof. dept. pathology Coll. Vet. Medicine, Iowa State U., 1960-63, asso. prof., 1963-66; prof., head dept. pathology and parasitology Coll. Vet. Medicine, U. Ga., 1966-71, head dept. pathology, 1971-79, prof., 1971—. Cub Scout master, 1967-69, scout com. chmn., 1970-72; mem. citizens com. to County Bd. Edn., 1968-70. Bd. dirs. Christian Coll. Ga., 1974-77. Served with AUS, 1946-48. Recipient Borden award Gail Borden Co., 1956; Norden Distinguished teaching award Norden Labs., 1964, 1969; Prof. of Year award Coll. Vet. Medicine, Iowa State U., 1965; Outstanding Prof. award Coll. Vet. Medicine, U. Ga., 1970, 76. Mem. Farm House, Am., Ga. vet. med. assns., Am. Coll. Vet. Pathologists (mem. council 1975-77), Am. Assn. Vet. Med. Colls. (chmn. com. teaching-learning materials 1975-77), Nat. Program for Instructional Devel. in Vet. Pathology (adv. com. 1976-77; apptd. discussant Charles L. Davis Found. for Advancement Vet. Pathology 1977—), Aghon, Sigma Xi, Phi Eta Sigma, Alpha Zeta, Gamma Sigma Delta, Phi Kappa Phi, Phi Zeta, Omega Tau Sigma. Mem. Christian Ch. (Disciples Christ) (elder 1968—, chmn. ch. bd. 1973-74). Home: 160 Sunnybrook Dr Athens GA 30605

TYLER, DAVID MALCOLM, lawyer; b. Detroit, Sept. 12, 1930; s. Alfred David and Esther May (Williams) T.; A.B., Wayne State U., 1952; J.D., U. Mich., 1959; m. Rose Lee Brunette, Dec. 17, 1954; children—Deborah, Claudia, David. Admitted to Mich. bar, 1959; research clk. U.S. Dist. Ct., Western dist. Mich., 1959-60; asso. firm Cholette, Perkins & Buchanan, Grand Rapids, 1960-61; mem. firm Sommers, Schwartz, Silver, Schwartz & Tyler, Detroit, 1961-77, Tyler & Canham, P.C., 1977—; vice chmn. negligance council State Bar Mich., chmn. Products Liability Task Force; lectr. continuing legal edn. Served with USNR, 1953-56. Mem. Am., Mich., Fed. bar assns., Fedn. Ins. Counsel, Internat. Assn. Ins. Counsel. Club: Grosse Pointe. Home: 566 Shelden St Grosse Pointe Shores MI 48236 Office: 400 Renaissance Center Suite 1010 Detroit MI 48243

TYLER, HAROLD RUSSELL, JR., lawyer, former govt. ofcl.; b. Utica, N.Y., May 14, 1922; s. Harold Russell and Elizabeth (Glenn) T.; grad. Philips Exeter Acad., 1939; A.B., Princeton, 1943; LL.B., Columbia, 1949; m. Barbara L. Eaton, Sept. 10, 1949; children—Bradley E., John R., Sheila B. Admitted to N.Y. bar, 1950; pvt. practice, N.Y.C., 1950-53, 55-60; mem. firm Gilbert & Segall, 1957-60, 61-62; asst. U.S. atty., 1953-55; asst. atty. gen. U.S. charge civil rights div., 1960-61; commr. N.Y.-N.J. Waterfront Commn., 1961-62; U.S. dist. judge So. Dist. N.Y., 1962-75; dep. atty. gen. U.S., 1975-77; mem. firm Patterson, Belknap, Webb & Tyler, N.Y.C., 1977—; adj. prof. law N.Y. U. Law Sch., 1966-75; vis. lectr. Inst. Criminology, Cambridge, 1968; vice chmn. Adminstrv. Conf. USA, 1975-77. Bd. dirs. Fed. Jud. Center, Washington, i968-72. Home: Indian Hill Rd Bedford NY 10506 Office: 30 Rockefeller Plaza New York City NY 10020

TYLER, LESLIE J., chem. co. exec.; b. Salamanca, N.Y., Nov. 2, 1919; s. Leslie Alvin and Sarah Freda (Henry) T.; B.S., U. Scranton, 1942; M.S., Pa. State U., 1947, Ph.D., 1948; m. Priscilla Jane Beatty, June 14, 1947; children—Leslie, Lewis, John, Amy, Priscilla, Bruce, Robert. With Dow Corning Corp., Midland, Mich., 1948—, bus. mgr., then dir. research, 1968-73, v.p. research and devel., 1973—. Served with USAAF, 1942-45. Decorated Air medal with oak leaf cluster; Am. Chem. Soc. predoctoral fellow, 1946-48. Mem. Am. Chem. Soc., Research Soc. Am., Phi Kappa Phi. Club: Midland Optimists (pres. 1967). Author publs., patentee in field. Address: 4523 Chatham Dr Midland MI 48640. *The two opposing, yet synergistic, essential ingredients of productive research are freedom and discipline. I attempt to practice freedom for others; discipline for myself.*

TYLER, LLOYD JOHN, lawyer; b. Aurora, Ill., May 28, 1924; s. Lloyd J. and Dorothy M. (Curtis) T.; B.A., Beloit Coll., 1948; J.D., U. Mich., 1951; m. Inez Chappell Busener, Feb. 25, 1970; children by previous marriage—Barbara Tyler Miller, John R., Benjamin C., Robert B., Amy C. Admitted to Ill., Mich. bars, 1951; mem. firm Sears, Street, Tyler and Dreyer and predecessors, Aurora, Ill., 1951-62; mem. firm Tyler, Peskind, Solomon & Hughes, P.A., Aurora, 1962—; lectr., speaker on profl. subjects, 1964—. Democratic precinct committeeman, 1954-59; mem. Batavia (Ill.) Sch. Bd., 1959-62. Served with USAAF, 1943-46. Fellow Am. Bar Found.; mem. Am. Bar Assn. (Ho. of Dels. 1975-79), Ill. Bar Assn. (gov. 1970-78, pres. 1978-79), Ill. Bar Found. (pres. 1972-75), Ill. Inst. Continuing Legal Edn. (dir. 1971-75, 77-79), Soc. Trial Lawyers Ill., Phi Beta Kappa, Omicron Delta Kappa. Presbyterian. Contbr. chpts. to profl. books, articles to profl. jours. Home: 701 Fargo Blvd Geneva IL 60134 Office: Tyler Peskind Solomon & Hughes PO Box 1425 Aurora IL 60507

TYLER, MAX EZRA, bacteriologist, educator; b. Groveland, N.Y., June 1, 1916; s. Leon Charles and Bessie L. (Dorn) T.; B.S., Cornell U., 1938; M.Sc., Ohip State U., 1940, Ph.D., 1948; m. Charlotte Dean Moelchert, May 3, 1945; children—Gail Ann, Scott Dean. Asst. bacteriology, grad. asst. Ohio State U., 1938-41; instr., research asso. bacteriology Colo. Coll. A. and M., 1941-42; research bacteriologist, br. chief, Camp Detrick, Md., 1946-53; chmn., prof. dept. bacteriology U. Fla., 1953-71, prof. microbiology, 1971—; cons. U.S. Chem. Corps, Biol. Warfare Center, 1953-56. Served to lt. San. Corps, AUS, 1943-46. Fellow A.A.A.S., Am. Pub. Health Assn.; mem. Am. Soc. Microbiology (pres. S.E. br. 1959, nat. councilor 1963—), Soc. for Gen. Microbiology (Eng.), Sigma Xi (pres. Fla. 1960), Gamma Sigma Delta (pres. Fla. 1960). Contbr. articles to nat., fgn. sci. jours. Home: 1800 NW 10th Ave Gainesville FL 32605

TYLER, MORGAN SEYMOUR, JR., ret. air force officer; b. Three Rivers, Mich., July 6, 1920; s. Morgan Seymour and Marian (Foote) T.; student U. Calif., Davis, 1938-39, Santa Monica City Coll., 1939-40, U. Md., 1949-51; m. Norma Louise Hawes, June 22, 1946; children—Morgan Seymour III, Pamela Hawes, Steven Gregory. Commd. 2d lt. USAAF, 1941, advanced through grades to brig. gen.; air attache U.S. embassy, Turkey, 1947-49; staff officer Tactical Air Command, SAC, USAF Hdqrs., 1961-64; comdr. Fighter Squadron, World War II, Tactical Air Command and Air Def. Command, 1951-55, Wing and Air Div., SAC, 1965-70; dep. chief of staff for combat ops. N.Am. Air Def. Command; dir. Combat Ops. Center, including Space Def. Center, Cheyenne Mountain, Colo., 1970-73; ret., 1973; pres., Tyler-Hawes, Inc., Ridge Air Inc., Ridge Air Leasing Corp.; v.p. Bartee Corp., Gen. Aviation; citrus and cattle interests. Decorated D.S.M., Legion of Merit with oak leaf cluster, D.F.C. with 2 oak lead clusters, Soldiers medal, Air medal with 14 oak leaf clusters; Vietnamese Distinguished Service Order 1st class. Mem. Air Force Assn., Daedalian Soc., Air Force Acad. Athletic Assn. (life), Zeta Xi. Republican. Methodist. Clubs: Omaha; Colorado Springs Perry Park Country; Broadmoor Golf, Eisenhower Golf; Echo Hills, Internat., Florida, Lake Region, Yacht and Country, Rotary. Home: 1776 6th St NW Winter Haven FL 33880

TYLER, MORRIS, lawyer; b. New Haven, May 28, 1901; s. Victor Morris and Jessie (Brooks) T.; grad. Phillips Andover Acad., 1920; B.A., Yale, 1924, LL.B., 1929, Sterling Research fellow, 1929-30; m. Eugenie Crosby, Sept. 5, 1925. Admitted to Conn. bar, 1930, since practiced law specializing trial work, New Haven; mem. firm Tyler, Cooper, Grant, Bowerman & Keefe. Chmn. Regional Planning Agy. South Central Conn., 1949-56, dir., 1956—; dir. Conn. Fedn. Planning and Zoning Agys., 1954-56, Conn. Assn. Mental Health. Fellow Am. Coll. Trial Lawyers, Am. Bar Found. (life); mem. Am., Conn., New Haven bar assns., Am. Judicature Soc. (dir.). Club: Century Assn. (N.Y.C.). Home: 22 Penrhyn Rd Woodbridge CT 06525 Office: 205 Church St New Haven CT 06509

TYLER, OTTIS JAN, lawyer; b. Abilene, Tex., Mar. 4, 1937; s. Ottis J.T. and Alle Mae (Bertelsen) T.; B.B.A. cum laude, North Tex. State U., 1958; J.D. cum laude, So. Meth. U., 1963; m. Virginia Nell Weatherford, Dec. 26, 1958; children—Michael Jan, Mitchell Jan, Marcus Jan, Martha Jo, Mary Jane. Jr. and sr. accountant firm Peat, Marwick, Mitchell, Dallas, 1958-60; admitted to Tex. bar, 1963; trial atty. tax div. U.S. Dept. Justice, Washington, 1963-67; partner firm Sands & Tyler, Dallas, 1967—. Cattle rancher; lectr. Southwestern Grad. Sch. Banking, So. Meth. U., U. Tex. Tax Inst., Tex. C.P.A. Tax Inst.; pres., dir. Dallas Factors Inc., Diamond C Land & Cattle Co., Weatherford & Assos., Vanguard Life Ins. Co., Tex. Med. Econs., Inc., Garland Med. Tower Corp. Trustee, Denton Kappa Sigma Ednl. Found., 1967-73, Law Sch., So. Meth. U., 1971, Sands & Tyler Profit-Sharing Plan, Weatherford & Assos. Employees Pension Plan, 1972—. C.P.A., Tex. Mem. Am., Dallas (chmn. sect. tax 1972-73) bar assns., State Bar Tex., Dallas Soc. C.P.A.'s, Dallas Estate Planning Council, Phi Delta Phi, Kappa Sigma. Methodist (trustee). Club: Lancer's. Articles editor S.W. Law Sch. Jour., 1962-63. Home: 4455

Mill Run Rd Dallas TX 75234 Office: 2030 Republic Bank Tower Dallas TX 75201

TYLER, RALPH SARGENT, JR., lawyer; b. Cleve., July 28, 1906; s. Ralph S. and Alice (Campbell) T.; A.B., Case Western Res. U., 1927; LL.B., Harvard, 1930; m. Marion K. Clark, Mar. 31, 1939; children—Alice C., William C., Rae S. (Mrs. Howard L. Millman), Ralph Sargent III. Admitted to Ohio bar, 1930; asso. firm Squire, Sanders & Dempsey, Cleve., 1930-40, partner, 1940-64, 72; spl. asst. counsel Fed. Res. Bd., 1933; officer, dir. Lubrizol Corp., Cleve., 1964-72, gen. counsel, vice chmn. bd., 1967-68, chmn. bd., 1968-72. Trustee Erie Lackawanna Ry. Co. in reorgn., 1972—; pres., dir. First Multi-Currency Bond Fund, Inc., N.Y.C.; dir. Liquid Capital Income, Inc., Cleve., Electric Furnace Co., Salem, Ohio. Mem. vis. com. Harvard Law Sch., 1965-71. Mem. Am. Ohio, Cleve. bar assns., Phi Beta Kappa, Delta Kappa Epsilon. Baptist. Club: Union (Cleve.). Home: 1 Bratenahl Pl Cleveland OH 44108 Office: Midland Bldg Cleveland OH 44115

TYLER, ROBERT, architect; b. Los Angeles, May 5, 1926; s. Frederick W. and Fanny E. (Boozer) T.; B.Arch., U. So. Calif., 1952; m. Eleanore C. Hines, Aug. 11, 1951; children—Linda C., Karen E., Robert F. Archtl. designer Welton Becket Assos., Los Angeles, 1952-60, asst. dir. design, 1960-65, dir. design for Los Angeles, 1965-69, dir. design for corp., 1969—. Served with USNR, 1944-46. Fellow AIA (Silver medal 1952). Presbyterian. Home: 19344 Rosita St Tarzana CA 91356 Office: 10000 Santa Monica Blvd Los Angeles CA 90067

TYLER, ROBERT N., lawyer, ins. co. exec.; b. Haymarket, Va., Mar. 2, 1921; s. Grayson and Sally Norton (Tyler) T.; LL.B., U. Va., 1950; children—Robert N., Penelope Nicholas. Individual practice law, 1950-58; mem. legal staff Ho. of Reps. Armed Services Com., Washington, 1958; with Old Republic Life Ins. Co., Chgo., successively atty. legal dept., counsel, 2d v.p., v.p., 1958-75, v.p., sec., counsel, 1975—; dir. Home Owners Life, Old Republic, N.Y.C., Old Republic Internat. Corp. Served to 1st lt. USAAF, World War II. Episcopalian. Clubs: Chgo. Athletic, Skyline; Fauquier (Va.). Home: 1350 N Astor St Chicago IL 60610 Office: 307 N Michigan Ave Chicago IL 60601

TYLER, ROGER BROWNE, lawyer; b. Bernardston, Mass., July 19, 1896; s. William J. and Susie Noyes (Browne) T.; grad. Boston Latin Sch., 1913; A.B., Harvard, 1917, LL.B., 1920; LL.D. (hon.), Emerson Coll., 1965; D. Jurisprudence (hon.), Suffolk U., 1968; m. Margaret L. Blakely, Oct. 4, 1924 (dec. 1955); children—William B., Martha Ann (Mrs. William K. Saunders), Margaret Connable (Mrs. John B. Stetson); m. 2d, Beatrice M. Lowell Colby, Aug. 29, 1956. Admitted to Mass. bar, 1920, since practiced in Boston; asso. firm Goodwin, Procter, Field & Hoar, 1920-26; asso. firm Rackemann, Sawyer & Brewster, 1926-30, partner, 1930—, sr. partner, 1971-78, of counsel, 1978—; pres. Workingmens Coop Bank, Boston, 1947- 52, chmn. bd., dir., 1923-71; past trustee Warren Instn. Savs.; past incorporator Union-Warren Savs. Bank; past corporator Newton Savs. Bank; trustee Thomas Thompson Trust, Ogden Codman Trust. Chmn. Brookline (Mass.) Bldg. Commn., 1945-53; pres. Brookline Community Council, 1955-58; mem. Brookline Bicentennial Commn. Mem. Brookline Town Meeting, 1955-74. Vice pres., dir. Bunker Hill Monument Assn.; corporator Brattleboro Meml. Hosp.; trustee, past chmn. Walnut Hills Cemetery, Emerson Coll.; past pres., trustee Rivers Country Day Sch.; past trustee Marlboro Coll., Beaver Country Day Sch.; sec. Harvard Class of 1917. Served to ensign USNR, 1918-19. Mem. Am., Mass. (past v.p.), Boston (past mem. council), Norfolk County bar assns., Am. Judicature Soc., Mass. Conveyancers Assn. (exec. com., past pres.), Bostonian Soc. (past pres., dir.), New Eng. Historic Geneal. Soc. (past mem. council), Boston Latin Sch. Assn. (trustee, past pres.), Soc. Cincinnati N.H. (standing com.), Soc. Colonial Wars Mass. (past lt. gov.), Am. Philatelic Soc. (life), Mass. Audubon Soc., Nantucket, Brookline, Bernardston, Dorchester hist. socs., Soc. Preservation New Eng. Antiquities, Navy League. Clubs: Union (Boston); The Country (Brookline); Curtis, Abstract. Republican. Unitarian Mason (mem. various orgns.). Home: 144 Independence Dr Chestnut Hill MA 02167 Office: 28 State St Boston MA 02109

TYLER, RONNIE CURTIS, museum curator, historian; b. Temple, Tex., Dec. 29, 1941; s. Jasper J. and Melba Curtis (James) T.; B.S.E., Abilene (Tex.) Christian Coll., 1964; M.A., Tex. Christian U., 1966, Ph.D. (Univ. fellow), 1968; m. Paula Eyrich, Aug. 24, 1974. Instr. history Austin Coll., Sherman, Tex., 1967-68, asst. prof., 1968-69; curator history, dir. publs. Amon Carter Mus. Western Art, Ft. Worth, 1969—; adj. prof. history Tex. Christian U., 1971-72; cons. visual materials; pres. Tarrant County (Tex.) Hist. Soc., 1975-77; Good Neighbor Commn. scholar Instituto Tecnologico Monterrey (Mex.), 1967. Am. Philos. Soc. grantee, 1970-71; recipient H. Bailey Carroll award, 1974; Coral H. Tullis award, 1976. Author: Santiago Vidaurri and the Confederacy, 1973; The Big Bend: The Last Texas Frontier, 1975; The Image of America in Caricature and Cartoon, 1975; The Cowboy, 1975; The Mexican War: A Lithographic Record, 1974; The Rodeo Photographs of John Addison Stryker, 1978; editor: (with Lawrence R. Murphy) The Slave Narratives of Texas, 1974; Posada's Mexico, 1979. Home: 3418 Worth Hills Dr Fort Worth TX 76109 Office: PO Box 2365 Fort Worth TX 76113

TYLER, SAMUEL LYMAN, librarian, historian; b. Attica, Ark., Mar. 27, 1920; s. Rufus Black and Mary Ann (Hogan) T.; B.S., U. Utah, 1949, Ph.D., 1951; m. Bessie Marie Rohde, Apr. 9, 1943; children—Marie, Michael, Susan, Steven. Prof. history Brigham Young U., 1952-66, dir. libraries, 1954-66; prof. history U. Utah, Salt Lake City, 1966—, curator Western History Collection, 1967-68, dean internat. programs, 1968-71, dir. Am. West Center, 1971—. Mem. Utah Bd. Indian Affairs. Research fellow history U. Utah, 1949-51, Social Sci. Research Council, 1951-52. Served with USNR, World War II. Mem. Am., Utah (pres.) library assns., Western Hist. Assn., Phi Alpha Theta, Phi Kappa Phi. Mem. Ch. of Jesus Christ of Latter-day Day Saints. Kiwanian. articles, bibliog. studies on Indians S.W. Home: 1017 Douglas Salt Lake City UT 84105

TYLER, VARRO EUGENE, univ. dean, pharmacognosist; b. Auburn, Nebr., Dec. 19, 1926; s. Varro Eugene and Venus (Leamer) T.; B.S., U. Nebr., 1949; postgrad. Yale, 1949-50; M.S., U. Conn., 1951, Ph.D., 1953; m. Virginia May Demel, Aug. 20, 1947; children—Jeanne, David. Asso. prof., chmn. dept. pharmacognosy U. Nebr. Coll. Pharmacy, 1953-57; asso. prof., chmn. pharmacognosy, dir. drug plant gardens U. Wash. Coll. Pharmacy, 1957-61, prof. pharmacognosy, 1961-66; research fellow Institut für Biochemie der Pflanzen, Halle/Saale, Germany, 1963-64; dean Purdue U. Sch. Pharmacy and Pharmacal Scis., West Lafayette, Ind., 1966—, Sch. Nursing, Sch. Health Scis., 1979—. Bd. dirs. Am. Council Pharm. Edn., 1972-78, pres., 1974-78; bd. dirs. Am. Found. Pharm. Edn., 1971-76. Recipient Lehn & Fink Products Corp. medal, 1949; Eli Lilly Research fellow, 1950-51; Gustavus A. Pfeiffer Meml. Research fellow, 1963-64. Fellow AAAS, Acad. Pharm. Scis. (past sec. chmn.); mem. Am. Assn. Colls. Pharmacy (exec. com., pres. 1970-71), Am. Soc. Pharmacognosy (past pres., past mem. exec. com.), Soc. for Econ. Botany, Die Gesellschaft für Arzneipflanzenforschung, Am. (Found. Research Achievement award 1966), Ind. pharm. assns., Sigma Xi, Rho Chi, Kappa Psi (Scholarship key 1949), Phi Gamma Delta. Author: (with A.E. Schwarting) Experimental Pharmacognosy, 1962; (with J.E. Robbers, L.R. Brady) Pharmacognosy, 1976. Mem. editorial adv. bd. Jour. Pharm. Scis., 1959-65, Lloydia, 1961—, Planta Medica, 1963-78. Contbr. articles to profl. jours. Home: 640 Ridgewood Dr West Lafayette IN 47906

TYNDALL, ALBERT FORBES, JR., business exec.; b. Kinston, N.C., Aug. 18, 1936; s. Albert Forbes and Katie Lou (Holland) T.; B.A. in Econs., Duke U., 1958; M.B.A. in Mgmt., N.Y. U., 1972; m. Louise Edwards, May 23, 1958; children—Daivd Clark, Mark Whitney. Sr. accountnat Price Waterhouse & Co., C.P.A.'s, N.Y.C. and Stamford, Conn., 1958-63; treas., controller Greenwich Gas Co. (Conn.), 1963-67; asst. treas. Emerson div. and subsidiaries Nat. Union Electric Corp., Jersey City, 1967-68; chief fin. officer Modern Talking Picture Service, Inc., N.Y.C., 1968-73; exec. v.p. Marcel Dekker, Inc., N.Y.C. and Basel, Switzerland, 1973-78; pres. Tynco, Inc., Old Greenwich, Conn., 1978—. C.P.A., N.C. Mem. Am. Inst. C.P.A.'s, Sales Execs. Club N.Y.C. Episcopalian. Club: Old Greenwich Yacht. Home: 31 Indian Head Rd Riverside CT 06878 Office: PO Box 230 Old Greenwich CT 06870

TYNDALL, DAVID GORDON, educator; b. Bangalore, India, Nov. 19, 1919; s. Joseph and Gladys E. (Pickering) T.; B.Comm., U. Toronto, 1940, M.A., 1941; Ph.D., U. Calif., 1948; m. Margaret Patricia Davies, Apr. 4, 1942; children—Caroline Lee, David Gordon, Benjamin. Asst. prof. bus. adminstrn. Cornell U., Ithaca, N.Y., 1947-49; asso. prof. Carnegie-Mellon U., Pitts., 1949-53; asso. prof., dir. analytical studies U. Calif., Berkeley, 1955-67, lectr., 1979—; v.p. fin. and adminstrn., investment officer U. Alta., Edmonton, 1967-74; prof. fin., 1974-79; investment adv., Berkeley, 1979—; dir. Great Western United. Served with Royal Can. Air Force, 1942-45. Fulbright fellow, 1952. Mem. Am. Econ. Assn., Am. Fin. Assn. Democrat. Unitarian. Home: 1417 Arlington Blvd El Cerrito CA 94530 Office: Univ of Calif Berkeley CA 94720

TYNE, GEORGE, television dir., actor; b. Phila., Feb. 6, 1917; s. Charles and Molly (Ostroff) Yarus; student CCNY, 1935; m. Ethel Chaplin, Dec. 27, 1950; 1 step dau., Judy Chaplin. Appeared in numerous films including: A Walk in the Sun, 1945; Sands of Iwo Jima, 1949; dialogue dir., acting coach numerous films including: Aimez Vous Brahms, 1960, My Geisha, 1961, 5 Miles to Midnight, 1964; various appearances in Broadway plays, also co-producer plays; dir. numerous TV shows, series, 1967—; now dir. Love Boat TV series. Mem. Screen Actors Guild, Dirs. Guild Am., Acad. Motion Pictures Arts and Scis., Acad. TV Arts and Scis., Am. Film Inst. Office: care Shapiro Lichtman Agy 9200 Sunset Blvd Los Angeles CA 90069

TYNER, GEORGE S., ophthalmologist, ednl. adminstr.; b. Omaha, Oct. 9, 1916; s. George S. and Ethel (Holmquist) T.; B.S., U. Nebr., 1940, M.D., 1942; M. Med. Sci., U. Pa., 1952; postgrad. Tex. Tech. U., 1971-73; m. Jean Walt, June 13, 1942; children—Holly Jean, Helen Tyner Thompson. Intern, Phila. Gen. Hosp., 1942-43, resident in ophthalmology, 1947-48; research fellow, resident in ophthalmology Hosp. U. Pa., 1948-51, asst. instr., 1948-52; practice medicine specializing in ophthalmology, Denver, 1952-61; with U. Colo., 1952-71, asst. clin. prof., 1952-61, chief glaucoma clinic, 1953-61, asso. prof. ophthalmology, 1964-71, asso. prof., preventive medicine, 1968-71, asso. dean, 1963-71; prof. ophthalmology Tex. Tech. U., Lubbock, 1971—, prof. preventive medicine and community health, 1973, prof. psychiatry, 1974, asso. dean adminstrn., 1971-72, chmn. dept. ophthalmology, 1971-74, asso. dean edn. and student affairs, 1973-74, dean Sch. Medicine, 1974—; staff St. Mary of the Plains Hosp., Health Scis. Center Hosp., Lubbock; dir. Colo. chpt. Soc. Prevention of Blindness, 1961-66; bd. dirs., 1st v.p. Lubbock Council on Alcoholism, 1973-74; mem. Colo. State Bd. Basic Sci. Examiners, 1962-67. Served with USN, 1943-47. Diplomate Am. Bd. Ophthalmology. Fellow A.C.S.; mem. AMA, Colo., Denver (past pres.) med. socs., Am. Assn. Ophthalmology (trustee 1961—), Colo. Ophthal. Soc. (past pres.), Assn. Univ. Profs. Ophthalmology, N.Y. Acad. Sci., Am. Acad. Ophthalmology and Otolaryngology, Tex. Med. Assn., Am. Med. Soc. on Alcoholism, Nat. Council on Alcoholism, Assn. Research in Vision and Ophthalmology, Sigma Xi. Alpha Omega Alpha. Contbr. articles to med. jours. Home: 4006 Flint Ave Lubbock TX 79413 Office: Texas Tech U Sch Medicine Lubbock TX 79430

TYNER, MACK, JR., educator; b. Laurel Hill, Fla., Feb. 1, 1917; s. Mack and Effie (Campbell) T.; B.S., U. Fla., 1938; M.S., U. Cin., 1940, Ph.D., 1941; m. Carolyn Vidal, June 14, 1946; children—Ruth Lynn, Mack III, Grace Nell. Research engr. Kimberly-Clark, Neenah, Wis., 1941-42, Armour Research Found., Chgo., 1942-43; prof. chem. engring. U. Fla., Gainesville, 1943—. Mem. Am. Inst. Chem. Engrs., Instrument Soc. Am. Author: Process Engineering Calculations, 1960; Process Engineering Control, 1968. Asso. editor Chem. Engring. Edn., 1968—. Home: 1421 SW 13th Ave Gainesville FL 32608

TYNER, NEAL EDWARD, ins. co. exec.; b. Grand Island, Nebr., Jan. 30, 1930; s. Edward Raymond and Lydia (Kruse) T.; B.B.A., U. Nebr., 1956; m. Leota Faye Butler, May 6, 1953; children—Karen Sue, Morgan Matthew. securities analyst Bankers Life Ins. Co. Nebr., Lincoln, 1956-62, asst. v.p.-securities, 1962-67, v.p. securities, treas., 1967-69, fin. v.p., treas., 1969-72, sr. v.p. fin.-treas., 1972—, pres., dir. Lincoln Gateway Shopping Center Inc.; mem. Lincoln Investment Adv. Bd., 1964—; vice-chmn. Lincoln Elec. System Adminstrv. Bd., 1967-70, chmn., 1971-73; mem. exec. com., chmn. audit com., dir. Spencer Foods, Inc., 1972-78. Trustee U. Nebr. Found., Lincoln Found.; bd. dirs., diplomat Nebr. Resources Found. Served with USMCR, 1950-54. Mem. Omaha, Lincoln socs. fin. analysts (treas. 1966-70), Chartered Financial Analysts Soc., Delta Sigma Pi. Republican. Lutheran. Clubs: Lincoln Country, Nebraska (Lincoln). Home: 2734 O'Reilly Dr Lincoln NE 68502 Office: Bankers Life Ins Co Cotner and O Sts Lincoln NE 68501

TYNG, ANNE GRISWOLD, architect; b. Kuling, Kiangsi, China, July 14, 1920; d. Walworth and Ethel Atkinson (Arens) Tyng (parents Am. citizens); A.B., Radcliffe Coll., 1942; M.Arch., Harvard U., 1944; Ph.D., U. Pa., 1975; 1 dau., Alexandra Stevens. Asso., Stonorov & Kahn, Architects, 1945-47, Louis I. Kahn, Architect, 1947-73; pvt. practice architecture, Phila., 1973—; adj. asso. prof. architecture U. Pa. Grad. Sch. Fine Arts, 1968—; asso. cons. architect Phila. Planning Commn. and Phila. Redevel. Authority, 1952-54, Mill Creek Redevel. Plan, 1954; vis. disting. prof. Pratt Inst., 1979-80; vis. critic architecture Pratt Inst., 1969, Rensselaer Poly. Inst., 1969, 78, Carnegie Mellon U., 1970, Drexel U., 1972-73, Cooper Union, 1974-75, U. Tex., Austin, 1976; lectr. Archtl. Assn. London, also numerous univs. throughout U.S. and Can.; subject of films Anne G. Tyng at Parsons School of Design, 1972, Anne G. Tyng at University of Minnesota, 1974, Connecting, 1976, Forming the Future, 1977; work included in Smithsonian Travelling Exhbt., 1979. Fellow Graham Found. for Advanced Study in Fine Arts, 1965, 79. Fellow AIA (Brunner grantee N.Y. chpt. 1964, dir., mem. exec. bd. Phila. chpt. 1976-78); mem. NAD (asso.), Nat. Assn. Archtl. Historians, C.G. Jung Center Phila. (planning com. 1979—). Democrat. Episcopalian. Contbr. articles to profl. publs. Patentee Tyng Toy. Prin. works include Walworth Tyng Farmhouse (Hon. mention award Phila. chpt. AIA 1953). Home: 2511 Waverly St Philadelphia PA 19146 Office: Dept Architecture Grad Sch Fine Arts U Pa Philadelphia PA 19107

TYNION, JAMES T., lawyer; b. Bklyn., Dec. 4, 1902 s. William and Mary (Huber) T.; grad Pulcifer Bus. Inst., Bklyn., 1920; LL.B., St. John's U., 1931; LL.D., St. Michael's Coll., Winooski, Vt., 1958; m. Julia L. Egan, Aug. 8, 1922; children—James T., Donald W., Louisemary (Mrs. John McDonald). With O'Brien, Boardman, Harper & Fox, 1917; law clk., sec. Justice M.J. O'Brien, 1920-32; admitted to N.Y. bar, 1932; mem. firm Conboy, Hewitt, O'Brien & Broadman, N.Y.C., 1943-72, sr. partner, 1965-72; pvt. practice, N.Y.C., 1972—. Chmn. bd., sec., dir. Hamilton Press. Bd. dirs. St. Vincent's Hall, Bklyn.; v.p., dir. Marquis George MacDonald Found., 1961—. Named knight of Malta, 1943 (sec. Am. chpt. 1951-78, dep. master sec. 1957—, bd. founders 1950—); knight grand cross Order Holy Sepulchre, 1951, bronze cross merit, 1954, (Eastern lt.-treas. 1951-78, sec.-treas., 1957-78, councilor 1951—). Mem. Am. Irish Hist. Soc., Ancient Order Hibernians, Friendly Sons St. Patrick. K.C. (4 deg.). Clubs: Lawyers (N.Y.C.); Montauk (Bklyn.). Home: 220 E 73d St New York City NY 10021 Office: 280 Park Ave New York City NY 10017

TYRE, NORMAN RONALD, lawyer; b. Boston, Aug. 28, 1910; s. Jack and Fannie (Spector) T.; student U. Calif. at Berkeley, 1926-28; B.A. with highest distinction Stanford, 1930; LL.B., Harvard, 1933; m. Margery Cayton, Mar. 10, 1935; children—Joy (Mrs. Sheldon Coburn), Patricia Ann (Mrs. Robert Tanenbaum). Admitted to Calif. bar, 1933, since practiced in Los Angeles; mem. firm Gang, Tyre & Brown, 1941—; v.p., dir. Motion Picture and TV Tax Inst. Mem. Fgn. Policy Assn. (nat. council). Club: Hillcrest Country. Home: 801 N Linden Dr Beverly Hills CA 90210 Office: Gang Tyre & Brown 6400 Sunset Bldg Los Angeles CA 90028

TYREE, ALAN DEAN, clergyman; b. Kansas City, Mo., Dec. 14, 1929; s. Clarence Tillman and Avis Ora (Gross) T.; B.A., U. Iowa, 1950; postgrad. U. Mo. at Columbia, 1956-58, at Kansas City, 1961-62; m. Gladys Louise Omohundro, Nov. 23, 1951; children—Lawrence Wayne, Jonathan Tama, Sharon Avis. Ordained minister Reorganized Ch. Jesus Christ Latter Day Saints, 1947; appointee minister, Lawrence, Kans., 1950-52; mission adminstr. Mission Sanito, French Polynesia, 1953-64; regional adminstr., Denver, 1964-66; mem. Council Twelve Apostles, Independence, Mo., 1966—, also mem. Joint Council and Bd. Appropriations; originator music appreciation broadcasts Radio Tahiti, 1962-64, Mission Sanito radio ministry, 1960-64. Bd. dirs. Outreach Internat. Found. Recipient Elbert A. Smith Meml. award for publ. articles, 1968, 72. Mem. Internat. Relations Council, Phi Beta Kappa, Phi Eta Sigma. Lion. Editor Cantiques des Saints French-Tahitian hymnal, 1965. Home: 18804 RD Mize Rd Independence MO 64057 Office: Box 1059 Independence MO 64051

TYREE, DAVID MERRILL, ret. naval officer, former expdn. assn. exec.; b. Washington, Jan. 23, 1904; s. Amos and Mabel Edith (Garrett) T.; B.S., U.S. Naval Acad., 1925; M.S. in Engring., U. Mich., 1934; m. Eleanor Yates Haddox, Dec. 21, 1927; children—Mary Lee (Mrs. Harold J. Deering), David Merrill. Commd. ensign USN, 1925, advanced through grades to rear adm., 1952; comdg. officer U.S.S. Renville, 1947-48, U.S.S. New Jersey, 1950-51; Nat. War Coll., 1948-50; asst. chief of naval ops. (materiel), 1952-54; comdr. Cruiser Div. One, 1954-55, supt. Naval Gun Factory, Washington, 1956-58; dep. comdr. Joint Task Force 7 and CTG 7.3, 1958; comdr. U.S. Naval Support Force, Antarctica and U.S. Antarctica projects officer, 1959-63, ret., 1963; lectr., 1963—; cons. Arctic Inst. N.Am., Washington, 1966-74, pres. Polar Expdns., Inc., Washington, 1968-74, chmn. bd., 1974-78. Decorated Legion of Merit with 2 oak leaf clusters, Bronze Star, Navy Commendation (2), Army Commendation; Korean UN; Order of Orange Nassau (Netherlands). Mem. Am. Legion, Mil. Order World Wars, Internat. Platform Assn., Phi Lambda Upsilon. Clubs: Ruritan, Explorers; Army-Navy. Home: Port Haywood VA 23138

TYREE, DONALD ANDREW, educator; b. St. Louis, Nov. 19, 1930; s. Wesley F. and Dena (Krieter) T.; B.S., B.A., Washington U., St. Louis, 1953, M.B.A., 1956; Ph.D. in Finance, U. Tex. at Austin, 1959; m. Sherry Johnson, Nov. 18, 1978; children by previous marriage—Wesley G., Thomas A. Research asso. Washington U., 1953; lectr. U. Tex., 1956-59; mem. faculty St. Louis U., 1959—, prof. finance, 1969—, chmn. dept., 1968—, asso. dean Sch. Bus. Adminstrn., 1973-74. Cons. in field. Mem. St. Louis County Ins. Com., 1962-68. Served with AUS, 1953-55. Wienhiemer fellow, 1955-56; Tex. Savs. and Loan Assn. fellow, 1956-59. Author: Small Loan Industry in Texas, 1960; School Insurance Administration, 1975. Home: 6 Southmoor Saint Louis MO 63105

TYREE, JOHN AUGUSTINE, JR., ret. naval officer; b. Blackstone, Va., Oct. 3, 1911; s. John Augustine and Nannie Grinnan (Kelly) T.; B.S., U.S. Naval Acad., 1933; grad. Nat. War Coll., 1954; m. Margaret Fletcher James, June 20, 1935; children—Judith Keith (Mrs. Burton M. Onofrio), Johanne (Mrs. James F. Beck); m. 2d, Nora McDavid Curren, Jan. 23, 1975. Commd. ensign U.S. Navy, 1933, advanced through grades to vice adm., 1968; served in carriers and submarines, 1933-41; exec. officer U.S.S. Finback, 1941-42, comdg. officer, 1943-44; asst. naval aide to Presidents Roosevelt and Truman, 1944-45; mem. staffs comdr.-in-chief, comdr. submarines Atlantic, CINCAtlantic Fleet, 1945-49; submarine div. comdr., 1949-50; submarine force operations officer, 1950-51; assigned Bur. Naval Personnel, 1951-53; comdg. officer U.S.S. Botetourt, 1954-55; comdr. Submarine Squadron 6, 1955-56; mem. faculty Nat. War Coll., 1957-58; comdr. Task Force 73, 1958-59; assigned ComNav Forces, Korea, 1959-60; asst. chief naval operations for Naval Res., 1960-62; comdr. S. Atlantic Force, 1962-64; dep. comdr. submarine force, Atlantic, 1964-66; dep. chief staff U.S. European Command, 1966-68; chief staff U.S. European Command, 1968-70; naval insp. gen., 1970-71; ret., 1971. Pres., United Way S.E. Conn., 1979-80. Decorated Navy Cross with gold star, D.S.M., Silver Star, Legion of Merit with gold star, Bronze Star with 2 gold stars and combat V, Navy Commendation medal with combat V; Order Mil. Merit Taeguk (Korea); grand star Naval Merit (Chile); comdr. Order Naval Merit (Brazil); Order Naval Merit 2d class (Venezuela). Mem. U.S. Naval Inst. Home: 14 Baldwin Dr Waterford CT 06385

TYREE, SHEPPARD YOUNG, JR., educator; b. Richmond, Va., July 4, 1920; s. Sheppard Young and Rosa Dove (Burton) T.; B.Sc. in Chemistry, Mass. Inst. Tech., 1942, Ph.D., 1946; m. Barbara Doris Jones, June 5, 1943; children—Susan Scott, Pamela Fore, Peter Burton, Sally Blair, Rebecca Young. Instr., Mass. Inst. Tech., 1943-46; asst. prof., then asso. prof. U. N.C., 1946-58; sci. officer Office Naval Research, 1954-55; prof. U. N.C., 1958-66; liaison scientist Office Naval Research, London, 1965-66; prof. chemistry Coll. William and Mary, 1966—, head dept., 1968-73; research chemist Oak Ridge Nat. Lab., summer 1949; lectr., operator Morehead Planetarium, 1951-52; gen. coll. adviser U. N.C., 1956-58; dir. 4th Summer Inst. Coll. Chemistry Tchrs., 1957; vis. prof. U. P.R., summer 1963; chem. cons. to pvt. industry, govt. agys. Chmn. Gordon Research Conf. Inorganic Chemistry, 1957, mem. com., 1955-56, 61, 67; lectr. NSF Summer Inst., 1956-68; mem. bd. Inorganic syntheses, Inc., 1957-73, sec.-treas., 1968-72; chmn. Council Oak Ridge Asso. Univs., 1973-76, bd. dirs., 1976—. Active local Boy Scouts Am. Served with USNR, 1942. Recipient Herty medal Am. Chem. Soc., 1964. Fellow AAAS; mem. Chem. Soc., Va. Acad. Sci., Am. Chem. Soc. (tour speaker 1959, 61, 64, 77; vis. scientist 1958-63; chmn. N.C. sect. 1960; councillor 1963-66), Phi Beta Kappa, Sigma Xi (pres. U. N.C. chpt. 1964-65), Alpha Chi Sigma, Phi Gamma Delta (purple legionnaire 1943-45, 63-65). Episcopalian. Author: (with K. Knox) Inorganic Chemistry, 1961. Editor: Inorganic Syntheses, Vol. IX, 1967. Home: 306 Indian Springs Rd Williamsburg VA 23185

TYRER, JOHN LLOYD, headmaster; b. Brockton, Mass., Jan. 16, 1928; s. Lloyd Perkins and Dorothy (Nicholson) T.; A.B., Bowdoin Coll., 1949; M.A., Middlebury (Vt.) Coll., 1959; m. Jeanne Irene Dunning, June 7, 1952; children—Alison Jane, John Lloyd, David Dunning, Jill Anne. Tchr., Wilbraham (Mass.) Acad., 1949-53; tchr., adminstr. Hill Sch., Pottstown, Pa., 1953-64; headmaster Asheville (N.C.) Sch., 1964—. Mem. adv. bd. Warren Wilson Coll.; mem. N.C. State Competency Test Commn. Bd. dirs. Asheville Country Day Sch., 1965-68, Asheville Community Concert Assn., St. Genevieve/Gibbons Hall Sch., 1970-77, Ind. Ednl. Services, 1970-75, Council Religion in Ind. Schs., 1969-78. Served with AUS, 1946-47. Mem. Nat. (chmn. com. on boarding schs.), So. (pres., bd. dirs.), N.C. (pres., bd. dirs.) assns. ind. schs., Headmasters Assn., So. Headmasters Assn., So. Assn. Colls. and Schs. (N.C. com.), English-Speaking Union (pres. Asheville br.), Theta Delta Chi. Episcopalian. Clubs: Asheville Rotary (dir. 1967-69), Mountain City (Asheville). Address: Asheville Sch Asheville NC 28806

TYROL, ROBERT SHERMAN, broadcasting exec.; b. Hartford, Conn., May 3, 1923; s. Otto Robert and Ethel Hollister T.; grad. U.S. Coast Guard Acad., 1943; m. Virginia Stoneburner, Jan. 11, 1944; children—Lee R., Bradford R. Announcer, WTIC-AM-FM (Broadcast-Plaza, Inc.), Hartford, Conn., 1940-56, salesman, 1956-57, asst. gen. sales mgr., 1957-58, gen. sales mgr., 1958-59, v.p., 1959-66; asst. corp. sec. WTIC-AM-FM-TV (Broadcast-Plaza, Inc.), Hartford, 1962-63, corp. sec., 1963-64, dir., 1963-74, v.p. adminstrn., 1966, v.p., gen. mgr., 1966-74; exec. v.p., gen. mgr. WTIC-AM-FM (The Ten Eighty Corp.), Hartford, 1974-78, pres., chief exec. officer, 1978—, dir., 1974—; mem. NBC Radio Affiliates Exec. Com.; past mem. adv. bd. Soc. for Savs.; cons. to univs. Past corporator Am. Sch. for Deaf; past bd. dirs. Travelers Aid Soc., Hartford Retail Trade Bur., Better Bus. Bur., Conn. Soc. for Prevention of Blindness; past chmn. State Industry Adv. Com.; vice chmn. 1970 fund campaign Charter Oak council Boy Scouts Am. Served with USCGR, 1942-46. Recipient Leadership award Boy Scouts Am., 1974. Mem. Broadcast Pioneers, Conn. Broadcasters Assn. (pres. 1962-63). Clubs: Rotary (pres. 1967-68), Hartford, Hartford Golf (Hartford, Conn.); Masons. Home: 925 Ridge Rd Wethersfield CT 06109 Office: WTIC-FM-AM 1 Financial Plaza Hartford CT 06103

TYSON, CHARLES ROEBLING, ins. exec.; b. Phila., Feb. 22, 1914; s. Carroll Sargent and Helen (Roebling) T.; ed. Episcopal Acad., Phila., Pa., Princeton, 1934-35; m. Barbara Kurtz, Oct. 12, 1935; children—Charles Roebling, Barbara, Helen R., Margaret, Sarah. Dir. John A. Roebling's Sons Co., Trenton, N.J., 1936-58, pres., exec. v.p., dir. Colo. Fuel Iron Corp. (now CF & I Steel Corp.), 1958-59; exec. v.p. Penn Mut. Life Ins. Co., 1959-61, pres., chief exec. officer, 1961-71, chmn., chief exec. officer, 1971-73, chmn. bd., 1971-78, chmn. exec. com., 1979—, also trustee; dir. Bell Telephone Co. Pa., CPC Internat., Inc.; trustee Mut. Assurance Co., Phila., Stock Ins. Co. of Greentree. Republican. Episcopalian. Clubs: Ivy (Princeton); Pine Valley Golf; Sunnybrook Golf; Philadelphia. Home: 225 Mathers Rd Ambler PA 19002 Office: Penn Mutual Life Ins Co Independence Sq Philadelphia PA 19172

TYSON, CICELY, actress; b. N.Y.C.; d. William and Theodosia Tyson; student N.Y. U., Actors Studio; hon. doctorates Atlanta U., Loyola U., Lincoln U. Former sec., model; stage appearances include The Blacks, 1961-63, Off-Broadway, 1961-63, Moon on a Rainbow Shaw, 1962-63, Tiger, Tiger, Burning Bright, Broadway; star film Sounder, 1972; other film appearances include: Twelve Angry Men, 1957, Odds Against Tomorrow, 1959, The Last Angry Man, 1959, A Man Called Adam, 1966, The Comedians, 1967, The Heart is a Lonely Hunter, 1968, The Blue Bird, 1976, The River Niger, 1976, A Hero Ain't Nothin' but a Sandwich, 1978; TV appearances include series East Side, West Side, 1963, spl. TV play, The Autobiography of Miss Jane Pittman, 1973, 1974, A Woman Called Moses, 1978; TV series Roots, 1977, King, 1978, TV movie Just An Old Sweet Song, 1976. Co-founder Dance Theatre of Harlem; bd. dirs. Urban Gateways; trustee Human Family Inst., Am. Film Inst. Recipient Vernon Price award, 1962; named best actress for Sounder, Atlanta Film Festival, 1972; Nat. Soc. Film Critics, 1972; nominee best actress for Sounder, Acad. awards, 1972; Emmy award for best actress in a spl., 1973; also awards NAACP, Nat. Council Negro Women; Capitol Press award. Address: care William Morris Agy 151 El Camino Dr Beverly Hills CA 90212*

TYSON, KENNETH ROBERT THOMAS, surgeon, educator; b. Houston, July 30, 1936; s. Howard Ellis and Myrtle Henrietta (Daunoy) T.; B.A., U. Tex., 1956; M.D., U. Tex. Med. Br., 1960; m. Sue Ann Delahoussaye, Nov. 20, 1971; children—Deborah, Kenneth, Michael, Jill. Intern, Ind. U. Med. Center, Indpls., 1960-61, resident in gen. and thoracic surgery, 1961-66; resident in pediatric surgery Children's Hosp. Med. Center, Boston, 1966-67; chief pediatric gen., thoracic surgery U. Tex. Med. Br., Galveston, 1967—, asst. prof. surgery, 1967-71, asso. prof., 1971-75, prof., 1975—, surgeon-in-chief Child Health Center, 1974—. Diplomate Am. Bd. Surgery, Am. Bd. Thoracic Surgery. Fellow A.C.S., Am. Acad. Pediatrics, Am. Coll. Cardiology; mem. Am. Assn. Thoracic Surgery, Soc. Surgery Alimentary Tract, So. Thoracic Surg. Assn., Am. Pediatric Surg. Assn., Tex. Surg. Soc., Soc. Univ. Surgeons, So. Surg. Assn., Sigma Xi, Alpha Omega Alpha, Delta Kappa Epsilon, Alpha Kappa Kappa. Episcopalian. Contbr. articles to profl. jours. Home: 2824 Dominique St Galveston TX 77551 Office: Dept Surgery U Tex Med Br Galveston TX 77550

TYSON, RALPH ROBERT, physician, educator; b. Phila., Dec. 14, 1920; s. Ralph M. and Hazel (Beeber) T.; B.A., Dartmouth, 1941; M.D., U. Pa., 1944; m. Eleanor M. Hare, Apr. 21, 1945; children—R. Michael, Virginia H., Leslie B. Intern Grad. Hosp. U. Pa., 1944-45; resident Grad. Hosp. U. Pa., 1945-46, U.S. Naval Hosp., Phila., 1946-48, Temple U. Hosp., 1948-51, asst. W. Emory Burnett Temple U. Hosp., 1951; prof. surgery, Temple U. Hosp., Phila., 1962—, chmn. dept., 1973—; asso. attending surgeon St. Christopher's Hosp., Phila.; cons. surgery Wilkes Barre VA Hosp., Phila. VA Hosp., Gen. Hosp. Monroe County, East Stroudsburg, Pa., Germantown Hosp., Phila., Chestnut Hill Hosp., Phila.; cons. peripheral vascular surgery Phoenixville (Pa.) Hosp. Served with USNR, 1946-48. Diplomate Am. Bd. Surgery, Pan Am. Med. Assn. (sect. surgery). Fellow A.C.S., Am. Surg. Soc.; mem. Am. Fedn. Clin. Research, Soc. Vascular Surgery, Internat. Cardiovascular Soc., N.Y. Acad. Sci., Phila. Acad. Surgery, Phila. Coll. Physicians, Nat. Bd. Med. Examiners, AMA, Pa. Med. Soc., Phila. County Med. Soc., Soc. Surg. Chairmen, Allen O. Whipple Soc., Sigma Xi. Club: Appalachian. Contbr. articles to med. jours. Home: 521 Jarden Rd Philadelphia PA 19118

TYSON, REMER HOYT, JR., writer; b. Statesboro, Ga., July 2, 1934; s. Remer Hoyt and Eva (NeSmith) T.; student Ga. So. Coll., Statesboro, 1952-54; A.B. in Journalism, U. Ga., 1957; Neiman fellow Harvard, 1966-67; m. Alyce Elizabeth McCord, July 17, 1955; children—Tera Elizabeth, Remer Dean. News reporter Columbus (Ga.) Ledger, 1956-57, 59-60; city editor Valdosta (Ga.) Daily Times, 1960-64; reporter Atlanta Constn., 1964-65, Washington corr., 1965-66; polit. editor Atlanta Constn., 1967-69; polit. cons., free-lance writer Burton-Campbell, Inc., Atlanta, 1969-70; polit. writer Detroit Free Press, 1970—. Served with AUS, 1957-59. Mem. Sigma Delta Chi. Home: 5565 Yorkshire Detroit MI 48224 Office: 321 W LaFayette Detroit MI 48226

TZIMAS, NICHOLAS ACHILLES, orthopedic surgeon; b. Greece, Apr. 18, 1928; s. Archilles Nicholas and Evanthia B. (Exarchou) T.; came to U.S., 1955, naturalized, 1960; M.D., U. Athens (Greece), 1952; m. Helen J. Papastylopoulos, Apr. 22, 1958; children—Yvonne, Christina. Intern, St. Mary's Hosp., Hoboken, N.J., 1955-56; resident in gen. surgery Misericordia Hosp., N.Y.C.; resident in orthopedic surgery Bellevue Hosp., N.Y.C., 1957-60; instr. orthopedic surgery N.Y. U. Sch. Medicine, 1961-63, asst. clin. prof., 1963-65, asso. clin. prof., 1965-71; clin. prof., 1971—; mem. staff Univ. and Bellevue Hosps.; chief children's orthopedics, 1966—; orthopedic cons. Inst. Rehab. Medicine, N.Y. U., 1966—, St. Agnes Hosp., White Plains, N.Y., 1972—; advisory com. Bur. Handicapped Children, N.Y.C., 1975—. Spl. invitations for teaching Osaka, Japan, 1970, Jerusalem, 1974, São Paolo, Brazil, 1976, Taranto, Italy, 1977, Bazi, Italy, 1978, Bazquisimeto, Venezuela, 1979. Served with M.C., Greek Army, 1952-55. Fellow Am., Internat. colls. surgeons; mem. N.Y. Acad. Medicine, N.Y. State, N.Y. County med. socs., Am. Acad. Orthopedic Surgeons, Am. Congress Rehab. Medicine, Am. Acad. Cerebral Palsy. Mem. Greek Orthodox Ch., Archon of the Ecumenical Patriarchate of Constantinople. Author articles on spina bifida child mgmt. Home: 33 Edgewood St Tenafly NJ 07670 Office: 566 1st Ave New York NY 10016

TZIMOULIS, PAUL JAMES, editor, pub.; b. N.Y.C., Nov. 16, 1936; s. James and Maria (Gress) T.; student public schs., Conn.; m. Doris Patricia Pecorino, Nov. 25, 1965; children—Jason, Tristin Marie. Pres., Diving Center, 1958-59, Underwater Sch. Sport Diving, 1959-60; customer service mgr. U.S. Divers Co., Stanford, Conn., 1960-61; eastern sales mgr. Sportsways, Inc., Jersey City, 1961-64; editor, pub. Skin Diver mag., Los Angeles, 1964—; tchr. underwater photography; diving travel cons.; master of ceremonies for underwater film festival. Recipient Arts award New Orleans Grand Isle, 1969, Hawaii Dive Council award, 1971, Diver of Yr. award Boston Sea Rovers, 1972, Our World Underwater, 1979. Mem. Profl. Assn. Diving Instrs., Nat. Assn. Underwater Instrs., Am. Littoral Soc., YMCA, Audubon Soc., Our World Underwater. Roman Catholic. Home: 1033 N Orlando Los Angeles CA 90069 Office: 8490 Sunset Blvd Los Angeles CA 90069

UBBELOHDE, CARL WILLIAM, educator; b. Waldo, Wis., Nov. 4, 1924; s. Carl William and Carrie S. (Stratton) U.; B.S., Oshkosh State Tchrs. Coll., 1948; M.A., U. Wis., 1950, Ph.D., 1954; m. Mary Jean Tipler, May 31, 1952; children—Mary Susan, Carrie Ellan, Libby Jean, Katherine Johanna. Instr. history U. Colo., Boulder, 1954-56, asst. prof., 1956-59, asso. prof., 1959-65; asso. prof. Case Western Res. U., Cleve., 1965-68, prof., 1968—, Henry Eldridge Bourne prof. history, 1975—, chmn. dept. history, 1973-76; vis. prof. univs. Tex., Wis., Vt., Pa., Del., Ohio State U. Served with AUS, 1943-45. Decorated Purple Heart. Recipient Herfurth award U. Wis., 1955; distinguished teaching awards U. Colo., 1963, Case Western Res. U., 1967, 73. Mem. Am. Hist. Assn., Orgn. Am. Historians, Ohio Acad. History, Western Res. Hist. Soc., A.A.U.P. Democrat. Unitarian (trustee). Author: The Vice-Admiralty Courts and the American Revolution, 1960; A Colorado History, 1965, 72, 76; (with Clifford L. Lord) Clio's Servant: The State Historical Society of Wisconsin, 1967; The American Colonies and the British Empire, 1968, rev. edit., 1975. Home: 2577 Overlook Rd Cleveland Heights OH 44106 Office: Dept History Case Western Reserve U Cleveland OH 44106

UBELL, EARL, TV sci. editor; b. Bklyn., June 21, 1926; s. Charles and Hilda (Kramer) U.; B.S., Coll. City N.Y., 1948; m. Shirley Leitman, Feb. 12, 1949; children—Lori Ellen, Michael Charles. With N.Y. Herald Tribune, 1943-66, successively messenger, asst. sec. to mng. editor, reporter, 1943-53, sci. editor, 1953-66, syndicated columnist, 1956-66; sci. commentator MBS, 1958-59; spl. sci. editor WNEW, N.Y., 1962; health and sci. editor WCBS-TV, N.Y.C., 1966-72, 78—; dir. TV news NBC News, N.Y.C., 1972-76, producer spl. broadcasts, 1976-78, producer documentaries: Medicine in America, 1977, Escape from Madness, 1977. Pres. Council Advancement Sci. Writing, Inc., 1960-66, bd. dirs., 1960—; chmn. Center Modern Dance Edn., Inc., 1962—; bd. dirs. Dance Notation Bur., 1968—, chmn. bd., 1975—; pres. North Jersey Cultural Council, 1966-72; bd. dirs. Sex Info. and Edn. Council U.S., 1967-69, YMHA, Bergen County, 1968-73, Nat. Center Health Edn., 1977. Served as aviation radioman USNR, 1944-46. Recipient Mental Health Bell award N.Y. State Soc. Mental Health, 1957, Albert Lasker med. journalism award, 1958; award for radio program Nat. Assn. Mental Health, 1962, Sci. Writers award Am. Psychol. Found., 1965; Westinghouse award AAAS, 1960; Empire State award, 1963; TV Reporting award N.Y. Asso. Press, 1969, 71; N.Y. Emmy award, 1971. Mem. Nat. Assn. Sci. Writers (pres. 1960-61), Nuclear Energy Writers Assn. (pres. 1965-66), Am. Crystallographic Assn., Phi Beta Kappa (pres. Gamma chpt. 1976-77). Home: 682 Broadway New York NY 10012 Office: 524 W 57th St New York NY 10019

UBELL, ROBERT NEIL, editor, publisher; b. Bklyn., Sept. 14, 1938; s. Charles and Hilda (Kramer) U.; B.A., Bklyn. Coll., 1961; student Acad. Fine Arts, Rome, Italy, 1959-60, City U. N.Y., 1961-62, Pratt Graphic Arts Workshop, N.Y.C., 1972-73; m. Rosalyn Deutsche, Sept. 24, 1976; children—Jennifer, Elizabeth. Asso. editor Nuclear Industry, Atomic Industrial Forum, 1962-64; editor Plenum Pub. Corp., N.Y.C., 1965-68, sr. editor, 1968-70, v.p., editor-in-chief, 1970-76; editor The Sciences, N.Y. Acad. Scis., N.Y.C., 1976-79; Am. pub. Nature, N.Y.C., 1979—. Mem. N.Y. Acad. Scis., Nat. Assn. Sci. Writers. Author (with Marvin Leiner) Children Are the Revolution, 1974. Contbr. articles to mags. Home: 198 St Johns Pl Brooklyn NY 11217 Office: 175 Fifth Ave New York NY 10010

UBERALL, HERBERT MICHAEL STEFAN, educator, physicist; b. Neunkirchen, Austria, Oct. 14, 1931; s. Michael and Stefanie (Hacker) U.; Ph.D., U. Vienna (Austria), 1953; Ph.D., Cornell U., 1956; m. Collette Bry, Sept. 23, 1957; children—Bernadette, Bertrand. Came to U.S., 1953, naturalized, 1963. Staff mem. Signal Corps Engring. Labs., Ft. Monmouth, N.J., 1953-54; research asst. Cornell U., 1954-56; research fellow Nuclear Physics Research Lab., U. Liverpool, Eng., 1956-57; Ford Found. fellow CERN, Geneva, Switzerland, 1957-58; research physicist Carnegie Inst. Tech., Pitts., 1958-60; asst. prof. U. Mich., Ann Arbor, 1960-64; asso. prof. Catholic U., Washington, 1964-65, prof. physics, 1965—; cons. Naval Research Lab., Washington, 1966—, Naval Surface Weapons Lab., Silver Spring, Md., 1976—. Fellow Am. Phys. Soc., Acoustical Soc. Am.; mem. A.A.U.P. Author: Electron Scattering from Complex Nuclei, 1971. Contbr. articles to profl. jours. Home: 6100 Landon Ln Bethesda MD 20034 Office: Physics Dept Catholic U Washington DC 20064

UBEROI, MAHINDER SINGH, educator; b. Delhi, India, Mar. 13, 1924; s. Kirpal Singh and Sulaksha (Kosher) U.; came to U.S., 1945, naturalized, 1960; B.S., Punjab U., Lahore, India, 1944; M.S., Calif. Inst. Tech., 1946; D.Eng., Johns Hopkins U., 1952. Mem. faculty U. Mich., 1953-63, prof. aeros., 1959-63, vis. prof., 1963-64; prof. aerospace engring. U. Colo., Boulder, 1963—, chmn. dept. aerospace engring., 1963-75; fellow F. Joint Inst. for Lab. Astrophysics, Boulder, 1963-74; hon. research fellow Harvard U., 1975-76; invited prof. U. Que. (Can.), 1972-74. Council mem. Ednl. TV, Channel 6, Inc., Denver, 1963-66. Guggenheim fellow Royal Inst. Tech., Stockholm, Sweden, 1958; exchange scientist U.S. Nat. Acad. Scis., Soviet Acad. Scis., 1966. Registered profl. engr. Mem. Am. Inst. Aeros. and Astronautics (mem. council Rocky Mountain sect. 1963-66), Am. Phys. Soc., Am. Soc. Engring. Edn., Air Force Assn., Tau Beta Pi. Home: 819 6th St Boulder CO 80302

UCCELLO, ANTONINA PHYLLIS, former govt. ofcl., ins. and real estate broker; b. Hartford, Conn.; d. Salvatore and Josephine (Bordonaro) Uccello; B.S., St. Joseph Coll., 1944; student U. Conn. Law Sch., 1953-54; L.H.D., St. Joseph Coll., 1971. Tchr. history, social studies East Hampton (Conn.) High Sch., 1944-45; with G. Fox & Co., Inc., Hartford, 1945-67, successively dept. mgr., asst. to div. mgr.; councilman City of Hartford, 1963-67, mayor, 1967-71; dir. Office Consumer Affairs, Transp. Dept., 1971—. Adv. bd. Am. Com. Italian Migration, 1966-71; adv. bd. U.S. Conf. Mayors, 1969-71; adv. bd., vice chmn. Capitol Region Council Govt., 1968-69; mem. Nat. Tourism Resources Rev. Commn., 1971-79; ins. and real estate broker The Gustafson Agys., Farmington, Conn., 1979—: sec. Conn. Conf. Mayors, 1970-71; mem. Dept. Def. Adv. Com. on Women in Service, 1969-72. Mem. Republican Town Com., 1955-63; candidate U.S. Congress, 1970. Bd. dirs. Hartford County Area Tb and Respiratory Disease Assn. Inc., Hartford Public Library, 1978—. Recipient Amita Achievement award in govt., 1967; Salvation Army Leadership award, 1971; Columbo award Italian-Am. Civic Club Md. and Md. Order Sons Italy, 1971; William Paca award Italian-Am. Execs. Am., 1969; Achievement award Greater Hartford capt. Nat. League Am. Pen. Women, 1969; Civic Achievement award Internat. Scandinavian Assn., 1969; named cavaliére Stella della Solidarieta Italiana, 1972; named Outstanding Woman of Year, Alverno Coll., Milw., 1971; Sec.'s award for meritorious achievement Transp. Dept., 1973. Mem. AAUW, LWV, Catholic Grads. Club Greater Hartford, St. Joseph Coll. Club (pres. 1959-60). Alpha Delta Kappa (hon.). Club: Pilot. Home: 219 Penn Dr West Hartford CT 06119 Office: 790 Farmington Ave Farmington CT 06032

UCELAY, MARGARITA, educator, author; b. Madrid, Spain, May 5, 1916; d. Enrique and Pura (Maortua) Ucelay; B.A., Inst. Escuela, Madrid, 1933; student U. Madrid Sch. Law, 1933-36; M.A., Columbia, 1942, Ph.D., 1950; m. Ernesto DaCal, Oct. 28, 1936 (div. 1965); 1 son, Enrique. Came to U.S., 1939, naturalized, 1945. Instr. Spanish, Vassar Coll., 1940-42, Hunter Coll., 1942-43; mem. faculty Barnard Coll., 1943—, prof. Spanish, 1967—, chmn. dept., 1962-70, 73-76, 78—; active exptl. theatre groups, 1933—. Recipient Hispanic medal Am. Assn. Tchrs. Spanish, 1942. Author: Los esp anoles pintados por sí mismos: estudio de un género constumbrista, 1951; (with E. DaCal) Literatura Del Siglo XX, 1968; (with A. del Río) Visión de España, 1968. Home: 300 Riverside Dr New York NY 10025

UCHENDU, VICTOR CHIKEZIE, educator; b. Nsirimo, Nigeria, Jan. 1, 1932; s. Aburonye Isaac and Sabina Ogbuisi (Enyidiya) U.; B.Sc., U. London, 1962; M.A., Northwestern U., 1963, Ph.D. (Rockefeller Found. fellow), 1965; m. Caroline Urasi Onuoha, Dec. 22, 1959; children—Carolyn Ijeoma, Chimela Victor, Clarita Uchechi, Chike, Chinturu, Chinwe. Asst. prof. Stanford (Calif.) U., 1966-69; research asso. Makerere U., Uganda, 1966-67; research asso. U. Ghana, 1967-68; sr. lectr. Makerere Inst. Social Research, Uganda, 1969-70, reader anthropology and dir., 1970-71; dir. African Studies Center, prof. anthropology U. Ill., Urbana, 1971—; cons. UNESCO, govt. and pvt. founds. Mem. vis. com. Afro Am. studies dept. Harvard U., 1974-77. Fellow Am. Anthropol. Assn.; mem. African Studies Assn. (v.p. 1975, pres. 1976), Assn. Applied Anthropology, Internat. African Inst. Britain, Royal Anthrop. Inst. Britain and Ireland, Assn. Current Anthropology. Club: Rotary. Author several books. Contbr. articles to profl. jours. Home: 2401 Barberry Dr Champaign IL 61820 Office: 1208 W California St Urbana IL 61801

UCHITELLE, LOUIS, journalist; b. N.Y.C., Mar. 21, 1932; s. Abraham and Alice Lee (Cronbach) U.; B.A., U. Mich., 1954; m. Joan Eva Shapiro, Oct. 7, 1966; children—Isabel Anne, Jennifer Emily. Reporter, Mt. Vernon (N.Y.) Daily Argus, 1955-57; with AP, 1957—, fgn. corr. and bur. chief AP, San Juan, P.R., 1964-67, Buenos Aires, Argentina, 1967-73, supervising editor AP Newsfeatures, N.Y.C., 1974-76, bus. news editor, 1977—; asso. prof. journalism Sch. Gen. Studies, Columbia U., 1976—. Home: 11 Ridgecrest W Scarsdale NY 10583 Office: AP 50 Rockefeller Plaza New York NY 10020

UCKO, KURT, fgn. trader; b. Frankfurt, Germany, Aug. 25, 1921 (parents Am. citizens) s. Felix E. and Eva (Beck) U.; student Goethe U. (Germany), 1940-42; m. Martha Kribben, June 24, 1947; children—Linda, Lloyd. Vice-pres. Transmares Corp., N.Y.C., 1948-52; v.p. Kurt Orban Co. Inc., Wayne, N.J., 1952-64, exec. v.p., 1964-76; pres. Ucko Machine Tools Co., Fairfield, N.J., 1976—. Served with AUS, 1942-46. Home: Box 1862 Wayne NJ 07470 also 12 Valley View Terr Packanack Lake NJ 07470 Office: Box 1388 Fairfield NJ 07006

UDALL, CALVIN HUNT, lawyer; b. St. Johns, Ariz., Oct. 23, 1923; s. Grover C. and Dora (Sherwood) U.; LL.B., U. Ariz., 1948; m. Doris Fuss, Dec. 11, 1943; children—Fredric, Margaret Udall Learn, Julie (Mrs. Blair M. Nash), Lucinda (Mrs. Douglas Johnson), Tina. Admitted to Ariz. bar, 1948; practice in St. Johns, 1948-49; asst. atty. gen. Ariz., 1949-51; practice in Phoenix, 1951—; partner firm Fennemore, Craig, von Ammon & Udall, and predecessor, 1953—. Chmn. Ariz. Jr. Bar Conf., 1954. Bd. dirs. Boys Clubs Phoenix, 1956-78; mem. co. Phoenix Musical Theatre, 1959-65. Fellow Am. Bar Found., Am. Coll. Trial Lawyers; mem. Am. (ho. dels. 1962—), Maricopa County (bd. dirs. 1954-58; pres. 1957) bar assns., State Bar Ariz. (bd. govs. 1960-65), Lawyers Club Phoenix (founding dir. 1961-65; 1st pres. 1961), U. Ariz. Alumni Assn. (bd. dirs. 1959-64), Ariz. Law Coll. Assn. (founding dir. 1967—, pres. 1978-79), Am. Judicature Soc. Served with USAAF, 1942-43. Home: Phoenix AZ Office: 100 W Washington St Suite 1700 Phoenix AZ 85003

UDALL, MORRIS KING, congressman; b. St. Johns, Ariz., June 15, 1922; s. Levi S. and Louise (Lee) U.; LL.B. with distinction, U. Ariz., 1949; m. Ella Royston, 1968; children (by previous marriage)—Mark, Judith, Randolph, Anne, Bradley, Katherine. Admitted to Ariz. bar, 1949; partner firm Udall & Udall, Tucson, 1949-61; chief dep. county atty. Pima County, 1950-52; county atty. Pima County, 1953-54; lectr. labor law U. Ariz., 1955-56; mem. 87th-96th Congresses, 2d Dist. Ariz.; chmn. House Com. on Interior and Insular Affairs; vice chmn. Com. on Post Office and Civil Service; chmn. Office Tech. Assessment. A founder Bank of Tucson, 1959, former dir.; former chmn. bd. Catalina Savs. and Loan Assn. Chmn. Ariz. Com. for Modern Cts., 1960. Del. Democratic Nat. Conv., 1956, chmn. Ariz. delegation, 1972; chmn. Ariz. Volunteers for Stevenson, 1956; candidate for Dem. nomination for Pres., 1976. Served to capt. USAAF, 1942-46; PTO. Mem. Am., Ariz. (bd. govs.), Pima County (exec. com.) bar assns., Am. Judicature Soc., Am. Legion, Phi Kappa Phi, Phi Delta Phi. Author: Arizona Law of Evidence, 1960; Education of a Congressman, 1972; co-author The Job of the Congressman, 1966. Office: Cannon House Office Bldg Washington DC 20515

UDALL, STEWART LEE, author, lawyer, former sec. of interior; b. St. Johns, Ariz., Jan. 31, 1920; s. Levi S. and Louise (Lee) U.; LL.B., U. Ariz., 1948; m. Ermalee Webb, Aug. 1, 1947; children—Thomas, Scott, Lynn, Lori, Denis, James. Admitted to Ariz. bar, 1948, practiced in Tucson, 1948-54, Washington, 1969—; mem. 84th-86th Congresses, 2d Dist. Ariz.; U.S. sec. of interior, 1961-69; of counsel firm Duncan, Brown, Weinberg and Palmer, Washington. Chmn. bd. Overview Corp., 1969—; writer syndicated column Udall on the Environment, 1970—. Served with USAAF, 1944. Mem. Am. Bar Assn. Mem. Ch. of Jesus Christ of Latter Day Saints. Author: The Quiet Crisis, 1963, 1976: Agenda for Tommorrow, 1968; America's Natural Treasures, 1971; (with others) The National Parks of America, 1972; co-author: The Energy Balloon, 1974. Office: care Duncan Brown Weinberg and Palmer 1775 Pennsylvania Ave Suite 1200 NW Washington DC 20006*

UDENFRIEND, SIDNEY, biochemist; b. N.Y.C., Apr. 5, 1918; s. Max and Esther (Tabak) U.; B.S., Coll. City N.Y., 1939; M.S., N.Y. U., 1942, Ph.D., 1948; D.Sc. honoris causa, N.Y. Med. Coll., 1974, Coll. Medicine and Dentistry of N.J., 1979; m. Shirley Frances Reidel, June 20, 1943; children—Alice, Elliot. Lab. asst. N.Y.C. Dept. Health, 1940-42; jr. chemist N.Y. U. Research Service, 1942-43, asst. chemist, 1943-44, research chemist, 1944-46, research asst. Med. Sch., 1946-47, instr., 1947-48; instr. Washington U. Med. Sch., 1948-50; biochemist Nat. Heart Inst., Bethesda, Md., 1950-53, head sect. cellular pharmacology lab. chem. pharmacology, 1953-56, chief lab. clin. biochemistry, 1956-68; now dir. Roche Inst. Molecular Biology, N.J.; professorial lectr. George Washington U., 1953-70; adj. prof. human genetics and devel. dept. Columbia U., 1969—; adj. prof. dept. biochemistry City U. N.Y., 1968—, dept. pharmacology Emory U., 1976—; mem. sci. adv. bd. Scripps Clinic and Research Found., 1974-78; mem. adv. com. to dir. NIH, 1976-78; mem. Sci. Adv. Com. for Cystic Fibrosis. Trustee Wistar Inst., 1968-71; mem. adv. bd. Weizmann Inst. Sci., 1978-79, bd. govs., 1979—. Recipient Cert. of Merit for studies on malignant carcinoid A.M.A., 1956, Arthur S. Flemming award, 1958; City of Hope research award, 1975; NIH fellow St. Mary's Hosp. Med. Sch., London, Eng., 1957; Harvey lectr., 1964; recipient Superior Service award Dept. HEW, 1965, Distinguished Service award, 1966; Gairdner Found. award, 1967; Heinrich Waelsch lectr. in neurosci., 1978. Fellow N.Y. Acad. Scis. (trustee 1978—); mem. Am. Soc. Biol. Chemists, Am. Soc. Pharmacology and Exptl. Therapeutics (sec.), A.A.A.S., Soc. Exptl. Biology and Medicine, Am. Assn. Clin. Chemists (Van Slyke award 1967, Ames award 1969), Am. Chem. Soc. (Hillebrand award 1962, Torald Sollmann award 1975), Nat. Acad. Scis., Am. Acad. Arts and Scis., Japanese Pharmacol. Soc. (hon.), Japanese Biochem. Soc. (hon.), Czechoslovak Pharmacology Soc. (hon.), Sigma Xi. Home: 22 Maple Dr North Caldwell NJ 07006 Office: Roche Inst Nutley NJ 07110

UDICK, ROBERT E., newspaper exec.; b. Colorado Springs, Colo., May 27, 1922; s. Albert Earl and Edna (Young) U.; student Colo. U. Staff corr. Rocky Mountain News, Denver, 1947-49, United Press Denver and Santa Fe, 1950-51; war corr. Korea, 1951-53, later became mgr. Hong Kong and Manila burs., then mgr. for Southeast Asia, hdqrs. Singapore; editor, pub. Bangkok World, until 1967; now pub. Pacific Daily News, Agana, Guam. Mem. civilian adv. bd. 8th Air Force; mem. Navy League, Guam Stock Exchange. Bd. regents U. Guam. Served with Coast Arty., Inf., Signal Corps, World War II. Mem. Fgn. Corr. Assn. Thailand (pres.), Phi Delta Theta. Rotarian. Address: Pacific Daily News PO Box DN Agana Guam 96910. *Given the opportunities and options actually available to you, you always do what you want to do most. "Most" is the operative word. Anyone who acts or makes a decision and says, "I didn't want to do that" is trying to fool someone, perhaps, tragically, himself.*

UDOVITCH, ABRAHAM LABE, historian, educator; b. Winnipeg, Man., Can., May 31, 1933; s. Benjamin Alexander and Minnie (Benson) U.; came to U.S., naturalized, 1966; B.S., Columbia, 1958, M.A., 1959; Ph.D., Yale, 1965; m. Joan Sheila Diamond, Sept. 9, 1956; children—Tamar, Miriam Esther. Asst. prof. Middle East history Brandeis U., 1964-65, Cornell U., 1965-67; asso. prof. Middle East history Princeton, 1968-71, prof., 1971—, chmn. dept. Nr. Eastern studies, 1973—. Bd. govs. Am. Research Inst. in Turkey, 1969—; dir. Middle East study panel Commn. on Critical Choices for Americans, 1974—. Trustee, N.E. Pooled Common Fund. Guggenheim fellow, 1970-71. Mem. Am. Oriental Soc. (chmn. Islamic sect. 1972—), Middle East Studies Assn., Econ. History Assn. Author: Partnership and Profit in Medieval Islam, 1970. Editor: Studia Islamica, 1975. Editorial bd. Jour. of Interdisciplinary History, 1970—, Internat. Jour. of Middle East Studies, 1975—; mem. exec. com. Ency. of Islam. Home: 7F Magie Apts Princeton NJ 08540

UDOW, MICHAEL WILLIAM, percussionist, composer; b. Detroit, Mar. 10, 1949; s. Jack B. and Madeline (Miller) U.; student Settlement Music Sch., 1963-64, Interlochen Arts Acad., 1965-66; B.A., U. Ill., 1971, M.Mus., 1975, D.M.A. in Percussion, 1978; m. Nancy Lee Wagner, Aug. 6, 1972. Prin. percussionist Santa Fe Opera Co., 1968-72, 74-79; percussionist New Orleans Phil., 1971; percussionist PWSM, Warsaw, Poland, 1972, Amerika, Haus, Berlin, 1973; charter mem., percussionist Blackearth Percussion Group, 1972—; mem. faculty No. Ill. U., 1973, U. Mo., Kansas City, 1979—; artist-in-residence U. Ill., 1975; touring internationally with Nancy Udow performing works for percussion and movement, 1976-79. Recipient Student Composers' award Broadcast Music Inc., 1971; Fulbright-Hays and Polish Govt. grantee, Poland, 1971; Creative Performing Arts fellow U. Ill., 1974-76; Edgard Varesé scholar, 1976. Mem. Broadcast Music Inc., Am. Composers Alliance, Am. Soc. Univ. Composers, Percussive Arts Soc., Phi Eta Sigma. Author: An Acoustical Notation for Percussively Generated Sounds; Rhythmic Source Book for Actors, Dancers, and Musicians, 1976. Composer: African Welcome Piece, 1971; Understanding, 1971; Seven Textural Settings of Japanese Poetry, 1970; Concerto for Percussion with String Quartet; Acoustic Composition #1 for 1-5 percussioninsts and monophonic tape, 1973; Acoustic Composition #2 for tenor trombone, 1974; Acoustic Study #1 for solo percussion, 1973; Music for Carillon and Concert Choir, 1974; Bog Music (1st prize Percussive Arts Soc. Internat. Competition), 1978. Inventor mus. instruments and mallets. Home: U Mo Conservatory of Music Kansas City MO 64110. *I am a percussionist-composer concerned with the precarious relationship between audiences and the contemporary arts. I try to compose and perform works which provoke thought and creative listening on the part of each member of an audience. I choose to view my workshops not as music education, but rather as education through music.*

UEBEL, J. JOHN, chemist, educator; b. Chgo., Dec. 25, 1937; s. Jacob and Elsie (Loibl) U.; B.A., Carthage Coll., 1959; M.S., U. Ill., 1962, Ph.D., 1964; m. Kathleen Ann Garman, Aug. 23, 1958; children—Virginia, John, Mark. Chemist, Ill. Water Survey, Urbana, 1958; research asso. U. Mich., 1964; asst. prof. U. N.H., 1964-68, prof. chemistry, 1972—; vis. prof. U. Calif., Riverside, 1971; vis. scientist Eastman Kodak Co., 1978-79; cons. to pubs. and chem. industry. Treas., Ch. Sch. Durham United Ch. of Christ, 1968-69, chmn. nomination com., 1976. Mem. Am. Chem. Soc., Sigma Xi, Gamma Kappa Alpha. Contbr. articles to profl. jours. Office: Parsons Hall Chemistry Dept Durham NH 03824

UEHLING, BARBARA STANER, univ. chancellor; b. Wichita, Kans., June 12, 1932; d. Roy W. and Mary Elizabeth (Hilt) Staner; B.A., U. Wichita, 1954; M.A., Northwestern U., 1956, Ph.D., 1958; hon. degree Wichita State U., 1978; children—Jeffrey Steven, David Edward. Mem. psychology faculty Oglethorpe U.. Atlanta, 1959-64, Emory U., Atlanta, 1966-69; adj. prof. U. R.I., Kingston, 1970-72; dean Roger Williams Coll., Bristol, R.I., 1972-74; dean arts scis. Ill. State U., Normal, 1974-76; provost U. Okla., Norman, 1976-78; chancellor U. Mo.-Columbia, 1978—; cons. higher edn. State of N.Y., 1973-74; cons. N. Central Accreditation Assn., 1975—; mem. nat. educator adv. com. to Comptroller Gen. U.S., 1978; mem. commn. on mil.-higher edn. relations Am. Council on Edn., 1978. Bd. dirs., chmn. Nat. Center Higher Edn. Mgmt. Statistics; bd. dirs. Am. Council on Edn., 1979-80; trustee Carnegie Found. for Advancement of Teaching, 1980-81. Social Sci. Research Council fellow, 19S4-55; NSF fellow, 1956-57; NIMH postdoctoral research fellow, 1964-67; named one of 100 Young Leaders of Acad., Change Mag. and ACE, 1978; recipient Alumni Achievement award Wichita State U., 1978. Mem. Am. Assn. Higher Edn. (dir. 1974-77, pres. 1977-78), Sigma Xi. Author: Women in Academe: Steps to Greater Equality, 1978; also articles in profl. jours. Office: Office of Chancellor Univ Mo-Columbia 105 Jesse Hall Columbia MO 65211

UELAND, KENT, physician, educator; b. Chgo., May 27, 1931; s. Lars Berthold and Gudrun (Pedersen) U.; student St. Olaf Coll., 1949-50; B.A., Carleton Coll., 1953; B.S., U. Ill., 1957, M.D., 1957; m. Theresa Mae Karshner, Aug. 9, 1971; children—Harold K., Philip C., Carl B., Frederick R. Intern, U. Oreg. Hosps. and Clinics, Portland, 1957-58, research fellow, 1964; resident in obstetrics and gynecology Harborview Med. Center, Univ. Hosp., Seattle, 1960-63; research fellow in cardiovascular research tng. program. dept. physiology and biophysics U. Wash., Seattle, 1963, instr. obstetrics and gynecology, 1964-65, asst. prof., 1965-69, asso. prof., 1969-74, prof., 1974-77; prof. Stanford (Calif.) U., 1977—; practice medicine specializing in obstetrics and gynecology, maternal and fetal medicine; mem. staff Univ. Hosp., Seattle, 1964-77, dir. obstetrics, 1968-77; asst. obstetrician, gynecologist-in-chief King County Hosp., Seattle, 1965-68; mem. staff Harborview Med. Center, Seattle, 1974-77; chief sect. maternal and fetal medicine Stanford U. Med. Center, 1977—, Santa Clara Valley Med. Center, 1977—; obstet. cons. Nat. Found. March Dimes, Internat. Childbirth Edn. Assn., Kaiser Found. Hosps. Served with M.C., U.S. Army, 1958-60. Diplomate Am. Bd. Obstetrics and Gynecology. Fellow Am. Coll. Obstetricians and Gynecologists; mem. Soc. for Gynecologic Investigation, Soc. for Obstet. Anesthesia and Perinatology, Soc. Perinatal Obstetricians, Calif. Perinatal Assn., Wash. Heart Assn., Shufelt Gynecologic Soc. Santa Clara Valley, San Francisco Gynecol. Soc., Peninsula Gynecol. Soc. Editorial referee Am. Jour. Obstetrics and Gynecology, 1970—, Anesthesiology, 1977—; editorial bd. Perinatal Medicine; guest editor Clin. Obstetrics and Gynecology; research in pregnancy and maternal cardiovascular physiology, heart disease and pregnancy, maternal-fetal medicine. Home: 13601 Paseo del Roble Los Altos Hills CA 94022 Office: Dept Gynecology and Obstetrics Stanford U Stanford CA 94305

UELNER, ROY WALTER, agrl. equipment exec.; b. Dubuque, Iowa, Aug. 24, 1936; s. Felix Hugo and Susan M. (Phillipp) U.; B.S. in Indsl. Engring., Iowa State U., 1957; m. Sandra S. Hammerand, Dec. 13, 1958; children—Steven Roy, Scott Michael. Various mfg. engring. and mgmt. positions Allen-Bradley, Inc., Milw., 1957-64; with Allis-Chalmers Corp., 1964—, indsl. engr. agrl. equipment div., La Crosse, Wis., 1964-65, gen. plant mgr., 1965-68; gen. mgr. Independence (Mo.) plant, 1968-70, mgr. combine operation, Independence, 1970-72; mgr. sales and mktg. agrl. equipment div., Milw., 1971-72, gen. mgr., 1972-73, v.p., 1973, group exec. and v.p. agrl. equipment group, 1974-76, exec. v.p., 1976—. Served with U.S. Army, 1958. Mem. Farm and Indsl. Equipment Inst. (chmn.), Am. Soc. Agrl. Engrs., Tau Beta Pi, Phi Kappa Phi. Home: 2775 Woodbridge Ct Brookfield WI 53005 Office: 1205 S 70th St Milwaukee WI 53201

UELSMANN, JERRY NORMAN, photographer; b. Detroit, June 11, 1934; s. Norman Charles and Florence Gertrude (Crossman) U.; B.F.A., Rochester (N.Y.) Inst. Tech., 1957; M.S., Ind. U., 1958, M.F.A., 1960; m. F. Diane Farris, Mar. 22, 1975. Mem. faculty U. Fla., Gainesville, 1960—, grad. research prof. photography, 1974—; one-man exhbns. include Mus. Modern Art, N.Y.C., 1967, Art Inst. Chgo., 1972, Phila. Mus. Art, 1970, San Francisco Mus. Modern Art, 1977; rep. permanent collections Mus. Modern Art, Nat. Gallery Can., Victoria and Albert Mus., London, Eogg Mus. at Harvard U., Mus. Fine Arts, Boston. Fellow Nat. Endowment Arts, 1972, Guggenheim Found., 1967; named Tchr.-Scholar of Year, U. Fla., 1975. Fellow Royal Photog. Soc. Gt. Britain; mem. Soc. Photog. Edn. (a founder), Friends of Photography, Internat. Mus. Photography at George Eastman House. Home: 5701 SW 17th Dr Gainesville FL 32608 Office: Art Dept Univ Fla Gainesville FL 32611

UFFEN, ROBERT JAMES, univ. dean, geophysicist; b. Toronto, Ont., Can., Sept. 21, 1923; s. James Frederick and Elsie May (Harris) U.; B.A.Sc., U. Toronto, 1949, M.A., 1950; Ph.D., U. Western Ont., 1952, D.Sc., 1970; D.Sc., Queen's U., 1967, Royal Mil. Coll., 1978; m. Mary Ruth Paterson, May 3, 1949; children—Joanne Grace, Robert Ross. Mem. faculty U. Western Ont., 1951-66, prin. Univ. Coll., 1961-65, dean Coll. Sci., 1965-66; vice chmn. Def. Research Bd., Ottawa, Can., 1966, chmn., 1967-69; chief sci. adviser to Cabinet, Ottawa, 1969-71; dean faculty applied sci. Queen's U., Kingston, Ont., 1971—; vis. fellow U. Sussex, 1976-77. Dir. Canadian Patents and Devel. Ltd., 1967-72; vice chmn. Ont. Hydro-Electric Power Corp., 1974—. Mem. NRC, 1963-66; del. Internat. Union Geologic Soc., New Delhi, India, 1964; chief del. for Can. Internat. Union Geodesy and Geophysics, 1967; mem. Sci. Council of Can., 1967-71, Club of Rome, 1968—; chmn. Canadian Engring. Manpower Council, 1972-74; mem. Fisheries Research Bd., 1975—. Mem. council regents Colls. Applied Arts and Tech., Ont., 1966-69, 73-76; mem. adv. bd. Canadian Mil. Colls., 1967-73. Research Council Ont. scholar, 1950, 51; research fellow Inst. Geophysics, U. Calif. at Los Angeles. Served to lt. Canadian Army, 1942-45. Fellow Royal Soc. Can., Geol. Soc. Am.; mem. Am. Inst. Mining, Metall. and Petroleum Engrs., Canadian Inst. Mining and Metallurgy, A.A.A.S., Soc. Exploration Geophysicists, Am. Geophys. Union, Canadian Assn. Physicists. Clubs: Rideau (Ottawa); Cataraqui Golf (Kingston). Mem. editorial bd. Earth and Planetary Science Letters, 1965-69, Tectonophysics, 1964—. Co-discoverer Lac Allard ilmenite, deposits; publs. on temperature of earth's interior, origin of volcanoes and influence of evolution of earth's interior on origin and evolution of geomagnetic field and evolution of life, radioactive waste mgmt. and sci. policy. Office: Dean Faculty Applied Science Queen's Univ Kingston ON Canada

UFHEIL, JOHN LLOYD, splty. chem. mfg. co. exec.; b. Pekin, Ill., Sept. 3, 1933; s. Albert Adolph and Leora Ellen (Flathers) U.; B.S. in Indsl. Engring., Bradley U., 1958; m. Rosemary, Feb. 8, 1958; children—Tracey Ellen, John Thomas, Patricia Anne. Area mng. dir. Baxter-Travenol Labs., Inc., Deerfield, Ill., 1959-75; v.p. mktg. and ops. C. R. Bard, Inc., Murray Hill, N.J., 1975-76; pres. Litton Med. Systems, Des Plaines, Ill., 1976-77; sr. v.p. Mallinckrodt, Inc., St. Louis, 1977—. Served with U.S. Army, 1953-55. Office: 675 Brown Rd PO Box 5840 Saint Louis MO 63134

UGGAMS, LESLIE, entertainer; b. N.Y.C., May 25, 1943; d. Harolde and Juanita (Smith) U.; student Juillard Sch. Music, 1961-63; m. Grahame Pratt, Oct. 17, 1965. Appeared on Beulah TV show, 1949; featured on Sing Along With Mitch, 1961-64; starred in Broadway play Hallelujah Baby, 1967, also nightclubs, top television mus. variety shows; appeared in film Skyjacked, 1972; appeared on ABC-TV's Roots, 1977. Recipient Tony award, 1968, Drama Critics award, 1968; Critics Choice award as best supporting actress in Roots, 1977; chosen Best Singer on TV, 1962, 63. Author: The Leslie Uggams Beauty Book, 1966. Address: care ICM 40 W 57th St New York NY 10019*

UHDE, GEORGE IRVIN, physician; b. Richmond, Ind., Mar. 20, 1912; s. Walter Richard and Anna Margaret (Hoopes) U.; M.D., Duke U., 1936; m. Maurine Elizabeth Whitley, July 27, 1935; children—Saundra Uhde Seelig, Thomas Whitley, Michael, Janice. Intern, Reading (Pa.) Hosp., 1936-37, resident in medicine, 1937-38; resident in otolaryngology Balt. Eye, Ear, Nose and Throat Hosp., 1938-40, U. Oreg. Med. Sch., Portland, 1945-47; practice medicine specializing in otolaryngology, Louisville, 1948—; asst. prof. otolaryngology U. Louisville Med. Sch., 1945-62, prof. surgery (otolaryngology), head dept., 1963—, dir. otolaryngology services, 1963—; mem. staffs Meth., Norton's-Children's, Jewish, St. Joseph's, St. Anthony's, St. Mary and Elizabeth's hosps.; cons. Ky. Surg. Tb Hosp., Hazlewood, VA Hosp., Louisville, U. Louisville Speech and Hearing Center. Bd. dirs. Easter Seal Speech and Hearing Center. Served to lt. col. M.C., U.S. Army, 1940-45; ETO. Recipient Disting. Service award U. Louisville, 1972. Diplomate Am. Bd. Otolaryngology. Fellow A.C.S., Am. Acad. Ophthalmology and Otolaryngology, So. Med. Soc.; mem. N.Y. Acad. Scis., Am. Coll. Allergists, Am. Acad. Facial Plastic and Reconstructive Surgery, AAAS, Assn. U. Otolaryngologists, AAUP, Assn. Mil. Surgeons U.S., Am. Laryngol., Rhinol. and Otol. Soc., Am. Audiology Soc., Soc. Clin. Ecology, Am. Soc. Otolaryngology Allergy, Centurian Otol. Research Soc. (Ky. rep.), Am. Council Otolaryngology (Ky. rep. 1968—), Hoopes Quaker Found., Alpha Kappa Kappa. Democrat. Methodist. Clubs: Filson, Big Spring Country, Jefferson. Author 4 books. Contbr. articles to profl. jours. Home: 708 Circle Hill Rd Louisville KY 40207 Office: Med Towers South Louisville KY 40202. *Esteemed should be all rational people striving to remain healthy, happy, and working with their maximum mental and physical ability in any honest occupation regardless of pecuniary reward but most of all in the care and education of youth. May we live to leave a better world.*

UHL, EDWARD GEORGE, mfg. exec.; b. Elizabeth, N.J., Mar. 24, 1918; s. Henry and Mary (Schiller) U.; B.S., Lehigh U., 1940, D.Sc. (hon.), 1975; m. Maurine B. Keleher, July 19, 1942; children—Carol Uhl Nordingler, Kim, Scott, Cynthia; m. 2d, Mary Stuart Brugh, Sept. 17, 1966. Engr. guided missiles Martin Co., 1946-51, chief project engr., 1951-53, v.p. engring., 1953-55, v.p. operations, 1955-56, v.p., gen. mgr. Orlando div. (Fla.), 1957-59; v.p. tech. adminstrn. Ryan Aero. Co., 1959-60, v.p., div. mgr., 1961; pres., chief exec. officer, dir. Fairchild Industries, 1961-76, chmn. bd., chief exec. officer, dir., 1976—; dir. Bunker Ramo Corp., Am. Satellite Corp., Md. Nat. Bank, Md. Nat. Corp. Trustee, Johns Hopkins U.; bd. nominations Aviation Hall Fame. Recipient Hamilton Holt award Rollins Coll., 1965. Served from 2d lt. to lt. col. Ordnance Corps, AUS, 1941-46. Fellow Am. Inst. Aeros. and Astronautics; mem. Air Force Assn., Am. Def. Preparedness Assn. (dir., John C. Jones award 1975), Soc. Automotive Engrs., Nat. Space Club (gov.), Phi Beta Kappa, Tau Beta Pi. Clubs: Assembly, Fountain Head Country (Hagerstown); Federal City (Washington); Burning Tree (Bethesda, Md.); Sky, Union League (N.Y.C.). Co-inventor bazooka. Home: 2105 Hillandale Rd Hagerstown MD 21740 Office: Sherman Fairchild Tech Center Germantown MD 20767. *Progress is keyed to the individual. It is most important that each of us do his job well, work to maximum capability, accept total responsibility for results. Today's trend to submerge the individual in a group or committee must be reversed. Without the pride, conscience, skill of the individual, a group, a society, a nation is doomed to mediocrity. Let's get back to building strong productive individuals and we will automatically create strong productive societies and nations.*

UHL, KENNETH PAUL, educator; b. Ames, Iowa, July 3, 1931; s. Edward G. and Caroline C. (Tweed) U.; B.S., U. Iowa, 1953, M.A., 1958, Ph.D., 1960; m. Eleanor Lock, Oct. 11, 1951; children—Jerrie R., Terrie R., Pamela K., Paul K., Robin A., Princetta. With Maytag Co., 1956-57; instr. U. Iowa, 1958-59, asst. prof., 1960-63, asst. dean, 1963-64, asso. prof. dept. bus., 1963-67, chmn. dept. bus., 1966-68, prof. dept. bus. adminstrn., 1967-72; asst. prof. U. Ariz., 1959-60; vis. prof. U. Wash., 1964-65; prof., head dept. bus. adminstrn. U. Ill., Urbana, 1972—; vis. prof. Australian Grad. Sch. Mgmt., 1978; mktg. cons., 1960—. Served to 1st lt. USAF, 1953-55. Research grantee U. Iowa, 1967-68, research award Consumers Research Inst., 1969-70, research prof. award U. Iowa, 1970. Ford Found. Mktg. Workshop fellow, 1963. Mem. Am. Inst. for Decision Scis. (v.p. membership 1970-71, 73-74, nat. program chmn. 1972-73, pres. 1975-76), Am. Mktg. Assn. (nat. program chmn. research tract 1972, nat. dir. 1975—), Alpha Iota Delta. Author: (with J. Carman) Marketing: Principles and Methods, 7th edit., 1973; (with T. Pogue) Direct State Taxes on Advertising Services: Economic Implications, 1973; Marketing Today, 1975; (with B. Schoner) Marketing Research: Information Systems and Decision Making, 2d edit., 1975. Home: 3203 Valley Brook Dr Champaign IL 61820 Office: Dept Bus Adminstrn U Ill 350 Commerce W Urbana IL 61801

UHL, WILFRED OTTO, utility co. exec.; b. N.Y.C., Sept. 8, 1927; s. Otto Jacob and Lucie Anna (Hardekopf) U.; B.E.E., Cooper Union, 1949; postgrad. Poly. Inst. Bklyn., 1953-55; m. Gloria Leona Lane, Dec. 14, 1948; children—Jeanette (Mrs. George Newton), Warren, David. With L.I. Lighting Co., Mineola, N.Y., 1949—, sr. v.p. engring., constrn., 1974-78, pres., 1978—. Mem. industry com. State U. at Stony Brook, 1973—, Hofstra U., 1975—. Bd. dirs. Nassau-Suffolk chpt. Am. Lung Assn. Served with USAAF, 1946-47. Mem. I.E.E.E., N.Y. Soc. Profl. Engrs. Office: Long Island Lighting Co 250 Old Country Rd Mineola NY 11501

UHLENHOPP, HARVEY HAROLD, state supreme ct. justice; b. Butler County, Iowa, June 23, 1915; s. Henry Harold and Charlotte Ellen Wade (Green) U.; A.B., Grinnell Coll., 1936, LL.D., 1971; J.D., U. Iowa, 1939; m. Elizabeth Christine Elliott, June 20, 1940; children—Elliott L., John C. Admitted to Iowa bar, 1939; practice in

Hampton, 1939-43, 46-53; county atty. Franklin County, Iowa, 1947-50; dist. judge Ia., 1953-70; justice Iowa Supreme Ct., 1970—. Mem. Iowa Legislature from Franklin County, 1951-52. Served with USCG, 1943-45. Mem. Am. Law Inst., Am. Judicature Soc., Inst. Jud. Adminstrn., Am., Iowa bar assns., Order of Coif. Mem. United Ch. Christ. Contbr. to legal jours. Home: 815 4th Ave SE Hampton IA 50441 Office: PO Box 341 Hampton IA 50441

UHLENHUTH, EBERHARD HENRY, psychiatrist, educator; b. Balt., Sept. 15, 1927; s. Eduard Carl Adolph and Elisabeth (Baier) U.; B.S. in Chemistry, Yale U., 1947; M.D., Johns Hopkins U., 1951; m. Helen Virginia Lyman, June 20, 1952; children—Kim Lyman, Karen Jane, Eric Rolf. Intern, King County Hosp., Seattle, 1951-52; resident in psychiatry Johns Hopkins Hosp. Balt., 1952-56, asst. psychiatrist-in-charge outpatient dept., 1956-61, psychiatrist-in-charge, 1961-62; chief, adult psychiatry clinic U. Chgo. Hosps. Clinics, 1968-76; instr. psychiatry Johns Hopkins U., 1956-59, asst. prof., 1959-67, asso. prof.. 1967-68; asso. prof. U. Chgo., 1968-73, prof., 1973—; cons. in field; mem. clin. psychopharmacology research rev. com. NIMH, 1968-72; mem. psychopharmacology advisory com. FDA, 1974-78. Recipient Research Career Devel. award USPHS, 1962-68, Research Scientist award, 1976-81. Fellow Am. Coll. Neuropsychopharmacology, Am. Psychiat. Assn.; mem. AAAS, Balt. Psychoanalytic Soc., Collegium Internationale Neuro-Psychopharmacologicum, Psychatric Research Soc. Contbr. articles to profl. jours. Mem. editorial bd. Jour. Affective Disorders, 1978—. Home: 6836 Euclid Ave Chicago IL 60649 Office: Dept Psychiatry Box 411 University of Chicago 950 E 59th St Chicago IL 60637

UHLIR, ARTHUR, JR., elec. engr., univ. adminstr.; b. Chgo., Feb. 2, 1926; s. Arthur and Helene (Houghteling) U.; B.S., Ill. Inst. Tech., 1945, M.S. in Chem. Engring., 1948; S.M. in Physics, U. Chgo., 1950, Ph.D. in Physics, 1952; m. Ingeborg Williams, July 24, 1954; children—Steven, Donald, David. Process analyst Douglas Aircraft, Chgo., 1945; asst. engr. Armour Research Found., Chgo., 1945-48; mem. tech. staff Bell Telephone Labs., Murray Hill, N.J., 1951-58; dir. semi- condr. research and devel., mgr. semicondr. div., group v.p. engring. Microwave Assos., Inc., Burlington, Mass., 1958-69; dir. research Computer Metrics, Rochelle Park, N.J., 1969-73; prof. elec. engring. Tufts U., Medford, Mass., 1970—, chmn. dept. elec. engring., 1970-75, dean of engring., 1973—. AEC fellow, 1949-51. Fellow IEEE; mem. Am. Phys. Soc., AAAS, Sigma Xi. Home: 45 Kendal Common Rd Weston MA 02193 Office: Elec Engring Dept Tufts Univ Medford MA 02155

UHLMAN, WES CARL, lawyer; b. Cashmere, Wash., Mar. 13, 1935; s. Werner and Dorcas (Zimmerman) U.; student Seattle Pacific Coll., 1952-54; B.A., U. Wash., 1956, LL.B., 1959; m. Laila Hammond, Dec. 28, 1957; children—Wesley Carl, Daniel Willard. Admitted to Wash. bar, 1960, since practiced in Seattle; mem. Wash. Ho. of Reps., 1958-70, chmn. com. higher edn., 1961-70, chmn. Senate jud. com.; mayor of Seattle, 1969-78; past pres. Puget Sound Govt. Conf.; cons. HUD, 1978—, NSF, 1977. Chmn. 32d Dist. Democratic Orgn., 1960-62; trustee U.S. Conf. Mayors; pres. Nat. Assn. Reg. Councils; mem. Fed. Council on Aging, 1978—; mem. bd. Nat. Endowment for Arts, Am. Council Arts, Japan-Am. Conf. Mayors; bd. dirs. Wallingford Boys' Club. Named Outstanding Young Man, Wash. Jr. C. of C., 1963. Mem. Am. Arbitration Assn. (panel arbitrators 1978—), Pi Sigma Alpha, Theta Delta Chi, Phi Alpha Delta. Methodist. Clubs: Kiwanis; Coll. (Seattle); Wallingford Comml. Office: 2720 Rainier Bank Tower Seattle WA 98101. *Nothing is more important in politics and government today than to convince young people that it is an honorable and worthy profession. Unless those of us who are involved in the political process use our influence and example to reaffirm the fundamental responsibility of government to serve the people—and not the office holder—then we have no hope of attracting the bright young idealistic leadership that our nation must have to meet its future.*

UHRICH, RICHARD LEE, former food co. exec.; b. Lebanon, Pa., Nov. 12, 1913; s. William Fisher and Virginia (Klick) U.; student U. Pa., 1940; m. Marylou Pattillo, Oct. 11, 1947; 1 son, Richard Lee. With Hershey Foods Corp., 1930—, asst. sec., 1947-61, sec., 1961-78, v.p., 1971-78, also dir.; former sec., dir. San Giorgio Macaroni, Inc., Cory Corp. Served to maj. AUS, 1942-46; ETO. Decorated Bronze Star; Croix de Guerre (France). Republican. Lutheran. Rotarian. Home: 343 E Granada Ave Hershey PA 17033

UHRIG, ROBERT EUGENE, engr., utility co. exec.; b. Raymond, Ill., Aug. 6, 1928; s. John Matthew and Anna LaDonna (Fireman) U.; B.S. with honors, U. Ill., 1948; M.S., Iowa State U., 1950, Ph.D., 1954; grad. Advanced Mgmt. Program, Harvard U., 1976: m. Paula Margaret Schnepf, Nov. 27, 1954; children—Robert John, Joseph Charles, Mary Catherine, Charles William, Jean Marie, Thomas Paul, Frederick James. Instr. engring. mechanics Iowa State U., 1948-51, asso. engr., research asst. Inst. Atomic Research at univ., 1951-54, asso. prof. engring. mechanics and nuclear engring., also group leader, 1956-60; prof. nuclear engring., chmn. dept. U. Fla., Gainesville, 1960-68, on leave, 1967-68, dean Coll. Engring., 1968-73; dep. asst. dir. research Dept. Def., Washington, 1967-68; dir. nuclear affairs Fla. Power & Light Co., Miami, 1973-74, v.p. for nuclear affairs, 1974-75, v.p. nuclear and gen. engring., 1976-78, v.p. advanced systems and tech., 1978—; dir. EFC Services, Miami. Rep. Dept. Def. to com. on acad. sci. and engring. Fed. Council Sci. and Tech., 1967; chmn. engring. adv. com. NSF, 1972-73; bd. dirs. Engring. Council Profl. Devel., 1968-72; mem. commn. edn. for engring. profession Nat. Assn. State Univs. and Land Grant Colls., 1969-72. Served to 1st lt. USAF, instr. engring. mechanics U.S. Mil. Acad., 1954-56. Recipient Sec. of Def. Civilian Service award, 1968, Outstanding Alumni award U. Ill. Coll. Engring., 1970, Alumni Profl. Achievement award Iowa State U., 1972, President's medallion U. Fla., 1973. Registered profl. engr., Iowa, Fla. Fellow Am. Nuclear Soc. (chmn. edn. com. 1962-64; chmn. tech. group for edn. 1964-66; dir. 1965-68, exec. com. of bd. 1966-68); mem. Am. Soc. M.E. (Richards Meml. award 1969), Am. Soc. Engring. Edn. (pres. S.E. sect. 1972-73; chmn. nuclear engring. div. 1966-67; research award S.E. sect. 1962), John Henry Newman Honor Soc., Sigma Xi, Tau Beta Pi, Pi Mu Epsilon, Pi Tau Sigma, Phi Kappa Phi. Author: Random Noise Techniques in Nuclear Reactor Systems, 1970, trans. into Russian, 1974. Home: 7480 SW 133d St Miami FL 33156 Office: Fla Power & Light Co PO Box 529100 Miami FL 33152

UITTI, KARL DAVID, educator; b. Calumet, Mich., Dec. 10, 1933; s. Karl Abram and Joy (Weidelman) U.; A.B., U. Calif. at Berkeley, 1952, A.M., 1952, Ph.D., 1959; student univs. Nancy and Bordeaux, 1952-54; m. Maria Esther Clark, Feb. 15, 1953 (div. Feb. 1973); children— Maria Elisabeth, Karl Gerard; m. 2d, Michelle Alice Freeman, Mar. 13, 1974; 1 son, David Charles. Instr. Princeton U., 1959-61, asst. prof., 1961-65, Class of 1936 preceptor, 1963-66, asso. prof., 1965-68, prof., 1968—, John N. Woodhull prof. modern langs., 1978—, chmn. dept. Romance langs., 1972-78; vis. prof. Universidad de P.R., U. Pa., Queens Coll., U. Iowa, U. Wash., Rutgers U., U. Calif. at Los Angeles, Johns Hopkins, École Normale Supérieure de Saint-Cloud, de Sèvres (Paris); corr. Romance Philology, 1970—; cons. Nat. Endowment for Humanities, 1976-78. Served with AUS, 1954-56. Decorated chevalier des Palmes Académiques (France); Guggenheim fellow, 1964-65; sr. fellow Nat. Endowment for Humanities, 1974-75; vis. fellow All Souls Coll., Oxford (Eng.) U., 1975. Mem. Modern Lang. Assn. Am., Linguistic Soc. Am., Medieval Acad. Am. Société linguistique romane, Phi Beta Kappa. Author: The Concept of Self in the Symbolist Novel, 1961; La Passion littéraire de Remy de Gourmont, 1962; Linguistics and Literary Theory, i969; Story, Myth and Celebration in Old French Narrative (1050-1200), 1973. Editor: Edward C. Armstrong Monographs on Medieval Literature; mem. editorial bd. Historiographica linguistica; mem. adv. council Dictionary of the Middle Ages. Home: 76 Alexander St Princeton NJ 08540

ULAM, ADAM BRUNO, educator, writer; b. Lwow, Poland, Apr. 8, 1922; s. Jozef and Anna (Auerbach) U.; came to U.S., 1939, naturalized, 1949; A.B., Brown U., 1943; Ph.D., Harvard, 1947; m. Mary Hamilton Burgwin, 1963; children—Alexander Stanislaw, Joseph Howard. Mem. faculty Harvard, 1947—, prof. govt., 1959—, Gurney prof. history and polit. sci., 1979—, research asso. Russian Research Center, 1948—, also dir.; research asso. Center for Internat. Studies, Mass. Inst. Tech., 1953-55. Guggenheim fellow, 1956, Rockefeller fellow, 1957, 60. Mem. Am. Polit. Sci. Assn., The Signet (Cambridge), Am. Acad. Arts and Scis. Democrat. Club: Badminton and Tennis. Author: Philosophical Foundations of English Socialism, 1951; Titoism and the Cominform, 1952; The Unfinished Revolution, 1960; New Face of Soviet Totalitarianism, 1963; The Bolsheviks, 1965; Expansion and Coexistence History of Soviet Foreign Policy, 1968; The Rivals: America and Russia Since World War II, 1971; The Fall of the American University, 1972; Stalin: The Man and His Era, 1973; A History of Soviet Russia, 1976; Ideologies and Illusions, 1976; In the Name of the People, 1977. Home: 17 Lowell St Cambridge MA 02138

ULANOV, BARRY, author, educator; b. N.Y.C., Apr. 10, 1918; s. Nathan A. and Jeanette (Askwith) U.; A.B., Columbia U., 1939, Ph.D., 1955; Litt.D., Villanova U., 1965; m. Joan Bel Geddes, Dec. 16, 1939; children—Anne, Nicholas, Katherine; m. 2d, Ann Belford, Aug. 21, 1968; 1 son, Alexander. Editor, Swing mag., 1939-41, Listen mag., 1940-42, Metronome mag., 1943-55, Metronome Yearbook, 1950-55; columnist Down Beat mag., 1955-58; instr. English Princeton U., 1950-51; instr. English Barnard Coll., 1951-56, asst. prof., 1956-59, asso. prof., 1959-66, prof., 1966—, chmn. dept., 1967-71, 79—, chmn. program in the arts, 1975-79; adj. prof. religion Columbia U., 1966; asso. editor The Bridge Yearbook of Inst. Judaeo-Christian studies, 1955-68. Guggenheim fellow, 1962-63. Mem. St. Thomas More Soc. (pres. 1955-56, 64-65), Cath. Renascence Soc. (pres. 1960-66), Conf. on Humanities (sec. 1957-58, chmn. 1958-59), Medieval Acad., MLA, The Keys (vice chmn. 1959). Author: The Recorded Music of W.A. Mozart, 1942; Duke Ellington, 1946; The Incredible Crosby, 1948; A History of Jazz in America, 1952; A Handbook of Jazz, 1957; Sources and Resources, 1960; Death: A Book of Preparation and Consolation, 1959; Makers of the Modern Theater, 1961; The Way of St. Alphonsus Liguori, 1961; Seeds of Hope in the Modern World, 1962; (with Robert C. Roby) Introduction to the Drama, 1962; Contemporary Catholic Thought, 1963; The Two Worlds of American Art, 1965; The Making of a Modern Saint, 1966; (with James B. Hall) Modern Culture and the Arts, 1967, 72; Where Swing Came From, 1970; (with Ann Ulanov) Religion and the Unconscious, 1975. Co-translator: The Last Essays of George Bernanos, 1955; Joy Out of Sorrow (by Mere Marie des Douleurs), 1958. Office: Barnard Coll Columbia Univ New York NY 10017

ULBRICHT, JOHN, artist; b. Havana, Cuba, Nov. 6, 1926; s. Tomlinson Carlile and Beatrice (Himely) U.; student Art Inst. Chgo., 1946-50; m. Angela von Neumann, July 25, 1950; children—Alexandra, John R. Asst. to dir. Denver Art Mus., 1952-54; exhbns. include: Spanish Contemporary Art, Brussels, Helsinki, Berlin, 1961, 63, Homage to Miro, Palma de Mallora, 1973; one-man shows: Pavilion of Spain, N.Y. World's Fair, 1965, Richard deMarco Gallery, Edinburgh, 1969, Iolas-Velasco Gallery, Madrid, 1972; represented in permanent collections: Denver Art Mus., Nat. Portrait Gallery, London, SUNY, Buffalo, Pasadena Art Mus., Columbus Gallery Fine Arts; portraits include: Mrs. Betty Ford, Chief Judge David Bazelon, Lord Mountbatten, Edward G. Robinson, Pablo Picasso, Sandy Calder, Duchess of Alba, Joan Miro, Robert Graves, others. Served with U.S. Army, 1945-46. Address: 85 Es Clapes Galilea Mallorca Spain. *I have always believed that the primary goal of life is simply the realization of its potentials and that each human being possesses the potential for some form of self-realization. My own road to this end is painting and therein I have dedicated my whole life. Perhaps the full attainment of this goal isn't possible, but certainly the striving towards it provides one of the most enriching experiences that life can offer.*

ULERICH, WILLIAM KEENER, publishing co. exec.; b. Latrobe, Pa., Apr. 18, 1910; s. William Wesley and Anna (Keener) U.; A.B., Pa. State U., 1931; LL.D., Dickinson Sch. Law, 1977; m. Edith O. Orton, May 26, 1934 (div. 1950); 1 dau., Constance K.; m. 2d, Alethea M. Jones, Aug. 23, 1950. Editor, Daily Times, State College, Pa., 1931-45; asso. prof. journalism Pa. State U., 1934-45; pub. Clearfield (Pa.) Daily Progress, 1946; pres., dir. Progressive Pub. Co., Clearfield, Centre Broadcasters, Inc., State College, 1947-77, chmn. bd., dir., 1964—; pres., dir. radio sta. WDAD, Inc., Indiana, Pa., 1949—; chmn. bd., dir. Collier Broadcasting Co., Naples-Marco Island, Fla., 1975—; dir. County Nat. Bank, Clearfield. Bd. dirs., past pres. Clearfield Meml. Hosp.; trustee Pa. State U., 1952-57, 64—, v.p. bd. trustees, 1973-76, pres. bd. trustees, 1976-79. Served with AUS, World War II. Mem. Pa. Newspaper Pubs. Assn. (pres. 1952). Methodist. Home: 724 S 2d St Clearfield PA 16830 also N-1003 Longboat Key Towers Longboat Key Club Rd Sarasota FL 33577 Office: 206 Locust St Clearfield PA 16830

ULEVICH, NEAL HIRSH, photojournalist; b. Milw., June 18, 1946; s. Ben and Leah Jean (Klitsner) U.; B.A. in Journalism, U. Wis., 1968; m. Maureen Ann Vaughan, Sept. 25, 1974; 1 son, Jacob Vaughan. Reporter, A.P., 1968-69, photographer, photo editor, 1971-78, Asia photo editor, 1978—: freelance writer, Vietnam, Hong Kong, 1969-71; fellow in journalism U. Wis.-Madison, 1971-72. Recipient Pulitzer prize for news photography, 1976. Jewish. Home: 2310 Bancroft Ct Mequon WI 53092 Office: Associated Press 50 Rockefeller Plaza New York NY 10020 also AP CPO Box 607 Tokyo Japan

ULFUNG, RAGNAR SIGURD, tenor; b. Olso, Feb. 28, 1927; s. Erling Thorbjorn and Sigrid Fredrike (Olsen) Myrvang; student Music Conservatory, Oslo; studied singing, Milan, Italy, 1950-54; m. Bjorg Flognfeldt, July 12, 1951; 4 children. Mem. Den Nationale Scene, Bergen, Norway, Stora Teatern, Goteborg, Sweden, Royal Opera House, Stockholm, Sweden, 1958—; artistic dir. Stora Teatern, Goteborg, 1977-78; guest appearances in major opera houses throughout the world; leading tenor Royal Opera House, Stockholm. Decorated comdr. Order St. Olav Iklasse (Norway); named Swedish Royal Ct. singer by King Carl Gustav XVI of Sweden. Home: Karlavagen 14A Stockholm Sweden 11431

ULICH, WILLIE LEE, engring. educator; b. Somerville, Tex., Nov. 10, 1920; s. William Daniel and Anna Marie (Schultz) U.; B.S. in Agrl. Engring., Tex. A. and M. U., 1943, M.S., 1947; D.P.A. (Littauer fellow 1951), Harvard, 1956; m. Esther Helen Schoppe, June 28, 1939; children—William Lloyd, Bobby Lee. Farm labor supr., asst. agrl. engr. Tex. Agrl. Extension Service, Dept. Agr. and Tex. A. and M. U., 1947-49; extension agrl. engr. Tex. Agrl. Extension Service, Tex. A. and M. U., 1949-61; prof., chmn. dept. agrl. engring. Coll. Agrl. Scis., Tex. Tech. U., Lubbock, 1961-74, univ. prof., 1974—. Project leader various agrl. investigations, 1962—; mem. farm mechanics seminar com. Nat. Thor Found., 1963-68; vice chmn. Tex. Air Control Bd., 1976-78. Served to 1st lt., pilot USAAF, 1943-46; ETO, CBI; col. Res. ret. Decorated D.F.C., Air medal with three oak leaf clusters, Presdl. citation; Chinese Meml. award; recipient Nat. Presdl. 4 H Leadership award, 1939; Design and Welding award Lincoln Found., 1949; Fellowship award Tex. Cottonseed Crushers, 1947; Nat. Safety award, 1950, Tex. Safety Edn. award, 1949, 54, Progressive Farmer Hall of Fame award, 1955. Registered profl. engr., Tex. Mem. Am. Soc. Agrl. Engrs. (vice chmn. S.W. region 1964—, chmn. 1965, chmn. Tex. sect. exec. com. 1964, mem., vice chmn. nat. dir. 1969—), Tex. Safety Assn. (chmn. farm and ranch sect. 1952—, v.p. 1956), Am. Soc. Engring. Edn. (editor newsletter 1971-72), So. Agrl. Workers Assn., Tex. Farm and Ranch Safety Council, Nat. Soc. Profl. Engrs., Soil Conservation Soc. Am., AAAS. Methodist. Rotarian (chmn. Lubbock agrl. com.). Editor books, bulls., reports. Home: 3424 60th St Lubbock TX 79413

ULINSKI, JOHN ANTHONY, JR., govt. ofcl.; b. Buffalo, June 24, 1923; s. John Anthony and Theresa Mary (Kuczmarski) U.; A.B., Cornell U., 1948; postgrad. in law Georgetown U., 1948-50; m. Anne Tallmadge Franke, Nov. 3, 1951; children—Carol Anne, Susan, John Anthony III, Judith, Matthew. Mgmt. analyst U.S. Bur. Budget, 1948-50; staff Point Four Program, 1950-53; ops. officer U.S. Tech. Assistance Program, Indonesia, 1954-57; loan officer S.E. Asian ops. Devel. Loan Fund, 1957-60, regional dir. South Asia ops., 1960-62; dir. Office of India, Ceylon and Nepal affairs AID, 1962-63; asst. dir. U.S. AID Mission to India, 1963-65; asso. dir. AID mission to Vietnam, Saigon, 1966-67; dir. AID mission to Liberia, 1967-69; dir. financial ops. for Near East and South Asia, Office Pvt. Resources AID, Washington, 1969-70, dep. dir. Office Pvt. Overseas Programs, 1970-72, dir. Office Pvt. and Vol. Coop., 1972—, dir. Adv. Com. on Voluntary Fgn. Aid, 1978—. Ford Found. fellow, Indonesia, 1953-54; fellow Woodrow Wilson Sch., Princeton, 1965-66. Mem. Phi Sigma Kappa. Home: 7009 Girard St McLean VA 22101 Office: AID Office for Private and Vol Coop Washington DC 20523

ULLESTAD, HAROLD NORMAN, credit co. exec.; b. Radcliffe, Iowa, Dec. 9, 1921; s. Elmer and Helen Marie (Stenberg) U.; student Iowa State U., 1940, Ind. U., 1942; B.S., Drake U., Des Moines, 1948; m. Cleone Maxine Grant, Oct. 30, 1942; children—James, Linda (Mrs. Gordon McCosh), Gary, Janis, Charles. Sr. auditor Baumann, Finney & Co., Chgo., 1948-52; with Sunamerica Corp. and predecessor co., Cleve., 1952—, now sr. v.p., treas., dir.; sr. v.p., treas., dir. Sunam. Fin. Corp.; treas., dir. Sun State Life Ins. Co., Gt. Lakes Ins. Co. Served with USNR, 1942-45. Mem. Fin. Forum (fin. com.), Nat. Consumer Finance Assn. Clubs: Exchange (pres. 1963) (Euclid, Ohio); Tanglewood Country (Bainbridge, Ohio). Home: 17516 Merry Oaks Trail Chagrin Falls OH 44022 Office: 1015 Euclid Ave Cleveland OH 44115

ULLMAN, ALBERT CONRAD, congressman; b. Great Falls, Mont., Mar. 9, 1914; s. Albert C. and Julia (Miller) U.; A.B., Whitman Coll., 1935; M.A., Columbia U., 1939; m. Audrey K. Manuel, Aug. 1972; 4 children. Pub. sch. tchr. Port Angeles (Wash.) High Sch., 1935-37; real estate broker, builder, Baker, Oreg., 1945-57; mem. 85th-96th congresses from 2d Dist. Oreg., chmn. House Budget Com., 1974, chmn. Ways and Means Com., 1975—, chmn. Joint Com. on Taxation, 1975, 77, 79. Served with USNR, 1942-45; capt. Res. Mem. Beta Theta Pi. Democrat. Presbyterian. Office: 1136 Longworth Office Bldg Washington DC 20515

ULLMAN, NORMAN VICTOR, profl. hockey player, orgn. exec.; b. Provost, Alta., Can., Dec. 26, 1935. Profl. hockey player, 1955—, with Detroit Red Wings Nat. Hockey League, 1955-68, Toronto Maple Leafs Nat. Hockey League, 1968-75, Edmonton Oilers, World Hockey Assn., 1975-77; former pres. Nat. Hockey League Players Assn. Address: 19 Averdon Crescent Don Mills ON M3A 1P4 Canada

ULLMAN, PIERRE LIONI, educator; b. Nice, France, Oct. 31, 1929 (parents Am. citizens); s. Eugene Paul and Suzanne (Lioni) U.; B.A., Yale U., 1952; diploma en estudios Hispanicos, U. Salamanca (Spain), 1955; M.A., Columbia U., 1956; Ph.D., Princeton U., 1962; m. Mary Meade McDowell, June 9, 1956; children—Katherine Meade Parker, Susan Randolph Johnson. Master, Choate Sch., Wallingford, Conn., 1956-57, St. Bernard's Sch., 1957-58; instr. Rutgers U., 1961-63; asst. prof. U. Calif. at Davis, 1963-65; asso. prof. U. Wis. at Milw., 1965-68, prof. Spanish, 1968—; vis. prof. U. Minn., 1970-71, U. Mich., summer 1975. Signatory convocation First Internat. Congress on Archpriest of Hita, Madrid, Spain, 1972, First Internat. Congress on Celestina, 1974. Served with U.S. Army, 1952-54. Mem. Modern Lang. Assn., Midwest Modern Lang. Assn., Am. Assn. Tchrs. Spanish and Portuguese, Wis. Assn. Fgn. Lang. Tchrs., Am. Assn. Tchrs. Esperanto, Universal Esperanto Assn. (asso. judge lit. contests 1975—), AAUP, Esperanto Studies Assn. (sec.-treas.), Sigma Delta Pi (state dir.). Author: Mariano de Larra and Spanish Political Rhetoric, 1971. Adv. editor Papers on Lang. and Lit., 1966—; Estudos Ibero-Americanos (Brazil), 1975—, Los Ensayistas. Contbr. articles, book revs. to profl. jours. Office: Dept Spanish and Portuguese U Wis Milwaukee WI 53201

ULLMAN, RICHARD HENRY, polit. scientist, educator, editor; b. Balt., Dec. 12, 1933; s. Jerome E. and Frances (Oppenheimer) U.; A.B., Harvard, 1955; B. Phil., Oxford (Eng.) U., 1957, D.Phil., 1960; m. Margaret Yoma Crosfield, July 4, 1959 (div.); children—Claire Frances, Jennifer Margaret; m. 2d, Susan Sorrell, May 6, 1977. Research fellow European history and politics St. Antony's Coll., Oxford U., 1958-59; instr. govt. Harvard, 1960-63, asst. prof., 1963-65; asso. prof. politics and internat. affairs Princeton, 1965-69, prof., 1969-77, 79—, asso. dean Woodrow Wilson Sch. Pub. and Internat. Affairs, 1968-71. Mem. policy planning staff Office Asst. Sec. Def., 1967-68; mem. staff Nat. Security Council, Exec. Office Pres., 1967; dir. studies Council Fgn. Relations, 1973-76, dir. 1980s project, 1974-77, sr. research fellow, 1978-79; mem. editorial bd. N.Y. Times, 1977-78; editor Fgn. Policy, Washington, 1978—. Rhodes scholar, 1955-58; recipient George Louis Beer prize Am. Hist. Assn., 1969. Fellow Am. Acad. Arts and Scis.; mem. Council Fgn. Relations, Internat. Inst. Strategic Studies. Author: Intervention and the War, 1961; Britain and the Russian Civil War, November 1918-January 1920, 1968; The Anglo-Soviet Accord, 1972, vols. I, II and III Anglo-Soviet Relations, 1917-21; also numerous articles. Co-editor: Theory and Policy in International Relations, 1972. Home: 12 Maple St Princeton NJ 08540 Office: Woodrow Wilson Sch Princeton U Princeton NJ 08544

ULLMANN, LIV, actress; b. Tokyo, Japan (parents Norwegian); attended a local pub. sch.; studied under a dramatic coach in London, Eng., for 8 months; m. Hans Stang (div.); 1 dau., Linn, by Ingmar Bergman. After dramatic tng. in London, returned to Norway to act; starred in Diary of Anne Frank with a small repertory troupe in Stavanger, Norway; became an established stage actress of classic roles in Norway, also played in Norwegian films; became Bergman's leading lady in film Persona, 1966; appeared in other films directed by Bergman including The Hour of the Wolf, Shame, The Passion of Anna, Cries and Whispers, 1972, Face to Face, Scenes from a Marriage, Serpents, Autumn Sonota; other films include: The Night Visitor, Pope Joan, The Emigrants (directed by Jan Troell), The New Land, and Hollywood films, Lost Horizon, 40 Carats, Zandy's Bride, and The Abdication; starred as Nora in A Doll's House in N.Y. Shakespeare Festival prodn. at Lincoln Center's Vivian Beaumont Theater, N.Y.C.; appeared on Broadway in Anna Christie, 1977, I Remember Mama, 1979. Recipient Best Actress award for Cries and Whispers, N.Y. Film Critics; was honored for performance in Scenes From a Marriage and Face to Face by N.Y. Film Critics and Nat. Soc. Film Critics; has won either Nat. Soc. Film Critics or N.Y. Film Critics best actress awards for 6 pictures in past 7 years. Author: Changing, 1978 (transl. 20 langs., Book-of-Month club). Office: care Robert Lantz 114 E 55th St New York NY 10022

ULLSTROM, L. BERWYN, lawyer; b. Memphis, Nebr., Sept. 18, 1919; s. LeRoy and Myrtle Estella (Parrish) U.; student Scottsbluff Coll., 1937-40; B.S., U. Mich., 1946; LL.B., U. Denver, 1948; m. Loine Evelyn Sloan, Sept. 11, 1942; children—Linda Louise Dixon, Jeanne Ann Cook, Bruce Richard. Admitted to Colo. bar, 1948, also U.S. Supreme Ct.; practice in Denver, 1948-51; instr. aviation law and legal subjects U. Denver, 1948-51; trial atty. CAA, 1951-54; asso. gen. counsel FCDA, 1954-56, dep. exec. asst. adminstr., 1956-58; observer Operation Redwing, Joint Task Force 7 Pacific Thermonuclear Test, 1956; exec. asst. dir. Office Civil and Def. Mblzn., Exec. Office Pres., 1958-61, cons. Dept. Def., 1961; pvt. practice law, Denver, 1961—. Served to comdr., aviation USNR, 1941-45, ret. from Res., 1962. Mem. Am., Colo., Denver, Lawyer-Pilots bar assns., Am. Judicature Soc., Am., Colo. Trial lawyers assns., Am. Soc. Pub. Adminstrs., Aircraft Owners and Pilots Assn., Phi Delta Phi. Licensed comml. pilot. Home: 13990 W 30th Ave Golden CO 80401 Office: Suite 200 601 Broadway Denver CO 80203

ULMAN, LEWIS HOLMES, lawyer, telephone co. exec.; b. Washington, Apr. 28, 1916; s. Leon Simon and Lilly Caudry (Hawkins) U.; A.B., Princeton, 1938; J.D., Georgetown U., 1942; m. Suzanne Preston, Apr. 5, 1941; children—Michael H., Craig H. Admitted to D.C. bar, 1941, N.Y. bar, 1968, Conn. bar, 1972; asso. Cravath, Swaine & Moore, N.Y.C., 1941-43; atty. NLRB, Washington, 1946-54; gen. atty. Chespeake & Potomac Telephone Cos., Washington, 1954-66; atty. AT&T, N.Y.C., 1966-70; v.p., gen. counsel So. New Eng. Telephone Co., New Haven, 1971—. Mem. D.C. Democratic Central Com., 1964-68; mem. Woodbridge (Conn.) Dem. Town Com., 1973—. Exec. v.p., bd. dirs. House of Mercy; bd. govs. St. Albans Sch. Served with AUS, 1943-46; ETO. Mem. Am., Conn., D.C., New Haven County, Fed. Communications bar assns. Episcopalian. Rotarian. Clubs: New Haven Lawn; Woodbridge; Met., Chevy Chase (Washington). Home: 16 Hunting Hill Rd Woodbridge CT 06525 Office: 227 Church St New Haven CT 06506

ULMAN, LLOYD, economist; b. N.Y.C., Apr. 22, 1920; s. Harry Richard and Ruth Langer (Glick) U.; A.B., Columbia U., 1940; A.M., U. Wis., 1941; Ph.D., Harvard U., 1950; m. Lassie A. Finck, July 4, 1948. Asst. prof. econs. U. Minn., 1950-52, asso. prof., 1952-56, prof., 1956-58; prof. U. Calif., Berkeley, 1958—, dir. Inst. Indsl. Relations, 1963—; sr. labor economist Council Econs. Advs., 1961-62. Served with USNR, 1942-46. Social Sci. Research Council fellow, 1953-54; Guggenheim fellow, 1966-67. Mem. Indsl. Relations Research Assn., Am. Econ. Assn., AAUP. Jewish. Author: The Rise of the National Trade Union, 1955; (with R. J. Flanagan) Wage Restraint: A Study of Incomes Policies in Western Europe, 1971. Home: 776 Creston Rd Berkeley CA 94708 Office: Inst Indsl Relations U Calif Berkeley CA 94720

ULMER, ALFRED CONRAD, JR., investment banker; b. Jacksonville, Fla., Aug. 26, 1916; s. Alfred C. and Ruth Clementine (Porter) U.; grad. Hill School, 1935; A.B., Princeton, 1939; m. Doris Lee Bridges, June 20, 1942 (div.); children—Alfred Conrad III, Marguerite, Nicholas Courtland. Reporter, Jacksonville (Fla.) Jour., 1935-37; pub. relations staff Benton & Bowles, advt. agy., 1939-41; attache Am. embassy, Vienna, 1945-47, Madrid, 1948-50, 1st sec. embassy, spl. asst. to ambassador, Athens, Greece, 1953-55; cons. Far Eastern Affairs, Dept. State, 1955-58; 1st sec. embassy, spl. asst. to ambassador, Paris, France, 1958-62; dir. Niarchos (London) Ltd., 1962-68; gen. partner Devon Securities, 1969-72; mng. dir. Jesup and Lamont Internat. Ltd., London, 1972-75; pres. Lombard, Odier et Cie, Geneva, 1980—; pres. Lombard Odier (Bermuda) Ltd., 1975—. Served from ensign to lt. comdr. USNR, 1941-45. Decorated Bronze Star; comdr. Order of Phoenix (Greece). Mem. Inst. Strategic Studies, Council Fgn. Relations. Presbyn. Clubs: Buck's, Boodle's, Pilgrims (London); Knickerbocker, Links (N.Y.C.). Office: Lombard Odier et Cie 11 rue de la Corraterie 1204 Geneva Switzerland also Lombard Odier (Bermuda) Ltd Airlie House Church St Hamilton Bermuda

ULMER, MELVILLE JACK, economist, educator; b. N.Y.C., May 17, 1911; s. Saul and Lillian (Ulmer) U.; B.S., N.Y. U., 1937, M.A., 1938; Ph.D., Columbia, 1948; m. Naomi Zinken, June 1, 1937; children—Melville Paul, Stephanie Marie. Writer, N.Y. Am., 1930-37; chief, price research sect. Bur. Labor Statistics, 1940-45; sr. economist Smaller War Plants Corp., 1945; chief financial analysis sect. Dept. Commerce, 1946-48, editor Survey of Current Bus., 1948-50; asso. prof. econs. Am. U., 1950-52, prof., 1952-61, chmn. dept., 1953-61; prof. econs. U. Md., 1961—; vis. prof. econs. Netherlands Sch. Econ., Rotterdam, 1958-59, 65-66; research asso. Nat. Bur. Econ. Research, 1950-60; cons. OAS, 1954, Dept. Commerce, 1955, Gen. Services Adminstrn., 1957, Dept. State, 1962, Bur. Budget, 1967-69. Sr. Fulbright award, 1958, 65; Merrill Found. fellow, 1957; Wilton Park fellow, Gt. Britain, 1966; Peoples Coll. fellow, Denmark, 1966; Nuffield fellow, Can., 1971; Nat. Endowment for Humanities sr. fellow, 1973; NSF grantee, 1973; State Dept. econ. specialist grantee, 1977, 78; recipient Outstanding Tchr. award U. Md., 1978. Fellow AAAS; mem. Am. Econ. Assn., Am. Statis. Assn., Econometric Soc., Assn. Evolutionary Econs. (exec. bd.), Artus Soc., Pi Gamma Mu. Club: Cosmos (Washington). Author numerous books, including Economics: Theory and Practice, 2d edit., 1965; Capital in Transportaton, Communications and Pub. Utilities, 1960; The Welfare State: U.S.A., 1969; The Economic Theory of Cost of Living Index Numbers, 1949; also articles. Contbg. editor New Republic, 1970—. Home: 10401 River Rd Potomac MD 20854 also Kezar Falls ME 04047 Office: Dept of Economics U Maryland College Park MD 20742. *Failure must be taken as an instructive experience that aids in exposing the pitfalls to achievement.*

ULRICH, BENJAMIN HARRISON, JR., educator; b. Olean, N.Y., Nov. 5, 1922; s. Benjamin Harrison and Gertrude Emma (Bauman) U.; B.S. in Aero. Engring., Pa. State U., 1944, M.S. in Aero. Engring., 1949; m. Mary Elizabeth Kuder, June 7, 1945; children—James Gregory, Robert Michael, Susan Elaine. Aero. research scientist NACA, Langley Field, Va., 1944-46; asso. prof. aero. engring. W. Va. U., 1951-64, dept., chmn., 1964; prof. aero. engring., also chmn. aerospace engring. and engring. sci. depts. Parks Coll., St. Louis U., 1964—. City councilman, Morgantown, W. Va., 1958-60, 61-63. Served with USNR, 1944-46. Registered profl. engr., W.Va. Mem. ASEE, Am. Inst. Aeros. and Astronautics, Soc. Exptl. Stress Analysis, VFW, Sigma Gamma Tau, Alpha Chi, Tau Beta Pi. Club: St. Louis Engineers. Home: 9144 Desmond Dr St Louis MO 63126 Office: Parks College Cahokia IL 62206

ULRICH, LARRY ADAIR, aviation exec.; b. Denver, Apr. 11, 1936; s. Fred Charles and Sarah Jean (Hanlin) U.; student, U. Colo., 1955-60; m. Kay Mackey, Sept. 2, 1961; children—T. Royal, Kriste Kae. Mgr. used plane div. Combs Aircraft, Denver, 1959-66, v.p. sales, 1966-72, exec. v.p., gen. mgr. Combs-Gates Denver, Inc., 1972-75; exec. v.p. fixed base div. Gates Learjet Corp., 1975-78; pres. Combs-Gates and Arapahoe Aviation, Inc., Denver, 1978—. Mem. Am. Mgmt. Assn. Clubs: Lions, Colo. Mountain. Home: 3621 E Geddes Pl Littleton CO 80122 Office: Combs-Gates Denver Inc Stapleton Internat Airport Denver CO 80207

ULRICH, MAX MARSH, exec. search cons.; b. Kokomo, Ind., Mar. 21, 1925; s. Max Dan and Esther Stone (Marsh) U.; B.S., U.S. Mil. Acad., 1946; M.S. in Civil Engring., Mass. Inst. Tech., 1951; m. Mary Ellen Fisher, Sept. 12, 1950; children—Max Dwight, Jeanne Nanette; m. 2d, Geraldine A. Kidd, Jan. 25, 1973. Comd. 2d lt. C.E., U.S. Army, 1946, advanced through grades to capt., 1950; resigned, 1954; asst. to mng. dir. Edison Electric Inst., 1954-58; with Consol. Edison Co., N.Y.C., 1958-71, asst. v.p., 1962-63, v.p. charge advt. and pub. relations, 1963-67, v.p. customer service, 1968-69, v.p. Bklyn. div., 1969-71; prin., dir. Ward Howell Assos., N.Y.C., 1971-74, pres., 1974—; dir. Environ. Research & Tech., Inc. Mem. Sigma Xi. Home: Kingswood Dr Orangeburg NY 10962 Office: 99 Park Ave New York City NY 10016

ULRICH, MYRON WILBUR, lawyer; b. Greenville, Iowa, Jan. 31, 1912; s. Otto Philip and Anna (Brubaker) U.; A.B., Western Res. U., 1934, LL.B., 1936; m. Beatrice J. Handy, Sept. 11, 1937 (dec. 1972); children—John C., Daniel R.; m. 2d, Marion W. Adams, July 13, 1973. Admitted to Ohio bar, 1936, since practiced in Cleve.; partner firm Roudebush, Brown, Corlett, Ulrich Co., and predecessor, 1945—; chief contract br. legal dept. Cleve. Ordnance Dist., 1942-45; instr. Cleve. Marshall Law Sch., 1945-54. Dir. Cuyahoga Savs. Assn. Co. Chmn., Ohio Legal Services Fund. Bd. govs. Western Res. U., 1966-67, chmn. vis. com. Adelbert Coll., 1966-70; bd. overseers Case Western Res. U., 1967-72; trustee Polyclinic Hosp., 1953—, pres., 1956-64; rep. Cleve. Welfare Fedn., 1956-64, Cleve. Hosp. Council, 1956-64. Fellow Am., Ohio bar founds.; mem. Ohio Bar Assn. (chmn. profl. econs. com. 1959-64, exec. com. 1967-73, pres. 1971-72), Am. Coll. Probate Counsel (Ohio rep.), Am., Cleve. (exec. com. 1950-53, 67-70, chmn. municipal ct. com. 1964, 66) bar assns., Am. Judicature Soc., Cleve. Growth Assn., Delta Upsilon. Republican. Presbyn. Home: 2202 Acacia Park Dr Apt 2308 Lyndhurst OH 44124 Office: Williamson Bldg Cleveland OH 44114

ULRICH, PAUL GRAHAM, lawyer; b. Spokane, Wash., Nov. 29, 1938; s. Donald Gunn and Kathryn (Vandercook) U.; B.A. with high honors, U. Mont., 1961; J.D., Stanford U., 1964; m. Virginia Rae Ragland, June 10, 1961; children—Kathleen Elizabeth, Marilee Rae, Michael Graham. Admitted to Calif. bar, 1965, Ariz. bar, 1966, U.S. Supreme Ct. bar, 1969; law clk. to judge U.S. Ct. Appeals, 9th Circuit, San Francisco, 1964-65; asso. firm Lewis and Roca, Phoenix, 1965-70, partner, 1970—; instr. Thunderbird Grad. Sch. Internat. Mgmt., 1968-69; cons. instr. legal writing Ariz. State U. Coll. Law, 1970-73, instr. on the legal profession, 1978; instr. in law office mgmt. Scottsdale Community Coll., 1975-77. Served with U.S. Army, 1956. Mem. Am. Bar Assn. (chmn. com. on nonlawyer personnel 1979—), State Bar Ariz. (co-chmn. Ariz. Appellate Handbook project 1976—, Continuing Legal Edn. award 1978), Maricopa County Bar Assn., State Bar Calif., Am. Law Inst., Am. Judicature Soc., Phi Kappa Phi, Phi Alpha Delta. Republican. Presbyterian. Club: Ariz. Contbr. articles to profl. jours. Office: 100 W Washington St Phoenix AZ 85003

ULRICH, PETER HENRY, banker; b. Munich, Germany, Nov. 24, 1922; s. Hans George and Hella (Muschweck) U.; student Northwestern U., 1941-42, U. Iowa, 1943, Sch. Mortgage Banking, 1954-56; m. Carol A. Peek, Oct. 21, 1944; children—Carol Jean (Mrs. D. Scott Hewes), Patricia Diane (Mrs. Damon Eberhart), Peter James. Escrow officer Security Title Ins. Co., Riverside, Calif., 1946-53; asst. cashier Citizens Nat. Trust & Savs., Riverside, 1953-57; v.p. Security First Nat. Bank, Riverside, 1957-63; sr. v.p. Bank of Calif., N.A., Los Angeles, 1963-72; pres. Ban Cal Mortgage Co., 1972-74, Ban Cal Tri-State Mortgage Co., 1974-75; cons., 1975-76; pres., dir. Beneficial Standard Mortgage Co., 1976—; instr. real estate and bus. San Bernardino Valley Coll., Riverside City Coll., Pasadena City Coll. Pres. Residential Research Com. So. Calif., 1965. Pres. Riverside Opera Assn., 1956-59, Riverside Symphony Soc., 1959-61; trustee Idyllwild Arts Found., 1957—, pres., 1970-73; adv. bd. Salvation Army, 1959—, vice chmn., 1971-74, chmn., 1975, chmn. Harbor Light com., 1965-68; convocator Calif. Luth. Coll., 1976—; bd. dirs. Lark Ellen Lions Charities, 1976—. Served with AUS, 1943-46. Recipient Resolution of Commendation, Riverside City Council, 1963; Resolution of Appreciation, Los Angeles City Council, 1968, 1973; licensed real estate broker, certified mortgage banker. Mem. Nat., Calif. (sec. 1965, dir. 1972-75), So. Calif. (dir. 1975), Inland Empire (past pres., hon. dir.) mortgage bankers assns., Town Hall, Los Angeles C. of C., Lambda Alpha (sec. 1967-71, pres. 1974-75). Lutheran (v.p. ch. council 1967-70, mem. ch. council 73-77, chmn. fin. com. 1979—). Club: Lions (bd. dirs. Los Angeles 1970—), Los Angeles Athletic. Home: 447 Fairview Ave Apt 2 Arcadia CA 91006 Office: 3700 Wilshire Blvd Los Angeles CA 90010. *Being of foreign birth, I particularly appreciate and cherish the American way of life. I am grateful for the opportunities which it has afforded me. I also feel strongly that we who have had the benefit of these opportunities owe something in return to our communities and to our country. I have tried to the best of my abilities to conduct myself and my business affairs in an honorable and forthright manner, thus helping to preserve what I feel is still the best life style in the world.*

ULRICH, ROBERT GARDNER, retail food chain exec.; b. Evanston, Ill., May 6, 1935; s. Charles Clemens and Nell Clare (Stanley) U.; LL.B. (Law Rev. key), Marquette U., Milw., 1960; m. Diane Mary Granzin, June 6, 1964; children—Robert Jeffrey, Laura Elizabeth, Meredith Christine. Admitted to Wis. bar, 1960, Ill. bar, 1960; law clk. to fed. dist. judge, Milw., 1961-62; atty. S.C. Johnson & Son, Inc., Racine, Wis., 1962-65, Motorola, Inc., Franklin Park, Ill., 1965-68; atty., then asst. gen. counsel Jewel Cos., Inc., Melrose Park, Ill., 1968-75; v.p., gen. counsel Gt. Atlantic & Pacific Tea Co., Inc., Montvale, N.J., 1975—. Mem. Am. Bar Assn Home: 500 Weymouth Dr Wyckoff NJ 07481 Office: 2 Paragon Dr Montvale NJ 07645

ULRICH, ROGER KEITH, astronomer; b. Berkeley, Calif., May 13, 1942; s. Albert and Jane (Murdock) U.; B.S., U. Calif., Berkeley, 1963, Ph.D., 1968; m. Sandra Lee Selders, June 15, 1963; children—Scott Roger, Christopher David, Marcus Robert. Research asso. Calif. Inst. Tech., 1969-70; asst. prof. astronomy UCLA, 1970-73, asso. prof., 1973-77, prof., chmn. dept. astronomy, 1977—; guest observer Hale Observatories, 1977—. NSF grantee, NASA grantee. Mem. Am. Astron. Soc., Internat. Astron. Union. Developed theory which led to field of solar seismology; demonstrated that some T Tauni stars accrete matter from space. Office: Dept Astronomy UCLA Los Angeles CA 90024*

ULRY, ORVAL LEE, former univ. dean; b. Westerville, Ohio, Aug. 23, 1917; s. E.A. and Lurana Catherine (McElwee) U.; B.S. in Edn., Ohio State U., 1938, M.A., 1944, Ph.D., 1953; m. Doris Helen Bevelhymer, Aug. 29, 1939; 1 dau., Diana Leigh. Exptl. tchr. Canal Winchester (Ohio) High Sch., 1939-44; supt. Hyatts Local Sch., Delaware, Ohio, 1944-45, Green Camp (Ohio) Local Sch., 1945-48; instr. Ohio State U., 1949-51; dir. student teaching Miami U., Oxford, Ohio, 1951-56; dir. summer sch. U. Md., 1956-62; tchr. edn. adviser AID mission, New Delhi, India, 1962-64; head dept. tchr. edn. Western Mich. U., Kalamazoo, 1965-69; asst. dean for grad. programs Coll. Edn., Western Ill. U., Macomb, 1969-78. Fellow A.A.A.S.; mem. N.E.A., Nat. Sci. Tchrs. Assn., Assn. Profs. Edn., Nat. Soc. Coll. Tchrs. Edn., Phi Delta Kappa, Kappa Phi Kappa, Kappa Delta Pi. Author reports and articles in field, contbr. to yearbooks. Home: 600 Wichita #107 McAllen TX 78501

ULRYCH, TADEUSZ JAN, geophysicist; b. Warsaw, Poland, Aug. 9, 1935; s. Juliusz August and Zofia Krystyna (Wilke) U.; came to Can., 1958, naturalized, 1963; B.Sc., U. London, 1957; M.Sc., U. B.C. (Can.), Vancouver, 1958, Ph.D. (NRC Can. fellow), 1963; m. Miriam Iris Owen, Oct. 9, 1959; children—Jason Andrew, Liza Megan. Lectr. in geophysics U. Western Ont., London, 1961-62, asst. prof. geophysics, 1962-64; asst. prof. U. B.C., 1968-74, prof. geophysics and astronomy, 1974—; postdoctoral fellow in geology Oxford (Eng.) U., 1964; postdoctoral fellow Bernerd Price Inst., Johannesburg, S. Africa, 1965; contracted prof. Petrobras, Salvedor, Brazil, 1967-68; cons. to mining and petroleum cos. Mem. Am. Geophys. Union. Contbr. articles on isotope studies, time series analysis to profl. publs. Home: 2950 W 43d St Vancouver BC V6N 3J3 Canada Office: Dept Geophysics and Astronomy U BC Vancouver BC V6T 1W5 Canada

ULSTROM, ROBERT ALGER, physician, educator; b. Mpls., Feb. 23, 1923; s. Alger Roy and Catherine Margaret (Dougall) U.; B.S., U. Minn., 1944, M.B., 1946, M.D., 1946; m. Mary Janet McGrath, June 7, 1946; children—Jane Elizabeth Ulstrom Brissett, Susan Jean Ulstrom Nierengarten, Cynthia Louise. Intern Strong Meml. Hosp., Rochester, N.Y., 1946-47, resident, 1947-48; mem. faculty pediatrics U. Minn., Mpls., 1950-53, asso. prof., 1956-61, prof., 1961-64, 67—, acting head dept., 1961-62, asso. dean Coll. Med. Scis., 1967-70; asst. prof. U. Calif. at Los Angeles Sch. Medicine, 1953-56, prof., 1964-67, chmn. dept. pediatrics, 1964-67. Mem. NRC, 1961-64; cons. NIH, 1964-68; mem. med. adv. bd. Group Health, Inc., 1967—, Mpls. Diabetes Edn. Center, 1969-72; track physician, Donnybrooke, 1968-73. Trustee Minn. Med. Found., 1968-78. Served from 1st lt. to capt. AUS, 1948-50. Markle scholar in med. scis., 1954-59. Recipient Wyeth Co. award for med. research, 1963. Diplomate Am. Bd. Pediatrics (examiner 1970—), subsplty. bd. endocrinology. Mem. Am. Pediatric Soc., Am. Soc. Clin. Investigation, Central, Western socs. clin. research, Endocrine Soc., Soc. Pediatric Research, Western Soc. Pediatric Research, Midwestern Pediatric Research Soc. (council 1961-64), Lawson Wilkins Pediatric Endocrine Soc., Soc. for Inherited Metabolic Disorders, Phi Rho Sigma, Alpha Omega Alpha. Presbyn. Editorial bd. Jour. Pediatrics, 1962-65. Contbr. articles to tech. jours., chpts. to books. Office: Dept Pediatrics U Minn Minneapolis MN 55455

ULTAN, LLOYD, educator, composer, author; b. N.Y.C., June 12, 1929; s. Carl and Blanche (Scheiner) U.; B.S., N.Y. U., 1951; M.A., Columbia, 1952; Ph.D., State U. Ia., 1956; m. Roslye Rita Benson, Sept. 8, 1956; children—Wendy June, Alicia Jill, Jacqueline Beth, Deborah Kim. Mem. faculty Dickinson Coll., Carlisle, Pa., 1956-62, asst. prof., 1957-62; mem. faculty Am. U., Washington, 1962-75, prof., 1965-75, chmn. dept. music, 1962-75; mem. faculty, chmn. depts. music and music edn. U. Minn., 1975—; mem. faculty Royal Coll. Music, London, Eng., 1968-69; guest lectr. Cambridge (Eng.) U., 1969; dir. composer's residency program Wolf Trap Am. U. Acad. for Performing Arts, summer 1971, 73, 74. Chmn. ad hoc com. on Renaissance music seminar Folger Library, Washington, 1970-71; adviser to music com. Corcoran Gallery Art, Washington, 1967-68; chmn. region IV, bd. dirs. Nat. Assn. Schs. Music, 1978—. Served with AUS, 1952-54. Fellow Bennington Composer Conf., 1961. Mem. Pa. Music Tchrs. Assn. (pres. 1961-62), Am. Composers Alliance, Coll. Music Soc., Am. Music Center, Am. Musicological Soc., Phi Mu Alpha Sinfonia (life). Composer numerous compositions including: Symphony Number 1, 1954; The Man with a Hoe (cantata for chorus and orch.), 1956; Symphony Number 2, 1961; String Quartet, 1964; Piano Sextet, 1970; Collaborations (tape and organ), 1973; Conflicts 74, 1974; Sonata for Viola and Piano, 1976; Wanaki Win, 1977; Concerto for Organ and Orchestra, 1978. Author: Music Theory: Compositional Problems and Practices in the Middle Ages and Renaissance and Accompaning Anthology, 1977; also articles. Home: 5249 Lochloy Dr Edina MN 55436

ULTMANN, JOHN ERNEST, physician, educator; b. Vienna, Austria, Jan. 6, 1925; s. Oskar and Hedwig (Schechter) U.; came to U.S., 1938, naturalized, 1943; student Bklyn. Coll., 1946, Oberlin Coll., 1946-48; M.D., Columbia, 1952; m. Ruth E. Layton, May 25, 1952; children—Monica, Michelle, Barry. Intern N.Y. Hosp.-Cornell Med. Center, N.Y.C., 1952-53; resident N.Y. Hosp., 1953-55; Am. Cancer Soc. fellow in hematology Columbia, 1955-56; practice medicine specializing in internal medicine, N.Y.C., 1956-68, Chgo., 1968—; mem. staff Francis Delafield Hosp., 1955-68, Presbyn. Hosp., 1956-68, Bellevue Hosp., 1961-68; career scientist Health Research Council City N.Y., 1959-68; cons. Harlem Hosp., N.Y.C., 1966-68; dir. clin. oncology Franklin McLean Meml. Research Inst., 1968—; prof. medicine Sch. Medicine, U. Chgo., 1970—, also dir. Cancer Research Center and asso. dean for research programs; chmn. bd. sci. counselors div. cancer treatment Nat. Cancer Inst., 1976—; mem. Adv. Bd. Cancer Control to Gov. of Ill. Bd. dirs. Assn. Am. Cancer Insts., 1974-75; bd. dirs. at-large Ill. div. Am. Cancer Soc.; pres. Ill. Cancer Council, 1976—. Served with AUS, 1943-46. Diplomate Nat. Bd. Med. Examiners, Am. Bd. Internal Medicine. Fellow A.C.P., Inst. Medicine Chgo.; mem. Am. Fedn. Clin. Investigation, Soc. Study Blood, Am. Assn. Cancer Research, Internat., Am. socs. hematology, A.A.U.P., A.A.A.S., Harvey Soc., Am. Soc. Clin. Oncology (dir. 1978—), Chgo. Soc. Internal Medicine, Central Soc. Clin. Research, Sociedad Chilena de Cancerologia, Sociedad Chilena de Hematologia, Phi Beta Kappa, Alpha Omega Alpha. Asso. editor Cancer Research, 1974-78; editorial bd. Annals Internal Medicine, 1974-77, Blood, 1975-77; cons. editor Am. Jour. Medicine, 1975—. Contbr. articles to profl. jours. Home: 5632 S Harper Ave Chicago IL 60637 Office: 950 E 59th St Chicago IL 60637

ULYSHEN, MICHAEL, diversified industry exec.; b. Saskatoon, Sask., Can., June 8, 1922; s. Nicholas and Anna (Pryma) U.; came to U.S., 1924, naturalized, 1943; B.S., U. Mich., 1948; m. Mary Alice Warner, Aug. 18, 1947; children—Thomas, James, Jane, Joan. Plant mgr. Ira Wilson Dairy, Detroit, 1950-58; div. gen. mgr. Dairypak, Champion Papers Co., 1958-62; exec. v.p. Dairypak div. U.S. Plywood Champion Co., 1962-68, pres. Lewers and Cooke div.,

Honolulu, 1968-73; exec. v.p. Alexander & Baldwin Inc., Honolulu, 1973—. Served to capt., pilot, USMCR, 1940-45, 52-53. Home: 46404 Hulupala Pl Kaneohe HI 96744 Office: 822 Bishop St Honolulu HI 96820

UMBACH, WILLIAM ECKHARD, univ. dean; b. Racine, Wis., Aug. 31, 1912; s. Eckhard and Anna (Lohr) U.; B.A., Denison U., 1934; M.A., U. Mich., 1935, Ph.D., 1950; m. Virginia Mae DeLong, June 16, 1937; children—Margaret Anne (Mrs. Gordon A. Clopine), David Richard, Kenneth William. From. instr. to asso. prof. German, Case Inst. Tech., 1936-52; prof. German, U. Redlands (Calif.), 1952-79, dir. div. langs. and lit., 1953-61, dean grad. studies, 1961-79, dir. summer sessions, 1963-68, 70-71, v.p. for adminstrn., 1968-71, coordinator fed. relations, 1971-73; moderator Family Forum of Air, sta. WSRS, Cleve., 1949-52; etymological editor World Pub. Co., 1942—. Mem. Cleveland Heights Bd. Edn., 1950-52, pres., 1951; mem. Cleveland Heights Joint Recreation Bd., 1951-52, Redlands Recreation Commn., 1971-78. Bd. dirs. Redlands YMCA, 1959-62, 63-66, 68-71, pres., 1966; bd. dirs. Redlands Community Chest, 1963-65, 67, 71; trustee Redlands Unified Sch. Dist., 1971—, pres., 1975-76. Mem. modern lang. assns. Am., So. Calif., Am. Assn. Tchrs. German, AAUP (pres. Case Inst. Tech. chpt. 1947-49, U. Redlands chpt. 1955), Philol. Assn. Pacific Coast, Am. Assn. Higher Edn., P.E.N., Phi Beta Kappa (councilor alumni So. Calif. 1964-67, 73—, pres. 1968-70, treas. Internat. Scholarship Fund alumni So. Calif. 1966-67, chmn. 1976-79), Tau Kappa Alpha (council 1950-52), Omicron Delta Kappa (sec. Redlands Circle 1955-68), Alpha Mu Gamma, Kappa Sigma. Democrat. Baptist. Contbr. to books, encys. Home: 23 E Highland Ave Redlands CA 92373

UMBREIT, WAYNE WILLIAM, bacteriologist, educator; b. Markesan, Wis., May 1, 1913; s. William Traugott and Augusta (Abendroth) U.; B.A., U. Wis., 1934, M.S., 1936, Ph.D., 1939; m. Doris McQuade, July 31, 1937; children—Dorayne Loreda, Jay Nicholas, Thomas Hayden. Instr. soil microbiology Rutgers U., 1937-38; faculty U. Wis., Madison, 1938-44, asst. prof. bacteriology and chemistry, 1941-44; faculty Cornell U., 1944-47, prof. bacteriology, 1946-47; head dept. enzyme chemistry Merck Inst., Rahway, N.J., 1947-58; asso. dir., 1958; chmn. dept. bacteriology Rutgers U., New Brunswick, N.J., 1958-75, prof. microbiology, dir. grad. programs, 1969—. Recipient Biochem. Congress Symposium medal, Paris, France, 1952. Fellow Am. Acad. Microbiology, N.Y. Acad. Sci., A.A.A.S.; mem. Am. Soc. for Microbiology (Eli Lilly award in bacteriology 1947, Carski Found. award for distinguished teaching 1968), Soc. Biol. Chemists, Am. Chem. Soc., Theobald Smith Soc. (Waksman award in microbiology 1957, past pres.), AAUP, Sigma Xi. Author: (with Burris, Stauffer) Manometric Techniques, 1945, 5th edit., 1972; (with Oginsky) An Introduction to Bacterial Physiology, 1954; Metabolic Maps, 1960; Modern Microbiology, 1962; Essentials of Bacterial Physiology, 1976. Editor: Advances in Applied Microbiology, vols. 1-10, 1959-68. Contbr. articles to profl. jours. Home: 498 Route 2 Flemington NJ 08822 Office: Dept Bacteriology Nelson Hall Rutgers U New Brunswick NJ 08903

UMLAUF, CHARLES JULIUS, sculptor; b. Mich., July 17, 1911; s. Christian Heinrich and Charlotte (Derouet) U.; student Chgo. Sch. Sculpture, 1932-34, Art Inst. Chgo., 1929-32, 34-37; m. Angeline McMorine Allen, July 13, 1937; children—Karl, Carolynn, Madelon, Louis, Arthur, Thomas. Artist, Fed. Art Project, Chgo., 1939-41; instr. art U. Tex., 1941-47, asst. prof. art, Austin, 1948-50, asso. prof., 1951-54, prof., 1955—; one-man shows include: Passedoit Gallery, N.Y.C., 1955, Valley House Gallery, Dallas, 1959, Galleria D'Arte Santacroce, Florence, Italy, 1966, U. Tex. Art Mus., Austin, 1967, T.V. Robinson Galleries, Houston, 1979; group shows include: Whitney Mus. Am. Art, 1946-56, Pa. Acad. Art, Phila., 1946-66, Internat. Religious Biennale, Salzburg, Austria, 1958-59, Princeton U., 1960, Speed Art Mus., Louisville, 1965; represented in permanent collections, including: Met. Mus. Art, N.Y.C., Des Moines Art Center, Santa Barbara (Calif.) Mus., Krannert Mus., U. Ill., Wichita (Kans.) Mus., Okla. Art Center, Oklahoma City, Library at Women's Coll., Greensboro, N.C., La. State U. Union Gallery, Baton Rouge, Lakeview Center for Arts and Scis., Peoria, Ill., La. Coll. Weathersby Fine Arts Bldg., Pineville, Nat. Collection Fine Arts, Washington; works include: marble relief St. Michael and All Angels Ch., Dallas, 1961; bronze fountain sculpture Love Field Airport, Dallas, 1961; U. Tex., Austin, 1963, Space Tech. Center, U. Kans., Lawrence, 1975, Houston Mus. Natural Sci., 1972, Fountain and Sculpture for Lobby of Cook County Hosp., Chgo., Angel for Entrance to City of Lubbock (Tex.) Cemetery, Fountain and Bronze Sculpture, Spirit of Flight, for Entrance to Love Field, Dallas, Witte Meml. Mus. Frontal Sculpture (2), San Antonio. Guggenheim fellow, 1949; U. Tex. grantee, 1966; Ford Found. grantee, 1979. Mem. Omicron Delta Kappa (hon.). Subject of book: Charles Umlauf, Sculptor, 1967. Home: 506 Barton Blvd Austin TX 78704 Office: Art Dept U Tex Austin TX 78712

UMSTEAD, WILLIAM LEE, newspaperman; b. Durham, N.C., July 23, 1921; s. William L. and Sally (Breeze) U.; student George Washington U., 1938-41; m. June L. Myers Feb. 18, 1949; children—Eric William, William Lee III, Robin Lynne. Reporter, then news editor Washington bur. Internat. News Service, 1941-58; mem. staff U.P.I. Washington bur., 1958-68, night editor, bur. mgr., 1966-68; asst. mng. editor N.Y. Daily News, 1968-74, night mng. editor, 1974—. Served with USAAF, 1943-45. Decorated Purple Heart, Air Medal with 3 oak leaf clusters. Mem. Sigma Phi Epsilon, Pi Delta Epsilon. Clubs: Nat. Press (Washington); Press of N.Y. Home: 5 Heatherbloom Rd White Plains NY 10605 Office: 220 E 42d St New York NY 10017

UNCAPHER, IVAN T., union ofcl.; b. Albany, N.Y., Apr. 14, 1924; s. Andrew I. and Iva Lee (Hollack) U.; m. Connie B. Andrews, 1966; 1 son, David. Pres., local 1000 Am. Flint Glass Workers Union, 1954, internat. rep., 1954-65, internat. asst. sec., Toledo, Ohio, 1965-73, internat. sec.-treas., 1973—. Democrat. Club: Elks. Home: 2220 Winterset Toledo OH 43614 Office: 1440 S Byrne Toledo OH 43614*

UNDERCOFLER, HIRAM K., judge; b. Pa., 1916; ed. Temple U., U. Ga.; m. Flora Gatewood; children—Hiram K., Dale. Mem. Ga. Gen. Assembly, 1959-62; state revenue commr. Ga., 1962-66; justice Ga. Supreme Ct., Atlanta, 1966—, now presiding justice. Served to lt. col. USAAF, 1940-46. *

UNDERHILL, EARLE CALVIN, banker; b. Salt Lake City, Jan. 28, 1914; s. Earle Raymond and Clara (Zengel) U.; m. Beth W. Wickham, Feb. 11, 1939; children—James E., David R., Patricia (Mrs. William T. Nutt), Joel B. With First Security Bank, Salt Lake City, 1933-39; nat. bank examiner, 1939-47; with Idaho 1st Nat. Bank, Boise, 1947-61, cashier, 1950-60, v.p., 1960-61; v.p. Peoples Nat. Bank Wash., Seattle, 1961-67, exec. v.p., 1967-79, dir. 1967—; pres. Pacific Coast Banking Sch., Seattle, 1964-66, trustee, 1955-61; instr. Am. Inst. Banking, Pacific Coast Banking Sch.; chmn. Seattle Com. on Fgn. Relations, 1969-70. Trustee Boise Ind. Sch. Dist., 1954-60. Mem. Wash. Bankers Assn. (pres. 1978-79). Home 10500 NE 47th Pl Kirkland WA 98033 Office: 1414 4th Ave Seattle WA 98171

UNDERHILL, FRANCIS TRELEASE, JR., former ambassador; b. Summit, N.J., Apr. 1, 1921; s. Francis and Edith (Raymer) U.; A.B., Wesleyan U., 1942; M.A., Fletcher Sch. Law and Diplomacy, Tufts U., 1943; m. Helen Savacool, Sept. 17, 1949; children—Francis S., Lisa H. Chief sect. Army-Navy Petroleum Bd., Washington, 1946-47; joined State Dept., 1947; fgn. service officer gen., Lisbon, Portugal, 1947-48; pub. affairs officer, Bilbao, Spain, 1948-51; assigned to Washington, 1951-52; polit. officer, Djakarta, Indonesia, 1952-55; officer in charge Indonesia and Pacific Islands affairs, Washington, 1955-59, intelligence research specialist, 1959; consular officer, Warsaw, Poland, 1959-61; polit. officer, Kuala Lumpur, Malaysia, 1961-63; detailed Army War Coll., Washington, 1963-64, dep. dir. Office South West Pacific Affairs, 1964-66, country dir., Indonesia, 1966-68; counselor polit. affairs, Manila, Philippines, 1968-71; dep. chief mission, counselor, Seoul, Korea, 1971-74; ambassador to Kuala Lumpur, 1974-77. Served to lt. USNR, 1943-46. Unitarian. Clubs: Royal Selangor Golf, Manila Yacht. Address: 622 G St NW Washington DC 20024

UNDERHILL, JACOB BERRY, III, ins. co. exec.; b. N.Y.C., Oct. 25, 1926; s. Jacob Berry, Jr. and Dorothy Louise (Quinn) U.; grad. Phillips Exeter Acad., 1944; A.B., Princeton, 1950; m. Cynthia Jane Lovejoy, Sept. 9, 1950 (div. Sept. 1962); children—David Lovejoy, Kate Howell Underhill Kerwin, Benedict Quinn; m. 2d, Lois Beachy, Nov. 2, 1963. Editor, Courier & Freeman, Potsdam, N.Y., 1950-53; reporter Democrat & Chronicle, Rochester, N.Y., 1953-56; chief editorial writer St. Petersburg (Fla.) Times, 1956-59; asso. editor McGraw Hill Publ. Co., N.Y.C., 1959-61; asso. editor Newsweek, N.Y.C., 1961-63; asst. press sec. to Gov. N.Y., 1963-67; dep. supt., 1st dep. supt. State N.Y. Ins. Dept., 1967-72; vice chmn. bd., v.p., sr. v.p., exec. v.p., dir. N.Y. Life Ins. Co., N.Y.C., 1972—. Bd. dirs. Manhattan Eye, Ear and Throat Hosp., Better Bus. Bur. of Met. N.Y.; trustee retirement system ARC, Nat. Trust for Hist. Preservation. Served with USNR, 1944-46. Clubs: Players, Links (N.Y.C.); Noyac Golf and Country (Sag Harbor, N.Y.). Office: 51 Madison Ave New York NY 10010

UNDERKOFLER, JAMES RUSSELL, utility exec.; b. Baraboo, Wis., Oct. 25, 1923; s. Ray Carr and Margaret (Thompson) U.; LL.B., U. Wis., 1950; m. Dorothy Paske, Nov. 16, 1947; children—James H., Thomas R., R. Craig, Kevin S., Cynthia M. With Wis. Power and Light Co., 1941—, pres., chief exec. officer, 1968—; pres., chief exec. officer South Beloit Water, Gas & Electric Co.; dir. First Wis. Nat. Bank Madison, Am. Family Mut. Ins. Co., Madison, H.C. Prange Co., Sheboygan, Wis., First Wis. Corp. Mem. Mayor Madison Adv. Com., 1964; chmn. budgets Madison United Givers Fund, 1966-67; pres. United Way, Madison 1971. Bd. dirs. Methodist Hosp., Madison, 1967-75, Nat. Assn. Electric Cos., Washington, 1975-77; bd. dirs., pres. Wis. Electric Utilities Research Found., 1970-77; mem. U. Wis. Alumni Bd., 1965; trustee Milton (Wis.) Coll., 1971-74. Served with inf. AUS, 1943-46. Decorated Purple Heart. Mem. Edison Elec. Inst. (dir. 1975—, adv. com., chmn. energy and environment com. 1973-75), Wis. Utilities Assn. (pres. 1972-73, chmn. 1973-74, dir. 1975—), Wis. Bar Assn., Wis. (dir. 1970-74), U.S. (ad hoc liaison com. on environment 1972-73) chambers commerce), Wis. Mfrs. and Commerce (dir.). Lutheran (pres. 1964). Rotarian (dir. Madison 1970-72). Clubs: Madison, Maple Bluff Country (Madison). Home: 6233 S Highlands Ave Madison WI 53705 Office: 222 W Washington Ave Madison WI 53701

UNDERWEISER, IRWIN PHILIP, mining co. exec., lawyer; b. N.Y.C., Jan. 3, 1929; s. Harry and Edith (Gladstein) U.; B.A., Coll. City N.Y., 1950; LL.D., Fordham U., 1954; LL.M., N.Y.U., 1961; m. Beatrice J. Kortchmar, Aug. 17, 1959; children—Rosanne, Marian, Jeffrey. Admitted to N.Y. bar, 1954; with firm Scribner & Miller, N.Y.C., 1951-54, 56-62; partner firm Feuerstein & Underweiser, 1962-73, Underweiser & Fuchs, 1973-77, Underweiser & Underweiser, 1977—; v.p., sec. Sunshine Mining Co., Kellogg, Idaho, 1965-70, chmn. bd., 1970-78, pres., 1971-74, 77, v.p., 1977—, also dir.; sec., dir. Berel Industries, Inc., N.Y.C., 1964—; vice chmn., dir. Underwriters Bank and Trust Co., N.Y.C., 1969-73; dir. Anchor Post Products, Inc. Bd. dirs. Silver Inst. Inc.; gen. counsel, mem. bus. council Friends City Center Music and Drama, N.Y.C., 1966-67; pres. W. Quaker Ridge Assn., 1969-70; treas. Scarsdale Neighborhood Assn. Presidents, 1970-71. Served with AUS, 1954-56. Mem. Am., N.Y. State bar assns., Bar Assn. City N.Y., Phi Beta Kappa, Phi Alpha Theta. Home: 7 Rural Dr Scarsdale NY 10583 Office: 405 Park Ave New York NY 10022 also 250 Park Ave New York NY 10017

UNDERWOOD, BENTON J., educator; b. Center Point, Iowa, Feb. 28, 1915; s. Willie B. and Blanche (Campbell) U.; B.A., Cornell (Iowa) Coll., 1936, D.Sc. (hon.), 1966; M.A., U. Mo., 1940; Ph.D., U. Iowa, 1942; m. Hazel Louise Olson, June 1, 1939; children—Judith (Mrs. John Maples), Kathleen (Mrs. Thomas F. Olsen). Mem. faculty Northwestern U., 1946—, prof. psychology, 1952—. Served with USNR, 1942-46. Recipient Warren medal Soc. Exptl. Psychologists, 1964; Distinguished Sci. Contbn. award Am. Psychol. Assn., 1973. Mem. Am. (pres. div. 3, 1960, div. 1, 1970), Midwestern (pres. 1957) psychol. assns., Nat. Acad. Sci. Author: Experimental Psychology, rev. edit., 1966; Psychological Research, 1957; Meaningfulness and Verbal Learning, 1960; Temporal Codes for Memories: Issues and Problems, 1977. Home: 1745 Stevens Dr Glenview IL 60025 Office: Dept Psychology Northwestern Univ Evanston IL 60201

UNDERWOOD, CECIL H., coal co. exec., former gov. W.Va.; b. Josephs Mills, W.Va., Nov. 5, 1922; s. Silas and Della (Forrester) U.; A.B., Salem (W.Va.) Coll., 1943; A.M., W.Va. U., 1952; research fellow Amelia Earhart Found., Ann Arbor, Mich., 1954-56; LL.D., Marietta (Ohio) Coll., Bethany (W.Va.) Coll., W.Va. U., W.Va. Inst. Tech., 1957, W.Va. State Coll., 1961, Concord Coll., 1960; Dr. of Humanics, Salem Coll.; Dr. Pub. Adminstrn., W.Va. Wesleyan Coll.; Litt.D., Western New Eng. Coll., 1969; m. Hovah Hall, July 25, 1948; children—Cecilia A., Craig Hall, Sharon. High sch. tchr., 1943-46; mem. staff Marietta Coll., 1946-50; v.p. Salem Coll., 1950-56; gov. State of W.Va., 1957-61; v.p. Island Creek Coal Co., 1961-64; dir. civic affairs Monsanto Co., 1965-67, v.p., 1967; pres. Cecil H. Underwood Assos., 1965—, Franswood Corp., 1968-75; dir. Huntington Fed. Savs. & Loan Assn.; pres. Bethany (W.Va.) Coll., 1972-75; field underwriter N.Y. Life Ins. Co., 1976-78; pres. Princess Coals, Inc., Huntington, 1978—; v.p. Burnwood Co., real estate. Mem. W.Va. Ho. Dels., 1944-56, minority floor leader, 1949, 51, 53, 55. Mem. exec. com. Gov.'s Conf., 1959; chmn. So. Regional Edn. Bd., 1959-60. Pres. Young Republican League of W.Va., 1946-50; parliamentarian Young Rep. Nat. Conv., Boston, 1951; del.-at-large Rep. Nat. Conv., 1960, 64, 72, 76, temporary chmn., 1960. Bd. dirs. W.Va. Found. Ind. Colls., Appalachian Regional Hosps.; bd. dirs. W.Va. div. Am. Cancer Soc., nat. bd. dirs., chmn. nat. crusade com., 1976-77, chmn. com. on legacies and planned giving, 1979; regional vice chmn. Boy Scouts Am., 1961-67; mem. governing council Nat. Municipal League. Served with U.S. Army Enlisted Res. Corps, 1942-43. Mem. Sigma Phi Epsilon, Pi Kappa Delta. Methodist. Mason (Shriner), Elk, Rotarian, Moose. Home: 609 13th Ave Huntington WV 25701 Office: Princess Coals Inc PO Box 1210 Huntington WV 25714

UNDERWOOD, DON, pub. relations and advt. exec.; b. Thomas, W.Va., Feb. 20, 1918; s. Roy L. and Helen (Brown) U.; student pub. schs., Indpls.; m. Miriam L. Ellison, Apr. 21, 1941 (div. 1960); 1 son, Donald M.; m. 2d, Nancy M. Costlow, May 28, 1966. News editor Indpls. News, 1936-42, chief polit. writer, 1945-47, chief Washington bur., 1947-49; v.p., Washington mgr. Bozell & Jacobs, Inc., 1949-56, exec. v.p., N.Y.C., 1956-64, pres., 1964—, chief exec. officer, 1967; co-founder, chmn. bd. Underwood Jordan Assos., 1968—; chmn. bd. Underwood Jordan McLeish, London, 1970—; dir. Inside Can. Pub. Relations Ltd.; founder, chmn. Pinnacle Group, internat. public relations, U.S., Can., Gt. Britain, Tokyo, 1976—. Served capt. AUS, 1942-45; ETO. Decorated Bronze Star. Mem. Internat. Public Relations Assn., Public Relations Soc. Am., Public Utilities Advt. Assn., Am. Legion, Sigma Delta Chi. Clubs: Nat. Press (Washington); N.Y. Athletic, Marco Polo (N.Y.C.); Indpls. Press; Poor Richard (Phila.); LeMirador Country (Vevey, Switzerland). Home: 2 Sutton Pl S New York NY 10022 Office: 230 Park Ave New York NY 10017. *Without compassion, your existence on earth is suspect.*

UNDERWOOD, JAMES MARTIN, business exec.; b. Pitts., Feb. 27, 1909; s. Fred P. and Jean (Martin) M.; B.S., U. Pitts., 1930; M.B.A., Harvard, 1932; m. Anne E. Saxman, Dec. 31, 1931 (dec. Mar. 1974); children—Ann Eliza (Mrs. G.N. Potts), James Martin, Thomas Saxman, Charles; m. 2d, Alice A. Clemens, Dec. 1976. Asst. sec.-tres. Vulcan Mold & Iron Co., 1935-40, pres., dir., 1946—, chmn. (name changed to Vulcan, Inc. 1967), 1968—; exec. v.p. Toyad Corp., Latrobe, 1941; founder, pres. Halund Co., 1941-45; gen. sales mgr. Latrobe Electric Steel Co., 1945-46, dir., 1948-75. Mem. Western Pa. Hosp. Council, 1969—, v.p., 1972-76; exec. com. Economy League Western Pa., 1974—. Republican nominee 28th Congl. Dist. Pa., 1940; councilman, Latrobe, 1943-69, pres., 1953-69; del. Rep. Nat. Conv., 1960, 68. Dir., Westmoreland Airport Authority, 1951-76, chmn., 1951-68. Bd. dirs. Latrobe Hosp., 1948—, pres., 1961-66; trustee Community Chest, St. Vincent Coll., 1954-71, U. Pitts., 1964-71. Mem. Am. Iron and Steel Inst., Young Presidents Orgn., Def. Orientation Conf. Assn. (dir.), Phi Delta Theta. Presbyn. (trustee). Mason (32 deg., Shriner, Jester), Elk. Clubs: Rolling Rock (Ligonier, Pa.); University, Duquesne, Oakmont Country (Pitts.); Latrobe Country; Sea Island (Ga.) Cottage Owners. Home: Saxman Dr Extension Latrobe PA 15650 also Sea Island GA 31561 Office: Vulcan Inc Box 70 Latrobe PA 15650

UNDERWOOD, MILTON R., investment banker; b. Orange, N.J., Aug. 17, 1901; s. Peter J. and Mary (Coffey) U.; student Roanoke Coll., 1921-23, Columbia, 1923-25; LL.B., Vanderbilt U., 1928; m. Catherine Fondren, Feb. 14, 1931 (dec.); children—Peter (dec.), David Milton; m. 2d, Sue D. Johnson, Sept. 3, 1970. With investment dept. Second Nat. Bank, Houston, 1928-31; agy. dir. Seaboard Life Ins. Co., 1931-34; investment banker Milton R. Underwood & Co., 1935-47, pres. Underwood, Neuhaus & Co., 1948-68, vice chmn., 1968—; v.p. Feliciana Co., Houston, 1946—; dir. Am. Liberty S.S. Co., Benjamin Franklin Savs. and Loan. Gov. N.Y. Stock Exchange, 1963-66. Trustee Fondern Found., Vanderbilt U.; bd. govs. Rice U.; pres. U. Houston Found. Mem. Nat. Assn. Security Dealers, Ind. Petroleum Assn., Investment Bankers Assn. Am. (gov.), C. of C. (sec., dir.), Delta Kappa Epsilon. Episcopalian. Clubs: Houston, River Oaks Country, Houston Country, Bayou, University, Ramada (Houston); Garden of Gods (Colorado Springs, Colo.). Home: 3711 San Felipe St Houston TX 77027 Office: 724 Travis St Houston TX 77002

UNDERWOOD, ROBERT CHARLES, state justice; b. Gardner, Ill., Oct. 27, 1915; s. Marion L. and Edith L. (Frazee) U.; B.A., Ill. Wesleyan U., 1937, LL.D., 1970; J.D., U. Ill., 1939; LL.D., Eureka Coll., 1970, Loyola U., Chgo., 1969; m. Dorothy Louise Roy, Feb. 2, 1939; 1 dau., Susan Louise (Mrs. John C. Barcalow III). Admitted to Ill. bar, 1939; pvt. practice, Bloomington, 1939-46; city atty., Normal, Ill., 1942-43; asst. state's atty., McLean County, Ill., 1942-46, county judge, 1946-62; justice Ill. Supreme Ct., 1962—, chief justice, 1969-75. Mem. Conf. Chief Justices, 1969-75, mem. exec. council 1971-75, vice chmn., 1974-75; Ill. rep. Council State Ct. Reps., Nat. Center for State Cts. Vice chmn. Ill. Commn. Children, 1953-55. Trustee Ill. Wesleyan U., 1957-59; past mem. bd. dirs. McLean County Mental Health Center, Bloomington; chmn. com. to survey legal edn. needs in Ill., Bd. Higher Edn., 1968; numerous other civic activities. Recipient Distinguished Service award U.S. Jr. C. of C., 1948, Good Govt. award, 1953; Outstanding Citizen award Normal C. of C., 1962; ann. citation for pub. service Ill. Welfare Assn., 1960; certificate of outstanding achievement U. Ill. Coll. Law, 1969. Fellow Pa. Mason Juvenile Ct. Inst.; mem. Am., Ill. (award of merit 1976), McLean County (past pres.) bar assns., Ill. County and Probate Judges Assn. (past pres.), Am. Judicature Soc. (dir. 1974—), Inst. Jud. Adminstrn., Sigma Chi, Pi Kappa Delta. Republican. Methodist. Mason (33 deg.). Clubs: Bloomington, Bloomington Country, Rotary (hon.), Kiwanis (hon.). Contbr. articles to profl. jours. Home: 11 Kent Dr Normal IL 61761 Office: 300 Peoples Bank Bldg Bloomington IL 61701

UNDLIN, CHARLES THOMAS, banker; b. Madison, Minn., Mar. 4, 1928; s. Jennings C. and Alice (Berg) U.; B.A., St. Olaf Coll., Northfield, Minn.; m. Lois M. Anderson, June 23, 1953; children—Sarah, Mary Lee, Margaret, Thomas. Asst. cashier Northwestern State Bank, Osseo, Minn., 1950-55, Northwest Bancorp., Mpls., 1955-57, Security Bank & Trust Co., Owatonna, Minn., 1957-59; pres. First Nat. Bank Black Hills, Rapid City, S.D., 1959—; dir. Black Hills Power & Light Co., Wyodak Resources Devel. Co., 1st N.W. Trust Co. Served with AUS, 1951-52. Mem. S.D. Bankers Assn. (pres.), Rapid City C. of C. (past pres.). Republican. Lutheran. Club: Arrowhead (Rapid City). Home: 1805 W Boulevard Rapid City SD 57701 Office: First Nat Bank Rapid City SD 57701

UNGAR, EDWARD WILLIAM, research orgn. exec.; b. N.Y.C., Feb. 6, 1936; s. Morris and Elizabeth (Czitrom) U.; B.M.E., CCNY, 1957; M.S., Ohio State U., 1959, Ph.D., 1966; m. Lois Cramer, July 9, 1978; children—Michele Ruth, Mark Steven, Elizabeth Ann. Mem. research staff Battelle Columbus Labs. (Ohio), 1957-66, div. chief, 1966-70, sect. mgr., 1970-73, dept. mgr., 1973-76, asso. dir., 1976-78, dir., 1978—; v.p. Battelle Meml. Inst., 1978—; dir. Olentangy Mgmt. Co. Trustee, Battelle Meml. Inst. Found.; mem. Devel. Com. for Greater Columbus; mem. steering com. (Com. for Tomorrow) Ohio State U. Mem. ASME, Newcomen Soc., Sigma Xi, Pi Tau Sigma, Tau Beta Pi. Office: 505 King Ave Columbus OH 43201

UNGAR, FRANK, biochemist, educator; b. Cleve., Apr. 30, 1922; s. Michael and Susan (Gelberger) U.; B.A., Ohio State U., 1943; M.S., Western Res. U., 1948; Ph.D., Tufts U., 1952; m. Shirley Ruth Katz, Sept. 26, 1948; children—Leanne Ruth, William Stephan, Barbara Louise, Joanne Sue. Research staff Cleve. Clinic, 1947-48, Worcester Found. for Exptl. Biology, Shrewsbury, Mass., 1951-58; faculty U. Minn. Med. Sch., Mpls., 1958—, prof. biochemistry, 1966—, dir. tng. program for steroid biochemistry, 1962-72; vis. asst. prof. Clark U., 1956-58; Fulbright sr. vis. prof. dept. biochemistry Univ. Coll. Cork (Ireland), 1974-75. Mem. Am. Assn. Biol. Chemists, Am. Chem. Soc., Soc. for Exptl. Biology and Medicine, AAAS, Endocrine Soc., Sigma Xi. Co-author: Metabolism of Steroid Hormones, 1953, 65. Contbr. articles to profl. jours. Home: 5232 Stevens Ave Minneapolis MN 55419

UNGAR, FREDERICK, publishing co. exec.; Vienna, Austria, Sept. 5, 1898; s. Moriz and Bertha (Kobler) U.; came to U.S., 1939, naturalized, 1945; Doctor of Law, U. Vienna, 1923; m. Hansi Beck, Apr. 17, 1948; 1 son, Bertrand Theodore. Founder Phaidon Verlag, Vienna, 1924, Saturn Verlag, 1926-38; pub. Frederick Ungar Pub. Co.,

Inc., N.Y.C., 1940—, Stephen Daye Press, N.Y.C., 1945—. Recipient Alexander Gode medal Am. Translators Assn., 1975; named hon. prof. Austrian govt., 1976. Mem. Ethical Soc. No. Westchester. Editor: To Mother with Love, 1951; What's Right with America, 1952; Friedrich Schiller, An Anthology for Our Time, 1959; Goethe's World View, 1963; (with Alexander Gode) Anthology of German Poetry through 19th Century, 1964; Handbook of Austrian Literature, 1973; The Last Days of Mankind (Karl Kraus), 1974; (with Lina Mainiero) Encyclopedia of World Literature in the 20th Century, Vol. 4, 1975; No Compromise: Selected Writings of Karl Kraus, 1977; Practical Wisdom: A Treasury of Aphorisms and Reflections from the German, 1977; editor, author foreword The Little Comedy and Other Stories (Arthur Schnitzler), 1978; author foreword The Eternal Feminine: Selected Poems of Goethe, bilingual edit., 1980. Office: 250 Park Ave S New York NY 10003

UNGARO, JOSEPH MICHAEL, newspaper editor; b. Providence, Nov. 4, 1930; s. Rocco and Lucy (Mott) U.; B.A., Providence Coll., 1952; M.S. in Journalism, Columbia, 1953; m. Evelyn Short, Apr. 15, 1961; children—Elizabeth Anne, Joseph Michael, Ellen Lucia. With Providence Jour.-Bull., 1951-73, mng. editor Eve. Bull., 1967-72, mng. editor Eve. Bull., also dir. planning and devel. Providence Jour. and Bull., 1972-73; mng. editor Westchester-Rockland Newspapers, White Plains, N.Y., 1974-75, v.p., exec. editor, 1975—. Bd. dirs. Am. Newspaper Pubs. Assn. Research Inst. Mem. Am. Soc. Newspaper Editors, AP Mng. Editors Assn. (exec. com.). Home: Ridgefield Ave South Salem NY 10590 Office: 1 Gannett Dr White Plains NY 10604

UNGER, DAVID GRANT, govt. ofcl.; b. Romulus, Mich., Feb. 20, 1932; s. Hugo and Elsie A. (Bolle) U.; B.A. in Earth Scis., Antioch Coll., Yellow Springs, Ohio, 1954; A.M. in Polit. Sci., U. Pa., 1962; M.P.A., Harvard U., 1964; m. Renee Marilyn Satz, Apr. 3, 1954; children—David Jordan, Christopher Blair. Exec. sec. Upper Susquehanna Watershed Assn., Norwich, N.Y., 1954-56; dir. Pa. Soil and Water Conservation Commn., 1956-63; exec. sec., then exec. v.p. Nat. Assn. Conservation Dists., Washington, 1964-78; dep. asst. sec. natural resources and environ. Dept. Agr., 1978—. Fels scholar, 1959-62; Littauer fellow, 1963-64. Fellow Soil Conservation Soc. Am.

UNGER, FERDINAND THOMAS, ret. army officer; b. Pitts., Oct. 28, 1913; s. Ferdinand and Ann (Sweeney) U.; student U. Pitts., 1932-33; B.S., U.S. Mil. Acad., 1937; grad. Command and Gen. Staff Coll., 1944; student Columbia U., 1946; grad. Armed Forces Staff Coll., 1948, Nat. War Coll., 1958; m. Evelyn Bayly Bucher, Oct. 28, 1942; children—James T., Charles K. Commd. 2d lt. U.S. Army, 1937, advanced through grades to lt. gen., 1966; various assignments camps in U.S., 1937-44; comdr. 718th F.A. Bn., 63d Inf. Div., France and Germany, 1945-47, 1st Corps Arty., Korea, 1953-54; staff Arty. Sch., Fort Sill, Okla., 1954-57; exec. to supreme allied comdr., Europe, SHAPE, Paris, France, 1958-59; comdr. 72d Arty. Group and 3d Inf. Div. Arty., Germany, 1960-61; chief staff Third U.S. Army, Fort McPherson, Ga., 1961-62; dir. operations Joint Chiefs Staff, Washington, 1962-64; comdg. gen. 7th Inf. Div., Korea, 1964-65; supr. army tng. Ft. Monroe, Va., 1965-66; high commr. Ryukyu Islands, comdg. gen. U.S. Army, Ryukyus, 1966-69; dir. plans and policy Joint Chiefs of Staff, Washington, 1969-70; ret., 1970; gov. U.S. Soldiers' and Airmen's Home, Washington, 1971—. Pres. bd. dirs. Army Distaff Found., 1973-75. Decorated D.S.M. with cluster, Legion of Merit with cluster; Croix de Guerre with star; knight Order St. Gregory. Mem. West Point Soc. D.C. (v.p. 1974—). Roman Catholic. Address: 4 N Dogwood Ln Charlottesville VA 22901

UNGER, GARRY DOUGLAS, profl. hockey player; b. Edmonton, Alta., Can., Dec. 7, 1947; s. Jack and Olive Lavina (Wheeler) U.; grad. high sch. Center, St. Louis Blues Profl. Hockey Team, 1971-79, Atlanta Flames, 1979—. Office: Omni Arena 100 Techwood Atlanta GA 30062

UNGER, HOWARD ROBERT, air force officer; b. Shamokin, Pa., July 2, 1927; s. Howard Smink and Florence Ida (Krieger) U.; A.A., George Washington U., 1947, B.A., 1949, M.D., 1952; M.P.H., Johns Hopkins, 1958; m. Patricia Anne Boyer, Mar. 21, 1953; children—Lori Colleen, Howard Robert, Cynthia Lynn, Kimberly Anne. Rotating intern Gallinger Municipal Hosp. (now D.C. Gen. Hosp.), Washington, 1952-53; commd. 1st lt. M.C., USAF, 1954, advanced through grades to brig. gen., 1974; resident in aerospace medicine USAF, 1958-60; service in Vietnam and U.S.; comdr. USAF Hosp., RAF, Lakenheath, Eng., 1972-74; command surgeon Hdqrs. USAF Europe, Ramstein, Ger., 1974-75; comdr. Aerospace Med. Div., Brooks AFB, Tex., 1975-78; command surgeon Mil. Airlift Command, Scott AFB, Ill., 1978—. Decorated Legion of Merit with 3 oak leaf clusters, Air medal with 2 oak leaf clusters, Joint Service Commendation medal, USAF Commendation medal with 2 oak leaf clusters. Diplomate aerospace medicine Am. Bd. Preventive Medicine (vice chmn. aerospace medicine 1971—). Mem. Am. Coll. Preventive Medicine (pres. 1976-77), Aerospace Med. Assn. (pres. 1977-78), Soc. USAF Flight Surgeons (pres. 1970). Episcopalian. Home: 153 W Goettler St Scott AFB IL 62225 Office: Command Surgeon Mil Airlift Command Scott AFB IL 62225

UNGER, IRWIN, historian, educator; b. Bklyn., May 2, 1927; s. Elias C. and Mary (Roth) U.; B.Social Scis., City Coll. N.Y., 1948; M.A., Columbia, 1949, Ph.D., 1958; student U. Wash., 1949-51; m. Bernate Myra Spaet, Feb. 1956 (div.); children—Brooke David, Miles Jeremy, Paul Joshua; m. 2d, Debi Irene Weisstein, May 11, 1970; stepchildren—Anthony Allen, Elizabeth Sarah. Instr., Columbia, 1956-58; vis. lectr. U. P.R., 1958-59; asst. prof. Long Beach (Calif.) State Coll., 1959-62; asso. prof. U. Calif. at Davis, 1962-66; prof. history N.Y.U., 1966—. Served with AUS, 1952-54. Recipient Pulitzer prize for history, 1965; Guggenheim fellow, 1972-73. Mem. Am. Hist. Assn., Orgn. Am. Historians, Econ. History Assn. Author: The Greenback Era: A Social and Political History of American Finance, 1865-1879, 1964; The Movement: A History of the American New Left, 1974; (with Debi Unger) The Vulnerable Years: The United States, 1896-1917. Home: 110 Bleecker St New York NY 10012

UNGER, JAMES FREDERICK, cartoonist; b. London, Jan. 21, 1937; came to Can., 1968; s. Cecil James and Lilian Maud (Hill) U.; student public grammar sch., London. Ins. clk., London, 1953-55; police officer Port of London, 1957-60; various positions and cos., Eng., 1960-68; worked as copywriter, graphic designer Minto Constrn., Ottawa, Ont. Can., 1968-71; art dir. Mississanga Times, Toronto, Ont., 1971-74; syndicated cartoonist, 1974—. Served with Brit. Army, 1955-57. Named Cartoonist of Yr., Ont. Weekly Newspaper Awards, 1972, 73, 74. Author: Apart from a little dampness, 1975; And you wonder why I don't want to go to Italian restaurants, 1976; Where's the kids, 1978; The 1st Treasury of Herman, 1979.

UNGER, LEONARD, educator, former U.S. ambassador; b. San Diego, Dec. 17, 1917; s. Louis Allen and Rachel (Seidman) U.; B.A., Harvard, 1939; m. Anne Louise Axon, Dec. 18, 1944; children—Deborah (Mrs. Duncan J. G. Mackintosh), Philip, Andrew, Anne Thomas, Daniel. With Nat. Resources Planning Bd., 1939-41; mem. staff Dept. State and Fgn. Service, from 1941, now ret.; with Council Fgn. Ministers and Commn. to Investigate Italo-Yugoslav Boundary, Paris Peace Conf., 1946; U.S. polit. adviser in Trieste, 1950-52; with NATO Command, Naples, 1952-53; rep. Trieste negotiations, London, 1954; officer-in-charge polit.-military affairs European bur. Dept. State, 1954-57; assigned Nat. War Coll., 1957-58; dep. chief of mission Am. embassy, Bangkok, Thailand, 1958-62; U.S. ambassador to Laos, 1962-64; dep. asst. sec. state for Far Eastern Affairs, chmn. Vietnam coordinating com., 1965-67; appointed career minister, 1966; U.S. ambassador to Thailand, 1967-73; U.S. ambassador to Republic of China, from 1974; faculty mem. Tufts U., Medford, Mass. Decorated Order of White Elephant (Thailand); recipient Distinguished Honor award Dept. of State, 1965. Mem. Assn. Am. Geographers, Am. Fgn. Service Assn., Am. Geog. Soc., Siam Soc., Phi Beta Kappa. Club: Cosmos. Contbr. articles to mags. Office: Tufts U Medford MA 02155

UNGER, LEONARD HOWARD, educator; b. N.Y.C., July 26, 1916; s. Joseph and Sadie (Friedman) U.; B.A., Vanderbilt U., 1937; M.A., La. State U., 1938, postgrad., 1938-39; Ph.D., State U. Iowa, 1941; m. Sherley Glasscock, July 3, 1946; children—Anne Elizabeth, Thomas Michael, Amy Catherine. English instr. Bemidji (Minn.) State Coll., 1941, Bard Coll., 1946-47; mem. faculty U. Minn., Mpls., 1947—, prof. English, 1956—, co-editor pamphlets on Am. writers, 1961—; Fulbright lectr. Am. lit. U. Rome, U. Florence (Italy), 1957-58, U. Athens, 1963-64. Served with USAAF, 1942-45. Guggenheim fellow, 1953; Ind. Sch. Letters fellow, summers 1957, 67. Mem. Phi Beta Kappa. Author: Donne's Poetry and Modern Criticism, 1950; The Man in the Name: Essays on the Experience of Poetry, 1956; (pamphlet) T.S. Eliot, 1961; T.S. Eliot: Moments and Patterns, 1966; also essays, poems. Editor: T.S. Eliot: A Selected Critique, 1948; (with W.V. O'Connor) Poems for Study, 1953; Seven Modern American Poets, 1967; Home: 135 Malcolm Ave SE Minneapolis MN 55414

UNGER, SHERMAN EDWARD, lawyer; b. Chgo., Oct. 9, 1927; s. Mel I. and Helen (Strong) U.; B.A., Miami U., Oxford, Ohio, 1950; J.D., U. Cin., 1953; m. Polly Van Buren Taylor, Dec. 29, 1953 (div. Feb. 1972); children—Cathleen Estelle, Peter Van Buren; m. 2d, Nancy McBryde Turnbull, Aug. 20, 1976. Admitted to Ohio bar, 1953, D.C. bar, 1972; partner firm Frost & Jacobs, Cin., 1956-69; gen. counsel Dept. Housing and Urban Devel., 1969-70; v.p. Am. Financial Corp., Cin., 1971-72; practice law, 1972—. Bd. dirs. Fed. Nat. Mortgage Assn., 1969-72; gen. counsel Govt. Nat. Mortgage Assn., 1969-70; mem. Adminstrv. Conf. U.S., 1969-71; mem. nat. adv. com. for legal services program Office Econ. Opportunity, 1969-71; chmn. bd. Modern Talking Picture Service Inc., 1968-69, Modern Media, 1968-69; mem. Ohio Water and Sewer Commn., 1965-69; mem. Nat. Adv. Council Econ. Opportunity, 1971-73; dir. Master Design Corp. Bd. dirs. Shared Med. Services, 1973—. Served to 1st lt. AUS, 1946-47, USAF, 1953-56. Mem. Am., Ohio, Cin. bar assns., World Peace Through Law Center, Beta Theta Pi. Presbyn. Mason. Clubs: Cincinnati Country, Queen City (Cin.); Metropolitan (Washington); Racquet and Tennis (New York). Home: 16 Corbin Dr Cincinnati OH 45208 Office: 2820 DuBois Tower Cincinnati OH 45202 also 1776 F St Washington DC 20006

UNGER, STEPHEN HERBERT, elec. engr., computer scientist; b. N.Y.C., July 7, 1931; s. Julius I. and Rebecca (Cooper) U.; B.E.E., Poly. Inst. Bklyn., 1952; S.M., Mass. Inst. Tech., 1953, Sc.D., 1957; m. Marion Ruth Baker, Apr. 8, 1960 (div. July 1978); children—Donald N., Debra Susan. Research asst. Mass. Inst. Tech. Research Lab. in Electronics, 1954-57; mem. tech. staff Bell Telephone Labs., Whippany, N.J., 1957-61; asso. prof. elec. engring. and computer sci. Columbia U., 1961-68, prof., 1968—; vis. prof. U. Calif., Berkeley, 1967; vis. prof. computer sci. Danish Tech. U., Lyngby, 1974-75; sr. research asso. Center for Policy Research, N.Y.C., 1970-74; cons. in field. Bd. dirs. Morris County (N.J.) Urban League, 1959-60. Guggenheim fellow, 1967; IEEE fellow, 1975; NSF grantee, 1966-70, 71-74, 79. Mem. IEEE (asso. editor Tech. and Soc. 1971—, chmn. working group on ethics and employment practices 1971-78, acting chmn. com. social implications of technology 1979), Assn. Computing Machinery, AAUP, AAAS, Sigma Xi, Eta Kappa Nu, Tau Beta Pi. Author: Asynchronous Sequential Switching Circuits, 1969; research, numerous articles in field; patentee parallel data processing apparatus. Home: 229 Cambridge Ave Englewood NJ 07631 Office: Dept Computer Sci Columbia U New York NY 10027. *Unless, in doubtful situations, we act as though good may triumph, it surely won't.*

UNGERER, JEAN TOMI, author, artist; b. Strasbourg, France, Nov. 28, 1931; s. Theo and Alice (Essler) U.; student French and German Schools; m. Miriam Lancaster; 1 dau., Phoebe Alexis. Came to U.S., 1957. Free-lance artist, illus., cartoonist for nat. mags.; illustrator children's books. Served with Mounted Police, Sahara, 1953. Recipient honors for books, N.Y. Herald Tribune; gold medal Soc. of Illustrators, 1960; International Children's Book Prize. Mem. Inst. Graphic Arts, P.E.N. Club. Internat. Platform Assn., Author's Guild, Audubon Soc., N.Y. Hist. Soc. Illustrator cartoon album, author children's books. Author: The Mellops Go Flying, 1957; Crietor, 1958; Adelaide, 1959; Emile, 1960; Inside Marriage, 1960; Horrible, 1960; Rufus, 1961; Three Robbers, 1962; Snail Where Are You, 1962; Herzinfarkt, 1962; The Mellops Go Underground, 1962; A Child-Phoebe Alexis, 1962; Underground Sketchbook, 1964; One Two Where Is My Shoe, 1964; The Party, 1966; Orlando, 1966; Zeralda's Ogre, 1967; Moon Man, 1967; Ask Me A Question, 1968; The Hat, 1969; The Fornicon, 1969; Compromises, 1969; Beast of Monsieur Racine, 1971; I Am Papa Snap and These Are My Favorite No Such Stories, 1971; No Kiss for Mother, 1972; Allumette, 1974; A. Great Song Book, 1978. Office: care Doubleday and Co Inc 245 Park Ave New York NY 10017*

UNGERLEIDER, HARRY EDUARDE, physician; b. Phila., May 24, 1895; s. Ignace and Kate (Rauscher) U.; M.D., Medico Chirurgical Coll., Phila., 1916; m. Marian Eleanor Rice, Dec. 28, 1925; children—Barbara Barnard, Ellen (Justus). Intern Phila. Gen. Hosp., 1916-20; instr. Temple U. Sch. Medicine, 1920-22, U. Pa. Grad. Sch. Medicine, 1920-22; med. dir. Eastern State Penitentiary, Phila., 1922-25; asst. physician Polyclinic and Meth. Hosp., 1925-29; asst. med. dir. Equitable Life Assurance Soc., 1930-45, asso. med. dir., N.Y.C., 1945-47, med. dir. research, 1947-59; cons., med. dir. N.Am. Reassurance Co., 1959—. Chmn. bd. Life Ins. Medicine; mem. health council U.S. C. of C.; bd. dirs. Nat. Health Council; hon. pres. XI Internat. Congress de Medicina del Seguro de Vida. Served as maj. M.C., U.S. Army, 1917-19. Recipient award of merit Am. Heart Assn., 1956; Alumni award Medico-Chirurg. Coll., Phila., 1965. Diplomate Am. Bd. Internal Medicine. Fellow AAAS, A.C.P., Am. Coll. Cardiology; hon. fellow Cardiol. Soc. Brazil, Soc. Life Ins. Physicians Mexico; mem. Pan-Am. Med. Assn. (hon.), Assn. Life Ins. Med. Dirs. (2d v.p. 1947, 1st v.p. 1948, pres. 1949), N.Y. Acad. Sci., Am. Heart Assn. (sec. 1947-48, dir. 1942-57), N.Y. Heart Assn. (dir. 1942—), Soc. Ex-Residents and Physicians Phila. Gen. Hosp. (pres.), AMA, N.Y. County Med. Soc., Am. Life Conv., Life Ins. Med. Research Fund, Acad. Medicine, Am. Soc. Study Arteriosclerosis, Am. Therapeutic Soc. (pres. 1960), Am. Pub. Health Assn., Health Ins. Council, Indsl. Med. Assn., Harvey Soc., N.Y. State Med. Soc., Am. Med. Writers Assn., Am. Soc. Clin. Pharmacology and Therapeutics. Mason. Club: Channel City (Santa Barbara). Author: Life Insurance and Medicine. Editor trans. Assn. Life Ins. Med. Dirs., 1937-47; asso. editor Geriatrics; mem. adv. editorial bd. Nat. Heart Bull. Contbr. sects. on roentgenology of heart in several text books; numerous articles on various aspects of heart disease to sci. jours. in U.S. and S.A., 1917-48. Home: 600 E Ocean Blvd Apt 1501 Long Beach CA 90802

UNGERMAN, IRVINE E., lawyer; b. Leavenworth, Kans., May 12, 1908; s. William and Rachel (Ettleman) U.; LL.B., Washburn U., 1930; m. Hanna Friedberg, Apr. 13, 1929; children—Maynard I., Rowena Mae (Mrs. David Galerston). Admitted to Okla. bar, 1930, since practiced in Tulsa; sr. mem. firm Ungerman, Conner, Little, Ungerman & Goodman, 1930—. Gen. counsel, dir. Union Nat Bank, Tulsa. Pres. Okla. Bd. Corrections, 1971-75, Tulsa Hebrew Sch., 1949-51, Congregation Bnai Emunah, 1951-53. Fellow Am. Coll. Trial Lawyers, Comml. Law Found. Am.; mem. Internat., Am., Okla. (bd. govs. 1978), Tulsa County bar assns., Am. Judicature Soc., Nat. Assn. Def. Counsel, Am., Okla. (pres. 1974-75) trial lawyers assns., Comml. Law League Am. Clubs: Meadowbrook Country (sec. 1952-65), University, Summit (Tulsa). Home: 2230 E 39th St Tulsa OK 74105 Office: Wright Bldg Tulsa OK 74103

UNGERMAN, MAYNARD IVAN, lawyer; b. Topeka, Dec. 5, 1929; s. Irvine E. and Hanna (Friedberg) U.; B.A. cum laude, Stanford, 1951, LL.B., 1953; m. Elsa Leiter, June 25, 1950; children—William Charles, Karla Beth, Rebecca Diane. Admitted to Okla. bar, 1953, since practiced in Tulsa; mem. firm Ungerman, Whitebook, Grabel & Ungerman, 1953-58, Ungerman, Grabel, Ungerman & Lieter, 1958—; labor relations cons. for cos. and unions, 1953—. Mem. Mayor's Sub-com. on Housing for Tulsa, 1964—; mem. nat. council Am. Jewish Joint Distbn. Com., 1963—; mem. Nat. Citizens Com. on Community Relations, 1964-68; v.p. Tulsa Jewish Community Council, 1961-66; vice chmn. Oklahoma City-Tulsa Catholic Diocese Social Action Bd., 1969-73; mem. exec. bd. Tulsa Family & Children's Service, 1963-69, treas., 1965-66, 1st v.p., 1967—; mem. exec. bd. S.W. Region Anti-Defamation League, 1962—, v.p., 1966—, chmn. Okla. sect., 1967—. Mem. finance com. Okla. Democratic Party, 1964; Tulsa County coordinator Okla. Dem. Central Com., 1964; alternate del. Dem. Conv., 1964; mem. inaugural com. inauguration of Pres. Johnson and Vice Pres. Humphrey, 1965; Tulsa County Dem. chmn., 1967-69. Served to 1st lt. USAF, 1953-55. Mem. Jr. Mems. Assn. Comml. Law League Am. (chmn., rec. soc. 1966-67), Tulsa County (mem. exec. com. 1964-65), Fed., Am., Okla. (vice chmn. labor law com. 1967—) bar assns., Am. Judicature Soc., Phi Alpha Delta. Editor: Stanford Law Rev., 1952-53. Home: 6959 S Delaware Pl Tulsa OK 74136 Office: Wright Bldg Tulsa OK 74103

UNGERS, OSWALD M., architect, educator; b. Kaisersesch, Germany, July 12, 1926; s. Anton and Maria (Mitchels) U.; Dipl. Tng., Tech. U., Karlsruhe, Germany, 1950; m. Lisselotte Gabler, July 4, 1956; children—Simon, Sibylle, Sophia. Came to U.S., 1969. Archtl. practice, Cologne, Germany, 1950-62, Berlin, 1962-69, Itahaca, N.Y., 1969—; prof. architecture Tech. U. Berlin, 1963-73, dean faculty architecture, 1965-67; prof. architecture Cornell U., Ithaca, 1968—, chmn. dept., 1968-74; vis. prof. Harvard U., 1972, 77, U. Calif. at Los Angeles, 1973; exhibited in biennale, Venice, Italy, 1976, also Berlin, London, N.Y.C.; organized 1st and 2d Berlin Summer Acads. for Architecture. Recipient prizes in several urban design competitions. Mem. A.I.A. Author: The Urban Block, The Urban Villa, The Urban Garden; (with wife) Utopian Comunes in the U.S.A.; Megastructure in Habitation; also numerous articles on architecture to internat. mags., numerous chpts. in books. Research on cast optimisation in large-scale housing, urban pattern devel. in N.Y. State, subsystems of cities. Designer large-scale pub. housing projects in Germany. Home: 627 Highland Rd Ithaca NY 14850 also 60 Belvederstrasse Cologne 41 West Germany

UNITAS, JOHN CONSTANTINE, profl. football player; b. Pitts., May 7, 1933; m. 2d, Sandra Unitas; 1 son, Francis Joseph; children by previous marriage—Janice, John Constantine, Robert, Christopher, Kenneth. Player, Pitts. Steelers, 1955, Balt. Colts, 1956-72, San Diego Chargers, 1973-74; sports analyst CBS, 1975. Owner Johnny Unitas Golden Arm Restaurant, Balt. Leading passer Nat. Football League; recipient Nat. Football League Man of Year award Vitalis Scholarship Fund, 1972; Gold medal award Pa. Broadcasters, 1972; named Nat. Football League Most Valuable Player, 1957, 64, 67; Greatest Quarterback of All Time Nat. Football League 50th Anniversary Com.; player of decade A.P., 1970; named All Pro; player Pro Bowl, 1957-59, 64-65, 67. Super Bowl, 1969-70. Address: Johnny Unitas Golden Arm Restaurant 6354 York Rd Baltimore MD 21212*

UNKLESBAY, ATHEL GLYDE, geologist, educator; b. Byesville, Ohio, Feb. 11, 1914; s. Howard Ray and Madaline (Archer) U.; A.B., Marietta Coll., 1938, D.Sc. (hon.), 1977; M.A., State U. Iowa, 1940, Ph.D., 1942; m. Wanda Eileen Strauch, Sept. 14, 1940 (dec. 1971); children—Kenneth, Marjorie, Carolyn, Allen; m. 2d, Mary Wheeler Myhre, June 8, 1973. Geologist, U.S. Geol. Survey, 1942-45, Iowa Geol. Survey, 1945-46; asst. prof. Colgate, 1946-47; mem. faculty U. Mo., Columbia, 1947—, prof. geology, 1954—, chmn. dept., 1959-67, v.p. adminstrn., 1967-79; exec. dir. Am. Geol. Inst., 1979—; cons. in field. Mem. Columbia Bd. Edn., 1954-70, Columbia Parks and Recreation Commn., 1954-57. Wilton Park fellow, 1968, 72, 76. Mem. Am. Assn. Petroleum Geologists, Paleontol. Soc. Am., Geol. Soc. Am., Econ. Paleontologists and Mineralogists, Nat. Assn., Sigma Xi. Methodist. Club: Cosmos. Author: Geology of Boone County, 1952; Common Fossils of Missouri, 1955; Pennsylvanian Cephalopods of Oklahoma, 1962; also articles. Home: 2113-S Skyline Tower 5597 Seminary Rd Falls Church VA 22041

UNNA, WARREN W., journalist; b. San Francisco, Sept. 14, 1923; s. Walter J. and Phyllis (Fleischer) U.; A.B. in Internat. Relations, U. Calif. at Berkeley, 1943; postgrad. in Chinese studies, Stanford, 1943-44. Reporter, San Francisco Chronicle, 1946-51; asso. editor Archtl. Forum, also House and Home, 1951-52; mem. staff Washington Post, 1952-70, South Asia corr., 1965-67; fgn. affairs commentator Channel 26, Washington, 1970-71; U.S. corr. The Statesman of India, 1971—. Served with AUS, 1943-46; CBI. Author: The Coppa Murals, 1951; also articles. Home: 121 6th St NE Washington DC 20002

UNRUH, HENRY CORNELIUS, life ins. co. exec.; b. Barmstedt, Holstein, Germany, Mar. 25, 1914; s. Cornelius and Martha (Woltmann) U.; B.S., Acadia U., 1933; A.M., Brown U., 1935; m. Mary Olive Facey, Oct. 4, 1941; children—Sandra Jane, David John. Came to U.S., 1946, naturalized, 1952. Actuarial clk. No. Life Assurance Co. Can., London, Ont., 1937-46; asst. actuary Provident Life & Accident Ins. Co., Chattanooga, 1946-48, actuary, 1948-55, chief actuary, 1955—, v.p., 1957-68, adminstrv. v.p., also chief actuary, 1968-70, pres., chief operating officer, 1970-72, chief exec. officer, 1972-79, chmn., 1972—. Fellow Soc. Actuaries. Presbyn. (elder). Home: 102 South Dr Signal Mountain TN 37377 Office: Provident Life & Accident Ins Co Fountain Sq Chattanooga TN 37402

UNRUH, JESSE MARVIN, state ofcl.; b. Newton, Kans., Sept. 30, 1922; s. Isaac P. and Nettie Laura (Kessler) U.; B.A., U. So. Calif., 1948, postgrad., 1949; LL.D., U. So. Calif., 1967; m. Virginia June

Lemon, Nov. 2, 1943; children—Bruce, Bradley, Robert, Randall, Linda Lu. Dist. staff dir. Fed. Census, 1950; with Pacific Car DeMurrage Bur., 1950-54; mem. Calif. Assembly, 1954-70, chmn. com. fin. and ins., 1957-59, chmn. ways and means com., 1959-61, speaker of assembly, 1961-68, Democratic leader, 1968-70, mem. adv. commn. on intergovtl. relations, 1967-70; vis. prof. polit. sci. San Fernando Valley State Coll., 1970; vis. prof. U. So. Calif. Sch. Law, 1971-72; now treas. State of Calif.; cons., prof. polit. sci. Eagleton Inst. Politics, Rutgers U., 1965—; co-chmn. Seminar Young Legislators, Carnegie Corp.; Chubb fellow Yale, 1962. Mem. Calif. Central Democratic Com., 1954—; So. Calif. mgr. John F. Kennedy presdl. campaign, 1960; So. Calif. co-chmn. gubernatorial campaign, 1962; statewide coordinator assembly, congl. campaigns, 1962; chmn. Robert F. Kennedy's Calif. presdl. campaign, 1968; chmn. Calif. del. Dem. Nat. Conv., 1968; pres. Nat. Conf. State Legis. Leaders, 1966; Dem. candidate for gov. Calif., 1970; bd. regents U. Calif., 1961-68; trustee Calif. State Colls., 1961-68, Inst. for Am. Univs., Citizens Conf. on State Legislatures, 1968—. Served with USNR, 1942-45. Home: 306 Bora Bora Way Marina Del Rey CA 90291 Office: State Capitol Sacramento CA 95814

UNSELL, LLOYD NEAL, journalist, trade assn. exec.; b. Henryetta, Okla., May 12, 1922; s. John William and Rhoda Elizabeth (Martinez) U.; student U. Ill., Kalamazoo Coll., 1942-43; m. Nettie Marie Rogers, Sept. 24, 1944; children—Lloyd Neal, Jonna Kay Unsell Wilhelm, James Allan. Mem. editorial staff Tulsa Daily World, 1947-48; successively staff writer, dir. communications, v.p. for pub. affairs, exec. v.p. and chief exec. officer Ind. Petroleum Assn. Am., Washington, 1948—; chmn. selection com. for Milburn Petty award Am. Petroleum Inst.-Assn. Petroleum Writers, 1972—. Served with U.S. Army, 1942-46; ETO; PTO. Recipient Spl. award as outstanding petroleum industry communicator Assn. Petroleum Writers, 1960. Mem. Nat. Press Club. Republican. Baptist. Club: Washington Golf and Country. Author reports and articles in field. Home: 6248 N Washington Blvd Arlington VA 22205 Office: 1101 16th St NW Washington DC 20036

UNSER, AL, auto racer; b. Albuquerque, May 29, 1939; s. Jerry H. and Mary C. (Craven) U.; student pub. schs., Albuquerque; m. Wanda Jesperson, Apr. 22, 1958 (div.); children—Mary Linda, Debra Ann, Alfred; m. 2d, Karen Barnes, Nov. 22, 1977. Auto racer U.S. Auto Club, Speedway, Ind., 1964—, placed 3d in nat. standings, 1968, 2d in 1969, 77, 78, 1st in 1971, 72, 4th in 1976; winner Indpls. 500, 1970, 71, 78, Pocono 500, 1976, 78, Ont. 500, 1977, 78; placed 3d in USAC SCCA Formula 5000, 1975, 2d place, 1976; IROC champion, 1978. Home: 7625 Central NW Albuquerque NM 87105

UNSER, BOBBY, profl. race car driver; b. Albuquerque, Feb. 20, 1934; 4 children. Former modified stock car race driver; now driver profl. racing cars. Winner Indpls. 500, 1968, 75; U.S. Auto Club champion, 1969, 74; winner Calif. 500, 1974, 76; winner Pike's Peak Auto Hill Climb, 12 times. Named Martini and Rossi Driver of Year, 1974. Address: 7700 Central Ave SW Albuquerque NM 87105

UNSWORTH, ARTHUR JAMES, lawyer, diversified co. exec.; b. Moncton, N.B., Can., Apr. 19, 1933; s. Arthur Darrell and Dorothy Evelyn (Kierstead) U.; student Dalhousie U., 1955-58; m. Gwendolyn Faye Tomblin, May 17, 1958 (div.); children—James Bradley, Shelley. Called to N.S. bar, 1959, N.B. bar, 1969, Que. bar, 1972; individual practice law, Kentville, N.S., Can., 1958-66; sec., gen. counsel Maritime Tel. & Tel. Co., Ltd., Halifax, N.S., 1966-69; gen. counsel K.C. Irving Cos., St. John, N.B., 1969-70; gen. counsel Genstar, Ltd., Montreal, Que., Can., 1970-73, v.p., gen. counsel, 1973—. Mem. N.S., N.B., Que. barristers socs. Anglican. Club: Montreal Amateur Athletic Assn. Home: 440 Bonsecours St Montreal PQ Canada Office: Suite 4105 1 Place Ville Marie Montreal PQ H3B 3R1 Canada

UNSWORTH, RICHARD PRESTON, clergyman, educator; b. Vineland, N.J., Feb. 7, 1927; s. Joseph Lewis and Laura (MacMillan) U.; B.A., Princeton, 1948; B.D., Yale, 1954; Th.M., Harvard, 1963; S.T.D., Dickenson Coll., 1971; L.H.D., Washington and Jefferson Coll., 1971; m. Joy Merritt, Aug. 20, 1949; children—Sarah, John, Mary, Lucy. Ordained to ministry Presbyn. Ch., 1953; tchr. Bible and English, Mt. Hermon Sch., 1948-50; asst. chaplain Yale, 1952-54; chaplain, asso. prof. Smith Coll., 1954-64; dean William Jewett Tucker Found., prof. religion Dartmouth, 1963-67; chaplain, prof. religion Smith Coll., 1967-80; head Northfield Mt. Hermon Sch., East Northfield, Mass., 1980—; cons. Ednl. Assos., Inc., 1967-69, U.S. Office Edn., 1969-77. Leader Operation Crossroads Africa unit in Nigeria, 1961, mem. adv. bd., 1961-66; adminstrv. com. Student Christian Movement of New Eng., 1964; mem. Mass. unit So. Christian Leadership Conf., 1968; trustee Conf. on Religion in Independent Schs., 1961-63; pres. Am. Friends of Coll. Cevenol, 1957-63; trustee, Am. rep. Coll. Cevenol, France, 1958—; bd. dirs. Family Planning Council Western Mass., 1972—. Mem. AAUP, Nat. Assn. Coll. and Univ. Chaplains, Am. Acad. Religion. Author: Sexuality and the Human Community, 1970; Dignity and Exploitation, Images of Sex in the 70's, 1974; (with Arnold Kenseth) Prayers for Worship Leaders, 1978. Contbr. to Sex Education and the Schools, 1967. Address: Mount Hermon Sch East Northfield MA 01354

UNTERBERG, THOMAS ISRAEL, investment banker; b. N.Y.C., Jan. 8, 1931; s. Clarence Ephraim and Marjorie (Kahn) U.; student Deerfield (Mass.) Acad., 1946-48; B.A., Princeton, 1952; M.B.A., U. Pa., 1956; m. Susan Appleman, Aug. 16, 1961; children—Ellen Rose, Emily Jane. Asso., C.E. Unterberg, Towbin Co., N.Y.C., 1956-60, partner, 1960-75, mng. partner, 1975-77; partner L.F. Rothschild, Unterberg, Towbin, N.Y.C., 1977—; dir. 509 Madison Ave., Unterberg Realty Co., LIN Broadcasting Corp., Thermo Electron Corp., Eberline Instrument Corp., Am. Internat. Pictures, Princeton Gamma-Tech. Chmn., Grand St. Settlement, 1963-72, chmn., 1972—; div. chmn. United Hosp. Fund, 1971—. Mem. finance com. N.Y. State Democratic Com., 1973—; trustee Montefiore Hosp., 1973—, treas., 1974—. Served with AUS, 1952-54. Mem. Nat. Assn. Securities Dealers (co-chmn. com. corp. fin. 1973-75), Investment Assn. N.Y., Security Traders Assn. N.Y. Jewish. Clubs: Hollywood Golf (v.p.); City Athletic, Bond (N.Y.C.); Princeton Key and Seal. Home: 784 Park Ave New York NY 10021 Office: 55 Water St New York NY 10041

UNTERECKER, JOHN EUGENE, educator, author; b. Buffalo, Dec. 14, 1922; s. John G. and Bertha (Ellinger) U.; B.A., Middlebury Coll., 1944; M.A., Columbia, 1948, Ph.D., 1958; m. Ann Apalian, Feb. 28, 1953 (div. 1973). Radio announcer sta. WBNY, Buffalo, 1944; Off-Broadway, stock and TV actor, 1945-46; instr. Coll. City N.Y., 1946-58; mem. faculty Columbia, 1958-74, prof. English lit., 1966-74; faculty dept. English, U. Hawaii, Honolulu, 1974—. Vis. prof. U. Hawaii, 1969, U. Tex., 1974; lectr. Yeats Internat. Summer Sch., Ireland, 1972, 73-75, 77, 78, 79; mem. book reviewer N.Y. Times, New Leader, Sat. Rev. Pres. Hawaii Lit. Council, 1975, mem. bd., 1975-78. Guggenheim fellow, 1964-65; grantee Am. Philos. Soc., 1962; Yaddo fellow, 1967, 68, 69, 70, 72, 74, 79; Am. Council Learned Socs. grantee, 1962, 72. Mem. Author's Guild, P.E.N., James Joyce Soc., Am. Com. Irish Studies, Am. Gloxinia Soc. Author: A Reader's Guide to W.B. Yeats, 1959; Lawrence Durrell, 1964; The Dreaming Zoo, 1965; Voyager: A Life of Hart Crane, 1969; Dance Sequence, 1975; Stone, 1977; editor (with Frank Stewart) Poetry Hawaii: A Contemporary Anthrology, 1979. Contbr. poetry to major mags. Address: Dept English University of Hawaii 1733 Donaghho Rd Honolulu HI 96822. *The value of life must always be seen in personal terms: my relationship with particular people -- friends, family, students -- never with an unidentifiable movement; my relationship with particular places -- cities, hills, houses -- never with such vast areas as countries or regions. Once I was told that I have a weakness for falling in love; the accusation -- and it was that -- is absolutely just. Abstractions have never meant anything to me; feelings, almost everything.*

UNTERKOEFLER, ERNEST, bishop; b. Phila., Aug. 17, 1917; s. Ernest L. and Anna Rose (Chambers) U.; A.B. summa cum laude, Catholic U. Am., 1940, S.T.L., 1944, J.C.D., 1950. Ordained priest Roman Cath. Ch., 1944; asst. pastor in Richmond, Va., 1944-47, 50-54, Arlington, Va., 1947-50; sec. Richmond Diocesan Tribunal, 1954-60; moderator Council Cath. Women and Council Cath. Nurses, 1956-61; sec. Diocesan bd. Consultors, 1960-64; founder Cath. Physicians Guild, Richmond, 1957-64; chancellor Richmond Diocese, 1960-64; papal chamberlain, 1961; aux. bishop Richmond, titular bishop Latapolis, vicar gen. Richmond Diocese, 1962-64; bishop of Charleston, S.C., 1964—; promoter IV Synod, Diocese Richmond, 1962-64; sec. Nat. Conf. U.S. Bishops, 1966-70, chmn. permanent diaconate com., 1968-71, 74—, chmn. Region IV, 1972-74, mem. adminstrv. com., 1974—; sec. adminstrv. bd. Nat. Cath. Conf., 1966-70; mem. Bishops' Com. on Ecumenical and Inter-religious Affairs, 1965-78, chmn., 1978—; mem. 2d Vatican Council, 1962-65; mem. Anglican-Roman Catholic subcommns. theology of marriage and mixed marriage; co-chmn. Anglican/Roman Cath. Commn. Theology of Marriage; chmn. Roman Cath.-Presbyn./Reformed Consultation; mem. com. social devel. and world peace U.S. Council Chs., 1971-74; mem. adminstrv. com. and bd. NCCB-USCC, 1978—; mem. Ad Hoc Com. Women in Ch. and Soc., 1971—; co-chmn. Charleston Bicentennial Commn. on Religious Liberty. Bd. dirs. CARA, 1969—, pres., 1972—; mem. alumni bd. govs. Cath. U. Am. Recipient Pax Christi award St. John's U., Collegeville, Minn., 1970; medal of U. Santa Maria La Antiqua, Panama, 1976; decorated grand cross Republic of Panama, 1976. Address: 119 Broad St Charleston SC 29401. *Where would I be without the love and care of God, our Father? Answers to that question I ponder. Indeed I am among people who share their gifts and strength; I live with them joyfully in their response to me in fellowship and common care. Life continues to be an adventure for the curious.*

UOTILA, URHO ANTTI KALEVI, educator, geodesist; b. Pöytyä, Finland, Feb. 22, 1923; s. Antti Samuli and Vera Justina (Kyto) U.; came to U.S., 1951, naturalized, 1957; B.S., Finland's Inst. Tech., 1946, M.S., 1949; Ph.D., Ohio State U., 1959; m. Helena Vanhakartano, Aug. 6, 1949; children—Heidi, Kirsi, Elizabeth, Julie, Trina, Caroline. Surveyor, geodesist Finnish Govt. 1944-46, 46-51; geodesist Swedish Govt., 1946; research asst. Ohio State U., 1952-53, research asso., 1953-58, research supr., 1959—, lectr. in geodesy, 1955-57, asst. prof., 1959-62, asso. prof., 1962-65, chmn. dept. geodetic sci., 1964—, prof., 1965—; mem. Solar Eclipse Expdn. to Greenland, 1954. Mem. adv. panel on geodesy U.S. Coast and Geodetic Survey, Nat. Acad. Sci., 1964-66; mem. geodesy and cartography working group, space sci. steering com. NASA, 1965-67, mem. geodesy/cartography working group, summer conf. lunar exploration and sci., 1965, mem. geodesy and cartography adv. subcom., 1967-72; mem. ad hoc com. on N.Am. datum div. earth scis. Nat. Acad. Scis.-N.A.E., 1968-70; bd. dirs. Internat. Gravity Bur., France, 1975—; mem. com. on geodesy Nat. Acad. Scis., 1975-78. Served with Finnish Army, 1942-44. Recipient Kaarina and W.A. Heiskanen award, 1962; Apollo Achievement award NASA, 1969. Fellow Am. Geophys. Union (v.p. geodesy sect. 1964-68, pres. 1968-70); mem. Am. Congress Surveying and Mapping (nat. dir. 1970-73, dir. control survey div. 1975-77, v.p. 1977-78, pres. 1979—), Am. Soc. Photogrammetry, Can. Inst. Surveying, Am. Soc. Engring. Edn., Internat. Assn. Geodesy (pres. spl. study group 5.30 1967-71, pres. sect. V 1971-75, exec. com. 1971—), Univs. Space Research Assn. (trustee 1973-75), Finnish Nat. Acad. Scis. (fgn.), Profl. Land Surveyors Ohio (hon.), Sigma Xi. Mem. editorial adv. com. Advances in Geophysics, 1968-77. Contbr. articles to profl. jours., encys. Research in geometric geodesy, phys. geodesy and statis. analysis of data. Home: 4329 Shelbourne Ln Columbus OH 43220

UPBIN, HAL JAY, real estate co. exec.; b. Bronx, N.Y., Jan. 15, 1939; s. David and Evelyn (Sloan) U.; B.B.A. in Accounting, Pace Coll., 1961; m. Shari Kiesler, May 29, 1960; children—Edward, Elyse, Danielle. Tax sr. Peat, Marwick, Mitchell & Co., C.P.A.'s, N.Y.C., 1961-65; tax mgr. Price Waterhouse & Co., C.P.A.'s, N.Y.C., 1965-71; dir. taxes Wheelabrator-Frye Inc., N.Y.C., 1971-72, treas., 1972-74; pres. Wheelabrator Financial Corp., N.Y.C., 1974-75; v.p., chief financial officer Chase Manhattan Mortgage and Realty Trust, N.Y.C., 1975-76, pres., 1976-78, pres., chmn., 1978—. C.P.A., N.Y. Mem. Am. Inst. C.P.A.'s, N.Y. State Soc. C.P.A.'s, Franklin (N.J.) Jaycees (v.p.). Jewish (pres. temple). Home: 45 E 89th St New York NY 10028 Office: One Pennsylvania Plaza New York NY 10001

UPCHURCH, THERON ACRIEL, ins. co. exec.; b. Apex, N.C., Oct. 25, 1915; s. Malpheus Gilbert and Lessie Helen (Upchurch) U.; B.S., U. N.C., 1936; m. Mabel Stuart Weatherspoon, June 17, 1939; 1 dau., Stuart (Mrs. William Thomas Buice, III). With Wachovia Bank & Trust Co., Raleigh, N.C., 1936-42; with Durham Life Ins. Co., Raleigh, 1942—, asst. treas., 1945-50, dir., 1950—, treas., 1951-56, v.p., treas., 1956-67, pres., chief exec. officer, chmn. exec. com., 1967-78, chmn. bd. dirs., 1976—; chmn. bd., exec. com. Durham Life Broadcasting Service, Inc., Raleigh, 1972—; chmn. bd. State Capital Ins. Co., Raleigh, 1976—. Served with AUS, 1943-46, 50-51. Mem. Raleigh C. of C. (past dir., treas.), Sigma Chi. Baptist. Kiwanian. Club: Carolina Country (Raleigh). Home: 1724 Canterbury Rd Raleigh NC 27608 Office: PO Box 27807 Raleigh NC 27611

UPDIKE, JOHN HOYER, writer; b. Shillington, Pa., Mar. 18, 1932; s. Wesley R. and Linda G. (Hoyer) U.; A.B., Harvard U., 1954; student Ruskin Sch. Drawing and Fine Art, 1954-55; m. Mary E. Pennington, June 26, 1953; children—Elizabeth, David, Michael, Miranda; m. 2d, Martha R. Bernhard, Sept. 30, 1977. With New Yorker mag., 1955-57. Recipient Rosenthal award Nat. Inst. Arts and Letters, 1960; O'Henry Prize Story award winner, 1967-68. Mem. Nat. Inst. Arts and Letters, Am. Acad. Arts and Scis. Democrat. Congregationalist. Author: The Carpentered Hen, 1958; The Poorhouse Fair, 1959; The Same Door, 1959; Rabbit, Run, 1960, Pigeon Feathers, 1962; The Centaur (Nat. Book award), 1963; Telephone Poles, 1963; Olinger Stories (selection), 1964; Of the Farm, 1965; Assorted Prose, 1965; The Music School, 1966; Couples, 1968; Midpoint, 1969; Bech: A Book, 1970; Rabbit Redux, 1971; Museums and Women, 1972; Buchanan Dying, 1974; A Month of Sundays, 1975; Picked-Up Pieces, 1975; Marry Me, 1976; Tossing and Turning, 1977; The Coup, 1978; Problems, 1979. Address: Georgetown MA 01833

UPLINGER, ROBERT JAQUA, power transmission equipment co. exec.; b. St. Francis, Kans., Aug. 14, 1912; s. James Edward and Magnolia (Jaqua) U.; student U. Kans., 1930-32, 33, 35, 36-37; m. Martha Rath, Aug. 20, 1939; children—Robert Jaqua, Karen Martha. With U.S. Coast and Geodetic Survey, 1934-35, Gates Rubber Co., Denver, 1937-43; pres. Uplinger & Sherman, Inc., Syracuse, N.Y., 1946-48; pres., treas. Robert J. Uplinger, Inc., distbrs. power transmission equipment, Syracuse, 1949-77; v.p. Robert J. Uplinger div. Kaman Bearing & Supply-East (merger), 1977—. Internat. pres. Lions, 1971-72, rep. at UN, 1977—. Co-organizer CAP, Syracuse, 1942, officer, 1942-43; pres. Syracuse Assn. Blind, 1959-61, dir., 1957-59, 62-63. Served with AUS, 1943-45. Recipient Internat. Solidarity Merit award VIIth Congress World Fedn. Deaf. Mem. Power Transmission Distbrs. Assn. (co-founder Chgo. 1959), U. Kans. Alumni Assn., Syracuse C. of C. (aviation com. 1969—, chmn. 1975—), Alpha Xi, Sigma Chi. Lutheran. Mason. Home: 909 Cumberland Ave Syracuse NY 13210 Office: 430 Oneida St Syracuse NY 13201

UPPMAN, THEODOR, concert and opera singer; b. San Jose, Calif., Jan. 12, 1920; s. John August and Hulda Maria (Thörnström) U.; student Coll. of Pacific, 1938-39, Curtis Inst. Music, 1939-41, Stanford, 1941-42, U. So. Calif., 1948-50; m. Jean Seward, Jan. 31, 1943; children—Margot, Michael. Profl. debut as baritone No. Calif. Symphony, 1941; appeared with San Francisco Symphony, 1947; performed in Pelleas et Melisande, City Center Opera Co., N.Y., 1948; debut San Francisco Opera Co., 1948; N.Y. recital Times Hall, 1950; appeared Billy Budd opera premiere, Royal Opera House, London, Eng., 1951; appeared Theatre de la Champs Elysees, Paris, France, 1952; performed in Billy Budd, NBC-TV Opera Theatre, 1952, Pelleas et Melisande, Met. Opera Co., 1953, Magic Flute, 1956-77, La Perichole, 1956-71, Don Giovanni, 1957-73, Madama Butterfly, 1961-76, Cosi fan Tutte, 1962-71, L'Italiana in Algeri, 1973-75; world premiere of the Passion of Jonathan Wade, N.Y.C. Opera, 1962, Villa Lobos' Yerma, Santa Fe Opera, 1971, Pasatieri's Black Widow, Seattle Opera, 1972; Barab's Philip Marshall, Chautauqua, 1974; Aix en Provence Festival, summer 1964, Aldeburgh Festival, summer 1975; Chgo. Lyric Opera debut, 1964; War Requiem by Britten, Dallas, Cleve., Cin. orchs., 1965; Damnation of Faust, N.Y. Philharmonic, 1966; Am. premiere Billy Budd, Chgo. Lyric Opera, 1970. Concert opera symphony appearances throughout U.S., also radio, TV; mem. profl. com. regional auditions Met. Opera. Address: care Columbia Artists Management Inc 165 W 57th St New York City NY 10019

UPSHAW, HARRY STEPHAN, educator; b. Birmingham, Ala., July 10, 1926; s. N.H. and Florence (Arnold) U.; student U. Ala., 1946-47; A.B., U. Chgo., 1949; M.A., Northwestern U., 1951; Ph.D., U. N.C., 1956; m. Paula Binyon, June 18, 1950; children—Alan Binyon, Phyllis, David Arnold, Stephan Lipner. Asst prof. psychology U. Ala., 1954-57; spl. instr. psychology Simmons Coll., Boston, 1957-58; research asso. Ednl. Research Corp., Cambridge, Mass., 1957-58; asst. prof., asso. prof. pub. health U. N.C., 1958-61, lectr., asso. prof. psychology, 1958-64; asso. prof. Bryn Mawr (Pa.) Coll., 1964-65; asso. prof., then prof. psychology U. Ill. at Chgo. Circle, 1965—, dept. head, 1968-72; guest prof. U. Mannheim (Germany), 1975; guest prof., Fulbright scholar Technische Universitaet Berlin, 1978-79; editorial cons. Jour. Exptl. Social Psychology, Jour. Exptl. Research in Personality, Jour. Applied Social Psychology, Jour. Personality Social Psychology. Served with AUS, 1944-46. Fellow Am., Midwestern psychol. assns., Psychometric Soc. Contbr. articles profl. jours. Home: 2025 Sherman Ave Evanston IL 60201 Office: U Ill at Chgo Circle Psychology Dept PO Box 4348 Chicago IL 60680

UPSON, HOWARD EDWIN, realtor; b. Newark, Ohio, Mar. 29, 1921; s. Howard Henry and Juliet (Besuden) U.; B.A., Harvard, 1943; M.B.A. in Marketing, Wharton Sch. Finance, U. Pa., 1948; m. Joyce Terry, June 1, 1957; children—Thomas Howard, Stuart Turner, Matthew Wright. Product advt. mgr. Gen. Electric Co., Bridgeport, Conn., 1949-52, 54-57, Louisville, 1952-54; account exec. McCann-Erickson, Inc., N.Y.C., 1957-64, v.p., account dir., 1964-67, sr. v.p., mng. dir., 1969-72; mng. partner Hastings Assos./Lesher-Glendinning, Georgetown, Conn., 1972—. Served with USNR, 1943-46. Home: 62 Hemmelskamp Rd Wilton CT 06897 Office: Hastings Assos/Lesher-Glendinning Georgetown CT 06829

UPSON, JAMES JULIAN, wallboard mfg. co. exec.; b. Barnesville, Minn., Feb. 7, 1919; s. William Harrison and Alma (Thompson) U.; B.S. in Econs., U. Pa., 1942; m. Elizabeth Fishburne, May 20, 1943; children—James Laurance, Elizabeth Ann. Adminstrv. v.p. The Upson Co., Lockport, N.Y., 1946-48, sec., 1948-52, exec. v.p., 1952-56, dir., 1953—, pres., 1956-77, chmn., 1977—; dir. chmn. bd. Jim Upson Corp.; dir. Lockport Exchange office Mfrs. & Traders Trust Co. Mem. Lockport, U.S. chambers commerce, N.A.M. Clubs: Rotary, Masons, Tuscarora, Lockport Town and Country, Buffalo. Home: 16 The Common Lockport NY 14094 Office: Upson Co Upson Point Lockport NY 14094

UPSON, STUART BARNARD, advt. exec.; b. Cin., Apr. 14, 1925; s. Mark and Alice (Barnard) U.; B.S., Yale, 1945; m. Barbara Jussen, Nov. 2, 1946; children—Marguerite Nichols, Anne English, Stuart Barnard. With Dancer, Fitzgerald, Sample, Inc., N.Y.C., 1946—, sr. v.p., 1963-66, exec. v.p., 1966-67, pres., 1967-74, chmn., 1974—; dir. Manhattan Life Ins. Co. Bd. dirs., pres. Fresh Air Fund, N.Y. Served with USNR, 1943-46. Mem. St. Elmo Soc. Clubs: Wee Burn Country (Darien); Minneapolis; Yale, Sky (N.Y.C.); Blind Brook Country, Pine Valley Country. Home: 68 Stephen Mather Rd Darien CT 06820 Office: 347 Madison Ave New York NY 10017

UPSTON, JOHN EDWIN, assn. exec., fgn. affairs officer; b. Maxwell AFB, Ala., Apr. 17, 1935; s. John E. and Claudia (Smith) U.; student Va. Mil. Inst., 1954-55; student in internat. relations Harvard U., 1957; A.B., Stanford, 1958; m. Barbara Craven, Aug. 23, 1969; children—John Edwin, III, Michael Gignoux, Bennet Colt, Leland Craven. Founding adminstr. Mental Research Inst., Palo Alto, Calif., 1959-61, dir., 1961—; bus. developer, N.Y.C., San Francisco, 1961—; mem. mgmt. planning policy implementation staff Dept. State, Washington, 1964-65, adv. Internat. Orgn. Affairs, 21st, 22d UN Gen. Assembly, mem. permanent U.S. Mission to UN, N.Y.C., 1966-69; exec. dir. Sec. of State's Com. Facilitate Internat. Travel, 1970—; spl. asst. dep. under sec. State for mgmt. 1970-72; exec. dir. Secretariat, U.S. Nat. Commn. to UNESCO, Bur. of Internat. Orgn. Affairs, Dept. of State, 1972-77, also exec. sec. nat. commn.; U.S. rep. regional meeting European Nat. Commn., Varna, Bulgaria and Bucharest, Rumania; U.S. adviser Gen. Conf. UNESCO, Paris, 1972, Nairobi, Kenya, 1976; gen. mgr. Mediphone, Inc., 1961; v.p., dir. Broadcast Devel. Corp., N.Y.C., 1962—; creator, producer Career, Westinghouse Broadcasting Network TV series, 1961; asso. Burnham & Co., investment bankers, N.Y.C., 1969-70; founder Nat. TV Sales, Inc., 1964; cons. Ithaca Gun Co., Gen. Recreation, Inc., Warner Bros. Record Co., Burbank, Calif. Past dir. Tolstoy Found.; founding pres., dir. Caribbeana Council, 1977; mem. Caribbean Conservation Assn., Barbados, W.I.; mem. task force on U.S. immigration policy Council on Fgn. Relations; hon. mem. Population Crises Com., Washington. Recipient Superior Honor award State Dept., 1973. Club: Knickerbocker (N.Y.C.); Olympic (San Francisco); Army Navy (Washington). Home: 4602 Tournay Rd Westmoreland Hill MD 20016 also 2 E 62d St New York NY 10021 Office: Caribbeana Council 1625 Eye St NW Washington DC 20006 also Regina Ct Maxwell Gardens Christchurch Barbados West Indies

UPTHEGROVE, WILLIAM REID, metallurgist, univ. dean; b. Ann Arbor, Mich., Nov. 10, 1928; s. Clair and Hazel Katherine (Platt) U.; B.S.E. in Metall. Engring., U. Mich., 1950, M.S., 1954, Ph.D., 1957; m. Margot Jeanne Mowatt, July 11, 1953; children—Amy Elizabeth, David Clair, Thomas Reid, Bruce Warren, Michael John. Mem. faculty U. Okla., 1956-62, chmn. Sch. Metall. Engring., 1956-62, asst. prof., 1956-60, asso. prof., metall. engring., 1960-62; supr. powder metallurgy Internat. Nickel Co. Research Lab., Bayonne, N.J., 1962-64; prof., chmn. dept. mech. engring. U. Tex., Austin, 1964-70; dean Coll. Engring., U. Okla., Norman, 1970—; materials cons., 1964—. Served to lt. (j.g.) USNR, 1950-53. Registered profl. engr., Okla., Tex. Mem. ASME, AAAS, Am. Soc. for Engring. Edn., Metall. Soc., Am. Soc. Metals, Nat. Soc. Profl. Engrs., Sigma Xi, Tau Beta Pi, Phi Lambda Upsilon, Phi Kappa Phi, Pi Tau Sigma, Phi Gamma Delta. Contbr. articles to profl. jours. Home: 3941 Warwick Dr Norman OK 73069

UPTON, ARTHUR CANFIELD, pathologist; b. Ann Arbor, Mich., Feb. 27, 1923; s. Herbert Hawkes and Ellen (Canfield) U.; grad. Phillips Acad., Andover, Mass., 1941; B.A., U. Mich., 1944, M.D., 1946; m. Elizabeth Bache Perry, Mar. 1, 1946; children—Rebecca A., Melissa P., Bradley C. Intern Univ. Hosp., Ann Arbor, 1947, resident, 1948-49; instr. pathology U. Mich. Med. Sch., 1950-51; pathologist Oak Ridge Nat. Lab., 1951-54, chief pathology-physiology sect., 1954-69; prof. pathology, State U. N.Y. Med. Sch. at Stony Brook, 1969-77, chmn. dept. pathology, 1969-70, dean Sch. Basic Health Scis., 1970-75; dir. Nat. Cancer Inst., Bethesda, Md., 1977-79; chmn. dept. environ. medicine N.Y. U. Med. Sch., N.Y.C., 1979—. Mem. various coms. nat. and internat. orgns. Served with AUS, 1943-46. Recipient Ernest Orlando Lawrence award for atomic field, 1965; Comfort-Crookshank award for cancer research, 1979. Mem. Am. Assn. Pathologists and Bacteriologists, Internat. Acad. Pathology, Radiation Research Soc. (councilor 1963-64, pres. elect 1964-65, pres. 1965-66), Am. Assn. Cancer Research (pres. 1963-64), Am. Soc. Exptl. Pathology (pres 1967-68), A.A.A.S., Gerontological Soc., Sci. Research Soc. Am., Soc. Exptl. Biology and Medicine, Phi Beta Kappa, Phi Gamma Delta, Alpha Omega Alpha, Nu Sigma Nu. Asso. editor Cancer Research; mem. editorial bd. Lab. Investigation, Nuclear Medicine, Excerpta Medica, Internat. Jour. Cancer, Internat. Union Against Cancer. 5206 W Cedar Ln Bethesda MD 20014 Office: NY U Sch Medicine 550 1st Ave New York NY 10016

UPTON, ARVIN EDWARD, lawyer, writer; b. Upton, Ky., Apr. 8, 1914; s. Arvin Edward and Jennie (Ferrill) U.; A.B., Western Ky. U., 1933; J.D., Harvard, 1940. Exec. asst. child welfare Ky. Dept. Welfare, 1936-39; practice law, mem. firm Ogden, Galphin, Tarrant & Street, Louisville, 1940-43; asst. exec. dir. Fgn. Liquidation Commn., 1946-47; asso. and dep. gen. counsel Air Force, 1950-53; former sr. Washington partner LeBoeuf, Lamb, Leiby & MacRae; professorial lectr. George Washington Nat. Law Center; chmn. Independent Curators Inc. Past chmn. D.C. Health and Welfare Council; past pres. United Community Services of Washington; bd. dirs. Episc. Center for Children. Served to maj. AUS, 1943-46. Recipient Commendation Ribbon, 1946, Air Force Exceptional Civilian Service award, 1953. Mem. Am. Bar Assn., Bar Assn. D.C., Internat. Nuclear Law Assn. Clubs: City Tavern (Georgetown); Harvard (N.Y.C.). Author: Lorenzino, 1977. Home: 1239 31st St NW Washington DC 20007

UPTON, ELDON CLAGGETT, JR., ins. broker; b. New Orleans, May 14, 1911; s. Eldon Claggett and Emily Massie Burton (Lewis) U.; B.B.A., Tulane U., 1932; m. Winifred Leone Suydam, Nov. 9, 1939; children—Leone Suydam, Claggett Coldham. Agt., instr. Travelers Ins. Co., 1932-35; agt., mgr. Sun Life Assurance Co. of Can., 1935-43, br. mgr., 1943-48; gen. agt. Mut. Benefit Life Ins. Co. of Newark, 1948-55; mem. Fed. Maritime Bd., 1953-54. Past pres. Met. Crime Commn. New Orleans, Inc.; v.p. Eye Found. Am.; past pres. YMCA. Mem. Am. Soc. C.L.U.'s (past pres.), Nat., New Orleans (past pres.) assns. life underwriters, Soc. Colonial Wars, Life Mgrs. Assn. New Orleans (past pres.), Nat. Tulane Alumni Assn. (past pres.), Delta Kappa Epsilon, Omicron Delta Kappa. Clubs: Boston, Recess, Tulane Alumni T., Tulane Commerce Alumni, Southern Yacht, Lakeshore. Home: 1550 2d St G-2 New Orleans LA 70150 Office: 135 St Charles Ave New Orleans LA 70130

UPTON, RICHARD F., lawyer; b. Bow, N.H., Sept. 3, 1914; s. Robert W. and Martha G. U.; grad. Phillips Exeter Acad., 1931; A.B., Dartmouth, 1935; LL.B., Harvard, 1938; m. Marie Audibert, Sept. 23, 1950 (dec. 1970); children—William W., Mathew H.; m. 2d, Shirley D. Knowland, May 17, 1975. Admitted to N.H. bar, 1938, practice law, Concord, 1938—. Dir. Concord Nat. Bank, Concord Group Ins. Co. Mem. N.H. State Housing Bd., 1946-48, N.H. War Records Com., 1946-51, N.H. Commn. Alcoholism, 1951-63, N.H. Commn. Interstate Cooperation, 1951-55; chmn. N.H. Civil Rights Adv. Commn., 1958-62, N.H. Lincoln Sesquicentennial Com., 1958-60; mem. N.H. Com. Study Pub. Schs., 1961-63; mem. N.H. Hist. Commn., 1963-68, chmn., 1965-68; chmn. N.H. Fish and Game Commn., 1968-74; chmn. com. environ. systems N.H. Citizens' Task Force, 1969-70; mem. N.H. Interstate Wetlands Commn., 1969-70; chmn. N.H. Environ. Council, 1970-71; mem. N.H. Interstate Boundary Commn., 1971-73, N.H. Am. Revolutionary Bicentennial Com., 1969-75. Mem. N.H. Legislature, 1941, 47, 49, maj. floor leader, 1947, speaker, 1949; pres. 15th N.H. Constl. Conv., 1964. Trustee N.H. Hosp., 1946-48. Served to capt. AUS, 1942-46. Fellow Am. Bar Found.; mem. Am., N.H. (pres. 1964-65) bar assns., N.H. Hist. Soc. (pres., trustee). Club: Concord Country. Author: Revolutionary New Hampshire, 1936. Editorial bd. N.H. Bar Jour., 1972—. Home: 110 Centre St Concord NH 03301 Office: 10 Centre St Concord NH 03301

UPTON, RICHARD THOMAS, artist; b. Hartford, Conn., May 26, 1931; s. Ray Granville and Helen Marie (Colla) U.; B.F.A., U. Conn., 1960; M.F.A., Ind. U., 1963; 1 son, Richard Thomas, II. Exhbns. include Westampe Contemporaine, Galerie Mansart, Bibliot Nat., France, 1969, 74, L'estampe aujourd'hui, 1973-78, Sala Internat., Palacio de Bellas Artes, Mexico City, 1969, Sept. Graveures un Sculpteur de Medailles, Mus. Deonon, Chalon-Sur Saone, France, 1973, Brit. Internat. Print Biennale, U.S. sect. touring Eng., 1973, Del. Water Gap, Corcoran Gallery Art, Washington, 1975, Everson Mus. Art, Syracuse, N.Y., 1975, Nat. Collection Prints and Poetry, Library of Congress, 1976-77, retrospective prints from Elvehejm Art Center, Atelier 17, Paris, 1977, Okla. Art Center, Oklahoma City, 1977, Tweed Mus. Art, Duluth, Minn., 1977, Weatherspoon Art Gallery, Greensboro, N.C., 1977; rep. permanent collections Nat. Coll. Fine Arts at Smithsonian Instn., Mus. Modern Art, N.Y.C., Victoria and Albert Mus., London, Bibliot Nat., Paris, Montreal (Que., Can.) Mus. Fine Arts; commns. include Eros Thanatos Suite (German poem and woodcuts), Interlaken Corp., Providence, 1967, Salamovka Poster (silkscreen), Oklahoma Art Center, 1974, (in collaboration) River Road Suite with poems by Stanley Kunitz, 1976, Robert Lowell at 66 (suite of drawings), 1977, Salmagundi mag. for humanities. Fulbright fellow, 1964; grantee NEA, Artists for Environ., 1972; recipient Interlaken Corp. Designer award, 1967. Served with USNR, 1950-54. Home: 113 Regent St Saratoga Springs NY 12866 Office: Art Dept Skidmore Coll Saratoga Springs NY 12866

UPUESE, GALOIA, Samoan judge; b. Vatia, Pago Pago, Am. Samoa, Aug. 12, 1912; s. Maua and Musu (Taito) Gaoteote; Diploma in Theology, Malua Theology Coll., 1936; m. Agiga Galoia, Jan. 19, 1935; children—Tereise, Eketone, Faavae, Avasa, Pulusila, Ta'ai, Evaline, Sipoloa, Iefata, Upuese, Uili, Musu;, Faulua, Sarai, Mareta, Likuone; m. 2d, Evaselita, Oct. 31, 1975; 1 son, Faamasino. Ordained to ministry Congregation Christian Ch. in Samoa, 1952; missionary vills., Am. Samoa, 1936-40, 51-59; mayor Village of Pava'ia'i (Am. Samoa), 1941-42, 61-68; rep. to Legis. of Am. Samoa, 1948-51; Samoan asso. judge High Ct. of Am. Samoa, Pago Pago, 1969-76, Samoan chief judge land and title div., 1977—. Scout master, 1946-47; youth leader, 1962-66; mem. bd. ministry to reverendhood Congregation Christian Ch. in Samoa; mem. village council Village of Pava'ia'i; chmn. Beautification Com. Western Dist., Am. Samoa. Mem. Bar Assn. Judges, Lawyers, Legal Practitioners of Am. Samoa. Club: Bar Assn. Home: Box 413 Pago Pago American Samoa 96799 Office: High Ct of Am Samoa Pago Pago American Samoa 96799

URBACH, FREDERICK, physician, educator; b. Vienna, Austria, Sept. 6, 1922; s. Erich and Josepha (Kronstein) U.; A.B. cum laude U. Pa., 1943; M.D., Jefferson Med. Coll., 1946; m. Nancy Ann Phillips, Dec. 20, 1952; children—Erich J., Gregory M., Andrew D. Intern Jefferson Hosp., 1946-47; fellow dermatology U. Pa. Hosp., 1949-52; fellow pediatric dermatology Children's Hosp., Phila., 1950-52; asst. vis. physician Phila. Gen. Hosp., Skin and Cancer Hosp., U. Pa. Hosp., 1952-54; asso. chief cancer research (dermatology) Roswell Park Meml. Inst., Buffalo, 1954-55, chief cancer research dermatology, 1955-58; asst. med. dir. Skin and Cancer Hosp. Phila., 1958-67, med. dir., 1967—; research prof. physiology U. Buffalo Grad. Sch., 1955-58; asso. prof. dermatology Temple U. Sch. Medicine, 1958-60, prof. research dermatology, 1960-67, prof., chmn. dept. dermatology, 1967—, dir. Center for Photobiology, 1977—; dep. dir. Health Research Inc. Buffalo, 1954-58. Mem. U.S. nat. com. photo-biology Nat. Acad. Sci., 1973—. Served with AUS, 1943-46, USAAF, 1947-49. Diplomate Am. Bd. Dermatology; fellow A.A.A.S.; mem. A.M.A., Am. Coll. Physicians, Am. Dermatologic Assn., Am. Acad. Dermatology, Am. Soc. Photobiology (councilor 1973-76, pres. 1977), Am. Assn. Cancer Research, Soc. Exptl. Biology and Medicine, Soc. Investigative Dermatology, Internat. Soc. Tropical Dermatology, N.Y. Acad. Sci., Royal Soc. Medicine, Internat. Assn. Photobiology (v.p. 1976-79, pres. 1980—), Danish (hon.), Swedish (hon.), Polish (hon.) socs. dermatology. Author: The Biology of Cutaneous Cancer, 1963; The Biologic Effects of Ultraviolet Radiation, 1969; contbr. articles to profl. jours.; research epidemiology of cancer, photobiology, phototherapy. Home: 438 Clairemont Rd Villanova PA 19085 Office: 3322 N Broad St Philadelphia PA 19140

URBAHN, MAXIMILIAN OTTO, architect; b. Burscheid, W. Germany, Feb. 2, 1912; s. Maximilian Otto and Hedwig (Hilbertz) U.; came to U.S., 1925, derivative citizenship; B.S., U. Ill., 1935; B.F.A., Yale, 1936, M.F.A., 1937; m. Marion Frank, Oct. 2, 1937; 1 son, Eric McGregor; m. 2d, Allyn Delano Smith, June 21, 1957; children—Maximilian Otto III, John Arthur; m. 3d, Bess Balchen, Mar. 17, 1979. Partner, Reisner & Urbahn, N.Y.C., 1946-50; sr. partner Urbahn & Brayton, N.Y.C., 1950-61; pvt. practice architecture, N.Y.C., 1961—, pres. Max O. Urbahn Assos., Inc.; asst. prof. design Yale, 1947-49; architect, mng. venturer Vehicle Assembly Bldg. and Launch Control Center, Cape Kennedy, Fla. Hon. chmn., past chmn., past pres. N.Y. Bd. Trade, v.p. urban and environmental affairs. Mem. White House Conf. Natural Beauty, 1965—. Vice chmn., dir. Madison Sq. Boys Club. Trustee, Doctor's Hosp.; bd. chancellors U. So. Calif.; bd. dirs. Nat. Energy Found.; trustee Akin Hall Natural History Mus. and Library. Served capt., C.E., AUS, 1942-46. Recipient award merit for design excellence of Launch Control Center, N.Y. State Assn. Arch., 1963. Garland Profl. award Yale, 1935, Ricker prize U. Ill., 1933; named Architect of Year, N.Y. Constrn. Inst., 1955. Allerton fellow U. Ill., 1933. Fellow AIA (pres. N.Y. chpt. 1965-67, nat. pres. 1971-72, regional dir. N.Y. region 1967-70), Soc. Am. Mil. Engrs. (past pres. N.Y. chpt.); mem. Fedn. Pan Am. Architectural Assns. (1st v.p. 1975-79), N.Y. State Assn. Architects, Am. Arbitration Assn. (dir.), Phi Gamma Delta. Episcopalian. Clubs: Metropolitan (past bd. govs.), Yale, Dutchess Valley Rod and Gun (pres.); Quaker Hill Country; Pine Valley Golf. Prin. works include Bronx State Hosp., Downstate Med. Center, Bklyn., Niagara U. Lewiston, VA Hosp., Wood, Wis., Nat. Security Agy. Complex, Ft. Meade, Md., Naval Air Sta., Lemoore, Calif., Our Lady of Angels Sem., Glenmont, N.Y., Sem. St. Vincent de Paul, Boynton Beach, Fla., Kings County Hosp., Bklyn., Nassau County Med. Center, East Meadow, L.I., Franklin Delano Roosevelt P. O., N.Y.C., Pub. Library, Greenburgh, N.Y., Hall of Sci., Flushing Meadow, N.Y., Lincoln Med. and Mental Health Center, Bronx, N.Y., Nat. Accelerator Lab., Batavia, Ill., Saudi Fund for Devel., Riyadn, Saudi Arabia, numerous others. Home: Aikendale Rd Pawling NY 12564 Office: 1250 Broadway New York NY 10001

URBAN, CARLYLE WOODROW, lawyer; b. Beverly, Kans., Dec. 14, 1914; s. Joseph William and Anna Bell (Murphy) U.; student Kans. Wesleyan U., 1931-33; LL.B., U. Tex., Austin, 1941; m. Lois Ball, June 10, 1946; children—Elizabeth Anne (Mrs. James E. Alexander), Michael Joseph. Admitted to Tex. bar, 1941; practiced in Austin, 1941-42, Houston, 1944—; asso. firm Powell, Wirtz, Rauhut & Gideon, Austin, 1941-42; partner firms Elledge, Urban & Bruce, Houston, 1944-62, Urban & Coolidge, Houston, 1963—. Gen. atty. Texas City Refining Inc. (Tex.), 1954—. Scoutmaster Sam Houston Area council Boy Scouts Am., 1959-61. Precinct committeeman Harris County (Tex.) Democratic Exec. Com., 1957-63. Served with USAAF, 1942-44. Mem. Order of Coif, Delta Theta Phi. Methodist (trustee, chmn. bd. trustees dist. conf.). Lion. Club: Houston Racquet. Home: 9311 Wickford Dr Houston TX 77024 Office: Urban & Coolidge 777 South Post Oak Rd Houston TX 77056

URBAN, EUGENE WILLARD, physicist; b. Omaha, Apr. 20, 1935; s. Willard Fred and Jean Marie (Ohler) U.; B.S., Harvard U., 1957; M.S., U. Ala., 1963, Ph.D., 1970; m. Barbara Joy Howard, May 27, 1960; children—Roxane, Nancy, Susan, Diane, Carl, Howard, Matthew, Christopher. Physicist, Army Ballistic Missile Agy., Huntsville, Ala., 1959-60; physicist NASA, Marshall Space Flight Center, Huntsville, 1960-70, supervisory physicist ES 63, 1970—. Served with U.S. Army, 1957-59. Recipient medal for Exceptional Sci. Achievement, NASA, 1975. Mem. Am. Phys. Soc., Sigma Xi. Presbyterian. Contbr. articles to sci. jours. Patentee in field. Home: 8020 Craigmont Rd Huntsville AL 35802 Office: ES 63 NASA Marshall Space Flight Center AL 35812

URBAN, GILBERT WILLIAM, banker; b. Silver Lake, Minn., Oct. 20, 1928; s. William and Alice (Polak) U.; B.B.A., U. Minn., 1949; m. Elvera Mattson, Feb. 23, 1954; children—Lisa Alice Marie, Leann Kay. Sr. accountant Price, Waterhouse & Co., Chgo., 1949-50; chief accountant Calif. Bank, Los Angeles, 1950-51; asst. controller 1st Nat. Bank, Mpls., 1951-63, controller, 1963-69; v.p., cashier La. Nat. Bank Baton Rouge, 1969-73, v.p. corp. planning, 1973—; instr. U. Minn. Eve. Sch., 1956-69; instr. Nat. Assn. Bank Auditors and Controllers Sch., U. Wis., 1960-63, sect. leader, 1963-69; instr. La. State U., 1970—; chmn. dept. controllership Bank Adminstrn. Inst., 1970—; course coordinator Banking Sch. of South, 1970. Mem. Beta Alpha Psi, Alpha Kappa Psi. Lutheran. Home: 12264 Queensbury Baton Rouge LA 70815 Office: PO Box 3399 Baton Rouge LA 70821

URBAN, HENRY ZELLER, newspaperman; b. Buffalo, July 11, 1920; s. George Pennock and Florence Lenhard (Zeller) U.; grad. Hotchkiss Sch., 1939; B.S., Yale U., 1943; m. Ruth deMoss Wickwire, Apr. 28, 1948; children—Ruth Robinson, Florence de Moss, Henry Zeller, Ward Wickwire. Treas., George Urban Milling Co., 1946-53; with Buffalo Eve. News, 1953—, asst. bus. mgr., 1957-62, bus. mgr., 1962-71, treas., dir., 1971-74, pres., pub., 1974—; dir. G. F. Zellers Sons, Inc., 1948-53. Bd. dirs. Travelers Aid Soc., 1953-59, Buffalo Fine Arts Acad., 1960-63, 70—, YMCA, 1955-68; trustee Elmwood-Franklin Sch., 1967-70, Canisius Coll., 1977—; bd. regents Canisius Coll., 1972—; adv. bd. Medaille Coll., 1968; chmn. parents council Hamilton Coll. Served to lt. USNR, 1942-46. Mem. Buffalo C. of C., N.Y. State Pubs. Assn. (dir. 1976—). Clubs: Mid-day, Tennis and Squash, Buffalo, Buffalo Country, Saturn Pack (Buffalo); Sankaty Head (Nantucket), Nantucket Yacht; Cragburn. Home: 57 Tudor Pl Buffalo NY 14222 Office: 1 News Plaza Buffalo NY 14240

URBAN, JAMES ARTHUR, lawyer; b. West Palm Beach, Fla., Feb. 18, 1927; s. Arthur Joseph and Elsie Elizabeth (Wespeaker) U.; A.B., Duke U., 1950; J.D. with high honors, U. Fla., 1953; m. Alice Burmah Steed, June 21, 1952; children—James Arthur, Katherine Elizabeth. Admitted to Fla. bar, 1953; since practiced in Orlando; mem. firm Urban, Williamson & Davis; dir. Fla. Legal Services, Inc., 1975-76. Bd. visitors Coll. Law Fla. State U., Tallahassee, 1973—, mem. council advisers, 1975—; mem. pres.'s council U. Fla., Gainesville, 1976-77. Served with U.S. Army, 1945-47. Recipient Outstanding Alumnus award U. Fla. Law Rev. Alumni Assn., 1975. Fellow Am. Coll. Probate Counsel, Am. Bar Found.; mem. Am. Bar Assn., Am. Law Inst., Fla. Bar (author, lectr. continuing legal edn. program 1968—, pres. 1974-75), Fla. Bar Found. (dir. 1975—, pres. 1977-79), Nat. Conf. Bar Founds. (dir. 1979—), Orlando C. of C. (dir. 1971-73), Phi Kappa Phi, Theta Chi. Episcopalian. Clubs: Kiwanis, Citrus, Univ. Country (Orlando). Home: 1614 Pepperidge Dr Orlando FL 32806 Office: PO Box 512 Orlando FL 32802 also 25 W Church St Orlando FL 32801

URBAN, JOSEPH, engr., educator; b. Bklyn., Mar. 6, 1921; s. Joseph and Marie (Katzensteiner) U.; B. Chem. Engring., Cooper Union, 1943; M. Chem. Engring., Poly Inst. Bklyn., 1947, Dr. Chem. Eng., 1950; m. Rose M. Rieker, Mar. 8, 1947; children—Joseph, Charles, Ronald, Mark. Research chemist Manhattan Project, Columbia, 1943-44; research engr. Manhattan Project, Kellex Corp., Jersey City, 1944-45; petroleum research M.W. Kellogg Co., Jersey City, 1945-47; instr. chemistry Adelphi Coll., 1947-50; prof. sci. Webb Inst. Naval Architecture, Glen Cove, N.Y., 1948—, dean, 1969—; cons. A. Pollak Co., 1951-53, J.L. Finck Labs., 1953-56. Registered profl. engr., N.Y. Mem. AAUP, Sigma Xi, Omega Delta Phi, Phi Lambda Upsilon. Home: 6964 64th St Glendale NY 11227

URBANEK, JAMES FRANK, mfg. co. exec.; b. Chgo., Jan. 23, 1925; s. James Frank and Mae A. (Krejsa) U.; B.S. in Bus. Adminstrn., Northwestern U., 1949; grad. Advanced Mgmt. Program, Harvard, 1965; m. Gladys A. Barbara, Sept. 7, 1946; children—Barbara Lynn, Susan Mae. With Arthur Andersen & Co., C.P.A.'s, Chgo., 1949-62, partner, 1959-62; with Brunswick Corp., Chgo., 1962—, corp. v.p., pres. tech. products div., 1967-74, group v.p. tech. bus., 1974—. Served with AUS, 1943-46. C.P.A., Ill. Mem. Am. Inst. C.P.A.'s, Financial Execs. Inst., Ill. Soc. C.P.A.'s. Mem. United Ch. of Christ. Clubs: University, Economic (Chgo.); Ridgemoor Country. (Chgo.). Home: Rt 2 Lexington Dr Long Grove IL 60047 Office: 1 Brunswick Plaza Skokie IL 60076

URBANOWSKI, FRANK, publishing co. exec.; b. Balt., Mar. 5, 1936; s. Frank and Tofilia (Jakubik) U.; B.S. in Ceramic Engring., Va. Poly. Inst.; postgrad. Columbia; m. Ferris Buck, Jan. 23, 1960; children—Alexandra, Tasha. Rep. Ronald Press, 1960-61; editor coll. dept. Macmillan Co., 1961-66; editorial dir. Glencoe Press, 1966-68, v.p., 1968-72, pub., 1972-73; dir. ednl. relations Ednl. Testing Service, 1973-75; dir. Mass. Inst. Tech. Press, Cambridge, 1975—; v.p., treas. Uniserv Corp., Littleton, Mass.; dir. Mass. Inst. Tech. Press Ltd., London, Eng.; chmn. exec. council TSM, 1979-81. Mem. Am. Assn. Pubs. (dir. 1979-81), Assn. Am. Univ. Press (dir. 1979-81). Home: 2 Munroe Rd Lexington MA 02173 also Wildcat Hill New Ipswich NH Office: 28 Carleton St Cambridge MA 02142

URBANSKI, JAMES FRANCIS, newspaper exec.; b. Bloomington, Ill., Oct. 4, 1927; s. Vincent S. and Celia Urbanski; B.S., U. Ill., 1950; m. (Marie) Ann Anderson, May 29, 1954; children—Cecelia, Elizabeth, William, Mark. Salesman, Jackson (Miss.) Daily News, 1951-54; retail advt. mgr. Jackson State Times, 1955-56; asst. advt. dir. Gary (Ind.) Post-Tribune, 1956-60; retail advt. mgr. Tribune Co., Tampa, Fla., 1960-68, advt. dir., 1968-73, bus. mgr., 1973-77, v.p., gen. mgr., 1977—. Pres., Gulf Ridge council Boy Scouts Am., 1977-79, recipient Silver Beaver award, 1979; bd. dirs. United Way of Tampa, 1975—, ARC, 1970-79, March of Dimes, 1961-63, Guidance Center, 1964-70, Tampa Philharm., 1963-68, Mchts. Assn., 1968-72; mem. Tampa Sports Authority, 1968-77, vice chmn., 1971-77; trustee St. Leo Coll., 1966-74; bd. dirs. Hillsborough County unit Am. Cancer Soc., 1968—, chmn., 1976-77, dir. Fla. div., 1978—. Served with AUS, 1946-47. Named Advt. Man of Year, Tampa Advt. Fedn., 1963, Sales Exec. of Year, Sales and Mktg. Execs. Tampa, 1967; recipient Am. Advt. Fedn. silver medal award, 1972. Mem. Internat. Newspaper Advt. Execs. (pres. 1975-76, hon. life), Newspaper Advt. Bur. (chmn. plans com. 1977-79), Sales and Mktg. Execs. (pres. 1968-69, Top Mgmt. award 1979), Tampa Advt. Fedn., Fla. Newspaper Advt. Execs. (pres. 1969-70), Greater Tampa C. of C. (dir., mem. exec. com. 1978—, chmn. Com. of 100, 1979-80), Alpha Delta Sigma. Roman Catholic. Clubs: Ye Mystic Krewe of Gasparilla, Tampa Yacht and Country, Univ. of Tampa, Kiwanis. Home: 4623 Lowell Ave Tampa FL 33609 Office: Tribune Co PO Box 191 202 S Parker St Tampa FL 33601

URBINA, RICARDO MANUEL, lawyer, educator; b. N.Y.C., Jan. 31, 1946; s. Luis Paulino and Ramona (Hernandez) U.; grad. cum laude (athletic scholar), Georgetown U., 1967, Law Center, 1970; m. Coreen Marie; children—Adrienne Jennifer, Ian Manuel. Law clk. firm Hogan & Hartson, Washington, from 1967; admitted to D.C. bar; staff atty. Pub. Defender Service, 1970-72; partner firm Urbina & Libby, 1972-73, Dowdey & Urbina, Washington, 1973—; prof. law Howard U., 1974—, dir. Criminal Justice Clinic, 1975—; gen. counsel Atlantic Real Title Corp. Bd. dirs. Law Student Consortium Program for D.C., 1975-76. Recipient awards for Outstanding Supervision, Class of 1974 Criminal Justice Clinic; named All-Am. Athlete, 1963, 65, 66, 67; NCAA indoor half-mile champion, 1966; named to Georgetown U. Athletic Hall Fame, 1978; named Prof. of Year Howard U., 1979. Mem. Bar Assn. D.C. (dir.). Litigated in landmark case of James E. McCall v. C.L. Swain, 1975. Home: 1437 Shepherd St NW Washington DC 20011 Office: 1819 H St NW Washington DC 20006

URBOM, WARREN KEITH, judge; b. Atlanta, Nebr., Dec. 17, 1925; s. Clarence Andrew and Anna Myrl (Irelan) U.; A.B. with highest distinction, Nebr. Wesleyan U., 1950; student Iliff Sch. Theology, Denver, 1950; J.D. with distinction, U. Mich., 1953; m. Joyce Marie Crawford, Aug. 19, 1951; children—Kim Marie, Randall Crawford, Allison Lee, Joy Renee. Admitted to Nebr. bar, 1953; mem. firm Baylor, Evnen, Baylor, Urbom, & Curtiss, Lincoln, Nebr.,

1953-70; judge U.S. Dist. Ct. for Dist. of Nebr., 1970-72, chief judge, 1972—. Mem. com. on practice and procedure Nebr. Supreme Ct., 1965—; mem. subcom. on fed. jurisdiction Judicial Conf. of U.S., 1975—. Bd. dirs. Lincoln YMCA, pres., 1965-67; bd. govs. Nebr. Wesleyan U., chmn., 1975—. Served with AUS, 1944-46. Fellow Am. Coll. of Trial Lawyers; mem. Am., Nebr. (mem. ho. of dels. 1966-70), Lincoln (pres. 1968-69) bar assns. United Methodist (bd. mgrs., bd. global ministries 1972-76). Club: Masons (33 deg.). Contbr. articles to profl. jours. Home: 4510 Van Dorn Lincoln NE 68506 Office: 586 Federal Bldg Lincoln NE 68501

URBON, VICTOR ANDREW, banker; b. Woodbury, N.J., Dec. 7, 1933; s. Victor Philip and Mary (Kubelczik) U.; B.S., Drexel U., 1957, M.B.A., 1968; postgrad. U. Wis., 1970; m. Kathryn Faye Childs, Dec. 19, 1959; children—Mark A., Michael A., Monica A. Trust adminstr. Bank of N.J., 1957-61; mgmt. trainee Boardwalk Nat. Bank (now First Nat. Bank South Jersey), Pleasantville, N.J., 1961-62, cost adminstr., 1962-64, asst. comptroller, 1964-67, auditor, 1967-73, v.p., gen. auditor, 1973—. Mem. U.S. Naval Acad. Found. Served to lt. comdr. USNR, 1957-60. Mem. Bank Adminstrn. Inst., Navy League U.S. (past pres., dir.), Pi Kappa Phi. Club: Drexel U. Alumni Varsity (Phila.). Home: 420 Jefferson Ave Linwood NJ 08221

URDAN, JAMES ALAN, lawyer; b. Milw., July 30, 1931; s. Henry Edward and Marion E. (Eisenberg) U.; A.B., Harvard U., 1953, J.D., 1956; m. Joan M. Rubinstein, May 30, 1958; children—Jennifer, Jonathan, Jeffrey. Admitted to Wis. bar, 1956; asso. firm Quarles & Brady, Milw., 1956-63, partner, 1964—; dir. M. & I. Marshall & Ilsley Bank. Treas., Milw. Performing Arts Center, 1976—; v.p. Mt. Sinai Med. Center, Milw., 1976—; pres. Jewish Vocat. Service of Milw., 1972-76. Mem. Am. Bar Assn., Wis. State Bar, Milw. Bar Assn., Am. Law Inst. Jewish. Clubs: Rotary, Univ., Town, Milw. Athletic. Home: 4732 N Wilshire Rd Milwaukee WI 53211 Office: 780 N Water St Milwaukee WI 53202

URETZ, ROBERT BENJAMIN, univ. dean; b. Chgo., June 27, 1924; s. Sol A. and Lottie (Kaplan) U.; B.S., U. Chgo., 1947, Ph.D., 1954; m. Vi Fogle, June 30, 1955; children—Jane Elizabeth, Alan Daniel. Mem. faculty U. Chgo., 1954—, prof. biophysics, 1964—, chmn. dept., 1966-69, asso. dean div. biol. sci. Sch. Medicine, 1969-70, dep. dean, 1970-77, asso. v.p. for Med. Center, 1976-77, dean div. biol. sci. and sch. medicine, v.p. for Med. Center, 1977—. Served to 1st lt. USAAF, 1943-46. Mem. Biophys. Soc., Radiation Research Soc., Am. Soc. Cell Biology, A.A.A.S., Sigma Xi. Home: 5637 S Woodlawn Chicago IL 60637

UREY, HAROLD CLAYTON, chemist; b. Walkerton, Ind., Apr. 29, 1893; s. Samuel Clayton and Cora Rebecca (Reinoehl) U.; B.S., U. Mont., 1917; Ph.D., U. Calif., 1923, LL.D., 1955; Am. Scandinavian Found. fellow, U. Copenhagen, 1923-24; D.Sc., U. Mont., Princeton, 1935, Rutgers U., 1939, Columbia, Oxford U., 1946, Washington and Lee U., 1948, U. Athens, 1951, McMaster U., 1951, Yale, 1951, Ind. U., 1953, Durham U., 1957, Birmingham U., 1957, U. Sask., 1960, Israeli Inst. Tech., 1962, Gustavus Adolphus Coll., 1963, U. Pitts., 1963, U. Chgo., 1963, U. Manchester (Eng.), 1966, U. Mich., 1967, Franklin and Marshall Coll., 1969, McGill U., 1970; LL.D., Wayne State U., 1958, U. Notre Dame, 1965; L.H.D., Hebrew Union Coll., 1959; m. Frieda Daum, June 12, 1926; children—Gertrude Elizabeth, Frieda Rebecca, Mary Alice, John Clayton. Tchr. rural schs., 1911-14; chemist Barrett Chem. Co., Phila., 1917-19; inst. chemistry U. Mont., 1919-21; asso. in chemistry Johns Hopkins, 1924-29; asso. prof. chemistry Columbia, 1929-34, prof., 1934-45, exec. officer dept. chemistry, 1939-42, dir. research S.A.M. Labs., 1940-45; distinguished service prof. chemistry Inst. Nuclear Studies, U. Chgo., 1945-52, Martin A. Ryerson distinguished service prof. chemistry, 1952-58; prof. chemistry-at-large U. Calif., 1958-70, Univ. prof. emeritus chemistry, 1970—; Bownocker lectr. Ohio State U., 1950; Silliman lectr. Yale, 1951; Montgomery lectr. U. Nebr., 1952; Hitchcock lectr. U. Calif., 1953; George Eastman vis. prof. Oxford U., 1956-57; Scott lectr. Cambridge U., 1957; Priestley lectr., 1963; Joseph Henry lectr., 1940, 70; John C. Lindsay lectr., 1970; vis. prof. univs. of U.K., 1971, others. Chmn. bd. Quadri-Sci., Inc.; dir. Deuterium Corp. Dir. Am. Scandinavian Found. Recipient Willard Gibbs medal Chgo. sect. Am. Chem. Soc., 1934; Nobel prize in chemistry, 1934; Davy medal Royal Soc. London, 1940; Franklin medal Franklin Inst., 1943; distinguished service award Phi Beta Kappa, 1950; Cordoza award, 1954; Honor Seroll award Chgo. chpt. Am. Inst. Chemists, 1954, gold medal award nat. soc., 1972; Priestley award, 1955; Alexander Hamilton award, 1961, J. Lawrence Smith medal, 1962; Remsen Meml. award, 1963; Medal of U. Paris, 1964; Nat. Medal Sci. award for astronomy, 1964, Gold Medal award Royal Astron. Soc. London, 1966; Am. Acad. Achievement award, 1966; Chem. Pioneer award Am. Inst. Chemists, 1969; Leonard medal Meteoritical Soc., 1969; Linus Pauling award Oreg. State U., 1970; Priestly medal Am. Chem. Soc., 1973; Exceptional Sci. Achievement award NASA, 1973; medallion, hon. mem. award Indiana Acad., 1974; V.M. Goldschmidt medal Geochem. Soc., 1975; Headliner award San Diego Press Club, 1974; medal, hon. council mem. Higher Council Sci. Research, Barcelona, Spain, 1973; Silver medal 50th Anniversary Internat. Fair Barcelona, 1973; 200th Anniversary plaque Am. Chem. Soc., 1976; named Knight of Malta, 1973. Fgn. mem. Royal Soc., Royal Swedish Acad. Scis., also other fgn. socs.; mem. A.A.A.S. (Johann Kepler medal 1971), Am. Chem. Soc., Nat. Acad. Scis., Am. Inst. Chemists (gold medal award 1972), Am. Philos Soc., Am. Phys. Soc., Am. Acad. Arts and Scis., Am. Geophys. Union, Geol. Soc. Am. (Arthur L. Day award 1969), Am. Astron. Soc., N.Y. Acad. Scis., Franklin Inst. (hon.), Geochim. Soc., Ill. Acad. Scis., Royal Irish Acad. (hon.), Royal Soc. Arts and Scis., Royal Astron. Soc. (asso.), French Chem. Soc. (hon.), Sigma Xi, Gamma Alpha, Phi Lambda Upsilon, Epsilon Chi, numerous others. Clubs: Quadrangle (Chgo.); Cosmos (Washington). Author: (with A.E. Ruark) Atoms, Molecules and Quanta, 1930; The Planets, 1952. Contbr. to Treatise on Physical Chemistry (edited by H.S. Taylor), 1931; chpt. in Physics and Astronomy of Moon (Z. Kopal), rev. edit., 1971. Editor Jour. Chem. Physics, 1933-40. Contbr. to sci. jours. Has specialized in structure of atoms and molecules, thermodynamic properties of gases, separation of isotopes, paleotemperatures, meteorites and the early solar system. Discoverer of hydrogen atom of atomic weight two; research for prodn. heavy water, and U235 for the atomic bomb. *

URICCHIO, WILLIAM ANDREW, educator; b. Hartford, Conn., Apr. 21, 1924; s. William and Mary (Donadio) U.; B.A., Cath. U. Am., 1949, M.S., 1951, Ph.D., 1953; m. Velma Mathias, June 12, 1950; children—William Charles, Mary Lynn, Barbara Ann, Robert John, Michael. Asst. prof., acting head, dept. biology Carlow Coll., Pitts., 1953-54, head, dept. biology, 1954—, prof., 1962—, asst. to pres., 1970—. Program dir. NSF, 1967-68; cons. scholars program Pitts. Pub. Schs., 1964—. Bd. dirs. Allegheny Cath. Social Service, Gilmary Sch. Girls, McGuire Meml., Human Life Found., Duquesne U. Served with AUS, 1943-46. NSF grantees, 1958—; knight of St. Gregory the Great. Fellow A.A.A.S.; mem. Nat. Assn. Sci. Tchrs., Nat. Assn. Biology Tchrs., Am. Inst. Biol. Scis., Pa. Acad. Sci. (past editor jour., past pres.), Sigma Xi, Delta Epsilon Sigma. Club: Pittsburgh Serra (past pres.). Author: Laboratory Manual in Microbiology, 1966; editor Procs. Research Conf. Natural Family Planning, 1973. Home: 1402 Murray Ave Pittsburgh PA 15217

URICH, ROBERT, actor; b. Toronto, Ohio, Dec. 19; B.A. in Radio and TV Communications, Fla. State U.; M.A. in Communications Mgmt., Mich. State U., 1971; m. Heather Menzies; 1 son. Formerly sales account sta. exec. WGN, Chgo.; 1st stage appearance in Lovers and Others Strangers, Pheasant Run Playhouse; other appearances at Ivanhoe Theatre, Chgo., Arlington Park (Ill.) Theatre; TV appearances in series Bob and Carol and Ted and Alice, 1973, S.W.A.T., 1975-76, Tabitha, 1977-78, Soap, 1977-78; star of TV series Vega$, 1978—; other TV appearances include The Love Boat, The FBI, Gunsmoke, Kung Fu, Owen Marshall, Macus Welby, M.D.; TV movies include Bunco, 1977, Leave Yesterday Behind, 1978, Vega$, 1978, When She Was Bad, 1979; film appearance in Magnum Force. Address: care Blake Agy Ltd 409 N Camden Dr Beverly Hills CA 90210*

URIE, JOHN JAMES, fed. judge Can.; b. Guelph, Ont., Can., Jan. 2, 1920; s. G. Norman and Jane A. U.; B.A., Queen's U.; LL.B., Osgoode Hall Law Sch.; m. Dorothy Elizabeth James. Children—David, Janet, Alison. Called to Ont. bar, 1948; partner firm Burke-Robertson, Urie, Weller & Chadwick, Ottawa, Ont., 1948-73; judge Fed. Ct. of Can., Ottawa, 1973—; gen. counsel to Joint Com. of Senate and House of Commons on Consumer Credit; chmn. planning com. First Nat. Conf. on Law, Ottawa, 1972; judge Ct. Martial Appeal Ct., 1973—. Vice pres. Children's Aid Soc. Served with Cameron Highlanders of Ottawa, Can. Army, 1942-45. Mem. Eastern Profl. Hockey League, Royal Can. Mil. Inst., Phi Delta Phi. Mem. United Ch. of Canada. Clubs: Gyro (past pres.), Cameron Highlanders, Ottawa Hunt and Golf, Rideau (Ottawa); Glebe Curling. Office: Fed Ct of Can Welling and Kent Sts Ottawa ON K1A 0H9 Canada

URIS, LEON, author; b. Balt., Aug. 3, 1924; s. Wolf William and Anna (Blumberg) U.; ed. Balt. City Coll.; m. Betty Katherine Beck, Jan. 5, 1945; children—Karen Lynn, Mark Jay, Michael Cady; m. 2d, Jill Peabody, Feb. 15, 1971. Served from pvt. to pfc., 2d Div., USMCR, 1942-46. Author: Battle Cry, 1953; The Angry Hills, 1955; Exodus, 1957; Exodus Revisited, 1959; Mila 18, 1961; Armageddon, 1964; Topaz, 1967; QB VII, 1970; Trinity, 1976; (with Jill Uris) Ireland: A Terrible Beauty, 1975; also screen writer. Home: Aspen CO 81611 also Hollywood CA 90028 Office: care Doubleday & Co 245 Park Ave New York NY 10017

UROFSKY, MELVIN IRVING, historian; b. N.Y.C., Feb. 7, 1939; s. Philip and Sylvia (Passow) U.; A.B., Columbia U., 1961, M.A., 1962, Ph.D., 1968; m. Susan Linda Miller, Aug. 27, 1961; children—Philip Eric, Robert Ian. Instr. history Ohio State U., 1964-67; asst. prof. history and edn., then asst. dean State U. N.Y., Albany, 1967-74; prof. history, chmn. dept. Va. Commonwealth U., Richmond, 1974—. Chmn. exec. com. Zionist Academic Council, 1976-79; mem. nat. bd. Am. Zionist Fedn., 1976-79; co-chmn. Am. Zionist Ideological Commn., 1976-78; nat. bd. Assn. Reform Zionists Am., 1978—. Mershon Found. fellow, 1965; sr. research fellow Nat. Endowment Humanities, 1976-77; recipient Kaplun award Jewish Book Council, 1976; grantee Nat. Endowment Humanities, Am. Council Learned Socs. Mem. Am. Jewish Hist. Soc., Orgn. Am. Historians, Soc. History Edn. Books: Big Steel and Wilson Administration, 1969; Why Teachers Strike, 1970; A Mind of One Piece, 1971; co-editor: Brandeis Letters, 5 vols., 1971-78; American Zionism from Herzl to The Holocaust, 1976; We Are One!, 1978. Home: 1500 Careybrook Dr Richmond VA 23233 Office: 912 W Franklin St Richmond VA 23284

URQUHART, MALCOLM CHARLES, economist; b. Islay, Alta., Can., Dec. 12, 1913; s. William Gordon and Mary Louise (Marlow) U.; B.A. with honors, U. Alta., 1940; postgrad. U. Chgo., 1940-42, 48-49; m. Mary Elizabeth Rowell, June 8, 1969; stepchildren—Elizabeth Anne Arrowsmith, John David Arrowsmith. Instr., M.I.T., 1942-43; mem. faculty dept. econs., Queen's U., Kingston, Ont., Can., 1945—, prof., now Sir John A. Macdonald prof. polit. and econ. sci., dir. Inst. Econ. Research, 1960-66, head dept. econs., 1964-68, acting head, 1970-71; mem. exec. com. of conf. on research in income and wealth Nat. Bur. Econ. Research, 1967-70; mem. subcom. on research grants Com. on Health Research, Ont. Council of Health, 1968-72. Treas., Art Collection Soc. Kingston, 1954-58, pres., 1958-60; chmn. budget com. Kingston Community Chest. Fellow Royal Soc. Can. (pres. Acad. II 1975-76, mem. gen. council 1974-77; mem. Can. Econ. Assn. (pres. 1968-69), Royal Econ. Soc., Econometric Soc. Anglican. Club: Cataraqui Golf and Country. Author, editor works in field including: Historical Statistics in Canada, 1965. Contbr. articles to profl. jours. Home: 94 Beverley St Kingston ON K7L 3Y6 Canada Office: Econs Dept Queen's Univ Kingston ON K7L 3N6 Canada

URQUIZA, NICOLAS, accounting firm exec.; b. Queretaro, Mex., 1921; C.P.A. with highest honors, U. Mex., 1946; Joined Mexico City office Arthur Andersen & Co., 1946, mgr., 1950-59, partner, 1959—, sr. partner, 1976—, coordinator, dir. tax dept., 1954-72, tax practice dir. for Mex. and C.Am., 1972—; mem. adv. com., 1961-64, mem. nominating com., 1968-69; coordinator, participant numerous tax confs. and seminars in Mex. and other countries; adj. prof. accounting U. Mex., 1955-63. Mem. Mex. Inst. Pub. Accountants (dir.), Mex. Coll. Pub. Accountants, Acad. Tax Studies of Accounting Profession Mex. (founding mem., past pres.), Am. Inst. C.P.A.'s. Author numerous articles on taxation. Office: Ruiz Urquiza & Cia SC reps of Arthur Andersen & Co Paseo de la Reforma 76 Mexico 6 DF Mexico

URRY, GRANT WAYNE, educator; b. Salt Lake City, Mar. 12, 1926; s. Herbert William and Emma (Swanner) U.; S.B., U. Chgo., 1947, Ph.D., 1953; m. Lillian Alibertini, Sept. 4, 1946; children—Lisa, Claudia, Serena, Anthony. Research asst., asso. U. Chgo., 1949-53, research asso., asst. prof., 1954-55; asst. prof. Washington U., St. Louis, 1955-58; asso. prof. Purdue U., 1958-64, prof., 1964-68; prof. chemistry Tufts U., Medford, Mass., 1968—, Robinson prof. chemistry, 1970—, chmn. dept., 1968-73; cons. E.I. du Pont de Nemours & Co., Inc., Coleman Instrument Co., 1960-66; cons. dir. Fusion, Inc., 1967—. Alfred P. Sloan fellow, 1956-58. Fellow N.Y. Acad. Scis., Am. Inst. Chemists, A.A.A.S.; mem. Am. Chem. Soc., Am. Soc. Sci. Glassblowers, Fedn. Am. Scientists, Sigma Xi, Phi Lambda Upsilon. Home: 2 Black Horse Terr Winchester MA 01890

URRY, WILBERT HERBERT, chemist, educator; b. Salt Lake City, Nov. 5, 1914; s. Herbert William and Irene (Swaner) U.; student U. Utah, 1932-34; B.Sc., U. Chgo., 1936, Ph.D., 1944; m. Dion Brown, Nov. 6, 1936; children—Wilbert Lynn, Steven Jay, Katherine, Janis. Lectr., curator chemistry Mus. Sci. and Industry, Chgo., 1936-44; mem. faculty U. Chgo., 1944—, prof. chemistry, 1960—; vis. prof. U. Calif. at Berkeley, 1958-59; cons. to govt. and industry, 1950—; mem. sr. postdoctoral panel NSF, 1967-70, chmn., 1970; mem. Com. on Recommendations for U.S. Army Basic Sci. Research, 1975—; expert witness in numerous chem. patent litigations. Bd. dirs. U. Chgo. Settlement, 1945-50. Daines Meml. lectr. U. Kans., 1954; Carbide and Carbon profl. fellow, 1956. Mem. A.A.A.S., Am. Chem. Soc., Phi Beta Kappa, Sigma Xi (Nat. Scholarship award 1934). Bd. editors Jour. Organic Chemistry, 1958-62. Contbr. articles on determination of structure and synthesis of RAL compounds, others in organic chemistry to profl. publs. Home: 1215 E 56th St Chicago IL 60637

URSANO, JAMES JOSEPH, army officer; b. Newark, N.Y., Apr. 13, 1921; s. Joseph and Virginia (Signorf) U.; B.S., Niagara U., 1943; M.B.A., Harvard, 1955; M.A. in Internat. Affairs, George Washington U., 1965; m. Neoma Faye Summers, Aug. 2, 1944; children—Barbara F., Robert J., Ronald J. Commd. 2d lt. U.S. Army, 1943, advanced through grades to maj. gen., 1971; chief classification and assignment br. AG sect. Hdqrs. Army Forces Far East, 8th U.S. Army, Korea, 1955-56, chief assignment br., Japan, 1956-57, chief publs. br. 8th U.S. Army UN Command, Japan, 1957-58; mgmt. analyst comptroller div. Adj. Gen.'s Office, Dept. Army, Washington, 1959-60, asst. chief gen. officer br. Office Dep. Chief of Staff for Personnel, 1960-61, chief, 1961-64; asst. chief plans and policy sect., dir. instrn. and research Army War Coll., Carlisle Barracks, Pa., 1965-66, chief, 1966-67; exec. officer, dep. chief staff personnel Hdqrs U.S. Army Europe and 7th Army, 1967-68, asst. dep. chief of staff personnel, 1968; dir. personnel systems Office Dep. Chief of Staff Personnel and CG PERSINS CMD, Dept. Army, Washington, 1968-70; dep. chief of staff personnel and adminstrn. Hdqrs. U.S. Army Vietnam, 1970-72; dep. chief staff personnel U.S. Army Pacific, 1972-74; dir. mgmt. Dept. Army, Washington, 1974-76, dir. Army Emergency Relief, 1976—. Decorated D.S.M. with 2 oak leaf clusters, Legion of Merit with 2 oak leaf clusters, Army Commendation medal. Home: 3915 Rive Dr Alexandria VA 22309 Office: Army Emergency Relief Dept of Army Washington DC 20314

URSE, VLADIMIR GEORGE, psychiatrist; b. Chgo., Jan. 18, 1906; s. Matthew and Marie (Marek) U.; student U. Chgo., 1923-25; B.S., B.M., Northwestern U., 1929, M.D., 1930; m. Ruth Bressler, Sept. 23, 1933 (dec.); children—Jean Val (Mrs. Frank P. Popoff), Linda Ruth (Mrs. Thomas N. Anton). Intern Cook County Hosp., Chgo., 1930-31, supt. Mental Health Clinic, 1959-70, asst. commr. mental health Chgo. Bd. Health, 1970-75, cons. in psychiatry, 1975—; resident Psychopathic Hosp., 1932-35, asst. psychiatrist, 1935-41, supt., 1941-59; practice medicine, specializing in psychiatry, Chgo., 1935—; clin. prof. psychiatry Med. Coll., U. Ill., 1961-73; prof. Rush. U., Chgo., 1973—; attending staff Presbyn.-St. Lukes Hosp., 1942; cons. staff VA Hosp., Hines, Ill., 1946—, Ill. Central Hosp., 1958-69; dir. div. psychiatry Cook County Hosp., 1968-70. Served to lt. col. M.C., AUS, 1944-46. Diplomate Am. Bd. Psychiatry and Neurology. Fellow Am. Psychiat. Assn. (life). Inst. Medicine Chgo.; mem. A.M.A., Central Neuropsychiatric Assn., Am. Psychopathological Assn. (life). A.A.A.S., Ill. Psychiat. Assn. (past pres.), Ill., Chgo. med. socs., Chgo. Neurol. Soc. (past v.p.), Phi Chi, Alpha Omega Alpha. Contbr. articles to med. jours. Home: 1447 Keystone Av River Forest IL 60305 Office: 8 S Michigan Ave Chicago IL 60603

URSHAN, NATHANIEL ANDREW, clergyman; b. St. Paul, Aug. 29, 1920; s. Andrew David and Mildred (Hammergren) U.; student Columbia U., 1936-39; Dr.Theology (hon.), Gateway Coll. Evangelism, 1976; m. Jean Louise Habig, Oct. 1, 1941; children—Sharon, Annette, Nathaniel, Andrew. Ordained to ministry, United Pentacostal Ch. Internat., evangelist, 1941-44; asso. pastor Royal Oak, Mich., 1944-46; asso. pastor, N.Y.C., 1947-48, Indpls., 1948-49; pastor Calvary Tabernacle, Indpls., 1949-78; presbyter Ind. Dist. United Pentacostal Ch., 1950-77, asst. gen. supt. United Pentecostal Ch. Internat., 1971-77, gen. supt., Hazelwood, Mo., 1977—; host radio show Harvestime, 1961-78. Mem. internat. com. YMCA, 1958-79; bd. dirs. Indpls. YMCA, 1961-79, world service chmn. Region L, YMCA, 1967-71; chmn. Heart Fund Campaign, 1968-69; mem. screening com. Marion County (Ind.) Republican Party, 1973-74; chmn. Ministerial Com. of Richard Lugar for Mayor of Indpls., 1968, William Hudnut for Mayor, 1975; chaplain Ho. of Reps., 1972; bd. dirs. Little Red Door, Cancer Soc., Indpls., 1974-77. Recipient Gold and brass medallion Heart Fund, Indpls., 1968-69; named Nathaniel A. Urshan Day Nov. 3, 1979 by Mayor Hudnut, Indpls., Mem. Indpls. Ministerial Assn. Author: Consider Him, 1962; These Men are Not Drunk, 1964; Book of Sermons of the Baptism of the Holy Spirit, 1968; Major Bible Prophecy, 1971. Home: 8821 Dunn Rd Hazelwood MO 63042 Office: 8855 Dunn Rd Hazelwood MO 63042

USDANE, WILLIAM MILLER, govt. ofcl.; b. Seattle, July 29, 1914; s. Louis and Jennie (Miller) U.; B.A., U. Wash., 1936, M.A., 1940; Ph.D., N.Y. U., 1955; m. Bernice Stusser, Dec. 5, 1943; children—Lynn Millard, Mark. Vocational adviser VA, Seattle, 1946-50; dir. vocational rehab. Inst. for Crippled and Disabled, N.Y.C., 1950-56; prof. rehab. counseling, San Francisco State Coll., 1956-63; div. chief research and demonstration HEW Social and Rehab. Service, Washington, 1963- 69; dir. office of research Dept. of Labor, Washington, 1969-70; asst. commr. rehab. services adminstrn. HEW, Washington, 1970—; mem. Pres.'s Com. Services to Severly Handicapped, 1971—. Pres. Woodly House, Washington, 1968-69; mem. research bd. Easter Seal Found., Nat. Soc. for Crippled Children and Adults, 1963-70. Served with AUS, 1942-45. Recipient Disting. Service award U. Wis.-Stout, 1953, Goodwill Industries of Chgo., 1973; Disting. Contbn. award Am. Personnel and Guidance Assn.-Am. Rehab. Counseling Assn., 1974; Disting. Service award Wis. Rehab. Facilities Assn., 1977; Disting. Alumnus award N.Y. U., 1978; Fulbright sr. research fellow London Sch. Econs., U. London, 1962-63. Mem. Am. Psychol. Assn. (pres. div. 22). Contbr. articles to profl. jours. Home: 20227 Laurel Hill Way Germantown MD 20767 Office: HEW 330 C St SW Washington DC 20201

USDIN, GENE LEONARD, physician, psychiatrist; b. N.Y.C., Jan. 31, 1922; s. I. L. and Eva (Miller) U.; student U. N.C., 1939-40, U. Fla., 1940-41; B.S., Tulane U., 1943; M.D., 1946; m. Cecile Weil, Nov. 8, 1947; children—Cecile Catherine Burka, Linda Ann, Steven William, Thomas Michael. Intern, Touro Infirmary, New Orleans, 1946-47; jr. asst. resident psychiatry Cin. Gen. Hosp., 1949-51; fellow psychiatry, Tulane Sch. Medicine, 1951-52; pvt. practice psychiatry, New Orleans, 1952—; asst. prof. clin. psychiatry Tulane U., 1959-62, asso. clin. prof., 1962-67; asso. clin. prof. La. State U., 1967-71, clin. prof., 1971—; prof. Notre Dame Sem., 1969-75; chief div. neurology and psychiatry Touro Infirmary, New Orleans, 1962-66, dir. psychiat. services, 1966-71; sr. vis. psychiatrist DePaul and Charity Hosps.; chmn. psychiat. cons. com. Am. Bar Found., 1970-73; asst. examiner Am. Bd. Psychiatry and Neurology, 1956—. Bd. trustees United Fund Greater New Orleans, 1966-70. Served to lt. (j.g.) USNR, 1947-49. Diplomate Am. Bd. Psychiatry and Neurology, Am. Bd. Legal Medicine. Fellow Am. (chmn. com. on psychiatry and law 1964-68, mem. com. on ethics 1970-74, com. on pub. affairs 1976-78, trustee 1978—), So. (bd. regents 1969-72, chmn. 1971-72, pres. 1973-74), La. (past pres.) psychiat. assns., Am. Coll. Psychiatrists (bd. regents 1967-70, pres. 1978-79), Acad. Psychosomatic Medicine (mem. exec. council 1974-76), New Orleans Soc. Psychiatry and Neurology (past pres.), Group Advancement Psychiatry (bd. dirs. 1970-77, treas. 1973-77); mem. La. (chmn. com. on mental health 1966-70) Orleans Parish med. socs., Nat. Assn. Mental Health (mem. profl. advisory council 1968—), Inst. of Mental Hygiene (pres. 1978—). Editor-in-chief Psychiatry Digest, 1964-71, 75—; mem. editorial bd. Mental Hygiene, 1969-76; Clin. Medicine, 1965-71, 75—, Med. Digest, 1965-71, Jour. Psychiat. Edn., 1975—, Jour. Hosp. and Community Psychiatry, 1975—, Jour. Ottawa Med. Sch., 1976—, Psychiatry Bookshelf, 1976—. Editor: Psychoneurosis and Schizophrenia, 1966; Practical Lectures in Psychiatry for the Medical Practitioner, 1966; Adolescence: Care and Counseling, 1967; Perspectives on Violence, 1972; (with Peter A. Martin and A.W.

Swipe) A Physician in the General Practice of Psychiatry, 1970; The Psychiatric Forum, 1973; Sleep Research and Clinical Practice, 1973; Psychiatry: Education and Image, 1973; Overview of the Psychotherapies, 1975; Schizophrenia: Biological and Psychological Perspective, 1976; Depression: Clinical, Biological and Psychological Perspectives, 1977; Psychiatric Medicine, 1977; Aging: The Process and the People, 1978; Psychiatry in General Medical Practice, 1979. Contbr. articles to profl. jours. Home: 3 Newcomb Blvd New Orleans LA 70118 Office: 1403 Delachaise St New Orleans LA 70115

USEEM, JOHN HEARLD, sociologist, anthropologist; b. Buffalo, Oct. 15, 1910; s. Abram and Sema (Ross) U.; B.A., U. Calif., Los Angeles, 1934; student Harvard, 1934-36; Ph.D., U. Wis., 1939; m. Ruth Marie Hill, June 6, 1940; children—Michael, Howard, Bert. Prof., U. S.D., 1939-42; vis. lectr. Barnard Coll., Columbia, 1946; asso. prof. U. Wis., 1946-49; prof. sociology and anthropology Mich. State U., 1949—, head dept., 1958-65; lectr., cons. Fgn. Service Inst., Dept. State, 1950—; cons. Nat. Inst. Growth and Devel.; adv. com. Edward W. Hazen Found., Social Sci. Research Council, NIMH, Conf. Bd. Asso. Research Council, Am. Commn. for UNESCO. Bd. govs. Arctic Inst. Served as lt. USNR, World War II; mil. gov. in South Pacific. Sr. fellow East-West Center, 1972, mem. internat. adv. panel, 1978-79. Honored by Internat. Soc. Ednl., Cultural and Sci. Interchanges, 1979. Mem. Am. Sociol. Assn., Am. Anthrop. Assn., North Central Sociol. Assn. (pres. 1971), Soc. Applied Anthropology, Sociol. Research Assn., Soc. Study Social Problems, Central States Anthrop. Soc., Phi Beta Kappa, Phi Kappa Phi, Alpha Kappa Delta, Pi Gamma Mu, Pi Sigma Alpha. Author: The Western-Educated Man in India, 1955. Contbg. author: Human Problems in Technological Change, 1952; Cultural Patterns and Technical Change, 1953; The Underdeveloped Area, 1957; Reconstituting the Human Community, 1972. Contbr. articles to profl. jours. Home: 227 Chesterfield Pkwy East Lansing MI 48823

USELDING, PAUL JOHN, economist; b. Port Washington, Wis., July 2, 1938; s. Edward Nicholas and Lucy (Scheftgen) U.; B.S.I.E., Northwestern U., 1961, Ph.D., 1970; M.B.A., Cornell U., 1963; m. Mary Claire Winkle, May 22, 1965; children—Justine, John. Asst. prof. econs. U. Ill., Urbana, 1968-70, asso. prof., 1973-76, prof., 1976—; asst. prof. Johns Hopkins U., 1970-73; gen. editor JAI Press Inc., Greenwich, Conn. Recipient Abbott Payson Usher prize Soc. History of Tech., 1975; Nat. Endowment for Humanities fellow, 1972-73; Charles Warren fellow, 1978-79; Guggenheim fellow, 1978-79. Mem. Econ. History Assn. (trustee), Bus. History Conf. (trustee), Am. Econ. Assn., Social Sci. History Assn., Soc. for History Tech. Roman Catholic. Editor: Bus. and Econ. History, 1975—, Research in Econ. History, 1976—, Quar. Rev. Econs. and Bus., 1979—; editorial bd., Social Sci. History Jour., 1976—, Bus. History Rev., 1977—, Tech. and Culture, 1979—; research in devel. precision metalworking tech. Home: 208 W Iowa St Urbana IL 61801 Office: 118 David Kinley Hall U Ill Urbana IL 61801. *Personal satisfaction comes from combining a career in which one can do what one does comparatively best with the need to serve some larger human purpose. External rewards and recognition then become only the "frosting on the cake," nice to have but not essential to continued progress and performance.*

USHER, ELIZABETH REUTER (MRS. HARRY T. USHER), librarian; b. Seward, Nebr.; d. Paul and Elizabeth (Meyer) Reuter; diploma Concordia Tchrs. Coll., Seward; B.S. in Edn., U. Nebr., 1942; B.S. in Library Sci., U. Ill., 1944; m. Harry Thomas Usher, Feb. 25, 1950. Tchr., Zion Luth. Sch., Platte Center, Nebr. and St. Paul's Luth. Sch., Paterson, N.J.; library asst. charge res. book reading room U. Nebr., 1942-43; asst. circulation librarian Mich. State U., 1944-45; librarian Cranbrook Acad. Art, Bloomfield Hills, Mich., 1945-48; catalog and reference librarian Met. Mus. Art, N.Y.C., 1948-53, head cataloger and reference librarian, 1953-54, asst. librarian, 1954-61, chief of art reference library, 1961-68, chief librarian, 1968—, acting librarian, 1954-57. Trustee N.Y. Met. Reference and Research Library Agy., 1968—, sec. to bd., 1971-77, v.p., 1977—. Mem. Spl. Libraries Assn. (pres. 1967-68, dir. 1960-63, 66-69), Coll. Art Assn. (chmn. libraries session 1972-73), N.Y. Library Club, Art Libraries Soc. N.Am., Archons of Colophon. Lutheran. Contbr. articles to profl. periodicals, library publs. Home: 5 Peter Cooper Rd New York City NY 10010 Office: Met Museum Art Fifth Ave and 82d St New York City NY 10028

USHER, LEONARD GRAY, news assn. exec.; b. Paeroa, New Zealand, May 29, 1907; s. Robert and Mary Elizabeth (Johnston) U.; tchrs. certificate Auckland Tng. Coll., 1926-27; B.A., Auckland U., 1934; m. Mary Gertrude Lockie Nov. 30, 1940 (div. 1962); children—Lala Athene Frazer, Miles Gray; m. 2d, Jane Hammond Derne, July 11, 1962. Headmaster schs. Fiji, 1930-43; pub. relations officer Govt. of Fiji, 1943-56; exec. dir. Fiji Times & Herald, Suva, 1956-73, dir., 1973-77; editor Fiji Times, 1958-73, organizing dir. Pacific Islands News Assn., 1974—; chmn. bd. Fiji Devel. Bank, 1978—: dep. chmn. Nat. Bank Fiji, 1974—, Fiji Times-Herald, 1975-77; dir. Bay Islands Hotel Ltd., Fiji Liquefied Gas Carriers Ltd., Australian Credit Register Pty., Ltd., Naviti Investments Ltd. Mem. Fiji Broadcasting Commn., 1954-56, Fiji Visitors Bur., 1953-56; pres. Fiji Bd. Fire Commrs., 1967-70, 75-76; councillor Suva, 1962-71, 75-77, mayor, 1967-70, 75-76; mem. council U. South Pacific, 1975-78. Trustee Fiji Crippled Children Soc., 1965—, pres., 1971-74. Served with inf. Fiji Army, 1942-45. Decorated comdr. Brit. Empire. Mem. Royal Commonwealth Soc. (pres. Fiji). Methodist. Mason (master Fiji 1949-50, 74-75). Clubs: Defence (trustee), Fiji Arts (trustee), Union, United (trustee) (Suva); Royal Automobile (Sydney); Grammar (Auckland). Home: 12 Kavika Pl Suva Fiji Office: Nat Bank Bldg Victoria Parade PO Box 1298 Suva Fiji. *I would like to be worthy of C.E. Montague's tribute to three friends: "They were not ruled by fear or desire, and you could believe what they said."*

USHIJIMA, JOHN TAKEJI, lawyer, state senator; b. Hilo, Hawaii, Mar. 13, 1924; s. Buhachi and Sano (Nitahara) U.; B.A., Grinnell Coll., 1950; J.D., George Washington U., 1952; m. Margaret Kunishige, June 6, 1954. Admitted to Hawaii bar, 1953; partner firm Pence & Ushijima, Hilo, 1953-61, Ushijima & Nakamoto, Hilo, 1961-69; mem. Hawaii Senate, 1959—, pres. pro tem, 1974—; dir. Am. Security Bank, Honolulu, Royal State Nat. Ins. Co., Ltd., Honolulu. Bd. dirs. Waiakea Settlement YMCA. Served with AUS, 1943-46; ETO. Mem. Am. Bar Assn., Phi Delta Phi. Democrat. Home: 114 Melani St Hilo HI 96720 Office: Box 964 Hilo HI 96720

USTINOV, PETER ALEXANDER, actor, producer; b. London, Eng., Apr. 16, 1921; s. Iona and Nadia (Benois) U.; student Westminster Sch., London Theatre Studio; m. Isolde Denham, 1940; 1 dau., Tamara; m. 2d, Suzanne Cloutier; children—Pavia, Andrea, Igor; m. 3d, Helena du Lau d'Allemans. Playwright, House of Regrets, 1940, Blow Your Own Trumpet, 1943; prod. play Squaring the Circle, 1941; prod. film School for Secrets, 1946, We're No Angels, 1955; writer, actor The Way Ahead, 1943-44; writer The Banbury Nose, 1944, Love of Four Colonels, 1951; actor Crime and Punishment, 1946; screen debut in Brit. motion picture Mein Kampf, My Crimes, 1941, others include Odette and Hotel Sahara, 1950, Quo Vadis, 1951, The Egyptian, 1954, We're No Angels, 1955, Photo Finish, 1963; John Goldfarb, 1965; Lady L.; also author and actor Romanoff and Juliet in 1958; dir., appeared films Billy Budd, 1962; author, dir. and actor Photo Finish, 1963; actor, dir. Hammersmith is Out, 1972; starred in Viva Max, 1970, Logan's Run, 1976, Treasure of Matacwmbe, 1976, The Last Remake of Beau Geste, 1977, The Mauve Taxi, 1977, Death on the Nile, 1978, Aslantic, 1978, Thief of Bagdad, 1978; collaborator Peter Jones, radio program In All Directions, BBC; guest appearances on TV. Rector, U. Durdee. Served with Royal Sussex Regt., Royal Army Ordnance Corps, 1942-46. Decorated comdr. Order Brit. Empire; recipient Emmy award for Dr. Johnson, 1957; Motion Picture Acad. award as best actor in Spartacus, 1961; Acad. award as best supporting actor in Topkapi, 1964; Emmy award for Barefoot in Athens, 1966; Emmy award for best dramatic actor in single program A Storm in Summer, 1971; UNICEF award for distinguished service at internat. level, 1978. Author: The Loser, 1960; We Were Only Human, 1961; Add A Dash of Pity, 1966; Frontiers of the Sea, 1966; Unknown Soldier and His Wife, 1967; Halfway up the Tree, 1968; Krumnagel, 1971; Dear Me, 1977. Clubs: Queens, Royal Automobile, Arts Theatre, Garrick Savage. Office: care William Morris Agy (UK) Ltd 167/169 Wardom St London W1 England

UTERMOHLE, CHARLES EDWARD, JR., utility exec.; b. Balt., Feb. 11, 1915; s. C. Edward and Edna (O'Neill) U.; B.S. in Mech. Engring., Johns Hopkins, 1942; m. Florence Mildred Wicks, Feb. 25, 1939; 1 son, Charles Edward III. With Balt. Gas & Electric Co., 1934—, asst. gen. supt. gas operations, 1957-65, v.p. mgmt. and staff services, 1965-68, pres., dir., 1968-74, chmn. bd., chief exec. officer, 1969-80; dir. U.S. Fidelity & Guaranty Co., 1st Nat. Bank Md. Mem. Community Action Commn., City of Balt., 1966-69. Bd. dirs. Augsburg Lutheran Home, 1965-74, Balt. regional chpt. ARC, Balt. Symphony Orch. Assn., Edison Elec. Inst., 1969-72, 75—, Southeastern Electric Exchange; trustee Goucher Coll., 1972-74, Johns Hopkins; Registered profl. engr., Md. Mem. Am. Gas Assn. (award of merit 1956, dir. 1973-77), ASME, Nat., Md. socs. profl. engrs., Engring. Soc. Balt., Nat. Assn. Electric Cos. (dir. 1976-78), Md. Acad. Sci. (trustee, mem. exec. com.), C. of C. of Met. Balt. (dir. 1970-74), Md. C. of C. (dir. 1974—), Greater Balt. Com. Lutheran (past congregation pres.). Clubs: Johns Hopkins, Center, Maryland, Baltimore Country (Balt.). Office: Balt Gas and Electric Co PO Box 1475 Baltimore MD 21203

UTHOFF, MICHAEL, dancer, choreographer, artistic dir.; b. Santiago, Chile, Nov. 5, 1943; s. Ernst and Lola (Botka) U.; came to U.S., 1962; grad. biology, high sch., Chile; dance tng. with Juilliard Sch., 1962-65, Martha Graham, 1962-63, Joffrey Ballet, 1965-68, Sch. Am. Ballet, 1962-64; 1 dau., Michelle. Leading dancer Jose Limon Dance Co., 1964-65, City Center Joffrey Ballet, 1965-68, N.Y.C. Opera, 1968-69; leading dancer, asst. dir. First Chamber Dance Co. N.Y., 1969—; mem. faculty Juilliard Sch. Music, N.Y.C., 1969—; choreographer, dancer-actor film Seafall, 1968, opera prodns. Aida and La Cererentola, Honolulu, 1972; choreographer Quartet, City Center Joffrey Ballet, 1968; The Pleasure of Merely Circulating, Juilliard Sch. Music, 1969; Windsong, Reflections, Dusk, Promenade, First Chamber Dance Co., 1969-70; Mozart's Idomeneo for Caramoor Music Festival, 1970; Concerto Grosso for Ballet Clasico 70 of Mexico, also restaged Dusk, 1972; guest artist, tchr. Princeton Ballet Soc.; prof. dance State U. N.Y. at Purchase, 1972-74; now artistic dir. Hartford Ballet Co., also choreographer Aves Mirabiles, 1973, Danza a Quattro, 1973, Marosszek Dances, 1973, Duo, 1974, Pastorale, 1974, Brahms Variations, 1974, Autumalal, 1975, Mir Ken Geharget Veren, 1976, Tom Dula, 1976, Unstill Life, 1977, Songs of a Wayfarer, 1977, White Mountains Suite, 1978, Bach Cantata, 1978; Nat. Endowment Arts commns. for choreography Primavera, Minn. Dance Theatre, 1975, Panvezitos, Greater Houston Civic Ballet, 1976, Sonata, The Prodigal Son, Hartford Ballet, 1977, 79. Home: 49 Shadow Ln West Hartford CT 06110 Office: Hartford Ballet Co 308 Farmington Ave Hartford CT 06105

UTIGER, ROBERT DAVID, physician; b. Bridgeport, Conn., July 14, 1931; s. David Alfred and Aldine (Frey) U.; A.B., Williams Coll., 1953; M.D., Washington U., 1957; m. Sally Baldwin, Nov. 23, 1953; children—Jane, David, Nancy. Intern, resident in medicine Barnes Hosp., St. Louis, 1957-61; investigator Nat. Cancer Inst., Bethesda, Md., 1961-63; asst. prof. medicine Washington U. Sch. Medicine, 1963-69; asso. prof. U. Pa. Sch. Medicine, Phila., 1969-73, prof., 1973-79; prof. medicine U. N.C. Sch. Medicine, Chapel Hill, 1979—. Mem. Am. Soc. Clin. Investigation, Assn. Am. Physicians, Am. Bd. Internal Medicine (bd. govs.), Endocrine Soc., Phi Beta Kappa, Alpha Omega Alpha. Home: Route 2 Box 160 Chapel Hill NC 27514 Office: Dept Medicine Univ NC Sch Medicine Chapel Hill NC 27514

UTLEY, CLIFTON GARRICK, news corr.; b. Chgo., Nov. 19, 1939; s. Clifton Maxwell and Frayn (Garrick) U.; B.A., Carleton Coll., 1961; postgrad. Free U. Berlin (Germany); 1962-63. TV corr. news dept. NBC, 1963—, assignments in Brussels, Belgium, 1963-64, Vietnam, 1964-65, Chgo., 1966, N.Y.C., 1966, 71-73, Berlin, Germany 1966-68, chief bur., Paris, France, 1968-71, London (Eng.) corr., 1973-79, N.Y.C., 1980—. Served wtih AUS, 1961-62. Home: 12 Hanover Terr NW 1 London England Office: care NBC 30 Rockefeller Plaza New York NY 10020

UTNIK, WILLIAM JOSEPH, hotel exec.; b. Niagara Falls, N.Y., June 18, 1921; s. Martin and Bertha (Dziewcz) U.; B.A., Mich. State U., 1953; m. Mary Elizabeth Viau, Feb. 5, 1966. Staff positions Niagara Falls Country Club (N.Y.), 1937-42, asst. mgr., 1946-48; with Hilton Hotels Corp., 1953—, Western sales mgr., San Francisco, 1958-59, dir. sales Dallas Statler Hilton, 1959-63, Eastern div. sales mgr., 1963-66, gen. mgr. Tarrytown Hilton (N.Y.), 1966-67, resident mgr. Shamrock Hilton, Houston, 1967-69, gen. mgr. Dallas Hilton Inn, 1969-70, Detroit Hilton, 1970-72, Washington Statler Hilton, 1972-74, Atlanta Hilton, 1974—, asst. sec. Hilton Hotels Corp., lectr. hotel mgmt. Wayne State U.; chmn. industry advisory bd. Ga. State U. Served with USMC, 1942-45. Mem. Atlanta Conv. Visitors Bur. (treas.). Hotel Sales Mgmt. Assn., Ga. Hospitality and Travel Assn. (dir., treas.), Ga. Bus. and Industry Assn. (gov.), Atlanta C. of C., Central Atlanta Progress. Roman Catholic. Clubs: Rotary, Lions, Farmington Golf and Tennis. Home and Office: Atlanta Hilton Hotel Courtland and Harris St NE Atlanta GA 30303

UTRECHT, JAMES C., lawyer; b. Cin., May 26, 1922; s. Arthur C. and Alma (Schnieders) U.; B.A., U. Cin., 1947, J.D., 1948; m. Zena B. Utrecht; children-James D., Steven T., Daniel S., Gregory F., Jonathan A., Teresa S. Admitted to Ohio bar, 1948, U.S. Ct. Mil. Appeals bar, 1953, U.S. Supreme Ct. bar, 1953; practiced in Cin., 1948-56, Troy, Ohio, 1956—; pres. Shipman, Utrecht & Dixon Co., L.P.A., 1956—; past asst. pros. atty. Hamilton County, Ohio; past spl. counsel atty. gen. Ohio. Past trustee Stouder Meml. Hosp., Troy. Served to lt. col. AUS, 1943-45, 51-53. Decorated Bronze Star. Fellow Am. Coll. Trial Lawyers, Ohio Bar Assn. Found.; mem. Am., Ohio (past council dels.), Miami County (past pres.), Cin. bar assns., Am. Judicature Soc., Am. Soc. Hosp. Attys., Internat. Assn. Ins. Counsel, Charles McMicken Soc. Roman Catholic. Rotarian (past pres. Troy). Home: 410 Ridge Ave S Troy OH 45373 Office: Cornwall Bldg 12 S Plum St Troy OH 45373

UTT, GLENN S., JR., pharm. co. exec.; b. Neodesha, Kans., Aug. 7, 1926; s. Glenn S. and Reba (White) U.; B.S. in Bus. Adminstrn., Kans. State U., 1949, B.S. in Elec. Engring., 1949; M.B.A., Harvard, 1951; m. Mary Lou Ford, Aug. 8, 1948; 1 dau., Jan Allison. Sales analyst Drexel Furniture Co., 1951-55; asso. Booz Allen & Hamilton, mgmt. cons., Chgo., 1955-59; v.p. Booz Allen & Hamilton Internat., Zurich, Switzerland, 1959-62; with Abbott Labs., North Chicago, Ill., 1962—, exec. v.p., 1970—, also dir. Served with USNR, 1944-46. Mem. Beta Theta Pi. Club: Knollwood, Bath and Tennis (Lake Forest, Ill.); Indian Wells (Calif.) Country. Home: 161 N Sheridan Rd Lake Forest IL 60045 Office: Abbott Park North Chicago IL 60064

UTTAL, WILLIAM R(EICHENSTEIN), scientist, educator; b. Mineola, N.Y., Mar. 24, 1931; s. Joseph and Claire (Reichenstein) U.; student Miami U. Oxford, Ohio, 1947-48; B.S. in Physics, U. Cin., 1951; Ph.D. in Exptl. Psychology and Biophysics, Ohio State U., 1957; m. Michiye Nishimura, Dec. 20, 1954; children—Taneil, Lynet, Lisa. Staff Psychologist, mgr. behavioral sci. group IBM Research Center, Yorktown Heights, N.Y., 1957-63; asso. prof. U. Mich., Ann Arbor, 1963-68, prof. psychology, 1968—, research scientist, 1963—; vis. prof Kyoto (Japan) Prefectural Med. U., 1965-66, Sensory Sci. Lab., U. Hawaii, 1968, 73, U. Western Australia, 1970-71, U. Hawaii, 1978-79. Pres., Nat. Conf. on On-Line Uses Computers in Psychology, 1974. Served to 2d lt. USAF, 1951-53. USPHS spl. postdoctoral fellow, 1965-65; NIMH research scientist award, 1971-76. Fellow Am. Psychol. Assn., A.A.A.S.; mem. Psychonomics Soc. Author: Real Time Computers: Techniques and Applications in the Psychological Sciences, 1968; Generative Computer Assisted Instruction in Analytic Geometry, 1972; The Psychobiology of Sensory Coding, 1973; Cellular Neurophysiology and Integration: An Interpretive Introduction, 1975; An Autocorrelation Theory of Visual Form Detection, 1975; The Psychobiology of Mind, 1978; also numerous articles. Editor: Readings in Sensory Coding, 1972; asso. editor Behavioral Research Method and Instruction, 1968—, Computing: Archives for Electronic Computing, 1963-75, Jour. Exptl. Psychology: Perception and Performance, 1974-79. Patentee in field. Home: 2096 Greenview Dr Ann Arbor MI 48103

UTTER, MERTON FRANKLIN, biochemist, educator; b. Westboro, Mo., Mar. 23, 1917; s. Merton Franklin and Gertrude (McMichael) U.; B.A., Simpson Coll., 1938; Ph.D., Iowa State U., 1942; m. Marjorie Fern Manifold, Sept. 2, 1939; 1 son, Douglas Max. Instr. bacteriology Iowa State U., 1942-44; asst. prof. physiol. chemistry U. Minn., 1944-46; asso. prof. biochemistry Case Western Res. U., 1946-56, prof., 1956—, chmn. dept. biochemistry, 1965-76. Mem. metabolic biology panel NSF; mem. biochem. study sect. NIH; mem. basic sci. adv. com. VA. Fulbright Research fellow, Australia, 1953-54; NSF Sr. research fellow, Oxford U., 1960-61, U. Leicester, 1968-69. Mem. Soc. Exptl. Biology and Medicine, Am. Soc. Biol. Chemists, Biochem. Soc. (Eng.), Am. Chem. Soc. (Paul-Lewis award in enzyme chemistry 1956), Soc. Am. Microbiologists, A.A.A.S., Am. Acad. Arts and Scis., Nat. Acad. Scis., Sigma Xi. Asso. editor Jour. Biol. Chemistry, 1971—. Research, numerous publs. on delineation of metabolic pathways in liver concerned with initial steps of carbohydrate synthesis from non-carbohydrate precursors and structure and mechanism of action of specific enzymes involved in this metabolic area. Home: 2569 Berkshire Rd Cleveland Heights OH 44106 Office: 2119 Abington Rd Cleveland OH 44106

UTTER, ROBERT FRENCH, judge; b. Seattle, June 19, 1930; s. John and Besse (French) U.; B.S., U. Wash., 1952; LL.B., 1954; m. Elizabeth J. Stevenson, Dec. 28, 1953; children—Kimberly, Kirk, John. Admitted to Wash. bar, 1954; pros. atty. King County, Wash., 1955-57; individual practice law Seattle, 1957-59; ct. commr. King County Superior Ct., 1959-64, judge, 1964-69; judge Wash. State Ct. Appeals, 1969-71; judge Wash. State Supreme Ct., 1971—, now chief justice; lectr. in field. Pres., founder Big Brother Assn., Seattle, 1955-67; pres., founder Job Therapy Inc., 1963-71. Named Alumnus of the Year Linfield Coll., 1973. Mem. Am. Bar Assn., Am. Judicature Soc. Baptist. Office: Temple of Justice Olympia WA 98504*

UTTERBACK, PRISCILLA WOOTEN, lawyer; b. Holly Springs, Miss., Dec. 10, 1902; d. William Elbert and Valerie (Burton) Utterback; B.A., Southeastern State Tchrs. Coll., 1924. Admitted to Okla. bar, 1929; asso. Utterback & Stinson, 1930-32; mem. firm Utterback, Stinson & Utterback, 1932-38, Utterback & Utterback, 1938-50; pvt. practice, Durant, Okla., 1950—. Life mem. Okla. Soc. for Crippled Children; mem. Five Civilized Tribes Mus., Thomas Gilcrease Inst. Am., Okla. Heritage Assn. (dir.); trustee Robert Lee Williams Pub. Library, Highland Cemetery. Fellow Am. Coll. Probate Counsel; mem. Am., Okla., Bryan County (past pres.) bar assns., Nat., Okla. (past v.p.) assns. women lawyers, Am. Judicature Soc. (life), Am. Legion Aux., Okla. Hist. Soc. (life), Okla. League Young Democrats (past v.p.), Kappa Delta Pi, Delta Kappa Gamma. Home: 409 N 4th St Durant OK 74701 Office: Utterback Bldg Box 126 Durant OK 74701. *It has been my desire to uphold principles and standards upheld by my father, as an attorney, in his practice of law. I believe that as a Christian I can witness for my Lord, in my conduct as an attorney, by serving my fellowman, by attempting to do justice, love mercy, and walk humbly. Any success I may have attained has been due to my dependence on my Lord, my training by my parents, my legal studies, and many fine clients and friends.*

UTTING, MARY EMOGENE, assn. exec.; b. Saranac Lake, N.Y., Apr. 10, 1927; d. George Arthur and Agnes Annie (Waldock) Utting; A.B., Cornell U., 1948. Copy editor Miami (Fla.) Daily News, 1949-55; with Charlotte (N.C.) Observer, 1955-74, asst. Feature editor, 1973-74; exec. dir. Women in Communications, Inc., Austin, Tex., 1974—. Mem. Austin World Affairs Council, Women in Communications, Inc., Sigma Delta Chi. Democrat. Presbyn. Home: 1111 Red Cliff Dr Austin TX 78758 Office: PO Box 9561 Austin TX 78766

UTZ, DAVID C., urologist; b. Rochester, Minn., Dec. 2, 1923; s. Gilbert C. and Marion (Hoy) U.; student State U. Iowa, 1941-42, U. Minn., 1942-44; M.D., St. Louis U., 1950; M.S. in Urology, U. Minn., 1957; m. Virginia Lou Nehring, June 26, 1954; children—David C., Mary Elizabeth, William J., Mark E., Jeffrey P. Intern, Geisinger Meml. Hosp., Danville, Pa., 1950-51; fellow in urology Mayo Found., Rochester, Minn., 1951-53, 1954-56, asst. to urology staff Mayo Clinic, 1957, mem. urology staff, 1958—, chmn. dept. urology, 1972—; prof. urology Mayo Med. Sch., 1973—, also Dr. Anson L. Clark prof. urology. Bd. regents U. Minn., Mpls., 1973-79, vice chmn., 1977-79. Served with USNR, 1944-46, USAF, 1953-54. Diplomate Am. Bd. Urology (trustee 1977—). Mem. A.C.S. (gov. 1979—), AMA, Am. Urol. Assn. (pres. N. Central sect. 1980—), Assn. Genitourinary Surgeons, Clin. Soc. Genitourinary Surgeons, Soc. Univ. Urologists, Soc. Pelvic Surgeons, Western Urologic Forum, Minn. Urol. Soc., Société Internat. d'Urologie. Editor: Clinical Urography, 1977; mem. editorial bd. Urol. Survey, 1969—, Urologic Radiology, 1979—. Office: 200 1st St SW Rochester MN 55901

UTZ, EDWARD JOSEPH, lawyer; b. Cin., Feb. 8, 1918; s. Edward Joseph and Frances (Kraemer) U.; B.B.A., U. Cin., 1943; LL.B., Chase Law Sch., Cin., 1944. Admitted to Ohio bar, 1944, Ky. bar, 1967; design engr. Cin. Bickford Tool Co., 1942-44; practice with C.B. DesJardins, Cin., 1944-48; individual practice, Cin., 1948—; instr. Chase Law Sch., 1960-71. Fellow Am. Coll. Trial Lawyers; mem. Internat. Assn. Ins. Counsel, Am. Bar Assn., Am. Patent Law Assn., Ohio Bar Assn., Ky. Bar Assn., Cin. Bar Assn., Cin. Patent Law Assn.

Republican. Clubs: Cin., Kenwood Country. Contbr. articles to legal jours. Home: 4975 Councilrock Ln Indian Hill OH 45243 Office: 1306 4th and Walnut Bldg 36 E 4th St Cincinnati OH 45202

UTZ, JOHN PHILIP, physician, med. educator; b. Rochester, Minn., June 9, 1922; s. Gilbert C. and Marion H. (Hoy) U.; student Notre Dame U., 1940-42; B.S., Northwestern U., 1943, M.D., 1946; M.S., Georgetown U., 1949; m. Dorothy Mary Griffin, July 2, 1947; children—Margaret, Christopher, Charles, Jonathan, Stephen. Intern Mass. Meml. Hosp., 1946-47; researcher Lab. Infectious Diseases, 1947-49, chief infectious disease service Lab. Clin. Investigation, Nat. Inst. Allergy and Infectious Diseases, NIH, Bethesda, Md., 1952-65; prof. medicine, chmn. dept. immunology and infectious disease Med. Coll. Va., Richmond, 1965-73; instr. Sch. Medicine, Georgetown U., Washington, 1952-56, asst. prof. medicine, 1956-62, asso. prof., 1962-65, prof., dean Sch. Medicine, 1973-78, prof., 1973—; lectr. dept. preventive medicine Howard U., 1960-73; fellow Mayo Found., Rochester, Minn., 1949-52; vis. investigator Pasteur Inst., Paris, France, 1962-63; cons. U.S. Dept. State, El Salvador, 1953, Costa Rica, 1954, Hoffmann-La Roche Co., Nutley, N.J., 1965—, Clin. Center, NIH, Bethesda, 1965—, VA, 1965—. Pres. Nat. Found. Infectious Diseases, 1972-75. Served with AUS, 1943-45. Diplomate Am. Bd. Internal Medicine; recipient Ruth Gray award, 1973; Distinguished Alumni award Northwestern U., 1977. Mem. Am. Fedn. Clin. Research, A.C.P., Am. Coll. Chest Physicians (gov. D.C. chpt. 1978—), Am. Clin. and Climatological Assn., Soc. Exptl. Biology and Medicine, Am. Thoracic Soc., Am. Assn. Immunologists, So. Soc. Clin. Investigation, Infectious Disease Soc. Am., Am. Soc. Microbiology, Am. Coll. Clin. Pharmacology and Chem. Therapy, Internat. Soc. Human and Animal Mycology, Soc. Clin. Investigation, Assn. Am. Physicians, Med. Mycol. Soc. Am. (council, pres. 1974-75), Academie Royale des Sciences D'Outre Mer (Belgium), Alpha Omega Alpha. Co-author: Medical Mycology, 1st, 2d, 3d edits. Bd. editors Jour. Infectious Diseases, Antimicrobial Agents and Chemotherapy. Address: Georgetown U Sch Medicine Washington DC 20007

UTZ, LOIS MARIE, gift shop exec.; b. Paterson, N.J., Jan. 4, 1932; d. Ralph August and Mary (Schumacher) Cook; student in bus. Berkeley Sch., East Orange, N.J., 1950-51, in Comml. Art Famous Artist Schs., 1960-62; B.S., Caldwell Coll.; m. Donald Utz, July 20, 1957; 1 dau., Heidi May. Receptionist Franklin Fader Co., advt., Newark, 1951-53; adminstrv. asst. Keafott Co., engring. firm, Little Falls and Clifton, N.J., 1953-59; artist, adminstrv. asst. Gen. Precision Co., Little Falls, 1959-61; owner, mgr. Lois Utz Originals, gift items for children, Little Falls, 1966—; v.p. Donald Utz Engring. Inc., Clifton, N.J., 1971—. Corr. sec. Mt. St. Dominic Acad. Grade Sch. Bd., Caldwell, N.J., 1973—; bd. dirs. Apostolate for Retarded, Mt. Carmel Guild, St. Catherine of Siena Ch., Cedar Grove, N.J. Freelance author; columnist Paterson Morning Call and Shopping Times, Morristown, N.J., 1955-64. Active in fields of emotionally disturbed children and animal welfare; vol. therapist Essex County Hosp. Center, Cedar Grove, N.J., 1977—. Author, illustrator: The Pineapple Duck with the Peppermint Bill, 1968; The Houndstooth Check, 1972; The Simple Pink Bubble that Ended the Trouble with Jonathan Hubble, 1972; A Delightful Day with Bella Ballet, 1972; The King, the Queen and the Lima Bean, 1974. Contbr. free verse to Modern Bride, Jack and Jill, and other mags. editor Children's House, Children's World Montessori Mag., 1978—. Home: 64 Stevens Ave Little Falls NJ 07424

UVILLER, H. RICHARD, educator; b. N.Y.C., July 3, 1929; B.A., Harvard U., 1951; LL.B., Yale U., 1953; m. Rena K. Uviller; 1 dau., Daphne R. Admitted to N.Y. State bar, 1954, U.S. Supreme Ct. bar; with office of legal counsel U.S. Dept. Justice, Washington, 1953-54; with dist. atty.'s office N.Y. County, N.Y.C., 1954-68; prof. Columbia Law Sch., N.Y.C., 1968—. Mem. Am. Law Inst. Author: Casebook, The Processes of Criminal Justice, 1974, 2d edit., 1979; contbr. articles to legal jours. Home: 51 Fifth Ave New York NY 10003 Office: 435 W 116th St New York NY 10027

UYEHARA, OTTO ARTHUR, mech. engr.; b. Hanford, Calif., Sept. 9, 1916; s. Rikichi and Umi U.; B.S., U. Wis., 1942, M.S., 1943, Ph.D., 1945; m. Chisako Suda, Aug. 12, 1945; children—Kenneth Otto, Susan Joy, Emi Ryu. Mem. faculty dept. mech. engring. U. Wis., Madison, 1945—, prof., 1957—; cons. in field. Fellow Soc. Automotive Engrs.; mem. ASME, Am. Soc. Engring. Edn. Methodist. Author works in field. Home: 1610 Waunona Way Madison WI 53713 Office: 1513 University Ave Madison WI 53706

UYEKI, EUGENE SHIGEMI, univ. provost; b. Seattle, May 26, 1926; s. Roger R. and Chisato (Hirai) U.; B.A., Oberlin Coll., 1948; M.A., U. Chgo., 1952, Ph.D., 1953; m. Martha C. Ono, Sept. 8, 1956; children—Timothy M., Robert H. Research asso., instr., asst. prof., asso. prof., prof. Case Inst. Tech., Cleve., 1952-67; prof. sociology Case Western Res. U., 1967—, Selah Chamberlain prof. sociology, 1977—, acting asso. provost, asso. provost social and behavioral scis., 1968-69, chmn. interdisciplinary programs in social sci., 1969-71, provost social and behavioral scis., 1971-76. Served with AUS, 1954-55. Mem. Am. Sociol. Assn., A.A.A.S., Am. Population Assn. Home: 2281 Woodmere Dr Cleveland Heights OH 44106 Office: Case Western Res U Cleveland OH 44106

UYTERHOEVEN, HUGO EMIL ROBERT, educator, bus. cons.; b. Eindhoven, Netherlands, Aug. 6, 1931; s. Willem and An (Von der Nahmer) U.; came to U.S., 1955, naturalized, 1967; Dr. Iur., U. Zurich, 1955; Dr. in law, U. Ghent, 1955; M.B.A., Harvard, 1957, D.B.A., 1963; m. Sandra Louise Bunt, June 20, 1959; children—Monique, An, Sonia, Laura. Mem. faculty Grad. Sch. Bus. Adminstrn. Harvard U., 1960—, Timken prof. bus. adminstrn., 1974—; dir. Am. Res. Corp., Schroders Inc., Bendix Corp., The Stanley Works. Mem. Planning Bd. Weston (Mass.), 1969-72, Conservation Commn., 1972-76; pres. Weston Forest and Trail Assn., 1970-77. Belgian-Am. Ednl. Found. fellow, 1955-57. Author: (with others) Strategy and Organization: Text and Cases in General Management, 1973, 2d edit., 1977. Office: Harvard Bus Sch Boston MA 02163

VACANO, WOLFGANG, orch. condr., educator; b. Cologne, Germany, Dec. 23, 1906; s. Stephen and Charlotte (Schirmann) V.; diploma, Berlin (Germany) State Acad. Music, 1928; Ph.D. (hon.), Marian Coll., Indpls., 1977. Came to U.S., 1951, naturalized, 1957. Condr. municipal opera houses in Germany and Switzerland, 1928-39; condr. Teatro Argentino, La Plata, 1947-51, Teatro Municipal, Santiago, Chile, 1942-43, Teatro El Sodre, Montevideo, Uruguay, 1945, Teatro Colon, Buenos Aires, Argentina, 1949-51, Nat. Symphony Orch., Nicaragua, 1977, Opera Co., Peoria, Ill., 1977-78; prof. music, opera condr. Ind. U. Sch. Music, 1951—, Aspen (Colo.) Festivals and Music Sch., 1952-54, 61-64; condr. Indpls. Philharmonic Orch., 1963—; vis. prof. music U. Wis. at Milw., 1967-68, also mus. dir. Music for Youth, Milw., 1967-70; artistic dir. Brigham Young U., Provo, Utah, 1972, 74. Named Hon. Citizen Indpls., 1966. Address: School of Music Indiana U Bloomington IN 47401

VACCA, JOHN JOSEPH, TV cons.; b. Chgo., Apr. 7, 1922; s. John Joseph and Caroline (Bain) V.; student Northwestern U., 1940-42, Internat. Corr. Schs., 1950-54; m. Alice Isabel Ure, May 2, 1944; children—John Joseph, Dawn Susan, Kim Frances. Editor, Midwest Times, Chgo., 1940-41; with prodn. dept. NBC Radio, 1946-47; news dir. sta. KECK, Odessa, Tex., 1947-49, chief announcer, 1948-49; program mgr. KOSA-Radio, Odessa, 1949-55, sta. mgr. KOSA-TV, 1955-61, gen. mgr. 1962-72; v.p., dir. Trigg Vaughn Stas., Inc., Odessa, 1962-67; sec. Odessa Broadcasting Co., 1950-72; asst. sec. Doubleday Broadcasting Co., 1967-77, v.p., 1967-75, sr. v.p., 1975-77; gen. mgr. KDTV, Dallas, 1972-73; TV cons., Dallas, 1978—. Bd. dirs. Odessa Community Chest, 1964-72, Better Bus. Bur., 1956-72; campaign maj. A.R.C., 1951-72; publicity adviser Ector County chpt. Nat. Found. for Infantile Paralysis, 1949-72; campaign coordinator Civic Music Assn., 1950-72; sponsor, adviser Permian Playhouse, 1959-72, v.p., bd. dirs. 1971-72. City councilman, Odessa, 1962-64. Bd. dirs. Am. Cancer Soc. Served with USAAF, 1942-46. Recipient Zeus award Epsilon Sigma Alpha, 1971. Mem. Nat., Tex. assns. broadcasters, Tex. AP Broadcasters Assn., Advt. Club Odessa (pres. 1960-61, dir. 1960-63), C. of C. (publicity adviser 1950-72), Holy Name Soc. Roman Catholic. K.C. (sec. Odessa 1950-51). Home and Office: 9872 Dale Crest Suite # 2116 Dallas TX 75220. *A philosophy of service, personal and through broadcasting, coupled with a sincere approach to excellent Human Relations have formed the keystone of my career. Consistent honesty and a constant effort to give and produce much more than required have always been guiding principles. My goals have been set with flexible policies to implement them, ever mindful that "change" is an integral part of life and progress.*

VACCARA, BEATRICE NEWMAN, economist, govt. ofcl.; b. N.Y.C., Sept. 20, 1922; d. Wilfred and Gussie (Tannlenbaum) Newman; B.A. cum laude, Bklyn. Coll., 1943; M.A. (Univ. scholar), Columbia U., 1944, postgrad., 1944-45; postgrad. Am. U., 1958; m. John Vaccara, June 15, 1944; 1 son, Richard John. Research asso. Brookings Instn., 1954-59; asst. chief nat. econ div. Dept. Commerce, Washington, 1959-65, coordinator econ. growth studies, 1965-71, chief economist growth div., 1971-73, asso. dir. Bur. Econ. Analysis, 1973-77; dep. asst. sec. for econ. policy Dept. Treasury, Washington, 1977—. Mem. exec. com. Montgomery County LWV, 1959-65. Recipient Adam Smith award Bklyn. Coll., 1943; Silver award Dept. Commerce, 1965, Gold Medal award, 1974. Fellow Am. Statis. Assn. (chmn. fellowship com. 1975-76, dir. 1975-78, v.p. 1979); mem. Am. Econ. Assn., Nat. Economist Club (dir. 1973), Washington Statis. Soc. (pres. 1971-72), Conf. on Research in Income and Wealth (exec. com. 1972-74), Internat. Assn. Research in Income and Wealth, Caucus for Women in Statistics. Author: Employment and Output in Protected Manufacturing Industries, 1960; (with Walter Salant) Import Liberalization and Employment, 1961; A Study of Fixed Capital Requirements of the U.S. Business Economy, 1971-80, 1975; editor: (with John Kendrick) New Developments in Productivity Measurement, 1980; contbr. numerous articles to profl. jours. Home: 2801 New Mexico Ave NW Washington DC 20007 Office: Dept of Treasury Washington DC 20220*

VACCARO, BRENDA, actress; b. Bklyn., Nov. 18, 1939; d. Mario and Christine (Pavia) Vaccaro; student Neighborhood Playhouse, 1958-60. Appeared in Broadway plays Everybody Loves Opal, 1961, The Affair, 1962, Children from Their Games, 1963, Cactus Flower, 1965, The Natural Look, 1967, How Now Dow Jones, 1968, The Goodbye People, 1968, Father's Day, 1971; motion pictures include Midnite Cowboy, Where it's At, I Love My Wife, Summer Tree, Going Home, Once Is Not Enough, Airport '77, House by the Lake, Capricorn One; TV appearances in The Greatest Show on Earth, 1963, Fugitive, 1963, Defenders, 1965, Doctors and Nurses, 1965, Coronet Blue, 1967, The FBI, 1969, The Psychiatrist, 1971, Name of the Game, 1971, Marcus Welby, M.D., 1972, Banacek, 1972, McCloud, 1972, McCoy, Streets of San Francisco, Sara, 1976, Dear Detective, 1979; TV movie appearances in Travis Logan, D.A., 1971, What's A Nice Girl Like You, 1971, Honor Thy Father, 1973, Sunshine, 1973, The Big Ripoff, 1975, Julius and Ethel Rosenberg, 1978. Recipient Theatre World award, 1961-62, 3 Tony nominations, 2 Hollywood Fgn. Press Assn. nominations, Emmy award as supporting actress in The Shape of Things, 1974. Address: care William Morris Agy 151 El Camino Blvd Beverly Hills CA 90212*

VACHON, BRIAN PETER, editor; b. Washington, Oct. 3, 1941; s. John Felix and Millicent (Leeper) V.; student Villanova U., 1959-61, U. Tenn., 1961-62; m. Nancy Virginia Cargill, Nov. 14, 1972. Newspaper reporter Bristol (Va.) Herald Courier, 1963-66, Suffolk (N.Y.) Sun, 1967, N.Y. Daily News, 1969-70; asst. mag. editor Careers Today, Del Mar, Calif., 1968-69; asso. editor Newsweek, N.Y.C., 1970; editor Charlie mag., N.Y.C., 1970-71; sr. editor Saturday Rev., N.Y.C., 1972-73; editor Vt. Life, Montpelier, 1973—. Lectr. history U. Vt., Montpelier, 1975—; mag. cons.; freelance writer; tchr. creative writing Norwich U.; lectr. Goddard Coll., 1977. Served with AUS, 1962. Author: A Time To Be Born, 1972. Home: Montpelier VT 05602 Office: 61 Elm St Montpelier VT 05602

VACHON, LOUIS ALBERT, bishop; b. St. Frederic, Que., Can., Feb. 4, 1912; s. Napoleon and Alexandrine (Gilbert) V.; D.Ph., Laval U., 1947; D.Th., St. Thomas Aquinas U., Rome, 1949; hon. degrees U. Montreal, McGill and Victoria, 1964, Guelph U., 1966, Moncton U., 1967, Bishop's, Queen's and Strasbourg U., 1968, U. Notre Dame, 1971, Carleton U., 1972. Superior, Grand Seminaire Québec, Quebec, 1955-59, superior gen., 1960-77; prof. philosophy Laval U., 1941-47, prof. theology, 1949-55, vice-rector, 1959-60, rector, 1960-72; protonotary apostolic, 1963; aux. bishop Que., 1977—; Past pres. Corp. Laval U. Med. Centre; hon. pres. La Société des etudes grecques et latines du Québec; asso. mem. bd. Quebec Symphony Orch.; bd. govs. Laval U. Found. Decorated officier de l'Ordre de la Fidelite francaise, companion Order of Can. Fellow Royal Soc. Can.; mem. Canadian Assn. French Lang. Educators (pres. 1970-72), Assn. Univs. and Colls. Can. (pres. 1965-66), Conf. Rectors and Prins. Quebec Univs. (pres. 1965-68), Internat. Assn. Univs. (dep. mem. adminstrv. bd. 1965-70), Assn. des universites partiellement ou entierement de langue francaise (adminstrv. bd. 1961-69), Internat. Fedn. Cath. Univs. (adminstrv. bd. 1963-70). Author: Espérance et Présomption, 1958; Verité et Liberte, 1962; Unité de l'universite, 1962; Apostolat de l'universitaire catholique, 1963; Memorial, 1963; Communauté universitaire, 1963; Progres de l'universite et consentement populaire, 1964; Responsabilite collective des universitaires, 1964; Les humanites aujourd'hui, 1966; Excellence et loyauté des universitaires, 1969. Home: Archbishop Residence PO Box 459 Quebec PQ G1R 4R6 Canada Office: 1073 Blvd Saint-Cyrille oeust Quebec PQ G1S 4R5 Canada

VACHON, ROGATIEN ROSAIRE, hockey player; b. Palmarolle, Que., Can., Sept. 8, 1945; s. Joseph and Lucia (Bellavance) V.; student pub. schs.; m. Nicole Blanchard, Nov. 30, 1971; children—Nicholas, Jade. Profl. hockey player Jr. Canadian Hockey Team, 1963, Jr. Thetford Mins Hockey Team, 1964-65, Houston Apollos Central Hockey League, 1966, Montreal Canadian, Nat. Hockey League, 1967-71, Los Angeles Kings, Nat. Hockey League, 1971-78, Detroit Red Wings, 1978—. Recipient Vezina trophy, 1968, Red Rose award Hosp. Charities Assn., 1975; named Los Angeles Kings Most Inspirational Player, 1972-73, Most Valuable Player, 1973, 74-75, 77; Hockey News Player of Year, 1974-75; Citizens Savs. Bank, Los Angeles Athlete of Month, 1974; Team Can. Most Valuable Player, 1976; Most Popular King Player, 1977; nominated Brian Piccolo award, 1976, Charles Conacher Meml. award, 1976; selected to All Star team, 1974-75, 76-77. Roman Catholic. Home: Bloomfield Hills MI 48013

VADAKIN, JAMES CHARLES, educator; b. Lima, Ohio, Mar. 8, 1924; s. James Charles and Grace (Miller) V.; B.A., Denison U., 1946; M.B.A., Harvard, 1947; Ph.D., Cornell U., 1952; m. Mary Ann Willoughby, Sept. 8, 1946; 1 son, Jeffrey J. Mem. faculty U. Miami (Fla.), 1947—, prof. econs., 1957—, chmn. dept., 1961—; coordinator Cuban Econ. Research Project, 1961—; arbitrator labor-mgmt., 1950—; frequent speaker. Mem. panel arbitrators Fed. Mediation and Conciliation Service; mem. Fed. Service Impasses Panel; mem. Presdl. Emergency Bd. 177, 1970; mem. Fla. Council Econ. Edn. Served with USNR, 1942-46. First hon. mem. Personnel Assn. Miami, 1954. Mem. Nat. Acad. Arbitrators (bd. govs.), Am. Arbitration Assn., Am., So. econ. assns., Phi Kappa Phi, Omicron Delta Kappa, Lambda Chi Alpha. Club: Harvard (Miami). Author: Family Allowances, 1958; Children, Poverty and Family Allowance, 1968; also articles. Home: 1450 Ancona Ave Coral Gables FL 33146

VAETH, JOSEPH GORDON, govt. ofcl.; b. N.Y.C., Feb. 12, 1921; s. Joseph Anthony and Sara (Billard) V.; A.B., N.Y. U., 1941; m. Joanne Corell, Dec. 30, 1950; 1 son, Gordon Corell. Instr., Adm. Billard Acad., New London, Conn., 1941-42, Lawrenceville (N.J.) Sch., 1946-47; project engr., tech. programs officer U.S. Naval Tng. Device Center, 1947-54, head new weapons and systems div., 1954-58; tech. staff mem. for man-in-space Advanced Research Projects Agy., Def. Dept., 1958-60; mgr. Washington operations Reflectone Eletronics, Inc., 1960-62; asst. to dir. Nat. Weather Satelite Center, U.S. Weather Bur., 1962-63, mgr. TIROS operational satellite system engring. div., 1963-66; dir. system engring. Nat. Environ. Satellite Service, Environ. Sci. Services Adminstrn., 1966-70, Nat. Oceanic and Atmospheric Adminstrn., 1970—, Served as officer USNR, 1942-46. Fellow Am. Inst. Aeros. and Astronautics (asso.); mem. British Interplanetary Soc., U. S. Naval Inst., Lighter-than-Air soc. Episcopalian. Author: Weather Eyes in the Sky, 1965; 200 Miles Up, 1951; Graf Zeppelin, 1958; To the Ends of the Earth, 1962; Langley: Man of Science and Flight, 1966; The Man Who Founded Georgia, 1968; also numerous articles. Contbr. to Ency. Brit. Office: care Nat Environmental Satellite Service Washington DC 20233*

VAFAKOS, WILLIAM PAUL, mech. engr., educator, lawyer; b. Bklyn., Oct. 12, 1927; s. Paul and Pauline (Kontolefas) V.; B.M.E. magna cum laude, Poly. Inst. Bklyn., 1951, M.M.E., 1955, Ph.D. in Applied Mechanics, 1960; J.D., Bklyn. Law Sch., 1976; m. Gloria Mary Albantides, Aug. 19, 1962; children—Constance Maria, Paul William, George William. Engr., Westinghouse Electric Corp., 1951-53; sr. engr. Ford Instrument Co., div. Sperry Rand Corp., 1953-57; research asso. Poly. Inst. N.Y. (formerly Bkyn.), 1957-60, asst. prof. applied mechanics, 1960-63, asso. prof., 1963-68, prof. mech. and aerospace engring., 1968—; admitted to N.Y. bar, 1977; asso. firm Pappas & Pappas, Esqs., N.Y.C., 1978—. Mem. Assn. Help Retarded Children, N.Y. Assn. Brain Injured Children. Served with AUS, 1945-47. Registered profl. engr., N.Y. State. Fellow Am. Inst. Aero. and Astronautics (asso.); mem. ASME, AAUP, Am. Bar Assn., N.Y. State Bar Assn., Kings County Bar Assn., N.Y. County Bar Assn., Am. Patent Law Assn., Tau Beta Pi, Pi Tau Sigma, Sigma Gamma Tau. Greek Orthodox. Author articles elasticity, shell theory, structures. Patentee in field. Home: 967 E 17th St Brooklyn NY 11230

VAGELOS, PINDAROS ROY, biomed. research exec.; b. Westfield, N.J., Oct. 8, 1929; s. Roy John and Marianthi (Lambrinides) V.; A.B., U. Pa., 1950; M.D., Columbia, 1954; m. Diana Touliatos, July 10, 1955; children—Randall, Cynthia, Andrew, Ellen. Intern medicine Mass. Gen. Hosp., 1954-55, asst. resident medicine, 1955-56; surgeon Lab. Cellular Physiology, NIH, 1956-59, Lab. Biochemistry, 1959-64, head sect. comparative biochemistry, 1964-66; prof. biochemistry, chmn. dept. biol. chemistry Washington U. Sch. Medicine, St. Louis, 1966-75, dir. div. biology and biomed. scis., 1973-75; sr. v.p. research Merck, Sharp & Dohme Research Labs., 1975-76, pres. 1976—; mem. molecular biology study sect. NIH, 1967-71, mem. physiol. chemistry study sect., 1973-75; mem. commn. on human resources NRC, 1973-76, Inst. Medicine, Nat. Acad. Scis., 1974—. Mem. Am. Chem. Soc. (chmn. div. biol. chemistry 1973; award enzyme chemistry 1967), Am. Soc. Biol. Chemists, A.A.A.S., Nat. Acad. Scis., Am. Acad. Arts and Scis. Discoverer of acyl-carrier protein. Mem. editorial bds. jours. in field. Home: 10 Canterbury Ln Watchung NJ 07060

VAGLIANO, ALEXANDER MARINO, banker; b. Paris, France, Mar. 15, 1927; s. Andre M. and Barbara (Allen) V.; came to U.S., 1940, naturalized, 1945; grad. St. Paul's Sch., Concord, N.H., 1944; B.A., Harvard, 1949; LL.B. cum laude, Harvard, 1952; m. Sarah Griesinger Findlay, June 14, 1974; 1 son, Justin C.; children by previous marriage—Barbara A., Andre M. Admitted to N.Y. bar, 1952; asso. firm White & Case, N.Y.C., 1952-58; asst. treas. J.P. Morgan & Co., Inc., N.Y.C., 1959; v.p. Morgan Guaranty Trust Co., N.Y.C., 1959-62, 65-66, sr. v.p., 1968-76, exec. v.p., 1976—; mng. dir. Banca Vonwiller, Milan, Italy, 1967-68; chmn. Morgan Guaranty Internat. Finance Corp., 1976—, J.P. Morgan Overseas Capital Corp., 1976—; dir. Texasgulf, Inc., Stamford, Conn.; dir. office of capital devel. and finance Near East and S. Asia, AID, 1963-65; adviser Yale Econ. Growth Center, 1973—. Pres. Parks Council N.Y.C., 1971-73; bd. dirs. French Am. Found., N.Y.C. Served with AUS, 1945-47. Mem. Council Fgn. Relations. Clubs: Brook (N.Y.C.); Travellers (Paris). Home: Sunset Ridge Norfolk CT 06058 Office: 23 Wall St New York City NY 10015

VAGLIO-LAURIN, ROBERTO, educator; b. Milan, Italy, Aug. 7, 1929; s. Guglielmo and Ester (Singrossi) V.; D.Eng., U. Rome, 1950, Dr. Aero. Engring., 1952; Ph.D., Poly. Inst. Bklyn., 1954; m. Norma A. Bonaventura, Jan. 4, 1958; children—Stefan J., Marc W. Came to U.S., 1952, naturalized, 1961. Profl. engr., Rome, 1950-52; mem. faculty Poly. Inst. Bklyn., 1955-64, prof. aerospace engring., 1960-64, asst. dir. aerospace research, 1962-64, dir., 1964; mem. staff Inst. Def. Analyses, Arlington, Va., 1964-65; prof. aeros. and astronautics N.Y.U., N.Y.C., 1965-73, prof. applied sci., 1974—; chief exec. officer Gen. Applied Sci. Labs., Inc., Westbury, N.Y., 1976—; vis. lectr. aerodynamics U. Rome, 1959—; cons. Inst. Def. Analyses, Aerospace Corp., other govt. and indsl. orgns. Fellow Am. Inst. Aeros. and Astronautics (asso. editor AIAA Jour. 1967-71; mem. fluid dynamics com. 1964-67); corr. mem. Internat. Acad. Astronautics of Internat. Astronautical Fedn.; mem. Am. Phys. Soc., AAAS, Sigma Xi, Tau Beta Pi. Contbr. articles to profl. jours. Home: 333 Hempstead Ave Rockville Centre NY 11570 Office: NY University New York City NY 10003

VAGTS, DETLEV FREDERICK, lawyer, educator; b. Washington, Feb. 13, 1929; s. Alfred and Miriam (Beard) V.; grad. Taft Sch., 1945; A.B., Harvard, 1948, LL.B., 1951; m. Dorothy Larkin, Dec. 11, 1954; children—Karen, Lydia. Admitted to N.Y. bar, 1952; asso. firm Cahill, Gordon, Reindel & Ohl, N.Y.C., 1951-53, 56-59; asst. prof. law Harvard Law Sch., 1959-62, prof., 1962—, mem. faculty Harvard Bus.

Sch., 1974—; counselor internat. law Dept. State, 1976-77. Served to 1st lt. USAF, 1953-56. Mem. Am. Bar Assn., Am. Soc. Internat. Law, Phi Beta Kappa. Author: (with others) Transnational Legal Problems, 1968, 2d edit., 1976; Basic Corporation Law, 1973, 2d edit., 1979. Co-editor: Secured Transactions Under the Uniform Commercial Code, 1963-64; asso. reporter Restatement of Foreign Relations Law. Home: 29 Follen St Cambridge MA 02138

VAHAN, RICHARD, marine scientist; b. N.Y.C., Oct. 23, 1927; s. Vahan Churghents and Minerva (Eknayan) V.; B.S., Boston U., 1951; children—Julia, Suzanne. Field mgr. circulation Courier Jour. and Louisville Times, 1951; reporter, staff writer Nashua (N.H.) Telegraph, 1952-53; sci. and med. writer Boston Herald-Traveler, 1954-65, also staff writer, reporter; curator New Eng. Aquarium, Boston, 1965-68, John G. Shedd Aquarium, Chgo., 1968-72; sr. editor Ocean World of Jacques Cousteau, N.Y.C., 1972-73; dir. Marlab, Miami, Fla., 1973-75; marine coordinator, asst. chmn. dept. marine sci. U. South Fla., St. Petersburg, 1975-77; partner Aquatic Exploration, Miami and St. Petersburg, 1975—. Mem. Gov.'s Conf. on Mental Health, Boston, 1961; mem. Gov.'s Com. on Safe Boating, Boston, 1959-68. Served with AUS, 1944-47. Mem. Am. Soc. Ichthyologists and Herpetologists, Am. Fisheries Soc., Internat. Assn. Profl. Diving Scientists (life), Underwater Soc. Am. (founding mem.), World Underwater Fedn. Unitarian-Universalist. Club: Club de Exploraciones y Deportes Acuaticos de Mexico Internat. (founding mem.) (Mexico City). Author: The Truth About the John Birch Society, 1962. Editor (with James Dugan) Men Under Water, 1965. Home: 136 Ricardo Way NE St Petersburg FL 33704

VAIL, CHARLES BROOKS, coll. pres.; b. Bessemer, Ala., Apr. 29, 1923; s. William Gordon and Flora (Platowsky) V.; student U. Ala., 1941-42, Howard Coll., 1943-44; B.S., Birmingham-So. Coll., 1942-43; M.S., Emory U., 1947, Ph.D., 1951; m. Emily Blake, July 21, 1944; children—Julie Winifred Vail Brown, Lise Frances. Instr., Armstrong Coll., Savannah, Ga., 1948; chemist So. Research Inst., Birmingham, Ala., 1951-53; prof. Coker Coll., Hartsville, S.C., 1953-56; asso. prof. Agnes Scott Coll., Decatur, Ga., 1956-57; acad. dean Hampden-Sydney (Va.) Coll., 1957-65; asso. exec. sec. Commn. on Colls., So. Assn. Colls. and Schs., Atlanta, 1965-68, acting exec. sec., 1967-68; dean Sch. Arts and Scis., Ga. State U., Atlanta, 1968-73; pres. Winthrop Coll., Rock Hill, S.C., 1973—. Mem. exec. com. S.C. United Way. Served to lt. (j.g.) USNR, 1943-46. Mem. Am. Chem. Soc., S.C. C. of C. (dir.), Sigma Xi, Omicron Delta Kappa, Phi Kappa Phi. Contbr. Handbook of Academic Administration, 1970. Home: 601 Oakland Ave Rock Hill SC 29730

VAIL, CHARLES ROWE, elec. engr., ednl. adminstr.; b. Glens Falls, N.Y., Oct. 16, 1915; s. Charles Herbert and Grace Evangeline (Rowe) V.; B.S., Duke U., 1937; M.S., U. Mich., 1946, Ph.D., 1956; m. Helen Hall Wilson, Sept. 4, 1939; children—Helen Winifred Vail Sites, Charles Wilson, Theodore Wakefield. Elec. engr. Gen. Electric Co., 1937-39, summers 1940, 41, 49; from instr. to prof. elec. engring. Duke U., 1939-67, chmn. dept. elec. engring., 1953-64, asso. dean Coll. Engring., 1964-67; prof. elec. engring. and electronic scis. So. Meth. U., Dallas, 1967-73, asso. dean Inst. Tech., 1967-70, v.p. univ., 1970-73; prof. elec. engring. Ga. Inst. Tech., Atlanta, 1973—, asso. dean Coll. Engring., 1973-79, dir. dept. continuing edn., 1979—; pres. Ga. Engring. Found., 1977. Recipient Disting. Alumnus award Duke U. Sch. Engring., 1967; Exceptional Service in Engring. Professionalism award Atlanta chpt. Am. Inst. Plant Engrs., 1975, Engr. of Yr. in Edn. award, 1976, others; Rackham Spl. fellow, 1945-46; Gen. Edn. Bd. fellow, 1950-51; registered profl. engr. Fellow IEEE (chmn. N.C. sect. 1963-64); mem. Am. Soc. Engring. Edn., Nat. Soc. Profl. Engrs., Ga. Soc. Profl. Engrs. (pres. Atlanta chpt. 1977-78, state pres.-elect 1979-80, Engr. of Year in Ga. 1976), AAAS, Soc. History Tech., Assn. for Media-Based Continuing Edn. for Engrs. (initial registered agt., corp. sec.), Phi Beta Kappa, Sigma Xi, Tau Beta Pi, Eta Kappa Nu, Phi Eta Sigma, Pi Mu Epsilon. Republican. Methodist. Author: Circuits in Electrical Engineering, 1950. Contbr. articles to tech. and profl. jours. Home: 2669 Peppermint Dr Tucker GA 30084 Office: Dept Continuing Edn Ga Inst Tech Atlanta GA 30332. *The intellectual stimulation and the emotional satisfaction to be derived from interacting synergistically with other persons have always been driving forces in my life. So also has been the not unrelated desire to contribute to the well-being of individual fellow human beings as well as to society as a whole.*

VAIL, HERMAN LANSING, lawyer; b. Cleve., July 6, 1895; s. Harry L. and Sarah A. (Wickham) V.; A.B., Princeton, 1917; LL.B., Harvard, 1922; m. Delia B. White, June 29, 1922 (dec.); children—Herman Lansing, Thomas Van Husen; m. 2d, Mary Louise Frackelton Gleason, Feb. 11, 1965. Admitted Ohio bar, 1922, since practiced in Cleve.; partner firm Vail, Steele, Howland & Olson, 1931—; former pres., dir. Holden Estates Co., Forest City Pub. Co., Art Gravure Corp. of Ohio; dir. Cleve. Trust Co., 1948-70, adv. dir., 1970-75; dir. Island Creek Coal Co., Occidental Petroleum Corp., 1968-79. Hon. trustee Western Res. Hist. Soc., Univ. Sch., Garden Center of Greater Cleve., No. Ohio Opera Assn., Cleve. Health Museum, St. Luke's Hosp., Hiram House; hon. trustee Cleve. Travelers Aid Soc., Friends of Cleve. Pub. Library; trustee, v.p. Horace Kelley Art Found., Norweb Found.; mem. Ohio Gen. Assembly, 1929-32. Served as 1st lt. 332d Inf., U.S. Army, 1917-19. Mem. Citizens League Cleve. (past pres.), Cleve. Council World Affairs (past pres.), Ohio, Cleve., Am. bar assns. Clubs: Country, Union. Home: 13467 N Park Blvd Cleveland Heights OH 44118 Office: 1615 Illuminating Bldg 55 Public Sq Cleveland OH 44113

VAIL, PETER ROBBINS, geologist; b. N.Y.C., Jan. 13, 1930; s. Donald Bain and Eleanor (Robbins) V.; A.B., Dartmouth, 1952; M.S., Northwestern U., 1955, Ph.D. (Shell fellow), 1959; m. Carolyn Flesher, Sept. 15, 1956; children—Andrea, Susan, Timothy Edward. Asst. geologist U.S. Geol. Survey, Spokane, Wash. and Evanston, Ill., 1952-56; research geologist Carter Oil Co., Tulsa, 1956-58; sr. research geologist Jersey Prodn. Research Co., Tulsa, 1958-62, sr. research geologist, 1962-65; sr. research specialist Esso Prodn. Research Co., Houston, 1965-66, research asso., 1966, research supr., 1966-70, sr. research asso., 1970-72, sr. research adv., 1972-74; sr. research adv. Exxon Prodn. Research Co., Houston, 1974-76, research scientist, 1976—; mem. Consortium for Continental Reflection Profiling Site Selection Com., 1974—, Internat. Subcom. Stratigraphic Classification, 1976—; mem. com. on geol. perspectives on climatic change Nat. Acad. Scis., 1977—; mem. Joint Oceanographic Insts Deep Earth Sampling Passive Margin Panel, 1978-79; William Smith lectr. Geol. Soc. London, 1978. Fellow Geol. Soc. Am. (research grants com. 1977-79, chmn. 1979); mem. Assn. Petroleum Geologists (disting. lectr. 1975-76, Pres.'s award for best paper 1979), Soc. Exploration Geophysicists (recipient Virgil Kaufmann Gold medal 1976), Am. Petroleum Inst., AAAS, Geol. and Geophys. Socs. Houston, Mayflower Soc., Sigma Xi. Contbr. articles to profl. jours. Home: 3745 Del Monte Dr Houston TX 77019 Office: Exxon Production Research Co Box 2189 Houston TX 77001

VAIL, THOMAS VAN HUSEN, newspaper pub. and editor; b. Cleve., June 23, 1926; s. Herman Lansing and Delia (White) V.; A.B. in Politics cum laude, Princeton U., 1949; H.H.D. (hon.), Wilberforce U., 1964; L.H.D., Kenyon Coll., 1969, Cleve. State U., 1973 m. Iris Jennings, Sept. 15, 1951; children—Siri, Thomas Van Husen, Lawrence Jennings White. Reporter, Cleve. News, 1949-53, polit. editor, 1953-57; with Cleve. Plain Dealer, 1957—, v.p., 1961-63, pub., editor, 1963—, pres., 1970—, also dir.; pres., dir. Art Gravure Corp. Ohio; dir. AP, 1968-74. Bd. dirs. Greater Cleve. Growth Assn.; bd. dirs., past pres. Cleve. Conv. and Visitors Bur.; mem. Nat. Adv. Commn. on Health Manpower, U.S. Adv. Commn. on Info.; mem. Pres.'s Commn. for Observance 25th Anniversary UN; trustee No. Ohio region NCCJ, nat. Brotherhood Week chmn., 1969, recipient Nat. Human Relations award, 1970; trustee Cleve. Council World Affairs, Cleve. Clinic Found., Downtown Cleve. Corp.; mem. distbn. com. Cleve. Found. Served to lt. (j.g.) USNR, 1944-46. Recipient Cleve. Man of Year award Sales and Mktg. Execs. Cleve., 1976. Mem. Sigma Delta Chi. Clubs: Cleve. Athletic, Union (Cleve.); Kirtland Country (Willoughby, Ohio); Cypress Point (Pebble Beach, Calif.); Nat. Press (Washington). Home: Hunting Valley Chagrin Falls OH 44022 Office: 1801 Superior Ave Cleveland OH 44114

VAILL, PETER BROWN, mgmt. cons.; b. St. Cloud, Minn., Nov. 5, 1936; s. Stanley Theodore and Elizabeth (Brown) V.; A.B., U. Minn., 1958; M.B.A., Harvard U., 1960, D.B.A., 1964; m. Margery Jean Barnes, Aug. 15, 1959 (div. 1978); children—Emily Susan, Timothy Dexter. Asst. prof. Harvard Bus. Sch., 1963-64; asst. prof. Grad. Sch. Mgmt., U. Calif. at Los Angeles, 1964-70, vice-chmn. dept. bus. adminstrn., 1969-70; asso. prof. Sch. Bus. Adminstrn., U. Conn., 1970-73, asso. dean, 1972-73; dean Sch. Govt. and Bus. Adminstrn., prof. human systems George Washington U., 1973-78; vis. prof. human systems Stanford (Calif.) U., 1980; pres. Mgmt. Art, Inc.; cons. numerous corps., govtl. agys. Bd. govs. VA Adminstrv. Scholars Program. Mem. Am. Soc. Tng. and Devel., Acad. Mgmt., Orgn. Devel. Network, Eastern Acad. Mgmt. (dir.), NTL Inst. Applied Behavioral Sci. (charter), Delta Tau Delta, Beta Gamma Sigma. Democrat. Episcopalian. Contbr. articles to profl. jours. Home: 1118 S 17 St Arlington VA 22202

VAILLANT, GEORGE EMAN, psychiatrist; b. N.Y.C., June 16, 1934; s. George Clapp and Mary Suzannah (Beck) V.; A.B., Harvard U., 1955, M.D., 1959; postgrad. Boston Psychoanalytic Inst., 1967-76; m. Caroline Brown, Apr. 17, 1971; children—George Emery, John Holden, Henry Greenough, Anne Liberty, Caroline Joanna. Resident in psychiatry Mass. Mental Health Center, Boston, 1960-63; from asst. prof. to asso. prof. psychiatry Tufts U. Sch. Medicine, 1966-71; asso. prof. psychiatry Harvard Med. Sch., 1971-77, prof., 1977—; dir. tng. Cambridge (Mass.) Hosp., 1976—; dir. study of adult devel. Harvard U. Health Services, 1972—. Bd. dirs. Justice Resource Inst., 1977—. Served with USPHS, 1963-65. Fellow Center for Advanced Study in Behavioral Scis., 1978-79. Fellow Am. Psychiat. Assn.; mem. Boston Psychoanalytic Soc. Episcopalian. Author: Adaptation to Life, 1977; contbr. articles to profl. jours. Home: 41 Holden St Cambridge MA 02138 Office: Cambridge Hosp 1493 Cambridge St Cambridge MA 02139

VAINSTEIN, ROSE, educator, librarian; b. Edmonton, Alta., Can., Jan. 7, 1920; d. Nathan and Jane (Simenstein) Vainstein; A.B., Miami U., Oxford, Ohio, 1941; B.L.S., Western Res. U., 1942; M.S., U. Ill., 1952. Jr. librarian Cuyahoga County Library, Cleve., 1942-43; young people's librarian Bklyn. Pub. Library, 1943-44; br. librarian Contra Costa County Library, Martinez, Calif., 1948-51; library cons. Calif. State Library, Sacramento, 1953-55; head extension dept. Gary (Ind.) Pub. and Lake County Library, 1955-57; pub. library specialist U.S. Office Edn., Washington, 1957-61; asso. prof. Sch. Librarianship, U. B.C., Vancouver, 1961-64; dir. Bloomfield Twp. Pub. Library, Bloomfield Hills, Mich., 1964-68; prof. library sci. U. Mich. at Ann Arbor, 1968—, dir. Middle Mgmt. Inst. for Pub. Librarians, 1969, 1st Margaret Mann Distinguished prof. library sci., 1974—; librarian U.S. Armed Forces, U.S., Hawaii, Japan, 1944-48; dir. B.C. (Can.) Pub. Libraries Research Study, 1963-64. Fulbright Research scholar, Eng., 1952-53; Council on Library Resources fellow, 1974-75. Mem. Am. Assn. U. Profs., A.L.A. (chmn. pub. library standards com. 1969-73, chmn. pub. library activities com. 1974-76, mem. council 1975-79, mem. council budget assembly 1975-79, chmn. nominating com. 1976-77), Mich., Canadian library assns., Spl. Library Assn., U. Mich. Women's Research Club (treas. 1971-72, chmn. loan fund com. 1976-79, Spl. 75th Anniv. award 1978), League of Women Voters, Phi Beta Kappa (Alumnus mem. Iota of Ohio chpt. 1976), Beta Phi Mu (dir. 1974-77). Contbr. articles to profl. jours. Home: Apt 261 2013 Medford Rd Ann Arbor MI 48104 Office: U Mich Ann Arbor Ann Arbor MI 48109

VAIRA, PETER FRANCIS, lawyer; b. McKeesport, Pa., Mar. 5, 1937; s. Peter Francis and Mary Louise (Bedogne) V.; B.A., Duquesne U., 1959, J.D., 1962. Admitted to Pa. bar, 1963, D.C. bar, 1968; atty. Chgo. Strike Force, Justice Dept., 1968-72, atty. in charge Phila. Strike Force, 1972-73, Chgo. Strike Force on Organized Crime, 1973-78; U.S. atty., Phila., 1978—. Served with USNR, 1963-68. Recipient Spl. Commendation award Justice Dept., 1976. Office: US Atty 3310 US Courthouse Independence Mall W 601 Market St Philadelphia PA 19106

VAIRO, PHILIP DOMINIC, univ. dean; b. N.Y.C., Aug. 4, 1933; s. Nicola and Rosana (Contino) V.; B.A., Hunter Coll., 1955; M.A., N.Y.U., 1958; Ed.D., Duke, 1963; m. Lillian Escalante, June 28, 1958; children—Mary E., Bonnie R. Tchr. social studies, chmn. dept. social studies, ednl. counselor N.Y.C. pub. schs., 1957-61; research asso. N.C. Bd. Higher Edn., Raleigh, 1962-63; instr., asst. coordinator student teaching Hunter Coll., City U.N.Y., 1963-64; asso. prof., chmn. dept. edn. U. N.C., Charlotte, 1964-67; asso. prof. edn., chmn. div. curriculum and teaching Sch. Edn., Fordham U., N.Y.C., 1967-69; dean profl. studies, prof. edn. U. Tenn., Chattanooga, 1969-73; prof. edn. Calif. State U., Los Angeles, 1973—, dean Coll. Edn., 1973—. Vis. prof. St. Lawrence U., Canton, N.Y., summer 1961, Coll. New Rochelle (N.Y.), summer 1968, So. Ill. U., Carbondale, summer 1968, Rollins Coll., summer 1969. Cons. Ednl. Testing Service, Princeton, N.J., 1969, Speech and Hearing Center, Chattanooga, 1970. Served with USNR, 1955-57. Mem. N.E.A., A.A.U.P., Kappa Delta Pi. Author: How to Teach Disadvantaged Youth, 1969; Urban Education: Problems and Prospects, 1969; Urban Education: Opportunity or Crisis?; contbr. articles to profl. jours. Home: 2041 Carolwood Dr Arcadia CA 91006 Office: Calif State University Los Angeles CA

VAISRUB, SAMUEL, physician, med. assn. editor; b. Russia, Sept. 15, 1906; s. Abraham and Kreina (Maley) V.; came to Can., 1924, naturalized, 1929; M.D., U. Man. (Can.), 1932; postgrad. VA Hosp., Winnipeg, Man., 1945-47; London Postgrad. Sch. Medicine, 1947-48; m. Judith Ida Maltz, Mar. 19, 1949; children—Naomi, Daniel. Intern St. Paul's Hosp., Saskatoon, Sask., Can., 1931-33; practice medicine, Sask., 1933-41; practice medicine specializing in internal medicine, Winnipeg, Man., 1949-65; asst. prof. Man. Med. Sch., 1950-65; editor Man. Med. Rev., 1955-65; sr. editor Jour. A.M.A., Chgo., 1965—; asso. editor Archives Internal Medicine, 1967—; asso. prof. medicine Chgo. Med. Sch., 1967—. Served with M.C., Royal Can. Army, 1941-45. Diplomate Canadian Bd. Internal Medicine. Fellow A.C.P., Royal Coll. Physicians Can.; mem. Royal Coll. Physicians London; Am. Soc. Internal Medicine, Am. Heart Assn., Assn. History Medicine, Soc. Med. History, Council Med. Editors, Am. Med. Writers Assn., Can. Med. Assn. Author: Medicine's Metaphors: Messages and Menaces; co-author: Diabetes and the Heart. Contbr. editorials and articles to med. jours. Home: 520 Knox Ave Wilmette IL 60091 Office: 535 N Dearborn Chicago IL 60601

VAJK, HUGO, mfg. exec.; b. Ljubljana, Yugoslavia, Mar. 26, 1928; s. Hugo and Magda (Slatnar) V.; came to Can., 1947, naturalized, 1953; student Institut Polytechnic, Grenoble, France, 1947; B.Eng. with honors, McGill U., Montreal, 1951; M.S., Carnegie Mellon U., Pitts., 1953; m. Barbara Louise Hallin, June 13, 1953; children—Tanja Astrid, Hugo Anthony, Madeleine Louise, Anita Marie, Nicolette Cecile, Moira Suzanne. Product mgr. Joy Mfg. Co., Buffalo, 1957-59, dir. gen., Paris, 1960-63; with Massey-Ferguson, Ltd., 1964-78, pres. Moteurs Perkins S.A., S. Am., Paris, 1964-65, Massey-Ferguson S.A., Paris, 1966-69, v.p. logistics parent co., Toronto, 1970-72, exec. v.p., 1973-78; dir. GEC Inc., N.Y. (subs. Gen. Electric Co. Eng., 1979—; chmn. English Electric Corp., Elmsford, N.Y., 1979—. Mem. ASME, Soc. Automotive Engrs., Assn. Profl. Engrs. Ont., Inst. Mgmt. Scis. Clubs: Univ., Royal Canadian Yacht (Toronto); Union Interalliée, Yacht de France (Paris); Royal Thames Yacht (London). Address: 33 Harbour Sq Toronto ON M5J 2G2 Canada

VAKY, VIRON PETER, fgn. service officer; b. Tex., Sept. 13, 1925; B.S., Georgetown U., 1947; M.A., U. Chgo., 1948; m. Luann Colburn. Vocat. appraiser VA, 1948-49; joined Fgn. Service, State Dept., 1949; consular officer, Guayaquil, 1949-51; econ. officer, Buenos Aires, 1951-54; internat. relations officer State Dept., 1955-57, info. specialist, 1958-59; polit. officer, Bogota, 1959-61; detailed Nat. War Coll., 1963-64; counsellor-dep. chief mission, Guatemala, 1964-67; mem. Polit. Plan Council, State Dept., 1967-68, dep. asst. sec. Bur. Inter-Am. Affairs, 1968-69, acting asst. sec. Inter-Am. affairs, 1969, detailed Nat. Security Council, 1959-70; diplomate-in-residence Georgetown U., 1970-71; ambassador to Costa Rica, San Jose, 1972-74, to Colombia, Bogota, 1974-76, to Venezuela, Caracas, 1976-78; asst. sec. for Inter-Am. affairs, Washington, 1978—. Served with AUS, 1944-46. Address: Bur Inter-Am Affairs Dept State Washington DC 20520

VALBUENA-BRIONES, ANGEL JULIAN, educator, author; b. Madrid, Spain, Jan. 11, 1928; s. Angel Valbuena and Francisca Briones; Licenciado summa cum laude, Murcia (Spain) U., 1949; Ph.D. with honors, Madrid U., 1952; m. Barbara Northrup Hobart, Nov. 9, 1957; children—Teresa, Vivian. Naturalized Am. citizen, 1963. Prof. Ayudante, Murcia U., 1949-51; lectr. Oxford (Eng.) U., 1953-55; prof. Ayudante, Madrid U., 1955-56; vis. lectr. U. Wis., 1956-58; asst. prof. Yale U., 1958-60; Elias Ahuja prof. Spanish lit. U. Del., 1960—; lecture tour S.Am., summer 1957; vis. summer prof. N.Y. U., 1960, 61; vis. prof. Madrid U., 1970-71, summer 1977. Fellow del Consejo Superior de Investigaciones Cientificas, 1951, 70-71, del Instituto de Cultura Hispanica, 1951-52. Mem. Am. Assn. Tchrs. Spanish and Portuguese, Modern Lang. Renaissance Soc. Am., Spanish Inst., Internat. Fedn. Modern Langs. and Lits., Internat. Linguistic Assn., Asociación Internacional de Hispanistas, S. Atlantic, Northeast modern lang. assns., Sigma Delta Pi (hon.), Phi Kappa Phi. Club: Greenville Country. Author: Nueva Poesia de Puerto Rico, 1952; Comedias de Capa y Espada de Calderon, 1954; Dramas de Honor de Calderon, 2 vols., 1956; Obras Completas de Calderon vol. I dramas, 1959, vol. II comedias, 1956; Ensayo sobre la obra de Calderon, 1954; Literature Hispanoamericana, 1962; Perspectiva critica de los dramas de Calderon, 1965; Ideas y Palabras, 1968; El alcalde de Zalamea de Calderon, 1971; Primera Parte de Comedias de Pedro Calderon de la Barca, Vol. I, 1974; La Dama Duende de Calderon, 1976; Calderon y la comedia nueva, 1977; also articles, reviews, lectures. Editorial bd. Arbor, Bull. Comediantes. Address: 203 Nottingham Rd Newark DE 19711

VALDES-DAPENA, MARIE AGNES, pathologist; b. Pottsville, Pa., July 14, 1921; d. Edgar Daniel and Marie Agnes (Rettig) Brown; B.S., Immaculata Coll., 1941; M.D., Temple U., 1944; m. Antonio M. Valdes-Dapena, Apr. 6, 1945; children—Victoria Maria Valdes-Dapena Grefe, Deborah Anne Valdes-Dapena, Maria Cristina Valdes-Dapena, Andres Antonio, Antonio Edgardo, Carlos Roberto, Marcos Antonio, Ricardo Daniel, Carmen Patricia, Catalina Inez, Pedro Pablo. Intern, Phila. Gen. Hosp., 1944-45, resident in pathology, 1945-49; asst. pathologist Fitzgerald Mercy Hosp., Darby, Pa., 1949-51; dir. labs. Woman's Med. Coll. Pa., Phila., 1951-55, instr. pathology, 1947-51, asst. prof., 1951-55, asso. prof., 1955-59; asso. pathologist St. Christopher's Hosp. for Children, Phila., 1959-76; dir. div. pediatric pathology Jackson Meml. Hosp., Miami, 1976—; cons., lectr. U.S. Naval Hosp., Phila., 1972-76; instr. pathology Sch. Medicine U. Pa., 1945-49, instr. Sch. Dentistry, 1947, instr. Grad. Sch. Medicine, 1948-55, vis. lectr., 1960-62; asst. prof. Temple U. Med. Sch., 1959-63, asso. prof., 1963-67, prof., 1967-76, prof. pediatrics, 1967-76; prof. pathology and pediatrics U. Miami, 1976—; cons. pediatric pathology div. med. examiner Dept. Pub. Health Phila., 1967-70; mem. perinatal biology and infant mortality research and tng. com. Nat. Inst. Child Health and Human Devel., NIH, 1971-73; mem. sci. adv. bd. Armed Forces Inst. Pathology, 1976—; asso. med. examiner, Dade County, Fla., 1976—, chmn. med. bd., 1970—. NIH grantee. Diplomate Am. Bd. Pathology. Mem. Internat. Acad. Pathology, Am. Assn. Pathologists and Bacteriologists, Pathol. Soc. Phila., Pediatric Pathology Club, Pediatric Pathology Soc. Gt. Britain and Ireland, Coll. Physicians Phila., Internat. Assembly Pediatric Pathology, Alpha Omega Alpha. Roman Catholic. Contbr. articles to profl. jours. Home: 418 Tamarind Dr Hallandale FL 33009 Office: Dept Pathology Jackson Meml Hosp Miami FL 33101

VALDEZ, JOEL DAVID, city ofcl.; b. Tucson, July 2, 1934; s. Luis F. and Miriam V.; B.S., U. Ariz., 1957; postgrad. Mass. Inst. Tech., 1972; m. Mary Lee Jacobs, May 30, 1958; children—David E., Laura Lisa. Dir. detention service Pima County Juvenile Ct., Tucson, 1958-66; adminstrv. asst. City of Tucson Library, 1966-70; asst., city mgrs. office City of Tucson, 1970-71, asst. city mgr., 1971-74, city mgr., 1974—. Mem. governing bd. Catholic Diocese of Tucson, Ariz. Mem. Ariz. internat. city mgrs. assns. Roman Catholic. Club: K.C. Home: 2045 Calle Armenta Tucson AZ 85705 Office: PO Box 27210 Tucson AZ 85726

VALDMAN, ALBERT, educator; b. Paris, France, Feb. 15, 1931; s. Jacques and Rose (Standman) V.; came to U.S., 1944, naturalized, 1953; A.B., U. Pa., 1953; A.M., Cornell U., 1955, Ph.D., 1960; m. Hilde Wieners, Aug. 19, 1960; 1 son, Bertrand Andre. Linguistic scientist Fgn. Service Inst., 1957-59; asst. prof. Romance langs. Pa. State U., 1959-60; mem. faculty Ind. U., Bloomington, 1960—, prof. French, Italian and linguistics, 1966—, chmn. dept. linguistics, 1963-68; vis. prof. Harvard, summer 1965; vis. lectr. U. West Indies, 1965-66; cons. in field, 1959—. Guggenheim fellow, 1968; Fulbright lectr. U. Nice (France), 1971-72, 75-76. Mem. Phi Beta Kappa. Author: Applied Linguistics-French, 1960; Drillbook of French Pronounciation, 1964, 70; Trends in Language Teaching, 1966; College French in the New Key, 1965, Saint-Lucian Creole Basic Course, 1969; Basic Course in Haitian Creole, 1970; First and Second Level High School French, 1972, 2d edit., 1977; Langue et Culture, 1975; Introduction to French Phonology and Morphology, 1976; Le Creole: Structure, Statut et Origine, 1978; Editor: Pidgin and Creole Linguistics, 1977; Le Francais hors de France, 1978. Office: Dept of Linguistics Indiana U Bloomington IN 47401

VALENCY, MAURICE, educator, playwright; b. N.Y.C., Mar. 22, 1903; s. Jacques and Mathilde (Solesme) V.; A.B., Coll. City N.Y., 1923; A.M., Columbia, 1924, LL.B., 1927, Ph.D., 1939; Litt.D., L.I. U., 1975; m. Janet Cornell, Dec. 25, 1936. Admitted to N.Y. bar, 1928; instr. philosophy Coll. City of N.Y., 1931-33; instr. English, Bklyn. Coll., 1933-42, asst. prof., 1942-46; asso. prof. comparative lit. Columbia, 1946-54, prof., 1954—, Brander Matthews prof. dramatic lit., 1968-71, emeritus prof., 1971—; dir. acad. studies Juilliard Sch., N.Y.C., 1971—; over-all adviser text-film div. McGraw-Hill Co. Recipient Ford Found. research fellow, 1958; Guggenheim fellow, 1961, 65. Mem. Internat. Assn. U. Profs. English, Authors League (council, sec. 1968-75, v.p. 1967, dir. Authors League Fund), Dramatists League Fund (v.p.), Dramatists Guild, Modern Lang. Assn., Acad. Lit. Studies, Renaissance Soc., Asia Soc., A.S.C.A.P. (awards 1964—), Am. Comparative Lit. Assn. (adv. bd.), Dante Soc., Writers Guild East. Club: Century Assn. (N.Y.C.). Author: The Tragedies of Herod, 1939; In Praise of Love, 1958; The Flower and the Castle, 1963; The Breaking String, 1966; The Cart and the Trumpet, 1973; The End of the World, 1980. Playwright: The Thracian Horses, 1940; Battleship Bismarck, 1945; The Reluctant Virgin, 1948; The Madwoman of Chaillot (after Giraudoux), 1949; The Enchanted, 1950; Ondine, 1954; The Virtuous Island, 1955; Feathertop, 1959; The Queen's Gambit, 1956; The Apollo of Bellac, 1954; The Visit (after Duerrenmatt), 1958; Savonarola, 1974; Electra, 1975; Conversation with a Sphinx, 1976; librettist: La Perichole, 1957, The Gypsy Baron, 1959, The Reluctant King, 1974; Feathertop, 1979. Editor: The Palace of Pleasure, 1960; Giraudoux, Four Plays, 1958. Adv. editor for humanities Ency. Americana. Home: 404 Riverside Dr New York NY 10025 also Dingle Ridge Rd North Salem NY 10560 also Point Salines Grenada West Indies Office: Juilliard School Lincoln Center Plaza New York NY 10023

VALENS, EVANS GLADSTONE, author, former TV producer-dir.; b. State College, Pa., Apr. 17, 1920; s. Evans G. and Mabel (Grazier) V.; B.A., Amherst Coll., 1941; m. Winifred A. Crary, Oct. 11, 1941 (div. 1976); children—Thomas Crary, Marc John, Jo Anne, Dan Malcolm. Reporter, El Paso Herald-Post, 1942-43; corr. UPI, Central Pacific, U.S. and Europe, 1943-48, bur. chief, Munich, 1946-48; producer-dir. KQED, San Francisco, 1954-62, 70-71; author, 1950—; non-fiction includes: A Long Way Up, The Story of Jill Kinmont, 1966; The Number of Things, 1963; (with others) Elements of the Universe (Thomas Alva Edison award), 1958; poetry includes: Cybernaut, 1968; The Attractive Universe, 1969; Viruses and the Nature of Life, 1961; People-reading, 1975; juvenile books include: Me and Frumpet, 1957; Wingfin and Topple, 1962; Wildfire, 1963; Magnet, 1965; Motion, 1965; The Other Side of the Mountain, 1975, Part II, 1978; writer numerous films and TV prodns. Decorated Purple Heart. Address: Mill Valley CA 94941

VALENSTEIN, SUZANNE GEBHART, art historian; b. Balt., July 17, 1928; d. Jerome J. and Lonnie Cooper Gebhart; m. Murray A. Valenstein, Mar. 31, 1951. With dept. Far Eastern art Met. Mus. Art, N.Y.C., 1965—, asso. curator Far Eastern art. Mem. Oriental Ceramic Soc. (London), Oriental Ceramic Soc. (Hong Kong), Asia Soc. Author: Ming Porcelains: A Retrospective, 1970; A Handbook of Chinese Ceramics, 1975; Highlights of Chinese Ceramics, 1975; (with others) Oriental Ceramics: The World's Great Collections, Vol. 12, The Metropolitan Museum, 1977. Office: Dept Far Eastern Art Met Mus Art Fifth Ave at 82d St New York NY 10028

VALENTE, BENITA, lyric soprano; b. Delano, Calif.: d. Lawrence Guiseppe and Severina Antonia (Masdonati) Valente; grad. Curtis Inst. Music, 1960; studied with Chester Hayden, Martial Singher, Lotte Lehmann, Margaret Harshaw; m. Anthony Phillip Checchia, Nov. 21, 1959; 1 son, Peter. Freiburg Opera debut, 1962, Met. Opera debut, 1973; leading roles in: Magic Flute, Rigoletto, Falstaff, Marriage of Figaro, La Traviata, Turandot, Abduction from the Seraglio, La Boheme, and Orfeo; appeared throughout U.S. and Europe in operas and symphonies. Winner Met. Opera Council Audition, 1960. Recs. for Columbia Records, Desmar Records. Address: c/o Thea Dispeker Artists Rep 59 E 54th St New York NY 10022

VALENTE, MAURICE REMO, corp. exec.; b. Racine, Wis., Nov. 25, 1928; s. Rocco B. and Rose (Guarascio) V.; B.S., DePaul U., 1951, M.B.A., 1958; m. Dolores Grant, Aug. 28, 1954; children—Candace, James, Steven. With ITT, 1967—, dir. N.Am. staff, N.Y.C., 1967-69, v.p., group exec., Nutley, N.J., 1969-71, sr. v.p., dir. ops., N.Y.C., 1971, pres. ITT Europe, Brussels, Belgium, 1974-78, exec. v.p. Office Chief Exec. Consumer Products and Services, N.Y.C., 1978—. Served with USMCR, 1950-52. Decorated Air medal with 2 gold stars. Mem. Work Factors Assos., Am. C. of C. in Brussels. Clubs: Upper Montclair Country; Elkview Country; Internat. Golf. Home: 337 Briarly Dr Franklin Lakes NJ 07417 Office: 320 Park Ave New York NY 10022

VALENTE, MICHAEL FEENEY, educator; b. Albany, N.Y.; s. Abel A. and Anna E. (Feeney); A.B. in Philosophy, Stonehill Coll., 1959; M.S. in Math., Notre Dame U., 1961, M.A. in Theology, 1962; Ph.D. in Religion, Columbia, 1968; M.S.L. in Law, Yale U., 1974. Mem. religion faculty Manhattanville Coll., 1962-63; mem. faculty religious studies Seton Hall U., South Orange, N.J., 1967—, asso. prof., 1970—, chmn. dept., 1968-71. Founder Inst. Study Ethical Issues, 1968, pres., 1968-73; mem. bd. consultants Nat. Com. for Sexual Civil Liberties. Mem. AAUP, Am. Acad. Religion, Am. Soc. Christian Ethics, Delta Epsilon Sigma. Club: Club at the World Trade Center (N.Y.C.). Author: Sex: The Radical View of a Catholic Theologian, 1970. Home: 332 Sandford Ave Newark NJ 07106 Office: Seton Hall U South Orange NJ 07079

VALENTI, JACK JOSEPH, motion picture exec.; b. Houston, Sept. 5, 1921; B.A., U. Houston, 1946; M.B.A., Harvard U., 1948; m. Mary Margaret Wiley, June 1, 1962; children—Courtenay Lynda, John Lyndon, Alexandra Alice. Co-founder, formerly exec. v.p. Weekley and Valenti, Inc., advt.; spl. asst. to Pres. Johnson, 1963-66; pres. Motion Picture Assn. Am., Inc., 1966—, Assn. Motion Picture and TV Producers, Inc., 1966—, Motion Picture Export Assn. Am.; dir. Am. Film Inst., 1967—, Trans World Airlines, Washington Star. Trustee John F. Kennedy Center for Performing Arts. Served with USAAF, 1942-45. Decorated D.F.C., Air medal with five oak leaf clusters. Author: The Bitter Taste of Glory; A Very Human President. Address: 1600 I St NW Washington DC 20006

VALENTINE, BARRY, bishop; b. Shenfield, Essex, Eng., Sept. 26, 1927; s. Harry John and Ethel Margaret (Purkiss) V.; B.A., St. John's Coll., Cambridge (Eng.) U., 1949, M.A., 1952; B.D., McGill U., 1951; L.Th., Montreal Diocesan Theol. Coll., 1951, D.D., 1970; D.D., St. Johns Coll., Winnipeg, Man., 1969; m. Mary Currell Hayes, Oct. 4, 1952; children—John Nugent, Lesley Claire, Guy Richard Neville, Michael Hayes. Ordained to ministry Anglican Ch.; curate Christ Ch. Cathedral, Montreal, 1952; incumbent Chateauguay-Beauharnois, 1954; dir. religious edn. Diocese of Montreal, 1957-61; rector St. Lambert Ch., 1961-65; exec. officer Diocese of Montreal, 1965-66, archdeacon, 1966-68; dean of Montreal and rector Christ Ch. Cathedral, 1968-69; coadjutor bishop of Rupert's Land (Winnipeg), 1969-70, bishop, 1970—; chancellor St. Johns Coll., Winnipeg, 1970. Office: 935 Nesbitt Bay Winnipeg MB R3T 1W6 Canada

VALENTINE, DEWAIN, artist; b. Ft. Collins, Colo., Aug. 27, 1936; s. Glenn and Rouine (Lass) V.; B.F.A., U. Colo., 1958, M.F.A., 1960; Yale Norfolk fellow Yale U., 1958; children—Christopher, Sean, Nelsen. One man. exhbns. include U. Colo., 1958, 60, The Gallery, Denver, 1964, Douglas Gallery, Vancouver, Wash., 1968, Ace Gallery, Los Angeles, 1968, Galerie Birschofberger, Zurich, Switzerland, 1969, Pasadena (Calif.) Mus. Modern Art, 1970, San Jose (Calif.) Mus., 1974, Long Beach (Calif.) Mus. Art, 1975, La Jolla (Calif.) Mus. Contemporary Art, 1975, Santa Barbara (Calif.) Mus. Art, 1977. group exhbns. include Whitney Ann. Exhibit, 1966, 68, 70, Am. Ann. Exhibit, Chgo. Art Inst., 1970, 74, Walker Art Center, Mpls., 1970, Milw. Art Center, 1970; rep. permanent collections Los Angeles County Mus. Art, Milw. Art Center, Whitney Mus. Am. Art, Chgo. Art Inst., Joslyn Mus. Art, others; instr. U. Colo., 1958-61, 64-67, U. Calif., Los Angeles, 1967-68; artist-in-residence Aspen (Colo.) Inst., 1964, 65, 68. Address: 69 Market St Venice CA 90291

VALENTINE, DORRIS LYNN, realtor; b. nr. Fulton, Ky., Jan. 11, 1906; s. Thomas O. and Mary Beatrice (Bowen) V.; grad. Chillicothe Bus. Coll., 1926; student La. State U., 1962, Okla. U., 1958; m. Eva Blanche Austin, Mar. 27, 1927; children—Thomas Logan, Max Lynn. Chief clk. Swift & Co., South Fulton, Tenn., 1929-41; office asst. Ford Motor Co., Memphis, 1941; treas., controller John Gerber Co., Memphis, 1941-54, Kerr's, Inc., Oklahoma City, 1954-59; pres. Rosenfield House of Fashion, Baton Rouge, 1959-65; mgr. Hartwell Bros., Memphis, 1965-69; adminstr. City of Memphis Hosp., 1969-78; sec. Memphis Hosp. Council, 1972-73, pres., 1973-74; prin. Valentine Realty Co., Memphis, 1979—. Pres., Downtown Assn. Baton Rouge; bd. dirs. Chickasaw council Boy Scouts Am., Memphis. Named hon. col. La., 1960, hon. mayor Baton Rouge, 1965, hon. atty. gen. La., 1964. Mem. Nat. Retail Mchts. Assn. (dir. Controllers Congress), La. Retailers Assn. (treas.), Nat. Assn. Accountants (pres. Memphis chpt.). Clubs: Sherwood Forest Country, City (Baton Rouge). Contbr. articles profl. jours. Home: 4270 Heatherwood Ln Memphis TN 38117 Office: 860 Madison Ave Memphis TN 38103

VALENTINE, FOY DAN, clergyman; b. Edgewood, Tex., July 3, 1923; s. John Hardy and Josie (Johnson) V.; B.A., Baylor U., 1944, LL.B., 1979; Th.M., Southwestern Baptist Theol. Sem., 1947, Th.D., 1949; D.D., William Jewell Coll., 1966; m. Mary Louise Valentine, May 6, 1947; children—Mary Jean, Carol Elizabeth, Susan Foy. Ordained to ministry Baptist Ch., 1942; dir. Bapt. student activities colls. in Houston, 1949-50; pastor First Bapt. Ch., Gonzales, Tex., 1950-53; dir. Christian life commn. Bapt. Gen. Conv. Tex., 1953-60; exec. sec.-treas. Christian life commn. So. Bapt. Conv., 1960—, chmn. So. Bapt. inter-agy. council, 1965-67; Willson lectr. applied Christianity Wayland Bapt. Coll., 1963; Christian ethics lectr. Bapt. Theol. Sem., Ruschlikon-Zurich, Switzerland, 1966; Layne lectr. New Orleans Bapt. Theol. Sem., 1974; Jones lectr. Union U., 1976. Co-chmn. commn. religious liberty and human rights Bapt. World Alliance, 1966-75, chmn. commn. Christian ethics, 1976—, mem. gen. council, 1976—; mem. Nashville Met. Human Relations Commn., 1966-78. Trustee, Ams. United for Separation of Church and State, 1960—; bd. dirs. Bapt. Joint Com. Pub. Affairs, 1960—, Chs. Center Theology and Pub. Policy, 1976—; bd. fellows Interpreter's House, 1967-78. Recipient Disting. Alumnus award Southwestern Bapt. Theol. Sem., 1970. Mem. Am. Soc. Christian Ethics. Democrat. Author: Believe and Behave, 1964; Citizenship for Christians, 1965; The Cross in the Marketplace 1966; Where the Action Is, 1969. Editor: Christian Faith in Action, 1956; Peace, Peace, 1967; contbr. to numerous anthologies, also autho articles. Home: 6354 Torrington Rd Nashville TN 37205 Office: 460 James Robertson Pkwy Nashville TN 37219

VALENTINE, GEORGE GORDON, retail co. exec.; b. Dumbarton, Scotland, Dec. 23, 1919; s. James Gordon and Isabella Beaton (Mac Kenzie) V.; brought to U.S., 1926, naturalized, 1930; B.B.A., U. Mich., 1947; student Albion Coll., 1939-42; m. Winifred Mae Christie, Sept. 29, 1951; children—Sally Jean, James Gordon, Douglas Michael, Roger Alan. Mgr. Lybrand, Ross Bros. & Montgomery, C.P.A.'s, Detroit, 1947-61; asst. controller Wickes Corp., San Diego, 1961—, v.p., 1978—. Bd. dirs. YMCA, Saginaw, Mich., Saginaw Art Mus., Planned Parenthood Assn., San Diego. Served to 1st lt. inf. AUS, 1942-46. C.P.A., Mich. Mem. Am. Inst. C.P.A.'s, Mich., Calif. assns. C.P.A.'s, Fin. Execs. Inst. Methodist. Home: 2267 Caminito Preciosa N La Jolla CA 92037 Office: 1010 2d Ave San Diego CA 92101

VALENTINE, HERMAN EDWARD, mgmt. cons.; b. Norfolk, Va., June 26, 1937; s. Frank and Alice Mae (Heigh) V.; B.S. in Bus. Adminstrn., Norfolk State Coll., 1967; grad. student Am. U., 1968, Coll. William and Mary; m. Dorothy Jones, Nov. 27, 1958; children—Herman Edward, Bryce, Thomas. Asst. bus. mgr. Grad. Sch., Dept. Agr., 1967, exec. officer, 1967-68; bus. mgr. Norfolk State Coll., 1968; pres. Systems Mgmt. Assos., Inc., Norfolk, 1969-75, Virginia Beach, 1975—. Mem. Gov. Va. Minority Econ. Devel. Council; mem. Va. Gov.'s Com. Minority Bus. Affairs; pres. Tidewater Area Bus. League, 1972-74; founder, chmn. Uptown Businessman's Assn.; mem. cluster program Elizabeth City State Coll.; mem. pres.'s council Am. Inst. Mgmt.; dir. Norfolk C. of C.; bd. dirs. Tidewater chpt. ARC, TV Corp. Va., Norfolk State Coll. Found., N.C. Bus. and Econ. Improvement Corp., Nat. Alliance Businessmen, Norfolk Community Hosp., Opportunities Industrialization Centers Am.; bd. visitors, mem. edn. com. Old Dominion U., 1973. Named Businessman of Yr., Tidewater Area Bus. League, 1972, Outstanding Young Man of Yr., Norfolk Jaycees, 1972, Outstanding Businessman of Yr., Va. State Office Minority Bus. Enterprise, 1976, Young Businessman of Yr., Norfolk C. of C.; recipient citation Hunton YMCA, Norfolk, 1972, Norfolk Distinguished Achievement award. Mem. Tidewater Area Bus. and Contractors Assn. (v.p., dir.), Nat. Assn. Businessmen, Tidewater Regional Polit. Assn. (chmn.), Nat. Bus. League (dir.), NAACP, Am. Mgmt. Assn. Home: 3401 Archer Ct Virginia Beach VA 23452 Office: Airport Exec Center Suite 105 5700 Thurston Ave Virginia Beach VA 23455

VALENTINE, WILLIAM NEWTON, physician, educator; b. Kansas City, Mo., Sept. 29, 1917; s. Herbert Spencer and Mabel (Watson) V.; student U. Mich., 1934-36, U. Mo., 1937; M.D., Tulane U., 1942; m. Martha Hickman Winfree, Aug. 31, 1940; children—William Newton, James W., Edward T. Successively intern, asst. resident, chief resident U. Rochester Sch. Medicine, 1942-44, instr. medicine, 1947-48; sect. chief hematology, atomic energy project U. Calif. at Los Angeles, 1948-50; mem. faculty U. Calif. Center Health Scis., Los Angeles, 1950—, prof. medicine, 1957—, chmn. dept., 1963-71. Served to capt. M.C., AUS, 1944-47. Diplomate Am. Bd. Internal Medicine. Master A.C.P.; mem. Am. Soc. Clin. Investigation (v.p. 1963), Assn. Am. Physicians, Western Soc. Clin. Research, Western Assn. Physicians (pres. 1969), Nat. Acad. Sci., Am., Calif., Los Angeles County med. assns., Am., Internat. (v.p. 1976—) socs. hematology. Home: 627 Ocampo Dr Pacific Palisades CA 90272 Office: Dept Medicine U California Center Health Scis Los Angeles CA 90024

VALERIANI, RICHARD GERARD, news broadcaster; b. Camden, N.J., Aug. 29, 1932; s. Nicholas and Christine (Camerota) V.; B.A., Yale U., 1953; postgrad. U. Pavia (Italy). Reporter, The Trentonian, Trenton, N.J., 1957; with AP, 1957-61, corr., Havana, Cuba, 1959-61; with NBC-TV News, 1961—, corr., Washington, 1964—; participant 2d Carter-Ford debate, 1976. Served with AUS, 1955-56. Recipient Overseas Press Club award for best radio reporting, 1965. Mem. Elihu Soc. Club: Yale (Washington). Author: Travels With Henry, 1979. Home: 3025 Arizona Ave NW Washington DC 20016 Office: 4001 Nebraska Ave NW Washington DC 20016

VALETTE, REBECCA MARIANNE, educator; b. N.Y.C., Dec. 21, 1938; d. Gerhard and Ruth Adelgunde (Bischoff) Loose; B.A., Mt. Holyoke Coll., 1959, L.H.D. (hon.), 1974; Ph.D., U. Colo., 1963; m. Jean-Paul Valette, Aug. 6, 1959; children—Jean-Michel, Nathalie, Pierre. Instr., examiner in French and German, U. So. Fla., 1961-63; instr. NATO Def. Coll., Paris, 1963-64, Wellesley Coll., 1964-65; asst. prof. Romance Langs., Boston Coll., 1965-68, asso. prof., 1968-73, prof., 1973—; lectr., cons. fgn. lang. pedagogy; Fulbright sr. lectr., Germany, 1974. Am. Council on Edn. fellow in acad. adminstrn., 1976-77. Mem. Modern Lang. Assn. (task force on commonly taught langs.), Am. Council on Teaching Fgn. Langs., Am. Assn. Tchrs. French, German, Phi Beta Kappa, Alpha Sigma Nu. Author books, including: Modern Language Testing, 1967, rev. edit., 1977; French for Mastery, 1975; Contacts, 1976; C'est comme ca, 1978; Spanish for Mastery, 1980; contbr. numerous articles to fgn. lang. pedagogy and lit. publs. Home: 16 Mount Alvernia Rd Chestnut Hill MA 02167 Office: Lyons 313 Boston Coll Chestnut Hill MA 02167. *One of the most challenging and rewarding activities in my life has been the study of foreign languages. Each new language opens broader horizons and gives one the opportunity to communicate with other people one would otherwise barely get to know.*

VALICENTI, MITCHEL JOSEPH, lawyer; b. N.Y.C., Apr. 5, 1909; A.B. magna cum laude, Holy Cross Coll., 1930; J.D., Harvard Law Sch., 1933; m. Mary Roth, Apr. 6, 1957; children—Joanne (Mrs. Edward Fischer), Michele (Mrs. Thomas B. Keal), Susan (Mrs. William Hogerty) (by previous marriage). Admitted to N.Y. bar, 1934; partner firm Hardin, Hess & Eder, N.Y.C., 1936-53, Spence & Hotchkiss, N.Y.C., 1954-55; sr. partner firm Valicenti Leighton Reid & Pine, N.Y.C., 1956-75, Cole & Deitz, N.Y.C., 1976—. Dir. Acme Electric Corp., Filtrol Corp., Pfister Chem., Inc., Trans World Life Ins. Co., Waddell & Reed, Inc., United Funds, Inc., United Vanguard Fund, United Continental Growth Fund, United Continental Income Fund, Continental Investment Corp., United Municipal Bond Fund. Trustee Charles Evans Hughes Meml. Found., Inc. Clubs: N.Y. Yacht; Saugatuck Harbor Yacht. Home: 155 E 49th St New York City NY 10017 Office: 40 Wall St New York City NY 10005

VALK, HENRY SNOWDEN, coll. dean, physicist; b. Washington, Jan. 26, 1929; s. Henry Snowden and Dorothy (Blencowe) V.; B.S., George Washington U., 1953, M.S. (Agnes and Eugene Meyer scholar), 1954; postgrad. Johns Hopkins, 1953-54; Ph.D. (Shell fellow), Washington U., St. Louis, 1957; m. Gillian Wedderburn, June 20, 1968; children—Alison Elizabeth, Diana Andrea. Profl. asst. NSF, 1957, asst. program dir. physics, 1959-60; asst. prof. physics U. Oreg., 1957-59; mem. faculty U. Nebr., 1960-70, prof. physics, 1964-70, chmn. dept., 1966-70; prof. physics, dean Coll. Scis. and Liberal Studies, Ga. Inst. Tech., Atlanta, 1970—. Cons. physics sect. NSF, 1961-62, program dir. theoretical physics, 1965-66; chmn. Gordon Research Conf. Photonuclear Reactions, 1969; vis. prof. U. Frankfurt/Main (Germany), 1970. Chmn. S.E. regional Marshall scholarship com., 1974—. Fellow Am. Phys. Soc.; mem. Am. Math. Soc., Am. Assn. Physics Tchrs., AAAS, Math. Assn. Am., Phi Beta Kappa, Sigma Xi. Club: Cosmos (Washington). Author: (with M. Alonso) Quantum Mechanics, Principles and Applications, 1973. Contbr. articles to profl. jours. Home: 3032 St Helena Dr Tucker GA 30084

VALK, ROBERT EARL, corp. exec.; b. Muskegon, Mich., Aug. 21, 1914; s. Allen and Lulu (Schuler) V.; B.S. in Mech. Engring., U. Mich., 1938; m. Ann Parker, August 9, 1941 (div. July 1959); children—James A., Sara C.; m. 2d, Alice Melick, Dec. 29, 1960; children—Marie and Susan. With Nat. Supply Co., 1938-55, plant mgr., Houston, 1945-48, works mgr., Toledo, Houston and Gainesville, Tex., 1949-55; asst. v.p. prodn. Electric Auto-Life Co., Toledo, 1956, v.p., group exec. gen. products, 1956-60; gen. mgr. mfg. automotive div. Essex Internat., Inc., 1960-66, v.p. corp., gen. mgr. automotive div., 1966-74; pres. I.T.T. Automotive Elec. Products Div., 1974—; dir. Woodstream Corp., Lititz, Pa. Trustee Samaritan Hosp., Cottage Hosp., Grosse Pointe; chmn. Mich. diocese Epis. Ch. Found.; bd. dirs. Inst. Advanced Pastoral Studies. Mem. Am. Soc. Naval Engrs., Soc. Automotive Engrs., Am. Ordnance Assn., Am. Mgmt. Assn., Air Force Assn., Am. Mfrs. Assn., Wire Assn., Nat. Elec. Mfrs. Assn., Engring. Soc. Detroit. Republican. Episcopalian. Clubs: Country, Yondotega, Economics (Detroit): Grosse Pointe; Bay View Yacht; Key Largo (Fla.) Anglers; Little Harbor (Harbor Springs, Mich.). Home: 80 Renaud Rd Grosse Pointe Shores MI 48236 Office: 13220 Cloverdale Ave Oak Park MI 48237

VALK, WILLIAM LOWELL, physician, educator; b. Muskegon, Mich., Aug. 23, 1909; s. Allen D. and Lulu B. (Schuler) V.; A.B., U. Mich., 1934, M.D., 1937; m. Mary E. Mixer, June 20, 1937; children—William Allen, Allen Michael. Rotating intern U. Mich. Hosp., 1937-38, gen. resident surgery, 1938-40, resident urology, 1940-43, instr. surgery, 1940-43; asso. prof. surgery U. Kans. Med. Center, 1947, prof. surgery, chmn. sect. urology, 1948—; cons. VA Hosp., Kansas City, Mo., 1953—. Regent Nat. Library Medicine. Served to maj. M.C., AUS, 1943-46. Diplomate Am. Bd. Urology (exec. sec. 1975—). Mem. Am. Surg. Assn., Am. Assn. Genito Urinary Surgeons (pres. 1978-79), Clin. Soc. Genito Urinary Surgeons, A.C.S., Soc. Univ. Surgeons, Am. Urol. Assn. (pres. 1966-67), Halstead Soc., A.M.A., Urologic Forum. Bd. editors Jour. Urology, 1960—. Home: 5401 W 81st St Prairie Village KS 66208 Office: Univ Kansas Med Center Kansas City KS 66203

VALLANCE-JONES, ALISTER, physicist; b. Christchurch, N.Z., Feb. 4, 1924; s. Frederick Edmund Jones and Nellie Marion Vallance; came to Can., 1949, naturalized, 1959; B.Sc., U. N.Z., 1945, M.Sc., 1946; Ph.D., Pembroke Coll., Cambridge (Eng.) U., 1949; m. Catherine Ferguson, Dec. 1, 1951; children—Elizabeth Marie, Catrina Anne, Alasdair Frederick. Postdoctoral fellow NRC Can., Ottawa, Ont., 1949-51, prin. research officer, 1976—; spl. lectr. in physics U. Sask. (Can.), Saskatoon, 1952-53, asst. prof. physics, 1953-56, asso. prof., 1956-64, prof., 1964-68. Fellow Royal Soc. Can.; mem. Can. Assn. Physicists, Club: Britannia Yacht. Author: Aurora, 1974. Home: 2145 Fillmore St Ottawa ON K1S 6A1 Canada Office: Nat Research Council Can Ottawa ON K1A 0R6 Canada

VALLBONA, CARLOS, physician; b. Granollers, Barcelona, Spain, July 29, 1927; s. Jose and Dolores (Calbó) V.; came to U.S., 1953, naturalized, 1967; B.A., B.S., U. de Barcelona, 1944, M.D., 1950; m. Rima Gretel Rothe, Dec. 26, 1956; children—Rima Nuria, Carlos Fernando, Maria Teresa, Marisa. Child health physician Escuela de Puericultura, Barcelona, 1952, Stagier Etranger Hôp. des Enfants Malades, Paris, 1952-53; intern, resident U. Louisville, 1953-55; resident Baylor U. Coll. Medicine, 1955-56, prof. rehab. medicine, 1967—, asso. prof. physiology and pediatrics, 1962-69, prof., chmn. dept. community medicine, 1969—; chief community medicine service Harris County Hosp. Dist.; staff gen. med. service Tex. Children's Hosp.; distinguished cons. med. staff Tex. Inst. Rehab. and

Research; staff St. Luke's Episcopal Hosp.; Fulbright vis. prof. U. Autónoma, Guadalajara, Mex., 1967. French Ministry of Edn. fellow, 1952; Children's Internat. Center fellow, 1953. Mem. Soc. Pediatric Research (emeritus), AMA, Am. Coll. Chest Physicians, Am. Pub. Health Assn., Am. Coll. Preventive Medicine, AAAS, Am. Congress Rehab. Medicine, Assn. Tchrs. Preventive Medicine, Sigma Xi. Roman Catholic. Home: 3002 Ann Arbor St Houston TX 77063 Office: 1200 Moursund St Houston TX 77030

VALLEE, BERT LESTER, biochemist, physician, educator; b. Hemer, Westphalia, Germany, June 1, 1919; s. Joseph and Rosa (Kronenberger) V.; Sc.B., U. Berne (Switzerland), 1938; M.D., N.Y. U. Coll. Medicine, 1943; A.M. (hon.), Harvard, 1960; m. Natalie T. Kugris, May 29, 1947. Came to U.S., 1938, naturalized, 1948. Research fellow Harvard Med. Sch., Boston, 1946-49, research asso., 1949-51, asso., 1951-56, asst. prof. medicine, 1956-60, asso. prof., 1960-64, prof. biol. chemistry, 1964—, Paul C. Cabot prof. biol. chemistry, 1965—; research asso. dept. biology Mass. Inst. Tech., Cambridge, 1948—; physician Peter Bent Brigham Hosp., Boston, 1961—; sci. dir. Biophysics Research Lab., Harvard Med. Sch., Peter Bent Brigham Hosp., 1954—. Founder, trustee Boston Biophysics Research Found., 1957—. Recipient Buchman Meml. award Calif. Inst. Tech., 1976. Fellow A.A.A.S., Nat. Acad. Scis., Am. Acad. Arts and Scis., N.Y. Acad. Scis.; mem. Am. Soc. Biol. Chemists, Am. Chem. Soc., Optical Soc. Am., Biophys. Soc., Swiss Biochem. Soc. (hon. fgn. mem.), Royal Danish Acad. Scis. and Letters, Alpha Omega Alpha. Author book. Contbr. articles and chpts. to sci. publs. Home: 56 Browne St Brookline MA 02146

VALLÉE, HUBERT PRIOR RUDY, orch. leader; b. Island Pond, Vt., July 28, 1901; s. Charles Alphonse and Katherine (Lynch) V.; student U. Maine, 1921; Ph.B., Yale, 1927; m. Fay Webb, July 6, 1931 (dec. Nov. 18, 1936); m. 2d, Bette Jane Greer, Dec. 1943 (div. 1944); m. 3d, Eleanor Kathleen Norris, Sept. 3, 1949. Played with Savoy Havana Band at Hotel Savoy, London, Eng., 1924-25, broadcast and recorded while there; played with band at Yale and led Yale football band during sr. year; toured U.S. with coll. band; formed Connecticut Yankees, 1928; first U.S. broadcasts, 1928; performed with orch. for 10 yrs. on NBC's Fleischmann Variety Hour; appeared at Paramount (N.Y.) and Paramount (Bklyn.) 10 weeks spring of 1929, returning in Oct. for run of nearly two years; starred in motion picture Vagabond Lover, 1929, George White's Scandals, 1934, Sweet Music, 1935, Gold Diggers in Paris, 1938, Second Fiddle, 1939, Time Out for Rhythm and Too Many Blondes, 1941, also Man Alive, People Are Funny, It's in the Bag, The Fabulous Suzanne, I Remember Mamma, The Bachelor and the Bobby Soxer, Beautiful Blonde from Bashful Bend, Father Was a Fullback, Mother Is a Freshman, The Admiral Was a Lady, Mad Wednesday, Ricochet Romance, Gentlemen Marry Brunettes, How to Succeed in Business Without Really Trying, Live a Little, Love a Little; appeared in stage show of George White's Scandals, 1931, 36; played Coronation Week engagement in London, 1937, Cocoanut Grove, Los Angeles, 1937, 38; broadcasted weekly, for Standard Brands, 1929-39, for Nat. Dairies, Sealtest program, 1940-41, Drene Show 1944-46, Philip Morris, 1946-47; Rudy Vallee Show, 1950; frequent night club appearances; appeared in musical comedy How To Succeed in Business Without Really Trying, N.Y.C., 1961-64; has appeared on TV variety shows; tours with one-man multi-media show. Composer of songs and musical numbers. Served in USN, World War I, USCG. World War II. Recipient N.Y. Critics award, 1962. Pres. Am. Fedn. Actors, 1937; mem. Am. Fedn. Musicians, Am. Soc. of Authors and Composers, Acad. Motion Picture Arts and Scis., Amateur Cinema League, Nat. Assn. Performing Artists, Screen Actors' Guild, Am. Arbitration Assn., Am. Legion, La Société des 40 Hommes et 8 Chevaux, Sigma Alpha Epsilon. Clubs: N.Y. Athletic, Lambs, Friars, Elks, Yale (N.Y.C.). Author: Vagabond Dreams Come True, 1930; Let the Chips Fall, 1975. Address: care William Meiklejohn Assos 9250 Wilshire Blvd Beverly Hills CA 90212

VALLEY, DORIS LORRAINE, former railroad exec.; b. Mpls., Feb. 1, 1919; d. Ulysses Aloysius and Mary Bell (Field) Valley; student Minn. Sch. Bus., 1938. With Soo Line R.R. Co., Mpls., 1940-79, corp. sec., sr. adminstrv. asst. to pres., 1974-79. Methodist. Club: Mpls. Athletic. Home: 8040 Russell Ave S Minneapolis MN 55431

VALLEY, GEORGE EDWARD, JR., physicist, educator; b. N.Y.C., Sept. 5, 1913; s. George Edward and Edith Ringgold (Cummins) V.; S.B., Mass. Inst. Tech., 1935; Ph.D., U. Rochester, 1939; m. Louisa King Williams, July 19, 1941 (div. Dec. 1960); children— George Cummins, John Williams, Katharine; m. 2d, Shea LaBonte. Optical engr. with Bausch & Lomb Optical Co., 1935-36; teaching asst. U. Rochester, 1936-39; research asso. Harvard, 1939-41, NRC fellow nuclear physics, 1940-41; project supr., sr. staff Radiation Lab., Mass. Inst. Tech., 1941-45, editorial bd. Radiation Lab. Tech. Series, 1945, successively asst. prof., asso. prof. Mass. Inst. Tech., 1946-57, prof. physics, 1957-78, now prof. emeritus, assisted founding Lincoln Lab., 1949, asso. dir., 1953-57, undergrad. planning prof., 1965-68. Mem. Air Force Sci. Adv. Bd., 1946-64; chmn. Air Def. Systems, Engring. Com. for Chief Staff USAF, 1950-51, chief scientist, 1957-58. Recipient U.S. Army certificate of appreciation; President's certificate of merit; Air Force Assn. Sci. award; exceptional civilian service medal, USAF, 1956, 58, 64. Fellow Am. Phys. Soc., Inst. Radio Engrs.; mem. Sigma Xi. Author and editor books and monographs. Address: 607 Main St Concord MA 01742

VALLI, FRANKIE (FRANK CASTELLUCCIO), singer; b. Newark, May 3, 1937; student pub. schs., Newark. With vocal group Four Lovers, 1956-61, Four Seasons, 1962—; solo performer, 1966—; records include: Sherry, Big Girls Don't Cry, Walk Like a Man, Rag Doll, I've Got You under My Skin, Can't Take My Eyes Off You, Grease. Office: care William Morris Agency Inc 1350 Ave of the Americas New York NY 10019*

VALLOTTON, WILLIAM WISE, surgeon, educator; b. Valdosta, Ga., Nov. 26, 1927; s. Joseph Edward and Mattie (Rouse) V.; A.B., Duke U., 1947; M.D., Med. Coll. Ga., 1952; postgrad. Harvard U., 1956; m. Hulda Roberta Jones, Sept. 3, 1950; children—Stephen Ralph, Amie, Mark Hugh, William Wise. Intern, U. Wis., 1952-53; resident in ophthalmology Duke U., 1953-55, instr., 1953-55, asso., 1955-56; asso. prof. ophthalmology Med. U. S.C., Charleston, 1958-65, prof., 1965—, dir. residency program ophthalmology, 1960-70, chmn. dept. ophthalmology, 1966—, dir. Storm Eye Inst., 1976—; v.p. Vallorbe Inc., Valdosta, 1955—; cons. USN Hosp., Charleston, 1962—, State Hosp. S.C., Columbia, 1963—, VA Hosp., Charleston, 1966—; faculty home study Am. Acad. Ophthalmology and Otolaryngology. Bd. dirs. S.C. Commn. for Blind, 1975-76. Served to lt. M.C., USNR, 1956-58. Diplomate Am. Bd. Ophthalmology. Fellow A.C.S.; mem. S.C. Ophthal. and Otolaryn. Soc. (pres. 1965), Assn. Research in Ophthalmology (chmn. S.E. sect. 1966-67), Am. Acad. Ophthalmology and Otolaryngology (Honors award 1968), Pan Am. Ophthalm. Assn., So. Med. Assn. (asso. councilor 1972-75, councilor 1975—), N.Y. Acad. Sics., Charleston Duke Alumni Assn. (past pres.), Pi Kappa Phi, Alpha Kappa Kappa, Alpha Omega Alpha. Republican. Methodist. Clubs: Charleston Country, James Island Yacht, Elks. Contbr. articles in field to profl. jours. Home: 15 Broughton Rd Charleston SC 29407 Office: Eye Inst Med U SC Charleston SC 29403

VALPEY, ROBERT GRAHAM, coll. dean; b. N.Y.C., Feb. 18, 1923; s. Frank Russell and Ethel (Sher) V.; B.S., U.S. Mil. Acad., 1945; B.M.E., Cornell U., 1950; M.S., U. Colo., 1958; Ph.D., U. Ill., 1962; m. Margaret Joy Smale, June 10, 1966; children—Raymond W., Kenneth R. Commd. 2d lt. USAAF, 1945, advanced through grades to lt. col. USAF, 1965; ret., 1965; dean Sch. Engring., Calif. State Coll., Fullerton, 1965-72; dean Sch. Engring. and Tech., Calif. Polytech. State U., San Luis Obispo, 1972—; cons. autonetics div. North Am. Rockwell, Inc.; pres., dir. Colorado Estates, Inc., 1957—. Mem. Am. Soc. Engring. Edn. (dir. mechanics div. 1970-71, mem. ethics com. 1968-69), Council Engring. Deans Calif. State Univs. (chmn. 1970-71), Engr. Liason Com. State Calif. (chmn. 1971-72). Home: 601 Skyline Dr San Luis Obispo CA 93401

VALTIN, HEINZ, educator; b. Hamburg, Germany, Sept. 23, 1926; s. Ernst Wiegelmesser and Eva Valentin; came to U.S., 1938, naturalized, 1945; A.B., Swarthmore Coll., 1949; M.D., Cornell U., 1953; m. Nancy Heffernan, June 12, 1953; children—Thomas Curt, Alison Eva. Intern, resident internal medicine Strong Meml. Hosp., Rochester, N.Y.; mem. faculty Dartmouth Med. Sch., 1957—, prof. physiology, 1967-73, Andrew C. Vail prof. physiology, 1973—, chmn. physiology, 1977—; cons. nephrologist Hitchcock Clinic and Hosp., Hanover, N.H., 1960—. Served with M.C., AUS, 1945-46. Mem. A.A.A.S., Am. Physiol. Soc., Am. Soc. Nephrology, Endocrine Soc., Am. Fedn. Clin. Research, Am. Soc. Clin. Investigation, Alpha Omega Alpha. Author: Renal Function. Mechanisms Preserving Fluid and Solute Balance in Health, 1973; Renal Dysfunction. Mechanisms Involved in Fluid and Solute Imbalance, 1979. Home: Bradley Hill Rd Norwich VT 05055 Office: Dept Physiology Dartmouth Med Sch Hanover NH 03755

VALTIN, ROLF, arbitrator; b. Hamburg, Germany, Jan. 4, 1925; s. Ernst Friedrich Wilhelm and Eva (Valentin) Wiegelmesser; came to U.S., 1938, naturalized, 1943; B.A. in Econs., Swarthmore Coll., 1948; M.A., U. Pa., 1950; m. Nancy Eberle, Nov. 26, 1948; children—Jane, Carol, Christopher, Matthew. Wage analyst Sharp & Dohme, Inc., Phila., 1948-49; tribunal clk. Am. Arbitration Assn., Phila., 1950-51; asst. labor advisor to Under Sec. Army, Washington, 1951-52; fed. mediator Phila. office Fed. Mediation and Conciliation Service, 1952-56; asst. arbitrator labor-mgmt. disputes to umpire for Bethlehem Steel and United Steelworkers Am., Washington, 1956-59, asso. arbitrator, 1959-65; practice arbitration, McLean, Va., 1965—. Mem. U.S. Olympic Soccer Team, 1948; coach baseball programs, McLean, 1970-75, also dir. Served with AUS, 1943-46, 51-52; ETO. Decorated Bronze Star, Silver Star. Mem. Indsl. Relations Research Assn., Am. Arbitration Assn. (affiliate), Fed. Mediation & Conciliation Service (affiliate), Nat. Acad. Arbitrators (pres. 1975-76). Contbr. articles to profl. jours. Umpire under nat. agreement between Gen. Motors and U.A.W., 1969-75, between Bituminous Coal Operators and United Mine Workers, 1975—. Home and Office: 1319 Woodside Dr McLean VA 22102

VAN, GEORGE PAUL, diversified co. exec.; b. Isle Maligne, Que., Can., Feb. 12, 1940; s. Raymond Murdoch and Germaine Marie (Brassard) V.; B.A., McGill U., 1961; D.H.A., U. Toronto, 1963; m. Janine Marie Irene Therese Yvette Boily, Sept. 15, 1962; children—John, Robert, Caroline. Sr. cons. Agnew Peckham and Assos., Toronto, Ont., Can., 1963-65; chief exec. officer, exec. dir. Misericordia Corp., Edmonton, Alta., Can., 1965-68; chief operationg officer, exec. v.p., dir. Texpack, Ltd., Brantford, Ont., 1968-70; group v.p. Will Ross, Inc., Milw., 1970-73; exec. v.p., dir. Nortek, Inc., Cranston, R.I., 1973-77; pres., chief operating officer, dir. Hosp. Affiliates Internat. Inc. subs. INA Corp., Nashville, 1977—. Recipient several scholarships. Mem. Am. Mgmt. Assn., Am. Coll. Hosp. Adminstrs., Am. Hosp. Assn., Am. Pub. Health Assn., Fedn. Am. Hosps., Internat. Hosp. Fedn. Clubs: Nashville Racquet, Seven Hills Swim. Hillwood Country. Contbr. articles to profl. jours. Home: 4509 Shy's Hill Rd Nashville TN 37215 Office: 4525 Harding Rd Nashville TN 37205

VAN AKEN, WILLIAM RUSSELL, lawyer; b. Shaker Heights, Ohio, Dec. 1, 1912; s. William J. and Florence E. (Swallow) Van A.; B.S., Lafayette Coll., 1934; LL.B., Western Res. U., 1937; m. Dorothy Harrison, Apr. 27, 1940; children—Nancy, William R. (dec.), Mary Alice, Dorothy Louise, William J. II. Admitted to Ohio bar, 1938, since practiced in Cleve.; mem. firm Van Aken, Bond, Withers, Asman & Smith, 1949—. Pres. William J. Van Aken Orgn., Inc., real estate, property mgmt., 1951-72; dir., v.p. Ohio Bar Title Ins. Co.; trustee, chmn. bd. Ohio Bar Automated Research Corp. Vice pres., trustee Ohio Info. Com.; mem. Ohio Legislature, 1943-44, 47-48, Shaker Heights City Council, 1951-55; mem. Ohio Republican Central and Exec. Com., 1954-64, Cuyahoga County Rep. Central Com., 1942-64. Pres. bd. trustees Heather Hill, Inc., 1970-78; trustee Shaker Hist. Soc., pres., 1964-66, 70-71; trustee Ohio Legal Center Inst., 1971-77; bd. mgrs. Heights YMCA, 1942-73. Fellow Am., Ohio (trustee, pres. 1971-77) bar founds.; mem. Am. Judicature Soc., Apt. and Home Owners Assn. (trustee, past pres.), Am., Ohio (council dels., pres. 1958-59) bar assns., Nat. Conf. State Bar Founds. (pres. 1977-79, trustee 1979—), Northeastern Ohio Intermus. Council (chmn. 1968-70, trustee 1968—, vice chmn. 1977), Cleve. Fedn. Realty Interests, Cleve. Real Estate Bd. (pres. 1957, trustee 1953-58), Greater Cleve. Growth Assn., Ohio, Western Res. hist. socs., Early Settlers Assn. (trustee), Phi Gamma Delta (gen. counsel 1969-72), Delta Theta Phi. Presbyn. (elder, former trustee). Rotarian. Clubs: Union, Mid-Day, Skating (Cleve.); Univ. (Columbus). Co-author: Ohio Practice-Real Estate Transactions; author: Buckeye Barristers - The First Hundred Years of the Ohio State Bar Association. Asso. editor: Baldwin's Ohio Legal Forms. Home: 22299 Douglas Rd Shaker Heights OH 44122 Office: Nat City Bank Bldg Cleveland OH 44114

VAN ALLEN, JAMES ALFRED, physicist, educator; b. Mt. Pleasant, Iowa, Sept. 7, 1914; s. Alfred Morris and Alma E. (Olney) Van A.; B.S., Iowa Wesleyan Coll., 1935, Sc.D., 1951; M.S., U. Iowa, 1936, Ph.D., 1939; Sc.D., Grinnell Coll., 1957, Coe Coll., 1958, Cornell Coll., 1959, U. Dubuque, 1960, U. Mich., 1961, Northwestern U., 1961, Ill. Coll., 1963, Butler U., 1966, Boston Coll., 1966, Southampton Coll., 1967, Augustana Coll., 1969; m. Abigail Fithian Halsey, Oct. 13, 1945; children—Cynthia Olney, Margo Isham, Sarah Halsey, Thomas Halsey, Peter Cornelius. Research fellow, physicist dept. terrestrial magnetism Carnegie Instn., Washington, 1939-42; physicist, group and unit supr., applied physics lab. Johns Hopkins, 1942, 1946-50; organizer, leader sci. expdns. study cosmic radiation, Peru, 1949, Gulf of Alaska, 1950, Greenland, 1952, 57, Antarctica, 1957; discoverer radiation belts around earth; Carver prof. physics, head dept. U. Iowa, 1951—; research asso. Princeton, 1953-54. Devel. radio proximity fuze Nat. Def. Research Council, OSRD; pioneer high altitude research with rockets, satellites and space probes. Served as lt. comdr. U.S. Navy, 1942-46, ordnance and gunnery specialist, combat observer. Received C.N. Hickman medal for devel. Aerobee rocket, Am. Rocket Soc., 1949; physics award Washington Acad. Sci., 1949; Guggenheim Meml. Found. research fellow, 1951; space flight award Am. Astronautical Soc., 1958; Louis W. Hill space transp. award Inst. Aero. Scis., 1959, Elliot Cresson medal Franklin Inst., 1961, John A. Fleming award Am. Geophys. Union, 1963, 64; Golden Omega award Elec. Insulation Conf., 1963; comdr. Order du Merit Pour la Recherche et L'Invention, 1964; Iowa Broadcasters Assn. award, 1964; Fellows award of merit Am. Cons. Engrs. Council, 1978. Fellow Am. Rocket Soc., IEEE, Am. Phys. Soc., Am. Geophys. Union (William Bowie medal 1977); mem. Iowa Acad. Sci., Nat. Acad. Scis., Internat. Acad. Astronautics (founding mem.), Am. Philos. Soc., Royal Astron. Soc. (U.K.) (gold medal 1978), Am. Acad. Arts and Scis., Sigma Xi, Gamma Alpha. Presbyn. Club: Cosmos (Washington). Contbg. author: Physics and Med. of Upper Atmosphere, 1952; Rocket Exploration of the Upper Atmosphere. Editor: Scientific Uses of Earth Satellites, 1956; asso. editor Jour. Geophysical Research, 1959-64, Physics of Fluids, 1958-62. Contbr. numerous articles to sci. jours. Office: 203 Physics Bldg U Iowa Iowa City IA 52242

VAN ALLEN, MAURICE WRIGHT, physician; b. Mt. Pleasant, Iowa, Apr. 3, 1918; s. Alfred Maurice and Alma E. (Olney) Van A.; B.A., Iowa Wesleyan Coll., 1939; M.D., U. Iowa, 1942; m. Jane Hunt, Aug. 20, 1949; children—David, Martha, Evalyn, Jonathan. Intern Pa. Hosp., Phila., 1942-43; tng. in neurology and neurosurgery; practice medicine specializing in neurology, Iowa City, Iowa, 1954—; chief neurol. sect. VA Hosp., Iowa City, 1954-59; asso. prof. dept. neurology Coll. Medicine, U. Iowa, 1959-65, prof., 1965—, head dept., 1974—; mem. council Nat. Inst. Dental Research. Served with M.C., U.S. Army, 1943-46. Diplomate Am. Psychiatry and Neurology, Am. Bd. Neurol. Surgery. Mem. AMA, Am. Acad. Neurology, Am. Neurol. Assn., Assn. for Research and Nervous and Mental Disease, Sigma Xi, Alpha Omega Alpha. Republican. Episcopalian. Author book in field; contbr. articles to profl. jours. Editor Archives of Neurology, 1976—. Home: 354 Lexington Ave Iowa City IA 52240 Office: Dept Neurology Univ Hosp Iowa City IA 52240

VAN ALLEN, WILLIAM KENT, lawyer; b. Albion, N.Y., July 30, 1914; s. Everett Kent and Georgia (Roberts) Van A.; A.B., Hamilton Coll., 1935; LL.B., Harvard U., 1938; m. Sally Schall, Nov. 11, 1944; children—William Kent, George Humphrey, Peter Cushing. Admitted to N.Y. bar, 1938, D.C. bar, 1939, U.S. Supreme Ct. bar, 1946, N.C. bar, 1951; with firm Hanson, Lovett & Dale, Washington, 1938-50; partner firm Lassiter, Moore & Van Allen and Moore and Van Allen, Charlotte, N.C., 1950—; permanent mem. Jud. Conf. 4th Jud. Circuit; dir. F.N. Thompson, Inc., Noll Constrn. Co., Wrenn Service, Inc. Vestryman, Episcopal Ch., 1957-60, 66-69; chmn. Mecklenburg County Bd. Public Welfare, 1957-59; bd. dirs. N.C. Found. Commerce and Industry, 1965-73, Found. U. N.C. at Charlotte, 1979—; bd. dirs. United Community Services, 1972-75, v.p., 1972; bd. mgrs. Charlotte Country Day Sch., 1956-61, chmn., 1959-61; trustee Spastics Hosp., 1951-60, Mint Mus. Art, 1976—, Surtman Found.; bd. visitors Johnson C. Smith U. Served to lt. comdr. USNR, 1941-45. Mem. Am. Bar Assn., Charlotte C. of C. (dir. 1971-75, v.p. 1972-75), Am. Arbitration Assn. (chmn. Charlotte area adv. com. 1967-76), Phi Beta Kappa, Chi Psi. Clubs: Charlotte Country, Charlotte City; Chevy Chase (Washington); Mullett Lake (Mich.) Country. Home: 265 Cherokee Rd Charlotte NC 28207 Office: 3000 NCNB Plaza Charlotte NC 28280

VAN ALLER, ROBERT THOMAS, univ. dean; b. Mobile, June 18, 1933; s. Godfrey Harry and Elsie (Swartz) Van A.; student Baylor U., 1951-53; B.S., U. Ala., 1960, M.S., 1962, Ph.D., 1965; student U. Miss., 1963-67; m. Beverly Ann Wilkins, Dec. 20, 1959; children—Geoffrey Thomas, Robert Merrick. Research chemist Tenn. Eastman Corp., Kingsport, 1963; research technologist NASA, Huntsville, Ala., 1967-68; research asso. U. Miss., 1965-67; dean Coll. Sci., U. So. Miss., 1970-71, dean Grad. Sch., 1971—. Trustee Gulf Univs. Research Corp. Served with USN, 1953-57. Mem. Am. Chem. Soc., AAAS, Sigma Xi, Sigma Chi, Phi Kappa Phi, Phi Delta Kappa. Rotarian. Contbr. articles to sci. jours. Home: 3004 Raphael Dr Hattiesburg MS 39401

VAN ALSTYNE, ARVO, univ. adminstr.; b. N.Y.C., May 4, 1922; s. Guy Chase and Alli (Luoma) Van A.; B.A., Yale, 1943, LL.B., 1948; m. Ruth Lamb, May 21, 1945; children—David, Peter, Laura, Philip, Sara, Kristina. Admitted to Calif. bar, 1949; research atty. State of Calif., Los Angeles, 1948-50; dep. county counsel, Los Angeles, 1950-53; prof. law U. Calif. at Los Angeles Law Sch., 1953-66; prof. law U. Utah, Salt Lake City, 1966—, exec. asst. to pres. univ., 1973—, v.p., 1975—; cons. Calif. Law Revision Commn., 1957—; reporter-draftsman uniform eminent domain code Nat. Conf. Uniform State Laws, 1972-74. Served with USNR, 1943-45. Mem. Phi Beta Kappa, Order of Coif. Mem. Ch. of Jesus Christ of Latter-day Saints. Author: California Pleading, 1961; California Government Tort Liability, 1964, 2d edit., 1979; State and Local Government Law, 1977; California Discovery Practice, 1972; Sum and Substance of Constitutional Law, 1975; also numerous articles. Home: 2530 E 1300 S Salt Lake City UT 84108

VAN ALTENA, WILLIAM FOSTER, astronomer; b. Hayward, Calif., Aug. 15, 1939; s. William Rogers and Eileen (Foster) van A.; B.A., U. Calif., Berkeley, 1962, Ph.D., 1966; M.A. (hon.), Yale U., 1975; m. Jean Whyte, Dec. 16, 1961; children—Paul David, Michael John. Instr., Yerkes Obs., U. Chgo., 1966, asst. prof., 1967-72, asso. prof., 1972-74, dir. Yerkes Obs., 1972-74; prof. astronomy dept. Yale U., New Haven, 1974—, chmn. astronomy dept., 1975—; pres. Yale So. Obs., Inc., 1976—. NSF grantee, 1969-80; NASA grantee, 1973—; Office Naval Research grantee, 1966-71. Mem. Internat. Astron. Union, Am., Pacific astron socs., Sigma Xi. Contbr. articles in field of astrometry to profl. jours. Office: Astronomy Dept Box 2023 Yale Station New Haven CT 06520

VAN ANDEL, JAY, corp. exec.; b. Grand Rapids, Mich., June 3, 1924; s. James and Nella (Vanderwoude) Van A.; student Pratt Jr. Coll., 1945, Calvin Coll., 1942, 46, Yale, 1943-44; D.B.A. (hon.), No. Mich. U., 1976; LL.D. (hon.), Ferris State Coll., 1977; m. Betty J. Hoekstra, Aug. 16, 1952; children—Nan, Stephen, David, Barbara. Formerly engaged in aviation, restaurant and mail order businesses; co-founder, chmn. bd. Amway Corp., Ada, Mich.; chmn. bd. Amway Can., Ltd., Amway Australia, Amway Mgmt. Co., 1970—, Amway U.K. Ltd., Amway Germany, Amway Hong-Kong, Amway France, Amway Malaysia, Amway Japan, Amway Netherlands, Amway Hotel Properties, Mut. Broadcasting System, Nutrilite Products Inc.; dir. Mich. Nat. Bank, Lansing, Van Andel & Flikkema Motor Sales, Grand Rapids. Mem. adv. council Citizens for Ednl. Freedom, Nat. 4H Found. Chmn. Mich. Republican Finance Com.; mem. Nat. Rep. Finance Com. Trustee, Calvin Coll. Found., Ferguson Hosp., Grand Rapids, Citizens Research Council Mich.; chmn. Citizens Choice; pres. Van Andel Found. Trustee Hillsdale Coll. Served to 1st lt. USAAF, 1943-46. Recipient Disting. Alumni award Calvin Coll., 1976. Mem. Soap and Detergent Assn. (dir.), U.S. C. of C. (chmn. bd.). Mem. Christian Reformed Ch. (elder). Clubs: Penisular; Cascade Hills; Lotus; Capitol Hill (Washington); Macatawa Bay Yacht (Holland, Mich.); Cat Cay (Bahamas); La Mirador (Switzerland). Home: 7186 Windy Hill Rd Grand Rapids MI 49506 Office: 7575 E Fulton Rd Grand Rapids MI 49355

VAN ANTWERPEN, FRANKLIN JOHN, cons., former assn. exec.; b. Paterson, N.J., Nov. 28, 1912; s. William and Frances (Wambach) Van A.; A.E., Newark Coll. Engring., 1935, B.S., 1938; grad. study Columbia U., 1938-40; Eng.D. (hon.), N.J. Inst. Tech., 1975; m. Dorothy Hoedemaker, June 3, 1939; children—Franklin Stuart, Virginia Evelyn (Mrs. Walter Rosenberger). Engaged as mgr. Munitex

Corp., 1935-38; mng. editor Indsl. and Engring. Chemistry, 1938-46; founder, pub. editor Chemical Engring. Progress, Am. Inst. Chem. Engrs., bus. mgr., 1946-54, pub., editor Monograph and Symposium Series, 1950-78, pub. Jour. Am. Inst. Chem. Engrs., 1954-78, Internat. Chem. Engring., 1961-78, sec., exec. sec., 1955-78, publisher, 1955-78, Washington cons., 1978—, recipient Founders award, honored by creation F.J. Van Antwerpen award for outstanding service, also 1st recipient, 1978. Fellow Am. Inst. Chem. Engrs. AAAS, Am. Inst. Chemists, Instn. Chem. Engrs. Gt. Britain; mem. Am. Chem. Soc., Am. Soc. Engring. Edn., Council Engring. and Sci. Soc. Execs. (pres. 1974-75), Interam. Confedn. Chem. Engring. (treas. 1969-73, v.p. 1973-75, pres. 1975-77), Tau Beta Pi, Chi Omega. Club: Chemists (trustee, past pres.) (N.Y.C.). Author articles and editorials chem. engring. mags. Co-author: Fifty Years of American Institute of Chemical Engineers. Home: 16 Son Rd West Millington NJ 07946 Office: PO Box 4241 Warren NJ 07060

VANARIA, LOUIS MICHAEL, educator; b. N.Y.C., Oct. 17, 1925; s. Raymond and Luisa (Bauso) V.; A.B., Columbia, 1948, M.A., 1949, Ph.D., 1958; m. Marianne Ficalora, June 4, 1949; children—Marianne (Mrs. Thomas Seilheimer), Linda (Mrs. Louis Melazzo), Kathy, Diane. Tchr. social studies Bedford Hills (N.Y.) High Sch., 1949-53; instr. Tchrs. Coll., Columbia, N.Y.C., 1953-57; prof., chmn. history dept. State U. N.Y. Coll., Cortland, 1957—. Served to 2d lt. USAAF, 1943-45. Mem. Am. Hist. Assn., Nat. Council for Social Studies. Home: 8 Westfield Park Cortland NY 13045

VAN ARK, JOAN, actress; b. N.Y.C.; d. Carroll and Dorothy Jean (Hemenway) Van A.; student Yale Sch. Drama; m. John Marshall, Feb. 1, 1966; 1 dau., Vanessa Jeanne. Appeared at Tyrone Guthrie Theatre, Washington Arena Stage, in London, on Broadway; appeared in plays Barefoot in the Park, School for Wives, Rules of the Game, Cyrano de Bergerac, Ring Round the Moon; appeared on TV series Temperatures Rising, We've Got Each Other, Dallas, Knots Landing. Recipient Theatre World award, 1970-71; Los Angeles Drama Critics Circle award, 1973. Mem. Actors Equity Assn., Screen Actors Guild, AFTRA. Club: San Fernando Valley Track. Office: care William Morris Agy 151 El Camino Dr Beverly Hills CA 90212

VAN ARSDALL, CLYDE JAMES, JR., naval officer; b. Indianola, Miss., July 22, 1913; s. Clyde James and Ida (Barnard) VanA.; B.S., U.S. Naval Acad., 1934; m. Polly Ann Austin, May 14, 1938; children—Anne, Clyde James, III, Robert B. Commd. ensign U.S. Navy, 1934, advanced through grades to rear adm., 1961; service in Japan, Germany; naval attaché, Paris; asst. chief staff U.S. European Command, 1970; comdt. 12th Naval Dist., San Francisco, 1972; governor Naval Home, Gulfport, Miss., 1976—. Decorated Navy Cross, Silver Star, Legion of Merit with 2 oak leaf clusters; Legion of Honor (France). Clubs: Bohemian (San Francisco); Army-Navy Country (Arlington, Va.). Address: Governor's House Naval Home 01800 E Beach Blvd Gulfport MS 39501

VAN ARSDALL, ROBERT ARMES, ret. air force officer, engr.; b. Omaha, Oct. 5, 1925; s. Samuel Peter and Althea (Armes) Van A.; B.S., U.S. Mil. Acad., 1948; postgrad. U. Colo., spring 1961; M.S., George Washington U., 1968; m. Margaret Cooper Kiersted, June 9, 1948; children—Robert Armes, Janet Althea, Susan DeBaun, Kathryn Ann. Commd. 2d lt. USAF, 1948, advanced through grades to col., 1968; grad. Randolph AFB, Tex., 1949; assigned 5th Air Rescue Group, Westover AFB, Mass., 1949-51; student USAF Squadron Officer Sch., Maxwell AFB, Ala., 1950; pilot, operations officer 9th Air Rescue Group, Burton-Wood, Manston and Bushy Park Eng., 1951-55; operations officer Hdqrs. Air Rescue Service, Orlando AFB, Fla., 1955-57; plans officer Hdqrs. Air Research and Devel. Command, Balt., also Andrews AFB, Md., 1957-60; grad. USAF jet qualification course Randolph AFB, 1959; tng.-with-industry Air Force Inst. Tech., Martin Co., Denver, 1960-61; chief plans div. Hdqrs. Space Systems Div., Los Angeles, 1961-63; exec. officer Office Space Systems, Office Sec. Air Force, 1963-67; asso. Air War Coll. program, Washington, 1964-66; student Naval War Coll., 1967-68; dep. dir. Dept. Def. Manned Space Flight Support Office, Patrick AFB, Fla., 1968-69, dir. range engring., 1969-70, dir. range operations, 1970-72; comdr. USAF Satellite Test Center, Sunnyvale, Calif., 1972-73; vice comdr. USAF Satellite Control Facility, Los Angeles, 1973-74, comdr., 1974-76; staff engr. Pan Am. World Airways, Cocoa Beach, Fla., 1976-78, project dir., 1978—. Decorated Air Force Commendation medal with two oak leaf clusters, Legion of Merit with oak leaf cluster. Life mem. Assn. Grads. U.S. Mil. Acad.; charter mem. Nat. Soujourners, USAF Acad. Athletic Assn. Republican. Methodist. Mason. Clubs: Burtonwood Air Force (gov.); Bushy Park Air Force (gov.); Orlando Air Force (gov.); Andrews Air Force (gov.); Space Systems Division Air Force (gov.). Home: 660 Cinnamon Ct Satellite Beach FL 32937 Office: 195 Brevard Ave Cocoa Beach FL 32931

VAN ARSDEL, PAUL PARR, JR., physician, educator; b. Indpls., Nov. 4, 1926; s. Paul P. and Ellen (Ewing) Van A.; B.S., Yale, 1948; M.D., Columbia, 1951; m. Rosemary Thorstenson, July 7, 1950; children—Mary Margaret, Andrew Paul. Intern, resident Presbyn. Hosp., N.Y.C., 1951-53; research fellow dept. medicine U. Wash. Med. Sch., Seattle, 1953-55; instr., 1956-58, asst. prof. medicine, 1958-62, asso. prof., 1962-69, prof. medicine, 1969—, head div. or sect. allergy, 1956—; cons. Seattle VA Hosp., Madigan Army Hosp., Seattle Pub. Health Hosp., Seattle Children's Med. Center; mem. staff Univ., King County hosps. Served with USNR, 1945-46. Diplomate Am. Bd. Internal Medicine and Allergy. Fellow A.C.P., Am. Acad. Allergy (pres. 1971-72, exec. com.); mem. A.A.A.S., A.M.A. (council allergy sect., alt. del. 1972—), Am. Fedn. Clin. Research, Assn. Am. Med. Colls., Phi Beta Kappa, Sigma Xi, Alpha Omega Alpha. Mem. editorial bd. Jour. Allergy, 1966-71. Contbr. articles profl. jours. Home: 4702 NE 39th St Seattle WA 98105 Office: Univ Hosp Seattle WA 98195

VAN ARSDELL, PAUL MARION, educator; b. Indpls., Sept. 25, 1905; s. Marion and Katherine (Palmer) Van A.; student Ind. U., 1923-24; B.S., U. Ill., 1927, M.S., 1929, Ph.D., 1935; m. Sophia Wilsford Smith, Sept. 15, 1946; children—Paul Marion, Stephen Cottrell. Mem. faculty U. Ill., Urbana, 1927—, successively asst. examiner Office of Registrar, teaching staff dept. econs., vice chmn. dept. econs., asso. dean Coll. Commerce and Bus. Adminstrn., 1927-57, prof. finance and head dept., 1957-71, prof. finance emeritus, 1971—; distinguished prof. finance Fla. Atlantic U., 1971-75; Armco alumni prof. finance Miami U., Oxford, Ohio, 1975—; cons. analysis of risk and profitability in Bell Telephone System, AT&T, 1955-59, 64-65, 69-70; prin. bus. economist, iron and steel price br. OPA, 1942-43. Chmn. U. Ill. YMCA, 1949-54; dir. Citizens Bldg. Assn., Urbana, 1967—; trustee Milliken U., 1970-73. Served from lt. (j.g.) to lt. comdr. USNR, 1943-46. Mem. Am. Finance Assn. (editorial bd. 1955-56, dir. investments 1957-58, pres. 1960, dir. and mem. adv. com. 1960-64), Midwest, So. (exec. com. 1972-73) finance assns., U.S. Savs. and Loan League (exec. com. ann. conf. on savs. and residential financing 1958-71), Am. Econ. Assn., Phi Kappa Phi, Beta Gamma Sigma, Beta Alpha Psi, Sigma Iota Epsilon, Omicron Delta Epsilon, Sigma Alpha Epsilon, Alpha Kappa Psi. Presbyn. (elder). Mason, Kiwanian (pres. Champaign-Urbana 1966). Author: Problem Manual in Security Analysis, 1940; Problem Manual in Corporation Finance, rev. edit., 1958; Corporation Finance: Policy, Planning, Administration, 1968. Editorial bd. Quar. Rev. Econs. and Bus., 1962-77. Contbr. articles to profl. jours. Home: 209 W Michigan Ave Urbana IL 61801

VAN ARTSDALEN, DONALD WEST, judge; b. Doylestown, Pa., Oct. 21, 1919; s. Isaac Jeans and May Mable (Danenhower) Van A.; student Williams Coll., 1937-40; LL.B., U. Pa., 1948; m. Marie Catherine Auerbach, June 20, 1953. Admitted to Pa. bar, 1948, U.S. Supreme Ct. bar, 1956; practiced in Doylestown, 1948-70; dist. atty. Bucks County (Pa.), 1954-58; U.S. dist. judge Eastern Dist. Pa., Phila., 1970—. Served with Canadian Army, 1940-42, AUS, 1942-45. Home: RD #2 Doylestown PA 18901 Office: US Courthouse 14614 6th and Market Sts Philadelphia PA 19106

VAN ARTSDALEN, ERVIN ROBERT, educator, phys. chemist; b. Doylestown, Pa., Nov. 13, 1913; s. Isaac J. and May M. (Danenhower) Van A.; B.S. in Chemistry cum laude, Lafayette Coll., 1935; Internat. Exchange fellow U. Munich (Germany), 1935-36; A.M., Harvard, 1939, Ph.D. in Phys. Chemistry, 1941; m. Mary Louise Naylor, June 14, 1945. Instr., then asst. prof. chemistry Lafayette Coll., 1941-45; on leave to Nat. Def. Research Com., Johns Hopkins Med. Sch., 1943-45; group leader Los Alamos Atomic Bomb Lab., 1945-46; asst. prof. chemistry Cornell U., 1946-51; adminstrv. group leader Oak Ridge Nat. Lab., 1951-56; asst. dir. research, basic lab. Union Carbide Corp., Cleve., 1956-63; John W. Mallet prof. chemistry, chmn. dept. U. Va., 1963-68; prof. chemistry U. Ala., 1968—, head dept., 1968-72; with Inst. Energy Analysis, Oak Ridge, 1975-76; cons. to govt. and industry. Mem. chemistry adv. com. USAF Office Sci. Research, 1958-72, chmn., 1963-70; spl. research reaction kinetics and photochemistry, thermodynamics, fused salts, nuclear energy, energy analysis; dir. High Sch. Students and Tchrs. Sci. Workshops and Seminars, Cleve., 1957-60. Bd. dirs. Oak Ridge Sch. Music, 1953-56, Oak Ridge Asso. Univs., 1969-75. Recipient Distinguished Alumni Sci. Tchr. citation Lafayette Coll., 1966. Fellow Am. Inst. Chemists; mem. Am. Chem. Soc., Am. Phys. Soc., Va. Acad. Sci., AAAS, Phi Beta Kappa, Alpha Chi Sigma, Gamma Alpha, Gamma Sigma Epsilon, Kappa Delta Rho. Mem. Evang. and Reformed Ch. Clubs: Oak Ridge Country; Indian Hills Country (Tuscaloosa, Ala.). Contbr. to profl. jours., govt. reports. Mem. editorial bd. Jour. Phys. Chemistry, 1958-62. Home: 14 Dunbrook Tuscaloosa AL 35406

VANATTA, JOHN CROTHERS, III, physician, educator; b. Lafayette, Ind., Apr. 22, 1919; s. John Crothers and Ida Lahr (Raub) V.; B.A., Ind. U., 1941, M.D., 1944; m. Carol Lee Geisler, July 30, 1944; children—Lynn Ellen Vanatta Dahl, Paul Richard. Intern, Wayne County Gen. Hosp., Eloise, Mich., 1944-45, resident in internal medicine, 1946-47; fellow in physiology, pharmacology Southwestern Med. Coll., Dallas, 1947-48, fellow in exptl. and internal medicine, 1948-49, instr. physiology U. Tex. Southwestern Med. Coll., 1949-50, asst. prof., 1950-53, asso. prof., 1953-57, prof. physiology, 1957—; prof. physiology So. Meth. U. Dallas, 1969—; mem. staff Parkland Meml. Hosp., Dallas, 1953-57, VA Hosp., Dallas, McKinney, Tex., 1956-58; cons. div. nuclear edn. tng. AEC, 1964-67. Scouter, Circle 10 council Boy Scouts Am., Dallas, 1963—; v.p. Luth. Health Care Council N. Tex., 1975—. Served as lt. (j.g.) M.C., USNR, 1945-46; PTO. Mem. AMA, AAAS, Am. Physiol. Soc., Soc. Exptl. Biology and Medicine, Phi Beta Pi, Sigma Xi, Delta Tau Delta. Lutheran (councilman 1951-79, v.p. 1974-75). Author: Oxygen Transport, Hypoxia and Cyanosis, 1974, Fluid Balance - A Clinical Manual, 1976. Contbr. articles to profl. jours. Home: 10416 Remington Ln Dallas TX 75229

VAN ATTA, ROBERT ERNEST, educator; b. Ada, Ohio, Feb. 29, 1924; s. Ernest A. and Agnes (Klingler) Van A.; student Ohio No. U., 1941-43, B.A., 1948; M.S., Purdue U., 1950; Ph.D., Pa. State U., 1952; m. Mary Ellen Koons, Jan. 20, 1946; children—John Robert, Richard Lewis, Matthew Ernest. Asso. prof. dept. chemistry Ohio No. U., Ada, 1952-54, also chmn. dept., dir. div. natural scis., 1953-54; mem. faculty So. Ill. U., Carbondale, 1954-69, asso. prof., 1959-67, prof., 1967-69; prof., head dept. chemistry Ball State U., Muncie, Ind., 1969—, dir. Inst. Environmental Studies, 1973-74; cons. bus., local govt. Served to 2d lt. AUS, 1943-46. Recipient numerous fed. agy. research grants; recipient Alumni Founder's Day award Ohio No. Univ., 1972. Fellow Am. Inst. Chemists, Ind. Acad. Sci. (sec. 1975—); mem. Am. Chem. Soc., AAAS, AAUP, Izaak Walton League, Sigma Xi, Phi Lambda Upsilon, Phi Mu Delta. Republican. Mem. Ch. Christ. Mason. Clubs: KOA (Billings, Mont.); Good Sam (Calabasas, Cal.); NCHA (Buffalo); WBCCI (Cerritas, Cal.). Author: Introduction to Analytical Chemistry, 1964; Experimental Chemical Analysis, 1973; Instrumental Methods of Analysis for Laboratory Technicians, 1978. Contbr. profl. jours. Home: 2605 W Berkshire Dr Muncie IN 47304 Office: Dept Chemistry Ball State U Muncie IN 47306

VAN BAALEN, CHASE, microbiologist; b. Detroit, Sept. 12, 1925; s. Harold and Lillian (Netzorg) Van B.; B.S., U. Ala., 1938; M.S., U. Detroit, 1950; Ph.D., U. Tex., 1957; m. Donna Gale Ems, June 20, 1954; children—Patricia, Aaron, Julie. Research scientist Kitchawan Research Lab., Bklyn. Bot. Garden, Ossining, N.Y., 1958-61; lectr. U. Tex. Marine Sci. Inst., Port Aransas, 1961-64, asst. prof. botany, 1965-67, asso. prof., 1968-72, prof. botany and marine studies Port Aransas Marine Lab., 1972—. NSF grantee, 1961—. Mem. Am. Soc. Microbiology, Am. Soc. Photobiology, Am. Soc. Plant Physiology, Phycological Soc. Am., Soc. Gen. Microbiology, Japanese Soc. Plant Physiology, Scandinavian Soc. Plant Physiology, Sigma Xi. Contbr. numerous articles, revs. to profl. publs.; editorial bd. Handbook Microbiology, 1978-79; asso. editor Jour. Phycology, 1979—. Home: PO Box 417 Port Aransas TX 78373 Office: PO Box 1267 Port Aransas TX 78373

VAN BAALEN, JACK LIT, lawyer; b. Phila., Apr. 2, 1930; s. Richard and Helene (Greenwald) Van B.; A.B. magna cum laude, Dartmouth Coll., 1952; LL.B. cum laude, U. Pa., 1955; m. Lynn Potamkin, Dec. 20, 1953; children—Jeffrey, Meg, James, Annette. Asso. firm Wolf, Block, Schnorr and Solis-Cohen, Phila., 1955-64, partner, 1964-74; prof. law U. Wyo., 1974—. Mem. Wyo. Bar Assn., Pa. Bar Assn., Am. Law Inst. Office: Coll of Law Laramie WY 82071*

VAN BERGEN, FREDERICK HALL, physician, educator; b. Mpls., Sept. 21, 1914; s. Frederick S. and Jeannette (Hall) Van B., student St. Thomas Coll., St. Paul, 1933-37; M.B., U. Minn., 1941, M.D., 1942, M.S., 1952; m. Nancy Thiel, July 9, 1964; Intern Bremerton (Wash.) Naval Hosp., 1941-42; resident U. Minn. Hosp., 1946-48; practice medicine, specializing in anesthesiology, Mpls., 1948—; instr. anesthesiology Med. Sch. U. Minn., 1948-53, asst. prof., asso. dir. anesthesiology, 1953-54, acting dir. anesthesiology, 1955-57, prof., chmn. dept. anesthesiology, 1957—; regional VA cons.; cons. Hennepin County Gen. Hosp. (Mpls.). Served to lt. comdr. M.C., USNR, 1941-46. Recipient Certificate of merit Am. Soc. Anesthesiologists, 1955. Mem. Am. (past dir.), Minn. (past pres.) socs. anesthesiologists, Assn. U. Anesthetists, Acad. Anesthesiology (pres. 1968), Am. Therapeutic Soc., N.Y. Acad. Scis., Phi Chi. Club: University of Minnesota Alumni. Developed Van Bergen Respirator. Home: 2005 Argonne Dr Minneapolis MN 55421

VAN BERGH, FREDERIC W., mfg. co. exec.; b. Rochester, N.Y., Nov. 4, 1926; s. Maurice H. and Helen Rose (Freeman) Van B.; B.S. in Acctg., Fordham U.; m. Ana Lucia Echevarria, Feb. 24, 1975; children—Frederic W., Michael Scott, Richard Lee. With United Mchts. & Mfrs., Inc., N.Y.C., 1949—, v.p., 1970-76, sr. v.p., 1976-77, exec. v.p., 1977—, treas., chief fin. officer, 1979—, also dir. Served with USN, 1943-44. Clubs: Sleepy Hollow Country, Scarborough-on-Hudson.

VAN BORTEL, FRANCIS JOHN, advt. exec.; b. Macedon, N.Y., June 2, 1921; s. Peter Marvin and Margaret (Blankenberg) Van B.; M.A., U. Chgo., 1952; m. Dorothy Matilda Greey, Aug. 18, 1953. Instr. U. Chgo., 1952-54; dir. research McCann-Erickson, Chgo., 1954-65; dir. Western Region Marplan, Chgo., 1965-69, pres., 1969-70; exec. v.p. McCann Erickson, Inc., N.Y.C., 1970—. Served with USAAF, 1942-46. Mem. Sigma Xi. Club: Coveleigh (Rye, N.Y.). Home: 55 Stuyvesant Ave Rye NY 10580 Office: 485 Lexington Ave New York City NY 10017

VAN BRONKHORST, EDWIN EARL, electronics co. exec.; b. Rio Linda, Calif., Feb. 21, 1924; s. Klaas and Ethel (Diebold) van B.; B.S., U. Calif. at Berkeley, 1944; m. Russella Diane Ball, Feb. 16, 1957; children—Kort, Jon, Derek. Accountant, partner F.W. Lafrentz & Co., San Francisco, 1950-53; with Hewlett-Packard Co., Palo Alto, Calif., 1953—, v.p., treas., 1963—, also dir.; dir. No. Calif. Savs. & Loan Assn., Rolm Corp. C.P.A., Calif. Home: 193 Meadowood Dr Portola Valley CA 94025 Office: 1501 Page Mill Rd Palo Alto CA 94304

VAN BRUNT, ALBERT DANIEL, advt. exec.; b. N.Y.C., Nov. 13, 1920; s. Ernest Robert and Helen (Rothschild) Isaacs; B.S. in Mktg., N.Y. U., 1942. Dir. advt. Air France, N.Y.C., 1947-50; v.p. Buchanan Advt. Agy., N.Y.C., 1951-57; pres. Van Brunt & Co., Advt.-Mktg., Inc., N.Y.C., 1958—; pres. IMAA, Inc., N.Y.C., 1965-70, sr. v.p., 1970—; exec. v.p. Van Brunt & Co., Chgo., Inc., 1969-76, Van Brunt/Schaeffer, 1979—; v.p. HBC/Van Brunt, Chgo., 1976-77. Trustee, N.Y. chpt. Leukemia Soc. Am., 1979—. Served to lt. USNR, 1942-46. Mem. Am. Assn. Advt. Agys. (dir. N.Y. council 1969-74), Aviation and Space Writers Assn., Internat. Advt. Assn. Clubs: Wings, Lotos (dir. 1966—, treas. 1975-76) (N.Y.C.); Sheldrake Yacht (Mamaroneck, N.Y.); Easthampton (N.Y.) Yacht. Home: 315 E 68th St New York NY 10021 also Jason's Ln East Hampton NY 11937 Office: 300 E 42d St New York NY 10017

VAN BRUNT, BERGEN HOUSTON, lawyer; b. Frankfort, Ind., Nov. 27, 1911; s. Geddes and Caroline (Houston) Van B.; student U. Utah, 1929-32, Northwestern U., 1932-33, Purdue U., 1934; LL.B., Ind. U., 1936; m. Cecile Marie Saunders, Apr. 24, 1953. Admitted to Ind. bar, 1937, Cal. bar, 1945; claims atty. Md. Casualty Co., Indpls., 1936-39; claims mgr. Ohio Casualty Ins. Co., Detroit, 1940-42, San Francisco, 1946; partner firm Jackson & Van Brunt, San Francisco, 1946-53, Bergen Van Brunt, San Francisco, 1953—. Pres. Am. Bd. Trial Advs., 1963. Pres. El Camino Assembly of Calif. Republican Assembly, 1963-64, Crystal-Camino Rep. Assembly, 1964—; mem. San Mateo County Rep. Central Com., 1957—. Served to lt. USNR, 1942-45. Mem. Am., Calif., Ind., San Francisco bar assns., Am. (pres. No. Calif. chpt. 1965—), Calif. (parlimentarian 1968-71, asso. editor Jour. 1969-73), San Francisco (pres. 1965) trial lawyers assns., Lawyers Club San Francisco (pres. 1964), SAR (chancellor Calif. 1964-74, Citizens Gold medal Nat. SAR 1969, Honor award 1975), Beta Theta Pi (pres. San Francisco 1958). Clubs: Big Ten Univ. (pres. 1961); Toastmaster (area gov. San Francisco 1959). Home: 1220 Cardigan Rd Hillsborough CA 94010 Office: 1255 Post St Suite 740 San Francisco CA 94109

VAN BRUNT, CONSTANCE, editor; b. Los Angeles, July 29, 1949; d. Godwin Augustus and Vida Lois (Milton) Van B.; B.A., Sarah Lawrence Coll., 1971; M.A., Harvard U., 1972; m. Robert F. McMillan, Jr.; 1 dau., Ayisha Nell. Program asst. for vis. African educators, escort/interpretor African Am. Inst., N.Y.C., summers 1969-71; tutor, tchr. METCO Program, Lincoln, Mass., 1971-72; mng. editor Ebony Jr. mag. Johnson Pub. Co., Chgo., 1972-77: sr. editor EMC Corp., St. Paul, 1977-79; dir. communications Wilson Learning, Mpls., 1979—. Bd. dirs. Chgo. UNICEF, Nat. Black Child Devel. Inst.; trustee, Chgo. Pub. Broadcasting Sta. WTTW. Named Outstanding Young Career Woman of Ill., 1976. John Hay Whitney fellow, 1971-72, Dwight D. Eisenhower scholar, 1971-72. Mem. Internat. Reading Assn., Children's Reading Roundtable. Presbyterian. Home: 2631 Kyle Ave N Golden Valley MN 55427

VAN BRUNT, EDWIN DAVID, advt. exec.; b. N.Y.C., Mar. 19, 1914; s. Ernest R. and Helen (Rothschild) Van B.; B.S., N.Y. U., 1935; m. Marion Rydholm, Mar. 11, 1944; children—Carl, Laurie. Partner Covent Co., N.Y.C., 1937-43; information officer OPA, Washington, 1943-46; advt. promotion dir. Butterick Co. Inc., N.Y.C., 1946-48; pres. Media Promotion Orgn., Inc., N.Y.C., 1948-58; exec. v.p. Van Brunt & Co., N.Y.C., 1958-66, chmn., 1966—, also chief exec. officer; pres. IMAA (Internat. Markets Advt. Agy.), Inc., hdqrs. N.Y.C., 1965-78; pres., dir. Potentials Corp., hdqrs. N.Y.C., 1978—; dir. Ecofin S.A., Luxembourg, 1978—. Mem. Internat. Advt. Assn. (dir. 1971—, treas. 1972-78, exec. com. 1972-78). Office: 300 E 42d St New York City NY 10017

VAN BRUNT, JOHN, JR., lawyer; b. N.Y.C., Oct. 5, 1915; s. John and Ethel D. (Roberts) Van B.; B.S., Haverford Coll., 1936; LL.B., Harvard, 1939; m. Margaret Dickson Blithe, Sept. 7, 1940; children—John, Margaret Lindsay (Mrs. James R. Booth), Nicholas, Albert. Admitted to Del. bar, 1941, N.Y. bar, 1939, also U.S. Supreme Ct.; asso., partner firm Hastings, Stockley & Layton, Wilmington, Del., 1940-44, Killoran & Van Brunt, Wilmington, 1944-70, 75-76; v.p., gen. counsel, dir. Robino-Ladd Co., Wilmington, 1970-75; gen. counsel James Julian, Inc., 1976—. Mem. Am., Del. bar assns. Clubs: Harvard, Holland Soc. of N.Y. Home: 1232 Grinnell Rd Wilmington DE 19803

VAN BUITENEN, JOHANNES ADRIAN BERNARD, educator, author; b. The Hague, Holland, May 21, 1928; s. Adrian and Johanna (van Rooyen) van B.; B.A., U. Utrecht (Holland), 1948, M.S., 1951, Ph.D., 1953; m. Cornelia M. Krapels, Oct. 29, 1952 (dec. 1973); children—Adrian Hans Benedict, Jeannette Louise Josephine. Came to U.S., 1961. Sub editor Sanskrit Dictionary, Poona, India, 1953-56; postdoctoral fellow Harvard, 1956-57; research asso. U. Chgo., 1957-59; reader Indian philosophy U. Utrecht, 1959-61; mem. faculty U. Chgo., 1961-79, prof. Sanskrit and Indic Studies, 1964-79, now Distinguished Service prof., chmn. dept. S. Asian langs., 1966-77; Radhakrishnam lectr. Oxford U., 1978; lectr., cons. Mem. Royal Acad. Arts Scis., Holland Assn., Inst. Indian Studies (chmn. publs. com. 1966-79), Am. Acad. Arts and Scis. Author: Tales of Ancient India, 1959; Two Plays of Ancient India, 1968; The Mahabharata, vols. I-III, 1973-78. Producer documentary film Vajapeya Sacrifice, 1961. Home: 1700 E 56th St Chicago IL 60637 Died Sept. 21, 1979.

VAN BUREN, ABIGAIL (PAULINE FRIEDMAN PHILLIPS), columnist, writer, lectr.; b. Sioux City, Iowa, July 4, 1918; d. Abraham and Rebecca (Rushall) Friedman; student Morningside Coll., Sioux City, 1936-39; Litt.D. (hon.), Morningside Coll., 1965; m. Morton Phillips, July 2, 1939; children—Edward Jay, Jeanne. Vol. worker for causes of better mental health, Nat. Found. Infantile Paralysis, tng. Gray Ladies A.R.C., 1939-56; pres. Minn.-Wis. council B'nai B'rith Aux., 1945-49; columnist Dear Abby, San Francisco Chronicle, 1956, syndicated Chgo.-Tribune, N.Y. News Syndicate, now appears in newspapers U.S., Brazil, Australia, Japan, Germany, Holland, Denmark, Can.; radio program CBS, 1963—. Mem. nat. adv. council on aging NIH, HEW, 1978—; hon. chairwoman 1st Nat. Women's Conf. on Cancer, Am. Cancer Soc., 1979; bd. dirs. Guthrie Theatre, Mpls., 1970-74, Dr. Franz Alexander Research Found., Los Angeles, nat. bd. Goodwill Industries, 1968-75. Nat. chmn. Crippled Children Soc., 1962. Recipient Mother of Year award, Los Angeles, 1958; Golden Kidney award, Los Angeles, 1960; Margaret Sanger award Nat. Planned Parenthood, 1974; Robert T. Morse award Am. Psychiat. Assn.; hon. life mem. Concern For Dying-Am. Ednl. Council; Paul Harris fellow Internat. Rotary Club; award NCCJ, St. Louis, 1968. Hon. mem. Women in Communications; mem. Sigma Delta Chi. Author: Dear Abby, 1957 (also translated Japanese, Dutch, German, Spanish); Dear Teen Ager, 1959; Dear Abby on Marriage, 1962. Contbr. McCall's mag. Home: Beverly Hills CA 90212 Office: 132 Lasky Dr Beverly Hills CA 90212. *I have learned the art of enlightened selfishness. If one permits others to waste his time, he will forever be fighting deadlines and working under pressure. When I learned how to say "no" graciously, life became immeasurably more productive.*

VAN BUREN, MARTIN LEROY, library planning cons.; b. Cleve., Feb. 24, 1921; s. Donald C. and Anne (Deyo) Van B.; student Ohio State U., 1939-40, Ga. Inst. Tech., 1940-43; m. Janie H. Lynch, Feb. 17, 1966; children by former marriage—Anne Lynn, Tye Wynn; 1 stepson, William Lynch, Jr. Propr. Van B. Assos., Inc., indsl. designer, Charlotte, N.C., 1946-48; with Knoll Asso., design reps., 1948-53; propr. M. Van Buren, Inc., planning cons., Charlotte, 1953—; planning cons. Nat. Library Nicaragua, 1971-72, Nat. Libraries, Libya, 1975. Served with AUS, 1943-46. Decorated Purple Heart, Bronze Star; UNESCO grantee, 1959; Ford Found. grantee, 1964, 66. Contbr. articles to profl. jours. Address: 1628 Jameston Dr Charlotte NC 28209

VAN BUREN, PAUL MATTHEWS, educator; b. Norfolk, Va., Apr. 20, 1924; s. Harold Sheffield and Charlotte (Matthews) van B.; B.A., Harvard U., 1948; B.D., Episcopal Theol. Sch., Cambridge, Mass., 1951; D. Theol., U. Basel (Switzerland), 1957; m. Anne Hagopian, Feb. 7, 1948; children—Alice, Ariane, Philip, Thomas. Ordained to ministry Episcopal Ch., 1951; minister in Detroit, 1954-57; asst., then asso. prof. theology Episcopal Sem. S.W., Austin, Tex., 1957-64; asso. prof. Temple U., Phila., 1964—, prof. religion, 1966—, chmn. dept. religion, 1974-76; cons. Detroit Indsl. Mission, 1956-66. Served with USCGR, 1942-43, USNR, 1943-45. Fellow Am. Assn. Theol. Schs., 1962-63; Fulbright sr. lectr. Oxford (Eng.) U., 1967-68; Guggenheim fellow, 1967-68. Fellow Soc. Values in Higher Edn.; mem. Am. Acad. Religion, NAACP, AAUP, ACLU, Am. Theol. Soc. Author: Christ in Our Place, 1957; The Secular Meaning of the Gospel, 1963; Theological Explorations, 1968; The Edges of Language, 1972; The Burden of Freedom, 1976; Discerning the Way, 1980. Home: 134 Chestnut St Boston MA 02108 Office: Dept Religion Temple Univ Philadelphia PA 19122

VAN BUREN, RAEBURN, illustrator; b. Pueblo, Colo., Jan. 12, 1891; s. George Lincoln and Luella (la Mar) Van B.; student Central High Sch., Kansas City, Mo., 1906-09, Art Students League, N.Y.C., 1913; m. Fern Rita Ringo, Dec. 8, 1920; 1 son, Richard. Sketch artist Kansas City Star, 1909-12; free lance illustrator, 1913—; has illustrated over 350 stories for the Sat. Evening Post; also regular contbr. to Colliers', Red Book, The New Yorker, Esquire, McCalls, McClure Syndicate and King Features Syndicate; creator of the comic strip, Abbie and Slats, syndicated in over 368 daily newspapers by United Feature Syndicate; permanent collection illustrations comic strips, Boston U. Library, Syracuse U. Served as volunteer 107th Regt., 27th Div., N.Y. N.G.; in World War I, 1917-19 with AEF 11 mos. Recipient award as Cartoonist of Year, Phila. B'nai B'rith, 1958; named Best Story Strip cartoonist Nat. Cartoonist Soc., 1976, named to Cartoonist Hall of Fame, 1978. Mem. Nat. Cartoonists Soc., Society Illustrators, Artists and Writers. Home-Studio: 21 Clover Drive Great Neck NY 11021

VAN BUREN, WILLIAM BENJAMIN, III, pharm. co. exec.; b. Bklyn., Mar. 25, 1922; s. William Benjamin and Dorothy Marjorie (Way) Van B.; B.A., Washington and Lee U., 1944; LL.B., Yale U., 1949; m. Joan Cottrell Whitford, Sept. 11, 1948; children—Susan (dec.), Patricia, William S., Richard W. Admitted to N.Y. bar, 1950; mem. firm Chadbourne, Hunt, Jaeckel & Brown, N.Y.C., 1949-51, Richard P. Jackson, N.Y.C., 1951-53, Spence & Hotchkiss, N.Y.C., 1953-55; mem. legal dept. Merck & Co., Inc., 1956-57; div. counsel Merck Sharp & Dohme div. Merck & Co., 1957-60, asst. to div. pres., 1960-62, dir. planning., 1963-64, dir. corp. devel. Merck & Co., Inc., 1964-76, v.p. and sec., 1976—. Mem. Watchung Bd. Adjustment, 1968—, chmn., 1977—; mem. Bd. Edn., Watchung Hills Regional High Sch., 1971-75, acting pres., 1975; trustee Bryn Mawr Hosp., 1961-64, Ind. Coll. Fund N.J., 1979—. Served with USNR, 1943-46. Mem. Bar Assn. City N.Y., Am. Soc. Corp. Secs., Stockholder Relations Soc. N.Y., Phi Beta Kappa. Clubs: Yale (N.Y.C.), Seaview Country (Absecon, N.J.). Home: 185 Knollwood Dr Watchung NJ 07060 Office: PO Box 2000 Rahway NJ 07065

VAN BUSKIRK, ALDEN LOTHROP, govt. ofcl.; b. Melrose, Mass., Mar. 4, 1914; s. Robert Long and Annie (Ruby) (Westman) Van B.; student Boston U., 1932-36; B.S., Air U., 1949; m. Kathleen M. Miller, Feb. 14, 1943; children—Robert Long, Priscilla Anne. Factory rep. Armstrong Cork Co., Lancaster, Pa., 1936-41; commd. officer USAAF, 1941, advanced through grades to col. USAF; command pilot, electronics staff officer; comdr. USAF Air Traffic Control Sqdn., Berlin Airlift, 1948; chief instrn., electronics course Air Command and Staff Coll., Air U., Maxwell AFB, Ala., 1950-54; dep. for communications Mil. Assistance Command, Vietnam, 1964; ret. 1966; with AID, 1967—, adviser to Govt. Vietnam, 1967-70, Air Vietnam, 1970-73, assigned Washington, 1973—, editor Engring. Newsletter; devel. single integrated telecommunications plan for Vietnam, 1970. Decorated Legion of Merit with oak leaf cluster, Air medal, Air Force and Army commendation medals. Mem. Armed Forces Communications Assn. Home: McLean VA Office: AID State Dept Washington DC 20523

VAN CAMPEN, JOSEPH ALFRED, educator; b. Trucksville, Pa., June 14, 1933; s. Joseph and Elise Geraldine (Wendel) Van C.; B.A., U. Chgo., 1953, M.A., 1955; Adenauer fellow U. Munich (W. Ger.), 1953-54; Fulbright grantee U. Leiden (Netherlands), 1956-57; Ph.D., Harvard U., 1961; m. Eleanor Sharples Vermette, May 4, 1963; children—James Joseph, Elise Marie. Instr., then asst. prof. Harvard U., 1960-66; mem. faculty Stanford U., 1966—, prof. Slavic langs., 1971—, chmn. dept. Slavic langs. and lits., 1969-78; IBM fellow Harvard U. Computing Center, 1964-65. Recipient Stanford U. Dean's award teaching, 1979. Mem. Am. Assn. Tchrs. Slavic and E. European Langs. Author computer based courses in Russian. Office: Dept Slavic Langs and Lits Stanford Univ Stanford CA 94305

VAN CASPEL, VENITA WALKER (MRS. JACOB T. VAN CASPEL), fin. planner; b. Sweetwater, Okla., Oct. 3, 1922; d. Leonard Rankin and Ella Belle (Jarnagin) Walker; student Duke, 1944-46; B.A., U. Colo., 1948, postgrad., 1949-51; postgrad. N.Y. Inst. Finance, 1962; m. Jacob T. Van Caspel, Dec. 7, 1963. Stockbroker, Rauscher Pierce & Co., Houston, 1962-65, A.G. Edwards & Sons, Houston, 1965-68; founder, pres., owner Van Caspel & Co., Inc., Houston, 1968—; owner, mgr. Van Caspel Planning Service, Van Caspel Advt. Agy.; owner Diamond V Ranch; dir. N. Loop Nat. Bank. Moderator Successful Texans CBS-TV; speaker Internat. Mut. Fund Conv., Chgo., 1964, Miami, Fla., 1967, San Francisco, 1974, Atlanta, 1975, Los Angeles, 1977, Investment Expo, Los Angeles, 1978; mem., speaker Million Dollar Mut. Fund Forum, N.Y.C., 1969; speaker Internat. Assn. Fin. Planners; condr. investment seminars, Houston, annually; 1st women mem. Pacific Stock Exchange. Mem. Gov.'s Commn. on Status Women; mem. adv. com. Houston Women's Leadership Council; adv. bd. Career Conf. for Kincaid Sch.; bd. dirs. Found. for Children, Certified Fin. Planners Found., Boy Scouts Am., Interface, San Jacinto Lung Assn.; mem. bd., exec. com. Better Bus. Bur. Recipient Matrix award Theta Sigma Phi, 1969. Cert. fin. planner. Mem. Internat. Assn. Financial Planners (charter; dir.), Mut. Fund Council Million Dollar Producers (charter), Houston C. of C. (mem. econ. devel. com.) Phi Gamma Mu, Phi Beta Kappa. Presbyterian. Author: Money Dynamics, 1975; Dear Investor; The New Money Dynamics, 1978; (video-cassette tapes) Money Dynamics. Editor, Fin. Planners Newsletter. Home: 165 Sage Rd Houston TX 77056 Office: 1540 Post Oak Tower Houston TX 77056

VANCE, CARL BRUCE, utility co. exec.; b. Bagnell, Mo., Apr. 12, 1915; s. Homer Benton and Hattie Fugitt (Hallar) V.; B.S. in Mech. Engring., U. Okla., 1936; postgrad. U. Mich., 1960, Columbia U., 1961, Am. Mgmt. Assn. Sr. Mgmt. Program, 1977; m. Ruth Brenneman, Mar. 11, 1939; children—Janet Vance Smith, Julia Vance Keller, Carl Bruce. Sales-service engr. Bailey Meter Co., Cleve., St. Louis and Kansas City, Mo., 1936-39; test engr. Gen. Electric Co., Schenectady, 1940; sr. engr. prodn. dept. Cleve. Electric Illuminating Co., 1940-42; mech. engr., supt. power and distbn. Mil. Chem. Works, Jayhawk Ordnance Works, Pittsburg, Kans., 1942-45; with Indpls. Power & Light Co., 1945—, mech. engr., supt. power prodn., 1957-62, asst. v.p. power prodn., 1962, v.p. power prodn., 1963-75, sr. v.p. ops., 1975-78, exec. v.p. ops., 1978—, dir., mem. exec. com., 1979—; dir. Property & Land Co., Tecumseh Coal Co. Chmn., City of Indpls. Air Pollution Adv. Com., 1966-67, City of Indpls. Air Pollution Control Bd., 1968-70, mem. bd., 1968-76; tech. cons. State of Ind. Air Pollution Control Bd., 1968-70, mem. Bd., 1969-70; mem. Environ. Quality Control Air Com., 1972—; bd. dirs. Indpls. Sci. and Engring. Found., 1971-74, mem. nominating com., 1973-76; mem. Mayor's Solid Waste Task Force, 1976—. Registered profl. engr., Ohio, Ind. Fellow ASME (vice chmn. air pollution standards com. 1964-68, chmn. exec. com. air pollution controls div. 1967-68); mem. Ind. Soc. Profl. Engrs., Edison Electric Inst. (chmn. prome movers com. 1963-65, mem. exec. com. engring. and operating div. 1965-70, chmn. air and water problems subcom. 1967-70), Assn. Edison Illuminating Cos. (power generation com. 1965—), East Central Area Reliability Group (chmn. generation adv. panel 1967-69), Ind. Electric Assn. (chmn. environ. policy com. 1969-72, 76-77), Engrs. Joint Council (commr. Nat. Engrs. Commn. on Air Resources 1970-71), Electric League Ind., Tau Beta Pi. Presbyterian. Clubs: Columbia, Indpls. Athletic, Meridian Hills Country. Home: 7520 Hoover Rd Indianapolis IN 46260 Office: Indpls Power & Light Co 25 Monument Circle Indianapolis IN 46206. *Every change does not mean an improvement, but you can't have an improvement without change.*

VANCE, CYRUS ROBERTS, sec. state, lawyer; b. Clarksburg, W.Va., Mar. 27, 1917; s. John Carl and Amy (Roberts) V.; student Kent Sch.; B.A., Yale, 1939, LL.B., 1942; LL.D., Marshall U., 1963, Trinity Coll., Hartford, Conn., 1966, Yale, 1968, W.Va. U., 1969, Brandeis U., 1971; m. Grace Elsie Sloane, Feb. 15, 1947; children—Elsie Nicoll, Amy Sloane, Grace Roberts, Camilla Vance Higgins, Cyrus Roberts. Admitted to N.Y. bar, 1947, U.S. Supreme Ct. bar, 1960; asst. to pres. Mead Corp., 1946-47; with Simpson Thacher & Bartlett, N.Y.C., 1947-56, partner, 1956-61, 67—; gen. counsel Dept. Def., 1961-62; sec. of army, 1962-63; dep. sec. def., 1964-67; spl. rep. of the Pres., Cyprus, 1967, Korea, 1968; U.S. negotiator Paris Peace Conf. on Vietnam, 1968-69; sec. state, 1977—. Spl. counsel, preparedness investigating subcom. Senate Armed Services Com., 1957-60; cons. counsel spl. Com. on Space and Astronautics, U.S. Senate, 1958; chmn. com. on adjudication of claims Adminstrv. Conf. of U.S.; mem. Com. to Investigate Alleged Police Corruption in N.Y.C., 1970-72; chmn. UN Devel. Corp., 1976. Dir. Pan Am. World Airways, One William St. Fund, N.Y. Times Co. Bd. dirs., chmn. bd. Union Settlement Assn., Inc., 1953-61; former trustee Yale, Urban Inst., N.Y. Presbyn. Hosp.; chmn. trustees Rockefeller Found., 1975-76. Served to lt. (s.g.) USNR, 1942-46. Recipient Medal of Freedom, 1969. Fellow Am. Coll. Trial Lawyers; mem. Am. Bar Assn., Assn. Bar City N.Y. (pres. 1974-76). Office: Dept of State 2201 C Street NW Washington DC 20520

VANCE, ELBRIDGE PUTNAM, educator; b. Cin., Feb. 7, 1915; s. Selby Frame and Jeannie (Putnam) V.; student Haverford Coll., 1932-33; A.B., Coll. Wooster, 1936; M.A., U. Mich., 1937, Ph.D., 1939; m. Margaret Gertrude Stoffel, Aug. 5, 1939 (div. 1975); children—Susan (Mrs. Timothy Griffin), Peter Selby, Douglas Putnam, Emily (Mrs. Charles Harold Beynon III); m. 2d, Jean Haigh, Jan. 1975. Asst. U. Mich., 1937-39; instr. U. Nev., 1939-41, asst. prof., 1941-43; vis. lectr. Oberlin (Ohio) Coll., 1943-46, asst. prof., 1946-50, asso. prof., 1950-54, prof., 1954—, chmn. dept., 1948—, acting Dean Coll. Arts and Scis., 2d semester, 1965-66, 1st semester, 1970-71; chmn. advanced placement com. Coll. Entrance Exam. Bd., 1961-65, chief reader, 1956-61; chmn. com. examiners math. Comprehensive Coll. Tests, Ednl. Testing Service, 1965-67. Mem. Oberlin Sch. Bd., 1952-60, pres. 1957-60. NSF Faculty fellow, 1960-61. Mem. Math. Assn. Am., Nat. Council Tchrs. of Math., Am. Math. Soc., Phi Beta Kappa, Sigma Xi, Phi Kappa Phi. Author: Trigonometry, 2d edit., 1969; Unified Algebra and Trigonometry, 1955; Fundamentals of Mathematics, 1960; Modern College Algebra, 3d edit., 1973; Modern Algebra and Trigonometry, 3d edit., 1973; An Introduction to Modern Mathematics, 2d edit., 1968; Mathematics 12, 1968; Solution Manual for Mathematics 12, 1968. Book review editor Am. Math. Monthly, 1949-57, asso. editor, 1964-67. Home: 290 Yorktown Pl B4 Vermilion OH 44089

VANCE, GRAHAM ALEXANDER, physician; b. Bristol, Tenn., July 16, 1919; s. Frederick Victor and Mary Helen (Gray) V.; B.S., La. State U., 1941; M.D., U. Va., 1944; m. Martha Gordon Miller, June 5, 1948; children—Mary Martha, Jane Marie, Graham Alexander, Patricia, Carol, Dorothy. Intern Johns Hopkins Hosp., 1944-45, resident physician, 1945-46; resident physician U. Chgo., 1947-48, J.H. Pratt Diagnostic Hosp., Boston, 1948-49; instr. dept. medicine Coll. Medicine, U. Ill., Chgo., 1949-52, adminstrv. asst. to dean, 1949-52; chief out-patient med. clinic U. Ill. Research and Edn. Hosp., 1949-52; practice medicine specializing in internal medicine, 1949—; chief medicine Holy Family Hosp., Des Plaines, Ill., 1967-70, pres. med. staff, 1974-76; formerly attending physician Research and Edn. Hosps., U. Ill., Lutheran Gen. Hosp., Park Ridge, Ill.; asso. clin. prof. medicine U. Ill., 1960-77; electrocardiographer, cons. in medicine West Plains (Mo.) Community Hosp., 1977—. Served as capt. O.R.C., M.C., AUS, 1951-53. Diplomate Am. Bd. Internal Medicine. Fellow A.C.P.; mem. Raven Soc., Scabbard and Blade, Alpha Omega Alpha, Sigma Chi, Nu Sigma Nu, Omicron Delta Kappa. Home: Box 0-36 Lanton Route West Plains MO 65775 Office: 805 Kentucky Ave West Plains MO 65775

VANCE, JAMES, mfg. co. exec.; b. Cleve., May 20, 1930; B.A. cum laude, Baldwin Wallace Coll., 1955; J.D. magna cum laude, Cleve. Marshall Law Sch., 1960; m. Dolores Bernadette Doyle, July 6, 1957; 1 son, James J. Asst. treas., asst. to v.p. fin. and adminstrn., financial analyst Republic Steel Corp., 1956-68; treas. Addressograph & Multigraph Corp., Cleve., 1968-72; v.p. fin. Cin. Milacron Inc., 1972-77; exec. v.p. fin., dir. Dayton-Walther Corp., 1977—; dir. Citation Cos., Amertool Corp., Gen. Automation, Min-Cer, S.A., Mexico, Dwisa of Paris, Dayton-Est of Vesoul, Fiday of Asnieres, France; lectr. bus. law Baldwin Wallace Coll., 1961-63. Vice chmn. United Appeal, 1959; mem. Citizens League Cleve., 1960—; mem. fin. com. YMCA, 1961—; mem. Greater Cleve. Growth Center, 1963—. Vice chmn. fin. com., Cuyahoga Republican Party, 1968-69. Served with inf., AUS, 1951-52. Decorated Bronze Star. Mem. Cleve. Soc. Security Analysts, Am., Ohio bar assns., Fin. Execs. Inst., Am. Ordnance Assn., Nat. Machine Tool Builders Assn., Machinery and Allied Products Inst., Am. Mgmt. Assn., Cin. Indsl. Inst., Ohio C. of C. Alpha Tau Omega, Delta Theta Phi. Club: Cleve. Treasurers (dir.). Home: 6600 Wyman Ln Cincinnati OH 45243 Office: PO Box 1022 Dayton OH 45401

VANCE, JAMES EARBEE, banker; b. Gadsden, Ala., Aug. 4, 1915; s. Winfield Scott and Laura (Earbee) V.; B.S., Auburn U., 1936; grad. Stonier Grad. Sch. Banking, 1950; m. Elizabeth Duke Bryant, Oct. 17, 1939; children—James Earbee, Elizabeth Duke (Mrs. Roy V. Bolyard, Jr.). With 1st Nat. Bank of Birmingham (Ala.), 1936—, v.p. advt., pub. relations and mktg., 1953-68, sr. v.p., 1968—. Vice-chmn. Med. Clinic Bd. City Birmingham (South), 1975—. Vice pres. Ala. Goodwill Industries, 1970-71, vice chmn., 1977-78; pres. Indsl. Health Council, 1972-75; treas. Jr. Achievement; bd. dirs. Gen. Retirement System Employees Jefferson County; mem. Mayor's Police-Community Relations Council; active Anti-Tb Assn. Served to lt. USNR, 1942-45; PTO. Mem. Birmingham Area C. of C. (v.p. 1957-58), Asso. Industries Ala. (treas.), Am. Bankers Assn. (state chmn. savs. bond com.), Ala. Bankers Assn. (state legis. com.), Phi Delta Theta, Omicron Delta Kappa, Phi Kappa Phi, Delta Sigma Pi. Anglican Catholic (vestryman; treas.). Clubs: Vestavia Country, Exchange, Downtown (Birmingham). Home: 3500 Redmont Rd Birmingham AL 35213 Office: PO Box 11007 Birmingham AL 35288

VANCE, JOHN THOMAS, lawyer, educator, former govt. ofcl.; b. Lexington, Ky., Oct. 12, 1921; s. John Thomas and Margaret Scott (Breckinridge) V.; A.B., U. Mont., 1947; LL.B., George Washington U., 1950; m. Camilla Fox McCormick, May 26, 1946 (div. 1969); children—Margaret Breckinridge, Katherine McCormick, Angela Fox, Mary Camilla Dudley. Admitted to Mont. bar. 1950; partner firm Toole, Leaphart and Vance, Missoula, 1950-52, Marchi, Sullivan, Vance and Leaphart, Helena, 1954, Vance and Leaphart, Helena, 1959-67; asso. prof. Sch. Law, U. N.D., 1966-67; mem. U.S. Indian Claims Commn., 1967-78, chmn., 1968-69; prof. law U. Toledo, 1978—; dep. county atty., Missoula, 1954; counsel Mont. Trade Commn., 1954-63; city atty., Helena, 1964-66. Sec. bd. mgrs., Chevy Chase, Md., 1948-50; commnr. pub. safety, Missoula, 1952-54; comdr. Mont. wing Civil Air Patrol, 1959-62, comdr. Rocky Mountain region, 1963-65. Served with AUS, 1942-46. Mem. Am., Mont. bar assns., Phi Delta Phi, Sigma Chi. Democrat. Presbyterian. Clubs: Metropolitan, Nat. Capital Democratic (Washington). Office: Coll Law U Toledo 2801 W Bancroft St Toledo OH 43606

VANCE, LEE, publishing co. exec.; b. Fremont, Nebr., Jan. 21, 1907; s. Clarence Warren and Rachel (Lee) V.; B.A., U. Nebr.. 1928; m. Frances Elizabeth Cook, Aug. 16, 1938; children—Judith Lee (Mrs. Wayne L. Earl), Patricia Lee (Mrs. Gerald R. Delaney). Mem. advt. dept. DuPont Cellophane Co., N.Y.C., 1928-32; sales promotion dept. Gugler Co., Milw., 1932-38; with David C. Cook Pub. Co., Elgin, Ill., 1938—, gen. mgr., 1944-76, pres., 1976—. Presbyterian. Clubs: Univ. (Chgo.); Barrington Hills Country; Fox River Valley Hunt. Office: 850 N Grove Ave Elgin IL 60120

VANCE, ROBERT SMITH, fed. judge; b. Talladega, Ala., May 10, 1931; s. Harrell Taylor and Mae (Smith) V.; B.S., U. Ala., 1950, J.D., 1952; LL.M., George Washington U., 1955; m. Helen Rainey, Oct. 4, 1953; children—Robert Smith, Charles R. Partner firm Vance, Thompson & Brown, Birmingham, Ala., 1956-77; U.S. circuit judge U.S. Ct. Appeals for 5th Circuit, Birmingham, 1978—; lectr. Cumberland Sch. Law, Samford U., 1967-69. Chmn., Ala. Democratic Com., 1966-77; pres. Nat. Assn. Dem. State Chairmen, 1973-75. Served to 1st lt. AUS, 1952-54. Fellow Internat. Soc. Barristers; mem. Am., Ala., Birmingham bar assns., Am. Judicature Soc., Newcomen Soc. N.Am., Omicron Delta Kappa, Beta Gamma Sigma, Delta Chi. Episcopalian. Clubs: Birmingham Kennel, Heart of Ala. Great Dane, Am. Saluki Assn. Home: 2824 Shook Hill Rd Birmingham AL 35223 Office: US Courthouse Birmingham AL 35203

VANCE, SHELDON BAIRD, lawyer, former diplomat; b. Crookston, Minn., Jan. 18, 1917; s. Erskine Ward and Helen (Baird) V.; A.B., Carleton Coll., 1939; J.D., Harvard, 1942; m. Jean Chambers, Dec. 28, 1939; children—Robert Clarke and Stephen Baird. Admitted to Mass. bar, 1942, also U.S. Supreme Ct. bar, D.C. bar, 1977; practiced in Boston, 1942; asso. firm Ropes, Gray, Best, Coolidge & Rugg; joined Fgn. Service; econ. analyst, 3d sec. Am. embassy, Rio de Janeiro, Brazil, 1942-46; U.S. vice consul, Nice, France and Monaco, 1946-49; U.S. consul, Martinique, W.I., 1949-51; Belgium-Luxemburg desk officer Dept. State, Washington, 1951-54, 1st sec. Am. embassy, Brussels, Belgium, 1954-58, chief personnel placement br. for Africa, Middle East and South Asia, 1958-60, student Sr. Seminar in Fgn. Relations, 1960-61, dir. Office Central African Affairs, 1961-62; dep. chief mission Am. embassy, Addis Ababa, Ethiopia, 1962-66; sr. fgn. service insp., 1966-67; U.S. ambassador to Republic of Chad, 1967-69, to Republic of Zaire, Kinshasa, 1969-74, career minister, 1971; sr. adviser to sec. state, coordinator internat. narcotics matters, also exec. dir. President's Cabinet Com. on Internat. Narcotics Control, Dept. State, 1974-77; partner firm Vance & Joyce, Washington, 1977—; dir. Sun Co., Inc., Radnor, Pa. Mem. Am., Fed., Mass. bar assns., Nat. Lawyers Club, Fgn. Service Assn. Presbyterian. Club: Columbia Country (Chevy Chase, Md.). Home: 8510 Lynwood Pl Chevy Chase MD 20015 Office: 1701 Pennsylvania Ave NW Washington DC 20006

VANCE, STANLEY CHARLES, educator; b. Minersville, Pa., May 5, 1915; s. Stanley and Margaret (Zelin) V.; A.B., St. Charles Sem., 1937, M.A., U. Pa., 1944, Ph.D., 1951; m. Regina Dober, Mar. 4, 1946. Instr., U. Pa., 1945-47; asst. prof. U. Conn., 1947-52; prof. U. Mass., 1952-56; dean Coll. Bus. Adminstrn., Kent State U., 1956-60; H.T. Miner prof. bus. adminstrn. U. Oreg., Eugene, 1960-75, head dept. personnel and indsl. mgmt., 1963-71, also acting dean Coll. Bus. Adminstrn.; William B. Stokely prof. mgmt. U. Tenn., Knoxville, 1975—. Mem. nat. council Nat. Planning Assn.; bd. dirs., pres. Inst. Adminstrv. Research. Mem. Eugene Budget Com. Fellow Nat. Acad. Mgmt. (pres. Western div., editor Jour. 1966-70, Newsletter 1971—, pres. 1975—), Internat. Acad. Mgmt.; mem. C. of C., A.I.M., Am.

Soc. Personnel Adminstrn., N.Am. Simulation and Gaming Assn. (dir.), Assn. for Bus. Simulation and Exptl. Learning (pres.), N.Am. Simulation and Gaming Assn. (gov.), Dirs. Council Corp. Bds., Nat. Assn. Corp. Dirs. Rotarian. Author: American Industries, 1955; Industrial Administration, 1959; Management Decision Simulation, 1960; Industrial Structure and Policy, 1961; Quantitative Techniques for Operations Management, 1962; Board of Directors Structure and Performance, 1964; The Corporate Director, 1968; Managers and Mergers, 1971. Editor book revs. Dirs. and Bds. Home: 1701 Cherokee Blvd Knoxville TN 37919

VANCE, WILLIAM SILAS, educator; b. Paradise, Tex., Feb. 14, 1901; s. Edward F. and Mary (Gunn) V.; A.B., Baylor U., 1922; A.M., Harvard, 1927; Ph.D., Chgo., 1941; m. Eleanor Graham, Nov. 22, 1945; children—Eleanor Margaret, Dale Lines. Asst. prof. English, Westminster Coll. (Pa.), 1926-28, asst. prof. English, Baylor U., 1929-31; instr. Northeastern U., 1932-36; asso. prof. English, Howard Coll. (Ala.), 1936-40; prof. English, Edinburg (Tex.) Coll. (now Pan-Am. U., 1941-46, 56—; head dept. speech, journalism and English, Northwestern State Coll., Alva, Okla., 1946-56. Bd. dirs. Urban Renewal. Mem. A.A.U.P., N.E.A., Nat. Council Tchrs. English. Independent. Author: Carlyle and Whitman (monograph), 1944. Contbr. to Folklore of Texan Cultures, 1974; also articles to scholarly and lit. mags. Home: 109 Austin Blvd Edinburg TX 78539

VANCIL, RICHARD FRANKLIN, educator, mgmt. cons.; b. St. Louis, Sept. 17, 1931; s. George K. and Pearl M. (Cochran) V.; B.S., Northwestern U., 1953; M.B.A., Harvard U., 1955, D.B.A., 1960; m. Emily Robinson, June 17, 1955; children—Robinson C., Richard C., Virginia. Mem. faculty Harvard Bus. Sch., 1958—, prof., 1968—, Lovett-Learned prof., 1977—; chmn. bd. Mgmt. Analysis Center, Cambridge, Mass., 1964—, The Terradux Co., Inc., 1978—. dir. Conn. Gen. Ins. Co., Trustee, Joslin Diabetes Found., Boston, 1965—. Served as lt. Fin. Corps, U.S. Army, 1955-58. C.P.A., Mass. Mem. Am. Inst. C.P.A.'s, Fin. Execs. Inst. Author: (with Treynor) Machine Tool Leasing, 1956; (with Harlan) Cases in Accounting Policy, 1961; (with Harlan and Christenson) Managerial Economics Text and Cases, 1962, rev. edit. (with Christenson and Marshall), 1973; (with Vandell) Cases in Capital Budgeting, 1962; Leasing of Industrial Equipment, 1963; (with Buzzell and Salmon) Product Profitability Measurement and Merchandising Decisions, 1965; (with de Vos) Cost Analysis for Pricing and Distribution Policies, 1965, Analysis for Purchase or Sale of a Business, 1967; (with Glover) Management of Transformation, 1968; (with Anthony and Dearden) Management Control Systems, rev. edit., 1972; (with Bruns) A Primer on Replacement Cost Accounting, 1976; (with Lorange) Strategic Planning Systems, 1977; Decentralization: Managerial Ambiguity by Design, 1979; others; contbr. articles to profl. jours. Home: 12 Lambert Rd Belmont MA 02178

VANCISIN, JOSEPH RICHARD, sports assn. exec.; b. Bridgeport, Conn., June 14, 1922; s. Stephen and Susan V.; B.A., Dartmouth Coll., 1944; M.A., U. Minn., 1956; m. Elizabeth Ann Butler, Apr. 21, 1951; children—Richard, Susan. Supr. Joseph Seagram & Sons, Relay, Md., 1946-47; asst. basketball coach U. Mich., 1947-48; asst. coach basketball and baseball U. Minn., 1948-56; head basketball coach Yale U., 1956-75, dir. Yale Golf Course, 1971-74; exec. dir. Nat. Assn. Basketball Coachs U.S., Branford, Conn., 1975—; trustee Basketball Hall of Fame; mgr. 1976 Olympic Basketball; chief of mission Intercontinental Cup.; asso. fellow Morse Coll., Yale U., Trustee, First Baptist Ch., Branford. Served as cpl. SAC, USAF. Mem. Am. Basketball Assn.-U.S.A., Dartmouth Alumni Assn., Nat. Assn. Basketball Coaches (pres. 1973-74), Beta Theta Pi. Club: Kiwanis. Editor Basketball Bull., 1975—. Office: 12 Pine Orchard Rd Branford CT 06405

VAN CITTERS, ROBERT LEE, physician, dean med. sch.; b. Alton, Iowa, Jan. 20, 1926; s. Charles J. and Wilhelmina (Heemstra) Van C.; A.B., U. Kans., 1949, M.D., 1953; m. Mary Ellen Barker, Apr. 9, 1949; children—Robert, Mary, David, Sarah Mary. Intern, U. Kans. Med. Center, Kansas City, 1953-54, Nat. Heart Inst. research fellow, 1955-56, resident internal medicine, 1957-58; trainee Nat. Heart Inst., USPHS, Kansas City, 1956-57; spl. research fellow NIH Cardiovascular Tng. Program physiology and biophysics U. Wash. Sch. Medicine at Seattle, 1958-59, postdoctoral research fellow, 1959-62, asst. prof. physiology and biophysics, 1963-65, Robert L. King chair cardiovascular research, 1963-68, core staff Regional Primate Research Center, 1964-68, asso. prof., 1965-70, prof. medicine, 1970—, prof. physiology and biophysics, 1970—, asso. dean, 1968-70, dean, 1970—, chmn. bd. health scis., 1970, dir. Cardiovascular Research Tng. Center. Research asso. Cardiopulmonary Inst., Scripps Clinic and Research Found., La Jolla, Calif., 1962; exchange scientist Joint U.S.-USSR Sci. Exchange Agreement, 1962; mem. various comms. NIH, 1967—; mem. spl. med. adv. com. VA, 1974—. Served with USAF, 1954-55. Fellow Am. Coll. Cardiology; mem. Am., Wash. heart assns., Am. Physiol. Soc., Am. Fedn. Clin. Research, AAAS, N.Y. Acad. Scis., Am. Assn. Med. Colls. (exec. council 1975—, various coms.), Inst. Medicine, Nat. Acad. Scis. Contbr. articles to profl. jours. Home: 9131 184th St SW Edmonds WA 98020 Office: Wash Sch Medicine Seattle WA 98195

VAN CLEEF, LEE, actor; b. Somerville, N.J., Jan. 9, 1925; s. Clarence LeRoy and Marion Levinia (Van Fleet) Van C.; student pub. schs., Sommerville; m. Barbara Hevelone, July 13, 1976; children by previous marriage—Alan, Deborah, David. Farm worker, N.J., 1942, 46; pvt. practice accounting, Somerville, 1946-50; motion picture actor, 1950—; appeared in: For A Few Dollars More, 1967, The Good, the Bad and the Ugly, 1967, El Condor, 1970, The Magnificent Seven Ride, 1972, Return of Sabata, 1971, The Stranger and the Gunfighter, 1976. Served with USN, 1942-46. Mem. Screen Actors Guild, Acad. Motion Picture Arts and Scis. Office: care Beakel and Jennings Agency 427 N Canon Dr Suite 205 Beverly Hills CA 90210*

VAN CLEVE, RUTH GILL, govt. ofcl.; b. Mpls., July 28, 1925; d. Raymond S. and Ruth (Sevon) Gill; student U. Minn., 1943; A.B. magna cum laude, Mt. Holyoke Coll., 1946, LL.D., 1976; LL.B., Yale, 1950; m. Harry R. Van Cleve, Jr., May 16, 1952; children—John Gill, Elizabeth Webster, David Hamilton Livingston. Intern Nat. Inst. Pub. Affairs, 1946-47; admitted to D.C. and Minn. bars, 1950; atty. Dept. Interior, 1950-54, asst. solicitor, 1954-64, dir. Office Territories, 1964-69, dir. Office Territorial Affairs, 1977—; atty. FPC, 1969-75, asst. gen. counsel, 1975-77. Trustee Mt. Holyoke Coll. Recipient Fed. Woman's award, 1966, Distinguished Service award Dept. Interior, 1968. Mem. Phi Beta Kappa. Unitarian. Author: The Office of Territorial Affairs, 1974. Home: 4400 Emory St Alexandria VA 22312 Office: Dept Interior Washington DC 20240

VAN COETSEM, FRANS CAMILLE CORNELIS, educator; b. Grammont, Belgium, Apr. 14, 1919; s. Paul and Helene (De Lil) van C.; Ph.D., U. Louvain (Belgium), 1952; m. Juliette De Bodt, Dec. 30, 1947; children-Paul, Anne-Marie. Came to U.S., 1968, naturalized, 1974. Research on Dutch Dictionary, Leiden, The Netherlands, 1947-57; asso. prof. U. Louvain, 1957-61, prof. 1961-67; prof. U. Leiden, 1963-68; vis. prof. Cornell U., 1965-66, prof. linguistics, 1968—; vis. prof. U. Vienna, spring 1976. Served with Belgium Army, 1945. Mem. Royal Netherlands Acad. Scis. Author books articles in field. Home: 329 Winthrop Dr Ithaca NY 14850

VAN DAM, HEIMAN, psychoanalyst; b. Leiden, The Netherlands, Feb. 5, 1920; s. Machiel and Rika (Knorringa) van D.; A.B., U. So. Calif., 1942, M.D., 1945; m. Barbara C. Strona, Oct. 6, 1945; children—Machiel, Claire Ilena, Rika Rosemary. Fellowship child psychiatry Pasadena (Calif.) Child Guidance Clinic, 1950; gen. practice psychiatry and psychoanalysis, Los Angeles, 1951—; instr. Los Angeles Psychoanalytic Inst., 1959—, co-chmn. com. on child psychoanalysis, 1960-67, tng. and supervising psychoanalyst, 1972—; cons. Reiss Davis Child Study Center, 1955-76, Neighborhood Youth Assn., Los Angeles, 1964-69; asso. clin. prof. psychiatry U. Calif. at Los Angeles Sch. Medicine, 1960—; vis. supr. child psychoanalysis San Francisco Psychoanalytic Inst., 1969—. Mem. adv. bd. Western State U. Coll. Law, Fullerton, Calif., 1965—. Trustee, mem. edn. com. Center for Early Edn., 1964—, v.p., 1978-79; bd. dirs. Child Devel. and Psychotherapy Tng. Program, Los Angeles, 1975—, pres., 1975-77. Served to capt. M.C., AUS, 1946-48. Mem. Am. Psychoanalytic Assn. (mem. com. on ethics 1977—), Assn. Child Psychoanalysis (councillor 1966-69, sec. 1972-74), Phi Beta Kappa. Contbr. articles to profl. jours. Office: 941 Westwood Blvd Los Angeles CA 90024

VANDAM, LEROY DAVID, physician, educator; b. N.Y.C., Jan. 19, 1914; s. Albert Herman and Esther (Cowan) V.; Ph.B., Brown U., 1934; M.D., N.Y.U., 1938; M.A. (hon.), Harvard, 1967; m. Regina Phyllis Rutherford, Nov. 30, 1939; children—Albert Rutherford, Samuel Whiting. Intern Beth Israel Hosp., Boston, 1938-40, resident, 1940-43; practice medicine, specializing in anesthesiology, Boston, 1954—; dir. dept. anesthesia Peter Bent Brigham Hosp., 1954—; mem. faculty Med. Sch. Harvard, 1954—, prof. anesthesia, 1967—. Chmn. subcom. on anesthesia NRC, 1965—; mem. various coms. NIH, 1963—. Mem. AMA, Am. Assn. Anesthesiologists, Assn. U. Anesthetists, Halsted Soc., Horace Wells Soc., Phi Beta Kappa, Sigma Xi, Alpha Omega Alpha. Author: (with R.D. Dripps, J.E. Eckenhoff) Introduction to Anesthesia, 1957; The Physiology and Clinical Pharmacology of Anesthetic Administration, 1965. Editor-in chief: Anesthesiology, 1962—. Contbr. articles to profl. jours. Home: 11 Holly Rd Waban MA 02168 Office: 721 Huntington Ave Boston MA 02115

VAN DEERLIN, LIONEL, Congressman; b. Los Angeles, July 25, 1914; s. Lionel and Gladys Mary (Young) Van D.; B.A. in Journalism, U. So. Calif., 1937; m. Mary Jo Smith, Oct. 8, 1940; children—Lionel James, Lawson John, Victoria, Elizabeth Louise, Mary Susan, Lawrence Jeffrey. Formerly reporter, editor San Diego Sun, Mpls. Tribune, Balt. Evening Sun, Stars and Stripes in MTO, San Diego Jour.; news dir. stas. KOGO and XETV, San Diego; contbg. editor San Diego mag.; mem. 88th-92d Congresses from 37th Dist. Calif., 93d Congress from 41st Dist. Calif., 94th-96th Congresses from 42d Dist. Calif., mem. com. on interstate and fgn. commerce, chmn. subcom. on communications. Democratic candidate for Congress, 1952, 58. Mem. San Diego Newspaper Guild (pres. 1948), Sigma Delta Chi, Sigma Alpha Epsilon. Episcopalian. Office: 2408 Rayburn Office Bldg Washington DC 20515*

VANDE HEY, JAMES MICHAEL, bus. exec., ret. air force officer; b. Maribel, Wis., Mar. 15, 1916; s. William Henry and Anna (Zimmerman) VandeH.; student U. Wis., 1947-49; B.A., U. Philippines, 1955; postgrad. Air War Coll., Maxwell AFB, Montgomery, Ala., 1956-57; m. Jean Margretta Schilleman, June 23, 1944; children—James Todd, Dale Michael, Dean Clark. Commd. 2d lt. USAAF, 1941, advanced through grades to brig. gen. USAF, 1967; fighter pilot PTO, 1941-45, including Hawaii, 1941; duty in command and USAF level including duty in Europe (NATO) and Philippines, 1945-69; dep. chief of staff Hdqrs. USMACV, Saigon, Vietnam, 1969-71; assigned Hdqrs. Tactical Air Command, 1971—; mem. faculty Air War Coll., 1957-59, dep. for academics, dean of faculty, 1959-61; ret., 1971; pres. Vanson Inc., 1971—. Decorated D.S.M., Legion of Merit with oak leaf cluster, D.F.C. with oak leaf cluster, Bronze Star, Air medal with 7 oak leaf clusters, decorations from Philippine, Vietnamese and Korean govts. Mem. USAF Hist. Found., Air Force Assn., Order of Daedalians, Sertoma. Roman Catholic. Clubs: Rotary, Elks. Home: 426 Eagle St Austin TX 78734 Office: 1200 Lakeway Austin TX 78734

VANDE LINDE, VERNON DAVID, univ. adminstr., elec. engr.; b. Charleston, W.Va., Aug. 9, 1942; s. Vernon Geno and Ava Mae (Scott) Vande L.; B.S., Carnegie-Mellon U., 1964, M.S., 1965, Ph.D., 1968; m. Marjorie Ann Park, Aug. 29, 1964; children—Robert Scott, Karen Elizabeth (dec.). Asst. prof. elec. engring. Johns Hopkins U., 1967-74, asso. prof., 1974-77, prof., 1977—, dean Sch. Engring., 1978—. Mem. IEEE (sr.), Soc. Indsl. and Applied Math., Am. Soc. Engring. Edn. Home: 605 W 40th St Baltimore MD 21211 Office: Johns Hopkins U Charles and 34th Sts Baltimore MD 21218

VANDELL, ROBERT FRANK, educator; b. Bklyn., June 22, 1928; s. Frank R. and Marjorie Drew (Pritchett) V.; B.S., Yale U., 1950; M.B.A., Harvard U., 1952, D.B.A., 1958; m. Margaret Edwards, Sept. 4, 1954; children—Robert Charles, Barbara Drew, Warren Edwards. Mem. faculty Harvard U. Bus. Sch., 1954-64, asso. prof., until 1964; prof. Darden Grad. Sch. Bus. Adminstrn., U. Va., Charlottesville, 1964-69, 70—, now Charles C. Abbott prof.; prof. Mgmt. Devel. Inst., Lausanne, Switzerland, 1969-70; research dir. Fin. Analyst Research Found.; dir. Landmark Communications, Inc.; prin. MAC Inc. Mem. pension adv. com. Va. State Retirement System. Served with AUS. Mem. Fin. Mgmt. Assn. (v.p., dir., program chmn. 1978), Eastern (dir.), So., Midwestern fin. assns. Episcopalian. Co-author: Case Problems in Finance, 1961; Cases in Capital Budgeting, 1961. Contbr. profl. jours. Home: 106 Cavalier Dr Charlottesville VA 22901 Office: Box 6550 Charlottesville VA 22906

VAN DELLEN, THEODORE ROBERT, physician, educator; b. Chgo., Aug. 15, 1911; s. Robert Lubert and Nettie (Ten Houten) Van D.; B.S., Northwestern U., 1933, M.D., 1936, M.S., 1939; m. Janet Wabich Fritzel, July 28, 1966; children by previous marriage—Theodore Robert, Jane, Julie Ann. Fellow in medicine Med. Sch., Northwestern U., 1937-40, instr. medicine, 1940-41, asso. medicine, 1941-47, asst. prof. medicine, 1947-49, asso. prof., 1949—, asst. dean Med. Sch., 1949—, head cardiac clinic, 1944-51; med. editor and dir. Chgo. Tribune, 1945-77; attending physician Passavant Pavilion of Northwestern Meml. Hosp.; sr. cons. internal medicine Hines VA Hosp. cons. internal medicine Ill. Pub. Aid Commn., 1950-59; mem. adv. com. on narcotics Ill. Dept. Pub. Health, 1951-52; mem. Ill. Hosp. Licensing Bd., 1954-70; mem. Chgo. Bd. Health, 1974-75; mem., v.p. Municipal Tb Sanitarium, 1969-74. Chmn. sports medicine com. Chgo. Pan. Am. Games. Mem. bd. regents Nat. Library Medicine, 1959-63. Served as 1st lt. M.C., AUS, 1942-43. Recipient Distinguished Service award Am. Med. Writers Assn., 1958. Diplomate Am. Bd. Internal Medicine, 1942, in cardiovascular, 1944. Fellow A.C.P., Am. Coll. Dentistry; mem. Am. Fedn. Clin. Research, Am. Heart Assn., AMA, Central Soc. Clin. Research, Ill., Chgo. (pres. 1961) med. socs., Chgo. Heart Assn. (bd. govs. 1951—), Chgo. Soc. Internal Medicine, Am. Med. Writers Assn. (pres. 1960-61), Inst. Med. Chgo. (dir.), Indsl. Med. Assn., Billings Med. and Med. Dirs. clubs, Northwestern U. Alumni Assn. (pres. 1956-57, life regent 1961), Nat. Assn. Sci. Writers, Sigma Delta Chi, Delta Tau Delta, Nu Sigma Nu, Pi Kappa Epsilon. Clubs: Lake Zurich Golf; Tavern, Arts (Chgo.). Editor Illinois Medical Jour., 1959-77. Contbr. articles to med. jours. Home: 5200 Brittany Dr S St Petersburg FL 33715 Office: 435 N Michigan Ave Chicago IL 60611

VAN DE MAELE, ALBERT CAMILLE LOUIS, business exec.; b. Ghent, Belgium, Nov. 24, 1914; s. Rene and Honorine (Slachmuylders) Van de M.; Licencie Sciences Commerciales Financieres et Consulaires, Inst. Superieur Commerce, Antwerp, 1935; m. Joan Florence Guggenheim, Aug. 1, 1947. Came to U.S., 1939, naturalized, 1942. Asst. to v.p. in charge finance Sofina Co., Brussels, Belgium, 1935-39; treas. Amitas, Ltd. (affiliate of Sofina Co.), N.Y.C., 1940-41; v.p. Amitas, Inc., 1946-48, pres., 1948-51; partner Guggenheim Bros., 1952—; vice-chmn. bd. Motor Parts Industries, Huntington, N.Y.; dir., pres. Anglo Co., Ltd.; chmn. bd. R.L. Manning Co., Denver; dir. Nabors Drilling Ltd., Calgary, Alta., Can. Printex Corp., Mountain View, Calif. Bd. dirs. Daniel and Florence Guggenheim Found., N.Y.C. Served as 1st lt., M.I., AUS, 1942-45. Mem. Pan Am. Soc. (dir.). Clubs: Met., River (N.Y.C.).

VAN DEMARK, NOLAND LEROY, physiologist, educator; b. Columbus Grove, Ohio, July 6, 1919; s. Daniel Leroy and Mary Frances (Bogart) VanD.; B.S., Ohio State U., 1941, M.S., 1942; Ph.D., Cornell U., 1948; m. Beda Alta Basinger, Aug. 18, 1940; children—Gary Lee, Judy Beth, Linda Kay. Asst. animal husbandry Ohio State U., 1941-42; vitamin chemist, div. plant industry Ohio Dept. Agr., 1942; livestock specialist U.S. Allied Commn. Austria, 1946-47; asst. animal husbandry Cornell U., 1942-44, 48; from asst. prof. to prof. physiology, dept. dairy sci. U. Ill., 1948-64; prof. dairy sci., chmn. dept. Ohio State U. and Ohio Agrl. Research and Devel. Center, 1964-73; dir. research N.Y. State Coll. Agr. and Life Scis., dir. Cornell U. Agr. Expt. Sta., Ithaca, 1974—. Cons. on reproductive biology study sect. Nat. Inst. Child Health, 1966-70. Mem. bd. Community Sch. Dist. 4, Champaign, Ill., 1956-64. Served to 2d lt., inf. and CIC, AUS, 1944-46. Recipient Borden award in dairy sci., 1959; Alpha Zeta Outstanding Agr. Tchr. award U. Ill., 1960; Italian Master Pioneer Gold Medal award 5th Internat. Congress Reprodn., Trento, 1964; Ivanov Centennial medal (Russia), 1975. Fellow AAAS; mem. Am. Physiol. Soc., Soc. Study Fertility, Am. Dairy Sci. Assn. (chmn. prodn. sect. 1969-70, dir. 1971-74), Soc. for Study Reprodn. (v.p. 1968-69, pres. 1969-70, dir. 1970-71), Am. Soc. Animal Sci., Sigma Xi, Gamma Sigma Delta. Methodist (lay leader). Author: (with G. W. Salisbury) Physiology of Reproduction and Artificial Insemination of Cattle, 1961, 78; co-editor, contbr. to The Testis, 3 vols., 1970. Office: 292 Roberts Hall Cornell University Ithaca NY 14853

VAN DEMARK, ROBERT EUGENE, orthopedic surgeon; b. Alexandria, S.D., Nov. 14, 1913; s. Walter Eugene and Esther Ruth (Marble) Van D.; B.S., U. S.D., 1936; A.B., Sioux Falls (S.D.) Coll., 1937; M.B., Northwestern U., 1938, M.D., 1939; M.S. in Orthopedic Surgery, U. Minn., 1943; m. Bertie Thompson, Dec. 28, 1940; children—Ruth Elaine, Robert, Richard. Intern, Passavant Meml. Hosp., Chgo., 1938-39; fellow orthopedic surgery Mayo Found., 1939-43; 1st asst. orthopedic surgery Mayo Clinic, 1942-43; orthopedic surgeon, Sioux Falls, 1946—; attending orthopedic surgeon McKennan Hosp., pres. med. staff, 1954, 70; attending orthopedic surgeon Sioux Valley Hosp., pres. staff, 1951-52; clin. prof. orthopedic surgery U. S.D., 1953—; med. dir. Crippled Children's Hosp. and Sch.; chief hand surgery clinic VA Hosp., Sioux Falls. Served from lt. to maj. U.S. Army, 1943-46. Recipient Humanitarian Service award United Cerebral Palsy, 1976; Alumni Achievement award U. S.D., 1977; Disting. Citizen award S.D. Press Assn., 1978. Diplomate Am. Bd. Orthopedic Surgery. Fellow A.C.S. (pres. S.D. chpt. 1952, 53); mem. Am. Assn. Med. Colls., Assn. Orthopaedic Chairmen, Am. Acad. Orthopedic Surgery, Clin. Orthopedic Soc., Am. Assn. Hand Surgery, Assn. Mil. Surgeons U.S., Am. Acad. Cerebral Palsy, S.D. Med. Assn. (pres. 1974-75, Robins award for outstanding community service 1971), Sioux Falls Dist. Med. Soc., SAR, 500 1st Families Am., Sigma Xi, Alpha Omega Alpha, Phi Chi. Lutheran. Clubs: Optimist; Minnehaha Country. Editor: S.D. Jour. Medicine. Contbr. articles to med. jours. Home: 2803 Ridgeview Way Sioux Falls SD 57105 Office: 1301 S 9th Ave Sioux Falls SD 57105

VANDEMARK, ROBERT GOODYEAR, retail co. exec.; b. Youngstown, Ohio, Sept. 1, 1921; s. Arthur Glenn and Lola (Goodyear) V.; B.Sc., Ohio U., 1943; m. Jean Chapman, Sept. 19, 1943; children—Ann (Mrs. William K. Butler), Peggy Lynn (Mrs. Michael Murray). Dept. mgr. F. & R. Lazarus, Columbus, Ohio, 1947-54; asst. controller Boston Store, Milw., 1954-57; v.p., treas. Cleland Simpson Co., Scranton, Pa., 1957-65; asst. to exec. v.p. Bergdorf Goodman, N.Y.C., 1965-68; treas. Garfinckel, Brooks Bros., Miller & Rhoads, Inc., Washington, 1968-69, v.p., 1969-73, exec. v.p., 1973—, also dir. Head dept. and specialty stores div. United Fund, Scranton, Pa., 1960-65. Bd. dirs. Goodwill Industries, 1964-65. Served to 1st lt. AUS, 1943-46; col. Res. Decorated Bronze Star with V and cluster, Mil. Order of Wilheim. Mem. Fin. Execs. Inst., Nat. Retail Mchts. Assn. (sec., treas., 1st v.p., pres., dir., mem. exec. com. financial exec. div.), Delta Tau Delta. Mason (32 deg.), Kiwanian. Clubs: University, Army-Navy (Washington); Springfield Country, Burning Tree Golf. Home: 670 Potomac River Rd McLean VA 22102 Office: 1629 K St NW Washington DC 20006

VAN DEN BERGH, SIDNEY, astronomer; b. Wassenaar, Netherlands, May 20, 1929; s. Sidney J. and Mieke (van den Berg) vandenB.; came to U.S., 1956; student Leiden (Netherlands) U., 1947-48; A.B., Princeton U., 1950; M.Sc., Ohio State U., 1952; Dr. rer. nat., Goettingen U., 1956; m. Gretchen Krause; children—Peter, Mieke, Sabine; Asst. prof. Perkins Obs., Ohio State U., Columbus, 1956-58; research asso. Mt. Wilson Obs., Palomar Obs., Pasadena, Calif., 1968-69; prof. astronomy David Dunlap Obs., U. Toronto (Ont., Can.), 1958-77; dir. Dominion Astrophys. Obs., Victoria, B.C., 1977—. Mem. Am., Royal astron. socs., Royal Soc. Can., Internat. Astron. Union (v.p.). Home: 418 Lands End Rd Sidney BC Canada Office: Dominion Astrophysics Observatory Victoria BC Canada

VANDENBURGH, EDWARD CLINTON, III, lawyer; b. Chgo., Sept. 27, 1915; s. Edward Clinton and Charlotte (Knowles) V.; B.S., Iowa State U., 1937; LL.B., Duke, 1940; M.P.L., John Marshall Law Sch., 1947; m. Mary M. Chandler, 1939; children—Edward C. IV, Lael, Jean, Anne; m. 2d, Beverly A. Hibbot, 1959; children—Lynn, John D. Admitted to Iowa bar, 1940, Ill. bar, 1946, since practiced patent law; mem. firm Darbo & Vandenburgh, 1961—; adj. prof. John Marshall Law Sch., 1959-78. Served with Transp. Corps, AUS, 1944-46. Recipient Jefferson medal for outstanding contbn. to field of patent, trademark and copyright law, 1978. Mem. Am. Patent Law Assn., Am. (editor 1963-69, sec. 1971-73, vice chmn. 1974, chmn. elect 1975, chmn. 1976, patent, trademark and copyright sect.), Ill. bar assns., Patent Law Assn. Chgo., Holland Soc. N.Y. Author: Trademark Law and Procedure, 2d edit., 1968. Contbr. Ency. Patent Practice and Invention Management, 1964. Home: 31 Elizabeth Ln Barrington IL 60010 Office: 120 W Eastman Arlington Heights IL 60006

VAN DEN HEUVEL, STANLEY, banker; b. Yonkers, N.Y., Nov. 10, 1917; s. Antoine Hubert and Elizabeth (Miller) van den H.; A.B., Princeton, 1940; LL.B., Harvard, 1947; m. Margaret Hosack Duff, Feb. 8, 1947; children—Susan, John, Elizabeth. Admitted to N.Y. bar, 1948; asso. firm Barr, Robbins & Palmer, N.Y.C., 1948-55; sec.

Hanover Bank, N.Y.C., 1955-61; v.p., sec. Mfrs. Hanover Trust Co., N.Y.C., 1961—; v.p., sec., dir. Gallatin Co., Inc., Mfrs. Hanover Internat. Finance Corp., Mfrs. Hanover Internat. Banking Corp.; dir., sec. Mfrs. Hanover Bank Internat., Los Angeles; treas., dir. Goodwill Industries Housing Corp., Inc.; v.p., sec. Mfrs. Hanover Corp. Treas., trustee Goodwill Industries Greater N.Y.; hon. sec., trustee Newcomen Soc. N.Am. Served to 2d lt. F.A., AUS, 1941-44; PTO. Home: 300 Hollow Tree Ridge Rd Darien CT 06820 Office: 350 Park Ave New York City NY 10022

VANDEN HEUVEL, WILLIAM J., diplomat; b. Rochester, N.Y., Apr. 14, 1935; s. Joost William and Alberta Marie (Demunter) vanden H.; B.A., Cornell U., 1950, LL.D., 1952; children—Katrina, Wendy. Admitted to N.Y. bar, 1952; asso. firm Leisure Newton Newton & Irvin, 1952-57; exec. asst. to ambassador to Thailand, 1953-54; spl. counsel to gov. N.Y., 1958; asso. firm Javits, Moore & Trubin, 1959-61; spl. asst. to Atty. Gen. U.S., 1963-64; acting regional adminstr. OEO, 1964-65; partner firm Stroock & Stroock & Lavan, 1965-77; U.S. ambassador to European Office UN, Geneva, 1977—. Vice pres. N.Y. State Constl. Conv. 1967; chmn. N.Y.C. Bd. Corrections, 1970-73, N.Y.C. Commn. on State-City Relations, 1971-73; v.p. Internat. Rescue Com.; vice chmn. Internat. League Human Rights; bd. dirs. P.R. Legal Def. and Edn. Fund, Fortune Soc. Co-author: On His Own: RFK, 1964-68. Contbr. articles to profl. jours. Office: 80 rue de Lausanne Geneva Switzerland*

VAN DEN NOORT, STANLEY, physician, coll. dean; b. Lynn, Mass., Sept. 8, 1930; s. Judokus and Hazel G. (Van Blarcom) van den N.; A.B., Dartmouth, 1951; M.D., Harvard, 1954; m. June Le Clere, Apr. 17, 1954; children—Susanne, Eric, Peter, Katherine, Elizabeth. Intern, then resident Boston City Hosp. Med. Center, 1954-56; resident neurology Boston City Hosp., 1958-60; research fellow neurochemistry Harvard, 1960-62; instr. medicine Case Western Res. U., Cleve., 1962-66, asst. prof., 1966-69, asso. prof., 1969-70; prof. neurology U. Calif. at Irvine, 1970—, chief dept. neurology, 1970-72, asso. dean Coll. Medicine, 1972-73, dean, 1973—. Mem. cons. staff St. Joseph Hosp., U. Calif. at Irvine Med. Center; mem. cons. staffs Long Beach (Calif.) Meml. Hosp., Long Beach VA Hosp., Children's Hosp. of Orange County; mem. med. adv. bds. Orange County Epilepsy Soc., 1971—, Nat. Multiple Sclerosis Soc./Myasthenia Gravis, 1971—, Orange County chpt. Nat. Multiple Sclerosis Soc., 1971—; mem. Orange County Health Planning Council, 1971—. Served to lt. MC, USNR, 1956-58. Fellow A.C.P.; mem. A.A.U.P., Am. Assn. Neurology, Am. Neurol. Assn., Am. Assn. Neurol. Surgeons, Calif. Med. Assn., Am. Cancer Soc., Am. Heart Assn. Home: 17592 Orange Tree Tustin CA 92680 Office: Coll of Medicine U of Calif Irvine CA 92664

VANDERBILT, GLORIA MORGAN, artist, actress, fashion designer; b. N.Y.C., Feb. 20, 1924; d. Reginald Claypoole and Gloria (Morgan) Vanderbilt; attended Mary C. Wheeler, Miss Porter's schs.; studied acting with dir. Sanford Meisner, beginning 1955; m. Pasquale di Cicco (div.); m. 2d, Leopold Stokowski, 1945 (div. 1955); children—Stanislaus, Christopher; m. 3d, Sidney Lumet, 1956 (div.); m. 4th, Wyatt Emory Cooper, 1963; children—Carter V., Anderson H. Exhibited in one-man shows at Rabun Studio, N.Y.C., 1948, Bertha Shaeffer Gallery, N.Y.C., 1954, Juster Gallery, N.Y.C., 1956, Hammer Gallery, N.Y.C., 1966, 68, Cord Gallery, N.Y.C., 1966, Washington Gallery Art, 1968, Neiman-Marcus, Dallas, 1968, Vestart Gallery, N.Y.C., 1969, Parish Museum, Southampton, N.Y., also in Nantucket, Mass., Houston, Reading, Pa., Monterey, Calif., Nashville; exhibited in group shows Washington Gallery Art, 1967, Hoover Gallery, San Francisco, 1971; stage career: acted in summer stock prodn. The Swan; made Broadway debut in The Time of Your Life, 1955; other stage appearances include Picnic, 1955, The Spa, 1956, Peter Pan, 1958, The Green Hat; made TV debut in Tonight At 8:30; other TV appearances include Colgate Comedy Hour, 1955, Flint and Fire on U.S. Steel Hour, 1958, Family Happiness on U.S. Steel Hour, 1959, Very Important People; appeared in film Johnny Concho, 1955; dir. design Riegel Textile Corp., N.Y.C., 1970—; designer stationary and greeting cards Hallmark Co.; designer fabrics Bloomcraft Co. designer bed linens Martex Co., table linens Leacock Co., Gloria Vanderbilt jeans, also china, glassware, scarves. Recipient Sylvania award, 1959, Fashion award Neiman-Marcus, 1969. Mem. Actors Equity, Screen Actors Guild, AFTRA, Authors League Am., Am. Fedn. Arts. Author: Love Poems, 1955; (with Alfred Allen Lewis) Gloria Vanderbilt Book of Collage, 1970; Woman to Woman; author play: Three by Two, early 1960's, author poems and short stories. Office: care Murjani USA 498 7th Ave New York NY 10009*

VANDERBILT, KERMIT, educator; b. Decorah, Iowa, Sept. 1, 1925; s. Lester and Ella (Qualley) V.; B.A., Luther Coll., Decorah, 1947, Litt. D. (hon.), 1977; M.A., U. Minn., 1949, Ph.D., 1956; m. Vivian Osmundson, Nov. 15, 1947; 1 dau., Karen Paige. Instr. English, U. Minn., 1954-57; instr. U. Wash., 1958-60, asst. prof. English, 1960-62; asst. prof. San Diego State U., 1962-65, asso. prof., 1965-68, prof., 1968—; vis. prof. Am. lit. U. B.C. (Can.), Vancouver, summer 1963, U. Oreg., summer 1968. Served with USNR, 1943-46. Named Outstanding Prof., San Diego State U., 1976; Guggenheim fellow, 1978-79; Am. Philos. Soc. grantee, 1964; Am. Council Learned Socs. grantee, 1972. Mem. Am. Studies Assn. (exec. council 1968-69), So. Calif. Am. Studies Assn. (pres. 1968-69). Philol. Assn. Pacific Coast (chmn. sect. Am. lit. 1968), MLA, United Profs. of Calif. (Disting. prof. 1978). Author: Charles Eliot Norton: Apostle of Culture in a Democracy, 1959; The Achievement of William Dean Howells: A Reinterpretation, 1968; editor: (with others) American Social Thought, 1972; April Hopes (W.D. Howells), 1975; editorial bd. U. Wash. Press, 1960-62, Twentieth Century Lit., 1969—. Contbr. numerous articles to profl. jours. Home: 6937 Coleshill Dr San Diego CA 92119 Office: English Dept San Diego State U San Diego CA 92182

VANDERBILT, OLIVER DEGRAY, financier; b. N.Y.C., Oct. 25, 1914; s. Oliver DeGray, Jr. and Madelon (Weir) V.; student St. Paul's Sch., Concord, N.H., 1929-33; A.B., Princeton, 1937; m. Frances Philips, Nov. 11, 1939; children—Oliver DeGray IV, Madelon Weir (Mrs. Charles S. Peck). With Tenn. Coal Iron & R.R. Co., Birmingham, Ala., 1939-40; v.p. Weir Kilby Corp., Cin., 1940-49; exec. v.p. Taylor Wharton Iron & Steel Co., Cin., 1949, pres., 1950-54; v.p. Harrisburg Steel Corp., 1954; pres. Twisco Corp., 1954-55; v.p., dir. Baldwin-Lima-Hamilton Corp., 1955-56; exec. v.p., dir. Blair & Co., Inc., Phila., 1957-62, chmn., 1963-70; founder, pres. Vanderbilt Corp., Phila., 1963-68, Capitol Mgmt. Corp., 1968—, Innovest Group, Inc., 1970—; pres., chief exec. officer Ecolaire Inc., 1971-74; founder, pres. Dorsey Corp., 1959, Standard Computers Inc., 1965; founder, chmn. Mfrs. Lease Plans, Inc., 1965, Systems Capital Corp., 1967, Marina City Corp., 1968; founder, chmn. bd. Vanderbilt Energy Corp., N.Y.C., 1978—; founder, chmn. bd. Tierra Corp., San Francisco, 1977—. Bd. dirs. Home of Merciful Savior for Crippled Chidren, Phila., United Cerebral Palsy Assn. Research and Ednl. Found. Served from 2d lt. to maj. AUS, 1942-45; ETO, NATOUSA. Decorated Croix De Guerre (France); Bronze Star medal. Republican. Episcopalian. Clubs: Racquet and Tennis, Links (N.Y.C.); Commonwealth (Cin.); Philadelphia, Racquet, Gulph Mills Golf (Phila.); Ivy, Nassau (Princeton, N.J.); Seminole (Palm Beach, Fla.); Maidstone (Easthampton, N.Y.). Home: 133 Old Gulph Rd Wynnewood PA 19096 Office: 1700 Market St Philadelphia PA 19103

VANDER DUSSEN, NEIL R., mfg. co. exec.; b. Kansas City, Mo., Sept. 22, 1931; s. Herman and Florence (Wallgrave) Vander D.; B.S., Kans. State U., Manhattan, 1955; M.S. (Alfred P. Sloan fellow) M.I.T., Boston, 1970; m. Geraldine McLaughlin, Aug. 9, 1953; children—Cathy, Carol. Mgr. studio equipment engring. and product mgmt. RCA Broadcast Systems, 1970-71; div. v.p., gen. mgr., 1971-77; div. v.p., gen. mgr. Comml. Communications Systems div. RCA, 1977-79, exec. v.p. RCA Corp., N.Y.C., 1979—; dir. RCA Ltd. (Australia), RCA North Ryde Pty. Ltd. (Australia), RCA Ltd. (U.K.), Banquet Foods Corp., Coronet Industries, Inc., Random House, Inc., Oriel Foods Group. Bd. dirs. Inst. Med. Research, 1974—, YMCA Camden County (N.J.), 1975-79, Greater Camden Movement, 1977-79, Camden County council Boy Scouts Am., 1978-79; mem. exec. com. Cooper Med. Center, 1977—. Served to 1st lt. Signal Corps, U.S. Army, 1955-57. Mem. Electronics Industry Assn. (dir. communications div. 1977-79). Club: Tavistock Country (Haddonfield, N.J.). Office: 30 Rockefeller Plaza New York NY 10020

VAN DER EB, HENRY GERARD, packaging co. exec.; b. Hartford, Conn., May 11, 1918; s. Henry Johan and Harriet (Krug) Van der Eb; B.S., Harvard, 1942; m. Janet Susan Land, Sept. 6, 1941; children—Janet Susan Van der Eb Greene, Henry Gerard, Peter Johan. With Container Corp., Am., 1946—, mem. mgmt. com., 1960—, exec. v.p., 1965-68, pres., 1968—, chief exec. officer, 1970—, chmn., 1974—, also dir.; dir. Nat. Blvd. Bank Chgo., Bell & Howell Co., Am. Hosp. Supply Corp., Mobil Corp. Chmn. gen. mfg. sect. Chgo. Crusade of Mercy, 1963; mem. com. on univ. resources Harvard U. Trustee Loomis-Chaffee Sch., 1972-73, Chgo. Zool. Soc.; trustee, chmn. operating bd. Paperboard Packaging Council, 1967; bd. dirs. Nat. Center for Resource Recovery, Inc. Served to lt. USNR, 1942-45. Mem. Folding Paper Box Assn. Am. (pres. 1966-67, dir., exec. com.), Am. Paper Inst. (dir., chmn. 1975-76). Clubs: Harvard (N.Y.C.); Mid-Am., Chicago, Mid-Day, Economic, Commercial, Chicago Commonwealth (Chgo.); Onwentsia (Lake Forest); Old Elm. Home: 811 N Hawthorne Pl Lake Forest IL 60045 Office: One 1st Nat Plaza Chicago IL 60603

VAN DER HEUVEL, GERRY BURCH, journalist; b. Alexandria, Minn.; d. John Selstine and Fay (Whitman) Burch; student Wayne State U., 1940-41, U. Mich., 1941-43; m. Kenneth Van der Heuvel, June 26, 1943 (dec. Mar. 1959); children—Claudia, Heidi, Jon; m. Robert J. Donovan, Mar. 17, 1978. Reporter, UPI, Detroit, Phila., 1943-46; corr. Pat Munroe News Bur., Washington, 1961-63; corr., columnist N.Y. Daily News, N.Y. News-Chgo. Tribune Syndicate, Washington, 1963-65; columnist Newhouse Nat. News Service, Washington, 1965-68; press sec. to Mrs. Richard Nixon, 1968-69; spl. asst. to U.S. ambassador to Italy, 1969-73; assigned to Washington, 1973—. Mem. Women's Nat. Press Club (sec. 1963-64, 1st v.p. 1965-66, pres. 1967-68). Home: 3031 Beechwood Ln Falls Church VA 22042

VANDERHOEF, LARRY NEIL, biologist; b. Perham, Minn., Mar. 20, 1941; s. Wilmar James and Ida Lucille (Wothe) V.; B.S., U. Wis., Milw., 1964, M.S., 1965; Ph.D., Purdue U., 1969; m. Rosalie Suzanne Slifka, Aug. 31, 1963; children—Susan Marie, Jonathan Lee. Postdoctorate, U. Wis., Madison, 1969-70, research asso., summers 1970-72; asst. prof. biology U. Ill., Urbana, 1970-74, asso. prof., 1974-77, prof., 1977—, head dept. botany, 1977—; vis. investigator Carnegie Inst., 1976-77, Edinburgh (Scotland) U., 1978; cons. in field. NRC postdoctoral fellow, 1969-70; Dimond travel grantee, 1975; NSF grantee, 1972, 74, 76, 77, 78, 79. Mem. AAAS, Am. Soc. Plant Physiology (bd. editors Plant Physiology 1977—). Home: 2506 Melrose Dr Champaign IL 61820 Office: 289 Morrill Hall U Ill Urbana IL 61801

VANDERHOOF, IRWIN THOMAS, life ins. co. exec.; b. Newark, Dec. 4, 1927; s. Irwin Arthur and Dora (Blanchard) V.; B.S., Worcester (Mass.) Poly. Inst., 1948; m. Ruth Elizabeth Green, Feb. 18, 1949; children—Thomas Arthur Irwin, Karen McNeill Brundage. Asst. actuarial supr. Met. Life Ins. Co., 1950-54; asst. actuary U.S. Life Ins. Co., 1954-59; exec. v.p., treas. Standard Security Life Ins. Co., 1959-73; sr. v.p. corp. devel. and fin. Equitable Life Assurance Soc. U.S., N.Y.C., 1973—; adj. asso. prof. Coll. Ins. Grad. Sch. Pres. Montville (N.J.) Twp. Bd. Edn., 1962. C.L.U.; chartered fin. analyst. Fellow Soc. Actuaries, Life Officer Mgmt. Inst.; asso. Casualty Actuarial Soc., Inst. Actuaries; mem. N.Y. Soc. Security Analysts. Republican. Episcopalian. Author papers in field. Office: 1285 Ave Americas New York NY 10019

VANDER JAGT, GUY, congressman; b. Cadillac, Mich., Aug. 26, 1931; s. Harry and Marie (Copier) Vander J.; A.B., Hope Coll., 1953; B.D., Yale U., 1957; LL.B., U. Mich., 1960; postgrad. U. Bonn (Germany), 1955-56; m. Carol Doorn, Apr. 4, 1964; 1 dau., Virginia Marie. Admitted to Mich. bar, 1960; practice in Grand Rapids; mem. firm Warner, Norcross & Judd, 1960-64; mem. Mich. Senate, 1964-66; mem. 89th-96th Congresses from 9th Mich. Dist.; mem. ways and means com., trade and select revenue measures subcoms.; chmn. Nat. Republican Congl. Com. Named One of Five Most Outstanding Young Men in Mich., Mich. Jr. C. of C., 1956. Republican. Mem. Hope Coll. Alumni Assn. Washington (pres.). Home: Luther MI 49656 Office: 2334 Rayburn House Office Bldg Washington DC 20515

VAN DER KLOOT, WILLIAM GEORGE, biologist, educator; b. Chgo., Feb. 18, 1927; s. Albert and Pearl (Schoenwerk) Van der K.; S.B., Harvard U., 1948, A.M., 1950, Ph.D., 1952; m. Barbara Wrigley, July 20, 1948 (div. 1963); m. 2d, Diane Munson, June 14, 1963; children—Peter Albert, Thomas Erik. Instr. Harvard U., 1953-56; asst. prof. Cornell U., 1956-57, asso. prof., 1957-58; prof., chmn. dept. pharmacology N.Y. U. Coll. Medicine, 1958-61, prof., chmn. dept. physiology and biophysics, 1961-71; prof., chmn. dept. physiology and biophysics State U. N.Y. at Stony Brook, 1971—, dean Sch. Basic Health Scis., 1976-78; cons. NSF, 1959-64, NIH, 1958—. Mem. Am. Soc. Zoologists, Soc. Exptl. Biology, Am. Physiol. Soc., AAAS. Author: Behavior, 1968; Readings in Behavior, 1974. Asso. editor Jour. Exptl. Zoology, 1967-71. Home: 17 Salt Meadow Ln Stony Brook NY 11790

VAN DER KROEF, JUSTUS MARIA, educator; b. Djakarta, Indonesia, Oct. 30, 1925; s. Hendrikus Leonardus and Maria Wilhelmina (van Lokven) van der K.; came to U.S., 1942, naturalized, 1952; B.A., Millsaps Coll., 1944; M.A., U. N.C., 1947; Ph.D., Columbia, 1953; m. Orell Joan Ellison, Mar. 25, 1955; children—Adrian Hendrick, Sri Orell. Asst. prof. fgn. studies Mich. State U., 1948-55; Charles Dana prof., chmn. dept. polit. sci. U. Bridgeport (Conn.), 1956—; vis. prof. Nanyang U., Singapore, U. Philippines, Quezon City, Vidyodaya U., Ceylon, Colombo; dir. Am.-Asian Ednl. Exchange, 1969—. Chmn. editorial bd. Communications Research Services, Inc., Greenwich, Conn., 1971—; mem. internat. adv. bd. Union Trust Bank, Stamford, Conn., 1974—; mem. nat. acad. adv. council Charles Edison Meml. Youth Fund; bd. dirs. WUBC-TV, Bridgeport, Conn. Served with Royal Netherlands Marine Corps, 1944-45. Sr. fellow Research Inst. Communist Affairs, Columbia, 1965-66; fellow U. Queensland, Brisbane, Australia, 1968-69. Mem. U. Profs. Acad. Order (nat. pres. 1970-71), Pi Gamma Mu, Phi Alpha Theta, Lambda Chi Alpha, Alpha Sigma Lambda. Author: Indonesia in the Modern World, 2 vols., 1954-56; Indonesian Social Evolution. Some Psychological Considerations, 1958; The Communist Party of Indonesia: Its History, Program and Tactics, 1965; Communism in Malaysia and Singapore, 1967; Indonesia Since Sukarno, 1971; The Lives of SEATO, 1976. Editorial bd. World Affairs, 1975—, Jour. Asian Affairs, 1975—; book rev. editor Asian Thought and Soc., 1976—. Home: 165 Linden Ave Bridgeport CT 06602

VANDERLIND, MERWYN RAY, physicist; b. Grand Rapids, Mich., June 30, 1936; s. Marvin and Janet (DeWitt) V.; B.A., Hope Coll., Holland, Mich., 1958; M.S., Ohio U., Athens, 1960, Ph.D., 1964; m. Martha Jane Scott, June 3, 1961; children—Gary Scott, Marcia Ann, Julie Renee. Research scientist Atomics Internat. Co., Canoga Park, Calif., 1960-61; polymer scientist Rohm & Haas Chem. Corp., Phila., 1964-65; mgr. phys. sci. sect. Battelle Meml. Inst., Columbus, Ohio, 1966—; cons. Materials Adv. Bd., Nat. Acad. Engring. NSF fellow, 1963. Mem. Am. Phys. Soc., Am. Inst. Physics. Am. Def. Preparedness Assn., Sigma Xi. Contbr. to profl. publs. Home: 118 Saint Julien Ct Worthington OH 43085 Office: 505 King Ave Columbus OH 43201

VAN DER MARCK, JAN, museum adminstr.; b. Roermond, Netherlands, Aug. 19, 1929; s. Everard and Anny (Finken) van der M.; B.A., U. Nijmegen (Netherlands), 1952, M.A., 1594, Ph.D. in Art History, 1956; postgrad. U. Utrecht (Netherlands), 1956-57, Columbia U., 1957-59; m. Ingeborg Lachmann, Apr. 27, 1961. Curator, Gemeentemuseum, Arnhem, Netherlands, 1959-61; dep. dir. fine arts Seattle World's Fair, 1961-62; curator Walker Art Center, Mpls., 1963-67; dir. Mus. Contemporary Art, Chgo., 1967-70; asso. prof. art history U. Wash., 1972-74; dir. Dartmouth Coll. Mus. and Galleries, 1974—; Netherlands Orgn. Pure Research fellow, 1954-55; Rockefeller Found. fellow, 1957-59. Mem. Am. Assn. Art Mus. Dirs., Am. Found. Arts (nat. exhbn. com.), Internat. Art Critics Assn., Internat. Council Mus.'s, Internat. Com. Modern Mus.'s. Author: Lucio Fontana, 1974; George Segal, 1975; contbr. articles to art jours. Home: Wildwood Dr West Lebanon NH 03784 Office: Dartmouth Coll Mus and Galleries PO Box 6034 Hanover NH 03755

VANDERMARK, ROBERT EARL, banker; b. Bklyn., Feb. 19, 1925; s. Harry J. and Martha E. (Mahoney) V.; grad. Am. Inst. Banking, 1950; B.B.A. cum laude, Adelphi U., 1960; postgrad. Stonier Grad. Sch. Banking, 1963; m. Josephine Blumenberg, Sept. 20, 1947; children—Robert Earl, Lois Jane. With Bank of N.Y., 1941-55; with credit dept. Mobil Oil Co., Inc., N.Y.C., 1955-57; with credit dept. Ft. Neck Nat. Bank, Seaford, N.Y., 1957-58; comml. loan adminstr., sr. v.p. Security Nat. Bank, Melville, N.Y., 1958-74; v.p. Chem. Bank, N.Y.C., 1975—. Served with AUS, 1943-46, U.S. Army, 1950-52. Mem. Robert Morris Assos., Asso. Retail Credit Men of N.Y.C., Huntington C. of C. (dir.), Alpha Sigma Lambda. Club: Elks (trustee) (Huntington). Home: 205 Syosset-Woodbury Rd Syosset NY 11791 Office: 115 Broadhollow Rd Melville NY 11747

VAN DER MEULEN, JOSEPH PIERRE, neurologist; b. Boston, Aug. 22, 1929; s. Edward Lawrence and Sarah Jane (Robertson) VanDer M.; A.B., Boston Coll., 1950; M.D., Boston U., 1954; m. Ann Irene Yadeno, June 18, 1960; children—Elisabeth, Suzanne, Janet. Intern, Cornell Med. div. Bellevue Hosp., N.Y.C., 1954-55, resident, 1955-56; resident Harvard U., Boston City Hosp., 1958-60, instr., fellow, 1962-66; asso. Case Western Res. U., Cleve., 1966-67, asst. prof., 1967-69, asso. prof. neurology and bioned. engring., 1969-71; prof. neurology, chmn. dept. U. So. Calif., Los Angeles, 1971—, also dir. dept. neurology Los Angeles County/U. So. Calif. Med. Center; v.p. for health affairs U. So. Calif., 1977—; vis. prof. Autonomous U. Guadalajara (Mex.), 1974. Mem. med. adv. bd. Calif. chpt. Myasthenia Gravis Found., 1971-75, chmn., 1974-75, 77-78; med. adv. bd. Amyotrophic Lateral Sclerosis Found., Calif., 1973-75, chmn., 1974-75; mem. Com. to Combat Huntington's Disease, 1973—. Served to lt. M.C., USNR, 1956-58. Nobel Inst. fellow Karolinska Inst., Stockholm, 1960-62; NIH grantee, 1968-71; diplomate Am. Bd. Psychiatry and Neurology. Mem. Am. Neurol. Assn., Am. Acad. Neurology, Los Angeles Soc. Neurology and Psychiatry (pres. 1977-78), Mass., Ohio, Calif. med. socs., Los Angeles Acad. Medicine, Alpha Omega Alpha (councillor). Editorial bd. Archives of Neurology. Contbr. articles to profl. jours. Home: 39 Club View Ln Rolling Hills Estates CA 90274 Office: 1200 N State St Los Angeles CA 90033

VANDERMOLEN, MIMI WILLEMINA, indsl. designer; b. Geleen, Netherlands, Apr. 20, 1946; d. John Henderikus and Julia (Hasper) Vandermolen; came to U.S., 1970; Intermediate certificate, John F. Ross Collegiate, 1963; diploma Royal York Collegiate, 1965; diploma Ont. Coll. Art, 1969. Sr. designer Ford Motor Co., Dearborn, Mich., 1970-74, Autodynamic Corp. Am., Madison Heights, Mich., 1974-76; designer Chrysler Corp., Highland Park, Mich., 1976; sr. designer Ford Motor Co., Dearborn, 1977—. Club: Dearborn Racquet. Home: 23123 Lodge Ln Dearborn MI 48128 Office: Ford Motor Co Dearborn MI

VAN DER POEL, CORNELIUS J., educator; b. Oud-Ade, Netherlands, Sept. 19, 1921; s. Jacobus and Laurentia (van der geest) Van der P.; B.A., Holy Ghost Fathers Sem., Weert, Netherlands, 1940; M.A., Theologate Holy Ghost Fathers, Germert, Netherlands, 1946; M.S.Ed., Iona Coll., New Rochelle, N.Y., 1968. Came to U.S., 1962. Prof. theology, Morogoro, Tanzania, 1948-58, Norwalk, Conn., 1963-69; co-dir. Clergy Devel. Center, La Crosse, Wis., 1970-74; dir. Family Life Bur., Detroit, 1974-78; tchr. theology St. John's Sem., Plymouth, Mich., 1975-78; dir. pastoral care St. Michael's Hosp., Stevens Point, Wis., 1978—. Cons. to Del. for the Clergy, Detroit, 1974-78. Mem. Canon Law Soc. Am., Acad. for Pastoral Counselors, Nat. Assn. Social Workers. Author: The Search for Human Values, 1971; Religious Life: A Risk of Love, 1972; God's Love in Human Language, 1969. Contbr. articles to mags. Home: 933 Illinois Ave Stevens Point WI 54481 Office: 900 Illinois Ave Stevens Point WI 54481. *After I began to experience that the utilization of my abilities for the benefit and happiness of others was a major factor for personal growth as well, my life began to take on a value that reaches far beyond myself into the development of others as a participation in God's creative love.*

VANDERPOOL, EUGENE, archaeologist; b. Morristown, N.J., Aug. 3, 1906; s. Wynant Davis and Cornelia Grinnell (Willis) V.; A.B., Princeton U., 1929; s. Joan Jeffery, June 11, 1935; children—Joan Vanderpool Gayley, Ann Vanderpool Levenduski, Eugene, Alice Vanderpool Evert. Fellow, Agora Excavations, Athens, Greece, 1932-49; prof. archaeology Am. Sch. Classical Studies, Athens, 1949-71, prof. emeritus, 1971—; vis. fellow Inst. Advanced Study, Princeton, N.J., 1944, 55. Decorated Greek Order of Phoenix. Mem. Archaeol. Inst. Am. (gold medal for distinguished achievement 1975), German. Archaeol. Inst., Archaeol. Soc. Athens. Republican. Episcopalian. Club: Holland Soc. N.Y. Contbr. articles to profl. jours. Home: 51-55 Kleomenous Athens 140 Greece Office: 54 Souidias Athens 140 Greece

VAN DERPOOL, JAMES GROTE, educator; b. N.Y.C., July 21, 1903; s. Jeremiah Franklin and Lucy (Grote) Van D.; N. Arch., Mass. Inst. Tech., 1927; research student Am. Acad. in Rome (Italy), 1928, Atelier Gromort of Ecole des Beaux Arts, Paris, France, 1929; M.A., Harvard, 1940; m. Margaret Lyons, June 6, 1932; children—Margaret Mary (Mrs. Chas. M. Grace), Van Buren J.L. Asso. with Blackall and Elwell, Boston, 1930-31; instr. history of architecture Rensselaer Poly. Inst., Troy, N.Y., 1931-32; asso. in architecture U. of Ill., 1932-34, asst. prof., 1934-36, asso. prof., 1936-38, prof. history of art and architecture, head of dept. art, 1939-46; head Avery and Associated Fine Arts libraries, prof. Columbia, 1946—, acting dean sch. of architecture, 1959-60, adv. bd. dept. of art history; asso. dean Sch. Architecture, Columbia, 1960-61; v.p. Lenygon and Morant, 1951-62; adviser U.S. Dept. Interior, 1954-60; exec. dir. Landmarks Preservation Commn., N.Y.C., 1962-65; nat. co-chmn. Save Venice Com. Adv. bd. Nat. Trust Lyndhurst, 1965-68, Am. Mus. Folk Arts; trustee Internat. Fund. for Monuments; bd. dirs., nat. co-chmn. Venice com. Dyckman House Mus. Assn. Recip. George McAnemy medal, 1965. Benjamin Franklin fellow, life fellow Royal Soc. Arts (London); Fellow AIA; mem. Holland Soc., Soc. Archtl. Historians (trustee 1949—, past nat. pres.), Am. Scenic and Historic Preservation Soc. (trustee), St. Nicholas Soc., Ulster Co. Hist. Soc. (dir.), Huguenot Soc., Municipal Art Soc. N.Y.C. Baptist. Clubs: Century, Grolier, St. Nicholas (N.Y.C.). Author works fields art and architecture. Contbr. periodicals and encys. Archtl. editor Columbia Ency., 2d edit. Home: 95 Ocean Way Santa Monica CA 90402 also 570 Park Ave New York City NY 10021 also (summer) Hobby Horse Hill Esopus NY 12429

VANDERPOOL, ROBERT LEE, JR., banker; b. Galveston, Tex., Nov. 10, 1918; s. R.L. and Fay (Hussey) V.; student Tex. A. and M. Coll., 1935-36; B.B.A., Tulane U., 1941; m. Mildred F. Loscalzo, Sept. 23, 1946; children—Janet Ann, R.L. III. Vice pres., dir. Citizens State Bank, Dickinson, Tex., 1949-50; v.p. Ouachita Nat. Bank, Monroe, La., 1951-52, pres., 1952—. Chmn. United Givers Fund, 1959-60. Served as lt. comdr. USNR, 1944-45. Mem. Monroe C. of C. (past pres.), La. Bankers Assn. (pres. 1972-73), Sigma Alpha Epsilon. Episcopalian. Clubs: Bayou DeSiard Country (pres. 1960), Lotus (Monroe); Boston (New Orleans). Home: 3410 Loop Rd Monroe LA 71201 Office: 130 DeSiard St Monroe LA 71201

VANDERRYN, JACK, govt. ofcl.; b. Groningen, Netherlands, Apr. 14, 1930; s. Herman Gabriel and Henrietta S.E. (Hartog) V.; came to U.S., 1939; B.A., Lehigh U., 1951, M.S., 1952, Ph.D., 1955; m. Margrit Wolfes, Mar. 18, 1956; children—David, Judith, Amy, Daniel. Research and grad. teaching asst. Lehigh U., Bethlehem, Pa., 1952-55; asst. prof. chemistry Va. Poly. Inst., Blacksburg, 1955-58; research participant Oak Ridge (Tenn.) Nat. Lab., 1957; chemist U.S. AEC, Oak Ridge, 1958-62, tech. adviser to asst. gen mgr. for research and devel., Washington, 1962-67, asst. to gen. mgr., Washington, 1971-72, tech. asst. to dir. div. applied tech., 1972-73, chief energy tech. br., div. applied tech., 1973-75; acting dir. div. energy storage ERDA, 1975, dir. Office Internat. Research and Devel. Programs, 1975-77; dir. Office Internat. Programs Dept. Energy, 1977—. Sr. sci. adviser U.S. Mission to Internat. Atomic Energy Agy., Dept. of State, Vienna, Austria, 1967-71; lectr. Brookings Instn., 1965-66. Mem., dep. pres. exec. bd. Am. Internat. Sch., Vienna, 1968-71; v.p. Oak Ridge Civic Music Assn., 1959-60. Fellow AAAS. Home: 8112 Whittier Blvd Bethesda MD 20034 Office: Dept Energy Washington DC 20585

VANDERSALL, JOHN HENRY, educator; b. Helena, Ohio, July 20, 1928; s. Clarence C. and Ida M. (Barnhope) V.; B.S., Ohio State U., 1950, M.S., 1954, Ph.D., 1959; m. Patricia L. King, May 11, 1963; children—Eric John, Karen Susan. Farm researcher Ralston Purina Co., 1950; from research asst. to instr. Ohio State U. Agrl. Expt. Sta., 1953-59; mem. faculty U. Md., 1959—, prof. diary sci., 1971—. Served with AUS, 1950-52. Mem. Am. Dairy Sci. Assn., Am. Soc. Animal Sci., AAAS, Sigma Xi. Contbr. profl. jours. Home: 10906 Ashfield Rd Adelphi MD 20783 Office: Dept Dairy Sci Univ Md College Park MD 20742

VANDERSLICE, GEORGE F., utility exec.; b. Phila., Mar. 2, 1922; student U. Pa.; LaSalle Coll., U. Mich.; m. Doris M. Vanderslice; children—Robert, William. Prin. accountant Haskins & Sells, Phila., 1945-58, mgr. auditing Pa. Power & Light Co., Allentown, 1958, now v.p., comptroller; v.p., comptroller Hershey Electric Co.; dir. Pa. Mines Co., Interstate Energy Co., Uranium Resources & Devel. Co. C.P.A., Pa. Mem. Am., Pa. insts. C.P.A.'s, Financial Execs. Inst., USCG Aux. (flotilla comdr.). Home: 764 Spruce St Emmaus PA 18049 Office: 2-N 9th St Allentown PA 18101

VANDERSLICE, JOSEPH THOMAS, chemist; b. Phila., Dec. 21, 1927; s. Joseph R. and Mae (Daly) V.; B.S. in Chemistry, Boston Coll., 1949; Ph.D. in Phys. Chemistry (Allied Chem. and Dye fellow), Mass. Inst. Tech., 1953; m. Patricia Mary Horstmann, Nov. 20, 1954; children—Sharon, Joseph, Julie, Peter, John, Polly, Jeffrey, Amy. Mem. faculty Cath. U. Am., 1952-56, asst. prof., 1955-56; mem. faculty U. Md., College Park, 1956-79, prof. chem. physics, 1963-79, dir. Inst. Molecular Physics, 1967-69, chmn. chemistry dept., 1968-76; research chemist Nutrition Inst., U.S. Dept. Agr., Beltsville, Md., 1978—. Recipient Disting. Alumni award Boston Coll., 1979. Fellow Washington Acad. Scis., Am. Phys. Soc.; mem. Am. Chem. Soc., Philos. Soc. Washington, Sigma Xi. Club: Cosmos. Author: (with Schamp and Mason) Thermodynamics, 1966; also articles. Home: 14801 W Auburn Rd Accokeek MD 20607 Office: Dept Chemistry Univ Md College Park MD 20740

VANDERSLICE, THOMAS AQUINAS, elec. mfg. co. exec.; b. Phila., Jan. 8, 1932; s. Joseph R. and Mae (Daly) V.; B.S. in Chemistry and Philosophy, Boston Coll., 1953; Ph.D. in Chemistry and Physics, Catholic U. Am., 1956; m. Margaret Hurley, June 9, 1956; children—Thomas Aquinas, Paul Thomas Aquinas, John Thomas Aquinas, Peter Thomas Aquinas. With Gen. Electric Co., 1956—, gen. mgr. electronic components bus. div., 1970-72, v.p., 1970—, group exec. spl. systems and products group, Fairfield, Conn., 1972-77, sr. v.p., sector exec. Power Systems Sector, 1977-79, exec. v.p., sector exec., 1979; pres., chief operating officer, dir. Gen. Telephone & Electronics Corp., Stamford, Conn., 1979—; mem. com. on energy Aspen Inst. for Humanistic Studies; mem. Oxford Energy Policy Club, Oxford U., mem. com. econ. devel., chmn. design com. on tech. policy. Trustee, Boston Coll., Fairfield U., Clarkson Coll., Potsdam, N.Y.; past trustee Oklahoma City U. Found.; mem. Okla. Bd. Corrections, 1966-68, Okla. Bd. Vocat. and Tech. Edn., 1968; pres. Frontiers Sci. Found. Okla., 1968; organizer Valley Forward Assn., Phoenix, 1968-70; trustee Com. Econ. Devel.; chmn. Design Com. on Tech. Policy; bd. dirs. Jr. Achievement Onondaga and Madison counties, N.Y., 1971-72, Phoenix, 1968-70. Fulbright scholar, 1953-56; recipient Golden Plate award Acad. Achievement, 1963; Bicentennial medallion Boston Coll., 1976. Mem. Conn. Acad. Sci. and Engring., Am. Vacuum Soc., ASTM, Am. Chem. Soc., Am. Inst. Physics, Sigma Xi, Tau Beta Pi, Alpha Sigma Nu, Sigma Pi Sigma. Clubs: Laurel Valley (Pa.); Aspetuck (Easton, Conn.); Patterson (Fairfield); Oxford U. Energy Policy. Co-author: Ultra High Vacuum and Its Applications, 1963; reviser: Scientific Foundations of Vacuum Technique, 1960. Contbr. to profl. jours. Patentee low pressure gas measurements and analysis, gas surface interactions and elec. discharge. Home: 41 Cherry Ln Fairfield CT 06430 Office: Gen Telephone & Electronics Corp 1 Stamford Forum Stamford CT 06904

VANDER VEEN, RICHARD FRANKLIN, lawyer, former congressman; b. Grand Rapids, Mich., Nov. 26, 1922; s. Frank R. and Nettie (Moerdyke) Vander V.; student U. of South, 1943-44; B.S., U.S.C., 1946; LL.B., Harvard, 1949; m. Marion P. Coward, June 29, 1946; children—Richard Franklin III, Lawrence James, Paul Allen. Admitted to Mich. bar, 1949, D.C. bar, 1979; practiced in Grand Rapids and Washington; sr. partner firm Vander Veen, Freihofer & Cook, 1951-74, Vander Veen & Gould, 1979—; mem. 93d-94th Congresses from 5th Dist. of Mich., mem. Ways and Means Com. Mem., chmn. Mich. Mental Health Commn., 1959-64; commr. Mich. Hwy. Commn., 1964-69; trustee E. Grand Rapids Sch. Bd., from 1968; former mem. nat. bd. missions Presbyn. Ch. U.S.A. Chmn. Mich. Democratic Conv., 1960; candidate for U.S. Congress, 1958, for lt. gov. Mich., 1960, for U.S. Senate, 1977, 78. Chmn. Urban Affairs Inst., Grand Valley Coll., 1969—. Served to lt. (j.g.) USNR, 1941-46, 51-52. Mem. Mems. Congress for Peace through Law. Democrat. Presbyn. (elder). Rare book dealer. Home: 1150 Gladstone SE Grand Rapids MI 49506 Office: 250 Frey Bldg Grand Rapids MI also 1333 New Hampshire Ave NW Washington DC

VANDERVELD, JOHN, JR., waste disposal co. exec.; b. Chgo., Oct. 24, 1926; s. John J. and Rose (Renkema) V.; Pres., Nat. Disposal Contractors, Barrington, Ill., 1952-71; sr. v.p., dir. Browning Ferris Industries, Houston, 1971-78; pres. Pioneer Equities, Inc., 1975—; dir. Am. Far East, Inc., Dallas and Tokyo. Vice chmn. adv. bd. Southwestern Legal Found. Mem. Nat. Solid Waste Mgmt. Assn. (former chmn. govt. industry coordinating council, mem. environ. research com.). Home: 7031 Brookshire Dr Dallas TX 75030 Office: World Trade Center #114 Dallas TX 75258

VANDER VELDE, JOHN CHRISTIAN, educator; b. Holland, Mich., Sept. 25, 1930; s. Otto and Margaret (Den Herder) Vander V.; B.A. magna cum laude, Hope Coll., 1952; Ph.D., U. Mich., 1958; m. Marilyn Veldman, Dec. 19, 1953; children—Mary Elizabeth, Alison, Jonathan. Instr. U. Mich., Ann Arbor, 1958-61, asst. prof., 1961-64, asso. prof., 1964-68, prof. physics, 1968—, co-dir. Bubble Chamber Project, 1972—; vis. scientist Ecole Polytechnique, Paris, 1966-67, C.E.N., Saclay, France, 1974. Fellow Am. Phys. Soc.; mem. Alliance Francaise of Ann Arbor (v.p. 1972—). Presbyterian (elder). Home: 400 Barton Shore Dr Ann Arbor MI 48105

VANDER VELDE, WALLACE EARL, educator; b. Jamestown, Mich., June 4, 1929; s. Peter Nelson and Janet (Keizer) Vander V.; B.S. in Aero Engring., Purdue U., 1951; Sc.D., Mass. Inst. Tech., 1956; m. Winifred Helen Bunai, Aug. 29, 1954; children—Susan Jane, Peter Russell. Dir. applications engring. GPS Instrument Co., Inc., Newton, Mass. 1956-57; mem. faculty Mass. Inst. Tech., 1957—, prof. aero. and astronautics, 1965—. Cons. to industry, 1958—. Served to 1st lt. USAF, 1951-53. Mem. Am. Inst. Aeros. and Astronautics, I.E.E.E. Author: Flight Vehicle Control Systems, Part VII of Space Navigation, Guidance and Control, 1966; (with Arthur Gelb) Multiple-Input Describing Functions, 1968; also papers. Home: 50 High St Winchester MA 01890 Office: Massachusetts Institute of Technology Cambridge MA 02139

VANDERVOORT, BENJAMIN HAYS, govt. ofcl., ret. army officer; b. Gasport, N.Y., Mar. 3, 1915; s. Benjamin F. and Marian A. (Hays) V.; A.B., Washington Coll., Chestertown, Md., 1938; student Ohio State U., 1946; grad. Armed Forces Staff. Coll., 1953; m. Nedra Marlin, Dec. 24, 1940; children—Benjamin Franklin, Nedra Marlin. Commd. 2d lt., inf., U.S. army, 1939, advanced through grades to col., 1946; as comdr. bns., parachuted into Sicily, Salerno, Normandy, Nimegen, World War II; severely wounded, 1945, ret., 1946; joined U.S. Fgn. Service, 1947; exec. officer Dept. Army, 1950-54, also joint polit. adviser to comdg. gen. UN Forces and U.S. ambassador, Korea, 1951-52, attache Am. embassy, Lisbon, Portugal, 1955-58; assigned Dept. State, 1958-60; exec. CIA, 1960-66, cons. politico-mil. affairs U.S. Army staff, 1960—; plans and program officer Army Staff, Dept. Def., 1964—. Decorated D.S.C. with oak leaf cluster, Purple Heart with 2 oak leaf clusters, Bronze star medal with one oak leaf cluster; Croix de Guerre with palm (France); Bronze Lion (Netherlands); Fourragere (Belgium). Mem. Army Airborne Assn., Assn. U.S. Army, 82d A.B. Div. Assn., Army-Navy Legion of Valor, Theta Chi. Episcopalian. Clubs: Sea Pines Plantation Golf, Inter-Course Ace Assn. (Hilton Head, S.C.); Army-Navy Country (Arlington Va.). Address: 13 Marsh Wren Rd Sea Pines Plantation Hilton Head Island SC 29928

VANDER VOORT, DALE GILBERT, textile co. exec.; b. Paterson, N.J., Feb. 7, 1924; s. Gilbert H. and Lillian (Hatton) Vander V.; B.M.E., Clemson U., 1944; m. Florine E. Storey, Aug. 6, 1944; children—Lydia Ann, Dale Gilbert, Roy Lee. Gen. mgr., dir. Stevens Line Assos., Webster, Mass., 1954-56; gen. mgr. Montreal Cottons Ltd., Valleyfield, Que., Can., 1951-54; supt. Mill #4 Dan River Mills, Danville, Va., 1946-51; sr. v.p. United Merchants & Mfrs. Inc., N.Y.C., 1972-77; chmn. bd. Asso. Textiles Can. Ltd., 1969-77; pres., chief exec. officer Arnold Print Works, Inc., Adams, Mass., 1977—; dir. Northwestern Bank, Asheville, N.C., Western Carolina Industries Inc., Brit. Silk Dyeing Co., Valchem Australia, Profile Sports Corp., West Lebanon, N.H. Served to lt. AUS, 1943-46. Decorated Bronze Star, Purple Heart. Mem. Am. Soc. M.E., Am. Assn. Textile Chemists and Colorists, Canadian Textile Inst. (dir.), Soc. Advancement of Mgmt. (nat. gov. 1961-62). Lutheran (council 1962—). Clubs: Metropolitan, Weavers, Faculty, Taconic Golf. Home: 110 Hill Province Rd Williamstown MA 01267 Office: Arnold Print Works Inc Adams MA 01220 also 267 Fifth Ave New York NY 10016

VANDERVORT, LOWELL MILLER, hosp. adminstr.; b. Danville, Ill., Dec. 27, 1922; s. Harold M. and Florence (Stickler) V.; A.B., Wheaton Coll., 1950; postgrad. U. Ill., 1951; M.H.A., U. Minn., 1958; m. Druscilla Skomp, Feb. 18, 1951. Personnel dir. Pines Engring. Co., Aurora, Ill., 1951-53; dir. personnel., pub. relations St. Barnabas Hosp., Mpls., 1953-56; adminstrv. resident Baylor Med. Center, Dallas, 1957-58; asst. adminstr. St. Luke's Hosp., Milw., 1958-63, asso. adminstr., 1964-68, adminstr., 1968-73; exec. dir. Eisenhower Med. Center, Rancho Mirage, Calif., 1974—. Dir. First Wis. Nat. Bank of Southgate (Milw.). Bd. dirs. Hosp. Council So. Calif., 1977—. Served with USAAF, 1942-46. Mem. Wis. Hosp. Assn. (bd. dirs. 1970-73), Hosp. Council Greater Milw. Area (pres. 1971-72), Am. Coll. Hosp. Adminstrs., Internat. Hosp. Fed. Baptist. Rotarian. Club: Ironwood Country. Home: 76181 Shawnee Circle Indian Wells CA 92260 Office: 39000 Bob Hope Dr Rancho Mirage CA 92270

VAN DER WAAG, WALTER E., banker; b. Bklyn., 1910; m. Catherine M. Koeppel, Feb. 12, 1935; children—Walter C., Kathleen (Mrs. John Bozzomo) Robert, Warren; m. 2d, Helen E. Valentine, Jan. 5, 1979; stepchildren—Linda, Nancy. With Chase Nat. Bank, 1929-40; with central credit com. Fed. Res. Bank of N.Y., 1940-50; with Nat. Bank N.Am., West Hempstead, N.Y., 1950—, former exec. v.p., pres., vice chmn. bd., dir. Bd. dirs. Nassau div. Am. Cancer Soc.; mem. adv. com. Legal Aid Soc. Nassau County; mem. Heart Fund; mem. adv. bd. Chaminade High Sch.; mem. fin. com., dir. emeritus St. Francis Hosp.; trustee Catholic Charities Diocese of Rockville Centre, United Fund of L.I.; past pres. Research Found. of L.I. Assn.; bd. sponsors Mercy Hosp.; mem. L.I. Planning Council; bd. mgrs. Nassau County Med. Center. Recipient Caritas award Catholic Charities Diocese of Rockville Centre, Humanitarian award Nassau div. Am. Cancer Soc.; Brotherhood award NCCJ. Mem. L.I. Bankers Assn. (past chmn.), L.I. Assn. Commerce and Industry (past pres., chmn. bd.), Nat. Alliance Businessman (adv. com.). Club: North Hempstead Country (Port Washington, N.Y.). Home: 62 Robbins Dr East Williston NY 11596

VANDERWERF, CALVIN ANTHONY, coll. ofcl.; b. Friesland, Wis., Jan. 2, 1917; s. Anthony and Anna (Schaafsma) V.; A.B., Hope Coll., 1937, Sc.D., 1963; Ph.D., Ohio State U., 1941; L.D., St. Benedict's Coll., Atchison, Kans., 1966; Sc.D., Rose Poly Inst., 1966; m. Rachel Anna Good, Aug. 22, 1942; children—Gretchen, Klasina, Julie, Lisa, Pieter, Marte. Instr., U. Kans., 1941-42, mem. faculty and staff, 1943-63; prof. chemistry, 1949-63, chmn. dept., 1961-63; pres. Hope Coll., Holland, Mich., 1963-70; vis. prof. Colo. State U., 1970-71; dean U. Fla. Coll. Arts and Scis., Gainesville, 1971—. Vis. scientist NSF, 1955—; guest lectr. Continental Classroom, 1959. Cons. U.S. Naval Ordnance Test Sta., China Lake, Calif., 1951-60; cons. editor organic and biochemistry Dowden, Hutchinson and Ross Pub. Co., 1970; cons. editor chemistry Burgess Pub. Corp., 1970—; mem. Petroleum Fund Adv. Bd., 1957-63; cons. Smith, Kline and French Co., 1947-63, Spencer Chem. Co., 1952-63, Pan Am. Petroleum Co., 1958-63; Western Conn. vis. scientist of year, 1967; rep. U.S. Dept. State, 9th Internat. Conf. on Higher Edn., Yugoslav Univs., Drubovnik; lectr. cons. on sci. edn. OAS, Buenos Aires, 1965. Dir. Kativo Chem. Co., Ltd., Costa Rica. Chmn. discipline com. in chemistry Ednl. Testing Service; mem. Danforth Grad. Fellowship Reading Com. Trustee, mem. exec. com. Research Corp. Grantee Petroleum Research Fund, 1962. Fellow N.Y. Acad. Scis.; mem. Am. Chem. Soc. (mem. com. chemistry and pub. affairs), Chem. Soc. London, Sigma Xi, Phi Lambda Upsilon, Gamma Alpha. Author: (with Sisler and Davidson) General Chemistry, 2d edit., 1959, Korean transl., 1959; A Systematic Approach, 2d edit., 1961, Korean transl., 1964, Asian edit., 1964; (with Brewster and McEwen) Unitized Experiments in Organic Chemistry, 3d edit., 1969, A Brief Course in Experimental Organic Chemistry, 1972; Acids, Bases and the Chemistry of the Covalent Bond, 1961; College Chemistry, A Systematic Approach, 3d edit., 1967; also Japanese, French, Spanish and Italian transls.; also numerous articles in field. Editor Organic Series. Mem. editorial bd. Jour. Chem. Edn. Office: College of Arts and Sciences University of Fla Gainesville FL 32611

VANDERWIER, CONSTANCE JEAN, food co. exec.; b. Muskegon, Mich., Feb. 27, 1921; d. John O. and Anna Marie (Olsen) Loberg; grad. high sch.; m. Henry M. Vanderwier, Mar. 13, 1946. Secretarial positions in law office, Muskegon, 1939-40, Brunswick Corp., Muskegon, 1940-42, Canadian Nat. Ry., Chgo., 1942-46; ct. reporter Marine Corps, 1946; secretarial positions Norge Corp., Muskegon, 1947-50; exec. sec. Gerber Products Co., Fremont, Mich., 1951-68, asst. sec., 1968-73, sec., 1973—. Mem. Am. Soc. Corporate Secs., Bus. and Profl. Women. Club: Ramshorn Country. Home: 1018 Leo St Fremont MI 49412 Office: 445 State St Fremont MI 49412

VAN DER ZEE, JAMES AUGUSTUS JOSEPH, photographer; b. Lenox, Mass., June 29, 1886; student Carlton Conservatory, N.Y.C., 1906; m. Kate Brown, 1906 (dec.); children—Rachael (dec.), Emil (dec.); m. 2d, Gaynella Greenlee, 1920 (dec.); m. 3d, Donna Mussenden, June 15, 1978. Dark room developer Gertz Dept. Store, Newark, 1907; 1st violinist John Wanamaker Orch.; opened Guarantee Photo Studio, N.Y.C., 1918 (name changed to GGG Photo Studio, 1932); exhibited Met. Mus. Art, N.Y.C., 1969, other maj. museums; represented in permanent collections Met. Mus. Art, other museums, also pvt. collections; publs. include: Harlem On My Mind, 1969, rev. edit., 1979; The World of James Van Der Zee, 1969; James Van Der Zee, 1973; The Harlem Book of the Dead, 1978; James Van Der Zee: The Picture Takin' Man, 1979; video prodns. include Uncommon Images, 1975. Recipient Pierre Toussaint award, 1978; Living Legacy award Pres. U.S., 1979. Address: 220 W 93d St New York NY 10025

VANDERZELL, JOHN HOWARD, educator; b. Rochester, N.Y., July 11, 1924; s. Neil and Dina (Bliek) V.; B.A., Miami U. (Ohio), 1949; Ph.D., Syracuse U., 1954; m. Beryl Jane Schelter, June 9, 1949; children—Susan Jane, John Burrell, David Jacob. Faculty dept. govt. Franklin and Marshall Coll., Lancaster, Pa., 1952-69, acad. dean of coll., 1969-74, now prof. polit. sci.; vis. prof. U. Pa., 1957-58, Bryn Mawr Coll., 1966-69. Dir. research Bur. Municipal Affairs, Commonwealth of Pa.; cons. Pa. Dept. Edn., Pa. Economy League. Chmn. Lancaster City Planning Commn., 1955-62. Served with inf. AUS, 1943-46; ETO. Mem. Am., N.E. polit. sci. assns., A.A.U.P., Am. Soc. Pub. Adminstrn., Pa. Polit. Sci. and Pub. Adminstrn. Assn., Phi Beta Kappa. Author: The Supreme Court and American Government, 1968. Home: 931 W Walnut St Lancaster PA 17603

VAN DER ZIEL, ALDERT, elec. engr.; b. Zandeweer, Netherlands, Dec. 12, 1910; naturalized U.S. citizen, 1955; s. Jan and Hendrika (Kiel) Van der Z.; B.A., U. Groningen, The Netherlands, 1930, M.A., 1933, Ph.D., 1934; m. Jantina J. deWit, Nov. 22, 1935; children—Jan P., Cornelia H., Joanna C. Research physicist Philips Labs., Eindhoven, Netherlands, 1934-47; asso. prof. physics U. B.C., Vancouver, Can., 1947-50; prof. dept. elec. engring. U. Minn., Mpls., 1950—; grad. research prof. U. Fla., Gainesville, 1968—. Recipient Vincent Bendix award Am. Soc. Engring. Edn., 1975. Fellow IEEE; mem. Am. Phys. Soc., Sigma Xi. Lutheran. Author 10 books in field; contbr. numerous articles to profl. jours.; patentee in field. Office: Elec Engring Dept Univ of Minn Minneapolis MN 55455

VAN DEUSEN, GLYNDON GARLOCK, author, historian; b. Clifton Springs, N.Y., Sept. 22, 1897; s. Frank F. and Jennie May (Garlock) Van D.; A.B., U. Rochester (N.Y.), 1925; A.M., Amherst Coll., 1926; Ph.D., Columbia U., 1932; m. Ruth Naomi Litteer, Aug. 1, 1931; children—Nicholas, Nancy. Instr. in history U. Rochester, 1930-33, asst. prof., 1933-42, asso. prof., 1942-47, prof., 1947-62, research prof. emeritus, 1962—; prof. Columbia U., summer 1939; Fulbright prof. Am. history, N.Z., 1951-52, chmn. dept. history, 1954-62, asso. dean grad. studies Coll. Arts and Sci., 1957-60. Mem. Soc. Am Historians, Orgn. Am. Historians, Phi Beta Kappa. Author: Sieyes, His Life and His Nationalism, 1932; The Life of Henry Clay, 1937; Thurlow Weed: Wizard of the Lobby, 1947; Horace Greeley: Nineteenth Century Crusader, 1952; The Jacksonian Era, 1828-1848, 1959; (with D. Perkins) The United States of America: A History, 1962, The American Democracy: Its Rise to Power, 1964; William Henry Seward, 1967; The Rise and Decline of Jacksonian Democracy, 1970; contbr. to various learned periodicals. Home: Ten Manhattan Sq Apt 3-G Rochester NY 14607

VANDEVENTER, BRADEN, lawyer; b. Norfolk, Va., Sept. 27, 1921; s. Braden and Phelan (Ruffin) V.; B.A., Va. Mil. Inst., 1943; LL.B., U. Va., 1948; m. Barbara Ann Lewis, June 11, 1954; children—Elizabeth Ann, Thomas Ruffin, William Lewis, Ann Braden. Admitted to Va. bar, 1949; practiced in Norfolk, 1950—; partner Vandeventer, Black, Meredith & Martin, 1951—, dir. Life Fed. Savs. & Loan Assn., Bank of Va.-Eastern, Hampton Rds. Maritime Assn. Bd. dirs., past pres. Norfolk Community Concerts, Inc.; past bd. dirs. Virginia Beach Art Center; trustee Mariners Mus.,

Newport News, Va. Served to maj., arty., AUS, 1944-46: ETO. Decorated Bronze Star medal. Mem. Holland Soc. N.Y., Newcomen Soc. N.Am., Maritime Law Assn. U.S. (exec. com. 1976—), Am., Va., Norfolk, Portsmouth bar assns., Assn. Average Adjusters U.S. Clubs: Propeller, Harbor, Virginia, Hampton Roads Fgn. Commerce (past pres.) (Norfolk); Princess Anne Country (Virginia Beach). Contbr. articles to profl. jours. Home: 1129 Chumley Rd Virginia Beach VA 23451 Office: 2050 One Commercial Pl Norfolk VA 23501

VAN DEVENTER, JOHN FRANCIS, investment exec.; b. Passaic, N.J., Aug. 30, 1909; s. William and Irma (Fowler) VanD.; A.B., Hamilton Coll., 1932; M.S., Columbia, 1935; m. Ellenor Sowerbutt Vandermade, Jan. 19, 1946; children—Tina Maillefert, John Francis. Trust dept. Bankers Trust Co., N.Y.C., 1935-41; with Van Alstyne, Noel & Co., 1946-47; treas. dept. Gen. Aniline & Film Corp., 1947-49, Southport Distbrs., Inc., 1950, investments Chem. Fund, Inc.; v.p., dir. F. Eberstadt & Co., Inc., N.Y.C., 1951-77, Mgr's. & Distbrs., Inc.; v.p., sr. investment officer, dir. Chem. Fund Inc.; hon. dir., vice chmn. trust investment com. First Nat. Bank of Litchfield. Served as lt. comdr. USNR, 1942-46; comdr. Res. Mem. Holland Soc. N.Y., Down Town Assn. Clubs: Hamilton; Washington (Conn.); University, University Glee (N.Y.C.); Down Town Athletic; Southampton, Southampton Yacht, Shinnecock Hills Golf, Meadow, Southampton (Southampton, N.Y.). Home: Meadow Springs Route 199 Washington CT 06793 Office: 61 Broadway New York City NY 10006

VANDEWALLE, GERALD WAYNE, justice N.D. Supreme Ct.; b. Noonan, N.D., Aug. 15, 1933; s. Jules C. and Blanche Marie (Gits) VandeW.; B.Sc., U. N.D., 1955, J.D., 1958. Admitted to N.D. bar, 1958, U.S. Dist. Ct. bar for N.D., 1959; spl. asst. atty. gen. State of N.D., Bismarck, 1958-75, 1st asst. atty. gen., 1975-78; justice N.D. Supreme Ct., 1978—; mem. faculty Bismarck Jr. Coll., 1972-76. Active Bismarck Meals on Wheels. Mem. State Bar Assn. N.D., Burleigh County Bar Assn., Am. Bar Assn., N.D. Jud. Council, Am. Contract Bridge League (dir. N.D. unit), Order of Coif, Phi Eta Sigma, Beta Alpha Psi, Beta Gamma Sigma, Phi Alpha Delta. Roman Catholic. Clubs: Elks, K.C. Editor-in-chief N.D. Law Rev., 1957-58. Office: Supreme Ct State Capitol Bismarck ND 58505

VAN DE WEGHE, RAYMOND FRANCIS, banker; b. Fort Morgan, Colo., July 17, 1934; s. Maurice and Marie (Rogers) Van D.; B.S. in Bus., U. Colo., 1956; student U. Hawaii, 1957-58; m. Joan Louise Kaszuba, Sept. 19, 1964; children—Louise Marie, Matthew Maurice, Benjamin Joseph, David Raymond. Sr. accountant Price Waterhouse & Co., C.P.A.'s, Chgo., 1956-65; dir. internal auditing C., R.I. & P. R.R., 1965-67; with N.C. Nat. Bank, Charlotte, 1967-73, v.p., controller, 1969-73; v.p. 1st Nat. Bank Chgo., 1973-74; sr. v.p. finance, sec., treas. Bankshares N.C., Inc., Raleigh, 1974-75; v.p., controller Huntington Bancshares Inc., Columbus, Ohio, 1975—. Served with AUS, 1957-59. Mem. Am. Inst. C.P.A.'s, Fin. Execs. Inst., Alpha Kappa Psi. K.C. Home: 4649 Barrymede Ct Columbus OH 43220 Office: 17 S High St Columbus OH 43215

VAN DE WETERING, JOHN E(DWARD), coll. exec.; b. Bellingham, Wash., Jan. 20, 1927; s. John and Jessie Van De W.; B.A. in History, U. Wash., 1950, M.A. in History, 1953, Ph.D. in History, 1959; m. Maxine Schorr, Mar. 7, 1961; 1 son, Josh. Instr., U. Idaho, 1959; instr. U. Wash., 1959-61, vis. asst. prof. history, 1963; asst. prof. U. Mont., 1961-64, asso. prof., 1964-69, prof., chmn. dept. history, 1969-76; acting pres. Eastern Mont. Coll., 1976-77, pres., 1977—; mem. Mont. Com. for Humanities, 1972-74; Danforth asso. Bd. dirs. Yellowstone Art Center. Served with C.E., U.S. Army, 1955-57. Mem. AAUP, Am. Hist. Assn. Author: (with Jack Bumsted) "What Must I Do to Be Saved?": The Great Awakening in Colonial America, 1976; contbr. articles to profl. jours. Home: 432 Silver Ln Billings MT 59101 Office: Eastern Mont Coll Billings MT 59101

VAN DE WETERING, RICHARD LEE, educator; b. Bellingham, Wash., Aug. 2, 1928; s. John and Jessie Priscilla (Straks) Van de W.; student Western Wash. Coll., 1946-48; B.S., U. Wash., 1950; postgrad. Western Wash. Coll., 1950-51; Ph.D., Stanford, 1960; m. Beatrice Arlene Milbrat, Aug. 21, 1960; children—Brian Lee, Eileen Marie. Asst. prof. San Diego State U., 1960-63, asso. prof., 1963-67, prof. math., 1967—; mem. faculty U. Santa Clara, summers, 1962, 64, 66, 70, Stanford, summer 1963; research asso. U. Groningen (Netherlands), 1973-74. Served with USNR, 1951-55. Research grantee Technische Hogeschool Delft (Netherlands), 1966-67. Mem. Am. Math. Soc., Math. Assn. Am. Contbr. articles to math. jours. Home: 4034 St James Pl San Diego CA 92103

VANDE WIELE, RAYMOND LAURENT, physician, educator; b. Kortryk, Belgium, Oct. 2, 1922; s. Jan B. and Marie Louise (Lampe) Vande W.; grad. St. Amands Coll., Belgium, 1940; M.D., Universite Catholique de Louvain (Belgium), 1947; m. Beatrice Silides, Sept. 25, 1954; children—Barbara, Carol, Margaret. Asst. prof. to prof. obstetrics and gynecology Columbia, also head dept. obstetrics and gynecology; chief Sloane Hosp. for Women; dir. Internat. Inst. Study Human Reprodn. Cons. St. Luke's Hosp., Roosevelt Hosp., Harlem Hosp., North Shore Hosp., Clin. Center NIH. Served with Belgian Army on the Rhine. Club: Century. Contbr. numerous articles to profl. jours. Home: Closter Dock Rd Alpine NJ 07620 Office: 622 W 168th St New York NY 10032

VAN DINE, VANCE, investment banker; b. San Francisco, July 2, 1925; s. Melvin Everett and Grace Winifred (Harris) Van D.; B.A., Yale U., 1949; LL.B., N.Y. U., 1955; m. Isabel Erskine Brewster, Sept. 8, 1956; 1 dau., Rose M. Asso. Morgan Stanley & Co., N.Y.C., 1953-59, 61-63, partner, 1963-75; mng. dir. Morgan Stanley & Co. Inc., N.Y.C., 1970—; cons. Internat. Bank for Reconstn. and Devel., 1959-61. Bd. dirs. Yale Alumni Fund, Rec. for Blind, Inc., N.Y.C.; trustee Cancer Research Inst., N.Y.C. Served with USN, 1943-46. Republican. Episcopalian. Clubs: Union, Creek, Piping Rock, Seawanhaka Corinthian Yacht, Church, Yale of N.Y.C., Met. Opera. Author: The Role of the Investment Banker in International Transactions, 1970; The U.S. Market After Controls, 1974. Office: 1251 Ave of Americas New York NY 10020

VANDIVER, FRANK EVERSON, coll. pres., author, educator; b. Austin, Tex., Dec. 9, 1925; s. Harry Shultz and Maude Folmsbee (Everson) V.; Rockefeller fellow in humanities U. Tex., 1946-47, Rockefeller fellow in Am. Studies, 1947-48, M.A., 1949; Ph.D., Tulane U., 1951; M.A., Oxford (Eng.) U., 1963; H.H.D. (hon.), Austin Coll., 1977; m. Carol Sue Smith, Apr. 19, 1952; children—Nita, Nancy, Frank Alexander. Apptd. historian Army Service Forces Depot, Civil Service, San Antonio, 1945, Air U., 1951; prof. history La. State U., summers 1954-57; asst. prof. history Washington U., St. Louis, 1952-55; asst. prof. history Rice U., Houston, 1955-56, asso. prof., 1956-58, prof., 1958-65, Harris Masterson Jr. prof. history, 1965-79, chmn. dept. history and polit. sci., 1962-63, dept. history, 1968-69, acting pres., 1969-70, provost, 1970-79, v.p., 1975-79; pres. N. Tex. State U., Denton and Tex. Coll. Osteo. Medicine, 1979—; Harmsworth prof. Am. history Oxford U., 1963-64. Vis. prof. history U. Ariz., summer 1961; master Margarett Root Brown Coll., Rice U., 1964-66. Harman lectr. Air Force Acad., 1963; Keese lectr. U. Chattanooga, 1967; Fortenbaugh lectr. Gettysburg Coll., 1974; Phi Beta Kappa asso. lectr., 1975—; vis. prof. mil. history U.S. Mil. Acad., 1973-74; hon. pres. Occidental U., St. Louis, 1975—; Confederate Inaugural Centennial speaker Va. Civil War Centennial, 1962; mem. adv. council Civil War Centennial Commn.; cons. Nat. Endowment Humanities, 1966—; mem. adv. council, office chief mil. history Dept. Army, 1969-74; exec. dir. Am. Revolution Bicentennial Commn. Tex., 1970-73; mem. selection com. Ft. Leavenworth Hall of Fame Assn. U.S. Army, 1971-72, 74-76; bd. dirs. Inst. Civil War Studies, 1975—; chmn. adv. council U.S. Mil. Hist. Research Collection, Carlisle Barracks, Pa., 1972—; mem. Nat. Council for Humanities, 1972-78, vice-chmn., 1976-78. Recipient research grants Am. Philos. Soc., 1953, 54, 60; Guggenheim fellow, 1955-56; Carr P. Collins prize Tex. Inst. Letters, 1957; Huntington Library research grant, 1961; Harry S. Truman award Kansas City Civil War Round Table; Jefferson Davis award Confederate Meml. Lit. Soc., 1970; Fletcher Pratt award N.Y. Civil War Round Table, 1970; laureate Lincoln Acad., Ill., 1973; First Outstanding Alumnus award Tulane U. Grad. Sch., 1974; Outstanding Civilian Service medal Dept. Army, 1974. Fellow Tex. Hist. Assn.; mem. Am., So. (asso. editor jour. 1959-62, pres. 1975-76) hist. assns., Tex. Inst. Letters (past pres.), Jefferson Davis Assn. (pres., chmn. adv. bd. editors of papers), Soc. Am. Historians (councillor), Tex. Philos. Soc. (pres. 1978), Civil War Round Table (Houston), Phi Beta Kappa. Club: Cosmos (Washington). Editor: The Civil War Diary of General Josiah Gogas, 1947; Confederate Blockade Running Through Bermuda, 1861-65, Letters and Cargo Manifests, 1947; Proceedings of First Confederate Congress, 4th Session, 1954; Proceedings of Second Confederate Congress, 1959; A Collection of Louisiana Confederate Letters; new edit. J.E. Johnston's Narrative of Military Operations; new edit. J.A. Early's Civil War Memoirs; The Idea of the South, 1964. Author: Ploughshares Into Swords: Josiah Gorgas and Confederate Ordnance, 1952; Rebel Brass: The Confederate Command System, 1956: Mighty Stonewall, 1957: Fields of Glory (with W. H. Nelson), 1960; Jubal's Raid, 1960; Basic History of the Confederacy, 1962; Jefferson Davis and the Confederate State, 1964; Their Tattered Flags: The Epic of the Confederacy, 1970; The Southwest: South or West?, 1975; Black Jack: The Life and Times of John J. Pershing (Nat. Book Award finalist 1978), 1977; also hist. articles. Mem. bd. editors U.S. Grant Papers, 1973—. Office: N Tex State U Denton TX 76203

VANDIVIERE, H(ORACE) MAC, physician; b. Dawsonville, Ga., Mar. 26, 1921; s. Lewis A. and Luna P. (Castleberry) V.; A.B., Mercer, U., 1941, M.A., 1944; postgrad. U. Mich., 1944-46; M.D., U. N.C., 1960; m. Margaret Reynolds, June 5, 1941 (dec. Feb. 1967); children—Christopher, Martin Mac; m. 2d, Irene Graham Melvin, Mar. 23, 1968. Instr., U. Mich., 1944-46; asst. prof. Mercer U., 1947-48; dir. spl. services lab. Ga. Dept. Public Health, 1948-51; dir. dept. research and clin. labs. N.C. Sanatorium System, Chapel Hill, 1951-67; asst. prof. Duke U., Durham, N.C., 1965-68; med. dir. Haitian Am. Tb Inst., Chapel Hill, also Jeremie Haiti, 1962—, pres., 1965—; clin. asso. prof. U. N.C. Sch. Public Health, 1967—; asso. prof. U. Ky., Lexington, 1967-71, prof., 1972—; dir. Tb div. Ky. Bur. Health Services, Dept. Human Resources, 1971-73, dir. adult remedial sers., 1973-74, dir. remedial services, 1975-76; vice chmn. dept. community medicine U. Ky., 1978—, acting chmn. dept., 1978—; cons. infectious diseases Sante Publique Dept., Republic of Haiti, 1964-73; cons. div. Tb Control Ky. State Dept. Health, 1971-72; vice chmn. Ky. Comprehensive Health Planning Tb Study Com., 1969-70. Decorated by Pres. of Haiti, 1963. Fellow Am. Public Health Assn, Am. Geriatrics Assn.; mem. Nat. Tb and Respiratory Disease Assn., Am. Thoracic Soc., Ky. Assn. Pub. Health Physicians (pres. 1973-75), Ky. Thoracic Soc. (pres. 1970-71), AMA, Assn. Am. Med. Colls., Soc. Epidimeol. Research, Fayette County Med. Soc. (com. community health-comprehensive com.) Ky. Med. Assn., N.C. Med. Assn. Editor: (with others) Bahama International Conference on Burns, 1964. Contbr. articles to profl. jours. Home: 3429 Brookhaven Dr Lexington KY 40502

VAN DORE, WADE (KIVEL), poet, environmentalist; b. Detroit, Dec. 12, 1899; s. Peter Francis and Laura (Pennington) Van D.; ed. Bollitat Music Sch., 1917-19; pupil Robert Frost, 1925-26; m. Edrie Frances MacFarland, May 21, 1932; m. 2d, Erma Mae Jones, Oct. 11, 1946; 1 son, Peter Francis. Housekeeper, hired man Robert Frost, 1929-43; poet-in-residence Marlboro Coll., 1950; free-lance author, piano technician; co-founder, v.p. Thoreau Fellowship, Inc. Trustee Thoreau Lyceum. Mem. Wilderness Soc., Natural Resources of Maine Council, Poetry Soc. Am. (recipient Alice Fay di Castagnola award). Author: Far Lake; Verse With a Vengeance; (with Richard Eberhart) Declaration of Dependence (on nature). Contbr. poems, essays, articles to mags. Home: 62 Somerset St Clearwater Beach FL 33515. *As an environmentalist, this is the thought that comes to me again and again: To focus attention on our national misuse of nature, America could not do better than proclaim a Declaration of Dependence on nature to supercede our 1776 Declaration of Independence from England. Along with this, Thoreau's Walden might be named our guidebook for attaining the ideal human-nature relationship.*

VAN DOREN, CHARLES, editor; b. N.Y.C., Feb. 12, 1926; s. Mark and Dorothy (Graffe) Van D.; B.A., St. Johns Coll., Annapolis, Md., 1947; M.A., Columbia, 1949, Ph.D. (Cutting fellow), 1959; m. Geraldine Bernstein, Apr. 17, 1957; children—Elizabeth, John C.L. Instr. English, Columbia, 1955-59; sr. asso. Inst. for Philos. Research, Chgo., 1960-67, asso. dir., 1967—; v.p. editorial Ency. Brit., Inc., 1973—; pres. Praeger Pubs., 1974-75. Served with USAAF, 1944-45. Mem. Authors Guild. Democrat. Author: The Idea of Progress, 1967. Editor: Annals of America, 20 vols., 1969; Webster's American Biographies, 1974; Great Treasury of Western Thought, 1977; others. Home: 335 W Menomonee St Chicago IL 60614 Office: Ency Brit Inc 425 N Michigan Ave Chicago IL 60611

VAN DREELEN, JOHN (JACQUES THEODORE VAN DRIELEN GIMBERG), actor; b. Amsterdam, Netherlands, May 5, 1922; s. Louis Th. van Drielen and Elise Cornelie (Labouchere) Gimberg; student Lyceum and Gymnasium The Hague, Netherlands; m. Adriana Maria Boon, 1949 (div. 1966). Debut at Royal Theatre in The Hague, 1939; appeared throughout Europe in numerous plays, including Arsenic and Old Lace, Romeo and Juliet and The Hasty Heart, 1948-50; appeared on London stage in Daphne Laureola, 1950, later at Music Box Theatre on Broadway; appeared in Am. stage prodns. of The Sound of Music, 1963-65, The Deputy, 1966, Private Lives, 1963, Marriage-Go-Round, 1962, Write Me A Murder, 1967, My Fair Lady, 1972; appeared in motion pictures A Time to Live, A Time to Die, Monte Carlo Baby, Madame X, Von Ryan's Express, The Wizard of Baghdad, The Enemy General, Feuerwerk, Nachtschatten, Dirty Business, Diamanten Party, Nachtfrost, Books of the Smaller Souls, Rufus, My Dog the Thief, The Flying Fontaines, Nous Irons a Monte Carlo, Brelan D'as; television appearances include 12 O'Clock High, The Man Who Never Was, The F.B.I. Story, Wild Wild West, Jericho, Voyage to the Bottom of the Sea, Tarzan, Run For Your Life, Mission Impossible, Garrison's Gorillas, Ironside, The Name of the Game, It Takes A Thief, Green Acres, Mod Squad, Bracken's World, The Man and the City, Twilight Zone, Marcus Welby, M.D.; guest star in The Rhineman Exchange, The Hardy Boys, Charlie's Angels, Switch, Six Million Dollar Man, Wonder Woman, The Great Wallendas, The Clone Master, 1979, The Ultimate Imposter, 1979, Swang Song, 1979; appeared in Dutch TV spl. Giovanni Bocchaccio, 1979, The Reluctant Past, 1979. Mem. Screen Actors Guild, AFTRA, Equity, Acad. Motion Picture Arts and Scis. Address: c/o Paul Kohner-Michael Levy Agy 9169 Sunset Blvd Los Angeles CA 90069

VAN DUSEN, ALBERT CLARENCE, univ. adminstr.; b. Tampa, Fla., Aug. 30, 1915; s. Charles H. and Maude E. (Green) Van D.; B.S., U. Fla., 1937, A.M., 1938; Ph.D., Northwestern, 1942; Litt.D., U. Tampa, 1959; L.H.D., Duquesne U., 1967; m. Margaret Davis, Jan. 3, 1943; children—Margaret Anne (Mrs. Joseph J. Pysh), Jane Katherine, Sally Elizabeth (Mrs. Daniel L. Brooks). Instr., asst. prof. dept. psychology U. Fla., 1938-41; asso. prof. psychology Northwestern U., 1946, dir. summer session, 1948-52, v.p., dir. pub. relations, 1952-56; prof. psychology, bus. adminstrn. and edn. U. Pitts., 1956—, asst. chancellor for planning and devel., 1956-59, vice chancellor The Professions, 1959-67, vice chancellor Program Devel. and Pub. Affairs, 1967-71, vice chancellor, sec. univ., 1971—. Trustee Dollar Savs.-Bank, Pitts. Bd. govs. Pinchot Inst. for Conservation Studies; bd. dirs. World Affairs Council Pitts., Duquesne U., Pitts. YMCA, ACTION-Housing, Inc.; bd. dirs., v.p. Pitts. Ednl. TV (WQED); trustee Pitts. History and Landmarks Found.; pres. H.C. Frick Ednl. Commn., United Way Pa.; pres., chmn., dir. Health and Welfare Planning Assn. Allegheny County, South Hills Child Guidance Center; chmn. self-care study Health Edn. Center. Served as lt. USNR, 1942-46, aviation psychologist. Fellow Am., Pa. psychol. assns.; mem. C. of C. (dir., 1953-55), Am. Coll. Public Relations Assn. (v.p. 1956-58), Assn. Deans and Dirs. Summer Sessions (sec. 1950-51), Profl. Schs. and World Affairs Com. (chmn. edn. and world affairs 1965-67), Am. Personnel and Guidance Assn., AAUP, Midwest, Eastern, Pitts. psychol. assns., Western Pa. Council Econ. Edn. (charter mem.), 100 Friends Pitts. Art, Internat. Assn. Applied Psychology, Phi Beta Kappa, Sigma Xi, Phi Kappa Phi, Omicron Delta Kappa, Beta Theta Pi. Clubs: Univ., Duquesne (Pitts.). Editor: Proc. Am. Coll. Personnel Assn. Contbr. articles to profl. jours. Home: 108 Blue Spruce Circle Pittsburgh PA 15243

VAN DUSEN, BRUCE BUICK, publisher; b. Toledo, Nov. 23, 1930; s. Bruce Buick and Helen (Campbell) Van D.; grad. Deerfield Acad., 1949; B.A., Williams Coll., 1953; postgrad. Wayne State U., 1956, Wesleyan U., Middletown, Conn., 1957; m. Carolyn Rick Perkins, Sept. 15, 1954; children—Carolyn Murray, Philip Campbell, Andrew Bruce. Tchr., Deerfield (Mass.) Acad., 1956-58; reporter Providence Jour., 1958-64; editorial writer Detroit News, 1965-68, Louisville Courier-Jour., 1968-69; editor Niles (Mich.) Daily Star, 1968; pres. Jefferson Pub., Inc., Matthews, Ky., 1971—; adminstrv. dir. Planned Parenthood, Louisville, 1969-70. Bd. dirs. Housing Opportunity Centers, Inc. Louisville, 1970-73, Ky. Pub. Health Assn. Served with CIC, AUS, 1953-56. Congl. fellow Am. Polit. Sci. Assn., 1962-63. Mem. Alpha Delta Phi. Democrat. Unitarian. Club: Owl Creek (Anchorage, Ky.). Address: 12345 Osage Rd Anchorage KY 40223

VAN DUSEN, FRANCIS LUND, U.S. circuit judge; b. Phila., May 16, 1912; s. Lewis H. and Muriel (Lund) Van D.; A.B., Princeton, 1934; LL.B., Harvard, 1937; m. Rhe Brooke Meserole, June 11, 1942 (dec. Nov. 1976); children—Rhe Van D. Jain, Muriel Van D. Berkeley, Francis Lund, Clinton Meserole; m. 2d, Margaret Brooks Goodenough, Aug. 19, 1978. Admitted to Pa. bar, 1938; asso. Dechert, Smith & Clark, 1937-41; with Barnes, Dechert, Price, Myers & Rhoads, 1945-55, partner, 1950-55; sr. atty. WPB, 1941-42; U.S. judge Eastern Dist. Pa., 1955-67, U.S. judge 3d U.S. circuit, 1967—. Vice chmn. exec. com. Crime Prevention Assn. Served as lt. comdr. USNR, 1942-45. Decorated Bronze Star medal (USN, USAAF), Mem. Am., Fed., Pa. (exec. com. 1953-56), Phila. bar assns., Harvard Law Sch. Assn. Phila. (past pres.), Hist. Soc. Pa., World Affairs Council Phila., Am. Legion, Mil. Order Fgn. Wars, Pa. Soc., S.A.R., Phi Beta Kappa. Clubs: Princeton (dir. 1947-52, 79, pres. 1978-79); Merion Cricket, Lawyers, Phila. (Phila.). Home: 507 Moreno Rd Wynnewood PA 19096 Office: 20613 US Court House Philadelphia PA 19106

VAN DUSEN, LEWIS HARLOW, JR., lawyer; b. Phila., Dec. 18, 1910; s. Lewis Harlow and Muriel (Lund) Van D.; A.B., Princeton U., 1932; student law Harvard, 1932-33; B.C.L. (Rhodes scholar), New Coll., Oxford U. (Eng.), 1935; m. Maria Pepper Whelen, Nov. 8, 1935; children—Duncan, Lewis Harlow, Michael Hillegas, Sally Pepper. Admitted to Pa. bar, 1935; with Drinker, Biddle & Reath, Phila., 1935-41, partner, 1942-52, sr. partner, 1952—. Pres. Rivierside Metal Co. (N.J.), 1947-49, dir., 1947-54; past dir. Kiwi Polish Co. (U.S.A.); dir. ITE-Imperial Corp., 1967-76, Campbell Soup Co., The Girard Bank, Phila., I.U. Internat. Corp.; dep. to U.S. rep. NATO, 1950-51; chief spl. FOA mission to Brazil, 1954; past solicitor Zoning Hearing Bd. of Lower Merion Twp. (Pa.), 1952—; spl. counsel Southeastern Pa. Transp. Authority; mem. Pa. Commonwealth Compensation Commn., 1971-72. Active United Fund, Vis. Nurse Assn. Bd. dirs. Greater Phila. Partnership; former chmn. Greater Phila. Movement; former trustee Princeton U., Episc. Acad., Phila., Phila. Div. Sch., World Affairs Council Phila.; chmn. men's bd. Ingils House; trustee Acad. Natural Scis. Phila. Served from lt. to lt. col. AUS, 1942-45. Decorated Purple Heart, Bronze Star medal, Legion of Merit (U.S.); Legion of Honor, Croix de Guerrre (France). Mem. Am. Bar Found., Am. (past mem. ho. dels.; chmn. standing com. on ethics and profl. responsibility, mem. standing com. fed. judiciary), Pa. (pres. 1974-75), Phila. (chancellor 1968) bar assns., Phila. Jud. Council (chmn.), Am. Coll. Trial Lawyers. Episcopalian. Club: Union League (Phila.) Home: 10 Righters Ferry Rd Bala PA 19004 Office: Phila Nat Bank Bldg Philadelphia PA 19107

VAN DUSEN, RICHARD CAMPBELL, lawyer; b. Jackson, Mich., July 18, 1925; s. Bruce Buick and Helen (Campbell) Van D.; B.S., U. Minn., 1945; LL.B., Harvard, 1949; m. Barbara Congdon, June 28, 1949; children—Amanda, Lisa, Katherine. Admitted to Mich. bar, 1949; asso. firm Dickinson, Wright, McKean, Cudlip & Moon, Detroit, 1949-57, partner, 1958-62, 64-68, 73—; mem. Mich. Ho. of Reps. from Oakland County, 1954-56; legal adviser to gov. Mich., 1963; undersec. housing and urban devel., 1969-72; dir. Detroit Automobile Inter-Ins. Exchange, chmn., 1978—; dir. Pennwalt Corp., Ticor, Ticor Mortgage Ins. Co., W.S. Butterfield Theatres, Inc. Del. Mich. Constl. Conv., 1961-62; mem. Mich. Law Revision Commn. Trustee Cranbrook, Kingswood and Brookside schs., 1966-72, Deerfield Acad., 1975—; bd. govs. Wayne State U., 1979—. Served with USNR, 1943-46. Mem. Fed., Am., Detroit (dir. 1965-69, trustee Found.) bar assns., State Bar Mich., Adminstrv. Conf. of U.S. (council 1969-72, 73—). Clubs: Econ. of Detroit, Automobile of Mich. (chmn. bd. dirs. 1978—). Republican. Episcopalian. Home: 32205 Bingham Rd Birmingham MI 48010 Office: 800 1st National Bldg Detroit MI 48226

VAN DUYN, MONA JANE, poet; b. Waterloo, Iowa, May 9, 1921; d. Earl George and Lora G. (Kramer) Van Duyn; B.A., U. No. Iowa, 1942; M.A., U. Iowa, 1943; D.Litt. (hon.), Washington U., St. Louis, 1971, Cornell (Iowa) Coll., 1972; m. Jarvis A. Thurston, Aug. 31, 1943. Instr. English, U. Iowa, 1943-46, U. Louisville, 1946-50; lectr. English, Univ. Coll., Washington U., 1950-67; poetry readings, 1970—; poetry editor, co-pub. Perspective, A Quar. of Lit., 1947-67; lectr. Salzburg (Austria) Seminar Am. Studies, 1973; poet-in-residence Breadloaf Writing Conf., Mass., 1974, 76. Recipient Bollingen prize, 1970, Nat. Book award, 1971, Eunice Tietjens award, 1956, Helen Bullis prize, 1964, 76, Harriet Monroe award, 1968, Hart Grane Meml. award, 1968, Borestone Mountains 1st prize, 1968;

Loines prize Nat. Inst. Arts and Letters, 1976; grantee Nat. Council Arts, 1967; Guggenheim fellow, 1972. Author: Valentines to the Wide World, 1959; A Time of Bees, 1964; To See, To Take, 1970, Bedtime Stories, 1972; Merciful Disguises, 1973. Address: 7505 Teasdale Ave St Louis MO 63130

VAN DUZER, ALBERT WIENCKE, clergyman; b. Newburgh, N.Y., July 15, 1917; s. Albert Barton and Clara Helen (Wiencke) Van D.; A.B., Trinity Coll., Hartford, Conn., 1940; Th.B., Gen. Theol. Sem., 1945, S.T.D., 1966; B.D., Phila. Div. Sch., 1954, D.D., 1967; m. Marion R. Lippincott, Apr. 31, 1939; children—Daryl (Mrs. Henry Gorczycki), Margaret Lynn (Mrs. Joseph A. Ryan), Marianne Gayle (Mrs. Joseph M. Carson). Ordained to ministry Episcopal Ch., 1946; curate Grace Ch., Merchantville, N.J., 1946-47, rector, 1949-66; rector Ch. of Advent, Cape May, N.J., 1947-49; suffragan bishop N.J. Diocese, 1966-72; bishop coadjutor of N.J., 1972-73, bishop of N.J., 1973—. Past youth dir., past pres. Youth Cons. Service N.J. Diocese; Camden (N.J.) County rep. White House Conf. Aging, 1957; mem. Bd. Examining Chaplains N.J., 1957-66; past chaplain Merchantville Fire Co.; mem. exec. council Episcopal Ch. Trustee Evergreen's Home Aged, Camden County Children's Shelter, Camden County council Girl Scouts Am. Named Man of Year Merchantville Fire Co.; recipient Medal of Honor, Diocese N.J., 1962, Boyle award citizenship and community service Camden County Bar Assn., 1965; Nat. Alumni Achievement award Trinity Coll., Hartford, 1976; named hon. canon Trinity Cathedral, Trenton, N.J., 1957. Mem. Camden County Health and Welfare Assn. (mem. bd.), Nat. Assn. Social Service. Mason (33 deg.; past grand chaplain N.J.), Kiwanian, Lion. Home: 31 Delaware Ave Trenton NJ 08628 Office: 808 W State St Trenton NJ 08618

VAN DYKE, DICK, TV actor, comedian; b. West Plains, Mo., Dec. 13, 1925; ed. high sch.; m. Marjorie Willett, Feb. 12, 1948; children—Christian, Barry, Stacey, Carrie Beth. Appeared school plays, civic theatre prodns.; with Wayne Williams, founded advt. agy., Danville, Ill., 1946; with Philip Erickson, appeared in pantomine act The Merry Mutes, Eric and Van, 1947-53; TV master ceremonies Merry Mutes Show, The Music Shop, Atlanta; TV variety show Dick Van Dyke Show, New Orleans; master ceremonies Morning Show, CBS, 1955, Cartoon Show, 1956; guest appearances nat. TV shows, 1958; host Flair, weekly TV show ABC, 1960; Broadway debut in The Girls Against the Boys, 1959, performed Broadway musical Bye Bye Birdie, 1960-61 (also motion picture version); weekly comedy program Dick Van Dyke Show, CBS-TV, 1961-66; star New Dick Van Dyke Show, 1971-74; performer Carol Burnett Show; host Van Dyke and Company, 1976; numerous TV guest appearances; performed in motion pictures including What a Way To Go, 1964, Mary Poppins, 1965, Divorce American Style, 1967, Chitty, Chitty, Bang, Bang, 1968, Comic, 1969, Some Kind of Nut, 1969, Cold Turkey, 1971, The Morning After, 1974. Served with USAAC, World War II. Recipient Theater World award, 1960; Antoinette Perry award for best mus. comedy actor, 1961; Emmy award for comedy Nat. Acad. TV Arts and Scis., 1962, 64, 65. Author: Faith, Hope, and Hilarity, 1970. *

VAN DYKE, MILTON DENMAN, educator; b. Chgo., Aug. 1, 1922; s. James Richard and Ruth (Barr) Van D.; B.S., Harvard, 1943; M.S., Calif. Inst. Tech., 1947, Ph.D., 1949; m. Sylvia Jean Agard Adams, June 16, 1962; children—Russell B., Eric J., Nina A., Brooke A. and Byron J. and Christopher M. (triplets). Research engr. NACA, 1943-46, 50-54, 55-58; vis. prof. U. Paris (France), 1958- 59; prof. aero. Stanford, 1959—; cons. aerospace industry, 1949—. Served with USNR, 1944-46. Guggenheim fellow, 1954-55. Mem. Am. Acad. Arts and Scis., Nat. Acad. Engring., Am. Phys. Soc., Phi Beta Kappa, Sigma Xi. Club: Sierra. Author: Perturbation Methods in Fluid Mechanics, 1964. Home: 506 Campus Dr Stanford CA 94305 Office: Div Applied Mechanics Stanford Univ Stanford CA 94305

VAN DYKE, WILLARD AMES, motion picture dir.; b. Denver, Dec. 5, 1906; s. Louis W. and Pearl (Ames) Van D.; m. Mary Gray Barnett, Jan. 2, 1938 (div. Mar. 1950); children—Alison (Mrs. Richard Shank), Peter; m. 2d, Margaret Barbara Murray Milikin, June 17, 1950; children—Murray, Cornelius. Photographer, PWA Art Project, San Francisco, 1934, Harpers Bazaar, 1935; co-founder Group f.64, 1932, dir. documentary films including The City, Valleytown, Rice; dir. TV programs including High Adventure, 1958, 20th Century, 1963-65, 21st Century, 1968; dir. dept. film Mus. Modern Art, N.Y.C., 1965-74; prof. State U. N.Y. at Purchase, 1973—; vis. prof. U. N.H., 1968, 69. Mem. Yale Art Council, 1976—; trustee Internat. Film Seminars, pres., 1965-72; mem. Brandeis Commn. for Awards in Creative Arts, 1977; bd. dirs. Anthology Film Archives, 1977. Mem. Screen Dirs. Internat. Guild (pres. 1960-62), N.Y. Film Council (pres. 1947), Am. Fedn. Arts (trustee 1976—). Democrat. Photographs exhibited in one-man shows De Young Meml. Mus., San Francisco, 1933, San Diego Mus., 1934, Pa. State U., 1970, Budapest, 1974, Witkin Gallery, N.Y.C., Wirtz Gallery, San Francisco, 1977, others. Recipient Spl. award Internat. Mus. Photography, 1978. Club: Century (N.Y.C.). Home: 505 West End Ave New York City NY 10024 Office: Univ State of NY Purchase NY. *My actions in life have been governed by the belief that artists are the keepers of humanity's conscience and their works the measure of a society's worth.*

VANEK, JAROSLAV, educator, economist; b. Prague, Czechoslovakia, Apr. 20, 1930; s. Josef and Jaroslava (Tucek) V.; degree in statistics, Sorbonne, Paris, 1951; license in econ., U. Geneva, 1954; Ph.D., Mass. Inst. Tech., 1957; m. Wilda M. Marraffino, Dec. 26, 1959; children—Joseph, Francis, Rosemarie, Steven, Teresa. Came to U.S., 1955, naturalized, 1960. Instr., then asst. prof. Harvard, 1957-63; adviser AID, 1964; mem. faculty Cornell U., 1964—, prof. econ., 1966—, Carl Marks prof. internat. studies, 1969—, dir. program comparative econ. devel., 1968-73, dir. program participation and labor-managed systems, 1969—. Mem. nat. adv. bd. econs. NSF, 1969-70. Mem. Fedn. Econ. Democracy (co-founder). Roman Catholic. Author: International Trade: Theory and Economic Policy, 1962; The Balance of Payments, Level of Economic Activity and the Value of Currency, 1962; The Natural Resource Content of United States Foreign Trade, 1950-1955, 1963; General Equilibrium of International Discrimination, 1965; Estimating Foreign Resource Needs for Economic Development, 1966; Maximal Economic Growth, 1968; The General Theory of Labor-Managed Market Economies, 1970; The Participatory Economy, 1971; Self-Management: Economic Liberation of Man, 1975; The Labor-Managed Economy, 1977. Home: 414 Triphammer Rd Ithaca NY 14850

VAN EKRIS, ANTHONIE CORNELIS, trading corp. exec.; b. Rotterdam, Netherlands, June 3, 1934; s. Cornelis and Evertje (Mulder) van E.; came to U.S., 1963; m. Heather Frances Button, Sept. 7, 1960; children—Anthonie Cornelis, Marijke Karin. Trainee Van Rees, Ltd., Rotterdam, 1952-57; mgr. African Coffee Trading Ops., Mombasa, E. Africa, 1957-63, mgr. Ralli Trading Co., N.Y.C., 1963-67; pres. Van Ekris & Stoett, Ltd., N.Y.C., 1967-70; pres., dir. Ralli-Am. Ltd., N.Y.C., 1970-72; pres., chief exec. officer Kay Corp., N.Y.C., 1972—, also dir.; chmn. Kay Jewelers, Inc., Balfour, Maclaine Internat. Ltd., Van Ekris & Stoett, Inc., Marcus & Co., Inc. Served with Royal Dutch Navy, 1951-53. Address: Hilltop Pl Rye NY 10580

VAN ELDEREN, MARLIN JAMES, editor; b. Modesto, Calif., Mar. 10, 1946; s. Bastiaan and Vivolyn Maxine (Ross) Van E.; A.B., Calvin Coll., Grand Rapids, Mich., 1966; postgrad. Harvard U., 1966-67; m. Meribeth Ann Yoder, July 22, 1966; children—Kimberly Anne, Amy Joy, Abigail Lynne. Editor, William B. Eerdmans Pub Co., Grand Rapids, Mich., 1967-68, gen. book editor, 1970-72, editor-in-chief, 1972—, v.p., 1979—. Cons., The Banner. Served with U.S. Army, 1968-70. Decorated Bronze Star medal, Army Commendation medal with oak leaf cluster; recipient awards for writing Evang. Press Assn., 1972, 76, 77, Asso. Ch. Press, 1975. Mem. Christian Ref. Ch. (del. denomination synod 1973, 75). Mng. editor The Ref. Jour., 1971-78, editor-in-chief, 1978—. Contbr. articles and revs. to periodicals. Home: 2303 Jefferson Dr SE Grand Rapids MI 49507 Office: 255 Jefferson Ave SE Grand Rapids MI 49503

VAN ESELTINE, WILLIAM PARKER, microbiologist, educator; b. Syracuse, N.Y., Aug. 21, 1924; s. Glen Parker and Florence Marie (Lamb) Van E.; A.B., Oberlin Coll., 1944; M.S., Cornell U., 1947, Ph.D., 1949; m. Marian Louise Vanderburgh, Aug. 25, 1948; children—Kenneth Leslie, Karen Elaine. Asst. in bacteriology N.Y. State Agrl. Expt. Sta., Geneva, 1944-45, summer 1946, N.Y. State Coll. Agr., Cornell U., Ithaca, 1946-48; asso. prof. bacteriology Clemson (S.C.) Agrl. Coll., 1948-52; asst. prof. vet. hygiene U. Ga., Athens, 1952-59, asso. prof. microbiology and preventive medicine, 1959-67, prof. med. microbiology, 1967—. Mem. Am. Soc. Microbiology, N.Y. Acad. Sci., Ga. Acad. Sci., Am. Leptospirosis Research Conf. (pres. 1973), AAAS, Sigma Xi, Phi Kappa Phi. Contbr. articles on microbiology to profl. jours. Home: 237 Woodlawn Ave Athens GA 30606

VAN FLEET, JAMES ALWARD, army officer (ret.), business exec.; b. Coytesville, N.J., Mar. 19, 1892; s. William and Medora Roxanne (Scofield) Van F; B.S., U.S. Mil. Acad., 1915; LL.D., U. Fla., 1946, Seoul (Korea) Nat. U., 1952, Columbia, 1954, L.I. U., 1958, Chung-ang U., Korea, 1962; m. Helen Hazel Moore, Dec. 25, 1915; children—Helen Elizabeth (Mrs. Edward Traywick McConnell), Dempsie Catherine (Mrs. Joseph Alexander McChristian), James Alward Jr. (capt. USAF; missing in N. Korea, 1952, presumed dead, 1954). Commd. 2d lt. inf. U.S. Army, 1915, and advanced through grades to gen., 1951; served in Mexican Border campaign, 1916-17, overseas, 1918-19; comd. 8th Inf. Regt., 4th Div., 90th Div. XXIII Corps and III Corps, 1941-45; comd. 2d Service Command, Governors Island, N.Y., 1947, dep. comdg. gen. 1st Army, 1947; dep. chief of staff European Command, Frankfurt, Germany, 1947-48; dir. joint mil. adv. and aid groups, Greece, 1948-50; comdr. UN and ROK Army Forces in Korea, 1951-53, ret., 1953; surveyed mil., econ. and polit. situation for Pres. Eisenhower, 1954. Cons. guerrilla warfare office Sec. Army, 1961-62. Pres. James A. Van Fleet Estates, Inc., Withlacoochee Ranch, Inc., Green Valley Ranch, Inc., Overseas Basic Industries, Inc., Ulen Mgmt. Co.; dir. 20th Century-Fox Film Corp., Sun Bank Auburndale, Société des Eaux (Greece), Motorola (Korea). Decorated D.S.C. with 2 oak leaf clusters, D.S.M. with 3 oak leaf clusters, Silver Star with 2 oak leaf clusters, Legion of Merit with oak leaf cluster, Bronze Star medal with 2 oak leaf clusters, Purple Heart with 2 oak leaf clusters, World War I Victory medal with 2 battle stars, World War II Victory medal, European Theater medal with arrowhead and 5 battle stars, Air Medal with oak leaf clusters, UN Korean Service ribbon, D.S.O., knight Brit. Empire (Gt. Britain), Legion of Honor, Croix de Guerre with palm (France), Croix de Guerre with palm (Belgium), grand cross Order of Phoenix, Distinguished Medal of Honor, grand comdr. Order of George 1st Air Force Cross (Greece), Royal Order, grade one (Iran), Taekuk D.S.M. with gold star (Rep. Korea), Orden de Boyaca (Columbia), Grand Cross Order Orange Nassau with swords (Netherlands), also honors and awards from various other fgn. countries; recipient Distinguished Am. award Nat. Football Found. and Hall of Fame, 1976. Home: South Beach Rd Jupiter Island Hobe Sound FL 33455 Office: Van Fleet Ranch Polk City FL 33868

VAN FOSSAN, ROBERT VIRGIL, ins. co. exec.; b. Breckenridge, Minn., Sept. 24, 1926; s. Virgil R. and Marie (Hogan) Van F.; grad. pub. schs.; m. Mary Jane Lake, Aug. 20, 1946; children—Deborah Van Fossan Bruers, Craig, Mark. Agency cashier Northwestern Nat. Life Ins. Co., Mpls., 1947-49, agt., 1949-51, supr. central div., Chgo., 1951, supt. agencies, Spokane, Wash., Mpls., v.p., agency dir., 1966-69, sr. v.p., agency dir., 1969-72; pres. Mut. Benefit Life Ins. Co., Newark, 1972-78, chmn. bd., chief exec. officer, 1978—; dir. Pub. Service Electric & Gas, Amerada Hess Corp. Mem. Gov. Byrne's Econ. Recovery Commn.; mem. planning com., dir. Am. Council Life Ins.; mem. advisory bd. Essex council Boy Scouts Am.; trustee Greater Newark Hosp. Devel. Fund, Greater Newark Urban Coalition, Newark Mus., United Way of Essex and West Hudson, N.J. Safety Council; bd. govs. N.J. State Opera; mem. exec. com. NCCJ; mem. exec. com. advisory council Coll. Bus. Adminstrn., U. Notre Dame; overseer N.J. Symphony Orch.; mem. advisory com. Pingry Sch. Mem. Greater Newark C. of C. (vice chmn.). Club: Two Hundred (trustee) (Essex County). Home: 33 Horizon Dr Mendham NJ 07945 Office: 520 Broad St Newark NJ 07101

VAN GAASBECK, HARRY ROBERT, investment exec.; b. Chemung, N.Y., Nov. 26, 1919; s. Harry Sage and Jessie (Lenox) Van G.; A.B., Middlebury Coll., 1941; student (fellow) Babson Inst., 1941-42; M.B.A., Harvard, 1947; m. Martha Clark Newton, May 6, 1944; children—Robert Clark, Margaret Newton. Asst. treas. investment sec. Springfield Ins. Co. (Mass.), 1951-65; investment sec., v.p. investment stocks, v.p. securities Monarch Life Ins. Co., Springfield, 1960—; pres., dir. Monarch Securities, Inc., 1968—; v.p., dir. Monarch Investment Mgmt. Corp., Springfield, 1974—; v.p., treas. Variable Stock Fund Inc., 1977—. Instr. evening div. U. Hartford, 1948-52, Western New Eng. Coll., 1952-63; mem. financial adv. com. Springfield Redevel. Authority, 1962—. Mem. finance com. United Way Pioneer Valley, 1967—. Served with USAAF, 1942-46. Mem. Nat. Assn. Security Dealers, Boston Security Analysts Soc., Chi Psi. Republican. Conglist. Rotarian. Home: 83 Duxbury Ln Longmeadow MA 01106 Office: 1250 State St Springfield MA 01101

VAN GELDER, RICHARD GEORGE, mus. ofcl., zoologist; b. N.Y.C. Dec. 17, 1928; s. Joseph and Clara DeHirsch (Goldberg) Van G.; B.S. with honors, Colo. A. and M. Coll., 1950; M.S., U. Ill., 1952, Ph.D., 1958; m. 2d, Rosalind Rudnick, July 1, 1962; children—Russell Neil, Gordon Mark, Leslie Gail. Lab. asst. Colo. A. & M. Coll., 1947-50; teaching asst. U. Ill., 1950-53; research asst. U. Kan., 1954-55, asst. prof., 1955; asst. curator Am. Mus. Nat. Hist., N.Y.C., 1956-61, asso. curator, 1961-69, curator, 1969—, acting chmn. dept. mammals, 1958-59, chmn. dept., 1959-74; also professorial lectr. Downstate Med. Center, State U. N.Y., 1970-73. Lectr. Columbia, 1958-59, asst. prof., 1959-63; with Huachuca Mountain Expdn., summer 1950, Graham Mountain Expdn., summer 1951, Spotted Skunk Expdn., 1953-54, Puritan Expdn., 1957, Uruguay Expdn., 1962-63, Bolivian Expdn. 1964, Bolivian Expdn. II, 1965, Bahama Biol. Survey, 1966, Mozambique Expdn., 1968, S.W. Africa Expdn., 1970, Nyala Expdn., 1971-74, Tsessebe Expdn., 1976-77. Mem. sci. adv. bd. Nat. History Mag., 1958-66, 72-74; mem. adv. bd. Archbold Biol. Sta., Lake Placid, Fla., 1958-74; mem. tech. and editorial adv. bd. Population Reference Bur., 1971-75; bd. dirs. Archbold Expdns., Inc., 1965-74, Quincy Bog Natural Area, 1977—; mem. sci. adv. bd. Found. Environ. Edn., 1972. Fellow N.Y. Zool. Soc.; mem. Am. Soc. Mammalogists (pres. 1968-70), Soc. Systematic Zoology, AAAS, Wildlife Soc., Sigma Xi, Beta Beta Beta, Phi Sigma, Alpha Gamma Rho. Author: Physiological Mammalogy, 1963, 65; Biology of Mammals, 1969; Animals and Man, 1972. Office: American Museum Natural History New York City NY 10024

VAN GELDEREN, BARBARA, advt. exec.; b. Long Beach, N.Y., Jan. 17, 1928; d. Sidney and Sadie (Fribourg) Van G.; m. Joseph E. Goldman, Mar. 22, 1947; children—Carlee Goldman Paddock, Richard. Portrait artist, 1947—; v.p. Adways, Inc., Jericho, N.Y., 1965-74, dir., 1965-72; v.p. Goldman Van Gelderen, Inc., Old Bethpage, N.Y., 1974—, also dir. Address: 297 M Pinecroft Dr Taylors SC 29687

VANGER, MILTON ISADORE, historian; b. N.Y.C., Apr. 11, 1925; s. Max Manuel and Rose (Rothstein) V.; A.B., Princeton U., 1948; M.A., Harvard U., 1950, Ph.D., 1958; m. Elsa M. Oribe, Sept. 10, 1956; children—John, Mark, Rachel. Teaching fellow history Harvard U., 1952-56; instr. Okla. State U., 1956-58; asst. prof. history Sacramento State Coll., 1958-62; mem. faculty Brandeis U., Waltham, Mass., 1962—, prof. history, 1973—, chmn. com. Latin Am. studies, 1971—; invited lectr. 50th anniversary conf. commemorating death of Batlle y Ordoñez, Montevideo, Uruguay, 1979. Served with AUS, 1943-45. Doherty Found. fellow, 1950-52; grantee Am. Philos. Soc., 1966. Mem. New Eng. Council Latin Am. Studies (sec.-treas. 1970-72), Am. Hist. Assn., Latin Am. Studies Assn., Phi Beta Kappa. Democrat. Jewish. Author: Jose Batlle y Ordonez of Uruguay: The Creator of His Times, 1963, Spanish translation, 1968; outside reviewer Nat. Endowment Humanities, Radcliffe Inst.; contbr. articles profl. jours. Home: 32 Gray St Cambridge MA 02138 Office: Brandeis Univ Waltham MA 02254

VAN GINKEL, BLANCHE LEMCO, architect, coll. adminstr.; b. London, Dec. 14, 1923; d. Myer and Claire Lemco; B.Arch., McGill U., 1945; M.C.P., Harvard U., 1950; m. H. P. Daniel van Ginkel, 1956; children—Brenda Renee, Marc Ian. Tech. asst. Nat. Film Bd. Can., 1943-44; mgr. City Planning Office, Regina, Sask., Can., 1946; architect Atelier Le Corbusier, Paris, 1948; asst. prof. architecture U. Pa., 1951-57; partner van Ginkel Assos., Montreal, Que., Can., also Toronto, Ont., Can., 1957—; dir. Sch. Architecture U. Toronto, 1977—; vis. critic Harvard U., 1958, 70; vis. prof. Universite de Montreal, McGill U. Recipient Lt. Gov.'s medal McGill U., 1945; Internat. Fedn. Housing and Planning Grand Prix, 1956; Massey medal, 1962; Mademoiselle Mag. award, 1957; Silver Jubilee medal, 1977. Fellow Royal Archtl. Inst. Can.; mem. Can. Inst. Planners, Assn. Royal Inst. Brit. Architects (asso.) Ordre des Architectes du Quebec, Royal Canadian Acad. Art. Contbr. articles to profl. jours. Home: 36 Summerhill Gardens Toronto ON M4T 1B4 Canada Office: 230 College St Toronto ON M5S 1A1 Canada

VAN GORKOM, JEROME WILLIAM, corp. mfg. exec.; b. Denver, Aug. 6, 1917; s. A.G. and Elizabeth (Laux) Van G.; B.S., U. Ill., 1939, J.D., 1941, C.P.A., 1950; m. Betty Jean Alexander, June 27, 1942; children—Gayle, Lynne. Admitted to Ill. bar, 1941; law asso. Kix Miller, Baar & Morris, Chgo., 1945-47; accountant Arthur Andersen & Co., 1947-54, partner, 1954-56; treas., controller Trans Union Corp., Chgo., 1956—, dir., 1957—, v.p., 1958-60, exec. v.p., 1960-63, pres., 1963-78, chmn. bd., 1978—; dir. Schering-Plough Corp., Champion Internat. Corp., Ill. Central Industries, Ill. Central Gulf R.R. Bd. dirs., chmn. Lyric Opera of Chgo., pres., 1962, chmn. bd., 1964-69, 79; trustee Tax Found. Served with USNR, 1941-45. Mem. Am. Bar Assn., Am. Inst. C.P.A.s. Clubs: Chicago, Mid America, Comml., Onwentsia, Old Elm, Pauma Valley Country. Home: 908 Ringwood Rd Lake Forest IL 60045 Office: 90 Half Day Rd Lincolnshire IL 60015

VAN GRAAFEILAND, ELLSWORTH ALFRED, judge; b. Rochester, N.Y., May 11, 1915; s. Ivan and Elsie (Gohr) VanG.; A.B., U. Rochester, 1937; LL.B., Cornell U., 1940; m. Rosemary Vaeth, May 26, 1945; children—Gary, Suzanne, Joan, John, Anne. Admitted to N.Y. bar, 1940; practiced in Rochester; now judge U.S. Ct. Appeals for 2d Circuit. Fellow Am., N.Y. bar founds.; mem. Am. (ho. dels. 1973-75), N.Y. State (v.p. 1972-73, pres. 1973-74) chmn. negligence compensation and ins. sect. 1968-69), Monroe County (past pres.) bar assns., Am. Coll. Trial Lawyers. Mason. Clubs: Kent; Oak Hill Country (Rochester). Home: 76 Ramsey Park Rochester NY 14610 Office: US Court House Rochester NY 14614

VAN GUNDY, GREGORY FRANK, lawyer; b. Columbus, Ohio, Oct. 24, 1945; s. Paul Arden and Edna Marie (Sanders) Van G.; B.A., Ohio State U., Columbus, 1966, J.D., 1969. Admitted to N.Y. bar, 1971; asso. atty. firm Willkie Farr & Gallagher, N.Y.C., 1970-74; v.p. legal, sec. Marsh & McLennan Cos., Inc., N.Y.C., 1974—. Mem. Am. Bar Assn., Phi Beta Kappa. Roman Catholic. Club: University (N.Y.C.). Home: 20 Beekman Pl New York NY 10022 Office: 1221 Ave of Americas New York NY 10020

VAN GYTENBEEK, RICHARD PETER, recreation orgn. exec.; b. Paterson, N.J., Feb. 5, 1933; s. Rudolph Johann and Carrie (Rist) Van G.; B.A., Princeton, 1955; m. Bette Fradd Tonge, June 18, 1955; children—Richard, Tony, Kate. Salesman, sales mgr. Kendrick Bellary, Denver, 1958-61; br. mgr., div. mgr. Kistler/Kwill, Colorado Springs, 1961-67, Denver, 1967-69; exec. dir. Trout Unlimited, Denver, 1969-74; pres. Am. Sportsman's Club, Inc., Denver, 1975—; v.p. Seal Furniture & Systems Inc. Pres., Chadwell Farms, Inc., 1966-69; chmn. bd. United Sportsmen's Council of Colo. Pres. Colorado Springs Symphony, 1964-67; chmn. Colorado Springs Planning Commn., 1965-67; pres., founder Colorado Springs Racquet Club, 1965-67. Bd. dirs. Rocky Mountain Center on Environment. Served to capt. AUS, 1956-58. Mem. South Park Sportsmen (chmn. bd.), Trout Unltd. (nat. dir.), Am. League Anglers (nat. dir.). Clubs: Alpine-Water Park Ski (v.p.) (Denver); El Paso (Colorado Springs); Arapahoe Tennis (Cherry Hills, Colo.). Author: The Way of a Trout, 1972; (with J. Michael Migrl) Streamside Conservation Guide, 1974. Home: 5 Belleview Pl Englewood CO 80110

VANHAEFTEN, CARL FREDERICK, cons. internat. devel.; b. Santa Cruz, Calif., Jan. 12, 1923; s. Karel August Rudolf and Anna Bartholda (Faure) van H.; B.S., Royal Coll. Tropical Agr., The Netherlands, 1945; m. Dorothy G. Wolthuis, Aug. 30, 1946 (div. July 1968); children—Karel A.R., Linda, Eileen; m. 2d, Roberta K. Taylor, Oct. 31, 1969. Investigator, U.S. Mil. Intelligence Unit, The Hague, 1946-47; German youth activities officer U.S. Army, Augsburg, 1947-48; edn. adviser 2d Armored Cav. Regt., Augsburg, 1948-50; chief information and edn. 2d Air Div., Landsburg, Germany, 1950-51; fgn. student adviser Coll. Agr., U. Maine, 1952-53; agrl. tng. specialist U.S. mission to European Regional and Other Orgns., 1953-54; chief FOA agrl. tng. br. Europe and Latin Am., 1954-56; dep., and acting chief div. econ. assistance to Spain for food and agr., 1956-60; dir. program econ. assistance for food and agr., Cambodia, 1960-63, Morocco, 1964-65; asst. dir. U.S. AID mission to Vietnam, 1965-68, spl. asst. war on hunger, Washington, 1968-70; mid-career tng. Johns Hopkins, 1970-71; chief rural devel. div. Latin Am. Bur., AID, 1972-75; cons. internat. devel., 1975—. Served with Underground Resistance Movement in Holland, World War II. Recipient U.S. Medal of Freedom 1946; Vietnam Agrl. medal, 1968.

Home: 2840 Linden Lane Falls Church VA 22042 Office: Experience Inc 1725 K St NW Suite 312 Washington DC 20006

VAN HAGEN, GEORGE ELY, III, rental co. exec.; b. Chgo., Apr. 11, 1923; s. George Ely and Ardietta (Ford) Van H.; student Cornell U. Sch. Mech. Engring., 1941-42, Northwestern U. Sch. Journalism, 1946-48; m. Barbara Kransz, Oct. 28, 1950 (div. 1965); 1 son, George E. IV; m. 2d, Sarah Bohannon, Aug. 30, 1969; 1 dau., Sarah Harrison. Account exec. Harry Coleman & Col, pub. relations, 1946-50; dir. personnel Peabody Coal Co., Chgo., 1950-53; mng. editor Home Guide, Inc., pubs., 1953-60; owner, pres. Van Hagen & Co., Chgo., 1960—; pres. Tri-Rental Co., Elk Grove Village, Ill., 1969—. Lectr. on history and use of jade to community orgns. Pres., Barrington Youth Services, 1971—. Bd. dirs. North Side Boys Clubs, 1950-67. Served with USNR, 1942-45; PTO. Mem. Alpha Delta Phi. Episcopalian. Clubs: Racquet (Chgo.); Barrington Hills Riding (past pres.), Barrington Hills Polo (past pres.). Explored Yukon Ty., Alaska, 1946-50, also numerous other trips for jade. Home: 123 Coolidge St Barrington IL 60010 Office: 660 Fargo Ave Elk Grove Village IL 60007

VAN HAMEL, MARTINE, dancer; b. Brussels, Nov. 16, 1945; student Nat. Ballet Sch. Can. Debut with Nat. Ballet Can., 1963; guest dancer Royal Swedish Ballet, Royal Winnipeg Ballet, Joffrey Ballet; with Am. Ballet Theatre, soloist, 1971-73, prin. dancer, 1973—. Office: Am Ballet Theatre 888 7th Ave New York NY 10019

VANHANDEL, RALPH ANTHONY, librarian; b. Appleton, Wis., Jan. 17, 1919; s. Frank Henry and Gertrude Mary (Schmidt) Van H.; B.A., U. Wis., 1946; A.B., U. Mich., 1947; m. Alice Catherine Hogan, Oct. 27, 1945; children—William Patrick, Karen Jean, Mary Jo. Head librarian Lawrence (Kans.) Free Pub. Library, 1947-51, Hibbing (Minn.) Pub. Library, 1951-54; library dir. Gary (Ind.) Pub. Library, 1954-74, Wells Meml. Pub. Library, Lafayette, Inc., 1974—; mem. Ind. Library Certification Bd., 1969—, Ind. Library Expansion Commn., 1973—. Named Ind. Librarian of Year, 1971. Mem. Anselm Forum (sec. 1964, v.p., 1965), ALA, Ind. (pres. 1963-64), Kans. (v.p. 1951) library assns. Clubs: K.C., Rotary. Home: 3624 Winter St Lafayette IN 47905 Office: 638 North St Lafayette IN 47901

VAN HAUER, ROBERT, health care co. exec.; b. Chgo., June 9, 1910; s. Francis Anthony and Della Agnes (Mulhern) Van H.; B.A. in Econs., B.B.A. in Accounting (Reiman scholar), U. Mont., Missoula, 1938; M.A. in Econs., U. Minn., Mpls., 1940; m. Elaine Greenwood, July 24, 1944 (dec. Nov. 1961); children—Peter, Jan, Mary, Christopher, Gretchen, Juliana; m. 2d, Margaret Ann St. Pierre Viehman, May 4, 1968; stepchildren—Gayle, Edwin, Thomas, John, Michael, Daniel. Jr. Auditor, Peat Marwick Mitchell, C.P.A.'s, Mpls., 1938-40; asst. sales mgr. North Star Woolen Mill, Mpls., 1940-42; dir. contracts Mpls. regional officer VA, 1946-51; with Health Central, Inc., Mpls., 1951-79, exec. v.p., 1965, pres., 1970-79; exec. dir. Health Found., Mpls., 1979—. Mem. planning commn., Golden Valley, Minn., 1959-66; past trustee St. Margaret's Acad., Benilde-St. Margaret's High Sch. Served to maj. AUS, 1941-46. Decorated Commendation ribbon; Rieman fellow, 1938-40. Mem. Am., Minn. (trustee, com. chmn. 1974) hosp. assns., War Meml. Blood Bank (pres., dir. 1967), Physicians Health Plan Mpls. (dir., exec. com.), Am. Legion. Republican. Roman Cath. Clubs: Mpls. Athletic, Minn. Valley Country, Elks. Home: 4105 Golden Valley Rd Golden Valley MN 55422 Office: 230 Brookdale Towers 2810 57th Ave N Minneapolis MN 55430

VAN HENGEL, MAARTEN, banker; b. Amsterdam, The Netherlands, Mar. 29, 1927; s. Adrianus J. and Helena (Gips) van H.; student Kennemer Lyceum, Bloemendaal, Holland, 1939-45; m. Drusilla Drake Riley, Dec. 1, 1951; children—Maarten, Virginia, Hugh, Drusilla. Came to U.S., 1950, naturalized, 1957. With tng. programs of Amsterdamsche Bank, N.V., Amsterdam, Lazard Bros. & Co. Ltd., London and Canadian Bank of Commerce, Montreal, 1945-49; with Brown Bros. Harriman & Co., 1950—, partner, 1968—; dir. Mission Ins. Group, Los Angeles. Served with AUS, 1951-53. Clubs: India House, Netherland (N.Y.C.); Shattemuc Yacht (Ossining, N.Y.); Hay Harbor (Fishers Island); Sleepy Hollow Country (Scarborough, N.Y.). Home: 99 Wilson Park Tarrytown NY 10591 Office: 59 Wall St New York City NY 10005

VAN HEUSEN, JAMES, composer; b. Syracuse, N.Y., Jan. 26, 1913; s. Arthur E. and Ida May (Williams) Van H.; student piano and voice, Syracuse U., 1930-32; m. Josephine Perlberg, Aug. 20, 1966. Announcer radio station WSYR, Syracuse, 1928; piano player Santly's and Remick, pub. house, 1934-38; composer songs and scores for motion pictures and musical comedies, 1940—; prodn. test pilot Lockheed Aircraft Corp., 1942; pres. Van Heusen Music Corp., music pubs., 1959—. Recipient citation and plaque for services in War Finance Program, 1945, Silver medal for services to Treasury Dept., 1946, plaque for better understanding through internat. lang. of Am. song, Los Angeles City Council, 1958, Plaque Saints and Sinners orgn. Los Angeles, 1958; named hon. Tex. citizen, 1958. Mem. A.S.C.A.P., Composers and Lyricists Guild, Am. Guild Authors and Composers. Authors League Am., Quiet Birdmen, OX-5 Club. Methodist. Clubs: Thunderbird Golf and Country, Racquet, Press (Palm Springs, Calif.). Composer: (motion picture scores) Love Thy Neighbour, 1940, (with Johnny Burke) Moonlight Becomes You, 1942, Sunday, Monday or Always, 1943, It Could Happen to You, 1944, It's Always You, 1941, Going My Way (Swinging on a Star recipient Acad. award), 1944; (TV score) Our Town (Love and Marriage recipient Emmy and Christopher award), 1955; (individual songs) Heaven Can Wait, 1939, (with Johnny Mercer) I Thought About You, 1939, Like Someone in Love, 1944, Tender Trap, 1955, All The Way (Acad. award, Cash Box award for most programmed record), 1957, Come Fly With Me (Cash Box award for most programmed album), 1958, To Love and Be Loved, 1958, High Hopes (Acad. award), 1959, Call Me Irresponsible (Acad. Award 1963 from picture Pappa's Delicate Condition). Address: Van Heusen Music Corp 301 E 69th St New York NY 10021

VAN HEUVELEN, WILLIS H., state ofcl.; b. Archer, Iowa, Apr. 18, 1914; s. Bernard and Kathryn Carrie (DeFyter) Van H.; B.A., Huron (S.D.) Coll., 1935; M.S., U. Colo., 1940; m. Ragna Odegand, Aug. 11, 1937; children—Alan, Sally Van Heuvelen Moen, Gary. Instr., Bismarck (N.D.) Jr. Coll., 1942-46; dir. N.D. Div. San. Chemistry and Bacteriology, 1946-49; exec. officer, chief environ. health and engring. services N.D. Dept. Health, Bismarck, 1957—. Mem. nat. environ. control adminstrn. adv. com. USPHS. Mem. Bismarck City Commn., 1956-68, Burleigh County Zoning Com., 1958-68. Mem. Conf. State San. Engrs. (chmn. 1965), Nat., N.D. (Merit award, 1966) socs. profl. engrs., Am. Water Works Assn. (Publ. award 1961, George Warren Fuller award 1966), Water Pollution Control Fedn. (Arthur Sidney Bedell award 1962), Am., N.D. (Merit award, 1966) pub. health assns., Am. Pub. Works Assn., N.D. Water and Pollution Conf. (sec. 1957—, editor ofcl. bull. 1957—). Lutheran. Contbr. articles to profl. jours. Home: 100 Cherokee St Bismarck NC 58501 Office: Dept Health State Capitol Bismarck ND 58505

VAN HOEFEN, HARI, architect, engr.; b. St. Louis, Mar. 20, 1905; s. S. A. and M. M. (Statler) Van H.; student Jackson Acad., Western Mil. Acad., Washington U., U. So. Calif., U. Tex., 1929, St. Louis Sch. Fine Arts, 1931; m. Jane Dietrich, Mar. 4, 1936; 1 dau., Mrs. T.W. Harrison. Owner, Advt. & Indsl. Designers, 1934, Hari Van Hoefen, Architect, 1935-51; partner Schwarz & Van Hoefen and predecessor firm, 1952-67; owner Hari Van Hoefen, Inc., design mgmt., architecture-engring.-product, Ladue, Mo., 1968—; pres. Twinx, Inc., 1947-64; designer Seei'n Stars Movie Exhibit, Hollywood, 1934, Shell Aero. Exhibit, 1935, Evangel. Synod Exhibit, Century of Progress, Chgo., 1935, Dallas Exposition, 1935; product design Am. Thermometer Series, 1937-39, Toastswell Toasters, 1938-40; exhibited painting Trial, 1941, Family, 1956, (sculpture) Delor Park Fountains, 1961, Ancient City, Medical Instrument Jazz Band, 1964. Mem. Mo. Bd. Architects and Engrs., 1951-65; pres. Nat. Archtl. Accrediting Bd., 1958-61; mem. pub. adv. panel GSA, 1967-70. Founder, Visualeague; archtl. advisor St. Louis Art Mus. Recipient awards for Ploeser-Watts Bldg., 1953, Hayes Residence, 1957, Mansion House Center, 1968. Fellow A.I.A.; enrolled mem. Cherokee Nation; mem. Scarab, Sigma Alpha Epsilon. Author: Illustrations, Ltd., 1932. Inventor: Lettering Guide, 1934, Pocket Size 5 Cell Flash Light, 1937, Am. Talisman, 1972. Prin. archtl. works include Forest Ct. Apts., 1936, HEC res., Albuquerque, 1941, Am. Zinc Smelter, Tex., 1942, Monolithic Concrete Bldg., 1948, Concordia Hist. Inst., 1950, 77, Northland Shopping Center, 1952, Louisville Fed. Res. Bank Bldg., 1953, Engrs. club St. Louis, 1959, Optimist Internat. Hdqrs., 1962, 77, Saint Louis Club, 1964, 70; movable seating platforms on track Busch Stadium Complex, 1966, Mansion House Center, 1967, MN Ranch, Ariz., 1972, Desert Caballeros Mus., Ariz., 1974. Home; 6308 E Hummingbird Ln Paradise Valley AZ 85253. *Don't crowd yourself - in time or populace.*

VAN HOEK, ROBERT, physician, med. adminstr., educator; b. N.Y.C., 1927; B.S., Coll. City N.Y., 1949; M.D., Columbia, 1953. Intern St. Luke's Hosp., N.Y.C., 1953-54; resident internal medicine Bronx (N.Y.) VA Hosp., 1954-57; with USPHS, 1963-76; asst. surgeon gen. USPHS, Dept. HEW; med. dir. Wishard Meml. Hosp., 1976-78; asso. dean Ind. U. Sch. Medicine, Indpls., 1976-78; med. dir. Group Health Assn., Inc., Washington. Served with USAF, 1955-63. Fellow A.C.P.; mem. Radiation Research Soc., Am. Fedn. Clin. Research, Alpha Omega Alpha. Address: 3836 N Tazewen St Arlington VA 22207

VAN HOLDE, KENSAL EDWARD, educator; b. Eau Claire, Wis., May 14, 1928; s. Leonard John and Nettie (Hart) Van H.; B.S., U. Wis., 1949, Ph.D., 1952; m. Barbara Jean Watson, Apr. 11, 1950; children—Patricia, Mary, Stephen, David. Research chemist E.I. du Pont de Nemours & Co., 1952-55; research asso. U. Wis., 1955-56, asst. prof. U. Wis. at Milw., 1956-57; mem. faculty U. Ill., Urbana, 1957-67; prof. dept. biochemistry and biophysics Oreg. State U., Corvallis, 1967— Am. Cancer Soc. research prof., 1977—; instr.-in-charge physiology course Marine Biol. Lab., Woods Hole, Mass., 1977—; mem. research staff Centre des Recherches sur les Macromolecules, Strasbourg, France, 1964-65; mem. study sect. USPHS, 1966-69. NSF sr. postdoctoral fellow, 1964-65; Guggenheim fellow, 1973-74; European Molecular Biology Orgn. fellow, 1975. Mem. AAAS, Biophys. Soc., Am. Soc. Biol. Chemists. Author: Physical Biochemistry, 1971. Editor: Biochemica Biophysica Acta, 1966-68; mem. editorial bd. Jour. Biol. Chemistry, 1968-75, Biochemistry, 1973-76. Contbr. profl. jours. Home: 229 NW 32d St Corvallis OR 97330

VAN HORN, KENT ROBERTSON, metallurgist; b. Cleve., July 20, 1905; s. Frank Robertson and Myra (Van Horn) van H.; B.S., Case Sch. Applied Sci., 1926; M.S., Yale, 1928, Ph.D. (Sterling Research fellow), 1929; D.Sc., Case Inst. Tech., 1955; m. Estelle Yost, July 23, 1932; children—Karl Robertson, Neil Yost. Research metallurgist Aluminum Co. Am., 1929-62, dir. research, 1952-62, v.p., 1962-70, ret., 1970; lectr. metallurgy Case Inst. Tech. 1930—, also trustee. Lectr. analysis Nat. Metal Congress, 1936; Inst. Metals lectr., 1953; Mehl Nonor lectr., 1957; Campbell Meml. lectr. Am. Soc. for Metals, 1954; mem. U.S. Navy Civilian Com. for Procurement, 1942-43; mem. minerals and metals adv. bd. NRC. Recipient Sainte Claire-Deville medal Societe Francaise de Metallurgic, 1965, gold medal Am. Soc. for Metals, 1970; Platinum medal Brit. Inst. Metals, 1973—. Fellow Am. Soc. for Metals (hon.; treas. 1939-41, trustee 1941-43, pres. 1944-45), Am. Inst. Mining and Metall. Engrs., Soc. for Non-Destructive Testing (hon.); mem. Brit. Inst. Metals, Am. Indsl. Radium and X-Ray Soc. (nat. dir. 1943-44, pres. 1944-45, chmn. Cleve. chpt. 1943), Sigma Xi, Tau Beta Pi, Theta Tau, Zeta Psi. Republican. Presbyn. Author: (with George Sachs) Practical Metallurgy 1940; (with George Case) Aluminum in Iron and Steel, 1953; Aluminum, 3 vols., 1967. Contbr. articles to tech. jours. Home: 373 Fox Chapel Rd Pittsburgh PA 15238 Office: Alcoa Bldg Mellon Sq Pittsburgh PA 15219

VAN HORN, VERNE HILE, III, retail stores exec.; b. Tulsa, July 27, 1938; s. Verne Hile and Vonnie Hoffman (King) Van H.; student U. Okla., 1957; B.S. in Bus., U. Tulsa, 1962; children—Tracy, Melissa. Salesman, Phillips Petroleum Co., Dallas, 1963-66; with Nat. Convenience Stores Inc., Houston, 1966—, v.p. stores div., 1971-75, exec. v.p., 1975, pres., dir., 1975—. Mem. Nat. Assn. Convenience Stores (dir., chmn. tng. sessions com.), Texans Pub. Safety (co-chmn.). Republican. Home: 1927 Stoneybrook St Houston TX 77079 Office: PO Box 758 Houston TX 77001

VAN HORNE, HARRIET, journalist; b. Syracuse, N.Y., May 17, 1920; d. Victor Cornelius and Gertrude (Theall) Van H.; B.A., U. Rochester (N.Y.); m. David Lowe, Apr. 20, 1956 (dec.). Columnist, N.Y. World-Telegram, then N.Y. Post, now syndicated by Los Angeles Times Syndicate; lectr., TV panelist, radio news analyst. Trustee Strange Preventive Medicine Inst., Corr. Fund. Author: Never Go Anywhere Without a Pencil, 1972; also mag. articles. Address: New York Post 210 South St New York NY 10002

VAN HORNE, JAMES CARTER, economist, univ. dean; b. South Bend, Ind., Aug. 6, 1935; s. Ralph and Helen (McCarter) Van H.; A.B., De Pauw U., 1957; M.B.A., Northwestern U., 1961, Ph.D., 1964; m. Mary A. Roth, Aug. 27, 1960; children—Drew, Stuart, Stephen. Comml. lending rep. Continental Ill. Nat. Bank Chgo., 1958-62; prof. finance Stanford U. Grad. Sch. Bus., 1965-75, A.P. Giannini prof. finance, 1976—, asso. dean, 1973-75, 76—; dep. asst. sec. Dept. Treasury, 1975-76; dir. Knudsen Corp., Golden State Sanwa Bank, Creative Strategies Internat.; dir. Nat. Bur. Economic Research, 1976—. Served with AUS, 1957. Mem. Am. Econ. Assn., Am. Fin. Assn. (dir.), Western Fin. Assn. (dir.), Fin. Mgmt. Assn. Author: Function and Analysis of Capital Market Rates, 1970; Fundamentals of Financial Management, 1980; Financial Management and Policy, 1980; Financial Market Rates and Flows, 1978; asso. editor Jour. Financial and Quantitative Analysis, 1969—, Jour. Finance, 1971-73. Home: 2000 Webster St Palo Alto CA 94305 Office: Grad Sch Bus Stanford U Stanford CA 94305

VAN HORNE, RALPH RICHARD, aluminum co. exec.; b. Milw., June 7, 1931; s. Ralph Rupert and Edna M. (Benson) Van H.; B.B.A., U. Wis., 1953; m. Elizabeth Dixon, July 3, 1954; children—Ann, Ross, Margaret. With Anaconda Co., 1955—, mgr. corporate planning Brass div., Waterbury, Conn., 1971-72, pres., 1972-74, pres. Aluminum div., Louisville, 1974—; dir. Citizens Fidelity Bank & Trust Co., Louisville. Bd. dirs. U. Louisville Internat. Center, Jr. Achievement. Served to 1st lt. U.S. Army, 1953-55. Clubs: Hunting Creek Country (Prospect, Ky.); Pendennis (Louisville). Home: 6521 Gunpowder Ln Prospect KY 40059 Office: PO Box 32860 Louisville KY 40232

VAN HORNE, ROBERT LOREN, univ. dean; b. Malvern, Iowa, Dec. 26, 1915; s. Paul E. and Nellie Ruth (Breeding) Van H.; B.Sc. in Pharmacy, U. Iowa, 1941. M.Sc., 1947, Ph.D., 1949; m. Alice Irene Cummings, June 2, 1941 (dec.); children—Colleen Alice, Robert Corwin, Roger Alan, Russell Edward; m. 2d, Geneva T. Penland, Aug. 18, 1962; 1 son, Paul L. Asst. prof. U. Iowa, 1950-52, asso. prof., 1953-56; prof. pharmacy Mont. State U., 1956—, dean, 1956-75. Mem. Mont. Commn. on Alcoholism and Drug Dependence, 1969—. Served to comdr. USNR, 1943-45. Registered pharmacist, Ia., Mont. Mem. Am., Iowa, Mont. pharm. assns., Res. Officers Assn. U.S. (pres. 1961-62), Am. Assn. Colls. Pharmacy, A.A.A.S., Sigma Xi, Rho Chi. Lutheran. Home: 4 Marthas Ct Missoula MT 59801

VAN HOUSEN, EDWARD IRVIN, banker; b. St. Paul, Mar. 4, 1922; s. William Ross and Ovidia (Iverson) Van H.; B.B.S., U. Minn., 1943; M.B.A., Harvard, 1947; m. Dorothy Puelicher, Sept. 13, 1947; children—Sandra Ann (Mrs. Charles Yanke), Barbara Ann, Peter Ross, Patricia Ann. Sr. clk. Marshall & Ilsley Bank, Milw., 1947-51, asst. cashier, 1951-54, asst. v.p., 1954-57, v.p., 1957-70, sr. v.p., 1970-72, exec. v.p., 1972—; dir. Richter Schroeder Co., 1st Nat. Leasing Co., Acme-Machell Co., Blower Application Co., Utility Products Co., Wenthe-Davidson Engrs., Milw. Bd. dirs. Citizens Govtl. Research Bur.; bd. dirs. United Way Greater Milw.; mem. adv. council U. Wis. at Milw.; trustee Lawrence U., Appleton, Wis., St. Joseph's Hosp., Milw. Served with USNR, 1943-46. Mem. Nat. Ski Patrol (sr.). Kiwanian. Clubs: Milwaukee, Milwaukee Country, Heiliger Huegel Ski. Home: 9090 N Range Line Rd Milwaukee WI 53217 Office: 770 N Water St Milwaukee WI 53201

VAN HOUTEN, FRANKLYN BOSWORTH, geologist, educator; b. N.Y.C., July 14, 1914; s. Charles Nicholas and Hessie Osborne (Bosworth) Van H.; B.S., Rutgers U., 1936; Ph.D., Princeton, 1941; m. Jean Oliver Sholes, Feb. 18, 1943; children—Jean S., F. Bosworth, David Gordon. Instr. dept. geology Williams Coll., 1939-42; asst. prof. Princeton, 1946-51, asso. prof., 1951-55, prof., 1955—; vis. prof. geology U. Calif. at Los Angeles, 1964, State U. N.Y. at Binghamton, 1971; geologist U.S. Geol. Survey, 1948-67; temporary geologist Geol. Survey Can., 1953, Yukon Expdn. geol. expdns. Morocco, Tunisia, Libya and Egypt. Served as lt. USN, 1942-46. Fellow Geol. Soc. Am., Explorers Club; mem. Am. Assn. Petroleum Geologists, Soc. Econ. Paleontologists and Mineralogists (hon. mem.), Internat. Assn. Sedimentologists, Colombia Geol. Soc. (hon.), Sigma Xi, Delta Upsilon. Author reports and articles on geology. Home: 168 Fitz Randolph Rd Princeton NJ 08540

VAN HOUTEN, LEONARD ERSKINE, engring. and constrn. co. exec.; b. Jersey City, Dec. 20, 1924; s. Leonard and Margaret Agnes (Molumby) Van H.; B.C.E., Rensselaer Poly. Inst., 1945, M.C.E., 1947; m. Marie K. Regan, Dec. 27, 1947; children—Elizabeth M., Peter J. Engr. to sr. v.p. Frederic R. Harris, Inc., N.Y.C., 1947-65; pres., chmn. bd. Van Houten Assos., Inc. and VHA Services, Inc., N.Y.C., 1965-76; with Dravo Corp., Pitts., 1976—, v.p. Dravo Internat., chmn. bd. dirs. Dravo Van Houten, Inc. Served with USNR, 1943-46. Fellow ASCE; mem. Nat. Soc. Profl. Engrs., Am. Inst. Mining, Metall. and Petroleum Engrs., Soc. Naval Architects and Marine Engrs., Soc. Am. Mil. Engrs., Am. Welding Soc., Am. Concrete Inst., U.S. Com. on Large Dams, The Moles. Club: N.Y. Yacht. Contbr. articles to tech. jours., Ency. Americana; co-inventor devices for mooring large ships and offshore structures. Home: 2208 Ben Franklin Dr Pittsburgh PA 15237 Office: One Oliver Plaza Pittsburgh PA 15222

VAN HOUWELING, CORNELIUS DONALD, veterinarian, former govt. ofcl.; b. Mahaska County, Iowa, July 19, 1918; s. Dirk Cornelius and Elbertha (Tysseling) Van H.; student Central Coll., Pella, Iowa, 1935-38; D.V.M., Iowa State Coll., 1942; M.S., Iowa State U., 1966; m. Roberta Irene Olson, Sept. 12, 1942; children—Douglas Edward, Cornelius Donald II, Bruce Robert, Dirk Alan, Susan Irene. Practice vet. medicine, Springfield, Ill., 1942-43; dir. dept. vet. med. relations Ill. Agrl. Assn., Chgo., 1946-48; dir. profl. relations also asst. exec. sec. Am. Vet. Med. Assn., 1948-53; faculty U. Ill., 1953-54; dir. Livestock Regulatory Programs, Agrl. Research Service, Dept. Agr., Washington, 1954-56, asst. adminstr., 1956-61; asst. dir. regulatory labs. Nat. Animal Disease Lab. Agrl. Research Service, Dept. Agr., Ames, Iowa, 1961-66; dir. Bur. Vet. Med. FDA, HEW, Washington, 1967-78, asst. to commr. FDA, 1978-79; cons., 1979—. Served from lt. to capt., AUS, 1943-46. Recipient award Am. Mgmt. Assn., 1957. Fellow AAAS; mem. Am. Vet. Med. Assn. (mem. council pub. health and regulatory vet. medicine, mem. ho. dels.), U.S. Animal Health Assn., Am. Coll. Vet. Preventive Medicine (organizing com.), Conf. Pub. Health Vets., Nat. Assn. Fed. Vets., D.C. Vet. Med. Assn., World Assn. Vet. Food-Hygienists, Sigma Xi, Gamma Sigma Delta. Kiwanian, Toastmaster. Home: 4303 Ballard Ct Fairfax VA 22030

VANICEK, PETR, geodesist; b. Susice, Czechoslovakia, July 18, 1935; s. Ivan and Irena (Blahovcova) V.; came to Can., 1969, naturalized, 1975; Ing. (Geodesy), Czech Tech. U., Prague, 1959; Ph.D. in Math. Physics, Czech Acad. Scis., Prague, 1968; m. Jana Vancurova, Apr. 9, 1960; children—Filip, Stepan, Anna. Geodesist, Inst. Surveying, Prague, 1959-63; computer cons. Czech Tech. U., 1963-67; Natural Environ. Research Council sr. research fellow Tidal Inst., U. Liverpool (Eng.), 1967-68; sr. sci. officer Natural Environ. Research Council, U.K., 1968-69; NRC Can. postdoctoral fellow Fed. Govt., Ottawa, 1969-71; prof. geodesy U. N.B., Fredericton, 1971—; vis. prof. U. Parana (Brazil), summers 1975-76, 79; vis. scientist U.S. Geol. Survey, Menlo Park, Calif., 1977; sr. vis. scientist U.S. Nat. Acad. Scis., 1977; sec. NRC Subcom. on Geodesy, 1972-73; mem. Can. Nat. Com. on Geodynamics, 1975-78; nat. corr. on geodesy Can. Geophys. Union, 1975-77, mem. exec. com., 1977—; mem. study groups on recent crustal movements, inertial positioning, large networks and determination geoid Internat. Union Geodesy and Geophysics, 1971, 73; Can. rep. Commn. on Recent Crustal Movements. Fellow Geol. Assn. Can., Explorers Club; mem. Am. Geophys. Union, N.Y. Acad. Scis., Can. Inst. Surveying, Czechoslovak Soc. Arts and Scis. in Am., Sigma Xi. Club: Can. Lawn Tennis Assn. Author: (with V. Pleskot and others) Zaklady Programovani Pro Ural, vol. I., 1964, (with J. Culik, T. Hruskova) vol. II, 1965; contbr. sect. Satellite Geodesy and Geodynamics to Ency. Soil Sci. and Applied Geology; editor: Procs. Internat. Symposium of N. Am. Geodetic Networks, 1974; Procs. Can. Geophys. Union Symposium on Satellite Geodesy and Geodynamics, 1975; mem. internat. editorial bd. Manuscripta Geodetica; contbr. articles to profl. jours. Home: 180 Charing Crescent Fredericton NB E3B 4R7 Canada

VANIER, KIERAN FRANCIS, bus. forms printing co. exec.; b. Alliance, Ohio, May 10, 1914; s. Joseph A. and Johanna Mary (McCarthy) V.; B.S., Loyola U., 1937; m. Marjory S. Kitche, 1937 (dec.); children—Denis K., Annette Vanier Kritzenkotter; m. 2d, June Day, 1975. Salesman, Moore Bus. Forms, to 1947; founder, chmn. bd. Vanier Graphics Corp., 1946—; vice chmn. bd. Am. Bus. Products, Atlanta. Founder, Amytotrophic Lateral Sclerosis Found.; chmn. San Diego chpt. Muscular Dystrophy. Clubs: San Diego Yacht, San Diego

Country, Kona Kai, Cuyamaca. Office: 8787 Olive Ln Santee CA 92071

VANIK, CHARLES A., congressman; b. Cleve., Apr. 7, 1913; s. Charles Anton and Stella (Kvasnicka) V.; A.B., Western Res. U., 1933; LL.B., 1936; m. Beatrice Marian Best, Feb. 2, 1945; children-Phyllis Jean, John Charles. Admitted to Ohio bar, 1936, since practiced in Cleveland; assn. judge Cleve. Municipal Ct. 1947-54; mem. 84th-90th, 91st-96th congresses from 22d Ohio Dist., mem. Ways and Means Com., chmn. subcom. on trade. Mem. Cleveland City Council, 1938-39; mem. senate Ohio Legislature, 1940-41; mem. Cleve. Bd. Edn., 1941-42. Trustee Cleve. Library, 1946. Served as lt. USNR, 1942-45, North Africa, Sicily and Okinawa. Mem. Cleve., Cuyahoga bar assns. Home: 26151 Lake Shore Blvd Euclid OH 44123 Office: Rayburn House Office Bldg Washington DC 20015

VAN ITALLIE, THEODORE BERTUS, physician; b. Hackensack, N.J., Nov. 8, 1919; s. Dorus Christian and Lucy M. (Pohle) Van I.; grad. Deerfield Acad., 1937; B.S., Harvard, 1941; M.D., Columbia, 1945; m. Barbara Cox, Sept. 25, 1948; children—Lucy M., Theodore Bertus, Christina M., Elizabeth B., Katharine R. Dir. nutrition and metabolism research lab. St. Luke's Hosp., N.Y.C., 1952-55; asso. Peter Bent Brigham Hosp., Boston, 1955-57; dir. medicine St. Luke's Hosp. Center, N.Y.C., 1957-75, dir. Obesity Research Center, 1974—; asst. prof. Sch. Pub. Health, Harvard, 1955-57; asso. clin. prof. medicine Columbia, N.Y.C., 1957-65, clin. prof., 1965-71, prof., 1971—; vis. prof. internal medicine Am. U. of Beirut, 1968-69, trustee, 1976—; mem. sci. adv. bd. Nutrition Found., 1967-71; pres. Am. Bd. Nutrition, 1968-71; mem. food and nutrition bd. NRC, 1970-76; med. adv. com. on cyclamates HEW, 1969-70; mem. gastrointestinal and nutrition tng. com. NIH, 1969-73, mem. nat. arthritis, metabolic and digestive diseases adv. council, 1978—; dir. Miles Labs. Mem. Englewood (N.J.) Bd. Edn., 1960-65, v.p., 1964-65. Diplomate Am. Bd. Internal Medicine. Fellow A.C.P.; mem. Am. Soc. Clin. Investigation, Am. Inst. Nutrition, Soc. Exptl. Biology and Medicine, Am. Clin. and Climatol. Assn., A.M.A. (council on foods and nutrition 1967-74, vice-chmn. 1974), Am. Soc. Clin. Nutrition (council 1970-73, pres. 1976-77), Century Assn. Mem. editorial bd. Diabetes, 1960-71; editor-in-chief designate Am. Jour. Clin. Nutrition, 1979—. Research and contbr. numerous publs. on obesity, body composition, pancreatic hormone, glucagon, mechanism of energy balance regulation, treatment of pruritus and hypercholesteremia in biliary cirrhois, physiology and clin. use of medium chain triglyceride. Office: St Luke's Hosp Center Amsterdam Ave at 114th St New York City NY 10025

VAN KLEECK, R. JOHN, newspaper pub.; b. Binghamton, N.Y., Dec. 31, 1924; s. Seba Golden and Marion Watrous (Burton) Van K.; grad. Drake Sch. Journalism, N.Y.C., 1945; m. Elizabeth J. Belden (dec.); children—Elaine Van Kleeck Tarsi, Katrina, John. Reporter, Binghamton Press and Binghamton Sun, 1945-47; with Ottaway Newspapers, Inc., 1947-55; pub. Twin Valley Publs., Inc., 1955-63; bus. mgr. Times Herald-Record, Middletown, N.Y., 1963-67; pub. Danbury (Conn.) News-Times, 1970-73; pres., pub. Middletown Times Herald Record, 1973—. Bd. dirs. Horton Meml. Hosp., Middletown, Orange County Arts Council; bd. dirs. Greater Orange YMCA, 1974, Mid Hudson Patterns, Inc., 1975. Mem. Am. Newspaper Pubs. Assn., N.Y. State Pubs. Assn., Am. Soc. Newspaper Editors, Internat. Newspaper Advt. Execs., Am. Press Inst. Office: 40 Mulberry St Middletown NY 10940

VAN KRANENDONK, JAN, physicist, educator; b. Delft, Netherlands, Feb. 8, 1924; s. Anthonius G. and Elisabeth M. Van K.; came to Can., 1958; Ph.D., U. Amsterdam, 1952. Lectr. physics U. Leiden (Netherlands), 1954-57; asso. prof. physics U. Toronto, 1958-60, prof., 1960—. E.W.R. Steacie prize, 1964; Can. Assn. Physicists Gold medal, 1976. Fellow Royal Soc. Can.; mem. Netherlands Acad. Scis., Am. Phys. Soc., Can. Assn. Physicists. Contbr. articles to profl. jours. Home: 141 Duncairn Rd Don Mills ON M3D 1C9 Canada Office: Dept Physics U Toronto Toronto ON M5S 1A7 Canada

VAN LANCKER, JULIEN LEON, educator; b. Belgium, Aug. 14, 1924; s. Maurice and Elisabeth Van L.; M.D., U. Louvain, 1950, M.S. in Pathology, 1956, M.S. in Radiol. Sci. and Oncology, 1970; M.A. ad eundem, Brown U., 1964; children—Catherine M., Peter J., Michael J. Came to U.S., 1953. Asst. pathology and radiotherapy U. Louvain, 1950-53, research asso., 1955-56; vis. instr. pathology-oncology U. Kans., 1953-54; Runyon fellow U. Wis., 1954-55, asso. prof., 1960-63, chief pathology sect., 1960-66; asst. prof. pathology U. Utah, 1956-60, prof. med. sci. Brown U., 1966-70; prof., chmn. dept. pathology and research molecular pathologist U. Calif. at Los Angeles, 1970—. Served with Belgian Army, 1944-46. Recipient NIH career awards. Mem. Am. Assn. Cancer Research, Radiation Research Soc., Soc. Exptl. Pathology, Internat. Acad. Pathology, Societe Belge de Biochimie, Am. Assn. Pathologists and Bacteriologists, N.Y. Acad. Sci., Am. Soc. Cell Biology, Los Angeles Acad. Medicine, Am. Assn. Study Liver Diseases, Am. Soc. Biol. Chemists, Am. Assn. Chmn. Pathology, Soc. Belge de Biologie. Contbr. articles to profl. jours. Home: 3355 Scadlock Ln Sherman Oaks CA 91403

VANLANDINGHAM, WILLIAM J., banker; b. Louisville, Sept. 10, 1937; s. Zack Jennings and Corinne (Brown) VanL.; B.Indsl. Engring., Ga. Inst. Tech., 1959; postgrad. Law Sch., Emory U., 1964-67, Program for Mgmt. Devel. Harvard U.; m. Mary Dell Cawley, Oct. 12, 1961; children—William Jennings II, Teri Leigh, Joseph Templeton. Prodn. mgr. Procter & Gamble Mfg. Co., 1959-64; asst. to v.p. Rich's, Inc., 1964-66; With The Citizens & So. Nat. Bank, Atlanta, 1966—, exec. v.p., 1971-77, asst. to pres., 1977—. Mem. Bd. Edn., Atlanta, 1971-73. Bd. dirs. Pub. Affairs Council, Ga. Safety Council, Research Atlanta, Inc.; trustee Met. Found. of Atlanta. Served to lt. (j.g.) USNR. Recipient Liberty Bell award Savannah (Ga.) Bar Assn. Mem. U.S. C. of C. (named Outstanding Young Man of Atlanta 1973, mem. urban and regional affairs com.), Am. Bankers Assn. (mem. urban affairs com.), Ga. Inst. Tech. Nat. Alumni Assn. (pres. 1975), Nat. Alliance Businessmen (chmn. met. Atlanta). Methodist. Clubs: Savannah Yacht and Country; Capital City, Commerce (Atlanta). Home: 835 Loridans Dr NE Atlanta GA 30342 Office: 99 Annex Atlanta GA 30399

VAN LEEUWEN, GERARD, physician, educator; b. Iowa, July 4, 1929; s. William and Rena (Slothouber) Van L.; B.A., Calvin Coll., 1950; M.D., U. Iowa, 1954; m. Wilma Van Leeuwen; children—Sheryl, Jeanine. Intern Butterworth Hosp., Grand Rapids, Mich., 1954-55; resident pediatrics U. Mo.-Columbia, 1957-59; practice medicine, specializing in pediatrics, Odessa, Tex., 1959-62; mem. faculty medicine U. Mo.-Columbia, 1962-68; mem. faculty medicine U. Nebr., 1968—, prof., 1969-77, chmn. dept. pediatrics, 1969-75, chmn. emergency dept., 1975-78; asso. med. dir. sect. med. care Mo. Div. Health, Jefferson City, 1978—. Served to capt. M.C., AUS, 1955-57. Mem. Am. Acad. Pediatrics, Am. Pediatric Soc., Alpha Omega Alpha. Author numerous articles field newborn medicine. Office: PO Box 570 Broadway State Office Bldg Jefferson City MO 65102

VAN LEUVEN, ARTHUR EDWIN, JR., credit corp. exec.; b. Redlands, Calif., Nov. 13, 1925; s. Arthur Edwin and Bessie Lee (Gotcher) Van L.; student Kans. State Coll. at Pittsburg, 1944-45, U. Kan., 1945-46; Exec. Degree in Credit and Financial Mgmt., Stanford, 1962-64; m. Charlotte Adele Miller, Apr. 21, 1946; children—Fred Arthur and Nancey Adele (twins). Field rep. Transam. Financial Corp. (previously Pacific Finance Corp.), Los Angeles, 1947-48, office mgr., 1948-52, credit supr., 1952-55, supr. operations, 1955-59, mgr. dist., 1959-62, various home office poistions, 1962-66, v.p. region, 1967-69, v.p. adminstrn., 1969-72, exec. v.p., 1972-77, pres., chief exec. officer, 1977—, mem. exec. com., 1972—, also dir.; dir. Lyon Moving & Storage Co. Inc., Los Angeles. Served with USNR, 1943-46. Mem. Nat. Consumer Finance Assn. Office: 1150 S Olive St Los Angeles CA 90015

VAN LOPIK, JACK RICHARD, geologist, educator; b. Holland, Mich., Feb. 25, 1929; s. Guy M. and Minnie (Grunst) Van L.; B.S., Mich. State U., 1950; M.S., La. State U., 1953, Ph.D., 1955; 1 son, Charles Robert. Geologist, sect. chief, asst. chief, chief geology br. U.S. Army C.E., Waterways Expt. Sta., Vicksburg, Miss., 1954-61; chief area evaluation sect., tech. dir., mgr. Space and Environ. Sci. Programs, tech. requirements dir. geosciences ops. Tex. Instruments, Inc., Dallas, 1961-68, chmn. dept. marine sci., 1968-74; prof. dept. marine sci., dir. sea grant devel., dean Center for Wetland Resources, La. State U., Baton Rouge, 1968—; chmn. Coastal Resources Directorate of U.S. Nat. Com. for Man and Biosphere, U.S. Nat. Commn. for UNESCO, 1975—; dir. Gulf South Research Inst., 1974—; mem. Nat. Adv. Com. Oceans and Atmosphere, 1978—; ofcl. del. XX Congreso Internacional, Mexico City, 1956, XII Gen Assembly Internat. Union Geodesy and Geophysics, Helsinki, 1960; chmn. panel on geography and land use Nat. Acad. Scis.-NRC, com. on remote sensing programs for earth resources surveys, 1969-77. Fellow Geol. Soc. Am., A.A.A.S.; mem. Am. Astronautical Soc. (dir. S.W. sect. 1967-68), Am. Soc. Photogrammetry (dir. 1969-72, chmn. photo interpretation com. 1960, 65, rep. earth scis. div. NRC 1968-71), Am. Geophys. Union, Am. Assn. Petroleum Geologists (acad. adv. com. 1973—), Assn. Am. Geographers, Soc. Econ. Paleontologists and Mineralogists (mem. research com. 1962-65), Am. Mgmt. Assn., Soc. Research Adminstrs., Marine Tech. Soc., Assn. Sea Grant Program Instns. (exec. bd. 1972-74), Nat. Ocean Industries Assn. (adv. council 1973—), Sigma Xi. Home: 5216 Claycut Rd Baton Rouge LA 70806 Office: Center for Wetland Resources La State U Baton Rouge LA 70803

VAN METER, ABRAM DEBOIS, banker; b. Springfield, Ill., May 16, 1922; s. A.D. and Edith (Graham) Van M.; B.S., Kings Point Coll., 1946; J.D., Northwestern U., 1948; m. Margaret Schlipf, Dec. 1, 1956; children—Andy, Alice, Ann. Admitted to Ill. bar, 1949; partner firm Van Meter, Oxtoby and Funk, Springfield, 1949—; adminstrv. asst. to treas. Ill., 1963; v.p. Ill. Nat. Bank, Springfield, 1964-65, pres., 1965—, also dir.; vice chmn. Ill. Bd. Investment, 1969—; dir. Toledo, Peoria & Western R.R. Co. Chmn., Ill. Housing Devel. Authority, 1977—; trustee So. Ill. U., 1975—; bd. dirs., mem. exec. com. Meml. Med. Center. Home: 6 Fair Oaks St Springfield IL 62704 Office: 1 Old State Capitol Plaza N Springfield IL 62701

VAN METER, CRAIG, lawyer; b. Charleston, Ill., Aug. 25, 1895; s. John and Ina (Craig) Van M.; LL.B., U. Ill., 1917; m. Eliza Haynes, Apr. 7, 1921; 1 dau., Alice. Admitted to Ill. bar, 1917; practiced in Mattoon, Ill., 1919—; partner firm Craig & Craig, 1923—; asst. atty. gen. Ill. Inheritance Tax Div., 1932-33; judge 5th Jud. Circuit Ill., 1933-36; master-in-chancery Fed. Ct. Eastern Dist. Ill., 1951-65; mem. legal com. Interstate Oil Compact Commn., 1951-52. Mem. Mattoon Bd. Edn., 1925-31; appeal agt. Draft Bd. 2, Coles County, 1941-45. Del. Democratic Nat. Conv., 1932. Vice pres., bd. dirs. United Fund, 1963-64; former pres. bd. trustees Meml. Methodist Hosp.; mem. U. Ill. Found. Served as 2d lt. U.S. Army, 1917-19; AEF. Mem. Mattoon Assn. Commerce (past dir. indsl. com.), Am., Ill. (chmn. exec. com. mineral law 1955-56), 7th Fed. Circuit bar assns., Am. Coll. Probate Counsel, Am. Judicature Soc., Soc. Trial Lawyers, Am. Legion (past comdr.), Order of Coif, Phi Delta Phi, Phi Delta Theta. Episcopalian. Club: Mattoon Country. Home: 300 Wabash Ave Mattoon IL 61938 Office: 1807 Broadway Mattoon IL 61938

VAN METER, THEODORE, lawyer; b. Cadillac, Mich., May 15, 1921; s. Morton Isaac and Esther Eunice (Wilson) Van M.; B.S., Mich. State U., 1948; J.D., Detroit Coll. Law, 1953; m. Gene English, Dec. 30, 1948; children—Elizabeth, Margaret, David. With Sperry Vickers div. Sperry Corp., Troy, Mich., 1948—, patent counsel, 1955-59, gen. counsel, 1959-62, v.p., gen. counsel, 1962—. Served with AUS, 1943-46. Mem. State Bar Mich., Am., Mich. (pres. 1969-70) patent law assns., Birmingham Power Squadron, Multi-Lakes Conservation Assn., Tau Beta Pi, Delta Theta Phi, Phi Delta Theta. Presbyn. Club: Orchard Lake (Mich.) Country. Patentee in field. Home: 1906 Kenwood Ct Birmingham MI 48009 Office: 1401 Crooks Rd Troy MI 48084

VANN, DAVID JOHNSON, mayor, lawyer; b. Roanoke, Ala., Aug. 10, 1928; s. Clyde Harold and Ruth (Johnson) V.; B.S., U. Ala., 1950, LL.B., 1951; LL.M., George Washington U., 1953; m. Lillian Foscue, Apr. 24, 1965; children—Lillian Ruth, Cora Elizabeth (dec.), Michael Lee. Admitted to Ala. bar, 1951; law clk. Justice Hugo Black, 1953-54; asso. firm Bradley, Arant, Rose & White, 1954-62; partner Vann & Patrick, 1963-65; partner Berkowitz, Lefkovits, Vann and Patrick, Birmingham, Ala., 1965-69; individual practice law, Birmingham, 1969-75; councilman, City of Birmingham, 1971-75, mayor, 1975—. Bd. dirs. Wesley Found., U. Ala.; dir. U. Ala. Law Sch. Found.; bd. dirs. Nat. League Cities; mem. adv. bd. U.S. Conf. Mayors; co-chmn. Commn. Race Religion N. Ala. Conf. United Meth. Ch. Served with U.S. Army, 1946-47, 51-53. Mem. Am., Ala., Birmingham bar assns., Am. Judicature Soc., V.F.W., Am. Legion. Democrat. Club: Lions. Home: 4201 Cliff Rd Birmingham AL 35222 Office: 710 N 20th St Birmingham AL 35203

VANNEMAN, EDGAR, JR., lawyer; b. El Paso, Ill., Aug. 24, 1919; s. Edgar and Fern (Huffington) V.; B.S., Northwestern U., 1941, J.D., 1947; m. Shirli Thomas, Apr. 29, 1951; children—Jill, Thomas. Admitted to Ill. bar, 1947; mem. firm Campbell, Clark & Miller, 1947-48; gen. atty. Chgo. and NorthWestern R.R. Co., 1949-62; gen. atty., asst. sec. Brunswick Corp., Skokie, Ill., 1962—; sec. Sherwood Med. Industries, Inc., 1976—. Pres., Northeastern Ill. Planning Commn., 1978—; dir. Suburban Health Systems Agy., 1976—; mayor City of Evanston (Ill.), 1970-77; alt. del. Republican Nat. Conv., 1952, 56. Served with USAF, 1942-46. Decorated Bronze Star. Mem. Ill. Bar Assn. (past bd. govs.), Chgo. Bar Assn., Am. Bar Assn., Soc. Trial Lawyers. Presbyterian. Club: Law (Chgo.). Home: 715 Monticello Pl Evanston IL 60201 Office: 1 Brunswick Plaza Skokie IL 60077

VAN NESS, EDWARD HARRY, assn. exec.; b. Chgo., Apr. 10, 1929; s. George R. and Grace E. (Wikoff) Van N.; student Loras Coll., 1947-49; Ph.B. magna cum laude, Coll. St. Thomas Aquinas, 1952; M.A. magna cum laude, Aquinas Inst., 1953; postgrad. Loyola U., 1953-54, U. Chgo., 1957-58. Asst. dir. Center for Programs in Govt. Adminstrn., U. Chgo., 1958-59; asso. dir. govt. exec. program N.Y. U., 1959-61; asst. sec. to Gov. Nelson A. Rockefeller, Albany, N.Y., 1961-66; exec. dir. N.Y. State Health Planning Commn., N.Y.C., 1967-73; exec. v.p. Nat. Health Council, N.Y.C., 1973—; vis. prof. health planning Sloan Inst. Hosp. Adminstrn., Cornell U., 1967-73; lectr. Columbia U., 1968-73; mem. faculty hosp. adminstrn. program Wagner Coll., N.Y.C., 1967-77. Chmn. Gov.'s Task Force on Universal Health Ins., 1965-70; chmn. Gov.'s Planning Com. for Narcotic Addiction Control, 1966-67; exec. sec. N.Y. State Joint Council on Regional Med. Programs, 1967. Served with U.S. Army, 1955-56. Mem. Nat. Council on Philanthropy (trustee), Am. Health Planning Assn. (dir.), Am. Soc. Assn. Execs., Am. Public Health Assn. Club: Univ. (N.Y.C.). Co-editor: Concepts and Issues in Administrative Behavior, 1962. Office: 1740 Broadway New York NY 10019

VAN NESS, HENDRICK CHARLES, educator; b. N.Y.C., Jan. 18 1924; s. Hendrick W. and Grace I (Mead) Van N.; B.S., U. Rochester, 1944, M.S., 1946; D. Engring., Yale, 1953; m. Virginia L. Crider, Oct. 14, 1950; 1 son, Kirk Charles. Instr., U. Rochester, 1945-47; chem. engr. M.W. Kellogg Co., Jersey City, 1947-48; asst. prof. Purdue U., 1952-56; mem. faculty Rensselaer Poly. Inst., 1956—, prof. engring., 1963—, Union Carbide prof., 1967-72, chmn. div., 1969-74; vis. Fulbright lectr. King's Coll., Newcastle upon Tyne, Eng., 1958- 59; vis. prof. U. Calif. at Berkeley, 1966, Institutet for Kemiteknik, Danmarks Tekniske Højskole, Lyngby, Denmark, 1977. Registered profl. engr., N.Y. Fellow Am. Inst. Chem. Engrs.; mem. Am. Chem. Soc., Am. Soc. Engring. Edn., Sigma Xi, Tau Beta Pi, Theta Delta Chi. Author: (with J.M. Smith) Introduction to Chemical Engineering Thermodynamics, 1959, rev. edit., 1975; Classical Thermodynamics of Non-Electrolyte Solutions, 1964; (with M.W. Zemansky) Basic Engineering Thermodynamics, 1966, rev. edit. (with others), 1975; Understanding Thermodynamics, 1969; (with M.M. Abbott) Schaum's Outline of Theory and Problems of Thermodynamics, 1972. Home: Brunswick Rd-Taylor Ln Troy NY 12180

VAN NESS, JAMES EDWARD, educator; b. Omaha, June 24, 1926; s. Hubert James and Jean (Woodruff) Van N.; B.S., Iowa State U., 1949; M.S., Northwestern U., 1951, Ph.D., 1954; m. Mary Ellen Dolvin, Dec. 28, 1948; children—Rebecca Ellen, Barbara Jean, Margaret Ann, Julie Lynn. Faculty elec. engring. dept. Northwestern U., 1952—, now prof., chmn. dept., 1969-72, dir. Computer Center, 1962-65; vis. asso. prof. U. Calif., Berkeley, 1958-59; vis. prof. Mass. Inst. Tech., 1973-74. Served with USNR, 1944-46. Mem. IEEE, Am. Soc. Engring. Edn., AAUP, Assn. Computing Machinery. Contbr. articles to profl. jours. Home: 2601 Noyes St Evanston IL 60201

VAN NEST, DEAN GILLETTE, advt. agy. exec.; b. Windom, Minn., Nov. 25, 1928; s. Leland Stanford and Ethel (Gillette) Van N.; B.S. in Elec. Engring., Northwestern U., 1948; M.B.A., Harvard, 1950; m. Maude Sinclair Haulenbeek, June 13, 1953 (dec.); children—Dean Gillette, Raymond Haulenbeek; m. 2d, Diana P. Jenney, Aug. 4, 1971; children—Ross Jenney, Kathleen Farkass. Exec. asst. Time, Inc., 1948-49; account exec. J. Walter Thompson, 1949-59; v.p. Doherty Clifford Steers & Shenfield, 1959-63; v.p. William Esty Co., Inc., 1963-65, sr. v.p., 1965— (all N.Y.C.); adj. asso. prof. Pace U., N.Y. U. Served to lt. (j.g.) USNR, 1944-50. Mem. Holland Soc. N.Y., St. Nicholas Soc. N.Y. (bd. mgrs. 1971—), Beta Theta Pi, Tau Beta Pi, Phi Eta Sigma. Presbyn. Clubs: Racquet and Tennis, Harvard (N.Y.C.); Point O Woods (L.I., N.Y.). Author: Across the Fence, 1965. Home: 25 Sycamore Bronxville NY 10708 Office: 100 E 42d St New York NY 10017

VAN NORDEN, LANGDON, lawyer; b. N.Y.C., Jan. 12, 1915; s. Ottomar Hoghland and Jeanie Belle (Duncan) Van N.; grad. Choate Sch., 1933; A.B., Princeton, 1937; LL.B., Yale, 1940; m. Gloria I. Barnes, June 19, 1948; 1 son, Langdon. Admitted to N.Y. bar, 1941, Conn. bar, 1977; with firm Davis, Polk, Wardwell, Sunderland & Kiendl, N.Y.C., 1940-42, 45-49; with H.A. Caesar & Co., N.Y.C., 1949—, partner, 1951—, now spl. counsel; resident counsel firm Winthrop, Stimson, Putnam & Roberts, Stamford, Conn. Pres., Met. Opera Guild, 1953-67; bd. dirs. Met. Opera Assn., chmn., 1975-77; pres. Nat. Orchestral Assn.; trustee Greenwich County Day Sch., 1968-74. Served to capt. AUS, 1942-45; ETO. Decorated Bronze Star medal. Mem. Yale Law Sch. Assn. (exec. com., past chmn. exec. com.). Clubs: Century Assn. (N.Y.C.); Round Hill (Greenwich, Conn.). Home: Cherry Valley Rd Greenwich CT 06830 Office: 260 Madison Ave New York NY 10017 also 21 Broad St Stamford CT

VAN NORMAN, CLARENDON ESS, musician; b. Galesburg, Ill., Aug. 23, 1930; s. Clarendon Ess and Marion V. Van Norman; student Eastman Sch. Music, 1948-49; B.S.M., M.S.M., Juilliard Sch. Music; M.A., Columbia U., 1957, Ed.D., 1965; m. Linda Barnes, July 8, 1978; children by previous marriage—Diane, Steven, Mark, Thomas. Solo French horn Buffalo Philharm., 1958-60; 3d and 1st horn Met. Opera Orch., N.Y.C., 1960-61, co-prin. French horn, 1961-63, 65—; solo French horn Chgo. Symphony Orch., 1963-65; instr. horn Northwestern U., 1963-65, Manhattan Sch. Music, N.Y.C., 1965-78. Served with USAF, 1950-54. Club: Rotary. Office: Box A73 Wantagh NY 11793

VAN NOSTRAND, MORRIS ABBOTT, JR., publisher; b. N.Y.C., Nov. 24, 1911; s. Morris Abbott and Margaret Adrianna (Edwards) Van N.; grad. St. Paul's Sch., 1930; B.A., Amherst Coll., 1934; m. Jane Alexander, Dec. 28, 1934 (dec. 1944); children—Pamela George, Patricia Abbott; m. 2d, Julia de La Roche Eaton, July 3, 1953; children—Deborah, Abbie. With Samuel French, Inc., N.Y.C., 1934—, sec., 1948-52, pres., 1952—; pres. Samuel French Canada, Ltd., Toronto, Ont., 1952—, Walter H. Baker Co., Boston and Denver, 1952—, Hugo & Luigi-Samuel French Music Pubs., Inc.; chmn. bd. Samuel French, Ltd., London; dir. Dyneer, Canton, Ohio; trustee Lincoln Savs. Bank, Bklyn. Vice pres. Forest Hills Garden Assn.; dir. New Dramatists Com., Travelers Aid Soc. Trustee Kew Forest Sch.; mem. council Friends of Amherst (Mass.) Library. Mem. ANTA (dir.), Chi Phi. Clubs: Lambs, Amherst, El Morocco (N.Y.C.); Nassau Country (gov.) (Glen Cove); Les Ambassadeurs (London). Home: 131 E 66th St New York NY 10021 Office: 25 W 45th St New York NY 10036

VANNOY, WALTER MONROE, JR., capital goods co. exec.; b. Lynchburg, Va., Jan. 13, 1928; s. Walter Monroe and Catherine Virginia (Beazley) V.; student Va. Mil. Inst., 1944-46; B.S., U.S. Mil. Acad., 1950; M.S. in Nuclear Engring., U. Va., 1957; m. Virginia Johnson McMillan, Dec. 1, 1951; children—Walter Monroe, Virginia Johnson. Instr. physics Va. Mil. Inst., 1954-56; nuclear engr. Babcock & Wilcox Co., Lynchburg, 1957-63, govt. market coordinator, 1963-65, utility market coordinator, 1964-65, program mgr., 1965-66, asst. mgr. nuclear and spl. products dept., 1966-67, plant mgr. Nuclear Fuel Plant, 1967-68, div. v.p., 1968-71, corp. v.p. naval nuclear fuel div., 1971-73, group v.p. power generation group, Barberton, Ohio, 1973-76, exec. v.p., N.Y.C., 1976-79; exec. v.p., chief administrv. officer J. Ray McDermott, New Orleans, 1979—; founder, dir. Jefferson Nat. Bank, Lynchburg; bd. dirs. Atomic Indsl. Forum, 1973-78, vice chmn., 1976-77; bd. dirs. Am. Nuclear Energy Council, 1975-78. Trustee, Va. Bapt. Hosp., 1971-73, Lynchburg Coll., 1970—. Served with U.S. Army, 1950-54. Mem. Am. Nuclear Soc. (past chmn. N.C.-Va. sect.), Newcomen Soc., Lynchburg C. of C. (past dir.). Episcopalian. Clubs: Boonsboro Country (past pres.), Piedmont (Lynchburg); Portage Country, Cascade (Akron, Ohio); Union League (N.Y.C.; Fairfield County (Conn.) Hunt. Home: 2858

Chestnut St New Orleans LA 70115 Office: PO Box 60035 New Orleans LA 70160

VANOCUR, SANDER, broadcasting exec.; b. Cleve., Jan. 8, 1928; s. Louis and Rose (Millman) Vinocur; grad. Northwestern U., 1950; postgrad. London (Eng.) Sch. Econs.; m. Edith Pick, Mar. 3, 1946; children—Nicholas, Christopher. City staff N.Y. Times, 1955-57; Brit. corr. CBS News; with NBC News, 1957-71, Washington, Midwestern, White House corr. nat. polit. corr., Washington corr. Today show, host First Tuesday TV show; sr. corr. Nat. Pub. Affairs Center for TV div. Pub. Broadcasting Service, 1971-77; TV columnist Washington Post, 1975-77; v.p. spl. reporting units ABC News and Sports, 1977—; former cons. Center for Study Democratic Instns.; former prof. communications Duke U. Served with U.S. Army, 1952-54. Office: care ABC News 1330 Ave of the Americas New York NY 10019*

VANONI, VITO AUGUST, hydraulic engr.; b. Calif., Aug. 30, 1904; s. Battitta and Mariana V.; B.S. in Civil Engring., Calif. Inst. Tech., 1926, M.S. in Civil Engring., 1932, Ph.D., 1940; m. Edith Maria Fulcinella, June 23, 1934. Supr. research lab. U.S. Soil Conservation Service, Pasadena, Calif., 1935-47; asst. prof. hydraulics Calif. Inst. Tech., 1942-49, asso. prof., 1949-55, prof., 1955-74, prof. emeritus, 1974—. Mem. ASCE, Internat. Assn. Hydraulic Research, Nat. Acad. Engring., Sigma Xi. Contbr. numerous articles on hydraulics and sedimentation to profl. jours.; editor: Sedimentation Engineering, 1975. Home: 3545 Lombardy Rd Pasadena CA 91107 Office: 1201 E California St Pasadena CA 91125

VAN OSDOL, PAUL, JR., lawyer; b. Brookfield, Mo., Aug. 16, 1915; s. Paul and Willie (Woodson) Van O.; A.B., U. Mo., Columbia, 1936, LL.B., 1938, J.D.; m. Evelyn Foreman, Nov. 15, 1942; children—Evelyn Van Osdol Edmonds, Paul, III. Admitted to Mo. bar; asso. firm Watson, Ess, Groner, Barnet & Whittaker, Kansas City, Mo., 1938-41; individual practice law, 1946-57; partner firm Terrell, Van Osdol and Magruder, Kansas City, Mo., 1957—; dir., gen. counsel Tower Properties Co., Kansas City; mem. jud. selection com. Circuit Ct. Jackson County (Mo.), 1958-63; cons. on nonpartisan ct. plan Am. Judicature Found. Bd. dirs. Mo. Public Sch. Redistricting Plan; mem. Mo. Gov.'s Com. on Higher Edn.; mem. Charter Com. for Drafting County Charter, Jackson County. Served with USAAF, 1941-46. Recipient citation of merit Sch. Law, U. Mo., Arts and Sci. Sch., U. Mo. Fellow Am. Bar Found.; mem. Kansas City Bar Assn., Lawyers Assn. Kansas City, Mo. Bar Assn., Am. Bar Assn. (del.), Am. Judicature Soc., Am. Law Inst., Kansas City C. of C. (dir. 1960-62). Republican. Mem. Christian Ch. (Disciples of Christ). Clubs: Mercury (Kansas City); Univ., Mission Hills Country. Home: 631 W 67th St Kansas City MO 64131 Office: 515 Commerce Bldg 922 Walnut St Kansas City MO 64106

VAN PALLANDT, NINA MAGDALENE, singer, actress; b. Copenhagen, July 15, 1932; d. Kaj and Clara Undset (Gyth) Moller; student U. So. Calif., 1951-53, Sorbonne, Paris, 1954-55; children—Nicolas Floris, Kirsa Eleonora Clara, Ana Maria Else. Debut (with B. Frederik Van Pallandt) at Tivoli, Copenhagen, 1957; appeared in movies: The Long Goodbye, Quintet, A Wedding, American Gigolo; cabaret and conert appearances including at Albert Hall, Festival Hall, Palladium; starred in TV series in Scandinavia, on BBC, Eng.; appeared in Royal Command Performance, London, 1960. Mem. Screen Actors Guild, AFTRA, Actors Equity, Musicians Union Eng. Office: care Paula Ceder Agy 9200 Sunset Blvd Suite 808 Los Angeles CA 90069

VAN PATTEN, DICK VINCENT, actor; b. Kew Gardens, N.Y., Dec. 9, 1928; s. Richard and Josephine (Acerno) Van P.; m. Patricia Poole, Apr. 25, 1954; children—Nels, Jimmy, Vince. Broadway debut in Tapestry in Gray, 1935; other stage appearances include: Ah, Wilderness!, 1939, 40, Watch on the Rhine, 1942, The Skin of Our Teeth, 1942, Mister Roberts, 1948, 51, 53, The Tender Trap, 1955, Will Success Spoil Rock Hunter?, 1957, Don't Drink the Water, Next, 1969; films include: Reg'lar Fellers, 1941, Charly, 1968, Joe Kidd, 1972, Westworld, 1973, Soylent Green, 1973, Superdad, 1974, Freaky Friday, 1976, High Anxiety, 1977; radio series Young Widder Brown, 1941, also radio plays Kiss and Tell, 1947, State Fair, 1950, 53, Father of the Bride, 1951, Good Housekeeping, 1951; regular TV series I Remember Mama, The Partners, 1971-72, The New Dick Van Dyke Show, 1973-74, When Things Were Rotten, 1975, Eight is Enough, 1977—; TV spl. Grandpa Max, 1975; drama Ladies of the Corridor, 1975, A Memory of Two Mondays, 1971; TV movie The Love Loat, 1976. Mem. Actors Equity, Screen Actors Guild. Office: MEW Co 151 N San Vicente Blvd Beverly Hills CA 90211*

VAN PELT, JOHN ROBERT, JR., univ. pres. emeritus; b. Denver, Apr. 2, 1896; s. John Robert and Ellen Russell (Warren) Van P.; A.B., Cornell Coll., 1918, D.Sc., 1942; B.S., Mich. Coll. Mines, 1922, E.M., 1923; LL.D., Chgo. Med. Sch., 1957; grad. study geology U. Chgo., 1926-28; m. Frances Church, Dec. 27, 1929 (dec. Aug. 1978); children—Peter, Richard Warren, Ellen Morgan (Mrs. Dennis T.P. Sears). Engaged in mining industry as mucker, tracklayer, motorman, surveyor, and mill hand, 1919-21; successively instr., asst. prof., prof. geology Cornell Coll., 1922-28, also exec. sec., 1922-23; ranger-naturalist Nat. Park Service, 1926; teaching fellow geology U. Chgo., 1926-28; asst. geologist Ill. State Geol. Survey, 1927, asso. geologist, 1928-29; chief div. geology, mining and metallurgy Mus. Sci. and Industry, Chgo., 1928-30, asst. dir., 1930-40, tech. dir. in charge planning and design exhibits, 1940-45; dir. research edn. and in charge Battelle research fellowships, also chmn. pub. relations com. Battelle Inst., Columbus, Ohio, 1945-51; pres. Mont. Sch. Mines, Butte, also ex-officio dir. Mont. Bur. Mines and Geology, 1951-56; pres. Mich. Technol. U., Houghton, 1956-64, chancellor, 1965-66, pres. emeritus, 1966—; pres. Western Soc. Engrs., 1936-37. Bd. dirs., mem. exec. com. Detroit & No. Savs. & Loan Assn., 1960-72. Mem. Mont. delegation Western Interstate Commn. for Higher Edn., 1951-56; expert cons. on tech. personnel War Dept., 1942-43; chmn. Sec. Interior's Survey Com. on U.S. Geol. Survey, 1953-54. Life trustee Cornell Coll. Served pvt. to 2d lt. F.A., U.S. Army, 1918-19. Registered profl. engr. Fellow A.A.A.S. (past mem. council); mem. Am. Inst. Mining and Metall. Engrs. (life; dir. 1941-47, v.p. 1944-47; chmn. mineral industry edn. div. 1954-55). Am. Soc. Engring. Edn., Engrs.' Council Profl. Devel., Gt. Lakes Hist. Soc., Explorers Club, Sierra Club, Phi Beta Kappa, Sigma Xi, Theta Tau, Gamma Alpha, Tau Beta Pi. Episcopalian. Club: Rotary. Author: Boston and Keweenaw, an Etching in Copper, 1945, 4th edit., 1964 also articles in ednl. and mining press. Address: 700 John Ringling Blvd Apt 709 Sarasota FL 33577 also summer Route 1 Box 190 Eagle Harbor MI 49951

VAN PELT, ROBERT, judge; b. Gosper County, Nebr., Sept. 9, 1897; s. Francis M. and Sarah (Simon) Van P.; A.B., Doane Coll., 1920, LL.D., 1959; LL.B., U. Nebr., 1922; L.H.D., Westmar Coll., 1960; m. Mildred Carter, June 17, 1925; children—Robert (dec.), Margery Van Pelt Irvin, Samuel. Admitted to Nebr. bar, 1922, practiced in Lincoln, 1922- 57; asst. U.S. atty., 1930-34; U.S. dist. judge Dist. Nebr., 1957-70, sr. judge, 1970—; lectr. Nebr. Law Coll., 1946-57; mem. com. to implement Fed. Magistrates Act; mem. adv. com. jud. activities, adv. com. fed. rules of evidence U.S. Jud. Conf. Del. Rep. Nat. Conv., 1940, 44, 48; trustee Doane Coll., 1928-68. Mem. Am. Coll. Trial Lawyers, Am. Coll. Probate Counsel, Phi Sigma Kappa, Phi Delta Phi. Congregationalist. Clubs: Masons (33 deg.), Rotary, Lincoln Country, Lincoln Univ. Home: 2323 Woodscrest Lincoln NE 68502 Office: Federal Bldg Lincoln NE 68508

VAN PETTEN, GARRY ROBERT, univ. adminstr.; b. Camrose, Alta., Can., Nov. 9, 1936; s. William Stewart and Alice Louella (Pierce) Van P.; B.Sc., U. Alta., 1957, M.Sc., 1959; Ph.D. in Pharmacology, U. Glasgow, 1962; m. Betty Irene Converse, Aug. 26, 1957; children—Stewart, Deane, Wayne. Asso. prof. div. pharmacology and therapeutics Faculty of Medicine, U. Calgary (Alta.), 1970-75, prof., 1976-78, acting head div., 1974-76, head div., 1976-78, dir. med. vivarium, 1974-78; dean Faculty Pharmacy and Pharm. Scis., U. Alta., Edmonton, 1978—. Recipient Harry Gold award Jour. Clin. Pharmacology, 1972. Mem. Pharm. Soc. Can. (pres.), Can. Soc. Toxicology, Western Pharm. Soc., Am. Soc. Clin. Pharmacology and Therapeutics. Contbr. articles to profl. jours. Home: Rural Route 4 Sherwood Park AB Canada Office: Faculty of Pharmacy and Pharm Scis Univ of Alberta Edmonton AB T6G 2N8 Canada

VAN PETTEN, HARRY O, JR., lawyer; b. Long Beach, Calif., May 19, 1920; s. Harry O and Blanche Ruth (Solomon) Van P.; B.A., Stanford, 1947; LL.B., 1949; m. Ione Wenzinger, July 1, 1944; children—Peter, Cyma. Admitted to Calif. bar, 1950, since practiced in Los Angeles; mem. firm Richards, Watson, Smith & Van Petten, 1954-60, Van Petten & Holen, 1961—. Chmn. bd. Jacquard Systems, computer mfrs., Santa Monica, Calif. Atty., Calif. Dem. Com., 1953-58; Dem. nominee for congress, 1964. Served to lt. AUS, 1943-46. Mem. Am., Calif. bar assns. Presbyn. Elk. Contbr. articles to legal, financial publs. Home: 10218 Lesterford Ave Downey CA 90241 Office: 1150 S Olive St Suite 1520 Los Angeles CA 90015

VANPOOLE, THOMAS BENNETT, JR., patent lawyer; b. Salisbury, N.C., Sept. 7, 1921; s. Thomas B. and Mary (Beaver) VanP.; A.B. cum laude, Catawba Coll., 1942; postgrad. Princeton, 1944; Mass. Inst. Tech., 1945; J.D., U. Va., 1948; m. Mary Gilmer Cocke, Oct. 1, 1949; children—Thomas Bennett III, Virginia Cromwell, Elizabeth Anne. Examiner, U.S. Patent Office, Richmond, Va., 1942-44; patent adviser Naval Research Lab., 1945-46; admitted to Va. and D.C. bars, 1949, since practiced in Washington; sr. partner firm Mason, Fenwick & Lawrence, 1969—. Served to lt. (j.g.) USNR, 1944-46. Mem. Am., Va., D.C., Fed. bar assns., Am. Patent Law Assn., Kappa Sigma, Delta Theta Phi. Rotarian. Home: 2219 N Roosevelt St Arlington VA 22205 Office: 1730 Rhode Island Ave NW Washington DC 20036

VAN PRAAG, ALEX, JR., cons. engr.; b. Little Falls, Minn., Jan. 29, 1896; s. Alexander and Rachel (Davis) Van P.; student James Millikin U., 1913-15; B.S. in Civil Engring., U. Ill., 1917; m. Bernice I. Metzger, Dec. 27, 1926; children—Roger C., James N. Asst. engr. Miller, Holbrook & Warren, Decatur, Ill., 1919-20; asst. to chief san. engr. Ill. Dept. Pub. Health, 1920-22; mem. firm Warren & Van Praag, Inc., cons. engrs., architects, Decatur, 1922—, pres., 1952-68, chmn. bd., 1968—; treas., dir. Midwest Computer Service, Decatur, 1958-64; dir. 1st Nat. Bank of Decatur, 1955—. Mem. Ill. Bd. Pub. Health Advisers, Springfield, 1962-69; mem. Ill. Bldg. Authority, 1961-65. Mem. pres.'s citizens advisory com. U. Ill., 1961—; mem. advisory com. St. Mary's Hosp., Decatur, 1963-68; trustee Millikin U., 1961-70; bd. dirs. United Fund of Decatur and Macon County, Ill., 1966-69. Served with U.S. Army, AEF, 1917-19. Recipient Loyalty award U. Ill. Alumni Assn., 1964; Alumni Merit Loyalty award Millikin U., 1973; Distinguished Alumnus award Civil Engring. Alumni Assn. U. Ill., 1975; registered profl. engr., Ill., Ind., Ohio, Ky., Mo., N.D., Iowa, Tenn., Wis. Fellow Am. Cons. Engrs. Council; mem. ASCE (life), Nat. (past pres.), Ill. (past pres., hon. mem.) socs. profl. engrs., Cons. Engrs. Council Ill., Ill. Registered Land Surveyors Assn., ASTM, Am. Rd. Builders Assn., Am. Water Works Assn., Water Pollution Control Assn. Central States, Decatur Assn. Commerce, Ill. C. of C. (chmn. water resources com. 1959-60), U. Ill. Alumni Assn., Am. Legion. Presbyterian. Clubs: Elks, Decatur. Home: 402 Southmoreland Pl Decatur IL 62521 Office: 253 S Park St Decatur IL 62523

VAN REEVEN, JAN PIETER, ret. oil co. exec.; b. Rotterdam, Netherlands, Sept. 6, 1921; came to U.S., 1976; s. Pieter Anthonie and Lijntne (van Harten) van R.; law grad. Amsterdam Municipal U., 1945; m. Theresia Maria van Leeuwen, Oct. 14, 1948; children—Johannes, Henri Wynand, Lijntje. With legal dept. N.V. De Bataafsche Petroleum Mij., The Hague, 1950-53; with legal dept. Compania Shell de Venezuela Ltd., Maracaibo and Caracas, 1953-56; sec. to bd. dirs., mgr. govt. agreement affairs Iranian Oil Operating Cos., Teheran, 1957-61; gen. mgr. Shell Co. of Ceylon, Ltd., 1963; chmn. bd. P.T. Shell Indonesia, 1964-66; regional coordinator Middle East, Shell Internat. Petroleum Co. Ltd., London, 1966-70; gen. mng. dir. Iranian Oil Operating Cos., Teheran, 1970-74; pres. dir. Shell Nederland B.V., Rotterdam, 1974-76; exec. v.p. adminstrn. Shell Oil Co., Houston, 1976-79. Presbyterian.

VAN RENSBURG, WILLEM CORNELIUS JANSE, mineral economist; b. Bloemfontein, South Africa, Nov. 28, 1938; s. Willem Cornelius Janse and Maria Katarina (Wandrag) van R.; came to U.S., 1978; B.Sc., U. Pretoria (South Africa), 1960, B.Sc. with honors, 1961, M.Sc., 1963; Ph.D., U. Wis., 1965; m. Jennifer Dawn Line, Aug. 4, 1962; children—Kathryn, Patricia, Jillian. Sr. geologist South African Geol. Survey, 1960-67; dep. dir. South African Dept. Planning, 1967-73; chief div. econs. and costing South African Nat. Inst. for Metallurgy, 1973-75; tech. dir. South African Minerals Bur., 1975-77; Brit. Petroleum prof. energy econs. Rand Afrikaans U., Johannesburg, 1977-78; prof. geol. scis., asso. dir. Bur. Econ. Geology, U. Tex., Austin, 1978—; dir. United Services Gold Fund; mem. Presdl. Commn. Inquiry into Conservation South Africa's Coal Resources, 1970-75. Mem. South African Coal Processing Soc. (chmn. 1978), Sigma Xi. Congregationalist. Author: (with D.A. Pretorius) South Africa's Strategic Minerals—Pieces on A Continental Chessboard, 1977; (with S. Bambrick) The Economics of the World's Mineral Industries, 1978. Home: 7619 Rockpoint Dr Austin TX 78731 Office: U Tex Austin TX 78712. *My father told me that one might kid others but if you kid yourself you are a fool. A man must know himself, his strengths and weaknesses. He must face up squarely to those weaknesses.*

VAN RENSSELAER, STEPHEN, banker; b. N.Y.C., Nov. 28, 1905; s. Charles August and Caroline Elizabeth (Fitzgerald) Van R.; grad. St. Mark's Sch., Southboro, Mass., 1924; A.B., Harvard, 1928, postgrad. Advanced Mgmt. Program, 1952; m. Lillie Langstroth, Aug. 1, 1946; 1 son, Stephen. Clk. First Nat. Bank, N.Y.C., 1928-46, mgr. credit dept., 1946-48, asst. v.p., 1948-53, dir. v.p., 1953-55; v.p. First Nat. City Bank of N.Y., 1955-70; investor, 1970—; dir. Upson Co., Lockport, N.Y., 1951-76. Bd. govs. N.Y. Coll. Osteo. Medicine of N.Y. Inst. Tech., Old Westbury, 1979—. Served as capt. USAAF, 1942-45. Mem. Robert Morris Assos. (pres. N.Y. chpt. 1951). Episcopalian. Mason. Club: Piping Rock (Locust Valley N.Y.). Home: Box 333 Locust Valley NY 11560

VAN RIPER, PAUL PRITCHARD, educator; b. Laporte, Ind., July 29, 1916; s. Paul and Margaret (Pritchard) Van R.; A.B., DePauw U., 1938; Ph.D., U. Chgo., 1947; m. Dorothy Ann Dodd Samuelson, May 11, 1964; 1 son, Michael Scott Samuelson. Instr. Northwestern U., 1947-49, asst. prof. polit. sci., 1949-51; mgmt. analyst Office Comptroller Dept. Army, 1951-52; mem. faculty Cornell U., 1952-70, prof., 1957-70, chmn. gov. bd., exec. com. Cornell Social Sci. Research Center, 1956-58; prof., head dept. polit. sci. Tex. A & M U., 1970-77, prof., 1977—; vis. prof. U. Chgo., 1958, Ind. U., 1961, U. Strathclyde (Scotland), 1964, U. Mich., 1965, U. Okla., 1969, U. Utah, 1979. Mem. exec. com. Civil Service Reform Assn. N.Y., 1960-64; mem. hist. adv. com. NASA, 1964-66. Bd. dirs. Brazos Valley Community Action Agy., 1975—. Served to maj. AUS, 1942-46. Decorated Croix de Guerre (France). Mem. Am., So., S.W. (exec. com. 1975-77) polit. sci. assns., Am. Soc. Pub. Adminstrn. (nat. adv. com. 1957-60), Pub. Personnel Assn., Internat. City Mgmt. Assn., Phi Beta Kappa, Beta Theta Pi (v.p. 1962, gen. sec. 1963-65), Pi Sigma Alpha, Phi Kappa Phi, Sigma Delta Chi. Republican. Baptist. Author: History of the United States Civil Service, 1958; Some Educational and Social Aspects of Fraternity Life, 1961; (with others) The American Federal Executive, 1963; Handbook of Practical Politics, 3d edit., 1967. Home: 712 E 30th St Bryan TX 77801 Office: Dept Polit Sci Tex A and M Univ College Station TX 77843

VAN SANT, GUS GREENE, apparel co. exec.; b. Mayfield, Ky., Mar. 23, 1927; s. Lewis Loving and Dorothy (Greene) Van S.; student Purdue U., 1946-50; m. Betty Seay, Feb. 11, 1950; children—Gus Greene, Malinda. With Merit Clothing Co., Mayfield, 1950-56; with McGregor-Doniger, Inc., N.Y.C., 1956-70, pres., 1967-70; pres. White Stag Apparel div. Warnaco, Inc., Portland, Oreg., 1970-71; sr. v.p. Warnaco, Inc., Bridgeport, Conn., 1971-73, exec. v.p., 1973-78; pres. Huk-A-Poo Sportswear, Inc., N.Y.C., 1978—. Home: 20 Inwood Rd Darien CT 06820 Office: One W 39 St New York NY 10018

VANSANT, NICHOLAS, advt. agy. exec.; b. Balt., Mar. 24, 1924; s. Wilbur and Mary Freeman (Garrett) VanS.; B.A., Cornell U., 1964; m. Harriette Procter, June 24, 1948; children—Nicholas P., Katherine P., Mary Pat, Craig G. With VanSant, Dugdale & Co., Balt., 1947—, dir., 1957—, v.p., 1960-67, sr. v.p., 1967-73, pres., 1973—, also, sec., treas. Bd. dirs. Goodwill Industries, 1950, YMCA, 1948, Police Boys' Clubs, 1965; mem. Jail Bd. Balt., 1975—. Served with AUS, 1943-46. Mem. Am. Assn. Advt. Agys. (mem. agy mgmt. com. 1972—), Kappa Sigma. Methodist (dir.). Clubs: Balt. Country, Mchts., Center (Balt.). Home: 118 Witherspoon Rd Baltimore MD 21212 Office: World Trade Center Baltimore MD 21202

VAN SANT, VERNON, JR., oil co. exec.; b. Morehead, Ky., May 27, 1921; s. Vernon and Jessie Milton (Jones) Van S.; student Berea (Ky.) Coll., LaSalle Extension U.; divorced; children—Frances H. Van Sant Cormack, Donna K., Jessie L. Van Sant Murray, Benjamin F., Rebecca A. Accounting clk., accountant Ashland Oil & Refining Co. (Ky.), 1942-52, mgr. exploration and prodn. Canadian div., Calgary, Alta., 1958-63; controller, treas., exec. v.p. Amurex Oil Co., Ashland, 1952-58; gen. mgr. Whitehall Canadian Oils Ltd., Calgary, 1963-66, exec. v.p., gen. mgr., 1966-69; exec. v.p. Ashland Oil Can. Ltd., Calgary, 1969-74, pres., 1974—, chief exec. officer, 1976-79, cons., 1979—, also dir.; chmn., chief exec. officer Francana Oil & Gas Ltd., Canadian Merrill Ltd., Calgary, 1979—; dir. Midhurst Corp., Whitehall Mining Co. Ltd., Brazeau Collieries Ltd., Kananaskis Exploration & Devel. Co. Ltd., Kananaskis Mines Ltd. Bd. mgrs. Grace Presbyn. Ch., Calgary; active United Fund Calgary and Dist. Served with USNR, 1943-46. Mem. Canadian Petroleum Assn. (gov.), Ind. Petroleum Assn. Can. (past treas., dir.), Calgary C. of C. (chmn. oil and gas com.). Clubs: Calgary Golf and Country, Glencoe, Petroleum, Ranchmen's, Gun (Calgary). Home: 24 Eagle Ridge Dr SW Calgary AB T2V 2V4 Canada Office: 700 2d St SW Suite 2900 Calgary AB T2P 2W2 Canada

VAN SCHILFGAARDE, JAN, govt. ofcl.; b. The Hague, Netherlands, Feb. 7, 1929; came to U.S., 1946, naturalized, 1957; B.S., Iowa State Coll., 1949, M.S., 1950, Ph.D. in Agrl. Engring. and Soil Physics, 1954; married; 3 children. Instr., asso. agrl. engr. Iowa State Coll., 1949-54; asst. prof. agrl. engring. N.C. State Coll., 1954-57, asso. prof., 1957-62, prof., 1962-64; drainage engr. Agrl. Research Service, U.S. Dept. Agr., Raleigh, N.C., 1954-64; chief water mgmt. engr. soil and water conservation research div. U.S. Dept. Agr., Beltsville, Md., 1964-67, asso. dir., 1967-71, dir., 1971-72, dir. Salinity Labs, Riverside, Calif., 1972—; vis. prof. Ohio State U., 1962. Mem. Am. Soc. Agrl. Engrs., Soil Sci. Soc., ASCE, Soil Conservation Soc. Am. Office: US Salinity Lab Agrl Research Ser US Dept Agr Riverside CA 92501

VAN SCHOONEVELD, CORNELIS HENDRIK, educator, editor; b. The Hague, Netherlands, Jan. 19, 1921; s. Daniel and Antje (Steenstra) Van S.; came to U.S., 1949, naturalized, 1961; ed. Leiden U., Netherlands, 1938-46; Ph.D., Columbia, 1949; m. Dorothy Jean Abel, Jan. 2, 1967; children—Daniel, Eleanor Anne, Anne Laetitia. Prof. Balto-Slavic langs. Leiden U., 1952-59; prof. Slavic langs. and lits. Stanford U., 1959-66; prof. dept. Slavic langs. and lits. Ind. U., Bloomington, 1966—, chmn. dept., 1973—. Mem. Linguistic Soc. Am., Société de Linguistique de Paris, Nederlandse Vereniging voor Algemene Taalwetenschap. Author: A Semantic Analysis of the Old Russian Finite Preterite System, 1959; (with J.E. Buning) The Sentence Intonation of Contemporary Russian as a Linguistic Structure, 1960; Semantic Transmutations, vol. 1, 1978; editor: Janua Linguarum, Slavistic Printings and Reprintings, De Proprietatibus Litterarum, Internat. Jour. of Slavic Linguistics and Poetics. Home: 200 E Atwater St Bloomington IN 47401

VAN SCOTT, EUGENE JOSEPH, physician; b. Macedon, N.Y., May 27, 1922; s. Charles J. and Eleanor (Du Pre) Van S.; student U. Mich., 1941-44; B.S., U. Chgo., 1945, M.D., 1948; m. Mary Louise Yox, Oct. 9, 1948; children—Christopher J., Stephen J., David J. Intern Millard Fillmore Hosp., Buffalo, 1948-49; resident dermatology U. Chgo. Clinics, 1949-52; asso. dermatology U. Pa. Hosp., 1952-53; mem. staff Nat. Cancer Inst., NIH, 1953-68, chief dermatology br., 1961-67. sci. dir. for gen. labs. and clinics, 1965-68; prof., also asso. dir. Skin and Cancer Hosp., Temple U., 1968—. Charter mem. trustee Dermatology Found., 1964-72. Served with USNR, 1943-45, Recipient Mr. and Mrs. J. N. Taub Internat. Meml. award for psoriasis research, 1964, James Clarke White award dermatologic medicine Assn. Mil. Surgeons, 1965; Meritorious Service medal USPHS, 1966; Albert Lasker award, 1972; Stephen Rothman award 1975). Mem. Am. Soc. Clin. Investigation, Soc. Investigative Dermatology (pres. 1965-66), Am. Acad. Dermatology, A.A.A.S., Am. Assn. Cancer Research, Am., Canadian (hon.) dermatol. assns., Swedish (hon.), Danish (hon.) dermatol. socs., A.M.A., Am. Soc. Exptl. Pathology. Mem. editorial bd. Jour. Nat. Cancer Inst., 1958-60, Jour. Investigative Dermatology, 1961-65, Archives Dermatology, 1964-71. Home: 1138 Sewell Ln Rydal PA 19046 Office: Skin and Cancer Hosp Philadelphia PA 19140

VANSELOW, NEAL ARTHUR, physician, coll. adminstr.; b. Milw., Mar. 18, 1932; s. Arthur Frederick and Mildred (Hoffman) V.; A.B., U. Mich., 1954, M.D., 1958, M.S., 1963; m. Mary Ellen McKenzie, June 20, 1958; children—Julie Ann, Richard Arthur. Intern, Mpls. Gen. Hosp., 1958-59; resident Univ. Hosp., Ann Arbor, Mich.,

1959-63; instr. medicine U. Mich., 1963-64, asst. prof., 1964-68, asso. prof., 1968-72, prof., chmn. dept. postgrad. medicine and health professions edn., 1972-74; dean Coll. Medicine U. Ariz., Tucson, 1974-77; chancellor Med. Center U. Nebr., Omaha, 1977—, v.p. univ., 1977—; Chmn. Joint Bd. Osteo. and Med. Examiners Ariz., 1974-77. Bd. dirs. Devel. Authority for Tucson's Economy, 1975-77; bd. dirs., mem. exec. com. Health Planning Council Midlands, Omaha, 1978—. Diplomate Am. Bd. Internal Medicine, Am. Bd. Allergy and Immunology. Fellow A.C.P., Am. Acad. Allergy; mem. Phi Beta Kappa, Sigma Xi, Alpha Omega Alpha, Beta Theta Pi, Nu Sigma Nu. Home: 8115 Jackson St Omaha NE 68114 Office: Coll of Medicine U Nebr Omaha NE 68105

VAN SETERS, JOHN, educator; b. Hamilton, Ont., Can., May 2, 1935; s. Hugo and Anne (Hubert) Van S.; B.A., U. Toronto, 1958; M.A., Yale U., 1959, Ph.D., 1965; B.D., Princeton Theol. Sem., 1962; m. Elizabeth Marie Malmberg, June 11, 1960; children—Peter John, Deborah Elizabeth. Asst. prof. dept. Near Eastern studies Waterloo Luth. U., 1965-67; asso. prof. Old Testament Andover Newton Theol. Sch., 1967-70; asso. prof. dept. Near Eastern studies U. Toronto, 1970-76, prof., 1976-77; James A. Gray prof. Bibl. lit., dept. religion U. N.C., Chapel Hill, 1977—. Woodrow Wilson fellow, 1958; J.J. Obermann fellow, 1962-64; John Simon Guggenheim fellow, 1979-80. Mem. Soc. Bibl. Lit., Am. Schs. Oriental Research, Soc. Study of Egyptian Antiquities, AAUP. Presbyterian. Author: The Hyksos: A New Investigation, 1966; Abraham in History and Tradition, 1975. Home: 303 Hoot Owl Ln Chapel Hill NC 27514 Office: 101 Saunders Hall Univ of NC Chapel Hill NC 27514

VAN SICKLE, BRUCE MARION, judge; b. Minot, N.D., Feb. 13, 1917; s. Guy Robin and Hilda Alice (Rosenquist) Van S.; B.S.L., U. Minn., 1941, J.D., 1941; m. Dorothy Alfreda Hermann, May 26, 1943; children—Susan (Mrs. Michael Cooper), John Allan, Craig Bruce, David Max. Admitted to Minn. bar, 1941, N.D. bar, 1946; practiced in Minot, 1947-71; judge U.S. Dist. Ct., 1971—. Mem. N.D. Ho. of Reps., 1957-61. Served with USMCR, 1941-46. Mem. Am., N.D., Northwest, Ward County bar assns., Am. Trial Lawyers Assn., Am. Coll. Probate Counsel, Am. Judicature Soc. Mason (Shriner), Elk. Office: US District Ct PO Box 670 Bismarck ND 58501

VAN SICLEN, DEWITT CLINTON, educator; b. Carlisle, Pa., Oct. 25, 1918; s. Clinton DeWitt and Mary (Coyle) Van S.; A.B., Princeton, 1940, A.M., 1947, Ph.D., 1951; M.S., U. Ill., 1941; m. Beverly Gale King, Apr. 10, 1949; children—Mary Chandos, Clinton DeWitt, Sally Jane, Henry King. Geologist, Consol. Natural Gas Co., Pitts., 1939-46, Drilling & Exploration Co., Abilene, Tex., 1947-50; cons. geologist, Snyder, Tex., 1950-51; geologist subsidiaries Standard Oil Co. of Ind., Houston, 1952-59; prof. geology U. Houston, 1959—, chmn. dept. geology, 1960-67. Geol. cons. Served to capt. USAAF, 1942-46, USAF, 1951-52. Mem. Am. Assn. Petroleum Geologists (former del.), Nat. Assn. Geology Tchrs. (former pres. Tex. sect.), Houston Geol. Soc., Assn. Profl. Geol. Scientists (former editor Tex. sect.), Phi Beta Kappa, Sigma Xi. Episcopalian. Home: 4909 Bellaire Blvd Bellaire TX 77401 Office: U Houston Houston TX 77004

VANSINA, JAN MARIA JOZEF, historian, anthropologist; b. Antwerp, Sept. 14, 1929; s. Dirk and Suzanna (Verellen) V.; B.A. in Law, U. Louvain, 1949, B.A., M.A. in History, 1951; postgrad. Univ. Coll., U. London, 1951-52; Ph.D., U. Louvain, 1957; m. Claudine Herman, Sept. 3, 1954; 2 son, Bruno. Researcher, Inst. for Research in Central Africa, Zaire, Rwanda and Burundi, 1952-60, head social sci., 1957-60; mem. faculty dept. history U. Wis.-Madison, 1960—, Vilas research prof., 1976—, prof. anthropology, 1963—; vis. prof. U. Louvain, 1973-75, U. Lovanium, Kinshasa, 1963, 66, 71; mem. UNESCO Com. for writing history of Africa, 1970—. Recipient Herskovits award African Studies Assn., 1966. Mem. Royal Acad. Overseas Sci., Belgium Internat. African Inst. (mem. bd. 1968-73), African Studies Assn. (bd. dirs. 1967-70), Am. Hist. Assn., Soc. Francaise Histoire d'outremer. Author 12 books in field including: Children of Woot: A History of the Kuba Peoples, 1978. Bd. editors Jour. African History, History in Africa, African Econ. History, Sprache und Geschichte. Home: 2810 Ridge Rd Madison WI 53705 Office: 455 N Park St Madison WI 53706. *Always be curious; alternate belief and doubt.*

VAN SINDEREN, ALFRED WHITE, telephone co. exec.; b. Bklyn., June 20, 1924; s. Adrian and Jean (White) Van S.; B.A., Yale U., 1945; M.B.A., Harvard U., 1947; m. Suzanne Petersen, Apr. 21, 1962; children—Alexander, David Cabot, Sylvia (Mrs. Van Sinderen Abbate), Jean White, Katherine. With So. New Eng. Telephone Co., New Haven, 1947—, v.p. No. area, Hartford, Conn., 1962-65, v.p. operations, 1965-67, pres., 1967—, also dir.; past dir. Fed. Res. Bank Boston; dir. United Techs., Hartford, Conn., Stanley Works, New Britain, Conn. Mem. adv. bd. Yale-U.S. Sch. Orgn. and Mgmt.; trustee Yale Library Assn.; co-chmn. Gov. Conf. Human Rights, 1967; pres. Conn. Econ. Devel. Corp., Hartford, Shirley Frank Found.; trustee Devereux Found., Devon, Pa. Served with USNR, 1943-46. Recipient Charter Oak Leadership medal Hartford, 1965; Conn. Man of Yr., New Eng. Council, 1976. Clubs: Quinnipiack (New Haven), New Haven Country. Home: 12 Highview Dr Woodbridge CT 06525 Office: 227 Church St New Haven CT 06506

VANSITTART, PETER, novelist, lectr., critic; b. Bedford, Eng., Aug. 27, 1920; s. Edward Morris and Mignon Therese Vansittart; student Worcester Coll., Oxford U., 1940-41. Author: I Am The World, 1942; Enemies, 1947; The Overseer, 1949; Broken Canes, 1951; A Verdict of Treason, 1953; A Little Madness, 1953; The Game and Ground, 1957; Orders of Chivalry, 1959; The Tournament, 1961; A Sort of Forgetting, 1961; Carolina, 1961; The Siege, 1962; Sources of Unrest, 1962; The Friends of God, 1963; The Lost Lands, 1964; The Dark Tower, 1965; The Shadow Land, 1967; Green Knights, Black Angels, 1967; The Storyteller, 1968; Pastimes of a Red Summer, 1969; Landlord, 1970; Vladivostock, 1972; Dictators, 1973; Worlds and Underworlds, 1974; Quintet, 1976; Lancelot, 1978; Flakes of History, 1978. Address: care Anthony Shiel Ltd 2 Morwell St London WC1B 3AR England

VAN SLYKE, HELEN, novelist; b. Washington, July 9, 1919; d. Frederic Vogt and Lenore Vogt (Lyon); Journalist, Washington Evening Star, 1938-43, Glamour Mag., 1945-60; v.p. Norman, Craig & Kummel Advt. Agy., 1961-63; pres. Givenchy Perfumes, N.Y.C., 1963-68; v.p. Helena Rubinstein, Inc., N.Y.C., 1968-72; author: All Visitors Must Be Announced, 1972; The Heart Listens, 1974; The Mixed Blessing, 1975; Always Is Not Forever, 1977; The Best Place To Be, 1976; The Rich and the Righteous, 1971; Sisters and Strangers, 1978; A Necessary Woman, 1979; contbr. nat. mags. Recipient Today's Woman award, 1977. Mem. Fashion Group (internat. pres. 1966-67), AFTRA. Fgn. reprints of books in 16 langs. Died July 3, 1979. *To be a contemporary novelist, with the response that evokes, seems to me the richest reward for a lifetime of work in many areas. Throughout my life I have sought respect, decency and the affection of friends, both business and personal. And have tried to return these qualities to the best of my ability. Identity with people is the key to a full and interesting life. An inquiring mind, a level head and a genuine appreciation of one's blessings are God's greatest gifts to me.*

VAN SMITH, HOWARD, writer; b. San Francisco, Apr. 6, 1910; s. Arthur Lockwood and Florence (Garrettson) S.; student Pennington Prep., 1927-29, Franklyn Union, 1936-37; m. Anne McCarron, June 21, 1938 (div. 1965); children—Garrett, Parris, Antony, William; m. 2d, Micheline Mathews, Nov. 26, 1965. Staff reporter N.Y. Times, 1930-32; free-lance writer, 1933-35; heating and hydraulics engr., 1935-42; civilian engr. Air Force, Warner-Robins Airfield, Ga., 1942-44; reporter Orlando (Fla.) Sentinel, 1944; Sunday editor Miami (Fla.) Daily News, 1945-57, spl. writer, 1957-65, Ft. Lauderdale (Fla.) News, 1965-77; adminstrv. asst. Fla. Dept. Agr., Davie, 1978—; lectr. U. Miami, 1948-54. Recipient Pulitzer prize for nat. reporting, 1959; meritorious award Fla. Pub. Health Assn., 1959; Service to Mankind award, 1961; named to Hort. Hall of Fame, 1976; named foremost gardening writer in Am. and Can., Am. Assn. Nurserymen, 1978; N.Y. State Center for Migrant Studies fellow N.Y. State U. at Geneseo. Author: (with C. Raymond Van Dusen) The New Speech-O-Gram Technique for Persuasive Public Speaking, 1962; The Education of Juan, 1973. Contbr. articles, short stories to nat. mags. Home: 905 SW 9th Terr Fort Lauderdale FL 33312 Office: Fla Dept Agr 4810 SW 47 Ave Davie FL 33314

VAN SOEST, BERT EDWARD, clergyman; b. Strasburg, N.D., July 31, 1921; s. Peter M. and Mary (Kamps) Van S.: A.B., Central Coll., Pella, Iowa, 1943, D.D., 1975; M.Div., Western Theol. Sem., Holland, Mich., 1946; postgrad. Oberlin Grad. Sch. Theology, 1947-50, McCormick Theol. Sem., Chgo., 1956, Iliff Theol. Sem., Denver, 1968; m. Barbara Stavast, Sept. 6, 1943; children—Mark, David, Janice, Linda. Ordained to ministry Reformed Ch. Am., 1946; pastor chs. in Ohio, Mich. and Ill., 1946-61; pastor Mountain View Community Ref. Ch., Denver, 1961-69, Pompton Ref. Ch., Pompton Lakes, N.J., 1969—; pres. Classis Ill., Ref. Ch. Am., 1959, W. Central Classis, 1964; v.p. Particular Synod Chgo., 1960; pres. Particular Synod of West, 1967; v.p. Gen. Synod Ref. Ch. Am., 1974-75, pres., 1975-76, mem. exec. com., 1974-79; chmn. Christian action Commn., 1964-68; mem. bd. Western Sem., Central Coll.; chmn. bd. trustees Central Ministries, Paterson, N.J., 1971—; pres. ministerial assns. West Side Cleve., 1948-49, Morrison, Ill., 1958, Pompton Lakes, 1971. Mem. personnel com. Bethesda Hosp., Denver, 1968-69; mem. exec. com. N.J. chpt. CROP, 1974-78; chmn. Ramapo Pompton Conservators, 1970-77; mem. Pompton Lakes Bicentennial Com., 1976. Recipient Outstanding Leadership award CROP, 1975. Author: The Surrendered Life, 1953; Basic Bible Knowledge Test, 1958; Study Guide on Basic Truths of the Bible, 1965; Prayer Time Booklet, 1958; Sermons for Temple Time, 1959; also articles. Home: 508 Lincoln Ave Pompton Lakes NJ 07442 Office: 59 Hamburg Turnpike Pompton Lakes NJ 07442. *I consider myself a Christian realist. One of my favorite quotes is "Expect great things from God, attempt great things for God."*

VANSTRUM, PAUL ROSS, mfg. co. exec.; b. Mpls., Aug. 3, 1920; s. Paul August and Ruth (Ross) V.; B.Chem. Engring., U. Minn., 1942; m. Kathleen W. Johnson, Sept. 26, 1942; children—Marilyn K. (Mrs. G. Frank Hood, Jr.), Richard W., Paul W. With Union Carbide Corp., 1942, 44—, tech. dir. nuclear div. prodn. plants, 1967-69, v.p., 1969—; chem. engr. Prest-O-Lite Co., 1942-44; design engr. SAM Labs., Columbia, 1944. Recipient Ernest Orlando Lawrence Meml. award AEC, 1966; Outstanding Achievement award U. Minn., 1966. Mem. Am. Nuclear Soc., AAAS, Am. Inst. Chemists, Sigma Xi, Tau Beta Pi. Home: 104 Ogden Ln Oak Ridge TN 37830 Office: PO Box Y Oak Ridge TN 37830

VAN TAMELEN, EUGENE EARLE, chemist, educator; b. Zeeland, Mich., July 20, 1925; s. Gerrit and Henrietta (Vanden Bosch) van T.; A.B., Hope Coll., 1947, D.Sc., 1970; M.S., Harvard, 1949, Ph.D., 1950; D.Sc., Bucknell U., 1970; m. Mary Ruth Houtman, June 16, 1951; children—Jane Elizabeth, Carey Catherine, Peter Gerrit. Instr., U. Wis., 1950-52, from asst. to asso. prof., 1952-59, prof., 1959-61, Homer Adkins prof. chemistry, 1961-62; prof. chemistry Stanford, 1962—, chmn. dept., 1974-78. Am.-Swiss Found. lectr., 1964. Recipient A.T. Godfrey award, 1947; G. Haight traveling fellow, 1957; Guggenheim fellow, 1965, 73; Leo Hendrik Baekeland award, 1965; Prof. Extraordinarius Netherlands, 1967-73. Mem. Am. Chem. Soc. (Pure Chemistry award 1961, Creative Work in Synthetic Organic Chemistry award 1970), Am. Acad. Arts and Scis., Nat. Acad. Sci. Mem. editorial adv. bd. Chem. and Engring. News, 1968-70, Synthesis, 1969—, Accounts of Chem. Research, 1970-73; editor Bioorganic Chemistry, 1971—. Home; 23570 Camino Hermoso Los Altos Hills CA 94022 also 127 Cormorant Way Pajaro Dunes CA also 1 Smugglers Cove Cap Estate Castries St Lucia West Indies also Sealodge Princeville Hanalei Kauai HI 96714 Office: Dept Chemistry Stanford U Stanford CA 94305

VAN TASSEL, DAVID DIRCK, educator; b. Binghamton, N.Y., Mar. 29, 1928; s. Walter Raymond and Etta May (Strathie) Van T.; A.B., Dartmouth Coll., 1950; M.S., U. Wis, 1951, Ph.D., 1955; m. Helen Hamilton Liddell, July 29, 1950; children—David Dirck Jr., Emily Field, Katharine Anne, Jonathan Judson, Jeanie Strathie. Instr. Am. history U. Tex., 1954-57, asst. prof., 1957-61, asso. prof., 1961-65, prof., 1965-69, prof. history and edn., 1967-69; vis. prof. history Case Western Res. U., 1968-69, prof., 1969—, chmn. dept. history, 1976—; vis. lectr. U. Wis., 1961; vis. prof. U. Hawaii, summer 1966. Served with AUS, 1946-47. Recipient Cherry Lawn Sch. Trustees award, 1968. Guggenheim fellow, 1963-64. Mem. Am. Hist Assn. (com. on Albert J. Beveridge award, 1966-69), Am. Studies Assn. (pres. Tex. chpt. 1967), Orgn. Am. Historians, Ohio Acad. History, Imigration History Soc. (dir. 1973—), Gerontol. Soc. (mem. council 1977-79), A.A.U.P. Democrat. Episcopalian. Author: Recording America's Past, 1960; author (with M.G. Hall.) Science and Society in the United States, 1966; (with others) Computer Assisted Research in Educational History, 1969; editor American Thought in the 20th Century, 1967; Rand McNally series On American Thought and Culture, 1969-76; Aging, Death, and the Completion of Being, 1979; co-editor European Origins of American Thought, 1969, Aging and the Elderly: Humanistic Perspectives in Gerontology, 1978. Home: 2940 Euclid Heights Blvd Cleveland Heights OH 44118 Office: 11201 Euclid Ave Cleveland OH 44106

VAN TASSEL, KARL RAYMOND, mfg. co. exec.; b. Geneva, N.Y., July 8, 1902; s. Reneaux Paul and Elizabeth Norman (Lord) Van T.; B.S. in Elec. Engring., Mass. Inst. Tech., 1925: m. Evelyn F. White, June 27, 1931; children—Carole A. (Mrs. Paul F. Donahue). Katrina (Mrs. Max D. Anderson). With Gen. Electric Co., Schenectady, 1925-56, gen. mgr. indsl. control dept., 1949-52, gen. mgr. Knolls Atomic Power Lab., 1952-56; exec. v.p. A.B. Dick Co., Chgo., 1956-61, pres., 1961-70, vice-chmn. bd.. 1970-71, pres., chief exec. officer, 1977—. dir., 1956—, also dir. fgn. subsidiaries in Can., Gt. Britain, Holland and S.Am. Bd. dirs., mem. exec. com. St. Johns Coll.; mem. bus. adv. council Northwestern U.; mem. devel. com. corp. Mass. Inst. Tech.; mem. adv. com. U. Ill. Coll. Bus. Adminstrn. Mem. IEEE (life), Ill. C. of C. (v.p.), Conf. Bd. (sr.), Lambda Chi Alpha, Beta Gamma Sigma. Episcopalian. Clubs: Chicago, Executives, Economic (Chgo.); Mohawk (Schenectady). Home: 255 E Illinois Rd Lake Forest IL 60045 Office: 5700 W Touhy Ave Chicago IL 60648

VAN TASSEL, ROGER CARLETON, educator; b. Germantown, N.Y., Nov. 27, 1924; s. Archie S. and Elizabeth (Whitney) Van T.; A.B., Union Coll., 1947; M.A., Cornell U., 1950; Ph.D., Brown U., 1956; m. Grace Evans, May 6, 1944; children—Richard, Linda. Chmn. dept. econs. Clark U., 1965—, dir. summer sch., 1958-62. Econ. adviser Conf. of N.E. Govs., 1962-65; exec. dir. N.E. Econ. Research Found., 1964-65, project devel. cons., 1965-68; cons. New Eng. Telephone Co., 1967-71; vis. prof. Calif. State Coll., Los Angeles, summer 1971-72, Katholieke Universiteit te Leuven, Belgium, 1972-73. Served to 2d lt. USAAF, 1943-45. Mem. Regional Sci. Assn. (pres. N.E. sect. 1965-66), Am. Econ. Assn. Author: Economic Essentials: a Core Approach, A Principle's Text, 1969; (with Constantine Michalopoulos) Commercial Uses of Gold in the United States, 1969. Home: Putnam Rd Holden MA 01520 Office: 950 Main St Worcester MA 01610

VAN TIL, CORNELIUS, clergyman, educator; b. Netherlands, May 3, 1895; s. Ite and Klazina (Van der Veen) Van T.; A.B., Calvin Coll., 1922; A.M., Princeton, 1924, Ph.D., 1927; Th.B., Princeton Theol. Sem., 1924, Th.M., 1925; Prof. Honoris causa, U. Debrecen (Hungary), 1938; m. Rena Klooster, Sept. 15, 1925; 1 son, Earl Calvin. Came to U. S., 1905, naturalized, 1911. Ordained to ministry Christian Ref. Ch., 1927; pastor, Spring Lake, Mich., 1927-28; instr. Princeton Theol. Sem., 1928-29; prof. apologetics Westminister Theol. Sem., Phila., 1929—. Author: The New Modernism, 1946; Common Grace, 1947; Christianity and Idealism, 1955; Christianity and Modern Theology, 1955; The Defense of the Faith, 1955; The Theology of James Doane, 1959; Christianity and Barthianism, 1962; The Case for Calvinism, 1963; The Confession of 1967: Its Theological Background and Ecumenical Significance, 1967; Christ and the Jews, 1968; The Sovereignty of Grace: An Appraisal of G.C. Berkouwer's View of Dordt, 1969; A Christian Theory of Knowledge, 1969; The Great Debate Today, 1970; The Reformed Pastor and Modern Thought, 1971; The God of Hope, 1978; The New Hermeneutics. Asso. joint editor Philosophia Reformata, Quar. Contbr. Westminster Theol. Jour. Home: 16 Rich Ave Philadelphia PA 19118

VAN TIL, WILLIAM, educator, writer; b. Corona, N.Y., Jan. 8, 1911; s. William Joseph and Florence Alberta (MacLean) Van T.; B.A., Columbia, 1933, M.A., Tchrs. Coll., 1935; Ph.D., Ohio State U., 1946; m. Beatrice Barbara Blaha, Aug. 24, 1935; children—Jon, Barbara, Roy. Tchr. N.Y. State Tng. Sch. for Boys, 1933-34; instr. dept. univ. schs. Coll. Edn., Ohio State U., 1934-36, asst. prof., 1936-43, on leave, 1943-45; researchist, writer Consumer Edn. Study NEA, 1943-44; dir. learning materials Bur. Intercultural Edn., 1944-47; prof. edn. U. Ill., 1947-51; prof. edn., chmn. div. curriculum and teaching George Peabody Coll. Tchrs., Nashville, 1951-57; prof. edn., chmn. dept. secondary edn. N.Y. U., 1957-66, head div. secondary and higher edn., 1966-67; Coffman distinguished prof. edn. Ind. State U., 1967-77, emeritus, 1977, dir. univ. workshops Writing for Profl. Publs., 1978—. Mem. Ill. Interracial Commn., 1948-51; moderator Nashville sch. desegregation meetings, 1955-57; adv. bd. jour. Teacher Edn., 1956-59; co-organized Nashville Community Relations Conf., 1956; cons. Phelps-Stokes Fund project, 1958-62; staff P.R. edn. survey 1958-59; staff of Iran tchr. edn. survey, 1962, V.I. edn. survey, 1964; lectr. abroad, 1974. Recipient Centennial Achievement award Ohio State U., 1970, awards N.J. Collegiate Press Assn., 1962, N.J. Assn. Tchrs. English, 1962. Mem. John Dewey Soc. (v.p. 1957-60, acting pres. 1958-59, pres. 1964-66, award 1977), Assn. Supervision and Curriculum Devel. (dir. 1950-54, 57-61, pres. 1961-62, chmn. rev. council 1972-73), United Educators (chmn. bd. educators 1969-77), Nat. Soc. Coll. Tchrs. Edn. (pres. 1967-68), Am. Edn. Studies Assn. (editorial bd. 1970-77), Asso. Orgn. Tchr. Edn. (adv. council 1967-73, chmn. issues tchr. edn. 1972-73), Nat. Soc. Study Edn. (editor Yearbook Issues in Secondary Edn. 1976). Author: The Danube Flows Through Fascism; Economic Roads for American Democracy; The Making of a Modern Educator; Modern Education for the Junior High School Years; The Year 2000: Teacher Education; One Way of Looking at It; Education: A Beginning; Another Way of Looking at It; Van Til on Education; Secondary Education: School and Community. Editor: Forces Affecting Am. Edn.; Curriculum: Quest for Relevance; co-editor: Democratic Human Relations; Intercultural Attitudes in the Making; Education in American Life; adv. editor Houghton Mifflin, 1964-70. Contbr. to Saturday Rev., Woman's Day, Parents and numerous other publs., author articles, reviews and editorials; columnist Ednl. Leadership, Contemporary Edn., Kappan. Home: Lake Lure Rural Route 32 Box 316 Terre Haute IN 47803 Office: Ind State U Terre Haute IN 47809. *As an educator and writer, I believe that mankind's best hope is education which meets individual needs, illuminates social realities, fosters democratic values and utilizes relevant knowledge.*

VAN UITERT, LEGRAND GERARD, chemist; b. Salt Lake City, May 6, 1922; s. Antone and Lambertha Maria (Groeneveld) Van U.; B.S., George Washington U., 1949; M.S., Pa. State U., 1951, Ph.D., 1952; m. Marion Emma Woolley, June 8, 1945; children—Robert, Bonnie, Craig. Union Carbide fellow Pa. State U., 1940-46; materials scientist Bell Telephone Labs., Murray Hill, N.J., 1952—; cons. to materials adv. bd. Nat. Acad. Sci. Served with USN, 1940-46. Co-recipient W.R.G. Baker award IEEE, 1971; recipient H. N. Potts award Franklin Inst., 1975, award Indsl. Research Inst., 1976. Mem. Am. Chem. Soc. (award for creative invention 1978), Sigma Xi. Research, numerous publs. in microwave ferrites, lasers, bubble domain memory, electro, non-linear and acusto-optic materials, luminescence, optical fibers, crystal growth and passive displays; patentee in field. Home: 2 Terry Dr Morristown NJ 07960 Office: Bell Labs Murray Hill NJ 07974

VAN UMMERSEN, CLAIRE A(NN), univ. exec., biologist; b. Chelsea, Mass., July 28, 1935; d. George and Catherine Courtovich; B.S., Tufts U., 1957, M.S. (Am. Cancer Soc. grantee), 1960, Ph.D., 1963; m. Frank Van Ummersen, June 7, 1958; children—Lynn, Scott. Research asst. Tufts U., 1957-60, research asso., 1960-67, grad. asst. in embryology, 1962, postdoctoral teaching asst., 1963-66, lectr. in biology, 1967-68; asst. prof. biology U. Mass., Boston, 1968-74, asso. prof., 1974—, asso. dean acad. affairs, 1975-76, asso. vice chancellor acad. affairs, 1976-78, chancellor, 1978—; asst. Lancaster Course in Opthalmology, Mass. Eye and Ear Infirmary, 1962-69, lectr., 1970—; reviewer HEW. Recipient Disting. Service medal U. Mass., 1979. Mem. AAAS, Am. Soc. Zoologists, Soc. Devel. Biology, Phi Beta Kappa, Sigma Xi. Mem. research team leading to establishment of safety standards for exposure to microwave radiation, 1958-65. Office: U Mass Harbor Campus Boston MA 02125

VAN URK, J. BLAN, author, pub. relations counsel; b. Mich., Apr. 15, 1902; s. Dr. Thomas and Rosalynde (Blan) van U.; grad. Culver Mil. Acad., 1920; B.S., Princeton, 1924; m. Virginia Nellis, Sept. 1, 1944. Mem. publicity com. Miami Beach C. of C.; mem. Miami City Planning Com; chmn. publicity and advt. com. Miami Beach Real Estate Bd.; originator of plan adopted for first ofcl. Fla. News Bur; mem. organizing com. Miami U., 1925-29; organizer and dir. Bur. Pub. Relations Commonwealth Bond Corp., N.Y., 1930-32; tax cons. Lewis, Garvin & Kelsey, attys. in disposition of certiorari proceedings 1932-36; spl. pub. relations assignment Anaconda Wire & Cable Co., 1934; drafted plans for two N.Y. World's Fair projects, 1938; mem. staff N.Y. Journal-American, 1942; mem. public relations dept. Young & Rubicam, 1942; mem. pub. relations and advt. depts. N.W. Ayer & Son, 1943-52; v.p. and bus. coordinator Dowd, Redfield & Johnstone, N.Y.C., 1953; exec. v.p., dir. Calkins & Holden, Inc., 1954-59; bus.

adviser corporate policy, pub. relations Wilmington Group, Inc.-consumer research Rockland Corp., 1959-61; chmn. Nat. Assn. Schs. and Pubs. Inc., 1961-68; pres. Nat. Pubs. Service Inc., 1968-74, chmn., 1975—; pub., editor Serendipity Press, 1974—; dir. Delfi Am. Corp. Was proponent of plan for Subsistence Homesteads provision Nat. Recovery Act, 1933; analysed slum clearance in large cities for Pres. Roosevelt's Decentralization of Industry Com., 1934; guest student horsemanship in European, Cav. Schs., hunted in Europe, India, New Zealand, Australia, 1926-28; Am. Pioneer hunting corr., touring and participating in hunts; wrote 2-year series of articles, Good Hunting, for Town and Country mag.; hunting corr. Middleburg (Va.) Chronicle; authority on hunting in Europe and N.A. for Ency. Brit., 1945—; book reviewer on horses, hounds, hunting, 1938-40. Decorated chevalier Confreie de la Chaine des Rotisseurs (Paris). Mem. Pa. Horse Breeders Assn., Nat. Steeplechase and Hunt Assn. (sr. mem., mem. racing com.), Rolling Rock Hunt Racing Assn., Netherland-Am. Found., Pub. Relations Soc. Am., Brandywine Polo Assn. Clubs: Springdale Hall (S.C.); University, Princeton, Grolier, Soc. of Amateur Chefs, Wine and Food Soc. (N.Y.); Rolling Rock (Ligonier, Pa.); Camp Fire Club of Am.; Royal Dutch Hunt (The Netherlands); Racquet (Phila.); Radnor Hunt (Pa.); Moore County Hounds (N.C.); Vicmead Hunt (Wilmington, Del.); Mr. Stewart's Cheshire Foxhounds (Pennsylvania); The Skeeters (pres.). Author: The Story of American Foxhunting (1650-1861), Vol. I, 1940 (chosen by Grolier Club as one of 150 finest written and pub. sporting books in 600 years), Vol. II (1865-1906), 1941; Little Charlie the Fox, 1945; The Horse, The Valley and The Chagrin Valley Hunt, 1948; The Story of Rolling Rock, 1950. Contbr. articles on econs., sociology and polit. economy. Article Norfolk-Our Worst War Town, Am. Mercury precipitated Fed. investigation of that city. Pen Names Jan Westergaard and dan Russel. Lectr. on fox-hunting and steeplechasing. Home: Sugar Tree Farm Unionville PA 19375 Office: 3801 Kennett Pike Wilmington DE 19807. *Formal education notwithstanding, one's education must continue, unceasingly, throughout one's lifetime. Without this self-imposed improvement of the mind, worthwhile objectives are unattainable. The tragedy of today's universal confusion is that people acquire a smattering of disconnected and irrelevant fragments of learning. There is little intellectual discipline. To be mature and genuinely successful, one must hunger for knowledge. Money and luxuries—the gadgets—often impede one's intellectual growth. With application, most goals are within reach. . . age is not a deterrent. "The soul's joy lies in doing."*

VAN VALKENBURG, MAC ELWYN, engring. educator; b. Union, Utah, Oct. 5, 1921; s. Charles Mac and Nora (Walker) Van V.; B.S. in Elec. Engring., U. Utah, 1943; M.S., Mass. Inst. Tech., 1946; Ph.D., Stanford, 1952; m. Evelyn J. Pate, Aug. 27, 1943; children-Charles Mac II, JoLynne, Kaye, David R., Nancy J., Susan L. With Radiation Lab., Mass. Inst. Tech., 1943-45, Research Lab. Electronics, 1945-46; mem. faculty U. Utah, 1946-55, U. Ill. 1955-66; prof. elec. engring. Princeton, 1966-74, chmn. dept., 1966-72; prof. elec. engring. U. Ill., 1974—; vis. prof. Stanford, U. Colo., U. Calif., Berkeley, U. Hawaii, Manoa, 1978-79. Mem. IEEE (v.p., dir. 1969-73); editor transactions 1960-63, proc. 1966-69, Edn. medal 1972), Am. Soc. Engring. Edn. (George Westinghouse award 1963, Benjamin Garver Lamme award 1978), Nat. Acad. Engring., Sigma Xi, Tau Beta Pi, Phi Kappa Phi. Author: Network Analysis, 3d edit., 1974; Introduction to Modern Network Synthesis, 1960; Introductory Signals and Circuits, 1967; Signals in Linear Circuits, 1974; Circuit Theory: Foundations and Classical Contributions, 1974. Home: 1606 W Healey Champaign IL 61820

VAN VALKENBURG, PAUL, lawyer; b. Mpls., Dec. 19, 1933; s. Horace and Julia (Patty) Van V.; B.A., Harvard, 1955; postgrad. in law U. Minn., 1955-57; J.D., U. Wis., 1959; m. Patricia Anne Meuler, Aug. 23, 1958; children—Sarah Lynn (dec.), Paul Douglas, Anne Louise, Peter Andrew, Elizabeth Ann. Admitted to Minn. bar, 1959; instr. legal writing U. Wis. at Madison, 1958-59; mem. firm Moss Flaherty Clarkson & Fletcher, and predecessor, Mpls., 1959—; asst. prof. bus. law, gen. extension div. U. Minn., 1960—. Mem. Hennepin County (Minn.) Personnel Bd., 1966-77. Bd. dirs. Citizen's Com. on Pub. Edn., 1970-76; pres. Mpls. Assn. for Retarded Children, 1968-70; bd. dirs. Alpha Tau Omega Found. Minn., 1967-76. Mem. Am., Minn., Hennepin County bar assns., U. Wis. Law Alumni Assn. (dir. 1976-79). Republican. Presbyterian (deacon 1967-73, pres. 1972-73, 76-78, trustee 1973—). Home: 5239 Girard Ave S Minneapolis MN 55419 Office: 2350 IDS Center Minneapolis MN 55402

VAN VEEN, STUYVESANT, artist, ret. educator; b. N.Y.C., Sept. 12, 1910; s. Arthur Lewis and Marcella Reutlinger (Marks) Van V.; student Pa. Acad. Fine Arts, summers, 1927-28, N.Y. Sch. Indsl. Art, 1928, N.A.D., 1929, Coll. City N.Y., Art Students League, 1933-34; m. Felicia Geffen, Aug. 10, 1962. Tchr. painting and drawing classes for writers, N.Y.C., 1932-34; lectr. Coll. Art Assn., 1940-41; supr., instr. Cin. Art Acad., 1946-49; asso. prof. City Coll., U. City of N.Y., 1949-74; ret., 1974; murals executed bldgs. throughout U.S.; numerous one-man exhbns. including ACA Gallery, N.Y.C., 1964, 68, 73, Maurice M. Pine Free Pub. Library, Fairlawn, N.J., 1978; exhibited in numerous group shows including Am. Water Color Soc., 1932, 34, 36, 40, 42, 56, 67, N.A.D., 1956, 65, Nat. Arts Club N.S.P.C. Ann., 1956, 58, 60, 62, 64, 65-67, 70, 73, Riverside Mus., 1955, 57, 59, 61, 64, 66, Plastics U.S.A. Year Tour of USSR, 1961-62, Eastern States Exhbn. Springfield (Mass.) Mus. Art, 1963, 64, Archtl. League of N.Y., 1965, New Deal for Art, 1977-78, N.Y. WPA Artists Then and Now, 1977; represented in permanent collections including U. Wichita, U. Minn., Coll. Fine Arts at Ohio U., Lincoln Center Mus. Performing Arts, Columbia, N.Y. State U. Mus., New Paltz, Norfolk Mus. Art, Newark Mus., Syracuse Mus., Smithsonian Instn. Contemporary Am. Art, Washington, Fairleigh Dickinson U., N.Y. U.; art dir., prodn. mgr. Fox Features Syndicate, 1940-41; art dir. Cin. Ordnance Dist., U.S. War Dept., 1942-43; publs. illustrator USAAF, 1944-45; reviewer Cin. Enquirer, 1946-49; stage designer Stage, Inc., Cin. Civic Theater, 1948-49; mural cons. Internat. Fair Consultants, 1961-62; art cons. Hall of Edn., N.Y. World's Fair 1964-65, 61-62. Pres., mem. adv. bd. Artists Tech. Research Inst., 1963—; co-founder Nat. Com. Arts and Govt., 1952. Served with USAAF, 1943-45. Recipient numerous awards including Childe Hassam Purchase award Am. Acad. Arts and Letters, 1961; Nelson Whitehead prize Am. Soc. Contemporary Artists, 1966; Hat Co. Am. award Silvermine Artist's Guild, New Eng. Ann., 1969. Mem. Am. Acad. and Inst. Arts and Letters, Artists Equity Assn. (pres. N.Y. chpt. 1958-59), Am. Watercolor Soc., Nat. Soc. Painters in Casein, Nat. Soc. Mural Painters, Art Students League (life), Am. Soc. Contemporary Artists, Art League Hudson Valley, Audubon Artists Soc. Illustrator 8 books including Gesture, Race and Culture, 1972. Address: 320 Central Park W New York City NY 10025

VAN VLACK, LAWRENCE HALL, educator; b. Atlantic, Iowa, July 21, 1920; s. Claude H. and Ruth (Stone) Van V.; B.S. in Ceramic Engring., Iowa State U., 1942; Ph.D. in Geology, U. Chgo., 1950; m. Frances E. Runnells, June 27, 1943; children-Laura R., Bruce H. With U.S. Steel Co., 1942-53; mem. faculty U. Mich., 1953—, prof. materials and metall. engring., 1958—, chmn. dept., 1967-73; cons. in field. Served with USNR, 1945-46. Registered profl. engr., Mich. Fellow Am. Soc. Metals (Sauveur lectr. 1979), Am. Ceramic Soc.; mem. Am. Inst. Metall. Engrs., Brit. Ceramic Soc., Am. Inst. Chem. Engrs., AAAS, Nat. Inst. Ceramic Engrs., Sigma Xi, Tau Beta Pi, Alpha Chi Sigma, Alpha Sigma Mu (hon.). Methodist. Author: Nature and Behavior of Engineering Materials, 1956; Elements of Materials Science, 2d edit., 1964; Physical Ceramics for Engineers, 1964; Materials Science for Engineers, 1970; Textbook of Materials Technology, 1973; Materials Science and Engineering, 1975; Aids for Introductory Materials Courses, 1977; Nickel Oxide, 1979. Home: 1510 Glen Leven Ann Arbor MI 48103

VAN VLECK, JOHN HASBROUCK, physicist; b. Middletown, Conn., Mar. 13, 1899; s. Edward Burr and Hester Laurence (Raymond) Van V.; A.B., U. Wis., 1920, Sc.D., 1947; A.M., Harvard U., 1921, Ph.D., 1922, Sc.D., 1966; Sc.D., Wesleyan U., 1936, U. Md., 1955, Rockford Coll., 1961, U. Chgo., 1968, U. Nancy (France), 1961, U. Minn., 1971; Dr. honoris causa, U. Grenoble, 1950, U. Paris, 1960; Sc.D. honoris causa, Oxford (Eng.) U., 1958; m. Abigail June Pearson, June 10, 1927. Instr. physics Harvard U., 1922-23, asso. prof. math. physics, 1934-35, prof., 1935—, chmn. physics dept., 1945-49, Hollis prof. math. and nat. philosophy, 1951-69, emeritus, 1969—, dean engring. and applied physics, 1951-57; asst. prof. physics U. Minn., 1923-26, asso. prof., 1926-27, prof., 1927-28; prof. theoretical physics U. Wis., 1928-34. Vis. lectr. Stanford, 1927, 34, 41, U. Mich., 1933, Columbia, 1934, Princeton, 1937; Lorentz prof., Leiden, 1960; Eastman prof. Oxford (Eng.) U., 1961-62; head theory group Radio Research Lab., Harvard, 1943-45; cons. Radiation Lab., Mass. Inst. Tech., 1942-45; asso. editor various phys. jour. Guggenheim Meml. Found. fellow, 1930. Decorated chevalier Legion of Honor (France); recipient Albert A. Michelson award Case Inst. Tech., 1963; Irving Langmuir award in chem. physics Gen. Elec. Found., 1965; Nat. Medal of Sci., 1966; Distinguished Service award U. Wis. Alumni Assn., 1967, Cresson medal Franklin Inst., 1971; Lorentz medal Netherlands Acad., 1974; co-recipient Nobel prize in Physics, 1977. Fellow Am. Phys. Soc. (councillor 1932- 35, pres. 1952-53), AAAS (v.p. 1960), Am. Acad. Arts and Scis. (v.p. 1956-57); mem. Nat. Acad. Sci., Am. Philos. Soc., Internat. Acad. Quantum Molecular Sci., Am. Math. Soc., Holland Soc. N.Y. (medal 1969), Netherlands Phys. Soc., Phi Beta Kappa, Sigma Xi; hon. mem. Societe Francaise de Physique; fgn. mem. Royal Netherlands Acad. Scis., Royal Acad. Sci. Uppsala, Royal Swedish Acad. Sci., Royal Soc. of London, Acad. des Sciences (France). Presbyn. Author: Quantum Principles and Line Spectra, 1926; The Theory of Electric and Magnetic Susceptibilities, 1932. Address: Lyman Lab Harvard U Cambridge MA 02138

VAN VLIET, CAREL MARINUS (KAREL), educator, physicist; b. Dordrecht, Netherlands, Dec. 27, 1929; s. Marinus and Jacoba (de Lange) van V.; B.S., Free U. Amsterdam (Netherlands), 1949, M.A., 1953, Ph.D. in Physics, 1956; m. Annette Joan Cappon, Dec. 29, 1953; children—Elsa Marianne, Mark Edward, Cynthia Joyce, Renata Annette Carolina. Came to U.S., 1960, naturalized, 1967. Research fellow Free U. Amsterdam, 1950-54, research asso., 1954-56, conservator, 1956-60; postdoctoral fellow U. Minn., Mpls., 1956-57, mem. faculty, 1957-58, 60-70, prof. elec. engring. and physics, 1965-70; sr. research mem., prof., centre recherches math. U. Montreal (Que.), 1969—; vis. prof. U. Fla., 1974, 78—. Research grantee NSF and Air Force OSR. Fellow Am. Sci. Affiliation; mem. Am., European, Dutch, Canadian phys. socs., IEEE (sr.), Sigma Xi, Tau Beta Pi. Contbg. author: Fluctuation Phenomena in Solids, 1965; also numerous articles. Home: 30 Normandy Dr Montreal 305 PQ Canada

VAN VLIET, CLAIRE, artist; b. Ottawa, Ont., Can., Aug. 9, 1933; d. Wilbur Dennison and Audrey Ilene (Wallace) Van V.; A.B., San Diego State Coll., 1952; M.F.A., Claremont Grad. Sch., 1954. Instr. printmaking Phila. Coll. Art, 1959-65; owner The Janus Press, 1954—; vis. lectr. printmaking U. Wis.-Madison, 1965-66; one-man exhbns. include: Print Club Phila., 1963, 66, 73, 77, Wiggin Gallery, Boston Public Library, 1977, Rutgers U. Art Gallery, 1978; group exhbns. include: Bklyn. Nat., Phila. Arts Festival, Kunst zu Kafka, Germany, Paper as Medium, Smithsonian Instn., Washington; represented in permanent collections: Lessing Rosenwald, Phila. Mus. Art, Boston Public Library, Library of Congress, Cleve. Mus. Art, Montreal Mus. Fine Arts. NEA grantee, 1976-78. Mem. Soc. Printers Boston. Address: RD 2 West Burke VT 05871. *...to feel, to understand; for that to take form in material; to realize within a framework of hand production which by its nature provides the slow time, the climate for organic fantasy, to feel, to understand, etc...*

VAN VOORHIS, JOHN, lawyer; b. Rochester, N.Y., June 14, 1897; s. Eugene and Allis Mozier (Sherman) Van V.; grad. Hill Sch., Pottstown, Pa., 1915; A.B., Yale, 1919; LL.D., Hobart Coll., 1953, Union U., 1954, U. Rochester, 1958, N.Y. Law Sch., 1966, Bklyn. Law Sch., 1967; m. Linda Lyon, June 2, 1928; children—Emily (Mrs. Edward R. Harris), Allis (Mrs. Louis D'Amanda), Eugene. Admitted to N.Y. bar, 1922; practiced in Rochester, 1922-36; justice Supreme Ct. 7th Jud. Dist. N.Y., 1937-53; asso. justice Appellate Div., N.Y. State Supreme Ct. in and for First Jud. Dept., N.Y.C., 1947-53; asso. judge N.Y. Ct. of Appeals, 1953-67; mem. firm Van Voorhis and Van Voorhis, Rochester and N.Y.C., 1967—. Fellow Am., N.Y. State bar founds., Phi Beta Kappa Assos.; mem. Am., N.Y. Rochester, N.Y.C. bar assns., Phi Beta Kappa. Episcopalian. Clubs: Century Assn., Recess, University (N.Y.C.); Genesee Valley, Rochester Country, University, Rochester Yacht. Home: 714 Rock Beach Rd Rochester NY 14617 Office: 1 Graves St Rochester NY 14614 also 120 Broadway Room 3017 New York NY 10005

VAN VOORHIS, WALTER ROE, mathematician, educator; b. Monogahela, Pa., July 23, 1904; s. Charles Elmer and Sallie (McConnell) Van V.; A.B., Pa. State U., 1930, M.A., 1931, Ph.D., 1941; m. June Roberta Fite, June 11, 1941; children—Jan Karl, Gretchen. Instr. pub. schs., Washington County, Pa., 1925-28; instr. math. Pa. State U., 1930-34, asst. prof. math., dir. Schuylkill Undergrad. br., 1934-41; mem. faculty Fenn Coll., Cleve., 1941-65, prof. math., chmn. dept., 1946-65; prof. math., chmn. dept. Cleve. State U., 1965—; vis. prof. engring. adminstrn. Case Inst. Tech., 1953, mem. ops. research group, 1953—. Served to capt. USAAF, 1945-46. Mem. Am. Math. Assn. (chmn. Ohio sect. 1960), Inst. Math. Statistics, Am. Soc. Engring. Edn., Pi Mu Epsilon, Phi Delta Kappa, Psi Chi, Kappa Phi Kappa. Co-author: Statistical Procedures and Their Mathematical Bases, 1940; Fundamentals of Business Mathematics, 1948; Basic Mathematics for Engineering and Sci., 1952. Editor: Operations Research in Industry, 1955. Contbg. author: Introduction to Operations Research, 1957. Home: 12 Bunker Hill Rd RD1 Stevens PA 17578

VAN VRANKEN, JOHN FREDERICK, JR., investment banker; b. N.Y.C., Aug. 22, 1935; s. John Frederick and Beatrice Inez Van V.; B.A., Middlebury Coll., 1957; postgrad. N.Y. U. Sch. Bus. Adminstrn., 1960-64; m. Nancy Jane Sharp, June 17, 1958; children—Virginia Elizabeth, Cynthia Dale. First v.p. Smith Barney & Co., Inc., N.Y.C., 1950-73, also dir.; chief operating officer Sogen-Swiss Internat. Corp., N.Y.C., 1973-78; sr. v.p. Smith Barney Harris Upham & Co. Inc., N.Y.C., 1978—, also dir.; dir. Equitable Fed. Savs. & Loan Assn. Served to 1st lt. arty. U.S. Army, 1958-60. Mem. Bond Club N.Y. Clubs: River, Piping Rock, Meadow Brook. Home: 138 E 65th St New York NY 10021 Office: 1345 Ave of Americas New York NY 10019

VAN VUNAKIS, HELEN, biochemist, educator; b. N.Y.C., June 15, 1924; d. Stavros Michael and Rose (Mountakis) Vanvunakis; B.A., Hunter Coll., 1945; Ph.D., Columbia, 1951; m. Lawrence Levine, Jan. 31, 1958; children—Stephanie Michel, Joanne R. Research asso. USPHS Postdoctoral fellow in biochemistry Johns Hopkins, 1951-54; sr. research scientist labs. biochemistry and immunology N.Y. State Dept. Health, Albany, 1954-58; prof. biochemistry Brandeis U., 1958—. Lectr. Albany Med. Coll., 1957-58. Recipient Research Career award USPHS, 1963. Mem. Johns Hopkins Soc. Scholars. Office: Dept of Biochemistry Brandeis U Waltham MA 02154

VAN WAGENEN, HAROLD WILLIAM, JR., lawyer; b. Mt. Vernon, N.Y., July 15, 1938; s. Harold William and Violet Berle (Mitchell) Van W.; A.B., Denison U., 1960; J.D., Ohio State U., 1963; m. Pamela Privette, June 24, 1967. Admitted to N.Y. bar, 1963; asso. atty. Breed, Abbott & Morgan, N.Y.C., 1963-68; asst. gen. counsel Indian Head, Inc., N.Y.C., 1968-70; v.p. legal affairs, sec. U.S. Home Corp., N.Y.C., 1970-74; gen. counsel Westinghouse Broadcasting, Learning and Leisure Time Co. div. Westinghouse Electric Corp., N.Y.C., 1974-79; asst. gen. counsel Norton Simon, Inc., N.Y.C., 1979—. Mem. alumni council Denison U., 1967—. Bd. dirs. Li Found., N.Y.C., Am. Found. for Learning Disabilities, N.Y.C. Mem. Assn. Bar N.Y.C., Delta Upsilon, Phi Delta Phi, Pi Sigma Alpha. Clubs: University (N.Y.C.); Pelham Country. Home: 121 Elderwood Ave Pelham NY 10803 Office: New York NY

VAN WAGNER, ALBERT EDWIN, advt. agy. exec.; b. Newburgh, N.Y., Jan. 23, 1915; s. William Edwin and Mary Alice (Gaffney) Van W.; A.B., Harvard U., 1937; m. Margaret Virginia Libby, Aug. 31, 1940 (dec. Feb. 6, 1978); children—James Arthur, Albert Edwin, Alana Libby; m. 2d, Marilynn Ennis Brown, Aug. 11, 1978. Claims adjuster Liberty Mut. Ins. Co., Boston, 1938-39; salesman Gillette Safety Razor Co., Boston, 1939-40; asst. sales mgr. Am. Writing Machine Stores div. Remington Rand, N.Y.C., 1940-43; asst. advt. mgr. Interchemical Corp., N.Y.C., 1943-47; account exec. St. Georges & Keyes, N.Y.C., 1947-50; v.p. Noyes & Co., Providence, 1950-63, Kenyon & Eckhardt, Providence, 1963-65; v.p. Culver Advt., Inc., Boston, 1965-68, exec. v.p., 1968-75; dir. corp. advt. Best Western Inc., Phoenix, 1975-80, B-W Advt. Agy., 1975-80; v.p. Van Wagner Assos., Inc., Phoenix, 1980—. Home: 6127 N 13th St Phoenix AZ 85014

VAN WAZER, JOHN ROBERT, chemist, educator; b. Chgo., Apr. 11, 1918; s. John Robert and Florence Ivy (Johnson) Van W.; B.S. magna cum laude, Northwestern U., 1940; M.A., Harvard U., 1941, Ph.D., 1942; m. Mary Elizabeth Ballou, July 15, 1940; 1 dau., Mary Elizabeth. Chemist, Eastman Kodak Co., 1942-44; group leader Oak Ridge Lab., 1944-46; phys. chemist Rumford Chem. Works, Providence, 1946-49; head physics research Great Lakes Carbon Corp., 1949-50; sr. scientist Monsanto Co., 1950-68, research dir., 1965-68, cons., 1968-70; prof. chemistry Vanderbilt U., Nashville, 1968—. NSF grantee, 1969—. Air Force Office of Sci. Research grantee, 1972—. Mem. Am. Chem. Soc., Soc. Rheology, AAAS, N.Y. Acad. Sci., Gesellschaft deutscher Chemiker, Chem. Soc. (London), Eposcatologic Soc., Am. Recorder Soc., Assn. Am. Chamber Music Players, Phi Beta Kappa, Sigma Xi, Alpha Chi Sigma. Clubs: University (Nashville); Percy Priest Yacht; Explorers (N.Y.). Author books, numerous articles in several field. Recent research in systemization phosphorus chemistry, devel. equilibrium-controlled structural chemistry, nuclear magnetic resonance, inner-orbital photoelectron spectroscopy, applied quantum chemistry, synthetic inorganic chemistry, nutrition. Home: 1121 Ridgeview Dr Nashville TN 37220. *Life appears to me dependent upon a complicated mixture of luck and foresight. Even in this modern world which is dominated by a host of narrow experts, it makes good sense to be as self-reliant and independent of authority as possible. A person who is adept at taking care of himself is often the best qualified to assist others and should do so.*

VAN WICKLER, JOHN HENRY, ins. co. exec.; b. Dayton, Ky., Feb. 20, 1929; B.S.C., Salmon P. Chase Coll., 1951; M.B.A., Miami U., Oxford, Ohio, 1952; m. Maria Therese Grimm, Dec. 30, 1950; children—Nancy, Richard. Vice pres. CNA Fin. Corp., Chgo., 1969-75, Union Central Life Ins. Co., Cin., 1975-76; sr. v.p., treas. Provident Life & Accident Ins. Co., Chattanooga, 1976—. Chartered fin. analyst. Mem. Investment Analysts Soc. Chgo. Office: Fountain Square Chattanooga TN 37402

VAN WOERKOM, DOROTHY O'BRIEN, author; b. Buffalo, June 26, 1924; d. Peter Simon and Helen Elizabeth (Miller) O'Brien; student Canisius Coll., 1948-50; m. John Van Woerkom, Feb. 22, 1961. Author children's books including: Stepka and the Magic Fire, 1974—; Journeys to Bethlehem, 1974, Meat Pies and Sausages, 1976, A Hundred Angels, Singing, 1976, The Queen Who Couldn't Bake Gingerbread, 1974, Abu Ali, 1976, Tit for Tat, 1977, Harry and Shellburt, 1977, The Friends of Abu Ali, 1978; Donkey Ysabel, 1978; Alexandra the Rock-Eater, 1978; series editor I Can Read a Bible Story, Concordia Pub. House, 1975. Recipient Best Religious Children's book Stepka and the Magic Fire, Catholic Press Assn., 1974. Mem. Authors Guild, Mystery Writers Am. Home: 8826 McAvoy Dr Houston TX 77074

VAN WORMER, BENJAMIN FRANCIS, corp. ofcl.; b. Charlotte, N.C., Aug. 1, 1915; s. David F. and Nancy C. (Heptinstall) Van W.; B.S., St. Lawrence U., 1937; M.B.A., N.Y. U., 1942; m. Margaret R. Garner, Mar. 29, 1952 (dec. 1967); children—Frances E., Laura E.; m. 2d, Marjorie L. Ault, Apr. 4, 1970; stepchildren—Robert L., Susan F. Ault. Traveling auditor, tax acct. Am. Standard Inc., 1937-42, acct., 1949-51, asst. sec., asst. treas., 1952-55, v.p. 1955, comptroller, 1956-62, dir. fin. administrv. services, 1962-65, dir. fin. and adminstrn. internat. ops., 1965-71, adminstr. econ. controls, 1971-74, staff v.p. corporate affairs, 1974-76, v.p. pub. affairs, 1976—; tax accountant Sylvania Electric Products, Inc., 1947-48. Bd. dirs. Jr. Achievement of N.Y., 1974—; trustee St. Lawrence U., 1968—, Coro Found., 1978—. Served as maj. Signal Corp, AUS, 1942-47. C.P.A., Pa. Mem. Am. Inst. C.P.A.'s, Pa. Soc. C.P.A.'s, Holland Soc. N.Y., Financial Execs. Inst., Pub. Affairs Council (dir. 1974—), Beta Theta Pi, Sigma Pi Sigma. Clubs: Pinnacle (N.Y.C.); Tokeneke, Wee Burn (Darien, Conn.). Home: Pin Oak Ln West Norwalk CT 06850 Office: 40 W 40th St New York NY 10018

VAN WYK, JUDSON JOHN, physician; b. Maurice, Iowa, June 10, 1921; s. John Cornelius and Amelia Susan (Menning) Van W.; A.B., Hope Coll., Holland, Mich., 1943; postgrad. in biochemistry St. Louis U., 1943-44; M.D., Johns Hopkins U., 1948; Sc.D. (hon.), Hope Coll., 1979; m. Persis Ruth Parker, June 6, 1944; children—Judith Parker, Persis Allen, Peter Menning, Judson John. Intern, Johns Hopkins Hosp., 1948-49, resident in pediatrics, 1949-50, fellow in pediatric endocrinology, 1953-55; resident in pediatrics Cin. Childrens Hosp., 1951-52; asst. prof. pediatrics U. N.C. Sch. Medicine, 1955-59, asso. prof., 1962—, Kenan prof. pediatrics, 1975—, chief div. endocrinology, 1955, dir. tng. program in endocrinology and metabolism, 1962—; mem. staff N.C. Meml. Hosp.; cons. Womack Army Hosp., Ft. Bragg, N.C., 1957—; vis. scientist Karolinska Institutet, Stockholm, 1968-69. Served with USPHS, 1951-53. Recipient numerous fellowships and grants. Diplomate Am. Bd. Pediatrics. Fellow Am. Acad. Pediatrics; mem. Endocrine Soc. (mem.

council 1975—), Soc. Pediatric Research, Am. Pediatric Soc., So. Soc. Clin. Investigation, Am. Fedn. Clin. Research, So. Soc. Pediatric Research, Lawson Wilkins Pediatric Endocrine Soc. (pres. 1976-77), La Sociedad Peruana de Pediatria (hon.), Sociedad Pediatrica de Trujillo (jon.), European Soc. for Pediatric Endocrinology (corr.). Presbyterian. Mem. editorial bd. Jour. Clin. Endocrinology and Metabolism, 1956-71, Pediatrics, 1969-70. Contbr. chpts. to books, articles to profl. jours. Home: 1020 Highland Woods Chapel Hill NC 27514 Office: Dept Pediatrics U NC Sch Medicine Chapel Hill NC 27514

VAN WYLEN, GORDON JOHN, coll. pres.; b. Grant, Mich., Feb. 6, 1920; s. John and Effa (Bierema) Van W.; A.B., Calvin Coll., 1942; B.S.E., U. Mich., 1942, M.S., 1947; Sc.D., M.I.T., 1951; m. Margaret E. DeWitt, Dec. 29, 1951; children—Elizabeth Ann Van Wylen Rudenga, Stephen John, Ruth Margaret, David Gordon, Emily Jane. Indsl. engr. duPont Co., 1942-43; instr. mech. engring. Pa. State U., 1946-48; asst. prof. mech. engring. U. Mich., 1951-55, asso. prof., 1955-57, prof., 1957-72, chmn. dept., 1958-65, dean Coll. Engring., 1965-72; pres. Hope Coll., Holland, Mich. 1972—. Served from ensign to lt. (s.g.) USNR, 1943-46. Fellow ASME, AAAS; mem. Sigma Xi, Tau Beta Pi, Phi Kappa Phi. Mem. Reform Ch. Am. Author: Thermodynamics, 1959; (with R.E. Sonntag) Fundamentals of Thermodynamics, 1965, Fundamentals of Statistical Thermodynamics, 1966, Introduction to Thermodynamics, 1971. Contbr. articles to profl. jours. Home: 92 E 10th St Holland MI 49423

VAN-ZANT, RONALD WAYNE (RONNIE), musician, vocalist; b. Jacksonville, Fla., Jan. 15, 1948; s. Lacy and Marion Virginia (Hicks) V.-Z.; student pub. schs., Jacksonville; m. Judith Seymour, Nov. 18, 1972; 1 dau., Melody Renee; 1 dau. by previous marriage, Tammy Michelle. Lead singer, major songwriter for Lynyrd Skynyrd Rock Group, 1965—; recordings include (Platinum albums) Pronounced Leh'nerd Skin-nerd, 1973, Second Helping, 1974, One More From the Road, 1976, Street Survivors, 1977; (Gold albums) Pronounced Leh'nerd Skin-nerd, 1973, Second Helping, 1974, Nuthin' Fancy, 1975, One More From the Road, 1976, Street Survivors, 1977. Recipient Ampex Golden Reel award; hon. mem. Ala. State Militia; hon. citizen Atlanta, Jacksonville. Mem. ASCAP, AFTRA, Nat. Assn. Rec. Arts and Scis., Broadcast Music Inc. Democrat. Club: Bass Anglers Sportsmen's Soc. Composer: Freebird, 1973; Sweet Home Alabama, 1974. Home: Brickyard Rd Doctors Inlet FL 32030 Office: 130 W 57th St Suite 6D New York City NY 10019

VAN ZANTE, SHIRLEY MAE, mag. editor; b. Elma, Iowa; d. Vernon E. and Georgene (Woodmansee) Borland; A.A., Grandview Coll., 1950; B.A., Drake U., 1952; m. Dirk C. Van Zante. Asso. editor Mchts. Trade Jour., Des Moines, 1952-55; copywriter Meredith Pub. Co., Des Moines, 1955-60, book editor, 1960-67, home furnishings editor Better Homes and Gardens Spl. Interest Publs., Meredith Corp., 1967-74, home furnishing and design editor Better Homes and Gardens mag., 1974—. Named Advt. Woman of Year, Des Moines, 1961; recipient Dorothy Dawe award, 1971, 73, 75, 76, 77. Mem. Nat. Home Fashion League, Am. Inst. Interior Designers (press affiliate), Am. Fedn. Advt., Alpha Xi Delta, Theta Sigma Phi. Club: Women's Advt. (Des Moines). Office: 1716 Locust St Des Moines IA 50336

VAN ZANTEN, FRANK VELDHUYZEN, library cons.; b. Heemstede, The Netherlands, Oct. 21, 1932; s. Adrian V. and Cornelia (Van Eesteren) Van Z.; came to U.S., 1946, naturalized, 1953; A.B., Calvin Coll., Mich., 1959; postgrad. U. Wash., 1960; M.A. in L.S., U. Mich., 1961; m. Lois Ruth Holkeboer, June 17, 1961; children—Kiki Maria, Lili Roxanne, Amy Suzanne. Cataloger, extension project asst. Mich. State Library, Lansing, 1961-62; dir. Dickinson County (Mich.) Library, 1962-65, Mid-Peninsula Library Fedn., Iron Mountain, Mich., 1963-65, St. Clair County (Mich.) Library, 1965-68, Tucson Pub. Library, 1968-73; library cons. Ill. State Library, Springfield, 1973-75, asso. dir. for library devel., 1975-78; dir. Mid-Hudson Library System, Poughkeepsie, N.Y., 1978—. Served with AUS, 1953-55. Mem. Am., N.Y. library assns. Presbyterian. Home: 138 Wilbur Blvd Poughkeepsie NY 12603 Office: 103 Market St Poughkeepsie NY 12601

VAN ZELST, THEODORE WILLIAM, civil engr., instrument co. exec.; b. Chgo., May 11, 1923; s. Theodore Walter and Wilhelmina (Oomens) VanZ.; B.S., U. Calif. at Berkeley, 1944; B.A.S., Northwestern U., 1945, M.S. in Civil Engring., 1948; m. Louann Hurter, Dec. 29, 1952; children—Anne, Jean, David, Pres. Soil Testing Services, Inc., Chgo., 1948-52; pres. Soiltest, Inc., Chgo., 1948-78, chmn. bd., 1978—; exec. v.p. Cenco Inc., Chgo., 1962-77, vice chmn., 1975-77, also dir., 1962-77; dir. Lab. Glass, Inc., 1970-78, Wilmad Glass, Inc., 1970-78, Virtis Co., Inc., 1974-78, Calumet Coach Co., 1969-78, Barber Greene Co., 1975—, Houghton Mfg. Co., 1967-78, Minann, Inc., Hoskin Sci. Co. Can., 1977—, Testing Scis. Inc., 1959—, Aparatos S.A., 1978—; pres., dir. Geneva-Pacific Corp., 1969—. Treas., Internat. Road Fedn., 1961-64, sec. 1964—, dir., 1973—; pres. Internat. Rd. Edn. Found., 1978—. Trustee Evanston Hist. Soc. Served to lt. (j.g.) USNR, 1942-45. Recipient Service award Northwestern U., 1973, Merit award, 1974; Service award U. Wis., 1973; La Sallian award, 1975. Registered profl. engr., Ill. Mem. ASCE, Am. Concrete Inst., Nat. Soc. Profl. Engrs., Soil Sci. Soc., ASTM, Western Soc. Engrs., Evanston C. of C. (v.p. 1969-73), Ovid Esbach Soc. (pres.), Tau Beta Pi. Clubs: Economic, North Shore; Univ. (Evanston); Netherland (N.Y.). Inventor engring. testing equipment for soil, rock concrete and asphalt. Home: 1213 Wagner Rd Glenview IL 60025 Office: 2205 Lee St Evanston IL 60202

VAN ZWOLL, CORNELIUS, educator; b. Rochester, N.Y., Nov. 12, 1916; s. John and Adriana (van der Pijl) van Z.; A.B., Calvin Coll., 1938; M.A., U. Mich., 1947; Ph.D., Mich. State U., 1965; m. Ruth de Beer, May 30, 1946; children—Wayne Cornell, Dean Calvin, Kim Ellen. Tchr., Eastern Acad., Paterson, N.J., 1938-41, 45-46; teaching asst. German, U. Mich., 1946-47; asst. prof. German, Carroll Coll., Waukesha, Wis., 1947-50; teaching fellow modern lang. Cornell U., 1950-52; crypto-linguist Nat. Security Agy., 1952-53; instr. modern langs. Eastern Christian High Sch., N. Haledon, N.J., 1953-55, prin., 1955-56; asst. prof. German, Calvin Coll., 1956-59; asst. prof. German and Russian, Albion (Mich.) Coll., 1959-64; prof., chmn. dept. Alma (Mich.) Coll., 1964-68; prof. German and Russian, head dept. DePauw U., Greencastle, Ind., 1968—. Served as officer AUS, 1941-45; maj. Res. ret. Recipient German Studies award Cornell U., 1952; West German Fgn. Study award Fed. Republic Germany, 1961; Nat. Def. Fgn. Lang. fellow U. Mich., 1960; Nat. Endowment for Humanities fellow U. Minn., 1975. Mem. Am. Assn. Tchrs. German, Modern Lang. Assn. Am., Am. Tchrs. Fgn. Langs., Res. Officers Assn. Author: Motifs and Themes in Broch's Die Schlafwandler, 1965. Home: 112 Northwood Blvd Greencastle IN 46135

VARCO, RICHARD LYNN, surgeon, educator; b. Fairview, Mont., Aug. 14, 1912; s. Lynn G. and Maurine V.; M.B., U. Minn., 1936, M.D., 1937, Ph.D., 1944; m. Louise Miller, June 4, 1940. Resident surgery U. Minn., to 1942, instr. dept. surgery, 1943-44, asst. prof., 1944-46, asso. prof., 1946-50, prof. surgery, 1950—, Regents' prof., 1974—. Mem. Am. Bd. Med. Spltys. Diplomate Am. Bd. Surgery, Am. Bd. Thoracic Surgery. Fellow A.C.S. (1st v.p. 1976-77); mem. Am. Assn. Thoracic Surgery, Am. Fedn. Clin. Research, A.M.A., Am. Surg. Assn., Soc. Univ. Surgeons (pres. 1958), Soc. Exptl. Biology and Medicine, Soc. Vascular Surgery (pres. 1964), Am. Heart Assn., Sigma Xi. Office: U Minn Hosps Box 495 Mayo Meml Bldg Minneapolis MN 55455

VARGA, RICHARD STEVEN, mathematician, educator; b. Cleve., Oct. 9, 1928; s. Steven and Ella (Krejcs) V.; B.S., Case Inst. Tech., 1950; A.M., Harvard, 1951, Ph.D., 1954; m. Esther Marie Pfister, Sept. 22, 1951; 1 dau., Gretchen Marie. With Bettis Atomic Power Lab., Westinghouse Electric Co., 1954-60, adv. mathematician, 1959-60; prof. math. Case Inst. Tech., 1960-69; Univ. prof. math. Kent (Ohio) State U., 1969—. Cons. to govt. and industry. Recipient Research award Sigma Xi, 1965. Guggenheim fellow, 1963; Fairchild scholar, 1974. Author: Matrix Iterative Analysis, 1962; Functional Analysis and Approximation Theory in Numerical Analysis, 1971. Editor: Numerical Solution of Field Problems in Continuum Physics, 1970; Padé and Rational Approximations: Theory and Applications, 1977. Mem. editorial bd. Numerische Mathematik, Linear Algebra and Its Applications, Soc. Indsl. and Applied Math., Aequationes Mathematicae, Jour. Approximation Theory, Utilitas Mathematica, Revue Française d' Automatique, Récherche Opérationelle, Jour. Math. and Math. Physics. Home: 7065 Arcadia Dr Cleveland OH 44129

VARGAS, GEORGE LELAND, lawyer; b. Winnemucca, Nev., Aug. 31, 1909; s. John Dorsey and Margaret Harriet (Wilkinson) V.; A.B., U. Nev., 1931; LL.B., Stanford, 1934; m. Phyllis Balzar, Aug. 1928 (div. 1943); children—Dell, George Leland II (dec.) Susan, Linda; m. 2d, Andrea Drumm, 1948 (div. 1950); m 3d, Josephine Berliner, Oct. 17, 1950; 1 dau., Nola. Admitted to Nev. bar, 1934, Calif. bar, 1934; r.r. pub. relations counsel, 1937-41; nat. counsel Nat. Bd. Fire Underwriters, 1944-46, Western gen. counsel, 1946-65; practice in Reno, 1934—; sr. partner Vargas, Bartlett & Dixon. Organizer, 1946-68, dir., counsel Bonanza Lines, 1946-68; dir. Johnson Controls, Inc., Milw., Valley Bank of Nev.; dir., mem. exec. com. Air West, 1968-70; gen. counsel Nev. Bankers Assn., 1978—, Nat. Jud. Coll. Fellow Am. Acad. Matrimonial Lawyers; mem. Stanford Assos., Am. Bar Assn., Internat. Assn. Ins. Counsel, Am. Coll. Trial Lawyers, Am. Coll. Probate Counsel, Alpha Tau Omega. Episcopalian. Elk (past exalted ruler Reno). Club: Balboa de Mazatlan (Mexico) (dir.). Home: 150 Greenridge Dr Reno NV 89501 Office: 201 W Liberty St Reno NV 89504 also Valley Bank Plaza Suite 500 300 S 4th St Las Vegas NV 89101

VARGAS, LESTER LAMBERT, surgeon, educator; b. Providence, May 20, 1921; A.B., Brown U., 1943; M.D. summa cum laude, George Washington U., 1945; m. Cynthia M. Baptist, Mar. 6, 1969; one son, Leslie H. Intern, R.I. Hosp., Providence, 1945-46, dir. cardiac surgery and cardiovascular surgery research lab., 1956-71, pres. staff assn., 1967, surgeon-in-chief, 1961-70, asso. surgeon-in-chief, 1970—; intern, resident gen., thoracic, pediatric and cardiovascular surgery Columbia-Presbyn. Med. Center, N.Y.C., 1948-55; asst. resident thoracic surgeon Bellevue Hosp., N.Y.C., 1949; Lambert fellow in cardiovascular surgery Coll. Physicians and Surgeons, Columbia U., 1954-55, asst. in surgery, 1950-55; asst. clin. prof. surgery Tufts U. Sch. Medicine, 1959-62, lectr., 1963—; prof. surgery R.I. Hosp. Brown U., 1963-67, prof. med. sci., 1968—. Served from 1st lt. to capt., M.C., U.S. Army, 1946-48. Recipient Disting. Lectr. award Providence Coll., 1961. Diplomate Am. Bd. Surgery, Nat. Bd. Med. Examiners. Fellow Am. Coll. Cardiology (bd. govs. and gov. for R.I. 1963-66), Am. Coll. Chest Physicians, A.C.S., Am. Geriatrics Soc.; mem. Titulaire Société Internationale de Chirurgie, Internat. Soc. Cardiovascular Surgery, New Eng. Surg. Soc., New Eng. Soc. Vascular Surgery, AAAS, Am. Heart Assn. (pres. R.I. chpt. 1963-65, Disting. Service medal), N.Y. Acad. Scis., R.I. Med. Soc. (Fiske prize), Allen O. Whipple Soc., Sigma Xi. Contbr. articles to med. jours. and books; author, producer med. edn. films. Office: Box G Brown U Providence RI 02903

VARI, VICTOR BENEDICT, educator; b. San Francisco, Feb. 22, 1920; s. August and Agnes (Proia) V.; A.B., San Francisco State U., 1942; student Sorbonne U., Paris, France, 1945; U. Lausanne (Switzerland), 1946, U. Mexico, 1949; M.A., Stanford, 1952; Ph.D., U. Madrid (Spain), 1961; m. Julia Botto, Oct. 22, 1952. Tchr. pvt. sch., San Francisco, 1937-41; prof. Romance langs. and lit. U. Santa Clara (Calif.), 1946—, chmn. dept. modern langs. and lits., 1949-59, 64—, dir. div. modern and classical langs. and lits., 1950-59; radio announcer, music dir., news commentator in Italian, KRE, Berkeley, Calif., 1941-42; lectr. Coll. Notre Dame, Belmont, Calif., 1953-62. Served with Mil. Intelligence, AUS, 1942-46. Spanish Govt. research grantee, 1960-61; Fulbright grantee, 1963. Mem. Internat. Assn. Study Italian Lang. and Lit., Hispania, Italica, Modern Lang. Assn., Internat. Assn. Hispanic Studies, Il Cenacolo, Fgn. Lang. Assn. No. Calif., Fgn. Lang. Assn. Santa Clara County. Author: Carducci y Espana, 1963. Contbr. articles to profl. jours. Home: 24600 Summerhill Rd Los Altos Hills CA 94022 Office: U Santa Clara Dept Modern Langs and Lits Santa Clara CA 95053

VARIAN, HAL RONALD, economist; b. Wooster, Ohio, Mar. 18, 1947; s. Max Ronald and Elaine Catherine (Shultzman) V.; S.B., M.I.T., 1969; M.A., U. Calif., Berkeley, 1973, Ph.D. (NSF fellow), 1973. Asst. prof. econs. M.I.T., 1973-76; vis. asst. prof. U. Calif., Berkeley, 1977, Stanford U., 1977; prof. U. Mich., 1977—. Guggenheim fellow, 1979-80. Mem. Am. Econ. Soc., Econometric Soc. Author: Microeconomic Analysis, 1978. Home: 1114 Woodlawn Ave Ann Arbor MI 48104 Office: Dept Econs U Mich Ann Arbor MI 48109

VARLEY, JOHN HERBERT, author; b. Austin, Tex., 1947; s. John Edward and Joan Francis (Boehm) V.; student Mich. State U., 1965-67; m. Anet Mconel, Oct. 10, 1970; children—Maurice McConnell, Roger McConnell, Stefan McConnell. Author: The Ophiuchi Hotline, 1977, The Persistence of Vision (collected stories), 1978, Titan, 1979. Recipient Nebula award for best novella, 1978; Hugo award for best novella, 1978. Mem. Sci. Fiction Writers Am. Address: 345 River Rd Eugene OR 97404

VARMA, RANBIR, educator; b. India, Nov. 29, 1928; s. Ananta Lal and Saraswati (Devi) Das; B.A., Patna U., 1949; M.A., Columbia, 1952; Ph.D., New Sch. for Social Research, 1957; m. Gopi Jagtiani, Dec. 20, 1957. Came to U.S., 1951. Script writer, narrator USIA, N.Y.C., 1953-66; chmn. econ. dept. L.I. U., Bklyn., 1963-76, prof., 1966—. Am. Philos. Soc. travel and research fellow, 1968; Sidney Hillman fellow, 1953-54. Mem. Am. Econ. Assn., Met. Econ. Assn., Soc. Internat. Devel. Contbr. articles to profl. jours. Home: 565 West End Ave New York City NY 10024 Office: Dept Econs Long Island U Brooklyn NY 11201. *To strive, to find, to see, but not to yield.*

VARNADORE, DONALD GENE, assn. exec.; b. San Angelo, Tex., Mar. 7, 1947; s. Henry Clell and Mary Theo (Lord) V.; B.S.E., U. Central Ark.; m. S. Renee White, Mar. 16, 1968; children—Lauri, Christy. Tchr. public schs., Little Rock, 1970-72; exec. dir. Ark. Youth Forum, 1972-73; exec. dir. mem. devel. com. U.S. Jaycees, Tulsa, 1973-78, exec. v.p., 1978—, nat. cons., 1972-73; sec. bd. trustees U.S. Jaycee War Meml. Bd.; dir. U.S. Jaycee Found.; mem. nat. adv. bd. Citizens Choice, Bus. Edn. Council; exec. pub. Future Mag., 1978—. Nat. v.p. Muscular Dystrophy Assn. Mem. Am. Soc. Assn. Execs., PTA. Republican. Author: Personal Dynamics, 1973; Leadership Dynamics, 1974. Home: 10129 E 29th St Tulsa OK 74129 Office: 4 W 21st St Tulsa OK 74121

VARNER, BARTON DOUGLAS, lawyer; b. Ida Grove, Iowa, May 2, 1920; s. Charles R. and Mary E. (Whinery) V.; student U. Nebr., 1938-42; LL.B., U. Mo. at Kansas City, 1951; m. Frances Elaine Seaton, May 9, 1943; children—Charles R., John A. Admitted to Mo. bar, 1951, since practiced in Kansas City; partner firm Gage and Tucker, and predecessors, 1955—. Sec., Marvin Warner Co. Bd. mgrs. Kansas City YMCA, 1958—, chmn., 1962; bd. dirs. Kansas City Goodwill Industries. Served with USNR, 1942-45. Mem. Am., Kansas City bar assns., Newcomen Soc., Lawyers Assn., Nebr. Alumni Assn. Kansas City (pres. 1960), Kansas City C. of C., Delta Sigma Pi, Delta Theta Phi. Methodist (steward 1964-66, trustee 1968-69). Clubs: Kansas City, Knife and Fork (pres. 1966) (Kansas City, Mo.); Brookridge Country (Overland Park). Home: 9933 Foster St Overland Park KS 66212 Office: Mut Benefit Life Bldg Kansas City MO 64108. *Ralph Waldo Emerson best expressed the principle that has helped me the most in attaining what success that I have attained when he stated in his Essay on Self Reliance the following: "There is a time in every man's education when he arrives at the conviction that envy is ignorance; that imitation is suicide; that he must take himself for better or worse as his portion; that though the wide universe is full of good, no kernel of nourishing corn can come to him but through his toil bestowed on that plot of ground which is given him to till. The power which resides in him is new in nature and none but he knows what that is which he can do, nor does he know until he has tried."*

VARNER, FRANK B., steel co. exec.; b. Newark, Ohio, Sept. 9, 1918; s. Frank R. and Irilla M. (Bolin) V.; B.S. in Indsl. Engring., Ohio State U., 1941; m. Marian Jean Wobbecke, Apr. 12, 1941; children—James A., William F. With U.S. Steel Corp., 1941—, gen. transp. mgr., Pitts., 1958-64, asst. gen. mgr. traffic and transp., 1964-71, gen. mgr. traffic and transp., 1971-78, v.p. traffic and transp., 1978—. Mem. bus. adv. com. Northwestern U. Transp. Center, 1978—. Mem. Transp. Assn. Am. (dir.), Am. Iron and Steel Inst., Nat. Freight Transp. Assn., Nat. Indsl. Traffic League, Traffic and Transp. Assn. Pitts., Pitts. Athletic Assn. Republican. Methodist. Clubs: Duquesne, South Hills Country, Traffic of Pitts. Home: 4571 Doverdell Dr Pittsburgh PA 15236 Office: US Steel Corp 600 Grant St Pittsburgh PA 15230

VARNER, ROBERT EDWARD, judge; b. Montgomery, Ala., June 11, 1921; s. William and Georgia (Thomas) V.; B.S., Auburn U., 1946; J.D., U. Ala., 1949; m. Carolyn Hood Self, Sept. 2, 1947; children—Robert Edward, Carolyn Stuart. Admitted to Ala. bar, 1949; atty. City of Tuskegee, 1951; asst. U.S. atty. Middle Dist. Ala., 1954-58; practice in Montgomery, 1958-71; partner firm Jones, Murray, Stewart & Varner, 1958-71; U.S. dist. judge, Montgomery, 1971—; guest lectr. bus. law Huntingdon Coll. Pres. Montgomery Rotary Charity Found., v.p., fin. chmn. Tukabatchee Area council Boy Scouts Am. Mem. Macon County Bd. Edn., 1950-54. Served with USNR, 1942-46. Recipient Silver Beaver award Boy Scouts Am. Mem. Am., Fed., Montgomery (pres. 1971), Macon County bar assns., Am. Trial Lawyers Assn., Jud. Conf. of U.S. (com. on operation of jury system), Phi Alpha Delta, Phi Delta Theta. Republican. Methodist. Rotarian (pres. 1961). Office: US District Ct PO Box 2406 Montgomery AL 36103*

VARNEY, CARLETON BATES, JR., interior designer, columnist; b. Lynn, Mass., Jan. 23, 1937; s. Carleton Bates and Julia (Raczkowskos) V.; B.A., Oberlin Coll., 1958; student U. Madrid (Spain), 1957; M.A., N.Y. U., 1969; m. Suzanne Maria Lickdyke, Dec. 25, 1969; children—Nicholas, Seamus, Sebastian. Sch. tchr., 1958-59; asst. to pres. Dorothy Draper & Co., Inc., 1959-63, exec. v.p., 1963-66, pres., 1966—; designer chairs, 1964, dinnerware and china, 1965, 76, crystal glassware, 1966, decorative fabrics, 1964, 65, 67, sheets, 1977, table linen, 1978, fragrances, 1978; interior designer Dromoland Castle, Ireland, 1963, Westbury Hotel, Belgium, 1964, N.Y. World's Fair, 1965, Clare Inn, Ireland, 1968, Greenbrier Hotel, White Sulphur Springs, Va., 1968, Westbury Hotel, San Francisco, 1973, Copley Plaza Hotel, Boston, 1976, The Grand Hotel, Mackinac Island, Mich., 1978, numerous others; designer White House party for celebration Israel-Egypt Peace Treaty, 1979; syndicated columnist Your Family Decorator, 1968—; designer charity movie premiers Lord Jim, 1965, Man for All Seasons, 1967, War and Peace, 1968. Recipient Shelby Williams award for design achievement, 1967. Mem. Nat. Soc. Indsl. Designers. Clubs: N.Y. Athletic; Shannon Rowing (Ireland); Millbrook (N.Y.) Golf and Tennis. Author numerous books including: Carleton Varney's Book of Decorating Ideas, 1970; Decorating With Color, 1971; Decorating For Fun, 1972; Be Your Own Decorator, 1979. Office: 60 E 56th St New York NY 10022. *Throughout my career, I have tried to achieve a perfection of details in my designs, be those designs for a hotel lobby or for a collection of china. The details always show-they separate excellent from ordinary design. My success, I believe in part, is due to my ability to understand and work in large spaces with vibrant color.*

VARNEY, ROBERT NATHAN, physicist; b. San Francisco, Nov. 7, 1910; s. Frank Hastings and Emily Patricia (Rhine) V.; A.B., U. Calif., 1931, M.A., 1932, Ph.D., 1935; m. Astrid Margareta Riffolt, June 19, 1948; children—Nils Roberts, Natalie Rhine. Instr., U. Calif., 1935-36, N.Y. U., 1936-38; asst. prof. Washington U., St. Louis, 1938-44, asso. prof., 1944-48, prof. physics, 1948-64; mem. tech. staff Bell Telephone Lab., Inc., Murray Hill, N.J., 1951-52 (leave of absence from Washington U.); sr. mem. research lab. Lockheed Missiles & Space Co., Palo Alto, Calif., 1964-75; ret., 1975; NSF sr. postdoctoral fellow Ballistic Research Labs., Aberdeen Proving Ground, Md., 1975-76. Vis. staff mem. research lab. Linde Air Products Co., 1954; Austrian-Am. Fulbright lectr. in atomic physics U. Innsbruck, 1971-72, 76-77, guest prof., 1977-78. Mem. Gov.'s Sci. Adv. Com. State of Mo., 1961-64. NSF sr. post-doctoral fellow dept. electronics Royal Inst. Tech., Stockholm, 1958-59. Served as comdr. USNR, 1941-45. Fellow Am. Phys. Soc., A.A.A.S.; mem. Phi Beta Kappa, Sigma Xi, Omicron Delta Kappa, Tau Beta Pi. Author: Lecture Notes in Engineering Physics, 1947; Laboratory Manual of Physics (with J.P. Davidson Jr.); articles on electronic and plasma physics. Home: 4156 Maybell Way Palo Alto CA 94306

VARNUM, JAMES WILLIAM, hosp. adminstr.; b. Grand Rapids, Mich., May 29, 1940; s. Robert Otto and Jeannette (Badger) V.; A.B., Dartmouth, 1962; M.Hosp. Adminstrn. with honors, U. Mich., 1964; m. Lucinda Hotchkiss, June 6, 1964; children—Kenneth James, Susan Lucinda. Adminstrv. asst. U. Wis. Hosps., Madison, 1963-64, asst. supt., 1964-68, asso. supt., 1968-69, supt., 1969-73; hosp. adminstr. U. Wash. Hosp., Seattle, 1973-78; exec. dir. Mary Hitchcock Meml. Hosp., Hanover, N.H., 1978—; v.p. Dartmouth-Hitchcock Med. Center, Hanover, 1978—; prof. Med. Sch., Dartmouth Coll., 1978—. Home: Woodcock Ln Etna NH 03750 Office: 2 Maynard Hanover NH 03755

VARNUM, LAURENT KIMBALL, lawyer; b. Chgo., Oct. 31, 1895; s. Clark and Irene (Galloway) V.; A.B., U. Mich., 1925, J.D., 1927; m. Maryellen Brown, June 7, 1930. (dec. Oct. 1955); children—Irene Varnum McLaughlin, Catherine Varnum Beaman; m. 2d, Zoe Shippen, Feb. 28, 1959. Admitted to Mich. bar, 1927, since practiced in Grand Rapids; mem. Varnum, Riddering, Wierengo & Christenson,

1935—; spl. counsel City of Grand Rapids, 1943-44; mem. Little Hoover Commn.; chmn. com. for balanced legislature and co-author constnl. amendment on reapportionment, adopted in Mich., 1952; chmn. Alien Enemy Hearing Bd., 1941-45; mem. bd. Kent County Dept. Aeros., 1958-67. Bd. dirs. Grand Rapids Symphony Soc., pres., 1955-56. Mem. citizens adv. commn. on Reorgn. State Govt. Fellow Am. Coll. Trial Lawyers; mem. Am. Law Inst., Am. Judicature Soc., Am. (ho. dels. 1947-50), Mich. (pres. 1946- 47), Grand Rapids bar assns., Internat. Assn. Ins. Counsel, Jud. Council Mich., Sixth Circuit Jud. Conf. (life mem.), Better Govt in Mich., Order of Coif, Phi Beta Kappa. Club: Everglades (Palm Beach, Fla.). Home: 220 Fairview Rd Palm Beach FL 33480 Office: Old Kent Bldg Grand Rapids MI 49503

VARRO, BARBARA JOAN, journalist; b. East Chicago, Ind., Jan. 25, 1938; d. Alexander R. and Lottie R. (Bess) V.; B.A., Duquesne U., 1959. Feature reporter, asst. fashion editor Chgo. Sun-Times, 1959-64, fashion editor, 1964-76, feature writer, 1976—. Recipient awards for feature writing Ill. Asso. Press, 1978-79. Mem. Chgo. Council on Fgn. Relations. Office: Chgo Sun-Times 401 N Wabash Ave Chicago IL 60611

VARRONE, ANGELO ROBERT, media sales exec.; b. Bklyn., Feb. 27, 1947; s. Albert Carl and Rose (Ferrara) V.; B.S., State U. N.Y., 1965; m. Diana Verga, Jan. 28, 1968; children—Danielle, Andrea. Sales rep. Prentice Hall Inc., N.Y.C., 1967-69, United Bus. Publs., N.Y.C., 1969-71; with Gralla Publs. Co., N.Y.C., 1971-79, asso. pub. Catalog Showroom Bus. mag., 1972-75, pub. Health Care Products News, 1975-79; exec. v.p. Sunbelt Media Sales, Inc., Coral Springs, Fla., 1979—. Mem. Pharm. Advt. Club N.Y.C., Health Care Exhibitors Assn., Health Industry Mfrs. Assn. Office: 10211 W Sample Rd Coral Springs FL 33065

VARSHNI, YATENDRA PAL, physicist; b. Allahabad, India, May 21, 1932; came to Can., 1960; s. Hari Pal and Bhagyawati V.; B.Sc., U. Allahabad, 1950, M.Sc., 1952, Ph.D., 1956. Asst. prof. U. Allahabad, 1955-60; postdoctoral fellow NRC, Ottawa Ont., Can., 1960-62; asst. prof. U. Ottawa, 1962-65, asso. prof., 1965-69, prof., 1969—. Fellow Am. Phys. Soc., Indian Phys. Soc., Royal Astron. Soc. (U.K.), AAAS, Inst. Physics U.K., Chem. Soc. U.K., Brit. Interplanetary Soc. (asso.); mem. Am. Astron. Soc., Can. Astron. Soc., Can. Assn. Physicists, Royal Astron. Soc. Can., Astron. Soc. India, Am. Assn. Physics Tchrs., European Phys. Soc. Contbr. numerous articles to profl. jours. Office: Dept Physics U Ottawa Ottawa ON K1N 6N5 Canada

VARTAN, VARTANIG GARABED, journalist; b. Pasadena, Calif., June 28, 1923; s. Garabed S. and Yeranig (Saxenian) V.; B.A., Yale, 1948; m. Cynthia Kirk Smith, Nov. 18, 1961; 1 son, Kirk Spencer. Reporter, Laurel (Miss.) Leader-Call, 1948-49, Tupelo (Miss.) Jour., 1949-52, United Press, 1952-55; financial writer N.Y. Herald Tribune, 1955-62; Wall St. columnist C.S. Monitor, 1957-62; financial writer N.Y. Times, 1963—: free-lance writer. Author: 50 Wall Street, 1968; The Dinosaur Fund, 1972. Served with AUS, 1943-45. Episcopalian. Home: 14 Sutton Pl South New York City NY 10022

VARTANIAN, SONA, ballet dancer; b. Alexandria, Egypt, Jan. 16, 1947; d. Petros and (Vartanouch) Vartanian; came to Can., 1973, naturalized, 1977; grad. Choreographic Acad. City of Yerevan (Armenia), 1964; m. Serge Kouyoumdjian, July 1, 1971 (dec. 1978). Prin. ballet dancer Yerevan's Spendiarov Acad. Opera House, 1964-73, including performances in Spartacus, Gayane, Don Quixote, Swan Lake, Giselle, Hamlet, Paquita, Romeo and Juliet; with Les Grands Ballets Canadiens, Montreal, 1973—, prin. dancer, 1975—; guest tchr., Wichita Falls, Tex., 1974, Montreal Acad. Les Grands Ballets Canadians, 1974, Les Ballets Russes de Montreal, 1976, 77. Recipient various prizes for competitions in USSR, 1967-68. Toured with Les Grands Ballets Canadiens in S.Am., U.S., Europe, Can. Home: 1721 Couvrette Ville St Laurent Montreal PQ H4L 4T7 Canada Office: 5415 Queen Mary Rd Montreal PQ H3X 1V1 Canada. *I was brought up in the Soviet Russian system, where our school taught us to consider dance as a holy vacation. Dance is part of my life without which I can never be. One might consider me a fanatic in my field; I consider it the only way to be. Dance is a total art of total expression, and the only way to be true to it is to give oneself wholly to it.*

VARTANIAN, VAHAN, state ofcl.; b. Boston, Nov. 11, 1917; s. Setrag and Victoria (Calusdian) V.; student Emerson Coll., 1938, Suffolk U., 1948-49, Boston U., 1950; m. Mary Nigohosian, Apr. 23, 1944; children—Kenneth, Richard, Robert. Tng. specialist U.S. VA, Boston, 1946-57; mgmt. analyst U.S. Army C.E., Waltham, Mass., 1946-60; program analyst electronic systems div. USAF, Bedford, Mass., 1960-72; adj. gen. Commonwealth of Mass., Boston, 1972—. Served with AUS, 1940-46. Decorated Army Commendation medal with oak leaf cluster; recipient Man of Yr. award Italian-Am. Civic League Am., 1976. Mem. N.G. Assn. U.S., N.G. Assn. Mass., Inc. (pres. 1971), Ancient and Hon. Arty. Co. Mass. (hon.). Mem. Armenian Apostolic Ch. Clubs: Masons (32 deg.); Shriners. Home: 9 Slocum Rd Jamaica Plain MA 02130 Office: 905 Commonwealth Ave Boston MA 02215

VAS, STEPHEN ISTVAN, educator; b. Budapest, Hungary, June 4, 1926; s. Gyula and Ilona (Rosenberg) V.; M.D., Med. Univ. Budapest, 1950, Ph.D., 1956; m. Magdalene Raditz, Apr. 23, 1953. Came to Can., 1957, naturalized, 1962. Asst. prof. U. Budapest, 1953-56; Rockefeller research fellow McGill U., 1957-59, mem. faculty, 1959-77, prof. microbiology, 1967-77, chmn. dept., 1972-77; prof. microbiology, asso. prof. medicine U. Toronto, 1977—. Mem. Canadian Med. Assn., Canadian, Am. assns. microbiology, Can., Am. socs. immunology, Soc. Gen. Microbiology. Contbr. articles to profl. jours. Home: 96 Princess Margaret Blvd Toronto ON M9B 2Y9 Canada

VASARELY, VICTOR, artist; b. Pecs, Hungary, 1908; student medicine; Dr. honoris causa in Humanities, State U. Cleve., 1977. Mem. Budapest Bauhaus; moved to Paris, 1930; one-man shows include Rose Fried Gallery, N.Y.C., 1958, World House Gallery, N.Y.C., 1961, 62, Met. Mus. Art, Montevideo, 1958, Hanover Gallery, London, Eng., Pace Gallery, Boston; group exhbns. major Paris Salons and Stadelijk Mus., Amsterdam, Documenta III Kassel, Carnegie Inst., Gallery Chalette, N.Y.C., Sidney Janis Gallery, N.Y.C., Guggenheim Mus., Sao Paolo, Rio de Janeiro, Montevideo; rep. permanent collections Mus. Modern Art, N.Y.C., Mus. St. Etienne, Paris, Mus. Modern Art, Paris, Albright-Knox Gallery, Harvard, Buenos Aires Mus., Montivideo Mus., Brussels Mus., Reyjavik Mus., Carnegie Inst., Stedelijk Mus., Sao Paulo Mus., Tate Gallery, London, Vienna Mus., Tel Aviv Mus., Guggenheim Mus., Rockefeller Found. Helsinki Mus. Decorated chevalier Legion of Honor, officer Nat. Order Merit (France); grand ribbon honor Order Andre Bello (Venezuela); medal Order of Flag (Hungary); recipient Guggenheim Internat. award Merit, 1964; named to Order Arts and Letters, France, 1965; grand prize 8th Biennal Art, Sao Paulo, Brazil, 1965; cert. distinction N.Y. U., 1978; Art prize City of Goslar, 1978; named hon. citizen of New Orleans, 1966; prize 9th Biennal, Minister Fgn. Affairs, Tokyo, 1967; Citoyen d'Honneur de la Ville d'Aix en Provence. Musée Vasarely at Château de Gordes, France, dedicated, 1971; Fondation Vasarely á Aix-en-Provence, opened 1976. Assn; France-Hungary (hon. pres. 1977—), Internat. Inst. Nuclear Engrs. (corres.). Address: 77410 Annet-sur-Marne France

VASEK, RICHARD JIM, educator; b. Wharton, Tex., June 23, 1935; s. James F. and Albina (Zapalac) V.; student Wharton County Jr. Coll., 1954-56; B.S., Tex. A. and M. U., 1958, M.Ed., 1960, Ed.D., 1967; m. Lou Ann Ponder, Oct. 29, 1955; children—Jeffrey, Donna, Blake, Carole, Laura. Instr., Ft. Worth Pub. Schs., 1958-59; instr. Ark. A. and M. Coll., College Heights, 1959-60; asst., then asso. prof. Miss. State U., 1960-66, 68-70, prof. indsl. edn., head dept., 1970—; research U.S. Office Edn., 1966-67; cons. indsl. arts curriculum in pub. schs. Mem. Am., Miss. (pres., bd. mem.) indsl. arts assns., Am. Vocat. Assn., Iota Lambda Sigma (pres.), Phi Delta Kappa (pres.). Roman Catholic. Contbr. articles to profl. jours. Home: 208 Woodlawn Starkville MS 39759 Office: Miss State U Dept Indsl and Occupational Edn Drawer NU Mississippi State MS 39762

VASILACH, SERGE, mathematician, educator; b. Fintina Mare, Rumania, July 26, 1904; s. Georges and Helen (Sopon) V.; licentiate phys. scis., U. Paris, 1927, licentiate sci. math., 1929, D.E.S. Phys. Math. and Calculus Probabilities, 1931; Dr. es Sciences Maths., U. Rennes, France, 1966; m. Louise Beauchemp, July 19, 1963. Research asst. U. Paris, 1928-35; research asst. Centre Nat. Recherches Scientifiques, Paris, 1935-40; dir. engring. Laboratoire Industriel d'Electricité, Paris, 1939-43; research asst. U. Bucharest, 1944-50; prof. Inst. Math. Rumanian Acad. Sci., 1950-65; asso. prof. U. Rennes, 1965-66; prof. math. Laval U, Quebec, Can., 1966—. Recipient Work Merit Order, Acad. Scis. Rumanian Socialist Republic. NRC Can. grantee, 1966—. Mem. Am. Math. Soc., Math. Assn. Am., Canadian Math. Congress, Soc. Math. de France. Author: Set Theory, 1956; Ensembles; Structures; Categories; Faisceaux, 1977. Contbr. articles profl. jours. Patentee electronics. Address: Laval U Dept Math Quebec 10 PQ Canada

VASINGTON, FRANK DANIEL, educator; b. Norwich, Conn., Nov. 3, 1928; s. Samuel and Carmela (Tempesta) V.; A.B., U. Conn., 1950, M.S., 1952; Ph.D., U. Md., 1955; m. Margaret Elizabeth Campbell, Aug. 16, 1952; children—Lynn, Gail, Mark, Philip. Asst. prof. biol. chemistry Sch. Medicine, U. Md., Balt., 1955-57; Nat. Found. research fellow McCollum-Pratt Inst.,. also Johns Hopkins, 1957-59; asst. prof. biochemistry Johns Hopkins, 1959-64; asso. prof. biochemistry U. Conn., Storrs, 1964-68, prof., 1968—, head biochemistry and biophysics sect., 1967-76, asso. dean Coll. Liberal Arts and Scis., 1976-78, asso. v.p. acad. affairs, 1978—, exec. officer biol. scis. group, 1967-71. NIH research grantee, 1964-69; NSF research grantee, 1969-71. Mem. Am. Soc. Biol. Chemists, Am. Chem. Soc., A.A.A.S. Contbr. articles to profl. jours. Research in field of biol. transport processes. Home: 16 Lynwood Rd Storrs CT 06268

VASLEF, IRENE, librarian; b. Budapest, Hungary, Mar. 23, 1934; d. Imre and Ilona (Selyebi-Kovats) Szabo; came to U.S., 1956, naturalized, 1960; B.A., San Jose (Calif.) State U., 1960; M.S., Simmons Grad. Sch. Library Sci., Boston, 1963; postgrad. Columbia U., 1968, U. Colo., 1961-62, U. Munich, 1967-68, Catholic U. Am., 1974—; m. Nicholas P. Vaslef, Sept. 2, 1956; children—Suzanne, Steven. Librarian, Cambridge (Mass.) Sch. System, 1962-64; librarian Colorado Springs (Colo.) Sch. System, 1964-67; head catalog librarian Colo. Coll., Colorado Springs, 1968-72; librarian Dumbarton Oaks Research Library, Trustees for Harvard U., Washington, 1972—. Mem. Spl. Libraries Assn., Art Libraries Assn. N.Am., Phi Gamma Mu. Book reviewer Colo. State Library publ., 1965-66. Home: 1405 Grady Randall Ct McLean VA 22101 Office: 1703 32d St NW Washington DC 20007

VASS, GUY BOYD, cable co. exec.; b. Galax, Va., Aug. 23, 1918; s. Dennis Shelby and Laura E. (Payne) V.; grad. bus. adminstrn. Jackson Bus. U., 1937; student Mich. State U.; m. Katherine S. Pittenger, Dec. 10, 1938; children—Suzanne Kay, Dennis Boyd, Carol Lynn. With Hayes Industries Inc., Jackson, Mich., 1937-69, exec. v.p. 1955-59, pres., 1959-69; pres. Thompson Industries, Inc. subsidiary ITT, Southfield, 1970-73; pres. Cova Corp., Jackson, 1973—; v.p. Am. Chain & Cable Co., Bridgeport, Conn., 1974—; pres. Fifty Plus Five Corp., West Unity, Ohio, 1957—, Plastigage Corp., Jackson, 1957—; exec. v.p. Hayes-Albion Corp.; dir. Macklin Co., Jackson, City Bank and Trust Co., Jackson. Past pres. dir. Jackson YMCA; trustee Hillsdale Coll. Mem. Am. Mgmt. Assn., Jackson C. of C. (dir.), Soc. Automotive Engrs., Indsl. Execs. Club (past pres., dir.), Mfrs. Assn. Jackson (past dir.) Presbyn. Mason. Clubs: Jackson Country, Recess; Detroit Athletic. Home: 3415 E Walmont Dr Jackson MI 49203 Office: One Jackson Sq Jackson MI 49203

VASSIL, PAMELA, graphic designer, mech. artist; b. N.Y.C., Nov. 29, 1943; d. George Peter and Lenora (Zablo) V.; B.S. in Art Edn., Hofstra U., 1965; M.A. in Art Edn., N.Y. U., 1968. Designer Columbia Records, N.Y.C., 1970-72; asso. art dir. Harper's Bazaar, N.Y.C., 1972-74; designer, mech. artist Album Graphics Inc., N.Y.C., 1974-75; freelance designer, mech. artist; prodn. dir. Push Pin Studios, N.Y.C., 1975-77; art dir. op. ed. page N.Y. Times, N.Y.C., 1977-79; freelance designer/art dir./mech. artist, 1979—; instr. mechs. Parson's Sch. Design, N.Y.C., 1974—.

VASSOS, JOHN, indsl. designer, painter, illustrator, lectr., author; b. Greece, Oct. 1898; s. Apostolos and Iphigenia (Mitaraki) V.; student Robert Coll., 1912-14, Art Students League, 1921-22; m. Ruth Carrier, Mar. 1923. Came to U.S., 1919, naturalized, 1924. Indsl. designer R.C.A., 1938—; intermittent work for Remington, Du Pont, Savage Arms, Imperial Cutlery, Perey Turnstiles, Am. Tel. & Tel. Co., and others; designer Room of Tomorrow, N.Y. World's Fair, Television Pavilion San Francisco Fair, 1939; inventor Multi-purpose furniture, 1939; designer archtl. light prins. for comml. bldgs.; con. RCA Internat. & Engring. Products; lectr. Pratt Inst., N.Y. U., Syracuse U., Vassar Coll. Illustrator alone and with Ruth Vassos numerous books and other publs., executed murals Riviera Theatre, N.Y.C., Egyptian Theatre, Los Angeles, Condado Beach Hotel, P.R., WCAU Sta. in Phila. Radio and TV Center, RCA, Washington, Syosset and Rivoli theatres, N.Y.C., Mil. Electronic Center, Van Nuys, Cal. and others; designed Am. pavilions for U.S. Govt. at India Trade Fair, New Delhi and Karachi, Pakistan, 1955; designer pavilion Am. Interiors World's Fair, 1964; cons. Fairfield County Mus. Art, Sci. & Industry, Prudential Grace Lines, 1970—; exhbn. Art Deco, Finch Coll. Mus., Cranbrook Acad., Mpls. Inst. Arts; represented permanent exhbn. Syracuse U. mem. adv. council Norwalk Community Coll., Gen. Studies, Columbia; mem. exec. historic com. Norwalk-Conn. Soc. Served as lt. col., OSS, AUS, 1942-45. Decorated Cross of Golden Phoenix (Greece); recipient numerous awards and medals including Indsl. Designers Inst., 1955; Paidea award Hellenic U. Club of N.Y., 1963; Am. Soc. Neo-Hellenic Studies award, 1973. Fellow Silvermine Guild Artists (past pres.), Indsl. Designers Soc. Am. (chmn. bd. 1965, award 1970). Pub. collection 90 illustrations, 1975. Home: Comstock Hill Ave Norwalk CT 06850

VASTA, BRUNO MORREALE, info. scientist, chemist; b. Washington, Apr. 1, 1933; s. John and Charlotte M. V.; B.S., Georgetown U., 1954; M.S., George Washington U., 1957; m. Dorothy Delaney, Aug. 18, 1956; children—Karen, Vicki, Charlotte, Robert. Research. asso. Nat. Heart Inst., Bethesda, Md., 1955-57; research biochemist Beltsville, Md., 1957-60; info. scientist FDA, 1963-70; chief toxicology info. services Nat. Library Medicine, Bethesda, 1970-76, chief bibliog. services div., 1976-77; dir. Chem. Info. div. Office Toxic Substances, EPA, 1977—; chmn. div. chem. info. Am. Chem. Soc., 1975-76. Recipient merit awards FDA, 1969, NIH, 1972. Mem. Am. Chem. Soc., Am. Soc. Info. Scis., Med. Library Assn., Chem. Notation Assn. Clubs: Salt Water Sportsmen, Stripus Unltd. Editor: Drug Interactions Bibliography, Vols. I and II, 1974-75. Home: 9111 Westerholme Way Vienna VA 22180 Office: Waterside Mall 401 M St NW Washington DC 20460

VATH, JOSEPH G., bishop; b. New Orleans, Mar. 12, 1918; ed. Notre Dame Sem., New Orleans, 1935-41; J.C.L., Catholic U. Am., 1948. Ordained priest Roman Catholic Ch., 1941; asst. pastor Ascension Ch., Donaldsonville, La., 1941-46, Incarnate Word Ch., New Orleans, 1948, St. Michael's Ch., 1948-49; vice-chancellor Archdiocese of New Orleans, 1948-66, sec. to bishop, 1949-62, sec. diocesan tribunal, 1955; adminstr. Our Lady of Perpetual Help Ch., Kenner, La., 1952; pastor Little Flower Ch., 1966-69; consecrated bishop, 1966; vicar gen., aux. bishop Mobile-Birmingham (Ala.) and titular bishop of Novaliciana, 1966-69, bishop of Birmingham, 1969—. Office: PO Box 2086 Birmingham AL 35201*

VAUGHAN, AUSTIN BERNARD, clergyman; b. N.Y.C., Sept. 27, 1927, s. Austin Bernard and Delia (Considine) V.; A.B., St. Josephs Sem., 1948; S.T.D., Gregorian U., 1954. Ordained priest Roman Catholic Ch., 1951; tchr. modern langs. Cathedral Coll., N.Y.C., 1955-56; prof. theology St. Josephs Sem., Yonkers, N.Y. 1956-73; rector St. Joseph's Sem., Yonkers, 1973-79; aux. bishop of N.Y., 1977—, vicar for Orange County, 1979—; chmn. Nat. Conf. of Cath. Bishops Com. on Human Values, 1977—. Mem. Cath. Theol. Soc. Am. (pres. 1968-69), Mariological Soc. Am. (pres. 1971-73), Coll. Theology Soc. Address: St Patrick's Ch 55 Grand St Newburgh NY 12550

VAUGHAN, DAVID LISLE, lawyer; b. Vancouver, B.C., Can., Feb. 15, 1922; s. William Randolph and Blanche (Park) V.; B.A., U. B.C., 1943, LL.B., 1948; m. Mavis Anne Carter, May 20, 1944; children—Michael David, Anna Teresa, Peter Christopher. Called to bar, B.C., 1948. Queens Counsel, 1967; since practiced in Vancouver; asso. Farris, Stultz, Bull & Farris, 1948-56, partner, 1956-64; partner Farris, Farris, Vaughan, Wills & Murphy and predecessor firm, 1964-77, asso. counsel, 1977—; lawyer in residence U.B.C. Law Faculty, 1977-78. Mem. B.C. Assessment Appeal Bd., 1978—. Dir., mem. exec. com. Festival Concert Soc., 1973; bd. dirs. Shawnigun Sch. Music and Fine Arts; mem. Vancouver Art Gallery; founder mem. Met. Coop. Theatre Soc.; hon. mem. Sculptors Soc. Can. Served to 1st lt. Canadian Army, 1943-45, comdg. officer B.C. Regt., 1960-63. Mem. Royal Canadian Armoured Corps Assn. (life), Canadian, Vancouver (past mem. exec. com.) bar assns., Assn. Canadian Pension Mgmt. (adv. council 1976). Clubs: Vancouver; West Vancouver Yacht. Home: Glendwyr Rural Route 4 Gibbons BC Canada Office: 700 W Georgia St Vancouver BC V7Y 1B3 Canada

VAUGHAN, EDWIN DARRACOTT, JR., urologist, surgeon; b. Richmond, Va., May 13, 1939; s. Edwin Darracott and Blanche V. (Bashaw) V.; B.S., Washington and Lee U., 1961; M.D., U. Va., 1965, M.S., 1969; m. Virginia Ann Lloyd, June 30, 1962; children—Edwin Darracott, III, Barbara Anderson. Intern, Vanderbilt U., 1965-66, asst. resident, 1966-67; chief resident in urology U. Va., 1970-71, asst. prof. urology, 1973-75, asso. prof., 1975-78, prof., 1978; clin. research fellow Columbia U., 1971-72, research asso. dept. medicine, 1972-73; James J. Colt prof. urology, chmn. div. urology Cornell U. Med. Coll., N.Y.C. and attending urologist-in-chief N.Y. Hosp., N.Y.C., 1978—; mem. sci. adv. bd. Nat. Kidney Found., 1977; sec.-treas. Urology Council, 1977; mem. med. adv. bd. Council High Blood Pressure, 1977. Recipient Research Career Devel. award NIH, 1976-78; NIH tng. grantee, 1967-68; USPHS grantee, 1971-73, 74-77; Am. Heart Assn. grantee, 1976-79. Mem. N.Y. Acad. Scis., AAAS, A.C.S., Soc. Univ. Urologists, Am. Urol. Assn. (chmn. research com.), So. Soc. Clin. Investigation, Soc. Exptl. Biology and Medicine, Société Internat. d'Urologie, Am. Assn. Genito-Urinary Surgeons, Sigma Xi, Alpha Omega Alpha (award 1976). Contbr. articles on obstructive uropathy, renal hemodynamics, hypertension to profl. jours.; asso. editor Investigative Urology, 1977-78, editorial bd., 1978—. Home: 1675 York Ave Apt 6-K New York NY 10021 Office: 525 E 68th St New York NY 10021

VAUGHAN, EUGENE H., JR., investment co. exec.; b. Brownsville, Tenn., Oct. 5, 1933; s. Eugene H. and Margaret (Musgrave) V.; B.A., Vanderbilt U., 1955; M.B.A. (J. Spencer Love fellow), Harvard, 1961; m. Susan Bolinger Westbrook, May 11, 1963; children—Margaret Corbin, Richard Bolinger. Investment analyst Putnam Mgmt. Co., Boston, 1961-64; v.p. research, dir. Underwood, Neuhaus & Co., Inc., mems. N.Y. Stock Exchange, Houston, 1964-70; pres. Vaughan, Nelson & Hargrove, Inc., Houston, 1970—; dir. Alliance Capital Reserves, Inc., Alliance Govt. Reserves, Inc., N.Y.C., Founders Growth Mut. Fund, Founders Spl. Mut. Fund, Denver, Moncrief-Lenoir Mfg. Bd. dirs. Goodwill Industries, Houston Grand Opera Assn.; trustee Vanderbilt U., 1972—, Financial Analysts Research Found., 1973-74. Served to lt. (j.g.) USN, 1955-58. Mem. Financial Analysts Fedn. (chmn. bd., chief exec. officer 1973-74, dir. 1969-76, exec. com. 1971-76, Disting. Service award 1978), Inst. Chartered Financial Analysts (trustee 1973-74), Houston Soc. Financial Analysts (pres. 1967-68, dir. 1966-70), Vanderbilt U. Alumni Assn. (dir. 1966-70), Sigma Alpha Epsilon. Presbyn. (elder). Clubs: Harvard Bus. Sch. Houston (pres. 1970-72, dir. 1966-73), Houston Country, Houston Athletic. Home: 3465 Inwood Dr Houston TX 77019 Office: 2150 Two Shell Plaza Houston TX 77002

VAUGHAN, HERBERT EDWARD, educator; b. Ogdensburg, N.Y., Feb. 18, 1911; s. Herbert Emmons and Caroline Ransom (Dillingham) V.; B.S. in Civil Engring., U. Mich., B.S. in Engring. Math., 1932, Ph.D. in Math., 1935; m. Irene Carroll Ford, Sept. 19, 1947; 1 son, Edward Carroll. Mem. faculty Brown U., 1935-36; fellow U. Mich., Ann Arbor, 1936-37; mem. faculty U. Ill., Champaign, 1937—, prof. math., 1960-79, prof. emeritus, 1979—. Mem. Math. Assn. Am., Am. Math. Soc., Assn. Symbolic Logic, Phi Beta Kappa, Sigma Xi. Home: 907 S Vine St Urbana IL 61801

VAUGHAN, JAMES HERBERT, JR., educator; b. Norfolk, Va., July 28, 1927; s. James Herbert and Beatrice (Spence) V.; B.A., U. South, 1950; M.A., U. N.C., 1952; Ph.D., Northwestern U., 1960; m. Ann Maxwell Richard, Sept. 9, 1950; children—Susan Guerry, Frank Richard. Asst. prof. anthropology U. Cin., 1961-64, asso. prof., 1964-67; asso. prof. Ind. U., Bloomington, 1967-70, prof. anthropology, 1970—, chmn. dept., 1969-75, 77—. Served with USCGR, 1945-46, USNR, 1952-62. Ford Found. fellow, 1959-60. Mem. Royal, Am., Central States (pres. 1967) anthrop. assns., Internat. African Inst., African Studies Assn., Alpha Tau Omega. Democrat. Home: 1627 Woodruff Ln Route 3 Bloomington IN 47401

VAUGHAN, JAMES ROLAND, educator; b. Allentown, Pa., June 7, 1928; s. Roland I. and Ann (Griffiths) V.; B.S., Muhlenberg Coll., 1952; M.S., Lehigh U., 1954, Ph.D., 1961; m. Joanne Elaine Evans, Sept. 16, 1950; children—Janice Lynn, Jill Aileen, Jeff Evans. Instr. Muhlenberg Coll., Allentown, 1956-60, asst. prof., 1960-62, asso. prof., 1962-65, prof. biology, 1966—, chmn. dept., 1965—; cons.

water microbiology. Served with USNR, 1946-48. Recipient A.P. Hitchens award Lehigh U., Bethlehem, Pa., 1954; Christian R. and Mary Lindbach Found. award Muhlenberg Coll., 1969. Mem. A.A.A.S., Am. Chem. Soc., Am. Soc. Cell Biology, Am. Soc. Microbiology, Sigma Xi. Republican. Lutheran. Research in mucopolysaccharides, pigmentation in bacteria, water microbiology. Home: 522 N Berks St Allentown PA 18104

VAUGHAN, JAMES SAMSON, mfg. co. exec.; b. Madison, Wis., July 7, 1915; s. Richard English and Amy Eloise (Samson) V.; B.S. in Civil Engring., U. Wis., 1938; postgrad. pub. adminstrn. Syracuse U., 1939-40; m. Kathryn Kuechenmeister, June 6, 1942; children—Frances, James Stephen. With Square D Co., Milw., 1946—, v.p., mgr. distbn. equipment div., 1955-59, v.p., mgr. circuit breaker div., Cedar Rapids, Iowa, 1959-64, mng. dir. Square D Ltd., London, Eng., 1964-69, v.p., group mgr., Milw., 1969-73, v.p., group mgr., Lexington, Ky., 1973-76, v.p. mfg., 1976—; dir. fgn. subsidiaries; dir. W.H. Brady Co., Milw., Chgo. Gear Works. Chmn., Cedar Rapids Urban Renewal Bd., 1961-64. Bd. dirs. United Way of Bluegrass, Lexington, Cedar Rapids YMCA; bd. dirs., v.p. U. Wis. Found. Served to lt. col., Signal Corps, AUS, 1940-46. Decorated Legion of Merit. Mem. Cedar Rapids C. of C. (dir. 1960-63), U. Wis. Alumni Assn. (v.p. 1964—), Am. Guild Organists, Guild Carilloneurs N.Am. Presbyn. (elder). Club: University (Milw.). Home: 21142 N Valley Rd Kildeer IL 60047 Office: Exec Plaza Palatine IL 60067

VAUGHAN, JOHN GEORGE, JR., developer; b. Nanchang, China, Oct. 27, 1911 (parents Am. citizens); s. John George and Daisy (Mathis) V.; B.S. in Mech. Engring., Purdue U., 1934; m. Eleanor Devine Thomas, June 28, 1935; children—Michael Thomas, Anthony Allen. Engring. rep. Am. Radiator Co., 1934-37; specification writer USES, 1938-39; asst. engr., asso. housing mgmt. supr. U.S. Housing Authority, 1939-42; sr. housing specialist Nat. Housing Agy., 1942-44; regional rep., Manhattan area rent dir., regional dir. ops., acting regional rent adminstr. OPA, N.Y.C., 1944-49; dir. devel. Chgo. Housing Authority, 1949-50; cons. engr. and contractor, Chgo., 1951-59; exec. dir. Better Housing League Cin., also Citizens for Better Housing, Washington, 1960-66; housing cons., Washington and Chgo., 1964-78; pres. Va. Devel. Asso., Inc., 1967-78; lectr. Ill. Inst. Tech., 1959-60, U. Cin., 1962, Loyola U., Chgo., 1968-69; cons. ACTION Inc. for Cleve. and Syracuse, N.Y., 1961-65, OEO, 1967-69, UN, 1969; rehab. officer D.C. Dept. Housing and Community Devel., 1971-78; pres. Vaughan Assos., Inc., 1978—; former v.p. Garden Hills Coop. Homes, Inc., Cin., 1963. Former mem. Met. Housing and Planning Council Chgo.; bd. dirs. Nat. Housing Conf.; sec.-treas. Washington Center for Visual Arts, Inc., 1976—; mem. Nat. Com. Against Discrimination in Housing. Registered profl. engr., Ill., D.C., Maine. Mem. ASHRAE, Nat. Trust Historic Preservation, Scabbard and Blade, Pi Tau Sigma, Kappa Sigma. Co-author: Guide to Urban Living, 1963. Contbr. articles to profl. jours. Home: Parker Point Rd Blue Hill ME 04614

VAUGHAN, JOHN THOMAS, veterinarian, educator; b. Tuskegee, Ala., Feb. 6, 1932; s. Henry Asa and Mary (Howard) V.; D.V.M., Auburn U., 1955, M.S., 1963; m. Ethel Evelyn Sell, July 7, 1956; children—John Thomas, Faythe, Michael Sell. Clin. resident U. Pa. Sch. Vet. Medicine, Phila., 1958; instr. Auburn (Ala.) U. Sch. Vet. Medicine, 1955-57, asst. prof., 1959-65, asso. prof., 1965-70, prof., head dept. large animal surgery and medicine, 1974-77, dean Sch. Vet. Medicine, 1977—; prof. vet. surgery, dir. Large Animal Hosp., N.Y. State Vet. Coll., Cornell U., Ithaca, N.Y., 1970-74. Chmn. ofcl. bd. Auburn Meth. Ch., 1968-69; pres. bd. dirs. United Fund, Auburn, 1968-69. Mem. Am. Vet. Med. Assn., Am. Assn. Equine Practitioners (v.p.), Am. Coll. Vet. Surgeons (pres.-elect), Assn. Am. Vet. Med. Colls. (council of deans), Ala. Vet. Med. Assn. Club: Rotary. Co-author textbook; contbr. chpts. to books, articles to profl. jours. Office: Auburn U Sch Vet Medicine Auburn AL 36830

VAUGHAN, JOSEPH BRYAN, communications counsel; b. Toronto, Ont., Can., June 19, 1914; s. Joseph McCarthy and Margaret (Stewart) V.; ed. univ. extension courses; m. Dorothy Truax, Nov. 20, 1937; children—Michael, Seanna, Jonathan, Alan, Julie, Timothy. From copy boy to city editor Toronto Star, 1941; dep. info. dir. Wartime Prices and Trade Bd., 1945; research and promotion dir. Maclean-Hunter, bus. publs., 1946; pres. Pub. & Indsl. Relations Ltd., 1954; pres. Vickers & Benson Ltd., 1966-74, chmn., 1974-76; chmn. Volco Mgmt. Ltd., 1976—. Home: 71 Clarendon Ave Toronto ON M4V 1J2 Canada Office: 22 St Clair E Toronto ON Canada

VAUGHAN, JOSEPH LEE, educator; b. Lynchburg, Va., Jan. 26, 1905; s. Ellis Lee and Anna Margaret (Worley) V.; A.B., U. Va., 1926, A.M., 1927, Ph.D., 1940; m. Ann Cleveland Doner, Aug. 3, 1938; children—Joseph Lee, Ann Ketchum. Instr. English, U. Va., Charlottesville, 1930-32, instr. English dept. engring., 1932-35, asst. prof., 1935-40, asso. prof., 1940-45, prof., 1945—, Joseph L. Vaughan prof. humanities, 1970—, provost, 1956-60, chancellor Community Colls., 1960-66, dir. studies Humanities Inst., 1968-70. Lectr., cons. Inst. Textile Tech., Charlottesville, 1947-56, 74, pres., 1951-53; asso. dir. sch. for tchrs. of English in engring. colls. U. Mich., 1941; prof. humanities Sch. Engring. and Applied Sci.; dir. Nat. Bank & Trust Co., Charlottesville. Mem. information council NSF; cons. Va.-Md. Bankers Assn., Fieldcrest Mills, Consumer Bankers Assn., State Farm Ins. Co., Va. Employment Commn. Recipient Significant Sig award, 1969, Raven award, 1970, Distinguished Prof. award, 1971. Mem. Albemarle Art Assn., Internat. Artists Assn., So. Art Assn., Am. Watercolor Soc., Phi Beta Kappa, Omicron Delta Kappa, Pi Delta Epsilon, Sigma Chi, Raven Soc. Presbyterian. Clubs: Colonnade, Farmington Country. Author: (with W. O. Birk, H. Melvin, F. Holmes) Basic Principles of Writing, 1937, rev. edit., 1943; sect. 19th Century Am. novel in Good Reading (editor H. H. Townsend), 1948; (with E. C. McClintock) Work Manual in English, Oral Communications for the Layman. Editor: English Notes sect. Jour. Engring. Edn., 1936-40, contbr. articles to jour. since 1940; asso. editor Report on Instruction in English in Engineering Colleges in the U.S., 1940; asso. editor and contbr. A Guide to Good Reading, 1942-48. Contbr. to prof. publs. Specialist in communication techniques. Home: 2109 Morris Rd Charlottesville VA 22903

VAUGHAN, JOSEPH ROBERT, dairy food co. exec.; b. Los Angeles, Jan. 28, 1916; s. Vincent B. and Lucille (Eichler) V.; A.B., Loyola U., 1937, LL.B., 1939; m. Margaret Koetters, Jan. 20, 1940; children—Barbara, Christine (Mrs. Roy Graham), Judith. Admitted to bar; mem. firm Vaughan, Brandlin, Robinson & Roemer, 1939-65; v.p. finance Knudsen Creamery Co. of Calif., Los Angeles, 1965, exec. v.p., 1965-69, pres. Knudsen Corp., 1969-71, pres., chief exec. officer, 1971-77, chmn., pres., 1977-78, chmn. bd., 1979—; dir. Los Angeles br. Fed. Res. Bank of San Francisco, 1973, chmn., 1974. Bd. dirs. Los Angeles Beautiful, 1957-65; trustee Pacific Legal Found., 1973—; bd. dirs. Daniel Freeman Hosp., 1955—, sec., 1959-60, pres., 1963-65; chmn. bd. visitors Loyola Law Sch., 1978-79; bd. regents Loyola Marymount U., 1973—. Mem. Calif. State, Los Angeles County bar assns., Am. Arbitration Assn., Nat. Panel of Arbitrators, Los Angeles C. of C. (bd. govs. 1971-73). Club: Rotary (Los Angeles). Home: 404 S Lorraine Los Angeles CA 90020 Office: Knudsen Corp PO Box 2335 TA Los Angeles CA 90051

VAUGHAN, ODIE FRANK, JR., bus. exec.; b. Camden, Ark., Feb. 3, 1936; s. Odie Frank and Bernece (May) V.; student South State Coll., 1954-55; B.S., La. Tech. U., 1959; m. Sandra Kay Beard, Sept. 8, 1962; children—Christopher Michael, Laura Elizabeth. Acct., Peat, Marwick, Mitchell & Co., Dallas, 1959-61; mgr. taxes Murphy Oil Corp., El Dorado, Ark., 1962-72; treas., chief fin. officer Ocean Drilling and Exploration Co., New Orleans, 1973—, v.p., treas., chief fin. officer, 1977—. Mem. Fin. Execs. Inst., Tax Exec. Inst., Am. Petroleum Inst. (chmn. tax com. 1977-78), Am. Inst. C.P.A.'s, Tex. Soc. C.P.A.'s. Baptist. Club: Lions. Home: 546 Topaz New Orleans LA 70124 Office: 1600 Canal St New Orleans LA 70112

VAUGHAN, PATRICK JOSEPH, govt. ofcl.; b. Dodge City, Kans., Mar. 17, 1929; s. John Joseph and Elsie Marie (Kimbrel) V.; B.A., Coll. Idaho, 1953; M.A., Boise State U., 1975; m. Cecelia A. Grove, Aug. 30, 1952; children—Patrick Joseph, II, Katherine M., Bridget A., Molly S. Mgmt. trainee Idaho First Nat. Bank, Boise, 1952-55; treas. City of Boise, 1955-61; profl. relations ofcl. Med. Assn., Boise, 1961-64; dir. profl. and pub. relations Blue Cross of Idaho, Boise, 1964-70; econ. devel. dir. Idaho Office Econ. Opportunity, Boise, 1970-72; spl. asst. to Gov. Cecil D. Andrus, Idaho, 1972-77; fed. co-chmn. Pacific N.W. Regional Commn., Washington, 1977—. Democrat. Roman Catholic. Home: 4098 Hawthorne Way Boise ID 83703 Office: 444 N Capitol St NW Washington DC 20001

VAUGHAN, RALPH THOMAS, airline exec.; b. Halifax, N.S., Can., July 12, 1919; s. Francis William and Lillian (Hemsworth) V.; B.A., St. Mary's U., 1941, LL.D., 1969; LL.B., Dalhousie U., 1944; m. Elinore Gavin, Oct. 28, 1950; children—Gavin, Scott, Martha, Patrick. News editor Halifax Herald (U.S., Can.), 1946-48; admitted to N.S. bar, 1948; partner firm Fielding, O'Hearn & Vaughan, Halifax, 1948-51; exec. asst. to premier N.S., 1951-54; with Canadian Nat. Rys., 1955—, asst. to pres., 1958-62, sec., 1962-66, v.p., sec., 1966—; also sec. subsidiary cos.; sec. Air Canada, 1962-71, v.p., asst. to chmn., 1971-73, pres., 1973-75, sr. v.p. corp. services, 1976-79, sr. v.p. corp. affairs, 1979—. Hon. v.p. Que. Provincial council Boy Scouts Can. Served to capt. Canadian Army, World War II. Decorated Order St. John Jerusalem. Mem. N.S. Barristers Soc. Clubs: St. James of Montreal, Summerlea Golf and Country (Montreal, Que., Can.). Home: 393 Devon Ave Town of Mount Royal Montreal PQ H3R 1C1 Canada Office: Air Canada Place Ville Marie Montreal PQ H3B 3P7 Canada

VAUGHAN, RICHARD PATRICK, clergyman, psychologist; b. Los Angeles, May 26, 1919; s. Vincent B. and Lucille E. (Eichler) V.; A.B., St. Louis U., 1943, M.A., 1945; S.T.L., Alma Coll., 1951; Ph.D., Fordham U., 1956. Clin. psychologist McAuley Clinic, St. Mary's Hosp., San Francisco, 1958-62, dir. psychol. service, 1960-65; prof., chmn. dept. psychology U. San Francisco, 1958-68, dean arts and scis., 1967-69; joined S.J., 1937; ordained priest Roman Catholic Ch., 1950; provincial for edn. Calif. Jesuit Province, 1969-71, regional provincial, 1971-76; adj. prof. Loyola Marymount U., 1977—; research asso. Center Applied Research in Apostolates, 1977. Author: Mental Illness and the Religious Life, 1962; Introduction to Religious Counseling, 1969. Contbr. chpt. to Religious Life in the Church Today, 1962; articles to profl. jours. Address: Loyola Marymount U 7107 W 80th St Los Angeles CA 90045

VAUGHAN, SAMUEL SNELL, editor, publisher; b. Phila., Aug. 3, 1928; s. Joseph and Anna Catherine (Alexander) V.; B.A., Pa. State U., 1951; m. Jo LoBiondo, Oct. 22, 1949; children—Jeffrey Marc, Leslie Jane, Dana Alexander, David Samuel. Deskman, King Features Syndicate, N.Y.C., 1951; asst. mgr. Doubleday Syndicate, 1952-54; advt. mgr. Doubleday & Co., Inc., N.Y.C., 1954-56, sales mgr., 1956-58, sr. editor, 1958-68, exec. editor, 1968-70, pub., pres. pub. div., 1970—, v.p. parent co., 1970—; Bowker lectr., 1976; faculty English dept. Columbia U., 1978—. Served with USMC, 1946-48. Mem. Assn. Am. Pubs. (chmn. edn. for pub. com.). Episcopalian. Clubs: Publishers Lunch; Coffee House, Dutch Treat (N.Y.C.); Tenafly (N.J.) Tennis. Author: (juveniles) Whoever Heard of Kangaroo Eggs?, 1957; New Shoes, 1961; The Two-Thirty Bird, 1965; (history) The Little Church, 1969; (satire) Little Red Hood, 1979; contbr. N.Y. Times, Sunday Times of London, The Writer, other mags. and newspapers. Home: 23 Inness Rd Tenafly NJ 07670 Office: 245 Park Ave New York NY 10017

VAUGHAN, SARAH LOIS, singer; b. Newark, Mar. 27, 1924; d. Asbury and Ada (Baylor) Vaughan; m. Waymon Reed, 1978; singer with orchestras lead by Earl Hines, 1943-44, Billy Eckstein, 1944-45, John Kirby, 1945-46; solo performer and recording artist, 1945—, now with Pablo Records. Recipient numerous Down Beat mag. awards. Address: care James Harper 13063 Ventura Blvd Los Angeles CA 91316

VAUGHAN, THOMAS JAMES GREGORY, historian; b. Seattle, Oct. 13, 1924; s. Daniel George and Kathryn Genevieve (Browne) V.; B.A., Yale U., 1948; M.A., U. Wis., 1950, doctoral residence, 1951-53; Litt.D., Pacific U., 1969; LL.D., Reed Coll., 1975; m. Elizabeth Ann Perpetua Crownhart, June 16, 1951; children—Meagan, Margot, Stephen, Cameron. Dir., Rock County (Wis.) Hist. Soc., 1953-54; exec. dir. Oreg. Hist. Soc., Portland, 1954—, editor-in-chief Oreg. Hist. Quar., 1954—; adj. prof. Portland State U., 1968—; pres., chmn. bd. Salar Enterprises, Ltd.; dir. Am. Heritage Pub. Co., 1976—; film producer, 1958-76; cons. Oreg. Am. Revolution Bicentennial Commn. First chmn. Oreg. State Com. for Humanities, Nat. Endowment for Humanities, 1969—; 1st chmn. Gov.'s Adv. Com. on Historic Preservation Oreg., 1970—, Oreg. Profl. Com. on Teaching of History; sec. Oreg. Geog. Names Bd., 1958—; adviser 1000 Friends of Oreg., 1972—; lay mem. Oreg. State Bar Disciplinary Rev. Bd., 1975—; vice chmn. adv. panel Nat. Endowment for Arts, 1975—; mem. Nat. Hist. Publs. and Records Commn. Matrix, 1975-76. Served with USMC, 1942-45. Decorated comdr. Order Brit. Empire; recipient Aubrey Watzek award Lewis and Clark Coll., 1975; Edith Knight Hill award, 1977; English Speaking Union grantee, 1961. Fellow Royal Geog. Soc.; mem. Am. Assn. State and Local History (dir. 1955-74, pres. 1976—), Am. Assn. Museums (council), Nat. Trust Historic Preservation (adv. council). Clubs: City (bd. govs.), Univ. (bd. govs.) (Portland). Author: A Bibliography of Pacific Northwest History, 1958; A Century of Portland Architecture, 1967; Captain Cook, R.N., The Resolute Mariner: An International Record of Oceanic Discovery, 1974; Portland, A Historical Sketch and Guide, 1976; Voyage of Enlightenment, Malaspina on the Northwest Coast, 1977; editor: Space, Style and Structure: Building in Northwest America, 2 vols., 1974; The Western Shore, 1975; Ascent of the Athabasca Pass, 1978; others. Mem. adv. bd. Am. Heritage Mag., 1977—. Home: 1634 SW Myrtle St Portland OR 97201 Office: 1230 SW Park Ave Portland OR 97205

VAUGHAN, VICTOR CLARENCE, III, physician, educator; b. Toledo, July 19, 1919; s. Warren Taylor and Emma Elizabeth (Heath) V.; A.B., Harvard, 1939, M.D., 1943; m. Deborah Cloud, Dec. 27, 1941; children—Jonathan, Judith (dec.), Sarah Fox, Joanna. Intern Mass. Gen. Hosp., Boston, 1943; resident in pediatrics New Haven Hosp., 1944-47; research fellow in pediatrics Harvard, Children's Hosp., Boston, 1947-49; Instr., then asst. prof. pediatrics Yale Sch. Medicine, 1949-52; asso. prof. pediatrics Temple U. Sch. Medicine, 1952-57, prof., 1964—, chmn. dept., 1964-76; prof., chmn. dept. pediatrics Med. Coll. Ga., Augusta, 1957-64; med. dir. St. Christopher's Hosp. for Children, Phila., 1964-76; sr. fellow Nat. Bd. Med. Examiners, 1977—; cons. Nat. Inst. Child Health and Human Devel., NIH, 1963-70. Diplomate Am. Bd. Pediatrics (dir. 1960-65, 68-73, sec. 1963-65, pres. 1973); sr. fellow Nat. Bd. Med. Examiners, 1977—. Mem. AMA, Am. Pediatric Soc., Soc. for Pediatric Research (v.p. 1964- 65), Am. Acad. Pediatrics, Am. Acad. Allergy, Am. Coll. Allergists, Am. Soc. for Human Genetics, Friends Med. Soc. Mem. Soc. of Friends. Research on hemolytic disease of newborn, childhood allergies, growth and devel. Home: 125 W Walnut Ln Philadelphia PA 19144 Office: Nat Bd Med Examiners 3930 Chestnut St Philadelphia PA 19104

VAUGHEY, WILLIAM MEAGHER, ret. oil producer; b. Marseilles, Ill., Sept. 16, 1904; s. Emmett A. and Margaret Theresa (Meagher) V.; student pub., parochial schs., Albuquerque; m. Genevieve Sara Cowman, Mar. 19, 1932 (dec. Oct. 1966); children—William Meagher, John Cowman, Genevieve Sandra, Patricia; m. 2d, Augusta Pipes Fitzhugh, Oct. 27, 1969. With Philmack Co., also successor Ind. Oil & Gas Co., 1925-30; procurer gas properties Elec. Bond & Share Co., Pa., 1930-32; organizer W. M. Vaughey, Inc., 1932; partner Vaughey & Vaughey in Houston, 1935-39, Jackson, Miss., 1939-73; dir. Deposit Guaranty Bank & Trust Co., Jackson, also v.p. petroleum dept., 1958-73. Chmn. adv. com. St. Dominic's Hosp., 1949-53. Mem. Independent Petroleum Assn. Am. (pres. 1954-55), Am. Petroleum Inst. (dir.), Mid-Continent Oil and Gas Assn. (dir. gen. bd. 1955; pres. Miss.-Ala. div. 1948-50), Nat. Petroleum Council, Gen. Mid-Continent Oil and Gas Assn. (pres. 1963). Clubs: Jackson Petroleum (pres. 1952-53, dir. 1954-55), Univ., Jackson Country (dir. 1962). Home: 7 Eastbrooke Jackson MS 39216

VAUGHN, CHARLES MELVIN, zoologist; b. Deadwood, S.D., Nov. 23, 1915; s. Roy Francis and May (Smith) V.; B.A., U. Ill., 1939, M.A. (scholar zoology 1939-40), 1940; Ph.D., U. Wis., 1943; m. Mattie Christine Isaacson, Sept. 6, 1941; children—Martha Frances, Richard Charles. Asst. prof., then asso. prof. zoology Miami U., Oxford, Ohio, 1946-51, prof., chmn. dept. zoology and physiology, 1965-71, prof., 1971—, chmn. dept. zoology, 1971-78, acting dean research, 1970-71; instr. parasitology Inst. Tropical Medicine, Bowman Gray Sch. Medicine, 1950-52, sr. parasitologist, 1950-52, asso dir. inst., 1951-52; sr. parasitologist, asso. dir. field service unit Am. Found. Tropical Medicine, N.Y.C., 1952-53; prof. zoology, head dept. U. S.D., 1953-61, prof., chmn. dept., 1961-64, dir. NSF acad. year inst. sci. and math. tchrs. at univ., 1958-64; program dir. coll. and elementary tchr. program inst. sect. NSF, Washington, 1964-65, program dir. acad. year research tng., 1965, cons., 1965-69; biology specialist AID, 1966, 67. China Med. Bd. fellow, C.A., summer 1956. Served to maj., San. Corps, AUS, 1943-46; now col. AUS (ret.). Fellow AAAS, Ohio Acad. Sci. (pres. 1977-78), Royal Soc. Tropical Medicine and Hygiene; mem. Am. Soc. Zoologists, Am. Soc. Parasitologists, Am. Microscopical Soc. (pres. 1972-73), Soc. Protozoologists, Am. Soc. Tropical Medicine and Hygiene, Assn. Acads. Sci. (pres. 1971-72), S.D. Acad. Sci. (pres. 1961-62), Assn. Midwestern Coll. Biology Tchrs., Wis. Acad. Scis., Arts and Letters, Res. Officers Assn., Brit. Soc. Parasitologists, Phi Beta Kappa, Sigma Xi, Phi Kappa Phi, Phi Sigma, Kappa Delta Pi, Gamma Alpha, Alpha Phi Omega. Presbyterian. Mason, Lion. Home: 6295 Devonshire Dr Oxford OH 45056

VAUGHN, DORRIS WELDON, utilities exec.; b. Sturgis, Ky., May 25, 1909; s. Guy L. and Pearl (Woodring) V.; B.S., U. Evansville, 1931; m. Alma R. Schuessler, Oct. 14, 1939; 1 dau., Laurel. Engr., Mead Johnson & Co., Evansville, Ind., 1931-35; truck salesman Hartmetz Bros., Evansville, 1935-37; agt. Sun Life Assurance Co., Evansville, 1937-41; engr., asst. gen. supt. T.H.M. Electric Co., Evansville, 1941-45; mgr. quality control, mgr. indsl. and community relations, gen. mgr. ice maker component div. Whirlpool Corp., Evansville, 1945-64; v.p., gen. mgr., pres., chmn. bd., chief exec. officer So. Ind. Gas & Electric Co., Evansville, 1964—; dir. Citizens Nat. Bank, Internat. Steel Co., Geo. Koch Sons, Ind. World Trade Center, Ohio Valley Electric Co., Ind.-Ky. Electric Co. Bd. dirs., v.p. Deaconess Hosp., Evansville Indsl. Found., Tri-State Regional Health Planning Council; chmn. bd. dirs. Historic New Harmony; bd. dirs. Evansville's Future, Evansville Goodwill Industries, Harmonie Assos., New Harmony, Ind., Ind. Sch. Religion, Vanderburgh County United Fund; mem. state of Ind. Commn. on New Harmony; chmn., trustee Ind. Vocat. Tech. Coll., S.W. Region; chmn. adv. bd. Salvation Army; mem. planning council Evansville Philharmonic Orch.; adv. council Evansville center Ind. U. Med. Sch.; trustee Robert G. Blaffer Trust, New Harmony. Mem. IEEE (life), Ind. (dir., v.p.), Evansville (dir., past pres.) chambers commerce, Ind. Electric Assn. (dir., past pres.), Ind. (pres., dir.), Midwest (dir.) gas assns. Mem. United Ch. of Christ. Elk. Home: Rural Route 8 Browning Rd Evansville IN 47711 Office: 2024 NW 4th St Evansville IN 47741

VAUGHN, JACK JOSEPH, hotel exec.; b. Portland, Oreg., Nov. 1, 1937; s. Jacob Joseph and Katherine Theresa (Gette) V.; student San Diego State Coll., 1958; degree Lewis Hotel Sch., 1959; student Portland State Coll., 1960-63; children by previous marriage—John Douglas, Deborah Ann. With Western Internat. Hotels, 1959-73, gen. mgr. Continental Plaza, Chgo., 1967-71, gen. mgr. Century Plaza, Los Angeles, 1971-73; mng. dir. Royal Inns Am., San Diego, 1974; gen. mgr. Opryland Hotel, Nashville, 1975—; v.p. WSM, Inc., Nashville, 1975—, also dir.; dir. Opryland U.S.A. Talent Agy.; mem. adv. bd. U. Tenn. at Knoxville Hotel and Restaurant Sch., 1979. Trustee Alcuin Montessori Sch., Chgo., 1969-72. Served to sgt. USMC, 1955-59. Recipient award Kiwanis, Los Angeles, 1967, Lions, Chgo., 1970, Hotel Sales Mgmt. Assn., Las Vegas, Nev., 1972, Boy Scouts Am., Los Angeles, 1973. Mem. Nashville Hotel and Motel Assn. (dir.), Tenn. Hotel and Motel Assn. (v.p.), Nashville C. of C. (gov. 1978—). Roman Catholic. Club: SKAL of Nashville. Home: 3806 Moss Rose Dr Nashville TN 37216 Office: 2800 Opryland Dr Nashville TN 37214

VAUGHN, JOHN ROLLAND, banker; b. Iola, Kans., Aug. 4, 1938; s. Ralph H. and Alice (Dille) V.; B.S. in Bus., Emporia State U., 1960; m. Doris K. Black, Sept. 4, 1960; children—Lisa Ann, Brian Douglas. Sr. auditor Arthur Andersen & Co., Kansas City, Mo., 1961-66; auditor First Nat. Bank Kansas City, 1966-69; auditor Commerce Bancshares, Inc., 1969-73; sr. v.p. Adminstrv. Services div. Peoples Trust Bank, Ft. Wayne, Ind., 1973-77; dep. gen. auditor, v.p. Crocker Nat. Bank, San Francisco, 1978-79; v.p., gen. auditor S.W. Bancshares, Houston, 1980—. Treas., Overland Park (Kans.) Jr. C. of C., 1965-66; outside dir. Overland Park Credit Union; controller Fort Wayne Bicentennial Commn., 1974-77. Mem. Mo. Air N.G., 1961-67. Mem. Inst. Internal Auditors (1st v.p. Kansas City 1969-70, pres. 1970-71, midwest regional v.p. 1971-72), Fin. Execs. Inst. (dir. Ft. Wayne 1976-77), Bank Adminstrn. Inst., Nat. Assn. Accts., Hartsmen, Soc. Preservation and Encouragement Barber Shop Quartet Singing in Am., Sigma Tau Gamma. Home: 505 Mt Davidson Ct Clayton CA 94517

VAUGHN, JOHN VERNON, banker, industrialist; b. Grand Junction, Colo., June 24, 1909; s. John S. and Alice Ann (Baylis) V.; A.B., U. Calif. at Los Angeles, 1932; m. Dorothy May Pickrell, Oct. 12, 1934; children—Dorothy (Mrs. Richard H. Stone), John Spencer.

Br. mgr. Nat. Lead Co., 1932-37; sales mgr. Sillers Paint & Varnish Co., 1937-46, pres., gen. mgr., dir., 1946-58; pres., chmn. Dartell Labs., Inc., 1959-70; vice chmn. bd. Crocker Nat. Bank and Crocker Nat. Corp., San Francisco, 1970-75, dir., 1970—; cons. Coopers & Lybrand, 1975—; dir. Pacific Lighting Corp., Calif. Fed. Savs. & Loan, O.K. Earl Corp., Forest Lawn Corp., IT Corp. Chmn. San Marino Recreation Commn., 1956-58; chmn. citizen's adv. Council Pub. Transp., 1965-67; commr. Los Angeles Coliseum Commn., 1971—; trustee Calif. Mus. Found., 1973—; bd. dirs. Orthopaedic Hosp., 1965—, pres., 1974-78, chmn. bd., 1978—; bd. dirs. YMCA, Los Angeles, 1965-77, Central City Assn., So. Calif. Visitors Council, 1970-76, NCCJ, Calif. Museum Sci. and Industry, Los Angeles County Heart Assn., Friends of Claremont Coll., 1973-78, Los Angeles Beautiful, 1972-74; regent U. Calif., 1958-59, Forest Lawn Meml. Park, 1968—; trustee U. Calif. at Los Angeles Found., 1967—, Claremont Men's Coll., 1970-71, Pepperdine U., 1972—; mem. bd. visitors Grad. Sch. Bus. Adminstrn. U. Calif. at Los Angeles, 1971—. Recipient Distinguished Service award U. Calif. at Los Angeles, 1965, Outstanding Community Service award, 1970, Alumnus of Year award, 1971; Brotherhood award NCCJ, 1971, Los Angeles Jaycees award merit, 1972, Most Distinguished Citizen, Los Angeles Realty Bd., 1972, other honors. Mem. Los Angeles Area C. of C. (bd. dirs. 1961, pres. 1969, chmn. 1970), World Affairs Council (chpt. v.p., treas. 1970—), Iranian-Am. Chamber Industry and Commerce (pres. 1971—), Paint, Varnish and Lacquer Assn. (past nat. v.p., past chpt. pres.), Town Hall Calif. (dir. 1973-75), Beta Theta Pi (pres. 1960). Presbyn. Mason. Clubs: Jonathan (pres. 1964), Los Angeles Country, California; (Los Angeles); San Gabriel (Calif.) Country (dir. 1964-68). Home: 1199 Sherwood Rd San Marino CA 91108 Office: 1000 W 6th St Los Angeles CA 90017

VAUGHN, KENNETH WILLARD, corp. exec.; b. Rushville, Ill., July 11, 1910; s. Chester J. and Mabel (Briggs) V.; B. Edn., Western Ill. U., 1937; M.A., State U. Ia., 1939, Ph.D., 1941; m. Estel M. Boyd, Oct. 7, 1933; children—Kenneth W., Lucy Anne, Paul M. Tchr. pub. schs., Ill., State U. Iowa, 1928-41; instr., research asso., dir. Carnegie Found. Advancement Teaching, N.Y.C., 1942-48; research dir., lectr. Grad. Sch. Edn., Harvard, 1948-50; partner Rohrer, Hibler & Replogle, mgmt. cons., N.Y.C., 1950-62; chmn. exec. com., dir. Ansul Co., Marinette, Wis., 1958-67, exec. v.p., 1964-67; pres. Ansul Internat. Corp., 1963-67; pres. Mgmt. EPD, Inc., Hyde Park, N.Y., 1968—. Pres. Hunting Hall Fame Found., 1972—, Am. Hunting Found., 1973—. mem. People-to-People Sports Council. Mem. Am. Psychol. Assn., AAAS. Home: PO Box 1493 Camino del Norte Rancho Santa Fe CA 92067 Suite 201 Pickfair Bldg PO 1493 Rancho Santa Fe CA 92067. *From early life I have been guided by three considerations: the conservation and development of America's resources—manpower and physical resources; education of our people, both youth and adult; and leadership within our major professions and industrial efforts and work. A personal goal: Study, Work, and Restudy!*

VAUGHN, ROBERT, (Francis), actor; b. N.Y.C., Nov. 22, 1932; s. Walter and Marcella Vaughn; B.S. in Theatre Arts, 1956, also M.A., Los Angeles State Coll.; Ph.D. in Communications, U. So. Calif., 1970; m. Linda Staab, 1974; 1 son, Cassidy. Appeared in local Calif. stage prodn. End as a Man, then small roles in several motion pictures; appeared as Napoleon Solo on TV in The Man From U.N.C.L.E., 1964-67; appeared in motion pictures Hell's Crossroads, 1957, No Time to be Young, 1957, Unwed Mother, 1958, Good Day for a Hanging, 1959, The Young Philadelphians, 1959, The Big Show, 1961, The Caretakers, 1963, To Trap a Spy, 1966, The Spy With My Face, 1966, One Spy Too Many, 1966, The Venetian Affair, 1967, The Bridge at Remagen, 1969, If It's Tuesday, This Must Be Belgium, 1969, The Towering Inferno, 1974, Bullitt, 1968, The Mind of Mr. Soames, 1970, The Assassination of Julius Caesar, The Statue, 1971, The Magnificent 7, 1960; stage appearances as Hamlet at Pasadena Playhouse, 1964; star one-man play F.D.R., 1978; portrayed Harry Truman in TV play The Man From Independence, 1974, Woodrow Wilson in TV movie Backstairs at the White House, 1979; appeared in TV mini-series Washington: Behind Closed Doors, 1977. Former chmn. registration and Speaker's Bur., Calif. Democratic Com. Recipient Acad. Motion Picture Arts and Scis. nomination for role in The Young Philadelphians, 1960. Mem. Am. Acad. Polit. and Social Scis. Democrat. Roman Catholic. Author: Only Victims, 1971. Address: care Internat Creative Mgmt 8899 Beverly Blvd Hollywood CA 90048*

VAUGHN, ROBERT ALLEN, lawyer; b. Dover, Ohio, Mar. 2, 1930; s. Charles Franklin and Bernice (Ralph) V.; A.B., Miami U., Oxford, Ohio, 1953; J.D., U. Mich., 1959; m. Clara Emma Morris, Nov. 25, 1953; children—Jonathan Ross, Robert Allen. Admitted to Ohio bar, 1959, N.J. bar, 1961; asso. firm Baker, Hostetler & Patterson, Cleve., 1959; clk., sr. judge appelate div. Superior Ct. N.J., 1959-61; practice in Springfield, Ohio, 1961—; partner Martin, Browne, Hull & Harper, 1967—. Bd. dirs. Mid-Ohio Health Planning Fedn., Clark Health Planning Council, Planned Parenthood Center; chmn. bd. dirs. Community Hosp. Springfield and Clark County. Served with USN, 1953-56. Mem. Phi Delta Theta. Club: Rotary. Home: 292 Brighton Rd Springfield OH 45504 Office: First Nat Bank Bldg Springfield OH 45502

VAUGHN, RUFUS MAHLON, psychiatrist; b. Ensley, Ala., Oct. 31, 1924; s. Rufus Samuel and Anna Martina (Fink) V.; student U. Mich., 1942-43, 46-47; A.B., Birmingham So. Coll., 1949; M.D., Med. Coll. Ala., 1953; children—Stephen Andrew, Alexander. Intern, USPHS Hosp., San Francisco, 1953-54; resident in psychiatry Ind. U. Hosp., Indpls., 1954-56, U. Calif. Hosp. at Los Angeles, 1956-57; dir. psychiatry Student Health Service, U. Mass., Amherst, 1958-59; researcher Boston State Hosp., 1959-61; asso. prof. psychiatry U. Fla., Gainesville, 1961-70; dir. Palm Beach County Mental Health Center, West Palm Beach, Fla., 1970-71; med. dir. Lake Hosp. and Clinic, Lake Worth, Fla., 1971-73; dir. tng., research So. Fla. State Hosp., Hollywood, 1973-74, supt., 1974; chief Bur. Mental Hosp. Services, Fla. Div. Mental Health, Tallahassee, 1974-75; pvt. practice medicine specializing in psychiatry, West Palm Beach, 1975—. Clin. prof. psychiatry U. Miami, 1973-75. Served with USNR, 1943-46. Diplomate Am. Bd. Psychiatry and Neurology (examiner 1974-75). Fellow Am. Psychiat. Assn.; mem. Am. Coll. Psychiatrists. Home: 3218 Spruce Ave West Palm Beach FL 33407 Office: 1897 Palm Beach Lakes Blvd West Palm Beach FL 33409

VAUGHN, THOMAS HUNT, chem. corp. exec.; b. Clay, Ky., Nov. 11, 1909; s. George Leamon and Beulah (Hunt) V.; B.S., U. Notre Dame, 1931, M.S., 1932, Ph.D., 1934; m. Ruby Wentworth, Sept. 13, 1930; children—Jolan Adele, Vicki Lee, Trudy Gail. Vice pres. Vitox Labs., 1933-34; head dept. organic research Union Carbide and Carbon Research Labs., Niagara Falls, N.Y., 1934-39; dir. organic research Mich. Alkali Co., Wyandotte, Mich., 1939-43; dir. research J. B. Ford Co., 1939-41, merged with Mich. Alkali, 1943, asst. dir. research of successor co., Wyandotte Chems. Corp., 1943-48, dir. research, 1948-49, v.p., 1949-53; v.p. Colgate-Palmolive Co., Jersey City, 1953-57; exec. v.p. Pabst Brewing Co., 1957—; pres. Myzon Labs., 1959-62; pres. Vaughn Assos., Inc., 1962—; v.p. planning and devel. Escambia Chems. Corp., 1966-68; pres. Thomas H. Vaughn & Co., 1962—. Mem. Scandinavian Research and Industry Tour, 1946; cons. to Sec. of Navy, Quartermaster Gen. of Army, 1943-53; mem. governing com. Ann. Conf. on Adminstrn. Research, 1950—, exec. com., 1952-58, conf. chmn., 1955; pres. tech. sect. on detergents, 1st World Conf. on Detergents, Paris, 1954; adv. bd. Office of Critical Tables, Nat. Acad. Scis., 1956; adv. bd. Coll. Sci. and Engring., U. Notre Dame, 1956—. Pres., Indsl. Research Inst., 1958; tech. cons. UN, 1970—. Mem. Am. Chem. Soc., Am. Inst. Chem. Engrs., Am. Inst. Chemists, Am. Oil Chemists Soc., AAAS, Engring. Soc. Detroit, Sigma Xi, Tau Beta Pi. Club: Chemist. Editor: Research Mgmt., 1958-69. Contbr. articles to profl. publs. Patentee in field. Home: 207 Jolly Roger Way Waretown NJ 08758

VAUGHT, JACK THOMAS, mgmt. cons.; b. Birmingham, Ala., June 16, 1908; s. Luther Vernon and Minnie (Hudgins) V.; student Tex. Christian U., 1942-43; grad. certificate, Am. Inst. Banking, 1931; student Rutgers U., Grad. Sch. Banking, 1949-50; m. Abbie Sue Dalton, May 31, 1938; 1 son, John Raymond. With First Nat. Bank, Ft. Worth, 1926-73, sr. v.p., cashier, until 1973; mgmt. cons. J.T. Vaught & Assos., Fort Worth, 1973—; tchr. banking courses Am. Inst. Banking. Served with AUS, 1943-45. Mem. Adminstrv. Mgmt. Soc. Ft. Worth (past pres.), Ft. Worth Personnel and Indsl. Relations Soc. (past pres.), Ft. Worth C. of C. Methodist. Mason. Home: 4013 Scenery Hill Ct Fort Worth TX 76103

VAUGHT, JAMES BENJAMIN, army officer; b. Conway, S.C., Nov. 3, 1926; s. John M. and Ruth (Thompson) V.; B.B.A., Ga. State Coll., 1960; M.S., George Washington U., 1966; grad. Nat. War Coll., 1967; m. Winifred V., Mar. 23, 1979; children—Cathryn A., James B. Jr., Stephen P. Commd. 2d lt. U.S. Army, 1946, advanced through grades to maj. gen., 1975; service in Ger., Japan, Korea, Vietnam and Turkey; comdr. 1st Corps Support Command, Ft. Bragg, N.C., 1971-73; chief staff XVIII Airborne Corps, Ft. Bragg, 1973-74; asst. div. comdr. 82d Airborne Div., Ft. Bragg, 1974-75; chief staff Allied Land Forces Southeastern Europe, Izmir, Turkey, 1975-77; comdr. 24th Inf. Div., Fort Stewart, Ga., 1977—. Decorated Silver Star with oak leaf cluster, Legion of Merit with 2 oak leaf clusters, D.F.C., Soldiers medal, Bronze Star with oak leaf cluster, Meritorious Service medal, Air medal (5), Joint Service Commendation medal, Army Commendation medal with oak leaf cluster, Purple Heart, Combat Inf. badge; Gallantry cross with silver star (2), Armed Forces Honor medal 1st class (2) (Vietnam). Home: 5206 Taro Leaf Circle Fort Stewart GA 31313 Office: Hdqrs 24th Inf Div Fort Stewart GA 31313

VAUPEL, MICHAEL CHRISTIAN, mfg. co. exec.; b. N.Y.C., May 30, 1936; s. Karl and Katherine Alice (Tuohy) V.; B.S., Holy Cross Coll., 1958; M.B.A., City U. N.Y., 1965; m. Jeanne Frances Shinners, Oct. 15, 1961; children—Juliet, Michael, Maureen. Supr., Touche Ross & Co., N.Y.C., 1961-65; v.p., controller Hewitt Robins, Inc., Stanford, Conn., 1965-70; corp. controller Norris Industries, Inc., Los Angeles, 1970—, v.p., 1973—; instr. bus. adminstrn. Saddleback Coll., 1976—. Served to 1st lt. USMCR, 1958-61. C.P.A., N.Y. Mem. Am. Inst. C.P.A.'s, Financial Execs. Inst., Am. Mgmt. Assn., Newcomen Soc. N.Am. Republican. Roman Catholic. Club: Niguel Country (Laguna Niguel, Calif.). Home: 74 Monarch Bay Laguna Niguel CA 92677 Office: One Golden Shore Long Beach CA 90802

VAUPEN, BURTON, advt. exec.; b. N.Y.C., Apr. 28, 1930; s. Alex and Betty (Stimell) V.; B.S., Columbia, 1952; M.A., Columbia Tchrs. Coll., 1954; children—Robert, Susan, Pamela, Jill; 1 stepson, Paul. Asst. dir. NBC, N.Y.C., 1953-54; researcher Benton & Bowles Advt., N.Y.C., 1954-56; with Young & Rubicam Inc., 1956—, mgr. adminstrn., San Francisco, 1958-69, sr. v.p., dir. domestic bus. affairs, N.Y.C., 1969-79, sr. v.p., treas., 1979—, sr. v.p. fin. and adminstrn. Y&R Affiliates, Inc. div., 1979—; dir. Aero-Flow Dynamics, Inc., N.Y.C. Home: Saddle River NJ 07458 Office: 285 Madison Ave New York NY 10017

VAUX, HENRY JAMES, forest economist, educator; b. Bryn Mawr, Pa., Nov. 6, 1912; s. George and Mary (James) V.; B.S., Haverford Coll., 1933; M.S., U. Calif., 1935; Ph.D., 1948; m. Jean Macduff, Jan. 11, 1937; children—Henry J., Alice J. Forest engr. Crown Willamete Paper Co., Portland, Oreg., 1936-37; instr. Sch. Forestry, Oreg. State Coll., Corvallis, 1937-42; asso. economist La. Agrl. Expt. Stat., Baton Rouge, 1942-43; economist U.S. Forest Service, Washington, also Berkeley, Calif., 1946-48; lectr. Sch. Forestry, U. Calif. at Berkeley, 1948-50, asso. prof., 1950-53, prof., 1953-78, prof. emeritus, 1978—, dean, 1955-65, asst. dir. Agrl. Expt. Sta., 1955-65; dir. Wildland Research Center, 1955-65; chmn. Calif. Bd. Forestry, 1976—. Served from ensign to lt. (j.g.), USNR, 1943-46. Fellow A.A.A.S., Soc. Am. Foresters; mem. Forest History Soc. (dir. 1971-75), Sigma Xi, Xi Sigma Pi. Mem. Soc. of Friends. Author tech. articles, bulls. Home: 622 San Luis Rd Berkeley CA 94707

VAVALA, DOMENIC ANTHONY, med. scientist, educator, ret. air force officer; b. Providence, Feb. 1, 1925; s. Salvatore and Maria (Grenci) V.; B.A., Brown U., 1947; M.S., U. R.I., 1950; M.A., Trinity U., San Antonio, 1954; Ph.D. in Physiology, Accademia di Studi Superiori Minerva, Italy, 1957; M.Ed., U. Houston, 1958; D.Sc. (hon), Nobile Accademia di Santa Teodora Imperatrice, Rome, Italy, 1966, D.M.S., 1970; D. Pedagogy, Studiorum Universitas Constantiniana of Sovrano Ordine Constantiniano di San Giorgio, Rome, 1966; D.Ed., Imperiale Accademia di San Crillo, Pomenzia, Italy, 1977. Research asst. tumor research U. R.I., also asst. entomol. research, 1950; research asst. pharmacology Boston U. Sch. Medicine, 1950-51; commd. 2d lt. med. service USAF, 1951, advanced through grades to lt. col., 1968; physiologist cold injury research team Army Med. Research Lab., Osaka (Japan) Army Hosp., 1951-52; research aviation physiologist USAF Sch. Aviation Medicine, Randolph AFB, Tex., 1952-54; research aviation physiologist 3605th USAF Hosp., Ellington AFB, Tex., 1955-57, chief physiol. tng., 1957; writer, producer TV Series, Your Body in Flight, sta. KUHT, Houston, 1956, Highway to Health series, Okinawa, 1965; cons. aviation physiology, film prodn. dept. U. Houston, 1956; research aviation physiologist, head acad. sect. dept. physiol. tng. USAF Hosp., Lackland AFB, Tex., 1957-58; vis. prof. physiology Incarnate World Coll., San Antonio, 1958; research aviation physiologist, chief physiol. tng. comdr. 832d Physiol. Tng. Flight, 832d Tactical Hosp., Cannon AFB, N.Mex., 1958-65; adj. faculty mem. Eastern N.Mex. U., Portales, 1959-64; instr. adult edn. div. Clovis (N.Mex.) municipal schs., 1960; research aviation physiologist, comdr. 15th Physiol. Tng. Flight, 824th USAF Dispensary, Kadena Air Base, Okinawa, 1965-66; research scientist, directorate fgn. tech., aerospace med. div. Brooks AFB, Tex., 1966-68, chief, research and devel. support and interface div., dep. dir. for fgn. tech., 1968-70; adj. faculty mem., asst. prof. humanities, coordinator biomed. and behavioral scis. Day Coll. div., psychology coordinator vets. div. Coll. Continuing Edn., asso. dean adj. faculty, dean faculty, coordinator academic devel., prof. nutrition and dietetics Johnson and Wales Coll., Providence, 1973—. Trustee, Gov. Center Sch., Providence, 1979—. Served with AUS, 1943-44. Recipient Distinguished Service award Clovis Jr. C. of C., 1959; academician div. scis. Accademia di Studi Superiori Minerva, 1960, also recipient Academic Palms Gold medal, 1960; decorated Air Force Commendation medal, Certificate of Achievement, Dept. Army, 1966, Knight Grand Officer Merit Class, knight of Grand Cross Justice Class, Sovereign Constantinian Order St. George, Italy; recipient citation from chief chaplains USAF, 1970, chief insignia, biomed. scis. corps, 1970. academician, Nobile Accademia di Santa Teodora Imperatrice, Rome, 1967, appointed Minister Plenipotentiry to U.S., 1967; named Magnificus Rector Studiorum Universitas Constantiniana, Italy. Fellow AAAS, Tex. Acad. Sci., Royal Soc. Health, Am. Inst. Chemists; mem. Assn. Mil. Surgeons U.S., Royal Soc. Health, Nat. Assn. Doctors U.S. (founder 1958, sec. treas. 1958—, exec. council 1958—), Accademia di San Cirillo Italy (hon.), Phi Sigma, Kappa Delta Pi, Phi Kappa Phi. Editor-in-chief NADUS Jour., 1963—. Compiled and edited Fifty Years of Progress of Soviet Medicine, 1917-67. Abstractor Am. Chem. Soc., 1963-74. Contbr. articles to profl. jours. Home: 210 Wentworth Ave Providence RI 02905

VAWTER, MARVIN L(EE), govt. adminstr.; B.A. in English and Theatre, U. Cin., 1962, M.A. in English Lit., 1966; Ph.D., U. Wis., Madison, 1970; participating fellow Harvard U. Inst. Ednl. Mgmt., 1976; cert. U. Chgo. Inst. Fund-Raising and Devel., 1975; married. Tchr. English and speech Anderson High Sch., Cin., 1962-64; teaching fellow in English, U. Cin., 1964-66, lectr. in theatre, dir. summer theatre inst. and summer theatre program, 1966; teaching asst., quiz sect. instr. U. Wis., 1966-68, master tchr. asst., 1968-69; asst. prof. English, U. Ill., 1969-74, asst. to v.p. for acad. affairs and public services, 1974-76; exec. dir. Ill. Humanities Council, Nat. Endowment for Humanities, Champaign, 1973—; speaker, lectr. in field for civic groups, univ. faculties, radio, TV; mem. Spl. Task Force on Arts in Edn. State Ill.; bd. advs. Georgetown (Ky.) Coll.; cons. in field. Mem. precinct com., Champaign, Ill. Recipient Undergrad. Instructional award U. Ill., 1971, named Excellent Tchr. and to Top Tchrs. on Campus, 1971, 72, 73; Ford Found. summer fellow, 1968; U. Ill. faculty fellow, 1970. Mem. Lambda Chi Alpha (dir. chpt., mem. nat. scholarship commn.). Research, publs. on Shakespeare; producer indsl., acad. media packages; designed numerous ednl. forums and symposia for adult edn. Ill. Home: 8 Briar Hill Circle Champaign IL 61820 Office: 201 W Springfield St Suite 205 Champaign IL 61820. *The Renaissance idea of the whole man who serves his fellowman while improving himself is my ideal. But ideals are like elusive butterflies.*

VAYDA, ANDREW PETER, educator; b. Budapest, Hungary, Dec. 7, 1931; s. Sándor and Zelma (Szentgyörgyi) Vajda; A.B., Columbia, 1952, Ph.D., 1956; m. Cherry Lowman, June 9, 1962 (div. Apr. 1976); 1 dau., Andrea. Lectr. anthropology U. B.C., 1958-60; asst. prof. Columbia U., 1960-64, asso. prof., 1964-68, prof., 1968-72, dir. human ecology tng. program, 1967-72; prof. anthropology and ecology Rutgers U., 1972—. Bd. dirs. Social Sci. Research Council. Fellow Am. Anthropol. Assn., A.A.A.S.; mem. Assn. Social Anthropologists, Man and Biosphere Program Directorate, Polynesian Soc. Author: Maori Warfare, 1960; War in Ecological Perspective, 1976. Editor: Man, Culture, and Animals (with Anthony Leeds), 1965; Peoples and Cultures of the Pacific, 1968; Environment and Cultural Behavior, 1969; Human Ecology: An Interdisciplinary Jour. Address: Human Ecology Cook Coll PO Box 231 Rutgers U New Brunswick NJ 08903

VAZAN, WILLIAM JOSEPH, artist; b. Toronto, Ont., Can., Nov. 18, 1933; s. John Joseph and Mary (Stochmal) V.; student Ont. Coll. Art, Ecole de Beaux Arts, Paris; B.A., Sir George Williams U. (Can.); m. Marthe Lise Perras, July 23, 1960; children—Danielle, Nathalie. represented in permanent collections: Musee des Beaux Arts, Montreal, Art Gallery Ont., Toronto, Power Gallery Contemporary Art, Sydney, Australia, Musee d'Art Contemporain, Montreal, Phila. Mus. Art, Compagnie Petroliere Imperiale Ltee, Toronto, Banque d'Art du Conseil du Canada, Ottawa, Ont., Galerie Nationale du Canada, Ottawa, Loyola de Montreal, Agnes Etherington Art Centre, Kingston, Ont., Ministeres des Affaires Exterieures, Ottawa, Ministere des Travaux Pulics, Terrebonne, Que., York U., Toronto, Teleglobe Can., Air Can., 1976 Olympics, Montreal, Can. Fed. Dept. Public Works, Ottawa, also pvt. collections; prof. Concordia U., Montreal. Can. Council grantee; Que. Dept. Cultural Affairs grantee. Mem. Conseil de la Peinture du Que., Conseil de la Sculpture du Que. Author: Worldline, 1971; Contacts, 1973.

VAZQUEZ, ALBERTO M., educator, former fgn. service officer; b. Yabucoa, P.R., Mar. 25, 1901; s. Modesto and Cristina (Rivera) V.; A.B., U. Idaho, 1925, A.M., 1926; postgrad. U. Florence, Italy, 1933. U. Paris, 1934; Ph.D. (Sterling fellow, Rockefeller grant), Yale, 1935; m. Hildegarde Wanous, Aug. 29, 1934; 1 son, Alberto Wanous. Instr. Romance langs. and lit. U. Idaho, 1925-31; instr. Romance langs. and lit. Dartmouth Coll., 1935-37, asst. prof., 1937-42; lectr. Spanish Am. lit. George Washington U., 1945-56; chief translator Dept. State, 1942-43, cons., research analyst OSS, 1943-44, sect. chief Office Internat. Information and Cultural Affairs, 1945-47, specialist Inter-Am. affairs, acting sect. chief div. research for Am. Republics, 1947-54, sect. chief div. research, 1954-56; fgn. service officer, 1956-61; 1st sec., consul, polit. officer Am. embassy, Mexico City, 1956-60; officer in charge Latin Am. area planning staff Bur. Ednl. and Cultural Affairs, 1960-61; vis. prof. Center Latin Am. Studies, Tulane U., New Orleans, 1962-77, prof. emeritus, 1977—, acting chmn. dept. Spanish and Portuguese, 1973, prof. charge Tulane-Newcomb jr. year abroad, Paris, France, 1974-75; vis. prof. Spanish and Spanish-Am. lit. Pan Am. U., Edinburg, Tex., 1977-79; vis. lectr. Loyola U., New Orleans; U.S. rep. OAS com. for cultural action, 1962-70, chmn. com., 1965-70; alternate U.S. mem. Inter Am. Indian Inst., 1957-59; directing council Inter-Am. Inst. Geography and History, 1959, conf. on financial and econ. control Hot Springs, Va., 1942, UNESCO Assembly, Paris, 1946; del. 3d meeting Inter-Am. Cultural Council, San Juan, P.R., 1959, 4th meeting, Washington, 1966, 5th meeting, Maracay, Venezuela, 1968, 6th meeting, Port of Spain, Trinidad and Tabago, 1969. Decorated Order of Petion-Bolivar, Haiti, Order Palmes Academiques, France. Mem. Phi Beta Kappa. Co-Author: Cartas de Don Diego de Mendoza, 1935; Spanish Grammar, 1940; Brief Spanish Course for Beginners, 1943. Editor Spanish publs. Home: 1436 N Inglewood St Arlington VA 22205

VAZQUEZ, JACINTO JOSE, educator, scientist; b. Havana, Cuba, Aug. 17, 1923; s. Francisco J. and Ramona (Lopez) V.; M.D., U. Havana Sch. Medicine, 1948; M.S., Ohio State U., 1954; m. Martha Delia Sierra, Aug. 19, 1948; children—Flavia (Mrs. Hanna Sarji), Rachel. Asso. mem. Scripps Clinic and Research Found., La Jolla, Calif., 1961-63, mem., asst. dir., 1974-77, asso. dir., 1977—; prof. dept. pathology Duke, 1963-70; prof. dept. pathology U. Ky., 1970-74, chmn. dept. pathology Med. Center, 1970-74, dir. Med. Research on Aging Inst., 1973-74. Chmn. med. and health com. Ky. Partners of Americas, 1971-74; mem. study sect. NIH, 1965-70, 75-78; mem. adv. com. Nat. Prostate and Bladder Cancer Project. Recipient Golden Apple award Student Am. Med. Assn., 1968, 72. Mem. Am. Assn. Immunology, Am. Soc. Exptl. Pathology, Am. Assn. Pathologists and Bacteriologists, Am. Acad. Allergy, Internat. Acad. Pathology, Soc. Exptl. Biology and Medicine. Mem. editorial bd. Jour. Lab. Investigation, 1964-67, Am. Jour. Pathology, 1967-78. Home: 2676 Caminito Prado La Jolla CA 92037

VAZSONYI, ANDREW, computer and mgmt. scientist; b. Budapest, Hungary, Nov. 4, 1916; came to U.S., naturalized, 1945; s. Maximilian and Hermine V.; Ph.D., U. Budapest, 1938; S.M., Harvard U., 1942; m. Laura Thalia Saparoff, Jan. 16, 1943; 1 dau., Beatrice Ann. Teaching fellow Harvard U., 1942-44; engr. Elliott Co., Jeanette, Pa., 1944-45; supr. N. Am. Aviation, Los Angeles, 1945-46; div. head Naval Ordnance Test Sta., Pasadena, Calif., 1947-51, Hughes Aircraft Co., Culver City, Calif., 1951-54; div. mgr. TRW, Los Angeles,

1954-58; partner Alderson Assos., Phila., 1959-60; div. dir. TRW, 1960-61; sci. adv. Rockwell Internat., Los Angeles, 1961-69; prof. computer sci. U. So. Calif., 1969-72; prof. computer and mgmt. sci. U. Rochester, 1972-79; Emil C.E. Jurica prof. computer mgmt. St. Mary's U., San Antonio, 1979—. Fellow AAAS; mem. Inst. Mgmt. Scis. (chmn. 1953-54), Ops. Research Soc. Am., Am. Inst. Decision Scis., Assn. Computing Machinery. Author: Scientific Programming in Business and Industry, 1958; Problem Solving by Digital Computers with PL/I Programming, 1970; Introduction to Electronic Data Processing, 1977; asso. editor Interfaces; contbr. numerous articles to profl. jours. Office: St Mary's U One Camino Santa Maria San Antonio TX 78284. *I started my career as a pure mathematician, but became interested in applying mathematics to practical problems. I have a profound faith in the success of applying science and mathematical techniques to the problem of choosing the right means to meet societal goals. Verbal discourse is inadequate to resolve complex issues, and mathematics is the language par excellence to come to grips with complexity, to dispel fog from the human mind and the most effective tool to triumph in the battle against confusion, ignorance and mismanagement.*

VEACH, CARSON WARD, educator, univ. ofcl.; b. Poughkeepsie, N.Y., June 26, 1930; s. Arthur Hiram and Hazel (Melius) V.; B.A. cum laude, St. Anselm's Coll., 1959; M.A. (Woodrow Wilson fellow), Harvard, 1967; Ph.D., Ind. U., 1967; m. Pauline G. Paquereau, Nov. 3, 1951; children—Carson Peter, Cynthia Marie, Cheryl Anne, Cathleen Mary, Carrie Lynn, Carter Ward. Teaching asst., tennis coach St. Anselm's Coll., Manchester, N.H., 1958-59; teaching asso. Ind. U., 1960-64; dir. forensics, asst. prof. English, Colgate U., 1964-67; acad. dean, prof. English, Notre Dame Coll. S.I., 1967-70; dean of coll., prof. English, Coe Coll., 1970-75, provost, 1974-75; dir., prof. English, Pa. State U., Altoona, 1975—, chief exec. officer, 1975—; cons., mem. charter evaluation and elementary and secondary certification evaluation team N.Y. State Edn. Dept., 1969-70; mem. So. Alleghenies Planning Commn., 1976—. Chmn. Asso. Colls. Midwest Council Deans, 1974—, Stillwater Conf. Acad. Deans, 1975. Served with M.C., AUS, 1951-53. Mem. Am. Assn. Higher Edn., A.A.U.P., Modern Lang. Assn. Am., Am. Assn. Coll. and Univ. Deans, Eastern Assn. Coll. Deans and Advisers of Students, Nat. Assn. Student Personnel Adminstrs., Nat. Debate Soc., N.Y.-New Eng. Forensics Assn. (chmn.), Delta Epsilon Sigma. Home: 2811 Edgewood Dr Altoona PA 16602

VEACH, HENRY HARRELL, retail food chain exec.; b. Willard, N.C., Feb. 7, 1915; s. Henry Jones and Effie May (Harrell) V.; student N.C. State Coll., Raleigh, 1932-33; m. Carolyn Elizabeth Bethea, Feb. 1, 1941; children—Sandra Kay Veach Ground, Barbara Lynn Veach Wood, Henry Harrell. Engaged in grocery bus., 1933—; exec. v.p. Bio-Lo, Inc., Mauldin, S.C., 1962-75, chmn. bd., 1975-78. Elder, Second Presbyn. Ch., Greenville, S.C. Home: 1401 Parkins Mill Rd Greenville SC 29607 Office: Bi-Lo Inc Industrial Blvd Mauldin SC 29662

VEALE, TINKHAM, II, corp. exec., profl. engr.; b. Topeka, Dec. 26, 1914; s. George W. and Grace Elizabeth (Walworth) V.; B.S., Case Inst. Tech., 1937, M.E., 1938; m. Harriett Alice Ernst, Sept. 6, 1941; children—Harriett Elizabeth (Mrs. Larry Lee Leedy), Tinkham III, Helen Ernst (Mrs. Robert Walter Gelbach). With Gen. Motors Corp., 1937-38, Avery Engring. Co., 1939, Reliance Electric Co., 1940-41; asst. to pres. Ohio Crankshaft Co., 1942-46; gen. mgr. Tocco Co., 1947-51; pres., dir. Ric Wil Corp., 1952-53; pres. Alco Chem. Corp., 1954-56, dir., 1954—; spl. partner Ball Burge & Kraus, investment bankers, 1957-60; chmn. bd. V. and V. Cos., Inc., 1960-65, also divs.; chmn. bd. Alco Standard Corp., 1965—, also subsidiaries. Home: Fair Elm Gates Mills OH 44040 Office: Alco Standard Corp Valley Forge PA 19482

VEALS, RALPH LANGDON, mfg. co. exec.; b. Carney's Point, N.J., Nov. 25, 1926; s. Ralph Cyril and Ada May (Langdon) V.; student Duke U., 1944-46; B.S., Columbia U., 1947; m. Barbara Maud Beardsley, Dec. 15, 1951; children—Pamela, Susan, John, Mark. Various fin. and adminstrv. positions Gen. Electric Co., Schenectady, Louisville, N.Y., and N.Y.C., 1949-63; v.p. Schieffelin & Co., N.Y.C., 1963, v.p., treas., 1964-69, sr. v.p., treas., 1969-75, dir., 1970-76; v.p., treas. Revere Copper & Brass Inc., N.Y.C., 1975—, dir., 1977—. Served with USNR, 1944-46. Mem. Chappaqua Internat. Exchange (dir. 1972-75), Fin. Execs. Inst. Clubs: Union League (N.Y.C.); Birchwood Swim and Tennis (Chappaqua). Home: 64 Paulding Dr Chappaqua NY 10514 Office: 605 3d Ave New York NY 10016

VEAR, JUDD GRAY, publisher; b. Albion, Mich., Aug. 23, 1923; s. Leonard Ray and Helen Marie (Gray) V.; student Purdue U., 1941-42; B.B.A., U. Mich., 1947; m. Rita C. Sullivan, Mar. 17, 1947; children—Timothy, Casey, Lynn, Jim, Kate, Matt. Salesman, Proctor & Gamble Co., Chgo., 1947-49; with Good Housekeeping mag. Hearst Mag. div. Hearst Corp., 1949—, nat. advt. dir., N.Y.C., 1968-73, v.p., pub., 1973-77, v.p., dir. corp. advt. sales Hearst mags., 1978—. Served with AC, U.S. Army, 1943-45. Decorated D.F.C., Air Medal. Republican. Roman Catholic. Club: Pelham Country. Home: 4 Bon Mar Rd Pelham Manor NY 10803 Office: 959 8th Ave New York City NY 10019

VECOLI, RUDOLPH JOHN, educator; b. Wallingford, Conn., Mar. 2, 1927; s. Giovanni Battista and Settima Maria (Palmerini) V.; B.A., U. Conn., 1950; M.A., U. Pa., 1951; Ph.D., U. Wis., 1963; m. Jill Cherrington, June 27, 1959; children—Christopher, Lisa, Jeremy. Fgn. affairs officer Dept. State, 1951-54; instr. history Ohio State U., 1957-59; instr. history Pa. State U., 1960-61; asst. prof. Rutgers U., 1961-65; asso. prof. U. Ill., Champaign, 1965-67; prof. history, dir. Immigration History Research Center, U. Minn., Mpls., 1967—; vis. prof. U. Uppsala, Sweden, 1970. Mem. exec. council Nat. Ethnic Studies Assembly, Inc.; bd. Am. Immigration and Citizenship Conf., Am. Council for Nationalities Service. Served with USNR, 1945-46. Recipient Am. Philos. Soc. grant-in-aid, 1970; Social Sci. Research Council fellow, 1959-60; Newberry Library fellow, 1964; Am.-Scandinavian Found. fellow, 1970; Fulbright-Hays sr. research scholar, Italy, 1973-74; Am. Council Learned Socs. grantee, 1974; Dept. State travel grantee, 1977. Mem. Am. Italian (pres., mem. exec. council), Am. hist. assns., Orgn. Am. Historians, AAUP, Immigration History Soc. (mem. exec. council). Author: The People of New Jersey, 1965; Foreword to Marie Hall Ets, Rosa: The Story of an Italian Immigrant, 1970; contbg. author: Perspectives in Italian Immigration and Ethnicity, 1977, Immigrants and Religion in Urban America, 1977, The State of American History, 1970, The Reinterpretation of American History and Culture, 1973; editor, contbg. author: The Other Catholics, 1978. Mem. editorial bd. Ethnicity, Internat. Migration Rev., Italian Americana. Contbr. articles to profl. jours. Home: 610 E 58th St Minneapolis MN 55417

VEDAM, KUPPUSWAMY, educator; b. Vedharanyam, India, Jan. 15, 1926; s. Tiruvarur Vaidyanathan and Saraswathi (Ramaseshan) K.; B.Sc. with Honors, Nagpur (India) U., 1946, M.Sc., 1947; research student Indian Inst. Sci., Bangalore, 1948-51; Ph.D., Saugor (India) U., 1953; m. Nalini Subramanyam, Sept. 14, 1956; children—Saraswathi, Subramanyam. Lectr. physics U. Saugor, 1947-48, 51-53; sr. research asst. Indian Inst. Sci., 1953-56; asst. prof. physics Pa. State U., 1956-59; sr. research officer Atomic Energy Establishment, Bombay, India, 1960-62; asso. prof. Pa. State U., University Park, 1962-70, prof. physics, 1970—. Fellow Am. Phys. Soc., Optical Soc. Am.; mem. Materials Research Soc., Soc. Photo-optic Instrumentation Engrs., Sigma Xi. Research and numerous publications on optical properties of materials under high pressure, surface physics and crystal physics. Home: 122 Harris Dr State College PA 16801 Office: Materials Research Laboratory Pa State U University Park PA 16802

VEDDER, BLAIR, advt. agy. exec.; b. Chgo., Dec. 4, 1924; s. Beverly B. and Helen (Morse) V.; B.A., Colgate U., 1946; m. Geraldine Bovbjerg, Feb. 1, 1947; children—Nicholas B., Nancy N., Richard D. Salesman, Radio Sta. WOSH, Oshkosh, Wis., 1947-48; asso. media dir. Needham, Louis & Brorby, Chgo., 1948-55; v.p., media dir. Needham, Harper & Steers Advt., Inc., Chgo., 1955-64, sr. v.p. adminstrn., corporate media, 1964-66, sr. v.p. internat., London, 1966-67, exec. v.p., Chgo., 1967-74, chmn. bd., 1974—, pres., 1976—; pres. Needham, Harper & Steers, Inc., 1976—. Dir. Nat. Outdoor Advt. Bur., N.Y.C., 1955-60. Served to lt. USNR, 1942-46; PTO. Clubs: Plaza (gov.), N.Y. Yacht, Chicago Yacht, Tavern. Home: 2714 Lincoln St Evanston IL 60201 Office: 401 N Michigan Ave Chicago IL 60611

VEDDER, BYRON CHARLES, newspaper exec.; b. Adrian, Mich., Feb. 9, 1910; s. Adelbert and Adah (Dibble) V.; A.B., U. Mich., 1933; m. Kathleen Fry, June 20, 1936 (dec. 1960); children—Richard Kent, Robert Allen; m. 2d, Helen Cochrane, Dec. 16, 1976. Grad. mgr. student publs. U. Mich., 1933-34; with Champaign-Urbana (Ill.) Courier, 1934-64, pub., 1960-64; v.p. ops. Lindsay-Schaub Newspapers, Inc., 1964-75; v.p. planning Lindsay-Schaub Newspapers, Inc., 1975-79, v.p. so. media sales, 1979—; dir. Comml. Savs. & Loan Assn., Urbana, v.p., 1975-76, chmn. bd., 1976—. Mem. Arrowhead council exec. bd. Boy Scouts Am., 1951—, pres., 1960-64; mem. Pres.'s Com. Traffic Safety, 1954-58. Recipient Silver Beaver award Boy Scouts Am., 1959; named Boss of Year, Champaign-Urbana chpt. Nat. Secs. Assn., 1958; Disting. Service to Journalism award U. Minn., 1979. Mem. Inland Daily Press Assn. (dir. 1950-53, pres. 1954, chmn. 1955), Central States Circulation Mgrs. Assn. (pres. 1944-46), Ill. Daily Newspaper Markets Assn. (pres. 1962-63, chmn. 1963-64), Am. Newspaper Pub. Assn. (com. chmn.), Urbana Assn. Commerce (v.p. 1946), Campus Bus. Men's Assn. (dir.), Champaign C. of C. (dir. 1955-57), Internat. Circulation Mgrs. Assn. (hon.). Presbyn. (trustee). Clubs: Kiwanis (pres. 1948, lt. gov. 1951, Kiwanian of Year 1971); Urbana Country (dir.); Champaign Country. Home: 3 Stanford Pl Champaign IL 61820 Office: 110 W University St Champaign IL 61820

VEDER, SAL, photographer; s. John B. and Ann K. V.; student Modesto Jr. Coll., Coll. of Pacific, Diablo Coll. (Calif.), Sacramento State Coll.; m. 3d, Petronella, Dec. 1973; stepchildren—Tom, Tim, Kathleen, Joni, Kathryn. Sportswriter, Richmond (Calif.) Ind.; newsroom staff Alameda (Calif.) Times-Star, 1949-52; asst. Sunday editor, Tulsa, 1952-58; photographer AP, San Francisco, 1961—. Recipient Pulitzer prize, 1974, awards World Press Assn., Nat. Press Photographers Assn. Office: AP The Fox Plaza 1390 Market St San Francisco CA 94102

VEECK, WILLIAM LOUIS, sports exec.; b. Chgo., Feb. 9, 1914; s. William L. and Grace Greenwood (De Forrest) V.; student Kenyon Coll.; m. Eleanor Raymond, Dec. 8, 1935 (div. 1949); m. 2d, Mary Frances Ackerman, Apr. 29, 1950; 9 children. With Chgo. Cubs Profl. Baseball Team, 1933-41, treas., asst. sec., 1940-41; pres., owner profl. baseball teams Milw. Brewers (Am. Assn.), 1941-45, Cleve. Indians, 1947-49, St. Louis Browns, 1951-53, Chgo. White Sox, 1959-61, 76—; sports announcer NBC-TV, 1957-58; pres., owner Suffolk Downs, Boston, 1969-71. Served with USMCR, 1943-45. Named Minor League Exec. of Year, Sporting News, 1942, Maj. League Exec. of Year, 1948, 77. Roman Catholic. Author: (with Ed Linn) Veeck-As in Wreck, 1962, The Hustler's Handbook, 1965, Thirty Tons a Day, 1972. Office: Comiskey Park Dan Ryan at 35th St Chicago IL 60616*

VEEDER, WILLIAM JOHN, assn. exec.; b. Amsterdam, N.Y., Nov. 16, 1923; s. Alexander H. and Alice V.; B.A. in Polit. Sci., Colgate U., 1947; postgrad. in internat. relations Oxford (Eng.) U., summer 1947; m. Ann Marsh; 1 dau., Kammie Lynn. Public adminstrv. intern N.Y. State Dept. Civil Service, Albany, 1947-48, jr. personnel technician, 1948-49, personnel technician, 1949-50; staff asst. Public Personnel Assn. U.S. and Can., Chgo., 1950-52; personnel dir., asst. city mgr. City of Ft. Lauderdale (Fla.), 1952-55, city mgr., 1955-59; city mgr. City of Charlotte (N.C.), 1959-71; exec. v.p. Carowinds Corp., Charlotte, 1971-75; pres. Greater Charlotte C. of C., 1975—. Served with U.S. Army, 1943-46. Home: 5811-D Sharon Rd Charlotte NC 28210 Office: PO Box 32785 129 W Trade St Charlotte NC 28232

VEENEMA, RALPH JAMES, surgeon, urologist, educator; b. Prospect Park, N.J., Dec. 13, 1921; s. Ralph and Sadie (Van Dyke) V.; B.A., Calvin Coll., 1942; M.D., Jefferson Med. Coll., 1945; m. Henriette Van Der Molen, Sept. 19, 1944; children—Shirley (Mrs. B. Smith), Lois, Ralph James, Kenneth. Intern Paterson (N.J.) Gen. Hosp., 1945-46, resident in pathology, 1948; resident in gen. surgery VA Hosps., Alexandria, La. and Jackson, Miss., 1946-48; asst. resident in urology VA Hosp., Bronx, N.Y., 1949; asst. resident urology Columbia-Presbyn. Med. Center, N.Y.C., 1950-51, resident, 1952; practice medicine specializing in urology, Ridgewood and Paterson, N.J., 1953-60, N.Y.C., 1953—; asst. in urology Columbia U. Coll. of Phys. and Surgs., N.Y.C., 1953-54, instr. urology, 1954-56, asso. in urology, 1956-58, asst. clin. prof. urology, 1958-60, asst. prof. urology, 1960-63, asso. prof. clin. urology, 1963-68, prof. clin. urology, 1968—; chief urol. out-patient clinic Columbia-Presbyn. Med. Center, N.Y.C., 1955-60, asst. attending urologist, 1955-63, attending urologist, 1968—; chief urology Francis Delafield Hosp., Cancer Research Inst. of Columbia-Presbyn. Med. Center, 1960-75; attending urologist Valley Hosp., Ridgewood, 1956-60, cons. urology, 1960—; cons. USPHS, S.I., N.Y., 1961—; cons. dept. surgery Harlem Hosp., N.Y.C., 1962—. Served with M.C., AUS, 1946-48. Diplomate Am. Bd. Urology. Fellow A.C.S., A.M.A.; mem. Am. Urol. Assn. (First prize research award 1955, 64), World Med. Assn., Acad. of Medicine (sec. 1960-61, chmn. 1961-62, adv. com. 1962-66), N.Y. State Med. Soc., Am. Assn. of Univ. Urologists, Internat. Soc. of Urology, Am. Assn. Clin. Oncology, Am. Assn. of Genito-Urinary Surgeons. Presbyn. Research in chemotherapy of bladder cancer, pathophysiology of genitourinary neoplasms. Home: 76 Concord Ave Glen Rock NJ 07452 Office: 161 Fort Washington Ave New York City NY 10032

VEENKER, CLAUDE HAROLD, educator; b. George, Iowa, July 31, 1919; s. Ralph C. and Fannie (Casjens) V.; B.A., U. No. Iowa, 1943; M.A., U. No. Colo., 1953; D. Health and Safety, Ind. U., 1957; m. Elizabeth Louise Higgins, Jan. 1, 1944; children—Jo Lee, Vicki Susan. Tchr., Osage (Iowa) High Sch., 1946-47, Mason City (Iowa) Pub. Schs., 1947-55; teaching asst. Ind. U., 1955-56, vis. lectr., 1956-57; asst. prof. Purdue U., Lafayette, Ind., 1957-61, asso. prof., 1961-66, prof., 1966—, chmn. health edn. sect., 1961-77. Chmn. health edn. test project Ednl. Testing Service, Princeton, 1965-74; cons. bur. research coop. research br. U.S. Office Edn., 1966-68; cons. healthful sch. environment AMA, NEA, Washington, 1969; mem. Ind. Council on Sch. Health, 1971—, Ind. Adv. Com. on Drug Edn., 1969-74, Ind. Gov.'s Regional Com. on Mental Health, 1966-67. Served to 1st lt. USMC, 1943-46. Decorated Purple Heart. Fellow Am. Sch. Health Assn., Am. Pub. Health Assn. (governing council 1974-76, mem. sch. health sect. council 1970-73); mem. Am. Alliance for Health, Phys. Edn. and Recreation (exec. council sch. health div. 1964-67, chmn. sch. health service sect. 1959-60), Mid-Am. Coll. Health Assn., Ind. Assn. Health Educators (pres. 1970), Phi Delta Kappa, Eta Sigma Gamma. Methodist. Club: Elks. Editor, contbr. author: Synthesis of Research in Selected Areas of Health Instruction, 1963; mem. editorial bd. Jour. Health, Phys. Edn. and Recreation, 1961-62, 64-66. Contbr. articles to profl. jours. Home: 224 E Knox Dr West Lafayette IN 47906 Office: Lambert Bldg Purdue U Lafayette IN 49707. *Life as a child during the Roaring 20's, as a young teen-ager during the Great Depression of the 30's, and as a young adult during World War II, was a great adventure. But the world is no easier now than it was then. It seems that living is a continual challenge: to seek, to find, to try, to conquer. To succeed, one must live with confidence and hope, fearing neither failure nor success. To live well is to live with self-discipline in the present, using the hard-learned lessons of the past to brighten one's prospects for the future.*

VEGA, MARYLOIS PURDY, editor; b. Chgo., Nov. 4, 1914; d. William Thomas and Mary Helene (Buggy) Purdy; B.A., U. Wis., Madison, 1935; m. Carlos Juan Vega, Sept. 4, 1965. With Time mag., N.Y.C., 1942—, editor Letters to the Editor, 1951-67, chief dept. reporters-researchers, 1967-76, asso. editor, 1976—. Mem. sr. adv. council on careers in bus. N.Y. U. Mem. Overseas Press. Roman Catholic. Home: 140 West End Ave New York NY 10023 Office: Time and Life Bldg Rockefeller Center New York NY 10020

VEINOTT, ARTHUR FALES, JR., ops. researcher; b. Boston, Oct. 12, 1934; s. Arthur Fales and Sally Pike (Quinn) V.; B.A., B.S., Lehigh U., 1956; Eng.Sc.D. in Indsl. Engring., Columbia U., 1960; m. Ruth Ann Chastain, June 4, 1960; children—Elizabeth Sharon, Michael Chastain. Asst. prof. indsl. engring. Stanford U., 1962-64, asso. prof., 1964-67, prof. ops. research, 1967—, chmn. dept ops. research, 1975—; vis. prof. Yale U., 1972-73; cons. in field; mem. NSF Research Initiation Grant Panel, 1971. Mem. mgmt. and fin. com. Palo Alto (Calif.) Coop. Soc., 1974—, chmn., 1974-75. Served to 1st lt. USAF, 1960-62. Guggenheim fellow, 1978-79; Office Naval Research grantee, 1964—; Western Mgmt. Sci. Inst. grantee, 1964-65; NSF grantee, 1967—. Fellow Inst. Math. Stats.; mem. Inst. Mgmt. Scis. (council 1971-73, v.p. publs. 1973-76), Ops. Research Soc. Am., Math. Programming Soc., Am. Math. Soc., Econometric Soc., Am. Stat. Assn., Phi Beta Kappa, Tau Beta Pi, Omicron Delta Kappa. Co-editor: Mathematics of the Decision Sciences, vols. I and II, 1968; editor Math. Studies in Mgmt. Sci., 1965; founding editor Math. of Ops. Research, 1974—; research in lattice programming, inventory theory, dynamic programming, network flows, math. programming. Home: 1004 Cathcart Way Stanford CA 94305 Office: Dept Ops Research Stanford U Stanford CA 94305

VEIS, ARTHUR, educator; b. Pitts., Dec. 23, 1925; s. Fred M. and Sarah (Landis) V.; B.S., U. Okla., 1947; Ph.D., Northwestern U., 1951; m. Eve Zenner, June 24, 1951; children—Judith, Sharon, Deborah. Instr. phys. chemistry U. Okla., 1951-52; research chemist Armour & Co., Chgo., 1952-60, head phys. chemistry dept., 1959-60; spl. instr. Crane Jr. Coll., Chgo., 1955-56, Loyola U., Chgo., 1957-58; mem. faculty Northwestern U. Med. Sch. Chgo.,, 1960—, prof. biochemistry, 1965—, asst. dean Grad. Sch., 1968-70, asso. dean Grad. Sch. and Med. Sch., 1970-76, chmn. dept. oral biology, 1977—. Chmn. dental insts. and spl. projects adv. com. Nat. Inst. Dental Research, 1974-78. Served with USNR, 1943-46. Recipient Fogarty Sr. Internat. Scholar award, 1977. Guggenheim fellow, 1967. Mem. Am. Chem. Soc., Am. Soc. Biol. Chemists, Biophys. Soc., N.Y. Acad. Scis., Sigma Xi, Phi Lambda Upsilon. Author: Macromolecular Chemistry of Gelatin, 1964. Editor: Biological; Polyelectrolytes, 1970; also articles. Patentee in field. Home: 7633 Lowell St Skokie IL 60076 Office: 303 E Chicago Ave Chicago IL 60611

VEIT, FRITZ, librarian; b. Emmendingen, Baden, Germany, Sept. 17, 1907; s. Samuel W. and Helene (Geismar) V.; student U. Berlin, 1927, Heidelberg U., 1928; J.U.D., U. Freiburg, 1932; B.L.S., Peabody Library Sch., Nashville, 1936; Ph.D., U. Chgo. Grad. Library Sch., 1941; m. Lucille Stearns, June 11, 1939; children—Joanne Grace, Mary Catherine. Came to U.S., 1935, naturalized, 1940. Research asst. Inst. History Law, U. Freiburg (Germany), 1932-33; librarian U. Chgo. Grad. Library Sch., 1937-42, Social Sci. Reading Room, 1942, acting librarian Law Sch., 1943; librarian Chgo. City Jr. Coll., Englewood evening br., 1941-48; law librarian U.S. R.R. Retirement Bd., Chgo., 1943-49; supr. library John Marshall Law Sch., 1949-57; vis. prof. library sci. Rosary Coll., River Forest, Ill., 1950—, Western Mich. U., summer 1959, Ariz. State U., summer 1964, 65, 67, 68, Emporia State U., summer 1977, Grad. Library Sch. U. Chgo., summer 1975, 78, fall 1977; dir. libraries Chgo. State U., 1949-73, also Kennedy-King Coll., 1949-72; chmn. adv. com. library tech. program Chgo. City Colls., 1968-74; mem. adv. council librarians U. Ill. Grad. Sch. Library Sci., 1971-74. Mem. ALA (sec., chmn. tchr. edn. libraries sect. ACRL 1959-61, asso. editor monographs 1952-60; local chmn. ACRL 1963 Conf.), Ill. Library Assn., Chgo. Library Club (pres. 1964-65), Pi Gamma Mu. Author: The Community College Library, 1975; contbr. articles to profl. jours. Home: 1716 E 55th St Chicago IL 60615

VEIT, KENNETH PHILLIP, ins. exec.; b. N.Y.C., Aug. 11, 1938; s. Paul E. and Helen M. (Muller) V.; B.S., Fordham U., 1960; m. Sandra A. Sporn, June 2, 1962. Actuarial asst. N.Y. Life Ins. Co., 1961-63; asso. actuary Wyatt Co., 1963-66, actuary, 1966-69; v.p. Aetna Variable Annuity Life, Falls Church, Va., 1969-78, dir., 1974—; v.p. Aetna Life Ins. Co., Hartford, Conn., 1978—. Fellow Soc. Actuaries; mem. Am. Acad. Actuaries, Inst. for Study of Econ. Systems (dir.). Office: 151 Farmington Ave Hartford CT 06156. *The person who strives too much, who must compete in every type of activity, will ultimately be unhappy and a failure in life. On the other hand, the person who strives too little, who fails to enter into the joy of competition, will be a failure and unhappy as well. The trick is to find the balance. Apparently the margin of error is large, since few do.*

VEIT, WERNER, publisher; b. Stuttgart, Germany, July 31, 1929; came to U.S., 1940, naturalized, 1949; s. Konrad David and Ida Sophie (Wolber) V.; student Grand Rapids (Mich.) Jr. Coll., U. Md.; m. Marianne DeWeese, Dec. 24, 1958; children—Anthony Michael, Andrea, Tamilyn. With Grand Rapids Herald, 1949-59, mng. editor, 1958-59; Sunday editor Grand Rapids Press, 1959-63, mng. editor, 1963-66; editor, 1966-78; pres. Booth Newspapers Inc., Grand Rapids, 1978—. Office: PO Box 2168 Grand Rapids MI 49501*

VEIT, WERNER, newspaper pub.; b. Stuttgart, Germany, July 31, 1929; s. Konrad David and Ida Sophie (Wolber) V.; came to U.S., 1940, naturalized, 1948; student U. Md.; m. Marianne DeWeese, Dec. 24, 1958; children—Anthony, Tamilyn, Andrea. With Grand Rapids (Mich.) Herald, 1949-59, mng. editor, 1958-59; Sunday editor Grand Rapids Press, 1959-63, mng. editor, 1963-66, editor, 1966-78; pres. Booth Newspapers, 1978—. Served with AUS, 1948-49. Mem. Am. Newspaper Pubs. Assn., Am. Soc. Newspaper Editors. Club: Kent Peninsular Torch (Grand Rapids). Home: 7361 Grachen SE Grand

Rapids MI 49506 Office: Grand Rapids Press Plaza-Vandenberg Center Grand Rapids MI 49502

VEITH, EDWIN THOMAS, bus. exec.; b. N.Y.C., Sept. 5, 1931; s. Edwin James and Mary Catherine (Flannery) V.; B.S., Fordham U., 1953; M.B.A., Pace U., 1962; m. Marie Theresa Leahy, Apr. 23, 1955; children—Ellen Marie, Edwin James, Anthony John, Brian Michael, David Thomas. Acct., IBM, N.Y.C., 1953-54; auditor Bigelow Sanford Co., N.Y.C., 1959-60; dir. mgmt. info. systems E.R. Squibb & Sons, N.Y.C., 1960-66; v.p., controller Hooker Chem. Co., N.Y.C., 1966-71; exec. v.p., chief fin. officer U.S. Filter Corp., N.Y.C., 1971—; dir. Resource Scis. Corp., Filtrol Corp., Drew Chem. Corp. Served to 1st lt. USAF, 1954-59. Mem. Am. Mgmt. Assn., Fin. Execs. Inst. Democrat. Roman Catholic. Clubs: N.Y. Athletic; Pelham (N.Y.) Men's, Pelham Manor Country. Office: 522 Fifth Ave New York NY 10036

VEITH, ILZA, educator; b. Ludwigshafen, Germany, May 13, 1915; came to U.S., 1937, naturalized, 1945; student med. schs., Geneva and Vienna, Austria, 1934-36; M.A., Johns Hopkins, 1944, Ph.D., 1947; Igaku hakase (M.D., D.M.S.), Sch. Medicine, Juntendo U., Tokyo, 1975; m. Hans von Valentini Veith, Oct. 20, 1935. Cons. Oriental medicine Armed Forces Med. Library, Washington, 1947-57; lectr. in history medicine U. Chgo., 1949-51; editor mag. Biology and Medicine, U. Chgo. Press, 1951-53; asst. prof. history medicine U. Chgo., 1953-57, asso. prof., 1957-63; vis. prof. Menninger Sch. Psychiatry, 1963; prof. history medicine, vice chmn. dept. U. Calif. at San Francisco Med. Center, 1964-79, prof. history psychiatry, 1967-79, prof. emeritus, 1979—; D.J. Davies Meml. lectr. U. Ill. Sch. Medicine, 1958: Sloan vis. prof. Menninger Found., 1963, 66; John Shaw Billings lectr. U. Ind. Sch. Medicine, Indpls., 1970; George W. Corner lectr. history medicine U. Rochester (N.Y.), 1970; Logan Clendenning lectr. history of medicine U. Kans. Sch. Medicine, 1971; spl. lectr. VI World Congress Psychiatry, 1977; Hideyo Noguchi lectr. Johns Hopkins U., 1977. Decorated officer Cross Merit, German Fed. Republic, 1971; recipient Gold-Headed Cane award U. Kans. Sch. Medicine, 1976. Hon. fellow Am. Psychiat. Assn.; mem. Am. Assn. History of Medicine (council mem. 1958-62, 73-77), AAAS, Soc. History of Medicine Chgo. (pres. 1954—), Soc. History Med. Scis. Los Angeles (hon.), History Sci. Soc., AMA (asso.), Marin Med. Soc. (hon.), Spanish Soc. History of Medicine (hon., corr. mem.), Bay Area Med. History Soc. (v.p. 1972), Johns Hopkins Alumni Assn. (past pres. Ill.), Royal Soc. Medicine (London), German Soc. History Medicine, Sci. and Tech. (corr.), Sigma Xi. Author: Medicine in Tibet, 1962; Hysteria; The History of a Disease, 1965; Yellow Emporer's Classic of Internal Medicine, 1966; co-author Great Ideas in the History of Surgery, 1961; Acupuncture Therapy: Current Chinese Practice, 1973, 2d rev. and enlarged edit., 1976; Histoire de l' hystérie 1974; Nei-Ching: Canone di Medicina Interna dell' Imperatore Giallo, 1976. Editorial bd. Jour. AMA; adv. bd. Ency. Britannica. Contbr. articles to profl. jours. Home: 2235 Centro East Tiburon CA 94920 Office: U Calif San Francisco Med Center San Francisco CA 94143

VELDE, GAIL PATRICK, TV producer; b. Birmingham, Ala., June 20; d. Lawrence C. and La Valle (Smith) Fitzpatrick; A.B. with honors, Howard Coll. (now Samford U.); m. John E. Velde, Jr., Sept. 28, 1974; children by previous marriage—Jennifer Stanley Jackson, Thomas Cornwell Jackson, Jr. Actress in motion pictures including My Man Godfrey, Stage Door, My Favorite Wife, Up in Mabel's Room, Claudia and David; propr. Gail Patrick's Enchanted Cottage, children's shop, Beverly Hills, Calif., 1945-54, Gail Patrick's Enchanted Weavers, Beverly Hills, 1950-51; exec. producer Perry Mason Show, Paisano Prodns., Hollywood, Calif., 1957-66; mng. partner Paisano Prodns., 1957—, pres., 1966—; exec. cons. The New Perry Mason, 1973-74. Treas., Los Angeles County chpt. Freedoms Found. at Valley Forge, 1967-68; 1st v.p. The Muses, Mus. Sci. and Industry, Los Angeles, 1967-68, 1st vice-chmn. bd. dirs., 1979-80; co-chmn. Mayor's Celebrity Com., Los Angeles, 1966—; nat. hon. chmn. Christmas Seal Campaign, 1970, Am. Lung Assn.; chmn. bd. dirs. Am. Diabetes Assn., 1973-74, bd. dirs., 1972-76, mem. nat. adv. council, 1979—, chmn. public affairs com., 1972-76, bd. dirs. So. Calif. affiliate, 1977—; mem. Nat. Commn. on Digestive Diseases, 1977-79; mem. bd. councilors Brain Research Inst., U. Calif. at Los Angeles, 1978—; mem. nat. arthritis, metabolism and digestive diseases adv. council NIH, 1972-76; mem. adv. council U. Mid Am., 1974—; regent Immaculate Heart Coll., Los Angeles, 1968-73; bd. dirs. Film Industries, Workshop, 1966-68; bd. dirs., co-chmn. bd. trustees Center for Ulcer Research and Edn. Found., 1977—; bd. dirs., mem. fin. com. YMCA Met. Los Angeles, 1974—; trustee Columbia Coll., 1963—; v.p. bd. dirs. Digestive Diseases Info. Center, 1978—. Named Woman of Year, Los Angeles Times, 1961. Businesswomen of Year, Nat. Assn. Accountants, 1962; recipient Muses award, 1966; Justica award Nat. Assn. Women Lawyers, 1960. Mem. Acad. TV Arts and Scis. (nat. trustee, bd. govs. 1959-63, chpt. pres. 1960-62, nat. v.p. 1960-62), Am. Women for Internat. Understanding, Les Dames de Champagne (Los Angeles), Delta Zeta (v.p. found. 1961-62, dir. 1961-65), Zeta Phi Eta. Home: 2003 LaBrea Terr Hollywood CA 90046

VELDE, JOHN ERNEST, JR., investor; b. Pekin, Ill., June 15, 1917; s. John Ernest and Alga (Anderson) V.; A.B., U. Ill., 1938; m. Shirley Margaret Walker, July 29, 1940 (dec. 1969); 1 dau., Drew; m. 2d, Gail Patrick Jackson, Sept. 28, 1974. Pres., Velde, Roelfs & Co., Pekin, Ill., 1955-60; dir. Herget Nat. Bank, 1948-75; dir. Kroehler Mfg. Co., 1974—. Trustee, Pekin Pub. Library, 1948-69, Pekin Meml. Hosp., 1950-69; chmn. Am. Library Trustee Assn. Found., 1976; trustee Am. Library Assn. Endowment, 1976—; trustee Everett McKinley Dirksen Research Center, 1965-74; co-chmn. trustees, bd. dirs. Center Ulcer Research and Edn. Found., 1977—; mem. bd. councilors Brain Research Inst. UCLA, 1977—; commr. Nat. Commn. on Libraries and Info. Sci., 1970-79; mem. adv. bd. on White House Conf. on Libraries, 1976-80; bd. trustees Joint Council on Econ. Edn., 1977—; bd. dirs. U. Ill. Found., 1977—; vice chmn. U. Ill. Pres.' Council, 1977-79, chmn., 1979— mem. fin. resources council steering com., 1976-78; pres. Ill. Valley Library System, 1965-69; dir. Lakeview Center for Arts and Scis., Peoria, Ill., 1962-73; mem. Nat. Book Com., 1969-74. Served as lt. (j.g.) USNR, World War II. Mem. Am. Library Trustee Assn. (regional v.p. 1970—, chmn. internat. relations com. 1973-76), Kappa Sigma. Clubs: Chgo. Yacht; Country (Peoria, Ill.); Capitol Hill (Washington); Calif. (Los Angeles). Home: 2003 La Brea Terr Hollywood CA 90046 and 501 Main St Peoria IL 61602

VELDER, ELI, educator; b. Balt., Nov. 9, 1925; s. Abraham and Rose (Nissel) V.; B.A., Johns Hopkins U., 1948, Ph.D., 1952; m. Jane Carol Kasper, Dec. 21, 1952 (dec. Mar. 1970); children—Ruth N., David M.; m. Zahava Brand Pearl, May 26, 1977. Asst. prof. edn. Balt. Hebrew Coll., 1952-57, asso. prof., 1957-63; mem. faculty Goucher Coll., Towson, Md., 1958—, asso. prof., 1965-71, prof., 1971—, dir. grad. program, 1972-75; lectr. history edn. Johns Hopkins Evening Coll., Balt., 1960—; tchr. English lit. Agrl. Secondary Sch., Pardess-Hannah, Israel, 1954-55. Served with AUS, 1944-46. Decorated Purple Heart. Mem. AAUP, History Edn. Soc. Home: 2119 Sulgrave Ave Baltimore MD 21209 Office: Dept Edn Goucher Coll Towson MD 21204

VELETSOS, ANESTIS STAVROU, educator; b. Istanbul, Turkey, Apr. 28, 1927; s. Stavros and Mathilde (Tjerahidou) V.; B.S., Robert Coll., Istanbul, 1948; M.S., U. Ill., 1950, Ph.D., 1953; guest scientist, Mass. Inst. Tech., 1958-59; m. Katherine Evangeline Economou, Aug. 19, 1966; children—Ann Marie Veletsos, Melinda Veletsos. Came to U.S., 1948, naturalized, 1960. Structural designer Frank L. Ehasz, N.Y.C., summer 1950, Skidmore, Owings and Merrill, Chgo., summer 1953; from asst. prof. to prof. civil engring. U. Ill. at Urbana, 1953-58, 58-60, 60-64; prof. civil engring., chmn. dept. Rice U., 1964-72, Brown and Root prof. engring., 1966—; vis. prof. civil engring. U. Calif. at Berkeley, spring 1977. Cons. to govt. and industry, since 1953—; asso. mem. Center Advanced Study, U. Ill., 1961-62; chmn. U.S. Joint Com. on Earthquake Engring.; NSF cons. Indian Inst. Tech., Bombay, summer 1969; vis. prof. Catholic U., Rio de Janeiro, summer 1970. Mem. ASCE (chmn. structural dynamics com. 1964-67, chmn. engring. mechanics div. 1970-71, chmn. com. on dynamic forces 1974—, Norman medal 1958, research prize 1961, Tex. sect. prizes 1973, Nathan M. Newmark medal 1978), Earthquake Engring. Research Inst. (dir., v.p. 1974-77), Seismol. Soc. Am., Internat. Assn. Bridge and Structural Engring., Sigma Xi, Tau Beta Pi, Phi Kappa Phi. Contbr. papers to profl. jours. Home: 5211 Paisley Houston TX 77096

VELICER, LELAND FRANK, microbiologist, virologist; b. Kewaunee, Wis., Oct. 16, 1939; s. George Matthew and Elsie (Cherney) V.; D.V.M., Iowa State U., 1964; Ph.D., U. Pa., 1969; m. Janet Francis Schafbuch, Aug. 17, 1963; children—Mark Allen, Gregory Jon, Daniel James. Asst. prof. microbiology Mich. State U., 1969-74, asso. prof., 1974-79, prof., 1979—; vis. scientist Center for Cancer Research, Mass. Inst. Tech., 1977-78. Served with U.S. Army, 1957. Recipient USPHS research career devel. award Nat. Cancer Inst., 1974-79. Mem. AVMA, Am. Soc. Microbiology, AAAS, Sigma Xi. Roman Catholic. Home: 2678 Blue Haven Ct East Lansing MI 48823 Office: Dept Microbiology and Pub Health Mich State U East Lansing MI 48824

VELICK, SIDNEY FREDERICK, research biochemist, educator; b. Detroit, May 3, 1913; s. Harry Alexander and Ella (Stocker) V.; B.S., Wayne State U., 1935; Ph.D., U. Mich., 1938; m. Bernadette Stemler, Sept. 5, 1941; children—William Frederick, Martha Elizabeth. Research fellow parasitology Johns Hopkins, 1939-40; research asso. chemistry Yale, 1941-45; mem. biol. chemistry dept. Washington U. Sch. Medicine, St. Louis, 1946-63, prof. biol. chemistry, 1958-64; prof., head dept. biol. chemistry U. Utah Coll. Medicine, 1964—. Mem. biochemistry study sect. NIH. Mem. Am. Soc. Biol. Chemists, Am. Chem. Soc., AAAS, Sigma Xi. Mem. editorial bd. Jour. Biol. Chemistry, Archives Biochemistry and Biophysics. Contbr. papers on enzyme chemistry to tech. lit. Home: 4183 Parkview Dr Salt Lake City UT 84117

VELIE, LESTER, journalist; b. Kiev, Ukraine, 1907; s. Samuel and Sarah (Spector) V.; B.A., U. Wis., 1929; m. Frances Rockmore, Oct. 29, 1932; children—Alan R., Franklin Bell. Brought to U.S. at age 5, naturalized 1922. Reporter Asso. Press, N.Y., 1931-32; suburban editor Bklyn. Eagle, 1932-35; asso. editor Jour. of Commerce, N.Y.C., 1937-46; radio analyst WQXR, N.Y.C., 1941-45; asso. editor Collier's, 1946-52; roving editor Reader's Digest, 1953-79. Recipient Distinguished Service award for mag. journalism, Sigma Delta Chi, 1949; Sch. Bell award for mag. journalism NEA, 1966; Silver Gavel award Am. Bar Assn., 1973. Author: Labor U.S.A., 1959; Labor U.S.A. Today, 1964; Countdown in The Holy Land, 1969; Desperate Bargain: Why Jimmy Hoffa Had To Die, 1977. Home and Office: 42 Pond Rd King's Point NY 11024

VELIKOVSKY, IMMANUEL, author, scientist; b. Vitebsk, Russia, June 10, 1895; s. Simon-Yehiel and Belia Rachel (Grodensky) V.; student Edinburgh U., Moscow Econ. Inst., Moscow U., Kharkov U.; M.D., U. Moscow, 1921; postgrad. Charité, Berlin, Monakow Brain Inst., Zürich; studied psychoanalysis under Wilhelm Stekel, Vienna, 1933; hon. doctorate in Arts and Sci., U. Lethbridge, 1974, m. Elisheva Kramer, Apr. 15, 1923; 2 daus. Practiced as M.D. then psychoanalyst, 1924-39. Pub., organizer, editor Scripta Universitatis atque Bibliothecae Hierosolymitanarum, 1921-24. Author: Thirty Days and Nights of Diego Pires on the Bridge of St. Angelo, 1935; Worlds in Collision, 1950; Ages in Chaos, Vol. I, 1952; Earth in Upheaval, 1955; Oedipus and Akhnaton: Myth and History, 1960; Peoples of the Sea, 1977; Ramses II and His Time, 1978; contbr. to sci. jours.; editorials on Middle East, New York Post, 1948-49. First to suggest characteristic brain waves in epileptics, 1930; cosmological postulations caused controversy in modern science: claimed Venus must be very hot, 1950, posited that Jupiter emits radio waves, 1953, suggested existence of terrestrial magnetosphere reaching to lunar orbit, 1956, claimed steep thermal gradient below lunar surface, significant magnetic remanence of lunar rocks and lavas, predicted sun's magnetosphere reaches to Pluto. Address: 78 Hartley Ave Princeton NJ 08540

VELIOTES, NICHOLAS ALEXANDER, ambassador; b. Calif., Oct. 28, 1928; s. Alexander John and Irene Frances (Kiskaskis) V.; A.B., U. Calif., Berkeley, 1952, M.A., 1954; m. Patricia J. Nolan, July 17, 1953; children—Christopher, Michael. Commd. fgn. service officer Dept. State, 1955; served in Italy, 1955-60, India, 1964-66, Laos, 1966-69, Israel, 1973-75; dep. asst. sec. Dept. State, Washington, 1976-78; ambassador Republic of Jordan, Amman, 1978—. Served with U.S. Army, 1946-48. Recipient Meritorious Honor award Dept. State, 1956, Superior Honor award, 1973, Disting. Honor award, 1977. Mem. Am. Fgn. Service Assn. Office: US Embassy Jebel Amman PO Box 354 Amman Jordan

VELIOTIS, PANAGIOTIS TAKIS, shipbldg. co. exec.; b. Kranidion, Greece, Aug. 11, 1926; s. Eleutherios George and Joanna (Zarifis) V.; B.A., St. Paul Coll., Greece; postgrad. Nat. U., Athens, Greece; degree in engring. Royal Naval Acad. Greece; m. Paulette Dupuis; children—Eleutherios George, Joanna. Engr., E. G. Veliotis Shipowners, 1948-53; engr., draftsman Davie Shipbldg. Ltd., Que., Can., 1953, supt. gen. engring. div., 1954, mgr. gen. engring. div., 1955-59, asst. gen. mgr., 1959-62, dir., gen. mgr., 1962-72, pres., gen. mgr., dir., 1972; v.p. Gen. Dynamics Corp., pres., gen. mgr. Quincy (Mass.) Shipbldg. div., 1973-77, gen. mgr. Electric Boat div., 1977—. Served as officer Royal Hellenic Navy, World War II. Mem. Soc. Naval Architects and Marine Engrs., Shipbuilders Council Am., Am. Bur. Shipping, Lloyd's Register of Shipping. Greek Orthodox. Clubs: Que. Garrison, Que. Yacht. Home: 1431 Brush Hill Rd Milton MA 02186 Office: Electric Boat Div Gen Dynamics Corp Eastern Point Rd Groton CT 06340

VELMANS, LOET ABRAHAM, pub. relations exec.; b. Amsterdam, Netherlands, Mar. 18, 1923; s. Joseph and Anna (Cohen) V.; grad. U. Amsterdam, 1947; m. Pauline Edith Van Hessen, Mar. 29. 1949; children—Marianne and Hester (twins), Jessica. Info. officer Dutch Govt. in Singapore, 1945-47; with Hill & Knowlton, Inc., 1953—, v.p. Hill Knowlton Internat., Geneva, 1959-60, pres., 1960-74, vice chmn., London, 1969-76, pres., N.Y.C., 1976—, chief exec. officer, 1979—. Bd. dirs. Lincoln Center Inst. Recipient Commendatore dell'Ordine Merito della Repubblica Italiana, 1976. Mem. Internat. Pub. Relations Assn., Legal Aid Soc. N.Y. (dir.). Contbr. articles on multinat. corps. to profl. jours. Home: 20 Sutton Pl S New York NY 10022 Office: Hill and Knowlton 633 3d Ave New York NY 10017

VELTMAN, PETER, coll. dean; b. Muskegon, Mich., Jan.29, 1917; s. Douglas and Minnie (Achterhof) V.; A.B., Hope Coll., Holland, Mich., 1938; M.A., Western Res. U., 1939; student U. Chgo., 1939-40, U. Amsterdam (Netherlands), 1949-50; Ph.D., Northwestern U., 1959; m. M. Marian Waalkes, Aug. 20, 1940; children—Virginia (Mrs. William Rice), Donna (Mrs. Richard Garcia), Marian, Michelle (Mrs. Robert Dulceak). Tchr., Chgo. Christian High Sch., 1939-40, Holland (Mich.) pub. schs., 1940-48; mem. English dept. Wheaton (Ill.) Coll., 1948-57, chmn. edn. dept., 1957-66, dean. coll., 1966—. Mem. Wheaton Pub. Library Bd., 1955-70, pres., 1967-70; mem. Wheaton Sister City Commn., 1974—. Bd. dirs. Grace Bible Coll., Grand Rapids, Mich. Fulbright grantee, 1949-50; Danforth grantee, 1957-58. Mem. AAUP, Am. Assn. Higher Edn., Phi Delta Kappa (past pres. Du Page County chpt.), Pi Kappa Delta (hon.). Mem. Wheaton Bible Ch. Club: Exchange (Wheaton) (pres. 1969-70). Author: (with others) Modern Journalism, 1962. Reviewer Dutch and Belgian lit. for Books Abroad. Home: 600 College Ave Wheaton IL 60187

VELTRI, ROBERT WILLIAM, microbiologist; b. McKeesport, Pa., Dec. 1, 1941; s. Anthony and Desdemona V.; A.B., Youngstown U., 1963; M.S., Ph.D., W.Va. U., 1968; m. Suzanne Jones, Apr. 15, 1961; children—Anthony Joseph, Katherine Marie dec., 4-13-79. Asst. prof., dir. otolaryngic research U. W.Va., Morgantown, 1968-72, asso. prof., 1972-76, prof. surgery, microbiology, 1976—, Named Outstanding Tchr., W.Va. U., 1976. Mem. Am. Assn. Immunologists, Soc. Exptl. Biologists, Am. Assn. Cancer Research, Am. Soc. for Microbiology, Am. Acad. Ophthalmology and Otolaryngology (award of merit 1978), Am. Soc. for Infectious Diseases, English Soc. for Infectious Diseases. Contbr. articles to profl. jours. Address: Route 4 Box 500-1 Morgantown WV 26506. *I have pursued my goals with a dedication and purpose equal to my energy and enthusiasm. I also get great satisfaction from taking an idea to its completion. I have a desire to accomplish something of value to society now and in years to come. Research and teaching are compatible.*

VELZEN, BERNARD HENRY, coll. adminstr.; b. The Netherlands, Nov. 13, 1919; s. Henry and Gerritdina (Messelink) V.; came to U.S., 1921, naturalized, 1929; A.B., Calvin Coll., Grand Rapids, Mich., 1941; postgrad. U. Mich., 1941-42; Ph.D., U. Ill., 1945; m. Jane Edna Ryskamp, Mar. 27, 1942; children—Patricia (Mrs. Gary Nederveld), Mary (Mrs. James Voogt), Virginia (Mrs. John Bylsma), Jack. Mem. faculty U. Ill., 1942-44; research chemist Upjohn Co., 1945-47; with Keebler Co., Elmhurst, Ill., 1947-63, pres. Hekman div., 1959-61, v.p. mfg., 1961-63, also dir.; pres. Milprint Inc., Milw., 1963- 67; exec. v.p. Standard Packaging Corp., Stamford, Conn., 1967-69; exec. v.p. Chocolate & Confection div. W.R. Grace Co., N.Y.C., 1969-70; pres. Kingsford Co., Louisville, 1970-72; exec. v.p. Sonnevelt Co., Grand Rapids, 1972-73; pres. Golden Dipt Co. div. DCA Food Industries Inc., Millstadt, Ill., 1973-75; dir. bus. and fin. Trinity Christian Coll., Palos Heights, Ill., 1975-79; sr. v.p. and v.p. fin. affairs McKendree Coll., Lebanon, Ill., 1979—. Active local Community Chest campaigns. Mem. Am. Chem. Soc., Sigma Xi, Alpha Chi Sigma, Phi Lambda Upsilon, Phi Alpha Kappa. Mem. Ref. Ch. (elder, deacon). Address: 906 Matthew Dr O'Fallon IL 62269

VELZY, CHARLES O., cons. sanitary engr.; b. Oak Park, Ill., Mar. 17, 1930; s. Charles R and Ethel B.; B.S., U. Ill., 1953, B.S. in Civil Engring., 1960, M.S. in San. Engring., 1959; m. Marilyn A. Gilman, Aug. 17, 1957; children—Charles Mark, Barbara Helen, Patricia Ethel. Design engr., project engr., Nussbaumer, Clarke & Velzy, N.Y.C., 1959-66; sec.-treas., dir. Charles R Velzy Assos., Inc., Armonk, N.Y., 1966-76, pres., 1976—. Mem. White Plains (N.Y.) Bldg. Code Appeals Bd., 1970—. Served with U.S. Army, 1954-56. Registered profl. engr., N.Y., 8 other states. Mem. ASME (v.p. 1978—, chmn. solid waste processing div. 1973-74, mem. policy bd. research 1974-78), Am. Nat. Standards Inst., ASTM (mem. exec. com. on methods of sampling and analysis of atmospheres), ASCE, Water Pollution Control Fedn., Am. Water Works Assn., Am. Public Works Assn., Nat. Water Well Assn., Am. Water Research Assn., Nat. Assn. Corrosion Engrs., Nat. Soc. Profl. Engrs., Air Pollution Control Assn., Am. Mgmt. Assn. Methodist. Contbr. articles to profl. jours. Home: 131 Woodcrest Ave White Plains NY 10604 Office: 355 Main St Armonk NY 10504. *After deciding on what is needed in a specific situation, based on the facts, establish your objectives and goals and persist to a successful conclusion.*

VENDLER, HELEN HENNESSY, educator; b. Boston, Apr. 30, 1933; d. George and Helen (Conway) Hennessy; A.B., Emmanuel Coll., 1954; Ph.D., Harvard, 1960; 1 son, David. Instr., Cornell U., Ithaca, N.Y., 1960-63; lectr. Swarthmore (Pa.) Coll. and Haverford (Pa.) Coll., 1963-64; asst. prof. Smith Coll., Northampton, Mass., 1964-66; asso. prof. Boston U., 1966-68, prof., 1968—; Fulbright lectr. U. Bordeaux (France), 1968-69; reviewer N.Y. Times Book Review, 1968—; poetry reviewer New Yorker, 1978—. Fulbright fellow, 1954; Guggenheim fellow, 1971-72; Am. Council Learned Socs. fellow, 1971-72; AAUW fellow, 1959; recipient Lowell prize 1969, Explicator prize, 1969, award Nat. Inst. Arts and Letters, 1975. Mem. Modern Lang. Assn. (exec. council 1972-75, 1st v.p. 1979), English Inst. (trustee 1977—), Am. Acad. Arts and Scis., Phi Beta Kappa. Author: Yeats's Vision and the Later Plays, 1963; On Extended Wings: Wallace Stevens' Longer Poems, 1969; The Poetry of George Herbert, 1975; Part of Nature, Part of Us, 1980. Home: 16 A Still St Brookline MA 02146 Office: 236 Bay State Rd Boston MA 02215

VENDLER, ZENO, educator; b. Devecser, Hungary, Dec. 22, 1921; s. Zeno Miklos and Vilma (Gubás) V.; S.T.L., Canisianum, Maastricht, Netherlands, 1952; Ph.D., Harvard, 1959; m. Semiramis Da Silva, May 28, 1964; children—David, Alexander. Asst. prof. Cornell U., Ithaca, N.Y., 1960-63; research asso. U. Pa., 1959-60, 63-64; asso. prof. Bklyn. Coll., 1964-65; prof. U. Calgary (Alta., Can.), 1965-73; Carolyn and Fred McManis prof. philosophy Rice U., Houston, 1973-74; prof. philosophy U. Calif. at San Diego, 1974—. Canada Council grantee, 1968-69; Nat. Endowment for Humanities grantee, 1979. Author: Linguistics in Philosophy, 1967; Adjectives and Nominalizations, 1968; Res Cogitans, 1972. Address: U Calif San Diego La Jolla CA 92037

VENEMAN, GERARD EARL, paper co. exec.; b. Wheeling, W. Va., June 30, 1920; s. F. Earl and Ethel Martha (Joyce) V.; student U. Detroit, Northwestern U.; m. Doris D. Alexander, Jan. 10, 1948; children—Stephanie Joyce, Dean Gerard, Leslie Ann, Nancy Ellen, Jill Edwards. Sales mgr. Agar Packing Co. Chgo., 1945-49; with Nekoosa Papers Inc., Port Edwards, Wis., 1949—, v.p., dir. sales, 1954-62, exec. v.p., dir. mktg., 1962-69, exec. v.p., 1969-70, pres., 1970—, also dir.; chmn. bd. dirs. Butler Paper Co., Port Edwards; dir. Wood County Nat. Bank, Wisconsin Rapids, Franklin Electric, Bluffton, Ind., Sentry Ins. Co., Stevens Point, Wis., Universal Foods Corp., Milw., Gt. No. Nekoosa Corp., Stamford, Conn., Nekoosa Envelopes, Inc., Denver. Pres. bd. Nekoosa-Edwards and Alexander Charitable Founds. Bd. dirs., v.p. South Wood County YMCA, Port Edwards; bd. regents U. Wis. System. Served with AUS, World War II. Decorated Bronze Star medal. Mem. Sales Assn. Paper Industry (pres. 1960, gov. 1964—), Writing Paper Mfrs. Assn. (exec. and finance coms. 1954—, chmn. sulphite bond group 1960-62, v.p. 1960-62, pres. 1963-65), Printing and Writing Assn. (chmn. 1975), Am. Paper Inst. (rep. bd. govs. 1963-65). Home: 311 1st St Port Edwards WI 54469 Office: 100 Wisconsin Dr Port Edwards WI 54469

VENEZIALE, CARLO MARCELLO, biochemist, physician; b. Phila., Oct. 2, 1932; s. Marcello and Mae V.; B.A., Haverford Coll., 1954; M.D., U. Pa., 1958; M.S., Mayo Clinic, U. Minn., 1965; Ph.D., U. Wis., 1969; m. Joyce Laubach, Jan. 15, 1959; children—Paula Joyce, Carla Jill. Intern, Grad. Hosp., Phila., 1958-59; resident Mayo Clinic, Rochester, Minn., 1961-65, staff cons., 1965—; prof. medicine and biochemistry Mayo Med. Sch., 1978—. Served with M.C., USN, 1959-61. Mem. Am. Diabetes Assn., Endocrine Soc., Am. Soc. Biol. Chemists, Am. Soc. Andrology, Soc. Study Reprodn., Soc. Exptl. Biology and Medicine, Central Soc. Roman Catholic. Asso. editor Jour. Lab. and Clin. Medicine, 1977—; editorial bd. Proc. Soc. Exptl. Biology and Medicine, 1976—, Advances in Sex Hormone Research, Ann. Series, 1978—; research in carbohydrate metabolism, male sex steroids. Office: Mayo Clinic 200 First St SW Rochester MN 55901

VENEZIAN, ANGELO RALPH, pub. co. exec.; b. Bklyn., May 12, 1912; s. Vincent and Prudence (Benfanti) V.; student Coll. City N.Y., 1929-31, N.Y.U., 1931-33, Pace Inst., 1933-34, also bus. and sales courses; m. Mathilda Winifred Garber, Sept. 18, 1938; children—Patricia (Mrs. Kenneth Daley), Arleen (Mrs. Howard Shafer), David, Amy, Richard. Employed with the McGraw-Hill Pub. Co., 1929-68, acting mgr. company research, 1935-43, mgr. advt. sales service, 1943-47, asst. to dir. advt., 1947-55, asst. to exec. v.p., 1955-57, v.p., circulation coordinator, 1957-63, v.p. marketing, 1963-66, v.p. prodn., 1966-68; pres. Specialized Information Co., N.Y.C., 1968—; v.p. market Creative Mailing Service, Inc., 1969—; pres. Angelo R. Venezian Inc., 1973—. Mem. Postmasters' Gen. Mailers Tech. Adv. Com., chmn. N.Y. Postal Customers Council. Mem. Bd. Direct Mail Mktg. Assn., 1961, gen. chmn. N.Y. Conv. 1961, chmn. bd. govs., 1962-64; past chmn. publishing mgmt. com. Am. Bus. Press. Active local Boy Scouts Am. Mem. Catholic Press Assn. Clubs: N.Y. Athletic, Chemists. Author reports. Home: 88-99 195th Pl Hollis NY 11423 Office: 10-64 Jackson Ave Long Island City NY 11101

VENEZKY, RICHARD LAWRENCE, educator; b. Pitts., Apr. 16, 1938; s. Bernard Jacob and Isabelle (Zeisel) V.; B.E.E., Cornell U., 1961, M.A., 1962; postgrad. U. Calif. at Berkeley, 1962-63; Ph.D., Stanford U., 1965; m. Karen F. Gauz, Aug. 2, 1964; children—Dina Yael, Elie Michael. Systems programmer, tech. writer Control Data Corp., Palo Alto, Calif., 1962-65; asst. prof. English and computer scis. U. Wis., Madison, 1965-69, asso. prof. computer scis., 1969-74, prof., 1974-77, chmn. dept., 1975-77; Unidel prof. ednl. founds. U. Del., Newark, 1977—; vis. research asso. Tel Aviv U., 1969-70, research fellow, 1973. Chmn. edn. commn. Madison Jewish Community Council, 1973-77; regional chmn. Am. Profs. for Peace in Middle East, 1968-73. Office of Edn. grantee, 1964-66; NSF grantee, 1966-74; Nat. Inst. Edn. grantee, 1973-77; Nat. Endowment Humanities grantee, 1978—. Mem. Am. Psychol. Assn., Am. Ednl. Research Assn., Internat. Reading Assn., Assn. Computing Machinery. Democrat. Jewish. Author: The Structure of English Orthography, 1970; Testing in Reading, 1974; contbr. chpts. to books, articles to profl. jours.; cons. Oxford English Dictionary Supplement; adviser for data processing Dictionary of Old English, 1971—; editorial/adv. com. Computers and the Humanities, 1974; Visible Language, 1976; Doubleday Dictionary, 1975-77. Home: 206 Hullihen Dr Newark DE 19711 Office: Room 211 Williard Hall Bldg U Del Newark DE 19711

VENTO, BRUCE FRANK, Congressman; b. St. Paul, Oct. 7, 1940; s. Frank A. and Ann V. (Sauer) V.; A.A., U. Minn., 1961; B.A., Wis. State U., River Falls, 1965; m. Mary Jean Moore, Oct. 24, 1959; children—Michael, Peter, John. Tchr. sci., social studies Mpls. Pub. Schs.; mem. Minn. Ho. of Reps., 1971-76, asst. majority leader, vice chmn. jud. com.; mem. 95th-96th Congress from 4th Minn. Dist. Mem. legis. rev. com. Minn. Commn. on Future Del., Democratic Farm Labor party Central Com., 1972, chmn. Ramsey County Com., 1972. NSF grantee, 1967-68. Mem. Minn. Fedn. Tchrs., Beta Beta Beta, Kappa Delta Phi. Office: 230 Cannon House Office Bldg Washington DC 20515

VENTULETT, THOMAS WALKER, III, architect; b. Albany, Ga., Oct. 29, 1935; s. Thomas Walker, Jr. and Edith Mae (Poole) V.; B.S., Ga. Inst. Tech., 1957, B.Arch., 1958; M.Arch., U. Pa., 1961; m. Elizabeth Paulick, Dec. 28, 1956; children—Suzanne, Thomas, Jonathan. With archtl. firms in Ga. and Fla., 1959-67; v.p., prin. charge design Thompson, Ventulett & Stainback, Inc., Atlanta, 1968-76; v.p., dir. design Thompson, Ventulett, Stainbeck & Assos., Inc., Atlanta, 1977—; mem. regional pub. adv. panel archtl. and engring. service GSA, 1975; mem. So. G.F. Design Awards Jury, 1974-76. Div. chmn. Atlanta United Way, 1974; exec. bd. Atlanta Area council Boy Scouts Am., 1977. Served as capt. AUS, 1958. Recipient Kawneer prize Student Design competition, 1957; Leadership and Merit medal Alpha Rho Chi, 1958; Wade meml. scholar, 1961; Archtl. award excellence Am. Inst. Steel Constrn., 1973, 77. Fellow AIA (pres. Atlanta 1976, mem. nat. coms. design and urban planning, various design awards juries; Honor award Ga. chpt. 1973, 76, 78, Nat. Bronze medal 1975, South Atlantic Region Conf. Honor award 1976, 78); mem. Tau Sigma Delta (hon.). Democrat. Presbyterian. Prin. works include Omni Arena, Atlanta, 1972, Omni Internat., 1975, N.C. Nat. Bank Plaza, Charlotte, 1974-77, Commerce Pl., Nashville, 1977, Ga. World Congress Center, Atlanta, 1976, IBM-GSD Hdqrs. Bldg., Atlanta, 1977, Merc. Bank Tower, St. Louis, 1974, IBM-SCD, Charlotte, 1980. Home: 4234 Conway Valley Atlanta GA 30327 Office: 1200 N Omni Internat Atlanta GA 30303

VENTURA, FRANK ROBERT, utilities co. exec.; b. Kansas City, Kans., Oct. 24, 1939; s. Frank R. and Eva (Warmington) V.; B.S., B.A. in Accounting, Rockhurst Coll., 1965; m. Carol A. Seufert, Oct. 29, 1960; Gen. accountant Jenkins Music Co., Kansas City, Mo., 1963-65; staff auditor Arthur Young & Co., Kansas City, 1965-66; staff accountant United Telecommunications, Inc., Shawnee Mission, Kans., 1966, mgr. consolidation accounting, 1966-67, asst. controller, 1967-68, controller, 1968—, v.p., 1972—. Office: 2330 Johnson Dr Shawnee Mission KS 66205

VENTURI, RICK JOSEPH, football coach; b. Taylorville, Ill., Feb. 23, 1946; s. Joseph Louis and Norma (Gherardini) V.; B.S. in Edn., Northwestern U., 1968, M.A., 1969; m. Cheri Marie Rotello, Dec. 7, 1967; children—Marin Elizabeth, Jason John. Asst. football coach Northwestern U., Evanston, Ill., 1968-72, head football coach, 1978—; asst. football coach Purdue U., 1972-76, U. Ill., 1977-78. Mem. Am. Football Coaches Assn. Roman Catholic. Home: 618 Colfax St Evanston IL 60201 Office: Dyche Stadium 1501 Central Ave Evanston IL 60201

VENTURI, ROBERT, architect; b. Phila., June 25, 1925; s. Robert C. and Vanna (Lanzetta) v.; grad. Episcopal Acad., 1943; A.B. summa cum laude, Princeton, 1947, M.F.A., 1950; D.F.A. (hon.), Oberlin Coll., 1977, Yale U., 1979; m. Denise (Lakofski) Scott Brown, July 23, 1967; 1 son, James Charles. Designer firms of Oskar Stonorov, Eero Saarinen and Assos., Louis I. Kahn, 1950-58; partner firm Robert Venturi, Cope & Lippincott, Phila., 1958-61, Venturi and Short, Phila., 1961-64, Venturi, Rauch & Scott Brown, Phila., 1964—; from asst. to asso. prof. architecture U. Pa., 1951-65; Charlotte Shepherd Davenport prof. architecture Yale, 1966-70; Trustee Am. Acad. Rome, 1966-71; pres. Venturi, Inc., 1960-73. Recipient various awards including Brunner award Nat. Acad. Arts and Scis., 1973; Medal of Achievement, Phila. Art Alliance, 1978. Fellow Am. Acad. Rome, 1954-56: fellow Graham Found. Advanced Studies Fine Arts, 1962; grantee State Dept. archt. specialist in USSR, 1965. Fellow AIA (awards 1974, 77, 78); mem. Phi Beta Kappa. Author: Complexity and Contradiction in Architecture, 1966; also articles. Co-author: Learning from Las Vegas, 1971. Prin. works include Guild House, Phila., 1963; Humanities Bldg. State U. N.Y., 1972; Franklin Ct., 1976; addition to Allen Meml. Art Bldg., Oberlin Coll., 1977, others; exhibited at Whitney Mus., 1971. Home: 6904 Wissahickon Ave Philadelphia PA 19119 Office: 4236 Main St Philadelphia PA 19102

VENZA, JAC, broadcast exec.; b. Chgo., Dec. 23, 1926. Producer, asso. producer, designer CBS, N.Y.C., 1950-64; exec. producer NET Playhouse (Peabody award 1968, Emmy award 1969); exec. producer for cultural programs NET, N.Y.C., 1964-69 (recipient Prix D'Italia 1966), exec. producer for drama, 1969-73, dir. Performance Programs, PBS WNET/13, N.Y.C., 1973—; exec. producer Adams Chronicles (Emmy award nomination 1976, Peabody award 1977), WNET's Great Performances series including Dance in America (Emmy award nomination 1976), Theater in America (Peabody award 1974), Fine Music spls. (Emmy award 1975, TV Critics Circle awards 1976-77); organizer, dir. Mus. Modern Art's TV USA-13 season, 1976; condr. workshop Creating Dramas for TV, Tarrytown, N.Y., 1976. Mem. Nat. Acad. TV Arts and Scis. Office: WNET-Channel 13 356 W 58th St New York City NY 10019

VENZKE, WALTER GEORGE, veterinarian, educator; b. White Lake, S.D., June 18, 1912; s. Carl John and Katherine Dorothea (Ebert) V.; D.V.M., Iowa State U., 1935, Ph.D., 1942; M.Sc., U. Wis., 1937; m. Elaine King, Apr. 15, 1939; children—Ann Rees, Thomas R. Groff. With Agrl. Research Service, Dept. Agr., 1935; research asst. U. Wis., 1935-37; ambulatory clinician Iowa State U., 1937, instr., then asst. prof. vet. anatomy, 1937-42; mem. faculty Coll. Vet. Medicine, Ohio State U., Columbus, 1946—, prof. vet. medicine, 1951—, chmn. dept., 1948-54, chmn. dept. vet. anatomy, 1954—, asst. dean student affairs, sec., 1960—; prof. vet. sci. Ohio Agrl. and Devel. Center, Wooster, 1948—. Mem. Columbus Bd. Health, 1968—. Served to maj. AUS, 1942-46. Recipient Distinguished Tchr. award Coll. Vet. Medicine, Ohio State U., 1969. Mem. Am., Ohio vet. med. assns., World Assn. Vet. Anatomists, Am. Assn. Anatomists, Conf. Research Workers Animal Diseases, Am. Legion. Republican. Club: Ohio State U. Faculty. Contbr. articles to profl. jours. Home: 2535 Andover Rd Columbus OH 43221

VERALDI, LEWIS C., automotive co. exec.; b. July 16, 1930; s. Luigi and Carmella (Bilotta) V.; B.S.M.E., Lawrence Inst. Tech., 1967; m. Irene Kuciemba, Oct. 23, 1954; children—William, Marcia, Lisa, Carla, Joseph, Cristina. With Ford Motor Co. and subs., 1949—, v.p. car engring. Ford of Europe, London, 1973-75, v.p. product devel. Ford of Europe, London, 1975-76, v.p. advanced vehicles devel. Ford Motor Co., Dearborn, Mich., 1976—. Served with AUS, 1948-49. Mem. Soc. Automotive Engrs., Engring. Soc. Detroit. Roman Catholic. Patentee vehicle chassis front suspension mechanism. Home: 550 Arlington Dr Birmingham MI 48009 Office: 21175 Oakwood Blvd Dearborn MI 48126

VERANO, ANTHONY FRANK, banker; b. West Harrison, N.Y., Jan. 4, 1931; s. Frank and Rose (Viscome) V.; student Am. Inst. Banking, 1956-60, Bank Adminstrn. Inst., U. Wis., 1962-64, RCA Programmers Sch., 1965, Burroughs Programmers Sch., 1965, N.J. Bankers Data Processing Sch., 1966-68, others; m. Clara Cosentino, July 8, 1951; children—Rosemarie, Diana Lynn. With County Trust Co., White Plains, N.Y., 1949-61, sr. auditor, 1960-61; with State Nat. Bank Conn., Bridgeport, 1961—, auditor 1962—; tchr. bank auditing Am. Inst. Banking, 1976-78. Mem. adv. bd. Norwalk Community Coll., 1968—. Served with USN, 1951-52. Mem. Bank Adminstrn. Inst. (dir. Stamford chpt. 1967-68, sec. Western Conn. chpt. 1968-69, treas. 1969-70, v.p. 1970-71, pres. 1971-72), Am. Accounting Assn., Inst. Internal Auditors. (chartered bank auditor 1970). Home: 59 Bugg Hill Rd Monroe CT 06468 Office: 2834 Fairfield Ave Bridgeport CT 06605 . *It is difficult to define the elements of success. There are those who say success is achieved through drive and ambition only. However, those who have achieved their goals in life using only these two principles have probably destroyed more than they have created. Success, I feel, is achieved when drive and ambition are tempered with honesty, fairness, and respect for others. An individual must have a sense of dedication not only to his work and for those with whom he works but, most importantly, for those who work for him. This has been my philosophy in achieving my success.*

VERBA, SIDNEY, polit. scientist; b. Bklyn., May 26, 1932; s. Morris Harold and Recci (Salman) V.; B.A., Harvard U., 1953; M.A., Princeton U., 1955, Ph.D., 1959; m. E. Cynthia Winston, June 17, 1955; children—Margaret Lynn, Ericka Kim, Martina Claire. Asst. prof. polit. sci. Princeton U., 1960-63, asso. prof., 1963-64; prof. Stanford U., 1964-68, U. Chgo., 1968-72; prof. govt., chmn. dept. govt. Harvard U., 1972—; mem. bd. syndics Harvard U. Press. Fellow Am. Acad. Arts and Scis.; mem. Am. Polit. Sci. Assn. (Woodrow Wilson Found. award 1976, exec. council 1971—), Internat. Polit. Sci. Assn. Jewish. Author: Small Groups and Political Behavior, 1961; The Civic Culture, 1963; Participation in America, 1972; The Changing American Voter, 1976; Participation and Political Equality, 1978; Injury to Insult, 1979. Home: 142 Summit Ave Brookline MA 02146 Office: Littauer M22 Harvard U Cambridge MA 02138

VERBECK, BRUNO JOSEPH, lawyer; b. Chgo., July 7, 1913; s. Anthony and Amelia (Ramanauskas) V.; B.S. in Chemistry, U. Ill., 1936; J.D., Loyola U., Chgo., 1942; m. Katherine Strubbe, June 28, 1941; 1 son, Daniel. Research chemist Wilson & Co., Chgo., 1936-42; admitted to Ill. bar, 1942, Calif. bar, 1971; practice firm Johnson, Dienner, Emrich, Verbeck & Wagner and predecessor, Chgo., 1949-74; practice in San Diego, 1971—; partner firm Verbeck & Haller, 1977. Served to maj. AUS, 1942-46. Mem. Am., Chgo., San Diego bar assns., Am., Chgo. patent law assns., Am. Chem. Soc., AAAS, Fine Arts Soc. San Diego (life), Am. Inst. Chemists, Phi Alpha Delta. Clubs: Union League, Adventurers (Chgo.). Home: 6502 Avenida Manana La Jolla CA 92037 Office: 1010 2d Ave San Diego CA 92101

VERBER, RICHARD WILLIAM, chess master; b. Cleve., June 4, 1944; s. Fred and Ann Mary (Piller) V.; B.S., Loyola, Chgo., 1967; postgrad. U. Chgo., 1967-70. Chgo. chess champion, 1966, 67, 69, Ill. chess champion, 1967, 68, 70; mem. 1st place U.S. Student Chess Team, World Student Team Chess Championship, Haifa, 1970; exec. chmn. U.S. Open Chess Tournament, Chgo., 1973; chief commentator Fischer Spassky match Ednl. TV, Chgo., 1972; tournament dir. Chgo.-U.S. Chess Fedn. internat. tournament, 1973; exec. chmn. U.S. Class Championship, Chgo., 1976; chmn., organizer U.S. Class Chess Championship, Chgo., 1978; co-sponsor, chmn., chief tournament dir. U.S. Open Chess Championship, 1979. Mem. U.S. Chess Fedn. (officer) Chgo. Chess Found. (v.p. 1964-73), Chgo. Chess Club (pres. 1968—). Home: 724 W Cornelia Chicago IL 60657 Office: Chicago Chess Club care No Exit Cafe 7001 N Glenwood Chicago IL 60626

VERBRUGGE, FRANK, educator; b. Chandler, Minn., Dec. 22, 1913; s. James and Maria (Vander Vliet) V.; B.A., Calvin Coll., Grand Rapids, Mich., 1934; M.A., U. Mo., 1940, Ph.D., 1942; m. C. Helen Roelofs, Dec. 27, 1940; children—Anne Louise, Lois Marie, Robert Roelofs, Martha Helen. Instr. physics U. Mo., 1940-41; prof. N.E. Mo. State Tchrs. Coll., Kirksville, 1941-43; from asst. prof. to prof. physics Carleton Coll., 1943-56; mem. staff radiation lab. Mass. Inst. Tech., 1944-46; asso. prof. physics U. Minn., 1956-59, prof., 1959—, asso. dean Inst. Tech., 1959-68, dir. University Computer Services, 1968—. Mem. Commn. Coll. Physics, 1961-63; cons. higher edn. Latin Am., West Africa, Ford Found. Mem. Am. Assn. Physics Tchrs. (sec. 1956-61, pres. 1962-63), Am. Phys. Soc., AAAS, Sigma Xi. Home: 1787 Shryer Ave St Paul MN 55113 Office: Space Sci Center U Minn Minneapolis MN 55455

VERDERY, JOHN DUANE, clergyman, educator; b. Berkeley, Calif., Mar. 4, 1917; s. Marion Jackson and Eleanor (Simonds) V.; student Blair Acad., 1931-35; A.B., Princeton, 1935-39, Litt.D. (hon.) 1963; postgrad. Union Theol. Sem., 1939-41; B.D., Episcopal Theol. Sem., 1942; D.D. (hon.), Hobart Coll., 1959; m. Suzanne Aldrich, June 17, 1942; children—Joan, Daniel, Donald, Benjamin. Ordained priest P.E. Ch., 1942; dir. St. Paul's Cathedral Camp, 1942; asst. St. Paul's Cathedral, Boston, 1942-43; headmaster Wooster Sch., 1943-76, rector, 1976—. Trustee Wooster Sch., Day Sch., N.Y.C., Palm Beach (Fla.) Day Sch. Decorated chevalier Ordre des Palmes Académiques. Mem. Nat. Assn. Episcopal Schs. (past pres., treas.), Conn. Assn. Ind. Schs. (trustee 1971-74), Headmasters Assn. (v.p. 1976), Nat. Assn. Ind. Schs. (past pres., treas.). Club: Century. Author: It's Better to Believe, 1964. Home: 620 Ridgebury Rd Ridgefield CT 06877

VERDEYEN, JOSEPH THOMAS, educator; b. Terre Haute, Ind., Aug. 15, 1932; s. George Francis and Josephine (Kelly) V.; B.S. (scholarship), Rose Poly. Inst., 1954; M.S., Rutgers U., 1958; Ph.D. (Bendix fellow), U. Ill., 1962; m. Kathryn A. Forbes, June 12, 1954; children—Mary, Joseph, Jean, Michael. With Bell Telephone Labs., Murray Hill, N.J., 1954-55; instr. Rutgers U., 1957-58; prof. elec. engring. and nuclear engring. U. Ill., Champaign, 1958—, now also dir. gaseous electronics lab.; cons. ITT, Ft. Wayne, Ind., 1967-68, Zenith Radio Corp., 1972-77, C.E. Research Labs., 1972-77, Gen. Electric, 1975—, Lawrence Livermore Labs., 1976—, Lucitron Corp., 1978—, Hurletron, 1978—. Mem. exec. com. Gaseous Electronic Conf., 1975-78. Mem. Bd. Edn., Champaign-Urbana Bd. for Cath. Edn., 1968-77. Served with U.S. Army, 1955-57. Mem. IEEE, Am. Phys. Soc., Sigma Xi, Tau Beta Pi. Roman Catholic. Contbr. articles to profl. jours. Home: 913 W White St Champaign IL 61820

VERDIER, LEONARD D'OOGE, JR., lawyer; b. Grand Haven, Mich., Aug. 1, 1915; s. Leonard D'Ooge and Anna (Carpenter) V.; A.B., U. Mich., 1937, J.D. with distinction, 1939; m. Anita B. Carvalho, July 27, 1940; children—Leslie (Mrs. David N. Armentrout), David D., Laurie M. Admitted to Mich. bar, 1939, since practiced in Grand Rapids; sec. Bissell, Inc. Served with USNR, 1943-46. Mem. Am., Mich., Grand Rapids bar assns., Sigma Phi. Republican. Conglist. Clubs: University, Kent Country (sec.) (Grand Rapids), Macatawa Bay Yacht (past commodore) (Holland, Mich.). Home: 2555 Chatham Woods SE Grand Rapids MI 49506 Office: Old Kent Bldg Grand Rapids MI 49503

VERDIER, PHILIPPE M(AURICE), art historian; b. Lambersart, France, Oct. 5, 1912; s. Georges and Berthe (Fort) V.; came to Can., 1965, naturalized, 1973; M.A., Sorbonne, Paris, 1935; mem. Ecole Française de Rome, 1938-39; Professeur Agrégé de l'Université, Ecole Normale Supérieure, Paris, 1936; m. Patricia Cowles, July 3, 1954; children—Francesca, Lisa, Caroline, Patrick. Prof., Institut Français, Barcelona, Spain, 1941, Madrid, 1943-44, Lycée R. Poincaré, Bar Le Duc, 1950-51; Henri Focillon fellow Yale U., 1951-52, guest prof., 1959, 61; guest prof. Bryn Mawr Coll., 1952-53, Johns Hopkins U., 1954, 65; prof. U. Poitiers (France), 1964; mem. Inst. Advanced Study, Princeton U., 1964-65; titular prof. U. Montréal (Qué., Can.), 1965-79; curator Walters Art Gallery, Balt., 1953-65, Mus. Art, Carnegie Inst., Pitts., 1963-64; guest prof. Harvard U., 1967; prof. Carleton U., 1972-74; mem. Commission des Programmes Universitaires du Qué., 1973-74; cons. curator Cleve. Mus. Art, 1979. U.S. fgn. policy reporter Marshall Plan, 1947-48. Served with French Air Force, 1937-38, 38-40, 45. Decorated Legion of Honor; Arts Council Can. Killam fellow, 1974-76. Mem. Internat. Center Medieval Art, Universities Art Assn. Can., Corpus Vitrearum Medii Aevi, Musée Des Beaux-Arts Montreal, Comité Internat. d'Histoire de l'Art, Menil Found. Roman Catholic. Author books, the most recent being: Limoges Painted Enamels, 1977; Le Couronnement de la Vierge, 1979. Home: 2626 Côte-Ste-Catherine Montreal PQ H3T 1B4 Canada Office: U Montréal History of Art CP 6128-A Montreal PQ H3C 3J7 Canada

VERDISCO, GEORGE MICHAEL, food co. exec.; b. Yonkers, N.Y., May 4, 1939; s. Samtine Joseph and Anna (Pagnillo) V.; A.B. in History, Georgetown U., 1961; M.B.A. in Fin., Fairleigh Dickinson U., 1970; m. Anne Marie Petrucione, Sept. 15, 1962; children—Amy, Michael, Sarah. Credit reporter Dun & Bradstreet, N.Y.C., 1964-66; sr. fin. analyst Warner Lambert Pharm. Co., Morris Plains, N.J., 1966-70; mgr. cash forecasting Bordens, Inc., N.Y.C., 1970-71; asst. treas. Welch Foods, Inc., Westfield, N.Y., 1971-75, treas., 1975—; lectr. Fredonia State U.; adv. bd. Erie County Savs. Bank. Adv. bd. Jamestown (N.Y.) Gen. Hosp.; mem. Real Estate Grievance Bd. Served with USAF, 1961-64. Mem. Fin. Execs. Inst. Roman Catholic. Clubs: N.Y. Athletic, Moon Brook Country, Livingston. Home: RD 4 Hillview Dr Jamestown NY 14701 Office: 2 S Portage St Westfield NY 14787

VERDON, GWEN (GWYNETH EVELYN), actress, dancer, choreographer; b. Los Angeles, Jan. 13, 1925; d. Joseph William and Gertrude (Standring) V.; ed. pub. schs.; m. James Henaghan, 1942 (div. June 1947); children—James O'Farrell, Nicole; m. 2d, Robert Louis Fosse, Apr. 3, 1960 (div.). Broadway debut in Alive and Kicking, 1950; appeared in musical plays including Can Can, 1953-54, Damn Yankees 1955-56, New Girl in Town, 1957; appeared motion picture Damn Yankees, 1958, On The Riviera, 1951; David and Bathsheba, 1952; appeared in play Sweet Charity, 1966; star play Chicago, N.Y.C., 1975; staged musical Dancin, also acted as dance mistress. Bd. dirs. Postgrad. Center for Mental Health. Recipient Donaldson award for acting and dancing, Lambs Gambol award for acting; Grammy award, 1959; Silver Bowl award Dance Mag., 1961; Antoinette Perry award for Can Can, 1954, Damn Yankees, 1956, New Girl in Town, 1958, Red Head, musical, 1959. Office: care Shapiro Taxon and Kopell 1180 Ave of the Americas New York NY 10036*

VERDUIN, JACOB, educator; b. Orange City, Iowa, Nov. 19, 1913; s. Peter and Jennie (Lagestee) V.; B.S., Iowa State Coll., 1939, M.S., 1941, Ph.D., 1947; m. Bethy Albertha Anderson, July 3, 1942; children—Lans, Jan, Charlotte, Leslie, Bethy. Farmer, 1933-35; head botany dept. S.D. State U., 1946-48; asso. prof. hydrobiology F. T. Stone Lab., Ohio State U., 1948-54; head biology dept. Bowling Green

State U., 1955-64; prof. botany So. Ill. U., Carbondale, 1964—. Cons. NIH, summer 1954, cons. water pollution control sect. TVA, summer 1957, Commonwealth Edison, 1972-79, EPA, 1975-79. Served to ensign USNR, 1942-45. Fellow Ohio Acad. Sci. (exec. v.p. plant sci. sect. 1958), AAAS; mem. Am. Inst. Biol. Scis., Societas Internationalis Limnologiae, Ecol. Soc. Am., Am. Fisheries Soc., Am. Assn. Limnologists and Oceanographers, Sigma Xi, Phi Kappa Phi, Beta Beta Beta, Gamma Sigma Delta, Omicron Delta Kappa. Episcopalian. Mem. editorial bd. Ecology, 1954-57, Limnology and Oceanography, Ohio Jour. Sci., Trans. Am. Fisheries Soc. Home: RFD 4 Carbondale IL 62901. *As a scientist, I have always believed that objectivity and integrity were more important than prestige. As a teacher I have believed that understanding is the goal and memorization should never be a substitute for it. As a person I have believed that most misunderstandings result from inadequate communication.*

VERDY, VIOLETTE, ballerina; b. Pont-L'Abbe, France, Dec, 1, 1933; d. Renan and Jeanne (Chateaureynaud) Guillerm; ed. in Paris. With Ballet des Champs Elysees, 1945-51, Ballet de Paris de Roland Petit; headed London Festival Ballet on tour U.S.; appeared La Scala, Milan, 1955-56, also Ballet Rambert Co., Eng., Am. Ballet Theatre on tour U.S., Europe and Iron Curtain countries, 1957-58; prin. ballerina N.Y. City Ballet, 1958-77; dir. Paris Opera Ballet, 1977-80; asso. artistic dir. Boston Ballet, 1980—; guest ballerina Royal Ballet, 1958; guest appearances include Munich, Stuttgart opera ballets, Jacob's Pillow Festival, others; roles include Miss Julie, Cinderella, Sleeping Beauty, Nutcracker, Romeo and Juliette, Carmen, Giselle; movie roles in Ballerina, 1948, The Glass Slipper, 1954; TV appearances in U.S., Eng., France, Belgium, Germany. Recipient Silver Medallion award Annual Dance Mag., 1968. Office: care Boston Ballet 19 Clarendon St Boston MA 02116*

VEREEN, BEN, actor, singer, dancer; b. Miami, Fla., Oct. 10, 1946; student High Sch. of Performing Arts; L.H.D. (hon.), Emerson Coll., 1977; married; children—Benjamin, Malaika, Naja, Kabara, Karon. Debuted off Broadway in The Prodigal Son, 1965; played Brother Ben in Sweet Charity, N.Y.C., Las Vegas, San Francisco, 1966, Daddy Brubeck in Sweet Charity, Can. tour, 1968; in Los Angeles co. of Hair, 1968, joined Broadway cast, 1969; played role of Judas in Jesus Christ Superstar, 1971 (Theatre World award); played role of Leading Player in Pippin, 1972 (Tony award; Drama Desk and Clio awards for comml.); hosted four-week mini series on TV, summer 1975; appeared in TV movie Louis Armstrong-Chicago Style, 1976; created role of Chicken George in Roots, 1977 (TV Critics award); appeared in TV spl. Ben Vereen-His Roots, 1978; film: Funny Lady, 1975; also nightclub appearances. Recipient George M. Cohan awards Am. Guild Variety Artists, 1976; Image award NAACP, 1977, 78; Israel's Cultural award, 1978, Humanitarian award, 1975. Office: care William Morris Agy 1350 Ave of Americas New York NY 10019. *I am like the turtle - determined and will stick my neck out; turtles also teach me patience.*

VEREEN, ROBERT CHARLES, editor; b. Stillwater, Minn., Sept. 8, 1924; s. George and Leona Lucille (Made) Wihren; grad. high sch.; m. Rose Catherine Blair, Nov. 5, 1945; children—Robin, Stacy, Kim. Mng. editor Comml. West Mag., Mpls., 1946-50; mng. editor Bruce Pub. Co., St. Paul, 1950-53, Nat. Retail Hardware Assn., Indpls., 1953-59; mng. dir. Liberty Distributors, Phila., 1959-63; editor Hardware Retailing, Indpls., 1963—. Lectr. mgmt. insts.; guest lectr. on distbn., pub. Served to sgt., AUS, 1943-46. Mem. Am. Soc. Bus Press Editors (dir., v.p. 1966-70), Soc. Nat. Assn. Publs. (dir., pres. 1970-75, chmn. journalism edn. liaison com. 1976-79), Toastmasters (v.p., treas., sec. 1955-59), Am. Hardware Mfrs'. Assn. (co-founder, sec.-treas. Young Execs'. Club 1958-59, 63-65), Hardware-Housewares Packaging Exposition (founder 1960, chmn. com. packaging 1960-62 chmn. judging com. Hardware-Packaging Expn. 1975-78), Packaging Inst. Author: (with Paul M. Doane) Hunting for Profit, 1965; The Computer Age in Merchandising, 1968; Perpetuating the Family-Owned Business, 1970; The How-To of Merchandising, 1975; The How-To of Store Operations, 1976; A Guide to Financial Management, 1976; Productivity: A Crisis for Management, 1978. Home: 4560 Lincoln Rd Indianapolis IN 46208 Office: 770 N High School Rd Indianapolis IN 46224

VERGE, PIERRE, coll. dean; b. Quebec City, Can., Jan. 9, 1936; s. Francis and Regina (Roy) V.; B.A., Laval U., 1956, LL.L., 1959, LL.D., 1971; M.A., McGill U., 1962, Cambridge U., 1977; LL.M., U. Toronto, 1968; 1971; m. Colette Habel, June 29, 1963; children—Marc, Caroline, Louis. Admitted to Que. bar, 1961; Queen's Counsel, 1976; pvt. practice law, Quebec City, Can., 1961-66; mem. faculty Laval U. Faculty of Law, 1966—, dean Faculty of Law, 1973—; Commonwealth fellow St. John's Coll., Cambridge U., 1977-78. Mem. Assn. Can. Law Tchrs. (pres. 1972-73; chmn. conf. law deans 1975-76), Que. Bar, Canadian Bar. Home: 2542 de la Falaise Sillery PQ G1T 1W3 Canada Office: Cite Universitaire Quebec PQ Canada

VERGER, DON MARSHALL, psychologist, educator; b. Rock Island, Ill., Oct. 17, 1926; s. John Oscar and Blanche (Sosna) V.; B.S., U. Ill., 1952; M.Ed., U. Ore., 1960, Ed.D., 1965; m. Wilma Rose Spacek, June 11, 1959; 1 dau., Lynn Rosel. Instr. psychology William Woods Coll., 1959-63; prof. psychology, chmn. dept. U. Wis., 1965—; faculty Alfred Adler Inst., Chgo., 1968—; post-doctoral fellow clin. psychology U. N.C. Sch. Medicine, 1970-71; pvt. practice psychology, Platteville, Wis., 1971—; cons. Southwest Wis. Mental Health Center, Lancaster, Wis., 1968-69. Served with AUS, 1944-46. Mem. Wis., Iowa, Am. psychol. assns., Am. Soc. Adlerian Psychology, Psi Chi. Home: 80 Preston Dr Platteville WI 53818

VERGER, MORRIS DAVID, architect, planner; b. Ft. Worth, Mar. 25, 1915; s. Joseph and Dora (Bunyan) V.; B.Arch., U. Calif., Berkeley, 1943; m. Florence Brown, June 21, 1939; children—Paul, Alice. Naval architect U.S. Navy Bur. Ships, San Pedro, Calif., 1943-45; draftsman various archtl. firms So. Calif., 1946-50; pvt. practice as architect and planner, Los Angeles, 1951—; works include Terman Engring. Center, Stanford U., 1974, Huntington Dr. Sch., Los Angeles, 1975, Flax Artist Materials Bldg., Los Angeles, 1976, Frank D. Lanterman High Sch., Los Angeles, 1978; lectr. architecture U. Calif. Los Angeles Extension; vis. critic Calif. State U. (San Luis Obispo); leader Seminar on Interactive Planning, San Francisco. Recipient design awards Westwood C. of C., 1974, 75. Fellow AIA (pres. So. Calif. chpt. 1975, v.p. environ. affairs Calif. council 1976, v.p. Calif. council 1979—, pres. designate Calif. council 1980, presdl. citation 1976). Inventor (with E.H. Porter) Interactive Planning; developed method for computer design of Interstitial Space. Home: 1362 Comstock Ave Los Angeles CA 90024 Office: 10880 Wilshire Blvd Los Angeles CA 90024

VERHEYEN, EGON, art historian, educator; b. Duisburg, Germany, Apr. 13, 1936; s. Franz and Klara (Läufer) V.; came to U.S., 1966; student U. Mainz (Germany), 1956-58; Ph.D., U. Würzburg (Germany), 1962; m. Hanne Schulten, Aug. 22, 1961; children—Peter David, Gero, Esther. With German Nat. Museum, Nuremberg, 1961; Herodotos mem. Inst. for Advanced Study, Princeton, N.J., 1962-63; research fellow Bayerische Staatsgemäldesammlungen, Munich, Germany, 1965-66, asst. prof. history of art U. Mass., Amherst, 1966; asst. prof. U. Mich., Ann Arbor, 1967-70, asso. prof., 1970-72; prof. dept history of art Johns Hopkins, 1972—, chmn. dept., 1972-76; research fellow Bibliotheca Hertziana, Rome, Italy, 1963-65. Max Planck Gesellschaft grantee, 1963-65; Horace H. Rackham Found. grantee, 1968, 70; Nat. Endowment for Humanities grantee, 1972, 76, 77; Fritz Thyssen Gesellschaft grantee, 1965-66; U. Mich. travel grantee, 1971-72, Office Research Adminstrn. grantee, 1971. Mem. Coll. Art Assn. Am., Renaissance Soc. Am., Soc. Archtl. Historians, A.A.U.P., Kunsthistorisches Institut Florence (Italy). Author: Minoritenkirche Duisburg, 1959; Goldene Evangelienbuch von Echternach, 1963; Studiolo of Isabella d'Este, 1971; Palazzo del Te in Mantua, 1977. Contbr. numerous articles to profl. jours. Home: 3953 Cloverhill Rd Baltimore MD 21218

VERHOOGEN, JOHN, educator; b. Brussels, Belgium, Feb. 1, 1912; s. Rene and Lucy (Vinçotte) V.; Mining Engr., U. Brussels, 1933; Geol. Engr., U. Liege, 1934; Ph.D., Stanford, 1936; m. Ilse Goldschmidt, Nov. 28, 1938; children—Robert H., Alexis R., Therese, Sylvie. Came to U.S., 1947, naturalized 1953. Asst. U. Brussels, Brussels and Belgian Congo, 1936-39; Fonds National Rocherche Scientifique, Belgian Congo, 1939-40; Mines d'or de Kilo-Moto, Belgian Congo, 1940-43; dir. prodn. Miniere de Guerre, Belgian Congo, 1943-46; asso. prof. U. Calif., 1947-51, prof., 1952-77, prof. emeritus, 1977—. Guggenheim fellow, 1953-54, 60-61. Mem. Nat. Acad. Scis., Am. Acad. Arts and Scis., Am. Geophys. Union, Geol. Soc. Am. (Day medal 1958). Club: Faculty (Berkeley). Author books, articles on petrology, volcanology, geophysics. Home: 2100 Marin Ave Berkeley CA 94707

VERITY, CALVIN WILLIAM, JR., steel co. exec.; b. Middletown, Ohio, Jan. 26, 1917; s. Calvin William and Elizabeth (O'Brien) V.; grad. Phillips Exeter Acad., 1935; B.A., Yale, 1939; m. Margaret Burnley Wymond, Apr. 19, 1941; children—Jonathan George, Peggy Wymond (Mrs. John Power), William Wymond. With Armco Steel Corp. (now Armco Inc.), Middletown, 1940—, dir. public relations, 1961-62, asst. to pres., 1962-63, v.p., gen. mgr., 1963-65, exec. v.p., dir., 1965, pres., chief exec. officer, 1965-71, chmn. bd., 1971—; dir. Chase Manhattan Bank, Mead Corp., Dayton, Ohio, Bus. Internat., N.Y.C., First Nat. Bank, Middletown, Boston Co., Taft Broadcasting Co., Cin. Chmn. bd. govs. Ford's Theater. Mem. Middletown C. of C. (past pres.), Cin. Council World Affairs, SAR. Clubs: Brown's Run Country (Middletown); Moraine (Dayton); Laurel Valley (Ligonier, Pa.); Queen City, Camargo (Cin.) Office: Armco Inc 703 Curtis St Middletown OH 45042*

VERITY, GEORGE LUTHER, lawyer; b. Oklahoma City, Jan. 3, 1914; s. George H. and Mae (Tibbals) V.; LL.B., Okla. U., 1937; m. Ellen Van Hoesen, Mar. 18, 1939; children-George Luther II, Grover Steven, David Webster, Mark Sidney. Admitted to Tex. bar, 1937, Okla. bar, 1939, N.M. bar, 1957; practice in Wichita Falls, Tex., 1939-40, 46-48, Oklahoma City, 1948-57, Farmington, N.Mex., 1957-64, Oklahoma City, 1964—; partner firm Verity, Brown & Verity and predecessor firm, 1964-77; of counsel Bay, Hamilton, Lee, Spears & Verity, 1978—; chmn. bd., dir. Big D Chem. Co.; pres., dir. Okla. Mgmt. Co.; pres., chmn. bd., dir. Progress Life & Accident Ins. Co. Trustee Rocky Mountain Mineral Law Found. Served to capt. USAAF, 1941-46; PTO; prisoner of war. Decorated Purple Heart. Mem. Am., Okla. bar assns., State Bar N.Mex. (chmn. mineral sect.), State Bar Tex., Assn. Trial Lawyers Am., Okla. Trial Lawyers Assn., Acacia. Mason, Elk. Author: The Modern Oil and Gas Lease. Home: 7107 Brentwood Terr Oklahoma City OK Office: 501 NW 13th St Oklahoma City OK 73103. *In a Japanese prison camp during World War II the love of God came into my life in a magnificant and dramatic way. The expression of this love has brought to my life, health, happiness, and success.*

VERITY, MAURICE ANTHONY, pathologist, neuropathologist; b. Bradford, Eng., Apr. 21, 1931; s. Arthur Maurice and Nora (Fox) V.; B.A., Denstone Coll., 1949, M.A., 1950; M.D., U. London, 1956; m. Valerie Ann, June 15, 1957; children—Michael, Neil, Gail. Intern, St. Mary's Hosp., London, 1956-57; clin. pathologist United Bristol (Eng.) Hosp., 1958; asst. prof. pharmacology UCLA, 1959-61, resident in pathology, 1961-63, asst. prof. pathology, 1963-67, asso. prof., 1968-74, prof., 1974—, mem. Brain Research Inst. and Mental Retardation Center, 1968—; cons. neuropathology Kaiser Permanente Found. NIH fellow Bristol U., 1968; recipient numerous fed., pvt. found. grants. Mem. Am. Soc. Exptl. Pathology, Am. Assn. Pathologists and Bacteriologists, Am. Neurochem. Soc., Histochem. Soc. Author: A Stereotaxic Atlas of the Mongolian Gerbil Brain, 1974; contbg. author Metabolic Conjugation and Hydrolysis, 1973; The Striated Muscle, 1973. Contbr. articles to profl. pubs. Home: 9431 Texhoma Ave Northridge CA 91325 Office: Dept of Pathology University of California Center for Health Sciences Los Angeles CA 90024

VERLANDER, WILLIAM ASHLEY, ins. co. exec.; b. Portsmouth, Va., Jan. 23, 1920; B.S., Ga. Inst. Tech.; married; 2 children. Accountant, W.W. Stribling Co., Atlanta; sr. examiner Ga. Ins. Dept.; partner firm Stribling, Blanton, Rintye & Verlander, Atlanta; co-organizer, exec. v.p., treas. Am. Heritage Life Ins. Co., Jacksonville, Fla., 1956-62, pres. after 1962, also dir.; pres., dir. Am. Heritage Life Investment Corp., Am. Century Advisers Inc.; chmn. bd., trustee Am. Century Mortgage Investors; dir. Varnett Bank of Jacksonville N.A., Fla. Pub. Co., Cain & Bultman, Inc., Barnett Investment Services Inc. Chmn. Downtown Devel. Council of Jacksonville; pres. Gator Bowl Assn.; mem. nat. advisory bd., then, chmn. Ga. Inst. Tech.; trustee Jacksonville U. Recipient Good Citizens award Jacksonville Jr. C. of C., 1965, C.G. Snead Meml. award as outstanding ins. man in Jacksonville area, 1968, Man of Yr. award Fla. Assn. Life Underwriters, 1970; honored in recognition of outstanding mgmt. accomplishments in commerce and industry Sales and Mktg. Execs. of Jacksonville, 1967; named Outstanding Alumnus Coll. Indsl. Mgmt. Ga. Inst. Tech., 1970. Mem. Jacksonville Area (pres.), Fla. State (dir.) chambers of commerce. Clubs: River, San Jose, Univ. (Jacksonville); Ponte Vedra (Ponte Vedra Beach, Fla.); Capital City (Atlanta). Office: Am Heritage Life Ins Co 11 E Forsyth St Jacksonville FL 32202*

VERLEGER, PHILIP KING, lawyer; b. Santa Clara, Calif., Sept. 26, 1918; s. Frederick and Mildred Frances (Thomas) V.; A.B., U. Calif. at Berkeley, 1940, LL.B., 1943; m. Hester Ann Wilkinson, June 6, 1942; 1 son, Philip King. Admitted to Calif. bar, 1943; law clk. Justice Roger Traynor, Calif. Supreme Ct., San Francisco, 1943-44; instr. comml. law U. Calif. at Berkeley, 1943-44; asso. atty. McCutchen, Black, Harnagel & Shea, and predecessor firms, San Francisco, 1944-45, Los Angeles, 1945-56; partner firm McCutchen, Black, Verleger & Shea, Los Angeles, 1956—; gen. counsel Western Oil & Gas Assn., Los Angeles, 1961—. Fellow Am. Coll. Trial Lawyers, Am. Bar Found.; mem. State Bar Calif., Am. Bar Assn. (chmn. natural resources law sect. 1975-76), Am. Law Inst., Maritime Law Assn., Order of Coif. Club: Calif. Editor-in-chief Calif. Law Rev., 1942-43. Contbr. articles on environ. and anti-trust law to profl. jours. Office: 3435 Wilshire Blvd Los Angeles CA 90010

VERMA, MANINDRA KISHORE, educator; b. Motihari, India, Jan. 31, 1931; s. Rajendra K. and Nanda (Rani) V.; M.A., Patna U., India, 1953; M.A., U. Mich., 1963, Ph.D., 1966; m. Sheela Prasad, June 4, 1956; children—Sanjay, Mona. Lectr. dept. edn. Bihar U., India, 1953-61; asst. prof. U. Wis., Madison, 1965-70, asso. prof., 1970-73, prof., chmn. dept. South Asian studies, 1973—; asst. prof. Indian Inst. Tech., Kanpur, 1967-69. Trustee Am. Inst. Indian Studies, 1973—. Fulbright fellow, 1961-64; Smith-Mundt fellow, 1961-62; Am. Council Learned Socs. fellow, 1962. Mem. Am., Gt. Britain, India linguistic socs., Assn. Asian Studies, Nepal Studies Assn. Author: The Comparative Structure of the Noun Phrasein English and Hindi, 1971; The Notion of Subject in South Asian Languages, 1976. Home: 13 Rye Circle Madison WI 53717 Office: 1240 Van Hise Hall U Wis Madison WI 53706

VERMA, SADANAND, mathematician; b. Muzaffarpur, Bihar, India, Jan. 24, 1930; s. Brinda Prasad and Ramiyou (Kuar) V.; came to U.S., 1955, naturalized, 1966; B.Sc. with honors, Patna U., 1950; M.Sc., Bihar U., 1952; M.S., Wayne State U., 1958, Ph.D., 1958; m. Joyce L. Moulton; children—Tammy, Tommy, Tony, Tonia. Hon. lectr. math. Bihar U., 1952-53, lectr. math., 1953-55, 58-60; teaching fellow math. Wayne State U., Detroit, 1955-58; asst. prof. U. Windsor (Ont.), 1960-65; asso. prof. math. Western Mich. U., Kalamazoo, 1965-67; prof. math. U. Nev., Las Vegas, 1967—, chmn. dept., 1968—. Mem. Math. Assn. Am., Can. Math. Congress, Assn. Computing Machinery, Sigma Xi (U.S. subcom. for Internat. Center Cybernetics and Systems). Contbr. articles to profl. jours. Home: 121 Rancho Vista Dr Las Vegas NV 89106

VERMEULE, CORNELIUS CLARKSON, III, museum curator; b. Orange, N.J., Aug. 10, 1925; s. Cornelius Clarkson, Jr. and Catherine Sayre (Comstock) V.; grad. Pomfret Sch., 1943; A.B., Harvard, 1949, M.A., 1951; Ph.D., U. London (Eng.), 1953; m. Emily Dickinson Townsend, Feb. 2, 1957; children—Emily D. Blake, Cornelius Adrian Comstock. Instr. fine arts, then asst. prof. U. Mich., 1953-55; asst. prof. classical archaeology Bryn Mawr (Pa.) Coll., 1955-57; curator classical art Mus. Fine Arts, Boston, 1957—, acting dir., 1972-73; asso. curator coins Mass. Hist. Soc., 1965-71, curator, 1971—. Lectr. fine arts Smith Coll., 1960-64, Boston U., Harvard, Wellesley Coll.; vis. prof. Yale, 1969-70, 72-73; Thomas Spencer Jerome lectr. U. Mich., 1975-76; vis. prof. Boston Coll., 1978—. Served to 1st lt. AUS, 1943-47. Recipient Bicentennial medal Boston Coll., 1976. Guggenheim fellow, 1968. Fellow Am. Numismatic Soc. (life), Royal Numis. Soc., Soc. Antiquaries, Am. Acad. Arts and Scis.; mem. Coll. Art Assn. (life), Archaeol. Inst. Am. (life), German Archaeol. Inst., Holland Soc. N.Y., Colonial Lords of Manors in Am. Republican. Episcopalian. Club: Tavern (Boston). Author: (with N. Jacobs) Japanese Coinage, 1948, 2d edit., 1972; Bibliography of Applied Numismatics, 1956; The Goddess Roma, 1959, 2d edit., 1974; Dal Pozzo-Albani Drawings, 1960; European Art and the Classical Past, 1964; Drawings at Windsor Castle, 1966; Roman Imperial Art in Greece and Asia Minor, 1968; Polykleitos, 1969; Numismatic Art in America, 1971; (with M. Comstock) Greek Etruscan and Roman Bronzes, 1972; (with N. Neuerburg) Catalogue of the Ancient Art in the J. Paul Getty Mus., 1973; Greek and Roman Sculpture in Gold and Silver, 1974; Greek and Roman Cyprus, 1976 (with M. Comstock) Sculpture in Stone, 1976; Greek Sculpture and Roman Taste, 1977; Roman Art: Early Republic to Late Empire, 1978; The Ernest Brummer Collections, Vol. II, 1979. Home: 47 Coolidge Hill Rd Cambridge MA 02138 Office: Museum Fine Arts Boston MA 02115. *To teach, collect and record the past, as exemplar for the present, as prologue to the future, can there be any better use of a historian's and archaeologist's life?*

VERMEULE, EMILY TOWNSEND, classicist, educator; b. N.Y.C., Aug. 11, 1928; d. Clinton Blake and Eleanor (Meneely) Townsend; A.B., Bryn Mawr Coll., 1950, Ph.D., 1956; student Am. Sch. Classical Studies, 1950-51, St. Anne's Coll., Oxford (Eng.) U., 1953; M.A., Harvard U., 1954; D.Litt., Douglass Coll., Rutgers U., 1968; LL.D., Regis Coll., 1971; D.F.A., U. Mass., Amherst, 1971; D.Litt., Smith Coll., 1972, Wheaton Coll., 1973, Trinity Coll., 1974; m. Cornelius C. Vermeule III, Feb. 2, 1957; children—Emily Dickinson Blake, Cornelius Adrian Comstock. Instr. in Greek, Bryn Mawr Coll., 1956-57; instr. Wellesley Coll., 1957-58, prof. art and Greek, 1965-70, chmn. dept. art, 1966-67; asst. prof. classics Boston U., 1958-61, asso. prof., 1961-65; fellow for research Boston Mus. Fine Arts, 1965—; James C. Loeb prof. classical philology Harvard U., 1969—, dir. univ. Cyprus expdn., 1971—; Samuel and Doris Zemurray Stone-Radcliffe prof. Harvard U., 1970—; Sather prof. U. Calif., Berkeley, 1975—. Recipient Gold medal for disting. achievement Radcliffe Coll. Grad. Soc., 1968; Guggenheim fellow, 1964-65. Fellow Soc. Antiquaries; mem. Am. Inst. Archaeology, Am. Acad. Arts and Scis., Am. Philos. Soc., Am. Philol. Assn., Classical Assn. New Eng., Hellenic Soc., Classical Assn. Author: Euripides V. Electra, 1959; Greece in the Bronze Age, 1964; Götterkult, 1974; Toumba tou Skourou, the Mound of Darkness, 1974; Death in Early Greek Art and Poetry, 1979; contbr. articles to profl. jours. Office: Dept Classics Boylston Hall Harvard U Cambridge MA 02138

VERMEULE, EMILY TOWNSEND (MRS. CORNELIUS C. VERMEULE III), classicist, educator; b. N.Y.C., Aug. 11, 1928; d. Clinton Blake and Eleanor (Meneely) Townsend; A.B., Bryn Mawr Coll., 1950; student Am. Sch. Classical Studies, Athens, 1950-51, St. Anne's Coll., Oxford U., 1953; M.A., Harvard, 1954; Ph.D., Bryn Mawr Coll., 1956; D. Litt., Douglass Coll., Rutgers U., 1968; LL.D., Regis Coll., 1971; D. Fine Arts, U. Mass, Amherst, 1971; D.Litt., Smith Coll., 1972, Wheaton Coll., 1973, Trinity Coll., 1974; m. Cornelius C. Vermeule III, Feb. 2, 1957; children—Emily Dickinson Blake, Cornelius Adrian Comstock. Instr. in Greek. Bryn Mawr Coll., 1956-57; instr. Wellesley (Mass.) Coll., 1957-58, prof. art and Greek, 1965-70, chmn. dept. art, 1966-67; asst. prof. classics Boston U., 1958-61, asso. prof. classics, 1961-65; fellow for research Boston Mus. Fine Arts, 1965—; James C. Loeb vis. prof. classical philology Harvard, 1969, dir. univ. Cyprus expdn., 1971—; Samuel and Doris Zemurray Stone-Radcliffe prof. Harvard, 1970—; Sather prof. U. Calif. at Berkeley, 1975—; judge Nat. Book Award, 1977. Recipient Gold medal for distinguished achievement Radcliffe Coll. Grad. Soc., 1968. Guggenheim fellow, 1964-65. Fellow Soc. Antiquaries; mem. Am. Inst. Archaeology, Am. Acad. Arts and Scis., Am. Philos. Soc. (v.p. 1978—), Am. Philol. Assn., Classical Assn. New Eng., Hellenic Soc., Classical Assn. Author: Euripides V. Electra, 1959; Greece in the Bronze Age, 1964; The Trojan War in Greek Art, 1964; Götterkult, 1974; Toumba tou Skourou, The Mound of Darkness, 1975; Death in Early Greek Art and Poetry, 1978. Contbr. articles to profl. jours. Excavations in Greece, Turkey, Libya, Cyprus. Office: Dept Classics Boylston Hall Harvard University Cambridge MA 02138

VERMEULEN, THEODORE, chem. engr.; b. Los Angeles, May 7, 1916; s. Aurele and Helen Scott (Douglas) V.; B.S., Calif. Inst. Tech., 1936, M.S., 1937; Ph.D., U. Calif., Los Angeles, 1942; m. Mary Dorothy Cole, June 24, 1939; children—Raymond, Bruce. Research chem. engr. Union Oil Co., Wilmington, Calif., 1937-40, Shell Devel. Co., Emeryville, Calif., 1941-47; asso. prof. chem. engring. U. Calif., Berkeley, 1947-51, prof., 1951—, chmn. div. chem. engring., 1947-53, Miller research prof., 1960-61, faculty scientist Lawrence Berkeley Lab., 1947—; Fulbright prof., Belgium, France, 1953-54; Guggenheim fellow, resident Cambridge (Eng.) U., 1963-64; vis. prof. Nat. U. Mexico, 1967, Syracuse U., 1971, U. Karlsruhe, 1974; Reilly lectr. U. Notre Dame, 1972; cons. in field; dir. Memorex Corp., 1963—.

Registered profl. engr., Calif. Fellow Am. Inst. Chem. Engrs. (William H. Walker award 1971); mem. Am. Chem. Soc. (nat. council 1975-77), Am. Inst. Aeros, Astronautics, Am. Meteorol. Soc., Am. Nuclear Soc., Combustion Inst., Catalysis Soc., AAAS, Am. Soc. Engring. Edn., Sigma Xi, Tau Beta Pi, Alpha Chi Sigma. Clubs: Commonwealth (San Francisco); Faculty (Berkeley). Sect. editor Chem. Engrs. Handbook, 1963—; co-editor Advances in Chem. Engring., 1964—; contbr. articles on and patentee in chem. processes, process principles; inventor Optel spelling. Home: 725 Cragmont Ave Berkeley CA 94708 Office: Chem Engring Dept U of Calif Berkeley CA 94720. *Idealism blended with realism—dreaming the impossible dream and fitting it into the art of the possible.*

VERMILYEA, DAVID AUGUSTUS, metall. research adminstr.; b. Troy, N.Y., Oct. 11, 1923; s. Wesley F. and Rebecca Lois (Warner) V.; B.S. in Metallurgy, Rensselaer Poly. Inst., 1947, M.S. in Metallurgy, 1950, Ph.D. in Metallurgy, 1953; m. Jane Elizabeth Tripp, July 29, 1950; children—Carol J., Barbara A., Mark E. Metallurgist E.I. du Pont de Nemours & Co., Wilmington, Del., 1947-48; instr. metallurgy Rensselaer Poly. Inst., Troy, N.Y., 1948-51, vis. prof. electrochemistry, 1972-73; chemist Gen. Electric Co., Schenectady, 1951—, mgr. chem. metallurgy sect., 1957-60, metallurgist, 1961-75. Served with AUS, 1943-46. Decorated Purple Heart; Coolidge fellow, 1971; recipient Willis R. Whitney award Nat. Assn. Corrosion Engrs., 1975. Mem. Electrochem. Soc. (hon., pres. 1974-75, Outstanding Achievement award corrosion div. 1975, Acheson medal and prize 1978), Am. Chem. Soc., Adirondack Mountain Club, Appalachian Mountain Club, Niskayuna Park Com., Sigma Xi, Phi Lambda Upsilon, Tau Beta Pi. Contbr. articles to profl. publs.; asso. editor Ann. Review Material Sci. Patentee in field. Home: 2505 Whamer Ln Schenectady NY 12309 Office: Bldg K-1 Room 5A64 General Electric Research Lab Schenectady NY 12301. *Although talents are given, behavior is chosen. Choose, therefore, that which is good, true, and beautiful, and eschew that which is degrading and vulgar.*

VERNBERG, FRANK JOHN, educator; b. Fenton, Mich., Nov. 6, 1925; s. Sigurd A. and Edna (Anderson) V.; A.B., DePauw U., 1949, M.A., 1950; Ph.D., Purdue U., 1951; m. Winona M. Bortz, Sept. 7, 1945; children—Marcia Lynn, Eric Morrison, Amy Louise. Prof. zoology Duke Marine Lab., Beaufort, N.C., 1951-69; Belle W. Baruch prof. marine ecology, dir. Belle W. Baruch Coastal Research Inst., U. S.C., Columbia, 1969—; vis. prof. U. Coll. West Indies, Jamaica, 1957-58, U. Sao Paulo (Brazil), 1965. Program dir. exptl. analytical biogeography of sea Internat. Biol. Program, 1967—; mem. com. manned orbital research lab., Am. Inst. Biol. Scis.-NASA, 1966—; pres. Estuarine Research Fedn., 1975-77. Served with USNR, 1944-46. Guggenheim fellow, 1957-58; Fulbright-Hayes fellow, 1965. Mem. Am. Soc. Zoologists (sec.-treas. div. comparative physiologists 1959-61, sec.-treas. edn. com. 1960—, mem. council 1965-67), Southeastern Estuarine Research Soc. (pres. 1974-76), AAAS. Contbr. articles to profl. jours. Spl. editor Am. Zoologist, 1963; mem. editorial bd. Biol. Bull., 1977—; editor Jour. Exptl. Marine Biology and Ecology, 1978—. Office: Belle W Baruch Coastal Research Inst U SC Columbia SC 29208

VERNER, HUGH DAVID, physician; b. Florence, S.C., Apr. 20 1919; s. Carl Hugh and Flora (Garner) V.; B.S., Davidson Coll., 1940; M.D., Johns Hopkins, 1943; m. Margaret Oberdorfer, July 22, 1945; children—David Carl, Scott Crawford, Jonathan Kent. Intern Johns Hopkins Hosp., 1944; resident Univ. Hosps., Cleve., 1944-45, Meml. Hosp., Charlotte, N.C., 1947-48; pvt. practice, Charlotte, 1949—; cons. staff Meml. Hosp., 1949—, pres. vis. med. staff, 1964-66; staff physician Presbyn. Hosp.; cons. staff Mercy Hosp.; clin. asst. prof. medicine U. N.C., 1970—. Pres. Mecklenburg unit Am. Cancer Soc., 1959. Chmn. schs. com. for N.C., Johns Hopkins Alumni, 1962-66, mem. nat. resources com., 1963-75. Trustee Davidson Coll., 1968-72, Montreat-Anderson Coll., Montreat, N.C., 1971-73; bd. regents Barium Springs Home For Children, 1968-72. Served as capt., M.C., AUS, 1945-47. Diplomate Am. Bd. Internal Med. Fellow A.C.P.; mem. N.C., Mecklenburg County (pres. 1978) med. socs., AMA, Am. N.C., Charlotte (pres. 1958) socs. internal medicine, Johns Hopkins (pres. N.C. 1961), Davidson Coll. (nat. pres. 1966-67) alumni assns., Charlotte C. of C. (dir. 1978), Mountain Retreat Assn. (dir. Montreat 1972-73), Newcomen Soc. Rotarian. Presbyn. (ruling elder). Clubs: Charlotte Country; Biltmore Forest Country (Asheville, N.C.). Home: 2439 Knollwood Rd Charlotte NC 28211 Office: Mecklenburg Med Group 3535 Randolph Rd Charlotte NC 28211

VERNER, JAMES MELTON, lawyer; b. Selma, Ala., Sept. 19, 1915; s. Singleton Foster and Jennie (Harris) V.; student Biltmore Coll., 1932-34; A.B., U. N.C., 1936, LL.B., 1938; m. Gretchen Gores, Aug. 12, 1939; children—Ann Verner Picardo, James Singleton, William Melton. Admitted to N.C. bar, 1938, Tenn. bar, 1947, D.C. bar, 1950; asso. firm Gover & Covington, Charlotte, N.C., 1938; law clk. atty. gen. N.C., 1938-40; atty. CAB, Washington, 1940-43; asst. gen. counsel Chgo. & So. Airlines, Memphis, 1946-47; atty. Air Transport Assn. Am., Washington, 1947-49; hearing examiner CAB, 1949-50, exec. asst. to chmn., 1950, exec. dir., 1950-53; atty. Turney & Turney, 1953—, partner, 1954-60; partner firm Verner, Liipfert, Bernhard & McPherson and predecessor firms, 1960—. Served as lt. (j.g.) USNR, 1943-46; legal officer Naval Air Transport Service, 1945-46. Mem. Am. Bar Assn., Order of Golden Fleece, Assn. ICC Practitioners, Nat. Aero. Assn. Clubs: Nat. Aviation; Aero of Washington, Nat. Lawyers, International. Asso. editor N.C. Law Rev., 1937-38. Home: 3618 N Nelson St Arlington VA 22207 Office: 1660 L St NW Washington DC 20036

VERNIER, ROBERT LAWRENCE, physician, educator; b. El Paso, Tex., July 29, 1924; s. William J. and Ada E. (McQuillen) V.; B.S., U. Dayton, 1948; M.D., U. Cin., 1952; m. Molly Katherine Bennett, Apr. 31, 1945; children—Katherine (Mrs. David Peterson), Patricia (Mrs. Louis DeMartino), Janet, Richard, Christine. Intern Univ. Hosp., Little Rock, 1952-53; resident U. Ark., 1952-54, U. Minn., 1954-58; asst. prof. U. Minn., 1959, asso. prof., 1963; prof. U. Calif., Los Angeles, 1964-68; prof. pediatrics U. Minn., Mpls., 1968—. Nat. cons. USAF, 1970—; established investigator Am. Heart Assn., 1959-64, mem. research com., 1966-71, chmn., 1970. Pres., Kidney Found. Upper-Midwest, 1968-71; mem. sci. rev. com. NIH, 1961-66. Served to 1st lt., inf. AUS, 1943-46. Guggenheim fellow, 1960-61. Mem. Am. Soc. Clin. Investigation, Am. Soc. Nephrology, Am. Soc. Pediatric Research (Mead Johnson award for research 1962). Contbr. sci. articles to jours., chpts. to books. Home: 2109 N Wilder St St Paul MN 55113

VERNON, DAVID HARVEY, lawyer, educator; b. Boston, Aug. 9, 1925; s. Bernard Nathan and Ida E. (Cohen) V.; A.B., Harvrd, 1949, LL.B., 1952; LL.M., N.Y. U., 1953, J.S.D., 1960; m. Rhoda Louise Sterman, June 1, 1947; children—Amy Lynne Charles Adam. Instr., N.Y. U., 1953-54; asst. prof. law U. Houston, 1954-55; from asst. prof. to prof. law U. N.Mex., Albuquerque, 1955-64; asso. dean, prof. law U. Wash., Seattle, 1964-66; prof. law U. Iowa, 1966—, dean Coll. Law, 1966-71; vis. prof. Sch. Law, Washington U., St. Louis, 1974-75. Bd. dirs. Wash. State affiliate A.C.L.U., 1964-66, Iowa Civil Liberties Union, 1966-72. Served with USNR, 1943-46. Mem. Am., Iowa bar assns., Assn. Am. Law Schs. (mem. exec. com. 1978—). Editor: (with Depew) General State Food and Drug Law, Annotated, 1955; Title XIV of the American Law of Mining, 1960; Conflict of Laws: Cases, Problems and Essays, 1973, supplement, 1979; Contracts: Theory and Practice, 1980. Home: 327 Koser Ave Iowa City IA 52240

VERNON, GLENN MORLEY, sociologist, educator; b. Vernal, Utah, Apr. 6, 1920; s. William Morley and Roseltha (Bingham) V.; B.S., Brigham Young U., 1947, M.S. in Sociology, 1950; Ph.D., Wash. State U., 1953; m. June Andersen, Dec. 24, 1941; children—Gregory Glenn, Rebecca, Paul Bingham. Asst. prof. Auburn U., 1953-54; asst. prof., then asso. prof. Central Mich. U., 1954-59; asso. prof. Brigham Young U., 1959-63; prof. sociology, head dept. sociology and anthropology U. Maine, 1963-68; prof. sociology U. Utah, 1968—, chmn. dept., 1970-73; vis. prof. McMaster U., Hamilton, Ont., Can., summer 1959, U. Utah, summer 1966, U. Maine and U. Del., summer 1976. Served as pilot USAAF, 1942-45. Fellow Am. Sociol. Assn.; mem. Insts. Religion and Health, Acad. Religion Mental Health, Found. of Thanatology, Soc. Sci. Study Religion, Internat. Conf. for Sociology of Religion, Religious Research Assn., Pacific Sociol. Assn., Utah. Sociol. Soc. (pres. 1976-77), Sigma Xi, Phi Kappa Phi. Mem. Ch. of Jesus Christ of Latter Day Saints. Author: Sociology of Religion, 1962; Human Interaction, An Introduction to Sociology, 1965, 2d edit., 1972; Sociology of Death, 1970; also articles. Home: 3646 E 3580 S Salt Lake City UT 84109

VERNON, LEO PRESTON, biochemist, educator; b. Roosevelt, Utah, Oct. 10, 1925; s. William M. and Roseltha (Bingham) V.; A.B. in Chemistry, Brigham Young U., 1948; Ph.D., Iowa State U., 1951; m. Marion Fern Trunkey, Sept. 5, 1946; children—Richard Leo, Marion Elise, Martin Preston, Jillaine, Eric Eugene. Research asso. Washington U., St. Louis, 1952-54; prof. chemistry dept. Brigham Young U., Provo, Utah, 1954-61, asst. acad. v.p. research, 1970—; dir. Charles F. Kettering Research Lab., Yellow Springs, Ohio, 1961-70; prof. chemistry Antioch Coll., Yellow Springs, 1962-70; prof. botany dept. Ohio State U., Columbus, 1962- 70. Research fellow Nobel Inst., Stockholm, Sweden, 1960. Served with AUS, 1944-46. Mem. Am. Soc. Photobiology, Am. Soc. Plant Physiologists, Am. Soc. Biol. Chemists. Author: (with H. Guest, A. San Pietro) Bacterial Photosynthesis, 1963; (with G. Seely) The Chlorophylls, 1966; (with R. Sanadi) Current Topics in Bioenergetics, Vol. 8. Asso. editor Bioenergetics, 1969—, Photochemistry and Photobiology, 1970-76. Contbr. numerous articles to sci. jours. Home: 1680 North 1550 East Provo UT 84601

VERNON, RAYMOND, economist, educator; b. N.Y.C., Sept. 1, 1913; s. Hyman and Lillian (Sonnenberg) V.; A.B. cum laude, Coll. City N. Y., 1933; Ph.D., Columbia U., 1941; M.A. (hon.), Harvard, 1959; m. Josephine Stone, Aug. 7, 1935; children—Heidi, Susan Patricia. Statistician, SEC, 1935-42, asst. dir. trading and exchange div., 1942-46; asst. chief internat. resources div. Dept. of State, 1946-48; became adviser on comml. policy, 1948; dep. dir. Office of Econ. Def. and Trade Policy, 1951, acting dir., 1954; staff mem. joint Presdl. Congl. Commn. on Fgn. Econ. policy, 1953- 54; planning and control dir. Hawley and Hoops, Inc., 1954-56; dir. N.Y. Metropolitan Region Study, 1956-59; prof. Harvard Bus. Sch., 1959-80, dir. Harvard Devel. Adv. Service, 1962-65, acting dir. Center for Internat. Affairs, 1966-68, dir. Center for Internat. Affairs, 1973-78; prof. internat. relations, 1978—; dir. Am. Gen. mut. fund complex; lectr. Am. U., 1946-48, Princeton U., 1954-55, Swarthmore Coll., 1955-56. Mem. Mission on Japanese Combines, Tokyo, 1946; mem. U.S. del. GATT, Geneva, 1950, Torquay, Eng., 1951, vice chmn. U.S. del., Geneva, 1952; spl. cons. to undersec. Treasury, 1978-79; participated UN Conf. on Regional Devel., Tokyo, 1958. Bd. govs. World Peace Found.; bd. overseers Florence Heller Sch., Brandeis U. Recipient Meritorious Service Award Dept. State, 1951. Fellow Am. Acad. Arts and Scis.; mem. Council on Fgn. Relations, UN Assn. (econ. council), Phi Beta Kappa. Author: Regulation of Stock Exchange Members, 1941; America's Trade Policy and GATT, 1954; Organizing for World Trade, 1956; (with Edgar M. Hoover) Anatomy of a Metropolis; 1959; Metropolis 1985, 1960; The Dilemma of Mexico's Development, 1963; Public Policy and Private Enterprise in Mexico, 1964; Myth and Reality of Our Urban Problems, 1965; Manager in The International Economy, 1968; Sovereignty at Bay, 1971; Storm over the Multinationals, 1976. Editor: How Latin America Views the U.S. Investor, 1966; The Technology Factor in International Trade, 1970; Big Business and the State, 1974; The Oil Crisis, 1976. Contbr. articles to profl. jours. Home: 1 Dunstable Rd Cambridge MA 02138 Office: Center Internat Affairs Harvard U Cambridge MA 02138

VERNON, SHIRLEY JANE, architect; b. Mt. Kisco, N.Y., Dec. 9, 1930; d. J.H. and M.R. (Maher) V.; B.Arch. cum laude, Pa. State U., 1953. Asso., coordinating architect for design, designer Vincent G. Kling and Assos., Phila., 1953-68; pvt. practice architecture, Phila., 1968-74; mgr. archtl. design Ballinger Co., Phila., 1974-75; prin. JC Assos., Phila., 1975—; instr. architecture Drexel U., 1956-58, adj. asst. prof., 1959-64, adj. asso. prof., 1965-69, adj. prof., 1970—. Fellow AIA (chpt. dir. 1973, 79, chpt. v.p. 1975); mem. Art Alliance Phila., Print Club Phila., Tau Beta Pi. Home: 1704 Delancey St Philadelphia PA 19103

VERNON, WESTON (WES), III, journalist; b. N.Y.C., Aug. 23, 1931; s. Weston, Jr. and Adelaide (Neilson) V.; student Utah State U., 1949-50, Brigham Young U., 1953-54; m. Alida Steinvoort, Oct. 5, 1951; children—Rosanne, Weston IV, Diane, John Randall. Reporter, producer KBUH, Brigham City, Utah, 1950-51, KVRS, Rock Springs, Wyo., 1952, KOVO, Provo, Utah, 1952-54, Intermountain Network, Salt Lake City, 1954, KLO, Ogden, Utah, 1954, KBMY, Billings, Mont., 1954-63; news dir.-polit. specialist KSL Radio-TV, Salt Lake City, 1963-68; bur. chief Bonneville Internat. Corp., Washington, 1968-72; corr. CBS Radio Stas. News Service, CBS Radio, Washington, 1972—. Program chmn. Washington chpt. Nat. Ry. Hist. Soc., 1974—. Bd. dirs. Winding-Orchard Citizens Assn., Wheaton-Glenmont, Md., 1974-77, pres., 1975-76; chmn. Metro Transit, 1974—. Mgr. nat. div. Magnum Force Volleyball. Served with AUS, 1951-52. Recipient Journalism awards Mont. A.P. Press Stas., 1960, Utah Bar Assn., 1965, Utah Broadcasters Assn., 1965-66. Mem. Internat. Platform Assn., Nat. Press Club, Radio-TV Corrs. Assn., Am. Legion (comdr. Yellowstone Post 4, 1962-63), 40 and 8, Railroad Enthusiasts (Chesapeake div.), Sigma Delta Chi. Home: 1605 Billman Ln Silver Spring MD 20902 Office: 2020 M St NW Washington DC 20036

VERON, EARL ERNEST, fed. dist. judge La.; b. Smoke Bend, La., Jan. 2, 1922; s. Dyer M. and Edna (Rodriguez) V.; B.A., McNeese State U., 1958; J.D., La. State U., 1959; m. Alverdy Heyd, Oct. 10, 1948; children—J. Michael, Douglas E. Admitted to La. bar, 1959; pvt. practice law, Lake Charles, La., 1959-67; judge 14th Jud. Dist., Lake Charles, La., 1967-77, U.S. Western Dist. of La., Lake Charles, 1977—; mem. Orleans Parish Criminal Ct., 1972; Circuit Ct. Appeal, 1974. Office: US Dist Ct PO Box 1404 Lake Charles LA 70602*

VERONIS, GEORGE, oceanographer, educator; b. New Brunswick, N.J., June 3, 1926; s. Nicholas Emmanuel and Angeliki (Efthimakis) V.; A.B., Lafayette Coll., 1950; Ph.D., Brown U., 1954; M.A., Yale, 1966; m. Anna Margareta Olsson, Nov. 8, 1963; children—Melissa, Benjamin. Staff meteorologist Inst. for Advanced Study, Princeton, 1953-56; staff mathematician Woods Hole (Mass.) Oceanographic Instn., 1956-64; asso. prof. Mass. Inst. Tech., 1961-64, research oceanographer, 1964-66; prof. geophysics and applied sci. Yale, New Haven, 1966—, chmn. dept. geology and geophysics, 1976-79. Served with USNR, 1943-46. Guggenheim fellow U. Stockholm (Sweden), 1960, 66. Fellow Am. Geophys. Union; mem. Am. Phys. Soc., Am. Acad. Arts and Scis., Phi Beta Kappa, Sigma Xi. Home: 183 Colony Rd New Haven CT 06511

VERONIS, JOHN JAMES, pub., publishing co. exec.; b. New Brunswick, N.J.; s. Nicholas E. and Anna (Eftimakis) V.; B.A., Lafayette Coll., 1948; postgrad. N.Y. U., 1960-63; L.H.D., Franklin Pierce Coll., 1972; m. Sarah Shepard, Mar. 1, 1960; children—Jane Shepard, John James, Nicholas O'Malley. With Popular Sci., Field and Stream, Woman's Day, N.Y.C., 1948-52, Am. Home Mag., N.Y.C., 1952-58; with Curtis Pub. Co., N.Y.C., 1958-64, v.p., 1959-63, pub. Am. Home, 1962-63, pub. Ladies Home Jour., 1962-64, sr. v.p., 1963-64, pres. Curtis mag. div., 1963-64; pres. Veronis Pub. Co., N.Y.C., 1964-66; exec. v.p. Interpublic Group of Cos., N.Y.C., 1966-67; co-founder Psychology Today mag., pres. Communications/Research/Machines, Inc., N.Y.C., 1967-71; pres. Saturday Rev. Industries, N.Y.C., 1971-73; founder, pres. Book Digest Mag., N.Y.C., 1973—. Office: Book Digest 730 Fifth Ave New York NY 10019

VERONIS, PETER, publisher; b. New Brunswick, N.J., June 15, 1923; s. Nicholas M. and Angeliki (Efthemakis) V.; student Columbia U., 1951-54; m. Dorothy E. White, Sept. 8, 1946; 1 dau., Judith Anne Veronis Rodgers. Nat. advt. mgr. Springfield (Mass.) Newspapers, 1954-57; v.p., gen. sales mgr. Ridder Johns Co., N.Y.C., 1957-62; corp. exec. Curtis Pub. Co., N.Y.C., 1963-64; asso. sales mgr. Look mag., 1964-68; v.p., advt. dir. Psychology Today mag., 1968-71; v.p. advt. Saturday Rev., N.Y.C., 1971-73; pub. Book Digest, N.Y.C., 1973—. Served with USN, 1941-51. Home: 42 Thornwood Rd Stamford CT 06903 Office: Book Digest 730 Fifth Ave New York City NY 10019

VERPLANCK, WILLIAM SAMUEL, psychologist, educator; b. Plainfield, N.J., Jan. 6, 1916; s. William Samuel and Kathryn (Tracy) V.; B.S., U. Va., 1937, M.A., 1938; Ph.D., Brown U., 1941. Asst. prof. Ind. U., 1946-50; asst. prof. Harvard, 1950-55, acting asso. prof., 1955-56; research asso. Stanford, 1956-57; asso. prof. Hunter Coll., 1957-59; prof. U. Md., 1958-62; prof. psychology U. Tenn., 1963—, head dept., 1963-73. Served to lt. USNR, 1943-46. Recipient travel grant Am. Philos. Assn., 1953. Fellow Am. Psychol. Assn., Assn. Study Animal Behavior, AAAS; mem. Eastern Psychol. Assn., Psychonomic Soc. (past sec.-treas., gov.), Sigma Xi, Sigma Alpha Epsilon. Author: (with others) Modern Learning Theory, 1953. Home: 4605 Chickasaw Ave Knoxville TN 37919. *The history of psychology is largely constituted of a succession of fads overlying the continuity given by a few plausible technological methods which have been progressively misapplied, with little critical concern for their social or scientific consequences. Can one person, working over a period of thirty years, make a difference? Well, I try.*

VERRECCHIA, ALFRED JOSEPH, toy mfr.; b. Providence, Feb. 19, 1943; s. Alfred A. and Elda L. (Tortolani) V.; B.A., U. R.I., 1967, M.B.A., 1971; m. Geraldine Macari, June 11, 1964; children—Michael, Michele, Melisa, Lisa. With Hasbro Industries, Inc., Pawtucket, R.I., since 1965, controller, 1971, treas., since 1974; dir. Hasbro Industries (Can.) Ltd., Romper Room Schs., Hasbro Devel. Corp. Mem. Nat. Accounting Assn., Am. Accounting Assn., Financial Execs. Inst., Am. Mgmt. Assn. Home: 140 Middle Rd East Greenwich RI 02818 Office: 1027 Newport Ave Pawtucket RI 02861

VERRETT, SHIRLEY, soprano; b. New Orleans, May 31, 1931; d. Leon Solomon and Elvira Sugustine (Harris) V.; A.A., Ventura (Calif.) Coll., 1951; diploma in voice (scholarship 1956-61), Juilliard Sch. Music, 1961; Mus.D. (hon.), Coll. Holy Cross, Mass., 1978; m. Louis Frank LoMonaco, Dec. 10, 1963; 1 dau., Francesca. Recital debut Town Hall, N.Y.C., 1958; appeared as Irinia in Lost in the Stars, 1958; orchestral debut Phila. Orch., 1960; operatic debut in Carmer, Festival of Two Worlds, Spoleto, Italy, 1962; debuts with Bolshoi Opera, Moscow, 1963, N.Y.C. Opera, 1964, Royal Opera, Covent Garden, 1966, Maggio Fiorentino, Florence, 1967, Met. Opera, 1968, Teatro San Carlos, Naples, 1968, Dallas Civic Opera, 1969, La Scala, 1970, Vienna State Opera, 1970, San Francisco Opera, 1972, Paris Opera, 1973, Opera Co. Boston, 1976; guest appearances with all major U.S. symphony orchs.; TV debut on Ed Sullivan Show, 1963; rec. artist RCA, Columbia, ABC (Westminster), Angel and Deutsche Grammophon records; mem. adv. bd. Opera Ebony. Recipient Marian Anderson award, 1955, Nat. Fedn. Music Clubs award, 1961, Walter Naumberg award, 1958, Blanche Thebom award, 1960; John Hay Whitney fellow, 1959; Ford Found. fellow, 1962-63; Martha Baird Rockefeller Aid to Music Fund fellow, 1959-61; grantee William Matteus Sullivan Fund, 1959; grantee Berkshire Music Opera, 1956; recipient Achievement award Ventura Coll., 1963, N.Y. chpt. Albert Einstein Coll. Medicine, 1975; 2 plaques Los Angeles Sentinel Newspaper, 1960, plaque Peninsula Music Festival, 1963; Los Angeles Times Woman of Yr. award, 1969. Mem. Mu Phi Epsilon. Address: care Edgar Vincent Assos 145 E 52 St Suite 804 New York NY 10022

VERRILL, CHARLES OWEN, JR., lawyer; b. Biddeford, Maine, Sept. 30, 1937; s. Charles Owen and Elizabeth (Handy) V.; A.B., Tufts U., 1959; LL.B., Duke, 1962; m. Mary Ann Blanchard, Aug. 13, 1960; children-Martha Anne, Edward Blanchard, Ethan Christopher, Elizabeth Handy, Matthew Lawton, Peter Goldthwait. Admitted to D.C. bar, 1962, since practiced in Washington; asso. Weaver & Glassie, 1962-64; asso. Barco, Cook, Patton & Blow, 1964-66, partner, 1967; partner Patton, Blow, Verrill, Brand & Boggs, 1967—; lectr. Duke Law Sch., 1970-73; adj. prof. Georgetown U. Law Sch., 1978—. Local dir. Tufts U. Ann. Fund, 1965-69; mem. Duke Law Alumni Council, 1972-75. Recipient Service citation Tufts U. Alumni Assn., 1968. Mem. Am., D.C. bar assns., Order of Coif, Theta Delta Chi, Phi Delta Phi. Clubs: Metropolitan (Washington); Tarratine (Dark Harbor, Maine). Home: 8205 Dunsinane Ct McLean VA 22101 Office: 2550 M St NW Washington DC 20037

VERRILL, F. GLENN, advt. agy. exec.; b. N.Y.C., Dec. 17, 1923; s. Ralph Francis and Rose (Verner) V.; A.B., Adelphi Coll., 1949; A.M., Harvard, 1950; m. Jean Demar, Aug. 25, 1946; children—Gary, Joan. With Batten, Barton, Durstine & Osborn, Inc., 1952—, v.p., 1964, creative dir. Burke Dowling Adams div., Atlanta, 1965-70, exec. v.p., gen. mgr., 1970-71, pres., 1971—, also dir. parent co. Mem. adv. bd. U. Ga.; bd. dirs. Atlanta Humane Soc. Served with USNR, 1943-46. Mem. Am. Assn. Advt. Agys. (nat. dir. 1973—). Episcopalian. Clubs: Atlanta Athletic, Cherokee, Harvard (Atlanta). Home: 3620 Cloudland Dr NW Atlanta GA 30327 Office: 3290 Northside Pkwy NW Atlanta GA 30327

VERROCHI, WILLIAM ANTHONY, utility co. exec.; b. Boston, Nov. 14, 1921; s. Antonio and Mary Rose (Di San Bernardo) V.; B.S. in Mech. Engring., M.I.T., 1947; m. Gloria Maria Todino, Oct. 3, 1953; children—Elizabeth A., Suzanne J., Kathryn J., Barbara M. Project engr. Jackson & Moreland, Boston, 1947-61; supt. prodn. Pa. Electric Co., Johnstown, 1961-69, asst. v.p. tech., Parsippany, N.J., 1969-71; v.p. design and construction GPU Service Corp., Parsippany, 1971-74, v.p. generation, 1974-77; pres. Pa. Electric Co.,

Johnstown, 1977—; dir. Utilities Mutual Ins. Co., U.S. Nat. Bank, GPU Service Corp. Chmn., Greater Johnstown Com.; bd. dirs. Greater Johnstown YMCA, Johnstown Symphony Orch., Mercy Hosp. Johnstown, Johnstown Area Econ. Devel. Corp.; mem. adv. bd. Johnstown Flood Mus. Served to 1st lt. U.S. Army, 1943-46. Recipient Outstanding Leadership award N.Y. chpt. ASME, 1975. Mem. Air Pollution Control Assn., ASME, Pa. Soc. Profl. Engrs., Pa. Electric Assn. (exec. com.), Pa. Council Econ. Edn. (mem. fin. com). Roman Catholic. Club: Sunnehanna Country. Office: 1001 Broad Johnstown PA 15907

VERSCHOOR, CURTIS CARL, educator; b. Grand Rapids, Mich., June 7, 1931; s. Peter and Leonene (Dahlstrom) V.; B.B.A. with distinction, U. Mich., 1951, M.B.A., 1952; Ed.D., No. Ill. U., 1977; m. Marie Emilie Kritschgau, June 18, 1952; children—Katherine Anne, Carolyn Marie, John Peter, Carla Michelle. Pub. accountant Touche, Ross, Bailey & Smart, C.P.A.'s, 1955-63; with Singer Co., 1963-68, asst. controller, 1965-68; controller Colgate-Palmolive Co., 1968-69; asst. controller bus. products group Xerox Corp., 1969-72; controller Baxter Labs., Inc., 1972-73; v.p. finance Altair Corp., Chgo., 1973-74; prof. DePaul U., Chgo., 1974—; part-time instr. Wayne State U., 1955-60. Served with AUS, 1953-55. Recipient Elijah Watts Sells award Am. Inst. C.P.A.'s, 1953. Mem. Financial Execs. Inst., Am. Inst. C.P.A.'s, Ill. Soc. C.P.A.'s, Am. Accounting Assn., Nat. Assn. Accountants, Beta Gamma Sigma, Beta Alpha Psi, Delta Pi Epsilon, Phi Kappa Phi, Phi Eta Sigma. Contbg. editor Jour. Accountancy, 1961-62. Home: 231 Wyngate Dr Barrington IL 60010 Office: Suite 1252 25 E Jackson Blvd Chicago IL 60604

VER STEEG, CLARENCE LESTER, historian, educator; b. Orange City, Iowa, Dec. 28, 1922; s. John A. and Annie (Vischer) Ver S.; A.B., Morningside Coll., Sioux City, Iowa, 1943; M.A., Columbia, 1946, Ph.D., 1950; m. Dorothy Ann De Vries, Dec. 24, 1943; 1 son, John Charles. Lectr., then instr. history Columbia, 1946-50; mem. faculty Northwestern U., Evanston, Ill., 1950—, prof. history, 1959—, dean Grad. Sch., 1975—. Vis. lectr. Harvard, 1959-60; vis. mem. Inst. Advanced Study, Princeton, 1967-68. Chmn. faculty com. to recommend Master Plan Higher Edn. in Ill., 1962-64; mem. council Inst. Early Am. History and Culture, Williamsburg, Va., 1961-64, 71—, chmn., 1970-71. Served with USAAF, 1942-45. Decorated Air medal with three oak leaf clusters; Nat. fellow econ. history Social Sci. Research Council, 1948-49; fellow George A. and Eliza Gardner Howard Found., 1954-55; research fellow Huntington Library, 1955; sr. fellow Am. Council Learned Socs., 1958-59, Nat. Endowment for Humanities, 1973. Guggenheim fellow, 1964-65. Mem. Am. Hist. Assn. (chmn. nominating com. 1967-68; Albert J. Beveridge prize 1952), Orgn. Am. Historians, So. Hist. Assn. (nominating com. 1970—), AAUP. Presbyn. Author: Robert Morris, Revolutionary Financier, 1954; Tailfer's A True and Narrative History of Georgia, 1960; The American People: Their History, 1961; The Formative Years, 1607-1763, 1964, pub. in Eng., 1965; The Story of Our Country, 1965; (with others) Investigating Man's World, 6 vols., 1970; (with Richard Hofstadter) A People and A Nation, 1971; The Origins of a Southern Mosaic: Studies in the Early Carolinas and Georgia, 1975; World Cultures, 1977. Editor: (with R. Hofstadter) Great Issues in American History, From Settlement to Revolution 1584-1776, 1969. Editorial bd. Jour. Am. History, 1968—. Contbr. articles to profl. jours. Home: 2619 Ridge Ave Evanston IL 60201

VERTES, VICTOR, physician, educator; b. Cleve., Sept. 10, 1927; s. Louis W. and Mary (Anscel) V.; B.S., Case Western Res. U., 1948, M.D., 1953; m. Merle Stephanie Schumann, Nov. 26, 1960; children—Keith Victor, Peter Louis, Adam Steven, Melissa Anscel. Intern Univ. Hosps. of Cleve., 1953-54; resident Mt. Sinai Hosp. of Cleve., 1954-56, asso. vis. physician, 1958-64, physician in charge outpatient clinic, 1959-64, dir. metabolic and endocrine lab., 1959-65, dir. dept. medicine, 1964—; fellow in metabolism and endocrinology N.Y. Hosp. Cornell Med. Center, 1956-57; instr. medicine Western Res. U., 1962-64, asst. clin. prof., 1964-68, asso. clin. prof., 1968-72, prof., 1972—. Mem. med. adv. bd. Cleve. chpt. Kidney Disease Found., 1965-68; cons. Kidney Disease Control Program Pub. Health Service, Arlington, Va., 1968-71; numerous vis. professorships. Mem. nominating com. Bd. Trustees Cleve. Med. Library Assn., 1975—. Served with M.C., AUS, 1946. Recipient Julius E. Goodman award Mt. Sinai Hosp., 1968. Fellow A.C.P., Am. Coll. Cardiology; mem. Central Soc. Clin. Research, European Dialysis and Transplant Assn., Am. Soc. Nephrology, Pan Am. Med. Assn., Soc. Critical Care Medicine, Council High Blood Pressure Research, Transplantation Soc. (pres. 1971), Phi Beta Kappa, Sigma Xi, Alpha Omega Alpha. Club: Oakwood Country. Mem. editors bd. Nephron; mem. editorial bd. Perspectives in Nephrology and Hypertension. Contbr. articles to profl. jours. Home: 21226 S Woodland Shaker Heights OH 44122 Office: Mt Sinai Hosp of Cleve 1800 E 105th St Cleveland OH 44106

VERTLIEB, RICHARD HARVEY, former baseball club exec., educator: b. Los Angeles, Oct. 7, 1930; s. Jack and Gertrude J. (Starkman) V.; B.S. in Econs., U. So. Calif., 1953; m. Joan Selenkow, Aug. 3, 1956; 1 son, Adam. Account exec. Merrill, Lynch, Hollywood, Calif., 1956-67; bus. mgr., gen. mgr. Seattle SuperSonics, 1967-70; registered rep. Kidder-Peabody, Seattle, 1970-72; pres. Trail Capital Corp., Seattle, 1972-74; gen. mgr. Golden State Warriors, Oakland, Calif., 1974-76; exec. dir., gen. mgr. Seattle Mariners, 1976-79; gen. mgr. NBA World Championship Basketball Team, 1974-75; affiliate prof. grad. program in sports adminstrn. Sch. Phys. Edn., U. Wash., Seattle, 1979—. Bd. dirs. Visitors and Conv. Bur. Served with U.S. Army, 1953-55. Mem. Nat. Basketball Assn. (Exec. of Year 1975). Clubs: Masons, Wash. Athletic, Friars. Home: 6280 W Mercer Way Mercer Island WA 98040

VERWOERDT, ADRIAAN, psychiatrist; b. Voorburg, Netherlands, July 5, 1927; s. Christopher and Juliana Margaretha (Busch) V.; came to U.S., 1953, naturalized, 1958; M.D., Med. Sch. of Amsterdam, 1952; m. Dorothy Jean Taylor, Oct. 9, 1965; children—Christopher Earl, Mark Adrian. Rotating intern Touro Infirmary, New Orleans, 1953-54; resident in psychiatry Duke U. Med. Center, Durham, N.C., 1954-55, 58-60, fellow in psychiat. research, 1960-61, asst. prof. psychiatry, 1963-67, asso. prof., 1967-71, prof., 1971—, dir. geriatric psychiatry tng. program, 1966—; dir. psychiat. residency tng. John Umstead Hosp., Butner, N.C., 1968—. Served as capt. M.C., U.S. Army, 1955-57. NIMH Career Tchr. Tng. grantee, 1964-66; diplomate Pan Am. Med. Assn. Fellow Am. Psychiat. Assn.; mem. AMA, Am. Geriatrics Soc., Am. Psychoanalytic Assn. Author: Communication with the Fatally Ill, 1966, Clinical Geropsychiatry, 1976. Contbr. articles to profl. jours. Office: Duke U Med Center Durham NC 27710

VERY, DONALD LEROY, lawyer; b. Pitts., Aug. 19, 1933; S. Rocco and Elizabeth (Garfold) V.; B.A., Duquesne U., 1955; J.D., U. Notre Dame, 1958; m. Norma Claire Wandrisco, June 30, 1956; children—Donald Leroy, Dianne, David, Daniel, Douglas, Dennis. Admitted to Pa. bar, 1959; asso. partner firm Campbell, Thomas, & Burke, Pitts., 1959-63, partner, 1964-70; partner firm Tucker, Arensberg, Very & Ferguson, Pitts., 1971—; asst. dir. In-Dev-Or, The Ins. Devel. Orgn. Bus. Sch.; mem. admiralty rules com. U.S. Dist. Ct. Western Dist. Pa., 1967—; examiner Pa. Bd. Law Examiners, 1968-72; lectr. U. Pitts. Sch. Gen. Studies, 1971-75; adj. prof. admiralty law, 1976—. Sec., Parks Commn. Bethel Park Borough, Pitts., 1966-68. Mem. Allegheny County (pres. elect 1977), Pa., Am., Allegheny County (pres, 1978) bar assns., Am. Judicature Soc., Am. Trial Lawyers Assn., Maritime Law Assn. U.S., Acad. Trial Lawyers Am. Club: Serra (pres. 1976). Author: The Law-Make It Work for You, 1974. Opinion editor Pitts. Legal Jour., 1964-67, editor-in-chief, 1968—; editor Pa. Bar Quar., 1969—. Home: 90 Redpath Trail Upper St Clair Twp Pittsburgh PA 15241 Office: Pittsburgh National Bldg Pittsburgh PA 15222

VESAK, NORBERT FRANKLIN, choreographer, dir.; b. Vancouver, B.C., Can., Oct. 22, 1936; came to U.S., 1971, naturalized, 1979; s. Frank and Norah Grace (Riley) V.; studied dance with Josephine Slater, 1957-60, Ted Shawn, 1960-63, La Meri, 1962, Pauline Koner, 1963, Margaret Craske, 1960-63, Merce Cunningham, 1964-66, Vera Volkova, 1969-72. Resident choreographer Playhouse Theatre, Vancouver, B.C., 1960-68; choreographer Can. Broadcasting Co. Television, 1965-67, Royal Winnipeg Ballet, 1970-80, San Francisco Opera, 1971-74; dir. ballet Met. Opera Co., N.Y.C., 1976—; choreographer Deutsche Oper, Berlin, 1975, Nat. Ballet Can., 1976, Scottish Ballet, 1976, Miami Opera, 1978-80, Joffrey II, 1975, N.C. Dance Theatre, 1973, 74, 79; dir. Forest Meadow Festival of the Arts, 1976; master tchr. Nat. Assn. for Regional Ballet, 1974—; dir. Nat. Craft of Choreography Conf., 1978, 79. Can. Council grantee; Nat. Endowment Arts grantee. Mem. Royal Acad. Dancing (London); Actors Equity (Can.), Am. Guild Musical Artists, Nat. Assn. Regional Ballet, Am. Fedn. TV and Radio Artists. Roman Catholic. Office: Lincoln Center Met Opera Ballet New York NY 10023

VESCOLANI, FRED JULIUS, coll. dean; b. Mich., Feb. 16, 1916; B.S. in Econs., St. Norbert Coll., DePere, Wis., 1938; M.A. in Ednl. Adminstrn., Mich. State U., 1953; Ed.D., Columbia U., 1954; Litt.D., Lawrence (Mass.) Inst. Tech., 1959; m. Mildred Hobbs, Oct. 16, 1962; children—Tony, Bill, Diane, Margaret. Elementary, then secondary sch. tchr., 1938-41; athletic coach, 1938-43; supt. schs., 1943-53; asso. coordinator Coop. Program Ednl. Adminstrn., Middle Atlantic Area, Columbia U., 1954-55; mem. faculty Mich. State U., 1955-70, profl. ednl. adminstrn. and higher edn., to 1970; dean Coll. Edn., U. Ark., Fayetteville, 1970—; sr. cons. Office of Overseas Schs., U.S. Dept. State, 1979; cons., lectr. in field. Fellow Ford Found., 1953-54; recipient Distinguished Alumni award edn. St. Norbert Coll., 1977. Mem. Am., Mich. (past dir.) assns. sch. adminstrs., Mich. Edn. Assn. (past pres.), Am. Acad. Polit. and Social Sci., Univ. Council Ednl. Adminstrs., Nat. Council Profl. Ednl. Adminstrs., Ark. Edn. Assn., Phi Delta Kappa, Kappa Delta Phi. Contbr. profl. publs. Address: 323 Coll Education Univ Ark Fayetteville AR 72701

VESELL, ELLIOT SAUL, pharmacologist, physician, educator; b. N.Y.C., Dec. 24, 1933; s. Harry and Evelyn (Jaffe) V.; grad. Phillips Exeter Acad., 1951; A.B., Harvard U., 1955, M.D., 1959; m. Kristen Paige Peery, Mar. 24, 1968; children—Liane Clark, Hilary Peery. Research asso. Rockefeller U., 1960-62; intern children's med. service Mass. Gen. Hosp., Boston, 1959-60; asst. resident Peter Bent Brigham Hosp., Boston, 1962-63; surgeon Nat. Inst. Arthritis and Metabolic Diseases, NIH, Bethesda, Md., 1963-65; head sect. on pharmacogenetics Lab. Chem. Pharmacology, Nat. Heart Inst., Bethesda, 1965-68; prof., chmn. dept. pharmacology, prof. genetics, prof. medicine Pa. State U., Hershey, 1968—, asst. dean grad. edn. Milton S. Hershey Med. Center, 1973—; William N. Creasy vis. prof. clin. pharmacology George Washington U., 1975, U. Conn., 1979; vis. prof. medicine U. Nebr., 1973; clin. asst. prof. medicine Georgetown U., 1964-68; vis. prof. biochemistry U. Ala., Birmingham, 1966—; cons. FDA, 1970—; Pfizer lectr. Med. Coll. Pa., 1976, U. Iowa, 1977, Med. Coll. Wis., 1978, Georgetown U., 1979; Rufus Cole lectr. Rockefeller U., 1979. Mem. sci. adv. bd. Nat. Center Toxicological Research, 1970-75, chmn., 1975-76; mem. study sect. pharmacology NIH, 1972-75; mem. com. on drug safety NRC-Nat. Acad. Sci., 1974—. Mem. Am. Soc. Clin. Investigation, Am. Soc. Pharmacology and Exptl. Therapeutics (clin. pharmacology award 1971), Am. Physiol. Soc., Am. Soc. Human Genetics, Am. Coll. Clin. Pharmacology, Am. Fedn. Clin. Research, Soc. Exptl. Biology and Medicine (Samuel J. Meltzer award 1967), Harvey Soc., Sigma Xi. Editor: Life and Works of Thomas Cole (Louis Legrand Noble), 1964; Annals of N.Y. Acad. Scis., 1968, 71, 76; Survey of Pharmacology in Medical Schools of North America, 1974. Office: Pa State U Coll Medicine Dept Pharmacology Hershey PA 17033

VESELY, WILLIAM JAMES, lawyer, business exec.; b. N.Y.C., June 15, 1923; s. William A. and Margaret A. (Lynch) V.; A.B., Colgate U., 1948; LL.B., Yale U., 1951; divorced; children—Marie Elizabeth, Susan A., William James, Robert H., Patricia A. Admitted to Ohio bar, 1951; atty., then partner, mem. exec. com. firm Thompson, Hine & Flory, Cleve., 1951-75; v.p., gen. counsel, sec. Pneumo Corp., Boston, 1975—; dir. Towlift, Pyronics, Jennings & Churella. Trustee Cleveland Heights (Ohio) Library. Served with USN, 1943-45. Mem. Am. Bar Assn., Ohio Bar Assn., Cleve. Bar Assn. Clubs: Shaker Heights (Ohio) Country; Kittansett (Marion, Mass.); Court of Nisi Prius (Cleve.). Contbr. articles to legal jours. Home: 1 Longfellow Pl Boston MA 02114 Office: Pneumo Corp 4800 Prudential Tower Boston MA 02199

VESIC, ALEKSANDAR SEDMAK, civil engr., educator; b. Resan-Bitolj, Yugoslavia, Aug. 8, 1924; s. Bozidar P. and Teofanija (Jancic) V.; B.C.E. with highest honor, U. Belgrade, 1950, C.E., 1952, D.Sc., 1956; postgrad. U. Manchester (Eng.), 1957, U. Ghent (Belgium), 1957-58, Mass. Inst. Tech., 1959; m. Milena Sedmak, May 5, 1946. Came to U.S., 1958, naturalized, 1964. Engring. aide Bur. Reclamation, Belgrade, 1942-44; instr. U. Belgrade, 1949-52; civil engr. large dam Drina I and Corps Engrs., Yugoslav Army, 1952-53; also cons. engr., Belgrade, 1952-56; lectr. U. Belgrade, also cons. Nat. Inst. Testing Materials, 1953-56; research engr. Nat. Geotech. Inst. Belgium, Ghent, 1956-58; asst. prof., then asso. prof. civil engring. Ga. Inst. Tech., 1958-64, also cons. engr., Atlanta; prof. civil engring. Duke, 1964-71, J.A. Jones prof., 1971—, chmn. dept., 1968-74, dean engring., 1974—; cons. engr., Durham, 1964—; fellow Churchill Coll., Cambridge (Eng.) U., 1971-72. Chmn. com. theory pavement design Hwy. Research Bd., 1965-70; mem. adv. panel pavements, nat. coop. hwy. research program Nat. Acad. Scis., 1967—; gen. reporter 3d Panam. Conf., Caracas, 1968, 5th Conf., Buenos Aires, 1975; v.p. main session 5th European Conf., Madrid, 1972. Recipient prize scholastic achievement Nat. Com. Univs. Yugoslavia, 1949; 3d prize competition design Sava River bridge, 1953; Chi Epsilon award as outstanding prof. civil engring., 1967; Hwy. Research Bd. award for paper spl. merit NRC, 1969; Overseas fellow Churchill Coll., Cambridge (Eng.) U., 1970. Fellow ASCE (chmn. com. deep founds. 1968-74, Thomas A. Middlebrooks award 1974); mem. Internat. Soc. Soil Mechanics, Internat. Assn. Bridge and Structural Engrs., Am. Soc. Engring. Edn., Am. Pub. Works Assn., Sigma Xi, Chi Epsilon (hon.), Tau Beta Pi (hon.); corr. mem. Venezuelan Soc. Soil Mech. Found Engring.; hon. mem. Colombian Geotech. Soc. Author: Bearing Capacity of Shallow Foundations, 1971; also papers. Editor, contbr.: Bearing Capacity and Settlement of Foundations, 1967. Home: 1722 Duke University Rd Durham NC 27701

VESPA, NED ANGELO, news photographer, photographer; b. Streator, Ill., May 31, 1942; s. Ned James and Evelyn Blanche (Flanigan) V.; B.S., So. Ill. U., 1965; m. Carol DeMasters, Sept. 11, 1976; 1 son by previous marriage, James Paul. Photographer Milw. Jour. Co., 1965—, Milw. Sentinel, 1965—. Mem. Nat. Press Photographers Assn., Wis. News Photographers Assn. (pres.), Milw. Press Photographers. Home: 7535 N Boyd Way Fox Point WI 53217 Office: 333 W State St Milwaukee WI 53202

VESPER, KARL HAMPTON, educator; b. San Marino, Calif., Aug. 12, 1932; s. Karl Conrad and Roxie (Armstrong) V.; B.S. in Mech. Engring., Stanford U., 1955; M.S. in Mech. Engring., 1965, Ph.D., 1969; M.B.A., Harvard U., 1960; m. Joan Frantz, June, 1964; children—Karen, Linda, Holly, Nancy. Casewriter, Harvard Bus. Sch., 1960-61; bus. mgr., mech. engr., Marine Advisers, 1961-62; cons. Dept. State, summer, 1963; dir. Hosmer Machine Co.. Contoock, N.H., 1966-67; dir. summer insts. Stanford U., 1966, 67, dir. case devel., research asso., lectr. mech. engring., 1963-69, research asso., NASA faculty fellow in air pollution research design project, summer 1970; editor mech. engring. series McGraw Hill Book Co., N.Y.C., 1966-74; prof. bus. adminstrn., mech. engring. and marine studies, U. Wash., Seattle, 1969—. Served with USAF, 1955-57. Mem. Am. Inst. for Decision Scis., Acad. Mgmt., Sigma Xi. Author: How To Write Engineering Cases, 1966, 73; Engineers at Work, 1975; Entrepreneurship Education, 1976; the Entrepreneurial Function, 1977. Contbr. articles to books and profl. jours. Home: 3721 47th Pl NE Seattle WA 98105 Office: Sch Business Administration University Washington Seattle WA 98195

VEST, GEORGE SOUTHALL, govt. ofcl.; b. Columbia, Va., Dec. 25, 1918; s. George Southall and Nancy Margaret (Robertson) V.; A.B., U. Va., 1941, M.A., 1947; m. Emily Barber Clemons, June 21, 1947; children—Jeannie Robertson, George Southall, Henry Clemons. Vice consul, Hamilton, Bermuda, 1947-49; 3d sec. embassy, Quito, 1949-51; 2d sec., Ottawa, Can., 1952-54; Canadian desk officer State Dept., 1954-57; staff asst. to asst. sec. state European affairs, 1957-58; mem. staff embassy, Paris, France, 1958-60, NATO internat. staff, Paris, 1961-63; assigned Nat. War Coll., 1963-64, State Dept., 1965-67; dep. chief U.S. mission European Communities, Brussels, Belgium, 1967-69; dep. U.S. permanent rep. to NATO, Brussels, 1970-72; negotiator to CSCE, Helsinki and Geneva, 1972-73; spl. asst. to sec. for press relations, 1973, dir. Bur. Polit.-Mil. Affairs, 1974-77; asst. sec. state for European affairs, 1977. Served to capt. AUS, 1941-46. Recipient Superior honor award Dept. of State, 1973. Mem. Am. Fgn. Service Assn., Phi Beta Kappa. Episcopalian. Home: 5307 Iroquois Rd NW Washington DC 20016 Office: Room 6226 Dept State 2201 C St NW Washington DC 20520

VEST, ROBERT WILSON, ceramic engr.; b. Lawrenceburg, Ind., Oct. 17, 1930; s. Wilson Purlee and Mildred Emily (Baker) V.; B.S., Purdue U., 1952; Ph.D., Iowa State U., 1957; m. Ariel Maxine Huffman, June 7, 1952; children—Gary Wilson, Gregory Robert, Scott Alden. Chemist, Nat. Lead Co., Fernald, Ohio, 1952-53; research asst. Inst. Atomic Research, Ames, Iowa, 1953-57; research chemist Monsanto Corp., Dayton, Ohio, 1957-61; sr. scientist Systems Research Labs., Dayton, 1961-66; Turner prof. engring. Purdue U., West Lafayette, Ind., 1966—; cons. in field. Fellow Am. Ceramic Soc. (Ross Coffin Purdy award 1969); mem. Nat. Inst. Ceramic Engrs., Ceramic Edn. Council, Internat. Soc. Hybrid Microelectronics, Am. Soc. Metals, Sigma Xi. Club: Rotary. Contbr. articles to profl. publs. Home: 810 Princess Dr West Lafayette IN 47906 Office: Potter Engring Center Purdue U West Lafayette IN 47907. *My goal has always been to do the best possible job on all endeavors, both personal and professional. The most effective method for me to approach this goal has been to always have a number of activities underway at any time, and not to force results on any of them.*

VESTAL, ALLAN DELKER, lawyer, educator; b. Indpls., Nov. 26, 1920; A.B., DePauw U., 1943; LL.B., Yale U., 1949. Admitted to Iowa bar, 1949; instr. law U. Iowa, Iowa City, 1949-50, asst. prof., 1950-53, asso. prof., 1953-57, prof., 1957-67, Murray prof., 1967-72, Carver prof., 1972—; vis. prof. Tex. Tech. U., Lubbock, summer 1974, U. Tenn., Knoxville, 1975, U. N.C., Chapel Hill, 1976, U. So. Calif., 1977. Mem. Johnson County Regional Planning Commn., 1965-78; mem. Nat. Conf. Commrs. on Uniform State Laws, 1964—. Mem. Order of Coif (v.p.). Author: Res Judicata/Preclusion, 1969, Iowa Practice, 1974, Iowa Land Use and Zoning Law, 79. Home: 1704 Glendale Rd Iowa City IA 52240 Office: Coll of Law U Iowa Iowa City IA 52242

VESTAL, LUCIAN LAROE, financier; b. Whitewright, Tex., Aug. 10, 1925; s. Rolla C. and Lora A. (Robinson) V.; student Baylor U., 1942-43; B.S., U. Pitts., 1947; postgrad. N.Y.U., 1948-50, Ill. Inst. Tech., 1960; m. Dorothy Millington Sing, Aug. 15, 1952; children—John William, Denise Millington. Security analyst Lionel D. Edie & Co., N.Y.C., 1947-54; asst. dir. finance Champion Papers, Inc., Hamilton, Ohio, 1954-55; dir. research Rotan, Mosle & Co., Houston, 1955-58; dir. planning Pure Oil Co., Palatine, Ill., 1958-63; dir. planning and fin. services Weyerhaeuser Co., Tacoma, 1963-65; treas. Sunray DX Oil Co., Tulsa, 1965-68; asst. treas. Sun Oil Co., Tulsa, 1968-69; group v.p. Tesoro Petroleum Corp., San Antonio, 1969-72; sr. v.p. affiliate banking Palmer Bank Corp., Sarasota, Fla., 1973-75; trustee Citizens Growth Properties, 1969-78; chmn., dir. Palmer banks of Siesta Key, Village Plaza, N.A., Gulf Gate (all Sarasota), Palmer Bank of Bradenton, N.A. (Fla.), Palmer Bank & Trust Co. Naples, N.A. (Fla.), Palmer Bank & Trust Co. Ft. Myers, N.A. (Fla.); pres., dir. Point Palma Sola, Inc., 1975-78, Cortez Yachts, Inc., 1975-78, So. Yachts, Inc., 1978—. Served to 1st lt., inf., USMCR, 1943-45, 50-51. Decorated Navy Cross, Purple Heart. Mem. N.Y. Soc. Security Analysts, U.S. Power Squadron, Delta Tau Delta. Republican. Baptist. Club: Sarasota Yacht. Home: 244 Cedar Park Circle Sarasota FL 33581

VESTLING, CARL SWENSSON, biochemist, educator; b. Northfield, Minn., May 6, 1913; s. Axel E. and Bertha (Swensson) V.; B.A., Carleton Coll., Northfield, Minn., 1934; Ph.D., Johns Hopkins, 1938; m. Christina Brunyate Meredith, Dec. 24, 1938; children—Martha M., Christina L. (Mrs. John William Copenhaver, Jr.), Anne S. (Mrs. Jaime J. Galdos). From instr. to prof. dept. chemistry and chem. engring. U. Ill., 1938-63; prof. biochemistry, U. Iowa, Iowa City, 1963—, head dept., 1963-76; cons. to govt. and industry, 1940—. Guggenheim fellow, 1954. Mem. Am. Soc. Biol. Chemists, Biochem. Soc. (Eng.), Am. Chem. Soc., A.A.A.S., Soc. Exptl. Biology and Medicine, Phi Beta Kappa, Sigma Xi, Phi Lambda Upsilon, Alpha Chi Sigma. Research on isolation and characterization liver enzymes, kinetics and mechanism action, enzymatic steroid transformations. Home: Rural Route 6 Fairview Knoll Iowa City IA 52240

VETTE, JAMES IRA, govt. ofcl.; b. Evanston, Ill., Mar. 4, 1927; s. Ira Charles and Alma (Ishmael) V.; student Northwestern U., 1944-45; B.A. in Physics, Rice Inst., 1952; Ph.D., Calif. Inst. Tech., 1958; m. Zoe Jane Cashmore, June 9, 1951; children—James Alden, Zoe Jane, Pamela Anne, Alan Frederick. Staff scientist, then sr. staff scientist Convair. Sci. Research Lab., 1958-62; mgr. nuclear physics Vela satellite program, also staff scientist space physics lab. Aerospace Corp., El Segundo, Calif., 1962-66; dir. Nat. Space Sci. Data Center, 1967—. Mem. panel information analysis center Com. Sci. and Tech. Information, 1967-71, chmn. task group synopit data centers,

1968-69, mem. data mgmt. adv. panel marine scis. council, 1967-68, chmn. COSPAR adv. com. data problems and Publ., 1974—. Served with USAAF, 1946-49. Recipient Exceptional Service award NASA, 1969. Dow Chem. Co., Gen. Electric Co., IBM fellowships Calif. Inst. Tech., 1954-57. Mem. Am. Phys. Soc., Am. Geophys. Union, A.A.A.S., Profl. Group Nuclear Sci., Phi Beta Kappa, Sigma Xi. Research high energy physics, accelerators, experiments on ballons, satellites and rockets in cosmic rays, solar physics, trapped radiation. Home: 12502 White Dr Silver Spring MD 20904 Office: Nat Space Sci Data Center Goddard Space Flight Center Greenbelt MD 20771

VETTER, BETTY MCGEE, orgn. assn.; b. Center, Colo., Oct. 25, 1924; d. William Allen and Bonnie Hunsaker McGee; B.A., U. Colo., 1944; M.A., Stanford U., 1948; m. Richard C. Vetter, Sept. 4, 1951 (div. 1971); children—David Bruce, Richard Dean, Robert Alan. Chemist, Shell Devel. Co., Emeryville, Calif., 1944-45; instr. Fresno State Coll., 1948-50; instr. Far Eastern div. U. Calif., 1950-51; adj. prof. Am. U., Washington, 1952-64, part-time U. Va., Arlington, 1952-64, U. Md. Ext. div., College Park, 1960-61; exec. dir. Sci. Manpower Commn., Washington, 1964—. Bd. dirs. Wider Opportunities for Women, Inc. Served with U.S. Naval Women's Res., 1944-45. Mem. Manpower Analysis and Planning Soc., AAAS. Editor Sci., Engring., Tech. Manpower Comments, 1965—. Home: 4779 N 33d St Arlington VA 22207 Office: 1776 Massachusetts Ave NW Washington DC 20036

VETTER, HERBERT, physician; b. Vienna, Austria, August 24, 1920; M.D., U. Vienna, 1948; m. Eleonore von Hacklaender, July 6, 1946 (div. 1969); 1 dau., Barbara Weber; m. 2d, Brigitte Frei, Dec. 20, 1973. Physician, Allgemeines Krankenhaus, Vienna, Austria, 1948-60; Brit. Council research fellow, 1951; research fellow Sloan-Kettering Inst. Cancer Research, N.Y.C., 1954; head radioisotopes lab. 2d Med. Univ. Clinic, Vienna, 1951-60; asso. prof. medicine U. Vienna, 1959-67, prof., 1967—; sr. officer Internat. Atomic Energy Agy., 1958—. Chmn. planning bd. IB, Internat. Commn. Radiation Units and Measurements, 1962-69, cons., 1969—. Recipient prize for art and sci. Republic of Austria, 1956. Affiliate Royal Soc. of Medicine; mem. Gesellschaft der Aerzte, Gesellschaft für Innere Medizin, Österreichische Roentgengesellschaft. Rotarian (pres. Vienna 1975-76). Author: (with N. Veall) Radioisotope Techniques in Clinical Research and Diagnosis, 1958. Editor: Radioaktive Isotope in Klinik und Forschung (Vol. I, II, III), 1955, 56, 58; (with E.H. Belcher) Radioisotopes in Medical Diagnosis, 1971; jour. Nuclear Medicine, 1959—, Internat. Jour. Biomed. Engring., 1971—. Home: Landesgerichtsstrasse 18 Vienna 1010 Austria Office: Internat Atomic Energy Agy Wagramerstrasse 5 Vienna 1400 Austria

VETTER, JAMES GEORGE, JR., lawyer; b. Omaha, Apr. 8, 1934; s. James George and Helen Louise (Adams) V.; B.S., Georgetown U., 1954; J.D., Creighton U., 1960; m. Mary Ellen Froelich, June 25, 1960; 1 son, James G. III. Admitted to Nebr. bar, 1960, Tex. bar, 1967; counsel IRS, Washington, 1960-64, Dallas, 1964-67; practiced in Dallas, 1967—; partner firm Vetter, Tibbals & Bates, 1979—; lectr. taxation seminars; dir. Gulf Tex Constrn., Inc., Monzingo Industries, Inc., Drake & Assos. Inc. Asst. sgt.-at-arms Tex. Democratic Conv., 1968; advisor selection com. Georgetown U., 1970—; scoutmaster Boy Scouts Am., 1974-75. Served with USAF, 1954-57. Mem. Nebr. Bar Assn., State Bar Tex., Dallas Legal Aid Soc., Creigton U. Alumni Assn. (pres. Dallas-Ft. Worth 1969-70), Delta Theta Phi. Independent. Roman Catholic. Clubs: Lancers, Brookhaven Country. Contbr. articles to profl. jours. Home: 11023 Rosser Rd Dallas TX 75229 Office: 2468 One Main Pl Dallas TX 75250

VEVIER, CHARLES, historian, univ. adminstr.; b. N.Y.C., June 15, 1924; s. Max and Sarah (Kramer) V.; B.A., U. Wis., 1948, M.A., 1949, Ph.D., 1953; m. Marcia Gold, Sept. 7, 1952; children—Ann, Ellen, John. Instr., U. Wis. Extension at Wausau, 1951-52, Rutgers U., 1952-54; asst. prof. U. Rochester, 1954-59; mem. faculty U. Wis. at Milw., 1959—, vice chancellor, 1963-69; pres. Adelphi U., 1969-71; exec. v.p. Coll. Medicine and Dentistry of N.J., 1971—. Cons. community action programs OEO, 1968—; cons. Urban Coalition, 1968—; participant, speaker program exn. and tng. A.M.A. U. Wis. rep. com. urban problems Nat. Assn. Land Grant Colls. and Univs.; mem., interim chmn. com. urban affairs Com. Instl. Coop.; mem. com. on non-traditional edn., com. on urban edn. Master Plan for Higher Edn. in N.J. Dir. NCCJ, Nassau-Suffolk Region; trustee Lexington Sch. for Deaf, Jackson Heights, N.Y., North Shore Hosp., Manhasset, N.Y., Newark Pub. Radio. Mem. L.I. Arts Study Com.; hon. mem. council for hearing impaired; spl. adv. cons. Bklyn. Inst. Council; exec. com. Council Higher Edn. in Newark; adv. com. Health Professions Edn. Master Plan N.J.; rep. N.J. Assn. Colls. and Univs. Served with USAAF, 1943-45. Decorated Air medal. Mem. Am. Hist. Assn., AAUP. Author: United States and China, 1906-16; also articles. Editor: A Voyage Down the Amur. Home: 9 Peter Lynas Ct Tenafly NJ 07670

VEYS, ALBERT LOUIS, mayor; b. Omaha, Jan. 10, 1919; s. Cyriel Leo and Mary Madeline (Vannest) V.; grad. Creighton Prep. Sch., 1936; m. Jean Blessing, Sept. 23, 1942; children—Janice, Mary Kathlee, Donald, Carol. Pres., Veys Foodland, Inc., Omaha; mem. Omaha City Council, 1957-73; mayor of Omaha, 1977—. Pres. Nebr. League Municipalities. Served with M.C., U.S. Army, 1942-45. Recipient Distinguished Service award U.S. Jaycees, 1954; IGA Internat. award for outstanding achievement, 1954; Nebr. Congress Parents and Tchrs. award, 1968. Mem. U.S. Conf. Mayors, C. of C., Am. Legion, VFW, DAV. Roman Catholic. Clubs: Kiwanis, K.C., Optimists. Office: 1819 Farnam St Omaha NE 68102*

VEYSEY, ARTHUR ERNEST, reporter, adminstr., writer; b. Boulder, Colo., Sept. 28, 1914; s. Ernest Charles and Lillian (Larson) V.; B.A., U. Colo., 1935; m. Florence Jones, 1937 (dec. 1940); 1 dau., Priscilla Joan; m. 2d, Gwendolyn Morgan, 1946. Reporter Denver Post, 1935-37, Scottsbluff (Neb.) Star-Herald, 1937-41, Omaha World-Herald, 1941-43; war corr. Southwest Pacific, Chgo. Tribune, 1943- 45, fgn. corr., 1946-50, chief London bur., 1950-75; gen. mgr. Cantigny Trust, 1975—. Author: Death in the Jungle, 1966; (with Gwen Morgan) Halas by Halas, 1979. Club: Lake Zurich Golf. Address: 1 S 151 Winfield Rd Wheaton IL 60187

VEZEAU, SISTER JEANNETTE EVA, coll. pres.; b. Rochester, N.H., May 11, 1913; d. Edward U. and Laura Ann (Richey) Vezeau; B.S., Boston U., 1948, M.Ed., 1955, Ed.D., 1960. Joined Sisters of Holy Cross, 1933; tchr. high sch., Manchester, N.H., 1937-45, North Grosvenordale, Conn., 1945-49, New Bedford, Mass., 1949-57; prin. St. George High Sch., Manchester, 1960-64; supr. schs. Sisters of Holy Cross in New Eng., Pittsfield, N.H., 1964-67; pres. Notre Dame Coll., Manchester, 1967—; mem. Christian Unity Commn., 1965-71; mem. Diocesan Sch. Bd. Manchester, 1965-71, adv. bd. Elliott Sch. Nursing, Manchester, 1968-76; mem. exec. bd. N.H. Coll. and Univ. Council, 1967—, treas., 1978—; mem. exec. bd. Council for Better Schs. in N.H., 1975—; bd. incorporators Cath. Med. Center, 1978; mem. Gov.'s Commn. on Post Secondary Edn., 1973—, vice chmn., 1977—. Recipient Woman of Achievement award N.H. Fedn. Bus. and Profl. Women's Clubs, Inc., 1974. Mem. Am. Council Edn. Author: (with others) 10,000 Legal Words, 1971. Address: 2321 Elm St Manchester NH 03104

VICK, HOMER JEROME, utility co. exec.; b. McFarland, Wis., Feb. 22, 1924; s. Homer L. and Della M. (Hjortland) V.; B.S. in Elec. Engring., Marquette U., 1946; M.S., U. Wis., 1949; m. Elaine Ruth Lippert, Mar. 2, 1946; children—Sherry Lee, Sue Ellen, Alan Jerome. With Wis. Power & Light Co., Madison, 1950—, v.p. rates and consumer services, sec., 1976—. Served to lt. (j.g.) USNR, 1943-46. Registered profl. engr., Wis. Mem. Nat., Wis. socs. profl. engrs., I.E.E.E. Methodist (lay speaker). Kiwanian. Home: 2751 Tower Rd McFarland WI 53558 Office: 222 W Washington Ave Madison WI 53703

VICKER, RAY, author; b. Wis., Aug. 27, 1917; s. Joseph John and Mary (Young) V.; student Wis. State U., Stevens Point, 1934, Los Angeles City Coll., 1940-41, Northwestern U., 1947-49; m. Margaret Ella Leach, Feb. 23, 1944. With Chgo. Jour. Commerce, 1946-50, automobile editor, 1947-50; mem. staff Wall St. Jour., 1950—, European editor, London, Eng., 1960—, now sr. internat. editor. Served with U.S. Merchant Marine, 1942-46. Recipient Outstanding Reporting Abroad award Chgo. Newspaper Guild, 1959; Best Bus. Reporting Abroad award E. W. Fairchild, 1963, 67, hon. mention, 1965. Mem. Soc. Auto. Engrs., Sigma Delta Chi. Catholic. Clubs: Overseas Press (Reporting award 1963, 67) (N.Y.C.); Press, Adventurers (Chgo.). Author: How an Election Was Won, 1962; Those Swiss Money Men, 1973; Kingdom of Oil, 1974; Realms of Gold, 1975; This Hungry World, 1976; also numerous articles. Home: Pnytagoras No 9 Flat 2 Engomi Nicosi Cyprus Office: Wall Street Jour London Internat Press Centre 76 Shoe Ln London EC4A 3JB England

VICKERS, JON, operatic tenor; b. Prince Albert, Sask., Can., 1926; studied with George Lambert, Royal Conservatory of music, Toronto; hon. doctorate U. Sask., Bishops U., Que., U. Western Ont.; m. Henrietta Outerbridge, 1953; children—Allison, William, Jonathan, Kenneth, Wendy. Operatic debut Rigoletto, Toronto Opera Festival, 1952; appeared with Stratford (Ont.) Festival, 1956—; also Covent Garden, London, Chgo. Lyric Opera, Vienna State Opera, Bayreuth Festival, Teatro Colón, Buenos Aires, San Francisco Opera Co., Met. Opera Co., La Scala, Milan Italy, numerous others. Recs. include Messiah, Otello, Aida, Die Walkure, Samson et Delilah, Fidelio, Italian Arias, Carmen, Les Troyens, Tristand und Isolde; appeared in films Carmen, Pagliacci, Otello. Recipient Can. Centennial medal, 1967; decorated companion Order of Can., 1968. Presbyn. Address: Metropolitan Opera Lincoln Center Plaza New York NY 10019*

VICKERS, ROGER SPENCER, research physicist; b. Hitchin, Hertfordshire, Eng., Nov. 13, 1937; s. John Hector and Corona (McCarthy) V.; came to U.S., 1963, naturalized, 1974; B.Sc. with honors, Southampton U. (Eng.), 1959, Ph.D., 1963; m. Solvi Loken, May 18, 1968; children—Michelle, Jacqueline. Physicist, Ill. Inst. Tech. Research Inst., Chgo., 1963-66; research asso. Stanford U., 1966-68; v.p. sci. and applications E.R.A., Inc., Houston, 1969-70; asso. prof. elec. engring. Colo. State U., 1970-73; sr. physicist Stanford Research Inst., Menlo Park, Calif., 1973—; cons. NSF. Mem. Inst. of Physics (London), Internat. Glaciological Soc. Home: 1143 Los Altos Ave Los Altos CA 94022 Office: Bldg 44 Stanford Research Inst Menlo Park CA 94025

VICKERY, EDWARD DOWNTAIN, lawyer; b. Ft. Worth, May 1, 1922; s. Charles Richard and Margaret (Downtain) V.; B.A., U. Tex., 1947, J.D. with honors, 1948; m. Dorothy Butler, Jan. 30, 1943; children—Anne Elise (Mrs. Hal C. Stevenson III), Edward Downtain. Admitted to Tex. bar, 1948, since practiced in Houston; asso. firm Royston, Rayzor, Vickery & Williams, 1948-54, partner, 1954-55, sr. partner, 1955—; dir. 1st Nat. Bank of Bellaire, Madison-So. Nat. Bank, Tex. Nat. Bank of Baytown, 1st Nat. Bank LaMarque, 1st Bank of Deer Park. Mem. permanent adv. com. and program and planning com. Tulane U. Sch. Law Admiralty Law Inst., lectr., 1977; trustee, vice chmn. Austin Presbyn. Theol. Sem. Fellow Am. Coll. Trial Lawyers, Internat. Acad. Trial Lawyers; mem. Maritime Law Assn. U.S. (mem. exec. com. 1977—), Am., Tex., Houston bar assns., Internat. Assn. Ins. Counsel, Tex. Assn. Def. Counsel, World Trade Assn. Presbyn. (deacon, elder). Clubs: Propeller of U.S. (past nat. pres., mem. exec. com.); Port of Houston Propeller (past pres.) (Houston). Home: 610 Wellesley Dr Houston TX 77024 Office: One Shell Plaza Houston TX 77002

VICKERY, WILLIAM MCCALL, advt. agy. exec.; b. Savannah, Ga., July 6, 1935; s. William Wallace and Bertha (McCall) V.; B.A., Amherst Coll., 1957; M.B.A., Harvard, 1959. With Dancer-Fitzgerald-Sample, Inc., N.Y.C., 1960—, v.p., 1965-70, treas., dir., 1970-75, exec. v.p., sec., treas., dir., 1975—. Club: Harvard (N.Y.C.). Home: 400 E 54th St New York City NY 10022 Office: 347 Madison Ave New York City NY 10017

VICKREY, JAMES FRANK, JR., univ. adminstr.; b. Montgomery, Ala., Feb. 6, 1942; s. James Frank and Mildred Ward (Murray) V.; A.B., Auburn U., 1964, M.A., 1965; Ph.D., Fla. State U., 1972; m. Suzanne M. Vickrey, June 5, 1965; 1 son, John Robert. Instr. speech communication Auburn U., 1965-68; asst. debate coach U. Ala., 1968-69; instr. bus. communications Fla. State U., 1969-70, adminstrv. asst. to exec. v.p., 1970-71; asst. to pres., dir. univ. relations U. South Fla., 1971-75; exec. asst. to chancellor, dir. public affairs State Univ. System of Fla., 1975-77; pres. U. Montevallo (Ala.), 1977—. Bd. dirs. United Way, Birmingham. Mem. Am. Assn. State Colls. and Univs., Am. Council Edn., Council Advancement and Support of Edn., Ala. Film Com. Democrat. Methodist. Clubs: Kiwanis, Rotary. Contbr. articles to profl. jours. Home: Flowerhill Montevallo AL 35115 Office: Calkins Hall Station 1 Univ of Montevallo Montevallo AL 35115. *As Dag Hammarskojold, I believe that true success in life is measured by what one gives to rather than by what one gets from others. Accordingly, I believe also that one should not aspire to specific positions of employment or levels of attainment but rather to types of contributing activity in which one is good or can be good at— and which is satisfying in and of itself.*

VICKREY, ROBERT REMSEN, artist; b. N.Y.C., Aug. 20, 1926; s. Claude Claire and Caroline (McKim) V.; studied with Victoria Huntley; B.A., Yale, 1947, B.F.A., 1950; student Art Students League; m. Marjorie Elizabeth Alexander, Sept. 18, 1950; children—Remsen Scott, Elizabeth Nicole, Wendy Caroline, Alexander Sean. One-man shows: Midtown Galleries, N.Y.C., 1954-58, 62, 65, 69, 70, 72, Columbia (S.C.) Mus. Art, 1959, Davison Art Center, Wesleyan U., 1966, Va. Mus. Fine Arts, 1965, retrospective U. Ariz. Mus. Art, 1973, San Diego Fine Arts Gallery, 1973; exhibited in nat. group shows; represented in permanent collections Whitney Mus., Corcoran Gallery of Art, Washington, Lakeland (Fla.) Mus., Museo Modern Art, Rio de Janeiro, Brazil, Sara Roby Found., Parrish Art Mus., Southampton, Isaac Delgado Mus., Dallas Mus., Munson-Williams-Proctor Inst., Utica, N.Y., Met. Mus. Art, Nat. Acad. Design, Butler Inst. Am. Art, New Britain Mus. Am. Art. Gallery of Modern Art, Birmingham Mus., Spelman Coll., Newark Mus., many others; illustrator mag. covers, books. Recipient award Edward Austin Abbey mural competition, 1949, top prize Fla. Internat. Art Exhbn., 1952, 2d prize Internat. Hallmark competition, 1955; Am. Artist mag. citation, 1956, Winsor and Newton award Am. Water Color Soc., 1956, S.J. Wallace Truman prize Nat. Acad. ann., 1958, Salmagundi Club award Audubon Artists, 1971, spl. prize Internat. Biennial of Sport in Fine Arts, Mus. Contemporary Art, Madrid, Spain, 1973. Mem. Audubon Artists, Am. Water Color Soc. Author: New Techniques in Egg Tempera, 1973; Robert Vickrey-Artist at Work, 1979. Home: Box 445 Orleans MA 02653 Office: Hirschl & Adler Galleries 21 E 70 St New York NY 10021

VICKREY, WILLIAM SPENCER, economist, educator; b. Victoria, B.C., Can., June 21, 1914; s. Charles Vernon and Ada Eliza (Spencer) V.; came to U.S., 1914; B.A. in Math. with high honors (scholar), Yale, 1935; M.A., Columbia, 1937, Ph.D., 1947; Social Sci. Research Council predoctoral field fellow, 1938-39; m. Cecile Montez Thompson, July 21, 1951. Jr. economist Nat. Resources Com., Washington, 1937-38; research asst. 20th Century Fund, 1939-40; economist OPA, 1940-41; sr. economist, div. tax research Treasury Dept., 1941-43; civilian pub. service assignee, 1943- 46; tax cons. to gov. P.R., 1946; mem. faculty Columbia, N.Y.C., 1946—, prof. econs., 1958—, chmn. dept., 1964-67, McVickar prof. polit. economy, 1971—. Cons. to govt. and industry, 1949—; participant numerous confs., seminars; Ford research prof. Columbia, 1958-59; instr. IBM Systems Research Inst., 1964; vis. lectr. Monash U., Melbourne, Australia, 1971 inter-regional adviser UN, 1974-75. Clk., Scarsdale (N.Y.) Friends Meeting, 1959-62. Fellow Inst. Advanced Study Behavioral Scis., Stanford, 1967-68. Fellow Am. Econ. Assn., Econometric Soc.; mem. Met. Econ. Assn., Am. Statis. Assn., Royal Econ. Soc. Club: City (N.Y.C.). Author: Agenda for Progressive Taxation, 1947; Microstatics: Metastatics and Macroeconomics, 1964. Home: 162 Warburton Ave Hastings-on-Hudson NY 10706 Office: 1009 Internat Affairs Bldg Columbia Univ New York City NY 10027

VICROY, FRANK MARION, sociologist, educator; b. Cleve., Mar. 22, 1911; s. Raymond B. and Minnie Lee (Roden) V.; B.S. in Elec. Engring., Case Inst. Tech., 1932; M.A. in Social Adminstrn., Ohio State U., 1937, Ph.D. in Sociology, 1951; m. Beatrice Mary Green, Apr. 23, 1938 (dec. Apr. 1976); children—Kathleen Patricia, Mary Elizabeth; m. 2d, Mary Bryant, Jan. 4, 1978. Case worker Cuyahoga County (Ohio) Relief Adminstrn., 1934-36; campaign dir. Beverly Hills (Calif.) Community Chest, 1937-38; adminstrv. asst. Portland (Oreg.) Council Social Agencies, 1938-39; exec. sec. Wis. Conf. Social Work, 1939-41, Rock Island (Ill.) Community Chest, 1941-42; asso. elec. engr. Pearl Harbor Navy Yard, 1942-46; mem. faculty U. Louisville, 1947—, prof. sociology, 1952-79, prof. emeritus, 1979—, chmn. dept., 1965-79; vis. scholar U. Chgo., 1960; Fulbright lectr. Teheran (Iran) Sch. Social Work, 1962. Fellow Am. Sociol. Assn.; mem. Ohio Valley Sociol. Soc. (mem. council 1967-69), Nat. Assn. Social Workers, Population Assn. Am., Eta Kappa Nu, Alpha Kappa Delta, Phi Pi Phi. Home: 2940 Swifton Rd Sarasota FL 33581

VICTOR, JANET MARSHALL (MRS. DONALD C. VICTOR), editor; b. Wichita, Kans., Jan. 27, 1914; d. Clifford Ormond and Claribel (Macomber) Bentley; A.A., Compton Coll., 1934; B.A., Whittier Coll., 1936, M.S. in L.S., 1938; m. Donald C. Victor, Oct. 22, 1961. Society editor, reporter Bell Indsl. Post, Calif., 1930-36; asst. br. librarian, head book reviewer Los Angeles County Library, 1930-41; propr. various photog. studios, also tchr., 1942-51; founder Rangefinder Mag., also editor, pub., Los Angeles, 1952—; lectr. on personal color harmony. Instr., Los Angeles Inst. Photog. Art, 1948-49. Mem. Whittier Alumni Found., 1948—, Los Angeles Press Club 8 Ball Found., 1954—, Los Angeles Mus. Art, 1971—. Recipient Achievement awards Profl. Photographers Am., Inc. Mem. Mont. Photographers Assn., Profl. Photographers Calif., Profl. Photographers West (exec. mgr.), Am. Soc. Mag. Photographers, Indsl. Photographers So. Calif., Greater Los Angeles Press Club, Western Pubs. Assn., others. Contbr. articles to photog. jours. Home: 14231 Cohasset Van Nuys CA 91405. *I guess I can say, without feeling subservient, that my success has been based on service. My career in publishing has been dotted with experiences of finding answers for those with questions.*

VICTOR, MARY O'NEILL, museum exec.; b. Boston, Dec. 27, 1924; d. James Daniel and Mary Ellen Beatty (McLaughlin) O'Neill; student Boston U., 1943-47; m. John Victor, Nov. 25, 1971. Adminstrv. asst. to dean Sch. Pub. Health Harvard, 1949-62; bus. mgr. Girl Scouts Am., Washington, 1963; registrar Mus. Fine Arts, Boston, 1964-69; dir., art adminstr. Mobile (Ala.) Art Gallery (name changed to Fine Arts Mus. of South at Mobile 1975), 1969—. Cons. Allied Arts Council, Mobile, 1969—. Bd. dirs. Friends of Mobile Pub. Library, Mobile Opera Assn. Mem. Mobile Area C. of C. Office: Langan Park Mobile AL 36608

VICTOR, ROBERT EUGENE, corp. exec.; b. N.Y.C., Dec. 17, 1929; s. Louis and Rebecca (Teitelbaum) V.; LL.B., St. John's U., 1953, J.D., 1968; m. Dorothy Saffir, Oct. 14, 1951; children—Priscilla Saffir Victor Dennis, Pandora Saffir. Admitted to N.Y. bar, 1953, Cal. bar, 1965; with firm Szold and Brandwen, N.Y.C., 1953-54; atty. Dept. Army, Phila., 1955-56; with Hughes Aircraft Co., Culver City, Calif., 1956-62; v.p., gen. counsel Packard Bell Electronics Corp., Los Angeles, 1962-70; sr. v.p., gen. counsel Cordon Internat. Corp., Los Angeles, 1970-78, also dir.; gen. counsel Am. Harp Soc., 1969—; pres. Vanowen Realty Corp., 1978—, also dir. Mem. Los Angeles County Bar Assn. Mason. Home: 722 N Walden Dr Beverly Hills CA 90210 Office: 10100 Santa Monica Blvd Los Angeles CA 90067

VICTORIN (VICTORIN URSACHE), archbishop; b. Manastioara-Siret, Dist. of Suceava, Romania, July 1912; grad. State Lyceum of Siret; L.Th., U. Cernauti (Romania); postgrad. Bibl. Inst. Jerusalem. Ordained deacon Romanian Orthodox Ch., 1937, priest, 1937, consecrated bishop, 1966, elevated to archbishop, 1973; prof. religion Orthodox Lyceum of the Romanian Orthodox Metropolis of Cernautsi, 1936-37; prof. theology Seminary of Neamtzu Monastery, 1937-46, asst. dir. sem., 1937-40, dir. sem., superior of monastery, 1940-44; rep. Romanian Orthodox Ch. at Holy Places in Jerusalem, 1946-56; bishop Romanian Orthodox Missionary Episcopate in Am., 1966-73; archbishop Romanian Orthodox Missionary Archdiocese in Am., 1973—. Mem. Holy Synod, Romanian Orthodox Ch. of Romania; bd. dirs. U.S. Conf., World Council Chs., mem. central com.; mem. Standing Conf. Canonical Orthodox Bishops in Ams. Editor: Locurile Sfinte. Address: 19959 Riopelle St Detroit MI 48203

VICTORY, ANTONY MICHAEL, investment banker; b. London, Eng., Nov. 3, 1934; s. Gerald Louis and Oonagh (Kealy) V.; B.S. magna cum laude, Providence Coll., 1956; M.B.A., Harvard U., 1960; m. Annemarie Waldner; children—Elizabeth Anne, Christopher Michael. Came to U.S., 1949, naturalized, 1954. Asso. corporate fin. dept. Shearson, Hammill & Co., Inc., N.Y.C., 1960-64, asst. v.p., 1964, v.p., dir., exec. v.p., 1968-70; gen. partner Cumberland Assos., 1970-76, Cumberland Investment Group, 1976—; dir. Berkey Photo, Inc.; chmn. The THH Corp., Pueblo Internat.; chmn., pres. Peerless Devel. Corp., Park Electrochem. Corp. Served to 1st lt. AUS, 1958-60. Clubs: N.Y. Athletic, Harvard. Home: 136 E 64th St New York NY 10021 Office: 10 E 53d St New York NY 10036

VIDAL, GORE, writer; b. West Point, N.Y., Oct. 3, 1925; s. Eugene L. and Nina (Gore) V.; grad. Phillips Exeter Acad., 1943. Author: (novels) Williwaw, 1946, In a Yellow Wood, 1947, The City and the Pillar, 1948, The Season of Comfort, 1949, A Search for the King, 1950, Dark Green, Bright Red, 1950, The Judgment of Paris, 1952,

Messiah, 1954, Julian, 1964, Washington, D.C., 1967, Myra Breckinridge, 1968, Two Sisters, 1970, Burr, 1973, Myron, 1974, 1876, 1976; Kalki, 1978; (stories) A Thirsty Evil, 1956; (plays) Visit to a Small Planet (for TV and Broadway), 1957; The Best Man, 1960; Romulus, 1966; Weekend, 1968; An Evening with Richard Nixon, 1972; (essays) Rocking the Boat, 1962, Reflections upon a Sinking Ship, 1969; (collected essays) Homage to Daniel Shays, 1973; Matters of Fact and of Fiction, 1977. Mem. Pres.'s Adv. Com. on Arts, 1961-63. Democratic-Liberal candidate for U.S. Congress, 1960; co-chmn. The New Party, 1970-71. Served with AUS, 1943-46. Address: care Random House 201 E 50th St New York NY 10022

VIDICH, ARTHUR JOSEPH, sociologist, educator; b. Crosby, Minn., May 30, 1922; s. Joseph and Pauline (Pesjak) V.; B.A., U. Mich., 1943; M.A., U. Wis., 1948; Ph.D., Harvard, 1953; postgrad. U. London, 1951; m. Mary Rudolph; children—Charles A., Paul., Andrew W., Joseph L., Max Z., Rosilind H. Research asst. NRC, Palau, Western Carolines, 1948; research asst. Social Relations Lab., Harvard, 1949; asst. prof., resident field dir. Cornell U., 1951-54; asso. prof., research cons. Social Sci. Research Center, Coll. Social Scis., U. P.R., 1954-57; asst. prof. dept. sociology, anthropology U. Conn., 1957-60; vis. asso. Florence Heller Grad. Sch. Advanced Studies in Social Welfare, Brandeis U., 1960—; prof. sociology, anthropology New Sch. For Social Research Grad. Faculty, N.Y.C., 1960—, chmn. dept., 1964—; vis. prof. Universidad Nacional, Bogota, Colombia, 1964, Clark U., 1966, U. Zagreb, 1973, U. Calif., La Jolla, 1977, Doshisha U., Japan, 1978; editorial adviser to social sci. editor Praeger Publishers, Inc. Served to 1st lt. USMCR, 1943-46. Fellow Am. Anthrop. Assn., Am. Sociol. Soc.; mem. Eastern Sociol. Soc., Am. Assn. U. Profs., Latin Am. Studies Assn. Contbr. articles to profl. jours. Home: 37 S Oxford St Brooklyn NY 11217 Office: 66 W 12th St New York NY 10011

VIDOR, KING WALLIS, motion picture dir. and producer; b. Galveston, Tex., Feb. 8, 1895; s. Charles Shelton and Kate (Wallis) V.; ed. high sch., Galveston, and Peacock Mil. Acad., San Antonio; m. 2d, Eleanor Boardman, Sept. 1926; children—Suzanne, Antonia, Belinda; m. 3d, July 26, 1937. Dir. many motion pictures, including The Big Parade; The Crowd; Hallelujah; Street Scene; The Citadel; Northwest Passage; H. M. Pulham, Esq.; The Fountainhead, War and Peace, Solomon and Sheba in 1959, and others; mem. cinema dept. U. So. Calif. Recipient of the Christopher award, 1957, and of the D. W. Griffith award, 1957, Golden Thistle award Edinburgh Film Festival, 1964, Outstanding Achievement award Dirs. Guild Am. 1957; decorated Order of Merit, Italian Gout., 1970. Mem. Acad. Motion Picture Arts and Sciences. Clubs: Bel Air Country. Author: (autobiography) A Tree is a Tree, 1953; Guerra e Pace, 1956; King Vidor on Film-Making, 1972. Office: Willow Creek Ranch PO Box 1935 Paso Robles CA 93446. *I have always believed that we cannot blame anyone for anything. I know that we make our own world, our own universe; and whenever a problem or conflict presents itself I turn to myself, to my own thoughts to search out the cause. In this way I have it in a place I can do something about it. Most of the problems in the world grow from a sense of dualism instead of oneness. In other words, "me" and "not me," the mistakings of humbling one's self when the self is divinity manifested. "Love thy neighbor as thyself" should never be interpreted to mean not loving one's self, because the self is our principle communication with God.*

VIEBRANZ, ALFRED COLVILLE, elec. mfg. co. exec.; b. New Rochelle, N.Y., Feb. 28, 1921; s. Alfred C. and Helen (Dyer) V.; B.S. in Physics, St. Lawrence U., 1942; m. Elaine Frailey, Oct. 8, 1947; children—Scott, Curt, Gayle, Joan. Mktg. exec. Young & Rubicam, Inc., 1954-59; with Sylvania Electric Products, Inc., 1946-54, 59—, sr. v.p. mktg., 1961-73, sr. v.p., gen. mgr. archtl. products group, 1973-79, electronic components group, 1974-79, lighting products group, 1976-79; sr. v.p. Gen. Telephone and Electronics Corp., Stamford, Conn., 1979—; dir. GTE Sylvania Inc., Unistrut Corp. Police commr., Westchester County, 1968-72. Trustee St. Lawrence U. Served to lt. USNR, 1942-46. Decorated Silver Star (2), Bronze Star; mem. honor legion N.Y.C. Police Dept. Home: 426 Frogtown New Canaan CT 06840 Office: One Stamford Forum Stamford CT 06902

VIEHMAN, JOHN W(ILLIAM), bldg. materials mfg. co. exec.; b. Pitts., July 24, 1929; s. Ralph G. and Margaret M. V.; B.B.A., U. Pitts., 1952, M.L., 1958; m. Donna M. Werner, Oct. 18, 1952; children—J. David, Mark D., Lori A. Asst. treas. Am. Inst. for Research, Pitts., 1954-59, bus. mgr., 1954-60; v.p. fin. H. H. Robertson Co., Pitts., 1960—; dir. IRD Mechanalysis Inc. Served with USMC, 1952-54. Club: Duquesne (Pitts.). Office: Two Gateway Center Pittsburgh PA 15222

VIEIRA DA SILVA, MARIE HELENE, painter; b. Lisbon, Portugal, June 13, 1908; d. Marcos and Maria (Graca) Vieira du Silva; student Portugal, Switzerland, Eng., France; m. Szenes, Feb. 22, 1930. Naturalized French citizen, 1956. Paintings exhibited Mus. Modern Art, Paris, N.Y.C., Met. Mus., Guggenheim Mus., Barns Found., Mus. U. Mich., Toledo Mus., Cin. Art Mus., Tate Gallery, London, museums Jerusalem, Israel, Amsterdam, Rotterdam, Holland, Lausanne, Switzerland, Venice, Italy, Grenoble, Rouen, Lyon, Reims, France, Essen, Germany, Helsinki, Finland, Dusseldorf, Germany, Rotterdam, Carnegie Inst., Pitts., Sao Paulo, Brazil, Australia, Mannheim Kunsthalle, Phillip's Art Gallery, Washington, Galeria d'Arte Moderna Turin. Decorated commandeur l'Ordre des Arts et des Lettres, Grand Croix de Santiago a Espada, 1977. Recipient of acquisition prize Biennale de Sao Paulo, 1953, Europe Afrique prize Guggenheim Found., 1957, annual mention prize Guggenheim Found., 1958, 4th prize Carnegie Inst., 1958; 1st prize for painting, Biennale of S ao Paulo, 1961; Nat. prize Fine Arts, France, 1963. Address: care of Guy Weelen 8 Ave Frochot Paris 9 ieme France

VIELEHR, JEROME EDWARD, soft drink co. exec.; b. Chgo., Jan. 16, 1932; s. Edward William and Dorothy Muriel (Coveney) V.; student Northwestern U., 1953-55; B.S. in Elec. Engring., Mass. Inst. Tech., 1956; M.B.A., Harvard U., 1959; m. Patricia Ware Driscoll, Mar. 30, 1957; children—Kurt, Errett, Antoinette, Byron, Ethan. Adminstrv. officer Indian Inst. Tech., Kanpur, India, 1962-65; new enterprises mgr. Coca Cola Co., N.Y.C., 1966-71, v.p. internat. trade, 1976—; fin. v.p. Aqua-Chem, Inc., Milw., 1971-72, pres., 1972-76; dir. Koss Stereophone Corp., Milw. Past chmn. Wis. Mass. Inst. Tech. Fund Drive; trustee Carroll Coll., Waukesha, Wis. Served with USMC, 1950-52. Registered profl. engr., Mass. Mem. Young Pres.'s Orgn. Presbyterian. Club: Atlanta Mass. Inst. Tech. (past pres.). Home: 117 W 58th St New York City NY 10019 Office: Coca Cola Co 515 Madison Ave New York City NY 10022

VIENER, JOHN DAVID, lawyer; b. Richmond, Va., Oct. 18, 1939; s. Reuben and Thelma (Kurtz) V.; B.A., Yale U., 1961; J.D., Harvard U., 1964; m. Karin Erika Bauer, Apr. 7, 1969; children—John David Jr., Katherine Bauer. Admitted to N.Y. State bar, 1965, U.S. Supreme Ct. bar, 1970, U.S. Tax Ct. bar, 1975; asso. firm Satterlee, Warfield & Stephens, N.Y.C., 1964-69; individual practice law, N.Y.C., 1969-76; partner firm Christy & Viener, N.Y.C., 1976—; gen. counsel, dir. Landmark Communities, Inc., 1970—. Founder, dir., gen. counsel Foxfire Fund, Inc., 1968—. Mem. Am., N.Y. State bar assns., Assn. Bar City N.Y. Clubs: Harmonie (N.Y.C.); Manursing Island (Rye, N.Y.). Home: 45 E 62d St New York City NY 10021 Office: 620 5th Ave New York City NY 10020

VIERBUCHEN, RICHARD CARL, utilities co. exec.; b. Washington, Nov. 21, 1927; s. Carl Lee and Olive (Braddy) V.; B.S., Washington and Lee U., 1950; m. Robin Love Stickle, Jan. 25, 1950; children—Richard C., Robin L., Thomas L., Catherine L. With Washington Gas Light Co., 1950—, v.p. mktg., 1964-73, v.p. consumer services and public affairs, 1973-77, exec. v.p., 1977—, pres. 6 subs. cos. Pres., Nat. Cherry Blossom Festival, Inc. Served with U.S. Army, 1946-47. Mem. Washington Bd. Trade, Washington Area Conv. and Visitors Assn. (pres. 1975-76), Am. Gas Assn., Met. Washington Builders Assn. Clubs: Washingtonian Country (past pres.), Advt. Club of Met. Washington (past pres.), Kiwanis (past pres.). Home: 4990 Sentinel Dr Sumner MD 20016 Office: 1100 H St NW Washington DC 20080

VIERECK, PETER, educator, poet; b. N.Y.C., Aug. 5, 1916; s. George S. and Margaret (Hein) V.; B.S. summa cum laude, Harvard, 1937, M.A., 1939, Ph.D., 1942; Henry fellow, Christ Church, Oxford U., Eng., 1937-38; L.H.D., Olivet Coll., 1959; m. Anya de Markov, June 1945 (div. May 1970); children—John-Alexis, Valerie Edwina (Mrs. John Gibbs); m. 2d, Betty Martin Falkenberg, Aug. 30, 1972. Teaching asst. Harvard, 1941-42, instr. German lit., tutor history and lit. dept., 1946-47; instr. history U.S. Army U., Florence, Italy, 1945; asst. prof. history Smith Coll., 1947-48, vis. lectr. Russian history 1948-49; asso. prof. Modern European, Russian history Mt. Holyoke Coll., 1948-55, prof., 1955—; vis. lectr. Am. Culture Oxford U., 1953; Whittal lectr. in poetry Library of Congress, 1954, 63, 79; Fulbright prof. Am. poetry and civilization, U. Florence, Italy, 1955; Elliston chair poetry lectr. U. Cin., 1956; vis. lectr. U. Calif. at Berkeley, 1957; Disting. William R. Kennan chair poetry lectr. Mt. Holyoke Coll., 1979; Charter mem. Council Basic Edn.; vis. poet Russian-Am. cultural exchange program Dept. State, USSR, 1961; vis. research scholar 20th Century Fund, USSR, 1962-63; vis. scholar Rockefeller Study Center at Bellagio (Italy), 1977; vis. artist and scholar Am. Acad. in Rome, 1978; dir. poetry workshop, N.Y. Writers Conf., 1965-67; research fellow Huntington Library, San Marino, Calif. Served with U.S. Army, Africa and Italy, 1943-45. Awarded Tietjens prize for poetry, 1948, Pulitzer prize for poetry, 1949; recipient Most Distinguished Alumnus award Horace Mann School for Boys, 1958; Poetry Translation award Translation Center, Columbia U., 1978; Sadin poetry prize N.Y. Quar., 1977. Guggenheim fellow, Rome, 1949-50; Rockefeller Found. researcher in history, Germany, summer 1958; Nat. Endowment for Humanities sr. research fellow, USSR, 1969; Artists Found. fellow, 1978. Mem. Am. Hist. Assn., Oxford Soc., Poetry Soc. Am., P.E.N., Phi Beta Kappa. Clubs: Harvard (N.Y.C. and London); Bryce (Oxford, Eng.). Author: Metapolitics—From the Romantics to Hitler, 1941 (Swedish edit., 1942, Italian, 1948); Terror and Decorum (poems), 1948, reprinted, 1972; Who Killed the Universe (novelette included in anthology New Directions Ten), 1948; Conservatism Revisited-The Revolt Against Revolt 1815-1949, 1949 (English edit, 1950); Strike Through the Mask, New Lyrical Poems, 1950, reprinted, 1972; The First Morning: New Poems, 1952, reprinted, 1972; Shame and Glory of the Intellectuals, 1953, rev. edit., 1978; Dream and Responsibility; The Tension Between Poetry and Society, 1953; The Unadjusted Man; a New Hero for Americans, 1956, reprinted, 1973; Conservatism: From John Adams to Churchill, reprinted 1978; The Persimmon Tree (poems). 1956; Inner Liberty; The Stubborn Grit in the Machine, 1957; The Tree Witch: A Verse Drama, 1961, reprinted, 1973; Meta-politics, The Roots of the Nazi Mind, 1961; Conservatism Revisited and The New Conservatives: What Went Wrong, rev. paperback edits., 1962, 65; New and Selected Poems, 1932-67, 1967; also author of selections in symposium books Towards a World Community, 1950; Midcentury American Poets, 1950; Arts in Renewal, 1951; The New American Right, 1955; Education in a Free Society, 1958; The Radical Right, 1962; Soviet Policy Making, 1967; Outside Looking In, 1972; A Question of Quality, 1976. Contbr. essays, monographs, poems to popular mags., and profl. jours., Ency. Brit., 1974. Home: 12 Silver St South Hadley MA 01075. *After 60 years of books, scars, and sugar plums, my rock-bottom thought on life is a line of Vachel Lindsay: "Courage and sleep are the principal things."*

VIERLING, BERNARD JULIUS, cons.; b. Bakersfield, Calif., Dec. 27, 1914; s. Bernard Julius and Elizabeth J. (Wilcox) V.; B.S. in Mech. Engring., Stanford U., 1936; m. Martha Jane Peairs, July 20, 1939; children—Lawrence Bernard, Bruce Wilcox, Karen Jane. Engr., Douglas Aircraft Co., 1936-39; chief engr., dir. engring. and maintenance Pa.-Central Airlines, 1939-47; pres. Aircraft Advisers, Inc., Washington, 1946-48, Aircraft Supply Corp., Washington, 1948-54, Helidusters, Inc., Washington, 1950-52; partner Aircraft Supply Co., Washington, 1954-62; dir. systems maintenance service FAA, 1962-65, dep. dir. supersonic transp. devel., 1965-71; dir. Morgantown program Urban Mass Transp. Adminstrn., Dept. Transp., 1971-73, spl. counselor to asso. adminstr. research and devel., 1973-74, dir. bus and rail research and devel., 1974-75, dir. bus. and paratransit tech. devel., 1975-79, cons., 1979—. Recipient Nat. award for economy achievement Pres. Johnson, 1964; Sec.'s award Dept. Transp., 1973. Mem. Nat. Aero. Assn., Air Force Assn., Phi Gamma Delta. Clubs: Nat. Aviation (life; gov. 1954—, v.p. 1954-56, pres. 1956-58), Aero (Washington); Belle Haven Country (Alexandria). Home: Locust Grove Flint Hill VA 22627 Office: PO Box 88 Flint Hill VA 22627. *One of my greatest rewards is the satisfaction of seeing the lasting contributions to mankind that have been made by those who have worked with me in many endeavors to make life more meaningful for all of us.*

VIESER, MILFORD AUGUST, financial exec.; b. Newark, Jan. 2, 1903; ed. Pace Coll.; LL.D., Fairleigh Dickinson U.; m. Vera Kniep; 1 son, William Milford. Chmn. finance com. Mut. Benefit Life Ins. Co., 1960-70, dir., 1960-72, now hon. dir.; past dir. U.S. Savs. Bank, Newark; dir. Triangle Industries, Inc., Holmdel, N.J., 1st Nat. State Bancorp. of N.J., 1st Nat. State Bank of N.J., Am. Gen. Bond Fund, Inc., Am. Gen. Bond Convertible Securities, Inc., Houston. U.S. del. Housing Com. of Econ. Commn. for Europe, 1957; mem. Fed. N.J. Tercentenary Celebration Commn., 1960; hon. co-chmn. Newark 300th Anniversary Corp.; chmn. N.J. Hist. Soc.; former chmn. N.J. Am. Revolution Bicentennial Celebration Commn. Mem. N.J. Republican Finance Com., former chmn.; del. Rep. Nat. Conv., 1956, 64. Hon. dir. Regional Plan Assn.; trustee, vice chmn. St. Barnabas Med. Center; trustee Newark Mus. Recipient Outstanding Citizen of N.J. award Advt. Club N.J., 1968. Mem. Greater Newark C. of C. (dir., past pres.), Mortgage Bankers Assn. of N.J. (pres. 1952). Conglist. Clubs: Essex (Newark); Baltusrol Golf (Springfield, N.J.); Tarratine Yacht (Dark Harbor, Maine). Home: 8 Shore Edge Ln Short Hills NJ 07078 also Dark Harbor ME

VIESER, RICHARD WILLIAM, elec. mfg. co. exec.; b. Newark, Nov. 14, 1927; s. William L. and Viola S. (Coltorti) V.; A.B., Lafayette Coll., 1951; m. Lois Barbara Johnson, Sept. 8, 1951; children—Richard, Cheryl, Cynthia, William, Jaime. Mgmt. trainee Western Electric Co., N.Y.C., 1951-52; sales mgr. Chatham Electronics Corp., Livingston, N.J., 1954-56; from asst. div. mgr. to gen. mgr. Tung Sol Electric, Livingston, 1957-66; div. gen. mgr. Wagner Electric Corp., Livingston, 1966-70, v.p., 1970, group v.p., 1971-73, pres., 1973-74, chief exec. officer, 1974-79; exec. v.p. McGraw-Edison, 1979—. Bd. dirs. Hwy. Users Fedn. Served with U.S. Army, 1946-48; Korea. Mem. Automotive Presidents Council, Soc. Automotive Engrs., Motor Equipment Mfrs. Assn. (dir.), Theta Delta Chi. Clubs: Rock Spring (West Orange, N.J.); Baltusrol (Springfield, N.J.); Seaview Country (Absecon, N.J.); St. Louis; Economic (N.Y.C.); Renaissance (bd. govs.) (Detroit).

VIEST, IVAN M(IROSLAV), steel co. exec.; b. Bratislava, Czechoslovakia, Oct. 10, 1922; s. Ivan and Maria (Zacharova) V.; came to U.S., 1947, naturalized, 1955; Ing., Slovak Tech. U., Bratislava, 1946; M.S., Ga. Inst. Tech., 1948; Ph.D., U. Ill., 1951; m. Barbara K. Stevenson, May 23, 1953. Research asst. U. Ill., Urbana, 1948-50, research asso., 1950-51, research asst. prof., 1955-57; bridge research engr. Am. Assn. State Hwy. Ofcls. rd. test Nat. Acad. Scis., Ottawa, Ill., 1957-61; structural engr. Bethlehem Steel Corp. (Pa.), 1961-67, sr. structural cons., 1967-70, asst. mgr. sales engring. div., 1970—; lectr. in field. Recipient Constrn. award Engring. News Record, 1972; registered profl. engr., Pa. Fellow ASCE (Research prize 1958, v.p. 1973-75), Am. Concrete Inst. (Wason Research medal 1956); mem. Am. Iron and Steel Inst., Internat. Assn. Bridge and Structural Engring., Nat. Acad. Engring., Transp. Research Bd. Club: Saucon Valley Country (Bethlehem). Author: Composite Construction, 1958; research, numerous publs. on various steel and concrete structures, especially bridges and bldgs., to profl. jours. Home: RD 4 Bethlehem PA 18015 Office: Bethlehem Steel Corp GSO Bethlehem PA 18016

VIESULAS, ROMAS, artist, educator; b. Lithuania, Sept. 11, 1918; s. Kazimieras and Juzefa (Kozukauskas) K.; diploma Ecole des Arts et Metiers, Freiburg, Germany, 1949; student Ecole Nat. Superieure des Beaux Arts, Paris, 1949-50; m. Jura Gailiusis, June 22, 1968; children—Romas-Tauras, Vytautas-Kostas, Auste-Neringa. Mem. faculty dept. printmaking Tyler Sch. Art, Temple U., Phila., 1960—, prof., 1969—, chmn. dept., 1960—; vis. artist Am. Acad. in Rome, 1964-65, 79; artist in resident Biennial of Venice, 1970; one man exhbns. include: Le Soleil dans la Tete, Paris, 1959, Yoseido Gallery, Tokyo, 1964, Il Torcoliere, Rome, 1965, Cin. Art Mus., 1967, Oxford (Eng.) Gallery, 1968, Venice Biennial, 1970; represented in permanent collections: Mus. Modern Art, N.Y.C., Met. Mus. Art, Nat. Gallery, Art Inst. Chgo., Biblioteque Nationale, Paris, Nat. Mus., Krakow, Poland, Mus. Modern Art, Kamakura, Japan, Mus. Contemporary Art, Skopje, Yugoslavia, Bklyn. Mus., 73, Library of Congress, others. Mem. AAUP, Soc. Am. Graphic Artists, Soc. Am. Graphic Artists, Inst. Lithuanian Stuides, Lithuanian Cath. Acad. Sci., Assn. Advancement Baltic Studies. Club: Print (Phila.). Office: Tyler Sch Art Temple Univ Beech and Penrose Aves Elkins Park PA 19126. *For thirty years of my creative life I have strived to be true to myself, regardless of the fads of the time. During my twenty years of teaching art I have asked my students to do the same.*

VIETH, WOLF RANDOLPH, educator; b. St. Louis, May 5, 1934; s. Hans W. and Hedy (Fahrig) V.; S.B. in Chem. Engring., Mass. Inst. Tech., 1956, Sc.D., 1961; M. Sc., Ohio State U., 1958; m. Peggy Schira, July 6, 1957; children—Jane, Linda, Christopher, Mark. From asst. prof. to asso. prof. chem. engring. Mass. Inst. Tech., 1961-68, dir. Sch. Chem. Engring. Practice, 1965-68; prof. chem. and biochem. engring., chmn. dept. Rutgers U., 1968—; cons. to govt. and industry; chmn. Gordon Research Conf. on Separation and Purification, 1975. Mem. econ. study subcom., planning bd. Montgomery (N.J.) Twp., 1970—. Served to 1st lt. AUS, 1961. Recipient DuPont Co. Invention award, 1960, St. Albert the Great medal for sci. Aquinas Coll., 1952; Vis. Fgn. Scientist award Japan Soc. for Promotion Sci., 1975. Ford postdoctoral fellow, 1961. Registered profl. engr., N.J. Fellow Am. Inst. Chemists; mem. Am. Inst. Chem. Engrs., Am. Chem. Soc., Am. Soc. Engring. Edn., N.Y. Acad. Scis., Sigma Xi, Phi Lambda Upsilon. Research on semipermeable membranes, enzyme engring. Home: RD 2 Box 253 Belle Mead NJ 08502 Office: Rutgers Univ Heights Campus New Brunswick NJ 08903

VIGDOR, JUSTIN LEONARD, lawyer; b. N.Y.C., July 13, 1929; s. Irving Barton and Ida (Devins) V.; LL.B. magna cum laude St. John's U., 1951; LL.M., N.Y. U., 1952; m. Louise Martin, Mar. 8, 1952; children—Robert, Jill Vigdor Feldman, Lisa, Wendy. Admitted to N.Y. bar, 1951, Fla. bar, also U.S. Supreme Ct.; partner firm Mousaw, Vigdor, Reeves Heilbronner and Kroll, Rochester, N.Y., 1958—. Dir. Bankers Trust Co. Western N.Y., Star Supermarkets, Inc., Computer Consoles, Inc., Flanigan Furniture, Inc., IEC Electronics Corp., Monroe Prepaid Legal Service Plan. Faculty, Nazareth Coll. Bd. dirs. Mary Carola Children's Center; bd. dirs., pres. Rochester Area Found. Monroe County Bar; v.p., bd. dirs. Jewish Community Fedn.; bd. dirs., past pres. Al Sigl Center for Rehab. Agys.: v.p., bd. dirs. United Community Chest Greater Rochester, ARC. Recipient Community Service award, 1960. Served with AUS, 1952-54. Fellow Am. Bar Found.; mem. Am., Fla., N.Y. State, Monroe County (past pres.) bar assns., Estate Planning Council, Am. Arbitration Assn. (nat. panel 1962—), N.Y. State C. of C. (Distinguished Service award 1964). Democrat. Jewish religion. Clubs: Irondequoit Country; Ski Valley. Contbr. articles to profl. jours. Home: 1880 Clover St Rochester NY 14618 Office: 6th Floor First Federal Plaza Rochester NY 14614

VIGIER, FRANCOIS CLAUDE DENIS, educator; b. Geneva, Switzerland, Oct. 14, 1931; s. Eugene Henri Rene and Francoise (Dupuy) V.; came to U.S., 1957; B.Arch., Mass. Inst. Tech., 1955; M.C.P., Harvard U., 1959, Ph.D., 1967. Architect, UN Relief and Works Agy., Jordan, 1955-57; designer Town Planning Cons., Cambridge, Mass., 1957-58; mem. faculty Harvard Grad. Sch. Design, Cambridge, 1960—, prof. city planning, 1968—; vis. lectr. art Dartmouth Coll., 1962, 64; vis. critic urban design U. N.C., 1963; cons. Ford Found. Latin Am. program, 1964-65, Ednl. Services, Inc., 1966; dir. Harvard Center Environ. Design Studies, 1967-69; pres. Nash-Vigier, Inc., planning cons., Cambridge, 1965—. Mem. Inst. Cert. Planners, Am. Planning Assn., Middle East Inst. Author: Change and Apathy: Liverpool and Manchester during the Industrial Revolution, 1970; also articles. Home: 27 Fayerweather St Cambridge MA 02138

VIGIL, CHARLES S., lawyer; b. Trinidad, Colo., June 9, 1912; s. J.U. and Andreita (Maes) V.; LL.B., U. Colo., 1936; m. Kathleen A. Liebert Jan. 2, 1943; children—David Charles Edward, Marcia Kathleen. Admitted to Colo. bar, 1936; dep. dist. atty. 3d Jud. Dist. Colo., 1937-42, asst. dist. atty., 1946-51; U.S. atty. Dist. Colo., 1951-53; pvt. practice law, Denver. Dir., sec. Las Animas Co. (Colo) ARC; bd. dirs. Family and Children's Service Denver; dir. Auraria Community Center; mem. Bishop's com. on housing. Served as ensign to lt. (s.g.) USCG, 1942-46. Recipient award of civil merit, Spain, 1960, Colo. Centennial Expn. Bd., 1976; award Colo. Chicano Bar Assn., 1979. Mem. Internat. Law Assn., Am., Fed., Colo. (bd. govs.), So. Colo., bar assns., Am. Judicature Soc., Internat. Bar Assn., Inter-Am. Bar, V.F.W. (comdr.), Am. Legion (comdr.), Nat. Assn. Def. Lawyers, Am. Trial Lawyers Assn., Lambda Chi Alpha, Elk, Eagle, Cootie. Clubs: Lions, Denver Athletic, Columbine Country, City of Denver; Trinidad Country. Author: Application of Psychology in Law; Saga of Casimiro Barela. Home: 1085 Sherman St Denver CO 80203 Office: 320 Capitol Life Center 225 E 16th Ave Denver CO 80203. *Desire to serve and achieve in all matters related to public* *good as promoted and espoused by thoughts of father and mother-and family-brothers and sisters.*

VIGILANTE, JOSEPH LOUIS, social worker, univ. dean; b. Phila., June 21, 1925; s. Pasqualino and Marion Theresa (Mercaldo) V.; A.B., Temple U. 1950; M.S. (student merit scholar), N.Y. Sch. Social Work, Columbia, 1951, NIMH scholar, 1958, D.S.W., 1968; m. Florence Wexler, Mar. 11, 1952; children—Amy Ruth, Grace Caroline, and Theodore Joseph. Child welfare worker div. children and youth Wis. Dept. Welfare, 1951-53; case worker, student supr. VA Hosp., Northport, L.I., N.Y., 1953-55; part-time case worker, case supr., chief social worker Mid-Nassau Community Guidance Clinic, Hicksville, L.I., 1955-60; dir. field work, asst. prof. Adelphi Univ. Grad. Sch. Social Work, 1955-60, asso. prof., 1961—, asst. dean, 1960-62, acting dean, 1962, dean, 1962—; exec. v.p. Inst. Child Mental Health; lectr., N.Y. State Insts. Pub. Welfare, Cornell U., 1962-64; vis. lectr. New Sch. for Social Research, N.Y.C.; cons. Bur. Family Services, HEW, OEO, 1966-67; mgmt. cons. Brookhaven Labs. Bd. dirs. Health and Welfare Council Nassau County, Community Council Greater N.Y., Adelphi U. Film Co., Adelphi U.; bd. dirs. Council Social Work Edn. Huntington Hosp. Served with OSS, USAAF, 1943-45. Mem. Nat. Assn. Social Workers, Acad. Certified Social Workers, Pi Gamma Mu. Author: Social Policy and Social Action Activity of National Social Welfare Organizations, 1960; (with M. Blanchard) Response to Change-The Educational Alliance and its Future, 1970; editor and chief: Ency. of Social Work; editor: (with D. Thursz) Social Service Delivery Systems, internat. ann.; contbr. to profl. jours. Home: 125 Midland St Cold Spring Harbor Long Island NY 11724 Office: Adelphi U Garden City Long Island NY 11530

VIGNESS, DAVID MARTELL, educator; b. La Feria, Tex., Oct. 12, 1922; s. Lewis Martell and Nina (Hegge) V.; B.A., U. Tex., 1943, M.A., 1948, Ph.D., 1951; m. Winifred Woods, Jan. 29, 1949; children—Margaret, Richard. Instr., U. Tex., 1951; prof. history, head dept. social scis. Schreiner Inst., Kerrville, Tex., 1951-55; mem. faculty Tex. Tech. Univ., 1955—, prof. history, 1961—, chmn. dept., 1961-78; Fulbright lectr. U. Chile, also Cath. U. Santiago, 1957-58; vis. prof. Pan Am. U., summer 1973, U. N.Mex., spring 1979. Cons. Peace Corps, 1965, 1966; participant Congress de Historia de Noreste de Mexico, 1971. Mem. Tex. Com. Humanities and Pub. Policy, 1971-78, vice chmn., 1976-77; mem. Nat. Endowment for the Humanities, also program cons. Trustee Austin Presbyn. Theol. Sem., 1973—. Served with USNR, 1943-46; PTO. Recipient H. Bailey Carroll award S.W. Hist. Quar., 1972. Fellow Tex. Hist. Assn.; mem. Am. Hist. Assn., Southwestern Council Latin Am. Studies (pres. 1972-73), Latin Am. Studies Association, Western History Association, Conf. Latin American History, Southwestern Social Sci. Assn. (exec. council 1964-65), Phi Kappa Phi, Phi Alpha Theta, Pi Sigma Alpha, Sigma Delta Pi. Rotarian. Presbyterian. Author: The Revolutionary Decades, 1965; (with others) Estudios de Historia del Noreste de Mexico, 1972. Staff writer, contbr. Handbook of Texas History, 1951; asst. editor Documents of Texas History, 1963; editorial cons. Arizona and The West: A Quar. Jour. of History, 1977—; mem. editorial adv. bd. N.Mex. Hist. Quar., 1978—. Contbr. articles to profl. jours. Home: 3523 58th St Lubbock TX 79413

VIGODA, ABE, actor; b. N.Y.C., Feb. 24, 1921; s. Samuel and Lena (Moses) V.; student Theatre Sch. Dramatic Arts, Am. Theatre Wing; m. Beatrice Schy, Feb. 24, 1968; 1 dau., Carol. Actor in numerous Broadway prodns. including The Man in The Glass Booth, 1968, Tough to Get Help, 1972, Marat-Sade, 1967, Inquest, 1970; film appearances include The Godfather, Part I, 1972, Part II, 1973, The Don is Dead, 1973, Newman's Law, 1973, The Cheap Detective, 1978; TV appearances include Barney Miller (Emmy award nomination 1975-76, 76-77), Fish (Emmy award nomination 1976-77), 1977. Mem. Actors Equity Assn., Screen Actors Guild, AFTRA. Address: care Contemporary-Korman Artists Ltd 132 Lasky Dr Beverly Hills CA 90212. *When I was a young man I was told success had to come in my youth. I found this to be a myth. My experiences have taught me that if you deeply believe in what you are doing, success can come at any age.*

VIGTEL, GUDMUND, mus. dir.; b. Jerusalem, Palestine, July 9, 1925; s. Arne Jonsen and Elisabeth (Petri) V.; came to U.S., 1948, naturalized, 1966; B.F.A., U. Ga., 1952, M.F.A., 1953; m. Carolyn Gates Smith, July 18, 1964; 1 dau., Catherine Higdon. Adminstrv. asst., asst. to dir. Corcoran Gallery Art, Washington, 1954-61, asst. dir., 1961-63; dir. High Mus. Art, Atlanta, Ga., 1963—. Served with Royal Norwegian Air Force, 1944-45. Mem. Am. Assn. Mus., Assn. Art Mus. Dirs. Author essays and articles in field. Home: 2082 Golf View Dr NW Atlanta GA 30309 Office: 1280 Peachtree St NE Atlanta GA 30309

VIGUERIE, RICHARD ART, direct mail mktg. co. exec.; b. Houston, Sept. 23, 1933; s. Arthur C. and Elizabeth M. (Stoufflet) V.; B.S., U. Houston, 1957; m. Elaine Adele O'Leary, Feb. 17, 1962; children—Renee, Michelle, Richard Ryan. Pres., Richard A. Viguerie Co., Inc., Falls Church, Va., 1965—, Prospect House, Inc., Falls Church, 1970—; chmn. bd. Diversified Mail Mktg., Inc., 1969—, Am. Mailing List Corp., 1972—; publisher Conservative Digest, The Right Report, Polit. Gun Newsletter. Exec. sec. Young Americans for Freedom, 1961-63. Mem. Direct Mail Mktg. Assn., Assn. Direct Mktg. Agencies, Direct Mail Advt. Club Washington. Ind. Conservative. Roman Catholic. Office: 7777 Leesburg Pike Falls Church VA 22043

VILA, BENITO, advt. agy. exec.; b. Havana, Cuba, Mar. 9, 1939; s. Benito Nicolas and Lucila Rensoli (Cancio-Bello) V.; came to U.S., 1964, naturalized, 1970; student (Rufus Choate scholar) Dartmouth Coll., 1954-57; m. Teresa Diaz-Arquelles, Sept. 3, 1960; children—Benito Nicolas, Teresa Mercedes, Maria de las Mercedes, Rosario Mercedes, Santiago Ramon. Copy chief J. Walter Thompson Chilena, 1960-61; partner, creative dir. LeBlanc & CIA LTDA, 1961-64; with Procter & Gamble Co., Cin., 1965-74, brand mgr., 1967-72, brand promotion mgr., 1972-74; mng. dir. Mktg. Corp. Am., Westport, Conn., 1974-77, v.p. cons. group, 1976-77; pres. MCA-Graham Advt., N.Y.C., 1977—; breeder Dalmation champions. Mem. Dalmatian Club Am. Dalmatian Club Greater N.Y., Dalmatian Club So. N. Eng. (pres. 1977-78), Longshore-Southport Kennel Club, Chicagoland Dalmatian Club. Republican. Roman Catholic. Home: Montjuic RFD 2 Monroe CT 06468 Office: 405 Lexington Ave New York NY 10017

VILA, GEORGE RAYMOND, mfg. co. exec.; b. Phila., Mar. 12, 1909; s. Joseph S. and Rachel P. (McCulley) V.; A.B., Wesleyan U., Middletown Conn., 1932; M.S. in Chem. Engring., Mass. Inst. Tech., 1933; student Advanced Mgmt. Program, Harvard U., 1952; D.Eng. (hon.), Clarkson Coll. Tech., 1967. Devel. and prodn. engr. Boston Woven Hose & Rubber Co., 1933-36; with U.S. Rubber Co. (name now Uniroyal, Inc.), 1936—, successively tech. salesman rubber chems. dept. Naugatuck Chem. div., research chemist, dir. synthetic rubber research and devel., asst. dir. research and devel., gen. sales mgr., asst. gen. mgr. div., 1953-57, gen. mgr. div. and v.p. co., 1957, group exec. v.p., 1957-60, pres., mem. exec. com., 1960—, chief exec. officer, 1961-75, chmn. bd., chmn. exec. com., 1965-75, also dir.; past chmn. bd. Uniroyal, Ltd.; dir. Bendix Corp., Inc., Church & Dwight Co., Inc., Chem. Bank. Mem. of tech. indsl. intelligence com. Joint Chiefs of Staff, World War II. Trustee Center Info. Am., Inst. Future, Wesleyan U., Kent Sch.; former mem. corp. Mass. Inst. Tech. Corp. Recipient certificate of appreciation U.S. Govt. Mem. Mfg. Chemists Assn. (past dir.), Nat. Agrl. Chem. Assn. (past dir.), Am. Chem. Soc., Rubber Mfrs. Assn. (past dir.), Soc. Automotive Engrs., Conf. Bd. (dir.), Pa. Soc. (mem. council), Pilgrims U.S., Fgn. Policy Assn., Newcomen Soc. N.Am., Psi Upsilon. Episcopalian. Clubs: Economic, University (N.Y.C.). Home: Sharon CT 06069 Office: 1230 Ave of Americas New York NY 10022

VILLAPIANO, PHILIP JAMES (PHIL), profl. football player; b. Long Branch, N.J., Feb. 26, 1949; B.S. in Phys. Edn., Bowling Green State U., 1971. With Oakland Raiders, NFL, 1971—; played NFL Championship Game, following 1976 season, Pro Bowl (NFL All Star Game), following 1973, 74, 75 seasons. Office: care Oakland Raiders 7811 Oakport St Oakland CA 94621*

VILLARD, OSWALD GARRISON, JR., educator; b. Dobbs Ferry, N.Y., Sept. 17, 1916; s. Oswald Garrison and Julia B. (Sandford) V.; A.B. with honors, Yale, 1938; E.E., Stanford, 1943, Ph.D., 1949; m. Barbara S. Letts, June 27, 1942; children—Thomas Houghton, Barbara Suzanne, John Sandford. Instr. elec. engring. Stanford, 1941-42, acting asst. prof., 1946-50, asst. prof., 1950-52, asso. prof., 1952-55, prof., 1955—, dir. Radioscience Lab., 1958-73; dir. ionospheric dynamics lab. Stanford Research Inst., 1970-72, sr. sci. adviser, 1972—; spl. research asso. Radio Research Lab., Harvard, 1941-42, mem. sr. staff, 1944-46; mem. Air Force Sci. Adv. Bd., 1963-75; mem. Naval Research Adv. Com., 1967-75, chmn., 1972-75. Dir. Flagg Fund, Inc., Calif. Microwave, Inc., United Sci. Corp. Named Outstanding Young Bay Area Engr., Engrs. Joint Council, 1955; recipient Morris Liebmann Meml. prize Inst. Radio Engrs., 1957. Fellow IEEE, AAAS; mem. Nat. Acad. Scis., Nat. Acad. Engring., Internat. Sci. Radio Union. Home: 2887 Woodside Rd Woodside CA 94062 Office: Radioscience Lab Stanford U Stanford CA 94305

VILLARREAL, CARLOS CASTANEDA, engr.; b. Brownsville, Tex., Nov. 9, 1924; s. Jesus Jose and Elisa L. (Castaneda) V.; B.S., U.S. Naval Acad., 1948; M.S., U.S. Navy Postgrad. Sch., 1950; LL.D. (hon.), St. Mary's U., 1972; m. Doris Ann Akers, Sept. 10, 1948; children—Timothy Hill, David Akers. Commd. ensign U.S. Navy, 1948, advanced through grades to lt., 1956; comdg. officer U.S.S. Rhea, 1951, U.S.S. Osprey, 1952; comdr. Mine Div. 31, 1953; resigned 1956; mgr. marine and indsl. operation Gen. Electric Co., 1956-66; v.p. mktg. and adminstrn. Marquardt Corp., 1966-69; head Urban Mass Transit Adminstrn., Dept. Transp., Washington, 1969-73; commr. Postal Rate Commn., 1973-79, vice chmn., 1975-79; v.p. Washington ops. Wilbur Smith and Assos., engring. design and cons. firm, 1979—; lectr. in field. Mem. devel. com. Wolftrap Farm Park for the Performing Arts, 1973-78. Recipient award outstanding achievement Dept. Transp. Mem. Am. Public Transit Assn., Am. Rds. and Transp. Builders Assn., Transp. Research Bd. Republican. Roman Catholic. Clubs: University, Army- Navy (Washington); University (Cin.). Contbr. to profl. jours. Office: 1100 Connecticut Ave NW Suite 440 Washington DC 20036

VILLARS, FELIX MARC HERMANN, physicist, educator; b. Biel, Switzerland, Jan. 6, 1921; s. Jean Felix and Alma (Engel) V.; diplome, Swiss Fed. Inst. Tech., Zurich, 1945, D.Sc.Nat., 1946; m. Jacqueline Dubois, June 25, 1949; children—J. Frederic, Cecile, Monique, Philippe. Came to U.S., 1949, naturalized, 1955. Research asst. Swiss Fed. Inst. Tech., 1946-49; vis. mem. Inst. Advanced Study at Princeton, 1949-50; research asso. Mass. Inst. Tech., 1950-52, asst. prof. physics, 1952-55, asso. prof., 1955-60, prof., 1960—; lectr. biophysics Harvard Med. Sch., 1974—; cons. Lincoln Lab. Served with Swiss Army, 1940-45. Fellow Am. Acad. Arts and Scis.; mem. Am. Phys. Soc. Home: 55 Orchard St Belmont MA 02178 Office: Center for Theoretical Physics 77 Massachusetts Ave Cambridge MA 02139

VILLECHAIZE, HERVE JEAN PIERRE, actor; b. Paris, Apr. 23, 1943; s. Andre and Eveline (Rechionne) V.; attended Beaux Art Sch., Paris. Films: Man With The Golden Gun, Crazy Joe, The Gang That Couldn't Shoot Straight, Seizure, The One and Only; stars as Tattoo in TV series Fantasy Island, 1976—; other TV appearances include: The Tonight Show, Dick Cavett Show. Active in Burbank (Calif.) Community Services, Public Service, Venice Anti-Crime Commn. Recipient Art award City of Paris. Mem. AFTRA, Screen Actors Guild, Actors Equity, Am. Film Inst., Tri Valley Horse Show Assn., Nat. Wildlife Assn., NRA.

VILLEE, CLAUDE ALVIN, JR., educator; b. Lancaster, Pa., Feb. 9, 1917; s. Claude Alvin and Mary Elizabeth (Nestel) V.; B.S., Franklin and Marshall Coll., 1937; Ph.D., U. Calif. at Berkeley, 1941; A.M. (hon.), Harvard U., 1957; m. Dorothy Theresa Balzer, Jan. 21, 1952; children—Claude Alvin III, Stephen Eric Fortney, Suzanne, Charles Andrew. Research fellow U. Calif. at Berkeley, 1941-42; asst. prof. U. N.C., 1942-45; mem. faculty Harvard, 1946—, prof. biol. chemistry, 1962-63, Andelot prof. biol. chemistry, 1964—, fellow Winthrop House, 1957—; tech. aide Nat. Acad. Scis., 1946-47; research asso. Boston Lying in Hosp., 1950-66; dir. lab. reproductive biology Boston Hosp., 1966—; distinguished vis. prof. U. Belgrade (Yugoslavia), 1974, 77; vis. prof. Mahidol U., Bangkok, Thailand, 1974; cons. NSF, Ford Found., Nat. Found./March of Dimes; mem. nat. adv. child health and human devel. council NIH; pres. Internat. Symposium Foeto-Placental unit, Milan, 1968. Trustee Forsythe Dental Center, Boston, Winsor Sch., Boston; bd. dirs. Moors Assn., Falmouth, Mass. Lalor fellow, 1946-47; Guggenheim fellow, 1949-50; recipient Ciba award, 1956, Rubin award, 1957. Fellow Am. Acad. Arts and Scis., Am. Gynecol. Soc. (hon.), Am. Coll. Obstetrics and Gynecology (hon.), Soc. for Gynecol. Investigation (hon.); mem. Moors Assn. Falmouth (pres.), Am. Soc. Biol. Chemists, Endocrine Soc. Am., Biochem. Soc. (Eng.) Am. Chem. Soc., Marine Biol. Lab. (Woods Hole, Mass). Author: Biology, 7th edit., 1977; General Zoology, 5th edit., 1978; Introduction to Animal Biology, 1979; Control of Ovulation, 1961; Mechanism of Action of Steroid Hormones, 1960; The Placenta and Fetal Membranes, 1960; Gestation, Vols. 2-5, 1955-58; Biological Principles and Processes, 1976; Human Reproduction, 1976; Respiratory Distress Syndrome, 1973; The Placenta: A Neglected Experimental Animal, 1979; also articles. Home: 43 Cottage Farm Rd Brookline MA 02416 Office: 25 Shattuck St Boston MA 02115

VILLELLA, EDWARD JOSEPH, ballet dancer; b. L.I., N.Y., Oct. 1, 1936; s. Joseph and Mildred (DeGiovanni) V.; B.S. in Marine Transp., N.Y. State Maritime Coll., 1959; div. Nov. 1970. Dancer, N.Y. City Ballet, 1957—; guest appearance in London, 1962, Royal Danish Ballet Co., 1963, Boston Ballet, 1968, 69, Miami Ballet, 1968-69, N.Y.C. Opera, 1969, White House, London, 1971; appearances on TV shows, summer theatres, festivals U.S. and abroad, 1957—. Mem. Nat. Council on Arts; chmn. Commn. for Cultural Affairs City N.Y., 1978—. Recipient Emmy award for program Harlequin on CBS Festival of Lively Arts, 1975. Address: NYC Ballet Lincoln Center Plaza New York City NY 10023

VILLEMONTE, JAMES RICHARD, civil engr.; b. Fennimore, Wis., May 11, 1912; s. James Roy and Eulalia Hannah (Pengilly) V.; B.S.C.E., U. Wis., Madison, 1935, M.S.C.E., 1941, Ph.D. in Civil and Mech. Engring., 1949; m. Helen Margaret Kotts, June 25, 1939; children—Mary Helen, James Richard, John Karl. Sr. engr. aide Wis. Hwy. Commn., Lancaster, 1935-36, jr. asst. hwy engr., 1938-40; asst. prof. civil engring. Pa. State Coll., 1941-46; asst. prof. U. Wis., Madison, 1949-51, asso. prof., 1952-56, prof., 1957—, chmn. dept. civil and environ. engring., 1972-76, dir. Wis. Water Resources Center, 1971-72, asst. coordinator U. Wis.-AID Program in India, Shibpur, 1954- coordinator, 1956-58, field coordinator U. Wis. contract with Indonesian Govt. to provide acad. services in devel. Inst. Tech., Surabaya, 1978-79; cons. in field, 1952-76; guest prof. applied mechanics Bengal Engring. Coll., Shibpur, 1954-58. Committeeman, Four Lakes council Boy Scouts Am., 1961-68, scoutmaster, 1966-68; mem. numerous coms. Bethany United Methodist Ch., Madison, 1948—, lay leader, 1952-53, 1964-65, trustee, 1950-53, 66-70; chmn. leadership tng. 4 Lakes council, Madison, 1968-70. Served to lt. (s.g.) USNR, 1943-45. Recipient Outstanding Tchr. award U. Wis., 1969, 77, Statuette award Boy Scouts Am., 1963; registered profl. engr., Wis., Pa. Mem. AAUP, Am. Soc. Engring. Edn., ASCE (Disting. Service award 1978), Nat. Soc. Profl. Engrs., Wis. Soc. Profl. Engrs., Wis. Acad. Arts and Scis., Internat. Assn. Hydrolic Research, Internat. Water Resources Assn., Sigma Xi, Pi Mu Epsilon, Tau Beta Pi, Chi Epsilon, Phi Kappa Phi. Research, numerous publs. on measurement of flow in closed and open ducts; research on effects of submergence of structures in open channels; designer spl. stream controls adopted for use by U.S. Dept. Agr. Home: 4209 Bagley Pkwy Madison WI 53705 Office: Dept Civil and Environ Engring U Wis Madison WI 53706

VILLERS, PHILIPPE, mech. engr.; b. Paris, France, June 20, 1935; s. Raymond and Garda (Schmidt) V.; came to U.S., 1940, naturalized, 1946; A.B. in Applied Scis. cum laude, Harvard U., 1955; S.M. in Mech. Engring., Mass. Inst. Tech., 1960; m. Annie Louise Young, July 13, 1957 (div. 1973); children—Jocelyn Anne (dec.), Renata Jane; m. 2d, Katherine Stephan, 1973; children—Noel Stephan, Carolyn Grace. Mem. mfg. tng. program Gen. Electric Co., 1955-58; project engr. Perkin-Elmer Corp., Wilton, Conn., 1959-62; project engr. Apollo Antenna pointings sensor Barnes Engring. Co., Stamford, Conn., 1962-65; project mgr. Advanced Products Center, Link Group, Gen. Precision, Inc., Binghamton, N.Y., 1965-67; mgr. advanced products Concord Control, Inc., Boston, 1967-69; sr. v.p., dir. Computervision Corp., Bedford, Mass., 1969-80; pres., dir. Automatix Inc., Concord, Mass., 1980—; mgmt. cons. Rautenstrauch & Villers, N.Y.C., 1954-55, 58-60. Mem. Democratic Town Com., Wilton, Conn., 1963, Concord, Mass., 1978. NSF grad. fellow, 1959-60. Mem. IEEE, ASME, Am. Inst. Aeros. and Astronautics, Sigma Xi. Patentee process welding aluminum liners to steel surfaces, horizon sensor for visible wavelength, infrared roughness testing instrument, improved thermopile constrn. thermal die marker; pioneer design and feasibility solar sail applications for interplanetary probe propulsion and stblzn. Home and Office: 20 Whit's End Rd Concord MA 01742

VILLONE, LOUIS DOMINICK, mfg. co. exec.; b. Balt., Nov. 8, 1934; s. James Vincent and Rose Conetta V.; B.S., Loyola Coll., 1959; LL.B., U. Balt., 1967; grad. Advanced Mgmt. Program, Harvard U., 1976; m. Oct. 4, 1964; 1 son, James D. With Roper Corp., v.p. mktg. Roper Eastern, 1976-77, exec. v.p., 1977, pres. Roper Eastern, exec. v.p. corp., 1977—. Office: Roper Corp 1905 W Court St Kankakee IL 60901*

VILTER, RICHARD WILLIAM, physician; b. Cin., Mar. 21, 1911; s. William Frederick and Clara (Bieler) V.; A.B., Harvard, 1933, M.D., 1937; m. Sue Potter, Aug. 17, 1935; 1 son, Richard William. Intern, resident internal medicine Cin. Gen. Hosp., 1937-42, dir. lab. hematology and nutrition, 1945-56, asst. dir. dept. internal medicine, 1953-56, dir., 1956-78, asso. prof. medicine U. Cin. Coll. Medicine, 1948-56, Gordon and Helen Hughes Taylor prof., 1956-78, prof. medicine on spl. assignment, 1978—, asst. dean, 1945-51; cons. VA, 1947—; cons. hematology Good Samaritan Hosp., Cin.; cons. physician Deaconess, Christ, Drake hosps., Cin. Mem. sci. adv. bd. Nat. Vitamin Found., 1953-56; spl. cons. nutrition and anemias in Egypt, WHO, 1954; chmn. hematology study sect. NIH, 1965- 69; chmn. nat. adv. com. anemia malnutrition Research Center, Chiengmai, Thailand, 1967-75. Recipient Joseph Goldberger award AMA, 1960. Diplomate Am. Bd. Internal Medicine. Fellow A.C. P. (past gov. for Ohio, bd. regents, sec. gen. 1973-78, pres. elect 1978-79, pres. 1979-80); mem. Federated Council for Internal Medicine (chmn. 1979-80), Clin. and Climatol Assn., Assn. Am Physicians, Am. Soc. Clin. Nutrition (pres. 1960-61), Am. Soc. Clin. Investigation, Central Soc. Clin. Research, Am. Soc. Hematology, Am. Bd. Nutrition, Internat. Soc. Hematology, Phi Beta Kappa, Alpha Omega Alpha, Nu Sigma Nu. Asso. editor Jour. Clin. Investigation, 1951-52. Contbr. to profl. publs. Home: 5 Annwood Ln Cincinnati OH 45206 Office: U Cin Med Center Cincinnati OH 45267

VIMOND, EDMUND GEORGE, JR., tobacco co. exec.; b. Toledo, Ohio, May 30, 1935; s. Edmund George and Bertha Olive (Squires) V.; B.S.B.A., Northwestern U., 1957, M.B.A., 1958; m. Pamela Jolie Thompson, Sept. 23, 1957; children—Edmund G., Frederick A., Cynthia D. With Procter & Gamble, Cin., 1958-63; brand mgr. Warner-Lambert Co., Morris Plains, N.J., 1963-69, products div. v.p. mktg., 1965, products div. pres., 1968-69; health care div. v.p., gen. mgr. Johnson & Johnson, New Brunswick, N.J., 1970-74, group v.p. domestic ops., 1974-76, pres. personal products co., 1976-78; group v.p. Am. Cyanamid Co., Wayne, N.J., 1978-79; pres., chief exec. officer R.J. Reynolds Tobacco Internat., Inc., Winston-Salem, N.C., 1980—. Trustee, Morristown Meml. Hosp., 1972-78. Served with USMCR, 1958. Mem. Proprietary Assn. (dir. 1971-77), Assn. Nat. Advertisers, Cosmetic, Toiletry and Fragrance Assn., Delta Tau Delta. Republican. Episcopalian. Club: Morris County Golf (Morristown, N.J.). Office: R J Reynolds Co Reynolds Blvd Winston-Salem NC 27102

VINCE, DENNIS JORDAN, pediatric cardiologist; b. Toronto, Ont., Can., Jan. 3, 1930; s. Anthony Joseph and Dorothy Margaret (Cowan) V.; M.D., U. Toronto, 1954; m. Elizabeth Anne Harland, June 20, 1953; children—Pauline Anne, Marilynne Anne, Janet Anne, Robert Anthony, William Dennis. Intern, Toronto Gen. Hosp., 1954-55, resident in pediatrics, 1955-57; resident Sunnybrook Hosp., Toronto, 1957-58; resident in pediatric cardiology Hosp. for Sick Children, Toronto, 1958-59; asst. prof. pediatrics U. B.C. (Can.), Vancouver, 1959-72, asso. prof., 1972-74, prof., 1974—, head sect. pediatric cardiology, 1974—; dir. pediatric cardiac catheterization lab. Vancouver Gen. Hosp.; founding chmn. B.C. Orton Soc., 1972-73, B.C. Parent Support Assn., 1976-79. Fellow Royal Coll. Physicians and Surgeons Can.; mem. Am. Heart Assn., B.C. Med. Assn. (founding chmn. sect. cardiology 1979-80), B.C. Pediatric Soc., Can. Cardiovascular Soc., Can. Med. Assn., Can. Paediatric Cardiology Soc. (founding chmn. 1972-73), Can. Paediatric Soc., Osler Soc. Mem. United Ch. Can. Author: Essentials of Paediatric Cardiology, 1974; contbr. articles to Can. Med. Assn. Jour., Circulation; participant in devel. B.C. Congenital Heart Museum, U. B.C. Paediatric Cardiology Learning Centre; developed: Essentials of Paediatric Cardiology, 80 slide-tape programs and self evaluation

univs., 1972—. Home: 455 Gordon Ave West Vancouver BC V7T 1T4 Canada Office: 715 W 12th Ave Vancouver BC V5Z 1M9 Canada

VINCE, ROBERT, educator; b. Auburn, N.Y., Nov. 20, 1940; s. George John and Betty (Colavito) V.; B.S., U. Buffalo, 1962; Ph.D., SUNY at Buffalo, 1966; m. Maureen Veronica Ramsey, Aug. 26, 1961; children—Susan Maureen, Sharon Mary. Asst. prof. med. chemistry U. Miss., Oxford, 1966-67; asst. prof. U. Minn., Mpls., 1967-71, asso. prof., 1971-76, prof., 1976—; vis. scientist Roche Inst. Molecular Biology, 1974-75. Recipient Lunsford Richardson Research award, 1966, Research Career award Nat. Cancer Inst., 1972-76; named Scholar of Yr., Phi Kappa Phi, 1979. Mem. Am. Chem. Soc., Am. Pharm. Assn., AAAS, Am. Assn. Cancer Research, Am. Soc. Biol. Chemists, Sigma Xi, Rho Chi. Contbr. numerous articles to profl. jours. Patentee antibiotics and antiviral agts. Home: 1723 Yorkshire Ave Saint Paul MN 55116 Office: Coll Pharmacy U Minn Minneapolis MN 55455

VINCENT, BURTON JUDSON, bus. exec.; b. Evanston, Ill., June 19, 1925; s. Harold Sellew and Frances Willard (Hill) V.; B.B.A., U. Mich., 1948; m. Marilyn Margaret Hall, June 12, 1947; children—Burton Judson, John Scott. Salesman, Julien Collins & Co., Chgo., 1948-51; v.p. Carl McGlone & Co., Chgo., 1951-54; pres. Burton J. Vincent & Co., Chgo., 1954-74; founder, chmn. bd., chief exec. officer Capitol Food Industries, Inc., Chgo., 1955—; chmn. bd., chief exec. officer Burton J. Vincent, Chesley & Co., 1974—; dir. Mojonnier Bros. Co., Chgo.; vice chmn. bd. govs. M.W. Stock Exchange; mem. N.Y. Stock Exchange; cons. Twin City Barge & Towing Co. Mem. exec. com. Chgo. Home Missionary and Ch. Extension Soc., 1964—; mem. Chgo. Crime Commn. and Police Com., 1974—; pres. Methodist Ministers' Pension Fund Bd., 1974—; chmn. Salvation Army Adv. Bd., 1977—. Served with USMC, 1943-46. Mem. Securities Industry Assn. Clubs: Chgo. Golf, Bond of Chgo., Union League, Attic. Office: 105 W Adams St Chicago IL 60603

VINCENT, CHARLES RIDGELY, mfg. and engring. exec.; b. Chgo., Nov. 19, 1912; s. Charles R. and Margaret (Tiffany) V.; B.A., Denison U., Granville, Ohio, 1938; postgrad. U. Okla., 1971-72; m. Charlotte Jane McCarroll, June 17, 1939; children—David Ridgely, Barbara Vincent Henares, Peter McCarroll, Patricia Tiffany Vincent Merkley. Jr. exec. First of Mich. Corp., Detroit, 1938-39; gen. sales mgr., exec. asst. to pres., dir. Ford-Ferguson, Inc., Detroit, 1939-46; mng. dir., bd. dirs. Harry Ferguson, Ltd., Coventry, Eng., 1946-48; owner Vinlee Co., Detroit, 1948-50; research and devel. engr. Willys-Overland Co., Toledo, 1950-52; owner Vincent & Co., King City, Calif., 1953-56; exec. v.p., dir. Rolligon, Inc., Monterey, Calif., 1956-59; engaged in patent research and devel., Monterey, 1960-64; math. researcher Stanford Research Inst., 1965-66; math. researcher, supr. data analysis, mgr. data processing project scientist advanced planning and analysis Litton Industries, 1966-71; cons. Bechtel, Inc., San Francisco, 1972-73, prin. engr., 1973—; mgr. Bechtel Rolligon Joint Venture, 1973-75; cons. engr. logistics Bechtel Internat. Inc., 1976—; project engr. Internat. Bechtel, Inc., 1977; adviser WPB, 1940-45. Decorated Commemorative War cross Royal Yugoslavian Army, 1945; recipient citation for distinguished service to English postwar effort, 1946-47. Mem. First Families Va., Mayflower Descendants, Soc. Colonial Wars, Soc. Am. Revolution, Soc. War 1812, Americans of Royal Descent, New Eng. Hist. Geneal. Soc., William the Conqueror Soc., Les Ambassadeurs (London). Patentee in field. Address: 26195 Mesa Place Carmel CA 93923

VINCENT, CLARK EDWARD, sociologist; b. Otis, Colo., May 13, 1923; s. Ralph Ellory and Lillian May (Auld) V.; A.B., U. Calif. at Berkeley, 1949, M.A., 1950, Ph.D. (NIMH fellow, Univ. fellow), 1952; m. Roseann Wagoner, Dec. 27, 1955. From instr. to asst. prof. family sociology U. Calif. at Berkeley, 1952-59; asso. prof. State U. Iowa, 1959-60; scientist administr. NIMH, 1960-64, mem. research rev. com. applied research br., 1975-77; prof. sociology Bowman Gray Sch. Medicine, 1964-78, dir. Behavioral Scis. Center, 1966-74, dir. Marital Health Clinic, 1972-77, chmn. dept. med. social scis. and marital health, 1974-75. Cons. to tng. and manpower resources br. Nat. Inst. Mental Health, 1964-65, 75-76, AID, Dept. State, 1969-71; spl. cons. to com. on family life Nat. Council Chs. Christ in U.S., 1963-66; mem. family life edn. com. Am. Coll. Obstetricians-Gynecologists. Co-founder, bd. dirs. Sex Edn. and Information Council U.S., 1964-70, 72-74; bd. dirs. Nat. Council Illegitimacy, 1967-70; nat. chmn. Groves Conf. Marriage and the Family, 1962-63, bd. dirs., 1963-67. Recipient Clark E. Vincent scholarly award Calif. Assn. Marriage and Family Counselors, 1975; Medallion of Merit Wake Forest U., 1978; Sperry award N.C. Family Life Council, 1978. Fellow Am. Assn. Marriage and Family Therapists (past v.p., exec. bd., pres. 1973-74, Disting. Pioneer award, 1978), Am. Sociol. Assn. (chmn. family sect. 1973-74), Soc. Sci. Study Sex; mem. Nat. Council Family Relations (chmn. counseling sect. 1961-62, exec. bd. 1962-65, pres. 1964-65); Sigma Xi. Author: Unmarried Mothers, 1961; Sexual and Marital Health, 1973. Asso. editor Social Problems, 1961-64, 67-69, Jour. Marriage and Family, 1965-69, 75-78, Jour. Marriage and Family Counseling, 1975-78, Jour. Sex and Marital Therapy, 1974-79. Editorial bd. Jour. Spl. Edn., 1967-78, Jour. of Divorce, 1977-79. Compiler, editor: Readings in Marriage Counseling, 1957; Human Sexuality in Medical Education and Practice, 1968; co-editor, compiler Psychosocial Aspects of Medical Training, 1971. Contbr. numerous articles to profl. publs. Home: Rural Route 3 Fox Trail Broken Arrow Estates Sedona AZ 86336

VINCENT, DIETRICH HERMANN, educator; b. Leszno, Poland, May 11, 1925; s. Hermann and Kaethe (Strempel) V.; diplom physiker, U. Göttingen (Germany), 1950, Dr. Rer. Nat., 1956; m. Elisabeth E. Schmidt, Dec. 28, 1954; children—Martin, Dorothea. Came to U.S., 1958, naturalized, 1967. Sci. asst. isotope lab. Max Planck Inst. Med. Research, Göttingen, 1951-58; resident research asso. physics div. Argonne (Ill.) Nat. Lab., 1958-60; asso. prof. nuclear engring. U. Mich. at Ann Arbor, 1960-64, prof., 1964—; Internat. Atomic Energy Agy. expert Nat. Tsing-Hua U., Hsinchu, Taiwan, 1968-69; vis. prof. physics Nat. Taiwan U., Taipei, 1969. Mem. Am. Phys. Soc., Am. Nuclear Soc., AAAS, Am. Soc. Metals, Sigma Xi. Asso. editor Radiochem. and Radioanalytical Letters, 1969-75. Home: 4795 Bridgeway Ann Arbor MI 48103

VINCENT, DONALD EDWARD PERRY, librarian; b. Martins Ferry, Ohio, Dec. 26, 1922; s. George Nicholas and Anne (Martochko) Perry; B.A., U. Buffalo, 1949; M.A. in L.S., U. Mich., 1952, M.A. in Polit. Sci., 1957, Ph.D. in Library Sci., 1974; m. Nancy Elizabeth Suliburk; children—Daniel, Jerett. Cataloger, Wayne State U., 1952-58, bibliographer, 1958-59, lectr. library sci., 1957-59; dir. library services U. Mich., Dearborn, 1959-62; univ. librarian U. N.H., 1962—. Mem. Gov. N.H. Com. Better Libraries, 1962-63. Co-founder, co-chmn. NELINET, 1964-68, chmn. exec. com., 1970—; mem. N.H. Adv. Council on Libraries, 1972-78; v.p. N.H. Library Council, 1970-71, pres., 1971—; mem. Regional Archives Adv. Council, 1971-72. Served to lt. (j.g.) USNR, 1943-47. Mem. A.L.A., New Eng. (v.p. 1975-76, pres. 1976-77), N.H. (treas., 1963, 1st v.p. 1963-65) library assns., Phi Kappa Phi, Phi Beta Mu. Home: Riverview Rd Durham NH 03824

VINCENT, DOUGLAS VAUGHAN, Can. city ofcl.; b. Gladstone, Man., Can. May 11, 1943; s. George Waldo and Norah Eileen (Clayton) V.; student Capilano Coll., North Vancouver, B.C., 1976-77, Can. Inst. Orgn. Mgmt., Western U., London, Ont., 1970-76; m. Therese Irene Gosselin, Oct. 25, 1969; children—Corrie Lee, Wendy Allison, Sarah Elizabeth. With Can. Imperial Bank of Commerce, 1961-63; in retail sales, 1963-65; officer in charge records and identification Corrections Br., Prince George, B.C., 1965-69; mgr. Jasper Park C. of C., Jasper, Alta., Can., 1969-71; gen. mgr. Thunder Bay (Ont., Can.) C. of C., 1971-74; pres. Ont. C. of C. Execs., 1974; dir. policy devel. Vancouver (B.C.) Bd. Trade, 1974—. Sec. West Vancouver Res. Police; mem. hon. adv. com. B.C. and Yukon Chamber of Mines; bd. dirs. N.W. Ont. Tourists Assn., 1973-74; mem. indsl. relations com. Employers' Council B.C. Mem. C. of C. Execs. of Can. (dir. for B.C.), Mem. United Ch. of Can. Editor: Facts and Trends in Industrial Relations, 1974-79; Starting a New Business in Greater Vancouver, 1974-79. Home: 2652 Chesterfield Ave North Vancouver BC V7N 3M2 Canada Office: 1177 W Hastings St 5th Floor Vancouver BC V6E 2K3 Canada

VINCENT, FRANCIS THOMAS, JR., entertainment co. exec.; b. Waterbury, Conn., May 29, 1938; s. Francis Thomas and Alice (Lynch) V.; B.A. cum laude, Williams Coll., 1960; LL.B., Yale U., 1963; m. Valerie McMahon, July 3, 1965; children—Anne, William, Edward. Admitted to Conn. bar, 1963, N.Y. State bar, 1964, D.C. bar, 1969; asso. firm Whitman & Ransom, N.Y.C., 1963-68; partner firm Caplin & Drysdale, Washington, 1968-78; asso. dir. div. corp. fin. SEC, Washington, 1978; pres., chief exec. officer Columbia Pictures Industries, Inc., N.Y.C., 1978—. Trustee, Williams Coll., 1970—; trustee Hotchkiss Sch., 1975—; mem. N.Y. Gov.'s Adv. Bd. on Film, 1979—. Mem. Motion Picture Assn. (bd. dirs.), Phi Beta Kappa. Roman Catholic. Clubs: University, Belle Haven. Home: 45 Bush Ave Greenwich CT 06830 Office: 711 Fifth Ave New York NY 10022

VINCENT, GERALD GLENN, chemist; b. Winnepeg, Man., Can., Apr. 13, 1934; s. Hubert Glenn and Alma (Webber) V.; came to U.S., 1963, naturalized, 1975; B.Sc., U. Man., 1958, M.Sc., 1960, Ph.D., 1963; m. Joan Pauline Grinke, Dec. 1, 1956; children—Erin Elizabeth, Mark Frederick, Kathryn Joan, David Arthur. Project mgr., research chemist Dow Chem. Co., Midland, Mich., 1963-67; sect. leader, tech. mgr., dept. mgr. DeSoto, Inc., Des Plaines, Ill., 1967-73; asst. dir. research Crown Zellerbach Corp., Camas, Wash., 1973-74, dir. research, 1974—. Mem. TAPPI, Indsl. Research Inst., Canadian Pulp and Paper Assn., Am. Paper Inst. Lutheran. Patentee in field. Home: 4507 DuBois Dr Vancouver WA 98661 Office: Central Research Div Crown Zellerbach Corp Camas WA 98607

VINCENT, HAL WELLMAN, marine corps officer; b. Pontiac, Mich., Sept. 27, 1927; s. Harold and Glenda (Wellman) V.; student Navy V-5 program Western Mich. Coll./Colgate U., 1945; B.S., U.S. Naval Acad., 1950; postgrad. Marine Officers Basic Sch., 1950, Flight Sch., 1952, Test Pilot Sch., 1955, Navy Fleet Air Gunnery Sch., 1958, Air Force Fighter Weapons Sch., 1959, Indsl. Coll., 1969; m. Virginia Bayler, June 9, 1951; children—David B., Dale W., Deborah K. Vincent Minder. Commd. 2d lt. U.S. Marine Corps, 1950, advanced through grades to maj. gen., 1974; rifle and machinegun platoon comdr., Camp Lejeune, N.C., 1951; fighter pilot, El Toro, Calif. and Korea, 1953-54; test pilot Flight Test Div., Patuxent River, Md., 1955-57; ops. officer, squadron asst. and fighter pilot, El Toro, 1958-59; conventional weapons project officer Naval Air Weapons Test Center, China Lake, Calif., 1960-62; squadron ops. and exec. officer El Toro and Japan, 1962-64; aviation specialist Marine Corps amphibious warfare presentation team and staff officer, Quantico, Va., 1965-66; comdg. officer 2d Marine Aircraft Wing fighter-attack squadron, Beaufort, S.C., 1967-68; exec. officer Marine Aircraft Group, Vietnam, 1969, logistics staff officer Fleet Marine Force Pacific, Hawaii, 1970-72; comdg. officer Marine Aircraft Group, Yuma, Ariz., 1972-73; chief of staff 3d Marine Aircraft Wing, El Toro, 1973-76; dep. chief. of staff plans and policy, to Comdr. in Chief Atlantic, Norfolk, Va., 1976-78; comdg. gen. 2d Marine Aircraft Wing, Cherry Point, N.C., 1978—; flight test pilot; preliminary pilot, evaluator new mil. aircraft. Decorated Legion of Merit with gold star, D.F.C., Bronze Star with combat V, Air medal with star and numeral 14, Joint Services Commendation medal (U.S.); Honor medal 1st class, Cross of Gallantry with gold star (Republic of Vietnam). Mem. SAR, Soc. Exptl. Test Pilots, Marine Corps Assn., Order of Daedelians, Marine Corps Aviation Assn., Mach 2 Club, 1000 miles per hour Club. Clubs: Army-Navy Country, Army-Navy Town. Contbr. numerous articles on tactics and conventional weapons delivery, flight test stability and control to various mil. publs.; invented Triple Ejector Rack for delivery of conventional bombs, 1961; devel. fighter tactics in F8 and F4 aircraft, 1958-69. Home: 317 Jefferson St MCAS Cherry Point NC 28533 Office: Comdg Gen 2d Marine Air Wing Cherry Point NC 28533. *In all 34 years in the service I am convinced that war is bad, and little is accomplished in the long term by warfare. However when national policy dictates a war, then we must not limit what can be done. We must win. My thought then remains: "Winning isn't everything, it's the only thing!" When I must go to battle I want to be allowed to fight to win.*

VINCENT, HARRY FLEMING, govt. ofcl.; b. Union City, Tenn., May 27, 1918; s. Harry Otis and Fannie (Fleming) V.; B.S. in Elec. Engring., Washington U., St. Louis, 1940; M.S., U. Ala., 1971; m. Rachel Boone, Nov. 14, 1942; children—Judith Lynn (Mrs. Michael Settle), Barbara Jo (Mrs. Joe H. Glover III), Engr., IBM Corp., 1940-41; radio engr. Bendix Radio, Townson, Md., 1946-47; project engr. Grebe project Naval Aviation Ordnance Test Sta., Chincoteague, Va., 1947-50; chief internat. instrumental sect., instrumentation engring. div. USAF Missile Test Center, Cocoa, Fla., 1950-51; chief electronics br. research and devel. div. Army Rocket and Guided Missile Agy., Redstone Arsenal, Ala., 1951-54, chief surface-to-air missile br., 1954-58, chief project engr., project mgmt. staff, 1958-59, chief engring. and research staff, 1959-60; dept. dir. research and devel. directorate, 1960-62; project dir., research and devel. directorate U.S. Army Missile Command, Redstone Arsenal, 1962—. Chmn. HAWK tech. steering com., 1955-58, Nike Hercules adv. panel, 1955-58, Nike Ajax product improvement com., 1954-57; mem. Signal-Ordnance Steering Com. Fire Integration Systems, 1955-57; chmn. tech. com. SAM-D Trade Off Study, 1965, tech. dir. Source Selection Evaluation Bd., 1967; exec. dir. Am. Diabetes Assn. of Ala.; cons. Army Research office, Durham, N.C., Lockheed Corp., Teledyne Brown. Served to maj. USAAF, 1941-46. Recipient Meritorious Civil Service award, 1966. Exceptional Civilian Service award, 1968. Registered profl. engr., Ala. Mem. IEEE (sr.), Profl. Group Engring. Mgmt., Assn. U.S. Army. Methodist (past chmn. bd. stewards, trustee). Clubs: Internat. Toastmasters (past pres. Mason-Dixon club.) Home: 2211 De Russey Rd SE Huntsville AL 35801 Office: 4717 University Dr Suite 106 Huntsville AL 35805

VINCENT, HELEN, editor; b. Elizabeth, N.J.; d. James Burlin and Eva Harriet (Winter) Vincent; B.A. with honors, Elmira Coll., 1942; student Columbia, 1940, N.Y. U., 1949. Asst. editor Your Life and Your Health mags., 1943-50; spl. editorial assignments Wilfred Funk, Inc., publisher, 1943-50; asso. editor Intimate Romances, Ideal Pub. Corp., N.Y.C., 1950-53; True Life Stories, Pines Publs., N.Y.C., 1953-54; free-lance editor, writer Pocket Books, Inc., N.Y.C., 1953-57; mng. editor True Confessions, Macfadden-Bartell Corp., N.Y.C., 1954-73, editor, 1973-75; editor True Story, 1975—. Home: 10 Mohawk Trail Westfield NJ 07090 Office: 205 E 42d St New York City NY 10017

VINCENT, JAMES LOUIS, pharm. co. exec.; b. Johnstown, Pa., Dec. 15, 1939; s. Robert Clyde and Marietta Lucille (Kennedy) V.; B.S., Duke U., 1961; M.B.A., U. Pa., 1963; m. Elizabeth Matthews, Aug. 19, 1961; children—Aimee Archelle, Christopher James. Sales mgr. Del., AT&T, 1965-68; gen. mgr. Germany Tex. Instruments, Inc., 1968-70; mgr. Far East div., pres. Asia, Tex. Instruments, 1970-73; v.p. diagnostic ops. Abbott Labs., North Chicago, Ill., 1973-76, group v.p., 1976-79, exec. v.p., chief operating officer, 1979—, also dir. Bd. dirs. Chgo. Hort. Soc. Office: Abbott Labs North Chicago IL 60064

VINCENT, JOSEPH SCOTT, ins. co. exec.; b. Mebane, N.C., Aug. 11, 1913; s. Joseph Shaw and Mary Edwin (Scott) V.; B.S., N.C. State U., 1934; postgrad. Exec. Program, U. N.C., 1969; m. Margaret Willene Yost, June 16, 1936; children—Joseph Scott, Anne (Mrs. James Ross Perry), Dorothy (Mrs. Dale Paul Wilson). With Liberty Mut. Ins. Co., various cities, 1934-43; ins. mgr. Curtiss Wright Corp., Buffalo, 1944-46; with Pilot Life Ins. Co., Greensboro, N.C., 1947—, sr. v.p., 1968—, also mem. exec. com., dir. Vice pres. N.C. State U. Edn. Found., 1974—. Mem. Sigma Pi. Presbyterian (elder, clk. of session). Home: 2502 W Market Greensboro NC 27403 Office: PO Box 20727 Greensboro NC 27420

VINCENT, LLOYD DREXELL, coll. adminstr.; b. DeQuincy, La., Jan. 7, 1924; s. Samuel and Lila (Dickerson) V.; student Rice U., 1946-47, 49-50; B.S., U. Tex., Austin, 1952, M.A., 1953, Ph.D., 1960; m. Johnell Stuart, Aug. 30, 1947; children—Drexell Stuart, Sandra. Asst. prof. U. Southwestern La., 1953-55, asso. prof., 1956-58; instr. Tex. A. and M. U., 1955-56; Danforth Found. tchr. study grantee, NSF Sci. faculty fellow. U. Tex., 1958-59; research scientist Tex. Nuclear Corp., Austin, 1959-60; prof., dir. physics dept. Sam Houston State U., 1960-65, asst. to pres., 1965-67; pres. Angelo State U., San Angelo, Tex., 1967—. Co-owner, mgr. ACME Glass Corp., Baytown, Tex., 1947-49; physics cons. Columbia U. Tchrs. Coll., U.S. AID, India, summer 1966; dir. W.Tex. Utilities Co., 1978—. Bd. dirs. W.Tex. Rehab. Center, 1977—. Served to 2d lt. USAAF, 1942-45. Named Citizen of Year San Angelo C. of C., 1975. Fellow Tex. Acad. Sci.; mem. Am. Phys. Soc., Am. Assn. State Colls. and Univs. (state rep. 1972-74), Am. Assn. Physics Tchrs. (sect. chmn. 1965-67), Sigma Xi, Sigma Pi Sigma. Democrat. Baptist. Rotarian. Home: 2602 Live Oak St San Angelo TX 76901

VINCENT, WILLIAM SHAFER, educator; b. Tupelo, Miss., Dec. 12, 1907; s. William Shafer and Jessie (Clark) V.; A.B., Coll. of William and Mary, 1936; A.M., Columbia, 1940, Ph.D., 1944; m. Janet Newton, Aug. 31, 1934 (dec. Aug. 27, 1976); m. 2d, Dorothy Averell, Mar. 21, 1978. Tchr., Virginia Beach (Va.) Sch. for Boys, also Norfolk Prep. Sch., 1930-36; tchr., adminstr. pub. schs., Hampton, Va., 1936-40, Danville, Va., 1941-43; research asso. Tchrs. Coll., Columbia, 1943-46, prof. edn., 1950-73, prof. emeritus, 1973—, dir. citizenship edn. project, 1950-60, dir. Inst. Adminstrv. Research, 1950-73; prof. edn. Pa. State U., 1946-49; exec. sec. Pa. Sch. Study Council, 1946-49, also cons. Ednl. Policies Commn.; asso. instrnl. film research project Pa. State U., 1947-49; cons. Ency. Brit. Films, Inc., 1945-46; exec. sec. Met. School Study Council, 1957-59, gen. sec., 1959-72; gen. sec. Asso. Pub. Sch. Systems, 1959-72; dir. Central Sch. Bds. Com. Ednl. Research, 1959-72; chmn. Vincent & Olson Sch. Evaluation Services, 1973—. Mem. NEA, Sigma Phi Epsilon. Episcopalian. Author: (with others) What Education Our Money Buys, 1943; What Schools Can Do, 1944; Emerging Patterns of Public School Practice, 1945; (with Paul R. Mort) A Look at Our Schools, 1946; (with others) Tools for Teaching, 1948, Interaction between Schools and Local Community Groups, 1949; (with Mort) Modern Educational Practice, 1950, Introduction to American Education, 1954; (with James E. Russell) You and the Draft, 1952; (with others) Building Better Programs in Citizenship, 1958; Roles of the Citizen, 1959; (with W. H. Hartley) American Civics, 1967; Indicators of Quality, 1968; Measurement School Quality and Its Determiners, 1972; Improbable Planet, 1976. Films produced: The Teacher as Observer and Guide, 1946; (with F.T. Matthewson) Integrated Art and Home Economics, 1946; (with others) Education for Citizenship, 1947; Teachers at Work, 1948; A Day in the Life of a Five-Year-Old, 1949. Home: Salisbury CT 06068 also Rio Verde AZ 85255

VINCENTI, LOUIS RUDOLPH, lawyer, savs. and loan assn. exec.; b. Balt., Feb. 27, 1906; s. Guido A. and Agnes (Nicholini) V.; A.B., Stanford, 1928, J.D., 1930; m. Luella Wadsworth, July 29, 1930 (dec. Aug. 1962); children—Louis R., Nataline V. (Mrs. G. Harris Hartman); m. 2d, Marion Gene Johnson, Sept. 28, 1963. Admitted to Calif. bar, 1930, since practiced in Pasadena; partner Hahn & Hahn, 1930-55; exec. v.p. Mut. Savs. & Loan Assn., Pasadena, 1955-61, pres., 1961—, chmn. bd., 1973—; exec. v.p. Wesco Financial Corp., 1959-61, pres., 1961—, chmn. bd., 1973—; dir. Investors Mortgage Ins. Co., Boston, 1968-71. Mem. Pasadena Redevel. Agy., 1966-73, chmn., 1968-73. Mem. bd. visitors U.S. Mil. Acad., 1970-72. Office: 315 E Colorado Blvd Pasadena CA 91109

VINCENTI, WALTER GUIDO, aero. engr., educator; b. Balt., Apr. 20, 1917; s. Guido A. and Agnes (Nicolini) V.; A.B., Stanford, 1938, Aero Engr., 1940; m. Joyce H. Weaver, Sept. 6, 1947; children—Margaret Anna, Marc Guido. Aero. research scientist NACA, 1940-57; prof. aero. and astronautics and history of tech. Stanford, 1957—. Cons to industry, 1957—; mem. adv. panel engring. sec. NSF, 1960-63. Served with USN, 1945-46. Recipient Gold medal Pi Tau Sigma, 1948; Rockefeller Pub. Service award, 1956; Guggenheim fellow, 1963. Fellow Am. Inst. Aero. and Astronautics; mem. Am. Phys. Soc., Internat. Acad. Astronautics (corr.), Soc. History Tech., Phi Beta Kappa, Sigma Xi, Tau Beta Pi. Author: (with Charles H. Kruger, Jr.) Introduction to Physical Gas Dynamics, 1965; (with Nathan Rosenberg) The Britannia Bridge, 1978; also papers. Co-editor: Annual Review of Fluid Mechanics, 1970-76. Home: 13200 E Sunset Dr Los Altos Hills CA 94022 Office: Stanford U Stanford CA 94305

VINCENZ, STANISLAW ALEKSANDER, geophysicist, educator; b. Oskrzesince, Poland, Feb. 4, 1915; s. Stanislaw Andrzej and Helena (Loeventon) V.; came to U.S., 1961, naturalized, 1971; B.S., Imperial Coll., U. London, 1937, D. Imperial Coll., 1939, Ph.D., 1952; m. Margit Annemarie Schwarz-Rehwald von Jochen, June 3, 1949; 1 son, Felix. Demonstrator in geophysics Imperial Coll., London, 1948-49, asst. lectr., 1949-52, research asst., 1952-53; head geophysics div. Indsl. Devel. Corp., Kingston, Jamaica, W.I., 1953-61; asso. prof. geophysics St. Louis U., 1961-67, prof., 1967—; vis. scientist U. Tex. at Dallas, 1965; sr. vis. fellow U. Colo., 1976; Nat. Acad. Sci. exchange scientist to Polish and Czechoslov acads. sci., 1976. NSF grantee, 1963—, U.S. Geol. Survey grantee, 1973-76. Fellow Royal Astron. Soc. London; mem. Am. Geophys. Union, Soc. Exploration Geophysicists, European Assn. Exploration Geophysicists, AAAS, Soc. Geomagnatism and Geoelectricity Japan, Nat. Geog. Soc., St. Louis Met. br. Am. Geophys. Union (pres. 1974-75), Astron. Soc. St. Louis, Sigma Xi. Roman Catholic. Contbr. articles to revs. to sci. publs. Home: 805 Pine Tree Ln Webster Groves MO 63119 Office: St Louis U PO Box 8099 Laclede Sta Saint Louis MO 63156. *Scientific* *honesty is the true honesty of the spirit. It is a measure of true success that is not always a worldly success, i.e., not one that hits the headlines. Hence the motto, "I know that I know very little" has been guidelight in my scientific work.*

VINCOW, GERSHON, educator; b. Bronx, N.Y., Feb. 27, 1935; s. Samuel and Minnie (Kurtzman) V.; A.B., Columbia, 1956, M.A., 1957, Ph.D., 1959; m. Dina Lichomanov, Mar. 14, 1964; children—Evelyn Sandra, Michelle Anita. Prof. chemistry U. Wash., Seattle, 1961-71; prof. Syracuse (N.Y.) U., 1971—, v.p. research and grad. affairs, 1977-78, dean Coll. Arts and Scis., 1978—. NSF predoctoral fellow, 1956-59, postdoctoral fellow, 1960-61, sr. postdoctoral fellow, 1970-71; Alfred P. Sloan Found. fellow, 1964-67. Mem. Am. Chem. Soc., Am. Phys. Soc., AAAS, Phi Beta Kappa, Sigma Xi, Phi Lambda Upsilon. Jewish. Contbr. to profl. jours. Office: 300 Hall of Languages Syracuse Univ Syracuse NY 13210

VINE, ALLYN COLLINS, oceanographer; b. Garrettsville, Ohio, June 1, 1914; s. Elmer James and Lulu (Collins) V.; B.A., Hiram (Ohio) Coll., 1936, Garfield scholar, 1972; M.S., Lehigh U., 1938, D.Sc. (hon.), 1973; m. Adelaide Ruth Holton, Nov. 16, 1940; children—Vivian (Mrs. Carl F. Dreisbach), Norman, David. Oceanographer, Woods Hole (Mass.) Oceanographic Instn., 1940—; part-time oceanographer Bur. Ships, Dept. Navy, 1947-50, Mem. panel engring. aids for oceanography Nat. Acad. Scis., 1958-64. Trustee Ocean Resources Inst., 1952-64. Internat. Oceanographic Found., 1960—. Recipient David B. Stone award New Eng. Aquarium, 1977. Fellow Marine Tech. Soc. (a founder, bd. dirs. 1964-65, Compass award 1969); mem. Acoustical Soc. Am., Am. Geophys. Union, Soc. Naval Architects and Marine Engrs., Am. Phys. Soc. Home: Juniper Point Woods Hole MA 02543

VINE, RICHARD DAVID, fgn. service officer; b. N.Y.C., Dec. 10, 1925; s. George Henry and Mary (Dooley) V.; B.S., Georgetown U., 1949; M.A., Yale, 1960; m. Dawn Dieces Vessa, Sept. 27, 1947; children—Gail Joan, Michael David. Commd. officer Fgn. Service; with Dept. State, 1948-50; mem. U.S. High Commn. for Germany, Bonn, 1951-54; assigned Tel Aviv, 1954-56, Paris, 1956-59; office charge European integration affairs State Dept., 1960-63; 1st sec., Bonn, 1963-65; counselor polit. affairs U.S. Mission to European Communities, Brussels, 1965-69; counselor, dep. chief mission, Bern, Switzerland, 1969-72; dir. Office of Western Europe Affairs, Dept. State, 1972-74, dep. asst. sec. European affairs, 1974-79; U.S. ambassador to Switzerland, 1979—. Served with AUS, 1943-46. Mem. Am. Fgn. Service Assn. Address: 3602 Macomb St NW Washington DC 20016

VINEBERG, PHILIP FISCHEL, lawyer; b. Mattawa, Ont., Can., July 21, 1914; s. Malcolm and Rebecca (Phillips) V.; B.A., McGill U., 1935, M.A., 1936, B.C.L., 1939; postgrad. Ecole Libre des Scis. Politiques, Paris, France, 1935-36; m. Miriam S. Schachter, Dec. 19, 1939; children—Robert S., Michael D. Called to bar, Que., 1939, since practiced in Montreal; mem. firm Phillips & Vineberg, 1939—; appointed Queen's Counsel, 1959; lectr. econs. Sir George Williams Coll., 1936-39; lectr. econs. McGill U., 1939, asst. dir. Sch. Commerce, 1940, sec. B.Com. Advisory Com., 1942-47, asst. prof. econs. and polit. scis. Faculty Arts, 1941-46, prof. comml. law Sch. Commerce, 1945-56, lectr. co. law Law Faculty, 1956-68; lectr. U. Montreal, U. Toronto, Queens U., Laval U., N.Y.U.; econ. cons. Canadian War Time Prices and Trade Bd., 1945; mem. consultative com. Que. Dept. Revenue. Mem. Ry. Conciliation Bd., 1958, 60; v.p. Canadian Friends of Alliance Israelite Universelle; trustee Jewish Gen. Hosp., Canadian Inst. Research Pub. Policy; chmn. bd. govs. Canadian Tax Found., 1966-67; bd. govs. YMHA; pres. fellows Found. for Legal Research in Can., 1973-76. Fellow Brandeis U., Bar-Ilan U., U.S. Coll. Trial Lawyers. Apptd. officer Order of Canada, 1974. Mem. Canadian Bar Assn. (pres. Que. br. 1973-74, nat. exec. com. 1974-75), Bar Province Que. (vice chmn. 1969-70), Bar of Montreal (batonnier 1969-70), Internat. Fiscal Assn. (pres. Canadian br. 1974-76; internat. exec.). Author: The French Franc and the Gold Standard, 1936. Contbr. chpts. to Money Credit and Banking, 1940, Studies in Canadian Company Law, 1968; contbg. editor Prentice Hall Income Taxation in Canada. Contbr. articles to profl. jours. Home: 32 Summit Crescent Westmount PQ H3Y 1L3 Canada Office: 1 Place Ville Marie Montreal PQ H3B 4A7 Canada

VINER, ARTHUR WILLIAM, real estate investment co. exec.; b. Chgo., Apr. 22, 1922; s. Jacob and Frances Viola (Klein) V.; S.B., Harvard U., 1942; m. Ann Welch, Aug. 2, 1947; 1 son, William Babcock. Security analyst G.H. Walker & Co., N.Y.C., 1946-48; mem. research staff Com. for Econ. Devel., Washington, 1948-54; nat. exec. sec. Voluntary Home Mortgage Credit Program, Washington, 1954-56; pres., chief exec. officer, dir. Investors Central Mgmt. Corp., N.Y.C., 1956—; mng. trustee ICM Realty, N.Y.C., 1968—; dir. ICM Cons., Inc. Served with USCGR, 1942-46. Mem. Nat. Assn. Real Estate Investment Trusts (past pres.), Mortgage Bankers Assn. Am., Nat. Assn. Realtors. Republican. Clubs: Union League, Harvard, New Canaan Field. Home: 109 Rosebrook Rd New Canaan CT 06840 Office: 600 3d Ave New York City NY 10016

VINES, DWIGHT DELBERT, univ. pres.; b. Jonesboro, La., Sept. 27, 1931; s. Dwight N. and Bessie (Barlow) V.; student Fla. State U., 1950-51; B.S., Northwestern State Coll., 1957; M.B.A., La. State U., 1958; D.B.A., U. Colo., 1966; m. Frances Imogene Varnado, June 4, 1956; children—Michael Allan, Timothy Wayne, David Ray. Sales rep. Burroughs Corp., Shreveport, La., 1956-57; instr., asst. prof. NE La. State Coll. (now NE La. State U.), Monroe, 1958-63, asso. prof. mgmt., 1964-69, dean Sch. Bus., 1964-69, prof., dean Sch. Bus. Adminstrn., 1969-75, pres. univ., 1975—; cons., 1960—. Served with USAF, 1950-55. Mem. Southwest Acad. Mgmt., Omicron Delta Kappa, Delta Sigma Pi, Pi Sigma Epsilon, Phi Kappa Phi, Sigma Iota Epsilon, Beta Gamma Sigma, Pi Omega Pi, Pi Kappa Delta. Home: 221 Bayou Dr Monroe LA 71203 Office: 700 University Ave NE La State U Monroe LA 71209

VINEYARD, GEORGE HOAGLAND, lab. adminstr.; b. St. Joseph, Mo., Apr. 28, 1920; s. George Hoagland and Mildred M. (Barkley) V.; B.S., Mass. Inst. Tech., 1941, Ph.D., 1943; Sc.D., L.I. U., 1977; m. Phyllis Ainsworth Smith, Feb. 3, 1945; children—John H., Barbara Gale. Mem. staff Radiation Lab., Mass. Inst. Tech., 1943-45; mem. faculty U. Mo., Columbia, 1946-54, prof., 1952-54; mem. staff Brookhaven Nat. Lab., Upton, N.Y., 1954—, sr. physicist, 1960—, chmn. dept. physics, 1961-66, dep. dir. lab., 1966-72, dir. lab., 1973—; cons. to govt. and industry; fellow Poly. Inst. N.Y., 1978—; mem. vis. com. materials Sci. Center, Cornell U., 1964-67, dept. physics Mass. Inst. Tech., 1969-73; mem. sci. and ednl. adv. com. Lawrence Berkeley Lab., U. Calif., 1977-81; adv. com. Nat. Magnet Lab., 1963-67; adv. com. math. and phys. scis. NSF, 1966-71, chmn., 1971; mem. sci. policy bd. Stanford Synchotron Radiation Project, 1977—; mem. solid state scis. panel NRC, 1954—, chmn., 1965-71, chmn. solid state scis. com., 1970-72; chmn. panel condensed matter, physics survey com. Nat. Acad. Scis., 1969-72; mem. materials research council ARPA, 1967—; mem. Sec. State ad hoc com. U.S. participation IAEA, 1970-72. Bd. dirs. L.I. Action Com., 1979—. Recipient award distinguished contbns. to higher edn. Stony Brook Found., 1975. Fellow Am. Acad. Arts and Scis., Am. Phys. Soc. (chmn. div. solid state physics 1972-73, councillor at large 1974-78); mem. AAAS, L.I. Assn. Commerce and Industry (dir. 1975-78), Sigma Xi. Co-editor: (series) Documents in Modern Physics, 1964-78; bd. asso. editors Am. Jour. Physics, 1948-50, Phys. Rev., 1959-61; bd. editors Physics, 1964-68, Jour. Computational Physics, 1966-70, Physics and Chemistry of Liquids, 1968—. Research on theory X-ray and neutron scattering; microwave devices; solid state; radiation damage; lattice defects; structure of liquids. Home: 10 Brewster Ln Bellport NY 11713 Office: Brookhaven Nat Lab Upton NY 11973

VINING, ELIZABETH GRAY, author; b. Phila., Oct. 6, 1902; d. John Gordon and Anne (Iszard) Gray; A.B., Bryn Mawr Coll., 1923; M.S. in L.S., Drexel Inst. Tech., 1926, Litt.D., 1951; Litt.D., Tufts Coll., 1952, Douglas Coll., 1953, Women's Med. Coll. Phila., 1953, Lafayette Coll., 1956; L.H.D., Russell Sage Coll., 1952, Haverford Coll., 1958, Western Coll. Women, 1959, Cedar Crest Coll., 1959, Moravian Coll., 1961, Wilmington Coll., 1962, Internat. Christian U., Tokyo, Japan, 1966; D.Ed., R.I. Coll. Edn., 1956; m. Morgan Fisher Vining, Jan 31, 1929 (dec. 1933). Tutor to Crown Prince of Japan, 1946-50; vice pres. bd. trustees Bryn Mawr Coll., 1952-71, vice chmn. bd. dirs., 1952-71. Decorated 3d Order Sacred Crown (Japan), 1950; recipient Skinner award Women's Nat. Book Assn., 1954. Mem. P.E.N. Club. Author: Windows for the Crown Prince, 1952; The World in Tune, 1954; The Virginia Exiles, 1955; Friend of Life,; The Biography of Rufus M. Jones, 1958; Return to Japan, 1960; Take Heed of Loving Me, 1964; Flora: A Biography, 1966; also I. Roberta, 1969; Quiet Pilgrimage, 1970; The Taken Girl, 1973; Mr. Whittier, 1974; Being Seventy: The Measure of a Year, 1978; also 14 juveniles under name Elizabeth Janet Gray, including Penn, 1938; Adam of the Road (John Newbery medal 1943), 1942, The Cheerful Heart, 1959. Address: Kendal at Longwood Box 194 Kennett Square PA 19348

VINING, LEO CHARLES, biologist; b. Whangarei, N.Z., Mar. 28, 1925; came to Can., 1955, naturalized, 1970; s. Charles Hildrup and Ruby Robina (Withers) V.; B.Sc., Auckland (N.Z.) U., 1947, M.Sc., 1948; Ph.D., Cambridge (Eng.) U., 1951; m. Norma Marie Krimmel, Aug. 22, 1953; children—Robert, Michael, Deborah, Russell. Instr., Rutgers U., 1954-55; research officer prairie regional lab. NRC Can., Saskatoon, Sask., 1955-62, head chem. biology sect. Atlantic regional lab., Halifax, N.S., 1962-71; prof. biology Dalhousie U., Halifax, 1971—. Served with Royal N.Z. Navy, 1943-46. 1851 Exhbn. scholar, 1949-52; Merck Sharp & Dohme lectr., 1965. Fellow Royal Soc. Can.; mem. Can. Soc. Microbiologists (award 1976), Chem. Inst. Can. (dir. 1972-77), Chem. Soc. (London), Am. Soc. Microbiology, AAAS, N.S. Inst. Sci. Contbr. numerous articles in chemistry, biochemistry and microbiology, especially on antibiotics, to profl. jours.; asso. editor Jour. Antibiotics, 1968—. Home: 5780 Ogilvie St Halifax NS B3H 1C2 Canada Office: Biology Dept Dalhousie U Halifax NS B3H 4J1 Canada

VINING, RICHARD ALFRED, automobile mfg. co. exec.; b. Detroit, Jan. 29, 1925; s. Merritt Alfred and Marian Monica (Armstrong) V.; B.S. in Mech. Engring., Purdue U., 1948; M.S. in Automobile Engring., Chrysler Inst., 1950; m. LaVohn Teckla Coleman, Aug. 21, 1948; children—R. Burce, Thomas, Paul, Gregg. With Chrysler Corp., Detroit, 1948—, group v.p. engring., product devel. and purchasing, 1976-77, exec. v.p. engring., product devel. and purchasing, 1977-78, exec. v.p. mfg. and purchasing, 1978—, also dir. Mem. Evansville (Ind.) Philharmonic Orch., 1940-42; elder Emmanuel Ch., Royal Oak, Mich., 1956-62, pres., 1961; trustee Birmingham (Mich.) Congregational Ch., United Ch. Christ, 1965-68, 75-76, moderator, 1971-72; nat. chmn. 17/76 Achievement Fund, United Ch. Christ, 1972-78; div. chmn. Detroit United Fund. Fund, 1972, indsl. unit chmn., 1975; chmn. Meadow Brook Fin. com. Oakland U., Rochester, Mich., 1972-78; chmn. Meadow Brook Music Festival and Theatre, 1978; bd. dirs. Nat. Minority Purchasing Council, 1978. Served as ensign USNR, 1943-45. Research fellow Purdue U., 1947-48, recipient Distinguished Engring. Alumnus award, 1975. Registered profl. engr., Ind. Mem. Soc. Automotive Engrs., Detroit Engring. Soc., Am. Inst. Indsl. Engrs., Greater Detroit Bd. Commerce, Purdue U. Alumni Assn., Detroit Econ. Club, Tau Beta Pi, Pi Tau Sigma, Delta Tau Delta. Clubs: Detroit Athletic; Bloomfield Hills (Mich.) Country. Address: PO Box 1919 Detroit MI 48288

VINK, PIETER CAREL, mfg. co. exec.; b. Eindhoven, Holland, Sept. 18, 1919; s. Hermanus and Catherina (Pellekaan) V.; grad. Lorenz Lyceum, Eindhoven, 1937; m. Thea Fluijt, June 7, 1945. With N.Am. Philips Corp., or subsidiary companies, 1939—, gen. mgr. Philips South Africa, chmn. mng. dir. operations Iran, India, Australia, 1948-65, pres. N.Am. Philips Co., 1965-69; pres. N.Am. Philips Corp., N.Y.C., 1969-78, chmn. chief exec. officer, 1978—, also dir.; dir. PEPI, Inc. Served with Brit. Army, 1944-45. Decorated Order Brit. Empire. Mem. Newcomen Soc. N.Am. Clubs: Stanwich (Greenwich, Conn.); Indian Harbor Yacht (Greenwich, Conn.); Blind Brook (Port Chester, N.Y.); Economic, Sky (N.Y.C.) Office: North America Philips Corp 100 E 42d St New York NY 10017*

VINOGRADE, BERNARD, educator, mathematician; b. Chgo., May 7, 1915; s. James and Rose (Epstein) V.; B.S., Coll. City N.Y., 1937; M.A., U. Mich., 1940; Ph.D., 1942; m. Ann Costikyan, Dec. 30, 1942; children—Polly Jean, Peter James, Alice, Barbara. Instr., U. Wis., 1942-44, Tulane U., 1944-45; mem. staff radiation lab. Mass. Inst. Tech., 1945; mem. faculty Iowa State U., Ames, 1946—, Distinguished prof. math., 1955—, chmn. dept., 1960-64; vis. prof. San Diego State Coll., 1959-60, Coll. City N.Y., 1964-65; spl. research in fields, rings and algebras; ops. analyst standby unit USAF, 1951—. Mem. Math. Assn. Am. (gov. 1957-59); Am. Math. Soc., AAUP. Author: Linear and Matrix Algebra, 1967; co-author Laplace Transform, 1959; Inseparable Extension Fields, 1970. Home: 1206 Michigan Ave Ames IA 50010

VINSON, BAILIE WALSH, oil exec.; b. Trinidad, Colo., Aug. 11, 1897; s. Bailie Cowan and Jenny (Walsh) V.; B.S. in Mech. Engring., U. Okla., 1921; m. Jewel E. Dougherty, Jan. 31, 1922; children—Marilyn (Mrs. Basil Georges), Jeanne (Mrs. Donald L. Brawner), Susie (dec. wife Baron Henri de la Bouillerie). Sales engring. Vinson Supply Co., Tulsa, 1922-25; founder Vinson Supply Co., 1925, pres., 1925—; chmn. bd. Vinson Investment Co., 1961—; founder Exploration Drilling Co., 1943, mng. partner, 1943-53, pres., 1954-58; dir. The First Nat. Bank & Trust Co. of Tulsa. Treas., Okla. State Republican Com., 1946-48, state finance chmn., 1946-49; mem. Rep. Nat. Com. for Okla., 1949-56, mem. arrangement com., chmn. housing com., 1952; regional vice chmn. Rep. Nat. Finance Com. Trustee Holland Hall Sch., Tulsa; dir. Gilcrease Inst. Am. History and Art, Tulsa; initial trustee of Robert A. Taft Meml. Found., Inc. Served as seaman USNRF, 1917-18. Mem. Tulsa C. of C. (dir. 1938-48), Southwestern Art Assn. (dir., 1942-50, v.p., 1948-50), Sigma Alpha Epsilon. Clubs: Tulsa, So. Hills Country (Tulsa); Eldorado Country (Palm Desert). Home: 2300 Riverside Dr Tulsa OK 74114 Office: 1st Nat Bldg Tulsa OK 74103

VINSON, FRED MOORE, JR., lawyer; b. Louisa, Ky., Apr. 3, 1925; s. Fred Moore and Roberta (Dixon) V.; A.B., Washington and Lee U., 1948, LL.B., 1951, LL.D. (hon.), 1968; m. Nell P. Morrison, Jan. 15, 1955; children—Fred Moore III, Carolyn. Admitted to D.C. bar 1951; partner firm Reasoner, Davis & Vinson, Washington, 1963-65, 69—; asst. atty. gen. criminal div. Dept. Justice 1965-69; dir. Lockheed Aircraft Corp., 1971—. Chmn. com. law and legislation D.C. Bd. Trade, 1964-65; mem. Jud. Conf. D.C. Circuit, 1960—, Adminstrv. Conf. U.S., 1963-65; gen. counsel Inaugural Com., 1961; chmn. com. admissions and grievances U.S. Ct. Appeals, D.C. Circuit, 1974-78; chmn. inquiry com. D.C. Bar, 1973-75, gov., 1975-78. Chmn. bd. trustees D.C. Pub. Defender Service, 1976-78. Served with USAAF, 1943-46. Mem. Am. Bar Assn. (ho. dels. 1971-74), Bar Assn. D.C. (pres. 1971-72), Phi Beta Kappa, Omicron Delta Kappa. Home: 5310 Carvel Rd Washington DC 20016 Office: 800 17th St NW Washington DC 20006

VINSON, JACK ROGER, mech. engr., educator; b. Kansas City, Mo., Nov. 10, 1929; s. Harry Roger and Myrtle (Kiple) V.; student Kansas City Jr. Coll., 1946-47; B.M.E., Cornell U., 1952; postgrad. Cambridge (Eng.) U., 1952-53; Ph.D., U. Pa., 1961; m. Gertrude Hovey, June 11, 1955 (dec. 1977); children—Jack Roger, Stephen Scott, Jeffrey Alan, Christopher Lee. Engr. analytical methods and materials Gen. Electric Co., Phila., 1956-61; v.p., sr. scientist Dyna/Structures, Cons., Phila., 1961-64; prof., chmn. mech. and aerospace engring. U. Del., Newark, 1964-79, H. Fletcher Brown prof. mech. and aerospace engring., 1979—; partner, Structural Mechanics Assos., Cons., Narberth, Pa. Recipient ONR-Am. Inst. Aeros. and Astronautics award, 1978. Served to 1st lt. USAF, 1954-56. Research grantee NSF, 1965-72, Air Force, 1969-78, Naval Civil Engring. Lab., 1970-72, Army Research Office, Durham, 1974-75, Office Naval Research, 1978, NASA, 1978. Rotary Internat. Found. fellow, 1952-53. Asso. fellow Am. Inst. Aeros. and Astronautics; mem. ASME (chmn. structures and materials nat. com. 1976-77; mem. exec. com. aerospace div. 1975—, chm. exec. com. 1979-80), Am. Acad. Mechanics, Am. Soc. Engring. Edn., Sigma Xi, Tau Beta Pi, Pi Tau Sigma. Episcopalian. Author: Structural Mechanics: The Behavior of Plates and Shells, 1974; (with T.W. Chou) Composite Materials and Their Use in Structures, 1975; also research articles. Home: 229 Cheltenham Rd Newark DE 19711

VINTON, BOBBY (STANLEY ROBERT), entertainer; b. Canonsburg, Pa., Apr. 16; s. Stanley and Dorothy (Studzenski) V.; student Duquesne U., Pitts.; m. Dolly Dobbin, Dec. 17, 1962; children—Robert, Kristin, Christopher, Jennifer, Rebecca. Leader own band, singer, night club entertainer; appearances on TV in Bobby Vinton Show, 1975—, also numerous guest appearances; single Gold records include Roses Are Red, Blue on Blue, Blue Velvet, Mr. Lonely, I Love How You Love Me, My Melody of Love; rec. artist Epic; dramatic roles in films Surf Party, Big Jake, 1971, The Train Robbers, 1973, also on TV; owner Tapestry Record Co., Feather Music Publishing Co., Acacia Music Pub. Co.; partner Vinton-Klein Film Prodn. Co. Served with U.S. Army. Named Number One Male Vocalist, Cash Box mag., 1965; Most Played Rec. Artist, Billboard mag., 1965; author: (autobiography) Polish Prince. Address: PO Box 49690 Los Angeles CA 90049

VIOLA, ALFRED, educator; b. Vienna, Austria, July 8, 1928; s. Isidore and Grete (Broch) V.; B.A., Johns Hopkins, 1949, M.A., 1950; Ph.D., U. Md., 1955; m. Joy Darlene Winke, Oct. 19, 1963. Research asso. Boston U., 1955-57, vis. lectr., 1956-57; asst. prof. chemistry Northeastern U., Boston, 1957-62, asso. prof., 1962-68, prof., 1968—; vis. prof. U. Munich, 1977. Mem. Am. Chem. Soc., Sigma Xi (pres. chpt. 1967-68). Contbr. articles to profl. jours. Home: 14 Glover Rd Wayland MA 01778 Office: Dept Chemistry Northeastern U Boston MA 02115

VIOLA, HERMAN JOSEPH, museum ofcl.; b. Chgo., Feb. 24, 1938; s. Joseph and Mary (Incollingo) V.; B.A., Marquette U., 1960, M.A., 1964; Ph.D., Ind. U., 1970; m. Susan Patricia Bennett, June 13, 1964; children—Joseph, Paul, Peter. Founding editor Prologue: Jour. of Nat. Archives, 1969-72; dir. nat. anthropol. archives Smithsonian Instn., Washington, 1972—. Served with USNR, 1960-62. Mem. Orgn. Am. Historians, Western History Assn., Am. Hist. Assn., Soc. Am. Archivists (program chmn. 1972). Author: Thomas L. McKenney, Architect of America's Early Indian Policy, 1816-1830, 1974; The Indian Legacy of Charles Bird King, 1976. Home: 7307 Pinewood St Falls Church VA 22046 Office: Nat Anthropological Archives Smithsonian Instn Washington DC 20560

VIORST, MILTON, writer; b. Paterson, N.J., Feb. 18, 1930; s. Louis and Betty (LeVine) V.; B.A. summa cum laude, Rutgers U., 1951; student (Fulbright scholar) U. Lyon (France), 1952; M.A., Harvard U., 1955; M.S., Columbia U., 1956; m. Judith Stahl, Jan. 30, 1960; children—Anthony, Nicholas, Alexander. Reporter, Bergen (N.J.) Record, 1955-56, Newark StarLedger, 1956-57, Washington Post, 1957-61; Washington corr. N.Y. Post, 1961-64; syndicated columnist Washington Evening Star, 1971-75. Chmn. Fund for Investigative Journalism, 1969-78; bd. dirs. Georgetown Day Sch., 1977—. Served as officer USAF, 1952-54. Woodrow Wilson sr. fellow, 1975—; Alicia Patterson fellow, 1979. Author: Hostile Allies: FDR and deGaulle, 1965; Great Documents of Western Civilization, 1965; Fall from Grace: The Republican Party and the Puritan Ethic, 1968; Hustlers and Heroes, 1971; Fire in the Streets: America in the 1960's, 1980; also articles. Address: 3432 Ashley Terr NW Washington DC 20008

VIPOND, DAVID SPRUKS, bank exec.; b. Scranton, Pa., July 3, 1909; s. Jonathan and Daisy Mildred (Wardell) V.; grad. Phillips Acad., 1927; B.A., Williams Coll., 1931; m. Florence Victoria Neumann, Oct. 3, 1942; children—Jonathan III, James M., Linda Ann, David W. With Scranton Tobacco Co., 1931-65, v.p., 1945-54, pres., 1954-65; chmn. bd. 3d Nat. Bank & Trust Co., Scranton, 1966—; dir. Anthracite Bridge Co., Scranton, Parco Fin. & Investment Co., Scranton, Scranton-Lackawanna Indsl. Bldg. Co., Lackawanna Indsl. Fund Enterprise. Bd. dirs. Lackawanna United Fund, 1953-60, Clarks Summit-Abington Sch. Dist., 1955-64, Health and Hosp. Planning Council N.E. Pa., 1967-76, Econ. Devel. Council N.E. Pa., 1971—, Philharmonic Orch. N.E. Pa., 1971—; trustee Keystone Jr. Coll., La Plume, Pa., 1949—. Named to Tobacco Industry Hall of Fame, 1963. Mem. Nat. Assn. Tobacco Distbrs. (chmn. 1963-64, dir. 1954-64), Scranton C. of C. (dir. 1959—), Phi Beta Kappa. Republican. Presbyn. Clubs: Country Scranton, Scranton; Williams (N.Y.C.); Waverly Country. Home: Waverly PA 18471 Office: 120 Wyoming Ave Scranton PA 18503

VIRDON, WILLIAM CHARLES, baseball mgr.; b. Hazel Park, Mich., June 9, 1931; s. Charles Neles and Bertha Mae (Marley) V.; student Drury Coll., Springfield, Mo.; m. Shirley Levern Shemwell, Nov. 17, 1951; children—Lisa Lee, Linda Sue Virdon Holmes, Deborah Ann (Mrs. Mark Miller). Baseball player St. Louis Cardinals, 1955-56, Pitts. Pirates, 1956-65; coach Pitts. Pirates, 1968-71, mgr., 1972-73; mgr. N.Y. Yankees, 1974-75, Houston Astros, 1975—. Named Nat. League Rookie of Yr., 1955; Major League Mgr. of Yr., 1974; Nat. League Mgr. of Yr., UPI, 1979. Clubs: Masons, Shriners, Lions. Office: Astrodome PO Box 288 Houston TX 77001

VIRGO, JULIE ANNE CARROLL, assn. exec.; b. Adelaide, South Australia, Australia, June 14, 1944; came to U.S., 1966; d. Archibald Henry and Norma Mae (Gillett) Noolan; M.A., U. Chgo., 1968, Ph.D., 1974; m. Daniel Thuering Carroll, Aug. 20, 1977. With State Library of South Australia, 1960-62, Repatriation Dept. South Australia, 1962-66; asst. librarian U. Chgo. Libraries, 1966-67; dir. edn. Med. Library Assn., Chgo., 1972-77; exec. dir. Assn. Coll. and

Research Libraries, Chgo., 1977—; mem. faculty U. Chgo., 1968—; dir. Continuing Library Edn. Network and Exchange. U. Chgo. fellow, 1967-68; Higher Edn. Act fellow, 1969-72; Nat. Library of Medicine trainee, 1968-69. Mem. ALA, Am. Soc. Assn. Execs., Am. Mgmt. Assn., Assn. Am. Library Schs., Spl. Libraries Assn., AAAS, Am. Soc. for Info. Scis. (doctoral award), Beta Phi Mu. Author: Continuing Education: Needs Assessment and Model Programs; contbr. articles to jours. Home: 900 Private Rd Winnetka IL 60093 Office: Assn Coll and Research Libraries 50 E Huron St Chicago IL 60611

VIRTUE, JOHN FRANCIS, journalist; b. Nelson, B.C., Can., Sept. 7, 1934; s. Abner C. and Edna E. (Coles) V.; came to U.S., 1962; B.J., Carleton U., Ottawa, Can., 1957; m. Anna Leduc, Nov. 10, 1956; 1 son, Mark David. With UPI, 1957—, mgr., Venezuela and Netherlands Antilles, 1970-75, mgr., No. div. Latin Am., 1975—. Home: Arrayanes 12 Secc Mirador Jardines de San Mateo Naucalpan Estado de Mexico Mexico Office: Apartado 91-Bis Mexico 1 DF Mexico

VIRZI, RICHARD A., metals distbn. exec.; b. Oak Park, Ill., Sept. 19, 1927; s. Al and Lee (Lamantia) V.; student U. Ill., 1948-50, Northwestern U., 1952; m. Winifred Ann Burke, Sept. 15, 1951; children—Richard A., Diane Marie, Peggy Ann, Robert J. Office mgr. H.D. Hudson Mfg., 1949-60; mgr. systems Dynalectron Co., 1960-63; v.p., sec. A.M. Castle & Co., Franklin Park, Ill., 1963-72, exec. v.p., dir., 1972-77, pres., chief exec. officer, 1977—. Served with AUS, 1946-48. Mem. Chgo. Assn. Commerce and Industry, Steel Service Center Inst., Nat. Assn. Aluminum Distbrs. (v.p., dir.). Home: 354 May St Elmhurst IL 60126 Office: 3400 N Wolf Rd Franklin Park IL 60131

VISCARDI, HENRY, JR., business exec.; b. N.Y.C., May 10, 1912; s. Henry and Anna (Esposito) V.; student Fordham U., 1930-33, LL.D. (hon.), 1954; law student St. John's U., 1933-36; LL.D. (hon.), L.I. U., 1956; L.H.D., Manhattanville Coll. Sacred Heart, 1958, Hofstra U., Ohio U., 1968, U. Bridgeport, 1970, Pfeiffer Coll., 1972; Sc.D., Clarkson Coll. Tech., 1966; Litt.D., Sung Kyun Kwan U., Seoul, Korea, 1966; m. Lucile Darracq, Nov. 16, 1946; children—Nina (Mrs. Brian Sharkey), Donna (Mrs. Patrick Shooltz), Lydia (Mrs. James Weisman), Lucille. Supr. taxation division of HOLC, 1933-42; field service officer, amputee rehab. ARC, 1942-43; spl. cons., adviser on employment disabled vets. to Surgeon Gen., USAF, also to dir. WPB, 1943-45; asst. dir., spl. events and sports MBS, N.Y.C., 1945-47; dir. personnel adminstrn. Burlington Mills, Inc., N.Y.C., 1947-49; exec. dir. Just One Break, Inc., Bellevue Hosp., N.Y.C., 1949, now exec. v.p. and mem. bd.; founder, trustee Abilities, Inc., Albertson, New York, 1942—; pres., chmn. of Human Resources Center, 1955—; asst. prof. clin. phys. medicine and rehab. N.Y. U. Coll. Medicine; faculty Inst. Phys. Medicine and Rehab., N.Y.C.; dir. Rosyln Savs. Bank, Ins. Co. N.Am., Old No. Co., Ltd., Life Ins. Co. N.Y. Mem. task force com. on utilization of handicapped ODM; appt. nat. adv. council HEW, dir. vocat. rehab., 1954; mem. N.Y. State Commr.'s Adv. Council for Children with Handicapped Children; mem. Pres.'s Task Force on Problems Physically Handicapped; exec. dir. MEND Inst.; chmn. White House Conf. Handicapped Individuals, 1975-76. Recipient of the Presidential Citation, 1954; recipient of the citation for outstanding service AMA, 1957; Gold Knight of Mgmt. award Nat. Mgmt. Assn., 1958; Internat. Humanity Service award Am. Overseas Assn., 1964. Mem. Nat. Rehabilitation Assn. Co-recipient (with Bernard M. Baruch) of Outstanding Citizen of the Year award by Jr. O.U.A.M., 1953; recipient Achievement in Rehab. award, 1962; Petrean medal St. Peter's Coll., 1962; Hofstra U. Edn. award, 1965; Theodore Roosevelt medal, 1966; Silver medal of the City of Paris (France), 1966; Medal Japan Gov. Tokyo, 1966; distinguished Social Service award Sophia U. Tokyo, 1966; citation Outstanding Service Sogang Coll., Seoul, Korea, 1966; Thanksgiving award Clarke Coll., Dubuque, 1964; citation Significant Contbrs. to Welfare of People. Hyde Park Lodge B'nai B'rith, 1967, Distinguished Citizen award, Dowling Coll., 1969; Rehab. award, AMVETS, 1969; Rizzuto award Unico Nat. Conv., Los Angeles, 1970; Achievement award Italian Dental Soc., 1972; Am. Exemplar medal Freedoms Found., Valley Forge, 1972; St. John Baptist de la Salle medal Manhattan Coll., 1975; James E. Allen, Jr. Meml. award for distinguished service to edn. N.Y. State Bd. Regents, 1975; Marion Mill Preminger award Pres.'s Com. Employment of the Handicapped, 1975; Pres.'s award Nat. Rehab. Assn., 1975. Benjamin Franklin fellow Royal Soc. Arts. Author: A Man's Stature, 1952; Give Us The Tools; A Laughter in the Lonely Night, 1961; A Letter to Jimmy, 1962; The School, 1964; The Abilities Story, 1967; But Not on Our Block, 1971; The Phoenix Child, 1975; also articles on utilization of disabled and overage workers in industry. Home: 305 Steamboat Rd Kings Point NY 11024 Office: Human Resources Center IU Willets Rd Albertson NY 11507

VISCUGLIA, FELIX ALFRED, musician; b. Niagara Falls, N.Y., Jan. 13, 1927; s. Felix and Josephine (Palermo) V.; Mus.B., New Eng. Conservatory Music, 1953; m. Deborah Hamilton, Nov. 16, 1974; children by previous marriage—Donna, Lisa. Clarinetist, Boston Symphony Orch., 1966—; mem. faculty New Eng. Conservatory Music, 1953—, Boston U., 1966—, Mass. Inst. Tech., 1963—; lectr.-clinician H.H. Selmer, Inc.; mem. faculty U. Nev., Las Vegas. Trustee New Eng. Conservatory Music. Served with USMCR, 1944-46. Mem. Alumni Assn. New Eng. Conservatory Music (pres. 1968-70), Pi Kappa Lambda. Home: PO Box 251 Henderson NV 89015 Office: Music Dept U Nev Las Vegas Maryland Pkwy Las Vegas NV

VISEK, WILLARD JAMES, scientist, educator; b. Sargent, Nebr., Sept. 19, 1922; s. James and Anna S. (Dworak) V.; B.Sc. with honors (Carl R. Gray scholar), U. Nebr., 1947; M.S.C. (Smith fellow in agr.), Cornell U., 1949, Ph.D., 1951; M.D. (Peter Yost Fund scholar), U. Chgo., 1957; m. Priscilla Flagg, Dec. 28, 1949; children—Dianna, Madeleine, Clayton Paul. Grad. asst., lab. animal nutrition Cornell U., 1947-51; AEC postdoctoral fellow, Oak Ridge, 1951-52, research asso., 1952-53; research asst. pharmacology U. Chgo., 1953-57, asst. prof., 1957-61, asso. prof., 1961-64; rotating med. intern U. Chgo. Clinics, 1957-58, 58-59, 59; prof. nutrition and comparative metabolism, dept. animal sci. Cornell U., Ithaca, N.Y., after 1964, mem. subcom. teratology Commn. Drug Safety, 1963; prof. clin. sci. (nutrition and metabolism) Sch. Basic. Med. Scis. and dept. food sci. U. Ill. at Urbana-Champaign, 1975—, prof. clin. sci. (nutrition) Sch. Clin. Medicine, 1978—; subcom. dog nutrition, com. animal nutrition NRC-Nat. Acad. Sci., 1965-71, adv. council Inst. Lab. Animal Resources, 1966-69; sub-com. animal care facilities Survey Inst. Lab. Animal Resources, 1967-70; cons., lectr. in field; mem. sci. adv. com. diet and nutrition cancer program Nat. Cancer Inst., 1976—; mem. nutrition study sect. NIH, 1980—; chmn. membership com. Am. Inst. Nutrition-Am. Soc. Clin. Nutrition, 1977-79; cons. VA, NSF, indsl. orgns. Nat. Cancer Inst. spl. fellow Mass. Inst. Tech., research fellow Mass. Gen. Hosp., 1970-71. Active local Boy Scouts Am. Served with AUS, 1943-46. Recipient Alumni award Neb. 4-H, 1967. Diplomate Nat. Bd. Med. Examiners, 1960. Mem. Am. Soc. Animal Sci. (chmn. subcom. antimicrobials, mem. regulatory agency com. 1973—), AAAS, Soc. Pharmacology and Exptl. Therapeutics, Am. Inst. Nutrition, Soc. Exptl. Biology and Medicine, Am. Soc. Clin. Nutrition, Am. Therapeutic Soc., Am. Gastroenterol. Assn., Am. Bd. Clin. Nutrition, Innocents Soc., Gamma Alpha (pres. 1948-49), Phi Kappa Phi, Alpha Gamma Rho (pres. 1946-47), Gamma Sigma Delta. Presbyterian (elder). Mason. Contbr. articles to profl. jours.; editorial bd. Jour. Nutrition, 1980—. Home: 1405 W William St Champaign IL 61820

VISGILIO, GEORGE RAYMOND, JR., food co. exec.; b. Westerly, R.I., Feb. 17, 1942; s. George Raymond and Mildred B. V.; B.A. in Internat. Relations cum laude, Lehigh U., 1963; M.B.A. in Fin. cum laude, U. Chgo., 1968; m. Linda Ellen Bach, June 15, 1963; children—Amy N., Jennifer A., Christopher G. Trainee customer service Inland Steel Co., Chgo., 1963-64, asst. mgr. sales div., 1967-69; with Ogden Corp., 1969—, dir. corp. planning, N.Y.C., 1974-76, pres. subs. Ogden Food Products Corp., Stockton, Calif., 1976—, and div. Tillie Lewis Foods, Stockton, 1978—, dir. sub. Ramirez & Feraud Inc., 1978—. Mem. Nat. Food Processors Assn. (dir.), Psi Upsilon. Office: Drawer J Stockton CA 95201

VISHNEVSKAYA, GALINA PAVLOVNA, soprano; b. Leningrad, USSR, Oct. 25, 1926; married; children—Ogla, Elena. Soprano, Bolshoi Opera, Moscow, to 1974; appeared throughout Europe, U.S., S. Am., including: Covent Garden, Paris Opera; also appears in concerts, recitals throughout the world. Recipient Lenin prize of USSR. Mem. Sigma Alpha Iota. Russian Orthodox. Office: care Columbia Artists Mgmt Inc 165 W 57th St New York NY 10019

VISICH, MARIAN, JR., educator; b. Bklyn., Jan. 8, 1930; s. Marian and Emily (Jonas) V.; B.Aero. Engring., Bklyn. Poly. Inst., 1951, M.Aero. Engring., 1953, Ph.D., 1955; m. Carol Susa, May 2, 1959; children—Michael, Carol Ann, Gregory William. Mem. faculty Bklyn. Poly. Inst., 1951-74, prof. aerospace engring. and applied mechanics, 1965-74; prof. engring. State U. N.Y. at Stony Brook, 1974—, chmn. program tech. and soc., 1976-77, asso. dean engring., 1977—. Active Local Boy Scouts Am. Asso. fellow Am. Inst. Aero. and Astronautics (mem. council L.I. sect. 1964-72, treas. L.I. sect. 1967-68, sec. L.I. sect. 1968-69, chmn. sect. 1970-71; Outstanding Faculty Adviser citation L.I. sect. 1964-67); mem. Am. Soc. Engring. Edn., Sigma Xi, Sigma Gamma Tau, Tau Beta Pi. Author numerous articles in field. Home: 8 Whitehall Dr Huntington NY 11743 Office: State U NY at Stony Brook Coll Engring Stony Brook NY 11794

VISKANTA, RAYMOND, mech. engr.; b. Lithuania, July 16, 1931; s. Vincas and Genovaite (Vinickas) V.; came to U.S., 1949, naturalized, 1955; B.S. in Mech. Engring., U. Ill., 1955; M.S., Purdue U., 1956, Ph.D., 1960; m. Birute B. Barpsys, Oct. 13, 1956; children—Renata, Vitas, Tadas. Asst., then asso. mech. engr. Argonne (Ill.) Nat. Lab., 1956-62; mem. faculty Purdue U., 1962—, prof. mech. engring., 1966—; vis. prof. U. Calif., Berkeley, 1968-69; guest prof. Tech. U.. Munich, Ger., 1976-77; cons. to industry. Recipient Sr. U.S. Scientist award Alexander von Humbolt Found., Bonn, Ger., 1975. Registered profl. engr., Ill. Fellow ASME (Heat Transfer Meml. award 1976); mem. AIAA (Thermophysics award 1979), AAUP, AAAS, Sigma Xi, Pi Tau Sigma, Tau Beta Pi. Contbr. to profl. publs. Home: 123 Pawnee Dr West Lafayette IN 47906 Office: Sch Mech Engring Purdue Univ West Lafayette IN 47907

VISOTSKY, HAROLD MERYLE, educator, physician; b. Chgo., May 25, 1924; s. Joseph and Rose (Steinberg) V.; student Herzl Coll., Chgo., 1943-44, Baylor U., 1944-45, Sorbonne, 1945-46; B.S., U. Ill., 1947, M.D. magna cum laude, 1951; m. Gladys Mavrich, Dec. 18, 1955; children—Jeffrey, Robin. Intern, Cin. Gen. Hosp., 1951-52; resident U. Ill., Ill. Research and Ednl. Hosp., also Neuropsychiat. Inst., Chgo., 1952-55; asst. prof. U. Ill. Coll. Medicine, 1957-61, asso. prof. psychiatry, 1965-69, dir. psychiat. residency tng. and edn., 1955-59; prof., chmn. dept. psychiatry, dir. Psychiat. Inst., Northwestern U. Med. Sch., Chgo., 1969—; chmn. dept. psychiatry Northwestern Meml. Hosp.; sr. attending Evanston Hosp. Polio respiratory center psychiat. cons. Nat. Found. Infantile Paralysis, U. Ill., 1955-59; dir. mental health Chgo. Bd. Health div. mental health services, 1959-63; dir. Ill. Dept. Mental Health, 1959-69; examiner Am. Bd. Psychiatry and Neurology, 1964—; dir. Center Mental Health and Psychiat. Services, Am. Hosp. Assn., 1979—; mem. 1st U.S. mission on mental health to USSR, State Dept. Mission, 1967; chmn. task force V, Joint Commn. on Mental Health of Children, 1967—; mem. adv. com. on community mental health service Nat. Inst. Mental Health, 1965—; mem. profl. adv. com. Jerusalem Mental Health Center; profl. adv. group Am. Health Services, Inc.; adv. com. joint commn. accreditation hosps. Council Psychiat. Facilities; mem. spl. panel mental illness for bd. dirs. ACLU; rector Lincoln Acad. of Ill. Faculty Social Service; mem. select com. psychiat. care and evaluation HEW; mem. faculty Practising Law Inst. Trustee, Erikson Inst. Early Edn., Ill. Hosp. Assn., Mental Health Project, Washington. Served with AUS, 1942-46. Decorated D.S.C., Purple Heart, Bronze Star; recipient Edward A. Strecker award Inst. Pa. Hosp., 1969; Med. Alumnus of Year award U. Ill., 1976; Disting. Service award Chgo. chpt. Anti-Defamation League, B'nai B'rith, 1978. Fellow Am. Orthopsychiat. Assn. (dir. v.p. 1970-71, pres. 1976), Am. Psychiat. Assn. (chmn. council on mental health services 1967—, v.p. 1973-74, chmn. council nat. affairs 1975—), AAAS, Am. Coll. Psychiatrists (charter; bd. regents 1976-79, v.p. 1980), Chgo. Inst. Medicine; mem. Am. Assn. Chmn. Dept. Psychiatry, Am. Assn. Social Psychiatry (mem. council, mem. constn. com.), Council Med. Splty. Socs., AMA, Ill. Psychiat. Soc. (pres. 1965-66). Contbr. articles to psychiat. jours., chpts. psychiat. textbooks. Home: 1128 Ridge Ave Evanston IL 60202 Office: 320 E Huron St Chicago IL 60611

VISSER, JOHN EVERT, univ. pres.; b. Orange City, Iowa, Apr. 24, 1920; s. Arthur J. and Frances (TePaske) V.; B.A., Hope Coll., 1942; M.A., U. Iowa, 1947, Ph.D., 1957; Dr. Honoris Causa, Universidad Industrial de Santander, Bucaramanga, Colombia, S.Am., 1968; m. Virginia Jean Schuyler, May 29, 1946; children—Betty Jean, Mary Frances, Nancy Ann, Martha Ellen. Asst. prof. history Hope Coll., Holland, Mich., 1949-56; asst. registrar Western Mich. U., 1956-57; asst. dean Ball State U., 1957-58, exec. asst. to pres., prof. history, 1962-67; dean Grand Rapids (Mich.) Jr. Coll., 1958- 62; pres. Emporia (Kans.) State U., 1967—. Served to capt. inf. AUS, 1942-46. Mem. Nat. Assn. Intercollegiate Athletics (exec. com.), Kans. Assn. Sch. Adminstrs., Am. Assn. State Colls. and Univs. (treas. 1971-75), Kans. Assn. Colls. and Univs. (pres. 1972-73), Blue Key, Phi Delta Kappa, Phi Alpha Theta. Presbyn. Rotarian. Home: 1522 Highland St Emporia KS 66801

VISTE, GERALD DELMAR, ins. co. exec.; b. Foley, Minn., Mar. 29, 1923; s. Martin N. and Mildred E. (Schwartz) V.; A.B., Harvard U., 1947, M.B.A., 1954; m. Marion C. Muller, June 14, 1947; children—Deborah Viste Brunton, John, Nathan. With Wausau Ins. Cos., now exec. v.p., dir. Gen. campaign chmn. United Way of Marathon County, 1979; mem. Wis. Humanities Com., 1973—, chairperson, 1978-80; trustee Performing Arts Found., 1979—. Served with USAAF, 1942-45. Mem. Ins. Acctg. and Statis. Assn., Soc. Ins. Accts. Unitarian. Club: Wausau. Home: 515 McIndoe St Wausau WI 54401 Office: 2000 Westwood Dr Wausau WI 54401

VITALE, ALBERTO ALDO, paperback book pub. co. exec.; b. Vercelli, Italy, Dec. 22, 1933; s. Sergio and Elena (Segre) V.; came to U.S., 1960; Dr. Econs. and Bus. Adminstrn., U. Turin (Italy), 1956, postgrad., 1956-57; postgrad. (Fulbright scholar) Wharton Sch. Finance, U. Pa., 1957-58; m. Gemma G. Calori, Oct. 11, 1961; children—Raffaele Robert, Alessandro David. With Olivetti Corp. Am., 1959-72, dir. corp. planning, N.Y.C., 1965-69, v.p. adminstrn., 1969-70, v.p. adminstrn., treas., N.Y.C., 1970-72; prin. officer IFI, Torino, 1972-75; exec. v.p., chief operating officer Bantam Books, Inc., N.Y.C., 1975—, also dir.; dir. Transworld Pubs. Ltd. Home: 505 Alda Rd Mamaroneck NY 10543 Office: Bantam Books Inc 666 Fifth Ave New York NY 10019

VITALE, ALFRED WILLIAM, chem. co. exec.; b. N.Y.C., Nov. 19, 1926; s. George and Frances (Longo) V.; B.S. in Accounting and Finance cum laude, Bryant Coll., 1952; m. Mary M. Barabas, Sept. 19, 1958; 1 dau., Maria F. Sr. accountant Price Waterhouse & Co., C.P.A.'s, 1952-58; v.p. finance Rumrill-Hoyt, Inc., Rochester, N.Y., 1958-63; v.p. finance Cap Roc Inc., Rochester, 1966-67; v.p. finance J. Hungerford Smith Co., Victor, N.Y., 1963-66; pres. Am. Recreation Services, N.Y.C., 1968-71; sr. v.p., treas., dir. STP Corp. Ft. Lauderdale, Fla., 1971—; dir. Longman Enterprises, Inc., Fort Lauderdale. Trustee, Holy Cross Hosp., Fort Lauderdale. Served with USNR, 1945-46. C.P.A., N.Y., D.C. Mem. Am. Inst. C.P.A.'s, Ft. Lauderdale C. of C., Financial Execs. Inst., Assn. Corporate Growth. Clubs: Coral Ridge Country, Tower (Ft. Lauderdale). Office: 1400 W Commercial Blvd Ft Lauderdale FL 33300

VITEK, VACLAV, materials scientist; b. Olomouc, Czechoslovakia, Sept. 10, 1940; came to U.S., 1978; s. Josef and Ruzena V.; B.Sc. in Physics, Charles U., Prague, 1962, RNDR., 1965; Ph.D. in Physics, Czechoslovakian Acad. Scis., Prague, 1966; m. Ludovita Stankovicova, Aug. 5, 1972. Research officer SKODA Research Inst., Pilsen, Czechoslovakia, 1962-64, Inst. Physics, Czechoslovakian Acad. Scis., 1964-67; research asso. dept. metall. materials sci. and research fellow Wolfson Coll., Oxford (Eng.) U., 1967-75; research officer Central Elec. Research Labs., Central Elec. Generating Bd., Leatherhead, Eng., 1975-78; prof. materials sci. and engring. U. Pa., 1978—. Fellow Inst. Physics (London); mem. Am. Phys. Soc., Am. Metal Soc. Research on atomistic models of lattice defects and interfaces, fracture processes and mechanisms, plastic deformation. Office: Dept Materials Sci and Engring U Pa 33d and Walnut Sts Philadelphia PA 19104

VITERBI, ANDREW JAMES, corp. exec.; b. Bergamo, Italy, Mar. 9, 1935; s. Achille and Maria (Luria) V.; brought to U.S., 1939, naturalized, 1945; S.B., Mass. Inst. Tech., 1957, S.M., 1957; Ph.D., U. So. Calif., 1962; m. Erna Finci, June 15, 1958; children—Audrey, Alan, Alexander. Research group supr. C.I.T. Jet Propulsion Lab., 1957-63; mem. faculty Sch. Engring. and Applied Sci., U. Calif. at Los Angeles, 1963-73, asso. prof., 1965-69, prof., 1969-73; exec. v.p. Linkabit Corp., 1973—. Cons. sci. adv. panel U.S. Army, 1968-74; adj. prof. U. Calif., San Diego, 1975—. Recipient award for valuable contbns. to telemetry, space electronics and telemetry group IRE, 1962; best original paper award Nat. Electronics Conf., 1963; outstanding paper award, info. theory group IEEE, 1968; Christopher Columbus Internat. Communications award, 1975. Fellow IEEE (past chmn. info. theory group); mem. Nat. Acad. Engring. Author: Principles of Coherent Communication, 1966; (with J.K. Omura) Principles of Digital Communication and Coding, 1979. Mem. bd. editors Proceedings IEEE, 1968-77, Information and Control, 1967, Transactions on Information Theory, 1972-75, Home: 2712 Glenwick Pl La Jolla CA 92037 Office: Linkabit Corp 10453 Roselle St San Diego CA 92121

VITT, SAM B., advt. co. exec.; b. Greensboro, N.C., Oct. 23, 1926; s. Bruno Caesar and Gray (Bradshaw) V.; A.B., Dartmouth, 1950; m. Marie Foster, Oct. 30, 1955; children—Joanne Louise, Michael Bradshaw, Mark Thomas. Exec. asst. TV film CBS, N.Y.C., 1950-52; broadcast media buyer Benton & Bowles, Inc., N.Y.C., 1952-54; broadcast media buyer Biow Co., N.Y.C., 1954-55, asso. account exec., 1955-56; broadcast media buyer Doherty, Clifford, Steers & Shenfield, Inc., N.Y.C., 1956-57, media supr., 1958-59, v.p. media supr., 1960, v.p., asso. media dir., 1960, v.p., media dir., 1960-63, v.p. in charge media and broadcast programming, 1963-64; v.p., exec. dir. media-program Ted Bates & Co., Inc., N.Y.C., 1964-66, sr. v.p., exec. dir. media-program dept., 1966-69; dir. Advt. Info. Services, Inc., 1964-65; founder, pres. Vitt Media Internat., Inc., N.Y.C., 1969—; advt. dir. Banking Law Jour., 1955-69; lectr. in field, 1967—; lectr. advt. media N.Y. U., 1973, 74, Am. Mgmt. Assn., 1974, 75, Assn. Nat. Advertisers, 1967, 69, 70, Advt. Age Media Workshop, 1975. Dir. N.Y.C. Comml. Devel. Corp., 1966-69; mem. com. Nat. UN Day Com., 1973, vice chmn., 1974, asso. chmn., 1975, co-chmn., 1976-77; bd. dirs. UN Assn. Am., 1977; chmn. radio-TV reps. div. Greater N.Y. Fund, 1962, chmn. consumer pub. div., 1963. Bd. govs. N.Y. Young Republican Club, 1957-58, editor Directory, 1956-57. Recipient Media award sta. WRAP, Norfolk, Va., 1962, award of Merit, Greater N.Y. Fund, 1963, Gold Key Advt. Leadership award Sta. Reps. Assn., 1967, ann. honors Ad Daily, 1967, certificate of merit Media/Scope, 1967, 69; named one of 10 Best Dressed Men of Advt. Community, Gentlemen's Quar., 1979. Mem. Am. Assn. Advt. Agys. (broadcast media com. corr. 1958-63, media operating com. on consumer mags. 1964-65), Internat. Radio and TV Soc. (timebuying and selling seminar com. 1961-62), Internat. Radio and TV Found. (faculty seminar 1974), Nat. Acad. Arts Sci., Media Dirs. Council, Sigma Alpha Epsilon. Clubs: Manor Park Beach (Larchmont, N.Y.); N.Y. Athletic (N.Y.C.); Roxbury Run (Denver, N.Y.). Presbyterian. Media columnist Madison Ave., 1963-68; editorial cons. Media/Scope, 1968-69. Contbg. editor: Handbook of Advertising Management, 1970. Contbr. to Advertising Procedure, 1969, rev. edit., 1973, 7th edit., 1977; Exploring Advertising, 1970; producer album The Body in the Seine; cover story guest editor Media Decisions, 1967. Home: 3 Roosevelt Ave Larchmont NY 10538 also Roxbury Run Denver NY 12421 Office: 1114 Ave of Americas New York NY 10036

VIVIAN, CORDY TINDELL, clergyman, sem. adminstr.; b. Howard County, Mo., July 30, 1924; s. Cordy Robert and Euzetta (Tindell) V.; A.B., Western Ill. U., 1953; B.D., Am. Baptist Theol. Sem., 1958; Ph.D. candidate Union Grad. Sch., 1975; m. W. Octavia Geans, Feb. 23, 1953; children—Denise, Cordy Tindell, Kira, Mark, Charisse, Albert. Ordained to ministry Bapt. Ch., 1955; editor religious materials, nat. dir. boys work and lay activities for Sunday Sch. Publ. Bd., Nat. Bapt. Conv., U.S.A., Inc., Nashville, 1955-61, editor Baptist Informer, 1956-61, The Baptist Layman, 1957-61; nat. dir. affiliates SCLC, Atlanta, 1963-67; dir. Ford Fellowships and Black Ministry Devel., Urban Tng. Center for Christian Mission, Chgo., 1967-71; pres. Black Center for Strategy and Community Devel., Chgo., 1972; lectr. Africana Study Center, Cornell U., 1973; dir. for Asia and community orgn. Nat. Council Chs., div. Overseas Ministries, Dept. Agr., N.Y.C., 1973; dir. Sem. Without Walls, Shaw U. Div. Sch., Raleigh, N.C., 1974, dean Div. Sch., dir. Sem. Without Walls, 1975—. Pres., Urban Potential; v.p. Nashville Christian Leadership Conf.; pres. Coalition for United Community Action, 1970-72; chmn. bd. Inst. of Black World, 1970-76; bd. dirs. Tenn. Voters Council, Joint Action for Community Service, SCLC, Nat. Council Indsl. Missions; mem. exec. com. Nat. Found. for Coop. Housing, 1968-72; mem. nat. exec. council Nat. Council Community Chs., 1967-68; mem. Black Caucus of Urban Coalition, 1971-72, Nat. Adv. Council for Black Econ. Devel., SBA; bd. dirs. SCLC, 1973—, acting exec. dir., 1979; founder, chmn. bd. Black Action Strategies and Info. Center, Atlanta, 1975—; v.p. Inst. Internat. Devel., Washington and Raleigh, N.C.,

1976—, exec. dir. Vision (prototype Upward Bound), 1965. Recipient Honored Alumni award Am. Bapt. Theol. Sem., 1960; C.T. Vivian Day named in his honor, Macomb, Ill. Ford Found. grantee 1967, Lilly Endowment grantee, 1974. Mem. Assn. Third World Theologians (co-founder). Author: Black Power and the American Myth (Ebony Book Club alternate selection), 1971. Office: Shaw U Div Sch 118 W South St Raleigh NC 27602 also BASIC Inc 595 Parsons St Atlanta GA 30314

VIVIAN, JOHNSON EDWARD, educator; b. Montreal, Que., Can., July 6, 1913; s. Edgar John and Mary Meade (McMahon) V.; B. Chem. Engring., McGill U., 1936; S.M., Mass. Inst. Tech., 1939, Sc.D., 1945; m. Florence Evelyn Frye, Feb. 10, 1940; children—John Edward, David James, Ann. Came to U.S., 1936, naturalized, 1942. Research engr. Canadian Pulp and Paper Assn., 1936; teaching asst. Mass. Inst. Tech., Cambridge, 1937-38, asst. dir. Bangor chem. engring. practice sch., 1938-41, dir. Buffalo chem. engring. practice sch. sta., 1941-43, research engr. govt. project, 1943-46, asso. prof. chem. engring., 1946-56, prof., 1956—, dir. chem. engring. practice sch., 1946-57, dir. Oak Ridge engring, practice sch., 1948-57. Cons. chem. engring., 1946—; vis. prof. Birla Inst. Tech. and Sci., Pilani (Rajasthan), India, 1972—, dir. Sch. Chem. Engring. Practice, 1974—, exec. officer dept. chem. engring., 1974—. Mem. Am. Inst. Chem. Engrs. (Colburn award 1948), TAPPI, Am. Chem. Soc., AAAS, Am. Soc. Engring. Edn., Nat. Soc. Profl. Engrs., Sigma Xi. Home: 35 Hutchinson Rd Arlington MA 02174 Office: Dept Chem Engring Mass Inst Tech Cambridge MA 02139

VIVIAN, WESTON EDWARD, educator; b. Hermitage Bay, Nfld., Can., Oct. 25, 1924; s. N. Gardner and Bess (Rowsell) V.; came to U.S., 1929, naturalized citizen; B.S., Union Coll., Schenectady, 1945; M.S., Mass. Inst. Tech., 1949; Ph.D., U. Mich., 1959; m. N. Anne Biggs, Aug. 17, 1946 (dec.) children—Byron G., Alice B., Leslie L., Sarah J. Electronics engr., 1946-60; v.p. Conductron Corp., Ann Arbor, Mich., 1961-64, 67, dir., 1961-65; mem. 89th Congress from 2d Dist. Mich.; cons. Nat. Council Marine Resources and Ocean Engring., Exec. Office Pres., 1967; v.p. KMS Industries, Ann Arbor, 1967-68; chmn. Spuntech Housing Corp., 1969-70; v.p. Vicom Industries, Inc., 1970-73; chmn., pres. Vicom Mfg. Co., 1971-73; cons., dir. I.A.M., Inc., Perrysburg, Ohio, 1972-74; adj. prof. U. Mich., 1973—, dir. program engring. for pub. systems, 1974—; mem. Mich. Hwy. Commn., 1976—; chmn. Com. Adminstrn. Tng. Programs, Washington, 1967-68; mem. Nat. Com. on U.S.-China Relations, 1968-76. Bd. dirs. United Fund Ann Arbor, 1962-64, United Fund Mich., 1964, Ann Arbor Community Devel. Corp., 1970-74; Chmn. Ann Arbor Democratic Com., 1959-60, vice chmn., 1964, 75-77. Served with USNR, 1943-46. Home: 1235 Morningside Rd Ann Arbor MI 48103

VIVIANO, BARTHOLOMEW JOSEPH, lawyer, railroad exec.;b. N.Y.C., Mar. 24, 1911; s. Louis A. and Lily (Cressiamano) V.; grad. Phillips Andover Acad., 1929; M.E., Cornell U., 1933. LL.B., 1936; m. Beulah Fisher, Nov. 14, 1942; children—Judith A., Patricia E., Thomas C. Admitted to N.Y. bar, 1936; with Whitman, Ransom, Coulson & Goetz, 1936, 40; gen. counsel Lehigh Valley R.R. Co., N.Y.C., 1946—, v.p. 1955-59, v.p. traffic, 1959-62; v.p. Pa. R.R., Washington, 1962-65, Phila. office, 1965-70, ret.; pvt. practice law also transp. cons., Plainfield, 1970—. Served as maj. Ordnance Corps, AUS, 1941-45. Mem. Am. Bar Assn. Clubs: Cornell, Traffic (N.Y.C.); Plainfield Country. Address: 901 Ocean Ave Sea Bright NJ 07760

VIVONA, STEFANO, vol. agy. exec.; b. St. Louis, Mar. 25, 1919; s. Francesco and Grazio (Larocca) V.; M.D., St. Louis U., 1943; M.P.H., Harvard U., 1952; m. Carol Louise Holtmann, May 14, 1950; children—Francis Stephen, William Phillip, Grace Carol, Stephen Roger, Christine Mabel. Intern, Deaconess Hosp., St. Louis, 1943-44, resident surgery, 1944-45; commd. 1st lt. U.S. Army, 1945, advanced through grades to col., 1969; chief gen. surgery 142d Sta. Hosp., 1945-47; pvt. practice medicine, specializing in gen. surgery, St. Louis, 1947-50; comdg. officer St. Louis Army Dispensary, 1950-51; preventive medicine officer V Corps, Germany, 1952-54, 7th Army, Germany, 1954-55; acting chief dept. biostatistics, div. preventive medicine Walter Reed Army Inst. Research, 1955-58; chief preventive medicine research br. U.S. Army Med. Research and Devel. Command, Office of Surgeon Gen., 1958-60; preventive medicine officer 8th Army, Korea, 1960-61; fellow biologics prodn. Walter Reed Army Inst. Research, Walter Reed Army Med. Center, Washington, 1962, acting dir., div. communicable diseases and immunology, 1962, dir. div., 1962-64; chief U.S. Army Med. Research Team, Vietnam, 1964-65; dir. U.S. Army Med. Comp. SEATO, 1965-67; dir. global medicine course, dep. dir., div. preventive medicine Walter Reed Army Inst. Research, 1967, dir. global medicine course, dir. div. preventive medicine, 1968-69; ret., 1969; research adminstr. Am. Cancer Soc., N.Y.C., 1969, asst. v.p. research, 1970, v.p. research grant awards, 1970-74, v.p. research, 1974—; clin. prof. preventive medicine N.Y. U., 1970-73. Decorated Legion of Merit with oak leaf cluster, Army Commendation medal with oak leaf cluster. Diplomate Am. Bd. Preventive Medicine. Fellow Am. Coll. Preventive Medicine, Am. Pub. Health Assn.; mem. AAAS, Am. Assn. Cancer Research, Alpha Omega Alpha, Delta Omega. Home: 25 Fanshaw Ave Yonkers NY 10705 Office: Am Cancer Soc Inc 777 3d Ave New York City NY 10017

VIZZA, ROBERT FRANCIS, educator; b. N.Y.C., Apr. 2, 1933; s. Saverio and Agatha (Costanzo) V.; B.B.A., Pace Coll., 1954; M.B.A., City U. N.Y., 1959; Ph.D., N.Y.U., 1967; LL.D. (hon.), LaSalle Coll., 1978; m. Joan Kilday, Dec. 11, 1954; children—Lorraine, Mary, Cathy, Robert. Account exec. Diebold Inc., N.Y.C., 1954-61; asst. prof. mktg. St. John's U., 1962-66; asso. prof. marketing, chmn. dept. bus. adminstrn. C. W. Post Coll., 1966-67; dean Sch. Bus., prof. mktg. Manhattan Coll., 1967—; cons. to industry. Bd. dirs. Am. Assembly Collegiate Schs. Bus.; Pres. St. Mary's Sch. Bd. Ford Found. fellow; Jerome Levy Found. award. Fellow Internat. Acad. Mgmt.; mem. Middle Atlantic Assn. Colls. of Bus. Adminstrn. (v.p. 1970-71, pres. 1972-73, exec. com. 1969—), Sales Execs. Club N.Y. (bd. dirs.), Am. Mktg. Assn., Delta Sigma Pi, Delta Mu Delta, Pi Sigma Epsilon. Author: Adoption of the Marketing Concept, 1967; Basic Facts in Marketing, 1966; New Handbook of Sales Training, 1967; Measuring the Value of the Field Sales Force; Training and Developing the Field Sales Manager, 1965; Improving Salesmen's Use of Time, 1962; Time and Territory Management, 1972, 2d edit., 1979; Time and Territorial Management-A Programmed Learning Course, 1975. Contbr. articles to profl. jours. Home: 3 Maria Ln Old Brookville NY 11545 Office: Manhattan Coll Manhattan Coll Pkwy Bronx NY 10471

VLASIN, RAYMOND DANIEL, agrl. economist; b. Wallace, Nebr., Aug. 7, 1931; s. John and Mary (Tabor) V.; B.S., U. Nebr., 1953, M.A., 1957; Ph.D., U. Wis., 1963; m. Helen Claire Pritchard, July 11, 1955; children—Theresa, Celia, Ilene, John, Marie. With natural resource econs. div. Econ. Research Service, Washington, 1959-65; prof., program leader community resource devel. U. Minn., St. Paul, 1965-67; asst. chancellor community outreach and research U. Wis., Green Bay, 1967-71, asst. chancellor extension, univ. extension, 1967-71; prof. resource econs., chmn. dept. recource devel. Mich. State U., E. Lansing, 1971-78, dean lifelong edn. programs, 1979—; mem. Mich. Sci. and Tech. Commn., 1976—, Nat. Task Force Research Related to Land Use Planning and Policy, 1975-76, Mich. Conservation Com., 1975-78, Mich.-U.S. Dept. Agr. Rural Devel. Com., 1975-78. Served with AUS, 1953-55. Recipient Superior Performance award Dept. Agr., 1966. Mem. Community Devel. Soc. Am. (dir. 1968-73, pres. 1972-73), Soil Conservation Soc. Am. (editorial bd. 1974—), Am., Western agrl. econs. assns., Mich. Acad. Sci., Arts and Letters, Mich. Soil Conservation Soc. Contbr. to profl. publns. Home: 687 Jaywood East Lansing MI 48823 Office: 114 Kellogg Center for Continuing Edn Mich State U East Lansing MI 48824. *In this highly organized and large scale society, the human value of each other individual ought to be central. There is no greater inner satisfaction than hearing beyond what is shared and then caring and responding beyond what is anticipated. Nor is there a greater gift than to see another become heartened and renewed.*

VLIET, ROLLIN DALE, lawyer, educator; b. Wichita, Kans., Mar. 4, 1914; s. Richard Marion and Gertrude May (Buck) V.; A.B., U. Kans., 1934; LL.B., U. Okla., 1938; LL.M., Harvard U., 1946, S.J.D., 1950; student Juilliard Inst. Mus. Arts, 1934-35; m. Genevieve Estelle Kern, June 15, 1949; children—Richard Frank, Marcia Lavonne, Kent Allen, Cynthia Kay. Admitted to Okla. bar, 1938: asso. Butler, Brown & Rinehart, Oklahoma City, 1938-39; pvt. practice law, Oklahoma City, 1940-42; asso. prof. law U. Okla., 1947-50, prof., 1950—, David Ross Boyd prof. law, 1955—; vis. prof. law U. Tex., summer 1953, U. So. Calif., 1954-55, summer 57, 60, La. State U., 1967, 76, 77-78; prof. faculté international de Droit Comparé, L' Université des Sciences Comparés Luxembourg, 1962-66, Oxford U., summers 1975, 77; Fulbright lectr. U. Helsinki (Finland), 1961-62. Served to col., AUS, 1942-46. Mem. Am., Okla. bar assns., Am. Judicature Soc., Phi Beta Kappa, Order of Coif, Phi Delta Phi, Phi Mu Alpha, Pi Kappa Alpha. Presbyn. (elder). Rotarian. Contbr. articles to legal jours. Home: 1216 Melrose Dr Norman OK 73069

VODICKA, RUTH KESSLER (CHAI), sculptor; b. N.Y.C.; d. Julius and Rachel Kessler; student Baruch Coll. Music Sch. Settlement, N.Y.C., Y Sch. Music, N.Y.C., Sculpture Center, N.Y.C.; student Oliver O'Connor Barrett, sculptor, Art Students League, New Sch., N.Y. U.; B.Profl. Studies, Empire State Coll., 1978; postgrad. Bklyn. Coll., 1978—; m. Otokar Vodicka; 1 dau., Phyllis Ellen. Exhibitor Art Alliance, Phila., Sculpture Center, San Francisco Mus., Tex. Travelling Exhibit, Whitney Mus., N.A.D., N.Y.C., Pa. Acad., Audubon Artists, N.Y.C., Sculptors Guild, Detroit Inst. Arts, Riverside Mus., N.Y.C., Dallas Mus., Corcoran Gallery, Washington, Albright Art Gallery, Buffalo, Cleve. Mus., Abilene (Tex.) Mus., J.B. Speed Mus., Louisville, Archtl. League N.Y., Am. Jewish Tercentenary Travelling Art Exhibit, Art Inst. Chgo., New Burlington Galleries, London, Eng., Am. Fedn. Art Travelling Exhibit, Galerie Claude Bernard, Paris, Hanover Gallery, London, Museo de Bellas Artes, Buenos Aires, Argentina, Mexican, Bd. Edn. travelling shows, N.Y. Cultural Arts Festival, N.Y. Cultural Center, Hudson River Mus., Yonkers, N.Y., 1973, 7th Congress Internat. Art Assn., Vrana, Bulgaria, Bergen County Mus., Women's Interart Center; 15 one person shows, 1956-79; former sculpture tchr. Queens Youth Center, Bayside, L.I., Emanu-El Midtown Y, N.Y.C., Great Neck Arrandale Sch., Hillside Sch., Hastings, N.Y., 1973-74; coordinator 8 O'Clock Art Forums, 1967-72; represented in permanent collections Norfolk Mus., Montclair State Coll., Women's Interart Center, others, also pvt. collections; commn. "Eternal Light" Temple of Jewish Community Center, Harrison, N.Y. Recipient Sculpture House prize Nat. Assn. Women Artists, 1954, Helen Foster Barnett prize N.A.D., 1955, Huntington Hartford Family prize, Nat. Assn. Women Artists, 1957, Silvermine Guild of Artists award and Top prize J.W. Beatman award, 1957, Bedi-Rossi award, 1958, Stuart Clay award, Bklyn. Soc. Artists, 1959, medal of honor Painters and Sculptors Soc. N.J., 1962, 1st prize, Am. Soc. Contemporary Artists, 1962, 1st prize, David Knapp Meml. award Painters and Sculptors Soc. N.J., 1963, Julia Ford Pew prize Nat. Assn. Women Artists, 1963, Pauline Law prize, 1966. Mem. Am. Soc. Contemporary Artists, Nat. Assn. Women Artists, Sculptors Guild, Jewish Visual Artists, Coll. Art Assn., Women's Interart Center. Author: (poetry) The Space Between, 1976. Home and Studio: 97 Wooster St New York NY 10012

VODOVNIK, RAYMOND FRANK, automobile parts mfg. co. exec.; b. Chisholm, Minn., Jan. 31, 1935; s. Joseph Anthony and Mary (Fierst) V.; B.Mech. Engring., U. Minn., 1961, J.D., 1964; m. Barbara Ann Berdice, July 13, 1963; children—Joseph, Mary, Robert. Admitted to Minn. bar, 1964; market research analyst Donaldson Co., Inc., Mpls., 1964-69, sec., 1969—. Asso. chmn. United Fund., Mpls. Area, 1972; mem. Bloomington Promotion & Devel. Commn., 1973—, chmn., 1976. Trustee Donaldson Found. Served with USMC, 1953-56; Korea. Mem. Bloomington C. of C., Am., Minn. bar assn., V.F.W. Home: 4642 Heritage Hills Dr Bloomington MN 55437 Office: 1400 W 94th St Minneapolis MN 55431

VOEGELI, VICTOR JACQUE, educator, univ. adminstr.; b. Jackson, Tenn., Dec. 21, 1934; s. Victor Jacque and Winnie Lou (Lassiter) V.; B.S., Murray State Coll., 1956; M.A., Tulane U., 1961, Ph.D., 1965; m. Anna Jean King, Oct. 14, 1956; children—Victor Jacque, Charles Lassiter. Instr. history Tulane U., 1963-65, asst. prof., 1965-67; asst. prof. history Vanderbilt U., 1967-69, asso. prof., 1969-73, prof., chmn. dept., 1973-76, dean Coll. Arts and Sci., 1976—. Served with U.S. Army, 1956-58. Nat. Endowment Humanities grantee, 1969-70, 72. Mem. Orgn. Am. Historians, So. Hist. Assn., Tenn. Hist. Soc. Presbyterian. Author: Free But Not Equal: The Midwest and the Negro During the Civil War, 1967. Home: 103 Monticello Rd Franklin TN 37064 Office: Vanderbilt U Nashville TN 37240

VOEGELIN, HAROLD STANLEY, lawyer, financier; b. Summit, N.J., Sept. 10, 1919; s. Frederick Ernest and Clara Aestelle (Dorland) V.; B.A., U. Mich., 1942, J.D., 1948; m. Winifred Nemec Martin, Dec. 24, 1962; children—Frederick P.; stepchildren—Jon F. Martin, Janis L. Kingaard. Teaching asst. constl. law, dept. polit. sci. U. Mich., 1947-48; admitted to Calif. bar, 1949; asso. firm McEntee, Willis & MacCracken, Los Angeles, 1948-52; asso., partner Brady & Nossaman, Los Angeles, 1952-57; partner Wood, Voegelin & Barton, 1957-60; sr. partner Voegelin, Barton, Harris & Callister, 1960-70, Voegelin & Barton, Los Angeles, 1970—. Pres., dir. Five-Thirty Corp.; chmn. bd. West Coast Commodity Exchange, Inc., Nesbitt Food Products, Inc.; dir. Smith Internat., Inc., Newport Beach, Calif., A.J. Bayer Co., Los Angeles; gen. counsel Trailer Coach Assn., Anaheim, Calif.; lectr. U. So. Calif. Inst. on Fed. Taxation, Title Ins. & Trust Co. Tax Forum, Internat. and Comparative Law Center, So. Methodist U. Vice pres., bd. dirs. United Cerebral Palsy Assn. of Los Angeles, Inc., 1958-62; bd. dirs. South Coast Child Guidance Clinic, Newport Beach; trustee Whittier (Calif.) Coll., Nesbitt Found., Los Angeles, Lluella M. Murphey Found., Los Angeles, So. Coast Repertory Theatre, Costa Mesa, Calif.; mem. exec. com. Pres.'s Club, U. Mich.; mem. adv. bd. Internat. and Comparative Law Center, Southwestern Legal Found., Dallas. Served with USNR, 1943-45; PTO. Mem. Am. (lectr. Nat. Inst. on Current Legal Aspects of Doing Bus. in Europe), Internat., Inter-Am., Orange County, Los Angeles County (chmn. com. on continuing edn. of bar 1961-62, 1st prize legal essay competition 1949) bar assns., State Bar Calif. (lectr. Continuing Edn. of Bar Program), Los Angeles Area C. of C. (dir., chmn. internat. commerce com., chmn. com. internat. trade devel. city of Los Angeles Econ. Advisory Council), Theta Delta Chi, Delta Theta Phi. Republican. Presbyn. Clubs: California (Los Angeles); Newport Harbor Yacht, Balboa Bay (Newport Beach); Capitol Hill (Washington). Home: 32 Harbor Island Newport Beach CA 92660 also 800 W 1st St Los Angeles CA 90012 Office: 606 S Olive St Los Angeles CA 90014 also 4343 Von Karman Blvd Newport Beach CA 92660

VOELKEL, ROBERT T(OWNSEND), coll. exec., educator; b. Cleve., Feb. 26, 1933; s. Elmer E. and Mercy (Townsend) V.; B.A., Coll. Wooster, 1954; postgrad. (Fulbright scholar) New Coll. U. Edinburgh (Scotland), 1954-55; B.D. in N.T. and Ch. History, 1957, Th.D. in Systematic Theology, 1962; m. Martha Ann Bousman, Dec. 21, 1955; children—Andrew, Thomas, James. Instr. in religion Coll. Wooster, 1957-59; instr. Pomona Coll., 1962-64, asst. prof. religion, 1964-67, asso. prof., 1967-73, prof., 1973—, chmn. dept. religion, 1969-75, v.p., dean of coll., 1975—. Mem. com. on ecumenics and liturgics So. Calif. Conf. United Ch. of Christ, 1966-68; sec. exec. com. United Ministries in Higher Edn. Regional Commn., So. Calif., 1966-68; mem. bd. deacons Claremont (Calif.) United Ch. of Christ, 1971-74, mem. bd. Christian edn., 1964-66; mem. corp. Pilgrim Pl., retirement center, Claremont, 1973-76. Recipient Wig Disting. Prof. award Pomona Coll., 1966; Fulbright travel grantee, 1975-76. Mem. Am. Soc. Ch. History, Am. Acad. Religion, Pacific Coast Theol. Soc., Phi Beta Kappa. Author: The Shape of the Theological Task, 1968; editor, author intro., critical notes and bibliography: The Communion of the Christian with God (Wilhelm Herrmann), 1971. Home: 910 Pomona Ct Claremont CA 91711 Office: Pomona Coll Sumner Hall 201 Claremont CA 91711

VOELKER, LARRY, corp. exec.; b. Akron, Ohio, July 15, 1933; s. Paul James and Pearl Betty (Jewell) V.; B.S., Franklin U., 1965; m. Marjorie Jean Radcliff, Oct. 26, 1957; children—Karen, David. Sr. tax specialist Columbus & So. Ohio Electric Co., 1959-65; tax mgr. Iowa So. Utilities, 1966-75; tax dir., asst. treas. SCOA Industries, Inc., Columbus, Ohio, 1967-75; treas., 1975—. Mem. devel. bd. Children's Hosp., Columbus. Served with U.S. Army, 1953-56. Mem. Nat. Assn. Accts., Fin. Execs. Inst., Nat. Retail Mchts. Assn. Methodist. Home: 4545 Helston Ct Columbus OH 43220 Office: 155 E Broad St 10th Fl Columbus OH 43215

VOGE, MARIETTA, educator; b. Yugoslavia, July 7, 1918; d. Bernard and Augusta (Meyer) Jirku; came to U.S., 1942; A.B., U. Calif. at Berkeley, 1944, M.A., 1946, Ph.D., 1950; m. Noel H. Voge, June 12, 1942; 1 son, Nicholas C. Mem. faculty Sch. Medicine U. Calif. at Los Angeles, 1952—, asso. prof.. infectious diseases, 1962-69, prof. dept. med. microbiology and immunology, 1969—. Cons. Cal. Dept. Pub. Health. Recipient many fellowships and travel grants for research in tropical diseases and parasitology. Mem. Am. Soc. Tropical Medicine and Hygiene, (council, v.p.), Am. Soc. Parasitologists (council, pres.), Helminthological Soc. Wash., Brazilian Soc. Tropical Medicine, British Soc. Parasitology, Phi Beta Kappa, Sigma Xi. Co-author: Medical Parasitology, 1958; Experiments and Techniques in Parasitology, 1970. Contbr. to profl. jours. Home: 2499 Corinth Ave Los Angeles CA 90064

VOGEL, ARTHUR ANTON, clergyman; b. Milw., Feb. 24, 1924; s. Arthur Louis and Gladys Eirene (Larson) V.; student U. of South, 1942-43, Carroll Coll., 1943-44; B.D., Nashotah House Theol. Sem., 1946; M.A., U. Chgo., 1948; Ph.D., Harvard, 1952; S.T.D., Gen. Theol. Sem., 1969; D.C.L., Nashotah House, 1969; D.D., U. of South, 1971; m. Katharine Louise Nunn, Dec. 29, 1947; children—John Nunn, Arthur Anton, Katharine Ann. Ordained deacon Episcopal Ch., 1946, priest, 1948; teaching asst. philosophy Harvard, Cambridge, Mass., 1949-50; instr. Trinity Coll., Hartford, Conn., 1950-52; mem. faculty Nashotah House Theol. Sem., Nashotah, Wis., 1952-71, asso. prof., 1954-56, William Adams prof. philosophical and systematic theology, 1956-71, sub-dean Sem., 1964-71; bishop coadjutor Diocese of West Mo., Kansas City, 1971-72, bishop, 1972—. Rector, Ch. St. John Chrysostom, Delafield, Wis., 1952-56; dir. Anglican Theol. Rev., Evanston, Ill., 1964-69; mem. Internat. Anglican-Roman Cath. Consultation, 1970—; mem. Nat. Anglican-Roman Catholic Consultation, 1965—, Anglican chmn., 1973—; mem. Standing Commn. on Ecumenical Relations of Episcopal Ch., 1957—; mem. gen. bd. examining chaplains Episcopal Ch., 1971-72; del. Episcopal Ch., 4th Assembly World Council Chruches, Uppsala, Sweden, 1968, and others. Vice chmn. bd. dirs. St. Luke's Hosp., Kansas City, Mo., 1971, chmn., 1973—. Research fellow Harvard, 1950. Mem. Am. Philos. Assn., Metaphys. Soc. Am., Soc. Existential and Phenomenological Philosophy, Catholic Theol. Soc. Am. Author: Reality, Reason and Religion, 1957; The Gift of Grace, 1958; The Christian Person, 1963; The Next Christian Epoch, 1966; Is the Last Supper Finished?, 1968; Body Theology, 1973; The Power of His Resurrection, 1976. Contbr. profl. jours. Home: 524 W 119th Terr Kansas City MO 64145 Office: 420 W 14th St PO Box 23216 Kansas City MO 64141

VOGEL, CHARLES A., JR., banker; b. Cheltenham, Pa., Mar. 7, 1925; s. Charles A. and Clara (Mack) V.; grad. Wharton Sch. Finance, U. Pa., 1950; postgrad. Bank Adminstrn. Inst., U. Wis., 1970; married Sept. 11, 1965. With Charter Bank Phila., 1942-50; with Bank of N.J., Camden, 1950—, now auditor, exec. officer. Mem. Bank Adminstrn. Inst. (past pres.), dir. So. N.J. chpt.). Home: Box 200 Rural Route 4 Sewell NJ 08080 Office: Route 38 East Gate Dr Moorestown NJ 08057

VOGEL, CHARLES JOSEPH, judge; b. Star Lake Twp., Otter Tail County, Minn., Sept. 20, 1898; s. Philip Francis and Anna Marie (Jenson) Vogel; ed. Huron (S.D.) Coll., 1917-18; LL.B., U. Minn., 1923; m. Fern Nesbitt. Admitted to Minn bar 1923, N.D. bar, 1924; practiced at Minot in office of Lewis & Bach; U.S. referee in bankruptcy, 1924; practiced in Fargo, N.D., 1925- 41; partner firm Vogel & Vogel, 1934-38, Thorp. Wattam & Vogel, 1938-41; U.S. dist. judge N.D., 1941-54, U.S. circuit judge, 1954-65; chief judge U.S. Ct. Appeals, 8th Circuit, 1965-68; judge U.S. Circuit Ct., 1968—. Democratic candidate for U.S. Senate, 1940. Served with U.S. Army, 1918-19. Episcopalian. Address: Box 3006 Fargo ND 58102

VOGEL, CYRIL J., bishop; student Duquesne U., St. Vincent's Sem., Latrobe, Pa. Ordained priest Roman Catholic Ch., 1931; bishop of Salina (Kans.), 1965—. Office: PO Box 999 Salina KS 67401*

VOGEL, EZRA F., educator; b. Delaware, Ohio, July 11, 1930; s. Joseph H. and Edith (Nachman) V.; B.A., Ohio Wesleyan U., 1950; M.A., Bowling Green State U., 1951; Ph.D., Harvard U., 1958; m. Suzanne Hall, July 5, 1953 (div.); children—David, Steven, Eva; m. 2d, Charlotte Ikels, Nov. 3, 1979. Research fellow Harvard for work in Japan, 1958-60; asst. prof. Yale U., 1960-61; research asso., lectr. Harvard U., 1961-67, prof., 1967—, asso. dir. East Asian Research Center, 1967-73, dir. East Asian Research Center, 1973-77, chmn. Council East Asian Studies, 1977—. Mem. Joint Com. on Contemporary China, 1968-75, Com. on Scholarly Communication with Peoples Republic China, 1973-75, Joint Com. Japanese Studies, 1977—. Trustee Ohio Wesleyan U., 1970-75. Served with AUS, 1951-53. Recipient Harvard faculty prize for book of year, 1970; Guggenheim fellow, 1972. Mem. Am. Sociol. Assn., Assn. Asian Studies (bd. dirs. 1970-72), Am. Acad. Arts and Scis. Author: Japan's New Middle Class, 1963; Canton Under Communism, 1969; Japan As Number One, 1979. Editor: (with Norman W. Bell) A Modern

Introduction to the Family, 1960; Modern Japanese Organization and Decision-Making, 1975. Home: 14 Sumner Rd Cambridge MA 02138

VOGEL, FERDINAND LINCOLN, JR., material scientist, educator; b. Phila., Nov. 30, 1922; s. Ferdinand Lincoln and Emma Alwiene Leipe V.; B.S., U. Pa., 1948, M.S., 1949, Ph.D., 1952; m. Sally Thomas, Sept. 4, 1946; children—Kathryn, Linda, Robert. Mem. tech. staff Bell Telephone Labs., Murray Hill, N.J., 1952-59; mgr. advanced material RCA, Somerville, N.J., 1959-63; dir. semicondr. research Sprague Electric Co., North Adams, Mass., 1963-68; group leader Exxon Research Engring. Labs., Linden, N.J., 1969-73; prof. elec. sci. U. Pa., Phila., 1968-69, 73—; cons. in field. Served with Signal Corps, AUS, 1942-45. Mem. Am. Inst. Metall. Engrs., Am. Phys. Soc., Metal Sci. Club. Presbyterian. Contbr. articles to profl. jours.; patentee in field. Home: RD 3 Whitehouse Station NJ 08889 Office: 322 Moore School U Pa Philadelphia PA 19104

VOGEL, HENRY ELLIOTT, univ. dean, physicist; b. Greenville, S.C., Sept. 16, 1925; s. Henry Lamprecht and Alice (Cousins) V.; B.S., Furman U., 1948; M.S., U. N.C., 1950, Ph.D., 1962; m. Barbara Argyle Gladden, Aug. 16, 1953; children—Alisabeth, Henry L. II, Barbara Alice, Susan Marie. Instr. dept. physics Clemson (S.C.) U., 1950-52, asst. prof. physics, 1952-59, asso. prof., 1959-65, prof., 1965-67, prof., head physics dept., 1967-71, prof., dean Coll. Scis., 1971—. Served with AUS, 1943-45. Decorated Purple Heart. Mem. Am. Phys. Soc., Am. Vacuum Soc., Am. Assn. Physics Tchrs., Sigma Xi, Sigma Pi, Alpha Epsilon Delta. Home: 222 Wyatt Ave Clemson SC 29631

VOGEL, HENRY JAMES, biochemist; b. Berlin, June 1, 1920; s. Paul Theodor and Erna (Italiener) V.; came to U.S., 1939, naturalized, 1943; M.S., N.Y. U., 1941, Ph.D., 1949; m. Ruth Hermine, May 17, 1946; 1 son, Stephen Mark. Asso. prof. microbial biochemistry Rutgers U., New Brunswick, N.J., 1957-60, prof. microbiology, 1960-68; prof. microbiology Coll. Physicians and Surgeons, Columbia U., N.Y.C., 1968—; cons. NIH, 1973-76. USPHS fellow, 1950-52; Damon Runyon Meml. fellow Yale U., 1952-56; recipient Lindback Found. award, 1967. Mem. Am. Soc. Biol. Chemists, Am. Soc. Microbiology, Genetics Soc. Am. Joint editor: Informational Macromolecules, 1963; Evolving Genes and Proteins, 1965; Organizational Biosynthesis, 1967; Neuronal Information Transfer, 1978; Cells of Immunoglobulin Synthesis, 1979; editor: Metabolic Regulation, 1971; Nucleic Acid - Protein Recognition, 1977; series editor P & S Biomed. Scis. Symposia, 1976—; editorial bd. Jour. Molecular Evolution, 1971—. Office: Coll Physicians and Surgeons 630 W 168th St New York NY 10032

VOGEL, HERBERT DAVIS, exec. engr.; b. Chelsea, Mich., Aug. 26, 1900; s. Lewis P. and Pearl M. (Davis) V.; B.S., U.S. Mil. Acad., 1924; M.S. in Civil Engring., U. Calif., 1928; Dr.-Ing., Berlin Tech. U., 1929; C.E., U. Mich., 1933; m. Loreine Elliott, Dec. 23, 1925; children—Herbert D., Richard E. Commd. 2d. lt. U.S. Army, 1924, advanced through grades to brig. gen.; founder, builder, dir. U.S. Army Engrs. Waterways Expt. Sta., Vicksburg, Miss., 1929-34; student Command and Gen. Staff Sch., 1934-36; with 3d Engrs., Hawaii, 1936-38; instr. Army Engrs. Sch., 1938-40; asst. to dist. engr., chief inspection div., Pitts., 1940-41; dist. engr., 1942-43; grad. Army-Navy Staff Coll., 1943; with S.W. Pacific Theatre Operations, 1944; chief of staff intermediate sect. (New Guinea), then base comdr. Base M (Philippines), 1944-45; with Army of Occupation, Yokohama, Japan, 1945; dist. engr. C.E., Buffalo, 1945-49, engr. maintenance Panama Canal, v.p., dir. Panama R.R. Co., 1949-50, lt. gov. C.Z. Govt., v.p. Panama Canal Co., 1950-52, div. engr. Southwestern div. C.E., 1952- 54; chmn. bd. TVA, 1954-62; engr. adviser World Bank, 1963-67, including Indus Basin project, 1964-67, resource devel. engring. cons., 1967—; 1st occupant George W. Goethals chair mil. constrn. U.S. Army Engr. Sch., 1973—. Dir. Internat. Gen. Industries, 1973—, Planning and Devel. Collaborative, 1968-74. Mem. Beach Erosion Bd., 1946-49, Internat. Boundary Commn., 1946-49; mem. Miss. River Commn., 1952-54, Bd. Engrs. for Rivers and Harbors, 1952-54; chmn. Ark., White, Red Basin Inter-Agy. Com., 1952-54; mem. permanent internat. com. Permanent Internat. Assn. Navigation Congresses, 1957-64, hon. mem., 1967; chmn. bd. consultants to Panama Canal, 1971-72; mem. cons. panel Ludington pumped storage project, 1969-73; engring. cons. GAO, 1977. Mem. visitors com. Sch. Engring., Vanderbilt U. Decorated D.S.M., Legion of Merit, Philippine Liberation and Independence medals, knight Grand Cross (Thailand), Colon Alfaro medal; recipient Distinguished Alumnus award U. Mich., 1953; Meritorious Service award for service to engring. profession Cons. Engrs. Council, 1967. Benjamin Franklin fellow Royal Soc. Arts. Registered profl. engr., N.Y., Tex., Tenn., D.C. Fellow Am. Cons. Engrs. Council; mem. U.S. Com. Large Dams, Am. Power Conf., ASCE (hon.; mem. nat. water policy com. 1971-74, chmn. 1974-76, mem. nat. energy policy com. 1976—, pres.'s award, 1979), Soc. Am. Mil. Engrs. (hon., nat. dir. 1956-62, 66, treas. 1974-76), Nat. Acad. Sci., Nat. Soc. Profl. Engrs., Pub. Works Hist. Soc. (hon.), Order of Carabao. Episcopalian. Clubs: Army-Navy, Cosmos (Washington). Writer numerous papers on hydraulic models and lab. procedures, 1930-40, articles and speeches on TVA, 1954-63, papers defining U.S. position on inland navigation. Home: 3033 Cleveland Ave NW Washington DC 20008 Office: 601-2 Washington Bldg Washington DC 20005

VOGEL, HOWARD H., JR., educator; b. N.Y.C., Nov. 30, 1914; s. Howard H. and Edith (Eiseman) V.; A.B., Bowdoin Coll., 1936; M.A., Harvard, 1937, Ph.D., 1940; m. Christine McKean, June 9, 1940 (dec. 1958); children—Nancy Edith, Diana Ellen; m. 2d, Barbara Russell, Sept. 23, 1961; children—Naomi Ruth, Thomas Howard. Mem. faculty dept. zoology Wabash Coll., Crawfordsville, Ind., 1940-47; chmn. biol. scis. Coll., U. Chgo., 1947-49; biologist div. biol.-med. research Argonne (Ill.) Nat. Lab., 1950-67; prof., head radiation biology U. Tenn. Coll. Medicine, Memphis, 1967—, prof. radiation oncology, physiology and biophysics Center Health Scis., 1967—. Pres. Hyde Park Coop. Soc., Chgo., 1957. Fellow AAAS; mem. Am. Inst. Biol. Scis. (governing bd.), Am. Soc. Zoologists, Radiation Research Soc., Transplantation Soc. Animal Behavior Soc., AAUP (chmn. state conf.), Phi Beta Kappa, Sigma Xi (Southeastern rep. nat. bd.). Co-editor: Medical Radiation Biology, 1973. Home: 280 Ben Avon Way Memphis TN 38111

VOGEL, JOHN H., banker; b. N.Y.C., 1917; ed. N.Y. U. Chmn., chief exec. officer Nat. Bank N.Am., also dir. Home: 18 Wynmor Rd Scarsdale NY 10583 Office: 60 Hempstead Ave West Hempstead NY 11552 also 44 Wall St New York NY 10005

VOGEL, JULIUS, actuary; b. N.Y.C., Jan. 22, 1924; s. Max and Bertha V.; B.A., Bklyn. Coll., 1943; postgrad. Johns Hopkins U., 1943-44; m. Corinne Iskowitz, Mar. 11, 1947; children—Robert, Charles. With Prudential Ins. Co. Am., Newark, 1946—, sr. v.p., chief actuary, 1977—. Served with U.S. Army, 1944-46. Recipient Disting. Public Service award Dept. Navy, 1976. Fellow Soc. Actuaries (pres. 1979-80); mem. Am. Acad. Actuaries. Club: Essex. Office: Prudential Plaza Newark NJ 07101

VOGEL, MANFRED HENRY, educator; b. Tel-Aviv, Israel, Sept. 15, 1930; s. Henry and Rachel (Fellman) V.; came to U.S., 1947, naturalized, 1954; B.A., Wayne State U., 1953; M.A., Columbia, 1955, Ph.D., 1964; M.Hebrew Lit., Jewish Theol. Sem., 1957; m. Susan A. Sugarman, Apr. 15, 1962; children—Evan James, Henry Michael. Hillel dir., adj. lectr. philosophy Brandeis U., 1958-62; Hillel dir. Northwestern U., Evanston, Ill., 1962-65, asst. prof. religion, 1965-67, asso. prof., 1967-71, prof., 1971—, chmn. dept., 1972—. Mem. Am. Theol. Soc., Am. Acad. Religion. Jewish. Translator: Philosophy of the Future (L. Feuerbach), 1966. Contbr. articles to profl. jours. Contbg. editor Christian Century, 1970-74. Home: 2517 Greenwood St Wilmette IL 60091 Office: 1940 Sheridan Rd Evanston IL 60201

VOGEL, MICHAEL JOHN, mfg. co. exec.; b. N.Y.C., Apr. 29, 1935; s. John and Elizabeth (Krebs) V.; B.I.E., N.Y. U., 1956; m. Bernice Blow, July 24, 1956; children—Diana G., Stephen M. Project engr. Alcoa, Pitts., 1956-57; sales engr. Spaulding Fibre Co., N.Y.C., 1958; gen. mgr., mktg. mgr. Joy Mfg. Co., Pitts., 1959-72; group v.p. Chgo. Pneumatic Tool Co., Chgo., 1972-75; group v.p. Masco Corp., Taylor, Mich., 1975—; dir. Turbonetics, Inc. Mem. Zeta Psi. Home: 493 Whippers In Ct Bloomfield Hills MI 48013 Office: 21001 VanBorn Rd Taylor MI 48180

VOGEL, ORVILLE ALVIN, agronomist; b. Pilger, Nebr., May 19, 1907; s. William and Emelia (Paege) V.; B.S., U. Nebr., 1929, M.S., 1931, Ph.D. (hon.), 1970; Ph.D., Wash. State U., Pullman, 1939; m. Bertha J. Berkman, July 14, 1931; children—Evelyn May, Richard Frank. With Agr. Research Service, U.S. Dept. Agr., Wash. State U., 1931-73, research agronomist, 1965-73, prof. agronomy, 1965-73; developed semidwarf winter wheats for high yield capabilities, equipment for efficiency wheat research. Recipient Superior Service award Dept. Agr., 1962; Nat. Sci. medal, 1976; Distinguished Alumnus award Wash. State U., 1977. Fellow Am. Soc. Agronomy (Crop Sci. award 1969, Edward Browning award 1972); mem. Sigma Xi, Alpha Zeta, Gamma Sigma Delta. Republican. Methodist. Author articles wheat breeding. Address: SE 733 Ridgeview Ct Pullman WA 99163

VOGEL, ROBERT, lawyer, educator; b. Coleharbor, N.D., Dec. 6, 1918; s. Frank A. and Louella (Larsen) V.; B.S., U. N.D., 1939; LL.B., Mpls. Coll. Law, 1942; m. Elsa Mork, May 29, 1942; children—Mary Lou, Sarah May, Frank, Robert. Admitted to N.D. bar, 1943, practiced in Garrison, 1943-54; state's atty. McLean County, 1948-54; U.S. atty., Fargo, 1954-61; mem. law firm Vogel, Bair & Brown, Mandan, N.D., 1961-73; judge N.D. Supreme Ct., 1973-78; prof. U. N.D. Law Sch., Grand Forks, 1978—. Democratic candidate for U.S. Ho. of Reps., 2d Dist. N.D., 1962. Mem., sec. Nonpartisan League State Exec. Com., 1952. Mem. N.D. Parole Bd., 1966-73. Fellow Am. Bar Found.; mem. Internat. Soc. Barristers, Am. Coll. Trial Lawyers. Home: 524 Harvard Grand Forks ND 58201 Office: U ND Law Sch Grand Forks ND 58202

VOGEL, ROBERT, ednl. adminstr.; b. Vienna, Austria, Nov. 4, 1929; B.A., Sir George Williams U., 1952, M.A., 1954, Ph.D., 1959. Lectr. history Sir George Williams U., Montreal, 1955-58; lectr. history McGill U., Montreal, 1958-61, asst. prof., 1961-64, asso. prof., 1964-69, prof., 1969—, chmn. dept. history, 1966-71, vice dean social scis., 1969-71, dean faculty of arts, 1971—. Recipient Silver Medal Lt. Gov. Que., 1952. Mem. Canadian Assn. Deans of Arts and Sci., Canadian, Am. hist. assns., Peace Research Inst., McGill Assn. Univ. Tchrs. (past mem. council). Author: A Breviate of British Diplomatic Blue Books, 1919-39, 1963. Contbr. articles to profl. jours. Home: 4800 de Maisonneuve Blvd W Apt 705 Montreal PQ H3Z 1M2 Canada Office: Faculty of Arts McGill U 853 Sherbrooke St W Montreal PQ H3A 2T6 Canada

VOGEL, WALTER, farm equipment mfg. co. exec.; b. Schwaebisch Hall, Ger., Apr. 28, 1928; s. Gustav and Rosa (Barger) V.; grad. Stuttgart U., 1954; Fulbright scholar, U. Mich., Ann Arbor, 1956; married; children—Birgit, Peter, Sabine. With Deere & Co., Moline, Ill., 1956—, mng. dir. for Europe, Africa and Middle East, 1975-77, v.p., 1977-79, exec. v.p., 1979—; adv. council Deutsche Bank, Mannheim, W. Ger. Mem. Am. Soc. Agrl. Engrs. Office: Deere & Co John Deere Rd Moline IL 61265

VOGELER, ALAN ROTH, lawyer; b. Cin., July 12, 1917; s. Karl Alfred and Frederique (Roth) V.; A.B., U. Ky., 1938, LL.B., 1940; LL.M. (Cook fellow 1940-41), U. Mich., 1941; m. Sara Robertson Biggs, Sept. 8, 1940; children—Alan Roth, Edwin Biggs, Douglas Malcolm, Sara King. Admitted to Mich. bar, 1941, Ohio bar, 1946; pvt. practice, Detroit, 1941-42, Cin., 1946—; partner firm Frost & Jacobs, 1978—, head tax/estate dept., 1979—; adj. prof. taxation Chase Coll. Law, Cin., 1958-63; mem. vis. com. U. Ky. Coll. Law, 1978—. Chmn. Village of Mariemont (Ohio) Town Meeting, 1952-56; pres. trustees Mariemont Community Ch., 1965-68. Served to capt. AUS, 1942-46. Fellow Ohio Bar Found.; mem. Am. Bar Assn., Ohio Bar Assn. (chmn. com. on taxation 1975-78), Cin. Bar Assn. (v.p. 1978-80), Cin. Bar Found. (pres. 1975-78), Order of Coif, Phi Delta Phi, Phi Delta Theta. Republican. Presbyterian. Clubs: University (pres. 1976-77), Cin. Country, Literary (Cin.). Contbr. articles profl. jours.; editor in chief Ky. Law Jour., 1939-40. Home: 3047 Ononta Ave Cincinnati OH 45226 Office: 201 E 5th St Cincinnati OH 45202

VOGT, ERICH WOLFGANG, physicist, ednl. adminstr.; b. Steinbach, Man., Can., Nov. 12, 1929; s. Peter Andrew and Susanna (Reimer) V.; B.S., U. Man., 1951, M.S., 1952; Ph.D., Princeton, 1955; m. Barbara Mary Greenfield, Aug. 27, 1952; children—Edith Susan, Elizabeth Mary, David Eric, Jonathan Michael, Robert Jeremy. Research officer Chalk River (Ont.) Nuclear Labs., 1956-65; prof. physics U. B.C., Vancouver, 1965—. Asso. dir. TRIUMF Project, U. B.C., 1968-73, v.p. univ., 1975—; chmn. Sci. Council B.C., 1978—. Decorated officer Order of Can.; recipient Centennial medal of Can., 1967. Fellow Royal Soc. Can., Am. Phys. Soc.; mem. Canadian Assn. Physicists (past pres.). Co-editor: Advances in Nuclear Physics, 1968—. Contbr. articles profl. jours. Home: 1816 Wesbrook Crescent Vancouver BC Canada

VOGT, EVON ZARTMAN, JR., anthropologist; b. Gallup, N.Mex., Aug. 20, 1918; s. Evon and Shirley (Bergman) V.; A.B., U. Chgo., 1941, M.A., 1946, Ph.D., 1948; m. Catherine Christine Hiller, Sept. 4, 1941; children—Shirley Naneen (Mrs. Geza Teleki), Evon Zartman III, Eric Edwards, Charles Anthony. Instr. Harvard, 1948-50, asst. prof., 1950-55, asso. prof., 1955-59, prof. anthropology, 1959—, dir. Harvard Chiapas project, 1957—, chmn. dept. anthropology, 1969-73, master Kirkland House, 1974—, asst. curator Am. ethnology Peabody Mus., 1950-59, curator Middle Am. ethnology, 1960—; vis. prof. U. Hawaii, 1972. Mem. div. anthropology and psychology NRC, 1955-57. Served from ensign to lt., USNR, 1942-46. Decorated Order Aztec Eagle (Mexico). Fellow Center for Advanced Study in Behavioral Sci., 1956-57. Fellow Am. Acad. Arts and Scis. (councilor 1974-78), Am. Anthrop. Assn. (exec. bd. 1958-60); mem. Nat. Acad. Scis., Soc. Am. Archaeology, Royal Anthrop. Inst. Gt. Britain and Ireland, Am. Folklore Soc. Clubs: Harvard (N.Y.C.); Harvard (Boston). Author: Navaho Veterans, 1951; Modern Homesteaders, 1955; (with W. A. Lessa) Reader in Comparative Religion, 1958; (with Ray Hyman) Water Witching U.S.A., 1959; Zinacantan: A Maya Community in The Highlands of Chiapas, 1969 (Harvard Press Faculty prize 1969, Republic of Mexico Bernardino de Sahagún prize 1969); The Zincantecos of Mexico: A Modern Maya Way of Life, 1970; Tortillas for the Gods: A Symbolic Analysis of Zinacanteco Rituals, 1976. Editor: Desarrollo Cultural de Los Mayas, 1964; Los Zinacantecos, 1966; People of Rimrock, 1966; Handbook of Middle American Indians, vols. 7, 8, 1969; Aerial Photography in Anthropological Field Research, 1974. Home: 85 Dunster St Cambridge MA 02138

VOGT, JAMES HENRY, communication co. exec.; b. Gary, Ind., May 19, 1934; s. William F. and Evelyn J. (Visconti) V.; B.S., Ill. Inst. Tech., 1958; m. Gloria O'Dell, Apr. 12, 1958; children—Michelle, Diane, Robert, James, Thomas, Kathleen. Student engr., asst. mgr. quality control, supt. mfg., supt. prodn. and inventory control Combustion Engring., Inc., East Chicago, Ind., Chattanooga, 1950-67; v.p., gen. mgr. apparatus div. ITT Telecommunications, Corinth, Miss., 1967-71, pres. equipment and systems div., Hartford, Conn., 1971-74; exec. v.p. ops. No. Telecom, Inc. subs. No. Telecom Ltd., Boston, 1974-77; exec. v.p. Stromberg-Carlson subs. Gen. Dynamics, St. Louis, 1977-79; pres. Lynch Communications Systems, Inc., Reno, 1979—. Registered profl. engr., Ind. Mem. ASME. Home: 2500 Lakeridge Shores W Reno NV 89509 Office: 204 Edison Way Reno NV 89502

VOGT, JOHN HENRY, found. exec.; b. Ft. Madison, Iowa, Dec. 31, 1918; s. John Andrews and Edith Elizabeth (Cramer) V.; B.S.C., Iowa U., 1940; m. Jean Hilleary, Aug. 4, 1942; children—John Hilleary, Linda Jean, Lisa Louise. Retail exec. trainee Sears Roebuck & Co., 1940-41; mgmt. trainee, then chief standards engr. Nat. Pressure Cooker Co., Eau Claire, Wis., 1946; sr. indsl. engr. Continental Can Co., 1950-51; with aircraft engine div. Ford Motor Co., Chgo., 1951-57, asst. to gen. mgr., 1956-57; exec. adminstr. Lions Internat., Chgo., 1957-71; exec. v.p. Dairy and Food Industries Supply Assn., Washington, 1971-73; pres. Nat. Eye Research Found., Chgo., 1973—. Mem. at large Nat. council Boy Scouts Am. Bd. dirs. Nat. Eye Research Found., 1972—. Served from pvt. to capt. USAAF, 1941-46. Mem. Am. Soc. Assn. Execs. Clubs: Toastmasters (past pres.) (Chgo.); Lions (Park Forest); Executives. Home: 2311 W 183d St Apt 303-B Homewood IL 60430 Office: 18 S Michigan Ave Chicago IL 60603

VOGT, ROCHUS EUGEN, physicist; b. Neckarelz, Germany, Dec. 21, 1929; s. Heinrich and Paula (Schaefer) V.; student U. Karlsruhe (Germany), 1950-52, U. Heidelberg (Germany), 1952-53; S.M., U. Chgo., 1957, Ph.D., 1961; m. Micheline Alice Yvonne Bauduin, Sept. 6, 1958; children—Michele, Nicole. Came to U.S., 1953. Mem. faculty dept. physics Calif. Inst. Tech., Pasadena, 1962—, asso. prof., 1965-70, prof., 1970—, chmn. faculty, 1975-77, chmn. div. physics, math. and astronomy, 1978—, chief scientist Jet Propulsion Lab., 1977-78. Fellow Am. Phys. Soc.; mem. Am. Assn. Physics Tchrs., AAAS, Sigma Xi. Research in astrophysics. Office: Calif Inst Tech Physics 103-33 Pasadena CA 91125

VOGTLE, ALVIN WARD, JR., utility exec.; b. Birmingham, Ala., Oct. 21, 1918; s. Alvin Ward and Ollie (Stringer) V.; B.S., Auburn U., 1939; LL.B., U. Ala., 1941; m. Kathryn Drennen, Apr. 20, 1945 (dec.); children—Kathryn D., Alvin Ward III, Anne Moore Baldwin; m. 2d, Rachael Giles, 1966; children—Bryant Wade, William Patrick, Rachel Giles, Robert Jackson. Admitted to Ala. bar, 1941; asso. firm Martin, Vogtle, Balch & Bingham and predessor firms, Birmingham, 1941-50, mem. firm, 1950-62; exec. v.p. Ala. Power Co., 1962-65; exec. v.p., dir. So. Co., 1966-69, pres., dir., 1969—; dir., chmn. bd. So. Co. Services, Inc.; dir. Protective Life Ins. Co., Seaboard Coast Line Industries, Inc., So. Electric Generating Co., Union Camp Corp.; v.p., dir. Ala. Power Co., Gulf Power Co., Miss. Power Co., Ga. Power Co. Trustee Tax Found., Inc., YMCA Met. Atlanta. Served from 2d lt. to capt., USAAF, 1941-45. Mem. Conf. Bd., Com. for Econ. Devel. (trustee), Newcomen Soc. N. Am., Ala. Hist. Soc., S.A.R., Soc. Colonial Wars, S.R., Auburn Alumni Assn., Sigma Nu. Episcopalian. Home: King's Lea Farms Batesville Rd Woodstock GA 30188 Office: 64 Perimeter Center E Atlanta GA 30346

VOHRA, RANBIR, polit. scientist; b. Lyallpur, Punjab, Pakistan, Mar. 5, 1928; came to U.S., 1964; s. Sualatram and Garuandevi Vohra; B.A. with honors, Govt. Coll., Lahore, 1946; diploma in Chinese, Peking (China) U., 1959; M.A. (Ford Found. fellow 1964-68, teaching fellow 1965-67, 68-69), Harvard U., 1965, Ph.D., 1969; m. Meena Vincent, Jan. 14, 1954. Program exec. All India Radio, 1947-64, head Chinese unit external services, 1959-64; instr., then lectr. history Harvard U., 1970-73; asso. prof. U. Calgary (Alta., Can.), 1971-73; mem. faculty Trinity Coll., Hartford, Conn., 1973—, Charles A. Dana prof. polit. sci., 1975—, chmn. dept., 1973—; tutor Dudley House, Harvard U., 1966-71, vis. univ. prof., summer 1972; vis. prof. Amherst Coll., spring 1974. Mem. Assn. Asian Studies, Am. Hist. Assn., Am. Polit. Sci. Assn., India Internat. Center. Author: Lao She and the Chinese Revolution, 1974; editor: The Chinese Revolution 1900-1950, 1974. Home: 4 Shepard Rd West Hartford CT 06110 Office: Trinity Coll Hartford CT 06106

VOHS, JAMES ARTHUR, health care program exec.; b. Idaho Falls, Idaho, Sept. 26, 1928; s. John Dale and Cliff Lucille (Packer) V.; B.A., U. Calif., Berkeley, 1952; postgrad. Harvard Sch. Bus., 1966; m. Janice Hughes, Sept. 19, 1953; children—Lorraine, Carol, Nancy, Sharla. Employed by various Kaiser affiliated orgns., 1952—, now pres. bd. dirs. Kaiser Found. Hosps. and Kaiser Found. Health Plan, Inc., Oakland, Calif. Mem. Sec. HEW's Task Force on Medicaid and Related Programs, 1969-70; vice chmn. Forum on Health Care Delivery, White House Conf. on Children, 1970; bd. regents Holy Names Coll., 1972—; pres. Marcus Foster Inst., 1979; vice chmn. Oakland Council Econ. Devel., 1976—. Served with AUS, 1946-48. Mem. Inst. Medicine. Home: 17 Westminster Dr Oakland CA 94618 Office: Ordway Bldg Kaiser Center Oakland CA 94612

VOHS, THOMAS RAYMOND, advt. exec.; b. N.Y.C., Jan. 21, 1920; s. Ernest J. and Gertrude C. (Moore) V.; B.A. cum laude, Colgate U., 1942; m. Marie C. Tierney, Dec. 13, 1944; children—Thomas J., James R., John L. With Chirurg & Cairns, Inc., Advt. (formerly John A. Cairns & Co.), N.Y.C., 1946—, v.p., 1951-55, exec. v.p., 1955-69, pres., also chief exec. officer, 1969—; chmn. bd. Advt. Crafts, Inc., N.Y.C., 1960—. Dir. Am. Assn. Advt. Agys., 1970-71. Served to lt. (s.g.) USNR, World War II. Mem. Delta Upsilon. Clubs: Union League (N.Y.C.); Huntington (N.Y.) Country Club.

VOIGHT, JON, actor; b. Yonkers, N.Y., Dec. 29, 1938; s. Elmer and Barbara (Camp) V.; grad. Cath. U.; studied with Sanford Meisner and Samantha Harper, N.Y.C.; m. Marcheline Bertrand, Dec. 12, 1971; children—James Haven, Angelina Jolie. Stage appearances include The Sound of Music, A View from the Bridge, Romeo and Juliet, The Tempest, A Streetcar Named Desire, Hamlet; TV appearances include Gunsmoke, Cimarron Strip; appeared in films Fearless Frank, 1969, Out of It, 1970, Midnight Cowboy, 1969, Catch-22, 1970, The Revolutionary, 1970, Deliverance, 1972, The All American Boy, 1973, Conrack, 1974, The Odessa File, 1974, End of the Game, 1976, Coming Home, 1978, The Champ, 1979. Winner Best Actor awards for Midnight Cowboy and Coming Home, Cannes Internat. Film Festival; Golden Globe award for Best Actor, Coming Home and The Champ; Acad. award for Best Actor, Coming Home, 1979; N.Y. Film Critics award, Los Angeles Film Critics award for Best Actor,

Midnight Cowboy, Coming Home. Address: care Laird Internat Studios 9336 W Washington Blvd Culver City CA 90230

VOIGT, ADOLF FRANK, educator, chemist; b. Upland, Calif., Jan. 31, 1914; s. Adolf Frank and Marie (Hirschler) V.; B.A., Pomona Coll., 1935; M.A., Claremont Coll., 1936; Ph.D., U. Mich., 1941; m. Mary London, Dec. 26, 1941; children—Maryanne, Richard L. Instr., Smith Coll., 1941-42; chemist Manhattan Dist., Iowa State U., Ames, 1942-46, faculty, 1946—, prof. chemistry, 1955—, sr. chemist Ames Lab., AEC, 1955—, asst. dir., 1959—, chief reactor div., 1968—, asst. dir. Inst. for Atomic Research (now Energy and Mineral Resources Research Inst.), 1959—. Mem. Am. Chem. Soc., Am. Phys. Soc., Am. Nuclear Soc., AAAS, Phi Beta Kappa, Sigma Xi, Phi Kappa Phi, Phi Lambda Upsilon. Contbr. articles to profl. jours., also chpts. on tracer methodology, thorium toxicology to books. Research on application radioactive tracers to chemistry, equilibrium problems, kinetics, activation analysis, behavior of energetic carbon atoms produced in nuclear reactions, radioactive decay properties of short-lived fission products. Home: 519 Oliver Circle Ames IA 50010

VOIGT, GARTH K., soil scientist; b. Merrill, Wis., Jan. 17, 1923; s. M.W. and Hattie (Krause) V.; B.S., U. Wis., 1948, M.S., 1949, Ph.D., 1951; m. Jane Wurster, Jan. 12, 1946; children—Timothy, Valerie, Jeffrey, Cabot. Mem. faculty U. Wis., Madison, 1950-54, asst. prof., 1953-54; faculty Yale, New Haven, 1955—, Margaret K. Musser Found. prof. forest soils, 1965—, acting dean Sch. Forestry, 1970-71, 75-76, dir. grad. studies Sch. Forestry, 1971-75. Collaborator U.S. Forest Service, 1952-55. Mem. Soil Sci. Soc. Am. (past divisional chmn., asso. editor proc. 1964-71), Am. Soc. Agronomy (dir. 1976—), Wis. Acad. Arts, Letters and Sci., Sigma Xi, Alpha Zeta. Author: Analysis of Soil and Plants, 1955, 58, 72. Contbr. articles to profl. jours. Research on ion uptake by trees. Office: 370 Prospect St New Haven CT 06511

VOIGT, KEITH MARION, soybean processing co. exec.; b. Iowa Falls, Iowa, Sept. 22, 1923; s. August E. and Luella V.; student pub. schs., Iowa Falls; m. Veloise D. Nolte, Apr. 22, 1944; children—Claudia, Vicky, Merle, John. Gen. mgr. Farmers Co-op, Iowa Falls, 1946-59; exec. v.p., gen. mgr. Boone Valley Co-op, Eagle Grove, Iowa, 1959—; dir. Farmland Ins. Co., Brenton Bank, Eagle Grove Indsl. Expansion Corp., Farmland Ind. Inc., Kansas City, Mo. Served with U.S. Army, 1944-46. Named Boss of Yr., Eagle Grove Jr. C. of C., 1972. Mem. Eagle Grove C. of C. (dir.). Clubs: Rotary, Elks. Home: Route 2 Eagle Grove IA 50533 Office: N Commercial St Eagle Grove IA 50533

VOIGT, MILTON, educator; b. Milw., Mar. 19, 1924; s. Arthur William and Esther (Bartelt) V.; Ph.B., U. Wis., 1948; M.A., U. Calif. at Berkeley, 1950; Ph.D., U. Minn., 1960; m. Leta Slack, July 27, 1947 (div. 1969); children—John Gregory, James Lewis, Andrew Charles. Asso. in subject A, U. Calif. at Berkeley, 1949-50; instr. English, U. Idaho, 1952-55; instr. U. Ky., 1956-60; asst. prof. U. Utah, Salt Lake City, 1960-64, asso. prof., 1964-68, prof., 1968—, asso. dean Coll. Letters and Sci., 1965-66, acting dean, 1966-67, dean, 1967-70, chmn. dept. English, 1971-75. Served to 2d lt. USAAF, 1943-45. John R. Park fellow U. Utah, 1970. Mem. Modern Lang. Assn., AAUP. Democrat. Episcopalian. Author: Swift and the Twentieth Century, 1964. Home: 1376 Princeton Ave Salt Lake City UT 84105

VOIGT, STUART ALAN, profl. football player; b. Madison, Wis., Aug. 12, 1948; s. Lester Preston and Alphilda (Brostrom) V.; B.B.A., U. Wis., 1969, M.B.A., 1974. Tight end, Minn. Vikings Profl. Football Club, 1970—. Hon. chmn. Whale of a Walk at Minn. Zool. Soc., Nat. Ataxia Found. Named Most Improved Player, Minn. Vikings, 1972; Madison's Favorite Son, Madison Pen and Mike Club, 1975; mem. Nat. Football Conf. Champion Team in Super Bowl, 1973, 74, 76. Mem. Nat. Football League Players Assn. Home: 454 Toepfer Ave Madison WI 53711 Office: 7110 France Ave S Edina MN 55435

VOINOVICH, GEORGE V., city ofcl.; b. Cleve., July 15, 1936; B.A., Ohio State U. 1958, J.D., 1961; m. Janet Voinovich; 4 children. Admitted to Ohio bar, 1961, U.S. Supreme Ct. bar, 1968; asso. firm Calfee, Halter and Griswold; asst. Ohio atty. gen., 1962-63; mem. Ohio Ho. of Reps., 1967-71; auditor Cuyahoga County (Ohio), 1971-76, commr., 1977-78; lt. gov. State of Ohio, 1979; mayor City of Cleve., 1979—. Recipient cert. of Merit award Ohio U.; named one of Outstanding Young Men in Ohio, Ohio Jaycees, 1970; one of Outstanding Young Men in Greater Cleve., Cleve. Jaycees. Mem. Omicron Delta Kappa, Phi Alpha Theta, Phi Delta Phi. Republican. Office: City Hall 601 Lakeside Ave E Cleveland OH 44114*

VOISINET, JAMES RAYMOND, bldg. materials mfg. co. exec.; b. Buffalo, June 18, 1931; s. Walter E. and Hildegarde M. (Opitz) V.; B.M.E., Cornell U., 1951; B.A. in Econs. cum laude, St. Lawrence U., 1954; m. Virginia M. Waud, Sept. 14, 1957; children—James Raymond, Sarah, Anne. Partner Weber, Loes, Weber Assos., Buffalo, 1956-62; dir. mktg. Gold Bond div. Nat. Gypsum Co., Charlotte, N.C., 1962-72, v.p. merchandising Gold Bond div., 1973-74; corp. group v.p., Dallas, 1974—; dir. Pregypan-Rigips, Marseille, France. Bd. dirs. Nat. Council World Affairs, 1979; mem. adv. council U. Tex., Dallas. Served to 1st lt. U.S. Army, 1954-56. Republican. Roman Catholic. Clubs: Dallas, Northwood. Home: 6938 Meadowcreek Dr Dallas TX 75240 Office: 4100 First Internat Bldg Dallas TX 75270

VOIT, RICHARD LOUIS, lawyer; b. Milw., June 16, 1917; s. Max L. and Alma (Harnisch) V.; B.S. in Elec. Engring. magna cum laude, U. Wis., 1939; J.D. with distinction (Larner medal, Ellsworth Patent Law prize), George Washington U., 1944; m. Grace H. Roden, Mar. 24, 1979; children—Holly Pose, Richard Jay, Steven Max. Engr., Gen. Electric Co., 1939-42, Bur. Ships Navy Dept., 1942-45; admitted to D.C. bar, 1943, Ill. bar, 1946, also U.S. Patent Office; atty. patent sect. Bur. Ships, 1945; mem. firm Leydig, Voit, Osann, Mayer & Holt, Chgo., 1945—. Mem. Am., Chgo. bar assns., Am., Chgo. (pres. 1972) patent law assns., Order of Coif, U.S. Power Squadrons, Tau Beta Pi, Eta Kappa Nu, Phi Delta Phi. Republican. Presbyterian. Home: 250 Maple Row Northbrook IL 60062 Office: One IBM Plaza Chicago IL 60611

VOJTA, CHARLES JOHN, JR., pub. co. exec.; b. Berwyn, Ill., July 28, 1927; s. Charles John and Lucille Virginia (Clouston) V.; B.B.A., Northwestern U., 1950; M.B.A., U. Chgo., 1958; m. Lorraine Ellen Weber, Feb. 7, 1953; children—John, Charles, Richard, Elizabeth. Jr. acct. Baumann Finney & Co., C.P.A.'s, 1950-53; acct. Lone Star Steel Co., 1953-55; controller Easterling Co., 1955-61; exec. v.p., chief operating officer Standard Rate and Data Service, Inc., Skokie, Ill., 1961—; pres., dir. Nat. Register Pub. Co. Inc.; dir. Standard Rate and Data Service Inc. Bd. dirs., treas. St. Mark Luth. Ch. Served with U.S. Army, 1945-47. Mem. Am. Inst. C.P.A.'s, Am. Bus. Press. Home: 118 S Kenilworth Mount Prospect IL 60056 Office: 5201 Old Orchard Rd Skokie IL 60076

VOKETAITIS, ARNOLD MATHEW, bass-baritone; b. East Haven, Conn., May 11, 1932; s. Mathew Joseph and Agnes Mary (Pilvelis) V.; B.S. in Bus. Adminstrn., Quinnipiac Coll., 1954; m. Nijole Julia Lipciute, Sept. 6, 1968; children—Arnold Mathew, Paul Stanley. Operatic Debut with N.Y.C. Opera, 1958; European debut at Liceo, Barcelona, Spain, 1968; appeared with maj. operatic and symphonic orgns., in U.S., Can., Mexico, Central Am.; mem. Lyric Opera of Chgo., 1966-79; rec. artist; recitalist; appearances on Pay-TV; tchr. voice and acting; condr. master classes in singing; mem. adv. panels in music and ethnic affairs Ill. Arts Council. Served with band U.S. Army, 1954-56. Winner, Conn. Opera Auditions of Air, 1957; Rockefeller grantee, 1964. Mem. Am. Guild Mus. Artists (gov.), AFTRA, Actors Equity.

VOLAND, KENNETH LEE, constrn. co. exec.; b. Nashville, Ind., Nov. 1, 1933; s. Lloyd Lewis and Olive (Tracey) V.; B.A. in Accounting, Ind. U., 1956; m. Sarah Lou Weddle, July 12, 1953; children—Bruce Allen, Douglas J., Suzzane. Cost accounting mgr. Cummins Engine Co., Columbus, Ind., 1953-59; regional controller Divco Wayne Corp., N.Y.C., 1959-68; v.p. finance, sec. Redman Mobile Home, Inc., Dallas, 1968-74; v.p. finance and adminstrn. Bendix Home Systems, Inc., 1974-79; v.p. mfg. Mobile Home Industries, Inc., Tallahassee, Fla., 1979—. Served with AUS, 1953-55. Elk. Home: 120 Honey Tree Ln Roswell GA 30341 Office: 1309 Thomasville Rd Tallahassee FL 32304

VOLCHOK, ZOLLIE MARC, corp. exec.; b. Salem, Oreg., Sept. 22, 1916; s. Abram and Luba V.; B.S., U. Oreg., 1939; m. Sylvia Helen Lebenzon, Aug. 5, 1939; children—Gary, Michael, Tony. Gen. mgr. Sterling Theatres, 1946-52; co-founder N.W. Releasing Corp., 1952-68; exec. v.p., gen. mgr. First N.W. Industries, Seattle, 1968—. Bd. dirs. March of Dimes, Jewish Fedn. and Council; Seattle B'nai B'rith Community Service Found.; mem. regional bd. Anti-Defamation League, B'nai B'rith. Served with USNR, 1943-45. Recipient Outstanding Citizen award Hebrew Acad., 1978. Mem. U. Oreg. Alumni Assn. (dir. 1962-68), Found. Motion Picture Pioneers. Club: Variety (past pres. Pacific N.W., internat. v.p., internat. fund raising chmn.). Office: 419 Occidental S Seattle WA 98104

VOLCKER, PAUL A., banker, govt. ofcl.; b. Cape May, N.J., Sept. 5, 1927; s. Paul A. and Alma Louise (Klippel) V.; A.B. summa cum laude, Princeton U., 1949; M.A., Harvard U., 1951; postgrad. London (Eng.) Sch. Econs., 1951-52; m. Barbara Marie Bahnson, Sept. 11, 1954; children—Janice, James. Economist, Fed. Res. Bank N.Y., 1952-57, pres., 1975—; economist Chase Manhattan Bank, 1957-61, v.p., dir. planning, 1965-68; with Dept. Treasury, 1961-65, 69-74, dep. under sec. monetary affairs, 1963-65, under sec., 1969-74; pres. Fed. Res. Bank of N.Y., N.Y.C., 1975-79; chmn. bd. govs. Fed. Res. System, 1979—. Sr. fellow Woodrow Wilson Sch. Pub. and Internat. Affairs, 1974-75. Office: Office Chmn Fed Res Bd 20th and Constitution Ave NW Washington DC 20551

VOLDSETH, EDWARD VICTOR, univ. ofcl.; b. Harlowton, Mont., May 29, 1922; s. Nels E. and Mina Berg (Grande) V.; B.A., U. Mont., 1944; M.A., Columbia, 1946; Ph.D., U. Ia., 1958; m. Elizabeth Annie Settle, Sept. 1, 1945; children—Nels Edward, John Eric, Karen Elizabeth, Kristin Jane. Asst. dean men, instr. bus. adminstrn. Carroll Coll., Waukesha, Wis., 1946-49; dir. student affairs for men Drake U., Des Moines, 1949-56; dean students, prof. psychology U. Alaska, 1958-64; dean students U. No. Iowa, Cedar Falls, 1964-71, v.p. univ. relations and devel., 1971-76, asst. to pres., 1977—; dir. Cedar Falls Savs. & Loan Assn., 1966—. Mem. bd. Clive Ind. Sch. Dist., Des Moines, 1953-56; Alaska del. White House Conf. on Children and Youth, 1960; Iowa del. White House Conf. on Youth, 1971; mem. nat. council for devel. ministry Episcopal Ch., 1976—. Bd. dirs. U. No. Iowa Found.; trustee Seabury Western Sem., Evanston, Ill., 1975—. Mem. Sigma Chi, Phi Delta Kappa. Republican. Episcopalian (diocesan council, standing com., del. gen. convs., vestryman, chmn. finance com.). Rotarian (past pres.). Club: Des Moines. Home: 1228 Grand Blvd Cedar Falls IA 50613

VOLK, DAVID LAWRENCE, state ofcl.; b. Mitchell, S.D., Apr. 12, 1947; s. Erwin John and Joan (Nieses) V.; B.S., No. State Coll., Aberdeen, S.D., 1969; m. Susan Tessier, May 31, 1969. State treas., State of S.D., Pierre, 1972—. Mem. adv. com. U.S. Commn. on Civil Rights; mem. exec. com. Boy Scouts Am. Served with U.S. Army, 1969-71; Vietnam. Decorated Bronze Star. Republican. Roman Catholic. Clubs: Elks, Am. Legion, VFW. Home: 223 N Pierce St Pierre SD 57501 Office: State Treasurer's Office Capitol Bldg Pierre SD 57501

VOLK, HARRY J., bank exec.; b. Trenton, N.J., July 20, 1905; s. Michael T. and Susan (Harkins) V.; A.B., Rutgers U., 1927, LL.B., 1930, L.H.D., 1958; m. Marion E. Waters, Oct. 12, 1931 (dec. 1972); children—Robert H., Richard R., Carolyn E. Volk Jacques; m. 2d, Marjorie L. Hale, Aug. 14, 1976. With Prudential Ins. Co., 1927-57, v.p. in charge Western ops., Los Angeles, 1947-57; pres. Union Bank of Los Angeles, 1957-69, dir., 1957—, chmn. 1974—; chmn., dir. Union Bancorp, Inc., 1969-79; dir. Standard Chartered Bancorp. Trustee, Rutgers U., 1942-47, Calif. Inst. Tech., Hosp. of Good Samaritan. Alumni trustee Rutgers U., 1942-47, pres. Nat. Alumni Assn., 1940-45. Served as div. chief, U.S. Strategic Bombing Survey, 1945. Mem. Los Angeles C. of C. (dir. 1949-52), Calif. Clearing House Assn., USC Assos., Los Angeles County Mus. Art, Assos. Calif. Inst. Tech. Clubs: The Founders, Los Angeles, Bohemian, Los Angeles Country, Calif. Office: Union Bank 445 S Figueroa St Los Angeles CA 90071

VOLK, ROBERT HARKINS, fin. holding co. exec.; b. E. Orange, N.J., Nov. 27, 1932; s. Harry J. and Marion (Waters) V.; B.A., Stanford, 1954, LL.B., 1958; m. Barbara June Klint, 1955. Admitted to Calif. bar, 1959; asso., then partner firm Adams, Duque & Hazeltine, Los Angeles, 1958-67; commr. corps. State of Calif., 1967-69; chmn. bd. Unionamerica, Inc., Los Angeles, 1969—; dir. Union Bank, Los Angeles, Union Bancorp, Host Internat., Western Airlines. Chmn. Calif. Bd. Investment, 1967; mem. Calif. World Trade Authority, 1969. Bd. overseers Hoover Instn. on War, Revolution and Peace. Served with USAF, 1955-57. Mem. Am., Calif., Los Angeles bar assns., Calif. C. of C. (dir. 1972—). Clubs: Los Angeles, Los Angeles Country, Cal. (Los Angeles); Beach (Santa Monica, Calif.). Co-author: Practice Under the Corporate Securities Law of 1968, 1969. Office: 445 S Figueroa Los Angeles CA 90071

VOLKART, EDMUND HOWELL, educator; b. Aberdeen, Md., Nov. 9, 1919; s. Ernest and Edna (Ripken) V.; B.A., St. John's Coll., 1939; M.A. in Sociology, Yale, 1942, Ph.D., 1947; m. Mary Ellen Drew, June 16, 1949; children—Karen Elaine, Kirsten. Instr. sociology Syracuse U., 1946-47; from instr. to asst. prof. Yale, 1947-54; from asst. prof. to prof. Stanford, 1954-62, exec. head dept. sociology, 1956-59, dir. program in medicine and behavioral scis., 1959-62; dean humanities and social scis. Oreg. State U., 1962-63, dean faculty, 1963-65; now prof. sociology U. Hawaii. Vis. research asso. Harvard Grad. Sch. Edn., 1950-52; nat. editor social psychology UNESCO project in social scis., 1957-64; mem. social sci. subcom. and policy and planning bd. NIMH, 1962-64. Served lt. USNR, 1942-45. Decorated Legion of Merit. Mem. Am. Sociol. Assn. (exec. officer 1965-70), Sociol. Research Assn., AAAS, Phi Kappa Phi. Editor: Social Behavior and Personality, 1951. Home: 750 Ululani St Kailua HI 96734. *If I had to single out one condition above all others for such modest success as has been mine, it would be luck - sheer luck. The happenstances of family environment, the chance encounters that led to inspired teachers and loyal friends, the countless combinations of the dice of history that put one in the right place at the right time - these are the stuff of which careers are made. When all is said and done, the aleatory element prevails.*

VOLKER, JOSEPH FRANCIS, univ. chancellor; b. Elizabeth, N.J., Mar. 9, 1913; s. Francis Joseph and Rose G. (Hennessey) V.; D.D.S., Ind. U., 1936; A.B., U. Rochester, 1938, M.S., 1939, Ph.D., 1941; D.Sc. (hon.), U. Med. Sci., Thailand, 1967; Dr. honoris causa, Lund U., Sweden, 1968, U. Louis Pasteur de Strasbourg, 1972; D.Sc. (hon.), Ind. U. 1970, U. Ala., 1970, Coll. Medicine and Dentistry N.J., 1973, U. Rochester, 1975, Georgetown U., 1978, Fairleigh-Dickinson U., 1978, U. Ariz., 1978; Prof. honoris causa, U. Fed. do Rio de Janeiro, 1977; m. Juanita Berry, Feb. 6, 1937; children—Joseph Francis, Juanita Anne, John Berry. Dental intern Mountainside Hosp., Montclair, N.J., 1936-37; Carnegie fellow in dentistry U. Rochester, 1937-41; asst. prof. biochemistry U. Rochester, 1941-42; prof. clin. dentistry Dental Sch., Tufts Coll., 1942-47, dean, 1947-49, dean Sch. Dentistry, U. Ala., 1948-62, dir. research and grad. study U. Ala. Med. Center, 1955-65; v.p. health affairs, 1962-66; v.p. Birmingham Affairs, 1966-68, dir. Med. Center, Birmingham, 1966-68, exec. v.p. U. Ala., Birmingham, 1968-69, pres., 1969-76; chancellor U. Ala. System, 1976—; dir. Ariz. Med. Sch. Study, 1960-61, U.S. Dept. State teaching specialist, Thailand, 1951; mem. Unitarian Service committee's med. teaching mission to Czechoslovakia, 1946, Germany, 1948. Bd. regents Nat. Library Medicine, 1973-77. Decorated Order White Lion (Czechoslovakia), 1946; Most Noble Order Crown (Thailand), 1959; comdr. Order Falcon, Republic Iceland, 1969; fellow in dental surgery Royal Coll. Surgeons Eng., 1961; fellow faculty dentistry Royal Coll. Surgeons Ireland, 1973. Diplomate Am. Bd. Oral Medicine. Mem. Inst. Medicine of Nat. Acad. Scis., Soc. for Exptl. Biology and Medicine, Am. Dental Assn., Am. Chem. Soc., Internat. Assn. for Dental Research, Sigma Xi, Omicron Kappa Upsilon, Alpha Omega Alpha. Club: Cosmos. Home: 8 Central Highlands Tuscaloosa AL 35404 Office: U Ala System PO Box BT University AL 35486

VOLKHARDT, JOHN MALCOM, food co. exec.; b. Pa., Apr. 13, 1917; s. George Thomas and Evelyn (Mitchell) V.; A.B. cum laude, Brown U., 1939; children—Jacqueline, Janet, Dana. Product mgr. Vick Chem. Co., N.Y.C., 1939-48; gen. mgr. N.O. Warren Co., Stamford, Conn., 1948-56; gen. mgr. Rit div. Best Foods Co., N.Y.C., 1956-58; with Best Foods div. CPC Internat. Inc., Englewood Cliffs, N.J., 1959-78, exec. v.p., 1968-72, Pres. 1972-78, pres. North Am. div. CPC Internat. and exec. v.p. CPC Internat., 1978—. Trustee Nutrition Found., N.Y.C.; chmn. Keep Am. Beautiful Inc. N.Y.C. Mem. Am. Mgmt. Assn., Grocery Mfrs. Assn., Conf. Bd., Phi Beta Kappa. Clubs: Knickerbocker Country, Met., Can. Office: Internat Plaza Englewood Cliffs NJ 07632

VOLKMAN, (ROSALYN) ELIZABETH, soprano; b. Wichita, Kans.; d. Harold William and Velma Katharine V.; Mus.B., U. Colo., 1965; postgrad. Juilliard Sch. Music, 1965-68; 1 son, Douglas Randall. European debut Geneva Grand Theatre, 1967; appeared with opera cos. throughout Europe, 1968-74; lead soprano Charlotte (N.C.) Opera Co., 1975, Kansas City (Mo.) Lyric Opera, 1976, Mich. Opera Co., Detroit, 1976, Met. Opera Co., N.Y.C., 1976—, Jackson (Miss.) Opera, 1977, Miami (Fla.) Opera Co., 1973, Houston Grand Opera, 1978; soloist numerous festivals and symphonies throughout U.S. and Europe; roles sang include: Cio-Cio-San in Madame Butterfly, Mimi and Musetta in La Boheme, Micaela in Carmen, Marenka in The Bartered Bride, Lisa in Pique Dame, Alice Ford in Falstaff, Antonia in Tales of Hoffman, Countess in Marriage of Figaro, title roles in Rusalka, Ariadne, Vanessa, also Giorgetta in Il Taliarro, Donna Elvira in Don Giovanni, others. Winner Liederkranz Found. Competition, 1966, Montreal Voice Competition, 1967, Balt. Opera Auditions, 1968, Internat. Opera Competition, Sofia, Bulgaria, 1967; Artists Adv. Council of Chgo. scholar, 1967; William Sullivan Found. grantee, 1968-77. Mem. Met. Opera Guild, Am. Guild Mus. Artists. Composer: Julia Smith; recording of opera Daisy, 1976, Cycle of Love, others. Address: 43 Amberson Ave Yonkers NY 10705

VOLKMANN, DANIEL GEORGE, JR., architect; b. San Francisco, June 3, 1924; s. Daniel George and Beatrice (Simpson) V.; B.A., Yale U., 1945; B.A. in Architecture, U. Calif. at Berkeley, 1950, M.A., 1951; m. Maruin Johnson, Sept. 1, 1949; children—Daniel G., William R., David R., Wendy. Practice architecture, San Francisco, 1952—; sec., dir. Bull, Field, Volkmann, Stockwell, architects, 1969—; ltd. partner Dean Witter & Co., San Francisco, 1967-69; dir. Pacific Lighting Corp. Mem. council Friends Bancroft Library, U. Calif. at Berkeley. Trustee San Francisco Mus. Art, Marin Country Day Sch., 1972-77; mem. Art Commn. City and County San Francisco, 1975—. Served with USNR, 1944-46. Recipient numerous awards in design AIA. Mem. AIA, San Francisco Planning and Urban Renewal Assn., Cow Hollow Improvement Assn. (dir., pres. 1970). Clubs: Bohemian, Olympic, McCloud River, Pacific Union (San Francisco). Home: 2616 Union St San Francisco CA 94123 Office: 350 Pacific St San Francisco CA 94111

VOLKMER, HAROLD L., congressman; b. Jefferson City, Mo., Apr. 4, 1931; student Jefferson City Jr. Coll., 1949-51, St. Louis U. Sch. Commerce and Finance, 1951-52; LL.B., U. Mo., 1955; m. Shirley Ruth Braskett; children—Jerry Wayne, John Paul, Elizabeth Ann. Admitted to Mo. bar, 1955; individual practice law, Hannibal, 1958—; asst. atty. gen. Mo., 1955; pros. atty. Marion County, 1960-66; mem. Mo. Ho. of Reps., 1966-76, chmn. judiciary com., mem. revenue and econs. com.; mem. 95th-96th Congresses from 9th Mo. Dist., mem. judiciary and sci. coms. Served with U.S. Army, 1955-57. Recipient award for meritorious pub. service in Gen. Assembly, St. Louis Globe-Democrat, 1972-74. Mem. Mo., 10th Jud. Circuit bar assns. Roman Catholic. Clubs: K.C., Hannibal Lions. Office: 1728 Longworth House Office Bldg Washington DC 20515

VOLLE, ROBERT LEON, educator; b. Houston, Pa., June 2, 1930; s. Leon Jacob and Ida (Volle) V.; B.S., W.Va. Wesleyan Coll., 1953; Ph.D., U. Kans., 1959; m. Adva Jean Runnels, Sept. 7, 1952; children—Linda Michelle, Robert Leon, Stephen, Lisa Marie, John. Mem. faculty U. Pa., Phila., 1959-65, asst. prof. pharmacology, 1960-64, asso. prof., 1964-65; prof., chmn. dept. Tulane U., New Orleans, 1965-67; prof. U. Conn. Health Center, Farmington, 1967-78, head dept., 1967-68, asso. dean preclin. edn., 1977—. Served with USAF, 1950-54. Pa. Plan scholar, 1960-63; recipient Career Devel. award USPHS, 1963. Mem. Am. Pharmacology Soc., Biophys. Soc., AAAS, Sigma Xi, Theta Chi. Research on autonomic nervous system. Home: 5 Wagon Hill Avon CT 06001 Office: U Conn Health Center Farmington CT 06032

VOLLEN, ROBERT JAY, lawyer; b. Chgo., Jan. 23, 1940; s. Ben N. and Rose (Belonsky) V.; A.B., U. Mich., 1961; J.D., U. Chgo., 1964; m. Judith Paula Spector Aug. 12, 1961; children—Steven, Neil, Jennifer. Admitted to Ill. bar, 1964, D.C. bar, 1965, U.S. Supreme Ct. bar, 1975; atty. appellate sect. Civil Div., U.S. Dept. Justice, Washington, 1964-65; asso. firm Schiff Hardin & Waite, Chgo., 1965-70, partner firm, 1971-72; gen. counsel BPI (Bus. and Profl. People for Pub. Interest), Chgo., 1972—. Mem. vis. com. U. Chgo. Law Sch., 1978—. Mem. Chgo. Council Lawyers (gov. 1972-76, 79—), Am. Bar Assn. (ho. of dels. 1974-76). Home: 661 Detamble Ave Highland Park IL 60035 Office: 109 N Dearborn St Chicago IL 60602

VOLLMAR, JOHN RAYMOND, elec. engr.; b. Phila., Nov. 8, 1929; s. William Gustav and Pauline Marie (Jesanker) V.; B.E.E., Drexel U., Phila., 1952; m. Sara Lois Jacob, Feb. 1, 1964; children—Paul Gary, Virginia Ann, Pamela Jean, Barbara Gayle, Thomas Edward. Sales and applicarion engr. Gen. Electric Co., Erie, Pa., 1955-59; rail transit and equipment engr. Louis T. Klauder & Assos., Phila., 1959-65, partner in charge r.r. and transit equipment engring., 1965—. Served with C.E., AUS, 1952-54. Decorated Army Commendation ribbon; registered profl. engr., Pa. Fellow Am. Cons. Engrs. Council; mem. Nat., Pa. socs. profl. engrs., IEEE, Am. Pub. Transit Assn., Transp. Research Bd. Presbyterian. Clubs: Union League, Engrs. (Phila.). Home: 225 Oak Hill Dr Hatboro PA 19040 Office: 2100 Phila Nat Bank Bldg Philadelphia PA 19107

VOLLUM, HOWARD, corp. exec.; b. 1913; B.A., Reed Coll., 1936; married. With Murdock Radio & Appliance Co., 1936-41; a founder, chmn. Tektronix, Inc., 1946—; dir. U.S. Nat. Bank Oreg., Pacific Power & Light Co. Served with U.S. Signal Corps, 1941-45. Office: Tektronix Inc PO Box 500 Beaverton OR 97005

VOLNER, JILL WINE, lawyer, former govt. ofcl.; b. Chgo., May 5, 1943; d. Bert Stanford and Sylvia Dawn (Simon) Wine; B.S., U. Ill., 1964; J.D., Columbia U., 1968; LL.D., Hood Coll., 1975; m. Ian David Volner, Aug. 21, 1965. Asst. dir. press and relations Assembly of Captive European Nations, N.Y.C., 1965-66; research asst. Columbia Law Sch., N.Y.C., 1967-68; admitted to N.Y. State bar, 1969, also D.C. bar, Supreme Ct. bar; spl. atty. criminal div. organized crime and racketeering sect. U.S. Dept. Justice, Washington, 1969-70, trial atty. criminal div. mgmt. and labor sect., 1970-73, trial atty. strike force 18 organized crime and racketeering sect., 1973, asst. spl. prosecutor Watergate spl. prosecution force, 1973-75; asso. firm Fried, Frank, Harris, Shriver & Kampelmen, 1975-77; gen. counsel Dept. Army, 1977-79; practice law, Chgo., 1979—. Recipient Spl. Achievement award for sustained superior performance U.S. Dept Justice, 1972, Meritorious award, 1973. Mem. D.C. Bar, Fed. Bar Assn.

VOLNY, JAMES GEORGE, librarian; b. Columbus, Ohio, Aug. 10, 1931; s. James and Anna (Hochmuth) V.; B.S., Kent State U., 1953; student Northwestern U., 1953-54; M.L.S., Western Res. U., 1963; m. Doris M. Karabek, May 17, 1958; children—Constance Marie, Laurie Ann, Christina Mae. Chemist, Standard Oil Co. (Ohio) Cleve., 1954-62; librarian U. Notre Dame, 1963-66; univ. librarian Loyola U., New Orleans, 1966-77, also tchr. eve. div.; dir. library services Centenary Coll. of La., Shreveport, 1977—. Mem. Am., La., Catholic (council 1968—) library assns., La. Conf. Colls. and Univs. (chmn. library sect. 1969-70), Library Assn., Beta Phi Mu. Club: K.C. Home: 4800 Tartan Dr Metairie LA 70003 Office: Magale Library Centenary Coll Shreveport LA 71104

VOLPE, EDMOND LORIS, coll. pres.; b. New Haven, Nov. 16, 1922; s. Joseph D. and Rose (Maisano) V.; A.B., U. Mich., 1943; M.A., Columbia, 1947, Ph.D., 1954; m. Rose Conte, May 20, 1950; children—Rosalind, Lisa. Instr., N.Y. U., 1949-54; mem. faculty City Coll. N.Y., 1954-74, prof. English, 1968-74, chmn. dept., 1964-70, pres. Richmond Coll., 1974-76; pres. Coll. S.I., 1976—. Fulbright prof. Am. lit., France, 1960-61. Bd. dirs. Staten Island United Way, 1975—, S.I. council boy Scouts Am., 1977—, S.I. Doctors Hosp., 1977-78, Snug Harbor Cultural Center, 1978—, St. Vincent's Hosp., 1979—. Served with AUS, 1943-46. Mem. MLA, Am. Studies Assn., Assn. Dept. English (exec. com. 1969-71). Club: Andiron N.Y. (pres. 1972-75). Author: A Reader's Guide to William Faulkner, 1964; also anthologies and coll. text books. Co-editor: Eleven Modern Short Novels.

VOLPE, ERMINIO PETER, educator, biologist; b. N.Y.C., Apr. 7, 1927; s. Rocco and Rose (Ciano) V.; B.S., City Coll. N.Y., 1948; M.A., Columbia, 1949, Ph.D. (Newberry award 1952), 1952; m. Carolyn Lawton Thorne, Sept. 1, 1955; children—Laura Elizabeth, Lisa Lawton, John Peter. Mem. faculty Newcomb Coll., 1952-60, prof. zoology, 1960-64; prof. biology, Tulane U., New Orleans, 1964—, chmn. dept., 1964-66, 69—, asso dean grad. sch., 1967-69. Cons., Nat. Commn. Undergrad. Edn. in Biol. Scis., 1964-71; mem. steering com. Biol. Scis. Curriculum Study, 1966-70; panelist NRC, 1967-70; mem. U.S. Nat. Commn. for UNESCO, 1968-72; regional lectr. Sigma Xi, 1970-72; chmn. Advanced Placement Test in Biology, Ednl. Testing Service, 1975—. Served with USNR, 1945-46. Fellow AAAS; mem. Genetics Soc. Am., Am. Soc. Zoologists, Am. Soc. Naturalists, Soc. Developmental Biology, Soc. Study Evolution, Phi Beta Kappa (v.p. Tulane U. chpt. 1962), Sigma Xi (pres. Tulane U. chpt. 1964, faculty award 1972). Author: (textbook) Understanding Evolution, 1967; Human Heredity and Birth Defects, 1971; Patterns and Experiments in Developmental Biology, 1973; Man, Nature, and Society, 1975. Mem. editorial bd. Copeia, 1962-63; asso. editor Jour. Exptl. Zoology, 1968-76; editor Am. Zoologist, 1975—. Contbr. articles to profl. jours. Home: 1591 Exposition Blvd New Orleans LA 70118

VOLPE, RAYMOND FRANCE, assn. exec.; b. N.Y.C., Aug. 14, 1939; s. Frank and Mildred (Lentini) V.; B.S., Fordham U., 1960-64; m. Susan Nan Oren, Dec. 21, 1968; children—Noel, Dana. Account exec. Doyle, Dane, Bernbach, Inc., advt. agy., N.Y.C., 1964-71; v.p. mktg. Nat. Hockey League, N.Y.C., 1972-75; commr. Ladies Profl. Golf Assn., N.Y.C., 1975—. Served with USMCR, 1956-59. Office: Ladies Profl Golf Assn 919 3d Ave New York City NY 10028

VOLPE, ROBERT, endocrinologist; b. Toronto, Ont., Can., Mar. 6, 1926; s. Aaron G. and Esther (Shulman) V.; M.D., U. Toronto, 1950; m. Ruth Vera Pullan, Sept. 5, 1949; children—Catherine, Elizabeth, Peter, Edward, Rose Ellen. Intern, U. Toronto, 1950-51, resident in medicine, 1952-52, 53-55, fellow in endocrinology, 1952-53, 55-57, sr. research fellow dept. medicine, 1957-62, McPhedran fellow, 1957-65, asst. prof., 1962-68, asso. prof., 1968-72, prof., 1972—; attending staff St. Joseph's Hosp., Toronto, 1957-66; active staff Wellesley Hosp., Toronto, 1966—, dir. endocrinology research lab., 1968—, physician-in-chief, 1974—. Recipient Goldie medal for med. research U. Toronto, 1971; Med. Research Council Can. grantee, 1955—. Fellow Royal Coll. Physicians (Can.), Royal Soc. Medicine, A.C.P.; mem. Can. Soc. Endocrinology and Metabolism (past pres.), Can. Soc. Clin. Investigation, Am. Thyroid Assn. (1st v.p. 1975-76), Endocrine Soc., Am. Fedn. Clin. Research, Soc. Nuclear Medicine, AAAS, N.Y. Acad. Sci., European Thyroid Assn., Latin Am. Thyroid Assn. Clubs: Donalda, Alpine Ski, U. Toronto Faculty; hon. mem. Soc. Endocrinology and Metabolism of Chile. Author: Systematic Endocrinology, 1973; also numerous research articles, especially on immunology of thyroid disease; editorial bd. Clin. Endocrinology. Home: 3 Daleberry Pl Don Mills ON M3B 2A5 Canada Office: Wellesley Hosp Toronto ON M4Y 1J3 Canada. *Rigid adherence to high standards and integrity is essential. Do what is worth doing now, not tomorrow.*

VOLPICELLI, LOUIS JOSEPH, TV producer and dir.; b. Scranton, Pa., Oct. 15, 1923; s. Vito Loreto and Clara (Aruta) V.; B.S., U. Scranton, 1949; postgrad. Catholic U. Am., 1949, Fordham U., 1950-51, Ohio State U., 1944; m. Susan Wright, Oct. 30, 1954; 1 dau., Elizabeth. Actor, 1951—; staff dir., dir. musicals, comedy, news, and other shows ABC-TV, 1953—, dir. Discovery, 1961-69, Mr. Imagination, 1954, Runy to Daylight docuemntary, 1962, Ancient Games film, 1972, producer-dir. ABC Sports, 1963—, dir. Hour of Commercials, Arthur Godfrey Spl., 1970, Olympics '68, '72, '76, dir. program planning 1980 Winter Olympics; dir. On the Carousel, CBS, 1953; tchr. in field. Served with U.S. Army, 1943-46. Recipient Peabody award; Western Heritage award Nat. Cowboy Hall of Fame, 1963, 66, 73; Golden Eagle award 1978. Mem. Nat. Acad. TV Arts and Scis. (Emmy 1968), Radio and TV Dirs. Guild. Democrat. Roman Catholic. Home: 38 Phillips Ln Darien CT 06820 Office: ABC Sports 1330 Ave of the Americas New York NY 10019

VOLPP, LOUIS DONOVAN, coll. adminstr.; b. Ida Grove, Iowa, Nov. 16, 1929; s. Herman Henry and Mary (Donovan) V.; B.S., Iowa State U., 1952; M.A., State U. Ia., 1956, Ph.D., 1958; m. Hollace Rae Saar, Jan. 29, 1956; children—Bryan, Denise, Diane, John. Mem. faculty U. Ill. at Urbana, 1957-67, asso. dir. Grad. Sch. Bus., 1961-65, asso. provost, 1965-67; prof. bus. adminstrn. Duke U., Durham, N.C., 1967-73, dean Grad. Sch. Bus. Adminstrn., 1969-73, chmn. dept. mgmt. scis., 1967-73; prof. Grad. Sch. Bus. Adminstrn., Columbia U., N.Y.C., 1973-76, dean, 1973-75; prof., v.p. acad. affairs Calif. State U., Fresno, 1976—; dir. Bache & Co., Diebold Venture Capital Co. Chief Div. Tech. Services Ill., 1965-66; chmn. Council on Community Services Ill., 1965-67; bd. Am. Council Germany, 1974—. Ex officio mem. bd. dirs. Am. Assembly, 1973-76. Served to lt. USMCR, 1952-54. Mem. Order Artus, Beta Gamma Sigma. Address: California State U at Fresno Fresno CA 93740

VOLRICH, JOHN JACK, mayor, lawyer; b. Anyox, B.C., Can., Feb. 27, 1928; s. Emil and Nana (Perlain) V.; B.A., LL.B., U. B.C.; m. Laverne Volrich, Oct. 16, 1954; children—Steven, Dana. Mayor, City of Vancouver (B.C.); chmn. Vancouver Police Commn.; chmn. Urban Transit Authority of B.C. Mem. Can. Fedn. Mayors (past pres.), Union B.C. Municipalities. Club: Lions. Office: City Hall 453 W 12th Ave Vancouver BC Canada

VOLWILER, WADE, educator, physician; b. Grand Forks, N.D., Sept. 16, 1917; s. Albert T. and Ada Ethel (White) V.; A.B., Oberlin Coll., 1939; M.D. cum laude, Harvard, 1943; m. Anna Catherine Davies, Mar. 13, 1943; children—Susan, Craig Davies, Timothy Davies. Intern, med. resident Mass. Gen. Hosp., Boston, 1943-45, asst. medicine research fellow gastroenterology, 1945-48; teaching fellow medicine Harvard, 1945-46, asst. medicine, 1946-48; instr. medicine U. Wash., 1949-50, asst. prof. medicine, 1950-54, head div. gastroenterology, 1950—, asso. prof. medicine, 1954-59, prof., 1959—; program dir. Clin. Research Center, 1960-64; attending physician King County Hosp. System, Seattle, 1950—, U. Wash. Hosp., 1959—; cons. gastroenterology VA Hosp., Seattle, 1951—, USPHS Hosp., Seattle, 1955—; vis. prof. University, Auckland, New Zealand, 1964. Research fellow Am. Gastroent. Assn., 1947; research asso. Mayo Found., 1948; med. scis. fellow NRC, 1948-49; Markle scholar U. Wash., 1950-55; Outstanding Achievement award U. Minn., 1964; mem. general medicine study sect. NIH, 1957-59, mem. gastroenterology tng. com. Nat. Inst. Arthristis and Metabolic Diseases, 1961-65. Diplomate Am. Bd. Internal Medicine (mem. subspecialty bd. gastroenterology 1970-76). Mem. AMA, Am. Fed. Clin. Research, Am. Soc. Clin. Investigation, Am. Gastroent. Assn. (sec. 1959-62, pres. 1967), Assn. Am. Physicians, Western Soc. Clin. Research (councillor 1956-59), Western Assn. Physicians (sec.-treas. 1959-62, pres. 1966), Am. Assn. Study Liver Diseases (councillor 1951-54, v.p. 1954, pres. 1956), Western Gastroenterology Research Group (chmn. 1957-58), King County Med. Soc. Editorial bd. Gastroenterologia (Basel), 1959-68, Gastroenterology, 1959-64. Author numerous med. and sci. articles. Home: 17004 37th Ave NE Seattle WA 98155 Office: U Washington Hospital Seattle WA 98195

VOLZ, CHARLES HARVIE, JR., lawyer; b. Richmond, Va., Sept. 15, 1925; s. Charles Harvie and Mary V. (Mallory) V.; B.S., U. Ala., 1950, LL.B., 1951, J.D., 1970; m. Constance A. Lewis, July 30, 1976; children—Charles Harvie III, Judith C. Spl. agt. FBI, 1951; admitted to Ala. bar, 1951; claim mgr. Allstate Ins. Co., 1952-54; claims atty. State Farm Ins. Co., 1954-57; pvt. practice, 1957-63, Montgomery, 1959—; asst. dir. Dept. Indsl. Relations, State of Ala., 1959-62; partner firm Volz, Capouano, Wampold & Sansone, 1963—. Campaign dir. March of Dimes, 1958, Am. Cancer Soc., 1967; exec. sec. Gov.'s Com. on Employment Physically Handicapped, 1959-62; mem. Pres.'s Com. on Employment Physically Handicapped, 1959-62. Pres., bd. dirs. Montgomery chpt. Am. Cancer Soc. Served to 2d lt. USAAF, 1943-45. Recipient Outstanding Service award Am. Cancer Soc., 1967. Mem. Am. Arbitration Assn. (mem. nat. panel), Am., Ala. bar assns., Assn. Trial Lawyers Am. (state committeeman 1973-75), Ala. Trial Lawyers Assn. (bd. govs.), Phi Alpha Delta. Methodist. Mason. Note editor Ala. Law Rev., 1950-51. Home: 6057 Monticello Dr TM 1 Montgomery AL 36117 Office: 350 Adams Ave Montgomery AL 36103

VOLZ, MARLIN MILTON, educator; b. Cecil, Wis., Sept. 3, 1917; s. Edwin A. and Mae C. (Winter) V.; B.A., U. Wis., 1938, LL.B., 1940, S.J.D., 1945; m. Esther R. Krug, Aug. 23, 1941; children—Marlin M., Karen D., Thomas A. Admitted to Wis. bar, 1940; mem. U. Wis. Law Sch. faculty, 1946-50; dean U. Kansas City Sch. Law, 1950-58; dean U. Louisville Sch. Law, 1958-65, prof., 1965—; probate judge Jefferson County, Ky., 1970-74. Mem. panel labor arbitrators Fed. Mediation and Conciliation Service and Am. Arbitration Assn.; reporter on legal draftsmanship Am. Law Inst.; adviser San Juan (P.R.) Sch. Law. Mem. Am., Fed., Ky., Wis. bar assns., Am. Judicature Soc. (dir.), C. of C. Methodist. Rotarian. Clubs: Conversation, Filson (Louisville). Co-author: Drafting Partnership Agreements, 1949; Wisconsin Practice Methods, 1949; Missouri Practice Methods, 1953; Iowa Practice Methods, 1954; Kansas Practice Methods, 1957; West's Federal Practice Manual, 1960, co-author, gen. editor 2d edit., 1970; Ky Legal Forms, vol. 3 and 4, 1965; Caldwell's Kentucky Form Book. Editor: Cases and Materials, Civil Procedure, 1975. Home: 1819 Woodfill Way Louisville KY 40205

VOM BAUR, FRANCIS TROWBRIDGE, lawyer; b. Riverton, N.J., Sept. 17, 1908; s. Carl H. and Edith V. (Trowbridge) vom Baur; B.A., Amherst Coll., 1929; LL.B., Harvard, 1932; m. Carolyn Bartlett Laskey, June 6, 1934; children—Nerissa, Daphne. Admitted to N.Y. bar, 1934, D.C. bar, 1948, Ill. bar, 1952; asso. firm Milbank, Tweed & Hope, N.Y.C., 1933-42; regional counsel Office Coordinator Inter-Am. Affairs, C.A., Panama, 1942-46; practiced law, Washington, also Chgo., 1947-53; gen. counsel Dept. of Navy, Washington, 1953-60; mem. firm Hensel, vom Baur & Heller, 1960-62; sr. partner vom Baur, Coburn, Simmons & Turtle, and predecessor firms, 1963—. Chmn. Republican finance com. D.C., 1975-77. Mem. Am. (mem. ho. of dels. 1957, chmn. post conv. com. to visit Germany, 1957, chmn. standing com. on unauthorized practice law 1958-62, chmn. sect. pub. contract law 1970-71, chmn. coordinating com. model procurement code), Fed. (pres. D.C. chpt. 1954-55, award for distinguished service 1972) bar assns., Assn. Bar City N.Y., Bar Assn. D.C., Am. Soc. Internat. Law, Amherst Alumni Assn. (pres. Washington chpt. 1969-70), Beta Theta Pi, Delta Sigma Rho. Clubs: Cosmos, City Tavern Assn. (Washington). Author: Federal Administrative Law, 2 vols., 1942; Standards of Admission for Practice before Federal Administrative Agencies, a Report for the Survey of the Legal Profession, 1953; The Practical Lawyer's Manual on Research, Writing and Indexing, 1979. Editor: Navy Contract Law, 2d edit., 1959. Contbr. articles to profl. jours. Office: 1700 K St NW Washington DC 20006

VON AMMON, PHILIP ERNST, lawyer; b. Evanston, Ill., Jan. 10, 1915; s. Ernst Carl and Ida (Kroeschell) von A.; student Williams Coll., 1931-33; A.B., Northwestern U., 1935; J.D., 1938; m. Barbara Sieck, Sept. 7, 1946; children—Hallie, Karla, Sara. Admitted to Ill. bar, 1938, Ariz. bar, 1952; with firm Sidley, McPherson, Austin & Burgess, Chgo., 1938-46; with law dept. A.T.&S.F. R.R., 1946-51; with firm Fennemore, Craig, von Ammon & Udall, Phoenix, 1952—, partner, 1953—. Mem. Maricopa County Planning and Zoning Commn., 1953-55; trustee, pres. Scottsdale (Ariz.) Bds. Edn., 1955-58. Councilman, Paradise Valley, Ariz., 1964-70. Mem. adv. bd. Phoenix Symphony Assn., 1959-65; bd. dirs. Ariz. Citizens for Strengthening Pub. Sch. Edn., 1959-66, Phoenix C. of C., 1969-72, Ariz. Zool. Soc., 1976—; trustee Ariz. Acad., 1969-75. Served to lt. comdr. USNR, 1942- 46. Fellow Am. Coll. Trial Lawyers. Mem. Am., Maricopa County (past pres., dir.) bar assns., State Bar Ariz. (bd. govs., pres. 1968-69), Ariz. State U. Law Soc. (pres. 1976—), Delta Upsilon, Phi Delta Phi. Clubs: Phoenix Lawyers; Paradise Valley Country; University; Arizona. Address: 1700 First Nat Bank Plaza Phoenix AZ 85003

VON AROLDINGEN, KARIN, dancer; b. Germany, July 9, 1941. Profl. debut, Frankfurt, Germany, 1958; with N.Y.C. Ballet, 1961—, soloist, 1967-72, prin. dancer, 1972—. Office: care NYC Ballet NY State Theatre Lincoln Center Plaza New York NY 10023*

VON AUW, ALVIN, communications co. exec.; b. Newton, Mass., Oct. 13, 1916; s. Ivan and Mary (McMahon) von A.; B.A., Wesleyan U., Middletown, Conn., 1937, M.A., 1938; m. Eleanor Flagg, Oct. 7, 1939; 1 dau., Eleanor II (Mrs. Richard Berry). With Western Electric Co., 1939-65, pub. relations dir., 1962-65; asst. v.p. info. dept. Am. Tel. & Tel. Co., 1965-69, v.p., asst. to chmn., 1969—; dir. So. New Eng. Telephone Co. Served to lt. USNR, 1942-45. Mem. Phi Beta Kappa, Beta Theta Pi. Home: Saw Mill Rd Stamford CT 06903 Office: 195 Broadway New York City NY 10007

VON BECKH, HARALD J., physician, aeromed. scientist; b. Vienna, Austria, Nov. 17, 1917; s. Johannes and Elisabeth (Flach-Hillé) von B.; M.D., U. Vienna, 1940. Came to U.S., 1957, naturalized, 1963. Staff mem., lectr. Aeromed. Acad., Berlin, Germany, 1941-43; lectr. Nat. Inst. Aviation Medicine, Buenos Aires, Argentina, 1947-56; mem. sci. staff Aeromed. Research Lab., Holloman AFB, N.Mex., 1957-64, chief scientist, 1964-70; dir. research Aerospace Med. Research dept. Naval Air Devel. Center, Warminster, Pa., 1970—; prof. physiology N.Mex. State U., 1959-70; mem. Armed Forces-NRC Com. on Bio-Astronautics, 1958-61; mem. bio-astronautics com. Internat. Astronautical Fedn., 1961—. Recipient Melbourne W. Boynton award Am. Astron. Soc., 1972. Fellow Am. Inst. Aeros. and Astronautics (asso.; Jeffries Med. Research award 1976), Brit. Interplanetary Soc., Aerospace Med. Assn. (Arnold D. Tuttle award 1972, Hubertus Strughold award 1976); mem. Internat. Acad. Aerospace Medicine, Internat. Acad. Astronautics, Assn. Mil. Surgeons U.S.; hon. mem. Hermann Oberth Soc. (Honor ring 1975), Med. Assn. Armed Forces Argentina, Center Astronautical Studies Portugal, Spanish Soc. Aerospace Medicine, Austrian Astronautical Soc. Author: Physiology of Flight, 1955. Contbr. numerous articles on aerospace medicine to sci. jours. in U.S., Germany, Eng., Argentina, Spain. Research on physiology of weightlessness, biodynamics of space flight. Address: PO Box 1220 Warminster PA 18974

VONBERG, WILLIAM GEORGE, corp. exec.; b. N.Y.C., May 8, 1919; s. William and Margaretha (Kreidler) vonB.; B.S. cum laude in Accounting, Syracuse U., 1940; m. Barbara J. Fleckenstein, May 3, 1947; children—William G., Susan C., Carol A., Barbara C., Steven E. Sr. accountant, audit staff Ernst & Ernst, 1939-42, 45-48; controller W.B. Coon Co., 1948-52; with Sybron Corp. (formerly Ritter Pfaudler Corp., Pfaudler Co., Pfaudler Permutit, Inc.), Rochester, N.Y., 1952—, controller, 1957-65, v.p., 1962-65, treas., 1965, v.p. fin., 1965-70, exec. v.p., 1970-71, pres., 1971-75, pres., chief exec. officer, 1975-78, chmn. bd., chief exec. officer, 1978—, also dir. subsidiaries; dir. Rochester Gas & Electric Corp. Lincoln First Bank Inc. Bd. dirs. United Community Chest Greater Rochester, chmn., chief exec. officer, 1978—; bd. dirs. Rochester Hosp. Service Corp., Genesee Valley Group Health Assn., Indsl. Mgmt. Council, Rochester Conv. and Publicity Bur.; trustee U. Rochester, Syracuse U. Served to capt. U.S. Army, 1942-45; ETO. C.P.A., N.Y. State. Mem. Fin. Execs. Inst. (past pres. Rochester chpt.), Conf. Bd., Rochester C. of C. (trustee, pres. 1977), Beta Gamma Sigma, Alpha Kappa Psi. Clubs: Rochester Country, Univ. (Rochester). Home: 8 Old Landmark Dr Rochester NY 14618 Office: Midtown Tower Rochester NY 14604

VON BOMHARD, MORITZ, opera dir.; b. Berlin, June 19, 1908; came to U.S., 1936, naturalized, 1942; s. Ernst and Hanna (Schmid) von B.; diploma, Conservatory Leipzig, 1932; diploma Juilliard Grad. Sch., 1941; M.A., Columbia U., 1947; Litt.D. (hon.), Ursuline Coll., 1958; Ph.D. in Fine Arts (hon.), Center Coll., Danville, Ky.; m. Elizabeth Riesley Aug. 31, 1962. Dir., Princeton U. Orch.-Glee Club, until 1942; founder The New Lyric Stage Opera Co.; founder, dir. Ky. Opera Assn., Louisville, 1952—; prof. music U. Louisville, 1952-78; guest conductor numerous European orchs. Served with USAAF, 1942-45. Recipient Giovanni Martini award Bellarmine Coll., Louisville. Roman Catholic. Composer songs, chamber music, two symphonies. Home: 1725 Cherokee Terr Louisville KY 40205 Office: Gardencourt Alta Vista Rd Louisville KY 40205

VONDERHAAR, WILLIAM PURCELL, physician; b. Davenport, Iowa, Oct. 21, 1930; s. Bernard Herman and Dorothy Elizabeth (Purcell) V.; A.B., U. Louisville, 1952, M.D., 1956; m. Elayne Elizabeth Roose, Sept. 8, 1954; children—Lisa Maret, Denys Laurent, Mark Roose, Niel Gerard, Gregory Jude, Julie Elayne, Kurt Barnard, Franz Purcell. Intern, U.S. Army Hosp., El Paso, Tex., 1956-57; gen. practice medicine Vine Grove, Ky., 1957-58, Louisville, 1972—; 1st chmn. dept. family medicine U. Louisville, 1972—, asst. v.p. health affairs, 1974—, prof., 1973—. Bd. dirs. Roman Catholic Sch., 1970—; chmn. County Sch. Bd., 1974—; bd. dirs. Community Action Commn., Neighborhood Health Assn. Served with USAF, 1950-52, Ky. Air N.G., 1952-56, U.S. Army, 1956-57. Named Man of Yr. WHAS, WHAS TV, 1963. Mem. AMA, Soc. Tchrs. Family Medicine, Am. Acad. Family Physicians, Am. Sch. Bds. Assn., Internat. Health Evaluation Assn. (v.p. Region I 1978—), Jefferson County Med. Soc. (pres. 1975). Democrat. Club: Kiwanis. Home: 1908 Tyler Ln Louisville KY 40205 Office: Vice Pres Health Affairs U Louisville Louisville KY 40201

VON DER HEYDEN, INGOLF MUELLER, mfg. co. exec.; b. Berlin, Germany, July 18, 1936; s. Werner and Erika (Mueller) von der H.; came to U.S., 1957, naturalized, 1967; student Free U., Berlin, 1959-61; B.A., Duke, 1962; M.B.A., Wharton Sch. U. Pa., 1964; m. Mary Ellen Terrell, Aug. 17, 1963; children—Ellen, Eric. Mgmt. trainee Berliner Bank, Berlin, 1955-57; sr. staff accountant Coopers & Lybrand, Phila., 1963-66; asst. comptroller, corporate comptroller Pitney-Bowes, Inc., Stamford, Conn., 1966-74; controller PepsiCo, Inc., Purchase, N.Y., 1974-76, v.p., controller, 1976-77; v.p. finance Pepsi-Cola Co., 1977-79, v.p. tech. ventures, 1979—. C.P.A., Pa.,

Mem. Am. Inst. C.P.A.'s, Fin. Execs. Inst. Club: Wilton Riding. Home: 8 Laurel Ln Wilton CT 06897 Office: Anderson Hill Rd Purchase NY 10577

VON DER HEYDT, JAMES ARNOLD, lawyer, U.S. dist. judge; b. Miles City, Mont., July 15, 1919; s. Harry Karl and Alice S. (Arnold) von der H.; A.B., Albion (Mich.) Coll., 1942; J.D., Northwestern, 1951; m. Verna E. Johnson, May 21, 1952. Admitted to Alaska bar, 1951; pvt. law practice, Nome, 1953-59; judge superior ct., Juneau, Alaska, 1959-66; U.S. dist. judge, Alaska, 1966—; U.S. commr., Nome, Alaska, 1951—; U.S. atty. div. 2, Dist. Alaska, 1951-53; mem. Alaska Ho. of Reps., 1957-59. Pres. Anchorage Fine Arts Mus. Assn. Mem. Alaska Bar Assn. (mem. bd. govs., 1955-59, pres. 1959-60), Wilson Ornithologists Soc., Am. Judicature Soc., Sigma Nu, Phi Delta Phi. Mason (32 deg., Shriner). Specializing study Arctic bird life. Address: PO Box 1080 Anchorage AK 99510

VON DER MEHDEN, FRED R., educator; b. San Francisco, Dec. 1, 1927; s. Fred G. and Margaret (de Valasco) von der M.; B.A., U. of Pacific, 1948; M.A., Claremont Grad. Sch., 1950; Ph.D., U. Calif. at Berkeley, 1957; m. Audrey Eleanor Whitehead, Dec. 27, 1954; children—Laura Ware, Victoria Margaret. Mem. faculty U. Wis. at Madison, 1957-68, chmn. East Asian studies, 1963-65, 67-68; Albert Thomas prof. polit. sci. Rice U., 1968—, dir. Center for Research, 1969-70, chmn. dept., 1975-78, dir. program devel. studies, 1978—; cons. AID, 1967—. Mem. Mid-West Conf. Asian Affairs (pres. 1968-69), Assn. Asian Studies, Am. Polit. Sci. Assn., S.E. Asia Devel. Adv. Group, SW Conf. Asian Affairs (pres. 1976-77). Author: Politics of the Developing Nations, 2d edit., 1969; Religion and Nationalism in Southeast Asia, 1963; Comparative Political Violence, 1973; co-author: Issues of Political Development, 1967; The Military and Politics of Five Developing Nations, 1970; Southeast Asia 1930-1970, 74; editor (with R. Soligo) Issues on Income Distribution, 1975. Home: 12530 Mossycup Dr Houston TX 77024

VONDRICK, ARTHUR FRANK, civil engr.; b. Chgo., Nov. 6, 1923; s. Frank J. and Antoinette (Pelikan) V.; B.S. in Civil Engring., U. Wis., 1949; children—Dean C. (dec.), Glen D. San. engr. Stream Pollution Control Bd. Ind., 1949; dist. engr. Ind. Bd. Health, 1950; engring. supr., sewage sect. Cook County (Ill.) Dept. Pub. Health, 1950-54; product mgr., dist. engr. Sewage Equipment div. Chgo. Pump Co., 1954-58; asst. dir. water and sewers Phoenix Water and Sewers Dept., 1958-71, dir. water and sewers, 1971-78; exec. v.p. Arthur Beard, Engrs., 1978—. Chmn. Gov.'s Task Group Emergency Planning for Water, 1966; mem. res. commn. USPHS; bd. dirs. Water Pollution Control Fedn., 1961-64, mem. exec. com., 1963-64, v.p., 1968-69, pres., 1970-71; mem. exec. bd. Ariz. Water Resources Com., 1973-78; bd. dirs. Central Ariz. Project Assn., 1974-78. Served with USAAF, 1943-45. Decorated Air medal with clusters; recipient Arthur Sidney Bedell award, 1960; named Hon. Citizen Tex., 1971; Water Utility Man of Year award, 1972; Distinguished Service award in support of water pollution control, 1972. Diplomate Am. Acad. Environ. Engrs. Mem. Am. Water Works Assn., ASCE, Am. Assn. Engrs. (pres. Phoenix 1961), Ariz. Water and Pollution Control Assn. Contbr. articles to profl. jours. Office: 4710 N 16th St Rd Phoenix AZ 85016

VON ECKARDT, WOLF, archtl. critic; b. Berlin, Germany, Mar. 6, 1918; s. Hans Felix and Gertrude (Lederer) E.; brought to U.S., 1936, naturalized, 1943; student New Sch. Social Research, 1936-38; m. Marianne Horney, June 28, 1941 (div.); children—Barbara (Mrs. Michael Klein), Marina (Mrs. Sander Gilman). Graphic artist, book designer, N.Y.C., 1936-41; info. officer Dept. State, Washington, 1945-53; free-lance pub. info. specialist, Washington, 1953-59; dir. pub. info. AIA, 1959-63; architecture critic Washington Post, 1963—; Albert A. Levin prof. urban studies and pub. service Coll. Urban Affairs, Cleve. State U., 1978—; lectr. Harvard, 1966, Mass. Inst. Tech., 1967. Served with AUS, World War II. Hon. mem. AIA; mem. Am. Inst. Graphic Arts (pres. Washington chpt. 1962-65), Soc. Archtl. Historians. Author: Eric Mendelsohn, 1960; The Challenge of Megalopolis, 1964; A Place to Live-The Crisis of the Cities, 1968; (with Sander Gilman) Bertolt Brecht's Berlin, 1975; Back to the Drawing Board! Planning Livable Cities, 1979; also articles. Home: 2014 Hillyer Pl NW Washington DC 20009 Office: The Washington Post 1150 15th St NW Washington DC 20005

VONESH, RAYMOND JAMES, bishop; b. Chgo., Jan. 25, 1916; s. Otto Francis and Mary Josephine (Brennan) V.; M.A., St. Mary of the Lake, Mundelein, Ill., 1939, S.T.L., 1941; J.C.L., Gregorian U., Rome, 1949. Ordained priest Roman Catholic Ch., 1941; instr. religion Sacred Heart High Sch., Chgo., 1941-45, Holy Name Cathedral, Chgo., 1945-47; with Chancery office Chgo. Notary, 1949-56; procurator St. Mary of the Lake Sem., 1956-67; vicar gen. Joliet, Ill., 1967; aux. bishop Joliet, 1968—; notary Met. Tribunal, 1949-56; defender of the bond, 1956-66; papal chamberlain, 1957; domestic prelate, 1959; pastor St. Patrick Ch., Joliet, 1970; titular bishop of Vanariona. Home: Holy Cross Church 901 Elizabeth St Joliet IL 60435

VON EULER, LEO HANS, research inst. adminstr.; b. Stockholm, Jan. 31, 1931; s. Ulf Svante and Jane von E.; B.A., Williams Coll., 1952; M.D., Yale U., 1959. Dep. dir. Nat. Inst. Gen. Med. Scis., Bethesda, Md., 1974—. Served with U.S. Army, 1953-55. Office: 5333 Westbard Ave Bethesda MD 20205

VON EULER, ULF SVANTE, physiologist; b. Stockholm, Sweden, Feb. 7, 1905; s. Hans and Astrid (Cleve) Von E.; M.D., Karolinska Inst., 1930; M.D. h.c., U. Dijon, 1963, U. Ghent, 1963, U. Tubingen, 1964, U. Rio de Janeiro, 1953, U. Buenos Aires, 1971, U. Edinburgh, 1971, U. Madrid, 1973, U. Manchester (Eng.), 1973; m. Jane Sodenstierna, Apr. 12, 1930; children—Leo, Christopher, Ursula (Mrs. L. Sjöberg), Marie (Mrs. Anthony John); m. 2d, Dagmar Cronstedt, Aug. 20, 1958. Asst. prof. Karolinska Inst., Stockholm, 1930-39, prof. physiology, 1939-71. Mem. Nobel Com. for Medicine, 1953-60, chmn., 1958-60, gen. sec., 1961-65, pres. Nobel Found., 1966-75; v.p. Internat. Union Physiol. Sci., 1965-72. Decorated comdr. Order North Star (Sweden), Cruzeiro do Sul (Brazil), Palmes academiques (France); recipient Gairdner award, 1961, Jahre award, 1965, Stouffer award, 1967, Nobel prize in physiol. medicine, 1970. Mem. Nat. Acad. Sci.; Am. Acad. Arts and Scis., Royal Soc., acads. sci. Sweden, Denmark, Belgium, Leopoldina of East Germany, U.S. Author: Noradrenaline, 1956; (with R. Eliasson) Prostaglandins, 1968; also articles. Home: 14 Sturegatan S-11436 Stockholm Sweden Office: Dept Physiology Karolinska Inst Stockholm Sweden

VON FELDT, ELMER, editor; b. Hays, Kans., Nov. 26, 1919; s. John G. and Anna (Wittman) Von F.; student St. Fidelis Coll., Herman, Pa., 1936-41, Capuchin Theol. Coll., Washington, 1941-43, Georgetown U., 1955-56; m. Mariacristina Beltranena, Sept. 19, 1954; children—Joan Marie, Marianne, Paul Francis. Reporter, rewrite man Nat. Catholic News Service, Washington, 1944-55, fgn. news editor, 1955-56, gen. news editor, 1956-65; editor Columbia mag., New Haven, 1965—; dir. pub. info. Supreme Council K.C., New Haven, 1965—. Spl. writer Def. Dept., 1952; dir. U.S. Cath. Bishops Press Panel, 2d Vatican Council, 1963-64. Decorated papal knight St. Gregory Great, 1960. Mem. Cath. Press Assn. U.S. and Can. (bd. dirs. 1967—), Nat. Frat. Congress U.S. and Can. (pres. press and pub. relations 1969—), U.S. Cath. Conf. (v.p. communications com.). K.C. (4 deg.). Contbr. articles various mags. Home: 502 Howellton Rd Orange CT 06477 Office: 1 Columbus Plaza New Haven CT 06507

VON FLUE, FRANK WALTER, engr., aerospace co. exec.; b. Los Angeles, Nov. 6, 1925; s. Leo and Eleonore (Claus) Von F.; B.S., U. So. Calif., 1950, M.B.A., 1967; m. Wanetah Lois Cunningham, July 7, 1945; children—Francine Ann, David Alan, Lisa Marie. With Garrett-AiResearch, Los Angeles, 1950-62; applications engr. Teledyne Corp., 1962-64; advanced programs tech. engring. mgmt. space div. Rockwell Internat., Downey, Calif., 1964—. Served with USAAF, 1944-45. Registered profl. engr., Calif. Fellow Inst. Advancement Engring.; mem. ASME (past chmn. Los Angeles sect., chmn. profl. devel. com., Church award 1976), Nat. Mgmt. Assn., Inst. Advancement of Engring. (dir.), Los Angeles Council Engrs. and Scientists (dir.), Indsl. Engring. and Mgmt. Council. Roman Catholic. Home: 921 E Walnut Ave El Segundo CA 90245 Office: 12214 Lakewood Blvd Downey CA 90241

VON FRANCKENSTEIN, BARONESS JOSEPH. see Boyle, Kay

VON FRISCH, KARL, zoologist; b. Vienna, Austria, Nov. 20, 1886; s. Anton Ritter and Marie (Exner) von F.; several years of pvt. tutoring at home; attended a convent sch. of Piarist Fathers and Schottengymnasium, a Benedictine secondary sch., Vienna; Dr. Phil., U. Vienna, 1910; Dr. honoris causa, U. Bern (Switzerland), 1949, Eidgenossiche Technische Hochschule, Zurich, Switzerland, 1955, U. Graz (Austria), 1957, Harvard, 1963, Tubingen (Germany) U., 1964, U. Rostock (East Germany), 1969; m. Margarethe Mohr, July 20, 1917; children—Johanna (Mrs. Theodor Schreiner), Maria, Helen (Mrs. Eckehard Pfluger), Otto. Mem. faculty U. Munich (Germany), 1912-21, 25-46, 50-58; prof. zoology U. Rostock, 1921-23, U. Breslau (Poland), 1923-25, U. Graz, 1946-50. Recipient Magellanic prize Am. Philos. Soc., 1956, Kalinga prize for popularization of sci. UNESCO, 1959, Balzan prize for biology, 1963, Nobel prize for physiology or medicine (shared with Konrad Lorenz and Nikolaas Tinbergen) recognizing maj. contbns. to relatively new sci. sociobiology, 1973; Orden pour le merite fur Wissenschaften und Kunste, 1952. Mem. Royal Entomol. Soc. London (Eng.), Royal Soc., acads. sci. Washington, Stockholm (Sweden), Vienna, Munich, Copenhagen (Denmark), Uppsala (Sweden), Helsinki (Finland), Boston, Gottingen (Germany). Author: Aus dem Leben der Bienen, 1927; Du und das Leben, 1936; Bees, 1954; The Dancing Bees, 1954; Man and the Living World, 1963; The Dance Language and Orientation of Bees, 1967; A Biologist Remembers, 1967; Animal Architecture, 1974. Contbr. numerous articles to profl. jours. Research in lang. of bees, color sense in bees and fish, sense of smell and taste in bees, hearing in fish, perception of polarized light in bees. Address: 10 Uber der Klause Munich 90 Federal Republic of Germany

VON FURSTENBERG, BETSY, actress; b. Neiheim Heusen, Germany, Aug. 16, 1932; d. Count Franz-Egon and Elizabeth (Johnson) von Furstenberg; attended Miss Hewitt's Classes, N.Y. Tutoring Sch.; prepared for stage with Sanford Meisner at Neighborhood Playhouse; m. Guy Vincent de la Maisoneuve (div.); 2 children. Made stage debut in Second Threshold, N.Y., 1951; appeared in Dear Barbarians, 1952; toured in The Petrified Forest, in Jason, in The Second Man, 1952; appeared in Josephine, 1953, subsequently toured; appeared in Oh, Men! Oh, Women!, N.Y., 1953; What Every Woman Knows, 1954, The Chalk Garden, 1955; toured in Oh, Men! Oh, Women!, summer 1955; appeared in Child of Fortune, 1956, Nature's Way, 1957, The Making of Moo, 1958, Say Darling, 1959, Wonderful Town, 1959, Season of Choice, 1959, Much Ado About Nothing, 1959, Mary, Mary, 1961, The Paisley Convertible, 1967, Wonderful Town, 1967, Beyond Desire, 1967, Avanti, 1968, Private Lives, 1968, The Gingerbread Lady, 1970; toured, appeared in Broadway prodn. Absurd Person Singular, 1976; appeared in off-Broadway prodn. Does Anyone Here Do The Peabody, 1976; appeared in motion picture Women Without Names, 1951; TV appearances include Pulitzer Prize Playhouse, Armstrong Circle Theatre, TV Sound Stage, Medallion Theatre, Omnibus, Appointment with Adventure, Robert Montgomery Presents, Kraft Theatre, Have Gun Will Travel, Alfred Hitchcock Presents, Playhouse 90, U.S. Steel Hour, Alcoa Presents, Play of the Week, the Fifth Column, Mystery Show, Adventures in Paradise, Golden Show, Defenders, Your Money or Your Wife. Contbr. articles to newspapers and mags. Office: care Lionel Larner Ltd 850 7th Ave New York NY 10019

VON FURSTENBERG, DIANE SIMONE MICHELLE, fashion designer; b. Brussels, Belgium, Dec. 31, 1946; d. Leon L. and Liliane L. (Nahmias) Halfin; came to U.S., 1969; student U. Madrid, 1965-66, U. Geneva, 1966-68; m. Eduard Egon von Furstenberg, July 16, 1969; children—Alexandre, Tatiana. Founder, pres. Diane von Furstenberg, Ltd., mfr. ladies clothing, N.Y.C., 1970—, Diane Von Furstenberg Cosmetics & Fragrance div. Diane Von Furstenberg, Inc. Office: 745 Fifth Ave New York NY 10021 . *Honesty in all ways—honest products, honest and straight approach to needs.**

VON FURSTENBERG, EGON EDVARD. see Furstenberg, Egon Edvard

VON GIERKE, HENNING EDGAR, govt. ofcl.; b. Karlsruhe, Germany, May 22, 1917; s. Edgar and Julie (Braun) Von G.; came to U.S., 1947; naturalized, 1977; Dipl. Ing., Karlsruhe Tech., 1943, Dr. Engr., 1944; married; 2 children. Asst. in acoustics Karlsruhe Tech., 1944-47, lectr., 1946; cons. Aerospace Med. Research Labs, Wright-Patterson AFB, Ohio, 1947-54, chief bioacoustics br., 1954-63, dir. biodynamics and bionics div., 1963—; asso. prof. Ohio State U., 1963—. Mem. com. hearing and bioacoustics Armed Forces NRC, 1953, bio-astronaut, com., 1959-61; mem. adv. com. flight medicine and biology NASA, 1960-61. Recipient Def. Disting. Civilian Service award, 1963. Fellow Acoustical Soc. Am. (pres. 1979-80), Aerospace Med. Assn. (v.p. 1966-67, E. Liljenkrantz award 1966, A.D. Tuttle award 1974), Inst. Environ. Scis. (hon.), Internat. Acad. Aviation and Space Medicine; mem. Inst. Noise Control Engring., Biomed. Engring. Soc., Nat. Acad. Engring. Author numerous tech. publs., book chpts.; researcher in bioacoustics, acoustics, biomechanics and bioengring. Home: 1325 Meadow Ln Yellow Springs OH 45387 Office: Biodynamics and Bionics Div Aerospace Med Research Lab USAF Wright Patterson AFB OH 45433

VON GRONICKA, ANDRÉ, educator; b. Moscow, Russia, May 25, 1912; s. Eduard and Nina (De Witt) von G.; came to U.S., 1926, naturalized, 1933; B.A., U. Rochester, 1933, M.A., 1935; Ph.D., Columbia, 1942; m. Hilde Stock, Oct. 1, 1935; children—Ingrid Nina, Andrea Elizabeth. Instr. German, Kan. U., 1937-40, U. Chgo., 1940-44; mem. faculty Columbia, 1944-62, prof. German lit. and lang., 1959-62; prof. German lit., chmn. German dept. U. Pa., 1962—; lectr. in field; spl. research modern German drama and novelle, Russo-German lit. relations, Thomas Mann. Guggenheim and Fulbright fellow, 1957-58; Social Sci. Research Coun. Fellow, 1957; guest Bundesrepublik Deutschland, summer 1964; Am. Council Learned Socs. grantee, 1965; Guggenheim fellow, 1969-70; Nat. Endowment for Humanities sr. fellow, 1976-77. Mem. Modern Lang. Assn. (hon. life mem., chmn. group V, 1950, group III, 1963), Am. Assn. Tchrs. German, Assn. Tchrs. Slavic and East European Langs., Am. Council German Studies, Thomas Mann Soc. (life), Acad. Lit. Studies, Phi Beta Kappa (mem. Christian Gauss award com. 1971-73, chmn. 1973), Delta Phi Alpha. Author: Henry von Heiseler, a Russo German Writer, 1944; (with Helen Yakobson) Essentials of Russian, 4th edit., 1964; The Russian Image of Goethe, 1968; Thomas Mann: Profile and Perspectives, 1970; editorial bd. Germano-Slavica, 1973—. Contbr. to profl. jours., encys., critical anthologies, Festschriften for H.O. Burger, C.F. Bayerschmidt, Walter Silz; A.D. Klarmann. Home: 4618 Osage Ave Philadelphia PA 19143

VONGROSSMANN, FREDERIC RICHARD (FRITZ), architect; b. Milw., Mar. 3, 1904; s. Frederic Paul and Pauline (Schok) vonG.; B.Arch., U. Minn., 1928; M.Arch. (U. fellow), Harvard, 1932; m. Leanore E. Danielson, Aug. 26, 1935; children—Nancy, Sue vonGrossman Broughton. Various engring. jobs in Minn., 1921-33; state architect S.D. Civil Works Adminstrn., Pierre, 1933-35; regional architect U.S. Dept. Agr. Resettlement Adminstrn., Lincoln, Nebr., 1935-37; staff architect Badger Ordnance Works, Wilmington, Del., 1941-42; architect-partner Bogner-von-Grossmann, 1948-50; prin. firm Fritz vonGrossmann, Milw., 1937-55; sr. partner von Grossmann, Burroughs & van Lanen, Milw., 1955-58, pres., 1958-66. Vice pres. Ace Foods, Inc., Milw., 1948-54; pres. Nassu Realty, Inc., Milw., 1958-70; city planner, cons. Dept. City Devel., Milw., 1966-70. Gov., Sch. Facilities Council, Mt. Vernon, N.Y., 1957-65; dir. Wis. Architects' Found., Milw., 1960-66. Co-chmn. Friends of Art Found., Milw., 1960; tech. coordinator Milw. World Festival (Summerfest) Inc., 1967-70; co-chmn. Model Cities Task Force Commn., Milw., 1969-70. Founder, bd. dirs. Milw. Symphony Bd., 1960-68; bd. dirs. Meml. Hosp., Milw., 1962-77; founding chmn. joint bd. and deaconite Northshore Congl. Ch., Milw., 1949-52. Served with USCGR, 1942-45. Recipient 1st medal Beaux Arts Inst. Design, N.Y.C., 1932; Milw. Civic Center-Kilbourn Mall competition, 1948-50; Golden Baton award Milw. Symphony League, 1967; One of Ten Best Steel Bldgs. in Am. award U.S. Inst. Steel Constrn., 1968, others. Fellow AIA (bd. dirs. Life Ins. Trust 1964-66); mem. Nat. Council Archtl. Registration Bds., Ch. Architects Guild, Am. Arbitration Assn. (panelist), Gambrinus Soc., Navy League, Am. Soc. Mil. Engrs., U. Minn. Alumni Assn., Alpha Rho Chi. Congregationalist. Clubs: Masons (32 deg.), Shriners, Elks, Kiwanis, Harvard; Royal Palm Yacht and Country (gov. 1974-77, vice commodore 1976-77) (Boca Raton, Fla.); Sarasota Yacht, Harvard (Sarasota, Fla.). Editor-contbr. to AIA Handbook Archtl. Practise, 1967-68; contbr. to ofcl. AIA jour. Prin. works include Kohl's Food Stores prototype, 1952, Masonic Grand Lodge Hdqrs., 1954, Covenant Luth. Ch. and Ednl. Wing, 1962, Wis. Synod Luth. Ch. Hdqrs., 1963, Milw. Gaslight Co. No. Service Center, 1961, Milw. Forest Home Library, 1968 (all winners of All-Wis. AIA Honor award competitions); A.O. Smith Research and Engring. Center (Glass House) (Indsl. Internat. award), 1929-31; Equitable Life Assurance Soc. Office Complex, 1955; corp. office bldg. for Allis-Chalmers Corp., West Allis, Wis., 1962; Harbor Commn. Milw. Port Harbor Terminal, 1963; Christopher Latham Sholes Jr. High Sch., Milw., 1964; U. Wis.-Milw. Classroom and Adminstrn. Center, 1964; Ripon (Wis.) High Sch., 1965. Address: Plymouth Harbor Suite 901 700 John Ringling Causeway Sarasota FL 33577

VON HIPPEL, ARTHUR ROBERT, univ. prof.; b. Rostock, Germany, Nov. 19, 1898; s. Robert and Emma (Bremer) von H.; Ph.D., Univ. Goettingen, Germany; m. Dagmar Franck, June 2, 1930 (dec. Sept. 1975); children—Peter H., Arndt R., Frank N., Eric A., Marianne M. Rockefeller Fellow, U. Cal. 1927-28; private dozent U. Jena, 1928-29. U. Goettingen, 1930-33; prof. Univ. Istanbul, 1933-34; guest prof. Univ. of Copenhagen, 1935-36; asst. prof. Mass. Inst. Technology, 1936-40, asso. prof., 1940-46, prof., 1947-62, Institute prof., 1962-64, Institute prof. emeritus, 1964—; dir. lab. for insulation research Mass. Inst. Tech. Chmn. conf. on electrical insulation, National Research Council, 1952. Recipient Arthur von Hippel prize, 1976. Fellow Am. Acad. Arts and Scis., Am. Physics Soc., Nat. Acad. Engring., Washington Acad. Scis., A.A.A.S., New York Acad. Sci. Author: Dielectrics and Waves, 1954; Molecular Science and Molecular Engineering, 1959. Editor: Dielectric Materials and Applications, 1954; The Molecular Designing of Materials and Devices, 1965. Contbr. articles to journals. Home: 265 Glen Rd Weston MA 02193 Office: Mass Inst Tech Cambridge MA 02139

VON HIPPEL, PETER HANS, educator; b. Goettingen, Germany, Mar. 13, 1931; s. Arthur Robert and Dagmar (franck) von H.; came to U.S., 1937, naturalized, 1942; B.S., Mass. Inst. Tech., 1952, M.S., 1953, Ph.D., 1955; m. Josephine Baron Raskind, June 20, 1954; children—David F., James A., Benjamin J. Phys. biochemist Naval Med. Research Inst., Bethesda, Md., 1956-59; asst. prof. to asso. prof. biochemistry Dartmouth, 1959-67; prof. chemistry, mem. Inst. Moledular Biology of U. Oreg., 1967—, dir. inst., 1969—. Mem. study sect. USPHS, 1963-67; chmn. biopolymers Gordon Conf., 1968; mem. trustees' vis. com. Mass. Inst. Tech. biology dept., 1973-76; mem. bd. sci. counsellors Nat. Inst. Arthritis, Metabolic and Digestive Diseases, NIH, 1974—. Served as lt. M.S.C., USNR, 1956-59. NSF predoctoral fellow, 1953-55; NIH postdoctoral fellow, 1955-56, NIH sr. fellow, 1959-67; Guggenheim fellow, 1973-74. Mem. AAAS, Am. Chem. Soc., Am. Soc. Biol. Chemists, Biophys. Soc. (mem. council 1970-73, pres. 1973-74), Nat. Acad. Scis. Soc. Gen. Physiology, Fedn. Am. Scientists, Sigma Xi. Editorial bd. Jour. Biol. Chemistry, 1967-73, 76—, Biochem. Biophys. Acta, 1965-70, Physiological Reviews, 1972-77, Jour. Biol. Chemistry, 1976—, Biochemistry, 1977—. Contbr. articles to profl. jours. and books. Home: 1900 Crest Dr Eugene OR 97405

VON HOFE, HAROLD, educator; b. Plainfield, N.J., Apr. 23, 1912; s. Henry G. and Claire (Lindemann) von H.; B.S., N.Y.U., 1936; Ph.D., Northwestern U., 1939; m. Lenore Doster Curtis, Feb. 27, 1947; children—Harold Edward, Eric Henry. Instr., asst. prof., then asso. prof. German, U. So. Calif., 1939-47, prof., 1947—, chmn. dept. German, 1945-56, 63-68, 71—, chmn. div. humanities, 1959-63, interim dean Grad. Sch., 1974-77, dir. U. So. Calif. program in Vienna, 1963—; prof. German School, Middlebury (Vt.) Coll., 1958; vis. prof. U. Calif. at Berkeley, 1959. Chmn. Fulbright Nat. Selection Com. for Germany, 1957-59; dir. Feucht wanger Inst. Exile Studies, 1978—. Fulbright research fellow, 1955-56; research fellow, Vienna, Austria, 1962-63. Decorated officer's cross Order of Merit (Germany). Christopher Longest lectr. U. Miss., 1964. Mem. Am. Assn. Tchrs. German (mng. editor German Quar. 1957-63), Modern Lang. Assn. Am., Philol. Assn. Pacific Coast (exec. council 1963-65), Modern Lang. Assn. So. Calif., AAUP, Delta Phi Alpha (nat. pres. 1962-63, nat. counselor and trustee invested funds 1936-68). Author: (L. Marcuse) A German Sketchbook, 1950; Im Wandel der Jahre, 3d edit., 1964, 5th edit., 1974, 6th edit., 1979; Im Wandel: Lesebuch für Ausländer, 1956; Der Anfang, 1958, rev. edit., 1963, 3d edit., 1968; Die Mittelstufe, 1961, rev. edit. 1966, 3d edit., 1971; also articles in field. Editor: The Heretic of Soana (Gerhart Hauptmann), 1958; Übungsbuch, rev. edit., 1963, 3d edit., 1968; Cultural History of the United States of America, 1963, 2d edit., 1972; Faust: Leben, Legende, Literatur, 1965; Deutsche Sprachlehre für Amerikaner, 1965, 2d edit., 1970; (J. Strelka) Lûgendichtung, 1966; (J. Strelka) Vorboten der Gegenwart, 1967; (M. Freitas) Deutschland ist anders, 1972; Kultur und Alltag, 1973; Briefe von und an Ludwig Marcuse, 1975; (with others) Fortschritt Deutsch, 1976; Texte zur deutschen Kultur, 1976; Marcuses Essays, Porträts, Polemiken, 1933-1971, 1979; (with others) Perspektiven Zu Aktuellen Fragen, 1978. Mem.

editorial bd. Europa Verlag, 1963—; German adv. editor Charles Scribner's Sons, 1961—; asso. editor Books Abroad, 1956-64. Contbr. Ency. Judaica. Home: 12733 Mulholland Dr Beverly Hills CA 90210

VON HOFFMAN, NICHOLAS, newspaperman; b. N.Y.C., Oct. 16, 1929; s. Carl and Anna (Bruenn) von H.; grad. Fordham Prep. Sch., 1948; m. Ann Byrne, 1950 (div.); children—Alexander, Aristodemos, Constantine. Asso. dir. Indsl. Area Found., Chgo., 1954-63; mem. staff Chgo. Daily News, 1963-66, Washington Post, 1966-76. Author: Mississippi Notebook, 1964; Multiversity, 1966; We Are The People Our Parents Warned Us Against, 1968; Two, Three, Many More, 1969; Left at The Post, 1970; (with Garry Trudeau) Fireside Watergate, 1973, (with Garry Trudeau) Tales From the Margaret Mead Taproom, 1976; Make-Believe Presidents: Illusions of Power from McKinley to Carter, 1978.

VON HOFFMANN, GEORGE, pub. co. exec.; b. St. Louis, Mo., July 3, 1908; s. Albert and Anna (Albrecht) von H.; A.B., Univ. of Mo., 1930; m. Dorothy Edna Rodenroth, Oct. 22, 1927; children—Jean Louise, Betty Ann, Carol Lee, George. Dir. and chmn. bd. Von Hoffmann Press and dir. Von Hoffmann Corp. Mem. Legion of Honor. Mason (Scottish rite, K.T., hon. mem. dirs. staff, Moolah Temple Shrine), Elk. Past pres. St. Louis Optimist Club. Home: 902 Forestlac Ct St Louis MO 63141 Office: 1000 Camera Ave St Louis MO 63126

VON KANN, CLIFTON FERDINAND, airline assn. exec.; b. Boston, Oct. 14, 1915; s. Alfred and Lyllian (Kaufman) Von K.; A.B. cum laude, Harvard, 1937, M.B.A., 1948; grad. Arty. Sch., 1942, Command and Gen. Staff Sch., 1945, Armed Forces Staff Coll., 1954, Nat. War Coll., 1957; m. Sallie Emery Flint, Oct. 6, 1938 (div. May 1965); children—Curtis Emery, Lisa Christine; m. 2d, Kathryn Heyne, July 18, 1965. Commd. 2d lt., F.A., U.S. Army, 1938, advanced through grades to maj. gen., 1962; attached to 77th F.A., then 631st F.A. bn., Ft. Sill, Oklahoma, North Africa, Sicily and Italy, 1937-45; member War Dept. gen. staff, 1945-46; staff Office Comptroller, Dept. of Army, 1948-51; with CIA, 1951-53, 7th Inf. Div. Arty., 8th Army, 1954, Korean Mil. Adv. Group, Korea, 1954-55; staff Hdqrs. Army Forces Far East and 8th Army, Japan, 1955-56; asst. div. comdr. 82d Airborne Div., Ft. Bragg, N.C., 1957-59; dir. Army aviation, Office Dep. Chief Staff Mil. Operations, Dept. Army, 1959-61; J-3 U.S. Strike Command, Tampa, Fla., 1961-62; comdg. gen. 1st cavalry div., Korea, 1962-63, U.S. Army Aviation Center, Ft. Rucker, Ala., 1963-65; ret.; v.p. operations and engring. Air Transport Assn. Am., 1965-70, sr. v.p. operations and airports, 1970—. Recipient Charles Edwin Webb Meml. medal Pa. Mil. Coll., 1964; Mil. Rev. award, Command and Gen. Staff Coll., 1964; decorated Silver Star, Legion of Merit; Cross of Mil. Valor (Italy). Mem. Am. Helicopter Soc. (chmn. bd. 1962-63, pres. 1961-62), Nat. Aero. Assn. (v.p. 1961, sr. v.p. 1980, dir.), Am. Inst. Aeros. Astronautics, Soc. Automotive Engrs. Clubs: Harvard Varsity (Cambridge); Metropolitan, Nat. Aviation (pres. 1974-75), Black Tie (pres. 1978-79), Aero (pres. 1969) (Washington). Home: 4807 Van Ness St NW Washington DC 20016 Office: 1709 New York Ave NW Washington DC 20006

VON KARAJAN, HERBERT, conductor; b. Salzburg, Austria, Apr. 5, 1908; s. Ernst and Martha von K.; student Prof. Ledwinka; grad. as condr. Vienna Coll. Music, 1929; married; children—Isabel, Arabel. Conducting debut in The Marriage of Figaro, Ulm, Germany, 1929, condr. opera, Ulm, 1929-34; gen. dir. music, Aachen, Germany, from 1935; debut with Vienna State Opera, 1937, artistic dir., 1957-64, condr. various operas, 1977; internationally recognized debut in Tristan and Isolde, Berlin State Opera, 1938, staatskapellmeister, 1941-44; condr. Prussian State Orch., until 1944; a founder London Philharmonia Orch., 1948, permanent condr., from 1950; dir. concerts Gesellschaft der Musikfreunde, Vienna, from 1949; lifetime dir. Berlin Philharmonic Orch., 1955—; artistic supr. Orchestre de Paris, 1969-71; instr. Internat. Condrs.' Course, Salzburg Festival, and guest condr. Vienna Symphony Orch., 1930-34; rec. artist with Deutsche Grammophon, Electric and Mus. Industries Ltd., London, Polydor Internat.; recs. include complete set of Beethoven's Nine Symphonies, 1977; numerous worldwide guest appearances, 1950—, including La Scala and Lucerene (Switzerland) Festival; numerous orchestral tours, mainly, in recent years, with Berlin Philharmonic and Vienna Singverein, including U.S. tour, 1976 and Japan tour, 1977; condr. Salzburg Festival, 1951—; dir. and condr. films of operas and concerts, 1965—. Herbert von Karajan Found. founded and named in his honor, 1968; recipient Art prize City of Lucerene, 1969, Franco-German prize Aix-en-Provence, France, 1970; named Hon. Citizen, City of Berlin, 1973. Roman Catholic. Office: Festspielhaus A 5010 Salzburg Austria

VON KLEMPERER, ALFRED HERBERT, fin. co. exec.; b. Berlin, Germany, July 22, 1915; s. Herbert Otto and Frieda (Kuffner) Von K.; student Banking Sch., Berlin, 1934-35; m. Nancy Church Logan, Mar. 26, 1943; children—William John, Diana, Marie. Came to U.S., 1937, naturalized, 1943. Apprentice, Berliner Handels-Gesellschaft, Berlin, 1934-37; clk. Mergenthaler Linotype Co., Bklyn., 1937-39, N.Y. Trust Co., N.Y.C., 1939-42; fgn. exchange trader, analyst Fed. Res. Bank N.Y., N.Y.C., 1946-51; with Morgan Guaranty Trust Co. N.Y., N.Y.C., 1951-76, sr. v.p., 1966-76; pres. Pvt. Export Funding Corp., N.Y.C., 1977—; asst. to U.S. sec. treasury, Washington, 1959-60. Treas., Village of Plandome, N.Y., 1956-59; treas. Village of Mill Neck, N.Y., 1976—, trustee, 1978—; pres. Buckley Country Day Sch., 1964-66; treas. Internat. Center in N.Y., 1971—. Served to 2d lt. U.S. Army, 1942-46. Mem. Council on Fgn. Relations, Bankers Assn. Fgn. Trade (pres. 1968). Clubs: Creek (Locust Valley, N.Y.); Metropolitan (Washington); Board Room (N.Y.C.). Home: Beaverbrook Rd Mill Neck NY 11765 Office: 280 Park Ave New York City NY 10017

VON KLEMPERER, KLEMENS, educator, historian; b. Berlin, Germany, Nov. 2, 1916; s. Herbert and Frieda (Kuffner) von K.; student Collège Francais, Berlin, 1924-33, U. Vienna, Austria, 1934-38; M.A., Harvard, 1940, Ph.D., 1949; m. Elizabeth Gallaher, Dec. 19, 1953; children—Catharine Lee, James Alfred. Came to U.S., 1938, naturalized, 1943. Teaching fellow, tutor Harvard, 1942-43, 46-49; mem. faculty Smith Coll., 1949—, L. Clark Seelye prof. modern European history, 1969—; vis. prof., Stanford U., summer 1960, Bonn (Germany) U., 1963- 64; acting dir. Seminar für Politische Wissenschaft, 1963-64; Overseas fellow Churchill Coll., Cambridge, Eng., 1973-74. Served to 1st lt. AUS, 1943-46. Guggenheim fellow, 1957-58; Fulbright fellow, 1957-58, 63-64. Author: Germany's New Conservatism, 1957; Mandate for Resistance: The Case of the German Opposition to Hitler, 1968; Ignaz Seipel, Christian Statesman in a Time of Crisis, 1972. Home: 23 Washington Ave Northampton MA 01060

VON KUTZLEBEN, SIEGFRIED EDWIN, engring. co. exec.; b. Veckerhagen, Germany, May 19, 1920; s. Erich Melchior and Katherina Helene (Klotz) von K.; came to U.S., 1926, naturalized, 1929; student U. Vienna, 1941-42; M.S., U. Hamburg, 1944; postgrad. N.Y. U., 1949-50; m. Ursula Herta Klotz, May 20, 1946; children—Bernd, Roy, Werner. Chief liaison engr. Allied Mil. Govt., Hamburg, Germany, 1945-47; design engr. Colgate Palmolive Co., Jersey City, 1949-50; engr. Lummus Co., N.Y.C., 1951-57, gen. mgr., The Hague, Netherlands, 1957-71, exec. v.p., Bloomfield, N.J., 1971-74, v.p. Lummus Group, Inc., 1974—; pres. Constrn. Equipment Internat. Inc., 1974—. Decorated Order Oranje-Nassau (Netherlands); Order Lion (Finland). Mem. ASME, ASCE, Am. Inst. Chem. Engrs. Club: Netherlands (N.Y.C.). Contbr. articles to profl. jours. Office: 1515 Broad St Bloomfield NJ 07003

VON LANG, FREDERICK WILLIAM, librarian, genealogist; b. Scranton, Pa., May 6, 1929; s. Frederick William and Carrie Della (Brundage) von Lang; B.S., Kutztown State Coll., 1951; M.S. in L.S., Syracuse U., 1955; m. Ilsabe von Wackerbarth, July 12, 1960; children—Christoph, Karl Philipp. Librarian, Broughal Jr. High Sch., Bethlehem, Pa., 1951-52; asst. librarian Bethlehem Pub. Library, 1952-55, Enoch Pratt Free Library, Balt., 1956-66; library dir. Lehigh County Community Coll. Library, Allentown, Pa., 1966-73, Auburn (Maine) Pub. Library, 1973-77; dir. St. Joseph (Mo.) Pub. Library, 1977—. Treas., mem. exec. bd. Friends of Bethlehem Pub. Library; treas., mem. steering com. Auburn City Bicentennial Com.; mem. exec. bd. Northampton County Assn. for Blind; ofcl. del. Gov.'s Conf. on Libraries and Info. Scis. Mem. Am. (councilor from Maine Library Assn. 1974-77), Maine (fed. coordinator A.L.A.) library assns., S.A.R., Maine Soc. Mayflower Descendents, Soc. Colonial Wars in Maine, Huguenot Soc. Maine, Bradford Family Compact. Lutheran. Clubs: Masons (32 deg.), K.T., Shriners, Kiwanis, Elks. Asso. editor: Genealogisches Handbuch des in Bayern immatrikulierten Adels, Vol. 4, 1954. Home: 2224 Jule St Saint Joseph MO 64501 Office: 10th and Felix Sts Saint Joseph MO 64501

VON LAUE, THEODORE HERMAN, educator; b. Frankfurt/Main, Germany, June 22, 1916; s. Max and Magda (Milkau) Von L.; came to U.S., 1937; student U. Freiburg (Germany), 1936-37; A.B., Princeton, 1939, Ph.D., 1944; certificate Russian Inst., Columbia, 1948; m. Hildegarde Hunt, Oct. 23, 1943 (div. 1976); children—Christopher (dec. 1968), Madeleine, Esther; m. 2d, Angela Turner, Nov. 13, 1976. Asst. prof. history U. Pa., 1948-49, Swarthmore (Pa.) Coll., 1949-51; lectr. Bryn Mawr and Swarthmore colls., 1952-54; asst. prof. U. Calif. at Riverside, 1955-59, asso. prof., 1959-60, prof., 1960-64; prof. Washington U., St. Louis, 1964-70; Frances and Jacob Hiatt prof. history Clark U., Worcester, Mass., 1970—. Sr. fellow Russian Inst., Columbia, 1951-52; Fulbright Research fellow, Finland, 1954-55; Guggenheim fellow, 1961-62, 74-75; recipient various Social Sci. Research Council grants. Mem. Am. Assn. Advancement Slavic Studies (bd. dirs. 1968-71), Am. Hist. Assn. Author: Leopold Ranke, The Formative Years, 1950; Sergei Witte and the Industrialization of Russia, 1963; Why Lenin? Why Stalin?, 1964; The Global City, 1969. Home: care History Dept Clark U Worcester MA 01610

VON LEDEN, HANS VICTOR, surgeon; b. Germany, Nov. 20, 1918; s. Peter Paul and Elizabeth (Freter) von L.; M.D., Loyola U., Chgo., 1941; m. Mary Louise Shine, Jan. 10, 1948; children—Jon Eric, Lisa Maria. Intern Mercy Hosp.-Loyola U. Clinics, Chgo. 1941-42; resident Presbyn. Hosp., Chgo., 1942-43; fellow otolaryngology and plastic surgery Mayo Found., Rochester, Minn., 1943-44, 1st asst. Mayo Clinic, 1945; practice medicine specializing in head and neck surgery, Chgo., 1947-61, Los Angeles, 1961—; clin. asso. Loyola U. Sch. Medicine, 1947-51; asso. prof. otolaryngology Cook County Grad Sch. Medicine, 1948-58; from asst. to asso. prof. otolaryngology Northwestern U. Med. Sch., 1952-61; asso. prof. surgery head and neck U. Calif. at Los Angeles, 1961-66; prof. biocommunications U. So. Calif., 1966—; cons. in laryngology Juilliard Sch. Music and Drama, N.Y.C., 1969—, Charles R. Drew Postgrad. Med. Sch., Los Angeles, 1972—; cons. staff White Meml. Med. Center, Rancho Los Amigos Hosp., Calif., Lenox Hill Hosp., New York Eye and Ear Infirmary, N.Y.C.; cons. otolaryngology and plastic surgery U.S. Navy, 1947—; mil. adv. staff Ill. Office Civil Def., 1954-61; cons. Fed. Republic Germany, 1960—. Pres. Inst. Laryngology and Voice Disorders, 1959-65, med. dir., 1966—; served as exec. v.p., med. dir. William and Harriet Gould Found., 1955-61; co-chmn. Internat. Voice Conf., 1957; v.p. Voice Found. Am., 1969-76; vis. prof., guest lectr. various univs. U.S. and fgn. countries. Served as lt. M.C., USNR, 1945-46; sr. surgeon USPHSR, 1967-77. Decorated knight's cross Internat. Constantinian Order; knight Royal Order of St. John; grand cross Mil. and Hosp. Order St. Lazarus; grand cross Order of St. John the Baptist; Ordensmarschall Orden Signum Fidei; caballero Real y Bienmer Orden de San Juan Bautista. Recipient Bronze plaque, Gold medal Ill. Med. Soc., 1954, 60; Gold medal Italian Red Cross, 1959; Bucranio, U. Padua, 1958, 60; Casselberry award Am. Laryngol. Assn., 1962, other awards for contbns. to med. sci., edn.; named companion Naval Order U.S., Mil. Order Fgn. Wars. Diplomate Am. Bd. Otolaryngology, Internat. Bd. Surgery. Fellow A.C.S., Internat. Coll. Surgeons (hon.; pres. U.S. sect. 1971-72, gov. 1972—), Am. Speech and Hearing Assn. (sci. awards 1960, 62, 65), Am. Acad. Facial Plastic and Reconstructive Surgery (dir. 1964-76), Am. Acad. Ophthalmology and Otolaryngology (certificate of merit 1953, award of honor 1959), AAAS, Am. Soc. Head and Neck Surgery, Academia Peruana de Cirugia (hon.); mem. A.M.A. (Hektoen award 1961, certificate merit 1962, 65), Calif. (del.), Los Angeles County (councilor 1969-74, v.p. 1974-75, sec.-treas. 1975-76, pres. 1977-78, trustee 1978—) med. assns., Am. Council Otolaryngology (dir. 1973-76), Am. Fedn. Clin. Research, Soc. Exptl. Biology and Med., Soc. Mil. Surgeons, Soc. Med. Consultants to Armed Forces, Pan-Am. Assn. Otolaryngology and Broncoesophagology (sec.-gen. 1966—), Mil. Order World Wars (surgeon-gen. 1954-59, vice comdr.-in-chief 1959-62, comdr.-in-chief 1962-63, Honor medal 1958), Sigma Xi; hon. mem. socs. otorhinolaryngology in U.S., Germany, Japan, Mex., Argentina, Colombia, Denmark, Chile, Peru, Panama, El Salvador, Greece. Republican. Roman Catholic. Clubs: Army-Navy (Washington); Mariner (San Francisco). Author med. textbooks and articles; producer med. motion pictures; chief editor Jour. Continuing Med. Edn. in Otorhinolaryngology. Home: 259 Tilden Ave Los Angeles CA 90049 Office: 10921 Wilshire Blvd Los Angeles CA 90024

VON LEHMDEN-MASLIN, ALYS AUGUSTA, med. sci. editorial cons.; b. Aug. 22, 1941; d. F. Ralph and Alice Curry (Ditz) von Lehmden; B.Sc., Ohio State U., 1959; student Harvard U., 1958; M.Sc., U. Rochester (N.Y.), 1961; postgrad. Washington U., St. Louis, 1961-62; m. Kirksey Brunswick Maslin, June 27, 1963; 1 dau., Kirsten Augusta Frances Brunswick von Lehmden. Research asso. U. Ill., Urbana, 1962-68; sr. editor, research asso. dept. drugs AMA, Chgo., 1968-71; sci. editor sch. dept. Harper & Row Pubs., Evanston, Ill., 1971-72; exec. editor Drug Therapy Med. Jour., Biomed. Info. Corp., N.Y.C., 1974-78; med. sci. editorial cons., 1978—; past mem. faculty U. Rochester, Washington U., St. Louis, U. Ill.; sci. judge Nat. Sci. competition, 1972. Mem. women's com. Kips Bay (N.Y.) Boys' Club, 1973—, exec. bd., 1977—; mem. aux. N.Y. Infirmary, 1977—; culture chmn. fund raising Chapin Sch., 1976-78. Research fellow Nat. Inst. Allergy and Infectious Diseases, 1965-68, Nat. Heart Inst., 1965-68, Mark L. Morris Found., 1965-68. Mem. AAAS, Am. Med. Writers Assn., Women in Communications, Jr. League N.Y.C. (Am. Debutante of Yr. 1954, co-chmn. Block Assn. 1972—), Sigma Delta Epsilon (hon.). Co-editor: Infectious Blood Diseases of Man and Animal, 1969; AMA Drug Evaluation, 1969; Teaching About Drugs, curriculum guide book, 1970; contbr. to med., vet. and sci. jours. Home: 177 E 78th St New York NY 10021

VON MEHREN, ARTHUR TAYLOR, educator, lawyer; b. Albert Lea, Minn., Aug. 10, 1922; s. Sigurd Anders and Eulalia Marion (Anderson) von M.; S.B., Harvard, 1942, LL.B., 1945, Ph.D., 1946; Faculty of Law, U. Zurich, 1946-47; Faculté de Droit, University of Paris, 1948-49; m. Joan Elizabeth Moore, Oct. 11, 1947; children—George Moore, Peter Anders, Philip Taylor. Editor in chief Harvard Law Review, 1944-45; law clk. to Chief Judge Calvert Magruder, U.S. Ct. Appeals, 1st Circuit, 1945-46; asst. prof. law Harvard, 1946-53, prof., 1953-76, Story prof., 1976—; acting chief legislation br., legal div. Occupation Mil. Govt. U.S., Germany, 1947-48, cons. legal div., 1949; admitted to Mass. bar, 1950; tchr. Salzburg Seminar in Am. Studies, summers 1953, 54; Fulbright research prof. U. Tokyo, Japan, 1956-57, Rome, Italy, 1968-69; cons. legal studies Ford Found., New Delhi, 1962-63; vis. prof. U. Frankfurt, summer, 1967; Ford vis. prof. Inst. Advanced Legal Studies, U. London, 1976; professeur associé U. Paris, 1977. Mem. U.S. delegation Hague Conf. pvt. internat. law, 1966, 68, 76. Guggenheim fellow, 1968-69. Mem. Am. Bar Assn., Am. Fgn. Law Assn., Internat. Academy Comparative Law, Japanese Am. Soc. Legal Studies, Am. Arbitration Assn. (mem. comml. panel), Am. Assn. Comparative Study Law (dir.), Am. Soc. Polit. and Legal Philosophy, Internat. Law Assn., Phi Beta Kappa. Author: The Civil Law System, 1957, 2d edit. (with J. Gordley), 1977. Co-author: The Law of Multistate Problems, 1965. Bd. editors Am. Jour. Comparative Law. Contbr. articles to profl. jours. Editor: Law in Japan-The Legal Order in a Changing Soc., 1963; mem. editorial com. Internat. Ency. Comparative Law, 1969—. Home: 68 Sparks St Cambridge MA 02138

VON MERING, OTTO OSWALD, educator; b. Berlin, Germany, Oct. 21, 1922; s. Otto O. and Henriette (Troeger) von M.; came to U.S., 1939, naturalized, 1954; grad. Belmont Hill Sch., 1940; B.A. in History, Williams Coll., 1944; Ph.D. in Social Anthropology, Harvard, 1956; m. Shirley Ruth Brook, Sept. 11, 1954; children—Gretchen, Karin, Gregory. Instr. Belmont Hill Sch., Belmont, Mass., 1945-47, Boston U., 1947-48, Cambridge Jr. Coll., 1948-49; research asst. lab. social relations Harvard, 1950-51, Boston Psychopathic Hosp., 1951-53; Russell Sage Found. fellow, N.Y.C., 1953-55; asst. prof. social anthropology U. Pitts., 1955-60, asso. prof., 1960-65, prof. social anthropology, 1965-71, prof. child devel. and child care, 1969-71; prof. anthropology and family medicine U. Fla., 1971—, prof. anthropology in Ob-Gyn, 1979—; lectr. Sigmund Freud Inst., Frankfurt, Germany, 1964, Pitts. Psychoanalytical Inst., 1960-71, Interuniversity Forum, 1967-71; cons. mental hosps.; tech. adviser Maurice Falk Med. Fund; Fulbright vis. lectr., 1962-63; Richard-Merton guest prof. Heidelberg U., Germany, 1962-63; vis. prof. Dartmouth, 1970-71; Am. Anthrop. Assn. vis. lectr., 1961-62, 71-74; dir. Tech. Assistance Research Assos., U. Fla., 1979—. Research grantee Wenner-Gren Found., N.Y., 1962-63, Am. Philos. Soc., 1962-63, Maurice Falk Med. Fund, 1970-71; Spl. fellow NIMH, 1971-72. Fellow Am. Anthrop. Assn. (mem. James Mooney award com.), Am. Sociol. Assn., AAAS, Am. Gerontol. Soc., Royal Soc. Health, Acad. Psychosomatic Medicine, Am. Ethnological Soc., Soc. Applied Anthropology, Royal Anthrop. Inst.; mem. Assn. Am. Med. Colls., Am. Fedn. Clin. Research, Am. Pub. Health Assn., Am. Psychiat. Assn., World Fedn. Mental Health, Internat. Assn. Social Psychiatry (regional counselor). Author: Remotivating the Mental Patient, 1957; A Grammar of Human Values, 1961; (with Mitscherlich and Brocher) Der Kranke in der Modernen Gesellschaft, 1967; (with Kasdan) Anthropology in the Behavioral and Health Sciences, 1970; also articles. Commentary editor Human Organization, 1974-76. Corr. editor. Jour. Geriatric Psychiatry; mem. editorial bd. Med. Anthropology, 1976—. Office: UF-LAS:GPA-B-370 Gainesville FL 32611. *Three guides to conduct I value most: the first step to wisdom is searching for the best fit of fact, argument, and experience. For every excess every first remedy must be amended quickly. When the past disturbs the present, more work on the future is needed.*

VON MOLTKE, WILHELM VIGGO, architect, urban designer; b. Kreisau, Silesia, Germany, May 8, 1911; s. Count Helmuth Adolf and Dorothy (Rose-Innes) von M.; came to U.S., 1940, naturalized, 1944; Dipl. Ing. Arch. magna cum laude, Technische Hochschule, Berlin, 1937; M.Arch., Harvard U., 1942; m. Veronica Maria Jochum, Nov. 15, 1961. Employed in archtl. offices, Eng., 1937-38, Stockholm, Sweden, 1938-40; with Marcel Breuer, architect, N.Y.C., 1948; designer Skidmore, Owings & Merrill, architects, N.Y.C., 1948-49; sr. designer Eero Saarinen & Assos., Bloomfield Hills, Mich., 1949-53; chief designer Phila. City Planning Commn., 1953-61; dir. urban design Guayana project Joint Center for Urban Studies, Mass. Inst. Tech. and Harvard U., 1961-64; prof. urban design, dir. urban design program Grad. Sch. Design, Harvard U., Cambridge, Mass., 1964-77, prof. emeritus, 1977—; commr. for edn. and research Boston Soc. Architects, 1976-78; mem. faculty Salzburg (Austria) Seminar in Am. Studies, 1972; urban design cons. to Quito, Ecuador, Managua, Nicaragua and Istanbul, Turkey, 1973-76, Ministry Community Devel., Devel., Saudi Arabia, 1979; adv. U. Autonoma Metropolitana, Mexico City, 1979; scholar in residence Centre Human Settlements, U. B.C., 1979; vis. prof. dept. architecture École Polytechnique Fédérale, Lausanne, Switzerland, 1979. Bd. dirs. Boston Archtl. Center, 1978—. Served to 1st lt. U.S. Army, 1943-46. Decorated Order of Merit, Fed. Republic Germany; recipient 1st prize internat. competition Mus. Modern Art, N.Y.C., 1941; 2d prize Carson-Pirie-Scott Internat. Competition for Design of Center City, Chgo., 1954. Fellow AIA; mem. Am. Inst. Planners, Boston Soc. Architects (dir. 1971-74), Bayerische Akademie der Schönen Künste (hon. corr.), Deutsche Akademie für Städtebau und Landesplanung (hon. corr.). Contbr. to publs. in field. Home: 14 Gray Gardens W Cambridge MA 02138 Office: Grad Sch Design Harvard U Cambridge MA 02138

VONNEGUT, KURT, JR., writer; b. Indpls., Nov. 11, 1922; s. Kurt and Edith (Lieber) V.; student Cornell U., 1940-42; student U. Chgo., 1945-47, M.A. in Anthropology, 1971; m. Jane Marie Cox, Sept. 1, 1945 (div. 1979); children—Mark, Edith, Nanette; adopted nephews—James, Steven and Kurt Adams; m. 2d, Jill Krementz, 1979. Reporter Chgo. City News Bur., 1946; pub. relations with Gen. Electric Co., 1947-50; free-lance writer, 1950-65; lectr. Writers Workshop, U. Iowa, 1965-67; lectr. in English, Harvard, 1970; distinguished prof. City Coll. N.Y., 1973-74. Served with inf. AUS, 1942-45. Guggenheim fellow 1967-68. Mem. Nat. Inst. Arts and Letters (recipient Lit. award 1970). Author: (novels) Player Piano, 1951, Sirens of Titan, 1959, Mother Night, 1961, Cat's Cradle, 1963, God Bless You, Mr. Rosewater, 1964; (story collection) Welcome to the Monkey House, 1968; (novel) Slaughterhouse-Five, 1969; (play) Happy Birthday, Wanda June, 1970; (TV script) Between Time and Timbuktu or Prometheus-5, 1972; Breakfast of Champions, 1973; (essays) Wampeters, Foma and Granfalloons, 1974; (novels) Slapstick, or Lonesome No More, 1976; Jailbird, 1979; also short stories, articles, revs. Address: care Donald C Farber Conboy Hewitt O'Brien & Broadman 600 Madison Ave New York NY 10022

VON RHEIN, JOHN RICHARD, music critic, editor; b. Pasadena, Calif., Sept. 10, 1945; s. Hans Walter and Elsa Maryon (Brossmann) Von R.; B.A., UCLA, 1967; B.A., Calif. State U., Los Angeles, 1970. Music reviewer Hollywood (Calif.) Citizen-News, 1968-70; music editor and critic, dance critic Akron (Ohio) Beacon Jour., 1971-77;

music editor and critic Chgo. Tribune, 1977—; tchr. music appreciation Rio Hondo Jr. Coll., 1970-71. Calif. Music Critics Assn. fellow, 1972, 75. Contbr. articles to Cleve. mag., Chgo. mag., High Fidelity, Musical Am., Opera News. Office: Chicago Tribune 435 N Michigan Ave Chicago IL 60611

VON RICHTHOFEN, ERICH BENEDIKT, educator; b. Hirschberg, Silesia, May 8, 1913; s. Friedrich Wilhelm and Sybilla Dorothea Von R.; came to Can., 1956, naturalized, 1961; Ph.D., U. Frankfurt am Main (Germany), 1940, Dr. HABIL, 1943; m. Eleanor Agnes Gruss; 1 son, Daniel Frederik. Privatdozent, U. Frankfurt am Main, 1943-51, ausserplanmassiger prof., 1951-56, dir. Internat. Summer Sch., 1952-56; asso. prof. Romance studies U. Alta. (Can.), Edmonton, 1956-61, prof., 1961-62; prof. Romance studies Boston Coll., 1962-64; prof. Hispanic and Italian studies U. Toronto (Ont., Can.), 1964-79, prof. emeritus, 1979—; vis. prof. U. Chgo., spring 1954. Can. Council research grantee, 1969, 71, 73, 75, travel grantee, 1964, 70, 72. Fellow Royal Soc. Can.; mem. Société Rencesvals, Société Internationale Arthurienne, Internat. Assn. Hispanists, Soc. Study of Names, Can. Soc. Italian Studies. Author books, most recent being: Limites de la critica literaria, 1976; Sincretismo literario, 1980. Home: 232 Panorama Pl Lions Bay BC V0N 2E0 Canada Office: Dept Spanish and Portuguese U Toronto Toronto ON M5S 1A1 Canada

VON RINGELHEIM, PAUL HELMUT, sculptor; b. Vienna, Austria; s. Henry and Rosita (Altschuler) von R.; B.S., Bklyn. Coll., 1956; M.A., Fairleigh Dickinson U., 1958; postgrad. Art Students League, N.Y.C., 1958-59; Fulbright scholar in sculpture, Acad. Fine Arts, Munich, 1960-61. Tchr. printmaking Bklyn. Mus. Sch., 1957-58; prof. sculpture Sch. Visual Arts, N.Y.C., 1967-71; one-man shows at Niveau Art Gallery, N.Y.C., 1958, Am. House, Berlin, Munich and Hamburg, 1960-61, Rose Fried Gallery, N.Y.C., 1964, 67, Fairleigh Dickinson U., 1964, New Vision Galleries, London, 1964, O.K. Harris Gallery, N.Y.C., 1971-73, Mitzi Landau Gallery, Los Angeles, 1974, N.Y. Cultural Center, 1975, OK Harris Gallery, N.Y.C., 1976, 78; exhibited in group shows at Bklyn. Mus. Ann., 1958, Gunther Franke, Munich, 1961, New Eng. Exhbn., Silver Mine Guild Council (Silver prize), 1962, Whitney Ann., 1963, 65, Mus. Modern Art, N.Y.C., 1964, Whitney Mus., 1964, O.K. Harris Gallery, Providence, 1964, Ben Uri Gallery, London, 1965, S.I. Mus., N.Y.C., 1965, Byron Gallery, N.Y.C., 1965, Jewish Mus., N.Y.C., 1966, 68, Cleve. Mus., 1966, Obelisk Gallery, Boston, 1967, Albright-Knox Gallery, Buffalo, 1967, Rose Art Mus., Brandeis U., 1967, Am. embassy, Brussels, 1967, Mus. Modern Art, N.Y.C., 1967, 69, Hessischeslanders Mus., Daensstadt, Germany, 1967, Mus. Paymons-Von Bellninger, Rotterdam, Netherlands, 1967, New Sch. Social Research, N.Y.C., 1968, Meml. Hall, Boston, 1968, Finch Coll., N.Y.C., 1968, Bridgehampton (L.I.) Galleries, 1968, Hardin Simmons U., Abilene, Tex., 1968, Cedar Rapids (Iowa) Art Assn., 1968, Decatur (Ill.) Art Center, 1968, Greenville County (S.C.) Mus., 1968, St. Cloud (Minn.) Coll., 1968, U. Tex., Austin, 1968, Roanoke (Va.) Art Center, 1968, Westmoreland County Mus., , Greensburg, Pa., 1969, Frick Mus., Pitts., 1969, Temple U. Music Festival, 1969, Dance Set for Chimera by Murray Louis, N.Y.C., 1969, Cultural Affairs Commn., N.Y.C., 1969-70, Internat. Sculpture Show, Govt. Center, Boston, 1971, Monumenta, Newport, R.I., 1974, Nebr. Bi-Centennial Interstate 80 Project, 1976, Flair, Columbia Mall, Columbia, S.C., Tex. Eastern, Houston, 1977, Moment, Taubman Center, Sterling Heights, Mich.; Endless Force, Pres. Gerald R. Ford, Palm Springs, Calif.; commd. Going My Way, Meml. to Bing Crosby, Los Angeles, 1978; designer cover Time mag. and Partisan Rev.; represented in permanent collections at Welton Becket Assos., Broadway Maintenance Corp., Carter Wallace Corp., N.Y.C., CBS, N.Y.C., Fairleigh Dickinson U., Haus Der Kunst, Munich, Martin Found., Mus. Modern Art, N.Y.C., Mus. Modern Art, Tel Aviv, Israel, Mus. Modern Art, Tokyo, Japan, Twentieth Century Fund, N.Y.C., Wheaton Coll., Whitney Mus. Am. Art, Hrsicher Landes Mus., Damstatd, Germany, Time and Life Collection, N.Y.C.; archtl. commns. include World Peace Monument, U.S. Pavilion, New York Worlds Fair, 1963-64, lands, 1967, New Sch. Social Research, N.Y.C., 1968, Meml. Hall, Boston, 1968, Finch Coll., N.Y.C., 1968, Bridgehampton (L.I.) Galleries, 1968, Hardin Simmons U., Abilene, Tex., 1968, Cedar Rapids (Iowa) Art Assn., 1968, Decatur (Ill.) Art Center, 1968, Greenville County (S.C.) Mus., 1968, St. Cloud (Minn.) Coll., 1968, U. Tex., Austin, 1968, Roanoke (Va.) Art Center, 1968, Westmoreland County Mus., Greensburg, Pa., 1969, Frick Mus., Pitts., 1969, Temple U. Music Festival, 1969, Dance Set for Chimera by Murray Louis, N.Y.C., 1969, Cultural Affairs Commn., N.Y.C., 1969-70, Internat. Sculpture Show, Govt. Center, Boston, 1971, Monumenta, Newport, R.I., 1974, Nebr. Bi-Centennial Interstate 80 Project, 1976, Flair, Columbia Mall, Columbia, S.C., Tex. Eastern, Houston, 1977, Moment, Taubman Center, Sterling Heights, Mich.; Endless Force, Pres. Gerald R. Ford, Palm Springs, Calif.; commd. Going My Way, Meml. to Bing Crosby, Los Angeles, 1978; designer cover Time mag. and Partisan Rev.; represented in permanent collections at Welton Becket Assos., Broadway Maintenance Corp., Carter Wallace Corp., N.Y.C., CBS, N.Y.C., Fairleigh Dickinson U., Haus Der Kunst, Munich, Martin Found., Mus. Modern Art, N.Y.C., Mus. Modern Art, Tel Aviv, Israel, Mus. Modern Art, Tokyo, Japan. Twentieth Century Fund, N.Y.C., Wheaton Coll., Whitney Mus. Am. Art, Hrsicher Landes Mus., Damstatd, Germany, Time and Life Collection, N.Y.C.; archtl. commns. include World Peace Monument, U.S. Pavilion, New York Worlds Fair, 1963-64, Bronx Park 11, Steel Directional #17, N.Y.C., 1968, Gateway, New York, Unimark Internat. Tangential 32, N.Y.C., 1969, Continum III, Worcester (Mass.) Center, Westinghouse Nuclear Center, Fulcrum, Pitts., 1971, Vortex in Red, Houston, 1975, numerous others. Dir. fine arts bd. Fairleigh Dickinson U., Fine Arts Commn., 1974-75. Recipient Outstanding Young Man of Year award for world peace sculpture Fed. Pavilion, New York Worlds Fair, 1964. Mem. Archtl. League City of N.Y. Clubs: Lambs (hon.), Explorers. Home: 9 Great Jones St New York NY 10012

VON STADE, FREDERICA, mezzo-soprano; b. Somerville, N.J., June 1, 1945; student Mannes Coll. Music, N.Y.C.; m. Peter Elkus. Former nanny, salesgirl; sec. Am. Shakespeare Festival; debut in Zauberfloete with Met. Opera, 1970, now resident mem.; appeared with opera cos., including Paris Opera, San Francisco Opera, Salzburg Festival, London Royal Opera, Spoleto Festival, Boston Opera Co., Santa Fe Opera, La Scala; recital artist, soloist with symphony orchs.; appeared in: The Marriage of Figaro, Faust, The Magic Flute, Don Giovanni, Tales of Hoffmann, Rigoletto. Mem. Am. Guild Mus. Artists. Roman Catholic. Albums: French Opera Arias; Frederica Von Stade Sings Mozart-Rossini Opera Arias. Office: care Columbia Artists Mgmt 165 W 57 St New York City NY 10019*

VON SUMMER, ALEXANDER CARL, JR., real estate exec.; b. Teaneck, N.J., Nov. 2, 1938; s. Alexander Carl and Edith Marion (Spencer) von S.; B.A., Dartmouth, 1960; m. Sally Louise Pierce, Sept. 21, 1963; children—Kristen Pierce, Alexander Carl III, Hollis Marion Dene. Propr. Alexander Summer Co., realtors and property devel., Teaneck and West Orange, N.J., 1962—; v.p. Alexander Summer Mortgage, Teaneck, West Orange, N.J., 1963-73, chmn. bd., 1973—; v.p. property mgmt. Alexander Summer, Inc., Teaneck, 1962-74, exec. v.p., 1974—; dir. United Jersey Bank, United Jersey Mortgage Co. Mem. legislative com. Bd. Realtors Eastern Bergen County, 1964-72, chmn., 1965-72, bd. dirs., 1970-75, pres., 1973—. Mem. Conservation Commn., Saddle River, N.J., 1970-71; jury commnr. Bergen County, 1971-75. Trustee Teterboro Aviation Hall of Fame; mem. real estate adv. com. Bergen Community Coll., 1977. Served with N.J. Nat. Guard, 1960-64. Mem. N.J. Builders, Owners and Mgrs. Assn. (pres. 1971—; dir. 1966—), N.J. Builders Assn. (dir. 1971—, mem. legislative com. 1971—), N.J. Assn. Realtors (mem. legis. com. 1969-75, dir. 1973-74), Am. Soc. Real Estate Counselors, Am. Arbitration Assn. (dir.), Chamber Commerce and Industry No. N.J., Alpha Delta Phi. Clubs: Dartmouth of Bergen County (v.p. 1959-60); Arcola Country (Paramus, N.J.). Home: 19 Pilot Rock Ln Riverside CT 06878 Office: 222 Cedar Ln Teaneck NJ 07666

VON SYDOW, MAX CARL ADOLF, actor; b. Lund, Sweden, Apr. 10, 1929; s. Carl Wilhelm and Greta (Rappe) von S.; student Royal Dramatic Theatre Acad. Stockholm, 1948-51; m. Kerstin Olin, Aug. 1, 1951; children—Clas Wilhelm, Per Henrik. Appearances with Municipal Theatre of Korrköping-Linköping, 1951-53, Municipal Theatre of Hälsingborg, 1953-55, Municipal Theatre of Malmö, 1955-60, Royal Dramatic Theatre Stockholm, 1960-62; Broadway debut in The Night of the Tribades, 1977; films include The Seventh Seal, 1956, The Magician, 1958, The Virgin Spring, 1959, The Hour of the Wolf, 1968, The Shame, 1969, A Passion, 1968, The Greatest Story Ever Told, 1963, Hawaii, 1965, The Reward, 1965, The Kremlin Letter, 1971, The Passion of Anna, 1971, The Immigrants, 1971, Night Visitor, 1971, The Emigrants, 1972, The New Land, 1973, Three Days of the Condor, 1975, Voyage of the Damned, 1976, Exorcist II: The Heretics, 1977, March Ordie, 1977, Hurricane, 1978. Served with Swedish Quartermaster Corps, 1947-48. Recipient Royal Found. Cultural award, 1954. Office: care Paul Kohner Inc 9169 Sunset Blvd Los Angeles CA 90069*

VON TERSCH, LAWRENCE WAYNE, educator; b. Waverly, Iowa, Mar. 17, 1923; s. Alfred and Martha (Emerson) Von T.; B.S., Iowa State U., 1943, M.S., 1948, Ph.D., 1953; m. LaValle Sills, Dec. 17, 1948; 1 son, Richard George. From instr. to prof. elec. engring. Iowa State U., 1946-56; dir. computer lab. Mich. State U. , 1956—, prof. elec. engring., chmn. dept., 1958-65, asso. dean engring., 1965-68, dean, 1968—. Mem. IEEE, Sigma Xi, Tau Beta Pi, Eta Kappa Nu, Phi Kappa Phi, Pi Mu Epsilon. Author: (with A. W. Swago) Recurrent Electrical Transients, 1953. Home: 4282 Tacoma Blvd Okemos MI 48864 Office: Coll Engring Michigan State U East Lansing MI 48823

VONTRESS, CLEMMONT EYVIND, educator; b. Bowling Green, Ky., Apr. 22, 1929; s. Benjamin Franklin and Elizabeth (Brown) V.; B.A., Ky. State U., 1952; M.S., Ind. U., 1956, Ph.D., 1965; m. Mary Delma Hockersmith, Apr. 12, 1951; 1 son, Amasa Delano. Instr. English, So. U., Baton Rouge, 1956-57; English tchr. George Washington High Sch., Indpls., 1957-58; dir. counseling Crispus Attucks High Sch., Indpls., 1958-65; asso. prof. edn. Howard U., 1965-69; prof. edn. George Washington U., 1969—, pres. Urban Learning, Tng. and Research Assos., Inc., 1975—. Served with U.S. Army, 1953-55. Mem. Nat. Capital Personnel and Guidance Assn., Am. Personnel and Guidance Assn., Nat. Vocat. Guidance Assn., AAUP, Assn. Counselor Educators and Suprs., D.C. Psychol. Assn., Phi Delta Kappa. Author: Counseling Negroes, 1971. Office: Dept Edn George Washington U Washington DC 20052

VON WYSS, MARC ROBERT, cement co. exec.; b. Zurich, Switzerland, Feb. 12, 1931; s. George H. and Mariejenny A. (Burckhardt) von W.; came to U.S., 1971; grad. Fed. Inst. Tech., Zurich, 1956; m. Marina V. Gygi, Sept. 4, 1963; children—George M., Martin C. Control systems design engr. Svenska Aeroplan AB, Joenkoeping, Sweden, 1957-60; control systems design engr., asst. dept. head Contraves, AG, Zurich, 1961-65; sr. v.p. Holderbank Mgmt. & Cons., Ltd. (Switzerland), 1966-71; pres., chief exec. officer Dundee Cement Co. (Mich.), 1971—. Home: 2526 Londonderry St Ann Arbor MI 48104 Office: PO Box 122 Dundee MI 48131

VOOK, FREDERICK LUDWIG, physicist; b. Milw., Jan. 17, 1931; s. Fred Ludwig and Hedwig Anna (Werner) V.; B.A. with honors, U. Chgo., 1951, B.S., 1952; M.S., U. Ill., 1954, Ph.D. in Physics, 1958; m. Frederica Jean Sandin, Aug. 16, 1958; children—Eric Robert, Dietrich Werner. With Sandia Labs., Kirtland AFB East, N.Mex., 1958—, div. supr., 1962-71, mgr. dept. research, 1971-78, dir. research, 1978—. U. Chgo. and U. Ill. scholar and fellow. Fellow Am. Phys. Soc. (chmn. study group on physics problems relating to energy techs.); mem. Phi Beta Kappa, Sigma Xi. Editor: Radiation Effects in Semiconductors, 1968; co-editor: Applications of Ion Beams to Metals, 1974. Editorial bds. Radiation Effects, Crystal Lattice Defects. Office: Sandia Labs Orgn 5100 Kirtland AFB East NM 87185

VOORDE, FRANCES, govt. ofcl.; b. South Bend, Ind., Oct. 28, 1939; d. Edward F. and Theresa (Muszik) Voorde; B.A., St. Mary's Coll., Notre Dame, Ind., 1961; M.A., George Washington U. Personnel and appointment sec. to U.S. Congressman J. Edward Roush of Ind., 1961-64; exec. sec. to U.S. Senator Birch Bayh of Ind., 1965-71; asst. chief Office Records and Registration, U.S. Ho. of Reps., 1972-75; spl. asst. Office Disclosure and Compliance, Fed. Election Commn., 1975-76; dep. dir. Office Voter Registration, Democratic Nat. Com., 1976; dir. scheduling and advance Carter Presdl. Campaign, 1976; dir. scheduling Office of the President, 1977-78, dep. appointments sec., 1978—. Roman Catholic. Address: The White House Washington DC 20500

VOORHEES, ALAN MANNERS, transp. and planning cons.; b. New Brunswick, N.J., Dec. 17, 1922; s. Ralph W. and Jane (Manners) V.; B. Civil Engring., Rensselaer Poly. Inst., 1947, D.Engring. (hon.), 1978; M. City Planning, Mass. Inst. Tech., 1949; certificate traffic engring. Yale U. Bur. Hwy. Traffic, 1952; m. Nathalie Potter, Apr. 30, 1949; children—Susan, Scott Whitaker, Nancy. City planner, traffic engr. City of Colorado Springs, 1949-51; traffic planning engr. Automotive Safety Found., Washington, 1952-61; pres. Alan M. Voorhees & Assos., Inc., McLean, Va., 1961-77; dean Coll. Architecture, Art and Urban Scis., U. Ill. at Chgo. Circle, 1977—; guest lectr. various univs., 1955—; dir. Planning Research Corp., Data Terminal Systems, Inc. Served to lt. USNR, 1943-45; Decorated Bronze Star, Silver Star. Mem. Am. Inst. Planners (pres. 1968-69), Inst. Traffic Engrs. (past pres. award 1955), ASCE (Harland Bartholomew award 1969), Transp. Research Bd. (exec. com. i969-72, chmn. exec. com. 1972; award 1959), Town Planning Inst. Can., Internat. Fedn. Housing and Planning, Lambda Alpha. Conglist. (trustee 1967-68). Club: Cosmos. Contbr. articles to profl. jours., handbooks. Home: 860 N Lake Shore Dr Chicago IL 60611 Office: Coll Architecture Art and Urban Scis U Ill at Chgo Circle Box 4348 Chicago IL 60680

VOORHEES, DONALD SHIRLEY, judge; b. Leavenworth, Kans., July 30, 1916; s. Ephraim and Edna Mary (Oliphint) V.; A.B., U. Kans., 1938; LL.B., Harvard U., 1946; m. Anne Elizabeth Spillers, June 21, 1946; children—Stephen Spillers, David Todd, John Lawrence, Diane Patricia, Richard Gordon. Admitted to Okla. bar, 1947, Wash. State bar, 1948; practiced law, Tulsa, 1946-47, Seattle, 1947-74; partner firm Riddell, Williams, Voorhees, Ivie, & Bullitt, Seattle, 1952-74; judge U.S. Dist. Ct., Western dist. Wash., 1974—. Bd. dirs. Fed. Jud. Center. Served with USN, 1942-46. Mem. Am., Washington State, Seattle-King County bar assns., Maritime Law Assn., Am. Judicature Soc., Phi Beta Kappa. Democrat. Unitarian. Office: 609 US Courthouse Seattle WA 98104

VOORHEES, ENDERS MCCLUMPHA, ret. steel exec.; b. Amsterdam, N.Y., Apr. 28, 1891; s. James and Margaret (McClumpha) V.; B.S., Dartmouth, 1914; student Amos Tuck Sch. of Finance, 1914, Bentley Sch. of Accounting (Boston), 1914-16; D.C.S. (hon.), N.Y.U., 1950; m. Blanche Pauline Andrews, Sept. 15, 1923. Jr. accountant Hollis H. Sawyer & Co., 1914-15; with Pacific Commercial Co., Manila, 1915-16; asst. comptroller U.S. Rubber Co., 1918-20; gen. auditor and asst. to pres., Ajax Rubber Co., 1921-25; with Sanderson & Porter & W.A. Harriman & Co., 1926-27; gen. auditor, later sec.-treas. and v.p., Johns-Manville Corp., 1927-37; vice chmn. finance com. U.S. Steel Corp., 1937-38, chmn. finance com., mem. exec. com., dir., 1938-56, dir., mem. finance and exec. coms., 1956-65. Served lt. 73d F.A., Camp Jackson, 1917-18. Mem. Holland Soc., St. Nicholas Soc. Clubs: Links, Dartmouth, Seminole, Jupiter Island. Home: 960 Fifth Ave New York City NY 10021

VOORHEES, WILLIAM DELANO, JR., psychiatrist, hosp. adminstr.; b. Bklyn., Dec. 29, 1920; s. William Delano and Thekla (Grimmell) V.; B.A., Johns Hopkins, 1942, M.D., 1945; m. Selma Jean Schurmann, Dec. 8, 1945; children—Carol Ann, Susan Jean, William Delano III, Intern Hartford (Conn.) Hosp., 1945-46; resident in psychiatry Payne Whitney Psychiat. Clinic, N.Y. Hosp., N.Y.C., 1948-53; asst. in psychiatry Cornell U., N.Y.C., 1949-51, instr., 1951-53; instr. psychiatry U. Wash., Seattle, 1953-56; dir. extramural services Western State Hosp., Ft. Steilacoom, Wash., 1956-60; supt. No. State Hosp., Sedro-Woolley, Washington, 1960-68; asso. commr. div. local services N.Y. State Dept. Mental Hygiene, 1968, 1st dep. commr., 1968-74, regional dir., 1974-77; dir. forensic unit Western State Hosp., Ft. Steilacoom, Wash., 1977—. Cons. Nat. Inst. Mental Health, 1963-71. Served to capt., M.C. AUS, 1946-48. Diplomate Am. Bd. Neurology and Psychiatry. Mem. Am. Psychiat. Assn. Home: 4034 Soundview Dr W Tacoma WA 98466 Office: Western State Hosp Ft Steilacoom WA 98494

VOORHIS, HORACE JERRY, ex-congressman, ret. exec.; b. Ottawa, Kans., Apr. 6, 1901; s. Charles Brown and Ella Ward (Smith) V.; A.B., Yale, 1923; M.A., Claremont Colls., 1928; LL.D. (hon.), St. Francis Xavier University, 1953, Claremont Grad. Sch., 1979; m. Alice Louise Livingston, Nov. 27, 1924; children—Alice Nell, Charles Brown, Jerry Livingston. Traveling rep. YMCA, Germany, 1923-24; worker Ford assembly plant, Charlotte, N.C., 1924-25; tchr. Allendale Farm Sch., Lake Villa, Ill., 1925-26; dir. Dray Cottage, Home for Boys, Laramie, Wyo., 1926- 27; headmaster and trustee Voorhis Sch. for Boys, 1928-38; spl. lectr. Pomona Coll., 1930-35; mem. 75th to 79th Congresses 12th Calif. Dist. Exec. dir. Cooperative League U.S., 1947-67, now cons., bd. dirs. Group Health Assn. Am., 1947—; chmn. The Co-op. Found., 1967—. Mem. Am. Country Life Assn., Pomona Valley Council Chs., Nat. Cath. Rural Life Conf., Adult Edn. Assn., Am. Pub. Health Assn., World Federalists, Phi Beta Kappa, Phi Delta Kappa. Democrat. Episcopalian. Author: Out of Debt, Out of Danger; Confessions of a Congressman; The Christian in Politics; American Cooperatives; Strange Case of Richard Milhous Nixon; Life and Times of Aurelius Lyman Voorhis; Confession of Faith. Home: 633 W Bonita Ave Claremont CA 91711 Office: 114B N Indian Hill Blvd Claremont CA 91711

VORDERBURG, MARVIN FRANKLIN, charitable trust adminstr.; b. Toledo, Ohio, Oct. 11, 1915; s. Frank H. and Margaret (Mayer) V.; student U. Toledo, 1933-34, U. S.C., 1935-37, Sch. Banking, U. Va., 1962-64; D.Sc. (hon.), Fla. Inst. Tech., 1978; m. Helen J. Goethe, Feb. 5, 1938; 1 son, Christopher. With City Loan & Savs. Co. Toledo, 1937-57; v.p., trust officer Palmer First Nat. Bank and Trust Co., (name now S.E. Banks Trust Co. N.A.), Sarasota, Fla., 1957-71; adminstr. William G. Selby and Marie Selby Found., Sarasota, 1971—, Karl Bickel Charitable Trust, 1973—, Cordelia Lee Beattie Found., 1974—. Bd. dirs. Internat. Amyotrophic Lateral Sclerosis Found., Sarasota Art Assn., So. Scholarship Found., Tallahassee, Community Found. Sarasota; trustee S.E. Council of Founds. Served with AUS, 1944-46; ETO. Mason (Shriner). Home: 7485 Mariana Dr Sarasota FL 33581 Office: 1401 Main St Sarasota FL 33577

VORENBERG, JAMES, educator, lawyer; b. Boston, Jan. 10, 1928; s. F. Frank and Ida (Muhlfelder) V.; A.B., Harvard, 1948, LL.B., 1951; m. Dorothy Greeley, Oct. 25, 1952; children—Jill, Amy, Eliza; m. 2d, Elizabeth Weiner Troubh, June 20, 1970. Law clk. to Justice Frankfurter, 1953-54; with firm Ropes & Gray, 1954-62, partner, 1960-62; prof. law Harvard, Cambridge, Mass., 1962—. Dir. Office of Criminal Justice, 1964-65; exec. dir. Pres.'s Commn. on Law Enforcement and Adminstrn Justice, 1965-67; asso. spl. prosecutor Watergate Spl. Prosecution Force, 1973-75. Bd. dirs. Police Found.; trustee NAACP, Legal Def. Fund, Mexican-Am. Legal Def. Fund; chmn. Mass. State Ethics Commn., 1978—. Served with USAF, 1951-53. Home: 9 Willard St Cambridge MA 02138

VOROS, GERALD JOHN, public relations co. exec.; b. Milw., May 13, 1930; s. Thomas Louis and Theresa Johanna (Huebler) V.; B.J., Marquette U., 1951; postgrad. U. Utah, 1956; m. Carla Marie Olson, Nov. 22, 1958; children—Bergen, John, Marta, Andrew, Matthew. Reporter, Blackfoot (Idaho) Daily Bull., 1953-54, Longview (Wash.) Daily News, 1954-56, Salt Lake Tribune, 1956-57, 58-61, Milw. Jour., 1957-58; writer E. & J. Gallo Winery, 1961; v.p., gen. mgr. William Kostka & Assos., Denver, 1958-64; account supr. N.W. Ayer & Sons, Inc., Chgo., 1964-66; with Ketchum MacLeod & Grove Public Relations, Pitts., 1966—, exec. v.p., 1977-78, pres., 1978—. Served with USMC, 1951-53. Mem. Public Relations Soc. Am., Sigma Delta Chi. Roman Catholic. Clubs: Duquesne, Pitts. Press. Home: 116 Bently Down Dr Coraopolis PA 15108 Office: 4 Gateway Center Pittsburgh PA 15222

VORSANGER, FRED S., univ. adminstr.; b. Calumet City, Ill., Apr. 20, 1928; s. Fred and Hannah (Steifel) V.; B.S. in Bus. Adminstrn., Ind. U., 1951; M.B.A., George Washington U., 1970; postgrad. U. Ark., 1971; m. Doreen D. Carter, Apr. 24, 1965; children—Diana, Bruce, Bob; 1 stepson, Mark Carter. Acct., Ernst & Ernst, Chgo., 1951-53; internal auditor Purdue U., Lafayette, Ind., 1953-59; treas., bus. mgr. Am. Council on Edn., Washington, 1959-68; v.p. U. Ark., Fayetteville, 1968—; lectr. U. Ky. Mgmt. Inst., 1976—, U. Calif. Mgmt. Inst., 1976—; trustee Common Fund, N.Y.C.; dir. Tyson Foods, Inc. Spl. cons. Meridian House Found., Washington, 1960-68; examiner North Central Commn. on Accrediting, 1971—. Pres., Washington County unit Am. Cancer Soc., 1971-72; bd. dirs. Nationwide Edn. Conf. Centers, N.W. Ark. Regional Planning Commn., Ark. Regional Med. Program, U. Ark. Found., Fayetteville Community Concert Assn. Served with U.S. Army, 1945-47. Mem. Nat. Assn. Land Grant Colls. and State Univs. (dir.), Nat. Assn. Ednl. Buyers (treas., dir.), Nat. Assn. Coll. and Univ. Bus. Officers, So. Assn. Coll. and Univ. Bus. Officers (pres.), Am. Council Edn., Fayetteville C. of C. (dir., 2d v.p.), Blue Key, Delta Sigma Pi, Sigma Phi Epsilon. Clubs: Rotary, Fayetteville Country; Capitol (Little Rock). Author: (with Julian H. Levi) Patterns of Giving to Higher Education, 1968; contbr. articles to profl. jours.; mem. editorial adv. bd. Commerce Clearing House, Inc., 1963-68; mem. editorial adv. com. Coll. and Univ. Bus. Mag. Home: 1315 E Ridgeway Dr Fayetteville AR 72701

From standing in a public welfare relief line to being listed in Who's Who; Thank God for America.

VORYS, ARTHUR ISAIAH, lawyer; b. Columbus, Ohio, June 16, 1923; s. Webb Isaiah and Adeline (Werner) V.; B.A., Williams Coll., 1945; LL.B., J.D., Ohio State U., 1949; m. Lucia Rogers, July 16, 1949; children—Caroline S., Adeline Vorys Eavenson, Lucy R., Webb I. Admitted to Ohio bar, 1949, since practiced in Columbus; asso., partner Vorys, Sater, Seymour & Pease, 1949—; dir. Beasley Energy, Inc., Beasley Investments, Inc., Beasley Industries, Inc., Celina Financial Corp., Celina Nat. Life Ins. Co., Ohio Casualty Corp., Ohio Casualty Ins. Co., Underwriters Investment Corp., Ohio Security Ins. Co., Pan-Western Life Ins. Co., Vorys Bros., Inc., other corps. Supt. of ins. Ohio, 1957-59. Sec., Capital South Task Force. Del. Republican Nat. Conv., 1968, 72. Trustee, pres. Children's Hosp., Greenlawn Cemetery Assn., Griffith Found. for Ins. Edn., Internat. Ins. Seminars, Met. Sch. Columbus, Franklin County Health Planning Fedn., Franklin County Hosp. Commn., Mid-Ohio Health Planning Fedn. Served as lt. USMCR, World War II. Decorated Purple Heart. Fellow Ohio State Bar; mem. Am., Columbus bar assns., Am. Judicature Soc., Am. Soc. Hosp. Attys., Columbus Area C. of C. (dir.), Phi Delta Phi. Chi Psi. Club: Rocky Fork Hunt and Country (Gahanna); Columbus Athletic. Home: 5826 Havens Corners Rd Gahanna OH 43230 Office: 52 E Gay St Columbus OH 43215

VOS, FRANK, advt. and mktg. exec.; b. N.Y.C., Dec. 1, 1919; s. George W. and Anna (Lewis) V.; student Mass. Inst. Tech., 1936-37, Columbia U., 1977—; m. Mary C. Dempsey, June 24, 1951; children—George Andrew, Julia Elizabeth. Copywriter firm Schwab & Beatty, N.Y.C., 1941-42, 46-48; sales promotion mgr. Doubleday & Co., N.Y.C., 1948-52; group head Kleppner Co., N.Y.C., 1952-57; founder, chmn. Vos & Co., N.Y.C., 1957, became Vos & Reichberg, 1965, Altman, Vos & Reichberg, Inc., 1970-76, Vos & White, Inc., 1976-79, Frank Vos Co. Inc., 1979—; vis. lectr. N.Y. U., 1961, 73, 75. Chmn. Direct Mktg. Day in N.Y., 1972. Served as 1st lt., inf. AUS, World War II; ETO. Decorated Bronze Star (U.S.); Knight's Cross Crown of Italy. Mem. Soaring Soc. Am., Aircraft Owners and Pilots Assn. Clubs: Lotos (chmn. lit. com. 1965-73, dir. 1971—) (N.Y.C.); Roxbury Swim and Tennis (Stamford, Conn.); Ski Club Ten (Warren, Vt.). Home: Windermere Ln Stamford CT 06901 Office: 485 Madison Ave New York City NY 10022

VOS, HUBERT DANIEL, health care exec.; b. Paris, Aug. 2, 1933 (parents Am. citizens); s. Marius and Aline (Porge) V.; B.A., Institut d'Etudes Politiques, U. Paris, 1954; M.P.A., Princeton U., 1956; m. Susan Hill, Apr. 18, 1958; children—Wendy, James. Internal auditor Internat. Packers Ltd., 1957-61, dir. fin., 1962-64; asst. to controller, Monsanto Co., 1964-66, controller internat. div., 1966-69; v.p. planning and fin. Smith Kline Corp., 1969-72; sr. v.p. fin. Comml. Credit Co., Balt., 1972-74; sr. v.p. fin. and adminstrn. Norton Simon Inc., N.Y.C., 1974-79; sr. v.p. fin. Becton Dickinson and Co., Paramus, N.J., 1979—; dir. Rowe Price New Era Fund, Rowe Price Prime Res. Fund, Inc., Leesona Corp. Mem. Am. Mgmt. Assn. (fin. council), Fin. Execs. Inst. Presbyterian. Clubs: Econ. of N.Y., Princeton of N.Y., Field of Greenwich. Home: 340 Lake Ave Greenwich CT 06830 Office: Becton Dickinson and Co Mack Centre Dr Paramus NJ 07652

VOSBECK, ROBERT RANDALL, architect; b. Mankato, Minn., May 18, 1930; s. William Frederick and Gladys (Anderson) V.; B.Arch., U. Minn., 1954; m. Phoebe Macklin, June 21, 1953; children—Gretchen, Randy, Heidi, Macklin. Various archtl. positions, 1956-62; partner, Vosbeck-Vosbeck & Assos., Alexandria, Va., 1962-66, VVKR Partnership, Alexandria, 1966—; mem. Nat. Capital Planning Commn., 1976—; chmn. sub.-com. on orgn. and tech. design US/USSR Joint Group on Bldg. Design and Constrn. Served as engr. officer USMC, 1954-56. Fellow AIA (dir. 1976-78, v.p. 1979); mem. Constrn. Specifications Inst., Council Ednl. Facility Planners, Soc. Coll. and Univ. Planning, Soc. Archtl. Historians, Nat. Trust Hist. Preservation, Alexandria C. of C. (pres. 1974-75), Alexandria Jaycees (pres. 1960-61), Va. Jaycees (v.p. 1962-63, Outstanding Local Pres. 1961, Disting. Service award as Outstanding Young Man in Va. 1963). Presbyterian. Club: Kiwanis (Alexandria). Archtl. works include: Thomas Jefferson Sch., Community Center, Arlington, Va., Yorktown (Va.) Visitors Center, 1976, No. Va. Community Coll., 1976, Fed. Bldg., Norfolk, Va., 1979. Home: 820 Rapidan Ct Alexandria VA 22304 Office: 720 N Saint Asaph St Alexandria VA 22314

VOSBECK, WILLIAM FREDERICK, JR., architect; b. Mankato, Minn., May 13, 1924; s. William Frederick and Gladys (Anderson) V.; student U. Notre Dame, 1943, Cornell U., 1945; B.Arch., U. Minn., 1947; m. Elizabeth Just, Aug. 2, 1947; children—Lee, William Frederick III, Lynn, James Stephen. Partner firm Vosbeck & Ward, Architects, Alexandria, Va., 1957-62; partner firm Vosbeck Vosbeck & Assos., (changed to Vosbeck Vosbeck Kendrick Redinger, Architects, Engrs., Planners), Alexandria, 1962-68, mng. partner, 1968—; dir. VEPCO, United Va. Bankshares. Mem. Gov.'s Com. Employment Handicapped, 1973; trustee Va. Found. Ind. Colls., Va. Mus. Fine Arts. Served with USMCR, 1943-50. Recipient Wash. Acad. Sci. Nat. Capital award for achievement in architecture; Nat. Rehab. Assn. citation tech. services; Gargoyle award; numerous honor and merit awards Va. chpt. AIA, Va. Mus. Fine Arts; Outstanding Achievement award Engring. News Record, 1977. Fellow AIA (pres. Va. chpt. 1971); mem. Am. Hosp. Assn. Clubs: Belle Haven Country, Cosmos. Home: 7512 Ft Hunt Rd Alexandria VA 22307 Office: 720 N St Asaph St Alexandria VA 22314

VOSBURGH, FREDERICK GEORGE, editor, writer; b. Johnstown, N.Y., Sept. 16, 1904; s. John Ross and Alice (Baker) V.; A.B., Syracuse U., 1925; grad. study George Washington U., 1938-39; m. Doris Kennedy, Jan. 2, 1929 (div. 1948); children—Richard Kennedy, Alan Frederick; m. 2d, Valerie Paterson, May 28, 1949. Reporter Syracuse (N.Y.) Jour., 1922-24, Syracuse Post- Standard, 1925-26, A.P., N.Y.C., Washington, 1927-33, covering sports, later nat. and fgn. affairs including U.S. Senate, Dept. State, Roosevelt campaign trip, 1932, World Econ. Conf., London, Eng., 1933; joined editorial staff Nat. Geog. Mag., 1933, asst. editor, 1951-56, sr. asst. editor, 1956. asso. editor, 1957-67, editor, 1967-70. Served to lt. col. USAAF, overseas, 1942-45. Decorated Bronze Star, Air medal. Mem. Nat. Geog. Soc. (v.p. 1958-70, trustee 1962-79, trustee emeritus 1979—), Phi Beta Kappa. Club: Nat. Press. Author numerous articles in various fields. Home: 8500 W Howell Rd Bethesda MD 20034

VOSE, CLEMENT ELLERY, polit. scientist, educator, archivist; b. Caribou, Maine, Mar. 18, 1923; s. Arthur G. and Florence (Murphy) V.; B.A., U. Maine, 1947; M.A., U. Wis., 1949, Ph.D., 1952; M.A., Wesleyan U., Middletown, Conn., 1961; m. Doris Foran, Dec. 27, 1947; children—John S., Celia L. Project mgr. French study tours on U.S., U. Wis. Indsl. Relations Center, Madison, 1951-52; instr. Beloit (Wis.) Coll., 1952-53; asst. prof. Western Res. U., Cleve., 1953-55; dir. Bur. for Research Municipal Govt., asso. prof. govt., Bowdoin Coll., Brunswick, Maine, 1955-58; asso. prof. govt. Wesleyan U., Middletown, 1958-61, prof., 1961—, chmn. dept. govt., 1961-67, 68-69, 72-73, 78—, John E. Andrus prof. govt., 1965—, dir. Collection on Legal Change, 1970—; research dir. study constl. change 20th Century Fund, 1969-70; mem. Nat. Archives Adv. Council, 1971-79, chmn., 1977-78; sr. fellow Yale Law, Yale U., 1958-59; vis. prof., 1962-63; sr. fellow Columbia U., 1968-69; prin. investigator Civil Rights Law Manuscripts Microfilm Project, 1974-80. Mem. Maine Gov.'s Com. on State Govt., 1956-58. Served with AUS, 1943-46; ETO. Decorated Purple Heart. Soc. Sci. Research Council grantee, 1956-58; Rockefeller Found. research grantee, 1958-59; Nat. Endowment Humanities fellow, 1976-77. Mem. Am. (exec. council 1977-78), New Eng. (exec. com. 1971-72, 76-79, pres. 1977-78) polit. sci. assns., AAAS, Soc. Am. Archivists. Author: Caucasians Only: The Supreme Court, the NAACP and the Restrictive Convenant Cases, 1959; Constitutional Change: Amendment Politics and Supreme Court Litigation since 1900, 1972; Guide to Library Sources in Political Science: American Government, 1975. Contbr. articles to profl. jours. Home: 20 Miles Ave Middletown CT 06457 Office: Dept Govt Wesleyan Univ Middleton CT 06457

VOSE, ROBERT CHURCHILL, JR., art gallery exec.; b. Boston, Mar. 30, 1911; s. Robert Churchill and Sarah Helen (Williams) V.; student Harvard, 1930-32; m. Ann Peterson, Mar. 8, 1941; children—Robert Churchill III, Abbot Williams. With Vose Galleries of Boston, Inc., 1932—, treas., 1953—, pres., 1976—; mem. Friends of Art, Boston U., 1957-59, Friends of Art, Colby Coll., 1959—; trustee Boston Arts Festival, 1955-59. Chmn. Community Fund drive, Dedham, Mass., 1952. Mem. Copley Soc. (dir. 1950-53), Back Bay Assn. (v.p. 1958, dir. 1964-66), New Eng. Historic Geneal. Soc. (mem. council 1958-77, pres. 1971-74), Dedham Hist. Soc. (corr. sec. 1958), Boston Mus. Fine Arts, Albany Inst. History and Art, Conn. Hist. Soc., Duxbury Rural and Hist. Soc., N.Y. State Hist. Assn., Colonial Soc. Mass., Back Bay Council, Pilgrim Soc. (life), Neighborhood Assn. Back Bay (dir. 1964-66). Republican. Unitarian (chmn. parish com. 1941). Clubs: Harvard (Boston); Duxbury Yacht. Contbr. articles to profl. jours.). Address: 238 Newbury St Boston MA 02116

VOSPER, ROBERT GORDON, librarian; b. Portland, Oreg., June 21, 1913; s. Chester Vivian and Anna (Stipe) V.; B.A., U. Oreg., 1937, M.A., 1939; library certificate U. Calif., 1940; LL.D., Hofstra U., 1967; m. Loraine Gjording, Aug. 20, 1940; children—Ingrid, Kathryn, Elinor, Stephen. Jr. librarian U. Calif., 1940-42; asst. reference librarian Stanford, 1942-44; head acquisitions dept., library U. Calif. at Los Angeles, 1944-48, asst. librarian, 1948-49, asso. librarian, 1949-52; dir. libraries U. Kans., 1952-61; prof. library sci. U. Calif. at Los Angeles, 1961—, librarian, 1961-73, dir. W.A. Clark Meml. Library, 1966—; Ann. library lectr. U. Tenn., 1957; Walters Meml. lectr. U. Minn., 1959; Fulbright lectr., Italy, 1960; Guggenheim fellow, 1959-60; hon. research fellow Sch. Library Studies, Univ. Coll., London, 1973-74; dir. Assn. Research Libraries Farmington Plan Survey, 1957-58; del. Princeton Conf. Internat. Exchanges, 1946, Mexico City Conf. Microfilming Archives, 1949. Sec. Gov.'s Commn. Kans. Territorial Centennial Celebration, 1954-55; mem. NSF Sci. Info. Council, 1965-70; facilities and resources Nat. Library Medicine, 1966-68; vis. com. Mass. Inst. Tech. Library, 1965-72, Stanford U., 1972-78; vis. prof. Columbia U., summer 1967; mem. govt. adv. com. on overseas book and library coms. Dept. State, 1970-75. Decorated officer Order of Crown of Belgium, 1977. Bd. dirs. Council on Library Resources, 1968—; mem. U.S. Com. to UNESCO, 1968-73. Fellow Internat. Fedn. Library Assns. (v.p. 1971-77); mem. Calif. (chmn. coll. and univ. sect. 1946-47), Mountain Plains (chmn. coll. and univ. sect. 1953-54), Kans., Am. (pres. assn. coll. and reference libraries 1955-56, chmn. bd. acquisition library materials 1954-55, mem. council 1960-72, pres. 1965-66) library assns., AAUP, Assn. Research Libraries (chmn. 1963, dir. 1962-64, 69-72), Library Assn. (Gt. Brit.) (hon. v.p. 1974—), Bibliog. Soc. Am., Phi Beta Kappa. Clubs: Zamorano, Rounce and Coffin (Los Angeles); Caxton, Grolier. Author or editor: Acquisitions Trends in American Libraries, 1955; The Acquisition of Latin American Library Materials, 1958; European University Libraries, 1964; National and International Library Planning, 1976; Building Book Collections, 1977; adv. bd. Chem. Abstracts, 1965-67; contbr. articles to profl. jours. Home: 10447 Wilkins Ave Los Angeles CA 90024 Office: Grad Sch Library and Info Sci U Calif at Los Angeles Los Angeles CA 90024

VOSS, CARL HERMANN, clergyman, educator, author; b. Pitts., Dec. 8, 1910; s. Carl August and Lucy (Wilms) V.; A.B., U. of Pitts., 1931, Ph.D., 1942; student Internat. People's Coll., Elsinore, Denmark and U. of Geneva, Switzerland, 1931; student Chicago Theol. Sem., 1931-32; M.Div., Union Theol. Sem., New York, 1935; student Yale Divinity Sch., 1938-40; m. Dorothy Katherine Grote, Nov. 25, 1940 (div. 1957); 1 dau., Carlyn (Mrs. Harold Iuzzolino); m. 2d, Phyllis MacKenzie Gierlotka, May 9, 1959; 1 dau., Christina Elisabeth Gierlotka. Minister United Church (Congl.-Christian-Friends), Raleigh, N.C., 1935-38; chaplain Cheshire (Conn.) Acad., 1938-40; asso. minister Smithfield Church (Conglist.), Pitts., 1940-43; extension sec. Ch. Peace Union and World Alliance for Internat. Friendship Through the Chs., 1943-49; editor World Alliance News Letter, 1944-49; exec. sec. Christian Council on Palestine, 1943-46; chmn. exec. council Am. Christian Palestine Com., 1946-57; minister Flatbush Unitarian Ch., Bklyn., 1953-57, N.E. Congl. Ch., Saratoga Springs, N.Y., 1957-64; Merrill research asso. Brandeis U., 1965-67; lectr. New Sch. for Soc. Research, 1948-56, lectr. dept. philosophy and religion, Skidmore College, Saratoga Springs, 1960-61, 65-66; vis. prof. theology and history religions Theol. Sch. St. Lawrence U., Canton, N.Y., 1964-65; prof. humanities Edward Waters Coll., Jacksonville, Fla., 1973-76, chmn. humanities div., 1974-76; NCCJ ecumenical-scholar-in-residence; resident scholar Ecumenical Inst. Advanced Theol. Studies, Tantur, Jerusalem, 1976-77, Centre Postgrad. Hebrew Studies, Oxford U., 1977—. Conducted European tours, 1930, 31, 35, Arab countries and Israel, 1949, 51, 53, 55, 58, 63, 66, 70, 73, 75, 79; lectr. tour Rhodesia, South Africa under auspices Good Will Council S.Africa, 1947. Recipient Nat. Brotherhood award NCCJ, 1978; hon. fellow Hebrew U., Jerusalem, 1979. Mem. Sigma Alpha Epsilon, Theta Alpha Phi, Druids. Unitarian Universalist. Author: The Rise of Social Consciousness in the Congregational Churches: 1865-1942; The Palestine Problem Today, 1953; (with Theodore Huebner) This Is Israel, 1956; Rabbi and Minister: The Friendship of Stephen S. Wise and John Haynes Holmes, 1964; In Search of Meaning: Living Religions of the World, 1968; Stephen S. Wise: Servant of The People-Selected Letters, 1969; A Summons unto Men: An Anthology of the Writings of John Haynes Holmes, 1971; Living Religions of the World: Our Search for Meaning, 1977. Editor: The Universal God: An Interfaith Anthology, 1953; Excalibur Books, 1964—; Quotations of Courage and Vision: A Source Book for Speaking, Writing and Meditation, 1972. Contbr. to mags. and religious jours. Home: 7783 Point Vicente Ct Baymeadows Jacksonville FL 32216

VOSS, CHARLOTTE ELIZABETH, nurse educator; b. Cleve., Feb. 15, 1917; d. Henry Emil and Mabel (Mann) Voss; grad. Mountainside Hosp. Sch. Nursing, Montclair, N.J., 1942; B.S., Temple U., 1949; M.S., U. Pa., 1950, Ed.D., 1957. Dir. nursing edn. Lancaster (Pa.) Gen. Hosp., 1950-52, Fitkin Hosp., Neptune, N.J., 1952-54, Met. Hosp., Cleve., 1956-63; clin. asst. prof. nursing Western Res. U., 1956-63; dean, prof. nursing Coll. Nursing Northeastern U., 1964-68; dir. nursing program Harrisburg (Pa.) Community Coll., 1968-71; prof., chmn. baccalaureate nursing program Thomas Jefferson U., Phila., 1971-79. Served with Nurse Corps, U.S. Navy, 1943-47. Mem. Am. Nurses Assn., Nat. League for Nursing, AAAS, Pi Lambda Theta, Phi Kappa Phi, Phi Sigma.

VOSS, FREDERICK JOSEPH, construction co. exec.; b. Mitchell, Ind., Aug. 13, 1913; s. Bernard Henry and Eliza Antle V.; B.S.C.E., Purdue U., 1936; m. Mildred Gangwer, Apr. 17, 1976; children—John Frederick, Richard Killer. Civil engr. Chgo. Dist. Electric Generating Co., 1936-38; engr. examiner Public Works Adminstrn., 1938; constrn. supt. Henry Pratt Co., 1939-42, v.p. constrn. 1946-60; pres. Power Systems, Inc., Schaumberg, Ill., 1960-78, chmn., 1978—; dir. Fischbach and Moore, Inc. Trustee, Village of Barrington, Ill., 1969-72, pres., 1972-74. Served to capt. AUS, 1942-45. Named Man of Yr., Barrington C. of C. Mem. ASME. Republican. Episcopalian. Clubs: Univ. (Chgo.); Barrington Hills Country. Home: 745 Concord Ln Barrington IL 60010 Office: 1211 E Tower Rd Schaumburg IL 60196

VOSS, JACK DONALD, bus. exec., lawyer; b. Stoughton, Wis., Sept. 24, 1921; s. George C. and Grayce (Tusler) V.; Ph.B., U. Wis., 1943; J.D., Harvard, 1948; m. Mary Josephine Edgarton, May 7, 1955; children—Julia, Jennifer, Andrew, Charles. Admitted to Ill. bar, 1949, Ohio bar, 1963; practiced in Chgo., 1949-62, Lancaster, Ohio, 1962—; mem. firm Sidley & Austin (formerly Leibman, Williams, Bennett, Baird & Minnow), 1948-62; gen. counsel Anchor Hocking Corp., 1962- 67, v.p., gen. counsel, 1967-72, v.p., 1972—; gen. mgr. Internat. div., 1970—, pres. Anchor Hocking Internat., 1972—. Mem. internat. council conf. Bd. Mem. Fairfield County Republican Exec. Com. Pres. Fairfield Heritage Assn., 1966-69; v.p. Lancaster Community Concert Assn., 1965-73; trustee, chmn. Ohio Information Com. Served with USNR, 1943-46; MTO, PTO. Soc. (sec.-treas. 1978-80), Am., Ohio (chmn. corp. counsel sect. 1966), Ill., N.Y. State, Chgo., Fairfield County bar assns., Harvard Law Sch. Assn., Ohio Mfrs. Assn. (trustee 1970-72), Symposiarch, Alpha Chi Rho. Lutheran. Rotarian (pres. Lancaster 1968). Clubs: Racquet (Chgo.); Lancaster Country. Home: Amanda Rd Route 6 Lancaster OH 43130 Office: 109 N Broad St Lancaster OH 43130

VOSS, JAMES FREDERICK, psychologist, educator; b. Chgo., Dec. 5, 1930; s. Leo Carl and Lydia (Isreal) V.; B.A., Valparaiso (Ind.) U., 1952; M.S., U. Wis., 1954, Ph.D., 1956; m. Marilyn Lydia Timm, June 20, 1953; children—Barbara Lynn, Katherine Ann, Mark Frederick, Carol Jean, David James. Instr., asst. prof. Wis. State Coll., Eau Claire, 1956-58; asst. prof., asso. prof. Coll. of Wooster (Ohio), 1958-63; asso. prof. U. Pitts., 1963-66, prof., 1966—, chmn. dept. psychology, 1968-70, also research asso. Learning Research and Devel. Center; prin. investigator Nat. Inst. Child Health and Human Devel., 1956-58, 59-70; Fulbright disting. prof., lectr., USSR, 1979; NSF fellow Ind. U., 1960; vis. prof. U. Wis., 1964; vis. prof. NIMH spl. fellow U. Calif., Irvine, 1970—. Recipient Disting. Alumni award Valparaiso U., 1979. Fellow Am. Psychol. Assn.; mem. Midwestern, Eastern psychol. assns., AAAS, N.Y. Acad. Sci., Psychonomic Soc. (sec.-treas. 1978-80), Am. Diabetes Assn. (chmn. bd. Western Pa. affiliate 1974-77), Sigma Xi. Author: Psychology as a Behavioral Science, 1974. Editor: Approaches to Thought, 1969; Topics in Human Performance, 1972. Cons. editor Jour. Exptl. Psychology, 1975—. Home: 115 Glen David Dr Pittsburgh PA 15238

VOSS, JAMES MILTON, petroleum co. exec.; b. Bastrop, Tex., Oct. 8, 1916; s. John Jake and Merle (Murchison) V.; m. Mildred Frances Pennell, Feb. 14, 1943 (dec. Nov. 1965); children—Phyllis, Susan (Mrs. Dan Brown Sedgwick, Jr.), James Milton; m. 2d, Mary Johnson, Mar. 17, 1970. Admitted to Tex. bar, 1939; atty. Aetna Casualty Surety Co., 1939-44; with Caltex Petroleum Corp., 1946—, legal work in Far East and Australia, 1946-61, pres., N.Y.C., 1964-70, chief exec. officer, chmn. bd., 1970—. Chmn. bldg. campaign Japan House, N.Y.C., 1970; mem. exec. com. Adv. Council on Japan-U.S. Econ. Relations. Bd. dirs. Japan Soc., 1964—, vice chmn., 1970; bd. dirs. Am. Bur. Med. Aid to China, 1970, U.S.-Korea Econ. Council; trustee Asia Soc., 1970, U.S. council Internat. C. of C. Served with USAAF, 1944-46; CBI. Mem. Am. Petroleum Inst. Clubs: Apawamis (Rye, N.Y.); Blind Brook (Port Chester, N.Y.). Home: Taylor Ln Harrison NY 10528 Office: 380 Madison Ave New York NY 10017

VOSS, JERROLD RICHARD, city planner; b. Chgo., Nov. 4, 1932; s. Peter Walter and Annis Lorraine (Hayes) V.; B.Arch., Cornell U., 1955; M. City Planning, Harvard U., 1959; Ph.D. (Bus. History fellow, Univ. fellow, IBM fellow), 1971; m. Jean Evelyn Peterson, Aug. 21, 1954; children—Cynthia Jean, Tania Hayes. Asst. prof. U. Calif., 1960-61; asst. prof., asso. prof. U. Ill., 1961-69; asso. prof. Harvard U., 1969-71; prof. city and regional planning Ohio State U., Columbus, 1971—, chmn. dept. city and regional planning, 1971—; UN advisor to Govt. Indonesia, 1964-65; social affairs officer UN Secretariat, 1970-71; project mgr. UN Task Force on Human Environment, Thailand, 1975-76; dir. research and devel. UN Center for Human Settlements (Habitat), 1979—; cons. Ill. Dept. Devel., J.S. Bolles & Assos., UN Office Tech. Cooperation, UN Devel. Program, and other pvt. and pub. orgns. Mem. pub. policy com. Smithsonian Instn., 1970-73; bd. dirs. Champaign County United Community Council, 1965-69, Columbus Theatre Ballet Assn., 1972-75. Served to 1st lt. U.S. Army, 1955-57. Mem. Acad. for Contemporary Problems (asso.), Am. Am. Inst. Planners, Am. Soc. Engring. Edn., Internat. Center for Urban Land Policy (London). Author: National Settlement Analysis and Policy Formulation; The Mitigation of Natural Disasters through Land Use Planning and Controls; Urban Land Policies and Land Use Control Measures; Human Settlements: Problems and Priorities. Contbr. articles to profl. jours. Home: 530 Riley St Worthington OH 43085 Office: 190 W 17th Ave Columbus OH 43210

VOSS, JOHN, assn. exec.; b. Albany, Oreg., July 7, 1917; s. Enoch George and Lulu (Porter) V.; A.B., Willamette U., 1938; S.T.B., Harvard U., 1942; m. Barbara Fischer, Sept. 8, 1945; children—Christopher, Caroline. Instr. history Tufts U., 1946-47, M.I.T., 1949-54; mgr. spl. projects Arthur D. Little, Inc., Cambridge, Mass., 1954-64; exec. officer Am. Acad. Arts and Scis., Boston, 1964—; mem. corp. Internat. Centre Insect Physiology and Ecology, Nairobi, Kenya, 1968—; trustee ICIPE Found., Stockholm, Sweden, 1977—; mem. U.S. Pugwash Com., 1966—; trustee, mem. exec. com., sec.-treas. Nat. Humanities Center, Research Triangle Park, N.C., 1975—; sec. Commn. on Yr. 2000, 1965-68. Fellow AAAS. Democrat. Unitarian. Clubs: St. Botolph's, Appalachian Mountain, Harvard Mountaineering, Mass. Audubon Soc. Editor: Confrontation and Learned Societies, 1970; (with others) When Values Conflict, 1976; (with A. Oleson) Organization of Knowledge in Modern America, 1860-1920, 1979. Home: 187 Garfield Rd Concord MA 01742 Office: 165 Allandale St Jamaica Plain MA 12130

VOSS, OMER GERALD, farm equipment co. exec.; b. Downs, Kans., Sept. 14, 1916; s. John and Grace (Bohlen) V.; A.B., Ft. Hays (Kans.) State Coll., 1937; J.D., U. Kans., 1939; m. Annabelle Katherine Lutz, June 20, 1940; children—Jerrol Ann, Omer Gerald. With Internat. Harvester Co., 1936-79, v.p. farm equipment div., 1962-66, exec. v.p., dir., 1966—, vice chmn., 1977-79; admitted to Kans. bar, 1939; dir. Ill. Tool Works, Northern Trust Co., Beatrice Foods Co. Trustee, Nat. 4-H Council. Served with USAAF, 1943-46. Club: Chicago; Commercial; Westmoreland Country.

VOSS, WILLIAM CHARLES, oil co. exec.; b. Buffalo, Sept. 22, 1937; s. William T. and Dorathea S. (Grotke) V.; A.B. with honors, Harvard, 1959, M.B.A. with honors, 1961; m. Marilyn Erickson, Sept. 6, 1958; children—William, John, Douglas. With Northwestern Refining Co., St. Paul Park, 1961-70, v.p. adminstrn., 1969-71; with Ashland Oil Inc. (Ky.), 1971—, v.p., 1973-79, adminstrv. v.p., 1979—, pres. Ashland-Warren Inc., 1979—. Home: 413 Country Club Dr Bellefonte Ashland KY 41101 Office: 1409 Winchester Ave Ashland KY 41101

VOTH, BEN, computer co. exec.; b. Enid, Okla., Apr. 21, 1899; s. John and Suzanne (Fast) V.; student Phillips U., Enid, 1919-20, Ind. U., 1920-21, Columbia U., 1922-23; LL.D., Phillips U., 1959; m. Yukola Gilbert, June 25, 1930; children—Suzanne (Mrs. Richard R. Dillenbeck), Janet (Mrs. Merrill Jerome Foote). Salesman, Powers Paper Co., Springfield, Mass., 1923-27; real estate and ins., Tulsa, 1927-35; partner Frates Co., 1935-40; partner Voth & Wright, ins., 1940-62; founder Standard Ins. Co., Tulsa, 1944, pres., 1944-60; v.p. Springfield Fire & Marine Ins. Co., 1960-61; v.p. Marsh & McLennan, Inc., ins., 1961-63; chmn. bd. Univ. Computing Co., Dallas, 1964-69, chmn. exec. com., 1969-72; chmn. bd., chief exec. officer Swift-Ohio Corp., 1972—. Pres. bd. trustees Hillcreast Med. Center, 1964-68, now trustee; pres. bd. govs. Tulsa Club, 1962; trustee Phillips U. Mem. Tulsa C. of C. Episcopalian. Clubs: Tulsa Southern Hills Country (Tulsa). Author: A Piece of the Computer Pie, 1973. Home: 7157 S Evanston St Tulsa OK 74105 Office: 2001 Nat Bank Tulsa Bldg Tulsa OK 74120

VOTH, MELVIN H., farm equipment mfg. co. exec.; b. Newton, Kans., Jan. 21, 1932; s. John F. and Helena (Hildebrand) V.; B.A. in Econs., Bethel Coll., 1955; M.B.A., U. Wichita, 1959; D. Bus. Adminstrn., Ind. U., 1964; m. Ellen Stucky, July 21, 1956; children—Patrick, Gina, Jeffrey. Staff accountant Arthur Young & Co., Wichita, Kans., 1958-59; instr. Kans. State U., Manhattan, 1959-61; asso. prof. accounting Wichita State U., 1963-70; asst. treas. Hesston Corp. (Kans.), 1970-74, treas., 1974-75, v.p. fin., treas., 1975—, also dir. Pres. Hesston Bd. Edn., 1975-76; chmn. bd. dirs. Bethel Coll., Newton, Kans., 1976—. Served with U.S. Army, 1955-57. Mem. Am. Accounting Assn., Am. Inst. C.P.A.'s, Kans. Soc. C.P.A.'s (exec. dir. Wichita chpt. 1963-66), Nat. Assn. Accountants (pres. Wichita chpt. 1970-71), Fin. Execs. Inst., Alpha Kappa Psi. Beta Alpha Psi, Beta Gamma Sigma. Home: 233 S College Dr Hesston KS 67062 Office: 420 W Lincoln Blvd Hesston KS 67062

VOULKOS, PETER, artist; b. Bozeman, Mont., Jan. 29, 1924; B.S., Mont. State Coll.; M.F.A., Calif. Coll. Arts and Crafts. Tchr. Archie Bray Found., Helena Mont., Black Mountain Coll., Los Angeles County Art Inst., Mont. State U., U. Calif. at Berkeley, Greenwich House Pottery, N.Y.C., Columbia Tchrs. Coll. One man exhbns. include Gump's Gallery, San Francisco, U. Fla., Hist. Soc. Mont., Felix Landau Gallery, Chgo. Art Inst., Bonniers, Inc., N.Y.C., Fresno State Coll., Scripps Coll., U. So. Calif., Pasadena (purchase prize) Art Mus., Scripps Coll., Syracuse/Everson, Nat. Ceramic Exhbn., U. Tenn., Brussel's World's Fair, 1958, de Young Mus., Seattle World's Fair, 1962, Whitney Mus. Art, Stanford, Denver Art Mus. (purchase prize), Smithsonian Instn. (purchase prize), Los Angeles County Mus. Art (purchase prize); rep. permanent collections Balt. Mus. Art, Denver Art Mus., U. Fla., U. Ill., Japanese Craft Mus., Los Angeles County Mus. Art, Mus. Contemporary Crafts, Oakland Art Mus., Pasadena Mus. Art, San Francisco Mus. Art, Smithsonian Instn., U. Wis. Recipient first prize RAC, Nat. Decorative Art Show, Wichita, Northwest Craft Show, Pacific Coast Ceramic Show; purchase prize Cranbrook Art Mus., Los Angeles County Fair, Ford Found.; Silver medal Internat. Ceramic Exhbn., Ostend, Belgium, 1954, Gold medal, Cannes, France; I Paris Biennial, 1959; Rodin Mus. prize in Sculpture. Address: care Art Dept University California Berkeley CA 94720

VOULTSOS-VOURTZIS, PERICLES COUNT, composer, condr., educator, author, former hon. consul Grenada; b. Athens, Greece, Jan. 26, 1910; s. Christos C. and Aspasia (Kambouroglou) V.; came to U.S., 1921, naturalized, 1932; student in mech. engring. N.Y. U., 1927; postgrad. N.Y. Coll. Music, 1934, tchr.'s diploma; Mus.B., U. Chgo., 1939; M.A., Staley Coll., Brookline, Mass., 1949; Ed.D., Calvin Coolidge Coll., Boston, 1956, Litt.D. (hon.), 1958; Ph.D. in Musicology, Milano Accademia, 1960; LL.D., (hon.), Emporia Coll., 1961; children by previous marriage—Chris, George; m. 2d, Countess Helene Fioravanti, Oct. 26, 1946; 1 son, Basil. Mem. faculty N.Y. Coll. Music, N.Y.C., 1937-67; dir. Am. Conservatory of Music, 1930—; hon. prof. Nat. Conservatory, Athens; composer many musical compositions; author lit. hist. works. Nat. chmn. Greek sect. All-Am. origins Citizens for Eisenhower-Nixon, 1952. Permanent observer to UN (N-G-O) Inst. Humaniste, Paris, France, 1952; royal envoy plenipotentiary and extraordinary for King Peter of Yugoslavia, 1964; ambassador good will to Greece, Gov. Burns and people, Fla., 1965; ambassador good will to Greece of Gov. Smith and people, Tex., 1970; personal ambassador of King Ntare V of Burundi, to U.S., 1969; brig. gen. gov. staff La., a.d.c. to gov., 1965, 73; hon. consul of Grenada, 1976-79. Served with SSS, World War II. Decorated medal in name of Congress, Pres. Truman, 1945, Silver medal City of Paris, France, 1953, Keys to City and Gold medal City of Athens, 1972; grand collar, grand master Sovereign Greek Order St. Dennis of Zante; decorations Yugoslavia, Panama, Cuba, Haiti, Burundi; comdr. Poland; Chevalier Cambodia, Brazil, San Marino; grand cross 1st grade St. Andrew, Order St. Mark, Order Saints Peter and Paul, Order Holy Sepulchre Orthodox, Order St. Catherine, Gold Lateran Cross; decorations and crosses of merit from Red Cross of govts. Greece, Japan, Spain, Portugal, Cuba, numerous others. Mem. Am. Mil. Engrs. Soc., N.Y. Acad. Scis., AAAS, SAR, Fils de la Revolution Americaine (Paris), Am. Internat. Inst. (pres.), Am. Soc. Greek Order St. Dennis of Zante, Greek Am. Nat. War Vets. (nat. comdr.), Vets. Arty. Corps, La Confrerie du Tastevin. Clubs: Hellenic, Army and Navy, Columbia Univ. (N.Y.C.); Army and Navy (Washington).

VOWLES, DONALD DEFOREST, electric utility exec.; b. Richfield, Ohio, Oct. 7, 1915; s. Levi DeForest and Anna (Rau) V.; student Bankes Inst. Commerce, 1935-36; m. Eileen E. Eastwood, June 10, 1939; children—Nancy (Mrs. Jerry P. Snowball), David D. Bookkeeper, Del's Cafes Inc., Akron, 1936-37; with Ohio Edison Co., Akron, 1937—, asst. sec., 1966-72, asst. treas., 1968-72, sec., 1972—. Clk. Richfield Twp., 1948-60; chmn. Richfield Twp. Zoning Commn., 1964-69; vice-chmn. Richfield Village Planning Commn., 1968-72. Mem. Am. Soc. Corp. Secs., Stock Transfer Assn. Republican. Mason. Home: 3569 Southern Rd Richfield OH 44286 Office: 76 S Main St Akron OH 44308

VOWLES, RICHARD BECKMAN, educator; b. Fargo, N.D., Oct. 5, 1917; s. Guy Richard and Ella (Beckman) V.; B.S., Davidson Coll., 1938; postgrad. U. N.C., 1938-39, U. Stockholm, 1939-40; M.A., Yale, 1942, Ph.D., 1950; m. Ellen Noah Hudson, Aug. 1, 1942 (div. 1969); children—Elizabeth Ellen, Richard Hudson. Engr., Hercules Powder Co., Wilmington, Chattanooga, 1941-43; chemist Rohm & Haas, Knoxville, Tenn., 1943-44; econ. cons. War Dept., 1944; Am. vice consul, Gotehorg, Sweden, 1945-46; asst. prof. English, Southwestern U., Memphis, 1948-50; asst. prof. English, Queens U., N.Y.C., 1950-51; asso. prof. English, U. Fla., 1951-60; prof. Scandinavian, comparative lit. U. Wis., Madison, 1960—, chmn. comparative lit., 1962-63, 64-67, 71-72, chmn. Scandinavian studies, 1977—; Am. specialist in Scandinavia Dept. State, summer 1963; vis. prof. N.Y.U., summer 1964, U. Helsinki, Finland, spring 1968, Stockholm, 1969; lectr. Sydney, Australia, 1975, Paris, 1975. Am.-Scandinavian Found. fellow, Stockholm, 1939-40, Fulbright fellow, Copenhagen, 1955-56; Strindberg fellow, Stockholm, 1973; Swedish govt. research award, 1978; Norwegian Govt. fellow, summer 1978. Mem. Modern Lang. Assn., Soc. Advancement Scandinavian Study (mem. exec. com.), Internat. Comparative Lit. Assn., Am. Comparative Lit. Assn. (adv. bd.), Strindberg Soc., Phi Beta Kappa. Editor: Eternal Smile, 1954; Dramatic Theory, 1956; Comparatists at Work, 1968. Adv. editor: Nordic Council Series, 1965-70. Adv. editor Herder Ency. of World Lit. Contbr. articles profl. jours. Home: 1115 Oak Way Madison WI 53705

VOXMAN, HIMIE, music educator; b. Centerville, Iowa, Sept. 17, 1912; s. Morris and Molly (Chapman) V.; B.S., U. Iowa, 1933, M.A., 1934; D.Mus. (hon.), Coe Coll., 1975; m. Lois Ruth Wilcox, Dec. 28, 1936; children—William Lloyd, James Herbert. Woodwind instr. Iowa City pub. schs., 1934-39; instr. U. Iowa, 1939, asst. prof. music, 1940-46, asso. prof., 1946-51, prof., 1951—, dir. Sch. Music, 1954—. Mem. Am. Musicol. Soc., Music Educators Nat. Conf., Music Library Assn., Nat. Assn. of College Wind and Percussion Instrs., Bruckner Soc. Am. (dir.). Author: (with Lyle Merriman) Woodwind Ensemble Music Guide, 1973, Woodwind Solo and Study Material Music Guide, 1975; also publs. for wind instrument pedagogy. Contbr. articles profl. jours. Home: 821 N Linn St Iowa City IA 52240

VOYE, JOSEPH JAMES, accountant; b. Klamath Falls, Oreg., Dec. 3, 1919; s. Arthur James and Louise (Lee) V.; student Mass. Inst. Tech., 1938-39, Stanford, 1940-42, 47; B.B.A., Golden Gate Coll., 1950; m. Elizabeth Patton Will, Nov. 22, 1943; children—Lee, Sally, Robert James, Anne. Mem. staff Farquhar & Heimbucher, C.P.A.'s, 1950-51; office mgr. Wunderlich Co., 1951-59; sec., controller Gordon H. Ball, Inc., Danville, Calif., 1960-70, bd. dirs., 1968-70; controller Heath Electric Co., Santa Clara, Calif., 1970-76, Western Traction Co., Hayward, Calif., 1976—. Served to 1st lt. USMCR, 1942-45. C.P.A., Calif. Mem. Am. Inst. C.P.A.'s, Delta Kappa Epsilon. Home: 231 Camille Ave Alamo CA 94507

VOYSEY, FRANK ERNEST, investment banker; b. Great Ormesby, Eng., Mar. 18, 1908; s. Walter Albert and Agnes (Derry) V.; student Grove Coll., Eng.; m. Betty Otte, July 1, 1943 (dec.); children—Peter D., Stephen O., m. 2d, Eleanor Page MacDonald, Nov. 18, 1972. Came to U.S., 1929. With Kidder, Peabody Co., Boston; 1932-50, Chgo., 1950—, partner, 1957—, v.p., 1960—. Served to capt. AUS, 1942-46. Decorated Order Brit. Empire. Mem. Investment Bankers Assn. Am. (gov.), Bond Club Chgo. (past pres., sec.). Clubs: Exmoor Country; Mid-Day (pres., trustee), Saddle and Cycle, Union League (Chgo.); Adventurers. Home: 656 Locust St Winnetka IL 60093 Office: 125 S Wacker Dr Chicago IL 60606

VRABLIK, EDWARD ROBERT, chem. co. exec.; b. Chgo., June 8, 1932; s. Steven Martin and Meri (Korbel) V.; B.S. in Chem. Engring., Northwestern U., 1956; M.B.A., U. Chgo., 1961; m. Bernice G. Germer, Jan. 25, 1958; children—Edward Robert, II, Scott S. Dir. indsl. mktg. Eimco Corp., 1956-61; dir. indsl. mktg. and planning Swift & Co., Chgo., 1961-68; v.p., gen. mgr. Swift Chem. Co., Chgo., 1968-73; pres., chmn. bd. Estech Gen. Chems. Corp. (formerly Swift Agrl. Chems. Corp.), Chgo., 1973—; dir. Estech, Inc., Swift Canadian, Ltd., Consol. Fertilizers, Ltd. Bd. dirs., v.p. Northwestern U. Tech. Inst. Registered profl. engr., Ill. Mem. Internat. Superphosphate Mfrs. Assn. (dir.), Am. Inst. Chem. Engrs., Fertilizer Inst. (dir.). Lutheran. Club: Rolling Green Country (Arlington Heights); Butler Nat. (Oak Brook, Ill.). Author, patentee in field. Home: 1404 N Walnut Ave Arlington Heights IL 60004 Office: 30 N La Salle St Chicago IL 60602

VREDENBURG, DWIGHT CHARLES, supermarket chain exec.; b. Lamoni, Iowa, Jan. 17, 1914; s. David Milton and Kate Emelyn (Putnam) V.; student Graceland Coll., 1931-34; B.S. in Commerce, U. Iowa, 1935; m. Ruth Irene Taylor, Apr. 25, 1937; children—John, Martha (Mrs. Gerald Wibe), Charles. Store mgr. Hy Vee Food Store Inc., Chariton, Iowa, 1935-38, pres., 1938—, chief exec. officer, chmn., 1978—, also dir.; dir. Iowa So. Utilities Co., Centerville, Nat. Bank and Trust Co. Chariton; pres. Chariton Storage Co.; pres., dir. Iamo Realty Co. Adv. com. Iowa Coll. Found.; bd. dirs. Indian Hills Community Coll., Ottumwa, Iowa, 1966-74; trustee Hy Vee Found., 1960—. Served with USCGR, 1942-44. Named citizen of year, 1965-66. Mem. Food Mktg. Inst. (sec. 1965-68, dir.). Mason (Shriner), Rotarian. Club: Des Moines. Home: Rural Route 5 Box 217 Chariton IA 50049 Office: Hy-Vee Food Stores Inc 1801 Osceola Ave Chariton IA 50049

VREDENBURGH, JOHN CULLODEN, former oil co. exec.; b. Park City, Mont., June 29, 1914; s. James Brinckerhof and Katharine Culloden (Matheson) V.; student elec. engring. Calif. Inst. Tech., 1931-32; student Rutgers U., 1933-35, Am. Inst. Banking, 1936-40; m. Barbara Jeanette Germain, July 10, 1948; children—Katharine Germain, Peter Matheson. Head teller Security First Nat. Bank, Santa Monica, Calif., 1935-41; supr. banking and fin. Douglas Aircraft Co., Eritrea, 1941-43; mem. jr. staff First Nat. City Bank, Cairo, 1944-45; fin. coordinator treasury Aramco, Saudi Arabia and N.Y.C., treas. Aramco Overseas Co., Holland, 1945-63; treas. Amoco Internat. Oil Co., 1963-68; fin. v.p. AIOC, Chgo., 1968-71; dir. fin. planning and financing Standard Oil Co. Ind., Chgo., 1971-73, treas., 1973-78; dir. Banco di Roma, Chgo., Zimmer Paper Products Inc., Indpls., ESP Systems Devel., Inc., Mt. Clemens, Mich.; fin. v.p. Biothermal Energy Corp., N.Y.C. Founding mem. Am. C. of C. in Netherlands, 1961; bd. overseers Rutgers U. Found., 1976—; asso. mem. Wildlife Preservation Trust Internat. Mem. Holland Soc. N.Y., U.S. Tennis Assn. (life), Delta Kappa Epsilon. Republican. Episcopalian. Clubs: Adventurers, Plaza, (Chgo.); Yale (N.Y.C.); Belfrey (London); Oranje Tennis (The Hague). Home: Racquet Club 3939 Ocean Dr Vero Beach FL 32960

VREELAND, DIANA DALZIEL, mag. editor; b. Paris, France; d. Frederick Y. and Emily Key (Hoffman) Dalziel; m. Thomas Reed Vreeland, Mar. 1, 1924; children—Thomas Reed, Frederick D. Brit. subject, until 1925. Fashion editor Harper's Bazaar, 1937-62; with Vogue mag., 1962—, editor-in-chief, 1962-71, cons. editor, 1971—. Cons. Costume Inst., Met. Mus. Art, 1972. Decorated Legion of Honor (France). Home: 550 Park Ave New York City NY 10021 Office: Metropolitan Museum Art 1000 Fifth Ave New York City NY 10028

VRENIOS, ANASTASIOS, lyric-spinto tenor; b. Turlock, Calif., Aug. 24, 1940; s. Nicholas and Despina (Vastis) V.; B.Mus., U. Pacific, 1962; M. in Voice, Ind. U., 1965, postgrad., 1965-67; m. Elizabeth Anne Kirkpatrick, July 14, 1963; children—Nicholas Andreas, Christopher Louis. Appeared with Washington Opera and Symphony, spring 1967; leading artist Spoleto (Italy) Festival of Two Worlds, summer 1967; leading tenor Am. Nat. Opera Co., touring throughout U.S.; London debut, Royal Albert Hall, 1968; lead tenor roles Phila. Lyric Opera, Am. Opera Soc., Milw. Opera, San Francisco Spring Opera, and others, 1968; world premiere Menotti's opera The Egg, Nat. Cathedral, 1976; leading tenor Spoleto Festival, Italy, summer 1978; choir dir. St. George Greek Orthodox Ch.; profl. concerts Nat. Cathedral, Am. Univ. Concert Series, Binghamton (N.Y.) Symphony, others, 1976. Grad. Asst. in voice Ind. U., 1962-67; appeared on TV in La Rondine; recorded Les Huguenots, 1969. Nat. winner student auditions, Nat. Fedn. Music Clubs, 1960; 1st place winner Auditions of Air, WGN-TV-Ill. Opera Guild, 1967; named Alumnus of Decade 1960-70, U. of Pacific. Mem. Am. Guild Mus. Artists. Greek Orthodox. Home: 6628 32d St NW Washington DC 20015

VROOM, VICTOR HAROLD, mgmt. cons., educator; b. Montreal, Que., Can., Aug. 9, 1932; s. Harold Heard and Avice May (Brown) V.; B.Sc., McGill U., Montreal, 1953, M.Sc., 1955; Ph.D., U. Mich., 1958; M.A. (hon.), Yale, 1972; m. Ann Louise Workman, June 12, 1956; children—Derek Alan, Jeffrey James. Lectr., study dir. U. Mich.. Ann Arbor, 1958-60; asst. prof. psychology U. Pa., Phila., 1960-63; asso. prof. psychology and indsl. adminstrn. Carnegie-Mellon U., Pitts., 1963-66, prof., 1966-72; John G. Searle prof. adminstrv. scis. Yale U., 1972—; trustee Conn. Savs. Bank; mgmt. cons. Recipient Ford Found. Doctoral Dissertation award, 1958-59; McKinsey Found. research design award, 1967; Fulbright lectr., U.K., 1967-68. Fellow Am. Psychol. Assn. (James McKeen Cattell award 1970). Author: Work and Motivation, 1964; Leadership and Decision-Making, 1973. Office: Yale Univ 56 Hillhouse Ave New Haven CT 06520

VROOMAN, WARREN TERRY, ins. co. exec.; b. Phila., Aug. 10, 1917; s. William B. and Ethel (Terry) V.; grad. U. Pa., 1942; m. Margaret E. Fulmer, June 28, 1941; children—Sandra E. McCormick, William B. II. With Fidelity Mut. Life Ins. Co., Phila., 1935—, asst. sec., 1947-61, sec., 1961-68, dept. head adminstrn., 1967, 2d v.p., sec., 1968-72, v.p., sec., 1972-76, sr. v.p., sec., 1976—; past pres., dir. Combined Shares, Inc. Chmn. Community Services dept. campaign United Way, Phila., past trustee; past pres., now bd. dirs. Phila. council Boy Scouts Am.; chmn. Phila. Presbytery Maj. Mission Fund. Recipient Disting. award of merit U. Pa. Fellow Life Office Mgmt. Assn. Inst. (past council chmn., dir.); mem. Am. Council Life Ins. (postal subcom.), Ins. Fedn. Pa. (various offices). Presbyn. Clubs: Rotary (dir.), Union League (Phila.). Home: 1634 Huntingdon Rd Abington PA 19001 Office: Fidelity Mut Life Ins Co Philadelphia PA 19101

VUITTON, HENRY-LOUIS, designer; b. Asnieres, Seine, France, Aug. 10, 1911; s. Gaston-Louis and Renee (Versillé) V.; student St. Louis, Paris; m. Josette Rateau, Oct. 15, 1935; children—Colette (Mrs. Jacques Novatin), Philippe-Louis (dec.), Daniele (Mrs. Philippe Masson). Comml. dir. Vuitton et Vuitton, Paris, 1945-75, pres. bd. mgrs., 1975-77; pres. bd. insps. Louis Vuitton S.A.; hon. pres. Chambre Syndicale Nationale des Fabricants d'Articles de Voyage, 1977—; hon. v.p. Fedn. Nat. des Industries de la Maroquinerie et Articles de Voyage, 1977—; sec. Ct. of Arbitration, Conseil Nat. du Cuir, 1977—; v.p. Preparatory Interunion Com. of Adv. Sects. Decorated officer Order Nat. of Merit (France); Grande Medaille d'Or du Travail.

VYKUKAL, EUGENE LAWRENCE, wholesale drug corp. exec.; b. Caldwell, Tex., June 26, 1929; s. Henry J. and Anna P. (Polansky) V.; B.S. in Pharmacy, U. Tex., Austin, 1952; m. Judith Anderson, Jan. 1, 1977; children—Anna K., Mark Roman, Laura Roman, Geni. Pharmacist, Scarborough's Pharmacy, Baytown, Tex., 1952-53, Gene Vykukal's Pharmacy, Clifton, Tex., 1953-57; with Southwestern Drug Corp., 1957—, gen. sales mgr., Dallas, 1966-67, v.p., dir. sales, 1967-75, exec. v.p., dir. sales, 1975—, dir., 1966—. Mem. adv. council Pharm. Found., U. Tex., chmn., 1978-79. Recipient Disting. Alumni award U. Tex. Coll. Pharmacy, 1979. Mem. Nat. Wholesale Druggists Assn. (chmn. sales mgmt. com. 1972-73), Am. Pharm. Assn., Tex. Pharm. Assn., Dallas County Pharm. Assn., Wholesale Druggist Assn. Tex. (pres. 1978-79), Drug Travelers Assn. Tex. (pres. 1977-78), Sales and Mktg. Execs. Dallas (dir. 1971-72), Dallas C. of C. Roman Catholic. Home: 2734 Wagonwheel Dr Carrollton TX 75006 Office: 8000 John Carpenter Freeway Dallas TX 75247

WAAGE, JOHN ARTHUR, banker; b. N.Y.C., Oct. 19, 1913; s. Benjamin and Ingeborg (Modal) W.; student Rutgers U. Grad Sch. Banking, 1950-52, Advanced Mgmt. Program, Harvard U., 1958; m. Doris Anna Barnes, Apr. 20, 1946; children—Judith Anna, Candace Anne. Vice pres. Mfrs. Trust Co., N.Y.C., 1946-63; sr. v.p. Mfrs. Hanover Trust Co., N.Y.C., 1963-72, exec. v.p., 1972-76, vice chmn., dir., 1976-78; vice chmn., dir. Mfrs. Hanover Corp., N.Y.C., 1976-78; chmn. bd. Republic Nat. Bank N.Y., 1978—, Republic N.Y. Corp., 1978—; dir. Suburban Propane Gas Corp. of N.J., Trade Devel. Bank Holding S.A., Luxembourg. Trustee, Near East Found. Served with USAAF, 1942-45. Home: 18 Country Club Dr Chatham NJ 07928 Office: 452 Fifth Ave New York NY 10018

WAAGE, KARL MENSCH, geologist, educator; b. Phila., Dec. 17, 1915; s. Frederick Oswin and Vinnie (Mensch) W.; B.A., Princeton U., 1939, M.A., 1942, Ph.D., 1946; student Yale U., 1939-40; m. Elizabeth Ann King, May 29, 1942; children—Jonathan King, Jeffrey King. Geologist U.S. Geol. Survey, 1942-46; instr. geology and geophysics Yale U., 1946-47, asst. prof., 1947-52, asso. prof., 1952-67, prof., 1967-77, Alan M. Bateman prof., 1977—; asso. curator invertebrate paleontology Peabody Mus. Natural History, 1947-59, curator, 1959—. Fellow Geol. Soc. Am.; mem. Paleontol. Soc., AAAS, Sigma Xi. Author: (with Carl O. Dunbar) Historical Geology, 3d edit., 1969. Home: 79 Bedford Ave Hamden CT 06517 Office: Peabody Museum New Haven CT 06520

WAALKES, T. PHILLIP, physician, govt. ofcl.; b. Belmond, Iowa, Oct. 30, 1919; s. Albert Herman and Grace (Prins) W.; A.B. magna cum laude, Hope Coll., 1941; Ph.D. in Chemistry, Ohio State U., 1945; M.D. with honors, George Washington U., 1951; m. Frances Elizabeth Brewster, Aug. 18, 1945; children—Richard Hugh, Steven Albert, Michael Phillip, Robert Louis Brewster, Kelly, Marion. From grad. asst. to instr. dept. chemistry Ohio State U., 1941-48; asst. scientist Res., USPHS, Nat. Cancer Inst., Bethesda, Md., 1948-51; intern USPHS Hosp., Balt., 1951-52, resident in medicine, 1952-55; clin. staff Nat. Heart Inst., Bethesda, 1955-58; spl. asst. to chief cancer chemotherapy Nat. Service Center, Bethesda, 1958-59, chief clin. br., 1959-63; asso. dir. charge collaborative research Nat. Cancer Inst., 1963-65, charge extramural ops., 1965—; prof. Med. Sch., John Hopkins U., 1976—. Served to med. dir. USPHS, 1959—. Mem. Am. Soc. Oncology, AMA, AAAS, Am. Pub. Health Assn., Internat. Histamine Club, Sigma Xi, Phi Lambda Upsilon, Phi Chi. Home: 4244 Norbeck Rd Rockville MD 20853 Office: Johns Hopkins Oncology Center Johns Hopkins U Hosp Baltimore MD 21205

WAAS, DAVID ASHER, educator; b. Burbank, Calif., Feb. 20, 1926; s. Elroy Robert and Lorraine Ellen (Douglas) W.; student Manchester Coll., 1947, Bethany Bib. Sem., 1947-48; M.A., U. Ill., 1949, Ph.D., 1958; m. Rebecca Mae Brightbill, Aug. 15, 1947; children—Martha Susan, Deborah Ann, Elizabeth, Lorraine Esther. Ordained to ministry Ch. of Brethren, 1945; asst. prof. history Cottey Coll., Nevada, Mo., 1949-53, dir. pub. relations, 1951-53; asst. to pres. Manchester Coll., 1953-54; teaching asst. U. Ill., 1954-58; asst. prof. history Western State Coll. Colo., Gunnison, 1958-60, acting chmn. grad. studies, 1959-60; prof. history, dean coll. Otterbein Coll., 1960-64; head dept. history-polit. sci., chmn. div. social scis. Manchester Coll., North Manchester, Ind., 1965—. Vis. prof. U. Malawi, 1971-72. Postdoctoral fellow African Studies Center, U.

Calif. at Los Angeles, 1968-69. Exec. dir. Ind. Consortium for Internat. Programs, 1975—. Mem. Membership Assn. Bethany Hosp., Chgo., Am. Hist. Assn., Orgn. of Am. Historians, African Studies Assn., Phi Alpha Theta (pres. Epsilon chpt. 1956-57). Rotarian (pres. Nevada, Mo. 1952-53). Address: 209 Damron Dr North Manchester IN 46962

WABER, JAMES THOMAS, educator; b. Chgo., Apr. 8, 1920; s. James Warren and Anna May (Cline) W.; B.S., Ill. Inst. Tech., Chgo., 1941, M.S., 1943, Ph.D., 1946; m. Santon Fotheringham, May 12, 1951; children—Lauriene, Sue Berenaise, Gay Ellen (dec.), John James. Research asst. prof. chemistry Ill. Inst. Tech., 1946; staff mem., sect. leader Los Alamos Sci. Lab., 1947-66; prof. materials sci. and engring., nuclear engring., Northwestern U., Evanston, Ill., 1967—; cons. Los Alamos Sci. Lab. Recipient Sr. U.S. Scientist award Alexander von Humboldt Found., 1975, Profl. Achievement award Ill. Inst. Tech. Alumni Assn., 1967, Willis Rodney Whitney award Nat. Assn. Corrosion Engrs., 1961. Fellow Am. Phys. Soc., Inst. Metallurgists (Gt. Britain); mem. Am. Inst. Mining and Metall. Engrs., Am. Soc. Metals. Editor: Compounds of Interest in Nuclear Reactor Technology, 1964; Energy Bands in Metals and Alloys, 1967; Magnetism in Alloys, 1972; contbr. articles to sci. jours.; patentee in field. Office: 2145 Sheridan Rd Evanston IL 60201

WACHAL, DAVID E., corp. exec.; b. Windom, Minn., May 23, 1939; s. Louis Leon and Virginia Eva (Rickert) W.; B.A., Mankato State U., 1962; m. Merry Dee Cummings, Aug. 13, 1960; children—Micheal, Susan. Mem. audit staff Arthur Andersen & Co., 1962-66, audit mgr., 1967-73; v.p., controller Ellerbe, Inc., Bloomington, Minn., 1973-76; v.p. fin. Am. Crystal Sugar Co., Moorhead, Minn., 1976—. Dep. comdr. N.D. Civil Air Patrol, 1978—. Served with U.S. Army, 1957-58. Mem. Am. Inst. C.P.A.'s, Fin. Execs. Inst. Republican. Lutheran. Home: 79 N Woodcrest Dr Fargo ND 58102 Office: 101 N 3d St Moorhead MN 56560

WACHENFELD, WILLIAM THOMAS, lawyer, found. exec.; b. Orange, N.J., Feb. 9, 1926; s. William A. and Ann (Weir) W.; A.B., Tufts U., 1947; LL.B., Duke, 1950; m. Mary Roberts; children—William S., Robin A., John C. Admitted to N.J. bar, 1949, since practiced in Newark; mem. firm Lum, Biunno & Tompkins, 1957-58; pres. Charles Hayden Found., N.Y.C., 1956—; prof. law Jersey City div. Rutgers U., 1954-56; v.p., asso. gen. counsel Prudential Ins. Co. Am., 1965—. Pres. Essex County Park Commn., 1960-65; commr. pub. affairs Orange, 1956-58. Pres., Newark Acad., 1972—; pres. standing com. Episcopal Diocese of Newark; mem. vestry St. Peter's Ch., Essex Fells, N.J. Served with USNR, World War II. Mem. Am., N.J., Essex County bar assns., N.J. Zool. Soc. Clubs: Essex (Newark); Essex Fells Country. Home: 40 Windsor Pl Essex Fells NJ 07021 Office: Prudential Plaza Newark NJ 07102

WACHMAN, HAROLD YEHUDA, educator; b. Tel Aviv, Israel, Dec. 2, 1927; s. Samuel and Jean (Kuselewitz) W.; came to U.S., 1940, naturalized, 1959; B.S., Coll. City N.Y., 1949; M.A., U. Mo., 1952, Ph.D., 1957; m. Barbara Uvlin, June 20, 1954; children—Alan, Joel, Joshua. Research scientist space scis. lab. Gen. Electric Co., King of Prussia, Pa., 1956-63, cons., 1963-70, cons. environ. systems div., 1978; vis. asso. prof. M.I.T., 1962-63, asso. prof., 1963-69, prof., 1969—; vis. sr. research fellow Jesus Coll., Oxford (Eng.) U., 1971-72. Co-chmn. VI Internat. Symposium on Rarefied Gas Dynamics, 1968, co-editor proc., 1969. Served with Chem. Corps, U.S. Army, 1952-54. Mem. Sigma Xi. Author: (with F.O. Goodman) Dynamics of Gas-Surface Scattering, 1976. Office: 77 Massachusetts Ave Cambridge MA 02139

WACHMAN, MARVIN, coll. pres.; b. Milw., Mar. 24, 1917; s. Alex and Ida (Epstein) W.; B.S., Northwestern U., 1939, M.A., 1940; Ph.D., U. Ill., 1942; LL.D., U. Pa., 1964, Lincoln (Pa.) U., 1970, Del. Valley Coll. Sci. and Agr., 1973; D.H.L., Gratz Coll., 1973; Litt.D., Jewish Theol. Sem. Am., 1973; L.H.D., Colgate U., 1975, Widener Coll., 1976; m. Adeline Lillian Schpok, Apr. 12, 1942; children—Kathleen M., Lynn A. Asst. in history U. Ill., 1940-42; instr. Biarritz Am. U., Biarritz, France, 1945-46; vis. asst. prof. San Diego State Coll., summer 1948, U. Minn., 1950; asso. prof. history U. Md. in Europe, 1952-53; from instr. to prof. Colgate U., 1946-61, dir. upper class core program, 1956-61; pres. Lincoln (Pa.) U., 1961-70; v.p. acad. affairs Temple U., 1970-73, pres., 1973—. Dir. Salzburg Seminar in Am. Studies, 1958-60; specialist in Africa for State Dept., 1965, 68. Dir. Bell Telephone Co. Pa.; trustee Phila. Saving Fund Soc. Mem. Pa. Higher Edn. Assistance Agy.; mem. adv. council Expt. in Internat. Living; mem. Colgate Nat. Council, Crime Commn. Corp. Phila., Phila. Com. Fgn. Relations. Bd. overseers Coll. V.I.; trustee Phila. Award, Middle States Assn. Colls. and Schs., Temple U., Abington Meml. Hosp., Acad. Music Phila., African Student Aid Fund, Jewish Publ. Soc. Am.; bd. dirs. African Acad. Arts and Research, Inc., Phila. Contributionship, Crime Prevention Assn. Phila., Phila. Orch. Assn., Jour. History Ideas. Greater Phila. Partnership. Served with AUS, 1942-46. Mem. NAACP, Am. Studies Assn. (past mem. exec. com.), AAUP (past pres. Colgate U. chpt.), Am. Hist. Assn., ACLU, Assn. Am. Colls. (commn. coll. adminstrn., 1967-69, task force presdl. selection and career devel. 1973—), Am. Assn. Higher Edn., Nat. Assn. State Univs. and Land-Grant Colls. (veterans affairs com., com. on voluntary support), Pa. Assn. Colls. and Univs. (past pres.), Phi Beta Kappa. Author: History of Social-Democratic Party of Milwaukee, 1897-1910, 1945. Contbr. articles to profl. jours. Home: 321 E Evergreen Ave Philadelphia PA 19118 Office: Temple U Philadelphia PA 19122

WACHOWSKI, THEODORE JOHN, physician, radiologist; b. Chgo., Nov. 20, 1907; s. Albert and Constance (Korzeniewski) W., B.S., U. Ill., 1929, M.D., 1932; m. Barbara Florence Benda, June 1, 1931; 1 son, Ted James. Intern, resident radiology Research and Ednl. Hosps., Chgo., 1931-35; radiologist Copley Meml. Hosp., Aurora, Ill., 1935-77; clin. prof. radiology U. Ill. Coll. Medicine, Chgo., 1949—. Mem. Radiol. Soc. N.A. (dir., pres., gold medal 1969), Am. Coll. Radiology (bd. chancellors, chmn. bd. chancellors 1961-62, pres. 1963, gold medal 1969), Polish Medical Soc. Chgo. (past pres.), Ill., Kane County, Aurora (past pres.) med. socs., AMA, Am. Roentgen Ray Soc. Home: 101 Tennyson Dr Wheaton IL 60187 Office: Med Clinic 1822 N Main St Wheaton IL 60187

WACHS, MOSES, geriatric facility adminstr.; b. Bklyn., Feb. 4, 1913; s. William and Lottie (Dickman) W.; student Coll. City N.Y., 1931-33; m. Evelyn Ossakow, Dec. 22, 1940; children—Rena Leslie (Mrs. Murray Cautin), Howard Sanford. Dir. personnel-employment dept. Bellevue Hosp. Center, N.Y.C., 1931-43; asst. exec. dir. Daughters of Jacob Geriatric Inst., Bronx, N.Y., 1943-52; adminstr. Parshelsky Pavilion Bklyn. Hebrew Home & Hosp. for Aged, 1952-67; exec. dir. Metropolitan Jewish Geriatric Center, Bklyn., 1967—. Mem. Coney Island Community Council, 1961—. Bd. dirs. Central Bur. Jewish Aged. Fellow Nat. Gerontol. Soc. Inc.; mem. Hosp. Exec. Club, Nat. Conf. Jewish Communal Service, Nat. Assn. Jewish Homes for Aged, Nat. Council on Aging, Am. Hosp. Assn., Am. N.Y. State assns. homes for aged. Home: 4012 Surf Ave Brooklyn NY 11224 Office: 4915 10th Ave Brooklyn NY 11219

WACHSLER, ROBERT ALAN, mktg. exec.; b. N.Y.C., Jan. 4, 1934; s. Norman and Giselle (Beer) W.; B.S., Coll. City N.Y., 1955; M.A., Ohio State U., 1957, Ph.D., 1958; m. Jane Baum, July 23, 1960; children—Anne, Elizabeth, Susan. Sr. research psychologist Gen. Motors Corp., Detroit, 1958-61; research account exec. Batten, Barton, Durstine & Osborn, N.Y.C., 1961-63, research account supr., 1963-64, asso. research dir., 1964-65, v.p., 1965-66, mgr. research dept., 1966-68, dir. research, 1968-69, dir. research and mktg. info. services, 1969-70, sr. v.p., 1972-77, mgmt. supr., dir. corp. communications group, 1974-77, also dir.; prin., dir. Canter, Achenbaum, Heekin, Inc., 1977—; dir., mem. fin. com. Ideal Mut. Ins. Co., 1978—; dir. Florafax Internat. Bd. dirs. Advt. Research Found., Vitam Drug Rehab. Center, 1975-76. Mem. Am. Psychol. Assn., Am. Mktg. Assn., Am. Assn. Pub. Opinion Research. Contbr. articles to profl. jours. Home: 14 Cob Dr Westport CT 06880 Office: 950 3d Ave New York NY 10022

WACHTEL, HARRY H., lawyer, chain store exec.; b. N.Y.C., Mar. 26, 1917; s. Samuel and Minnie (Herzhaft) W.; B.S. in Social Sci., Coll. City N.Y., 1938; LL.B., Columbia, 1940; m. Leonora Golden, July 30, 1939; children—Alan B., Susan M., William B. Admitted to N.Y. bar, 1940, since practiced in N.Y.C.; sr. partner firm Rubin, Wachtel, Baum & Levin, until 1975; exec. v.p., gen. counsel, dir. McCrory Corp., 1959-75, exec. asst. to pres., 1975—; vice chmn., exec. v.p. Rapid Am. Corp., 1960-65; gen. counsel, dir. Lerner Stores Corp., 1961-75. Vis. prof. polit. sci. Hofstra U., 1967-71; adj. prof. polit. sci. Columbia, 1973—, fellow Urban Center, 1972—; dir. Vanguard Nat. Bank, Hempstead, N.Y., 1972-74. Mem. exec. com. N.Y. State Com. Am. Vets. Com., 1947. Dir. North Shore Community Arts Center, Roslyn, N.Y., 1960-72; v.p., dir., counsel Martin Luther King Jr. Center For Social Change; exec. v.p., counsel Am. Found. Nonviolence, 1964-72; trustee So. Christian Leadership Conf.; past mem. council Hofstra U. Served with AUS, 1942-45. Decorated Bronze Star medal. Mem. Phi Beta Kappa. Home: 211 Central Park W New York NY 10024 Office: 888 7th Ave New York NY 10019

WACHTELL, RICHARD LLOYD, engring. exec.; b. N.Y.C., Feb. 18, 1920; s. Theodore and Bertha (Trompeter) W.; B.S., Columbia U., 1941; m. Clara Hirsch, June 28, 1941; 1 dau., Nancy D. Asst. metallurgist Republic Aviation Corp., Farmingdale, L.I., N.Y., 1941-44, metallurgist Quality Control Lab., 1944-46; metall. engr. tech. services sect. Air Reduction Co., Murray Hill, N.J., 1945-48; metallurgist, project engr., asst. dir. research Am. Electro Metals Corp., Yonkers, N.Y., 1948-52; chief metallurgist, tech. dir. Chromalloy Corp., West Nyack, N.Y., 1952-60, v.p., gen. mgr., 1960-66, merged to form Chromalloy Am. Corp., 1966, exec. v.p. tech., pres. research and tech. div., 1962-80, chmn. bd., chief exec. officer, 1980—, pres. turbine support div., 1966—, dir. corp.; chmn. Chromalloy Metal Tectonics Co., 1976-80. Mem. Am. Ceramic Soc., Metal Sci. Club, Am. Inst. Metall. Engrs., Am. Soc. Metals, Iron and Steel Inst., Am. Ordnance Assn., Am. Soc. Corrosion Engrs. Contbr. articles profl. jours. Patentee in field. Home: Circuit Rd Tuxedo NY 10987 Office: 641 Lexington Ave New York NY 10022

WACHTLER, SOL, judge; b. N.Y.C., Apr. 29, 1930; s. Philip Henry and Fay (Sobel) W.; B.A., Washington and Lee U., 1951, LL.B., 1952; LL.D., Albany Law Sch., Union Coll., 1978, Bklyn. Law Sch., 1978. m. Joan Wolosoff, Feb. 23, 1952; children—Lauren Jane, Marjorie Dru, Alison Toni, Philip Henry. Admitted to N.Y. bar, 1956; justice N.Y. State Supreme Ct., 1968-72; judge N.Y. State Ct. Appeals, Albany, 1972—; guest lectr. Yale U. Sch. Law, Albany Law Sch., St. John's Law Sch., 1968-77, USIS, Munich, Germany, 1973, Stuttgart, Germany, 1977. Councilman, Town of N. Hempstead (N.Y.), 1963-65, chief exec., 1965-67; mem. Nassau County Bd. Suprs., 1965-67, chmn. com. pub. safety, 1965-67; trustee L.I. Jewish-Hillside Med. Center, 1970—; dist. chmn. Boy Scouts Am., 1968-69; trustee Cerebral Palsy Assn. and Assn. for Help of Retarded Children, 1966-67. Served with JAGC, U.S. Army, 1953-55. Mem. Am. Law Inst., Assn. N.Y. State Supreme Ct. Justices, Am.. N.Y. State, Nassau County bar assns., Phi Delta Phi. Jewish. Club: Masons. Contbr. articles to legal jours. Home: 6 Beech Ln Great Neck NY 11024 Office: Court of Appeals Hall Eagle St Albany NY 12207. *As a people, we are fond of the observation that ours is a nation of laws and not of men. It too, like the words of our great laws, seems to lend security, a sense of certainty, and a predictability to the paths we travel. In the law particularly, the thought that past generations have separated right from wrong and good from evil can be comforting. Yet, here again, if we will just scratch the surface, we will find that the greatest responsibility for our national welfare does not rest with statutes carved in stone but with the principles, conscience, and morality of the individuals who constitute this generation.*

WACHTMAN, JOHN BRYAN, JR., govt. ofcl.; b. Conway, S.C., Feb. 6, 1928; s. John Bryan and Ruby Lee (Moore) W.; B.S. in Physics, Carnegie-Mellon U., 1948, M.S., 1949; Ph.D., U. Md., 1961; m. Edith Virginia Matheny, Aug. 27, 1955. Research asso. Carnegie-Mellon U., 1949-51; with Nat. Bur. Standards, Dept. Commerce, Washington, 1951—, sect. chief, 1962-68, chief inorganic materials div., 1968-78, dir. center Materials Sci., 1978-79; vis. prof. materials sci. Northwestern U., 1971; mem. advisory com. Ames Lab, AEC, 1973-74; program mgr. Congl. Office Tech. Assessment, 1974-75; mem. ceramic advisory bd. U. Ill., 1973-75, Alfred U., 1974—, Pa. State U., 1976—, Northwestern U., 1977—, MIT, 1978-80, SUNY, Stony Brook, 1979; mem. Nat. Materials Advisory Bd., 1976—; chmn. Henniher Conf. Nat. Materials Policy, 1976, Internat. Materials Congress, 1979. Trustee Orton Found., Columbus, Ohio. Recipient gold medal Dept. Commerce, 1971; Samuel Wesley Stratton award, Nat. Bur. Standards, 1975. Fellow Am. Ceramic Soc. (trustee 1969-72, pres. 1978-79), Fedn. Materials Soc. (pres. 1975; Hobart N. Craner award in ceramics 1978); mem. Nat. Acad. Engring. Editor: (with A.D. Franklin) Mass Transport in Oxides, 1966; Mechanical and Thermal Properties of Ceramics, 1969; series editor Ceramics and Glass: Science and Technology, 1969—; editorial bd. Ency. Solid State, 1969—; contbr. articles to profl. jours. Cosmos. Home: 802 Rollins Ave Rockville MD 20852 Office: Center Materials Sci Nat Bur Standards Washington DC 20234

WACKENHUT, GEORGE RUSSELL, security services exec.; b. Phila., Sept. 3, 1919; s. William Henry and Frances (Hogan) W.; student U. Pa. Wharton Evening Sch., 1937-38, State Tchrs. Coll., West Chester, Pa., 1938-41; B.S., U. Hawaii, 1942; postgrad. Temple U., 1946; M.Ed., Johns Hopkins U., 1949; m. Ruth Johann Bell, Apr. 8, 1944; children—Janis Lynn, Richard Russell. Dir. phys. edn. profl. program tchrs. tng. Johns Hopkins, 1946-50; civilian cons. recreational sports br. Office Spl. Services, U.S. Army, Washington, 1950-51; spl. agt. FBI, 1951-54; dir. personnel, security and safety Giffin Industries, Inc., Miami, Fla., 1954; pres., chmn. bd. Spl. Agt. Investigators, Inc., Spl. Agts. Security Guards, Inc., Security Services Corp. (all Miami), 1954-58; pres., chmn. bd., dir. Wackenhut Corp., Coral Gables, Fla., 1958—, Wackenhut Services, Inc., Coral Gables, 1960—; chmn. bd. Wackenhut Electronics, Inc., 1966-68; chmn. bd., dir. Gor-Buc Security Systems, Inc., 1967-69, Wackenhut Protective Systems, Inc., 1967—; dir. Wackenhut of Can., Ltd., Wackenhut de Colombia, S.A., Wackenhut del Ecuador, S.A., Venezolana de Seguridad y Vigilancia, C.A., Wackenhut Belgium, S.A. Mem. law enforcement council Nat. Council Crime and Delinquency, 1971—. Bd. dirs. Heart Assn. of Greater Miami, 1965-66, Gov.'s War on Crime, Fla., 1967-70; bd. visitors U.S. Army M.P. Sch., 1972-74. Served with AUS, 1941-45. Mem. Soc. Former Spl. Agts. FBI, Inc., Am. Soc. for Indsl. Security, AIM (pres.'s council 1964-66). Christian Scientist. Clubs: Ocean Reef (Key Largo, Fla.). Home: 20 Casuarina Concourse Gables Estates Coral Gables FL 33143 Office: 3280 Ponce de Leon Blvd Coral Gables FL 33134

WACKENHUT, RUTH J. (MRS. GEORGE R. WACKENHUT), business exec.; b. Phila., 1922; m. George Russell Wackenhut, Apr. 8, 1944; children—Janis Lynn, Richard Russell. Sec., Spl. Agt. Investigators, Inc., Miami, 1954-58, Spl. Agts. Security Guards, Inc., Miami, 1954-58, Security Services Corp., Miami, 1954-58; sec. Wackenhut Corp., Coral Gables, Fla., 1958—; dir. Wackenhut Services, Inc., 1960—. Designer. Clubs: Ocean Reef (Key Largo, Fla.); Coral Gables Yacht. Home: 20 Casuarina Concourse Gables Estates Coral Gables FL 33143 Office: 3280 Ponce de Leon Blvd Coral Gables FL 33134

WACKER, FRED P., govt. ofcl.; b. Washington, Dec. 3, 1926; s. Fred W. and Marguerite A. (Dommel) W.; B.A. in Econs. magna cum laude, Am. U., 1950; M.A. in Fin. Mgmt., George Washington U.; m. Louise Ginn, Nov. 3, 1951; children—Robin, Susan, Lisa. With GAO, Washington, Dept. Commerce; with Dept. Navy, Washington, from 1951; now asst. sec. def. (comptroller) Dept. Def.; mem. Cost Acctg. Standards Bd., 1977—. Served with U.S. Army, 1944-46. Recipient Disting. Public Service medal Sec. Def.; Disting. Civilian Service medal; Meritorious Civilian Service medal. Mem. Am. Soc. Mil. Comptrollers. Home: 1733 Dalewood Pl McLean VA 22101 Office: Pentagon Washington DC 20301

WACKER, FREDERICK GLADE, JR., mfg. co. exec.; b. Chgo., July 10, 1918; s. Frederick Glade and Grace Cook (Jennings) W.; grad Hotchkiss Sch., 1936; B.A., Yale, 1940; student Gen. Motors Inst. Tech., 1940-42; m. Ursula Comandatore, Apr. 26, 1958; children—Frederick Glade III, Wendy, Joseph Comandatore. With AC Spark Plug div. Gen. Motors Corp., 1940-43 efficiency engr., 1941-43; with Ammco Tools, Inc., N. Chicago, Ill., 1947—, pres., 1948—, chmn. bd., 1948—; founder, 1954, since pres., chmn. bd. Liquid Controls Corp., N. Chicago; limited partner Francis I. DuPont & Co., N.Y.C., 1954-70; dir. Hydro-Air Engring., Inc., Zenith United Corp., Moehlenpah Industries Inc. Exec. council Cof. Bd., 1971—. Condr. of Freddie Wacker and His Orch., 1955-69; orch. has appeared on television and radio, recs. for Dolphin, Cadet records. Bd. govs. United Republican Fund Ill.; trustee Lake Forest Acad., 1956-71, Warren Wilson Coll., 1973—, Chgo. chpt. Multiple Sclerosis Soc.; bd. govs. Lyric Opera Chgo., 1963-66; bd. advisers Nat. Schs. Com., 1966—; mem. adv. council Trinity Evang. Div. Sch., 1977—. Served to lt. (j.g.) USNR, 1943-45. Mem. N.A.M., Chief Execs. Forum, Young Pres. Orgn. (chmn. Chgo. chpt. 1965-66), Sports Car Club Am. (pres. 1952-53), Ill. Mfrs. Assn. (chmn. bd. 1975—), Chgo. Presidents Orgn. (pres. 1972-73), Automotive Orgn. Team (life, dir. 1976—), Soc. Automotive Engrs., World Bus. Council, Waukegan C. of C. (dir. 1965-68), Chgo. Fedn. Musicians (life). Presbyterian. Clubs: Chgo., Racquet (pres. 1960-61), Casino, Mid-Am. (Chgo.) Shoreacres; N.Y. Yacht; Onwentsia (Lake Forest). Home: 1600 Green Bay Rd Lake Bluff IL 60044 Office: 2100 Commonwealth Ave North Chicago IL 60064

WACKER, JOHN AUGUST, constrn. co. exec.; b. Temple, Tex., Oct. 24, 1920; s. John August and Charlotte (Dickson) W.; student Tex. Technol. U., 1938-40; B.S., U. Tex. at Austin, 1943; m. Lee Ida Pinkston, Oct. 20, 1950; children—Lisa, Lauren. Chmn. bd., chief exec. officer, dir. J.W. Bateson Co., Inc., Dallas, 1974—; pres. Centex Enterprises, Inc., 1974—; dir. Centex Corp., Prestonwood Nat. Bank, Dallas, Centex Constrn. Co., Inc.; chmn. bd. Frank J. Rooney, Inc., Ft. Lauderdale; pres., dir. Cardinal Contracting Co., Inc. Served with USAF, 1943-46. Mem. Assn. Children with Learning Disabilities (nat. bd. dirs.). Phi Kappa Sigma. Home: 10848 Strait Ln Dallas TX 75229 Office: Box 20445 Dallas TX 75220

WACKER, PETER OSCAR, geographer; b. Orange, N.J., Aug. 7, 1936; s. Franz Oscar and Linnea Ingeborg (Zackariasson) W.; B.A., Montclair State Coll., 1959; M.A., La. State U., 1961, Ph.D., 1966; m. Arlene Mae Gibbs, Aug. 25, 1962; children—Jill, Craig. Instr., La. State U., New Orleans, 1962-64; mem. faculty Rutgers U., New Brunswick, N.J., 1964—, prof., chmn. dept. geography, 1972-77, chmn. New Brunswick Dept. Environ. Studies, 1977—; mem. panel on advanced studies N.J. Dept. Edn., 1978. Trustee East Jersey Olde Towne, Inc., 1973-75; mem. N.J. State Rev. Bd. Hist. Sites, 1976—. Recipient certificate of commendation Am. Assn. State and Local History, 1968; Author award N.J. Tchrs. of Eng., 1968, 75; Alumni citation Montclair State Coll., 1976; award of recognition N.J. Hist. Commn., 1977; Gottlieb fellow, 1961-62; Guggenheim fellow, 1971-72; N.J. Hist. Soc. fellow, 1972. Mem. Assn. Am. Geographers, Am. Geog. Soc., N.J. Hist. Soc., Pioneer Am. Soc., Gamma Theta Upsilon, Phi Kappa Phi. Author: The Musconetcong Valley of New Jersey: A Historical Geography, 1968; Land and People: A Cultural Geography of Preindustrial New Jersey, 1975; The Cultural Geography of Revolutionary New Jersey, 1975. Home: 1321 Mallard Dr Martinsville NJ 08836

WACKER, WARREN ERNEST CLYDE, physician, educator; b. Bklyn., Feb. 29, 1924; s. John Frederick and Kitty Dora (Morrissey) W.; student Georgetown U., 1946-47; M.D., George Washington U., 1951; M.A. (hon.), Harvard, 1968; m. Ann Romeyn MacMillan, May 22, 1948; children—Margaret Morrissey, John Frederick. Intern, George Washington U. Hosp., 1951-52, resident, 1952-53; resident Peter Bent Brigham Hosp., Boston, 1953-55; Nat. Found. Infantile Paralysis fellow, 1955-57; investigator Howard Hughes Med. Inst., Boston, 1957-68; mem. faculty Harvard Med. Sch., Boston, 1955—, asso. prof. medicine, 1968-71, Henry K. Oliver prof. hygiene, 1971—, dir. univ. health services, 1971—, acting master Mather House, 1974-75, Kirkland House, 1975-76, master South House; dir. Millipore Corp., Bedford, Mass. Bd. dirs. Harvard Community Health Plan, Boston, Bishop Rhinelander Found., Cambridge, 1973-76; pres. bd. overseers Peter Bent Brigham Hosp., Boston; trustee Affiliated Hosp. Center, Boston. Served to 1st lt. USAAF, 1942-45. Decorated Air medal, D.F.C. Named Distinguished Alumnus George Washington U., 1963. Mem. Am. Chem. Soc., Am. Soc. Biol. Chemistry, Am. Soc. Clin. Investigation, AMA, Mass. Med. Soc., A.C.P. Democrat. Episcopalian. Club: Harvard (Boston). Sec., editorial adv. bd. Biochemistry, 1962-76. Home: 87 Perry St Brookline MA 02146 Office: 75 Mt Auburn St Cambridge MA 02138

WACTOR, JAMES WESLEY, bishop; b. near Lumber Bridge, N.C., Sept. 13, 1908; s. Henry Lee and Anne Bell (Campbell) W.; A.B., Livingstone Coll., 1936, D.D. (hon.), 1955; postgrad. Union Theol. Sem., 1942, Chaplain's Sch., Harvard U., 1943; m. Hildred Anita Henry, July 3, 1934. Licensed to preach African Methodist Episcopal Zion Ch., 1930, ordained deacon, 1935, elder, 1935, consecrated as bishop, 1972; pastor chs. N.C., Tenn., N.Y., 1931-43; pastor Hood Meml. Ch., N.Y.C., 1948-60, Big Zion Ch., Mobile, Ala., 1960-64, Met. Ch., Birmingham, Ala., 1964-72, bishop 7th Episcopal dist. A.M.E. Zion Ch., Fayetteville, N.C., 1972—, also chmn. bd. statistics and records and ministerial relief, vice chmn. bd. temperance and law relief; mem. Commn. Evangelism of Protestant Council Chs., 1955-56; mem. interracial commn. Billy Graham Crusade, 1956; dir.

Citizens Fed. Savs. and Loan Assn. Bd. dirs. A.G. Gaston Boys Club; trustee Lomax-Hannon Jr. Coll., Greenville, Ala., Livingstone Coll. Recipient award of merit Beta Psi, 1967, award for leadership in Christian service and edn. Booker T. Washington Bus. Coll., Birmingham, 1972. Mem. N.C. (dir.), Fla. (dir.) councils chs., Nat. Council Chs. of Christ in U.S.A., NAACP. Home: 709 Edgehill Rd Fayetteville NC 28302*

WADA, GEORGE T., food co. exec.; b. Honolulu, Oct. 19, 1931; s. I. and A. (Muraoka) W.; B.B.A., U. Hawaii, 1953; grad. Exec. Program, Stanford, 1969; m. Betty Nomura, June 1956. Controller, treas. Hawaiian Airlines, Honolulu, 1958-65; financial analyst Dole Co., Honolulu, 1965-67, controller, 1967-73; controller Hawaii Pineapple div. Castle & Cooke Foods, 1973—. Served as 1st lt. USAF, 1953-55. Mem. Nat. Assn. Accountants. Office: 650 Iwilei Rd Honolulu HI 96817

WADA, HARRY NOBUYOSHI, assn. exec.; b. North Platte, Nebr., Nov. 29, 1919; s. Gosaku and Hina (Arakawa) W.; B.S., Ill. Inst. Tech., 1954, M.S., 1956; m. Carol Tanaka, July 30, 1950; children—Sharon, Leslie, Gregg. Owner, Palace Cafe, North Platte, 1946-50; mgr. purchases IIT Research Inst., Chgo., 1954-65, materials mgr., 1965-76; dir. continuing edn. Nat. Assn. Purchasing Mgmt., 1976—; instr. Ill. Inst. Tech., Roosevelt U. Mem. Bd. Standardization Cook County, Health and Hosps. Governing Commn. Served with AUS, 1942-46. Recipient J. Shipman Gold medal, 1976. Mem. Purchasing Mgmt. Assn. Chgo. (pres. 1969), Nat. Assn. Purchasing Mgmt. (chmn. dist. III profl. devel. 1970-71, program chmn. Internat. Conf. 1971, pres. 1974—, Brueggemann award 1974), Ill. C. of C., Ill. Inst. Tech. Alumni (bd. dirs.), Phi Eta Sigma, Sigma Iota Epsilon. Editor chpt. George Aljians Handbook, 1973. Contbr. articles profl. jours. Home and office: 336 Oswego St Park Forest IL 60466

WADDELL, ALFRED MOORE, JR., bldg. constrn. co. exec.; b. Chattanooga, Tenn., Jan. 30, 1939; s. Alfred Moore and Harriet Belseth Aplin W.; B.A. in Econs., U. of South, 1961; M.B.A., Harvard U., 1968; m. Clara Teresa Saxon, Jan. 3, 1961; children—Virginia Martin, Alfred Moore III, David Sewall. Various positions IBM, Tenn., Ark., Mass., 1962-68; pres. UC Leasing, Memphis, 1968-71; v.p. fin. Gable Industries Inc., Atlanta, 1971-74, chmn. bd., 1974-76, also dir.; sr. v.p. Flintkote Co., Stamford, Conn., 1976-78, also dir.; pres., chmn., chief exec. officer Hajoca Corp. (formerly Gable Industries), Ardmore, Pa., 1978—. Mem. Fin. Execs. Inst. Home: 409 Hillbrook Rd Bryn Mawr PA 19010 Office: 127 Coulter Ave Ardmore PA 19103

WADDELL, C(HARLES) EUGENE, artist, writer; b. Charlottesville, Va., Oct. 7, 1923; s. John Boyd and Mary Gertrude (Mack) W.; student Duquesne U., 1940, Art Inst. Pitts., 1940, U. Pitts., 1944, Art Students League, N.Y.C., 1950, Cooper Union, 1955; m. Patricia Colbourne, Dec. 4, 1959. Numerous one-man and group shows in U.S. and Europe, 1944—; painting and murals represented in numerous pvt. and corporate collections, Am. embassies; copy dir. Clyne Maxon, Lennen & Newell, Dancer-Fitzgerald-Sample, Warwick & Legler, Geyer, Morey & Ballard, 1945-68; pres. Waddell Group, N.Y.C., 1967—, Eastright Waddell, N.Y.C., 1967—, Pyap Internat. Ltd., 1969—; creative cons. for numerous corps., 1966—. Radio and TV script writer, 1944—; lectr. N.Y. U., 1970-71, also clubs, assns., 1966—. Mem. Nat. Council Arts and Govt., 1962—. Life fellow Royal Soc. Arts (London); mem. Archtl. League, Berkshire, Dutchess County, Kent, Washington art assns., Artists Equity Assn., Allied Artists Am., Art League Hudson Valley, Artists/U.S.A. (asso.), Inst. Contemporary Arts (London), Communities Activities League, Westchester Art Soc., Direct Mktg. Writers Club (v.p. 1968-70), Holiday Hills, De Mena, Spectrum, Nantucket, Waddell galleries, Pawling Art Center. Club: Lambs (N.Y.C.). Author: Your Family's Health, 1965. Contbr. numerous articles to various publs., radio and TV. Inventor, author do-it-yourself art course and kit. Address: 200 Diplomat Towers Mount Kisco NY 10549

WADDELL, WILLIAM JOSEPH, pharmacologist; b. Commerce, Ga., Mar. 16, 1929; s. John Daniel and Lillian Marie (Vollrath) W.; A.B. in Chemistry, U. N.C., 1951, M.D., 1955; m. Grace Carolyn Marlowe, Oct. 19, 1974; children—William Joseph, James Glenn, Martin Christie, Amy Alison. Postdoctoral research fellow U. N.C. Sch. Medicine, 1955-58, asst. prof. pharmacology, 1958-62, asso. prof., 1962-72, asso. prof. oral biology Dental Research Center, 1967-69, prof., 1969-72, asso. dir., 1968-72; prof. pharmacology U. Ky. Coll. Medicine, Louisville, 1972-77; prof., chmn. dept. pharmacology and toxicology U. Louisville, 1977—; Centennial Alumni Disting. vis. prof. U. N.C. Sch. Medicine, 1979. Mem. Am. Soc. for Pharmacology and Exptl. Therapeutics, Am. Physiol. Soc., Am. Teratology Soc., Internat. Soc. for Quantum Biology, Soc. for Exptl. Biology and Medicine, Soc. Toxicology, Sigma Xi. Contbr. articles to profl. jours. Home: 6604 Gunpowder Ln Prospect KY 40059 Office: Dept Pharmacology U Louisville PO Box 35260 Louisville KY 40232

WADDINGHAM, JOHN ALFRED, newspaperman, artist; b. London, Eng., July 9, 1915; s. Charles Alfred and Mary Elizabeth (Coles) W.; came to U.S., 1927, naturalized, 1943; student Coronado (Calif.) Sch. Fine Arts, 1953-54, Portland Art Mus., 1940-65, U. Portland, 1946-47; pupil Rex Brandt, Eliot Ohara, George Post; m. Joan Lee Larson, May 3, 1952; children—Mary Kathryn, Thomas Richard. Promotion art dir. Oreg. Jour., Portland, 1946-59; with The Oregonian, Portland, 1959—, editorial art dir., 1959—; rep. mus. rental collections Portland Art Mus., Bush House, Salem, Ore., U. Oreg. Mus., Vincent Price collection, Ford Times collection, also Am. Watercolor Soc. Travelling Show; judge art events, 1946—; over 36 one-man shows; ofcl. artist Kiwanis Internat. Conv., 1966; designed, dir. constrn. cast concrete mural Genesis, St. Barnabas Episcopal Ch., Portland, 1960; tchr. watercolor Ore. Soc. Artists, 1954-56; spl. work drawings old Portland landmarks and houses; propr. John Waddingham Hand Prints, fine arts serigraphs and silk screen drawings, 1965—. Served with USAAF, 1942-46. Recipient gold medal Salone Internazionale dell' Umorismo, Italy, 1974, 76. Artist mem. Portland Art Mus.; mem. Portland Art Dirs. Club (past pres.). Featured artist Am. Artist mag., May 1967. Home: 955 SW Westwood Dr Portland OR 97201 Office: The Oregonian Portland OR 97201

WADDINGTON, RAYMOND BRUCE, JR., educator; b. Santa Barbara, Calif., Sept. 27, 1935; s. Raymond Bruce and Marjorie Gladys (Waddell) W.; B.A., Stanford U., 1957; Ph.D., Rice U., 1963; postdoctoral (Univ. fellow in Humanities) Johns Hopkins U., 1965-66; m. Linda Gayle Jones, Sept. 7, 1957; children—Raymond Bruce, Edward Jackson. Instr. English U. Houston, 1961-62; instr. U. Kans., 1962-63; asst. prof., 1963-65; asst. prof. English lit. U. Wis., Madison, 1966-68, asso. prof., 1968-74, prof., 1974—. Huntington Library fellow, 1967, 75; Inst. Research in Humanities fellow, 1971-72; Guggenheim fellow, 1972-73; Nat. Endowment for Humanities fellow, 1977; Newberry Library fellow, 1978; Am. Philos. Soc. grantee, 1965. Mem. Modern Lang. Assn., Milton Soc. Am., Friends of Bemerton. Club: Logos. Author: The Minds Empire, 1974; co-editor: The Rhetoric of Renaissance Poetry, 1974; editorial bd. Sixteenth Century Jour., 1975—, Lit. Monographs, 1974—. Home: 4010 Paunack Ave Madison WI 53711 Office: 600 N Park St Madison WI 53706

WADDLE, JOHN FREDERICK, retail chain exec.; b. Somerset, Ky., July 1, 1927; s. Lewis Everett and Anna Hall (Prather) W.; B.S., U. Ky., 1949; M.S., N.Y. U., 1952; m. Catherine Joan Osborn, June 3, 1977; children—Lewis Victor, Joan Catherine. With Sears, Roebuck and Co., 1949—, nat. mgr. toys, 1969-72, asst. to sr. exec. v.p. merchandising, 1972-76, group nat. merchandising mgr., 1977-78, v.p. children's apparel, 1978—. Served with USN, 1945-46. Republican. Baptist. Club: Metropolitan (Chgo.). Office: Sears Tower Chicago IL 60684

WADDLES, CHARLESZETTA LINA CAMPBELL, clergywoman, mission exec.; b. St. Louis, Oct. 7, 1912; d. Henry and Ella (Brown) Campbell; student pub. schs., St. Louis; m. Payton Waddles, Jr., Dec. 27, 1957; children—Beatrice, Lathet L., Latheda, Annette, Lorraine, Andrea, Roosevelt, Charles, Dennis, Theresa. Founder, nat. dir. Mother Waddles Perpetual Mission, Inc., Detroit, 1956—. Mem. Detroit Mayor's Task Force Com., Detroit Bicentennial Com.; hon. chmn. Women's Conf. of Concern. Recipient over 75 awards including Bell Ringer award Ford Motor Co., Lane Bryant citation, Sojourner Truth award, Religious Heritage award, spl. tributes State of Mich., Mich. Ho. of Reps., Humanitarian award Pres. Nixon, Vol. Leadership award Gov. of Mich. Mem. NAACP (life), 3d Order Interfaith Orgn., Alpha Phi Zeta. Home: 638 W Pingree St Detroit MI 48202 Office: 3700 Gratiot St Detroit MI 48207

WADE, ADELBERT ELTON, educator; b. Hilliard, Fla., Apr. 29, 1926; s. Adelbert Elton and Esther (Sundberg) W.; B.S., U. Fla., 1954, M.S., 1956, Ph.D., 1959; m. Mary Lucy Cooper, Jan. 22, 1950; children—William Elton, James Howard. Research asst. U. Fla., 1954-59, asst. prof. pharmacology, 1959-62; asso. prof. pharmacology Sch. Pharmacy, U. Ga., 1962-67, prof., 1967—, head dept., 1968—. Served with USNR, 1944-46. Mem. Am. Soc. Pharmacology and Exptl. Therapeutics, Internat. Soc. Biochem. Pharmacology, Soc. Exptl. Biology and Medicine, Am. Assn. Colls. Pharmacy, Sigma Xi, Rho Chi, Gamma Sigma Epsilon, Phi Kappa Phi, Gamma Sigma Delta. Democrat. Baptist. Mason. Research biochem. pharmacology, role of nutrition in drug metabolism and chem. carcinogenesis. Home: 120 Rivermont Rd Athens GA 30606

WADE, CHARLES BYRD, JR., indsl. exec.; b. Morehead City, N.C., July 8, 1915; s. Charles Byrd and Elizabeth (Ormond) W.; A.B., Duke U., 1938; m. Margaret Patterson, July 26, 1942; children—Ruth E. (Mrs. J. David Ross), Mary M. (Mrs. Malcolm W. Jones, Jr.), Charles Byrd III. With R. J. Reynolds Tobacco Co., Winston-Salem, N.C., 1938—, asst. personnel mgr., 1946-47, asst. supr. mfg., 1948-49, personnel mgr., 1949-59, v.p. personnel and pub. relations, 1959-70, sr. v.p., 1970—, dir., 1955—; sr. v.p. R.J. Reynolds Industries, Inc. (parent co.), 1973-76, dir., 1970-76, sec. internat. adv. bd., 1975—; bd. mgrs. Wachovia Bank, 1949-76; dir. Spector Industries, Atlantic & East Carolina Ry. Co. Former mem. adv. council personnel adminstrn. Nat. Indsl. Conf. Bd.; former chmn. Urban Redevel. Commn. of Winston-Salem; former pres. Old Salem, Inc.; mem. President's Adv. Council on Youth Opportunity, N.C. Ednl. Council on Nat. Purposes, Winston-Salem Mayor's Bi-racial Goodwill Com.; founding mem. N.C. Council on Crime and Delinquency; trustee N.C. Ch.-Related Colls. Found.; former mem. N.C. Bd. Conservation and Devel.; former head YMCA, United Fund, Winston-Salem. Alderman, Winston-Salem, 1950-51; trustee Salem Coll.; trustee, chmn. N.C. Symphony; former bd. visitors Sch. Bus. Adminstrn., Duke U., trustee, former chmn. bd.; adv. dir. Met. Opera; former trustee Brevard Coll.; chmn. adv. bd. Duke Hosp.; bd. dirs., past pres. N.C. Citizens Assn.; former trustee N.C. Assn. Ind. Colls. and Univs. Served from pvt. to maj. AUS, World War II. Decorated Legion of Merit. Mem. U.S., Winston-Salem (past dir.) chambers of commerce, Am. Mgmt. Assn. (adv. council), Tobacco Inst. (chmn. communications com.), NAM (past v.p., dir.). Methodist. Clubs: Rotary; Forsyth Country (Winston-Salem.); Univ. (N.Y.C.); City (Raleigh); Coral Bay (Morehead City). Home: 756 Pine Valley Rd Winston-Salem NC 27106 Office: RJ Reynolds Industries Inc Winston-Salem NC 27102

WADE, GLEN, educator, elec. engr.; b. Ogden, Utah, Mar. 19, 1921; s. Lester Andrew and Nellie (Vanderwerff) W.; B.S. in Elec. Engring., U. Utah, 1948, M.S., 1949; Ph.D., Stanford U., 1954; m. LaRee Bailey, Mar. 20, 1945; children—Kathleen Ann, RaLee, Lisa Jean, Mary Sue. Research group leader, asso. prof. elec. engring. Stanford U., 1955-60; asso. dir. engring., microwave and power tube div. Raytheon Co., 1960-61, asst gen. mgr. research div., 1961-63; dir. Sch. Elec. Engring., Cornell U., 1963- 66, J.P. Levis prof. engring., 1963-66, prof. elec. engring. U. Calif. at Santa Barbara, 1966—. Indls. adviser U. R.I., 1961-63; vis. lectr. Harvard, 1963; cons. to industry, 1956—; vis. prof. Tokyo. U., 1971; Fulbright-Hays lectr., Spain, 1972-73; cons. mem. Dept. Def. Adv. Group Electron Devices, 1966-73. U.S. del. Tech. Cooperation Program internat. meeting, 1970. Served with USNR, 1944-46. Recipient annual award Nat. Electronics Conf., 1959, Outstanding Teaching award Acad. Senate, U. Calif., Santa Barbara, 1977. Fellow IEEE (mem. adminstrv. com. profl. group election devices 1960-71, mem. publs. bd., chmn. info. processing com., mem. exec. com. 1971-72, dir. 1971-72, chmn. ednl. activities bd. 1971-72, now editor proc.); mem. Am. Phys. Soc., Phi Kappa Phi, Tau Beta Pi, Sigma Xi, Eta Kappa Nu (Outstanding Young Elec. Engr. award 1955). Editor: Transactions on Electron Devices, 1961-71, IEEE Jour. Quantum Electronics, 1965-68; series editor Harcourt Brace and World, 1964—. Contbr. to profl. jours. Home: 1098 Golf Rd Santa Barbara CA 93108

WADE, HARRY VAN NUYS, ins. co. exec.; b. Lafayette, Ind., Apr. 8, 1902; s. Harry and Anna E. (Fullenwider) W.; B.Arch., Cornell U., 1927; m. Agnes Throop Lester, June 16, 1928; children—Elizabeth Wade Freiberger, Harry V., Douglas M. Architect, Shreve, Lamb & Harmon, N.Y.C., 1927-31; asst. to pres. United Mut. Life Ins. Co., 1931-36; v.p. charge operations Am. United Life Ins. Co., 1936-41; pres. Standard Life Ins. Co. of Ind., 1941-67, chmn. bd., 1962-79; dir. Gen. Grain, Acme Evans Milling Co., Early Daniel Grain Co., Tidewater Grain Corp.; pres. Advisers Fund Mgmt. Corp. Chmn., Indpls. Housing Authority, 1948-50. Trustee Hanover Coll.; bd. dirs. Indpls. Symphony Orch., Civic Theatre. Mem. Cornell U. Alumni Assn. (past nat. pres.), Sigma Chi (past nat. pres.). Clubs: Masons, Shriners. Died June 23, 1979. Home: 6335 Riverview Dr Indianapolis IN 46220

WADE, JAMES FRANCIS, security and commodity broker; b. Chgo., May 23, 1927; s. James Francis and Helen (O'Neill) W.; B.S., Loyola U., Chgo., 1950; m. Joan Fanning, Aug. 9, 1952; children—Eileen, Kathleen, James, Hugh. With Harris Trust & Savs. Bank, Chgo., 1950-51; Lamson Bros. & Co., 1951-59; partner Lamson Bros. & Co., Chgo., 1959-76; exec. v.p., dir. Shearson Hayden Stone Inc., 1976-78; chmn. Julien Collins & Co., 1978—. Served with AUS, 1945-47. Mem. Midwest Stock Exchange (gov. 1972-76), Chgo. Bd. Trade. Home: 200 We Go Trail Mount Prospect IL 60056 Office: 230 W Monroe St Chicago IL 60606

WADE, JAMES O'SHEA, publisher; b. Atlanta, June 17, 1940; s. Richard J. and Mary Clare (O'Shea) W.; A.B. magna cum laude, Harvard, 1962; m. Linda Norman, June 19, 1971; 1 son, Christopher Scott. Editor Blaisdell Pub. Co., N.Y.C., 1963-65; asst. to pres., sr. editor Macmillan Co., 1966-69; editor-in-chief World Pub. Co., 1969-71; v.p., editorial dir. David McKay Co., 1971-74; founder, pres. Wade Pub. Co., Inc., N.Y.C., 1975-78; exec. v.p. Rawson, Wade Pubs., Inc., N.Y.C., 1978—. Democrat. Clubs: Harvard, Dutch Treat (N.Y.C.); Iroquois/D.U., Hasty-Pudding Inst. 1770 (Harvard). Home: RD 1 Baptist Church Rd Yorktown Heights NY 10598 Office: 630 3d Ave New York NY 10017

WADE, JAY PAUL, utilities exec.; b. Port Arthur, Tex., Dec. 28, 1919; s. Jay Paul and Myra (Davis) W.; student La. State U., 1937-38; La. Tech., 1938-40; m. Clarice S. Smith, Dec. 12, 1942; children—William Allan, Nikki Ann Orton. News editor Ruston (La.) Daily Leader, 1940-41; editor, pub. various weekly newspapers in La., 1945-48; exec. editor Minden (La.) Herald, Webster Rev., 1953-54; gen. mgr. Webster Printing Co., 1953-54; pub. relations rep. Bozell & Jacobs, Inc., Shreveport, 1948-50, sr. account exec., N.Y.C., 1954-56; mgr. advt. and pub. relations Central Ill. Pub. Service Co., Springfield, 1956-66, v.p. marketing, 1966-77, v.p. pub. relations, 1977—. Mem. or former mem. all utility industry maj. advt., pub. relations and mktg. coms. Publicity dir. St. Johns Hosp. bldg. fund drive, 1969—, Springfield and Sangamon County United Fund Campaign, 1972-73, 78. Served to 1st lt. USMCR, 1941-45, to capt., 1950-52; maj. Res. ret. Recipient La. Pub. Affairs Research Council 1st ann. award for outstanding editorial on govt., 1953, Distinguished Service award U.S. Jr. C. of C., 1955; named Outstanding Young Man of Year, Owensboro (Ky.) Jr. C. of C., 1955; recipient Printers Ink Silver Medal award Springfield Advt. and Pub. Relations Club, 1966. Mem. Am. Legion (past vice comdr. La. dept.). Home: 29 Greencastle Circle Springfield IL 62703 Office: 607 E Adams St Springfield IL 62701

WADE, JOHN EDWARD, lawyer, supermarket exec.; b. Fostoria, Ohio, Sept. 8, 1918; s. Ora Raymond and Minnie (Miller) W.; B.A. cum laude Findlay Coll., 1939; student U. Mich. Law Sch., 1939-40; J.D., Ohio No. U., 1942; LL.M., Cleve. Marshall Law Sch., 1961, S.J.D., 1962; LL.M., Western Res. U., 1966; m. Marie Greenwood, Aug. 26, 1942; children—Patricia Lynn (dec.), David Warner. Admitted to Ohio, bar, 1942; pvt. practice, Fostoria, 1945-55; asst. title officer Cuyahoga Title Co., Cleve., 1955-56; atty. Great Atlantic & Pacific Tea Co., Cleve., 1956-61; atty. Cook United, Inc., Cleve., 1961-75, sec., 1967-75, v.p., 1973-75; sec. Pick-N-Pay Supermarkets, Inc., Maple Heights, Ohio, 1975-78, corp. atty., 1975-77, v.p., gen. counsel, 1977-78; sr. v.p. legal affairs, sec. 1st Nat. Supermarkets, Inc., Maple Heights and Hartford, 1978—. Served to 1st lt., Med. Administrv. Corps, AUS, 1942-45. Mem. Delta Theta Phi. Mason (32 deg., Shriner). Home: 17420 Edgewater Dr Lakewood OH 44107 Office: 17000 Rockside Rd Maple Heights OH 44137 also One Myrtle St Hartford CT 06105

WADE, JOHN WEBSTER, educator; b. Little Rock, Mar. 2, 1911; s. John William and Sarah Vista (Webster) W.; A.B., U. Miss., 1932, J.D., 1934; LL.M., Harvard U., 1935, S.J.D., 1942; m. Mary Moody Johnson, June 1, 1946; children—John, Mary, William, Ruth. Asst. prof. law U. Miss., 1936-38, asso. prof., 1938-40, prof., 1940-47; vis. prof. law U. Tex., 1946-47; prof. law Vanderbilt U., 1947—, distinguished prof. law, 1971—, dean, 1952-72; vis. research prof. law Columbia U., 1964-65; vis. prof. Cornell U., 1972, U. Mo.-Columbia, 1976-77; chmn. Southeastern Conf. Law Tchrs., 1963-64; admitted to Miss. bar, 1934, Tenn. bar, 1947; uniform laws commr. State Tenn., 1961—, v.p. Nat. Conf. Commrs. Uniform State Laws, 1977-79. Trustee Southwestern at Memphis. Served as lt. USMC, 1943-45. Mem. Am. Bar Assn., Am. Law Inst. (council 1960-70), Nashville, N.Y.C. bar assns., Am. Judicature Soc. (dir. 1962-66), Assn. Am. Law Schs. (exec. com. 1957), Tenn., Miss. (pres. jr. bar sect., 1945-46) bar assns., Sigma Nu, Order of Coif (nat. pres. 1973-76), Phi Alpha Delta, Omicron Delta Kappa, Phi Eta Sigma, Eta Sigma Phi, Sigma Upsilon, Blue Key, Phi Kappa Phi. Presbyn. (permanent judicial commn. Presbyn. Church U.S. 1952-58, 62-66, chmn. 1954-58, 62-66, permanent nominating com. 1969-72, chmn. 1971-72). Author: Cases and Materials on Restitution, 1958, 2d edit., 1966; (with others) Cases and Materials on Legal Methods, 1969; Cases and Materials on Torts, 6th edit., 1976. Reporter: Restatement of Torts (2d), 1970—. Editor: Miss. Law Jour., 1933-34; faculty editor Vanderbilt Law Rev., 1948-52. Contbr. articles to law revs., other publs. Home: 215 Arden Pl 4400 Belmont Park Terr Nashville TN 37215

WADE, JOHN WILLIAM, educator; b. Florence, Ala., Dec. 25, 1925; s. Alex Chisolm and Myrtle Esther (Kent) W.; B.A. magna cum laude, Harvard U., 1949, B.Arch., 1952; postgrad. town planning (Fulbright scholar) Univ. Coll., London, 1952-53; M.Arch., U. Pa., 1964; m. Flora W. Fay, Mar. 1952 (div. Mar. 1960); children—Mark, Bret, Paul; m. 2d, Donna White, Sept. 30, 1965. Designer, Perry, Shaw & Hepburn, Boston, 1952; designer, job capt. Eero Saarinen & Assos., Bloomfield, Mich., 1953-56; job capt. Hideo Sasaki & Assos., landscape architects, Somerville, Mass., 1956-57; ind. practice architecture, Hilton Head, S.C., 1957-63; asso. prof., head div. architecture Tuskegee (Ala.) Inst., 1964-68; dean Sch. Architecture and Urban Planning, U. Wis.-Milw., 1968-75, prof. architecture, 1975-77; prof. architecture Va. Poly. Inst. and State U., Blacksburg, 1978—; co-chmn. Wis. Exam. Bd. for Architects, Engrs., Land Surveyors and Designers, 1968-75. Served with USAAF, 1944-45. Recipient grant Irwin Sweeney Miller Found., 1972-73. Registered architect, Wis., Ala., S.C. Mem. AIA, Assn. Collegiate Schs. Architecture, Nat. Council Archtl. Registration Bds., Environ. Design Research Assn. Author: Architecture, Problems, and Purposes, 1976. Office: Coll Architecture and Urban Studies Va Poly Inst and State U Blacksburg VA 24060

WADE, RICHARD ARCHER, research co. exec.; b. Fitchburg, Mass., Aug. 16, 1930; s. Burleigh Allison and Anne (Archer) W.; student U. Fla., 1952-53; B.S. magna cum laude, U. Miami, 1956, M.A., 1962, Ph.D., 1968; m. Molly Price, Mar. 8, 1976; children—Debra, Donna. Instr. U. Miami Inst. Marine Sci., 1959-62, 64-66; aquatic biologist Dade County (Fla.) Dept. Pub. Health, 1962-64; marine biologist Ayerst Labs., N.Y.C., 1966-68; head dept. ecology/pollution Va. Inst. Marine Sci., Gloucester Pt., 1969-70; asso. prof. U. Va., 1969-72; chief Bears Bluff Lab., Charleston, S.C., 1970-71; exec. sec. Sport Fishing Inst., Washington, 1971-72; exec. dir. Am. Fisheries Soc., Washington, 1972-75; pres. Environ. Scis. Research Corp., Miami, 1972—; sec.-treas. Seacamp, Inc., Miami, 1970—; adj. prof. U. Miami, 1971-73; cons. IBM Corp. Trustee Sport Fishery Research Found., Washington; bd. dirs. Renewable Natural Resources Found. Served with USMCR, 1948-49, 50-52. Rust Found. fellow; Sport Fishery Research Found. fellow; USPHS grantee, 1966. Mem. Am. Fisheries Soc., Sport Fishery Research Found., Marine Tech. Soc., Am. Soc. Limnology and Oceanography, Am. Soc. Ichthyologists and Herpetologists, Alpha Kappa Kappa. Presbyn. (deacon 1962). Editor: Am. Fisheries Soc. Newsletter, 1973—; asst. editor Exec. News Service, 1972. Home: 14229 Mocho Ave Albuquerque NM 87123 Office: US Fish and Wildlife Service 75 Spring St SW Atlanta GA 30303

WADE, RICHARD CLEMENT, educator, historian; b. Des Moines, July 14, 1922; s. Clement F. and Henrietta (Bush) W.; B.A., U. Rochester, 1944; Ph.D., Harvard, 1954; m. Cynthia H. Whitaker, July 1, 1975. From instr. to prof. history U. Rochester, 1948-61; prof. history Washington U., St. Louis, 1961-62, U. Chgo., 1962-70; prof. Grad. Center City U. N.Y., 1971—. Vis. prof. Emory U., 1966; Barry Bingham vis. prof. U. Louisville, 1967; Harmsworth prof. modern history Oxford (Eng.) U., 1974-75; lectr. Salzburg Seminar Am. Studies, 1955; State Dept. specialist to Australia and New Zealand, 1966; Harmsworth prof. Am. history Queen's Coll., Oxford, Eng., 1974-75. Chmn. N.Y. State Bd. Historic Preservation; mem. N.Y. State Commn. on Archives and Records; bd. dirs. Regional Plan Assn. Mem. Am. Hist. Assn., Orgn. Am. Historians, Urban History Group. Author: The Urban Frontier, 1959; Slavery in the Cities, 1964; (with H. Wilder and L. C. Wade) A History of the United States, 1966; (with Harold Mayer) Chicago: The Growth of a Metropolis, 1969. Editor: Urban Life in America Series; Rise of Urban America Series, 1973; Rise of Metropolitan America, 1974; Negroes in American Life; Cities in American Life; The Cities, 1976. Office: Grad Center City U NY 33 W 42d St New York City NY 10036

WADE, ROBERT HIRSCH BEARD, assn. exec., former govt. ofcl.; b. Tamaqua, Pa., Oct 5, 1916; s. Edgar Gerber and Annabelle (Hirsch) W.; A.B. magna cum laude, Lafayette Coll., 1937; diplome d'etudes universitaires Bordeaux U., 1938; Ph.D., Yale, 1942; m. Eleanor Marguerite Borden, Sept. 14, 1946; 1 son, Gregory Borden. Instr. French, Yale, 1939-42; chief Far Eastern analyst Office Naval Intelligence, 1946-54; asst. dir. Office Nat. Security Council Affairs, Dept. Def., Washington, 1954-56, dir., 1956-61; dir., coordinating staff NSC and Collateral Affairs, 1961; spl. asst. to asst. sec. state for ednl. and cultural affairs, 1962; dir. multilateral and spl. activities Bur. Ednl. and Cultural Affairs, Dept. State, 1962-64; U.S. permanent rep. to UNESCO, with rank of minister, 1964-69; asst. dir. U.S. Arms Control and Disarmament Agy., Washington, 1969-73; exec. dir. Fgn. Student Service Council, Washington, 1974-77; dir. Washington office Am. Assembly Collegiate Schs. Bus., 1977—. Mem. U.S. del. to UNESCO Gen. Confs., 1962, 1964, 1966, 68; dep. U.S. mem. exec. bd. UNESCO, 1964-69, mem. U.S. Nat. Commn. for UNESCO, 1977—, chmn., 1978—; trustee Am. Coll. in Paris, 1967-78, chmn. bd., 1967-69. Served to lt. USNR, World War II. Recipient Merit Citation award Nat. Civil Service League. Mem. Phi Beta Kappa, Kappa Delta Rho. Christian Scientist. Clubs: Union Interalliee, Racing (Paris); Chevy Chase (Washington). Home: 3049 W Lane Keys NW Washington DC 20007 Office: 1755 Massachusetts Ave NW Washington DC 20036

WADE, ROBERT PAUL, lawyer, govt. ofcl.; b. Atlantic City, Aug. 22, 1936; s. John Joseph and Irene Madeline (Saxon) W.; A.B., George Washington U., 1963, J.D., 1968; m. Jeanne Krohn, Aug. 5, 1979; 1 son, Elliott Saxon. Admitted to D.C. bar, 1968; mem. firm Denning & Wohlstetter, Washington, 1968-69; atty. Office Comptroller Gen. U.S., Washington, 1969-72; gen. counsel Nat. Endowment for Arts, Washington, 1972—; vis. lectr. Stanford U., N.Y. U., George Washington U. Served with U.S. Army, 1955-58. Mem. Phi Sigma Tau. Home: Box 467 Rt 1 Bluemont VA 22012 Office: 2401 E St NW Washington DC 20506

WADE, WILLIAM HAMPTON, chemist; b. San Antonio, Nov. 3, 1930; B.S., St. Mary's U., 1951; Ph.D., U. Tex. at Austin, 1955; m. Lillian Alice Stephens, Sept. 10, 1951. Postdoctoral research U. Calif. at Berkeley, 1955-58; postdoctoral research chemistry dept. U. Tex. at Austin, 1958-61, asst. prof., 1961-66, asso. prof., 1966-72, prof., 1972—, chmn., 1974—; mem. Nat. Colloid Symposium Com., 1968. Mem. Faraday Soc., Am. Chem. Soc. (chmn. div. coolloid and surface chemistry, 1976, vice-chmn. 1974-76), Soc. Petroleum Engrs., Sigma Xi. Home: 2707 Valley Springs Rd Austin TX 78746 Office: U Tex Dept Chemistry WEL 2-204 Austin TX 78712

WADKINS, CHARLES LEROY, biochemist; b. Joplin, Mo., May 8, 1929; s. Arthur Roy and Alice Marie (Montgomery) W.; B.A., U. Kans., 1951, Ph.D., 1956; m. Patricia True, July 13, 1952; children—Melanie, Patrik. Fellow dept. physiol. chemistry Johns Hopkins U. Med. Sch., 1956-57, instr., 1957-59, asst. prof. physiol. chemistry, 1959-63, asso. prof., 1963-66; prof. biochemistry, chmn. dept. biochemistry U. Ark., 1966—; mem. NSF Adv. Panel; sect. organizer Gordon Conf.; chmn. Orgn. Com. for Toxicology Tng. Program; mem. NSF Program Com. to Stimulate Competitive Research. Recipient Career Devel. award NIH, 1960-66; NIH postdoctoral fellow, 19565-7; NIH grantee, 1960—; NSF grantee, 1969-73. Mem. Am. Soc. Biol. Chemists, Am. Chem. Soc., Biochem. Soc., Internat. Assn. Dental Research. Research numerous publs. biochemistry. Home: 2400 Dogwood Ln Little Rock AR 72210 Office: 4301 W Markham St Little Rock AR 72201

WADLEIGH, JOHN REMEY, former naval officer; b. Washington, Sept. 24, 1915; s. John Winthrop and Mary (Remey) W.; B.S., U.S. Naval Acad., 1937; m. Ray Williams, June 3, 1939; children—Anne Winthrop, Marjorie Terry. Commd. ensign USN, 1937, advanced through grades to rear adm., 1965; various assignments in ships, 1937-40; watch and div. officer U.S.S. Yorktown, 1940-42; flag lt. to comdr. cruisers Task Force 16, 1942-43; assigned U.S. Naval Postgrad. Sch., 1943-44; staff communications officer on staff comdr. cruisers-destroyers Pacific Fleet, 1944-45; ops. officer on staff comdr. Cruiser Div. 16, 1945-46; gunnery officer U.S.S. N.C., 1946-47; student Armed Forces Staff Coll., 1947-48; instr. communications Gen. Line Sch., Newport, R.I., 1948-50; comdr. U.S.S. John R. Pierce, 1950-51; asst. head Europe, Africa and Middle E. br., internat. affairs div. Office Chief Naval Ops., 1951-54; comdr. Escort Squadron 16, 1954-55; readiness and tng. officer, asst. chief staff ops. on staff comdr. Destroyer Force, Atlantic Fleet, 1955-58; comdr. U.S.S. Grand Canyon, 1958-59; communications plans officer on joint staff U.S. Comdr. in Chief, Europe, 1959-62; comdg. officer U.S.S. Springfield, 1962-63; chief of staff, aide to comdr. Cruiser-Destroyer Force, Atlantic Fleet, 1963-64; dep. dir. naval communications for communications Navy Dept., 1964-65; asst. dep. dir. def. communication system Def. Communications Agy., 1965-67; comdr. Cruiser-Destroyer Flotilla 4, also comdr. Cruiser-Destroyer Force, U.S. Atlantic Fleet rep. in Norfolk, Va., 1967-69, also comdr. Cruiser Destroyer Flotilla 12, 1968; comdr. Tng. Command, U.S. Atlantic Fleet, Norfolk, Va., 1969-71; sr. analyst Analytic Adv. Group, McLean, VA., 1971—. Pres. Seaport '76 Found., Ltd., Newport, R.I., 1974-77. Decorated Silver Star, Legion of Merit (3), Commendation ribbon. Clubs: Army Navy (Washington); Army-Navy Country (Arlington, Va.); N.Y. Yacht; Reading Room, Newport Country, Clambake (Newport). Home: Jamestown RI 02835 also 313 Swan's Wharf Rd Brick Market Pl Newport RI 02840

WADLEIGH, KENNETH R., coll. dean; b. Passaic, N.J., Mar. 27, 1921; s. Wilfred Russell and Myrtle (Labaugh) W.; S.B. and S. M. in Mech. Engring., Mass. Inst. Tech., 1943, Sc.D. in Mech. Engring., 1953; M.A. (hon.), U. Cambridge (Eng.), 1954; m. Jeanne Stockbarger, Sept. 10, 1948; children—Gregg Robert, Karen Jeanne. Instr. mech. engring. Mass. Inst. Tech., 1946-49, asst. prof., 1950-53, asso. prof., 1953-61, prof., 1961—, dean student affairs, 1961-69, v.p., 1969—, dean Grad. Sch., 1975—. Bd. dirs. Harvard Community Health Plan, Mass. Heart Assn. Served with USNR, 1943-46. Recipient Goodwin medal for conspicuously effective teaching Mass. Inst. Tech., 1952, Bronze Beaver award Mass. Inst. Tech. Alumni Assn., 1969. Mem. ASME, Sigma Xi, Pi Tau Sigma, Tau Beta Pi. Club: St. Botolph (Boston). Home: 44 Clairemont Rd Belmont MA 02178 Office: 3-136 Mass Inst Tech Cambridge MA 02139

WADLEIGH, WINTHROP, lawyer; b. Milford, N.H., Jan. 23, 1902; s. Fred Tilton and Alice Bancroft (Conant) W.; A.B. magna cum laude, Dartmouth, 1923; J.D., Harvard, 1927; m. Sylvia Moore Leach, June 11, 1932 (dec. Sept. 1967); children—Theodore, James L.; m. 2d, Faith Preston, Dec. 19, 1970. Admitted to N.H. bar, 1927; practiced in Concord, 1927-29, Manchester, 1931—; asso. Robert W. Upton, Esq., 1927- 29; asst. atty. gen. N.H., 1929-31; partner Wadleigh, Starr, Peters, Dunn & Kohls, 1931—, now sr. partner. Dir. Mchts. Nat. Bank of Manchester, 1938-74, Osceola Shoe Co., Inc. Del. N.H. Constl. Conv., 1930; mem. Commn. to Revise Corp. Laws of N.H., 1932; moderator Ward I, Manchester, 1942-46; sec. Amoskeag Co., 1957-65, now hon. sec.; chmn. Christian Friends Drive, United Jewish Appeal, 1964; pres. Manchester br. NAACP, 1965-67; treas. Fund for Animals, Inc., N.Y.C., 1967-75; chmn. investment com. N.H. Conf. United Ch. of Christ, 1967—; vice-chmn., bd. dirs. N.H. Civil Liberties Union, 1967—; mem. N.H. Commn. for Human Rights, 1967-70; chmn. Brotherhood Week in N.H., 1968; chmn. SPACE, 1968-75; treas. ACLU, N.Y.C., 1969-75, bd. dirs., 1967-73. Bd. dirs. N.H. chpt. NCCJ, 1965-75; trustee White Pines Coll., Chester, N.H., Gale Home, Cogswell Benevolent Trust, Blanche A. Bruce Charitable Trust. Recipient Brotherhood award N.H. chpt. Nat. Conf. Christians and Jews, 1970. Mem. Am., N.H., Manchester bar assns., Dartmouth Assn. of Manchester (pres.), Audubon Soc. N.H. (life), Soc. for Protection N.H. Forests (life), Phi Beta Kappa Assos. (life), Phi Beta Kappa. Conglist. (trustee, deacon). Mason, Kiwanian. Contbr. chpt. to Religion Ponders Science, 1964. Home: Walnut Hill Chester NH 03036 Office: 95 Market St Manchester NH 03101

WADLEY, ELLEN PEARL, broadcasting producer; b. Little Rock, Dec. 6, 1924; d. Theodore C. and Effie Pearl (Ritchie) Wadley; B.A. with honors, U. Ark., 1945. Clk., Am. embassy, London, 1945-46; writer, broadcaster Sta. WAFS, Wiesbaden, Ger., 1946-47; chief script writer Sta. WTOP, Washington, 1948-51; asst. to dir. spl. events CBS News, Washington, 1951; radio and TV writer, network contact with Pub. Info. Office, A.R.C., Washington, 1951-53; partner Wilson-Wadley Pub. Relations, Washington, 1953-56; press info. officer CBS News, Washington, 1956-60, producer weekly news programs, 1960-67; producer, dir. pub. affairs CBS Radio News, Washington, 1967—. Recipient Eastman award Outstanding Woman in Broadcasting, 1964. Mem. Am. Women in Radio and TV (past chpt. pres.), Radio and TV Corr. Assn., Am. Newspaper Women's Club, Phi Beta Kappa, Sigma Delta Chi, Kappa Kappa Gamma. Club: Washington Press (pres. 1976-77). Home: 4201 Cathedral Ave NW Washington DC 20016 Office: CBS News 2020 M St NW Washington DC 20036

WADLIN, GEORGE KNOWLTON, JR., assn. exec.; b. New Haven, Sept. 20, 1923; s. George Knowlton and Laura (Mason) W.; B.S. in Civil Engring., Pa. State U., 1948; M.S., U. Maine, 1953; Ph.D., Carnegie Inst. Tech., 1959; m. Nora Elizabeth Thompson, July 29, 1944 (div. Dec. 1974); children—Gail Thompson, George Knowlton III, Lela Mason; m. 2d, Josephine C. Perkins, Aug. 2, 1975 (div. Apr. 1977); m. Ruth Feldman Schwartz, Oct. 1977. Mem. faculty U. Maine, 1948-69, prof. civil engring., 1961-69, head dept., 1958-69; research prof. engring. George Washington U., 1967-68; prof., head dept. civil engring. Mich. Tech. U., 1969-78; dir. edn. services and continuing edn. ASCE, N.Y.C., 1978—. cons. civil and structural engr., 1953—. Served with AUS, 1942-46; ETO. Registered profl. engr., Maine. Fellow ASCE; mem. Am. Soc. Engring. Edn. (chmn. civil engring. div. 1970-71, chmn. profl. interest council I, dir. 1976-78), Sigma Xi, Lambda Chi Alpha, Tau Beta Pi, Chi Epsilon, Phi Kappa Phi. Contbr. articles to profl. jours. Home: 10 Geneva Rd Norwalk CT 06850 Office: 345 E 47th St New York NY 10017

WADLINGTON, WALTER JAMES, legal educator; b. Biloxi, Miss., Jan. 17, 1931; s. Walter and Bernice (Taylor) W.; A.B., Duke, 1951; LL.B., Tulane U., 1954; m. Ruth Miller Hardie, Aug. 20, 1955; children—Claire Hardie, Charlotte Taylor, Susan Miller, Derek Alan. Admitted to La. bar, 1954, Va. bar, 1965; practice law, New Orleans, 1954-55, 58-59; asst. prof. Tulane U., 1960-62; mem. faculty U. Va., 1962—, prof law, 1964—, James Madison prof., 1970—; Fulbright fellow, tutor civil law U. Edinburgh (Scotland), 1959-60. Served to capt. AUS, 1955-58. Mem. Va. Bar Assn., Am. Law Inst., Order Coif. Author: (with Paulsen) Cases and Materials on Domestic Relations, 1970, 3d edit., 1978. Home: 1620 Keith Valley Rd Charlottesville VA 22901

WADMOND, LOWELL CURTIS, lawyer; b. Racine, Wis., Mar. 16, 1896; s. Christian George and Celia (Jensen) W.; Mus.B. cum laude, Chgo. Mus. Coll., 1921; Ph.B. cum laude, U. Chgo., 1922, J.D. cum laude, 1924; m. Mary Elita Cason, July 27, 1938. Admitted to Ill. bar, 1924, Wis. bar, 1925, N.Y. bar, 1926, U.S. Supreme Ct. bar, 1940; with Tolman, Sexton & Chandler, Chgo., 1924-26; asst. U.S. atty. for So. dist. N.Y., 1926-30; spl. asst. atty. gen. N.Y. State, 1929-31; spl. asst. to atty. gen. of U.S., 1930; mem. com. character and fitness, appellate div. Supreme Ct. of N.Y., 1st dept., 1934—, chmn., 1959—; mem. firm White & Case, N.Y.C., 1935—; dir. Texasgulf, Inc., 1949-73, hon. dir., 1973—; dir. Canrad Hanovia, Inc. Trustee Robert A. Taft Meml. Found.; trustee, vice chmn. Robert A. Taft Inst. Govt. Pres., dir. Met. Opera Assn. N.Y.C., 1951-56, vice chmn., dir., 1956-70, chmn. bd., dir., 1970-74, hon. pres., dir., 1974-75, chmn. emeritus, 1975-76, hon. life dir., 1976—; dir. The Villas, Inc., Palm Beach, Fla. Chmn. exec. com. Nat. Rep. Club, 1943-49; del. Nat. Rep. Conv., 1952. Trustee Grant Monument Assn., Parker Sch. Fgn. and Comparative Law, Columbia U.; trustee William M. Sullivan Musical Found., Inc.; bd. dirs. Lincoln Center for Performing Arts, 1970-75. Served with 340th Inf., U.S. Army, World War I. Decorated comdr. Royal Order North Star (Sweden), Order St. Dennis of Zente, Societe d'Encouragement Au Progres; recipient Pub. Service citation U. Chgo. Fellow Am. Bar Found.; mem. Am. Soc. Internat. Law, Bagby Music Lovers' Found. (pres. 1955-65, chmn. 1965-72, trustee emeritus), Assn. Bar City N.Y., N.Y. County Lawyers Assn., N.Y. State, Am., Internat. bar assns., Am. Coll. Trial Lawyers, Internat. Law Assn., Consular Law Soc., Am. Bible Soc. (v.p.), Am. Law Library Middle Temple (hon.), N.Y. Lawyers Club (pres. 1945-57, gov.), Order of Coif. Presbyterian (life elder, trustee emeritus). Mason. Clubs: University, Metropolitan Opera (pres. 1945-47), Downtown Assn. (N.Y.C.); Everglades, Bath and Tennis (Palm Beach). Home: 1192 Park Ave New York NY 10028 also The Villas 425 Worth Ave Palm Beach FL 33840 Office: 14 Wall St New York NY 10005

WADSWORTH, CHARLES WILLIAM, pianist, artistic dir.; b. Barnesville, Ga., May 21, 1929; s. Charles and Ethel (Capps) W.; student U. Ga., 1946-48; B.S., Juilliard Sch. Music, 1951, M.S., 1952; m. Susan Popkin, June 5, 1966; 1 dau., Rebecca; children from previous marriage—David, Beryl. Founder, artistic dir. Noon Day Chamber Music Concerts of Spoleto (Italy) Festival, 1960-77; founder, artistic dir. Chamber Music Soc., of Lincoln Center, N.Y.C., 1969—; pianist in recitals with Beverly Sills, Hermann Prey, Jennie Tourel, Shirley Verrett, Pinchas Zuckerman; founder, artistic dir. Spoleto/USA Festival Chamber Music Concerts, Charleston, S.C., 1977. Decorated Cavaliere Officiale nel Ordine di Merito dall Reppublica Italiana, 1975; recipient Mayors award for excellence in the arts, N.Y.C., 1979. Office: Chamber Music Soc Alice Tully Hall 1941 Broadway New York NY 10021

WADSWORTH, CHRISTOPHER, headmaster; b. Boston, June 18, 1940; s. Philip Pearson and Elizabeth (Shaffer) W.; B.A., Harvard, 1962, M.A.T., 1966, M.A., 1969; m. Lori Ann Dingman, July 27, 1963; children—Benjamin, Thomas Pearson. Andover teaching fellow Phillips Acad., Andover, Mass., 1962-63; asst., admissions office Harvard, 1963-65, asst. dir. advanced standing, 1965-67, dir. advanced standing, sr. adviser faculty arts and scis., 1967-69; headmaster Nichols Sch., Buffalo, 1969-79, Belmont (Mass.) Hill Sch., 1979—. Bd. advisers Buffalo Council World Affairs, 1970—; mem. Camp Becket com. New Eng. area council YMCA, 1968-73. Trustee N.Y. State Assn. Ind. Schs. (v.p.), Andover Alumni Council Phillips Acad.; bd. dirs. Buffalo Zool. Soc. Mem. Assn. Country Day Sch. Headmasters, Headmasters Assn., Phi Delta Kappa. Clubs: Pundits, Harvard of Buffalo (pres. 1975). Home: 350 Prospect St Belmont MA 02178

WADSWORTH, DYER SEYMOUR, co. exec.; b. N.Y.C., June 16, 1936; s. Seymour and Phoebe Armistead (Helmer) W.; B.A., Yale Coll., 1959; J.D., Harvard U., 1962; m. Beverley Allen Dunn Barringer, Feb. 2, 1963; children—Sophia, Jennifer. Admitted to N.Y. bar, 1963; asso. firm Humes, Andrews & Botzow, N.Y.C., 1962-64; with Inco Ltd. and its U.S. subs., N.Y.C., 1964—; now v.p., chief counsel, dir. ESB Ray-O-Vac Corp.; dir. Universal Electric Co., Owosso, Mich.; v.p., dir. Barringer Crater Co., Princeton, N.J. Mem. Am., N.Y. State bar assns., Assn. Bar City N.Y. (lawyers adv. council), Am. Soc. Corporate Secs., Inc., Meteoritical Soc., Nat. Assn. Mfrs. Club: Down Town Assn. (N.Y.C.). Home: 215 E 48th St New York NY 10017 Office: 5 Penn Center Plaza PO Box 8109 Philadelphia PA 19101

WADSWORTH, FRANCIS THOMAS, oil co. exec.; b. Ralls County, Mo., May 12, 1916; s. William Henry and Julia Ann (megown) W.; B.S. in Chemistry, NE Mo. State U., 1939; M.S., U. Mo., 1941, Ph.D., 1947; m. Marian Simmons, Dec. 21, 1941; children—Charlotte Ann, William Matthew, Thomas Marion. Research chemist Am. Oil Co., Texas City, Tex., 1942-46, research supr., 1948-57, asst. research dir., 1957-60; lab. mgr. Cities Service Co., Lake Charles, La., 1960-67, dir. chem. research and devel., Cranbury, 1967-71, dir. petroleum products and process dept., 1971-76, dir. chem. research, 1976—. Mem. Am. Chem. Soc., N.Y. Chemists Club. Methodist. Patentee in field. Contbr. articles to profl. jours. Home: 6 Empress Ln Lawrenceville NJ 08648 Office: Drawer 4 Cranbury NJ 08512

WADSWORTH, FRANK WHITTEMORE, educator; b. N.Y.C., June 14, 1919; s. Prescott Kingsley and Elizabeth Browning (Whittemore) W.; grad. Kent Sch., 1938; A.B., Princeton, 1946, M.A. (Woodrow Wilson fellow 1946-47), 1948, Ph.D. (Scribner fellow 1948-49), 1951; m. Roxalene Harriet Nevin, Oct. 22, 1943; children—Susan W. Emmons, Roxalene W. Taylor. Instr. English, Princeton U., 1949-50; from instr. to asso. prof. English. U. Calif. at Los Angeles, 1950-61; prof. English, dean div. humanities U. Pitts., 1962-67; acad. v.p. State U. N.Y. Coll. at Purchase, 1967-78, prof. lit., 1967—; vis. prof. Trinity Coll., Hartford, Conn., summer 1960. Nat. rep., cons. Woodrow Wilson Nat. Fellowship Found., 1958-61, trustee, 1973—; trustee Wenner-Gren Found., 1970—, chmn., 1977—; trustee Rye Country Day Sch., 1970-76. Served as aviator USNR, 1942-45. Folger Shakespeare Library fellow, 1961; Guggenheim fellow, 1961-62. Mem. Malone Soc., Modern Lang. Assn., Am. Soc. Theater Research, Phi Beta Kappa (hon.). Clubs: Century; Conanicut (R.I.) Yacht; Princeton (N.Y.C.). Author: The Poacher from Stratford, 1958; also articles. Home: 20 Stonehedge Dr S Greenwich CT 06830

WADSWORTH, HOMER CLARK, found. exec.; b. Pitts., Apr. 3, 1913; s. Leon Kearns and Ethel (Raynor) W.; A.B., U. Pitts., 1935; grad. student U. Chgo., 1935-36, U. Minn., 1936-37; LL.D., Tarkio (Mo.) Coll., 1961; Ed.D., Avila Coll., Kansas City, Mo., 1963; LL.D., U. Mo., 1964; m. Alice Pilkington Crutchfield, Nov. 11, 1939; children—Robert Raynor, Harriet Crutchfield, Alice Wadsworth Pasini, Homer Clark, Ethel Raynor, Marjorie Jane, James Leon. Teaching asst. U. Minn., 1936-37; adminstrv. asst. Office Mayor Pitts., 1937-39; exec. dir. Pitts. Planning Commn., 1939-42; supt. Pitts. Bur. Recreation, 1942-44; dir. Pitts. Dept. Parks and Recreation, 1945-46; v.p. New Sch. Social Research, N.Y.C., 1947-48; exec. dir. Kansas City (Mo.) Assn. Trusts and Founds., 1949-64, pres., dir., 1964-74; dir. Cleve. Found., pres. Cleve. Found. Resources, 1974—, Council on Founds., 1965—; cons. pub. affairs program Ford Found., USPHS, Greater Kansas City Mental Health Found., Nat. Endowment Humanities, Nat. Inst. Mental Health, HEW, Battelle Inst.; v.p., dir. Kansas City Gen. Hosp. and Med. Center, Community Research Assos., N.Y.C. Pres. Kansas City Bd. Edn., 1962-70; mem. Gov. Mo. Com. Arts, 1962-72; chmn. President's Council Youth Fitness, 1958-62; mem. Nat. Health Manpower Council, 1967-70. Chmn. bd. trustees Park Coll., Parkville, Mo., 1967-70. Served with USNR, 1944-45. Recipient Chancellor's medal U. Kansas City, 1965. Mem. Mo. Acad. Squires. Office: 700 National City Bank Bldg Cleveland OH 44114

WADSWORTH, JEFFERY PAGE REIN, ins. co. exec.; b. Toronto, Ont., Can., July 27, 1911; s. William Rein and Mildred (Jeffery) W.; student Lakefield Coll. Sch., Upper Can. Coll.; m. Elizabeth Cameron Bunting, Sept. 21, 1940; 1 dau. With Canadian Bank of Commerce, 1928-61, v.p., dir., 1957-61; bank merged with Imperial Bank of Can., 1961; v.p., gen. mgr. Canadian Imperial Bank Commerce, 1961-63, pres., 1963-64, vice chmn., 1964-70, dep. chmn., 1970-71, dep. chmn., pres., 1971-73, chief exec. officer, 1971-76, chmn., 1973-76; dir. Can. Imperial Bank Commerce, Campbell Soup Co., Massey-Ferguson Ltd., Holt Renfrew & Co., Ltd., MacMillan Bloedel Ltd., Bayer Fgn. Investments Ltd.; chmn. bd. dirs. Confedn. Life Ins. Co., Toronto, 1977—. Bd. govs. Lester B. Pearson Coll. Pacific, Lakefield Coll. Sch.; chmn. bd. govs. U. Waterloo. Clubs: York, Toronto (Toronto); Mt. Royal, St. James's (Montreal); Ranchmen's (Calgary, Alta.); Hamilton (Ont.). Home: Apt 4 7 Austin Terrace Toronto ON M5R 1Y2 Canada Office: Head Office Commerce Ct Toronto M5L 1A2 ON Canada

WADSWORTH, JOSEPH ALLISON CANNON, physician; b. Charlotte, N.C., Mar. 22, 1913; s. Joseph Allison Cannon and Mary (Henkel) W.; B.S., Davidson Coll., 1935, D.Sc. (hon.), 1977; M.D., Duke U., 1939; m. Martha Toms Buchanan, June 27, 1942; children—Martha (Mrs. Robert Haley), Mary (Mrs. Thomas S. White III), Joseph Allison Cannon III. Intern Bellevue Hospital, N.Y.C., 1939-42; resident Inst. Ophthalmology, Columbia Presbyn. Hosp., N.Y.C., 1945-48; pvt. practice ophthalmomgy, N.Y.C., 1949-65; attending ophthalmologist Presbyn. Hosp. and Vanderbilt Clinic, 1959-65; attending surgeon Roosevelt Hosp., 1961-64; asso. clin. prof. ophthalmology Columbia, 1959-65; prof. ophthalmology, chmn. dept. Duke Med. Center, 1965-78, chmn. emeritus, 1978—; cons. VA Hosp., Durham, Durham County Gen. Hosp., Durham, Nat. Society for Prevention of Blindness; spl. research ophthalmol. pathology; lectrs. in field. Bd. dirs. Nat. Soc. Prevention Blindness, vice chmn. med. adv. com. N.C. soc.; bd. visitors Davidson Coll. Served as flight surg. USAAF, 1942-45. Diplomate Am. Bd. Ophthalmology (chmn. 1973-74), Nat. Bd. Med. Examiners. Mem. Ill. Soc. Ophthalmology and Otolaryngology (hon.), Pacific Coast Soc. Ophthalmology and Otolaryngology (hon.), N.Y. Ophthal. Soc. (hon.), W.Va. Soc. Ophthalmology and Otolaryngology (hon.); A.C.S., Am. Acad. Opthalmologists and Otolaryngologists (1st v.p. 1974), Am. Ophthalmol. Soc. (pres. 1975-76), N.Y. Acad. Medicine, Verhoeff Soc., N.C. Soc. Ophthalmology, N.C. Bd. Med. Examiners, Assn. U. Profs. Ophthalmology, So. Med. Assn. (chmn. sect. on ophthalmology 1972), Soc. Eye Surgeons, N.Y. State Med. Soc., N.Y. Acad. Scis., Am. Assn. Ophthalmology, N.Y. Acad. Medicine, Med. Soc. County N.Y., Assn. Research in Vision and Ophthalmology, Pan Am. Assn. Ophthalmology, Sigma Xi, Sigma Alpha Epsilon, Omicron Delta Kappa, Alpha Omega Alpha, Nu Sigma Nu, Sigma Upsilon. Co-author: Atlas of Ophthalmic Surgery, 2d edit.; editorial cons.: Welcome Trends in Ophthalmology. Home: 112 Montrose Dunbarton Durham NC 27707

WADSWORTH, PHILIP ADRIAN, educator; b. Youngstown, Ohio, Dec. 2, 1913; s. Roscoe Conkling and Avis (Hamersly) W.; A.B., Yale, 1935, Ph.D. (fellowship for study in France 1938), 1939; m. Charlotte Louise Riley, Feb. 28, 1942; children—George (dec.), Adrian R., Avis H. (Mrs. Michael Rumney). Instr., then asst. prof. French, Yale, 1939-42, 45-50; asso. prof. Northwestern U., 1950-51; prof. French, U. Ill., 1954-64; prof. French, chmn. dept., dean humanities Rice U., 1964-65, prof. French, 1965-73; prof. French, U. S.C., Columbia, 1973—. Served to comdr. USNR, 1942-45, 52-53. Guggenheim fellow, 1949-50; fellow Folger Shakespeare Library, 1971. Mem. Modern Lang. Assn., Am. Assn. Tchrs. French, Modern Lang. Tchrs. Assn. Author: The Novels of Gomberville, 1942; Young La Fontaine, 1952; Poésies de Tristan l'Hermite, 1962; Molière and the Italian Theatrical Tradition, 1977. Home: 101 Shannondale Ct Columbia SC 29209

WADSWORTH, ROBERT HAIGH, investment firm exec.; b. Bklyn., Jan. 29, 1940; s. James Alfred and Julia (Pitt) W.; A.B., Princeton U., 1962; M.B.A., Pace U., 1971; m. Nina Susan Jansson, Aug. 10, 1963; children—Susan Haigh, James Jansson. Accountant Coopers & Lybrand, N.Y.C., 1962-65; with Calvin Bullock Ltd., N.Y.C., 1965-79, asst. v.p., 1971-73, v.p., treas., 1973-79; with Bache Halsey Stuart Shields Inc., N.Y.C., 1979, v.p., 1979—; v.p., sec., treas. Money Mart Assets Inc., 1979—, chancellor High Yield Fund, Inc., 1979—, Chancellor Tax-Exempt Daily Income Fund, Inc., 1979—. Served to lt. AUS, 1963-65. Mem. Princeton Alumni Assn. (pres. 1977—). Clubs: Princeton (N.Y.C.); Montclair Golf. Home: 93 Overlook Rd Upper Montclair NJ 07043 Office: 100 Gold St New York NY 10038

WAECHTER, ARTHUR JOSEPH, JR., lawyer; b. New Orleans, Nov. 20, 1913; s. Arthur Joseph and Elinor (Reckner) W.; A.B., Tulane U., 1934, LL.B., 1936; m. Peggy Weaver, Feb. 20, 1939; children—Susan Porter Waechter McClellan, Sally Ann Waechter McGehee, Robert. Admitted to La. bar, 1936, since practiced in New Orleans; partner firm Jones, Walker, Waechter, Poitevent, Carrere & Denegre, 1942—; prof. law Tulane U. Sch. Law, 1947-68. Dir. Bank of New Orleans & Trust Co., Canal Barge Co., Inc., Central Marine Service, Inc., Eugenie and Joseph Jones Family Found. Bd. visitors Tulane U., 1959-64; bd. advisers to editors Tulane Law Rev. Assn., 1960—; bd. adminstrs. Tulane Ednl. Fund, 1968—. Served to lt. (j.g.) USNR, 1943-46. Mem. Am., La. (gov. 1968- 70), New Orleans (pres. 1961-62) bar assns., Tulane U Alumni Assn. (pres. 1962-63), Nat. Assn. Coll. and U. Attys., Newcomen Soc., Order of Coif, Phi Kappa Sigma, Phi Delta Phi. Clubs: Pickwick, Boston, Stratford, International House, Round Table, Southern Yacht, Louisiana, The Plimsoll (New Orleans); Pinnacle (N.Y.C.). Home: 1210 Webster St New Orleans LA 70118 Office: 225 Baronne St New Orleans LA 70112

WAEHLER, FRANK JAMES, architect; b. Jersey City, June 23, 1920; s. Frederick and Josephine (Barry) W.; B.Arch., Cooper Union, 1948; student N.Y. U. Sch. Architecture, 1940-41; m. Catherine Patricia Caivano, Nov. 7, 1942; children—James, Kathleen (Mrs. Chester Nosal), Steven Patrick. Architect, designer, project mgr. Voorhees, Walker, Smith & Smith, N.Y.C., 1945-60; asso. Voorhees, Walker, Smith, Smith & Haines, 1960-62; partner Haines Lundberg Waehler, N.Y.C., 1962—. Trustee Cooper Union, 1970. Served to 2d lt. USAAF, 1942-45. Mem. A.I.A., N.Y. State Assn. Architects, Bldg. Research Inst., Regional Plan Assn. N.Y., N.Y. Bldg. Congress, Archtl. Assn. London, Nat. Football Found. and Hall of Fame, N.Y., Peter Cooper Soc. Roman Catholic. Clubs: Union League (N.Y.C.); Echo Lake Country (Westfield). Home: 760 Lawrence Ave Westfield NJ 07090 Office: 2 Park Ave New York NY 10016

WAELSCH, SALOME GLUECKSOHN, geneticist; b. Danzig, Germany, Oct. 6, 1907; came to U.S., 1933, naturalized, 1938; d. Ilyia and Nadia Gluecksohn; student U. Konigsberg (Ger.), U. Berlin; Ph.D., U. Freiburg (Ger.), 1932; m. Heinrich B. Waelsch, Jan. 8, 1943; children—Naomi Barbara, Peter Benedict. Research asso. in genetics Columbia U., 1936-55; asso. prof. anatomy Albert Einstein Coll. Medicine, 1955-58, prof., 1958-63, prof. genetics, 1963—, chmn. dept. genetics, 1963-76; mem. study sects. NIH. Mem. Am. Soc. Zoologists, Am. Assn. Anatomists, Genetics Soc., Soc. Devel. Biology, Am. Soc. Naturalists, Am. Soc. Human Genetics, Nat. Acad. Scis., Sigma Xi. Research, numerous publs. on devel. genetics. Office: Dept Genetics Albert Einstein Coll Medicine 1300 Morris Park Ave Bronx NY 10461

WAETJEN, WALTER BERNHARD, univ. pres.; b. Phila., Oct. 16, 1920; s. Walter E. and Marguerite D. (Dettmann) W.; B.S., State Coll., Millersville, Pa., 1942; M.S., U. Pa., 1947; Ed.D., U. Md., 1951; m. Betty Walls, Sept. 28, 1945; children—Walter Bernhard, Kristi (Mrs. Richard Jenkins), Daniel G. Profl. football player with Detroit Lions and Phila. Eagles, 1942-45; tchr. Sch. Dist. Phila., 1945-48; research fellow U. Md., 1948-50, mem. faculty, 1950-73, prof. ednl. psychology, 1957-65, dir. Bur. Ednl. Research and Field Services, 1962-65, gen. dir. Interprofl. Research Commn. Pupil Personnel Services, 1963-65, v.p. adminstrv. affairs, 1965-70, v.p. gen. adminstrn., 1970-73; pres. Cleve. State U., 1973—; Patty Hill Smith meml. lectr. U. Louisville, 1964; psychol. cons. to sch. systems, 1951—; dir. Union Commerce Bank Cleve. Trustee Downtown Cleve. Corp., Gray Drug Stores, Inc. Bd. dirs. Greater Cleve. Growth Assn., Ohio World Trade Center, Cleve. Council on World Affairs, 1974—, Cleve. Internat. Program, 1974—, Cleve. Scholarship Programs, Inc., 1974—, United Way Cleve., 1973—; trustee Am. Nat. Red Cross; mem. exec. com. Boy Scouts Am., 1976—; mem. adv. com. Cleve. Arts Council. Recipient Disting. Alumni award Pa. State Coll., 1972. Mem. NEA, Assn. Supervision and Curriculum Devel., Soc. Research Child Devel., AAAS, Am. Edn. Research Assn., Blue Key, Iota Lambda Sigma, Phi Delta Kappa, Phi Kappa Phi. Clubs: 50; Rotary of Cleve., Union; Masons (33 deg.). Co-author sourcebooks in field. Contbr. ednl. jours. Home: 14706 Larchmere Blvd Shaker Heights OH 44120 Office: Cleve State Univ Cleveland OH 44115

WAGENER, HOBART DEAN, architect; b. Sioux Falls, S.D., May 10, 1921; s. Frank Samuel and Beatrice (Hobart) W.; student Augustana Coll., 1939-41; B.Arch., U. Mich., 1944; m. Violet LaVaughn Whipple, Dec. 16, 1944; children—Diane Kay, Jeffrey Scott, Shaw Bradley. Archtl. draftsman Eggers & Higgens, architects, N.Y.C., 1946-47; archtl. designer Pietro Belluschi, architect, Portland, Oreg., 1947-50; practice architecture as Hobart D. Wagener Assos., Boulder, Colo., 1953-77, Wagener Vandervorste Architects, 1977—. Mem. Colo. Supreme Ct. Selection Com., 1970; chmn. Boulder City Planning Commn., 1966; pres. Boulder Jr. Achievement, 1964. Served to lt. (j.g.) USNR, 1944-46. Recipient numerous nat. and regional archtl. design awards. Fellow AIA (pres. Colo. 1972); mem. Boulder C. of C. (pres. 1971). Lion (pres. Boulder 1965). Co-author: The School Library. Home: 2965 Baylor Ave Boulder CO 80303 Office: 737 29th St Boulder CO 80303

WAGENER, JAMES WILBUR, univ. pres.; b. Edgewood, Tex., Mar. 18, 1930; s. James W. and Ima (Crump) W.; B.A., So. Methodist U., 1951; M.A., U. Tex., Austin, 1967, Ph.D. (Ellis fellow 1967-68), 1968; m. Ruth Elaine Hoffman, May 31, 1952; children—LuAnn Wagener Powers, Laurie Kay. Instr. edn. U. Tex., Austin, 1967-68, asst. prof., 1970-74; asst. prof. U. Tenn., Knoxville, 1968-70; asst. to chancellor acad. affairs U. Tex. System, 1974; asso. prof. U. Tex., San Antonio, 1974-78, acting pres., 1978, pres., 1978—, prof. div. edn. Coll. Multidisciplinary Studies, 1978—; asst. to pres., then exec. asst. to pres. U. Tex. Health Sci. Center, San Antonio, 1974-78, acting dean Dental Sch., 1976-78. Bd. govs. Southwest Found. Research and Edn., San Antonio, 1978—; bd. dirs., trustee Southwest Research Inst., San Antonio, 1978—. Mem. Am. Ednl. Studies Assn., Assn. Instl. Research, Soc. Profs. Edn., Soc. Coll. and Univ. Planning, Greater San Antonio C. of C., Phi Delta Kappa, Phi Theta Kappa. Clubs: Rotary, Torch. Author articles, book revs. in field. Home: 209 Sir Arthur Ct San Antonio TX 78213 Office: Univ Tex San Antonio TX 78285

WAGENKNECHT, EDWARD, author; b. Chgo., Mar. 28, 1900; s. Henry E. and Mary (Erichsen) W.; Ph.B., U. Chgo., 1923, M.A., 1924; Ph.D., U. Wash., 1932; m. Dorothy Arnold, Aug. 3, 1932; children—Robert Edward, David Arnold, Walter Chappell. Prof. of English, Boston U., 1947-65, prof. emeritus, 1965—, editor Boston U. Studies in English, 1954-57; Lowell lectr., 1958. Author many critical and biog. works, including: The Man Charles Dickens, 1929, rev. edit., 1966; Mark Twain, The Man and His Work, 1935, rev., 1961, 67; Cavalcade of the English Novel, 1943, rev. edit., 1954; Cavalcade of the American Novel, 1952; A Preface to Literature, 1954; Longfellow, A Full Length Portrait, 1955; The Seven Worlds of Theodore Roosevelt, 1958; Nathaniel Hawthorne, Man and Writer, 1961; Washington Irving: Moderation Displayed, 1962; The Movies in the Age of Innocence, 1962; Edgar Allan Poe: The Man Behind the Legend, 1963; Chicago, 1964; Seven Daughters of the Theater, 1964; Harriet Beecher Stowe, The Known and The Unknown, 1965; Dickens and the Scandalmongers, 1965; Merely Players, 1966; Nine Before Fotheringhay: A Novel about Mary Queen of Scots (under pseud. Julian Forrest), 1966; Henry Wadsworth Longfellow: Portrait of an American Humanist, 1966; John Greenleaf Whittier: A Portrait in Paradox, 1967; The Personality of Chaucer, 1968; As Far As Yesterday: Memories and Reflections, 1968; William Dean Howells: The Friendly Eye, 1969; The Glory of The Lilies, A Novel about Joan of Arc (under pseud. Julian Forrest), 1969; The Personality of Milton, 1970; James Russell Lowell: Portrait of a Many-Sided Man, 1971; Ambassadors for Christ: Seven American Preachers, 1972; The Personality of Shakespeare, 1972; Ralph Waldo Emerson: Portrait of a Balanced Soul, 1974; (with Anthony Slide) The Films of D.W. Griffith, 1975; A Pictorial History of New England, 1976; Eve and Henry James: Portraits of Women and Girls in His Fiction, 1978; editor: Mrs. Longfellow: Selected Letters and Journals, 1956; The Supernaturalism of New England (John Greenleaf Whittier), 1969; The Letters of James Branch Cabell, 1974; also numerous anthologies including: The Fireside Book of Christmas Stories, 1945; The Collected Tales of Walter de la Mare, 1950; An Introduction to Dickens, 1952; Chaucer: Modern Essays in Criticism, 1959; Stories of Christ and Christmas, 1963. Home: 233 Otis St West Newton MA 02165

WAGENKNECHT, ROBERT EDWARD, librarian; b. Seattle, Dec. 8, 1935; s. Edward and Dorothy (Arnold) W.; A.B., Harvard, 1958; M.S. in L.S., Simmons Coll., 1959; M.A., Sangamon State U., 1975; m. Therese Mueller, June 11, 1965; children—George Robert, Caroline Therese. Reference asst. Detroit Pub. Library, 1959-61; head librarian Stoneham (Mass.) Pub. Library, 1961-63; head librarian Winchester (Mass.) Pub. Library, 1963-67; dir. Lincoln Library, Springfield, Ill., 1967-78, City Library, Springfield, Mass., 1978—; mem. Ill. State Library Adv. Com., 1972-77. Mem. Springfield Area Council for Pub. Broadcasting, 1974-78. Bd. dirs. Springfield Symphony Orch., 1969-78; mem. adv. council U. Ill. Grad. Sch. Library Sci., 1976-78; adv. com. minimum standards state aid Mass. Bd. Library Commrs., 1979—; alumni award com. Simmons Coll. Sch. Library Sci., 1979; bd. dirs. Adult Edn. council, Springfield, Mass., 1979—. Mem. Am. (mem. nominating com. reference and adult services div. 1976, chmn. history sect. 1978-79), Ill. (fed. coordinator 1969-71, chmn. pub. library sect. 1971-72, exec. bd. 1971-72, legis.-library devel. com. 1976-77), Music (program chmn. summer conf. 1971) library assns., Sangamon County (Ill.) Hist. Soc. (pres. 1978). Rotarian. Editor: Bay State Librarian, 1964-66. Home: 342 Forest Park Ave Springfield MA 01108 Office: City Library 220 State St Springfield MA 01103

WAGER, WALTER HERMAN, author, editor, pub. relations exec.; b. N.Y.C., Sept. 4, 1924; s. Max Louis and Jessie (Smith) W.; B.A., Columbia, 1943; LL.B., Harvard, 1946; LL.M., Northwestern U., 1949; m. Sylvia Liebowitz Leonard, May 6, 1951 (div. May 1975); 1 dau., Lisa Wendy; m. 2d, Winifred McIvor, June 1975. Editor, Aviation Law Studies, 1947-48; research fellow air law Northwestern U., 1948-49; Fulbright fellow internat. air law U. Paris (France), 1949-50; spl. asst. to Israel dir. Civil Aviation, 1951-52; free-lance writer, 1953; editor UN, 1954-56; writer for TV documentary films and mags., 1956-63; editor of the Playbill, 1963-66; sr. editor of Show, 1965; editorial cons. ASCAP Today, 1965-72, dir. pub. relations, 1972-78; tchr. Northwestern U., 1949, Columbia, 1955-56. Spl. asst. to atty. gen. N.Y. State investigation hate lit. in elections, 1962. Pres. Columbia Coll. Class 1944. Mem. Writers Guild Am., Drama Desk N.Y., Author's League, Nat. Acad. Popular Music (dir.). Democrat. Jewish. Author: (novels) Death Hits the Jackpot, 1954, Operation Intrigue, 1956, I Spy, 1965; (non-fiction) Camp Century, 1962, Masterstroke, 1966, Superkill, 1966, Wipeout, 1967; Countertrap, 1967; (non-fiction) The Playwrights Speak, 1967; Death Twist, 1968; The Girl Who Split, 1969; Sledgehammer, 1970; Viper Three, 1971 (screenplay as Twilight's Last Gleaming, 1977); Swap, 1972 (screenplay 1974); Telefon, 1975 (screenplay 1977); My Side-By King Kong, 1976; Time of Reckoning, 1977; Blue Leader, 1979; Blue Moon, 1979.

WAGER, WILLIS JOSEPH, educator; b. Pittsburg, Kans., July 24, 1911; s. Holmes and Joda (Smith) W.; A.B., Washington U., 1931; A.M., 1932; diploma Kroeger Sch. Music, 1933; exchange fellow U. Frankfurt am Main, 1933-34; Ph.D., N.Y. U., 1943; m. Adah Allen, June 30, 1936 (dec. June 1970); children—Holmes, Geoffrey, Joseph; m. 2d, Inez Morton, May 30, 1971. Asst. English and journalism Washington U., 1932-33; instr. English, N.Y. U., 1935-43; asso. prof. English, Berea Coll., 1943-45; prof. English and humanities Boston U., 1945-77, chmn. dept., 1945-49, prof. emeritus, 1977—; spl. lectr. Am. lit. King Coll., 1977—. Ednl. radio broadcasting Lowell Inst. Coop. Broadcasting Council, Boston, 1945-51; Fulbright prof. Pädagogische Hochschule, Berlin, 1963-64, Istanbul U., 1966-68, Teheran U., 1968-70. Recipient Alumni and Dramatics prize Washington U., 1931. Mem. Modern Lang. Assn. Am., Am. Musicological Soc., Nat. Collegiate Players, Phi Beta Kappa, Sigma Chi, Sigma Upsilon, Delta Simga Rho, Kappa Phi Sigma, Eta Sigma Phi, Sinfonia. Democrat. Presbyterian. Club: Andiron (N.Y.C.). Author: From the Hand of Man, 1963, American Literature, A World View, 1968; Musician's Guide to Copyright and Publishing, 1977. Co-author: Liberal Education and Music, 1962; History of Music, 1973. Author sect. in Gustave Reese, Music in Middle Ages, 1940; Living History of World, 1971. Editor: Life on the Mississippi, 1943. Contbr. articles to scholarly mags. Home: 133 Tadlock Rd Bristol TN 37620 also Ashville ME 04607

WAGGENER, ROBERT GLENN, physicist, educator; b. Benton, Ky., June 12, 1932; s. Virgil Glenn and Dorothy (Shemwell) W.; B.A. in Math., U. Tex., 1954, M.A. in Physics, 1963, Ph.D. in Biophysics, U. Tex. Grad. Sch. of Biomed. Scis., 1967; m. Marcia Ann Voyles, June 27, 1959; children—Jeff, Catherine. Tchr., Taylor (Tex.) High Sch., 1960; research asst. U. Tex., Austin, 1960-61; chief scientist Nucleonics Research & Devel. Corp., Austin, 1961-62; radiol. health specialist Tex. Dept. of Health, Austin, 1962-64; post-doctoral fellow in physics M.D. Anderson Hosp. & Tumor Inst., Houston, Tex., 1967-68; asst. prof. dept. radiology div. med. physics U. Tex. Health Sci. Center, San Antonio, 1968-72, asso. prof., 1972-78, prof., 1978—, radiation safety officer, 1969-76; grant reviewer NSF; cons. in med. and health physics to various med. community and indsl. firms. Served with U.S. Army, 1954-56. Diplomate Am. Bd. Radiology. Mem. Am. Assn. of Physicists in Medicine (pres. S.W. chpt. 1972-73, dir. 1974-77, pres. elect 1979, pres. 1980), Am. Coll. Radiology (mem. physics com. 1977—), Radiol. Soc. N.Am. (mem. sci. exhibits com. 1974—), Biophysics Soc., Radiation Research Soc., Health Physics Soc., IEEE, AAAS, Tex. Radiol. Soc., Soc. of Applied Spectroscopy, Soc. of Photo-Optical Instrumentation Engrs. Republican. Episcopalian. Club: Masons. Contbr. articles on med. physics, radiology and spectroscopy to sci. jours.; mem. editorial bd. 2 jours. in field; co-editor Handbook of Medical Physics. Home: Route 2 PO Box SH 306 Boerne TX 78006 Office: Radiology Dept Univ of Texas Health Science Center 7703 Floyd Curl Dr San Antonio TX 78284

WAGGONER, EUGENE BENJAMIN, cons. engring. geologist; b. Kansas City, Mo., Jan. 7, 1913; s. Benjamin Critchelow and Mary Lavinia (Carpenter) W.; B.A. in Geology, U. Calif., Los Angeles, 1937, M.A., 1939; m. Winifred Margaret Wishart, Aug. 28, 1938; children—Alan Stuart, Diana Margaret, Teresa Mary. Petroleum engr., geologist Tidewater Associated Oil Co., also Superior Oil Co., 1940-45; engring. geologist U.S. Bur. Reclamation, Denver, 1945-54; engring. geologist cons., Denver, 1954-60; exec. v.p., co-mgr. Woodward-Clyde & Assos., Denver, 1960-67, pres., chief exec. officer, San Francisco, 1968-71; pres. parent co. Woodward-Clyde Cons., San Francisco, 1971-73; spl. cons. engring. geology, San Jose, Calif., 1973—; mem. exec. com. U.S. Nat. Com. on Tunneling Tech., 1977-79. Treas. Lakewood (Colo.) Bd. Edn., 1949-50. Registered engr. or geol. engr., Calif., 8 other states. Fellow Am. Cons. Engrs. Council (pres. 1966-67), ASCE, Assn. Soil and Found. Engrs.; mem. Cons. Engrs. Council Colo. (pres. 1961-62), Cons. Engrs. Assn. Calif., Am. Inst. Cons. Engrs., Assn. Engring. Geologists, U.S. Commn. Large Dams, U.S. Nat. Commn. Irrigation and Drainage, Sigma Xi, Sigma Gamma Epsilon, Phi Delta Kappa. Republican. Clubs: Villages Golf and Country, Masons. Contbr. to profl. publns.

WAGGONER, GEORGE RUBLE, coll. adminstr.; b. Wagoner, Okla., Feb. 4, 1916; s. George F. and Verna (Ruble) W.; B.A., U. Kans., 1936, M.A., 1939; Ph.D., U. Wis., 1947; Dr. Edn. and Humanities, U. East, Venezuela, 1969; m. Helen L. Talbert, June 4, 1941 (dec.); children—Jane Catherine, Margaret Louise, Sarah Verna; m. 2d, Barbara F. Ashton, June 9, 1962; stepchildren—Thomas Edward Ashton III, Laura Jennifer Ashton-Lilo. Instr. English, U. Kans., 1938-41; instr. English lit. Pa. State Coll., 1947, asst. prof., 1947-48; asst. prof. English, Ind. U., 1948-53, asst. dean Coll. Arts and Scis., 1948-52, asso. dean, 1952-54, asso. prof. English, 1952-54; prof. English, U. Kans., 1954—, dean Coll. Liberal Arts and Studies, 1954-75; asso. vice-chancellor acad. affairs, 1975—; on leave as adviser Office of Planning, Univ. Sector, Nat. Council Univs., Caracas, Venezuela, 1973. Cons. to Latin Am. Univs., also internat. orgns., dir. Seminar on Higher Edn. in the Americas, 1963-75. Served with USNR, 1942-44. Mem. AAUP, Modern Lang. Assn. Am., Renaissance Soc. Am., Latin Am. Studies Assn., Comparative and Internat. Edn. Soc., Phi Beta Kappa (senator United chpts. 1970-76), Sigma Delta Pi, Sigma Chi. Author: (with Barbara Waggoner) Education in Central America, 1971. Contbr. articles to profl. jours. Home: 726 Louisiana St Lawrence KS 66044

WAGGONER, JAMES NORMAN, physician; b. Elgin, Ill., Nov. 10, 1925; s. Ernest C. and Madeline Ann (Sadler) W.; B.S., Ind. U., 1946; M.D., Ind. U., 1949; m. Patricia Ann Dougherty, Feb. 1, 1947; children—Steven James, Kimberly Ann. Intern, U.S. Naval Hosp., Oakland, Calif., 1950; resident U.S. Navy Sch. Aerospace Medicine, 1950-51; practice medicine, specializing in preventive medicine, Los Angeles, 1957—; flight surgeon United Air Lines, Chgo., Los Angeles, 1952-59; dir. medicine, safety and life scis. The Garrett Corp., 1959—; adj. prof. aviation physiology U. So. Calif., 1958—; sr. med. adviser Western U.S., Air France, 1971—; mem. staff Daniel Freeman Hosp., Inglewood, Calif.; chancellor Internat. Acad. Aviation and Space Medicine, 1977-82. Mem. Gov.'s Com. for Employment Handicapped, Sacramento, 1960—. Served to lt., M.C., USNR, 1949-52. Recipient Spl. citation AMA, 1962; Louis H. Bauer award for most significant contribution to space medicine, 1968. Fellow Aerospace Med. Assn. (pres.). Home: 3352 Via La Selva Palos Verdes Estates CA 90274 Office: 9851 S Sepulveda Blvd Los Angeles CA 90009

WAGGONER, JAMES VIRGIL, plastics co. exec.; b. Judsonia, Ark., Oct. 29, 1927; s. Loren Dye and Vera Wilma (Meacham) W.; B.S. in Chemistry, Ouachita U., 1948; M.A. in Chemistry, Tex. U., 1950; m. Marjorie Elizabeth June Howell, Aug. 22, 1948; children—Liz Ann, Jay Howell. With Monsanto Co., St. Louis, 1950—, gen. mgr. cycle safe div. Monsanto Comml. Products Co., 1976-77, v.p., mng. dir. Monsanto Plastics & Resin Co., 1977-78, group v.p., mng. dir., 1978—. Mem. Soc. Plastics Industry, Mfg. Chemists Assn. Club: Bellerive Country (St. Louis). Home: 109 Frontenac Forest Saint Louis MO 63131 Office: 800 N Lindbergh Blvd Saint Louis MO 63166. *There is nothing so singularly significant toward individual achievement as an early dedication to succeed. Put another way, an individual must have that strong "dedication to excellence" as a basic ingredient of his or her everyday life.*

WAGGONER, LELAND TATE, ins. co. exec.; b. Greensboro, Ga., Feb. 5, 1916; s. Andrew B. and Blanche (Proffitt) W.; A.B., Maryville Coll., 1938; M.B.A. with honors, N.Y. U., 1972; C.L.U., 1941; m. Florence Adelaide Gee, Feb. 15, 1942; children—Frederick Charles, Leonora Blanche. Mgr. Mut. of N.Y., Boston, 1946-54, v.p. Western sect., San Francisco, 1954-57; v.p. sales Life Ins. Co. N.Am., Phila., 1957-63; v.p. sales Home Life Ins. Co., N.Y.C., 1963-69, sr. v.p., dir., 1969—; pres. Home Life Equity Sales Corp., 1970—; instr. Boston U., 1946-49, Stanford Grad. Sch. Bus. Adminstrn., 1957, Past mem. bd.

CLU Inst.; mem. agy. officers round table Life Ins. Mktg. and Research Assn.; life ins. pub. relations council Inst. Life Ins.; adv. bd. N.Y. State Ins. Dept.; mem. life ins. adv. com. Coll. Ins. Bd. mgrs. Am. Bible Soc.; bd. dirs. Maryville Coll., Foster Parents Plan. Served to lt. comdr. USNR, 1942-45. Recipient Walter A. Craig award; Leland T. Waggoner distinguished lecture series in life and health ins. established at Ga. State U. Mem. Am. Soc. C.L.U.'s, Tenn Soc., Newcomen. Soc. Episcopalian. Clubs: Merchants (N.Y.C.); Baltusrol Golf. Author: You Can See the World in Forty Days!; contbg. author Life Ins. Sales Mgmt. Handbook, other booklets. Asso. editor CLU Jour., 1946—; co-editor The Life Insurance Policy Contract; cons. editor, contbg. author: Life and Health Insurance Handbook. Home: 83 Slope Dr Short Hills NJ 07078 Office: 253 Broadway New York NY 10007

WAGGONER, LYLE WESLEY, actor; b. Kansas City, Kans., Apr. 13, 1935; s. Myron and Marie W.; student Washington U., St. Louis; m. Sharon Adele Kennedy, Sept. 17, 1960; children—Jason Kennedy, Beau Justin. With MGM Talent Program, 1964, 20th Century Fox, 1966; actor Carol Burnett show, 1968-74; host star It's Your Bet, 1969; star TV series The New Adventures of Wonder Woman, 1977-79; stage appearances include Teahouse of the August Moon, Born Yesterday, Boeing-Boeing. Served with AUS, 1954-56. Address: care J Carter Gibson Agy 19000 Sunset Blvd Los Angeles CA 90069. *Never expect anything from anyone, but always be grateful when you get it.**

WAGGONER, MARGARET ANN, coll. pres., physicist, educator; b. Centerville, Iowa, Aug. 27, 1926; d. Walter Loyal and Kathryn (Maring) Waggoner; B.A., State U. Iowa, 1946, M.S., 1948, Ph.D., 1950. Instr. physics Vassar Coll., Poughkeepsie, N.Y., 1950-54, asst. prof., 1954-58; asst. prof. Stanford, 1958-61; asso. prof. U. Md., College Park, 1961-65; asso. prof. physics U. Iowa, Iowa City, 1965-70; dean Smith Coll., Northampton, Mass., 1970-73, prof. physics, 1970-75; pres., prof. physics and history and philosophy of sci. Wilson Coll., Chambersburg, Pa., 1975-79; vis. scholar, spl. cons. to pres. for planning Radcliffe Coll., Cambridge, Mass., 1979—. Mem. Am. Phys. Soc., Am. Assn. Physics Tchrs., AAAS, Phi Beta Kappa, Sigma Xi. Office: Radcliffe Coll 10 Garden St Cambridge MA 02138

WAGGONER, PAUL EDWARD, scientist; b. Appanoose County, Iowa, Mar. 29, 1923; s. Walter Loyal and Kathryn (Maring) W.; S.B., U. Chgo., 1946; M.S., Iowa State Coll., 1949, Ph.D., 1951; m. Barbara Ann Lockerbie, Nov. 3, 1945; children—Von Lockerbie, Daniel Maring. With Conn. Agrl. Expt. Sta., 1951—, vice dir., 1969-72, dir., 1972—; lectr. Yale Forestry Sch., 1962—; dir. N.E. Bancorp Inc., Union Trust Co. Mem. Conn. Environ. Policy Com., 1970; mem. Conn. Com. Rev. Laws Governing Pesticides, 1963, Conn. Clean Water Task Force, 1966, Conn. Task Force for Preservation Agrl. Land, 1974—. Served with USAAF, 1943-46. Fellow Am. Soc. Agronomy, AAAS, Am. Phytopathol. Soc.; mem. Am. Acad. Arts and Sci., Am. Meteorol. Soc. (award outstanding achievement biometerology 1967), Am. Soc. Plant Physiology, Nat. Acad. Scis., Conn. Acad. Sci. and Engring. (v.p. 1976—). Club: Grads. (New Haven). Guggenheim fellow, 1963. Contbr. to profl. jours. Home: 314 Vineyard Rd Guilford CT 06437 Office: 123 Huntington St New Haven CT 06511

WAGGONER, RAYMOND WALTER, neuropsychiatrist; b. Carson City, Mich., Aug. 2, 1901; s. Charles W. and Anna J. (Herrick) W.; student Highland Park (Mich.) Jr. Coll., 1918-19; student U. Mich., 1919-20, M.D., 1924; Sc.D., U. Pa. Grad. Sch. Medicine, 1930; m. Marion Donnelly, Apr. 12, 1930; children—Raymond Walter, Karen. Intern, Harper Hosp., Detroit, 1924-25; resident Phila. Orthopedic Hosp., and Infirmary for Nervous Diseases, 1925-26; lab. intern Pa. Hosp., Phila., 1926; asso. with grad. course Pa. Hosp. for Nervous and Mental Diseases, 1927-28; Commonwealth Fund fellow, 1926-29; with U. Mich., 1929—, asst. prof. of neurology and asst. neurologist Univ. Hosp., 1929-32, asso. prof. and neurologist, 1932-36, prof. psychiatry, 1937—, dir. Neuropsychiat. Inst., 1937-70, chmn. dept. psychiatry, 1937-70, prof. emeritus, 1970—; pvt. practice psychiatry, 1970—; cons., Reproductive Biology Research Found., St. Louis, 1970—; disting. vis. prof. psychiatry U. Louisville Med. Sch., 1974—; chmn. liaison com. Am. Psychiat. Assn. and Am. Hosp. Assn., 1957-67; U.S. com. World Fedn. for Mental Health, 1959; cons. surg. gen. U.S. Army, 1958-76; adv. to dir. SSS, 1943-48; mem. commn. Mich. Dept. Mental Health, 1945-49, sr. clin. cons., 1974—. Bd. dirs. Masters and Johnson Found., 1970—, Behavioral Sci. Found., 1978—. Recipient Disting. Faculty Achievement award U. Mich., 1968, Med. Alumni award, 1974. Fellow AAAS, Am. Psychiat. Assn. (mem. council 1943-47, 1954-57, pres. 1969-70); mem. Am. Neurol. Assn., Soc. for Biol. Psychiatry, Central Neuropsychiat. Assn. (pres. 1951-52), Am. Geriatrics Soc., Group for Advancement of Psychiatry, Assn. Research in Nervous and Mental Diseases, AMA, Am. Psychopathol. Assn. (councillor 1946), Mich. Epilepsy Center and Assn. (past dir.), Acad. Psychoanalysis, Mich. Soc. for Pastoral Care (dir. 1945, v.p. 1947-49), Mich. Assn. Professions, Washtenaw County Med. Soc., Mich. Med. Soc. (mental hygiene com.), World Med. Assn., Mich. Soc. Neurology and Psychiatry (pres. 1941-42), Mich. Acad. Sci., Mich. Soc. for Mental Health (dir.), Am. Coll. Psychiatrists (pres. 1966-67, E.B. Bowis award 1968), Am. Assn. Chairmen Depts. Psychiatry (pres). Club: Cosmos. Contbr. sect. to comprehensive textbook Psychiatry, also Medicine; contbr. articles to profl. jours. Home: 3333 Geddes Rd Ann Arbor MI 48105 Office: U Hosp Ann Arbor MI 48104

WAGMAN, FREDERICK HERBERT, librarian, educator; b. Springfield, Mass., Oct. 12, 1912; s. Robert and Rebecca (Gaberman) W.; A.B. summa cum laude, Amherst Coll., 1933; A.M., Columbia, 1934, Ph.D., 1942; L.H.D., Amherst Coll., 1958; LL.D. (hon.), Alderson Broaddus Coll., 1967; Litt.D., Luther Coll., 1969; m. Ruth Jeannette Wagman, Nov. 21, 1941; children—Elizabeth L., William G. Instr. Columbia Extension, 1933-35; Ottendorfer Meml. fellow N.Y.U., 1935-36; teaching fellow Amherst, 1936-37; instr. U. Minn., 1937-42; head planning unit postal div. U.S. Office Censorship, Washington, 1942-43, head regulations and training sect., 1943-45, regulations officer, 1945; successively acting dir. personnel and acting dir. adminstrv. services Library of Congress, 1945-46, asst. dir. reference dept., 1946-47, dir. processing dept., 1947-51, dep. chief asst. librarian, 1951- 52, dir. adminstrn., 1952-53; dir. U. Mich. library, Ann Arbor, 1953-78, prof. library sci., 1953—; librarian Mich. Acad. Arts, Sci., Letters, 1953-78; vice chmn. com. mgmt. Wm. L. Clements Library, 1973-78; exec. com. Mich. Hist. Collections, 1953-78; cons. UN Library, 1959-62, Hebrew U. of Jerusalem, 1969. Vice chmn. Nat. Commn. on Obscenity and Pornography, 1968-70; pres. Midwest Region Library Network, 1975-76. Bd. dirs. Council on Library Resources, 1956—; bd. regents Nat. Library of Medicine, 1967-71. Mem. Am. (pres. 1963-64), Mich. (pres. 1960) library assns., Phi Beta Kappa, Phi Kappa Phi. Democrat. Author: Magic and Natural Science in German Baroque Literature, 1942. Home: 2979 Hickory Ln Ann Arbor MI 48104

WAGMAN, ROBERT JOHN, journalist; b. Chgo., Nov. 11, 1942; s. Albert Alan and Rosamond (Horner) W.; A.B., St. Louis U., 1966, M.A., 1968, J.D., 1971; m. Carol Ann Mueller, Jan. 30, 1965; children—Jennifer, Robert, Patricia, Marilyn. Analyst, Dun & Bradstreet, 1965-67; with CBS News, 1967-71, 74-77; asst. to dean St. Louis U. Sch. Law, 1971-74; Washington bur. chief N. Am. Newspaper Alliance, 1977—. Recipient Thomas Stokes award in journalism, 1977. Author: (with Sheldon Engelmayer) Hubert Humphrey, The Man and His Dream, 1978, Citizens Guide to the Tax Revolt, 1979. Office: 890 National Press Bldg Washington DC 20045

WAGNER, ALAN CYRIL, broadcasting co. exec.; b. N.Y.C., Oct. 1, 1931; s. Joseph and Isabelle (Chanson) W.; A.B., Columbia, 1951, M.A. in English, 1952; m. Martha Celia Dreyfus, Mar. 11, 1956; children—David Mark, Susan Jill, Elizabeth Celia. Mgr. network programs Benton & Bowles, Inc., N.Y.C., 1957-61; producer, dir. host program Living Opera, WNYC/WNYC-FM, N.Y.C., 1958-68; with CBS, N.Y.C., 1961—, dir. program devel., 1965-68, v.p. program devel., Hollywood, Calif., 1968-73, v.p. program planning and devel., N.Y.C., 1973-75, v.p. nighttime programs, 1975-78, v.p. programs, 1978—: host radio broadcasts N.Y.C. Opera Co. Served to lt. (j.g.) USNR, 1953-57. Mem. Am. Arbitration Assn., Acad. TV Arts and Scis., Internat. Radio and TV Soc., Columbia Coll. Alumni Assn., Columbia Coll. Grad. Faculty Alumni Assn. Author: Prima Donnas and Other Wild Beasts, 1961; also articles. Home: 205 E 63d St New York NY 10021 Office: 51 W 52d St New York NY 10019. *A decent and abiding respect for the opinions and talents of the creative community on one hand, and the consuming community on the other, has always served as the necessary framework for any decision making in both my professional and personal life. The doers and the thinkers are crucially important, but no more so than those for whom they do and think. If I can serve as an effective middle man, a good part of my life's objective is realizable.*

WAGNER, CARRUTH JOHN, physician; b. Omaha, Sept. 4, 1916; s. Emil Conrad and Mabel May (Knapp) W.; A.B., Omaha U., 1938, B.Sc., U. Nebr., 1938, M.D., 1941, D.Sc., 1966. Intern, U.S. Marine Hosp., Seattle, 1941-42; resident gen. surgery and orthopaedic surgery USPHS hosps., Shriners Hosp., Phila., 1943-46; med. dir. USPHS, 1952-62; chief orthopaedic service USPHS Hosp., San Francisco, 1946-51, S.I., N.Y., 1951-55, health mblzn., 1959-62, asst. surgeon gen. dep. chief div. hosps. UPHS, 1957-59, chief div. USPHS, 1962-65, chief div. Indian Health, 1962-65, dir. Bur. Health Services, 1965—. Served with USCGR, World War II. Recipient Pfizer award, 1962; Meritorious award Am. Acad. Gen. Practice, 1965; Distinguished Service medal, 1968. Diplomate Am. Bd. Sugery, Am. Bd. Orthopaedic Surgery. Fellow A.C.S. (bd. govs.), Am. Soc. Surgery Hand, Am. Assn. Surgery Trauma, Am. Geriatrics Soc., Am. Acad. Orthopaedic Surgeons; mem. Nat. Assn. Sanitarians, Am. Pub. Health Assn. Sanitarians, Am. Pub. Health Assn., Washington Orthopaedic Club, Am. Legion, Alpha Omega Alpha. Lutheran. Mason (Shriner). Contbr. articles to med. jours. Home: 6234 Silverton Way Carmichael CA 95608 Office: PO Box 638 Carmichael CA 95608. *My success can best be summarized as the result of efforts of other people. First my family, particularly my mother, then my teachers and perceptors, and finally my associates. Throughout my life there has been a key individual who created an environment where I could exercise my maximum capabilities. Later in life when it became possible for me to provide similar opportunities for associates I found the benefits I derived far exceeded anything I could have achieved on my own. In summary, success means getting things done, getting planned things done, and getting planned things done largely through other people.*

WAGNER, CHARLES ABRAHAM, journalist, poet; b. N.Y.C., Mar. 10, 1901; s. Morris and Fannie (Haut) W.; student L.I. Med. Coll., 1918-19; A.B., Columbia U., 1924; m. Ruth Waters, 1920; m. 2d, Celia Wagner, July 9, 1930; children—Carl and Caryl (twins). Journalist, Lit. Supplement, Morning World, 1925-26; drama revs. Morning Telegraph, 1926-29; book rev. editor Bklyn. Times, 1930-32; lit. editor Daily and Sunday Mirror, N.Y.C., 1932—; book, art critic, editor in chief N.Y. Sunday Mirror Mag. for King Features Syndicate, 1957-63; instr. journalism N.Y. U. Winner Poetry Mag. 1st award for "The Unknown Soldier," 1929; Stratford mag. poetry award, 1930; Edwin Markham poetry award, 1933; Harvard Nieman fellowship in Journalism, 1945. Mem. Am. Newspaper Guild, Authors League, Poetry Soc. Am. (First prize 1971, exec. sec. 1964—), Am. Acad. Polit. and Social Sci. Clubs: Harvard, Nat. Arts (N.Y.C.). Author: Poems of the Soil and Sea, 1923; Nearer the Bone (poems), 1929; Rhymes Out of School, 1941; editor: Prize Poems, 1930; Freemen of the Press (biography), 1940; Harvard: Four Centuries and Freedoms (history), 1950; Hades on Hudson and Other Poems; contbr. to Poetry, Am. Mecury, Forum, Nation, N.Y. Times, Chgo. Tribune, Atlantic, Sat. Rev. Lit. Rep. poet U.S. for UNESCO, Internat. Biennale Poetry, Belgium, 1968. Home: 106 Morningside Dr New York NY 10027 Office: 15 Gramercy Park New York NY 10003

WAGNER, CHARLES W., gen. merchandise co. exec.; b. Santa Fe, Apr. 30, 1919; s. M. and Flora M. W.; student Coll. Mines and Metallurgy, El Paso, Tex., 1937-39, Tex. A. and M. U., 1940-41; m. Harriett Marie Haninger, Feb. 1, 1939; children—Sandra Adamek, Charlene Devine, Roger, Craig. With Montgomery Ward, 1941—, v.p., gen. mgr. South Central region, Kansas City, 1969-75, dir., Chgo., 1970—, sr. v.p., 1975-77, exec. v.p., 1977—; dir. Frank Paxton Co., Kansas City, Bank of Commerce, Ft. Worth. Fin. adv. Ft. Worth Jr. League; mem. adv. bd. Boy Scouts Am., United Way. Mem. Am. Mgmt. Assn., Chgo. Assn. Commerce and Industry, Newcomen Soc. N.Am. Roman Catholic. Clubs: Chgo., Mid-Am.; Club Internat.; Fort Worth, Shady Oaks Country (Ft. Worth). Home: 626 Roaring Springs Rd Fort Worth TX 76114 Office: Montgomery Ward Plaza Chicago IL 60671

WAGNER, CHRISTIAN NIKOLAUS JOHANN, engr., educator; b. Saarbrucken-Dudweiler, Ger., Mar. 6, 1927; came to U.S., 1959, naturalized, 1969; s. Christian Jakob and Regina (Bungert) W.; student U. Poitiers, France, 1948-49; Licence es Sci., U. Saar (Ger.), 1951, Diplom-Ingenieur, 1954, Dr.rer.nat., 1957; m. Rosemaria Anna Mayer, Apr. 5, 1952; children—Thomas Martin, Karla Regina, Petra Susanne. Research asst. Inst. fur Metallforschung, Saarbrucken, 1953-54; vis. fellow M.I.T., 1955-56; research asso. Inst. fur Metallforschung, 1957-58, teaching, research asst. U. Saarbrucken, 1959; asst. prof. Yale U., New Haven, Conn., 1959-62, asso. prof., 1962-70; prof. dept. materials engring. UCLA, 1970—, chmn. dept., 1974-79; vis. prof. Tech. U., Berlin, 1969. Mem. Am. Phys. Soc., Am. Crystallographic Assn., Am. Inst. Metall. Engrs., Am. Soc. Metals, Sigma Xi. Contbr. articles to profl. jours. Home: 20407 Seaboard Rd Malibu CA 90265 Office: 6531 Boelter Hall Univ of Calif Los Angeles CA 90024

WAGNER, CLARENCE J., lawyer; b. St. Paul, July 9, 1905; s. George H. and Helen Marie (Jasper) W.; grad. St. Thomas Coll., 1928; LL.B., Minn. Coll. Law, 1932; m. Hilaria Pontius, July 13, 1935; children—Thomas George, Mary Helen, Charles Joseph. Admitted to Minn. bar, 1932; pvt. law practice, Mpls., 1932—; partner Wagner, Johnston, Falconer, Ltd.; formerly gen. counsel Credit and Fin. Mgmt. Assn.; formerly v.p. Murray's, Inc.; past sec. Kausel Foundry Co.; past treas. Service Ideas, Inc.; past pres. State Bank Mound.; past v.p. Mo Vu Devel. Co.; past treas. Northeast Plaza Inc.; past editor, pub. Robbinsdale Post-Post Pub. Co., past dir. Kodiak, Inc. Treas., Lighthouse Point Fedn. Police Assos.; past pres. De La Salle Alumni Assn. Mem. Comml. Law League Am. (past nat. pres.), Minn., Hennepin Co. (past sec.) bar assns., Sigma Delta Kappa. Clubs: K.C., Em Cee (past pres.), Deer Creek Golf, St. Croix Yacht; Deerfield Country (past pres.). Home: 5221 N E 27th Ave Pompano Beach FL 33064 Office: 620 Nat City Bank Bldg Minneapolis MN 55402

WAGNER, DURRETT, publisher, picture service exec.; b. El Paso, Tex., Feb. 27, 1929; s. Francis and Florence (Durrett) W.; B.A., Baylor U., 1950; M.Div., Yale, 1954; postgrad. U. Chgo., 1954-59; m. Betty Jane Brown, June 7, 1951; children—Gordon, Velma, Kendra. Chmn. social sci. div. Kendall Coll., Evanston, Ill., 1959-63, dean, 1963-67; owner, partner Swallow Press Inc., Chgo., 1967—; owner, partner, pres. Hist. Pictures Service, Inc., Chgo., 1975—. Home: 614 Ingleside Pl Evanston IL 60201 Office: 811 W Junior Terr Chicago IL 60613 also 17 N State St Chicago IL 60602

WAGNER, EDWARD FREDERICK, former ins. co. exec., cons.; b. Ironton, Ohio, Feb. 18, 1908; s. Thomas and Estelle (Hickey) W.; student Aquinas Coll., 1924-27, Ohio State U., 1934-35; H.H.D., Ohio Dominican Coll., 1968; m. Margaret Ann List, Dec. 30, 1932 (dec. June 1973); children—Gretchen (Mrs. Charles A. Gooding), Margaret Ellen (Mrs. Edwin J. Olsen), Edward Frederick; m. Yvonne Davis, Mar. 3, 1979. Retail petroleum bus., 1930-41; dist. rent dir. OPA, Central and S.E. Ohio, 1941-50; dir. community relations Nationwide Ins. Co., Columbus, Ohio, 1950-58; v.p., gen. mgr. Nationwide Devel. Co., Columbus, 1958-66, pres., 1966-73; pres. affiliated cos. Nationwide Ins. Co., 1966-73, sr. cons. to gen. chmn. and chief exec. officer, 1973—; former pres. Nationwide Communications, Inc., Nationwide Consumer Services, Inc., Heritage Securities, Inc. Chmn. Regional Planning Commn., 1960-65, Devel. Com. Greater Columbus, 1967-68, Ohio Inaugural Com. for 1961 Kennedy-Johnson and 1965 Johnson-Humphrey. Chmn. bd. dirs. St. Ann's Hosp., Columbus; bd. dirs. Found. for Coop. Housing, Washington; chmn. Ohio State U. Devel. Fund. Recipient Gold medal for distinguished internat. service City of Genoa, Italy, 1960; Columbus award for distinguished community service Columbus C. of C., 1973; Distinguished Service award Ohio State U., 1978. Mem. Am. Soc. Planning Ofcls., Nat. Planning Assn., Newcomen Soc. N.Am., Ohio Soc. N.Y. (v.p.), Exec. Order Ohio Commodores. Clubs: Press of Ohio; Athletic (Columbus); President's, Faculty (Ohio State U.). Home: 3850 Galt Ocean Dr Fort Lauderdale FL 33308 Office: One Nationwide Plaza Columbus OH 43216

WAGNER, EDWARD HARRISON, publisher; b. N.Y.C., Apr. 11, 1922; s. Aberaham and Jeanne Wagner; ed. L.I. U.; m. Frances Winstein, Sept. 12, 1948; children—Robin Joy, Karen Beth. Advt. mgr. Gellert Pub. Corp., N.Y.C., 1946-55; v.p. United Bus. Pub. Corp., N.Y.C., 1955-62; advt. mgr. Ziff-Davis Pub. Corp., N.Y.C., 1962-64; partner, pub. PTN Pub. Corp., Hempstead, N.Y., 1964—. Bd. dirs. Internat. Photog. Council. Served to maj. USAAF, World War II. Decorated Air medal with oak leaf cluster, D.F.C. Club: Woodcrest. Home: 874 Cedar Swamp Rd Old Brookville NY 11545 Office: 250 Fulton Ave Hempstead NY 11550

WAGNER, EDWARD KURT, publishing co. exec.; b. N.Y.C., Sept. 29, 1936; s. Kurt Henry and Julia Marie (Selesky) W.; B.B.A., St. Francis Coll., 1961; m. Ann Marie Philbin, Jan. 31, 1959; children—Denise, Steven, Kenneth, Jeanne. With Pitman Pub. Corp., N.Y.C., 1952-75, v.p., treas., 1968-71, exec. v.p., 1971-75; financial mgr. Dun-Donnelley Pub. Corp., N.Y.C., 1975-76, controller gen. book div., 1976-77; sr. mgr. controller's dept. Dun & Bradstreet, Inc., 1977-78; asst. controller, 1978—. Home: 18 Riley Rd Morganville NJ 07751 Office: 99 Church St New York NY 10007

WAGNER, FREDERICK EARL, cartoonist, feature artist; b. Memphis, Nov. 14, 1941; s. James Earl and Dotty Blanche (Hill) W.; student Memphis Acad. Arts, 1960-64; pvt. student Henry Hensche, 1963; m. Linda Worthy, Nov. 4, 1963; children—James Earl, Lesley Dow. Artist, mgr. Specialties Inc., custom wall decor and interiors, Memphis, 1964-67; artist, mgr. Florestone of Fla., Orlando, 1967-69; editorial artist Orlando Sentinel Star, 1969—; syndicated cartoonist Grin and Bear It, Fields Newspaper Syndicate, 1974—. Recipient award for best editorial cartoon of year Greater Orlando Press Club, 1971; Editor and Pub. award for best color illustration, 1976; Fla. Mag. Assn. award for best graphics, 1976. Republican. Methodist. Home: 144 Stirling Ave Winter Park FL 32789 Office: Orlando Sentinel Star 633 Orange Ave Orlando FL 32801

WAGNER, FREDERICK WILLIAM (BILL), lawyer; b. Daytona Beach, Fla., Apr. 13, 1933; s. Adam A. and Nella (Schroeder) W.; B.A., U. Fla., 1955, LL.B. with honors, 1960; m. Joan Handley, Jan. 24, 1955; children—Alan Frederick, Darryl William, Thomas Adam. Admitted to Fla. bar, 1960, U.S. Supreme Ct. bar, 1967; pvt. practice law, Miami, Fla., 1960-63, Orlando, Fla., 1963-65, Tampa, Fla., 1965—; partner law firm Nichols, Gaither, Beckham, Colson, Spence & Hicks, Tampa, Fla., 1965-67; partner law firm Wagner, Cunningham, Vaughan & Genders, P.A. and predecessor names, 1967—, pres., 1967—. Mem. Gov.'s Judicial Nominations Commn., 1971-72, Constnl. Judicial Nominations Commn., 1972-75; mem. Fla. Bd. Bar Examiners, 1974-77; chmn. Civil Procedure Rules Com. Fla. Bar, 1977-78; bd. govs. Fla. Bar, 1978—. Served to capt. USAF, 1955-57. Roscoe Pound fellow Am. Trial Lawyers Found. Fellow Assn. Trial Lawyers of Am. (bd. govs. 1973—, exec. com. 1975-78, chmn. nat. membership com. 1975-76, dir. internal affairs 1976-77), Am. Coll. Trial Lawyers; mem. Acad. Fla. Trial Lawyers (pres. 1972-73), Bay Area Trial Lawyers Assn. (v.p. 1966-68), Lawyer-Pilots Bar Assn., Judge Advocates Assn., N.Y. State, Calif. trial lawyers assns., U. Fla. Law Center Assn., U. Fla. Alumni Assn., Order of Coif, Fla. Blue Key, Beta Theta Pi. Democrat. Methodist. Club: Commerce Club of Tampa. Contbr. articles to profl. jours. Home: 1001 Bayshore Blvd Tampa FL 33606 Office: 708 Jackson St Tampa FL 33602

WAGNER, HARVEY ARTHUR, cons. engr.; b. Ann Arbor, Mich., Jan. 2, 1905; s. Emanuel M. and Emma (Kiebler) W.; B.S. in Mech. Engring., U. Mich., 1927; D. Engring., Lawrence Inst. Tech., 1969; m. Eleanor Mary Bond, July 6, 1929. With Proctor & Gamble Co., 1927-28; with Detroit Edison Co., 1928-70, exec. v.p., 1969-70; cons. engr., 1970—; v.p., dir. Overseas Adv. Assos., Inc., 1974—. Mem. Detroit Bd. Water Commrs., 1952-60. Trustee Nat. Sanitation Found. 1965—. Recipient Distinguished Alumnus award U. Mich. Coll. Engring., 1953; Sesquicentennial award as outstanding exec. and nuclear power cons. U. Mich., 1967; certificate pub. service Fed. Power Commn., 1964. Fellow ASME, Am. Nuclear Soc., Engring. Soc. Detroit (pres. 1968-69); mem. Nat. Acad. Engring., Tau Beta Pi, Phi Kappa Phi. Author papers in field. Home: 12900 E Outer Dr Detroit MI 48224 Office: Washington Blvd Bldg Detroit MI 48226

WAGNER, HARVEY MAURICE, educator; b. San Francisco, Nov. 20, 1931; s. Max and Bernice Wagner; B.S. in Statistics, Stanford, 1953, M.S., 1954; Ph.D. in Econs., Mass. Inst. Tech., 1960; m. Ruth G. Glesby, June 26, 1954; children—Caroline Beth, Julie Lynne. Teaching asst. Stanford, 1951-54, Cambridge (Eng.) U., 1954-55; instr. Sch. Indsl. Mgmt., Mass. Inst. Tech., 1955-57; mem. faculty Stanford, 1957-67, prof. mgmt. sci. Grad. Sch. Bus., 1963-67, dir. doctoral, prof. adminstrv. sci. Yale, 1967-76; dean Sch. Bus. Adminstrn., U. N.C., Chapel Hill, 1976-78, prof., 1970—; cons. to govt. and industry; cons. RAND Corp., 1953-78, McKinsey & Co., 1960—, U.S. Dept. Energy, 1978-79. U.S. chmn. State-of-the-Art Survey Project Internat. Inst. Applied Systems Analysis, Vienna,

Austria, 1975—. Chmn. allocations com. United Fund San Mateo County, 1963-65. Governing bd. Computer Research Center Econs. and Mgmt. Sci. Nat. Bur. Econ. Research, 1970-76; pres. N.C. Symphony Soc., 1977—; mem. N.C. Gov.'s Commn. on Productivity, 1978—. Oxford (Eng.) U. Summer Sch. fellow, 1952; Stanford Honors fellow statistics, 1953-54; Marshall scholar, 1954-55; research grantee Western Mgmt. Sci. Inst., 1960-65, NSF, 1962-72, Office Naval Research, 1973—, Army Research Office, 1974-77; Ford Found. Faculty Research fellow, 1963-64. Recipient Lanchester prize Ops. Research Soc. Am., 1969; Maynard Book award A11E, 1970. Fellow Am. Statis. Assn.; mem. Econometric Soc., Inst. Mgmt. Scis. (pres. No. Cal. chpt. 1961-62, council mem. 1969-71, 72-75, nat. pres. 1973-74), Ops. Research Soc. (chmn. edn. com. 1963-64, chmn. Western sect. 1965-66, council mem. 1972-75), Phi Beta Kappa, Sigma Xi. Author: Statistical Management of Inventory Systems, 1962; (with John Haldi) Simulated Economic Models, 1963; Principles of Operations Research, 1969, 2d edit., 1975; Principles of Management Science, 1970, 2d edit., 1975. Editor: (with C. Bonini and R. Jaedicke) Management Controls; New Directions in Basic Research, 1964; asso. editor Jour. Am. Statis. Assn., 1963-69; departmental editor Mgmt. Sci., 1969-72, editorial bd. Naval Research Logistics Quar., 1977—. Office: Sch Bus Adminstrn Univ NC Chapel Hill NC 27514

WAGNER, HENRY NICHOLAS, JR., physician; b. Balt., May 12, 1927; s. Henry N. and Gertrude Loane W.; A.B., Johns Hopkins U., 1948, M.D., 1952; m. Anne Barrett Wagner, Feb., 1951; children—Henry N., Mary Randall, John Mark, Anne Elizabeth. Chief med. resident Osler Med. Service, Johns Hopkins Hosp., Balt., 1958-59, asst. prof. medicine, radiology Johns Hopkins Med. Instns., 1959-64, asso. prof., 1964-65, prof., dir. divs. nuclear medicine and radiation health sci., 1965—. Served with USPHS, 1955-57. Recipient Georg von Hevesey medal, 1976. Fellow A.C.P.; mem. Balt. City Med. Soc. (pres.-elect), World Fedn. Nuclear Medicine and Biology (past pres.), Am. Bd. Nuclear Medicine (founding mem.), Soc. Nuclear Medicine (past pres.), Am. Fedn. Clin. Research (past pres.), Research Socs. Council (past pres.), Assn. Am. Physicians, Am. Soc. Clin. Investigation, Phi Beta Kappa. Author numerous books in field. Contbr. articles to med. jours. Home: 3410 Guilford Terr Baltimore MD 21218 Office: 615 N Wolfe St Baltimore MD 21205

WAGNER, HERMAN BLOCK, educator; b. Balt., Dec. 25, 1923; s. Henry N. and Gertrude L. (Loane) W.; B.E., Johns Hopkins, 1944, M.A., 1946, Ph.D., 1948; m. Mary Louise Hagel, June 5, 1946; children—Joseph, Marita, Stephen, Mary Lou, Gertrude. Asst. prof. chemistry Loyola Coll. at Balt., 1949-50; research chemist E.I. duPont Co., Phila., 1950-55; asso. research prof. Rutgers U., 1955-57; dir. chem. research TCA Research Center, Princeton, 1957-61; prof. chemistry Drexel U., Phila., 1961—; cons. Dow Chem. Co., TCA Research Center. Recipient research grants NSF, 1964-65, Dupont Co., 1962-64, Dow Chem. Co., 1963-77, Glycerin Research award for 1958. Mem. Am. Chem. Soc., A.A.A.S., Am. Inst. Chemists, Sigma Xi, Phi Lambda Upsilon. Patentee in field. Home: 1009 Forest Rd Perkasie PA 18944 Office: Chemistry Dept Drexel U Philadelphia PA 19104

WAGNER, JAMES DENNIS, communications co. exec.; b. N.Y.C., Dec. 13, 1938; s. Cyril Dennis and Lois (Gill) W.; B.S. in Econs., Wharton Sch., U. Pa., 1962; M.S. in Adminstrn., George Washington U., 1969; m. Mary Helen Tillman, Feb. 3, 1968; children—Todd, Craig. With Landmark Communications, Inc., Norfolk, Va., 1966—, fin. analyst, asst. treas., 1975-77, treas., 1977—. Treas. Redwood Civic League, Virginia Beach, Va., 1978. Served to lt. USNR, 1963-66. Mem. Inst. Newspaper Controllers and Fin. Officers (chmn. membership), com. 1970), Nat. Assn. Accountants (dir. Roanoke chpt. 1970). Presbyterian. Office: 150W Brambleton Ave Norfolk VA 23501

WAGNER, JOHN ADDINGTON, JR., lawyer; b. Battle Creek, Mich., Jan. 22, 1914; s. John A. and Alice M. (Goucher) W.; student Hillsdale Coll., 1932-34, LL.D., 1956; LL.B., Washington and Lee U., 1937; m. Virginia Dare Beagle, July 27, 1940 (div. 1961); 1 son, John Addington III; m. 2d, Dorothy E. Breuer, Aug. 24, 1963 (dec. Oct. 1977); m. 3d, Mary Ellen Turbeville, Aug. 18, 1978. Admitted to Mich. bar, 1937; partner Wagner, Wagner & Wagner, Battle Creek, 1937-56, Wagner & Greene, 1959-69; pvt. practice, 1969-77; partner firm Wagner & Jordan, 1977—. Asst. atty. gen. for Mich., 1940-41, chief asst. city atty., Battle Creek, 1946-48. Former mem. exec. bd. Battle Creek area council Boy Scouts; former dir. Community Chest, Battle Creek Area Devel. Corp.; bd. dirs., exec. com. United Community Service, 1965-71, pres., 1971. Recipient Quasquicentennial Alumni award Hillside Coll., 1969. Served as lt. comdr., USNR, 1942-46; P.T.O. Decorated Purple Heart. Mem. Am. Legion (nat. comdr. 1955-56), Mich., Calhoun County (pres. 1965-66) bar assns. Am. Judicature Soc., Am., Mich. trial lawyers assns., Battle Creek Area C. of C. (former dir.), Delta Tau Delta, Phi Delta Phi. Episcopalian. Clubs: Battle Creek Country, Kalamazoo Country. Home: 3644 Woodcliff Dr Kalamazoo MI 49008 Office: 134 W Van Buren St Battle Creek MI 49014

WAGNER, JOHN GARNET, educator; b. Weston, Ont., Can., Mar. 28, 1921; s. Herbert William and Coral (Cates) W.; Pharm.B., U. Toronto (Ont.), 1947; B.S. in Pharmacy, U. Sask., Can., 1948, B.A., 1949; Ph.D., Ohio State U., 1952; m. Eunice Winona Kelsey, July 4, 1946; children—Wendie Lynn, Linda Beth. Came to U.S., 1949. Asst. prof. pharm. chemistry Ohio State U., 1952-53; with Upjohn Co., Kalamazoo, 1953-68, head pharmacy research sect. 1956-63, sr. research scientist med. research div., 1963-68; prof. pharmacy Coll. Pharmacy, U. Mich. at Ann Arbor, 1968—; asst. dir. R. and D. Pharmacy Service, Univ. Hosp., 1968-72; mem. staff Upjohn Center for Clin. Pharmacology, 1973—; cons. Bur. of Drugs, FDA, Washington, 1971-73, Upjohn Co., 1968—, McNeil Labs., Ft. Washington, Pa., 1972—. Served with RCAF, 1941-45. Recipient Lt. George R. Parke Meml. scholarship and silver medal, 1946; John Roberts Gold medal for pharmacy and chemistry U. Toronto, 1947; Dr. William E. Upjohn award, 1960; Ebert prize Am. Pharm. Assn., 1961; Centennial Achievement award Ohio State U., 1970; Høst-Madsen medal Fédération internationale pharmaceutique, 1972; fellow Am. Found. Pharm. Edn., 1949-51; FDA grantee, 1969-76. Fellow Am. Coll. Clin. Pharmacology and Chemotherapy, Acad. Pharm. Sci., AAAS; mem. Am. Soc. Clin. Pharmacology and Therapeutics (bd. regents 1968-72, v.p. 1972, vice chmn. sect. on pharmacokinetics 1970-74), Am. Pharm. Assn., N.Y. Acad. Scis., Sigma Xi, Phi Lambda Upsilon, Rho Chi. Author: Biopharmaceautics and Relevant Pharmacokinetics, 1971; Fundamentals of Clinical Pharmacokinetics, 1975; also numerous articles. Editorial bd. Internat. Jour. Clin. Pharmacology, 1967—, Clin. Pharmacol. Therapeutics, 1973—; cons. editor Jour. Pharmacokinetics and Biopharmaceatics. Contbg. editor Drug Intelligence and Clin. Pharmacy. Home: 2142 Spruceway Ln Newport W Ann Arbor MI 48103

WAGNER, LEONARD GEORGE, journalist; b. Theresa, Wis., Dec. 25, 1936; s. Wilmar Michael and Mary (Lyons) W.; B.S., St. Norbert Coll., 1958; m. Agnes Marie Moore, Aug. 17, 1957; children—Carole, Peter, Michael, Barbara, Teresa, Patricia, Mary. Dir. news bur. St. Norbert Coll., 1957-58; news reporter WJPG Radio, Green Bay, Wis., 1958; sportswriter Green Bay Press-Gazette, 1961-67, sports editor, 1968—, news editor, 1977-79, features editor, 1979—. Pres., Green Bay Lions West Side Little League, Green Bay Parochial Sch. Basketball League. Served to 2d lt. AUS, 1959. Named Wis. Sportswriter of Year, 1974; Green Bay Sports Personality of Year, 1977. Mem. Profl. Football Writers Am., Nat. A.P. Sports Editors Assn., Wis. A.P. Sportswriters Assn. (pres. 1966, 77), Home: 620 St Jude St Green Bay WI 54303 Office: 435 E Walnut St Green Bay WI 54305

WAGNER, LINDSAY J., actress; b. Los Angeles, June 22, 1949; d. Bill Nowels and Marilyn Louise (Thrasher) W.; student U. Oreg., 1967; m. Michael Brandon, Dec. 1976 (div.). Actress numerous TV shows Universal Studios, Universal City, Calif., 1971-74; actress motion pictures Two People, by Robert Wise, 1972, The Paper Chase, 1973, Second Wind, 1975; tchr. acting children Founders Sch. Los Angeles, 1975; TV series Bionic Woman, 1976-78; in TV miniseries Scruples, 1980, TV film The Two Worlds of Jennie Logan, 1979. Office: Ron Samuels Enterprises 4000 Warner Ave Burbank CA 91505*

WAGNER, LOUIS CARSON, JR., army officer; b. Jackson, Mo., Jan. 24, 1932; s. Louis Carson and Margaret Marie (Macke) W.; B.S., U.S. Mil. Acad., 1954; M.S. in Applied Mechanics, U. Ill., 1961; grad. U.S. Naval War Coll., 1971; m. Judith Gifford, Sept. 24, 1955; children—Susan, Stephen, Amy. Commd. 2d lt. U.S. Army, 1954, advanced through grades to maj. gen., 1979; service in Vietnam, Germany and Alaska; dep. dir. materiel plans and programs Office Dep. Chief Staff Research, Devel. and Acquisition, Washington, 1976-78, dir. combat support systems, 1978—. Decorated D.S.C., Silver Star, Legion of Merit (2), Bronze Star, Air medal, Meritorious Service medal, Army Commendation medal (3), Purple Heart, Combat Inf. badge. Mem. Assn. Grads. U.S. Mil. Acad., Armor Assn., Assn. U.S. Army. Home: Quarters 14 Woodlawn Dr Fort Belvoir VA 22060 Office: HQDA DAMA-CSZ-A Washington DC 20310

WAGNER, MARJORIE COOGAN DOWNING, coll. pres.; b. N.Y.C., Mar. 16, 1917; d. Charles A. and Marguerite C. (Ohland) Coogan; B.A., Coll. Mt. St. Vincent, 1938; M.A., Cath. U. Am., 1939; Ph.D., Yale, 1942; LL.D., Chapman Coll., 1975; m. M. John Wagner, June 6, 1974; children—Francis, Margaret (Mrs. Philip Harrington), Nicholas. Dean, Sarah Lawrence Coll., Bronxville, N.Y., 1961-65; dean of faculty Scripps Coll., Claremont, Calif., 1965-71, Frederick Hard prof. English Lit., 1971-74; pres. Calif. State Coll. Sonoma, Rohnert Park, 1974-76; vice chancellor faculty-staff affairs Calif. State U., Long Beach, 1976—. Cons. Edml. Inst. Bd. dirs. United Way, 1975; trustee Mt. St. Mary's Coll., Los Angeles, 1979—. Mem. Western Coll. Assn. (dir. 1969-71), Western Assn. Schs. and Colls. (sr. commn. 1968-71, 76—), Am. Council Edn. (dir. 1977-79, commn. on leadership). Home: 28411 Lomo Dr Palos Verdes CA 90274 Office: 400 Golden Shore Long Beach CA 90802

WAGNER, NORMAN ERNEST, univ. exec.; b. Edenwold, Sask., Can., Mar. 29, 1935; s. Robert Eric and Gertrude Margaret (Brandt) W.; B.A., U. Sask., 1958, M.Div., 1958; M.A., U. Toronto (Ont., Can.), 1960, Ph.D. in Near Eastern Studies, 1965; m. Catherine Hack, May 16, 1957; children—Marjorie Dianne, Richard Roger, Janet Marie. Asst. prof. Near Eastern studies Wilfrid Laurier U., Waterloo, Ont., 1962-65, asso. prof., 1965-69, prof., 1970-78, dean grad. studies and research, 1974-78; pres. U. Calgary (Alta., Can.), 1978—. Can. Council grantee; recipient other grants. Mem. Soc. Bibl. Lit., Can. Archaeol. Assn., Can. Soc. Bibl. Studies. Lutheran. Author: (with others) The Moyer Site: A Prehistoric Village in Waterloo County, 1974. Home: 1356 Montreal Ave SW Calgary AB T2T 0Z5 Canada Office: U Calgary Calgary AB T2N 1N4 Canada

WAGNER, PETER EWING, educator; b. Ann Arbor, Mich., July 4, 1929; s. Paul Clark and Charlotta Josephine (Ewing) W.; student Occidental Coll., 1946-48; A.B., U. Calif. at Berkeley, 1950, Ph.D. (with honors), 1956; m. Caryl Jean Veon, June 23, 1951; children—Ann Frances, Stephen Charles. Teaching, research asst. U. Calif., 1950-56; research physicist Westinghouse Research Labs., Pitts., 1956-59; asso. prof. elec. engring. Johns Hopkins, 1960-65, prof., 1965-73; dir., prof. U. Md. Center for Environmental and Estuarine Studies, 1973—. Spl. projects engr. State of Md., 1971-72; mem. Gov.'s Sci. Adv. Council, 1973—; mem. Md. Power Plant Siting Advisory Com., 1972—; cons. in field. Trustee Chesapeake Research Consortium, 1974—. Guggenheim fellow Oxford U., 1966-67. Mem. Am. Phys. Soc., AAAS, AAUP, Md. Acad. Scis. (mem. sci. council 1960-77), Phi Beta Kappa, Sigma Xi, Sigma Alpha Epsilon. Contbr. articles to profl. jours. Patentee in field. Home: 2 Willis St Cambridge MD 21613

WAGNER, PHILIP MARSHALL, writer; b. New Haven, Feb. 18, 1904; s. Charles Philip and Ruth (Kenyon) W.; A.B., U. Mich., 1925; m. Helen Crocker, Apr. 16, 1925; children—Susan, Philip; m. 2d, Jocelyn McDonough, Sept. 4, 1940. With publicity dept. Gen. Electric Co., Schenectady, N.Y., 1925-30; editorial writer Baltimore Evening Sun, 1930-36; London corr., Baltimore Sun, 1936-37; editor Evening Sun, 1938-43; editor Baltimore Sun, 1943-64; writer syndicated newspaper column, 1964—; lectr. U. Calif., 1961, 64. Am. delegate Federation Nationale de la Viticulture Nouvelle. Named Officer Ordre du Merite Agricole, France. Mem. N.Y. Fruit Testing Coop. Assn. Democrat. Clubs: National Press, Overseas Writers (Washington); Hamilton St. (Balt.). Author: American Wines and How to Make Them, 1933; Wine Grapes and How to Grow Them, 1937; The Wine-Grower's Guide, 1945, rev. 1965; American Wines and Wine Making, 1963; H.L. Mencken, 1966; Grapes into Wine, 1976. Editor (with Dr. Sanford V. Larkey); Turner on Wines, 1941. Contbr. articles to numerous mags. Maintains an experimental vineyard devoted to adaptation of wine grapes to Am. conditions. Address: Boordy Vineyard Box 38 Riderwood MD 21139

WAGNER, RALPH CHARLES, ednl. film co. exec.; b. Wheaton, Ill., June 16, 1915; s. Val A. and Rose C. (Haig) W.; B.A. in Edn., Western Ill. U., Macomb, 1941; m. Laura J. Hagan, Dec. 31, 1937; children—Larry, Richard, Ralph M. With du Pont Co., 1941-44; coach, tchr. schs. in Ill., 1945-52; salesman, then Midwest Regional sales mgr. E.B. Films, Wilmette, Ill., 1952-60; with Ency. Brit. Ednl. Corp., Chgo., 1960—, exec. v.p. mktg., 1973-77, pres., from 1977, also chief exec. officer. Bd. dirs. Western Ill. U. Found., 1971—. Recipient Alumni Achievement award Western Ill. U., 1976. Mem. NEA, Assn. Edn. and Communications Tech., Nat., Ill. audio-visual assns., Assn. Am. Pubs., ALA, Assn. Media Producers. Lutheran. Clubs: Carlton, Thorngate Country, Bardmoor Country. Address: 425 N Michigan Ave Chicago IL 60611*

WAGNER, RICHARD, baseball exec.; b. Central City, Nebr., Oct. 19, 1927; s. John Howard and Esther Marie (Wolken) W.; student pub. schs., Central City; m. Gloria Jean Larsen, May 10, 1950; children—Randolph Greg, Cynthia Kaye. Gen. mgr. Lincoln (Nebr.) Baseball Club, 1955-58; mgr. Pershing Municipal Auditorium, Lincoln, 1958-61; exec. staff Ice Capades Inc., Hollywood, Calif., 1961-63; gen. mgr. Sta. KSAL, Salina, Kans., 1963-65; dir. promotion and sales St. Louis Nat. Baseball Club, 1965-66; gen. mgr. Forum, Inglewood, Calif., 1966-67; asst. to exec. v.p. Cin. Reds, 1967-70, asst. to pres., 1970-74, v.p. adminstrn., 1975, exec. v.p., 1975-77, exec. v.p., gen. mgr., 1977-79, now pres., chief exec. officer; pres., dir. N. Platte (Nebr.) Broadcasting Inc., 1972—. Served with USNR, 1945-47, 50-52. Named Exec. of Year Minor League Baseball, Sporting News, 1958. Mem. Internat. Assn. Arena Mgrs. Republican. Methodist. Office: 100 Riverfront Stadium Cincinnati OH 45202*

WAGNER, RICHARD, business exec.; b. N.Y.C., June 15, 1896; s. Richard and Emma (Rinker) W.; student Chgo. night high schs., night courses Northwestern U. and Am. Inst. Banking; m. Grace L. Sommer, Mar. 28, 1917; children—Grace Margaret (Mrs. Raymond G. Hanson), John Donald, Richard, James Arthur. Runner, Continental-Comml. Nat. Bank (now Continental Ill. Nat. Bank), Chgo., 1910-11, stenographer, 1911-14, sec. to pres., 1914-26, 2d vice pres., 1926-30; v.p. Chgo. Corp. (name changed to Champlin Oil & Refining Co.), 1930-38, became pres. and dir., 1938, chmn. and chief exec. officer, 1954-61, chmn. exec. com., 1961-63, vice chmn. bd., now cons.; chmn. Tenneco, 1943-45; dir. First Nat. Bank of Barrington (Ill.). Bus. adviser Am. delegation 13th session GATT, Geneva, 1958; adviser U. S. Bus. del., 44th Session, ILO, Geneva, 1960; U.S. Employer del., 45th-49th sessions ILO, 1961, 62, 63, 64, 65, mem. governing body ILO; mem. U.S. mgmt. com. OECD. Chmn. bus. div., Community and War Fund, Chgo., 1944. Mem. U. Chgo. citizens com.; dir., v.p., chmn. policy com., mem. polit. participation, natural resources coms. C. of C. of U.S., pres., 1961-62, chmn. bd., 1962—, chmn. exec. com., 1963-64, chmn. nominating com., 1966—, mem. sr. council. Mem. Mid-Continent Oil and Gas Assn., Ind. Natural Gas Assn., Chgo. Assn. Commerce and Industry, Am. Petroleum Inst. (dir.,) Tax Inst., Ill. C. of C., Nat. Export Expansion Council. Republican. Lutheran. Mason. Clubs: Economic (pres. 1943, 44), Chicago (Chgo.); Park Ridge (Ill.) Country; Barrington Hills (Ill.) Country; De Anza Desert Country. Address: 79 Brinker Rd Barrington IL 60010. *Small incidents alter and shape the course of one's life. In my case, at the age of 13, a shorthand manual came into my possession. More out of curiosity than plan, I studied it and became adept. As a result, at 17 I was secretary to the head of the leading bank in Chicago. By then I had set for myself the following principles and rules of conduct. Study and learn as rapidly as possible every aspect of the business in which you are employed.... Continue to broaden your knowledge not only of the activities in which you are engaged, but, also, in related activities, and in areas which shape broad economic forces. Knowledge is power, to attain it requires effort—it pays off. A sense of integrity and ethical conduct are important. Once lost a good reputation is hard to recover.*

WAGNER, ROBERT, actor; b. Detroit, Feb. 10, 1930; m. Natalie Wood, 1957, div., 1962, remarried, 1972; 1 dau., Courtney; m. Marian Donnen (div.); 1 dau., Kate. Films include: Halls of Montezuma, The Frogmen, Let's Make it Legal, With a Song in My Heart, What Price Glory, Stars and Stripes Forever, The Silver Whip, Titanic, Star of Tomorrow, Beneath the 12-Mile Reef, Prince Valiant, Broken Lance, White Feather, A Kiss Before Dying, The Mountain, The True Story of Jesse James, Stopover Tokyo, In Love and War, Say One For Me, Between Heaven and Hell, The Hunters, All the Fine Young Cannibals, Sail a Crooked Ship, The Longest Day, The War Lover, The Condemned of Altona, Harper, Banning, The Biggest Bundle of Them All, The Pink Panther, Winning, The Affair, The Towering Inferno, Cat on A Hot Tin Roof, 1976, Critical List, 1978, Pearl, 1978; starred in TV series It Takes A Thief, Switch, 1975—; produced, starred in Madame Sin; formed Robert Wagner Prodns.; TV appearances The Ox-Bow Incident, Gun in His Hand, And Man Created Vanity, The Enemy on the Beach, Runaway Bay, How I Spent My Summer Vacation, Name of the Game, City Beneath the Sea, Cable Car Mystery, Streets of San Francisco. Address: care Internat Creative Management Ltd 8899 Beverly Blvd Hollywood CA 90069

WAGNER, ROBERT EARL, educator; b. Balt., July 30, 1920; s. Robert Earl and Emma Katherine (Simpson) W.; B.S. in Chem. Engring., Drexel U., 1946; M.S., Princeton, 1948, Ph.D., 1955; m. Ruth Ann Svejda, Sept. 1, 1949; children—Heidi, Susan, Bonnie. Mem. faculty Worcester (Mass.) Poly. Inst., 1949—, prof. chem. engring., 1962—. Cons. chem. engr., 1949—. Served with USAAF, 1943-46. Decorated D.F.C., Air medal (5). Mem. Am. Chem. Soc., Am. Inst. Chem. Engrs., Sigma Xi, Tau Beta Pi, Phi Lambda Upsilon. Club: Appalachian Mountain (Worcester). Home: 41 North St Shrewsbury MA 01545 Office: Dept Chemical Engineering Worcester Poly Inst Worcester MA 01609

WAGNER, ROBERT EARL, agronomist; b. Garden City, Kans., Mar. 6, 1921; s. Fay Arthur and Margaret (Longbottom) W.; B.S., Kans. State Coll., 1942; M.S., U. Wis., 1943, Ph.D., 1950; m. Bernice Bittner, Aug. 7, 1948; children—Robert Earl, James Warren, Douglas Alan. Forage crops specialist Ft. Hays Expt. Sta., Hays, Kans., 1943-45; asso. agronomist Plant Industry Sta., U.S. Dept. Agr., Beltsville, Md., 1945-48, research agronomist, asst. project leader pasture and range project, 1951-54, research agronomist, project leader western pasture and range project, 1954-56; prof., head dept. agronomy U. Md., 1956-59; regional dir. American Potash Inst., 1959-66, also Found. for Internat. Potash Research, v.p. both orgns., 1966-67; dir. Coop. Extension Service, U. Md., 1967-75; pres. Potash Inst., 1975-77, Potash and Phosphate Inst., 1977—. Chmn. Nat. Extension Com. on Orgn. and Policy; mem. U.S. delegation 7th Internat. Grassland Congress, New Zealand. Recipient Medallion award Am. Forage and Grassland Council, award Md. Farm Bur. Fellow Am. Soc. Agronomy (chmn. grassland improvement steering com., past bd. dirs., mem. exec. com.; bd. dirs., pres. N.E. br.), A.A.A.S.; mem. Am. Grassland Council (pres.), Am. Soc. Range Mgmt., Sigma Xi, Alpha Zeta, Gamma Sigma Delta, Phi Kappa Phi. Presbyterian. Clubs: Cosmos (Washington); Atlanta Athletic. Author tech., popular publs. Editor Proc. Sixth Internat. Grassland Congress. Home: 1934 Mountain Creek Dr Stone Mountain GA 30087 Office: Potash and Phosphate Inst 1649 Tullie Circle NE Atlanta GA 30329

WAGNER, ROBERT F., lawyer, diplomat; b. N.Y.C., Apr. 20, 1910; s. Robert F. Wagner; A.B., Yale, 1933, LL.B., 1937; postgrad. Harvard Sch. Bus. Adminstrn., 1934; LL.D., L.I. U., Fordham U., Bklyn. Law Sch., St. John's Law Sch.; m. Susan Edwards (dec. 1964); 2 sons; m. 2d, Barbara Joan Cavanagh, July 1965 (div. June 1971); m. 3d, Phyllis Fraser Cerf, Jan. 1975. Mem. N.Y. State Assembly, 1938-41; city tax commn., N.Y.C., 1946; commr. housing and buildings, 1947; chmn. City Planning Commn., 1948; pres. Borough of Manhattan, Greater N.Y.C., 1949-53; mayor N.Y.C., 1954-65; partner firm Finley, Kumble, Wagner, Heine & Underberg, 1972—; U.S. ambassador to Spain, 1968-69; personal envoy of Pres. U.S. to Vatican, 1978—. First v.p., del. Constl. Conv., 1967; chmn. bd. United Neighborhood Houses; mem. Pres.'s Crime Commn., 1965-66. Chmn. Nat. Democratic Com. Compliance Rev. Commn.; bd. dirs. N.Y. Landmarks Conservancy; mem. N.Y.C. Temporary Commn. City Finances; chmn. jud. nominating com. First Jud. Dept., N.Y. State, also mem. commn. on jud. nominations; vice chmn. Port Authority N.Y. and N.J. Served to lt. col. 85th Air Force, 1942-45; now col. ret. Address: 425 Park Ave New York NY 10022

WAGNER, ROBERT RODERICK, scientist, educator, physician; b. N.Y.C., Jan. 5, 1923; s. Nathan and Mary (Mendelsohn) W.; A.B., Columbia, 1943; M.D., Yale, 1946; m. Mary Elizabeth Burke, Mar. 23, 1967. Intern, asst. resident physician Yale-New Haven Med.

Center, 1946-47, 49-50; research fellow Nat. Inst. Med. Research, London, Eng., 1950-51; instr., then asst. prof. medicine Yale, 1951-55; asst., then asso. prof. medicine Johns Hopkins, 1956-59, asso. prof. microbiology, 1959-64, asst., then asso. dean med. faculty, 1957-63, prof. microbiology, 1964-67; vis. fellow, mem. Common Room All Souls Coll., Oxford U., 1967, 76; prof., chmn. dept. microbiology U. Va., 1967—. Cons. Am. Cancer Soc. Mem. coms. USPHS, NSF, Assn. Am. Med. Colls., AMA, Nat. Bd. Med. Examiners. Served to lt. USNR, 1947-49. Rockefeller Found. resident scholar Villa Serbelloni, Bellagio, Italy, 1976; Macy Found. Faculty scholar Oxford U., 1976. Fellow AAAS (councillor); mem. Assn. Am. Physicians, Am. Soc. Clin. Investigation, Am. Soc. Biol. Chemists, Am. Assn. Immunologists, Am. Soc. for Microbiology (councillor), Assn. Med. Sch. Microbiology Chmn. (pres. 1974). Editor-in-chief Jour. Virology, 1966—. Office: Dept Microbiology U Va Charlottesville VA 22908

WAGNER, ROBERT WANNER, coll. dean; b. Nesquehoning, Pa., May 5, 1913; s. Alvin E. and Lilian (Wanner) W.; A.B., Ohio U., 1934; M.A., U. Mich., 1935, Ph.D., 1937; m. Sally I. Marsh, July 4, 1942; children—Marsha Lynn, Judith Ann, Barbara Jean. Instr. U. Wis., 1937-39; from instr. to asso. prof. Oberlin Coll. 1939-50; prof. U. Mass., 1950—, asso. dean Coll. Arts and Sci., 1961-70, acting dir. Office Instl. Studies, 1970-73. Served from lt. (j.g.) to lt. comdr. USNR, 1942-46. Mem. Am. Math. Soc., Am. Assn. U. Profs., Math. Assn. Am., Phi Beta Kappa, Sigma Xi, Phi Kappa Phi, Delta Tau Delta. Author coll. math. textbooks. Home: 47 Red Gate Lane Amherst MA 01002

WAGNER, ROBERT WAYNE, mgmt. cons.; b. Kiowa, Okla., Aug. 30, 1926; s. Leroy E. and Elizabeth (Armstrong) W.; B.S. in Bus. Adminstrn., Okla. U., 1949; m. Barbara Jean Shirley, Jan. 29, 1949; children—Carol Elizabeth, Sharon Ann. With IBM Corp., 1949-65, sales trainee, br. mgr. at Joplin, Mo. office, computer sales mgr., br. mgr. Oklahoma City, Indpls., Kansas City, Mo. offices; asst. to pres., also v.p. systems and corporate Planning Waddell & Redd, Inc., Kansas City, Mo., 1965-67, exec. v.p. sales, 1967-68, pres., 1968-69; founder, pres. Adv. Assos., Inc., mgmt. cons., Kansas City, Mo., 1969-70; pres., chmn. bd. Tech. Resources Corp., Kansas City, Mo., 1969—; pres. Marlennan Mgmt. Systems, Inc., Kansas City, 1970-76; v.p. Marsh & McLennan, 1973-76; owner, pres. Qintar Agy. Systems, Oklahoma City, 1974—. Mem. Kappa Alpha (chpt. pres. 1948). Home: 4417 W 111th Terr Leawood KS 66211

WAGNER, ROGER, choral dir.; b. LePuy, France, Jan. 16, 1914; s. Francis W.; came to U.S., 1921; B.A., Coll. of Montmorency, France; Ph.D. cum laude, U. Montreal; hon. doctorates, Westminster Choir Coll., Princeton U., St. Norbert Coll., Wis. Organist, choir master St. Josephs Ch., 1937-45; organizer Bur. of Music, 1945; founder Roger Wagner Chorale, 1946, nat. tours, 1956, Dept. State tours Central Am., Mexico, S.Am., 1959, 64, Middle East, 1966; tours to Japan, 1965, 67; head choral activities U. Calif., Los Angeles, 1949—, also prof.; formerly head music dept. Marymount Coll.; guest condr. Los Angeles Philharmonic Orch., Detroit Symphony, Royal Philharmonic, London, Orchestre des Conservatoires, Paris, Bolshoi Orch., Moscow, Concertgebouw Orch., Amsterdam, New Philharmonic, Paris; founder Los Angeles Master Chorale and Sinfonia Orch., 1965; condr. Phila. Orch. and Los Angeles Master Chorale at Kennedy Center for presdl. inaugural concert, 1973, Symphony Orch. in S.Am., Sao Paulo, 1973; toured Soviet Union with Soviet Orch. and Los Angeles Master Chorale, 1974; condr. symphony concerts in Montevideo, Uruguay and Sodre Symphony, 1974; toured Japan, 1978; recordings with Allegro and Capitol Records, 1951—; condr. New Philharmonic and Radio France Chorale in Royal Chapel of Versailles. Decorated knight Pope Paul VI, Order St. Bridgette; recipient Grammy award for album Virtuoso. Address: 1401 Stone Canyon Rd Los Angeles CA 90024

WAGNER, STANLEY PAUL, educator; b. Ambridge, Pa., Mar. 22, 1923; s. Stephan and Anna (Wojtkowski) W.; B.A., U. Pitts., 1947, M.A., 1949, Ph.D., 1953; m. Diana Mills, Oct. 20, 1945; 1 dau., Kathleen Anne (Mrs. James E. Lawler). Instr. social scis. Muskingum Coll., 1950-54; asst. prof. Allegheny Coll., 1954-62; prof. history and polit. sci., chmn. dept., asso. dean arts and scis. Oklahoma City U., 1962-68; vice-chancellor acad. affairs Minn. State Colls., 1968-69; pres. East Central Okla. State U., Ada, 1969—; cons. Allegheny Coll. Guidance Clinic, summers 1955-69. Mem. Commn. Orgn. Govt. for Conduct Fgn. Policy, 1972-75. Chmn. Ada Community Chest drive, 1970. Pres. East Central Okla. State U. Found. Served with AUS, 1942-45. Episcopalian. Rotarian. Author: The End of Revolution, 1970. Home: 230 S Francis St Ada OK 74820

WAGNER, THOMAS HERMAN, mgmt. cons.; b. Marquette, Mich., Oct. 31, 1915; s. Herman Charles and Mae (Smith) W.; A.B., U. Mich., 1937; m. Dorothy Jane Thompson, June 29, 1940; children—Dorothy Ann, Thomas Herman. With Nat. Bank Detroit, 1937-40; v.p., treas. Eureka Williams Corp., 1940-51; treas. Campbell, Wyant & Cannon Foundry Co., Muskegon, Mich., 1951-54; pres., gen. mgr. Rite-o-Tool & Gage Co., Hazel Park, Mich., 1953-64; pres. Ritoloy, Inc., Hazel Park, 1956-64, Detroit Boring Bar Co., 1957-64, Bennington Realty Co., 1960-65, Wagner Promotion Co., 1960- 65, Wagner Products Co., 1958-65; former vice-chmn. Bank of Commonwealth, Detroit; pres. Resources Planning Corp., 1971—; past chmn., dir. Peoples Bank, Pt. Huron, Mich., Monroe Bank & Trust; v.p., dir. Creative Capital Mich., Inc., 1962-68; pres., dir. Litchfield Plantation Assn., Planned Auto Mgmt. Co., 1972—, N.Am. Trading Co. Mem. Phi Beta Kappa, Delta Upsilon, Phi Eta Sigma, Beta Gamma Sigma, Phi Kappa Phi. Clubs: Old (Harsens Island, Mich.); Ocean Reef (Key Largo, Fla.); Palm Beach (Fla.) Tennis. Home: 2945 Woodward Apt 74 Bloomfield Hills MI 48013 Office: 777 Bowers St Birmingham MI 48008 also 319 Clematis West Palm Beach FL 33480

WAGNER, WARREN HERBERT, JR., educator, botanist; b. Washington, Aug. 29, 1920; s. Warren Herbert and Harriet Lavinia (Claflin) W.; A.B., U. Pa., 1942; Ph.D., U. Calif. at Berkeley, 1950; spl. student Harvard, 1950-51; m. Florence Signaigo, July 16, 1948; children—Warren Charles, Margaret Frances. Instr., Harvard, summer 1951; faculty U. Mich. at Ann Arbor, 1951—, prof. botany, 1962—, curator pteridophytes, 1961—, dir. Bot. Gardens, 1966-71, chmn. dept. botany, 1975-77, spl. research higher plants, origin and evolution ferns, methods accurate deduction phylogenetic relationships fossil and living plants. Panelist systematic biology NSF, 1962-65, prin. investigator project evolutionary characters ferns, 1960—; dir. bot. research aeroallergens NIH, 1957-64; chmn. Mich. Natural Areas Council, 1958-59; mem. Smithsonian Council, 1967-72, hon. mem., 1972—; cons. mem. Survival Service Commn., Internat. Union for Conservation of Nature and Natural Resources, 1971—. Trustee Cranbrook Inst. Scis. Recipient Distinguished Faculty Achievement award U. Mich., 1975. Fellow AAAS (sec. sect. bot. scis., v.p. sect. 1968); mem. Am. Fern Soc. (sec. 1952-54, curator, librarian 1957-77, pres. 1970, 71), Am. Soc. Plant Taxonomists (council 1958-65, pres. 1966), Soc. for Study Evolution (v.p. 1965-66, council mem. 1967-69, pres. 1972), Am. Soc. Naturalists, Bot. Soc. Am. (pres. 1977, merit award 1978), Mich. (pres. 1967-71), Torrey, New Eng. bot. clubs, Internat. Soc. Plant Morphologists, Internat. Assn. Plant Taxonomy, Sigma Xi, Phi Kappa Tau. Club: Explorers. Home: 2111 Melrose Ave Ann Arbor MI 48104

WAGNER, WIENCZYSLAW JOSEPH, educator; b. Poland, Dec. 12, 1917; s. Joseph Wienczyslaw and Margaret Maria (Ferrein) W.; LL.M., U. Warsaw (Poland), 1939; certificate Acad. Internat. Law, The Hague, Netherlands, 1939, 47; diploma Inst. Comml. Sci., Warsaw, 1940; LL.D., U. Paris, 1947; LL.M., Northwestern U., 1950, J.D., 1953, S.J.D., 1957; m. Danuta M. Moc, July 29, 1950; children—Joseph W., Alexandra D., Margaret E.; m. 2d, Magdalena M. Pomian-Niezychowska, 1978. Came to U.S., 1948, naturalized, 1956. Officer legal problems Zieleniewski & Fitzner—Gamper, Poland, 1939-44; jr. atty., Warsaw, 1940-44; research asso. French Inst. Air Transport, Paris, 1947-48; vis. prof. Fordham U., 1948-49; teaching fellow Northwestern U., 1950-53; instr. Notre Dame U., 1953-54, asst. prof., 1954-57, asso. prof., 1957-61, prof., 1961-62; admitted to Ind. bar, 1964; prof. law Ind. U., 1962-71; prof. law U. Detroit, 1971—. Vis. prof. Cornell U., 1961, 64; lectr. Am. specialists program Dept. State, 1962, USIA, Africa, Asia, Latin Am.; lectr. Europe. Co-founder Paderewski Found., N.Y.C., Am. Relief Com. Free Poland, South Bend, Ind., 1954; legal counsel German Consulate Gen., Ind., 1966-68; pres. Polish Am. Congress Bicentennial Com. for Mich. Served with Polish Underground Army, 1941-44, Polish Army Abroad, 1945-48. Decorated Golden Cross Merit, Polish mil. medals. Mem. Am. Fgn. Law Assn. (past v.p.), Council Polish Inst. Arts and Scis. in Am. (pres.), Am. Council Polish Cultural Clubs (past pres.), Internat. Acad. Comparative Law (asso.), Inst. High Internat. Studies (Nice and Paris, France), Am. Assn. Comparative Study Law (dir.), Pax Romana Jurists (internat. v.p.), Delta Theta Phi. Author or editor 6 books. Bd. editors Am. Jour. Comparative Law, 1962—; asst. to editor Natural Law Forum, 1958-62. Contbr. articles to profl. jours. Home: 28530 Eldorado Pl Lathrup Village MI 48076 Office: 651 E Jefferson Ave Detroit MI 48226

WAGNER, WILLIAM CHARLES, veterinarian; b. Elma, N.Y., Nov. 12, 1932; s. Frederick George and Doris Edna (Newton) W.; D.V.M., Cornell U., 1956, Ph.D., 1968; m. Donna Ann McNeill, Aug. 14, 1954; children—William Charles, Elizabeth Ann, Victoria Mary, Kathryn Farrington. Gen. practice vet. medicine, Interlaken, N.Y., 1956-57; research veterinarian Cornell U., 1957-65, NIH postdoctoral fellow dept. animal sci., 1965-68; asst. prof. vet. medicine Vet. Med. Research Inst., Iowa State U., Ames, 1968-69, asso. prof., 1969-74, prof., 1974-77; prof. physiology, head dept. vet. bioscis. U. Ill., Urbana, 1977—. Pres., Ames Community Theater, 1972-73, 76-77. Recipient Alexander von Humboldt U.S. Scientist award Humboldt Stiftung, Freising-Weihenstephan, W. Ger., 1973-74. Mem. Am. Coll. Theriogenologists (diplomate), AVMA, Physiol. Soc., Am. Soc. Animal Sci., Soc. Study Reprodn., Soc. Study Fertility, N.Y. Acad. Scis., Sigma Xi, Phi Kappa Phi, Phi Zeta, Gamma Sigma Delta, Alpha Zeta. Lutheran. Home: 306 W Florida Ave Urbana IL 61801 Office: U Ill Coll Vet Medicine Urbana IL 61801. *I believe that it is important to be friendly to others, to try to understand the other person's position or feelings and deal with colleagues and subordinates in an impartial and fair manner. One should always remember that talents are a gift to be used wisely and to the fullest extent possible.*

WAGNER, WILLIAM CHARLES, mag. editor; b. Swanton, Ohio, June 24, 1937; s. William Leon and Lona Jane (Jacobs) W.; m. Janet Constance Royt, Sept. 10, 1956; children—Donna, Gina, Fredrick, Stelle, Lawrence, Lynn. Naturalist, Toledo Met. Park Dist. 1966-71; editor Jack and Jill mag., Saturday Evening Post Co., Indpls., 1971—; freelance writer, lectr. Served with USN, 1955-58. Recipient distinguished achievement award Ednl. Press Am., 1973, 74, 75, Freedom Found. award, 1974. Mem. Outdoor Writers Ohio, Toledo Naturalists Assn. (pres. 1968-69). Contbr. articles to mags., newspapers. Office: Jack and Jill 1100 Waterway Blvd Indianapolis IN 46206

WAGNER, WILLIAM FREDERICK, educator; b. Canton, Mo., Sept. 13, 1916; s. William C. and Lilly (Giegerich) W.; A.B., Culver-Stockton Coll., 1938; M.S., U. Chgo., 1940; Ph.D., U. Ill., 1947; m. Jean Lois Rosselot, July 27, 1945; children—Jennie Ann, Lenore Elizabeth, Russell William. Research chemist Ill. Geol. Survey, Urbana, 1940-45; asst. prof. chemistry Hanover (Ind.) Coll., 1947-49; mem. faculty U. Ky., 1949—, prof. chemistry, 1958—, chmn. dept., 1965-68, 76—; cons. to industry, 1956—. Recipient Distinguished Alumni award Culver-Stockton Coll., 1962. Mem. Am. Chem. Soc., AAAS, AAUP, Sigma Xi, Alpha Chi Sigma. Unitarian. Contbr. profl. jours. Home: 1252 Summit Dr Lexington KY 40502

WAGNER, WILLIAM GERARD, univ. dean, physicist; b. St. Cloud, Minn., Aug. 22, 1936; s. Gerard C. and Mary V. (Cloone) W.; B.S., Calif. Inst. Tech., 1958, Ph.D. (NSF fellow, Howard Hughes fellow), 1962; m. Janet Agatha Rowe, Jan. 30, 1968; children—Mary, Robert, David, Anne. Cons. Rand Corp., Santa Monica, Calif., 1960-65; sr. staff physicist Hughes Research Lab., Malibu, Calif., 1960-69; asst. prof. physics U. Calif. at Irvine, 1965-66; asso. prof. physics U. So. Calif., Los Angeles, 1966-69, prof. depts. elec. engring. and physics, 1969—, dean div. natural scis. and math., Coll. Letters, Arts and Scis., 1973—, spl. asst. automated record services, 1975—. Chmn. bd. Malibu Securities Corp., Los Angeles, 1971—; cons. to Janus Mgmt. Corp., Los Angeles, 1970-71, Croesus Capital Corp., Los Angeles, 1971-74. Richard Chase Tolman Postdoctoral fellow, 1962-65. Mem. Am. Phys. Soc., Nat. Assn. Student Financial Aid Adminstrs., Financial Mgmt. Assn., Nat. Assn. Security Dealers, Sigma Xi. Contbr. articles on physics to sci. publs. Home: 2828 Patricia Ave Los Angeles CA 90064 Office: 200 Administration Bldg University of Southern California Los Angeles CA 90007

WAGONER, DAVID RUSSELL, author, educator; b. Massillon, Ohio, June 5, 1926; s. Walter Siffert and Ruth (Banyard) W.; B.A. in English, Pa. State U., 1947; M.A. in English, Ind. U., 1949; m. Patricia Lee Parrott, July 8, 1961. Instr. English DePauw U., 1949-50, Pa. State U., 1950-53; asst. prof. U. Wash., 1954-57, asso. prof., 1958-66, prof., 1966—; elliston lectr. U. Cin., 1968; editor Poetry NW, 1966—; poetry editor Princeton U. Press, 1977. Guggenheim fellow, 1956; Ford fellow, 1964; Nat. Inst. Arts and Letters grantee, 1967; recipient Morton Dauwen Zabel prize Poetry mag., 1967, Blumenthal-Leviton-Blonder prize, 1974, Tietjens prize, 1977; two Fels prizes Coordinating Council Lit. Mags., 1975; Nat. Endowment for Arts grantee, 1969. Mem. Acad. Am. Poets (chancellor 1978—), Soc. Am. Magicians, Nat. Assn. Blackfeet Indians (asso.). Author poetry books: Dry Sun, Dry Wind, 1953; A Place to Stand, 1958; The Nesting Ground, 1963; Staying Alive, 1966; New and Selected Poems, 1969; Working Against Time, 1970; Riverbed, 1972; Sleeping in the Woods, 1974; Collected Poems, 1976; Who Shall Be the Sun?, 1978; In Broken Country, 1979; author novels: The Man in the Middle, 1954; Money, Money Money, 1955; Rock, 1958; The Escape Artist, 1965; Baby, Come on Inside, 1968; Where Is My Wandering Boy Tonight?, 1970; The Road To Many A Wonder, 1974; Tracker, 1975; Whole Hog, 1976. editor: Straw for the Fire: From the Notebooks of Theodore Roethke, 1943-63, 1972. Home: 1075 Summit Ave E Seattle WA 98102

WAGONER, HAROLD EUGENE, ch. architect; b. Pitts., Feb. 27, 1905; s. Jesse L. and Hariett (Hess) W.; A.B., Carnegie Inst. Tech., 1926; postgrad. U. Pa., 1933; m. Ruth Cecelia McClatchy, July 6, 1936; 1 dau., Cynthia Suzanne. Staff mem. Meth. Bur. Architecture in Phila., 1927-33; critic archtl. design Drexel Tech. Eve. Coll., 1930; pvt. archtl. practice, 1933-40; nationwide eccles. archtl. practice, 1944—; received Shrine of Ages commn. for design Protestant, Cath., Jewish chapel on rim of Grand Canyon, Ariz., 1953. Chmn. commn. architecture Luth. Soc. Worship, Music, Arts. Civilian chief camouflage dept. C.E., AUS, 1942-44 (Phila. Dist. Engrs. Office). Recipient award of merit Carnegie Inst. Tech., 1956; Distinguished Achievement award Carnegie-Mellon U., 1970. Fellow A.I.A. (pres. Phila. chpt. 1963); mem. Stained Glass Assn. Am., Art Alliance, Ch. Archtl. Guild Am. (1st award for large chs. 1952, 53; small chs. 1956, dir., pres. 1957), Pi Kappa Alpha, Tau Sigma Delta, Scarab. Designer chapel furnishings Christian Peace bldg. at UN, Protestant chapel USAF Colo. Home: 331 Lindsey Dr Berwyn PA 19312 Office: Architects Bldg Philadelphia PA 19103

WAGONER, JOHN LEONARD, editor; b. Claremore, Okla., July 16, 1927; s. Silvanus and Vivian (Nicholson) W.; B.A. (McMahon fellow), U. Okla., 1951. Writer, editor Kansas City (Mo.) Star, 1953-60; various editorial positions Chgo. Tribune, 1961—, sr. news editor, 1972—. Served with USNR, 1945-46. Mem. Phi Beta Kappa, Sigma Delta Chi. Clubs: Chgo. Headline, Chgo. Press. Office: Chgo Tribune 435 N Michigan Ave Chicago IL 60611

WAGONER, PORTER, country music singer, composer; b. nr. West Plains, Mo., Aug. 12, 1927; s. Charles and Bertha Wagoner; married; children—Richard, Denise, Debra. Former clerk, butcher; singer, composer, radio and TV personality, 1950—; rec. artist RCA Record Co.; radio and TV appearances include radio KWPM, West Plains, Mo., 1950, KWTO, Springfield, Mo. 1951, Jubilee, U.S.A., ABC-TV, 1955, radio WSM Grand Ole Opry, Nashville, Tenn., 1957—, Porter Wagoner TV Show. Recipient (with Dolly Parton) Vocal Group of Year award, 1968, Vocal Duo of Year award (all from Country Music Assn.), 1970, 71. Records include: A Satisfied Mind, Skid Row Joe, Green Green Grass of Home, Cold Hard Facts of Life, Company's Comin', Sorrow on the Rocks, Julie, Carroll County Accident, Porter Wagoner Today. Composer: Look What Followed Me Home Tonight; (with others) Love at First Sight, Be Glad That You Ain't Me, Trademark. Address: 813 18th Ave S Nashville TN 37203

WAGONER, ROBERT VERNON, astrophysicist; b. Teaneck, N.J., Aug. 6, 1938; s. Robert Vernon and Marie Theresa (Clifford) W.; B.M.E., Cornell U., 1961; M.S., Stanford U., 1962, Ph.D., 1965; m. Lynne Ray Moses, Sept. 2, 1963; children—Alexa Frances, Kim Stephanie. Research fellow in physics Calif. Inst. Tech., 1965-68, Sherman Fairchild Disting. scholar, 1976; asst. prof. astronomy Cornell U., 1968-71, asso. prof., 1971-73; asso. prof. physics Stanford U., 1973-77, prof., 1977—; George Ellery Hale Disting. vis. prof. U. Chgo., 1978. Sloan Found. research fellow, 1969-71; Guggenheim Meml. fellow, 1979; NSF grantee, 1973—. Mem. Am. Phys. Soc., Am. Astron. Soc., Internat. Astron. Union, Sigma Xi, Tau Beta Pi, Phi Kappa Phi, Alpha Sigma Phi. Contbr. articles on theoretical astrophysics and gravitation to profl. publs., mags.; patentee in field. Home: 984 Wing Pl Stanford CA 94305 Office: Dept Physics Stanford U Stanford CA 94305

WAGONER, WILLIAM HAMPTON, univ. chancellor; b. Washington, N.C., May 12, 1927; s. William Gotha and Lossie Bell (Barrington) W.; B.S. cum laude, Wake Forest U., 1949; M.A., East Carolina U., 1953; Ph.D. in Ednl. Adminstrn. and Polit. Sci., U. N.C., Chapel Hill, 1958; m. June 3, 1952; children—William Michael, David Robin, Mark Hampton. Tchr., Washington (N.C.) High Sch., 1950-53; asst. prin. Elizabeth City (N.C.) High Sch., 1953-55; prin. Hattie Harney Elementary Sch., Elizabeth City, 1956; instr. U. N.C., 1957; asso. exec. sec. N.C. State Sch. Bds. Assn., 1958-59; supt. Elizabeth City Schs., 1959-61; supt. Wilmington-New Hanover County Schs., 1961-68; pres. Wilmington Coll., 1968; chancellor U. N.C., Wilmington, 1969—. Speaker before various profl. groups at confs., convs. Pres., N.C. Div. Supts., 1967-68; chmn. bd. govs. N.C. Advancement Sch., 1967; mem. Gov.'s Tech. Coordinating Com. for Marine Sci. Council. Served with USNR, 1945-46. Recipient East Carolina Alumni award as Univ.'s Outstanding Alumni Award Winner, 1968. Mem. N.E.A. (life). Democrat. Episcopalian. Club: Kiwanis. Office: PO Box 3725 Wilmington NC 28406 Home: 1705 Market St Wilmington NC 28403

WAGONSELLER, JAMES MYRL, real estate exec.; b. Zanesville, Ohio, July 29, 1920; s. Myrl H. and Florence L. (Pfeiffer) W.; grad. high sch.; m. Mary J. McCauley, Nov. 16, 1943; children—Thomas James, John Myrl, Anne Elizabeth (Mrs. Elwood Kim). Draftsman apprentice machinist Hermann Mfg. Co., Lancaster, Ohio, 1945-47; advt. sales Lancaster (Ohio) Eagle-Gazette, 1947-50, classified mgr., 1950-52, dir. advt. sales, 1952-54; real estate salesman Larkin Durdin, Realtor, Lancaster, 1954-60; partner Lancaster Realty Co., 1960-65, Simons & Wagonseller, Realtors, Lancaster, 1965-77, Wagonseller & Rife, Realtors, 1977—. Pres., Lancaster Bd. Realtors, 1965; mem. Bd. Zoning Appeals Lancaster, 1972-74. Pres., Community Service Council, 1944, United Appeal, 1968. Mem. central, exec. coms. Fairfield County Democratic Com., 1960-70, mem. exec. com., 1976—. Served with USAF, 1941-45. Decorated D.F.C., Air medal with 3 clusters. Mem. Lancaster C. of C. (pres. 1970), Nat., Ohio assns. real estate brokers, Am. Legion (nat. comdr. 1974-75). Kiwanian (pres.), Elk (Ann. Citizen award 1975). Democrat. Roman Catholic. Home: 1973 Coldspring Dr Lancaster OH 43130 Office: 622 E Wheeling St Lancaster OH 43130

WAGSTAFF, ROBERT WILSON, bottling co. exec.; b. Independence, Kans., Nov. 16, 1909; s. Thomas E. and Jane M. (Wilson) W.; A.B., Kans. U., 1930; LL.B., Harvard, 1933; m. Katherine Hall, Nov. 28, 1936; children—Katherine Tinsman, Robert Hall, Thomas Walton. Atty., Sinclair Refining Co., Kansas City, Mo., 1935-45; gen. counsel, later vice chmn., chief exec. officer Vendo Co., Kansas City, Mo., 1947-61; pres. Coca-Cola Bottling Co. Mid-Am., Inc., Shawnee Mission, Kans., 1961-77, chmn., 1961—; pres. Mid-Am. Container Corp., Lenexa, 1969-77, chmn., 1977—; chmn. bd. Fed. Res. Bank Kansas City, Mo., 1970-74; dir. Employers Reins. Corp., Commerce Bank of Kansas City, Los Angeles Coca-Cola Bottling Co. Bd. dirs. Kansas City Crime Commn., Am. Royal; pres. St. Luke's Hosp., Kansas City, Mo.; trustee Kans. Public Employee Retirement System, 1975-79; chancellor Episcopal Diocese W. Mo., 1956-71. Office: 9000 Marshall Dr PO Box 500 Shawnee Mission KS 66201

WAHBA, GRACE, statistician, educator; b. Washington; d. Harry and Anne Goldsmith; B.A., Cornell U., 1956; M.A., U. Md., 1962; Ph.D., Stanford U., 1966; m. A. J. Wahba, 1956 (div. 1964); 1 son, Jeffrey A.; m. 2d R.E. Moore, 1972 (div. 1976). Research mathematician Ops. Research, Inc., Silver Spring, Md., 1957-61; systems analyst IBM, 1962-66; prof. statistics U. Wis., Madison, 1967—; vis. prof. Math Research Center, U. Wis., Stanford U., U. Calif., Santa Cruz; fellow Weizmann Inst., Israel, St. Cross Coll., Oxford (Eng.) U.; Lady Davis fellow Technion, Israel; cons. to industry and govt. Fellow Inst. Math. Statistics; mem. Soc. Indsl. and Applied Math., Bernoulli Soc., Am. Math. Soc., Sigma Xi. Asso. editor Annals of Statistics, 1975—; mem. internat. editorial bd. Communications in Statistics. Contbr. articles to profl. jours. Developer methods of curve and surface smoothing. Address: Dept Statistics U Wis 1210 W Dayton St Madison WI 53705

WAHL, ARTHUR CHARLES, chemist; b. Des Moines, Sept. 8, 1917; s. Arthur C. and Mabel (Mussetter) W.; B.S., Iowa State Coll., 1939; Ph.D., U. Calif., 1942; m. Mary E. McCauley, Dec. 1, 1943; 1 dau., Nancy Jean. Chemist, Manhattan Project, 1942-46; asso. prof. chemistry Washington U., 1946-53, Farr prof. radio-chemistry, 1953—; cons. Los Alamos Sci. Lab., 1950—; NSF Sr. Postdoctoral fellow, 1967. Recipient Am. Chem. Soc. award for nuclear applications in chemistry, 1966, Humboldt award, 1977. Mem. Am. Chem. Soc. Editor, contbr.: Radioactivity Applied to Chemistry, 1951. Author tech. articles. Home: 7400 Teasdale University City MO 63130 Office: Washington U St Louis MO 63130

WAHL, EBERHARD WILHELM, educator; b. Berlin, Germany, May 24, 1914; s. Edmund and Gertrud (George) W.; Ph.D., U. Berlin, 1937; m. Lore Johanne Rading, Mar. 15, 1946; children—Gisela A., Dorothee M. Came to U.S., 1949, naturalized, 1957. Sci. asst. U. Berlin, 1937-45; councilor N.W. German Weather Service, Hamburg, 1946-49; project scientist USAF Cambridge Research Center, 1949-58; tech. dir., astronomer AF Elec. System div., Bedford, Mass., 1958-63; prof. meteorology U. Wis., 1963—, chmn. dept., 1970-73; cons. U.S. Army Missile Command. Trustee, mem. rep. Univ. Corp. of Atmospheric Research, 1967—. Served with German Air Force, World War II. Fellow A.A.A.S.; mem. Am. Meteorol. Soc., Am. Astron. Soc., Am. Geophys. Union, German Meteorol. Soc., Audubon Soc., Nature Conservancy, Sigma Xi. Contbr. articles profl. jours. Home: 5718 Tolman Terrace Madison WI 53711

WAHL, PAUL, writer, photographer; b. Union City, N.J., Jan. 17, 1922; s. Frank Joseph and Anne (Frechen) W.; grad. high sch. Partner, Wahl Arms Co., Bogota, N.J., 1948-68; propr. Wahl Co., Bogota, 1962-68; partner Frank J. Wahl Co., 1968—. Mem. Nat. Assn. Sci. Writers, Authors League Am., Am. Inst. Aeros. and Astronautics, Am. Soc. Mag. Photographers, Authors Guild, Aviation/Space Writers Assn., Outdoor Writers Assn. Am., Am. Soc. Journalists and Authors, Am. Def. Preparedness Assn., Nat. Rifle Assn., AAAS, Am. Med. Writers Assn., Nat. Press Club, Soc. Photog. Scientists and Engrs. Author: Gun Traders Guide, 1953-78; Arms Trade Yearbook, 1955, 1956; Single Lens Reflex Guide, 1959; Subminiature Technique, 1960; Press/View Camera Technique, 1962; The Candid Photographer, 1963; Carbine Handbook, 1964; The Gatling Gun, 1965. Cons. editor Popular Sci., 1976—; contbr. to other mags. Designer, Gatling Gun Centennial medal, 1961, Grant and Lee commemorative medals, 1962. Address: PO Box 6 Bogota NJ 07603

WAHLEN, EDWIN ALFRED, lawyer; b. Gary, Ind., Mar. 12, 1919; s. Alfred and Ethel (Pearson) W.; student U. Ala., 1936-38; A.B., U. Chgo., 1942, J.D., 1948; m. Alice Elizabeth Condit, Apr. 24, 1943; children—Edwin Alfred, Virginia Elizabeth, Martha Anne. Admitted to Ill. bar, 1948, since practiced in Chgo.; mem. firm Haight, Goldstein & Haight, 1948-55; partner Goldstein & Wahlen, 1956-59; partner Arvey, Hodes, Costello & Burman and predecessor, 1959—. Served to 2d lt. AUS, 1942-46. Decorated Silver Star medal. Mem. Am., Ill., Chgo. bar assns., Order of Coif, Phi Beta Kappa, Phi Alpha Delta. Author: Soldiers and Sailors Wills: A Proposal For Federal Legislation, 1948. Home: 3750 N Lake Shore Dr Chicago IL 60613 Office: 180 N LaSalle St Chicago IL 60601

WAHLER, WILLIAM ALBERT, engring. cons.; b. Boulder, Colo., Nov. 5, 1925; s. Joseph August and Alice V. Kelling; B.S. in Civil Engring., U. Colo., 1950, M.S., 1952; postgrad. Harvard U., M.I.T., 1953-54; m. Joyce Benson, Sept. 3, 1949; children—Mark J., Diana J., Lance S. Soil mechanics engr. U.S. Bur. Reclamation, Denver, 1949-53; partner Woodward, Clyde & Assos., Cons. Engrs., Denver, 1953-55; sr. soil engr. Bechtel Corp., Los Angeles, 1955-61; founder, pres. W.A. Wahler & Assos., Palo Alto, Calif., 1961-79, W.A. Wahler, Inc., Palo Alto, 1979—; chmn. USCOLD Com. for Tailings Embankments. Served to lt. USNR, 1944-46. Mem. Internat. Com. on Large Dams, U.S. Com. on Large Dams, ASCE, Assns. Engring. Geologists, Nat. Soc. Profl. Engrs. Contbr. articles on dams to profl. jours.

WAHLERT, ROBERT HENRY, meat packing co. exec.; b. Dubuque, Iowa, Jan. 19, 1939; s. Robert Charles and Celeste Joan (Canepa) W.; B.Sc., U. Iowa, 1963; m. Donna Jane Allendorf, June 3, 1961; children—Robert C., Amy, Kathleen, Marni, Mark. Sales trainee Dubuque Packing Co., 1961-63, advt. mgr., 1963-65, gen. sales mgr., 1965-69, v.p. sales, 1969-73, exec. v.p., 1973-77, chmn. bd., chief exec. officer, 1977—; dir., founder Key City Bank, Dubuque; dir. Rigid-Pak Corp., San Juan, P.R. Edelcar Corp., San Juan, Banks of Iowa. Bd. dirs., treas. Wahlert Found.; v.p. Dubuque Symphony Orch., 1967-74. Republican. Roman Catholic. Club: Dubuque Golf and Country (past pres.). Home: 600 Sunset Ridge Dubuque IA 52001 Office: 16th and Sycamore Dubuque Packing Co Dubuque IA 52001

WAHLGREN, ERIK, educator; b. Chgo., Nov. 2, 1911; s. Oscar G. and Marion I. (Wilkins) W.; Ph.B., U. Chgo., 1933, Ph.D., 1938; M.A., U. Neb., 1936; m. Dorothy Sly, Nov. 9, 1939 (div. 1951); children—Nils, Arvid; m. 2d, Beverly Pont, Dec. 18, 1952 (div. 1969); children—Siri, Thor; m. 3d, Helen Gilchrist-Wottring, July 2, 1971; 2 step-children. Mem. faculty U. Calif. at Los Angeles, 1938—, prof. Scandinavian Langs., 1955-70, Scandinavian and Germanic langs., 1970-77, prof. emeritus, 1977—, vice chmn. dept. Germanic langs., 1963-69, dir. U. Calif. study centers at Univs. Lund (Sweden) and Bergen (Norway), 1972-74; lectr. Uppsala U., also vis. prof. Stockholm Sch. Econs., 1947-48; exchange instr. U. B.C., summer 1940; vis. prof. Augustana Coll., summer 1946, U. Calif. at Berkeley, 1968, U. Wash., 1970, Portland State U., 1979—. U.S. mem. Commn. Ednl. Exchange U.S.-Sweden, 1973-74; sr. fellow, cons. Monterey Inst. Fgn. Studies, 1977-78; adv. Nat. Endowment Humanities, 1978—; German lang. dir. Army Specialized Tng. Program, 1943-44; mem. Mayor's Community Adv. Com., 1964-73. Am.-Scandinavian Found. fellow, Sweden, 1946-47, grantee to Scandinavia, Am. Philos. Soc., 1954-55; Guggenheim Meml. Found. fellow, Scandinavia, 1961-62; recipient pub. citation Icelandic Community Los Angeles, 1964, Gold medal Am.-Scandinavian Found., 1975. Decorated knight Royal Swedish Order of Polar Star; knight Order Lion of Finland. Fellow Internat. Inst. Arts and Letters (life); mem. Swedish Cultural Soc. Am. (dir. 1940-48, pres. Los Angeles 1941-46), Modern Lang. Assn. So. Calif. (exec. bd. 1950-53), Am.-Scandinavian Found. (pres. Los Angeles chpt. 1958-60), Modern Lang. Assn. Am. (chmn. Scandinavian sect. 1955, 67), Soc. Advancement Scandinavian Study (asso. editor, 1947-57, 70-73, asso. mng. editor 1957-69), Am. Assn. Tchrs. German (nat. exec. council 1957-59, 60-63), Finlandia Found., Medieval Acad. Am., Am. Swedish Hist. Mus., Swedish-Am. Hist. Soc. Calif., World Affairs Council Oreg., Tau Kappa Epsilon, Delta Sigma Rho, Delta Phi Alpha. Author: The Kensington Stone: A Mystery Solved, 1958; Fact and Fancy in the Vinland Sagas, 1969; also several other books, translations and numerous articles on Scandinavian philology. Home and Office: 752 Lake Forest Dr Lake Oswego OR 97034. *In struggling to impose intellectual and moral authority on the seeming chaos of experience, the human race as a whole makes no enduring progress. But the wise individual learns—alas! for himself alone—that the most honest answers to life's dilemmas are the direct and simple ones.*

WAHLKE, JOHN CHARLES, educator; b. Cin., Oct. 29, 1917; s. Albert B.C. and Clara J. (Ernst) W.; A.B., Harvard, 1939, M.A., 1947, Ph.D., 1952; m. Virginia Joan Higgins, Dec. 1, 1943; children—Janet (Mrs. Michael Parmely), Dale. Instr., asst. prof. polit. sci. Amherst (Mass.) Coll., 1949-53; prof. polit. sci. Vanderbilt, 1953-63; prof. polit. sci. State U. N.Y. at Buffalo, 1963-66; prof. polit. sci. U. Iowa, 1966-71; prof. polit. sci. State U. N.Y. at Stony Brook, 1971-72, U. Iowa, Iowa City, 1972-79, U. Ariz., Tucson, 1979—. Served to capt., F.A., AUS, 1942-46. Decorated Air medal with 2 oak leaf clusters. Mem. Am. (past pres.), Internat., So., Midwest (past pres.), Western, Southwestern polit. sci. assns., Soc. for Psychophysiol. Research. Author: (with others) The Legislative System, 1962, Government and Politics, 1966, The Politics of Representation, 1978. Editor: Causes of the American Revolution, 1950; Loyalty in a Democratic State, 1952; co-editor: Legislative Behavior, 1959; The American Political System, 1967; Comparative Legislative Behavior, 1973. Home: 5462 N Entrada Catorce Tucson AZ 85718 Office: Dept Polit Sci U Ariz Tucson AZ 85721

WAHLSTROM, ERNEST EUGENE, coll. adminstr.; b. Boulder, Colo., Dec. 30, 1909; s. Charles S. and Christine (Dahlin) W.; B.A., U. Colo., 1931, M.A., 1933; M.A., Harvard, 1936, Ph.D., 1939; m. Kathryn E. Kemp, Sept. 23, 1931; children—David Kemp, Karen Jean (Mrs. Steven V. Guzak). Mem. faculty U. Colo., 1936—, prof. geology, 1947–, chmn. dept. geol. scis., 1967-68, dean faculties, 1968-70, vice provost, 1970-71; cons. in field, 1939—. Fellow Geol. Soc. Am., Mineral Soc. Am., AAAS; mem. Soc. Econ. Geologists, Assn. Engring. Geologists, Assn. Profl. Geol. Scientists. Author six books in field. Contbr. profl. jours., encys. Home: 1566 Greenbriar Blvd Boulder CO 80303

WAHLSTROM, LAWRENCE FERDINAND, educator; b. Aurora, Wis., Feb. 4, 1915; s. Gust Hjalmar and Anna Sofia (Olsson) W.; B.A., Lawrence Coll., 1936; M.A., U. Wis., 1937, Ph.D., 1950; m. Dorothy A. Stegman, July 13, 1938; children—Linda Kay, Jon Lewis. Tchr. math. Loves Park (Ill.) Sch., 1937-41; chmn. math. dept. Lincoln Jr. High Sch., Rockford, Ill., 1941-45, Elgin (Ill.) Acad., 1945-47; grad. asst. math. U. Wis.-Madison, 1947-48; chmn. math. dept. U. Wis.-Eau Claire, 1948—. Pres., Cerebral Palsy Orgn., Eau Claire, 1954-55; pres. Midwest Inst. Scandinavian Culture, 1960—; chmn. Eau Claire County Democratic Com., 1951-52. NSF grantee to study in Scandinavian countries, 1957-58. Mem. Am. Math. Assn. (sec. Wis. sect. 1948—, chmn. 1953-54). Home: 110 Skyline Dr Eau Claire WI 54701

WAHN, IAN GRANT, lawyer; b. Herbert, Sask., Can., Apr. 18, 1916; s. Edgar Valentine and Margaret Florence (Reid) W.; LL.B., U. Sask., 1936; B.A. (Rhodes scholar), Oxford (Eng.) U., 1939, M.A., 1940; Barrister and Solicitor, Osgoode Hall Law Sch., 1942; m. Pearl Helen Lychak, Dec. 15, 1942; children—Ian Grant, Gordon Douglas. Called to Ont. bar, 1942, practiced in Toronto, 1946—; partner firm Borden, Elliot, Kelley & Palmer, 1956-62; partner firm Wahn, Mayer, Smith, Creber, Lyons, Torrance & Stevenson (now Smith, Lyons, Torrance, Stevenson & Mayer), 1962-69, counsel, 1969—; M.P. for St. Pauls, 1962-72, chmn. Ho. of Commons standing com. on external affairs and nat. def., 1968-72; chmn. Ont. Liberal Caucus, 1967-69. Chmn., dir. Alwinsal Potash of Can., Ltd.; dir. Potash Co. of Can., Ltd., Canadian Badger Co. Ltd. Served with Queens Own Rifles of Can., World War II. Recipient Univ. Gold medal, 1936. Mem. Deer Park Residents Assn., St. Pauls, St. Patricks liberal assns., Canadian Bar Assn., Queens Own Rifles of Can. Assn., Canadian Lawn Tennis Assn., U. Sask. Alumni Assn., Rhodes Scholars Found., Rhodes Scholars Assn. Clubs: Nat., Cricket, Skating and Curling (Toronto). Home: 62 Heath St W Toronto ON M4V 1T4 Canada Office: Toronto Dominion Centre Toronto ON M5K 1C7 Canada

WAHRSAGER, SIGMUND, investment co. exec.; b. N.Y.C., Oct. 26, 1925; s. Sam and Sadie (Koback) W.; A.B., Princeton, 1947; M.B.A., N.Y. U., 1950; m. Karel Fierman, Mar. 3, 1955; children—Eve, Erika, Kay. With Prudential Ins. Co. Am., 1947-50, Kuhn, Loeb Co., 1950-53; partner Bear, Stearns & Co., N.Y.C., 1953—; dir. Fla. Water & Utilities Co., Midland Glass Co., Inc., Sonderling Broadcasting Corp., S.E. Nichols, Inc., Hartford-Zodys Corp., and others; pres. Danbury River Properties, Inc. Bd. dirs. Wahrsager Found. Served with USNR, 1944-46. Home: 700 Park Ave New York NY 10005 Office: 55 Water St New York NY 10041

WAID, JAMES BYNUM, judge; b. Boaz, Ala., Mar. 25, 1919; s. Luther Pinckney and Roxie Ophelia (Bynum) W.; student Snead Jr. Coll., 1936-38; LL.B., U. Ala., 1948; m. LuVerna McKenna, June 2, 1946; children—Susan (Mrs. Randy Brown), Gerald, Walter, Richard. Admitted to Ala. bar, 1949; practice law, Gadsden, Ala., 1949-65; city atty. City of Gadsden, 1965-66; circuit judge 16th Jud. Circuit, Gadsden, 1966—. Chmn. adv. bd. Salvation Army, 1968-70. Served to capt., USAAF, 1942-46. Methodist. Club: Gadsden Civitan (past pres., past gov. No. Ala. dist.). Home: 431 Country Club Dr Gadsden AL 35901 Office: Etowah County Courthouse Gadsden AL 35901

WAIDELICH, CHARLES J., oil co. exec.; b. Columbus, Ohio, May 2, 1929; s. Bernard Howard and Alberta (Poth) W.; B.S., Purdue U., 1951; m. Margaret Ellen Finley, Jan. 26, 1952; children—Michael Brian, Sharon Ann. Engr., Cities Service Oil Co., Bartlesville, Okla., 1951-54; asst. to pres. Cities Service Pipeline Co., Bartlesville, Okla., 1956-59; pipeline coordinator Cities Service Co., N.Y.C., 1959-65, transp. coordinator, 1965-66, staff v.p. ops. coordination, 1966-68, exec. v.p. ops., dir., 1970-71, pres., 1971—; v.p. ops. Tenn. Corp., N.Y.C., 1968-70; chmn. bd. Colonial Pipeline Co., Atlanta, 1967-70; dir. Bank of Okla. Bd. dirs. Transp. Assn. Am.; pres. Tulsa Area United Way; mem. Pres.'s Council Purdue U. Served with C.E., AUS, 1954-56. Mem. Am. Petroleum Inst., Am. Inst. Mining Engrs., Theta Xi. Clubs: Economic, Sky (N.Y.C.); Southern Hills Country, Tulsa, Summit (Tulsa); Internat. (Washington). Mason. Office: Cities Service Bldg Box 300 Tulsa OK 74102*

WAINER, STANLEY ALLEN, diversified industry exec.; b. Los Angeles, May 10, 1926; s. Calman and Katherine (Copeland) W.; B.S., U. Calif. at Los Angeles, 1950, grad. exec. program, 1958; m. Shirlene Joy Goldberg, Feb. 3, 1949; 1 son, William Edward. Accountant, Price Waterhouse & Co., Los Angeles, 1950-55; chief financial and adminstrv. officer Paramount Pictures Corp. and subsidiaries, 1955-60; v.p., sec.-treas. Royal Industries, Pasadena, Calif., 1960-61; with Wyle Labs., El Segundo, Calif., 1962—, pres., 1970—; dir. Redwing Carriers, Inc., Elmar Electronics, Inc. Pres., dir. UCLA Bus. Sch. Alumni Assn., 1968-69; trustee UCLA Found., 1970—, dir. bd. overseers, 1972—; mem. dean's mgmt. council U. Calif. Los Angeles Grad. Sch. Mgmt.; bd. dirs. NCCJ, 1973—, Los Angeles Urban League, 1979—; trustee Orthopaedic Hosp., Los Angeles, 1975—. Served with USNR, 1944-46. Mem. Financial Execs. Inst., Am. Inst. C.P.A.'s, Calif. Soc. C.P.A.'s, C. of C. of U.S., Calif. C. of C., Los Angeles C. of C., UCLA Alumni Assn. (v.p. 1970-72, pres.-elect 1979—), Soc. Order Blue Shield, Town Hall, Beta Gamma Sigma. Home: 1151 Hilary Ln Beverly Hills CA 90210 Office: 128 Maryland St El Segundo CA 90245

WAINERDI, RICHARD ELLIOTT, bus. exec.; b. N.Y.C., Nov. 27, 1931; s. Harold Roule and Margaret (Greenhut) W.; B.S. in Petroleum Engring., Okla. U., 1952; M.S., Pa. State U., 1955, Ph.D., 1958; m. Angela Lampone, June 2, 1956; children—Thomas Joseph, James Cooper. Research asst., fellow petroleum engring. Pa. State U., 1953-55; mem. faculty Tex. A. and M. U., College Station, 1957-77, prof. chem. engring., 1961-77, asso. v.p. acad. affairs., 1974-77, also founder, head activation analysis lab., 1957-77; sr. v.p. 3D/Internat., Houston, 1977—, coordinator nuclear activities Dresser Industries Inc., Dallas, 1956-57; head Nuclear Sci. Center Tex. Engring. Experiment Sta., 1957-59; regional editor Internat. Jour. Radioanalytical Chemistry; contbg. editor Producers Monthly, 1957-69; asso. editor Radiochemical and Radioanalytical Letters; mem. editorial adv. bd. Talanta jour., 1969. Dir. First Nat. Bank, Bryan, Tex. Mem. Tex. Energy Adv. Com., 1964—. Served with USAF, 1952-53. Recipient 1st place presentation award Am. Inst. Chem. Engrs. and Chem. Inst. Can., 1961, disting. research award Tex. A. and M. U., 1962, George Hevesy medal, 1977, and others. Registered profl. engr., Tex. Mem. Am. Nuclear Soc. (chmn. isotopes and radiation div. 1964), Internat. Union Pure and Applied Chemistry, Am. Soc. Engring. Edn., Am. Chem. Soc., Sigma Xi, Tau Beta Pi, Phi Kappa Phi, Sigma Tau, Pi Epsilon Tau, Phi Eta Sigma. K.C. Author: Analytical Chemistry in Space; Modern Methods of Geochemical Analysis. Contbr. to profl. jours. Patentee in field. Home: 1635 Warwickshire Dr Houston TX 77077

WAINIO, WALTER, biochemist, educator; b. Astoria, Oreg., Sept. 8, 1914; s. Waldemar and Wilhelmina (Taipale) W.; B.S., U. Mass., 1936; M.S., Pa. State U., 1940; Ph.D., Cornell U., 1943; m. Betty Dent Hill, June 30, 1949; 1 dau., Marguerite. Instr., Pa. State U., 1938-41, Cornell U. Med. Coll., 1941-43; faculty N.Y. U. Coll. Dentistry, 1943-48, asst. prof., 1944-48; faculty Rutgers U., New Brunswick, N.J., 1948—, prof. bio-chemistry, 1959—, chmn. dept. physiology and biochemistry, 1960-63, chmn. dept. biochemistry, 1966-72, 75-78. Fellow N.Y. Acad. Scis.; mem. Am. Soc. Biol. Chemists, A.A.A.S., Am. Chem. Soc., Biochem. Soc. (Eng.). Contbr. articles to profl. jours. Home: 477 Walnut Ln Princeton NJ 08540 Office: Box 1059 Nelson Biol Labs Rutgers U Piscataway NJ 08854

WAINWRIGHT, BILL C., savs. and loan assn. exec.; b. Tampa, Fla., Nov. 20, 1913; s. Truby L. and Mabel A. (Britt) W.; B.S. in Bus., U. Fla., 1937; LL.B., Atlanta Law Sch., 1947; postgrad. Ind. U., 1956, Dartmouth, 1963; m. Rebecca Ann Bethel, June 27, 1942; children—Rebecca Ann Amos, Bill C. Chmn. bd. Ga. Fed. Savs. & Loan Assn., 1945—, also dir. mem. exec. com.; dir. United Family Life Ins. Co. Mem. Atlanta Bd. Edn., 1966-71, pres., 1968-69; pres. Atlanta Traffic and Safety Council, 1967, Northside Hosp., 1964-65; v.p. Better Bus. Bur. Atlanta. Bd. dirs. Am. Cancer Soc. Served as lt. col. AUS, 1941-46. Mem. State Bar. Ga., Atlanta Bar Assn., Am. Savs. and Loan Inst. (nat. pres. 1961), Ga. Savings and Loan League (pres. 1959), Atlanta C. of C. (dir. 1963-65), Am. Legion, Grand Jurors Assn., Lambda Chi Alpha (nat. dir.). Presbyn. Kiwanian. Clubs: Commerce, Cherokee Town and Country. Home: 3213 Old Mill Trace SE Marietta GA 30067 Office: 20 Marietta St NW Atlanta GA 30303

WAINWRIGHT, CARROLL LIVINGSTON, JR., lawyer; b. N.Y.C., Dec. 28, 1925; s. Carroll Livingston and Edith Katherine (Gould) W.; B.A., Yale U., 1949; LL.B., Harvard U., 1952; m. Nina Walker, July 2, 1948; children—Delos Walker, Mark Livingston. Admitted to N.Y. bar, 1953; with firm Milbank, Tweed, Hadley & McCloy, and predecessor, N.Y.C., 1952-58, 60-62, partner, 1963—; asst. counsel Gov. N.Y., 1959-60; mem. State Commn. Jud. Conduct, 1974—. Trustee Am. Mus. Natural History, Cooper Union Advancement Sci. and Art, Boys' Club N.Y.; trustee Ch. Pension Fund and Affiliates, treas., 1974-78; mem. univ. council Yale U. Served with USMCR, 1943-46. Mem. Am., N.Y. State bar assns., Assn. Bar City N.Y. (treas. 1970-73, v.p. 1975-76), Am. Coll. Probate Counsel. Clubs: Century Assn., Union, River (N.Y.C.); Maidstone (pres. 1970-73) (East Hampton, N.Y.). Home: 1120 Fifth Ave New York NY 10028 Office: 1 Chase Manhattan Plaza New York NY 10005

WAINWRIGHT, CHARLES ANTHONY, advt. agy. exec.; b. Los Angeles, Sept. 14, 1933; B.A. in Journalism, U. Colo., 1955; m. Mary Beth Halbmaier, Jan. 10, 1975; children—Colleen Ann, Elizabeth Ann. Vice pres. Tatham-Laird & Kudner, Inc., Chgo., 1964-69; pres. Wainwright, Spaeth & Wright, Inc., Chgo., 1969-77; sr. v.p. Grey Advt., Inc., Phoenix, 1977-78; exec. v.p. Marsbhalk Co. Inc., N.Y.C., 1978—; dir. Gamut of Games, Inc. Served with USN, 1956-58. Recipient Clio award, 1966, 67, Internat. Broadcast award, 1964, award Venice Film Festival, 1962, Chgo. Advt. Club, 1965, Outstanding Grad. award U. Colo., 1976. Roman Catholic. Club: Pelham (N.Y.) Country. Author: Television Commercials, 1962; Successful Management of New Products, 1964. Office: 1345 Ave Americas New York NY 10019

WAINWRIGHT, JAMES, actor; b. Danville, Ill., Mar. 5, 1938; s. Leo and Esther (Hembry) W.; student U. So. Calif.; divorced; 1 dau., Beth. TV series include Daniel Boone, 1968, Jigsaw, 1973; television movies President's Plane Is Missing, Man On The Move, Once Upon A Death, Killdozer, A Woman Called Moses, others; film appearances in Hoover, Joe Kidd, 1978, Mean Dog Blues, 1978; TV movies include Woman Called Moses, Freedom Riders; Beyond Westworld; over 100 guest star appearances; television series Beyond Westworld, 1980—; cons. Oxnard (Calif.) Police Dept. Served with USMC, 1954-58. Recipient Medal of Valor, Ventura County (Calif.) Peace Officers Assn., 1976. Mem. AFTRA, Screen Actors Guild, Actors Guild.

WAINWRIGHT, STUYVESANT, II, lawyer; b. N.Y.C., Mar. 16, 1921; s. Carroll L. and Edith Catherine (Gould) W.; LL.B., Yale U., 1947; m. Janet Parsons, June 12, 1941; children—Stuyvesant III, Jonathan Mayhew, Janet Snowden Waring, Laura Livingston. Admitted to N.Y. bar, 1948; with Satterlee, Warfield & Stephens, N.Y.C., 1947-49; partner firm Evarts, Balzell, Wainwright & Baker, N.Y.C., 1949-52, partner Wainwright & Matthews, Huntington, N.Y., 1953-64, Walker, Beale, Wainwright & Wolf, N.Y.C., 1965-70; partner Battle, Fowler, Lidstone, Jaffin, Pierce & Kheel, N.Y.C., 1970-75; chmn. bd. Miltope Corp., Plainview, N.Y., 1975-79; Authur T. Vanderbilt prof. polit. sci., Rutgers, 1961-62; mem. 83d-86th Congresses, 1st Dist. N.Y.; spl. congl. mission to Far East, 1953. Served in Office Strategic Services, U.S. Army, 1942-45; spl. mission to Vietnam with Lt. Gen. James Gavin, 1967. Mem. Phi Delta Phi. Republican. Mason. Clubs: Union, Maidstone (L.I.); Royal Bermuda Yacht. Home: Box 199 Wainscott NY 11975 Office: 521 Park Ave New York NY 10017

WAIT, JAMES RICHARD, educator, scientist; b. Ottawa, Ont., Can., Jan. 23, 1924; s. George Enoch and Doris Lillian (Browne) W.; came to U.S., 1955, naturalized, 1960; B.A.Sc., U. Toronto (Ont.), 1948, M.A.Sc., 1949, Ph.D. in Electromagnetic Theory, 1951; m. Gertrude Laura Harriet, June 16, 1951; children—Laura, George. Research engr. Newmont Eploration, Ltd., N.Y.C., 1948-51; sect. leader Def. Research Telecommunications Establishment, Ottawa, 1952-55, sr. scientist, 1970-71; scientist Nat. Bur. Standards, Boulder, Colo., 1955—; adj. prof. elec. engring. U. Colo. at Boulder, 1961—, fellow Coop. Inst. Research Environ. Scis., 1968—; sr. scientist Office of Dir. Environ. Research Labs., Boulder, 1967-70, 71—. Vis. research fellow lab. electromagnetic theory U. Denmark, Copenhagen, 1961; vis. prof. Harvard, 1966-67, Catholic U., Rio de Janeiro, Brazil, 1971;

mem.-at-large U.S. nat. com. Internat. Sci. Radio Union, 1963-65, 69-72, del. gen. assemblies, Boulder, 1957, London, 1960, Tokyo, 1963, Ottawa, 1969, Warsaw, Poland, 1972, Lima, Peru, 1975, Helsinki, Finland, 1978, sec. U.S. nat. com., 1976-78. Served with Canadian Army, 1942-45. Recipient Gold medal Dept. Commerce, 1958; Samuel Wesley Stratton award Nat. Bur. Standards, 1962; Arthur S. Flemming award Washington C. of C., 1964; Outstanding Publ. award Office Telecommunications, Washington, 1972; Research and Achievement award Nat. Oceanic and Atmospheric Adminstrn., 1973; Van der Pol gold medal, 1978. Fellow IEEE (mem. adminstrv. com. on antennas and propagation 1966-73; Harry Diamond award 1964), Instn. Elec. Engrs. (Gt. Britain), Sci. Research Soc. Am. (Boulder Scientist award 1960), AAAS; mem. Nat. Acad. Engring. Founder, Jour. Radio Sci., 1959-68; editor: Radio Science, 1969-72, Pure and Applied Geophysics, 1964-75; editor internat. series monographs on electromagnetic waves Pergamon Press, 1961-73, Instn. Elec. Engrs., London, 1974—. Home: 450 13th St Boulder CO 80302 Office: US Dept Commerce Research Bldg 1 Room 242 Boulder CO 80303

WAITE, CHARLES MORRISON, food co. exec.; b. Chgo., Oct. 1, 1932; s. Norman and Lavinia M. (Fyke) W.; B.A., Yale, 1954; M.B.A., Harvard, 1958; m. Barbara Chowning Wham, Aug. 21, 1954; children—Susan R., Charles M., John B., David T. Mgr. planning and analysis Standard Fruit & Steamship Co., New Orleans, 1958-62, v.p., exec. v.p., 1969-72, dir., 1972-76, div. mgr. Standard Fruit Co., La Ceiba, Honduras, 1962-69, dir. Standard Fruit Tropical Charities, Inc., 1970-76; sr. v.p. Castle & Cooke, Inc., Honolulu, 1972-76, exec. v.p. Castle & Cooke Foods, San Francisco, 1974-76; pres. United Fruit Co., Boston, 1976-77; sr. v.p. United Brands Co., Boston, 1976-77; pres. Genoa Packing Co., Boston, 1977-78; pres. Catelli Inc., 1979—. Served to 1st lt. USAF, 1955-57. Mem. Zeta Psi. Republican. Episcopalian. Club: Harvard (Boston). Home: Cherry Valley Rd Gilford NH 03246 Office: Commercial St Manchester NH 03101

WAITE, DANIEL ELMER, oral surgeon; b. Grand Rapids, Mich., Feb. 19, 1926; s. Charles Austin and Phoebe Isabel (Smith) W.; A.A., Graceland Coll., 1948; D.D.S., State U. Ia. Coll. Dentistry, 1953, M.S., Grad. Coll., 1955, certificate oral surgery, certificate residency univ. hosps., 1955; m. Alice Darlene Carlile, June 20, 1948; children—Christine Ann, Thomas Charles, Peter Daniel, Julie Marilyn, Stuart David. Resident oral surgery State U. Ia. Hosps., 1953-55; instr. oral surgery State U. Ia. Coll. Dentistry, 1955-56, asst. prof., 1956-57, asso. prof., acting head dept. oral surgery, 1957-59, prof. head dept., 1959-63; mem. staff Mayo Clinic, Mayo Grad. Sch. Medicine, Rochester, Minn., 1963-68; prof., also chmn. div. oral surgery U. Minn., 1968—. Active, People to People Found.; served with Project HOPE, Peru, 1962, Sri Lanka, 1969, Egypt, 1975. Trustee Graceland Coll., Lamoni, Iowa, 1970-78, Park Coll., Parkville, Mo., 1972-78; bd. dirs. Hennepin County unit Am. Cancer Soc., 1970-73. Served with USAAF, 1944-46; sr. dental surgeon USPHS(R). Recipient Novice award Internat. Assn. Dental Research, 1955. Diplomate Am. Bd. Oral Surgery. Fellow Am. Coll. Dentists, Am. Soc. Oral Surgeons; mem. Midwestern. Ia. (sec. 1958-61, pres. 1962) socs. oral surgeons, Am. Dental Assn., Internat. Assn. Dental Research (sec. Ia. sect. 1957-62), Sigma Xi, Omicron Kappa Upsilon. Mem. Reorganized Ch. of Jesus Christ of Latter Day Saints. (patriarch, mem. med. council). Author: Textbook of Practical Oral Surgery, 1972, 2d edit., 1978. Contbr. numerous articles to profl. jours. Home: 1801 Pennsylvania Ave N Golden Valley MN 55427

WAITE, MARY GEORGE JORDAN, banker; b. Centre, Ala., Aug. 8, 1918; d. James Oleus and Louise (Smith) Jordan; A.B., Huntingdon Coll., 1939, LL.D., 1974; grad. Sch. Banking of South, La. State U., 1960, grad. Sr. Mgmt. Sch., 1977; m. Dan Waite, Jr., Aug. 22, 1940; 1 dau., Betty Graves. Tchr. English, Cherokee County (Ala.) High Sch., 1944-49; pres., chmn. bd. Farmers & Mchts. Bank of Centre, 1957—; mem. Ala. Banking Bd., 1980—. Mem. exec. com. Choccolocco council Boy Scouts Am., 1972-75, pres., 1980, dist. chmn. Sequoyah Dist., bd. dirs. regional dist.; pres. Ala. sect. Am. Legion Aux., 1950, nat. v.p. So. div., 1960; past chmn. pub. edn. Ala. div. Am. Cancer Soc., 1971-75, crusade chmn., 1973, chmn. bd. dirs., 1980; chmn. Ala. Future Farmers Am. Found., Ala. Adv. Council on Vocat. Edn., 1976. Bd. dirs. Ala. 4-H Found., Ala. Dept. Pensions and Security, 1970-71, Little Theatre, Cherokee County, Ala. Women's Hall of Fame, Judson Coll., 1973-75, Wesley Found., Jacksonville State U., 1974—; mem. adv. bd. Sch. Bus., Auburn U.; mem. pres.'s cabinet U. Ala.; trustee Internat. House, Jacksonville State U., sec., treas., 1965-69, chmn., 1969—; trustee Huntingdon Coll., 1974—; nat. trustee Future Farmers Am. Found., 1974-76; bd. visitors Sch. Commerce, U. Ala., 1980. Recipient Outstanding Bank Women in the U.S. award Nat. Assn. Bank Women, 1961; State Woman of Achievement award Bus. and Profl. Womens Club, 1968; 4-H Nat. Alumni Key award, 1970; Alumni award Huntingdon Coll., 1973; Silver Fawn award Boy Scouts Am., 1974; hon. Am. Farmer degree Future Farmers Am., 1971. Mem. Am. (dir. 1973-75, mem. exec. council mktg. div. 1974-75, exec. council community bankers div. 1980, banker adv. 1980, mem. task force on regulation 1980), Ala. Bankers Assn. (state banking bd. 1970—, state legis. and resolutions com. 1968—, v.p. 1970, pres. 1971-72, finance com. 1972—, dir. ind. bankers div.), Nat. Assn. Bank Women (dir. 1960, regional v.p. So. div. 1965, pres. Ala. div. 1960), Bank Adminstrn. Inst. (community bank council), U.S. C. of C. (mem. urban affairs com. 1970-75), Centre C. of C. (pres. 1968-70), Future Farmers Am. (dist. chmn. 1965-75, state found. chmn. 1971-75, award 1970), Ala. Fedn. Womens Clubs (pres. 1968-70, 1st. v.p. Southeastern council 1972-73), Huntingdon Coll. Alumni Assn. (pres. 1973). Methodist (tchr. Sunday sch. 1965-75, pres. Wesleyan Service Guild 1966). Home: 310 College St PO Box 220 Centre AL 35960 Office: Farmers and Merchants Bank 130 Main St Centre AL 35960

WAITE, NORMAN, lawyer; b. Boston, Mar. 21, 1905; s. Frederick Caruth and Annie Hollis (Rogers) W.; A.B., Yale, 1927; LL.B., Harvard, 1930; m. Lavinia M. Fyke, Dec. 21, 1929; children—Charles Morrison, Norman. Admitted to Ill. bar, 1932, since practiced in Chgo.; with firm Schiff Hardin & Walte and predecessors, 1932—, partner, 1940—. Mem. Am., Ill., Chgo. bar assns., Chgo. Law Club, Chgo. Legal Club. Clubs: University (Chgo.); Indian Hill (Winnetka, Ill.); Bird Key Yacht (Sarasota, Fla.). Home: 512 North Spoonbill Dr Sarasota FL 33577 Office: 7200 Sears Tower Chicago IL 60606

WAITE, PETER BUSBY, historian; b. Toronto, Ont., Can., July 12, 1922; s. Cyril and Mary Henrietta (Craig) W.; B.A. with honors, U. B.C. (Can.), 1948, M.A., 1950; Ph.D., U. Toronto, 1954; m. Masha Anna Maria Gropuzzo, Aug. 22, 1958; children—Nina, Anya. With Dominion Bank, St. John, N.B. and Toronto, 1937-41; faculty Dalhousie U., Halifax, N.S., Can., 1951—, prof. history, 1962—; sr. prof. Can. history U. Western Ont., 1963-64; vis. prof. Can. history Dartmouth Coll., Hanover, N.H., 1967. Chmn., Humanities Research Council Can., 1968-70; vice chmn. Halifax Landmarks Commn., 1970-73; N.S. mem. Historic Sites and Monuments Bd. Can., 1968-77. Served with Royal Can. Navy, 1941-45. Fellow Royal Soc. Can.; mem. Can. Hist. Assn. (pres. 1968-69), Athenaeum (hon.). Author: The Life and Times of Confederation, 1864-1867, 1962; The Confederation Debates, 1865, 1963; Canada 1874-1896: Arduous Destiny, 1971; John A. Macdonald: His Life and World, 1975; editor: Parliamentary Debates of Canada 1867-1874. Home: 960 Ritchie Dr Halifax NS B3H 3P4 Canada

WAITE, RALPH, actor; b. White Plains, N.Y., June 22, 1929; B.A., Bucknell U.; B.D., Yale U.; m. Kerry Shear; children—Kathleen, Suzanne. Social worker, Westchester County, N.Y.; Presbyterian minister, Garden City, N.Y.; publicity dir. and asst. religious books editor Harper & Row Pub. Co., N.Y.C.; founder Los Angeles Actors Theatre, 1975, artistic dir., 1975—; stage appearances include: Hogan's Goat, 1965, Watering Place, 1969, The Trial of Lee Harvey Oswald, 1967, Blues for Mr. Charlie; films include: A Lovely Way to Die, 1968, Five Easy Pieces, 1970, Lawman, 1971, The Grissom Gang, 1971, The Sporting Club, 1971, The Stone Killer, 1973; regular TV series The Waltons, 1972—; on ltd. dramatic series Roots, 1977; other TV appearances include: Waiting for Godot, Red Alert, The Secret Life of John Chapman. Office: care Creative Artists Agy 9300 Wilshire Blvd Suite 535 Beverly Hills CA 90212*

WAITE, ROBERT GEORGE LEESON, educator; b. Cartwright, Manitoba, Can., Feb. 18, 1919; s. George Lloyd and Alice (Carter) W.; A.B., Macalester Coll., 1941; M.A., U. Minn., 1946; M.A., Harvard, 1947, Ph.D., 1949; postgrad. U. Munich, 1953-54; m. Anne Barnett, Sept. 8, 1943; children—Geoffrey, Peter. Came to U.S., 1929, naturalized, 1943. Teaching asst. Macalester Coll., 1941; Emerton fellow history Harvard, 1947, teaching fellow, 1947-49; asst. prof. history Williams Coll., 1949-53, asso. prof., 1953-58, prof., 1958—, Brown prof., 1960—, chmn. dept., 1967-72, dir. History Insts., 1968, 69; vis. prof. U. Minn., summer 1957, U. Tex., Austin, 1974; staff lectr. Inst. in Humanities (John Hay Found.), 1959, 1961-65; staff mem. Nat. Humanities Faculty, 1970—; sr. mem. St. Antony's Coll. Oxford U., 1978. Guggenheim fellow, 1953-54; sr. Fulbright research fellow, Germany, 1953-54; Am. Council Learned Socs. grantee, 1967; grantee Social Sci. Research Council, 1967. Mem. Am. Hist. Assn., Central European Study Group (sec.-treas. 1970-72). Conglist. (bd. deacons). Author: Vanguard of Nazism: The Free Corps Movement in Postwar Germany, 1918-23, 1952, 69, The Psychopathic God: Adolf Hitler, 1977. Editor, contbr.; Hitler and Nazi Germany, 1965, 69. Editorial bd. Jour. Modern History, 1957-60. Contbr. World Book, 1958, Collier's Ency., 1961, Psychoanalytic Interpretations of History, 1971, Jour. Interdisciplinary History, 1971; Afterword to the Mind of Adolf Hitler, 1972. Co-translator: (Erich Eyck) A History of the Weimar Republic, 2 vols., 1962, 70. Home: Talcott Rd Williamstown MA 01267. *For the intellectual, industry, creativity, and integrity are all important, but they are not enough; one needs also the courage to take a stand on social and moral issues.*

WAITE, ROBERT MONTROSE, communications co. exec.; b. Freetown, Sierra Leone, Sept. 14, 1928; s. Montrose and Ella (Puddler) W.; came to U.S., 1937, naturalized, 1946; B.A., Western Res. U., 1953; M.B.A., N.Y. U., 1963; m. Joan Berry, May 30, 1959; children—Robin, Montrose, Robert. Indsl. engr. Pitney Bowes, Inc., Stamford, Conn., 1956-60; gen. mgr. Nigerian Electronics, Ltd., Lagos, Nigeria, 1960-63; indsl. devel. adviser Arthur D. Little, Inc., Cambridge, Mass., 1963-65; v.p., product line mgr. ITT Corp., N.Y.C., 1967—; dir. Maiden Electronics, Ltd., Lagos. Past nat. dir. Interracial Council for Bus. Opportunities; exec. dir. Mayor's Task Force for Econ. Redevel. of Harlem, 1966-67; commr. Redevel. Agy., Twp. of Teaneck, N.J., 1976—. Served with U.S. Army, 1946-47. Office: ITT Corp 320 Park Ave New York NY 10022*

WAITE, STEPHEN HOLDEN, banker; b. Rochester, N.Y., Dec. 5, 1936; s. Richard Holden and Judith H. (Lapp) W.; B.A., Amherst Coll., 1958; J.D., Yale, 1961; m. Sarah T. Caswell, Aug. 20, 1960; children—Sarah T., Richard H. Admitted to N.Y. bar, 1961; mem. firm Nixon, Hargrave, Devans & Doyle, Rochester, N.Y., 1961-69; v.p., counsel Lincoln First Banks Inc., Rochester, 1969-73, sr. v.p., 1973-77, exec. v.p., 1978—, chief fin. officer, 1973—; exec. v.p., chief fin. officer Lincoln First Bank, N.A., 1979—. Bd. dirs. Highland Hosp., Rochester Area Hosps. Corp., Rochester Center for Govtl. Research, Rochester Regional Research Library Council; past bd. dirs. Harley Sch., Hearing and Speech Center of Rochester. Served with U.S. Army, 1962. Mem. Fin. Execs. Inst. Clubs: Genesee Valley, Country (Rochester). Home: 115 Pelham Rd Rochester NY 14610 Office: 1 Lincoln First Sq Rochester NY 14643

WAITER, SERGE-ALBERT, physicist; b. Belleville, Paris, France; Bachelier ès Sciences Mathematiques, Lycée Voltaire, Paris, France, 1948; License ès Sciences, Facultes des Sciences de Lille and Paris, 1948-53; Doctorat, Faculté des Sciences de Paris, Sorbonne, 1954; 1 son, Thomas-Bernard. Came to U.S., 1959, naturalized, 1965. Mgr., Sud Aviation, Paris, France, 1953-59; research scientist U. So. Calif., 1959-62; staff scientist hypersonic gasdynamics and plasma physics, mem. space shuttle team with responsibility for aerothermodynamics from design to flight Space div. Rockwell Internat., 1962—. Recipient 13 NASA awards for tech. devel. Fellow Am. Inst. Aeros. and Astronautics (asso.); mem. Société des Ingénieurs Civils de France, Research Soc. Am. Research, lectures, publs. on gasdynamics, plasmadynamics, aerothermodynamics and re-entry physics. Home: 801 Crest Vista Dr Monterey Park CA 91754 Office: Rockwell Internat Co Downey CA 90241

WAITH, EUGENE MERSEREAU, English scholar, educator; b. Buffalo, Dec. 29, 1912; s. William Sereno and Edith Almira (Mersereau) W.; B.A., Yale, 1935, Ph.D., 1939; postgrad. Cambridge (Eng.) U., 1935-36; m. Margaret Cecelia Deakers, June 7, 1939. Instr., English, Yale U., 1939-43, successively asst. prof., asso. prof., prof., 1946-70, Douglas Tracy Smith prof. English Lit., 1971—. Bd. dirs. Long Wharf Theatre, New Haven, 1972—. Served with AUS, 1943-46, OSS, 1944-46. Mem. English Inst., Shakespeare Assn. Am., Renaissance Soc. Am., Elizabethan Club Yale U. Author: Pattern of Tragicomedy in Beaumont and Fletcher, 1952; Herculean Hero, 1962; Ideas of Greatness, 1971; editor: Macbeth and Bartholomew Fair (Ben Jonson), Yale edits. Office: Yale Univ English Dept New Haven CT 06520

WAKATSUKI, JAMES HIROJI, state legislator; b. Honolulu, Aug. 17, 1929; s. Shichizaemon and Sachi (Kobayashi) W.; student U. Hawaii, 1947-48, Bowling Green State U., 1949-51; LL.B., U. Wis., 1954; m. Irene Natsuko Yoshimura, Feb. 17, 1957; children—Janie T., Stuart K., Cora A. Admitted to Hawaii bar, 1956; asso. firm Wakatsuki, Kawamoto and Wada, Honolulu, 1956—; mem. Hawaii Ho. of Reps. from 18th Dist., 1958—, speaker, 1975—; dir. Internat. Savs. & Loan Assn., Honolulu, Star Markets Ltd. Served with AUS, 1948-49. Mem. Am., Hawaii bar assns. Democrat. Club: Lions. Home: 1462 Ala Mahamoe St Honolulu HI 96819 Office: State Capitol Honolulu HI 96813*

WAKEFIELD, BENTON MCMILLIN, JR., banker; b. Monroe, La., Apr. 8, 1920; s. Benton McMillin and Adele (Rhodes) W.; B.S. in Commerce, Washington and Lee U., 1941; postgrad. Grad. Sch. Banking, U. Wis., 1949-51; m. Cindy Walton, May 19, 1951; children—Benton McMillin, III, Will Walton. Asst. v.p. First Nat. Bank Memphis, 1946-52; v.p. Ouachita Nat. Bank, Monroe, La., 1952-63; pres. Merc. Nat. Bank Ind., Hammond, Ind., 1963-72; also dir.; pres. 1st Bank and Trust Co., South Bend, Ind., 1972-75, chmn. bd., dir., chmn. exec. com., 1975-79; pres. FBT Bancorp., 1972-79; chmn., chief exec. officer First Nat. Bank of Jefferson Parish, 1979—; dir. Channel 34 Broadcasting, Carpetland U.S.A., Inc.; cons. 1st Nat. Bank of S.W. Mich.: Bd. dirs. Meml. Hosp., South Bend Civic Center Bldg. Authority, United Way St. Joseph County, Michiana Econ. Devel. Found., Parking Facilities of South Bend, Art Center Inc. Served to lt. comdr. USNR, 1941-46. Mem. South Bend C. of C. (dir.), Phi Beta Kappa, Sigma Alpha Epsilon, Omicron Delta Kappa. Methodist. Home: 5301 Marcia Ave New Orleans LA 70124 Office: PO Box 369 Gretna LA 70054

WAKEFIELD, DAN, writer; b. Indpls., May 21, 1932; s. Benjamin H. and Brucie (Ridge) W.; B.A., Columbia Coll., 1955; Nieman fellow Harvard U., 1963-64. News editor Princeton (N.J.) Packet, 1955; staff writer Nation mag., 1956-59; free lance writer, 1959—; staff Bread Loaf Writers Conf., 1964, 66; vis. lectr. U. Mass., Boston, 1965-66; vis. lectr. journalism U. Ill., 1968; creator, story cons. TV show James at 15, 1977-78; author: Island in the City: The World of Spanish Harlem, 1959; Revolt in the South, 1961; The Addict, an anthology, 1963; Between the Lines, 1966; Supernation at Peace and War, 1968; Going All the Way, 1970; Starting Over, 1973; All Her Children, 1976; Home Free, 1977; contbg. editor Atlantic Monthly, 1969—. Bernard DeVoto fellow Bread Loaf Writers Conf., 1957. Mem. Authors Guild Am. Clubs: Examiner, Women's City of Boston (asso.). Address: Atlantic Monthly 8 Arlington St Boston MA 02171*

WAKEFIELD, HOWARD, physician; b. Balt., Aug. 20, 1892; s. Antonio and Elizabeth E. (Brooke) W.; B.S., U. Chgo., 1917; M.D., Rush Med. Coll., 1924; m. Thelma Isabel Roach, Dec. 31, 1933; children—Isabel Elizabeth (Mrs. David Chilton Oppen), Howard Roach. Research asso. U. Chgo., 1917-22, asst. anatomy, 1919-21, asst., later asso. dept. medicine Rush Med. Coll., 1926-32; practice of medicine, 1924—; asst. to Dr. James B. Herrick, 1926-32; intern Cook County Hosp., Chgo., 1925-26; asst. attending physician St. Luke's Hosp., 1932-40, asso. attending physician, 1940-47, sr. attending physician, 1947-56, chmn. dept. med., 1956—; cons. physician Presbyn. Saint Lukes Hosp.; also asso. prof. medicine U. Ill.; emeritus prof. medicine Rush Med. Coll., Chgo.; chief staff, attending physician Old Peoples Home, City of Chgo. Chmn. conf. com. Grad. Tng. Internal Medicine in U.S.; mem. reviewing com. Homes for Aged; adv. com. USN, 1917-19; adv. bd. cardiac div. SSS. Trustee Sugar Island, Thousand Islands. Diplomate Am. Bd. Internal Medicine (ofcl. examiner; chmn. subspecialty bd. cardiovascular disease, chmn. residency review com. for internal medicine for U.S.). Fellow Inst. Medicine Chgo., A.C.P. (gov. No. Ill., gen. chmn. ann. session, Chgo. 1954, regent, 2d v.p., master 1969), A.A.A.S. (life); mem. A.M.A., Ill., Chgo. med. socs., Chgo. (v.p. 1943-44, pres. 1957—, mem. exec. com.), Internat. socs. internal medicine, Assn. Am. Med. Coll., Am. Soc. Tropical Medicine, Am. Assn. History Medicine, Am. Therapeutic Soc. (2d v.p., treas.), Soc. Med. History Chgo., Am. (founder, mem. sci. council). Chgo. heart assns., Gerontological Soc., N.A. Yacht Racing Assn., Am. (commodore 1931), Lake Mich. yachting assns., Am. Occupational Therapy Assn. (mem. med. adv. com.), Alumni Assn. U. Chgo. (life), Am. Canoe Assn. (commodore 1931), Sigma Xi, Alpha Omega Alpha. Phi Beta Pi. Republican. Episcopalian. Club: Chicago Yacht. Contbr. med. jours. Home: Apt 1818 2801 King Dr Chicago IL 60616

WAKEFIELD, STEPHEN ALAN, lawyer; b. Olney, Ill., Oct. 18, 1940; s. George William and Blanche Lucille (Sheesley) W.; LL.B., U. Tex., 1965; m. Charlotte Ellen Branch, Oct. 2, 1965; children—Melissa Lee, Tracy Anne, Stephen Alan. Admitted to Tex. bar, 1965; mem. firm Baker & Botts, Houston, 1965-70; asst. to gen. counsel FPC, Washington, 1970-72; dep. asst. sec. interior for mineral resources, 1972-73, asst. sec. interior energy and minerals, 1973-74; mem. firm Baker & Botts, Houston, 1974—. Asst. adminstr. Fed. Energy Office, 1973-74. Mem. Am. Bar Assn., State Bar Tex., Com. Fgn. Relations, Sigma Phi Epsilon, Phi Delta Phi. Republican. Methodist. Club: River Oaks Country. Home: 25 Westlane Houston TX 77019 Office: 3000 One Shell Plaza Houston TX 77002

WAKEHAM, HELMUT RICHARD RAE, tobacco co. exec.; b. Hamburg, Germany, Apr. 15, 1916; s. Rae G. and Augusta (Beiss) W.; B.A., U. Nebr., 1936, M.A., 1937; Ph.D., U. Calif. at Berkeley, 1939; m. Kathleen Ferguson, June 22, 1939; children—Stuart, Susan, Rosemary. Research chemist Standard Oil Co. Calif., 1939-41, So. Regional Research Lab., U.S. Dept. Agr., 1941-47; research asso. Inst. Textile Tech., Charlottesville, Va., 1947-49; project head chem.-physics sect. Textile Research Inst., also research dir., 1949-56; dir. Ahmedabad (India) Textile Industries Research Assn., 1956-58; staff asst. for research to v.p. Philip Morris, Inc., 1958-59, dir. research and devel., 1959-61, v.p., dir. research and devel., 1961-65, v.p. corporate research and devel., 1965-75, v.p. sci. and tech., 1975—. Mem. Sci. Commn. of CORESTA, internat. tobacco research orgn., 1966-72; gen. chmn. CORESTA/TCRC Conf., Williamsburg, Va., 1972; chmn. Nat. Conf. Adminstrn. Research, 1970; mem. gen. adv. com. Textile Research Inst., 1961-65; mem. tobacco working group Nat. Cancer Inst., 1967-76; session chmn. Nat. Cancer Plan Workshop, 1971. Pres. Robert E. Lee council Boy Scouts Am., 1972-75; pres. Sci. Mus. of Va. Found., 1974-77; exec. v.p. Richmond Symphony, 1976-79, pres., 1979-80. Va. Cultural Laureate, Sci. and Tech., 1977. Fellow Am. Inst. Chemists, Textile Inst. (Great Britain); mem. Am. Chem. Soc. (chmn. local program sect. 1943-45), Fiber Soc. (program chmn., councilor 1950-55), AAAS, Am. Inst. Physics. Home: 8901 Brieryle Rd Richmond VA 23229 Office: PO Box 26583 Richmond VA 23261

WAKELAND, HENRY H., govt. ofcl.; b. Rochester, Pa., Oct. 20, 1922; s. Ray Warren and Eva (Hice) W.; B.S. in Mech. Engring., Purdue U., 1943, M.S. in Mech. Engring., 1954; M.A. in Govt., N.Y. U., 1960; m. Barbara Wyatt Primm, May 19, 1962; children—Charles Warren, Eva Catherine. Asst. devel. engr. Nash-Kelvinator Corp., 1947-52; engr. Engring. Expt. Sta., Purdue U., 1952-54; sr. engr. aero. equipment Sperry Gyroscope Co., 1954-61; interdivisional marketing coordinator gyro group Sperry Rand Corp., 1961-65; project dir. safety car program N.Y. Dept. Motor Vehicles, 1965-66; cons. Fairchild-Hiller Corp., 1966-67; dir. bur. surface transp. safety Nat. Transp. Safety Bd., Washington, 1967-76, dir. Bur. Plans and Programs, 1976-78, chief scientist, 1978—; staff cons. joint legis. com. on vehicles and safety N.Y. State Legislature, 1961-67. Chmn. N.Y. Legislative-Industry Adv. Com. on Tire Safety, 1964; N.Y. County Republican committeeman, 1956-63. Served to 1st lt. AUS, World War II. Recipient spl. commendation Am. Assn. Automotive Medicine, 1964; Edward J. Speno award Nat. Motor Vehicle Safety Adv. Council, 1976. Registered profl. engr., Wis. Mem. Am. Polit. Sci. Assn., ASME, Am. Inst. Aeros. and Astronautics, Internat. Soc. Tech. Assessment, System Safety Soc., Am. Assn. Automotive Medicine, Soc. Automotive Engrs. (mem. gov. bd. Milw. and Met. sects.). Presbyterian. Contbr. articles to profl. jours.; bd. editors Jour. Safety Research. Patentee in field. Home: 9013 Cherbourg Dr Potomac MD 20854 Office: 800 Independence Ave SW Washington DC 20594

WAKELEY, JOHN HALBERT, psychologist, educator; b. Bucyrus, Ohio, Nov. 2, 1932; s. John Matthews and Winifred Florence (Kanable) W.; B.A., Coll. Wooster, 1954; M.S., N.C. State Coll., 1958; Ph.D. (NSF fellow), Mich. State U., 1961; m. Esther Sue Reed, Sept. 9, 1956; children—Susan Elaine, Daniel Reed, Joel Richard, Sara Diane. Asso. personnel research Corning Glass Works (N.Y.), 1961-64; asst. prof. psychology Mich. State U., East Lansing,

1964-72, prof., 1972—, Am. Council Edn. fellow, 1969-70, chmn. dept. psychology, 1973—. Dir.-ex-officio Scanlon Assos. Served with AUS, 1954-56. Mem. Am. Psychol. Assn., Sigma Xi. Author: Psychology of Industrial Behavior, 1972; The Scanlon Plan, 1974. Home: 1602 Clifton Ave Lansing MI 48910 Office: Dept Psychology Michigan State Univ East Lansing MI 48824

WAKELIN, JAMES HENRY, JR., research adminstr.; b. Holyoke, Mass., May 6, 1911; s. James Henry and Abbie Shattuck (Hobart) W.; A.B., Dartmouth Coll., 1932; B.A., Cambridge U., 1934, M.A., 1939; Ph.D., Yale, 1940; m. Margaret C. Smith, July 29, 1938 (dec. Apr. 1973); children—James Henry III, Alan Blanchard, David Shattuck; m. 2d, Carol Ackiss Holman, Oct. 19, 1974. Sr. physicist B. F. Goodrich Co., 1939-43; dir. research Engring. Research Assos., Inc., Washington, 1946-48; asso. dir. research Textile Research Inst., Princeton, 1948-51, dir. research, 1951-54, research asso., 1954-59; propr. ind. cons. bus., Princeton, 1954-59; asst. sec. navy for research and devel., 1959-64, chmn., 1964-69; mem. adv. bd. Teledyne-Ryan Aero. Co., San Diego, 1964-71, Continental Motors Corp., Detroit, 1964-71; asst. sec. commerce (sci. and tech.), 1971-72; pres., chmn. bd. Research Analysis Corp., McLean, Va., 1972—; a founder, 1954, Chesapeake Instrument Corp., Shadyside, Md., v.p., cons., 1954-59. Chmn. interagy. com. oceanography Fed. Council Sci. and Tech., 1959-64; chmn bd. Oceanic Found., Honolulu, 1965-71; chmn. Pres.' Task Force on Oceanography, 1969; spl. asst. to Gov. Del. for marine and coastal affairs, 1970-71; mem. Corp. Woods Hole Oceanographic Instn. Head of U.S. delegation Intergovtl. Conf. Oceanographic Research, Copenhagen, Denmark, 1960, to 1st session Intergovtl. Oceanographie Commn. UNESCO, Paris, France, 1961. Chmn. bd. overseers Thayer Sch. Engring., Dartmouth Coll., 1966-70; mem. vis. com. dept. astronomy Harvard U., 1970-78, dept. ocean engring. Mass. Inst. Tech., 1970-73. Mem. Naval Research adv. com., 1964-71; mem. bd. advisers to pres. Naval War Coll., 1970-73; chmn. interagy. com. atmospheric scis. and interdeptl. com. patent policy Fed. Council Sci. and Tech., 1971-72. Bd. dirs. Harbor Br. Found., 1973—; chmn. com. phys. scis. Yale U. Council, 1973—. Served from lt. (s.g.) to lt. comdr., USNR, 1943-46. Recipient Distinguished Pub. Service award U.S. Navy, 1961, 64; Rear Adm. William S. Parsons award, Navy League U.S., 1965; Wilbur Lucius Cross medal Yale Grad. Sch., 1976; Robert Fletcher award Thayer Sch. Engring. Dartmouth Coll., 1977. Benjamin Franklin fellow Royal Soc. Arts; mem. Am. Phys. Soc., Nat. Geog. Soc. (trustee), N.Y. Acad. Scis., Textile Research Inst., Marine Tech. Soc. (hon.; pres. 1966-68), Nat. Security Indsl. Assn. (hon.), Assn. Yale Alumni, Yale Grad. Sch. Assn. (pres. 1972-74), Sigma Xi. Congregationalist. Clubs: Explorers; Chevy Chase, Cosmos (Washington). Author: (with Tompkins and Stifler, Jr.) High-Speed Computing Devices, 1950. Home: 1809 45th St NW Washington DC 20007

WAKEMAN, FRED JOSEPH, paper co. exec.; b. St. Louis, Mar. 19, 1928; s. Fred Otis and Blossom Marie W.; B.Sc., St. Norbert Coll., 1950; postgrad. U. Wis., 1952-53; m. Carol Ann Muraski, Sept. 15, 1958; children—Julie, Jennifer, John, Jill. With Green Bay Packaging Corp. (Wis.), 1954—, v.p., regional mgr., 1975-77, exec. v.p. converting ops., 1977—. Served with U.S. Army, 1950-52. Decorated Purple Heart, Bronze Star. Mem. Fibre Box Assn. (mem. exec. bd.), Container Industry Devel. Assn. (mem. exec. bd.), Am. Paper Inst. (mem. exec. bd. container div.), Am. Mgmt. Assn., TAPPI. Clubs: Wausau, Oneida Country, Western Racquet. Office: PO Box 1107 Green Bay WI 54305

WAKEMAN, RICK, entertainer, composer; keyboard and composition tng. Royal Acad. Music, 1968; Performed with group Strawbs, 1970-71, with Yes, 1971-72, 77—; formed own group, 1973—; rec. artist A & M Records, 1971—; composed film score based on works of Liszt for film Lisztomania 1975, original film score White Rock, 1976; major pieces include Journey to the Center of the Earth, 1974; Six Wives of Henry VIII, 1974; Myths and Legends of King Arthur, 1975; No Earthly Connection, 1976; toured U.S. with Nat. Philharmonic Orch. and Chorus, 1974, with own group, 1975, with Yes, 1976, 78. Address: Beldock Levine & Hoffman 565 Fifth Ave New York NY 10017

WAKERLIN, GEORGE EARLE, educator, med. adminstr.; b. Chgo., July 1, 1901; s. George and Emma (Kenzig) W.; B.S., U. Chgo., 1923. Ph.D., 1926, M.D., Rush Med. Coll., 1929; M.S., U. Wis., 1924; m. Ruth Billings Coleman, 1952; children—Susan, George Earle. Surg. house officer Johns Hopkins Hosp., 1928-29, med. house officer, 1929-30; asst. in pharmacology U. Chgo., 1923, asso. in physiology, 1925-26, fellow, 1926-28; instr. pharmacology U. Wis., 1923-25; asst. prof. physiology and pharmacology U. Louisville (Ky), 1931-32, asst. prof. and acting head dept. physiology and pharmacology, 1932-33, asso. prof. and head dept., 1933-35, prof. and head dept., 1935-37; prof. and head dept. physiology U. Ill. Coll. of Medicine, 1937-58, asst. dean Rush-Presbyn. div., 1945-46; med. dir. Am. Heart Assn., 1958-66; adj. prof. physiology Coll. Phys. and Surg., Columbia, 1959-66; prof. medicine U. Mo. Sch. Medicine, Columbia, 1966-71, prof. medicine emeritus, 1971—; state coordinator Mo. Regional Med. Program, 1966-68, dir. planning 1968-71, central dist. cons., 1971-73; free lance med. writer, 1973—. Chmn. pub. health com. City Club of Chgo., 1940-45; chmn. med. and sci. com. Ill. Div. Am. Cancer Soc., 1945-50. mem. exec. com., 1945-58; pres. Chgo. Nutrition Assn., 1949-50. Served with Chem. Warfare Res., U.S. Army. as 1st lt., 1924-35; Med. Corp. Res., USN, as sr. lt., 1935-45. Recipient Disting. Alumni award U. Chgo., 1965, Gold medal Am. Heart Assn., 1966. Fellow Am. Pub. Health Assn., A.C.P., AAAS; mem. Am. Physiol. Soc. (distinguished mem., past chmn. circulation sect.), Am. Soc. Pharmacology and Exptl. Therapeutics, Soc. Exptl. Biology and Medicine, Central Soc. Clin. Research, Nat. Soc. Med. Research (dir. 1966-69), AAUP, Boone County Med. Soc., Mo. Med. Assn., Inst. Medicine of Chgo., Am. Heart Assn. (hon. fellow council clin. cardiology 1966—), AMA, So. Med. Assn., Sociedad Espanola de Cardiologica (hon.), Societe de Nephrologie (hon.), Phi Beta Kappa, Sigma Xi, Alpha Omega Alpha, Alpha Sigma Phi, Alpha Kappa Kappa. Author: A Laboratory Textbook of Human Physiology, parts I, II and III, 1937-52. Contbr. numerous articles to med. and sci. publs. Home and office: 231 El Bonito Way Millbrae CA 94030

WAKLEY, JAMES TURNER, mfg. co. exec.; b. Springfield, Ohio, Feb. 17, 1921; s. James Henry and Edith Lynn (Welsh) W.; student pub. schs., Springfield; m. Mary Pennell, May 18, 1945; children—Ruth Nadine, Gary James, Martin Pennell. Regional sales mgr. Nat. Supply Co., 1947-54; exec. v.p. Kanawha Sand Co., 1956-60; pres. Ohio River Sand & Gravel Co., Parkersburg, W.Va., 1960-77; v.p., dir. McDonough Co., Parkersburg, 1960—, also dir. Chmn., Parkersburg Urban Renewal Authority, 1968-75; trustee Ohio Valley Improvement Assn. Served with USAAF, 1942-45. Decorated D.F.C., Air medal. Mem. Nat. Sand and Gravel Assn. (dir. 1976-79). Lutheran. Home: 2000 Washington St Parkersburg WV 26101 Office: PO Box 1174 Parkersburg WV 26101

WAKOSKI, DIANE, poet; b. Whittier, Calif., Aug. 3, 1937; d. John Joseph and Marie Elvira (Mengel) W.; B.A. in English, U. Calif., Berkeley, 1960. Author books: Coins and Coffins, 1962, Discrepancies and Apparitions, 1966, Inside The Blood Factory, 1968, The George Washington Poems, 1967, The Magellanic Clouds, 1969, The Motorcycle Betrayal Poems, 1971, Smudging, 1972, Dancing On The Grave of A Son Of A Bitch, 1973, Trilogy, 1974, Virtuoso Literature For Two and Four Hands, 1976, Waiting For the King of Spain, 1977, The Man Who Shook Hands, 1978, Cap of Darkness, 1980; vis. writer Calif. Inst. Tech., 1972, U. Va., 1972-73, Wilamette U., 1973, Lake Forest Coll., 1974, Colo. Coll., 1974, U. Calif., Irvine, 1974, Macalester Coll., 1975, U. Wis., 1975, Hollins Coll., 1974, U. Wash., 1978, U. Hawaii, 1979, Whitman Coll., 1977, Emory U., 1980; writer-in-residence Mich. State U., 1976—. Cassandra Found. grantee, 1970; N.Y. State Cultural Council grantee, 1971-72; Nat. Endowment for Arts grantee, 1973-74; Guggenheim grantee, 1972-73. Office: 323 Morrill Hall Mich State U East Lansing MI 48823

WAKSMAN, BYRON HALSTED, educator, scientist; b. N.Y.C., Sept. 15, 1919; s. Selman A. and Bertha (Mitnik) W.; B.S., Swarthmore Coll., 1940; M.D., U. Pa., 1943; m. Joyce Ann Robertroy, Aug. 11, 1944; children—Nan, Peter. Intern Michael Reese Hosp., Chgo., 1944; fellow Mayo Found., 1946-48; NIH fellow Columbia Med. Sch., 1948-49; asso., then asst. prof. bacteriology and immunology Harvard Med. Sch., 1949-63; research fellow, then asso. bacteriologist (neurology) Mass. Gen. Hosp., 1949-63; prof. microbiology Yale U., 1963-72, prof. pathology, 1974-78, chmn. dept., 1964-70, 72-74, adj. prof. pathology and biology, 1979—; dir. research programs Nat. Multiple Sclerosis Soc., N.Y.C., 1979—; adj. prof. pathology N.Y. U., 1979—; mem. expert panel immunology WHO, 1962—; mem. numerous adv. panels and study sects. NIH, 1961—. Served as psychiatrist AUS, 1944-46. Mem. Am. Assn. Immunologists (councillor 1965-70, pres. 1970-71), British Soc. Immunology, Am. Soc. Microbiology (councillor 1967-69). Author numerous articles on thymus, cell-mediated immunity, tolerance, lymphokines, lymphocyte stimulation mechanisms, auto immunity. Editor Progress in Allergy, 1960—; editorial adv. bd. Cellular Immunology, 1970—, Immunol. Communications, 1972—, Annales d'Immunologie, 1973—, Pathologie et Biologie, 1975—, Inflammation, 1975—; asso. editor Bacteriological Revs., 1963-67, Jour. Immunology, 1962-66, Internat. Archives Allergy and Applied Immunology, 1962—. Home: 45 Rock Hill Rd Woodbridge CT 06525 Office: 205 E 42d St New York NY 10017

WALAN, ALFONS W., mfg. co. exec.; b. Kenosha, Wis., May 17, 1914; Ph.B., U. Wis., 1940; m. Audrey M. Benjamin, Feb. 14, 1942; children—Jeffrey, Cynthia, Valerie, Constance, Marcia, Gregory. With Lyon Metal Products Co., Aurora, Ill., 1940—, sec., treas. after 1957, pres., chmn. bd., chief exec. officer, 1976—, dir., 1969—; dir. Mchts. Nat. Bank. Bd. dirs. Mercy Center. Served with C.E., AUS, 1942-45. Mem. Nat. Assn. Accts. (past pres. Fox Valley chpt.), Am. Mgmt. Assn., Ill. C. of C., Aurora C. of C., Am. Soc. Corp. Secs. Clubs: Aurora Country, Moose. Office: PO Box 671 Aurora IL 60507

WALASZEK, EDWARD JOSEPH, educator; b. Chgo., July 4, 1927; B.S., U. Ill., 1949; Ph.D. in Pharmacology, U. Chgo., 1953; married, 1955; two children. Research fellow U. Edinburgh, 1953-55; asst. prof. neurophysiology and biochemistry U. Ill., 1955-56; asst. prof. pharmacology U. Kans. Sch. Medicine, Kansas City, 1957-59, asso. prof., 1959-62, prof., 1962—, chmn. dept., 1964—; USPHS spl. research fellow, 1956-61. Mem. health study sec. med. chemistry NIH, 1962-66, mem. health study sect. on research career devel. award, 1966-70, mem. health study sect. on pharmacology-toxicology, 1974-78, research career award, 1963; mem. com. teaching of sci. Internat. Council Sci. Unions; mem. adv. council Internat. Union Pharmacology, 1972—, chmn. sect. teaching, 1975—. Recipient vice-chancellor's award U. Kans., 1974; medal Polish Pharm. Industry for Service to Pharmacology, 1976; Bela Issekutz medal Hungarian Acad. Scis., 1979. Fellow Am. Coll. Clin. Pharmacologists; A.A.A.S., Am. Chem. Soc., Soc. Pharmacology, Soc. Neurosci., Finnish Acad. Sci. and Letters (fgn.), Sigma Xi, Alpha Omega Alpha, Rho Chi. Editorial bd. Med. Biology, 1974. Office: Dept Pharmacology Sch Medicine U Kans Kansas City KS 66103

WALBA, HAROLD, educator; b. Chelsea, Mass., Mar. 10, 1921; s. Joseph and Anna (Kamenetsky) W.; B.S., Mass. State Coll., 1946; Ph.D., U. Calif. at Berkeley, 1949; m. Beatrice Alpert, Oct. 12, 1945; children—David Mark, Jeffrey Howard. Teaching fellow U. Calif., 1946-48, DuPont research fellow, 1948-49; from instr. to asso. prof. San Diego State U., 1949-58, prof. chemistry, 1958—, chmn. dept. chemistry, 1960-64; research asso. Scripps Instn. Oceanography, 1951; part-time research chemist Narmco, Inc., 1956-59. Served to 1st lt. USAAF, 1943-45. Decorated D.F.C. Mem. Am. Chem. Soc. (chmn. San Diego sect. 1958-59), AAUP, AAAS, Calif. Assn. Chemistry Tchrs., Sigma Xi, Phi Kappa Phi, Alpha Epsilon Pi. Contbr. articles to chem. jours. Home: 3870 Carancho St La Mesa CA 92041 Office: San Diego State Univ San Diego CA 92182

WALBERT, DAVID EUGENE, former business exec.; b. Allentown, Pa., June 13, 1909; s. Franklin J.L. and Eda (Miller) W.; B.S. in Elec. Engring., Lehigh U., 1930; m. Helen Heggeman, July 12, 1972; children by previous marriage—Susan, David F. Indsl. engr. Westinghouse Electric & Mfg. Co., 1930-36; chief indsl. engr. N.J. Zinc Co., 1936-46, Brunswick Corp., 1946-48; v.p. mfg. Eigin Sweeper Co. (Ill.), 1948-53; asst. div. mgr. Murray Corp. Am., 1953-55; div. mgr. Dura Corp., 1955-56; v.p. Midland-Ross Corp., Owosso, Mich., 1956-60, group v.p., 1960-61, exec. v.p., 1962-65, pres., dir., 1965-69, chief exec. officer, 1967-69, now ret. Mem. Pi Mu Epsilon. Republican. Methodist. Mason (32 deg., Shriner). Clubs: Boca Raton (Fla.); Yacht and Country (Stuart, Fla.); Hound Ears (N.C.). Home: 3051 SE Fairway W Stuart FL 33494

WALBESSER, HENRY HERMAN, JR., univ. adminstr.; b. Buffalo, May 9, 1935; s. Henry Herman and Florence (Schoenl) W.; B.S. summa cum laude, State U. N.Y., Buffalo, 1958; M.A., U. Md., 1960, Ph.D., 1965; m. Diane L. Walker, Aug. 16, 1958; children—Henry Herman III, Kathleen Rae, James Jay. Asst. prof. math. and edn. U. Tex., Austin, 1960-62; dir. evaluation A.A.A.S., Washington, 1962-68; dir. Math. Projects, U. Md., College Park, 1968-73, dir. Bur. Ednl. Research and Field Service, 1972-73, asst. dean charge grad. studies and research, 1973—. Vice chmn. bd. dirs. Current Information Assos., Inc., Beltsville, Md., 1971—. Recipient Distinguished Achievement award for excellence in ednl. journalism Ednl. Press Assn. Am., 1973. Fulbright Hays fellow, 1968-69. Fellow Southeastern Asian Ministers Edn. Orgn., Am. Math. Soc., AAAS; mem. Nat. Council Tchrs. Math., Nat. Assn. for Research in Sci. Teaching, Math. Assn. Am., AAUP. Author: An Evaluation Model, 1968; Science-A Process Approach, 1969; Constructing Behavioral Objectives, 1969; How to Meet Accountability (with J.M. Cook), 1973. Home: 3415 Sonehall Ct Beltsville MD 20705 Office: Coll Edn U Md College Park MD 20742

WALBORSKY, HARRY M., chemist, educator; b. Lodz, Poland, Dec. 25, 1923; s. Israel and Sarah (Miedowicz) W.; B.S., Coll. City N.Y., 1945; Ph.D., Ohio State U., 1949; children—Edwin, Eric, Lisa, Irene. Research asso. AEC project U. Calif., Los Angeles, 1949-50; faculty chemistry Fla. State U., Tallahassee, 1950—, prof. chemistry, 1958—. Mem. Am. Chem. Soc., Chem. Soc. London. Contbr. articles profl. jours. Home: 2223 Ruadh Ride Tallahassee FL 32303

WALBOT, VIRGINIA, plant biochemist; b. Los Angeles, June 27, 1946; d. Henry Charles and Mary Elizabeth (Wehrly) W.; A.B. with distinction and honors in Biology, Stanford, 1967; M.Phil., Yale, 1969, Ph.D., 1972. NIH postdoctoral fellow U. Ga., Athens, 1972-74; asst. prof. biology Washington U., St. Louis, 1975—. Mem. Soc. Developmental Biology. Editorial bd. Plant Physiology, 1974—, Women in Cell Biology, 1970—. Research orgn. DNA, role of chloroplast DNA, origins cytoplasmic sterility in corn. Office: Dept Biology Box 1137 Washington U St Louis MO 63130

WALBRIDGE, SMITH STARR, civil engr.; b. Stockbridge, Vt., June 30, 1906; s. Ralph William and Kate Emelia (Starr) W.; student Rensselaer Poly. Inst., 1923-26; m. Dorothy Marie Hovey, June 20, 1937; 1 son, Starr Hovey. Surveyor, Del. & Hudson R.R., Oneonta, N.Y., 1926-27; jr. engr. N.Y. State Div. Hwys., Babylon, 1927-37; engr. N.Y. World's Fair, N.Y.C., 1939; chief engr. hwys. Andrews & Clark, N.Y.C., 1938-60; chief hwy. engr. Brown Engrs., N.Y.C., 1960-62; chief engr. Vollmer Assos., N.Y.C., 1962-65; partner designate, chief engr. hwys. Hardesty & Hanover, N.Y.C., 1965-74; ret., 1975-76; chief hwy. engr. Greenman-Pedersen Assos., P.C., Babylon, N.Y., Annapolis, Md., Worcester, Mass., and Albany, N.Y., 1976—. Comdr. North River squadron U.S. Power Squadron, 1964-65, nat. del., 1964-80, treas., 1960-64, chmn. coop. charting, 1972-80. Recipient Fletcher Sci. award, 1923, Radio News Innovation award, 1926, adult leadership award Boy Scouts Am., 1957, landscape certificate State of Israel, 1966; registered profl. engr., Del., Conn., Fla., Ga., Ind., Md., Mass., N.J., N.Y., Ohio, Va.; registered profl. planner, N.J.; registered land surveyor, Ind. Fellow ASCE (life, Frank M. Masters Transp. Engring. award), Inst. Transp. Engrs.; mem. N.J. Soc. Profl. Planners, Met. Assn. Urban Designers, Environ. Planners, Soc. Am. Mil. Engrs., Smithsonian Assos., Rensselaer Poly. Inst. Alumni Assn. (past dir. N.Y.C. chpt.), N.Y. State Assn. Hwy. Engrs. (dist. del., treas.), Theta Chi. Inventor directional grade-separated hwy. traffic interchange, 1931, triple-cantilever sect. Bklyn. Queens Expressway, 1943, interchange for Cross Bronx and Maj. Deegan Expressways, 1951; contbr. to designs of Detroit City Plan, UN Plaza, 1st Ave Tunnel, Westway, freeways in Que., Can., Minn., Ky., Miss., Ohio, Del., Md., Conn., Mass., Ind., N.J. and N.Y., Saratoga Performing Arts site, Voice of Am. Relay Sta. site in Liberia, parks, playgrounds and bridges. Home: Box 109 Bay Point Panama City FL 32407 Office: 100 W Main St Babylon NY 11702

WALBRIDGE, WILLARD EUGENE, broadcasting co. exec.; b. Republic, Pa., Mar. 11, 1913; s. Peter D. and Anna (Higbee) W.; A.B., U. Mich., 1936; m. Marietta H. Arner, Nov. 15, 1941; 1 son, Peter F. Salesman, Detroit Edison, 1936-39, radio sta. WWJ, Detroit, 1939-43; mgr. sta. WWJ-TV, Detroit, 1946-53; exec. v.p., gen. mgr. Sta. WJIM AM-TV, Lansing, Mich., 1953-54, Sta. KTRK-TV, Houston, 1954-70; sr. v.p. corp. affairs Capital Cities Communications, Inc., 1970-78, cons., 1978—; dir. Houston Lighting & Power Co., Tex. Commerce Med. Bank. Vice pres. Greater Houston Community Found.; bd. dirs. Soc. for Performing Arts, Salvation Army, Houston Area council Boy Scouts Am., Conv. and Tourist Bur., Houston Grand Opera Assn., Maximum Service Telecasters, Washington; mem. nat. bd. govs. ARC, 1974—, also bd. dirs. Houston chpt., 1965-72, chmn. Houston chpt., 1972-75; chmn. bd. TV Info. Office, N.Y.C., 1965-70; trustee Mus. Broadcasting, N.Y.C., 1978—. Served from ensign to lt. USNR, 1943-46. Decorated Silver Star. Mem. Maximum Service Telecasters (dir. 1972—), Houston Assn. Community TV (dir. 1972—), Internat. Radio and TV Fedn. (dir. 1969-76), Nat. Assn. Broadcasters (dir. 1965-70, chmn. bd. 1970-71), U.S. (dir. 1975—), Houston (dir. 1971—, chmn. bd. 1975-76) chambers commerce, Houston Council Fgn. Relations (chmn. 1977-78). Home: 3460 Piping Rock Ln Houston TX 77027 Office: Capital Cities Communications Inc Suite 330 Two Greenway Plaza Houston TX 77046

WALBURN, ROSWELL LEE, pub. relations exec.; b. LaGrange, Ga., Mar. 9, 1937; s. Jesse Forrest and Myrtle Elizabeth (Tucker) W.; student West Ga. Coll., 1955-57; B.A., LaGrange Coll., 1959; m. Jacquelyn Irma Miller, June 8, 1958; children—Shannon Leigh, Steven Patrick, David Terry. Sports editor LaGrange Daily News, 1958-59; asst. sport editor Macon (Ga.) Telegraph, 1959-61; sports writer Atlanta Jour., 1961-66; dir. pub. relations and promotions Atlanta Braves, Inc., 1966-72; v.p. Ball, Cohn & Weyman, 1972-73; pres. Walburn & Assos., Atlanta, 1973-75; pres. Walburn & Assos./J. Walter Thompson, Atlanta, 1975-78; div. mgr. adminstrn. and gen. services Oglethorpe Power Corp., Decatur, Ga., 1978—. Mem. Central Atlanta Progress Public Relations Task Force, 1976-77. Mem. Public Relations Soc. Am. (dir. Ga. chpt.). Baptist. Home: 2991 Hembree Rd Marietta GA 30062 Office: 3951 Snapfinger Pkwy Decatur GA 30095

WALCH, DAVID BEAN, univ. dean; b. La Grande, Oreg., May 19, 1936; s. Charles Lloyd and Lila (Bean) W.; B.S., Eastern Oreg. Coll., 1960; M.S. in L.S., U. Ill., 1962, cert. advanced studies, 1969; Ph.D., U. Utah, 1973; m. Phyllis Collins, June 23, 1959; children—Shane, Shawna, Sherece, Curt, Shalene. Tchr., LaGrande, 1960-61; asso. librarian Ch. Coll. of Hawaii, Laie, 1962-64, dir. library services, 1965-67; asst. prof. library sci. U. Utah, Salt Lake City, 1967-74; dean acad. services SUNY, Buffalo, 1974—; cons. library orgn. C&W Library Cons., 1969—. Katerine Sharp fellow, 1960-61. Mem. ALA, Utah Library Assn. Mem. Ch. of Jesus Christ of Latter-day Saints (bishop 1965—). Home: 246 Sprucewood St Williamsville NY 14221 Office: State Univ NY at Buffalo 1300 Elmwood Ave Buffalo NY 14221

WALCH, JOHN WESTON, pub. co. exec.; b. Brunswick, Maine, Nov. 27, 1901; s. John Thomas and Bessie Linn (Lowell) W.; B.S., Bowdoin Coll., 1925, D.Ed. (hon.), 1975; M.Ed., Bates Coll., 1940; m. Ruth Dyer Sanborn, Dec. 19, 1931; children—Carolyn Ruth Walch Slayman, Peter Sanborn. Tchr. Farmington (Maine) High Sch., 1925; submaster Wakefield (Mass.) Jr. High Sch., 1925-26; social studies dept. Portland (Maine) High Sch., 1926-53; founder, pres. J. Weston Walch, Publishing Co., Portland, 1927—; vis. lectr. debate, Bates Coll., 1955. Mem. Portland City Council, 1963-68, chmn., 1965, 66; mem. Portland City Charter Rev. Commn., 1977. Named Outstanding Citizen Portland City Council, 1977. Mem. Maine Hist. Soc. (bd. dirs. 1976—), Portland Tchrs. Assn. (past pres.), Phi Beta Kappa. Congregationalist. Author numerous publications in debate and other ednl. fields. Home: 116 Bradley St Portland ME 04102 Office: 321 Valley St Portland ME 04104

WALCH, W. STANLEY, lawyer; b. Sedalia, Mo., Mar. 23, 1934; s. Harry William and Martha (Inge) W.; B.A. cum laude, Kenyon Coll., Gambier, O., 1956; J.D., U. Mich., 1959; m. Valerie Bouton Marvin, Apr. 9, 1957; children—Gretchen Lynne, Charles Marvin, John Stanley. Admitted to Mo. bar, 1959; asso. firm Thompson, Mitchell, Thompson & Douglas, St. Louis, 1959-65; mem. firm Thompson, Mitchell, Douglas & Neill, St. Louis, 1965-69; with Chromalloy Am. Corp., St. Louis, 1969—, exec. v.p., gen. counsel, 1971-76, also dir.; partner firm Thompson & Mitchell, St. Louis, 1976—. Active local YMCA, United Fund, Heart Assn. Mem. Am., Mo., Met. St. Louis bar assns., Order of Coif, Delta Tau Delta. Episcopalian. Clubs: Mo. Athletic (St. Louis); Algonquin. Home: 5 Wild Rose St Ladue MO 63124 Office: One Mercantile Center St Louis MO 63101

WALD, GEORGE, biochemist; b. N.Y.C., Nov. 18, 1906; s. Isaac and Ernestine (Rosenmann) W.; B.S., N.Y. U., 1927; M.A., Columbia U., 1928, Ph.D., 1932; M.D. (hon.), U. Berne, 1957; D.Sc., Yale U., 1958, Wesleyan U., 1962, N.Y. U., 1965, McGill U., 1966, Amherst Coll., 1968, U. Rennes, 1970, U. Utah, 1971, Gustavus Adolphus U., 1972; m. Frances Kingsley, May 15, 1931 (div.); children—Michael, David; m. 2d, Ruth Hubbard, 1958; children—Elijah, Deborah. NRC fellow at Kaiser Wilhelm Inst., Berlin and Heidelberg, U. Zurich, U. Chgo., 1932-34; tutor biochem. scis. Harvard U., 1934-35, instr. biology, 1935-39, faculty instr., 1939-44, asso. prof. biology, 1944-48, prof., 1948—, Higgins prof. biology, 1968-77, prof. emeritus, 1977—; vis. prof. biochemistry U. Calif., Berkeley, summer 1956; Nat. Sigma Xi lectr., 1952; chmn. divisional com. biology and med. scis. NSF, 1954-56; Guggenheim fellow, 1963-64; Overseas fellow Churchill Coll., Cambridge U., 1963-64; participant U.S.-Japan Eminent Scholar Exchange, 1973; guest China Assn. Friendship with Fgn. Peoples, 1972. Recipient Eli Lilly prize Am. Chem. Soc., 1939; Lasker award Am. Pub. Health Assn., 1953; Proctor medal Assn. Research in Ophthalmology, 1955; Rumford medal Am. Acad. Arts and Scis., 1959; Ives medal Optical Soc. Am., 1966; Paul Karrer medal in chemistry U. Zurich, 1967; co-recipient Nobel prize for physiology, 1967; T. Duckett Jones award Helen Hay Whitney Found., 1967, Bradford Washburn medal Boston Mus. Sci., 1968; Max Berg award, 1969; Priestley medal Dickinson Coll., 1970. Fellow Nat. Acad. Sci., Am. Acad. Arts and Scis., Am. Philos. Soc. Co-author: General Education in a Free Society, 1945; Twenty Six Afternoons of Biology, 1962, 66; also sci. papers on vision and biochem. evolution. Home: 21 Lakeview Ave Cambridge MA 02138. *"A scientist lives with all reality. There is nothing better. To know reality is to accept it, and eventually to love it. A scientist is in a sense a learned child. There is something of the scientist in every child. Others must outgrow it. Scientists can stay that way all their lives." (Remarks on receiving the Nobel Prize, Stockholm, 1967)*

WALD, HASKELL PHILIP, govt. ofcl.; b. Worcester, Mass., Sept. 6, 1916; s. Joseph A. and Minnie (Bernstein) W.; A.B., Clark U., 1938; A.M., Harvard, 1942, Ph.D., 1950; m. Ruth Jacobs, July 2, 1939; children—Sharon Anne (Mrs. Ronald Krauss), Alan Maynard, Michael Ellis. Economist with various fed. agencies, 1938-53; research asso. Harvard Law Sch., 1953-55; economist Fed. Res. Bank N.Y., 1955-62; UN econ. cons., Korea, 1953; UN tech. assistance expert, Greece, 1958- 59; chief economist FPC, 1963-77, Fed. Energy Regulatory Commn., 1977—; vis. prof. grad. faculty New Sch. Social Research, 1957-62. Littauer fellow, 1941-42, 49. Mem. Am. Econ. Assn., Phi Beta Kappa. Author: Taxation of Agricultural Land in Underdeveloped Economies, 1959. Home: 9528 Starmont Rd Bethesda MD 20034 Office: 825 N Capitol St NE Washington DC 20426

WALD, NIEL, medical educator; b. N.Y.C., Oct. 1, 1925; s. Albert and Rose (Fischel) W.; A.B., Columbia, 1945; M.D., N.Y. U., 1948; m. Lucienne Hill, May 24, 1953; children—David, Phillip. Sr. hematologist Atomic Bomb Casualty Commn., Hiroshima, Japan, 1954-57; head biologist health physics div. Oak Ridge Nat. Lab., 1957-58; practice and teaching medicine and pub. health, specializing in radiation medicine and cytogenetics, Pitts., 1958—; mem. faculty U. Pitts. Grad. Sch. Pub. Health and Med. Sch., 1958—, prof. radiation health, 1962—, prof. radiology, 1965—, chmn. dept. radiation health, 1969-76, 77—, chmn. dept. occupational health, 1975-76, chmn. dept. indsl. environ. health scis., 1976-77; dir. radiation medicine dept. Presbyn.-Univ. Hosp., 1966—; cons. U.S. Nuclear Regulatory Commn., U.S. Dept. Energy, U.S. Navy, nuclear industries and utilities. Chmn. radiol. health study sect. USPHS, 1967-71; mem. Nat. Council Radiation Protection and Measurements, 1969—; mem. Gov. Pa. Adv. Com. Atomic Energy Devel. and Radiation Control, 1966—, chmn., 1974-76. Served to capt. M.C., USAF, 1952-54. Mem. Health Physics Soc. (pres. 1973-74), Am. Pub. Health Assn. (governing council 1971-73, program devel. bd. 1973-74), Radiation Research Soc. (asso. editor jour. 1965-68), Soc. Nuclear Medicine (asso. editor jour. 1959-69), Am. Soc. Human Genetics, Am. Occupational Med. Assn., AAAS, AMA, Internat. Soc. Hematology. Contbr. numerous articles to sci. and med. publs. Home: 5422 Normlee Pl Pittsburgh PA 15217

WALD, PALMER BERNARD, mus. adminstr., lawyer; b. Newport, R.I., Nov. 5, 1930; s. Palmer B. and Lillian R. (Morgan) W.; B.Ed., R.I. Coll., 1953; LL.B., Bklyn. Law Sch., 1966; postgrad. N.Y. U., 1958-61. Tchr. English pub. schs., N.Y.C., 1957-68; admitted to N.Y. State bar, 1966; asst. atty. gen. N.Y. State Dept. Law, N.Y.C., 1968-74; adminstr., sec. Whitney Mus. Am. Art, N.Y.C., 1974—. Lectr. law, mus. activities. Served with AUS, 1953-55. Mem. Assn. Bar City N.Y. Contbr. articles to profl. jours. Home: Nevada Towers 2025 Broadway New York NY 10023 Office: Whitney Museum American Art 945 Madison Ave New York NY 10021

WALD, PATRICIA MCGOWAN, lawyer, govt. ofcl.; b. Torrington, Conn., Sept. 16, 1928; d. Joseph F. and Margaret (O'Keefe) McGowan; B.A., Conn. Coll., 1948; LL.B., Yale, 1951; m. Robert L. Wald, June 22, 1952; children—Sarah, Douglas, Johanna, Frederica, Thomas. Admitted to D.C. bar, 1952; clk. U.S. Ct. of Appeals Judge Jerome Frank, 1951-52; asso. firm Arnold, Fortas & Porter, Washington, 1952-53; mem. D.C. Crime Commn., 1964-65, Dept. of Justice, 1967, Neighborhood Legal Service, D.C., 1968-70; co-dir. Ford Found. Project on Drug Abuse, 1970, Center for Law and Social Policy, 1971-72, Mental Health Law Project, 1972-77; asst. atty. gen. for legis. affairs U.S. Dept. Justice, Washington, 1977-79; judge U.S. Ct. of Appeals, D.C. circuit, 1979—. Trustee, Ford Found., 1972-77, Phillips Exeter Acad., 1975-77, Agnes Meyer Found., 1976-77, Conn. Coll., 1976-77; mem. Carnegie Council on Children, 1972-77. Mem. Am. Bar Assn. (bd. editors ABA Jour. 1978—), D.C. (dir.) Bar Assn., Am. Law Inst. (council 1978—), Inst. Medicine. Author: Law and Poverty, 1965; co-author: Bail in the United States, 1964; Dealing with Drug Abuse, 1973. Home: 107 Quincy St Chevy Chase MD 20015 Office: US Courthouse John Marshall Pl Washington DC 20530

WALD, RICHARD C., broadcasting exec.; b. N.Y.C.; s. Joseph S. and Lily (Forstate) W.; B.A., Columbia, 1952, M.A., 1953; B.A., Clare Coll., Cambridge, 1955; m. Edith May Leslie, June 7, 1953; children—Matthew Leslie, Elizabeth Tole, Jonathan Simon. From reporter to mng. editor N.Y. Herald Tribune, 1955- 66; asst. mng. editor Washington Post, 1967; exec. v.p. Whitney Communications Corp., N.Y.C., 1968—; exec. v.p., pres. NBC News, 1968-78; sr. v.p. ABC News, 1978—; dir. Columbia Daily Spectator. Mem. Coffee House. Annotator: (with James Bellows) The World of Jimmy Breslin, 1967. Office: 7 W 66th St New York NY 10023

WALD, ROBERT LEWIS, lawyer; b. Worcester, Mass., Sept. 9, 1926; s. Lewis and Freda (Rosenfield) W.; A.B., Harvard, 1947; LL.B., Yale, 1951; m. Patricia Ann McGowan, June 22, 1952; children—Sarah Elizabeth, Douglas Lewis, Johanna Margaret, Frederica Nora, Thomas Robert. Admitted to Mass. bar, 1951, D.C. bar, 1959; asst. to gen. counsel FTC, 1954-56; pvt. practice, Washington, 1956-61; partner firm Wald, Harkrader & Ross and predecessors, Washington, 1961—. Served to lt. USNR, 1944-46, 52-53. Home: 107 Quincy St Chevy Chase MD 20015 Office: 1300 19th St NW Washington DC 20036

WALD, SYLVIA, artist; b. Phila., Oct. 30, 1915; ed. Moore Inst. Art, Sci. and Industry. Exhibited one-woman shows: U. Louisville, 1945, 49, Kent State Coll., 1945, Nat. Serigraph Soc., 1946, Grand Central Moderns, N.Y.C., 1957, Devorah Sherman Gallery, Chgo., 1960, New Sch., 1967, Book Gallery, White Plains, N.Y., 1968, Benson Gallery, Bridgehampton, L.I., 1977, Knoll Internat., Munich, Germany, 1979, Amerika Havs, Munich, 1979; group shows: Nat. Sculpture Soc., 1940, Sculpture Internat., Phila., 1940, Chgo. Art Inst., 1941, Bklyn. Mus., 1975, Library of Congress, 1943, 52, 58, Smithsonian Instn., 1954, Internat. Print Exhbn., Salzburg and Vienna, 1952, 2d Sao Paulo Biennial, 1953, N.Y. Cultural Center, 1973, Mus. Modern Art, N.Y.C., 1975, others; represented in permanent collections: Aetna Oil Co., Am. Assn. U. Women, Ball State Tchrs. Coll., Bibliotheque Nationale, Paris, Bklyn. Mus., Howard U., State U. Iowa, Library of Congress, U. Louisville, Nat. Gallery, Mus. Modern Art, Phila. Mus., N.C. Mus., Rose Mus. Art at Brandeis U., Whitney Mus., N.Y.C., Finch Coll. Mus., N.Y.C., U. Nebr., Ohio U., U. Okla., Princeton, Victoria and Albert Mus., Walker Gallery, Worcester (Mass.) Art Mus., Guggenheim Mus., N.Y.C. Contbr. to profl. publs. Address: 37 E 4th St New York NY 10003

WALDAU, WALTER F., lawyer; b. N.Y.C., May 1, 1901; s. Ferdinand and Helene (Jurgens) W.; A.B., Brown U., 1923; LL.B., Harvard, 1926; m. L. Clara Gaertner, Jan. 15, 1935 (dec. Feb. 1948); children—Cynthia Lou (Mrs. Wayne B. Andrus), William Gaertner; m. 2d, Mary Berry Maroney, Feb. 6, 1954. Admitted to N.J. bar, 1927, U.S. Supreme Ct. bar; practiced in Newark, 1927—; partner firm Stryker, Tams & Dill, and predecessors, from 1935, now counsel. Chmn. Summit (N.J.) Zoning Bd. Adjustment. Mem. Am., N.J., Essex County bar assns., Delta Sigma Rho, Phi Sigma Kappa. Presbyn. Clubs: Essex (Newark); Canoe Brook Country; Sky Top. Home: 17 Rowan Rd Summit NJ 07901 Office: 33 Washington St Newark NJ 07102

WALDBAUER, GILBERT PETER, educator; b. Bridgeport, Conn., Apr. 18, 1928; s. George Henry and Hedwig Martha (Gribisch) W.; student U. Conn., 1949-50; B.S., U. Mass., 1953; M.S., U. Ill., Urbana, 1956, Ph.D., 1960; m. Stephanie Margot Stiefel, Jan. 2, 1955; children—Gwen Ruth, Susan Martha. Instr. entomology U. Ill., 1958-60, asst. prof., 1960-65, asso. prof., 1965-71, prof., 1971—, prof. agrl. entomology Coll. Agr., 1971—. Cons. Ill. Natural History Survey. Served with AUS, 1946-47; PTO Agrl. Research Service U.S. Dept. Agr. grantee, 1966-71; Nat. Geog. Soc. grantee, 1972-74; NSF grantee, 1976-79. Mem. AAAS, Am. Soybean Assn., Animal Behavior Soc., Entomol. Soc. Am., Sigma Xi, Phi Kappa Phi. Contbg. author: Insect and Mite Nutrition, 1972; Introduction to Insect Pest Management, 1975. Contbr. numerous articles to profl. jours. Home: 1806 Maynard Dr Champaign IL 61820 Office: Department of Entomology 320 Morrill Hall University of Illinois Urbana IL 61801

WALDEN, AMELIA ELIZABETH (MRS. JOHN WILLIAM HARMON), author; b. N.Y.C.; d. William A. and Elizabeth (Wanner) Walden; B.S., Columbia, 1934; certificate Am. Acad. Dramatic Arts; m. John William Harmon, Feb. 9, 1946 (dec. 1950). Author: Gateway, 1946; Waverly, 1947; Sunnycove, 1948; Skymountain, 1950; A Girl Called Hank, 1951; Marsha, On-Stage, 1952; Victory for Jill, 1953; All My Love, 1954; Daystar, 1955; Three Loves Has Sandy, 1955; The Bradford Story, 1956; I Found My Love, 1956; My Sister Mike, 1956; Palomino Girl, 1957; Flight Into Morning, 1957; Today is Mine, 1958; Queen of the Courts, 1959; (duo of novels) An American Teacher: Where Is My Heart?, 1960, How Bright the Dawn, 1962; A Boy to Remember, 1960; Shadow on Devils Peak, 1961; (trilogy) The American Shakespeare Festival: When Love Speaks, 1961, So Near the Heart, 1962, My World's the Stage, 1964; My Dreams Ride High, 1963; To Catch A Spy, 1964; The Spy on Danger Island, 1965; Race the Wild Wind, 1965; The Spy with Five Faces, 1966; In Search of Ophelia, 1966; A Spy Called Michel-E, 1967; A Name for Himself, 1967; The Spy Who Talked Too Much, 1968; Walk In A Tall Shadow, 1968; A Spycase Built For Two, 1969; Same Scene, Different Place, 1969; The Case of the Diamond Eye, 1969; Basketball Girl of the Year, 1970; What Happened to Candy Carmichael?, 1970; Valerie Valentine is Missing, 1971; Stay to Win, 1971; Play Ball, McGill, 1972; Where was Everyone when Sabrina Screamed?, 1973; Go, Phillips, Go, 1974; Escape on Skis, 1975; Heartbreak Tennis, 1977. Amelia Walden collection personal, profl. papers, original manuscripts, research data established at Case Western Res. U., Cleve., 1971; pioneer young adult novel. Home: 89 N Compo Rd Westport CT 06880. *Cultivate staying power. Persistence serves one better than talent or genius. Finish everything you begin. Even if the result is not what you had hoped it would be (when is it ever!), what really counts is the fact that you have done it. Above all, cultivate laughter. Laughter is a weapon against a legion of foes, including frustration and discouragement. Laughter is contagious, and thus blesses our friends, and possibly our enemies too. But more even than this, laughter is a medicine for the mind.*

WALDEN, OMI GAIL, govt. ofcl.; b. Alma, Ga., Dec. 25, 1945; d. Banner H. and Naomi (Thomas) Lee; A.B.J. in Journalism, U. Ga., 1967; m. Ralph Edward Walden, Apr. 27, 1968. Asst. dir. pub. relations Ga. Ports Authority, Savannah, 1968-69; dir. pub. relations U.S. HUD Model Cities Program, Alma, 1970-73, citizens participation coordinator, 1970, dir. research and evaluation, 1971-72; fed./state relations coordinator, policy adviser on energy and environ. issues to former Gov. Jimmy Carter, Gov. George Busbee, 1973-76; dir. Ga. Office Energy Resources, 1976-78; asst. sec. for conservation and solar energy applications U.S. Dept. Energy, 1978-79, adv. to sec. for conservation and solar energy mktg., 1980—. Mem. Ga. Gov.'s Task Force on the Transp. of Nuclear Wastes; mem. various energy-related coms., bds. and task forces of state govt. assns., pub. interest groups and environ. orgns. Democrat. Baptist. Author: Enabling Legislation for Georgia Office of Energy Resources, Two Solar Tax Exemption Laws, 1976; contbr. articles to profl. jours. Office: Dept Energy 1000 Independence Ave SW Washington DC 20585

WALDEN, PHILIP MICHAEL, rec. co. exec., pub. co. exec.; b. Greenville, S.C., Jan. 11, 1940; s. Clemuil Barto and Carolyn Hayes (McClendon) W.; A.B. in Econs., Mercer U., 1962; m. Peggy Hackett, Sept. 13, 1969; children—Philip Michael, Amantha Starr. Pres., Phil Walden Artists & Promotions, 1961, Walden Artists & Promotions, 1963-69, Phil Walden & Assos., 1965—, Capricorn Records, Inc., 1969—, Rear Exit and No Exit Music Pub. Co., 1969—. Campaign chmn. Macon Muscular Dystrophy Assn., 1975; chmn. Macon Heritage Found.; mem. In-Town Macon Neighborhood Assn. Mem. nat. finance com. Jimmy Carter for Pres.; mem. Com. for Preservation of the White House; mem. nat. adv. bd. NORML; bd. dirs. Brandywine Conservancy; mem. Presdl. Inaugural Com., 1977; trustee Ga. Trust for Historic Preservation. Served to 1st lt. Adj. Gen. Corps, AUS, 1963-65. Recipient Gold and Platinum Record awards, pub. awards; Big Bear award Mercer U., 1975; Martin Luther King, Jr. Humanitarian award, 1977; Human Relations award Am. Jewish Com., 1978; founder Otis Redding Scholarship Fund, Mercer U., Phil Walden scholarship. Mem. Common Cause, Middle Ga. Hist. Soc., Nat. Assn. Rec. Arts and Scis., Rec. Industry Assn. Am. (dir.), Nat. Assn. Rec. Merchandisers, Phi Delta Theta Alumni Assn. Clubs: Gov.'s of Ga.; Pres.'s of Mercer U.; River North Golf and Country; Sea Pines; Elks. Home: 1121 S Jackson Springs Rd Macon GA 31201 Office: 535 Cotton Ave Macon GA 31201

WALDEN, ROBERT, actor; b. N.Y.C., Sept. 25, 1943; s. Max and Hilda (Winokur) Wolkowitz; B.A., CCNY, 1964. Appeared in: (films) All the President's Men, 1975, Hospital, 1971, Rage, 1972, Audrey Rose, 1976, Capricorn I, 1976; appeared in television series Bold Ones, 1972, Our Time, 1974, Lou Grant, 1977—. Mem. AFTRA, ACLU, Screen Actors Guild. Office: Guild Mgmt 9911 W Pico Blvd Los Angeles CA 90035

WALDEN, ROBERT EDISON, psychiatrist; b. Boston, Apr. 5, 1920; s. Charles W. and Mary (James) W.; student Northeastern U., 1937-38; A.B., Lincoln U., 1942, postgrad., 1942-45; M.D., Meharry Med. Coll., 1945; m. Ethel Lee Bazar, June 23, 1953; children—Kenneth E., Roberta E., Robert Edison, Mark E., Mary E. Intern Kansas City (Mo.) Gen. Hosp., 1945-46, resident, 1946-47; acting clin. dir., tng. psychiatrist Taft (Okla.) State Hosp., 1950-53; tng. psychiatrist Tuskegee (Ala.) VA Hosp., 1955-57; resident psychiatrist Brockton (Mass.), also Boston VA hosps., 1957-60; staff psychiatrist Leech Farm Rd. VA Hosp., Pitts., 1960-62; supt. Lakin (W.Va.) State Hosp., 1962-65; psychiatrist dir. Oakland County Community Mental Health, Pontiac, Mich., 1965-68; asso. prof. depts. psychiatry and social medicine Med. Coll. of Ohio, Toledo, 1968—, psychiat. dir psychiat. in-patient service, 1977—; adj. asso. prof. psychiatry U. Toledo; founder, med. dir. Cordelia Martin Interim Health Center, Toledo, 1970-72; psychiat. cons. Toledo Soc. Handicapped, East Toledo Mental Health Center; project dir. Community Health and Screening Program. Mem. W.Va. Gov.'s Adv. Council for Emotionally Disturbed Children, 1963-65; mem. Ohio Rehab. Services Commn., 1972-79, Toledo Mental Hygiene Clinic Bd., 1968-74, Community Planning Council N.W. Ohio; mem. adv. council Ohio Regional Med. Program. Served with M.C., AUS, 1943-46; capt. M.C., USAF Res., 1953-55; now col. M.C., USAR. Diplomate Am. Bd. Psychiatry and Neurology. Fellow Am. Psychiat. Assn.; mem. Ohio Psychiat. Assn. (program chmn., sec.), N.W. Ohio Psychiat. Assn. (pres.), Sigma Pi Phi, Kappa Alpha Psi. Home: 1931 Mount Vernon Dr Toledo OH 43607 Office: CS 10008 Toledo OH 43699

WALDEN, STANLEY, composer, clarinetist; b. Bklyn., 1932; B.A. with honors in Music, Queens Coll.; student composition with Ben Weber, clarinet with David Weber. Pianist for Martha Graham, Anna Sokolow; music dir. Tamiris-Nagrin Dance Co., Horseman, Pass By, 1969; solo clarinet Contemporary Chamber Ensemble, Bennington Composers Conf., Penn Contemporary Players; guest artist N.Y. Woodwind Quintet. Faculty, C.W. Post Coll.; guest lectr. U. Wis., Yale Drama Sch.; mem. dance faculty (music) Juilliard Sch., N.Y.C., 1965-71; faculty Sarah Lawrence Coll., 1973-75, State U. N.Y., Purchase, 1973—; commns. include Dance Sonata for Daniel Nagrin, Stretti for Group for Contemporary Music Columbia, Image for Harkness Ballet, ballet with Anna Sokolow for Manhattan Festival Ballet; composer incidental music Off-Broadway prodn. Scuba Duba, 1967; music for Pinkville, Am. Place Theater, 1970, The Kid, 1972; Sigmunds Freude, Bremen Stadt Theater, 1975; Weewis for Joffrey Ballet, 1971; film The Crazy American Girl, 1975; as mem. The Open Window Trio: solo recitals, albums for Vanguard; Three Views, commd. and recorded Louisville Orch., 1969; incidental music for World War 2 1/2, 1969; music and lyrics Oh Calcutta!, 1969; new score The Caucasian Chalk Circle, 1978; musical Back Country, 1978, Shylock, 1978, My Mother's Courage, 1979. Address: Route 3 Box 438 Hopewell Junction NY 12533

WALDFOGEL, MORTON SUMNER, plywood co. exec.; b. Somerville, Mass., Nov. 5, 1922; s. Benjamin and Gertrude (Levins) W.; A.B., Harvard U., 1944; M.B.A., Boston U., 1948; m. Lillian Thelma Gouse, June 16, 1949; children—Peter Douglas, Jane Leslie. Asso. prof. math. econs. Boston U., 1947-48; mgr. Roddis Plywood Co., Cambridge, Mass., 1948-51; partner East Coast Mill Sales, 1951—; chmn. bd., chief exec. officer Allied Industries Inc., Charlestown, Mass., 1961—. Served with USNR, 1942-47. Decorated Letter of Commendation. Jewish. Home: 16 Brown Rd Swampscott MA 01907 Office: PO Box 56 Charlestown MA 02129

WALDHAUSEN, JOHN ANTON, cardiothoracic surgeon; b. N.Y.C., May 22, 1929; s. Max. H. and Agnes H. (Stettner) W.; B.S. magna cum laude, Coll. Great Falls, 1950; M.D., St. Louis U., 1954; m. Marian Trescher, June 4, 1957; children—John H., Robert Rodney, Anthony Gordon Scarlett. Intern, Johns Hopkins Hosp., 1954-55, resident, 1955-57; clin. asst. Nat. Heart and Lung Inst., NIH, 1957-59; resident Hosp. U. Pa., 1959, Ind. U. Med. Center, 1960-62; practice medicine specializing in cardiothoracic surgery, Indpls., 1962-66, Phila., 1966-70, Hershey, Pa., 1970—; mem. staff Milton S. Hershey Med. Center, 1970—; from instr. to asst. prof. Ind. U. Med. Center, 1962-66; asso. prof. surgery U. Pa., Phila., 1966-70; prof., chmn. dept. surgery Pa. State U. Coll. Medicine, Milton S. Hershey Med. Center, 1970—, sr. mem. grad. faculty, 1970—, vice chmn. med. policy bd. 1971-72, interim provost, dean, 1972-73, asso. dean health care, 1973-75. Served with USPHS, 1957-59. Recipient Career Devel. award USPHS, 1964; diplomate Am. Bd. Surgery, Am. Bd. Thoracic Surgery. Mem. Allen O. Whipple Surg. Soc., Am. Acad. Pediatrics, AAAS, Am. Assn. Surgery of Trauma, Am. Coll. Cardiology, A.C.S. (chpt. pres. 1974-75, gov. 1979—), Am. Fedn. Clin. Research, Am. Heart Assn., AMA, Am. Physiol. Soc., Am. Soc. Artificial Internal Organs, Am. Assn. Thoracic Surgery, Am. Surg. Assn., Central Surg. Assn., Internat. Cardiovascular Soc. (chpt. recorder, 1969-74), Pa. Assn. Thoracic Surgery (pres. 1977-78), Thoracic Surgery Dirs. Assn. (pres. 1977-79), Societe International de Chirurgie, Soc. Clin. Surgery (treas. 1972—), Soc. Surg. Chairmen, Soc. Thoracic Surgeons, Soc. Univ. Surgeons, Soc. Vascular Surgery, Sigma Xi, Alpha Omega Alpha. Mem. editorial bd. Jour. Pediatric Surgery, 1972-78; cons. editor Archives of Surgery, 1972-74; contbr. chpts. to books, articles to med. jours. Home: RD 1 PO Box 158G Annville PA 17003 Office: MS Hershey Med Center Hershey PA 17033

WALDHEIM, KURT, sec.-gen. UN; b. Sankt Andrä-Wördern, Austria, Dec. 21, 1918; s. Walter and Josefine (Petrasch) W.; doctor juris., Vienna U., 1944; LL.D., Fordham U., 1972, Carleton U., Ottawa, Can., 1972, U. Chile, Santiago, 1972, Rutgers U., 1972, Jawarharlal Nehru U., New Delhi, 1973, U. Bucharest, 1973, Wagner Coll., N.Y., 1973, Catholic U. Am., 1974, Wilfred Laurier U., Waterloo, Can., 1974, Catholic U. Leuven (Belgium), 1975, Charles U., Prague, Czechoslovakia, 1975, Hamilton Coll., Clinton, N.Y., 1975, U. Denver, 1976, U. Philippines, 1976, U. Nice, 1976, Vanderbilt U., 1976, Am. U., 1977, Kent State U., 1977, Warsaw U., 1977, Moscow State U., 1977, Mongolian State U., 1977; m. Elisabeth Ritschel, Aug. 19, 1944; children—Liselotte, Gerhard, Christa. Entered Austrian Fgn. Service, 1945; served Ministry Fgn. Affairs; mem. Austrian del. to Paris, London and Moscow for negotiations on Austrian State Treaty, 1945-47; 1st sec. Austrian embassy, Paris, 1948-51; head personnel div. Ministry Fgn. Affairs, 1951-55; permanent Austrian observer to UN, 1955-56; minister to Canada, 1956-58, ambassador to Canada, 1958-60; dir. gen. for polit. affairs Ministry Fgn. Affairs, 1960-64; permanent rep. to UN, 1964-68, 70-71, chmn. outer space com., 1965-68, sec. gen., 1971—; fed. minister for fgn. affairs Austria, 1968-70. Candidate for Pres. of

Austria, 1971. Author: The Austrian Example, 1971, English edit., 1973. Address: UN Secretariat UN New York NY 10017

WALDHORN, HERBERT FRANCIS, physician; b. N. Y.C., Aug. 28, 1919; s. Edward Elliott and Rose (Siltzbach) W.; A.B., Columbia, 1939; M.D., N.Y.U., 1942; certificate, N.Y. Psychoanalytic Inst., 1952; m. Miriam Rosenbloom, June 15, 1941; children—Jane, Richard Edward, Amy Ruth. Intern Queens Gen. Hosp., 1942-43; resident psychiatry Bklyn. State Hosp., 1946-48; practice medicine, specializing in psychiatry, psychoanalysis, N.Y.C., 1948—; psychiatrist out-patient dept. Israel Zion Hosp., Bklyn., 1947-48; staff psychoanalyst N.Y. Psychoanalytic Inst. Treatment Center, 1950-60; psychiat. cons. N.Y. Guild for Jewish Blind, 1950-57; instr. psychiatry State U. Downstate Med. Center, 1955-59; asst. psychiatrist Kings County Hosp., 1955-59; cons. psychiatrist Hillside Hosp., 1968—; tng. analyst, instr. N.Y. Psychoanalytic Inst., 1972—; asso. prof. clin. psychiatry State U. N.Y. Stony Brook Med. Sch., 1977—; mem. Center for Advanced Psychoanalytic Studies, Princeton, N.J. Served to capt., M.C., AUS, 1943-46. Mem. Am. Psychiat. Assn., N.Y. Soc. Clin. Psychiatry, Am. Psychoanalytic Assn. (sec.), N.Y., L.I. psychoanalytic socs., Nassau Neuro-Psychiat. Soc. Co-editor monograph series Kris Study Group, N.Y. Psychoanalytic Inst. Contbr. articles profl. jours. Home: 12 Wilshire Dr Great Neck NY 11020 Office: 10 Cutter Mill Rd Great Neck NY 11021

WALDMAN, ANNE LESLEY, poet, editor, pub., ednl. adminstr.; b. Millville, N.J., Apr. 2, 1945; d. John Marvin and Frances (Le Fevre) W.; B.A., Bennington Coll., 1966. Asst. dir. The Poetry Project, St. Marks Ch. In-the-Bowery, N.Y.C., 1966-68, project dir., 1968-78; co-dir. Jack Kerouac Sch. of Poetics at Naropa Inst., Boulder, Colo., 1974—; author books of poetry: Baby Breakdown, 1970, Giant Night, 1970, No Hassles, 1971, Life Notes, 1973, Fast Speaking Woman, 1975, Journals and Dreams, 1976; editor anthologies: The World Anthology, 1969, Another World, 1972; Talking Poetics From Naropa Institute vol. 1, 1978, vol. 2, 1979; publisher Angel Hair Books, N.Y.C., Full Ct. Press, N.Y.C. Recipient Dylan Thomas Meml. award New Sch., N.Y.C., 1967; Cultural Artists Program grantee, 1976-77; Nat. Endowment for Arts grantee, 1979-80. Mem. PEN Club. Office: care Naropa Inst 1111 Pearl St Boulder CO 80302

WALDMAN, ANNE LESLEY, poet; b. Apr. 2, 1945; d. John Marvin and Frances (Le Fevre) Waldman; B.A., Bennington Coll. Dir. poetry project St. Marks Ch. In-the-Bowery, N.Y.C. Co-dir. Kerouac Sch. of Disembodied Poetics, Naropa Inst., Boulder, Colo.; co-editor Full Ct. Press, N.Y.C., Bombay Gin mag., Boulder, Rocky Ledge mag., Eldora, Coll. Bd. dirs. Giorno Poetry Systems Inst. Author: Life Notes, 1970; Giant Night, 1970; No Hassles, 1971; Life Notes, 1973; Fast Speaking Woman, 1975; Journals and Dreams, 1976; Co-editor; Talking Poetics, 1978; editor; The World Anthology, 1969; Another World, 1971. Office: care The Poetry Project St Marks Ch 10th St and 2d Ave New York City NY 10005

WALDMAN, BERNARD, educator; b. N.Y.C., Oct. 12, 1913; s. Joseph and Mollie (Rothman) W.; A.B., N.Y. U., 1934, Ph.D., 1939; m. Florence Finley, June 13, 1942 (dec. June 1961); children—John William, Nancy Karen (Mrs. John L. Melcher); m. 2d, Glenna Frank Ryan, Mar. 21, 1964; stepchildren—Tawny Ryan (Mrs. Robert G. Nelb II), Sharon Ryan (Mrs. Clark A. Hickman). Grad. asst. N.Y. U., 1935-38; research asso. U. Notre Dame, 1938-40, instr., 1940-41, asst. prof. physics, 1941-48, asso. prof. physics, 1945-51, prof. 1951—, dir. nuclear physics research lab., 1946-64, asso. dean Coll. Sci., 1964-67, dean, 1967-79; prof. Mich. State U., East Lansing, 1979—. Ofcl. investigator OSRD 1942-43; dir. lab. Midwestern Univs. Research Assn., 1960-65; staff mem. Los Alamos Sci. Lab., 1943-45. Trustee Univs. Research Assn., 1965-71. Mem. Gov.'s Commn. on Med. Edn., 1971-74. Fellow Am. Phys. Soc.; mem. Am. Assn. Physics Tchrs., AAUP, Sigma Xi, Sigma Pi Sigma, Alpha Epsilon Delta. Home: 2060 Tamarack Dr Okemos MI 48864 Office: Cyclotron Lab Mich State U East Lansing MI 48824

WALDMAN, DIANE, museum curator; b. N.Y.C., Feb. 24, 1936; B.F.A., Hunter Coll., 1956; M.A., Inst. Fine Arts, N.Y. U., 1965, postgrad., 1965-74; m. Paul Waldman, 1957. With Solomon R. Guggenheim Mus., N.Y.C., 1965—, organizer various exhbns., asso. curator, 1969-71, curator exhbns., 1971—. Contbr. articles profl. jours.; author monographs. Office: 1071 Fifth Ave New York City NY 10028

WALDMAN, JEFFREY, metallurgist, educator; b. Phila., Jan. 10, 1941; s. Albert Berger and Rita Joanne (Weitzenkorn) W.; B.S. in Metall. Engring., Drexel Inst. Tech., 1963; Sc.D. in Metallurgy (Whitney fellow), M.I.T., 1967; m. Judith Shulman, Dec. 23, 1962; children—Stacey, Jonathan, Karen. Drexel Inst. Tech. coop. student RCA, Somerville, N.J., 1959-61; metallurgist Frankford Arsenal, Phila., summers 1963, 64, 68-77, U.S. Army Armament Research and Devel. Command, Dover, N.J., 1977—; sr. research engr. Western Electric Co., Princeton N.J., 1967-68; instr. evening coll. Drexel U., 1968-71, prof., 1975—, adj. prof. metallurgy, 1973. Recipient Spl. Act awards Frankford Arsenal, 1969, 71, also Suggestion award, 1969. Mem. Research Soc. N.Am. (treas. Frankford Arsenal chpt.), Frankford Arsenal Mgmt. Assn., Am. Soc. Metals, AIME, Am. Def. Preparedness Assn. (Liaison), Sigma Xi. Tau Beta Pi, Phi Kappa Phi, Alpha Sigma Mu. Contbr. articles to profl. jours.; patentee in field. Home: 3894 Donna Dr Huntingdon Valley PA 19006 Office; US Army Armament Research and Devel Command Dover NJ 07801

WALDMAN, MARTIN HERBERT, pub. co. exec.; b. Jersey City, Dec. 27, 1927; s. Julius and Rose (Rich) W.; B.A., Rutgers U., 1949; m. Sallie Brasky, Dec. 24, 1953; children—Nancy, Daniel, Amanda. Los Angeles rep. MacFadden Publs., N.Y.C., 1949-50; western rep. Pubs. Distbg. Corp., N.Y.C., 1950-51; circulation mgr. Los Angeles Sentinel, 1951-52; advt. salesman Daily Variety, Los Angeles, 1952-53; Hollywood Reporter, Los Angeles, 1953-54; dir. sales, advt., pub. relations Consol. Film Industries, Los Angeles, 1954-58; pres. Tech. Pub. Corp. (name now Brentwood Pub. Corp.), Los Angeles, 1958—, pub. Applied Radiology, Assn. and Soc. Mgr., CVP, Respiratory Therapy, Perinatology/Neonatology, Incentive Travel Mgr., Med. Imaging, Rx Home Care. Office: 825 S Barrington Ave Los Angeles CA 90049

WALDMEIR, PETER NIELSEN, journalist; b. Detroit, Jan. 16, 1931; s. Joseph John and Helen Sarah (Nielsen) W.; student Wayne State U., 1949-58; m. Marilyn C. Choma; children—Peter William, Patti Ann, Lindsey Marilyn. With Detroit News, 1949—, sports columnist, 1962-72, gen. columnist, 1972—. Served with USMC, 1951-53. Recipient Headliners award Nat. Headliners Club, 1971; named Mich. Sports Writer of Year, Nat. Sportscasters and Sportswriters, 1967, 69, 71. Mem. Sigma Delta Chi. Episcopalian. Office: 615 W Lafayette St Detroit MI 48231

WALDO, ALBERT LEON, cardiologist; b. N.Y.C., Nov. 25, 1936; s. Maxim and Susan Gertrude (Cohen) W.; B.A. (N.Y. State scholar, Schoelkopf scholar, LeFevre scholar), Cornell U., 1958; M.D., SUNY, 1962; m. Rosa Ines Torres Rodriguez, Dec. 28, 1973; children—Miguel A., Richard E., Eric W. Intern, Kings County Hosp., Bklyn., 1962-63, chief resident in medicine, 1965-66; asst. med. resident Balt. City Hosps., fellow in medicine Johns Hopkins U. Sch. Medicine, 1963-65; postdoctoral fellow in cardiac electrophysiology Coll. Physicians and Surgeons, Columbia U., N.Y.C., 1966-68, vis. fellow in medicine, 1968-69; practice medicine specializing in cardiology, N.Y.C., 1969-72, Birmingham, Ala., 1972—; asst. physician Vanderbilt Clinic, Presbyn. Hosp., N.Y.C., 1966-69, asso. in cardiovascular lab., 1969-70, asst. surgeon, 1969-72; asso. dept. pharmacology Coll. Physicians and Surgeons, 1969-70, asst. prof., 1970-72; asso. prof. dept. medicine U. Ala., Birmingham, 1972-76, prof., 1976—, scientist Cardiovascular Research and Tng. Center, 1972-76, sr. scientist, 1976—; staff physician Univ. Hosp. Mem. exec. bd. Birmingham Music Club, 1973—. Diplomate Am. Bd. Cardiology, Am. Bd. Internal Medicine. Fellow A.C.P., Am. Coll. Cardiology, Council on Clin. Cardiology; mem. Birmingham Cardiovascular Soc., Cardiac Electrophysiol. Soc., Am. Physiol. Soc., Am. Soc. for Clin. Investigation, So. Soc. for Clin. Investigation, Assn. Univ. Cardiologists, Jefferson County Med. Soc., Am. Heart Assn., Ala. Heart Assn., AAAS, N.Y. Acad. Sci., Alpha Epsilon Delta. Editorial bd. Circulation, 1974—, PACE, 1978—, Heart and Lung, 1978—. Office: U Ala Med Center Birmingham AL 35294

WALDO, BURTON CORLETT, lawyer; b. Seattle, Aug. 11, 1920; s. William Earl and Ruth (Corlett) W.; B.A., U. Wash., 1941, J.D., 1948; m. Margaret Jane Hoar, Aug. 24, 1946; children—James Chandler, Bruce Corlett. Admitted to Wash. bar, 1949, since practiced in Seattle, partner in firm Keller, Rohrback, Waldo & Hiscock and predecessors, 1953—. Mem. bd. theatre suprs. City Seattle, 1958-61; mem. Municipal League Seattle and King County, 1949—. Served to capt. AUS, 1942-46. Mem. Am., Wash., Seattle-King County (trustee 1965-68) bar assns., Fedn. Ins. Counsel, Internat. Assn. Ins. Counsel, Delta Tau Delta, Phi Delta Phi, Alpha Kappa Psi. Republican. Clubs: Wash. Athletic, Rainier (Seattle). Home: 3715 E Union St Seattle WA 98122 Office: IBM Bldg Seattle WA 98101

WALDO, (CLIFFORD) DWIGHT, educator; b. DeWitt, Nebr., Sept. 28, 1913; s. Cliff Ford and Grace Gertrude (Lindley) W.; B.A., Nebr. State Tchrs. Coll., Peru, 1935, M.A., U. Nebr., 1937; Ph.D., Yale, 1942; m. Gwen Payne, Sept. 17, 1937; children—Mary Grace, Martha Gwen, Margret Ann. Instr. polit. sci. Yale, 1941-42; price analyst OPA, 1942-44; adminstrv. analyst Exec. Office Pres., 1944-46; mem. faculty U. Calif. at Berkeley, 1946-67, prof. polit. sci., 1953—, dir. Inst. Govt. Studies, 1958-67; Albert Schweitzer prof. humanities Syracuse U., 1967-79, emeritus prof., 1979—; resident fellow Woodrow Wilson Internat. Center for Scholars, Smithsonian Instn., Washington, 1979—. Mem. Am. Polit. Sci. Assn. (v.p. 1961-62), Am. Soc. Pub. Adminstrn., Internat. Inst. Adminstrv. Scis., Internat. City Mgmt. Assn. (hon. life), Nat. Assn. Schs. Pub. Affairs and Adminstrn. (v.p. 1976-77, pres. 1977-78). Author: The Administrative State, 1948; The Study of Public Administration, 1955; Perspectives on Administration, 1956; Political Science in the U.S.A., 1956. Editor: Public Administration in a Time of Turbulence, 1972, others; editor-in-chief Pub. Adminstrn. Rev., 1966-77. Home: 3711 S George Mason Dr 1411-W Falls Church VA 22041

WALDO, TOMMY RUTH BLACKMON (MRS. SELDEN FENNELL WALDO), educator; b. Dallas, Jan. 14, 1916; d. Gulie Hargrove and Mary Lee (Craig) Blackmon; B.A., Agnes Scott Coll., 1938; M.A., U. Fla., 1955, Ph.D., 1961; m. Selden Fennell Waldo, Oct. 28, 1941 (dec. Nov. 1950); children—George Selden (dec.), Andrew Blackmon. Grad. asst. U. Fla., Gainesville, 1952-55, instr., 1955-61, asst. prof. English, 1961-68, asso. prof. English, 1968-76, prof., 1976—; pvt. tchr. piano and organ, 1938-55. Mem. So. Atlantic Modern Lang. Assn., Modern Lang. Assn., Fla. Music Tchrs. Assn., Gainesville Music Tchrs. Assn., Southeastern Renaissance Conf., Phi Beta Kappa, Sigma Alpha Iota (patroness), Delta Kappa Gamma. Author book on Shakespeare. Contbr. articles to profl. jours.

WALDOCK, PETER JOHN, publishing co. exec.; b. Lincoln, Eng., Feb. 26, 1945; came to Can., 1967, naturalized, 1979; s. Norman Bruce and Norah (Dransfield) W.; B.A. with honors, Keele U., Staffordshire, Eng., 1967; m. Gillian Irene Rigg, May 23, 1970; children—Christopher James, Sarah Elizabeth. Sales rep. coll. div. Longman Can. Ltd., Don Mills, Ont., 1967-69, sales dir./mgr. Penguin div., 1969-74; pres. Penguin Books Can. Ltd., Markham, Ont., 1974—. Mem. Can. Book Publs. Council (1st v.p.), Can. Booksellers Assn., Am. Booksellers Assn., Book Pubs. Profl. Assn. Office: 2801 John St Markham ON L3R 1B4 Canada

WALDON, DAVID GEORGE, ret. oil pipe line co. exec.; b. Toronto, Ont., Can., Aug. 24, 1916; s. Charles D. and Ethel (Park) W.; m. Mary Eileen Moore, Oct. 21, 1944; 1 son, Robert. With Andian Nat. Corp., 1935-49; with Interprovincial Pipe Line Co., 1950-78, pres., chief exec. officer, 1967—, also dir.; pres. Lakehead Pipe Line Co., Inc.; past v.p., dir. Mackenzie Valley Pipe Line Research Ltd.; dir. Royal Trustco, Union Gas Ltd., Nat. Life Assurance Co. Trustee, Toronto Western Hosp. Clubs: Nat., York Downs Golf (Toronto): Home: 469 Oriole Pkwy Toronto ON M59 2H5 Canada

WALDRON, CHARLES MARCIAN, dept. store exec.; b. Phila., Oct. 24, 1920; s. Michael Jerome and Mary Ellen (Daley) W.; B.S. in Econs., Wharton Sch., U. Pa., 1942; m. Kathryn Frances Schmid, Jan. 12, 1946; children—Joseph, Charles, Mary Ellen, Francis Denise, Kathleen. Exec. v.p. Waldron & Co., Inc., Phila., 1946-63; controller Midstates Mdse. Co., Dayton, Ohio, 1963; with Elder Beerman Stores Corp., Dayton, 1963—, exec. v.p., gen. mdse. mgr., 1971-76, vice chmn., chief adminstrv. officer, 1976—, pres., 1978—, also dir. Served to lt. USNR, 1942-46. Roman Catholic. Home: 347 Pleasant Hill Dr Dayton OH 45459 Office: 3155 Elbee Rd Dayton OH 45401

WALDRON, ELLIS LEIGH, educator; b. Denver, Feb. 21, 1915; s. Grover C. and Maud M. (Dolbeer) W.; B.A., Ohio State U., 1936; M.A., U. Wis., 1939, Ph.D., 1952; student Duke, 1939-40; m. Phyilis Schwoegler, May 16, 1941; 1 dau., Jean Madelene. Staff polit. corr. U.P., Columbus, Ohio, 1941-44; instr. polit. sci. extension div. U. Wis., 1946-49, fellow polit. sci., 1949-50; faculty dept. polit. sci. U. Mont., 1950—, prof. polit. sci., 1957—, dean Graduate Sch., 1957-61; fellow law and polit. sci. Harvard Law Sch., 1963-64. Mem. Mont. Constl. Conv. Commn., 1971-72. Served with AUS, 1944-46. Mem. Am. Polit. Sci. Assn. (council 1969-71), Am. Assn. U. Profs., Phi Beta Kappa, Kappa Sigma, Phi Kappa Phi. Author: (with Paul Wilson) Atlas of Montana Elections, 1889-1976, 1978; compiler Mont. Politics Since 1864; An Atlas of Elections, 1958. Home: 2345 S 7th St W Missoula MT 59801

WALDRON, HICKS BENJAMIN, food and beverage co. exec.; b. Amsterdam, N.Y., Oct. 31, 1923; s. Hicks Benjamin and Dorothy (Clearwater) W.; student Green Mountain Jr. Coll., 1941-42, U. Mich., 1943; B.S., U. Minn., 1944; m. Evelyn Rumstay; children—Janet Waldron Ambrose, Hicks Benjamin III. With Gen. Electric Co., 1946-73, v.p., group exec. consumer products group, 1971-73; pres., chief operating officer Heublein, Inc., Farmington, Conn., 1973—, also dir.; dir. Conn. Gen. Ins. Corp., Conn. Bank & Trust Co. Chmn., pres. Jr. Achievement No. Central Conn. Bd. dirs. Greater Hartford Arts Council, United Way, Hartford Hosp.; trustee Green Mountain Coll., Hartford Grad. Center. Served to ensign USNR, 1944-46. Mem. Greater Hartford C. of C. (dir.), Phi Gamma Delta. Episcopalian. Clubs: Hartford Golf; Country of Farmington. Home: 88 Prattling Pond Rd Farmington CT 06032 Office: Heublein Inc Munson Rd Farmington CT 06032

WALDRON, MARK A., JR., food co. exec.; b. Chgo., Jan. 18, 1937; s. Mark A. and Mary C. (Moylan) W.; B.S. in Acctg., Loyola U., Chgo., 1959; m. Theresa Mary Bennett, Jan. 31, 1959; children—Mark, Paul, Daniel, John, Mary Beth, Michael, Theresa, Thomas, Ann Marie. With Arthur Young & Co., Chgo., 1959-70; asst. corp. controller Consol. Foods Corp., Chgo., 1970-73, chief fin. officer Fuller Brush div., 1973-76; chief acctg. officer Cordura Corp., Chgo., 1976-77; asst. dir. corp. devel. (acquisitions) Beatrice Foods Corp., Chgo., 1977-78; exec. v.p., chief fin. officer, dir. Scot Lad Foods, Lansing, Ill., 1978—. Mem. Am. Inst. C.P.A.'s. Office: 1 Scot Lad Ln Lansing IL 60438

WALDRON, RODNEY K., librarian; b. Newberg, Oreg., Feb. 15, 1919; s. James Roscoe and Margaret (Wertman) W.; B.A., U. Denver, 1950, M.S. in L.S., 1950; m. Virginia E. Lay, Jan. 30, 1946; 1 son, John Stuart. With REA, 1939-42, Colo. Archives, Denver, 1950; cataloger Mo. Hist. Soc., 1951; gen. asst., archivist U. Idaho, 1951-53, asst. librarian, head readers services, 1953- 54; adminstrv. asst. to dir., asst. librarian, then asso. librarian Oreg. State U., 1954-65, dir. libraries, 1965—; cons. in field; chmn. interinstl. library council Oreg. State System Higher Edn., 1976-79. Served with inf. AUS, 1942-45; PTO. Decorated Bronze Star. Mem. Am., Oreg., Pacific Northwest (pres. 1965-66) library assns. Rotarian. Author: Use of Technical Library, 1964; Introductions for Preparation of the Thesis, 3d edit., 1966; also articles. Home: 445 NW 31st St Corvallis OR 97330

WALDRON, WILLIAM AUGUSTUS, lawyer; b. Schenectady, Aug. 1, 1913; s. Charles Newman and Dorothy (Waterman) W.; A.B., Union Coll., Schenectady, 1935, A.M., 1937, LL.D., 1979; LL.B., Harvard, 1941; m. Gertrude Lill Nelson, Mar. 13, 1948 (div.); children—Arthur Nelson, Dorothy Waterman; m. 2d, Sybil Jay Kinnicutt, June 25, 1969. Admitted to Mass. bar, 1941; practiced in Boston, 1941—; mem. staff Nat. War Labor Bd., 1942-45; gen. counsel Mass. Gen. Hosp., Boston, 1976—; full-time and part-time offices Mass. state govt., 1950-74; part-time offices Town of Wayland (Mass.), 1953-68; part-time lectr. Boston U., 1956, Harvard U., 1962-63. Bd. dirs. or trustee several charitable, ednl. or profl. orgns., 1951-75; trustee Edmund Niles Huyck Found., 1959—. Mem. Phi Beta Kappa, Alpha Delta Phi. Home: 15 Larch Rd Cambridge MA 02138 Office: Mass General Hospital Boston MA 02114

WALDROP, FRANCIS NEIL, physician, govt. adminstr.; b. Asheville, N.C., Oct. 5, 1926; s. Troy Lester and Emma Louise (Ballard) W.; A.B., U. Minn., 1946; M.D., George Washington U., 1950; m. Eleanor Dorothy Wickes, June 10, 1950; children—Mark Lester, Barbara Louise. Intern, George Washington U. Hosp., Washington, 1950-51; resident St. Elizabeth's Hosp., Washington, 1951-54, med. officer, 1951-71; dir. manpower and tng. programs NIMH, Rockville, Md., 1972-75; dep. adminstr. Alcohol, Drug Abuse and Mental Health Adminstrn., HEW, Rockville, 1975—; clin. prof. psychiatry George Washington U. Recipient Superior Service award HEW, 1962, Disting. Service award, 1964. Fellow Am. Psychiat. Assn.; mem. AAAS. Research, publs. in field. Home: 1775 Elton Rd Silver Spring MD 20903 Office: 5600 Fishers Ln Rockville MD 20857

WALDROP, GIDEON WILLIAM, composer, conductor; b. Haskell County, Tex., Sept. 2, 1919; s. Gideon W. and Margaret (Pierson) W.; Mus.B., Baylor U., 1940; Mus. M., U. Rochester, 1941, Ph.D., 1952. Conductor Shreveport Symphony, 1941-42, Waco-Baylor U. Symphony Orch., 1946-51; asso. prof. Baylor U., 1946-51; editor Rev. Recorded Music, N.Y.C., 1952-54, Musical Courier, 1954-58; cons. div. arts and humanities Ford Found., 1958-61; asst. to pres. Juilliard Sch. Music, 1961-63, dean, 1963—. Mem. advisory committee Toscanini Archives. Served to major USAAF, 1942-46. Decorated Bronze Star. Mem. A.S.C.A.P., Phi Mu Alpha. Democrat. Clubs: Players, Bohemians, N.Y. Athletic (N.Y.C.). Composer symphony, overture, prelude and fugue for orch., chamber music, choral works and songs. Commd. by San Antonio Symphony Soc., 1958, 63. Home: 160 Riverside Dr New York NY 10024

WALDSCHMIDT, PAUL EDWARD, clergyman; b. Evansville, Ind., Jan. 7, 1920; s. Edward Benjamin and Olga Marie (Moers) W.; B.A., U. Notre Dame, 1942; student Holy Cross Coll., Washington, 1942-45; S.T.L., Laval U., Que., Can., 1947; S.T.D., Angelicum U., Rome, Italy, 1948. Ordained priest Roman Catholic Ch., 1946; prof. apologetics and dogmatic theology Holy Cross Coll., 1949-55; v.p. U. Portland, 1955-62, dean faculties, 1956-60, pres., 1962-78; aux. bishop of Portland, 1978—. Bd. dirs. NCCJ, St. Vincent de Paul Rehab. Center. Mem. Cath. Theol. Soc. Am. (v.p. 1954-55), NEA, Delta Epsilon Sigma. K.C. (4 deg.). Clubs: University, City. Address: 5402 N Strong St Portland OR 97203

WALDSTEIN, SHELDON SAUL, physician, educator; b. Chgo., June 23, 1924; s. Herman S. and Sophia (Klapper) W.; student Harvard, 1941-43; M.D., Northwestern U., 1947; m. Jacqueline Sheila Denbo, Apr. 2, 1952; children—Sara Jean, Peter Denbo, David John. Intern Cook County Hosp., 1947-48, resident in internal medicine, 1948-51, chief Northwestern Med. Service, 1954-62, exec. dir. dept. medicine, 1962-64, chmn. dept. medicine, 1964-69; exec. dir. North Suburban Assn. Health Resources, 1969-72; mem. faculty Northwestern U. Med. Sch., 1954-61, asso. prof. medicine, 1961-66, prof. medicine, 1966—, asso. dean health services, dir. Northwestern U. Med. Assos., 1974-77; exec. dir., asso. dean, trustee Cook County Grad. Sch. Medicine, Chgo., 1977—. Served to capt. M.C., AUS, 1952-54. Diplomate Am. Bd. Internal Medicine. Mem. A.M.A., Chgo. Med. Soc., Central Soc. Clin. Research, Endocrine Soc., Am. Fedn. Clin. Research, Am. Assn. for Study Liver Disease, A.A.A.S., Inst. Medicine Chgo., Chgo. Soc. Internal Medicine, Sigma Xi, Alpha Omega Alpha. Contbr. articles to med. jours. Home: 265 Walden Dr Glencoe IL 60022 Office: 222 E Superior St Chicago IL 60611

WALECKA, JOHN DIRK, educator, physicist; b. Milw., Mar. 11, 1932; s. John A. and Charlotte (Haun) W.; B.A. summa cum laude, Harvard, 1954; Ph.D., Mass. Inst. Tech., 1958; m. Kathryn Alice Bayles, Aug. 28, 1954; children—John Lawrence, Ann Charlotte, James Dirk. Postdoctoral fellow NSF, CERN Geneva, Switzerland, also Stanford, 1958-60; mem. faculty Stanford, 1960—, prof. physics, 1966—, asso. dean humanities and scis., 1970-72, chmn. faculty senate, 1973-74, chmn. adv. bd., 1975-77, chmn. dept. physics, 1977—, recipient Gores award for teaching, 1972. Mem. ad hoc panel on the future of nuclear sci. Nat. Acad. Scis.-NRC, 1975-77; mem. Nuclear Sci. Adv. Com., 1977-79. Sloan Found. fellow, 1962-66. Fellow Am. Phys. Soc. (exec. com. div. nuclear physics 1976-78); mem. Phi Beta Kappa. Home: 942 Casaneuva Pl Stanford CA 94305

WALES, GWYNNE HUNTINGTON, lawyer; b. Evanston, Ill., Apr. 18, 1933; s. Robert Willett and Solace (Huntington) W.; A.B., Princeton U., 1954; J.D., Harvard U., 1961; m. Janet McCobb, Feb. 8, 1957; children—Thomas Gwynne, Catherine Anne, Louise Carrie. Admitted to N.Y. bar, 1962; asso. firm White & Case, N.Y.C., 1961-69, partner, 1969—, resident partner, Brussels, 1969-75. Served with USN, 1954-58. Mem. Am. Bar Assn., Assn. Bar City N.Y., N.Y. State Bar Assn., Downtown Assn. N.Y.C. Club: Round Hill

(Greenwich, Conn.). Home: 29 Oakwood Ln Greenwich CT 06830 Office: 14 Wall St New York NY 10005

WALES, HAROLD WEBSTER, lawyer; b. Seattle, June 23, 1928; s. John Harold and Clara (Webster) W.; B.C.S. cum laude, Seattle U., 1950; J.D., U. San Francisco, 1958; m. Dorothy C. Kotthoff, July 15, 1955; children—Elizabeth Marie, Mary Celine. Admitted to Calif. bar, 1959, Ariz. bar, 1959; practiced in Phoenix, 1959—; pres. Central Ariz. Estate Planning Council, 1964-65; lectr. Tax Inst., Ariz. State U., 1962, 64, Nat. Automobile Dealers Assn., 1975-76; lectr., income tax Scottsdale (Ariz.) Community Coll., 1971—. Pres., Cath. Social Service, Phoenix, 1964; Ariz. chmn. Nat. Found. March Dimes, 1969. Bd. dirs. A.R.C. Maricopa County. Served with USAF, 1950-54. Mem. Internat., Am., Maricopa County bar assns., State Bar Ariz. (chmn. taxation sect., 1966-67), Ariz. Acad., Alpha Sigma Nu. Republican. Rotarian. Home: 7102 N 1st St Phoenix AZ 85020 Office: 1830 1st Nat Bank Plaza Phoenix AZ 85003

WALES, HUGH GREGORY, educator, bus. exec.; b. Topeka, Feb. 28, 1910; s. Raymond Otis and Nola V. (Chestnut) W.; A.B., Washburn Coll., 1932; M.B.A., Harvard, 1934; Ph.D., Northwestern U., 1944; D.Sc., Washburn Municipal U., 1968; m. Mary Alice Fulkerson, June 11, 1938. Dean men N.W. Mo. State Tchrs. Coll., 1935-38, dean students, head dept. econs., 1938-39; dean students, dir. summer sch., vets. bur., head dept. econs. Washburn U., 1939-46; asso. prof. marketing U. Ill., 1946-53, prof., 1953-70, prof. emeritus, dir. micro-precision projects, 1970—; prof. marketing and mgmt., head dept. Roosevelt U., 1970—; pres. Decisions, Evaluations & Learning, Internat. Assos. Vis. prof. marketing U. South Africa, Pretoria, 1962; lectr. U. Stellenbosch, South Africa, 1973, 75, 76; cons. South African Govt., Pretoria, 1974; participant internat. confs.; bus., marketing research cons.; internat. pres. Micro-precision Miniaturization Inst., 1970—, dir., program chmn., Chgo., 1970—. Pres., Civic Symphony Soc., 1964-65. Mem. Am. Econ. Assn., Am. Marketing Assn. (sec., acad. v.p.), Am. Watchmakers Inst. (dir. research and edn. 1963-66), Internat. Platform Assn., Assn. Edn. Internat. Bus., Soc. Internat. Devel., Am. Statis. Assn., Nat. Assn. for Mgmt. Educators. Acad. Mgmt. Presbyterian. Club: Rotary. Author: Changing Perspectives in Marketing, 1951; Marketing Research, 1952, 4th edit., 1974; Marketing Research-Selected Literature, 1952; Cases and Problems in Marketing Research, 1953; (with Robert Ferber) Basic Bibliography in Marketing Research, 1956, 3d edit., 1974; Motivation and Market Behavior (with Ferber), 1958; Advertising Copy, Layout, and Typography (with Gentry and M. Wales), 1958; (with R. Ferber) The Champaign-Urbana Metropolitan Area; (with Engel and Warshaw) Promotional Strategy, 1967, 3d edit., 1975; (with Dik Twedt and Lyndon Dawson) Personality Theory in Marketing Research: A Basic Bibliography, 1976; (with Sharon Abrams) English as a Second Language in Business, 1978; (with Luck, Taylor and Rubin) Marketing Research, 1978; numerous others; works transl. several langs. Contbr. articles to profl. jours. Home: 2021 S LaRosa Dr Tempe AZ 85282

WALES, WALTER D., physicist, educator; b. Oneonta, N.Y., Aug. 2, 1933; s. Walter D. and Anna Laura (Brockway) W.; B.A., Carleton Coll., 1954; M.S., Calif. Inst. Tech., 1955, Ph.D., 1960; m. Margaret Irene Keiter, June 19, 1955; children—Stephen Dirk, Carolyn Sue. Instr. physics U. Pa., Phila., 1959-62, asst. prof., 1962-64, asso. prof., 1964-72, prof., 1972—, chmn., 1973—; asso. dir. Princeton-Pa. Accelerator, Princeton, N.J., 1968-71; staff physicist AEC, 1972-73. Fellow Am. Phys. Soc.; mem. Am. Assn. Physics Tchrs. Research in exptl. particle physics. Home: 404 Drew Ave Swarthmore PA 19081 Office: 209 S 33d St Philadelphia PA 19104

WALFRED, HUGO ANDERSON, lawyer; b. Jackson, Mich., May 9, 1925; s. Hugo Anderson and Karin Elizabeth (Froberg) W.; A.B., U. Mich., 1950, J.D., 1952; m. Marian A. Busch, Mar. 17, 1951; children—Steven, Anthony, Kelly Ann. Admitted to Mich. bar, 1952; atty. law dept. AMP Inc., Harrisburg, Pa., 1951-65, asst. to vice-chmn., 1965-68, asst. sec. AMP Inc., 1971-72, sec., gen. legal counsel, 1972—; gen. mgr. AMP of Can., Toronto, Ont., 1968-71. Pres. Boys Club of Harrisburg, 1974-76; pres. Tri-County br. Pa. Assn. for Blind; bd. dirs. Capital Blue Cross. Served with AUS, World War II. Home: 4484 Nantucket Rd Harrisburg PA 17112 Office: AMP Inc Harrisburg PA 17105

WALGENBACH, PAUL HENRY, educator; b. Peru, Ill., May 3, 1923; s. Martin F. and Marie G. (Haas) W.; B.B.A., Northwestern U., 1948, M.B.A., 1952; Ph.D., U. Ill., 1958. Auditor, Martin, Johnson & Bolton, C.P.A.'s, Chgo., 1948-50; asst. prof. Butler U., 1950-53; asst. prof. commerce U. Wis., Madison, 1953-55, asso. prof., 1957-63, prof., 1963—. Served to 1st lt. USAAF, World War II. C.P.A., Ill. Mem. Am. Accounting Assn. (sec.-treas. 1960—), Am. Finance Assn., Nat. Assn. Accountants, Am. Inst. C.P.A.'s, Wis. Soc. C.P.A.'s. Author: Retail Credits and Collections, 1959; Accounting: An Introduction, 1977; Principles of Accounting, 1976. Contbr. articles to profl. jours. Home: 5010 Milward Dr Madison WI 53711

WALGREEN, CHARLES RUDOLPH, III, retail store exec.; b. Chgo., Nov. 11, 1935; s. Charles Rudolph and Mary Ann (Leslie) W.; B.S. in Pharmacy, U. Mich., 1958; m. Kathleen Bonsignore Allen, Jan. 23, 1977; children—Charles Richard, Tad Alexander, Kevin Patrick, Leslie Ray, Chris Patrick. With Walgreen Co., Chgo., 1952—, globe liaison mgr., 1963, adminstrv. asst. to v.p. store operations, 1965-66, dist. mgr., 1967-68, regional dir., 1968-69, v.p., 1969, pres., 1969-75, chmn., 1976—, also dir.; dir. Sanborn Hnos., Mexico City. Mem. bus. adv. council Chgo. Urban League. Bd. dirs. Jr. Achievement Chgo., Chgo. Crime Commn., Internat. Coll. Surgeons Hall Fame and Mus. Surg. Scis.; trustee Nat. Jewish Hosp., Denver. Mem. Am. Found. Pharm. Edn. (chmn., dir. 1971—), Nat. Assn. Chain Drug Stores (dir.), Ill. Retail Mchts. Assn. (dir. 1966—), Young Pres.' Orgn., Am., Ill. pharm. assns., Delta Sigma Phi. Clubs: Economic, Commercial, Tavern (Chgo.); Great Lakes Cruising; Yacht and Country (Stuart, Fla.). Office: 200 Wilmot Rd Deerfield IL 60015

WALGREN, DOUG, congressman; b. Rochester, N.Y., Dec. 28, 1940; s. Bob and Margaret Lee W.; B.A., Dartmouth Coll., LL.B., Stanford U.; m. Carmala Vincent, Jan. 6, 1973. Staff atty. Neighborhood Legal Services, 1967-68; individual practice law, Pitts., 1969-72; corp. counsel Behavioral Research Labs., Inc., Palo Alto, Calif., 1972-76; mem. 95th and 96th Congresses from Pa.; tchr. pre-law Central Cath. High Sch. Chmn. West Pa. Area chpt. Muscular Dystrophy Assn., 1977, 78. Democrat. Roman Catholic. Office: 117 Cannon House Office Bldg Washington DC 20515

WALING, JOSEPH LEE, educator; b. Brook, Ind., Mar. 17, 1916; s. Floyd and Rose (Clark) W.; B.S. in Civil Engring. with distinction, Purdue U., 1938, M.S. in Structural Engring., 1940; Ph.D. in Structural Engring., U. Ill., 1952; m. Isabel Weishaar, May 31, 1942; children—Stephen Joe, Linda Lee (Mrs. Jack Pfunder), Isabel Sue, Stanley Reed. Grad. asst. applied mechanics Purdue U., 1938-40, instr., 1940-41, asst. prof. engring. mechanics, 1945-47, asso. prof., 1947-54, prof. engring. scis., 1954-55, prof. structural engring., 1955-63, asst. dean Grad. Sch., 1960-63, asso. dean Grad. Sch., 1963—, dir. div. sponsored programs, 1966—; naval architect Norfolk Naval Shipyard, 1941-45. Registered profl. engr., Ind. Mem. Nat. Council U. Research Adminstrs., AAAS, ASCE, Am. Soc. Engring. Edn., Am. Concrete Inst., Internat. Assn. Shell Structures, Internat. Assn. Housing Sci., Sigma Xi, Tau Beta Pi, Chi Epsilon. United Methodist. Rotarian, Elk. Contbr. to profl. jours. Home: 3731 Capilano Dr West Lafayette IN 47906

WALINSKI, NICHOLAS JOSEPH, judge; b. Toledo, Nov. 29, 1920; s. Nicholas Joseph and Helen Barbara (Morkowski) W.; B.S. in Engring., U. Toledo, 1949, LL.B., 1951; m. Vivian Melotti, June 26, 1954; children—Marcianne, Barbara, Deanna and Donna (twins), Nicholas Joseph III. Admitted to Ohio bar, 1951; law dir., Toledo, 1953, police prosecutor, 1953-58, municipal ct. judge, 1958-64, common pleas ct. judge, 1964-70; judge No. dist. Ohio Western div. U.S. Dist. Ct., Toledo, 1970—. Served to capt. USNR, 1942-48. Mem. Am., Toledo, Lucas County bar assns., Am. Legion, V.F.W., Cath. War Vets, Toledo Jr. Bar Assn. (Order of Heel 1970). Home: 4561 Penridge St Toledo OH 43615 Office: 1716 Speilbusch St US Courthouse Toledo OH 43624

WALK, FRANK HUMPHREY, cons. engr.; b. Decatur, Ala., Aug. 30, 1920; s. Francis Albert and Laura Adeline (Humphrey) W.; B.S. in M.E., La. State U., 1942; m. Consuelo Faust, Sept. 6, 1947; children—Wendlyn, Karen, Frank Humphrey, Edmond Wade, Wesley Albert. Vice pres., chief engr. Dunham-Wilson Mfg. Co., Baton Rouge, 1946-52; mng. asso. Wayne & Assos., New Orleans, 1953-58; pres., dir. Walk, Haydel & Assos., Inc., New Orleans, 1959—; dir. Walk-Haydel Devel. Co. Vice pres. Met. Area Council, 1976-78; chmn. bd. Econ. Devel. Council New Orleans Area, 1974-76, award of appreciation, 1976; co-chmn. Met. Forum for Econ. Action, 1975—. Served as officer with C.E., U.S. Army, 1942-47. Mem. La. Engring. Soc. (Lockett award for pub. service 1977), Soc. Am. Mil. Engrs. (Outstanding Service award 1972, Nat. Service award 1974, pres. La. post 1967, regional v.p. 1977—), Am. Cons. Engrs. Council, Nat., Miss. socs. profl. engrs., ASME (chmn. New Orleans sect. 1965, petroleum div. 1977-78), ASCE, Am. Petroleum Inst., Cons. Engrs. Council La. (pres. 1974). Republican. Roman Catholic. Clubs: Plimsoll, Petroleum, Internat. House, Lakeshore, New Orleans Lawn Tennis, New Orleans Serra (pres. 1967) (New Orleans); Baton Rouge City, Camelot (Baton Rouge). Home: 1543 Henry Clay Ave New Orleans LA 70118 Office: 600 Carondelet St New Orleans LA 70130. *God has been on my side throughout my life. Any success that I have attained is attributed to Him and to the wonderful wife He gave me.*

WALKEN, CHRISTOPHER, actor; b. Astoria, N.Y., Mar. 31, 1943; s. Paul W.; attended Hofstra U.; studied with Wynn Handman, David Craig, Marion Rich, Jamie Rogers, Eve Collyer. Stage appearances on and off-Broadway, regional theatres throughout U.S., Can.; Broadway debut in J.B., 1959; other stage appearances include: Best Foot Forward, West Side Story, Baker Street, The Lion in Winter (Clarence Derwent award 1966), Measure for Measure, The Rose Tatoo (Theatre World's Most Promising Personality 1966-67), Romeo and Juliet, A Comedy of Errors, Lemon Sky, The Night Thoreau Spent in Jail (Joseph Jefferson award 1970-71), Metamorphosis, The Judgement, Miss Julie, Sweet Bird of Youth, The Wild Duck; movies include: The Anderson Tapes, The Happiness Cage, Next Stop Greenwich Village, Roseland, Annie Hall, The Deer Hunter (N.Y. Film Critics award for best supporting actor 1978, Acad. award as best supporting actor 1979), The Last Embrace. Office: care Bill Treusch 853 7th Ave New York NY 10019

WALKER, AGESILAUS WILSON, JR., lawyer; b. Denison, Tex., June 10, 1901; s. Agesilaus Wilson and Rosa (Reeder) W.; B.A., U. Tex., 1921, LL.B., 1923; postgrad. summers Columbia, 1922, Yale, 1926; m. Ina Josephine Williams, Sept. 13, 1923; 1 dau., Maria Pearl (dec.). Admitted to Tex. bar, 1923, practice at Dallas, 1923-25, 1948—; prof. law U. Tex., 1925-33, 34-48; sr. atty. Petroleum Adminstrv. Bd., U.S. Dept. Interior, Washington, 1933-34; mem. law firm Jackson, Walker, Winstead, Cantwell & Miller, 1948—. Pres., Tex. Petroleum Council, 1933. Served as lt. comdr. USNR, World War II. Fellow Am. Bar Found., Tex. Bar Found.; mem. Am., Tex., Dallas (hon. life) bar assns., Am. Law Inst., Am. Judicature Soc., Phi Beta Kappa, Phi Delta Phi, Phi Delta Theta, Order of Coif. Presbyn. Mason (Shriner). Clubs: Dallas Petroleum, Brookhollow Golf. Author: Case and Notes on the Law of Oil and Gas, 1948; co-author: Cases on Oil and Gas, 1960. Contbr. numerous articles on law of oil and gas to profl. jours. Home: Apt 14-F 3131 Maple Ave Dallas TX 75201

WALKER, ALBERT LYELL, educator; b. Oklahoma City, Jan. 20, 1907; S. James Francis Docetti and Neva (Roberts) W.; A.B., Park Coll., 1929; M.A., U. Iowa, 1930, Ph.D., 1936; m. Jauvanta Maurine Young, Sept. 1, 1948; children by previous marriage—Judith Lyell, Anthony Lyell. Gen. Edn. Bd. fellow U. Chgo., 1941-42; faculty Ia. State U., Ames, 1935—, chmn. curriculum com. Coll. Scis. and Humanities, 1944-59, capital improvements com., 1963-72; prof. English, 1942-77, prof. emeritus, 1977—, chmn. dept. English and speech, 1959-69, chmn. dept. English, 1959-72. Recipient Mu Phi Epsilon award in piano, 1928, Alumni-Faculty citation Iowa State U., 1974. Mem. Modern Lang. Assn., Nat., Iowa councils tchrs. English, Iowa Colls. Council English, Am. Assn. U. Profs., Lampos, Phi Kappa Phi. Co-author: Essentials of Good Writing, rev., 1959; The Range of Literature, 1960, rev., 1967, 73. Contbr. articles on edn., Shakespeare to profl. jours. Home: 3620 Story St Ames IA 50010

WALKER, ANGUS LIGHTFOOT, mfg. exec., financial exec.; b. Newport, Eng., July 28, 1909; s. Fred and Margaret (McCuaig) W.; came to U.S., 1946, naturalized, 1951; student Victoria U. Coll., Wellington, N.Z., 1926-27, Canterbury U. Coll., N.Z., 1927-29; asso. Sydney (Australia) Tech. Coll. and Newcastle Sch. Mines, 1931; m. Amber Jacombe, Oct. 17, 1941; 1 son, Christopher Angus. With Broken Hill Pty. Ltd., Australia, 1929-31; sales mgr. John Lysaght Ltd., Australia, 1932-37; gen. mgr. Rheem Australia Pty., Ltd., 1937-45; with Rheem Mfg. Co., N.Y.C., 1946-74, pres., chief exec. officer, 1956-67, chmn., chief exec. officer, 1967-74, also dir., also officer numerous subs.; chmn. City Investing Co., N.Y.C., 1970-74, chmn. exec. com., 1974—, also dir.; dir. Marine Midland Bank, Inc.; advisory com. Marine Midland Internat. Mem. Council Fgn. Relations N.Y.C.; mem. advisory bd. Inst. World Affairs. Mem. Am. Arbitration Assn., Nat. Fgn. Trade Council, Internat. C. of C. (trustee U.S. Council), NAM, Pan Am. Soc. Home: 784 Park Ave New York NY 10021 also Gin Ln Southampton NY Office: City Investing Co 767 Fifth Ave New York NY 10022

WALKER, AUBREY MAX, telephone co. exec.; b. Hinton, W. Va., Apr. 25, 1922; s. Audrey Oakley and Nannie E. (Dobbins) W.; student U. Richmond, 1940-42; B.S. in Bus. Adminstrn., U.S.C., 1948; m. Patricia Koger, Sept. 2, 1954; children—Mark Koger, Susan Lynn, Terri Anne. With comptroller dept. So. Bell Tel.&Tel. Co., Nashville, 1948-58, 63-65, v.p., treas., Atlanta, 1968—; comptroller dept. Am. Tel.&Tel. Co., N.Y.C., 1959-62, regulatory dept., 1966-67; chmn. bd. Hatteras Income Securities, Inc., Charlotte, N.C.; dir. Liquid Capital Income, Inc., Cleve., Blue Cross and Blue Shield of Ga., Ga. Telco Credit Union, Atlanta; mem. pres.'s nat. advisory council U. S.C. Trustee, Atlanta Acad. and Inst. Reading. Served to lt. USNR, 1943-46. Mem. Financial Execs. Inst., So. Pension Conf., Blue Cross-Blue Shield (nat. benefits and compensation com., Chgo., Ill.), Theta Chi. Baptist. Clubs: Capital City, Commerce, Stadium (Atlanta). Home: 6215 Riverwood Dr Atlanta GA 30328 Office: So Bell Tel & Tel Co PO Box 2211 Atlanta GA 30301

WALKER, B.J., health products co. exec.; b. Erie, Pa., July 26, 1919; s. Edward E. and Florence Trutman (Keil) W.; student Cornell U., Ithaca, N.Y., 1938-42, Pa. State U., 1947-48; m. Barbara A. H. Walker, Sept. 17, 1951; children—John, Sally, David. With Am. Sterilizer Co., Erie, 1946—, now exec. v.p., also dir.; dir. Gen. Telephone Pa., Lakeview Forge Co., Amsco de Mexico. Past pres. adv. bd. Behrend Coll. Served to capt. AUS, 1942-46. Recipient award Erie C. of C. Clubs: Erie, Kahkwa. Office: 2222 W Grandview Blvd Erie PA 16509

WALKER, BARTH POWELL, lawyer; b. Cotton Plant, Ark., Oct. 2, 1914; s. Fred Tom and Mamie (Powell) W.; LL.B., U. Okla., 1940, B.S. in Geology, 1940; m. Josephine Lucile Brotherton, Apr. 9, 1916; children—Russell James, John Powell. Admitted to Ark. bar, 1939, Okla. bar, 1940, Tex. bar, 1941; practice in Oklahoma City, 1952—; lawyer Pan Am. Petroleum Corp. (now Amoco Prodn. Co.), 1940-52; mem. firm Walker & Walker, 1952—; v.p., gen. counsel Nat. Found. Life Ins. Co.; chmn. bd. NFC Corp.; pres. NFC Petroleum Corp.; dir. Newbridge Capital Corp. Served to lt. col. USAAF, World War II. Named Silver Anniversary Football All Am., Sports Illustrated Mag., 1962. Mem. Am., Tex., Okla., Ark. bar assns., Phi Beta Kappa, Sigma Gamma Epsilon, Omicron Delta Kappa, Phi Delta Phi. Home: 1709 Elmhurst St Oklahoma City OK 73120 Office: Nat Found Life Bldg Oklahoma City OK 73112

WALKER, BETH BREADY, publisher; b. Phila., Mar. 13, 1934; d. Frank T. and Evelyn V. (Appenzeller) Bready; A.A., Finch Jr. Coll., 1954; student Yale Drama Sch., 1955; m. Samuel Sloan Walker, Oct. 28, 1961; children—Sloan, Ramsey, Timothy. Formerly with Max Liebman Prodns., N.Y.C.; with Orion Press, N.Y.C., 1958-60; pub. Walker & Co., N.Y.C., 1960—. Mem. nat. bd. dirs. Med. Coll. Pa. Club: Cosmopolitan (N.Y.C.). Office: 720 Fifth Ave New York NY 10019

WALKER, BROOKS, JR., finance co. exec.; b. Oakland, Calif., Apr. 28, 1928; s. Brooks and Marjory (Walker) W.; B.A., U. Calif. at Berkeley, 1950; M.B.A. in Finance, Harvard, 1957; m. Margaret Myles Kirby, May 21, 1955; children—Kirby, Brooks III, Leslie. Financial analyst Shasta Forest Corp., San Francisco, 1956; with U.S. Leasing Internat., Inc., San Francisco, 1957—, asst. to treas., asst. to pres., treas., v.p. and treas., sr. v.p., dir., 1957-63, pres., 1963-69, chmn. bd., 1969—; chmn. bd. trustees San Francisco Real Estate Investors; dir. Bank of Calif., System Devel. Corp., The Gap Stores, Inc., Dillingham Corp. Chmn. distbn. com. San Francisco Found. Bd. dirs. San Francisco Opera Assn., Planned Parenthood Assn., Smith Kellewell Eye Research Found.; trustee Santa Catalina Sch. Served to lt. (j.g.) USNR, 1951-55. Mem. Delta Kappa Epsilon. Office: 615 Battery St Suite 600 San Francisco CA 94111

WALKER, BRUCE EDWARD, educator; b. Montreal, Que., Can., June 17, 1926; s. Robinson Clarence and Dorothea Winston (Brown) W.; B.S., McGill U., 1947, M.S., 1952, Ph.D., 1954; M.D., U. Tex. at Galveston, 1966; m. Lois Catherine McCuaig, June 26, 1948; children—Brian Ross, Dianne Heather, Donald Robert, Susan Lois. Instr. anatomy McGill U., 1955-57; asst. prof. anatomy U. Tex. Med. Br., 1957-67; prof. anatomy Mich. State U., East Lansing, 1967—, chmn. dept., 1967-75. Mem. Am. Assn. Anatomists, Teratology Soc., Internat. Assn. Dental Research. Contbr. articles to profl. jours. Office: Anatomy Dept Mich State U East Lansing MI 48824

WALKER, CHARLES ALLEN, chem. engr., educator; b. Wise County, Tex., June 18, 1914; s. Jackson Lamar and Eula (Hamilton) W.; B.S., U. Tex., 1938, M.S., 1940; D.Engring., Yale, 1948; m. Bernice Rolf, Dec. 24, 1942; children—Allen Rolf, John Lamar, Laurence Gordon. Faculty, Yale, 1942—, prof. chem. engring., 1956—, master Berkeley Coll., 1959-69, chmn. dept. engring. and applied sci., 1974-76, Raymond John Wean prof., 1979—, mem. staff Yale Instn. for Social and Policy Studies, 1970—; cons. chem. engr., 1942—. Bd. dirs. Conn. Fund for the Environ., 1978—. Fellow A.A.A.S.; mem. Sci. Research Soc. Am. (past nat. dir., treas 1968-73), Am. Chem. Soc. (petroleum research fund adv. bd. 1970—, chmn. 1972—), Am. Inst. Chem. Engrs., Am. Soc. Engring. Edn., Sigma Xi (dir. 1976-78), Tau Beta Pi, Phi Lambda Upsilon. Club: Yale (New Haven). Home: 29 Meadow Brook Rd Hamden CT 06517

WALKER, CHARLES ARTHUR, JR., cork co. exec.; b. Aldrich, Ala., Oct. 19, 1927; s. Charles Arthur and Ruth Acenath (Jones) W.; B.S., U. Ill., 1951; m. Marjorie Lou Ardis, July 25, 1953; children—Cynthia Ardis, Bradford Charles. Accountant Armstrong Cork Co., Pitts., Lancaster, Pa., Braintree, Mass., 1951-55, asst. treas., gen. credit mgr., Lancaster, 1963-67, sr. asst. treas., 1968-74, v.p., treas., 1974—; v.p., treas. Deltox Rug Co., Oshkosh, Wis., 1956-63. Served with USNR, 1946-47. Mem. U. Ill. Alumni Assn., Alpha Kappa Psi, Alpha Sigma Phi. Republican. Presbyn. Club: Lancaster Country. Home: 151 Wilson Dr Lancaster PA 17603 Office: Armstrong Cork Co Liberty and Charlotte Sts Lancaster PA 17604

WALKER, CHARLES LELAND, fin. exec.; b. Chgo., Apr. 14, 1926; s. Charles Leland and Marie (Weige) W.; student Iowa State Coll., 1943-44; B.S. in Bus. Adminstrn., Northwestern U., 1946; postgrad. Harvard Bus. Sch., 1947; m. Dorothy Jean Duncanson, Jan. 12, 1948; children—Wendy Leland, Carol Ann, Thomas Duncanson. With Merck, Sharpe & Dohme, Phila., 1954-57; with Merck & Co., Rahway, N.J., 1957-63, mgr. accounting and reports, 1961-63; gen. auditor Standard Brands, Inc., N.Y.C., 1963-66, asst. comptroller, 1966-70, comptroller, 1970-76; v.p., chief fin. officer Indsl. Nat. Corp., 1976—. Served to lt. (j.g.) USN, 1943-53. Mem. Financial Execs. Inst., Sigma Alpha Epsilon. Republican. Presbyterian. Clubs: R.I. Country, Rumson Country, Barrington Yacht, Turks Head. Home: 1 Mathewson Ln Barrington RI 02806 Office: 55 Kennedy Plaza Providence RI 02826

WALKER, CHARLES MONTGOMERY, lawyer; b. St. Louis, Sept. 30, 1915; s. Charles J. and Gertrude (Zoll) W.; A.B., U. Mo., 1937, LL.B., 1939; m. Gertrude E. Acton, Apr. 30, 1943. Admitted to Calif. bar, 1941, D.C. bar, 1977; practiced in Los Angeles, 1941—; mem. firm Brady, Nossaman & Walker, 1941-62; partner firm Paul, Hastings, Janofsky & Walker, 1962-75, 77—; asst. sec. treasury for tax policy, Washington, 1975-77. Bd. councilors U. So. Calif. Law Center. Served with AUS, 1942-46. Decorated Bronze Star. Fellow Am. Bar Found.; mem. Am. (officer, mem. council, taxation sect.), Los Angeles bar assns., Am. Law Inst., Am. Judicature Soc., Internat. Acad. Estate and Trust Law, State Bar Calif., Order of Coif, Sigma Chi. Republican. Clubs: California; Los Angeles Country; Chevy Chase; Metropolitan. Home: 9255 Doheny Rd Los Angeles CA 90069 Office: 555 S Flower St Los Angeles CA 90071

WALKER, CHARLS EDWARD, cons.; b. Graham, Tex., Dec. 24, 1923; s. Pinkney Clay and Sammye D. (McCombs) W.; B.B.A., U. Tex., 1947, M.B.A., 1948; Ph.D. in Econs., U. Pa., 1955; m. Harmolyn Hart, June 24, 1949; children—Carolyn, Charls Edward. Instr. finance U. Tex., 1947-48, asst., then asso. prof., 1950-54; instr. finance U. Pa. Wharton Sch., 1948-50; financial economist Fed. Res. Bank Phila., 1953; with Fed. Res. Bank Dallas, 1954-61, v.p., econ. adviser,

1958-61; economist Republic Nat. Bank Dallas, 1955-56; asst. to sec. treasury, 1959-61; exec. v.p. Am. Bankers Assn., N.Y.C., 1961-69; under sec. treasury, 1969-72, dep. sec., 1972-73; pres. Charls E. Walker Assos., Inc., Washington, 1973—. Trustee, Joint Council on Econ. Edn.; chmn. Am. Council for Capital Formation; co-founder, treas. Com. on the Present Danger; co-chmn. Presdl. Debates, 1976; bd. overseers Wharton Sch. Fin., U. Pa. Served to 2d lt. USAAF, 1943-45. Recipient Alexander Hamilton award U.S. Treasury Dept.; award Urban League. Clubs: Union League (N.Y.C.); Burning Tree, Congressional (Bethesda, Md.); Federal City (Washington). Contbr. articles to profl. jours. and newspapers, chpts. in books. Co-editor: The Bankers Handbook. Home: 10120 Chapel Rd Potomac MD 20854 Office: 1730 Pennsylvania Ave NW Washington DC 20006. *What's good for the public interest ultimately is good for every person, business, or other group in the nation. This, combined with modern application of the Golden Rule, about sums it up.*

WALKER, CLINTON W., mfg. co. exec.; b. Fall River, Mass., Dec. 3, 1917; s. Harry and Effie E. (Mercer) W.; student Tufts U.; m. Janet E. Harris, Apr. 16, 1966; children—Kristine, Hilary, Marion, Soame. Civilian with Navy Dept., 1937-42; with Howe Scale Co., Rutland, Vt., 1945-47; with Ethan Allen Inc., Danbury, Conn., 1947—, now pres. Served with USAAF, 1943-45. Mem. Nat. Assn. Furniture Mfrs. (dir.). Address: Ethan Allen Inc Ethan Allen Dr Danbury CT 06810

WALKER, CORA T., lawyer; b. Charlotte, N.C., June 20, 1926; d. William H. and Benetta Jones; B.S. in Econs., St. John's U., 1944, J.D., 1946; m. Lawrence Randolph Bailey, June 28, 1948 (div.); children—Lawrence Randolph, Bruce Elliott. Admitted to N.Y. bar, 1946; since practiced in N.Y.C.; prin. Cora T. Walker, atty., until 1954; mem. firm Doles, Sandifer & Walker, 1954-58; partner firm Doles & Walker, 1958-60; now partner with Lawrence R. Bailey, Jr. Spl. counsel to N.Y. State Legis. Joint Subcom. on Pub. Welfare, 1960-61; gen. counsel Radio Free Africa, Inc., Morningside Heights Consumers Co-op., Inc., African Stock Exchange and Devel. Corp.; spl. dep. to Atty. Gen. of N.Y. State. Mem. Bronx adv. council N.Y. State Commn. Against Discrimination, 1951-57; mem. N.Y. State's Citizen's Council, Citizen's Union, N.Y.C.; mem. Women United for Civil Action; coordinator Harlem Improvement Program; sec., treas. Mid-Eastern Co-ops., Inc., 1962-69; chmn. Manhattanville Citizens Urban Renewal Com., 1964-68. Mem. law com. of Republican County Com., 1961-64; co-chmn. Com. for Polit. Equality, N.Y.C., 1959-60; chmn. law com. Central Republican Club, 11th Dist. Assembly, N.Y., 1959-64; pres. City-Wide Republican Women's Club, 1957-63. Bd. dirs. N.Y. State Polit. Workshops, Inc., 1961-64; mem. exec. bd. Youth March for Integrated Schs.; trustee UN Internat. Sch., vice chmn., 1952-56. Recipient Outstanding Community Service award Women for Achievement; Hall of Fame Alumni award James Monroe High Sch., 1967; N.Y. Club Profl. award, 1969; Malcolm X award, 1969, others. Mem N.Y. County, Harlem (past pres.) lawyers assns., Nat. (chmn. com. on human rights, v.p.), N.Y.C. bar assns. Home: 501 W 123d St New York City NY 10027 Office: Walker & Bailey 270 Lenox Ave New York City NY 10027

WALKER, DAVID ALLEN HATCH, dancer, choreographer; b. Edmonton, Alta., Can., Mar. 14, 1949; s. Dennis and Iona (Loveseth) H., Leslie Walker (stepfather); came to U.S., 1969, permanent resident, 1974; student Nat. Ballet Sch. Can., Toronto; m. Takako Asakawa, Dec. 22, 1970. Mem. Martha Graham Co., 1970-76; toured Am., Europe and Asia with Graham Co.; ind. concert dancer U.S. and Asia; co-artistic dir. Asakawalker Dance Co., N.Y.C., 1977-78; USIS tour of Japan and Philippines, 1975. Fellow Can. Council, 1965-69. Mem. Am. Guild Mus. Artists. Address: 77 Greene St New York NY 10012. *Success to a dancer means to enter a new state, to discover a new area of oneself where expression comes from the center of being, outward, more clearly and with more power than one ever dreamed was possible.*

WALKER, DAVID HARRY, author; b. Dundee, Scotland, Feb. 9, 1911; attended Shrewsbury (Eng.) Sch., Shropshire, 1924-29; studied at Royal Mil. Coll., Sandhurst, Surrey, Eng., 1929-30; D.Litt., U. N.B. (Can.), Fredericton, 1955; m. Willa Magee, 1939; 4 children. Served with Black Watch, Brit. Army, 1931-47; served in India, 1932-36, Sudan, 1936-38; aide-de-camp to Gov.-Gen. of Can., 1938-39; prisoner-of-war, Germany, 1940-45; instr. Staff Coll., Camberley, Surrey, 1945-46; comptroller to Viceroy of India, 1946-47; ret. as maj., 1947; author, 1947—; author novels: The Storm and the Silence, 1949, Geordie, 1950, The Pillar, 1952, Digby, 1953, Harry Black, 1956, Where the High Winds Blow, 1960, Winter of Madness, 1964, Mallabec, 1965, Come Back, Geordie, 1966, Cab-Intersec, 1968, Pirate Rock, 1969; The Lord's Pink Ocean, 1972, Black Dougal, 1974, Ash, 1976; Pot of Gold, 1977; author book of short stories: Storms of Our Journey and Other Stories, 1962; author: (for children) Sandy Was a Soldier's Boy, 1957; Dragon Hill, 1962; Big Ben, 1970. Mem. Can. Council, 1957-61; Can. commr., Roosevelt Campobello Internat. Park Commn., 1965—, chmn., 1970-72. Mem. Order of Brit. Empire, 1946; recipient Gov. Gen.'s award, 1953, 54. Fellow Royal Soc. Lit. Club: Royal and Ancient. Address: Strathcroix St Andrews NB E0G 2X0 Canada

WALKER, DAVID TUTHERLY, educator, mathematician; b. Huntington, W.Va., July 10, 1922; s. Archbald and Florence Letitia (Dale) W.; B.S., Wofford Coll., 1949; M.S., U. Ga., 1951, Ph.D., 1955; m. Mary Elizabeth Douglass, June 1, 1957; 1 dau., Natalie Elizabeth. Instr. U. S.C., 1953-54; asst. prof. math. Memphis State U., 1955-63, asso. prof., 1963-67, prof., 1967—. Served with AUS, 1943-48. Mem. Tenn. Math. Tchrs. Assn. (pres. 1969-71), S.A.R. (pres. Memphis chpt. 1966-67), Sigma Xi, Phi Kappa Phi. Presbyterian (elder). Home: 4344 Tuckahoe Rd Memphis TN 38117

WALKER, DONALD ANTHONY, educator; b. Mar. 6, 1934; s. Timothy Anthony and Helen (Walker) W.; A.B., S.W. Tex. State U., 1952; M.A., U. Tex., 1956; Ph.D., Harvard, 1961; m. Patricia Ann McKeage, Feb. 14, 1961; 1 dau., Valerie Alana. Instr. Boston U., 1958-60; asst. prof. Boston Coll., 1960-61; asst. prof. Miami U., Oxford, Ohio, 1961-67, asso. prof., 1967-69; prof., chmn. dept. econ. Indiana U. Pa., 1969—. Recipient Commonwealth of Pa. Distinguished Acad. Service award, 1974. Harvard fellow, 1956-57, 57-58; Henry Lee Meml. fellow, 1957-58. Contbr. articles to profl. jours. Home: 48 Shady Dr Indiana PA 15701

WALKER, DONALD EZZELL, univ. ofcl.; b. Springfield, Mo., July 13, 1921; s. Edward Everett and Cecilia (Ezzell) W.; A.B., U. So. Calif., 1943, M.Th., 1947; Ph.D., Stanford, 1954; m. Ann Lathrop, Dec. 17, 1943; 1 son, Craig Lathrop. Recreational dir. club work All Nations Found., Los Angeles, 1941-42, Wilshire Meth. Ch., Los Angeles, 1942-43; asst. minister Vincent Meth. Ch., Los Angeles, 1943-44; minister Encinitas Meth. Ch., 1945-47; teaching asst. Stanford, 1947-49; instr. sociology San Diego State Coll., 1949-51, asst. prof. sociology, 1951-54, asso. dean students, counseling, 1954-56, dean counseling, 1956-58, v.p. for acad. affairs, 1968-71, acting pres., 1971-72; dean students San Fernando State Coll., Northridge, Calif., 1958-60; pres. Idaho State U., 1960-64; dean students Sonoma State Coll., Rohnert Park, Calif., 1964-66; vice chancellor student affairs U. Calif. at Irvine, 1966-68, sr. lectr. Grad. Sch. Adminstrn., 1967-68, fellow Univ. Coll., 1967-68; pres. Southeastern Mass. State U., Dartmouth, 1972—. Author: (with others) Readings in American Public Opinion; The Effective Administrator: A Practical Approach to Problem-Solving, Decision-Making, and Campus Leadership, 1979; contbr. articles to profl. jours. Home: 128 Chase Rd North Dartmouth MA 02747

WALKER, DUARD LEE, med. educator; b. Bishop, Calif., June 2, 1921; s. Fred H. and Anna Lee (Shumate) W.; A.B., U. Calif. at Berkeley, 1943, M.A., 1947; M.D., U. Calif. at San Francisco, 1945; m. Dorothea Virginia McHenry, Aug. 11, 1945; children—Douglas Keith, Donna Judith, David Cameron, Diane Susan. Intern, U.S. Naval Hosp., Shoemaker, Cal., 1945-46; asst. resident Stanford U. Service San Francisco Hosp., 1950-52; asso. prof. med. microbiology and preventive medicine U. Wis., Madison, 1952-59, prof. med. microbiology, 1959—, prof., chmn. med. microbiology, 1970-76, Paul F. Clark prof. med. microbiology, 1977—; cons. Naval Med. Research Unit, Gt. Lakes, Ill., 1958-74; mem. microbiology tng. com. Nat. Inst. Gen. Med. Scis., 1966-70; mem. nat. adv. Allergy and Infectious Diseases Council, 1970-74. Served to lt. comdr. USNR, 1943-46, 53-55. NRC postdoctoral fellow virology Rockefeller Inst. Med. Research, N.Y.C., 1947-49; USPHS fellow immunology George Williams Hooper Found. U. Calif. at San Francisco, 1949-50. Fellow Am. Pub. Health Assn., Am. Acad. Microbiology; mem. Am. Assn. Immunologists, Infectious Diseases Soc. Am., Am. Soc. Microbiology, AAAS, Soc. Exptl. Biology and Medicine (editorial bd. Procs.), Reticulendothelial Soc. AAUP, Wis. Acad. Scis., Arts and Letters. Mem. editorial bd. Infection and Immunity, 1975—. Home: 618 Odell St Madison WI 53711

WALKER, E. CARDON, motion picture co. exec.; b. Rexburg, Idaho, Jan. 9, 1916; s. Esmond Levier and Violet (Cardon) W.; B.A., U. Calif. at Los Angeles, 1938; m. Winifred L. Watkins, June 26, 1948; children—Mignonne, Marnie, John Cardon. Pres., Walt Disney Prodns., 1971—, dir., mem. exec. com., 1960—, chief exec. officer, 1976—, dir./officer various subs.'s. Trustee, Calif. Inst. Arts, UCLA Found., Verdugo Hills Hosp.; bd. dirs. Calif. C. of C., Bleitz Found.; chmn. licensing and merchandising adv. commn. Los Angeles Olympic Organizing Com. Served to lt. USNR, 1942-46. Mem. Acad. Motion Pictures Arts and Scis., Acad. TV Arts and Scis., Phi Kappa Sigma. Office: 500 S Buena Vista Burbank CA 91521

WALKER, E. JERRY, clergyman; b. Seattle, May 31, 1918; s. Septimus and Mae Ruth (Roys) W.; A.B., Seattle Pacific Coll., 1940; B.D., Garrett Theol. Sem., 1945; D.D., Wiley Coll., Marshall, Tex., 1958; Northland Coll., 1971; m. Holly Rae Harding, Nov. 10, 1941; children—Jerrianne (Mrs. Dale Hubred), Dale Harding, Barbara Rae. Ordained to ministry Meth. Ch.; teaching fellow State Coll. Wash., 1940-41; edn. dir. Prairie Farmer sta. WLS, Chgo., 1942-45; radio dir. Internat. Council Religious Edn., 1945-48; free-lance daily commentary radio station WGN, Chgo., 1948-49, KDAL-TV, Duluth, Minn., 1964—; staff writer-dir. CBS, Chgo., 1948-49; free-lance writer-dir. sta. WBKB-TV, Chgo., 1945-49; mgr. Trado, Inc., Chgo., 1949-53; pastor St. James Meth. Ch., Chgo., 1953-62, First United Meth. Ch., Duluth, 1962-74; exec. dir. Center for Family Studies, Duluth, 1972—; lectr. Redpath Bur., Chgo.; appearances on nat. and regional radio and TV series. Mem. Gov. Ill. Adv. Commn. on Aged, 1958- 62, Chgo.-Cook County Citizens Com. To Study Aid to Families with Dependent Children, 1960-62, S.E. Chgo. Commn., 1958-62, Kenwood-Ellis Community Renewal Com., Chgo., 1957-62; co-chmn. Duluth Citizens Com. Secondary Edn., 1963-64; hon. chmn. White House Conf. Rural Edn., 1945; mem. Model Cities Com., 1967-72, United Fund Survey Com., 1968-70; mem. gen. assembly Nat. Council Chs., 1955-67, mem. gen. bd., 1955-67. Bd. dirs. Chgo. chpt. Nat. Conf. Christians and Jews, 1955-62, mem. nat. bd. trustees, 1974-77. Recipient award nat. religious radio program Victorious Living, Inst. Edn. by Radio, 1945, 47; Human Relations award Chgo. Commn. Human Relations, 1954; Friend of Youth award Southside Community Com., Chgo., 1955; Chicagoan of Year award in religion Chgo. Jr. C. of C., 1962; Distinguished Citizen award Com. of One Hundred, Chgo., 1962; Achievement award Freedoms Found., 1963-65; Broadcast Journalism award Minn. Council Chs., 1971; Silver Venus Grand Medallion award Greater Miami Internat. Film Festival, 1978. Mem. Internat. Platform Assn. Author: Five Minute Stories from the Bible, 1948; Stories from the Bible, 1955; Seeking a Faith of Your Own, 1961; Sinner's Parish, 1963; Seven Who Saw Him, 1977; (plays) Checkerboard, Kyrie, The Unpainted Wall; also numerous articles. Home: 15800 Lexington Ave Minnetonka MN 55343 Office: 810 S 1st St Hopkins MN 55343

WALKER, EDWARD BULLOCK, III, petroleum co. exec.; b. Norfolk, Va., Jan. 10, 1922; s. Edward Bullock, Jr., and Mary Rennick (Ray) W.; B.S., Mass. Inst. Tech., 1946, M.S., 1947; m. Katherine Evelyn Miller, Sept. 5, 1953; children—Edward Bullock, Richard Miller. Exploration mgr. Mene Grande Oil Co., Venezuela, 1947-62, v.p., 1962-67; exploration coordinator Gulf Eastern Co., London, Eng., 1962-67; dir. exploration div. Gulf Research & Devel. Co., Harmarville, Pa., 1967; pres. Gulf Mineral Resources Co., Denver, 1968-71; v.p. Gulf Oil Corp., Pitts., 1971, exec. v.p., 1971-75, exec. v.p., Houston, 1978—, also dir., pres. Gulf Energy and Minerals Co. div., Houston, 1975-78; dir. Tex. Commerce Bancshares, Inc. Mem. corp. devel. com. Mass. Inst. Tech.; mem. bus. advisory council Coll. Bus. Adminstrn. U. Denver. Served with AUS, 1943-46. Decorated Bronze Star with oak leaf cluster. Fellow London Geol. Soc.; mem. Am. Assn. Petroleum Geologists, Assn. Profl. Geol. Scientists. Clubs: Duquesne, Fox Chapel Golf (Pitts.); Rolling Rock (Ligonier, Pa.); Cherry Hills (Denver); River Oaks, Ramada, Houston Met. Racquet (Houston). Office: PO Box 2100 Houston TX 77001

WALKER, ERIC ARTHUR, cons. engr.; b. Long Eaton, Eng., Apr. 29, 1910; s. Arthur and Violet Elizabeth (Haywood) W.; came to U.S., 1923, naturalized, 1937; B.S., Harvard, 1932, M.S., 1933, Sc.D., 1935; LL.D., Temple U., 1957, Lehigh U., 1957, Hofstra Coll., 1960, Lafayette Coll., 1960, U. Pa., 1960, U. R.I., 1962; L.H.D., Elizabethtown Coll., 1958; D.Litt., Jefferson Med. Coll., 1960; D.Sc., Wayne State U., 1965, Thiel Coll., 1966, U. Notre Dame, 1968, U. Pitts., 1970; m. L. Josephine Schmeiser, Dec. 20, 1937; children—Gail (Mrs. Peter Hearn), Brian. Instr. math. Tufts Coll. 1933-34, asst. prof., asso. prof. elec. engring., 1935-38, head elec. engring. dept. 1935-40; head elec. engring. dept. U. Conn., 1940-43; asso. dir. Harvard Underwater Sound Lab., 1942-45; dir. Ordnance Research Lab., Pa. State U., 1945-52, head elec. engring. dept., 1945-51, dean Sch. Engring., 1951-56, v.p. univ., 1956, pres., 1956-70; v.p. sci. and tech. Aluminum Co. Am., 1970-76; dir. Girard Trust Bank, Armstrong Cork Co., Gould, Inc. Exec. sec. Research and Devel. Bd., 1950-51; cons. NRC, 1949-50, mem. and past chmn. com. on undersea warfare; chmn. Pres.'s Com. on Tech. and Distbn. Research for Benefit of Small Bus., 1957; chmn. nat. sci. bd. NSF, 1964-66; chmn. Naval Research Adv. Com., 1963-65, 71—, Army Sci. Adv. Panel 1956-58; vice chmn. Pres.'s Com. Scientists and Engrs., 1956-58; adv. panel on engring. and tech. manpower Pres.'s Sci. Adv. Com.; mem. Gov.'s Com. of 100 for Better Edn., 1960-61. Trustee Inst. for Def. Analysis; bd. dirs. Engring. Found. United bd. visitors U.S. Naval Acad., 1958-60, U.S. Mil. Acad., 1962-64. Recipient Horatio Alger award, 1959, Tasker H. Bliss award Am. Soc. Mil. Engrs., 1959; Golden Omega award Am. Inst. E.E and Nat. Elec. Mfg. Assn., 1962; DoD Pub. Service medal, 1970; Presdl. citation, 1970. Registered profl. engr., Pa. Fellow IEEE, Am. Acoustical Soc., Am. Inst. E.E., Am. Phys. Soc.; mem. Am. Inst. Physics, Am. Soc. Engring. Edn. (Lamme award 1965, pres. 1961-62), Pa. Assn. Colls. and Univs. (pres. 1950- 60), Middle States Assn. Colls. and Secondary Schs. (commn. higher edn. 1958-61), Engrs. Joint Council (pres. 1962-63), Nat. Assn. State Univs. and Land-Grant Colls. (exec. com. 1958-62), Nat. Acad. Engring. (pres. 1966-70), Am. Acad. Arts and Scis., Newcomen Soc., Royal Soc. Arts, Sigma Xi, Tau Beta Pi, Phi Kappa Phi. Clubs: Duquesne, Cosmos. Contbr. to tech. mags. Home: Rock Spring Farm Pennsylvania Furnace PA 16865

WALKER, ERNEST WINFIELD, educator, fin. cons.; b. McComb, Miss., Sept. 14, 1917; s. Jefferson Winfield and Ida Eugenia (Brumfield) W.; A.A., Jones County Jr. Coll., 1938; B.B.A., U. Miss., 1948, M.B.A., 1948; D.B.A., Ind. U., 1953; m. Margaret Ruth Marshall, June 5, 1949; children—Marshall Winfield, Eledith Lucinda. Asst. prof. fin. Drake U., Des Moines, 1951-54; asso. prof. mgmt. U. Tex., Austin, 1954-58; fin. examiner Tex. Commn. on Higher Edn., 1956-59; asso. prof. dept. fin. U. Tex., Austin, 1958-61, prof., 1961-78, chmn. dept., 1961-65, Lawrence D. Gale prof., 1978—; chair of fin. U. Va., 1973-74; pres., chmn. bd. Detectogas Instruments, Inc., 1958-61; cons. Tracor, Inc., 1962-72, Hill Chems. Inc., 1966-67, Mesa Instruments, 1968-73, Traders Compress Industries, Inc., 1968-69, Pan Tex Corp., 1970; economist Nat. Assn. Credit Mgmt., 1969-72; cons., bd. dirs. Longhorn Disposal System, Inc., 1976-77; mem. faculty of Grad. Sch. of Credit and Fin. Mgmt., Dartmouth Coll., 1965-74, Williams Coll., 1975-77, Stanford U., 1978. Served with AUS, 1941-45. Mem. Fin. Mgmt. Assn. (pres. 1975-76, bd. dirs. 1976—), Austin Investment Assn. (pres. 1969), Austin-San Antonio Soc. Fin. Analysts (pres. 1974), Eastern Fin. Assn., Am., Southwestern fin. assns., Knights of the Symphony, Beta Gamma Sigma, Sigma Iota Epsilon, Delta Sigma Pi, Omicron Delta Kappa. Baptist. Clubs: Austin Country; Rotary; Farmington (Va.) Country; Masons. Editor: (with Harry L. Johnson) Monetary Issues of the 1960's, 1968; Dynamic Small Firm: Selected Readings, 1975. Author: (with William H. Baughn) Financial Planning and Policy, 1961; Case Problems in Financial Management, 1968; Essentials of Financial Management, 2d edit., 1971; (with J. William Petty II) Financial Management of the Small Firm; also articles. Home: 3402 Taylors Dr Austin TX 78703

WALKER, ESTELLENE PAXTON, librarian; b. Bristol, Va., Sept. 13, 1911; d. John Camp and Willie (Ropp) W.; B.A., U. Tenn., 1933; B.L.S., Emory U., 1935; Litt.D., Presbyn. Coll., Clinton, S.C., 1975. Head county dept. Lawson McGhee Library, Knoxville, Tenn., 1935-41; post librarian, Ft. Jackson, S.C., 1941-45; materials supply librarian Army Spl. Services, ETO, 1945-46; dir. S.C. Library Bd., 1946-69; librarian S.C. State Library, Columbia, 1969—; mem. adv. com. on library services program U.S. Office Edn., 1956-57; chmn. Southeastern States Co-op. Library Survey, 1972-76. Mem. S.C. Adv. Com. Adult Edn., S.C. Com. Welfare Children and Youth, S.C. Com. for Humanities, S.C. Child Devel. Council, S.C. Com. Primary Prevention in Mental Health; sec. Interdepartmental Council State Agys.; adv. mem. S.C. Confederate Centennial Commn.; del. White House Conf. Children and Youth, 1960. Mem. ALA (council 1952-56, adv. com. recruiting project 1962—), S.C. (v.p. 1972-73, pres. 1973-75), Southeastern (chmn. county and regional library sect. 1940) library assns., Am. Assn. State Libraries (pres.), Caroliniana Soc., Phi Kappa Phi, Order Palmetto. Editor S.C. Library Bull., 1946-56; contbr. articles to library, ednl. periodicals. Office: 1500 Senate St Columbia SC 29201

WALKER, EVERETT, newspaper editor; b. Bklyn., Aug. 18, 1906; s. Milton Everett and Elizabeth Ann (Bandholtz) W.; student Cooper Union, 1924; m. Frances Elizabeth Lander, Oct. 18, 1930; children—Shirley Ann, Carol Joan, Barbara Jean. Reporter, feature writer N.Y. Herald Tribune, 1924-37, Sunday sections editor, 1937-39, asst. to mng. editor, 1939-41, asst. mng. editor, 1941-44, sent to Paris to arrange republication European edit., 1944, war corr. 9th Army, Feb.-Mar. 1945, mng. editor, 1953-55, Sunday editor, 1955-61, asst. editor 1961-62, dir. N.Y. Herald Tribune div. Pubs. Newspaper Syndicate, 1963-66; mng. editor Washington Star Syndicate, 1967-68, Newsweek, N.Y.C., 1968-70; exec. editor Daily Mirror, 1971-72; cons. editor, asst. mgr. N.Y. Times Spl. Features, 1972-73; editorial cons. econs. dept. Citibank, NA, N.Y.C., 1973-78, cons., 1978—. Trustee Hood Coll., 1955-61. Member of the Society of Siulrians, Overseas Press Club, Pi Delta Epsilon. Clubs: Essex County Country (West Orange, N.J.); Dutch Treat. Home: 44 Wilber Terr Bloomfield NJ 07003

WALKER, EVERITT DONALD, univ. chancellor; b. Haynesville, La., Apr. 27, 1922; s. Samuel Bethel and Marjorie Lavada Walker; B.B.A., Sam Houston State U., Huntsville, Tex., 1948; M.B.A., U. Tex., Austin, 1950; LL.D., Southwestern U., 1976; m. Kathryn Marie Keneaster, Sept. 17, 1943; 1 son, Everitt Donald. Auditor, Sam Houston State U., 1950-51, Tex. Tech. U., Lubbock, 1951-55; bus. mgr. U. Tex. Med. Br., Galveston, 1955-59, bus. mgr., 1959-65, comptroller hosps., 1964-65; mem. adminstrv. staff U. Tex. System, Austin, 1965—, dep. chancellor, then pres., chief operating officer, 1975-78, chancellor, 1978—; asst. prof., then asso. prof. acctg. and fin. San Houston State U., 1949-51; prof. preventive medicine and community health U. Tex. Med. Br., 1972—; treas. 10th Internat. Cancer Congress, 1970; mem. coordinating bd. com. master planning for colls. and univs. Tex. Coll. and Univ. System, 1967; dir. Univ. State Bank, Austin, 1974—. Bd. dirs. Blue Cross-Blue Shield, 1977-78. Served to maj. USAF, 1942-47. Recipient Disting. Alumnus award Sam Houston State U., 1978, named to univ. Hall of Honor, 1974; C.P.A., Tex. Mem. Council Tex. Public Sr. Coll. and Univ. Presidents (chmn. 1977-79), Nat. Assn. State Univs. and Land-Grant Colls. (chmn. region II fed. legis. network 1978—), Assn. Am. Univs., Am. Council Edn., Tex. Soc. C.P.A.'s. Home: 1909 Hill Oaks Ct Austin TX 78703 Office: 601 Colorado St Austin TX 78701

WALKER, FLOYD LEE, lawyer; b. Kiefer, Okla., Mar. 27, 1919; s. Willis and Sarah Josephine (McFarland) W.; LL.B., Tulsa U., 1949; m. Virginia Gifford Raines, Oct. 8, 1971; children by previous marriage—Mary Lea (Mrs. John Byrd), Cheryl Sue (Mrs. Mark B. Newman), James M. Admitted to Okla. bar, 1949; practiced in Tulsa, 1953—; claims atty. Standard Ins. Co., Tulsa, 1949-53. Served as 1st lt. USAAF, 1942-45. Decorated Air medal with three oak leaf clusters, D.F.C. Fellow Am. Coll. Trial Lawyers; mem. Am., Okla. (bd. govs. 1979—), Tulsa County (pres. 1973) bar assns., Okla. Trial Lawyers Assn., Assn. Trial Lawyers Am. Home: 142 Lakeshore Dr W Westport OK 74020 Office: 2200 4th National Bldg Tulsa OK 74119

WALKER, FRANCIS GENE, paper mfg. co. exec.; b. Havre, Mont., Apr. 13, 1928; s. Robert R. and Marie (Conn) W.; B.S.E.E., Catholic U. Am., 1952; M.S., Carnegie Inst. Tech., 1954; m. Mary Donoghue, June 3, 1950; children—Nancy Walker Parmelee, Robert F., Cynthia. With Nekoosa Papers Inc., 1957-65, v.p. mcht. ops., 1964-65; v.p. Butler Paper Co., Port Edwards, Wis., 1965-67, exec. v.p., 1967-70, pres., 1970—, also dir.; dir. Nekoosa Papers Inc., 1970—, v.p. mcht. and converting ops., 1973—; chmn. bd. Pak-Well Corp., 1976—. Served with USNR, 1946-48. Mem. Nat. Paper Trade Assn. (treas. 1974-75, v.p. 1975-77). Office: Butler Paper Co 100 Wisconsin River Dr Port Edwards WI 54469*

WALKER, FRED COLLINS, advt. exec.; b. Ridgely, Tenn., Mar. 15, 1921; s. Paul Excell and Carmen (Collins) W.; B.S., U. Tenn., 1947; m. Jo Ann Terry, May 3, 1952; children—Fred Collins, Joan Terry, Mary Carmen. Advt. and sales promotion mgr. Sterchi Bros. Furniture, Knoxville, Tenn., 1947-48; exec. program, advt. and sales mgr. Sears Roebuck & Co., Greenville, S.C., 1948-55; with Henderson Advt. Agy., Inc., 1955—, v.p., mgr. Charlotte office, 1962-65, adminstrv. v.p., 1966-68, exec. v.p., 1969-76, pres., chief operating officer, 1976-79, vice chmn., 1979—, also sec., dir.; v.p., sec., dir. New South Devel. Corp.; dir. Five Forks Enterprises, Rockwood Corp. Past pres. Friends of Greenville Library, United Speech and Hearing Service; past pres. Greenville Community Planning Council; mem. Regional United Way Am.; pres. United Way Greenville County, 1979, chmn., 1980. Trustee Greenville United Fund. Served to maj. USAAF, 1942-45, USAF, 1961-62. Mem. Am. Assn. Advt. Agys. (dir., chmn. SE council, mem. account service com.), Greenville Advt. Club (past pres., dir.), U.S. (mem. communications com.), Greenville (chmn. image com., pres. 1980, dir.) chambers commerce, Alpha Tau Omega. Presbyn. (deacon). Clubs: Poinsett (gov.), Greenville Country. Home: 47 Partridge Ln Greenville SC 29601 Office: 60 Pelham Pointe PO Box 2247 Greenville SC 29602

WALKER, GEORGE BROWN, educator; b. Thankerton, Scotland, Jan. 27, 1919; s. Alexander Michie and Janet Fergusson (Johnston) W.; M.A., U. Glasgow, 1940; Ph.D. (Turner & Newall fellow), Imperial Coll., U. London, 1950; m. Eva Baird, June 12, 1943; children—Alexander Crawford, Ruth (Mrs. Terence Philip Glancy). Mem. research staff Mullard Radio Valve Co., Eng., 1940-46; lectr. U. Sheffield, 1950-52, Queen Mary Coll., U. London, 1950-59; research prof. U. B.C., 1959-64; chmn., prof. dept. elec. engring. U. Alta., Edmonton, 1964-74, univ. prof., 1975—. Mem. Profl. Engrs. Alta., Inst. Elec. Engrs., Engring. Inst. Can. (chmn. tech. ops. bd., mem. council). Club: Mayfair Golf and Country. Contbr. articles to profl. jours. Patentee in field. Home: 11815 93d Ave Edmonton AB T6G 1B7 Canada

WALKER, GEORGE GHOLSON, corp. officer; b. Staten Island, N.Y., Sept. 21, 1902; s. Norman S. and Minnie A. (Wiman) W.; ed. St. Paul's Sch., Concord, N.H., 1915-20, Harvard, 1920-24; m. Elizabeth L. Schroeder, May 5, 1928 (div.); children—George G., Diana L.; m. 2d, Caroline S. Dickson, Oct. 29, 1953 (dec.); m. 3d, Emily S. Lee, Feb. 9, 1974. Rate clk. Electric Bond & Share Co., 1924; with Fla. Power & Light Co., 1925-26; asst. to exec. v.p. Electric Bond & Share Co. (name changed to Ebasco Industries), 1927, head gen. dept., 1935-40, operating sponsor, 1940-41, v.p., dir., 1941-44, pres., dir., 1944-67, chmn. bd., 1967-68. Trustee, St. Luke's-Roosevelt Hosp. Center; chmn. Commn. on Resources, Harvard Med. Sch.; chmn. Correctional Assn. N.Y. Clubs: Brook, Links Golf, Harvard, Piping Rock, Recess, Maidstone, Nat. Golf Links; Century. Home: 1900 Muttontown Rd Syosset NY 11791 Office: 437 Madison Ave Room 2009 New York NY 10022

WALKER, GEORGE HERBERT, III, lawyer, investment banking co. exec.; b. St. Louis, Mar. 16, 1931; s. George H. and Mary (Carter) W.; B.A., Yale, 1953; LL.B., Harvard, 1956; m. Sandra E. Canning, Dec. 23, 1955 (div. Oct. 1962); children—Mary Elizabeth, Wendy, Isabelle; m. 2d, Kimberly Gedge, July 27, 1968 (div. Jan. 1977); children—George H. IV, Carter. Admitted to Conn. bar, 1956; registered rep. firm G.H. Walker & Co. (later G.H. Walker, Laird Inc.), St. Louis, 1958-61, gen. partner, 1961-65, founder, mgr. Chgo. office, 1963-71, mng. partner, 1965-71, chmn. exec. com., 1971-73, chmn. bd. dirs., 1973-74; sr. v.p. White, Weld & Co. Inc. (merger G.H. Walker, Laird Inc. with White Weld & Co.), St. Louis, 1974-75, also dir.; exec. v.p. Stifel Nicolaus & Co., 1976-78, pres., chief exec. officer, 1978—, also dir.; dir. Lafayette Fed. Savs. & Loan Assn., Measuregraph Corp., Laidlaw Corp. Civilian aide to Sec. U.S. Army for Eastern Mo., 1973—. Bd. dirs. Downtown St. Louis Inc., St. Louis Regional Commerce and Growth Assn., Episcopal Ch. Found., St. Louis Childrens Hosp., Arts and Edn. Council; vice chmn., bd. dirs. Webster Coll. Served with USAF, 1956-58. Mem. Conn. Bar Assn., Assn. U.S. Army (dir. chpt.). Clubs: Log Cabin, St. Louis Country, Noonday, Racquet, Yale of St. Louis, Yale of N.Y., Univ. of Chgo. Home: 8104 Kingsbury Clayton MO 63105 Office: 500 N Broadway St Louis MO 63102

WALKER, GEORGE THOMAS, mgmt. cons.; b. Wyatt, La., Mar. 2, 1913; s. William Thomas and Mary Elizabeth (Stovall) W.; B.A., Northwestern State (La.) U., 1935; M.S., La. State U., 1936, Ph.D., 1948; m. Mary Ellen Neal, May 28, 1938; children—George Thomas, Ellen Claire. Retail store mgr., Amite, La., 1931-32; instr. bus. La. State U., N.E. La. Jr. Coll., Southeastern La. U., U. Southwestern La., 1935-40; supr. bus. edn. State of La., 1940-43; dir. civilian tng. and employee relations New Orleans Port Embarkation, 1943-45; dir. counseling for men, jr. div. La. State U., 1945-48; prof. bus., dean Sch. Applied Arts and Scis. Northwestern State U., 1948, dean adminstrn., 1954-58; pres. N.E. La. U., Monroe, 1958-76; mgmt. cons., 1976—. Pres., La. Coll. Conf., 1957-58. Pres., United Givers Ouachita Parish, 1962-63. Bd. dirs. Ouachita chpt. A.R.C., Ouachita council Boy Scouts Am., Little Theatre Monroe. Found. for Econ. Edn. Edn. fellow, 1952. Mem. Am. Accounting Assn., La. League Nursing, Southwestern Social Sci. Assn. (pres. 1961-62), Beta Gamma Sigma, Beta Alpha Psi, Delta Pi Epsilon, Phi Delta Kappa, Kappa Delta Pi, Omicron Delta Kappa. Presbyn. (elder). Lion. Author: Correct Typewriting Style, 1938. Contbr. articles to profl. jours. Home: 2713 Pargoud Blvd Monroe LA 71201

WALKER, GLENN DAVID, ret. army officer, former adj. gen. Miss.; b. Rapides Parish, La., Jan. 21, 1916; s. Holt and Bertie (Hines) W.; B.A., Miss. Coll., 1939; grad. Inf. Sch., 1942, Command and Gen. Staff Coll., 1951, Army War Coll., 1955, Nat. War Coll., 1963; m. Margaret Hays, June 7, 1941; children—Glenn D., Michael J., Keith C. Commd. 2d lt. U.S. Army, 1942, advanced through grades to lt. gen., 1971; co. officer 22d Inf. Regt., Camp Gordon, Ga., 1942-44; comdr. 3d Bn., 22d Inf. Regt., France, Germany, 1944-45; mem. faculty Inf. Sch., 1945-47; G-3 sect. Army Adv. Group, Nanking, China, 1947-48; G-2 sect. GHQ FEC, Tokyo, 1948-50; mem. faculty Command and Gen. Staff Coll., 1951-54; comdr. 6th Inf. Regt., Europe, 1956-58; asst. div. chief Office Dep. Chief Staff Operations, Dept. Army, Washington, 1958-60; mem. Joint Staff, Washington, 1960-62; asst. chief staff G-1, Hdqrs. 8th Army, Korea, 1963-64, G-1, U.S. Army Pacific, Hawaii, 1964-65; asst. div. comdr. 25th Inf. Div., Hawaii, 1965-66; comdr. 3d Brigade Task Force, Vietnam, 1966; asst. comdr. 4th Inf. Div., Vietnam, 1966-67; dep. chief staff mil. operations and res. forces Continental Army Command, Ft. Monroe, Va., 1967-69; comdg. gen. 4th Inf. Div., Vietnam, 1969-70; asst. dep. chief staff mil. ops. Dept. Army, Washington, 1970-71; comdg. gen. I Corps, 8th U.S. Army, Korea, 1971-72; spl. asst. for tng., chief staff Dept. Army, Washington, 1972-73; comdg. gen. 1st U.S. Army, Ft. Meade, Md., 1973-74; ret., 1974; adj. gen. State of Miss., 1976-79. Decorated D.S.M. with oak leaf cluster, Silver Star with oak leaf cluster, Legion of Merit with 2 oak leaf clusters, D.F.C., Bronze Star, Air medal with 22 oak leaf clusters, Purple Heart; Croix de Guerre (France); Order Mil. Merit, Choong Mu (Korea); Army Distinguished Service Order 1st class, Gallantry Cross with palm, Gallantry Cross with gold star, Nat. Order 5th class, Armed Forces Honor medal 1st class, Ethnic medal, Armed Forces Honor medal 1st class (Vietnam); several others. Baptist. Mason. Home: Route 4 Box 21 Union MS 39365

WALKER, GORDON ARLON, mfg. co. exec.; b. St. Paul, Feb. 2, 1928; s. Lloyd W.D. and Minnie E. (Lundeen) W.; B.A. in Math., Hamline U., St. Paul, 1951; m. Fang Mei Huang, Feb. 2, 1973; children—Gordon Arlon, Ronald, Debra, Douglas. High sch. tchr., coach, Anoka, Minn., 1953-56; mgmt. trainee Gen. Electric Co., 1953-56, mgr. mfg. data control SAE dept., Lynn, Mass., 1956-58, cons. mfg. services, N.Y.C., 1958-60; mgr. systems and procedures ITT-Kellogg Co., Chgo., 1960-68; v.p. mfg. Reliable Electric Co., Franklin Park, Ill., 1968-69; exec. v.p. Whitney Blake Co., Hamden, Conn., 1968-69; pres. Colt's small arms div. Colt Industries, Hartford, Conn., 1969-71; with U.S. Industries, Inc., 1971—, v.p., then exec. v.p. indsl. group, Oak Brook, Ill., 1973-77, pres., N.Y.C., 1977—, also dir. Served with U.S. Army, 1946-47. Mem. Midwest Indsl. Mgmt. Assn. (past dir.), Am. Mgmt. Assn., Chgo. Assn. Commerce and Industry, Newcomen Soc. Clubs: Greenwich (Conn.) Country; Board Room (N.Y.C.). Home: 380 North St Greenwich CT 06830 Office: 250 Park Ave New York NY 10017

WALKER, GORDON ARTHUR HUNTER, scientist; b. Kinghorn, Scotland, Jan. 30, 1936; s. Frederic Thomas and Mary Taylor (Hunter) W.; B.Sc., Edinburgh U., 1958; Ph.D., Cambridge U., 1962; m. Sigrid Helen Fischer, Apr. 21, 1962; children—Nicholas Ian, Eric G.T. Research scientist Dominion Astrophys. Obs., Victoria, B.C., Can., 1963-69; mem. faculty Inst. Astronomy and Space Sci., U. B.C., Vancouver, 1969—, prof., 1974—. Killam fellow, 1974-75. Fellow Royal Soc. Can. Office: Geophysics and Astronomy Dept U British Columbia Vancouver BC V6T 1W5 Canada

WALKER, H(ERBERT) LESLIE, JR., architect; b. Wilmington, N.C., July 6, 1918; s. Herbert Leslie and May Bell (Sellers) W.; student N.C. State Coll., Raleigh, 1939-40, Duke U., 1948-49; m. Elnita Frances Sellers, June 18, 1939 (dec.); children—Judy S., Robert L.; m. 2d, Ernie Katherine Watson, July 20, 1973. Apprentice architect, 1946-56; partner Walker & Jackson, architects and engrs., Tampa, Fla., 1959-61; propr. H. Leslie Walker & Assos., architects, Tampa, 1961-65, 66-71; partner Walker & Weilage, Tampa, 1965-66, Walker & McLane, Architects, Engrs. & Planners, Inc., Tampa, 1972-75; pres. H. Leslie Walker, Architect, Inc., Tampa, 1975—. Fellow AIA (dir. Fla. region 1973-75, chmn. govtl. affairs commn. 1975, chmn. architect-engr. com. fedn. constrn. 1975, chmn. fed. agencies com. 1976-77, pres. Fla. Central chpt. 1962-63; Pullara Meml. award Fla. Central chpt. 1973, medal of honor 1974, pres. Fla. assn. 1969; Design Competition Honor award Fla. assn. 1965, Design Competition award merit 1966). Democrat. Clubs: Palma Ceia Golf and Country; Tampa Commerce (pres. 1964); Interbay Sertoma. Home: 4645 Baycrest Dr Tampa FL 33615 Office: 5200 W Kennedy Blvd Suite 250 Tampa FL 33609

WALKER, HAROLD BLAKE, clergyman; b. Denver, May 7, 1904; s. Herbert R. and Ethel G. (Blake) W.; A.B., U. Denver, 1925, D.D., 1952; A.M., Boston U., 1927; B.D., McCormick Theol. Sem., 1932; postgrad. U. Chgo., 1933-34; D.D., Emporia Coll., 1944, Hamilton Coll., 1949, Rocky Mountain Coll., 1971; L.H.D., Lake Forest U., 1959; Nat. Coll. Edn., 1970; S.T.D., Northwestern U., 1970; m. Mary Alice Corder, Feb. 1, 1930; children—Herbert Elwood, Howard Deane, Timothy Blake. Editor, writer A.P., Kansas City, 1927-30; ordained to ministry Presbyn. Ch., 1932; minister Fullerton-Covenant Ch., Chgo., 1932-36, First Ch., Utica, N.Y., 1936-42, Oklahoma City, 1942-47, 1st Presbyn. Ch., Evanston, Ill., 1947-69; columnist Splty. Salesman mag., 1954-67, Chgo. Tribune-N.Y. News syndicated columnist, 1954—. Lectr. homiletics McCormick Theol.; cons. W. Clement Stone Enterprises, 1970-74. Sem. v.p. Bd. Fgn. Missions Presbyn. Ch. U.S.A.; Nat. Commn. Evangelism, 1946-47; dir. Presbyn. Tribune, 1943-55; mem. Presbyn. Commn. on Consolidation, 1957-58, Commn. on Ecumenical Mission Relations, 1958-61. Bd. dirs. Nat. Presbyn. Ch. and Center, Washington; bd. dirs. McCormick Theol. Sem., pres., 1953-55, 57-71; bd. dirs. Ill. Masonic Med. Center, Chgo., Lake Forest Coll.; trustee Maryville Coll. Recipient DeMolay Legion of Honor; Freedoms Found. sermon prize, 1950, 55, 77; citations Protestant Found. Greater Chgo., 1970, Chgo. Friends of Lit., 1971; Disting. Alumnus award McCormick Theol. Sem., 1979. Mem. Utica Council Chs. (pres. 1940), Am. Theol. Soc. Chgo. Cleric, Pi Kappa Alpha. Mason (Shriner, 33 deg., grand chaplain N.Y. 1940-41). Clubs: University (Chgo., Evanston); Glenview. Author: Going God's Way, 1946; Ladder of Light, 1951; Upper Room on Main Street, 1954; Power to Manage Yourself, 1955; (with wife) Venture of Faith, 1959; Heart of the Christian Year, 1962; Faith for Times of Tension, 1963; Thoughts to Live By, 1965; To Conquer Loneliness, 1966; Prayers to Live By, 1966; Memories to Live By, 1968; Inspirational Thoughts for Everyday, 1970; Days Demanding Courage, 1978; contbr. to religious publs. Home: 425 Grove St Evanston IL 60201

WALKER, HAROLD WILLIAM, lawyer; b. Danville, Ky., Mar. 8, 1915; s. Arthur William and Rena Elizabeth W.; B.A., Centre Coll., Danville, Ky., 1936; LL.B., U. Cin., 1939; m. Claire Clayton Wilson, Feb. 19, 1943; children—Mary Sheridan, Harold William, Elizabeth Winslow. Admitted to Ky. bar, 1938, Ohio bar, 1939; mem. firm Murphy, Lanier & Quinn, Cin., 1936-55; partner firm Walker & Chatfield, and predecessor firms, Cin., 1955—, now mng. partner; dir. Parker Internat., LaBoiteaux Co., Maintenance Methods, Inc. Served with USAAF, 1942-46. Mem. Am. Bar Assn., Ohio Bar Assn., Ky. Bar Assn., Cin. Bar Assn. Episcopalian. Clubs: Cin. Country, Bankers, University. Author: (with Ward) Ohio and Federal Estate and Tax Planning. Office: 522 Dixie Terminal Bldg Cincinnati OH 45202

WALKER, HARRY GREY, justice Miss. Supreme Ct.; b. Ovett, Miss., Sept. 30, 1924; s. Chester A. and Ina (Mangum) W.; LL.B., U. Miss., 1952; m. Carrie Thorne Lang, Apr. 4, 1953; children—Harry Grey, Fred Wallace. Admitted to Miss. bar, 1952; practiced in Gulfport, Miss., 1952-64; judge Harrison County (Miss.) Ct., 1964-68; judge Circuit Ct., 2d Dist. Miss., 1968-72; asso. justice Miss. Supreme Ct., 1972—. Mem. Miss. Ho. of Reps., 1964. Served with USCG, 1942-44. Mem. Am. Judicature Soc., Miss. State Bar, DAV, Paralyzed Vets. Am., Phi Alpha Delta, Kappa Alpha. Democrat. Methodist. Clubs: Am. Legion, Elks, Gulfport Yacht, Magnolia Hunting. Home: 2107 Plantation Blvd Jackson MS 39211 Office: Miss Supreme Ct Bldg Jackson MS 39205

WALKER, HENRY ALEXANDER A., JR., corp. exec.; b. Honolulu, Mar. 5, 1922; s. Henry Alexander and Una (Craig) W.; student Harvard, 1940-42, Columbia, 1946-47; m. Nancy Johnston, Mar. 10, 1946; children—Henry Alexander III, Susan Walker Kowen. With AMFAC, Inc., Honolulu, 1947—, v.p., operations, 1966, exec. v.p., 1966-67, pres., 1967, also chief exec. officer, chmn. bd., 1974—; dir. Am. Factors Assos. of Australia, Inc., Calif. & Hawaiian Sugar Co., Kekaha Sugar Co., Ltd., Oahu Sugar Co., Ltd., Pioneer Mill Co., Ltd., Puna Sugar Co., Ltd., Bank Calif. N.A., Hawaiian Telephone Co., Hawaiian Trust Co., Ltd., Rhodes Western; chmn. bd. Lihue Plantation Co., Island Holidays, Joseph Magnin Co. Bd. dirs. Hawaii chpt. ARC, Hawaii Emplohers Council; trustee Lewis and Clark Coll., Oceanic Found. Served with USNR, 1944-46. Mem. Jud. Council Hawaii, Hawaiian Sugar Planters Assn. Clubs: Oahu Country Pacific (Honolulu); Kaneohe Yacht; Pacific Union (San Francisco); Phoenix S.K.; Chicago. Office: Amfac Inc PO Box 3230 Honolulu HI 96801*

WALKER, HENRY GARY, real estate developer, mgmt. exec.; b. Alta., Can., Oct. 1, 1921 (parents Am. citizens); s. Henry and Amalia (Nagel) W.; ed. pub. schs.; m. Alma Jane Eichinger, Oct. 1, 1951; children—Cynthia Louise, Henry Gary III, Catherine Ann. Photographer, Silver Screen mag., 1939-41, San Francisco Examiner, 1941; White House photographer Life mag., 1949-59, fgn. corr. in Berlin, U.K., Paris, Japan and Korea, 1948, 51, 60; with Curtis Pub. Co., 1962-65, mem. editorial bd., 1963-65, mng. dir. Photography, 1963-65, asst. mng. editor Sat. Eve. Post, 1962-65; pres. Walker Broadcasting Co., Ft. Pierce, Fla., owner radio sta. WARN AM-FM, 1965-68; coordinator Manned Spaceflight Still Photo Pool, Cocoa Beach, Fla., 1965-68; sr. v.p. C.V.R. Industries, Inc.; pres. Scottie Craft Boat Corp. Am., 1968-72, Congress Industries; v.p., dir. Outdoor Supply Corp., Servinational Inc., 1972-79; owner I&W Properties Ltd., 1972—. Served with USMCR, World War II. Home: 1424 W 28th St Sunset Island I Miami Beach FL 33140 Office: 20340 NE 15th Ct Miami FL 33179

WALKER, HERMAN, JR., educator, former fgn. service officer; b. Nashville, Nov. 21, 1910; s. Herman and Georgia Elizabeth (Graham) W.; A.B., Duke, 1931, M.A., 1933, Ph.D., 1937; student U. Paris, 1934-35; M.A., Harvard, 1938; m. Betty Friemel, Oct. 17, 1936; 1 son, Steven F.; m. 2d, Evelyn Acomb, Jan. 26, 1969. Economist, legislative analyst Resettlement Adminstrn., Dept. Agr., 1936-38, 39-46; instr. govt. La. State U., 1938-39; treaty adviser Dept. State, 1946-56, became cons. fgn. service, 1955; vice chmn. U.S. delegation to GATT Tariff Conf. (Geneva), 1960-62, chmn. Trade Agreements Com., 1961-62, ret., 1962; cons. Dept. State, 1962-67; vis. prof. Duke U., 1962-63; prof. internat. affairs George Washington U., Army War Coll., 1964-65; chmn. div. history, polit. economy State U. Coll., New Paltz, N.Y., 1965-69, chmn. dept. econs. and polit. sci., 1969-77, emeritus, 1977—. Served with USAAF, 1943-45. Rockefeller Found. grantee, 1963-64. Mem. Am. Soc. Internat. Law, Am., So. polit. sci. assns., Phi Beta Kappa. Address: State U Coll New Paltz NY 12561

WALKER, HOWARD, lawyer, fin. and mgmt. co. exec.; b. Chgo., May 17, 1939; s. Benjamin and Lillian (Davis) W.; B.S., U. Ill., 1961, J.D., 1963; m. Ethel Gordon, Jan. 28, 1962 (div.); children—Dina Lynn, Gordon Daniel. Admitted to Ill. bar, 1963; mem. firm Marks, Katz, Walker & Blatt, Chgo., 1964-78; v.p. Equity Fin. and Mgmt. Co., Chgo., 1978—; instr. real estate Mallinckrodt Coll. Legal Asst. Program, spring 1975. Served with AUS, 1964. Mem. Am., Ill., Chgo. bar assns., Chgo. Council Lawyers. Democrat. Clubs: Atrium (N.Y.C.); Monroe (Chgo.). Author chpt. in manual. Home: 1314 N Dearborn Chicago IL 60610 Office: 10 S LaSalle St Chicago IL 60608

WALKER, JAMES BARRETT, life ins. co. exec.; b. Toronto, Ont., Can., July 22, 1919; s. James Morley George and Mary Ellen (Barrett) W.; honors grad. U. Toronto, 1942; m. Doris June Riddell, Dec. 25, 1944; children—James Barrett, June Anne, Candace Marion. With Can. Life, 1946—, group exec., 1961-68, v.p., dir. group, 1968-70, v.p., dir. U.S. div., Toronto, 1970-77, exec. v.p., dir. U.S. div., 1977—. Served to lt. comdr. RCNVR, 1945. Fellow Soc. Actuaries, Can. Inst. Actuaries; mem. Am. Acad. Actuaries. Clubs: National; Lambton Golf and Country. Home: 43 Abilene Dr Islington ON M9A 2N1 Canada Office: Canada Life Assurance Co 330 University Ave Toronto ON M5G 1R8 Canada

WALKER, JAMES BENJAMIN, educator; b. Dallas, May 15, 1922; s. James Benjamin and Dorothy (Doran) W.; B.S., Rice U., 1943; M.A., U. Tex., Austin, 1949, Ph.D., 1952; m. Margaret Ann Skorvaga, June 8, 1956; children—Julia Dorothy, James Michael, John Benjamin. Research scientist Clayton Biochemical Inst., U. Tex., Austin, 1952-55; postdoctoral fellow Nat. Cancer Inst., U. Wis., 1955-56; asst. prof. biochemistry Baylor Coll. Medicine, 1956-59, asso. prof., 1959-64; prof. biochemistry Rice U., Houston, 1964—. Served to lt. (j.g.) USNR, 1943-46. Mem. Am. Soc. Biol. Chemists, Am. Chem. Soc., Am. Soc. Microbiology, Phi Beta Kappa, Sigma Xi, Phi Delta Theta, Tau Beta Pi. Contbr. articles profl. jours. Home: 5658 Chevy Chase St Houston TX 77056

WALKER, JAMES CALVIN, educator; b. Mooresville, N.C., Jan. 16, 1935; s. James Clay and Lois Swaim (Brower) W.; A.B., Harvard, 1956; Ph.D., Princeton, 1961; m. Patricia Anne Wilan, June 14, 1958; children—Duncan Randal, Danial Clay, Kathleen Rebecca. Instr. Princeton, 1960-61; mem. faculty Johns Hopkins U., Balt., 1964—, prof. physics, 1969—. Cons. Army Ballistic Research Labs., 1964-68. NSF postdoctoral fellow, Oxford, 1961-63; Sloan Found. fellow, 1966-70; Shaw Travelling fellow, 1956-57. Fellow Am. Phys. Soc., Phi Beta Kappa. Home: 531 W 40th St Baltimore MD 21211

WALKER, JAMES CARTER, comedian, actor; b. Bronx, N.Y.; s. James Walker and Lorena (Perryman) W.; student City Coll. N.Y. Comedian appearing in clubs, theatres, TV variety shows; appeared as J.J. in TV series Good Times, 1974-79; costar TV series The B.A.D. Cats, 1980; dramatic TV debut in The Greatest Thing That Almost Happened, 1977; movie roles include Let's Do It Again, Rabbit Test. Hon. chmn. Los Angeles Free Clinic, 1977. Named Most Popular TV Performer, Family Circle mag., 1975. Mem. AFTRA, AGVA, Screen Actors Guild. Office: care Mgmt Consultants Co 9100 Wilshire Blvd Suite 1070 Beverly Hills CA 90212

WALKER, JAMES KENNETH, lawyer; b. Decatur, Tex., Jan. 10, 1936; s. James Bluford and Elmer Vernice (Clark) W.; LL.B., Baylor U., 1960; m. Mary Frank Garrett, July 9, 1960 (dec. Nov. 1976); children—James Garrett, Steven Wade; m. 2d, Jo Beth Robertson, July 28, 1978. Admitted to Tex. bar, 1960; practice law, Lubbock, Tex., 1960-63, Morton, Tex., 1963—; Cochran County atty., 1965-72. Dir. Morton Indsl. Found. Mem. Am., Tex. bar assns. Methodist. Lion. Home: 507 SE 9th St Morton TX 79346 Office: 109A W Washington St Morton TX 79346

WALKER, JERALD CARTER, coll. pres., clergyman; b. Bixby, Okla., May 22, 1938; s. Joseph Carter and Trula Tosh (Jackson) W.; B.A. in Sociology, Oklahoma City U., 1960; B.Div., U. Chgo., 1964; D.Religion, Sch. Theology at Claremont, 1966; m. Virginia Canfield, Apr. 14, 1963; children—Elisabeth Katherine, Anne Carter. Ordained to ministry Methodist Ch.; dir., campus minister Campus Christian Assn., Chgo., 1961-64; minister of outreach Temple Meth. Ch., San Francisco, 1965-66; chaplain, asst. prof. religion Neb. Wesleyan U., 1966-69; pres. John J. Pershing Coll., 1969-70; v.p. univ. relations, asso. prof. Southwestern U., Georgetown, Tex., 1970-74; pres. Baker U., Baldwin, Kans., 1974-79; pres. Oklahoma City U., 1979—; cons. div. higher edn. United Meth. Bd. Edn., Rocky Mountain Coll., Baldwin-Wallace Coll., Southwestern Coll., Winfield, Kans., all 1968-69, Rice U., 1973. Recipient Pres.'s Creative Young Prof. award Nebr. Wesleyan U., 1968; Alumni Recognition award Nebr. 4H Club, 1970; Distinguished Alumnus award Oklahoma City U., 1974; Student Commn. Outstanding Person of Yr. award Baker U., 1977. Mem. Am. Soc. Christian Ethics, Kansas East Conf. United Methodist Ch. Rotarian. Contbr. articles to profl. jours. Home: 2500 N Blackwelder Oklahoma City OK 73106 Office: Oklahoma City U Oklahoma City OK 73106

WALKER, JOHN ALEXANDER, mcht.; b. Phila., June 10, 1922; s. John Anthony and Dorothy (Morrison) W.; student Muhlenberg Coll., 1941-42, U. Pa., 1942-43, Northwestern U., 1944; m. Beryl

Audrey Lienhard, Apr. 21, 1946; children—Charolyn Walker Riker, Dorothy Walker Moynihan, Gail Ann Walker Owen, Deborah Sue Walker Blackwell, Mary Morrison. With Hotpoint Distbg. div., Gen. Electric Co., 1946-58, dist. mgr., 1958—; with Lowe's Cos., Inc., North Wilkesboro, N.C., 1958—, mng. dir., 1971—; dir. Brad Ragan, Inc. Mem. plywood adv. council Chgo. Bd. Trade, 1970—. Chmn. N. Wilkesboro Housing Authority, 1967—. Mem. Republican Nat. Finance Com., 1967—; Rep. candidate for lt. gov. N.C., 1972; chmn. finance com. N.C. Rep. Com., 1968-72, mem. central com., 1968-72, exec. com., 1968-72; mem. exec. com. Wilkes County Rep. Com., 1968-70. Bd. dirs. Lowe's Profit-Sharing Plan and Trust, Lowe's Charitable and Trust Found., Wilkes Devel. Corp.; bus. adv. council of Appalachian State U., Wilkes YMCA; trustee Northwestern Financial Investors, So. States Fund, Inc. Served to lt. USNR, 1942-46; PTO, ETO. Recipient Meritorious award N.C. Home Builders, 1971; Pres.'s award Gen. Electric Co., 1955, Man of Half-Century award Home Center Industry, 1975; named Man of Yr. in Home Center Industry, B'nai B'rith, 1978. Mem. N.C. Home Builders Assn. (dir. 1968—), Phi Kappa Sigma. Mason (32 deg., Shriner), Elk. Clubs: Oakwoods Country (N. Wilkesboro); Roaring Gap (N.C.); Charlotte (N.C.) City. Contbr. articles to various publs.; also poems. Home: 104 Coffey St North Wilkesboro NC 28659 Office: Hwy 268 E North Wilkesboro NC 28659

WALKER, JOHN BYRNES, pub. relations exec.; b. Fayetteville, Ark., Aug. 23, 1898; s. Jacob Wythe and Mayme Marie (Byrnes) W.; student U. Ark., 1916-19; m. Constance Marie Haslam, Apr. 6, 1938; 1 dau., Doreen Virginia. Copywriter to editor-in-chief all catalogs Montgomery Ward & Co., Chgo., 1919-23; copywriter, account exec., v.p. Ferry-Hanly, Critchfield, Potts Turnbull, advt. agys., Chgo., 1924-29; sales mgr., then v.p. sales Greyhound Lines, 1929-34; v.p., TWA, 1934-38; asst. to pres. United Airlines, 1939-44; a founder John B. Walker & Assos., 1944, reorgn. as Walker & Crenshaw, Inc., internat. pub. relations, 1950; v.p. Braniff Airways, 1949; pres., dir. Airlines Terminal Corp.; v.p., dir. U.S. Aviation Exhibits; pres. Relamex, Coastal Enterprises, Delray Beach, Fla.; chmn. Globe Press, Inc.; dir. Surface Freight Corp., Hunter Mfg. Co., Walker & Crenshaw, Inc., Gen. Aviation Equipment Co., Aircraft Accessories Corp., Aireon Mfg. Co., Avemco Corp. Col., a.d.c. Gov.'s Staff, Ky. and N.M. Served as 2d lt. U.S. Army. Mem. Soc. Automotive Engrs., Pub. Relations Soc. Am., Am. Legion, N.Y. Aviation Assn. (past pres.), Ox-5 Aviation Pioneers. Clubs: Conquistadores del Cielo (pres. 1951), Nat. Aviation (Washington); Wings, Quiet Birdmen (N.Y.C.). Author: How to Get into Aviation, 1939; War in the Air, 1940; War Planes of the World, 1939. Home: Star Route 1 Box 44 Yankeetown FL 32698

WALKER, JOHN LUTHER, lawyer; b. Lynnwood, Va., Aug. 3, 1905; s. Luther V. and Sarah V. (Hopkins) W.; A.B., Roanoke Coll., 1925; LL.B., U. Va., 1928; m. Katherine E. Crawford, Oct. 6, 1934; children—John Luther, Jane C. Admitted to Va. bar, 1927, Fla. bar, 1928, also to U.S. Supreme Ct. bar; practiced with Wideman & Wideman, West Palm Beach, Fla., 1928-30; asso. with Woods, Chitwood, Coxe & Rogers (now Woods, Rogers, Muse, Walker & Thornton), 1930—, mem., 1937—. Lectr. ins. law U. Va. Law Sch., spring 1957. Mem. Va. Bd. Bar Examiners, 1964—. Chmn. Roanoke City-County Pub. Forum, 1943-44; trustee Elks Nat. Found., 1962—, vice chmn., acting chmn., 1966, chmn. 1966—; bd. mgrs. U. Va. Alumni Assn. 1951-54. Fellow Am. Coll. Trial Lawyers, Am. Bar Found.; mem. U. Va. Law Sch. Alumni Assn. (pres. 1975-77), C. of C. (dir. 1950, 51), Am., Va. (life mem., pres. 1947-48), Roanoke (pres. 1948-49), W. Va. (hon.) bar assns., Am. Judicature Soc. (dir. 1952-57), Am. Law Inst. (life mem.), Jud. Conf. 4th U.S. Circuit, Raven Soc., Order of Coif, Phi Beta Kappa, Phi Delta Phi, Tau Kappa Alpha. Democrat. Presbyn. Elk. (pres. Va. state assn. 1941-42, dist. dep. Va., West, 1945-46. Grand Lodge judiciary com. 1947-50, mem. Grand Forum 1950—, chief justice 1954-55, grand exalted ruler 1955-56, mem. adv. com. 1956—, chmn. 1961-66, mem. nat. service commn. 1957-60, sec. 1960-74). Clubs: Shenandoah, Kiwanis (Roanoke); Farmington Country (Charlottesville, Va.). Home: 3248 Brightwood Pl Roanoke VA 24014 Office: 105 Franklin Rd SW Roanoke VA 24004

WALKER, JOHN MOORE, electronics co. exec.; b. Albany, Ga., May 19, 1921; s. John Moore and Julia (Benedict) W.; B.S. in Elec. Engring., Ga. Inst. Tech., 1943; M.B.A., Harvard, 1948; m. Carol Vander Voort, Oct. 28, 1944; children—John Moore, Elisabeth Essex. Asst. to treas. Metals & Controls Corp., Attleboro, Mass., 1954-58; with Tex. Instruments, Inc., 1958—, v.p., controller, 1967-75, v.p., treas., prin. financial officer, 1975—. Served with USNR, 1944-46. Mem. Financial Execs. Inst. Home: 5215 Westgrove Pl Dallas TX 75240 Office: PO Box 5474 Dallas TX 75222

WALKER, JOHN MORT, JR., lawyer; b. New Orleans, Feb. 10, 1904; s. John Mort and Nellie (Quealy) W.; B.E., Tulane U., 1925; LL.B., Loyola U. of South, 1936; m. Marie de los Reyes, Nov. 12, 1929; 1 dau., Mary Margaret (Mrs. John V. Baus). Admitted to La. bar, 1936; practiced in New Orleans, 1942—; mem. firm Jones, Walker, Waechter, Poitevent, Carrère & Denègre, 1943—; prof. law Loyola U. of South, 1936-44; mem. council La. State Law Inst., 1936-44; dir., former chmn. bd. Jefferson Bank & Trust Co.; dir. Canal Barge Co., Central Marine Service, Inc. Mem. New Orleans City Planning Com., 1946-62. Bd. dirs. Council for a Better La. Mem. Am. Law Inst., C. of C. New Orleans, Am., La. (gov. 1942-43, 44-45), New Orleans bar assns. Clubs: Lake Shore, Pickwick, Stratford, Petroleum, New Orleans Country. Home: 519 Betz Pl Metairie LA 70005 Office: 225 Baronne St New Orleans LA 70112

WALKER, JOHN REX, banker; b. St. Louis, July 22, 1922; s. Virgil Sylvester and Genevieve (Hart) W.; student U. Kans., 1941-43, Washington U., St. Louis, 1951-52; m. Mary Fearn Tucker, Aug. 5, 1950; children—Jeffrey Alan Gentle, Mark Evan. Staff accountant H. Stoller & Co., C.P.A.'s Dallas, 1946-48; asst. gen. ledger accountant Hunt Oil Co., Dallas, 1948-50; with Ernst & Ernst, C.P.A.'s, 1950-65, mgr., Ft. Worth, 1956-65; v.p. Ft. Worth Nat. Bank, 1965-72, sr. v.p., chief fin. officer, 1972—; former mem. faculty Southwestern Grad. Sch. Banking, So. Meth. U. Mem. adv. council Southwestern Bapt. Theol. Sem. Served with AUS, 1943-46, 50-52. C.P.A., Tex. Mem. Am. Inst. C.P.A.'s, Tex. Soc. C.P.A.'s (John Burnis Allred award 1952, sec. Tex. 1963-64, pres. Ft. Worth 1962-63), Nat. Assn. Accountants (pres. Ft. Worth 1961-62), Assn. for Systems Mgmt. (pres. Ft. Worth chpt. 1968-69), Am. Mgmt. Assn., Ft. Worth Art Assn., Am. Inst. Banking, Am. Automobile Assn. (dir. Tex. div.), Alpha Tau Omega. Baptist (deacon). Mason (Shriner), Rotarian (pres. North Ft. Worth 1970-71, dir. Ft. Worth 1979). Club: Century II. Author: Bank Costs for Decision Making, 1970. Home: 3840 Arroyo Rd Fort Worth TX 76109 Office: PO Box 2050 Fort Worth TX 76101

WALKER, JOHN T., bishop; b. Barnesville, Ga., 1925; B.D., Va. Theol. Sem., 1954; m. Rosa Maria Flores; 3 children. Ordained to ministry Episcopalian Ch.; rector St. Mary's Ch., Detroit, 1955-57; tchr. St. Paul's Sch., 1957-66; canon Washington Cathedral, 1966-71; suffragan bishop Diocese of Washington, 1971-76, bishop coadjutor, 1976-77, bishop, 1977—; tchr. Bishop Tucker Theol. Coll., Mukono, Uganda, 1964-65; dean Washington Cathedral; chmn. Urban Bishops Coalition; pres. Interfaith Conf. Greater Washington. Trustee, Absalom Jones Theol. Inst., St. Paul's Sch., Va. Theol. Sch.; chmn. citizens adv. council D.C. Chief of Police, 1976—. Office: Episcopal Ch House Mount Saint Alban Washington DC 20016

WALKER, JOSEPH, lawyer, dept. store exec.; b. N.Y.C., Mar. 19, 1912; s. Benjamin and Celia (Margulies) W.; B.A., Coll. City N.Y., 1931; LL.B., Columbia, 1937; m. Eleanor Junger, Mar. 3, 1938; children—Mark, Robert. Admitted to N.Y. bar, 1937, since practiced in N.Y.C.; chief price atty. N.Y. dist. OPA, 1945-46; sec., gen. counsel S. Klein Dept. Stores, Inc., Grayson-Robinson Stores, Inc., 1953-60; v.p., counsel, sec., dir. S. Klein Dept. Stores, Inc., N.Y.C., 1960—, exec. v.p., 1974—; sr. v.p. McCrory Corp., 1975—; dir. Lerner Stores Corp., 1971-73. Past chmn. Apparel Chain Store Credit Com. Mem. Mayor's Com. N.Y.C. Shakespeare Festival, 1966-70; co-chmn. lawyer's div. Anti-Defamation League, N.Y., 1967-69. Mem. Phi Beta Kappa, Kappa Delta Pi. Home: 350 Central Park W New York NY 10025 also Roughland Rd Norfolk CT Office: 888 7th Ave New York NY 10019

WALKER, JOSEPHINE DENNING, assn. exec.; b. Orlinda, Tenn.; d. Frank and Maude Ann Denning; student Lambuth Coll., Peabody Coll.; m. Charles Walker (dec.); 1 dau., Michelle. Formerly with Crescent Amusement Co., Nashville; former office mgr. Goldhill Food Corp., New Orleans; mem. staff, pub. relations rep. G. Edward Friar, Nashville, 1956-58; exec. dir. Country Music Assn., Nashville, 1958—; organized Country Music Assn.-UN tour New Zealand, Australia, Japan for Bangladesh; spl. events chmn. Tenn. div. Am. Cancer Soc.; active Nashville Cerebral Palsy Telethon; bd. dirs. Communication Arts Council Ednl. Television; mem. Met. Nashville Tourist Commn., 1976-78. Recipient Metronome award City of Nashville, 1970. Mem. Nat. Assn. Rec. Arts and Scis., Am. Women in Radio and TV, Nashville Area C. of C. (bd. govs. 1977—, chmn. conv., visitors com., membership com. Nashville First Club all 1971). Presbyterian. Address: Country Music Association 7 Music Circle N Nashville TN 37203*

WALKER, LANNON, fgn. service officer; b. Los Angeles, Calif., Jan. 17, 1936; s. James Orville and Esther W.; B.S., Georgetown U., 1961; m. Arlette Daguet, July 14, 1954; children—Rachelle, Anne. Commd. fgn. service officer Dept. State, 1961; polit. officer, Rabat, Morocco, 1962-64; prin. officer, Constantine, Algeria, 1964-66; assigned Exec. Secretariat, Dept. State, 1966-69; econ. counselor, Tripoli, Libya, 1969-70; dep. chief mission, Yaounde, Cameroon, 1971-73; adminstrv. counselor, Saigon, Viet Nam, 1973-74; dep. chief mission, Kinshasa, Zaire, 1974-77; dep. asst. sec. African Affairs, Washington, 1977—. Served with USAF, 1953-58. Mem. Am. Fgn. Service Assn. (chmn. 1966-69). Roman Catholic. Home: 5911 Overlea Rd Bethesda MD 20016 Office: Dept State 21st and C Sts NW Washington DC 20520

WALKER, LAURENCE ALBERT, univ. dean; b. Gillette, Wyo., Nov. 13, 1919; s. Marion A. and Ruth Elizabeth (Spielman) W.; B.A., U. Wyo., 1949, M.A., 1951; Ed.D. (Grad. fellow), U. Fla., 1964; m. Mathilda Martha Michalek, June, 1946; 1 son, David Laurence. Tchr., Campbell County (Wyo.) Rural Schs., 1937-42, Albin (Wyo.) Pub. Sch., 1942-43, Torrington (Wyo.) Pub. Schs., 1943-45; elementary prin. Jackson (Wyo.) Pub. Schs., 1945-49; tchr. lab. sch. U. Wyo., Laramie, 1949-53, dir. lab. sch., 1954-56, 59-60, coordinator extension classes, 1960-63, prof. elementary edn. and curriculum, 1964—, asst. dean, 1956-59, asso. dean, 1964-66, 67-70, acting dean, 1966-67, 70-71, dean, 1971—; cons. Lear Sigler Corp.; vis. lectr. U. No. Colo., U. Fla., Fla. Inst. Continuing Edn. Studies; sch. cons. or evaluator, S.D., Nebr., Nev., Colo., Fla., Tex., Ohio, Wyo., P.R. Pres., Albany County (Wyo.) Hist. Soc., 1975-79; mem. Laramie Parks Recreation Bd. Recipient Distinguished Service award Future Farmers Am.; Silver Beaver award Boy Scouts Am.; Luther Wesley Smith Edn. award Am. Bapt. Chs., 1978; Laramie Community Service award, 1978. Republican. Baptist. Author: School Camping, 1952; (with Dorris Sander) First Grade Entrance Requirements, 1951. Contbr. to edn. jours. and curriculum guides. Home: 1059 Colina Dr Laramie WY 82070

WALKER, LELAND JASPER, civil engr.; b. Fallon, Nev., Apr. 18, 1923; s. Albert Willard and Grayce (Wilkinson) W.; B.S. in Civil Engring., Iowa State U., 1944; m. Margaret Frances Noble, Jan. 21, 1946; children—Thomas, Margaret, Timothy. Engr. with various govtl. depts., 1946-51, 53-55; v.p. Wenzel & Co., cons. engrs. Gt. Falls, Mont., 1955-58; pres., chmn. bd. No. Testing Labs., Gt. Falls, 1958—; v.p., dir. Service Corp. Mont.; pres. Ind. Labs. Assurance Co., 1977-79; dir. Gt. Falls Savs. & Loan Assn. Pres., trustee Endowment and Research Found., Mont. State U., 1969—, Mont. Deaconess Hosp., Gt. Falls, 1959-67; trustee Rocky Mountain Coll., 1977—; chmn., bd. dirs. Mont. Tech. Services Adv. Council; bd. dirs. Mont. State Fair, Engring. Socs. Commn. on Energy, 1977—. Served with USNR, 1943-46, 51-53. Fellow ASCE (pres. 1976-77), Cons. Engrs. Council (pres. Mont. 1971); mem. Am. Council Ind. Labs. (sec. 1973-76), Engrs. Council Profl. Devel. (v.p. 1978-80), Chi Epsilon (hon.), Tau Beta Pi (hon.). Republican. Methodist. Clubs: Kiwanis (pres. Gt. Falls chpt. 1970), Mont., Meadowlark Country, Black Eagle Country. Home: 2819 8th Ave S Great Falls MT 59405 Office: 528 Smalter Ave PO Box 951 Great Falls MT 59403*

WALKER, LELAND JASPER, civil engr.; b. Fallon, Nev., Apr. 18, 1923; s. Albert Willard and Grayce (Wilkinson) W.; B.S. in Civil Engring., Iowa State U., 1944; m. Margaret Frances Noble, Jan. 21, 1946; children—Thomas, Margaret, Timothy. Engr. with various govtl. depts., 1946-51, 53-55; v.p. Wenzel & Co., cons. engrs., Great Falls, Mont., 1955-58; pres., chmn. bd. No. Testing Labs., Great Falls, 1958—; v.p., dir. Service Corp. Mont.; pres. Ind. Labs. Assurance Co., 1977-79; dir. Great Falls Savs. & Loan Assn.; v.p. Engr.'s Council for Profl. Devel., 1978-79. Pres., trustee Endowment and Research Found., Mont. State U., 1969—, Mont. Deaconess Hosp., Great Falls, 1959-67; trustee Rocky Mountain Coll., 1977—; chmn., dir. Mont. Tech. Services Adv. Council; bd. dirs. Mont. State Fair, Engring. Socs. Commn. on Energy, 1977—. Served with USNR, 1943-46, 51-53. Fellow ASCE (pres. 1976-77), Cons. Engrs. Council (pres. Mont. 1971), AAAS; mem. Am. Council Ind. Labs. (sec. 1973-76), Chi Epsilon (hon.), Tau Beta Pi (hon.). Republican. Methodist. Clubs: Kiwanis (pres. Great Falls 1970), Montana, Meadowlark Country, Black Eagle Country. Home: 2819 8th Ave S Great Falls MT 59405 Office: 528 Smelter Ave PO Box 951 Great Falls MT 59403

WALKER, LEROY TASHREAU, educator, coach; b. Atlanta, June 14, 1918; s. Willie and Mary Elizabeth (Thomas) W.; B.S., Benedict Coll., 1940; M.A., Columbia U., 1941; Ph.D., N.Y. U., 1957; m. Katherine McDowell, Dec. 31, 1938 (dec.); children—LeRoy, Carolyn. Chmn. dept. phys. edn., coach basketball, football, track and field Benedict Coll., Columbia, S.C., 1941-42, Bishop Coll., Marshall, Tex., 1942-43, Prairie View State U., 1943-45; chmn. dept. phys. edn. and recreation, coach basketball, football, track and field N.C. Central U., Durham, 1945-73, vice-chancellor for univ. relations, 1974—; ednl. specialist Cultural Exchange Program, Dept. State, 1959, 60, 62; dir. program, planning and tng. Peace Corps, Africa, 1966-68; coach Ethiopian and Israeli Olympic teams, Rome, 1960; adviser Jamaican Nat. Team in track and field Carreras Games, 1962, Trinidadian Olympic Team, Mexico City, 1968; track and field coach Western Hemisphere Team, Germany, Eng., 1969; head coach U.S. Nat. Track and Field Team, France, Germany and Russia, 1970; organizer, coordinator Pan-Africa vs. U.S.A. Internat. Track and Field Meet, Durham, 1971, U.S.A. Nat. Track and Field Team, Germany, Italy, Russia and W.Africa, 1973, U.S.A. vs. USSR Internat. Track and Field Meet and Arts Festival, Durham, 1974, U.S.A.-Pan-Africa-Germany Internat. Track and Field Meet, Durham, 1975; tech. cons. Kenyan Olympic Team, Munich, 1972; commr. Mid-Eastern Athletic Conf., 1971-74; mem. U.S. Collegiate Sports Council, 1971; chmn. Coll. Commrs. Assn., 1971-74; chmn. Athletic Union of U.S.A. Track and Field Com., 1973-75; head coach U.S.A. Olympic Track and Field Team, Montreal, 1976; bd. dirs. U.S. Olympic Com., U.S.A.-China Relations Com. Recipient Hamilton Watch Co. award for James E. Shepard Outstanding Tchr. at N.C. Central U., 1964, Achievement award Central Intercollegiate Athletic Assn., 1967, Distinguished Alumni Service award Benedict Coll., 1968, Distinguished Service awards Kiwanis Internat., 1971, City of Durham, 1971, Durham C. of C., 1973, Gov.'s Ambassador of Goodwill award, 1974, O. Max Gardner award, 1976, N.C. Distinguished Citizen award, 1977, Achievement in Life award Ency. Brit., 1977; elected to N.C. Hall of Fame, 1975, S.C. Hall of Fame, 1977, Nat. Assn. Sport and Phys. Edn. Hall of Fame, 1977. Mem. AAHPER (nat. pres., Honor award 1972), NEA, U.S. Track Coaches Assn. (Nat. Track Coach of Year award 1972), Nat. Assn. Intercollegiate Athletics, Nat. Collegiate Athletic Assn. (Nat. Coach of Year award 1972), N.C. Assn. for Health, Phys. Edn. and Recreation (Honor award 1971, v.p. phys. edn. div., dir.), Internat. Assn. Athletic Fedns. (U.S. rep. 1976—), Sigma Delta Psi, Alpha Phi Omega, Omega Psi Phi. Episcopalian. Author: Manual of Adapted Physical Education, 1960; Physical Education for the Exceptional Students, 1965; Championship Techniques in Track and Field, 1969. Contbr. articles to profl. jours. Home: 1208 Red Oak Ave Durham NC 27707 Office: NC Central U Durham NC 27707

WALKER, LUTHER LONEITH, writer; b. Rockingham, N.C., Jan. 23, 1939; s. Lonnie Luther and Dora Josephine (Watts) W.; student U. N.C., 1957-60, 67; m. Daphne Mae Norton, Sept. 6, 1959; children—Michael Todd, David Norton. Stock mgr. A&P Tea Co., Chapel Hill, N.C., 1960-61; copy editor State-Record Pub. Co., Columbia, S.C., 1965-68; asso. editor The Nat. Guardsman, publ. N.G. Assn. U.S., Washington, 1968-74, editor, 1974-78; freelance writer, 1978—. Treas. Ridgeview (Va.) Civic Assn., 1973. Served with USAF, 1961-65. Recipient Valley Forge honor certificate Freedoms Found. at Valley Forge, 1975, George Washington honor medal, 1976. Mem. Soc. Nat. Assn. Publs., N.G. Assn. U.S. (life), Mt. Vernon-Lee C. of C. Mem. Assembly of God. Club: Masons. Editor: The Militia in The Revolutionary War, 1976. Home: 4106 Javins Dr Alexandria VA 22310

WALKER, M. LUCIUS, JR., mech. engr.; b. Washington, Dec. 16, 1936; s. M. Lucius and Inez L. W.; student Morehouse Coll., 1952-54; B.S.M.E. summa cum laude, Howard U., 1957; M.S.M.E., Carnegie Inst. Tech., 1958, Ph.D., 1966; m. Oswaldene E. Cocking, Feb. 13, 1961; children—Mark, Monique. Instr., Howard U., 1958-63, asst. prof., 1963-67, asso. prof., 1967-70, prof. mech. engring., 1970—, asst. dean Sch. Engring., 1965-66, chmn. dept. mech. engring., 1966, 68-73, asso. dean Sch. Engring., 1973-74, acting dean, 1977-78, dean, 1978—; vis. prof. U. Mass., summer 1968; vis. sr. staff mem. Internat. Research and Tech. Corp., 1969-70; mem. engring. manpower commn. Engrs.' Council Profl. Devel.; reviewer NRC Postdoctoral Fellowship Evaluation Panels; mem. biotech. resources rev. com. NIH; cons. in field. Recipient Ralph R. Teetor award Soc. Automotive Engrs.; Ford teaching fellow; Ford faculty-in-engring. resident, 1969-70; registered profl. engr., Washington. Mem. Am. Soc. Engring. Edn., ASME, Sigma Xi, Tau Beta Pi, Pi Mu Epsilon, Kappa Alpha Psi. Episcopalian. Contbr. articles to profl. publs. Office: 2300 6th St NW Washington DC 20059

WALKER, MALLORY ELTON, tenor; b. New Orleans, May 22, 1935; s. James Hugh and Edith Mamie (Gilmore) W.; B.A., Occidental Coll., 1957; m. Carolyn Pryor, Dec. 21, 1956; children—Maria Vanessa, Anthony Hugh, Jamie Eugene. Soloist Robert Shaw Chorale, 1960; appeared with Dallas Opera, Cologne Opera, Stuttgart Opera, Miami Opera, Metropolitan Opera; soloist with Los Angeles Philharmonic, Cleve. Symphony, Boston Symphony, Phila. Orch. Chgo. Symphony; vocal instr. Boston Conservatory of Music, 1974-77. Served with U.S. Army, 1957-60. Rockefeller Found. grantee, 1962-63; Ford Found. grantee, 1963. Mem. Am. Guild Musical Artists, AFTRA. Office: care of Thea Dispeker 59 E 54th St New York City NY 10022

WALKER, MORT, cartoonist; b. El Dorado, Kans., Sept. 3, 1923; s. Robin A. and Carolyn (Richards) W.; student Kansas City Jr. Coll., 1941-42, Washington U., St. Louis, 1943-44; B.A., U. Mo., 1948; m. Jean Marie Suffill, Mar. 12, 1949; children—Greg, Brian, Polly, Morgan, Marjorie, Neal, Roger. Designer, Hallmark Greeting Cards, 1941; editor Dell Pub. Co., 1948-49; free lance cartoonist Sat. Eve. Post; other popular mags., 1948-50; comic strip artist King Features, 1950—; creator Beetle Bailey, 1950, Hi and Lois, 1954, Sam's Strip, 1961, Boner's Ark, in 1968, Sam and Silo, 1977. Mem. Pres.'s Com. to Hire Handicapped, People to People Com. Exhbt. touring group show Met. Mus. Art, N.Y.C., 1951. Pres., Mus. Cartoon Art. Served to 1st lt. AUS, 1943-46; ETO. Recipient award as outstanding cartoonist The Banshees, 1955; Il Secolo XIX award, Italy, 1972; Adamson award, Sweden, 1975; Segar award, 1977; 4th Estate award Am. Legion, 1978. Mem. Nat. Cartoonists Soc. (pres. 1959-60, Reuben award 1953; award for best humor strip of 1966, 69), Artists and Writers, Comics Council, Authors Guild, Kappa Sigma. Clubs: Silvermine (Norwalk, Conn.); Belle Haven Beach. Author: Beetle Bailey and Sarge, 1958; Trixie, 1960; National Cartoon Society Album, 1965; Beetle Bailey and Friends, 1968; Sam's Strip Lives, 1968; Fall Out Laughing, 1969; Hi and Lois, 1970; Most, 1971; Land of Lost Things, 1973; Backstage at the Strips, 1975; contbr. to numerous anthologies and textbooks. Home: Greenwich CT Office: care King Features Syndicate 235 E 45th St New York NY 10017. *If I enjoy my own life that's one life enjoyed. But if I can help others enjoy their lives more, many lives are made more enjoyable.*

WALKER, NANCY (ANN MYRTLE SWOYER), actress; b. Phila., May 10, 1921; d. Dewey and Myrtle (Lawler) Berto; ed. Bentley Sch., Profl. Children's Sch., both N.Y.C.; m. David Craig, Jan. 29, 1951; 1 dau., Miranda. Actress, appearing in Broadway shows Best Foot Forward, 1941-42, On the Town, 1944-46, Barefoot Boy with Cheek, 1947, Look, Ma I'm Dancing, 1948, Along Fifth Avenue, 1948-49, Pal Joey, 1952-53, Phoenix 55, 1955, Fallen Angels, 1956, The Girls Against the Boys, 1959; Do Re Mi, 1960; UTBU, 1966; motion pictures include Best Foot Forward, Girl Crazy, Broadway Rhythm, Lucky Me, Stand Up and Be Counted, 1972, Forty Carats, The World's Greatest Athlete, 1973, Murder by Death, 1976, Won Ton Ton, The Dog Who Saved Hollywood, 1976; dir. Discoland; TV appearances include Mary Tyler Moore Show, Rhoda, McMillan & Wife, Nancy Walker Show, Blansky's Beauties; also TV movies; with APA, N.Y.C., 1968-69, appeared in The Cherry Orchard, The Show-Off, The Cocktail Party, A Funny thing Happened on the Way to the Forum, 1971, Sondheim: A Musical Tribute, 1973. Recipient Genii award Am. Women in Radio and TV, 1975. Office: care Contemporary Korman Artists Ltd Contemporary Artists Bldg 132 Lasky Dr Beverly Hills CA 90212

WALKER, NORMA ELIZABETH PEDEN, educator; b. Grove City, Pa., Sept. 26, 1921; d. David Stanton and Mary Louella (Giebner) Peden; B.S., Indiana (Pa.) U., 1958; M.S., Pa. State U., 1961, Ph.D., 1968; m. Charles Linn Walker, May 14, 1940 (dec.); children—Edward Erdman, Charles Linn, Rebecca Walker Mihelcic, Ellen Walker Torrey, Esther Walker Habla, Charlotte Corl. Homemaking tchr., Marion Center (Pa.) Area High Sch., 1958-60, tchr., head homemaking dept., 1961-63; grad. research asst. Pa. State U., 1960-61, instr., 1963-68; asso. prof. clothing and textiles Tex. Technol. U., Lubbock, 1968-69, asso. prof., chmn. clothing and textiles, 1969-70, prof., chmn., 1970-75, Margaret W. Weeks prof., 1975-77; prof. consumer services Indiana (Pa.) U., 1977—. Mem. AAUW, Am. Home Econs. Assn., ASTM, Assn. Coll. Profs. Textiles and Clothing, Kappa Delta Pi, Kappa Omicron Phi, Delta Kappa Gamma. Republican. Methodist. Club: Current Events (pres.). Home: 10 La Vista Dr Indiana PA 15701. *To try and succeed is gratifying, but to try and fail is the best learning experience that one can have. There are at least a thousand ways for doing something wrong, but very few for doing it right. Is it any wonder that humans make so many mistakes before they achieve success?*

WALKER, NORMAN ARTHUR, choreographer, educator; b. N.Y.C., June 21, 1934; s. Norman Arthur and Mary Elizabeth (Krutovich) W.; student modern dance Gertrude Shurr, May O'Donnell, Martha Graham; student ballet Robert Joffrey, Don Farnworth, Valentina Pereyslavic, Rochelle Zide-Booth. Lead dancer May O'Donnel & Co., 1952-57; instr. Utah State U., 1959-60; artistic dir., choreographer Norman Walker Dance Co., N.Y.C., 1961-71, lead dancer, 1961-67; dir. dept. modern dance Jacob's Pillow Dance Festival and Sch., Becket, Mass., 1967-69, 71, dir., 1974-79, chmn. bd. advisors, 1979—; artistic dir. Batsheva Dance Co., Tel-Aviv, Israel, 1970; tchr. dance Adelphi U., 1972—, chmn. dept. dance, 1972—; ballet master Harkness Ballet Co., N.Y.C., 1973-74; tchr. dance High Sch. Performing Arts, N.Y.C., 1955-57, 60-69, 71, 72, mem. adv. commn., 1979—; guest artist various prodns. Pearl Lang & Co., 1962-63, N.Y. Philharmonic, 1966; guest tchr. Dance Acad., Stockholm, 1965, Summer Dance Acad., Cologne, Ger., 1965, 72, others; dancer-actor various prodns. Utah State U.; dancer, actor, choreographer Dark of the Moon at McCarter Theatre, Princeton U., 1962; dancer-choreographer CBS-TV prodns., 1962, 64, 65, 67, 68, 69; opera dir. prodns. of Orfeo, Madame Butterfly, Archy and Mehitabel, Illumnations, The Coronation of Poppea, The Music Master, Pelleas and Melisande; cons. on dance N.J. Bd. Higher Edn., 1973-74, Thomas A. Edison Coll., 1975—; leading architect dance curriculum Sch. of Arts, Balt. Served with U.S. Army, 1957-59. Office: Adelphia U Garden City NY 11530

WALKER, OLIVER MALLORY, mortgage banker and realtor; b. Alpine, Ala., Sept. 1898; s. Samuel and Ella Belle (Mallory) W.; student U. Ala., 1917, Marion (Ala.) Mil. Inst., 1917-18; B.S., U.S. Naval Acad., 1922; m. Elizabeth Powell Dunlop, June 11, 1932; children—Elizabeth Dunlop (Mrs. Arthur B. Edgeworth, Jr.), Ann Mallory (Mrs. Richard W. Gaffney), O. Mallory. Advt. salesman Am. Bur. Trade Extension, 1922, advt. mgr., 1923; organizer Washington Concrete Products Corp., 1924, sales mgr., 1924-30, v.p., 1930-43; sec., dir. Union Market Terminal, Washington, 1928-35; organizer, pres. Walker & Dunlop, Washington and Balt., 1935—; now chmn. bd.; dir. mem. exec. com. Title Guarantee Co., Balt., 1941-75; pres. Am. Standard Life Ins. Co., 1953-58; lectr., speaker mortgage financing. Pres., Washington Real Estate Bd., 1949-50; pres. mortgage council Nat. Assn. Real Estate Bds., 1954-55, chmn. com. real estate econs. 1956-60. Chmn. bd. zoning appeals, Montgomery County, Md., 1943-47. Trustee, pres. Whitehall Country Sch., 1944-46; trustee Landon Sch., 1950-52, Naval Acad. Found., 1968-79. Recipient Realtor of Yr. award Washington Bd. Realtors, 1967. Mem. Mortgage Bankers Assn. Am. (gov. 1952-60, v.p. 1960—, dir. 1961-69, Certified Mortgage Bankers award 1974, dir.). Clubs: Metropolitan, Chevy Chase, Army and Navy (Washington); Army and Navy Country (Arlington, Va.); Rehoboth Beach Country; Balboa (Mazatlan, Mexico). Author: Servicing Mortgage Loans, 1951. Co-author: Quar. Mortgage Market Reports, Nat. Assn. Real Estate Bds., 1955-65. Home: 4522 Jamestown Rd Washington DC 20016 Office: 1156 15th St NW Washington DC 20005. *Having been born just before the beginning of this century, I have had the pleasure and satisfaction of participating in the development of modern civilization. The most important being the airplane, communications, television, automobile, exploration of space, nuclear power, a great advance in medical science, computers and many other achievements, which have greatly improved but, also, complicated modern civilization.*

WALKER, PHILIP LEROY, JR., educator, materials scientist; b. Balt., Jan. 10, 1924; s. Philip L. and Mary Belle (Heaps) W.; B.Engring., Johns Hopkins, 1947, M.S., 1948; Ph.D., Pa. State U., 1952; m. Virginia Lee Strobel, July 14, 1949; children—Page, John, Lawrence. Control chemist Lever Bros. Co., 1948-49; mem. faculty Pa. State U., 1952—, prof. fuel tech., 1955-68, prof. materials sci., 1968—, Evan Pugh prof., 1973—, head dept. fuel sci. 1954-59, chmn. div. mineral tech., 1959-64, head dept. materials sci., 1967-78; dir. C-Cor Electronics, Inc., State College, Pa.; cons. fuels and carbon industry, 1955—; chmn. Am. Carbon Com., 1963-69. Recipient Henry H. Storch award, 1969; George Skakel Meml. award, 1971. Mem. Am. Chem. Soc., Am. Phys. Soc., Am. Ceramic Soc., Am. Inst. Chem. Engring., Sigma Xi, Phi Lambda Upsilon. Author: Chemistry and Physics of Carbon, vols. 1, 2, 4, 12, 1966, 68, 75. Asso. editor Carbon, 1963—; editor Chemistry and Physics of Carbon, 1966—; editorial bd. Fuel. Contbr. articles to profl. jours. Home: 210 Seneca Circle State College PA 16801 Office: Pa State U Coll Earth and Mineral Scis University Park PA 16802

WALKER, PINKNEY CALVIN, educator, former govt. ofcl.; b. Graham, Tex., Nov. 2, 1917; s. Pinkney Clay and Sammye D. (McCombs) W.; B.B.A., U. Tex., 1939; M.B.A., U. Pa., 1940, Ph.D. in Econs., 1955; m. Vera Helen Abernathy, Nov. 2, 1939; children—Pinkney Clay, Anne, John Abernathy. Faculty, U. Mo., Columbia, 1940—, prof. econs., 1955—, chmn. dept., 1960-62, dean Sch. Bus. and Pub. Adminstrn., 1964-71; commr. Fed. Power Commn., 1971-73, vice chmn., 1972; dir. Commerce Bank of Columbia, USLIFE Corp., N.Y.C.; participant Gov.'s Bicentennial Econ. Conf., 1975. Bd. dirs. Inst. for Study Regulated Industry. Served to lt. USNR, 1943-46. Named Ky. col. adm. Tex. Navy, Top-Displaced W. Texan; recipient Mo. Faculty Alumni Distinguished Service award. Mem. QEBH, Omicron Delta Epsilon, Alpha Kappa Psi, Beta Gamma Sigma, Omicron Delta Kappa. Author: The Interest Theories of Boehm-Bawerk, Fisher and Keynes: A Critique, 1955; The Economics of Income Distribution, 1960, 2d edit., 1962. Editor: Essays in Honor of Harry Gunnison Brown, 1950; Essays in Monetary Theory in Honor of Elmer Wood, 1965. Contbr. articles to profl. jours. Home: 300 Lindell Dr Columbia MO 65201

WALKER, RICHARD DAVID, civil engr., educator; b. Washington, Feb. 19, 1931; s. Stanton and Amelia (Ramseyer) W.; B.C.E., U. Md., 1953; M.C.E., Purdue U., 1955, Ph.D., 1961; m. Alice Patricia Davis, June 6, 1953; children—Patricia Vawn, Jean Brianne, Sharyl Elise. Instr., Purdue U., 1957-61; asst. prof. Va. Poly. Inst., 1961-62, asso. prof., 1962-68, prof., 1968—, head dept. civil engring., 1970—. Mem. Montgomery County Republican Com. Served to lt. USAF, 1955-57. Mem. ASTM (sec. com. C-9 on concrete and concrete aggregates 1970-76), Transp. Research Bd., Am. Concrete Inst., ASCE, Am. Soc. for Engring. Edn., Sigma Xi, Chi Epsilon. Presbyterian (elder 1973—). Author (with R.D. Krebs) Highway Materials, 1971. Home: 701 Broce Dr Blacksburg VA 24060. *Have respect for others, their opinions and beliefs. At the same time, stand firm for what you believe. Remember, even a firmly rooted tree stands because it is flexible and can bend with the wind. Concerning goals, avoid rigidity; include service to others, then set goals sufficiently general to embrace the total purpose God has for you in this life.*

WALKER, RICHARD HAROLD, pathologist; b. Cleve., Dec. 2, 1928; s. Harold Deford and Bernice Margaret (Wright) W.; B.S., Emory U., 1950, M.D., 1953; m. Carolyn Franklin, Sept. 28, 1954; children—Bruce, Lynn, Cara, Leah. Intern, City Memphis Hosps., 1953-54; resident in pathology U. Tenn. Coll. Medicine, Memphis, 1954-55, 57-59, Am. Cancer Soc. clin. fellow, 1957-59; med. dir. blood bank and transfusion service City of Memphis Hosps., 1961-70; prof. pathology Coll. Medicine, U. Tenn., Memphis, 1966-70; chief of blood bank and transfusion service William Beaumont Hosp., Royal Oak, Mich., 1970—, dir. Sch. Med. Tech., 1970—. Served in USNR, 1955-57. Recipient Murray Thelin Humanitarian award Memphis chpt. Nat. Hemophilia Found., 1968. Mem. AMA, Coll. Am. Pathologists, Am. Soc. Clin. Pathologists (Disting. Service award 1977), Am. Assn. Blood Banks (pres. 1976-77), Internat. Soc. Blood Transfusion, Am. Assn. for Clin. Histocompatibility Testing. Republican. Presbyterian. Contbr. articles on blood transfusion, blood group genetics and blood banking to med. jours. Home: 22301 Nottingham St Birmingham MI 48010 Office: Blood Bank William Beaumont Hosp Royal Oak MI 48072

WALKER, RICHARD LOUIS, educator; b. Bellefonte, Pa., Apr. 13, 1922; s. Robert Shortlidge and Genevieve (Bible) W.; B.A., Drew U., 1944; certificate Chinese lang. and area, U. Pa., 1944; M.A., Yale, 1947, Ph.D., 1950; m. Celeno Claypole Kenly, Mar. 29, 1945; children—Geoffrey Kenly, Dorothy Anne, Stephen Bradley. Asst. prof. history Yale, 1950-57; prof. internat. studies U. S.C., 1957—, James F. Byrnes prof. internat. relations, 1959—; vis. asso. prof. Nat. Taiwan U., Taipei, China, 1954-55; vis. prof. U. Wash., 1959, 65; prof. polit. affairs Nat. War Coll., 1960-61; spl. research internat. relations Far East; lectr., cons. U.S. Govt., 1953—, Dept. Def., 1969—; rep. Dept. State, SEATO meeting, Philippines, 1957; lectr. Nat. War Coll., Fgn. Service Inst., Army War Coll., Armed Forces Staff Coll., Air War Coll., Naval War Coll., Australian Nat. U., Hong Kong U.; cons. to standing com. edn. about communism Am. Bar Assn., 1961-69; cons. spl. studies project Rockefeller Bros., 1956-57; vis. lectr. Fgn. Service Inst., Dept. State, 1971—; cons., lectr. USIS, 1973-74. Bd. dirs. Aid Refugee Chinese Intellectuals, 1952-70, Am. Bur. for Med. Advancement in China, 1955—, Am.-Asian Ednl. Exchange, 1957—, Inst. Am. Strategy, 1958—; adv. council U.S. Army Inst. Mil. Assistance, 1971-73; adv. bd., also research council Center for Strategic and Internat. Studies, 1968—. Bd. dirs. Nat. Com. U.S.-China Relations, 1968—, U.S. Strategic Inst., 1977—, U. S.C. Ednl. Found., 1958—, Conf. on European Problems, 1967—. Served with AUS, 1942-46; PTO. Recipient Alumni Achievement award in arts Drew U., 1958; Disting. Service award Air U., 1970; Fgn. Service Inst. award, 1971; Armed Forces Staff Coll. award, 1978; Fulbright-Social Sci. Research Council research scholar Academia Sinica, Republic China, 1965-66. Mem. Assn. Asian Studies, Am. Hist. Assn., Am. Polit. Sci. Assn., Internat. Studies Assn., Pi Gamma Mu. Omicron Delta Kappa, Aurelian Honor Soc. Episcopalian. Clubs: Forest Lake, Torch, Summit. Author: Western Language Periodicals on China, 1949; Multi-State System of Ancient China, 1954; China Under Communism, 1955; China and the West, 1956; The Continuing Struggle, 1958; Democracy Confronts Communism in World Affairs, 1965; Edward R. Stettmius, Jr., 1965; The China Danger, 1966; Ancient China, 1969; Prospects in the Pacific, 1972; Ancient Japan, 1975. Editorial bd. Orbis, 1974—, Asian Survey, 1978—, Jour. Internat. Relations, 1977—. Contbr. to various symposium vols., learned jours. Home: 700 Spring Lake Rd Columbia SC 29206

WALKER, ROBERT ALANDER, publisher; b. Syracuse, N.Y., Apr. 30, 1912; s. Forrest Alander and Lena Rebecca (Orman) W.; student U. Ill., 1932, Wheaton Coll., 1933; B.S., Northwestern U., 1936, M.S., 1941; Litt.D., John Brown U., 1947; LL.D., Taylor U., 1962; m. Jean Browning Clements, Oct. 1, 1937; children—Gwyneth, Telford, Rob, Kent, Cherry. Telegraph, sports editor Menominee (Mich.) Herald Leader, 1936; advt. agy. copy writer Rosenow Co., Chgo., 1937-38, gen. sec. Christian Workers Found., Chgo., 1940—; founder, editor His Mag., Chgo., 1941-43; dir., asst. to pres. Club Aluminum Products Co., Chgo., 1941-45; asst. prof. journalism Wheaton Coll., 1941-51; dir., distbn. mgr. Scripture Press Found., Chgo., 1945-56; pres. Christian Life, Inc., 1945—, Christian Writers Inst., 1946—, Christian Life Missions, 1956—. Recipient award distinguished service in religious journalism Okla. Bapt. U., 1948. Mem. Evang. Covenant Ch. Rotarian. Home: 515 E Oak Ave Wheaton IL 60187 Office: 396 E Saint Charles Rd Wheaton IL 60187. *I have discovered a new dimension to my life through commitment to Jesus Christ. It's the greatest discovery I have ever made.*

WALKER, ROBERT BRUCE, savs. and loan assn. exec.; b. Phila., Jan. 8, 1923; s. J. Howard and Gertrude (Caddy) W.; student Pierce Bus. Coll., 1946, Exec. Devel. Sch., U. Ga., 1964, Grad. Sch. Savs. and Loan, Ind. U., 1967; m. Jean C. Hillegass, Jan. 17, 1943; children—Jayne L., Ann Walker Lacy, Robert Bruce, II. Exptl. machinist U.S. Gauge Co., Sellersville, Pa., 1941-44; asst. sec., fire ins. underwriter Union Mut. Ins. Co., Norristown, Pa., 1946-48; mgr. Forrest J. Henry, Ins. Agy., Red Hill, Pa., 1948-56; asst. sec., sec. Red Hill Savs. & Loan Assn., 1948-68, pres., 1968—. Sch. dir., Red Hill, 1952-53, Upper Perkiomen Sch. Dist., 1959-71; mayor City of Red Hill, 1954-58; bd. dirs. Lutheran Sem., Mt. Airy, Pa.; pres., dir. numerous charitable orgns. Mem. Montgomery County Savs. and Loan League (pres.), Insured Savs. Assn. Delaware Valley (pres.), Pa. Savs. League (1st v.p.). Clubs: Lions, Masons. Home: Box 528 RD 1 Perkiomenville PA 18074 Office: 400 Main St Red Hill PA 18076*

WALKER, ROBERT HAROLD EARLE, lawyer; b. Davos, Switzerland, Feb. 2, 1912; s. Harold Earle and Hazel (Hart) W.; student Royal Mil. Coll. Can., 1929-33; B.C.L., McGill U., 1936; m. Kathleen Ryan, June 10, 1936; children—David, Ann (Mrs. Glenn Williams), Christine (Mrs. Graham Bagnall). Called to bar, 1936, Queen's counsel, 1949; with firm Martineau & Walker, and predecessors, Montreal, Que., Can., 1936-39, 45—, partner, 1946—; dir. Dominion Electric Protection Co., Am. Express Can., Inc., Martin-Black Inc., Commerce Capital Corp. Chmn., Can. Tax Found., 1974-75. Served to lt. col. Can. Army, 1939-45. Decorated companion Disting. Service Order; Efficiency Decoration. Mem. Am. Coll. Probate Counsel (bd. regents 1968-73), Canadian Bar Assn. (v.p. Que. 1970-71), Delta Upsilon. Club: Saint James' (Montreal). Home: 4089 Highland Ave Montreal PQ H3Y 1R4 Canada Office: 800 Victoria Sq Montreal PQ H4Z 1E9 Canada

WALKER, ROBERT HARRIS, educator; b. Cin., Mar. 15, 1924; B.S., Northwestern U., 1945; M.A., Columbia U., 1950; Ph.D., U. Pa., 1955; m. Grace Burtt; children—Amy, Rachel, Matthew. Edn. specialist U.S. Mil. Govt., Japan, 1946-47; instr. Carnegie Inst. Tech., 1950-51, U. Pa., 1953-54; asst. prof., dir. Am. studies U. Wyo., 1955-59; asso. prof. George Washington U., 1959-63, prof. Am. civilization, 1963—, dir. Am. studies program, 1959-66, 68-70; dir. edn. and pub. program Nat. Endowment for Humanities, 1956-68; fellow Woodrow Wilson Internat. Center, 1972-73; Fulbright and specialist grants to Japan, Germany, Sweden, Thailand, Iran, Greece, 1964-75; Am. Council Learned Socs. alt. del. UNESCO Gen. Info. Program, 1978—. Mem. Japan-U.S. Friendship Commn., 1977—. Served with USNR, 1943-46, 50. Mem. Am. Studies Assn. (nat. pres. 1970-71), Phi Beta Kappa. Club: Cosmos. Author: American Studies in teh U.S., 1958; Poet and Gilded Age, 1963; Life in the Age of Enterprise, 1967; American Studies Abroad, 1975; Reform Spirit in America, 1976; American Studies: Topics and Sources, 1976; editor Am. Quar., 1953-54; sr. editor Am. Studies Internat., 1970—; Am. studies series for Greenwood Press, 1972—. Office: Am Studies Program George Washington U Washington DC 20052

WALKER, ROBERT KIRK, lawyer; b. Jasper, Tenn., May 22, 1925; s. Jerry A. and Clemmie (Turner) W.; student U. of South, 1943-44; J.D., U. Va., 1948; m. Miriam Joyce Holt, Aug. 11, 1945; children—Robert Kirk, Marilyn Joy, James Holt. Admitted to Va. bar, 1948, Tenn. bar, 1948; practice in Chattanooga, 1949—; partner firm Strang, Fletcher, Carriger, Walker, Hodge & Smith, 1955—. Mayor City Chattanooga, 1971-75. Gen. counsel Tenn. Credit Union League, 1956—; sec.-treas., dir. McLaughlin Devel. Corp., Chattanooga, 1959—; sec., dir. Southland Fabrics, Inc., Chattanooga, 1959—; spl. counsel to atty. gen. Tenn. depts. banking, hwys., 1968-71; sec. Pepsi-Cola Bottling Co. Chattanooga, 1969-74, TCUL Service Corp., 1969—. Mem. exec. bd. Cherokee Area council Boy Scouts Am., 1958—, commr., 1959-60, mem.-at-large nat. council, 1966-76, v.p., 1967-69; mem. exec. bd. Hamilton County Law Enforcement Commn., 1962-67; mem. Chattanooga Area Heart Assn., 1966-75; pres. McCallie Sch. Patrons Assn., 1967-68; vice chmn. adv. bd. U. Tenn. Govt.-Industry-Law Center, 1965-66; mem. Law Revision Commn. Tenn., 1970-71, Tenn. Law Enforcement Planning Commn., 1972-75, Tenn. Manpower Council, 1972-75; chmn. Tenn. Local Govt. Study Commn., 1973-74; life mem. U.S. 6th Jud. Circuit Conf., 1966—; mem. adv. bd. Chattanooga-Hamilton County Health Dept., 1967-71; v.p. Tenn. Municipal League, 1971-75; pres. Chattanooga Area Regional Council Govts., 1971-74; col. staff of Tenn. Gov., 1966-75. Bd. dirs. Chattanooga Urban Coalition, 1968-71, Tenn. River Valley Assn., 1973-75, So. Bapt. Conv. Home Mission Bd., 1969-74, Tenn. Bapt. Children's Home, 1975—, Met. Council Community Services, 1971-75, Chattanooga-Hamilton County Regional Planning Commn., 1971-75; chmn. Miller Park Bd. 1974—, Greater Chattanooga Bicentennial Commn., 1974-76; treas. Human Services Inst. for Children and Families. Served to lt. USNR, 1943-46, 51-52. Recipient Silver Beaver award Boy Scouts Am., 1966; Citizenship award Chattanooga Realtors, 1966, George Washington Honor medals for addresses Freedom Found., 1966-70; Outstanding Salesman at Large award Chattanooga Sales and Mktg. Execs., 1969; Sertoma Internat. Service to Mankind award, 1969; Citizen of Year award Chattanooga Edn. Assn., 1970; Patriotic Civilian Service award Dept. Army, 1975. Fellow Am. Bar Found.; mem. Nat. Conf. Bar Presidents, Tenn. (pres. 1965-66, gov. 1963-67), Chattanooga (gov. 1959-64, pres. 1962-63) bar assns., Chattanooga C. of C. (dir. 1969-75), Estate Planning Council Chattanooga (exec. bd. 1960-62), Internat. Platform Assn., Order of Coif, Sigma Nu Phi. Baptist (deacon). Clubs: Mountain City, Optimist (pres. 1958-59, dist. lt. gov. 1959-60, Man of Year award 1956 Chattanooga). Home: 3019 Brownwood Dr Chattanooga TN 37404 Office: Maclellan Bldg Chattanooga TN 37402

WALKER, ROBERT MOWBRAY, educator, physicist; b. Phila., Feb. 6, 1929; s. Robert and Margaret (Seivwright) W.; B.S. in Physics, Union Coll., 1950, D.Sc., 1967; M.S., Yale, 1951, Ph.D., 1954; D.h.c., Université de Clermont-Ferrand, 1975; m. Alice J. Agedal, Sept. 2, 1951 (div. 1973); children—Eric, Mark; m. 2d, Ghislaine Crozaz, Aug. 24, 1973. Physicist, Gen. Electric Research Lab., Schenectady, 1954-62, 63-66; McDonnell prof. physics Washington U., St. Louis, 1966—, dir. McDonnell Center for Space Scis., 1975—. Vis. prof. U. Paris, 1962-63; adj. prof. metallurgy Rensselaer Poly. Inst., 1958, adj. prof. physics, 1965-66; vis. prof. physics and geology Calif. Inst. Tech., 1972. Pres., Vols. for Internat. Tech. Assistance, 1960-62, 65-66, founder, 1960, bd. dirs., 1961—; mem. Lunar Sample Analysis Planning Team, 1968-70, Lunar Sample Rev. Bd., 1970-72; adv. com. Lunar Sci. Inst., 1972-75; mem. temporary nominating group in planetary scis. Nat. Acad. Scis., 1973-75, bd. on sci. and tech. for internat. devel. 1974—, com. planetary and lunar exploration, 1978—. Bd. dirs. Univs. Space Research Assn., 1969-71. Recipient Distinguished Service award Am. Nuclear Soc., 1964, Yale Engring. Assn. award for contbn. to basic and applied sci., 1966, Indsl. Research awards, 1964, 65; Exceptional Sci. Achievement award NASA, 1970; E.O. Lawrence award AEC, 1971; NSF fellow, 1962-63. Fellow Am. Phys. Soc., Meteoritical Soc., AAAS; mem. Am. Geophys. Union, Am. Astron. Soc., Nat. Acad. Scis. Research and publs. on cosmic rays, nuclear physics, geophysics, radiation effects in solids, particularly devel. solid state track detectors and their application to geophysics and nuclear physics problems; discovery of fossil particle tracks in terrestrial and extra-terrestrial materials and fission track method of dating; application of phys. scis. to art and archaeology. Home: 3 Romany Park Ln Olivette MO 63132

WALKER, ROBERT SMITH, congressman; b. Bradford, Pa., Dec. 23, 1942; s. Joseph Eddman and Rachel Viola (Smith) W.; B.S., Millersville (Pa.) State Coll., 1964; M.A. in Polit. Sci., U. Del., 1968; m. Sue Ellen Albertson, Apr. 13, 1968. Tchr., Penn Manor High Sch., Lancaster, Pa., 1964-67; legis. asst. to Congressman Edwin D. Eshleman, 1967-74, adminstrv. asst., 1974-76; mem. 95th-96th Congresses from 16th Dist. Pa. Pres. trustees Bethany Presbyn. Ch., Lancaster, 1975; mem. exec. com. Lancaster County Young Republicans, 1964-67; vice chmn. Lancaster County Rep. Party, 1975-76; dir. Inaugural Ball, 1973; press room dir. Rep. Nat. Conv., 1973. Recipient award in writing Freedoms Found., 1973. Am. Legion, Lancaster County Hist. Soc. Clubs: Capitol Hill, Old Hickory Racquet, Elks, Kiwanis (hon.). Co-author: Congress—The Pennsylvania Dutch Representatives, 1774-1974, Can You Afford This House, 1978; author articles. Home: 6065 Parkridge Dr East Petersburg PA 17520 Office: 1028 Longworth House Office Bldg Washington DC 20515. *When you decide to seek public office, you accept a trust. The responsibilities of that trust involve not only your talents, your wisdom and your energies, but also your integrity, your character and your commitment to a better tomorrow.*

WALKER, RONALD EDWARD, educator, psychologist; b. East St. Louis, Ill., Jan. 23, 1935; s. George Edward and Marnella (Altmeyer) W.; B.S., St. Louis U., 1957; M.A., Northwestern U., 1959, Ph.D., 1961; m. Aldona M. Mogenis, Oct. 4, 1958; children—Regina, Mark, Paula, Alexis. Lectr. psychology Northwestern U., 1959-61; faculty dept. psychology Loyola U., Chgo., 1961—, asst., then asso. prof., 1961-68, prof., chmn. dept., 1965—, acting dean Coll. Arts and Scis., 1973-74, dean, 1974—. Cons. VA, Chgo., 1965—; Am. Psychol. Assn.-NIMH vis. cons., 1969; vis. scientist Am. Psychol. Assn. NSF, 1968; Cook County (Ill.) rep. from Ill. Psychol. Assn., 1969—. Mem. Am. (council rep., 1970-72), Ill. (chmn. student devel. com. 1965-67, chmn. acad. sec. 1966-67), Midwestern psychol. assns., AAAS, Sigma Xi, Psi Chi. Contbr. articles to profl. jours. Home: 2712 Park Pl Evanston IL 60201 Office: 6525 N Sheridan Rd Chicago IL 60626

WALKER, RONALD H., event mgmt. and polit. cons. co. exec.; b. Bryan, Tex., July 25, 1937; s. Walter Hugh and Maxine (Tarver) W.; B.A., U. Ariz., 1960; m. Anne Lucille Collins, Aug. 8, 1959; children—Lisa, Marjorie, Lynne. With Allstate Ins. Co., Pasadena, Calif., 1964-67, Hudson Oxygen Therapy Sales Co., Los Angeles, 1967-69; asst. to sec. interior, 1969-70; staff asst. to Pres. U.S., dir. White House Advance Office, 1970-72, spl. asst. to Pres., 1972-73; dir. Nat. Park Service, Washington, 1973-75; cons. Saudi Arabia, 1975; asso. dir. World Championship Tennis, 1975-77; pres. Ron Walker & Assocs., Inc., Dallas, 1977—. Served with U.S. Army, 1961-64. Recipient Distinguished Citizen award U. Ariz., 1973, Outstanding Service award Dept. Interior, 1975. Mem. Phi Delta Theta. Republican. Methodist. Home: 7231 Hillwood Ln Dallas TX 75248 Office: 2731 Lemmon Ave E Suite 320 Dallas TX 75204

WALKER, RUSSELL T., lawyer, corp. exec.; b. Ft. William, Ont., Can., Sept. 9, 1914; s. Joseph Henry and Elissa Jane (Mutart) W.; A.B., U. Mich., 1936, J.D., 1939; m. Miriam O'Loughlin, Apr. 5, 1941; children—Margaret Ellen, Terry Jo, Mary Elissa, Wendy Ann. Admitted to Mich., N.Y., Ill., Pa., Iowa bars; legal research clk. Michigan Supreme Court, 1939-40; law clk. N.Y. Central R.R., Detroit, 1941-42, atty. 1942-45, asst. gen. atty., 1945-51, asst. to sec. N.Y. Central, 1951-52, asst. sec., 1952, sec., 1952-54 gen. counsel Mcht. Despatch Transp. Corp. and Northern Refrigerator Line, Chgo., 1954-55; treas. Nat. U.S. Radiator Corp., Johnstown, Pa., 1955-60; v.p., gen. mgr. Montgomery Ward Credit Corp., 1960-61; v.p. adminstrn. A. Y. McDonald Mfg. Co., Dubuque, Iowa, 1961-62, pres., treas., dir., 1962-69; chmn. bd. Brock-McVey, Inc., 1969; v.p., gen. mgr. Acme Industries (Rheem Mfg. Co.), Jackson, Mich., 1971—; v.p. Midwest Bank, 1974—. Mem. Am. Bar Assn., Phi Sigma Kappa. Club: Jackson Country. Home: 5500 Browns Lake Rd Jackson MI 49203 Office: One Midwest Center Jackson MI 49202

WALKER, SAMUEL SLOAN, JR., publishing co. exec.; b. N.Y.C., Nov. 2, 1926; s. Samuel Sloan and Audrey (Riker) W.; student Buckley Sch., 1932-39; grad. with honors Groton Sch., 1944; B.A. with honors, Yale, 1948; m. Beth Bready, Oct. 28, 1961; children—Samuel Sloan III, Randolph Ramsey, Timothy Taggart. Vol. ambulance driver Am. Field Service, France and Germany, 1945; war corr. N.Y. Post, Paris, 1945-46; asst. to research dir. Time, Inc., N.Y.C., 1949-51; v.p. Free Europe Com., N.Y.C., dir. Free Europe Press, 1951-59; pres. Walker & Co., N.Y.C., 1959—, Tennfort Corp., N.Y.C. Bd. dirs., chmn. exec. com. Am. Field Service; trustee, sec. St. Bernard's Sch. Mem. Brookfield Hist. Soc., Phi Beta Kappa. Clubs: Century, Yale (N.Y.C.); Rumson (N.J.) Country. Home: 17 Old Bridge Rd Brookfield CT 06804 Office: Walker Pub Co Inc 720 Fifth Ave New York NY 10019

WALKER, SANDRA, mezzo soprano; b. Richmond, Va., Oct. 1, 1946; d. Phillip Loth and Mary Jane Walker; Mus.B., U. N.C., 1969; m. Melvin Brown, May 17, 1975. Debut, San Francisco Opera, 1972, Chgo. Lyric Opera, 1973, Washington Opera Soc., 1973, Phila. Lyric Opera, 1973; leading mezzo soprano at N.Y.C. Opera, 1974—; singer in major U.S. and European music festivals Tanglewood, Caramoor, Spoleto-U.S.A. and Spoleto Festival of Two Worlds in Italy; appeared in Pub. Broadcasting System nat. telecasts Live From Lincoln Center series The Saint of Bleecker Street, Manon and The Ballad of Baby Doe, on Great Performances in The Consul; orchestral appearances with Nat. Symphony, Washington, St. Louis Symphony, Chgo. Symphony, Richmond (Va.) Symphony; recorded Ned Rorem's song cycle King Midas on Desto Records, 1974. Recipient Nat. Endowment for Arts Affiliate Artist grant sponsored by Va. Opera Assn. and Sears Roebuck Co., 1978. Office: care Kuzuko Hillyer Internat Inc 250 W 57th St New York NY 10019

WALKER, THEODORE ROSCOE, educator; b. Madison, Wis., Feb. 8, 1921; s. Theodore and Hazel (Tetzlaff) W.; Ph.B., U. Wis., 1947, Ph.D., 1952; m. Barbara Ann Simonsen, June 11, 1949; children—Lynn Diane, Bruce David, Scott Cameron, Ann Leslie. Geologist, Ill. Geo. Survey, 1952-53; mem. faculty U. Colo., Boulder, 1953—, prof. geology, 1965—, chmn. dept. geol. scis., 1972-75. Vis. research prof. Geologisches Institut, Eidg. Technische Hochschule, Zurich, Switzerland, 1968-69. Served from ensign to lt. (j.g.) USNR, 1944-46. Recipient U. Colo. Research Lectureship award, 1973. NSF sr. fellow Scripps Instn. Oceanography, 1962-63. Fellow Geol. Soc. Am., AAAS; mem. Am. Assn. Petroleum Geologists (Distinguished lectr. 1965), Soc. Econ. Paleontologists and Mineralogists. Home: 2805 16th St Boulder CO 80302

WALKER, VINCENT HENRY, govt. ofcl.; b. Lowell, Mass., Oct. 14, 1915; s. Daniel Henry and Annie Jane (Gookin) W.; J.D., Boston Coll. Law, 1939; B.C.S., Benjamin Franklin U., 1951; m. Irene Iris Johnson, Nov. 16, 1946; children—Patricia Anne (Mrs. John Armstrong III), J. Melinda (Mrs. Gaetano Monterosso). Admitted to Mass. bar, 1940, Fed. Tax Ct. bar, 1952, U.S. Supreme Ct. bar, 1965, D.C. bar, 1980; partner firm, 1940-42; gen. mgr., counsel, joint venture land and subdiv. devels. and sales South and Southwestern U.S., 1946-60; FHA regional atty., Southeastern U.S. and Virgin Islands, later FHA Washington Hdqrs. and Mid Atlantic region, 1960, zone ops. exec. asst., Southwestern U.S., 1960-61; AID State Dept. contract specialist, chief comml. contracts br., adviser to Govt. of Sudan for contract negotiations, developed conversion of AID contracts to Automatic Data Processing System in Vietnam, AID Office of Contract Services, Washington, 1961-69; internat. trade policy specialist, chief trade policy br., dir. (acting) indsl. resources div., AID Office of Procurement, 1969-72; internat. trade specialist, agrl. commoditiies mgr., procurement support div. Office of Commodity Mgmt., AID, 1972-75; contract specialist, mem. interagency procurement policy com. Office Contracts Mgmt., 1975—. Hon. mem. bd. dirs. Am. Opera Scholarship Soc.; contbr. incorporating atty. Lowell Light Opera Guild, 1942. Served to lt. comdr. USNR, Overseas, 1942-46. Named hon. citizen City of Lexington (Ky.), 1970. Mem. Lowell, Middlesex County, Mass., D.C. bar assns., Nat. Trust for Historic Preservation, Smithsonian Assos., Wolf Trap Assos., D.A.V. Author and interagy. collaborator AID govt. and world-wide legal and regulatory publs., export program directives, notices to U.S. industry, internat. posts and orgns., 1970—; author, pub. weekly Agrl. Commodity Supply, Price, Trends, Report, 1972-75. Founding editor Keith Acad. Alumni mag., 1940-42. Photog. works published various media in U.S. and fgn. countries. 1970—. Home: 9908 Julliard Dr Bethesda MD 20034 Office: AID State Dept SER/CM Washington DC 20523. *I have so far discerned only one essential ingredient in most prescriptions for "success." The essential ingredient is persistence. While this means that you never give up, it is not the mindless determination of he who "picks himself up, dust himself off, and starts all over again" — probably to get knocked down again, and so establish a pattern of failure if not self destruction. No, persistence toward success means persistence in flexible responses, resourceful efforts, or creative solutions, — that move you toward your goal.*

WALKER, WADE HAMPTON, athletic dir.; b. Mocksville, N.C., Nov. 29, 1923; s. George Goode and Ella Pauline (Hendricks) W.; B.A., U. Okla., 1949; m. Nancy Jean Herman, Aug. 5, 1948; children—Carol, Ronald, Gary, Anne, Winfield. Asst. football coach N.C. State U., 1950; asst. football coach Tex. Tech. U., 1950-53; asst. football coach Miss. State U., 1954-57, head coach, 1957-63, athletic dir., 1965-70; athletic dir. U. Okla., Norman, 1970—. Served with USNR, 1943-46. Democrat. Presbyterian. Home: 1810 Thorton Norman OK 73069 Office: 180 W Brooks Norman OK 73019

WALKER, WALDO SYLVESTER, coll. dean; b. Fayette, Iowa, June 12, 1931; s. Waldo S. and Mildred (Littelle) W.; B.S. cum laude, Upper Iowa U., Fayette, 1953, M.S., 1957; Ph.D., U. Iowa, 1959; m. Marie J. Olsen, July 27, 1952; children—Martha Lynn, Gayle Ann. Mem. faculty Grinnell (Ia.) Coll., 1958—, prof. biology, 1968—, asso. dean coll., 1963-65, dean adminstrn., 1969-73, exec. v.p., 1973-77, dean coll., 1973—, provost, 1977—. Served with AUS, 1953-55. Mem. Am. Assn. Higher Edn., Am. Assn. Colls., Am. Conf. Acad. Deans (nat. chmn. 1977-78), Sigma Xi. Author articles on plant physiology, ultrastructural cytology. Home: 1702 Country Club Dr Grinnell IA 50112

WALKER, WARREN STANLEY, educator; b. Bklyn., Mar. 19, 1921; s. Harold Stanley and Althea (Luscher) W.; B.A., State U. N.Y., Albany, 1947, M.A., 1948; Ph.D., Cornell U., 1951; m. Barbara Jeanne Kerlin, Dec. 9, 1943; children—Brian, Theresa. Prof., chmn. dept. English, Blackburn Coll., Carlinville, Ill., 1951-59; prof., dean arts and scis. Parsons Coll., Fairfield, Iowa, 1959-64; Fulbright lectr. Am. lit. Ankara (Turkey) U., 1961-62; prof. English, Tex. Tech U., Lubbock, 1964—, Horn prof., 1972—; dir. Archive Turkish Oral Narrative, 1971; adv. council Tex. Cultural Alliance, 1975. Served with USAAF, 1943-45. Recipient Tex. Writers award, 1967; citation Turkish Ministry Edn., 1967, Turkish Ministry State, 1973; research grantee Am. Council Learned Socs., 1973, 79, Am. Philos. Soc., 1974, Tex. Tech U., 1971-74, 76. Mem. Modern Lang. Assn., Am. Folklore Soc., Nat. Council Tchrs. English, Internat. Soc. Folk Narrative Research, Middle East Studies Assn., Turkish Studies Assn. Author: Nigerian Folktales, 1961; Twentieth-Century Short Story Explocation, 7 vols., 1961-77; James Fenimore Cooper, 1962; Leatherstocking and the Critics, 1965; Tales Alive in Turkey, 1966; Archive of Turkish Oral Narrative: Catalogue 1, 1975; Plots and Characters in the Fiction of J.F. Cooper, 1978; editorial bd. Definitive Edit. Works of James Fenimore Cooper, 1968; bibliographer Studies in Short Fiction, 1973. Home: 3703 66th St Lubbock TX 79413 Office: Dept English Tex Tech U Lubbock TX 79409

WALKER, WESLEY M., lawyer; b. Union, S.C., Jan. 28, 1915; s. John Frost and Cornelia (Greer) W.; A.B., U. S.C., 1936, LL.B., 1938; m. Martha Bratton, Nov. 8, 1941; children—Martha Bratton, Wesley M., Nancy F. Admitted to S.C. bar, 1938; now partner firm Leatherwood, Walker, Todd & Mann, Greenville, S.C.; city atty., Greenville, 1949-51; spl. circuit judge York County, 6th Jud. Circuit, 1962. Served to lt. USNR, 1941-45. Mem. Am. (ho. of dels. 1952-54, 72—, mem. com. law lists 1955-68, chmn. 1965-68), S.C. (state del. 1973-77, gov. 1976—), Greenville (pres. 1973) bar assns., Phi Delta Phi. Home: 233 Camille Ave Greenville SC 29605 Office: 217 E Coffee St Greenville SC 29602

WALKER, WILBERT ALDEN, steel co. exec.; b. Pitts., July 26, 1910; s. Alden B. and Anna C. (Miller) W.; B.S., U. Pitts., 1931; m. Ruth V. Kercher, Apr. 17, 1938; 1 dau., Virginia Ann. Chief accounting officer Pitts. Meat Packing Co., 1931-34; audit staff Ernst & Ernst, 1934-40; sales and systems staff IBM Corp., 1940-41; with Carnegie-Ill. Steel Corp., 1941—, v.p. accounting, 1949—, also dir.; v.p. accounting U.S. Steel Corp., Pitts., 1951—, v.p., comptroller, N.Y.C., 1956-59, adminstrv. v.p., controller, 1959-67, exec. v.p., comptroller, 1959-69, vice chmn. finance com., comptroller, 1969—, chmn. finance com., 1970-73, pres., 1973-75, now dir.; dir. Marsh McLennon Corp., Moller S.S. Co., Chem. N.Y. Corp., Chem. Bank, Am. Standard Inc. C.P.A., Pa. Mem. Fin. Execs. Inst., Am., Pa. insts. C.P.A.'s. Author: (with W.R. Davies) Industrial Internal Auditing, 1951. Home: Belleair FL 33516 Office: US Steel Corp Gen Motors Bldg 767 Fifth Ave New York NY 10022

WALKER, WILBUR GORDON, educator, physician; b. Lena, La., Sept. 18, 1926; s. Daniel Clark and Ettie (Hodnett) W.; student La. State U., 1942-44, 46-47, La. Coll., 1947; M.D., Tulane U., 1951; m. Betty Couch, Aug. 23, 1947; children—Wilbur Gordon, Martha Jane, Joseph Marshall, Carla Frances. Intern, Johns Hopkins Hosp., Balt., 1951-52, asst. resident 1953-54, fellow in medicine, 1954-56, resident physician, 1956-57, physician, 1957—, dir. Clin. Research Center, 1960—; resident Charity Hosp., New Orleans, 1952-53; faculty Johns Hopkins U. Sch. Medicine, 1956—, prof., 1968—, chmn. com. on clin. investigation, 1964-71, ednl. policy com., 1976—, dir. renal div., 1958—; attending physician Balt. City Hosp., 1960—; dir. Dept. Research Medicine Good Samaritan Hosp., Balt., 1968—, chmn, med. bd., 1972-74. Mem. clin. research centers com. NIH, mem. renal disease and urology grants com., 1968-76, chmn. clin. research centers com., 1975-76, hon. cons. physician Royal Prince Alfred Hosp., Sydney NSW Australia, 1968—; chmn. Council on Research Md. Heart Assn., 1963-64; chmn. Med. adv. bd. Md. Kidney Found., 1966-68; mem. Md. Gov.'s Commn. on Kidney Disease, 1970—; chmn. Md. Kidney Commn., 1975—. Trustee Md. Heart Assn. Served with USNR, 1944-45. Mem. Am. Fedn. Clin. Research, Am. Physiol. Soc., Am. Soc. Clin. Investigation, Am. Soc. Nephrology, Council for High Blood Pressure Research, Am. Clin. and Climatol. Assn., Am. Coll. Physicians, Interurban Clin. Club. Club: Peripatetic. Author articles on renal physiology, capillary permeability, electrolyte metabolism, hypertension and clin. medicine. Editorial adv. bd. Am. Jour. Medicine, 1975—; editorial bd. Kidney Internat., 1978—; sect. editor Principles and Practice of Medicine, 17th-19th edits. Home: 3812 Fenchurch Rd Baltimore MD 21218

WALKER, WILLIAM, baritone; b. Waco, Tex., Oct. 29, 1931; s. William Wallace and Ruby (Barton) W.; B.Mus., Tex. Christian U., 1956; m. Marci Martin, May 25, 1957; children—Nancy, David, Thomas, John. Performer various Broadway, summer stock and indsl. shows, 1951-62; appeared with Met. Opera, N.Y.C., 1962—; roles include Figaro in Barber of Seville, Ashton in Lucia, Valentin in Faust, Germont in La Traviata, Marcello in La Boheme, Luna in Trovatore, Malatesta in Don Pasquale, High Priest in Samson, Sharpless in Madam Butterfly, Yeletsky in Queen of Spades, Lescaut in Manon Lescaut; solo concerts with N.Y.C., Cleve., Chgo., Pitts., Denver, Minn., Milw., San Antonio, Ft. Worth symphonies, 1965—; on tour with Met. Opera, Japan, 1975, with State Dept., Sweden, Denmark, Iceland, 1976; 1st Am. to sing at Grand Teatr, Lodz, Poland, 1976. Served with AUS, 1952-54. Decorated Bronze Star; named Distinguished Alumnus, Tex. Christian U., 1970. Clubs: Dutch Treat, Lotos (N.Y.C.); Canyon Creek Country (San Antonio). Home: 209 Lariat Dr San Antonio TX 78216 Office: Met Opera House New York NY 10023

WALKER, WILLIAM BOND, librarian; b. Brownsville, Tenn., Apr. 15, 1930; s. Marshall Francis and Mary Louise (Taylor) W.; B.A., State U. Iowa, 1953; M.L.S., Rutgers U., 1958, Librarian-trainee Donnell br. N.Y. Public Library, N.Y.C., 1955-57; reference librarian/cataloger Met. Mus. Art, N.Y.C., 1957-59; chief librarian Bklyn. Mus., 1959-64; chief librarian Library of Nat. Collection Fine Arts and Nat. Portrait Gallery, Smithsonian Instn., Washington, 1964—. Ralph Beals Meml. scholar N.Y. Public Library, 1956. Mem. Art Libraries Soc. N.Am. (nat. chmn. 1975), ALA, Spl. Libraries Assn., Coll. Art Assn., Phi Beta Kappa. Author: annotated bibliography: American Sculpture, 18th-20th Century, 1979. Home: 3325 N 23d Rd Arlington VA 22201 Office: Library Nat Collection Fine Arts and Nat Portrait Gallery NCFA/NPG Bldg Smithsonian Instn Washington DC 20560

WALKER, WILLIAM D., electronics co. exec.; b. Howell County, Mo., Sept. 28, 1930; s. Earl T. and Grace Millicent W.; B.S. in Elec. Engring., U. Mo., Rolla, 1958; m. Lula F. DeBoard. With Tektronix Inc., Beaverton, Oreg., 1958—, v.p. engring. and product planning, 1969-71, group v.p. research and engring., 1971-75, group v.p. test and measurement group, 1975-79, exec. v.p., chief operating officer, 1979—; dir. SONY/Tektronix Corp; mem. Internat. Electrotech. Com.; tech. adviser NSF; bd. dirs. Grass Valley group Oreg. Grad. Center for Study and Research. Served with USAF, 1951-55. Mem. Sci. Apparatus Mfrs. Assn. (dir.), Am. Electronics Assn., Electro Sci. Industries, IEEE. Office: Tektronix Inc PO Box 500 Beaverton OR 97077

WALKER, WILLIAM DELANY, educator; b. Dallas, Nov. 1923; s. William Delany and Mildred (Ramsey) W.; B.A., Rice U., 1944; Ph.D., Cornell U., 1949; m. Suzanne Porter, Dec. 23, 1946; children—Nancy, Elizabeth, Samuel; m. 2d, Constance Kalbach, Oct. 10, 1975. Asst. prof. Rice U., 1949-52; lectr. U. Calif. at Berkeley, 1951-52; asst. prof. U. Rochester, 1952-54; prof. physics U. Wis., Madison, 1954-71, chmn. dept., 1964-66, Max Mason prof., 1968-71; prof. physics Duke, 1971—, chmn. dept., 1975—. Chmn., ZGS user's group Argonne Lab., 1964-66; mem. physics panel NSF, 1965-67; mem. exec. com. Users Group, Fermi Nat. Accelerator Lab., 1972-75, chmn., 1973-74; bd. dirs. Oak Ridge Asso. Univs., 1980—. Served as ensign USNR, 1944-45. Mem. Am. Phys. Soc. (exec. com. div. particles and fields), Phi Beta Kappa, Sigma Xi, Phi Kappa Phi. Episcopalian (deacon). Home: 907 Green St Durham NC 27701. *My life was renewed and rebuilt at age 35 by Jesus Christ. Any success I may have had is due to him.*

WALKER, WILLIAM LAURENS, lawyer, educator; b. Spartanburg, S.C., Feb. 11, 1937; s. William Laurens and Georgia B. W.; A.B., Davidson Coll., 1959; J.D., Duke U., 1963; S.J.D., Harvard U., 1970; m. Marjo Vogl, Mar. 13, 1965; children—Helgard, Margit. Admitted to Ga. bar, 1964, D.C. bar, 1966, N.C. bar, 1972; asso. firm Sutherland, Asdill and Brennan, Atlanta, 1963, 65-67; Eaton prof. law U. N.C., 1968-78; prof. law U. Va., Charlottesville, 1978—. Served to capt., U.S. Army, 1963-65. Author: (with John Thibaut) Procedural Justice, 1975. Office: Sch of Law Univ of Va Charlottesville VA 22901

WALKER, WILLIAM NICKERSON, lawyer, former diplomat; b. Newton, Mass., Apr. 3, 1938; s. Albert Nickerson and Helen Faye (Jackson) W.; B.A. cum laude, Wesleyan U., Middletown, Conn., 1960; J.D., U. Va., 1963; m. Janet Mason Smith, June 21, 1961; children—Gilbert Nickerson, Helen Anne. Admitted to Ill. bar, 1963, D.C. bar, 1978, N.Y. State bar, 1978: asso. firm Price, Cushman, Keck & Mahin, Chgo., 1963-69; chief evaluation and planning Office Legal Services, OEO, Washington, 1969-70, spl. counsel, 1970, acting dep. gen. counsel, 1970-71; dep. dir. White House Office Consumer Affairs, 1971-72; gen. counsel Cost of Living Council, Washington, 1972-74; gen. counsel Fed. Energy Office, Washington, 1974; dir. Presdl. Personnel Office, White House, 1974-75; ambassador, dep. spl. rep. for trade negotiations, Geneva, Switzerland, 1975-77; counsel firm Mudge, Rose, Guthrie & Alexander, N.Y.C., 1977-78, partner, 1978—; Founder, pres. Chgo. Lions Rugby Football Club, 1963-65; founder, exec. sec. Midwest Rugby Football Union, Chgo., 1963-65. Mem. Am., Chgo. bar assns., Psi Upsilon. Republican. Clubs: Mystical Seven; Larchmont Yacht. Home: 1 Dundee Rd Larchmont NY 10538 Office: 20 Broad St New York NY 10005

WALKER, WILLIAM TIDD, JR., investment banker; b. Detroit, Sept. 5, 1931; s. William Tidd and Irene (Rhode) W.; student Stanford, 1950; m. Patricia Louise Frazier, Sept. 10, 1953; children—Donna Louise, Carol Ann, Sally Lynn, Alyssa Jane. Rep., William R. Staats & Co., Los Angeles, 1952-57, sales mgr., 1957-58, syndicate partner, 1958-65; sr. v.p. Glore Forgan, William R. Staats Inc., N.Y.C., 1965-68; partner, exec. com. Lester, Ryons & Co., Los Angeles, 1968; sr. v.p., dir. Bateman Eichler, Hill Richards Inc., Los Angeles, 1969—, mng. dir., 1978—; pres., dir. Delhi Co., Los Angeles, 1973—; pres., dir. Kingo Farms Inc., Los Angeles, 1973—; dir. Bayliner Marine Corp. Served with USAF, 1949-52. Mem. Securities Industry Assn. (nat. syndicate com., chmn. Calif. Dist. 10), Pacific Coast Stock Exchange (bd. govs. 1971-72), Investment Bankers Assn. (nat. pub. relations com. 1966—), Nat. Assn. Security Dealers, Bond Club Los Angeles (pres. 1973—), Stock Exchange Club Los Angeles. Clubs: Calif. Yacht, St. Francis Yacht, Newport Harbor Yacht. Home: 812 Birchwood Dr Los Angeles CA 90024 Office: Bateman Eichler Hill Richards Inc 700 S Flower St Los Angeles CA 90017

WALKER, WYATT TEE, clergyman; b. Brockton, Mass., Aug. 16, 1929; s. John Wise and Maude (Pinn) W.; B.S. magna cum laude, Va. Union U., 1950, M.Div. summa cum laude, 1953, L.H.D., 1967; Ph.D., Colgate-Rochester Div. Sch., 1975; m. Theresa Edwards, Dec. 24, 1950; children—Ann Patrice, Wyatt Tee, Jr., Robert Charles, Earl Maurice. Ordained to ministry Baptist Ch., 1952; minister Historic Gillfield Baptist Ch., Petersburg, Va., 1953-60; chief of staff to Dr. Martin Luther King, Jr., v.p. bd., exec. dir. So. Christian Leadership Conf., Atlanta, 1960-64; minister Abyssinian Baptist Ch., N.Y.C., 1965-66; spl. asst. on urban affairs to Gov., N.Y.C., 1965-75; resident minister, chief exec. officer Cannan Baptist Ch. of Christ, N.Y.C., 1967—; pub. Negro Heritage Library, Yonkers, N.Y., 1965-67; vis. prof. Princeton Theol. Sem., 1970-72, 77; vis. prof. polit. sci. N.Y. U., 1971-72, 74-75; adj. prof. N.Y. Theol. Sem., N.Y.C., 1973-74, 74-75. Del. World Conf. on Religion and Peace, Japan, 1969; mem. World Peace Council, 1971—. Recipient numerous human rights awards including Elks, 1963; Nat. Alpha award in civil rights, 1965; Nat. Civil Rights award Shriners, 1974; Civil Rights award Am. Dental Assn., 1975. Author: Black Church Looks at the Bicentennial; Hush, Somebody's Calling My Name. Home: 108 W 120th St New York City NY 10026 Office: 132 W 116th St New York City NY 10026

WALKER-HURST, JOAN, psychologist; b. Macomb, Ill., Apr. 15, 1924; d. Ricey Allen and Clara (Harlan) Walker; B.S. in Edn., Western Ill. U., 1944; M.A. in English, U. Chgo., 1957; M.S. in Psychology, Roosevelt U., 1972; Ph.D. in Psychology, Ill. Inst. Tech., 1974; children by previous marriage—Natalie H. Hurst, Kevin W. Hurst, Jason T. Hurst. Reporter, feature writer Champaign (Ill.) News-Gazette, 1944-46; tchr. English public jr. high schs., Berwyn, Ill., 1946-48, Blue Island, Ill., 1948-50; TV script writer Schwimmer and Scott Agy., Chgo., 1950-53; analyst, editor, 1st v.p. Worthington Hurst and Assos., Inc., Chgo., 1963-73; lectr. Roosevelt U. and North Central Coll., 1973-76; counselor dept. psychology Ill. Inst. Tech., 1974-76, affirmative action officer, inst. archivist, 1976—. Mem. AAAS, Am. Psychol. Assn., Midwest Psychol. Assn., Ill. Psychol. Assn., Chgo. Farmers, AAUW, Sigma Xi. Home: 3100 S Michigan Ave Chicago IL 60616 Office: Room 223 Perlstein Hall Ill Inst Tech Chicago IL 60616

WALKONEN, HELVI ESTHER, librarian; b. Skandia, Mich., Dec. 16, 1925; d. William and Selma (Lindbergh) W.; A.B., No. Mich. U., 1946; M.A. in English, U. Mich., 1951, M.L.S., 1955. Tchr., Manistique (Mich.) High Sch., 1946-47, 49-52, Ishpeming (Mich.) High Sch., 1947-49, Munich, Germany, 1953-54; head librarian

Grosse Pointe (Mich.) High Sch., 1955-63; reference librarian No. Mich. U., 1963-64, head librarian, 1964—, asso. prof. Mem. Am., Mich. library assns., Marquette County Hist. Soc., Zonta, Alpha Delta Kappa, Delta Kappa Gamma, Phi Delta Kappa. Club: Marquette Economic. Home: 1947 Granite St Marquette MI 49855

WALKUP, BRUCE, lawyer; b. Berkeley, Calif., Sept. 26, 1914; s. William Wallace and Florence L. (Fitch) W.; B.A., U. Calif., 1935; LL.B., Boalt Hall Law, Berkeley, 1938; m. Betty Makins, Mar. 31, 1939; 1 dau., Joan Walkup Richardson. Admitted to Calif. bar, 1939; pvt. practice, Oakland, 1939-41, San Francisco, 1941—; partner firm Walkup, Downing, Shelby, Bastian, Melodia, Kelly & O'Reilly, and predecessors, 1959—. Diplomate Am. Bd. Trial Advocates (named Trial Lawyer of Year 1969). Fellow Am. Coll. Trial Lawyers, Internat. Acad. Trial Lawyers; mem. Am., San Francisco bar assns., Calif. State Bar, Am. Trial Lawyers Assn., Inner Circle Advocates (pres. 1977-78), Am. Bd. Product Liability Attys., Beta Theta Pi, Phi Delta Phi. Republican. Clubs: San Francisco Golf, Olympic, Lakeside Golf, Bankers. Contbr. articles to profl. jours., lectr., panelist trial procedures. Address: 650 California St 30th Floor San Francisco CA 94108. *I have 2 basic beliefs: A deal is a deal; nothing is too good for a friend.*

WALKUP, JOHN HARPER, educator; b. Jackson, Miss., Jan. 20, 1915; s. Robert Lee and Margaret (Caldwell) W.; A.B., Westminster Coll., Fulton, Mo., 1937; student U. Miss., 1937-39; Ph.D., Western Res. U., 1943; m. Iveene Jackson, Feb. 20, 1943; 1 son, John Harper. Research chemist Pa. Salt Co., 1943-45; mem. faculty Centre Coll., Danville, Ky., 1945—, prof. chemistry, 1952—, head dept., 1961-67. Moderator Transylvania Presbytery. Mem. Danville City Council, 1954-56. Trustee Presbyn. Children's Homes, 1952-60. Petroleum research grantee, 1960-67; NSF grantee, 1962—; T.A.P.P.I. grantee, 1961—. Mem. Am. Chem. Soc., Am. Electro-Chem. Soc., Faraday Soc., Ky. Acad. Sci., Sigma Xi, Phi Beta Kappa, Phi Delta Theta, Omicron Delta Kappa. Presbyterian. Patentee continuous starch enzymatic conversion process. Office: Centre Coll Danville KY 40422

WALKUP, WILLIAM EDMONDSON, business exec.; b. Nashville, May 31, 1918; s. John Pegram and Marion (Edmondson) W.; student U. Calif. at Los Angeles, 1936-38; m. Dorothy Elizabeth Sanborn, Sept. 2, 1939; children—William Sanborn, Marion Elena, Frank Sanborn. With Signal Oil & Gas Co., Los Angeles, 1939—, dir. finance dept., 1955—, group v.p. staff, 1962-64, sr. exec. v.p., 1964-68; vice chmn. bd., exec. v.p. Signal Cos., Inc., 1968-69, chmn. bd., exec. v.p., 1969—. Clubs: Los Angeles Country; California. Home: 1140 Brooklawn Dr Los Angeles CA 90024 Office: 9665 Wilshire Blvd Beverly Hills CA 90212

WALL, ALEXANDER JAMES, mus. cons.; b. N.Y.C., Sept. 12, 1912; s. Alexander James and Lillian Bertha (Hashagen) W.; A.B., Columbia, 1934, postgrad. Am. history, 1937; m. Fannie Elizabeth Lerch, Oct. 11, 1941; 1 son, Alexander James III. Gen. asst. Met. Mus. Art, N.Y.C., 1934-35; mus. and library asst. N.Y. Hist. Soc., 1935-39, charge edn. and pub. relations, 1939-51, asst. dir., 1947-51; dir. N.J. Hist. Soc., 1951-56; curator Old Sturbridge (Mass.) Village, 1956-57, asst. dir., 1957-60, v.p., 1960-66, pres., 1966-78; cons., 1978—; dir. Savers' Coop. Bank. Mem. Scandinavian Museums Seminar, 1965. Trustee Harrington Meml. Hosp., 1960—, bd. mgrs. 1965—, v.p., 1975-78, pres., 1978—; mem. vis. com. Eleutherian Mills-Hagley Found., 1971-74, Mystic Seaport, 1976-79; adv. com. Mus. Our Nat. Heritage, Lexington, Mass. Served from pvt. to capt. USAAF, 1942-46. Recipient Gary Melchers gold medal, 1969. Mem. Am. Assn. for State and Local History (sec. 1953-60, mem. council 1960-76, v.p., 1968-70, pres. 1970-72, nat. chmn. awards com. 1964-68), Am. Antiquarian Soc., Am. Assn. Museums (council 1970-76, accreditation commn. 1970—, chmn. 1973-76), N.Y., N.J. hist. socs., Psi Upsilon. Rotarian. Clubs: Worcester (Mass.); Princeton U. (N.Y.C.). Author: William Bradford, Colonial Printer. Home: Sturbridge MA 01566

WALL, ARTHUR EDWARD PATRICK, editor; b. Jamestown, N.Y., Mar. 12, 1925; s. George Herbert and Doris (Olmstead) W.; student pub. schs.; LL.D., Rosary Coll., River Forest, Ill., 1979; m. Marcella Joan Petrine, Nov. 5, 1954; children—John Wright, Marie Ann, David Arthur Edward. Copy editor Worcester (Mass.) Telegram, 1958; Sunday editor Hawaii Island Corr., Honolulu Star-Bull., 1958-59; editor Hilo (Hawaii) Tribune-Herald, 1960-63; Sunday editor Honolulu Advertiser, 1963-65, mng. editor, 1971-72; mng. editor Cath. Rev., Balt., 1965-66, editor, 1966-71; dir. Bur. Info. Archdiocese Balt., 1965-66; dir., editor-in-chief Nat. Cath. News Service, Washington, 1972-76; editor-in-chief Origins and Cath. Trends, 1972-76, Am. Cath. Who's Who, 1974-76; editor, gen. mgr. Chgo. Cath. (formerly New World), 1976—; pres. New World Pub. Co., Inc., 1978—; dir. Our Sunday Visitor, Inc. Chmn., Hawaii Gov.'s Com. on Ednl. TV, 1964-65. Trustee, St. Mary's Seminar and U., Balt., 1975-77; bd. regents Chaminade Coll. of Honolulu, 1959-65, chmn., 1963-65. Named Hilo Young Man of Year, Jaycees, 1960; Father of Year, Honolulu C. of C., 1964. Mem. Internat. Fedn. Cath. Press Agys. (v.p. 1972-74, pres. 1974-77), Internat. Cath. Union of Press (council 1972—), Cath. Press Assn. (dir. 1977—, St. Francis de Sales award 1977), Internat. Fedn. Cath. Journalists (pres. 1977—), Sigma Delta Chi (past chpt. pres.). Roman Catholic. Clubs: Nat. Press (Washington); Overseas Press (N.Y.C.); Chgo. Press. Author: The Big Wave, 1960. Contbr. articles to mags. Home: 2100 Lincoln Park W Chicago IL 60614 Office: 155 E Superior St Chicago IL 60611. *Most of my life has consciously involved words; almost everyone is a captive of words ("fatso, nigger, turncoat, buy-now-pay-later, stupid, I love you") that trigger moods and actions almost in themselves. I guess it is the power of words, and especially the power of what most Christians call the Word, that has influenced me since a fortunate childhood in a literate household. I learned from my grandfather that a loud word limps (although I forget that once in a while), that decibel doesn't equal impact. I sometimes forget something else he taught me, that kinky four-letter words are weak and express a weakness inside. There are stronger words of the same size, such as soul and love, life and holy, good and idea, hear and talk. One who listens for those words hears something special; or to put it in a different vocabulary, God guides, and following that Guide leads to the only success there is.*

WALL, BENNETT HARRISON, educator; b. Raleigh, N.C., Dec. 7, 1914; s. Bennett Louis and Evie David (Harrison) W.; A.B., Wake Forest Coll., 1933; M.A., U. N.C., 1941, Ph.D., 1946; m. Neva White Armstrong, Sept. 7, 1968; children by previous marriage—Maie (Mrs. John E. Clark), Diana (Mrs. John Freckman), Ann Bennett. Instr., N.C. State U., 1942-43; instr. U. N.C., 1943-44; instr. U. Ky., 1944-46, asst. prof., 1946-52, asso. prof., 1952-64; prof. history dept. Tulane U., New Orleans, 1968—, head dept., 1968-73, dir. Tulane Center Bus. History Studies, 1974—. Mem. Orgn. Am. Historians, Agrl. History Soc., Bus. History Soc., Econ. History Assn., Newcomen Soc., Western History Assn., La. (pres. 1974-75), So. (sec.-treas. 1953—) hist. assns., Omicron Delta Kappa, Phi Alpha Theta. Co-author: Teagle of Jersey Standard, 1974. Contbr. numerous articles to profl. jours. Home: 6320 S Claiborne New Orleans LA 70125

WALL, BRIAN ARTHUR, sculptor; b. London, Sept. 5, 1931; s. Arthur Francis and Dorothy (Seymour) W.; student Luton (Eng.) Coll. Art, 1951; m. Sylvia Brown, Oct. 27, 1973; children—Nathaniel, Gideon. First asst. to Dame Barbara Hepworth, St. Ives, Cornwall, Eng., 1954-59; instr. Ealing Coll. Art, Middlesex, Eng., 1961-62; prin. lectr. Central Sch. Art and Design, London, 1962-72, head dept. sculpture, 1962-72; vis. lectr. U. Calif., Berkeley, 1969-73, lectr., 1973-75, asst. prof., 1975-77, asso. prof. art, 1977—; exhibited in one-man shows U. Nev., Las Vegas, 1976, Braunstein Gallery, San Francisco, 1974, 76, 78, Sculpture Now, N.Y.C., 1977, 78, Max Hutchinson Gallery, Houston, 1979; group shows include Mus. Modern Art, 1961, U. Tex., Dallas, 1976, Crocker Art Mus., Sacramento, 1979; works represented in collections at Tate Gallery, London, Mus. Art, Dublin, Art Gallery of New South Wales (Australia), Univ. Art Mus., Berkeley, Calif., U. Houston; works include Thornaby, 1968, Ali, 1978; mem. Arts Council Gt. Brit., 1969-72; trustee San Francisco Art Inst., 1974-77; mem. San Francisco Twin Bicentennial Arts Com., 1975-76. Served with RAF, 1950-52. Recipient prize BART Sculpture Competition, 1975; U. Calif. at Berkeley Humanities Research Fellowship Program grantee, 1978-79. Subject of numerous profl. articles. Home: 1824 Grant Ave San Francisco CA 94133 Office: Art Dept U Calif Berkeley CA 94720

WALL, CARROLL EDWARD, librarian, pub. co. exec.; b. Cherokee, Iowa, Mar. 3, 1942; s. Clifford R. and Mabel B. (Tjossem) W.; B.A. with distinction, U. Iowa, 1964; postgrad. in Chinese mil. history U. Mich., 1964-65, M.A. in L.S., 1966; m. Mary Ellen Stratton, Sept. 1, 1962; children—Annette, Jannette, Heather, Christopher. Reference librarian U. Mich., Dearborn, 1966-67, head librarian, 1967—; founder, pub. Pierian Press., pub. reference books, Ann Arbor, Mich., 1968—; speaker, cons. in field. Mem. exec. com. Mich. region Am. Friends Service Com., 1968-73; mem. Dearborn Hist. Commn., 1971-73; vice chmn., chmn. Fairlane Music Guild, 1971-73. Recipient Loleta Fyan award Mich. Library Assn., 1971; Ford Found. scholar, 1963. Mem. ALA, Mich. Library Assn. (chmn. acad. div. nominating com. 1971), Assn. Ednl. Communications and Tech., Ednl. Film Library Assn., Phi Beta Kappa, Beta Phi Mu. Editor books, the most recent being: Author Index to Public Affairs Information Service, 1965-69, 1971; Author Index to A.L.A.'s Index to General Literature, 1972; contbr. articles to profl. jours.; editor Media Rev. Digest, 1970—, Reference Services Rev., 1972—, Consumers Index, 1972—, Serials Rev., 1975—, Index to Free Periodicals, 1976—. Home: 3196 Maple Dr Ypsilanti MI 48197 Office: 4901 Evergreen Rd Dearborn MI 48128 also 5000 Washtenaw St Ann Arbor MI 48104

WALL, DONALD REED, publishing co. exec.; b. New Bedford, Mass., Aug. 30, 1926; s. Allan Clinton and Dorothy Adelaide (Whitehead) W.; student Boston U. Coll. Bus. Adminstrn., 1947-50; m. Eleanor Frances Dougherty, Sept. 7, 1968; children—Nance R., Peter A. Asst. advt. mgr. Bostitch, Inc., Westerly, R.I., 1950-54; dir. advt. and pub. relations Atlas Plywood Corp., Boston, 1954-57; various positions from dist. sales mgr. to group v.p. McGraw-Hill, Inc., N.Y.C., 1957-70; v.p. Cahners Pub., Chgo., 1970-71; pres. mag. div. Whitney Communications Corp., N.Y.C., 1971—; dir. Am. Bus. Press. Served with AUS, 1944-46. Clubs: N.Y. Athletic; Hickory Hill Assn. (Bedford, N.Y.). Home: 301 E 64th St New York NY 10021 also 12 Fox Run East Sandwich MA 02537 Office: 850 E 3d Ave New York NY 10022

WALL, (HERMON) DUNCAN, librarian; b. Tulsa, Okla., Aug. 6, 1933; s. Hermon Duncan and Ruby Prunella (Jones) W.; B.A., Wesleyan U., 1957; M.S., Columbia U., 1960; m. Carol A. Carter, June 10, 1957; children—Suzanne, Marianne, Matthew. With Library of Congress, 1956-57, Columbia U. Libraries, 1957-59; head catalog dept. Curtis Meml. Library, Meriden, Conn., 1960-63; tech. librarian United Aircraft Corp. Systems Center, 1963-65; systems engr. United Aircraft Corp., 1966-67; systems cons. Ont. Council Univ. Librarians, 1968-69; asst. dir. libraries Kent (Ohio) State U., 1969-75; dir. univ. libraries Cleve. State U., 1975—; mem. cons. team. computer systems survey for Univ. libraries Western Can. Provinces, 1969-70. Mem. ALA, AAUP, Assn. Coll. Research Librarians, Am. Soc. Info. Sci. Democrat. Office: Cleveland State U University Libraries Cleveland OH 44115

WALL, FRED GRAHAM, mfg. co. exec.; b. New Burlington, Ohio, May 15, 1934; s. George Robert and Helen Marie (Graham) W.; B.S., Miami U., Oxford, Ohio, 1956; m. Shirley A. Schoenherr, June 30, 1956; children—Tami Lyn, Scott Devin, Wendy Lee. With Ernst & Ernst, Dayton, Ohio, 1959-65, supr., 1962-65; asst. to pres. Robbins & Myers, Inc., Springfield, Ohio, 1965-68, v.p., 1968-70, exec. v.p., 1970-72, pres., 1972—, also dir.; dir. First Nat. Bank Springfield, Sweet Mfg. Co., Ponderosa Systems, Inc., Dayton, Danis Industries Corp., Huffy Corp. Instr. accounting Wright State U., Dayton, 1963-64, Wittenberg U., Springfield, 1962-63. Trustee Robbins & Myers Found., 1966—, Wittenberg U., 1976—. Served with AUS, 1957-59. Mem. Am. Inst. C.P.A.'s, Ohio Soc. C.P.A.'s, Springfield C. of C. (dir. 1971-75), Delta Upsilon. Republican. Methodist. Mason. Clubs: Springfield Country, Dayton Racquet, Van Dyke, Dayton. Home: 2800 Cottonwood Dr Springfield OH 45504 Office: 1400 Winters Bank Tower Dayton OH 45423

WALL, FREDERICK THEODORE, educator; b. Chisholm, Minn., Dec. 14, 1912; s. Peter and Fanny Maria (Rauhala) W.; B.Chemistry, U. Minn., 1933, Ph.D., 1937; m. Clara Elizabeth Vivian, June 5, 1940; children—Elizabeth Ann Wall Ralston, Jane Vivian Wall Meinike. Instr. chemistry U. Ill., 1937-39, asso., 1939-41, asst. prof., 1941-43, asso. prof., 1943-46, prof. chemistry, 1946-64, acting dean grad. coll., 1951-52, head div. phys. chemistry, 1953-56, dean grad. coll., 1955-63; prof., chmn. dept. chemistry U. Calif., Santa Barbara, 1964-66, vice chancellor research, 1965-66; vice chancellor grad. studies and research, prof. chemistry U. Calif. at San Diego, 1966-69; exec. dir. Am. Chem. Soc., Washington, 1969-72; prof. chemistry Rice U., Houston, 1972-78, San Diego State U., 1978—. Pres., Assn. Grad. Schs., 1961; trustee Inst. Def. Analyses, 1962-64. Mem. governing bd. Nat. Acad. Scis.-NRC, 1963- 67; mem. adv. com. for math. and phys. scis. NSF, 1964-68, chmn., 1967; chmn. bd. trustees Univs. Space Research Assn., 1970-73, chmn. council instns., 1974; mem. sci. adv. com. U. Calif. concerning Los Alamos and Livermore Labs., 1972—. Mem. Am. (Pure Chemistry award 1945, dir. 1962-64), Finnish (corr.) chem. socs., Am. Acad. Arts and Scis., Nat. Acad. Scis., Am. Phys. Soc., AAAS, Sigma Xi, Phi Kappa Phi, Phi Lambda Upsilon (hon.). Author: Chemical Thermodynamics, 1958. Editor: Jour. Phys. Chemistry, 1965-69. Contbr. articles on phys. chemistry of polymers and statis. mechanics to sci. jours. Home: 2468 Via Viesta La Jolla CA 92037 Office: Dept Chemistry San Diego State U San Diego CA 92182

WALL, HOWARD ELDEN, bus. service co. exec.; b. Heber, Utah, Dec. 29, 1929; s. Cecil Isaac and Mabel V. (Mair) W.; student Weber Coll., 1948-49; B.S., U. Utah, 1955; m. Deloris K. Blumke, Apr. 7, 1950; children—Edward H., David E. Accountant Ackerson & Howerton, Salt Lake City, 1954-55; auditor Arthur Andersen & Co., Los Angeles, 1955-56; mgr. accounting Convair div. Gen. Dynamics Corp., San Diego, 1956-64, mgr. accounting, N.Y.C., 1964-66, asst. controller, N.Y.C., 1966-68, controller Quincy (Mass.) Shipyard div., 1968-70, asst. comptroller, N.Y.C., 1970-71; controller Dun & Bradstreet Cos., Inc., N.Y.C., 1971-75, v.p., 1974-75, v.p., treas., 1975-78; exec. v.p., chief fin. officer Field Enterprises, Inc., Chgo., 1978—. Served to sgt. USMCR, 1950-52. Home: 100 E Bellevue Pl Chicago IL 60611 Office: 401 N Wabash Ave Chicago IL 60611. *I have always enjoyed a statement made by Brigham Young: "Work like everything depended upon you, pray like everything depended upon the Lord."*

WALL, JAMES MCKENDREE, clergyman, editor; b. Monroe, Ga., Oct. 27, 1928; s. Louie David and Lida (Day) W.; student Ga. Sch. Tech., 1945-47; A.B., Emory U., 1949, B.D., 1955; M.A., U. Chgo., 1960; Litt. D., Ohio No. U., 1967; L.H.D., Willamette U., 1978; m. Mary Eleanor Kidder, Sept. 11, 1953; children—David McKendree, Robert Kidder, Richard James. Staff writer Atlanta Jour., 1947-50; asst. dean students Emory U., 1954-55; ordained to ministry Meth. Ch., 1955; minister Moreland (Ga.) Meth. Charge, 1955-57, Bethel Meth. Ch., Chgo., 1957-59; asso. editor Together mag., 1959-60; mng. editor Christian Adv., Park Ridge, Ill, 1960-64, editor, 1964-72; editor Christian Century, Chgo., 1972—; mem. Pres.'s Commn. on White House Fellows, 1977—; vis. lectr. Claremont (Calif.) Sch. Theology. Vice chmn. Ill. delegation Democratic Nat. Conv., 1972; candidate U.S. Congress, 14th Dist. Ill., 1972; Ill. alt. del.-at-large Dem. Nat. Conf., 1974, del., 1976; chmn. Ill. Carter Presdl. Campaign, 1976; mem. Dem. Nat. Com., 1976—; Dem. state central committeeman, 14th Dist. Ill., 1974—; mem. Ill. Humanities Council, 1978—, Council on Religion and Internat. Affairs, 1977—. Served to 1st lt. USAF, 1950-52. Mem. Sigma Delta Chi, Alpha Tau Omega. Author: Church and Cinema, 1971; Three European Directors, 1973. Home: 451 S Kenilworth St Elmhurst IL 60126 Office: 407 S Dearborn St Chicago IL 60605

WALL, JOSEPH FRAZIER, educator; b. Des Moines, July 10, 1920; s. Joseph Frazier and Minnie Ellen (Patton) W.; B.A., Grinnell Coll., 1941, LL.D. (hon.), 1978; M.A., Harvard, 1942; Ph.D., Columbia, 1951; LL.D. (hon.), Simpson Coll., 1978; m. Beatrice Mills, Apr. 16, 1944; children—April Ane, Joseph Frazier, Julia Mills. Faculty, Grinnell (Iowa) Coll., 1947-78, prof. history, 1957-78, James Morton Roberts honor prof., 1960-61, Parker prof., 1961-78, Earl Strong Distinguished prof., 1972-78, chmn. dept. history, 1954-57, 58-60, chmn. div. social studies, 1956-57, 59-60, chmn. div. history, philosophy and math., 1965-66, chmn. faculty, 1966-69, dean coll., 1969-73; prof. history, chmn. dept. SUNY, Albany, 1978—; spl. assignment to asst. oral history project Columbia, 1957; sr. research Fulbright scholar U. Edinburgh (Scotland), 1957-58; Fulbright prof. U. Gothenburg (Sweden), 1964-65. Served to lt. USNR, 1942-46. Mem. Am., Iowa (chmn. 1955-56) assns. univ. profs., Am. Hist. Assn., Orgn. Am. Historians (exec. bd. 1974-77), Soc. Am. Historians, Phi Beta Kappa, Sigma Delta Chi. Democrat. Author: (with Robert Parks) Freedom (ann. Iowa Civil Liberties Union award 1956), 1955; Henry Watterson; Reconstructed Rebel (hon. mention John A. Dunning prize 1956), 1956; Andrew Carnegie (Bancroft prize 1971), 1970; Iowa, 1978; Policies and People, 1979. Home: 40 Tierney Dr Delmar NY 12054

WALL, KELVIN A., bus. cons., educator; b. N.Y.C., June 14, 1933; s. George D. and Ivy (Phoenix) W.; B.B.A., St. John's U., 1953; M.B.A., N.Y. U., 1957. Dir. advt. N.Y. Amsterdam News, N.Y.C., 1958-62; merchandising mgr. Ebony mag., N.Y.C., 1962-66; v.p. market devel. Coca-Cola USA, Atlanta, Ga., 1966-71; sr. cons. Arthur D. Little, 1970-71; pres. Thursday Devel. Corp., 1971—, Kabon Consulting, Inc., 1972—, Black Creative Group, Inc., 1973—, Kabon Advt., Inc., 1975—; v.p. Leber Katz Advt. Agy., 1978-79; lectr. bus. policies Ga. Inst. Tech., 1968-70; lectr. bus. adminstrn. Harvard, 1970—, mem. recruiting com. Harvard Bus. Sch., vis. com. U. Center for Internat. Affairs. Founding bd. dirs., pres. Atlanta chpt. Southeastern Fair HARYOU-ACT Poverty Program; bd. dirs., v.p. Interracial Council Bus. Opportunities. Mem. U.S. C. of C. (communication com. 1970-71), Am. Mgmt. Assn., Am. Marketing Assn., Inst. Mgmt. Sci., Nat. Soc. for Study Communication, Nat. Assn. Market Developers, Sales Exec. Club. Author: Marketing to Low Income Neighborhoods: A Systems Approach, 1969; A Critical Analysis: Advertising Agency's Utilization of Special Media, 1970; Communication Barriers: Bias by Race of Interviewer, 1970; Interracial Communication in Business, 1968; Positioning Your Brand in the Black Market, 1973. Office: 275 Madison Ave New York NY 10017

WALL, MATTHEW JOSEPH, constrn. co. exec.; b. Jersey City, May 26, 1929; s. Matthew Joseph and Mary Etta (Jaggs) W.; B.S. in Mech. Engring., Newark Coll. Engring., 1950; M.S. in Chem. Engring., Stevens Inst. Tech., 1958; m. Annie Veronica Connolly, Sept. 7, 1957; children—Matthew, Eileen, William, Kathleen. Constrn. engr. J.P.O. Donnell Co., N.Y.C., 1949-50; with Pullman Kellogg Co., Houston, 1950—, project mgr., mgr. projects, mgr. devel., then v.p. research and devel., 1973-75, v.p. contract mgmt., 1975—. Served with AUS, 1954-56. M.W. Kellogg Co. Grad. fellow, 1958.

WALL, MAURICE STANLEY, coll. adminstr.; b. Humphrey, Ky., Nov. 11, 1915; s. George Washington and Verniece (Durham) W.; B.S. in Agr., Berea Coll., 1938; M.S. in Edn., U. Ky., 1947, Ed.D., 1955; m. Ruby Hammn, June 4, 1939; children—Michael, Maureen, Phyllis, Kathleen, Barbara. Tchr. vocat. agr., Ky., 1938-46; faculty U. Ky., 1946—, asso. prof. agr. edn., 1956—, asso. dean Coll. Agr. and Home Econs., 1956—, dir. univs.'s summer session, 1965—, asso. dean univ.'s community coll. system, 1966-70, v.p. community colls., 1970—; adv. bd. ERIC Clearinghouse, 1979. Trustee, Cin. Bible Sem., 1975—. Named hon. farmer Ky. Future Farmers Assn., 1956; recipient Distinguished Alumnus award Berea Coll., 1973; Master Builder of Men award Nat. Farm House Fraternity, 1974; award Coop. Edn. Assn. Ky., 1976. Mem. Ky. Vocat. Assn. (past pres.), Nat. Council State Dirs. Community Jr. Colls. (treas. 1974, chmn. 1978), Commn. Govtl. Affairs, Phi Delta Kappa (past pres. Ky.), Gamma Sigma Delta, Omicron Delta Kappa, Phi Kappa Phi, Alpha Zeta. Mem. Christian Ch. Mason. Author: (with Carsie Hammonds) Food for Home Use, 1951; A More Effective FFA, 1956, 3d edit., 1968. Home: 128 Edgemoor Dr Lexington KY 40503

WALL, NATHAN SANDERS, educator; b. Chgo., May 25, 1925; s. Peter and Sara (Melnick) W.; B.S., Rensselaer Poly. Inst., 1949; Ph.D., Mass. Inst. Tech., 1954; m. Charlotte Katz, Jan. 28, 1951; children—David, Johanna. Research asso. Ind. U., 1954; asst. prof. Mass. Inst. Tech., 1956-63; asst. prof. U. Rochester, 1955; prof. physics U. Md., 1963-79; vis. prof. Cath. U. Louvain (Belgium), 1978; cons. to bus., industry and govt. Bd. dirs. Montgomery County (Md.) chpt. ACLU. Served with AUS, 1943-45. Decorated Bronze Star. NSF sr. postdoctoral fellow, 1961; NATO fellow, 1971; Weizmann Inst. fellow, 1971. Fellow Am. Phys. Soc. Contbr. articles to profl. jours. Home: 12607 Davan Dr Silver Spring MD 20904 Office: Dept Physics Univ Md College Park MD 20742 Died Sept. 2, 1979.

WALL, SHANNON JEROME, union ofcl.; b. Portland, Oreg., Mar. 4, 1919; s. Edward C. and Hope C. (Scartum) W.; student U. Wash., 1939-41; m. Lucy Mildred Davis, May 10, 1952; children—Sean Michael, Maureen Hope, Kevin Edward. Bus. agt. Nat. Maritime Union, 1951-58, v.p., 1958-69, sec.-treas., 1969-73, pres., 1973—. Vice pres. indsl. union dept. AFL-CIO; mem. exec. bd. AFL-CIO, chmn. maritime com., co-chmn. labor/mgmt. com., Washington; vice chmn. Seafarers sect. Internat. Transport Workers Fedn., London, Eng. Served with U.S. Mcht. Marine, 1942—. Office: 346 W 17th St New York NY 10011*

WALL, WILLIAM E., utility exec.; b. 1928; B.S., U. Wash., 1951, LL.B., 1954. Asst. atty. gen. State of Wash., 1956-59, chief examiner Pub. Service Commn., 1959; sec., house counsel Cascade Natural Gas Corp., 1959-64; pres. United Cities Gas Co., 1964-65; exec. v.p. Cascade Natural Gas Corp., 1965-67; spl. asst. to chmn. bd. Consol. Edison Co., N.Y., 1967-68, v.p., 1968-70, sr. v.p. gas ops., 1970-71, exec. v.p. div. ops., 1971-73; gen. mgr. public affairs Standard Oil Co., 1973-74; exec. v.p. Kans. Power and Light Co., 1974-75, pres., 1975—, chief exec. officer, 1976—, chmn., 1979—, also dir. Served with AUS, 1954-56. Office: Kans Power and Light Co 818 Kansas Ave Topeka KS 66612*

WALL, WILLIAM MONROE, advt. exec.; b. St. Louis, Jan. 11, 1926; s. Virgil D. and Mabel (Wilson) W.; B.A., U. Mo., 1948; m. Lou Ann Trexler, May 1, 1949; children—Eric Wilson, Jonathan Scott, Melanie. Writer, Cities Service Co., 1948-50, Batten, Barton, Durstine & Osborn, 1950-51; writer-producer Cunningham & Walsh, 1951-52; creative dir. Doner Advt., Detroit, 1952-54, Compton Advt., 1954-55, Doner Advt., Balt., 1955-56; dir. Doherty, Clifford, Steers & Shenfield, 1956-64; copy supr. Ogilvy, Benson & Mather, 1964-65; exec. v.p. Rockwell, Quinn & Wall, N.Y.C., 1965-71, Manor House, Inc., Phoenix, 1971—. Served with USAAF, World War II. Recipient Carl Stepp Meml. award Sigma Alpha Epsilon, 1948. Home: 5215 E Lafayette Blvd Phoenix AZ 85018 Office: 5301 N 16th St Phoenix AZ 85016

WALLACE, ANDREW GROVER, physician; b. Columbus, Ohio, Mar. 22, 1935; s. Richard Homes and Eleanor Bradley (Grover) W.; B.S., Duke, 1958, M.D., 1959; m. Kathleen Barrick Altvater, June 22, 1957; children—Stephen Andrew, Michael Bradley, Kathleen Claude. Intern medicine Duke, Durham, N.C., 1959-60, jr. asst. resident, 1960-61, research fellow, 1961, fellow Nat. Heart Inst., 1961-63, chief resident medicine, 1963-64, asst. prof. medicine, 1965-67, asso. prof., 1967-71, asst. prof. physiology, 1969, asst. dir. grad. med. edn., 1970-71, chief, div. cardiology, 1970, prof. medicine, 1971—, Walter Kempner prof. medicine, 1973—. Cons. program project com. pharmacology study sect. Nat. Heart and Lung Inst.; mem. cardiovascular merit rev. bd. VA. Pres. Durham YMCA Swim Assn., 1975-77, AAU age group swim team. Markle scholar, 1965-70. Diplomate Am. Bd. Internal Medicine. Mem. Am. Fedn. for Clin. Research, So. Soc. for Clin. Investigators, Am. Heart Assn. (council on clin. cardiology), A.A.A.S., Am. Physiol. Soc., Biomedical Engring. Soc., Am. Soc. for Clin. Investigation, Assn. U. Cardiologists, Assn. Am. Physicians, Am. Clin. and Climatol. Assn. Mem. editorial bd. Am. Jour. of Physiology, 1965-70, Jour. of Pharmacology and Exptl. Therapeutics, 1966-71, Jour. of Molecular and Cellular Cardiology, 1970-75, Circulation, Jour. of Clin. Investigation, 1973-78. Home: 3413 Rugby Rd Durham NC 27707

WALLACE, ANDREW HUGH, educator; b. Glasgow, Scotland, June 14, 1926; s. Andrew and Elizabeth (Arnott) W.; M.A., U. Edinburgh (Scotland), 1946; Ph.D., U. St. Andrews, 1949; postgrad. U. Chgo., 1952. Came to U.S., 1959. Lectr., St. Andrews U., 1946-50, 52-53, U. Coll. of North Staffordshire (Eng.), 1953-57; asst. prof. U. Toronto, 1957-59; asso. prof., then prof. Ind. U., 1959-64; mem. Inst. for Advanced Study, 1964-65; prof. math. U. Pa., 1965—. Visitor, Pahlavi U. under U. Pa.-Pahlavi Devel. Program, Shiraz, Iran, 1971-72, 74-75. Mem. London, Am. math. socs., Can. Math. Congress. Author: Introduction to Algebraic Topology, 1957; Homology Theory on Algebraic Varieties, 1958; Differential Topology, 1969; Algebraic Topology, 1970; also articles. Home: 1212 Waverly Walk Philadelphia PA 19147

WALLACE, ANTHONY EDWARD, utility exec.; b. Stamford, Conn., Dec. 6, 1915; s. Anthony John and Ann (Bordus) W.; B.S., U. Cal. at Los Angeles, 1941; postgrad. Harvard Sch. Bus. Adminstrn., 1942-43; m. Helen Barton, Oct. 19, 1941; children—Richard Anthony, Anthony Edward. Faculty, Hillyer Coll., U. Hartford (Conn.), 1946-52; asst. dir. research and planning div. Conn. Devel. Commn., 1943-52; with Conn. Light & Power Co., 1952—, exec. v.p., 1964-68, pres., 1968—, also dir.; trustee corp. Soc. for Savs., Hartford; exec. v.p., dir. N.E. Utilities Service Co., Holyoke Water Power Co.; dir., exec. v.p. Hartford Electric Light Co.; dir. N.E. Nuclear Energy Co., Conn. Water Service, Inc., Conn. Mut. Life Ins. Co., Western Mass. Electric Co., Mohasco Corp. Chmn., Conn. Bd. Pesticide Control, 1964-68; mem. Citizens Commn. Conn. Gen. Assembly, Conn. Regional Med. Program; Conn. chmn. U.S. Savs. Bonds Vol. Com., 1969-78; mem. exec. com. Natural Resources Council Conn.; mem. nat. emergency com. Nat. Council Crime and Delinquency; mem. com. fed. finance Council State Chambers Commerce. Mem. Conn. Ho. of Reps., 1956-62, speaker, 1961-62. Trustee, 1st vice chmn. Conn. Ednl. TV Corp., 1967-75; trustee Conn. Pub. Expenditure Council, 1969-75, Samuel I. Ward Tech. Coll., Sterling Opera House Found., 1972-75; corporator Mt. Sinai Hosp., Hartford, Inst. Living, New Britain Gen. Hosp.; bd. dirs. Bus.-Industry Polit. Action Com., U. Conn. Found., 1968-74, hon. life dir.; bd. dirs. Am. Sch. Deaf; mgmt. adv. com. Hartford Grad. Center, Rensselaer Poly. Inst. Conn.; mem. exec. com., regional bd. dirs. NCCJ. Mem. Conn. Electric and Gas Assn. (pres., chmn. exec. com.), C. of C. U.S. (dir. 1968-75), Conn. C. of C. (chmn. bd. 1967-68), Conn. Bus. and Industry Assn., New Eng. Gas Assn., Electric Council New Eng. Clubs: Shuttle Meadow Country; Economic (N.Y.C.); Hartford; Harvard Business School No. Conn. Home: 201 Andrews St Southington CT 06489 Office: 107 Selden St Berlin CT 06037

WALLACE, ANTHONY FRANCIS CLARKE, anthropologist, educator; b. Toronto, Ont., Can., Apr. 15, 1923; s. Paul A.W. and Dorothy Eleanor (Clarke) W.; B.A., U. Pa., 1948, M.A., 1949, Ph.D., 1950; m. Betty Louise Shillott, Dec. 1, 1942; children—Anthony, Daniel, Sun Ai, Samuel, Cheryl, Joseph. Instr. anthropology Bryn Mawr Coll., 1948-50; asst. instr. anthropology U. Pa., research sec. Behavioral Research Council, 1951-55, research asst. prof. anthropology, 1952-55, vis. asso. prof. anthropology, 1955-61, prof. dept. anthropology, 1961—, chmn., 1961-71; sr. research asso. anthropology Eastern Pa. Psychiat. Inst., 1955-60, dir. clin. research, 1960-61, med. research scientist III, 1961—. Mem. tech. adv. com. N.J. Psychiat. Inst., 1958; cons. disaster studies NRC, 1956-57; cons. Phila. Housing Authority, 1952; mem. research adv. com. Commonwealth Mental Health Research Found., 1960-61; mem. research adv. com. U.S. Office Edn., 1965-68; mem. behavioral scis. study sect. NIMH, 1964-68; mem. NRC, 1963-66; mem. various adv. coms. NIMH, 1962—; mem. social sci. adv. council NSF, 1969-72. Bd. mgrs. Founds. Fund for Research in Psychiatry, 1969-71. Served AUS, 1942-45. Recipient Bancroft prize in Am. History, 1979; Guggenheim fellow, 1978-79. Fellow Am. Anthrop. Assn. (pres. 1971-72), AAAS; mem. Nat. Acad. Scis., Am. Philos. Soc., Am. Acad. Arts and Scis. Author: King of the Delawares: Teedyuscung, 1700-1763; 1949; Culture and Personality, 1961, rev. edit., 1970; Religion: An Anthropological View, 1966; Death and Rebirth of the Seneca, 1970; Rockdale: The Growth of an American Village in the Early Industrial Revolution, 1978. Office: Dept Anthropology U Pa 33d and Spruce Sts Philadelphia PA 19174

WALLACE, BRUCE, educator; b. McKean, Pa., May 18, 1920; s. George Egbert and Rose Irma (Paterson) W.; B.A., Columbia, 1941, Ph.D., 1949; m. Miriam Jane Covalla, Nov. 3, 1945; children—David Bruce, Roberta Scott. With dept. genetics Carnegie Instn. of Washington, Cold Spring Harbor, N.Y., 1947-49, Biol. Lab., Cold Spring Harbor, 1949-58; faculty Cornell U., Ithaca, N.Y., 1958—, prof. genetics, 1961—. Bd. dirs. Biol. Scis. Curriculum Study, Boulder, Colo., 1968-78. Served with AAC, 1943-46. USPHS spl. research fellow, Brazil, 1960; NSF sr. postdoctoral fellow, Greece and Netherlands, 1965. Mem. Am. Soc. Naturalists (sec. 1956-58, pres. 1971), Genetics Soc. Am. (sec. 1968-70, v.p. 1973, pres. 1974), Soc. Study Evolution (pres. 1974), Am. Acad. Arts and Scis. Author: (with Th. Dobzhansky) Radiation, Genes, and Man, 1959; (with A.M. Srb) Adaptation, 1961; Chromosomes, Giant Molecules, and Evolution, 1966; Topics in Population Genetics, 1968; Genetic Load, 1970; Essays in Social Biology, 3 vols., 1972. Home: 416 Mitchell St Ithaca NY 14850

WALLACE, CARL S., business exec.; b. Ontario, Wis., Sept. 27, 1918; s. David Wallace and Mae (McQueen) W.; Ph.B., U. Wis., 1943; m. Marian E. Jones, Feb. 22, 1941; children—Carl S., Mary Ann Green. Mgr. Wausau (Wis.) office Wis. Employment Service, 1951-53, Stevens Point (Wis.) Area C. of C., 1953-65; adminstry. asst. to U.S. rep. Melvin Laird, 1965-69; spl. asst. to sec. and dep. sec. def., 1969-72, asst. sec. manpower and res. affairs U.S. Army, 1973-74; corp. v.p. Purolator, Inc., 1974—; mem. Bus. Govt. Relations Council. Served with AUS, 1943-45. Decorated Bronze Star (2); recipient medal for distinguished service Dept. of Def., 1973; Distinguished Civilian Service medal Dept. of Army, 1974. Mem. Am. Legion. Republican. Methodist. Elk, Kiwanian. Home: 8315 Ashwood Dr Alexandria VA 22308 Office: 1800 K St NW Suite 614 Washington DC 20006

WALLACE, CATHERINE THERESE, coll. pres.; b. Lawrence, Mass., Mar. 10, 1917; d. Michael and Sarah Alice (Watson) Wallace; B.A., Dalhousie U., Halifax, N.S., 1939, LL.D., 1974; Tchr.'s diploma, Mt. St. Vincent Normal Sch., 1940; M.A., St. John's U., N.Y.C., 1945, Ph.D., 1952; D.C.L., U. King's Coll., 1971; LL.D., St. Thomas U., 1969, Mt. Allison U., 1971, U. N.B., 1973, McMaster U., 1974, Meml. U., 1974, U. Western Ont., 1975; Ed.D., Laval U., 1974. Tchr. jr. and sr. high sch., N.Y.C., 1939-53; prin. Notre Dame High Sch., Vancouver, B.C., 1953-59; prof. English Mt. St. Vincent Coll., 1959-65; pres. Mt. St. Vincent U., Halifax, 1965—; now chmn. Maritime Provinces Higher Edn. Commn., Fredericton, N.B. Dir. Canadian Imperial Bank Commerce, Maritime Telegraph & Telephone Co. Ltd., Can. Devel. Corp. Supr. edn. Congregation Sisters of Charity, 1962. Mem. com. on role of women in ch. and society Canadian Cath. Conf., 1972; mem. Canadian Govt. Adv. Council on Status of Women, 1973; mem. Exec. Com. on Status of Women, 1975—. Bd. dirs. Canadian Orgn. for Peace and Devel., 1966, Canadian Univ. Students Overseas, 1970—, Service for Admission to Coll. and Univ., 1971—; Atlantic bd. dirs. Canadian Council Christians and Jews, 1976—; chmn. exec. heads N.S. univs., 1972; trustee Inst. for Research on Pub. Policy, 1972; mem. hon. adv. com. Netherwood, Rothesay, N.B., 1972. Recipient medal of service Order of Can., 1972; Woman of Yr. award B'nai B'rith Women's Council Toronto, 1974; Vanier award Inst. Pub. Adminstrn. Can., 1977. Mem. Canadian Fedn. U. Women, Assn. Univs. and Colls. Can. (dir., chmn. standing com. on status of women 1971-72, v.p. 1972, pres. 1973), Assn. Commonwealth Univs. (council and exec. 1972). Mem. editorial Bd. Stoa, 1973—. Home: 10 Sherwood Ct Fredericton NB Canada. *I believe my life has been, free, committed, and really worth living. It seems to me anything is possible if a person is strongly motivated, flexible, and ready to risk. It seems to me also that failure, opposition, hardship are also essential parts of growth. Perhaps I have been the right person, in the right place, at the right time. In a time of woman's reaching for freedom, I feel I have been free, and any bounds to my achievements are merely a result of my own personal limitations.*

WALLACE, CHARLES EDWARD, educator; b. Portland, Oreg., Apr. 19, 1929; s. Charles Stuart and Myrtle Alice (Young) W.; student Oreg. State U., 1947-48, Reed Coll., 1948-49; B.S., Lewis and Clark Coll., 1951; M.S., Oreg. State U., 1954; Ph.D., Stanford, 1959; m. Theresa Mueller, July 31, 1965; children—Edward Stuart, Anne Marie. Engr., Douglas Aircraft Co., Long Beach, Calif., 1953-55; mem. faculty Ariz. State U., Tempe, 1958—, prof. engring., 1964—, chmn. engring. sci. faculty, 1961-67, engring. mechanics, 1967-71, engring. mechanics and materials, 1971-73, mechanics materials and measurement engring., 1973-75, engring. sci., 1975-78, aerospace engring. and engring. sci., 1978—; engring. cons. on acoustic fatigue N.Am. Aviation, 1960-64, AiResearch, 1971-72, Rockwell Internat., 1973-74, 79—, HUD, 1975-77. Sr. postdoctoral resident research asso. NRC, 1968-69. Grantee Title I Higher Edn. Act, 1965. Mem. Am. Soc. Engring. Edn., Am. Inst. Aeros. and Astronautics, Acoustical Soc. Am., Am. Acad. Mechanics, Assn. Chmn. Depts. Mechanics, Sigma Xi, Tau Beta Pi, Sigma Pi Sigma. Home: 533 E Erie Dr Tempe AZ 85282

WALLACE, CHARLES LESLIE, food co. exec.; b. Monmouth, Ill., Dec. 26, 1945; s. Leslie and Harriet Elizabeth Wallace; B.S. (Arthur J. Mellinger Found. scholar), No. Ill. U., 1967; M.B.A. (Chase Manhattan Bank Careers for Blacks in Mgmt. fellow), U. Chgo., 1973; m. Marie Elizabeth Lancaster, June 24, 1967; children—Allison Marie, Bryan Charles. Sr. accountant Arthur Andersen & Co., Chgo., 1967-74; fin. analyst Joseph Schlitz Brewing Co., Milw., 1974-76; asst. treas. Universal Foods Corp., Milw., 1976-78, treas., 1978—. Bd. dirs. Milw. Urban League, 1975—, treas., 1975-78, v.p., 1979—; bd. dirs. Planned Parenthood Assn. Wis., 1977—; cons. Nat. Alliance Businessmen, 1977—, Milw. Inroads, 1976—, Project Bus., 1976—. Served with USMCR, 1967-68. C.P.A. Mem. Am. Inst. C.P.A.'s, Fin. Execs. Inst., Milw. Forum, Kappa Alpha Psi. Home: 1150 W Duchess Ct Milwaukee WI 53217 Office: Universal Food Corp 433 E Michigan St Milwaukee WI 53202

WALLACE, DALLAS LANE, indsl. distbn. co. exec.; b. Greensboro, N.C., Oct. 31, 1931; s. K. C. and Laura (Hinshaw) W.; B.S. Engring., U.S. Naval Acad., 1954; m. Linda Curry, Sept. 6, 1970; children—Stephen, Kelle. Commd. ensign U.S. Navy, 1954, advanced through grades to lt., 1961; served aboard nuclear submarines, 1954-62, resigned, 1962; project mgr. manned space flight Pan Am. World Airways, Cape Canaveral, Fla., 1962-66; v.p. mktg. McMaster-Carr Supply Co., Chgo. and Los Angeles, 1966-72; group v.p. Internat. Utilities, Phila., 1972-76; pres., chief exec. officer Distbn. Enterprises, Lancaster, Pa., 1976—. Mem. Am. Mgmt. Assn., Naval Inst. Clubs: Lancaster Country, Hamilton. Home: 748 Orchard Rd Lititz PA 17543 Office: 1560 Lititz Pike Lancaster PA 17601

WALLACE, DAVID ALEXANDER, architect, educator; b. Chgo., Aug. 30, 1917; s. David A. and Grace (Eaton) W.; B.Arch., U. Pa., 1940, M.Arch., 1941; M.City Planning, Harvard, 1950, Ph.D., 1953; m. Joan Heatly Dulles, Oct. 23, 1954; 1 stepson, Robert N. Cunningham III. With various archtl. offices, 1941, 46-48; supervising planner Chgo. Housing Authority, 1951; asst. dir. Marshall Field Found. Study of Housing of Low Income Groups, 1952; asst. prof. U. Chgo., 1952; dir. planning Phila. Redevel. Authority, 1953-57, Council Greater Balt. Com., 1957-61; prof. city planning U. Pa. Sch. Fine Arts, Phila., 1961-72, adj. prof., 1972-76. Partner, Wallace, McHarg, Roberts & Todd, Phila., 1963—. Served to maj. AUS, 1941-46. Fellow AIA; mem. Am. Planning Assn. (bd. govs. 1961-63). Home: 7316 Elbow Ln Philadelphia PA 19119 Office: 1737 Chestnut St Philadelphia PA 19103

WALLACE, DAVID WILLIAM, bus. exec.; b. N.Y.C., Feb. 23, 1924; s. Fergus Ferguson and Isabelle Taylor (Wilson) W.; B.S., Yale Sch. Engring., 1948; J.D., Harvard, 1951; m. Jean Ives McLean, June 20, 1953; children—Mary H., Anne S. Admitted to N.Y. bar, 1952; asso. White & Case, N.Y.C., 1951-54; gen. counsel Alleghany Corp., 1954, sec.-treas., 1954-56, v.p., 1956-58, exec. v.p., 1958-59; exec. v.p. chmn. exec. com. United Brands Corp. until 1967; dir. Bangor Punta Corp., 1967—, pres., 1967-78, chief exec. officer, 1969—, chmn. bd., 1973-78; dir., mem. exec. com., chmn. audit com. Lone Star Industries, Inc.; dir., chmn. exec. com. Piper Aircraft Corp.; dir. Intext, Inc., Producers Cotton Oil Co. Vice pres., trustee Robert R. Young Found.; trustee Greenwich Acad.; bd. govs. N.Y. Hosp. Served as 1st lt., inf. U.S. Army, 1943-46. Mem. St. Andrew's Soc. N.Y. Presbyterian (elder). Clubs: Pinnacle, Yale, Economic, Greenwich Country. Home: Deer Park Greenwich CT 06830

WALLACE, DEWITT, ret. publisher; b. St. Paul, Nov. 12, 1889; s. James and Janet (Davis) W.; student Macalester Coll., 1907-09, U. Calif., 1909-11; m. Lila Bell Acheson, Oct. 15, 1921. With book dept. Webb Pub. Co., St. Paul, 1911-15, Brown & Bigelow, St. Paul, 1916; publicity dept. Westinghouse Electric & Mfg. Co., 1920-21; founder Reader's Digest Assn., Inc., 1921, ret., 1973. Served as sgt. 35th Div., U.S. Army, 1917-19. Home: 543 Byram Lake Rd Mount Kisco NY 10549

WALLACE, DONALD GORDON, educator; b. Bklyn., Feb. 15, 1919; s. William H. and Evelyn (Hope) W.; student N.Y.U., 1937-38; B.S., Ithaca Coll., 1941; M.S., Syracuse U., 1947, Ed.D., 1949; m. Genevieve Treichler, Apr. 5, 1947 (div. 1973); children—Rebecca, Paul J., Stuart D. Supr. music W. Valley (N.Y.) Central Sch., 1941-42; dir. instl. studies, asso. prof. edn. Drake U., 1949-54, dean grad. div., prof. edn., 1954-57, dean Coll. of Edn., 1957-64, prof. edn., 1957—, dir. summer session and instl. research, 1964-67, dir. instl. research, 1967-74, asso. dean for summer sessions, 1974—. Served with USAAF, 1942-46. Mem. Nat. Council Measurements Used in Edn., Am. Ednl. Research Assn., Midwestern, Iowa psychol. assns., N.Am. Assn. Summer Sessions (v.p. 1976-80), North Central Conf. Summer Schs. (dir. 1978-80), Phi Delta Kappa, Phi Mu Alpha, Phi Kappa Phi. Presbyn. (elder). Author: (with Schwartz, Tiedeman) Judging Progress of Secondary School Students, 1957. Contbr. articles to profl. jours. Home: 1201 Office Park Rd Apt 2011 West Des Moines IA 50265

WALLACE, DONALD SHERIDAN, architect; b. Spokane, Wash., Oct. 24, 1915; s. John Sheridan and Laura Grace (Smith) W.; student Eastern Wash. State Coll., 1933-34, Kinman Bus. U., 1936; B.A. in Architecture, U. Wash., 1952; m. Patricia Haggart Wilson, Feb. 19, 1973. Draftsman, Hovind, Harthorne & Smith, Architects, Seattle, 1952-53, Paul Hayden Kirk & Assos., Seattle, 1954-59; partner Kirk, Wallace, McKinley & Assos., Seattle, 1960—; v.p. The McKinley Architects, Seattle, 1978—. Served with AUS, 1943-46. Mem. A.I.A. (treas. Seattle chpt. 1970). Republican. Mason (Shriner), Elk. Home: 10905 SE 1st St Bellevue WA 98004 Office: 2000 Fairview Ave E Seattle WA 98102

WALLACE, DWANE L., aircraft mfr.; b. Belmont, Kans., Oct. 29, 1911; s. Dr. Eugene and Grace Opal (Cessna) W.; B.S., U. Wichita, 1933; m. Velma Ruth Lunt, Sept. 8, 1941; children—Linda, Karen, Diana, Sarah. Gen. Mgr. Cessna Aircraft Co., Wichita, 1934—, pres., 1935—, chmn. bd., chief exec. officer, 1964—; sr. cons. CEA, 1975—. Mem. C. of C. Club: Rotary. Home: 5 Willowbrook Rd Eastborough Wichita KS 67207 Office: 750 Fourth Financial Center Wichita KS 67202

WALLACE, GEORGE CORLEY, former gov. Ala.; b. Clio, Ala., Aug. 25, 1919; s. George C. and Mozell (Smith) W.; LL.B., U. Ala., 1942; m. Lurleen Burns, May 23, 1943 (dec.); children—Bobbie Jo, Peggy Sue, George Corley, Janie Lee; m. 2d, Cornelia Ellis Snively, Jan. 1971 (div. Jan. 1978). Admitted to Ala. bar, 1942; asst. atty. gen. Ala., 1946-47; mem. Ala. Legislature from Barbour County, 1947-53; judge 3d Jud. Dist. Ala., 1953-58; pvt. practice, Clayton, Ala., 1958-62; gov. Ala., 1963-66, 71-79; dir. rehab. resources U. Ala., 1979—; counselor to Gov. of Ala., 1979—. Sponsor, Wallace Act for state trade schs., 1947; candidate for pres. Am. Ind. party, 1968, Democratic primary, 1972, 76; bd. dirs. Ala. Tb Assn. Served with USAAF, 1942-45; PTO. Mem. Am. Legion, VFW, DAV. Democrat. Methodist (past Sunday sch. tchr. and supt.). Clubs: Masons, Shriners, Moose, Elks, Modern Woodman of World, Order Eastern Star, Civitan Internat. Office: Dept Rehab Resources U Ala University AL 35486 also Celebrity Mgmt 50 Music Sq W Suite 401 Nashville TN 37203*

WALLACE, GEORGE EDWARD, ins. co. exec.; b. Chatham, Ont., Can., May 18, 1917; s. Joseph Andrew and Effie Ann (Mills) W.; came to U.S., 1953, naturalized, 1961; B.A., U. Western Ont., 1939; postgrad. Advanced Mgmt. Program, Harvard U., 1965; m. Janet E. MacNearney, Sept. 6, 1946 (div. Jan. 1972); children—Douglas, Jill, Meredith (dec.), Shelagh; m. 2d, Marjorie A. Robbins, Oct. 6, 1974. Tchr., Leaside High Sch., Toronto, Ont., Can., 1947-53; with John Hancock Mut. Life Ins. Co., Boston, 1954—, mem. data processing staff, 1954-75, sr. v.p., 1975—; mem. advisory com. on dataprocessing Lowell (Mass.) U. Served to capt. Can. Army, 1942-46. Fellow Soc. Actuaries. Unitarian. Clubs: Sandy Bay Yacht, Brae Burn Country. Home: 23 Nantucket Rd Wellesley MA 02181 Office: John Hancock Pl Box 111 Boston MA 02117

WALLACE, GEORGE MAGOUN, II, army officer; b. Washington, Jan. 15, 1924; s. Fred Clute and George Butler (Magoun) W.; B.S., U.S. Mil. Acad., 1945; M.S. in Internat. Affairs, George Washington U., 1966; m. Beverley Bonnycastle Bender, June 21, 1947; children—Jane Bonnycastle, Anne Churchill, Melissa Jordan. Commd. 2d lt. U.S. Army, 1945, advanced through grades to maj. gen., 1973; battalion comdr., Vietnam, 1966; staff officer Joint Chiefs of Staff, 1968-69; dir. ops. So. Command, C.Z., 1969-71; asst. div. comdr., Korea, 1972; dir. Inter-Am. region Dept. Def., 1973-75; chief of staff 5th Army, Fort Sam Houston, Tex., 1975-79; comdr. Readiness Region VII, Fort Sam Houston, 1979—. Decorated Silver Star, Legion of Merit, D.F.C., Bronze Star, Air medal, others. Mem. Assn. U.S. Army, Assn. 1st Infantry Div., Sigma Chi. Home: 8 Staff Post Rd Fort Sam Houston TX 78234 Office: Hdqrs Readiness Region VII Fort Sam Houston TX 78234

WALLACE, GEORGE ROBERTS, ret. fisheries exec.; b. Morehead City, N.C., Oct. 13, 1906; s. Charles Slover and Nina (Webb) W.; A.B., Duke, 1927; m. Laura Abernathy Mace, Oct. 21, 1936; children—George Roberts (dec.), William Borden. Trustee emeritus Duke U. Mem. Lambda Chi Alpha. Republican. Episcopalian. Clubs: Masons, Shriners, Coral Bay, Dunes. Home: 213 Land's End Rd Route 2 Morehead City NC 28557

WALLACE, HAROLD JAMES, JR., physician; b. South Hadley Falls, Mass., Aug. 15, 1930; s. Harold James and Evelyn (Mason) W.; B.A., U. Vt., 1954, M.D. cum laude, 1958; m. Dorothy Ann Green, July 4, 1959; children—Harold James III, Elizabeth Marie, John Hill. Intern, Mary Fletcher Hosp., Burlington, Vt., 1958-59, resident, 1959-62; practice medicine specializing in oncology, Buffalo, 1970-79, Rutland, Vt., 1979—; asso. chief dept. medicine Roswell Park Meml. Inst., Buffalo, 1970-75, dir. Cancer Control Rehab. and Adolescent Program, 1976-79; oncologist Rutland Hosp., 1979—; asst. prof. medicine and pharmacology U. Vt. Coll. Medicine, 1964-70; research asso. prof. medicine and exptl. pathology SUNY Sch. Medicine, Buffalo, 1970-79. Recipient Appleton-Century Croft prize, 1956. Mem. Am. Cancer Soc. (dir. N.Y. State div., Nat. div. award 1969), Am. Assn. for Cancer Research, Am. Assn. for Cancer Edn., Am. Soc. Clin. Oncology, Alpha Omega Alpha. Presbyterian. Office: 92 Allen St Rutland VT 05701

WALLACE, HAROLD LEW, educator, historian; b. Montgomery, Ind., Nov. 9, 1932; s. Lewis Alfred and Winifred Maria (Summers) W.; A.B., Ind. U., 1961, M.A. (Univ. grantee), 1964, Ph.D., 1970; m. Janice June Inman, June 22, 1957; children—Stefanie Ann, Stacy Elizabeth. Tchr. history and English, Mooreseville (Ind.) High Sch., 1961-63; teaching asst. Ind. U., 1963-64, univ. fellow, 1964-65; asst. prof., then asso. prof. history Murray (Ky.) State U., 1965-71; prof. history, head social sci. div. No. Ky. State Coll., Highland Heights, Ky., 1971—; mem. continuing seminar community edn. Ball State U. and Mott Found., 1973—. Mem. advisory com. pub. documents State of Ky. Bd. dirs. Coll. Programs for No. Ky. Sr. Citizens. Served with USNR, 1952-56. Recipient Service award State Ind., 1957. Eli Lilly fellow, 1962, 63; Harry S. Truman research scholar, 1965, 71; grantee Murray State U., 1967, 71, No. Ky. State U., 1973, Mott Found., 1973, No. Ky. State U., 1976, 78. Mem. Am., So. hist. assns., Orgn. Am. Historians, Polit. Sci. Acad., AAUP, Center Study Democratic Instrn., Mensa, Sierra Club, Alpha Epsilon Delta, Phi Delta Kappa, Phi Alpha Theta. Author: Coal in Kentucky, 1975. Contbr. articles to profl. jours. Editorial bd. U. Ky. Press, 1971—; cons., reviewer Oceana Press, Inc., 1973—. Home: 22 Orchard Terr Cold Springs KY 41076 Office: No Ky State Coll Highland Heights KY 41076

WALLACE, HARRY LELAND, lawyer; b. San Francisco, June 26, 1927; s. Leon Harry and Anna Ruth (Haworth) W.; A.B. in Govt., B.S. in Bus., Ind. U., 1949; J.D., Harvard U., 1952; m. Mary Lue Eckels, Apr. 16, 1951; 1 dau., Mary Ann Wallace Frantz. Admitted to Wis. bar, 1953; law clk. U.S. Supreme Ct. Justice Sherman Minton, Washington, 1952-53; asso. firm Foley & Lardner, Milw., 1953-61, partner, 1961—; officer and/or dir. various corps. Treas., Mequon-Thiensville Sch. Bds., 1966-67, 71-73, pres., 1965-66, 67-71, 73-75; bd. dirs. Milwaukee County Assn. for Mental Health, 1970-76; bd. dirs. Citizens for Wis. Ltd., 1978—, pres., 1978—; chmn. financing policies com. Gov.'s Commn. on Edn., 1969-70; mem. Gov.'s Task Force on Sch. Financing and Property Tax Reform, 1972-73; chmn. Gov.'s Commn. on State-Local Relations and Fin. Policies, 1975-76. Served with USN, 1945-46. Mem. Am., Wis., Milw. bar assns., Am. Law Inst. Methodist. Clubs: Wis., Milw. Home: 2104 W Quincy Ct Mequon WI 53092 Office: 777 E Wisconsin Ave Milwaukee WI 53202

WALLACE, HELEN MARGARET, physician, educator; b. Hoosick Falls, N.Y., Feb. 18, 1913; d. Jonas and Ray (Schweizer) Wallace; A.B., Wellesley Coll., 1933; M.D., Columbia, 1937; M.P.H. cum laude, Harvard, 1943. Intern, Bellevue Hosp., N.Y.C., 1938-40; child hygiene physician Conn. Health Dept., 1941-42; successively jr. health officer, health officer, chief maternity and new born div., dir. bur. for handicapped children N.Y.C. Health Dept., 1943-55; prof., dir. dept. pub. health N.Y. Med. Coll., 1955-56; prof. maternal and child health U. Minn. Sch. Pub. Health, 1956-59; chief profl. tng. U.S. Childrens Bur., 1959-60, chief child health studies, 1961-62; prof. maternal and child health U. Calif. Sch. Pub. Health, Berkeley, 1962—. Cons. WHO, Uganda, 1961, Philippines, 1966, 68, 75, Turkey, 1968, India, Geneva, 1970, Iran, 1972, Burma, India, Thailand, Sri Lanka, 1975, East Africa, 1976, Australia, 1976, Burma, 1977, India, Indonesia, Thailand, Burma, 1978, Ford Found., Colombia, 1971. Traveling fellow WHO. Diplomate Am. Bd. Pediatrics, Am. Bd. Preventive Medicine. Fellow Am. Acad. Pediatrics, Am. Pub. Health Assn. (officer sect.; Martha May Eliot award 1978); mem. AMA, Am. Women's Med. Assn. (asst. editor Jour. Human Sexuality, Advances in Planned Parenthood), Assn. Tchrs. Maternal and Child Health, Calif. League for Nursing (pres. elect). Author 3 textbooks. Home: 1515 Oxford St Berkeley CA 94708

WALLACE, HUGH DONALD, ins. co. exec.; b. Madison, Wis., Oct. 30, 1921; s. Robert Joseph and Genevieve Margaret (Gunning) W.; Ph.B. in Finance, U. Wis., 1947; m. Jeanne Elizabeth Gaffney, Feb. 12, 1949; children—Daniel, Mary, Michael, Robert, James, Lawrence, John. With Wis. Ins. Dept., 1947-51, 52; with Am. Family Mut. Ins. Co., Madison, 1953—, controller, 1959-66, treas., 1961—, v.p. finance, 1966—, also dir.; dir. Am. Family Life Ins. Co., Am. Standard Ins. Co., Am. Family Financial Services Co.; guest lectr. U. Wis. extension. Trustee Am. Family Incentive and Thrift Plan. Bd. dirs. Wis. Assn. Alcoholism and Other Drug Abuse. Served with AUS, 1942-46, 51-52. Mem. Nat. Assn. Ind. Insurers, U. Wis. Assn. for Continuing Edn. in Bus. (dir.). Republican. Roman Catholic. Club: Madison East Rotary (dir. club and found.). Home: 2314 Hollister Ave Madison WI 53705 Office: 3099 E Washington Ave Madison WI 53704

WALLACE, IRVING, author; b. Chgo., Mar. 19, 1916; s. Alexander and Bessie (Liss) W.; student Williams Inst., Berkeley, Calif., 1935; m. Sylvia Kahn, June 3, 1941; children-David, Amy. Freelance writer articles, short stories Sat. Eve. Post, Cosmopolitan, Reader's Digest, Collier's, Esquire, others, 1931-53. Served with USAAF, Signal Corps, AUS, 1942-46. Mem. Authors Guild Am., Writers Guild Am., PEN, Soc. Authors (London). Author: The Fabulous Originals, 1955; The Square Pegs, 1957; The Fabulous Showman, 1959; The Sins of Philip Fleming, 1959; The Chapman Report, 1960; The Twenty-Seventh Wife, 1961; The Prize, 1962; The Three Sirens, 1963; The Man (George Washington Carver Inst. award, Commonwealth Club of Calif. Lit. award; Nat. Bestsellers Inst. 1965 Paperback of Year award), 1964; The Sunday Gentleman, 1965; The Plot, 1967; The Writing of One Novel, 1968; The Seven Minutes, 1969; The Nympho and Other Maniacs, 1971; The Word, 1972; The Fan Club (Popular Culture Assn. award of excellence), 1974; The People's Almanac, 1975; The R Document, 1976; The Book of Lists, 1977; The Two, 1978; The People's Almanac 2, 1978; The Pigeon Project, 1979; The Book of Lists 2, 1980; The Second Lady, 1980; contbr. to Am. Oxford Ency., Collier's Ency., Ency. Brit. Address: PO Box 49328 Los Angeles CA 90049

WALLACE, J. CLIFFORD, fed. judge; b. San Diego, Dec. 11, 1928; s. John Franklin and Lillie Isabel (Overing) W.; B.A., San Diego State U., 1952; LL.B., U. Calif., Berkeley, 1955; m. Virginia Lee Schlosser, Apr. 8, 1957; children—Paige, Laurie, Teri, John. Admitted to Calif. bar, 1955; with firm Gray, Cary, Ames & Frye, San Diego, 1955-70; U.S. judge for So. Dist. Calif., 1970-72; U.S. judge 9th Circuit Ct. Appeals, 1972—. Served with USN, 1946-49. Mem. Am. Bar Assn., Am. Law Inst., Am. Bd. Trial Advocates. Mormon (stake pres. San Diego East 1962-67, regional rep. 1967-74, 77—). Address: US Courthouse Room 4N25 940 Front St San Diego CA 92189. *My principles, ideals and goals and my standard of conduct are embodied in the Gospel of Jesus Christ. They come to fruition in family life, service, industry and integrity and in an attempt, in some small way, to make my community a better place within which to live.*

WALLACE, JAMES BREVARD, organist, orch.-choral dir., educator; b. Westminster, S.C., July 17, 1915; s. Joseph Edward and Mary (Reynolds) W.; A.B., U. Miss., 1936; B.Mus., Westminster Choir Coll., Princeton, N.J., 1939, D.Fine Arts, 1967; Mus.M., U. Mich., 1947; D.Mus., Hillsdale (Mich.) Coll., 1961. Organist, choir dir. various chs. N.Y., Pa., Miss., Mich., 1937-60; tchr. music, Phila., 1937-39; concert organist U.S., Europe, 1939-46; dean music Belhaven Coll., Jackson, Miss., 1939-42; prof. music U. Mich., Ann Arbor, 1949—, asso dean Sch. Music, 1950-60, dean, 1960-70, Guest lectr., tchr. U.S. Army Chaplain's Sch., 1947-48; cons. music and fine arts. Trustee Nat. Music Camp and Interlochen Arts Acad. Co-chmn. Mich. Council Arts, 1961-70. Bd. dirs. United Fund Ann Arbor; trustee Westminster Choir Coll. Served with AUS, 1942-46. Mem. Nat. Assn. Schs. Music, Music Educators Nat. Conf., Bohemians Detroit, Nat. Music Execs. of State Univs., Pi Kappa Lambda, Phi Mu Alpha, Kappa Kappa Psi. Presbyterian. Rotarian. Co-author: (textbooks) Richard Wagner and the Music Drama, 1954; Masterpieces of Music Literature, 1958. Home: 2226 Vinewood Blvd Ann Arbor MI 48104

WALLACE, JANE YOUNG (MRS. DONALD H. WALLACE), editor; b. Geneseo, Ill., Feb. 17, 1933; d. Worling R. and Margaret C. (McBroom) Young; B.S. in Journalism, Northwestern U., 1955, M.S. in Journalism, 1956; m. Donald H. Wallace, Aug. 24, 1959; children—Robert, Julia. Editor house organ Libby McNeill & Libby, Chgo., 1956-58; prodn. editor Instns. Mag., Chgo., 1958-61, food editor, 1961-65, mng. editor, 1965-68, editor-in-chief, 1968—, editor Instns./Volume Feeding Mag., 1970—, editorial dir. Service World Internat. Mag., 1971—, Foodservice Distbr. Salesman Mag., 1975—. Cons. Nat. Restaurant Assn., dir., 1977—; cons. Nat. Inst. for Foodservice Industry. Mem. com. investigation vocat. needs for food service tng. U.S. Dept. Edn., 1969; mem. Instnl. Food Editors' Conf., 1959—, pres., 1967; mem. hospitality industry edn. adv. bd. Ill. Dept. Edn., 1976, mem. adv. bd. Ill. sch. foodservice, 1978. Recipient Jesse H. Neal award for best bus. press editorial, 1969, 70, 73, 76, 77. Mem. Soc. for Advancement Foodservice Research (dir. 1975—), Internat. Foodservice Mfrs. Assn., Nat. Assn. Foodservice Equipment Mfrs., Am. Bus. Press Assn. (chmn. editorial com. 1978), Am. Inst. Interior Designers (asso.), Women in Communications (v.p. Chgo. 1957-58), Gamma Phi Beta, Kappa Tau Alpha. Editor: The Professional Chef, 1962; The Professional Chef's Book of Buffets, 1965. Contbr. restaurant chpt. World Book Ency., 1975, Food Service Trends, American Quantity Cooking, 1976. Home: 186 Signal Hill Rd Barrington IL 60010 Office: 5 S Wabash Ave Chicago IL 60603

WALLACE, JOAN EDAIRE SCOTT, social scientist, govt. ofcl.; b. Chgo., Nov. 8, 1930; d. William Edouard and Esther (Fulks) Scott; A.B. with honors, Bradley U., 1952; M.S.W. (Episcopal Youth Service fellow), Columbia U., 1954; postgrad. U. Chgo. Sch. Social Service Adminstrn., 1963-64; Ph.D. in Psychology (fellow), Northwestern U., 1973; D.Hum., U. Md., 1979; m. John H. Wallace, June 12, 1954 (div. Mar. 1977); children—Mark Scott, Eric Matthew, Victor Paul; m. 2d, Maurice A. Dawkins, Oct. 14, 1979. Social worker St. Mary's Home for Children, Chgo., 1954-58, casework dir., 1965-67; social worker United Charities Family Service Bur., Chgo., 1959-61; social work analyst Midway research project U. Chgo. Sch. Social Service Adminstrn., 1962-65; asso. prof. social work Jane Addams Grad. Sch. Social Work, U. Ill., Chgo. Circle, 1967-73; asso. prof. psychology Barat Coll., U. Ill., 1970-72; asso. dean, prof. Howard U. Sch. Social Work, Washington, 1973-76; asst. sec. Dept. Agr., Washington, 1977—; dep. exec. dir. Nat. Urban League, 1975-76; v.p. bd. execs. Morgan State U., 1976-77; mem. Pres.'s Com. on Handicapped, N.Y.C. Mayor's Com. on Aging; cons. in field. Trustee, St. Mary's Services for Children; bd. dirs. Travelers Aid Soc. Recipient Robert S. Abbott award, 1948; Disting. Alumni award Bradley U.; Links Paragon award, others. Office: Dept Agr 14th St and Independence Ave SW Washington DC 20250

WALLACE, JOHN CLEMENTS, metal co. exec.; b. Pitts., July 4, 1920; s. George R. and Jaquetta (Clements) W.; B.E., Yale, 1942; m. Carolyn Cresson, May 26, 1951 (dec. May 1956); 1 dau., Helen L.; m. 2d, Mary Willson, June 14, 1958; children—John Clements, Melissa W. Draftsman with Bessemer & Lake Erie R.R. Co., 1946-48; design engr. Lima Hamilton Corp., 1946-51; from chief engr. to v.p., gen. mgr. Hunt Spiller Mfg. Corp., Boston, 1951-57; v.p. mfg. Walworth Co., N.Y.C., 1957-58. v.p., gen. mgr., 1958-59, pres., 1959-60; sr. v.p., dir. John Wood Co., metal fabrications, N.Y.C., 1960-71, Anthes Imperial Ltd., 1967-69, Multiplex Co., 1966-70; pres. Struthers Nuclear & Process Co. div. Struthers Wells Corp., 1971, pres., dir. corp., 1972—. Served from ensign to lt., USNR, 1942-46. Mem. Yale Engring. Assn. Clubs: Union League (N.Y.C.); Short Hills (N.J.); Conwango (Warren, Pa.); Duquesne (Pitts.). Home: 500 3d Ave W Warren PA 16365 Office: 1003 Pennsylvania Ave W Warren PA 16365

WALLACE, JOHN DUNCAN, banker; b. Princeton, N.J., Feb. 12, 1933; s. John H. and Margaret (Cook) W.; B.A., Princeton U., 1955; m. Marjorie Goebel, Sept. 12, 1959; children—John, Christian, Marjorie. With fgn. dept. Hanover Bank, N.Y.C., 1959-62, Morgan Stanley Investment Bankers, N.Y.C., 1962-65; with N.J. Nat. Bank, Trenton, 1965—, sr. v.p., 1972-74, exec. v.p., 1974-76, pres., 1976—. Mem. Princeton Twp. Com., 1966-72; mayor, Princeton, 1969, 70-72; bd. trustees Princeton Day Sch., 1978—; exec. com. Council Princeton Univ. Community, 1978—; trustee Princeton Youth Fund, Princeton Battlefield Assn. Served with USN, 1955-59. Republican. Episcopalian. Clubs: Bedens Brook Country, Nassau, Trenton, Cap and Gown. Office: 1 W State St Trenton NJ 08603

WALLACE, JOHN FRANCIS, educator; b. Boston, Oct. 26, 1919; s. John Joseph and Ellen Gertrude (Organ) W.; B.S., Mass. Inst. Tech., 1941, M.S., 1953; m. Agnes Teresa Fitzgerald, July 17, 1943; children—Susan, Sally, Nancy. Metallurgist, head metal processing lab. div. Watertown Arsenal (now Army Materials and Mechanics Research Center), Watertown, Mass., 1941-54; metallurgist, chief heat treatment div., dir. Rodman Lab., Case Western Res. U., Cleve., 1954—, prof. metallurgy and materials sci., 1961—, Republic Steel prof. metallurgy, 1979—, chmn. dept., 1974—; cons. to industry; Hoyt Meml. lectr. Am. Foundrymen's Soc., 1975. Served with AUS, 1942-46. Decorated Bronze Star medal. Recipient Pangborn Gold medal Am. Foundrymen's Soc., 1962; award of honor Steel Founders Soc. Am., 1967; Nyselius award, Am. Die Casting Inst., 1967; Gold medal Gray and Ductile Soc., 1970. Fellow British Foundrymen's Soc.; mem. Am. Foundrymen's Soc. (hon. life, pres. tech. council 1972-74, chmn. gray iron div. 1970-72), Am. Inst. Mining and Metal Engrs., Am. Soc. Metals, Soc. Die Casting Engrs. (hon. life), Reserve Officers Soc., Sigma Xi. Author 3 books, editor 3 books; contbr. articles to profl. jours. Home: 3326 Braemar Rd Cleveland OH 44120

WALLACE, JOHN HOWARD, microbiologist; b. Cin., Mar. 8, 1925; s. John Howard and Lygia J. (Kaufman) W.; B.S., Howard U., 1947; M.S., Ohio State U., 1949, Ph.D., 1953; m. Kathryn E. Kennedy, July 21, 1979; children—John Howard III, Gloriajean L. Research asst. Cin. Children's Hosp., 1947-51; asst. instr. Ohio State U., Columbus, 1951-53, NIH fellow, 1954-55, prof. Coll. Biol. Scis., 1970-72; research asso. Harvard Med. Sch., Boston, 1955-59, bacteriologist, 1955-59; asso. prof. Meharry Med. Coll., Nashville, 1961-66, Tulane U. Med. Sch., New Orleans, 1966-70; prof., chmn. dept. microbiology and immunology U. Louisville Sch. Medicine, 1972—; organizer Conf. on Immunology of Aging, Nat. Inst. on Aging; mem. task force on immunization NIH. Mem. Commonwealth of Ky. Commn. on Human Rights. Mem. Am. Soc. Microbiology (pres. Ky.-Tenn. br.), Am. Assn. Immunologists, Sigma Xi, Kappa Alpha Psi. Office: Dept Microbiology and Immunology U Louisville Health Scis Center PO Box 35260 Louisville KY 40232*

WALLACE, JOHN MALCOLM, educator; b. London, Eng., Feb. 28, 1928; s. John Alfred Victor and Margery (Humphries) W.; B.A., Trinity Coll., Cambridge U., 1950, M.A., 1955; certificate edn., London U., 1952; Ph.D., Johns Hopkins, 1960; m. Justine Cecilia Cappola, Feb. 25, 1966 (div. 1976); 1 dau., Audrey Margery. Came to U.S., 1955, naturalized, 1964. Instr. English, Cornell U., 1960-63; asst. prof., then asso. prof. English, Johns Hopkins, 1963-67; prof. English, U. Chgo., 1967—; lectr., Clark Library, 1972, 76; chmn. Renaissance Seminar, 1976-79; dir. summer seminar Nat. Endowment Humanities, 1977; sr. research asso. Clark Library, 1980. Summer fellow Folger Library, 1961, Newberry Library, 1964, Huntington Library, 1976; Guggenheim fellow, 1969-70; overseas fellow Churchill Coll., Cambridge U., 1969-70; grantee Am. Council Learned Socs., summer 1973. Mem. Renaissance Soc. Am., Tudor and Stuart Club, Phi Beta Kappa. Author: Destiny His Choice: The Loyalism of Andrew Marvell, 1968; also articles, revs. Address: English Dept Univ Chicago Chicago IL 60637

WALLACE, JOHN MCCHRYSTAL, ret. banker; b. Salt Lake City, Dec. 14, 1893; s. William Ross and Annie (McChrystal) W.; B.A., U. of Utah, 1916; M.B.A., Harvard, 1921; LL.D., U. Utah, Westminster Coll., Brigham Young U.; m. Glenn Walker, Sept. 18, 1920; children—Matthew Henry Walker, John McChrystal. With Walker Bank & Trust Co., Salt Lake City, 1921—, dir., 1921-68, pres., 1944-57, chmn. bd., 1957-66, hon. chmn. bd., 1966-67, now advisory dir; pres., dir. United Park City Mines Co., 1955-64; v.p., dir. Banner Mining Co., 1953-71; v.p., dir. Ariz. Ranch & Metals Co.; former dir. Western Bancorp., Western Air Lines, Salt Lake City; Transam. Corp., Firstam. Corp., KSL Inc., Newhouse Realty Co., Salt Lake City Union Depot & R.R. Co. Civilian aide to sec. of army 1952-56; mem. Utah Senate, 1933-35. Mayor Salt Lake City, 1938-39. Mem. lay adv. bd., former chmn. Holy Cross Hosp.; trustee, former chmn. bd. trustees Westminster Coll. Named Businessman of Year Harvard Bus. Sch. Club, Utah, 1966; recipient Giants in our City award Salt Lake Area C. of C., 1977. Mem. Assn. Res. City Bankers (trustee banking research fund 1950-53), Utah Bankers Assn. (pres. 1946-47), Salt Lake City C. of C., Hon. Colo. Corps, Utah Nat. Guard, Chevaliers du Tastevin, Am. Soc. Order of St. John of Jerusalem (asso. knight), Sigma Chi. Presbyterian. Mason (33 deg. Shriner). Clubs: Alta, Cottonwood, Country (Salt Lake City); Los Angeles Country. Home: 2520 Walkers Ln Salt Lake City UT 84107 Office: 1600 Walker Bank Bldg Salt Lake City UT 84111

WALLACE, JOHN R., lawyer; b. Miami, Okla., Nov. 24, 1913; s. Arthur C. and Grace (VanMatre) W.; A.B., U. Okla., 1934; J.D., Harvard, 1937; m. Louise Bailey, Sept. 15, 1951; children—Ann Louise, John Robert. Admitted to Okla. bar, 1937, since practiced in Miami; partner firm Wallace & Wallace, 1937-41; sr. partner firm Wallace & Owens, 1946—. Dir., Security Bank & Trust Co., Welch State Bank, Exchange State Bank, Miami Savs. & Loan Assn. Chmn. bd. trustees Coll. of Ozarks, 1966-68. Served with AUS, 1942-46: ETO. Decorated Legion of Merit. Fellow Am. Bar Found., Am. Coll. Trial Lawyers, Am. Coll. Probate Counsel; mem. Am. (bd. govs. 1976-77), Okla. (pres. 1973) bar assns., Miami C. of C. Presbyterian (elder). Home: 2021 Yale Ave Miami OK 74354 Office: 21 S Main Box 1168 Miami OK 74354

WALLACE, KENNETH DONALD, lawyer; b. Spokane, Wash., Oct. 2, 1918; s. Donald and Adillah (Mason) W.; A.B. summa cum laude, Wash. State U., 1940; LL.B., Columbia, 1946; m. Ida H. Harvey, June 6, 1946 (div., 1965); children—Ann H., Jane B.; m. 2d, Betty Casey Major, July 31, 1965. Admitted to N.Y. bar, 1947, Conn. bar, 1971, since practiced in N.Y.C. and Conn.; with Cahill, Gordon, Reindel & Ohl, 1946-60; gen. counsel, sec. Bigelow-Sanford, Inc., 1960-70; v.p., dir. Oconee Realty Corp.; of counsel firms Ryan & Silberberg, N.Y.C., Bryan & Bollo, Stamford, Conn.; gen. counsel Johnson Assos., Inc., JAI Press, Inc., Alpen Pantry, Inc. Trustee Bigelow-Charitable Trust. Served to 1st lt. USAAF, 1942-46. Decorated D.F.C. with oak leaf cluster, Air medal with oak leaf cluster. Mem. Am. Acad. Polit. Sci., Am., N.Y. State, Conn. (vice chmn. antitrust sect.) bar assns., Assn. Bar City N.Y., Am. Soc. Corporate Secs., Phi Beta Kappa, Phi Sigma Kappa. Clubs: Union League (N.Y.C.); Landmark (Stamford, Conn.); New Canaan Field. Editor: Columbia Law Review, 1946. Home: Smith Ridge Rd New Canaan CT 06840 Office: 200 Park Ave New York NY 10016 also 2 Landmark Sq Stamford CT 06901

WALLACE, LEIGH ALLEN, JR., bishop; b. Norman, Okla., Feb. 5, 1927; s. Leigh Allen and Nellie Elizabeth (Whittemore) W.; B.A., U. Mont., 1950; M.Div., Va. Theol. Sem., 1962, D.Div., 1979; m. Alvira Kinney, Sept. 2, 1949; children—Jenny Leigh, Richard Kinney, William Paul. Ordained priest Episcopal Ch.; vicar chs., Sheridan, Virginia City, Jeffers, Mont., 1962-65; rector St. Luke's Ch., Billings, Mont., 1965-71; rector Holy Spirit Parish, Missoula, Mont., 1971-78; bishop of Spokane, 1979—. Served with USNR, 1945-46. Address: E 245 13th Ave Spokane WA 99202

WALLACE, LEON HARRY, educator; b. Terre Haute, Ind., Jan. 24, 1904; s. Harry Seymour and Leona A. (Wagoner) W.; student U. Ill., 1921-23; A.B., Ind. U., 1925, J.D., 1933; m. Anna Ruth Haworth, Aug. 21, 1926; children—Harry L., Susan J., Leona A. Prodn. mgr. Rand McNally & Co., S.F., 1927-30; admitted to Ind. bar, 1933; Supreme Ct. U.S., 1950; mem. Wallace, Handel & Wallace, 1933-44, Randel & Wallace, Terre Haute, 1944-45; asso. prof. law Ind. U., 1945-47, prof., 1947-74, acting dean 1951-52, dean sch. law, 1952-66, Charles McGuffey Hepburn prof. law, 1966-74, dean and prof. emeritus, 1974—. Chmn. adv. panel U.S. Dist. Ct. legislative apportionment; spl. hearing officer U.S. Dept. of Justice, 1964-68; Gov.'s rep. Ind. Constn. Revision Commn., 1967-69; spl. master U.S. Dist. Ct., No. Dist. Ind., 1969-72; cons. State of Ind., Ind.-Ky. border, 1966—. Mem. Am. (chmn. local govt. law section), Ind., Indpls. bar assns., Am. Judicature Soc., Am. Law Inst., Am. Acad. Social and Polit. Sci., Acad. Polit. Sci., Inst. Jud. Adminstrn., Ind. Bar Found. (dir., sec., treas., 1951-76, emeritus 1976—), Ind. Continuing Legal Edn. Forum, Phi Beta Kappa, Order of Coif, Phi Delta Phi (v.p. 1947-49, pres. 1949-51), Sigma Delta Chi, Delta Tau Delta. Democrat. Presbyn. Author works on legal subjects. Contbr. articles profl. pubs. Home: 939 S High St Bloomington IN 47401. *I have tried to achieve my goals and carry out my assignments in life by deciding, as objectively as I can, what is the right thing to do, both legally and* *morally. In this way, I can look at my children without apology, and, in their turn, they can remember me in the same way.*

WALLACE, LILA ACHESON, publisher; b. Virden, Man., Can.; d. T. Davis and Mary E. (Huston) Acheson; student Ward-Belmont Coll., Nashville, Tenn.; A.B., U. Oreg.; m. DeWitt Wallace, Oct. 15, 1921. Co-founder, past co-chmn. with husband, Reader's Digest. Recipient medal freedom Pres. U.S., 1972. Presbyterian. Home: High Winds Mount Kisco NY 10549 Office: Pleasantville NY 10570

WALLACE, MALCOLM VINCENT TIMOTHY, educator; b. Pittsfield, Mass., Oct. 3, 1915; s. Robert Emmett and Rachel Mary (Mooney) W.; A.B., St. Bonaventure Coll., 1936, postgrad., 1936-37; postgrad. U. Notre Dame, 1938-39; Ed.M., U. Buffalo, 1947; A.M., Harvard, 1949, postgrad., 1949-50, Ph.D., 1955; m. Kathryn Teresa Meyer, June 5, 1943; children—Michael William, Edmund Anthony, Mary Clare. Clk., Liberty Bank of Buffalo, 1937-38, cashier's office Buffalo Gen. Hosp., 1939-42; instr. St. Bonaventure (N.Y.) U., 1950-51, prof. classics, 1951—. Vis. prof. classics U. Ia., summer 1974. Served with AUS, 1942-45; ETO. Named Man of Year, Buffalo Council Catholic Men, 1960. Mem. Allegany Meml. Library Assn. (pres. 1962—), Am. Assn. U. Profs., Am. Philol. Assn., Classical Assn. Atlantic States, Vergilian Soc., Vergil Soc. (Eng.). Democrat. Roman Catholic. K.C. Founding editor, Cithara: Essays in the Judaeo-Christian Tradition, 1960-63, mng. editor, 1966-78. Home: 3276 W State Rd Olean NY 14760 Office: PO Box 61 St Bonaventure NY 14778

WALLACE, MARCIA, actress; b. Creston, Iowa, Nov. 1; B.A. in Drama and English, Parsons Coll. Started career in summer stock, later appeared off-Broadway with improvisational comedy group Fourth Wall; made TV comml.; TV appearances include Bob Newhart Show, 1972-78, Merv Griffin Show, Columbo, Brady Bunch, Love, American Style, Bewitched, Storefront Lawyers; appeared in motion picture Lady Sings the Blues, 1972, stage plays Fun City, Last of the Red Hot Lovers. Mem. AFTRA.*

WALLACE, MARTHA REDFIELD, found. exec.; b. Omaha, Dec. 27, 1927; d. Ralph J. and Lois (Thompson) Redfield; B.A. (Durant scholar), Wellesley Coll., 1949; M.A., Fletcher Sch. Law and Diplomacy, Tufts U., 1950; Litt. D. (hon.), Converse Coll., 1975; LL.D. (hon.), Occidental Coll., 1975, Pace U., 1975, Manhattan Coll., 1977. Instr. in econs., asst. to dean Fletcher Sch. Econs., Tufts U., 1950-51; economist Dept. State, Washington, 1951-53; with RCA Internat., 1954-55; mem. editorial staff Fortune mag., 1955-57; with IBM, 1960-61; asst. dir. corp. devel. Time, Inc., 1963-67; exec. dir., bd. dirs. Henry Luce Found., Inc., N.Y.C., 1967—; dir. Am. Can Co., Am. Express Co., Bristol-Myers Co., Chem. N.Y. Corp., N.Y. Stock Exchange, N.Y. Telephone Co.; trustee Bowery Savs. Bank; mem. Conf. Bd., 1974—; mem. Nat. Com. on U.S.-China Relations, 1975—; mem. Temporary Commn. on City Fins., 1975-77; mem. Brit.-N.Am. Com., 1976—, Trilateral Commn., 1978—; chmn., trustee Trust for Cultural Resources of City N.Y. Trustee, Williams Coll., 1974—, Citizens Budget Commn., 1976—; bd. dirs. Greater N.Y. Fund/United Way, 1975—. Mem. Am. Judicature Soc. (v.p., exec. com., dir. 1978), Council Fgn. Relations (dir. 1972—), Council on Founds. (dir. 1971-77), Found. Center (dir. 1971-77), Japan Soc. (dir. 1975—), N.Y. Racing Assn. (dir. 1976—), Acad. Polit. Scis., Phi Beta Kappa. Clubs: River, Millbrook Golf and Tennis, Bd. Room, Hemisphere. Office: 111 W 50th St New York NY 10020

WALLACE, MARY ELISABETH, polit. scientist; b. Oak Park, Ill., July 27, 1910 (parents Can. citizens); d. Malcolm William and Lily May (Pitkin) W.; B.A., U. Toronto (Ont., Can.), 1931, Oxford (Eng.) U., 1934; Ph.D., Columbia U., 1950. Asst. prof. polit. sci. U. Toronto, 1947-59, asso. prof., 1959-66, prof., 1966-76, prof. emeritus, 1976—. Recipient medal for popular biography U. B.C. (Can.), 1957. Mem. Can. Assn. Internat. Affairs, Can. Polit. Sci. Assn. Mem. United Ch. of Can. Author several books, the most recent being: The British Caribbean, 1977. Home: 421 Heath St E Toronto ON M4G 1B4 Canada

WALLACE, MIKE, TV interviewer and reporter; b. Brookline, Mass., May 9, 1918; s. Frank and Zina (Sharfman) W.; A.B., U. Mich., 1935-39; m. Lorraine Perigord, July 21, 1955; children—Peter (dec.), Christopher. Asso. with radio, 1939—, TV, 1946—; commentator CBS-TV, 1951-54, TV interviewer, reporter, 1951—, CBS news corr., 1963—; co-editor 60 Minutes, CBS. Recipient Robert Sherwood award, ATVAS Emmy award, 1971, 72, 73, George Foster Peabody awards, 1963-71, DuPont Columbia Journalism award, 1972, Carr Van Anda award, 1977, Thomas Hart Benton award, 1978. Mem. Sigma Delta Chi. Author: Mike Wallace Asks, 1958. Office: CBS News 524 W 57th St New York NY 10019

WALLACE, MIMI, advt. co. exec.; b. Englewood, N.J., Apr. 7, 1932; d. Jerome and Helen (Hirsch) Kolberg; B.A., N.Y. U., 1954; 1 son, David. Asst. radio-TV comml. bus. mgr. Batten, Barton Durstine & Osborne, Inc., N.Y.C., 1955-62; talent agt. Lester Lewis Assos., N.Y.C., 1964-68; with Ted Bates & Co., Inc., N.Y.C., 1968—, v.p. in charge radio-TV comml. bus. affairs, 1973, pres., 1975—; pres. Channelex, Inc., Calla Music, Inc., N.Y.C., 1973—. Home: 165 E 32d St New York NY 10016 Office: Ted Bates & Co Inc 1515 Broadway New York NY 10036

WALLACE, PHILIP RUSSELL, educator; b. Toronto, Ont., Can., Apr. 19, 1915; s. George Russell and Mildred (Stillwaugh) W.; B.A., U. Toronto, 1937, M.A., 1938, Ph.D., 1940; m. Jean Elizabeth Young, Aug. 15, 1940; children—Michael David, Kathryn Joan, Robert Philip. Instr. math. U. Toronto, 1938-40, U. Cin., 1940-42, Mass. Inst. Tech., 1942-43; asso. research scientist atomic energy div. NRC, 1943-46; mem. faculty McGill U., Montreal, Que., 1946—, prof. theoretical physics, 1949—, MacDonald prof. physics, 1976—, dir. Inst. Theoretical Physics, 1966-71, dir. Summer Sch. on Semicondrs., 1971. Vis. prof. Laboratoire de Physiques des Solides Universite Paul Sabatier de Toulouse, 1972-73; mem. physics research grants com. Nat. Research Council Can., 1972-75. Fellow Royal Soc. Can.; mem. Canadian Assns. Physicists (founder theoretical physics div. 1957, chmn. div. 1957-59), Am., European phys. socs., Canadian, McGill (pres. 1964-65) assns. univ. tchrs., Am. Assn. Physics Tchrs., Sigma Xi. Club: McGill Faculty (pres. 1960). Author: Mathematical Analysis of Physical Problems, 1972; Superconductivity 1-11, 2 vols., 1968; New Developments in Semiconductors, 1972; Editor: Canadian Jour. Physics, 1973—; mem. editorial bd. McGill-Queen's Press. Contbr. articles to profl. jours., Ency. Dictionary of Physics. Home: 125 Spartan Crescent Point Claire PQ Canada Office: McGill University PO Box 6070 Station A Dept Physics Montreal PQ Canada

WALLACE, PHYLLIS ANN, educator; b. Balt.; d. John L. and Stevella (Parker) Wallace; B.A., N.Y. U., 1943; M.A., Yale, 1944, Ph.D., 1948. Economist, statistician Nat. Bur. Econ. Research, 1948-52; lectr. Coll. City N.Y., 1948-51; asso. prof. econs. Atlanta U., 1953-57; econ. analyst U.S. Govt., 1957-65; chief tech. studies U.S. Equal Employment Opportunity Commn., Washington, 1966-69; v.p. research Met. Applied Research Center, N.Y.C., 1969-72; now prof. Sloan Sch. Mgmt. Mass. Inst. Tech., Cambridge; dir. State St. Bank and Trust Co., Boston. Trustee Brookings Instn., Washington; bd. dirs. Boston Mus. Fine Arts, Manpower Demonstration Research Corp.; mem. Minimum Wage Study Commn.; mem. Pres.'s Pay Adv. Com. Home: 780 Boylston St Boston MA 02199 Office: Sloan Sch Mgmt Mass Inst Tech Cambridge MA 02139

WALLACE, RALPH HOWES, engring. co. exec.; b. Williamsburg, Iowa, Feb. 25, 1916; s. John Rea and Lois Mary (Howes) W.; B.S., Iowa State U., 1946; m. Dorothea Lee Dexheimer, Dec. 28, 1941 (div. 1976); children—John F., Mary Helene; m. 2d, Muriel W. Nangle, 1976. Engr. bldgs and grounds Iowa State U., 1946; project engr. L.W. Malone, cons. engrs., Clear Lake, Iowa, 1946-48; cons. engr., Mason City, Iowa, 1948-56; partner Wallace & Holland, cons. engrs., Mason City, 1956-64; pres. Wallace Holland Kastler Schmitz & Co., Mason City, 1969—; dir. 1st Nat. Bank, Mason City; mem. Iowa State Bd. Regents, 1967-73; mem. Iowa Bd. Engring. Examiners, 1958-67, chmn., 1962, 63, 67; dir. Nat. Council State Bds. Engring. Examiners, 1965-67. Mem. Mason City Ind. sch. Bd., 1952-64, pres., 1964; mem. adv. bd. Center Indsl. Research and Service, Iowa State U., 1965-66; mem. adv. bd. Engring. Coll., U. Iowa, 1971-77; mem. adv. council Engring. Coll., Iowa State U., 1973—; bd. dirs. Iowa Ednl. Radio and TV Facility, 1972-76, Iowa Good Rds. Assn. Served to capt. AUS, 1941-46. Decorated Bronze Star, Croix de Guerre with Etoile d'Argent; registered profl. engr., Iowa, Minn. Fellow ASCE (dir. 1970-72, v.p. 1976, 77), Am. Cons. Engrs. Council; mem. Nat. Soc. Profl. Engrs., Iowa Engring. Soc., Am. Geophys. Union, AAAS (life), Am. Soc. for Engring. Edn., Am. Rd Builders Assn., Am. Legion, VFW. Republican. Mem. United Ch. Christ. Clubs: Rotary, Euchre and Cycle (Mason City); Embassy (Des Moines). Home: 718 E State St Mason City IA 50401 Office: Box 1467 Mason City IA 50401

WALLACE, ROBERT, poet, educator; b. Springfield, Mo., Jan. 10, 1932; s. Roy Franklin and Tincy (Stough) W.; A.B. summa cum laude, Harvard, 1953; B.A. with honours, St. Catharine's Coll., Cambridge (Eng.) U., 1955, M.A., 1959; m. Janeen Ann Weaver, July 24, 1965. Instr. English, Bryn Mawr Coll., 1957-61; asst. prof. English, Sweet Briar Coll., 1961-63, Vassar Coll., 1963-65; prof. English, Case Western Res. U., 1965—; reader Ednl. Testing Service, 1961-74, Book-of-Month Club 1964—. Served with AUS, 1955-57. Recipient William Rose Benet Meml. award, 1957, Bragdon prize, 1965; Fulbright scholar, 1953-55; Woodrow Wilson fellow, 1953-54. Author: This Various World and Other Poems, 1957; Views From a Ferris Wheel, 1965; Ungainly Things, 1968; Critters, 1978; Swimmer in the Rain, 1979. Editor: Poems on Poetry, 1965. Address: care Dept English Case Western Res U Cleveland OH 44106

WALLACE, ROBERT ASH, business exec.; b. Cordell, Okla.; s. John Marshall and Allie Beryl (Stewart) W.; student Okla. State U., 1938-42; B.A., U. Wash., 1945; Ph.D., U. Chgo., 1956; m. Lillian Rachel Simone Heine, 1977. Legis. asst. to U.S. Senator Paul Douglas, 1949-55; staff dir. U.S. Senate Banking and Urban Affairs, 1955-59; cons. to U.S. Senator John F. Kennedy, 1959-61; asst. sec. treasury, 1961-69; vice chmn. bd. Exchange Nat. Bank of Chgo., 1969-74, pres., 1974-76; research dir. spl. study on econ. change Joint Econ. Com., U.S. Congress, Washington, 1977-79; chmn. bd. PSM Internat. Corp., Chgo., 1979—; lectr. Adult Edn. Council Greater Chgo., 1957-58; staff dir. U.S. Joint Congl. Com. R.R. Retirement Legislation, 1952, mem. U.S. del. Internat. Textile Conf., Geneva, Switzerland, 1962; chmn. U.S. Assay Commn., Phila., 1962. Trustee Abraham Lincoln Centre, Chgo., Meadville-Lombard Theol. Sem.; del. Dem. Nat. Conv., 1972. Recipient U.S. Treasury Exceptional Service award, 1965, Alexander Hamilton award, 1968. Mem. Am. Bankers Assn., Chgo. Council Fgn. Relations. Democrat. Author: Factors Affecting the Stock Market, 1955; Congressional Control of Federal Spending, 1960. Contbr. articles to profl. jours. Home: 1623 Judson Ave Evanston IL 60201 Office: 200 W Monroe 1607 Chicago IL 60606

WALLACE, ROBERT BRUCE, surgeon; b. Washington, Apr. 12, 1931; s. William B. and Anne E. Wallace; B.A., Columbia U., 1953, M.D., 1957; m. Betty Jean Newel, Aug. 28, 1955; children—Robert B., Anne E., Barbara N. Chmn., prof. dept. surgery Mayo Clinic and Mayo Med. Sch., Rochester, Minn.; bd. govs. Mayo Clinic, 1968—; trustee Mayo Found., 1970—. Diplomate Am. Bd. Surgery, Am. Bd. Thoracic Surgery. Mem. A.C.S. (bd. govs. 1975—), Am. Surg. Assn., Soc. Clin. Surgery, Am. Assn. Thoracic Surgery, Internat. Cardiovascular Soc., Soc. Vascular Surgery. Home: 2816 Merrihills Dr Rochester MN 55901 Office: Dept Surgery Mayo Clinic Rochester MN 55901*

WALLACE, ROBERT FERGUS, banker; b. Bklyn., Oct. 5, 1934; s. Fergus F. and Isabelle Taylor (Wilson) W.; B.A., Colgate U., 1956; m. Florence S. Faminow, Dec. 18, 1959; children—Douglas F., Barbara E. Asst. v.p. Chem. Bank N.Y., N.Y.C., 1956-68; with First Nat. Bank Oreg., 1968—, pres., 1972—, chmn., 1975—; dir. Fed. Res. Bank San Francisco, Portland br. Bd. dirs. Boys Clubs Am.; trustee Western Forestry Center, Lewis and Clark Coll., Catlin Gabel Sch., Portland. Served to lt. (j.g.) USNR, 1957-60. Mem. Oreg. Hist. Soc. (trustee). Republican. Presbyterian. Clubs: Waverley Country, Arlington (Portland). Office: 1300 SW 5th Ave Portland OR 97208

WALLACE, ROBERT FRANCIS, business exec.; b. Chgo., Sept. 11, 1917; s. Peter A. and Helen Jeanne (Georres) W.; student U. Ill., 1935-37; B.S., Loyola U., Chgo., 1943; m. Harriet Jane Scales, Feb. 9, 1963; children—Warren L., David S. Staff auditor Arthur Andersen & Co., Chgo., 1943-49; exec. v.p., dir. Outboard Marine Corp., Waukegan, Ill., 1949—. Police magistrate, Winthrop, Ill., 1951-55. Bd. dirs. Ole Evinrude Found. Mem. Boating Industry Assn., Internat. Trade Club, Phi Eta Sigma. Home: Route 2 Box 97 Mundelein IL 60060 Office: 100 Sea Horse Dr Waukegan IL 60085

WALLACE, ROBERT GLENN, petroleum co. exec.; b. Webb City, Okla., Oct. 8, 1926; s. Glenn McKinsey and Sarah Elizabeth Wallace; B.S., Tex. A&M U., 1950; grad. Advanced Mgmt. Program, Harvard U.-U. Hawaii, 1972; m. Kelmor Wallace, Oct. 9, 1954; 1 son, John. Mgr. internat. sales and devel. Phillips Petroleum Co., 1970-71; pres. Sealright Co., Inc., Kansas City, Mo., 1972-73; v.p. plastics Phillips Petroleum Co., Bartlesville, Okla., 1974-78, sr. v.p., 1978—; dir. Applied Automation, Inc., Pier 66 Corp. Served with USNR 1944-46. Republican. Home: 2640 Williamsburg Bartlesville OK 74003 Office: Phillips Petroleum Co Phillips Bldg Bartlesville OK 74004

WALLACE, SPENCER MILLER, JR., hotel exec.; b. Portland, Maine, Aug. 17, 1923; s. Spencer M. and Caroline (Clark) W.; m. Margaret Keeler, May 12, 1956; 1 son, Daniel Walker. With Hotels Statler, 1944-54, Hilton Hotels Corp., 1954-57, Hilton Hotels, Internat., 1957-61; exec. v.p., dir. Hotel Syracuse Corp. (N.Y.), 1961—. Mem. Syracuse Govtl. Research Bur. Mem. N.Y. State Hotel Assn., Am. (past dir.), N.Y. State (past pres.), Syracuse (past pres.) hotel and motel assns., Syracuse C. of C. (dir.). Episcopalian. Mason (Shriner, Jester). Home: 5 Wheeler Ave Fayetteville NY 13066 Office: 500 S Warren St Syracuse NY 13201

WALLACE, THOMAS C(HRISTOPHER), editor; b. Vienna, Austria, Dec. 13, 1933 (parents Am. citizens); s. Don and Julia (Baer) W.; grad. Peddie Sch., 1951; B.A., Yale, 1955, M.A. in History, 1957; m. Lois Kahn, July 19, 1962; 1 son, George Baer. Editor, G.P. Putnam Sons, N.Y.C., 1959-63; with Holt, Rinehart & Winston, N.Y.C., 1963—, editor-in-chief gen. books div., 1968—. Bd. dirs. Roger Klein Found. Mem. P.E.N. Clubs: Yale, Century Assn. (N.Y.C.); Pound Ridge (N.Y.) Tennis. Home: 45 E 82d St New York City NY 10028 Office: 383 Madison Av New York City NY 10017

WALLACE, THOMAS P., univ. dean; b. Washington, Apr. 11, 1935; B.S., State U. N.Y. at Potsdam, 1958; M.S., Syracuse U., 1961; M.S., St. Lawrence U., 1964; fellow Mellon Inst. Sci., 1967-68; Ph.D. in Phys. Chemistry, Clarkson Coll. Tech., 1968; married 1959; 3 children. Asst. prof. chemistry State U. N.Y. at Potsdam, 1961-67; mem. faculty Rochester (N.Y.) Inst. Tech., 1968—, asso. prof., 1970—, head dept. chemistry, 1970-72, asso. dean Coll. Sci., after 1972, dean, 1973-78; prof. chem. scis. Old Dominion U., Norfolk, Va., 1978—, dean sci. and health professions, 1978—. Mem. Am. Chem. Soc. Contbr. articles to profl. jours. Address: Office of Dean Old Dominion U Coll Scis Norfolk VA 24011

WALLACE, WALTER L., sociologist, educator; b. Washington, Aug. 21, 1927; s. Walter L. and Rosa Belle (Powell) W.; B.A., Columbia, 1954; M.A., Atlanta, 1955; Ph.D., U. Chgo., 1963; children—Jeffrey Richard, Robin Claire, Jennifer Rose. Instr. Spelman Coll., Atlanta U., 1955-57; from lectr. to prof. sociology Northwestern U., Evanston, Ill., 1963-71; prof. sociology Princeton, 1971—; staff sociologist Russell Sage Found., N.Y.C., 1969-77, vis. scholar, 1968; cons. World Book, 1977—; fellow Center for Advanced Study in Behavioral Scis., Stanford, Calif., 1974-75. Mem. council Found. for Child Research, N.Y.C. Served with AUS, 1950-52. Mem. Am. Sociol. Assn. (council 1971-74), Caucus of Black Sociologists, Sociol. Research Assn. Author: Student Culture, 1966; Logic of Science in Sociology, 1971; (with James E. Conyers) Black Elected Officials, 1975. Editor-author: Sociological Theory, 1969. Address: Dept Sociology Princeton University Princeton NJ 08540

WALLACE, WESLEY HERNDON, broadcaster, educator; b. Denver, Apr. 18, 1912; s. William Harvey and Lillian Frances (Parker) W.; B.S., N.C. State U., 1932; M.A., U. N.C., 1954; Ph.D., Duke U., 1962; m. Mary Carolyn Andrews, Feb. 23, 1956; 1 dau., Sue Daniels. Broadcaster, writer, producer, announcer Sta. WPTF, Raleigh, N.C., 1934-42; gen. mgr. Manila Broadcasting Co., Philippines, 1948-50; lectr. in radio and TV, U. N.C., Chapel Hill, 1952-54, asst. prof., 1954-57, asso. prof., 1957-66, prof., 1966—, chmn. dept. radio, TV, motion pictures, 1962-74, acting chmn., 1976-77; cons. So. Regional Edn. Bd., 1964-67; mem. Gov.'s Ednl. TV Commn., 1962-64, also mem. central steering com. of commn.; cons. U.S. GAO, 1977-78; adminstrv. bd. sta. WUNC-FM, also adv. council sta.; v.p. Triangle Advt. Fedn., 1977-78. Bd. dirs. Orange County Chpt. N.C. Symphony Soc. Served with U.S. Army, 1942-47. Decorated Bronze Star, Army Commendation medal with oak leaf cluster. Mem. N.C. Assn. Broadcasters (Earle Gluck Disting. Service award 1975, Broadcasting Hall of Fame 1976), Broadcasting Edn. Assn., Nat. Assn. Ednl. Broadcasters, Radio-TV News Dirs. Assn., Radio-TV News Dirs. of Carolinas, Nat. Assn. TV Program Execs., Internat. Radio and TV Soc., Triangle Advt. Fedn. (Silver medal 1978), N.C. Hist. Soc., So. Hist. Assn., Kappa Phi Kappa, Phi Kappa Phi. Democrat. Baptist. Writer, producer, dir. program Compact Day, 1953; contbr. articles to profl. and hist. publs. Home: 102 Carol Woods Chapel Hill NC 27514 Office: 209A Swain Hall 044A U North Carolina Chapel Hill NC 27514

WALLACE, WILLIAM, III, cons. engring. co. exec.; b. Bklyn., June 6, 1926; s. William and Ruth (Fitch) W.; B.E.E., Union Coll., Schenectady, 1947; m. Dorothy Ann Reimann, Aug. 2, 1969; 1 son, Andrew William. Test engr. Gen. Electric Co., Schenectady, 1947; engr. Ebasco Services, Inc., N.Y.C., 1948-67, chief elec. engr., 1967-70, mgr. projects, 1970-73, v.p. Atlanta office, Norcross, Ga., 1973-76, exec. v.p., N.Y.C., 1976—, also dir. Deacon, Fifth Ave. Presbyterian Ch., N.Y.C. Registered profl. engr., Ark., Conn., Del., Ga., Fla., Ind., Iowa, Kans., La., Mich., Minn., Mo., N.H., N.Y., N.C., Ohio, Pa., S.C., Tex., Va., Vt., Wyo. Mem. IEEE (sr.), Delta Upsilon (dir.). Republican. Home: 84 Buckhaven Hill Upper Saddle River NJ 07458 Office: 2 Rector St New York NY 10006

WALLACE, WILLIAM EDWARD, scientist, educator; b. Fayette, Miss., Mar. 11, 1917; s. James D. and Mattie (Rogers) W.; B.S., Miss. Coll., 1936; Ph.D., U. Pitts., 1940; m. Helen Meyer, June 21, 1947; children—Richard Glen, Donald Alan, Marcia Louise. Teaching asst. U. Pitts., 1936-40, research asso. chemistry, 1945-49, mem. faculty, 1949—, prof. chemistry, chmn. dept., 1963-77, prof. materials and metall. engring., 1973—, prof. chem. engring., 1977—; research asso. Ohio State U., 1944-45; cons. Wright-Patterson AFB, 1962—, Du Pont, 1977—, Gen. Motors, 1974—, Amoco, 1977—. Mem. Pa. Gov.'s Sci. Com., Pa. Sci. and Engring. Found. Bd. Fellow Carnegie Instn., Washington, 1940-42; Buhl fellow, 1942-44; Guggenheim fellow, 1954-55. Mem. AAAS, Am. Chem. Soc. (dir. Pitts.), Sigma Xi, Phi Lambda Upsilon. Research on metals and intermetallics, hydrogen as a fuel, solar energy utilization, coal gasification. Home: 201 Pinecrest Dr Pittsburgh PA 15237

WALLACE, WILLIAM HUSTON, educator; b. Chgo., Dec. 10, 1924; s. Leow Huston and Barbara (Keizer) W.; B.S. in Geology, Beloit Coll., 1948; M.S. in Geography, U. Wis., 1950, Ph.D. in Geography, 1956; m. Faith Dunning Morgan, Sept. 2, 1950; children—Holly, Hope. Lectr. geography U. Auckland, New Zealand, 1952-54; instr. Rutgers U., New Brunswick, N.J., 1954-56, asst. prof. geography, 1956-57; mem. faculty U. N.H. at Durham, 1957—, prof. geography, 1965—, chmn. dept., 1968—; Fulbright lectr. U. Oslo, Norway, 1971. Mem. com. geography Grad. Record Exam., 1965-72, chmn., 1970-72. Mem. Sch. Bd., Barrington, N.H., 1965-68, chmn., 1967-68; mem. Planning Bd., Barrington, 1970-76, chmn., 1974-76. Served with USMC, 1943-46. Guggenheim fellow, 1963. Mem. Assn. Am. Geographers (pres. New Eng. div. 1968-69, councillor 1971-75), Canadian Assn. Geographers, Am. Geog. Soc. Contbr. articles to profl. jours. Home: Star Route Barrington NH 03825

WALLACE, WILLIAM RAY, fabricated steel mfg. co. exec.; b. Shreveport, La., Mar. 25, 1923; s. Jason Mohoney and Mattie Evelyn (Adair) W.; B.S. in Engring., La. Tech., 1944; m. Minyone Milligan Rose, Oct. 5, 1966; children—Jayne Cecile Rose McDearman, Susan Rose, H. Robert Rose; children by previous marriage—Patrick Scott, Michael B., Timothy, Shelly. Field engr. Austin Bridge Co., Dallas, 1944-45; core analyst Core Labs., Bakersfield, Calif., 1945-46; chief engr., then sec.-treas., exec. v.p. Trinity Industries, Inc., Dallas, 1946-58, pres., 1958—, also dir.; dir. Redman Industries, Inc., Lomas & Nettleton Financial Corp., Republic Nat. Bank, Dallas, Tex. Employers Ins. Assn., ENSERCH Corp. Methodist. Home: Dallas TX Office: 4001 Irving Blvd Dallas TX 75207

WALLACH, ALLAN HENRY, drama critic; b. N.Y.C., Oct. 23, 1927; s. Julius and Beatrice (Markowitz) W.; B.A. magna cum laude, Syracuse (N.Y.) U., 1951; m. Shirley Meyrowitz, Nov. 26, 1953; children—Jonathan, Mark, Paul. Tech. writer H.L. Yoh Co., Phila., 1951-53; reporter Patchogue (N.Y.) Advance, 1953-54; reporter, copy editor New Haven Register, 1954-56; successively reporter, copy editor, asst. night city editor, news feature editor, entertainment editor Newsday, Garden City, N.Y., 1957-71, drama critic, 1972—. Served with USNR, 1946-47. Mem. N.Y. Drama Critics Circle, New Drama Forum Assn., Am. Theatre Critics Assn., Deadline Club,

Sigma Delta Chi. Home: 64 Long St Huntington Station NY 11746 Office: Long Island NY 11747

WALLACH, ANNE JACKSON, actress; b. Pitts.; d. John Ivan and Stella Germaine (Murray) J.; grad. high sch.; m. Eli Wallach, Mar. 5, 1948; children—Peter, Roberta, Katherine. Profl. debut Cherry Orchard; mem. Am. Repertory Co.; Broadway plays include Summer and Smoke, Magnolia Alley, Love Me Long, The Last Dance, Oh Men, Oh Women, Major Barbara, Middle of the Night, Promenade All; nat. touring co. Waltz of the Toreadors; films include The Journey, Tall Story, How to Save a Marriage. . . And Ruin Your Life, The Secret Life of an American Wife, Zig-Zag, Lovers and Other Strangers, Dirty Dingus Maggee, Nasty Habits; Equity Library Theatre prodn. This Property is Condemned; also The Tiger Makes Out, Inquest, The Front Page; TV appearances include Armstrong Circle Theatre, G.E. Playhouse, Gunsmoke, Marcus Welby, M.D., Sticks and Stones, 84, Charing Cross Road, 20 Shades of Pink. Recipient Obie award.

WALLACH, EDWARD ELIOT, physician, educator; b. N.Y.C., Oct. 8, 1933; s. David Abraham and Madeleine (Spiro) W.; B.A., Swarthmore Coll., 1954; M.D., Cornell U., 1958; M.A. (hon.), U. Pa., 1970; m. Joanne Levey, June 24, 1956; children—Paul, Julie. Intern 2d med. div. Bellevue Hosp., N.Y.C., 1958-59; resident obstetrics and gynecology Kings County Hosp., Bklyn., 1959-63; asst. instr. State U. N.Y. Downstate Med. Center, Bklyn., 1962-63; mem. faculty U. Pa. Sch. Medicine, 1965—, prof. obstetrics and gynecology, 1971—, chief endocrinology sect., div. human reprodn., dept. obstetrics and gynecology, 1968-71, mem. admissions com., 1970-73, mem. community health com., 1966-71, mem. student adv. com., 1966—, mem. com. for appointments and promotions, 1972—, chmn., 1974-77; dir. dept. obstetrics and gynecology Pa. Hosp., 1971—, sec., treas. profl. staff, 1972-75. Trustee Marriage Council Phila., 1970-78; chmn. finance com. Phila. Coordinating Council for Family Planning, 1972-73, chmn. med. adv. com., 1973-76. Served as surgeon USPHS, 1963-65. Grantee USPHS, 1961-62; recipient Lindback Found. Distinguished Teaching award U. Pa., 1971. Diplomate Am. Bd. Obstetrics and Gynecology. Fellow Am. Coll. Obstetricians and Gynecologists, Am. Fertility Soc. (dir. 1977—); mem. Am. Gynecol. Soc., Endocrine Soc., Soc. Gynecol. Investigation, Phila. Endocrine Soc., Obstet. Soc. Phila. (program chmn. 1969-70, 70-71, 71-72, mem. council 1972—, v.p. 1976-77, pres. 1979-80), AAAS, Soc. Study Reprodn., Alpha Omega Alpha. Asso. editor Fertility and Sterility, 1974—. Contbr. to med. jours. Editorial bd. Fertility and Sterility, 1970—; Obstetrics and Gynecology, 1976—, Contemporary Obstetrics and Gynecology, 1976—, Biology of Reprodn., 1978—. Home: 27 Wiltshire Rd Overbrook Hills PA 19151 Office: Dept Obstetrics and Gynecology Pennsylvania Hosp Philadelphia PA 19107

WALLACH, ELI, actor; b. Bklyn., Dec. 7, 1915; s. Abraham and Bertha (Schorr) W.; A.B., U. Tex., 1936; M.S. in Edn., Coll. City N.Y., 1938; student Neighborhood Playhouse Sch. of Theatre, 1940; hon. degree Emerson Coll., Boston; m. Anne Jackson, Mar. 5, 1948; children—Peter Douglas, Roberta Lee, Katherine Beatrice. Actor, 1945—: Broadway plays include Antony and Cleopatra, 1948, Mr. Roberts, 1949-50, Rose Tatoo, 1950-52, Camino Real, 1953, Mademoiselle Colombe, 1953, Teahouse of the August Moon, 1954-55 (London prodn. 1954), Major Barbara, 1956, Rhinoceros, 1961, Luv, 1964; Promenade All, 1972; appeared off-Broadway prodn. Typists and the Tiger, 1962-63, London prodn., 1964; Saturday, Sunday, Monday, 1974; appeared in nat. tour co. Waltz of the Toreadors, 1973-74; appeared TV shows; motion pictures include Baby Doll, Line-Up, Magnificent 7, Misfits; Hemingway's Adventures of a Young Man, How the West Was Won, The Victors, 1962, Lord Jim, 1964, How To Steal a Million, The Good, the Bad and the Ugly, The Tiger Makes Out, Band of Gold, Zig-Zag, Cinderella Liberty, 1973, Crazy Joe, 1973, Movie, Movie, 1976. Corp. mem., dir. Neighborhood Playhouse Sch. Theatre. Served to capt. Med. Adminstrn. Corps, AUS, World War II. Recipient Donaldson, Theatre World, Variety, Antoinette Perry awards; Brit. Film Acad. award, 1956. Original mem. Actors Studio.

WALLACH, IRA, writer; b. N.Y.C., Jan. 22, 1913; s. Morris David and Rose (Sims) W.; student Cornell; m. Devera Sievers, Jan. 25, 1941; 1 dau., Leah B.S.; m. 2d, Lillian Opatoshu, June 4, 1970. Author: The Horn and the Roses, 1947; How to be Deliriously Happy, 1949; Hopalong-Freud, 1951; Hopalong-Freud Rides Again, 1950; Gutenberg's Folly, 1954; How to Pick a Wedlock, 1956; Muscle Beach, 1959; The Absence of a Cello, 1960; Horatio, 1954, Phoenix 55, 1955, (with A.S. Ginnes) Drink To Me Only, 1958; (play) Smiling, the Boy Fell Dead, 1961; (screen play) Boys' Night Out, 1962; (with George Goodman) The Wheeler-Dealers (screen-play); Absence of a Cello (play), 1964; (with Peter Ustinov) screen-play Hot Millions (Motion Picture Acad. nomination 1968, Writers Guild of Gt. Britain award for best Brit. comedy screenplay 1968); Five Thousand Years of Foreplay, 1976; (play) Phoenix 76. Mem. Authors Guild Am., Dramatists Guild, Writer's Guild Am., Aircraft Owners and Pilots Assn., P.E.N. Home: 345 W 58th St New York NY 10019

WALLACH, IRA DAVID, lawyer, bus. exec.; b. N.Y.C., June 3, 1909; s. Joseph and Della (Kahn) W.; A.B., Columbia, 1929, J.D., 1931; m. Miriam Gottesman, Dec. 25, 1938. Admitted to N.Y. bar, 1932; practiced in N.Y.C., 1932-45; exec. v.p. Gottesman & Co., Inc., N.Y.C., 1952-56, pres., 1956-74, chmn., chief exec. officer, 1974-79, chmn., 1979—, dir., 1947—; exec. v.p. Central Nat. Corp., N.Y.C., 1952-56, pres., 1956-74, chmn., chief exec. officer, 1974-79, chmn., 1979—, dir., 1948—; exec. v.p. Eastern Corp., Bangor, Maine, 1951-52, dir., 1947-58; dir. Interstate Paper Corp., N.Y.C., Allied Maintenance Corp., N.Y.C., Canadian Cellulose Co. Ltd., Vancouver, B.C., Stora Kopparberg Sales Co., Inc., N.Y.C.; mem. Grand Central adv. bd. Chem. Bank, N.Y.C. Pres., D.S. and R. H. Gottesman Found., 1956—, bd. dirs., 1941—; pres. and dir. Miriam and Ira D. Wallach Found., 1956—. Served to lt. USNR, 1943-46. Mem. Am. Bar Assn., Assn. Bar City of N.Y., N.Y. Co. Lawyers Assn. Home: 5 Sherbrooke Rd Scarsdale NY 10583 Office: 100 Park Ave New York NY 10017

WALLACH, JOHN S(IDNEY), library adminstr.; b. Toronto, Ohio, Jan. 6, 1939; s. Arthur M. and Alice I. (Smith) W.; B.S. in Edn., Kent State U., 1963; M.L.S., U. R.I., 1968; M.P.A., U. Dayton, 1977; m. Jane F. Springett, Sept. 21, 1963; children—John Michael, Wendy Anne, Bethany Lynne, Kristen Michele. Dir., Mercer County (Ohio) Library, 1968-70, Greene County (Ohio) Library, 1970-77; asso. dir. Dayton and Montgomery County (Ohio) Library, 1978, dir., 1979—; del. White House Conf. on Libraries and Info. Sci., 1979. Active health div. United Way, Dayton; bd. dirs. Dayton Mus. Natural History, Family Service Assn. Dayton. Served with USN, 1963-68; comdr. USNR. Mem. ALA (council), Ohio Library Assn. (exec. bd.), Naval Res. Assn., Res. Officers Assn. Club: Kiwanis (Dayton). Office: 215 E Third St Dayton OH 45402

WALLACH, LUITPOLD, educator, author; b. Munich, Germany, Feb. 6, 1910; s. Karl and Rosa (Schneeweis) W.; student Berlin U., 1929-30; Ph.D., U. Tuebingen, 1932, Cornell U., 1947; m. Barbara Jean Price, Aug. 22, 1970. Came to U.S., 1939, naturalized, 1947; Asst. prof. Hamilton Coll., 1951-52, U. Oreg., 1953, Cornell U., 1953-55, U. Okla., 1955-57, Harpur Coll., 1957-62; prof. classics Marquette U., Milw., 1962-67, faculty fellow, 1967, mem. bd. grad. studies, 1964-67; prof. classics U. Ill., Urbana, 1967-78, prof. emeritus, 1978—, asso. Center Advanced Study, 1969-70. Fund for Advancement Edn. fellow, 1952; Am. Council Learned Socs. grantee, 1960; fellow Leo Baeck Inst., 1967—. Mem. Am. Hist. Assn., Am. Philol. Assn., Medieval Acad. Am., N.Am. Patristic Soc. (exec. com. 1970-72), Phi Beta Kappa, Phi Kappa Phi, Sigma Tau Delta, Eta Sigma Phi. Author: Berthold of Zwiefalten's Chronicle, 1958; Alcuin and Charlemagne, 1959, 2d edit., 1968; Liberty and Letters, 1959; The Classical Tradition, 1966; Diplomatic Studies in Documents, 1977; Die Zwiefalter Chroniken, 1978; Alcuin's Libri Carolini, 1980; mem. editorial adv. com. Ill. Classical Studies, 1973-77; contbr. articles to profl. jours. Festschrift für Luitpold Wallach dedicated in his honor, 1975. Home: 708 S Urbana Ave Urbana IL 61801 Office: 4072 FLB U Ill Urbana IL 61801

WALLACH, MORTON BERTRAM, physician; b. N.Y.C., July 13, 1921; s. Joseph I. and Rose (Bernstein) W.; B.A., N.Y. U., 1940; M.D. summa cum laude, L.I. Coll. Medicine, 1943; D.Sc., L.I. U., 1972; m. Shirley Schmones, June 11, 1944; children—Joelle Marsha, Lee Anne. Rotating intern Jewish Hosp. of Bklyn., 1944; asst. resident medicine Goldwater Meml. Hosp., 1945, resident in neurology, 1946; practice medicine specializing in internal medicine and psychiatry, N.Y.C., 1946—; med. officer FDA, 1955; resident in psychiatry Creedmoor State Hosp., 1960-64, asst. supervising psychiatrist, 1964—, now clin. dir.; asst. vis. psychiatrist St. Vincents Hosp., 1963—; dir. Meyer Psychiat. Hosp., 1968-69, Bklyn. State Hosp., 1969-79, Middletown (N.Y.) Psychiat. Center, 1979—; asst. prof. psychiatry N.J. Coll. Medicine, 1967—; prof. psychiatry Downstate Med. Coll., 1969—; clin. prof. psychiatry N.Y. Sch. Psychiatry, 1969—; cardiac cons. N.Y.C. Dept. of Health, 1954—; asst. adj. in medicine Beth Israel Hosp., N.Y. Served as capt. USAF, 1952-54. Diplomate Am. Bd. Internal Medicine, Am. Bd. Psychiatry and Neurology. Fellow Am. Geriatrics Soc., Acad. Psychosomatic Medicine, A.C.P., Am. Psychiat. Assn.; mem. Am. Med. Writers Assn., AMA, N.Y. State, Queens County med. socs., Phi Beta Kappa. Author articles in field. Address: 141 Monhagen Ave Middletown NJ 10940

WALLACH, PHILIP, mfg. co. exec.; b. N.Y.C., May 29, 1928; s. Morris and Lillian (Levy) W.; B.S., U.S. Mcht. Marine Acad., 1950; postgrad. N.C. State Grad. Sch. Engring., N.Y. U. Grad. Sch. Bus.; m. Florence O'Neil, Apr. 8, 1951; children—Ruth, Sandra, Louis, David. Sales mgr. Nordberg Mfg. Co., 1955-67; v.p. mktg., pres. Engine div. Fairbanks Morse subs. Colt Industries, Inc., N.Y.C., 1967-71, corporate v.p., group exec., 1971, group v.p., 1972—; pres. Colt Industries Internat., Inc.; dir. Famoven, Caracas, Venezuela. Served to lt. USNR, 1953-55. Recipient Outstanding Profl. Achievement award U.S. Mcht. Marine Acad., Marine Man of the Yr. award. Mem. Am. Soc. Naval Engrs., Soc. Naval Architects and Marine Engrs. Club: Economic (N.Y.C.). Home: 3211 Montlake Dr Rockford IL 61111 Office: 701 Lawton Ave Beloit WI 53511

WALLACH, ROBERT CHARLES, physician; b. Bklyn., Jan. 2, 1935; s. Irving T. and Saralta W.; B.A. with honors (N.Y. State Regents scholar), Swarthmore Coll., 1956; M.D., Yale U., 1960; m. Judith Leffert, Apr. 1, 1968. Intern, Beth Israel Hosp., N.Y.C., 1960-61, resident in Ob-Gyn, 1961-65; fellow in gynecol. oncology SUNY, Bklyn., 1965-66; practice medicine specializing in Ob-Gyn, N.Y.C., 1966—; chief Ob-Gyn, Gouverneur Hosp., N.Y.C., 1966-76; dir. Ob-Gyn, Beth Israel Med. Center, N.Y.C., 1977—; prof. clin. Ob-Gyn, Mt. Sinai Sch. Medicine, N.Y.C., 1977—; lectr. SUNY, Bklyn. Fellow Am. Coll. Obstetricians and Gynecologists, A.C.S.; mem. Soc. Gynecol. Oncologists, Am. Fertility Soc., N.Y. Acad. Medicine, N.Y. Acad. Sci., N.Y. Cancer Soc., Am. Public Health Assn., N.Y. Obstetrical Soc., Internat. Soc. for Study Vulvar Disease. Office: 10 Perlman Pl New York NY 10003

WALLECHINSKY, DAVID, author; s. Irving and Sylvia (Kahn) Wallace. Author: (with Frank C. Bucaro) Chico's Organic Gardening and Natural Living, 1972; (with Irving Wallace) The People's Almanac, 1975, The People's Almanac Presents: The Book of Lists, 1977; (with Michael Medved) What Really Happened to the Class of '65, 1976; (with Irving Wallace) The People's Almanac No. 2, 1978. Office: care William Morrow and Co Inc 105 Madison Ave New York NY 10016*

WALLEIGH, ROBERT SHULER, assn. exec.; b. Washington, Mar. 31, 1915; s. Charles Henry and Martha (McDaniel) W.; B.S. in Elec. Engring., George Washington U., 1936; m. Catherine Richarde Coulon, Feb. 22, 1938; children—Margaret Coulon (Mrs. Shaffer), Catherine Richarde (Mrs. Carnevale). Test engr. Gen. Electric Co., 1936-38; rating examiner Civil Service Commn., 1938-39; adminstrv. asst. Pub. Roads Adminstrn., Washington, 1939-42; elec. engr. to dep. asst. dir. for adminstrn. Nat. Bur. Standards, 1943-53, asso. dir for adminstrn., 1955-75, asso. dir. emeritus, cons., 1975-79, acting dep. dir., 1975-79, sr. adv. internat. affairs, 1978-79; asst. for adminstrn. Diamond Ordnance Fuze labs. Dept. Army, 1953-55; cons. IEEE, Washington, 1979—. Trustee emeritus Govt. Services, Inc. Recipient Naval Ordnance Devel. award, 1945; Exceptional Service award with gold medal Dept. Commerce, 1967; Engr. Alumni Achievement award George Washington U., 1975, others. Methodist. Home: 5701 Springfield Dr Washington DC 20016 Office: IEEE 1111 19th St NW Washington DC 20036

WALLENDORF, PAUL E., business exec.; b. 1909; B.S., Northwestern U., 1931; m. With Gen. Electric Co., 1931-74, v.p., treas., 1968-74; pres. Pvt. Export Funding Corp., N.Y.C., 1974-77. C.P.A., Ill. Home: 2 Mead St New Canaan CT 06840 also 1225 S Ocean Blvd Delray Beach FL 33444 Office: 280 Park Ave New York City NY 10017

WALLENSTEIN, ALFRED FRANZ, condr.; b. Chgo., Oct. 7, 1898; s. Franz Albrecht Von and Anna (Klinger) W.; ed. pub. schs.; hon. Mus.D., Wooster Coll., 1943, U. So. Calif., 1951, Redlands U. Calif., 1954, Peabody Inst., Balt., 1962; m. Virginia Wilson, May 10, 1924. Began playing cello in pub. at age 9; made concert tours through Europe, S.Am., N.Am.; solo cellist Chgo. Symphony Orch., 1923-29, N.Y. Philharmonic Orch., 1929-36; head cello dept. Chgo. Mus. Coll., 1927-29. Has made many transcriptions for cello. Mus. dir. Radio Station WOR, 1935-45; condr., mus. dir. Los Angeles Philharmonic Orch., 1943-56; condr. Symphony of the Air, 1961-63; vis. condr. Juilliard Sch. Music, 1966—. Head Ford Found. project for young Am. condrs., 1962-64. Decorated Legion of Honor (France). Address: 200 E 66th St New York NY 10021

WALLER, A. BRET, III, mus. dir.; b. Liberal, Kans., Dec. 7, 1935; s. A. Bret and Juanita M. (Slawson) W.; B.F.A., Kansas City Art Inst., 1957; M.F.A., U. Kans., 1958; postgrad. U. Oslo, 1963-64; m. Mary Lou Dooley, Sept. 3, 1959; children—Bret, Mary Elizabeth. Dir., Citadel Mus., Charleston, S.C., 1960-63; curator to dir. U. Kans. Mus. Art, Lawrence, 1964-71; dept. head public edn.-higher edn. Met. Mus. Art, N.Y.C., 1971-73; dir. U. Mich. Mus. Art, Ann Arbor, 1973—. Mem. Historic Dist. Commn., Ann Arbor, 1978—; panel chmn. Mich. Council for the Arts, 1977-79. Fulbright scholar, 1963-64. Mem. Intermuseum Conservation Assn. (v.p. 1976-77, pres. 1977-79), Am. Assn. Museums, Coll. Art Assn., Assn. Art Mus. Dirs., Mich. Museums Assn. Home: 1046 Baldwin Ann Arbor MI 48104 Office: Museum of Art Univ of Mich Ann Arbor MI 48109

WALLER, EDWARD CARSON, III, naval officer; b. Chgo., Jan. 24, 1926; s. Edward Carson, Jr. and Miriam (Hall) W.; B.S., U.S. Naval Acad., 1949; B.S. in Aero. Engring., M.S. in Elec. Engring., U.S. Naval Postgrad. Sch., 1957; m. Margaret Clifford Gelly, May 27, 1950; children—Marcia, Edward, Margaret, Kristen. Commd. ensign U.S. Navy, 1949, designated naval aviator, 1951, advanced through grades to vice adm., 1975; service in China, Korea and Vietnam; comdr. Fleet Air Wings, Pacific, 1971-72, Anti-submarine Systems Project Office, 1973-74; dir. weapons systems evaluation group Office Sec. Def., 1975-76, dir. anti-submarine warfare programs Office Chief Naval Ops., 1976-78; comdr. U.S. Third Fleet, 1979—. Decorated Legion of Merit with 2 oak leaf clusters, Navy Air medal with 2 oak leaf clusters. Sec. Navy Commendation medal, Disting. Service medal. Roman Catholic. Home: Quarters K Ford Island Honolulu HI 96818 Office: Comdr Third Fleet Pearl Harbor HI 96860

WALLER, GEORGE MACGREGOR, historian, educator; b. Detroit, June 7, 1919; s. George and Marguerite (Rowland) W.; grad. Deerfield Acad., 1937; A.B., Amherst Coll., 1941; M.A., Columbia, 1947, Ph.D., 1953; m. Martha Huntington Stifler, Oct. 16, 1943; children—Susan, Marguerite, Elizabeth, Donald, Richard. Comml. rep. Detroit Edison Co., 1941-42; lectr. Hunter Coll., 1946-47; instr. Amherst Coll., 1948-52; chief Am. history research center Wis. Hist. Soc., 1952-54; prof., head dept. history and polit. sci. Butler U., Indpls., 1954—. Fulbright sr. scholar U. Southampton, Eng., 1961-62; vis. prof. Ind. U., 1967-69. Mem. Ind. Am. Revolution Bicentennial Commn., 1971—. Served to lt. comdr. USNR, 1943-46. Mem. Ind. Hist. Soc., Am. Hist. Assn., Orgn. Am. Historians, Ind. Acad. Social Scis., English Speaking Union (dir.), AAUP, Am. Studies Assn. (v.p. Ohio-Ind. chpt.), Ind. Mus. Soc. (past pres.), Internat. Platform Assn., Phi Beta Kappa (past pres. Ind. chpt.), Phi Kappa Phi, Phi Alpha Theta. Club: Literary (past pres.) (Indpls.). Author: Samuel Vetch. Colonial Enterpriser, 1960; The American Revolution in the West, 1976. Editor: Puritanism in Early America, 1950, rev. 1973; Pearl Harbor, Roosevelt and the Coming War, 1953, 65, 3d edit., 1976; mem. editorial adv. com. Ind. Mag. of History; contbr. to World Book Ency., Dictionary Canadian Biography, Vol. II. Home: 1701 W 51st St Indianapolis IN 46208

WALLER, JOHN HENRY, govt. ofcl.; b. Paw Paw, Mich., May 8, 1923; s. George and Marguerite (Rowland) W.; B.A., U. Mich., 1946; m. Barbara Steuart Hans, July 2, 1947; children—Stephanie S., Gregory R., Maria de Bernabeu. Vice consul U.S. Fgn. Service, State Dept., Tehran, 1946-49, vice consul, Meshed, Iran, 1949-50, attache, Tehran, 1950-53; fgn. affairs officer Def. Dept., Washington, 1953-55; attache U.S. embassy, New Delhi, India, 1955-59; staff planning officer Army Dept., Washington, 1959-60; 2d sec. U.S. embassy, Khartoum, 1960-62; polit. analyst State Dept., Washington, 1962-68; 1st sec. Am. embassy, also spl. asst. to ambassador, New Delhi, 1968-71; insp. gen. CIA, McLean, Va., 1976—. Mem. Am. Fgn. Service Assn. Club: Cosmos (Washington). Author: (under pseudonym John MacGregor) Tibet; A Chronicle of Exploration, 1970. Home: 4900 Sedgwick St NW Washington DC 20016 Office: CIA McLean VA 22101

WALLER, JOHN OSCAR, educator; b. Los Angeles, Oct. 29, 1916; s. David Oscar and Susan Veva (Williams) W.; B.A., San Diego State Coll., 1941; M.A., U. So. Calif., 1949; Ph.D., 1954; m. Elaine Louise Johnson, Jan. 6, 1946. Instr. San Diego State Coll., 1946-48; dir. publs. Oxnard (Calif.) Union High Sch., 1951-52; mem. faculty Walla Walla Coll., College Place, Wash., 1952-60; prof. English, Andrews U., Berrien Springs, Mich., 1960—, chmn. dept., 1963-79. Served with USNR, 1941-45. Mem. Mich. Acad. Sci., Arts and Letters, Modern Lang. Assn. Am., English Assn., Research Soc., Victorian Periodicals, Tennyson Soc., Nat. Council Tchrs. English, Conf. Coll. Composition and Communications, Conf. Brit. Studies. Mem. Seventh Day Adventist Ch. Editorial bd. Abstracts of English Studies, 1967—. Author articles on lit. history. Home: 121 N George St Berrien Springs MI 49103

WALLER, MICHAEL REGINALD, petroleum co. exec.; b. Mornington, Victoria, Australia, Nov. 10, 1927; s. Hector McDonald Laws and Nancy (Bowes) W.; came to U.S., 1950; B.Sc., U. Melbourne (Australia), 1949; M.Sc., U. Tulsa, 1952; m. Diana Margaret Field, June 16, 1952; children—Richard, Stephen, Andrew. Mining geologist Western Mining Corp., Kalgoorlie, Australia, 1949-50; with Amoco Prodn. Co., 1952—, mgr. research Amoco Prodn. Research Center, Tulsa, 1970-73, v.p. research, 1973—; bd. dirs. Okla. Petroleum Council. Pres. Jr. Achievement of Greater Tulsa, 1974-77; co-chmn. oil div. Tulsa United Way. Mem. Am. Assn. Petroleum Geologists, Soc. Petroleum Engrs., Geol. Soc. Australia, Soc. Canadian Petroleum Geologists, Soc. Exploration Geophysicists. Republican. Christian Scientist. Clubs: Petroleum of Tulsa, Harvard, Tulsa. Home: 2860 E 39th St Tulsa OK 74105 Office: Amoco Prodn Research Center 4502 E 41st St Tulsa OK 74115

WALLER, RICHARD CONRAD, ret. research exec.; b. Victory, Wis., Sept. 24, 1915; s. Benjamin Kenneth and Ruby Sybil (Spaulding) W.; B.S. in Chem. Engring., Wash. State U.; Ph.D. in Phys. Chemistry, Iowa State U., Ames, 1942; m. Blanche Adrienne Ratcliffe, Nov. 1, 1948; children—Susan Waller Dawson, Richard Michael, Kenneth Edward, Richard Conrad, Patricia Waller Smith. With E.I. duPont de Nemours & Co., 1942-48; with Goodyear Tire & Rubber Co., Akron, Ohio, 1948-80, v.p. research, 1976-80. Mem. Am. Chem. Soc., Soc. Chem. Industry, Fiber Soc., Alpha Chi Sigma. Club: Atwood Yacht. Home: 123 Leland St NE Port Charlotte FL 33952

WALLER, THEODORE, publisher; b. Oakland, Calif., Apr. 25, 1916; s. Thomas Lewis and Margaret (Little) W.; student U. Chgo., 1933-37; m. Ruth Cornish, 1943; m. 2d, Helen Heitt, Mar. 28, 1948; children—Jonathan Hiett, Mark Thomas, Margaret Ann; m. 3d, Irene Martin Kitzing, Jan. 1, 1962; m. 4th, Hilda Lindley, June 2, 1977. Staff various social agencies, San Francisco, 1931-33; student work officer of Nat. Youth Adminstrn., Fed. Security Agy., 1938-41; community activities dir. Tule Lake relocation project, War Relocation Authority, 1942, spl. rep. of dir., 1942-43; exec. officer, chief UNRRA mission to Byelorussia, 1946-47; Washington rep. United World Federalists, 1948-49; asst. to pres., exec. sec. com. on reading devel., later mng. dir. Am. Book Pubs. Council, 1950-53; editorial v.p. New Am. Library World Lit., Inc., 1953-54; v.p., dir. instnl. relations, dir. sch. and library div., dir. Grolier, Inc., exec. v.p., 1977—; v.p. Franklin Watts, Inc., 1954—; pres. Teaching Materials Corp., 1960-66, Groiler Ednl. Corp., 1966-77, also dir. Dir. Am. Book Pubs. Council; mem. Nat. Adv. Commn. on Libraries, 1966—; exec. com. Nat. Book Com., also Franklin Book Programs; mem. steering com. Nat. Library Week; U.S. co-chmn., mem. internat. support com. Internat. Book Year, 1972; chmn. internat. book com. UNESCO. Chmn. nat. adv. com. Hampshire Coll.; bd. visitors U. Pitts. Grad. Sch. Library and Info. Scis., 1977—. Mem. ALA (com. on intellectual freedom 1953-56, internat. relations com. 1956-62, 76—). Clubs: Grolier; Sierra of Calif.; N.Y. Athletic. Office: Danbury CT 06816

WALLER, WILHELMINE KIRBY (MRS. THOMAS MERCER WALLER), civic worker, orgn. ofcl.; b. N.Y.C., Jan. 19, 1914; d. Gustavus Town and Wilhelmine (Claflin) Kirby; ed. Chapin Sch., N.Y.C.; m. Thomas Mercer Waller, Apr. 7, 1942. Conservation chmn. Garden Club Am., 1959-61, pres., 1965-68, chmn. nat. affairs, 1968-74, dir. 1969-71; mem. adv. com. N.Y. State Conservation Commn., 1959-70; mem. Nat. Adv. Com. Hwy. Beautification, 1965-68; trustee Mianus River Gorge Conservation Com. of Nature Conservancy, 1955—, Arthur W. Butler Meml. Sanctuary, 1955-79; mem. Rachel Carson council Nat. Audubon Soc., 1964—; v.p. Bedford (N.Y.) Farmers Club, 1954-74; dir. Westchester County Soil and Water Conservation Dist., 1967-74; adviser N.Y. Gov.'s Study Commn. Future of Adirondacks, 1968-70; adv. com. N.Y. State Parks and Recreation Commn., 1971-72; adv. com. to sec. state UN Conf. Human Environment, 1971-72; mem. Pres.'s Citizens Adv. Com. on Environ. Quality, 1974-78. Mem. planning bd., Bedford, 1953-57; mem. Conservation adv. council, Bedford, N.Y., 1968-70, Westchester County Planning Bd., 1970—; bd. govs. Nature Conservancy, 1970-78. Mem. Lyndhurst council Nat. Trust for Historic Preservation, 1965-74; mem. steering com. Rene Dubos Forum, 1977—. Recipient Frances K. Hutchinson medal Garden Club Am., 1971, Holiday mag. award for beautiful Am., 1971, Conservation award Am. Motors Corp., 1975. Mem. Nat. Soc. Colonial Dames, Huguenot Soc. Am., Daus. of Cincinnati Address: Tanrackin Farm Bedford Hills NY 10507

WALLER, WILLIAM, lawyer; b. Nashville, Oct. 28, 1898; s. Claude and Martha Armistead (Nelson) W.; student Wallace U. Sch., 1911-14; B.S., Vanderbilt U., 1918; LL.B. magna cum laude, Yale, 1922; m. Elizabeth Warner Estes, Dec. 31, 1924; 1 son, William; m. 2d Milbrey Warner, Sept. 11, 1935; 1 dau., Mrs. Thomas G. Andrews, Jr. Admitted to Tenn. bar, 1922; asst. to gen. counsel N.C. & St.L Ry., 1922-27; gen. practice law, Nashville, 1927—; mem. firm Waller, Lansden, Dortch & Davis; lectr. Vanderbilt Law Sch., 1924, 50-56. Trustee Vanderbilt U., 1956—, Harpeth Hall Sch., 1950-66, Ladies Hermitage Assn., 1959—. Served as 2d lt., C.A.C., U.S. Army, 1918-19; AEF. Mem. Am. Law Inst., Mont Pelerin Soc., Tenn. Hist. Commn., Order of Coif, Phi Beta Kappa, Phi Delta Theta, Phi Delta Phi. Clubs: Round Table, Belle Meade Country, University (Nashville). Editor, compiler Nashville in the 1890's, 1970; Nashville, 1900 to 1910, 1972. Home: 4419 Chickering Ln Nashville TN 37215 Office: 2100 One Commerce Pl Nashville TN 37239

WALLER, WILLIAM KELLY, JR., ins. exec.; b. Dallas, Feb. 8, 1915; s. William Kelly and Elizabeth Tillman (Moore) W.; student So. Meth. U., 1933-34; m. Phyllis Leone Ross, Sept. 3, 1948; children—William Kelly (dec.), Ceneth Elizabeth, Kevin Kelly. Partner, So. Gen. Ins. Agy., Dallas, 1936-40; with Gen. Ins. Co. of Am. (name changed to Safeco Ins. Cos.), 1940—, pres. Safeco Life Ins. Co., Safeco Investment Co., also dir. Bd. dirs. N.W. Hosp., Seattle U., Stanford Prep. Sch., YMCA. Served with USAAF, 1942-45. Recipient Disting. Eagle scout award Boy Scouts Am., 1978. Mem. Am. Council Life Ins. (past mem. exec. com.), Health Ins. Inst. Am. (chmn. 1978-79). Club: Seattle Golf (past pres.). Office: SAFECO Plaza Seattle WA 98185

WALLER, WILLIAM WEAVER, banker; b. LaGrange, Ga., Sept. 17, 1932; s. William Thomaston and Annie (Weaver) W.; B.S. in Indel. Mgmt., Ga. Inst. Tech., 1955; m. Barbara Hudson, Sept. 21, 1973; children by previous marriage—Leslie, Vince. With Sears Roebuck & Co., 1954-55; with Fulton Nat. Bank, Atlanta, 1958-76; gen. mgr. SE region First Data Resources, Inc., Omaha, 1976—. Pres., Ga. Automated Clearing House. Bd. dirs. Atlanta Com. on Paperless Entry. Served with USMCR, 1956-58. Mem. Am. (operations and automation com.), Ga. (chmn. automation com.) bankers assns., Chi Phi. Presbyterian. Home: 60 Lanier Dr Cumming GA 30130

WALLERSTEDT, ROBERT W., banker; b. Kansas City, Mo., Aug. 9, 1928; s. John F. and Mary Frances (McLaughlin) W.; A.B., Rockhurst Coll., 1949; M.A., Catholic U. Am., 1950; m. Mary Louise Barnhart, 1962; children—Erin Michelle, Laurel Annette, Maureen Elizabeth. Regional mgr. Gen. Electric Credit Corp., 1954-63; pres., chief exec. officer J.I. Case Credit Corp., Racine, Wis., 1963-64; pres., chief exec. officer, dir. Met. Bank & Trust Co., Chgo., 1964-69, Amal. Trust & Savs. Bank, Chgo., 1966-69, Columbia Union Nat. Bank & Trust Co., Kansas City, Mo., 1969—; pres. Columbia Union Bancshares. Gen. chmn. Friends of Girl Scouts, 1970; chmn. Concerned Citizens for Sound Pub. Transp., 1971; maj. firms team capt. Kansas City Philharmonic, 1971-74; mem. Mayors Corps of Progress for Greater Kansas City, Internat. Council, Citizens Assn. Kansas City, Civic Council Greater Kansas City, Kansas City Transit Adv. Com. Bd. dirs. Better Bus. Bur., Heart of Am. Boys Clubs; bd. dirs., chmn. promotion com. Downtown, Inc.; bd. dirs., mem. publicity and pub. relations com. Jr. Achievement; adv. bd., chmn. finance com., mem. exec. com. St. Mary's Hosp.; exec. com., chmn. urban renewal com. Citizens Capital Improvement Program; mem. Kansas City Bd. Election Commrs., 1977—. Served with USCG, 1950-54; lt. comdr. Res. ret. Mem. Am. (governing council 1972), Mo., Installment, Independent bankers assns., Young Pres.'s Orgn., Greater Kansas City C. of C., Central Indsl. Dist. Assn., Mil. Order World Wars, Ret. Officers Assn., Rockhurst Coll. Hon. Dirs. Assn., Newcomen Soc. N.Am., Am. Royal Assn. (gov.). Clubs: Kansas City, Carriage; Woodside Racquet. Office: 900 Walnut St Kansas City MO 64106

WALLERSTEIN, DAVID B., cons.; b. Richmond, Va., May 13, 1905; s. David B. and Hattie (Pfaelzer) W.; B.S., U. Va., 1924; M.B.A. Harvard, 1926; m. Caroline Rieser, Dec. 28, 1931; children—John M., Michael R., David L. With Balaban & Katz Corp., Chgo., 1926-66, v.p., gen. mgr., 1950-57, pres., 1957-66, past dir.; cons. Bell & Howell Corp.; dir. McDonald's Corp., Opelika Mfg. Corp. Chmn., dir. State St. Council, Chgo., 1952-65; dir., mem. exec. com. Theatre Owners Am., 1950-65; bd. dirs. Chgo. Better Bus. Bur. Pres., chmn. bd. Francis W. Parker Sch., Chgo., 1951-58, trustee, 1946—; life trustee Michael Reese Hosp. and Med. Center. Mem. Chgo. Assn. Commerce and Industry. Club: Standard (Chgo.). Home: 2440 Lakeview Ave Chicago IL 60614 Office: 175 N State St Chicago IL 60601

WALLERSTEIN, RALPH OLIVER, physician; b. Dusseldorf, Germany, Mar. 7, 1922; s. Otto R. and Ilse (Hollander) W.; came to U.S., 1938, naturalized, 1944; A.B., U. Calif., Berkeley, 1943, M.D., San Francisco, 1945; m. Betty Ann Christensen, June 21, 1952; children—Ralph Oliver, Richard, Ann. Intern, San Francisco Hosp., 1945-46, resident, 1948-49; resident U. Calif. Hosp., San Francisco, 1949-50; research fellow Thorndike Meml. Lab., Boston City Hosp., 1950-52; chief clin. hematology San Francisco Gen. Hosp., 1953—; faculty U. Calif., San Francisco, 1952—, clin. prof. medicine, 1969—. Served to capt. M.C. AUS, 1946-48. Diplomate Am. Bd. Internal Medicine (bd. govs. 1975—). Mem. Am. Soc. Hematology (pres. 1978), Am. Coll. Physicians (gov. 1977—), San. Francisco Med. Soc., AMA, Am. Fedn. Clin. Research, Am. Soc. Internal Medicine, Am. Assn. Blood Banks, Calif. Acad. Medicine, Internat. Soc. Hematology, Western Soc. Clin. Research, Western Assn. Physicians. Republican. Home: 3447 Clay St San Francisco CA 94118 Office: 3838 California St Suite 707 San Francisco CA 94118

WALLERSTEIN, ROBERT SOLOMON, psychiatrist; b. Berlin, Germany, Jan. 28, 1921; s. Lazar and Sarah (Guensberg) W.; B.A., Columbia, 1941, M.D., 1944; postgrad. Topeka Inst. Psychoanalysis, 1951-58; m. Judith Hannah Saretsky, Jan. 26, 1947; children—Michael Jonathan, Nina Beth, Amy Lisa. Asso. dir., then dir. research Menninger Found., Topeka, 1954-66; chief psychiatry Mt. Zion Hosp., San Francisco, 1966-78; tng. and supervising analyst San Francisco Psychoanalytic Inst., 1966—; clin. prof. U. Calif. Sch. Medicine, Langley-Porter Neuropsychiat. Inst., 1967-75, prof., chmn. dept. psychiatry, also dir. inst., 1975—; vis. prof. psychiatry La. State U. Sch. Medicine, also New Orleans Psychoanalytic Inst., 1973-73, Pahlavi U., Shiraz, Iran, 1977. Mem., chmn. research scientist career devel. com. NIMH, 1966-70. Served with AUS, 1946-48. Recipient Heinz Hartmann award N.Y. Psychoanalytic Inst., 1968; Distinguished Alumnus award Menninger Sch. Psychiatry, 1972; J. Elliott Royer award U. Calif. at San Francisco, 1973. Fellow Center Advanced Study Behavioral Scis., Stanford, Calif., 1964-65. Fellow Am. Psychiat. Assn., A.C.P., Am. Orthopsychiat. Assn.; mem. Am. Psychoanalytic Assn. (pres. 1971-72), Internat. Psychoanalytic Assn. (v.p. 1977—), Group Advancement Psychiatry, Phi Beta Kappa, Alpha Omega Alpha. Author books and monographs. Mem. editorial bd. 8 profl. jours. Contbr. articles to profl. jours. Home: 290 Beach Rd Belvedere CA 94920 Office: Langley-Porter Neuropsychiat Inst 401 Parnassus St San Francisco CA 94143

WALLHAUSER, GEORGE MARVIN, former congressman, investment exec.; b. Newark, Feb. 10, 1900; s. Dr. Henry Joseph Frederick and Rachel Apolonia (Vogt) W.; A.B., U. Pa., 1922; student real estate appraising, Columbia, 1942; m. Isabel Towne, May 26, 1926; children—George Marvin, Henry Towne. With U.S. Realty & Investment Co., Newark, 1928—, treas., 1947—, sr. v.p., 1956—, dir., 1940; dir. Maplewood Bank & Trust Co.; mem. 86th-88th Congresses, 12th Dist. Chmn. planning bd, Maplewood, 1946-54, mem. twp. com., 1954-57; commr. N.J. Hwy. Authority, 1970-75, chmn., 1972-75. Past pres. Bur. Family Service, Oranges and Maplewood. Served with USNRF, World War I. Mem. Am. Legion, Phi Sigma Kappa. Methodist. Republican. Mason, Elk. Clubs: Baltusrol Golf (Springfield, N.J.). Home: 31 Kensington Terrace Maplewood NJ 07040 Office: 972 Broad St Newark NJ 07102

WALLICH, HENRY CHRISTOPHER, economist, govt. ofcl.; b. Berlin, Germany, June 10, 1914; s. Paul and Hildegard J. (Rehrmann) W.; grad. Bismarck Gymnasium, Berlin, 1932; student Oxford U., 1932-33; M.A., Harvard, 1941, Ph.D., 1944; m. Mable Inness Brown, Dec. 2, 1950; children—Christine Wallich de Hakim, Anna Hildegard, Paul Inness. Came to U.S., 1935, naturalized, 1944. Export bus., Argentina, 1933-35; with Chem. Bank & Trust Co., N.Y.C., 1935-36, Hackney Hopkinson & Sutphen, securities, N.Y.C., 1936-40; with Fed. Res. Bank N.Y., 1941-51, chief fgn. research div., 1946-51; prof. econs. Yale, 1951-74; mem. Bd. Govs. Fed. Res. System, Washington, 1974—. Sr. cons. to sec. Treasury, 1969-74; mem. Pres.'s Council Econ. Advisers, 1959-61; cons. Mut. Security Adminstrn., 1952, U.S. Treasury, 1951-52, White House, 1954-55. Mem. Am. Econ. Assn. Clubs: Harvard (N.Y.C.); University (Washington). Author: Monetary Problems of an Export Economy, 1950; (with John Adler) Public Finances of a Developing Country, 1951; Mainsprings of the German Revival, 1955; The Cost of Freedom, 1960; also articles. Editorial contbr. to Washington Post, 1961-64; columnist Newsweek mag., 1965-74. Address: Bd Govs Fed Reserve System Washington DC 20551

WALLIN, FRANKLIN WHITTELSEY, coll. pres.; b. Grand Rapids, Mich., Jan. 22, 1925; s. Franklin Whittelsey and Agnes (Sarles) W.; B.S., U. Wis., 1948; M.A., U. Calif. at Berkeley, 1950, Ph.D., 1953; m. Florence Gilbert Evans, Feb. 21, 1948; children—Susan Q. (Mrs. Ray Michael Hively), Thomas E., Elizabeth W., Franklin B. From instr. to asso. prof. history Wayne State U., 1953-68, asst. to pres., 1958-60; provost, dean faculty Colgate U., 1968-73, acting pres., 1969; pres. Inst. for World Order, 1973-74, bd. dirs., 1972—; pres. Earlham Coll., Richmond, Ind., 1974—; European dir. internat. seminars Am. Friends Service Com., 1964-66; chmn. steering. com. Internat. Conflict and Am. Orgns. Project. Commr., Highland Park (Mich.) Human Relations Commn., 1962-64; mem. Hamilton (N.Y.) Human Relations Com., 1968-74. Bd. dirs. Friends Sch., Detroit, 1962-68, chmn., 1962-64, 67-68; bd. dirs. Jamestown Coll., 1972-75, Global Perspectives in Edn., 1976—. Served with U.S. Navy, 1942-46. Fellow Am. Council Edn., Swarthmore Coll., 1966-67. Mem. Societe D'Histoire Moderne, French Hist. Soc., UN Assn. (com. on youth 1972), Assn. Colls. Ind. (dir. 1974—), Gt. Lakes Colls. Assn. (dir. 1974—, chmn. 1978—), Am. Council on Edn. (dir. 1978—), New Directions (dir. 1978—). Mem. Soc. Friends. Home: 712 College Ave Richmond IN 47374

WALLIN, WINSTON ROGER, mfg. co. exec.; b. Mpls., Mar. 6, 1926; s. Carl A. and Theresa (Hegge) W.; B.B.A., U. Minn., 1948; m. Maxine Houghton, Sept. 10, 1949; children—Rebecca, Brooks, Lance, Bradford. With Pillsbury Co., 1948—, v.p. commodity ops., 1971-76, exec. v.p., 1976, pres., chief ops. officer, 1977—; dir. Medtronic, Inc., Soo Line R.R., 1st Mpls. Bank. Bd. dirs. United Way, Mpls., 1977, Downtown Council Mpls., 1977. Served with USN, 1944-46. Mem. Chgo. Bd. Trade, Mpls. Grain Exchange (bd. dirs. 1977—), Kansas City Bd. trade. Clubs: Mpls., Interlachen, Minikahda. Home: 7022 Tupa Circle Edina MN 55435 Office: 608 2d Ave S Minneapolis MN 55435

WALLING, ROBERT HAROLD, lawyer; b. Fernandina, Fla., Sept. 13, 1927; s. Robert and Mary Lee (Smith) W.; B.S., Ga. Inst. Tech., 1951; LL.B., Emory U., 1957; LL.M. (Sterling fellow), Yale U., 1960; m. Mildred Bruce Fraser, Oct. 4, 1952; children—Carol Leigh, Lynne Elizabeth, Robert Fraser (dec.), Gregory Bruce. Law clk. to U.S. Dist. Ct. Judge Frank Hooper, 1957-58; asst. atty. gen. State of Ga., 1958-59; asst. prof. Emory U. Law Sch., 1960-63; partner firm Haas, Holland, Levison & Gibert, Atlanta, 1964-72; judge Superior Cts., Stone Mountain Circuit, 1972; partner firm Jones, Bird & Howell, Atlanta, 1973—; mem. Ga. Ho. of Reps., 1966-68; mem. Ga. State Senate, 1969-72; mem. Ga. Criminal Justice Council, 1974—, chmn., 1975-76. Mem. Democratic Nat. Com., 1978—; vice chmn. Dem. Party of Ga., 1978—, gen. counsel, 1974-78; bd. dirs. DeKalb unit Am. Cancer Soc., 1964—, pres., 1969, chmn. bd., 1970; bd. dirs. Atlanta Legal Aid Soc., 1963-64, pres., 1970; trustee Callanwolde Found., 1971—, Ga. Conservancy, 1973-75; dir. Atlanta Area council Boy Scouts Am., 1975—; bd. dirs. DeKalb Ct. Devel. Authority, 1974—. Served with USN, 1945-46, 51-54. Mem. Am. Bar Assn., State Bar Ga., Atlanta Bar Assn., Decatur-DeKalb Bar Assn., Am. Law Inst. Presbyterian. Club: Druid Hills Kiwanis (past pres.). Mem. editorial bd. Ga. State Bar Jour., 1975-77, editor-in-chief, 1976-77. Home: 1001 Oxford St Atlanta GA 30306 Office: Haas-Howell Bldg Atlanta GA 30303

WALLING, W(ILBUR) DONALD, educator; b. Hudson Falls, N.Y., Sept. 14, 1915; s. William D. and Julia (Griffin) W.; A.B., Union U., 1937; M.A., Columbia U., 1940, Ed.D., 1951; m. Jean Marion Sears, Dec. 30, 1950; children—Michael, William, Peter, Jon, Richard. Tchr., West Orange (N.J.) High Sch., 1940-42; research asso. N.Y. State Edn. Dept., Albany, 1947-53; dir. research N.Y. State Commn. on Sch. Bldgs., Albany, 1954; asst. supt. for bus. affairs Hicksville (N.Y.) Public Schs., 1955; prof., dir. field studies and research Rutgers U., 1956—; ednl. cons., 1950—; cons. N.J. Sch. Bldg. Guide Adv. Com. Served to capt. USAAF, 1942-46. Mem. Council Ednl. Facility Planners, N.E. Council Schoolhouse Constrn., AAUP, Phi Delta Kappa. Home: 2 Louise Dr Milltown NJ 08850 Office: Rutgers U New Brunswick NJ 08903

WALLIS, CARLTON LAMAR, librarian; b. Blue Springs, Miss., Oct. 15, 1915; s. William Ralph and Tellie (Jones) W.; B.A. with spl. distinction, Miss. Coll., 1936; M.A., Tulane U., 1946; B.L.S., U. Chgo., 1947; m. Mary Elizabeth Cooper, Feb. 22, 1944; 1 son, Carlton Lamar. English tchr., coach Miss. Pub. Schs., 1936-41; teaching fellow Miss. Coll. and Tulane U., 1941-42; chief librarian Rosenberg Library, Galveston, Tex., 1947-55; city librarian Richmond (Va.), 1955-58; dir. Memphis Pub. Library, 1958—. Trustee Belhaven Coll., 1978—. Served as chief warrant officer, AUS, 1942-46. Decorated Bronze Star. Mem. ALA (chmn. library mgmt. sect. 1969-71), Pub. (dir. 1973-77), Tex. (pres. 1952-53), Va. Southwestern (exec. bd. 1950-55), Southeastern (chmn. pub. library sect. 1960-62), Tenn. (pres. 1969-70) library assns. Presbyterian (elder). Clubs: Egyptian (pres. 1973-74); Holly Hills Country. Author: Libraries in the Golden Triangle, 1966; contbr. articles to library jours. Home: 365 Kenilworth Pl Memphis TN 38112 Office: 1850 Peabody Memphis TN 38104

WALLIS, CHARLES LANGWORTHY, educator, clergyman; b. Hamilton, N.Y., May 1, 1921; s. Robert Scott and Caroline (Langworthy) W.; B.A., U. Redlands, 1943; M.A., U. Rochester, 1945; M.Div., Colgate Rochester Div. Sch., 1945; m. Betty Barbe Watson, Aug. 16, 1947. Ordained to ministry Baptist Ch., 1944; minister, Canandaigua, N.Y., 1943-47; chaplain VA Hosp., 1944-46; from instr. to prof. English, Keuka (N.Y.) Coll., 1945—, chmn. dept. English, 1959-70, lectr. philosophy, 1952-61, coordinator publs., 1975—, lectr. religion, 1976—; minister Keuka Coll. Ch., 1947-65, Keuka Park Bapt. Ch., 1965—; adj. prof. Elmira (N.Y.) Coll., 1975-76. Chmn. Yates County (N.Y.) Republican Com., 1965—; mem. exec. com. N.Y. State Rep. Com., 1976—; del. N.Y. State Conv., 1962, 66, Nat. Convention, 1968, 72. Mem. 33d Congl. Mil. Acad. Selection Com., 1971—, chmn., 1975—; nat. com. Japan Internat. Christian Found., 1972—. Recipient medallion Civil War Centennial Commn., 1965; Ministers Research Found. research fellow, 1955-58. Mem. Am. Baptist Hist. Soc. (dir. 1961-67), AAUP, Coll. English Assn., N.Y. Hist. Assn., Am. Acad. Religion, Nat. Council Tchrs. English, Soc. Bibl. Lit., Poetry Soc. Am., Am., N.Y. folklore socs. Sigma Tau Delta, Pi Delta Epsilon, Delta Alpha. Mason (past master), Rotarian (past pres., Rotarian of Year award 1976); mem. Order Eastern Star (past patron). Editor: Selected Poems of John Oxenham, 1948; Poems of Edwin Markham, 1950; Treasury of Sermon Illustrations, 1950; The Funeral Encyclopedia, 1953; Stories on Stone: A Book of American Epitaphs, 1954; Worship Resources for the Christian Year, 1954; Speakers Illustrations for Special Days, 1956; Treasury of Story-Sermons for Children, 1957; Riverside Sermons, 1958; Table of the Lord, 1958; Notable Sermons from Protestant Pulpits, 1958; (with others) 20th Century Bible Commentary, 1955; (with Dr. Charles L. Allen) Christmas in Our Hearts, 1957, Candle, Star and Christmas, 1959, When Christmas Came to Bethlehem, 1963, A Treasury of Poems for Worship and Devotion, 1959; (with J. Ferguson) Prayers for Public Worship, 1958; Lenten-Easter Sourcebook, 1961; 1010 Sermon Illustrations from the Bible, 1962; 88 Evangelistic Sermons, 1964; The Treasure Chest, 1965; Speakers Illustrations from Contemporary Literature, 1965; Flapdoodle, Trust and Obey, 1966; Words of Life, 1966; The Eternal Light, 1966; 365 Table Graces for the Christian Home, 1967; Close Your Eyes When Praying, 1968; Holy Holy Land, 1969; The Charles L. Allen Treasury, 1970; Our American Heritage, 1970; American Epitaphs: Grave and Humorous, 1973; Worship Resources for Special Days, 1976; Christmas, 1977; A Complete Source Book for the Lord's Supper, 1978; editor: Pulpit Preaching, 1951-72, Pulpit Digest, 1972—, N.Y. Folklore Quar., 1955-63; asso. editor Ministers Manual 1955-67, editor, 1967—; daily radio broadcast For Heaven's Sake, Finger Lakes Radio Network, 1967—; columnist Lakeside Pulpit, 1968—, Religion Beat, 1976—; contbg. editor Harper & Row, 1952—. Home: E Bluff Dr Keuka Park NY 14478

WALLIS, EARL L., coll. dean; b. Los Angeles, Dec. 25, 1924; s. LeRoy J. and Eleanor (Subith) W.; student St. Mary's Coll., 1942-43; B.S., U. So. Calif., 1948, M.S., 1949, Ed.D., 1957; m. Beatrice R. Bayley, June 24, 1950; children—Walter J., Chris A. Instr. U. So. Calif., 1954-57; asst. prof. U. Calif. at Los Angeles, 1957-59; prof. Calif. State U., Northridge, 1959-65, dean students, 1968-70, dean Sch. Fine Arts and Profl. Studies, 1970-72, dean Sch. Communication and Profl. Studies, 1972—. Served with AUS, 1943-45. Decorated Bronze Star, Purple Heart. Author: Toward Better Teaching in Physical Education, 1961; Figure Improvement, 1965; Exercise for Children, 1966; Foundations of Conditioning, 1970. Home: Box 1452 Pebble Beach CA 93953 Office: California State U Northridge CA 91324

WALLIS, GEORGE EDWARD, broadcasting exec.; b. Phila., Nov. 25, 1915; student Western Res. U., 1934-36, Stanford. With Westinghouse Broadcasting Co. Inc., 1953—, area v.p. for WIND, Chgo., KDKA and KDKA-TV, Pitts., and WOWO, Ft. Wayne, 1966—, vice chmn. Group W Broadcasting, 1977—, also dir. co. Chmn., Allegheny County Human Services Commn.; bd. dirs. Pitts. Symphony, Civic Light Opera. Mem. Pa. Assn. Broadcasters, Ill. Broadcasters Assn. (past pres.), Broadcast Advertisers Club (past pres.), Am. Coll. Radio Arts Crafts and Sci. (past pres.). Address: care KDKA 1 Gateway Center Pittsburgh PA 15222

WALLIS, GORDON TODD, banker; b. Salt Lake City, Aug. 15, 1919; s. James Benjamin and Jessie (McAlister) W.; B.A., Columbia, 1940; LL.B., N.Y. U., 1948; m. (Dorothy) Jean Merrill, June 15, 1946; children—Judith (Mrs. Clifton Fenton), Deborah (Mrs. Joseph Rei). With Irving Trust Co., N.Y.C., 1940—, asst. sec., 1948-53, asst. v.p., 1953-55, v.p., 1955-64, sr. v.p., 1964-65, exec. v.p., 1965-69, vice-chmn., 1969-70, chmn., 1970—, dir., 1969—; pres. Irving Bank Corp., 1970-72, chief exec. officer, 1970—, chmn., 1972—, also dir.; dir. Gen. Telephone & Electronics Corp., J. Walter Thompson Co., Wing Hang Bank, Ltd., Sterling Drug, Inc., F.W. Woolworth Co., Internat. Comml. Bank, Ltd. Bd. dirs. United Way N.Y.C., Downtown-Lower Manhattan Assn., Inc., Econ. Devel. Council N.Y.C.; chmn., bd. dirs. United Way Tri-State. Served to capt. USAAF, 1942-46. Mem. Council Fgn. Relations, UN Assn. (dir.), Conf. Bd., N.Y. C. of C. and Industry, Internat. (trustee U.S. council), N.Y. chambers commerce. Club: Links (N.Y.C.). Home: New York NY Office: 1 Wall St New York NY 10015

WALLIS, HAL BRENT, motion picture producer; b. Chgo., Sept. 14; s. Jacob and Eva (Blum) W.; student Gregg Bus. Sch.; m. Louise Fazenda, Nov. 24, 1927 (dec. 1962); 1 son, Hal Brent; m. 2d, Martha Hyer. Office boy Cobe & McKinnon, Chicago, 1912; asst. sales and advt. mgr. Edison Gen. Electric Co., Chgo., 1916-22; mgr. Garrick Theatre, Los Angeles, 1922-23; with Warner Bros. Pictures, from 1923, exec. producer in charge prodn., 1933-1944. Ind. producer as Hal Wallis Prodns. releasing through Paramount Pictures, 1944-69, through Universal Pictures, 1969—. Recipient Acad. Thalberg award for best prodns., 1938, 43. Clubs: Masons (32 deg.), Shriners. Home: Beverly Hills CA Office: 9200 Sunset Blvd Los Angeles CA 90069

WALLIS, WILSON ALLEN, economist, univ. chancellor; b. Phila., Nov. 5, 1912; s. Wilson Dallam and Grace Steele (Allen) W.; A.B., U. Minn., 1932, postgrad., 1932-33; postgrad. fellow U. Chgo., 1933-35, Columbia, 1935-36; D.Sc., Hobart and William Smith Colls., 1973; LL.D., Roberts Wesleyan Coll., 1973; L.H.D., Grove City Coll., 1975; m. Anne Armstrong, Oct. 5, 1935; children—Nancy (Mrs. Carl R. Ingling, Jr.), Virginia (Mrs. Jack Solsman Cates). Economist Nat. Resources Com., 1935-37; instr. econs. Yale, 1937-38; asst., later asso. prof. econs. Stanford, 1938-46; Carnegie research asso. Nat. Bur. Econ. Research, 1939-40, 41; dir. research Statis. Research Group, Columbia (OSRD project), 1942-46; prof. statistics and econs. U. Chgo., 1946-62, chmn. dept. statistics, 1949-57, dean Grad. Sch. Bus., 1956-62; pres., trustee U. Rochester (N.Y.), also prof. econs. and statistics, 1962-70, chancellor, trustee, prof., 1970—. Dir. Macmillan, Inc., Lincoln First Banks, Rochester Telephone Corp., Eastman Kodak Co., Trans Union Corp., Lincoln 1st Bank, Bausch & Lomb, Inc., Met. Life Ins. Co., Standard Oil Co. (Ohio). Staff Ford Found., 1953-54; mem. math. div. NRC, 1958-60; dir. Nat. Bur. Econ. Research, 1953-74; spl. asst. Pres. Eisenhower, 1959-61; pres. Nat. Commn. for Study Nursing and Nursing Edn., 1967-70; chmn. Commn. on Presdl. Scholars, 1969-78; mem. Pres.'s Commn. on all All-Vol. Armed Force, 1969-70; chmn. Pres.'s Commn. on Fed. Statistics, 1970-71; mem. Nat. Council Ednl. Research, 1973-75; chmn. Adv. Council Social Security, 1974-75; mem. Corp. for Pub. Broadcasting, 1975-78, chmn., 1977-78. Trustee Tax Found., chmn. bd., 1972-75; trustee Robert A. Taft Inst. Govt., 1973-77; bd. overseers Hoover Instn. War, Revolution and Peace, 1972-78; trustee Eisenhower Coll., 1969-79, Nat. Opinion Research Center, 1957-62, 64-68, Com. for Econ. Devel., 1965-71, Colgate Rochester Div. Sch., Center for Govtl. Research, Inc., Internat. Mus. Photography at George Eastman House. Fellow Am. Soc. for Quality Control, Inst. Math. Statistics, Am. Statis. Assn. (editor Jour. 1950-59, pres. 1965), Am. Acad. of Arts and Scis.; mem. Am. Econ. Assn. (exec. com. 1962-64), Rochester C. of C. (trustee 1963-68, 70-75), Mont Pelerin Soc. (treas. 1949-54), Phi Beta Kappa, Chi Phi, Beta Gamma Sigma. Clubs: Cosmos (Washington); University (N.Y.C.); Bohemian (San Francisco): Genesee Valley; Country (Rochester); Pundit, Fortnightly. Author (with others): Consumer Expenditures in the United States, 1939; A Significance Test for Time Series and Other Ordered Observations, 1941; Techniques of Statistical Analysis, 1947; Sampling Inspection, 1948; Sequential Analysis of Statistical Data: Applications, 1945; Acceptance Sampling, 1950; Statistics: A New Approach, 1956; The Nature of Statistics, 1962; Welfare Programs: An Economic Appraisal, 1968; An Overgoverned Society, 1976. Co-compiler: The Ethics of Competition and Other Essays by Frank H. Knight, 1935. Chmn. editorial adv. bd. Internat. Ency. Social Scis., 1960-68. Contbr. articles to profl. jours. Home: 255 Allens Creek Rd Rochester NY 14618

WALLOP, MALCOLM, U.S. Senator; b. N.Y.C., Feb. 27, 1933; s. Oliver M. and Jean (Moore) W.; B.A., Yale U., 1954; m. Judith Warren, Mar. 26, 1967; children—Malcolm, Matthew, Amy, Paul. Owner, operator Polo Land & Livestock, Big Horn, Wyo., 1957—; mem. Wyo. Ho. of Reps., 1969-73, Wyo. Senate, 1973-77; mem. U.S. Senate from Wyo., 1976—, mem. Com. on Energy and Natural Resources, Com. on Fin., Com. on Intelligence, Com. on Ethics. Bd. dirs. All-Am. Indian Days; chmn. fund-raising com., local council Boy Scouts Am.; active No. Wyo. Mental Health Center. Served to lt. U.S. Army, 1955-57. Mem. Wyo. Stockgrowers Assn., Am. Nat. Cattleman's Assn., Am. Legion. Republican. Episcopalian. Office: US Senate Washington DC 20510

WALLOT, JEAN-PIERRE, educator; b. Valleyfield, Que., Can., May 19, 1935; s. Albert and Adrienne (Thibodeau) W.; B.A., Coll. Valleyfield, 1954; lic. es lettres U. Montreal, 1957, M.A. in History, 1957, Ph.D. in History, 1965; m. Rita Girard, Oct. 19, 1935; children—Normand, Robert, Sylvie. Reporter, Le Progres de Valleyfield, 1954-61; lectr. U. Montreal, 1961-65, asst. prof., 1965-66, prof. dept. history, 1973—, chmn. dept., 1973-75, vice dean studies faculty arts and scis., 1975-78, vice dean research Faculty Arts and Scis., 1979—; historian Nat. Mus. Man, Ottawa, Ont., 1966-69; asso. prof. U. Toronto, 1969-71; prof. Concordia U., Montreal, Que., 1971-73; dir. Etude Associé Ecole Pratique des Hautes Etudes en Sciences sociales, Paris, 1975-79. Recipient Marie Tremaine medal, 1973. Fellow Royal Soc. Can.; mem. Institut d'histoire de l'Amerique française (pres. 1973-77), Can. Hist. Assn. Roman Catholic. Author: (with John Hare) Les Imprimés dans le Bas-Canada, 1967, Confrontations, 1971; (with G. Paquet) Patronage et Pouvoir dans le Bas-Canada, 1973; Un Quebec qui bougeait, 1973. Office: Dept History U Montreal CP 6128 Montreal PQ H3C 3J7 Canada

WALLRAPP, YUSTIN JOHN, advt. agy. exec.; b. N.Y.C., Jan. 4, 1932; s. John W. and Eva (Sirutis) W.; B.A., Bklyn. Coll., 1953; M.A., U. Md., 1954; m. Marilyn Rogers, Dec. 5, 1959; children—Tracy Rae, Lisa Eve, Holly Beth. Exec. v.p. Canvas Products Assn., pubs. Canvas Products Rev., St. Paul, 1960-63; v.p. N.W. Ayer & Son, Inc., N.Y.C., 1963-71; pres. Bozell, Jacobs & Wallrapp, Inc., N.Y.C., 1972-74; sr. v.p. J. Walter Thompson Co., N.Y.C., 1974—; dir. Wallrapp Enterprises, N.Y.C.; cons. in Communications, 1964—. Trustee St. Luke's Sch., New Canaan, Conn. Served with U.S. Army, 1953-55. Mem. Public Relations Soc. Am. (Silver Anvil award 1969), Nat. Investor Relations Inst. Clubs: Lake Shore (Chgo.); Princeton (N.Y.C.). Home: Spring Valley Rd Ridgefield CT 06877 Office: 420 Lexington Ave New York NY 10017

WALLS, CARMAGE, newspaper pub.; b. Crisp County, Ga., Oct. 28, 1908; s. Benjamin Gaff and Anna (Byrd) W.; ed. pub. schs., Fla.; m. Odessa Dobbs, June 7, 1928 (div.); children—Carmage Lee, Mark Thomas, Jean; m. 2d, Martha Ann Williams, Jan. 2, 1954; children—Byrd Cooper, Lissa Williams. Bus. mgr. Orlanda (Fla.) Newspaper, Inc., 1934-40; pub. Macon (Ga.) Telegraph News, 1940-47; pres. Gen. Newspapers, Inc., Macon, 1945-59; pres. So. Newspapers, Inc., Montgomery, Ala., 1951-69, also dir.; pub. Montgomery (Ala.) Advt.-Jour., 1963-69; chmn. bd. Jefferson-Pilot Publs., Inc. (N.C.); v.p., dir. Houma (La.) Newspapers Inc.; chmn. bd., dir. Galveston Newspapers, Inc. (Tex.), dir. Jefferson Standard Life Ins. Co., Greensboro, N.C., Jefferson Pilot Corp., Greensboro; owner Walls Investment Co., Houston. Pres. Macon Area Devel. Commn., 1943-44, Macon C. of C., 1945; trustee Birmingham-So. Coll., 1971-77. Mem. So. Newspaper Pubs. Assn., Sigma Delta Chi. Episcopalian. Clubs: Columbia Lakes (West Columbia, (Tex.); Bob Smith Yacht (Galveston). Home: 623 Shartle Circle Houston TX 77024 Office: 7700 San Felipe Suite 111 Houston TX 77063

WALLS, DWAYNE ESTES, writer; b. Morganton, N.C., May 16, 1932; s. William Roy and Dora (Buchanan) W.; student Lenoir Rhyne Coll., 1950, 53-54, U. N.C., 1954-57; m. Judith Ann Michaels, Sept. 20, 1958; children—Helen Elizabeth, Dwayne Estes. Staff writer Durham (N.C.) Sun, 1955, Durham Morning Herald, 1956-58; news editor Chapel Hill (N.C.) Weekly, 1958-60; staff writer Charlotte (N.C.) Observer, 1961-67; free-lance writer, 1962—; research asso. Duke, 1972-73; lectr. N.C. State U., 1977-79, U. N.C., Chapel Hill, 1979—. Served with USAF, 1951-53. Recipient awards Sidney Hillman Found., L.I. U., NCCJ, Am. Polit. Sci. Assn., U.S. Office Econ. Opportunity, N.C. Press Assn., Sigma Delta Chi; travel and research grantee Ford Found., Louis M. Rabinowitz Found., So. Regional Council. Mem. Am. Polit. Sci. Assn. Unitarian. Author: The Chickenbone Special, 1970; The Kidwells, 1980. Address: Route 3 Box 105 Pittsboro NC 27312

WALLS, FORREST WESLEY, educator; b. Yale, Okla., Apr. 23, 1916; s. E. Wilbur and Elsie (Jackson) W.; student Central Coll., 1933-35; B.A., Greenville Coll., 1937; M.A., U. Wash., 1943, Ph.D., 1958; m. Elizabeth Jane Pickering, Oct. 17, 1937; children—Forrest Wesley, Burton Howard, Francine Elizabeth, Sylvia Jeannette. Prof. polit. sci. Seattle Pacific U., 1941-50, 1952-67, dean liberal studies, 1970-72, chmn. dept. polit. sci., 1972-78, dir. Sch. Bus., 1978—; dean acad. affairs Spring Arbor Coll., 1967-69. Mem. exec. council A.R.C., Jackson, Mich., 1967-69; mem. Am. Assn. UN, 1958—. Served to capt. AUS, 1944-46, 50-51. Danforth Tchr. Study grantee, 1957-58; Fulbright-Hayes fellow to Inst. on Indian Civilization, New Delhi, India, 1964. Mem. Am. Assn. for Internat. Law, Am., Western (mem. exec. council 1967-69), Northwest polit. sci. assns. Home: 824 W Etruria St Seattle WA 98119

WALLS, JOHN WILLIAM, assn. exec.; b. Knightstown, Ind., Mar. 25, 1927; s. Otto F. and Ruth (Miller) W.; A.B., Ind. U., 1949; M.P.A. (Upson-Volker fellow), Wayne State U., 1956; m. Phyllis Jean Hardin, June 20, 1948; children—Ann Walls Ponce, Kathryn Walls Roudebush, Elizabeth, Timothy. In various assn. and state and local govt. positions, Indpls., 1949-62; dep. planning dir. City of Pitts., 1962-65; exec. dir. Greater Indpls. Progress Commn., 1965-68; sr. dep. mayor City of Indpls., 1968-73; v.p. Mchts. Nat. Bank, Indpls., 1973-78; pres. Ind. State C. of C., Indpls., 1978—; vis. lectr./instr. in field; former pres. bd. Public Transit Corp.; pres. bd. dirs. Indpls. Met. Devel. Commn.; mem. Ind. Tourism Adv. Commn., Ind. Mass. Transp. Commn.; bd. dirs. Greater Indpls. Progress Com. Bd. dirs. Westview Hosp., Indpls. Served with USAAR, 1945-46. Recipient Good Govt. award Indpls. Jaycees, 1970, Brotherhood award NCCJ, 1972. Mem. Council State Chambers of Commerce, Am. Planning Assn., Ind. Commerce Execs. Assn. Quaker. Clubs: Columbia, Meridian Hills Country. Home: 1111 Fairway Dr Indianapolis IN 46260 Office: 143 N Meridian St Indianapolis IN 46204

WALLS, MARTHA ANN WILLIAMS (MRS. B. CARMAGE WALLS), newspaper exec.; b. Gadsden, Ala., Apr. 21, 1927; d. Aubrey Joseph and Inez (Cooper) Williams; student pub. schs., Gadsden; m. B. Carmage Walls, Jan. 2, 1954; children—Byrd Cooper, Lissa Williams. Pres., dir. Walls Newspapers, Inc., 1969-70; sec., treas. Summer Camps, Inc., Guntersville, Ala., 1954-69, also dir.; pres., dir. So. Newspapers, Inc., Baytown, Tex., 1970—; v.p., dir. Ft. Payne Newspapers, Inc. (Ala.), Dixie Newspapers, Inc., Gadsden, Ala., Rev. Publs. Inc., Freeport, Tex., Reidsville Newspapers, Inc. (N.C.), Scottsboro Newspapers (Ala.), Brenham (Tex.) Banner, Angleton (Tex.) Times, Rockport (Tex.) Pilot; sec.-treas., dir. Cedartown Newspapers, Inc. (Ga.); dir. LaMarque (Tex.) Times, Port Lavaca Newspapers, Inc. (Tex.), Franklin County Newspapers, Inc., Russellville, Ala., Madisonville Newspapers, Inc. (Tex.). Bd. dirs. Montgomery Acad., 1970-74. Episcopalian. Home: 623 Shartle Circle Houston TX 77024 Office: Suite 111 7700 San Felipe Houston TX 77063

WALLWORK, GEALY WESTON, coal mining co. exec.; b. Sewickley, Pa., June 18, 1930; s. Andrew C. and Anna Margaret (Myers) W.; B.S. in Mining Engring., Lehigh U., Bethlehem, Pa., 1952; M.B.A., U. Pitts., 1968; m. Betty Ann Boone, June 28, 1952; children—Andrew C., II, Jayne H., Todd W. Engring. and mgmt. positions Bethlehem Mines Corp., 1952-71; mgr. mining Am. Electric Power Service Corp., 1971-74; pres. Florence & Helen Mining Co., Seward, Pa., 1974-78; v.p. Underground Mining N.Am. Coal Corp., 1978—; dir. Florence Mining Co., Helen Mining Co., Quarto Mining Co., Nacco Mining Co. Mem. King Coal Club, AIME, Pitts. Coal Mining Inst., Assn. M.B.A. Execs. Presbyterian. Clubs: Masons, Canterbury Golf. Home: 2924 Carlton Rd Shaker Heights OH 44122 Office: 12800 Shaker Blvd Cleveland OH 44120

WALPOLE, RONALD NOEL, educator; b. Monmouthshire, Eng., Dec. 24, 1903; s. George W. and Florence M. (Blew) W.; B.A. in French with 1st class honors, Univ. Coll. Cardiff, 1925; M.A., U. Wales, 1936; Ph.D., U. Calif. at Berkeley, 1939; m. Doris G. Hoyt, Aug. 9, 1934; 1 dau., Mary R. (Mrs. Robert F. Marzke). Faculty, U. Calif. at Berkeley, 1939—, prof. French, 1950—, chmn. dept., 1957-63. Decorated chevalier de la Légion d'Honneur, 1962. Guggenheim fellow. 1949-50. Mem. Medieval Acad. Am., Internat. Arthurian Soc., Philol. Assn. Pacific Coast, Am. Acad. Arts and Scis., Phi Beta Kappa. Clubs: Faculty, Kosmos (U. Calif.). Author: Charlemagne and Roland; A Study of the Sources of Two Mediaeval English Romances, Roland and Vernagu and Otuel and Roland, 1944; Phillippe Mouskés and the Pseudo-Turpin Chronicle, 1947; The Old French Johannes Translation of the Pseudo-Turpin Chronicle: A Critical Edition, 2 vols., 1976. Contbr. articles, revs. to Am., fgn. periodicals and encys. Home: 1680 La Loma Ave Berkeley CA 94709.
My (Welsh) school had a motto, borne all over school and on our caps, blazers and prizes!-Nid da lle gellir gwell (Nothing is good where better is possible). It has always been to me a stimulus to effort and a constant lesson in humility.

WALRATH, JOHN FREDERICK, diversified mfg. exec.; b. Evans Mills, N.Y., May 18, 1916; s. Edson J. and Emma (Hoffer) W.; B.S. in Accounting cum laude, Syracuse (N.Y.) U., 1937; m. Ruth Marian Pease, Nov. 3, 1945; 1 dau., Lisa Ann. With Gen. Electric Co., 1937-63; v.p., controller Univac div. Sperry Rand Corp., N.Y.C., 1963-66; v.p. finance, sec., treas. Escambia Chem. Corp., N.Y.C., 1966-68; v.p. finance, treas., dir. Andrew Jergens Co., Cin., 1968-71; with Am. Brands, Inc., N.Y.C., 1971—, pres., 1977—, chief operating officer, 1974—, also dir. Mem. Fin. Execs. Inst., Nat. Assn. Accountants, Beta Gamma Sigma (dirs. table), Alpha Kappa Psi, Phi Kappa Phi. Methodist. Clubs: Burning Tree Country (Greenwich); Queen City (Cin.); Pinnacle (N.Y.C.); Shriners. Home: 25 Stepping Stone Ln Greenwich CT 06830 Office: 245 Park Ave New York NY 10017

WALSER, MACKENZIE, physician, educator; b. N.Y.C., Sept. 19, 1924; s. Kenneth Eastwood and Jean (Mackenzie) W.; grad. Phillips Exeter Acad., 1941; A.B., Yale, 1944; M.D., Columbia, 1948; m. Lynne Margaret White, Aug. 8, 1965; children—Karen D., Jennifer McK., Cameron M., Eric H. Intern Mass. Gen. Hosp., Boston, 1948-49, asst. resident in medicine, 1949-50; resident Parkland Hosp., Dallas, 1950-52; staff mem. Johns Hopkins Hosp., Balt., 1957—; instr. U. Tex. at Dallas, 1950-51, asst. prof., 1951-52; investigator Nat. Heart Inst., Bethesda, Md., 1954-57; asst. prof. pharmacology, Johns Hopkins Med. Sch., 1957-61, asso. prof., 1961-70, prof., 1970—, asst. prof. medicine, 1957-64, asso. prof., 1964-74, prof., 1974—. Med. dir. USPHS, 1970—, pharmacology study sect., 1968-72. Served with USNR, 1942-45; to lt. M.C., USNR, 1952-54. Recipient Research Career Devel. award USPHS, 1959-69. Diplomate Am. Bd. Internal Medicine. Mem. Am. Soc. Clin. Investigation, Assn. Am. Physicians, Am. Fedn. Clin. Research, AAAS, Am. Physiol. Soc., AAUP (pres. Johns Hopkins 1970), Biophys. Soc., Am. Soc. Pharmacology and Exptl. Therapeutics (Exptl. Therapeutics award 1975), Am. Soc. Nephrology, Council Renal Disease, Am. Heart Assn., Sigma Xi, Zeta Psi, Nu Sigma Nu. Co-author: Mineral Metabolism, 2d edit., 1969; Handbook of Physiology, 1973; The Kidney, 1976; also articles. Home: 7513 Club Rd Ruxton MD 21204 Office: Johns Hopkins U Sch Medicine Baltimore MD 21205

WALSH, BRYAN O., clergyman; b. Portarlington, Ireland, June 19, 1930; s. Richard and Catherine (Cummins) W.; student Sacred Heart Coll., 1946-48, Mungret Coll., Limerick, Ireland, 1948-50; S.T.L., St. Mary's Sem., 1954; M.A., U. No. Colo., 1974. Ordained priest Roman Catholic Ch., 1954; diocesan dir. Cath. Charities, Miami, Fla., 1957-65, 75—. Mem. Community Relations Bd. Dade County, 1973—; mem. Public Health Trust, 1979—; bd. dirs. Dade County Manpower Area Planning Council, 1972-76; chmn. Pub. Health Trust, 1977—. Named papal chaplain with title of monsignor, 1962. Home: 11450 Biscayne Blvd Miami FL 33132 Office: 4949 NE 2d Ave Miami FL 33132

WALSH, CHRISTOPHER THOMAS, chemist, biologist; b. Boston, Feb. 16, 1914; s. Christopher Thomas and Mary Louise (Fallon) W.; B.A., Harvard U., 1965; Ph.D., Rockefeller U., 1970; m. June 18, 1966; 1 dau., Allison. Asst. prof. chemistry and biology M.I.T., Cambridge, 1972-76, asso. prof., 1976-78, prof., 1978—; mem. study sect. NIH. Alfred P. Sloan fellow, 1975-77; Camille and Henry Dreyfuss fellow, 1976-80. Mem. Am. Chem. Soc. (Eli Lilly award in biol. chemistry 1979), Am. Soc. Microbiology, Am. Soc. Biol. Chemists (editorial bd. Jour. Biol. Chemistry 1978—). Author: Enzymatic Reaction Mechanisms, 1979; contbr. numerous articles to profl. jours. Office: Room 18-288 Chemistry Dept MIT Cambridge MA 02139

WALSH, CORNELIUS STEPHEN, business exec.; b. N.Y.C., Dec. 27, 1907; s. William Francis and Frances (Murphy) W.; student Eastman-Gaines Sch., 1924-25; m. Edwyna Lois Senter, May 1, 1930; children—Jane Linda (Mrs. Walsh Weed), Richard Stephen, Suzanne Patricia. Asso. with Dyson Shipping Co., Inc., 1925-27, Interocean Steamship Corp., 1928-30; sec. States Marine Corp., 1931-38, v.p., 1938-53, pres., 1953-65, dir., 1950-65; pres., dir. States Marine Corp. Del., 1946-65; chmn. Waterman Steamship Corp., N.Y.C., 1965—, Waterman Industries Corp., 1965—, Hammond Leasing Corp., 1967—; dir. Oliver Corp. Mem. Far East-Am. Council Commerce and Industry (dir.), Soc. Naval Architects and Marine Engrs. (asso.), Soc. of Four Arts (Palm Beach), Japan Soc. (hon. dir.), Am. Bur. Shipping. Clubs: Wall Street, Yacht, Met. Opera (N.Y.C.); Seawanhaka Corinthian Yacht (Oyster Bay, L.I., N.Y.); N. Am. Sta. Royal Scandinavian Yacht; Pine Valley Golf (Clementon, N.J.); Everglades, Bath and Tennis, Sailfish of Fla. (Palm Beach, Fla.). Home: 220 El Bravo Way Palm Beach FL 33480 Office: 120 Wall St New York NY 10005

WALSH, DENNY JAY, newspaperman; b. Omaha, Nov. 23, 1935; s. Gerald Jerome and Muriel (Morton) W.; B.J., U. Mo., 1962; m. Peggy Marie Moore, Feb. 12, 1966; children by previous marriage—Catherine Camille, Colleen Cecile; 1 son, Sean Joseph. Staff writer St. Louis Globe-Democrat, 1961-68; asst. editor Life mag., N.Y.C., 1968-70, asso. editor, 1970-73; reporter N.Y. Times, 1973-74, Sacramento Bee, 1974—. Served with USMCR, 1954-58. Recipient Con Lee Kelliher award St. Louis chpt. Sigma Delta Chi, 1962; award Am. Polit. Sci. Assn., 1963; award Sigma Delta Chi, 1968; Pulitzer prize spl. local reporting, 1969; 1st prize San Francisco Press Club, 1977. Home: 5558 Coronado Way Rocklin CA 95677 Office: 21st and Q Sts Sacramento CA 95813

WALSH, EDWARD JOSEPH, food co. exec.; b. Mt. Vernon, N.Y., Mar. 18, 1932; s. Edward Aloysius and Charlotte Cecilia (Borup) W.; B.B.A., Iona Coll., 1953; M.B.A., N.Y. U., 1958; m. Patricia Ann Farrell, Sept. 16, 1961; children—Edward Joseph, Megan, John, Robert. Sales rep. M & R Dietetic Labs., Columbus, Ohio, 1955-60; with Armour & Co., 1961—, v.p. toiletries div. Armour Dial Co., Phoenix, 1973-76, exec. v.p. Armour Dial Co., 1976-77, pres. Armour Internat. Co., Phoenix, 1978—. Pres., Mt. Vernon Fire Dept. Mems. Assn., 1960-61. Served with U.S. Army, 1953-55; Germany. Mem. Am. Mgmt. Assn., Nat. Meat Canner Assn. (pres. 1971-72). Republican. Roman Catholic. Office: 111 W Clarendon Phoenix AZ 85077

WALSH, ETHEL BENT, govt. ofcl.; b. Bridgeport, Conn., Dec. 29, 1923; d. William Woodworth and Corrine Ethel (Secor) Bent; student Katherine Gibbs, Boston, 1941-42; m. Robert John Walsh, Feb. 19, 1943; children—Diane (Mrs. Alfred M. Broch), Robert John. Vice pres. aerosol techniques, Inc., Bridgeport, 1955-63; plant mgr. Lavin-Charles of the Ritz, Holmdel, N.J., 1967-69; dir. office adv. councils SBA, Washington, 1969-71; mem. Equal Employment Opportunity Commn., Washington, 1971—, vice chmn., 1975-77, acting chmn., 1975, 76-77. Adv. bd. project on noncollegiate-sponsored instrn. Am. Council Edn.; adv. mem. Washington regional selection panel Pres.'s Commn. on White House Fellows. Chmn., adv. mem. Republican Women Fed. Forum; former bd. dirs. Vis. Nurses Assn., Bridgeport. Mem. Washington Forum, Exec. Women in Govt. (founding mem., past chmn.). Home: 318 Independence Ave SE Washington DC 20003 Office: Equal Employment Opportunity Commn 2401 E St NW Washington DC 20506

WALSH, GEORGE WILLIAM, editor; b. N.Y.C., Jan. 16, 1931; s. William Francis and Madeline (Maass) W.; B.S., Fordham U., 1952; M.S., Columbia U. Sch. Journalism, 1953; m. Joan Mary Dunn, May 20, 1961; children—Grail, Simon. Copy editor, reporter Cape Cod Standard-Times, Hyannis, Mass., 1955; communications specialist IBM, N.Y.C., 1955-58; editorial trainee Time, Inc., 1958-59; writer-reporter Sports Illus., N.Y.C., 1959-62; book editor Cosmopolitan, N.Y.C., 1962-65, mng. editor, 1965-74; editor-in-chief, v.p. Ballantine Books div. Random House, N.Y.C., 1974-79; editor-in-chief Macmillan Pub. Co., N.Y.C., 1979—. Served with AUS, 1953-55. Mem. Assn. Am. Pubs. Democrat. Roman Catholic. Clubs: Univ. (N.Y.C.); Pamet Harbor Yacht and Tennis (Truro, Mass.). Author: Gentleman Jimmy Walker, 1974; Public Enemies, 1980; contbr. articles to popular mags. Home: 597 4th St Brooklyn NY 11215 Office 866 Third Ave New York NY 10022

WALSH, GRACE JAYNE KELLEHER (MRS. JOHN EDWARD WALSH), statistician; b. Sarasota, Fla., Aug. 8, 1927; d. Harney Henry and Nella (Yarbrough) Walker; M.A. in Statistics, Am. U., 1955; B.S. in Pub. Adminstrn. and Mil. Sci., U. Md., 1952; postgrad. in math. econs., 1965-68; postgrad. in econs. So. Methodist U., 1969-71; M.S. in Indsl. Engring., U. Tex. at Arlington, 1974; m. Frank J. Kelleher, 1951 (div. 1968); children—Eileen, Linda; m. 2d, John Edward Walsh, Sept. 18, 1969 (dec. Aug. 1972). Statistician, Dept. Navy, Washington, 1945-50; statistician, logistician Hdqrs. U.S. Air Force, Washington, 1952-63; sr. research staff, econs. and systems analysis Inst. for Def. Analyses, Arlington, Va., 1964-69; lectr. econs. So. Meth. U., Dallas, 1969-70; asst. prof. mgmt. sci. U. Tex. at Arlington, 1970-72; ind. operations research cons., Tex., also Washington, 1972-73; operations research analyst Def. Communications Engring. Center, Reston, Va., 1973-77; ind. cons. mgmt. sci., ops. research, stats. and econs., Washington, 1978—. Served to capt. USAF, 1951-52. Recipient Meritorious Civilian Service award USAF, 1957. Fellow A.A.A.S.; mem. Operations Research Soc. Am. (chmn. long range planning com. 1974—), Inst. Mgmt. Scis. (vice chmn. Washington chpt. 1968-69), Am. Statis.

Assn. Co-author, editor: The Challenge to Systems Analysis: Public Policy and Social Change, 1970. Home: 6513 Beverly Ave McLean VA 22101

WALSH, H. ROBERT, advt. agy. exec.; b. Boston, Jan. 21, 1925; s. Henry Patrick and Mary Edith (Winchester) W.; A.B. magna cum laude, Harvard U., 1949; postgrad. U. Paris, 1950; M.B.A., Columbia U., 1952; m. Deirdre A. Ahearn, Nov. 7, 1964; children—Meredith Winchester, Eliot Winchester. With Young & Rubicam, Inc., N.Y.C., 1952—, sr. v.p., dir. research, chmn. strategy rev. bd. Served to 2d lt., inf., U.S. Army, 1942-46. Mem. Am. Mktg. Assn., Advt. Research Found., Am. Assn. Advt. Agys. Clubs: Harvard (N.Y.C.); Rockaway Hunting, Lawrence Beach, Cedarhurst Yacht. Office: 285 Madison Ave New York NY 10017

WALSH, JAMES A., dept. store exec.; b. 1923; ed. Fordham U., N.Y. U. Clk. Am. Cyanamid Co., 1942-43; officer mgr. Harper Megee Inc., 1946-48; with Allied Stores Corp., 1948—, asst. controller Bon Marche, Seattle, 1955-57, v.p., controller, 1957-65, exec. v.p., 1965-68, pres., mng. dir., 1968-71, v.p. parent co., 1968-78, sr. v.p. parent co., exec. group mgr. The Bon, Seattle, Donaldson's, Mpls., Block's, Indpls., 1978—. officer Bon Marche. Office: The Bon 3d and Pine Sts Seattle WA 98181

WALSH, JAMES ALOYSIUS, rubber co. exec.; b. Passaic, N.J., Mar. 23, 1921; s. James A. and Mary (Riley) W.; grad. Choate Sch., 1939; B.S. in Indsl. Adminstrn., Yale, 1943; m. Mary Fitzgerald, June 15, 1942 (div. Mar. 1965); children—Michael A., Tyla Ann; m. 2d, Sandra Spear, July 1970; children—Diana Lynn, Meaghan E., James F., Patrick O. With Armstrong Rubber Co., West Haven, Conn., 1942—, v.p. prodn., 1966-71, pres., 1971—, also dir.; dir. Copolymer Rubber & Chem. Co., Baton Rouge. Clubs: New Haven Country, Yale (New Haven). Office: 500 Sargent Dr New Haven CT 06507

WALSH, JAMES AUGUSTINE, judge; b. Westfield, Mass., Sept. 17, 1906; s. Thomas and Hannah (Shea) W.; student St. Anselm's Coll., Manchester, N.H., 1923-24; LL.B., Georgetown U., 1928; m. Mary Ficca, Feb. 17, 1930 (dec. Dec. 1966); children—James, Georgeanne, Geraldine, Thomas, Michael. Admitted to D.C., Ariz. bars, 1928; practice law, Mesa, 1928-41; city atty., Mesa, 1936-40; asst. U.S. atty. Dist. Ariz., 1943; co. atty., Maricopa County, Ariz., 1943-44; judge Superior Ct., 1945-47; mem. firm Snell & Wilmer, Phoenix, 1947-52; chief counsel Ariz. Code Commn., 1951-52; U.S. dist judge, 1952—. Mem. Ariz. Bar Assn. Home: 6674 E Broadway Tucson AZ 85710 Office: US Dist Ct Tucson AZ 85702

WALSH, JAMES CLEMENT, mgmt. cons.; b. Chgo., May 31, 1918; s. Karin E. and Loretto (Callahan) W.; B.S.C., U. Notre Dame, 1939; m. Jane Burnham, 1938; children—Barbara (Mrs. Richard S. Wilson), James B., Carol (Mrs. James J. Moran), Mary Ellen (Mrs. Robert Reinhold), Kathleen, Betsy Lyons, Gerald, Susan, Thomas. With Marshall Field & Co., Chgo., 1939-53, asst. to gen., mgr. Fieldcrest div., N.Y.C., 1949-52; sec.-treas. Fieldcrest Mills, Inc., 1953-55; v.p., treas. Hecht Co., Balt., 1955-58; sec., asst. treas. May Dept. Stores Co., St. Louis, 1959-60, v.p., treas., 1960-66, v.p. adminstrn. and control, 1967-68, exec. v.p., 1968-75, sr. exec. v.p., 1975-78, also dir.; pres. James C. Walsh, Inc., St. Louis, 1978—. C.P.A., Ill. Home: 2120 S Warson Rd Ladue MO 63124 Office: 515 Olive Sts Saint Louis MO 63101

WALSH, JAMES EDWARD, clergyman; b. Cumberland, Md., Apr. 30, 1891; s. William E. and Mary (Concannon) W.; A.B., Mt. St. Mary's Coll., Emmittsburg, Md., 1910, LL.D., 1937; student Maryknoll (N.Y.) Sem., 1912-15. Entered Cath. Fgn. Missions Soc. Am., Sept. 15, 1912; ordained priest Roman Cath. Ch., 1915; dir. Maryknoll Prep. Coll., Clarks Summit, Pa., 1916-18; assigned to mission in China, 1918; apptd. superior Maryknoll Mission China, 1919; consecrated titular bishop Sata and vicar apostolic of Kongmoon, China, May, 1927; Superior General Cath. Fgn. Mission Soc., Maryknoll, N.Y., 1936-46; gen. sec. Cath. Central Bur., Shanghai, China, 1948-58, imprisoned by Peoples Republic of China; with Maryknoll Fathers, 1971—. Founder, Little Flower Sem., 1926, Native Congregation of Sisters of Immaculate Heart of Mary, 1927, both Kongmoon, South China. Author: Father McShane of Maryknoll, 1932, 2d edit. as The Man on Joss Stick Alley, 1947; Tales of Xavier, 1946; Maryknoll Spiritual Directory, 1947; Church's Worldwide Mission, 1948; The Young Ones, 1958. Contbr. to Field Afar mag. Address: Maryknoll Fathers Maryknoll NY 10545

WALSH, JAMES JEROME, educator; b. Seattle, May 23, 1924; s. John Jerome and Agnes (Counihan) W.; B.A., Reed Coll., 1949; B.A., Oxford (Eng.) U., 1951, M.A., 1956; Ph.D., Columbia, 1960; m. Carol Jean Paton, Sept. 16, 1946; children—John Jerome II, James Paton. Mem. faculty Columbia, 1954—, prof. philosophy, 1966—, dir. grad. studies philosophy dept., 1963-66, 73—, chmn. dept., 1967-73; vis. instr. U. Calif. at Berkeley, 1958, cons. TV series G.E. Coll. Bowl, 1965-70. Mem. Rockland County Democratic Com., 1960-63. Served with AUS, 1943-45. Decorated Purple Heart. Rhodes scholar, 1949; Ford Found. fellow, 1958; Am. Council Learned Socs. fellow, 1962; Guggenheim fellow, 1966. Mem. Am. Philos. Assn., Soc. Medieval and Renaissance Philosophy (adv. to pres.). Author: Aristotle's Conception of Moral Weakness, 1963; Philosophy in the Middle Ages 1967. Editor: Jour. Philosophy, 1965—. Home: 50 Haverstraw Rd Suffern NY 10901 Office: Philosophy Hall Columbia Univ New York City NY 10027

WALSH, JAMES LOUIS, ret lawyer, ins. co. exec.; b. Parsons, Kan., Feb. 24, 1909; s. James Louis and Catharine (Nolan) W.; A.B., U. Notre Dame 1930; LL.B., So. Meth. U., 1933. Admitted to Tex. bar, 1933; asst. counsel Home Owners Loan Corp., Dallas, 1934-35, counsel, 1935-40, div. counsel, 1940-44; asso. law firm Hamilton, Lipscomb, Wood & Swift, Dallas, 1944-45; with legal dept. Southwestern Life Ins. Co., Dallas, 1945—, asso. gen. counsel, 1951-65, v.p., 1965-70, gen. counsel, 1965—, sr. v.p., 1970-73, exec. v.p., 1973-74. Mem. Dallas Estate Council, 1947—, pres., 1955-56; pres. Catholic Charities, Dallas, 1962-63. Dir. Community Council Greater Dallas, 1962-68. Decorated knight grand comdr. Order Holy Sepulchre, Knight of Malta. Mem. Am., Tex., Dallas bar assns., Assn. Life Ins. Counsel (mem. emeritus), Phi Alpha Delta. Roman Catholic. Club: Calyx (Dallas). Home: 5323 Monticello Ave Dallas TX 75206. *I thank God for America. The opportunity to dedicate oneself to something worthwhile, and the discipline it inevitably brings, is a great reward.*

WALSH, JAMES PATRICK, JR., ins. cons., actuary; b. Ft. Thomas, Ky., Mar. 7, 1910; s. James Patrick and Minnie Louise (Cooper) W.; comml. engr. degree, U. Cin., 1933; m. Evelyn Mary Sullivan, May 20, 1939. Accountant, Firestone Tire & Rubber Co., also Gen. Motors Corp., 1933-36; rep. A.R.C., 1937, A.F.L., 1938-39; dir. Ohio Div. Minimum Wages, Columbus, 1939-42; asst. sec.-treas. union label trades dept. A.F.L., Washington, 1946-53; v.p. Pension and Group Cons., Inc., Cin., 1953—. Mem. Pres.'s Commn. Jud. and Congl. Salaries, 1953, Ohio Gov.'s Commn. Employment of Negro, 1940, Hamilton (O.) County Welfare Bd., 1955—, council long term illness and rehab. Cin. Pub. Health Fedn., 1957-68. Bd. dirs. U. Cin., 1959-67; bd. govs. St. Xavier High Sch., Cin.; trustee Brown Found., Newman Cath. Center, Cin. Served to lt. col. AUS, 1942-46; col. Res. ret. Decorated Legion of Merit; named Ky. col., 1958, Ky. adm., 1968; recipient Distinguished Alumni award U. Cin., Insignis award St. Xavier High Sch., 1973. Fellow Am. Soc. Pension Actuaries; mem. Am. Arbitration Assn. (nat. community disputes panel), Res. Officers Assn., Am. Legion, Q.M. Assn., V.F.W., Ret. Officers Assn. (pres. Cin. chpt. 1973-74), Nat. Football Found. and Hall of Fame, Am. Fedn. State, County and Employees Union, Internat. Alliance Theatrical Stage Employees (past sgt. at arms,) Internat. Hodcarriers, Bldg. and Common Laborers Union, Ins. Workers Internat. Union, Office Employees Internat. Union, Cooks and Pastry Cooks Local, Friendly Sons St. Patrick (past pres.), Ret. Officers Assn. (past pres.), Convington Latin Sch. Alumni Assn. (past pres.), Soc. for Advancement Mgmt., Defense Supply Assn., Ancient Order Hibernians (past pres.). Assn. U.S. Army (trustee), Am. Ordnance Assn., Soc. Am. Mil. Engrs., Order of Alhambra, Internat. Assn. Health Underwriters, Allied Constrn. Industries, Scabbard and Blade, Nat. Council of Cath. Men, Indsl. Relations Research Assn., Zoo Soc. of Cin., Millcreek Valley Assn., Alpha Kappa Psi. Republican. Roman Catholic. K.C. (4 deg.), Elk. Clubs: C. Cincinnati (past pres.), Queen City, American Irish, Insiders, Touchdown, Blue Liners, Roundtable, Scuttlebuts, Newman, Bankers, Military (Cin.). Home: 5563 Julmar Dr Cincinnati OH 45238 Office: 6 E 4th St Cincinnati OH 45202

WALSH, JAMES PAUL, engr.; b. Fall River, Mass., Apr. 3, 1917; s. James Patrick and Cecila (Lowe) W.; M.E., Stevens Inst. Tech., 1938, D. Engring., 1958; M.S., U. Md., 1950; m. Joan Edwards, Apr. 11, 1942; children—Joanne, James Paul, William Joseph. Staff Naval Research Lab., 1943-59, project officer Operation Crossroads, Bikini, 1946, head structures br., 1949-55, project officer Operation Castle, Eniwetock, 1954, Operation Wigwam, 1955; project mgr. shock and vibration U.S.S. Nautilus; dep. dir. Project Vanguard, 1955; dir., v.p. Space Weapons Systems div. C-E-I-R, Inc., Arlington, Va., 1960-63; pres. Matrix Corp., Arlington, 1963-70, chmn. bd. 1965-70; supt. ocean tech. Naval Research Lab., Washington, 1970—. Registered profl. engr., D.C. Mem. Nat. Soc. Profl. Engrs., Research Soc. Am., Washington Philos. Soc. Home: Sherwood Forest MD 21405 Office: Naval Research Lab Washington DC 20375

WALSH, JOHN, mus. curator; b. Mason City, Wash., Dec. 9, 1937; s. John J. and Eleanor (Wilson) W.; B.A., Yale U., 1961; M.A., Columbia U., 1965, Ph.D., 1971; postgrad. U. Leyden, Netherlands; m. Virginia Alys Galston, Feb. 17, 1962; children—Peter Wilson, Anne Galston, Frederick Matthiessen. Lectr., curatorial asst. Frick Collection, N.Y.C., 1966-68; asso. for higher edn. Met. Mus. Art, N.Y.C., 1968-70, asso. curator, then curator dept. European paintings, 1970-75; prof. art history Barnard Coll., Columbia U., 1975-77; Mrs. Russell W. Baker curator of paintings Mus. of Fine Arts, Boston, 1977—; vis. prof. fine arts Harvard U., 1977—. Mem. Democratic County Com., N.Y., 1968-72. Served with USNR, 1957-59. Fulbright fellow, 1965-66. Mem. Coll. Art Assn. Am. (dir.), Yale U. Art Gallery (governing bd.), Am. Assn. Museums. Club: Century Assn. Contbr. articles to profl. jours. Office: Museum of Fine Arts Boston MA 02115*

WALSH, JOHN CHARLES, metallurgical co. exec.; b. Indpls., Sept. 8, 1924; s. John Charles and Nell (O'Neil) W.; B.S., Notre Dame U., 1949; m. Mary Louise Dreiss, Feb. 5, 1949; children—Michael S., Carolyn Ann, Anne D. Auditor, Herdrich Boggs & Co., Indpls., 1949-50; v.p. fin. Contact, Metals and Welding Inc., Indpls., 1950—. Served with USMCR, 1943-45. Mem. Financial Execs. Inst., Newcomen Soc. N.Am., Indpls. C. of C. Clubs: World Trade of Ind.; Economic (Indpls.); Notre Dame. Home: 7365 Huntington Rd Indianapolis IN 46240 Office: 70 S Gray St Indianapolis IN 46206

WALSH, JOHN JOSEPH, physician, educator; b. N.Y.C., July 31, 1924; s. Patrick J. and Elizabeth (Lawless) W.; student Fordham U., 1941-43, Cornell U., 1943-44; M.D., L.I. Coll. Medicine, 1948; m. Gloria Paolini, June 19, 1948 (dec. 1971); children—Maureen, John Joseph, Kathleen. Intern, USPHS Hosp., S.I., N.Y., 1948-49; resident USPHS Hosp., Seattle, 1951-54; practice medicine specializing in internal medicine, New Orleans, 1954—; commd. lt. (j.g.) USPHS, 1948, advanced through grades to rear adm., 1959; med. dir., med. officer in charge USPHS Hosp., New Orleans, 1964-66, now chmn. adv. com.; asst. surgeon gen. USPHS Hosp., dir. div. Direct Health Services, 1966-68; ret., 1968; instr., prof. medicine Tulane U., 1957—, dean, coordinator health scis. and programs, 1968-69, v.p. health affairs, 1969—; chancellor Tulane Med. Center, 1972—; vis. physician Charity Hosp., New Orleans, 1957—; cons. internal medicine VA Hosp., New Orleans. Served with USNR, 1943-45. Recipient Commendation medal USPHS, 1968. Diplomate Am. Bd. Internal Medicine. Fellow Am. Coll. Cardiology, A.C.P., Am. Coll. Clin. Pharmacology and Chemotherapy, Am. Coll. Chest Physicians; mem. Am. Cancer Soc., La. Tb and Respiratory Disease Assn. (past pres.), La. Thoracic Soc. (past pres.), Commd. Officers Assn. and Clin. Soc. USPHS (past nat. pres.), AMA (com. emergency health service), Am. Lung Assn. La. (life, hon.), Alpha Omega Alpha, Phi Chi, Delta Omega, Alpha Epsilon Delta. Home: 834 Audubon St New Orleans LA 70118 Office: Tulane Med Center 1430 Tulane Ave New Orleans LA 70112

WALSH, JOHN ROBERT, mfg. co. exec.; b. Boston, Apr. 17, 1930; s. Edward Robert and Alice Imelda (McMahon) W.; B.S. in Engring., M.I.T., 1953, postgrad. in process metallurgy, 1953; m. Christiane Bernadette Septier, Feb. 25, 1955; children—Mary Anne, John Robert, Marie-Noelle, Thomas M. Sr. partner Stephenson Walsh & Assos., cons. engrs., Paris, 1958-61; with Borg-Warner Corp. and sub's., 1961—, v.p. internat. ops. York div. (Pa.), 1967-68, pres. York Europe div., Geneva and Brussels, 1969-77, pres. York Internat. div., 1978—; chmn. mgmt. com., dir. Brown Boveri-York Kalte-Und Klimatechnik GmbH (Ger.); chmn. bd., dir. Borg-Warner A.G., Zug, Switzerland; joint mng. dir., dir. Borg-Warner Ltd. (U.K.); dir. Le Froid Industriel York, S.A. (France), York Internat. Corp. (U.S.A), York Aire, S.A. (Mexico), Recold S.A. De C.V. (Mexico), Refrigeracion York, S.A., (Venezuela), McFarland Co., Harrisburg, Pa. Served to 1st lt. C.E., U.S. Army, 1954-58. Registered prof. engr., Mass. Mem. Am. Mgmt. Assn. (pres's. council), Machinery and Allied Products Inst. (internat. ops. council). Roman Catholic. Club: Country of York, Lafayette, Rose Tree Fox Hunting, Beaufort Hunt. Home: 1100 Grantley Rd York PA 17403 Office: PO Box 1592 York PA 17405

WALSH, JOHN WALTER, physician, hosp. adminstr.; b. Bklyn., July 6, 1918; s. John Leo and Rose (Folles) W.; B.S. magna cum laude, St. Francis Coll., 1938; M.D., Downstate N.Y. Med. Center, 1942; m. Janet England, Nov. 24, 1943; 1 son, Christopher Strattan. Intern, St. John's Hosp., Bklyn., 1942-43; resident Bronx (N.Y.) VA Hosp., 1946-48; practice internal medicine, Wilkes Barre, Pa., 1952-55, Boston, 1955-57, Washington, 1957-69, Phila., 1967-71, Bronx, N.Y., 1974-75, Washington, 1975—; with VA, 1946—; dir. VA Hosp., Phila., 1969-71, San Juan, P.R., 1971-74, Bronx, N.Y., 1974-75; ops. rev. and analysis VA Central Office, 1975—; faculty Tufts U., 1956-58, George Washington U., 1958-69; asso. clin. prof. medicine Med. Coll. Pa., 1969-71, Mt. Sinai Med. Sch., 1975, George Washington U., 1975—; lectr. community medicine U. Pa., 1969-71. Mem. Surgeon Gen.'s Adv. Council Health Care, 1960-69, Gov.'s Adv. Council Comprehensive Health, 1971-74; 1st dir. planning programming budgeting system for health VA; mem. Interagy. Com. Emergency Med. Service HEW, 1975—. Pres., Locust Hills Citizens Assn., 1959-60. Club: Lakewood Country (Rockville, Md.). Contbr. articles to med. jours. Address: 4600 Connecticut Ave NW Washington DC 20008

WALSH, JOSEPH FIDLER, recording artist, record producer; b. Wichita, Kans., Nov. 20, 1947; s. George William and Helen Alice (Bowen) W.; student Kent (Ohio) State U. Recording artist with James Gang, to 1971, Barnstorm, 1971-74, Eagles, 1976—, also solo artist; songs include: Funk 49, In the City, Life's Been Good, Walk Away; albums include: Barnstorm Featuring Joe Walsh, The James Gang, The James Gang Rides Again, The Smoker You Drink, The Player You Get, So What?, You Cant's Can't Argue With a Sick Mind, But Seriously Folks. Mem. Amateur Radio Relay League. Research electronic music synthesizers. Office: care Front Line Mgmt 8380 Melrose Ave Los Angeles CA 90069*

WALSH, JOSEPH MICHAEL, bus. exec.; b. N.Y.C., Jan. 19, 1943; s. John Redmond and Bridget Judith (O'Donovan) W.; B.B.A. in Acctg., Iona Coll., 1964; m. Theresa Rose Vericker, Oct. 3, 1964; children—Joseph, Matthew, Teresa Ann, John, James. With Peat, Marwick, Mitchell & Co., C.P.A.'s, N.Y.C., 1964-70, audit supr., until 1970; asst. to chmn. bd. and pres. Cadence Industries Corp., West Caldwell, N.J., 1970-71, v.p., 1971-74, exec. v.p., 1974—, pres. subs. Curtis Circulation Co., 1972-74, subs. Data Services for Health, 1976-77, subs. U.S. Pencil and Stationery Co., 1977—. Mem. N.Y. State Soc. C.P.A.'s, Am. Inst. C.P.A.'s. Clubs: Lions, K.C. Home: 9 Pond Rd Woodcliff Lake NJ 07675 Office: 21 Henderson Dr West Caldwell NJ 07006

WALSH, JULIA MARGARET CURRY (MRS. THOMAS M. WALSH), investment co. exec.; b. Akron, Ohio, Mar. 29, 1923; d. Edward A. and Catharine V. (Skurkay) Curry; B.B.A. magna cum laude, Kent (Ohio) State U., 1945; postgrad. N.Y. Inst. Fin., 1956; grad. Advanced Mgmt. Program, Harvard, 1962; LL.D., Hood Coll., 1969, Regis Coll., 1973; m. John G. Montgomery, Apr. 7, 1948 (dec. Dec. 1957); children—John, Stephen, Michael, Mark; m. 2d, Thomas M. Walsh, May 18, 1963; 1 dau., Margaret; stepchildren—Mary Francis (Mrs. Steven Ferencie), Patrick Joseph, Kathleen, Thomas D., Joan, Daniel, Ann. Personnel officer Am. consulate gen., Munich, Ger., 1945-48; probation officer Wash. State Sch. Girls, Centralia, 1948-50; exec. officer U.S. Ednl. Commn., Ankara, Turkey, 1952-54; registered rep. Ferris & Co., Inc., Washington, 1955-59, gen. partner, 1959-70, sr. v.p., 1970-74, vice chmn., 1974-77, chmn. Julia M. Walsh & Sons, Inc., 1977—, dir. Pitney Bowes, Stamford, Ct.; mem. nat. adv. com. to Controller of Currency, 1975—; mem. Am. Stock Exchange, 1965, bd. govs., 1972, exchange ofcl., 1973—; advisory bd. Union 1st Bank Washington. Mem. Sec. State's Spl. Advisory Com. on Pub. Opinion; mem. advisory com. loan guarantee programs in health HEW; mem. Advisory Com. to the Sec. of the Treas. consolidated Fin. Statements, mem. Nat. Advisory Commn.; Assn. of Women in the Professions, mem. Advisory Com. Nat. Women's Polit. Caucas, mem. Nat. Com. on Ethics (AMA). Bd. dirs. Bus. Resources Center, Kent State U. Found., Christ Child Soc., Nat. Shrine Immaculate Conception, St. Mary of the Woods Coll., Georgetown U., Med. Coll. Pa., The East-West Center, Honolulu; dir.-at-large Met. Washington Bd. Trade; mem. Washington bd. Nat. Multiple Sclerosis Soc.; mem. Tax Revision Commn. D.C. Recipient Distinguished Alumna award Kent State U., 1967; Bus. and Profl. Leader in Fin. award Religious Heritage Am., 1973. Mem. Fin. Analysts Soc. Washington (chmn. women's conv. program, 1965), Bus. and Profl. Women's Club Potomac, AAUW, U.S. C. of C. (nat. dir.), Harvard Bus. Sch. Assn. (exec. council). Clubs: Women's Nat. Democratic, Am. Newspaper Women's, Harvard Bus. Sch. (past pres.), Zonta, Internat. (Washington). Home: 5001 Millwood Ln NW Washington DC 20016 Office: Julia M Walsh & Sons Inc 910 17th St NW Suite 717

WALSH, LAWRENCE EDWARD, lawyer; b. Port Maitland, N.S., Can., Jan. 8, 1912; s. Dr. Cornelius Edward and Lila May (Sanders) W.; brought to U.S., 1914, naturalized, 1922; A.B., Columbia, 1932, LL.B., 1935; LL.D., Union U., 1959, St. John's U., 1975, Suffolk U., 1975, Waynesburg Coll., 1976, Vt. Law Sch., 1976; m. Mary Alma Porter; children—Barbara Marie, Janet Maxine (Mrs. Wiggins), Sara Porter, Dale Edward, Elizabeth Porter. Admitted to N.Y. bar, 1936; spl. asst. atty. gen. Drukman Investigation, 1936-38; dep. asst. dist. atty. N.Y. County, 1938-41; asst. counsel to gov. N.Y., 1943-49, counsel to gov., 1950-51; counsel Pub. Service Commn., 1951-53; gen. counsel, exec. dir. Waterfront Commn. of N.Y. Harbor, 1953-54; U.S. judge So. Dist. N.Y., 1954-57; U.S. dep. atty. gen., 1957-60; partner firm Davis, Polk & Wardwell, 1961—. Trustee Mut. Life Ins. Co. N.Y.; dir. Richardson-Merrell, Inc. Trustee Columbia U., William Nelson Cromwell Found.; pres. Columbia Alumni Fedn., 1968-69; chmn. N.Y. State Moreland Commn. Alcoholic Beverage Control Law, 1963-64; chmn. Mayor's Task Force Law Enforcement, 1965-66; dep. head with rank of ambassador U.S. delegation meetings on Vietnam, Paris, 1969; counsel to N.Y. State ct. on judiciary, 1971-72; 2d circuit mem. U.S. Circuit Judge Nominating Commn., 1978—. Fellow Am. Bar Found., Am. Coll. Trial Lawyers; mem. Am. Law Inst. (council), Am. (pres. 1975-76), N.Y. State (pres. 1966-67), Internat. bar assns., Assn. Bar City of New York, N.Y. County Lawyers Assn.; hon. mem. Law Soc. Eng. and Wales, Can. Bar Assn., Mexican Bar Assn., Beta Theta Pi. Clubs: India House, The Century. Home: 320 E 72d St New York NY 10021 Office: 1 Chase Manhattan Plaza 44th Floor New York NY 10005

WALSH, LOREN MELFORD, jour. editor; b. Valparaiso, Ind., July 22, 1927; s. Melford Lee and Lois Ada (Beehler) W.; B.S., Valparaiso U., 1951; m. Shirley B. Hepner, June 21, 1944; children—Lauren Jo (Mrs. Earl T. Brushwood), Cindy Harper, Robin, Jeannette, Cathy. Quality engr. Stephens Adamson Co., Aurora, Ill., 1951-54, mgr. quality assurance, Spherco. div., 1954-59, dir. quality assurance Sealmaster bearing div., 1959-68, dir. tech. services, 1968-69; editor Quality Mag., Hitchcock Pub. Co., Wheaton, Ill., 1970—. Dir. Aurora Bearing Co., Batavia, Ill., 1972—. Served with AUS, med. corps, 1945-47. Mem. Am. Soc. Quality Control. Home: Route 1 Box 640 Batavia IL 60510 Office: Quality Management and Engineering Magazine Hitchcock Bldg Wheaton IL 60187

WALSH, MASON, pub.; b. Dallas, Nov. 27, 1912; s. Herbert C. and Margaret (Hayes) W.; B.A. in Polit. Sci., So. Meth. U., 1934; m. Margaret Anne Calhoun, Mar. 7, 1947; children—Margaret Anne, Timothy Mason, Kevin Calhoun. Staff, Dallas Evening Jour., 1929-37; profl. musician, 1929-35; staff Dallas Dispatch-Jour. (later Dallas Jour.), 1938-42; editor Austin (Tex.) Tribune, 1942; dir. employee relations N.Am. Aviation, Dallas, 1942-45; with Dallas Times-Herald, 1945-60, mng. editor, 1952-60; mng. editor Phoenix Gazette, 1960-66; gen. mgr. Phoenix Newspapers, Inc., 1966-75, asst. pub., 1975, pub. Ariz. Republic and Phoenix Gazette, 1978—. Chmn. Ariz. Dept. Econ. Planning and Devel. Bd., 1968-71; bd. dirs. Western Newspaper Found. Mem. A.P. Mng. Editors Assn. (dir. 1956-63, pres. 1963), A.P. Assn. Calif., Ariz., Hawaii and Nev. (pres. 1976-77), Sigma Delta Chi. Episcopalian. Clubs: Phoenix Press, Ariz. Press, University, Phoenix Country, Arizona. Home: 4102 N 64th Pl Scottsdale AZ 85251 Office: 120 E Van Buren St Phoenix AZ 85001

WALSH, MASON, JR., lawyer; b. Phila., Oct. 23, 1935; s. Mason and Alice Elizabeth (Breneman) W.; B.S. in Chem. Engring., Pa. State U., 1957; LL.B., Harvard U., 1960; m. Carole Henderson Krick, Dec. 23, 1961; children—Richard S., Constance. Admitted to Pa. bar, 1961; asso., partner firm Reed, Smith, Shaw & McClay, Pitts., 1960-67; with T. Mellon & Sons, Pitts., 1967-71; sr. v.p., gen. counsel Richard K. Mellon & Sons, Pitts., 1971—; trustee Richard King Mellon Found., R.K. Mellon Family Found., Richard King Mellon Charitable Trusts. Mem. Pa. State U. Alumni Council, 1977—; trustee Valley Sch. of Ligonier, Pa., Western Pa. Conservancy, Pitts.; v.p., trustee Children's Hosp., Pitts.; vice chmn. bd. trustees Nature Conservancy, Washington. Served with U.S. Army Res., 1961. Mem. Am. Bar Assn., Pa. Bar Assn., Allegheny County Bar Assn., Am. Law Inst., Tau Beta Pi, Sigma Tau, Sigma Alpha Epsilon. Republican. Episcopalian. Clubs: Harvard-Yale-Princeton, Duquesne (Pitts.); Rolling Rock (bd. govs.), Laurel Valley Golf (bd. govs.) (Ligonier). Home: 7545 Graymore Rd Pittsburgh PA 15221 Office: Richard K Mellon & Sons PO Box 1138 Pittsburgh PA 15230

WALSH, MAURICE DAVID, JR., librarian; b. N.Y.C., Dec. 24, 1924; s. Maurice David and Helen Merlyn (Flynn) W.; B.J., U. Mo., 1949; M.S. in Library Sci., La. State U., 1963; grad. U.S. Army Command and Gen. Staff Coll., 1967; m. Alice Louise Flynn, Oct. 18, 1952; children—Maud Maureen, Michael Sean, James Liam, Douglas Padraic. With Jefferson Parish Library, Metairie, La., 1959—, library adminstr., head librarian, 1963—. Served with AUS, 1943-45, 50-52; col. Army Res. Mem. La., Southwestern, Am. library assns., Assn. U.S. Army, First Cav. Div. Assn., 11th Armored Div. Assn., Alpha Delta Sigma. Republican. Roman Catholic. Elk, Rotarian. Contbr. articles mil. and library publs. Home: 4536 Folse Dr Metairie LA 70002 Office: Jefferson Parish Library Hdqrs PO Box 7490 3420 N Causeway Blvd Metairie LA 70010

WALSH, MICHAEL H., govt. ofcl.; b. Binghamton, N.Y., July 9, 1942; B.A. in Econs., Stanford U., 1964, J.D., Yale U., 1969. Admitted to Calif. bar, 1970; asst. dir. admissions Stanford U., 1964-65; White House fellow U.S. Dept. Agr., 1965-66; sr. staff atty. Defenders Inc., San Diego, 1969-72; mem. firm Sheela, Lightner, Hughes, Castro & Walsh, San Diego, 1972-77; U.S. atty. for Calif., 1978—. Trustee Stanford U. Mem. San Diego County Bar Assn., State Bar Calif. Contbr. articles to profl. jours. Office: US Courthouse 940 Front St San Diego CA 92189*

WALSH, PATRICK CRAIG, urologist; b. Akron, Ohio, Feb. 13, 1938; s. Raymond Michael and Catherine N. (Rodden) W.; A.B., Case Western Res. U., 1960, M.D., 1964; m. Margaret Campbell, May 23, 1964; children—Christopher, Jonathan, Alexander. Intern in surgery Peter Bent Brigham Hosp., Boston, 1964-65, asst. resident in surgery, 1965-66; asst. resident in pediatric surgery Children's Hosp. Med. Center, Boston, 1966-67; resident in urology U. Calif.-Los Angeles Med. Center, 1967-71; dir. Brady Urol. Inst., urologist-in-chief Johns Hopkins Hosp., Balt., 1974—; prof., dir. dept. urology Johns Hopkins U. Sch. Medicine, 1974—. Served to comdr. M.C., USN, 1971-73. Fellow A.C.S.; mem. Soc. Univ. Surgeons, Am. Assn. Genito-Urinary Surgeons, Clin. Soc. Genito-Urinary Surgeons, Am. Urol. Assn., Endocrine Soc., Alpha Omega Alpha. Roman Catholic. Contbr. articles to med. jours. Home: 13910 Cuba Rd Cockeysville MD 21030 Office: Johns Hopkins Hosp Baltimore MD 21205

WALSH, PETER JOSEPH, educator; b. N.Y.C., Aug. 21, 1929; s. Peter and Mary Ellen (Kelly) W.; B.S., Fordham U., 1951; M.S., N.Y.U., 1953, Ph.D., 1960; m. Rosemarie Imundo, May 13, 1952; children—Kathleen, Mary Ellen, Susan, Carole, Karen. Research physicist Westinghouse Elec. Co., Bloomfield, N.J., 1951-60; supervisory physicist Am. Standard, Piscataway, N.J., 1960-62; prof. physics Fairleigh Dickinson U., 1962—; cons. physics. Mem. Am. Phys. Soc., AAAS, N.J. Acad. Sci., Sigma Xi (sec. 1969). Author: Dark Side of Knowledge. Home: 40 St Joseph Dr Stirling NJ 07980 Office: Fairleigh Dickinson U Teaneck NJ 07666

WALSH, PHILIP CORNELIUS, mining co. exec.; b. Harrison, N.J., May 23, 1921; s. Philip Cornelius and Frances Walsh (Prendergast) W.; B.A., Yale U., 1944; m. Alexandra Somerville Tuck, May 19, 1945; children—Eugenie Philbin Walsh Flaherty, Philip C.C., Frances Cornelia Walsh Cummings, Alexander Tuck, Nicholas Holladay, Elizabeth Marshall. With W.R. Grace & Co., 1946-71, v.p. parent co., chief operating officer Latin Am. group, 1968-70, group exec. corp. adminstrv. group, 1970-71; v.p. Cerro Corp., 1972-74; v.p. Newmont Mining Corp., 1974—; chmn. bd. Foote Mineral Co., N.Y.C., 1979—; dir. So. Peru Copper Corp. Mem. Bd. Edn., Harding Twp., N.J., 1960-66; mem. Harding Twp. Com., 1966-72, police commr., 1966-72; trustee Morristown Meml. Hosp., 1969-79. Served with U.S. Army, 1942-46. Decorated Purple Heart. Mem. Am. Inst. Mining, Metall. and Petroleum Engrs., Pan Am. Soc. U.S. (dir.), Sigma Xi, Phi Beta Kappa. Republican. Roman Catholic. Clubs: Racquet and Tennis, Mining, Edgartown Yacht. Home: 170 E 77th St New York NY 10021 Office: 300 Park Ave New York NY 10022

WALSH, ULYSSES (JIM), author; b. Richmond, Va.; s. William Ernest and Katie Lillian (Wrenn) W.; student pub. schs. Va. Contbr. short stories and articles to Lone Scout boys mag. in early teens; head music dept. Boggs-Rice Furniture Co., Marion, Va., 1929-31; clk. Marion Post Office, 1932-34; reporter Johnson City (Tenn.) Press, 1934-36, feature writer, columnist and editorial writer, 1936-43; staff writer Roanoke (Va.) World News, 1943-47; news editor, writer radio-TV sta. WSLS, Roanoke, 1947-63; staff writer Roanoke Times, 1963-70; mag. writer, specializing in research on recorded music history for Phonograph Monthly Rev., The Gramophone, London, Eng., Music Lover's Guide, Am. Music Lover and Hobbies mag., 1929—; condr. Favorite Pioneer Recording Artists dept. Hobbies mag., 1942—; host radio program of old-time popular recordings WJHL, Johnson City, 1939-43, WDBJ and WSLS, Roanoke, 1943-60; writer on recorded music and old popular music history for Variety, 1949-79; extensive writings about Charles Dickens and Mark Twain in The Dickensian, Hobbies and other publs. Mem. Dickens Fellowship, Elbeetian Legion. Republican. Address: 225 N Maple St Box 476 Vinton VA 24179

WALSH, WILLIAM BERTALAN, physician; b. Bklyn., Apr. 26, 1920; s. Joseph W. and Irene (Viola) W.; B.S. St. John's U., 1940; M.D., Georgetown U., 1943, D.Sc. (hon.), 1962; L.H.D. (hon.), Beaver Coll. (Pa.), 1967; D.Sc., St. John's U., 1968, Howard U., 1969; LL.D., Trinity Coll., 1969; D.H.L., Clarkson Coll. Tech., 1975, Carthage Coll., 1970; m. Helen Rundvold, Dec. 19, 1943; children—William Bertalan, John Thomas, Thomas Stephen. Intern L.I. Coll. Hosp., 1943-44; resident internal medicine Georgetown U. Hosp.; 1946-48; practice medicine specializing in internal medicine, Washington, 1946-64; clin. prof. internal medicine Georgetown U. Med. Sch., 1958—; dir. Gen. Tire & Rubber Co. Pres., People-to-People Health Found., founder Project HOPE, 1958—; cons. surgeon gen. USAF, surgeon gen. USPHS; mem. Pres.'s Adv. Com. Physical Fitness Youth, 1956-59; vice chmn. Pres.'s Adv. Com. Selection Doctors and Dentists and Allied Specialists for SSS, 1959-60; vice chmn. health resources adv. com. OCDM, 1956-59, chmn., 1960; cons. diseases chest NIH, 1954-61; mem. Pres.'s Com. on Employment Handicapped; vice chmn. Fedn. People-to-People Programs. Bd. govs. John Carroll Soc.; mem., life regent emeritus Georgetown U.; trustee Landon Sch. Boys, Washington. Served to lt., M.C., USNR, 1943-46; PTO. Decorated Knight Magisterial Palms, Knight Order Daniel A. Carrion (Peru); Star of October, Al Merito (Ecuador); Order of Ruben Dario, Grand Ofcl. Grade (Nicaragua); officer Order Tunisian Republic; Gold medal (Medallo de Oro), City of Trujillo, Peru; Order San Carlos (Colombia), Order So. Cross (Brazil), comdr. Cross of Merit, So. Assn. Sovereign Mil. Order Malta, Papal Knighthood of St. Gregory, others; recipient Georgetown U. Alumni award, 1961; Health U.S.A. award, 1961; Distinguished Service award USIA, 1961; Detroit Internat. Freedom Festival award, 1961; Humanitarian of Year award Lions, 1961; Sertoma Internat. Service to Mankind award, 1962; Nat. Citizenship award Mil. Chaplains Assn., 1963; Theodore Roosevelt Distinguished Service medal, 1967; Americas award, Americas Found., 1967; Freedom Leadership medal, Freedom Founds. at Valley Forge, 1967; Lawrence C. Kline World Peace award, 1968; Stritch medal Stritch Sch. Medicine, Loyola U., 1970; Leatare medal U. Notre Dame, 1970; Simon Le Moyne award Le Moyne Coll., 1970; Distinguished Service award Am. Coll. Cardiology, 1971; Good Samaritan award St. Joseph Hosp., Albuquerque, 1972; Distinguished Service medal People-to-People Program, 1967; Alumni Achievement award Georgetown U. Alumni Club of Met. Washington, 1967; Magna Charta award Baronial Order Magna Charta, 1974; Bellarmine Coll. medal, 1974; Sovereign Mil. Order Malta, 1975; gold medal Nat. Inst. Social Scis., 1977; named to St. John's U. Alumni Hall of Fame, 1970. Fellow Internat. Coll. Dentists (hon.); mem. AMA (mem. council nat. def. 1954-56), Am. Soc. Internal Medicine (exec. com., chmn. legislative com. 1957-59), D.C. Med. Soc., Nat. Med. Vets. Soc. (pres. 1952), ADA (hon.). Clubs: University (Washington); Columbia Country (Chevy Chase, Md.); Circumnavigators (Magellan medal 1965) (N.Y.C.). Author: A Ship Called Hope, 1964; Yanqui, Come Back, 1966; Hope in the East: The Mission to Ceylon; co-author: Medicine and the Satellite. Home: 5101 Westpath Way Washington DC 20016 Office: The HOPE Center Millwood VA 22646

WALSH, WILLIAM DESMOND, printing, forest products and splty. food packaging co. exec.; b. N.Y.C., Aug. 4, 1930; s. William J. and Catherine Grace (Desmond) W.; B.A., Fordham U., 1951; LL.B., Harvard, 1955; m. Mary Jane Gordon, Apr. 5, 1951; children—Deborah, Caroline, Michael, Suzanne, Tara Jane, Peter. Admitted to N.Y. State bar, 1955; asst. U.S. atty. So. dist. N.Y., N.Y.C., 1955-58; counsel N.Y. Commn. Investigation, N.Y.C., 1958-61; mgmt. cons. McKinsey & Co., N.Y.C., 1961-67; sr. v.p. Arcata Corp., Menlo Park, Calif., 1967—; dir. DPF, Inc., Hartsdale, N.Y. Bd. dirs. Herbert Hoover Meml. Boys Club. Mem. Am., N.Y. State bar assns. Club: Sharon Heights Golf Country. Home: 279 Park Ln Atherton CA 94025 Office: 2750 Sand Hill Rd Menlo Park CA 94025

WALSH, WILLIAM RAYMOND, JR., found. exec.; b. Elizabeth, N.J., June 10, 1927; s. William Raymond and Mildred M. (Precheur) W.; B.A., Rutgers U., 1953; m. Helen Torsiello, Aug. 26, 1950; children—Karen, William Raymond III, Colleen. Bus. adminstr. Piscataway Twp. (N.J.) Sch. Dist., 1954-66; v.p. fin. and adminstrn. Middlesex County (N.J.) Coll., 1966-72; v.p., treas. Robert Wood Johnson Found., Princeton, N.J., 1972—; mem. adj. faculty Rutgers U. Grad. Sch., 1969-72; past guest lectr. Columbia U. Grad. Sch. Edn. Trustee, vice chmn. bd., chmn. fin. com. Middlesex County Coll., Edison, N.J.; trustee, chmn. bd. Middlesex Gen. Hosp., New Brunswick, N.J.; trustee Middlesex-Somerset chpt. Nat. Multiple Sclerosis Soc. Served with USAAF, 1947-49. Roman Catholic. Club: Kiwanis (past chpt. pres.). Home: 112 Wyckoff Ave Piscataway NJ 08854 Office: PO Box 2316 Princeton NJ 08540

WALSKE, M(AX) CARL, JR., physicist; b. Seattle, June 2, 1922; s. Max Carl and Margaret Ella (Fowler) W.; B.S. in Math. cum laude, U. Wash., 1944; Ph.D. in Theoretical Physics, Cornell U., 1951; m. Elsa Marjorie Nelson, Dec. 28, 1946; children—C. Susan, Steven C., Carol A. Staff mem., then asst. theoretical div. leader Los Alamos Sci. Lab., 1951-56; dep. research dir. Atomics Internat., Canoga Park, Calif., 1956-59; sci. rep. AEC in U.K., London, Eng., 1961-62; theoretical physicist RAND Corp., 1962-63; sci. attache U.S. missions to NATO and OECD, Paris, France, 1963-65; staff mem. Los Alamos Sci. Lab., 1965-66; asst. to sec. def. (atomic energy), 1966-73; pres., chief operating officer Atomic Indsl. Forum, Inc., Washington, 1973—. Chmn. Dept. Def. Mil. Liason Com. to U.S. AEC, 1966-73. Mem. U.S. delegation Conf. Suspension Nuclear Tests, Geneva, Switzerland, 1959-61. Served to lt. (j.g.) USNR, 1943-46. Recipient Distinguished Civilian Service medal Dept. Def. Fellow Explorers Club; mem. Am. Phys. Soc., Am. Nuclear Soc., Phi Beta Kappa, Sigma Xi. Clubs: Union League (N.Y.C.); University (Washington). Home: 10125 Bevern Ln Potomac MD 20854 Office: Atomic Indsl Forum 7101 Wisconsin Ave Washington DC 20014. *To seek out positions which appeared the most challenging and personally satisfying; to gain my reward through self-respect rather than public recognition; to expend extra effort as an offset to my limitations.*

WALSTER, GEORGE WILLIAM, statistician, educator; b. Palo Alto, Calif., Apr. 13, 1941; s. Don Bernard and Alda Ruth (Lehman) W.; B.A., Stanford, 1963; Ph.D., U. Minn., 1968. Asst. prof. ednl. psychology U. Wis., Madison, 1968-71, asso. prof. sociology, 1971-77, prof. sociology, 1977-78 (on leave); sr. research analyst Control Data Corp., Mpls., 1978—. Mem. Am. Statis. Assn., Inst. Math. Statistics, Am. Math. Soc., Soc. Indsl. and Applied Math., Soc. Exptl. Social Psychology. Contbr. articles to profl. jours. Home: 2207 E 34th St Minneapolis MN 55407 Office: Control Data Corp HQN060 8100 34th Ave S Box 0 Minneapolis MN 55440. *Believe in yourself, no matter what!*

WALSTON, RAY, actor; b. Laurel, Miss., Nov. 2, 1914; s. Harry Norman and Mittie (Kimball) W.; grad. high sch.; m. Ruth Calvert, Nov. 3, 1943; 1 dau., Katharine Ann. Appeared at Margo Jones Theatre, Houston, 1938-43, Cleve. Playhouse, 1943-45; Broadway appearances include GI Hamlet, 1945, Front Page, 1946, The Survivors, 1947, The Insect Comedy, 1948, Richard III, 1949, Summer and Smoke, 1949, The Rat Race, 1949, South Pacific, 1950, Me and Juliet, 1953, House of Flowers, 1954, Damn Yankees, 1955; films include The Apartment, 1959, Kiss Them for Me, 1957, South Pacific, 1957, Damn Yankees, 1958, Tall Story, 1958, Paint Your Wagon, 1968, Kiss Me Stupid, 1964, also Portrait in Black, Wives & Lovers, Who's Minding the Store, Caprice, The Sting, The Silver Streak; dir. Broadway musical Damn Yankees, 1974; TV series My Favorite Martian, 1963-66. Recipient Tony award for Damn Yankees, 1955, Clarence Derwent award for Summer and Smoke, 1949. Office: care Fred Amsel 321 S Beverly Dr Suite R Beverly Hills CA 90212. *Regarding success in any field, two of the most important words in the English language, or any language for that matter, are persistence and determination. They are all-powerful; nothing can match them.*

WALSTROM, MILTON CARL, exec. cons. co. exec.; b. Oakland, Calif., May 24, 1920; s. Carl Emmanuel and Nana Elizabeth (Blomquist) W.; student U. Uppsala (Sweden), 1937; B.A., U. Calif., 1942; postgrad. U. Hawaii, 1944, Am. U., Beirut, Lebanon, 1955; m. Elizabeth Anne Bown, Aug. 12, 1944; children—Thomas Carl, Kathryn Anne. Surveyor, Pacific Naval Air Bases, 1942; with U.S. Army Engrs., 1943-45; vice consul, Kingston, Jamaica, B.W.I., 1945-48; tng. Arabic lang., area studies Fgn. Service Inst., Dept. State, 1948; 3d sec., asst. pub. affairs officer Am. embassy, Baghdad, Iraq, 1949-51, 2d sec., pub. affairs officer, 1951-52; chief econ. sect. consulate gen., Algiers, Algeria, 1952-55; attache, consul Am. embassy, Beirut, 1955-56; chief polit. sect. Am. embassy, Amman, Jordan, 1956-58, acting dep. chief mission, 1958-59; acting officer-in-charge Central Treaty Orgn. affairs Dept. State, 1959-60, supervisory internat. relations officer Office Near Eastern Affairs, 1960-62, mem. policy planning staff Office Asst. Sec. Def. (Internat. Security Affairs), Washington, 1962-64; chief polit.-mil. affairs sect. Am. embassy, Bangkok, Thailand, 1964-66, counselor of embassy, 1966; dep. dir. Office East Asian and Pacific Regional Affairs, Dept. State 1967-68, supr. sr. officer career mgmt. and assignments, 1968; chief politico-mil. affairs Am. embassy, Saigon, Vietnam, 1969-70; dep. polit. adviser to comdr.-in-chief Pacific, Honolulu, 1970-73; dir. Dept. State Reception Center, Honolulu, 1973-78; mng. dir. internat. exec. cons. co., Kailua, Hawaii, 1978—. Recipient Honor award Dept. State. Mem. Am. Fgn. Service Assn., U. Calif. Alumni Assn., Delta Phi Epsilon. Clubs: Dacor House Washington); Rotary. Home and office: 333 Dune Circle Kailua HI 96734

WALT, ALEXANDER JEFFREY, surgeon, educator; b. Cape Town, South Africa, June 13, 1923; s. Isaac and Lea (Garb) W.; came to U.S., 1961, naturalized, 1966; M.B., Ch.B., U. Cape Town, 1948; M.S., Mayo Clinic, 1956; m. Irene Lapping, Dec. 21, 1947; children—John R., Steven D., Lindsay J. Asst. surgeon Groote Schuur Hosp., Cape Town, 1957-61; asst. chief surgery VA Hosp., Dearborn, Mich., 1961-62; chmn. dept. surgery Wayne State U., Detroit, 1966—; chief of surgery Detroit Receiving Hosp., 1965—, Harper-Grace Hosps., Detroit, 1972—. Served with South Africa Armed Forces, 1943-45. Diplomate Am. Bd. Surgery, bd. dirs., 1979—. Fellow Royal Coll. Surgeons (Can.), Royal Coll. Surgeons (Eng.), A.C.S.; mem. Am. Surg. Assn., Central Surg. Assn. (pres. 1977-78), Western Surg. Assn., Soc. Surgery of Alimentary Tract, Am. Assn. Surgery of Trauma (pres. 1976-77), A,A, Internat. Soc. Surgery, Alpha Omega Alpha. Author: (with R.F. Wilson) Management of Trauma: Pitfalls and Practice, 1975. Office: 540 E Canfield St Detroit MI 48201

WALT, DICK K., editor; b. Thayer, Kans., Nov. 28, 1935; s. Asa Bartlett and Vivian (Russell) W.; B.J., U. Kan., 1957; m. Bonnie Gregory, Sept. 15, 1967; 1 dau. by previous marriage, Sarah Margaret. With Topeka Daily Capital, 1957-58, 60-61; with Am. Med. News, publ. AMA, Chgo., 1961—, mng. editor, 1965-71, exec. editor, 1971—. Home: 551 W Deming Pl Chicago IL 60614 Office: 535 N Dearborn St Chicago IL 60610

WALT, HAROLD RICHARD, educator; b. Berkeley, Calif., Jan. 30, 1923; s. Ralph Sidney and Frances Kathryn (Leahy) W.; B.S. in Forestry, U. Calif., Berkeley, 1948, B.S. in Bus. Adminstrn., 1950, M.B.A. in Corp. Fin., 1953; m. Kathleen Dorothy O'Connell, Dec. 20, 1947; children—Michael Lowney, Timothy Gordon, Kimberly Ann, Patrick Randolph, Jennifer Joan, Carolyn Marie. Vice chancellor fin., lectr. bus. adminstrn. U. Calif., Berkeley, 1948-60; asst. budget dir. Kaiser Industries Corp., Oakland, Calif., 1961-64; dep. dir. fin. State of Calif., 1965-66; dir. civil systems Aerojet-Gen. Corp., El Monte, Calif., 1967-68; exec. v.p. SysteMed Corp., Newport Beach, Calif., 1969-71; pres. William L. Pereira Assos., Los Angeles, 1972-74; dean Coll. Bus. Adminstrn., U. San Francisco, 1974-78, prof. mgmt., 1978—; vis. prof. fin. San Francisco State U., 1978; mem. bd. Fed. Home Loan Bank, San Francisco. Mem. Calif. Gov.'s Commn. Ocean Resources, 1965-66, Gov.'s Com. Econ. Devel., 1965-66; chmn. bd. Children's Hosp., Stanford, Calif., 1974—. Served with USMCR, 1942-47. Fellow Fund Adult Edn., 1958. Mem. Fin. Execs. Inst., Bay Area Pub. Affairs Council, Beta Gamma Sigma, Pi Sigma Alpha, Alpha Zeta, Xi Sigma Pi, Theta Delta Chi, Delta Sigma Pi, Beta Alpha Psi. Republican. Roman Catholic. Club: Bohemian (San Francisco). Home: 18033 Skyline Blvd Woodside CA 94062 Office: McLaren Coll Bus Adminstrn U San Francisco San Francisco CA 94117

WALT, SHERMAN ABBOTT, musician; b. Virginia, Minn., Aug. 22, 1923; s. Ben and Pearl (Siegel) W.; student Curtis Inst. Music, 1945-46, U. Minn., 1941-43; children—Stephen, Barbara, Nancy. Bassoonist, Chgo. Symphony Orch., 1946-51; prin. bassoonist Boston Symphony Orch., 1953—; mem. Boston Symphony Chamber Players; prof. Boston U. Served with inf. AUS, 1943-45. Home: 31 Dundee Rd North Quincy MA 02171 Office: Symphony Hall Boston MA

WALTEMADE, HENRY GEORGE, banker; b. N.Y.C., Aug. 24, 1905; s. Henry and Helen (Hollander) W.; student Columbia, 1926-27; hon. letter real estate U. Mich., 1955; m. Jeannette A. Rae, June 23, 1937. Pres., Henry Waltemade, Inc., realtors, N.Y.C., 1938—65; trustee Dollar Savs. Bank, N.Y.C., 1947—, pres., 1965-74, chmn., 1973—; dir. Manhattan Life Ins. Co., N.Y.C., Instl. Securities Corp., Savings Banks Assn. N.Y. State, Savings Banks Trust Co.; chmn. Fordham Rd. Area Devel. Corp.; gov. Bronx Bd. Realtors; mem. N.Y. State Banking Bd. Bd. mgrs., past chmn. Westchester-Bronx YMCA; trustee Wartburg Orphan Farm Sch., Mt. Vernon, N.Y., 1942—; pres. Lutheran Soc. N.Y., 1939-40. Hon. bd. dirs. Bronx County Soc. Prevention Cruelty Children; bd. dirs. Econ. Devel. Council N.Y.C. Mem. Nat. (pres. 1955), N.Y. State (pres. 1944) assns. realtors, Am. Soc. Real Estate Appraisers, Am. Soc. Real Estate Counselors, Soc. Indsl. Realtors, Bronx C. of C., N.Y. C. of C. (dir.). Clubs: Union League; Wykagyl Country (pres. 1965-66) (New Rochelle, N.Y.); Winged Foot Golf (Mamaroneck, N.Y.). Home: 5 Hidden Green Ln Larchmont NY 10538 Office: 2530 Grand Concourse Bronx NY 10458

WALTEMEYER, ROBERT VICTOR, beverage co. exec.; b. Dallastown, Pa., June 8, 1934; s. Howard James and Helen Susan (Siltzer) W.; B.S. in Chem. Engring., Pa. State U., 1956; M.S. in Chem. Engring., Northwestern U., 1958; m. Gloria Hoover, Mar. 28, 1956. Various positions in plant design and ops., process devel., project mgmt. Standard Oil (N.J.), U.S., India, Malaysia, 1957-68; with Coca-Cola Co., Atlanta, 1968—, sr. v.p. tech., 1979—. Mem. adminstrv. bd. Northside Meth. Ch., 1974—; bd. trustees YWCA, Atlanta, 1978—. Mem. Am. Mgmt. Assn., Am. Inst. Chem. Engrs., Ga. Soc. Profl. Engrs., Nat. Soc. Profl. Engrs. Clubs: Capital City, Commerce.

WALTER, C. RICHARD, cons. civil engr.; b. N.Y.C., Apr. 17, 1929; s. John and Josephine Marie (Schloegel) W.; B.C.E., Manhattan Coll., 1950; M.S., Northwestern U., 1951; m. Patricia Ann McCafferty, Dec. 27, 1952; children—Mark, Gregory, Stephanie, Lisa, Valerie, Deirdre, Tara. Indsl. waste engr. Lederle Labs., Pearl River, N.Y., 1951-52; with Hazen & Sawyer, cons. environ. engrs., N.Y.C., 1952—, asso., 1958-62, partner, 1962—; cons. Manhattan Coll. Pres. Eastchester Home-Sch. Assn., 1975; chmn. parish council Immaculate Conception Roman Cath. Ch., Eastchester, 1971. Fellow Am. Acad. Environ. Engrs.; mem. ASCE, N.Y. Assn. Cons. Engrs. (pres. 1976-78), N.Y. Water Pollution Control Assn. (bd. control 1975-78; Brigham award 1975), Water Pollution Control Fedn. (dir. 1977—), Am. Water Works Assn. Republican. Clubs: Chemists (N.Y.C.); Coveleigh (Rye, N.Y.). Contbr. articles to profl. jours. Home: 53 Highland Ave Eastchester NY 10707 Office: 360 Lexington Ave New York NY 10017

WALTER, FRANK SHERMAN, hosp. adminstr.; b. Denver, June 23, 1926; s. Frank J. and Nancy (Sherman) W.; student U. Colo., 1944; B.S., U. Ore., 1950; M.B.A., U. Chgo., 1951; m. Carolyn May Cox, July 29, 1949; children—Douglas, Steven, Nancy. Adminstrv. resident Grad. Hosp. U. Pa., 1950-51, adminstrv. asst., 1951-52, asst. dir., 1952-55; adminstr. Meth. Hosp., Phila., 1955-63, St. Barnabas Hosp., Mpls., 1962-70; pres. Met. Med. Center, Mpls., 1970—; clin. preceptor U. Minn., 1965—; trustee Blue Cross/Blue Shield of Minn., 1977—. Bd. dirs. Mpls. War Meml. Blood Bank, 1964-70, Health Manpower Mgmt., 1972-77. Served with USAAF, 1944-46. Fellow Am. Coll. Hosp. Adminstrs.; mem. Twin City (dir., pres. 1970-71), Minn. (trustee 1970-78, treas. 1973-74, pres. 1975-76), Am. hosp. assns., Upper Midwest Hosp. Conf. (dir. 1977—), Downtown Council (dir. 1977—). Episcopalian (vestryman 1966-69). Kiwanian. Home: 6129 Blake Ridge Rd Edina MN 55436 Office: 900 S 8th St Minneapolis MN 55404

WALTER, FRANKLIN BURRITT, state ofcl.; b. LaGrange, Ind., Sept. 16, 1929; s. Rollo N. and Lola A. (Baker) W.; B.S., Manchester Coll., 1951; M.E., Miami U., Oxford, Ohio, 1955; Ph.D., Ohio State U., 1965; m. Jane Weber, Dec. 31, 1950; children—Ronald Lynn, Robert Lee. Tchr., Northwestern Local Schs., Springfield, Ohio, 1951-55; prin. New Lebanon (Ohio) High Sch., 1955-56; supt. New Lebanon Schs., 1956-61; research asso. Ohio State U., Columbus, 1961-63; supt. schs. Westlake (Ohio) City Sch., 1963-68; asst. supt. pub. instruction Ohio Dept. Edn., Columbus, 1968-70, dep. supt., 1970-77, supt. pub. instruction, 1977—; prof. Nat. Acad. Sch. Execs., Washington, 1970—; vis. prof. ednl. adminstrn. Bowling Green State U., 1976. Active United Appeal, Boy Scouts Am. Recipient E.E. Lewis award in Sch. Adminstrn., 1963; Centennial award Ohio State U. Coll. Edn., 1970; Distinguished Service award Miami U., 1972; named Vocat. Man of Yr., 1978. Mem. Am., Buckeye assns. sch. adminstrs., Phi Delta Kappa. Clubs: Lions, Rotary, Kiwanis. Contbr. articles to profl. jours. Home: 1357 Fishinger Rd Upper Arlington OH 43221 Office: State Supts Office 65 S Front St Columbus OH 43215

WALTER, JAMES ELIAS, educator, economist; b. Delmar, N.Y., Feb. 26, 1922; s. Floyd Jay and Iva Gertrude (Vock) W.; A.B., Duke, 1942; Indsl. Adminstr., Harvard, 1943; Ph.D., U. Calif. at Berkeley, 1953; m. Amy Buesing, Feb. 10, 1948; children—Marc Stuart, Barbara Lee, Randall James. Financial analyst War Dept., Tokyo, Japan, 1946-47; instr. econs. Duke, 1950-53; asst. prof. U. Calif. at Berkeley Sch. Bus. Adminstrn., 1953-56; vis. asst. prof. Carnegie Inst. Tech. Grad. Sch. Indsl. Adminstrn., 1956-57; asso. prof. bus. adminstrn. Harvard, 1957-62; prof. finance U. Pa., Phila., 1962—, chmn. grad. group bus. and applied econs., 1963-72, chmn. finance dept., 1975-77. Vis. prof. U. B.C., 1972. Served with AUS, 1943-46. Mem. Am. Accounting Assn., Am. Econ. Assn., Am. Finance Assn., Econometric Soc., Fin. Mgmt. Assn., Phi Beta Kappa, Pi Gamma Mu. Author: Role of Regional Securities Exchanges, 1957; The Investment Process, 1962; (with others) Case Problems in Finance, 1962; Dividend Policy and Enterprise Valuation, 1967. Contbr. to study Saving and Loan Industry, 1969. Home: 641 Sussex Rd Wynnewood PA 19096 Office: Wharton Sch Finance and Commerce U Pa Philadelphia PA 19104

WALTER, JAMES W., mfg. co. exec.; b. Lewes, Del., 1922; m. Monica Saraw, 1946; children—James W., Robert. Chmn. bd., chief exec. officer, dir. Jim Walter Corp., 1955—; dir. Walter E. Heller Internat. Corp., Gen. Telephone & Electronics Co., Biejerinvest, Sweden. Home: 2611 Bayshore Blvd Tampa FL 33609 Office: 1500 N Dale Mabry Tampa FL 33607

WALTER, JESSICA, actress; b. Bklyn., Jan. 31; student Bucks County Playhouse, Neighborhood Playhouse. Broadway debut in Advise and Consent, 1961; films include: Lilith, 1964, The Group, 1966, Grand Prix, 1966, Bye Bye, Braverman, 1968, Number One, 1969, Play Misty for Me, 1971; regular TV series Love of Life; ltd. series Amy Prentiss (Emmy award for Outstanding Lead Actress in Ltd. Series), 1974-75; other tv appearances include: The FBI, Mission: Impossible, Cannon, Medical Center, Mannix, Visions, Barnaby Jones, Hawaii Five-O, Wheels; TV movies Hurricane, 1974, Having Babies, 1976. Office: care William Morris Agy Inc 151 El Camino Beverly Hills CA 90212*

WALTER, KARL LOUIS, JR., lawyer; b. Denver, Mar. 29, 1931; s. Karl Louis and Fay (McKinster) W.; B.A., Colombia, 1953; LL.B., U. Colo., 1959; m. M. Gaile Gallwas, Sept. 17, 1966; children—Erich Russell, Mark Geoffrey, Brett Karl, Russell Dietrich. Law clk. Superior Ct., Fairbanks, Alaska, 1960; admitted to Alaska bar, 1961; practiced in Fairbanks, 1961-65, Anchorage, 1969—; atty. City of Anchorage, 1965-69; acting city mgr., 1966. Mem. Alaska Pub. Service Commn., 1960-64, chmn., 1963-64. Mem. Am., Alaska (gov. 1962-66, pres. 1965-66), Anchorage bar assns., Nat. Inst. Municipal Law Officers (Alaska chmn. 1967-69), Anchorage Civic Opera Assn. (pres. 1975). Home: 2441 Wellington Ct Anchorage AK 99503 Office: 301 W Northern Lights Blvd Anchorage AK 99501

WALTER, PAUL WILLIAM, lawyer; b. Cleve., Apr. 18, 1907; s. Carl F. and Leda (Scheidemantel) W.; A.B., Western Res. U., 1928, J.D., 1932; m. Susan Elizabeth Hamilton, Mar. 19, 1938; children—Susan E. (Mrs. Michael Cargile), Paul William. Admitted to Ohio bar, 1932, since practiced in Cleve.; partner firm Walter, Haverfield, Buescher & Chockley, 1932—; sec., dir. Sheet Metal Products Co., Euclid, Ohio. Chmn. steel inequity panel War Labor Bd., 1942-46. Chmn. Cleve. Farm Works Projects Com., 1932-33; chmn. Mayor's Work Relief Com., 1935-40. No. Ohio campaign chmn. Robert A. Taft, 1938-53; Northeastern Ohio campaign chmn. Robert Taft, Jr., 1964; del. Rep. Conv., 1952, alt. del., 1976. Pres., chmn. exec. com. Greater Cleve. YMCA; bd. dirs Cleve. Zool. Soc.; trustee Hiram House (pres.), Greater Cleve. Neighborhood Centers Assn. Mem. Am., Ohio, Cleve., Cuyahoga County bar assns., Am. Arbitration Assn., Indsl. Relations Research Assn., Am. Judicature Soc., Nat. Acad. Arbitrators (charter), Am. Acad. Polit. and Social Sci., United World Federalists (nat. pres. 1961-64, chmn. nat. adv. bd. 1964—), Western Res. Hist. Soc. (trustee). Home: 2 Bratenahl Pl Bratenahl OH 44108 Office: Terminal Tower Cleveland OH 44113

WALTER, RICHARD LAWRENCE, physicist; b. Chgo., Nov. 1, 1933; s. Lawrence Barnabas and Marie Ann (Boehmer) W.; B.S., St. Procopius Coll., 1955; Ph.D., Notre Dame U., 1960; m. Carol Elizabeth Goethals, Dec. 27, 1958; children—Timothy, Susan, Matthew. Teaching asst., research asst. Notre Dame U., 1955-59; research asso. dept. physics U. Wis., 1960-61, instr., 1961-62; asst. prof. physics Duke U., Durham, N.C., 1962-67, asso. prof., 1967-74, prof., 1974—; vis. staff mem. Los Alamos Sci. Lab., 1964, 70, 75; vis. prof. Max Planck Inst. fur Kernphysik, Heidelberg, Germany, 1970-71; staff mem. Triangle Univs. Nuclear Lab., 1970—. Fulbright scholar, 1970-71. Mem. Am. Phys. Soc., Sigma Xi, Sigma Pi Sigma (nat. council 1964-68, environ. metals group council 1973-76). Contbr. articles to profl. jours. Home: 2818 McDowell St Durham NC 27705 Office: Dept Physics Duke Univ Durham NC 27706

WALTER, ROBERT IRVING, educator, chemist; b. Johnstown, Pa., Mar. 12, 1920; s. Charles Weller and Frances (Riethmiller) W.; A.B., Swarthmore Coll., 1941; M.A., Johns Hopkins, 1942; Ph.D., U. Chgo., 1949. Instr., U. Colo., 1949-51, U. Conn., 1953-55; research asso. Rutgers U., 1951-53; asso. physicist Brookhaven Nat. Lab., 1955-56; faculty Haverford Coll., 1956-68, prof. chemistry, 1963-68; prof. U. Ill., Chgo., 1968—. Vis. lectr. Stanford, winter 1967; acad. guest U. Zurich, 1976; spl. research preparation, proof of structure, chem. and phys. properties stable aromatic free radicals. Mem. Adv. Council Coll. Chemistry, 1966-70. Served with USNR, 1944-46. Grantee U.S. Army Signal Research and Devel. Lab., NIH, NSF; NSF fellow, 1960-61. Mem. Am. Chem. Soc. (vis. scientist div. chem. edn. 1964-73), AAAS, Sigma Xi Home: 1130 S Michigan Ave Chicago IL 60605

WALTER, RONALD ALLEN, mech. engr.; b. McCook, Nebr.; s. Harold Carl Henry and Verla (Knappert) W.; B.S. with high distinction in Mech. Engring., U. Nebr., 1971; M.S. in Mech. Engring., Oreg. State U., 1976; m. Barbara Ann Gary, June 12, 1971. Mem. staff Battelle Northwest Lab., Richland, Wash., 1972—, lab. program mgr. geothermal energy research, 1976-78, mgr. waste-geoligic interactions sect., 1978—. Mem. ASME, Internat. Soc. Geothermal Engring., Geothermal Resources Council, Pi Tau Sigma. Author papers in field. Home: 1211 S Young St Kennewick WA 99336 Office: PO Box 999 Battelle Northwest Labs Richland WA 99352

WALTERS, BARBARA, newscaster; b. Sept. 25, 1931; d. Lou and Dena (Selett) W.; grad. Sarah Lawrence Coll., 1953; L.H.D. (hon.), Ohio State U., Marymount Coll., Tarrytown, N.Y., 1975; m. Lee Guber, Dec. 8, 1963 (div. 1976); 1 dau., Jacqueline Dena. Former writer-producer WNBC-TV, then with sta. WPIX and CBS-TV; joined Today Show, 1961, regular panel mem., 1963-74, co-host, 1974-76; newscaster ABC Evening News (now ABC World News Tonight), 1976—; appears on prime-time entertainment spls. and Issues and Answers; moderator syndicated TV program Not For Women Only. Hon. chmn. Nat. Assn. Help for Retarded Children, 1970. Recipient award of yr. Nat. Assn. TV Program Execs., 1975; Mass Media award Am. Jewish Com. Inst. Human Relations, 1975; Emmy award Nat. Acad. TV Arts and Scis., 1975; Hubert H. Humphrey Freedom prize Anti-Defamation League-B'nai B'rith, 1978; Matrix award N.Y. Women in Communications, 1977; Barbara Walters' Coll. Scholarship in Broadcast Journalism established in her honor Ill. Broadcasters Assn., 1975; named to 100 Women Accomplishment Harper's Bazaar, 1967, 71; Am.'s 75 Most Important Women Ladies' Home Jour., 1970, Woman of Year in Communications, 1974; Woman of Year, Theta Sigma Phi; named one of 200 Leaders of Future, Time Mag., 1974. Author: How To Talk With Practically Anybody About Practically Anything, 1970. Contbr. to Good Housekeeping, Family Weekly, Reader's Digest. Office: ABC News 1330 Ave of Americas New York NY 10019*

WALTERS, CHARLES, motion picture dir.; b. Pasadena, Calif., Nov. 17; ed. U. So. Calif. Appeared in Fanchon & Marco stage shows, 1934, in dance team Versailles Club, 1935; appeared in stage shows including Musical Parade, Jubilee, The Show Is On, Between the Devil, New Faces, I Married an Angel, Du Barry Was a Lady; choreographer stage shows Let's Face It, Banjo Eyes; dir. dance sequences in movies including Best Foot Forward, Du Barry Was a Lady, Meet Me in St. Louis, Abbott & Costello in Hollywood, Ziegfeld Follies; dir. motion pictures including Good News, Easter Parade, Lili, Dangerous When Wet, Torch Song, Easy to Love, Glass Slipper, Tender Trap, High Society, Walk Don't Run, others; dir. TV Shows Here's Lucy, Governor & J.J. Home: 23922-A DeVille Way Malibu CA 90265

WALTERS, DAVID MCLEAN, lawyer; b. Cleve., Apr. 4, 1917; s. William L. and Marguerite (McLean) W.; B.A., Baldwin-Wallace Coll., 1938; LL.B., Cleve. Sch. Law, 1943; J.D., U. Miami, 1950; M. Betty J. Latimer, Mar. 25, 1939; 1 dau., Susan Patricia (Mrs. James Edward Smith). Admitted to Fed. bar, 1950, Fla. bar, 1950; judge adminstrv. practices U.S. Dept. Justice, Washington, 1940-50; sr. law partner firm Walters & Costanzo, Miami, Fla., 1950—; personal envoy of Pres. U.S. to Vatican, 1976-77, ambassador, 1977-78. Chmn. Fla. Harbor Pilot Commn., 1952-54; chmn. City of Miami Seaport Commn., 1953-54; spl. bond counsel Dade County, 1957-58; gen. counsel Dade County Port Authority, 1975-58; vice-chmn. Nat. Democratic Finance Council, 1960—; mem. Gov.'s Adv. Bd. on Health and Rehabilitative Service, 1976-77; sec.-treas. Inter-Am. Center Authority, 1960-74; chmn. Nat. Leukemia Soc., 1965-66; chmn. Archbishops Charities Drive, 1975—; bd. dirs. Barry Coll.; chmn. bd. trustees Variety Children's Hosp. Served with CIC U.S. Army, 1943-46. Decorated Bronze Star medal. Mem. Am., Fla., Fed., Interam. bar assns. Democrat. Roman Catholic. Clubs: Jockey, Ocean Reef, Serra, Sovereign Mil. Order Malta (master knight 1975—). Home: 5273 SW 71st Pl Miami FL 33155 Office: 100 Biscayne Blvd N Suite 1001 Miami FL 33132

WALTERS, DONALD E., ednl. adminstr.; b. Feb. 22, 1934; A.B., Catholic U. Am., 1962; J.D., U. Md., 1969; m. Mary Clifford; 6 children. Asst. to pres. Mt. St. Agnes Coll., Balt., 1962-64; dir. estate planning Johns Hopkins U., Balt., 1964-65, asst. to pres., 1965-67; exec. asst. to chancellor state colls., dir. planning and devel. R.I. System Higher Edn., 1967-70; dep. provost Mass. State Coll. System, 1970-74, acting provost, dir., 1974-75; exec. dir. bd. govs. Ill. State Colls. and Univs., 1975—; chmn. Ill. Ednl. Consortium, 1978-79; cons. U. Man. (Can.), Winnipeg, 1974, Cal. State U. and Coll. System, 1974; lectr. in field. Mem. adv. com. Hubert H. Humphrey Fellowship Program, 1979—. Served with USAF, 1953-56. Mem. Acad. Acad. Personnel Adminstrn. (pres. 1974-75), Am. Acad. Polit. and Social Scis., Acad. Polit. Sci. Contbr. articles to profl. jours. Mem. editorial policy bd. Coll. Mgmt. mag., 1973-74. Home: 1122 Woodland Ave Springfield IL 62704

WALTERS, EVERETT, educator, author; b. Bethlehem, Pa., Apr. 4, 1915; s. Raymond and Elsie (Rosenberg) W.; A.B., U. Cin., 1936; M.A., Columbia, 1940, Ph.D., 1947; m. Jane C. Schrader, Apr. 23, 1938; children—Diane Colley (Mrs. Patrick B. Hearne), Everett Garrison. Instr., Finch Jr. Coll., 1940-43; rep. U.S. Civil Service Commn., 1943-44; instr. history Ohio State U., 1946-48, asst. prof., 1948-54, asso. prof., 1954-63, asst. dean Grad. Sch., 1954-55, acting dean, 1956-57, dean, 1957-63, chmn. editorial bd. Ohio State U. Press; Vis. prof. Whittier Coll., summer 1950; dir. grad. fellowship program U.S. Office Edn., 1962-63; v.p. acad. affairs Boston U., 1963-69, sr. v.p., dean faculties, 1969-71; dean faculties U. Mo.-St. Louis, 1971-75, vice chancellor community affairs, 1975-79, prof., 1979—, interim chancellor, 1972-73. Chmn., Grad. Conf. on Grad. Study and Research, 1961-62. Chmn. bd. dirs. Sta. KETC-TV, St. Louis Bach Soc., 1975—. Served as lt. USNR, 1944-46; Naval Officers Candidate Sch., Newport, R.I., 1950-52. Recipient Centennial Achievement award Ohio State U., 1970. Mem. Am. Hist. Assn., Ohio Hist. Soc., Assn. Grad. Schs. (sec.-treas. 1960-61, editor Procs. Jour. 1959-63), St. Louis Council World Affairs (chmn. bd.), Phi Delta Theta. Episcopalian. Club: Cosmos. Author: Joseph Benson Foraker; An Uncompromising Republican, 1948. Editor, contbr; Graduate Education Today, 1965. Contbr. articles to hist., ednl. jours. Home: 3 Fair Oaks Saint Louis MO 63124 Office: 8001 Natural Bridge Rd Saint Louis MO 63121

WALTERS, FREDERICK J(AMES), mgmt. cons.; b. N.Y.C., Feb. 18, 1906; s. Frederick J. and Laura Patricia (O'Connor) W.; A.B., Princeton, 1927; m. Virginia Cross, Jan. 18, 1934; children—Rosa Lee (Sister Marie Virginia O.P.), Virginia (Mrs. R. M. Stormont), Frederick James (dec.), James Anthony. With Gen. Motors Corp., 1927-45; mem. exec. staff Gen. Electric Co., 1945-46; v.p. Hotpoint, Inc., 1946-52; v.p. Packard Motor Car Co., 1952-53; pres. Fred Walters Oldsmobile, Atlanta, 1953-62; v.p. Boyden Assos., Inc., 1962-73; pres. Walters & Co., mgmt. cons., Atlanta, 1973—; dir. Flex-Comm Internat., Vital Products Co. Roman Catholic. Clubs: Capital City, Rotary (Atlanta); Princeton. Author: Handbook for District Representatives, 1939; A Summary of Veterans' Reemployment Rights, 1944. Home: 4418 Davidson Dr Atlanta GA 30319 Office: 3390 Peachtree Rd Atlanta GA 30326

WALTERS, GEOFFREY KING, physicist, educator; b. Baton Rouge, Aug. 23, 1931; s. Robert King and Harriett (Fuller) W.; B.A., Rice U., 1953; Ph.D., Duke, 1956; m. Jeanette Long, June 17, 1954; children—Terry Lynne, Jeffrey, Gina. Research asso. Duke, 1956-57; mem. tech. staff Tex. Instruments, Inc., Dallas, 1957-62, corporate research asso., 1962-63; prof. physics and space sci. Rice U., Houston, 1963—, chmn. physics dept., 1973-77, acting dean engring. and sci., 1968-69, 72-73; acting chief fire tech. div. Nat. Bur. Standards, Gaithersburg, Md., 1971-72; dir. Research Corp., 1977—. Guggenheim fellow Stanford U., 1977-78. Fellow Am. Phys. Soc. (chmn. div. electron and atomic physics 1972-73, div. councillor 1974-79); mem. Am. Geophys. Union, Am. Astronom. Soc., AAAS, Phi Beta Kappa. Contbr. articles on low temperature, solid state, atomic collision, nuclear physics, solar-terrestrial relationships radio astronomy to profl. jours. Home: 5102 Jackwood St Houston TX 77096

WALTERS, GEORGE MERLE, state ofcl.; b. Akron, Ohio, Jan. 29, 1919; s. George Dewey and Ruth (Mitchell) W.; B.B.A., Western Res. U., 1952; m. Helen J. Cerny, May 6, 1943; children—Robert E., Lucille G. Walters Hoenig, Donald M. With Ernst & Ernst, C.P.A.'s, Cleve., 1945-65, partner, 1960-65; controller Reynolds Metals Col., 1965-71, fin. v.p., dir., 1971-73, exec. v.p., 1973-75, pres., 1975-78, vice chmn., 1978-78; ret., 1978; sec. transp. State of Va., 1979—; dir. Struthers Oil and Gas Corp., N.Y. Bd. sponsors Coll. William and Mary Sch. Bus., Williamsburg, Va. Served with USAAF, 1942-45, C.P.A., Ohio, Va. Mem. Am. Inst. C.P.A.'s, Ohio, Va. socs. C.P.A.'s. Presbyterian (deacon). Clubs: Country of Virginia, Commonwealth (Richmond); Virginia Yacht, Indian Creek Yacht and Country (Kilmarnock, Va.); Burning Tree (Bethesda, Md.); University (N.Y.C.). Home: 308 Virginia Ave Richmond VA 32226 Office: Commonwealth of Va 9th St Office Bldg Richmond VA 23219

WALTERS, JESS HOYT, govt. ofcl.; b. Richmond, Va., Apr. 10, 1931; s. William Roy and Rosamond (Hill) W.; B.A., U. Richmond, 1952; M.A., Emory U., 1953; postgrad. U. Cal. at Los Angeles, 1953-56; m. Charlotte Stebbins Pole, July 26, 1958; children—Mary Evelyn, Nancy Rosamond, Amy Elizabeth, Martha Miriam, Charlotte Cary, William Lanier, Anne Christine, Catherine Joy. Research asst. U. Va., 1956-57; asst. prof., research asst. U. Hawaii, 1957-58; legis. asst. to gov. Hawaii, 1958-62; budget officer, research coordinator U. Hawaii, 1963-65; with Dole Co., Honolulu, 1965-72, v.p., sec., 1969-72; supervising legis. analyst Office Legislative Auditor, State of Hawaii, 1972—. Trustee, pres. U. Hawaii Found. Mem. Am. Soc. Pub. Adminstrn. (pres. Honolulu chpt.), Phi Beta Kappa. Mem. United Ch. of Christ. Home: 72 Dowsett Ave Honolulu HI 96817 Office: State Capitol Honolulu HI 96813

WALTERS, JOHN SHERWOOD, newspaperman; b. Junction City, Ark., May 15, 1917; s. John Thomas and Cora (McBride) W.; B.A., La. Tech. Inst., 1939; M.A., La. State U., 1941; m. Claire Dailey, June 1, 1941; children—Elizabeth Claire, Mary Dailey (dec.). Editor, Ruston (La.) Daily Leader, 1940; reporter Baton Rouge Morning Adv., 1941; rating examiner Jacksonville Naval Air Sta., 1941-42; reporter Fla. Times-Union, Jacksonville, 1943, 44-53, city editor, 1953-60, exec. editor Times-Union and Jacksonville Jour., 1960-78, asso. pub., 1978—; asst. prof. journalism La. Tech. Inst., 1943-44; mem. jud. Nominating Commn., 1st Dist. Ct. Appeals of Fla. Bd. dirs. Duval County chpt. A.R.C., chmn. 1966-67; charter trustee U. North Fla. Found., Inc., pres., 1973-75; chmn. council advisers U. North Fla., 1975—; bd. dirs. Health Planning Council, N.E. Fla. Cancer Program. Mem. Am., Fla. (pres. 1971-72) socs. newspaper editors, Alpha Lambda Tau, Sigma Delta Chi. Democrat. Methodist. Rotarian (Jacksonville, sec. 1970-71, pres. 1971-72). Clubs: University Timuquana Country, River. Home: 1750 Dogwood Pl Jacksonville FL 32210 Office: Times-Union Jour One Riverside Ave Jacksonville FL 32202

WALTERS, JOHNNIE MCKEIVER, lawyer; b. nr. Hartsville, S.C., Dec. 20, 1919; s. Tommie Ellis and Lizzie Lee (Grantham) W.; A.B., Furman U., 1942, LL.D., 1973; LL.B., U. Mich., 1948; m. Donna Lucile Hall, Sept. 1, 1947; children—Donna Dianne Walters Nelson, Lizbeth Kathern Walters Kukorowski, Hilton Horace, John Roy. Admitted to Mich. bar, 1948, N.Y. bar, 1955, S.C. bar, 1961, D.C. bar, 1973; atty. office chief counsel IRS, Washington, 1949-53; atty., asst. mgr. tax div. of law dept. Texaco, Inc., N.Y.C., 1953-61; partner firm Geer, Walters, & Demo, Greenville, S.C., 1961-69; asst. atty. gen. tax div. Dept. Justice, Washington, 1969-71; commr. IRS, 1971-73; partner firm Hunton and Williams, Washington, 1973-79, firm Leatherwood, Walker, Todd & Mann, Greenville, 1979—. Active Boy Scouts Am., PTA; bd. dirs. Greenville Art Assn., Greenville United Fund, Greenville Little Theater, Greenville Symphony Assn. Served with USAAF, 1942-45. Mem. Am. (taxation sect.), D.C., S.C. bar assns. Club: Rotary (pres. 1968-69). Home: 1804 N Main St Greenville SC 29609 Office: 217 E Coffee St Greenville SC 29602

WALTERS, LEE JOSEPH, advt. agy. exec.; b. Chgo., Sept. 19, 1930; s. Leo and Agnes Theresa W.; grad. Ray-Vogue Sch. Advt., 1951; Degree in Advt., Northwestern U., 1954-56; m. Carol Ann Brakesman, Mar. 26, 1977; children—Michael L., David J. Co-founder, exec. v.p. Stern, Walters & Simmons, Chgo. and Los Angeles, 1954-77; vice chmn. Stern Walters/Earl Ludgin Inc. (Stern, Walters & Simmons acquired Earle Ludgin & Co.), 1977-79; vice chmn. Stern Walters/Earle Ludgin Inc., Chgo. and Los Angeles, (acquired by Ted Bates & Co.), 1979—. Chmn., Com. Against Communist Activities in U.S., 1958-60. Served with CIC, U.S. Army, 1952-54; Korea. Mem. Am. Assn. Advt. Agys. (gov.). Democrat. Roman Catholic. Club: Chgo. Advt. (exec. v.p. 1969-71). Office: 9911 W Pico Blvd Los Angeles CA 90035. *Success is akin to a boxing match. You generally can win if you can get up one more time than you've been knocked down.*

WALTERS, MARY DAWSON, librarian; b. Mitchell County, Ga., Oct. 6, 1923; d. William Henry and Carrie Lou (Richardson) Dawson; B.S.H.E., Savannah (Ga.) State Coll., 1949; M.S. in L.S., Atlanta U., 1957; postgrad. in Russian Ohio State U., Columbus, 1963; m. William Gantt, 1977; children by previous marriage—Marjorie (Mrs. Quentin Ted Smith), Robert H. McCoy. Librarian Carver Jr. High Sch., Albany, Ga., 1956-57; dir. Albany State Coll. Library, 1957-61; vis. prof. Sch. Library Services Atlanta U., 1964; asst. prof. library adminstrn., head div. processing Ohio State U. Library, 1961-71, asso. prof., head dept. acquisitions, 1971-74; asso. librarian, chief acquisitions librarian Calif. State U. at Los Angeles, 1974-77, librarian, collection devel. officer, 1977—. Recipient Dir's. Citation of Merit award Ohio State U. Libraries, 1963. Mem. Am., Calif. library assns., So. Calif. Tech. Processing Group. Democrat. Published A Catalog of the Exhibition of Selected Private Presses in the U.S., 1965; Black History Holdings of the Ohio State University Libraries; Afro-Americana, 1969. Participant in collection of data Seventeen University Libraries classification Titles Classified by the Library of Congress, 1973. Home: 1659 W 81st St Los Angeles CA 90047

WALTERS, MORGAN LEIGH, ret. publisher; b. Wellsville, Utah, Aug. 19, 1912; s. Thomas Poppleton and Jennie Baxter (Maughan) W.; A.B., Stanford, 1933; M.A., U. Buffalo, 1940; Ph.D. in English Philology, Harvard, 1943; m. Marguerite F. McFarland, Oct. 22, 1948 (dec. May 1971); children—Barbara (Mrs. George Felton), Priscilla Anne (Mrs. Leroy Clark Jr.). Dir. parts catalog Sikorsky Aircraft Co., 1943-46; geography editor, then exec. editor Macmillan Co., N.Y.C., 1946-57; editorial dir. Ency. Internat., Grolier, Inc., N.Y.C., 1957-60; free-lance editor, 1960; cons. editor, editor-in-chief dictionary Holt, Rinehart & Winston, 1960-62; mgr. spl. projects div. T.Y. Crowell Co., N.Y.C., 1963; dir. U. Ala. Press, 1967-77; ret., 1977. Mem. Nat. Hist. Records Adv. Bd. Ala., 1977-78. Am. Chem. Soc. scholar 1929-33. Mem. Assn. Am. U. Presses (dir. 1975-76), Phi Beta Kappa. Editor: Holt's Intermediate Dictionary of American English, 1963-66. Home: 6 Chestnut Hills Estate Route 4 Box 84 Northport AL 35476

WALTERS, RAYMOND, JR., editor, author; b. Bethlehem, Pa., Aug. 23, 1912; s. Raymond and Elsie (Rosenberg) W.; A.B., Swarthmore Coll., 1933; postgrad. Princeton, 1933-35; M.A., Columbia, 1937, Ph.D., 1942. Editorial staff Current History mag., 1937-39; editorial staff Saturday Rev., 1946-58, book rev. editor, 1948-58; editor Encore mag., 1946-48; asso. editor N.Y. Times Book Rev., 1958—. Mem. fiction jury Pulitzer Prize adv. bd., 1968. Served with USAAF, 1942-46; hist. office hdqrs. USAAF, 1943-46. Mem. Am. Hist. Assn., Soc. Am. Historians (v.p.), P.E.N. Episcopalian. Author: Alexander James Dallas: Lawyer, Politician, Financier, 1943; Albert Gallatin: Jeffersonian Financier and Diplomat, 1957 (named One of Notable Books of Year, ALA); The Virginia Dynasty, 1965. Contbr. articles to profl. jours. Home: 315 E 68th St New York NY 10021 Office: 229 W 43d St New York NY 10036

WALTERS, ROBERT EUGENE, savs. and loan assn. exec.; b. Paola, Kans., Nov. 7, 1937; s. James Burton and Helen Lucile (Wiseman) W.; B.S. in Econs., Central Mo. U., Warrensburg, 1963; m. Jacqueline June Rowland, June 2, 1958; children—Machelle Rene, Casey Shawn, Alecia Nicole. Asst. v.p. Central Mortgage Co., Inc., Springfield, Mo., 1966-68, Amortibanc Investment Co., Inc., Wichita, Kans., 1968-70; v.p. Farm and Home Savs. Co., Nevada, Mo., 1970-75, sr. v.p., 1978—; pres. Home Fed. Savs. & Loan Assn., Greensboro, N.C., 1976-77. Served with USCGR, 1956-60. Mem. U.S. League Savs. Assn., Am. Inst. Real Estate Appraisers (asso.). Home: Route 1 Nevada MO 64772

WALTERS, ROBERT LEO, pub. co. exec.; b. Franklin, N.J., Sept. 18, 1924; s. Vivian Owen and Anna T. (Osborne) W.; student Rutgers U., 1948-50; m. Phyllis Georgia Kassack, Oct. 22, 1966; 1 son, Daniel Owen. Report and survey officer VA, Newark, 1945-50; chief statis. service br. USAF, N.Y.C., 1951-53; chief adminstrn. div. IRS, N.Y.C., 1954-56; gen. mgr. real estate and gen. services div., N.Y.C., 1957-63, asst. v.p., 1964, v.p., 1965-69, exec. v.p., 1969, pres., 1970—; v.p., dir. Rock-McGraw, Inc. Mem. Real Estate Bd. N.Y. Mem. Regional Plan Assn., N.Y.C., 1969-70. Served with USMCR, 1943-45. Mem. Bldg. Owners and Mgrs. Assn., Office Execs. Assn. Club: Glen Ridge (N.J.) Country. Home: 17 Vera Pl Montclair NJ 07042 Office: 1221 Ave of the Americas New York NY 10020

WALTERS, ROBERT LEVI, naval officer; b. Oblong, Ill., June 25, 1926; s. Otto and Helen Mae W.; B.S., U.S. Naval Acad., 1949; B.S.E.E., U.S. Naval Postgrad. Sch., 1956; student Armed Forces Staff Coll., 1964; M.B.A., Air War Coll./Auburn U., 1972; m. Diana Frances Moomau, Nov. 12, 1949; children—Andrew Robert, John Philip. Commd. ensign U.S. Navy, 1949, advanced through grades to rear adm., 1975; div. officer U.S.S. Missouri, 1949-51; gunnery officer U.S.S. Keppler, 1952-54; gunnery/readiness officer BATDIVTWO Staff, Norfolk, Va., 1956-57; asst. missile officer Cruiser Force, U.S. Atlantic Fleet Staff, 1957-59; weapons officer U.S.S. Norfolk, 1958-60; asst. for surface missile systems readiness Office Chief of Naval Ops., Washington, 1960-62; exec. officer U.S.S. Berkeley, 1962-64; prospective comdg. officer/comdg. officer U.S.S. Brooke, 1964-67; exec. officer U.S.S. Providence, 1967-69; program mgr. anti-ship missile def. Naval Ordnance Systems Command, Washington, 1969-71; comdg. officer U.S.S. Belknap, 1972-74, Naval Ship Weapon Systems Engring. Sta., Port Hueneme, Calif., 1974-75; project mgr. surface ship constn. project Naval Material Command, Washington, 1975-76; dep. comdr. surface combatants Naval Sea Systems Command, Washington, 1975-77; comdr. Cruiser-Destroyer Group Eight, Norfolk, Va., 1977—. Decorated Legion of Merit with gold star, Bronze Star, Navy Commendation medal with bronze V, Joint Service Commendation medal. Mem. U.S. Naval Inst. Club: Army-Navy Country. Home: Maryland House W 453 Dillingham Blvd Norfolk VA 23511 Office: Comdr Cruiser-Destroyer Group Eight FPO NY 09501

WALTERS, WALTER HENRY, univ. dean; b. Troy, Ala., Dec. 19, 1917; s. Walter Henry and Julia (Coleman) W.; B.S., Troy State Coll., 1939; Ph.M., U. Wis., 1947; M.F.A., Western Res. U., 1949, Ph.D., 1950; m. Geraldine Ross, Sept. 18, 1947; children—Ross Atwell, Ann Coleman, Kirk Madison. Tchr. pub. schs., Ala., 1939-42; faculty U. Wis., 1946-48; faculty Pa. State U., 1950—, chmn. dept. theatre arts, 1954-66, producer Mateer Playhouse, 1958-62, Pa. State Festival Theatre, 1963-66, dean Coll. Arts and Architecture, 1968—, dir. univ. arts services, 1973—. Cons. in field, 1955—; mem. adv. council Am. Acad., Rome, 1968—. Mem. Commonwealth Pa. Council on Arts, 1969-71; chmn. Theatre Adv. Panel Pa. Council Arts, 1972; chmn. fine arts commn. Nat. Assn. State Univs. and Land-Grant Colls., 1975—, mem. internat. affairs com., 1979—; bd. dirs., sec.-treas. Am. Research Inst. for Arts, 1975—. Served with USNR, World War II. Fellow Am. Theatre Assn. (pres. Univ. and Coll. Theatre Assn. 1970-71, chmn. chief adminstrs. program 1978—), U.S. Inst. Theatre Tech. (bd. dirs. 1976-80, editor newsletter 1966-68, 1st v.p. 1970-71, pres. 1971-72); mem. Internat. Council Fine Arts Deans (chmn. 1974). Home: 1358 Greenwood Circle State College PA 16801 Office: Arts Bldg Pa State Univ University Park PA 16802

WALTERS, WALTMAN, surgeon; b. Cedar Rapids, Ia., July 29, 1895; s. Frank and Mellie (Phipps) W.; B.S., Dartmouth, 1917; M.D., Rush Med. Coll., 1920; M.Sc. in Surgery, U. Minn., 1923; D.Sc. (h.c.), Dartmouth, 1937; LL.D., Hahnemann Med. Coll., Phila., 1942; m. Phoebe, d. Dr. Willian James Mayo, Feb. 5, 1921; children—Phoebe Mayo, Joan (dec.), Waltman Mayo, James Mayo, Carolyn Damon. Asst. surgeon Mayo Clinic, 1922-24; surgeon, head of a div. surgery, 1924-60, ret.; asso. prof. surgery Mayo Found., U. Minn., 1930-36, prof. surgery, 1936-60, prof. surgery emeritus, 1960—. Rear adm. Med. Corps, USNR, 1955-57, ret., chief surg. and exec. officer USN Hosp., Corona, Cal., 1942-44; chief surgery USN Hosp., Phila., 1945; inactive duty, 1945; mem. adv. panel med. scis. research and Engring. Office Asst. Sec. Def., 1954-60, cons. D.C. Balfour lecture, Toronto, 1949, Lord Moynihan lecture, Leeds, Eng., 1951; Bevan lectr., Chgo., 1953; John Stewart lectr. Dalhousie U., 1954; Walter Estelle Lee lectr. U. Pa., 1955; Phi Beta Pi lectr. U. Miami, 1956, W.J. Mayo lectr. U. Mich., C.H. Mayo lectr. Northwestern, 1960; Frank H. Lahey lectr., 1959; Roy McClure lectr., 1963. Recipient commendations (Navy); Gold Medal award AMA, 1941, Miss. Valley Med. Soc., 1954; certificate of Merit, AMA, 1955; A.C.S. award for films, 1958; Commendation award U. Chiba, Japan, 1959; Distinguished Surgeons award Am. Soc. Abdominal Surgeons, 1969; Distinguished Alumnus award Dartmouth, 1950, Rush Med. Coll., 1970. Diplomate Am. Bd. Surgery, Am. Bd. Urology. Fellow A.C.S., Am., So., Central, Western surg. assns., Internat. Soc. Surgery, Soc. Clin. Surgery, AMA (chmn. sect. surgery, gen. and abdominal, 1956, chmn. exec. com. surg. sect. 1958), German Surg. Soc., German Acad. Natural Scis., Czechoslovak Med. Soc. (hon.); mem. or hon. mem. numerous profl., med., surg., sci. socs. and assns. Congregationalist. Clubs: University (Chgo. and Rochester); Tucson Country; Rochester Country, U.S. Senior Golf Assn. Author several books; spl. chpts. in books on surgery, articles in profl. jours. Chief editor A.M.A. Archives of Surgery, 1938-62; editor-in-chief Lewis-Walters' Practice of Surgery, 1936—. Home: 304 8th Ave SW Rochester MN 55901 Office: Mayo Clinic Rochester MN 55901

WALTERS, WILLIAM LEROY, univ. adminstr.; b. Racine, Wis., Mar. 30, 1932; s. Robert N. and Elsie (Ahrens) W.; B.S., U. Wis., 1954, M.S., 1958, Ph.D., 1961; m. Darlene A. Kessenich, Feb. 5, 1955; children—Judy, Sandra, Robert, James. Asso. dean scis. Coll. Letters and Sci., U. Wis., Milw., 1965-67, spl. asst. to chancellor, 1967-68, exec. asst. chancellor, 1968-69, asst. chancellor, acting dean Coll. Applied Sci. and Engring., 1969-70, vice chancellor univ., 1971—. Served with U.S. Army, 1954-56. Mem. AAAS, Am. Assn. Physics Tchrs., Am. Phys. Soc., Am. Vacuum Soc., Nat. Assn. of State Univs. and Land Grant Colls (mem., chmn. exec. com. council academic affairs 1978), Physics Club Milw. (dir. 1964-67). Contbr. articles to physics jours. Home: 4301 N Morris Blvd Milwaukee WI 53211

WALTHALL, WILSON JONES, JR., educator, psychologist; b. San Antonio, July 7, 1918; s. Wilson Jones and Nina (Trimble) W.; B.A., U. Tex., 1944, M.A., 1944, Ph.D., 1948; m. Annie Marie Joekel, Sept. 2, 1944; children—Anne, Wilson Jones III. Faculty, U. Wyo., Laramie, 1947—, prof., 1957—, head dept. psychology, 1965—, acting dean Coll. Arts and Sci., 1973, 77—. Fulbright lectr. U. Coll., Mandalay, Burma, 1954-55. Mem. Am., Rocky Mountain (pres. 1959-60), Wyo. (pres. 1961) psychol. assns., NEA, Wyo. Edn. Assn., AAUP, Phi Beta Kappa, Sigma Xi, Psi Chi. Contbr. articles to profl. jours. Home: 1314 Steele St Laramie WY 82070

WALTHER, JOHN HENRY, banker; b. Hartford, Conn., June 13, 1935; s. George N. and Etta (Aschenbach) W.; B.A., Wesleyan U., Middletown, Conn., 1957; m. Jo Ann Hearne, June 6, 1959; children—John Henry, Jerome Hearne, Joshua Kirk. Asst. sec. Mfrs. Hanover Trust Co., N.Y.C., 1957-63; with N.J. Nat. Bank, Trenton, 1963—, exec. v.p., 1969-72, pres., 1972-76, chmn. bd., 1976—; chmn. N.J. Nat. Corp.; dir. Yates Industries, Inc. Home: 3 Aqua Terr Pennington NJ 08534 Office: 1 W State St Trenton NJ 08603

WALTON, ALAN GEORGE, educator; b. Birmingham, Eng., Apr. 3, 1936; s. Thomas George and Hilda (Glover) W.; Ph.D., U. Nottingham (Eng.), 1960, D.Sc., 1973; m. Jasmin Yvonne Christensen, Sept. 1, 1958 (dec. Nov. 1970); children—Kimm A., Keir D.A.; m. 2d, Elenor Jean McElliott, Aug. 6, 1977; children—Kristin M., Sherri L. Research asso. Ind. U., Bloomington, 1960-62; asst. prof. chemistry Case Inst., Cleve., 1962-66, asso. prof. chem. Case Western Res. U., Cleve., 1966-69, asso. prof. macromolecular sci., 1969-71, prof. macromolecular sci., 1971—; vis. lectr. biol. chemistry Harvard Med. Sch., 1971. Mem. Pres. Carter's Task Force Sci. and Tech., U.S. project officer Rudjer Boskovic Inst., Zagreb, Yugoslavia, 1967-75. Asso. Royal Inst. Chem. (London); mem. Biophys. Soc., Am. Chem. Soc., N.Y. Acad. Scis., Sigma Xi (Research award 1973). Pi Kappa Alpha. Author: Formation and Properties of Precipitates, 1967; Biopolymers, 1973. Home: 4114 Giles Rd Moreland Hills OH 44022 Office: Macromolecular Sci Dept Case Western Res U Cleveland OH 44106

WALTON, CHARLES MILTON, banker; b. Lumpkin, Ga., Dec. 21, 1935; s. Henry Taylor and Mary Allie (Geeslin) W.; student Ga. Southwestern Coll., Americus, 1953-55, Ga. State Coll., Atlanta, 1955-57; grad. U. Wis., 1964; m. Velma Louise Davis, Feb. 21, 1959; 1 son, Charles Milton. Account clk. Fulton Nat. Bank, Atlanta, 1955-56, audit clk., 1957-64, asst. auditor, 1964-70, auditor, 1970—, gen. auditor Fulton Nat. Corp., 1979—. Vice pres. J.H. House P.T.A., 1970—. Served with AUS, 1960. Chartered bank auditor; certified internal auditor. Mem. Am. Inst. Banking, Bank Adminstrn. Inst. Home: 2761 Valleydale Dr Conyers GA 30207 Office: 55 Marietta St Atlanta GA 30302

WALTON, CHARLES WHITNEY, III, machinery co. exec.; b. Hackensack, N.J., Jan. 12, 1927; s. Charles Whitney and Delfreda (Filandino) W.; B.S. in Engring., U. Mich., 1946; J.D., Columbia, 1948; M.B.A., Western Mich. U., 1963; m. Patricia Jane Coryell, May 29, 1948; children—Ann Whitney, Charles Coryell, David Sherman, Sarah Brinsmaid. Time study engr. Am. Seating Co., Grand Rapids, Mich., 1948-50; admitted to Mich. bar, 1949; pvt. practice law, Grand Rapids, 1950-52; mgr. patent dept. Gardner-Denver Co., Grand Haven, Mich. and Denver, 1952-57; asst. v.p., gen. solicitor KVP Sutherland Paper Co., Kalamazoo, 1957-64; sec., treas. McCord Corp., Detroit, 1964-65, sec., gen. counsel, 1965-69; sec., gen. counsel Koehring Co., Milw., 1969—, v.p., 1972—; instr., Western Mich. U. Sch. Bus., 1963-64. Mem. Am., Wis., Milw. bar assns., Am. Patent Law Assn. Mason, Rotarian. Club: Milw. Athletic. Home: 1835 Steeple Chase Brookfield WI 53005 Office: 200 Executive Dr Brookfield WI 53005

WALTON, CLARENCE, educator; b. Scranton, Pa., June 22, 1915; s. Leo and Mary (Southard) W.; B.A., U. Scranton, 1937; M.A., Syracuse U., 1938; Ph.D., Cath. U., 1951; m. Elizabeth Kennedy, June 1, 1946; children—Thomas Michael, Mary Elizabeth. Social sci. instr. Duquesne U., 1940, dean Sch. Bus. Adminstrn., 1954-58; asso. dean, prof. Columbia Grad. Sch. Bus., 1958-64, dean Sch. Gen. Studies, 1964-68, prof. Grad. Sch. Bus., 1978—; pres. Cath. U. Am., 1968-78; prof., chmn. dept. history and polit. sci. U. Scranton, 1946-53; Penfield fellow Inst. Advanced Internat. Studies, Geneva, Switzerland, 1951-52; vis. prof. U. Helsinki, Finland, summer 1959, U. Buenos Aires, summer 1961, U. Calif., Berkeley, 1963-64, Oreg. State U., 1969. Dir. GEICO, Peavey Co. Mem. Scranton Sch. Bd., 1948-52; bd. dirs. Am. Assembly. Served as lt. USNR, 1940-46, with Naval Intelligence, communications officer U.S.S. Wis. Mem. Acad. Polit. Sci. (bd. dirs.). Author: Corporate Social Responsibilities, Big Government and Big Business, 1968; Ethos and The Executive, 1969. Editor: Ethics of Corporate Conduct, 1977; Inflation and National Survival, 1979; co-editor: Disorder in Higher Education, 1979; contbr. articles to profl. jours. Home: The Radwyn Fll 245 Bryn Mawr Ave Bryn Mawr PA 19010

WALTON, CLYDE CAMERON, librarian, historian; b. Chgo., Mar 8, 1925; s. Clyde Cameron and Helen L. (Williams) W.; A.B., Cornell Coll., Iowa, 1948; A.M., U. Chgo., 1950; Litt.D., Lincoln Coll., 1956; m. Anne Hoover, 1946 (div. 1979); children—James R., Jean A., Julia L.; m. 2d, Patricia Senn Breivik, July 7, 1979. Asst. in charge Serials-Res. Library, State U. Iowa, 1950-51, curator rare books, univ. archivist, instr. bibliography, 1951-55, head reference dept., asst. prof., 1955-56; state historian Ill. Hist. Library, 1956-67; exec. dir. Ill. Hist. Soc., 1956-67; asso. prof., dir. libraries No. Ill. U., 1967-77, chmn. athletic bd., 1969-74; dir. libraries, prof. U. Colo., Boulder, 1977—; sec. Civil War Centennial Commn. Ill., 1959-65; chmn. Springfield Hist. Sites Commn., 1961-67; mem. Capitol City Plan Commn., 1965-67; mem. Ill. Historic Sites Adv. Council, 1971-77, chmn., 1975-77; chmn. Ill. State Archives Adv. Bd., 1973-77. Trustee Ill. State Hist. Library, 1975-77; bd. dirs. Springfield Central Area Devel. Assn., 1966-67, pres., 1963-64; sec., dir. U.S. Grant Assn., 1959—. Served with inf. AUS, World War II. Decorated Bronze Star, Purple Heart, Combat Inf. badge. Mem. Assn. Coll. and Research Libraries (exec. com. rare books and manuscripts sect. 1973-76; mem. manuscripts com. 1971-76, chmn. 1973-76), Am., Ill. (exec. bd. 1974-75, 76-77) library assns., Ill. Assn. Coll. and Research Libraries (chmn. 1974-75), Ill. Hist. Soc., Chgo. Civil War Round Table (pres. 1969-70), Abraham Lincoln Assn. Methodist. Clubs: Rotary; Caxton (Chgo.). Founder, past editor Civil War History; editor Jour. Ill. State Hist. Soc., 1956-67; Indian War of 1864, 1960; An Illinois Gold Hunter in the Black Hills, 1960; John Francis Snyder: Selected Writings, 1962; Behind the Guns: The History of Battery I, 1965; Mr. Lincoln Opens His Mail, 1967; Illinois Reader, 1970. Home: 4320 Butler Circle Boulder CO 80303

WALTON, EDWARD HAVILAND, mech. engr.; b. New Rochelle, N.Y., Jan. 3, 1913; s. Joseph Barnard and Louise (Haviland) W.; B.S. with high honors, Swarthmore Coll., 1933; m. Anne Gray Mode, June 22, 1935 (dec. June 1976); children—Linda Walton Doede, Edward Mode, Chandler Mode; m. 2d, Ruth Holl Reichelt, Mar. 19, 1977. Engr., Am. Radiator Co., N.Y.C., 1935-39; tech. analyst Babcock & Wilcox Co., N.Y.C., 1939-42; with United Illuminating Co., New Haven, 1942-69, engring. mgr., 1953-59, v.p., 1959-69; dep. exec. dir. ASME, N.Y.C., 1969-78, ret., 1978. Chmn., Hamden (Conn.) Town Plan and Zoning Commn., 1950-55; treas. Quinnipiac council Boy Scouts Am., 1956-64, v.p., 1964-70; pres. United Fund of Greater New Haven, 1968-70. Registered profl. engr., N.Y. State, Conn. Fellow ASME (v.p. 1962-66); mem. IEEE, Nat. Soc. Profl. Engrs. Quaker. Club: New Haven Country. Home: 144 Knoll Dr Hamden CT 06518

WALTON, FRANCIS RAY, architect; b. New Smyrna Beach, Fla., July 26, 1910; s. George and Mercy (Negus) W.; B.S., U. Fla., 1934; m. Elsie Eleanora Koglin, Sept. 1940; children—Patricia (Mrs. Duane Williamson), Suzanne (Mrs. Russell S. Hoadley). Pvt. practice architecture, Daytona Beach, Fla., 1940—. Mem. Halifax Area Study Commn., 1970—; chmn. Daytona Beach Downtown Devel. Authority, 1972—. Fellow A.I.A. (Pulara award Fla. assn. 1965, gold medal Fla. assn. 1970). Home and studio: 2740 S Atlantic Ave Daytona Beach FL 32018

WALTON, HAROLD FREDERIC, educator, chemist; b. Aug. 25, 1912, Tregony, Eng.; s. James and Martha Florinda Jane (Harris) W.; B.A., Exeter Coll., Oxford U., 1934, D.Phil., 1937; postgrad. Princeton, 1937-38; m. Sadie Goodman, June 17, 1938; children—James, Elizabeth Louise, Daniel Goodman. Came to U.S., 1937, naturalized, 1948. Research chemist Permutit Co., 1938-40; instr., asst. prof. Northwestern U., 1940-46; vol. Brit. Red Cross, 1946-47; faculty U. Colo., Boulder, 1947—, prof. chemistry, 1956—, chmn. dept., 1962-66. Vis. prof. (Fulbright lectr.) U. Trujillo, Peru, 1966-67, 70; hon. prof. U. Trujillo. Mem. regional com. Woodrow Wilson Fellowships, 1957-69. Mem. Am. Chem. Soc. (chmn. Colo. sect. 1957, Colo. sect. award 1976), AAAS, Chem. Soc. (London), Colo.-Wyo. Acad. Scis., Chem. Soc. Peru (corr.). Clubs: American Alpine (chmn. Rocky Mountain sect. 1958-61, central v.p. 1965-68), Colorado Mountain; Explorers (N.Y.C.). Author: Inorganic Preparations, 1948; Principles and Methods of Chemical Analysis, 2d edit., 1964; Elementary Quantitative Analysis, 1958; (with W. Rieman) Ion Exchange in Analytical Chemistry, 1970; (with J. Reyes) Modern Chemical Analysis and Instrumentation, 1973; Benchmark Papers in Ion-Exchange Chromotography, 1976. Home: 750 6th St Boulder CO 80302

WALTON, JAMES M., instl. exec.; b. Pitts., Dec. 18, 1930; grad. Yale; postgrad. Harvard Sch. Bus. Adminstrn.; m. Ellen Carroll; 4 children. With Gulf Oil Corp., Pitts., Houston, Tokyo, Japan, Rome, Italy, other locations, from 1956-67; pres. Carnegie Inst., Carnegie Library (both Pitts.), 1968—. Dir. Gulf Oil Corp. Mem. exec. com. Three Rivers Arts Festival, One Hundred Friends of Pitts. Art. Corporator Western Pa. Sch. Blind Children; bd. dirs. Pitts. Chamber Music Soc., Pitts. Regional Planning Assn., Carnegie Hero Fund Commn.; trustee Yale U. Art Gallery, Carnegie-Mellon U., Am. Acad. in Rome, Allegheny Found.; mem. Pa. Council on Arts, also chmn. visual arts adv. panel; exec. com. Allegheny Conf. on Community Devel.; adv. com. Pitts. Plan for Art, Jr. League Pitts.; mem. fine arts com. Dept. State. Served as 1st lt. AUS, 1954-56. Address: Carnegie Inst 4400 Forbes Ave Pittsburgh PA 15213

WALTON, JEAN B., coll. adminstr.; b. George School, Pa.; d. George A. and Emily W. (Ingram) Walton; A.B., Swarthmore Coll., 1935; A.M., Brown U., 1940; Ph.D., U. Pa., 1948. Tchr. math. Moorestown Friend's Sch., 1935-38; head dormitory Pembroke Coll., 1938-40; part-time instr. math., part-time asst. to deans Swarthmore Coll., 1940-42, asst. to deans, 1942-43, instr., 1943-45, acting dean women, summer 1945; instr. U. Pa., 1947-49; dean women Pomona Coll., Claremont, Calif., 1949-69, dean students, 1969-76, v.p. student affairs, 1976-79, emerita, 1979—; women's studies coordinator Claremont Colls., 1979—; adj. prof. dept. edn. Claremont Grad. Sch., 1979—; lectr. Japan Women's U., Tokyo, 1955-56; cons. Danforth Found., 1962-63. Mem. Nat. Assn. Women Deans, Adminstrs. and Counselors (chmn. coll. sect. 1963-65, treas. 1967-69), Nat. Assn. Student Personnel Adminstrs. (Scott-Goodnight award 1974), Calif. Assn. Women Adminstrs. and Counselors (pres. 1957-59), Mortar Bd., Phi Beta Kappa. Mem. Soc. of Friends. Home: 562 Baughman Ave Claremont CA 91711

WALTON, JOHN, educator; b. Fleming County, Ky., Nov. 17, 1910; s. Thomas and Ida (Bristow) W.; A.B., Transylvania Coll., Ky., 1932; M.A., U. Ky., 1936; Ph.D., Johns Hopkins, 1950; postgrad. summers Cornell U., U. So. Calif., Colo. U.; m. Elizabeth Keene, June 3, 1946. Instr. Latin, Manchester (Ohio) High Sch., 1934-35, prin., 1935-36; supt. schs., Manchester, 1936-42, 46-47; chmn. div. profl. subjects, dir. adult edn., dir. summer sch. Queen's Coll., Charlotte, N.C., 1950-51; prof. edn., head dept. Wesleyan Coll., 1951-53; asst. prof. edn. Johns Hopkins, Balt., 1953-56, asso. prof., 1956-60, chmn. dept. edn., 1956-68, prof. edn., 1960-76, prof. emeritus, 1976—. Past pres. Balt. Bd. Sch. Commrs. Trustee Va. Theol. Sem., St. Pauls Schs., Md.; chmn. bd. Ecumenical Inst., St. Mary's Sem., Balt.; mem. com. on edn. Nat. Council Chs. Served as spl. agt. CIC, AUS, 1942-46. Mem. Am. Assn. U. Profs., Md. Assn. Higher Edn. (pres.) Phi Beta Kappa. Democrat. Episcopalian. Clubs: Tudor and Stuart, Johns Hopkins. Author: John Filson of Kentucky, 1955; Adminstration and Policy-Making in Education, 1960; Toward Better Teaching in the Secondary Schools, 1966. Editor, contbr. The Discipline of Education, 1963, Introduction to Education, 1971. Contbr. articles to profl. jours. Home: 3435 Guilford Terr Baltimore MD 21218. *I have attempted to combine a genuine interest in people with a frank and* *straightforward manner. It has been my ambition to be able to cultivate the social graces and good manners and, at the same time, to be honest and forthright in the expression of my opinions.*

WALTON, LLOYD BARKER, writer, photographer; b. Indpls., July 30, 1919; s. Frank and Ruby Elizabeth (Barker) W.; student Ind. U., 1944; m. Barbara Jean Fagan, July 31, 1953; children—Bruce Lee, Vicki Sue, Ginger Ann. Photographer Indpls. Times, 1943; chief color photographer, 1945-46, roving reporter-photgrapher, 1947-50, real estate editor, 1951-53, reporter-photographer, 1954-60, chief photographer, 1960-65; lobbyist state legislature, Ind., 1966; copy editor Indpls. Star, 1967-69, writer-photographer Indpls. Star mag., 1969—; lectr. journalism Butler U., 1963-64. Mem. pub. relations com. Marion County chpt. Am. Heart Assn., 1977—; candidate Ind. Legislature, 1960. Served with AUS, 1940-41. Recipient certificate of merit, Internat. Reading Assn., 1971; Farm writing citation Ind. Farm Bur. Coop., 1972; first place award Nat. Soc. Profl. Engrs., 1973, citations, 1974, 75; Nat. Council for Advancement Edn. Writing award, 1974; Meritorious Service award Ind. Optometric Assn., 1974; Pub. Service award Ind. Podiatry Assn.; Casper award Indpls. Community Service Council, 1975, 78, spl. commendation, 1976; Gold Heart award Am. Heart Assn., 1978, Citation, 1979. Mem. Ind. News Photographers Assn. (founder, sec.-treas. 1957, pres. 1958), Nat. Press Photographers Assn. (President's award 1954, citation 1960), Soc. Profl. Journalists-Sigma Delta Chi. Republican. Methodist. Mason (Shriner). Club: Indpls. Press (sec. 1979, 1st place award for best continuous coverage 1974, Sweepstakes award for 1st 5 places 1975, Best Feature Story award 1977). Inventor newspaper color photography printing process, 1946, Maze Word, ednl. game, 1969. Home: 3014 N Richardt Indianapolis IN 46226 Office: Indianapolis Star 307 N Pennsylvania St Indianapolis IN 46206. *Work life hell, pray like Heaven, and treat your fellow man by the Golden Rule. Remember that those you pass on the way up will be waiting for you on the way down.*

WALTON, MATT SAVAGE, geologist, educator; b. Lexington, Ky., Sept. 16, 1915; B.A., U. Chgo., 1936; M.A. (James Furman Kemp fellow), Columbia U., 1947, Ph.D., 1951; m. Kay Ann Thorson, June 21, 1970; children—Matt Savage III, Kate Johns, Lisa Baar, Anne Elizabeth, Owen Hardwick. Geologist, U.S. Geol. Survey, 1942-46; asso. prof. Yale U., New Haven, 1948-65; geologist N.Y. State Geol. Survey, summers, 1947-57; cons. environ. geology, 1947-65; cons. geologist, 1965-73; regents lectr. environ. sci. and engring. UCLA, 1970-71; dir. Minn. Geol. Survey, U. Minn., 1973—, prof. geology and geophysics, 1973—. Pres., Old Town Restorations, Inc., St. Paul, 1974-79; bd. dirs. Summit Hill Assn., St. Paul, 1974-79. Fellow Geol. Soc. Am.; mem. Assn. Am. State Geologists. Contbr. articles on engring. geology to sci. jours. Home: 30 Crocus Pl Saint Paul MN 55102 Office: U Minn Minn Geol Survey 1633 Eustis St Saint Paul MN 55108

WALTON, MILLER, lawyer; b. Hephzibah, Ga., Aug. 10, 1901; s. William Robert and Mary Orlean (Carswell) W.; LL.B., U. Ga., 1922; m. Mary Virginia Howell, Nov. 7, 1922; 1 dau., Susan Howell (Mrs. Lemuel H. Gibbons). Admitted to Ga. bar, 1922, Fla. bar, 1924; practicing lawyer, Augusta, Ga., 1922-23; clk. law office, Palatka, Fla., 1923-24., asso. law firm, 1924-25; asso. atty., Ft. Lauderdale, Fla., 1925-26; mem. Baxter, Byrd & Walton, 1926-28, Baxter & Walton, 1928-34; mem. law firm Walton Lantaff Schroeder & Carson, and predecessors, Miami, Fla., 1934—. Chmn. bd., exec. com. Lawyers' Title Services, Inc. of Dade County, 1960-76; chmn. bd. Fla. Title Co., 1960-76, Miami Beach Abstract & Title Co., 1965-76; dir. Lawyers Title Services, Inc., 1976—. Chmn. bd. trustees Rollins Coll., Winter Park, Fla., 1953-69; trustee, chmn. exec. com. Bapt. Hosp. of Miami, 1957-61, chmn. adminstrv. com., 1962-63, chmn. bd. trustees, 1963—. Mem. Fla. Bar, Am., Dade County bar assns., Internat. Assn. Ins. Counsel, Fedn. Ins. Counsel, Assn. Fraternal Benefit Counsel, Phi Delta Phi, Lambda Chi Alpha. Baptist (bd. deacons chmn. finance com.). Kiwanian. Clubs: Miami; Bankers, Coral Gables Country. Home: 3644 SW Third Ave Miami FL 33145 Office: Alfred I duPont Bldg Miami FL 33131

WALTON, RICHARD EUGENE, educator; b. Pulaski, Iowa, Apr. 15, 1931; s. Lee Richard and Florence (King) W.; B.S., Purdue U., 1953, M.S., 1954; postgrad. Victoria U., New Zealand, 1953; D.B.A., Harvard, 1959; m. Sharon Claire Doty, Apr. 13, 1952; children—John, Elizabeth, Margaret, Andrew. Faculty, Harvard Bus. Sch., 1968—, Edsel Bryant Ford prof. bus., 1970-76, dir. research div., 1970-76; cons. various indsl. firms, govt. agys. including Dept. State; dir. Berol Corp., Graphic Controls Corp. Served with AUS, 1954-56. Ford Found. faculty grantee U. Mich., 1962-63. Author: A Behavioral Theory of Labor Negotiations: An Analysis of a Social Interaction System, 1965; (with R.B. McKersie) The Impact of the Professional Engineering Union, 1961, Interpersonal Peacemaking, 1969. Home: 109 Beaver Rd Weston MA 02193 Office: Harvard Bus Sch Boston MA 02163

WALTON, ROBERT EDWARD, cons. engr.; b. Chgo., July 11, 1923; s. William Charles and Martha (Walshon) W.; student Ind. U. Extension, 1942-43; diploma Bliss Elec. Engring. Coll., 1943; B.S., U. Tex., 1945; m. Edna Colson, June 9, 1945; children—Robert Edward, Martha C., James B., Nancy K., m. 2d, Sandra A. Cidylo, Aug. 31, 1968. Research in guided missiles Kellex Corp., Silver Spring, Md., 1946; v.p., chief engr. Sweney Electric Co., Gary, Ind., 1949-57; exec. v.p. Boese-Hilburn Electric Co., Kansas City, Mo., 1957-61; pres., dir. Kaighin & Hughes, Inc., Toledo, 1961-63; pres. Walton-Abeyta and Assos., Inc., 1955-77; v.p., mgr. bank properties div. Seattle 1st Nat. Bank, 1977-79; pres. Walton Assos., Inc., 1979—, Am. Resources Equity Corp., 1979—. Served with USNR, 1942-46, USMC, 1946-51. Registered profl. engr., Ohio, Mich., Ind., Ill., Pa., N.Y., Fla., Tenn., Nev., Tex., Colo., Idaho, Mont., Minn., Wis., Mo., Sask., Mass., Ariz., Calif., N.D., S.D., Iowa, Oreg., Utah, Wyo., Kans., N.Mex., Nebr., Hawaii, Wash., Conn., N.J., La., Miss. Mem. IEEE (sr.), Nat. Soc. Profl. Engrs., Cons. Engrs. Colo., Sigma Alpha Epsilon. Episcopalian. Clubs: Denver Athletic, Rainier, Pinery Country. Home: 6401 Ponderosa Way Parker CO 80134 Office: Denver Energy Center Suite 2640 717 17th St Denver CO 80202

WALTON, STEVEN DOUGLAS, corp. exec.; b. Salt Lake City, Jan. 14, 1938; s. Douglas Porter and Dora (Norton) W.; B.S., U. Utah, 1960; postgrad. DePaul U., 1964-65, U. Chgo., 1968, Harvard U., 1969; m. Ursula Auer, July 18, 1961; children—Ellen, Christina, Eric. Sr. acct. Arthur Andersen & Co., Chgo., 1961-64; v.p. fin. Keystone Industries, Inc., Chgo., 1964-73; with Ace Hardware Corp., Chgo., 1973—, now exec. v.p. Vice-pres. Olympia Fields Homeowners Assn., 1973-74. Mem. Fin. Execs. Inst., Nat. Soc. Accts. for Coops., Mgmt. Devel. Alumni Assn. U. Chgo. (past dir., pres.). Clubs: Harvard Bus. Sch. (Chgo.); Olympia Fields Country. Home: 106 Indian Trail Dr Oak Brook IL 60521 Office: 2200 Kensington Ct Oak Brook IL 60521

WALTON, WILLIAM BOWEN, lawyer, motel exec.; b. Pine Bluff, Ark., Jan. 24, 1920; s. William Bowen and Katherine (Walters) W.; LL.B., Memphis State U., 1942; m. Geneva Louise Chase, Oct. 21, 1944; children—William B., Richard Russell, Katherine Louise, Geneva Chase. Admitted to Tenn. bar, 1942; pvt. practice, 1946-55; with Holiday Inns Inc., 1955—, exec. v.p., 1955-69, pres., 1969—, vice chmn. bd.. 1973—, dir., mem. exec. com., 1955—; dir., dep. chmn. Fed. Res. Bank, St. Louis. Mem. bus. and industry adv. com. President's Council on Phys. Fitness and Sports. Sponsor, Mayo Found. Memphis chmn., trustee Freedoms Found. at Valley Forge; exec. com. Mayor's Prayer Breakfast; trustee Memphis State U. Found., U.S. Travel Data Center; bd. dirs. Shelby United Neighbors, Billy Graham Evangelistic Assn. Served as instr. USAAF, 1943-46. Mem. Am., Tenn., Shelby County, Memphis bar assns. Memphis Area C. of C. (gen. chmn. conv. and tourist bur.). Kiwanian. Home: 2710 Forest Hill Rd Germantown TN 38138 Office: 3742 Lamar Ave Memphis TN 38118

WALTON, WILLIAM C., geologist; b. Trenton, Mo., Apr. 7, 1924; s. Clarence C. and Irene (Loveland) W.; B.S. in Civil Engring., Lawrence Inst. Tech., 1948; postgrad. U. Wis., 1950-52, Ohio State U., 1954-56, Ind. U., 1942; m. Ellen Grace Shelton, June 13, 1948; children—Cynthia Ann, Louise Janet. Civil engr. U.S. Bur. Reclamation, 1948-49; hydraulic engr. U.S. Geol. Survey, 1949-58; engr. charge groundwater research Ill. Water Survey, 1958-64; prof. geology and geophysics, dir. Water Resources Research Center, U. Minn., Mpls., 1964-74; exec. dir. Upper Miss. River Basin Commn., 1974-79; geohydrologist Camp Dresser and McKee, Urbana, Ohio, 1979—; cons. groundwater hydrologist, Columbus, Ohio, 1955-57; water resources planning dir. Minn. Planning Agy., 1967-69. Mem. U.S. nat. com. Internat. Hydrological Decade, 1965-67. Served with AUS, 1942-45. Mem. Nat. Water Well Assn. (hon. life), Am. Soc. C.E. (past chmn. groundwater com., hydraulic div.). Home: 3 Spring Lake Mahomet IL 61853

WALTON, WILLIAM GRIFFIN, ins. co. exec.; b. Cheyenne, Wyo., June 25, 1928; s. Albert Douglass and Harriet Goodrich (Lund) W.; student U. Colo., 1948-50; LL.B., U. Wyo., 1953; m. Susan Ellen Buchanan, Feb. 4, 1956; children—Elizabeth Ann, Carol Susan. Admitted to Wyo. bar, 1953; individual practice law, Cheyenne, 1953-55, 59-67; asst. U.S. atty. Dist. Wyo., 1955-59; commr. ins. State of Wyo., 1967-70; with Royal Globe Ins. Cos., N.Y.C., 1970—, now sr. v.p., dir., mem. exec. com.; dir., mem. exec. com. Royal Globe Life Ins. Co.; dir. Ins. Info. Inst.; bd. govs. Ins. Inst. for Hwy. Safety, 1975-76. Mem. Laramie County (Wyo.) Republican Central Com., 1958-70; mem. exec. com. Nat. Assn. Ins. Commrs., 1968-70. Served with U.S. Army, 1946-47. Mem. Am. Bar Assn., Newcomen Soc. Congregationalist. Clubs: Masons (32 deg.); Shriners; Scarsdale Golf; Passe Internat. Home: 347 Old Colony Rd Hartsdale NY 10530 Office: 150 William St New York NY 10038

WALTON, WILLIAM (BILL) THEODORE, basketball player; b. La Mesa, Calif., Nov. 5, 1952; s. Theodore and Gloria W.; grad. U. Calif. at Los Angeles, 1974; 1 son, Adam. Team center Portland Trail Blazers, 1974-79, capt., 1976-77; with San Diego Clippers, 1979—. Recipient James E. Sullivan Meml. award, 1974; James Naismith award, 1972, 73, 74; Adolph Rupp trophy, 1972, 73, 74. Office: care San Diego Clippers San Diego Internat Sports Arena 3500 Sports Arena Blvd San Diego CA 92110*

WALTON, SIR WILLIAM TURNER, composer; b. Oldham Lancs, Eng., Mar. 29, 1902; s. Charles Alexander and Louisa Maria (Turner) W.; student Christ Ch. Cathedral Choir Sch., 1912, Christ Church Oxford, 1918-21, hon. student, 1950; Mus.D. (hon.), Durham, 1937, Oxford, 1940, Trinity Coll., Dublin, 1946, Manchester, 1953, Cambridge, 1955, London, Sussex, U. Ireland, Cork; m. Susana Gil Passo, Jan. 20, 1949. Recipient gold medal Royal Philharmonic Soc., 1947; Worshipful Co. of Musicians, knight bachelor, 1951; Order of Merit, 1967. Fellow Royal Coll. Music, Royal Acad. Music (hon.); hon. mem. Swedish Acad. Music. Clubs: Athenaeum, Garrick (London, Eng.). Compositions include: Piano Quartet, 1918, rev., 1974; Facade, 1923; Viola Concerto, 1929; Belshazzar's Feast, 1931; Symphony No. I, 1935; Coronation March Crown Imperial, 1937; Violin Concerto, 1939; String Quartet, 1947; Coronation Te Deum, 1953; Orb and Sceptre, 1953; Troilus and Cressida (opera), 1954; Cello Concerto, 1956; Partita, 1957; Anon in Love, 1960; Symphony Number II, 1960; Gloria, 1961; Variations on a Theme by Hindemith, 1963; The Twelve, 1965; The Bear, 1967; Capriccio Burlesco, 1968; Improvisations on an Impromptu of Benjamin Britten, 1970; Jubilate Deo, 1972; Sonata for String Orch., 1972; Cantico del Sole, 1974; Magnificat and Nunc Dimittis, 1974; Varii Capricci, 1976; Facade 2, 1978. Films: Henry V, Hamlet, Richard III. Home: care Oxford U Press 37 Dover St London W1 England

WALTRIP, DARRELL LEE, stock car driver; b. Owensboro, Ky., Feb. 5, 1947; s. Leroy and Margaret Jean (Evans) W.; student Ky. Wesleyan Coll.; m. Stephanie Hamilton Rader, Aug. 15, 1969. Owner, Waltrip's Racing Center, Franklin, Tenn.; driver for Digard-Gatorade Racing Co. Named Driver of the Year Nat. Motorsports Press Assn., 1977. Mem. NASCAR. Republican. Baptist. Office: 131 1st Ave S PO Box 591 Franklin TN 37064

WALTS, ROBERT WARREN, educator; b. New Albany, Ind., Apr. 1, 1921; s. William H. and Alma Ethel (Hixon) W.; A.B., Rutgers U., 1950, A.M., 1951, Ph.D. (Queens fellow), 1953; m. Gloria Halsey Denton, Jan. 22, 1944; children—Robert Denton, Anne Sawyer, Caroline Burns. Mem. faculty U. Mo., Columbia, 1952-53, U. Ga., Atlanta, 1953-56, Ga. State Coll., Atlanta, 1953-59; prof. English S.W. Tex. State U., San Marcos, 1959—, chmn. dept., 1965-72. Commr. urban renewal, San Marcos, 1963-69. Served with USNR, 1942-45. Mem. AAUP, Modern Lang. Assn., S. Central Modern Lang. Assn., Conf. Coll. Tchrs. English (councillor), Coll. English Assn. Kiwanian (pres. 1967). Author: William Dean Howells And The House Of Harper, 1957; Study Guide: The Rise Of Silas Lapham, 1963. Contbr. articles on Howells and Shakespeare to profl. jours. Home: 408 Walnut St San Marcos TX 78666

WALTZ, JON RICHARD, lawyer, educator, author; b. Napoleon, O., Oct. 11, 1929; s. Richard R. and Lenore (Tharp) W.; B.A., with honors in Polit. Sci., Coll. Wooster, 1951; J.D., Yale, 1954. Admitted to Ohio bar, 1954, Ill. bar, 1965; asso. firm Squire, Sanders & Dempsey, Cleve., 1954-64; chief prosecutor City of Willowick, O., 1958-64; asso. prof. law Northwestern U. Sch. Law, Chgo., 1964-65, prof. law, 1965-78, Edna B. and Ednyfed H. Williams prof. law, 1978—, instr. med. jurisprudence Med. Sch., 1969—. Book critic Washington Post, Chgo. Tribune, others; Distinguished vis. prof. law Ill. Inst. Tech.-Chgo.-Kent Coll. Law, 1974; lectr. Mem. Ill. adv. com. U.S. Commn. on Civil Rights, 1971-74, Ill. Criminal Justice System Policy and Planning Com., 1973-74; Republican candidate Ill. Appellate Ct., 1978. Served to 1st lt. AUS, 1955-58. Decorated Commendation medal; recipient Distinguished Service award Soc. Midland Authors, 1972. Mem. Am. Arbitration Assn., Assn. Am. Law Schs., Judge Adv.'s Assn., Nat. Assn. Def. Lawyers in Criminal Cases, Bar Assn. 7th Jud. Circuit, Am., Chgo. bar assns., Chgo. Council Lawyers, Law-Medicine Soc., Soc. Am. Law Tchrs., Order of Coif, Phi Alpha Delta, Pi Sigma Alpha. Independent. Presbyn. Co-author: The Trial of Jack Ruby, 1965; Cases and Materials on Evidence, 1968; Principles of Evidence and Proof, 1968, Medical Jurisprudence, 1971; author: The Federal Rules of Evidence-An Analysis, 1973; Criminal Evidence, 1975; Evidence: A Summary Analysis, 1976. Note, comment editor Yale Law Jour., 1953-54; mem. editorial adv. bd. Harcourt Brace Jovanovich Law Group, 1978—; contbr. numerous articles to profl. jours. Home: 421 W Melrose St Chicago IL 60657 also Eagle Crest Holland MI 49423 Office: 357 E Chicago Ave Chicago IL 60611

WALTZ, JOSEPH MCKENDREE, neurosurgeon; b. Detroit, July 23, 1931; s. Ralph McKinley and Bertha (Seelye) W.; student U. Mich., 1950; B.S., U. Oreg., 1954, M.D., 1956 m. Janet Maureen Journey, June 26, 1954; children—Jeffrey McKinley, Mary Elaine, David Seelye, Stephen McKendree; m. 2d, Marilyn Liska, June 5, 1967; 1 dau., Tristana McKendree. Surg. intern U. Mich. Hosp., 1956-57, gen. surg. resident, 1957-58, clin. instr. neurosurgery, 1960-63; neurosurg. asso. St. Barnabas Hosp., N.Y.C., 1963—, asso. dir. Inst. Neurosci., 1974—, dir. dept. neurol. surgery, 1977—; asso. cons. neurosurgery Englewood (N.J.) Hosp., 1964—; asso. prof. neurosurgery N.Y. U. Med. Center, 1974—; spl. research neurophysiology epilepsy, basal ganglia, abnormal movement disorders, cerebral palsy, also neurosurg. application cryogenic surgery and implantation brain stimulator. Served to capt. M.C., AUS, 1958-60. Recipient bronze award Am. Congress Rehab. Medicine, 1967. Diplomate Am. Bd. Neurol. Surgery. Mem. Nat. Ski Patrol, Soc. for Cryobiology, AMA, N.Y. State, Bronx County med. socs., N.Y. State Neurosurg. Soc., Phi Beta Pi. Author (with Dr. I.S. Cooper) papers on surg. treatment abnormal movement disorders stroke, cerebral palsy, cryothalamectomy-cryopulvinectomy and implantation brain pacemakers; chpt. in book on cryogenic surgery; developer spinal cord stimulator for treatment cerebral palsy, torticollis, dystonia musculorum deformans and stroke. Home: Four B Island South 720 Milton Rd Milton Harbor Rye NY 10580 Office: St Barnabas Hosp 4422 3d Ave Bronx NY 10457

WALTZ, KENNETH NEAL, educator; b. Ann Arbor, Mich., June 8, 1924; s. Christian Benjamin and Luella (Braun) W.; A.B., Oberlin Coll., 1948; M.A., Columbia, 1950, Ph.D., 1954; m. Helen Elizabeth Lindsley, June 4, 1949; children—Kenneth L., Thomas E., Daniel E. Instr., then asst. prof. Columbia, 1953-57; from asso. prof. to prof. politics Swarthmore Coll., 1957-66; research asso. Center Internat. Affairs, Harvard, 1963-64, 68-69, 72; prof. politics Brandeis U., Waltham, Mass., 1966-71, Adlai E. Stevenson prof. internat. politics, 1967-71; Ford prof. polit. sci. U. Calif., Berkeley, 1971—. Cons. govt. agys. Served to 1st lt. AUS, 1944-46, 51-52. NSF grantee, 1968-71; Guggenheim fellow, 1976-77. Mem. Am. Polit. Sci. Assn. (sec. 1966-67). Internat. Studies Assn. (pres. New Eng. sect. 1966-67), Council on Fgn. Relations, Phi Beta Kappa. Author: Man, The State and War, 1959; Foreign Policy and Democratic Politics, 1967; Theory of International Politics, 1979; co-author, co-editor: Conflict in World Politics, 1971. Mem. editorial bd. Jour. Politics; World Politics. Home: 70 Oak Ridge Rd Berkeley CA 94705 Office: Polit Sci Dept U Calif at Berkeley Berkeley CA 94720

WALTZER, HERBERT, educator; b. Bklyn., May 29, 1930; s. Samuel and Pearl (Bernstein) W.; B.A., N.Y. U., 1951, M.A. (Penfield fellow), 1954, Ph.D., 1959; m. Marilyn L. Fishchvogt, June 11, 1962; children—Adam Koehler, Sarah Lee, Samuel John. Program prodn. coordinator Radio Free Europe, 1951; instr. polit. sci. N.Y. U., 1954-55; faculty polit. sci. Miami U., Oxford, Ohio, 1957—, prof., 1966—, chmn. dept., 1970—. Vice chmn. Oxford Village Planning Commn., 1962-64. Bd. advisers Ohio Center Edn. in Politics, 1958-64, 72-74; dir. S.W. Ohio Center for Edn. in Politics, 1972-74. Served to capt. USAF, 1955-57. Faculty research fellow Rockefeller Found. Project on Constl. Democracy, 1964-65; Social Sci. Research Council Faculty fellow, 1968; Nat. Conv. Faculty fellow, 1964. Mem. Am., Midwest (exec. council 1977—) polit. sci. assns., Ohio Assn. Polit. Scientists and Economists (v.p. 1971-72, pres. 1972-73), Internat. Communicaton Assn. Author: American Government: Principles, Institutions and Processes, 1962, 63, 65; (with others) Ideologies and Modern Politics, 1971, rev. edit., 1975; The Job of Academic Department Chairmen, 1975. Contbr. to Politics Of Reapportionment, 1963; also articles to Pub. Opinion Quar., Western Polit. Quar., Midwest Rev. Pub. Adminstrn. Home: 3 Bull Run Dr Oxford OH 45056

WALVOORD, JOHN FLIPSE, educator; b. Sheboygan, Wis., May 1, 1910; s. John Garrett and Mary (Flipse) W.; A.B., Wheaton Coll., 1931, D.D., 1960; B.Th., Dallas Theol. Sem., 1934, M.Th., 1934, D.Th., 1936; A.M., Tex. Christian U., 1945; m. Geraldine Lundgren, June 28, 1939; children—John Edward, James Randall, Timothy, Paul. Registrar, Dallas Theol. Sem., 1935-45, asso. prof. systematic theology, 1936-52, prof., 1952—, regent, 1940—, asst. to pres., 1945-52, pres., 1952—, editor Sem. Bull., 1940-53; pastor Ft. Worth, 1935-50; editor Bibliotheca Sacra, 1952—. Mem. Evang. Theol. Soc., Wheaton Coll. Scholastic Honor Soc. Author: The Doctrine of the Holy Spirit, 1943; The Holy Spirit, 1954; The Return of the Lord, 1955; The Thessalonian Epistles, 1956; The Rapture Question, 1957; The Millennial Kingdom, 1959; To Live Is Christ, 1961; Israel in Prophecy, 1962; The Church in Prophecy, 1964; The Revelation of Jesus Christ, 1966; The Nations in Prophecy, 1967; Jesus Christ Our Lord, 1969; Philippians, 1971, Daniel, 1971; The Holy Spirit at Work Today, 1973; Major Bible Themes, 1974; Armageddon, Oil and the Middle East Crisis, 1974; Matthew: Thy Kingdom Come, 1975; The Blessed Hope and the Tribulation, 1976. Editor: Inspiration and Interpretation, 1957; Truth for Today, 1963. Home: 1302 El Patio Dr Dallas TX 75218

WALWORTH, ARTHUR, author; b. Newton, Mass., July 9, 1903; s. Arthur Clarence and Ruth Richardson (Lippincott) W.; grad. Phillips Andover Acad., 1921; B.A., Yale, 1925. Ednl. dept. Houghton Mifflin Co., 1927-43; staff OWI, 1943. Staff Medomak Camp, Washington, Maine, summers 1943-63. Recipient Pulitzer prize in biography, 1958. Clubs: Cosmos; Graduates (New Haven). Author: School Histories at War, 1938; Black Ships Off Japan, 1946; Cape Breton, 1948; The Medomak Way, 1953; Woodrow Wilson, 2 vols., 1958, 1 vol., 1967, 78; America's Moment: 1918, 1977. Home: Graduates Club 155 Elm St New Haven CT 06508

WALWORTH, EDWARD HENRY, JR., mfg. co. exec.; b. Wilkinsburg, Pa., Sept. 8, 1915; s. Edward Henry and May (Wilson) W.; A.B., U. Rochester, 1937; LL.B., U. Mich., 1940; m. Nancy Knowlton Zinsser, Feb. 5, 1944; children—Edward Z., Joyce K., Seth, Cornelia. Admitted to Ill. bar, 1940: with firm Isham, Lincoln & Beale, Chgo., 1940-47; with William Zinsser & Co., Inc., N.Y.C., 1947—, v.p., 1956-64, pres., 1964—, chmn., 1973—, also dir.; dir. Allegheny Power System, Inc. Trustee New Canaan Library. Served to capt. AUS, 1942-45, 50-51. Mem. Am. Bleached Shellac Mfrs. Assn. Clubs: New Canaan Country; Nassau. Home: 263 Oenoke Ridge New Canaan CT 06840 Office: 39 Belmont Dr Somerset NJ 08873

WALWORTH, THEODORE HOLTON, JR., broadcasting co. exec.; b. Greenwich, Conn., July 19, 1924; s. Theodore Holton and Janet R. (Warford) W.; student Nichols Coll., Dudley, Mass., 1946; m. Joan L. Petersen, Oct. 15, 1949; children—Wendy Joan, Theodore Holton III. With ABC, 1946-50, Edward Petry Co., 1951-52; with NBC, 1953—, sta. mgr. WRCV-TV, 1960-61, v.p., gen. mgr. WNBC-TV, 1961-71, pres. NBC TV stas. div., 1971-79, exec. v.p. NBC TV Stas./Radio, 1979—, also dir.; dir. Selchow & Righter Co. Mem. Internat. Radio and TV Soc. Club: Greenwich Country. Home: Saw Mill Ln Greenwich CT 06830 Office: 30 Rockefeller Plaza New York NY 10020

WALZAK, MYRON PAUL, JR., urologist; b. Cleve., Jan. 17, 1930; s. Myron Paul and Elizabeth Catherine (Rusnak) W.; M.D., Yale U., 1955; m. Mary Christina Provan, Nov. 24, 1954; children—Kevin, Keith, Katherine, Christine, Myron Paul, Mary, Maura, Michael. Intern, Ohio State U. Hosp., Columbus, 1955-56; resident in surgery St. Alexis Hosp., Cleve., 1956-57, Yale-New Haven Hosp., New Haven, 1957-58; resident in urology N.Y. Hosp.-Cornell U., N.Y.C., 1958-62; asst. prof. urology U. Va., Charlottesville, 1964-69, asso. prof., 1969-71; prof., chmn. dept. urology Creighton U. Sch. Medicine, Omaha, 1971—; mem. staffs St. Joseph, Omaha VA, Bergan-Mercy, Children's hosps. (all Omaha). Served with M.C., U.S. Army, 1962-64. Diplomate Am. Bd. Urology. Fellow Am. Acad. Pediatrics; mem. Assn. Am. Med. Colls., Soc. Univ. Urologists, A.C.S., AMA, Am. Urol. Assn. Office: Creighton U Health Center 601 N 30th St Omaha NE 68131

WALZER, MICHAEL LABAN, educator; b. N.Y.C., Mar. 3, 1935; s. Joseph P. and Sally (Hochman) W.; B.A., Brandeis U., 1956; Ph.D., Harvard, 1961; m. Judith Borodovko, June 17, 1956; children—Sarah, Rebecca. Fulbright fellow Cambridge (Eng.) U., 1956-57; asst. prof. Princeton, 1962-66; faculty Harvard, 1966—, prof. govt., 1968—. Bd. govs. Hebrew U., Jerusalem, 1975—; chmn. faculty adv. cabinet United Jewish Appeal, 1977—. Mem. Soc. Ethical and Legal Philosophy, Conf. Study Polit. Thought. Author: The Revolution of the Saints, 1965; Obligations: essays on disobedience, war and citizenship, 1970; Political Action, 1971; Regicide and Revolution, 1974; Just and Unjust Wars, 1977. Editorial bd. Dissent mag., 1960—; contbg. editor New Republic, 1976—. Home: 23 Bellevue Ave Cambridge MA 02140

WALZER, STANLEY, psychiatrist; b. N.Y.C., Aug. 23, 1929; s. Joseph and Sadie (Gootenberg) W.; A.B. magna cum laude, Syracuse U., 1951; M.D., U. Vt., 1955; m. Sarita Goodman, Apr. 14, 1957; children—Jonathan Holden, Elizabeth Ann. Intern, Cornell Med. Service, Bellevue Med. Center, N.Y.C., 1955-56; asst. resident psychiatry Cin. Gen. Hosp., 1956-58; fellow child psychiatry Judge Baker Guidance Center, Boston, 1958-60, psychiatrist (part-time), 1960-62, asst. to dir., 1972-77; research fellow in genetics Children's Hosp. Med. Center, Boston, 1964-65, asso. in psychiatry, 1967-69, sr. asso. psychiatry, 1969—; practice medicine specializing in psychiatry, Boston, 1964—; instr. psychiatry Harvard Med. Sch., Boston, 1965-67, asst. prof. psychiatry, 1969-77, lectr. psychiatry, 1977—; dir. Research Genetics Lab., Boston Hosp. for Women, 1968-75; prof., chmn. dept. psychiatry U. Mass. Med. Sch., Worcester, 1977—; psychiatrist-in-chief U. Mass. Med. Center, Worcester, 1977—; sr. asso. clin. genetics Children's Hosp. Med. Center, 1974-77. Served with USN, 1960-62. Recipient Career Research award NIMH, 1968-77; diplomate Am. Bd. Psychiatry. Mem. Am. Psychiat. Assn., Mass. Med. Soc., Sigma Xi, Phi Beta Kappa, Alpha Omega Alpha. Jewish. Contbr. articles on genetics, child devel. and psychiatry to sci. jours.; editorial bd. Seminars in Psychiatry, 1970-75. Home: 21 Renee Terr Newton Center MA 02159 Office: Univ of Mass Medical Center 55 Lake Ave North Worcester MA 01605

WALZER, STUART BERNARD, lawyer; b. Chgo., July 12, 1924; s. Leo A. and Frieda (Laskin) W.; B.S., U. Calif. at Los Angeles, 1948; J.D., Harvard, 1951; m. Paula Silverston, Dec. 2, 1951; children—Peter, David, Andrew, Lloyd. Admitted to Calif. bar, 1952, since practiced in Los Angeles; prin. Stuart B, A Law Corp., Los Angeles, 1957—; instr. advanced domestic relations practice U. So. Calif. Law Center, 1974-79; instr. extension div. U. Calif. at Los Angeles, 1972-78. Served with AUS, 1943-45. Mem. Am. Bar Assn., State Bar Calif., Am. Acad. Matrimonial Lawyers, Calif. Trial Lawyers Assn. Author: California Marital Termination Settlements, California Continuing Education of the Bar, 1971; contbr. articles to profl. jours. Office: 1888 Century Park E Suite 800 Los Angeles CA 90067

WALZER, WILLIAM CHARLES, former ch. ofcl., pub. co. exec.; b. Rochester, N.Y., July 20, 1912; s. William Frederick and Mable Beatrice (McElroy) W.; B.A., U. Rochester, 1935; M.A., 1937; B.D., Colgate-Rochester Div. Sch., 1941; Ph.D., U. Chgo., 1944; postgrad. Syracuse U. Sch. Journalism, 1951; m. Dorothy Mae Kramer, Aug. 28, 1938; children—Carolyn Walzer Dennis, Lorraine Walzer Harbaugh, William T. Tchr. high sch., 1935-38; ordained to ministry United Methodist Ch., 1941; pastor Stafford (N.Y.) Meth. Ch., 1938-41; asst. pastor Hyde Park Meth. Ch., Chgo., 1941-43; asst. prof. Garrett Theol. Sem., Evanston, Ill., 1943-45; prof. Scarritt Coll. for Christian Workers, Nashville, 1945-51; mem. staff Bd. Missions, Presbyn. Ch. in U.S.A., N.Y.C., 1951-54; exec. dir. dept. edn. for mission Nat. Council Chs., N.Y.C., 1954-77; exec. dir. Friendship Press, N.Y.C., 1954-77; interim pastor Westminster Presbyn. Ch., N.Y.C., 1955-59, 66-68, 75-77; cons. div. world mission and ecumenism Luth. Ch. in Am., N.Y.C., 1978—; chmn. Eastern Ecumenical Conf. on World Mission, Silver Bay, N.Y., 1978—; pres. Religious Pub. Relations Council, 1959-61; bd. dirs. Religion in Am. Life, 1965-68; del. World Council Christian Edn., Tokyo, 1958, Lima, Peru, 1971; cons. Pacific Council of Chs., Suva, Fiji, also Joint Bd. Christian Edn. Australia and N.Z., 1972; staff World Council Chs. Assembly, New Delhi, 1961, Uppsala, Sweden, 1968. Mem. U.S. Nat. Commn. for Unesco, 1972-78. Mem. Am. Soc. Ch. History, Internat. Soc. Missiology, Gray Panthers Phi Beta Kappa, Phi Sigma Iota. Author: American Denominations, 1953; Your World, Your Mission, 1963; Great Protestant Leaders, 1965. Home: 5 Bluebell Ct Garden City NY 11530. *I am committed to educating people for interracial, intercultural and international understanding and concern. To that end a major goal has been a better educated church and community, leading to social justice, world peace and human mutual helpfulness, all of which I feel are demands of my religious heritage.*

WALZL, FLORENCE LEDUC LITCHFIELD (MRS. EDWARD MCCOLGAN WALZL), educator; b. Mpls., Nov. 19, 1909; d. John Thomas and Agnes A. (LeDuc) Litchfield; B.A., U. Minn., 1930, M.A., 1931, Ph.D., 1935; postgrad. Johns Hopkins, 1940-41; vis. scholar Columbia, 1950-51; summer study Oxford (Eng.) U., 1956; m. Edward McColgan Walzl, Aug. 27, 1940 (dec. Aug. 1950). Asst. in English, U. Minn., 1930-34; instr. English, Eastern Ill. State Tchrs. Coll., Charleston, 1934-36; asst. prof. English, Bowling Green (Ohio) State U., 1936-40, Coll. Notre Dame of Md., 1951-54; asso. prof. English, U. Wis., Milw., 1954-65, prof. English, 1965—. Mem. Modern Lang. Assn., Nat. Council Tchrs. English, Milton Soc. Am., English Assn. Greater Milw. (past exec. v.p.), Poetry Soc. Milw. (past pres.), AAUP, Am. Com. for Irish Studies, James Joyce Found., Am. Assn. U. Women, Phi Beta Kappa, Lambda Alpha Psi, Sigma Tau Delta, Phi Mu, Phi Kappa Phi. Democrat. Roman Catholic. Contbr. articles to profl. jours. Home: 3041 N Stowell Ave Milwaukee WI 53211

WAMBAUGH, JOSEPH, author: b. East Pittsburgh, Pa., Jan. 22, 1937; s. Joseph Aloysius and Anne (Malloy) W.; B.A., Calif. State Coll., Los Angeles, 1960, M.A., 1968. Police officer, Los Angeles, 1960-74; creator television series Police Story, 1973. Served with USMC, 1954-57. Author: The New Centurions, 1971; The Blue Knight, 1972; The Onion Field, 1973 (screenwriter, producer motion picture 1979); The Choirboys, 1975; The Black Marble, 1978. Home: PO Box 8657 San Marino CA 91108

WAMPLER, CHARLES EDWIN, cons., ret. telephone exec.; b. Clinton, Ill., May 23, 1908; s. Thomas Calvin and Elizabeth (Cloud) W.; A.B., U. Ill., 1929; M.S. (Sloan fellow), M.I.T., 1940; postgrad. New Sch. for Social Research, 1971-77; m. Janet Brown, Sept. 25, 1937. With Ill. Bell Telephone Co., Chgo., 1929-49, asst. v.p., 1948-49; with Am. Tel.&Tel. Co., N.Y.C., 1949-53, 63-69, v.p., 1951-53, v.p., sec., 1963-69; pres., dir., mem. exec. com. Wis. Telephone Co., Milw., 1954-63; propr. Charles Wampler & Assos., econs. letter and cons. services, 1969—; with OPM-WPB, 1941-42; dep. adminstr. Def. Prodn. Adminstrn., 1951; cons. USIA, 1970-71; mem. program adv. com. Office Emergency Preparedness, 1971-73, Fed. Preparedness Agy., 1976. Served to lt. col. Signal Corps, AUS, World War II. Decorated Legion of Merit. Mem. Population Crisis Com., Am. Econ. Assn., Am. Acad. Polit. and Social Sci., Pub. Mems. Assn. Fgn. Service, Telephone Pioneers Am., U. Ill. Found. (pres.'s club), Phi Beta Kappa (life asso.), Sigma Xi, Beta Gamma Sigma. Clubs: Delray Dunes Golf and Country (Boynton Beach, Fla.); Baltusrol Golf (Springfield, N.J.). Home: 4919 King Palm Circle Delray Dunes Boynton Beach FL 33436 Office: PO Box 2235 Delray Beach FL 33444 also care Am Tel and Tel Co 195 Broadway New York NY 10007

WAMPLER, G. V., marketing exec.; b. Bloomington, Ind., Oct. 10, 1914; s. Harvey and Lenora R. (Hawkins) W.; ed. Ind. U., 1932-36; m. Dorothy Travis, June 2, 1940; 1 dau., Rebecca Sue. Advt. mgr., sales dept., field supr. Atlantic & Pacific Tea Co., Indpls., Cin., 1936-50; advt. and sales promotion mgr. Humpty Dumpty Super Markets, Oklahoma City, 1950-55; advt. dir., div. mgr., v.p., gen. dir. merchandising Fleming Co., Topeka, 1955-67, exec. v.p., 1967-70; pres. Marketing Analysts, Inc., 1970—. Served with USAAF, 1943-46. Congregationalist. Club: Quail Creek Country. Office: PO Box 8477 Naples FL 33941

WAMPLER, WILLIAM CREED, congressman; b. Pennington Gap, Va., Apr. 21, 1926; s. John Sevier and Lillian (Wolfe) W.; B.B.A., Va. Poly. Inst., 1948; postgrad. law U. Va., 1948-50; m. Mary Elizabeth Baker, Aug. 29, 1953; children—Barbara Irene, William Creed. Reporter, Bristol Va.-Tennessean, 1950-51; reporter, editorial writer Big Stone Gap (Va.) Post, 1951; reporter, copy editor Bristol Herald Courier, 1951-52; asst. campaign mgr. congl. candidate, 1948; keynote speaker, conv. chmn. 9th Dist. Va., Republican Conv., 1950, nat. vice chmn. congl. campaign com.; mem. 83d, 90th-96th Congresses, 9th Dist. Va.; ranking minority mem. com. on agr. Mem. at large Sequoyah council Boy Scouts Am. Pres., Young Rep. Fedn. Va., 1950; chmn. 9th Va. Rep. Dist., 1965-66. Bd. visitors Emory and Henry Coll., Emory, Va.; bd. dirs. Youth Devel. Found. Served as air cadet USNR, 1943-45. Recipient Freedoms Found. award, 1954; Watchdog of Treasury award Nat. Assn. Businessmen; Appreciation plaque Va. State Letter Carriers Assn., 1968; Outstanding Citizen of Year award Bristol VFW Sesquicentennial award U. Va., 1969; Distinguished Service award Ams. for Constl. Action, 1969. Mem. Am. Legion, Travelers Protective Assn., 40 and 8, Sigma Nu Phi. Moose, Lion. Home: 84 Kingsbridge Bristol VA 24201 Office: 2422 Rayburn House Office Bldg Washington DC 20515

WAMPOLD, CHARLES HENRY, JR., lawyer; b. Montgomery, Ala., Oct. 21, 1925; s. Charles Henry and Selma (Manasse) W.; B.A., U. Ala., 1946, LL.B., 1948, J.D., 1950; m. Babette Levy, Mar. 14, 1954; children—Jerre Lynn, Carolyn M., Charles Henry III. Admitted to Ala. bar, 1948; practice in Montgomery, 1949—; partner Volz, Capouano, Wampold & Sansone, 1960—. Dir. Real Estate Assos., Inc., Capitol, Inc., Maison, Inc., Barbados, Inc. Bd. dirs. Griel Meml. Hosp. Mem. Am., Ala. bar assns., Montgomery Jr., Montgomery Chambers Commerce, Zeta Beta Tau. Jewish. Home: 3113 Jasmine Rd Montgomery AL 36111 Office: 350 Adams Ave Montgomery AL 36104

WAN, HENRY YORK, JR., economist; b. Hankow, China, Dec. 16, 1931; s. Henry York and Hilda (Tzang) W.; came to U.S., 1966; B.A., Nat. Taiwan U., 1952; M.S., Bucknell U., 1958; Ph.D., M.I.T., 1961; m. Simone Clemhout, June 11, 1965; 1 son, Vincent. Jr. prof. Nat. Taiwan U., 1961-63; lectr. U. New South Wales (Australia), 1963-64; asst. prof. econs. U. Wash., 1964-65; asso. prof. U. Calif., Davis, 1965-70; prof. Cornell U., 1970—. Mem. Econometric Soc. Buddhist. Author: Economic Growth, 1971; contbr. articles to profl. jours. Office: Econs Dept Cornell U Ithaca NY 14850*

WANAMAKER, ROBERT JOSEPH, advt. co. exec.; b. Oak Park, Ill., Nov. 24, 1924; s. Daniel John and Mabel (Maloney) W.; ed. Northwestern U., 1949; m. Carol Anne George, Apr. 20, 1968; children—Stacey Lynne, Bethanne. Vice pres., copy dir. Edward H. Weiss & Co., Chgo., 1957-62; sr. v.p., creative dir. Clinton E. Frank, Inc., Chgo., 1962-72; sr. v.p., creative dir. Grey-North, Inc., Chgo., 1972-76; sr. v.p., dir. creative services Y & R/Buchen, Reincke, Chgo., 1976-79; dir. creative services Pollenex, Chgo., 1979—. Served with AUS, 1943. Named one of 100 top advt. creative people in U.S.A. Ad Dayl U.S.A., 1975. Mem. Chgo. Council Fgn. Relations. Clubs: Execs.; Oak Park Country. Home: 7225 Division St River Forest IL 60305 Office: 111 N Canal St Chicago IL 60606. *One of the biggest problems with success in worldly things is keeping your sense of values in proper perspective. Affluence can dull your sensitivity to the needs and aspirations of those less fortunate. You can become obsessed with building your own financial assets. The misguided fear of losing your status, your luxuries, your comforts can be abnormally painful. Every once in awhile you have to chasten your thinking and remind yourself that the only three riches in life are love, health, and being at peace with yourself and your God.*

WANAMAKER, SAM, actor, dir.; b. Chgo., June 14, 1919; s. Maurice and Molly (Bobele) W.; ed. Drake U., Goodman Theatre Sch.; m. Charlotte Holland, 1940; 3 daus. Dir. Jewish Peoples Inst., Chgo., 1939-40; radio actor, N.Y., 1940-41, also acted in Cafe Crown and Counterattack; actor, dir., 1946—; artistic dir. New Shakespeare Theatre, Liverpool, Eng., 1957-59; prin. acting roles include: My Girl Tisa, 1947, Christ in Concrete, 1949, Denning Drives North, 1951; films: Taras Bulba, 1962, Those Magnificent Men in Their Flying Machines, 1964, The Spy Who Came In From The Cold, 1965, The Law, 1974, Spiral Staircase, 1974, The Sell-Out, 1976, Voyage of the Damned, 1976, Billy Jack Goes to Washington, 1977, From Hell to Victory, 1978, Death on the Nile, 1978; dir. film: Sinbad & the Eye of the Tiger, 1977; actor, producer play: The Watergate Tapes; dir. plays: War and Peace, The Ice Breaks; actor, dir. Joan of Lorraine, 1946, The Winter Journey, The Shrike, The Rainmaker, Threepenny Opera, The Big Knife, A Hatful of Rain, A View From the Bridge, Reclining Figure, Othello, The Rose Tattoo, A Far Country, 1961, Macbeth, 1964; dir. Gentlemen From Athens, 1948, Goodby My Fancy, 1949, Caesar and Cleopatra, Revival of Gardsman, Children From Their Games, 1962, Case of Libel, 1963, (operas) King Priam, 1963, Forza del Destino, 1963; dir. and/or actor TV series The Defenders, For the People, Lancer, Gunsmoke, The Baron, Cimmarron Strip; TV films: The Day the Fish Came Out, 1966, Warning Shot, 1966, The Eliminator, 1967, Custer, The Hawk, Lassiter, Court Martial, The Champions, The Chinese Visitor, 1968, The File of the Golden Goose, 1968, The Executioner; actor, dir. TV shows: Holocaust, 1977, Return of the Saint, 1978; actor in TV: Blind Love, 1976; founder, exec. dir. Globe Playhouse Trust Ltd., World Centre for Shakespeare Studies Ltd. Served with AUS, 1942-45. Office: care Internat Creative Mgmt 8899 Beverly Blvd Los Angeles CA 90048*

WANDA, DIMITRY, savs. and loan assn. exec.; b. Chgo., Mar. 11, 1914; s. Mitro and Mary (Gaydos) W.; B.B.A. Roosevelt U., 1936; postgrad. Ind. U., 1953; m. Catherine Mihalko, June 7, 1941; children—Judy, Gregory, Amy. Mem. firm Talman Fed. Savs. and Loan Assn. of Chgo., 1939—, chmn. bd., 1977—, also pres.; dir. Talman Services Corp., Fed. Savs. and Loan Council of Ill. Bd. dirs., treas. Beverly Art Center; bd. dirs. Ill. chpt. Arthritis Found.; bd. govs. Ill. Council Econ. Edn.; trustee, treas., chmn. sch. mgmt. and finance com. Morgan Park Acad. Served with USNR, 1941-43. Author: Teller Operations, 1962. Office: 5501 S Kedzie Ave Chicago IL 60629

WANDERONE, RUDOLF WALTER (MINNESOTA FATS), pocket billiards player; b. N.Y.C., Jan. 19, 1913; s. Rudolf Walter and Rosa Wanderone; m. Evelyn Inez, May 7, 1941. Formerly host TV shows Minnesota Fats Hustles the Pros, Celebrity Billiards. Adviser Rozel Industries Inc. Author: (with Tom Fox) The Bank Shot and Other Great Robberies, 1966. Home: Dowell IL 62927 Office: 6501 Lincoln Ave Lincolnwood IL 60645*

WANDERS, HANS WALTER, banker; b. Aachen, Germany, Apr. 3, 1925; s. Herbert and Anna Maria (Kusters) W.; came to U.S., 1929, naturalized, 1943; B.S., Yale, 1947; postgrad. Rutgers U. Grad Sch. Banking, 1961-64; m. Elizabeth Knox Kimball, Apr. 2, 1949; children—Crayton Kimball, David Gillette. With Gen. Electric Co., 1947-48, Libbey-Owens-Ford Glass Co., 1948-53, Allied Chem. Co., 1953-55, McKinsey & Co., Inc., 1955-57; asst. cashier, then 2d v.p., v.p. No. Trust Co., Chgo., 1957-65; v.p. Nat. Blvd. Bank, Chgo., 1965-66, pres., 1966-70, also dir.; exec. v.p. Wachovia Bank & Trust Co., N.A., Winston-Salem N.C., 1970-74; pres., dir. Wachovia Corp., 1974-76, chmn., dir., 1977—; chmn., dir. Wachovia Bank & Trust Co., N.A., 1977—; v.p., dir. Winton Mineral Co.; dir. Hanes Dye & Finishing Co.; trustee Wachovia Realty Investments. Mem. com. on bank relationships Council on Founds., Inc., 1973-74; mem. com. Winston-Salem Found.; bd. dirs. N.C. Textile Found., N.C. Engring. Found., Inc. Served to lt. USNR, 1943-46, 51-53. Mem. Am. Bankers Assn. (chmn. mktg. div., dir. 1971-73), Assn. Res. City Bankers, Internat. C. of C. (trustee U.S. council), Conf. Bd. (So. regional adv. council), Newcomen Soc. in N.Am. Clubs: Commonwealth, Chicago (Chgo.); Old Town (Winston-Salem); Roaring Gap (N.C.). Home: 2210 Brookfield Dr Winston-Salem NC 27106 Office: 301 N Main St Winston-Salem NC 27101

WANDMACHER, CORNELIUS, civil engr., educator; b. Bklyn., Sept. 1, 1911; s. Frederick Cornelius and Louise Meta (Jensen) W.; B.C.E., Poly. Inst. Bklyn., 1933, M.S., 1935, D.Engring. (hon.), 1969; D.Engring. (hon.), Rose Hulman Inst., 1976; postgrad. Columbia Tchrs. Coll. 1948-50; m. Mary Elizabeth Royce, Nov. 28, 1936; children—Richard Royce, William Neil, James Lewis. Civil engr. plant engring. dept. W.Va. Pulp & Paper Co., Mechanicville, N.Y., 1936-37; instr. dept. civil engring. Poly. Inst. Bklyn., 1937-42, asst. prof., 1943-45, asso. prof., 1945-51, dir. evening session, mem. adminstrv. council, 1944-51; designer and detailer, office engr. of structures N.Y.C. R.R., summer 1939; engring. examiner Municipal Civil Service Commn., N.Y.C., summers 1939-51; structural designer Morenci works devel. Phelps Dodge Corp., summer 1940; prof. civil engring., head dept. U. Cin., 1951-58, asso. dean Coll. Engring., 1957-62, dean, 1962-74, prof. Engring. Edn., 1974—. Mem. Ohio Bd. Registration Engrs., 1962-72. Named Cin. Engr. of Year, 1963; recipient Distinguished Service award Nat. Council Engring. Examiners, 1970. Registered profl. engr., Ohio, N.Y., Ky. Fellow Inst. C.E. (U.K.), ASCE (hon. mem.); mem. Engrs. Council Profl. Devel. (chmn. profl. tng. com. 1952-54, 57-59, dir. 1966-73, mem. edn. and accreditation com. 1968-72), Am. Soc. Engring. Edn. (hon. mem.; council 1949, v.p. 1963-65, pres. 1974-75), Am. Nat. Metric Council (dir. 1976—), Nat. Soc. Profl. Engrs., Engring. Soc. Cin. (dir., pres. 1959), Sigma Xi, Omicron Delta Kappa, Alpha Sigma Phi, Tau Beta Pi, Chi Epsilon, Pi Tau Sigma, Triangle. Club: Cosmos. Author: Metric Units in Engineering—Going SI, 1978. contbr. articles to profl. jours. Home: 2930 Scioto St Cincinnati OH 45219

WANDYCZ, PIOTR STEFAN, educator; b. Krakow, Poland, Sept. 20, 1923; s. Damian Stanislaw and Stefania (Dunikowska) W.; B.A., Cambridge U., 1948, M.A., 1952; Ph.D., London, U., 1951; M.A. (hon.), Yale, 1968; m. Maria Teresa Chrzaszcz, Aug. 13, 1963; children—Anna, Joanna, Antoni. Instr. to asso. prof. history Ind. U., 1954-66; fellow Harvard's Russian Research Center, 1963-65; asso. prof. history Yale, 1966-68, prof., 1968—, chmn. Russian and East European council, 1974-76; vis. prof. history Columbia U., 1967, 69, 74. Served as 2d lt. Polish Army, 1942-45. Recipient Alfred Jurzykowski Found. award in history, 1977. Fellow, Guggenheim Found., Ford Found., Rockefeller Found., Am. Philos. Soc., Am. Council Learned Socs., Social Sci. Research Council, Internat. Research and Exchanges Bd. Mem. Am. Hist. Assn. (George Louis Beer prize, 1962), AAAS, Polish Inst. Arts and Scis., Czechoslovak Soc. Arts and Scis. Author: Czechoslovak-Polish Confederation and Great Powers, 1956; France and Her Eastern Allies, 1962; Soviet-Polish Relations, 1969; The Lands of Partitioned Poland, 1974; United States and Poland, 1979; contbr. articles to profl. jours. Home: 27 Spring Garden St Hamden CT 06517 Office: Yale New Haven CT 06520

WANG, AN, computer and word processing systems co. exec.; b. Shanghai, China, Feb. 7, 1920; s. Yin Lu and Zen Wan (Chien) W.; B.S., Chiao Tung U., 1940; M.S., Harvard, 1946, Ph.D., 1948; D.Sc. (hon.), Lowell Inst. Tech, 1971; m. Lorraine Chiu, July 10, 1949; children—Frederick A., Courtney S., Juliette L. Came to U.S., 1945, naturalized, 1954. Tchr., Chiao-Tung U., China, 1940-41; engr. Central Radio Works China, 1941-45; engr. Chinese Govt. Supply Agy., Ottawa, Ont., Can., 1946-47; research fellow Harvard, 1948-51; owner Wang Labs., Cambridge, Mass., 1951-55; chmn. bd., pres., dir. Wang Labs., Inc., Lowell, Mass., 1955—; dir. First Nat. Bank Boston. Mem. corp. Mus. Sci., Boston. Fellow IEEE; mem. Sigma Xi. Patentee in field. Home: Bedford Rd Lincoln MA 01773 Office: Wang Labs Inc 1 Indsl Ave Lowell MA 01851

WANG, ARTHUR WOODS, publisher; b. Port Chester, N.Y., Oct. 7, 1918; s. Israel and Madolin (Woods) W.; B.S., Bowdoin Coll., 1940; postgrad. Columbia U., 1949-51; m. Mary Ellen Mackay, Aug. 13, 1955; 1 son, Michael Anthony. Advt. research McCann-Erickson, Inc., 1940-41; editor Doubleday & Co., 1942-43, Alfred A. Knopf, Inc., 1943, T.Y. Crowell, Pub., 1943-47; with E.M. Hale & Co., Eau Claire, Wis., 1947-52; editor A.A. Wyn, Inc., 1952-56; pres., editor-in-chief Hill & Wang, Inc., 1956-71; editor-in-chief Hill & Wang div. Farrar, Straus & Giroux, Inc., N.Y.C., 1971—, also v.p., dir. corp. Mem. Am. Book Pubs. Council (dir. 1968-70). Club: Players (N.Y.C.). Home: 1035 Fifth Ave New York NY 10028 Office: 19 Union Sq W New York NY 10003

WANG, HAO, philosopher, educator; b. Tsinan, Shantung, China, May 20, 1921; s. Chuchen and Tsecheng (Liu) W.; B.Sc., Southwestern Asso. U., China, 1943; M.A., Tsing Hua U., China, 1945, Balliol Coll., Oxford, 1956; Ph.D., Harvard, 1948; postgrad. Zurich, 1950-51; m. Yenking Kan, June 22, 1948 (div. Mar. 1977); children—Sanyu, Yiming, Jane Hsiaoching; m. 2d, Yu-Shih Chen.

Tchr. math., China, 1943-46; research engr. Burroughs Corp., 1953-54; asst. prof. philosophy Harvard, 1951-56, Gordon McKay prof. math. logic, applied math., 1961-67; John Locke lectr. philosophy U. Oxford, 1954-55, reader philosophy of math., 1956-61; prof. Rockefeller U., 1967—; cons. U. Mich., summers 1956, 57, IBM, summer, 1957, 58, Mass. Inst. Tech., summer 1960, Bell Telephone Labs., 1962-64; mem. tech. staff Bell Telephone Labs., 1959-60; vis. prof. Rockefeller U., 1966-67; vis. scientist IBM Research Labs., 1973-74; visitor Inst. for Advanced Study, 1975-76; lectr. on math. logic, 1979. Jr. fellow Soc. of Fellows, Harvard, 1948-51; fellow Rockefeller Found., 1954-55. Mem. Assn. Symbolic Logic, Am. Acad. Arts and Sci., Brit. Acad. (fgn.). Author: A Survey of Mathematical Logic, 1962; Reflections on China (in Chinese), 1973; From Mathematics to Philosophy, 1974. Contbr. articles to math. philos. jours. Home: 1230 York Ave New York NY 10021

WANG, JAW-KAI, educator; b. Nanking, China, Mar. 4, 1932; s. Shuling and Hsi-Ying (Lo) W.; B.S., Nat. Taiwan U., 1953; M.S. in Agrl. Engring., Mich. State U., 1956, Ph.D., 1958; m. Kwang Mei Chow, Sept. 7, 1957; children—Angela C.C., Dora C.C., Lawrence C.Y. Faculty agrl. engring. dept. U. Hawaii, Honolulu, 1959—, asso. prof., chmn. dept., 1964-68, prof., 1968—, chmn. dept. agrl. engring., 1968-75; pres. Wang & Assos., 1979—; co-dir. internat. sci. and ednl. council U.S. Dept. Agr.; vis. asso. dir. internat. programs and studies office Nat. Assn. State Univs. and Land-Grant Colls., 1979. Vis. prof. Nat. Taiwan U., 1965; cons. U.S. Army Civilian Adminstrn., Ryukus, Okinawa, 1966, Internat. Rice Research Inst., Philippines, 1971, Pacific Concrete and Rock Co. Ltd., 1973, AID, 1973; sr. fellow East-West Center Food Inst., 1973-74. Registered profl. engr., Hawaii. Mem. Am. Soc. Agrl. Engrs. (chmn. Hawaii sect. 1962-63, chmn. grad. instrn. com. 1971-73, chmn. aquacultural engring. com. 1977-79, chmn. Pacific region 1976-77, engr. of yr. 1975, 76, Tech. Paper award 1978), Chinese Soc. Agrl. Engrs., Sigma Xi, Gamma Sigma Delta (pres. Hawaii chpt. 1974-75), Pi Mu Epsilon. Home: 1503 Uluhaku Pl Kailua HI 96734 Office: Dept Agrl Engring U Hawaii Honolulu HI 96822. *To be allowed a continuing search for truth even when you are doubting its existence, is to be blessed.*

WANG, L. EDWIN, ch. ofcl.; b. Medford, Oreg., Nov. 2, 1919; s. Lorang Edwin and Laura (Thomas) W.; extension student U. Calif., 1947-48, U. Minn., 1956-65; L.H.D., Midland Luth. Coll., Fremont, Nebr., 1970; C.L.U., 1960; m. Astrid H. Wikander, Sept. 4, 1942; children—David M., Linnea M., Judith L. Field underwriter, then asst. mgr. Mut. of N.Y., 1943-51; mgr. Standard Ins. Co., Oakland, Calif., 1951-56; exec. sec. Augustana Pension & Aid Fund, Mpls., 1956-62; adminstr. bd. pensions Luth. Ch. Am., 1962—; Acting ins. commr. Minn., 1967; part-time ins. instr. Oakland Jr. Coll., Contra Costa Jr. Coll., 1954-56. Pres., Oakland-East Bay Life Underwriters Assn., 1951, Oakland Mgrs. and Gen. Agts. Assn., 1955, Ch. Pensions Conf., 1967; mem. pensions com. Nat. Council Chs., 1964—; mem. pension research council U. Pa. Wharton Sch. Finance, 1971—; elector of candidates Ins. Hall of Fame. Recipient Outstanding Service award Gov. Minn. Mem. Am. Risk and Ins. Assn., Mpls. Chpt. C.L.U.'s (pres. 1973-74, dir.). Club: Mpls. Athletic (chmn. pension com.). Home: 6013 St Johns Ave Minneapolis MN 55424 Office: 608 2d Ave S Minneapolis MN 55402

WANG, PAUL PAO-SHIH, educator; b. Hsien-Yu, Fukien, China, May 8, 1936; s. Shih Ni and Shih Mei (Lin) W.; came to U.S., 1962, naturalized, 1971; B.Sc., Nat. Taiwan U., 1958; M.Sc., U. N.B. (Can.), 1963; Ph.D., Ohio State U., 1965; m. Julia Yu Haun Yang, Oct. 1, 1962; children—Samuel Wei Teh, George Wei Ben. Teaching asst., research asst. Ohio State U., 1962-65; mem. tech. staff Bell Labs., Inc., 1965-68; asst. prof. Duke U., Durham, N.C., 1968-70, asso. prof., 1970-75, prof. elec. engring., 1975—; cons. safeguard Anti-ballistic missile program Western Electric Corp., 1969-72; advising cons. Chantor Electronics, Inc., Taipei, Taiwan, 1973—; cons. electronics, space div. Emerson Electric Co., St. Louis, 1975; cons. adviser computer energy mgmt. Dept. Adminstrn. State of N.C., 1976—; cons. naval ship nav. problems Western Electric Co., 1978—. Served with Chinese Air Force, 1958-60. NASA-Am. Soc. Engring. Edn. summer faculty fellow 1972-73; NSF summer faculty fellow 1975. Mem. IEEE (sec. treas. chpt. 1970-71; chmn. 1972-73). Editor energy systems Internat. Jour. Public Policy and Info. Sci., 1976—. Contbr. articles to profl. jours. Home: 2709 Montgomery St Durham NC 27706

WANG, PING CHUN, educator; b. Kiangsu, China, Mar. 10, 1920; s. Chin-Shie and Shu-Inn (Shu) W.; came to U.S., 1947, naturalized, 1962; M.S., U. Ill., 1948, Ph.D., 1951; B.S., Nat. Central U. China, 1943; m. Aili Catherine Liu, Aug. 6, 1955; children—Paula, Elise. Jr. engr. China Bridge Co., Chungking, 1943-47; supervising engr. Seelye Stevenson Valvue & Knecht, N.Y.C., 1951-60; asso. prof. Stevens Inst. Tech., 1960-63; faculty N.Y. Poly. Inst., 1963—, prof. civil engring., 1963—. Cons. computer systems in structural engring, 1960—. Fellow ASCE; mem. Am. Concrete Inst., Am. Soc. Engring. Edn., N.Y. Acad. Sci., Sigma Xi. Author: Numerical and Matrix Methods in Structural Mechanics, 1966. Home: 36 East Dr Garden City NY 11530 Office: 333 Jay St Brooklyn NY 11201

WANG, SHIH CHUN, physiologist, educator; b. Tientsin, China, Jan. 10, 1910; s. Yen Sun and Hsi (Han) W.; B.S., Yenching U., 1931; M.D., Peking Union Med. Coll., 1935; Ph.D., Northwestern U., 1940; m. Mamie Kwoh, Jan. 10, 1939; children—Phyllis M., Nancy E. Came to U.S., 1937, naturalized, 1949. Practice medicine specializing in physiology and pharmacology, N.Y.C., 1940—; faculty Columbia Coll. Phys. and Surgs., 1941—, prof. physiology, 1954-56, prof. pharmacology, 1956—, Pfeiffer prof., 1975-79, Pfeiffer prof. emeritus, 1979—; vis. prof. China Med. Bd. Rockefeller Found., Taiwan, 1958. John Guggenheim fellow, 1951; Commonwealth fellow U. Goteborg, Sweden, 1966. Mem. Am. Physiol. Soc., Am. Pharmacol. Soc., N.Y. Acad. Scis., N.Y. Acad. Medicine, Assn. for Research on Nervous and Mental Diseases, Soc. Exptl. Biology and Medicine, Harvey Soc., AAAS, N.Y. State Soc. Med. Research, Sigma Xi. Contbr. chpts. to Handbook of Physiology, 1965, Physiological Pharmacology, 1965. Research, numerous publs. primarily in field physiology and pharmacology of automatic nervous system. Address: 18 Kent Rd Tenafly NJ 07670

WANG, SHIH YI, educator; b. Peking, China, June 15, 1923; s. Yen Chao and Li Hwa (Kung) W.; B.S., Nat. Peking U., 1944; Ph.D., U. Wash., 1952; m. Chun Lien Chi, Aug. 17, 1947; children—Robert Tung-hsing, Ethylin Tung-ying. Came to U.S., 1948, naturalized, 1962. Postdoctoral fellow Boston U., 1952-54; research fellow Harvard, 1954-55; asst. prof. Tufts U. Med. Sch., 1955-61; faculty Johns Hopkins, 1961—, prof. biochemistry, 1966—, prof., dir. div. radiation chemistry, 1976-78, prof., head program in environ. chemistry, dept. environ. health scis., 1977—. Mem. Am. Chem. Soc., Chem. Soc. London, AAAS. Home: 14 Windemere Pkwy Phoenix MD 21131 Office: 615 N Wolfe St Baltimore MD 21205

WANG, WILLIAM KAI-SHENG, educator, lawyer; b. N.Y.C., Feb. 28, 1946; s. Yuan-Chao and Julia Ying-Ru (Li) W.; B.A., Amherst Coll., 1967; J.D., Yale U., 1971; m. Kwan Kwan Tan, July 29, 1972. Admitted to Calif. bar, 1972; asst. to mng. partner Gruss & Co., N.Y.C., 1971-72; asst. prof. law U. San Diego, 1972-74, asso. prof., 1974-77, prof., 1977—; vis. prof. law U. Calif., Davis, 1975-76; cons. to White House Domestic Policy Staff, Washington, 1979. Mem. State Bar Calif., San Diego County Bar Assn., Pan-Asian Lawyers San Diego (founding mem.), Phi Beta Kappa. Contbr. articles to newspapers, mags., scholarly jours. Home: 5225 Edgeworth Rd San Diego CA 92109 Office: U San Diego Sch of Law Alcala Park San Diego CA 92110

WANG, WILLIAM SHI-YUAN, educator; b. Shanghai, China, Aug. 14, 1933; s. Harper and Lily W.; came to U.S., 1948, naturalized, 1960; A.B., Columbia U., 1955; M.A., U. Mich., 1956, Ph.D., 1960; m. Mary Streeter, June 21, 1972; children—Eugene, Yulun, Yumei, Yusi. Asso. prof., chmn. dept. linguistics Ohio State U., Columbus, 1963-65; prof. linguistics U. Calif., Berkeley, 1966—; fellow Center Advanced Studies in Behavioral Scis., 1969-70. Guggenheim Found. fellow, 1978-79. Mem. Linguistic Soc. Am., Acoustical Soc. Am. Editor: The Lexicon in Phonological Change, 1977; co-editor: Individual Differences in Language Ability and Language Behavior, 1979; asso. editor Language, 1967-73; editor Jour. Chinese Linguistics, 1973—; contbr. numerous articles to profl. jours. Office: U Calif 2222 Piedmont Ave Berkeley CA 94720

WANGAARD, ARTHUR CARL, JR., retail food co. exec.; b. Mpls., Aug. 28, 1927; s. Arthur Carl and Mabel Lillian (Gravem) W.; student Case Sch. Applied Sci., 1945-46, U. Louisville, 1946; B.S. in Law, U. Minn., 1950, J.D., 1952; m. Grace M. Lewis, July 21, 1951; children—Deborah, David, John. Admitted to Minn. bar, 1952, U.S. Supreme Ct. bar, 1968; claims adjuster State Farm Mut. Automobile Ins. Co., 1952-55; pvt. practice law, Mpls., 1955-63; With Nash-Finch Co., Mpls., 1955—, asst. sec., gen. counsel, 1963-72, v.p., 1973—. Chmn. Bloomington (Minn.) Liquor Study Commn., 1962; active Boy Scouts Am. Dir. Bloomington Sch. Bd., 1964-67. Served with USNR, 1945-47. Mem. Am., Minn. bar assns., Minn. Corporate Counsel Assn., Minn., Minn. Law Sch. alumni assns., Delta Theta Phi. Republican. Lutheran. Home: 5530 W 93d St Bloomington MN 55437 Office: 3381 Gorham Ave Minneapolis MN 55426

WANGBERG, LOU, lt. gov. Minn.; b. Bemidji, Minn., Mar. 27, 1941; B.S., U. N.D., Grand Forks, 1963, M.S. in Geography, 1964, Ed.D. in Sch. Adminstrn., 1970; m. Jane; 3 children. Tchr. and asst. prin., public schs., Granite Falls, Minn., 1964-66; prin. Cosmos High Sch., Cosmos, Minn., 1966-68; asst. supt. Worthington (Minn.) Public Schs., 1970-72; supt. schs. Bemidji Public Schs., 1972-79; lt. gov. State of Minn., 1979—. Bd. dirs. No. Minn. Public TV. Mem. NAACP, Bemidji C. of C., Bemidji State U. Found., Am. Assn. Sch. Adminstrs., Minn. Assn. Sch. Adminstrs. Independent Republican. Clubs: Masons (past master), Shriners, Rotary, Elks, Sons of Norway. Office: Office lt Gov State Capitol Saint Paul MN 55101*

WANGELIN, HARRIS KENNETH, judge; b. Des Moines, May 10, 1913; s. Fred G. and Pearl Clymer (Harris) W.; grad. Iberia Acad. and Jr. Coll., 1932; student Drury Coll., 1932-33; J.D., U. Mo., 1936; m. Freda Alice Buffington, June 27, 1939; 1 dau., Judith Arleen. Admitted to Mo. bar, 1936, since practiced in Poplar Bluff; judge U.S. Dist. Ct., St. Louis, 1970-79, chief judge Eastern Dist. Mo., 1979—. Mem. Mo. Republican State Com., 1952-66, chmn., 1957-62; chmn. Butler County Rep. Central Com., 1950-58; sec.-treas. Rocky Mountain Midwest Rep. State Chmns. Assn., 1958-62; vice chmn. Mo. Senatorial Re-districting Commn., 1965. Trustee U. Mo. Law Sch. Found., 1972-78. Served as lt. USNR, 1942-45. Decorated Silver Star. Mem. Am., Mo. bar assns., VFW, Amvets, Am. Legion, Delta Theta Phi. Conglist. Home: 10374 Chimney Rock Dr Creve Coeur MO 63141 Office: US Court and Custom House 12th and Market Sts Saint Louis MO 63101

WANGEMAN, FRANK G., hotel exec.; b. Frankfurt-on-Main, Germany, Apr. 20, 1912; s. Franz and Anna Maria (Gruenig) W.; student pub. and pvt. schs. Germany, Switzerland and Eng.; Bachelier es Lettres, Sorbonne U. (Paris); postgrad. work Zaragoza (Spain) U.; Advanced Mgmt Program Harvard; D.Sc. in Bus. Adminstrn. honoris causa, Bryant Coll., 1968; came to U.S., 1934; m. Marie Moyle, May 31, 1946; children—Alberta Ann, Frank Moyle (dec.), Henry Moyle, Marie, Conrad. With hotels in Europe; asst. mgr. Waldorf-Astoria, N.Y.C., 1934-43, exec. v.p., vice chmn. bd. dirs., gen. mgr., 1961—; mgr. Plaza Hotel, N.Y.C., 1943-45; gen. mgr. Town House, Los Angeles, 1945-47, Plaza Hotel, N.Y.C., 1947-49; exec. Hilton Corp., 1945- -, mem. operating com., 1945—, sr. v.p. charge Eastern div., 1962—, also dir. corp.; v.p., gen. mgr. Caribe Hilton, San Juan, P.R., 1949-51; v.p., dir., gen. mgr. Roosevelt Hotel Corp., 1951-53; gen. mgr. Hotel New Yorker, N.Y.C., 1954-56; sr. v.p., dir. Hilton Hotels Corp., Beverly Hills, Calif., 1956-61; dir. Utah Hotel Corp., Fifth Avenue Assn., N.Y.C. Bd. dirs. Radio N.Y. Worldwide; mem. exec. com. Better Bus. Bur. Met. N.Y., N.Y. Conv. and Visitors Bur.; hon. trustee Bryant Coll.; mem. nat. adv. council of exec. com. Hampshire Coll.; mem. com. L'Ecole Hoteliere Lausanne (Switzerland). Mem. Am. Hotel and Motel Assn. (dir.), N.Y.C. Hotel Assn. (past dir.), Wine and Food Soc. N.Y., Confrerie des Chevaliers du Tastevin (officier comdr.), La Chaine des Rotisseurs, Chancellier du Baillage National des U.S.A., Culinary Inst. Am. Lutheran. Club: Quaker Hill Country (Pawling, N.Y.); Bohemian (San Francisco). Contbr. articles to profl. jours. Address: Waldorf Astoria New York NY 10022

WANGSGARD, ROBERT LOUIS, retail food co. exec.; b. Brigham City, Utah, Dec. 22, 1915; s. Louis and Ione (Maughan) W.; B.S., Utah State U., 1938; M.B.A., Harvard, 1940; m. Patricia Wallace, Sept. 6, 1939; children—Robert Kent, Lynne (Mrs. Richard Sadler), Jo Ann (Mrs. Alan Crane), Ruth (Mrs. Dan Vaughan). Pub. accountant, Ogden, Utah, 1940-48; pres. Stimson's Inc., Ogden, 1948—; vice chmn. bd. Asso. Food Stores, Inc., Salt Lake City, 1964—; chmn. bd. Mchts., Inc., Salt Lake City, 1958—. Mem. Ogden Execs. Assn. (pres. 1954—), Ogden C. of C. Kiwanian (pres. 1970-71). Club: Ogden Knife and Fork (pres. 1962—). Home: 3055 Circle Way Ogden UT 84403 Office: 2784 Jefferson St Ogden UT 84403

WANGSNESS, ROALD KLINKENBERG, educator, physicist; b. Sleepy Eye, Minn., July 24, 1922; s. Gudbrand K. and Katherine (Fromm) W.; student St. Olaf Coll., 1940-41; B.A. summa cum laude, U. Minn., 1944; Ph.D. (AEC predoctoral fellow), Stanford, 1950; m. Cleo M. Abbott, July 29, 1944; children—Peter A.A., Steven J. Asst. prof. U. Md., College Park, 1950-51, prof., 1953-59; physicist U.S. Naval Ordnance Lab., Silver Spring, Md., 1950-59; prof. U. Ariz., Tucson, 1959—. Recipient Meritorious Civilian Service award USN, 1957. Fellow Am. Phys. Soc., AAAS; mem. Am. Assn. Physics Tchrs., Phi Beta Kappa, Sigma Xi. Author: Introduction to Theoretical Physics, 1963; Introductory Topics in Theoretical Physics, 1963; Electromagnetic Fields, 1979. Home: 5035 E Scarlett St Tucson AZ 85711

WANK, GERALD SIDNEY, dentist; b. Bklyn., Jan. 20, 1925; s. Joseph and Sadie (Ikowitz) W.; B.A., N.Y. U., 1945, D.D.S., 1949; cert. in orthodontia, Columbia U., 1951, cert. in periodontia, 1956; m. Gloria Baum, June 4, 1949; children—David, Stephen, Daniel. Intern in oral surgery Bellevue Hosp., 1949-50; practice dentistry specializing in oral rehab. and periodontal prosthetics, N.Y.C., Great Neck, N.Y., 1949—; instr. dept. periodontia, oral medicine N.Y. U. Dental Sch., 1956-63, asst. clin. prof. dept. periodontia, 1963-67, asst. prof. periodontia, oral medicine, former postgrad. dir. periodontal-prosthesis dept. fixed partial prosthesis, clin. asso. prof. periodontia, oral medicine, 1970-77, clin. prof., 1977—, postgrad. dir. periodontia, 1968-71; staff lectr. periodontology Harvard U. Sch. Dental Medicine, 1973-74; vis. lectr. Albert Einstein Coll. Medicine, N.Y.C. Community Coll. Sch. Dental Hygiene; asst. attending staff North Shore Univ. Hosp., 1974-77, sr. asst. attending div. surgery, 1977—; cons. orthodontic panel N.Y. State, N.Y.C. depts. health; former postgrad. instr. 1st Dist. Dental Soc. Postgrad. Sch.; lectr. various socs., N.Y. U.; mem. com. admissions N.Y. U. Coll. Dentistry, 1975—, chmn. fund raising, 1976—. Served to capt. USAF, 1953-55. Fellow Acad. Gen. Dentistry, N.Y. Acad. Dentistry, Internat. Coll. Dentists, Am. Coll. Dentists, Am. Acad. Oral Medicine (pres. N.Y. sect. 1971-72), Am. Public Health Assn.; mem. N.Y. Coll. Dentists (dir.), Dental Soc. N.Y.C. (dir. 1st dist.), Fedn. Dentaire Internat., Am. Assn. Dental Schs., N.Y. State Public Health Assn., AAUP, Pan Am. Med. Assn. (life), AAAS, ADA, Am. Acad. Periodontology, Sci. Research Soc. Am., Northeastern Soc. Periodontia, Am. Acad. Dental Medicine, Acad. Gen. Dentistry, Internat. Acad. Orthodontia, N.Y. U. Coll. Dentistry Alumni Assn. (dir., sec. 1973-74, v.p. 1974-75, pres. 1976-77), Am. Soc. Anesthesiology, Am. Assn. Endodontists, N.Y. U. Coll. Dentistry Dental Assos. (charter), Acad. Oral Rehab. (hon.), N.Y. U. Gallatin Assos., Alumni Fedn. N.Y. U. (dir. 1976-80), Omicron Kappa Upsilon, Alpha Omega. Jewish. Clubs: Fresh Meadow Country (Great Neck, N.Y.); N.Y. U, Century (charter N.Y. U. Coll. Dentistry), Masons. Contbr. to Practice of Periodontia, 1960; Dental Clinics of North America, 1972; Manual of Clinical Periodontics, 1973; contbr. articles to profl. jours. Home: 40 Bayview Ave Great Neck NY 11021 Office: 40 Bayview Ave Great Neck NY 11021 also 14 E 60th St New York NY 10022

WANKELMAN, WILLARD FRED, educator; b. Cin., May 21, 1916; s. Fred and Alma (Hammler) W.; B.Sc., Ohio State U., 1938, M.A., 1940; m. Jane Sargeant, Sept. 21, 1940; children—Willard Warren. Asst. instr. art Ohio State U., 1940-41; supr. art Port Clinton (Ohio) Pub. Schs., 1941-44; asst. prof. State Coll. Wash., 1944-46; dir. Sch. Art Bowling Green State U., 1946-72, trustee prof., 1972—. Guest prof. U. Hawaii, summer 1959; art editor William C. Brown Pub., Dubuque, Iowa; dir. 1st Fed. Savs. & Loan Assn., Bowling Green. named hon. alumnus Bowling Green State U., hon. letterman, 1978. Mem. Mid-Am. Coll. Art Assn. (pres. 1970), NEA, Ohio Edn. Assn., Ohio Art Educators, Am. Assn. U. Profs., Bowling Green C. of C., Phi Delta Theta, Delta Phi Delta, Omicron Delta Kappa. Mason, Kiwanian. Club: Internat. Torch. Author: Birds, 1942; Big Things, 1942; My First Book, 1942. Co-author: Arts and Crafts for Elementary Teachers. 1954; A Handbook of Arts and Crafts, 1960, 4th edit., 1977. Home: 864 Scott Blvd Bowling Green OH 43402

WANN, ANDREW JACKSON, educator; b. Humansville, Mo., Oct. 2, 1919; s. Homer Bell and Dora (George) W.; A.B. summa cum laude, Drury Coll., 1940; postgrad. Johns Hopkins, 1941-42; Ph.D., U. Mo., 1961; m. Anneliese Scheidacher, June 18, 1948; children—Lotti Ann, Kristin Kay. News commentator radio stas. KWTO, Springfield, Mo., 1939-41; instr. Coll. William and Mary, 1946-48, U. Mo., 1948-51; dir. inter-univ. program govt. and labor U. Wis., 1951-52; asst. prof., then asso. prof. U. Ill., 1952-64; prof., dir. labor edn. and research Ohio State U., 1964-68; prof., dept. polit. sci. U. Utah, Salt Lake City, 1968—, chmn. dept., 1968-74. Lectr., South Africa and S.W. Africa, State Dept., 1959-60; spl. Investigator Germany and France, Com. Fgn. Affairs U.S. Ho. of Reps., 1947-48; labor arbitrator Am. Arbitration Assn., Fed. Mediation and Conciliation Service, 1965—. Bd. dirs. Ohio Council Econ. Edn., 1965-68, Utah Soc. Pub. Adminstrn., 1970-72. Served to capt. AUS, 1942-46. Mem. Am., Western (exec. council 1971-74), Internat. polit. sci. assns., Indsl. Relations Research Assn., Am. Soc. Pub. Adminstrn., Am. Assn. U. Profs. (mem. exec. bd. Utah chpt. 1976-78), Pi Gamma Mu, Sigma Tau Delta, Kappa Alpha. Democrat. Author: The American Federation of Labor and International Affairs, 1952; (with others) The Philosophy and Policies of Woodrow Wilson, 1958; Unions and Politics in the United States, 1959; The Illinois Legislature Faces Reapportionment, 1963; The President as Chief Administrator, 1968. Home: 2628 E 13th S Salt Lake City UT 84108

WANNAMAKER, WILLIAM WHETSTONE, JR., former engr., gen. contractor; b. Orangeburg, S.C., May 18, 1900; s. William Whetstone and Lyall (Matheson) W.; B.S., The Citadel, 1919, C.E., 1929, D.Engring. (hon.), 1966; C.E., Cornell U., 1921; m. Evelyn Townsend, Sept. 3, 1925; children—William III, Mary (Mrs. George Morris), Evelyn (Mrs. J.T. Richards). Draftsman, insp., resident engr. S.C. Hwy. Dept., 1921-27; pres. Wannamaker & Wells, Inc., gen. contractors, Orangeburg, S.C., 1928-58, chmn. bd., 1959-69; v.p. Wateree Chem. Co., Inc., Lugoff, S.C. Mem. Republican Nat. Com., 1956-66; del. Rep. Nat. Conv., 1956, 60, 64. Bd. visitors The Citadel, 1946-66, vice chmn., 1960. Recipient Algernon Sidney Sullivan award, 1957. Served with C.E.C., USNR, 1940-45. Mem. ASCE (life), Assn. Governing Bds. (v.p. 1961-62), Sigma Alpha Epsilon. Club: Army and Navy (Washington). Author: A Story of American Flags, 1971; Long Island South, 1975. Home: 1225 Broughton St NW Orangeburg SC 29115

WANNER, JAMES EMERSON, fin. co. exec.; b. Marion, Ohio, Sept. 7, 1930; s. William Peter and Edith Marie (Hecker) W.; B.A., Miami U., Oxford, Ohio, 1952; J.D., Western Res. U., 1955; m. Peggy Louise Clary, June 15, 1952; children—Leslie Ann, Peggy Sue, Jani Beth, Heidi Jo. Admitted to Ohio bar, 1955; with Sunamerica Fin. Corp. and affiliates, Cleve., 1955—; gen. counsel, sr. v.p., sec., dir. Sunamerica Corp. and subsidiaries, 1967—. Active local Boy Scouts Am., Girl Scouts; fin. chmn. Olmsted Community Ch., Olmsted Falls, Ohio, 1963-64, 68-70, council chmn., 1966-67, 77-78. Mem. Nat. Consumer Fin. Assn. (law com.), Ga. Consumer Fin. Assn. (dir.), Ohio Bar Assn., Tax Club Cleve., Phi Alpha Delta. Republican. Club: Olmsted Falls Kiwanis (chmn. internat. relations com. 1978-79). Office: 1015 Euclid Ave Cleveland OH 44115

WANNIER, GREGORY HUGH, physicist, educator; b. Basel, Switzerland, Dec. 30, 1911; s. Eugene Oskar and Clara (Stachelin) W.; came to U.S., 1937, naturalized, 1943; student U. Basel, 1930-35, Ph.D., 1935; Univ. student Louvain (Belgium), 1930-31, Cambridge (Eng.) U., 1933-34; m. Carol Goodman, Sept. 21, 1939; 1 son, Peter Gregory. Exchange fellow Princeton U., 1936-37; instr. U. Pitts., 1937-38; lectr. U. Bristol (Eng.), 1938-39; instr. U. Tex., 1939-41; lectr. U. Iowa, 1941-46; mem. staff Socony-Facuum Labs., 1946-48; mem. tech. staff Bell Telephone Labs., Murray Hill, N.J., 1948-60; prof. U. Geneva, 1955-56; prof. physics U. Oreg., Eugene, 1961-77, prof. emeritus, 1977—. Recipient Humboldt Found. award, 1974. Fellow Am. Phys. Soc.; mem. Swiss Phys. Soc. Author: Elements of Solid State Theory, 1959; Statistical Physics, 1966. Home: 2000 University St Eugene OR 97403

WANOUS, EDWARD ELMER, publishing exec.; b. Owatonna, Minn., Jan. 31, 1920; s. Samuel A. and Rose (Stursa) W.; student U. Ariz., 1939-41; B.A., Minn. State U., 1942; postgrad. U. Calif., Los Angeles, 1945-46; m. Kathryn Magnetti, Dec. 18, 1949; 1 dau., Deborah. Pres., treas., chmn. bd. Southwestern Pub. Co., Cin., 1947—. Served with USNR, 1943-45. Club: Kenwood Country (Cin.). Author: Introduction to Data Processing, 1967; Fundamentals of Data Processing, 1971; Automation Office Practice, 1966; Basic Typing Drills, 1967. Home: 8375 Arapalo Ln Cincinnati OH 45243 Office: 5105 Madison Rd Cincinnati OH 45227

WANTY, VERNON, community coll. pres.; b. Sheffield, Eng., May 18, 1918; came to U.S., 1950, naturalized, 1952; s. Harry and Emma (Bennett) W.; B.A., Westminster (Pa.) Coll., 1954; M.A., Mich. State U., 1957, Ph.D. (Kellogg Found. fellow 1963-64), 1967; m. Mary Margaret Blackwood, June 27, 1945; 1 dau., Margaret Blackwood. Partner, Wanty & Co., Catcliffe, Eng., 1946-50; editor New Wilmington (Pa.) Globe, 1952-54; public relations dir. Westminster Coll., 1954-57; dean Middlesex County (N.J.) Coll., 1967-70; mem. faculty Kellogg Community Coll., Battle Creek, Mich., 1958-60, Towson (Md.) State Coll., 1960-67; pres. Essex Community Coll., Balt., 1970—; pres. Health and Edn. Council, Balt.; mem. health services com. Md. Health Coordinating Council. Served with Brit. Army, 1939-46. Gen. Foods Corp. faculty fellow, summer 1959; Danforth Found. faculty fellow, summer 1962. Mem. Am. Assn. Community and Jr. Colls., Md. Assn. Jr. Colls., Md. Council Community Coll. Presidents, Md. Hist. Soc., St. George's Soc. Govs. (pres. bd. govs. 1979-80), Balt. County C. of C. (dir.), Essex-Middle River C. of C. (dir.), Phi Delta Kappa, Sigma Delta Chi. Democrat. Presbyterian. Club: Hopkins. Author papers in field. Home: 315 Dixie Dr Towson MD 21204 Office: Essex Community Coll Baltimore MD 21237

WAPIENNIK, CARL FRANCIS, planetarium, sci. inst. ofcl.; b. Donora, Pa., Oct. 10, 1926; s. Karl and Rose (Kidzinski) W.; B.S., U. Pitts., 1953; m. Elva Louise Bartron, Nov. 27, 1953; children—Carl Eric, Ellen Louise. Prodn. supr. RCA, Canonsburg, Pa., 1953-54; staff physicist Buhl Planetarium and Inst. Popular Sci., Pitts., 1954-64, exec. dir., 1964—. Mem. Rostraver Twp. Planning Commn., 1965-67; adv. bd. Allegheny C. of C. (formerly North Side Pitts. C. of C.), 1966-67, dir. 1968—, pres., 1970; mem. adv. council Salvation Army, 1978—. Served with USNR, 1945-46. Recipient Man of the Year award in sci. Pitts. Jaycees, 1969. Mem. Pitts. Bapt. Assn. (bd. dirs. 1976—), Phi Beta Kappa, Sigma Pi Sigma. Patentee means for controlling liquid flow. Home: Salem Church Rd RD 4 Box 227 Belle Vernon PA 15012 Office: Buhl Planetarium Inst Popular Sci Allegheny Sq Pittsburgh PA 15212

WARD, AILEEN, author, educator; b. Newark; d. Waldron Merry and Aline Toppin (Coursen) Ward; A.B., Smith Coll., 1940; M.A., Radcliffe Coll., 1942, Ph.D., 1953; Litt.D., Skidmore Coll., 1973. Teaching fellow Radcliffe Coll., 1943-45; instr. English, Wellesley Coll., 1946-47, Barnard Coll., 1947-49; asso. Inst. Internat. Edn., 1952, Fund Advancement Edn., 1953; asst. prof. Vassar Coll., 1954-58; faculty Sarah Lawrence Coll., 1960-64; prof. English, Brandeis U., Waltham, Mass., 1964-75, 78-79; prof. English, N.Y. U., 1975-78, Albert Schweitzer prof. humanities, 1980—. Fulbright fellow Girton Coll., Cambridge (Eng.) U., 1949-50; Shirley Farr fellow Am. Assn. U. Women, 1958-59; Guggenheim fellow, 1966-67; Radcliffe Inst. fellow, 1970-71. Author: John Keats: The Making of a Poet (Duff Cooper meml. prize non-fiction 1963, Nat. Book award arts and letters 1964, Rose Mary Crawshay prize Brit. Acad. 1964), 1963. Office: NY Inst Humanities 19 University Pl New York NY 10003

WARD, ARTHUR ALLEN, JR., educator, neurol. surgeon; b. Manipay, Ceylon, Feb. 4, 1916; s. Arthur A. and Alice (Bookwalter) W.; B.A., Yale, 1938, M.D., 1942; m. Janet L. Miller, Dec. 20, 1941; children—Sally L., Linda A. Intern, Mary Imogene Bassett Hosp., Cooperstown, N.Y., 1942-43; neuropathol. fellow McGill U., 1943, neurosurg. intern, 1944, resident neurology and neurosurgery, 1944-45; research asst. physiology Yale, 1945; instr. neurosurgery U. Louisville Sch. Medicine, 1946-47; faculty U. Wash. Sch. Medicine, 1948—, prof. neurol. surgery, 1965—, chmn. dept., 1965—; chief neurol. service Univ. Hosp., Harborview Med. Center; cons. VA Hosp. (all Seattle). Cons. Dept. Health, Edn. and Welfare, NIH, NSF. Diplomate Am. Bd. Neurol. Surgery, Nat. Bd. Med. Examiners. Mem. Harvey Cushing Soc., Am. Acad. Neurol. Surgery (pres. 1977-78), Am. Neurol. Assn. (v.p. 1972-73), Am. Acad. Neurology, Am. Electroencephalographic Soc. (pres. 1960), Am. Physiol. Soc., Assn. Research Nervous and Mental Disease, Soc. Neurol. Surgery (pres. 1974-75), Am. Bd. Neurol. Surgery, Am. Epilepsy Soc. (pres. 1971-72), Western Inst. Epilepsy, AAAS, Western Neurosurg. Soc. (pres. 1966), Western Soc. Electroencephalography (pres. 1957), N.W. Soc. Neurology and Psychiatry, Seattle Neurol. Soc., Seattle Surg. Soc., Research Soc. Neurol. Surgeons, Sigma Xi, Alpha Omega Alpha. Editor-in-chief Epilepsia; mem. adv. bd. Jour. Neurosurgery, Neurology, Rev. Surgery. Home: 4001 NE Belvoir Pl Seattle WA 98105

WARD, ARTHUR GEORGE, advt. agy. exec.; b. N.Y.C., Feb. 1, 1927; s. Arthur G. and Genevieve (De Phillips) W.; student Amherst Coll., 1945, U.S. Mil. Acad., 1945; A.B., Pa. State U., 1949; m. Rita A. Close, July 2, 1951 (dec.); children—Kevin Gerard, Heather Patricia, Jeffrey Regan; m. Adeline Petito, Feb. 1, 1976; stepchildren—Margaret Rose, Barbara Ann, Caroline Annellen, Catherine. Advt. asst. Nassau Daily Rev. Star, 1949; asst. advt. mgr. Montgomery Ward, 1950-51; account exec. Hallicy & Harper, 1951-52; co-founder, gen. partner Gamut Advt., Hempstead, N.Y., 1952-55; pres., chmn. bd. Gamut Internat., Ltd., Hempstead, 1955—, Gamut de P.R., Inc., San Juan, 1970—; chmn. bd., pres. Gamut Agy., Inc., Hempstead, 1972—; pres., owner Simultest, Inc., Hempstead, 1968—, Res. Equities, Ltd., 1970—, Hendrickson Pub. Co.; pub. World Conv. Dates Mag.; dir. Communiplex, Inc., Gamut-Mitchell, Inc.; cons. Nassau County, Suffolk County, Tri-State Transp. Commn., N.Y. Dept. Transp., Dowling Coll., Molloy Coll., WOR N.Y. Radio and Suburban Broadcasting Corp., L.I., L.I. R.R., Newsday. Exec. dir. L.I. Festival of Arts, 1966; bd. dirs. Nassau Conv. and Visitors Bur. Mem. L.I. Advt. Club (co-founder, 1st sec. 1953—, past dir.), L.I. Pub. Relations Assn., Sigma Delta Chi. Home: Woodedge Brookville NY 11545 Office: 79 Washington St Hempstead NY 11550

WARD, BALDWIN HELFRICH, editor, pub.; b. Toledo, June 14, 1912; s. Harry Jacob and Grace Dell (Barker) W.; B.A. (Cleve. Yale Alumni scholar, Sterling Meml. scholar), Yale U., 1934; m. Kathryn Cleveland, June 27, 1934; children—Joanne Morse, Tom Ward, Wendy McGrath. Editor, East Orange (N.J.) Record, 1934-35; with Time, Inc., 1935-42, 45-58; West Coast mgr. Fortune Mag., 1945-57; editor, pub. Founded Year Inc., pub. News Front Mag., Year Pictorial News, history books, News Front Databank, N.Y.C., 1958—. Trustee Yale in China, Internat. YMCA. Served to 1st lt., USMCR, 1942-45. Clubs: Yale of N.Y., University, Los Angeles Country. Editor: Year's Ency. News Annual Series; Pictorial History of America; Pictorial History of the World; Pictorial History of Religions; Science and Engineering; Pictorial History of the Black American; Turbulent 20th Century; Nostalgia; Incredible Decade (1960-1970); The Great Innovators: The Anatomy of Change; Historic Decade (1950-60); Image of the Future (1970-2000); Contest for Power; News Front Directory of the 40,000 Leading Corporations. Home: 286 Sunnyslope Rd Petaluma CA 94952 Office: News Front Mag Box 380 Petaluma CA 94952

WARD, BERNARD JAMES, lawyer; b. New Orleans, Aug. 31, 1925; s. Albert James and Maude Marie (Bernard) W.; A.B., Loyola U., New Orleans, 1944, LL.B., 1949; LL.M., Yale U., 1954; m. Elaine McMurray, Aug. 5, 1948; children—Bernard James, Margaret Eleanor. Admitted to La. bar, 1949; asst. prof. law U. Notre Dame, 1954-58, asso. prof., 1958-62, prof., 1962-68; prof. U. Tex., Austin, 1968—, Thomas Watt Gregory prof. law, 1970—; reporter to adv. com. on appellate and civil roles Jud. Conf. U.S., 1961-78, mem. com. on roles, 1978—. Served to lt. (j.g.) USNR, 1944-46. Mem. La. Bar Assn., Am. Law Inst. Roman Catholic. Author: (with J.W. Moore) U.S. Courts of Appeals: Jurisdiction and Practice, 1970. Home: 4308 Far West Austin TX 78731 Office: 2500 Red River Austin TX 78705

WARD, CHARLES, actor, singer, dancer; b. Los Angeles, Aug. 24, 1952; s. Lee Charles and Olive Hannah (Conboy) W.; student pub. schs. With Houston Ballet, 1970-72; mem. Am. Ballet Theatre, N.Y.C., 1972—, mem. corps de ballet, 1972-74, soloist, 1974-76, prin. dancer, 1976—; film appearance in The Turning Point, 1977; star musical Dancin', Broadway, 1978; guest appearances throughout U.S. Mem. Am. Guild Mus. Artists, Screen Actors Guild, Actors Equity. Office: 888 7th Ave New York NY 10019

WARD, DANIEL P., justice Ill. Supreme Ct.; b. Chgo., Aug. 30, 1918; s. Patrick and Jane (Convery) W.; student St. Viator Coll., 1936-38; J.D., DePaul U., 1941, L.H.D., 1976; LL.D., John Marshall Law Sch., 1972; m. Marilyn Corleto, June 23, 1951; children—Mary Jane, John, Susan, Elizabeth. Admitted to Ill. bar, 1941; asst. prof. law Southeastern U., 1941-42; pvt. practice law, 1945-48; asst. U.S. atty. No. Dist. Ill., 1948-54, chief criminal div., 1951-54; with Eardley & Ward, Chgo., 1954-55; dean DePaul U. Coll. Law, 1955-60; states atty. Cook County, Ill., 1960-66; judge Supreme Ct. Ill., 1966—, chief justice, 1975-78; chmn. Ill. Cts. Commn., 1969-73. Served with AUS, 1942-45. Mem. Am. Fed., Ill., Chgo. bar assns. Roman Catholic. Office: Richard J Daley Center Chicago IL 60602

WARD, DAVID HARRIS, petroleum co. exec.; b. Kansas City, Mo., May 13, 1933; s. John Harris and Mary Godwin (Van Etten) W.; grad. Phillips Exeter Acad., 1951; B.A., Harvard, 1955, LL.B. cum laude, 1960; m. Rosemary Spencer, Sept. 2, 1968; 1 dau., Vanessa; children by previous marriage—April, David. Admitted to Ill. bar, 1960; law clk. to Justice Walter Schaefer, Supreme Ct. Ill., 1960-61; asso. firm Sidley & Austin, Chgo., 1961-69; dep. undersec. army internat. affairs, Washington, 1970-71; spl. rep. U.S. with rank of ambassador for Interoceanic Canal Negotiations, 1972-73; ofcl. Mobil Oil Corp., N.Y.C., 1973—. Governing mem. Chgo. Orch. Assn., 1965—; pres. men's council, trustee Art Inst. Chgo., 1968-69; dir., mem. exec. com. Planned Parenthood Chgo., 1963-66. Served as lt. (j.f.) USNR, 1955-57. Mem. Am., Chgo. bar assns. Author: The Legal Effect of Merger and Asset Sale Agreements before Shareholder Approval. Home: 136 E 79th St New York City NY 10021 Office: 150 E 42d St New York City NY 10017

WARD, DONALD BUTLER, clergyman; b. Boston, June 15, 1919; s. Donald Butler and Emma (Lyons) W.; student Yankton Coll., 1937-39; B.S., Northwestern U., 1942; M.Div., U. Chgo., 1959; D.D., Lakeland Coll., 1964; LL.D., Morningside Coll., 1964; m. Vera Barbara Bantz, June 10, 1944; children—Vera Margaret Ward McCarty, Laura Ann, Christopher Donald. Radio performer-producer, 1942-49; television performer-producer, 1949-51; television account exec. Blair TV Assos., Chgo., 1951-54, mgr., 1954-56; ordained to ministry Congl. Ch., 1959; minister First Congl. Ch. of Ravenswood, Chgo., 1958-60, Kirk of Bonnie Brae, Denver, 1960-62, First Congl. Ch., Evanston, Ill., 1970-79; v.p. Alaska Pacific U., Anchorage, 1979—; commentator Viewpoint, daily radio program, 1978-79. Pres., Yankton (S.D.) Coll., 1962-70; past pres. Tri-State Conf., S.D. Found Pvt. Colls.; chmn. bd. Colls. of Mid-Am., Consortium of Ten Colls. Bd. dirs. Chgo. Theol. Sem., Mental Health Assn. Named Man of Year, First Congl. Ch. Evanston, 1956. Mem. Evanston Hist. Soc., Aircraft Owners and Pilots Assn., Nat. Speakers Assn., Sigma Chi (gov.; Constantine award). Mason (32 deg., Shriner), Kiwanian. Club: University (Chgo.). Author: Not The Scabbard But The Blade, 1965; The Underground Church Is Nonsense, 1969; Master Sermon Series, 1973. Composer: The Bell In The Tower, 1965. Home: 6944 Gemini Dr Anchorage AK 99504 Office: Alaska Pacific U Anchorage AK 99504

WARD, DONOVAN FREDERICK, surgeon; b. Dubuque, Iowa, Nov. 30, 1904; s. Marmaduke and Margaret (Goard) W.; student U. Dubuque, 1923-25; M.D., U. Iowa, 1930; m. Marjorie Mary Plass, Jan. 23, 1927; children—Janice Louise (Mrs. John W. Kinder), Sarah Ann (Mrs. Richard M. Wilke), John Thomas. Intern, St. Mary's Hosp., Detroit, 1930-31; practice medicine specializing in surgery, Dubuque, 1931-34, 37-41, 45—; staff Finley Hosp.; med. cons. adv. bd. Bur. Vet. Medicine, U.S. FDA. Dir. Life Investors, Inc.; sec., dir. Life Investors Ins. Co. Am.; pres. Key City Bank & Trust Co., 1970-74, chmn. bd., 1971-73. Co-organizer, pres. Dubuque council Navy League, 1964. Mem. adv. bd. Salvation Army, YWCA. Served to comdr. M.C., USNR, 1942-46. Recipient Distinguished Service award U. Iowa, 1965; named Ky. col., adm. Nebr. Navy; mem. De Molay Legion of Honor, Fellow A.C.S., Internat. Coll. Surgeons; mem. AMA (past pres., v.p. 1963-64), Iowa, Dubuque County (past pres.) med. socs., Iowa Clin. Surg. Soc. (past pres.), Assn. Mil. Surgeons U.S., Am. Soc. Abdominal Surgeons, Assn. Am. Physicians and Surgeons, Am. Cancer Soc., Iowa Dental Assn. (hon.), U. Iowa Alumni Assn. (past pres.), Ret. Officers Assn., Mil. Order World Wars, VFW (past post comdr.), Sagamore of Wabash (chief), Am. Legion. Lion (past pres.), Elk (exalted ruler, trustee, hon. life). Club: Dubuque Golf and Country. Co-author: Effective Medical Assisting. Co-editor: Iowa Cancer Manual, 1949. Home: 2355 Coventry Park Dubuque IA 52001 Office: Dubuque Bldg Dubuque IA 52001

WARD, DOUGLAS ALAN, lawyer; b. Cleve., Oct. 23, 1946; s. Benjamin Henry and Lillian Ann (Holzheimer) W.; A.B., Duke U., 1968; J.D., U. Fla., 1971; m. Judith Ann Hanna, Aug. 3, 1968; children—Shanna Kerry, Kristen Ann. Admitted to Fla. bar, 1971, since practiced in Jacksonville; partner firm Rogers, Towers, Bailey, Jones & Gay, 1977—; sec. Gulf Life Ins. Co., Jacksonville, 1974—. Mem. Am., Jacksonville bar assns. Clubs: Deerwood, University (Jacksonville). Contbr. articles to legal jours. Home: 1740 Challen Ave Jacksonville FL 32205 Office: 1300 Florida Title Bldg Jacksonville FL 32202

WARD, DOUGLAS TURNER, actor, playwright; b. Burnside, La., May 5, 1930; student U. Mich. Broadway participation A Raisin in the Sun, 1959, One Flew Over the Cuckoo's Nest, OB in The Iceman Cometh, The Blacks, Pullman Car Hiawatha, Bloodknot, Happy Ending, Day of Absence, Kongi's Harvest, Ceremonies in Dark Old Men; Author: Day of Absence, 1965, Happy Ending, 1965 (Vernon Rice award and Obie awards); The Harangues; The Reckoning; River Niger; The Bronsville Raid; The Offering. Address: care Actors Equity Assn 165 W 46th St New York NY 10036*

WARD, DUDLEY AVERY, corp. exec.; b. Hingham, Mass., Sept. 30, 1922; s. Charles G. and Cornelia A. (Avery) W.; B.S., U. Pa., 1947; M.B.A., Harvard, 1955; m. Betsy Doble, Sept. 18, 1943; children—Sarah Abby, Jonathan Dudley. With Scott Paper Co., 1947-64, cashier, 1952-55, asst. treas., 1955-58, treas., 1958-64; v.p. finance and adminstrn. Budd Co., 1964-74, vice chmn. bd., 1974—, also dir.; dir. No. States Bancorp., A.V.C. Corp., Phila., Phila. Mfrs. Mut. Ins. Co., Pneumatic Scale Corp., Quincy, Mass., City Nat. Bank, Detroit. Trustee, William Beaumont Hosp., Royal Oak, Mich., Wells Coll., Aurora, N.Y. Served from ensign to lt. (j.g.) USNR, 1942-45. Mem. Citizens Research Council Mich. (dir.), Sigma Alpha Epsilon. Clubs: Bloomfield Hills Country; Detroit, Economic (Det.). Home: 130 Lake Park Dr Birmingham MI 48009 Office: 3155 W Big Beaver Rd Troy MI 48084

WARD, ELMER L., apparel exec.; b. Boston, Mass., Feb. 25, 1898; s. Lawrence Stephen and Mary (O'Connell) W.; grad. Boston English High Sch., 1916; m. Alice G. Brown, Aug. 14, 1924; children—Elmer L., Lawrence W., William A., Robert B. Mem. firm Forte-Moran Co., Boston, 1921-24, Campbell-Ward Co., Boston, 1924-31; gen. mgr. Goodall Co., Sanford, Me., 1931-35, pres., 1935-44, pres. Goodall-Sanford, Inc. (merger Sanford Mills and Goodall Worsted Co.), 1944-54; pres. Goodall Fabrics, Inc., 1944-54; pres. Palm Beach Co. (Goodall Co.), 1955-68, chmn. bd., chief exec. officer, 1968—. Knight, Order Malta. Mem. Men's Fashion Assn. Am. (dir.). Republican. Roman Catholic. Clubs: Algonquin (Boston); New York Athletic (N.Y.C.); Seminole Golf, Everglades (Fla.). Won N.E. amateur golf championship, 1930. Home: Kennebunk Beach ME 04045 Office: Palm Beach Co 400 Pike Cincinnati OH 45202 also: New York City NY

WARD, GEORGE HENRY, educator, botanist; b. Withrow, Wash., Nov. 28, 1916; s. Clyde Eric and Laura (Fournie) W.; B.S. in Agr., Wash. State Coll., 1940, M.S. in Botany, 1948; Ph.D. in Biology, Stanford, 1952; m. Anne Markgraf, Dec. 22, 1946; children—Karen Anne, Barbara Lynne. Tchr. vocational agr. Columbia Union High Sch., White Salmon, Wash., 1940-42; acting instr. biology Stanford, 1952-54; faculty Knox Coll., Galesburg, Ill., 1954—, prof. biology, 1966—, chmn. dept., 1955-71. Vis. prof. botany Wash. State U., summers 1962, 64, 66, 70. Served with AUS, 1943-45. Mem. Bot. Soc. Am., Calif. Bot. Soc., Calif., Ill. acads. sci., AAAS, Sigma Xi. Contbr. articles to profl. jours. Research plant taxonomy, especially genus Artemisia. Home: 1036 Jefferson St Galesburg IL 61401

WARD, GEORGE THORPE, former paper co. exec.; b. DeFuniak Springs, Fla., Dec. 7, 1907; s. George Washington and Ella (Jernigan) W.; B.S. in Civil Engring., Va. Mil. Inst., 1928; m. Alberta Poppell, May 11, 1931; children—Janis Ward Phillips, Frances Ward Oppenheimer, George T. With Fla. Rd. Dept., 1929-30; with Internat. Paper Co., 1930-72, v.p., 1958-62, exec. v.p., 1962-72, dir., 1963-72. Methodist. Clubs: Country of Mobile, Lake Forest Country, Dennis Lake (Mobile). Home: 126 Eaton Sq Mobile AL 36608

WARD, HAROLD GORDON, corp. exec.; b. Pasadena, Calif., Dec. 20, 1923; s. Max Ralph and Ellen Marie (Medley) W.; m. Marilyn L. Dahlstead, July 22, 1945; children—Leslie A., Linda C. Exec. v.p. Food Giant Markets, Inc., Los Angeles, 1961-64; pres., dir. Purity Stores, Inc., Burlingame, Calif., 1965-69; pres. Title Assets Mgmt., Inc., Long Beach, Calif., 1969—. Bd. dirs. Boys Club, Long Beach Youth Home, Long Beach council Boy Scouts Am.; pres. Long Beach Conv. and News Bur.; chmn. bd. dirs. Exec. Action, Inc. Mem. Sigma Chi. Lion. Contbr. articles to profl. jours. Home: 4255 Virginia Vista Ct Long Beach CA 90807 Office: 2101 E 4th St Santa Ana CA 92705

WARD, HARRY PFEFFER, physician, univ. chancellor; b. Pueblo, Colo., June 6, 1933; s. Lester L. and Alysmai (Pfeffer) W.; A.B., Princeton, 1955; M.D., U. Colo., 1959; M.S., U. Minn., 1963; m. Betty Jo Stewart, Aug. 20, 1955; children—Stewart, Leslie, Elizabeth, Mary Alice, Amy. Intern Bellevue Hosp., N.Y.C., 1959; resident Mayo Clinic, Rochester, Minn., 1960-63; practice medicine specializing in hematology; chief medicine Denver VA hosp., 1968-72; dean, asso. v.p. U. Colo. Sch. Medicine, 1972-78, prof. medicine, 1978; chancellor U. Ark. Med. Sci. Campus, Little Rock, 1979—; mem. adv. council Leukemia Soc., 1967—; med. adv. com. Hemophilia Soc., 1967—; clin. investigator VA, 1964-67. Mem. Am. Fedn. Clin. Research, Central Soc. Clin. Investigation, Am. Soc. Hematology, Internat. Soc. Hematology, AMA, Western Soc. Clin. Research. Home: 369 Valley Club Circle Little Rock AR 72212 Office: 4301 W Markham Little Rock AR 72201

WARD, HILEY HENRY, journalist, educator; b. Lafayette, Ind., July 30, 1929; s. Hiley Lemen and Agnes (Fuller) W.; B.A., William Jewell Coll., 1951; M.A., Berkeley (Cal.) Bapt. Div. Sch., 1953; M.Div., McCormick Theol. Sem., Chgo., 1955; summer, evening student Northwestern U., 1948, 54, 56-57; Ph.D., U. Minn., 1977; m. Charlotte Burns, May 28, 1951 (div. 1971); children—Dianne, Carolee, Marceline, Laurel; m. 2d, Joan Bastel, Aug. 20, 1977. News asst. Christian Adv., 1953-55; editor jr. publs. David C. Cook Pub. Co., 1956-59; editor Record, Buchanan, Mich., 1960; religion editor Detroit Free Press, 1960-73; asst. prof. journalism Mankato (Minn.) State Coll., 1974-76; asso. prof. journalism Wichita (Kans.) State U., 1976; dir. news-editorial sequence journalism dept. Temple U., 1977—, chmn. journalism dept., 1978—; instr. journalism Oakland U., Rochester, Mich., evenings 1963-66. Recipient citations Religious Heritage Am., 1962; Leidt award, 1969. Religious Pub. Relations Council fellow, 1970. Mem. Religion Newswriters Assn. (pres. 1970-72). Author: Creative Giving, 1958; Space-Age Sunday, 1960; Documents of Dialogue, 1966; God and Marx Today, 1968; Ecumania, 1968; Rock 2000, 1969; Prophet of the Black Nation, 1969; The Far-out Saints of the Jesus Communes, 1972; Religion 2101 A.D., 1975. Contbr. articles to profl. jours.

WARD, HIRAM HAMILTON, fed. judge; b. Thomasville, N.C., Apr. 29, 1923; s. O.L. and Margaret A. Ward; student Wake Forest Coll., 1945-47; J.D., Wake Forest U., 1950; m. Evelyn M. McDaniel, June 1, 1947; children—William McDaniel, James Randolph. Admitted to N.C. bar, 1950; practiced law, Denton, N.C., 1950-51; staff atty. Nat. Prodn. Authority, Washington, 1951-52; partner firm DeLapp, Ward & Hedrick, Lexington, N.C., 1952-72; U.S. dist. judge Middle Dist. N.C., 1972—; bd. visitors Wake Forest U. Sch. Law, 1973—. Mem. N.C. Bd. Elections, 1964-72; trustee Wingate Coll., 1969-72. Served with USAAF, 1940-45. Decorated Air medal, Purple Heart. Mem. Am., N.C. bar assns., Am. Judicature Soc., N.C. State Bar, Jud. Conf. Fourth Circuit, Phi Alpha Delta (hon. life). Republican. Baptist. Clubs: Lions, Masons (Denton). Contbr. legal opinions to Fed. Reporter System, 1972—. Home: Forest Park Dr Denton NC 27239 Office: 246 Fed Bldg and US Courthouse Winston-Salem NC 27101

WARD, HOWARD HOFFMAN, ins. co. exec.; b. Champaign. Ill., Nov. 24, 1920; s. Frank Howard and Fern (Hoffman) W.; B.S. in Marketing, U. Ill., 1946; m. Eleanor Dieckmann, June 26, 1942; children—Barbara Ellen, Pamela Jo. Howard F. Dir. edn., mgr. bus. research Olin Industries, 1946-54; chief accounting officer, chief financial officer Ball Bros., Inc., 1954-68; with Borden, Inc., 1968-73, financial v.p., 1968-73, also dir.; exec. v.p. finance Comml. Union Assurance Cos., Boston, 1973—, also dir. Served with AUS, World War II. Mem. Financial Execs. Inst., U.S. C. of C., Theta Chi. Presbyn. Mason. Clubs: Board Room, Economic (N.Y.C.); Illinois Athletic (Chgo.). Home: 168 Front St Marblehead MA 01945 Office: 1 Beacon St Boston MA 02108

WARD, HOWARD KENNETH, diversified industries exec.; b. Los Angeles, May 30, 1929; s. Howard F. and Grace Lucille (McDowell) W.; B.A., Claremont (Calif.) Men's Coll., 1952; m. Joan Tavernetti, Feb. 3, 1951; children—Michael Kenneth, Joanne Marie, Thomas Howard. Pres. Ward & Son Inc., Industry, Calif., 1952-75, Ward Assos., Inc., 1967—; with Elixir Industries, Gardena, Calif., 1971—, pres., 1973-75, also dir.; pres. Seaward Products Inc., South El Monte, Calif., 1976—; dir. Mansion Industries. Trustee Claremont Men's Coll. Mem. Recreation Vehicle Industry Assn. (dir. 1971—). Office: Seaward Products Inc 1431 Portrero Ave South El Monte CA 91744

WARD, HOWARD LEON, periodontist; b. N.Y.C., July 24, 1921; s. Edward M. and Min (Brenner) W.; B.A., N.Y. U., 1946, D.D.S., 1949, M.A. in Higher Edn., 1969; postgrad. Tufts U. Coll. Dentistry, 1950, Columbia, 1951; m. Leona Auster, Aug. 8, 1946; children—Richard Lee, Kenneth Andrew. Practice periodontics, N.Y.C., 1951—; prof. dept. periodontia and oral medicine, chmn. dept. N.Y. U. Coll. Dentistry, 1970-72, prof., chmn. dept. preventive dentistry and community health Brookdale Dental Center of N.Y. U., dir. hosp. dentistry program, 1972—, head div. health service mgmt., 1977, dir. continuing dental edn. program N.Y. U. Coll. Dentistry, N.Y.C., asst. dean clin. affairs, 1978—, prof. periodontics, 1979—; attending dept. surgery N.Y. U. Med. Center; former head periodontics sect. L.I. Jewish Med. Center; former cons., lectr. periodontology U.S. Naval Hosp., St. Albans, L.I.; now cons. dentistry Goldwater Meml. Hosp-N.Y. U. Coll. Medicine; cons. periodontics Nassau County Med. Center; Berkshire asso. in periodontia and oral medicine Tufts Coll. Dentistry; spl. cons. U.S. Dept. Pub. Health. Served with M.C., AUS, 1942. Recipient numerous awards, honors including S.C. Miller Meml. award oral medicine, Alumni Meritorious award N.Y. U.; Hirshfeld award. Diplomate Am. Bd. Periodontology, Am. Bd. Oral Medicine. Fellow Am. Coll. Dentists, N.Y. Acad. Dentistry, AAAS, Am. Pub. Health Assn.; mem. N.Y. Acad. Scis., Am. Acad. Oral Medicine, Nassau County (past pres.), 10th Dist. (past pres.) dental socs., L.I., Nassau-Suffolk (past pres.) acads. dentistry, NE Soc. Periodontists (past pres.), Am. Assn. Dental Examiners, N.Y. State Bd. Dentistry, NE Regional Bd. Dental Examiners, N.Y. U. Alumni Assn. (past pres.), Omicron Kappa Upsilon (past pres. Omega chpt.). Editor texts Manual of Clinical Periodontics (Mosby), edit. I and II; Periodontal Point of View (Thomas); Preventive Point of View (Thomas). Contbr. articles to profl. jours. Home: 150 Central Park S New York NY 10019 Office: NY U Dental Center of 345 E 24th St New York NY 10010 also 150 Central Park S New York NY 10019

WARD, JAMES MUNCIE, radio sta. exec.; b. Nashville, Dec. 28, 1928; s. James Truman and Mary Geneva (Muncie) W.; B.E., Vanderbilt U., 1950; m. Mary Jane Bolling, Apr. 10, 1953; children—Trudy, Janie. With WLAC Radio, Nashville, 1950—, sales dept. staff, 1953-66, gen. mgr., 1966—; dir. Nashville City Bank. Pres., Nashville Better Bus. Bur., 1967; pres. Nashville Y.M.C.A., 1970; chmn. Nashville chpt. ARC, 1975. Mem. Nashville Advtg. Fedn. (pres. 1969), Am. Advtg. Fedn. (chmn. bd. govs. 1976), Sales and Mktg. Execs. Ch. Christ. Clubs: Exchange Club of Nashville (pres. 1975). Nashville City (pres. 1969). Home: Old Hickory Blvd Brentwood TN 37027 Office: WLAC Radio 159 4th Ave N Nashville TN 37219

WARD, JAMES MYRON, newspaper editor; b. Montrose, Miss., Jan. 7, 1919; s. William Joseph and Myra (Anderson) W.; grad. Millsaps Coll., 1941; m. Bobbye Terry Ward, Dec. 11, 1941; children—Patricia, James Myron, Myra Annette. With Jackson (Miss.) Daily News, 1932—, photographer and reporter, city editor, mng. editor, 1932-57, editor, 1957—. Past mem. Miss. Agrl. and Indsl. Bd.; v.p. Natchez Trace Assn. Past mem. bd. dirs. Goodwill Industries Miss. Served as capt. USAAF, World War II. Decorated Air medal with nine oak leaf clusters. Mem. Am. Soc. Newspaper Editors, Miss.-La. Mng. Editors Assn., Jackson C. of C., A.P. Mng. Editors Assn., Am. Legion, V.F.W., Lambda Chi Alpha, Sigma Delta Chi. Rotarian. Club: Press (past pres. Jackson). Home: 327 Naples Rd Jackson MS 39206 Office: 311 E Pearl St Jackson MS 39205

WARD, JAMES RICHARD, ins. co. exec.; b. Tucumcari, N.Mex., Sept. 25, 1910; s. James Franklin and Mary Alta (Dodson) W.; student U. N.Mex., 1928-29; m. Bertha Hil Walker, June 19, 1934. Agt., Union Central Life Ins. Co. 1928-34; with Equitable Life Ins. Co. Iowa, Des Moines, 1934-74, v.p., dir. agys., 1959-69, sr. v.p., 1969-74, also mem. exec. com., ret., 1974. Served with AUS, 1943-45. Mem. Nat. Assn. Life Underwriters, Gen. Agts. and Mgrs. Assn., Internat. Sales Execs., C. of C., Pi Kappa Alpha. Presbyn. (elder). Rotarian. Home: 2318 Calle Tranquilo Santa Fe NM 87501

WARD, JASPER DUDLEY, III, architect; b. Flemington, N.J., Oct. 8, 1921; s. Jasper Dudley and Constance Fargis (Allen) W.; B.Arch., Mass. Inst. Tech., 1948; m. Lucretia Baldwin; children—Lucretia B., James R., Michael D., Alexander A., Abigail B. Designer, Skidmore, Owings & Merrill, N.Y.C., 1948-50; partner Ward-Knight, N.Y.C., 1950; architect Kelly & Gruzen, N.Y.C., Knappen, Tippetts, Abbott & McCarthy, N.Y.C., Gen. Electric Co., Reynolds Metals Co., Louisville, 1951-58; pvt. practice architecture, Louisville, 1958—. Vis. critic archtl. design Pratt Inst., 1954-56, Columbia, 1955, U. Ky., 1960-71. Served to 1st lt. C.E., AUS, 1943-46. Recipient AIA award of merit for Swain House, Watching, N.Y., 1956; 1st Honor awards Ky. Soc. Architects for CIT Bldg., 1961, Neighborhood House, 1964, Portland Sch., 1968, Ky. Sch. for Blind, Recital Hall and Music Bldg., 1977, Alice Lloyd Coll. Sci. Bldg., 1977; White Cement award of excellence for Dr.'s Office Bldg., Louisville, Portland Cement Assn., 1971. Prin. works include St. Francis Sch., Goshen, Ky., 1000 Car Fed. Parking Garage, Louisville, Alice Lloyd Coll. Boy's and Girl's dormitory, Pippa Passes, Ky., John F. Kennedy Library, West Liberty, Ky., U. Louisville Radiation Center, Jefferson County Elementary Sch., Okolona, Ky., Ballard Mills Silo Apts. and Redevel. of Big 4 Bridge. Home: 601 Riverwood Dr Louisville KY 40207 Office: 819 W Main St Louisville KY 40202

WARD, JOHN MILTON, educator; b. Oakland, Calif., July 6, 1917; s. John Milton and Maud (Van Alstyne) W.; B.A., San Francisco State Coll., 1941; M.Mus., U. Wash., 1942; Ph.D., N.Y. U., 1953; A.M. (hon.), Harvard, 1955; m. Ruth Marie Neils, Jan. 9, 1945. Instr. lit. and fine arts Mich. State U., 1947-53; asst., later asso. prof. music U. Ill., 1953-55; asso. prof. music Harvard, 1955-58, prof., chmn. dept., 1958-62, William Powell Mason prof., 1961—. Trustee Longy Sch. Music. Mem. Am. Acad. Arts and Scis., Am. Musicol. Soc., Internat. Musicological Soc., Internat. Folk Music Council, Cambridge Soc. for Early Music (dir.), Soc. Ethnomusicology, Renaissance Soc., Royal Mus. Assn. Author: The Dublin Virginal Manuscript, 1954. Contbr. articles to profl. jours. Home: 20 Follen St Cambridge MA 02138

WARD, JOHN ROBERT, physician, educator; b. Salt Lake City, Nov. 23, 1923; s. John I. and Clara (Elzi) W.; B.S., U. Utah, 1944, M.D., 1946; M.P.H., U. Calif. at Berkeley, 1967; m. Norma Harris, Nov. 5, 1948; children—John Harris, Pamela Lyn, Robert Scott, James Alan. Intern, Salt Lake County Gen. Hosp., 1947-48, asst. resident, 1949-50, resident physician internal medicine, 1950-51, asst. physician, 1957-58, asso. physician, 1958-69; instr. medicine U. Utah Med. Sch., 1954-58, asst. prof., 1958-63, asso. prof., 1963, prof., chmn. dept. preventive medicine, 1967-70, prof., 1969—, chief arthritis div., 1957—; clin. fellow medicine Harvard, 1955-57; attending physician internal medicine Salt Lake City VA Hosp., 1957—. Served as capt. M.C., AUS, 1951-53. Diplomate Am. Bd. Internal Medicine. Fellow A.C.P.; mem. Am. Rheumatism Assn., N.Y. Acad. Scis., Salt Lake County, Utah med. assns., Sigma Xi. Home: 1249 E 3770 S Salt Lake City UT 84106

WARD, JOHN WESLEY, pharmacologist; b. Martin, Tenn., Apr. 8, 1925; s. Charles Wesley and Sara Elizabeth (Little) W.; A.A., George Washington U., 1948, B.S., 1950, M.S., 1955; Ph.D., Georgetown U., 1959; m. Martha Isabelle Hendley, Dec. 7, 1947; children—Henry Russell, Judith Carol, Charles Wesley, Richard Little. Research asso. in pharmacology Hazleton Labs., Falls Church, Va., 1950-55, head dept. pharmacology, 1955-58, chief depts. biochemistry and pharmacology, 1958-59; with A. H. Robins Co., Richmond, Va., 1959—, dir. good lab. practices, 1977-78, dir. biol. research, 1978—; lectr. in pharmacology Med. Coll. Va., 1960-64; guest lectr. Seminar on Good Lab. Practices, FDA, Washington, 1979, Chgo., 1979, San Francisco, 1979. Served with USMC, 1943, USN, 1944-46, U.S. Army, 1944. Mem. AAAS, N.Y. Acad. Sci., Va. Acad. Sci., Am. Chem. Soc., Soc. Toxicology (charter), Am. Soc. Pharmacology and Exptl. Therapeutics, Pharm. Mfrs. Assn. (chmn. color additive toxicology com. 1978—), Am. Assn. for Accreditation Lab. Animal Care (chmn. bd. trustees 1976-80), Sigma Xi. Clubs: Willow Oaks (Richmond); Cosmos, Masons (Washington). Contbr. articles on pharmacology, toxicology and medicinal chemistry to profl. publs.; patentee in field. Home: 10275 Cherokee Rd Richmond VA 23235 Office: 1211 Sherwood Ave Richmond VA 23220

WARD, JOHN WILLIAM, coll. pres.; b. Boston, Dec. 21, 1922; s. John J. and Margaret (Carrigan) W.; B.A., Harvard, 1945, M.A., U. Minn., 1950, Ph.D., 1953; m. Barbara Carnes, Mar. 19, 1949; children—David, Christopher, Andrew. Mem. faculty Princeton, 1952-64; asso. prof. history, chmn. program Am. civilization, 1960-64; mem. faculty Amherst Coll., 1964—, prof. history and Am. studies, chmn. history dept., 1967-70, pres., 1971—. Guggenheim fellow, 1958, 68. Author: Andrew Jackson: Symbol for an Age, 1955; Red, White and Blue, 1969. Office: Office of Pres Amherst Coll Amherst MA 01002*

WARD, JOSEPH SIMEON, cons. engr.; b. N.Y.C., Jan. 23, 1925; s. Joseph Simeon and Kathryn Madelene (Winkler) W.; B.C.E., Manhattan Coll., 1946; M.S., Rutgers U., 1948; m. Ellin B. Callahan, Jan. 20, 1951; children—Ellin, Kathryn, Anne Marie, Joseph, Timothy, Christopher, John, Mary, Thomas, Jane, Robert. Grad. asst. Rutgers U., 1946-48; from instr. to asst. prof. civil engring. Cooper Union, 1948-57; cons. geotech. engr., Caldwell, N.J., 1950—; pres. Joseph S. Ward, Inc., 1957-78; partner Joseph S. Ward and Assos., 1957-78; pres. Converse Ward Davis Dixon, Caldwell, 1978—. Chmn. bd. trustees St. Vincent's Hosp., Montclair, N.J. Served to 1st lt. C.E., AUS, 1948-52. Recipient A.F. Davis Welding award Lincoln Arc Welding Found., 1946; Robert Ridgway award ASCE, 1946. Registered profl. engr., N.J., N.Y., Conn., Mass., W.Va., D.C., Pa., Fla., Tex., Calif., Md., Va., Ind. Fellow ASCE (v.p. 1975-77 pres. 1979-80); mem. Am. Cons. Engrs. Council (dir. 1969-70; Excellence award 1974), Nat. Soc. Profl. Engrs., Transp. Research Bd., Chi Epsilon, Tau Beta Pi. Roman Catholic. Clubs: N.Y. Athletic; Essex Fells Country, K.C. Contbr. articles to profl. jours. Home: 61 Norwood Ave Montclair NJ 07043 Office: 91 Roseland Ave PO Box 91 Caldwell NJ 07006

WARD, JUDSON CLEMENTS, JR., former coll. dean, hist. soc. exec.; b. Marietta, Ga., Apr. 13, 1912; s. Judson Clements and Bertie (Arnold) W.; A.B., Emory U., 1933, M.A., 1936; postgrad. Columbia, 1943, Am. U., 1945; Ph.D., U. N.C., 1947; m. Susan-Jane Weyant, Apr. 3, 1946; children—Peter, Michael, Rebecca, Jonathan. Tchr. English, history Fitzgerald (Ga.) High Sch., 1934-37; instr. social scis. Ga. Tchrs. Coll., 1939-40, pres., 1947-48; instr. dept. history Birmingham-So. (Ala.) Coll., 1940-42; asst. chancellor Univ. System Ga., 1948; dean Emory U. Coll. Arts and Scis., 1948-57, v.p., dean faculties, 1957-70, exec. v.p., dean faculties, 1970-79; dir. Atlanta Hist. Soc., 1979—; dir. Decatur Fed. Savs. & Loan Assn. Trustee, Wesleyan Coll., Morris Brown Coll., Pace Acad. Served as 2d lt. F.A., U.S. Army, 1942; instr. dept. econs., govt. and history U.S. Mil. Acad., 1943-46. Mem. So. Hist. Assn., Phi Beta Kappa, Omicron Delta Kappa, Kappa Phi Kappa, Sigma Pi. Democrat. Home: 1534 Emory Rd NE Atlanta GA 30306. *I am convinced that whatever hope there is for a better world, education must have an important role in it.*

WARD, LEE, lawyer, lectr.; b. Piggott, Ark., Dec. 13, 1906; s. Thomas Henry and Ida Elnora (Hughes) W.; student Washington U., St. Louis, 1927-29, Ark. Law Sch., 1935-38; m. Pearl Fulks, Oct. 13, 1929; 1 dau., Carol Lee (Mrs. William D. Jenness III). With Shell Petroleum Corp., 1929-33; law clk. to atty. O.T. Ward, Rector, Ark., 1933-35; admitted to Ark. bar, 1938, U.S. Supreme Ct. bar, 1956; pvt. practice, Little Rock, 1938-42, Paragould, Ark., 1947-54, Jonesboro, Ark., 1961-71; trial judge 12th Chancery Dist. Ark., 1955-60. Pres., Abundant Life Inst. Bd. dirs. Ozark Creative Writers, Inc. Served with USNR, 1943-45. Mem. Am., Ark. bar assns., Am. Judicature Soc., Am. Legion (past dept. comdr.), Am. Acad. Polit. and Social Sci., Internat. Platform Assn. Democrat. Methodist (tchr. men's Bible class). Lion (past dist. gov.). Club: Sugar Creek Country. Author weekly newspaper column About Your U.S. Constitution and Supreme Court. Editor-pub. The Spoken Word Newsletter. Home: Route 2 Box 62 Piggott AR 72454 Office: PO Box 341 Piggott AR 72454

WARD, LOUIS EMMERSON, physician; b. Mt. Vernon, Ill., Jan. 19, 1918; s. Henry Ben Pope and Aline (Emmerson) W.; A.B., U. Ill., 1939; M.D., Harvard, 1943; M.S. in Medicine, U. Minn., 1949; m. Nan Talbot, June 5, 1942; children—Nancy, Louis, Robert, Mark. Intern, Ill. Research and Ednl. Hosp., Chgo., 1943; fellow medicine Mayo Found., 1946-49; cons. medicine, rheumatology Mayo Clinic, 1950—, chmn. bd. govs., 1964-75. Dir., Northwestern Bell Telephone Co., Bankers Life, Des Moines. Vice chmn. bd. trustees Mayo Found., 1964-76; past bd. dirs. Fund for Republic; bd. dirs. Center for Study Democratic Instns.; past bd. dirs. Arthritis Found.; mem. Nat. Council Health Planning and Devel., 1976—. Recipient U. Ill. Alumni Achievement award, 1968. Mem. Inst. Medicine (Nat. Acad. Scis.), AMA, Am. Rheumatism Assn. (pres. 1969-70), Nat. Soc. Clin. Rheumatologists (pres. 1967-69), Central Soc. Clin. Research, Minn., Zumbro Valley med. socs., So. Minn. Med. Assn., Phi Beta Kappa, Sigma Xi, Alpha Omega Alpha, Phi Delta Theta. Contbr. articles to profl. jours. Home: 1110 10th St SW Rochester MN 55901 Office: 200 1st St Rochester MN 55901

WARD, LOUIS LARRICK, candy co. exec.; b. Kansas City, Mo., Nov. 18, 1920; s. Carter William and Fern Alpha (Larrick) W.; student U. Kans., 1937-38; B.S. in Chem. Engring., Stanford, 1941; m. Adelaide Selby Cobb, Dec. 17, 1955; children—Scott Hardman, Thomas Selby, Linda Larrick. With Drexel, Harriman & Co., 1946-47, Spencer Chem. Co., 1947-50, Ward Paper Box Co., 1950-60; with Russell Stover Candies, Inc., Kansas City, Mo., 1960—, pres., chmn. bd., 1960—; dir. First Nat Bank, Rival Mfg. Co., Ward Paper Box Co. (all Kansas City, Mo.), Bankers Life Ins. Co. Nebr., Lincoln. Served with USNR, 1941-46. Mem. Kappa Sigma. Clubs: Kansas City Country, River, University (Kansas City, Mo.). Home: 1240 W 57th Terr Kansas City MO 64113 Office: 1004 Baltimore St Kansas City MO 64105

WARD, LYND KENDALL, artist, illustrator; b. Chgo., June 26, 1905; s. Harry Frederick and Daisy (Kendall) W.; B.S., Columbia Tchrs. Coll., 1926; postgrad. Staatliche Akademic fuer Graphische Kunst, Leipzig, Germany, 1926-27; m. May Yonge McNeer, June 11, 1926; children—Nanda Weedon (Mrs. Robert E. Haynes), Robin Kendall (Mrs. Michael T. Savage). Illustrator, 1927—; prints represented in permanent collections Library of Congress, Smithsonian Inst., Neward Mus., Met. Mus., Victoria and Albert Mus., others; dir. graphic arts div. Fed. Art Project, N.Y.C., 1937-39. Recipient Zella de Milhan prize, 1947; award for wood engraving Library of Congress, 1948, N.A.D., 1949; Caldecott medal, 1953; silver medal Limited Edits. Club, 1954; John Taylor Arms Meml. prize, 1962; Samuel F.B. Morse gold medal, 1966; Rutgers medal, 1969; U. So. Miss. Silver medal, 1973; co-recipient Regina medal Catholic Library Assn., 1975. Mem. N.A.D., Soc. Am. Graphic Artist (pres. 1953-59). Author-illustrator: (novels in wood cuts) Gods' Man, 1929; Madman's Drum, 1930; Wild Pilgrimage, 1932; Prelude to a Million Years, 1933; Song Without Words, 1936; Vertigo, 1937; Storyteller Without Words—The Wood Engravings of Lynd Ward; children's books: The Biggest Bear, 1952, Nic of the Woods, 1965; The Silver Pony, 1973. Home: Lambs Ln Cresskill NJ 07626

WARD, NORMAN, educator; b. Hamilton, Ont., Can., May 10, 1918; s. Arthur Bramwell and Rachel (McQueen) W.; B.A., McMaster U., 1941, LL.D., 1974; M.A., U. Toronto, 1943, Ph.D., 1949; LL.D., Queen's U., 1977; m. Betty Edith Davis, Sept. 11, 1943; children—Nora Ward Russell, Nancy Ward Johnson, Rick, Donald, Colin, Michael. Mem. faculty U. Sask., 1945—, asso. prof., 1951-55, prof. polit sci., 1955—; free lance writer, broadcaster, 1941—, also editor, publisher's reader, pub. affairs commentator. Vice-chmn. Sask. Electoral Boundaries Commn., 1964-66, 72-73, 74-75, also Sask. Archives Bd.; mem. adv. com. Election Expenses, 1964-66; mem. Saskatoon adv. bd. Soc. Study Heritage of Can.; mem. Can. Council. Recipient Leacock medal, 1961; decorated officer Order Can.; Skelton Clark fellow, 1958-59. Fellow Royal Soc. Can., Can. Polit. Sci. Assn. Author: The Canadian House of Commons: Representation, 2d edit., 1963; Government in Canada, 2d edit., 1964; The Public Purse: A Study in Canadian Democracy, 1962; Mice in the Beer, 2d edit., 1970; The Fully Processed Cheese, 1964; Her Majesty's Mice, 1977; co-author: A Party Politician: The Memoirs of Chubby Power, 1966; Bilingualism and Biculturalism in the Canadian House of Commons, 1970; The Government of Canada, 5th edit., 1970; Democratic Government in Canada, 4th edit., 1971. Co-editor: Politics in Saskatchewan, 1968. Home: 412 Albert Ave Saskatoon SK S7N 1G3 Canada

WARD, PAUL HUTCHINS, educator, physician; b. Lawrence, Ind., Apr. 24, 1928; s. Howard Hutchins and Lillian (Anderson) W.; B.A., Anderson Coll., 1953; M.D., Johns Hopkins, 1957; m. Lois Ellen Ward, Apr. 13, 1952 (div. Nov. 1974); children—Walter Hutchins, Judy Ellen; m. 2d, Suzanne Fowler, Feb. 1975. Resident U. Chgo. Hosp., 1958-61, Career Devel. fellow, 1961-64, asst. prof. surgery, 1962-64; asso. prof. surgery, chmn. Vanderbilt U. Med. Sch., Nashville, 1964-68; prof. surgery, chief div. head and neck surgery U. Calif. at Los Angeles Med. Sch., 1968—; cons. VA, Harbor Hosp. Mem. various coms. and chmn. deafness research rev. com. NIH, 1956—. Bd. dirs., v.p. Hope for Hearing Found., Los Angeles, 1971—, Blalock Found., Los Angeles, 1972—. Served with M.C., AUS, 1946-49, 50-51. Recipient Gold medal Ill. Med. Soc., 1963, Ethicon Spectacular Problems in Surgery Cine award, 1963, Ignacio Barraquer award, 1969-72. Diplomate Am. Bd. Otolaryngology (mem. bd. examiners 1978—). Mem. Am. Council Otolaryngology, Acoustical Soc. Am., Am. Acad. Opthalmology and Otolaryngology (Gold Medal 1974-75), A.C.S., Barany Soc., Cleve. Otolaryngology Soc. (hon.), Internat. Soc. Lymphology, Med. Research Calif., Los Angeles County Med. Assn., Calif. Med. Assn., AMA (Billings silver medal 1975), Soc. Univ. Otolaryngologists (pres. 1976), Otological Soc., Pan-Am. Assn. Oto-Rhino-Laryngology, Triological Soc., Am. Broncho-Esophogological Assn. (pres. 1977-78), Am. Acad. Facial Plastic and Reconstructive Surgery, Am. Laryngological Assn., Collegium Otorhinolaryngologicum Sacrum, Pacific Coast Oto-Ophthal. Soc. (v.p. 1975-76), Am. Soc. for Head and Neck Surgery (council 1979—), Sigma Xi. Author: Deafness in Childhood, 1967; cons. editor Western Jour. Medicine, 1970—, Annals Otology, Rhono and Laryngology, 1968—; asso. editor Laryngoscope, 1979—. Home: 1 North Star Marina del Rey CA 90291 Office: School Medicine Univ Calif Los Angeles CA 90024

WARD, PHILIP HENRY, III, lawyer; b. Phila., Aug. 7, 1920; s. Philip Henry Jr. and Ruth Coke (MacNamara) W.; A.B. cum laude, Princeton U., 1942; J.D., Harvard U., 1948; m. Margaretta Dodge, Aug. 25, 1967; children—Philip Henry IV, Susan Ward Stitzer. Admitted to Pa. bar, 1949; since practiced in Phila.; partner firm Montgomery, McCracken, Walker & Rhoads, 1960—; permanent del. Jud. Conf. 3d Circuit; v.p. Phila. Crime Commn. Trustee Phila. Coll. Art, Chestnut Hill Acad., 1963-70, Springside Sch., 1963-69. Served to capt. U.S. Army, World War II; PTO. Decorated Silver Star, Bronze Star, Purple Heart. Mem. Phila. Bar Assn. (chmn. sect. corp. banking and bus. law 1967-70), Am. Arbitration Assn., Wilderness Club (past pres.), Com. of 70 (past chmn.), Wissahickon Valley Watershed Assn. (past chmn.), Juristic Soc., Pa. Soc., Newcomen Soc. N. Am., Pohoqualine Fish Assn. Clubs: Phila. Cricket, Racquet (sec.), Lawyers, Cohorts Gun, Union League, Anglers (trustee). Home: 8605 Seminole Ave Philadelphia PA 19118 Office: 3 Parkway Philadelphia PA 19102. *The problem is not building better mousetraps - the problem is killing mice.*

WARD, RALPH E., JR., diversified mfg. exec.; b. Scotch Plains, N.J., 1921. Chmn. bd., pres., chief exec. officer Chesebrough-Pond's, Inc.; dir. Stauffer Chem. Co., CPC Internat., 1969-73. Trustee Lafayette Coll. Home: Quail Rd Greenwich CT 06830 Office: 33 Benedict Pl Greenwich CT 06830

WARD, RICHARD GUERIN, lawyer; b. Detroit, Oct. 13, 1929; s. Robert William and Hazel Ellen (Hall) W.; B.S., Mich. State U., E. Lansing, 1952; J.D., Wayne State U., Detroit, 1959; m. Helen Marie Stone, Feb. 10, 1951; children—Susan Marie, Mark Douglas. With Prudential Investment Corp., Detroit, 1954-56, Fed. Homes Corp., Detroit, 1956-60; owner Holiday Homes Corp., Detroit, 1960-62; admitted to Mich. bar, 1960; partner firm Sullivan, Ranger, Ward & Bone, Detroit, 1966—; mem. faculty Oakland U., Mich. Served to 1st lt. AUS, 1952-54. Mem. Am., Mich., Detroit bar assns. Presbyterian. Club: Forest Lake Country. Home: 5815 Bloomfield Glens Rd West Bloomfield MI 48033 Office: 220 W Congress Detroit MI 48226

WARD, RICHARD THEODORE, educator; b. Avoca, Nebr., Sept. 10, 1925; s. Guy Theodore and Mae (Lemon) W.; B.Sc., U. Nebr., 1948; M.Sc., U. Minn., 1951; Ph.D., U. Wis., 1954; m. Barbara Ruth Johnson, Sept. 14, 1953; children—Justin R., Patricia L. Asst. prof. Beloit Coll., 1954-57; faculty Colo. State U., 1957—, prof. plant ecology, 1967—, chmn. dept. botany and plant pathology, 1966-75. Mem. Colo. Gov.'s Sci. and Tech. Adv. Council, 1975-79; chmn. Colo. Mined Land Reclamation Bd., 1976—. Served to ensign USNR, 1943-46. Mem. Ecol. Soc. Am., Nature Conservancy, Can. Reclamation Assn., Sigma Xi. Contbr. articles to profl. jours. Home: 120 Yale Way Fort Collins CO 80521

WARD, ROBERT, composer, condr., educator; b. Cleve., Sept. 13, 1917; s. Albert E. and Carrie (Mollenkopf) W.; B.Mus., Eastman Sch. Music, 1939; certificate Juilliard Grad. Sch. Music, 1946; student composition with Bernard Rogers, Howard Hanson, Frederick Jacobi,

Aaron Copland; conducting with Albert Stoessel, Edgar Schenkman; D.F.A., Duke, 1972; Mus.D., Peabody Inst., 1975; m. Mary Raymond Benedict, June 19, 1944; children—Melinda, Johanna, Jonathon, Mark, Timothy. Tchr., Juillard Sch. Music, 1946-56; mng. editor, mem. bd. Galaxy Music Corp. until 1967, dir., 1967—; exec. v.p. Highgate Press, 1967; pres. N.C. Sch. Arts, Winston-Salem, 1967-74, tchr. composition, 1974-79; prof. composition Duke U., Durham, N.C., 1978—. Bd. dirs. Martha Baird Rockefeller Fund for Music, 1971—; mem. music com. Henry St. Settlement. Bd. dirs. Winston-Salem Arts Council. Served with AUS, 1942-46. Decorated Bronze Star. Recipient Juilliard Pub. award, 1942; Fine Arts award State of N.C., 1975. MacDowell Colony fellow, 1938; Alice M. Ditson fellow Columbia, 1944; $1,000 grantee Am. Acad. Arts and Letters, 1946; Guggenheim fellow, 1950, 51, 66-67. Mem. Nat. Inst. Arts and Letters. Composer: 1st Symphony, 1942; Hush'd Be the Camps Today, 1943; Second Symphony, 1947; Third Symphony, 1951; Fourth Symphony, 1958; Divertimento for Orchestra, 1961; Earth Shall Be Fair, 1960; He Who Gets Slapped (Pantaloon) (opera in 3 acts); The Crucible (opera in 4 acts) (Pulitzer Prize in music), 1962; Hymn and Celebration (for orch.), 1962; Music for Celebration, 1963; The Lady From Colorado (opera in 2 acts), 1964; Let the Word Go Forth, 1965; Sweet Freedom's Song (cantata), 1965; Hymn To The Night, 1966; First String Quartet, 1966; Concerto for Piano and Orchestra, 1968; Claudia Legare (opera), 1974; Fifth Symphony-Canticles for America, 1976. Contbr. articles, revs. to Modern Music, Juilliard Rev., Nat. Fedn. Music Clubs Mag. Home: 308 Monticello Ave Durham NC 27707

WARD, ROBERT GEORGE, ins. co. exec.; b. Upland, Pa., July 10, 1924; s. Harry G. and Emma (Raetzer) W.; student U. Pa., 1942-43, 46-47; B.S., N.Y. U., 1947; M.A., U. Mich., 1948; m. Janice MacDonald, Nov. 29, 1952; children—John F., Susan J., Jeffrey D. With Provident Mut. Life Ins. Co. of Phila., 1948—, asso. actuary, 1958-61, dir. policy services, 1961-63, dir. ins. operations, 1963-64, v.p. ins. operations, 1964-71, v.p., sec., 1971-74, sr. v.p., sec., 1975-77, sr. v.p. ins. ops., 1977—. Served to 1st lt. USAAF, 1943-46. C.L.U. Fellow Soc. Actuaries, Acad. Actuaries. Home: 440 Woodland Circle Radnor PA 19087 Office: 4601 Market St Philadelphia PA 19139

WARD, ROBERT JOSEPH, judge; b. N.Y.C., Jan. 31, 1926; s. Joseph G. and Honor V. (Hess) W.; S.B., Harvard, 1945, LL.B., 1949; m. Florence C. Maisel, Apr. 15, 1951; children—Laura Alice, Carolyn. Admitted to N.Y. State bar, 1949, practiced in N.Y.C., 1949-51, 61-72; asst. dist. atty. N.Y. County, 1951-55; asst. U.S. atty. So. Dist. N.Y., 1956-61; judge U.S. So. Dist. N.Y., 1972—. Served with USNR, 1944-46. Mem. Am., N.Y. State bar assns., Assn. of the Bar of City of N.Y. Office: US Courthouse Foley Sq New York NY 10007

WARD, ROBERT LYLE, ret. copper co. exec.; b. Bklyn., May 23, 1915; s. Robert Henry and Etta (Lyle) W.; B.S. in Accounting cum laude, N.Y. U., 1950; m. Helen Gamble, June 29, 1941; children—Christine Helen Gwydir, Carolyn Anne Werner. With Kennecott Copper Corp., 1933-77, comptroller, 1968-77. Served with USNR, 1942-45. Mem. Tax Execs. Inst. (v.p. N.Y. chpt. 1965-66), Am. Mining Congress (tax com.), Fin. Execs. Inst., Beta Gamma Sigma. Republican. Presbyn. Club: Cloud (N.Y.C.). Home: 6 Harriet Ct Malverne NY 11565

WARD, ROBERTSON, JR., architect; b. Boston, Sept. 7, 1922; s. Robertson and Sylvia (Whiting) W.; A.B. cum laude, Harvard Coll., 1944, M.Arch., 1951; m. Sara Weeks, June 2, 1948 (div. 1953). Mem. faculty dept. advanced bldg. research Ill. Inst. Tech., Chgo., 1951-52; research designer Arnold Rosner, Chgo., 1952; architect Skidmore, Owings & Merrill, Tokyo, 1953; architect Breuer, Nervi and Zehrfuss, UNESCO, Paris, 1953-54; head dept. design research Skidmore, Owings & Merrill, Chgo, 1954-60; individual practice architecture, Chgo., 1960—. Rep., cons. UNESCO archtl. environ. info. system, 1976—, U.S. Nat. Com./Council Internat. Bldg. Research, 1973—; rep. from U.S. Econ. Commn. for Europe, 1972; mem. Chgo. Urban Renewal Rev. Commn., 1965; mem. tech. adv. bd. U.S. Dept. Commerce, 1967. Served with USNR, 1944-46. Recipient Gov. of Calif.'s Design award, 1966; Graham Found. fellow, 1963, 65. Fellow AIA; mem. Illuminating Engring. Soc., U.S. Inst. Theater Tech., Environ. Design Research Assn., Design Methods Group. Archtl. works include Sci., Visual and Performing Arts Centers Bennington Coll.; Exptl. Theater, Vassar Coll.; Sci. Center Deerfield Acad. Home: 175 E Delaware St Chicago IL 60611 Office: 21 W Elm St Chicago IL 60610

WARD, RODMAN, JR., lawyer; b. Wilmington, Del., Apr. 8, 1934; s. Rodman and Dorcas (Andrews) W.; B.A., Williams Coll., 1956; LL.B., Harvard, 1959; m. Susan Speakman Hill, Oct. 10, 1959; children—Margery, Emily Tatnall, Rodman III, Jenifer Janvier. Admitted to Del. bar, 1959, D.C. bar, 1959; asso. Prickett & Prickett, Wilmington, 1959-64, partner, 1965-67; partner firm Prickett, Ward, Burt & Sanders, Wilmington, 1967-79; partner firm Skadden, Arps, Slate, Meagher & Flom, Wilmington, 1979—. Chmn. New Castle County Housing Authority, 1972-73; co-founder, dir. Wilmington World Affairs Council; bd. dirs. Del. Hist. Soc., U. Del. Library Assos.; v.p., trustee Lalor Found.; trustee, mem. finance and investment coms. Wilmington Med. Center. Served to capt. USAF, 1960-63. Mem. Am., Del. (chmn. com. on profl. ethics), D.C. bar assns., Assn. Bar City N.Y., Am. Judicature Soc. Clubs: Wilmington, Wilmington Country, Vicmead Hunt. Mem. editorial bd. Nat. Law Jour. contbr. articles to profl. jours. Home: 52 Selborne Dr Wilmington DE 19807 Office: 1310 King St Wilmington DE 19899

WARD, ROGER COURSEN, lawyer; b. Newark, June 19, 1922; s. Waldron Merry and Aline (Coursen) W.; grad. Phillips Exeter Acad., 1940; A.B., Princeton, 1943; LL.B., Columbia, 1949; m. Katharine More Stevens, Oct. 22, 1949; children—James Olney, Alexander More. Admitted to N.J. bar, 1949, since practiced in Newark, Morristown, N.J.; partner firm Pitney, Hardin & Kipp, 1959—. Bd. dirs. United Hosps. Newark, 1965-78, pres., 1973; trustee, v.p. Newark Mus. Assn., 1969—; bd. dirs. Better Bus. Bur. Greater Newark, 1970—; mem. Summit Zoning Bd. Adjustment, 1966-70; trustee Eye Inst. N.J., 1973, Pingry Sch., 1966-68, Summit YMCA, 1960-62, Newark Council Social Agys., 1956-60; vice chmn. Newark Mayor's Commn. on Youth, 1958-60. Served to lt. (j.g.) USNR, 1943-46. Mem. Am., Fed., N.J., Essex County bar assns., Phi Beta Kappa. Clubs: Princeton (N.Y.C.); Essex (Newark); Short Hills (N.J.); Morristown (N.J.). Home: 91 Highland Ave Short Hills NJ 07078 Office: 163 Madison Ave Morristown NJ 07960

WARD, SYLVAN DONALD, educator, music condr.; b. Rock Springs, Wyo., July 7, 1909; s. Samuel and Hannah (Davis) W.; B.Mus., Chgo. Mus. Coll., 1931, M.Mus., 1932; M.S. in Edn., Northwestern U., 1934, M.Edn., 1946; D.Mus. Edn., Chgo. Mus. Coll., 1954; student violin John Brueggemann, Leon Sametini; m. Beatrice Dorrell Stackhouse, June 27, 1936; children—Dorrell Deen (Mrs. Gordon H. Williams), Susan Diane (Mrs. William D. Johnston), Jill Dawn (Mrs. George L. Manderino), Jack Donald, Nancy Deborah. Advt. mgr. Edn. Music mag., Chgo., 1931-36, asso. editor edn., 1937-43; asst. gen. mgr. edn. Music Bur., 1936-37; tchr. instrumental, vocal music Farragut High Sch., Chgo., 1936-49; instr. music Chgo. Mus. Coll., 1946-51, Chgo. Tchrs. Coll., 1949-58, Wilson Jr. Coll., part-time 1951-63, Crane Jr. Coll., Loop Jr. Coll., 1965; vis. prof. U. Ill., summers 1959-61; prof. music, Chgo. State U., 1958-77, chmn. dept., 1958-71; tchr. Vandercook Coll. Music, 1975—; dir. Chgo. Regional Mormon Choir, 1935—; condr., mus. dir. Chgo. Bus. Men's Orch., 1963-68, 77—; mem. Chgo. State Coll. String Quartet, 1952-77, Chgo. String Trio, 1960—, stage orch. Chgo. Lyric Opera Co., 1960-69. Bishop, Ch. of Jesus Christ of Latter-day Saints, 1963-72, mem. high council Chgo. Heights Stake, 1973. Served with USAAF, 1943-45. Mem. NEA, Music Educators Nat. Conf., Ill. Music Educators Assn., Music Tchrs. Nat. Assn., Am. Choral Dirs. Assn., Am. Fedn. Musicians, Am. String Tchrs. Assn. (pres. Ill. unit 1959-63, editor Scroll 1961-63), Phi Mu Alpha. Author: Elementary and Intermediate Methods for Viola; Elementary and Intermediate Methods for Cello; Elementary Method for String Bass; Instrumental Director's Handbook. Contbr. articles to profl. jours. Home: 2131 W 107th St Chicago IL 60643

WARD, THOMAS GREYDON, physician; b. Athens, La., Sept. 25, 1911; s. Joe Miller and Sarah Alice (Finley) W.; student So. Meth. U., 1928-31; M.D., Baylor U., 1935; Dr.P.H., Johns Hopkins, 1941; m. Opal Queen Doss, Sept. 11, 1934; children—Greydon, Moneen, Clayron. Practicing physician, Coushatta, La., 1935-37; health officer State of La., 1937-39; with Johns Hopkins, 1939-41, 45-56, asso. prof. microbiology, 1950-56; prof. virology U. Notre Dame, 1956-60; research dir. Microbiol. Assos., Inc., 1960-74; dir. med. edn. Montgomery Found. for Med. Care, 1974—; med. dir. Whittaker Corp., 1973—; practice medicine specializing in geriatrics, 1974—. Served with AUS, 1941-45. Mem. N.Y. Acad. Scis., Soc. Exptl. Biology and Medicine, Am. Assn. Immunologists, Am. Epidemiological Soc., Sigma Xi. Home and Office: 6116 Robinwood Rd Bethesda MD 20034

WARD, THOMAS MARTIN, JR., naval officer; b. Pontiac, Mich., Dec. 4, 1928; s. Thomas Martin and Edith Elsie (Crouch) W.; student Va. Mil. Inst., 1946-47; B.S., U.S. Naval Acad., 1951; B.S. in Elec. Engring., U.S. Naval Postgrad. Sch., 1957; M.S., M.I.T., 1958; M.M.A., U. R.I., 1970; m. Peggy Jane Dunn, Sept. 12, 1951; children—David, Vickey Ward Brown, Jim, Suzanna, Natalie. Commd. ensign U.S. Navy, 1951, advanced through grades to rear adm., 1977; comdr. U.S.S. Cardinal AMS-4, 1954-55, U.S.S. Berkeley (DDG-15), 1967-69, project mgr. NATO Seasparrow Surface Missile System Project, 1970-74; Destroyer Squadron 7, 1974-76; ordnance engring. sub-specialist, 1958—; dir. surface combat systems div. Office of Chief Naval Ops., Navy Dept., Washington, 1977-79; comdr. Naval Surface Group, Middle Pacific, Pearl Harbor, Hawaii, 1979—; mem. faculty, weapons dept. U.S. Naval Acad., Annapolis, Md., 1965-67. Active local troops Boy Scouts Am. Decorated Legion of Merit, Bronze Star with combat V and gold star. Presbyterian. Home: 37 Halawa Dr Honolulu HI 96818 Office: Comdr Naval Surface Group Midpacific Pearl Harbor HI 96860

WARD, THOMAS NELSON, electric utility exec.; b. Chambersburg, Pa., July 16, 1923; s. Thomas N. and Mary (Gilbert) W.; B.S., U. Ill., 1947; student Rutgers U., 1943- 44, U. Mich., 1956, 68; m. Jean R. Oyler, June 12, 1948; children—Marilyn J., Thomas G., Barbara B. Sr. accountant Arthur Andersen & Co., C.P.A.'s, N.Y.C., 1947-54; v.p., sec., treas. Ohio Valley Electric Corp., Piketon, Ohio, 1954—, Ind.-Ky. Electric Corp., Piketon, 1954—. Served with inf. AUS, 1943-45. Decorated Bronze Star. C.P.A., N.J., Ohio. Mem. Am. Inst. C.P.A.'s. Home: 34 Tecumseh Dr Chillicothe OH 45601 Office: PO Box 468 Piketon OH 45661

WARD, VIRGIL SCOTT, educator; b. Union, S.C., Mar. 19, 1916; s. John Lewis and Beatrice (Scott) W.; A.B., Wofford Coll., 1939; M.Ed., Duke, 1947; Ph.D., U. N.C., 1952; m. Sarah Alyne McNeill, Mar. 19, 1942; children—Patricia Ann, Rebecca Joan, William Milan. Tchr. English, Pub. Schs. Rock Hill, S.C., Durham, N.C., 1939-42, 45; from asst. prof. to prof., chmn. dept. edn. and psychology Wofford Coll., 1947-56; faculty U. Va., 1956—, prof. edn., 1962—, chmn. dept. ednl. founds., 1964-68, prof. dept. ednl. founds., 1968—. Vis. summer prof. Johns Hopkins, 1962, Tulane U., 1964, U. Calif. at Los Angeles, 1967. Project dir. So. Regional Project Edn. of Gifted, 1960-61, Gov. Sch. N.C., 1963-65. Pres., S.C. Assn. Mental Health, 1954; mem. Spartanburg (S.C.) Bd. Edn., 1952. Chmn. trustees Spartanburg Mental Health Clinic, 1953; chmn. bd. dirs. Wesley Found., U. Va., 1963-65. Served with USAAF, 1942-45. Mem. Council Exceptional Children (Va. rep. bd. govs. 1961-64, pres. Assn. Gifted 1965), NEA, Am., S.C. (pres. 1956) psychol. assns., Philosophy Edn. Soc., Am. Ednl. Research Assn. Author: Educating the Gifted: An Axiomatic Approach, 1961; (with others) The Gifted Student: A Manual for Program Improvement, 1962. Home: 301 Kent Rd Charlottesville VA 22903

WARD, WALLACE DIXON, educator; b. Pierre, S.D., June 30, 1924; s. Edmund Dixon and Thelma Marie (Hill) W.; B.S. in Physics, S.D. Sch. Mines and Tech., 1944, D.Sc., 1971; Ph.D. in Exptl. Psychology, Harvard, 1953; m. Edith Marion Bystrom, Dec. 27, 1949; children—Edith Marion IV, Laurie Elizabeth, Kathryn Christine, Holly Lydene. Research engr. Baldwin Piano Co., Cin., 1953-54; research asso. Central Inst. for Deaf, St. Louis, 1954-57; asso. dir. research Noise Research Center, Am. Acad. Ophthalmology and Otolaryngology, Los Angeles, 1957-62; prof., depts. communication disorders, otolaryngology, public health and psychology U. Minn., Mpls., 1962—. Mem. com. on hearing, bioacoustics and biomechanics NRC, 1960—, exec. council, 1970-75, chmn., 1971-73; mem. communicative scis. study sect. div. research grants NIH, 1969-73; sci. adviser Callier Hearing and Speech Center, Dallas, 1968—; cons. U.S. Army, 1972—, Environmental Protection Agy. Office Noise Abatement and Control, 1973; mem., co-chmn. Internat. Sci. Noise Teams, 1973—. Served with USNR, 1944-46. Recipient Research Career Devel. award NIH, 1962. Fellow Acoustical Soc. Am. (exec. council 1978-81), Am. Speech and Hearing Assn.; mem. AAAS, Am. Audiology Soc. (v.p. 1973-75, pres. 1976), Am. Acad. Ophthalmology and Otolaryngology, Internat. Audiology Soc. (governing bd., pres. 1978-80), Psychonomic Soc., Am. Otol. Soc., Am. Indsl. Hygiene Assn., Mensa, Sigma Xi, Sigma Tau, Triangle. Libertarian. Editor: Noise as a Public Health Hazard, 1969; Noise as a Public Health Problem, 1974. Contbr. articles to tech. jours. Home: 246 Maple Hill Rd Hopkins MN 55343 Office: 2630 University Ave SE Minneapolis MN 55414

WARD, WALTER GEORGE, steel co. exec.; b. Peterborough, Ont., Can., Dec. 8, 1914; s. Eldin Victor and Ethel Grace (Forsyth) W.; B.Engring., McGill U., 1942; m. M. Grace Strange, May 17, 1937; children—Nancy, John, Susan, Janet. With Canadian Gen. Electric Co., Ltd., 1931-64, 70-77, v.p., 1959-64, pres., 1970-72, chmn., chief exec. officer, 1972-77; chmn. Algoma Steel Corp., 1977—; gen. mgr. area div. Europe Gen. Electric Co., 1964-70, v.p., 1965-70, also dir. subsidiaries. Bd. govs. Trent U., Peterborough. Served to lt. comdr. Royal Canadian Navy. Mem. Assn. Profl. Engrs. Clubs: National (Toronto, Can.); Union Interalliee (Paris, France); Golf, Canadian (Geneva, Switzerland). Office: 503 Queen St E Sault Sainte Marie ON P6A 2A2 Canada

WARD, WALTER LEROY, JR., banker; b. Homer, La., Mar. 30, 1902; s. Walter Leroy and Virginia (Madden) W.; student Tulane U., Washington and Lee U.; m. Naomi Terry, Sept. 10, 1966; children (by previous marriage)—Walter Leroy III, Swan Sullivan. Chief clk. La. Banking Dept., 1923-27; engaged in bond and brokerage bus., also mem. New Orleans Cotton Exchange, 1928-31; bank examiner La., 1934-39; with Fidelity Nat. Bank Baton Rouge, 1939—, pres., 1954-72, chmn. bd., 1960-78, chmn. emeritus, adv. dir., 1978—. Mem. bd. Greater Baton Rouge Port Commn., 1962—, Downtown Baton Rouge Assn., 1962—, Baton Rouge Better Bus. Bur., 1942—. Bd. dirs. Baton Rouge Little Theatre, Baton Rouge Parish Libary, 1960-62; mem. La. State U. Found. Mem. Financial Pub. Relations Assn., Am., La. bankers assns., La. State Sr. Golf Assn. (dir.), Baton Rouge C. of C. (dir., exec. com. econ. devel. council). Clubs: Baton Rouge Country (past pres., dir.), Rotary, City, Boston (New Orleans). Home: 7031 Boyce Dr Baton Rouge LA 70809 Office: 440 3d St Baton Rouge LA 70821

WARD, WARREN HAYDEN, publisher, banker; b. Saginaw, Mich., Aug. 29, 1893; s. Louis E. and Hattie (Hayden) W.; student Northwestern U.; m. Helen Wold, Jan. 11, 1915; children—Louise (Mrs. Louis Ewing), Warren Hayden, Helen J. (Mrs. Donald Hall), Phillip (dec.). Tchr. country sch., 1910-12; with Standard Edn. Corp., Chgo., 1912—, v.p. 1920-40, pres., 1940-66, chmn. bd., 1966—; pres. Nat. Bank of North Evanston, 1961-63, chmn. bd., 1963-68, also dir. Mem. Am. Textbook Pubs. Inst. (sec. 1962). Clubs: Chicago Athletic Assn.; North Shore Country. Home: 2963 Payne St Evanston IL 60201 Office: 200 W Monroe St Chicago IL 60606. *Among my many pieces of good fortune, I now believe one of the greatest was being born poor.*

WARD, WILLIAM BINNINGTON, agriculturist; b. Idaho Falls, Ida., July 16, 1917; s. William A. and Daisy (Binnington) W.; B.S., Utah State Agrl. Coll., 1940; M.S., U. Wis., 1941; m. Thora Bracken, Sept. 12, 1939; children—Ann Lyn, William Bracken, Cristen Lee, Alan Miller. With editorial dept. Post Register daily newspaper, Idaho Falls, 1935-36; asst. to extension editor Utah State Agrl. Coll., Logan, 1937-40; corr. A.P. and Rocky Mountain newspapers, 1938-40; asst. to extension editor, grad. instr. agrl. journalism U. Wis., 1940-41; information specialist dairy marketing, handling pub. relations on milk marketing agreements and orders U.S. Dept. Agr., 1941-42; chief information sect. Agrl. Marketing Adminstrn., then Food Distbn. Adminstrn., 1943-44; prof., head dept. communication arts, editor, chief of publs. N.Y. State Coll. Agr. Life Scis. and Human Ecology, Cornell U., Ithaca, N.Y., 1945-72, prof., 1973—. Chmn. nat. adv. com. on information U.S. Dept. Agr., 1953-55; agr. adviser U. Philippines, 1956-57, 65; communcations adviser Argentine Govt., 1961-62; agr. communications cons. Ford Found., India, 1968-69, 70; communication adviser, chief of party U. Tenn./U.S. AID India Agrl. Programs, 1972; cons. ICRISAT, India, 1973, World Bank, Bangladesh, 1974—; vis. scientist Internat. Inst. Tropical Agr., Africa, 1976-77; communications cons., Indonesia, 1978-79. Mem. Am. Assn. Agrl. Coll. Editors (pres.), Am. Assn. Agr. Editors, Sigma Delta Chi, Blue Key. Rotarian. Author: Agricultural News in the Daily Press, 1941; Reporting Agriculture, 2d edit., 1959. Contbr. articles to internat., nat., regional agrl. publs. Home: 102 Forest Dr Ithaca NY 14850

WARD, WILLIAM FRANCIS, JR., publishing co. exec.; b. Everett, Mass., Aug. 23, 1928; s. William Francis and Helen (Schriber) W.; B.S., U.S. Mil. Acad., 1950; M.B.A., Harvard, 1956; m. Elaine L. Wilson, June 11, 1950; children—Jeffrey W., Gary T., Michelle A., Gregory W., Suzanne M. Econ. analyst E.I. duPont de Nemours & Co., Inc., Wilmington, Del., 1956-58; sec. N.Y. State Bridge Authority, Poughkeepsie, 1958-60; div. controller, dir. marketing services GAF Corp., N.Y.C., 1960-63; asst. to pres. Grosset & Dunlap, Inc., 1963-65, v.p., 1965-67; controller Dun & Bradstreet, 1967-71, v.p., 1968-71; chmn. bd., pres. Dun-Donnelley Pub. Corp., 1971-77; dir. Quotron Electronics, Inc., Empire Nat. Bank; dir., sec. Buy & Large Corp., 1963-65. Faculty, N.Y. U. Sch. Commerce, 1960-64. Pres., Ramapo Central Sch. Dist., 1966-72. County chmn. Citizen for Kennedy and Johnson, 1960; Democratic candidate for Ho. of Reps., 1962; chmn. Young Citizens for Johnson and Humphrey, 55 counties N.Y., 1964; exec. v.p. Am. Cancer Soc., 1976—; bd. dirs. Aerospace Edn. Found. Served to capt. AUS, 1950-54; brig. gen. Res. Decorated Legion of Merit, Meritorious Service medal, Air medal with 3 oak leaf clusters, Army Commendation medal, Purple Heart. Mem. West Point Soc. N.Y., Antrim Players, Soc. Harvard Engrs. and Scientists, Newcomen Soc., Res. Officers Assn., Am. Friends of Viet Nam (nat. chmn.), VFW, Am. Legion. Roman Catholic. K.C. Clubs: Army and Navy (Washington); University, Harvard (N.Y.C.). Home: 1 Bruce Ct Suffern NY 10901 Office: 19 W 56th St New York NY 10019

WARD, WILLIAM FRAZEE, life ins. co. exec.; b. Newark, July 13, 1911; s. Warren Daniel and Nellie Thompson (Frazee) W.; B.S., Rutgers U., 1933; m. Marjory Ann Knight, June 27, 1936; children—Carol, Susan, William Frazee. With Mut. Benefit Life Ins. Co., Newark, 1933-76, v.p., 1952-62, exec. v.p., 1962-76. Chmn., Montclair (N.J.) Community Chest drive, 1954, trustee, 1955-60; v.p. N.J. chpt. Arthritis and Rheumatism Found., 1954-64; mem. No. N.J. com. Am. industry Nat. Fund Med. Edn., 1954-64; mem. N.J. Med. Assistance Adv. Council, 1969—; chmn. Gov. Hughes' Com. to Study Blue Cross, 1965-67; mem. N.J. Health Planning Council, 1968-77; chmn. Newark UN Week, 1975; mem. adv. com. Newark Housing Authority. Bd. dirs. Essex Council com. Planned Parenthood, 1958-64; trustee United Hosps. of Newark, 1968-79, Symphony Hall, Newark. Mem. Greater Newark C. of C. (dir. 1971-73), Soc. Actuaries, Actuaries Club N.Y., Am. Acad. Actuaries. Club: Glen Ridge Country. Home: 21 College Ave Upper Montclair NJ 07043 Office: 520 Broad St Newark NJ 07101

WARD, WILLIAM RALPH, JR., clergyman; b. Boston, Oct. 16, 1908; s. William Ralph and Janie (Johnston) W.; A.B., Baker U., 1929, D.D., 1950; S.T.B., Boston U., 1932, S.T.M., 1933; LL.D., Mt. Union Coll., 1960; S.T.D., Syracuse U., 1961; D.D., Boston U., 1963; L.H.D., Keuka Coll., 1963; m. Arleen Burdick, June 3, 1933; children—Ralph A., David B., Gerald W. R. Ordained to ministry Meth. Ch., 1933; pastor, Mass., R.I., Conn., 1930-48, Mt. Lebanon Ch., Pitts., 1948-60; bishop Northeastern Jurisdictional Conf., Syracuse, N.Y. area, 1960-72, N.Y. area, 1972-80. Pres. program council United Meth. Ch.; pres. Bd. Nat. Missions; v.p. Gen. Bd. Missions; mem. Bd. Christian Concerns Meth. Ch. Chmn. bd. OPA, Manchester, Conn.; pres. United Meth. Devel. Fund, N.Y. State Council Chs., 1970-73, Council Bishops United Meth. Ch., 1975-76; mem. Bd. Ch. and Soc. Trustee Hartford Sem. Found., Syracuse U., Bethune-Cookman Coll., Folts Home, Drew U., St. Paul's Sch. Theology, Bethel Meth. Home, Mt. Union Coll., Troy Conf. Geriatric Found., Saratoga Springs, N.Y., Meth. Hosp. Bklyn. Recipient Freedoms Found. award, 1950; Man of Year award B'nai B'rith, Pitts., 1954. Mem. Pitts. Council Chs. (pres.), Theta Chi Beta, Zeta Chi. Mason (33 deg.), Kiwanian, Rotarian. Home: 190 North St Harrison NY 10528 Office: United Meth Center 210 Boston Post Rd Rye NY 10580

WARD, WILLIAM REED, composer, educator; b. Norton, Kans., May 20, 1918; s. Joseph Aloysius and Maude (Jones) W.; Mus.B., Mus.Edn.B., U. Kans., 1941; Mus.M., Eastman Sch. Music, 1942, Ph.D., 1954; student Charles S. Skilton, L.E. Anderson, Robert Palmer, Bernard Rogers, Howard Hanson; m. Elizabeth Jane Adam,

Aug. 8, 1943; children—Claudia Christine, Joseph Andrew, John David. Instr. music Colo. State U., 1942-44; asst. prof. music, head composition and theory curriculum Lawrence U., 1944-47; faculty San Francisco State U., 1947—, head music dept., 1954-69, prof. music, 1959—, asso. dean Sch. Creative Arts, 1977—. Lectr. panelist music Idyllwild Inst. Arts, Cal. Music Tchrs. Assn., Choral Condrs. Guild Calif., Am. Guild Organists, Music Educators Nat. Conf., Music Tchrs. Nat. Assn.; choir dir. First Christian Ch., Ft. Collins, Colo., 1942-44, Meml. Presbyn. Ch., Appleton, Wis., 1944-47, First Bapt. Ch., Burlingame, Calif., 1949-63, United Meth. Ch., 1967—; dir. Asian Arts Acad. and Music of Whole Earth Festival, San Francisco, 1978; compositions performed by Eastman-Rochester, Indpls. Oklahoma City, San Francisco symphony orchs., numerous others. Recipient Nat. Arrangers contest award, 1947. Mem. Assn. Univ. Composers, ASCAP, Music Tchrs. Nat. Assn., Music Educators Nat. Conf., Choral Condrs. Guild, AAUP. Composer: Lullaby for a Pinto Colt, 1941; A Vision of the World, 1955; Psalm 136, 1959; Fray Junipero Serra, The Great Walker (dramatic oratorio), 1960; Symphony 1, 1938, 2, 1947, 3, 1954; Variations on a Western Tune, 1948; Suite for Woodwind Quintet, 1954; A Psalm of Praise, 1964; The Crucufixion, 1971; Fun; Love; Joy; Trains, 1971; In Town Again, 1973; Arcs, 1973; O For A Thousand Tongues, 1973; others. Author: Examples for the Study of Musical Style, rev. edit., 1970; American Bicentennial Song Book, 2 vols., 1975. Home: 120 Occidental Ave Burlingame CA 94010 Office: 1600 Holloway Ave San Francisco CA 94132

WARD, YVETTE HENNIG, advt. exec.; b. St. Paul, June 15, 1910; d. Leo J. and Adele (Hennig) Borer; m. Charles Saunders, Nov. 30, 1931 (div.); 1 dau., Charlene; m. 2d, Charles Allen Ward, Feb. 29, 1940 (dec. May 1959); children—Allen, Vida, Herbert. Profl. dancer, 1918-28; free-lance interior decorator, 25 yrs.; publisher Hudson (Wis.) Star-Observer, 1952-58; with Brown & Bigelow, 1942—, pres., 1959—, also dir.; dir. Summit Nat. Bank, St. Paul, Arts and Sci. Bldg., Surety Savs. & Loan, Phoenix, Scottsdale, Yuma, Ariz. Chmn. fine arts and jewelry funding Compas 6, Phoenix. Chmn. bd. Hudson Meml. Hosp.; founding chmn. Scottsdale Meml. Hosp.; bd. dirs. Florence Crittenton Home. Mem. Nat. Fedn. Press Women, Minn. Press Women, Minn., Wis. editorial assns., Am. Hosp. Assn., Phoenix Zoo Aux., Phoenix Symphony Aux., Phoenix Art Mus., Western Arts, Costume Design Inst. Mem. Order Eastern Star. Clubs: Overseas Press; Women's Aid (Mpls.) Author: Russia Through Women's Eyes, 1956; Around the World in 32 Days, 1958. Home: Rancho Roca Roja Rimrock AZ also 106 E San Miguel St Phoenix AZ 85012

WARDE, GEORGE ANDRES, aviation exec.; b. Chgo., Nov. 22, 1921; s. George F. and Mabel W. (Eriksen) W.; student U. Ala., 1938-40, Hofstra Coll., 1950-54; m. Doris Rose Darius, June 6, 1943; 1 dau., Valerie. Pres., Airbus Industrie N.Am., N.Y.C., 1974-79, chief exec. officer, 1977-79; sr. v.p. customer support Airbus Industrie, Toulouse, France, 1975—; mechanic Am. Airlines, Inc., N.Y.C., 1940-42, gen. prodn. mgr., Tulsa, 1960-65, v.p. maintenance, 1965-66, v.p. maintenance and engring., 1966-68, sr. v.p. operations, N.Y.C., 1968-71, exec. v.p., gen. mgr., 1971-72, pres., chief operating officer, 1972-74, also dir., cons., 1974-76; foreman Am. Export Airlines, N.Y.C., 1942-45; maintenance supt. Am. Overseas Airlines, N.Y.C. and Eng., 1945-50; supt. line maintenance Pan Am. World Airways, N.Y.C., 1950-56, prodn. supt., San Francisco, 1957-60; chmn. bd. Flight Safety Found., 1978-79; sr. v.p. commerciae Airbus Industrie, Toulouse, France, 1979—. Trustee Nat. Cowboy Hall Fame, Oklahoma City; bd. regents Tex. Luth. Coll., Sequin, Tex. Mem. Soc. Licensed Aircraft Engrs. and Technologists, Newcomen Soc. N.Am. Home: Cedex 2121 31490 Leguevin France Office: Airbus Industrie North Am 630 Fifth Ave New York NY 10020 also Airbus Industrie Ave Lucien Servanty 31700 Blagnac France

WARDEBERG, HELEN L., educator; b. Barnesville, Minn.; d. Anton O. and Lillie (Bredemeier) Wardeberg; B.S., State Tchrs. Coll., Moorhead, Minn., 1945; M.A., U. Minn., 1948, Ph.D., 1951. Tchr. supr. Clay County, Minn., 1939-42; tchr. Elementary sch. Browns Valley, Minn., 1942-43; elementary supr. Winona (Minn.) State Tchrs. Coll., 1944-47; asst. prof. elementary edn., supr. student tchrs. Cortland (N.Y.) State Tchrs Coll., 1951-54; prof. edn. Cornell U., Ithaca, N.Y., 1954—, chmn. dept. edn. 1969-77, asso. dir. resident instrn., 1977—. Mem. Am. Ednl. Research Assn., Assn. Supervision and Curriculum Devel., Internat. Reading Assn., N.E.A., Nat. Soc. Study of Edn., Pi Lambda Theta. Contbr. articles to profl. jours. Home: 6-B Wildflower Dr Ithaca NY 14850

WARDEN, CHARLES BROWNE, JR., economist, univ. dean; b. Englewood, N.J., Jan. 15, 1931; s. Charles Browne and Margaretta Weymouth (Weed) W.; diplome superieure, U. Paris, 1951; A.B., Swarthmore (Pa.) Coll., 1953; Ph.D., Harvard U., 1964; m. Katherine Dolfis, June 9, 1962; children—Stacia Antigone, Gregory Charles. Instr., Georgetown U., 1958-60; economist Joint Econ. Com., U.S. Congress, 1959-60; lectr., then instr. Harvard U., 1961-64; program asst. Ford Found., 1964-65; spl. asst. to chmn. Council Econ. Advisers, 1966-69; v.p. Data Resources, Inc., 1969-77; dean Whittemore Sch. Bus. and Econs., U. N.H., Durham, 1977—; pres., chmn. bd. T.G.C., Inc. Chmn. local Boy Scouts Am., 1978-79, Monroe Hist. House Com., 1972-74, N.H. Revenue Rev. Com., 1979; bd. advisers MAGUS Theatre Group, 1979—; adv. Forum on N.H. Future, 1977—. Served to lt. comdr. USN, 1953-57. Mem. Am. Econ. Assn., Nat. Assn. Bus. Economists. Office: McConnell Hall Univ NH Durham NH 03824

WARDEN, CLARENCE ARTHUR, JR., mfg. co. exec.; b. Phila., Oct. 27, 1904; s. Clarence A. and Helen (Corning) W.; grad. Hill Sch., Pottstown, Pa., 1922; student Sheffield Sci. Sch., Yale, 1926; LL.D., Ursinus Coll.; m. Katharine B. Chase, Apr. 24, 1930 (dec. Jan. 1958); children—William G. III, Sally; m. 2d, Anna M. F. Thompson, Oct. 24, 1959. Student, Nat. City Co., N.Y.C., 1926; various office, sales positions Brown Bros. (later Brown Bros. Harriman & Co.), Phila., 1926-32; pres., dir. Superior Tube Co. and affiliated cos., 1948-67, chmn., 1967—; dir., mem. exec. com. Germantown Trust Co., 1936-47; dir. 1st Pa. Co., 1959-74, Peter A. Frasse & Co., Inc., N.Y.C., Williams & Co., Inc., UGI. Corp., 1947-77, Phila. Suburban Corp., 1969-75. Bd. dirs. Big Bros. Assn., Phila., 1939-45, Bryn Mawr (Pa.) Hosp., 1951-77, Ursinus Coll., 1957-76, Legal Aid Soc., 1953-76; chmn. bd. dirs. Del. Valley Hosp. Council, 1958-73; bd. dirs. Phila. Maritime Mus. Hon. fellow Am. Coll. Hosp. Adminstrs. Clubs: Sunnybrook Golf (Plymouth Meeting, Pa.); Yale, Racquet, Corinthian (Phila.); N.Y. Yacht; Merion Golf (Ardmore); Gulph Mills Golf; Cruising of America; New Bedford (Mass.) Yacht. Home: Cottesmore Haverford PA 19041 Office: 7 E Wynnewood Rd Wynnewood PA 19096

WARDEN, GAIL LEE, hosp. exec.; b. Clarinda, Iowa, May 11, 1938; s. Lee Roy and Juanita (Haley) W.; B.A., Dartmouth, 1960; M.H.A., U. Mich., 1962; m. Lois Jean Johnson, Oct. 9, 1965; children—Jay Christopher, Janna Lynn, Jena Marie. Adminstrv. asst. Blodgett Meml. Hosp., Grand Rapids, Mich., 1962, Dewitt Hosp., Ft. Belvoir, Va., 1963-65; adminstrv. asst. Presbyn.-St. Luke's Hosp., Chgo., 1965-68, asst. to pres., 1968, v.p. adminstrn., 1968-69; exec. v.p. Rush-Presbyn.-St. Luke's Med. Center, Chgo.; exec. v.p. Am. Hosp. Assn., Chgo., 1976—; lectr. U. Chgo., Washington U., St. Louis, 1968—; mem. adv. com. Ill. Regional Med. Programs, 1969—, Ill. State Bd. Vocat. Edn. and Rehab., 1968-69; preceptor in hosp. adminstrn. Trinity U., Xavier U., U. Chgo., Washington U., U. Mich.; mem. bd. Commn. on Profl. and Hosp. Services, Ann Arbor, Mich. Bd. dirs. South Suburban Hosp., Hazel Crest, Ill. Served to capt. AUS, 1965. Named one of Ten Outstanding Young Men in Chgo., Jr. Assn. Commerce and Industry, 1968. Mem. Am. Coll. Hosp. Adminstrs. (named Young Adminstr. of Year, 1972), Am. Pub. Health Assn., Alpha Chi Rho. Contbr. articles to profl. jours. Home: 20624 Corinth Rd Olympia Fields IL Office: 840 N Lake Shore Dr Chicago IL 60611

WARDEN, JACK, actor; b. Newark, Sept. 18, 1920; s. Jack Warden and Laura M. (Costello) Lebzelter; student pub. schs., Newark, acting classes, N.Y.C.; m. Vanda Warden; 1 son, Christopher. With Margo Jones Theatre, Dallas; appeared in numerous dramatic TV shows, including Studio One, Playhouse 90; appeared in Broadway plays A Very Special Baby, A View From The Bridge, The Body Beautiful, Sing Me No Lullaby, Golden Boy, The Man in The Glass Booth; motion pictures include Edge of The City, 12 Angry Men, Bachelor Party, Run Silent, Run Deep, That Kind of Woman, The Sound and the Fury, Darby's Rangers, The Sporting Club, Come Join the Club, Who Is Harry Kellerman And Why Is He Saying Those Terrible Things About Me?, The Man Who Loved Cat Dancing, Shampoo, White Buffalo; appeared in TV series N.Y.P.D., The Wackiest Ship in the Army, Jigsaw John, TV motion picture A Memory of Two Mondays, Nat. Ednl. TV, Topper, 1979, Bad News Bears; appeared in motion pictures Heaven Can Wait, Justice for All, Being There, Death on the Nile. Served with USN, 1938-41, U.S. Army, 1942-46; China, ETO. Recipient Obie award, 1963, Emmy award, 1972. Mem. Screen Actors Guild, AFTRA, Actors Equity. Democrat. Office: care Agy for Performing Arts Inc Suite 315 9000 Sunset Blvd Hollywood CA 90069

WARDEN, JOHN CHARLES, fashion designer; b. Niagara Falls, Ont., Can., Dec. 28, 1939; s. Jack Stewart and Maude Lily (Pocknell) W.; student Parsons Sch. of Design, N.Y.C., 1961-64; 1 son, Mark Steven. Asst. designer apparel for Bob Bugnand and Assos., N.Y.C.; fashion designer A. Sanft & Co., Montreal, Que., Can., Croydon Mfg. Co., Montreal, Hudson Cloak Co., Toronto, Ont., Chicard Ltd.; propr., mgr. Boutique Shop, Montreal; designer men's apparel for Bagatelle of Montreal; apparel designer for numerous projects including Canadian Walk-out Uniforms, Olympic Games at Munich, 1971, uniforms for Mirabelle airport hosts and hostesses, 1975, uniforms for Canadian Olympic team, 1975; propr. John Warden store, Yorkville, Toronto, Ont., 1975—. Recipient numerous awards and prizes including Designer of the World award Australia; Excellence of Design award Hudson Cloak Assn.; Cotton Council awards, Edee awards. Mem. Fashion Designer Assn. Can. (past v.p.). Home: 410 Place Jacques Cartier Montreal PQ Canada Office: 674 Victoria Ave Westmount PQ Canada*

WARDEN, JOHN L., lawyer; b. Evansville, Ind., Sept. 22, 1941; s. Walter Wilson and Juanita (Veatch) W.; A.B., Harvard U., 1962; LL.B., U. Va., 1965; m. Phillis A. Rodgers, Oct. 27, 1960; children—Anne, John, W. Carson. Admitted to N.Y. State bar, 1966, U.S. Supreme Ct. bar, 1972; asso. firm Sullivan & Cromwell, N.Y.C., 1965-72, partner, 1973—. Mem. Am. Law Inst., Am. Bar Assn., N.Y. State Bar Assn., Assn. Bar City N.Y., N.Y. County Lawyers Assn. Republican. Episcopalian. Clubs: Knickerbocker, Bedford Golf and Tennis, Down Town Assn. Editor-in-chief Va. Law Rev., 1964-65. Home: 531 Bedford Center Rd Bedford Hills NY 10507 Office: 125 Broad St New York NY 10004

WARDEN, RICHARD DANA, govt. ofcl.; b. Missoula, Mont., Dec. 10, 1931; s. Robert Dickinson and Helen (Leach) W.; B.A., Mont. State U., 1957, M.A., 1958; m. Barbara Freeman; children—Denise, Michael, Joseph, Jerome. Reporter, then state editor Gt. Falls (Mont.) Tribune, 1959-61; legis. asst. to U.S. Senator Lee Metcalf of Mont., 1962-63; adminstrv. asst. to U.S. Congressman James G. O'Hara of Mich., 1963-67; dep. dir. Office Civil Rights, HEW, 1967-68; legis. rep. AFL-CIO, 1969-70; dir. Washington Research Project Action Council, 1970-72; legis. rep. UAW, 1972-75, legis. dir., 1975-77; asst. sec. legis. HEW, 1977—. Served with USN, 1951-54. Congressional fellow, 1961-62; recipient Pub. Affairs Reporting award Am. Polit. Sci. Assn., 1960. Home: 3100 Connecticut Ave NW Apt 137 Washington DC 20008

WARDLAW, FRANK HARPER, JR., former publisher; b. Indiantown, S.C., Aug. 16, 1913; s. Frank Harper and Margaret Whitefield (Hudgens) W.; student U. S.C., 1931-33; m. Jane Wallace Williamson, Aug. 10, 1940 (dec. 1969); children—Frank Patterson, Harriet Ervin, George Williamson, Margaret Caroline; m. 2d, Rosemary Leonard Boynton, 1970. Reporter, Columbia (S.C.) Record, 1933-36, A.P., Charlotte, N.C., 1936-37; dir. news service, instr. journalism U. S.C., 1938-44, asso. prof. journalism, 1944-50, mng. editor U. S.C. Press, 1945-49, dir., 1949-50; dir. U. Tex. Press, 1950-74; dir. Tex. A. and M. U. Press, 1974-78. Mem. exec. bd. Centro Interamericano de Libros Academicso, Mexico City, Mexico; mem. adv. com. on publs. Winterthur Mus., Wilmington, Del. Bd. dirs. Franklin Book Program. Fellow Text. Inst. Letters (pres. 1958-60), Tex. Hist. Assn.; mem. Assn. Am. U. Presses (pres. 1961-63), Philos. Soc. Tex., S.C. Hist. Soc., Blue Key, Block C, Alpha Tau Omega, Sigma Delta Chi. Presbyn. (elder, deacon). Club: Town and Gown (Austin). Home: 777 Marlin Dr Fripp Island SC 29920

WARDLE, ORRIN DERMONT, educator; b. Victor, Idaho, June 22, 1913; s. William Haston and Annie Sorena (Sorenson) W.; student Idaho State Coll., 1933-35; B.S., Utah State U., 1946, M.S., 1950; Ed.D., U. Calif. at Berkeley, 1957; m. Viorene Eleanor Walker, Mar. 30, 1934; children—Joan (Mrs. Perry J. Bingham), Sharon (Mrs. Gary W. Steadman), Clayton Barry, Rosanne. Elementary sch. tchr., Clementsville, Idaho, 1935-38, Virginia, Idaho, 1938-42; elementary prin., tchr. high sch. Arimo, Idaho, 1942-45; prin. high sch., dist. supt., McCammon, Idaho, 1945-48; dist. supt. Snake River Schs., Moreland, Idaho, 1948-55; lectr. ednl. adminstrn. U. Calif. at Berkeley, 1956-57; asso. prof. edn., adminstrv. asst. to pres. Fresno State Coll., 1957-59, exec. dean, 1959-67, dir. instnl. studies, 1963-67, prof. edn. adminstrn., 1964—. Staff mem. Master Plan for Higher Edn. in Calif., 1960-75; cons., mem. survey teams for sch. dists., county edn. offices, edn. assns., in Calif. Mem. Fresno City Planning Commn., 1967-70. Mem. Calif., Am. assns. sch. adminstrs., Assn. for Higher Edn., Nat., Idaho (exec. com.), S.E. Idaho (pres.), Bannock-Caribou Counties (pres.) edn. assns., Phi Delta Kappa. Democrat. Mem. Ch. of Jesus Christ of Latter-day Saints. Contbr. articles to ednl. publs. Home: 3357 E Richert St Fresno CA 93726

WARDLOW, ELWOOD M., editor; b. Freeport, Ill., Mar. 5, 1924; s. Samuel M. and Jessie Mae (Kryder) W.; B.A., U. Wis., 1948; m. Rosemary E. Fonken, Sept. 24, 1949; children—Ann, Jane. Wire editor, state editor Freeport (Ill.) Jour.-Standard, 1948-52; copy editor Buffalo Evening News, 1952-58, asst. chief copy editor, 1958-65, asst. mng. editor, 1965-69, mng. editor, 1969—. Faculty, Canisius Coll., Buffalo, 1969, mem. Coll. Publs. Bd. Mem. journalism adv. council, also faculty St. Bonaventure U., 1975-76. Served as 2d lt. USAAF, 1943-45. Mem. Am. Soc. Newspaper Editors, A.P. Mng. Editors Assn., N.Y. Editors Soc., N.Y. A.P. Assn. (pres. 1970), Newcomen Soc., Sigma Delta Chi. Home: 33 Fox Chapel Rd Williamsville NY 14221 Office: 1 News Plaza Buffalo NY 14240

WARDLOW, ERVIN EUGENE, retail co. exec.; b. Fillmore, Mo., Sept. 22, 1921; s. LeRoy and Floy (Burns) W.; student Mich. State U., 1942-43, Harvard Bus. Sch. Advanced Mgmt. Program, 1961; m. Jean Anita Brandt, May 25, 1946; children—Daniel L., Mary Jean, Thomas A., Jeffrey W. With S.S. Kresge Co. (now K Mart Corp.), Troy, Mich., 1939—, store and dist. mgr., 1955-61, dir. sales, 1961-67, v.p. sales, gen. mdse. mgr., 1967-70, exec. v.p. mdse., dir., 1970-72, pres., chief operating officer, 1972—, also dir.; dir. S.S. Kresge Co. Ltd., K Mart (Australia) Ltd., Holly Stores, Inc., K Mart Enterprises. Served with USAAF, 1942-46. Clubs: Harvard Bus. Sch., Detroit Athletic (Detroit); Edgewood Country. Office: 3100 W Big Beaver Troy MI 48084*

WARDROPPER, BRUCE WEAR, educator; b. Edinburgh, Scotland, Feb. 2, 1919; s. Joseph Blair and Edna (Bruce) W.; student King Edward's Sch., Birmingham, Eng., 1932-36; B.A., U. Cambridge, 1939, M.A., 1942; Ph.D., U. Pa., 1949; m. Joyce Vaz, Dec. 15, 1942 (dec. Mar. 1959); 1 son, Ian Bruce; m. 2d, Nancy Hélène Palmer, July 19, 1960. Came to U.S., 1945. Head modern lang. dept. Wolmer's Sch., Kingston, Jamaica, 1940-45; instr. U. Pa., 1945-49; asst. prof. Johns Hopkins, 1949-53, asso. prof., 1953-55, chmn. dept. Romance langs., 1954-55, prof. Spanish, 1959-62; William H. Wannamaker prof. Romance langs. Duke, 1962—; prof. Spanish, Ohio State U., 1955-59; vis. Andrew Mellon prof. Romance langs. U. Pitts., 1965; vis. prof. U. N.C., 1967-68; cons. bd. overseers U. Louisville, 1976-78; NEH Fellowships in Residency Program, 1977-78; seminar dir. Nat. Endowment for Humanities Summer Seminars for Coll. Tchrs., 1975, 76; mem. ednl. adv. bd. John Simon Guggenheim Meml. Found., 1978—. Guggenheim fellow, 1952, 59. Recipient award Am. Philos. Soc., 1957, Am. Council Learned Socs., 1959, fellow, 1969. Mem. Modern Lang. Assn. (editorial bd. PMLA 1973-75), Internat. Assn. Hispanists (exec. com. 1971-77), Renaissance Soc. Am., South Atlantic Modern Lang. Assn. Am., Acad. Lit. Studies (membership com. 1973-78), Assn. Hispanists Gt. Britain and Ireland, Modern Humanities Research Assn. (Am. com. 1976—). Author: Introducción al teatro religioso, 1953; Historia de la poesía lírica a lo divino, 1958; Critical Essays on the Theatre of Calderón, 1965; Poesía elegíaca española, 1967; Teatro español del Siglo de Oro, 1970; Spanish Poetry of the Golden Age, 1971; co-author: Teoría de la comedia: La comedia española del Siglo de Oro, 1978; mem. editorial bd. PMLA (Modern Lang. Assn.), 1962-69, 73-75; asso. editor Purdue U. Monographs in Romance Langs., 1978—. Home: 3443 Rugby Rd Hope Valley Durham NC 27707

WARD-SMITH, KENNETH, ins. co. exec.; b. Atlanta, Oct. 22, 1916; s. Kenneth and Elizabeth (Dallas) W.; A.B., Harvard, 1938; m. Mildred Harris, Dec. 7, 1944; children—Kenneth, Mildred Linn. Adjuster, Liberty Mut. Ins. Co., N.Y.C., 1938-39; underwriter U.S. Guarantee Co., 1939-40; actuarial asst. Life & Casualty Ins. Co. Tenn., Nashville, 1940-48, asst. actuary, 1948-52, asso. actuary, 1952-56, chief actuary, 1956-61, v.p., 1962-66, sr. v.p., 1966—. Served to 1st lt. USAAF, 1942-45. Decorated D.F.C., Air medal (Army) (U.S.), Croix de Guerre (France); Mem. Am. Soc. Chartered Life Underwriters, Am. Acad. Actuaries, Southeastern Actuaries Club. Home: 1031 Balmoral Dr Nashville TN 37220 Office: Life and Casualty Tower Nashville TN 37219

WARDWELL, ALLEN, museum exec.; b. N.Y.C., Jan. 18, 1935; s. Edward Rogers and Lelia (Morgan) W.; grad. Groton Sch., 1953; B.A., Yale, 1957; M.A., N.Y. U., 1960; m. Sarah Williams Tilghman, June 29, 1957; children—William Thomas, Lelia Morgan, Alexander Tilghman. Asst. curator primitive art dept. Art Inst. Chgo., 1960-62, curator, 1962-73, acting curator decorative arts dept., 1963-70, asst. dir. mus. services, 1969-72; dir. Asia House Gallery, N.Y.C., 1974—. Trustee Yale Art Gallery. Adv. council U. Notre Dame Art Gallery, 1970; mem. exhbns. com. Am. Fedn. Arts; mem. mus. panel Indo-U.S. Subcommn. Edn. and Culture, 1975—. Mem. Coll. Art Assn., Am. Mus. Assn., Assn. Art Mus. Dirs. Home: 88 Central Park W New York City NY 10023 Office: Asia House Gallery 112 E 64th St New York City NY 10021

WARE, HARRIS OLIVER, paper co. exec.; b. Cleve., Sept. 23, 1913; s. Harris Oliver and Martha (Kuhn) W.; student Western Mich. U., 1934-37; m. Marion Antoinette Dennert, Mar. 23, 1940; children—Dennert Oliver, Mary (Mrs. Paul Brant), Kathryn (Mrs. Robert Thiede), Margaret. Chemist in paper chems. Hercules Powder Co., Kalamazoo, 1934-48, product mgr., Wilmington, Del., 1949-56; tech. mgr. Beveridge Paper Co., Indpls., 1956-61; v.p. Brown Co., Berlin, N.H., 1961-64; exec. v.p. Premoid Corp., West Springfield, Mass., 1964-73, also dir.; exec. v.p. Lincoln Pulp & Paper Co. (Me.), 1968-73, also dir.; exec. v.p. Precon Corp., Ludlow, Mass., 1968-73, also dir.; dir. Brownville Paper Co. (N.Y.), 1973—; chmn. bd. dirs. Preco Corp., West Springfield, 1973—. Fellow TAPPI (recipient Sci. medal 1966, pres. 1975-77); mem. New Eng. Profl. Guidance Com. (chmn. 1965), U. Maine Pulp and Paper Found. (dir. at large), Am. Chem. Soc., Paper Industry Mgmt. Assn., Non-Woven Materials Council. Contbg. author: Ency. Chem. Tech., 1949. Patentee in field. Home: 26 Randall Dr Suffield CT 06078 Office: Front St West Springfield MA 01089

WARE, HENRY HALL, JR., lawyer; b. Heard County, Ga., Mar. 30, 1903; s. Henry Hall and Mary E. (Allen) W.; student Mercer U.; U. LL.D, 1974; LL.B., Atlanta Law Sch., 1926, LL.D., 1970; m. Katherine F. Catchings, June 1, 1929; children—Margaret Virginia Ware Deimling, Henry Hall III. Admitted to Ga. bar, 1926, since practiced in Atlanta; mem. firm Ware, Hopkins, Dunlevie & McNairy; dir., mem. exec. com. Southeastern Capital Corp.; gen. counsel So. Fed. Savs. and Loan Assn. Alumni trustee Mercer U., 1938-43, 69, trustee, 1938-43, 69-75, mem. president's council, 1976—. Mem. Am. Judicature Soc., Mercer Alumni Assn. (past nat. pres.), Am., Ga. (past chmn. real estate sect.), Atlanta bar assns., Alpha Tau Omega (past pres. Atlanta; nat. dir. 1956). Presbyn. (elder, trustee). Clubs: Lawyers (past exec. com.), Commerce (Atlanta). Home: 404 Blackland Rd NW Atlanta GA 30342 Office: 101 Marietta Tower Suite 3301 Atlanta GA 30303

WARE, JAMES EDWIN, mfg. co. exec.; b. Athens, Ga., Jan. 27, 1925; s. James Edwin and Marguerite (McCue) W.; student St. Petersburg Jr. Coll., Fla., 1942-43, Rutgers U., 1943-44; M.E., Stevens Inst. Tech., 1948; m. Petronella J. Knoors, Dec. 13, 1952; children—Marguerite Linda, Jennifer Ellen. Salesman, Chgo. Pneumatic Tool Co., N.Y.C., N.Y., 1948-61; gen. sales mgr. Hoke, Inc., Cresskill, N.J., 1961-63; mgr. instrument systems sales McKiernan Terry div. Litton Industries, Clifton, N.J., 1963-66; dir. marketing, mining and constrn. div. Joy Mfg. Co., Claremont, N.H., 1966-67; v.p., gen. mgr. Picker X-Ray Co., White Plains, N.Y., 1967-70; pres., gen. mgr. Northrop Archtl. Systems, City of Industry, Calif., 1971—; v.p. Northrop Corp.; dir. Shinko-Northrop, Japan, Societe d'Etudes et de Prefabrication, France. Dir., Industry Mfrs. Council, City of Industry, Calif., 1971—. Served with inf., AUS, World War II; ETO. Decorated Combat Inf. badge. Office: 999 S Hatcher Ave City of Industry CA 91748

WARE, KARL ELLIS, mfg. co. exec.; b. Cleve., Nov. 19, 1926; s. Clyde and Lucy M. (Garforth) W.; student Oberlin (Ohio) Coll., 1945; B.A., Miami U., Oxford, O., 1948; LL.D., Cleveland Marshall Law Sch., 1959; m. Nancy Reese, June 27, 1953; 1 dau., Karla Reese. Pres.,

Strong, Carlisle & Hammond, Cleve., 1961-68; pres. Whitin Machine Works, Charlotte, N.C., 1968-69; group v.p. White Consol. Industries, Inc., Cleve., 1969-71, exec. v.p., 1972-74, sr. exec. v.p. ops., 1975-76, exec. v.p., chief operating officer, 1976—; dir. Oatey Co., Cleve., Americold Compressor Corp., Cullman, Ala., Soc. Nat. Bank, Cleve., WCI Can. Ltd., Guelph. Trustee Lakewood Hosp., Lakewood Hosp. Found., Kenneth Beck Center for Cultural Arts. Served with USNR, 1944-46. Mem. Cleve. Indsl. Distbrs. Assn. (pres. 1964-65), Ohio Bar Assn. Presbyn. (elder, deacon). Clubs: Pepper Pike, Union, Westwood Country, Cleve. Yachting, Catawba Island. Home: 21853 Lake Rd Rocky River OH 44116 Office: 11770 Berea Rd Cleveland OH 44111

WARE, MARCUS JOHN, lawyer; b. Yakima, Wash., Mar. 17, 1904; s. Marcus Clark and Ruby Marie (Cross) W.; LL.B., U. Idaho, 1927; m. Helen Gorton, June 6, 1933; children—Robert Gorton, Donald Frank (dec.), Barbara Jean (Mrs. Wray W. Featherstone, Jr.), Mary Elizabeth. Admitted to Idaho bar, 1927, since practiced in Lewiston; with firm Ware, Stellmon & O'Connell, 1927—, sr. partner, 1955—; pros. atty. Nez Perce County, Idaho, 1943-44. Chmn., Lewis-Clark Sesquicentennial Celebration, Lewiston, also Clarkston, Wash., 1955-56; chmn. Lewiston Centennial Celebration, 1961; former vice chmn. Lewis and Clark Trail Commn.; mem. Idaho Hist. Sites Rev. Bd., 1969—, Idaho Bi-Centennial Commn., 1972-76, Lewiston Bi-Centennial Commn., 1973-76; mem. nat. adv. council on ethnic heritage studies Office Edn., HEW, 1975-76. Bd. dirs. Pacific NW Nat. Parks Assn., 1976—; past dir. Lewis and Clark Trail Heritage Found. Recipient award of merit Am. Assn. State and Local History, 1961, citation Idaho Recreation and Park Soc., 1973. Mem. Am., Idaho (commr. 1959-62, pres. 1961-62), Clearwater bar assns., Am. Coll. Trial Lawyers, Idaho (past chmn. bd. trustees), Mont., Nev. hist. socs., C. of C., S.A.R. (past state pres.), Soc. Mayflower Descs. (past gov. Idaho soc., dep. gov. gen.), Luna House Hist. Soc. (past pres.), Phi Kappa Phi, Phi Alpha Delta, Delta Tau Delta. Republican. Mason (Shriner, K.T., 33 deg., past grand master Idaho), Elk. Kiwanian (past pres.). Club: Outlook (Lewiston). Home: 308 Prospect Blvd Lewiston ID 83501 Office: 1219 Idaho St Lewiston ID 83501

WARE, MITCHELL, state ofcl.; b. Chgo., Dec. 27, 1933; s. Robert A. and Bertha (Peete) W.; B.A., St. Ambrose Coll., 1955; J.D., DePaul U., 1967; m. Patricia R. Ford, Oct. 26, 1955 (div. Dec. 1967); children—Pamela Marie, Mitchell Gregory Robert; m. 2d, Nancy J. Herrmann, Dec. 20, 1973; 1 son, Michael Paul. Narcotic agt. Ill. Div. Narcotic Control, 1960-66; law clk. U.S. Dist. Ct., 1966-67; TV news reporter WBBM-TV, Chgo., 1967-68; admitted to Ill. bar, 1967; partner firm Mazza, Mazzio & Ware, Chgo., 1967-77; supt. Ill. Div. Narcotic Control, 1968-69, Ill. Bur. Investigation, Springfield, 1970-72; dep. supt. Chgo. Police Dept., 1972-78; individual practice law, 1978—; div. dir. Regional Transp. Authority, 1978—; mem. Pres. Nixon's Nat. Commn. Marijuana and Drug Abuse, 1971—; prof. criminal law DePaul U., 1967-71; lectr., 1974—. Area chmn. Boy Scouts Am., 1969-71, exec. bd. 1972—; trustee Fed. Defender Program; bd. dirs. Easter Seal Soc., Michael Reese Hosp. Served with AUS, 1955-57. Mem. Chgo. (criminal law com. 1967-69), Am., Ill., Nat., Fed., Cook County bar assns., Am. Judicature Soc., Sisters of Blessed Sacrament Alumni Assn. (chmn. 1969—), Phi Alpha Delta. Author: Operational Handbook for Narcotic Law Enforcement Officers, 1975. Office: 33 N Dearborn Suite 1011 Chicago IL 60602. *Throughout my life, I have sought to try always to lead by example; to maintain high standards of principles and integrity; to develop the wisdom to make fair, judicious, and proper decisions, along with the strength, courage and fortitude to carry out those decisions in the face of obstacles. Coming from a humble background, if my limited success will help inspire other underprivileged human beings, especially members of my race, to join in efforts to improve our society, then my endeavors will have been worthwhile.*

WARE, RICHARD ANDERSON, found. exec.; b. N.Y.C., Nov. 7, 1919; s. John Sayers and Mabelle (Anderson) W.; B.A., Lehigh U., 1941; M. Pub. Adminstrn., Wayne State U., 1943; m. Lucille Henney, Mar. 20, 1942 (div. 1972); children—Alexander W., Janet M., Bradley J., Patricia E.; m. 2d, Beverly G. Mytinger, Dec. 22, 1972. Research asst. Detroit Bur. Govt. Research, 1941-42; personnel technician Lend-Lease Adminstrn., Washington, 1942-43; research asso. to asst. dir. Citizens Research Council, Detroit, 1946-56; sec. Earhart and Relm Founds., Ann Arbor, Mich., 1956-70, trustee, pres., 1970—; prin. dep. asst. sec. Def. for internat. security affairs, Washington, 1969-70, cons. Office Asst. Sec. Def., 1970-73; dir. Ann Arbor Trust Co. Vice pres. Ann Arbor United Fund and Community Services, 1968, pres., 1969; asst. dir. Mich. Joint Legis. Com. on State Reorgn., 1950-52; sec. Gov.'s Com. to Study Prisons, 1952-53; com. to chmn. Ann Arbor City Planning Commn., 1958-67; mem. Detroit Com. on Fgn. Relations, 1971—; mem. adv. council Woodrow Wilson Internat. Center for Scholars, 1973—; vis. com. div. social scis. U. Chgo., 1977—; mem. adv. com. The Citadel, 1977—; polit. analyst Republican Nat. Com., Washington, 1964; trustee Greenhills Sch., 1973—, Ann Arbor Area Found., 1977—. Served with USAAF, 1943-46. Recipient Civilian Meritorious Service medal Dept. Def., 1970. Mem. Govtl. Research Asso. (trustee, v.p. 1955-56), Am. Polit. Sci. Assn., Am. Soc. Pub. Adminstrn., Mont Pelerin Soc., Phi Beta Kappa, Phi Alpha Theta. Congregationalist. Clubs: Ann Arbor; Barton Hills Country; Cosmos (Washington). Home: 16 Haverhill Ct Ann Arbor MI 48105 Office: 904 1st Nat Bldg Ann Arbor MI 48108

WARE, THADDEUS VAN, govt. ofcl.; b. High Point, N.C., Mar. 31, 1935; s. Elsec and Irene (Myers) W.; B.A. cum laude, Va. Union U., 1957; J.D., Howard U., 1960; m. Doretha Ardella Lee, June 18, 1960; children—Kimberly Melissa, Chrystal Lynn. Admitted to Va. bar, 1961, D.C. bar, 1970, U.S. Supreme Ct. bar; gen. atty. Office Solicitor Labor-Mgmr. Reports, Dept. Labor, 1961-66; trial counsel Chief Counsel's Office, Fed. Hwy. Adminstrn., 1966-69; staff asst. to Pres. Richard M. Nixon, 1969-70; adminstrv. judge Bd. Contract Appeals, Dept. Transp., 1970—. Served with AUS, 1960-61. Mem. Va., D.C., U.S. Supreme Ct., Fed. bar assns., Urban League, NAACP, Nat. Conf. Bd. Contract Appeal Mems., Alpha Phi Alpha, Sigma Delta Tau, Alpha Kappa Mu. Home: 12906 Morningside Lane Silver Spring MD 20904 Office: 400 7th St SW Washington DC 20011

WARF, JAMES CURREN, educator; b. Nashville, Sept. 1, 1917; s. James Curren and Susie (McCord) W.; B.S., U. Tulsa, 1939; Ph.D., Iowa State U., 1946; m. Kyoko Sato, Dec. 28, 1965; children—Sandra Louise, Curren Walter, Barnbay Louis. Group leader Manhattan Project Atomic Energy Program, Ames, Iowa, U. Chgo., Oak Ridge, 1942-47; Guggenheim fellow, Berne, Switzerland, 1947-48; prof. chemistry, research chemist U. So. Calif., 1948—; vis. prof. U. Indonesia, Jakarta, 1957-59, Airlangga U., Indonesia, 1962-64, Nat. U. Malaysia, Kuala Lumpur, 1974-75, Sabah br., 1976; research prof. Tech. U. Vienna (Austria), 1969-70, Hasanuddin U., Andalas U. (Indonesia), 1978-79. Office Naval Research grantee, 1952; Office Ordnance Research grantee, 1955; Research Corp. grantee, 1953; Austrian Ministry Edn. stipend grantee, 1969; NSF grantee, 1970, 78. Mem. Fedn. Am. Scientists (chmn. Los Angeles chpt. 1967-69), Am. Chem. Soc., Sigma Xi. Author: Physical Chemistry for Medical Students, 1964; Reference Book of Inorganic Chemistry, 1975; Textbook of Inorganic Chemistry, 1976; Inorganic Chemistry, 1979; English-Indonesian Dictionary for Chemists, 1979. Home: 3930 Franklin Ave Los Angeles CA 90027

WARFEL, RUTH ELIZABETH, ednl. adminstr.; b. Lancaster, Pa., Aug. 13, 1920; d. G. Earle and Mary (Breuninger) Warfel; B.S., State Tchrs. Coll., Millersville, Pa., 1941; M.S., Ind. U., 1948; postgrad. Tchrs. Coll. Columbia. Tchr. elementary schs., Lancaster, 1941-44; dean of women State U. Tchrs. Coll., Potsdam, N.Y., 1948-51, asso. dean students, 1948-61; dean women Miami U., Oxford, Ohio, 1961-64; dean students Mount Holyoke Coll., South Hadley, Mass., 1964—. Served as ensign USNR, 1944-46. Member AAUW, Am. Coll. Personnel Assn., Nat., Mass. assns. women deans adminstrs. and counselors, Pi Lambda Theta, Kappa Delta Pi. Club: Zonta (v.p. Potsdam). Home: 15 Ashfield Lane South Hadley MA 01075

WARFIELD, CHARLES HORACE, lawyer; b. Clarksville, Tenn., Oct. 18, 1924; s. Charles Percy and Georgia Ruth (Edmondson) W.; B.A., Vanderbilt, 1947, LL.B., 1949; student U. South, 1943; m. Martha Ezell Hardcastle, July 22, 1950; children—Charles Horace, Walter Miles, William Montgomery. Admitted to Tenn. bar, 1949, since practiced in Nashville; mem. firm Farris, Warfield & Kanaday; former chmn. Tenn. Law Revision Commn.; vis. tchr. Vanderbilt U. Sch. Law, 1958-61. Bd. govs. nat. ARC, Washington, 1970-76, 1st vice chmn., 1975-76; bd. govs. Children's Mus.; trustee United Givers Fund, Battle Ground Acad.; bd. dirs. YMCA, Nashville Symphony; adv. bd. Jr. League. Served with USNR, 1943-46. Mem. Am., Tenn., Nashville bar assns., Nashville Better Bus. (pres., 1969), Nashville C. of C. (past v.p., dir. 1971-72, exec. com. 1971-72, pres. elect 1976-78, pres. 1978—). Democrat. Presbyterian. Clubs: Belle Meade County, Nashville City. Mem. Met. Charter Commn., Nashville, 1962. Home: 4208 Estes Ave Nashville TN 37215 Office: 3d Nat Bank Bldg Nashville TN 37219

WARFIELD, EDWIN, state ofcl.; b. Balt., June 3, 1924; s. Edwin and Katharine Leee W.; student Cornell U., 1942, Johns Hopkins U., 1947-48; B.S. in Agr., U. Md., 1950; married; children—Edwin, Elizabeth, Diana, John. Served as enlisted man AC, U.S. Army, 1942-44, commd. 2d lt., 1944, advanced through grades to maj. gen., 1970; fighter pilot, Iwo Jima, 1945; mem. 104th Tactical Fighter Squadron, Md. Air N.G., Balt., 1950, unit comdr., 1950-57, chief of staff, 1957-65; asst. adj. gen. State of Md., Balt., 1965-70, maj. gen. and adj. gen., 1970—; chmn. bd. The Daily Record, Md. legal newspaper, Balt., 1972—; owner, operator farm, Howard County, Md.; mem. Md. Ho. of Dels., 1963-70. Democrat. Episcopalian. Clubs: Md., South River, Howard County Hunt, Am. Legion, VFW. Office: Adj Gen's Office Fifth Regt Armory Baltimore MD 21201

WARFIELD, GEORGE, research inst. exec.; b. Piombino, Italy, Apr. 21, 1919 (parents U.S. citizens); s. Vincent and Ada (Donati) W.; B.S., Franklin and Marshall Coll., 1940; Ph.D., Cornell U., 1949; m. Lauraine Serra, July 14, 1945; children—Cheryl Mitchell, Pamela, Richard. Asst. prof. Princeton, 1949-57, asso. prof., 1957-66, prof. elec. engring., 1966-72; cons. RCA Labs., Princeton, 1950-74; exec. dir. Inst. Energy Conversion, U. Del., 1974-77; asst. dir. Solar Energy Research Inst., Golden, Colo., 1977-79, dir. tech. dissemination, 1979—. Mem. IEEE (sr.), Am. Phys. Soc., Phi Beta Kappa, Sigma Xi. Research in MOS systems, insulator physics. Home: 1445 Lunnonhaus Dr Golden CO 80401

WARFIELD, GERALD ALEXANDER, composer; b. Ft. Worth, Feb. 23, 1940; s. George Alexander and Geraldine (Spencer) W.; student Tex. Christian U., 1958-61; B.A., North Tex. State U., 1963, M.Mus., 1965; M.F.A., Princeton, 1967; postgrad. Tanglewood, summers 1963-64. Instr., Princeton, 1968-71; asso. dir. Index of New Mus. Notation, N.Y.C., 1971-75; dir. notation project for contemporary music U. Ill., 1976-77; lectr. contemporary music notation. Mem. conf. com. Internat. Conf. on New Mus. Notation, Belgium, 1974; chmn. program com. 2d Nat. Conf. Music Theory, 1977. Mem. Am. Soc. Univ. Composers (chmn. exec. com. 1972-74, conf. chmn. 9th Ann. Conf. 1974, treas. 1974-76, founding editor Jour. of Music Scores), Am. Composers Alliance (gov. 1978—, treas. 1979—), Am. Musicol. Soc., Music Library Assn., Coll. Music Soc. (council), Soc. Music Theory, Broadcast Music Inc. Author: A Beginner's Manual of Music 4B, 1967; Layer Analysis: a Primer of Elementary Tonal Structures, 1976; Writings on Contemporary Music Notations, 1977; How to Write Music Manuscript, 1977; (with others) Layer Dictation, 1978; Composer: Three Movements for Orchestra, 1966; Thirteen Ways of Looking at a Blackbird (1st prize N.J. chpt. Nat. Soc. Arts and Letters), 1967; Variations and Metamorphoses (1st prize Ariz. Cello Soc.), 1973; (filmstrip) Introduction to Musical Notation, 1976; Music for Hippolytos, 1977; Fantasy Quintet (2d prize New Music for Young Ensembles), 1978; A Trophy, 1979. Contbr. to Grove's Dictionary of Music and Musicians, 1976; editor Longman Music Series, 1976—. Contbr. articles to profl. jours. Home: 205 W 22d St New York NY 10011

WARFIELD, SANDRA, mezzo-soprano; b. Kansas City, Mo.; grad. Kansas City Conservatory Music; m. James McCracken; 1 dau., Ahna. Appeared with maj. opera cos., including: Vienna Staatsoper, Met. Opera, Zurich (Switzerland) Opera, Berlin Staatsoper, San Francisco Opera, New Orleans Opera Co., Seattle Opera, N.J. State Opera; N.Y.C. recital debut at Alice Tully Hall, 1978; recitals throughout country; appeared with symphony orchs., including: Phila. Orch., Erie Philharm., N.W. Indpls. Symphony Orch., L.I. Symphony, Bergen Philharm. Orch.; performed at White House (with James McCracken) in Presdl. salute to 25th Anniversary of UN; leading roles in: Samson et Dalila, Ballo in Maschera, Carmen, Cosi fan tutte, Il Trovatore, Der Rosenkavalier, Greek Passion, Le Prophete, Ring cycle, La Gioconda; recs.: Duets of Love and Passion, London Records. Author: (with James McCracken) A Star in the Family, 1971. Office: care Columbia Artists Mgmt Inc 165 W 57th St New York NY 10019

WARFIELD, WILLIAM CAESAR, singer, actor, educator: b. West Helena, Ark., Jan. 22, 1920; s. Robert Elza and Bertha (McCamery) W.; B.M., Eastman Sch. Music, 1942; LL.D. (hon.), U. Ark., 1972; D.Mus. (hon.), Lafayette Coll., 1978; m. Leontyne Price, Aug. 31, 1952 (div. Dec. 1972). Mem. nat. co. Call Me Mister, 1946-47; Broadway plays include Set My People Free, Regina, 1948-49; Town Hall debut, 1950; tour of Australia, 1950; motion picture Showboat, 1951; toured with govt. sponsored European prodn. Porgy and Bess, singing role of Porgy, 1952; concerts, radio and TV appearances, Symphony soloist, recitals, 1950—; concert tour for Dept. State, as soloist with Phila. Orch. for its continental debut, 1955, tour Africa, Nr. East, Europe, 1956, Asia, Australia, 1958, Cuba, 1959, Europe, 1966, recital Brussels Fair, 1958; starred as De Lawd in Green Pastures, NBC-TV, 1957, 59; star N.Y.C. Opera revival Porgy and Bess, 1961, 64, also Vienna prodn., 1965-72; featured soloist Casals Festival, P.R. and N.Y.C., 1962-63, Athens Festival (Greece), 1966; starred in Richard Rodgers' prodn. Show Boat for Music Theater of Lincoln Center, 1966, German lang. Show Boat for Vienna Volksoper, 1971-72; soloist with Pablo Casals, Geneva, Switzerland, Pacem in Terris II Convocation, 1967; title role in Mendelssohn's Elijah, 1969; presented by Central City Opera (Colo.) as star prodn. Puccini opera Gianni Schicchi, 1972; performed concert Carnegie Hall, 1975. Prof. music dept. U. Ill., Champaign, 1974—. Bd. dirs. N.Y. Coll. Music, also trustee; trustee Berkshire Boys Choir, 1966-70, Nat. Assn. Negro Musicians. Recipient hon. citation Eastman Sch. Music, 1954. Mem. Actors Equity, Am. Guild Mus. Artists, Screen Actors Guild, AFTRA, NAACP (life), Phi Mu Alpha Sinfonia (life). Office: Dept of Music Univ of Illinois 2136 Music Bldg IL 61801

WARGA, JACK, mathematician; b. Warsaw, Poland, Dec. 5, 1922; s. Herman and Czarna (Lichtenstein) W.; came to U.S., 1943, naturalized, 1944; student Brussels (Belgium) U., 1939-40; B.A., Carleton Coll., 1944; Ph.D., N.Y. U., 1950; m. Faye Kleinman, Feb. 27, 1949; children—Charna Ruth, Arthur David. Chief engring. computing sect. Republic Aviation Corp., Farmingdale, N.Y., 1952-53; head math dept. Burroughs Corp., Pasadena, Cal., 1954-56; mgr., math dept. Avco Research and Devel., Wilmington, Mass., 1957-66; prof. math. Northeastern U., Boston, 1966—. Served with AUS, 1944-46. Weizmann Meml. fellow, 1956-57. Fellow AAAS; mem. Am. Math. Soc., Soc. Indsl. and Applied Math. (editor Jour. on Control and Optimization 1966—). Author: Optimal Control of Differential and Functional Equations, 1972. Contbr. articles to profl. jours. Home: 233 Clark Rd Brookline MA 02146 Office: Dept Math Northeastern University Boston MA 02115

WARHOL, ANDY, artist, filmmaker; b. Pitts.; s. James and Julia (Von) W.; student Carnegie Inst. Tech. One-man exhbns. include Leo Castelli Gallery, N.Y.C., Ferus Gallery, Los Angeles, Stable Gallery, N.Y.C., Morris Gallery, Toronto, Can., Rubbers Gallery, Buenos Aires, Sonnebend Gallery, Paris; dir., producer, photographer movies: Eat, 1963, Sleep, 1963, Kiss, 1963, Empire, 1964, Harlot, 1964, My Hustler, 1965, Chelsea Girls, 1966, Bike Boy, 1967, Lonesome Cowboys, 1968, Blue Movie, 1969, Imitation of Christ, 1969, Flesh, 1969, Trash, 1971, Women in Revolt, 1972, Andy Warhol's Bad, 1977, L'Amour, 1978; producer films: Heat, 1972, Blood for Dracula, 1974, Andy Warhol's Frankenstein, 1975; producer recs. of rock group Velvet Underground; pub. Interview mag. Recipient Art Dirs. Club medal, 1957; 6th Film Culture, award 1964; Los Angeles Film Festival award, 1964. Author: Andy Warhol's Mother's Book of Cats; Andy Warhol's Index; The Philosophy of Andy Warhol: From A to B and Back Again, 1975; Andy Warhol's Exposures, 1979. Address: 860 Broadway New York NY 10003*

WARIN, EDWARD GEORGE, U.S. atty.; b. Des Moines, Feb. 16, 1947; s. Roger F. and Mary A. (Gray) W.; B.S., Creighton U., 1969; J.D., Georgetown U., 1973; m. Colleen Walsh, Aug. 6, 1971; children—Edward Walsh, Kathleen Hall, Mary Colleen. Admitted to D.C. bar, Nebr. bar; dep. county atty. Douglas County, Omaha, 1973-77; U.S. atty., Omaha, 1978—; instr. criminal law U. Nebr. at Omaha. Mem. Am., D.C., Nebr., Omaha bar assns., Nat. Dist. Attys. Assn. Democrat. Roman Catholic. Home: 10006 Seward St Omaha NE 68114 Office: PO Box 1228 US Post Office and Courthouse Omaha NE 68101

WARING, EDWARD GRAHAM, JR., educator; b. Kansas City, Mo., Feb. 27, 1924; s. Edward Graham and Flora (Basye) W.; B.A., So. Meth. U., 1943; B.D., U. Chgo., 1946, Ph.D. 1950; m. Carobeth Elaine McIntire, June 8, 1945; children—Judith Elizabeth, Linda Louise, Christopher Andrew. Ordained to ministry Conglist. Ch., 1946; minister, Pecatonica, Ill., 1946-48, West Chicago, Ill., 1948-50; acting chaplain Asso. Colls. Claremont (Calif.), 1950-51; faculty Lawrence U., 1951—, chmn. dept. religion, 1953-68, 75—, prof. religion, 1962—, asso. dean faculty, 1969-75. Vis. prof. Dartmouth, summer 1967; dir. Lawrence U. German Study Center, Bonningheim, Germany, 1968-69. Mem. Am. Acad. Religion, Phi Beta Kappa. Editor, author introduction: (Schleiermacher) On Religion, 1955, (Feuerbach) Essence of Christianity, 1957, Deism and Natural Religion, 1967. Home: 2900 S Carpenter St Appleton WI 54911

WARING, FRED M., musical condr.; b. Tyrone, Pa., June 9, 1900; s. Frank and Jessie (Calderwood) W.; student engring. Pa. State U.; m. Evalyn Nair, 1933; children—Dixie, Fred, Bill; m. 2d, Virginia Gearhart, 1954; children—Paul, Malcolm. Writer numerous coll. songs; appeared in several mus. shows on Broadway; in motion picture Varsity Show; mus. condr. The Pennsylvanians; conducted his orch. in Paris; first appeared in Balaban Theatre, Chgo., 1923; on radio, 1933—; owner Shawnee Press, Inc., music pubs.; long interested in choral work and includes glee club with radio show program; organized and trained choral groups for The Seven Lively Arts (produced by Billy Rose) and for Laffing Room Only (Olsen and Johnson); organized Fred Waring Music Workshop for Choral Dirs., 1948; condr. TV program The Fred Waring Show for several seasons; producer, dir. Hear! Hear!, mus. revue, 1955; numerous recs.; former owner Shawnee Inn and Shawnee Country Club, Shawnee-on-Delaware, Pa. Hon. mem. Nat. Cartoonists Soc. Clubs: Lambs, Athletic (N.Y.C.). Developer Waring blender. Office: Fred Waring Show Delaware Water Gap PA 18327

WARING, WALTER WEYLER, educator; b. Sterling, Kans., May 13, 1917; s. Walter Wray and Bonnie Laura (Weyler) W.; B.A., Kans. Wesleyan U., 1939; M.A., U. Colo., 1946; Ph.D., Cornell U., 1949; m. Mary Esther Griffith, Feb. 8, 1946; children—Mary Laura, Helen Ruth, Elizabeth Anne, Claire Joyce. Tchr., English and chemistry, Belleville (Kan.) High Sch., 1939-41; instr. U. Colo., Boulder, 1941-42, 46-47; mem. faculty Kalamazoo Coll., 1949—, prof. English, 1955—, chmn. dept., 1953-78, dir. humanities, 1978—. Served to 1st lt. AUS, World War II; PTO. Decorated Legion of Merit. Mem. Phi Beta Kappa. Ednl. TV lectr. Author: Thomas Carlyle, 1978; also articles. Home: 156 Monroe St Kalamazoo MI 49007

WARK, ROBERT RODGER, art curator; b. Edmonton, Can., Oct. 7, 1924; s. Joseph Henry and Louise (Rodger) W.; B.A., U. Alta., 1944, M.A., 1946; A.M., Harvard, 1949, Ph.D., 1952. Came to U.S., 1948, naturalized, 1970. Instr. art Harvard, 1952-54; instr. history art Yale, 1954-56; curator art Henry E. Huntington Library and Art Gallery, San Marino, Calif., 1956—. Lectr. art Calif. Inst. Tech., 1960—, U. Calif. at Los Angeles, 1966—. Served with RCAF, 1944-45, RCNVR, 1945. Mem. Coll. Art Assn., Assn. Art Mus. Dirs., Am. Museums Assn. Author: Sculpture in the Huntington Collection, 1959; French Decorative Art in the Huntington Collection, 1961; Rowlandson's Drawings for a Tour in a Post Chaise, 1963; Rowlandson's Drawings for the English Dance of Death, 1966; Isaac Cruikshank's Drawings for Drolls, 1968; Early British Drawings in the Huntington Collection 1600-1750, 1969; Drawings by John Flaxman, 1970; Ten British Pictures 1740-1840, 1971; Meet the Ladies: Personalities in Huntington Portraits, 1972; Drawings from the Turner Shakespeare, 1973; Drawings by Thomas Rowlandson in the Huntington Collection, 1975; British Silver in the Huntington Collection, 1978; editor: Sir Joshua Reynolds: Discourses on Art, 1959. Home: 1330 Lombardy Rd Pasadena CA 91106 Office: Huntington Library San Marino CA 91108

WARKANY, JOSEF, physician; b. Vienna, Austria, Mar. 25, 1902; s. Jacob and Hermine (Buchwald) W.; student Real-Gymnasium, Vienna, 1912-20; M.D., U. Vienna, 1926; D.Sc. (hon.), Thomas Jefferson Med. Coll., 1974, U. Ill., 1975; m. Suzanne Blanche Buhlman, Apr. 24, 1937; children—Joseph Henry, Stephen Fred. Came to U.S., 1932, naturalized, 1938. Intern, Children's Clinic, Vienna, 1926-27; asst. Reichsanstalt for Mothers and Children, 1927-31; scholar Children's Hosp. Research Found., Cin., 1931-34, fellow, 1935—; dir. mental retardation research Inst. for Developmental Research, 1966-77; asst. attending pediatrician Children's Hosp., Cin., 1934-35, attending pediatrician, 1935—;

attending pediatrician, pediatric and contagious divs. Cin. Gen. Hosp., 1935—; prof. research pediatrics, 1953—. Recipient Mead-Johnson award, 1944; Borden award, 1950; award medal Am. Assn. Plastic Surgeons, 1962; Distinguished Achievement award Modern Medicine, 1964; Honors award Am. Cleft Palate Assn., 1966; Max Weinstein-Cerebral Palsy award United Cerebral Palsy Assns., 1969; Charles H. Hood Found. award, 1972; Research award Am. Assn. Mental Deficiency, 1976; Recognition award Cin. Pediatric Soc., 1976; George Rieveschl Jr. award U. Cin., 1976. Diplomate Am. Bd. Pediatrics, Ohio Med. Bd. Mem. Am. Pediatric Soc. (Howland award 1970), Soc. Pediatric Research, Ohio Med. Assn., Acad. Medicine Cin., Am. Acad. Pediatrics (hon.), Harvey Soc., Teratology Soc. (1st pres. 1960), Soc. de Pédiatrie (Paris), European Teratology Soc. (hon.). Home: 3535 Biddle St Cincinnati OH 45220 Office: Children's Hosp Research Found Cincinnati OH 45229

WARKOV, ESTHER, artist; b. Winnipeg, Man., Can., Oct. 12, 1941; d. Morris and Sarah (Schulman) W.; student Winnipeg Sch. Art, 1958-61; m. Frans Johannes Visscher, Sept. 6, 1966; 1 dau., Jenny Visscher. Exhbns. include: Expo '67, Montreal, 1967, Marlborough Godard Exhibition, 1973, Mus. Modern Art, Paris, 1973, Albright-Knox Gallery, Buffalo, 1974; represented in permanent collections: Nat. Gallery, Ottawa, Can., Mus. Fine Arts, Montreal, Vancouver Art Gallery, Winnipeg Art Gallery, Beaver Brook Art Gallery, Fredricton, N.B., Can. Recipient Can. Council grants. Democrat. Address: 341 Matheson Winnipeg MB R2W 0C9 Canada*

WARKOW, STEWART J., arts adminstr.; b. Bklyn., Sept. 9, 1934; s. Hyman and Edith (Kramer) W. Asst. mgr. Symphony of the Air, 1954-60; on tour with artists for Columbia Artists, also S. Hurok, 1960-61; mgr. Am. Symphony, N.Y.C., 1962-68; house mgr. Carnegie Hall, N.Y.C., 1968-78, exec. dir. Carnegie Hall Corp., 1978—. Mem. Am. Symphony Orch. League, League for N.Y. Music. Office: Carnegie Hall Corp 881 7th Ave New York NY 10019

WARLICK, ROBERT PATTERSON, investment mgmt. co. exec., mayor; b. Durham, N.C., July 25, 1924; s. Louis F. and Katie Alene (Maynard) W.; A.B. cum laude, Brown U., 1948; M.B.A., Harvard U., 1950; m. Margaret-Anne Buchanan, Oct. 22, 1960; children—Elizabeth Baetjer, Peter Maynard. Gen. investment mgr. Prudential Ins. Co., 1960-68; chmn. bd. First Morris Bank, Morristown, N.J., 1968-69, dir., 1969—; with Lord, Abbett & Co., N.Y.C., 1969—, partner charge investment div., 1972-74; pres., dir., portfolio mgr. Lord Abbett Bond-Debenture Fund, 1974—. Mem. planning bd. Chester Twp., N.J., 1975—, councilman, 1976-78, mayor, 1978—; past vestryman Episcopal Ch. of St. John on Mountain, Bernardsville, N.J. Served with USAAF, 1943-46. Decorated Bronze Star. Mem. N.Y. Soc. Security Analysts, Harvard Bus. Sch. Club N.Y.C. Republican. Clubs: Somerset Hills (N.J.) Country; Harvard, Broad St. (N.Y.C.). Home: Three Brook Farm Old Chester Rd Chester NJ 07930 Office: 63 Wall St New York NY 10005

WARMACK, JOHN LEE, utility co. exec.; b. Hope, Ark., Jan. 19, 1928; s. Robert Lee and Birdie Jane (Huckabee) W.; B.S., La. State U., 1951; m. Mary Allen, Jan. 4, 1951; children—Patricia, John Lee, Mary Jane, Robert, Andrew. With Gulf States Utilities Co., Beaumont, Tex., 1952-67; with So. Ind. Gas & Electric Co., Evansville, 1967-78, exec. v.p., gen. mgr., 1975-76, pres., gen. mgr., 1976-78; exec. mgr. LEMCO Engrs., Inc., St. Louis, 1979—; dir. Nat. City Bank. Bd. dirs. Vanderburgh County Soc. for Crippled Children and Adults, 1973-77, Jr. Achievement of Southwestern Ind., 1973-74; exec. bd., dist. chmn. Boy Scouts Am., 1976—, pres., 1978. Registered profl. engr., La., Tex. Mem. Ind. Electric Assn. (dir. 1970-74, pres. 1972-73), Constrn. Users Council, IEEE, Evansville C. of C. (dir. 1967-78) v.p. transp. and environ. mgmt. div. 1972-78). Clubs: Masons, Shriners, Petroleum (Evansville), Columbia (Indpls.). Home: 327 Woodmar Ct Ballwin MO 63011 Office: 11933 Westline Industrial Dr Saint Louis MO 63141

WARMAN, C. DALE, retail co. exec.; b. Springfield, Colo., July 4, 1929; s. William Thomas and Ella (Nagel) W.; student Warner Pacific Coll., Portland State U.; m. Marilyn Trudgeon, Feb. 14, 1950; children—Douglas, Sharon, Ronald. With Fred Meyer, Inc., Portland, Oreg., 1949-72, 75—, successively mdse. mgr., supr. mktg., exec. v.p., 1975—; exec. v.p. Allied Supermarkets, Detroit, 1973-75. Trustee, Warner Pacific Coll.; past chmn. United Way. Republican. Mem. Ch. of God. Club: Toastmasters. Home: 395 N Lotus Beach Dr Portland OR 97217 Office: 3800 SE 22d Portland OR 97242

WARMAN, JOHN BOYLE, clergyman; b. Uniontown, Pa., Apr. 9, 1915; s. Robert Densmore and Minnie Lillian (Conaway) W.; A.B., Western Md. Coll., 1937; B.D., Andover Newton Theol. Sch., 1941; Ed.M., U. Pitts., 1951; D.D., Allegheny Coll., 1958, Western Md. Coll., 1962, Lebanon Valley Coll., 1974; m. Annie Owings Sansbury, June 15, 1939; children—John Sansbury, Irene (Mrs. Vernard Taulbee, Jr.), Oden Robert. Ordained to ministry Meth. Ch., 1941; pastor 1st Meth. Ch., Butler, Pa., 1950-58, 1st Meth. Ch., Pitts., 1958-62, Baldwin Community Ch., Pitts., 1965-72; bishop Harrisburg (Pa.) area United Meth. Ch., 1972—; supt. Pitts. dist. Meth. Ch., 1962-65. Mem. Pitts. Human Relations Commn., 1962-67. Trustee Mt. Union Coll., 1962-65, Lebanon Valley Coll., 1974—, Dickinson Coll., 1974—. Served with USNR, 1945-46. Mem. Tau Kappa Alpha. Democrat. Mason (33 deg.). Home: 1 Frances Dr Harrisburg PA 17109 Office: 900 S Arlington Ave Harrisburg PA 17109

WARMBROD, JAMES ROBERT, educator; b. Belvidere, Tenn., Dec. 13, 1929; s. George Victor and Anna Sophia (Zimmerman) W.; B.S., U. Tenn., 1952, M.S., 1954; Ed.D. (Univ. fellow), U. Ill., 1962; m. Catharine P. Phelps, Jan. 30, 1965. Instr. edn. U. Tenn., Knoxville, 1956-57; tchr. high sch., Winchester, Tenn., 1957-59; asst. prof. U. Ill., Urbana, 1961-66, asso. prof., 1966-67; prof. agrl. edn. Ohio State U., Columbus, 1968—, chmn. dept., 1978—; vis. prof. Pa. State U., 1970, U. Minn., 1971, Iowa State U., 1974; vis. scholar Va. Poly. Inst. and State U., 1976. Served with USAF, 1954-56. Recipient Distinguished Teaching award Ohio State U. Alumni, 1972; Teaching award Ohio State U chpt. Gamma Sigma Delta, 1977. Mem. Am. Vocat. Assn. (v.p. 1976-79), Am. Ednl. Research Assn., Am. Vocat. Edn. Research Assn. (pres. 1976), Am. Assn. Tchr. Educators in Agr. (Distinguished Service award 1974; Distinguished lectr. 1974), Nat. Soc. for Study of Edn. Author: Review and Synthesis of Research on the Economics of Vocational Education, 1968; the Liberalization of Vocat. Education, 1974; editor Agrl. Edn. mag., 1968-71. Home: 3867 Mountview Rd Columbus OH 43220

WARNE, COLSTON ESTEY, economist, consumer leader; b. Romulus, N.Y., Aug. 14, 1900; s. Clinton Arlington and Harriet Ellsworth (Estey) W.; B.A., Cornell U., 1920, M.A., 1921; Ph.D., U. Chgo., 1925; M.A. (hon.), Amherst Coll., 1942; m. Frances Lee Corbett, Oct. 27, 1920; children—Clinton Lee, Margaret C. Nelson, Barbara Newell. Clk., Tompkins County Nat. Bank, Ithaca, N.Y., 1919; with accounting dept. Fed. Res. Bank N.Y., 1919-20; asst. econs. Cornell U., 1919-20, instr., 1920-21; instr. econs. U. Pitts., 1921-22, U. Chgo., 1922-25; asso. prof. U. Denver, 1925-26; asst. prof. econs. U. Pitts., 1926-30, Bryn Mawr Summer Sch. Indsl. Workers, 1927-29, 31, 32, 34; asso. prof. Amherst Coll., 1930-42, prof., 1942-70, prof. emeritus, 1970—. Vis. lectr. Wesleyan U., Middletown, Conn., 1938, 46; vis. prof. Smith Coll., 1939, Conn. Coll. for Women, 1940-42, 45-46, 48. Pres., Consumers Union U.S., 1936—; pres. Internat. Orgn. of Consumers Unions, 1960-70, treas., 1970-72, exec. com., 1972—. Am. specialist cultural exchange program U.S. Dept. State, 1962; mem. Industry Panels, Wage and Hour Adminstrn., U.S. Dept. Labor, 1943-44; cons. U.S. Coordinator of Fisheries, 1943; mem. consumers adv. com. OPA, 1944, regional consumer adviser, 1946; bd. dirs. Coop. League U.S.A., 1926-29; bd. dirs. Nat. Assn. Consumers, 1947; consumer adv. com. N.Y. State, 1955-59, Commonwealth of Mass., 1959-64; mem. Pres.'s Com. in Consumer Interests, 1946-65; pres. People's Lobby, Washington, 1934-36, v.p., 1941; hon. v.p. Nat. Consumers League, 1941; mem. consumer adv. com. Pres.'s Council Econ. Advisers, 1947-51, vice chmn., 1948; mem. prep. commn. White House Conf. on Aging, 1970; mem. Nat. Consumer Energy com. Fed. Energy Office, 1973-74; mem. consumer adv. com. Fed. Energy Adminstrn., 1974-76. Chmn. acad. freedom com. Am. Fedn. Tchrs., 1936-37; chmn. Pitts. br. ACLU, 1927-30, Western Mass. Civil Liberties Com., 1938-41. Served as apprentice seaman USNRF, 1918. Mem. Am. Econ. Assn., Am. Arbitration Assn. (panel arbitrators 1945—), AAUP (council 1938-42), Am. Marketing Assn., Artus. Author: The Consumers' Co-operative Movement in Ill.; The Pullman Boycott; Industry-Wide Collective Bargaining-Promise or Menace?; co-author: Labor Problems in Am.; chmn. bd. editors, contbr. Yearbook of Am. Labor; contbr. Materials for the Study of Bus., Consumer ED., Ency. Social Sci., Commonwealth Ency., Ency. Brit. Yearbook, Annals, Nation, New Republic; contbg. editor Current History. Home: 45 Oak Knoll Amherst MA 01002 Office: Consumers Union US Mount Vernon NY 10550

WARNE, WILLIAM ELMO, irrigationist; b. nr. Seafield, Ind., Sept. 2, 1905; s. William Rufus and Nettie Jane (Williams) W.; A.B., U. Calif., 1927; D.Econs., Yonsei U., Seoul, 1959; LL.D., Seoul Nat. U., 1959; m. Edith Margaret Peterson, July 9, 1929; children—Jane Ingrid (Mrs. David C. Beeder), William Robert, Margaret Edith (Mrs. John W. Monroe). Reporter, San Francisco Bull. and Oakland (Calif.) Post-Enquirer, 1925-27; news editor Brawley (Calif.) News, 1927, Calexico (Calif.) Chronicle, 1927-28; editor, night mgr. Los Angeles bur. A.P., 1928-31, corr. San Diego bur., 1931-33, Washington corr., 1933-35; editor, bur. reclamation Dept. Interior, 1935-37; on staff Third World Power Conf., 1936; asso. to reviewing com. Nat. Resources Com. on preparation Drainage Basin Problems and Programs, 1936, mem. editorial com. for revision, 1937; chief of information Bur. Reclamation, 1937-42; co-dir. (with Harlan H. Barrows) Columbia Basin Joint Investigations, 1939-42; chief of staff, war prodn. drive, WPB, 1942; asst. dir. div. power Dept. Interior, 1942-43, dept. dir. information, 1943, asst. commr. Bur. Reclamation, 1943-47, apptd. asst. sec. Dept. Interior, 1947, asst. sec. Water and Power Devel., 1950-51; U.S. minister charge tech. cooperation, Iran, 1951-55, Brazil, 1955-56; U.S. minister and econ. coordinator for Korea, 1956-59; dir. Cal. Dept. Fish and Game, 1959-60, Dept. Agr., 1960-61, Dept. Water Resources, 1961-67; v.p. water resources Devel. and Resources Corp., 1967-69; resources cons., 1969—; Distinguished Practitioner in Residence, Sch. Pub. Adminstrn., U. So. Calif. at Sacramento, 1976-78; adminstr. Resources Agy. of Calif., 1961-63. Chmn., Pres.'s Com. on San Diego Water Supply, 1944-46, chmn. Fed. Inter-Agy. River Basin Com., 1948, Fed. Com. on Alaskan Devel., 1948; pres. Group Health Assn., Inc., 1947-51; chmn. U.S. delegation 2d Inter-Am. Conf. Indian Life, Cuzco, Peru, 1949; U.S. del. 4th World Power Conf., London, Eng., 1950; mem. Calif. Water Pollution Control Bd., 1959-67; vice chmn., 1960-62; mem. water pollution control adv. bd. Dept. Health, Edn. and Welfare, 1962-65, cons., 1966-67; chmn. Calif. delegation Western States Water Council, 1965-67. Served as 2d lt. O.R.C., 1927-37. Recipient Distinguished Service award Dept. Interior, 1951; Distinguished Pub. Service Honor award FOA, 1955; Order of Crown, Shah of Iran, 1955; Outstanding Service citation UN Command, 1959. Mem. Nat. Acad. Pub. Adminstrn. (chmn. standing com. on environ. and resources mgmt. 1971-78), Nat. Water Supply Improvement Assn. (pres. 1978-79), Sigma Delta Chi, Lambda Chi Alpha. Clubs: Sutter (Sacramento); Nat. Press (Washington); Explorers (N.Y.C.). Author: Mission for Peace—Point 4 in Iran, 1956; The Bureau of Reclamation, 1973; How the Colorado River Was Spent, 1975; The Need to Institutionalize Desalting, 1978; prin. author: The California Experience with Mass Transfers of Water over Long Distances, 1978. Home: 2090 8th Ave Sacramento CA 95818

WARNECKE, JOHN CARL, architect; b. Oakland, Calif., Feb. 24, 1919; s. Carl I. and Margaret (Esterling) W.; A.B., Stanford U., 1941; M.A., Harvard U., 1942; children by previous marriage—John Carl, Rodger Cushing, Margaret Esterling, Frederick Pierce. Asso., Miller & Warnecke, architects, 1944-46; prin. John Carl Warnecke, A.I.A., 1947-58; partner Warnecke & Warnecke, 1954-62; pres., dir. design John Carl Warnecke & Assos., 1958—. Mem. Fine Arts Commn., Washington, 1963-67. Recipient Arnold Brunner prize in architecture, Nat. Inst. Arts and Letters, 1957; also 60 nat., regional awards for excellence. Fellow AIA; asso. N.A.D. Works include U.S. Naval Acad. Master Plan, Michelson and Chauvenet Halls, Annapolis, Md.; U. Calif. at Santa Cruz Master Plan and Library; Lafayette Sq., Washington; Georgetown U. Library, Washington; Kaiser Center for Tech., Pleasanton, Calif.; bldgs. Stanford U.; Hawaii State Capitol, Honolulu; Philip A. Hart Senate office bldg.; U.S.S.R. Embassy; Hennepin Govt. Center, Mpls.; J.F. Kennedy Meml. Grave, Arlington Nat. Cemetery (Va.); Neiman Marcus and Bergdorf Goodman Stores, Logan Airport, Boston; Am. Hosp., Paris; The Sun Co. Hdqrs., Radnor, Pa.; King Abdulaziz U. Med. Center, Jedda, Saudi Arabia. Office: 61 New Montgomery St San Francisco CA 94105 also 1 Farragut Sq S NW Washington DC 20006 also 745 Fifth Ave New York NY 10022 also 2029 Century Park E Los Angeles CA 90069

WARNEKE, HEINZ, sculptor; b. Bremen, Germany, June 30, 1895; s. Heinrich and Anna (Ritterhof) W.; student Staatliche Kunstgewerbe Schule and Akademie, Berlin, 1912-15, 18-23; m. Jessie Jay Gilroy Hall, Mar. 16, 1927. Came to U.S., 1923, naturalized, 1930. Represented by works in many large cities of U.S.; latest works include: Nat. Collection Fine Arts, Washington; War Meml., Lyme, Conn.; decorations Mellon Chapel of Washington Cathedral, also tympanum South Portal, entire decoration clerestory South Transcept, statues St. Alban and Prodigal Son; granite Elephant Group for Phila. Zool. Garden, 1963; carved oak pulpit, interior decorations Trinity Ch., Upperville, Va.; portrait Allen C. Dulles for C.I.A. bldg., Langley, Va.; Wildcat statue Pottstown (Pa.) High Sch. Complex; Nittany Lion statue Pa. State U.; Mountain Lion in bronze, Altoona, Pa.; unicorn statue Upperville garden Mrs. Paul Mellon; decorations of entire baptistry ceiling Washington Cathedral; portrait bust Judge John Bassett Moore, U. Va., Charlottesville; Pelican bronze Norfolk (Va.) Mus.; Immigrant, Samuels Meml., Phila.; Railway Mail Clerk, Anteroom Postmaster Gen.'s Office, Washington; large stone panel Lewis and Clark Expdn., Dept. Interior Bldg., Washington; OurangUtang Thinking, Addison Gallery, Andover, Mass.; Percheron Colts, U. Nebr., Omaha; Wild Boars and Hissing Geese, Art Inst. Chgo.; head sculpture dept. Corcoran Sch. Art, ret. Recipient numerous prizes, 1925—. Fellow Internat. Inst. Arts and Letters (life), Nat. Sculpture Soc., NAD; mem. New Eng. Sculptors So., Conn. Acad. Fine Arts, Associe de Salon des Tuileries, N.A. Address: East Haddam CT 06423

WARNER, ARTHUR E., educator; b. Garrett, Ind., May 30, 1922; s. Vern H. and Ethel (Button) W.; B.S. with distinction, Ind. U., 1949, M.B.A., 1950, D.Bus., 1953; m. Ann J. Bradin, July 11, 1941; children—Linda Ann (Mrs. William E. Holzwart), Arthur E. II, Patricia Joan, Melissa Jane. Faculty, Ind. U., 1948-53, instr., research asst. to dean Sch. Bus., 1949-53, asst. dir. Bur. Bus. Research, 1952; faculty Mich. State U., 1953-64, acting chmn. dept. ins., law and real estate adminstrn., 1958, dir. M.B.A. program, 1960, dir. programs for doctoral degree in bus. adminstrn., 1961-64, prof. bus. adminstrs., 1964; dean Coll. Bus. Adminstrn., U. Tenn., Knoxville, 1964-74, Am. U., Washington, 1974; Chair prof. real estate and property finance U. S.C., Columbia, 1974—. Dir. revenue accounting and statistics, pub. relations and informations Ind. Dept. Revenue, 1949; mem. higher edn. adv. com. HHFA, 1960; adviser Ministry Edn., Getulio Vargas Found. Sao Paulo, Brazil, 1958-60; cons. Hwy. Traffic Center, Mich. State U., 1956-58, Am. Inst. Real Estate Appraisers, 1953-57, Mich. Savs. and Loan League, 1954-57; adviser Mich. Real Estate Assn., 1954-58; mem. com. edn. Nat. Assn. Real Estate Bd., 1961-62; mem. com. grad. study Assn. State Univs. and Land Grant Colls., 1963-64; mem. adv. council Nat. Thrift Com., 1963-65; pres. Council Profl. Edn. for Bus., 1963-64; mem. gen. adv. com. Center for Govt., Industry and Law, Tenn., 1964—; mem. Atlanta Export Expansion Council, 1965-67. Served with AUS, 1942-45. Mem. Am. Statis. Assn., Am. Econ. Assn., Phi Eta Sigma, Beta Gamma Sigma, Alpha Kappa Psi. Address: University of SC Columbia SC 29208

WARNER, BRADFORD ARNOLD, banker; b. Locust Valley, N.Y., 1910; s. Henry Wolcott and Estelle Emma (Hawkins) W.; A.B., Yale, 1932; M.S., Columbia, 1935; m. Nancy Hill, June 9, 1932; children—Bradford Arnold, Miner Hill. Trainee, Mfrs. Trust Co., 1932-35; mem. pres. staff Gen. Motors Corp. overseas operations, 1935-40; rep. Fortune mag., 1940-54; v.p. Mfrs. Hanover Trust Co., 1954-62; sr. v.p., dir. Belgian-Am. Bank & Trust Co., Belgian-Am. Banking Corp., 1962-68, European-Am. Bank & Trust Co., 1968—, European-Am. Banking Corp., 1968-75; dir. corporate communications Instrument Systems Corp., 1975-76; v.p. corp. planning Gilman Paper Co., 1977—; dir. Colonial Surety Co., Fin. Guaranty Ins. Co., Applied Devices Corp., Buildex, Inc., Comml. Alliance Corp., Datatrol Inc., Bishop's Service, Inc.; trustee First Mortgage Investors, Central Savs. Bank. Mem. lay council, trustee Internat. Cardiology Found., 1968-74. Trustee N.Y. Pub. Library, Woodlawn Cemetery, Knickerbocker Hosp., 1955-58, Allen-Stevenson Sch., 1946—; hon. dir. Am. Found. for Blind; bd. dirs. Speech Rehab. Inst., 1955-75, Inst. for Crippled and Disabled, 1975, ARC of N.Y., 1970-76; chmn. Nat. Soc. Prevention Blindness, 1960-79, trustee, hon. chmn., 1979—. Andrew Wellington Cordier fellow Sch. Internat. Affairs, Columbia. Mem. Mayflower Soc. (former gov.), Pilgrims. Clubs: Piping Rock, (L.I.), Links, Anglers, Economic, Yale (N.Y.C.). Home: Tiffany Rd Oyster Bay NY 11771 Office: Gilman Paper Co 111 W 50th St New York NY 10020

WARNER, CECIL FRANCIS, mech. engr.; b. Parker, Ind., June 13, 1915; s. Leslie Clyde and Dollie May (Cecil) W.; B.S.M.E., Purdue U., 1939, Ph.D., 1945; M.S., Lehigh U., 1941; m. Melda M. Needler, Dec. 27, 1939; children—Robert Earl, James Bruce. Instr., Lehigh U., 1940-42; instr. Purdue U., 1942-45, asst. prof. mech. engring., 1945-50, asso. prof., 1950-55, prof., 1955—; engring. specialist Aerojet Gen. Corp., 1953-54, sr. engr., 1963-65; cons. in field. Registered profl. engr., Ind. Mem. ASME (pres. local sect. 1955-56), Air Pollution Control Assn., Sigma Xi. Methodist. Club: Kiwanis (pres. Lafayette club 1974-75). Author: (with C. W. Messersmith) Mechanical Engineering Laboratory, 1950; (with K. Wark) Air Pollution, Its Origin and Control, 1976; contbr. articles on rocket jet propulsion to profl. jours. Home: 124 Georgeton Ct West Lafayette IN 47906 Office: Mech Engring Bldg Purdue U West Lafayette IN 47907

WARNER, CHARLES ARTHUR, hydraulic cranes mfg. co. exec.; b. Waynesboro, Pa., Apr. 22, 1928; s. Charles Anderson and Helen (DeLawter) W.; B.S., Maryville Coll., 1950; grad. program mgmt. devel. Harvard U., 1960; m. Undine Cleonette Bridgers, Jan. 23, 1954; children—Melissa Beth, Rebecca Jane, Charles Anderson, III. Controller, Landis Tool Co., Waynesboro, Pa., 1951-64; exec. v.p. Grove Mfg. Co., Shady Grove, Pa., 1964—; dir. Circle Steel Corp., Taylorville, Ill., Grove Internat. Corp., Shady Grove, Contractors Machinery & Equipment Ltd., Hamilton, Ont. Club: Waynesboro Country. Home: 10204 Amsterdam Rd Waynesboro PA 17268 Office: PO Box 21 Shady Grove PA 17256

WARNER, DWAIN WILLARD, ornithologist, ecologist; b. Revere, Minn., Sept. 1, 1917; s. Louis and Marie (Enstad) W.; B.A., Carleton Coll., 1939; Ph.D., Cornell U., 1947; m. Dorothy H. Holway, Sept. 1, 1940 (dec. 1965); m. 2d, 1966 (div. 1979); children—Dwain Willard, Betsy, Robert, Bonnie, Richard. Asst. prof. U. Minn., Mpls., 1947-57, asso. prof., 1957-67, prof. ecology and behavioral biology, 1967—, curator ornithology Bell Mus. Natural History, 1947—; cons. ecol. problems. Served with U.S. Army, 1943-45. Grantee NIH, NSF, Office Naval Research, U. Minn. Office Internat. Programs, U. Minn. Grad. Sch. Mem. Am. Ornithol. Union, Minn. Ornithol. Union. Contbr. articles on ornithology and ecology to profl. publs. Home: 1798 Ashland Ave Apt 10 Saint Paul MN 55104 Office: Bell Mus Nat History U Minn 10 Church St SE Minneapolis MN 55455

WARNER, FRANCIS JAMES, physician, neuropathologist; b. Warsaw, Poland, Oct. 3, 1897; came to U.S., 1903, naturalized, 1925; s. Samuel and Molly (Smith) W.; B.A., U. Ia., 1922; M.A. in Anatomy, U. Mich., 1925; M.D., Loyola U. Med. Sch., 1919. Postgrad. student in anatomy (in lieu of internship) U. Mich., 1924-25, instr. clin. neurology, 1931-32; instr. clin. neurology U. Md., 1938-39; research asso. in neuro-anatomy U. Cal., 1943-44; lectr. neuroanatomy U. Utah, 1946-48; resident in neurology Henry Ford Hosp., Detroit, 1951-52; guest investigator in neuro-pathology Nat. (Queen's Sq.) Hosp., London, 1954-56; instr. neurology Temple U., 1957-75, asst. prof., 1975—. Diplomate in neuropathology Am. Bd. Pathology. Fellow Zool. Soc. of London, Royal Soc. Medicine (London), AAAS; mem. Am. Micros. Soc., Am. Assn. Anatomists, Am. Soc. Ichthyologists and Herpetologists, Am. Soc. Zoologists, Anat. Soc. Gt. Britain and Ireland, Assn. Research in Nervous and Mental Disease, Am. Psychiat. Assn., Ill. Acad. Sci., AMA, Am. Assn. Neuropathologists, N.J. Soc. Clin. Pathologists, Sigma Xi. Home: PO Box 523 Philadelphia PA 19105 Office: Sch Medicine Temple U Philadelphia PA 19122

WARNER, FRANK A., physician; b. Pierceville, Kans., Feb. 16, 1906; s. Clarence A. and Nellie (Bardo) W.; B.Sc., U. Idaho, 1931; M.D., Harvard, 1935; m. Elizabeth Murphy, Mar. 20, 1934; 1 son, Frank Amel. Intern, Balt. City Hosp., 1935-36; postgrad. Harvard, Mallory Inst. Pathology, Lahey Clinic, all Boston, 1946-48; asst. med. dir. John Hancock Mut. Life Ins. Co., Boston, 1948-51, asso., 1951-54, med. dir., 1954-71, v.p., 1956-71; asst.-in-medicine Mass. Gen. Hosp., 1950-68. Bd. dirs. Gritman Meml. Hosp., Moscow, Idaho; bd. dirs. Idaho div., pres. Latah County unit Am. Cancer Soc. Served from lt. to col. USAAF, 1939-46. Diplomate Bd. Life Ins. Medicine. Fellow Am. Geriatric Soc.; mem. AMA, Mass. Med. Soc. (councillor), Suffolk Dist. Med. Soc. (pres. 1969-70, 70-71), Am. Heart Assn., Assn. Life Ins. Med. Dirs., Phi Gamma Delta. Club: Harvard. Address: 721 Park Dr Moscow ID 83843

WARNER, HAROLD CLAY, JR., banker; b. Knoxville, Tenn., Feb. 24, 1939; s. Harold Clay and Mary Frances (Waters) W.; B.S. in Econs., U. Tenn., 1961, Ph.D., 1965; m. Patricia Alice Rethorst, Sept. 1, 1961; children—Martha Lee, Carol Frances. Asst. to pres. First Fed. Savs., Savannah, Ga., 1965-67; v.p. and economist No. Trust Co., Chgo., 1967-73; sr. v.p. and chief economist Crocker Nat. Bank, San Francisco, 1974—; lectr. dept. econs. U. Tenn., 1962-63, Grad. Sch. Bus., Loyola U., Chgo., 1969-73. Bd. dirs. Chgo. Commons Assn., 1973-74. NDEA fellow, 1961-64. Mem. Am. Econ. Assn., Am. Fin. Assn., Am. Statis. Assn. (past chpt. pres.), Nat. Assn. Bus. Economists (past pres. Chgo. chpt. 1971-72, San Francisco chpt. 1976-77), Phi Gamma Delta, Phi Eta Sigma, Omicron Delta Kappa, Phi Kappa Phi. Clubs: Peninsula Golf and Country (San Mateo, Calif.). Home: 350 Georgetown Ave San Mateo CA 94402 Office: 1 Montgomery St San Francisco CA 94104

WARNER, HARRY HATHAWAY, found. exec.; b. Staunton, Va., Nov. 30, 1935; s. Morris Thompson and Virginia Drury (Worthington) W.; B.A., Va. Mil. Inst., 1957; grad. U. Va. Sch. Bank Mgmt., 1963, Stonier Grad. Sch. Banking, 1969; m. Mary Elizabeth Patrick, Sept. 24, 1960; children—Harry Hathaway, Cabell Worthington, Ann Morris, Morris Patrick. With Met. Nat. Bank, Richmond, Va., 1965-71, exec. v.p., 1969-71; pres., dir. Transohio Fin. Corp., Cleve., 1971-78; exec. v.p. VMI Found., Lexington, Va., 1978—; dir. Chesapeake Corp. Va. Served as 2d lt. AUS, 1957. Recipient Distinguished Service award Richmond Jaycees, 1969. Episcopalian. Club: Country of Va. Address: PO Box 932 Lexington VA 24450

WARNER, HELENE BLISS, landscape architect; b. Middletown, Conn., Aug. 28, 1900; d. Howard H. and Nellie (Bliss) W.; student Bradford Coll., 1917-20, Cambridge Sch. Landscape, 1920-23. Designer, Thomas H. Desmond, Simsbury, Conn., 1923-27; partner Desmond, Eddy & Warner, 1927; pvt. practice landscape architecture, Middletown, 1932—. Mem. Middletown City Planning Commn., 1962-65; corporate emeritus Middlesex Meml. Hosp. Fellow Am. Soc. Landscape Architects; mem. Conn. Hort. Soc., Middlesex County Hist. Soc., Internat. Fedn. Landscape Architects, DAR. Club: Soroptimists Internat. Home and Office: 11 Lorraine Terr Middletown CT 06457

WARNER, HUBER RICHARD, educator; b. Glendale, Ohio, May 16, 1936; s. Richard Lyman and Katharine (Root) W.; B.A., Ohio Wesleyan U., 1958; B.S., Mass. Inst. Tech., 1958; Ph.D. (NSF fellow), U. Mich., 1962; m. Patricia Wellwood Campbell, July 8, 1961; children—Geoffrey, Peter. NSF postdoctoral fellow Mass. Inst. Tech., 1962-64; asst. prof. dept. biochemistry U. Minn., St. Paul, 1964-68, asso. prof., 1968-73, prof., 1973—. Active Boy Scouts Am., St. Paul Community Assn. Research Career Devel. award NIH, 1970-75. Contbr. articles to profl. jours. Home: 2243 Hillside Ave St Paul MN 55108

WARNER, J. KEITH, wholesale baking co. exec.; b. Sioux City, Iowa, Mar. 22, 1935; s. Karl R. and Lucille (Shea) W.; B.S., Morningside Coll., 1957; m. Patricia Caldwell, Sept. 3, 1955; children—Linda, Brian, Kevin, Lori, Lisa. With ITT Continental, 1957-74, bakery plant mgr., Wichita, Kans., Milw., 1967-74; exec. v.p. baker div. Heileman Brewery, 1974-75, pres., 1976; pres. Metz Baking Co., Sioux City, Iowa, 1976—. Council pres. Girl Scouts U.S.A., 1978—; council bd. dirs. Boy Scouts Am. Mem. Am. Inst. Baking (trustee). Republican. Roman Catholic. Club: Rotary. Office: 1014 Nebraska St PO Box 448 Sioux City IA 51102

WARNER, JACK, JR., motion picture-TV producer, writer; b. San Francisco, Mar. 27, 1916; s. Jack Leonard and Irma Warner (Rogell); A.B. cum laude, U. So. Calif., 1938; m. Barbara Ann Richman, May 30, 1948; children—Elizabeth Susan, Sally Jo (dec.), Deborah. Home office Warner Bros. Pictures, Inc., distbn. and exhbn. of films, U.S., Can.; produced short subject films, Warner Bros. Studios, Burbank, Calif., in theatre dept. and distbn. Warner Bros., 1946-49; producer in London, 1948-49; returned to U.S., organized own co., Jack M. Warner Prodns., Inc., 1949; former exec. television div. Warner Bros. Pictures, Inc., past v.p. charge TV commls. and indsl. films div. Past pres. Los Angeles County Assn. Mental Health; v.p. Mental Health Found. Served as 2d lt. Signal Corps Photog. Co.; advanced through grades to col.; photo officer on staff Gen. Omar Bradley, World War II; col. Res. ret. Mem. Acad. Motion Picture Arts and Scis. (asso.), Assn. U.S. Army, 12th Army Group Assn., Zeta Beta Tau, Pi Sigma Alpha. Democrat. Jewish.

WARNER, JAMES DANIEL, clergyman; b. Sheridan, Wyo., May 1, 1924; s. Stephan Daniel and Grace Margaret (Caple) W.; B.S., Northwestern U., 1950; M.Div., Seabury Western Theol. Sem., 1953, D.D., 1977; m. Barbara A. Wallgren, Sept. 6, 1952 (dec. 1957); m. 2d Marcy Walk Swan, Feb. 8, 1960; children—Stephen, David, Cheryl, Mark, Kathryn, James, Tammy. Vicar, St. James Ch., Mosinee, Wis., 1953-56; rector St. Paul's Ch., Marmette, Wis., 1956-60; asst. chaplain St. James Ch., U. Wichita (Kans.), 1960-62; rector St. Stephen's Ch., Wichita, 1962-70, Trinity Ch., Oshkosh, Wis., 1970-77; bishop Diocese of Nebr., Omaha, 1977—; pres. St. Com., Diocese of Kans., 1966-68. Pres. Community Planning Council, Wichita, 1965-66; police chaplain several community social agencies. Served in USN, 1942-46; PTO. Episcopalian. Home: 64 Ginger Cove Valley NE 68064 Office: 200 North 62d Omaha NE 68132

WARNER, JOHN ANDREW, foundry exec.; b. Kansas City, Mo., Jan. 1, 1924; s. Richard G. and Margaret (Falconer) W.; m. Patricia Pooley, Feb. 25, 1950; children—Katherine, Amanda. Sec., Warner Oil Co., Oklahoma City, 1948-50; pres., chief exec. officer Tyler Pipe Industries (Tex.), 1950—; dir. Tyler Corp., Peoples Nat. Bank, Tyler, Tex. Power & Light Co., Dallas. Past chmn. East Tex. Hosp. Found.; bd. dirs. East Tex. Fair Assn., Med. Center Hosp., Tyler Salvation Army, Am. Cancer Soc., Tex. Research League; trustee Tex. Chest Found.; mem. Tex. Gov.'s Commn. on Phys. Fitness. Served with USCGR, 1942-46. Named Tyler's Most Outstanding Citizen, 1973. Mem. Tyler C. of C. (dir., past pres.), Cast Iron Soil Pipe Inst. (dir., past pres.), Am. Foundrymen's Soc., East Tex. (dir.), Tyler Area (pres. 1973) chambers commerce, Tex. Assn. Taxpayers (regional v.p.), Sigma Alpha Epsilon. Presbyn. Mason (Shriner). Club: Willow Brook Country (dir., past pres. Tyler). Home: 608 Rosemont Pl I Tyler TX 75701 Office: PO Box 2027 Tyler TX 75710

WARNER, JOHN EDWARD, advt. exec.; b. Troy, N.Y., Mar. 26, 1936; s. George Edward and Ann Frances (Teson) W.; B.S. in Chemistry and Philosophy, Coll. Holy Cross, 1957; m. Anne Elizabeth Hibbard, Sept. 19, 1959; children—Matthew J., Barbara A., Peter J., Christopher J. Promotion mgr. Union Carbide Corp., N.Y.C., 1957-61; account exec. McCann-Erickson, Inc., N.Y.C., 1961-62; pres. Warner, Bicking & Fenwick, Inc., N.Y.C., 1962—. Chmn. bd. govs. Transworld Advt. Agy. Network; speaker confs. advt. mktg. assns. Columnist advt. and mktg. publs. Home: 706 Hillcrest Rd Ridgewood NJ 07450 Office: 866 United Nations Plaza New York City NY 10017

WARNER, JOHN WILLIAM, senator; b. Washington, Feb. 18, 1927; s. John William and Martha Stuart (Budd) W.; B.S., Washington and Lee U., 1949; LL.B., U. Va., 1953; m. Elizabeth Taylor, Dec. 4, 1976; children by previous marriage—Mary Conover, Virginia Stuart, John William IV. Law clk. to U.S. judge, 1953-54; spl. asst. to U.S. atty., 1956-57; asst. U.S. atty. Dept. Justice, 1957-60; partner firm Hogan & Hartson, 1960-68; undersec. of navy, 1969-72, sec. of navy, 1972-74; adminstr. Am. Revolution Bicentennial Adminstrn., 1974-76; U.S. senator from Va., 1979—. Trustee Washington and Lee U. Served with USNR, 1944-46; to capt., USMCR, 1949-52. Mem. Bar Assn. D.C., Washington Inst. Fgn. Affairs, Beta Theta Pi, Phi Alpha Delta. Republican. Episcopalian. Clubs: Metropolitan; Burning Tree; Chevy Chase; Alfalfa; Alibi. Home: Atoka Farm PO Box 1320 Middleburg VA 22117 also 3240 S St NW Washington DC 20007 Office: US Senate Washington DC 20510

WARNER, JOHN WILLIAM, lawyer; b. Amarillo, Tex., June 4, 1936; s. Arthur Greeley and Janet Karen (Miller) W.; B.A., Tex. A. and M. U., 1958; LL.B., U. Tex., 1962; m. Judith Diane Mumma, Dec. 30, 1961; children—Michael Allan, Sandra Kay, Melanie Diane, Patricia Karen. Admitted to Tex. bar, 1962; practice law, Pampa, Tex., 1962—; judge Municipal Ct., 1963-68; county atty. Gray County, Tex., 1969-76. Dir. Tri-City Office Supply, Inc.; instr. Dale Carnegie courses. Dist. commr. Boy Scouts Am., 1968-70; incorporator Pampa Youth Council, Inc., S.W. Indian Orgn., Inc., Masters Home for Children, Inc.; trustee Happy Haven Children's Home, 1970-71; coach Little League, 1974—; pres. Gray County chpt. Am. Cancer Soc., 1976-77. Recipient Adult Leader of Year award Pampa High Sch. Key Club, 1966, Distinguished Service award Pampa Jr. C. of C., 1969, Tru-Teens leader of year award, 1972. Mem. Am., Tex., Gray County bar assns., Assn. Trial Lawyers Am., Tex. Criminal Def. Lawyers Assn., Tex. Trial Lawyers Assn., Tex. (legal counsel 1970-71), Pampa (pres. 1969-70) jaycees, Pampa C. of C. Kiwanian, Optimist. Home: 2111 Dogwood St Pampa TX 79065 Office: Box 645 Pampa TX 79065. *The epitaph on my grandfather's grave reads: "He lived to serve." I have tried to live my life according to that philosophy.*

WARNER, KENNETH WILSON, JR., editor, assn. publs. exec.; b. Chgo., Dec. 22, 1928; s. Kenneth Wilson and Ann S. (Knapp) W.; B.S.Ed., No. Ill. U., 1950; m. Gail Marjorie Halling, Mar. 30, 1968 (separated 1979); children—Sara, Seth. Staff editor Bldg. Supply News, Chgo., 1953-56, Elec. Merchandising, 1956-60; freelance writer, Sarasota, Fla., 1960-66; editor Gunsport Mag., Alexandria and Falls Church, Va., 1966-67; editor, pub. Gunfacts Mag., Arlington, Va., 1968-70; exec. editor Am. Rifleman Nat. Rifle Assn., Washington, 1971-78, asst. dir. publs. div., 1972-78, editor Am. Hunter, 1973-78, editor Am. Rifleman, 1976-78, dir. publs., 1977-78; editor-in-chief Gun Digest, Handloader's Digest, Cartridges of the World, DBI Books Inc., Northfield, Ill., 1979—. Served to cpl. U.S. Army, 1951-53. Mem. Nat. Rifle Assn. (life), Outdoor Writer's Assn. Am., Knifemaker's Guild Am. (asso.). Author: The Practical Book of Knives, 1976; The Practical Book of Guns, 1978. Editor: The Bolt Action, 1976. Contbr. numerous articles on outdoors themes to profl. jours., popular mags. Home and Office: 3403 Surrey Ln Falls Church VA 22042 Office: DBI Books Inc 540 Frontage Rd Northfield IL 60093

WARNER, LAWRENCE ALLEN, educator; b. Monroe, Ohio, Apr. 20, 1914; s. Clarence Foster and Mary Bachelor (Wones) W.; A.B., Miami U. at Oxford, Ohio, 1937; Ph.D., Johns Hopkins, 1942; m. Elizabeth Robinson, Oct. 17, 1942; children—Garett Robinson, Susan Elizabeth. Geologist U.S. Antarctic Service, Marie Byrd Land, Antarctica, 1939-41; geologist U.S. Geol. Survey, Alaska, 1942-46; mem. faculty U. Colo., Boulder, 1946—, asso. prof. geology, 1952-58, prof., 1958—. Cons. U.S. Geol. Survey, 1946-52, USAF, 1952-56, Denver Bd. Water Commrs., 1956—. Recipient Congl. medal for sci. and exploration, 1946, Robert L. Stearns award for univ. service U. Colo., 1959. Mem. Geol. Soc. Am., Am. Geophys. Union, Mineral. Soc. Am., AAAS, Nat. Assn. Geology Tchrs., Colo. Sci. Soc., Sigma Xi, Phi Beta Kappa, Phi Kappa Tau. Conglist. Contbr. articles to profl. jours. Home: 2455 Kenwood Dr Boulder CO 80303

WARNER, MARVIN LEON, former ambassador, business exec.; b. Birmingham, Ala., June 8, 1919; s. Albert and Rose (Randman) W.; B.S. in Commerce, U. Ala., 1939, LL.B., 1941; LL.M., George Washington U., 1942; m. Jane Marie Blach, 1942 (div. June 1967); children—Marlin (Mrs. Stephen Arky), Alyson (Mrs. Herbert Kuppin, Jr.), Marvin Leon; m. 2d, Susan G. Goldwater, May 1979. Partner, Warner-Kanter Cos., Birmingham, Ala. and Cin., 1948-57; chmn. bd. Marvin Warner Co., real estate devel., Cin., 1959—, Home State Savs. Assn., Cin., 1958—; pres. Warner Nat. Corp., Cin., 1968—; chmn. Am. Bancshares, Miami, Fla., Com Banks Corp., Orlando, Fla.; ambassador to Switzerland, 1977-79; formerly an owner N.Y. Yankees; owner Warnerton Thoroughbred Farms, Cin.; former co-owner Tampa Bay Buccaneers, Nat. Football League. Mem. Ohio Gov.'s Commn. on Housing, 1972; mem. U.S. delegation to UN, 23d Gen. Assembly, 1968. Pres., Jewish Community Center, 1957-60. Mem. Nat. Dem. Party Policy Com., 1970-72, Dem. Nat. Com., 1975—. Trustee Miami U., Oxford, Ohio, 1970-72; bd. dirs. Ohio Thoroughbred Breeders and Owners Assn.; bd. govs. Hebrew Union Coll., 1961-73; bd. dirs. Drake Meml. Hosp., pres., 1972; bd. dirs. Nat. Conf. Christians and Jews; adv. com. Ohio Thoroughbred Race Fund; mem., chmn. Ohio Bd. Regents. Served to maj. AUS, 1941-46. Recipient Ohio Gov.'s award, 1970. Mem. Greater Cin. C. of C. (dir.), Ohio Assn. Commodores (grand comdr. 1972-73), Jewish Fedn. of Cin. (pres. 1967-69). Clubs: Army-Navy (Washington); Queen City (Cin.). Office: 601 Main St Cincinnati OH 45202

WARNER, NANCY ELIZABETH, pathologist; b. Dixon, Ill., July 8, 1923; d. Henry Chester and Lucile (Mertz) Warner; B.S., U. Chgo., 1944, M.D., 1949. Intern, U. Chgo. Clinics, 1949-50, asst. resident in pathology, 1950-53; resident in pathology Cedars of Lebanon Hosp., Los Angeles, 1953-54, asst. pathologist, 1954-58, asso. dir. div. labs., 1965-66; asst. prof. pathology U. Chgo., 1958-59, asso. prof., 1959-65, dir. Lab. Surg. Pathology, 1959-65; asso. prof. U. Wash. Sch. Medicine, Seattle, 1966-67; asso. prof. pathology U. So. Calif. Sch. Medicine, 1967-69, prof. pathology, 1969—, chmn. dept., 1972—, asso. dean for academic affairs, 1977—; attending physician Med. Center, U. So. Calif.; chief pathologist Womens Hosp. Los Angeles County/U. So. Calif. Med. Center, 1968-72, dir. labs. and pathology, 1972—; cons. Barlow Sanatorium and Hosp., 1968—. Fellow Coll. Am. Pathologists, Am. Soc. Clin. Pathologists; mem. AAAS, AMA U. Chgo. Alumni Assn., D.A.R., Daus. Founders and Patriots, Am. Assn. Pathologists, Calif. Soc. Pathologists, Am. Assn. Anatomists, Endocrine Soc., Los Angeles Soc. Pathologists, Am. Soc. Cytology, Microcirculatory Soc., European Soc. Microcirculation, Internat. Acad. Pathology, Los Angeles Acad. Medicine, Colonial Dames Am., Nat. Soc. Magna Charta Dames, Nat. Soc. U.S. Daus. 1812, Sigma Xi, Alpha Omega Alpha. Office: Univ Southern Calif Sch Medicine 2025 Zonal Ave Los Angeles CA 90033

WARNER, RAWLEIGH, JR., oil co. exec.; b. Chgo., Feb. 13, 1921; s. Rawleigh and Dorothy (Haskins) W.; grad. Lawrenceville (N.J.) Sch., 1940; A.B. cum laude, Princeton, 1943; m. Mary Ann deClairmont, Nov. 2, 1946; children—Alison W. Pyne, Suzanne W. Parsons. Sec., treas. Warner Bard Co., Chgo., 1946-48; with Continental Oil Co., 1948-53, asst. treas., Houston, 1952-53; treas. Socony-Vacuum Overseas Supply Co., 1953-55; asst. treas. Mobil Overseas Oil Co., 1955-56; mgr. econs. dept., then mgr. Middle East dept. Socony Mobil Oil Co. Inc., 1956-59; regional v.p. Mobil Internat. Oil Co., 1959-60, exec. v.p., 1960-63, pres., 1963-64; exec. v.p., dir. Mobil Oil Corp. (formerly Socony Mobil Oil Co., Inc.), 1964, pres., 1965-69, chmn. bd., chief exec. officer, 1969—; dir. Caterpillar Tractor Co., Chem. Bank-Chem. N.Y. Corp., Am. Tel. & Tel. Co., Am. Express Co., Am. Express Internat. Banking Co., Wheelabrator Frye Co. Chmn. council on univ. resources Princeton U.; trustee Woodrow Wilson Internat. Center for Scholars. Served to capt. F.A., AUS, 1943-46. Decorated Purple Heart, Bronze Star, Silver Star. Mem. Am. Petroleum Inst. (dir.). Republican. Presbyn. Clubs: Augusta (Ga.) Nat. Golf; Links, Pinnacle (N.Y.C.); New Canaan Country; Blind Brook (Port Chester, N.Y.); Jupiter Island (Hobe Sound, Fla.); Chicago; Seminole (North Palm Beach, Fla.). Office: 150 E 42d St New York City NY 10017

WARNER, ROBERT MARK, archivist, historian; b. Montrose, Colo., June 28, 1927; s. Mark Thomas and Bertha Margaret (Rich) W.; student U. Denver, 1945; B.A., Muskingum Coll., 1949; M.A., U. Mich., 1953, Ph.D., 1958; m. Eleanor Jane Bullock, Aug. 21, 1954; children—Mark Steven, Jennifer Jane. Tchr. high sch., Montrose, Colo., 1949-50; lectr. dept. history U. Mich., 1958-66, asso. prof., 1966-71, prof., 1971—, prof. Sch. Library Sci., 1974—; asst. in research Mich. Hist. Collections, 1953-57, asst. curator, 1957-61, asst. dir., 1961-66, dir., 1966—; bd. visitors Sch. of Library Sci., Case Western Res. U., 1976—; chmn. Gerald R. Ford Presdl. Library Bldg. Com., 1977-79. Served with U.S. Army, 1950-52. Fellow Soc. Am. Archivists; mem. Am. Hist. Assn., Orgn. Am. Historians, Am. Assn. State and Local History, Hist. Soc. Mich. (trustee 1960-66, v.p. 1972-73, pres. 1973-74), Soc. Am. Archivists (mem. council 1967-71, sec., exec. dir., 1971-73, v.p. 1974-75, pres. 1976-77), Phi Alpha Theta. Presbyterian. Clubs: Rotary, U. Mich. Research. Author: Chase S. Osborn, 1860-1949, 1960; Profile of a Profession, 1964; (with R. Bordin) The Modern Manuscript Library, 1966; (with C.W. Vanderhill) A Michigan Reader: 1865 to the Present, 1974. Home: 1821 Coronada Dr Ann Arbor MI 48103 Office: Bentley Hist Library U Mich Ann Arbor MI 48109

WARNER, ROBERT S., co. dir., former accountant; b. Erie, Pa., Apr. 9, 1907; s. Spencer Roycraft and Anna Edith (MacDonald) W.; Litt.B., Rutgers U., 1928; m. Doris Jean Squarey, June 29, 1931; children—Elizabeth S. (Mrs. Richard W. Bakenhus), Robert S. (dec.). With Lybrand, Ross Bros. & Montgomery, C.P.A.'s, N.Y.C., 1928-72, charge St. Louis office, 1936-49, Los Angeles, 1949-72, mem. firm, 1944-72, mem. exec. com.; exec. com. Coopers & Lybrand; dir. Bixby Ranch Co., Mattel, Inc., Monarch Bank, Laguna Niguel, Calif.; cons. prof. acctg. U. So. Calif., 1972—. Trustee J.B. and Emily Van Nuys Charities, Los Angeles. Mem. Calif., N.Y. socs. C.P.A's, Am. Inst. C.P.A.'s. Clubs: Bohemian (San Francisco); Big Canyon Country (dir. Newport Beach, Calif.). Home: 32 N LaSenda South Laguna CA 92677 Office: 610 Newport Center Dr Newport Beach CA 92660

WARNER, SAM BASS, JR., educator; b. Boston, Apr. 6, 1928; s. Sam Bass and Helen Binninger (Wilson) W.; A.B., Harvard, 1950, Ph.D., 1959; postgrad. Yale, 1950-51; M.Journalism, Boston U., 1952; m. Lyle S. Lobel, June 20, 1952; children—Rebecca Helen, William Eaton, Kate Sydney, Alice Louise. Editor, pub. Watertown (Mass.) Sun, 1952-53; tutor in history Harvard, 1954-56, instr., 1960-63, research asso. Mass. Inst. Tech.-Harvard Joint Center for Urban Studies, 1959-63; asst. prof. history and architecture Washington U., St. Louis, 1963-65, asso. prof. history, 1965-67; asso. prof. history U. Mich., Ann Arbor, 1967-68, prof., 1968-72; prof. history and social sci. Boston U., 1972—. Social Scis. Research Council rep. to Nat. Archives Adv. Council, 1968-72; council Inter-Univ. Consortium for Polit. Research, 1973-75. Recipient Albert J. Beveridge prize Am. Hist. Assn., 1969. Charles Warren Center for Studies in Am. History fellow, Harvard, 1974; Guggenheim fellow, 1976; Rockefeller Found. humanities fellow, 1977. Mem. Am. Hist. Assn., Orgn. Am. Historians. Author: Streetcar Suburbs, The Process of Growth in Boston 1870-1900, 1962; The Private City: Philadelphia in Three Periods of Its Growth, 1968; The Urban Wilderness, A History of the American City, 1973. Editor: Planning for a Nation of Cities, 1966; The American Experiment: Perspectives on 200 Years, 1976. Home: 24 W Cedar St Boston MA 02108

WARNER, SETH L., educator, mathematician; b. Muskegon, Mich., July 11, 1927; s. Seth Lemoine and Agnes (Brustad) W.; B.S., Yale, 1950; M.A., Harvard, 1951, Ph.D., 1955; m. Susan Emily Rose, June 16, 1962; children—Susan Emily, Sarah Southall, Seth Lawrence. Research instr. Duke, 1955-57, asst. prof., 1957-61, asso. prof., 1961-65, prof. math., 1965—, dir. grad. studies math., 1960-68, chmn., 1968-70, 73—. Served with Med. Service Corps, AUS, 1946-48. Mem. Phi Beta Kappa, Sigma Xi. Episcopalian. Author: Modern Algebra, vols. I and II, 1965; Classical Modern Algebra, 1971. Home: 2433 Wrightwood Ave Durham NC 27705

WARNER, THEODORE KUGLER, JR., lawyer; b. Phila., Sept. 13, 1909; s. Theodore Kugler and Anna (Allen) W.; A.B., U. Pa., 1931, LL.B. cum laude, 1934; m. Dorothy Wark Hoehler, Nov. 23, 1935; children—Betsy Ann (Mrs. Douglas R. Bulcher), Peter Joyce. Admitted to Pa. bar, 1934; with Pa. R.R., Phila., 1934-70, chief tax counsel, 1952-58, dir. taxation, 1958-68, v.p. taxes, 1968, v.p. accounting and taxes, 1968-69, v.p. corp. adminstrn., 1969-70; pres. Can. So. Ry., 1968-70; v.p. Pitts. & Lake Erie R.R., 1968-70; officer, dir. other Penn Central cos., 1968-70; counsel Duane, Morris & Heckscher, Phila., 1970-71; counsel Harper, George, Buchanan & Driver, 1975—; lectr. on consol. returns various tax forums. Bd. suprs. Easttown Twp., Pa., 1962-70, chmn., 1966-70. Mem. Nat. Tax Assn. (pres. 1965-66), Am. Law Inst. (life mem.), Am., Pa. bar assns., Order of Coif, Tau Kappa Epsilon. Republican. Lutheran. Mason (33 deg., mem. com. on masonic homes 1970—, chmn. 1975-77). Clubs: Aronimink Golf Club, Union League Club. Home: Sugar Knoll Sugartown and Berkeley Rds Devon PA 19333 Office: Western Savs Bank Bldg Philadelphia PA 19107

WARNER, BROTHER THOMAS WILLIAM, librarian; b. Woodbury, N.J., Aug. 20, 1919; s. Daniel Patrick and Nellie (Phelan) Warner; student Cath. U., 1937-40; B.A., LaSalle Coll., 1941; B.S. in Library Sci., Drexel Inst., 1944; grad. study George Washington U., 1945-46. Mem. Brothers of the Christian Schs., 1936—; instr. West Phila. Cath. High Sch., 1940-42; asst. librarian LaSalle Coll., Phila., 1942-43, librarian, 1946—; librarian LaSalle Coll. High Sch., 1943-44, St. John's Coll., 1944-46. Mem. A.L.A., Cath. (rep. Nat. Conf. on UNESCO 1947, nat. parliamentarian 1967-71), Pa. library assns., Assn. Coll. and Research Libraries, Tri-State Coll. Library Coop. (dir. 1967—). Address: 20th St and Olney Ave Philadelphia PA 19141

WARNER, VOLNEY F., army officer; b. Woonsocket, S.D.; B.S., U.S. Mil. Acad., 1950; M.A. in Psychology, Vanderbilt U., 1958; M.S. in Internat. Affairs, George Washington U., 1969. Served as enlisted man U.S. Navy; enlisted in U.S. Army, commd. 2d lt., 1950, advanced through grades to gen., 1979; mil. asst. to spl. asst. to the Pres. on Vietnam affairs, Washington, 1967-68; comdg. officer 3d Brigade, 4th Inf. Div., Vietnam; asst. chief of staff II Field Force; chief of staff 82d Airborne Div., 1972-73, asst. div. comdr. for ops., 1973-74; asst. dep. chief of staff ops. Hdqrs. U.S. Army Forces Command, Ft. McPherson, Ga., 1974-75; comdr. 9th Inf. Div., Ft. Lewis, Wash., 1975-77; comdr. 18th Airborne Corps, Ft. Bragg, N.C., 1977;

comdr.-in-chief U.S. Readiness Command, dir. Joint Deployment Agy., MacDill AFB, Fla., 1979—. Office: CINC Readiness Command MacDill AFB FL 33608

WARNER, WALTER EDWARDS, JR., lawyer; b. Bklyn., Apr. 14, 1908; s. Walter E. and Clara L. (Frost) W.; B.A., Princeton, 1928; LL.B., Columbia, 1931; m. Gertrude H. Warner, Nov. 22, 1946. Admitted to N.Y. bar, 1932, U.S. Supreme Ct. bar; practice law, N.Y.C., 1932—, specializing corp., estate litigation law; mem. firm Chambers, Clare & Gibson, 1944—. Dir. Crum & Forster; chmn. Dudley Mgmt. Corp. Mason. Club: University (N.Y.C.). Home: 3 Briar Close Larchmont NY 10538 Office: 61 Broadway New York City NY 10006

WARNER, WELLMAN JOEL, social psychologist, ret. educator; b. Lyndonville, Vt., Jan. 13, 1897; s. George A. and Rose Mary (Monahon) W.; A.B., George Washington U., 1921; B.D., Yale, 1924; Ph.D., U. London, 1929; m. Miriam Saint, Nov. 26, 1930; children—Wellman Joel, Linda. Ordained to ministry Meth. Ch.; dir. field work Yale, 1922-24; prof. social ethics Ohio Wesleyan U., 1930-38; prof. sociology, head dept. social scis. Dickinson Coll., Carlisle, Pa., 1938-46; prof. sociology U. Coll., head all-univ. dept. sociology and anthropology N.Y. U., 1946-59, prof. sociology and anthropology Grad. Sch. Arts and Scis., 1959-63, emeritus prof. sociology and anthropology, 1963—. Chmn. bd. dirs. Pub. Affairs Com. N.Y., 1962-70, then dir.; chmn. Internat. Congress for Group Psychotherapy, Toronto, Can., 1954, 2d Internat. Congress, Zurich, 1957, Internat. Council for Group Psychotherapy, 1954-62. Pres. bd. trustees Moreno Inst. Served with U.S. Army, 1917-19; AEF, France. Hooker-Dwight fellow Yale, London, Eng., 1924-26. Fellow AAAS, Am. Soc. Group Psychotherapy, Am. Anthrop. Assn., Am. Sociol. Assn. (sec. 1954-58); mem. Soc. Sci. Study Religion, Am. Civil Liberties Union (acad. freedom com.), Eastern Sociol. Soc., Soc. Psychol. Study Social Issues, Casa Materna Soc. (v.p.). Author: The Wesleyan Movement in the Industrial Revolution, 1930. Adv. editor: Social Problems; cons. editor Group Psychotherapy, Social Psychiatry; contbr. editor Psychotherapy and Psychosomatics (Switzerland). Contbr. to books, articles to jours. Home: 707 Wilson St Carlisle PA 17013

WARNER, WILLIAM HAMER, applied mathematician; b. Pitts., Oct. 6, 1929; s. John Christian and Louise (Hamer) W.; student Haverford Coll., 1946-48; B.S., Carnegie Inst. Tech., 1950, M.S., 1951, Ph.D., 1953; m. Janet Louise West, June 29, 1957; 1 dau., Katherine Patricia. Research asso. grad. div. applied math. Brown U., Providence, 1953-55; asst. prof. dept. aerospace engring. and mechanics U. Minn., Mpls., 1955-58, asso. prof., 1958-68, prof., 1968—. Mem. Am. Math. Soc., Soc. for Indsl. and Applied Math., Math. Assn. Am., Soc. Natural Philosophy. Author: (with L.E. Goodman) Statics, 1963, Dynamics, 1964. Contbr. articles to profl. jours. Office: 107 Aero Engring Bldg U Minn Minneapolis MN 55455

WARNER, WILLIAM WHITESIDES, author, Smithsonian Instn. exec.; b. N.Y.C., Apr. 2, 1920; s. Charles Jolly and Leonora (Haberle) W.; A.B., Princeton U., 1943; m. Kathleen Berryman McMahon, June 14, 1951; children—John B., Alletta B., Georgiana B., Alexandra DeP., Elizabeth S., Andrew. With USIA, Dept. State, 1951-62; exec. sec., program coordinator for Latin Am., Peace Corps, Washington, 1962-63; dir. Office of Internat. activities Smithsonian Instn., Washington, 1964-67, asst. sec. for pub. service, 1967-73, research asso., 1973—. Served with USNR, 1944-46. Author: Beautiful Swimmers: Watermen, Crabs and the Chesapeake Bay (recipient Phi Beta Kappa Book award, Christopher award, Pulitizer Prize for gen. non-fiction), 1976. Mem. Rachel Carson Trust for the Living Environment (v.p. 1966-73), Audubon Naturalist Soc. for Central Atlantic States (v.p. 1961-64), Sigma Xi. Episcopalian. Clubs: Federal City. Contbr. articles to mags. Home: 2243 47th St NW Washington DC 20007 Office: Office of Asst Sec Sci Smithsonian Instn Washington DC 20460

WARNKE, PAUL CULLITON, lawyer; b. Webster, Mass., Jan. 31, 1920; s. Paul Martin and Lillian (Culliton) W.; A.B., Yale U., 1941; LL.B., Columbia U., 1948; m. Jean Farjeon Rowe, Sept. 9, 1948; Fed. children—Margaret Farjeon, Georgia Culliton, Thomas Martin, Stephen August, Benjamin Hyatt. Admitted to D.C. bar, 1948; asso. firm Covington & Burling, Washington, 1948-57, partner, 1957-66; gen. counsel Dept. Def., 1966-67, asst. sec. for internat. security affairs, 1967-69; partner firm Clifford, Warnke, Glass, McIlwain & Finney, 1969-77; dir. ACDA, Washington, 1977-78; chief negotiator SALT, 1977-78; partner firm Clifford & Warnke, Washington, 1978—; spl. cons. to sec. state, 1978—; mem. Md. and D.C. adv. coms. to U.S. Commn. Civil Rights, 1962-66; trustee Lawyers Com. for Civil Rights Under Law; dir. Internat. Vol. Services, 1973-76; exec. com. Trilateral Commn., 1973-77; mem. China council Asia Soc., 1976-77; mem. disciplinary bd. D.C. Bar, 1973. Trustee Potomac Sch., 1958-66, chmn. bd., 1965-66; bd. dirs. Health and Welfare Council Nat. Capital Area, 1966-67; trustee Northland Coll., 1970-76; bd. dirs. Georgetown U., 1979—, Wolftrap Found.; chmn. bd. visitors Georgetown Sch. Fgn. Service, 1971-76; adv. com. Yale Econ. Growth Center; bd. visitors Columbia U. Sch. Law; bd. govs. Antioch Sch. Law, 1973-76. Served to lt. USCGR, 1942-46. Mem. Am., Fed., bar assns., D.C. Bar (disciplinary com. 1973, gov. 1976-77), Am. Soc. Internat. Law, Council Fgn. Relations (dir.). Democrat. Clubs: Met. (Washington); Yale (N.Y.C.). Home: 5037 Garfield St NW Washington DC 20016 Office: 815 Connecticut Ave Washington DC 20006

WARNKEN, DOUGLAS RICHARD, publisher; b. N.Y.C., Apr. 17, 1930; s. Richard William and Juliette (Lindsay) W.; A.B., Norwich U., 1952; m. Virginia M. Thompson, Sept. 16, 1957; 1 son, William Monroe. Sales rep. Prentice-Hall, Inc., Nashville, 1954-56; regional sales mgr. Wadsworth Pub. Co., Inc., Chgo., 1957-59, nat. sales mgr., Belmont, Calif., 1960-64, v.p., marketing mgr., Belmont, 1964-68, exec. v.p., 1968-77, pres., 1977-78, dir., 1971-78; pres., dir. Wadsworth, Inc., 1978—; chmn. bd. Wadsworth Pubs. of Can., Ltd., 1975—; dir. CBI Pub. Co. Inc. Active Boy Scouts Am. Served to 1st lt. AUS, 1952-54. Mem. Vols. for Internat. Tech. Assistance, Belmont C. of C. (dir. 1970—, pres. 1972-73), Western Book Pubs. Assn. (dir. 1971—). Republican. Presbyn. Clubs: Carmel Valley Golf and Country, Peninsula Golf and Country. Office: Wadsworth Inc 10 Davis Dr Belmont CA 94002

WARNOCK, FRANK MCLEOD, food distbn. co. exec.; b. Scotland, Mar. 8, 1925; s. John McLeod and Joan Walker (Connel) W.; immigrated to Can., 1947, naturalized, 1951; student Univ. Coll., London, 1941-42; m. Eleanor Jackson, Apr. 10, 1950; children—Eleanor Anne, John Robert, James Hamish, Alastair Alexander. With Scott Paper Co. Ltd., 1957-69, dir. mktg., 1968-69; v.p. sales and mktg. Dominion Dairies Ltd., 1969-72, pres., 1972-75; pres. M. Loeb Corp. (U.D.), 1975—; pres., chief exec. officer M. Loeb, Ltd., Ottawa, Can., 1975—; dir. Nat. Drug and Chem. Ltd., Horne & Pitfield Foods Ltd.; dir. market Wholesale Grocery Co. Inc. Served with RAF, 1942-47. Home: 7 Jackson Ave Ottawa ON K1S 4K7 Canada Office: 400 Industrial Ave Ottawa ON K1G 3K8 Canada

WARNOCK, WILLIAM KIRKPATRICK, apparel co. exec.; b. San Francisco, Feb. 23, 1921; s. James and Matilda (McClarty) W.; B.S., U. Calif., Berkeley, 1943; m. Guinevere Petrie Gunthorp, Feb. 28, 1942; children—William Kirkpatrick, Kerry, Robert D. With Koret of Calif. and parent co. Koracorp Industries Inc. (now D.A.E.), 1945—, pres. Women's Group, San Francisco, 1968-74, pres. parent co., San Francisco, 1975—, also dir. Served with USAAF, 1943-45. Republican. Episcopalian. Home: 20 Upland Rd Kentfield CA 94904 Office: 617 Mission St San Francisco CA 94105

WARNS, RAYMOND H., judge; b. St. Paul, July 24, 1920; s. Henry John and Veronica (Jennings) W.; student U. Minn., 1941-42, 45-47; B.S.L., J.D., St. Paul Coll. Law, 1948-52; m. Ruth Elenor Fuhrman, Nov. 22, 1947; children—Stephen F., Mark J., Michael T., Raymond H. With law dept. Soo Line R.R., Mpls., 1952-57; with firm Battle, Neal, Harris, Minor & Williams, Charlottesville, Va., 1962-63; with Greyhound Corp., Chgo., 1957-61, 63-69, v.p. claims Greyhound Lines, Inc., 1969; gen. atty. Household Finance Corp., 1969-71; adminstrv. law judge HEW, 1971—. Served as pilot USAAF, World War II. Mem. Minn. Bar Assn., Am. Arbitration Assn. Home: 1890 Willow Ave Bainbridge Island WA 98110 Office: Fed Bldg Seattle WA 98104

WARNTZ, WILLIAM, theoretical geographer, educator; b. Berwick, Pa., Oct. 10, 1922; s. Sterling Adrian and Lillian (Grey) W.; B.S., U. Pa., 1949, M.A., 1951, Ph.D., 1955; m. A. Minerva Mosdell, June 19, 1947; children—Christopher William, Pamela Mary Elizabeth. Instr. to asst. prof. U. Pa., 1949-56; Carnegie Found. grantee McGill U., 1950; mem. bd. advisers Wharton Sch., 1950-56; dir., chief researcher Behavioral Res. Council Sub-project, 1954-55; research asso. Am. Geog. Soc., N.Y.C., 1956-66; prof. theoretical geography and regional planning Harvard, Cambridge, Mass., 1966-71, dir. lab. computer graphics and spatialanalysis, 1968-71; prof., 1971—, chmn. dept. geography U. Western Ont., London, 1971-76; vis. prof. Cambridge U., 1976-77, fellow Clare Hall, 1976-77, life asso. Clare Hall, 1977—; lectr. in geog. grad. sch. Hunter Coll., 1956-66; research asso. astro-phys. sci. Princeton, 1957-65, mem. adv. council. dept. graphics, 1965-67; lectr. in regional sci. U. Pa. Grad. Sch., 1958-66; faculty seminar asso. Columbia, 1964-66; mem. adv. council Bur. Census, 1957-66; cons. NSF, 1959—, Ednl. Services, Inc., 1962-66, Learning Center, Princeton, 1962-67, Brookings Instn., 1961—, Can. Council, 1969—. Served to lst lt. USAAF, 1943-48; ETO. Decorated Air medal with two oak leaf clusters. Purple Heart. Fellow Royal Soc. Can., Explorers Club (N.Y.C.); mem. Regional Sci. Assn. (pres.), AAUP, Can. Assn. U. Tchrs., Assn. Am. Geographers, Internat. Geog. Union, AAAS (Council), Alpha Sigma Phi. Episcopalian. Clubs: University (London, Ont.); Royal Over-Seas League (London, Eng.); U. Pa. Author: Toward a Geography of Price, 1959; Geography, Geometry and Graphics, 1963; Geographers and What They Do, 1964; Geography Now and Then, 1964; Macrogeography and Income Fronts, 1965; Breakthroughs in Geography, 1971; author TV series on geography, Phila., 1957, Boston, 1968. Contbr. articles to profl. jours. Home: Wendling 85 Argilla Rd Andover MA 01810 also Hutton Rd London ON Canada Office: 2411 Social Sci Center U Western Ont London ON Canada

WARREN, ALBERT, editor; b. Warren, Ohio, May 18, 1920; s. David and Clara (Fersky) W.; B.A. in Journalism, Ohio State U., 1942; m. Margaret Virginia Yeomans, Jan. 9, 1947; children—Ellen, Paul, Claire, Daniel, Thomas, Joan. Mem. staff Television Digest, Washington, 1945—, chief Washington bur., 1958-61, editor and pub., pres., treas., 1961—; pres. Factbook Research, Inc., 1973—. Served with USNR, 1942-45; PTO. Mem. Ind. Newsletter Assn. (co-founder 1962, pres. 1963), Broadcasters Club, Broadcast Pioneers, Internat. Radio and TV Soc., White House Corr. Assn. Club: Lakewood Country. Home: 26 W Kirke St Chevy Chase MD 20015 Office: 1836-A Jefferson Pl NW Washington DC 20036

WARREN, CHARLES MARQUIS, dir., writer, producer; b. Balt., Dec. 16; s. Charles and Beatrice (Porter) W.; grad. Balt. City Coll.; m. Anne Crawford Tootle, Oct. 4, 1941; children—Anne Crawford, Jessica Porter, Victoria Lance. Dir., writer motion pictures Little Big Horn, 1951, Hellgate, 1952, Arrowhead, 1952; dir. Seven Angry Men, 1955, Tension at Table Rock, 1956, Trooper Hook, 1957; dir., producer, writer Charro!, 1969; created TV series Gunsmoke, 1955, Rawhide, 1958, The Virginian, 1962; pres. Comdr. Films Corp., Beverly Hills, Calif., 1951—, CMW Prodns., Beverly Hills, 1960—, Emirau Prodns., Beverly Hills, 1962—; dir. CMW, Inc. Served to comdr. USNR, 1942-46; PTO. Decorated Purple Heart, Bronze Star; recipient Brit. Critics award, 1956, Western Heritage award, 1959. Mem. Acad. Motion Picture Arts and Scis., Screen Dirs. Guild, Writers Guild Am., Screen Producers Guild. Republican. Episcopalian. Author: Wilderness, 1940; Only the Valiant, 1943; Valley of the Shadow, 1948; Deadhead, 1950; (screenplays) Beyond Glory, 1948, Springfield Rifle, 1952, Pony Express, 1952. Contbr. short stories, serials nat. mags. Home and office: 1130 Tower Rd Beverly Hills CA 90210*

WARREN, EARL FRANCIS, publishing co. exec.; b. Weatherford, Tex., Sept. 6, 1933; s. June B. and Marie Vaughan (Dobbs) W.; B.F.A., U. Tex., 1956; m. Evelyn Loraine Whitley; 1 dau., Dina Marie. Dir. pub. relations, editor assn. mag. North Tex. Milk Producers Assn., 1957-58; account mgr. Jack Holmes Advt., Fort Worth, 1959; merchandising mgr. Sta. KNOK, 1960-64; owner Earl Warren & Assos., Photojournalism and Pub. Relations/Advt., 1964-72; editor Make It With Leather mag., Fort Worth, 1972—; dir. Four Graphics, Inc., Fort Worth. Served to Capt. AUS, 1956-57, 60-61. Mem. Alpha Phi Omega, Alpha Epsilon Rho. Republican. Presbyn. Contbr. articles and photog. sets to trade and profl. mags.; designer children's books and toys, also cartoon series. Home: 1507 Marshalldale St Arlington TX 76013 Office: 2617 W 7th St Fort Worth TX 76107

WARREN, EDUS HOUSTON, JR., investment broker; b. Danville, Va., Dec. 9, 1923; s. Edus Houston and Edith (Farley) W.; A.B., Harvard, 1946; m. Roberta Ruth Lounsbury, June 24, 1949; children—Ann Warren Burcham, Ralph Lounsbury, Sarah Randolph, Edus Houston III. With Spencer Trask & Co., Inc., N.Y.C., 1951-77, gen. partner, 1959-68, pres., chief exec. officer, dir., 1974-77; vice chmn. Hornblower, Weeks, Noyes & Trask, Inc. (merger Spencer Trask & Co., Inc. and Hornblower-Weeks-Hemphill-Noyes), 1977—; exec. v.p., mem. fin. com., mem. exec. com. Loeb Rhoades, Hornblower & Co.; vice chmn. Capital Research Co., N.Y.C., 1978—; dir. Capital Guardian Trust Co. Trustee, Pingry Sch. Served to 1st lt. USAAF, 1943-45. Decorated D.F.C., Air medal. Mem. N.Y. Soc. Security Analysts, Securities Industry Assn., Inst. Chartered Financial Analysts. Republican. Episcopalian. Home: 100 Rotary Dr Summit NJ 07901 Office: 280 Park Ave New York NY 10017

WARREN, EDWARD WILLARD, educator; b. San Francisco, Jan. 20, 1929; s. Edward Hiram and Anne (Merkle) W.; B.A., Stanford, 1950; postgrad. U. Toronto, 1950-51, U. Calif., Berkeley, 1954-56; Ph.D., Johns Hopkins, 1961; m. Mary Jane Molsbergen, Dec. 26, 1955; children—Edward Willard, Diane Elizabeth, Richard John. Instr., asst. prof. philosophy Syracuse (N.Y.) U., 1959-63; successively asst. prof., asso. prof., prof. San Diego State U., 1963—, chmn. dept. classical and oriental langs., 1969-71. Served with AUS, 1951-54; lt. USNR, Ret. Mem. Am. Assn. U. Profs. (chpt. pres., Calif. conf. pres. 1972-73, vice chmn. assembly state confs. 1973-75, mem. com. D 1979—), Am. Philos. Assn., Soc. for Greek Philosophy, Inst. for Greek Philosophy, Neoplatonic Soc. Roman Catholic. Home: 9929 Waldgrove Pl San Diego CA 92131

WARREN, FERDINAND E., painter, educator; b. Independence, Mo., Aug. 1, 1899. Resident artist U. Ga., 1950-51; head dept. art Agnes Scott Coll., Decatur, Ga., 1951-69. Represented in collections Met. Mus., Bklyn. Mus., Rochester (N.Y.) Meml. Gallery, Butler Inst., Youngstown, O., High Mus., Atlanta, Currier Gallery, Manchester, N.H., NASA, Washington, Supreme Ct. D.C. Art Trust Collection, others. Recipient 2d Julius Hallgarten prize N.A.D., 1935, William Palmer Meml. prize, 1962; Opaque Water color prize S.E. Artists Exhbn., 1950; Water Color purchase award Butler Art Inst., 1954; Watercolor prize Assn. Ga. Artists, 1956. Nat. academician. Mem. Am. Watercolor Soc. (Osborn Water Color prize 1944), Ga. Artists Assn. (pres. 1956-57), Audubon Artists, other assns. Home: 227 E Hancock St Decatur GA 30030

WARREN, FRANK M., electric co. exec.; b. 1915; grad. Stanford, also Harvard Grad. Sch. Bus. Adminstrn.; married. With Portland Gen. Electric Co. 1937—, v.p., 1942, exec. v.p., 1946-55, dir. 1949—, pres., 1955-77, chief exec. officer, 1966—, chmn., 1977—; dir. U.S. Nat. Bank of Oreg., Tektronix, Inc. Bd. dirs., v.p. Portland Library Assn. Mem. Portland C. of C. (dir.). Address: Portland Gen Electric Co 121 SW Salmon St Portland OR 97204*

WARREN, FREDERICK HAYES, cons. engr.; b. Orange, N.J., Apr. 15, 1910; s. Frederick Hayes and Ruth (Spencer) W.; student Cornell U., 1926-27; B.S., U.S. Mil. Acad., 1931; C.E., Princeton U., 1934; m. Marie McIntyre, Oct. 26, 1935; children—Linda Lithgow Warren Hessel, Sandra Spencer. Examiner, regional engr. Def. Plants Corp., RFC, Washington, 1936-42, asst. dir. Office Def. Plants, 1946-47; successively asst., dir. production, dep. dir. constrn. and supply div. AEC, Washington, 1947-53, also mem. industry evaluation advisory bd. to Sec. Commerce; cons. engr. atomic energy devel., Washington, 1953-54; asst. to exec. v.p. for atomic energy Gen. Dynamics Corp., Washington, 1954-56; partner Pickard-Warren-Lowe Assos., Washington, 1956-64; co-founder, chmn. bd. NUS Corp., Rockville, Md., 1960-69, sr. v.p., 1972-75; chmn. bd. Hydrospace Research Corp., Rockville, 1962-66; advisor environ. quality FPC, Washington, 1970-72; adv. So. States Energy Bd., 1972—; dir. Atomic Devel. Mut. Fund, Steadman Sci. and Growth Fund, Steadman Shares Am. Industry, 1954-69. Pres. Kenwood Citizens Assn., Chevy Chase, Md., 1964-65; mem. Fed. City Council, Washington, 1968-78. Served to 2d lt. C.E., U.S. Army, 1931-35, to col. C.E., 1942-46. Decorated Legion of Merit. Fellow ASCE, Am. Cons. Engrs. Council; mem. Am. Nuclear Soc., Delta Tau Delta. Clubs: Chevy Chase, Met., Royal Poinciana. Co-author: A Growth Study of the Atomic Industry 1955-65, 1958-68; co-editor: Power Reactor Technology, 1961, National Power Survey, 1970. Home: 5816 Brookside Dr Chevy Chase MD 20015 Office: NUS Corp 4 Research Pl Rockville MD 20850

WARREN, FREDERICK MARSHALL, former army officer, judge; b. Newport, Ky., Aug. 23, 1903; s. William Ulysses and Katherine (Lampe) W.; A.B., LL.B., LL.M., LL.D. (hon.), U. Cin.; L.D., No. Ky. U., m. Peggy Beaton, Feb. 20, 1926; 1 son, Frederick Marshall. Various positions with lumber and millwork cos., 1926-32; police judge, Southgate, Ky., 1932-35; admitted to Ky. bar, 1935; city atty., Southgate, 1935-50; city solicitor, Newport, 1950-52; county judge Campbell County, 1954-58; cons. to under sec. army, 1958; spl. asst. to asst. sec. army for manpower personnel and res. forces, 1959; recalled to active duty as maj. gen. U.S. Army, 1959; chief U.S. Army Res. and ROTC Affairs, 1959-63; circuit judge 17th Jud. Dist. Ky., 1963-77. Field rep. Alcoholic Beverage Control Bd. Ky., 1949; mem. U.S. Army Gen. Staff com. N.G. and army res. policy, 1953-56; mem. res. forces policy bd. Dept. Def., 1958-59. Served to col. AUS. World War II. Decorated Combat Infantryman's badge, D.S.M., Silver Star, Bronze Star, Army Commendation medal (U.S.); Criox de Guerre (France, Belgium). Mem. Am., Ky., Campbell County (past pres.) bar assns., Am. Legion, VFW, DAV, Assn. U.S. Army, Res. Officers Assn. (past nat. v.p.), Mil. Order World Wars. Mason, Elk. Home: 20 Crow Hill Fort Thomas KY 41075

WARREN, GERALD EMERY, educator, economist; b. Lyons, Kans., Feb. 21, 1914; s. Albert W. and Laura Ellen (Umberger) W.; B.A., Southwestern Coll., Winfield, Kans., 1935; M.A., Ph.D., U. Iowa; m. Genevieve Walts, Aug. 3, 1940; children—Judith Rae, Joyce Elaine. Store asso. J.C. Penney Co., 1931-35; teaching fellow U. Iowa, 1935-38; instr., then asst. prof. econs. DePauw U., 1938-41, asso. prof. econs., 1946-47; state price exec. OPA, 1942-43, OPS, 1951-53; asso. prof., prof. econs. Tulane U., 1947-56; econ. adviser ICA, China, 1956-59, Korea, 1959-62; vis. prof. econs. Temple U., 1962-63, prof. econs., 1963-66; prof., head dept. econs. DePauw U., Greencastle, Ind., 1966-79, prof. emeritus, 1979—. Served as lt. comdr. USNR, 1943-46; comdr. Res., ret. Mem. Am., So. econs. assns., Am. Finance Assn., Am. Legion, S.W. Social Sci. Assn., Beta Gamma Sigma, Pi Gamma Mu, Pi Kappa Delta, Alpha Delta Sigma, Omicron Delta Kappa, Order of Artus. Methodist. Home: 710 Dogwood Ln Greencastle IN 46135

WARREN, GERALD LEE, newspaper editor; b. Hastings, Nebr., Aug. 17, 1930; s. Hie Elias and Linnie (Williamson) W.; A.B., U. Nebr., 1952; m. Euphemia Florence Brownell, Nov. 20, 1965 (div.); children—Gerald Benjamin, Euphemia Brownell. Reporter Lincoln (Nebr.) Star, 1951-52; reporter, asst. city editor San Diego Union, 1956-61; bus. rep. Copley News Service, 1961-63; city editor San Diego Union, 1963-68, asst. mng. editor, 1968-69, editor, 1975—; dep. press sec. to Pres. Nixon, 1969-74, Pres. Ford, 1974-75. Served to lt. (j.g.) USNR, 1952-56. Mem. Am. Soc. Newspaper Editors, Sigma Delta Chi, Sigma Nu. Republican. Episcopalian. Home: Apt A-301 2420 Torrey Pines Rd La Jolla CA 92037 Office: PO Box 191 San Diego CA 92112

WARREN, JACK HAMILTON, banker; b. Apr. 10, 1921; student Queen's U., Kingston, Ont., 1939-41; m. Hilary J. Titterington; children—Hilary Warren Nicolson, Martin, Jennifer, Ian. Joined Dept. External Affairs, 1945; assigned London, 1948-51; fin. counsellor, Washington, 1954-57; asst. dep. minister trade and commerce, 1958-64; dep. minister industry, trade and commerce, 1964-71; high commr. to U.K., 1971-75; ambassador to U.S., 1975-77; Can. coordinator for multilateral trade negotiations, 1977-79; vice chmn. Bank of Montreal (Que., Can.), 1979—. Served with Royal Canadian Navy, 1941-45. Office: Bank of Montreal Head Office 129 St James St Montreal PQ H2Y 1L6 Canada

WARREN, JAMES CALDWELL, educator, physician; b. Oklahoma City, May 13, 1930; s. William Bland and Geraldyn (Caldwell) W.; A.B., Wichita U., 1950; M.D., U. Kans., 1954; Ph.D., U. Neb., 1961; m. Mary Ann Carpenter, Dec. 27, 1951; children—Richard Bruce, Jamie Ann, James Douglas, Allison Jean. Intern, U. Kans. Hosp., 1954-55; resident U. Nebr. Hosp., 1957-60; practice medicine specializing in obstetrics and gynecology, Kansas City, Kans., 1961-71, St. Louis, 1971—; from asst. prof. to prof. obstetrics, gynecology and biochemistry U. Kans. Sch. Medicine, 1961-71; prof., head obstetrics and gynecology, prof. biochemistry Washington U.

Sch. Medicine, St. Louis, 1971—. Cons. NIH. Served to lt. M.C., USNR, 1955-57. Markle scholar med. sci., 1961. Fellow Am. Coll. Obstetricians and Gynecologists; mem. Am. Soc. Biol. Chemists, Sigma Xi, Alpha Omega Alpha. Contbr. articles to profl. jours. Office: 4911 Barnes Hosp Plaza St Louis MO 63110

WARREN, JAMES VAUGHN, physician, educator; b. Columbus, Ohio, July 1, 1915; s. James Halford and Lucile (Vaughn) W.; B.A., Ohio State U., 1935; M.D., Harvard, 1939; D.Sc., Emory U., 1974; m. Gloria Kicklighter, May 27, 1954. Med. house officer Peter Bent Brigham Hosp., 1939-41, asst. resident medicine, 1941-42; research fellow medicine Harvard, 1941-42; med. investigator problems of shock and vascular injuries OSRD, 1942-46, instr. medicine Emory U. Med. Sch., 1942-46, asso. prof. medicine, prof. physiology, chmn. dept. physiology, 1947-51, prof. medicine, 1951-52; asst. prof. medicine Yale Med. Sch., 1946-47; prof. medicine Duke Sch. Medicine, 1952-58; prof. medicine, chmn. dept. internal medicine U. Tex. Sch. Medicine, 1958-61; prof. medicine, chmn. dept. Ohio State U. Med. Sch., 1961—. Mem. cardiovascular sect. USPHS, 1952-56; mem. tng. grant com. Nat. Heart Inst., 1961-64; mem. Nat. Acad. Medicine-Inst. Medicine, 1971. Recipient Distinguished Alumnus award Duke U. Med. Center, 1970; Columbus Mayor's award for vol. service, 1978; diplomate Am. Bd. Internal Medicine (sec.-treas. 1970-71, vice chmn. 1971-72). Master A.C.P.; mem. AMA (chmn. sect. internal medicine 1964-65), Assn. Profs. Medicine (pres. 1967-68, Williams disting. chmn. medicine award 1979), Am. Clin. and Climatol. Assn., Soc. Univ. Cardiologists, Am. Heart Assn. (pres. 1962-63, Gold Heart award, James B. Herrick award 1976), Am. Soc. Clin. Investigation, Am. Fedn. Clin. Research (nat. pres. 1952-53), Am. Physiol. Soc., Soc. Exptl. Biology and Medicine, Assn. Am. Physicians, So., Central socs. clin. research, Sigma Xi, Alpha Omega Alpha. Conglist. Clubs: Cosmos; Explorers; Harvard. Author: Cardiovascular Physiology, 1975. Editorial bd. Am. Heart Jour., Excerpta Medica, Circulation (jour.), Med. Opinion, 1971. Contbg. author: Pre-Eclamptic and Eclamptic Toxemia of Pregnancy, 1941; Methods in Medical Research, vol. VII. Contbr. numerous articles to profl. publs. Home: 5526 Ashford Rd Dublin OH 43017 Office: Ohio State U Hosp Columbus OH 43210

WARREN, JOHN RUSH, educator; b. Columbus, Ohio, July 20, 1919; s. John Rush and Martha (Jewell) W.; A.B., Marietta Coll., 1941; postgrad. Ohio U., 1941-42; M.S., Ohio State U., 1947, Ph.D., 1950; m. Ruth Spargo (div.; children—Penelope, John; m. 2d, Aida Martinez (div.); children—Juana, Ricardo, Felicity; m. 3d, Carolyn Cox. Asst. plant pathologist Ohio Agrl. Exptl. Sta., Columbus, 1942-44, 46; asst. prof. botany Duke, 1946-52; plant pathologist Midwest Research Inst., La Ceiba, Honduras, 1952; plant pathologist Standard Fruit Co., Honduras, 1953-55, dir. tropical research, 1955-59; asso. prof. Tenn. Poly. Inst., 1960-61, prof., chmn. dept. biol. scis., 1961-64; prof. botany Marshall U., Huntington, W.Va., 1964—, dean Grad. Sch., 1964-72; cons. environ. scis. br. AEC. Fulbright lectr., chmn. dept. biology Nat. Autonomous U., Republic Honduras, 1968-69; Fulbright lectr. U. Guayaquil (Ecuador), 1980-81. Served with AUS, 1944-46. Mem. Sigma Xi, Phi Delta Kappa. Mason. Author sci. publs. on mycology, bacteriology, plant pathology, isotopes, antibiotics, archaeology. Office: Marshall U Huntington WV 25701

WARREN, KENNETH S., physician; b. N.Y.C., June 11, 1929; A.B., Harvard U., 1951, M.D., 1955; m. Sylvia Marjorie Rothwell, Feb. 14, 1959; children—Christopher Harwood, Erica Marjorie. Intern, Harvard service Boston City Hosp., 1955-56; research asso. Lab. Tropical Diseases, NIH, Bethesda, Md., 1956-62; asst. prof. medicine Case Western Res. U., 1963-68, asso. prof., 1968-75, prof., 1975-77, prof. library sci., 1974-77; dir. health scis. Rockefeller Found., N.Y.C., 1977—; cons. WHO; mem. com. internat. health Inst. Medicine, Nat. Acad. Scis. Recipient Career Devel. award NIH, 1966-71. Fellow A.C.P.; mem. Am. Soc. Clin. Investigation, Assn. Am. Physicians, Am. Assn. Immunologists, Am. Soc. Tropical Medicine and Hygiene (Bailey K. Ashford award 1974), Infectious Diseases Soc. Am. (Squibb award 1975), Royal Soc. Tropical Medicine and Hygiene. Author books, including: Schistosomiasis: The Evolution of a Medical Literature. Selected Abstracts and Citations, 1852-1972, 1973; Geographic Medicine for the Practitioner, 1978; contbr. numerous articles to profl. jours.; patentee diagnostic methods, drugs. Office: 1133 Ave of Americas New York NY 10036

WARREN, L.D., editorial cartoonist; b. Wilmington, Del., Dec. 27, 1906; s. Robert L. and Annie (Melvin) W.; ed. pub. schs.; m. Julianne Bussert Baker, May 9, 1958; children—Joy (Mrs. Don Haines), L.D. II. Cartoonist, Camden (N.J.) Courier Post, 1925-28, Phila. Record, 1928-47, Cin. Enquirer, 1947—; numerous cartoon illustrations for books, mags. and brochures; exhibited in group shows at Met. Mus. Art, N.Y.C., 1954; Internat. Pavillion of Humor, Montreal, Que., Can., 1968-74, World Cartoon Gallery, Skopje, Yugoslavia, 1969, 71, Nat. Portrait Gallery, London, 1970; one-man shows and represented in permanent collections Pub. Library Cin. and Hamilton County, U. Cin., Lyndon B. Johnson Library, Austin, Tex., Mus. Cartoon Art, Port Chester, N.Y.; represented in permanent collections Smithsonian Instn., numerous univ., libraries, museums in U.S., also pvt. collections of Presidents Truman, Eisenhower, Kennedy, Johnson, Nixon, and Ford, numerous others; guest instr. cartooning Art Acad. Cin., 1957. Recipient over 25 awards Freedoms Found., 1949-73, award Nat. Headliners Club, 1961, Best Cartoon of Sixties award Nat. Found. Hwy. Safety, 1971, Mass Media Brotherhood awards NCCJ, Nat. Comdr.'s citation Am. Legion, 1974. Mem. Assn. Am. Editorial Cartoonists (v.p. 1960, 75), Nat. Cartoonists Soc., Cin. Art Mus. Illustrator: Penny Penguin, 1935, Terry and Bunky Play Football (Japanese edit. 1949), Terry and Bunky Play Basketball series, 1945-51; (with Walter C. Langsam) The World and Warren's Cartoons (Martha Kinney Cooper Ohioana Book award 1977), 1977. Home: 1815 William Howard Taft Rd Cincinnati OH 45206 Office: Cin Enquirer 607 Vine St Cincinnati OH 45202

WARREN, LEROY JOHN, educator; b. Nyssa, Oreg., Apr. 1, 1926; s. LeRoy and Edna (Deno) W.; B.A., Coll. Idaho, 1950; M.A., U. Oreg., 1953, Ph.D., 1955; m. Patricia E. Ward, Aug. 13, 1954; children—Eric, Bruce, Brent. Faculty, San Diego State Coll., 1955—, prof. math., 1963—. Served with AUS, 1944-46. Mem. Am. Math. Soc., Math. Assn. Am. Contbr. articles in number theory to math. jours. Home: 4810 Campanile St San Diego CA 92115

WARREN, LOUIS BANCEL, lawyer; b. Monmouth Beach, N.J., Aug. 30, 1905; s. Schuyler Neilson and Alice (Binsse) W.; A.B., M.A., Trinity Coll., Oxford U., 1927; J.D., Columbia, 1930; m. Rosalie Warren, June 9, 1934; children—Hope Wilberforce (Mrs. Charles Shaw), Rosalie Starr (Mrs. Paul Byard), Louis Bancel. Admitted to N.Y. bar, 1930, since practiced in N.Y.C.; asso. Larkin, Rathbone & Perry, now Kelley & Drye & Warren, 1930-40, mem. firm, 1940—. Dir., mem. compensation com. Chrysler Corp., 1957-76; dir. Chrysler U.K. Ltd., Chrysler Espana S.A., Hammersons Holdings (U.S.A.), Inc.; dir. Chrysler France S.A.; dir., sec. Am. European Assos. Inc. Mem. exec. com. Correctional Assn. N.Y. Treas., trustee Homeland Found.; bd. dirs., pres. Lutece Found., Inc.; mem. bd. visitors Columbia Law Sch., pres., 1962-72; bd. dirs. Am. Ditchley Found., 1962-72; chmn. bd. dirs. Mgmt. Inst. for Nat. Devel. Participant U.S. Naval War Coll. global strategy discussions, 1966. Served with N.Y. N.G., 1927-30; with USCG(T), 1943-45. Decorated knight comdr. Order St. Gregory the Gt. (Vatican), 1957; officers cross merit Sovereign Order Malta, 1968; chevalier French Legion Honor, 1971; comdr. Order Brit. Empire, 1972; officier L'Ordre des Arts of Lettres (France), 1978; Morgan Library fellow; hon. fellow Trinity Coll., Oxford U., 1978. Mem. Am., N.Y. bar assns., Assn. Bar City N.Y., Am. Soc. Internat. Law, Am. Judicature Soc., St. Nicholas Soc., Alliance Francaise de N.Y., French Inst., English-Speaking Union, Internat. Bar Assn., France Am. Soc., Pilgrims Soc., St. Georges Soc., Phi Delta Phi. Republican. Roman Catholic. Clubs: Detroit; Knickerbocker, Century Assn. (N.Y.C.); Somerset Hills Country Somerset Hills Lake and Game (N.J.); Racquet and Tennis (N.Y.C.). Contbr. articles to legal jours. Home: Ballantine Rd Bernardsville NJ 07924 Office: 350 Park Ave New York NY 10022

WARREN, LUCIAN CRISSEY, journalist; b. Jamestown, N.Y., Feb. 12, 1913; s. Lucian Jason and Bernice (Scofield) W.; A.B., Denison U., 1936; m. Katherine Smith, June 17, 1939; children—Sylvia, Lucian James, Katherine, Nancy. Reporter, Jamestown (N.Y.) Evening Jour., 1929-31, 34; reporter Chautauquan (N.Y.) Daily, 1935-37, editor, 1938-39; reporter Buffalo Courier-Express, 1937-43, chief Washington bur., 1945-68; chief Washington bur. Buffalo Evening News, 1969-78; Washington corr. Frederick (Md.) News-Post and Roanoke (Va.) Time & World-News, 1979—; pub. relations dir. Colonial Radio Corp., Buffalo, 1944; editor World Hwys., 1966-71; free-lance writer, lectr. Recipient Distinguished Alumnus citation Denison U. Mem. Overseas Writers of Washington, Standing Com. of Corrs. Washington (chmn. 1967), Phi Beta Kappa Assos., Phi Beta Kappa, Sigma Delta Chi, Phi Gamma Delta (editor 1961-62), Omicron Delta Kappa. Clubs: Gridiron (pres. 1975), Nat. Press (pres. 1955) (Washington). Contbr. articles to mags. Home: 1034-N Crystal Towers 1600 S Eads St Arlington VA 22202 Office: 1296 National Press Bldg Washington DC 20045

WARREN, MARK EDWARD, television dir.; b. Harrodsburg, Ky., Sept. 24, 1938; s. Mark Edward and Mary Wallace (Wade) W.; student Lincoln Inst., 1951-55; m. Barbara Anne Rudy, Aug. 20, 1958; children—Andre Mark, Brian Rudy, Christopher. Stage mgr., performer CTV Network, Ottawa, Ont., Can., 1957-61; stage mgr. CBC TV Network, Toronto, Ont., Can., 1961-62, producer-dir., 1962-68; dir. TV programs Soul, T.C.B., Grammy Awards, Rowan and Martin's Laugh-In, Diahann Carroll Show, Turn-On, 1968—, The New Bill Cosby Show, Sanford & Son, Barney Miller, Sammy & Co., What's Happening, Get Christie Love, Black Achievement Awards, Fish, Beverly Sills and Friends; dir. films Come Back Charleston Blue, The Legend of Isaac Murphy; dir. for stage Selma (The Martin Luther King Story). Served with USAF. Recipient Emmy award for Rowan and Martin's Laugh-In, 1970-71; named Ky. col. Home: 1830 Outpost Dr Hollywood CA 90028

WARREN, MATTHEW, orgn. exec.; b. Pueblo, Colo., Aug. 12, 1918; s. Marshall Henry and Lola Maude (Gentry) M.; student Kan. State Coll. Architecture, 1937; m. Dorothy Florence Meeks, Aug. 2, 1940; children—D. Sharon, Marcia Louise, Kenneth W. Information officer Anglo-Am. Carribbean Commn., State Dept., Washington, 1944-45; news commentator Mut. Broadcasting System-WOL, Washington, 1945-46; program mgr. Arlington-Fairfax Broadcasting Co., Arlington, Va., 1946-50; dir. news and pub. affairs Dumont-Metromedia Corp., Washington, 1951-62; dir. pub. affairs Evening Star Broadcasting Corp., WMAL, Washington, 1962-64; bur. chief RKO-Gen. Corp. Broadcasting div., Washington, 1964-67; nat. dir. pub. relations Goodwill Industries Am., Inc., Washington, 1968—; pres. Warren Properties, 1961—. Cons., Johns Hopkins, 1966—; mem. Pres.'s Nat. Indsl. Adv. Com., FCC, 1966-70. Mem. Donaldson Run Citizens Assn., Arlington, Va. Served as civilian with C.E., AUS, 1941-44. Recipient Sylvania award for exceptional pub. service in broadcasting; Emmy award for best locally produced documentary in Am. Mem. Pub. Relations Soc. Am., Nat. Pub. Relations Council Health and Pub. Welfare Services. Club: National Press (Washington). Producer numerous documentaries on aspects of Washington for TV, 1963-64. Home: 3806 N 25th St Arlington VA 22207 Office: 9200 Wisconsin Ave Washington DC 20014

WARREN, RENNY DEBEVOISE, mfg. co. exec.; b. Flushing, N.Y., Aug. 4, 1942; s. Edward L. and Helen Q. Warren; B.S., U. Conn., 1964; grad. Advanced Mgmt. Program, Harvard U., 1979; m. Susan J. Ferguson; children—Timothy Scott, Christopher Edward. From trainee to asst. v.p. Citibank, N.A., N.Y.C., 1966-72; mgr. banking, then asst. treas. Phelps Dodge Corp., N.Y.C., 1972-79, treas., 1979—. Served to capt. USAR, 1964-66. Mem. AIME, Sigma Alpha Epsilon. Clubs: Wee Burn Country (Darien); Mining (N.Y.C.). Home: 16 Fox Hill Ln Darien CT 06820 Office: 300 Park Ave New York NY 10022

WARREN, RICHARD, surgeon; b. Brookline, Mass., May 12, 1907; s. Joseph and Constance M. (Williams) W.; grad. Milton (Mass.) Acad., 1925; A.B., Harvard, 1929, M.D. cum laude, 1934; m. Cora Lyman, Apr. 1, 1933; children—Janet (Mrs. George C. Buell), Constance (Mrs. Richard W. Warton), Richard Agassiz, John Collins. Surg. intern Mass. Gen. Hosp., Boston, 1934-36; surg. resident Peter Bent Brigham Hosp., Boston, 1936-38; fellow gastroenterology U. Pa., 1938-39; pvt. practice, Boston, 1940-80; cons. VA, 1946-80; mem. faculty Harvard Med. Sch., 1940-80, prof. surgery, 1969-80. Served to lt. col., M.C., AUS, 1942-45. Mem. New Eng. Surg. Soc. (pres. 1968-69), Soc. Vascular Surgery (pres. 1962). Author: Procedures in Vascular Surgery, 1960; Surgery, 1962; Lower Extremity Amputations for Arterial Insufficiency, 1967; also articles. Chief editor Archives of Surgery, 1970-77. Home: 200 Highland St Dedham MA 02026

WARREN, RICHARD KEARNEY, publisher; b. N.Y.C., Apr. 13, 1920; s. George Earle and Anna (Kearney) W.; B.S., Yale, 1942; Litt.D., Ricker Coll., 1971; m. Joanne Jordan, Sept. 18, 1943 (div. Oct. 1969); children—Richard J., Carolyn; m. 2d, Susan Atwood Thibodeau, Oct. 1, 1970. Shift supt. W.Va ordnance works Gen. Chem. Co., Point Pleasant, 1942-43; v.p., dir. Bangor Pub. Co. (Maine); pub., editor Bangor News, 1955—; pres. Rockland Courier-Gazette, Inc., 1974—, also dir.; dir. N.E. Pub. Co., Merrill Bankshares, Merrill Trust Co., Bangor & Aroostook R.R. Co. Past trustee Ricker Coll.; past bd. dirs. Bangor YMCA. Mem. devel. council U. Maine. Served to lt. (j.g.) USNR, 1943-46. Mem. Maine (pres. 1953-54, 73-74), N.E. (pres. 1959-60) daily newspaper assns., Am. Newspaper Pubs. Assn., New Eng. Council, Maine (dir.), Bangor (past dir.) chambers commerce, New Eng. Newspaper Advt. Bur. (past dir.), New Eng. Soc. N.Y., Sigma Delta Chi. Rotarian. Clubs: University (N.Y.C.); Penobscot Valley Country (Orono, Maine); Northeast Harbor (Maine) Fleet; Bar Harbor (Maine). Home: 28 W Broadway Bangor ME 04401 Office: Bangor Daily News 491 Main St Bangor ME 04401

WARREN, RICHARD M., exptl. psychologist, educator; b. N.Y.C., Apr. 8, 1925; s. Morris and Rae (Greenberg) W.; B.S. in Chemistry, Coll. City N.Y., 1946; Ph.D. in Organic Chemistry, N.Y. U., 1951; m. Roslyn Pauker, Mar. 31, 1950. Flavor chemist Gen. Foods Co., Hoboken, N.J., 1951-53; research asso. psychology Brown U., Providence, 1954-56; Carnegie sr. research fellow Coll. Medicine, N.Y. U., 1956-57, Cambridge (Eng.) U., 1957-58; research psychologist applied psychology Research Unit, Cambridge, 1958-59; research psychologist Nat. Inst. Mental Health, Bethesda, Md., 1959-61; chmn. psychology Shimer Coll., Mt. Carroll, Ill., 1961-64; asso. prof. psychology U. Wis. at Milw., 1964-66, prof., 1966-73, research prof., 1973-75, distinguished prof., 1975—. Vis. scientist Inst. Exptl. Psychology, Oxford (Eng.) U., 1969-70, 77-78. Mem. Am. Psychol. Assn., Accoustical Soc. Am., Am. Chem. Soc., AAAS, Am. Speech and Hearing Assn., Sigma Xi. Author: (with Roslyn Warren) Helmholtz on Perception: Its Physiology and Development, 1968. Contbr. articles on sensation and perception to profl. jours. Office: Dept Psychology U Wis-Milw Milwaukee WI 53201

WARREN, RICHARD MOORE, apparel co. exec.; b. Erwin, N.C., July 8, 1930; s. James Oliver and Marjorie (Godwin) W.; B.B.A., Wake Forest Coll., 1952, LL.B., 1960; m. Alice Clarke Warner, June 12, 1971; children—Marjorie Elizabeth, Anne Gertrude, Dianne Marie, Richard M., Colby Alden, Kristin Clarke. Admitted to N.C. bar, 1960; asso. Block, Meyland & Lloyd, Attys., Greensboro, N.C., 1960-62; gen. counsel Anderson Industries, Inc., Greensboro, 1962-63; sec., gen. counsel Blue Bell, Inc., Greensboro, 1963—. Served with AUS, 1952-54. C.P.A., N.C. Mem. Am., N.C., Greensboro, bar assns. Home: 4907 Kingswood Dr Greensboro NC 27410 Office: 335 Church St Greensboro NC 27401

WARREN, ROBERT CARLTON, mfg. exec.; b. Portland, Oreg., Apr. 13, 1918; s. Floyd Carlton and Ethel (Wright) W.; grad. Stanford, 1940; m. Nani Marie Swigert, June 23, 1945; children—Catharine K., Robert Carlton, Wendy W., William S., Elizabeth B. With U.S. Steel Corp., Portland, 1940, Esco Corp., Portland, 1941, Oreg. Shipbldg. Corp., 1941-43; gen. mgr., dir. Cascade Corp., Portland, 1944-54, pres., chief exec. officer, 1954-71, chmn., chief exec. officer, 1971—; dir. Esco Corp. Pres., Portland Art Assn., 1979—. Mem. NAM (dir. 1958-75, regional v.p., 1974—), Chi Psi. Office: care Cascade Corp PO Box 25240 Portland OR 97225

WARREN, ROBERT PENN, writer, ret. educator; b. Guthrie, Ky., Apr. 24, 1905; s. Robert Franklin and Anna Ruth (Penn) W.; B.A. summa cum laude, Vanderbilt U., 1925; M.A., U. Calif., 1927; postgrad. Yale, 1927-28; B.Litt. (Rhodes scholar), Oxford U., 1930; Litt.D., U. Louisville, Colby Coll., U. Ky., Swarthmore Coll., Harvard, Yale, Fairfield U., Wesleyan U., Southwestern Coll. at Memphis, U. South, U. New Haven, Johns Hopkins U.; L.H.D., Kenyon Coll.; LL.D., U. Bridgeport; m. Emma Brescia, Sept. 12, 1930 (div. 1950); m. 2d, Eleanor Clark, 1952; children—Rosanna, Gabriel Penn. Mem. Fugitive Group of Poets, 1923-25; asst. prof. English, Southwestern Coll., Memphis, 1930-31; acting asst. prof. Vanderbilt U., 1931-34; asst. prof. La. State U., 1934-36, asso. prof., 1936-42; prof. English, U. Minn., 1942-50; prof. playwrighting Yale, 1951-56, prof. English, 1961-73, prof. emeritus, 1973—. Chair of poetry Library of Congress, 1944-45; mem. staff Writer Conf. U. Colo., 1936, 37, 40, Olivet Coll. 1940; vis. lectr. U. Ia., 1941; Jefferson lectr. Nat. Endowment for the Humanities, 1974. Recipient Houghton Mifflin Lit. Fellowship award, 1936; Levinson prize Poetry: A Mag. of Verse, 1936; Caroline Sinkler prize Poetry Soc. S.C., 1936, 37, 38; Guggenheim fellow in writing, 1939-40, 47-48; Shelley prize for poetry, 1942; Pulitzer prize for fiction, 1947; Robert Meltzer award Screen Writers Guild, 1949; Sidney Hillman award, 1957; Edna St. Vincent Millay prize Am. Poetry Soc., 1958, Nat. Book award for poetry, 1958; Pulitzer prize in poetry, 1958; Irita Van Doren Lit. award N.Y. Herald Tribune, 1965; Bollingen prize in poetry Yale, 1967, Van Wyck Brooks award for poetry, 1970; Nat. medal for lit., 1970, award for lit. U. S.C., 1973; Emerson-Thoreau award Am. Acad. Arts and Scis., 1975; Copernicus prize Am. Acad. Poets, 1975; Pulitzer prize for poetry, 1979; Harriet Monroe award for poetry, 1979. Mem. Am. Acad. Arts and Letters, Acad. Arts and Scis., Am. Philos. Soc., Acad. Am. Poets (chancellor). Author of several books, 1929—; latest: World Enough and Time (novel), 1950; Brother to Dragons (poem), new version, 1979; Band of Angels (novel) 1955; Segregation, 1956; Promises (poems), 1957; Selected Essays, 1958; The Cave, 1959; You, Emperors and Others (poetry), 1960; The Legacy of the Civil War, 1961; Wilderness (novel), 1961; Flood, 1964; Who Speaks for the Negro, 1965; Selected Poems New and Old, 1923-1966, 1966: Incarnations (poems), 1968; Audubon: A Vision (poetry), 1969; Homage to Theodore Dreiser, 1971; Meet Me in The Green Glen (novel), 1971; Or Else-Poem/Poems 1968-74, 1975; Democracy and Poetry, 1975; Selected Poems: 1923-75, 1977; A Place To Come To (novel), 1977; Now and Then: Poems 1976-78. Editor or co-editor other books; a founder and editor The So. Rev., 1935-42. Home: 2495 Redding Rd Fairfield CT 06430

WARREN, ROBERT WILLIS, judge; b. Raton, N.M., Aug. 30, 1925; s. George R. and Clara (Jolliffe) W.; B.A. magna cum laude, Macalester Coll., 1950; M.A., U. Minn., 1951; J.D., U. Wis., 1956; postgrad. Fgn. Service Inst., 1951-52; m. Laverne D. Voagen, Aug. 23, 1947; children—Cheryl Lynn, Iver Eric, Gregg Alan, Treiva Mae, Lyle David, Tara Rae. Admitted to Wis. bar, 1956; mem. firm Godfrey, Godfrey & Warren, Elkhorn, 1956-57; partner firm Warren & Boltz, Attys., Green Bay, 1957-59, Smith, Will & Warren, 1965-69; asst. dist. atty. Brown County, Wis., 1959-61, dist. atty., 1961-65; mem. Wis. Senate, 1965-69; atty. gen. Wis., 1969; now U.S. dist. judge, Milw. Mem. Gt. Lakes Commn., Wis. Council on Criminal Justice, Wis. Bd. Commrs. Pub. Lands, Four Lakes council Boy Scouts Am., Wis. Controlled Substances Bd., Wis. Council on Drug Abuse, Wis. State Urban Affairs. Served with AUS, 1943-46; ETO. Decorated Purple Heart. Mem. Wis. Bar Assn., Nat. Assn. Attys. Gen. (pres. 1973—), Midwestern Conf. Attys. Gen., Wis. Dist. Attys. Assn., VFW, DAV, Republican. Methodist. Optimist. Office: 382 Federal Bldg Milwaukee WI 53202

WARREN, SHIELDS, physician; b. Cambridge, Mass., Feb. 26, 1898; s. William Marshall and Sara Bainbridge (Shields) W.; A.B., Boston U., 1918; M.D., Harvard, 1923; S.D., Boston U., 1949; D.Sc., Western Res. U., 1952, Case Inst. Tech., 1956; LL.D., Tulane U., 1953; D.Sc. (hon.), Northwestern U., 1959; Dr. honoris causa, U. Brazil, 1964; D.M.S., Brown U., 1969; m. Alice Springfield, Aug. 11, 1923; children—A. Emilie (Mrs. Guy C. McLeod), Patricia (Mrs. David R. Palmer). Instr. in pathology Harvard Med. Sch., 1925-36, asst. prof., 1936-48, prof., 1948-65, prof. emeritus, 1965—; pathologist New Eng. Deaconess Hosp., 1927-63, cons. pathology, 1963—; dir. Mass. Tumor Diagnosis Service, 1928-55, cons., 1955-71; pathologist New Eng. Bapt. Hosp., to 1963; dir. Mallinckrodt, Inc.; dir. biology and medicine U.S. AEC, 1947-52, mem. adv. com., 1952-58; cons. Dept. Energy, 1959—; spl. adviser, acting U.S. rep. to 2d Internat. Conf. on Peaceful Uses of Atomic Energy, Geneva, 1958; mem. sci. adv. bd. consultants Armed Forces Inst. Pathology, 1952-68; mem. Nat. Adv. Cancer Council, 1946-50; U.S. rep. UN Sci. Com. on Effects Atomic Radiation, 1955-63; sr. statesman, sci. adv. bd. USAF, 1961-62; chmn. life scis. com. NASA, 1971-74, mem. space program adv. council. Chmn. corp., trustee Boston U., 1953-69. Served as capt. USNR; res. cons. pathology USN. Recipient Ward Burdick award Am. Soc. Clin. Pathology, 1949; William Proctor award Sci. Research Soc. Am., 1952; Modern Medicine award, 1953; Banting medal Am. Diabetes Assn., 1953; Charles V. Chapin medal City of Providence, 1958; Order of So. Cross in degree of comdr. Brazilian govt., 1961; Albert Einstein medal and award, 1962; Enrico Fermi award AEC, 1972. Life trustee Am. Bd. Pathology. Mem. Nat. Acad. Scis., Am. Philos. Soc., Am. Cancer Soc. (medal 1950, Nat. award 1968, hon. life mem., dir., pres. Mass. div. 1958-60), AAAS,

AMA, Am. Acad. Arts and Scis., Am. Assn. Patholgists (past pres.), Am. Soc. Exptl. Pathology (past pres.), Soc. Exptl. Biology and Medicine, Am. Assn. Cancer Research (ex-pres.), Phi Beta Kappa. Methodist. Clubs: Cosmos, Harvard, Waquoit Yacht. Author: Medical Science for Everyday Use, 1927; Pathology of Diabetes Mellitus, 1930, 3d edit., 1952; (with O. Gates) A Handbook for the Diagnosis of Cancer of the Uterus, 1947, 48, 49; (with S.P. Hicks) Introduction to Neuropathology; (with A.W. Oughterson) Medical Effects of the Atomic Bomb in Japan, 1956; The Pathology of Ionizing Radiation, 1961; (with P.M. LeCompte, M.A. Legg) Pathology of Diabetes Mellitus, 4th edit., 1966. Contbr. articles to profl. jours. Home: 301 Otis West Newton MA 02165 Office: 194 Pilgrim Rd Boston MA 02215

WARREN, SKIP OWEN, constrn. co. exec.; b. Tulsa, Nov. 25, 1931; s. Clarence Albert and Mary Elizabeth (Palmer) W.; B.A., Okla. State U., 1953; J.D., U. Tulsa, 1960; m. Carol Ann Smith, Dec. 8, 1961; children—Skip R., Gary D., Scott A., Storme L. Admitted to Okla. bar, 1960; with U.S. Army C.E., 1960-73, chief counsel Cin. div., 1967-73; v.p., gen. counsel Perini Corp., Framingham, Mass., 1973—; lectr., speaker in field. Bd. dirs. Algonquin council Boy Scouts Am., 1978. Served with USAF, 1955-58. Named Fed. Profl. Employee of Year, Fed. Exec. Bd., Cin., 1971. Mem. Am. Bar Assn., Am. Arbitration Assn., Fed. Bar Assn., Mass. Bar Assn., Okla. Bar Assn., Soc. Am. Mil. Engrs. Democrat. Presbyterian. Home: 19 Woodland St Sherborn MA 01770 Office: 73 Mt Wayte St Framingham MA 01701

WARREN, THOMAS WAYNE, oil co. exec.; b. Electra, Tex., Apr. 30, 1923; s. Lester Paul and Jamie (Stansbury) W.; B.S. in Chem. Engring., U. Tex., Austin, 1944; m. Dona Marie Cunningham, Sept. 1, 1944; children—Deborah, Russell Conner, Margaret. With Pennzoil Co., Houston, now group v.p. mfg. and mktg., also dir., mem. exec. com. Served to lt. (j.g.) USN, 1944-46. Registered profl. engr., Tex. Mem. Am. Petroleum Inst., Soc. Automotive Engrs., Am. Inst. Chem. Engrs., Nat. Soc. Profl. Engrs., Tau Beta Pi, Omega Chi Epsilon, Phi Lambda Upsilon. Episcopalian. Club: Houston. Address: PO Box 2967 Houston TX 77001

WARREN, WILLIAM DAVID, educator; b. Mt. Vernon, Ill., Nov. 13, 1924; s. Arthur and Dorothy Davis (Phillips) W.; A.B., U. Ill., 1948, J.D., 1950; J.S.D., Yale, 1957; m. Susan C. Audren, Nov. 15, 1965; children—John David, Sarah Hartwell. Asst. prof. law Vanderbilt U., 1951-53, Ohio State U., 1953-54; asst. prof., then asso. prof., prof. law U. Ill., 1954-59; prof. law U. Calif. at Los Angeles, 1959-72, dean Law Sch., 1975—; William Benjamin Scott and Luna M. Scott prof. law Stanford, 1972-75. Cons., Fed. Res. Bd. (chmn. consumer adv. council 1979—), Nat. Commn. on Consumer Fin., Calif. Legislature, Calif. Law Revision Commn. Served with USAAF, 1943-45. Mem. Am. Bar Assn., Order of Coif, Phi Beta Kappa, Phi Kappa Phi, Phi Delta Phi. Co-author: California Commercial Law III, 1966; Attorney's Guide to Truth in Lending, 1968; Cases and Materials on Commercial and Consumer Law, 1972, 2d edit., 1978; Cases and Materials on Debtor Creditor Law, 1974. Office: U Calif Law Sch Los Angeles CA 90024

WARREN, WILLIS BURNEY, gas co. exec.; b. Cutler, Calif., Dec. 1, 1914; s. John Willis and Jonny (Burney) W.; m. Evelyn Lea Roberts, Aug. 9, 1978; 1 son, Charles Burney. Office mgr. Surbest Bakers, El Paso, 1929-42; with El Paso Co. (Tex.), 1946—, asst. sec., asst. treas., 1956-66, treas., 1966—, v.p. bd. dirs., 1969-73, exec. v.p., dir., 1973-79, pres., dir., 1979—. Served to capt., inf., AUS, 1942-46. Mem. Interstate Natural Gas Assn. Am., Pacific Coast, So. gas assns. Home: 870 Broadmoor Dr El Paso TX 79912 Office: El Paso TX

WARRINER, CHARLES KING, educator; b. Coloma, Mich., Aug. 26, 1920; s. Harold Charles and Dorothy Alice (Baker) W.; A.B., Hillsdale Coll., 1942; M.A., U. Chgo., 1948, Ph.D., 1953; m. Marian Elizabeth Ford, Aug. 20, 1942; children—Douglas Alan, David Philip, Ruth Eleanor. Research asso. Social Research, Inc., Chgo., 1947-48; faculty U. Kan., Lawrence, 1948—, prof. sociology, 1963—, chmn. dept., 1962-68. Fulbright grantee to Philippines, 1958-59. Mem. Am. Social Assn., Midwest Sociol. Soc. (pres. 1977-78), Soc. Applied Anthropology, Current Anthropology. Home: 701 Tennessee St Lawrence KS 66044

WARRINER, DAVID DORTCH, fed. judge; b. Brunswick County, Va., Feb. 25, 1929; s. Thomas Emmett and Maria Clarke (Dortch) W.; B.A. in Polit. Sci., U. N.C., 1951; LL.B., U. Va., 1957; m. Barbara Ann Jenkins, Jan. 31, 1959; children—Susan Wells, David Thomas Dortch, Julia Cotman. Admitted to Va. bar, 1957, U.S. Supreme Ct. bar, 1970; partner firm Warriner & Outten, Emporia, Va., 1957-74; U.S. dist. judge Eastern Dist. Va., Richmond, 1974—. Mem. Va. Republican Central Com., 1963-74, gen. counsel, 1972-74. Served as lt. USNR, 1951-54. Mem. Am., Va. bar assns. Home: Route 2 Box 280 Brodnax VA 23920 Office: US Courthouse 10th and Main Sts Richmond VA 23219

WARRINGTON, HOWARD MOODY, pub. co. exec.; b. Pocahontas, Iowa, Nov. 6, 1912; s. Winfield W. and Nell (Robinson) W.; B.A., Grinnell Coll., 1934; m. Mary Hathaway Spencer, May 8, 1937; children—Howard Moody, Robert Spencer. With Prentice-Hall, Inc., Englewood Cliffs, N.J., 1935—, editor, 1939-45, editor in chief, 1945-65, pres. coll. div., 1965-71, exec. v.p., 1971-74, chmn. bd., 1974—, also dir.; chmn. bd. Prentice-Hall of Can., Robert J. Brady Co., Goodyear Pub. Co., Reston Pub. Co. Mem. Assn. Am. Pubs. (dir.), Am. Ednl. Pubs. Inst. (pres.). Clubs: Bronxville Field; Princeton (N.Y.C.). Home: Perry Ave Silvermine Norwalk CT 06850 Office: Prentice-Hall Inc Englewood Cliffs NJ 07632

WARRINGTON, JOHN WESLEY, lawyer; b. Cin., June 6, 1914; s. George Howard and Eliza (Holmes) W.; A.B., Yale, 1936; postgrad. Cambridge (Eng.) U., 1937; LL.B., Harvard, 1940; m. Suzanne Mooney, May 5, 1951; children—Anne McGrath, George Howard, John Wesley, Mary Holmes, Elizabeth Mooney, Sarah Henley, Rachel Gaff. Admitted to Ohio bar, 1940, since practiced in Cin.; partner firm Graydon, Head & Ritchey, 1951—. Dir. Fifth Third Bank. Chmn. planning commn. Indian Hill, Ohio, 1959—; pres. Cin. Music Hall, Cin. Mus. Assn.; trustee emeritus Cin. Union Bethel, Am. Schs. Oriental Research, Seven Hills Schs.; trustee Cin. Inst. Fine Arts, Cin. Natural History Mus. Served to capt. Am. Field Service, 1942-45. Mentioned in dispatches (Brit.). Mem. Am., Ohio, Cin. bar assns., Phi Beta Kappa. Republican. Episcopalian. Home: 8625 Camargo Dr Cincinnati OH 45243 Office: Fifth-Third Center 511 Walnut St Cincinnati OH 45202

WARRINGTON, RICHARD WAYNE, publishing co. exec.; b. Sac City, Iowa, Sept. 15, 1924; s. Charles Wayne and Sarah Anna (Harter) W.; B.A., U. Cal. at Berkeley, 1950; m. Lydia Potter, Mar. 23, 1968; children—Wendy, Richard, Robert. Br. mgr. Radio Corp. Am., Seattle, 1950-62; field rep. Ginn and Co., San Francisco, 1962-64; with W.H. Freeman and Co., San Francisco, 1964—, pres., 1973—; dir. Sci. Am., Inc. Served with USN, 1942-45. Club: Olympic. Home: 2180 Carmelita Ave Hillsborough CA 94010 Office: 660 Market St San Francisco CA 94104

WARRINGTON, WILLARD GLADE, univ. adminstr.; b. Macomb, Ill., Oct. 24, 1920; s. Henry K. and Farie V. (Prather) W.; B.Ed., Western Ill. State Tchrs. Coll., 1941; M.S., U. Ill., 1949, M.S., 1950, Ed.D., 1952; m. A. Irene Windser, Aug. 9, 1945 (dec. 1969); m. 2d, Janette Moffatt Cooper, Apr. 26, 1972; children—David, Steven, Douglas, Jane Ann. Tchr. public high schs., Ill., 1941-42, 45-48; mem. faculty Mich. State U., 1952-58, dir. office evaluation services, 1958-74, asso. dean Univ. Coll., 1974-78, acting dean Univ. Coll., 1978—; cons. edn.; Ford Found. cons. U. Philippines. Active Boy Scouts Am., 1957-68. Served to lt. col. USAAF, 1942-45. Mem. Nat. Council on Measurement in Edn. (pres. 1973-74), Am. Ednl. Research Assn., Assn. for Gen. and Liberal Studies (sec.-treas. 1973-79). Methodist. Contbr. articles on ednl. measurement to profl. publs.; editorial bd. Ednl. and Psychol. Measurement, 1968—. Home: 1125 Old Hickory Ln East Lansing MI 48823 Office: 276 Ernst Bessey Hall Mich State U East Lansing MI 48824

WARSCHAWSKI, STEFAN EMANUEL, educator, mathematician; b. Lida, Russia, Apr. 8, 1904; s. Solomon and Olga (Lowenstein) W.; student U. Koenigsberg (Germany), 1924-26, U. Goettingen (Germany), 1926-27; Ph.D., U. Basel (Switzerland), 1930; m. Ilse Kayser, Mar. 24, 1947. Came to U.S., 1934, naturalized, 1941. Research asso. math. Columbia, 1934-35; research asso. elec. engring. Cornell U., 1935-37; instr. math. U. Rochester, 1937-38, Brown U., 1938-39; asst. prof., then asso. prof. math. Washington U., St. Louis, 1939-44; prof. math. U. Minn., 1945-63, head dept. math. Inst. Tech., 1952-63; prof., chmn. dept. math. U. Calif. at San Diego, 1963-67, prof. math., 1967—; sr. research mathematician applied math. group Brown U., 1944-45. Sr. mathematician Inst. Numerical Analysis, Nat. Bur. Standards, U. Calif. at Los Angeles, summer 1949; vis. prof. U. Calif. at Los Angeles, 1958-59. Mem. Am. Math. Soc., Math. Assn. Am. Home: 8902 Nottingham Pl La Jolla CA 92037 Office: Dept Math U Cal San Diego CA 92093

WARSHAW, LEON J., physician; b. N.Y.C., July 20, 1917; s. Samuel and Bessie (Olken) W.; A.B., Columbia U., 1938, M.D., 1942; m. Mona Glassman, Aug. 31, 1941; children—Peter M., David C. Intern, house physician 1st med. div. Bellevue Hosp., N.Y.C., 1942-44, from clin. asst. vis. physician to asso. vis. physician, 1942-59; clin. asst., then adj. Beth Israel Hosp., N.Y.C., 1944-49, asso. attending physician, 1949—, chief adult cardiac clinic, 1950-62; gen. practice medicine, N.Y.C., 1944-55; med. dir. and/or med. cons. various corps. in N.Y.C., 1944-69; with Equitable Life Assurance Soc., N.Y.C., 1967—, v.p., chief med. dir., 1970-75, v.p., corp. med. dir., 1975—; on leave as dep. dir. N.Y.C. Mayor's Office of Ops., 1978—; dir. Miller Communications, Norwalk, Conn.; mem. faculty Columbia U. Coll. Physicians and Surgeons 1944-60, N.Y. U. Med. Sch., 1945-47; chmn. bd. Equitable Environ. Health, Inc., Woodbury, N.Y., 1973-75, dir., 1975-78; trustee Ins. Med. Scientist Scholarship Fund, 1975-78; mem. nat. adv. com. Pres.'s Com. Employment Handicapped, 1965—; mem. Pres.'s Council Phys. Fitness and Sports, 1970—; bd. sponsors Twin Cities Health Care Devel. Project, 1972-75; chmn. med. adv. com. Washington Bus. Group Health, 1977-79; mental health adv. bd. Cornell U., 1970—; Sappington Meml. lectr. Indsl. Med. Assn. Diplomate Am. Bd. Internal Medicine, Am. Bd. Preventive Medicine (occupational medicine). Fellow Am. Acad. Occupational Medicine, Am. Coll. Cardiology, A.C.P., Am. Coll. Preventive Medicine, Am. Occupational Med. Assn. (past dir.), N.Y. Acad. Scis.; mem. AMA, Assn. Life Ins. Med. Dirs., N.Y. State, N.Y. County med. socs., Am. Arbitration Assn. (adv. health council 1972—), Am. Heart Assn. (chmn. heart industry com. 1966-68, dir. 1969-73), Conf. Board, Nat. (dir. 1972-74, v.p. research 1972-74), Greater N.Y. 1970—) safety councils, N.Y. C. of C., N.Y. Heart Assn. (dir. 1968-70, 76—), Occupational Health Inst. (dir. 1970—), N.Y. Acad. Medicine (chmn. sec. occupational medicine 1944-66), N.Y. State Soc. Occupational Medicine (pres. 1965-67, exec. com. 1967-77), Occupational Psychiatry Group, Soc. Occupational and Environ. Health, Alpha Omega Alpha, Beta Sigma Rho, Phi Delta Epsilon. Contbr. articles to profl. jours.; mem. editorial bds. jours. Home: PO Box 249 Route 1 Accord NY 12404 Office: 250 Broadway New York NY 10007

WARSHAW, MARTIN RICHARD, educator; b. N.Y.C., Sept. 17, 1924; s. Irving Gregg and Adelaide (Klein) W.; A.B., Columbia U., 1947; M.B.A., U. Mich., 1957, Ph.D., 1960; m. Alice M. Present, Mar. 28, 1948; children—Gregg, Mark, Lynn, Laurie. Salesman, Daniels Jewelry Co., Battle Creek, Mich., 1947-50, store mgr., 1950-55, v.p., dir., Lansing, Mich., 1955-64; instr. mktg. U. Mich., 1957-60, asst. prof., 1960-64, asso. prof., 1964-67, prof., 1967—, chmn. mktg. faculty, 1973-79; asso. Mgmt. Analysis Center, Cambridge, Mass., 1970—. Served with C.E., U.S. Army, 1943-46. Mem. Am. Mktg. Assn. (past pres. Detroit chpt.). Author: (with Rewoldt and Scott) Introduction To Marketing Management, 3d edit., 1977; (with Engel and Kinnear) Promotional Strategy, 4th edit., 1979. Home: 2279 Mershon Dr Ann Arbor MI 48103 Office: U Mich Sch Bus Adminstrn Ann Arbor MI 48109

WARSHAW, STANLEY IRVING, scientist; b. Boston, Nov. 5, 1931; s. Alec and Sarah (Laserson) W.; B.S. in Ceramic Engring., Ga. Tech. Inst., 1957; Sc.D. in Ceramics, M.I.T., 1961; grad. Advanced Mgmt. Program, Harvard Bus. Sch., 1978; m. Rosalyn Elaine Goldberg, Sept. 8, 1955; children—Glenn Stuart, Karen Beth. Sr. scientist research div. Raytheon Co., Waltham, Mass., 1961-64; with Am. Standard, Inc., New Brunswick, N.J., 1964-75, gen. mgr. engring. and devel., 1972-75; dir. Center for Consumer Product Tech., Nat. Bur. Standards, Dept. Commerce, Washington, 1975—. Vice pres. Bridgewater-Raritan (N.J.) Bd. Edn., 1969-72. Served to capt. U.S. Army, 1951-53. Fellow N.Y. Acad. Scis., Washington Acad. Scis.; mem. Am. Ceramic Soc. (chmn. 1971-73), ASTM. Home: 1519 W Kersey Ln Potomac MD 20854 Office: Nat Bur of Standards Washington DC 20234

WARTELL, C. ROBERT, lawyer; b. Detroit, Mar. 2, 1936; s. Irving Harry and Mynne G. (Franzblau) W.; A.B., U. Mich., 1957, J.D. with distinction, 1960; m. Susan Wallach, Sept. 24, 1960; children—Jeffrey Howard, Julie Dara, David Ross. Admitted to Mich. bar, 1960; practiced in Detroit, 1960-74, Southfield, Mich., 1974—; instr. Wayne State U., 1965—; dir. various bus., real estate corps. Mem. Am., Detroit, Oakland County bar assns., State Bar Mich., Order of Coif. Editor Mich. Law Rev., 1960—. Home: 30655 Pebblestone Ct Birmingham MI 48010 Office: 26600 Telegraph Rd Suite 100-A Southfield MI 48076

WARTH, ROBERT DOUGLAS, educator; b. Houston, Dec. 16, 1921; s. Robert Douglas and Virginia (Adams) W.; B.S., U. Ky., 1943; M.A., U. Chgo., 1945, Ph.D., 1949; m. Lillian Eleanor Terry, Sept. 18, 1945. Instr. history U. Tenn., Knoxville, 1950-51; instr. Rutgers U., Newark, 1951-54, asst. prof., 1954-58; vis. prof. Paine Coll., Augusta, Ga., 1960; asso. editor Grolier, Inc., N.Y.C., 1960-62, 63-64; lectr. Hunter Coll., N.Y.C., part time, 1962-63; asso. prof. S.I. Community Coll., 1964-68; prof. history U. Ky., Lexington, 1968—. Served with AUS, 1943-44. Mem. Am. Hist. Assn., Am. Assn. Advancement Slavic Studies, Am. Assn. U. Profs. Author: The Allies and the Russian Revolution, 1954; Soviet Russia in World Politics, 1963; Joseph Stalin, 1969; Lenin, 1973; Leon Trotsky, 1977. Home: 640 W Cooper Dr Lexington KY 40502 Office: Dept History U Ky Lexington KY 40506

WARTHEN, HARRY JUSTICE, JR., surgeon; b. Port Norfolk, Va., Sept. 30, 1901; s. Harry Justice and Marian (Sheppard) W.; M.D., U. Va., 1925; m. Martha Winston Alsop, Sept. 1, 1938; children—Harry Justice III, Benjamin P.A., George A. II. Intern St. Elizabeth's Hosp., Richmond, 1925-27; asst. resident, resident surgeon Johns Hopkins Hosp., 1927-32; research U. Freiburg, Germany, 1932-33; mem. staff Med. Coll. Va., 1933-65; staff Richmond Meml. Hosp., chief surgery, 1956-59, chief staff, 1961-63; attending, courtesy staff various Richmond hosps.; sr. surg. cons. McGuire VA Hosp., 1947-65; chief surg. cons. Commonwealth of Va., 1972—; cons. Armed Forces, 1948—, mem. council cons., 1960-64; lectr. Civil War medicine. Mem. Richmond Bd. Health, 1950-60, chmn., 1955-60; chmn. Confederate Med. Exhibit, Richmond, 1961-65; chmn. Va. Med. BiCentennial Commn., 1976—; trustee Historic Richmond Found., 1962—; mem. Commn. Archtl. Rev., 1969-79, Monument Ave. Commn., 1969—. Served to lt. col. USAAF, World War II; flight surgeon, cons. to Air Surgeon. Recipient A.H. Robins Community Service award, 1978. Diplomate Am. Bd. Surgery, Am. Bd. Plastic Surgery. Fellow Am., So. surg. assns.; mem. U. Va. Med. Alumni Assn. (pres. 1961), Richmond Surg. Soc. (pres. 1964-65), Richmond Acad. Medicine (pres. 1949-50), Soc. Va. Creepers, Soixant Plus, Va. Hist. Soc., Antiquarian Soc. Richmond, Mil. Order World Wars (comdr. Richmond chpt.), Raven Soc., Phi Beta Kappa, Sigma Xi, Alpha Omega Alpha, Delta Sigma Phi, Nu Sigma Nu. Presbyn. (elder). Clubs: Commonwealth, Surgeons. Editor: Va. Med. Monthly, 1955-75. Contbr. articles to profl. and hist. jours. Address: 2304 Monument Ave Richmond VA 23220

WARTIK, THOMAS, coll. dean; b. Cin., Oct. 1, 1921; s. Abraham and Lena (Monnes) W.; A.B., U. Cin., 1943; Ph.D., U. Chgo., 1949; m. Louise Dreifus, Apr. 8, 1952; children—Nancy, Steven Philip. Chemist, Manhattan project U. Chgo., 1944-46; faculty Pa. State U., University Park, 1950—, prof. chemistry, 1960—, chmn. dept., 1960-71, dean Coll. Sci., 1971—. Vis. scientist U. Calif. Radiation Labs., 1957, 59, 61; cons. in field. Mem. adv. bd. Petroleum Research Fund, Am. Chem. Soc., 1968-71; mem. Fulbright Scholar Selection Com. in Chemistry, 1966-72, chmn., 1969-72; mem. N.Y. State Doctoral Evaluation Com., 1974; chmn. chemistry vis. com. Tex. A. and M. U., 1979—. Mem. Am. Chem. Soc. (councillor 1967-69), AAAS, Phi Beta Kappa, Sigma Xi. Club: Lake Glendale Sailing (dir.). Contbr. profl. articles to jours. Editor: Borax to Boranes, 1961. Home: 939 Ringneck Rd State College PA 16801 Office: 211 Whitmore Lab University Park PA 16802

WARTLUFT, DAVID JONATHAN, assn. exec.; b. Stouchsburg, Pa., Sept. 22, 1938; s. Cleaver Milvard and Dorothy (Stump) W.; A.B. (Trexler scholar), Muhlenberg Coll., 1960; Div.M. (Danforth scholar), Lutheran Theol. Sem., Phila., 1964; A.M. (scholar), U. Pa., 1964; M.S. (Lily Found. scholar), Drexel U., 1968; m. Joyce Claudia Dittmer, June 15, 1963; children—Elizabeth Marie, Deborah Joy, Rebecca Janet, Andrew Jonathan. Asst. chaplain, instr. religion Springfield (Mass.) Coll., 1962-63; ordained minister Luth. Ch., 1964; pastor Jerusalem Luth. Ch., Allentown, Pa., 1964-66; cataloger, reference librarian Luth. Sem. Phila., 1966-68, asst. librarian, 1968-77, dir. library archives, 1977—, chaplain, 1978-79; exec. sec. Am. Theol. Library Assn., Phila., 1971—, also editor procs.; archivist Northeastern Pa. Synod, Luth. Ch. Am., 1970—, mem. communications com., 1967-78, sec., 1975-78, mem. conv. com., 1976. Active Boy Scouts Am., 1964-66. Mem. ALA, Theol. Librarians S.E. Pa. (sec. 1970-73), Luth. Hist. Conf., Assn. Theol. Schs. in U.S. and Can. (selection panel for library grants), Eta Sigma Phi, Phi Sigma Tau, Beta Phi Mu. Republican. Editor: Teamwork, 1970—; The Periodical (Luth. Hist. Soc. Eastern Pa.); contbr. articles to profl. jours. Home: 7328 Rural Ln Philadelphia PA 19119 Office: 7301 Germantown Ave Philadelphia PA 19119

WARWICK, DIONNE, singer; b. East Orange, N.J., Dec. 12, 1941; ed. Hartt Coll. Music, Hartford, Conn.; m. Bill Elliott (div. 1975); 2 sons. As a teen-ager formed Gospelaires, then sang background for rec. studio; debut Philharmonic Hall, N.Y. Lincoln Center, 1966; appearances include London (Eng.) Palladium, Olympia, Paris, France, Lincoln Center Performing Arts, N.Y.C.; records include: Alfie, Do You Know the Way to San Jose, Valley of the Dolls, What the World Needs Now, I'll Never Love This Way Again; albums include: Valley of the Dolls and Others, 1968, Promises, Promises, 1975, Dionne, 1979, Then Came You, screen debut The Slaves, 1969. Address: care Paul Cantor Enterprises 144 S Beverly Dr Beverly Hills CA 90212

WARWICK, JOHN PETERSEN, advt. exec.; b. New Rochelle, N.Y., Mar. 20, 1926; s. H. Paul and Hortense (Petersen) W.; grad. Taft Sch., 1944; B.A., Dartmouth, 1948; m. Janet Mick, Sept. 29, 1962; children—Brian John, Jennifer Jean. With sales dept. Hoffman Beverage Co., 1948-49; with Warwick, Welsh & Miller, Inc., advt., and predecessor firm, 1949—, pres., chief exec. officer, 1964—. Trustee Met. Savs. Bank, N.Y.C. Served with USNR, 1944-46. Mem. Kappa Sigma. Republican. Presbyn. Clubs: Westhampton (N.Y.) Country; Winged Foot Golf (Mamaroneck, N.Y.); Nat. Links (Southampton, N.Y.). Home: Hobart Ln Quioque NY 11978 Office: 375 Park Ave New York NY 10022

WARWICK, RONALD EUGENE, solar heating exec.; b. Scranton, Pa., Dec. 26, 1935; s. Frank Patrick and Catherine Elizabeth (Stull) W.; B.S. in Indsl. Engring., Lafayette Coll., 1957; M.S. in Physics, Drexel U., 1960; m. Virginia Baden Homisak, Oct. 24, 1953; children—Frank, Kim, Lisa, Michael, David, Rachel, Andrew. Research engr. Bell Labs., Allentown, Pa., 1957-58; mfg. mgr., v.p. Diotron, Inc., Phila., 1958-62; mfg. mgr. Concord Semiconductor div. Sprague Elec., Concord, N.H., 1964-66; mgr. components div. ITT, Australia, 1966-71; pres. ETC div. ITT Cleve., 1971-74; pres. Mallory Capacitor Co. div. P.R. Mallory & Co., 1974-78, Solar Heating & Woodburning, Inc., 1979—. Hon. guest Am. Chem. Soc., Toronto, Ont., Can., 1963. Served with USMCR, 1954-60.

WARWICK, WILLIAM BERTRAM, naval officer; b. Columbus, Ohio, Apr. 28, 1929; s. Chester Clendenning and Mary Althea (Manchester) W.; student Purdue U., 1946-48; B.S. in Math., U.S. Naval Postgrad. Sch., 1961; student Air War Coll., 1966-67; children—Dianne Elizabeth, Robert William, James Edward. Commd. ensign U.S. Navy, 1950, advanced through grades to rear adm., 1975; comdr. Attack Aircraft Squadrons 75 and 128, 1965-69, U.S.S. Ponce, 1973-74, Carrier U.S.S. Independence, 1974-75; asst. chief of naval personnel for enlisted personnel Bur. Naval Personnel, Washington, 1975-76; comdr. Carrier Group Four, Norfolk, Va., 1977—; participant air combat ops., Korea, 1950-52, Vietnam, 1965. Decorated Legion of Merit, D.F.C., Meritorious Service medal, Air medal, Navy Commendation medal. Mem. U.S. Naval Inst., Flying Midshipman Assn., Tailhook Assn. Methodist. Home: 2364 Leeward Shore Dr Virginia Beach VA 23451 Office: Comdr Carrier Group Four FPO NY 09501

WASAN, DARSH TILAKCHAND, educator; b. Sarai, Salah, West Pakistan, July 15, 1938; s. Tilakchand Gokalchand and Ishari Devi (Obhan) W.; B.S. in Chem. Engring., U. Ill. at Urbana, 1960; Ph.D., U. Cal. at Berkeley, 1965; m. Usha Kapur, Aug. 21, 1966; children—Ajay, Kern. Came to U.S., 1957, naturalized, 1974. Asst. prof. chem. engring. Ill. Inst. Tech., Chgo., 1964-67, asso. prof.,

1967-70, prof., 1970—, chmn. dept., 1971-77, 78—, acting dean Armour Coll. Engring., 1977-78; cons. Chgo. Bridge & Iron Co., 1967-71, Ill. EPA, 1971-72, Continental Can Co., 1972, Inst. Gas Tech., 1965-70, Ill. Inst. Tech. Research Inst., 1967—, NSF, 1971, 78-79, Nelson Industries, 1976—, B.F. Goodrich Chem. Co., 1976-78, Donnelley & Sons Co., 1976, Exxon Research & Engring. Co., 1977—. Recipient Western Electric Fund award Am. Soc. Engring. Edn., 1972, Excellence Teaching award Ill. Inst. Tech., 1967. Mem. Am. Inst. Chem. Engrs., Am. Chem. Soc., AAAS, Am. Soc. Engring. Edn., Am. Physics Inst., Sigma Xi. Mem. publs. bd. Chem. Engring. Edn. Jour.; mem. adv. bd. Internat. Jour. Powder Technology, 1969—; adv. bd. Jour. Internat. Inst. Bulk and Solids Handling. Contbr. profl. jours. Home: 237 W 57th St Westmont IL 60559

WASBY, MILTON CHARLES, lawyer; b. East Liverpool, Ohio, Oct. 19, 1907; s. Mendel and May (Rosenthal) W.; A.B., Antioch Coll., 1929; LL.B. (Harvard Legal Aid Bur.), Harvard, 1932; m. Pauline Bunshaft, Feb. 7, 1934; children—Stephen Lewis, Roger Allan. Admitted to Mass. bar, 1932; asso. firm Guterman & Guterman, Boston, 1932-42; with N.E. region OPA, 1942-46; asso. firm Mintz, Levin & Cohn, and successor, Mintz, Levin, Cohn, Glovsky & Popeo, Boston, 1946-51, partner, 1951—. Pres., Belmont (Mass.) Sr. High Sch. PTA, 1958-59; mem. Belmont Town Meeting, 1958-73, Belmont Capital Budget Com., 1968-78, chmn., 1973-78. Mem. investment adv. com. Antioch Coll., 1966-70, trustee, 1961-67; trustee Recuperative Center Assn., 1968—. Recipient Recognition award Antioch Coll., 1960. Mem. Am., Mass., Middlesex, Boston bar assns., Mass. Bar Found., Antioch Coll. Alumni Assn. (pres. 1956-58). Democrat. Jewish. Home: 35 Pequossette Rd Belmont MA 02178 Office: 1 Center Plaza Boston MA 02108

WASHA, GEORGE WILLIAM, educator; b. Milw., May 6, 1909; s. Louis and Anne (Wargowsky) W.; B.S., U. Wis., 1930, M.S., 1932, Ph.D., 1938; m. Janet E. Brown, June 23, 1934; children—Lawrence K., Craig R., Jon K. From instr. to asso. prof. mechanics U. Wis., Madison, 1930-47, prof., 1952—, chmn. dept., 1953-74. Trustee Village of Shorewood Hills, 1950-54. Recipient Benjamin Smith Reynolds teaching medal U. Wis., 1977; registered profl. engr., Wis. Mem. Am. Concrete Inst. (dir., trustee, Wason research medal 1940, 77), Am. Soc. Testing Materials, Nat. Soc. Profl. Engrs., Sigma Xi, Tau Beta Pi, Chi Epsilon, Gamma Alpha. Methodist (chmn. ofcl. bd.). Club: Technical (pres. Madison 1943). Author: (with E.R. Maurer, R.J. Roark) Mechanics for Engineers, 1945; (with M.O. Withey) Materials of Construction; contbr. Concrete Construction Handbook. Home: 1114 Shorewood Blvd Madison WI 53705

WASHBURN, ABBOTT MCCONNELL, pub. relations exec., govt. ofcl.; b. Duluth, Minn., Mar. 1, 1915; s. Abbott McConnell and Ruby Leslie (Frisk) W.; B.A., Harvard, 1937; m. Mary Brennan, May 12, 1939 (div. 1959); children—Abbott Michael, Daniel Norton; m. 2d, Wanda Allender, Aug. 3, 1963; 1 dau., Julie. Mgr. dept. pub. services Gen. Mills, Inc., Mpls., 1937-52; exec. vice chmn. Crusade for Freedom, Inc., nat. hdqrs. N.Y.C., 1950-52; dir. orgn. Nat. Hdqrs. Citizens for Eisenhower, N.Y.C., 1952, corr. sec., mem. personal staff Gen. Eisenhower, Denver, N.Y.C., 1952; exec. sec. Pres.'s Com. on Internat. Information Activities. Washington, 1953; dep. to spl. asst. to Pres., 1953; dep. dir. USIA, 1954-61; v.p. internat. operations Carl Byoir & Assos., 1961-62; pres. Washburn, Stringer Assos., Inc., Washington, Mexico City, 1962-69; dep. chmn. U.S. delegation Conf. on Definitive Arrangements for Internat. Telecommunications Satellite Orgn., 1969-70, chmn. with rank ambassador, 1970-71; cons. to dir. Office Telecommunications Policy, Exec. Office Pres., 1972-74; commr. Fed. Communications Commn., 1974—. Served from ensign to lt. USNR, 1942-45. Recipient Distinguished Service medal USIA, 1960. Mem. Pub. Relations Soc. Am., Council on Fgn. Relations, Washington Inst. Fgn. Affairs. Clubs: Harvard (N.Y.C.); International, National Press (Washington). Home: 4622 Broad Branch Rd N W Washington DC 20008 Office: Fed Communications Commn 1919 M St NW Washington DC 20554

WASHBURN, ALBERT LINCOLN, educator; geologist; b. N.Y.C., June 15, 1911; s. Albert Henry and Florence Belle (Lincoln) W.; A.B., Dartmouth, 1935; Ph.D., Yale, 1942;; m. Barbara Tahoe Talbot, Sept. 14, 1935; children—Nuna Lincoln, Land Lincoln, Sila Talbot. Mem. Harvard-Dartmouth Mt. Crillon Expdn., Alaska, 1934, Nat. Geog. Soc. Mt. McKinley Expdn., Alaska, 1936, Louise A. Boyd East Greenland Expdn., 1937, expdns. to Arctic N.Am., 1938-41, 43, 47, 49; geomorphic investigations in Greenland, 1954, N.E. Greenland, 1955-58, 60, 64, Antarctic, 1957-58, USNC IGY, 1957-58; mem. com. polar research Nat. Acad. Sci., 1958-59, 63-73, chmn. polar research bd., 1978—; v.p., hon. mem. Internat. Quaternary Union, 1973—; exec. dir. Arctic Inst. N.Am., 1945-51; hon. lectr. geography McGill U., 1948-51; dir. Snow, Ice and Permafrost Research Establishment, U.S. Army C.E., 1951-52; cons. Research and Devel. Bd., Washington, 1947-53, U.S. Army C.E., 1952-61; mem. Army Sci. Adv. Panel, 1958-59; prof. no. geology Dartmouth, 1953-59; prof. geology Yale, 1960-66, sr. research asso., 1966-70; prof. geology U. Wash., Seattle, 1966-76, prof. emeritus, 1976—, also dir. Quaternary Research Center, 1967-76. Mem. U.S. Olympic Ski Team, 1936. Served as officer AUS, 1942-45. Recipient medal U. Liege (Belgium), 1971. Fellow Am. Geog. Soc., Geol. Assn. Can., Geol. Soc. Am. (Kirk Bryan award 1971); mem. Arctic Inst. N.Am. (hon.), Am. Geophys. Union, Am. Quaternary Assn. (pres. 1970), Geol. Soc. Belgium (corr., André H. Dumont medal 1973), Internat. Glaciological Soc. (hon.), Sigma Xi. Clubs: American Alpine, Cosmos (Washington); Explorers (N.Y.C.). Author several books, papers. Editor: Quaternary Research, 1970-75. Specialist in geomorphology (periglacial), glacial geology. Home: 9414 Points Dr NE Bellevue WA 98004

WASHBURN, HENRY BRADFORD, JR., museum ofcl.; b. Cambridge, Mass., June 7, 1910; s. Henry Bradford and Edith (Hall) W.; grad. Groton Sch., 1929; A.B., Harvard, 1933, A.M., 1960, D.H.L., 1975; postgrad. Inst. Geog. Expdn., 1934-35; hon. Ph.D., U. Alaska, 1951; D.Sc., Tufts U., 1957, Colby Coll., 1957, Northeastern U., 1958; D.F.A., Suffolk U., 1965, U. Mass., 1972, Boston Coll., 1974; m. Barbara T. Polk, Apr. 27, 1940; children—Dorothy Polk, Edward Hall, Elizabeth Bradford. Instr., Inst. Geog. Exploration, Harvard, 1935-42; dir. Mus. Sci., Boston, 1939—. Dir. N.E. Tel. & Tel. Co., John Hancock Life Ins. Co.; mem. Corp. Boston Five Cents Savs. Bank; mem. trust bd. First Nat. Bank, Boston. Mountaineer in Alps, 1926-31; explorer Alaska Coast Range, 1930-40; leader 1st ascent Mt. Crillon, Alaska, 1934, Nat. Geog. Soc. Yukon Expdn., 1935; leader 1st aerial photog. exploration Mt. McKinley, 1936, ascended its summit, 1942, 47, 51; leader 1st aerial exploration St. Elias range, 1938, 1st ascents Mount Sanford and Mount Marcus Baker in Alaska, 1938, Mt. Lucania, Yukon, 1937, Mt. Bertha, Alaska, 1940, Mount Hayes, Alaska, 1941; served as leader numerous mountain, subarctic area explorations; cons. various govtl. agys. on Alaska and cold climate equipment; leader in spl. expdns. investigating high altitude cosmic rays, Alaska, 1947; rep. Nat. Geog. Soc., 17th Internat. Geog. Congress, 1952; leader Nat. Geog. mapping expdns. to Grand Canyon, 1971-75. Chmn., Mass. Com. Rhodes Scholars, 1959-64; chmn. arts and scis. com. UNESCO conf., Boston, 1961. Bd. overseers Harvard, 1955-61; trustee Smith Coll., 1962-68. Recipient Royal Geog. Soc. Cuthbert Peek award for Alaska Exploration and Glacier Studies, 1938; Burr prize Nat. Geog. Soc., 1940, 65; Stratton prize Friends of Switzerland, 1970; named Bus. Statesman of Year, Harvard Bus. Sch. Assn. Boston, 1970; New Englander of Year, 1974. Fellow Royal Geog. Soc. London, Harvard Travelers Club (Gold medal 1959), A.A.A.S., Am. Acad. Arts and Scis., Am. Geog. Soc. (hon.), Cal. Acad. Sci.; mem. Arctic Inst. N.Am., French Alpine (Groupe de Haute Montagne, Paris). Clubs: Commercial, Harvard Varsity, Harvard Mountaineering (hon., past pres.) (Boston): American Alpine (hon.), Explorers (N.Y.C.); Alpine (hon.) (London); Sierra of San Francisco (hon.); Mountaineers (hon.) (Seattle); hon. mem. several clubs. Lectr., London at Royal Geog. Soc. on work of Yukon Expdn., 1936, 37. Contbr. articles, photographs on Alaska, glaciers and mountains to mags., books. Editor, pub. 1st large scale map Mt. McKinley, Am. Acad. Arts and Scis.-Swiss Found Alpine Research, Bern, 1960; mapped Mt. Kennedy for Nat. Geog. Soc., 1965; editor new chart Squam Lake, N.H., 1968, new Grand Canyon map, 1978; pub. Tourist Guide to Mt. McKinley, 1971. Home: 220 Somerset St Belmont MA 02178 Office: Science Park Boston MA 02114

WASHBURN, JACK, metallurgist, educator; b. Mt. Vernon, N.Y., Apr. 30, 1921; s. Morgan and Marjory (Peck) W.; B.S., U. Calif. at Berkeley, 1949, M.S., 1950, Ph.D., 1954; m. Gertrudes Gastelum, June 22, 1947; children—Jo Ann, Kenneth, Melissa. Research engr. Inst. Engring. Research, U. Calif. at Berkeley, 1949-52, faculty, 1952—, prof. metallurgy, 1960—, chmn. dept. materials sci. and engring, 1966-70; prin. investigator Lawrence Berkeley Lab., 1960—. Research prof. Miller Inst. for Basic Research in Sci., Berkeley, 1962-63. NSF fellow Cambridge (Eng.) U., 1959-60, U. Paris Faculty Sci., Orsay, France, 1965. Mem. AAAS, Am. Inst. Mining and Metall. Engrs. (Mathewson Gold medal 1956), AAUP (pres. Berkeley chpt. 1973-75), Am. Soc. Metals, Sigma Xi, Tau Beta Pi. Editor: (with Gareth Thomas) Electron Microscopy and Strength of Crystals, 1963; also numerous articles. Research on stress induced motion small angle boundaries in zinc crystals proving existence dislocations, 1952, etch pit and transmission electron microscopy experiments for understanding behavior dislocations, other defects in crystals.

WASHBURN, JOHN HENRY, ins. co. exec.; b. N.Y.C., May 20, 1911; s. Ives and Elisabeth (Crane) W.; B.A., Amherst Coll., 1934; postgrad. N.Y. U. Sch. Bus., 1935-36; m. Rene Dillingham, Dec. 27, 1940 (div. 1970); children—Alexander D., Elisabeth C., J. Jeffery, Abigail G. With Home Ins. Co., 1934—, v.p. loss and claim div., 1959-68, pres., 1968-73, chief exec. officer, 1969—, chmn., 1973-76, chmn. exec. com., 1976—; dir. Home Ins., Home Indemnity, Seaboard Surety Co., City Investing Co. Bd. dirs. N.Y. Bd. Fire Underwriters Bldg. Corp. Bd. dirs. Francis Asbury Palmer Fund, Ins. Info. Inst., Alpha Delta Phi Found.; trustee Manhattan Eye, Ear and Throat Hosp., Coll. Ins., Inst. Property and Casualty Underwriters. Served to lt. comdr. USNR, 1943-46. Mem. Alpha Delta Phi (chmn. exec. council 1956-59). Republican. Episcopalian. Clubs: Down Town Assn., Union, University (N.Y.C.). Home: 535 Park Ave New York NY 10021 Office: 59 Maiden Ln New York NY 10038

WASHBURN, PAUL, bishop; b. Aurora, Ill., Mar. 31, 1911; s. Eliot Arthur and Lena (Buhrnsen) W.; B.A., N. Central Coll., Naperville, Ill., 1936, L.H.D., 1970; B.D., Evang. Theol. Sem., 1938; D.D., Ind. Central Coll., Indpls., 1954, Wiley Coll., Marshall, Tex., 1975; D.C.L., Westmar Coll., LeMars, Iowa, 1972; m. Kathryn Elizabeth Fischer, Jan. 12, 1937; children—Mary Kathryn Washburn Smith, Jane Anne Washburn Eigenbrodt, Frederick Paul, John Arthur. Teller, bookkeeper First Nat. Bank, Aurora, 1929-32; ordained to ministry Evang. Ch., 1938; pastor in Chenoa, Ill., 1934-39, Rockford, Ill., 1939-52, Naperville, 1952-64; exec. sec. EUB Commn. Ch. Union, 1964-68; bishop United Meth. Ch., Mpls., 1968-72, Chgo. area, 1972—; mem. exec. com. World Meth. Council, 1971—; mem. United Meth. del. to gen. bd. Nat. Council Chs., 1970—; pres. Bd. Global Ministries, United Meth. Ch., 1972-76. Pres., Council Social Ags., Rockford, 1948-49, Family Service Orgn., Rockford, 1948-50; mem. exec. com. and plan Union Commn. Consultation Ch. Union; trustee Garrett-Evang. Theol. Sem., Evanston, Ill., 1972—, N. Central Coll., Naperville, Kendall Coll., Evanston, 1972—, Northwestern Meml. Hosp., Chgo., 1972—. Author: The United Methodist Primer, 1968; also articles. Office: 77 W Washington St Chicago IL 60602. *I have wanted to give functional presence in the world to the love, justice, peace and joy revealed in Jesus Christ.*

WASHBURN, SHERWOOD LARNED, anthropologist, educator, editor; b. Cambridge, Mass., Nov. 26, 1911; s. Henry Bradford and Edith (Hall) W.; grad. Groton Sch., 1931; B.A., Harvard, 1935, Ph.D., 1940; m. Henrietta Pease, Sept. 10, 1938; children—Sherwood, Stanley. Instr., asst. prof. anatomy Columbia, 1939-47; asso. prof., prof. anthropology U. Chgo., 1947-58, chmn. dept., 1953-55; prof. anthropology U. Calif., Berkeley, 1958-79, Univ. prof., 1975-79, chmn. dept., 1961-63; research asso. Wenner-Gren Found. Anthrop. Research. Fellow Center Advanced Study in Behavioral Scis., 1956-57, 62. Mem. Am. Anthrop. Assn. (pres. 1962), Nat. Acad. Scis., Am. Assn. Phys. Anthropologists (pres. 1951-52), Am. Assn. Anatomists. Editor: Am. Jour. Phys. Anthropology, 1955-57; Viking Fund Publs. in Anthropology, 1956-60. Home: 2797 Shasta Rd Berkeley CA 94708

WASHBURN, WILCOMB EDWARD, educator, historian; b. Ottawa, Kans., Jan. 13, 1925; s. Harold Edward and Sidsell Marie (Nelson) W.; grad. Phillips Exeter Acad., 1943; A.B. summa cum laude, Dartmouth, 1948; M.A., Harvard, 1951, Ph.D., 1955; m. Lelia Elizabeth Kanavarioti, July 14, 1951; children—Harold Kitsos, Edward Alexandros. Teaching fellow history and lit. Harvard, 1954-55; fellow Inst. Early Am. History and Culture, Williamsburg, Va., 1955-58; instr. Coll. William and Mary, 1955-58; curator div. polit. history Smithsonian Instn., U.S. Nat. Mus., Washington, 1958-65, chmn. dept. Am. studies, 1965—. Professorial lectr. Am. U., 1961-63, adj. prof., 1963-69; cons. in research Grad. Sch. Arts and Scis., George Washington U., 1966—; adj. prof. U. Md., 1975—. Civil info. and edn. officer Toyama Mil. Govt. Team, Toyama Prefecture, Japan, 1946-47. Served with USMCR, 1943-46, 51-52. Fellow Am. Anthrop. Assn.; mem. Am. Soc. Ethnohistory (past pres.), Soc. History Discoveries (past pres.), Am. Studies Assn. (pres.), Columbia Hist. Soc. (pres.), Colonial Soc. Mass., Am., So., Western, Va., N.H. hist. assns., Am. Antiquarian Soc., Assos. John Carter Brown Library, Assos. James Ford Bell Library, Orgn. Am. Historians, Nat. Trust Historic Preservation, AAAS, Japan-Am. Soc. Washington (trustee), Instituto Histórico e Geográfico Brasileiro, Anthrop. Soc. Washngton, Phi Beta Kappa. Club: Cosmos (Washington). Author: The Governor and the Rebel: A History of Bacon's Rebellion in Virginia, 1957; Red Man's Land/White Man's Law: A Study of the Past and Present Status of The American Indian, 1971; The Assault on Indian Tribalism: General Allotment Law (Dawes Act) of 1887, 1975; The Indian in America, 1975; (with others) The Federal City: Plans and Realities, The Exhibition, 1976; Editor: The Indian and the White Man, 1964; Proc. of the Vinland Map Conf., 1971; The American Heritage History of the Indian Wars, 1977. Contbr. articles to profl. jours. Office: Smithsonian Instn Washington DC 20560

WASHINGTON, BENNETTA BULLOCK, govt. ofcl.; b. Winston-Salem, N.C., May 1, 1918; d. George Oliver and Rebecca (Burgess) Bullock; A.B., Howard U., 1937, M.A., 1939; Ph.D., Cath. U. Am., 1951; LL.D., Wilson Coll., 1969, Smith Coll., 1970, Rider Coll., 1974, Trinity Coll., Washington, 1974; L.H.D., Dunbarten Coll., 1970, Mt. Vernon Coll., 1977; m. Walter Edward Washington, Dec. 26, 1941; 1 dau., Bennetta Bullock Washington Jules-Rosette. Tchr., counselor, prin. pub. schs., Washington and Balt., 1939-64; dir. Women's Center, Job Corps, OEO, 1964-70; asso. dir. women's programs and edn. Job Corps, U.S. Dept. Labor, Washington, 1970-73, spl. asst. to asst. sec. for employment and tng., 1974—; vis. prof. counseling and guidance N.Y. U., 1952-63; dir. Cardozo Project in Urban Edn. Pres.'s Commn. Juvenile Delinquency, 1960-64, mem. commn., 1962-64; mem. Mayor N.Y.C. panel for decentralization of schs., 1966-67; dir. N.Y. U. Inst. Tchrs. and Counselors, V.I., 1967; selected to attend Brookings Inst. Conf. Fed. Execs., 1967; prof. Washington Sch. Psychiatry, 1968; mem. White House Conf. on Food Nutrition and Hunger, 1969, on Children, 1970, on Youth, 1971; mem. Pres.'s Commn. Employment of Handicapped, 1969—; Martin Luther King scholar in residence Rutgers U., 1969; mem. steering com. Nat. Reading Council, 1970—; mem. nat. com. Radcliffe Coll.; govt. rep. on diplomatic missions to Japan, Russia, France, Eng., 1969, Africa, 1971, Mex., 1973, Jamaica, 1974; cons. and lectr. on edn. and inter-group relations. adv. council midwifery program Georgetown U. Sch. Nursing, 1976—; bd. dirs. Internat. Student House, Sex Info. and Edn. Council U.S., Nat. Symphony Bd., Washington Opera Soc., Mt. Vernon Coll., Ch. Youth Research; trustee Henry M. Strong Found., Trinity Coll., D.C.; trustee Am. Field Service, 1969-70, Meridian House Internat., 1967—, Am. U., 1970—; founder, exec. Women in Govt., 1974; active Prevention of Blindness Soc., Florence Crittendon Home, United Fellowship of Chs. Recipient awards and citations for achievement in community service D.C. unit Nat. Council Jewish Women, 1964, Nat. Assn. Negro Bus. and Profl. Women's Clubs, 1965, Roosevelt U., 1966, P.O.E., 1966; alumni achievement award Howard U., 1969, Am. U., 1974, Cath. U., 1974; Human Rights and Fundamental Freedoms award, 1978; named D.C. Mother of Yr., 1978. Mem. Consortium of Univs., Alpha Kappa Alpha. Author: Background Factors and Adjustment, 1951; Youth in Conflict, 1963; Colored by Prejudice, 1964; Counseling the Disadvantaged Girl, 1968; contbr. articles to profl. jours. Developed spl. program Boys' Jr.-Sr. High Sch., Washington, 1956; Inderdisciplinary Cordoza Project, 1961. Home: 408 T St NW Washington DC 20001 Office: 601 D St NW Washington DC 20210

WASHINGTON, GROVER, JR., musician; b. Buffalo, Dec. 12, 1943; attended Wurlitzer Sch. Music; m. Christine; 2 children. Played with musical group Four Clefs, to 1963, with Keith McAllister, 1963-65; played with various groups in Phila. and with Billy Cobham; with Don Gardner's Sonotones, 1967-68; worked for record distbr., 1969-70; played with Charles Earland, 1971; rec. for Kudo records, C.T.I., now Elektra Records as leader of group; plays tenor, alto, soprano, baritone saxophones, clarinet, bass and piano; albums include: Mister Magic, Inner City Blues, Soul Box, Breakout, (with Don Sebesky) Giant Box, (with Randy Weston) Blue Moses, Paradise. Office: care Gt Eastern Mgmt 1913 Walnut St Philadelphia PA 19103*

WASHINGTON, JAMES WINSTON, JR., artist, sculptor; b. Gloster, Miss., Nov. 10, 1909; s. James and Lizie (Howard) W.; student Nat. Landscape Inst., 1944-47; D.F.A., Center Urban-Black Studies, 1975; m. Janie R. Miller, Mar. 29, 1943, Exhibited one man shows U.S.O. Gallery, Little Rock, 1943, Foster-White Gallery, Seattle, 1974; group shows Willard Gallery, N.Y.C., 1960-64, Feingarten Galleries, San Francisco, 1958-59, Grosvenor Gallery, London, Eng., 1964, Lee Nordness Gallery, N.Y.C., 1962, Woodside Gallery, Seattle, 1962-65, Foster-White Gallery, Seattle, 1974, 76, Smithsonian Instn., 1974, San Diego, 1977, others; represented in permanent collections Seattle, San Francisco, Oakland art museums, Seattle First Nat. Bank, Seattle Pub. Library YWCA, Seattle, Meany Jr. High Sch., Seattle World's Fair, Expo 70 Osaka, Japan. Recipient Spl. Commendation award for many contbns. to artistic heritage of state Gov., 1973, plaque City of Seattle, 1973, Benefit Guild, Inc., 1973. Mem. Internat. Platform Assn. Baptist. Mason (33 deg.). Home: 1816 26th Ave Seattle WA 98122

WASHINGTON, KENNETH STRICKLAND, coll. adminstr.; b. Chgo., Oct. 19, 1922; s. Louis Curtis and Velma (Strickland) W.; B.S., Roosevelt U., 1948; M.A., Calif. State U., 1954; Ph.D., U. So. Calif., 1970; m. Henrietta Dunn, Oct. 5, 1974; children—Lori, Marcella, Henry, Corine, Kim, Kent. Tchr. high sch., 1951-60; head counselor high sch., 1960-66; asst. to chancellor UCLA, 1966-68; asst. dean Calif. State Colls. and Univs., 1968-71; asst. supt. public instruction, State of Calif., 1971-75; pres. City Coll. of San Francisco, 1975—; trustee Los Angeles Community Coll. Bd., 1969-75. Bd. dirs. Sta. KQED-TV, Public Broadcasting, San Francisco Museum Soc., San Francisco Fund. Served with U.S. Army, 1944-46. Mem. Assn. Calif. Community Coll. Adminstrs., Western Assn. Council Black Am. Affairs, NAACP, Black Educators Assn., Black Leadership Forum. Office: 50 Phelan Ave San Francisco CA 94112

WASHINGTON, WALTER, coll. pres.; b. Hazlehurst, Miss., July 13, 1923; s. Kemp and Mable (Comous) W.; B.A., Tougaloo Coll., 1948; M.S., Ind. U., 1952; Edn. Specialist, Peabody Coll., 1958; postgrad. Yale, 1953; Ph.D., U. So. Miss., 1969; LL.D., Tougaloo Coll., 1972; m. Carolyn Carter, July 31, 1949. Tchr., Holtzclaw High Sch., Crystal Springs, Miss., 1948-49; asst. prin., tchr. Parrish High Sch., Hazlehurst, 1949-51; prin. Utica Jr. Coll. High Sch., Miss., 1951-54; dean Utica Jr. Coll., 1954-55, pres., 1957-69; pres. Alcorn (Miss.) State U., 1969—; prin. Sumner Hill High Sch., Clinton, Miss., 1955-57; dir. Miss. Power & Light Co., Middle South Utilities. Pres., Nat. Pan-Hellenic Council, 1964-67, Nat. Alumni Council of United Negro Coll. Fund, 1959-60; mem. adv. council Miss. Commn. on Hosp. Care; past mem. adv. council Miss. Vocational Edn. Program; past mem. adv. council Miss. Regional Med. Programs; mem. Miss. Econ. Council; mem. S.E. regional exec. com. Boy Scouts Am., mem. exec. com. Andrew Jackson council; mem. adv. council Miss. 4-H Clubs. Bd. dirs. Miss. Mental Health Assn., Miss. Easter Seal Soc. Mem. So. Assn. Colls. Secondary Schs. (dir., past chmn. secondary commn., trustee), Am. Assn. Sch. Adminstrs., Nat. Assn. State Univs. and Land Grant Colls., NEA, Miss. Educators Assn. (pres. 1964-65), Miss. Tchrs. Assn., Tougaloo Nat. Alumni Assn. (pres. 1960), Nat. Soc. for Study Higher Edn., John Dewey Soc., Assn. for Supervision and Curriculum Devel., Alumni Assn. George Peabody Coll. (past v.p. exec. com.), Delta Kappa Pi, Phi Delta Kappa, Alpha Kappa Mu, Alpha Phi Alpha (gen. pres. 1974-76). Address: Alcorn State U Office of President Lorman MS 39096

WASHINGTON, WALTER E., lawyer, former mayor Washington; b. Dawson, Ga., Apr. 15, 1915; s. William L. and Willie Mae (Thornton) W.; A.B., Howard U., 1938, J.D., 1948; postgrad. Am. U., 1939-43; LL.D., Fisk U., Georgetown U., 1968, Cath. U., Boston U., 1969, George Washington U., Princeton, 1970; L.H.D., Bishop Coll., 1970; J.D., Washington Coll. (Md.), 1972, Ind. Central Coll., 1972, Boston Coll., 1972, Carnegie-Mellon U., 1973, Howard U., 1974, Trinity Coll., 1974, Colgate U., 1976; m. Bennetta Bullock; 1 dau., Bennetta Jules Rosette. Admitted to D.C. bar, 1948, U.S. Supreme Ct. bar, 1952; with Nat. Capital Housing Authority, Washington, 1941-66, exec. dir., 1961-66; chmn. N.Y.C. Housing Authority, 1966-67; apptd. mayor commr. Washington, 1967-75, elected mayor, 1975-79; partner firm Burns, Jackson, Miller, Summit, 1979—. Mem. adv. bd. U.S. Conf. of Mayors; vice chmn. Nat. League of Cities. Mem. ins. panel Nat. Adv. Commn. on Civil Disorders; v.p. United

Community Funds and Councils Am. Trustee John F. Kennedy Center for Performing Arts; bd. dirs. Washington Council Chs., Washington area Boy Scouts Am., United Planning Orgn., Big Bros. Am. Recipient Alumni award Howard U., 1963; Career Service award Nat. Civil Service League, 1965; Archdiocesan award, 1968; award NCCJ; Nat. Bar Assn. award; Health and Welfare Council award; Distinguished Service awards Howard U. Law Alumni Assn., 1974, Capitol Press Club, 1974; Silver Beaver award Boy Scouts Am., 1973; Nat. Jewish Hosp. award for outstanding service, 1973. Mem. Am. Bar Assn., Washington Urban League (dir.), Order of Coif. Democrat. Mason (32 deg.). Club: Cosmos, Federal City (Washington), Nat. Lawyers; City N.Y. Office: 1025 15th St NW Washington DC 20005

WASHINGTON, WARREN MORTON, meteorologist; b. Portland, Oreg., Aug. 28, 1936; s. Edwin and Dorothy Grace (Morton) W.; B.S. in Physics, Ore. State U., 1958, M.S. in Meteorology, 1960; Ph.D. in Meteorology, Pa. State U., 1964; m. LaRae Herring, July 30, 1959 (div. Aug. 1975); children—Teri, Kim, Marc, Tracy; m. Joan Ann, July 3, 1978. Sr. scientist Nat. Center Atmospheric Research, Boulder, Colo.; affiliate prof. meteorology oceanography U. Mich. at Ann Arbor, 1968-71; mem. Nat. Adv. Com. for Oceans and Atmospheres, 1978-80. Mem. Boulder Human Relations Commn., 1969-71; mem. Gov.'s Sci. Adv. Com., 1975-78. Fellow Am. Meteorol. Soc.; mem. AAAS, Am. Geog. Union Contbr. articles to meteorol. jours. Home: 1480 Landis Ct Boulder CO 80303 Office: PO Box 3000 Boulder CO 80303

WASIELE, HARRY W., JR., diversified elec. mfg. co. exec.; b. Chgo., June 29, 1926; s. Harry W. and Antoinette (Tuleja) W.; grad. high sch.; m. Loretta K. Anderson, Jan. 3, 1948; children—Kathleen Ann, Brian David, Larry Scott, Mark Thomas. Asst. sales mgr. Drake Mfg. Co., Chgo., 1950-55; sales engr. AMP, Inc., Chgo., 1955, Detroit, 1956-57, product mgr., Harrisburg, Pa., 1958-61, industry mgr., 1961-67, dir. marketing, 1967-68; div. gen. mgr. Brand-Rex div. Am. Enka Corp., Willimantic, Conn., 1968-70; pres. Brand-Rex Co., subs. Akzona Inc., 1970—; chmn. Brand-Rex Ltd., Glenrothes, Scotland. Bd. dirs. Eastern Conn. State Coll. Found.; trustee Conn. Pub. Expenditure Council, Windham Community Hosp., Willimantic. Served with USNR, 1944-46. Mem. Nat. Elec. Mfrs. Assn. (dir., exec. com. wire and cable div.), Conn. Bus. and Industry Assn. (dir. emeritus). Republican. Roman Catholic. Clubs: New Seabury Country (Mashpee, Mass.); Union League (N.Y.C.). Home: 125 Hillyndale Rd Storrs CT 06268 Office: PO Box 498 W Main St Willimantic CT 06226

WASIOLEK, EDWARD, educator; b. Camden, N.J., Apr. 27, 1924; s. Ignac and Mary (Szczesniewska) W.; B.A., Rutgers U., 1949; M.A., Harvard, 1950, Ph.D., 1955; postgrad. U. Bordeaux (France), 1950-51; m. Emma Jones Thomson, 1948; children—Mark Allan, Karen Lee, Eric Wade. Teaching fellow Harvard, 1953-54; research fellow Harvard Russian Research Center, 1952-54; instr. English, Ohio Wesleyan U., 1954-55; asst. prof. English, U. Chgo., 1955-60, asso. prof. English and Russian, 1960-64, prof. Russian and comparative lit., 1964-69, Avalon prof. comparative lit. and Russian, 1969-76, disting. services prof., 1976—, chmn. comparative lit. program, 1965—, chmn. dept. Slavic langs. and lit., 1971-77; vis. prof. Slavic and comparative lit. Harvard, 1966-67. Served with USNR, 1943-46. Recipient Quantrell teaching prize U. Chgo., 1961; Laing Press prize, 1972. Research fellow USSR, 1963. Mem. Modern Lang. Assn., Phi Beta Kappa, Lambda Chi Alpha. Author: (with R. Bauer) Nine Soviet Portraits, 1955; Crime and Punishment and the Critics, 1961; Dostoevsky: The Major Fiction, 1964; The Notebooks for Crime and Punishment, 1967; The Brothers Karamazov and the Critics, 1967; The Notebooks for the Idiot, 1968; The Notebooks for the Possessed, 1968; The Notebooks for A Raw Youth, 1969; The Notebooks for the Brothers Karamazov, 1970; The Gambler, with Paulina Suslova's Diary, 1972; Tolstoy's Major Fiction, 1978. Home: Butterfield Ln Flossmoor IL 60422 Office: Univ Chicago Chicago IL 60637. *I believe in the life of the mind and I believe with Albert Camus that man's dignity lies in his lucidity: in seeing his fate clearly and in having the courage to accept it. Man is capable of sensitivity, courage, love, and compassion, and all of these are more human because he can think. He is also capable of cruelty, hatred, and destruction, and these are more tolerable because he can reason. Man is not man without reason.*

WASKOW, ARTHUR IRWIN, social analyst; b. Balt., Oct. 12, 1933; s. Henry B. and Hannah (Osnowitz) W.; B.A., Johns Hopkins, 1954; M.A., U. Wis., 1956, Ph.D., 1963; m. Irene Elkin, 1956 (div. 1978); children—David, Shoshana. Legis. asst. Ho. of Reps., Washington, 1959-61; sr. staff mem. Peace Research Inst., Washington, 1961-63; fellow Inst. Policy Studies, Washington, 1963-77; colleague Pub. Resource Center, Washington, 1977—. Alt. del. Democratic nat. conv., 1968. Mem. Fabrangen, Breira (exec. com.), Phi Beta Kappa. Jewish. Author: The Limits of Defense, 1962; (with Stanley L. Newman) America in Hiding, 1962; Worried Man's Guide to World Peace, 1963; From Race Riot to Sit-In, 1966; The Freedom Seder, 1969; Running Riot, 1970; The Bush Is Burning, 1971; Godwrestling, 1978. Editor: Debate Over Thermonuclear Strategy, 1965; Menorah Jour., 1979—. Address: Public Resource Center 1747 Connecticut Ave NW Washington DC 20009

WASMUTH, CARL ERWIN, physician, lawyer; b. Pitts., Feb. 16, 1916; s. Edwin Hugo and Mary Blanche (Love) W.; B.S., U. Pitts., 1935, M.D., 1939; LL.B., Cleve.- Marshall Law Sch., 1959; m. Martha Conn, Aug. 25, 1939; children—Carl Erwin. Intern, Western Pa Hosp., Pitts., 1939-40, fellow anesthesiology Cleve. Clinic Found., 1949-51; admitted to Ohio bar, 1959; pvt. practice medicine, Dry Run, Pa., 1942-45, Scottdale, Pa., 1945-49; mem. dep. anesthesia Cleve. Clinic, 1951—, head dept., 1967-69; asso. prof. law Cleve.-Marshall Law Sch., 1959-66, adj. prof. Cleve. Marshall Law Sch., 1966-73. Trustee Cleve.- Marshall Law Sch., chmn., 1969-71; bd. dirs. Scottdale Hosp. Found; chmn. bd. govs. Cleve. Clinic, 1969-77; trustee Cleve. Clinic Found., 1969—, v.p., 1973—; trustee Cleve. Clinic Ednl. Found., 1969—, v.p., 1973—; chmn. bd. trustees, pres. Cleve. Marshall Ednl. Found., 1972—; bd. overseers Coll. Law, Cleve. State U., 1972; vis. com. Coll. Law, Case-Western Res. U., 1973—; trustee United Torch Services; trustee Santa Cruz Med. Found., 1977, pres., 1978; bd. govs. Ohio World Trade Center; trustee Cancer Center Cleve., Ohio Coll. Podiatric Medicine, 1976; mem. U. Ariz. Found., 1978; mem. World Congress Med. Law, 1967—, Keynoter 3d World Congress, 1971; sec. Commn. Med. Malpractice, HEW, 1972-73. Diplomate Am. Bd. Anesthesiology; named Distinguished Eagle Scout, Nat. council Boy Scouts Am., 1977, Outstanding Citizen Eagle, Cuyahoga council, 1976; Citizen of Year, Cleve. Area Bd. Realtors, 1976. Fellow Am. Coll. Anesthesiologists, Am. Coll. Legal Medicine (pres. bd. govs. 1966-69), A.C.P., Am. Coll. Chest Physicians, Law Sci. Acad.; mem. Am. (dir., pres. 1968), Ohio (dir.), Cleve. (pres. 1963), socs. anesthesiologists, Internat. Anesthesia Research Soc., World Fedn. Soc. Anesthesiologists (vice chmn. Am. delegation 1967), Acad. Anesthesiology (chmn. program com. 1967), Am., Ohio med. assns., N.Y. Acad. Scis., Nat. Acad. Sci., NRC, Com. Cadaver Utilization, Cleve. Acad. Medicine, AAAS, Transplantation Soc. (charter), Am., Ohio, Cuyahoga County, Cleve. bar assns., Phi Rho Sigma, Delta Theta Phi. Clubs: Masons (32 deg., Shriner), Lions (past pres. local clubs), Union, Cleve., Midday, Old Pueblo, Tucson, Country of Green Valley (Ariz.), Pleasant Valley Country (Scottdale, Pa.). Author: Anesthesia and the Law, 1961; Law for the Physician, 1966; Law and the Surgical Team, 1968. Editor: Legal Problems in the Practice of Anesthesiology, 1973; contbg. editor Ency. Brit., Medicine, Surgery Specialties; Lawyer's Med. Cyclopedia; Hale's Anesthesiology; editorial bd. Med. Group News, Legal Medicine, Med. World News. Contbr. articles to profl. jours. Home: 727 Paseo el Paso Green Valley AZ 85614 Office: Cleveland Clinic Found Clinic Center Cleveland OH 44106

WASSER, HENRY, educator; b. Pitts., Apr. 13, 1919; s. Nathan and Mollie (Mendelson) W.; B.A., M.A., Ohio State U., 1940; Ph.D., Columbia, 1951; m. Solidelle Felicité Fortier, Aug. 20, 1942; children—Michael Frederick (dec.), Eric Anthony (dec.), Frederick Anthony, Felicity Louise. Teaching fellow George Washington U., 1940-42; analyst USAAF intelligence, 1941-43; chemist Goodyear Synthetic Rubber Co., 1943-45; tutor, asso. prof. City Coll., City U. N.Y.C., 1946-66, prof. English, dean faculties Richmond Coll., City U. N.Y., 1966-73; v.p. for acad. affairs Cal. State U., Sacramento, 1973-74; prof. English, City U. N.Y., Richmond, 1974—, dir. Center for European Studies, Grad. Sch., 1979—. Fulbright prof. U. Salonika (Greece), 1955-56; seminar asso. Columbia, 1961—, Colloquium on Higher Edn., Yale, 1974-75; Fulbright prof. Am. lit. U. Oslo (Norway), 1962-64, dir., prof. Am. Inst., 1963-64; lectr. univs. in Sweden, Norway, Eng., Germany, Poland, Yugoslavia, Italy, 1961-64, Norway, 1972; vis. prof. U. Sussex (Eng.), 1972; cons. in field, 1967—. Bd. dirs. Scandinavian Seminar, 1978—. Recipient Am. Scandinavian Found. award, 1969, 71; German Acad. Exchange Service award, 1973, 76. Mem. Am. Studies Assn. (pres. Met. N.Y. chpt. 1961-62, mem. nat. exec. council, 1968-74), Melville Soc. Am. (historian 1969-74), Modern Lang. Assn., Am. Scandinavian Found. (fellow 1971), Internat. Assn. U. Profs. English, Assn. Upper Level Colls. and Univs. (2d v.p. 1971-72), Phi Beta Kappa (sec. City Coll. chpt. 1957-62, 64-67). Author: The Scientific Thought of Henry Adams, 1956; co-author Higher Education in Western Europe and North America: A Selected and Annotated Bibliography, 1979. Editor: (with Sigmund Skard) Americana Norvegica; Norwegian Contributions to American Studies, 1966. Contbr. articles to newspapers and profl. jours. Home: 5517 Fieldston Rd New York NY 10471 Office: City U NY (Richmond) Staten Island NY. *I have seen the importance of intellect and industry, humor and shrewdness, poise and gentle grace, but as the years go by, it seems to me that moral integrity is most significant.*

WASSER, LEONARD, assn. exec.; b. N.Y.C., Apr. 4, 1918; s. Samuel and Rebecca S.; B.A., Bklyn. Coll., 1938; M.A., N.Y. U., 1951; m. Liisa Vuoristo, Dec. 15, 1977; children—Tina S., Jeremy S. Contracting officer Dept. Def., N.Y.C., 1947-59; contracting officer AEC, 1959-71; exec. dir. Writers Guild Am.-East, N.Y.C., 1971—. Mem. adv. council for Motion Pictures and TV, N.Y.C.; bd. dirs. Astoria Motion Picture and TV Center Found. Served with U.S. Army, 1942-46. Mem. Conf. Motion Picture and TV (bd. trustees), Nat. Acad. Television Arts and Scis. (bd. govs. 1975-79). Home: 60 Sutton Pl S New York NY 10022 Office: 555 W 57th St New York NY 10036

WASSERBURG, GERALD JOSEPH, educator, geologist; b. New Brunswick, N.J., Mar. 25, 1927; s. Charles and Sarah (Levine) W.; B.Sc. in Physics, U. Chgo., 1951, M.Sc. in Geology, 1952, Ph.D., 1954; m. Naomi Z. Orlick, Dec. 21, 1951; children—Charles David, Daniel Morris. Cons. Argonne Nat. Lab., 1952-55; research asso. Enrico Fermi Inst. Nuclear Studies, Chgo., 1954-55; mem. faculty Calif. Inst. Tech., 1955—, prof. geology and geophysics, 1962—; vis. prof. U. Kiel (Germany), 1960, Harvard, 1962, U. Bern (Switzerland), 1966, Swiss Fed. Tech. Inst., 1967. Served with AUS, 1943-46. Decorated Purple Heart, Combat Inf. Badge. Recipient Group Achievement award NASA, 1969, 73, Exceptional Sci. Achievement award, 1970, Distinguished Pub. Service medal, 1972; Distinguished Pub. Service medal with cluster, 1978; J.F. Kemp medal Columbia, 1973; Leonard medal Meteoritical Soc., 1975; V.H. Goldschmidt medal Geochem. Soc., 1978. Fellow Am. Acad. Arts and Scis., Am. Geophys. Union, Geol. Soc. Am. (Arthur L. Day medal 1970); mem. Nat. Acad. Sci. (chmn. com. lunar and planetary exploration). Home: 2100 Pinecrest Dr Altadena CA 91001 Office: Div Geol and Planetary Scis Cal Inst Tech Pasadena CA 91125

WASSERMAN, ALBERT, writer, dir.; b. N.Y.C., Feb. 9, 1921; s. Martin S. and Beatrice (Schaffer) W.; B.S., Coll. City N.Y., 1941; m. Della Newmark, Aug. 5, 1943 (div. Mar. 1965); children—Paul, Vicki; m. 2d, Barbara Alson, June 19, 1968. Writer documentary, ednl. and indsl. films, 1946-53; free lance writer, dir. TV documentary films, 1953-55; staff writer, dir., producer CBS-TV, 1955-60; producer, dir., writer NBC News, 1960-67; pres. Wasserman Prodns., Inc., N.Y.C., 1968-75; producer CBS News, 60 Minutes, 1976—; writer, prod., dir. Out of Darkness; writer film First Steps; writer, dir. films for The Search, CBS Pub. Affairs Series; prod., writer dir. NBC White Paper programs; prod., dir. The Making of the President, TV Spl., 1972. Recipient Lasker Med. Journalism awards (2); Sylvania TV award; Robert Flaherty film award; Acad. award, 1947; Edinburgh Film Festival silver medal, 1948; Peabody award CBS Pub. Affairs series. Mem. Writers Guild Am. East (treas. 1965-66), Dirs. Guild Am. (eastern regional council 1965-66, 69-70). Home: 259 W 11th St New York NY 10014

WASSERMAN, DALE, playwright; b. Rhinelander, Wis., Nov. 2, 1917; s. Samuel and Hilda (Paykel) W. Writer, prod., dir. for TV, motion pictures, theatre; author: (stage plays) (with Bruce Geller) Livin' the Life, 1957; The Pencil of God, 1961; 998, 1962; One Flew Over the Cuckoo's Nest, 1963; Man of La Mancha, 1965 (Tony award, Critics' Circle award, Outer Circle award, Variety award, Spanish Pavilion award, also recipient numerous other awards); Play with Fire, 1978; (motion pictures) World of Strangers, 1955, The Vikings, 1958, Two Faces to Go, 1959, Aboard the Flying Swan, 1962, Jangadeiro, 1962, Cleopatra, 1963, Quick Before It Melts, 1964; writer also co-producer (motion pictures) Mister Buddwing, 1965, A Walk With Love and Death, 1969, Man of LaMancha, 1972; also numerous TV plays for programs including Kraft Television Theatre, Matinee Theatre, Studio One, Dupont Show of Month; founder, artistic dir. Midwest Profl. Playwrights Lab. Trustee, founding mem. Eugene O'Neill Meml. Theatre Center. Recipient awards for TV plays The Fog, 1957, I, Don Quixote, 1960, The Lincoln Murder Case, 1961 (all Writers Guild Am.); play Elisha and the Long Knives voted Top TV Play of Year, 1954. Mem. Writers Guild Am., East (nat. council 1960-64), Dramatists Guild, ALA, French Soc. Authors and Composers. Club: Players. Contbr. short stories, articles to Redbook, True, Argosy, N.Y. Times, Variety. Office: DW Katz & Co 10 E 40th St New York NY 10016

WASSERMAN, EDEL, chemist, research exec.; b. N.Y.C., July 29, 1932; s. Abraham and Ida (Ulano) W.; B.A., Cornell U., 1953; M.A., Harvard, 1954, Ph.D. (NSF fellow 1953-56, Coffin fellow 1956-57), 1959; m. Zelda L. Rakowitz, Jan. 29, 1955; children—Stephen, Diane. Mem. tech. staff Bell Telephone Labs., Murray Hill, N.J., 1957-76; prof. chemistry Rutgers U., New Brunswick, N.J., 1967-76; dir. Chem. Research Center, Allied Chem. Co., 1976-78, dir. Corp. Research Center, 1978—. Regent's lectr. U. Calif., Irvine, 1973. Mem. Am. Chem. Soc. (adv. editor jour. 1971-75), Am. Inst. Physics. Research in complex organic systems. Adv. editor Chem. Physics Letters, 1967-79. Home: 71 Hillcrest Ave Summit NJ 07901

WASSERMAN, JACK, educator, art historian; b. N.Y.C., Apr. 27, 1921; s. William and Pearl (Bajcz) W.; B.A., N.Y. U., 1949, M.A., 1953, Ph.D., 1961; m. Ambra Amati, July 6, 1952; children—Shara, Talya. Instr., N.Y. U., 1952-53, U. Conn., 1953-60; faculty Ind. U., 1960-62; faculty U. Wis. at Milw., 1962-75, prof., curator Art History Gallery, 1964-75, chmn. dept. art history, 1962-75; prof. art history Tyler Sch. Art, Temple U., Phila., 1975—, dean, 1975-77. Mem. Archaeol. Research Fund, N.Y. U. with excavation at Samothrace, Greece, 1949; cons. Choice and Cultura, 1967—; mem. ednl. adv. bd. Milw. Sch. Arts; mem. fgn. fellowship selection com. Samuel H. Kress Found., 1972-74. Served with USAAF, 1942-45. Recipient Fulbright award, 1952-53, Fels Fund award, 1959-60. Am. Philos. Soc. Research grantee, 1970; Am. Council Learned Socs. research grantee, 1971; Samuel H. Kress research grantee, 1975. Fellow Royal Soc. Arts; mem. Amici di Brera (hon.), Coll. Art Assn. (chmn. area com. to rescue Italian art 1963—, co-chmn. film com.), Soc. Archtl. Historians (dir., archtl. preservation com.). Author: Ottaviano Mascarino, 1966; Leonardo da Vinci, 1975. Contbr. numerous articles to profl. jours. Home: 551 General Patterson Dr Glenside PA 19083 also Via L di Montreale 3 Rome Italy 00152

WASSERMAN, LEW R., business exec.; b. Cleve., Mar. 15, 1913; m. Edith Beckerman, July 5, 1936; 1 dau., Lynne Kay. Nat. dir. advt. and publicity Music Corp. Am., 1936-38, v.p., 1938-39, became v.p. charge motion picture div., 1940; now chmn. bd., dir., chief exec. officer, mem. exec. com. MCA, Inc., also chmn. bd., chief exec. officer, dir. subsidiary corps.; dir. Am. Airlines. Chmn. emeritus Assn. Motion Picture and TV Producers. Trustee John F. Kennedy Library, John F. Kennedy Center Performing Arts, Cal. Inst. Tech.; hon. chmn. bd. Center Theatre Group Los Angeles Music Center; bd. dirs. Research to Prevent Blindness; mem. nat. com. Lyndon Baines Johnson Meml. Grove on Potomac; mem. Rockefeller U. Council; mem. adv. bd. Presdl. Election Campaign Fund; mem. Radio Free Europe Com.; bd. dirs. Lyndon Baines Johnson Found. Recipient Jean Hersholt Humanitarian award Acad. Motion Picture Arts and Scis., 1973. Democrat. Office: MCA Inc 100 Universal City Plaza Universal City CA 91608*

WASSERMAN, LOUIS ROBERT, educator, physician; b. N.Y.C., July 11, 1910; s. Jacob and Ethel (Ballin) W.; A.B., Harvard, 1931; M.D., U. Chgo., 1935; m. Julia B. Wheeler, Feb. 20, 1957. Intern, Michael Reese Hosp., Chgo., 1935-37; research fellow hematology Mt. Sinai Hosp., N.Y.C., 1937-39, research asst., 1940-42, dir. dept. hematology, 1953-72, hematologist to hosp., 1950-72; research fellow med. physics U. Cal. at Berkeley, 1946-48, cons. radiation labs., 1948-51; asst. prof. Columbia Coll. Phys. and Surg., 1950-60, asso. clin. prof., 1960-66; prof. medicine Mt. Sinai Sch. Medicine, 1966-72, chmn. dept. clin. sci., 1967-72, Distinguished Service prof., 1972-79, emeritus, 1979—, Albert A. and Vera G. List prof. medicine, 1977-79, emeritus, 1979—. Research collaborator Brookhaven Nat. Labs., 1960-71; cons. practice specializing in hematology, N.Y.C., 1950—. Mem. nat. cancer planning com., chmn. polycythemia vera study group Nat. Cancer Inst., NIH, 1967—, mem. diagnostic research adv. com., 1972-75, co-chmn., 1975-77, chmn. bd. sci. counselors div. cancer treatment, 1974-76. Served to maj. AUS, 1942-46. Diplomate Am. Bd. Internal Medicine. Fellow A.C.P., AMA, N.Y. Acad. Medicine, N.Y. Acad. Sci., Internat. Soc. Hematology (v.p. 1972, counselor at-large 1973—); mem. Assn. Am. Physicians, Am. Soc. Hematology (exec. com. 1964-66, pres. 1968-69, adv. council 1969-74), Soc. Nuclear Medicine, Societe de Hopitaux de Paris, Soc. Exptl. Biology and Medicine, Harvey Soc., Soc. Study Blood, Am. Fedn. Clin. Research, Am. Soc. Clin. Nutrition, Am. Assn. Cancer Research, Am. Soc. Clin. Oncology, N.Y. Cancer Soc., Reticulo-Endothelial Soc., Alpha Omega Alpha. Office: Mount Sinai Hosp 19 E 98th St New York NY 10029

WASSERMAN, PAUL, educator; b. Newark, Jan. 8, 1924; s. Joseph and Sadie (Ringelescu) W.; B.B.A., Coll. City N.Y., 1948; M.S. in L.S., Columbia, 1949, M.S., 1950; Ph.D., U. Mich., 1960; postgrad. Western Res. U., 1963-64; m. 2d, Krystyna Ostrowska, 1973; children—Jacqueline R., Steven R. Advt. mgr. Zuckerberg Co., N.Y.C., 1946-48; asst. to bus. librarian Bklyn. Pub. Library, 1949-51, chief sci. and industry div., 1951-53; librarian, asst. prof. Grad. Sch. Bus. and Pub. Adminstrn., Cornell U., 1953-56, librarian, asso. prof., 1956-62, librarian, prof., 1962-65; dean U. Md. Coll. Library and Information Services, 1965-70, prof., 1970—. Vis. prof. U. Mich., summers 1960, 63, 64; Isabel Nichol lectr. Denver U. Library Sch., 1968; market research cons. Laux Advt., Inc., 1955-59, Gale Research Co., Detroit, 1959-60, 63-64; research planning cons. Ind. U. Sch. Bus., 1961-62; profl. cons. Spl. Libraries Assn., 1961—; cons. USPHS as mem. Nat. Library Medicine Manpower Tng. Rev. Com., 1966-69, Ohio Bd. Regents, 1969. Dir. Documentation Abstracts, Inc., 1970—, v.p., 1971—. Served with U.S. Army, 1943-46. Decorated Purple Heart, Bronze Star. Mem. Am. Soc. Information Sci., Md. Library Assn., AAUP, ALA, Spl. Libraries Assn. (editor, chmn. publ. project.). Author: Information for Adminstrators, 1956; (with Fred Silander) Decision Making, 1958; Measurement and Evaluation of Organization Performance, 1959; Sources of Commodity Prices, 1960, 2d edit., 1974; Sources for Hospital Administrators, 1961; Decision Making: An Annotated Bibliography, supplement, 1958-63, 1964; Librarian and the Machine, 1965. Book rev. editor: Adminstrv. Sci. Quar., 1956-61; editor Service to Bus., 1952-53; Directory of University Research Bureaus and Institutes, 1960; Health Organizations of the U.S. and Canada, 1961, 2d edit., 1965, 3d edit., 1974, 4th edit., 1977; Statistics Sources, 1962, 4th edit., 1974, 5th edit., 1977; (with Bundy) Reader in Library Adminstration, 1968, Reader in Research Methods in Librarianship, 1969. Mng. editor Mgmt. Information Guide Series, 1963—; Consultants and Consulting Organizations, 1966, 4th edit., 1979; Who's Who in Consulting, 1968, 2d edit., 1974; Awards, Honors and Prizes: A Sourcebook and Directory, 1969, 2d edit., 1972, 4th edit. Vol. 1, 1978; International and Foreign Awards, 1975; New Consultants, 1973-74, 76-77, 78-79; Readers in Librarianship and Information Science, 1968—; Ency. Bus. Information Sources, 1971, 3d edit., 1976; Library and Information Services Today, 1971-75; Museum Media, 2d edit., 1979; Consumer Sourcebook, 1974, 2d edit., 1978; series editor Contributions in Librarianship and Information Science, 1969—; coordinating mgmt. editor Information Guide Library, 1971—; The New Librarianship-A Challenge for Change, 1972; mng. editor Museum Media, 1973, Library Bibliographies and Indexes, 1975; Ethnic Groups in the United States, 1976; Training and Development Organizations, 1978; Speakers and Lecturers: How to Find Them, 1979; Learning Independently, 1979; Recreation and Outdoor Life Directory, 1979. Home: 3501 Duke St College Park Woods MD 20740 Office: College Library and Information Services U Md College Park MD 20742

WASSERMAN, ROBERT HAROLD, educator; b. Schenectady, Feb. 11, 1926; s. Joseph and Sylvia (Rosenberg) W.; B.S., Cornell U., 1949, Ph.D., 1953; M.S., Mich. State U., 1951; m. Marilyn Mintz, June 11, 1950; children—Diane Jean, Arlene Lee, Judith Rose. Research asso. AEC project U. Tenn., Oak Ridge, 1953-55; sr. scientist med. div. Oak Ridge Inst. Nuclear Studies, 1955-57; asso. prof. dept. phys. biology N.Y. State Vet. Coll. Cornell U., 1957-63, prof., 1963—, acting head phys. biology dept., 1963-64, 71, 75—. Vis.

fellow Inst. Biol. Chemistry, Copenhagen, 1964-65; chmn. Conf. on Calcium Transport, 1962; co-chmn. Conf. on Cell Mechanisms for Calcium Transfer and Homeostasis, 1970; chmn. symposium Calcium-Binding Proteins, 1977; cons. NIH, Oak Ridge Inst. Nuclear Studies. Mem. pub. affairs com. Fedn. Am. Socs. Exptl. Biology, 1974—. Served with U.S. Army, 1944-45. Recipient Mead Johnson award, 1969. Guggenheim fellow, 1964-65, 72; NSF-OECD fellow, 1964-65. Mem. Am. Physiol. Soc., Biophys. Soc., Soc. Exptl. Biology and Medicine, Am. Inst. Nutrition, AAAS, Sigma Xi, Phi Kappa Phi. Bd. editors Calcified Tissue Research, 1977—; editor monographs Contbr. articles to profl. jours. Bd. editors Procs. Soc. Exptl. Biol. Medicine, 1970-76, Cornell Veterinarian. Home: 207 Texas Ln Ithaca NY 14850

WASSERSTROM, RICHARD ALAN, educator; b. N.Y.C., Jan. 9, 1936; s. Alfred Howard and Gertrude (Kopp) W.; B.A., Amherst Coll., 1957; M.A. in Philosophy, U. Mich., 1958, Ph.D., 1960; LL.B., Stanford, 1960; m. Phyllis Ann Levin, June 16, 1957; children—Sara Ellen, Jeffrey Nathan, William Louis, Harold Levin. Instr. philosophy Stanford, 1959-60, asst. prof. law and Philosophy, 1960-62, asst. prof., asso. prof. law, 1962-64; dean Coll. Arts and Scis., Tuskegee Inst., 1964-67; prof. law and philosophy UCLA, 1967-79; prof. philosophy, chmn. philosophy bd. U. Calif., Santa Cruz, 1979—; vis. prof. U. Mich. Law Sch., summer 1961; atty. civil rights div. Justice Dept., 1963-64; vis. fellow All Souls Coll., Oxford U., 1970-71. Mem. regional selection com. Woodrow Wilson Found., 1962-63, 64-65, Council for Philos. Studies, 1964-70; mem. Ala. adv. com. U.S. Commn. Civil Rights, 1965-66, Calif. Council Humanities and Public Policy, 1977—. Woodrow Wilson fellow, 1957-58; U. Mich. fellow, 1958-59; Guggenheim fellow 1970-71. Mem. State Bar Assn. Calif., Order of Coif, Phi Beta Kappa, Phi Kappa Phi. Author: The Judicial Decision, 1961; Philosophy and Social Issues: Five Studies, 1980; author, editor: Morality and the Law, 1971; War and Morality, 1970; Today's Moral Problems, 1975, rev. edit., 1979; editorial bd. Monist, 1972—; Social Theory and Practice, 1976—; Humanities and Society, 1978; Environmental Ethics, 1978; contbr. articles to profl. jours. Home: 538 Escalona Dr Santa Cruz CA 95060

WASSON, EDWARD HORNSBY, research inst. ofcl.; b. Montague, Tenn., Apr. 29, 1905; s. James Edward and Lula (Hornsby) W.; student McCallie Sch., Chattanooga, 1918-22; A.B., U. Chattanooga, 1926; Sc.D. (hon.), Monmouth Coll., 1963; m. Regina Donnelly, May 7, 1933 (div. 1964); children—Edward Hornsby, Louellen; m. 2d, Eleanor Carver Clair, Feb. 1, 1964. With So. Bell Tel. and Tel. Co. Hdqrs., Atlanta, 1926-50; v.p. pub. relations Northwestern Bell Telephone Co., Omaha, 1950-51, v.p., gen. mgr. for Minn., Mpls., 1951-52; v.p. Am. Tel.&Tel. Co., 1952-59; pres., dir. N.J. Bell Telephone Co., 1959-65; pres., dir. Pacific Tel.&Tel. Co., 1965-68, Bell Telephone Co., Nev., 1965-68, chmn. bd., chief exec. officer both cos., 1968-70; chmn. bd. Stanford Research Inst., 1971-75, vice chmn. bd., 1975-77, dir. emeritus, 1977—; dir. Am. Potato Co., 1968-76; cons. Aerospace Corp.; dir. Bekins Co., Rockcor, Inc., Avantek Inc.; hon. dir. Carter Hawley Hale Stores Inc. Trustee McCallie Sch., 1957-69, U. Chattanooga, 1961-69, Newark Coll. Engring., 1963-65, United Hosps. Newark, 1960-65; bd. dirs. Deafness Research Found., 1960-65, asso. dir., 1965—. Mem. U.S. (dir. 1960-70, chmn. bd. 1969-70), San Francisco, Calif. chambers commerce, Newcomen Soc. N.Am., Delta Chi. Clubs: Bankers, Bohemian, Golf (San Francisco); Cypress Point (Pebble Beach). Home: Hillsborough CA 94010 Office: 2525 Crocker Plaza San Francisco CA 94104

WASSON, TED DECKER, hosp. adminstr.; b. Bluffton, Ind., Mar. 26, 1939; s. Paul Edwin and Vera Grace (Decker) W.; B.A., Mich. State U.; M.H.A., U. Mich., 1963; m. Patricia A. Perkins, May 6, 1961; children—Julie, Jennifer, Paul. Adminstrv. asst. Beaumont Hosp., 1963-65; asst. adminstr. Port Huron (Mich.) Hosp., 1965-66; asst. dir. Beaumont Hosp., Royal Oak, Mich., 1967-68, asso. dir., 1968-76, dir., 1976—. Office: 3601 W 13 Mile Royal Oak MI 48072*

WATANABE, MICHAEL SATOSHI, educator; b. Tokyo, Japan, May 26, 1910; s. Tchifuyu and Yoshiko (Motoo) W.; B.S., U. Tokyo, 1933, D.Sc., 1940; D.Sc., U. Paris, 1935; postgrad. U. Leipzig, 1937-39; m. Dorothea W. Dauer, Sept. 7, 1937; 1 son, Francis W. Dauer. Came to U.S., 1950. Asso. prof. Tokyo U., 1941-46, Wayne U., 1950-52; prof. U.S. Naval Postgrad. Sch., 1952-56; sr. physicist IBM Research Lab., Yorktown Heights, N.Y., 1956-64; vis. prof. Yale, Columbia, Fordham U., 1959-69; prof. U. Hawaii, 1966—. Fellow IEEE, Am. Phys. Soc.; mem. Internat. Soc. Study Time (pres. 1969-73), Internat. Acad. Philosophy Sci. (v.p.). Author: Knowing and Guessing, 1969. Contbr. articles to profl. jours. Home: 242 Kaalawai Pl Honolulu HI 96816

WATCHMAN, WILLIAM SURTESS, JR., food co. exec.; b. Englewood, N.J., Jan. 9, 1934; s. William S. and Avis (Rand) W.; B.S. in Bus. Adminstrn., Lehigh U., 1955; m. Mary Lou Brachman, June 11, 1955; children—William S. III, Gregory Rand, Sarah Link. Product mgr. Lehn & Fink Products Corp., N.Y.C., 1959-60; v.p., account supr. Kenyon & Eckhardt Advt. Co., N.Y.C., 1960-63; with Colgate-Palmolive Co., 1963-76, v.p., gen. mgr. personal care products div., 1972-74, v.p., gen. mgr. U.S. consumer div., N.Y.C., 1974-76; pres., chief exec. officer Swift & Co., Chgo., 1976—. Served with USNR, 1955-58. Mem. Am. Meat Inst. (bd. dirs. 1977—), Phi Beta Kappa, Lambda Mu Sigma, Alpha Kappa Psi, Beta Gamma Sigma. Clubs: Univ. (N.Y.C.); Saddle and Cycle, Chgo. (Chgo.). Home: 2430 N Lakeview Ave Chicago IL 60614 Office: 115 W Jackson Blvd Chicago IL 60604

WATERBURY, LESTER ELBA, ret. lawyer; b. LaGrange, Ill., May 17, 1895; s. Walton Cleveland and Luzora Venepha (Plass) W.; A.B., U. Mich., 1917, J.D., 1921; m. Jean Grosvenor Parker, Apr. 17, 1949; children—Walton Whitwell, Jonathan Ainsworth, Holly Arundel. Admitted to N.Y. bar, 1922; joined law dept. Am. Sugar Refining Co., 1921; with law dept. Gen. Foods Corp. (then Postum Co., Inc.), 1927-56, asst. sec., 1928-49, gen. atty., 1943-49, gen. counsel, 1949-56, sec., 1949-55, v.p., 1951-60, dir., 1954-61; pres. Gen. Foods Fund, Inc., 1956-60. Mem. adv. council Marine Midland Bank N.Y., 1965-72. Trustee, Gardens Nursery School-Kindergarten, 1957-65, Collegiate Sch., 1961-63. Enlisted in Army (U.S.S.E.R.C.), 1917, overseas 1917-19; commd. 1st lt. U.S. AS, 1918, with 99th Aero Squadron, 1918-19. Mem. Assn. Gen. Counsel, Order of Coif, Phi Beta Kappa, Sigma Delta Chi, Delta Upsilon, Phi Delta Phi. Home: The Apple House Norway Hill Rd Hancock NH 03449

WATERHOUSE, JOHN PERCIVAL, educator; b. Anerley, Kent, Eng., Dec. 4, 1920; s. Percival and Josephine (Williams) W.; M.B., B.S., U. London, 1951, B.D.S., 1956, Dr. Med. Pathology, 1963; m. Kathleen Hazel Wallington Tilley, June 7, 1944; children—Richard, Stella, Julia. with London Hosp. Med. Coll., U. London, 1963-66, reader in oral pathology U. London, 1966-67; prof., head dept. oral pathology Coll. Dentistry U. Ill. Med. Center, Chgo., 1967—, prof. pathology Coll. Medicine, 1968—, acting head dept. histology Coll. Dentistry, 1968-70. cons. West Side VA Hosp., Chgo., 1971—; mem. med. staff U. Ill. Hosp., 1972—. Served as flying officer RAF Vol. Res., 1943-46. Fellow Royal Coll. Pathologists (London); mem. Am. Acad. Oral Pathology, AAAS, Internat. Assn. Dental Research (asst. sec.-treas. 1973-77, asst. sec. 1978-79), Sigma Xi, Omicron Kappa Upsilon. Club: Chgo. Lit. Mem. editorial bds. Archives Oral Biology, 1966—, Jour. Oral Pathology, 1971—. Contbr. articles to profl. jours. Home: 2S151 Stratford Rd Glen Ellyn IL 60137 Office: Dept Oral Pathology U Ill PO Box 6998 Chicago IL 60680

WATERHOUSE, KEITH, surgeon; b. Derby, Eng., May 10, 1929; s. Arthur R. and Marion (Tock) W.; came to U.S., 1953, naturalized, 1964; B.A., Cambridge (Eng.) U., 1950; M.D., Oxford U. Med. Sch., 1953, M.A., 1957; m. Anne Therese Milotzky, Jan. 14, 1955; children—Katherine Anne, Vincent, Maria Ursula, Isabelle, Christopher. Intern, Bklyn. Hosp., 1953-54; resident Kings County Hosp., Bklyn., 1957-59; practice medicine specializing in urol. surgery, Bklyn., 1959—; instr. surgery State U. N.Y., Bklyn., 1959-61, asst. prof., 1961-62, asso. prof., 1962-65, prof., surgery, 1965-69, head div. urology, 1962-69, prof., chmn. dept. urology, 1969—; dir. urology Kings County Hosp., Bklyn., 1962—; cons. urology St. Mary's Hosp., Passaic, N.J., Samaritan Hosp., Bklyn., St. Charles Hosp., Port Jefferson, N.Y., Bklyn. VA Hosp., St. Francis Hosp., Poughkeepsie, N.Y., Arden Hill Hosp., Goshen, N.Y., Brookhaven Meml. Hosp., Patchogue, N.Y., Jewish Hosp. Bklyn., Luth. Med. Center, Columbus Hosp., N.Y.C., Wyckoff Hosp. Bklyn. Served to capt. M.C., Royal Army, 1955-57. Recipient William H. Burpeau award N.J. Acad. Medicine, 1973. Diplomate Am. Bd. Urology. Fellow N.Y. Acad. Medicine (pres. sect. on urology 1967); mem. Clin. Soc. Genitourinary Surgeons, Italian Urol. Soc. (hon.), Panamanian Urol. Soc. (hon.); Am. Acad. Pediatrics (pres. sect. on urology 1976), Bklyn. Urol. Soc. (pres. 1966-67), N.Y. State Med. Soc., Internat. Soc. Urology (chmn. exec. com. U.S. sect.), Am. Urol. Assn. (pres. N.Y. sect. 1971-72, mem. coordinating council 1975-76), Genitourinary Surgeons. Club: Univ. (N.Y.C.). Contbr. articles to med. jours. Office: 450 Clarkson Ave Brooklyn NY 11203

WATERHOUSE, WILLIAM JAMES, violinist, orch. exec.; b. Winnipeg, Man., Can., Aug. 15, 1917; s. John Fereday Preston and Mary Cecelia (Naughton) W.; came to U.S., 1946, naturalized, 1955; student Royal Acad. Music, London, Eng., 1934-39; B.Mus., Boston U., 1950, M.Mus., 1950; m. Ruth Elizabeth Moss, May 27, 1977; children by previous marriage—John David, Caitlin Cecelia, John Paul Jason; stepchildren—Judy and Kathy McKee. Mem. Winnipeg Symphony Orch., 1933-34; 2d violinist Silverman Quartet, 1935-38; concertmaster People's Palace Orch., 1935-39; mem. London String Orch., 1936-39, Boyd Neel String Orch., 1936-39; 2d violinist Stornaway Players, 1937-39; solo violinist London Ballet Co., 1937-39; mem. Montreal Orch., 1939-40; prin. 2d violinist, alternate concertmaster Springfield (Mass.) Symphony Orch., 1947-51; prin. 2d violinist Cambridge Festival Orch., 1948-51; mem. Boston Symphony Orch., 1951-75; concertmaster, guest condr. N.H. Philharmonic Orch., 1968-75; mem. Winnipeg Symphony Orch., 1975—; prin. 2d violinist Boston Pops Esplanade Orch., 1976—. Organizer, lectr., performer Winnipeg Chamber Music Soc., 1944-46; faculty South End Music Center, Boston, 1947-51; pvt. tchr., 1952—; recording artist Allegro Records, 1949-51; lectr., corr. Winnipeg Free Press; solo and chamber music performer in Eng., Can. and U.S.; automobile salesman, 1948-50; franchised new car dealer, 1950-52; pres. Canadian Music Students Club, London, Eng., 1937-39. Chmn., Boston Symphony Orch. String Players Assn., 1971-75, Winnipeg Symphony Orch. Players Assn., 1978—; pres. Boston Symphony Orch. Employees Fed. Credit Union, 1971-75; founder, organizer Boston Symphony Blood Donor Program, 1972-75. Served with Canadian Army, 1940-46. Asso. bd. exhibitioner Royal Acad. Music, 1934-38, Gowland Harrison exhibitioner, 1938-39, recipient 4 Bronze medals, 2 Silver medals, certificate of merit with distinction; recipient Gold medal London Mus. Competition Festival, 1939, Spl. distinction Boston U. Coll. Music, 1950. Asso. Royal Acad. Music; mem. Aircraft Owners and Pilots Assn. Roman Catholic. Home: 359 Elmhurst Rd Winnipeg MB R3R 0T8 Canada

WATERMAN, BERNARD EUGENE, broadcasting exec.; b. Strasburg, Va., Aug. 26, 1921; s. Harry H. and Isabelle M. (Burke) W.; B.J., U. Mo., 1949; m. Edith N. Bryant, Apr. 24, 1946. Sports editor Ill. State Register, Springfield, 1949-55; owner radio stas. WAAB and WAAB-FM, Worcester, Mass., 1956-65; v.p., gen. mgr. WSMW-TV, Worcester, 1969-72; pres., owner KTSA and KTFM Radio, San Antonio, 1965—, WBBH-TV, Ft. Myers, Fla., 1979—; dir. Home Fed. Savs. and Loan Assn., Worcester. Served with USN, 1942-45. Clubs: Oyster Harbors (Osterville, Mass.); San Antonio Country, Argyle (San Antonio); Worcester Country. Home: 13 Montclair Dr Worcester MA 01609 also Seapuit Rd Oyster Harbors MA 02655 Office: PO Box 627 Worcester MA 01613

WATERMAN, JOHN THOMAS, educator; b. Council Bluffs, Iowa, Aug. 1, 1918; s. Charles Murray and Edith (Clark) W.; abitur Concordia Coll., 1934-38; B.A., Concordia Theol. Sem., 1940; M.A., Washington U., 1945; Ph.D., U. Cal. at Los Angeles, 1949; postgrad. Yale, 1947; m. Mary Catherine Adams, Oct. 10, 1942; children—John Robert, Teresa Kathleen. Prof. linguistics U. So. Cal., 1948-68, dept. head, 1958-67; vis. prof. linguistics U. B.C., 1967; prof. German, chmn. dept. Germanic and Slavic langs. U. Cal. at Santa Barbara, 1968—. Linguistic cons. CBS, 1963—; lang. cons. Los Angeles City Sch. System, 1955—, Ventura County Sch. System, 1958—. Served with USAAF, 1941-44. Recipient award for creative research and scholarship U. So. Calif., 1967. Mem. Modern Lang. Assn. Am., Linguistic Soc. Am., Philol. Assn. Pacific Coast, Order St. Lazarus of Jerusalem, Delta Phi Alpha (hon.). Republican. Anglo-Catholic. Author: Sayri Dar Zaban Shinasi, 1969; Perspectives in Linguistics, 2d edit., 1970, Spanish edit., 1971; Die Linguistik und ihre Perspektiven, 1966; Breve Storia della linguistica, 1968; A History of the German Language, 2d edit., 1975; Gendei Gengogaku No Haikeli—Tenbo to Genjo, 1975; Leibniz and Ludolf on Things Linguistic, 1978. Home: 130 W Alamar 4 Santa Barbara CA 93105

WATERMAN, RICHARD D., shipping and agrl. co. exec.; b. Boston, Apr. 14, 1921; s. Ralph Brigham and Marjorie (Waterman) W.; A.B. cum laude, Princeton U., 1943; M.B.A., Harvard U., 1947. Adminstr., Macadamia Nut. div. Castle & Cooke, Inc., Honolulu, 1949-57; v.p., treas. Kentron Hawaii, Ltd., Honolulu, 1958, exec. v.p., 1959, pres., 1960-61; with Alexander & Baldwin, Inc., Honolulu, 1962—, asst. treas., 1964—, dir. corp. planning, 1967—, sec., 1974—, v.p., 1979—; dir. A & B Agribus. Corp., Tropic Sands Apts., Inc. Bd. dirs. Armed Services YMCA, 1977—, chmn., 1978. Served with USNR, 1943-46. Mem. C. of C. of Hawaii. Mem. Central Union Ch. Home: 91-303 Pupu Pl Ewa Beach HI 96706 Office: Alexander & Baldwin Inc 822 Bishop St Honolulu HI 96813

WATERMAN, RONALD FREDERICK, lawyer; b. Newark, Jan. 5, 1944; s. Frederick John and Elizabeth Ann (Heid) W.; student Washington and Jefferson Coll., 1962-63; B.A., U. Mont., 1966, J.D., 1969; m. Mignon Loretta Redfield, Sept. 11, 1965; children—Briar Kensington, Kyle Drew. Admitted to Mont. bar, 1969, U.S. Supreme Ct. bar, 1976; law clk. to U.S. sr. dist. judge, Billings, Mont, 1969-70; asso. firm Gough, Shanahan, Johnson & Waterman and predecessor, Helena, Mont., 1970-79, partner, 1972—; state bar examiner State of Mont., 1978. Mem. bd. adminstrn. St. Paul's United Meth. Ch., Helena, 1975-76; chmn. bd. trustees United Meth. Ch., 1978; gen. campaign chmn. United Way, 1977, bd. dirs. Fellow Am. Bar Found.; mem. State Bar Mont., Young Lawyers Assn. (pres. Mont. chpt. 1976-77), Am. Bar Assn. (Mont. membership chmn. 1973-78), Am. Judicature Soc., Am. Law Inst., Phi Delta Phi (magister 1968-69). Club: Mont. Home: 1221 9th Ave Helena MT 59601 Office: 301 First Nat Bank Bldg Helena MT 59601

WATERMAN, STERRY ROBINSON, judge; b. Taunton, Mass., June 12, 1901; s. Zeno Sterry and Sarah Wood (Robinson) W.; A.B., Dartmouth Coll., 1922, LL.D., 1963; postgrad. Harvard Law Sch., 1922-23, George Washington U. Law Sch., 1923-26, LL.D., 1969; J.D., Vt. Law Sch., 1977; LL.D., N.Y. Law Sch., 1979, U. Vt., 1973; LL.D., N.Y. U., 1979; m. Frances Chadbourne Knight, May 13, 1932 (dec.); children—Robert Sterry, Thomas Chadbourne. Admitted to D.C. bar, 1926, Vt. bar, 1926, U.S. Supreme Ct. bar, 1935; practice law, St. Johnsbury, Vt., 1926-55; mem. firm Waterman & Downs, 1949-55; chmn., gen. counsel Vt. Unemployment Compensation Commn., 1937-41; mem. Vt. Uniform State Laws Commn., 1938-58; judge U.S. Ct. of Appeals, 2d Circuit, St. Johnsbury, 1955—, sr. judge, 1970—. Trustee St. Johnsbury Acad., 1956—, pres., 1973—; trustee, pres. Vt. Law Sch., 1974—. Fellow Am. Bar Found.; mem. Am. Acad. Jud. Edn. (dir. 1971-75, 77—, pres. 1977-78), Vt. Hist. Soc. (trustee, v.p. 1972—), Am. Law Inst., Am. Judicature Soc. (past pres.), Fed. Bar Assn., Vt. Bar Assn. (past pres.), Caledonia County Bar Assn., Assn. Bar City N.Y., Nat. Conf. Commrs. Uniform State Laws, Am. Bar Assn., Nat. Lawyers Club, Inst. Jud. Adminstrn., Selden Soc., U.S. Supreme Ct. Hist. Soc. Republican. Congregationalist. Clubs: Century, Dartmouth (N.Y.C.); Rotary, Sphinx, Masons (33d degree), Elks. Office: PO Box 368 Saint Johnsbury VT 05819

WATERS, DAVID ROGERS, retail exec.; b. Akron, Ohio, Apr. 27, 1932; s. Herbert H. and Winifred Elsie (Kearns) W.; B.S. in Econs., Wharton Sch., U. Pa., 1954; children—Ann S., David Rogers, Thomas J., Peter M., Christopher C., Elizabeth E., Jeffrey P. Trainee, asst. to controller W.R. Grace & Co., N.Y.C., 1954-55; buyer M. O'Neil Co., Akron, 1957-62; div. mdse. mgr. May-Cohens, Jacksonville, Fla., 1962-66, Rich's, Atlanta, 1967; pres., gen. mdse. mgr. DePinna, N.Y.C., 1967-69; gen. mdse. mgr., then pres. Garfinckel's, Washington, 1969-73; pres. Garfinckel, Brooks Bros., Miller & Rhoads, Inc., Washington, 1972-76, pres., chief exec. officer, 1976—, chmn. bd. dirs., 1978—; vice chmn., dir. Frederick Atkins, Inc. Trustee, mem. exec. com. Federal City Council; bd. dirs. Greater Washington Bus. Center; bd. visitors Sch. Bus. Adminstrn., Georgetown U. Served with U.S. Army, 1955-57. Mem. Presidents Assn., Am. Mgmt. Assn. Clubs: Georgetown, Columbia Country, University.

WATERS, EUGENE PAUL, utility exec.; b. Olean, N.Y., July 8, 1932; s. Ray John and Gertrude (Dollard) W.; B.A., Colgate U., 1954, M.B.A., Cornell U., 1961; m. Sandra Ann Shay, June 27, 1959; children—Kevin, Michael, Elizabeth, William. Marketing rep. Procter & Gamble Distbg. Co., Syracuse, N.Y., 1957-60; mgr. accounting Dewey & Almy chem. div. W.R. Grace & Co., Cambridge, Mass., 1961-63; with N.Y. State Elec. & Gas Corp., Binghamton, 1963—, treas., 1971—, v.p. finance, 1976-78, sr. v.p., treas., 1978—; chmn. GAEL Assos., 1974-76; treas. Lancaster Towers Redevel. Corp., 1971-74, NYSEG Housing Corp., 1971-74; dir. Tompkins County Trust Co., Ithaca, N.Y. Mem. ednl. needs com. Homer (N.Y.) Sch. System, 1970-73; v.p. Homer PTA, 1972-73; mem. Homer Housing Commn., 1976. Treas., trustee Phillips Free Library, 1971-79; v.p., treas., trustee Phi Kappa Psi Alumni Corp., 1967-74; mem. Coll. Devel. Found. Cortland, 1973-79; trustee Tompkins-Cortland Community Coll., 1978-79; bd. dirs. George Jr. Republic, Freeville, N.Y., 1976-79. Served with USMCR, 1954-57. Mem. Phi Kappa Psi. Republican. Roman Catholic. (lay reader 1968-79). Clubs: Country of Cortland, Univ. Home: 25 Alpine Dr Apalachin NY 13732 Office: 4500 Vestal Pkwy E Binghamton NY 13902

WATERS, GEORGE WILBUR, travel and financial co. exec.; b. North Madison, Ind., Jan. 9, 1916; s. George Wilbur and Nellie (Wray) W.; B.S., U. Ind., 1938; postgrad. sr. execs. program Mass. Inst. Tech., 1956; m. Pauline Wasson, Feb. 19, 1942; children—Diane, Lawrence, Pauline. Data processing sales rep. IBM, Cin., 1938-41; dir., pres. Mass. S.S. Lines, Boston, 1946-48; v.p., dir. Colonial Stores, Inc., Atlanta, 1949-61; v.p. Am. Express Co., N.Y.C., 1961—, pres. travel related services, 1977-78, exec. v.p., 1968—, also chmn. Office of Strategic Devel.; dir. Am. Express Internat., Inc., Am. Express Internat. Banking Corp., Am. Express Pub. Corp., Am. Express Ltd., Payment Systems, Inc.; mem. Nat. Commn. on Electronic Fund Transfers, 1976-77. Served to col. USAAF, 1941-45. Decorated Legion of Merit. Mem. Acad. Alumni Fellows of Ind. U. Sch. Bus. Republican. Presbyterian. Clubs: Sandy Lane Country (St. James, Barbados); Navesink Country (Middletown, N.J.); Cherokee (Atlanta); Rumson (N.J.) Country. Home: 72 Pine Cove Rd Fair Haven NJ 07701 Office: Am Express Co American Express Plaza New York City NY 10004

WATERS, HERBERT OGDEN, artist; b. Swatow, China. Nov. 15, 1903; s. George Henry and Mary Kay (Scott) W.; student Shanghai Am. Sch., 1916-22; Ph.B., Denison U., 1926; postgrad. Pa. Mus. Sch. Indsl. Art, summer 1927, Art Inst. Chgo., 1929-31, Harvard, 1932-33; m. Bertha Margaret Adams, Aug. 22, 1932. Wood engraving prints exhibited N.Y. World's Fair, 1939, Phila. Print Club, 1948, Carnegie Mus., 1949, Boston Art Festival, 1952; works include mural Campton (N.H.) Bapt. Ch., 1954, meml. bookplate Denison U. Library, 1955, 72; prints in permanent collections Addison Gallery Am. Art, R.I. Sch. Design Mus., U. N.H., Dartmouth, Middlebury Coll., Pa. State Coll., Boston and N.Y. pub. libraries, N.A.D., Met. Mus. Art, Library of Congress, Bklyn. Mus., others; asst. in art Brown U., 1942; art tchr. Holderness Sch., Plymouth, N.H., 1946-61; tchr. U. N.H. summer sch., 1948-60; asso. prof. art Alderson-Broadus Coll., 1965-69, prof., 1969-72, prof. emeritus, 1973—. Recipient awards Ind. Soc. Printmakers, 1945, N.H. Art Assn., 1951, 54, 55, 65, 78, Soc. Am. Graphic Artists, 1955, Acad. Artists, Springfield, Mass., 1955, alumni citation Denison U., 1956, Clarksburg Realistic Centennial Art Exhbn., 1963, Elkins (W.Va.) Forest Festival, award in graphic art Appalachian Corridors Exhbn., Charleston, W.Va., 1968, 70, others; 1st Distinguished Teaching award Alderson-Broadus Coll., 1972. Mem. Soc. Am. Graphic Artists, Boston Printmakers Soc., NAD, N.H. Art Assn. (pres. 1960-61), Am. Commons Club, Phi Beta Kappa. Baptist. Illustrator: (wood engravings) New England Year (Muriel Follett), 1939; New England Days (Herbert Waters), 1940; Fragments (C.A. Wynem), 1941. Home: Upper Mad River Rd Campton NH 03223

WATERS, JAMES LOGAN, analytical instrument mfg. co. exec.; b. Lincoln, Nebr., Oct. 7, 1925; s. Leland L. and Marian L. (Yungblut) W.; B.S., Columbia U., 1946; m. Faith C. Pigors, Sept. 17, 1948; children—Richard C., Barbara F. Project mgr. Baird Assos., Inc., Cambridge, Mass., 1947; pres. James L. Waters, Inc., Framingham, Mass., 1947-58; pres. Waters Assos., Inc., Milford, Mass., 1958-72, chmn. bd., 1972—; pres. Waters Bus. Systems, Inc., Framingham, 1978—; dir. Markem Corp., Keene, N.H., 1971—, Transtek, Ellington, Conn., 1969—, Wellesley Motor Coach Co., Framingham, 1977—. Mem. Framingham Town Meeting, 1952-61; mem. Framingham Sch. Com., 1961-70, chmn., 1962, 64; trustee Babson Coll., Wellesley, Mass. Served as ensign USNR, 1943-46. Patentee in field. Home: 1153 Grove St Framingham MA 01701 Office: 12 Maple St Milford MA 01747

WATERS, LAUGHLIN EDWARD, fed. judge; b. Los Angeles, Aug. 16, 1914; s. Frank J. and Ida (Bauman) W.; A.B., U. Calif., Los Angeles, 1939; J.D., U. So. Calif., 1946; m. Voula Davanis, Aug. 22, 1953; children—Laughlin Edward, Maura Kathleen, Deirdre Mary, Megan Ann, Eileen Brigid. Admitted to Calif. bar, 1946; dep. atty. gen. Calif., Los Angeles, 1946; individual practice law, Los Angeles, 1947-53, 61-76; U.S. atty. So. Dist. Calif., 1953-61; judge U.S. Dist. Ct. for Calif. Central Dist., 1976—. Mem. Calif. Legislature, 1947-53. Served as capt. U.S. Army, 1942-46. Decorated Bronze Star medal, Purple Heart with oak leaf cluster, Combat Inf. badge. Fellow Am. Bar Found., Am. Coll. Trial Lawyers; mem. Am. Judicature Soc., U. So. Calif., U. Calif. at Los Angeles law assns., Am. Legion, U. So. Calif. Legion Lex, Order Blue Shield, Town Hall, Soc. Friendly Sons St. Patrick. Republican. Roman Catholic. Clubs: Knights of Malta; Newman; Anchor; Calif. Office: 243 US Courthouse 312 N Spring St Los Angeles CA 90012

WATERS, MUDDY (MCKINLEY MORGANFIELD), singer; b. Rolling Fork, Miss., Apr. 4, 1915. Learned to play harmonica and guitar as child; discovered by folklorist Alan Lomax while working in cotton fields; moved to Chgo., 1943, since played various clubs there; first toured Eng., 1958; first performed Carnegie Hall, 1959; rec. artist Chess Records, 1947-75, Blue Sky Records, 1977—; recs. include The Best of Muddy Waters, 1958, Folk Singers, 1964, Real Blues, 1966, They Call Me Muddy Waters (Grammy award), 1971, London Sessions (Grammy award), 1972, McKinley Morganfield a/k/a Muddy Waters, 1973, Muddy Waters Woodstock Album (Grammy award), 1975, Hard Again (Grammy and Rolling Stone Mag. Critics awards), 1977; I'm Ready (Grammy award), 1978, Muddy "Mississippi" Waters Live, 1979; appeared film The Last Waltz. Named to Ebony Black Music Hall of Fame, 1973; numerous other awards. Address: care Cameron Orgn 320 S Waiola Ave La Grange IL 60525

WATERS, WILLIAM WADSWORTH, ins. co. exec.; b. Orange, Mass., Oct. 7, 1920; s. Frank Thayer and Lue Mable (Smith) W.; B.A., Wesleyan U., Middletown, Conn., 1946; m. Geraldine A. McKenna, Sept. 28, 1946; children—Laura Gay, Nancy Jean. With Aetna Life & Casualty Co., Hartford, Conn., 1947—, asst. v.p., then v.p. claim dept., 1968-77, v.p. group div., 1977—. Served with USAAF, 1943-45. Decorated Purple Heart. Mem. Internat. Claim Assn. (pres. 1977-78), Health Ins. Assn. Am., Hartford Claim Assn. Club: Masons. Home: 77 Pheasant Hill Dr West Hartford CT 06107 Office: 151 Farmington Ave Hartford CT 06156

WATERSTON, SAMUEL ATKINSON, actor; b. Cambridge, Mass., Nov. 15, 1940; s. George Chychele and Alica Tucker (Atkinson) W.; B.A., Yale U., 1962; student Sorbonne, 1960-61; m. Lynn Louisa Woodruff, Jan. 26, 1976; 1 dau., Elisabeth P.; 1 son from previous marriage, James S. Appeared in numerous off Broadway and Broadway plays including: Indians, Oh Dad Poor Dad, Halfway Up the Tree; appeared with N.Y. Shakespeare Festival in numerous prodns. including Hamlet, The Tempest, Measure for Measure, Much Ado About Nothing; films include: The Great Gatsby, 1975, Rancho Deluxe, 1976, Capricorn I, Interiors, 1978, Sweet William, 1978, Heaven's Gate, 1979; TV films include: Much Ado About Nothing, 1974, The Glass Menagerie, 1975, Diabolique, 1975, Friendly Fire, 1978. Recipient Obie. Mem. Actors Equity Assn., Screen Actors Guild, AFTRA. Office: care Agy for the Performing Arts Inc 9000 Sunset Blvd Suite 315 Los Angeles CA 90069

WATERSTONE, TIMOTHY JOHN S., pub.; b. Beariden, Scotland, May 30, 1939; s. Malcolm Stuart and Sylvia Catherine W.; M.A., Cambridge U., 1961; m. Clare Peakins, Oct. 2, 1972; children—Richard, Martin, Sylvia, Amanda, Maya. Mktg. mgr. Grants of St. James, 1965-70; asst. mng. dir. J.R. Phillips & Co., 1970-73; div. dir. W.H. Smith and Son, Ltd., 1973—, pres. W.H. Smith & Son (U.S.A.) Holdings, Inc. Mem. Ch. of Eng. Home: 103 E 75th St New York NY 10021 Office: Suite 2403 575 Lexington Ave New York NY 10022*

WATKIN, LAWRENCE EDWARD, educator, author; b. Camden, N.Y., Dec. 9, 1901; s. George Edward and Caroline Harriet (Covert) W.; A.B., Syracuse U., 1924; A.M., Harvard, 1925; student Columbia, summer sessions; m. Dorothy Edwards Parke, Sept. 1, 1926; children—Lawrence Parke, Margaret Jean, Anne Caroline. Instr. English, Syracuse U., 1925-26; asst. prof. Washington and Lee U., 1926-38, asso. prof., 1938-42; screenwriter, Hollywood, Cal., 1945-65, 70—, with Disney Studio, 1947-60, 70—; prof. English Cal. State U. at Fullerton, 1965-70, prof. emeritus, 1970—. Served as lt. comdr. USNR, 1942-45; head Aviation Tng. Manuals Unit under Dep. Chief of Naval Operations for Air, Dept. Navy, Washington. Mem. Phi Gamma Delta, Sigma Upsilon. Author: (novels) On Borrowed Time, 1937, Geese in the Forum, 1940; The Gentleman from England, 1941; (juveniles) Thomas Jones and His Nine Lives, 1941; Marty Markham (basis for TV series Spin and Marty), 1941; screenplays include Beaver Valley, Treasure Island, Robin Hood, Sword and the Rose, Rob Roy, Light in the Forest, Darby O'Gill and the Little People, Ten Who Dared, The Biscuit Eater; writer, producer The Great Locomotive Chase. Address: 3450 W Benjamin Holt Dr Stockton CA 95209. *I worked a twelve-hour day at something I liked. I never tore my mind apart searching for my identity—our phoniest word. Who you are is what you do. Exchew all gurus, shun self-analysis, a form of status-seeking. (I'm a more sensitive person than you; I have more hang-ups, more compulsive urges, greater fears and bigger doubts.) Most existentialists are dismal—hopeless, helpless, licked. The village atheist in my home town was a better atheist. He got some fun out of it.*

WATKIN, VIRGINIA GUILD, lawyer; b. Clinton, Mass., July 28, 1925; d. George Cheever and Dorothy Louise (Springer) Guild; A.B., Wellesley Coll., 1946; LL.B., Columbia U., 1949; m. Donald Morgan Watkin, June 22, 1946; children—Henry, Mary Ellen, Edward, Ann Kymry. Admitted to D.C. bar, 1952, Mass. bar, 1963, N.Y. bar, 1949; research asst. Columbia U. Sch. Law, 1949-51; asso. firm Covington & Burling, Washington, 1952-58; asso. counsel Mass. Crime Commn., Boston, 1963-64; spl. cons. firm Herrick, Smith, Donald, Farley & Ketchum, Boston, 1965-66, asso. firm 1966-72, partner firm, 1973-74; partner firm Covington & Burling, Washington, 1974—; cons. Inter-Am. Tax Research Ltd. bd. visitors Columbia U. Law Sch., 1977—; trustee Norwich U., 1977—, Northfield Mt. Hermon Sch., 1978—. Radcliffe Inst. scholar, 1962-65. Mem. Am. Bar Assn., Soc. Women Geographers, Am. Law Inst. Club: Cosmopolitan (N.Y.C.). Author works on real property, tax law. Office: 888 16th St NW Washington DC 20006

WATKINS, CARLTON GUNTER, pediatrician; b. Wilmington, N.C., Aug. 25, 1919; s. Edison Lee and Maysie (Gunter) W.; A.B., U. N.C., 1939; M.D., Washington U., St. Louis, 1943; m. Charlotte Jean Metcalf, Mar. 21, 1943; children—Lloyd Dixon Hollingsworth, Carlton Gunter, Mary Melissa, Charlotte Lou. Rotating intern, asst. resident, resident pediatrics St. Louis City Hosp., 1943-45; resident pediatrics Duke Hosp., 1945-46; pvt. practice, Charlotte, N.C., 1946-51, 53-73; chmn. dept. pediatrics Charlotte Meml. Hosp., 1958-61, 63-67; founder, sr. mem. Charlotte Pediatric Clinic, 1963-73; med. dir. Mecklenburg Center for Human Devel., Charlotte, 1973—. Mem. Charlotte-Mecklenburg Bd. Edn., 1966-74, Charlotte Model City Commn., 1968-69; pres. N.C. Family Life Council, 1966, Charlotte-Mecklenburg Assn. for Children with Learning Disabilities, 1971-73; mem. profl. adv. bd. Epilepsy Assn. N.C., 1976—. Served to capt. M.C., AUS, 1951-53, Fellow Am. Acad. Pediatrics; mem. AMA, N.C., Mecklenburg County med. socs., N.C., Charlotte (founder, 1st sec. 1950, pres. 1962) pediatric socs., N.C. PTA (life), Alpha Kappa Kappa. Club: Old Catawba (Charlotte). Contbr. articles to med. jours. Home: 6724 Constitution Lane Charlotte NC 28210 Office: 3500 Ellington St Charlotte NC 28211

WATKINS, DANIEL JOSEPH, civil engr.; b. Albia, Iowa, Dec. 18, 1923; s. Thomas Joseph and Theresa Alice (O'Connor) W.; B.S., Iowa State U., 1947; m. Barbara Lorraine Van Cleve, Sept. 9, 1946; children—Daniel, Robert, Alice, John, Marianne, Jeanne, Thomas, James, Barbara, William, Margaret, Paul Gerard (dec.), Frances, David, Patrick. Design engr., dept. head Howard, Needles, Tammen & Bergendoff, cons. engrs., architects, planners, Kansas City, Mo., 1947-70, partner, 1970—; incorporator Citizens State Bank, Shawnee Mission, Kans., 1973. Mem. Prairie Village (Kans.) City Council, 1965-71; bd. dirs. Mayor Kansas City (Mo.) Corps Progress, 1972—; mem. bd. dirs. St. Joseph's Hosp., Kansas City, Mo.; mem. civil engring. adv. council Iowa State U., Ames, 1976. Served to lt. (j.g.) USNR, 1944-46; PTO. Named Councilman of Year, City of Prairie Village, 1970. Fellow ASCE, Am. Cons. Engrs. Council; mem. Nat., Mo. (pres. Western chpt. 1965, chmn. state profl. conduct com. 1967-70), socs. profl. engrs., Cons. Engrs. Council Mo. (v.p. 1971-72), Am. Pub. Works Assn., Am. Roadbuilders Assn., Internat. Bridge, Tunnel and Turnpike Assn., Am. Inst. Planners, Transp. Research Bd., Greater Kansas City C. of C. (life; bd. dirs.), Tau Beta Pi. Roman Catholic. Rotarian. Home: 3511 W 73d St Prairie Village KS 66208 Office: 1805 Grand Ave Kansas City MO 64108

WATKINS, DAVID HYDER, surgeon; b. Denver, Nov. 26, 1917; s. David Milroy and Mary Rose (Hyder) W.; A.B., U. Colo., 1937, M.D., 1940; M.S. in Surgery, U. Minn., 1947, Ph.D., 1949; m. Lucile Maxine Pingel, Sept. 27, 1941; children—John David Hyder, Bryan David Pingel. Intern, U. Iowa Hosps., Iowa City, 1940-41; resident Mayo Clinic, Rochester, Minn., 1942-44, asst. surg. staff, 1945-49; instr. surgery Ohio State U., Columbus, 1949-50; asso. prof. surgery U. Colo., Denver, 1951-56, prof., 1956-67; practice medicine specializing in surgery, Des Moines, 1967—; mem. staff Iowa Meth Hosp., Broadlawns Hosp., VA Hosp.; clin. prof. surgery U. Iowa, Iowa City, 1967—. Diplomate Am. Bd. Surgery, Am. Bd. Thoracic Surgery. Fellow A.C.S.; mem. Am. Assn. for Thoracic Surgery, Central, Western surg. assns., S.W. Surg. Congress, Soc. Univ. surgeons, Societe Internationale de Chirurgie, Am. Heart Assn., Am. Coll. Cariology, Am. Coll. Chest Physicians, Am. Fedn. for Clin. Research, Am. Geriatrics Soc., Am. Soc. for Artificial Internal Organs, Priestley Soc., S.A.R., Phi Beta Kappa, Sigma Xi, Alpha Omega Alpha. Club: Univ. (Denver). Contbr. articles in field to med. jours. Home: 6039 N Waterbury Rd Des Moines IA 50312 Office: 1420 Woodland Ave Des Moines IA 50309. *The historical imperative is as valid in science as in politics. Knowledge of the past is essential to predict the future.*

WATKINS, DAVID ROY, librarian; b. Rock Island, Ill., Apr. 23, 1915; s. David Warren and Alma Rose (Brumswig) W.; A.B., St. Ambrose Coll., 1937; B.S. in L.S., U. Ill., 1941; M.A., U. Minn., 1957. Instr., St. Bede Coll., Peru, Ill., 1942-44; librarian St. Thomas Coll., St. Paul, 1944-52; prin. reference librarian U. Minn., 1953-56; William Robertson Coe reference librarian Yale U., 1956-66; dean univ. libraries Fordham U., 1966-70; librarian Brandeis U., Waltham, Mass., 1970—; cons. New Haven Coll., Cath. U. of P.R., U. Wis. Library, Hobart Coll., Boston Coll., USCG Acad. Library. Mem. Am., New Eng. library assns., Assn. Coll. and Research Libraries. Club: Grolier. Contbr. articles to profl. jours. Home: 146 Richdale Rd Needham MA 02194 Office: Brandeis U Waltham MA 02154

WATKINS, DEAN ALLEN, educator, electronics exec.; b. Omaha, Oct. 23, 1922; s. Ernest E. and Pauline (Simpson) W.; B.S., Iowa State Coll., 1944; M.S., Calif. Inst. Tech., 1947; Ph.D., Stanford, 1951; m. Bessie Ena Hansen, June 28, 1944; children—Clark Lynn, Alan Scott, Eric Ross. Engr., Collins Radio Co., 1947-48; mem. staff Los Alamos Lab., 1948-49; tech. staff Hughes Research Labs., 1951-53; asso. prof. elec. engring. Stanford, 1953-56, prof., dir. Electron Devices Lab., 1956-64, lectr. elec. engring., 1964-70; co-founder, pres., chief exec. officer, dir. Watkins Johnson Co., Palo Alto, Calif., 1957-67, chmn., chief exec. officer, dir., 1967-80, chmn., dir., 1980—; cons. Dept. Def., 1956-66. Legis. chmn., dir. San Mateo County Sch. Bds. Assn., 1959-69; gov. San Francisco Bay Area Council, 1966-75. Republican precinct capt. Portola Valley, 1964; vice chmn. San Mateo County Finance Com., 1967-69; mem. Calif. Rep. Central Com., 1964-68; trustee Stanford, 1966-69; regent U. Calif., 1969—, chmn., 1972-74; mem. governing bd. Sequoia Union High Sch. Dist., 1964-68, chmn., 1967-68; mem. governing bd. Portola Valley Sch. Dist., 1958-66; mem. bd. overseers Hoover Instn. on War, Revolution and Peace, Stanford, 1969—, chmn., 1971-72. adv. policy commn. Santa Clara County Jr. Achievement; trustee Nat. Security Indsl. Assn., 1965-78. Served from pvt. to 1st lt. C.E., O.R.C., AUS, 1943-46. Fellow IEEE (7th region Achievement award 1957); mem. Am. Phys. Soc., Am. Mgmt. Assn., Western Electronic Mfrs. Assn. (chmn. San Francisco council 1967, v.p., dir.), Calif. C. of C. (dir. 1965—, treas. 1978, 2d v.p. 1979, 1st v.p 1980), Nat. Acad. Engring., Mounted Patrol San Mateo County (spl. dep. sheriff 1960-70), San Mateo County Horsemen's Assn., San Benito County Farm Bur., Calif. Cattlemen's Assn., Delta Upsilon. Clubs: Palo Alto, University (Palo Alto); Shack Riders (San Mateo County); Commonwealth, (San Francisco); Rancheros Visitadores. Contbr. articles to profl. jours. Patentee in field. Office: 3333 Hillview Ave Palo Alto CA 94304

WATKINS, ELLIS HERRIN, public transit exec.; b. Dallas, May 27, 1919; s. Matthew C. and Myrtie (Meredith) W.; student So. Methodist U., 1947-53; m. Maxine Lillian Gano, Aug. 18, 1941; 1 son, David. Dir. personnel Dallas Transit System, 1940-60, asst. gen. mgr., 1964-73, gen. mgr., 1974—; mgr. personnel adminstrn. Collins Radio Co., Dallas, 1960-64; chmn. Tex. Transit Industry Adv. Com., State Dept. Hwys. and Pub. Transp., Austin, 1979-80. Past pres. Dallas Midget Baseball League, Dallas Ch. Athletic Assn.; past pres. N.E. Tex. chpt. Muscular Dystrophy Assn. Am., mem. adv. council Greater Dallas chpt., 1980. Served with USAAF, 1943-45. Recipient Man with a Heart award Dallas Community Service Bur., 1959; Distinguished Service award Dallas County chpt. Muscular Dystrophy Assn. Am., 1959. Mem. Am. Pub. Transit Assn. (dir.), Dallas C. of C. (vice chmn. membership), Transit Data Summaries Group, Am. Soc. Tng. Dirs. Baptist. Clubs: Masons, Rotary. Home: 4415 Abrams Rd Dallas TX 75214 Office: 101 N Peak St Dallas TX 75226

WATKINS, FREDERICK DAVIS, ins. co. exec.; b. Little Rock, Sept. 13, 1915; B.S. in Econs., U. Pa., 1937; C.P.C.U. Underwriter, Aetna Ins. Co., Hartford, Conn., 1937-39, spl. agt., 1939-41, state agt., Ark., 1946-48, home office gen. agt., Hartford, 1948-50, asst. sec., 1950-55, sec., 1955-60, v.p., 1960-64, sr. v.p., 1964-66, pres., 1966-79; exec. v.p. Conn. Gen. Ins. Corp., 1979—, also dir.; dir. Conn. Gen. Life Ins. Co., Aetna Ins. Co., Hartford Nat. Corp., Kaman Corp., Internat. Reins. Corp., Trenwyck Ltd. Served with AUS, 1941-45. Mem. Beta Gamma Sigma, Beta Theta Pi. Home: 48 Westwood Rd West Hartford CT 06117 Office: 55 Elm St Hartford CT 06115

WATKINS, GLENN ELSON, musicologist, educator; b. McPherson, Kan., May 30, 1927; s. George Earl and Orpha Marie (Andes) W.; student U. Okla., 1944, U. Pa., 1945, U. Minn., 1945-46, N. Tex. State U., 1947; A.B., U. Mich., 1948; Ph.D., U. Rochester, 1953; postgrad. Fontainebleau, France, 1956. Asst. prof. So. Ill. U., Carbondale, 1954-58; asso. prof. U. N.C., Chapel Hill, 1958-63; asso. prof. music U. Mich., Ann Arbor, 1963-66, prof., 1966—, vis. prof., 1961-62. Vis. prof. Eastman Sch. Music, 1962-63. Served with AUS, 1944-46. Fulbright scholar, London and Oxford, 1953-54; Am. Council Learned Socs. grantee; Nat. Endowment for Humanities grantee. Mem. Am. Musicol. Soc. Author: Gesualdo: The Man and His Music (Nat. Book award nominee 1974), 1973. Editor: Complete Works of Carlo Gesualdo, 1959-66; Complete Works Sigismondo d'India, 1975—. Contbr. articles to Groves Dictionary of Music. Home: 2200 Fuller Rd Ann Arbor MI 48105

WATKINS, HAYS THOMAS, r.r. exec.; b. Fern Creek, Ky., Jan. 26, 1926; s. Hays Thomas and Minnie Catherine (Whiteley) W.; B.S. in Accounting, Western Ky. U., 1947; M.B.A., Northwestern U., 1948; m. Betty Jean Wright, 1950; 1 son, Hays Thomas III. With C.&O. Ry. Cleve., 1949—, v.p. finance, 1964-67, v.p. adminstrv. group, 1967-71; pres., chief exec. officer, 1971-73, chmn. bd., chief exec. officer, 1973—; with B.&O. R.R., 1964—, v.p. finance, 1964-71, pres., chief exec. officer, 1971-73, vice chmn. bd., chief exec. officer, 1973—; chmn., chief exec. officer Chessie System, Inc., 1973—; dir. Black & Decker Mfg. Co., Westinghouse Electric Corp., Fed. Res. Bank Cleve. Sponsor, William and Mary Coll. Sch. Bus. Adminstrn., 1971—. Trustee St. Luke's Hosp., Johns Hopkins U. Mus. Arts Assn. (Cleve. Orch.), Baldwin-Wallace Coll. Served with AUS, 1945-47. C.P.A. Mem. Nat. Assn. Accts., Am. Inst. C.P.A.'s, Ohio Soc. C.P.A.'s. Clubs: Center (Balt.); Commonwealth (Richmond, Va.); Sky (N.Y.C.); Pepper Pike, Union (Cleve.). Home: 70 Quail Hollow Dr Moreland Hills OH 44022 Office: 3600 Terminal Tower Cleveland OH 44101

WATKINS, JACK LEWIS, air force officer; b. Russelton, Pa., Aug. 11, 1928; s. Charles B. and Helen (Lewis) W.; B.A., U. Pitts., 1954; student U.S. Army Command and Gen. Staff Coll., 1964-65, Indsl. Coll. Armed Forces, 1968-69; m. Mary Ann Kring, May 28, 1955; 1 son, Mark Steven. Served as enlisted man U.S. Army, 1946-48, officer, 1950-52; commd. 1st lt. USAF, 1955, advanced through grades to maj. gen., 1978; served with Tactical Air Command and Mil. Air Transport Service, 1956-61; with Office Dep. Chief of Staff for Research and Devel., Hdqrs., Washington, 1961-63; a.d.c. to comdr. Bolling AFB, Washington, 1963-64; ops. officer, Albuquerque, 1965-68; prof. aerospace studies Air Force ROTC, U. Pitts., 1969-70; vice comdt. Air Force ROTC, Maxwell AFB, Ala., 1971-73; vice comdr. 410 Bombardment Wing, K. I. Sawyer AFB, Mich., 1973-74, acting comdr., 1974; comdr. 416 Bombardment Wing, Griffiss AFB, N.Y., 1974-75, 45th Air Div., Pease AFB, N.H., 1975-77; asst. dep. chief of staff ops. Hdqrs SAC, Offutt AFB, Nebr., 1977-78, dep. chief of staff ops., 1978—. Decorated Legion of Merit with 2 oak leaf clusters, Meritorious Service medal, Joint Service Commendation medal, Air Force Commendation medal with oak leaf cluster. Mem. Mil. Order World Wars, Order of Daedallians, Pi Sigma Alpha, Phi Gamma Delta. Methodist. Home: 789 Penn Ave Pittsburgh PA 15221 Office: Hdqrs SAC/DO Offutt AFB NE 68113

WATKINS, JERRY WEST, oil co. exec., lawyer; b. Vernon, Tex., Dec. 10, 1931; s. Terrell Clark and Daisy (West) W.; student Hendrix Coll., 1949-50, La. Poly. Inst., 1950-51; LL.B., U. Ark., 1954; m. Elizabeth Jill Cole, Sept. 3, 1955; children—Jennifer Leigh, Jay West, Julie Elizabeth. Admitted to Ark. bar, 1954; law clk. Supreme Ct. Ark., 1954-55; with Murphy Oil Corp., El Dorado, Ark., 1955—, sec., gen. atty., 1966-71, sec., gen. counsel, 1971—, v.p., 1975—, also dir. Mem. Ark. Bd. Law Examiners, 1969-74. Mem. Am., Ark., Union County bar assns., Am. Soc. Corp. Secs. Home: 111 Watkins Dr El Dorado AR 71730 Office: 200 Jefferson Ave El Dorado AR 71730

WATKINS, JOEL SMITH, geophysicist; b. Poteau, Okla., May 27, 1932; s. Joel Smith and Eva (Byers) W.; student U. Wis., Madison, 1956-58; B.A. in Geology, U. N.C., Chapel Hill, 1953; Ph.D. in Geology, U. Tex., 1961; m. Billie K. Dore, Mar. 28, 1971; children—Catherine, Victoria. Geophysicist U.S. Geol. Survey, Washington and Flagstaff, Ariz., 1961-66; research asso. Mass. Inst. Tech., 1967; asso. prof. U. N.C., 1968-70, prof., 1970-72; prof. marine studies U. Tex.-Austin, 1975-77, research scientist Marine Sci. Inst., 1973-77; sr. research asso. Gulf Oil Co., 1977-79, mgr. geol. interp. dept., 1979—; investigator explosion seismic expts. Apollos 14, 16, 17, 1965-73; co-chief sci. Glomar Challenger Leg 66, 1979; cons. marine geophysics. Served with USMC, 1953-56. Recipient U.S. Geol. Survey Outstanding Performance award, 1966, Exceptional Sci. Achievement medal NASA, 1973. Mem. Am. Geophys. Union, Soc. Exploration Geologists, Geol. Soc. Am. (Spl. commendation 1973), Assn. Engring. Geologists (Best Paper award 1968, editorial bd. 1970-76), Am. Assn. Petroleum Geologists, AAAS, Phi Beta Kappa, Sigma Xi. Contbr. numerous articles to profl. jours. Home: 2633 Glenchester Rd Wexford PA 15090 Office: Gulf Sci and Tech Co PO Box 2038 Pittsburgh PA 15230

WATKINS, JOHN CHESTER ANDERSON, newspaper publisher; b. Corpus Christi, Tex., Oct. 2, 1912; s. Dudley Warren and Ruth (Woodruff) Watkins; student pub., pvt. schs.; Litt.D., Bryant Coll.; m. Helen Danforth, Nov. 20, 1943 (div. 1959); children—Fanchon Metcalf, Robert Danforth, Stephen Danforth, Jane Pierce; m. 2d, Izetta Jewel Smith, Feb., 1960. Reporter, makeup editor, aviation editor Dayton (Ohio) Jour. and Herald, 1934-35; reporter, aviation editor, mil. corr. Balt. Sun, 1935-41; asst. to pub., asso. pub. Providence Jour.-Bull., 1945-54, pub., 1954-79; chmn., chief exec. officer, dir. Providence Jour. Co.; chmn. bd. Providence Gravure, Inc., 1961—, Colony Communications; pres. Interam. Press Assn., 1971-72, also mem. adv. council; dir. R.IHT Corp., R.I. Hosp. Trust Nat. Bank. Served as fighter pilot USAAF, 1941-45; operations officer 325th Fighter Group; MTO. Decorated D.F.C., Air medal with 9 oak leaf clusters; knight comdr. Order of Merit (Italy). Mem. Air Force Assn., Mil. Order Fgn. Wars, New Eng. Daily Newspaper Assn. (pres. 1966-68). Clubs: National Press, Army-Navy Country (Washington); Hope, Agawam Hunt (Providence); Cruising Am.; New Bedford (Mass.) Yacht; Brook, N.Y. Yacht (N.Y.C.); Spouting Rock Beach Assn. (Newport, R.I.); La Jolla (Cal.) Beach and Tennis. Home: PO Box 1085 Providence RI 02901 Office: Providence Jour Co Providence RI 02902

WATKINS, JOHN GOODRICH, educator, psychologist; b. Salmon, Idaho, Mar. 17, 1913; s. John Thomas and Ethel (Goodrich) W.; student Coll. Idaho, 1929-30, 31-32; B.S., U. Ida., 1933, M.S., 1936; Ph.D., Columbia, 1939; m. Evelyn Elizabeth Browne, Aug. 21, 1932; m. 2d, Doris Wade Tomlinson, June 8, 1946; m. 3d, Helen Verner Huth, Dec. 28, 1971; children—John Dean, Jonette Alison, Richard Douglas, Gregory Keith, Rodney Philip, Karen Ann Eiblmayr, Marvin R. Huth. Instr. high sch., Idaho, 1933-39; faculty Ithaca Coll., 1939-40, Ala. Poly. Inst., 1941-43, Wash. State Coll., 1945-46; chief clin. psychologist U.S. Army Welch Hosp.; clin. psychologist VA Hosp., American Lake, Wash., 1949-50; chief clin. psychologist VA Mental Hygiene Clinic, Chgo., 1950-53, VA Hosp., Portland, Oreg., 1953-64; prof. psychology, dir. clin. tng. U. Mont., Missoula, 1964—. Lectr. numerous univs.; clin. asso. U. Oreg. Med. Sch., 1957; pres. Am. Bd. Examiners in Psychol. Hypnosis, 1960-62.

Mem. Internat. (co-founder, pres. 1965-67, recipient awards 1960-65), Nat. (Morton Prince award, pres. 1969-71) socs. clin. and exptl. hypnosis, Am. Psychol. Assn. (pres. div. 30 1975-76), Sigma Xi, Phi Delta Kappa. Author: Objective Measurement of Instrumental Performance, 1942; Hypnotherapy of War Neuroses, 1949; General Psychotherapy, 1960; The Therapeutic Self, 1978. Contbr. articles to profl. jours. Home: 413 Evans St Missoula MT 59801. *For a complete life one needs a job, a home, a love, a friend, and an enemy. My "enemies" are injustice, war, poverty, illness, and suffering, not people. Make your existence as meaningful as possible. Enjoy life fully, and when it comes time to leave, have no fear or regrets. Seek to leave this world a little better off because you lived. These are my values. Would that I were mature enough always to live up to them.*

WATKINS, JOHN PIERCE, coll. pres.; b. Brownsville, Pa., Mar. 19, 1931; s. John Britton and Gwendolyn (Pierce) W.; B.S. in Edn., Calif. (Pa.) State Coll., 1953; M.A., W.Va. U., 1955; Ph.D., U. Pitts., 1964; m. Carole Ann Ruch, Sept. 7, 1957; children—John G.W., Jennifer A. Tchr. public schs., Pitts., 1953-57; prof. English, Calif. (Pa.) State Coll., 1957-73, chmn. dept. English, 1967, v.p. acad. affairs, 1973-77, pres., 1977—; dir. Atlas Corp. Bd. dirs. Monongahela Valley YMCA, Monongahela Valley Progress Council, Monongahela Valley United Way. Danforth fellow. Mem. Am. Assn. State Colls. and Univs., Pa. Commn. State Coll. and Univ. Presidents, Pa. Assn. Colls. and Univs. Clubs: Lions, Elks. Home: 200 College Ave California PA 15419 Office: Calif State Coll California PA 15419

WATKINS, LLOYD IRION, univ. pres.; b. Cape Girardeau, Mo., Aug. 29, 1928; s. Herman Lloyd and Lydia Mina (Irion) W.; B.Ed., Southeast Mo. State U., 1949; M.S., U. Wis., 1951, Ph.D., 1954; D.H., U. Dubuque, 1974; m. Mary Ellen Caudle, Aug. 14, 1949; children—John Lloyd, Joseph William, Robert Lawrence. Tchr. Jackson (Mo.) High Sch., 1948-50; asst. prof. Moorhead State Coll., 1954-56; asso. prof., asst. to academic v.p. Ohio U., 1956-66; exec. v.p. Ida. State U., 1966-69; pres. Ia. Assn. Pvt. Colls. and Univs. Des Moines, 1969-73; pres. West Tex. State U., 1973-77, Ill. State U., Normal, 1977—; dir. Bloomington Fed. Savs. and Loan Assn. Bd. dirs. Ill. State U. Found.; trustee Lincoln Acad. Recipient Baker grant for Research, Ohio U., 1963, Alumni Merit award Mo. State U., 1978. Mem. McLean County Assn. Commerce and Industry (dir.), Am. Assn. State Colls. and Univs., Speech Communication Assn., Kappa Delta Pi, Phi Delta Kappa, Phi Alpha Theta, Alpha Kappa Psi. Presbyterian. Clubs: Rotary (Normal). Contbr. articles to profl. jours. Home: 1000 W Gregory St Normal IL 61761 Office: Office of Pres Ill State U Normal IL 61761. *Any success I may have achieved has been made possible by the patience and assistance of others. I had parents who encouraged and supported me, and I have been blessed with a helpful and understanding wife and family. The list of those who have helped me along the way is too long to give—they know who they are and that I am grateful. We do not achieve alone! I hope I can help others as they have helped me.*

WATKINS, RALPH JAMES, economist; b. San Marcos, Tex., Dec. 31, 1896; s. Calvert and Martha (Smith) W.; B.B.A., U. Tex., 1921, A.B., 1922, postgrad. Universidad Nacional de Mexico, summer 1921; M.S., Columbia, 1924, Ph.D., 1927; m. Willye Ward, June 20, 1918 (dec. July 1979); children—Calvert Ward, John William James. Instr. bus. adminstrn. U. Tex., 1924-25, prof. statistics, statistician Bur. Bus. Research, 1927-28; asst. prof. statis. research Bur. Bus. Research, Ohio State U., 1925-27, asso. prof. 1928-29; mem. research staff Nat. Bur. Econ. Research, N.Y.C., 1929-30; dir. Bur. Bus. Research, prof. statistics U. Pitts, 1930-38; asst. adminstr. wage and hour div. Dept. Labor, 1939; econ. adviser Nat. Resources Planning Bd., Exec. Office Pres., 1939-40, asst. dir. 1940-43; chief lend-lease div. civil affairs sect. Allied Force Hdqrs., Algiers, 1943-44; econ. advisor WPB, 1944; dir. marketing and research div. Dun & Bradstreet, Inc., 1944-48. dir. research, 1948-57; dir. econ. studies Brookings Instn., 1957-62; v.p. Surveys & Research Corp., 1962-71, project dir. successor firm Exotech Systems, Inc., 1971-72, sr. asso., 1972—. Lectr. econs. Columbia, 1947-56; Barbara Weinstock lectr. U. Cal. at Berkeley, 1951; spl. cons. sec. army, 1950-52, spl. mission to Japan and Korea on politico-mil. policy, 1952; politico-mil. adviser to Gen. Van Fleet Presdl. Mission, Japan, Korea, Taiwan, Philippines, 1954; chmn. adv. com. on statis. policy Office Mgmt. and Budget, 1956-72; dir. Social Sci. Research Council, 1955-58; dir. Kobe-Nagoya Expressway Survey, Japanese Ministry Constrn., 1956; chmn. adv. panel for econ. and statis. studies of sci. and tech. NSF, 1961-66; dir. or condr. fgn. econ. surveys in Vietnam, 1960-63, Taiwan, 1961, Mexico and Ecuador, 1963, Tunisia, 1964, Malawi, 1965; sr. mem. World Bank team with Indian Planning Commn., Calcutta, 1965-67; study adviser Sarabhai Operations Research Group, Baroda, India, 1968-71; team leader state planning program Ford Found., also sr. cons. Indian Planning Commn., New Delhi, 1969-71; project dir. farm mechanization project Republic Korea, 1971-72; economist Tippetts-Abbett-McCarthy-Stratton on Egyptian reconstrn. and devel. program, Cairo, 1975-79; guest lectr. Internat. Devel. Center, Japan, Tokyo, 1976. Served as 1st sgt. U.S. Army, 1918-19; AEF in France. Decorated 3d class Order of Sacred Treasure (Japan). Fellow Am. Statis Assn. (dir. 1951-53, pres. 1955); mem. Am. Econ. Assn., Royal Econ. Soc. Mason. Clubs: Cosmos, National Economists. (Washington). Home: 2908 R St NW Washington DC 20007 (summer) RFD Passumpsic VT 05861

WATKINS, REYNOLD KING, educator; b. Garland, Utah, Jan. 15, 1920; s. George Reynold and Rhoda Evaline (King) W.; B.S. in Civil Engring., U. Utah, 1944; M.S. in Structural Engring., Mass. Inst. Tech., 1947; Ph.D. in Soil Engring. and Applied Mechanics, Iowa State U., 1957; m. Annie Elaine Haymore, Dec. 21, 1944; children—Adonna (Mrs. Ronald L. Schow), Elizabeth (Mrs. Noel C. Gill), Susan, Glen Reynold, Phyllis (Mrs. Kim Leavitt), Wayne Haymore, Nadine (Mrs. Boyd F. Edwards), Elaine, Kaye, Aldon Tanner, Paula. Faculty, Utah State U., 1947—, prof. mech. engring., 1958—, head dept. 1959-70, asso. dir. engring. expt. sta., 1970-75. Cons. in field, 1958—. Chmn. coms. culverts and buried structures Hwy. Research Bd., 1959-70; cons. pavement and soils div. Waterways Expt. Sta., 1962-77; sec.-treas. Western Admixture Co. Served to comdr. USNR, World War II. Recipient award for outstanding paper, distbn. div. Am. Water Works Assn. Mem. Ch. Jesus Christ Latter-day Day Saints (pres. Utah State U. 2d Second Stake 1967-73). Home: 1236 E 1900 North St Logan UT 84321. *The greatest satisfaction is found in doing for others what they want but cannot do for themselves. This requires special skills that may be found through education. But caution-as one gains special skills he also gains power with which he is prone to manipulate others.*

WATKINS, ROBERT DORSEY, judge; b. Balt., Sept. 27, 1900; s. Joseph Marion and Harriett Isabelle (Strong) W.; A.B., Johns Hopkins, 1922, Ph.D., 1925; LL.B., U. Md., 1925; m. Marion Turner, July 1, 1933; 1 dau., Eileen Roberta Dorsey. Admitted to Md. bar, 1925, since practiced in Balt. Instr. law sch. U. Md., 1925-68; instr. comml. law Johns Hopkins, 1926-55; U.S. dist. judge Dist. of Md., 1955—. Fellow Am. Coll. Trial Lawyers; mem. Am., Md., Balt. (pres. 1948-49); bar assns., Order of Coif, Phi Beta Kappa, Omicron Delta Kappa. Author: The State as a Party Litigant, 1925. Home: 11 S Belle Grove Rd Baltimore MD 21228 Office: US Ct House Baltimore MD 21201

WATKINS, STEPHEN EDWARD, accountant; b. Oklahoma City, Sept. 1, 1922; s. Ralph Bushnell and Jane (Howell) W.; B.B.A., U. N.Mex., 1944; m. Suzanne Fowler, Aug. 16, 1976; children—Elizabeth Ann Watkins Racicot, Stephen Edward. Jr. accountant firm Peat, Marwick, Mitchell & Co., Albuquerque, 1944-62, mgr. office, Santa Fe, 1962-67; v.p., treas. New Mexican, Santa Fe, 1967-70, pres., gen. mgr., 1970-78, also dir.; now practice accounting; dir. El Crepusculo, Inc., El Nuevo Mexicano, Inc. vice pres. Orch. of Santa Fe, Robert Moody Found. C.P.A., N.Mex. Mem. N.Mex. Soc. C.P.A.'s, Am. Inst. C.P.A.'s, S.A.R. Home: 1325 Don Gaspar St Santa Fe NM 87501 Office: 223 E Palace St Santa Fe NM 87501

WATKINS, THOMAS PRESCOTT, life ins. co. exec.; b. Youngstown, Ohio, Aug. 23, 1917; s. Thomas Webb and Carlena (Prescott) W.; A.B., Harvard U., 1939; m. Anne Wright, Aug. 11, 1945; children—Thomas, Elizabeth. With John Hancock Mut. Life Ins. Co., Boston, 1945—, dir. field adminstrn., 1967-69, 2d v.p., 1969-72, v.p., 1972—; dir. Sharon Corp. Bank (Mass.). Mem. Sharon Sch. Com., 1953-63; mem. Sharon Housing Authority, 1977—; mem. sch. com. Southeastern Regional Vocat. Sch., 1961-64. Served to maj., USAAF, 1942-45. Mem. Nat. Assn. Life Underwriters. Republican. Congregationalist.

WATKINS, WESLEY WADE, congressman; b. DeQueen, Ark., Dec. 15, 1938; s. L. V. and Mary J. Watkins; B.S., Okla. State U., 1960, M.S., 1961; m. Elizabeth Lou Rogers, June 9, 1963; children—Sally, Martha, Wade. With Dept. Agr., Washington, 1963; asst. dir. admissions Okla. State U., 1963-66; exec. dir. Kiamichi Econ. Devel. Dist. of Okla., 1966-68; residential constrn. bus., 1968-76; mem. Okla. Senate, 1975-76; mem. 95th and 96th Congresses from Okla.; pres. Higher Edn. Alumni Council of Okla.; Okla. chmn. Nat. Future Farmers Am. Found.; mem. Okla. Health Planning Council. Pres. Ada (Okla). Growth and Devel. Assn. Served with Air N.G., 1961-67. Recipient Okla. 4-H Alumni Recognition award, 1978; Disting. Alumnus award Okla. State U. Alumni Assn., 1978, others; named 1 of 3 Outstanding Young Men in Okla., Okla. Jaycees, 1968. Mem. C. of C. Democrat. Presbyterian. Clubs: Masons, Lions. Home: 521 S Broadway St Ada OK 74820 Office: 424 Cannon Bldg Washington DC 20515

WATLINGTON, JOHN FRANCIS, JR., banker; b. Reidsville, N.C., Mar. 23, 1911; s. John Francis and Frances (Byers) W.; A.B., Washington and Lee U., 1933; m. Margaret Jones, Feb. 22, 1947; children—John Francis III, Anne Wilson. With Wachovia Bank & Trust Co., Winston-Salem, N.C., 1933—, transit clk., asst. cashier, asst. v.p., v.p., sr. v.p., 1933-56, pres., 1956-74, chmn., 1974-76, chmn. exec. com., 1977—, also chmn. Charlotte office, 1946-56; chmn. Wachovia Corp., 1968-76; chmn. exec. com., 1977—; dir. Carolina Power & Co., Piedmont Natural Gas Co., Inc., Piedmont Airlines, Inc., Ga.-Pacific Corp., Mass. Mut. Life Ins. Co., Akzona, Inc. Trustee Tax Found., Union Theol. Sem., Va. Found. for Ind. Colls.; chmn. bd. visitors Bowman Gray Sch. Medicine. Mem. Winston-Salem C. of C. (pres. 1958-59, dir. 1957), N.C. Citizens Assn. (dir.). Presbyn. Home: 2020 Virginia Rd Winston-Salem NC 27104 Office: 301 N Main St Winston-Salem NC 27101

WATREL, ALBERT ADAM, ednl. adminstr.; b. Bklyn.; Dec. 23, 1927; s. John C. and Julia (Rock) W.; B.S., M.S., Syracuse U., 1951, Ph.D., 1961; m. Carole Fabend, June 30, 1956; children—Jane Carole, Susan Elizabeth, Nancy Lee, Robert Howard, William Carl. Asso. v.p. acad. affairs, prof. chemistry, chmn. chem. dept. State U. Coll. at Cortland, N.Y., 1954-68, pres. Slippery Rock State Coll., 1968-77, Dickinson (N.D.) State Coll., 1977—; sci. cons. N.Y. State Dept. Edn., 1960-61. Grantee NSF, 1961, AEC, 1962-63. Mem. Am. Chem. Soc. Am. Council Edn., Am. Assn. Higher Edn., AAAS, AAUP, Nat. Assn. Research Sci. Teaching, N.Y. Acad. Sci., Sigma Xi. Clubs: Masons, Rotary, Elks, Exchange (Cortland, N.Y.). Home: 1071 W 5th St Dickinson ND 58601

WATROUS, JAMES SCALES, educator, artist; b. Winfield, Kans., Aug. 3, 1908; s. Lester Durward and Daisy Belle (Scales) W.; B.S., U. Wis., 1931, M.A., 1933, Ph.D., 1939; student Pa. Acad. Fine Arts, 1931; m. Margaret L. Modie, Aug. 22, 1933; children—Stephen D., Lynne, Tom A. Prof. art history U. Wis., 1941-76, prof. emeritus, 1976—, chmn. dept., 1953-61, Oskar Hagen prof. art history, 1964-76, chmn. div. humanities, 1965-68, chmn. arts council, 1966-68; executed mural Webcrafter Printing Co., Madison, Wis., 1951, mosaic murals Commerce Bldg., U. Wis., 1956-57, archtl. sculpture Wis. Bar Assn., 1957, mosaic mural Engring. Bldg., Washington U., 1958, archtl. sculpture with mosaic Dean Clinic, Madison, 1961, Social Studies Bldg., U. Wis., 1962, mosaic mural Vilas Communications Bldg., U. Wis., 1973, Meml. Library, U. Wis., 1977; paintings and graphics in permanent collections Milw. Art Center, Lawrence U., Kans. State U. Served to lt. USNR, 1943-46. Ford Found. fellow, Italy, 1954-55. Recipient award of merit Wis. chpt. AIA, 1962; Wis. Gov.'s award for arts, 1969. Mem. Mid-Am. Coll. Art Assn. (pres. 1960), Coll. Art Assn. (dir. 1960-64, pres. 1962-64), Nat. Soc. Mural Painters, Midwest Art History Soc. (dir. 1973-75), Phi Beta Kappa (hon.). Author: The Craft of Old-Master Drawings, 1957. Contbr. articles to profl. jours. Home: 2809 Sylvan Ave Madison WI 53705

WATROUS, WILLIAM RUSSELL, trombonist, composer, conductor; b. Middletown, Conn., June 8, 1939; s. Ralph Jarvas and Edna (Little) W.; student pub. schs., New London, Conn. Trombonist with bands of Woody Herman, Quincy Jones, Count Basie; leader own band Manhattan Wildlife Refuge, 1970—; lectr. jazz edn., participant music seminars, brass confs.; bd. dirs. Internat. Trombone Workshop; rec. artist Columbia; composer Fourth Floor Walkup, Dee-Dee, Dirty Dan. Served with USNR, 1956-60. Voted Number One, Trombonist, Downbeat Reader's Poll, 1975, 76, 77, 78, Internat. Critics Poll, 1976, 77. Mem. ASCAP, Am. Fedn. Musicians. Address: care Willard Alexander 660 Madison Ave New York NY 10021*

WATSON, ALFRED MICHAEL, bishop; b. Erie, Pa., July 11, 1907; s. Thomas and Catherine (Fahey) W.; student Gannon Coll., Erie, 1925-27; A.B., St. Mary U., Balt., 1928, A.M., 1930, S.T.B., 1934. Ordained priest Roman Cath. Ch., 1934; prof. Mercyhurst Coll., Gannon Coll., 1934-44; rector St. Peter Cathedral, 1944-69; aux. bishop, Erie, 1965-69, bishop, 1969—. Address: 205 W 9th St Erie PA 16501*

WATSON, ALFRED NELSON, business exec., lawyer; b. Columbus, Ohio, Nov. 22, 1910; s. Alexander Livingston and Adaline (Kershner) W.; A.B., Ohio State U., 1931, M.S., 1932; Ph.D., 1934; LL.B., J.D., Capital U., 1955; Social Sci. Research Council fellow U. London (Eng.). 1937-38; m. Elizabeth Dixon, Sept. 15, 1934; children—Keith Stuart, Andrew Graham. Econ. and statis. research positions U.S. Govt., 1934-39; with Curtis Pub. Co., 1940-52, pres. market research subsidiary Nat. Analysts, Inc., 1946-52; admitted to Ohio bar, 1955, U.S. Supreme Ct. bar, 1958; bus. cons., pvt. practice law, 1953-58; pres. Bus. Investment Corp., Columbus, O., 1955—, also dir.; v.p. Alfred Politz Research, Inc., N.Y.C., 1958-61; v.p. U.S. Rubber Co., N.Y.C., 1961-63; dir. Pathe Industries, Inc., 1963-65, Lionel Corp., 1963-67; dir. ABC Industries, Inc., 1965-67; chmn., chief exec. officer, dir. Living Care Centers, Inc., 1968—. Prof. bus. Columbia Grad. School Bus., 1963-65; cons. WPB, 1941-42; chief statistician SSS, 1942. Pres., bd. dirs. N.Y. Fertility Research Found.; pres. N.Y. chpt. Epilepsy Found. Am., also nat. bd. dirs.; trustee Children's Hosp., Columbus. Served to maj. USAAF, 1943-45. Fellow AAAS, Am. Statis. Assn. (v.p. 1942), Am. Coll. Nursing Home Adminstrs.; mem. Am. Mktg. Assn., Am., N.Y.C. bar assns., Market Research Council N.Y. Contbr. articles to profl. publs. Home: 5700 Karl Rd Columbus OH 43229

WATSON, ARTHEL (DOC), vocalist, guitarist, banjoist, rec. artist; b. Deep Gap, N.C., Mar. 2, 1923; m. Rosa Lee Carlton; 1 son, Merle. Made first appearance at Boone (N.C.) Fiddler's Conf.; rec. for Folkways in 1960's; signed with Vanguard Records, 1964; also recorded for United Artists, Columbia, Poppy, and Verve Folkways labels; at Newport Folk Festival, 1963; albums include: Doc Watson, Doc Watson and Son, Elementary Doc Watson, Essential Doc Watson, Old Time Music at Clarence Ashley's, vols. 1 and 2, Jean Ritchie and Doc Watson at Folk City, Doc Watson and Family, Home Again, In Nashville, On Stage, Southbound, Then and Now, Two Days in November, Doc Watson and the Boys, Memories, Progressive Bluegrass and other Instrumentals. Office: care Manny Greenhill Mgmt 1671 Appian Way Santa Monica CA 90401*

WATSON, ARTHEL LANE (DOC), singer, guitarist; b. Deep Gap, N.C., Mar. 3, 1923; s. General Dixon and Annie (Greene) W.; ed. Morehead (N.C.) Sch. for Blind; hon. doctorate folk art Appalachian State U., 1973; m. Rosa Lee Carlton, June 8, 1946; children—Eddy Merle, Nancy Ellen. Performed with various bands, N.C., Tenn.; with Clarence (Tom) Ashley's Bands, 1960-62; soloist maj. U.S. folk festivals; tour Dept. State, Africa; appeared maj. Am. cities; rec. artist United Artists Records; recs. include Doc Watson & the Boys; Memories Rd. Recipient Grammy award for best ethnic or traditional rec., 1973, 74. Home: Route 1 Box 34 Deep Gap NC 28618 Office: care Folklore Prodns 1671 Appian Way Santa Monica CA 90401*

WATSON, ARTHUR ALLEN, broadcasting co. exec.; b. Bklyn., May 4, 1930; s, Arthur Martin and Marie (Scholl) W.; B.S., Fordham U. Sch. Bus., 1952; L.H.D. (hon.), St. John's U., 1978; m. Maryalesia Breslin, June 13, 1953; children—Arthur Allen, Keith, Lisa, Scott. With NBC, Inc., N.Y.C., 1956—, exec. v.p., gen. mgr. Sta. WNBC-TV, 1971-76, exec. v.p. TV Stas. Div., 1976-79, exec. v.p. NBC-TV Network, 1979, pres. NBC Sports, 1979—. Served to lt. (j.g.) USN, 1952-54. Named Man of Year, Fordham U. Sch. Bus., 1970. Mem. Advt. Council (dir. 1970—), Internat. Radio and TV Soc. (dir. 1974—), TV Bur. Advt. (dir. and mem. exec. com. 1973-79, sec.-treas. 1973-78), Catholic Apostolate of Radio, TV and Advt., Bedside Network (bd. govs.). Club: Ridgewood Country. Home: 70 Twin Brooks Rd Saddle River NJ 07458 Office: 30 Rockefeller Plaza New York NY 10020

WATSON, ARTHUR RICHARD, zoo dir.; b. Cleve., June 25, 1915; s. George Henry and Martha Helen (Ratensperger) W.; student Cleve. Coll., Western Res. U., 1940-46; m. Marybeth Wiemer Anderson, Nov. 2, 1967; 1 dau. by previous marriage, Lois Ruth Watson Ferber. Asst. to dir. Cleve. Zoo, 1942-48; dir. Balt. Zoo, 1948-79, emeritus, 1979—; master ceremonies, producer TV program This Is Your Zoo, 1949-59, 71-72, radio zoo program, 1966-76; incorporator, trustee Wild Animal Propagation Trust; expdns. to Africa, 1954, 66. Bd. mem.-at-large local Boy Scouts Am., 1976. Recipient McCormick award McCormick & Co., Inc., 1949; certificate of merit TV Guide, 1953; Notable Service award Advt. Club Balt., 1954; commendation Am. Legion, 1958, 68. Mem. Am. Assn. Zool. Parks and Acquariums, Balt. Zool. Soc., Audubon Soc., Sierra Club, Balt. Pub. Relations Council, St. George's Soc. Balt., Timber Ridge Bassets Club, Six Napoleons. Unitarian. Clubs: Order DeMolay (past chpt. master; Hats Off award 1956, Meritorious Service award 1956); Md. Sportsmen's Luncheon (pres. 1977-78). Home: 4700 Forest Park Ave Baltimore MD 21207 Office: Balt Zoo Druid Hill Park Baltimore MD 21217

WATSON, BARBARA M., lawyer; b. N.Y.C., Nov. 5; d. James S. and Violet (Lopez) W.; A.B., Barnard Coll., 1943; LL.B., N.Y. Law Sch., 1962; LL.D., U. Md.; L.H.D., Mt. St. Mary Coll. Admitted to N.Y. bar, 1962; atty. N.Y.C. Bd. Statutory Rev., 1962-63; asst. atty. law dept. Office Corp. Counsel, N.Y.C., 1963-64; exec. dir. N.Y.C. Commn. to UN, 1964-66; spl. asst. to dep. under sec. state for adminstrn., 1966; dep. adminstr. Bur. Security and Consular Affairs, State Dept., 1966-67, acting adminstr., 1967-68, adminstr., 1968-74, asst. sec. state, 1977—; pvt. practice law, 1975-76; mem. ex-officio women's adv. bd. Office Econ. Opportunity. Bd. dirs. Wolf Trap Found. for Performing Arts, Mus. African Art, Washington, Greater Washington Ednl. Telecommunications Assn.; trustee Fed. Women's Award, Barnard Coll. Recipient Hadassah Myrtle Wreath Achievement award, 1968, Am. Caribbean Scholarship Fund Inc. award, 1969, Service award Women's Div. United Hias, 1970, Service award United Seamen, 1970, award of merit Internat. Aviation Club, Washington, 1971, Black Women's Distinguished Service award Nat. Council Negro Women, Inc., 1971, Woman of Year award Deliverance Evangelistic Center, Inc., 1971, certificate of Recognition Washington Urban League, 1971, Rev. Hirsch Masliansky award, 1972, Am. Immigration and Citizenship Conf. award, 1972, Jr. Citizens Corps Achievement award, 1972, Woman of Yr. award State Beauty Culturalist Assn., 1973, Luther I. Replogle award State Dept., 1974; decorated Nat. Order Ivory Coast Republic, 1973; Internat. Consular Acad. fellow, 1971. Mem. N.Y. County Lawyers Assn., Am. Bar Assn., Fed. Women's Bar Assn., Assn. Am. Fgn. Service Women, Internat. Women's Lawyers Assn., Urban League Guild, Fed. Women's Assn., Delta Sigma Theta (hon., Social Action award 1974). Clubs: Women's, Cosmopolitan (N.Y.C.); Internat. (Washington); Business and Professional Women's. Home: 2521 Queen Anne's Ln NW Washington DC 20037

WATSON, C. GORDON, dentist; b. Rexburg, Idaho, July 2, 1921; grad. Ricks Coll., Rexburg, Brigham Young U.; D.D.S., Northwestern U., 1946; postgrad. U. Chgo., U. Santa Clara; married; 3 sons. Formerly practiced dentistry, San Diego; exec. dir. So. Calif. Dental Assn., 1965-69; exec. dir. Am. Dental Assn., 1970-78; pvt. practice dentistry, Palm Springs, Calif., 1978—. Served with Dental Corps, USNR, 1946-48; capt. Res. Recipient Award of Merit, Northwestern U. Alumni Assn., 1972. Mem. Am., Internat. colls. dentists, Nat. Acad. of Scis. (Inst. of Medicine), Am. Soc. Assn. Execs. (dir. 1969-73; named Certified Assn. Exec. 1971; key award 1972), Am. Pub. Health Assn., Am. Assn. Dental Editors, Alpha Omega, Omicron Kappa Upsilon, Xi Psi Phi (life). Home: 3 Fordham Ct Rancho Mirage CA 92270

WATSON, CATHERINE ELAINE, journalist; b. Mpls., Feb. 9, 1944; d. Richard Edward and LaVonne (Slater) Watson; B.A. in Journalism, U. Minn., 1967; M.A. in Teaching, Coll. of St. Thomas, 1971. Reporter, Mpls. Tribune, 1966-72, editor Picture mag., 1972-78; editor Tribune Travel/Adventure, 1978—. Recipient Minn. School Bell award for edn. writing NEA, 1968, 69; Newspaper Mag. Picture Editor's award Pictures of Year Competition, Nat. Press Photographers Assn. and U. Mo. Sch. Journalism, 1974, 75. Mem. Am. Newspaper Guild, Phi Beta Kappa, Kappa Tau Alpha, Alpha Omicron Pi. Author film scripts: This is Courage for Minn. Soc. Crippled Children and Adults, 1967; How Much Do You Care promotional film for Twin Cities United Fund, 1970. Contbr. articles to ednl. and historic preservation mags. Office: 425 Portland Ave Minneapolis MN 55488

WATSON, CLARENCE JOSEPH, c. of c. exec.; b. Robstown, Tex., Mar. 7, 1913; s. Russell Nathaniel and Inez Lucille (Emery) W.; student Southwestern U., 1929-32; B.A., U. Tex., Austin, 1935, M.A., 1937; m. Lou Marion Grace, Oct. 15, 1943; 1 son, Joseph Steven. Prin., Moran (Tex.) High Sch., 1935-37; supt. Moran pub. schs., 1937-41; dept. mgr. Ft. Worth C. of C., 1946-55, asst. gen. mgr., 1955-60; exec. v.p. Corpus Christi (Tex.) C. of C., 1960—. Served to lt. comdr. USNR, 1942-46. Mem. C. of C. Mgrs. and Secs. Assn. S.Tex. (pres. 1964-65), Tex. C. of C. Mgrs. Assn. (pres. 1969-70), Am. C. of C. Execs. Rotarian. Home: 317 Cape Cod St Corpus Christi TX 78412 Office: 1201 N Shoreline St Corpus Christi TX 78403

WATSON, DENNIS WALLACE, educator; b. Morpeth, Ont., Can., Apr. 29, 1914; s. William and Sarah (Verity) W.; came to U.S., 1938, naturalized 1946; B.S.A., U. Toronto, 1934; M.S., Dalhousie U., 1937; Ph.D., U. Wis., 1941; m. Alicemay Whittier, June 15, 1941; children—Catherine W., William V. Research asso. U. Wis., 1942, asst. prof., 1946-49; vis. investigator Rockefeller Inst., 1942; investigator Connaught Lab. for Med. Research U. Toronto, 1942-44; asso. prof., prof. head dept. microbiology U. Minn., Mpls., 1949—; vis. prof. Med. Sch. U. Wash., 1950; mem. Commn. Immunization Armed Forces Epidemiology Bd., 1946-59; mem. bd. sci. counselors, div. biol. standards NIH, 1957-59, mem. allergy and immunology study sect., 1954-58; chmn. tgn. grant com. Inst. Allergy and Infectious Diseases, 1964, mem. adv. council, 1967-71; mem. microbiology panel Office Naval Research, 1963-66. Vice chmn. Am. Soc. for Microbiology Found., 1973; bd. dirs. Nat. Found. Infectious Diseases, 1976-79. Served with AUS, 1944-46. Recipient USPHS Research Career award, 1962-64. Spl. research fellow USPHS, 1960-61. Mem. Am. Assn. Immunologists, Am. Chem. Soc., AAAS, Am. Acad. Microbiology (vice chmn. bd. govs. 1967), Am. Soc. for Microbiology (pres. 1969, v.p. Found. 1972-73), Soc. Exptl. Biology and Medicine (council 1977-79, pres. 1976-77), Sigma Xi, Phi Zeta. Editorial bd. Infection and Immunity, 1971-72; editorial cons. Medcom Faculty Medicine, 1973—. Home: 2106 Hendon Ave St Paul MN 55108 Office: Dept Microbiology U Minn Hosp Minneapolis MN 55455

WATSON, DONALD N., forest industry co. exec.; b. Winnipeg, Man., Can., 1921; grad. St. James Coll. Pres., chmn., chief exec. officer Canadian Cellulose Ltd.; dir. Canadair Ltd., Ins. Corp. B.C., B.C. Ry., B.C. Cellulose Co. Ltd., Canadair Ltd. Bd. dirs. Can. Aviation Hall of Fame. Decorated companion Order of Icarus; companion Order of Flight; Order St. Lazarus of Jerusalem; brotherhood of Silver Wings; mem. Order of Polaris. Mem. Air Transp. Assn. Can. (hon.; dir., life mem.). Clubs: Scottish Rite; Masons. Office: 1200-1111 W Hastings St Vancouver BC V6E 2K2 Canada*

WATSON, DONALD STEVENSON, educator; b. Greenwood, B.C., Can., Oct. 28, 1909; s. James Livingstone and Roberta (Stevenson) W.; B.A. U. B.C., 1930; Ph.D., U. Calif. at Berkeley, 1935; m. Liselotte Bunge, Oct. 4, 1935; children—Margot (Mrs. Thomas A. Zener), Wendy. Came to the U.S., 1930, naturalized, 1938. Teaching asst. U. B.C., 1929-30, U. Calif. at Berkeley 1930-33; apptd. to faculty George Washington U., 1935—, prof. econs., 1948—, exec. head dept., 1945-51, 56-60, coordinator research project for USAF, 1951-52, instrn. program for USAF, 1954-56; cons. Operations Research Office, 1950-60, also govt. agys., trade assns., bus. firms; vis. prof. U. Hawaii, summer 1964; dir. research project for NASA, 1963-66. Author: Economic Policy; Business and Government, 1960, Spanish edit., 1965; (with Burns and Neal) Modern Economics, 2d edit., 1953; (with Burns) Government Spending and Economic Expansion, 1940; Price Theory and Its Uses, 1963, Indian edit., 1967, Taiwan edit., 1968, Philippines edit., 1971, Tamil edit., 1974, Portuguese and Spanish edits., 1976, (with Holman) 4th edit., 1977; (with Holman) evaluation of NASA's Patent Policies, 1966; also articles in profl. jours. Editor Price Theory in Action, 1965, 3d edit., 1973. Home: 1850 Finn Hall Rd Port Angeles WA 98362

WATSON, EDDY MERLE, guitarist; b. Deep Gap, N.C., Feb. 8, 1949; s. Arthel Lane (Doc) and Rosa Lee (Carlton) W.; grad. pub. schs.; m. Geneva Sara Greene, Jan. 15, 1966; children—Richard, Karen. Guitarist, appearances include Newport Folk Festival, 1964, numerous concerts; rec. artist Vanguard and United Artists Recs. Office: care Folklore Prodns 1671 Appian Way Santa Monica CA 90401

WATSON, EDWIN F., social welfare agy. exec.; b. Togo, Sask., Can., Jan. 28, 1927; s. Edwin Jay and Ellen (Allbright) W.; B.A., United Coll., U. Man. (Can.), 1948; B.S.W., U. B.C. (Can.), 1949, M.S.W., 1955; m. Nettie Isabelle Proven, Apr. 30, 1955; 1 son, David Mark. Social worker and dist. supr. B.C. Dept. Health and Welfare, 1949-56; exec. sec. family and child welfare div. Community Chest and Councils, Vancouver, B.C., 1956-60; exec. sec. Commn. on Edn. and Personnel, Can. Welfare Council, Ottawa, Ont., 1960-66; exec. dir. Family Service Assn. Met. Toronto (Ont.), 1966-74; exec. dir. Children's Aid Soc. Met. Toronto, 1974-78; exec. dir. Child Welfare League Am., Inc., N.Y.C., 1978—; bd. dirs. Internat. Union for Child Welfare, Council on Social Work Edn., Nat. Assembly. Mem. Vanier Inst. of Family (past dir.), Canadian Council Social Devel. (past dir.), Child and Youth Centered Info. System (chmn.). Contbr. numerous articles to profl. jours. Home: 10 Waterside Plaza New York NY 10010 Office: 67 Irving Pl New York NY 10003

WATSON, GEOFFREY STUART, educator; b. Bendigo, Victoria, Australia, Dec. 3, 1921; B.A. with honors (Dixon research scholar) U. Melbourne, 1942; postgrad. Inst. Statistics, N.C. State Coll., 1947-49, Ph.D., 1952, D.Sc., 1967; m. Shirley Elwyn Jennings, 1953; children—Michael Geoffrey, Catharine Helena, Rebecca Sarah, Madeleine Claire. Research officer aerodynamics sect., div. aero. Commonwealth Sci. and Indsl. Research Orgn., 1943; tutor math. Trinity Coll., Melbourne U., 1944-47; tutor, lectr. math. U. Melbourne, 1944-47, sr. lectr. dept. statistics, 1951-54, acting head dept., 1952; research officer dept. applied econs. U. Cambridge (Eng.), 1949-51; sr. fellow dept. statistics Australian Nat. U., Canberra, 1955-58; vis. univs. in Eng., 1958; vis. prof. N.C. State Coll., 1958, 59, Rockefeller U., Utah U., 1976-77; research asso. dept. math. Princeton, 1958-59; asso. prof. dept. math. U. Toronto, 1959-62; cons. Ontario (Can.) Research Found., 1959-62; cons. Research Triangle Inst., Durham, N.C. 1960-62; prof. math. statistics, dept. statistics, prof. dept. biostatistics Johns Hopkins, 1962-70, chmn. dept. statistics, 1966-70; prof. Princeton U., 1970—, chmn. dept. statistics, 1970-79. Asso. editor statis. series John Wiley & Sons, Inc., N.Y., 1964—. Served as maj. Operations Research Sect., Royal Australian Army, 1953-58. NIH spl. fellow U. Pavia (Italy), 1968-69; Guggenheim fellow, 1976-77. Fellow Internat. Statis. Inst., Inst. Math Statistics, Royal Statis. Soc., AAAS, Am. Statis. Assn.; mem. Biometrics Soc. Contbr. numerous articles to profl. publs. Home: 24 Maclean Circle Princeton NJ 08540

WATSON, GEORGE HENRY, broadcast exec., journalist; b. Birmingham, Ala., July 27, 1936; s. George Henry and Grace Elizabeth (Carr) W.; B.A., Harvard U., 1959; M.S., Columbia U., 1960; m. Ellen Havican Bradley, July 13, 1979. Reporter, Washington Post, 1960-61; corr. ABC News, 1962-75, Moscow bur. chief, 1966-69, London bur. chief, 1969-75, v.p., Washington bur. chief, 1976—. Served with U.S. Army, 1958. Mem. Radio Television News Dirs. Assn., Soc. Profl. Journalists, Nat. Press Club, Overseas Press Club (award for best television documentary, 1971, citation for excellence 1974), Washington Press Club. Club: Fed. City. Office: ABC News 1124 Connecticut Ave NW Washington DC 20036

WATSON, GEORGE HENRY, coll. pres.; b. Chrisman, Ill., Sept. 29, 1915; s. P.M. and Margaret E. (Moore) W.; A.B., Miami U., Oxford, O., 1936; M.A., U. Ill., 1937; Ph.D., U. Chgo., 1942; m. Elizabeth Grill, July 18, 1937; children—Sara Elizabeth, Jean Margaret, John Woolman, Carol Ruth. Fellow Social Sci. Research Council, 1936-38; instr. So. Ill. Normal, 1939-41; research dir. Fedn. Tax Adminstrs., 1941-42, acting exec. dir., 1942-44, exec. dir., 1944-45; with Civilian Pub. Service, 1945-46; asso. prof. Roosevelt U., 1946-48, prof., 1948-72, chmn. dept. polit. sci., 1946-57, dean students, 1957-67, dir. grad. program pub. adminstrn., 1963-67, dean Coll. Arts and Scis., 1967-71; moderator Friends World Coll., Huntington, N.Y., 1972—; faculty mem. numerous ednl. TV series; faculty fellow Fund for Advancement Edn., Ford Found., 1953-54; lectr. Northwestern U., 1955-56; cons. U.S. Adv. Commn. on Intergovernmental Relations, 1970—; mem., cons. numerous govtl. commns. Chmn. Ind. Voters Ill., 1962-65, Chgo. regional office Am. Friends Service Com., 1969-72. Mem. Am. Soc. Pub. Adminstrn. (pres. Chgo. chpt. 1967-70, pres. Central States conf. 1970-71), Am. Assn. for Higher Edn., Phi Beta Kappa. Mem. Soc. of Friends. Contbr. to profl. publs. Home: Friends World Coll Plover Ln Lloyd Harbor Huntington NY 11743

WATSON, GEORGE NELSON, cons. actuary; b. Toronto, Ont., Can., Oct. 21, 1914; s. Harold and Alice Florence (Elliott) W.; B.A., U. Toronto, 1936; m. Hylda Hayhurst, Dec. 4, 1937; 1 son, Cameron Nelson. With Crown Life Ins. Co., Toronto, 1936—, group v.p., 1957-64, v.p., dir. group ins., 1964-71, sr. v.p., 1971-76; pres. G.N. Watson Ltd., 1977—, Fraser Watson Actuaries Ltd. (Can.); dir. Crown Life Pensions Ltd., Crown Life Assurance Co. Ltd., Kelsey Nat. Corp., Buckley & Kelling Computer Consultants, Ltd.; mem. Met. Toronto Bd. Trade. Fellow Soc. Actuaries, Canadian Inst. Actuaries; mem. Am. Acad. Actuaries, Internat. Congress Actuaries. Clubs: Ontario (Toronto). Author: The Elements of Group Insurance. Home: Rural Route 1 Palgrave ON Canada Office: 203 1 Eva Rd Etobicoke ON M9C 4Z5 Canada

WATSON, GLENN R., lawyer; b. Okla., May 2, 1917; s. Albert Thomas and Ethel (Riddle) W.; student East Central State Okla., 1933-36; LL.B., Okla. U., 1939; m. Dorothy Ann Mosiman, Feb. 25, 1945; 1 dau., Carol Ann. Admitted to Okla. bar, 1939, Cal. bar, 1946; pvt. practice law, Okla., 1939-41; partner firm Richards, Watson, Dreyfuss & Gershon, Los Angeles, 1946—; city atty. Industry, Calif., 1958-65, 78—, Commerce, Calif., 1960-61, Cerritos, Calif., 1956-64, Victorville, Calif., 1962-63, Carson, Calif., 1968—, Rosemead, Calif., 1960-76, Seal Beach, Calif., 1972-78, South El Monte, Calif., 1976-78, Avalon and Artesia, Calif., 1976—. Served with USNR, 1942-46. Mem. Los Angeles County, Am. bar assns., Am. Judicature Soc., Lawyers Club of Los Angeles (past pres.), La Canada C. of C. (past pres.), Order of Coif, Phi Delta Phi, Delta Chi. Home: 800 W 1st St Los Angeles CA 90012 Office: 333 S Hope St Los Angeles CA 90071

WATSON, JACK H., JR., mem. staff Exec. Office of Pres.; b. El Paso, Tex., Oct. 24, 1938; B.S., Vanderbilt U., 1960; LL.B., Harvard U., 1966; m. Carol Jones; children—Melissa Woodward, Lincoln Hearn; m. 2d, Teena Stern Mohr, July 1, 1977. Admitted to Ga. bar, 1965; asso. firm King & Spalding, Atlanta, 1966-71, partner, 1972-77; asst. to Pres. for intergovtl. affairs and sec. to cabinet, Washington, 1977—. Counsel, Met. Atlanta Commn. Crime and Juvenile Delinquency, 1966-67, chmn. Steering Com. Treatment and Rehab. Chronic Alcoholic Ct. Offenders, 1967-68; mem. Fulton County Mental Health Adv. Com., 1968-70, Citizens Adv. Council Urban Devel., 1970-72; pres. Met. Atlanta Mental Health Assn., 1971-72; chmn. Gov.'s Study Commn. Alcohol, 1971-72, Ga. Alcoholism Adv. Council, 1972; chmn. bd. Ga. Dept. Human Resources, 1972-77. Served as officer USMC. Named One of Atlanta's Five Outstanding Young Men, Jaycees, 1970. Mem. Atlanta Lawyers Club, Am., Atlanta bar assns., State Bar Ga., Phi Beta Kappa, Phi Eta Sigma, Omicron Delta Kappa. Author articles proverty, alcoholism, other health problems. Office: Exec Office of Pres White House 1600 Pennsylvania Ave NW Washington DC 20500

WATSON, JACK MCLAURIN, educator; b. Dillon, S.C., Nov. 22, 1908; s. John Reynolds and Maxie (McLaurin) W.; Mus.B., Cin. Coll. Conservatory Music, 1930, Mus.D. (hon.), 1958; Mus.M., U. So. Calif., 1940; M.A., Columbia U., 1945, Ph.D., 1947; L.H.D., Geneva Coll., 1971; m. Corinne Robertson, Feb. 18, 1937. Profl. musician, singer, 1930-39; instr. Winthrop Coll., 1939-41, asst. prof., 1941-45, asso. prof., 1945-47; asso. prof. N.Y. U., 1947-49; cons. music editor Silver Burdett Co., N.Y.C., 1948-49, adminstrv. music editor, 1949-53; vis. prof. U. So. Calif., 1953; prof. music, chmn. music edn. dept. Ind. U., 1953-62, dir. grad. studies and research, 1962-63; dean Coll. Conservatory of Music, U. Cin., 1963-74, univ. prof. creative and performing arts, 1974-77, dean and univ. prof. emeritus, 1977-78; acting pres. Mannes Coll. Music, 1978-79. Mem. Am., Internat. musicol. socs., AAUP, Bohemians. Author: (with others) Music for Living, 1956; (with wife) A Concise Dictionary of Music, 1965; also numerous articles profl. jours., yearbooks. Adv. music editor Dodd, Mead & Co., N.Y.C., 1957-74; cons. editor, bd. dirs. Princeton Book Co. Home: 68 Pine St Princeton NJ 08540

WATSON, JAMES A., supermarket chain exec.; b. 1919; B.A., U. Minn., 1942; chmn. bd. Red Owl Stores, 1946-72; pres., dir. Gamble Skogmo Inc., 1960-72; v.p.-retail and wholesale ops. George Weston Ltd., 1972-73, now dir.; pres., chief exec. officer Nat. Tea Co., Des Plaines, Ill., 1973—, also chmn. bd., dir.; pres. Watson-Plummer Inc.; dir. K-Tel Internat. Office: Nat Tea Co 9701 W Higgins Rd Des Plaines IL 60018*

WATSON, JAMES DEWEY, educator, molecular biologist; b. Chgo., Apr. 6, 1928; s. James Dewey and Jean (Mitchell) W.; B.S., U. Chgo., 1947, D.Sc., 1961; Ph.D., Ind. U., 1950; D.Sc., 1963; LL.D., U. Notre Dame, 1965; D.Sc., L.I. U., 1970, Adelphi U., 1972, Brandeis U., 1973, Albert Einstein Coll. Medicine, 1974, Hofstra U., 1976; m. Elizabeth Lewis, 1968; children—Rufus Robert, Duncan James. Research fellow NRC, U. Copenhagen, 1950-51; Nat. Found. Infantile Paralysis fellow Cavendish Lab., Cambridge U., 1951-53; sr. research fellow biology Calif. Inst. Tech., 1953-55; asst. prof. biology Harvard, 1955-58, asso. prof., 1958-61, prof., 1961-76; dir. Cold Spring Harbor Lab., 1968—. Hon. fellow Clare Coll., Cambridge U. Recipient (with F. H. C. Crick) John Collins Warren prize Mass. Gen. Hosp., 1959; Eli Lilly award in biochemistry Am. Chem. Soc., 1959; Albert Lasker prize Am. Pub. Health Assn., 1960; (with F.H.C. Crick) Research Corp. prize, 1962; (with F.H.C. Crick and M.H.F. Wilkins) Nobel prize in medicine, 1962. Mem. Nat. Acad. Scis. (Carty medal 1971), Danish Acad. Arts and Scis., Am. Assn. Cancer Research, Am. Acad. Arts and Sci., Am. Soc. Biol. Chemists. Author: Molecular Biology of the Gene, 1965, 2d edit., 1970, 3d edit., 1976; The Double Helix, 1968. Home: Bungtown Rd Cold Spring Harbor NY 11724

WATSON, JAMES EDGAR, cons. engr.; b. Waterloo, Iowa, Aug. 10, 1914; s. George R. and Anna Frances (McGrath) W.; B.S. in Mech. Engring., U. Iowa, 1936; m. Jean Bronson, Oct. 6, 1938; children—Stephen George, Mary Jean (Mrs. David Howard), Nina Patricia (Mrs. Nelson Head), Antoinette. With exptl. labs. Viking Pump Co., 1935; elec. engr. TVA, 1936-47, chief power contracts, 1947-50, asst. dir. power utilization, 1950-52, dir. power utilization, 1952-60, dir. power mktg., 1960-62, asst. mgr. power, 1962-70, mgr. power, 1970-76, sr. adviser power, 1976-77; vice chmn. Project Mgmt. Corp., 1971-77; v.p. So. Comfort Insulation, 1977—; cons. engr., 1977—; cons. P.R. Water Resources Authority, Panama C.Z. Mem. Southeastern regional adv. com. FPC, 1963-70; chmn. Southeastern Electric Reliability Council, 1971; bd. dirs. Nat. Electric Reliability Council; vice chmn. bd., then chmn. bd. Electric Power Research Inst., 1973-76; mem. indsl. adv. com. Def. Electric Power Adminstrn.; mem. U.S. nat. com. Internat. Conf. on Large Elec. Systems; mem. sr. utility tech. adv. panel AEDC. Registered profl. engr., Tenn. Mem. IEEE, Atomic Indsl. Forum (bd.), Argonne Univs. Assn. (rev. com.), Pi Tau Sigma, Tau Beta Pi, Delta Chi. Home: 126 Norvell Dr Signal Mountain TN 37377

WATSON, JAMES LOPEZ, U.S. judge; b. N.Y.C., May 21, 1922; s. James S. and Violet (Lopez) W.; B.A. in Govt., N.Y. U., 1947; LL.B., Bklyn. Law Sch., 1951; m. D'Jaris Hinton Watson, July 14, 1956; children—Norman, Karen, Kris. Admitted to N.Y. bar, 1951; mem. N.Y. Senate from 21st Senatorial Dist., 1954-63; judge Civil Ct. N.Y., 1964-66; acting judge N.Y. State Supreme Ct., 1965; judge U.S. Customs Ct., 1966—. Bd. dirs. N.Y.C. Police Athletic League. Served with inf. AUS, World War II; ETO. Decorated Purple Heeart, Combat Inf. badge. Mem. Am., N.Y. State bar assns., Fed. Bar Council, World Peace Through Law. Home: 676 Riverside Dr New York NY 10031 Office: 1 Federal Plaza New York NY 10007

WATSON, JOHN R., landscape illuminating co. exec.; b. Temple, Tex., Feb. 22, 1922; s. J. Elmer and Florence Catherine (Granger) W.; B.Landscape Architecture, Tex. A. and M. U., 1943, M.Landscape Architecture, 1946; postgrad. Sorbonne, Paris, Biarritz, France, 1945; studied under Andrew Dasberg, Taos, N.Mex., 1954; m. Mary Adele Aspoas, Nov. 2, 1963; children—Suzanne Elizabeth, John Shannon. Lighting designer Gen. Electric Co., Nela Park, Cleve., 1948-52; pres., owner John R. Watson Landscape Illumination, Dallas, Houston, Austin, Tex., New Orleans, Atlanta, Mexico, Can., 1953—. Mem. com. on exterior lighting U.S. nat. com. Commn. Internat. de L'Eclairage. Served with AUS, 1942-45. Recipient Design award Nat. Soc. Interior Designers, 1965, various others. Mem. Illuminating Engring. Soc. Methodist. Mason. Clubs: Brookhollow Golf, T Bar M Racquet (Dallas); Argyle (San Antonio). Contbr. articles to Time, House & Garden, Reader's Digest, Houston Post, Dallas Times Herald, London Mirror, numerous other publs. Home: 4110 Cochran Chapel Rd Dallas TX 75209 Office: 1933 Regal Row Dallas TX 75235

WATSON, K. BERT, gas co. exec.; b. Ranger, Tex., June 22, 1925; s. Max K. and Elizabeth (Slaughter) W.; B.Ch.E., U. Colo., LL.B., 1948; postgrad. Grad. Sch. Bus. Columbia U.; m. Joy Willhoite, Dec. 29, 1947; children—Sandra (Mrs. M. Lewis Browder), Randall, Kenneth, Delk, David. Admitted to Tex. bar, 1948; asst. atty. gen. State of Tex., 1949-52; atty. Amarillo (Tex.) Oil Co., 1952-53; corp. sec., atty. Pioneer Natural Gas Co., Amarillo, 1955-65, dir., 1965—, v.p., gen. counsel, 1965-71, exec. v.p., 1971-73, pres., 1973—; chmn. bd. Pioneer Gas Products Co.; chmn. bd., chief exec. officer Pioneer Corp.; dir. Amarillo Oil Co., Pioneer Nuclear Inc., Pinaga, Pioneer Transmission Corp., Pioneer Prodn. Corp.; mem. exec. com. Water, Inc. Active Boy Scouts Am. Served with USNR, 1942-45. Mem. West Tex., Amarillo chambers commerce, So., Am. (dir.) gas assns., Tex. Tech. Law Sch. Found., Phi Delta Phi, Pi Kappa Alpha. Home: 209 N Shore Dr Lake Tanglewood TX 79105 Office: PO Box 511 Amarillo TX 79163

WATSON, KENNETH DE PENCIER, educator, geologist; b. Vancouver, B.C., Can., July 19, 1915; s. Charles Burton and Winnifred Mary (De Pencier) W.; B.A.Sc., U. B.C., 1937; Ph.D., Princeton, 1940; m. Mary Rita Crotta, Dec. 23, 1941; children—Douglas Lawrence, Rita Ann, Marcia Joan. Came to U.S., 1950, Instr. geology Princeton, 1940-43; asso. mining engr. B.C. Dept. Mines, 1943-46; asso. prof., then prof. geology U. B.C., 1946-50; mem. faculty U. Calif. at Los Angeles, 1950—, prof. geology, 1952—, chmn. dept., 1960—; chief geologist Dome Exploration (Can.) Ltd., 1957-58, cons. geologist, 1947—; dir. Sigma Mines Ltd. Fellow Geol. Soc. Am., Mineral. Soc. Am.; mem. Soc. Econ. Geologists, Canadian Inst. Mining and Metallurgy, Mineral. Assn. Can., Sigma Xi. Home: 14931 Bestor Blvd Pacific Palisades CA 90272 Office: Dept Earth Space Sciences Univ California Los Angeles CA 90024

WATSON, KENNETH MARSHALL, physicist, educator; b. Des Moines, Sept. 7, 1921; s. Louis Erwin and Irene Nellie (Marshall) W.; B.S., Iowa State U., 1943; Ph.D., U. Iowa, 1948; Sc.D. (hon.), U. Ind., 1976; m. Elaine Carol Miller, Mar. 30, 1946; children—Ronald M., Mark Louis. Research engr. Naval Research Lab., Washington, 1943-46; mem. staff Inst. Advanced Study Princeton (N.J.) U., 1948-49; research fellow Lawrence Berkeley (Calif.) Lab., 1949-52, mem. staff, 1957—; asst. prof. physics U. Ind., Bloomington, 1952-54; asso. prof. physics U. Wis., Madison, 1954-57; prof. physics U. Calif., Berkeley, 1957—; dir. Phys. Dynamics Inc.; trustee LaJolla Inst.; cons. Stanford Research Inst.; mem. U.S. Pres's. Sci. Adv. Com. Panels, 1962-71; adviser Nat. Security Council, 1972-75. Author: Collision Theory (with M.L. Goldberger), 1964; (with J. Welch and J. Bond) Atomic Theory of Gas Dynamics, 1966; (with J. Nutall) Topics in Several Particle Dynamics, 1970; (with Flatté, Munk, Dashen) Sound Transmission Through a Fluctuating Ocean, 1979. Home: 2191 Caminito Circulo Norte La Jolla CA 92037 Office: Univ Calif Physics Dept Birge Hall Berkeley CA 94720

WATSON, MAX POWELL, gas co. exec.; b. Marion, La., Sept. 9, 1915; s. Boyd Kite and Minnie (Stewart) W.; B.S. in Mech. and Elec. Engring., La. Poly. Inst., 1936; m. Robbie Laverne Auger, Mar. 12, 1938; children—John Stewart, Max Powell, Janet Laverne. With U.S. C.E., Vicksburg, Miss., 1936-37; with United Gas Pipe Line Co., 1937-59, 68—, v.p., 1968-69, sr. v.p. 1969—, dir., 1960-70; with United Gas Corp., 1959-68, asst. to pres., v.p., 1964-68; v.p., pres., dir. Sea Robin Pipeline Co., 1968-73; v.p. United Offshore Co., 1968-69, sr. v.p., 1969—. Bd. dirs. Community Chest Caddo and Bossier parishes, 1960-63; successively treas., v.p., pres. Jr. Achievement of Shreveport and Bossier City, Inc., 1964-67. Registered profl. engr., La. Mem. La. Engring. Soc., Nat. Soc. Profl. Engrs., Natural Gas Men of Houston (dir.), Tau Beta Pi (life). Methodist (adminstrv. bd. 1970—). Clubs: Shreveport (past sec.-treas., v.p., pres.), Houston. Home: 10206 Briar Dr Houston TX 77042 Office: 700 Milam St Houston TX 77001

WATSON, MILLS, actor; b. Oakland, Calif., July 10, 1940; s. Thomas L. and Myrtle Lucille (Mills) W.; student San Francisco State Coll., 1958-59; A.A. (Acad. scholar), Royal Acad. Dramatic Arts, London, 1965-67; 1 son, Mason. TV debut in Gunsmoke episode, 1967; appeared in over 100 TV shows, including: The Migrants, Amy Prentiss, Supertrain, Gunsmoke; movies include: Dracula's Castle, 1970, Charlie and the Angels, 1971, Midnight Man, 1976, Up in Smoke, 1978; appeared as Dept. Perkins in TV series BJ and the Bear,

NBC, 1978-79, in TV series The Misadventures of Sheriff Lobo, NBC, 1979—. Mem. Screen Actors Guild. Democrat.

WATSON, RAYMOND LESLIE, architect; b. Seattle, Oct. 4, 1926; s. Leslie Alexander and Olive (Lorentzen) W.; B.A., U. Calif. at Berkeley, 1951, M.A., 1953; m. Elsa Constance Coito, Sept. 18, 1954; children—Kathy Ann, Bryan Frederich, Lisa Marie, David John. Architect firm Donald Haines & Assos., San Francisco, 1955-60; mgr. planning The Irvine Co., Newport Beach, Calif., 1960-64, v.p. planning, 1964-66, sr. v.p. land devel., 1966-70, exec. v.p., 1970-73, pres., 1973-77; pres., partner Newport Devel. Co., 1977—; dir. Disney Corp., Pacific Mut. Life Ins. Co. Trustee Occidental Coll. Served with USAAF, 1944-45. Fellow AIA. Home: 2501 Alta Vista Dr Newport Beach CA 92660 Office: 900 Cagney Ln Newport Beach CA 92663

WATSON, ROBERT EARL, controls mfg. co. exec.; b. Cleve., Jan. 28, 1925; s. Earl and Alice Marie (Evans) W.; B.Indsl. Engring., Ohio State U., 1949; postgrad. Harvard U. Sch. Bus., 1967; m. Eileen C. Fulton, Nov. 18, 1950; children—Susan Evans, William Earl, Richard Edward. With Ranco Inc., 1949—, v.p. mfg., then v.p. planning, 1970-74, exec. v.p. N. Am., Columbus, Ohio, 1974-77, exec. v.p. planning, 1977—, dir., 1975—. Served with USN, 1943-46. Recipient Disting. Alumnus award Ohio State U., 1979. Mem. Nat. Elec. Mfrs. Assn. (exec. com. residential controls 1977—), Ohio Mfrs. Assn., Columbus Indsl. Assn. Club: Catawba Island. Office: 701 W 5th Ave Columbus OH 43201

WATSON, ROBERT FLETCHER, physician, educator; b. Charlottesville, Va., Jan. 24, 1910; s. Thomas L. and Adelaide (Stephenson) W.; M.D., U. Va., 1934; m. Frances Helen Donahue, July 12, 1946; children—Margaret Ann, Francis Daniel. Intern, House of Good Samaritan, Boston, 1934, West Med. Service, Mass. Gen. Hosp., Boston, 1935-36; asst. resident N.Y. Hosp., 1936-38, resident, 1938-39, asso. attending physician, 1946-50, attending physician, 1950—; practice medicine, specializing in internal medicine, N.Y.C., 1946—; asst. in medicine Cornell U. Med. Coll., 1936-38, instr., 1938-39, asso. prof., 1946-50, asso. prof. clin. medicine, 1950-61, clin. prof. medicine, 1961-75, emeritus, 1975—; asst. resident physician Hosp. of Rockefeller Inst. for Med. Research, 1939-41, resident physician, 1941-46, asst. sci. staff Rockefeller Inst. for Med. Research, 1939-44, asso. sci. staff, 1944-46; chief-of-service Vincent Astor Diagnostic Service, 1950-75; clin. prof. medicine U. Va., 1975-78. Served from lt. (j.g.) to lt. comdr., M.C., USNR, 1941-46. Mem. numerous profl. orgns. Club: Men's (Pelham, N.Y.). Contbr. articles to profl. jours. Home: Westover Hills Route 2 Box 18 Charlottesville VA 22901

WATSON, ROBERT TANNER, phys. scientist; b. Columbus, Ohio, Sept. 25, 1922; s. Rolla Don and Gladys (Tanner) W.; B.A. DePauw U., 1943; Ph.D., Mass. Inst. Tech., 1951; m. Jean Mehlig, Oct. 7, 1944; children—Melinda Jean, Parke Tanner, John Mehlig, Todd Pennell, Kate Ann. With photo products dept. E. I. duPont de Nemours & Co., Inc., Parlin N.J., 1951-55; with electron tube div. RCA, Marion, Ind. 1955-59; with Internat. Tel. & Tel. Corp., 1959-71, v.p., gen. mgr. indsl. labs. div., 1962-63, pres., 1963-71, dep. tech. dir. Aerospace and Def. Group; gen. phys. scientist U.S. Dept. Commerce, 1971—. Mem. Gov.'s Air Pollution Control Bd., 1966-70; Allen County chmn. Ind. Sesquicentennial, 1965; mem. Gov.'s Com. Atomic Energy Installations. Bd. dirs. YMCA of Greater Ft. Wayne and Allen County. Served to lt. USNR, 1943-46; PTO. Mem. Am. Inst. Mgmt. (fellow pres.'s council), Ft. Wayne C. of C. (dir. 1966-68), Allen County-Ft. Wayne Hist. Soc. (Old Fort com.), Am. Phys. Soc., IEEE, Sigma Xi, Phi Eta Sigma, Beta Theta Pi. Presbyterian. Research in x-ray diffraction, radioactive scattering, solid state energy levels, electron emission, magnetic and photog. media, electro-optical, Laser and telecommunication systems. Inventor alpha numeric indicators, cathode ray tube systems. Home: 24 Williams Dr Annapolis MD 21401 Office: 179 Admiral Cochrane Dr Annapolis MD 21401

WATSON, ROBERT WINTHROP, educator, poet; b. Passaic, N.J., Dec. 26, 1925; s. Winthrop and Laura Berdan (Trimble) W.; B.A., Williams Coll., 1946; postgrad. U. Zurich, 1947; M.A., Johns Hopkins, 1950, Ph.D. in English, 1955; m. Elizabeth Ann Rean, Jan. 12, 1952; children—Winthrop, Caroline. Instr. English, Williams Coll., 1946, 47-48, 52-53, Johns Hopkins, 1950-52; mem. faculty U. N.C., Greensboro, 1952—, prof. English, 1963—; vis. poet, prof. English, Calif. State U., Northridge, 1968-69. Swiss-Am. exchange fellow, 1947; grantee Nat. Endowment Arts, 1973; recipient Am. Scholar Poetry prize, 1959; Lit. award Am. Acad. Inst. Arts Letters, 1977. Author: (poems) A Paper Horse, 1962, Advantages of Dark, 1966, Christmas in Las Vegas, 1971, Selected Poems, 1974; (poems) Island of Bones, 1977; (novel) Three Sides of the Mirror, 1966; (novel) Lily Lang, 1977. Home: 527 Highland Ave Greensboro NC 27403

WATSON, ROY, hotel exec.; b. Rochester, Minn., Oct. 22, 1921; s. Roy and Jane (Powers) W.; B.S., Cornell U., 1948; B.A., Dartmouth, 1943; m. June Hope Bandoli, Feb. 6, 1944 (div. Apr. 1956); children—Roy Steven, Michael; m. 2d, Beverly Jane Wilder, Jan., 1957; children—Kimberly Dianne, William Wilder. Apprentice, Kahler Corp., 1935; various capacities Palmer House, Chgo., 1945; asst. instr. Cornell U., 1946-48; mgr. Hotel Winfield Scott, Elizabeth, N.J., 1948-49; dir. personnel Kahler Corp., Rochester, Minn., 1949-50, dir., v.p., 1952-55, pres., gen. mgr., 1955-77, chmn. bd., 1977—; v.p. central div. Internat. Hospitality Advisors, Inc., N.Y.C.; v.p., dir. Ranfranz Funeral Home, Rochester, N.W. Nat. Bank. Bd. dirs. Rochester Meth. Hosp.; past mem. bd. overseers Hanover (N.H.) Inn; pres. Rochester Bd. Park Commrs. Served as lt. USNR, World War II. Mem. Cornell Soc. Hotel Men (past pres.), Am., Northwestern (past pres.), Minn. (past pres.), Internat. (v.p., mem. council) hotel assns., C. of C. (past pres.) Am. Hotel Ednl. Inst. (past pres., trustee), Inter Am. Hotel Assn. (past pres.), Am. Hotel and Motel Assn. (pres. 1964), Am. Legion, VFW. Elk. Mason (Shriner). Republican. Presbyn. (elder). Club: Tavern of N.Y. Author articles on hotel operation. Home: 620 Memorial Pkwy Rochester MN 55901 Office: The Kahler Hotel Rochester MN 55901

WATSON, ROY GARRETT, ret. pres. Christian Sci. Ch.; b. Houston, Dec. 27, 1890; s. Julius Lewis and Nettie May (Phillips) W.; student in So. France, 1902-03; grad. Lawrenceville (N.J.) Acad., 1909; Litt.B., Princeton, 1914; C.S.B., Christian Sci. Bd. Edn., 1940; m. Kathleen Timolat McNutt, Dec. 8, 1956. pres., publisher editor Houston Post, 1919-24; founder Houston Eve. Post; retired from business and traveled, 1924-27; became active in br. church work in Christian Sci., 1915, reader and practitioner, 1931; mem. Christian Science Com. on Publn. for Tex., 1935; became Chrstian Sci. tchr., 1940; treas. The Mother Church, The First Ch. of Christ Scientist, Boston, 1941-73, pres., 1974. Home: Longwood Towers Brookline MA 02146 also Eastern Point Blvd Gloucester MA 01930 also Warwick Hotel Houston TX 77001

WATSON, STERL ARTHUR, JR., judge; b. Hot Springs, Ark., July 11, 1942; s. Sterl Arthur and Pauline (Thrasher) W.; student Harding Coll., 1960-61, N.E. La. State Coll., 1961-62; J.D., U. Ala., 1966; m. Wanda Batt, May 2, 1968; children—Angel Lynn, Clinton Jeremy. Admitted to Ala. bar, 1967, U.S. Supreme Ct. bar, 1970; asst. dist. atty., Huntsville, Ala., 1968-69; chief asst. dist. atty., Huntsville, 1969-72; judge. Gen. Sessions Ct. Madison County, 1972-74; judge 23d Jud. Circuit, Huntsville, 1974—. Pres. Planned Parenthood Assn., 1968-70; mem. steering com. Police Ranger Corps, 1970-71; mem. adv. com. Ala. Youth Leadership Program, 1970-72; mem. legis. adv. com. Ala. Conservancy, 1971-72. Bd. dirs. Huntsville Boys Club, 1972—, Epilepsy Found. Am., Huntsville, 1972-76. Mem. Ch. of Christ. Home: 1313 Big Cove Rd Huntsville AL 35801 Office: Madison County Courthouse Huntsville AL 35801

WATSON, STUART DADE, beverage co. exec.; b. Decatur, Ill., Nov. 6, 1916; s. Dade O. and Lois (Stevens) W.; B.A., DePauw U., 1938: M.B.A., Northwestern U., 1939; grad. advanced mgmt. program, Harvard, 1951; m. Jane Preston, Nov. 23, 1940; children—Beth Ellen Watson Noujaim, Sarah Anne Watson DeCew, Stephen H., Margaret Jane. Asst. dir. advt. Standard Oil Co., Inc., 1939-52; advt. mdse. dir. S.C. Johnson, Racine, Wis., 1952-56; v.p. media, research, mktg. services McCann-Erickson, Inc., 1956-57; exec. v.p. McCann-Marschalk Co., N.Y.C., 1957-59, pres., chmn. bd., 1960-65, Interpub. Inc., 1966; chmn. bd. Heublein, Inc., Farmington, Conn., 1966—, also chmn. exec. com.; dir., bd. trustees Trinity Coll.; chmn. bd. dirs. Inst. of Living; chmn. fin. com. Advt. Council, Inc.; dir. Mohasco Ind., Amsterdam, N.Y., Conn. Bank and Trust Assn., Nashua Corp. (N.H.), Stanley Works, New Britain, Conn., Conn. Mut. Life Ins. Co., Hartford, Harte-Hanks Communications, Inc., San Antonio, Allied Breweries Ltd., London. Served to capt. U.S. Army, 1942-46. Home: 5 Sunny Reach Dr West Hartford CT 06117 Office: Heublein Inc Farmington CT 06032

WATSON, (MURIEL) SUSAN, journalist; b. Detroit, May 19, 1943; d. Horace Herman and Susie Frances (Perry) Holmes; B.A. with honors, U. Mich., 1965; postgrad. Howard U., 1967-69; m. Julius Allen Watson, Dec. 22, 1967; 1 son, Allen Perry. Speech writer U.S. Senator Philip A. Hart, Washington, 1967; reporter Free Press, Detroit, 1968-72; adminstrv. asst. to pres. New Detroit Inc., 1972-74; reporter Detroit Free Press, 1974—. Recipient Merit award UPI, 1974, 76, 1st pl. award, 1978; 1st pl. award Mich. Press Assn., 1978; medallion Detroit Press Club Found., 1978; Hayward Broun award Newspaper Guild Internat., 1979.

WATSON, THOMAS J., JR., ambassador; b. Dayton, Ohio, Jan. 8, 1914; s. Thomas J. and Jeanette (Kittridge) W.; B.A., Brown U., 1937; hon. degrees from following univs.; Brown, Columbia, Harvard, Oxford, Yale, Cath. U. Am., Lafayette, Notre Dame, Pace, R.P.I., Syracuse, U. Colo., Trinity; m. Olive Field Cawley, Dec. 15, 1941; children—Thomas J., Jeanette, Olive, Lucinda, Susan, Helen. With IBM, 1937-40, 46-79, pres., 1952-61, chmn., 1961-71, chmn. exec. com., 1971-79; U.S. ambassador to USSR, 1979—; dir. Mut. Life Ins. Co. N.Y., 1947-59, Bankers Trust Co., 1947-74, Time, Inc., 1958-74, 65-79, Bankers Trust N.Y. Corp., 1965-74, Pan Am. World Airways, 1970-79; mem. Pres.'s Commn. Nat. Goals, 1960-61, Pres.'s Adv. Com. Labor-Mgmt. Policy, 1961-69, Adv. Com. Troop Info. and Edn., Dept. Def., 1962, Pres.'s Task Force on War Against Poverty, 1964-68, Nat. Commn. on Tech., Govt., Automation and Econ. Progress, 1965-66, Pres.'s Commn. on Income Maintenance Programs, 1968-70, Am. Com. on East-West Accord, 1975-78. Pres., Greater N.Y. Councils, Boy Scouts Am., 1953-56, pres. Nat. Council, 1964-68; trustee Brown U., 1947—, vice chancellor, 1979—; trustee Am. Mus. Nat. History, 1955-78, hon. trustee, 1978—; trustee M.I.T., 1957-62, George C. Marshall Research Found., 1958—, Calif. Inst. Tech., 1960-79, Rockefeller Found., 1963-71, John F. Kennedy Library, 1964—, Mystic Seaport, Inc., 1967-69, Inst. Advanced Study, Princeton, 1958-75, World Wildlife Fund, 1974-78, Mayo Found., 1975-79; sr. fellow Woodrow Wilson Nat. Fellowship Found., 1973-79; dir. Alliance to Save Energy; mem. Com. of Ams. for the Canal Treaties, 1977-78. Served to lt. col. USAF, 1940-45. Decorated Air medal; Presdl. medal of Freedom; comdr. Order of Merit, Rep. of Italy; officer Legion of Honor (France); officer Order of Leopold II (Belgium); comdr. Al Mérito por Servicios Distinguídos (Peru); Grand Cross, Equestrian Order of St. Sylvester (Vatican); comdr. Royal Order of Vasa (Sweden); officer Order of So. Cross (Brazil); recipient Silver Antelope, Buffalo, Beaver awards Boy Scouts Am., 1958; Rosenberger medal Brown U., 1968; Gold medal Nat. Inst. Social Scis., 1971; Citation of Merit, Salvation Army, 1972; Gold medal Electronic Industries Assn., 1972; Public Service award Advt. Council, 1972; Herbert Hoover Meml. award Boys Clubs Am., 1975; Nat. Bus. Hall of Fame award for bus. leadership, 1976; Medallion, Sch. of Bus., Coll. of William and Mary, 1976. Mem. Council on Fgn. Relations, Bus. Council, Internat. C. of C. (trustee U.S. Council 1949-64, chmn. 1955-57), Psi Upsilon. Clubs: Links, River, N.Y. Yacht (N.Y.C.); Metropolitan (Washington); Round Hill, Hope (Providence); Cruising of Am., Royal Yacht Squadron, Ocean Cruising. Home: Spaso House Spasopesovskaya Ploshchad Moscow USSR Office: US Embassy Moscow USSR

WATSON, THOMAS J., JR., corp. exec.; b. Dayton, Ohio, Jan. 8, 1914; s. Thomas J. and Jeannette (Kittridge) W.; B.A., Brown U., 1937; hon. degrees from Brown U., Columbia, Harvard, Oxford, Yale, other univs. m. Olive Field Cawley, Dec. 15, 1941; children—Thomas J. III, Jeannette, Olive, Lucinda, Susan, Helen. With IBM, 1937-40, 46—, pres., 1952-61, chmn., 1961-71, chmn. exec. com., 1971—. Dir. Pan Am. World Airways, Inc., Time, Inc. Citizen regent Smithsonian Instn.; chmn. gen. advisory com. Arms Control and Disarmament Agy., 1978—; mem. nat. advisory council Boy Scouts Am. Trustee Brown U., Calif. Inst. Tech., John F. Kennedy Library, Mystic Seaport, Inc., Mayo Found. Served to lt. col. USAF, 1940-45; sr. pilot. Decorated Air medal, Army commendation ribbon; recipient Presdl. Medal of Freedom. Sr. fellow Woodrow Wilson Nat. Fellowship Found. Mem. Council Fgn. Relations, Bus. Council (grad. mem.). Office: Old Orchard Rd Armonk NY 10504

WATSON, THOMAS STURGES, profl. golfer; b. Kansas City, Mo., Sept. 4, 1949; s. Raymond Etheridge and Sarah Elizabeth (Ridge) W.; B.S., Stanford U., 1971; m. Linda Tova Rubin, July 8, 1973. Profl. golfer, 1971—; winner Western Open, 1974, 1977, Byron Nelson Tournament, 1975, 78, Brit. Open, 1975, 77, World Series, 1975, Bing Crosby Pro-Am., 1977, 78, Andy Williams San Diego Open, 1977, El Prat, 1977, Masters, 1977, Bing Crosby Nat. Pro-Am Golf Tournament, 1977, 78, Tucson Open, 1978, Colgate Hall of Fame Classic, 1978, Anheuser Busch Golf Classic, 1978. Recipient Vardon Trophy, 1977, 78, Byron Nelson award, 1977-78; named to Ryder Cup Team, 1977; named Player of Year, Profl. Golf Assn., 1977, 78 Mem. U.S. Golf Assn., Profl. Golfers Assn. Clubs: Butler Nat. Golf, Steamboat Springs Country, Kansas City Country, Par. Office: 1726 Commerce Tower Kansas City MO 64105

WATSON, WILLIAM, educator; b. Clydebank, Dunbartonshire, Scotland, Jan. 5, 1917; s. Thomas and Jessie (Brockett) W.; B.A., Cambridge U., Eng., 1947, M.Sc., 1949; Ph.D., Manchester U., Eng., 1952; m. Julie Ann Dixon, Jan. 12, 1973; children from previous marriage—Hamish Brockett, Calum Macfarlane, Angus Clark. Came to U.S., 1963. Anthropologist, Med. Research Council of U.K., 1948-51; research fellow Rhodes-Livingstone Inst., Zambia, 1951-56; prof. anthropology Manchester U., 1956-63; prof. anthropology U. Va., Charlottesville, 1963-69; prof., chmn. dept. sociology U. Okla., Norman, 1969—. Cons. sociologist Med. Research Council of U.K., 1959-63; mem. Youth Service Devel. Council of U.K., 1960-63. Served with RAF, 1939-45. Decorated D.F.C. Fellow Assn. Social Anthropologists of U.K.; mem. African Studies Assn., Royal African Inst., Brit. Sociol. Assn., Am. Sociol. Assn. Author: Tribal Cohesion in a Money Economy, 1958; Sociology in Medicine, 1962; also articles. Home: 1847 Rolling Hills Norman OK 73069

WATSON, WILLIAM GEORGE, electronics co. exec.; b. Chgo., Apr. 16, 1934; s. William Green and Julia Hunt (Baird) W.; A.A., Wright Coll., 1959; B.Sc. magna cum laude (Mences scholar), Iowa U., 1961; M.B.A. (Laverne Noyes scholar), U. Chgo., 1963; m. Mari Mabe Kuwahara, July 13, 1962; 1 dau., Julia Mako. Fin. analyst Ford Motor Co., Dearborn, Mich., 1963-67; controller Fairchild Camera and Instrument Co., Mountain View, Calif., 1967-69, mng. dir., Singapore, 1969-73; v.p. ops. Fairchild Camera and Instrument/TKD, Tokyo, 1973-75; pres. Gen. Instrument of Taiwan Corp., Taipei, 1975-76, Gen. Instrument Internat. Corp., Gen. Instrument Overseas Corp., Tokyo, 1976-79, Gen. Instrument of Taiwan, 1978-79, Gen. Instrument Internat. & Overseas, Tokyo, 1976-79; dir. Gen. Instrument Internat. Corp., N.Y.C., sr. dir. fin. adminstrn., 1979—. Served with U.S. Army, 1954-56. Recipient Bus. award Wall St. Jours., 1961. Mem. Am. C. of C. Clubs: Am. (Tokyo, Taipei, Singapore), Japan (Singapore), Internat. Bus. in China. Contbr. numerous articles on bus. and econs. in Singapore, Taiwan and Japan to profl. jours. Home: 4-13-9 Shirobane Minato-Ku Tokyo 108 Japan Office: Fukide Bldg 1-13 Toranomon 4 Chome Minato-Ku Tokyo 105 Japan also 77 Pao Chiao Rd Hsin Tien Taipei Taiwan. *Comprehend yourself; contemplate the outcome of your actions on others deeply. However, when the moment arrives to act, do so, intuitively, uninhibitedly without fear of loss or desire of gain.*

WATSON, WINSOR HAYS, JR., mining co. exec.; b. N.Y.C., June 2, 1919; s. Winsor Hays and Alice (Koch) W.; A.B. cum laude, Dartmouth, 1941; m. Janet Lois Burns, June 12, 1943; children—Claire Loretta (Mrs. Garcia), Winsor Hays III. Reporter, Bridgeport Post Pub. Co. (Conn.), 1941-42; asso. editor, promotion mgr. U.S. Camera Pub. Co., N.Y.C., 1945-47; account exec. Newell-Emmett Co., N.Y.C., 1947-50; v.p. Cecil & Presbrey, Inc., N.Y.C., 1950-53; sr. v.p., dir. Basford, Inc., N.Y.C., 1953-66; v.p. Am. Stock Exchange, N.Y.C., 1966-68, sr. v.p., 1968-71, exec. v.p., 1971-78; v.p. Kennecott Copper Corp., Stamford, Conn., 1978—. Served to lt. USAAF, 1942-45. Mem. Phi Beta Kappa, Phi Delta Theta. Clubs: Sky (N.Y.C.); Landmark (Stamford); Darien Country. Home: 60 Myanos Rd New Canaan CT 06840 Office: Ten Stamford Forum Stamford CT

WATT, ANDREW J., corp. exec.; b. Pitts., Sept. 26, 1916; s. Andrew and Edith Irene (Mann) W.; m. Thelma M. Prince, Oct. 5, 1940; children—James A., William A. With U.S. Gypsum Co., Chgo., 1938—, beginning as salesman, successively dist. mgr., sales mgr., mdse. mgr., v.p. merchandising, 1938-58, v.p. promotion and advt., 1958-60, v.p. marketing, 1962-65, sr. v.p., 1965- 69, exec. v.p., 1969—, also dir.; asst. to pres. Masonite Corp., Chgo., 1961, v.p. marketing, 1961-62. Presbyn. (elder). Home: 143 S Fernandez Ave Arlington Heights IL 60005 Office: 101 S Wacker Dr Chicago IL 60606

WATT, DEAN DAY, educator; b. McCammon, Idaho, Sept. 21, 1917; s. George Willaim and Mary Amelia (Day) W.; student Idaho State U., 1936-37, 38-40; B.S., U. Idaho, 1942; Ph.D., Iowa State U., 1949; postgrad. Case-Western Res. U., 1946-47; m. Frances Elaine Murdock, Aug. 23, 1945; children—Sharon (Mrs. William E. Shull, Jr.), Nola Jean (Mrs. Thomas E. Barzee, Jr.), Barbara (Mrs. Robert Lauritzen), David, Stuart. Research chemist Westvaco Chlorine Products, Newark, Calif., 1942-44; instr. Iowa State U., 1947-49; asst. prof. Purdue U., 1949-53; head dept. physiol. scis. Southeast La. Hosp., Mandeville, 1953-60; asso. prof. Tulane U., 1955-60; asso. prof. Ariz. State U., 1960-63; prin. biochemist Midwest Research Inst., Kansas City, Mo., 1963-69; prof. biochemistry Creighton U., 1969—. Fellow A.A.A.S.; mem. Internat. Soc. Toxinology (founding mem.), Am. Soc. Human Genetics, Mem. Ch. of Jesus Christ of Latter-day Saints. Research on animal venoms, biochemistry mental diseases. Home: 618 S 130th St Omaha NE 68154

WATT, DOUGLAS (BENJAMIN), writer; b. N.Y.C., Jan. 20, 1914; s. Benjamin Douglas and Agnes Rita (Neimann) W.; A.B., Cornell U., 1934; m. Ray Mantel, Nov. 5, 1937 (div.); children—Richard David, James Douglas; m. 2d, Ethel Madsen, Aug. 13, 1951; children—Patricia, Katherine. Copy boy N.Y. News, 1936-37, radio columnist, 1937-40, drama reporter, 1940-71, sr. drama critic, 1971—; staff writer New Yorker mag., 1946—; profl. song writer; columnist Small World, 1955-70. Pres. Hampton Animal Shelter, 1965—. Served with USAAF, World War II. Mem. ASCAP, N.Y. Drama Critics Circle (pres. 1975-77). Club: Dutch Treat (bd. govs.) (N.Y.C.). Home: 27 W 86th St New York NY 10024 Office: 220 E 42d St New York NY 10017. *To say one has achieved success, except perhaps in isolated instances, is an exercise in vanity and contrary to man's experience. At best, some satisfaction can be gained in one's career, and then almost always because of intense effort.*

WATT, GEORGE WILLARD, educator, chemist; b. Bellaire, Ohio, Jan. 8, 1911; s. Robert Whitefield and Grace (Korell) W.; B.A., Ohio State U., 1931, M.S., 1933, Ph.D., 1935; m. Pauline Ila Price, June 11, 1934; children—Susan Kathleen, George Winfield, Joseph Michael. Research chemist Goodyear Tire & Rubber Co., Akron, Ohio, 1935-37; asst., then asso. prof. chemistry U. Tex., Austin, 1937-43, prof., 1945—. With Manhattan Project, U. Chgo., 1943-45; cons. Gen. Electric Co., 1947-70, E.I. DuPont de Nemours & Co., 1950—, Exxon Nuclear Co., 1970—; expert witness patent and product liability litigation. Recipient Renaud Found. award, 1961, Standard Oil of Ind. Found. award, 1968, S.W. regional award Am. Chem. Soc., 1974. Fellow Am. Inst. Chemists; mem. Am. Chem. Soc. (dir.-at-large 1969-73), Sigma Xi, Phi Lambda Upsilon, Phi Kappa Phi. Contbr. articles to profl. jours. Patentee in field. Home: 3708 Meadowbank Dr Austin TX 78703

WATT, GRAHAM WEND, govt. ofcl.; b. Elizabeth, N.J., Oct. 23, 1926; s. William Harrison and Carolyn (Wend) W.; A.B. in Econs., Washington Coll., Chestertown, Md., 1949; M.A. in Govt. Adminstrn., U. Pa., 1951; m. Mary Aldridge Irish, Sept. 10, 1949; children—Terrence Graham, Laurie Frederika. Adminstrv. analyst City of Kansas City, Mo., 1950-54, chief asst. to city mgr., 1954-57; city mgr., Alton, Ill., 1958-62, Portland, Maine, 1962-67, Dayton, Ohio, 1967-70; dep. mayor, Washington, 1970-73; asst. to sec., dir. Office Revenue Sharing, U.S. Dept. Treasury, Washington, 1973-75; pres. Nat. Tng. and Devel. Service for State and Local Govts., 1975-79; county adminstr. Broward County (Fla.), 1979—. Mem. Pub. Service Commn. D.C., 1970-73; participant White House Conf. on Health, 1966, White House Conf. on Inflation, 1975; mem. urban devel. adv. com. to sec. U.S. Dept. Housing and Urban Devel., 1967-68; mem. Pub. Ofcls. Adv. Council Office Econ. Opportunity, 1966-68; mem. com. on fire dept. orgn. Nat. Fire Protection Assn., 1963-68; mem. com. on regional emergency med. communications sytems Nat. Acad. Scis.-NRC, 1973-78; mem. com. urban info. service Nat. Acad. Engring.-NRC, 1974-78. Bd. advisers Grad. Program in Pub. Adminstrn. Nova U., 1975—; mem. grad. adv. com. Wharton Sch. U. Pa. Served with USNR, 1944-46. Recipient Mgmt. Innovation award Internat City Mgmt. Assn., 1969; Man of Year award Wharton Sch. Club of Washington, 1971; Alumni citation Washington Coll., 1970. Mem. Fels Inst. Alumni Assn. (past pres.),

Internat. City Mgrs. Assn. (pres. 1971-72), Am. Soc. Pub. Adminstrn. (pres. chpt. 1975-76, nat. council 1976-79), Nat. Acad. Pub. Adminstrn. (dir. 1972—), Met. Washington Council Govts. (v.p. 1970-73). Address: 248 Broward County Courthouse Fort Lauderdale FL 33301

WATT, IAN PIERRE, educator; b. Windermere, Westmorland, Eng., Mar. 9, 1917; s. Thomas and Renée (Guitton) W.; B.A., St. John's Coll., Cambridge U., 1938, M.A., 1946; postgrad. Sorbonne, Paris, 1939, U. Calif. at Los Angeles, 1946-47, Harvard, 1947-48; m. Ruth Mellinkoff, July 14, 1947; children—George, Josephine. Fellow St. John's Coll., 1948-52; asst. prof. English, U. Calif. at Berkeley, 1952-55, asso. prof., 1955-58, prof., 1958-62; dean Sch. of English Studies, U. East Anglia, Norwich, Eng., 1962-64; prof. English, Stanford, 1964—, Eli Jackson Reynolds prof. humanities, 1971—; vis. prof. U. Hawaii, 1967-68, Williams Coll., 1970, U. Nice, U. Paris, 1975-76; Alexander lectr. U. Toronto (Ont., Can.), 1974; broadcaster BBC. Served with Brit. Army, 1939-46; PTO. Fellow Am. Acad. Arts and Scis. Author: The Rise of the Novel: Studies in Defoe, Richardson and Fielding, 1957. Editor: Jane Austen: A Collection of Critical Essays, 1963; Tristram Shandy (Laurence Sterne), 1965; The Augustan Age, 1968; The Victorian Novel: Modern Essays in Criticism, 1971; Conrad, The Secret Agent, A Casebook, 1973; The British Novel: Scott through Hardy, A Goldentree Bibliography, 1973; adv. editor Nineteenth Century Fiction, 1960—; Eighteenth Century Studies, 1968—, Style, 1968—, Novel, 1968—, also scholarly editions Defoe, Sterne, Smollett. Home: 35 Roan Pl Woodside CA 94062 Office: Dept of English Stanford Univ Stanford CA 94305

WATT, JAMES ARTHUR, chem. co. exec.; b. Peoria, Ill., Oct. 6, 1925; s. Clarence Jay and Fern Ione (Wingate) W.; B.S., U. Calif., Berkeley, 1949; m. Mary Ruth Mobley, Mar. 30, 1947; children—Charles, Joan, Judith. Tech. sales rep. Martin Hoyt Milne, San Francisco, 1949-51; chemist H.B. Fuller, San Francisco, 1951-59, tech. dir., St. Paul, 1959-64, v.p., regional mgr., South San Francisco, 1964-72; exec. v.p., St. Paul, 1972—, mem. exec. com., 1972—, dir., 1969—. Served with USNR, 1943-46. Mem. Adhesive Mfrs. Assn. Am. (pres. 1977—). Mem. St. Paul Athletic, N. Oaks Golf. Home: 29 Pheasant Ln St Paul MN 55110 Office: 2400 Kasota St St Paul MN 55108

WATT, JAMES GAIUS, legal found. exec.; b. Lusk, Wyo., Jan. 31, 1938; s. William G. and Lois M. (Williams) W.; B.S., U. Wyo., 1960, J.D., 1962; m. Leilani Bomgardner, Nov. 2, 1957; children—Erin Gaia, Eric Gaius. Admitted to Wyo. bar, 1962, U.S. Supreme Ct. bar, 1966; sec. to natural resources com. and environ. pollution adv. panel C. of C. of U.S., 1966-69; legis. asst., counsel to Senator Simpson of Wyo., 1962-66; dep. asst. sec. water and power devel. Interior Dept., 1969-72; dir. Bur. Outdoor Recreation, Washington, 1972-75; mem. Fed. Power Commn., 1975-77; pres., chief legal officer Mountain States Legal Found., Denver, 1977—; instr. Coll. Commerce and Industry, U. Wyo. Recipient Thomas Arkle Clarke award Alpha Tau Omega, 1960. Mem. Phi Kappa Phi. Home: 9950 E Grand Ave Englewood CO 80110 Office: Mountain States Legal Found Denver CO 80203

WATT, RICHARD FRYE, lawyer; b. Seattle, July 13, 1917; s. Paul Harris and Roberta (Frye) W.; A.B., U. Wash., 1937; M.A. (Rhodes scholar), Corpus Christi Coll., Oxford (Eng.) U., 1944; LL.B., U. Chgo., 1942; m. Sherry B. Goodman, Aug. 24, 1972; children by previous marriage—Douglas, Alan, Roberta (dec.). Admitted to Ill. bar, 1942; asst. prof. law U. Chgo. Law Sch., 1946-48; practiced in Chgo., 1949—; mem. firm Cotton, Watt, Jones, King and Bowlus and predecessor firm, 1951—. Lectr. Loyola U., 1965-66, Chgo.-Kent, Ill. Inst. Tech. Law Sch., 1973. Bd. dirs. Ill. div. ACLU, 1970-75, gen. counsel, 1973-75. Served with AUS, 1942-46. Decorated Bronze Star. Mem. Chgo. Bar Assn., Chgo. Council Lawyers, Phi Beta Kappa. Home: 5201 S Cornell Ave Chicago IL 60615 Office: Suite 4750 1 IBM Plaza Chicago IL 60611

WATT, STUART GEORGE, engring. contracting co. exec.; b. Warsaw, N.Y., Apr. 26, 1934; s. George James and Elizabeth Fern (Fullington) W.; B.S. in Mineral Engring., Pa. State U., 1956, M.S. in Mineral Engring. (NSF fellow), 1958; m. Dorothy Elayne McLeod, Aug. 13, 1957; children—Stuart George II, Eric Duncan. Ops. research cons. Lukens Steel Co., Coatesville, Pa., 1959; sr. research engr. Internat. Minerals & Chems. Co., Mulberry, Fla., 1959-62, project mgr., Skokie, Ill., 1962-64, prodn. mgr., Carlsbad, N.Mex., 1964-66; exec. engr. Davy Powergas, Inc., Lakeland, Fla., 1966-69, v.p. bus. devel., 1970-71, sr. v.p., 1972-74, exec. v.p., chief exec. ops., Houston, 1974-78; exec. v.p. Davy Internat. Inc., 1978—, also dir.; exec. v.p. Davy McKee, 1979—; dir. Hallanger Engrs., Tex. Bank and Trust. Mem. Am. Inst. Mining and Metal. Engrs., Pa. State Alumni Assn., Toastmasters Club, Jr. Achievement, Sigma Gamma Epsilon. Republican. Lutheran. Clubs: Houston Univ., Lone Palm Golf; Lakeside Country (Houston); University (Salt Lake City); Walden Golf. Home: 672 Glen Eden Ct Aurora OH 44202 Office: 6200 Oak Tree Blvd Independence OH 44131

WATT, WILLIAM JOSEPH, coll. dean; b. Carbondale, Ill., Dec. 15, 1925; s. Phillip Clement and Ella (Dickey) W.; student U. Mich., 1943; B.S. in Chemistry, U. Ill., 1949; M.S., Cornell U., 1951, Ph.D., 1956; m. Helen Stevens Gravatt, Sept. 1, 1956; children—John Gravatt, Phyllis Cary, William Joseph. Asst. prof. chemistry Davidson (N.C.) Coll., 1951-53; mem. faculty Washington and Lee U., 1955—, prof. chemistry, 1965—, asso. dean of coll., 1968-71, dean, 1971—; vis. prof. NSF Inst. High Sch. Tchrs., Ala. Coll., summers 1959-61, U. Va., summers 1964-66. Summer research participant Cornell U., 1956; Oak Ridge Nat. Lab., 1957, 58, U. Va., 1962. Pres. Rockbridge chpt. Va. Mus. Fine Arts, 1963-65; bd. dirs. Rockbridge Concert Theater Series, 1960—, pres., 1971-77; trustee Episcopal High Sch., 1974—; vestryman, sr. warden Episcopal Ch.; bd. dirs. Botetourt-Rockbridge Regional Library, chmn., 1975; sec.-treas. Conf. Acad. Deans of So. States, 1978-79. Served with AUS, 1944-46. Mem. Am. Chem. Soc., N.Y. Acad. Sci., Soc. Chimique de France, AAAS, Va. Acad. Sci., Phi Eta Sigma, Alpha Chi Sigma. Democrat. Contbr. articles to profl. jours. Home: 7 Providence Pl Lexington VA 24450

WATTEL, HAROLD LOUIS, educator, economist; b. Bklyn., Sept. 30, 1921; s. David Max and Carolyn (Abrams) W.; B.A., Queens Coll., 1942; M.A., Columbia, 1947; Ph.D. magna cum laude, New Sch. Social Research, 1954; m. Sara Gordon, Sept. 1, 1946; children—Karen, Jill. Jr. economist WPB, 1942; economist Dept. Agr., 1946; econ. cons. Boni, Watkins & Mounteer, 1952; economist Bur. Bus. and Community Research, Hofstra U., 1954, 57, dir., 1957-58, prof. econs. 1957—, chmn. dept. econs., 1957-61, chmn. div. bus., 1961—, dean Sch. Bus., 1965-73; dir., econ. cons. to consumer counsel, staff Gov. N.Y., 1956-58; cons. N.Y. State Moreland Commn. on Alcoholic Beverage Control Law, 1963-64, Legislative Reference Bur., U. Hawaii, 1966, Schenley Industries, 1967—, Ralston Purina Co., 1967—, Am. Can Co., 1965—; econ. cons. Nat. Millinery Planning Bd., 1959-70, author ann. publ. The Millinery Industry; ednl. cons. U.S. Mcht. Marine Acad., Kings Point, 1972, Bulova Watch Co., 1975—. Mem. Comprehensive Health Planning Council, 1970-75. Bd. dirs., v.p. N.Y. State unit Am. Lung Assn., pres. Nassau-Suffolk unit; bd. dirs. Comprehensive Health Planning Council, Nassau-Suffolk, N.Y., N.Y. State Citizen Council, Consumer Farmer Found., Found. for Econs., Regional Med. Program Nassau-Suffolk, Edn. fellow, 1949; Hazen Found. fellow, 1952; Ford Found. regional fellow, 1960. Served to lt. USNR, 1942-46. Mem. Middle Atlantic Assn. Colls. Bus. Adminstrn. (pres. 1970-71), Am., Met. econs. assns., Am. Assn. U. Profs. (chpt. pres. 1953), N.Y. State Environ. Health Assn. (v.p.), Coop. Extension Assn. Nassau County, Pi Gamma Mu, Omicron Chi Epsilon, Beta Gamma Sigma (hon. asso.). Editor: Voluntarism and the Business Community; Planning in Higher Education, 1975; (with Virginia Sugden) A Group Approach to the Master's Essay; Chief Executive Officer Compensation, 1978. Contbr. chpts. to books, encys., also reports. Editor, contbr. L.I. Bus., 1954-59. Home: 181 Shepherd Ln Roslyn Heights NY 11577 Office: Hofstra U Hempstead NY 11550

WATTENBERG, ALBERT, physicist, educator; b. N.Y.C., Apr. 13, 1917; s. Louis and Bella (Wolff) W.; B.S., Coll. City N.Y., 1938; M.A., Columbia, 1939; Ph.D., U. Chgo., 1947; m. Shirley Hier, Sept. 5, 1943; children—Beth, Jill, Nina Diane. Spectroscopist, Schenley Distilleries, N.Y.C., 1939-42; physicist Manhattan Project, Metall. Lab., Chgo., 1942-46; group leader Argonne Nat. Lab., Chgo., 1946-50; asst. prof. U. Ill., Urbana, 1950-51, prof. physics, 1958—; research physicist Mass. Inst. Tech., 1951-58. Recipient award for 1st nuclear reactor Am. Nuclear Soc., 1962. NSF fellow U. Rome, 1962-63. Pioneered controlled nuclear reactor. Home: 701 W Delaware St Urbana IL 61801

WATTENBERG, BEN J., author; b. N.Y.C., Aug. 26, 1933; s. Judah and Rachel (Gutman) W.; B.A., Hobart Coll., 1955; LL.D. (hon.), Hobart and William Smith Colls., 1975; m. Marna Hade, June 24, 1956; children—Ruth, Daniel, Sarah. Asst. to Pres. Johnson, Washington, 1966-68; aide to Vice Pres. Hubert Humphrey, Mpls., 1970; campaign adviser Senator Henry Jackson, 1972, 76; mem. presdl. advisory bd. on ambassadorial appointments, 1977—; bus. cons., Washington, 1968-79. Eminent scholar, prof.-at-large Mary Washington Coll., 1973-74; narrator, essayist In Search of Real Am., nat. TV series, Public Broadcasting Service, 1977-78; distinguished vis. prof. U.S. Internat. U., 1978, 79; narrator, essayist Ben Wattenberg's 1980, nat. TV series Public Broadcasting Service, 1980. Co-founder, chmn. Coalition for a Democratic Majority, 1972—; bd. dirs. Reading Is Fundamental; fellow, trustee, Hudson Inst., 1976—; sr. fellow Am. Enterprise Inst., 1977—. Served with USAF, 1956-58. Democrat. Jewish. Club: Federal City (Washington). Author: This U.S.A., 1965; (with R. Scammon) The Real Majority, 1970; The Real America, 1974; (with Ervin Duggan) Against All Enemies, 1977; (with Richard Whalen) The Wealth Weapon, 1980. Co-editor: Public Opinion Mag., 1977—. Contbr. articles to mags. Home: Office: American Enterprise Inst 1150 17th St NW Washington DC 20036

WATTERS, DAVID JEROME, lawyer; b. Detroit, Sept. 2, 1931; s. David Jerome and Maryclaire Bacon (Meldrum) W.; Ph.B., U. Detroit, 1954; LL.B., Detroit Coll. Law, 1957; m. Joyce E. Esposti, Aug. 26, 1956; children—David Jerome III, Janet Claire, Patricia F. Admitted to bar; now partner firm Plunkett, Cooney, Rutt, Watters, Stanczyk & Pedersen, Detroit. Fellow Am. Coll. Trial Lawyers; mem. Am. Bar, State Bar Mich., Detroit Bar Assn., Assn. Def. Trial Counsel (pres. 1970-71), Internat. Assn. Ins. Counsel, Nat. Health Lawyers Assn., Am. Soc. Law and Medicine, Soc. Chartered Property, Casualty Underwriters, Am. Soc. Hosp. Attys. Club: Detroit. Home: 26625 Captain's Ln Franklin Village MI 48025 Office: 1000 Guardian Bldg Detroit MI 48226

WATTERS, FRANK CARLETON, cons.; b. National Mine, Mich., Feb. 7, 1908; s. Rev. Frank Cole and Alice Luella (Molloy) W.; A.B., U. of Mich., 1930; student Am. U. (Washington), 1943-44; m. Nan McGurk, Jan. 3, 1936; children—Suzanne Alice, Kathryn Molloy, Elizabeth Lathrop. With Mich. Relief Commn., 1933-35; Works Progress Adminstrn., 1935-42; asst. regional dir. W.P.B., Detroit, 1942-43; cons. adminstrn. and finance, U.N. (New York), 1946; Housing and Home Finance Agency (successor to Nat. Housing Agency), 1946-48, asst. adminstr., 1947-48; dir. Fiscal Affairs, Oak Ridge Operations, Atomic Energy Commn., 1948-50; instr. govtl. accounting, Peoples U. Movement, Lansing, Mich., 1938-41; mem. Mich. Adv. Council, Citizenship Edn., 1939-41; asst. sec. 5th com, U.N. gen. assembly, New York, 1946; mem. bd. dirs., Mich. Rural Rehabilitation Corp., 1935-48; budget div. Office Chief Staff, Dept. Army, 1950-56; controller, dept. medicine and surgery VA, 1956-59; exec. dir. Group Health Assn., Inc., 1959-71; cons., 1971—. Pres. Fairfax Co. Fedn. of Citizens Assns., 1955-56, Idylwood Citizens Assn.; pres. adv. bd. Fairfax Falls Ch. Mental Health Center; treas. Community Group Health Found., Washington, Camp Tapawingo for Retarded Children, Alexandria, Va.; past pres. bd. No. Va. Mental Health Assn. Served as major, AUS, Finance Dept., 1943-46. Awarded Army Commendation in connection with budget for Army Service Forces, 1946; recipient Man of the Year, Washington Evening Star Cup award, Fairfax County, Va., 1958. Member Phi Kappa Sigma. Democrat. Presbyn. Home: Idylwood Rd Falls Church VA 22043 Office: 7627 Idylwood Rd Falls Church VA 22043

WATTERS, JAMES I(SAAC), educator; b. Broadus, Mont., Apr. 4, 1908; s. James O. and Hilda C. (Erickson) W.; student U. Fla., 1926-28, U. Calif. at Berkeley, 1928-29; B.S., U. Minn., 1931, Ph.D., 1943; m. Louise G. Chambers, Aug. 28, 1938; children—Louise Emilie, Molly Marie, James Norman, Kathryn Verne. Tchr., Anoka pub. schs., 1931-38; instr. Cornell U., 1941-43; chief analytical chemistry on atom bomb project U. Chgo., 1943-45; asso. prof. U. Ky., 1945-48; asso. prof. Ohio State U., 1948-58, prof. chemistry, math. and phys. scis., 1958—; summer cons. U.S. AID, Punjab U., 1965, Annamalai U., 1966, Ujjain U., 1967 (all India). Mem. Am. Chem. Soc., AAAS, Sigma Xi, Zeta Psi, Phi Lambda Upsilon. Lutheran. Editor: Analytical Chemistry of Atomic Energy Project, 1951. Contbr. chpts. to Treatise on Analytical Chemistry; also articles on polarography and spectrophotometry to tech. jours. Home: 1470 Ridgeview Rd Columbus OH 43221. *Any success I have enjoyed has been due to encouragement from my teachers and professors throughout my education and my fundamental interest in helping my students achieve their goals. I must not forget my parents who tried to guide me throughout my youth and inspired me to work to achieve my goals. Last but not least, my wife and children have been an inspiration.*

WATTERS, LORAS JOSEPH, bishop; b. Dubuque, Iowa, Oct. 15, 1915; s. Martin James and Carolyn R. (Sisler) W.; B.A., Loras Coll., Dubuque, 1937; S.T.B., Gregorian U., Rome, Italy, 1940; S.T.L., Cath. U. Am., 1941, M.A., 1947, Ph.D., 1954. Ordained priest Roman Cath Ch., 1941; asst. pastor St. Martin's Ch., Cascade, Iowa, 1941-45; mem. faculty Loras Coll., 1945-56; prin. Loras Acad., Dubuque, 1947-52, head edn. dept., 1954-56; spiritual dir. N.Am. Coll., Rome, 1956-60; dir. Am. Martyrs Retreat House, Cedar Falls, Iowa, 1960-65; aux. bishop of Dubuque, 1965-69; pastor Ch. of Nativity, Dubuque, 1965-69; archdiocesan supt. schs., 1967-69; bishop of Winona, Minn., 1969—. Mem. bishops' com. on priestly formation Nat. Conf. Cath. Bishops, 1970-78, chmn., 1972-75. Home: 55 W Sanborn Winona MN 55987 Office: 55 W Sanborn Box 588 St Winona MN 55987

WATTERSON, RAY LEIGHTON, educator; b. Greene, Iowa, Apr. 15, 1915; s. George Robert and Alice (Hesalroad) W.; A.B., Coe Coll., 1936, grad. student 1936-37; Ph.D., U. Rochester, 1941; grad. student Johns Hopkins, 1940-41; m. Evelyn Lily Goddard, July 30, 1941; children—Richard Dean (dec.), James Robert, Donald Kent (dec.), Jean Marie. Instr. zoology Dartmouth, 1941-42; asst. prof. zoology U. Calif. at Berkeley, 1942-46; asst. prof., then asso. prof. U. Chgo., 1946-49; faculty Northwestern U., 1949-61, prof. biology, 1955- 61, chmn. adminstrv. com., 1956-58, chmn. dept., 1958-61; prof. zoology U. Ill. at Urbana 1961-72, prof. genetics, devel. and basic med. scis., 1972—; instr. Marine Biol. Lab., Woods Hole, Mass., summers 1942, 44, 47, Frank R. Lillie fellow exptl. embryology, summer 1952; asst. prof. Hopkins Marine Sta., Stanford, summers 1945, 46; vis. prof. Friday Harbor Labs., U. Wash., summer 1954, U. Iowa, summer 1968; guest lectr. Bermuda Biol. Sta., summer 1966. Sec. subcom. on embryology Internat. Anat. Nomenclature Com., 1971-72. Fellow AAAS; mem. Am. Assn. Anatomists, Am. Soc. Zoologists (exec. com. 1960-63, 66, chmn. div. developmental biology 1966, policy com. 1975), Soc. Developmental Biology, Soc. Exptl. Biology and Medicine, Internat. Soc. Developmental Biologists, Am. Soc. Cell Biology, Sigma Xi. Research devel. in avian embryos, pigment cells, nervous system, glycogen body, endocrine activity after hypophysectomy, liver, kidney and heart after aminoguanidine treatment, ribs, hatching muscle, pigment patterns in tunicate embryos. Home: 1717 Lincoln Rd Champaign IL 61820 Office: Dept Genetics and Devel U Ill Urbana IL 61801

WATTLES, GEORGE M., fin. cons.; b. Mpls., Jan. 1, 1917; s. George M. and Janet (Hamilton) W.; B.A., Carleton Coll., 1939; student Harvard Grad. Sch. Bus. Adminstrn., 1939-40; Ph.D., U. Va., 1964; m. Louise Summerfelt, May 16, 1942; children— Jeffrey H., Janet Louise (Mrs. Charles Hoeveler), Thomas George; m. 2d, Margaret Louise O'Brien, 1973. With Ingersoll Milling Machine Co., 1940-41, Sperry Gyroscope Co., 1941-42; prin. J. Wattles & Assos., Rockford, Ill., 1946-60; chmn. econ. and bus. adminstrn. dept. Rockford Coll., 1962-76, v.p., dean, 1968-74; West Coast cons. N. Central Capital Corp., 1974-76; John David Campbell prof. Am. bus. Am. Grad. Sch. Internat. Mgmt., 1976—. Dir. Rockford Spring Co., Strong Products Corp., True Data Corp., Ramtek Corp. Chief econ. adviser Postal Rate Commn., 1971—. Research scholar, law sch. U. Chgo., 1971. Alderman, Rockford, 1967—. Bd. dirs. Rockford United Fund, Rockford Jr. Achievement. Served with USNR, 1942-46. Mem. Am. Econ. Assn., Mt. Pelerin Soc., Phi Beta Kappa. Presbyterian. Rotarian (dir. 1966-67). Club: Rockford Country. Home: 4602 E Sunset Dr Phoenix AZ 85028

WATTON, JAMES AUGUSTUS, archbishop; b. Southampton, Ont., Can., Oct. 23, 1915; s. George Augustus and Ada May (Lewis) W.; B.A., U. Western Ont., 1938; postgrad. Huron Coll., 1938, D.D., 1955; D.D., Wycliffe Coll., 1975; m. Irene A. Foster, Aug. 14, 1941; children—Dian, David, Mary. Ordained priest Anglican Ch.; parish priest in Huron, Moosonee and Toronto; dean of Moosenee, 1954-58, bishop, from 1963, now archbishop; metropolitan Province Ont., 1974—; publisher quar. The Northland. Club: Rotary. Address: Box 841 Schumacher ON P0N 1C0 Canada

WATTS, AMOS HOLSTON, lawyer; b. Nashville, Ill., Nov. 24, 1896; s. William Wadsworth and Laura (Holston) W.; A.B., U. Ill., 1919, LL.B., 1921; m. Lida Hough, 1921; 1 son, Dey Wadsworth; m. Gladys F. Brewer, Oct. 8, 1960. Admitted to Ill. bar, 1921, since practiced in Chgo.; ret. sr. partner firm Chapman & Cutler. Lectr., Sch. Banking, U. Wis., 1947-57. Pres., dir. U. Ill. Found., 1959-62. Pres. Glencoe (Ill.) Park Dist., 1934-43; mem. Ill. Commn. for Revision Park Laws for Dists. under 500,000, 1947-49. Mem. Am., Ill., Chgo. bar assns., Civic Fedn. Chgo., Chgo. Assn. Commerce, Ill. C. of C., Delta Phi, Phi Delta Phi. Republican. Mem. Union Ch. Mason. Clubs: University, Executives Mid-Day (Chgo.); Skokie Country (Glencoe, Ill.). Home: 508 Jefferson St Glencoe IL 60022 Office: 111 W Monroe St Chicago IL 60603

WATTS, ANDRÉ, concert pianist; b. Nüremberg, Germany, June 20, 1946; s. Herman and Maria Alexandra (Gusmits) W.; grad. Peabody Conservatory, Balt.; hon. doctorate Yale, 1973; H.H.D., Albright Coll., 1975. First pub. appearance at age 9, Phila. Orch. Children's Concerts, 1955; performed with Phila. Orch., 1956, with Leonard Bernstein and the N.Y. Philharmonic, 1963; European debut London Symphony Orch., 1966; made world concert tour to 16 Asian and Western European cities for U.S. State Dept., 1967, including an appearance at the Berlin Festival, Soviet Union tour with San Francisco Symphony, 1973; ann. appearances as soloist with all major U.S. and European orchs.; ann. solo tours, Europe, U.S., Japan, Israel; TV appearances include Camera Three, Live from Lincoln Center; on Great Performers series Lincoln Center, 11 years; NET TV Spl. with Zubin Mehta and Los Angeles Philharmonic; rec. artist CBS Records. Recipient Grammy award Nat. Acad. Rec. Arts and Scis., 1963; Lincoln Center medallion, 1974; decorated Order of Zaire (Congo), 1970. Address: care Columbia Artists Mgmt 165 W 57 St New York NY 10019

WATTS, CHARLES DEWITT, surgeon, corporate med. dir.; b. Atlanta, Sept. 21, 1917; s. Lewis G. and Ida H. (Hawes) W.; B.S., Morehouse Coll., 1938; M.D., Howard U., 1943; m. Constance Merrick, Jan. 5, 1945; children—Eileen Constance Watts Welch, Deborah Hill, Charles D., Winifred Anita. Practice medicine specializing in surgery, Durham, N.C., 1950—; med. dir. N.C. Mut. Life Ins. Co., Durham, 1960—; mem. faculty dept. surgery Howard U. Coll. Medicine, 1947-50; instr. surgery Howard U., Washington; asst. clin. prof. surgery Duke Med. Center; attending surgeon Durham County Gen. Hosp.; chmn. bd. Capital Health Systems Regional Agy., 1976. Trustee Howard U., Washington. Diplomate Am. Bd. Surgery. Fellow A.C.S.; mem. Inst. of Medicine of NSF. Home: 829 Lawson St Durham NC 27701

WATTS, CHARLES HENRY, II, univ. ofcl.; b. N.Y.C., Oct. 17, 1926; s. Charles Henry and Mabel (Lamborn) W.; A.B., Brown U., 1947, Ph.D., 1953, LL.D., 1975; M.A., Columbia, 1948; Litt.D. Franklin Coll., 1965; LL.D., Dickinson Sch. Law, 1968; H.H.D. Alderson-Broaddus Coll., 1969; L.H.D., Bucknell U., 1979; m. Patricia Dorothy McQuillen, June 9, 1951; children—Katharine Watts Morton, Caroline Moore, Charles Henry III. Mem. faculty Brown U., 1953-62, successively instr. English, asst. prof., 1955-57, asso. prof., 1957-62, prof., 1962, dean coll., 1958-62; exec. asso., dir. commn. on adminstrv. affairs Am. Council on Edn., 1962-64; pres. Bucknell U., 1964-76; pres., chief exec. officer Wolf Trap Found. Performing Arts, 1976-77; cons., 1977-78; dir. campaign Brown U., 1978—; dir. Beneficial Corp., Wilmington, Del., Weis Markets, Inc., Sunbury, Pa. Trustee Bucknell U., Lewisburg, Pa., Peddle Sch., Hightstown, N.J. Served to ensign USNR, World War II. Clubs: Hope (Providence, R.I.); University, Century (N.Y.C.); Duquesne (Pitts.). Author: Thomas Holley Chivers: His Literary Career and His Poetry, 1956; (with S. Foster Damon) Complete Works of T. H. Chivers, vol. 1, 1957; (with A.D. Van Nostrand) The Conscious Voice. Home: 708 Belgrove Rd McLean VA 22101

WATTS, CHARLES ROBERT, musician; b. Islington, Eng., June 2, 1941; attended Harrow Art Sch.; m. Shirley Shepherd, 1964; 1 dau., Serafina. Drummer with musical group The Rolling Stones, 1963—; appeared in films: Sympathy for the Devil, 1970, Gimme Shelter, 1970, Ladies and Gentlemen the Rolling Stones, 1974. Author: Ode to a High-flying Bird, 1964. Office: care Rolling Stones Records 75 Rockefeller Plaza New York NY 10019•

WATTS, DANIEL THOMAS, coll. dean, pharmacologist; b. Wadesboro, N.C., July 31, 1916; s. James Cyrus and Blanche (Rogers) W.; A.B., Elon Coll., 1937; Ph.D., Duke, 1942; m. Margaret Montgomery, Sept. 12, 1942 (dec. 1963); children—Daniel Thomas, Margaret Peyton; m. 2d, Ann M. Brewbaker, June 12, 1965; stepchildren—Carol Kay, Susan. High sch. tchr., Yanceyville, N.C., 1937-38; grad. asst. Duke, 1938-42; physiologist Naval Air Expt. Sta., 1946-47; mem. faculty U. Va., 1947-53, asso. prof. pharmacology, 1949-53; prof. pharmacology, chmn. dept. W.Va. U., 1953-66; dean Sch. Basic Scis. Med. Coll. Va., Va. Commonwealth U., 1966—; cons. pharmacology Walter Reed Army Med. Center, 1959-69; pres. Morgantown Planning Commn., 1963-66. Served with USNR, 1942-46; capt. Res. Mem. Am. Soc. Pharmacology and Exptl. Therapeutics, Soc. Exptl. Biology and Medicine. Democrat. Presbyn. Rotarian (pres. Morgantown 1958, Richmond, 1977). Home: 504 Ridge Top Rd Richmond VA 23229

WATTS, DAVID E., lawyer; b. Fairfield, Iowa, June 13, 1921; B.A., U. Iowa, 1941, J.D., 1942; postgrad. Columbia Law Sch., 1946-47. Admitted to Iowa bar, 1942, Mass. bar, 1950, N.Y. State bar, 1954; instr. U. Iowa, 1947-48; asst. prof. U. Pa., 1948-49, Harvard Law Sch., 1949-52; adj. asso. prof. N.Y. U., 1952-55; mem. firm Dewey, Ballantine, Bushby, Palmer & Wood, N.Y.C., 1952-58, partner, 1958—; vis. lectr. Columbia U., 1954. Trustee Collegiate Sch. N.Y.C. Mem. Am., N.Y. State bar assns., Assn. Bar City N.Y., N.Y. County Lawyers Assn., Am. Law Inst. Contbr. articles to legal jours. Home: 33 W 74th St New York NY 10023 Office: 140 Broadway St New York NY 10005

WATTS, EDWARD EVERETT, JR., lawyer; b. Springfield, Ill., Aug. 22, 1899; s. Edward Everett and Louise O. (Gros) W.; A.B., Princeton, 1921; J.D., Columbia, 1924; m. Isabella R. Hardy, Sept. 14, 1940; children—Elizabeth Hardy (Mrs. Nicholas P. Boileau), Edward Everett III, Isabella King. Admitted to N.Y. bar, 1925, U.S. Supreme Ct., 1942; asso. Cravath, de Gersdorff, Swaine & Wood, N.Y.C., 1924-29, Mitchell, Taylor, Capron & Marsh and predecessor firm, 1929-38; partner firm Turk, Marsh, Kelly & Hoare, and predecessor firm, 1938-75, counsel to firm, 1975—. Trustee, chmn. exec. com. Broadway Savs. Bank, 1943-70. Pres. Travelers Aid Soc., N.Y., 1947-57, chmn. hon. bd., 1957—; pres. Internat. Film Found., 1945—; dir. Legal Aid Soc. N.Y., 1938-71, officer, 1939-70, bd. chmn., 1967-70; chmn. com. corps. Commerce and Industry Assn. N.Y., 1956-71; incorporator Eye-Bank for Sight Restoration, 1945, bd. 1945—, sec., 1947-70; trustee United Bd. Christian Higher Edn. in Asia, 1952-67, vice chmn. 1958-67, counselor, 1974—; dir. Princeton in Asia, Inc., 1938-74, N.Y.C. Mission Soc., 1961-67; co-founder, chmn. Leap Year Assemblies, N.Y.C., 1924—; trustee, mem. corp. Harvard-Yenching Inst., 1963-78; trustee Tobey Hosp., Wareham, Mass., 1971—, v.p., 1977-79; pres. Princeton Class of 1921, 1941-51, Columbia Law Sch. Class of 1924; mem. Princeton Grad. Council, 1941-63. Recipient Columbia U. Alumni medal, 1954, Distinguished Service award Princeton Class of 1921, 1957, Distinguished Service citation Mayor, N.Y.C., 1957. Mem. Am., N.Y.C., N.Y. State bar assns., Delta Phi. Episcopalian. (trustee, clk., sr. warden). Clubs: Century, University (council), Down Town Assn., Princeton (council), Manursing Island, Pilgrims, Church (pres. 1964-66); Mattapoisett Casino; Nassau, Tower (Princeton); Metropolitan Opera (former officer; dir. 1932-42). Home: Shipyard Lane Mattapoisett MA 02739 Office: 575 Lexington Ave New York NY 10022

WATTS, EMILY STIPES, educator; b. Urbana, Ill., Mar. 16, 1936; d. Royal Arthur and Virginia Louise (Schenck) Stipes; student Smith Coll., 1954-56; A.B., U. Ill., 1958, M.A. (Woodrow Wilson Nat. fellow), 1959, Ph.D., 1963; m. Robert Allan Watts, Aug. 30, 1958; children—Benjamin, Edward, Thomas. Instr. in English, U. Ill., Urbana, 1963-67, asst. prof. English, 1967-73, asso. prof., 1973-77, prof., dir. grad. studies dept. English, 1977-79; bd. dirs. U. Ill. Athletic Assn. John Simon Guggenheim Meml. Found. fellow, 1973-74. Mem. Author's Guild, Ill. Writers' Assn., Phi Beta Kappa, Phi Kappa Phi, Republican. Presbyterian. Author: Ernest Hemingway and The Arts, 1971; The Poetry of American Women from 1632 to 1945, 1977; contbr. articles on Jonathan Edwards, Anne Bradstreet to lit. jours. Home: 1009 W University Ave Champaign IL 61820 Office: 100 English Bldg U Ill Urbana IL 61801

WATTS, ERNST JOHN, lawyer, ednl. adminstr.; b. Delavan, Wis., Apr. 29, 1924; s. Harold W. and Elizabeth (von Seussmilch) W.; B.A., U. Wis., 1949, LL.B., 1950. Admitted to Wis. bar, 1950, Nev. bar, 1977; practiced law, Delavan, 1950-60; judge Walworth County (Wis.) Ct. and Juvenile Ct., 1961-64, 26th Jud. Circuit Ct. Wis., 1964-74; dean Nat. Jud. Coll., Reno, 1974—, mem. faculty, 1969-79; mem. adv. bd. to study performance measures in criminal prosecution and adjudication progress Rand Corp., Santa Monica, Calif.; charter bd. dirs. Inst. for Study of the Trial, Fla. Tech. U.; mem. Nat. Bd. Trial Advocacy, Washington; mem. adv. bd. for research grante U. Minn., Duluth; lectr. in field. Served to capt. AC, U.S. Army, 1942-46. Named Hon. Alumni U. Nev., Revno, 1978; Nat. Jud. Coll. Class of 1965 fellow, 1978. Fellow Am. Bar Found., Inst. Jud. Adminstrn.; mem. Am. Bar Assn., Nat. Council Juvenile and Family Ct. Judges, Am. Judicature Soc., Wis. State Bar Assn., State Bar Nev., Walworth County Bar Assn., Am. Law Inst. Episcopalian. Author: Special Problems in the Judicial Function; contbr. articles on continuing jud. edn. and tng. to profl. publs. Home: 100 N Arlington Ave Reno NV 89501 Office: Jud Coll Bldg U Nev Reno NV 89557

WATTS, GLENN ELLIS, union ofcl.; b. Stony Point, N.C., June 4, 1920; s. George Dewey and Nellie Viola (Ellis) W.; student Wilson Tchrs. Coll., 1938-41; m. Bernice Elizabeth Willett, Nov. 8, 1941; children—Glenn Ellis II, Sharon Elizabeth Ann Watts Cardany, Marianne Elizabeth Watts Cardany. With Chesapeake & Potomac Telephone Co., Washington, 1941-48; with Communications Workers Am. (formerly Nat. Fedn. Telephone Workers), 1942—, pres. div. 36, Washington, 1948-51, dir. dist. 2, 1951-56, asst. to pres., 1956-65, v.p., 1965-69, sec.-treas. union, 1969-74, pres., 1974—; v.p. exec. council AFL-CIO, 1974—, v.p. indsl. union dept., 1968—, mem. exec. bd. maritime trades dept., 1974—; mem. Nat. Labor Com. for U.S. Savs. Bonds, 1975—; nat. advisory bd. Labor Council for Latin Am. Advancement, 1975—; mem. labor policy advisory com. for trade negotiations Dept. Labor, 1975—; mem. industry-labor council White House Conf. on Handicapped Individuals, 1976—; chmn. labor subcom. Pres.'s Com. on Employment of Handicapped, 1977—; mem. sec.'s adv. council Dept. Commerce, 1976-77; mem. Pres.'s Commn. on Mental Health, 1977-78, Pres.'s Commn. on The Holocaust, 1978-79. Past treas. Washington Housing Assn.; past mem. D.C. Appeals and Rev. Bd., D.C. Wage and Hour Rev. Panel, Home Rule for D.C. Com.; mem. nat. advisory com. Nat. Congress Community Econ. Devel., 1974; past chmn. community chest relations com. Nat. Capital Area council Boy Scouts Am., past chmn. James E. West Dist., 1969-71, Silver Beaver award, 1965; pres. Health and Welfare Council of Nat. Capital Area, 1967-69; mem. Inter-Am. adv. com. Postal Tel. and Tel. Internat., 1968-74, mem. exec. com., 1977—, v.p., 1978—; gen. chmn. United Giver's Fund, 1968, pres., 1971-75; sec. United Way of Am., 1971-76; bd. dirs., treas. United Way Internat., 1974-78. Mem.-at-large Democratic Nat. Com., 1974—, mem. incomes policy study group of domestic affairs task group, 1974-76. Trustee, sec.-treas. Am. Inst. Free Labor Devel., 1974—; mem. U.S. Assn. for Club of Rome, 1978—; trustee Human Resources Devel. Inst., 1974—, George Meany Center for Labor Studies, Inc., 1976—, Ford Found., 1976—, Aspen Inst. for Humanistic Studies, Nat. Planning Assn., 1974—; governing bd. Common Cause, 1974-77, sec.-treas. Center for Mgmt. Services, 1974; hon. vice chmn. Am. Trade Union Council for Histadrut, 1974—; mem. nat. adv. council Ariz. Heart Inst., 1974—; bd. dirs. Am. Arbitration Assn., 1975-79, Am. Productivity Center, 1978—, New Directions, 1977—, Alliance to Save Energy, 1977—; mem. nat. com. on coping with interdependence Aspen Program of Humanistic Studies, 1975—; bd. dirs. Initiative Com. for Nat. Econ. Planning, 1975-76; trustee, mem. exec. com. Joint Council Econ. Edn., 1976-79; mem. Commn. on a Nat. Inst. Justice, 1976—; mem. Trilateral Commn., 1977—; mem. Helsinki Watch, 1978—. Recipient Urban Trade Unionist award Nat. Urban Coalition, 1978. Democrat. Methodist. Clubs: Touchdown (Washington); Nat. Democratic. Office: 1925 K St NW Washington DC 20006

WATTS, HAROLD WESLEY, educator; b. Salem, Ore., Sept. 30, 1932; s. Elton L. and Claire (Collard) W.; B.A., U. Ore., 1954; M.A., Yale, 1955, Ph.D., 1957; m. Doris A. Roth, Sept. 28, 1951 (div. Jan. 1974); children—Michael, Suzanne, Jane, Kristin. Mem. econs. faculty Yale, 1957-62, Irving Fisher Research prof., 1971-72; asso. prof. U. Wis., 1963-66; prof. econs., 1966-76, dir. Inst. for Research on Poverty, 1966-71; prof. econs. Columbia, 1976—, dir. Center for Social Scis., 1976-79; cons. Urban Inst., Stanford Research Inst. Mem. Am. Econ. Assn., Econometric Soc., NARC, Carnegie Council on Children. Guggenheim fellow, 1975-76. Author: (with Dernberg and Rossett) Studies in Household Economic Behavior, 1958. Home: 448 Riverside Dr Apt 82 New York NY 10027 Office: Dept Econs Columbia U New York NY 10027

WATTS, HENRY MILLER, JR., stock broker; b. Phila., Mar. 13, 1904; s. Henry Miller and Laura Esther (Barney) W.; grad. St. Paul's Sch., 1921; A.B., Harvard, 1925; m. Maxine Wieczorek, 1935; m. 2d, Anna Harris Pepper, 1952. With Robert Glendinning & Co., Phila., 1925-29; mem. N.Y. Stock Exchange, 1929—, gov., 1958-61, vice chmn. bd. govs., 1961-62, chmn. bd. govs., 1962-65; sr. partner Mitchel Schreiber, Watts & Co., N.Y.C., 1931; pres., chmn. bd. Independence Sq. Income Securities Inc., 1972—; dir. Teradyne Corp., Temporary Investment Fund, Inc.; trustee Trust for Short-Term Fed. Securities; mng. gen. partner Chestnut St. Exchange Fund; trustee Income Trust for U.S. Govt. Guaranteed Securities, 1977—. Bd. dirs. Muscular Dystrophy Assn. Am., 1965—, pres., 1968-75, chmn. exec. com., 1975—. Served lt. (j.g.) to comdr. USNR, 1941-45; capt. Res. (ret.). Decorated Bronze Star with combat V. Mem. Soc. Cincinnati of Pa. (pres. 1968-71), Mil. Order Fgn. Wars, 1st Troop Phila. City Cav. (hon.). Episcopalian. Clubs: Racquet & Tennis (N.Y.C.); Philadelphia. Home: 219 Spruce St Philadelphia PA 19106 Office: 20 Broad St New York City NY 10005

WATTS, LINDA HEATHER, ballet dancer; b. Long Beach, Calif., Sept. 27, 1953; d. Keith Nevin and Sheelagh Maud (Woodhead) W.; student (Ford Found. scholar), Sch. Am. Ballet, 1967-70; mem. N.Y.C. Ballet, 1970—, soloist, 1978, prin. dancer, 1979—. Office: New York City Ballet NY State Theater New York NY 10023

WATTS, MABEL, author; b. London, May 20, 1906; d. Ernest Henry and Edith Mary (Elias) Pizzey; ed. in Eng. and Can.; m. William Watts. Feb. 22, 1936; 1 dau., Patricia Linda Watts Babcock. Came to U.S., 1927, naturalized, 1943. Works include: Jr. Lit. Guild selections Cow in the House, 1956, Everyone Waits, 1959, Weeks and Weeks, 1962; also Henrietta and the Hat, 1962; The Boy Who Listened to Everyone, 1963; The Narrow Escapes of Solomon Smart, 1966; (film) The Story of Zachary Zween, 1967; The King and the Whirly Bird, 1969; The Elephant that Become a Ferryboat, 1971; The Basket That Flew Over the Mountain, 1972; While the Horses Galloped to London, 1973 (Soc. Illustrators show 1974, Children's Book Showcase 1974), Molly and the Giant, 1973 (Book of Yr. award Child Study Assn.); Knights of the Square Table, 1973. Home: 1520 Ralston Ave Burlingame CA 94010

WATTS, MALCOLM S.M., physician; b. N.Y.C., Apr. 30, 1915; s. Malcolm S.M. and Elizabeth (Forbes) W.; A.B., Harvard, 1937; M.D., 1941; m. Genevieve Moffitt, July 12, 1947; children—Pauline, Elizabeth, Malcolm, James. Group practice internal medicine, San Francisco, 1948-76; clin. prof. medicine U. Calif. Sch. Medicine, 1972—, asso. dean, 1966—, dir. Extended Programs in Med. Edn., 1973—, dir. Central San Joaquin Valley Area Health Edn. Center, 1974—; chmn. bd. trustees San Francisco Consortium, 1968-74, trustee, 1974—; dir. Soc. Med. Coll. Dirs. Continuing Med. Edn., 1975—, pres., 1980—; trustee Hospice of San Francisco; pres. Alliance Continuing Med. Edn. Served to capt. M.C., AUS, 1942-46. Recipient Outstanding Community Leadership citation United Community Funds and Councils Am., 1964. Diplomate Pan Am. Med. Assn. Fellow A.C.P., Am. Coll. Hosp. Adminstrs. (hon.); mem. AMA, Calif. Acad. Scis., AAAS, Am. Med. Writers Assn., San Francisco Med. Soc. (pres. 1961), Am. Soc. Internal Medicine (pres. 1964-65), Calif. Med. Assn. (dir. 1962—), Nat. Inst. Medicine, Soc. Med. Friends Wine, Council Biology Editors, San Francisco Med. Soc. Health Plan Inc., Academia Mexicana de Ciencias Mexicano de Cultura (corr.). Editor Western Jour. Medicine. Home: 270 Sea Cliff Ave San Francisco CA 94121 Office: U Calif Sch Medicine San Francisco CA 94143

WATTS, MAURICE LYNN, adj. gen. Utah; b. Murray, Utah, Nov. 20, 1917; s. William Eugene and Ethel Gertrude (Park) W.; B.S., U. Utah, 1940; m. Donna Mae Christensen, Apr. 24, 1946; children—Kim, Brad, Cory, Melinda, Todd. Accountant, U.S. Rubber Co., Salt Lake City, 1940-41; partner Watts Floral & Nursery Co., Salt Lake City, 1946-48; staff asst., then asst. adj. gen. Utah N.G., 1948-64, maj. gen., adj. gen., 1964—. Bd. dirs. Utah Soc. Crippled Children and Adults, 1961-75; Mem. bishopric Mormon Ch., 1956-61, mem. gen. bd. Young's Men Mut. Improvement, 1961-71. Served with AUS, 1940-45. Decorated Legion of Merit, Bronze Star; recipient Silver Beaver award Boy Scouts Am., 1977. Mem. N.G. Assn. U.S., Assn. U.S. Army, Adj. Gens. Assn. U.S. (pres. 1968-71), Utah N.G. Assn. (pres. 1963), U. Utah Alumni Assn. (pres. 1961-63). Home: 2855 Carole Dr Salt Lake City UT 84121 Office: 1543 Sunnyside Ave Salt Lake City UT 84105

WATTS, OLIN ETHREDGE, lawyer; b. Bartow, Fla., Aug. 27, 1899; s. Olin Ethredge and Frances (Allen) W.; A.B., U. of Fla., 1925, LL.B., 1928, J.D., 1928, LL.D. (hon.), 1966; m. Cornelia Colson, June 23, 1926; children—Margaret Cornelia (Mrs. H. Darby Perry), Frances Eloise (Mrs. Edgar W. McCurry, Jr.), Jane. Admitted to the Fla. bar, 1928; mem. law firm Kent, Watts, Durden, Kent & Mickler, Jacksonville, since 1931; mem. Circuit Ct. Commn. Duval Co., Fla., 1942-48; dir. Stockton, Whatley, Davin & Co., Fidelity Fed. Savs. & Loan Assn., Jacksonville, Mem. Welfare bd. Duval Co., 1942-45; chmn. Fla. Bd. Bar Examiners, 1949-56; bd. trustees U. Fla. Law Center. Fellow Am. Bar Found. Mem. Am. Law Inst., Am. Judicature Soc., Nat. Conference Bar Examiners (past chmn.), Am. (past chmn. sect. legal edn. and admissions to the bar), Fla., Jacksonville bar assns., Jacksonville C. of C. (past pres.), Jacksonville Symphony Assn. (past pres.), U. Fla. Alumni Assn. (past pres.), Phi Delta Theta, Phi Delta Phi, Phi Kappa Phi, Phi Beta Kappa, Blue Key Soc., Order of Coif. Clubs: River, Rotary, Ponde Vedra, Yacht, Deerwood. Home: 1876 River Rd Jacksonville FL 32207 Office: Fla Nat Bank Bldg Jacksonville FL 32202

WATTS, ROBERT BURNHAM, lawyer, clergyman; b. Portland, Maine, May 28, 1901; s. Irving Spencer and Almira Kittredge (Roberts) W.; A.B., Bates Coll., Lewiston, Maine, 1922, LL.D., 1957; J.D., Yale, 1925; D.D., Williamette U., 1958; m. Helen Thomson Berry, June 20, 1925; 1 son, Robert Burnham. Admitted to N.Y. bar, 1925; Cal. bar, 1944; asst. U.S. atty., Southern Dist. of N.Y., 1925-27, chief asst. atty., 1927-31; partner Brown, Brenton & Watts, New York, 1931-34; spl. counsel Nat. Labor Relations Bd., Washington, D.C., 1934-35, asso. gen. counsel, 1935-40, gen. counsel, 1941-43; partner, Pruitt, Hale & Coursen, 1943-48; v.p., gen. counsel Consolidated Vultee Aircraft Corp., 1948-54; v.p., gen. counsel Convair div. Gen. Dynamics Corp., 1954-62, dir., 1954-57, mgmt. bd. 1954-62; legal cons. Gen. Dynamics Corp., 1962-73; ordained deacon P.E. Ch., 1957, priest, 1958; asst. minister St. James-by-the-Sea Episcopal Ch., La Jolla, Calif.; columnist Copley News Service, 1966-70. Bd. dirs. Scripps Meml. Hosp., La Jolla, 1947-57, pres. 1948; trustee Bishop's Sch., 1957-69, also Bates Coll., 1960—, S.R. Found. Calif., 1965—; bd. dirs., pres. E.T.B. Healing Prayer Fellowship, 1970—. Recipient George Washington medal Freedoms Found. at Valley Forge, 1966, 67, 68, 69. Mem. Am., Calif. bar assns., Phi Beta Kappa, Delta Sigma Rho, Phi Alpha Delta. Mason (33 deg., grand chaplain, grand cross, past grand orator and grand chaplain Calif., dir. edn. So. Jurisdiction 1969-79). Bd. editors Yale Law Jour. Contbr. legal jours. Home: 7949 Princess St La Jolla CA 92037 Office: 1733 16th St NW Washington DC 20009

WATTS, RONALD LAMPMAN, educator, univ. adminstr.; b. Japan, Mar. 10, 1929; B.A., U. Toronto, 1952; B.A. (Rhodes scholar), Oxford U., 1954, M.A., 1959, D.Phil. (Can. Council fellow), 1962; married Donna Paisley, 1954. Mem. faculty Queen's U., Kingston, Ont., 1955—, prof. polit. studies, 1965—, asst. dean Faculty of Arts and Scis., 1964-66, asso. dean, 1966-69, dean, 1969-74, prin. and vice chancellor, 1974—; tutor Balliol Coll., Oxford U., 1961; Can. Commonwealth Exchange scholar to Australia, 1968; vis. fellow Australian Nat. Univ., Canberra, 1968; Ford Found. vis. prof. Inst. Adminstrn., U. Ife, Ibadan, Nigeria, 1969; vis. lectr. U.K., U.S.A., Australia, New Zealand, Africa, Asia and Can.; cons. New Guinea Govt., 1974, 75; commr. Task Force on Can. Unity. Mem. Assn. Univs. and Colls. Can. (mem. exec. com.), Donner Found. Can. (gov.), Council Deans Arts and Scis. Ont. (past chmn.), Council Ont. Univs. (chmn. 1979—). Club: Kingston Yacht. Author: New Federations: Experiments in the Commonwealth, 1966, rev. edit., 1968; Administration in Federal Systems, 1970; contbr. chpts. to books, articles to profl. jours. Home: Summerhill East Wing Kingston ON K7L 3N6 Canada Office: Queen's Univ Kingston ON K7L 3N6 Canada

WATTS, ROOSEVELT, labor union ofcl.; b. Charlotte, N.C., June 21, 1915; s. Corley and Mora (Jackson) W.; B.A., Cornell U., 1964; m. Sadie Lane, Sept. 15, 1939; children—Roosevelt, Juanita, Wendlin. Streetcar and bus operator N.Y.C. Transit Authority, 1941-58; v.p. Transport Workers Union, Local 100, 1958-64, internat. v.p., 1965-74, internat. sec.-treas., 1974—. Bd. dirs. N.Y. Urban League, 1970-76; co-chmn. ad hoc fin. com. NAACP. Recipient Adam Clayton Powell Achievement award, 1975; Achievement award Hispanic Soc., 1975; Spl. Achievement award N.Y.C. Labor Council, 1976. Mem. Black Trade Unionists City of N.Y. Baptist. Club: Masons. Home: 168-04 Linden Blvd Jamaica NY 11434 Office: 1980 Broadway New York NY 10023

WATTS, VERVON ORVAL, econ. counsel; b. Chesley, Ont., Can., Mar. 25, 1898; s. Theophilus J. and Jennie (Williams) W.; A.B., U. Man., Can., 1918; M.A., Harvard, 1923, Ph.D., 1932; LL.D., Northwood Inst., 1973; m. Juanita Huntley, 1924; children—Joan, Carol, Thomas; m. 2d, to Mrs. Charles A. Phipps, 1949. Came to U.S., 1903, citizen, 1929. Instr. prep. dept., Brandon (Can.) Coll. 1919; asst. prin., high sch., Gilbert Plains, Man., 1919-21; instr. econs., Clark U., Worcester, Mass., 1924-26, Harvard U., 1927-29; lectr. econs. Wellesley (Mass.) Coll., 1929-30; asso. prof. econs. Antioch Coll., Yellow Springs, Ohio, 1930-36, Carleton Coll., Northfield, Minn., 1936-39; vis. prof. econs. Claremont Men's Coll., 1949-51; Burrows T. Lundy prof. philosophy of bus. Campbell Coll., Buies Creek, N.C., 1975-76; econ. counsel, Los Angeles C. of C., 1939-46, So. Calif. Edison Co., 1949-64, Northrop U., 1978; econ. editor, The Found. for Econ. Edn., 1946-49; mem. Economists Nat. Com. on Monetary Policy, 1949—; vis. lectr. Pepperdine Coll., Los Angeles Pacific Coll., 1961-63; dir. econ. edn. Northwood Inst., Midland, Mich., 1963—, also chmn. div. of social studies. Pres. Nat. U. Library Fund, 1959—. Mem. research div., Rep. Nat. Com., Wash., 1936. Recipient Gov. Gen.'s Gold Medal in Polit. Economy, 1918. Mem. Mont Pelerin Soc. Author: Why Are We So Prosperous?, 1938; Production for Use, 1939; Do We Want Free Enterprise?, 1944; The Bretton Woods Agreements, 1945; The Full Employment Act of 1945; Away From Freedom, 1952; Union Monopoly, 1954; United Nations: Planned Tyranny, 1955; Should We Strengthen the United Nations?, 1961; Economize Or Perish., 1964; Free Markets or Famine, 1967; Politics vs. Prosperity, 1976. Vis. editor Nat. Econ. Council Rev. of Books, 1950. Contbr. articles and revs. in jours., mags. Address: 600 Hillcrest Flintridge CA 91011

WAUD, MORRISON, lawyer; b. Oak Park, Ill., Nov. 19, 1910; s. Ernest Peyster and Olive Butler (Morrison) W.; grad. Hill Sch., 1928; A.B., Princeton, 1932; J.D., Northwestern U., 1935; m. Anne Byron Smith, Apr. 24, 1935; children—Diana Birnie, Ernest Peyster III, Cornelius Byron, Morrison, David Butler, Deborah Anne. Admitted to Ill. bar, 1935; asso. Gardner, Carton, Douglas, Chilgren & Waud, Chgo., 1935-41, partner, 1942—. Dir. Am. Bakeries Co., Chgo., Hartford Plaza Bank, Chgo. Alderman, City of Lake Forest, 1950-54, mayor, 1957-60; pres. Lake Forest Caucus, 1963. Bd. dirs. Marie G. Dennett Found.; trustee Northwestern Meml. Hosp., Chgo.; mem. citizens bd. U. Chgo., 1952—, mem. vis. com., social sci. div., 1960—. Served from 1st lt. to maj., USAAF, 1942-45. Decorated Legion of Merit. Mem. Am., Ill., Chgo. bar assns., U.S. Golf Assn. (exec. com. 1963-68), Phi Delta Phi. Republican. Episcopalian (vestryman). Clubs: Collectors, Princeton, Law, Legal, University, Chicago, Commercial (sec. 1963-65), Commonwealth (Chgo.); Onwentsia Golf (Lake Forest); Old Elm Golf (Fort Sheridan, Ill.); Pine Valley (N.J.) Golf; Augusta Nat. Golf (Ga.); Royal Poinciana (Fla.) Golf. Author: New York Foreign Mail Cancellations, 1870-1876, 1968. Home: 501 Oakwood Ave Lake Forest IL 60045 Office: 1 First Nat Plaza Chicago IL 60603

WAUGH, BUTLER HUGGINS, educator; b. Pitts., May 9, 1934; s. Butler Huggins and Olive (Tunnecliffe) W.; B.A., Washington and Jefferson Coll., 1955; postgrad. (Danforth fellow) Johns Hopkins, 1955-56; Ph.D. (Danforth fellow), Ind. U., 1959; m. Dolores Lindley, Sept. 20, 1953 (div. Jan. 1972); children—Butler Huggins III, Olivia, Charles, Eliza, Rebekah; m. 2d, Jennie Jerome, Mar. 29, 1972 (div. Jan. 1976); 1 son, William. Instr. English, U. Kan., Lawrence, 1959-61; asst. prof. U. Fla., Gainesville, 1961-67, asso. prof., 1967-70; exec. asst. to pres. Fla. Internat. U., Miami, 1969-70, prof. English,

1970—, dean Coll. Arts and Scis., 1970-75; coordinator humanities and fine arts div. acad. affairs State Univ. System Fla., Tallahassee, 1968-69. Mem. South Atlantic Modern Lang. Assn., Modern Lang. Assn., Am. Folklore Soc., Phi Beta Kappa. Home: 720 NW 132 St North Miami FL 33168

WAUGH, JAMES CORWIN, airline exec.; b. Huntington, W.Va., Aug. 20, 1921; s. James B. and Ruth Helen (Lady) W.; B.B.A. cum laude, U. Miami (Fla.), 1953; m. Maxine Prockter, July 29, 1944; children—Barbara, James Stephen, Elizabeth, Meghan. Civil engring. aide Corps U.S. Engrs., 1939-42; with Pan Am. World Airways, 1942—, check capt., 1965—, dir. flight standards Pacific, then v.p. flight ops., 1974-75, sr. v.p. flight ops., 1975—, sr. v.p. maintenance and engring., 1978—. Mem. Am. Inst. Aeros. and Astronautics. Club: Wings (N.Y.C.). Address: Pan Am World Airways JF Kennedy Internat Airport Jamaica NY 11430

WAUGH, JOHN STEWART, educator, chemist; b. Willimantic, Conn., Apr. 25, 1929; s. Albert E. and Edith (Stewart) W.; A.B., Dartmouth, 1949; Ph.D., Cal. Inst. Tech., 1953; children—Alice Collier, Frederick Pierce. Research fellow physics Cal. Inst. Tech., 1952-53; mem. faculty Mass. Inst. Tech., 1953—, prof. chemistry, 1962—, Albert Amos Noyes prof., 1973—. Vis. prof. U. Cal. at Berkeley, 1963-64. lectr. Robert Welch Found., 1968; Falk-Plaut lectr. Columbia, 1973; DuPont lectr. U. S.C., 1974; Lucy Pickett lectr. Mt. Holyoke Coll., 1978; Reilly lectr. U. Notre Dame, 1978; Spedding lectr. Iowa State U., 1979; sr. fellow Alexander von Humboldt-Stiftung, also vis. prof. Max Planck Inst., Heidelberg, 1972; mem. chemistry adv. panel NSF, 1966-69, vice chmn., 1968-69; mem. rev. com. Argonne Nat. Lab., 1970-74; exchange visitor USSR Acad. Scis., 1962, 75; mem. vis. com. Tufts U., 1966-69, Princeton, 1973-78; mem. fellowship com. Alfred P. Sloan Found., 1977—. Recipient Irving Langmuir award, 1976 Sloan fellow, 1958-62; Pitts. award Spectroscopic Soc. Pitts., 1979. Guggenheim fellow, 1963-64, 72 Fellow Am. Acad. Arts and Scis., Am. Phys. Soc.; mem. Nat. Acad. Scis., Unamerican Chem. Soc. (pres. 1962-), AAAS, Phi Beta Kappa, Sigma Xi. Author: New NMR Methods in Solid State Physics, 1978. Editor: Advances in Magnetic Resonance, 1965—; asso. editor Jour. Chem. Physics, 1965-67, Spectrochimica Acta, 1964-78; editorial bd. Chem. Revs., 1978—. Home: Conant Rd Lincoln MA 01773 Office: 77 Massachusetts Ave Cambridge MA 02139

WAUGH, THEODORE ROGERS, orthopedic surgeon; b. Montreal, Que., Can., Sept. 21, 1926; s. Theodore Rogers and Anne Maude (Lawlor) W.; B.A., Yale U., 1949; M.D., C.M., McGill U., 1953; D.Med.Sci., U. Goteborg (Sweden), 1968; m. Frances Stewart Patch, Sept. 12, 1952; children—Susanne Rogers, Margaret Stewart, Theodore Rogers. Intern, Royal Victoria Hosp., Montreal, 1953-54; asst. resident in pathology McGill U., 1954-55; asst. resident in surgery N.Y. U. Bellevue Med. Center, 1955-56; asst. resident, resident, fellow N.Y. Orthopedic Hosp., Columbia U., 1958-62, instr., clin. asst. prof. orthopedic surgery, 1962-68; asst. attending Presbyn. Hosp., N.Y.C., 1962-68; chmn., chief div. orthopedic surgery U. Calif., Irvine, 1968-78; prof., chmn. dept. orthopedic surgery N.Y. U. Med. Center, 1978—. Served to capt., M.C., USAF, 1956-58. Fellow A.C.S., Royal Coll. Surgeons (Can.), Am. Coll. Sports Medicine; mem. AMA, Med. Soc. State N.Y., Med. Soc. County N.Y., Am. Acad. Orthopaedic Surgeons, Scoliosis Research Soc., Can. Orthopaedic Assn., Assn. Bone and Joint Surgeons, Assn. Orthopaedic Chmn., Am. Orthopaedic Assn., Am. Orthopaedic Soc. for Sports Medicine. Diplomate Am. Bd. Orthopaedic Surgery. Republican. Presbyterian. Clubs: Interurban Orthopaedic, 20th Century Orthopedic. Contbr. numerous articles to profl. jours. Designer surg. devices used in orthopaedic surgery. Office: NY U Med Center 550 1st Ave New York NY 10016

WAUGH, WILLIAM HOWARD, physician, educator; b. N.Y.C., May 13, 1925; s. Richey Laughlin and Lyda Pearl (Leamer) W.; student Boston U., 1943, W.Va. U., 1944; M.D., Tufts U., 1948, postgrad., 1949-50; m. Eileen Loretta Garrigan, Oct. 4, 1952; children—Mark Howard, Kathleen Carey, William Peter. Intern, L.I. Coll. Hosp., Bklyn., 1948-49, asst. resident 1950-51; asst. resident U. Md. Hosp., Balt., 1951-52; cardiovascular research trainee Med. Coll. Ga., Augusta, 1954-55, asst. research prof. physiology, 1955-60, asso. medicine, 1957-60, USPHS Sr. Research fellow physiology, 1959-60; asso. prof. medicine, U. Ky. Coll. Medicine, Lexington, 1960-69, Ky. Heart Assn. prof. cardiovascular research, 1963-71, head renal sect. dept. medicine, 1960-68, prof. medicine, 1969-71; prof. medicine and physiology East Carolina U. Sch. Medicine, Greenville, 1971—, dir. dept. clin. scis., 1971-76. Mem. med. adv. bd. Kidney Found. Ky., 1967-71, chmn., 1969-70. Served with AUS, 1943-46; from 1st lt. to capt. USAF, 1952-54. Fellow A.C.P.; mem. Am. Physiol. Soc., Am. Heart Assn., Am. Soc. Nephrology, AAAS, Microcirculatory Soc., AMA, N.C. Med. Soc., So. Salt, Water and Kidney Club; Sigma Xi. Contbr. articles in cardiovascular research, muscle and renal physiology, internal medicine to life sci. and med. jours. Home: 119 Oxford Rd Greenville NC 27834

WAWZONEK, STANLEY, educator; b. Valley Falls, R.I., June 23, 1914; s. John and Sophie (Krol) W.; B.S., Brown U., 1935; Ph.D., U. Minn., 1939; m. Marian L. Matlock, Sept. 2, 1943; children—Ann Elizabeth, Lucile Kay, Mary Louise. Chemist, U. Minn., 1939-40; NRC fellow, 1940-41; instr. U. Ill., 1941-43, U. Tenn., 1943-44; asst. prof. State U. Iowa, 1944-47, asso. prof., 1947-52, prof., 1952—, chmn. dept. chemistry, 1962-68. Recipient Iowa award, 1960, Outstanding Achievement award U. Minn., 1975, Midwest award, 1976. Mem. Am. Chem. Soc., Electrochem. Soc., Am. Assn. Advancement Sci., Iowa Acad. Sci. (pres. 1971-72), Phi Lambda Upsilon, Alpha Chi Sigma. Conglist. Rotarian. Divisional editor Jour. Electrochem. Soc.; mem. editorial bd. Organic Prep. Proc. Internat. Home: 2014 Ridgeway Dr Iowa City IA 52240

WAX, BERNARD, historian; b. Phila., Apr. 4, 1930; s. Samuel and Anna (Kaminker) W.; B.A., U. Chgo., 1950, M.A., 1955; postgrad. U. Wis., 1955-59; m. Dolores Helen Nemchek, Mar. 21, 1953; children—Ann Susan, Steven Albert, Stuart Michael, Rebecca Mara. Field rep., field services supr. Ill. State Hist. Library, 1959-66; dir. Am. Jewish Hist. Soc., Waltham, Mass., 1966—; mem. Ill. State Records Commn., 1961-66, Cook County State Records Commn., 1961-66. Served with Signal Corps, U.S. Army, 1953-55. Mem. Am. Hist. Assn., Bay State Hist. League (editor, bd. dirs. 1971-76, pres. 1976-78), Am. Assn. for State and Local History, Orgn. Am. Historians. Editor: Assn. Jewish Libraries Bull., 1970-72, Bay State Hist. League Bull., 1971-73. Home: 21 Blake Rd Brookline MA 02146 Office: 2 Thornton Rd Waltham MA 02154

WAX, EDWARD LEWIS, advt. agy. exec.; b. Lowell, Mass., Jan. 3, 1937; s. Morris and Helen (Arenson) W.; B.S. in Chem. Engring., Northeastern U., 1959; M.B.A., Wharton Grad. Div., U. Pa., 1961; m. Susan Goldman, May 29, 1966; children—Elizabeth, Alexander. With E.I. duPont de Nemours, Del., 1961-63, Compton Advt., Inc., N.Y.C., 1963-77; pres., chief operating officer Manoff Geers Gross Inc., N.Y.C., 1977—. Served to 1st lt. Signal Corps, U.S. Army, 1961-63. Home: 251 E 51st St New York NY 10022 Office: 845 3d Ave New York NY 10022*

WAX, STEPHEN MARTIN, record co. exec.; b. Long Island City, N.Y., Jan. 31, 1943; s. Walter and Theresa W.; B.B.A., Pace Coll., 1964; m. Roberta Wax, Mar. 27, 1965; children—Lisa, Jodi. Nat. promotion dir. Jubilee Records, N.Y.C., 1964-68; v.p. promotion Bell Records, N.Y.C., 1968-73; pres. Elektra/Asylum Records, Los Angeles, 1973—. Home: Tarzana CA 91356 Office: 962 N La Cienega Blvd Los Angeles CA 90069

WAXENBERG, ALAN M., publisher; b. Davenport, Iowa, Mar. 1, 1935; s. George and Rose W.; B.A., U. Iowa, 1956; m. Suzanne C. Ecker, Oct. 26, 1958; children—Robin Lynn, Scott Stephen. Formerly central advt. dir. Look mag., nat. advt. dir. Petersen Pub. Co., pub. Motor mag. Hearst Pub. Co.; now pub. Sports Afield mag. Hearst Pub. Co., N.Y.C. Active United Jewish Appeal-Fedn., Anti-Defamation League, Jr. Achievement, United Fund. Served with U.S. Army, 1956-58. Mem. Mag. Pubs. Assn., Adcraft Club Detroit, U. Iowa Alumni Assn. Clubs: Franklin Hills Country (Franklin, Mich.); Recess (Detroit); Metropolis Country (White Plains, N.Y.). Office: Sports Afield Mag 250 W 55th St New York NY 10019

WAXMAN, ALBERT SAMUEL, actor, writer, producer, dir.; b. Toronto, Ont., Can., Mar. 2, 1935; s. Aaron and Tobie (Glass) W.; B.A., U. Western Ont., 1957; postgrad. U. Toronto Law Sch., 1957-58; student Neighbourhood Playhouse Sch. of Theatre N.Y., 1958-59, London Sch. Film Technique, 1963, Sch. Motion Picture Prodn., N.Y.C., 1964; m. Sara Shapiro, Oct. 24, 1968; children—Tobaron, Adam. Pres., Tobaron Prodns., Ltd., Toronto, 1967—; actor theatre West End, London, 1962, Off Broadway, N.Y.C., 1965, Repertory Theatre, Eng., 1961-62; summer stock in New Eng. states, 1958-59; actor in films Columbia Pictures, 20th Century Fox, Independents, 1961-71, also TV, U.S. and Canada, 1961-77; star of series King of Kensington, 1975—; dir. films: The Crowd Inside, 1971, My Pleasure is My Business, 1974; dir. TV films, 1968, 69, 77 dir. theatrical short Tviggy, 1968; dir. commls. and documentaries; author screenplays: The Crowd Inside, 1969, Big Joe, Little Joe, 1972; guest lectr. univs., colls. and high schs. Active United Jewish Appeal, United Way, Big Bros.; nat. campaign chmn. Can. Cancer Soc., 1979. Recipient ACTRA award for Best Performance in Continuing TV Series King of Kensington, 1976; Clio awards certificate for Advt. Excellenc-World-Wide, 1975; Her Majesty Queen Elizabeth's Silver Jubilee medal, 1979. Mem. Assn. Canadian TV and Radio Artists, Screen Actors Guild, Actors Equity, Brit. Actors Equity, Dirs. Guild Can., Canadian Assn. Motion Picture Producers, Acad. Canadian Cinema. Club: Variety. Address: 15 Roxborough St E Toronto ON M4W 1V5 Canada. *Life to me is a process just as learning is. I have some distance to go yet in this process so I will not comment now, other than to say "Making it" is happily, a never-ending process of making it.*

WAXMAN, HENRY ARNOLD, congressman; b. Los Angeles, Sept. 12, 1939; s. Louis and Esther (Silverman) W.; B.A. in Polit. Sci., U. Calif., Los Angeles, 1961, J.D., 1964; m. Janet Kessler, Oct. 17, 1971; children—Carol Lynn, Michael David. Admitted to Calif. bar, 1965; mem. Calif. State Assembly, 1969-74; mem. 94th-96th Congresses from 24th Calif. Dist. Pres., Calif. Fedn. Young Democrats, 1965-67. Mem. ACLU, Guardians Jewish Home for Aged, Am. Jewish Congress, Sierra Club. Jewish. Club: B'nai B'rith. Office: 1721 Longworth House Office Bldg Washington DC 20515*

WAY, ALVA OTIS, elec. mfg. co. exec.; b. Schenectady, Apr. 27, 1929; s. Alva Otis and Margaret L. (Sigsbee) W.; A.B. in Economics, Brown U., 1951; m. Eleonore Maurer; children—Peter, Karin Andrea, Cynthia Helena. With Gen. Electric Co., 1951-70, 73-79, traveling auditor, 1957-61, audit adminstr., 1961-62, various managerial positions domestic ops. and fgn. affiliates, Venezuela, Brazil, France, 1962-70, v.p., v.p. fin., chief fin. officer, Fairfield, Conn., 1973-79, named mem. corp. policy bd., 1974, also dir. Gen. Electric Credit Corp., Can. Gen. Electric Co. Ltd., Utah Internat. Inc.; v.p. Honeywell Info. Systems Inc., 1970-73, sr. v.p. fin., 1977-79; vice chmn., dir., chmn. fin. com. Am. Express Co., 1979—; Trustee Brown U. Served with U.S. Army, 1952-54. Mem. Fin. Execs. Inst. (trustee Fin. Execs. Research Found., trustee Fin. Acctg. Found., mem. fin. acctg. standards br.), Conf. Bd. (mem. council fin. execs.), Sigma Chi. Home: 87 N Wilton Rd New Canaan CT 06840 Office: Office Vice Chmn Am Express Co Am Express Plaza New York NY 10004

WAY, E. LEONG, pharmacologist, toxicologist; b. Watsonville, Calif., July 10, 1916; s. Leong Man and Lai Har (Shew) W.; B.S., U. Calif., Berkeley, 1938, M.S., 1940, Ph.D., San Francisco, 1942; m. Madeline Li, Aug. 11, 1944; children—Eric, Linette. Pharm. chemist Merck & Co., Rahway, N.J., 1942; instr. in pharmacology George Washington U., 1943-46, asst. prof., 1946-49; asst. prof. pharmacology U. Calif., San Francisco, 1949-52, asso. prof., 1952-57, prof., 1957—, chmn. dept. pharmacology, 1973-78; USPHS spl. research fellow U. Berne (Switzerland), 1955-56; vis. prof., China Med. Bd. research fellow U. Hong Kong, 1962-63; mem. disulfiram-methadone coop. study planning com. VA, 1976—; mem. sci. adv. com. Pharm. Mfrs. Assn. Found., 1968—; bd. dirs. Li Found., 1969—. Recipient 1st Achievement award in Pharmacodynamics Am. Pharm. Assn. Found., 1962, Faculty Research Lectr. award U. Calif., San Francisco, 1974, San Francisco Chinese Hosp. award, 1976; Cultural citation and Gold medal Ministry of Edn., Republic of China, 1978; Nathan B. Eddy award Com. on Problems in Drug Dependence. Fellow Am. Coll. Neuropsychopharmacology, AAAS, Am. Coll. Clin. Pharmacology (hon.); mem. Am. Soc. Pharmacology, Exptl. Therapeutics (bd. editors 1957-65, pres. 1976-77), Fedn. Am. Socs. Exptl. Biology (exec. bd. 1975-78, pres. 1977-78), Am. Pharm. Assn. (life; co-recipient Ebert prize certificate 1962), AMA (affiliate), Soc. Aid and Rehab. Drug Addicts (Hong Kong; life), Western Pharmacology Soc. (pres. 1963-64), Council Sci. Soc. Presidents (exec. com. 1979—), Sigma Xi. Contbr. numerous articles and revs. to profl. publs.; editor: New Concepts in Pain, 1967; (with others) Fundamentals of Drug Metabolism and Drug Disposition, 1971; Endogenous and Exogenous Opiate Agonists and Antagonists, 1979; research on drug metabolism, analgetics, developmental pharmacology, drug tolerance and dependence; editorial bd. Internat. Jour. Addictions, 1966—, Clin. Pharmacology, Therapeutics, 1975—, Drug, Alcohol Dependence, 1976—, Progress in Neuro-psychopharmacology, 1977—, Research Communications in Chem. Pathology and Pharmacology, 1978—. Office: Dept Pharmacology U Calif San Francisco CA 94143

WAY, WALTER LEE, anesthetist, pharmacologist; b. Rochester, N.Y., June 27, 1931; s. Kenneth F. and Mary F. (Faulkner) W.; B.S. in Pharmacy, U. Buffalo, 1953; M.D., SUNY, Syracuse U., 1957; M.S., U. Calif., San Francisco, 1962; m. Elizabeth J. Folwell, July 9, 1955; children—Barbara, Jonathon, Jeffrey. Intern, Highland Hosp., Rochester, N.Y., 1957-58; resident U. Calif., San Francisco, 1958-60, trainee, 1960-62, instr. anesthesia and oral medicine, 1960-64, asst. prof. anesthesiology, 1962-64, asst. prof. anesthesiology and pharmacology, 1964-68, asso. prof. anesthesiology and pharmacology, 1968-74, prof. anesthesiology and pharmacology, 1974—; vis. prof. various univs. cons. in field. Fellow N.Y. Acad. Sci.; mem. Am. Soc. Anesthesiologists, Calif. Soc. Anesthesiologists, Assn. Univ. Anesthesiologists, Am. Soc. Pharmacology and Exptl. Therapeutics. Office: U Calif S-436 San Francisco CA 94143

WAYLAND, J(AMES) HAROLD, biomed. scientist, educator; b. Boise, Idaho, July 2, 1909; s. Charles William and Daisy (McConnell) W.; B.S., U. Idaho, 1931, D.Sc. (hon.), 1977; M.S., Calif. Inst. Tech., 1935, Ph.D., 1937; m. Virginia Jane Kartzke, June 24, 1933; children—Ann Marie Peters, Elizabeth Jane (Mrs. Paul T. Barber). Am. Scandinavian Found. fellow U. Copenhagen, 1937; asst. prof. physics U. Redlands, 1938-41; mil. research in mine warfare and torpedo devel., 1941-48; asso. prof. applied mechanics Calif. Inst. Tech., Pasadena, 1949-57, prof., 1957-63, prof. engring. sci., 1963-79, prof. emeritus, 1979—. U.S. coordinator U.S.-Japan Coop. Seminars on Peripheral Circulation, 1967, 70; mem. cardiovascular and renal study sect. NIH, 1973-77; vis. prof. Shinshu U., Matsumoto, Japan, 1973, U. Limburg, Maastricht, The Netherlands, 1979. Recipient Ordnance Devel. award U.S. Navy, 1945; Certificate of Recognition, NASA, 1975. Guggenheim fellow, 1953-54; research grantee NIH, NSF, John A. Hartford Found., Kroc Found. Mem. Microcirculatory Soc. (pres. 1971-72), AAAS (chmn. med. scis. sect. 1976), Am. Phys. Soc., Am. Physiol. Soc., European Microcirculatory Soc., Internat. Soc. Biorheology, Am. Inst. Archeology, Am. Soc. Enologists, AAUP, Playing Card Soc., Sigma Xi, Phi Beta Kappa, Sigma Tau. Democrat. Unitarian. Club: Athenaeum. Author: Differential Equations Applied in Science and Engineering, 1957; Complex Variables Applied in Science and Engineering, 1970. Contbr. articles to profl. publs.; also books and articles on history of playing cards. Patentee in field. Home: 361 S Greenwood Ave Pasadena CA 91107 Office: Calif Inst Tech Pasadena CA 91125

WAYLAND, RUSSELL GIBSON, JR., govt. ofcl.; b. Treadwell, Alaska, Jan. 23, 1913; s. Russell Gibson and Fanchon (Borie) W.; B.S., U. Wash., 1934; A.M., Harvard, 1937; M.S., U. Minn., 1935, Ph.D., 1939; m. Mary Mildred Brown, 1943 (div. 1964); children—Nancy, Paul R.; m. 2d, Virginia Bradford Phillis, Dec. 24, 1965. Engr., geologist Homestake Mining Co., Lead, S.D., summers 1930-39; with U.S. Geol. Survey, 1939-42, 1952—, chief conservation div., 1966-78, research phys. scientist Office of Dir., 1978—. With Army-Navy Munitions Bd., 1942-45, Office Mil Govt. and Allied High Commn., Germany, 1945-52; instr. geology U. Minn., 1937-39. Served to lt. col. AUS, 1942-46. Decorated Army Commendation medal; recipient Distinguished Service award Dept. Interior. Mem. Am. Inst. Mining, Metall. and Petroleum Engrs., Mineral. Soc. Am., Geol. Soc. Am., Assn. Profl. Geol. Scientists, Geochem. Soc., Soc. Econ. Geologists, Assn. Engring. Geologists, Sigma Xi, Tau Beta Pi, Phi Gamma Delta, Sigma Gamma Epsilon, Gamma Alpha, Phi Mu Alpha (Sinfonia). Club: Cosmos. Author sci. bulls. in field. Home: 4660 N 35th St Arlington VA 22207 Office: U S Geol Survey National Center Reston VA 22092

WAYLAND, SLOAN RIGDON, sociologist; b. Conway, Ark., Nov. 6, 1918; s. Edward Theodore and Sue (Koontz) W.; B.A., Hendrix Coll., Conway, Ark., 1940; M.A., La. State U., 1941; Ph.D., Columbia U., 1951; m. Mayneal McCoy, 1943; children—Edward, Kenneth, Joanna. Mem. faculty Columbia U. Tchrs. Coll., 1947—, prof. sociology, 1951—, asso. dean, 1976—; vis. prof. Am. U. Beirut, 1957-58; ednl. adviser Ford Found., Middle East Regional Office, Beirut, 1958-59; cons. in field. Democratic committeeman Rockland County, N.Y., 1950-56. Served with USAAF, 1942-46. Grantee Social Sci. Research Council, 1956. Mem. Am. Sociol. Assn., Rural Sociol. Soc., Am. Ednl. Research Assn., AAAS. Author: Social Patterns of Farming, 1951; Educational Characteristics of American People, 1958. - Coordinating editor: Population Education in Asia: A Source Book, 1976. Home: Schuyler Rd Central Nyack NY 10960 Office: Box 174 Teachers Coll Columbia Univ New York City NY 10027

WAYNE, DONALD, editor; b. N.Y.C., May 13, 1913; s. Benjamin and Rose (Frank) W.; B.A., Cornell U., 1934; m. Elaine Pailthorpe, Nov. 23, 1938 (dec. July 1972); children—Arthur, Christina, Victoria, Alistair; m. 2d, Helena Paula Malinowska Burke, June 29, 1974. Stage mgr. Broadway theatricals, Ethan Frome, St. Helena, 1934-37; novelist, radio writer, 1937-40; editor Victory, Photo Review, overseas br. OWI, 1942-45; screen writer Selznick Studios, Hollywood, 1945-46; free lance writer nat. mags., 1945-56; asst. mng. editor Parade mag., 1956-58, mag. editor, 1958-65; mng. dir. Roto Publs., Ltd., London, Eng.; editor-pub. Friday mag.; pub. Southeast Living mag.; editor The Am.; mng. dir. Am. Weekly Newspapers, Ltd.; pub. Historic London for Ams. Author: Fine Flowers in the Valley, 1937; screen Adaptation Thomas Wolfe's Look Homeward, Angel. Home: Old High Hall Wickhambrook Newmarket Suffolk CB8 8XX England

WAYNE, JOEL ROBERT, advt. exec.; b. N.Y.C., Sept. 9, 1938; s. Al and Evelyn (Levine) W.; grad. Sch. Visual Arts, N.Y.C.; m. Kika Epstein, Feb. 19, 1961; children—April, Douglas, Leslie. Free-lance animation designer; asst. art dir. Benton & Bowles, advt., N.Y.C., 1961-62; with Grey Advt., N.Y.C., 1962—, now exec. v.p., creative dir. Bd. dirs. Phoenix House, drug rehab. Recipient awards N.Y. Art Dirs. Club, also Clio award. Address: 777 3d Ave New York City NY 10017

WAYNE, JUNE C., artist; b. Chgo., Mar. 8, 1918; d. Albert and Dorothy Alice (Kline) LaVine; D.F.A. (hon.), 1976. Indsl. designer, N.Y.C., 1939-41; radio writer, mem. staff sta. WGN, Chgo., 1942-43; founder, 1959, since dir. Tamarind Lithography Workshop, Inc., funded by Ford Found., Los Angeles; adviser Tamarind Inst., U. N.Mex., 1970—; mem. vis. com. Sch. Visual and Environ. Studies, Harvard, 1972-74; mem. chancellors adv. com., arts mgmt. program Grad. Sch. Adminstrn., U. Calif. at Los Angeles, 1969—. Numerous one-woman exhbns., 1935—, latest being Art Mus., U. N.Mex., 1968, Cin. Art Mus., 1969, Iowa Art Mus., U. Iowa, 1970, Grunwald Graphics Arts Found., U. Calif. at Los Angeles, 1971, Municipal Art Gallery, Barnsdale Park, Los Angeles, 1973, Van Doren Gallery, San Francisco, 1974, La Demeure, Paris, 1974, Musée de Brest (France), 1976, Montgomery Gallery, Pomona Colls., Calif., 1978, Ariz. State U. Galleries, 1978, ICA travelling exhbn., Rennes, 1976, Nancy, 1977, Brussels, 1978, Reims, 1978, Lyons, 1979; rep. permanent collections Library of Congress, Mus. Modern Art, N.Y.C., Art Inst. Chgo., Houghton Library at Harvard, Smithsonian Instn., Rosenwald Collection, Nat. Gallery Art, N.Y. Pub. Library, Cin. Art Mus., Pasadena (Cal.) Mus. Art, Phila. Mus. Art, Phila. Print Club, Walker Art Center, Mpls.; bd. dirs. Grunwald Center Graphic Arts, 1965—. Recipient numerous prizes, 1950—, latest being Prix de la Biennal Internat. de L'Estampe d'Epinal, France, 1971, Purchase prize Biennal d'Epinal, 1973; Golden Eagle Cine award and Acad. award nomination for film Four Stones for Kanemitzu, 1974. Mem. Writers Guild Am., Women in Film, AFTRA, Women's Caucus for Art, Soc. Am. Graphic Artists, Soc. Washington Printmakers, Los Angeles Printmakers Soc. Contbr. articles to profl. publs.; subject TV programs. Address: 1108 N Tamarind Av Los Angeles CA 90038

WAYNE, PATRICK JOHN, actor; b. Los Angeles, July 15, 1939; s. John and Josephine Alicia (Saenz) W.; B.S. in Biology, Loyola U., Los Angeles, 1961; m. Margaret Hunt, Dec. 11, 1965 (div.); children—Michael Ian, Melanie Margaret, Anthony Andrew. Films include: Rio Grande, 1950, The Quiet Man, 1951, Mr. Roberts, 1954, The Searchers, 1955, The Alamo, 1960, The Comancheros, 1961, Cheyenne Autumn, 1962, McClintock, 1963, Shenandoah, 1965, The Green Berets, 1968, Sole Survivor, 1969, Big Jake, 1970, Beyond

Atlantis, 1972, Mustang Country, 1975, Sinbad III, 1975, Texas Detour, 1977, The People that Time Forgot, 1978; TV series: The Rounders, 1967, Shirley, 1979; TV movies: Yesterday's Child, The Last Hurrah, Three on a Date, Grizzly Adams; appearances on TV shows include: Twelve O'Clock High, Have Gun Will Travel, Alcoa Theatre, FBI, Police Woman, McCloud, Marcus Welby, M.D.; rec. artist That's Why, Love in the Country; also commls. Served with USCG, 1961. Republican. Roman Catholic. . *I have tried to live by the Golden Rule, to take responsibility for my life, and my fellow man. And never to be afraid to make a mistake.*

WEADOCK, DANIEL P., corp. exec.; b. N.Y.C., June 21, 1939; B.S. in Fin., Fordham U., 1967; m. Florence Towey, Oct. 5, 1961; children—Daniel, Bryan, Kevin, Ann. With central bookkeeping Chase Manhattan Bank, 1957-61; with ITT, 1961—, spl. asst. to office of pres., 1969-75, dir. ops. ITT Africa and Middle East, Brussels, 1975-79, pres. ITT Africa and Middle East, 1979—, v.p. ITT, 1979—.

WEAKLAND, REMBERT G., archbishop; b. Patton, Pa., Apr. 2, 1927; s. Basil and Mary (Kane) W.; A.B., St. Vincent Coll., 1948; student Julliard Sch. Music, N.Y.C., 1954; grad. studies Sch. Music, Columbia U., 1954-56; L.H.D., Duquesne U., 1964, Belmont Coll., 1964, Cath. U. Am., 1975, St. Joseph's Coll., Rensselaer, Ind., 1979. Joined Benedictines, Roman Cath. Ch., 1945; ordained priest, 1951; mem. faculty music dept. St. Vincent Coll., 1957-63, chmn., 1961-63, chancellor chmn. of bd. of Coll., 1963-67; elected co-adjutor archabbot, 1963, abbot primate Benedictine Confederation, 1967-77; archbishop of Milw., 1977—. Mem. Ch. Music Assn. Am. (pres. 1964-66), Am. Guild Organists. Office: 345 N 95th St Milwaukee WI 53226

WEAN, RAYMOND JOHN, JR., steel mill equipment exec.; b. Warren, Ohio, May 30, 1921; s. Raymond John and Sara Ritner (Boone) W.; B.S., Yale, 1943; m. Adelaide Chave McCracken, May 22, 1943; children—Thomas Frederick, Raymond John III, Gordon Beekman, Sara Rebecca. Pres., chief exec. officer Wean United, Inc.; chmn. bd. Wean United Can., Ltd., Galt, Ont.; dir. 2d Nat. Bank of Warren, Wean Japan Co., Ltd., Tokyo, Stedman Foundry & Machine Co., Aurora, Ind.; dir., corporator Pitts. Nat. Bank. Trustee Palm Beach (Fla.) Day Sch. Served as lt. USNR, World War II. Mem. Am. Iron and Steel Inst., Assn. Iron and Steel Engrs., N.A.M., Machinery and Allied Products Inst., Trumbull County Mfrs. Assn., Chi Phi. Clubs: Trumbull Country, Youngstown (Ohio); Union (Cleve.); Edgeworth, Allegheny Country, Sewickley Hts. Golf (Sewickley, Pa.); Duquesne (Pitts.); Everglades, Bath and Tennis (Palm Beach, Fla.); Capitol Hill (Washington). Home: Scaife Rd Sewickley PA 15143 Office: 948 Fort Duquesne Blvd Pittsburgh PA 15222

WEANER, KARL HULL, lawyer; b. Defiance, Ohio, May 2, 1907; s. Karl A. and Zora E. (Hull) W.; student Defiance Coll., 1926-27; LL.B., Ohio State U., 1931; m. Dorothy G. Houck, Feb. 1, 1933; children—Zora Weaner Matson, John W. Admitted to Ohio bar, 1931, U.S. Supreme Ct. bar, 1957; mem. firm Weaner, Hutchinson, Zimmerman & Bacon, Defiance, 1949—; dir. State Bank & Trust Co., 1938—, chmn. bd., 1970—; dir., v.p. Ohio Bar Title Ins. Co., Dayton; pros. atty.; common pleas judge. Trustee, Trinity United Meth. Ch., Defiance Coll., Toledo Soc. Crippled Children; chmn. Defiance County Republican com., 1939—. Served with USNR, 1942-46. Fellow Am. Coll. Probate Counsel; mem. Am., Ohio, Defiance County bar assns., Am. Judicature Soc., Internat. Assn. Ins. Counsel, Nat. Assn. Railroad Trial Counsel. Clubs: Elks, Mason, Eagles. Home: 722 E High St Defiance OH 43512

WEAR, JAMES SMITH, publisher; b. Beaver Meadows, Pa., Jan. 21, 1914; s. James and Mary Carter (Wear) Smith; student pub. schs.; m. Minnie M. Eichinger, Nov. 18, 1933; children—Richard C., William H., Prudence H. Advt. dir. Jersey Jour., Jersey City, 1952-55, pub., 1967—; advt. dir. Star-Ledger, Newark, 1956-64; gen. mgr. Post-Standard, Syracuse, N.Y., 1964-67. Served to 2d lt. USAAF, 1944-46. Home: Troy Towers 380 Mountain Rd Union City NJ 07087 Office: 30 Journal Sq Jersey City NJ 07306

WEARLY, WILLIAM LEVI, cons. engr., b. Warren, Ind., Dec. 5, 1915; s. Purvis Gardner and Ethel Ada (Jones) W.; B.S., Purdue U., 1937, Dr. Engring. (hon.), 1959; m. Mary Jane Riddle, Mar. 8, 1941; children—Patricia Ann, Susan, William Levi, Elizabeth. Student career engr. C.A. Dunham Co., Michigan City, Ind., 1936; mem. elec. design staff Joy Mfg. Co., Franklin, Pa., 1937-39, v.p., gen. sales mgr., 1952-56, exec. v.p., 1956-57, pres., dir., 1957-62; v.p., dir. Ingersoll-Rand Co., 1964-66, exec. v.p., 1966-67, chmn., chief exec. officer, 1967—; dir. Bank of N.Y., Am. Smelting & Refining, Sperry Corp., Am. Cyanimid Co. Bd. dirs. Boys Clubs Am. Mem. IEEE, NAM (dir.), Am. Inst. Mining, Metall. and Petroleum Engrs., Machinery and Allied Products Inst. (exec. com.), C. of C., Eta Kappa Nu, Tau Beta Pi, Beta Theta Pi. Republican. Methodist. Mason (Shriner). Clubs: Mining, Sky (N.Y.C.); Duquesne; Blind Brook Golf. Author tech. publs. relating to mining; speaker before engring. groups; patentee. Home: 170 Round Hill Rd Greenwich CT 06830 Office: Ingersoll-Rand Co Woodcliff NJ 07675

WEARN, WILSON CANNON, media co. exec.; b. Newberry, S.C., Oct. 7, 1919; s. George F. and Mary (Cannon) W.; B.E.E., Clemson U., 1941; m. Mildred Colson, Feb. 21, 1948; children—Jean Wearn Held, Joan Wearn Gilbert, Wilson Cannon. Engr. Westinghouse Electric Corp., Pitts., 1941; engr. FCC, Washington, 1946-48; asso. cons. electronic engr. firm Weldon & Carr, Washington, 1948-50; partner firm Vandivere, Cohen & Wearn, cons. engrs., Washington, 1950-53; with Multimedia Broadcasting Co., Greenville, S.C., 1953—, organizer of corp., 1953, became corp. officer, 1960, pres., 1966—; pres., chief exec. officer Multimedia, Inc., Greenville, 1976—. Instr. electronic engring. Clemson U., 1946; bd. dels. NBC-TV Affiliates, 1972; mem. Am. Broadcasters visiting Japan Broadcast Execs. Joint Confs., fall 1972; pres., chief exec. officer, dir. Multimedia Inc., Greenville; dir. Bankers Trust of S.C., Broadcast Music, Inc. Mem. S.C. Hosp. Adv. Council, 1969-71. Bd. dirs. Family and Children Service of Greenville County, 1967-69, pres., 1969; trustee United Fund of Greenville County, 1959-61, chmn. campaign, 1961, bd. dirs., 1974—; trustee Greenville Symphony Assn., 1960-62, 71—, pres., 1977—; trustee Greenville Hosp. System, 1964-70, chmn., 1968-70; trustee Broadcast Rating Council; trustee Clemson U. Found., pres., 1978. Served to capt. Signal Corps, AUS, 1941-45; PTO. Decorated Bronze Star; recipient Outstanding Alumni award Clemson U., 1972. Mem. Nat. Assn. Broadcasters (chmn. bd. 1975-77), S.C. Broadcasters Assn. (pres. 1967), Nat. Broadcasters Club, Greater Greenville C. of C. (pres. 1972). Presbyn. (elder). Kiwanian. Clubs: Poinsett, Green Valley Country (Greenville). Home: 17 Round Pond Rd Greenville SC 29607 Office: PO Box 1688 Greenville SC 29602

WEARY, DANIEL CROFT, lawyer; b. Junction City, Kan., June 3, 1927; s. Ulysses S. and Ina (Kirkpatrick) W.; A.B. magna cum laude, Harvard, 1949, J.D., 1952; m. Barbara Ann Tindall, June 28, 1952; children—Alison, Catherine, Thomas, Eileen. Admitted to Mo. bar, 1952; practice in Kansas City, 1952—; partner firm Blackwell, Sanders, Matheny, Weary & Lombardi, 1958—. Dir., sec. Puritan-Benett Corp. Mem. city council, Leawood, Kan., 1968-70. Trustee Parker B. Francis Found., Parker B. Francis III Found. Served with USNR, 1945-46. Mem. Am., Mo., Kansas City bar assns. Clubs: Mission Hills Country, Univ., Pauma Valley Country. Home: 8502 Cherokee Pl Leawood KS 66206 Office: 2480 Pershing Rd Kansas City MO 64108

WEATHERBEE, ARTEMUS EDWIN, assn. exec.; b. Bangor, Maine, Feb. 9, 1918; s. (stepfather) Ray Wellman Sherman and Lola (Yelland) W.; A.B. with honors, U. Maine, 1939; intern Nat. Inst. Pub. Affairs, 1939-40; m. Pauline Jellison, June 18, 1940; children—Sue (Mrs. William C. Polini), Richard Charles, Steven Sherman. Chief of classification, chief of placement F.C.A., 1941-42; sr. personnel officer Office Emergency Mgmt., 1942-43; dir. personnel Nat. War Labor Bd., 1943. W.S.B., 1946; chief exec. selection War Assets Adminstrn., 1946; chief fgn. service recruitment Dept. State, 1946-48, asst. chief allowances staff, 1948-49, chief, 1949-50, asst. chief deptl. personnel div., 1950-51, spl. asst. to dir. personnel, 1951-52, dep. dir. personnel, 1952-53; exec. dir., dep. asst. postmaster gen. Bur. Personnel, P.O. Dept., 1954-59; adminstrv. asst. sec., asst. sec. for adminstrn. Treasury Dept., 1959-70; U.S. dir. Asian Devel. Bank-Manila with personal rank of ambassador, 1970-73; exec. dir. Kennebunk-Kennebunkport C. of C., 1975-78; corporator Kennebunk Savs. Bank, 1978—; cons. Maine Mgmt. and Cost Survey Commn., 1974. Mem. nat. adv. com. Am. Security Council, 1978—; mem. Nat. Tax Limitation Com., 1979—; chmn. U. Maine Devel. Council, 1975-77; mem. Gov.'s adv. com. on U. Maine, 1975-78, Kennebunk Budget Bd., 1974-77; bd. dirs. Kennebunk Area Indsl. Corp., 1976-79, York County Community Concert Assn., 1978—; mem. Nat. Rights to Work Com., 1975—; trustee U. Maine, 1975—; candidate for Maine Senate, 1978. Served to lt. (j.g.), USN, 1943-45; ret. comdr. Res., 1967. Recipient Meritorious Service award Dept. State, 1950, Arthur S. Flemming award U.S. Junior C. of C., 1956; Exceptional Service award Treasury Dept., 1965; Career Service award Nat. Civil Service League, 1965; Rockefeller Pub. Service award, 1968; Alexander Hamilton award Treasury Dept., 1970; Alumni Career Service award U. Maine, 1972. Mem. U. Maine Alumni Assn., World Wide Acad. Scholars, Maine Assn. C. of C. Execs. (pres. 1978), Portland Com. on Fgn. Relations, Naval Res. Assn., Phi Beta Kappa, Beta Theta Pi, Phi Kappa Phi, Sigma Mu Sigma. Republican. Mem. Christ Ch. Clubs: Webhannet Golf, Kennebunkport Men's (pres. 1976-77), Lions (dir. 1975-77), Rotary (chmn. internat. service com. 1978—). Address: 14 Constitution Rd Kennebunk ME 04043

WEATHERBEE, DONALD EMERY, polit. scientist; b. Portland, Maine, June 21, 1932; s. Perley Emery and Ruby Francis (Smith) W.; A.B. magna cum laude, Bates Coll., 1954; M.A., Johns Hopkins U. Sch. Advanced Internat. Studies, 1956, Ph.D. (Earhart dissertation fellow), 1968; m. Mary Ellen Bailey, Sept. 4, 1954; children—Mercy Meria, Donald Bailey, Thais Elizabeth, Amy Francesca, Oliver Parks Emery. Spl. lectr. Gajah Mada State U., Jogjakarta, Indonesia, 1957-61; Ford Found. fellow, The Hague, Netherlands, 1962-64; asst. prof. to prof. U. S.C., 1964-74, Donald S. Russell prof. contemporary fgn. policy, asso. dir. Inst. Internat. Studies, 1977—; asst. dean Coll. Social Scis., 1972; Henry L. Stimson prof. polit. sci. U.S. Army War Coll., 1974-77; vis. asst. prof. U. R.I., 1965; exchange prof. Free U. Berlin, 1969; panelist reviewer Nat. Endowment for Humanities; cons., lectr. for U.S. govt. agys. Recipient Disting. Civilian Service decoration Dept. of the Army, 1977. Fellow Inter-Univ. Seminar on Armed Forces and Soc.; mem. Assn. Asian Studies, Internat. Studies Assn., Koninklijke Instituut voor Taal-, Land- en Volkenkunde (Leiden, Netherlands). Author: Ideology in Indonesia, 1965; The United Front in Thailand, 1970; Ancient Indonesia, 1974; Indonesian Security Policy and Perceptions, 1978; contbr. numerous articles, revs. to publs. on S.E. Asian politics and internat. relations; editorial bd. Asian Survey. Home: 2310 Roper St Columbia SC 29206 Office: Inst Internat Studies U SC Columbia SC 29208*

WEATHERBY, MEREDITH, book publisher; b. Waco, Tex., Feb. 25. 1915; s. Oscar M. and Aline (Rogers) W.; A.B., Baylor U., Waco, 1936; B.S. in Fgn. Service, Georgetown U., 1938; postgrad. in Japanese Lit., Harvard U., 1947-50. Joined U.S. Fgn. Service, 1939, served in Cuba, Japan, Ceylon, Korea and Washington; ret., 1949; editor-in-chief Charles E. Tuttle Co., Tokyo, 1951-61; founder, 1961, since pres., editor-in-chief John Weatherhill, Inc., N.Y.C. and Tokyo; book designer, typographer; transl. from Japanese: Sound of Waves, Confessions of a Mask, Birds of Sorrow; one-man exhbns. of collages, Tokyo. Served with AUS, 1943-45. Address: 7-6-13 Roppongi Minato-ku Tokyo Japan

WEATHERFORD, HARRISON MARK, lawyer; b. Albany, Ore., Dec. 23, 1925; s. Mark Vern and Emmaline (Kuhn) W.; student Ore. State U., 1943, 46-48, Willamette U., 1948-50; J.D., Northwestern, 1952; m. Lillian Irene Odberg, July 24, 1952; children—Mark Harrison, Alice Vaughn, Joyce Verne. Wheat rancher, Arlington, Ore., 1944, 46-52; admitted to Ore. bar, 1952, since practiced in Albany; partner Weatherford, Thompson, Horton, Brickey & Powers, and predecessor firm, 1953—; wheat and cattle rancher, Arlington and Condon, 1966—. Chmn. Benton County Sch. Dist. reorgn. com., 1957-62; mem. Gov.'s Conf. on Edn., 1958; mem. Albany Zoning Commn., 1960-62; mem. adv. com. Intermediate Edn. Dist. Commn. of Ore. Legislature, 1967-69; dir. Rock Creek Water Control Dist., 1974—. Pres., sec., bd. dirs. Albany Boys Club; pres., trustee McDowell-Catt Found.; v.p., bd. dirs. Willamette Osteo. Hosp. Served with AUS, 1944-46: PTO. Named Gilliam County and Ore. Co-Conservation Farmer of Year, 1962. Mem. Ore., Linn County bar assns., Air Force Assn., Ore. Wheat, Cattlemens and Rye grass Growers Assn., Aircraft Owners and Pilots Assn., Am. Legion, Phi Delta Theta. Democrat. Presbyn. (deacon, elder). Elk. Home: 2834 NW Pineview Dr Albany OR 97321 also PO Box 595 Condon OR 97823 Office: 130 W 1st Ave Albany OR 97321

WEATHERFORD, WILLIS DUKE, JR., coll. pres.; b. Biltmore, N.C., June 24, 1916; B.A., Vanderbilt U., 1937; B.D., Yale, 1940; postgrad. U. N.C., 1940-41; M.A., Harvard, 1943, Ph.D. in Econs., 1952; LL.D., Carleton Coll., 1969; m. Anne Smith, 1954; children—Edith, Julia, Willis III, Susan, Alice. Dir. youth work Methodist Commn. World Peace, 1943-44; relief worker Am. Friends Service Com., Europe, 1944-47; asst. prof. econs. Swarthmore Coll., 1948-54, asso. prof., 1954-64; acad. dean Carleton Coll., 1965-67; pres. Berea (Ky.) Coll., 1967—. Rural devel. specialist Am. Friends Service Com., India, 1959-60, UN, Malaya, 1959-60. Bd. dirs. Nat. Assn. Ind. Colls. and Univs., Frontier Nursing Service, Pine Mountain Settlement Sch. Ford Found. tng. fellow, India, 1954-55. Mem. Am. Econ. Assn., Assn. Asian Studies, AAUP (pres. chpt. 1965), Phi Beta Kappa, Phi Delta Kappa. Club: University. Author: Geographic Differentials in Agricultural Wages, 1957; co-author Economies of the World Today, 1962, 65; contbg. author Labor in Developing Countries, 1962. Editor The Goals of Higher Education, 1960. Address: Berea Coll Office of Pres Berea KY 40404

WEATHERLY, ROBERT STONE, JR., aluminum co. exec.; b. Birmingham, Ala., May 12, 1929; s. Robert Stone and Gladys (Manning) W.; A.B., Princeton U., 1950; LL.B., Harvard U., 1953, grad. advanced mgmt. program, 1972; m. Mary Anne Burr, May 1, 1955; children—Robert Stone, III, Henry, William. Admitted to Ala. bar, 1953; asso. firm Burr, McKamy Moore & Thomas, Birmingham, 1955-62; asst. gen. atty. Vulcan Materials Co., Birmingham, 1962-69, v.p. chems. div., Wichita, Kans., 1969-71, treas., 1971-74, v.p. and controller, 1974-77, pres. metals div., Birmingham, Ala., 1977—; disting. lectr.-practitioner U. Ga. Served with U.S. Army, 1953-55. Mem. Am. Bar Assn., Fin. Exec. Inst., Nat. Assn. Accts. (cert. mgmt. acct.). Presbyterian. Club: Country of Birmingham. Home: 4608 Old Leeds Rd Birmingham AL 35213 Office: 1 Metroplex Dr Birmingham AL 35223

WEATHERSBY, GEORGE BYRON, state edn. ofcl.; b. Albany, Calif., Dec. 9, 1944; s. Byron and Fannie A. W.; B.S., U. Calif., Berkeley, 1965, M.S., 1966, M.B.A., 1967; S.M., Harvard U., 1968, Ph.D., 1970; m. Linda Rose W., June 29, 1979; 1 dau., Deborah Jane. Asso. dir. analytical studies U. Calif., Berkeley, 1969-72, also dir. Ford Found. research program, mem. faculty, 1969-72; spl. asst. to U.S. Sec. of State, Washington, 1972-73; dir. research Nat. Commn. on Financing Higher Edn., Washington, 1973-74; asso. prof. mgmt. Harvard U., 1974-78; commr. higher edn. Ind., 1977—. Calif. Regents scholar, 1963-65; NSF fellow, 1966-67; AEC fellow, 1966-67; Kent fellow, 1967-70; White House fellow, 1972-73; named 1 of 100 Outstanding Young Leaders in Higher Edn., Change Mag., 1978, One of Outstanding Young Men of 1976. Mem. Am. Council Edn., Ops. Research Soc. Am., Inst. Mgmt. Scis., Econometrica, Democrat. Author books including: Financing Postsecondary Education in the U.S., 1974; Colleges and Money, 1976; contbr. numerous articles to profl. jours., 1967—; cons. editor Jour. Higher Edn., 1974—. Office: 143 W Market St Indianapolis IN 46208

WEAVER, A. VERNON, govt. ofcl.; b. Miami, Fla.; B.E.E., U.S. Naval Acad.; m. Joyce McCoy; 3 daus. Vice-pres., So. Venetian Blind Co., 1949-60; pres. Lanotan, 1960-61; registered rep. Stephens, Inc., investment banking, 1960-63; pres. Union Mgmt. Corp., mut. funds mgmt., 1964-69; v.p. sec. Intersci. Capital Mgmt. Corp., 1969-71; v.p. Union Life Ins. Co., 1971-72, pres., 1972-77; adminstr. SBA, Washington, 1977—; Served to lt. j.g. USN, 1946-49, 51-53. Office: SBA 1441 L St NW Washington DC 20416*

WEAVER, ADELE TOMBRINK (MRS. JAMES BAIRD WEAVER), lawyer; b. Omaha; d. Martin Joseph and Marie (Dworak) Tombrink; B.S. in Edn., U. Nebr., 1935; J.D., cum laude, U. Miami, 1960; m. James Baird Weaver, Apr. 17, 1941; children—Beatrice Anne, Kathryn Louise. Admitted to Fla. bar, 1960; partner Pepper Clements, Hopkins & Weaver, Miami Beach, Fla., 1960-79. Hearing examiner Dade County Sch. Bd., 1969-76. Mem. Council for Internat. Visitors, Miami. Pres. Fla. Women's Polit. Caucus, 1971-73. Mem. Am., Inter-Am., Dade County bar assns., Fla. Bar, Fla. (pres.), Nat. (pres.) assns women lawyers, Internat. Fedn. Women Lawyers, Fla. Fedn. Bus. and Profl. Woman's Club (legislative chmn. 1968-70), Fla. Women's Polit. Caucus (chmn. policy council), Kappa Beta Pi, Phi Kappa Phi. Contbr. articles to profl. jours. Home: 8820 SW 51st St Miami FL 33165 Office: 370 Minorca Ave Suite 6 Coral Gables FL 33134

WEAVER, ALBERT BRUCE, univ. adminstr.; b. Mont., May 27, 1917; s. John B. and Myrtle (Dragstedt) W.; student Mont. Sch. Mines, 1935-37; A.B., U. Mont., 1940; M.S., U. Ida., 1941; student U. Minn., 1941-42; Ph.D., U. Chgo., 1951; m. Adeline Okerberg, Sept. 1945; children—Janet, Gail, John, Physicist, Naval Ordnance Lab., 1942-45; research asso. U. Chgo., 1952, U. Wash., 1952-54; mem. faculty U. Colo., 1954-58, asso. prof., 1957-58, chmn. dept. physics, 1956-58; prof., head dept. physics U. Ariz., 1958-70, asso. dean, 1961-70, provost acad. affairs, 1970-72, exec. v.p., 1972—. Fellow Am. Phys. Soc., AAAS; mem. Am. Assn. Physics Tchrs., Ariz. Acad. Sci., Sigma Xi. Home: 5726 E Holmes St Tucson AZ 85711

WEAVER, ARTHUR GORDON, fin. services exec.; b. Toronto, Ont., Can., June 21, 1915; s. S. Roy and Edith (Pratt) W.; B.A. with honours in Math., McGill U., 1936; grad. Advanced Mgmt. Program, Harvard, 1959; m. Melba L. Trombley. Sept. 27, 1941; children—David Roy, Arthur Bruce. With Prudential Assurance Co., 1936-39, Montreal Life Ins. Co., 1945-49; with John Hancock Mut. Life Ins. Co., 1949-70; managing dir. Exec. Services Ltd., 1978—; dir. Eaton-Bay Fin. Services Ltd., Eaton-Bay Life Assurance Co., Eaton-Bay Ins. Co., Eaton-Bay Trust Co., eight Eaton-Bay mut. funds, Fidmor Investors Corp. Served as flight lt. RCAF, 1939-45. Fellow Soc. Actuaries, Canadian Inst. Actuaries. Baptist. Home: 44 Jackes Ave Toronto ON M4T 1E5 Canada also Rural Route 2 Site E Box 8 Sutton West ON L0E 1R0 Canada. *God has given talents to each of us. It is our duty and privilege to use these talents, few or many, to His honour and glory. He, in turn, will honour us.*

WEAVER, BARBARA FRANCES, librarian; b. Boston, Aug. 29, 1927; d. Leo Francis and Nina Margaret (Durham) Weisse; B.A., Radcliffe Coll., 1949; M.L.S., U. R.I., 1968; Ed.M., Boston U., 1978; m. George B. Weaver, June 6, 1951; 1 dau., Valerie Susan. Head librarian Thompson (Conn.) Public Library, 1961-69; dir. Conn. State Library Service Center, Willimantic, 1969-72; regional adminstr. Central Mass. Regional Library System, Worcester, 1972-78; asst. commr. of edn., state librarian N.J. Dept. Edn., Trenton, 1978—; lectr. Simmons Coll., Boston, 1976-78. Mem. ALA, N.J. Library Assn., Chief Officers State Library Agys., Aircraft Owners and Pilots Assn. Home: 32 Twin Rivers Dr N East Windsor NJ 08520 Office: 185 W State St Trenton NJ 08625

WEAVER, CARLTON DAVIS, oil co. exec.; b. Grantsville, W.Va., May 27, 1921; s. Arley Ezra and Grace (Davis) W.; B.S., Engr. Mines, W.Va. U., 1948; m. Nancy Mason McIntosh, Mar. 21, 1951; children—Nancy Mason. Office engr. E.I. du Pont de Nemours & Co., 1941-42, tech. service rep., 1948-51; with Ashland Oil, Inc. (Ky.), 1951—, exec. asst., 1960-67, v.p., 1967-72, sr. v.p., 1972—, group operating officer, 1976—, pres. Ashland Resources Co. div., 1970-74. Chmn. vis. com. Coll. Mineral and Energy Resources, W.Va. U. Served to maj. USMCR, 1942-46, 52-53. Mem. Nat. Coal Assn. (dir.). Home: 509 Country Club Dr Ashland KY 41101 Office: 1409 Winchester Ave Ashland KY 41101

WEAVER, CHARLES EDWARD, educator; b. Lock Haven, Pa., Jan. 27, 1925; s. Clair William and Kathryn (Best) W.; B.S., Pa. State U., 1948, M.S., 1950, Ph.D., 1952; m. Janice Beatrice Hartland, Nov. 29, 1946; children—Alaine Robin, Patrice Kathryn, Allison Hartland, Research geologist Shell Oil Co., Houston, 1952-59; research group leader Continental Oil Co., Ponca City, Okla., 1959-63; prof. Ga. Inst. Tech., 1963-70, dir. sch. geophys. scis., 1970—; cons. cos., fed. govt., Nat. Acad. Scis., 1963—. Bd. dirs. Ponca Play House; pres. Cochise Riverview Club, 1971. Served to lt. (j.g.) USNR, 1943-46. Fellow Geol. Soc. Am., Am. Mineral. Soc. (hon. life; award 1958-; mem. Clay Minerals Soc. (pres. 1968), Ga. Geol. Soc. (pres. 1966), Soc. Econ. Paleontology and Mineralogy, Internat. Assn. Geochemists and Cosmochemists, Geochem. Soc. Am., Nat. Assn. Geology Tchrs., Soc. Environ. Geochemistry and Health, Internat. Assn. for Study of Clays, Sigma Xi (Research award 1972). Author: The Chemistry of Clay Minerals; Miocene of the S.E. United States. Contbr. articles profl. jours. Home: 3276 Craggy Point Atlanta GA 30339

WEAVER, CHARLES HADLEY, univ. adminstr.; b. Murfreesboro, Tenn., Jan. 27, 1920; s. Charles Preston and Carrie (Hadley) W.; student Vanderbilt U., 1938-40; B.S. in Elec. Engring., U. Tenn., 1943, M.S., 1948; Ph.D., U. Wis., 1956; m. Ann Hope Hampton, July 10, 1944; children—Hope Hampton, Charles Hadley, Jess Donelson, Amy Ann. Coop. student So. Bell Tel. & Tel. Co., 1940-43; supr., engr.

Tenn. Eastman Corp., Oak Ridge, 1943-46; from instr. to prof. elc. engring. U. Tenn., 1946-59; Westinghouse prof. elec. engring., head dept. Auburn U., 1959-65; dean engring. U. Tenn., 1965-68, chancellor U. Tenn. at Knoxville, 1968-71, v.p. continuing edn. U. Tenn. System, 1971—, dean Space Inst., Tullahoma, 1975—; cons. in feedback control, 1950—. Registered profl. engr., Ala., Tenn. Fellow IEEE; mem. Am. Soc. Engring. Edn., Sigma Xi, Tau Beta Pi, Eta Kappa Nu, Phi Kappa Phi. Presbyterian (elder). Author numerous articles in field. Address: Communications Bldg U Tenn Knoxville TN 37916

WEAVER, CHARLES HENRY, business exec.; b. Phila., Aug. 10, 1914; s. Charles Henry and Isabel (Walker) W.; B.S., U. Pa., 1936; m. Louise Schildecker, Sept. 7, 1940 (dec. Nov. 1977); children—Patricia Ann Weaver Telkins, William Schildecker, Peter Charles; m. 2d, Lois S. Amper, May 20, 1979. With Westinghouse Electric Corp., 1936-79, beginning as trainee, successively sales dept. transp. and generator div., sales engr. marine sect., mgr. marine sect., mgr. marine dept., mgr. marine and aviation sales dept., indsl. mgr. central dist. sales office, Pitts., mgr. atomic power div., 1948-55, v.p. charge atomic power activities, 1955-62, group v.p. atomic, def. and space group, 1962-67, v.p. govt. affairs, 1967-71, pres. world regions, 1971-75, exec. v.p. corp. world relations, 1975-79; pres. Pitts. Cons. Group, Inc., 1979—; dir., vice chmn. IEM, S.A., Mexico, 1973-78. Trustee Moore Sch. Elec. Engring. of U. Pa., also bd. overseers Coll. Engring. and Applied Sci. Recipient order of merit Westinghouse Elec. Corp., 1948; ann. Nat. Transp. award for outstanding contbns. transp. industry, 1955. Mem. Council on Fgn. Relations, Atomic Indsl. Forum (hon. dir., past pres.), Soc. Naval Architects and Marine Engrs., IEEE, ASME, Am. Nuclear Soc., Nat. Security Indsl. Assn. (past chmn.), Aerospace Industries Assn. (past gov.), Council Def. and Space Industry Assns. (past chmn.), Nat. Fgn. Trade Council (past dir.), World Affairs Council Pitts (dir., past pres.), Pitts. Council Internat. Visitors (trustee), Bus. Council Internat. Understanding (past vice chmn.), Internat. C. of C. (past dir. U.S. council), Advisory Council Japan-U.S. Econ. Relations, U.S.-Korea (past vice chmn.), U.S.-Yugoslav (past chmn.), Polish-U.S. econ. councils. Clubs: Duquesne, Concordia (Pitts.); Rolling Rock (Ligonier, Pa.); Internat. (Washington); Sky (N.Y.). Home: 540 N Neville St Pittsburgh PA 15213

WEAVER, CHARLES STEELE, cons. investments; b. Bluefield, W.Va., Nov. 17, 1918; s. Edward H. and India (Spencer) W.; student U. Cin., 1938-41; m. Louise Marsh, Jan. 30, 1954; 1 dau., Leslie J. Vocational tng. elec. design Appalachian Electric Power Co., 1936-38, developing, installation and maintenance carrier telephone and telemetering system, 1938-41; chief electronics and sci. equipment sect. tech. indsl. intelligence div. U.S. Dept. Commerce, Germany, 1947; indsl. engr. reparations br. Office Mil. Govt., Germany, 1948-49; intelligence specialist Dept. Def., 1949-70, dir. Office Fgn. Programs, Office Asst. Sec. Def. for Research and Engring., 1957-62, dep. asst. dir. (planning) Office of Dir. Def. Research and Engring., 1962-67, spl. asst. (policy planning) to dir. def. research and engring., 1967-70; pvt. cons. and investment bus., 1970—. Served from 2d lt. to maj., AUS, 1942-46; electronics engr. Air Def. Research and Devel. Establishment, Brit. Ministry and Supply, 1942- 43; U.S. Army engring. rep. to signal planning com. SHAEF, 1943-45; electronics engring. officer Field Information Agy., Technical Germany, 1945-46. Home: 2241 Meridian St Falls Church VA 22046

WEAVER, CLARK EVEREST, lawyer; b. Green Bay, Wis., Oct. 8, 1940; s. Norman Everett and Ruth Marguerita (Everest) W.; B.A., Stanford U., 1964; J.D., U. Colo., 1969; m. Elaine Estelle Hill, Apr. 12, 1963; children—Kelly Cybelle, Jessica May. Admitted to Colo. bar, 1969; asso. firm Holme, Roberts & Owen, Denver, 1969-71; gen. counsel Monfort of Colo., Inc., Greeley, 1971-74, v.p., gen. counsel, 1974-76, sr. v.p., gen. counsel, 1976—; mem. adv. bd. Midland Fed. Savs. Mem. Colo. Health Care Adv. Bd., 1979—; 1st v.p. United Way of Weld County, 1978—; bd. dirs. Colo. 4-H Found., 1973-76. Served with U.S. Army, 1964-66. Mem. Am. Bar Assn., Colo. Bar Assn., Denver Bar Assn., Weld County Bar Assn. (chmn. corp. banking and bus. law sect.), Greeley Area C. of C. (dir. 1974-77). Home: 1206 3d Ave Longmont CO 80501 Office: PO Box G Greeley CO 80632

WEAVER, DAVID ANDREW, educator; b. Ball Ground, Ga., Jan. 6, 1902; s. Andrew Jackson and Malinda (Chamlee) W.; A.B., Mercer U., 1927; M.A., Columbia, 1929; Ed.D., N.Y.U., 1935; postdoctoral work, Columbia, U. Pa., U. Mich., U. Cal., Harvard; m. Elsie E. Jacobson, Aug. 30, 1930; children—David Andrew, Walter William, Asst. prin. Central Jr. High Sch., Poplar Bluff, Mo., 1922-23; supt. schs., Bismarck, Mo. 1923-24; teaching fellow N.Y.U., 1929-30; instr. Coll. City N.Y., 1930-40, asst. prof., 1940-42; dean Baylor U., 1942-45; pres. Shurtleff Coll., Alton, Ill., 1945-55; lectr. Washington U., St. Louis, 1957, asst. dean admissions, 1958-67; coordinator Southeast Mo. State Co., 1967-68; prof. edn. Southwest Baptist Coll., Bolivar, Mo., 1968—; lectr. edn. U. Ga., summers 1936, 37, 38, U. Richmond, 1939, 40. Mem. commn. on higher edn. Nat. Council Chs. of Christ in U.S.A., 1950-55. Recipient Freedoms Found. award, 1953; John Mason Peck plaque, 1971; Distinguished Service award S.W. Bapt. Coll., 1971. Mem. AAUP, Nat. Soc. Study Edn., NEA, Nat. Soc. Coll. Tchrs. Edn., Phi Delta Phi, Phi Delta Kappa, Pi Kappa Alpha. Mason (Shriner). Baptist. Rotarian. Editor: Builders of American Universities, Vols. I, II, III; Butler's Commencement Address. Home: 105 E Freeman St Bolivar MO 65613

WEAVER, DENNIS, actor; b. Joplin, Mo., June 4, 1924; s. Walter and Lenna W.; B.F.A., U. Okla., 1948; m. Gerry Stowell, Oct. 20, 1945; children—Rick, Robby, Rusty. Appeared on New York stage, 1948-52; appeared in Streetcar Named Desire, Hollywood, Calif., 1953; under contract to Universal Internat., Hollywood, 1952-53; freelance actor, Hollywood, 1953-55; appeared on TV series Gunsmoke, 1955-64, Kentucky Jones, 1964-65, Gentle Ben, 1967-69, McCloud, 1970-77, Stone, 1980—, also Movies of the Week, Duel, 1971, Forgotten Man, 1971, Rolling Man, 1973, Terror on the Beach, 1973, Female Artillery, 1973, Patty Hearst, 1979; appeared on spls. Intimate Strangers, 1977, Police Story-A Cry for Justice, 1977, Pearl, 1978, Ishi, 1978, Islander, 1978, Centennial—The Longhorns, 1978, Amber Waves, 1979, His Name is Mudd, 1979. Mem. Screen Actors Guild, Dirs. Guild, AFTRA. Office: Universal Studios Universal City CA 91608

WEAVER, DOUGLAS WILLIAMS, athletic dir.; b. Goshen, Ind., Oct. 15, 1930; s. Robert Bartow and Dorothy (Williams) W.; student Yale U., 1948; B.A., Mich. State U., 1953; J.D., U. Kans., 1970; m. Nancy Doty Weaver; children—Amy Weaver Rice, Douglas, Matthew. Head freshman football coach Mich. State U., 1956, varsity asst. football coach, 1957; line coach, 1st asst. U. Mo., 1958-59; head football coach Kans. State U., 1960-66; asst. football coach U. Kans., 1967-69; admitted to Kans. bar, 1970; mem. firm Stevens, Brand, Brand, Lawrence, Kans., 1970; asst. head coach UCLA, 1971-72; head football coach So. Ill. U., 1974-75, athletic dir., 1973-75; athletic dir. Ga. Inst. Tech., 1976—. Served with USAF, 1953-55. Mem. Am. Bar Assn., Kans. Bar Assn., Nat. Assn. Coll. Dirs. Athletics (chmn. 1977 facilities conf.), Am. Football Coaches Assn., Coll. Football Assn. (chmn. athletic dirs. com.), Div. 1 Football Independents (pres. 1977-78). Episcopalian. Clubs: Indian Hills Country, Peachtree Racquet (Atlanta). Home: 3404 Clubland Dr Marietta GA 30067 Office: Ga Tech Athletic Assn Atlanta GA 30332

WEAVER, EARL SIDNEY, profl. baseball mgr.; b. St. Louis, Aug. 14, 1930; s. Earl Milton and Ethel Genieve (Wakefield) W.; children by previous marriage—Michael Earl, Rhonda Lee, Theresa Ann; m. 2d, Marianna Osgood, Sept. 26, 1964. Mgr. Balt. Orioles 1968—. Named Maj. League Mgr. of Yr., 1977, 79; Sporting News Mgr. of Yr., 1979; managed Orioles to 4 pennants, 1969-71, 79, world championship, 1971. Author: Winning, 1971. Office: Memorial Stadium Baltimore MD 21218*

WEAVER, EDWIN SNELL, educator; b. Hartford, Conn., Jan. 30, 1933; s. Elbert Cook and Grace Gavina (Kelsey) W.; B.S., Yale, 1954; Ph.D., Cornell, 1959; m. Dretta Leah Shorkey, July 2, 1955; children—Frances, Thomas, Janet, Patricia, David. Mem. faculty Mt. Holyoke Coll., South Hadley, Mass., 1958—, prof. chemistry, 1972—, chmn. dept., 1972-78; vis. prof. U. Conn., 1972; vis. fellow Yale U., 1978-79. NSF fellow, 1954; Sci. faculty fellow, 1964, 78-79. Mem. Am. Chem. Soc., AAAS, Sigma Xi. Author: Laboratory Introduction to Chemistry, 1962. Home: 115 Woodbridge St South Hadley MA 01075

WEAVER, FREDERICK S., pub. relations co. exec.; b. Hampton, Va., May 3, 1914; s. David Douglass and Estelle Irene Weaver; A.B., Howard U., 1935, LL.B., 1937; m. Carol Maria Hasbourne, Apr. 23, 1965; children—Frederick S., Lloyd, Edward, Thea, James Anastasia, Maria. Recorder of deeds D.C., Washington, 1940-46; pres. Frederick S. Weaver & Assos., N.Y.C., 1947-50; commr. of housing N.Y.C., 1950-54; clk. of Municipal Ct., N.Y.C., 1955-60; account exec. Thomas J. Deegan Co., Inc., N.Y.C., 1963-65; cons. N.Y. World's Fair, N.Y.C., 1963-65; chmn. Pub. Relations Enterprises, Inc., N.Y.C., 1965-77; chmn. Frederick S. Weaver & Assos., N.Y.C., 1977—. Founder, 1st pres. Community of Harlem Civic Assn., 1948, Frederick Douglass Dem. Club, N.Y.C. Bd. dirs. Catholic Big Bros., N.Y.C. Recipient achievement award Howard U. Sch. Communications; award N.Y. Press Club. Mem. Pub. Relations Soc. Am., Nat. Assn. Market Developers, Nat. Urban League, NAACP, Omega Psi Phi (Achievement award). Democrat. Roman Catholic. Clubs: Howard U. Alumni (N.Y.C.). Home: 70 W 95th St New York NY 10025 Office: 17 Battery Pl New York NY 10004

WEAVER, FRITZ WILLIAM, actor; b. Pitts., Jan. 19, 1926; s. John Carson and Elsa (Stringaro) W.; m. Sylvia Short, Feb. 7, 1953; children—Lydia Charlotte, Anthony Ballou. Mem. Barter Theatre Va., 1951, 52, Group 20 Players, Wellesley, Mass., 1953, 54, Stratford Shakespeare Festival, 1956, 58, Vancouver Festival, 1961, Phoenix Theatre, N.Y.C., 1959-60, Ednl. TV Channel 13, N.Y.C., 1960, 65; Off-Broadway appearances include Doctor's Dilemma, 1953, The Way of the World, 1954, L'Histoire du Soldat, 1954, Family Reunion, 1958, Power and Glory, 1958, Peer Gynt, 1959, Henry IV, parts I and II; Broadway appearances include White Devil (Carence Derwent award), 1955, Chalk Garden, 1955, Miss Lonelyhearts, 1957, A Shot in the Dark, 1962, Protective Custody, 1958, All American, 1962, Lorenzo, 1962-63, The White House, 1964, Baker Street, 1965, Child's Play, 1969-70, The Price, 1979; appearances with Am. Shakespeare Festival, 1955, 56, 57, 58, 73, Cambridge Drama Festival, 1960, N.Y. Philharmonic, 1962; motion pictures include The Crimson Curtain, 1955, Fail-Safe, 1963, The Guns of August, 1965, The Borgia Stick, 1966, The Maltese Bippy, 1969, A Walk in the Spring Rain, 1969, The Day of the Dolphin, 1973; numerous TV appearances, including Holocaust, 1978; starred in world premiere Sorrows of Frederick, Los Angeles, 1967; Absurd Person Singular, 1975; Lincoln, 1976; films Marathon Man, Demon Seed, Black Sunday, 1976-77. Recipient Antoinette Perry award; Drama Desk award, Outer Critics Circle, also Variety. Home: 161 W 75th St New York NY 10023 Office: care Lucy Kroll Agy 390 West End Ave New York NY 10023

WEAVER, GALBRAITH MCFADDEN, oil co. exec.; b. Moundsville, W.Va., Mar. 28, 1905; s. William Fairman and Elizabeth (McFadden) W.; m. Elizabeth Eudora James, Oct. 26, 1932; children—Galbraith McFadden, William Richard. With Southland Royalty Co., Fort Worth, 1955—, pres., 1964-67, chmn. bd., 1967-—, chief exec. officer, 1967-74, chmn. bd., 1974—. Bd. dirs. Ft. Worth Fat Stock Show. Trustee Tex. Wesleyan Coll. Episcopalian. Mason (32). Home: 1725 Hulen St Fort Worth TX 76107 Office: Southland Royalty Co 1000 Fort Worth Club Tower Fort Worth TX 76102

WEAVER, JIM, congressman; b. Brookings, S.D., Aug. 8, 1927; s. Leo C. and Alice (Flittie) W.; B.S. in Polit. Sci., U. Oreg., 1952; m. Sally Cummins, June 11, 1955; children—Regan, Allison, Sarah. Mem. 94th-96th Congresses from 4th Oreg. dist. Served with USNR, World War II. Office: 1226 Longworth House Office Bldg Washington DC 20515

WEAVER, JOHN BORLAND, organist, composer; b. Palmerton, Pa., Apr. 27, 1937; s. David Williams and Bertha Brownlee (Borland) W.; diploma Curtis Inst. Music, Phila., 1959; M.Sacred Music, Union Theol. Sem., N.Y.C., 1968; m. Marianne Carol Gruhn, Apr. 30, 1942; children—Jonathan Kirk, Kirianne Elizabeth. Organist, choirmaster Holy Trinity Lutheran Ch., N.Y.C., 1959-70; dir. music Madison Ave. Presbyn. Ch., N.Y.C., 1970—; head organ dept. Curtis Inst. Music, 1973—; organist Temple Beth-El, Manhattan Beach, N.Y., 1970—; mem. faculty Westminister Choir Coll., Princeton, N.J., 1968-69, 71-72, Union Theol. Sem. Sch. Sacred Music, 1970-73; solo organ recitalist, U.S., Can., Ger. Served with AUS, 1961-63. Decorated Army Commendation medal, 1963. Mem. Am. Guild Organists, Presbyterian. Club: St. Wilfrid (N.Y.C.). Composer: Psalm 100, 1958; Toccatafor Organ, 1959; Epiphany Alleluias, 1967; Rhapsody for Flute and Organ, 1968; Good Christian Men, Rejoice, 1978. Address: 921 Madison Ave New York NY 10021. *By hard work and good fortune I have been able to do that which I decided, at age ten, to do with my life.*

WEAVER, JOHN BOYD, ins. co. exec.; b. Staunton, Va., Mar. 5, 1925; s. Charles Dwight and Edna Marie (Sayers) W.; student Dunsmore Bus. Coll., 1946-47; B.S. in Bus., U. Richmond, 1951; m. Addie Jane Samples, Oct. 17, 1952. Jr. accountant Leach Calkins & Scott, C.P.A.'s, Richmond. Va., 1951-54; audit clk. Life Ins. Co. of Va., Richmond, 1954-60, asst. to treas., 1960-64, asst. treas., 1964-68, treas., 1968—; asst. treas. Richmond Corp., 1972-77, Richmond Co., mem. Continental Fin. Services Co., 1977—. Served with U.S. Navy, 1943-45. Fellow Life Office Mgmt. Assn. Methodist. Home: 3105 Comet Rd Richmond VA 23229 Office: 6610 W Broad St Richmond VA 23230

WEAVER, JOHN CARRIER, univ. pres. emeritus; b. Evanston, Ill., May 21, 1915; s. Andrew Thomas and Cornelia Myrta (Carrier) W.; A.B., U. Wis., 1936, A.M., 1937, Ph.D., 1942; LL.D., Mercer U., 1972, L.H.D., St. Scholastica, 1973; Litt.D., Drury Coll., 1973; m. Ruberta Louise Harwell, Aug. 8, 1940; children—Andrew Bennett, Thomas Harwell. Mem. editorial and research staff Am. Geog. Soc. of N.Y., 1940-42; mem. research staff Office of Geographer, U.S. Dept. State, 1942-44; asst. prof. dept. geography U. Minn., 1946-47, asso. prof., 1947-48, prof., 1948-55; prof. geography, dean Sch. Arts and Sci., Kans. State U., 1955-57; prof. geography, dean grad. coll. U. Nebr., 1957-61, v.p. research, dean grad. coll., prof. geography State U. Iowa, 1961-64; v.p. academic affairs, dean faculties, prof. geography Ohio State U., Columbus, 1964-66; pres., prof. geography U. Mo., 1966-70, U. Wis., 71; pres. U. Wis. System, 1971-77, emeritus, 1977—; prof. geography U. Wis. Milw., Madison, Green Bay, 1971-78; hon. prof. geography U. Wis. at Oshkosh; Distinguished vis. prof. U. So. Calif., 1977—, exec. dir. Center for Study of Am. Experience, 1978—; research cons. Midwest Barley Improvement Assn., Milw., 1946-50; expert cons. to Com. on Geophysics and Geography, Research and Devel. Bd., Washington, 1947-53; mem. adv. com. on geography Office Naval Research, NRC, 1949-52, chmn., 1951-52; vis. prof. U. Oreg., summer 1951, Harvard U., summer 1954; cons. editor McGraw-Hill series in geography, 1951-67; mem. adv. com. to sec. HEW, 1958-62; mem. Mid-Am. State U. Assn., 1959-70, chmn., 1959-61, 70-71; chmn. Council Grad. Schs. U.S., 1961-62; mem. Woodrow Wilson fellow selection com., 1961-70; mem. com. instl. coop. Univs. Western Conf. and Chgo., 1962-66, chmn., 1964-66; pres. Assn. Grad. Schs. in Assn. Am. Univs., 1963-64; Wilton Park fellow Brit. Fgn. Office, 1965, 67, 70, 74, 76; mem. Mo. Commn. of Higher Edn., 1966-70; mem. White House Task Force on Priorities in Higher Edn., 1969-70; mem. Edn. Commn. of States, 1971-77. Bd. dirs. Harry S. Truman Library Inst. Nat. and Internat. Affairs, 1967-70, trustee Nat. Com. on Accreditation, 1966-76, Johnson Found., Racine, Wis., 1971-77, Am. Univs. Field Service, 1971-75, Nat. Merit Scholarship Corp., 1971-77. Served as lt. (j.g.) USNR, 1944-46; assigned specialist Hydrographic Office, Office of Chief of Naval Ops., Washington. Recipient Vilas medal U. Wis., 1936, Letter Commendation from Chief of Naval Ops., 1946; Carnegie Found. adminstrv. fellow, 1957-58. Fellow Am. Geog. Soc. (trustee 1974—), AAAS; mem Assn. Am. Geographers (council 1949-51, Nat. Research award 1955), Am. Geophys. Union, Arctic Inst. N.Am. (charter asso.) Am. Polar Soc., Internat. Geog. Union, Am. Council Pharm. Edn., Am. Pharm. Assn. (hon.), Wis. Hist. Soc., Am. Friends of Wilton Park, Inc., Newcomen Soc. N.Am., Phi Beta Kappa, Sigma Xi, Phi Kappa Phi, Delta Sigma Rho, Phi Eta Sigma, Chi Phi, Alpha Kappa Psi. Congregationalist. Author: Ice Atlas of the Northern Hemisphere, 1946; American Barley Production; A Study in Agricultural Geography 1950; A Statistical World Survey of Commercial Production; A Geographical Sourcebook (with Fred E. Lukerman), 1953; The American Railroads, 1958; Minnesota and Wisconsin, 1961; illustrator: Quiet Thoughts, 1972; contbr. articles to books and profl. periodicals; contbg. editor Geog. Rev., 1955-70. Home: 2978 Crownview Dr Rancho Palos Verdes CA 90274

WEAVER, KENNETH NEWCOMER, govt. ofcl.; b. Lancaster, Pa., Jan. 16, 1927; s. A. Ross and Cora (Newcomer) W.; B.S., Franklin and Marshall Coll., 1950; M.A., Johns Hopkins, 1952, Ph. D., 1954; m. Mary Elizabeth Hoover, Sept. 9, 1950; children—Wendy Elaine, Matthew Owen. Instr. geology Johns Hopkins, 1953- 54; operations analyst Operations Research Office, Washington, 1954-56; chief geologist, then mgr. geology and quarry dept. Medusa Portland Cement Co., Wampum, Pa., 1956-63; dir., state geologist Md. Geol. Survey, Balt., 1963—; chmn. Md. Land Reclamation Com., 1967-76. Gov.'s rep. Interstate Oil Compact Commn., Interstate Mining Compact Commn.; chmn. Md. Mining Council, Md. Topographic Mapping Com.; mem. com. on surface mining and reclamation Nat. Acad. Scis., 1978; mem. subcom. on mgmt. of maj. underground constrn. projects Nat. Acad. Engring. Served with AUS, 1954-56. Fellow Geol. Soc. Am.; mem. Am. Inst. Mining Engrs., AAAS, Assn. Profl. Geol. Scientists, Am. Geol. Inst. (governing bd. 1973), Am. Water Well Assn., Geol. Soc. Washington, Assn. Am. State Geologists (pres. 1973), Sigma Xi. Republican. Presbyn. (elder). Club: Johns Hopkins (Balt.). Home: 14002 Jarrettsville Pike Phoenix MD 21131 Office: Johns Hopkins U Baltimore MD 21218

WEAVER, LAWRENCE CLAYTON, educator; b. Bloomfield, Ia., Jan. 23, 1924; s. Wilber C. and Faye (Ballew) W.; B.S., Drake U., 1949; Ph.D. (Foxbilt fellow), U. Utah, 1953; m. Delores Hillman, Sept. 8, 1949; children—Karen Celeste, Kevin Neal, Gordon Douglas, Elizabeth. With Pitman-Moore Research (became div. Dow Chem. Co., 1961), Indpls., 1953-66, pharmacologist to asst. gen. mgr., 1965-66; dean, prof. U. Minn. Coll. Pharmacy, Mpls., 1966—, dir. drug info. and edn. U. Minn. System, 1973—. Dir. Zinpro Corp. Chmn., Minn. Adv. Council Comprehensive Health Planning; pres. Am. Assn. Colls. Pharmacy, 1973-74. Recipient Research Achievement award Am. Pharm. Assn. Found., 1963; Alumni Distinguished Service award Drake U., 1966. Fellow AAAS; mem. Am. Soc. Pharmacology and Exptl. Therapeutics, Soc. Exptl. Biology and Medicine, Biometric Soc., Am. Pharm. Assn., Soc. Toxicology, Research Soc. Am., Sigma Xi, Phi Delta Chi, Rho Chi. Editorial bd. Jour. Toxicology and Applied Pharmacology. Contbr. articles profl. jours. Home: 703 Forest Dale Rd New Brighton MN 55112

WEAVER, NARVIN BLAKE, lawyer; b. Castleberry, Ala., Jan. 16, 1914; s. Allen T. and Lois (Atkisson) W.; student U. of Ala., 1930-33, Nat. U., 1942. Columbus, 1943; A.B., Southeastern U., 1941, LL.B., 1942; m. Martha Elizabeth Roberston, June 11, 1938; children—Narvin Leon, Patricia Elaine (twins). With Govt. of D.C. and U.S. Secret Service, 1939-42; admitted to D.C. bar, 1941, Va. bar, 1946, U.S. Supreme Ct., 1949, U.S. Customs Ct., 1956; atty., Office of Atty. Gen. U.S., 1942; counsel RFC, 1943-46, tax counsel, 1946-48, asst. chief counsel Office Def. Supplies, 1945-48, asst. gen. counsel U.S. Comml. Co., 1946-48, asst. to pres. U.S. Comml. Co., 1945-48, v.p., 1947-48; asst. mgr. Office of War Activity Liquidation, 1948, mgr., 1948-49; asst. mgr. Office of Loans, 1949-50; asst. mgr. Office of Prodn., 1950; pvt. practice law, 1950-58, 61-70; counsel Cities Service Co., 1957-61; sr. litigation atty. Dept. Commerce, 1970-75. Mem. Va., D.C. bar assns., Ala. State Soc., Sigma Delta Kappa. Clubs: Nat. Press, Country of Fairfax, Country of South Hill. Home: PO Box 331 South Hill VA 23970

WEAVER, PAUL RAYMOND, ins. co. exec.; b. Ellsworth, Iowa, Oct. 3, 1915; s. Herbert C. and Sylvia C. (Madole) W.; B.A., U. No. Iowa, 1938; postgrad. Northwestern U. Sch. Commerce, 1942-43, Harvard U., 1939-41, Columbia U., 1966; m. Mildred A. Kuschel, Oct. 10, 1943; children—Susan Weaver Sullivan, Jane Weaver Muse, Richard P. Tchr. pub. high schs., Cedar Falls, Iowa, 1938-42, Monmouth, Ill., 1945-47; with John Hancock Mut. Life Ins. Co., 1947—, sr. v.p., Boston, 1971-75, exec. v.p. individual ops., 1975—; chmn. bd., dir. Hanseco Ins. Co., Hanseco (U.K.) Ins. Co.; dir. John Hancock Mut. Life Ins Co., John Hancock Advisers, Maritime Life Assurance Co.; chmn. bd. Profesco, 1970-74; chmn. bd. John Hancock Distbrs., Inc., 1970-74. Served with USN, 1942-45. Mem. Am. Soc. Chartered Life Underwriters, Nat. Assn. Life Underwriters, Boston Life Underwriters, Smithsonian Instn., Columbia Execs. Assn. Club: Algonquin (Boston). Home: 20 Edgewater Dr Needham MA 02192 Office: John Hancock Pl PO Box 111 Boston MA 02117

WEAVER, ROBERT CLIFTON, educator, economist; b. Washington, Dec. 29, 1907; s. Mortimer G. and Florence (Freeman) W.; B.S., Harvard, 1929, M.A., 1931, Ph.D., 1934, also LL.D.; L.H.D., Temple U., Pratt Institute; LL.D., Howard U., Washington, Morehouse Coll., Amherst Coll., Boston Coll., Rutgers U., So. Ill. U., Columbia, Harvard U., U. Mich., U. Pa.; D.C.L., U. Ill.; D.S.S., Duquesne U.; m. Ella V. Haith, July 19, 1935; 1 son, Robert (dec.). Adviser Negro affairs Dept. Interior, 1933-37; spl. asst. to adminstr. U.S. Housing Authority, 1937-40; adminstrv. asst. OPM, WPB.

1940-42; vis. prof. Columbia Tchrs. Coll., 1947, N.Y.U. Sch. Edn., 1947-49; dir. opportunity fellowships J.H. Whitney Found., 1949-54; dep. commr. N.Y. State Div. Housing 1954-55; rent adminstr. N.Y. State, 1955-59; cons. Ford Found., 1959-60; vice chmn. Housing and Redevel. Bd., N.Y.C., 1960-61; adminstr. HHFA, 1961-66; sec. HUD, 1966-68; pres. Bernard M. Baruch Coll., 1969-70; distinguished prof. urban affairs Hunter Coll., 1970-78; dir. urban programs Brookdale Center on Aging, Hunter Coll., 1978—. Mem. Conciliation and Appeals Bd. N.Y.C. Rent Stblzn. Bd., 1974—, Municipal Assistance Corp. N.Y.C., 1975—; mem. com. transp. NRC; mem. vis. com. Sch. Design, Harvard U. Trustee Bowery Savs. Bank, Met. Life Ins. Co., 1969-78; bd. dirs. Legal Def. Fund. Former chmn. NAACP; overseer Grad. Sch. Fine Arts U. Pa. Recipient Springarn medal NAACP, 1962. Author: Negro Labor: A National Problem, 1946; The Negro Ghetto, 1948; The Urban Complex, 1964; Dilemmas of Urban America, 1965. Home: 215 E 68th St New York NY 10021

WEAVER, SYLVESTER LAFLIN, JR., communications cons.; b. Los Angeles, Dec. 21, 1908; s. Sylvester Laflin and Isabel (Dixon) W.; B.A. magna cum laude, Dartmouth Coll., 1930; m. Desiree Mary Hawkins, Jan. 23, 1942; children—Trajan Victor Charles, Susan Sigourney. Writer, producer CBS, Los Angeles, 1932, program dir., San Francisco, 1933-35; supr. programs, mgr. Young & Rubicam, N.Y.C., 1935-38, v.p., mem. exec. com., 1946-49; advt. mgr. Am. Tobacco Co., 1938-46; v.p. television, vice chmn., pres., chmn. NBC, N.Y.C., 1949-56; chmn. McCann Erickson, N.Y.C., 1958-63; pres. Subscription TV, Los Angeles, 1963-66; cons. Wells, Rich, Greene, others, Santa Barbara, Calif., 1967—; TV cons. Hon. Nelson A. Rockefeller, 1958, 60, 62, 66, 72, Com. on Critical Choices, 1973-75. Chmn., Am. Heart Assn., 1959-63; bd. dirs. Muscular Dystrophy Assn., 1967—, pres., 1975—. Served with USN, 1942-45. Recipient Peabody award, 1956, Emmy award, 1967, also Sylvania, Look and Variety awards. Mem. Phi Beta Kappa. Republican. Episcopalian. Clubs: University, Seawanhaka Corinthian Yacht (N.Y.C.); Thunderbird Country (Palm Springs); Valley (Montecito). Creator, Today Show, Tonight Show, TV spl.-spectacular Monitor, Wisdom, Wide Wide World, Matinee Theater, mag. concept of TV, others. Home: 818 Deerpath Rd Santa Barbara CA 93108

WEAVER, THOMAS, educator; b. Grenville, N.Mex., May 1, 1929; s. Joseph M. and Juanita (Archuleta) W.; B.A., U. N.Mex., 1955, M.A., 1960; Ph.D., U. Calif., Berkeley, 1965; m. Dora Edith Martinez, Oct. 21, 1950; children—Thomas Brian, Kathleen, Denise. Exec. sec. Calif. Commn. on Indian Affairs, Sacramento, 1964; asst. prof. depts. behavioral sci. and anthropology U. Ky., 1964-67; asst. prof., Maurice Falk Sr. faculty fellow depts. psychiatry and anthropology U. Pitts., 1967-69; asso. prof. anthropology U. Ariz., Tucson, 1969-75, prof., 1975—, dir. Bur. Ethnic Research, 1969-77; vis. prof. Northwestern U., 1975, vis. Disting. prof. So. Meth. U., summer 1978; cons. Calif. Commn. Indian Affairs, 1965-66. Fellow Am. Anthrop. Assn. (chmn. com. minorities and anthropology 1970-74), Soc. Applied Anthropology (exec. com. 1969-70, sec. 1971-74, pres. 1975-78); mem. S.W. Anthrop. Assn. (past pres.), Am. Ethnol. Soc., Latin Am. Studies Assn., Council on Anthropology and Edn., Am. Assn. Phys. Anthropology, AAAS (nominating com. sect. H 1973-76), Soc. Am. Archaeology, Sigma Xi. Author-editor: (with A. Magid) Poverty: New Interdisciplinary Perspectives, 1969; Medical Anthropology, 1968; Indians in California Rural and Reservation Areas, 1966; Arizona Indian People and Their Relationship to the State's Total Structure, 1971; Political Organization and Business Management in the Gila River Indian Community, 1971; (with D. White) The Anthropology of Urban Environments, 1972; To See Ourselves: Anthropology and Modern Social Issues, 1973; Indians of Arizona, 1974; Tribal Management Procedures Study of Seven Reservations, 1974; Mexican Migration, 1976; (with E.A. Hoebel) Anthropology and the Human Experience, 5th edit., 1979. Home: 6644 Donna Beatrix Circle Tucson AZ 85718

WEAVER, WARREN, JR., newspaperman; b. Madison, Wis., Feb. 7, 1923; s. Warren and Mary (Hemenway) W.; B.A., Amherst Coll., 1943; M.S., Columbia U., 1947; LL.B., Albany (N.Y.) Law Sch., 1958; m. Barbara J. Woodall, July 8, 1950 (div. Feb. 1975); children—Carolyn, Sally, Melissa, Anne; m. 2d, Marianne Means, Feb. 10, 1977. Reporter, then asst. state editor Watertown (N.Y.) Daily Times, 1947-48; mem. staff N.Y. Times, 1948—, bur. chief Albany, 1959-62, mem. staff Washington bur., 1962—, nat. polit. corr., 1966-68, Congressional corr., 1969-72, 79—, Supreme Ct. corr., 1973-75, 77-78; admitted to N.Y. bar, 1959. Mem. N.Y. State Legis. Corrs. Assn. (pres. 1957). Author: Making Our Government Work, 1964; Both Your Houses, 1972; contg. author: The Kennedy Years, 1964; The New York Times Election Handbook, 1964, 2d edit., 1968; The Road to the White House, 1965; Washington D.C.: Guide to the Nations Capital, 1967. Home: 1521 31st St NW Washington DC 20007 Office: NY Times 1000 Connecticut Ave NW Washington DC 20036

WEAVER, WARREN ELDRED, coll. dean; b. Sparrows Point, Md., June 5, 1921; s. Charles Harrison and Mary (Deaver) W.; B.S., U. Md., 1942, Ph.D., 1947; m. Virginia June Burkholder, July 21, 1945 (dec. Sept. 1968); children—Glenn H., Karen J., Janet S., Julie H.; m. 2d, Esther Schiesser McDaniel, Aug. 2, 1969. Research asst. Nat. Def. Research Com., U. Md., 1942-45; chemist Naval Research Lab., 1945-50; part-time research asso. George Washington U., 1948-49; mem. faculty Med. Coll. Va., 1950-54, chmn. dept. chemistry and pharm. chemistry. 1952-56, prof. pharm. chemistry, 1954—, dean Sch. Pharmacy, 1956—. Bd. visitors Sch. Pharmacy, U. Pitts., 1969-72. Named Pharmacist of Year in Va., Va. Pharm. Assn., 1963. Fellow AAAS; mem. Am. Chem. Soc. (chmn. Va. 1963), Va. (treas. 1960-62), Am. (trustee 1970-73) pharm. assns., Va. Soc. Hosp. Pharmacists, Am. Inst. History Pharmacy, Am. Assn. Colls. Pharmacy (v.p. 1967, pres. 1968, chmn. exec. com. 1973—), Friends of History Pharmacy (sec.-treas. 1960-66, pres. 1966-67), Am. Council on Pharm. Edn., Am. Found. Pharm. Edn. (bd. 1968—). Methodist. Contbr. articles to profl. jours. Home: 7607 Horsepen Rd Richmond VA 23229

WEAVER, WILLIAM MERRITT, JR., investment banker; b. Jenkintown, Pa., Jan. 7, 1912; s. William Merritt and Frances (Jones) W.; grad, Phillips Exeter Acad., 1930; B.A., Princeton, 1934; m. Rosemary R. Fine, May 9, 1972; children by previous marriage-Judith (Mrs. Ross Campbell), Patricia (Mrs. Clarence Wurts), Wendy, Alison M. Partner, Nathan Trotter & Co., Phila., 1934-40; pres., dir. Frank Samuel & Co., Inc., Phila., 1945- 59, Haile Mines, N.Y.C., 1957-58; pres. Howmet Corp., N.Y.C., 1958-65, chmn. bd., 1965-66; partner Alexander Brown & Sons, 1966—; dir. UMC Corp., Allen Group, Inc., Columbus Dental Co., IU Internat. Corp. Served to col. AUS, 1941-45. Decorated Legion of Merit, Bronze Star (U.S.); Croix de Guerre (France and Belgium). Mem. Phi Beta Kappa Assos. Clubs: River, Downtown Assn. (N.Y.C.); Lyford Cay (Nassau); Fairfield (Conn.) Country. Home: Smith NV 89430 Office: 72 Wall St New York NY 10005

WEAVER, WINSTON ODELL, constrn. co. exec.; b. Harrisonburg, Va., Dec. 15, 1921; s. Marion Ralston and Annie (Shank) W.; student Eastern Mennonite Coll., 1939-41; B.A., Bridgewater Coll., 1947, L.H.D., 1975; m. Phyllis Livengood, July 18, 1942; children—Winston Odell, M. Steven, M. Gregory. With Rockingham Constrn. Co., Inc., Harrisonburg, 1946—, pres.. gen. mgr., 1956—; pres. Rockingham Builders, Inc., Harrisonburg. 1959—; gen. partner Rockingham Rentals, Harrisonburg, 1972—; owner Mariann Meadows Farms; dir. Mennonite Broadcasts, Inc., Harrisonburg, 1957-67, v.p., 1962-67; adv. bd. Va. Nat. Bank, Harrisonburg, 1970-79, vice chmn., 1975-79; dir. First Nat. Bank, Harrisonburg, 1958-70. Pres. Harrisonburg-Rockingham chpt. Mental Health Assn., 1960-61; chmn. Cancer Crusade, Harrisonburg, 1966; mem. chmn. nat. alumni fund chmn. Bridgewater (Va.) Coll., 1966, 67, also trustee, mem. exec. com.; bd. dirs. World Vision, Inc., U.S., 1978—; bd. dirs. World Vision Internat., Los Angeles, 1964—, project dir. design and constrn. hosp., Cambodia, 1972-75; bd. visitors James Madison U., Harrisonburg, 1973—; campaign chmn. Harrisonburg/Rockingham United Way, 1976, pres., 1977. Recipient Distinguished Service awards Mental Health Assn., 1961, Cancer Crusade, 1966; named Alumnus of Year, Bridgewater Coll., 1968; Outstanding Service award World Vision Internat., 1970; Harrisonburg-Rockingham C. of C. Businessman of Year award, 1977. Mem. Power and Communications Contractors Assn. (dir. 1975—), Internat. Platform Assn. Rotarian (v.p. 1974-75, pres. 1975-76). Clubs: University, Capitol Hill (Washington). Home: 875 Summit Ave Harrisonburg VA 22801 Office: PO Box 808 Harrisonburg VA 22801

WEBB, CHARLES ALBERT, lawyer; b. Eagle Rock, Va., Mar. 26, 1917; s. Harold H. and Leonora (Woltz) W.; B.S., U. Iowa, 1938; LL.B., U. Va., 1941; m. Elinor June Anderson, June 10, 1941; children—Sandra, Stephen, Charles, Thomas. Admitted to D.C. bar, 1942, Va. bar. 1958; asso. Covington & Burling, 1941- 42, Kilpatrick, Ballard & Beasley, 1946-48; legislative asst. Sen. John W. Bricker of Ohio, 1949-58; commr. Interstate Commerce Commn., 1958-67, chmn. 1965; pres. Nat. Assn. Motor Bus Owners, 1967-77; mem. firm Vorys, Sater, Seymour & Pease, Washington, 1978—. Served to lt. USNR, 1942-45. Mem. Am. Bar Assn., Sigma Alpha Epsilon, Phi Delta Phi, Order of Coif. Republican. Notes editor Va. Law Rev., 1940-41. Home: The London House 1001 Wilson Blvd Arlington VA 22209 Office: 1800 M St NW Room 800 South Washington DC 20036

WEBB, CHARLES HAIZLIP, JR., univ. dean; b. Dallas, Feb. 14, 1933; s. Charles Haizlip and Marion (Gilker) W.; A.B., So. Meth. U., 1955, M.Mus., 1955; D.Mus., Ind. U., 1964; m. Kenda McGibbon, June 21, 1958; children—Mark, Kent, Malcolm, Charles Haizlip III. Asst. to dean Sch. Music, So. Meth. U., 1957-58; mem. faculty Sch. Music, Ind. U., 1960—, dean, 1973—; dir. Indpls. Symphony Choir, 1967—; guest condr. chorus and orch. festivals throughout U.S.; duo-pianist with Wallace Hornibrook in U.S. and Australian tour, 1973; organist First Meth. Ch., Bloomington, 1961—; music dir. ann. conf. Meth. Ch., Bloomington, 1961. Chmn. advisory bd. Internat. Festivals, Inc.; commr. Ind. Arts Commn.; mem. advisory panel The Music Found.; mem. recommendation bd. Avery Fisher Prize Program. Served with U.S. Army, 1955-57. Decorated D.S.M. Mem. Pi Kappa Lambda, Phi Mu Alpha, Phi Delta Theta. Home: 648 Woodscrest Dr Bloomington IN 47401

WEBB, CHARLES RICHARD, JR., coll. pres.; b. Berkeley, Calif., Oct. 4, 1919; s. Charles Richard and Adele (McDaniel) W.; A.B., U. Calif. at Berkeley, 1942, M.A., 1944; M.A., Harvard, 1947, Ph.D., 1949; m. Andrée Bonno; 1 son, Charles Richard III. Faculty, San Diego State Coll., 1949-64, prof., 1958-64, chmn. dept. history, 1956-58; dean acad. affairs Stanislaus State Coll., Turlock, Cal., 1964-66; prof. history San Diego State Coll., 1966-70; pres. Eastern Conn. State Coll., Willimantic, 1970—; former asso. dean acad. planning Cal. State Colls., former dep. state coll. dean acad. planning. Bd. dirs. Conn. Faculty Talent Search, New Eng. Program in Tchr. Edn., Conn. Higher Edn. Television Assn., Eastern Conn. Drug Action Program. Served with USNR, 1941-45. Mem. Am., New Eng. hist. assns., Assn. Am. U. Profs., Assn. Cal. State Coll. Profs. (v.p. 1958-60), Cal. Tchrs. Assn., Save the Redwoods League, Conn. Employees Assn., Fine Arts Soc. of San Diego, Am. Assn. State Colls. and Univs., Phi Alpha Theta, Kappa Delta Pi. Clubs: University San Diego, Commonwealth of Cal.; Willimantic Country. Author: Workbook in Western Civilization, 2 vols., 1959; Western Civilization vol. 1 (with Schaefer), vol. 2 (with Palm), 1958; (with Crosby) The Past as Prologue, 2 vols., 1973. Contbr. articles to profl. jours. Home: Gurleyville Rd Storrs CT 06268 Office: Eastern Conn State Coll Willimantic CT 06226

WEBB, DONALD ARTHUR, coll. exec.; b. Wales, May 4, 1926; s. Arthur and Emily W.; came to U.S., 1958; student Queen's Coll., Cambridge (Eng.) U., 1944-45; B.A., Ohio Wesleyan U., 1960; M.Div. Methodist Theol. Sch. in Ohio, 1963; Ph.D., Drew U., 1966; postdoctoral Lincoln Coll., Oxford (Eng.) U., 1969, 72; m. Renee Mowbray, May 18, 1946; children—Cheryl, Marian, Christopher, Alison, Ian. Insp., Brit. Social Services, 1953-58; ordained to ministry Methodist Ch., 1960; pastor various chs., Ohio and N.J., 1958-68; dean admissions, asst. prof. theology and lit. Meth. Theol. Sch. in Ohio, 1968-75, v.p. adminstrn., 1975-77; pres. Centenary Coll. La., 1977—. Served with Brit. Royal Navy, 1945-53. Mem. Shreveport (La.) C. of C. (dir. 1978-79). Author plays: The Flame and Dusty Miller, 1970; We Hold These Truths, 1960; author: Dostoevsky and Christian Agnosticism, 1971; contbr. articles, revs. to profl. jours. Home: 256 Symphony Ln Shreveport LA 71105 Office: 2911 Centenary Blvd Shreveport LA 71104

WEBB, EUGENE, educator; b. Santa Monica, Calif., Nov. 10, 1938; s. Eugene and Marguerite (Rufi) W.; B.A., U. Calif., Los Angeles, 1960; M.A., Columbia U., 1962, Ph.D., 1965; m. Marilyn Teruko Domoto, June 4, 1964; children—Alexandra Mariko, Christina Sachiko. Asst. prof. English, Simon Fraser U., 1965-66; asst. prof. U. Wash., Seattle, 1966-70, asso. prof., 1970-75, prof. comparative literature and comparative religion, 1975—. Mem. Am. Acad. Religion, Modern Lang. Assn., Phi Beta Kappa. Episcopalian. Author: Samuel Beckett: A Study of His Novels, 1970; The Plays of Samuel Beckett, 1972; The Dark Dove: The Sacred and Secular in Modern Literature, 1975. Home: 6911 57th Ave NE Seattle WA 98115 Office: Thomson Hall DR05 University Washington Seattle WA 98195

WEBB, EUGENE JOHN, educator; b. Albany, N.Y., July 18, 1933; s. John Joseph and Alice (Cussin) W.; A.B., SUNY, Albany, 1954; Ph.D., U. Chgo., 1956; m. Mary Ann Reiling, June 24, 1955; children—L. Geoffrey, Alison, Gregory. With E.H. Weiss & Co., Chgo., 1955-56; with Chgo. Tribune, 1956-60; mem. faculty Northwestern U., Evanston, Ill., 1960-68; prof. Grad. Sch. Bus., Stanford U., 1968—. Mem. Am. Psychol. Assn. Democrat. Co-author: Unobtrusive Measures, 1966; Organization of the Future, 1972. Home: 897 Southampton Palo Alto CA 94303 Office: Stanford Univ Stanford CA 94305

WEBB, GEORGE HENRY, conveyor mfr.; b. Detroit, Feb. 26, 1920; s. Jervis Bennett and Maureen (Campbell) W.; B.S. in Mech. Engring., U. Mich., 1942; m. Barbara L. McCain, Sept. 16, 1944; children—Barbara Alice (Mrs. George H. Bufford, Jr.), Dianne M. (Mrs. George A. Abbott), Ann M. (Mrs. Jimmy L. Tuck), Patricia M. With Jervis B. Webb Co., Detroit, 1942—, exec. v.p., 1970—, also dir.; sec., dir. Webb Forging Co., Webb Electric Co., Control Engring. Co., Ann Arbor Computer Co., Jervis B. Webb Internat. Co., Jervis B. Webb Co. Ga., Can. and Calif. Webb World Wide, Inc., Jervis B. Webb Continental Co. Mem. ASME, Soc. Automotive Engrs., Engring. Soc. Detroit. Mason (Shriner, K.T.). Clubs: Detroit Athletic; Bloomfield Hills (Mich.); Orchard Lake (Mich.); The Springs (Rancho Mirage, Calif.); Del Safari Country (Palm Desert, Calif.). Home: 140 Harlan St Bloomfield Hills MI 48013 also 75-711 Temple Ln Palm Desert CA 92260 Office: One Webb Dr Farmington Hills MI 48018

WEBB, HARRY CHARLES, cons.; b. Felsenthal, Ark., Sept. 30, 1905; s. Victor Leach and Lillian Zenobia (Stinnett) W.; student U. Tex.; m. Ruth Alene Brown, July 5, 1959; children—Harry Charles, Richard C. With Tex. Gulf Sulpher Co., Houston, 1929-53, exec. asst., asst. to v.p., dir. pub. relations; pres. Pan Am. Sulphur Co., Houston, 1954-70, dir., 1953-70, ret.; now cons. Mem. Am. Inst. M.E. Clubs: Houston Country, Petroleum, Coronado River Oaks Country.

WEBB, HOWARD WILLIAM, JR., educator; b. Dayton, Ohio, June 23, 1925; s. Howard William and Martha (Brown) W.; B.A., Denison U., 1947; M.A., State U. Iowa, 1950, Ph.D., 1953; m. Joyce Moore Cooper, Nov. 20, 1947; children—Howard William (dec.), Amy Forrest, Sarah Winship. Asst. prof. English, Central Mo. State Coll., 1953-56; asst. prof. So. Ill. U., Carbondale, 1956-62, asso. prof. English, 1962-67, prof. English, 1967—, dir. grad. studies in English, 1961-67, acting chmn., 1968, chmn., 1968-72, acad. affairs officer on bd. trustees staff, 1974-79, system acad. officer on chancellor's staff, 1979—. Served with USNR, 1943-46. Mem. Modern Lang. Assn., Am. Studies Assn., Midwest Modern Lang. Assn., Midcontinent Am. Studies Assn. Editor: Illinois Prose Writers: An Anthology, 1968. Contbr. articles to profl. jours. Home: 904 S Oakland Ave Carbondale IL 62901

WEBB, JACK, radio, TV producer, writer, dir., actor; b. Santa Monica, Calif., Apr. 2, 1920; s. Samuel Chester and Margaret (Smith) W.; student pub. schs.; m. Julie Peck, July 1947 (div.); children—Stacy, Lisa; m. 2d, Dorothy Thompson, Jan. 1955 (div. 1957); m. 3d, Jackie Loughery, June, 1958 (div. 1964). Starred radio show Pat Novak for Hire, San Francisco, 1945, Johnny Modero Pier 23, 1947; created radio show Dragnet, 1949, began TV show, 1951; producer-dir. TV series Noah's Ark; created radio show Pete Kelly's Blues, 1950, True Series, 1961; now owner; owner releasing firm Mark VII, Ltd., music pub. firms Mark VII Music, Pete Kelly Music; exec. charge TV prodn. Warner Studios, 1963; producer, dir., star Dragnet, 1967-70; exec. producer, creater Adam-12, 1968-71; exec. producer The D.A., 1971, O'Hara, U.S. Treasury, 1971, Emergency, Mobile One, 1975; narrator TV show Escape, 1973; exec. producer TV show Sam, 1977, Project U.F.O., 1978-79; feature roles in films The Men, Halls of Montezuma, He Walked by Night, You're in the Navy Now, Sunset Boulevard; producer, dir. motion picture Archie, 1959; actor-dir. motion picture Dragnet, 1954, 66, Pete Kelly's Blues, 1955, The D.I., 1957, All About Archie, 1960. Author: The Badge, 1958. Hon. chmn. United Cerebral Palsy Assn. Holder over 100 commendations of merit, award by radio, TV critics. Served with USAAF, World War II; named hon. sgt. USMC. Mem. Screen Actors Guild, Screen Dirs. Guild, Am. Soc. Cinematographers, Am. Fedn. Radio Actors. Club: San Francisco Press. Maintains large pvt. collection phonograph records, photographs, periodicals, etc., pertaining to U.S. in 1920s. Office: care Mark VII Ltd Samuel Goldwyn Studio 1041 N Formosa Los Angeles CA 90046*

WEBB, JACK M., mining co. exec.; b. Monroe, La., Feb. 23, 1936; s. Sam L. and Lillian Etta (McCowen) W.; B.S., Centenary Coll. La., 1957; J.D., Tulane U., 1960; m. Diane Adele Waterman, Aug. 22, 1964; children—Julia Lillian, Kathryn Joy, Samuel Logan. Admitted to La. bar, 1960, Tex. bar, 1963; atty. Standard Oil Co. Tex., Houston, 1961-66; staff atty. Trunkline Gas Co., Houston, 1966-71; sr. atty. M.W. Kellogg Co., Houston, 1971-73; sec., asst. gen. counsel Gulf Resources and Chem. Corp., Houston, 1973-78, v.p. govt. relations, adminstrv. asst. to chmn. bd., 1978—. Served to capt. U.S. Army, 1960-61. Mem. Am., Tex., La., Houston bar assns. Methodist. Home: 3434 Locke Ln Houston TX 77027 Office: Gulf Resources Chem Corp 47th Floor 1100 Milam Bldg Houston TX 77002

WEBB, JAMES EDWIN, lawyer; b. Granville County, N.C., Oct. 7, 1906; s. John Frederick and Sarah (Gorham) W.; A.B., U.N.C., 1928; student George Washington U. Law Sch., 1933-36; LL.D., U.N.C., 1949, Syracuse U., Colo. Coll.; Sc.D., U. Notre Dame, 1961, Brown U., 1976, also other hon. degrees; m. Patsy Aiken Douglas, May 14, 1938; children—Sarah Gorham, James Edwin, Jr. Exec. asst. to under-sec. of treasury, 1946; dir. Bur. of Budget, 1946- 49; undersec. of state, 1949-52; pres., gen. mgr. Republic Supply Co., 1953- 58, chmn. bd., 1958; asst. to pres. and dir. Kerr-McGee Oil Industries, Inc., Oklahoma City, 1952-61, 69-78; dir. McDonnell Aircraft Co., 1952-61, Fidelity Nat. Bank, 1957-59; adminstr. NASA, 1961-68; practice of law, Washington, 1968—. Dir. McGraw-Hill, Inc. Mem. Govt. Procurement Commn., 1972-73; mem. Comptroller Gen.'s Cons. Panel. Regent Smithsonian Instn., 1970—. Served to lt. col. as comdg. officer, 1st Marine Air Warning Group, 1944-45; lt. col. USMC Res. Recipient Robert J. Collier trophy, 1966; Distinguished Service medal NASA, 1968; Presdl. Medal of Freedom, 1969; Goddard Meml. trophy, 1971; N.C. Pub. Service award, 1971; Okla. State U. Bennett Service award, 1973; Gen. Accounting Office award for pub. service, 1973; named to Okla. Hall of Fame, 1967. Mem. Nat. Geog. Soc. (trustee, Hubbard medal 1979), Marine Corps Res. Officers Assn., Am. Soc. Pub. Adminstrn. (pres. 1966-67), Nat. Acad. Pub. Adminstrn. (treas. 1969-73), Soc. Advancement Mgmt., Am., D.C. bar assns., Acad. Polit. Sci., Nat. Planning Assn., Phi Beta Kappa, Phi Delta Phi. Presbyn. Democrat. Mason. Clubs: University (N.Y.C.); University, Chevy Chase, Metropolitan (Washington); Alfalfa. Home: 2800 36th St NW Washington DC 20007 Office: 1707 H St NW Washington DC 20006

WEBB, JAMES LEWIS ADRIAN, educator, chemist; b. Webb, Miss., Nov. 17, 1917; s. Lewis Daniel and Margaret (Turner) W.; B.S., Washington and Lee U., 1939; Ph.D., Johns Hopkins, 1943; m. Jeanne Eleanor DeHoff, June 6, 1946; children—Lewis Daniel (dec.), Mary Josephine, James Lewis Adrian, Jeanne Eleanor. From asst. prof. to prof. Southwestern at Memphis, 1945-59; research chemist Chapman Chem. Co., 1951-59; mem. faculty Goucher Coll., 1959—, prof. chemistry, chmn. dept., 1965—. Mem. Am. Chem. Soc. (chmn. Memphis 1959), Phi Beta Kappa, Sigma Xi. Episcopalian. Author articles, book. Patentee in field. Home: 1915 Eastridge Rd Timonium MD 21093 Office: Dept Chemistry Goucher Coll Towson MD 21204

WEBB, JAMES OKRUM, JR., ins. co. exec.; b. Cleve., Nov. 25, 1931; s. James Okrum and Bessie Ruth (Eubanks) W.; B.A., Morehouse Coll., Atlanta, 1953; M.B.A. in Actuarial Sci., U. Mich., 1955-57; m. Frankie L. Lowe, Feb. 19, 1954; children—Pamela Ruth, Lisa Suzanne. Actuarial asst. Mut. of N.Y., N.Y.C., 1957-62; asst. to pres., actuary Supreme Life Ins. Co. Am., Chgo., 1962-64, v.p., actuary, 1964-66; asst. actuary Health Care Service Corp. (Blue Cross and Blue Shield), Chgo., 1966-68, asst. v.p. product devel., 1968-69, v.p. product and project mgmt., 1969-73, v.p. finance, asst. treas., 1973-74, v.p. finance, treas., 1974-75, v.p. corp. planning and devel., 1975-79, sr. v.p. planning and devel., 1979—; dir. South Shore Nat. Bank Chgo. Mem. Ill. Ins. Adv. Com., 1965-67; mem. Ill. Commn. Urban Area Govt., 1970-72. Mem. Glencoe (Ill.) Sch. Bd., 1970-77, pres., 1976-77; pres. Glencoe Human Relations Com., 1970-71. Bd. dirs., mem. budget and finance com. Mid-Am. chpt. ARC, 1974-75; v.p., mem. exec. com., chmn. devel. com. Chgo. Black United Fund,

1974-76; pres., bd. dirs. Chgo. Caucus; founder, past pres. bd. dirs. Home Investments Fund, now chmn. bd.; bd. dirs. United Charities Chgo., Leadership Council for Met. Open Communities, Scholarship and Guidance; asso. Presbyn.-St. Luke's Hosp.; mem. New Trier Twp. Mental Health Adv. Bd.; bd. advsiers U. Ill. at Chgo. Circle Campus Bus. Sch. Served with C.E., AUS, 1953-55. Mem. Am. Acad. Actuaries (dir., treas. 1975-78), Conf. Actuaries in Pub. Practice (asso.), Assn. Corporate Growth, Nat., Midwest planning assns., N.Am. Soc. Corp. Planning, Planning Execs. Inst., Alpha Phi Alpha. Clubs: Economics, Execs. (Chgo.). Home: 260 Wentworth Glencoe IL 60022 Office: 233 N Michigan Ave Chicago IL 60601

WEBB, JAMES SIDNEY, JR., mfg. co. exec.; b. Salt Lake City, Oct. 14, 1919; s. James Sidney and Josephine Isabel (Hornung) W.; B.S. in Bus. Adminstrn., San Jose (Calif.) State U., 1941; m. Lucille Marian Gardner, June 28, 1941; children—Janet Webb Sippl, James Sidney. With Shell Chem. Co., 1945-48, U.S. Steel Corp., 1948-52, Varian Assos., 1952-54; with TRW Inc., 1954—, gen. mgr. electronics group, corp. v.p., 1963-66, exec. v.p., 1966-78, vice chmn. bd., 1978—, also dir.; dir. DeSoto, Inc., May Dept. Stores Co. Bd. dirs. Los Angeles Philharmonic Assn., TRW Found., Ind. Colls. of So. Calif., Estelle Doheny Eye Found.; trustee City of Hope; bd. govs. Hugh O'Brian Youth Found. Served to lt. USNR, 1942-45. Office: 10880 Wilshire Blvd Suite 1700 Los Angeles CA 90024

WEBB, JERVIS CAMPBELL, engring. exec.; b. Mount Vernon, N.Y., Mar. 22, 1915; s. Jervis Bennett and Maurene (Campbell) W.; B.S., Mass. Inst. Tech., 1937; m. Patricia D. Lyeth, 1977. In engring., sales depts. Jervis B. Webb Co., Detroit, 1937-52, pres, gen. mgr., 1952—; pres. Jervis B. Webb Co. of Can., Ltd., Hamilton, Ont., Jervis B. Webb Co. of Calif., Los Angeles, Webb Forging Co., Belleville, Michigan, Jervis B. Webb Co. of Ga., Webb Electric Co., Detroit, Control Engring. Co., Detroit, Campbell, Henry & Calvin, Inc., Detroit, Webb World Wide, Inc., Detroit, Jervis B. Webb Internat. Co., Detroit; v.p. Ann Arbor Computer (Mich.); sec., dir. Huron Forge & Machine Co., Jervis B. Webb (U.K.) Ltd., London; pres., dir. Jervis B. Webb Continental Co., Wilmington, Del. Mem. Nat. council Boy Scouts Am. Trustee Nat. Sanitation Found., Traffic Safety for Mich., Industry Adv. Com. on Adv. Com. on Automation, Detroit Country Day Sch., Detroit Inst. Tech. Mem. ASME, Engring. Soc. Detroit, Material Handling Inst., Am. Materials Handling Soc., Conveyor Equipment Mfrs. Assn. (pres. 1935), Am. Ordnance Assn., Employers Assn. Detroit (dir.), Foundry Equipment Mgrs. Assn. (dir.), Mich. C. of C. (dir.), Mich. Mfrs. Assn. (dir.), N.A.M., Soc. Automotive Engrs., Greater Detroit Bd. Commerce, Newcomen Soc. N.Am. Mason, Rotarian. Clubs: Engineers (N.Y.C.); Detroit Athletic (past pres., dir.), Detroit Economic, Hundred, Detroit Golf (Detroit); Huron River Hunting and Fishing, Lake Shore (Chgo.); Bloomfield (Mich.) Open Hunt. Contbr. mumerous articles to trade mags. Patentee bracket for overhead trolley chain conveyors. Home: 1436 Kirkway Bloomfield Hills MI 48013 Office: Webb Dr Farmington Hills MI 48018

WEBB, JIMMY LAYNE, composer; b. Elk City, Okla., Aug. 15, 1946; s. Robert Lee and Sylvia Ann (Killingworth) W. Propr., Canopy Music Films Prodns.; music dir. TV spl. Rolling Stone 10th Anniversary, 1977; recs. include Jim Webb Sings Jim Webb, Jimmy L. Webb: Songs and Music, And So On, Letters, Land's End, Mirage. Recipient Grammy award, 1967, 68. Mem. ASCAP, Am. Fedn. Musicians, Nat. Acad. Rec. Arts and Scis. (bd. dirs.), Composers and Lyricists Guild, AFTRA, Phi Mu Alpha (hon.). Composer: Up, Up and Away, 1966; By the Time I Get To Phoenix, 1966; MacArthur Park, 1967; Wichita Lineman; Galveston; All I Know. Address: care Katz-Gallin-Leffler 9255 Sunset Blvd Los Angeles CA 90069*

WEBB, JULIAN, judge; b. Byromville, Ga., Oct. 2, 1911; s. Vester Otis and Flossie (Woddruff) W.; A.B., J.D., Mercer U., 1932; m. Jo Smith, Sept. 25, 1935; children—Joanna Webb Custer, Julianna Webb Cheshire. Admitted to Ga. bar, 1932, practiced in Augusta, until 1933; mem. legal dept. Farm Credit Adminstrn., 1933-42; practice law, Donalsonville, Ga., 1943-74; judge Ga. Ct. Appeals, Atlanta, 1974—; city atty. City of Donalsonville, 1945-74; county atty. Seminole County, 1971-74. Mem. Ga. Senate, 1963-74, asst. floor leader, 1963, floor leader, 1964, pres. pro tem, 1967-69; mem. Ga. Constn. Revision Commns., 1963, 69; mem. Ga. Bar Disciplinary Bd., 1964-67; mem. Ga. Gov.'s Jud. Processes Commn., 1971-73; mem. Criminal Law Study Commn., 1972-74; mem. Gov.'s Commn. on Ct. Orgn. and Structure, 1975-79; Ga. mem. Nat. Council State Ct. Reps., 1975-78; chmn. Jud. Council Ga., 1978-79. Chmn. bd. trustees Thomasville dist. Methodist Ch., del. world conf.; trustee, chmn. So. Ga. Home for Aging, Americus. Mem. Am., Ga. (gov.), Pataula Circuit bar assns., Am. Judicature Soc., Am. Law Inst., C. of C. (dir.), Blue Key, Sigma Pi, Phi Alpha Delta. Democrat. 1966. Clubs: Masons, Shriners, Lions. Office: 420 State Judicial Bldg Atlanta GA 30334

WEBB, KEMPTON EVANS, geographer, educator; b. Melrose, Mass., Dec. 28, 1931; s. Winthrop Lambert and Margaret (Evans) W.; A.B., Harvard, 1953; M.A., Syracuse U., 1955, Ph.D., 1958; m. Nancy Ann Boyd, Sept. 3, 1955; children—Rachel Drake, Scott Winthrop. Tech. cons. Banco do Nordeste do Brasil, Ceara, 1957; asst. prof. geography Ind. U., Bloomington, 1958-61; asst. prof. geography, asst. dir. Inst. Latin Am. Studies, Columbia U., 1961-65, asso. prof., 1965-71, prof., 1971—, asso. dir. inst., 1965-69, dir., 1970-74, chmn. dept. geography, 1974-79, dir. world resources program Sch. Internat. Affairs, 1976—; pres. Champlain Windjammer Co. Mem. screening com. Fgn. Area Fellowship Tng. Program, 1965-68, Accion, 1964-67; head steering com. Consortium Latin Am. Studies Programs, 1973; cons. World Book Ency., 1971—. Fulbright-Hays Research grantee, 1968-69. Mem. Latin Am. Studies Assn. (exec. council 1965-68), Assn. Am. Geographers (v.p. Middle States div. 1980). Democrat. Unitarian. Author: Geography of Food Supply in Central Minas Gerais, 1959; Suprimento dos Generos Alimenticios para a Cidade de Fortalaza, 1957; Brazil, 1964; Geography of Latin America 1972; The Changing Face of Northeast Brazil, 1974; All Possible Worlds, 1980. Editor: Latin America: A Geographic Commentary, 1966; cultural geography series. Contbg. editor, mem. adv. bd. Handbook of Latin American Studies, 1959—; editorial bd. Latin Am. Research Rev., 1974—. Contbr. articles to profl. jours. Home: 468 Overbrook Rd Ridgewood NJ 07450 Office: Dept Geography Internat Affairs 1028 Columbia U New York NY 10027

WEBB, LANCE, bishop; b. Boaz, N.Mex., Dec. 10, 1909; s. John Newton Shields and Delia (Lance) W.; B.A. with highest honors, McMurry Coll., 1931, D.D., 1948; B.D., So. Meth. U., 1934, M.A., 1934; summer student Union Theol. Sem. 1939, 47; D.D., Ohio Wesleyan, U., 1960, MacMurray Coll., 1967, McKendree Coll., 1970, Morningside Coll., 1977; H.H.D., Ill. Wesleyan U., 1966; LL.D., So. Meth. U., 1966; Litt.D., Simpson Coll., 1979; m. Mary Elizabeth Hunt, June 30, 1933; children—Gloria (Mrs. David B. Davis), Mary M. (Mrs. Lee Edlund), Ruth Elizabeth (Mrs. Allan Lindstrom). Ordained to ministry Meth. Ch., 1935; pastor McCullough-Harrah Meth. Chs., Pampa, Tex., 1934-37; chaplain prof. religion McMurry Coll., Abilene, Tex., 1937-38; pastor, Shamrock, Tex., 1938-40, Eastland, Tex., 1940-41, University Park Meth. Ch., Dallas, 1941-52, North Broadway Meth. Ch., Columbus, Ohio, 1953-64; bishop Meth. Ch., 1964—, resident bishop Ill. area, 1964-76, resident bishop Iowa area, 1976—. Chmn. com. on worship Meth. Ch., 1964-72, mem. gen. and jurisdictional coms., co-chmn. world Meth. com. worship and liturgy, 1966-71; mem. World Meth. Council, 1966-71, sec., vice chmn. com. worship and liturgy, 1971—, chmn. com., 1976; mem. bd. higher edn. and ministry United Meth. Ch., 1972—; pres. north central jurisdiction Coll. of Bishops, 1979—; conducted goodwill tours Middle East and Round the World, 1961, 63; Nat. Council Chs. interchange preacher in Britain, 1959; chancellor Disciplined Order of Christ, 1964—. Mem. Columbus Mayor's Com on Human Relations, 1953-64; chaplain Ohio Senate, 1963; internat. chaplain Civitain Internat., 1951. Trustee Meth. Sch. Theology in Ohio, Garrett Evang. Theol. Sch., Evanston, Ill., McKendree Coll., Lebanon, Ill., Ill. Wesleyan U., MacMurray Coll.; chmn. bd. Wesley Found., U. Ill., 1964-76, Morningside Coll., Simpson Coll., Cornell Coll., Iowa Wesleyan Coll., Westmar Coll., 1976—, Rust Coll., 1978—. Clubs: Masons (33 deg.), Torch (Columbus). Author: Conquering the Seven Deadly Sins, 1955; Discovering Love, 1959; Point of Glad Return, 1960; Art of Personal prayer, 1962; On the Edge of the Absurd, 1965; When God Comes Alive, 1968; Disciplines for Life in the Age of Aquarius, 1971; God's Surprises, 1976. Home: 3005 Patricia Dr Des Moines IA 50322 Office: 1019 Chestnut St Des Moines IA 50309. *My life has been one continuous series of surprises in which the worst that has happened to me has turned out for the best. Since the age of 18 I have consciously lived by the faith that the spirit creating, sustaining, and ruling our universe is like the spirit that was seen in Jesus. Whenever I have given myself to love and to serve upon this living faith, I have found my darkest nights turn into brightest dawns.*

WEBB, NEIL JOHN, coll. pres.; b. Fond du Lac, Wis., June 21, 1929; s. Everett Thomas and Alice Louise (Nettekoven) W.; B.S. in Sociology and Psychology, Marquette U., 1952; M.A. in Psychology, Loyola U., 1958, Ph.D. in Psychology, 1959; grad. Inst. Ednl. Mgmt., Harvard, 1970; m. Mary Mae Moore, Sept. 18, 1954; children—Terrance, Maureen, Erin, Kevin, Colleen, Kathleen. Teaching fellow Loyola U., 1957; research asso. project religion and mental health NIMH, 1957-59; instr. to prof. psychology St. Norbert Coll., De Pere, Wis., 1959-66, dean coll., 1967, adminstrv. v.p., 1967-73, pres., 1973—; vis. lectr. Catholic U., 1960; vis. prof. Loyola U., 1963; cons. Brown County Ct. and Hosp., 1960-65; pres. Wis. Found. Ind. Colls., 1977-79; dir. Peoples Marine Bank, Wis. Pub. Service Co. Mem. Wis. Mental Health Task Force, 1964, Wis. Task Force Higher Edn., 1969, Wis. Task Force '70, 1970; mem. adv. com. Coop. Institutional Research Program, Am. Council on Edn. Mem. adv. bd. St. Vincent Hosp., 1977—. Served with M.C., AUS, 1952-54. Hill Found. grantee, 1962, U.S. Office Edn. grantee, 1965-67. Mem. Am. Psychol. Assn., Am. Assn. Higher Edn., Green Bay C. of C. (dir. 1975-79). Author: Student-Led Discussion, 1967; Psychodynamics of Personality Development, 1965. Contbr. to Casebook in Psychopathology, 1964. Home: 1116 Fox River Dr De Pere WI 54115 Office: St Norbert Coll De Pere WI 54115

WEBB, OMRI KENNETH, JR., univ. dean; b. Greymount, Ga., Feb. 25, 1926; s. Omri Kenneth and Lenora (Jordan) W.; B.A., The Citadel, 1948; B.D., So. Bapt. Theol. Sem., 1952; Ph.D., Duke, 1964; m. Betty Sue Jenkins, Aug. 11, 1962; children—Kenneth, Walter, Kirk, Susan. Instr. philosophy Furman U., Greenville, S.C., 1955-58, asst. prof. philosophy, 1958-62; asst. prof. Appalachian State U., Boone, N.C., 1962-63, asso. prof., 1963-68, prof. philosophy, religion, 1968—, dean student affairs, 1964-70, dean gen. coll., 1969—. Served to 2d lt. AUS, 1944-46. Mem. Am. Personnel and Guidance Assn., So. Soc. Philosophy and Psychology. Democrat. Baptist. Office: Gen Coll Appalachian State U Boone NC 28608

WEBB, RICHARD CREER, banker; b. Pocatello, Idaho, Oct. 10, 1939; s. Arch G. and Lucille C. W.; B.S., U. Utah, 1964; m. Kathleen Burke Hale, Dec. 18, 1964; children—Elizabeth Hale, Richard Hale. With Mich. Nat. Bank of Detroit, 1968—, group v.p. comml. loans, 1974-75, adminstrv. v.p. exec. offices, 1975-76, sr. v.p., 1976, exec. v.p., 1976—; dir. Mich. Nat. Bank-Farmington, Transport Warehouse, Computer Profls. Unlimited, Mich. Nat. Bank-West Oakland, Condamtic, Internat. Carriers, United Broadcasting Co. Served to capt. U.S. Army, 1965-68. Mem. Robert Morris Assos. Mormon. Clubs: Rotary, Econ. (Detroit). Office: 1000 W Maple PO Box 1059 Troy MI 48099

WEBB, RICHARD GILBERT, business exec.; b. Tulsa, May 11, 1932; s. William Leslie and Cora (Kroshus) W.; student Okla. U., 1950-52; B.B.A., So. Meth. U., 1954; M.B.A., Harvard, 1956; m. Patricia Helen Wagdin, Apr. 13, 1959 (div. Sept. 1974); children—Catherine, Andrea, Nicholas. Cons. McKinsey & Co., N.Y.C., 1959-61; new bus. analyst Mobil Oil Co., N.Y.C., 1961-64; subsidiary controller Internat. Tel. & Tel., N.Y.C., Chgo., also Montreal, Que., Can., 1964-66; v.p., mgr. corp. devel. Ill. Tool Works, Chgo., 1966-70; v.p. planning, treas., chief fin. officer Interstate Brands Corp., Kansas City, Mo., 1970-78; v.p., treas., chief fin. officer Gen. Host Corp., Stamford, Conn., 1978—. Served to lt. AUS, 1956-59. C.P.A., Okla. Mem. Okla. Soc. C.P.A.'s, Assn. Corp. Growth, Kappa Alpha. Unitarian. Club: Harvard. Home: 22 Rice's Ln Westport CT 06880 Office: Gen Host Corp 22 Gate House Rd Stamford CT 06902

WEBB, RICHARD PIERCE, diversified industry exec.; b. Paterson, N.J., July 25, 1941; s. James R. and Mary P. (Pierce) W.; B.A., Colgate U., Hamilton, N.Y., 1963; M.B.A., Columbia, 1965; m. Diane T. Doviak, Aug. 29, 1964; children—Geoffrey R., Kyle. Mgr. Arthur Andersen & Co., N.Y.C., 1965-74; treas. Carrier Corp., Syracuse, N.Y., 1974—, v.p., chief financial officer, 1975—. Served with AUS, 1966-68. Mem. Am. Inst. C.P.A.'s, N.Y. Athletic Club. Home: 37 Chenango St Cazenovia NY 13035 Office: Carrier Corp Carrier Tower PO Box 4800 Syracuse NY 13221

WEBB, ROBERT KIEFER, educator; b. Toledo, Nov. 23, 1922; s. Charles Ellis and Melva Marie (Kiefer) W.; A.B., Oberlin Coll., 1947; A.M., Columbia, 1948, Ph.D., 1951; postgrad. London Sch. Econs., 1949-51; m. Patty Bradburn Shull, Dec. 28, 1957; children—Emily, Margaret. Instr. history Wesleyan U., 1951-53; from asst. prof. to prof. history Columbia, 1953-70, adjunct prof., 1970—; editor Am. Hist. Rev., Washington, 1968-75; prof. history U. Md. Baltimore County, 1975—, acting vice-chancellor for acad. affairs, 1978-79; vis. professorial fellow Victorian Studies Centre of U. Leicester, Eng., 1967. Served with AUS, 1943-46. Fulbright scholar, 1950-51; Guggenheim fellow, 1959-60, 73-74; Am. Council Learned Socs. fellow, 1966-67; Nat. Endowment for Humanities research grantee, 1978-80. Mem. AAUP (1st v.p. 1970-72, editor bull. 1975-78, editor Academe 1979—). Democrat. Club: Cosmos (Washington). Author: The British Working-Class Reader, 1790-1848: Literacy and Social Tension, 1955; Harriet Martineau, a Radical Victorian, 1960; Modern England, from the Eighteenth Century to the Present, 2d edit., 1980; (with Peter Gay) Modern Europe, 1973. Home: 3309 Highland Pl NW Washington DC 20008 Office: Dept History Univ Md Baltimore County Baltimore MD 21228

WEBB, ROBERT WALLACE, educator, geologist; b. Los Angeles, Nov. 2, 1909; s. Robert Remme and Sharlie Jeannette (Ward) W.; A.B., U. Cal. at Los Angeles, 1931; postgrad. U. Wash., 1931, U. So. Cal., 1931-32; M.S., Cal. Inst. Tech., 1932, Ph.D., 1937; m. Evelyn Elaine Gourley, June 28, 1933; children—Robert Ian Arthur, Leland Frederick, Donald Gourley. Mem. faculty U. Cal. at Los Angeles, 1932-48; mem. faculty U. Cal. at Santa Barbara, 1948—, prof. geology, 1951—, chmn. dept. phys. scis., 1953-59; dir. Ford Found. Exptl. Program Instrs. for Colls., 1960-63. Coordinator vets. affairs univs. Cal., 1947-52; exec. sec. NRC div. geology and geography, 1953; dir. Am. Geol. Inst., 1953. Recipient Neil Miner award Nat. Assn. Geology Tchrs., 1973, Robert Wallace Webb award Far Western sect. Assn. Geol. Tchrs., 1973. Fellow Geol. Soc. Am., Mineral Soc. Am., Meteoritical Soc. (sec. 1937-41); mem. Nat. Assn. Geology Tchrs. (pres. Far Western sect. 1959, 72). Author: (with Joseph Murdoch) Minerals of California, 1966; (with Robert M. Norris) Geology of California, 1977; also bulls. Calif. Div. Mines and Geology. Contbr. articles to profl. jours. Home: 898 Via Campobello Santa Barbara CA 93111

WEBB, ROSS ALLAN, educator; b. Westchester, N.S., Can., July 22, 1923; s. William Oswald and Permilla Madge (Purdy) W.; B.A. with honours, Acadia U., Wolfville, N.S., 1949; M.A., U. Pitts., 1951, Ph.D., 1956; m. Ruth Evangeline Keil, June 19, 1954; children—Eric Seth, Alan George. Came to U.S., 1928, naturalized, 1954. Lectr. history U. Pitts., 1950-56; asso. prof., dir. undergrad. studies history U. Ky., 1956-57; prof., chmn. dept. history, govt. and geography Winthrop Coll., Rock Hill, S.C., 1967-68, dean faculty, 1968-71, prof. history, 1968-71, 75—, v.p. acad. affairs, 1971-75; vis. prof. Canadian history, dir. grad. studies history Acadia U., summers 1951-64; vis. prof. Inst. Am. Studies, W.Va. Wesleyan U., summer 1966. Mem. S.C. Commn. Archives History, 1967-68. Served as officer RCAF, 1941-45. Mem. Am. Hist. Soc., So. Hist. Soc., Canadian Hist. Assn., Phi Beta Kappa, Phi Alpha Theta, Phi Kappa Phi. Author: The Alaskan Boundary Dispute, 1779-1903, 1951; A Book of Remembrance, 1956; Benjamin Helm Bristow: Border State Politician, 1969; Kentucky in the Reconstruction Era, 1979; also articles; contbg. author: Radicalism, Racism and Party Realignment, 1969. Home: 2534 Shiland Dr Rock Hill SC 29730

WEBB, THOMPSON, univ. press dir.; b. Los Angeles, Mar. 16, 1917; s. Thompson and Vivian (Howell) W.; A.B., Princeton, 1939; A.M., Harvard, 1940; m. Diana Stimson, July 12, 1941; children—Thompson III, Gordon. Instr., Phillips Acad., Andover, Mass., 1940-41, Catalina Island Sch., Santa Catalina Island, Calif., 1941-42; sales mgr. U. Calif. Press, Berkeley, 1946, asst. editor, 1947; dir. U. Wis. Press, Madison, 1947—, prof., 1959—. Served to lt. (s.g.) USNR, 1942-45. Mem. Assn. Am. U. Presses (pres. 1973-74), Wis. Acad. Scis., Arts and Letters (pres. 1980), Phi Beta Kappa. Home: 4878 Wakanda Dr Waunakee WI 53597 Office: 114 N Murray St Madison WI 53715

WEBB, WATT WETMORE, physicist, educator; b. Kansas City, Mo., Aug. 27, 1927; s. Watt, Jr. and Anna (Wetmore) W.; B.S., Mass. Inst. Tech., 1947, Sc.D., 1955; m. Page Chapman, Nov. 1950; children—Watt III, Spahr C., Bucknell C. Research engr., asst. dir. research Union Carbide Metals Co., Niagara Falls, N.Y., 1947-52, 55-61; asso. prof., prof. applied physics Cornell U., Ithaca, N.Y., 1961—. Cons. applied sci.; asso. editor Phys. Rev. Letters, 1975—; mem. adv. panels Materials Adv. Bd., 1958-59, 63-64, NSF, 1974—. Guggenheim fellow, 1974-75. Fellow Am. Phys. Soc. (exec. com. div. biol. physics); mem. Biophys. Soc., Am. Inst. E.E., Metall. Soc. Clubs: Ithaca Yacht; Rochester Yacht. Mem. editorial bd. Biophys. Jour., 1975—, Phys. Rev., 1977—. Contbr. articles to profl. jours. Office: Clark Hall Cornell University Ithaca NY 14853

WEBB, WILLIAM DUNCAN, lawyer, utility co. exec.; b. Dayton, Ohio, Feb. 14, 1930; s. Herbert Henry and Dorothy (Chamberlain) W.; A.B., U. Mich., 1952, J.D., 1956; m. Nancy Helen Regester, June 12, 1953; children—Joseph Chamberlain (dec.), Mary Helen, Nancy Katherine, Sarah Elizabeth, Lucy Ellen. Admitted to Mo. bar, 1956, Kans. bar, 1958, U.S. Supreme Ct. bar, 1969—; asso. law firm Stinson, Mag, Thomson, McEvers & Frizzell, Kansas City, Mo., 1956-58; sec. Kansas City (Mo.) Power & Light Co., 1960—, asst. treas., 1969—, asst. v.p. communications, 1978-79, asst. v.p. fed. affairs, 1979—. Legal counsel Fellowship of Christian Athletes. Mem. city council Roeland Park, Kans., 1960-62. Chmn. Kansas City Myasthenia Gravis Found., 1965-67; bd. dirs. Boys Club of Kansas City, Mo., 1969-74, Greater Kansas City YMCA, Greater Kansas City chpt. ARC; chmn. bd. councilors Avila Coll., 1969-70, trustee, asst. sec., 1970. Mem. Internat. Maine-Anjou Assn. (dir., sec.-treas. 1969-76), Theta Delta Chi, Phi Alpha Delta. Presbyn. Home: 37000 W 155th St Gardner KS 66030 Office: 1330 Baltimore Kansas City MO 64141

WEBB, WILLIAM HESS, lawyer; b. Scottdale, Pa., Sept. 10, 1905; s. Austin Allison and Gertrude (Hess) W.; B.S., U. Pitts 1926, LL.B., 1929; m. Marian Elizabeth Wellings, Nov. 26, 1931; children—John M., Patricia Ann (Mrs. Terence S. Small). Admitted to Pa. bar, 1929, since practiced in Pitts.; sr. partner Webb, Burden, Robinson & Webb and predecessor firm, Pitts., 1948—. Bd. dirs. Pitts. Opera Soc.; mem. adv. bd. Civic Light Opera Assn.; mem. Pitts. Symphony Soc. Served to 1st lt. U.S. Army Res., 1926-34. Mem. Am. Patent Law Assn. (bd. mgrs. 1953-62), pres. 1959-60, Am. (ho. of dels. 1961-65), Pa., Inter-Am. Allegheny County bar. assns., Am. Law Inst., Licensing Execs. Soc., Nat. Assn. Bar Presidents, Internat. Assn. Protection Indsl. Property, Civic Light Opera Soc., Delta Theta Phi. Theta Chi. Clubs: Duquesne, University (Pitts); Edgeworth (Sewickley, Pa.); Allegheny Country; Skyline Country (Tucson); Seaview (N.J.) Country. Home: Apt 305 201 Grant St Sewickley PA 15143 Office: Oliver Bldg Pittsburgh PA 15222

WEBB, WILLIAM LOYD, JR., army officer; b. Mineral Wells, Tex., Sept. 30, 1925; s. William Loyd and Francis (Mayer) W.; student Tex. A. and M. Coll., 1942-44; B.S., U.S. Mil. Acad., 1947; M.A., U. Pa., 1958; m. Muriel Emma Hinson, Dec. 27, 1947; children—George Sidney, William Loyd II, Lucinda Adrienne, Alicia Muriel. Commd. 2d lt. U.S. Army, 1947, advanced through grades to maj. gen., 1974; co. comdr., Korea, 1950, Ft. Riley, Kans., 1951-52, Germany, 1953-54; asso. prof. English, U.S. Mil. Acad., West Point, N.Y., 1958-61, regimental comdr., dep. comdt. of cadets, 1969-71; squadron comdr. 14th Armored Calvary, Germany, 1963-64; mem. faculty U.S. Army War Coll., 1965-68; comdr. support command 1st Inf. Div., Vietnam, 1969; dep. comdg. gen., Ft. Ord, Calif., 1971-73; ops. officer 8th Army, U.S. Forces Korea, UN Command, Korea, 1973-75; sr. mem. UN Command Mil. Armistice Commn., Korea, 1975; comdr. 1st Armored Div., U.S. Army Europe, W.Ger., 1975-78; dep. comdg. gen. V Corps, U.S. Army Europe, W. Ger., 1978; asst. dep. chief of staff for personnel Dept. Army, Washington, 1978—. Decorated Legion of Merit with oak leaf cluster, D.F.C., Bronze Star medal with oak leaf cluster, Air medal with 5 oak leaf clusters, Army Commendation medal with 2 oak leaf clusters, Purple Heart. Mem. Assn. U.S. Army, Armor Assn. Episcopalian. Home: Post TX 79356 Office: Asst Dep Chief Staff for Personnel Hdqrs Dept Army Washington DC 20310

WEBB, WILLIAM ROBERT, III, ednl. adminstr.; b. Knoxville, Tenn., Feb. 8, 1919; s. Daniel Clary and Julia Hannah (McCulley) W.; A.B., U. Tenn., 1941, M.S., 1947; m. Julia Dossett, July 28, 1949; children—Julia Jennings, Susan Hunter. Tchr., Webb Sch., Bell Buckle, Tenn., 1946-54, Webb Sch. of Calif., Claremont, 1954-55; founder, pres. Webb Sch. of Knoxville, 1954—. Mem. Knox County Library Bd., 1961-64, chmn., 1964. Bd. dirs. Nat. Study Sch.

Evaluation; trustee So. Assn. Colls. and Schs. Served to 1st lt. USAAF, 1942-46. Mem. Nat. (sec., dir.), Tenn. (pres. 1974) assns. ind. schs., Sigma Alpha Epsilon (pres. local chpt. 1941). Democrat. Presbyn. (elder). Home: 11501 Nassau Dr Concord TN 37720 Office: Webb School of Knoxville Route 21 Knoxville TN 37919

WEBB, WILSE BERNARD, psychologist; b. Hollandale, Miss., Oct. 13, 1920; s. Wilse Lent and Estelle Turner (Bernard) W.; B.A., La. State U., 1941; M.A., U. Iowa, 1942, Ph.D., 1947; m. Mary Elizabeth Hayward, July 23, 1942; children—Ann Farren, Jean, Thomas Hayward, Molly Estelle. Asst. prof. psychology U. Tenn., 1947-48, Washington U., St. Louis, 1948-53; head aviation psychology U.S. Navy Sch. Aviatio Medicine, 1953-58; chmn. dept. psychology U. Fla., 1958-69, grad. research prof., 1969—; fellow Cambridge (Eng.) U., 1965-66, 69-70. Served with USAAF, 1942-46. Mem. Am. Psychol. Assn. (dir.), AAAS, S.E. Psychol. Assn., Assn. Psychophysiol. Study Sleep. Episcopalian. Author: Sleep, An Action Process, 1974; Sleep, The Gentle Tyrant, 1976; contbr. numerous articles to profl. publs. Home: 405 NE 4th Ave Gainesville FL 32601 Office: Dept Psychology U Fla Gainesville FL 32611

WEBBER, CHRISTOPHER A., lawyer; b. Rutland, Vt., 1905; B.S., Middlebury (Vt.) Coll., 1929; LL.B., Harvard, 1932; m. Esther L. Ladue, 1932; children—John B., Mary R., Christopher A. Admitted to Vt. bar. 1932; now partner firm Webber & Costello, Rutland; judge Rutland Municipal Ct., 1937-41. Pres. Rutland County Nat. Bank, 1948-67, also dir. sr. v.p., dir. Howard Nat. Bank and Trust Co., (merged with Rutland County Bank), 1967-72, chmn. exec. com., 1972—; trustee Marble Savs. Bank, 1940-64. Alderman, Rutland, 1935-39; chmn. Vt. Legis. Apportionment Bd., 1965-72. Fellow Am. Bar Found. Am. Coll. Trial Lawyers, Am. Coll. Probate Counsel; mem. Vt. Bankers Assn. (pres.), Am., 1961-62, lst v.p. 1962-63, pres. 1963-64), Vt. (pres. 1963), Rutland County bar assns., Internat. Soc. Barristers. Home: 10 Billings Ave Rutland VT 05701 Office: Marble Savs Bank Bldg Rutland VT 05701

WEBBER, DONALD WEDGWOOD, lawyer; b. Auburn, Maine, Nov. 19, 1906; s. George Curtis and Fannie (Saunders) W.; A.B., Bowdoin Coll., 1927; LL.B., Harvard, 1931; D.H.L., Bates Coll., 1962, Defiance Coll., 1964; LL.D., Bowdoin Coll., 1970, U. Maine, 1975; m. Lucy Merriam Nourse, Sept. 21, 1929; children—George Curtis II, Faith Merriam. Admitted to Maine bar, 1930; gen. practice law George C. & Donald W. Webber, Auburn, 1931-48; mem. Maine Bd. Bar Examiners, 1946-48; justice Superior Ct. Maine, 1948-53; asso. justice Supreme Jud. Ct., Maine, Auburn, 1953-73; practice law, Auburn, 1973—. Overseer Bowdoin Coll.; trustee Westbrook Jr. Coll.; trustee Congl. Christian Conf. of Maine, 1956—, pres., 1969-70; moderator United Church Christ, 1961-63. Served as lt. USNR, 1943-45. Mem. Am., Maine bar assns., Am. Legion, Delta Upsilon. Conglist. (deacon). Home: 39 Wedgwood Rd Auburn ME 04210 Office: 83 Pleasant St Auburn ME 04210

WEBBER, EVERARD LELAND, museum dir.; b. Chgo., Jan. 27, 1920; s. Leland Bacon and Harriet Gaylord (Peck) W.; B.B.A., U. Cin., 1942; C.P.A., U. Ill., 1949; m. Ellen Gowen Duer, Mar. 30, 1946 (dec. 1974); children—Leland Duer, James Randall, Ellen Robinson; m. 2d, Joan Wray Malloch. With Procter & Gamble Co., Cin., 1939-42, Ernst & Ernst, C.P.A.'s, Chgo. 1945-50; with Field Mus. Natural History, 1950—, exec. asst. to dir., 1951-60, asst. dir. 1960-62, dir. 1962—, trustee, 1966—, pres., 1976—; mem. Nat. Council on Arts, 1970-76, Nat. Mus. Services Bd., 1977—. Mem. Nat. 4H Service Com., 1972-76; bd. dirs. YMCA Hotel, Chgo., 1954-78, chmn., 1961-62; mem. bd. Ill. State Mus., 1965-70; bd. govs. Ill. State Colls. and Univs., 1967-75. Served to lt. USNR, 1942-45. Mem. A.A.A.S., Am. Assn. Museums (v.p. 1966-70), Beta Theta Pi. Episcopalian. Clubs: Tavern, Univ., Arts, Caxton, Michigan Shores, Comml., Econ., (Chgo.). Home: 1224 Elmwood Ave Wilmette IL 60091 Office: Field Mus Natural History Roosevelt Rd and Lake Shore Dr Chicago IL 60605

WEBBER, GORDON, author, ret. advt. exec.; b. Linden, Mich., Oct. 25, 1912; s. Roy Eugene and Dorothea (Boyd) W.; A.B., Jamestown Coll., 1933; M.A., U. Mich., 1936; m. Jeanne Carol Curtis, June 29, 1940 (dec.); children—Jacqueline, Dorothea, Laura. Radio, TV writer NBC, N.Y.C., 1938-48; free-lance writer TV plays, 1948-56; writer I Remember Mama, TV Show, 1950-55; with Benton & Bowles, Inc., advt., 1948-75, ret. as sr. v.p., mgr. creative dept., 1975; instr. Parsons Sch. Design, 1975-76. Exec. producer TV film The Endless War, 1970; producer Unsell the War nat. campaign, 1971; producer-dir. film The Jogger, 1971 (Cine Golden Eagle, Edinburgh Festival). Chmn. comml. prodn. com. Am. Assn. Advt. Agys., 1965-69. Public relations dir. Rye Red Cross Fund, 1960-64; co-chmn. Rye Council Human Rights, 1963-64. Served to lt. (s.g.) USNR, 1942-45. Recipient Navy Commendation, 1944; citation in field of lit. Jamestown Coll., 1959. Mem. P.E.N., Authors League Am. Club: Classic Car Am. (founding pres.). Author: Years of Eden, 1951; The Far Shore (citation Friends Am. Writers), 1954; What End But Love (award Mich. Hist. Soc.). 1959; The Great Buffalo Hotel, 1979; Our Kind of People: The Story of The First Fifty Years at Benton & Bowles, 1979; also short stories. Home: 7 E 86th St New York NY 10028 also Cleveland Dr Montauk NY

WEBBER, HOWARD RODNEY, pub. co. exec.; b. Berlin, N.H., Oct. 20, 1933; s. Robert Alfred and Amelia (Rousseau) W.; A.B., Dartmouth, 1956; postgrad. Lehigh U., 1956-57; m. Helen Margaret McCubbin, May 6, 1959; children—Benjamin James, Adam Brooks, Holly Isabella. Editor in chief U. N.C. Press, Chapel Hill, 1960-63, Johns Hopkins Press, Balt., 1963-65; dir. Case Western Res. U. Press Cleve., 1965-70, Mass. Inst. Tech. Press, Cambridge, 1970-74; v.p., gen. mgr., pub. Open Court Pub. Co., LaSalle, Ill., 1974—. Served with AUS, 1957-59. Mem. Phi Beta Kappa. Democrat. Episcopalian. Home: 1407 S Main St Princeton IL 61356 Office: 1058 8th St LaSalle IL 61301

WEBBER, HUGH E., physicist; b. Ludlow, Ill., July 11, 1914; s. Hugh E. and Louise (Armstrong) W.; B.A., Ohio State U., 1937; postgrad. Case Inst. Tech., 1941, Bklyn. Poly. Inst., 1943; m. Genevieve Downes, Aug. 4, 1940 (div. 1964); children—Winona Louise, Beverly Jean, Janet Kathleen, Hugh E., Douglas Elliott; m. 2d, Jeannine Doran, Nov. 27, 1964; children— Katherine, Nancy. Physicist, Western Res. Med. Sch., 1938-41; with Sperry Gyroscope Co., Great Neck, N.Y., 1941-58, chief engr. microwave electronics div., 1956-58; mgr. ground systems Martin Co., Orlando, Fla., 1958-60, dir. engring. support, 1960-61, dir. advanced tech., 1961-62, dir. research and devel., 1962-64; corp. dir. research techniques Sanders Assos., Inc., Nashua, N.H., 1964-66; mgr. new products div. EIMAC div. Varian Assos., Inc., San Carlos, Calif., 1967-68; gen. mgr. Gordon L. Ness Assos., Palo Alto, Calif., 1968—, exec. v.p. Ness Industries, Inc., Palo Alto, Calif., 1968-71, Pacific Assemblers Co., Ltd.; pres. Consumer Tech. Corp., Webber Assos.; chmn. bd., pres. Allex Corp., 1972—; dir. Computer Power Systems, Leaming Industries, NCA, Inc., Arno Assos., Inc.; nat. vice-chmn. profl. Group Aerospace & Electronics Systems, 1965—; gen. chmn. AESCON, 1967—. Mem. Pentagon Guided Missile Equipment Research and Devel. Bd., 1949-53; chmn. Met. Profl. Group Engring. Mgmt. 1957-58. Fellow IEEE (nat. chmn. group space, electronics and telemetry, vice chmn. group aerospace and electronic systems); mem. Am. Inst. Aeros. and Astronautics, Am. Ordnance Assn. (cons. to adv. panel electronics com.). Methodist (bd.). Author: (with others) Microwave Theory and Techniques Handbook, 1944. Home: 2031 Manzanita Ave Menlo Park CA 94025 Office: Allex Corp 7280 Blue Hill Dr San Jose CA 95129

WEBBER, PAYSON REX, architect; b. Rutland, Vt., Mar. 22, 1903; s. Marvelle Christopher and Mary (Rex) W.; student Middlebury Coll., 1920-22; S.B. magna cum laude, Harvard, 1924, M.Arch., 1929; m. Mary Elizabeth Williams, Nov. 29, 1934; 1 son, Robert Ames; m. 2d, Martha Humphrey Myer, Feb. 17, 1973. Practice architecture, Rutland, 1936—; partner firm Webber & Wilson, 1972—. Mem. Vt. Bd. Registration Architects, 1951-62, 77—, chmn., 1962-63, 78—. Chmn. Rutland Bd. Zoning Adjustment, 1953-56, Rutland Planning Commn., 1964-76. Mem. bd. aldermen Rutland, 1949-52. Mem. exec. com., bd. trustees Calvin Coolidge Meml. Found., Inc., 1962—; trustee emeritus Vt. Symphony Orch. Fellow A.I.A. (past pres. Vt.); mem. Rutland C. of C. (past pres.). Republican. Episcopalian. Club: Ekwanok Country (Manchester, Vt.). Designer, restorer several chs., including Baptist Ch., East Poultney, Vt., 1937; pub. bldgs., including nurses home, kitchen dining hall, auditorium, ward bldgs., State Hosp., Waterbury, Vt., 1945-61. Home: 240 Grove St Rutland VT 05701 Office: 198 N Main St Rutland VT 05701

WEBBER, ROBERT, actor; b. Santa Ana, Calif., Oct. 14; s. Robert and Alice W.; student Compton Jr. Coll., 1946; m. Miranda Jones, Oct. 1, 1953 (div.); m. 2d, Del Mertens, Apr. 23, 1972. Acting debut in high sch. prodn. A Night at an Inn, 1941; profl. stage debut in Ah, Wilderness!, 1947; Broadway debut in Two Blind Mice, 1949; other stage appearances: Goodbye, My Fancy, 1949, The Royal Family, 1951, No Time for Sergeants, 1955, Orpheus Descending, 1957, Wonderful Town, 1958, Fair Game, 1958, A Loss of Roses, 1959, A Period of Adjustment, 1960; films include: Highway 301, 1950, 12 Angry Men, 1957, The Stripper, 1963, The Sandpiper, 1965, Harper, 1966, The Silencers, 1966, The Hired Killer, 1967, Dead Heat on a Merry-Go-Round, 1966, Don't Make Waves, 1967, The Dirty Dozen, 1967, The Great White Hope, 1970, Dollars, 1971, Midway, 1976, The Choirboys, 1977, Revenge of the Pink Panther, 1978, 10, 1979, Bring Me the Head of Alfredo Garcia, 1974, Casey's Shadow, 1978; numerous TV guest appearances. Served in USMC, 1943-45. Mem. Actors Equity Assn., AFTRA, Screen Actors Guild. Office: care Jay Julien 91 E 41st St New York NY 10017

WEBBER, WILLIAM ALEXANDER, univ. adminstr., physician; b. Nfld., Can., Apr. 8, 1934; s. William Grant and Hester Mary (Constable) W.; M.D., U. B.C. (Can.), Vancouver, 1958; m. Marilyn Joan Robson, May 17, 1958; children—Susan Joyce, Eric Michael, George David. Intern, Vancouver Gen. Hosp., 1958-59; postdoctoral fellow Cornell U. Med. Coll., N.Y.C., 1959-61; asst. prof. medicine U. B.C., 1961-66, asso. prof., 1966-69, prof., 1969—, dean Faculty Medicine, 1977—. Mem. B.C. Med. Assn., Can. Assn. Anatomists, Am. Assn. Anatomists, Can. Nephrological Soc. Research on renal structure and function. Home: 2478 Crown St Vancouver BC V6R 3V8 Canada Office: Deans Office Faculty of Medicine U BC Vancouver BC V6T 1W5 Canada

WEBER, ALFONS, educator; b. Dortmund,, Germany, Oct. 8, 1927; B.S., Ill. Inst. Tech., 1951, M.S., 1953, Ph.D., 1956; married, 1955; 3 children. Asst. in physics Ill. Inst. Tech., Chgo., 1951-53, instr., 1953-56, fellow Nat. Research Council Can., 1956-57; asst. prof. Fordham U., Bronx, N.Y., 1957-61, asso. prof., 1961-66, prof., 1966—, chmn. dept. physics, 1964-70, prof. physics chemistry, 1976—; ofcl. Nat. Bur. Standards, 1977—. Fellow Am. Phys. Soc.; mem. Am. Assn. Physics Tchrs., Optical Soc. Am. Office: Dept Physics Fordham U Bronx NY 10458 also Molecular Spectroscopy Div 545 Nat Bur Standards Washington DC 20234

WEBER, ALFRED, ins. co. exec.; b. N.Y.C., June 16, 1911; s. Morris and Rebecca (Golub) W.; student N.Y. U., 1930-32; m. Beatrice Hartman, Sept. 4, 1937; children—Jill Susan Weber Radler, William Michael. With Am. Internat. Underwriting Co., 1931-55, 60-75, exec. v.p., 1969-75, vice chmn., 1975-78; pres. Transatlantic Reins. Co., N.Y.C., 1978-79; ret., 1979. Clubs: Drug and Chem., Shackamaxon Golf and Country. Office: 70 Pine St New York NY 10005

WEBER, ANNEMARIE, biochemist, educator; b. Rostock, Germany, Sept. 11, 1923; d. Hans Hermann and Marga (Oltmanns) Weber; came to U.S., 1954, naturalized, 1960; abitur Med. Schs. Gottingen, Konigsberg, Tubingen, 1942-48; M.D., Med. Sch. Tubingen, 1950. Postdoctoral fellow U. London, 1950-51, Harvard Med. Sch., 1952, Columbia Med. Sch., 1954-58; Rockefeller fellow U. Tubingen, 1953-54; asst. mem., asso. mem. Inst. Muscle Disease, N.Y.C., 1958-65; prof. biochemistry St. Louis U., 1965-72; prof. biochemistry U. Pa., Phila., 1972—; mem. NIH study sect., 1968-72, 76—. Trustee, Marine Biol. Lab., Woods Hole, Mass., 1977-78. Mem. Am. Physiol. Soc., Am. Soc. Biol. Chemists, Soc. Gen. Physiologists (council 1972-73, pres. 1977-78), Biochemical Soc., Harvey Soc., Biophys. Soc. (council, exec. bd. 1970-73), N.Y. Acad. Scis., Am. Acad. Arts and Scis., Leopoldina, Sigma Xi. Mem. editorial bd. Jour. Gen. Physiology, 1968-75, Jour. Biophysics, 1975-76, Circulation Research, 1975-77. Home: 3900 Ford Rd Philadelphia PA 19131

WEBER, ARTHUR, publisher; b. Chgo., Feb. 1, 1926; s. Philip and Mary (Arlinsky) W.; student Ill. Inst. Tech., 1943-44; B.S. in Elec. Engring., Northwestern U., 1946; m. Sylvia Zollinger, Aug. 19, 1950; children—Randy, Lori. Elec. design engr. Corn Products Refining Co., 1946-48, Naess & Murphy, architects & engrs., Chgo., 1949-51, Ford Motor Co., 1952-53, Skidmore, Owings & Merill, Chgo., 1954-57, Shaw, Metz & Dolio, Chgo., 1958-59; pub. Consumers Digest mag., Chgo., 1959—. Served with USNR, 1944-46. Office: 5705 N Lincoln Ave Chicago IL 60659

WEBER, BEN BRIAN, composer; b. St. Louis, July 23, 1916; s. Irwin and Eleanor Isabelle (Dew) W.; student U. Ill. 1934-35, DePaul U., 1937. Mem. faculty N.Y. Coll. Music, 1966—. Recipient award Nat. Inst. Arts and Letters, 1950; Guggenheim award, 1950, 53; From Found. award, 1953, 55; $3000, award Ford Found. Program Performing Artists; Phoebe Ketchum Thorne music award, 1965; Koussevitsky award of $3000 for orch. work, 1967. Mem. Internat. Soc. Contemporary Music, Am. Composer's Alliance (pres. 1959—), Nat. Inst. Arts and Letters (life mem.). Composer: Fantasia opus 25, Piano solo, 1946; Concerto opus 32, piano, winds, cello, 1950; Ballet, Pool of Darkness, opus 26, 1950; Symphony on Poems of William Blake, opus 34, baritone and 12 instruments; Concerto for Violin and Orchestra, opus 41; Prelude and Passacaglia for Orchestra opus 42; Rapsodie Concertante (for viola and chamber orch.), opus 47; Three Songs for Soprano and Strings, opus 48; Concerto for Piano and Orchestra, opus 52; L. Bernstein conductor W. Masselos, soloist, 1961; premiere performance of Chamber Fantasie for violin solo and six instruments, opus 51, Carnegie Hall, 1959: Dolmen for winds and strings, 1964; The Enchanted Midnight for orch., 1967; Concert Piece for solo violin and Orch., opus 61, 1970; Sinfonia Clarion, opus 62 (for chamber orch.); Consort of Winds, opus 66, 1974; 3 Cappricios for cello and piano, 1977. Home: 418 Central Park W New York NY 10025

WEBER, BERTRAM ANTON, architect; b. Chgo., Oct. 1, 1898; s. Peter Joseph and Bertha M. (Werkmeister) W.; student Northwestern, 1916-18; B.S., Mass. Inst. Tech., 1922; m. Dorothea Brammer, May 9, 1928; children—Dorie W. Hechler, John B. Independent practice architecture, 1923; partner White & Weber, 1924-36; propr. Bertram A. Weber, architect, 1936-73; Weber & Weber, 1973—; gen. practice. Works include pvt. residences, devels., comml. bldgs., chs., hosps., schs., multiple housing, Georgian Ct. Apts., Barrington, Inverness Countryside, Palatine, Ill., Julia Lathrop Apt., Chgo., DeKalb Pub. Library, Highland Park Pub. Library, Oak Park (Ill.) Post Office; YMCA, Winona, Minn. and Aurora, Ill., Doctors Hosp., Columbus, Ohio, Osteo. Hosp. of York, Pa., Chgo. Osteo. and Coll. Sci. bldgs., Detroit Osteo. Hosp. and Doctors Office Bldg., Riverside Osteo. Hosp., Trenton, Mich., Bi- County Community Hosp. and Med. Office Bldg. Warren, Mich., Bapt. Retirement Home, Maywood, Ill., Adm. Retirement Home, Chgo., St. James Episcopal Ch. at Northbrook, Ill., Highland Park Presbyn. Ch., Trinity Ch., Highland Park, Deerfield Presbyn. Ch., St. Gregory's, Deerfield, St. Timothy's, Griffith, Ind., Ill. All Saints Ch., Western Springs, Ill., St. Davids Episcopal Ch., Glenview, Ill., Kildeer Sch., Long Grove, Ill., Lake Forest Acad., Highland Park Dists. 107, 108, Deerfield State Bank, Nat. Bank N. Evanston, Duraclean Co. plant and office bldg., Deerfield, Am. Legion and Recreation Bldgs., Highland Park, Ill., Officers Quarters Glenview Air Base 1943, Scholl Mfg. Co., Chgo., Standard Am. Ins. Co. Bldg., Park Ridge, Ill., Gen. Finance Corp. Home Office Bldg., Calumet and Hecla office Bldg., Evanston, Ill., Evans Scholars Found. Bldg., Golf, Ill., Exmoor Country Club, Prestwick Country Club, Inverness Country Club, Aurora Country Club, others; asso. architect Julia Lathrop Housing Project, Chgo.; partner Central States Architects & Engrs., Kropp Forge Aviation Corp., 1942. Bd. dirs. Highland Park Hosp., Ravinia Festival Assn.; mem. Highland Park Park Dist. Bd., 12 yrs., pres., 3 yrs.; mem. Highland Park Plan Commn., 8 yrs. Served with R.O.T.C., Ft. Sheridan, 1918, S.N.T.C., 1918. Fellow AIA; mem. Ill. Soc. Architects, Delta Tau Delta, Scarab. Presbyn. Clubs: Exmoor, Executive, Builders, Adventurers, Dairymen's Country, Safari Internat., Anglers of Chgo. Home: 545 Groveland Ave Highland Park IL 60035 Office: 228 N LaSalle St Chicago IL 60601

WEBER, BROM, educator; b. N.Y.C., May 14, 1917; s. Kalman and Nadia (Svonkin) W.; B.S.S., Coll. City N.Y., 1938; M.A. (Coe fellow), U. Wyo., 1955; Ph.D. (Carnegie fellow), U. Minn., 1957; m. Nettie Held, Mar. 21, 1939; children—Eden Elizabeth, Kyle Maxson. Writer, editor Hist. Records Survey, N.Y., 1938-39; writer, adminstr. govt. agys., Washington, also Jersey City, 1940-45; instr. English, Coll. City N.Y., 1945-50; lectr. lit. and writing New Sch. Social Research, N.Y.C., 1948-54; asst. prof. English, Purdue U., 1957-58; asso. prof. English, sec. Am. Studies program U. Minn., 1958-63; prof. English, U. Calif. at Davis, 1963—, acting chmn. dept. English, 1964-65, vice chmn., 1965-70, chmn. Am. studies program, 1969-70, chmn. dept. English, 1977-78; vis. prof. English, De Pauw U., 1958, U. Wash., summer 1965, U. Wyo., summer 1966, U. Colo., summer 1968; vis. prof. Conf. on Am. Lit. and History, Mussoorie, India, 1963; cons. Nat. Endowment for Humanities, 1974—. Fulbright prof., France, 1966-67, Korea, 1973; Yaddo fellow Trask Found., 1949; recipient McKnight Humanities award McKnight Found., 1962; sr. non-resident fellow Can. Council, 1963; Am. Philos. Soc. grantee, 1976; U. Calif. Regents humanities fellow, 1976. Mem. MLA, Am. Humor Studies Assn. (pres. 1977). Author: Hart Crane: A Biographical and Critical Study, 1948; The Letters of Hart Crane, 1916-32, 1952; Sut Lovingood, 1954; An Anthology of American Humor, 1962; Sherwood Anderson, 1964; The Complete Poems and Selected Letters and Prose of Hart Crane, 1966; Sense and Sensibility in Twentieth- Century Writing, 1970. Co-editor: American Vanguard, 1953; American Literature: Tradition and Innovation, 1969. Asst. editor Twice a Year, 1946-48; asso. editor Tiger's Eye, 1949-51; adv. editor The Lovingood Papers, 1962-67, Modern Fiction Studies, 1957-58, Early Am. Lit., 1966-69; editorial bd. The Hollins Critic, 1965-66; adv. editor Studies in American Humor, 1973—, MELUS, 1976—. Home: 23 Almond Ln Davis CA 95616

WEBER, CHARLES EDWARD, educator; b. Chgo., Feb. 21, 1930; s. Edward W. and Augusta (Lonk) W.; student Marquette U., 1948-50; B.A., U. Ill., 1952, M.A. in Labor and Indsl. Relations, 1953; M.A. in Econs. (Hicks fellow), Princeton, 1954, Ph.D. in Econs., 1958; m. Suzanne Brodseller, Sept. 6, 1952; children—Paul Andrew, Mark Francis. Mem. research staff Princeton, 1954-56; from instr. to asso. prof. bus. U. Pitts., 1956-66, research asso. adminstrv. sci., 1961-63, acting dir. Adminstrv. Sci. Center, 1963-66; dean Sch. Bus. Adminstrn., U. Wis.-Milw., 1966-76, prof. policy and mgmt. studies, 1976—; cons. Arthur D. Little, 1964-66, Wis. Cons. Assos., 1979—; field reader U.S. Office Edn., 1966-74; organizer, dir. Univ. Nat. Bank, Milw., 1970-76; commr. pub. debt City of Milw., 1976—. Co-chmn. com. to advise on reorgn. Milw. City Govt., 1968-72; mem. Gov.'s Council for Econ. Devel., 1972-74. Bd. dirs. Citizens' Govt. Research Bur., 1974—. Ford Found. fellow, 1959-60, 62-63. Weber Exec. Alumni Assn. of U. Wis.-Milw. named in his honor. Mem. Inst. Mgmt. Sci., Am. Econ. Assn., Indsl. Relations Research Assn., Coll. on Orgns. (sec.-treas. 1963-65), Acad. Mgmt., Met. Milw. Assn. Commerce (vice chmn. legislative com.). Author: Management Action: Models of Administrative Decision, 1969; also articles. Home: 3453 N Hackett Ave Milwaukee WI 53211

WEBER, DAVID C(ARTER), librarian; b. Waterville, Maine, July 25, 1924; s. Carl J. and Clara (Carter) W.; A.B., Colby Coll., 1947; student Bowdoin Coll., 1946; B.S., Columbia, 1948; A.M., Harvard, 1953; postgrad. Rutgers U., 1956; m. Natalie McLeod, Dec. 26, 1952; children—L. Jefferson, Christopher Q., Douglas McL., Sarah N. Cataloger, asst. to dir., asst. dir. libraries Harvard, 1948-61; asst. dir., asso. dir. Stanford, 1961-69, dir. libraries, 1969—; cons. to acad. libraries, 1960—. Served with AUS, 1943-46. Council on Library Resources fellow, 1970. Mem. Assn. Coll. and Research Libraries, Am. Library Assn. Clubs: Roxburghe, Book of Calif. (San Francisco). Author: (with others) College and University Accreditation Standards, 1958; (with R.D. Rogers) University Library Administration, 1971. Compiler, editor: University Library Buildings, 1969. Editor: Studies in Library Administrative Problems, 1960. Contbr. articles to profl. jours. Office: Stanford U Libraries Stanford CA 94305

WEBER, DELBERT DEAN, univ. chancellor; b. Columbus, Nebr., July 23, 1932; s. Charles and Ella (Hueschen) W.; B.A., Midland Coll., 1954; M.Ed., U. Nebr., 1959, Ed.D., 1962; m. Lou Ann Ross, Dec. 29, 1954; children—William Dean, Bethany Ellen, Kelly Ann. Social studies and English tchr., prin. Creston (Nebr.) High Sch., 1956-58; instr. ednl. founds. U. Nebr., 1958-60, instr., coordinator jr. high lab. sch., 1960-62; asst. and asso. prof. edn. Ariz. State U., 1962-65; asst. to pres., sec. to bd. trustees Cleve. State U., 1965-69, acting provost, 1967-68; dean, prof. edn. Ariz. State U., 1969-77; chancellor U. Nebr. at Omaha, 1977—. Mem. exec. bd. Mid-Am. council Boy Scouts Am.; pres.'s adv. bd. Greater Omaha C. of C.; trustee Omaha Indsl. Found., Joslyn Art Mus. Served with CIC, U.S. Army, 1954-56. Mem. Assn. Tchr. Educators, Am. Assn. Colls. Tchr. Edn., Phi Delta Kappa. Club: Rotary. Author: Secondary Education Today. Home: 1553 Skylark Dr Omaha NE 68144 Office: PO Box 688 Omaha NE 68101

WEBER, EUGEN, educator, historian, author; b. Bucarest, Romania, Apr. 24, 1925; s. Emanuel and Sonia (Garrett) W.; student Institut d'etudes politiques, Paris, 1948-51; M.A., Emmanuel Coll., Cambridge U., 1954, M.Litt. 1956; m. Jacqueline Brument-Roth, June 12, 1950. Came to U.S., 1955. History supr. Emmanuel Coll., 1953-54; lectr. U. Alta., 1954-55; asst. prof. U. Iowa, 1955-56; asst. prof. history U. Calif. at Los Angeles, 1956, asso. prof., 1959-63, prof., 1963—, chmn. dept. 1965-68, dir. study center, France, 1968-70, dean social scis., 1976—, dean Coll. Letters and Scis., 1977—; Ford faculty lectr. Stanford, 1965. Served as capt. inf. Brit. Army, 1943-47. Decorated Ordre Nat. des Palmes Academiques (France); Fulbright fellow, 1952; research fellow Am. Philos. Soc., 1959, Social Sci. Research Council, 1959-61, Am. Council Learned Socs., 1962; Guggenheim fellow, 1963-64; sr. fellow Nat. Endowment for Humanities, 1973-74; fellow Netherlands Inst. Advanced Studies, 1977-78. Fellow Assn. française de science politique, Am. Acad. Arts and Scis.; mem. Am. Hist. Assn., Soc. d'histoire moderne, Soc. French Hist. Studies, Phi Beta Kappa (hon., Ralph Waldo Emerson prize 1977). Author: Nationalist Revival in France, 1959; The Western Tradition, 1959; Paths to the Present, 1960; Action Franc aise, 1962; Satan Franc-Maçon, 1964; Varieties of Fascism, 1964; (with H. Rogger) The European Right, 1965; A Modern History of Europe, 1970; Europe Since 1715, 1972; Peasants into Frenchmen, 1976 (Commonwealth prize Calif. 1977). Advisory editor of Jour. Contemporary History, 1966—, Reviews in European History, 1973—, French Hist. Studies, 1973-77; Stanford French Rev., 1977—. Home: 11579 Sunset Blvd Los Angeles CA 90049

WEBER, EUGENE WILLIAM, civil engr.; b. Stacyville, Iowa, Dec. 8, 1910; s. Matthew Nicholas and Gertrude (Wolf) W.; student St. Thomas Mil. Acad., St. Paul, 1922-26; B.C.E., U. Minn., 1930; m. Mary Adams, Jan. 14, 1938; 1 son, Charles Adams. Engr., Corps Engrs., U.S. Army, Duluth, Minn., 1931-33, Detroit, 1933-35, Boston, 1936-39, Washington, 1940-41; specialist on engring.-econ. policies and internat. water problems Office of Chief Engrs., U.S. Army, Washington, 1946-65; commr. U.S. sect. Internat. Joint Commn. under Boundary Waters Treaty of 1909 between Can. and U.S., 1948-73; fed. rep. interstate commn. Potomac River Basin, 1956. Served to lt. col. C.E., AUS, 1942-46; overseas service hdqrs. ETO, London, Normandy and Paris, 1944-45. Decorated Legion of Merit, Bronze Star, Army Commendation ribbon (U.S.), Croix de Guerre (France); recipient Rockefeller Pub. Service award, 1963; Dept. Army Exceptional Civilian Service award, 1963; Dept. Def. Distinguished Civilian Service award, 1964; Superior Honor award Dept. State, 1973; Outstanding Achievement award U. Minn., 1979. Mem. Washington Acad. Scis., Nat. Soc. Profl. Engrs., ASCE (hon.), Soc. Am. Mil. Engrs., Am. Geophys. Union, Nat. Acad. Engring., Phi Kappa Sigma, Chi Epsilon, Scabbard and Blade. Club: Cosmos (Washington). Home: 2700 Virginia Ave NW Washington DC 20037

WEBER, GERALD JOSEPH, U.S. judge; b. Erie, Pa., Feb. 1, 1914; s. Joseph J. and Ruth M. (Sullivan) W.; A.B., Harvard, 1936; LL.B., U. Pa., 1939; m. Berta M. Drechsel, Aug. 21, 1947; children—Thomas, William, Mary. Admitted to Pa. bar, 1940; civilian with U.S. Forces in Austria, 1946-47; practice law, Erie, 1947-64; city solicitor Erie, 1951-61; U.S. dist. judge Western Dist. Pa., 1964—, now chief judge. Served with AUS, 1942-45. Decorated Bronze Star. Home: 4207 Beech Ave Erie PA 16509 Office: US Court House Erie PA 16501 also US Court House Pittsburgh PA 15219*

WEBER, GUSTAVE WALTER, univ. pres.; b. Austria, Sept. 27, 1907; s. Joseph and Theresa (Bauer) W.; came to U.S., 1913, naturalized, 1920; B.A., Wagner Coll., 1928, D.D., 1962; B.D., Luth. Theol. Sem., Phila., 1931, S.T.M., 1933; Th.D., Phila. Div. Sch., 1937; LL.D., Hartwick Coll., 1965, Susquehanna U., 1977; Litt.D., Thiel Coll., 1973; m. Laura Winifred Shearer, Aug. 15, 1933; children—Richard Downing, Carol Shearer (Mrs. Don H. McLucas, Jr.). Ordained to ministry Lutheran Ch. Am., 1931; teaching fellow Phila. Sem., 1931-33; pastor in Pottstown, Pa., 1933-44; dir. religious studies Hill Sch., Pottstown, 1944-50; dir. human relations Doehler-Jarvis Corp., 1950-53, v.p. personnel, 1953; sr. pastor Glenwood Luth. Ch., Toledo, 1954-59; pres. Susquehanna U., 1959—; dir. Forest Home Systems Inc. Vice pres. Pottstown Sch. Bd., 1949-50; pres. Pottstown Recreation Commn., 1940-50; pres. Susquehanna Indsl. Devel. Corp., 1973. Pres. bd. Pottstown Meml. Hosp., 1934-41; bd. dirs. Luth. Theol. Sem., Gettysburg, Pa., Capitol Blue Cross, Luth. Ch. Found. Am., 1953-58, Pocono Lake Preserve. Mem. Central Pa. (dir.), Central Susquehanna Valley (pres. 1972) chambers commerce. Rotarian. Club: Susquehanna Valley Country. Home: PO Box 116 Spruce Hill Selinsgrove PA 17870

WEBER, HARM ALLEN, coll. pres.; b. Pekin, Ill., Sept. 28, 1926; s. Harm Allen and Hilda (Meyer) W.; B.A., Bethel Coll., St. Paul, 1950; B.D., Bethel Sem., 1954; M.R.E., Christian Theol. Sem., Indpls., 1959; postgrad. Ball State U., Muncie, Ind., 1961-62; D.D., Judson Coll., Elgin, Ill., 1964; m. Arlene Olson, Dec. 18, 1948; children—Jan Christine, Harm Allen III, Matthew Karl. Ordained to ministry Baptist Ch., 1953; pastorates at Isle (Minn.) Bapt. Ch., 1950-53, Central Bapt. Ch., Indpls., 1954-60, First Bapt. Ch., Muncie, 1960-64, Covenant Bapt. Ch., Detroit, 1964-69; pres. Judson Coll., Elgin, 1969—, also vice chmn. bd. trustees. Chmn. Indpls. Fedn. Chs., 1955-59; pres. Delaware County (Ind.) Council Chs., 1963-64; chmn. evangelism Detroit Council Chs., 1967-69; v.p. Am. Bapt. Home Mission Soc., 1969—; mem. exec. com. Gt. Lakes Council on Ministry, 1969—; mem. Ministers and Missionaries Benefit Bd., 1974-75. Mem. Ind. gov.'s Multiple Sclerosis Bd., 1957-60; bd. dirs. Camp Isongal, Delaware County Crippled Children's Assn.; chmn. bd. dirs. Galloway Meml. Youth Camp, Wahkon, Minn.; mem. state exec. bd. Vols. of Am.-Minn., 1976—. Mem. Elgin Area C. of C. (dir. 1975-78). Rotarian. Home and office: 1151 N State St Elgin IL 60120

WEBER, HAROLD CHRISTIAN, educator; b. Boston, Mar. 20, 1895; s. Christian and Ellen (Arnold) W.; B.S., Mass. Inst. Tech., 1918; Sc.D., Edgennosiche Technische Hochschule, Zurich, Switzerland, 1935; Sc.D., Suffolk U., 1963; m. Madeleine A. Duffy, Nov. 14, 1931 (dec. Apr. 1960); m. 2d, Marian F. Shaughness, Apr. 18, 1963. Cons., Walker, Lewis, McAdams & Knowland, Boston, 1919-20; prof. chem. engring. Mass. Inst. Tech., 1920-65, prof. emeritus, 1965—; cons. in oil, textiles, paper, mech. and electronic equipment, 1925—. Tech. adviser Chem. Warfare Service, 1941-45; chief sci. adviser U.S. Army, 1958-66; mem. Army Sci. Adv. Panel, 1954-74. Served as 2d lt. Chem. Warfare Service, U.S. Army, 1918-19. Recipient Presdl. certificate of merit for work in World War II, 1947, Chem. Corps certificate of merit, 1958, Army Meritorious Civilian Service award, 1959, Army Distinguished Service award, 1966. Fellow A.A.A.S., Am. Acad. Arts and Scis.; mem. Am. Inst. Chem. Engrs., Am. Chem. Soc., Sigma Xi, Tau Beta Pi. Roman Catholic. Author: Thermodynamics for Chemical Engineers, 1939, 2d edit., 1958; also thermodynamics sect. in Marks' Mechanical Engineers Handbook, 1950. Patentee in field of electronics and petroleum. Home: La Hacienda Apt F179 10333 W Olive Peoria AZ 85345

WEBER, HULDA. see Katz, Hilda

WEBER, JULIAN L., publishing and entertainment co. exec.; b. Des Moines, July 19, 1929; s. Milton and Zelda (Robinson) W.; B.A., UCLA, 1951; J.D., Harvard U., 1955; m. Idelle Feinberg, Apr. 17, 1957; children—Jonathan Todd, Suzanne. Admitted to N.Y. bar, 1956; asso. firm Dewey, Ballantine, Bushby, Palmer & Wood, N.Y.C., 1955-62, Botein, Hays, Sklar & Herzberg, N.Y.C., 1962-64, partner, 1964-79; pres. Nat. Lampoon, Inc., N.Y.C., 1979—, also dir. Mem. Bar Assn. City N.Y., Am. Bar Assn. Clubs: Harvard (N.Y.C.); Friars.

WEBER, LAVERN E., N.G. officer; b. Lone Wolf, Okla., Sept. 3, 1923; student U. Okla., La. Polytechnic Inst.; B.S., E. Central State Coll., 1948; m. Bette Ruth Weber; 4 children. Commd. 2d lt., Okla. Army N.G., 1948, advanced through grades to lt. gen.; state adj. gen. of Okla., 1965-71; dir. Army N.G., Washington, 1971-74, chief N.G. Bur., 1974—. Served to lt. USMCR, 1942-48. Decorated Legion of Merit, others. Mem. N.G. Assn. of U.S., 45th Inf. Div. Assn. Club: Rotary. Office: Pentagon Rm 2E 394 Washington DC 20310

WEBER, MORTON M., microbial biochemist, educator; b. N.Y.C., May 26, 1922; s. Morris and Mollie (Scherer) W.; B.S., Coll. City N.Y., 1949; Sc.D., Johns Hopkins, 1953; m. Phyllis Stern Levy, July 31, 1955; children—Stephen Abbott, Ethan Lenard. Instr. microbiology Sch. Medicine, Johns Hopkins, 1951-55; Am. Cancer Soc. fellow in biochemistry McCollum-Pratt Inst., 1953-56; instr. bacteriology and immunology Med. Sch., Harvard, 1956-59; asst. prof. Sch. Medicine, St. Louis U., 1959-61, asso. prof., 1961-63, prof., 1963—, chmn. dept. microbiology, 1964—; vis. prof. dept. biochemistry Oxford (Eng.) U., 1970-71. Mem. microbial chemistry study sect. NIH, USPHS, 1969-73. Served with USAAF, 1942-46. Fellow A.A.A.S., Am. Acad. Microbiology; mem. Am. Soc. Biol. Chemists, Am. Soc. Microbiology (sec. physiology div. 1964-65, vice chmn. 1965-66, chmn. 1966-67), Soc. Gen. Microbiology, N.Y. Acad. Scis., St. Louis Biochemistry Group (pres. 1968-69), Sigma Xi. Research in biochemistry of microorganisms, with emphasis on pathways and mechanisms of electron transport, enzymatic regulatory mechanisms, and mode of action of antimicrobial drugs and antibiotics. Home: 7068 Waterman Ave University City MO 63130 Office: Dept Microbiology St Louis U Sch Medicine St Louis MO 63104

WEBER, PHILIP JOSEPH, mfg. co. exec.; b. Chgo., Mar. 15, 1909; s. Joseph and Theresa (Zollner); B.B.A., Northwestern U., 1938; m. Esther P. White, Aug. 29, 1941; 1 dau., Patricia G. With Ernst & Ernst, Chgo., 1938-41; with Doall Co., Des Plaines, Ill., 1941—, exec. v.p., 1960-69, pres., 1969-74, chmn. bd., 1974—; dir. 1st Nat. Bank Des Plaines. Mason (Shriner), Elk. Club: Park Ridge Country. Home: 709 N Merrill Ave Park Ridge IL 60068 Office: 254 N Laurel Ave Des Plaines IL 60016

WEBER, ROBERT COLLINS, diversified mfg. co. exec.; b. Lakewood, Ohio, Aug. 31, 1930; s. Walter Eric and Hope Vivian (Hendrichsen) W.; B.A., Kent State U., 1952; J.D., Case Western Res. U., 1956; 1 son, Eric Sherman. Admitted to Ohio bar, 1956; atty. East Ohio Gas Co., Cleve., 1956-63; atty., asst. sec. True Temper Corp., Cleve., 1963-71; sec., gen. counsel Scott & Fetzer Co., Lakewood, 1971—; dir. First Fed. Savs. & Loan Assn. of Lakewood. Bd. mgrs. Cleve. West Side YMCA. Mem. Am., Ohio, Cleve. bar assns., Phi Delta Phi. Clubs: Lakewood Rotary; Westwood Country. Home: 1102 1/2 Forest Rd Lakewood OH 44107 Office: 14600 Detroit Ave 15th Floor Lakewood OH 44107

WEBER, RONALD GILBERT, coll pres.; b. Bergholz, Ohio, Feb. 18, 1916; s. George John and Elizabeth (Davis) W.; A.B., Mt. Union Coll., 1938; D.B.A., Ohio No. U., 1963; LL.D., Baldwin-Wallace Coll., 1976; m. Mary Evelyn Cook, May 25, 1940; children—Constance (Mrs. Norman G. Coates), Judith L. (Mrs. Charles C. Watts). Loan rep., comml. rep., mgr. Household Finance Corp. & Beneficial Mgmt. Corp., Canton, O., Pitts., and McKeesport, Pa., 1938-43; alumni sec., dir. admissions and publicity Mt. Union Coll., Alliance, O., 1943-44, bus. mgr., sec. trustees, 1945-50, v.p., sec., 1950-67, acting pres., 1967-68, pres., 1968—; comml. rep. First Nat. Bank McKeesport, 1944-45; dir. First Nat. City Bank Alliance. Past bd. dirs. United Fund Alliance; past treas. Alliance Citizens Hosp. Assn.; chmn. Ohio Five Coll. Commn. United Meth. Ch., 1963—; past vice-chmn. Commn. High Edn. Trustee Ohio Found. Ind. Colls., Assn. Ind. Colls. and Univs. Ohio (past vice chmn. mem. exec. com.); past pres. East Central Coll. Consortium. Recipient alumni award Mt. Union Coll., 1943. Mem. Council for Advancement and Support Edn., Eastern, Ohio assns. coll. and univ. bus. officers, Alliance C. of C. (dir.), Blue Key, Psi Kappa Omega, Pi Gamma Mu, Alpha Tau Omega. Methodist (adminstrv. bd.; lay del. annual conf.). Kiwanian. Club: Alliance Country. Home: 1304 S Union Ave Alliance OH 44601

WEBER, ROY EDWIN, savs. and loan assn. exec.; b. Ann Arbor, Mich., Aug. 17, 1928; s. Edwin J. and Ruth E. (Nichols) W.; student Mich. State U., 1946-48; m. Carol Warren, Oct. 29, 1948; children—Michael R., Douglas J. With Great Lakes Fed. Savs. & Loan Assn., 1948—, v.p., treas., 1959-68, exec. v.p., treas., 1968-69, pres., 1969—, chmn. bd., 1973—; dir. Fed. Home Loan Bank, Indpls., 1977—. Mem. city council, Ann Arbor, 1969-71. Bd. dirs. Washtenaw County A.R.C.; trustee Ann Arbor Found. Mem. Mich. (dir. 1970, pres. 1976), U.S. (legislative com. 1969—) savs. and loan leagues, Ann Arbor C. of C. (past dir.). Republican. Lutheran. Club: Barton Hills Country. Office: 401 E Liberty St Ann Arbor MI 48108 Home: 3332 Riverbend Dr Ann Arbor MI 48103

WEBER, SAMUEL, editor; b. N.Y.C., July 31, 1926; s. Bernard and Gertrude (Ellenberg) W.; B.S. in Elec. Engring., Va. Poly. Inst., 1947; m. Eileen Gloria Hornstein, Mar. 5, 1950; children—Bruce Jay, Robert Matthew. Engr., N.Y. Bd. Transp., 1948-50, U.S. Naval Shipyard, Bklyn., 1950-52, Barlow Engring. Co., N.Y.C., 1952-54; engring. supr. Curtiss Wright Corp., Woodridge, N.J., 1954-56; electronics engr. Loral Electronics Corp., N.Y.C., 1957-58; with Electronics mag., N.Y.C., 1958-67, 68—, asso. mng. editor, 1968-70, exec. editor, 1970-79, editor-in-chief, 1979—; editor-in-chief Electrotech. mag., N.Y.C., 1967. Served with AUS, 1944-46. Mem. IEEE. Author: Modern Digital Circuits, 1964; Optoelectronic Devices and Circuits, 1968; Large and Medium Scale Integration, 1974; Circuits for Electronics Engineers, 1977. Home: 261 Van Buren Ave Teaneck NJ 07666 Office: 1221 Ave of Americas New York NY 10020

WEBER, WALTER JACOB, JR., educator; b. Pitts., June 16, 1934; s. Walter Jacob and Anne Mae (Chando) W.; B.Sc., Brown U., 1956; M.S.E., Rutgers U., 1959; A.M., Harvard, 1961, Ph.D., 1962; children—Wendilyn Ruth, Elizabeth Anne, Pamela Jean, Linda Lorraine. Engr., Caterpillar Tractor Co., Peoria, Ill., 1956-57; instr. Rutgers U., 1957-59; engr. Soil Conservation Service, New Brunswick, N.J., 1957-59; research, teaching asso. Harvard, 1959-63; faculty U. Mich., Ann Arbor, 1963—, prof., chmn. water resources program, 1968—, Disting. prof., 1978—. Internat. cons. to industry, govt. Registered profl. engr., R.I. Recipient Distinguished Faculty awards U. Mich., 1967, 78, Assn. Environ. Engring. Profs., 1968; Faraday lectr., U. Mich., 1970; Engr. of Distinction, Engrs. Joint Council, 1973; Assn. Environ. Engring. Profs.-NALCO research award, 1979. Diplomate Am. Acad. Environ. Engrs. Mem. Am. Chem. Soc. (cert. of merit 1962), Am. Inst. Chem. Engrs., ASCE, Am. Water Works Assn., Assn. Environ. Engring. Profs., Nat. Soc. Profl. Engrs., Water Pollution Control Fedn. (John R. Rumsey Meml. award 1975), Tau Beta Pi, Sigma Xi, Chi Epsilon, Delta Omega. Author: (with K.H. Mancy) Analysis of Industrial Wastewaters, 1971; Physicochemical Processes for Water Quality Control, 1972; editor-author: (with E. Matijevic) Adsorption from Aqueous Solution, 1968. Contbr. numerous articles and chpts. to tech., profl. jours. and books. Home: 1700 South Grove Rd Ypsilanti MI 48197 Office: Water Resources Program Coll Engring U Mich Ann Arbor MI 48109

WEBER, WENDELL WILLIAM, pharmacologist; b. Maplewood, Mo., Sept. 2, 1925; s. Theodore William and Flora Ann (Holt) W.; A.B., Central Coll., 1945; Ph.D. in Phys. Chemistry, Northwestern U., 1950; M.D., U. Chgo., 1959; m. La Donna Tavis, Sept. 29, 1952; children—Jane Holt, Theodore Wendell. Asst. prof. chemistry U. Tenn., Knoxville, 1949-51; mem. ops. research staff U.S. Army Chem. Center, Edgewood, Md., 1951-55; successively instr., asst. prof., asso. prof., prof. pharmacology N.Y. U. Sch. Medicine, N.Y.C., 1963-74; prof. U. Mich., Ann Arbor, 1974—; mem. pharmacology-toxicology com. NIH, 1969-73, rev. coms., 1968—. NIH spl. fellow, 1962-65, research grantee, 1967—; recipient Career Scientist awards N.Y.C. Health Research Council, 1965-70, 70-74; licensed M.D., Mich., N.Y. Fellow N.Y. Acad. Scis.; mem. Am. Soc. Pharmacology and Therapeutics, Am. Chem. Soc., Am. Soc. Human Genetics, AAAS, Sigma Xi, Phi Lambda Upsilon. Home: 14 Geddes Heights Ann Arbor MI 48104 Office: Dept Pharmacology U Mich Ann Arbor MI 48109

WEBSTER, ALBERT KNICKERBOCKER, orch. exec.; b. Bklyn., Oct. 14, 1937; s. Albert Noyes and Janet (Knickerbocker) W.; B.A., Harvard Coll., 1959; student L'Ecole de Musique de Fontainebleau, summers 1958-59; m. Sara Beyer, Feb. 19, 1961; children—Albert Van Berghen, Katherine Lee. Asst. to mgr., asst. mgr. New York Philharmonic, 1962-71, mng. dir., exec. v.p., 1975—; gen. mgr. Cin. Symphony Orch., 1971-75; mem., co-chmn. planning sect., music panel Nat. Endowment for Arts, 1975-79. Mem. Am. Symphony Orch. League (v.p.), Am. Arts Alliance (dir.). Office: Avery Fisher Hall Broadway and 65th St New York NY 10023

WEBSTER, BETHUEL MATTHEW, lawyer; b. Denver, June 13, 1900; s. Bethuel Matthew and Anna Laura (Davidson) W.; grad. Culver Mil. Acad., 1918; A.B., U. Colo., 1922, LL.D., 1972; LL.B., Harvard, 1925; m. Eleanor Ashton Wilson, Mar. 16, 1929 (dec. June 28, 1967); children—Elizabeth (Mrs. William H. Hogeland, Jr.), Anna Clarissa (Mrs. William C. Atkinson), Eleanor Alice (Mrs. Bernard Shakin); m. 2d, Elizabeth W. Case, Nov. 1969. Admitted to N.Y. State bar, 1927, and D.C. bar, 1929; asst. U.S. atty. So. Dist. N.Y., 1926-27; spl. asst. to Atty. Gen. of U.S. antitrust div., Dept. of Justice, 1927-29; gen. counsel Fed. Radio Commn., 1929; cons. U.S. High Commr. for Germany, 1949, 51; practicing lawyer, N.Y.C., 1930—; mem. Webster & Sheffield and predecessor law firms, 1934—. Served as mem. Permanent Ct. Arbitration, under the Hague Convs., 1959-65; mem. com. sci. aids learning NRC, 1937-47; mem. com. internat. rules of jud. procedure; asst. to Dr. Vannervar Bush, dir. OSRD, report to Pres. of U.S. on postwar research, July 1945; mem., cons. Com. Scientists Supporting Bush Report; chmn. adv. com. project effective justice; mem. Armstrong research project Columbia Law Sch.; mem. mgmt. and selection coms. Arthur Goodhart Vis. Professorship in Legal Sci., Cambridge U.; mem. com. role patents indsl. research NAS-NRC; chmn. pub. health service. hosp. study com. Office Sci. and Tech., Exec. Office of Pres., 1965; ambassador representing U.S.A. to mediate dispute between U.K. and Guatemala over Brit. Honduras, 1965-68. Trustee Ford Found., 1961-70, William Nelson Cromwell Found., N.Y. Pub. Library (hon.), Inst. Pub. Adminstrn.; dir. Overbrook Found.; mem. overseers com. to visit Harvard Library; chmn. Drug Abuse Council; dir. Inst. Philos. Research; counsel N.Y. State Soc. Med. Research; deptl. com. on ct. adminstrn, 1st dept. jud. conf. of New York, N.Y.C. Health Research Council; mem. N.Y.C. Municipal Art Commn., 1960-64; mem. Mayor's Com. on Judiciary, 1962-65. Served as 2d lt. inf. U.S. Army, 1918-19. Recipient Norlin award U. Colo., 1968. Fellow Am. Coll. Trial Lawyers, Am. Bar Found., Aspen Inst. Humanistic Studies; mem. Assn. Bar City of N.Y. (pres. 1952-54), Am. Law Inst., N.Y. Co. Lawyers Assn., Am., N.Y. State bar assns., Am. Arbitration Assn. (dir.), Am. Judicature Soc., Fed. Bar Assn. N.Y., N.J. and Conn. (hon.) bar assns., Harvard Law Sch. Assn. of N.Y.C. (pres. 1948-49), Harvard Alumni Assn. (dir. 1952-54), Pub. Edn. Assn. (chmn. bd. of trustees, 1954-58), Council on Fgn. Relations, Pilgrims of U.S. Clubs: Century, Harvard, Coffee House, Metropolitan (Washington). Home: 200 E 66th St New York City NY 10021 also Grantville Rd Winchester CT 06098 Office: One Rockefeller Plaza New York City NY 10020

WEBSTER, COLIN WESLEY, business exec.; b. Quebec, Can., Nov. 29, 1902; s. Lorne C. and Muriel (Taylor) W.; B.A., McGill U., 1924; LL.D., Sir George William U., 1966; m. Jean Frosst, Dec. 1, 1927; children—Lorne C., Donald C., Beverley F. Webster Rolph. Chmn. St. Lawrence Stevedoring Co. Ltd., Internat. Paints (Can.) Ltd.; dir. Canadian Gen. Ins. Co., St. Lawrence Cement Co., C.G.T.X., Canadian Liquid Air Co., Ltd., Massey-Ferguson Ltd., Massey-Ferguson (Gt. Britain) Ltd., Montreal Shipping Co., Ltd., Montship Lines Ltd., Napierville Junction Ry. Co., Liquid Air Corp. N.Am., Little Long Lac Gold Mines Ltd., Ultramar Can. Inc., Stewart, Smith (Can.) Ltd., Toronto, Hamilton & Buffalo Ry. Co. Mem. Met. bd. Montreal YMCA, Old Brewery Mission. Mem. United Ch. Can. Home: 52 Gordon Crescent Montreal PQ H3Y 1M6 Canada Office: 5250 De Maisonneive Blvd Montreal PQ H4A 1Y7 Canada

WEBSTER, DAVID ARTHUR, life ins. co. exec.; b. Downs, Ill., July 20, 1937; s. Harold Sanford and Carmen Mildred (Moore) W.; B.S., U. Ill., 1960; m. Anna Elizabeth Prosch, June 10, 1956; children—Theodore David, Elizabeth Anna, Arthur Lee, William Harold. Actuarial asst. Mass. Mut. Life Ins. Co., Springfield, 1960-64; cons. actuary George Stennes & Assos., Mpls., 1964-68; v.p., actuary Piedmont Life Ins. Co., Atlanta, 1968-72, Pacific Fidelity Life Ins. Co., Los Angeles, 1972-74; v.p., chief actuary U.S. Life Corp., N.Y.C., 1974-76, exec. v.p., 1976-78, dir., 1976-78; sr. v.p., dir. Beneficial Standard Life, 1978—; v.p., dir. Beneficial Pension Services; v.p., treas., dir. Beneficial Assurance Co., BPS Agy., Inc.; asst. sec., dir. Beneficial Computer Services; treas. Tel-Assurance Corp. Am.; pres. Am. Exec. Life, 1978—. Fellow Soc. Actuaries; mem. Am. Acad. Actuaries. Clubs: Actuaries of Pacific States; Woodland Hills Country. Home: 5131 Encino Ave Encino CA 91316 Office: 3700 Wilshire Blvd Los Angeles CA 90010

WEBSTER, DWIGHT ALBERT, educator; b. S. Manchester, Conn., Feb. 2, 1919; s. Royal Dwight and Harriet (Brown) W.; student U. Conn., 1936-37; B.S., Cornell U., 1940, Ph.D., 1943; m. Priscilla Copley, Sept. 6, 1941; children—Dwight Albert, Mark Copley, Dianne Copley; m. 2d, Julia Chrystie Pitney, Oct. 4, 1978. Mem. faculty Cornell U., 1942—, instr. limnology, 1942-45, asst. prof. limnology and fisheries, 1946-48, asso. prof. fishery biology, 1949-56, prof., 1957—, chmn. dept. conservation, 1967-71. Recipient Trout Conservation award Trout Unlimited, 1965; Outstanding Prof. award, 1978-79; Vetlesen Skandinavian travel fellow, 1961. Mem. Am. Soc. Limnology and Oceanography, Am. Soc. Ichthyology and Herpetology (treas. 1949-51), Am. Fisheries Soc. (award of Merit,

N.E. div. 1979; program chmn. 1951, pres. N.E. 1962, 69), Sigma Xi, Phi Kappa Phi. Home: 62 Burdick Hill Rd Ithaca NY 14850

WEBSTER, ELEANOR RUDD, educator; b. Cleve., Oct. 11, 1920; d. George Davis and Mary (Spink) Webster; A.B., Wellesley (Mass.) Coll., 1942; M.A., Mt. Holyoke Coll., 1944; M.A., Radcliffe Coll., 1951, Ph.D., 1952. Chemist, Eastman Kodak Co., Rochester, N.Y., 1944-47; instr. Wellesley Coll., 1952-53, asst. prof., 1953-60, asso. prof., 1961-67, prof., 1967—, chmn., 1964-67, dir. Inst. Chemistry, 1964-72, dir. continuing edn., 1969-70. Mem. Am. Chem. Soc., History of Sci. Soc., A.A.A.S., A.A.U.P., Brit. Soc. History of Sci., New Eng. Assn. Chemistry Tchrs., Phi Beta Kappa, Sigma Xi. Home: 162 Western Ave Sherborn MA 01770 Office: Chemistry Dept Wellesley Coll Wellesley MA 02181

WEBSTER, FREDERICK ELMER, JR., ednl. adminstr., educator; b. Auburn, N.Y., Oct. 22, 1937; s. Frederick Elmer and Evelyn May (Dudden) W.; A.B., Dartmouth Coll., 1959, M.B.A. (Gulf Oil fellow), 1960, A.M. (hon.), 1974; Ph.D. (U.S. Steel Found. fellow 1961-63, Nat. Assn. Purchasing Agts. fellow 1963-64), Stanford U., 1964; m. Mary Alice Powers, Dec. 27, 1957; children—Lynn Marie, Mark Andrew, Lisa Ann. Acting instr., research asso. Stanford U., 1963-64; asst. prof. mktg. Columbia U., 1964-65; asst. prof. bus. adminstrn. Amos Tuck Sch. Bus. Adminstrn., Dartmouth Coll., 1965-68, asso. prof., 1968-72, prof., 1972-79, E.B. Osborn prof. mktg., 1979—, asso. dean, 1976—; mem. faculty Centre d'Etudes Industrielles, Geneva; dir. Garrison Stove Works, TLHC Inc. Trustee, Alice Peck Day Meml. Hosp., Lebanon, N.H., 1970—; firefighter Town of Hanover (N.H.), 1970—, mem. fin. com., 1973-78, chmn. com., 1977-78; bd. dirs., treas. Vt. Public Radio, 1978—; mem. fin. com. Dresden Sch. Dist., Hanover, N.H., 1973-78, chmn., 1976-77; vestryman St. Thomas Episcopal Ch., Hanover, 1967-70, 75-78. Mem. Am. Mktg. Assn. (dir. 1972-74). Republican. Author books, the most recent being: Social Aspects of Marketing, 1974, Marketing for Managers, 1974, Industrial Marketing Strategy, 1979; contbr. numerous articles to profl. jours.; editor: Series on Marketing Management, 1975—; editorial bd., sect. editor Jour. Mktg., 1968—. Home: Deer Run Farm Stevens Rd Etna NH 03750 Office: Amos Tuck Sch Bus Adminstrn Dartmouth Coll Hanover NH 03755

WEBSTER, GEORGE BURBANK, JR., investment co. exec.; b. Mpls., Feb. 13, 1917; s. George Burbank and Helen (Holton) W.; student U. Minn., 1936-39, U.S. Army Command and Gen. Staff Coll., Ft. Leavenworth, Kans., 1949-50, U.S. Armed Forces Staff Coll., 1953-54, U.S. Army War Coll., 1957-58; m. Nancy Strother Davis, July 19, 1940; 1 dau., Helen Burr (Mrs. Richard William Toward). Commd. 2d lt. U.S. Army, 1939, advanced through grades to brig. gen. 1966; ret., 1970; v.p., dir. Lake States Corp.; dir. Snowbird Corp.; dir. Webster Lumber Co., Villages Homeowners Corp. Decorated Army Commendation medal, Bronze Star, Legion of Merit, D.S.M.; Medal of Merit with rank of officer (Italy). Mem. Assn. U.S. Army, Theta Delta Chi. Republican. Episcopalian. Club: Garden of the Gods (Colorado Springs, Colo.). Home: 8236 Claret Ct San Jose CA 95135 Office: Box 292 Wayzata MN 55391

WEBSTER, GEORGE DRURY, lawyer; b. Jacksonville, Fla., Feb. 8, 1921; s. Geroge D. and Mary Gaines (Walker) W.; B.A., Maryville Coll., 1941; LL.B.; Harvard, 1948; m. Ann Kilpatrick; children—Aen Walker, George Drury, Hugh Kilpatrick. Admitted to Tenn. bar, 1948, D.C. bar, 1952, Md. bar, 1976; atty. tax div. Dept Justice, 1949-51; sr. partner Webster & Chamberlain, Washington; lectr. numerous tax. insts.; dir. 1st Western Financial Corp., Las Vegas, 1st Western Savs. & Loan Assn., Las Vegas, Nittany Ins. Ltd., Bermuda. Mem. Tenn. Indsl. and Agrl. Devel. Commn.; bd. dirs. Maryville (Tenn.) Coll.; trustee U.S. Naval Acad. Found., Annapolis, Md. Served to lt. USNR, 1942-46. Mem. Am. Law Inst., Am. Bar Assn. Clubs: Chevy Chase (Md.); Harvard (N.Y.C. and Washington); Metropolitan (Washington); Racquet and Tennis (N.Y.C.). Author: Business and Professional Political Action Committees, 1979; The Law of Associations, 1980. Home: 5305 Cardinal Ct Washington DC 20016 also Webster Angus Farms Rogersville TN 37857 Office: 1747 Pennsylvania Ave NW Washington DC 20006

WEBSTER, GEORGE VAN O'LINDA, plastic surgeon; b. Carthage, N.Y., July 11, 1911; s. George V. and Klara Jane (Love) W.; grad. Phillips Exeter Acad., 1928; A.B., Stanford, 1932, M.D., 1937; m. Elizabeth Jane Neuser, Oct. 26, 1944; children—George Van O'Linda, Alison Culver, Meridith Anne, John Brian. Intern Stanford U. Hosps., 1936-37, resident gen. surgery, 1940; intern Columbia-Presbyn. Med. Center, N.Y.C., 1940-41; resident plastic surgery Columbia-Presbyn. Med. Center, 1941; pvt. practice, Pasadena, Calif., 1946—; cons. plastic surgery Long Beach (Calif.) Naval Hosp., 1946-49; sr. cons. VA Hosp., Sawtelle, Calif., 1950—, Orthopaedic Hosp., Los Angeles, 1946—; sr. cons. head and neck cancer Orange County (Calif.) Gen. Hosp., 1946-60; mem., sr. cons. staff Methodist Hosp., 1956-; mem. sr. staff Huntington Meml. Hosp., 1948—; sr. staff St. Luke's Hosp., Pasadena, 1946—, chief gen. surgery, 1957; established plastic surg. service U. Calif. at Los Angeles Med. Sch., 1955, sr. cons., clin. prof. plastic surgery, 1955—. Mem. breakfast forum Calif. Inst. Tech., 1960—, sec.-treas., 1964—, pres., 1967-68. Bd. dirs. Pasadena Beautiful Found. Served to comdr., M.C., USNR, World War II. Diplomate Am. Bd. Surgery, Am. Bd. Plastic Surgery (mem. bd.). Fellow A.C.S. (adv. council plastic surgery); mem. Am. Soc. Plastic and Reconstructive Surgery (chmn. membership com. 1955-58, mem. exec. com. 1954-58, pres. 1964-65), Calif. (pres. 1959), British socs. plastic surgeons, Am. Found. Plastic and Reconstructive Surgery (dir. 1964-69), French Soc. Plastic Surgeons, Am. Soc. Surgery Hand (pres. 1958), Los Angeles Surg. Soc., Mexican-Am. Invitational Plastic Surg. Seminars (v.p. 1971—), Pan Pacific Surg. Assn. (v.p.), Japanese Soc. Plastic Surgery (corr.), Am. Assn. Plastic Surgeons (trustee). Internat. Confedn. Plastic Surgeons, Spanish Soc. Plastic and Reconstructive Surgery (corr.), Maestro's, Sheriff's Rythm Posse, Kappa Sigma, Alpha Kappa Kappa. Club: Valley (Santa Barbara). Contbr. articles to profl. jours. Office: 1145 E Green St Pasadena CA 91101

WEBSTER, H. MAX, union ofcl.; b. Fayette County, Ala., Feb. 15, 1931; s. Vandiver and Theoda (Still) W.; student Moline (Ill.) Inst. Commerce, 1955-56, George Meany Labor Inst. Center, 1971; m. Nell Ward, Apr. 25, 1952; children—Deborah K., Pamela J. Local union pres. Aluminum Workers Internat. Union, 1956-62, internat. rep., 1962-65, v.p., 1959-75, regional dir., 1965-75, sec.-treas., 1975—. Served with U.S. Army, 1949-50, 51-52. Office: 818 Olive St St Louis MO 63101

WEBSTER, HENRY DEFOREST, exptl. neuropathologist; b. N.Y.C., Apr. 22, 1927; s. Leslie Tillotson and Emily (deForest) W.; A.B. cum laude, Amherst Coll., 1948; M.D., Harvard U., 1952; m. Marion Havas, June 12, 1951; children—Christopher, Henry, Sally, David, Steven. Intern, Boston City Hosp., 1952-53, resident, 1953-54; resident Mass. Gen. Hosp., 1954-56, research fellow in neuropathology, 1956-59; prin. investigator NIH research grants for electron microscopic studies of peripheral neuropathy, 1959-69; mem. staffs Mass. Gen., Newton-Wellesley hosps.; instr. neurology Harvard Med. Sch., 1959-63, asso. in neurology, 1963-66, asst. prof. neuropathology, 1966; asso. prof. neurology U. Miami Sch. Medicine, 1966-69, prof., 1969; head sect. cellular neuropathology Nat. Inst. Neurol. and Communicative Disorders and Stroke, NIH, Bethesda, Md., 1969—, asso. chief Lab. of Neuropathology and Neuroanat. Scis., 1975—; Distinguished scientist and lectr., dept. anatomy Tulane U. Sch. Medicine, 1973. Recipient Weil award Am. Assn. Neuropathologists, 1960; Superior Service award USPHS, 1977. Mem. Am. Assn. Neuropathologists (v.p. 1976-77; pres. 1978-79), Internat. Soc. Neuropathology (councillor), Internat. Congress Neuropathology (sec. gen. VIII 1978), Peripheral Nerve Study Group (ad hoc com. 1975—), Am. Neurol. Assn., Am. Acad. Neurology, Am. Soc. Cell Biologists, Am. Assn. Anatomists, Soc. for Neurosci., Phi Beta Kappa, Sigma Xi. Author: (with A. Peters and S.L. Dalay) The Fine Structure of the Nervous System, 1970, 76. Mem. editorial bd. Jour. Neuropathology and Exptl. Neurology, Jour. Neurocytology, Tissue and Cell, Muscle and Nerve. Home: 9223 Burning Tree Rd Bethesda MD 20034

WEBSTER, JAMES C., govt. ofcl.; b. Grand Island, Nebr., Feb. 9, 1938. Mgr. for S.D., UPI, 1961-63; mng. editor Madison (S.D.) Daily Leader, 1963-68; editor East River Guardian, 1968-69; dir. pubs. Am. Public Power Assn., 1970-73; press sec., legis. asst. to U.S. Senator George McGovern, 1973-75; pres. sec. to U.S. Senate Com. on Agr. and Forestry, 1975-77; dir. Office Congressional and Public Affairs, Dept. Agr., 1977-79, asst. sec. agr., 1979—. Address: Dept Agriculture 14th and Independence Ave SW Washington DC 20250*

WEBSTER, JAMES CARSON, educator; b. Bloomfield, Ohio, June 27, 1905; s. James G(illespie) C(arson) and Maude (Kelly) W.; A.B., Princeton, 1929, M.F.A., 1933, Ph.D., 1939; Brevet de l'historire de L'art. U. Paris (France), 1931; m. Elizabeth Linard Webster, June 13, 1935; 1 son, James C(arson). Mem. faculty Northwestern U., 1934—, prof. art, 1949—, chmn. dept., 1960-64. Pres. Midwestern Coll. Art Conf., 1947-48; mem. Nat. Com. History Art, 1953-56; mem. com. criteria and selection Landmarks Commn. Chgo., 1951-54; com. selection Chgo. project Historic Am. Bldgs. Survey, 1963-65; Fellow Inst. Advanced Study, 1938. Mem. AAUP, Coll. Art Assn., Am. Soc. for Aesthetics, Soc. Archtl. Historians. Author monographs, articles. Editor for book revs. Coll. Art Jour., 1943-49; editor-in-chief Art Bull., 1953-56, editorial com. and editorial bd., 1956—. Home: 129 Dupee Pl Wilmette IL 60091

WEBSTER, JOHN HAMILTON, radiation oncologist; b. Belleville, Can., Dec. 17, 1928; s. Frederick and Katherine Margaret (Hamilton) W.; M.D., Queen's U., 1955, C.M., 1955; m. Doreen Elizabeth Beatrix, Aug. 17, 1953; children—Diana, Lorna, Patrick, Geoffrey. Intern, Meml. Hosp., Manchester, Conn., 1955-56; resident Roswell Park Meml. Inst., Buffalo, 1956-59; practice medicine specializing in therapeutic radiology, Buffalo, 1956-74; sr. cancer research radiologist dept. therapeutic radiology Roswell Park Meml. Inst., Buffalo, 1959-62, asso. cancer research radiologist, 1962-63, asso. chief cancer research radiologist, 1963-64, chief therapeutic radiology, 1964-74; prof., chmn. dept. radiation oncology Faculty Medicine McGill U., Montreal, Que., Can., 1974-79; prof. dept. radiology Joint Radiation Oncology Center, U. Pitts. Health Center, 1979—; therapeutic radiologist in chief Royal Victoria Hosp., Montreal Gen. Hosp., Montreal Children's Hosp., Jewish Gen. Hosp. Fellow Royal Coll. Physicians and Surgeons Can.; mem. Am. Coll. Radiology, Am. Soc. Therapeutic Radiologists, Can. Oncology Soc., Internat. Assn. Study Lung Cancer. Home: 302 Bank St Sewickley PA 15143

WEBSTER, LARRY RUSSELL, artist; b. Arlington, Mass., Mar. 18, 1930; s. James Burpee and Ethel (Hughes) W.; B.F.A., Mass. Coll. Art, 1952; M.S., Boston U., 1953; m. Rosemary Siekman, June 13, 1953; children—Wendy Lyn, Ricky Stewart, Holly Jean. Package designer Union Bag & Paper Co., N.Y.C., 1953-54; art dir., graphic designer, v.p., dir. Thomas Todd Co., Boston, 1956-78; asst. prof. design Mass. Coll. Art, 1964-66. Paintings in permanent collections including DeCordova Mus., Lincoln, Mass., Grand Rapids (Mich.) Art Mus., Springfield (Mo.) Art Mus., Davenport (Iowa) Municipal Gallery, Colby Coll. Art Mus., Waterville, Maine. Served with U.S. Army, 1954-56. Recipient Silver medal Am. Watercolor Soc., 1968, 72, C.F.S. award, 1963, Ed Whitney award, 1973; Rhinehold award, 1967, Ranger Fund Purchase prize, 1965, Adolph and Clara Obrig prize in watercolor NAD, 1970; gold medal Allied Artists Am., 1971; Washington Sch. Art award, 1977; Lena Newcastle award, 1978; Colo. Watermedia award, 1978; Golden award Rocky Mountain Nat. Watermedia Exhbn., 1979. Mem. Soc. Printers Boston (past mem. council), Am., Boston (pres. 1974-75) watercolor socs., Guild of Boston Artists, NAD (asso.). Home: 116 Perkins Row Topsfield MA 01983

WEBSTER, LEE DAVIS, corp. exec.; b. Vicksburg Miss., Oct. 22, 1923; s. Samuel D. and Lorena M. (Thompson) W.; B.S.C., Creighton U., 1950; student So. Meth. U. Law Sch., 1957-58; m. Sandra K. Collins; children—Lee Davis, Lisa, Michelle. Vice pres., sec.-treas. Ling-Temco Vought, Inc., Dallas, 1958-62; exec. v.p., dir., mem. exec. com. Electro-Science Investors, Inc., Richardson, Tex., 1962-63, pres., dir., chmn. exec. com., 1963-68; pres., chief exec. officer, chmn. exec. com. LTV Ling Altec, Inc., 1968-69; chmn. bd., pres., chief exec. officer Whitehall Corp., 1969—. Served with USAAF, 1943-46. C.P.A., Nebr., Tex. Mem. Tex. Soc. C.P.A.'s. Home: 9323 Preston Rd Dallas TX 75225 Office: 2659 Nova Dr PO Box 29709 Dallas TX 75229

WEBSTER, LESLIE TILLOTSON, JR., pharmacologist, educator; b. N.Y.C., Mar. 31, 1926; s. Leslie Tillotson and Emily (de Forest) W.; B.A., Amherst Coll., 1947; student Union Coll., 1944; M.D., Harvard, 1948; m. Alice Katharine Holland, June 24, 1955; children—Katharine White, Susan Holland, Leslie Tillotson III, Romi Anne. Intern Cleve. City Hosp., 1948-49, jr. asst. resident, 1949-50; asst. resident medicine Bellevue Hosp., N.Y.C., 1952-53; research fellow medicine Harvard and Boston City Hosp. Thorndike Meml. Lab., 1953-55; demonstrator Case Western Res. U. Sch. Medicine, 1955-56, sr. instr. biochemistry, 1959-60, asst. prof. medicine, 1960-70, asst. prof. biochemistry, 1960-65, asst. prof. pharmacology, 1965-67, asso. prof., 1967-70, prof., 1976—, chmn. pharmacology dept., 1976—; prof., chmn. pharmacology dept. Northwestern U. Med. Sch., 1970-76; cons. NIH, WHO, Rockefeller Found. Served to lt. USNR, 1950-52. Russell M. Wilder fellow Nat. Vitamin Found., 1956-59; Sr. USPHS Research fellow, 1959-61, Research Career Devel. awardee, 1961-69. Diplomate Am. Bd. Internal Medicine. Mem. Am. Assn. Study Liver Diseases, A.C.P., Central Soc. Clin. Research, Am. Soc. Clin. Investigation, Am. Soc. Biol. Chemists, Assn. Med. Sch. Pharmacology, Am. Soc. Pharmacology and Exptl. Therapeutics. Contbr. articles to med. and sci. jours. Home: 2728 Leighton Rd Shaker Heights OH 44120 Office: Dept Pharmacology Case-Western Res U Sch Med 2119 Abington Rd Cleveland OH 44106

WEBSTER, LUTHER DENVER, JR., steel co. exec.; b. Lubbock, Tex., June 10, 1910; s. Luther Denver and Johncy (Hardin) W.; student So. Meth. U. 1930-33; children—Lydia Hayes (Mrs. Frankie Dell Green), Rebel. Sports editor, pub. relations dir. Dallas Dispatch, 1932-41; gen. mgr. Air Force Contract Flight Sch., 1941-44; exec. v.p. Red Arrow Freight Lines, Houston, 1944-47; owner Red Webster & Assos., advt agy., 1947-49; v.p. Lone Star Steel Co., Dallas, 1950—; v.p., dir. Marshall Broadcasting Corp. Mem. Tex. Commn. on Alcoholism. Mem. Am. Petroleum Inst., Am. Iron and Steel Inst. (pub. relations com.), Pub. Relations Soc. Am., Soc. Am. Indsl. Editors, Sigma Delta Chi. Democrat. Methodist. Mason (Shriner). Author: I Saw Russia, 1958; The Red Whip. Home: 5823 Woodland St Dallas TX 75225 Office: 2200 W Mockingbird Ln Dallas TX 75235

WEBSTER, MARION ELIZABETH, biochemist; b. Ottawa, Ont., Can., Apr. 9, 1921; d. Arthur and E. May (McAllister) Webster; came to U.S., 1934, naturalized, 1944; B.S., Fla. State U.; M.S., Georgetown U., 1948, Ph.D., 1950; m. Alexis P. Bukovsky, Feb. 19, 1952. Research chemist So. Phosphate Corp., Bartow, Fla., 1942-43; jr. chemist Bur. Entomology and Plant Quarantine, Dept. Agr., Orlando, Fla., 1944-45; research biochemist U.S. Indsl. Chems. Co., Balt., 1946-47; chief biochemistry sect., dept. biologics research Walter Reed Army Inst. Research, Washington, 1947-58; research biochemist NIH, Bethesda, 1958-76; vis. prof. Escola Paulista de Medicine, Sao Paulo, Brazil, 1968-69, 77-79; vis. scholar Henry Ford Hosp., Detroit, 1979—. Recipient Disting. Service award Dept. Arg., 1947; Superior Accomplishment award Dept. Army, 1957; NIH spl. fellow, 1969. Mem. Am. Chem. Soc., AAAS, Am. Assn. Clin. Chemists, Am. Physiol. Soc., Am. Soc. Pharmacology and Exptl. Therapeutics, Internat. Soc. Biochem. Pharmacology, N.Y. Acad. Scis., Soc. Exptl. Biology and Medicine (Emeritus award D.C. chpt. 1978), Assn. Women in Sci. (pres. 1976-78), Sigma Delta Epsilon (pres. 1976-77). Author articles, chpts. in books. Address: 1071 Lakeview Dr Winter Park FL 32789. *As one goal is achieved another goal is always ahead of you.*

WEBSTER, MAURIE, broadcast sales, research, mgmt. cons.; b. Gibbon, Nebr., Apr. 22, 1916; s. George Corban and Lyllian Evalina (Weldin) W.; student Coll. Puget Sound., 1933-36, U. Calif. at Los Angeles, 1938-39; m. Judith Peairs, Apr. 18, 1940; children—Scott E., Susan A. With CBS, 1937-73, v.p., gen. mgr. KCBS, San Francisco, 1958-61, v.p., gen. mgr. radio spot sales, N.Y.C., 1961-67, v.p. devel., 1967-69, v.p. div. services, N.Y.C., 1969-73; exec. v.p. Compu/Net, N.Y.C., 1973-75; pres. Webster Group, N.Y.C., 1975—; exec. dir. N.Y. Market Radio Broadcasters Assn., N.Y.C., 1976—; mem. steering com. N.Am. broadcast sect. World Assn. Christian Communication, 1971-74; founder San Francisco Plant a Tree Week, 1959; pres. Internat. Radio and TV Found., 1970-73; bd. mgrs. broadcasting and film commn. Nat. Council Chs. Served with USNR, 1941-45. Recipient Notable Nebraskan's award, 1967. Mem. Internat. Radio and TV Soc. (pres. 1973-75), San Francisco Radio Broadcaster's Assn. (founder 1959), N.Y. Market Radio Broadcaster's Assn. (founder 1968). Presbyn. (mem. session 1973—). Club: Port Elco (Greenwich, Conn.). Home: 35 Sutton Pl New York City NY 10022 Office: 575 Lexington Ave New York City NY 10022

WEBSTER, PAUL FRANCIS, songwriter; b. N.Y.C., Dec. 20, 1907; s. Myron Lawrence and Blanche Pauline (Stonehill) W.; student Horace Mann Sch., also N.Y.U., 1924-27, Cornell U., summer 1925; m. Gloria Lenore Benguiat, June 10, 1937; children—Guy Michael, Roger Edmund. Composer songs: Masquerade, 1932, Reflections in the Water, My Moonlight Madonna, 1933, Two Cigarettes in the Dark, 1934; co-author scores for motion pictures: Giant, Friendly Persuasion, Rose Marie, Student Prince, Merry Widow, Calamity Jane, Great Caruso, The Alamo, Guns of Navarone, Tender Is the Night, Mutiny on the Bounty, Raintree County, The Sandpiper, also others; songs for the stage musical Jump for Joy, 1940; songs for films and stage include Love is a Many Splendored Thing, Somewhere, My Love, I'll Walk with God, Secret Love, I Got it Bad and That Ain't Good, Lamplighter's Serenade, Loveliest Night of the Year, The Green Leaves of Summer, A Certain Smile, The Twelfth of Never, April Love, The Shadow of Your Smile; also collaborated with Oscar Strauss and Rudolph Friml and Hoagy Carmichael, Franz Lehar, Sammy Fain, Jerome Kern, others. Recipient Best Song Award A.S.C.A.P., 1934; Acad. Award, 1953, 55, 65; gold medal Photoplay mag., 1955; bronze plaque Down-Beat mag., 1955, Best Song, 1956; Song Hit of the Year, Radio and TV Daily award, 1956: Diploma di Onore Messina, Italy, 1956; Limelight Film Critics award, 1961; Grammy award, 1965; Laurel award, 1965; elected to Songwriter's Hall Fame, 1972. Mem. A.S.C.A.P. (award of Merit 1966), Writers Guild Am. (hon. life), Songwriter's Protective Assn., Acad. Motion Picture Arts and Scis., Author's League, Dramatist's Guild. Author: The Children's Music Box, 1945. Home: 709 N Crescent Dr Beverly Hills CA 90210*

WEBSTER, REGINALD HOWARD, newspaper exec.; b. Que., Can., 1910; s. Lorne Campbell and Muriel Warren (Taylor) W.; B.A., McGill U., 1931; postgrad. Babson Inst. Chmn. bd., pres. Toronto (Ont., Can.) Globe & Mail; pres., dir. Annis Furs, Detroit, Detroit Marine Terminals, Inc., Canadian Fur Investments, Ltd.; chmn. Penobscot Bldg., Detroit, Windsor Hotel Ltd.; chmn., dir. F.P. Publs., Ltd.; pres. Imperial Trust Co., Durand Corp.; dir. Holt Renfrew & Co., Burns Foods Ltd. Office: Globe & Mail 444 Front St W Toronto ON M5V 2S9 Canada

WEBSTER, RONALD LEE, psychologist; b. Pitts., Sept. 1, 1937; s. Harry M. and Laura Verne (Anderson) W.; B.A., U. Maine, 1959; M.A., La. State U., Baton Rouge, 1962, Ph.D., 1964. Mem. faculty Hollins Coll., Roanoke, Va., 1964—, prof. psychology, 1975—; dir. Hollins Communications Research Inst., 1973—; pres. Communications Devel. Corp., Ltd., Roanoke, 1973—; pres. Communications Reconstruction Centers, N.Y.C. Recipient Sci. Exhibit award Am. Speech and Hearing Assn., 1974. Mem. Am., Southeastern, Va. psychol. assns., Psychonomic Soc., Am. Assn. Advancement Behavior Therapy, Am. Assn. Advancement Tension Control, Sigma Xi. Author: The Precision Fluency Shaping Program: Speech Reconstruction for Stutterers, 3 vols., 1974. Address: PO Box 9737 Hollins Coll Roanoke VA 24020

WEBSTER, SHIRLEY ALTON, lawyer; b. Minburn, Iowa, Sept. 21, 1909; s. Marion A. and Ruth (Shirley) W.; B.A., State U. Iowa, 1930, J.D., 1932; m. Marie E. Drews, Sept 19, 1935; children—Jane, Ann. Admitted to Iowa bar, 1932, since practiced in Winterset; mem. law firm Webster, Jordan, Olivera & Walters; county atty. Madison County, 1939-44. Served as lt. USNR, 1944-46. Recipient award of Merit, Ia. State Bar Assn., 1964. Fellow Am. Bar Found., Am. Coll. Probate Counsel (mem. bd. of regents, treas.). Mem. Am. (ho. of dels. 1958-69), Iowa (pres. 1957-58, chmn. spl. com. probate law 1958-73), 5th Jud. Dist., Madison County (sec. 1935-54) bar assns., Am. Legion, Order of Coif. Republican. Mason. Home: 214 N 8th Ave Winterset IA 50273 Office: Farmers & Mchts State Bank Bldg Winterset IA 50273

WEBSTER, STOKELY, painter; b. Evanston, Ill., Aug. 23, 1912; s. Henry Kitchell and Mary Ward (Orth) W.; ed. Yale, U. Chgo.; studied art with Lawton Parker, Paris and Wayman Adams, N.Y.C.; m. Iva Kitchell, Aug. 23, 1933; 1 dau., Stephanie T. Landscape painter, Chgo., 1932; textile designer, N.Y.C., 1934-35; exhibited portraits and landscapes, Corcoran Biennial Exhbn. Washington, Allied Artists and N.A.D., N.Y.C., Art Inst. Chgo., Ill. State Mus., Albany (N.Y.) Inst. Art, Salon des Indépendants, Paris, Salon des Artistes Francais, Paris; rep. The Phillips Collection, Washington, Mus. City N.Y., Fitchburg (Mass.) Art Mus., Ill. State Mus., Nat. Collection Fine Arts, Smithsonian Instn., Washington, Phillips Collection, Washington, Newark Mus., Northwestern U. Spl. Collection, Am. Tel. & Tel. Co.; one-man shows James St. Lawrence O'Toole Gallery, N.Y.C., 1940,

Albert Roullier Gallery, Chgo., 1940, Vallombreuse Gallery, Biarritz, 1970, Vallombreuse Gallery, Palm Beach, Fla., 1973, Hobe Sound (Fla.) Gallery, 1974, Eric Galleries, N.Y.C., 1975, 78; Recipient First Hallgartin prize N.A.D., 1941. Home: 309 Deer Park Ave Dix Hills NY 11746

WEBSTER, WILLIAM HEDGCOCK, govt. ofcl.; b. St. Louis, Mar. 6, 1924; s. Thomas M. and Katherine (Hedgcock) W.; A.B., Amherst Coll., 1947, LL.D., 1975; J.D., Washington U., 1949, LL.D., 1978; LL.D., William Wood Coll., 1978, DePauw U.; 1978; m. Drusilla Lane, May 5, 1950; children—Drusilla Lane Busch, William Hedgcock, Katherine Hagee. Admitted to Mo. bar, 1949; with firm Armstrong, Teasdale, Kramer and Vaughan, and predecessors, St. Louis, 1949-50, 52-59, partner, 1956-59, 61-70; U.S. atty. Eastern Dist. Mo., 1960-61; mem. Mo. Bd. Law Examiners, 1964-69; judge U.S. Dist. Ct., Eastern Mo. dist., 1971-73, U.S. Ct. Appeals, 8th Circuit, 1973-78, dir. FBI, 1978—. Mem. adv. com. on criminal rules, 1971-78, mem. ct. adminstrs. com., 1975-78. Trustee Washington U., 1974—. Served as lt. (j.g.), USNR, 1943-46, lt. (s.g.), 1951-52. Recipient citation Washington U. Alumni, 1972; Disting. Alumnus award Washington U., 1977. Fellow Am. Bar Found.; mem. Am. (chmn. sect. on corp. banking and bus. law 1977-78), Fed., Mo., St. Louis bar assns., Am. Law Inst. (council 1978—), Washington U. Alumni Fedn. (pres. 1956-57), Washington U. Law Alumni (pres. 1961). Big Brother Orgn. St. Louis (dir. 1958-66, pres. 1965-66, hon. life pres.), Big Brothers of Am. (dir. 1966, hon. dir. 1978—), Mo. Assn. Republicans (pres. 1958), Order of Coif, Psi Upsilon. Delta Sigma Rho, Phi Delta Phi. Clubs: Rotary; St. Louis Country, Noonday (St. Louis); Alfalfa, St. Alban's Tennis (Washington). Home: 9409 Brooks Dr Bethesda MD 20036 Office: FBI J Edgar Hoover Bldg Washington DC 20535

WEBSTER, WILLIAM MERLE, JR., electronics co. exec.; b. Warsaw, N.Y., June 13, 1925; s. William Merle and Carrie Melinda (Luce) W.; B.S. in Physics, Union Coll., Schenectady, 1945; Ph.D. in Elec. Engring., Princeton, 1954; m. Mary Lambert Tourison, May 3, 1947; children—Melissa, Cecelia. With RCA Corp., 1946—, v.p. labs., Princeton, N.J., 1969—; dir. Horizon Bancorp., Princeton Bank & Trust Co. Trustee Med. Center Princeton, Carrier Clinic. Served to lt. (j.g.) USNR, 1942-46. Fellow IEEE; mem. Nat. Acad. Engring., Sigma Xi. Home: 11 Morven Pl Princeton NJ 08540 Office: RCA Laboratories Princeton NJ 08540

WEBSTER, WILLIS HARRY, airplane mfg. co. exec.; b. Howard, Kans., Apr. 21, 1921; s. Samuel Harrison and Hazel (Bell) W.; accounting degree Wichita Bus. Coll., 1941; m. Melva Bell Hargadine, July 16, 1949; children—Gregory Lynn, Jeffrey Dean, Lyle Harry. Clk., Fourth Nat. Bank, Wichita, Kans., 1942-49; cost accountant Beech Aircraft Corp., Wichita, 1949-62; treas., asst. gen. mgr. Westholt Mfg. Inc., Wichita, 1962; treas., chief fin. officer Gates Learjet Corp., Wichita, 1962—. Trustee Wesley Med. Center, Wichita, Wichita United Way, Jr. Achievement, Leukemia Soc. Served with USAAF, 1942-46. Mem. Wichita C. of C. Republican. Methodist. Clubs: Rolling Hills Country, Wichita. Home: 142 Brendonwood Ct Wichita KS 67206 Office: PO Box 7707 Wichita KS 67277

WECHSBERG, JOSEPH, writer; b. Moravska-Ostrava, Aug. 29, 1907; s. Siegfried and Hermine (Krieger) W.; student Vienna State Acad. Music, 1925-30, Sorbonne, 1926-29; grad. summa cum laude, Prague U. Law Sch., 1930; m. Jo-Ann Novak, Mar. 24, 1934; 1 dau., Poppy. Came to U.S., 1938, naturalized, 1944. Musician, lawyer, journalist in Europe; free-lance writer, U.S., 1938—; writer New Yorker mag., 1943—, mem. staff, 1948—, fgn. corr., 1949—. Served as lt. Czechoslovak Army, 1938; as tech. sgt. psychol. warfare div., AUS, World War II. Recipient lit. fellowship award Houghton Mifflin, 1944; ann. mag. award Sidney Hillman Found., 1953. Mem. Authors Guild. Author: Looking for a Bluebird, 1945; Homecoming, 1946; Sweet and Sour, 1948; The Continental Touch, 1948; Blue Trout and Black Truffles, 1953; The Self-Betrayed, 1955; Avalanche, 1958; Red Plush and Black Velvet, 1961; Dining at the Pavillon, 1962; The Best Things in Life, 1964; Journey Through the Land of Eloquent Silence, 1964; The Merchant Bankers, 1966; Vienna, My Vienna, 1968; The Voices, 1969; The First Time Around, 1970; Prague, The Mystical City, 1971; The Opera, 1972; The Glory of the Violin, 1972; The Waltz Emperors, 1973; Verdi, 1974; Dream Towns of Europe, 1976; In Leningrad, 1977; Schubert, 1977; The Vienna I Knew, 1979. Contbr. nat. mags. Office: care Paul R Reynolds Inc 12 E 41st St New York City NY 10017. *To be able to smile at oneself when one fails; to be able to live with oneself when one succeeds.*

WECHSLER, HENRY, research psychologist; b. Warsaw, Poland, Aug. 16, 1932; s. William and Lucy (Fryd) W.; came to U.S., 1941, naturalized, 1953; A.B. summa cum laude, Washington and Jefferson Coll., 1953; M.A. (Harvard Found. for Advanced Study fellow, resident fellow), Harvard, 1955, Ph.D. in Social Psychology, 1957; m. Joan Goldstein, Oct. 16, 1955; children—Stephen Bruce, Pamela Jane, Peter Thomas. USPHS postdoctoral research fellow, 1957; research asso. Joint Commn. on Mental Illness and Health, 1957-58; research asso., asst. prof. Clark U., 1958-59; research social psychologist Mass. Mental Health Center, 1959-65; research asso. in psychology Med. Sch., Harvard, 1960-66, Sch. Pub. Health, 1963-66, lectr. social psychology, 1966—; dir. research Med. Found., Inc., Boston, 1965—; vis. lectr. Boston U., 1967-68; pres. SocioTech. Systems, 1969-74; lectr. in research Simmons Coll. Sch. Social Work, 1969—. Fellow Am., Mass. (treas. 1967-68) psychol. assns., Am. Sociol. Assn., Am. Pub. Health Assn.; mem. Mass. Pub. Health Assn., A.A.A.S., Phi Beta Kappa. Club: Harvard (Boston). Author, editor: The Threat of Impending Disaster; contbr. to Psychology of Stress, 1964, Social Psychology and Mental Health, 1970, Emergency Medical Services: Behavioral and Planning Perspectives, 1973, Social Work Research in the Human Services, 1976, Handbook of Medical Specialties, 1976; The Horizons of Health, 1977; Explorations in Nursing Research, 1978. Contbr. numerous articles to profl. jours. Home: 148 Puritan Dr Quincy MA 02169 Office: 29 Commonwealth Ave Boston MA 02116

WECHSLER, HERBERT, educator; b. N.Y.C., Dec. 4, 1909; s. Samuel and Anna (Weisberger) W.; A.B., Coll. of City of N.Y., 1928; LL.B., Columbia, 1931, LL.D., 1978; LL.D., U. Chgo., 1962, Harvard U., 1967; m. Elzie S. Stix, May 29, 1933 (div. 1957); m. 2d, Doris L. Klauber, Apr. 13, 1957. Admitted to N.Y. bar, 1933; editor Columbia U. Law Review, 1929-31, instr. in law, 1931-32, asst. prof., 1933-38, asso. prof., 1938-45, prof., 1945—, on leave 1940-46; law sec. to Mr. Justice Harlan F. Stone, 1932-33; counsel to minority leader N.Y. State Constl. Convention, 1938; asst. atty. gen. of N.Y. (assigned Bklyn. investigation), 1938-40; exec. sec. U.S. Bd. Legal Examiners, 1941-42; mem. adv. com. on rules criminal procedure U.S. Supreme Ct., 1941-45; spl. asst. to atty. gen. of U.S., 1940-44: asst. atty. gen. of U.S., in charge war div. U.S. Dept. Justice, 1944-46; tech. adviser to U.S. mems. Internat. Mil. Tribunal, 1945-46; vis. prof. Harvard Law Sch., 1956-57, Oliver Wendell Holmes lectr., 1958-59; Harlan Fiske Stone prof. constl. law Columbia, 1957-78, emeritus, 1978—. Am. Law Inst. reporter Model Penal Code, 1952-62; exec. dir. Am. Law Inst., 1963—; dir. Social Sci. Research Council, 1953. Mem. Pres.'s Commn. on Law Enforcement and Adminstrn. of Justice, 1965-67, N.Y. Temporary Commn. Rev. Penal Law and Criminal Code, 1961-70; mem. permanent com. for Oliver Wendell Holmes Devise, 1966-74; mem. com. on rev. fed. ct. appellate system, 1973-75; chmn. N.Y. Jud. Nomination Commn., 1978—. Fellow Am. Acad. Arts and Scis., Brit. Acad. (corr.); mem. Am. Bar Assn., Assn. Bar City of N.Y. (past v.p.). Democrat. Club: Century Assn. Author: Criminal Law and Its Administration (with J. Michael), 1940; The Federal Courts and the Federal System (with H. Hart Jr.), 1953, 2d edit. (with others), 1973; Principles, Politics and Fundamental Law, 1961; The Nationalization of Civil Liberties and Civil Rights, 1969. Home: 179 E 70th St New York NY 10021 Office: Box 36 435 W 116th St New York NY 10027

WECHSLER, NANCY FRAENKEL, lawyer; b. N.Y.C., Dec. 12, 1916; d. Osmond Kessler and Helene (Esberg) Fraenkel; B.A., Barnard Coll., 1937; LL.B. (James Kent scholar), Columbia U., 1940; m. James A. Wechsler, Oct. 4, 1934; children—Michael (dec.), Holly Wechsler Schwartztol. Admitted to N.Y. bar, 1941, U.S. Supreme Ct. bar, 1948; asso. firm Hays, St. John, Abramson & Schulman, 1940-41; asso. Bd. Econ. Welfare, Office Price Adminstrn., Office Econ. Stblzn., Office War Moblzn. and Reconversion and Labor Dept., 1942-48; counsel Pres.'s Com. on Civil Rights, 1946-47; asso. firm Greenbaum, Wolff & Ernst, N.Y.C., 1955-68, partner, 1968—. Bd. dirs. ACLU, N.Y.C., 1964-67, Nat., 1978—. Recipient Ordronaux prize Columbia U. Law Sch., 1940. Mem. Am. Bar Assn. (governing bd., forum com. on sports and entertainment industries), Assn. Bar City N.Y. (communications law com.), Am. Law Inst., Alumni Columbia Law Sch. (asso.), Barnard Coll. Alumnae Assn. (trustee 1971-74), Copyright Soc. U.S.A. (trustee 1973-77), Women's Media Group. Contbr. articles on lit. property, reproductive freedom to profl. jours.; editorial bd. Columbia U. Law Rev., 1938-40. Office: 437 Madison Ave New York NY 10022

WECHT, CYRIL HARRISON, educator, coroner Allegheny County (Pa.); b. Pitts., Mar. 20, 1931; s. Nathan and Fannie W.; B.S. cum laude, U. Pitts., 1952, M.D., 1956, J.D., 1962; LL.B., U. Md., 1962; m. Sigrid Ronsdal, Oct. 20, 1961; children—David, Daniel, Benjamin, Ingrid. Intern, St. Francis Gen. Hosp. and Rehab. Inst., Pitts., 1956-57; resident pathology VA Hosp., Pitts., 1957-59; research fellow forensic pathology, asso. pathologist Office Chief Med. Examiner, Balt., 1961-62; pathologist N. Charles Gen. Hosp., Balt., 1961-62; acting chief lab. service Leech Farm VA Hosp., Pitts., 1962-64; admitted to Pa. bar, 1963; dir. Pitts. Pathology and Toxicology Lab., 1964—; pathologist Charleroi-Monessen (Pa.) Hosp., 1964-65; asst. dist. atty., med. legal adviser to dist. atty. Allegheny County (Pa.), 1964-65; asso. pathologist St. Clair Meml. Hosp., Pitts., 1966-68; coroner Allegheny County, 1969—; teaching fellow pathology U. Pitts. Sch. Medicine, 1957-59, mem. faculty legal medicine anf forensic pathology, 1962—, clin. asso. prof. pathology Sch. Medicine and Sch. Dentistry, 1973—, adj. asso. prof. epidemiology Grad. Sch. Public Health; mem. faculty Duquesne U. Sch. Law, 1962-78, research prof. law, 1964-78 dir. Inst. Forensic Scis., 1964-78, adj. prof. pathology Sch. Pharmacy. Trustee Pitts. chpt. Am. Jewish Com., Jewish Chronicle; bd. dirs. YM-YWHA Assn., Pitts. dist. United Cerebral Palsy Assn., Nat. Com. Labor Israel, Squirrel Hill Urban Coalition, St. John's Hosp. Spl. Drug Treatment Unit. Served as capt. MC USAF, 1959-61. Diplomate Am. Bd. Pathology. Fellow Am. Acad. Compensation Medicine, Coll. Am. Pathologists, Am. Soc. Clin. Pathologists, Am. Acad. Forensic Scis. (pres. 1971-72), Law-Sci. Acad. Am. (vice-chancellor, trustee 1966-70), Internat. Acad. Law and Sci. (regent 1966-69), Am. Coll. Legal Medicine (pres. 1969-72), Am. Soc. Law and Medicine (hon.), French, Spanish, Belgian, Mexican, Columbian nat. socs. legal medicine (hon.); mem. Pa. Med. Soc., A.M.A., Pitts. Pathology Soc., Balt. Pathology Soc., Pa. Acad. Sci., Pa. Assn. Clin. Pathologists (co-chmn. legis. com. 1965-66), Pitts. Acad. Medicine, Pitts. Med. Forum, AAAS, Pan-Am. Med. Assn., Allegheny Council Emergency Medicine and Health Services (dir.), Pa., Allegheny County (chmn. med.-legal com. 1974-78), Fed. (chmn. tort sect. Pitts. 1967) bar assns., Assn. Trial Lawyers Am. (chmn. com. liaison with med. assns.), Am. Judicature Soc., Am. Arbitration Assn., Assn. Trial Lawyers Criminal Ct. Allegheny County, Nat. Soc. Hosp. Attys., Soc. Legal Writers, Allegheny County Med. Soc. (chmn. med.-legal com. 1971-72), Internat. Assn. Forensic Scis. (v.p. 1975-78), Nat. Assn. Med. Examiners (dir.), Am. Assn. Automotive Medicine, Am. Soc. Testing and Materials (chmn. com. forensic scis.), British Acad. Forensic Scis., Forensic Soc. Eng., Pitts. Inst. Legal Medicine (dir.), Internat. Acad. Legal Medicine and Social Medicine (v.p.), Internat. Assn. Accident and Traffic Medicine (sec. gen. 1966-69, v.p. 1969-72). Author: numerous articles; editor: Legal Medicine Annual; Legal Aspects of Medical Practice; mem. editorial bds. in field. Home: 5420 Darlington Rd Pittsburgh PA 15217 Office: 542 4th Av Pittsburgh PA 15219

WECHTER, VIVIENNE THAUL, artist; b. N.Y.C.,; d. Samuel Joshua and Hilda (Thaul) Rosenthal; b. Pedagogy, Jamaica Tchrs. Coll.; postgrad. Columbia U., N.Y. U., New Sch. for Social Research, Art Students League, Sculpture Center, Pratt Inst. Graphic Center; Ph.D. in Interarts and Psychology of Creativity, Union Grad. Sch.; m. Nathan Wechter; 1 dau., Robyrta Joan Wechter Rapoport. One woman shows: Castellane Gallery, East Hampton Gallery, N.Y.C., Cornell U., Ithaca, N.Y., Neville Pub. Mus., Green Bay, Wis., Nashville Fine Arts Center, Fairleigh Dickinson U., Rutgers U., Waterloo (Iowa) Municipal Galleries, Bodley Gallery, Gloria Cortella Gallery, N.Y.C., Everson Mus. Art, Syracuse, N.Y., B.R. Kornblatt Gallery, Balt., also Paris, Rejik, Yugoslavia, multimedia show Everson Mus. Fine Art, Syracuse, 1979; represented in permanent collection Corcoran Gallery, Washington, Houston Mus. Fine Arts, Jewish Mus. N.Y.C., Fordham U., N.Y.C., Univ. Art Museum Berkeley, Calif., Museum Art and Sci., Norfolk, Va., N.Y. U., Ohio State U., Phoenix Mus. Fine Arts, Fairleigh Dickinson U., Madison, N.J., UN, and others; monumental outdoor sculpture The Emerging Sun commd. for Manhattan Psychiat. Center, Ward's Island, N.Y.C.; artist in residence Fordham U., 1964—, asst. prof. art and esthetics, 1964, now prof. interdisciplinary creative arts, chmn. acquisitions and exhbns.; vis. poet-artist Kansas City Art Inst., 1975, Md. Inst. Coll. Art, 1975, New Sch., N.Y.C., 1976, Marist Coll., Poughkeepsie, N.Y., 1977; moderator weekly radio broadcast Today's World, WFUV, 1951—; past chmn. coll. liaison div. Bronx Council on Arts. Bd. dirs. Urban Arts Corps; founder, trustee, past pres. Bronx Mus. Art. Recipient awards Am. Acad. Arts and Letters, Am. Soc. Contemporary Art. Mem. AAUP, Coll. Art Assn., Artists Equity Assn., Am. Soc. Contemporary Artists, Urban League Center Grater N.Y. (dir.; mem. advisory bd. 1952—), United World Federalists (1st chmn.), Fedn. Modern Painters and Sculptors (v.p.), Alpha Mu Gamma, Kappa Pi. Illustrator book cover Park of Jonas (Alfeo Marzi), 1965; author: A View from the Ark, 1973; contbr. articles to profl. jours. Home: 4525 Henry Hudson Pky New York NY 10071. *To be an artist-poet who requires solitude in order to create yet has the urgent need to be actively involved in the human community is a frightening challenge. Yet I know that to live one without the other will be for me, neither.*

WECKESSER, ERNEST PROSPER, JR., publisher, educator; b. Akron, Ohio, Mar. 23, 1933; s. Ernest Prosper and Sadie (Liken) W.; B.A., Bowling Green State U., 1955, M.A., 1960; Ph.D., Mich. State U., 1963; m. Mary B. Hunter, Jan. 12, 1959; children—Jeffrey, Franz, Kathleen, Lynne. Asst. prof. speech State U. N.Y. at Oneonta, 1962-63, Kent State U., 1963-64; mem. faculty Purdue U., 1964-70, asso. prof., 1968-70; prof. speech Montclair Coll., 1970-; asso. prof. speech Pa. State U., 1971-72; dir. Ernest Weckesser Assos.; chmn. bd. dirs. Green Tree Press, Inc., Dunkirk, N.Y.; pres. Bierhaus Internat., Inc., Erie, Pa. Bd. dirs. Florerence Crittenden Home, Erie. Served to capt. USAF, 1955-59. Mem. Speech Communication Assn. Author: The Radio Rhetoric of John L. Lewis, 1963; How To Succeed in College, 1971; The 12,000 Housewife, 1975; Dollars in Your Mailbox, 1975. Home: 5370 Wolf Rd Erie PA 16505

WECKSTEIN, DONALD THEODORE, univ. dean; b. Newark, Mar. 15, 1932; B.B.A., U. Wis., 1954; J.D., U. Tex., 1958; LL.M., Yale U., 1959. Admitted to Tex. bar, 1957; adminstrv. practice law, Newark, 1958; asst. prof. U. Conn., 1959-62; asso. prof. law U. Tenn., 1962-66, prof., 1966-67; prof. law U. Conn., 1967-72; prof. law, dean Sch. of Law, U. San Diego, 1972—; cons. in field. Mem. Am., Tex., San Diego bar assns., Motor Carrier Lawyers Assn., Am. Law Inst., Assn. Am. Law Schs. (sect. chmn.), Am. Arbitration Assn. (panel), AAUP, ACLU, Indsl. Relations Research Assn. Editor Education in the Professional Responsibilities of the Lawyer, 1970; author: (with J. W. Moore and others) Moore's Federal Practice, 1948—; contbr. articles to law revs. Home: 8685 Nottingham Pl LaJolla CA 92037 Office: U San Diego Sch Law Alcala Park San Diego CA 92110

WECLEW, THADDEUS VICTOR, dentist; b. Chgo., Oct. 7, 1906; s. Victor Thomas and Mary Mae (Tadrowski) W.; D.D.S., U. Ill., 1930; m. Marguerite Helen Pfister, Jan. 1931 (dec. Jan. 1964); 1 dau., Marilyn Dootson Storm; m. 2d, Priscilla Joan Glenicki, Jan. 2, 1965; Pvt. practice dentistry, Chgo., 1930—; asso. prof. U. Ill. Dental Coll.; founder Acad. Gen. Dentistry, Acad. Continuing Edn. Bd. dirs. Ill. Good Govt. Inst., 1950—. Served with USCG, 1945. Named Distinguished Alumnus U. Ill., 1969; officer Ordre Palmes Académique, French Govt., 1976. Fellow Acad. Gen. Dentistry (pres. emeritus 1965; Master), Am. Coll. Dentistry, Acad. Dentistry Internat. (hon.), Internat. Coll. Dentistry; mem. ADA, Ill Good Govt. Inst., U. Ill. Dental Alumni Assn. (pres. 1967), Chgo., Dental Soc. (dir. 1969-73), Psi Omega, Omicron Kappa Upsilon. Roman Catholic. Founder, editor Acad. Gen. Dentistry Jour., 1952-74, editor emeritus, 1974—, exec. dir., 1965-69. Contbr. articles to profl. jours. Home: 6423 N Nokomis St Chicago IL 60646 Office: 6007 N Sauganash Chicago IL 60646

WEDDIG, LEE J(OHN), trade assn. exec.; b. Fon du Lac, Wis., Sept. 22, 1935; s. Edward K. and Rose M. Weddig; B.S. in Journalism, Marquette U., 1956; m. June M. Hennig, Jan. 28, 1956; children—Andrew J., Lisa M. Reporter, UP, Milw., 1956, Fairchild Publs., Chgo., 1957; nat. merchandising mgr. Motorola, Inc., Chgo., 1957-67; exec. dir. Nat. Fisheries Inst., Washington, 1967-73, exec. v.p., 1975—; pres. C.L. Watt, Inc., and Fin. Mgmt. Services, Inc., Dayton, Ohio, 1973-74; v.p., dir. Smith Bucklin & Assos., Chgo. and Washington; mem. marine fisheries adv. com. Dept. Commerce Mem. Am. Soc. Assn. Execs. Republican. Roman Catholic. Club: Internat. Office: 1101 Connecticut Ave NW Suite 700 Washington DC 20036

WEDDINGTON, SARAH RAGLE, lawyer, govt. ofcl.; b. Abilene, Tex., Feb. 5, 1945; d. Herbert Doyle and Lena Catherine (Morrison) Ragle; B.S., magna cum laude, McMurry Coll., 1965; LL.B., U. Tex. at Austin, 1967. Admitted to Tex. bar, 1967; individual practice law, Austin, 1967-77; gen. counsel Dept. Agr., Washington, 1977-79; spl. asst. to Pres., Washington, 1979—, chmn. Interdepartmental Task Force on Women. Mem. Tex. Ho. of Reps., 1972-77. Recipient Woman of Year award Tex. Womens Polit. Caucus, 1973. Mem. Am., Tex. bar assns., Nat. Orgn. Women, AAUW, Womens Equity Action League. Office: White House Washington DC 20500

WEDDLE, STEPHEN SHIELDS, mfg. co. exec.; b. Boston, Nov. 9, 1938; s. Harold Mansfield and Esther Letha (Bales) W.; A.B., Harvard, 1960; LL.B., Columbia, 1963; m. Meredith Baldwin, June 10, 1961; children—Christopher, Timothy, Justin, Jamien. Admitted to N.Y. bar, 1966; lectr. in law (supported by Ford Found. Project for Staffing African Instns. for Legal Edn. and Research) Ahmadu Bello U., Zaria, Nigeria, 1963-65; asso. firm Debevoise, Plimpton, Lyons & Gates, N.Y.C., 1965-71; corporate counsel Technicon Corp., Tarrytown, N.Y., 1971-74, sec., 1972-78, sr. v.p., gen. counsel, 1974-78; v.p., gen. counsel Stanley Works, New Britain, Conn., 1978—. Mem. Assn. Bar City N.Y. (sec. com. on fgn. and comparative law 1968-70), Am., Conn., N.Y. bar assns., Am. Soc. Corp. Secs. Mem. Soc. of Friends. Office: 195 Lake St New Britain CT 06050

WEDEL, CYNTHIA CLARK, civic worker; b. Dearborn, Mich., Aug. 26, 1908; d. Arthur Pierson and Elizabeth (Haigh) Clark; B.A., Northwestern U., 1929, M.A., 1930; Ph.D. in Psychology, George Washington U., 1957; L.H.D., Western Coll. Women, 1958, Elmhurst Coll., 1970, Moravian Coll., 1971, Fordham U., 1971, Smith Coll., 1972, Miami U., 1976; D.D., Gen. Theol. Sem., 1976, Bridgewater Coll., 1976; m. Theodore O. Wedel, May 4, 1939 (dec. July 1970). Profl. ch. work Episcopal Ch., 1931-39; tchr. Nat. Cathedral Sch., 1939-48; nat. exec. bd. Woman's Aux., Episcopal Ch., 1946-52, mem. nat. council Episcopal Ch., 1955-62; asst. gen. sec. Nat. Council Chs., 1962-65, asso. gen. sec., 1965-69; asso. dir. Center for a Vol. Soc., 1969-74; lectr. Am. U., 1958-60. Cons. Office Vols. A.R.C., nat. chmn. vols., 1973—; nat. bd. Girl Scouts U.S.A., 1960-66; mem. President's Commn. on Status of Women, 1961-63, Citizen's Adv. Council Status Women, 1963-68; pres. World Council of Chs., 1975—. Mem. United Ch. Women (nat. pres. 1955-58), Nat. Council Chs. gen. bd. 1954-62; v.p. 1957-60, pres. 1969-72), Am. Psychol. Assn., Nat. Urban Coalition (exec. com.), Common Cause, Phi Beta Kappa, Kappa Delta. Episcopalian. Author: Citizenship, Our Christian Concern, 1952; The Glorious Liberty, 1958; Employed Women and the Church, 1959; (with Janet Tulloch) Happy Issue, 1962; Faith or Fear and Future Shock, 1974; also articles in mags. Home: 4800 Fillmore Ave Alexandria VA 22311 Office: ARC 17th and D St NW Washington DC 20006

WEDEL, PAUL GEORGE, hosp. adminstr.; b. Elizabeth, N.J., Jan. 1, 1927; s. Paul John and Helen (Cleary) W.; grad. Peddie Sch., Hightstown, N.J., 1944; B.S. in Bus. Adminstrn., Am. U., 1952; M.S. in Hosp. Adminstrn., Northwestern U., 1955; m. Jean Marie Martin, June 18, 1949; children—Dana Lyn, Laurie Ann Wedel Musser, Paul John II, Kurt Frederick. Adminstrv. resident Harrisburg (Pa.) Polyclinic Hosp., 1953-54; asst. adminstr. Williamsport (Pa.) Hosp., 1954-59, adminstr., 1959-64; pres. Lancaster (Pa.) Gen. Hosp., 1964—. Bd. dirs. Inter-County Hospitalization Plan, Inc., 1966—, James Buchanan Found., Preservation Wheatland, 1968—; sr. warden St. Thomas Episcopal Ch. Served with USNR, 1944-46, 5O-51. Named Outstanding Young Man, Williamsport Jr. C. of C., 1957. Fellow Am. Coll. Hosp. Adminstrs.; mem. Am. Hosp. Assn., Hosp. Assn. Pa. (bd. dirs. 1970-73, Lancaster Assn. Commerce and Industry (bd. dirs.). Clubs: Rotary (pres. 1978-79), Masons, Hamilton. Home: 203 Riveredge Dr Rock Rimmon Ridges RD1 Leola PA 17540 Office: 555 N Duke St Lancaster PA 17604

WEDEMEYER, ALBERT COADY, ret. army officer, industrialist, author; b. Omaha, July 9, 1897; s. Albert Anthony and Margaret E. (Coady) W.; B.S., U.S. Mil. Acad., 1919; grad. Gen. Staff Sch., Ft. Leavenworth, 1936, German War Coll., Berlin, 1938; LL.D., Rollins Coll., DePauw U., U. Pa., Creighton U., U. San Francisco, U. So. Calif.; L.H.D., Temple U.; Ph.D., China Acad.; m. Elizabeth Dade

Embick, Feb. 5, 1925; children—Albert Dunbar, Robert Dade. Commd. 2d lt. U.S. Army, 1919, advanced through grades to gen., 1954; served, India, China, Philippines, Europe, War Dept. Gen. Staff, 1941-43; comdr. China Theater, 1944-46, also chief staff to Generalissimo Chiang Kai-Shek; made survey for Pres. U.S., rank of ambassador, China and Korea, 1947; comdg. gen. 2d Army, 1946-47; dir. plans and ops. div. G.S., 1947-48; dep. chief of staff for plans and combat ops. Gen. Staff, 1948; comdg. gen. 6th Army, Presidio, San Francisco, 1949-51; ret. from active service, 1951; v.p., dir. Avco Mfg. Corp., 1951-54, Rheem Mfg. Co., 1954-56; dir. Nat. Airlines, Inc. Decorated D.S.M. with 2 clusters, D.F.C., Comdr. of the Bath (Brit.), White Sun and Blue Sky (China), Grand Cross, Order of Phoenix (Greece), Polania Restitude Comdrs. Cross (Poland), Order of Mil. Merit (Brazil). Clubs: Army and Navy, Chevy Chase (Washington); Bohemian (San Francisco); Metropolitan, Dutch Treat (N.Y.C.). Author: Wedemeyer Reports. Home: Friends Advice Boyds MD 20720 also Metropolitan Club New York NY 10023. *Ever loyal to friend and principle but devoid of arrogance.*

WEDGEWORTH, ANN, actress; b. Abilene, Tex., Jan. 21; attended U. Tex.; B.A. in Drama, So. Methodist U.; m. Rip Torn (div.); 1 child, Danae; m. 2d, Ernest Martin; 1 dau., Dianna. Broadway debut in Make A Million, 1958; other Broadway appearances: Thieves, Blues for Mr. Charlie, The Last Analysis, Chapter Two (Tony award); off-Broadway appearances: Chapparal, The Crucible, Days and Nights of Beebee Fenstermaker, Ludlow Fair, Line; toured with nat. cos. of The Sign in Sidney Brustein's Window and Kennedy's Children; appeared in TV series: The Edge of Night, Another World, Somerset, Three's Company; other TV appearances: The Defenders, Bronk, All That Glitters; TV film The War Between the Tates; movies: Thieves, Bang the Drum Slowly, Scarecrow, Catamount Killing, Law and Disorder, Dragon-Fly, Birch Intervals, Handle With Care (Nat. Soc. Film Critics award). Office: care ABC Public Relations 1330 Ave of Americas New York NY 10019*

WEDGEWORTH, ROBERT, JR., assn. exec.; b. Ennis, Tex., July 31, 1937; s. Robert and Jimmie (Johnson) W.; A.B., Wabash Coll., 1959; M.S., U. Ill., 1961; Litt. D., Park Coll., 1973; m. Chung Kyun, July 28, 1972; 1 dau., Cicely Veronica. Cataloger, Kansas City Pub. Library, 1961-62; asst. librarian, acting librarian Park Coll., Parkville, Mo., 1962-64; librarian Meramec Community Coll., Kirkwood, Mo., 1964-66; acquisitions librarian Brown U. Library, 1966-69; asst. prof. Rutgers U., 1971-72; exec. dir. Am. Library Assn., Chgo., 1972—; mem. Nat. Commn. on New Technol. Uses of Copyrighted Works, 1975-78; mem. biomed. library rev. com. Nat. Library Medicine, 1975-78, chmn., 1978-79; mem. network adv. com. Library of Congress, 1977—, nat. adv. bd., exec. com. Center for Book, 1978—. Chmn. U.S. Nat. Com. for UNESCO PGI; bd. dirs. Newberry Library, Public Service Satellite Consortium; bd. visitors U. Pitts. Libraries, Air U.; adv. council Princeton U.; alumni bd. Wabash Coll. Council on Library Resources fellow, 1969. Mem. ALA, Am. Soc. Info. Sci., Am. Assn. Advancement Humanities (dir. 1978—). Editor: Library Resources and Tech. Services, 1971-73; editor-in-chief ALA Yearbook, ALA Ency. Home: 2626 N Lakeview St Chicago IL 60614 Office: 50 E Huron St Chicago IL 60611

WEDGWOOD, RALPH JOSIAH PATRICK, pediatrician, educator; b. London, Eng., May 25, 1924; s. Josiah and Dorothy Mary (Winser) W.; came to U.S., 1940, naturalized, 1951; M.D., Harvard, 1947; m. Virginia Lloyd Hunt, Oct. 25, 1943; children—Josiah Francis, James Cecil (dec.), Jeffrey Galton, John Christopher Ralph. Intern pediatrics Bellevue Hosp., N.Y.C., 1947-48, resident, 1948-49; research fellow pediatrics Harvard Med. Sch., 1949-51; sr. instr. pediatrics and biochemistry Western Res. U. Med. Sch., 1953-57, asst. prof. pediatrics and preventive medicine, 1957-62; asso. prof. pediatrics U. Wash. Sch. Medicine, 1962-63, prof., 1963—, chmn. dept., 1963-72. Spl. cons., mem. gen. clin. research center com. NIH, 1962-66; mem. Nat. Adv. Research Resources Council, 1966-70; pres. Assn. Med. Sch. Pediatric Chairmen, 1966-68; chmn. Joint Council Nat. Pediatric Socs., 1967-69; mem. basic, clin. and behavioral research adv. coms. Nat. Found., 1969—; mem. sci. adv. bd. St. Jude Children's Research Hosp., Memphis, 1970-76. Served to capt. M.C., AUS, 1944-46, 51-53. Spl. USPHS research fellow Microbiol. Research Establishment, Porton, Eng., 1960-61; John and Mary Markle scholar med. scis., 1960-65; vis. fellow St. John's Coll., Cambridge (Eng.) U., 1969-70. Distinguished service mem. Assn. Am. Med. Colls.; mem. numerous profl. socs. Editorial bd. Pediatrics, 1966-73. Contbr. numerous articles to profl. jours. Home: 3717 41st Ave NE Seattle WA 98105

WEDMAN, ELWOOD EDWARD, veterinarian; b. Harper, Kans., Aug. 22, 1922; s. Pete Edward and Ivah Ione W.; D.V.M., Kans. State U., 1941; M.P.H., U. Minn., 1958, Ph.D., 1964; m. Eula Rachel Jacob, June 1, 1946; children—Edward A., John C., Joel F. Practice vet. medicine, Kans., 1945-47; veterinarian in charge foot and mouth disease lab., Mexico City, 1947-49; veterinarian in charge Wichita Union Stockyards, 1952-54; research asso. U. Minn., 1954-58; staff veterinarian Agrl. Research Service, Washington, 1958-61; chief veterinarian Nat. Animal Disease Lab., Ames, Iowa, 1961-64; prof., asso. dir. Vet. Med. Research Inst., Ames, 1964-71; prof., head vet. medicine Oreg. State U., 1971-75, dean Sch. Vet. Medicine, 1975—; cons. U.S. Dept. Agr., Pan Am. Health Orgn. Served to capt. U.S. Army, 1950-52. Mem. Assn. Am. Vet. Med. Colls., Oreg. Vet. Med. Assn. (chmn. continuing edn. com. 1973-75), Oreg. Public Health Assn., Conf. Research Workers in Animal Diseases, AAAS, Am. Coll. Vet. Microbiologists (bd. govs. 1969-73, chmn. 1973), Am. Assn. Vet. Lab. Diagnosticians, U.S. Animal Health Assn., AVMA (council on research 1969-74), Alpha Zeta, Gamma Sigma Delta. Methodist. Contbr. articles to profl. jours. Home: 8100 NW Ridgewood Corvallis OR 97330 Office: Sch Veterinary Medicine Oregon State Univ Corvallis OR 97331

WEED, FREDERIC AUGUSTUS, educator; b. Potsdam, N.Y., Sept. 9, 1918; s. Frederic Barker and Marion Grace (Sisson) W.; B.A., N.Y. State Coll. for Tchrs., 1940; M.A., Columbia, 1941, J.D., 1948, Ph.D., 1949; m. Ruth Marjorie Head, Mar. 26, 1944: children—Mary Alison, Joseph Barker, Katherine Jane, Frederic Augustus. Tutor, Coll. City N.Y., 1946-48; instr., supr. social studies N.Y. State Coll. Tchrs., 1948-50; asst., then asso. prof. polit. sci. No. Ill. U., 1950-56; asst., asso. prof. polit. sci. San Jose State U., 1956-60, head dept. polit. sci. and pub. adminstrn., 1960-65, prof. polit. sci., 1965—, interim chmn. dept. polit. sci., 1970-71, coordinator internat. programs, 1971-73; Fulbright lectr. polit. sci. and Am. law, Lima, Peru, 1966-67; admitted to Calif. bar. Mem. DeKalb County Democratic Central Com., 1952-56, DeKalb City Council, 1954-56, Santa Clara County Dem. Central Com., 1958-64, 72-73. Served with AUS, 1942-45; lt. col. Res. (ret.). Mem. Am., Western, No. Calif. polit. sci. assns., NEA, Am. Soc. Internat. Law, Calif. Tchrs. Assn. Author: (with Dorothy B. Robins) The UN Story, 1947. Contbr. articles and book reviews to profl. publs. Home: 4225 Bloomfield Dr San Jose CA 95124

WEED, HERBERT M., metal co. exec.; b. Houghton, Mich., 1921; B.A., Washington and Lee U., 1942. With The Anaconda Co., N.Y.C., 1946—, v.p. mktg., 1966—; dir. Kawecki Berylco Ind., Brit. Am. Metals Co., Cuivre & Metaux Rares, Atomic Indsl. Forum. Served with USNR, 1942-46. Home: 3805 S Dahlia Englewood CO 80110 Office: 555 17th St Denver CO 80217

WEED, HERMAN ROSCOE, educator; b. Union City, Pa., Aug. 5, 1922; s. Roscoe Conklin and Leta Venettie (Bryner) W.; B.S. in Elec. Engring., Pa. State U., 1945; M.S. in Elec. Engring., Ohio State U., 1948; m. Sylvia Kathryn Yearick, Apr. 20, 1946; children—David Herman, Douglas Leonard, Kathryn Marie. Instr. elec. engring. Pa. State U., State College, 1943-46; instr. dept. elec. engring. Ohio State U., Columbus, 1946-49, asst. prof., 1949-55, asso. prof., 1955-59, prof., 1959—, dir., chmn. bio-med. engring. center, 1971—; cons., vis. prof. Punjab (India) Agrl. U., 1966, 72, 78, U. Cairo, 1977, 78, 79; vis. prof. U. Karlsruhe (W. Ger.), 1979; cons. in field. Chmn. task force assessment of indsl. activity in biomed. engring. Nat. Acad. Engring., 1969; chmn. Automation Research Council Group on Health Care. Recipient Top Ten Engring. Achievement award Nat. Soc. Profl. Engrs., 1971; Ronald E. Thompson award for meritorious achievement, 1970. Registered profl. engr., Ohio. Mem. IEEE, Am. Soc. Engring. Edn., Internat. Fedn. Automatic Control, Am. Automatic Control Council, Ohio Acad. Sci., Sigma Xi, Eta Kappa Nu (Disting. Teaching award 1965), Phi Kappa Phi, Tau Beta Pi (Robert M. Critchfield award for meritorious service 1973). Author: (with W.L. Davis) Industrial Electronic Engineering, 1953, Fundamentals of Electronic Devices and Circuits, 1959; asso. editor Automatica, 1969—; patentee in field. Home: 425 E Kanawsha Ave Columbus OH 43214

WEED, ITHAMAR DRYDEN, life ins. co. exec.; b. Pomeroy, Ohio, Sept. 3, 1914; s. Ithamar B. and Besse (Smith) W.; A.B., Ohio U., 1938; J.D. summa cum laude, Ohio State U., 1939; m. Sally Lemert, July 5, 1941; children—Judith Lynne (Mrs. G. Rodger Crowe), Charles Boyd, Donald Lemert. Admitted to Ohio bar, 1939; clk. U.S. Dist. Ct. So. Dist. Ohio, Columbus, 1939-41; asso. firm Vorys, Sater, Seymour and Pease, Columbus, 1946-54; asso. counsel Western and So. Life Ins. Co., Cin., 1954-63, v.p., chief counsel, 1963-73, sr. v.p., chief counsel, 1973—; sec., dir Eagle Savs. Assn., Cin., 1970—, West Ad, Inc., Cin., 1970—; lectr. Coll. Law, Ohio State U., 1949-53. Served to lt. col. AUS, 1941-46. Mem. Order of Coif, Beta Theta Pi, Phi Delta Pi. Home: 3753 Harvard Acres Cincinnati OH 45227 Office: 400 Broadway Cincinnati OH 45202

WEED, MAURICE JAMES, music educator, composer; b. Kalamazoo, Oct. 16, 1912; s. Frank Eugene and Ella May (Britton) W.; A.B., Western Mich. U., 1934; B.Mus., Eastman Sch. Music, U. Rochester, 1940, M.Mus., 1952, Ph.D., 1954; m. Berneice Laverne Pope, Aug. 23, 1937; children—Allison Gilbert (Mrs. Walter D. Herrick), Laurice Ellen (Mrs. Samuel L. Rich). Supr. instrumental music pub. schs., Ionia, Mich., 1934-36, Three Rivers, Mich., 1937-43; asst. prof. music, dir. instrumental music, tchr. music theory Ripon Coll., 1946-51; music teaching theory fellow Eastman Sch. Music, 1951-54, tchr., summer 1954; prof., head dept. music No. Ill. U., 1954-61, prof. music, 1961-74; adj. prof. music Western Carolina U., 1974-75; ret., 1975; composer in residence MacDowell Colony, 1961; performances include Serenity for Chamber Orch., Eastman-Rochester Symphony, 1953, Symphony Number 1, Nat. Symphony Orch., Washington, 1956, also Symphony of the Air, Carnegie Hall, 1957, Wonder of the Starry Night, 1st ann. symposium Contemporary Am. Music, U. Kans., 1959, Serenity and Fanfare for Two Trumpets and Organ, performed 8th ann. symposium Univ. Composers Exchange, Valparaiso, Ind., 1959, Sept. Cinquains for Soprano Voice and chamber instrumental group No. Ill. U., 1964, 67, Symphonie Breve, 9th ann. symposium Contemporary Am. Music U. Kans., 1964, Oklahoma City Symphony Orch. MBS broadcast, U. Redlands, Asheville (N.C.) Symphony Orch., 1979; condr. symposium of 8 sacred choral and 2 organ works by 6 coll., univ., high sch. and ch. choirs, Atlanta, 1975; Serenity, Asheville Symphony Orch., 1977. Recipient Benjamin award, 1954, 25th Anniv. award Nat. Symphony Orch., 1956, Ostwald award, 1959, J. Fisher & Bro. Centennial award, 1964, Pedro Paz award, 1966. Mem. Nat. Assn. Composers U.S.A., Am. Music Center, Music Edn. Nat. Conf., N.C. Music Educators, Am. Soc. Univ. Composers, A.S.C.A.P., Phi Mu Alpha. Methodist. Composer over 55 works including: Ships, Witchery (songs for soprano and piano), 1937; Rain, for contralto and piano, 1940; Three Preludes for Organ, 1945; Introduction and Scherzo, symphonic band, 1948; Gratitude, for contralto with organ, 1950; An After Easter Prayer, 1950: Serenity, for chamber orchestra, 1953; Wonder of the Starry Night, a capella choir, 1958; Symphonie Breve, 1959; Trio for violin, cello and piano, 1961: Concertino for cello and orch., 1962; Psalm XIII (mixed choir and organ), 1964; Hopkins Park, concert march, 1966; Triptych for Voices, a cappella choir, 1966; Vestigia Nulla Retrorsum, processional march, 1968; Praise Ye the Lord (mixed choir), 1968; A Wedding Song (soprano and organ), 1969; In the Midnight Hour (soprano and organ), 1970; In Te, Domini, Speravi (mixed choir), 1970; 4 Anthems for Mixed Choir, 1973; Postlude for Organ, 1974; The Catamounts, concert march for band, 1974; Duo for Viola and C Trumpet, 1977; Choral Fanfare No. 2, 1977; An Appalachian Celebration for Choir and Band, 1978; numerous others. Home: Rural Route 1 Box 641 Timberlane Rd Waynesville NC 28786

WEED, WILLIAM HENRY, advt. agy. exec.; b. Saginaw, Mich., Aug. 27, 1930; s. Rolland W. and Berenice (Hoheisel) W.; B.A., Carleton Coll., 1952; M.B.A., Harvard, 1954; m. Bette Bardsley, Dec. 5, 1969; children—William Henry, Elizabeth Bardsley. Brand mgr. toilet goods div. Procter & Gamble, Cin., 1955-59; with Ogilvy & Mather, N.Y.C., 1959—, exec. v.p., 1974—, now chmn. Europe, London; dir. Ogilvy & Mather Internat. Clubs: Univ., Harvard Bus. Sch. (N.Y.C.). Home: 16 Mallord St London SW3 England Office: Brettenham House Lancaster Pl London WC2 England

WEEDEN, ALAN NORMAN, investment banker; b. Oakland, Calif., May 16, 1924; s. Frank and Mabel (Henrickson) W.; B.A., Stanford, 1947; m. Barbara Elliott, Mar. 19, 1950; children—Donald Alan, Robert Elliott, Helen Leslie. With Weeden & Co. Inc., N.Y.C., 1949-79, v.p., 1958-66, pres., 1967-76, chmn. exec. com., 1977-79; now v.p., dir. Moseley, Hallgarten, Estabrook & Weeden Holding Co., N.Y.C. Mem. Mcpl. Securities Rulemaking Bd.; trustee Stanford U. Served to lt. (j.g.) USNR, 1943-46. Club: Explorers. Home: Upper Dogwood Ln Rye NY Office: One New York Plaza New York NY 10004

WEEDEN, MORRIS SKIFF, pharm. co. exec.; b. Syracuse, N.Y., Dec. 25, 1919; s. Walter Longfellow and Emma Loomis (Skiff) W.; A.B., Syracuse U., 1941; M.B.A., Harvard U., 1943; m. Jane Alys Senter, Oct. 14, 1944; children—Anna N., Charles S., Jane M., Robert R. With Bristol Labs. div. Bristol-Myers Co., Syracuse, 1946-72, treas., 1951-62, v.p., 1962-65, exec. v.p., 1965-68, pres., 1968-72; pres. Norwich Internat. div. Morton-Norwich Products, Inc., Chgo., 1973-75; group v.p. Morton Norwich Products, Inc., 1975-77, exec. v.p., 1977—. Trustee, Syracuse U., 1969—. Served to capt. U.S. Army, 1943-46. Decorated Army Commendation Ribbon. Mem. Pharm. Mfrs. Assn., Proprietary Assn. (dir.), Syracuse U. Alumni Assn. (pres. 1969-73). Republican. Episcopalian. Club: Onwentsia (Lake Forest, Ill.). Home: 5 E Laurel Ave Lake Forest IL 60045 Office: Morton Norwich Products Inc 110 N Wacker Dr Chicago IL 60606

WEEDON, WILLIAM STONE, educator; b. Wilmington, Del., July 5, 1908; s. William S. and Mary Covington (Brown) W.; B.S., U. Va., 1929, M.S., 1931, Ph.D., 1936; M.A., Harvard, 1933; M.A., Wesleyan U., 1962; m. Elizabeth duPont Bayard, June 25, 1934; children—Ellen B., Mary C., Elizabeth B., Jennifer M.E. Asst. math. U. Va., 1929-30, instr. philosophy, 1934-39, asst. prof., 1939-46, asso. prof., 1946-52, prof. philosophy, 1952-61, chmn. Corcoran dept. philosophy, 1954-61, chmn. liberal arts seminars, 1956-59, mem. univ. senate, 1955-58, 59-61, 65-68, 73-77, pres. Assembly of Profs., 1964-70; vis. prof. philosophy Wesleyan U., Middletown, Conn., 1959, William Griffin prof. philosophy, chmn. dept., 1961-63; Univ. prof. U. Va., 1963-79, Univ. prof. emeritus, 1979—; vis. prof. philosophy U. Tex., Austin, 1968; chmn. bd. Va. Metalcrafters, Inc., 1964-71, Sprigg Lane Investment Corp., 1971—. Cons. Dept. Def. Pres. Ellen Bayard Weedon Found.; mem. bd. U. Va. Press, Va. Center for Creative Arts; fellow Va. Mus. Fine Arts. Served from lt. (s.g.) to comdr. USNR, 1942-46, 50-52; capt. Res., 1959-68. Decorated Bronze Star; recipient Raven award U. Va., 1959, Algernon Sydney Sullivan award, 1961, Thomas Jefferson award, 1976, Disting. Tchr. award, 1978. Mem. Am., Va. (pres. 1957) philos. assns., So. Soc. Philosophy and Psychology (pres. 1956), Metaphys. Soc. Am. (councillor), Raven Soc., Phi Beta Kappa, Omicron Delta Kappa. Clubs: Lotus (N.Y.C.); Colonnade (U. Va.). Adv. bd. Va. Quar. Rev., 1953-61, chmn., 1963-79; editorial bd. Philosophy East and West, Insight. Home: 214 Sprigg Ln Charlottesville VA 22903

WEEGAR, EDWIN ALEXANDER, JR., newspaperman; b. Riverside, Calif., July 21, 1921; s. Edwin Alexander and Hannah Elizabeth (McDonald) W.; B.J., U. Mo., 1947; m. Freda Jean Elmore, Jan. 19, 1951; children—Sally Diane, Donald Elmore, Molly Ann. With Pomona (Calif.) Progress-Bull., 1947, Covina (Calif.) Argus-Citizen, 1948-50, Riverside Daily Press, 1950-51, San Diego Evening Tribune, 1951-53; mem. staff Los Angeles Times, 1953—, telegraph and news editor, 1955-60, acting chief Washington bur., 1963, nat. editor, 1963-64, asst. mng. editor, 1964-69, mng. editor Orange County edit., 1968-70, asst. mng. editor, 1970—; lectr. journalism U. Calif. at Los Angeles, 1961-62. Adv. com. LaVerne U., Mt. San Antonio Coll. Served with AUS, World War II; PTO. Decorated Bronze Star, Combat Inf. badge. Mem. U. Mo. Journalism Alumni (nat. pres. 1974-76), Pi Kappa Alpha. Republican. Presbyn. Home: 333 S Grand Ave West Covina CA 91791 Office: 202 W 1st St Los Angeles CA 90053

WEEKES, MICHAEL MANNING, lawyer; b. Leon, Iowa, July 12, 1938; s. Pearl Wilson and Marie Arvilla (Manning) W.; B.S., Drake U., 1960, J.D., 1963. Admitted to Iowa bar, 1963, Calif. bar, 1964, U.S. Dist. Ct. bar, 1964, U.S. Ct. Appeals bar, 1966, U.S. Supreme Ct. bar, 1973; practiced law, Los Angeles, 1964-76; asso. firm Dillavou & Cox (later Dillavou, Cox, Castle & Nicholson), Los Angeles, 1964-68, Cox, Castle & Nicholson, Los Angeles, 1968-71; partner Cox, Castle, Nicholson & Weekes, Los Angeles, 1972-76; lectr. Christian Legal Soc., 1977-78, Oral Roberts U., 1978. Bd. dirs. Hollywood Presbyn. Med. Center, Los Angeles, 1976—. Mem. Calif., Iowa bar assns., Beta Gamma Sigma, Delta Theta Phi. Presbyn. Author Manual for Application of Uniform Commercial Code for Surety Industry, 1964; editor Words to Live By, 1969, Bible Riches, 1970. Home: 691 S Irolo St Los Angeles CA 90005. *Success is a word of measurement. The true criterion is how we have been able to serve God and man, according to God's will. I have found that, whatever be the field of endeavor, no power to achieve can truly be effective, apart from Christ and the Holy Spirit.*

WEEKS, CHARLES CARSON, steel co. exec.; b. Sault Ste. Marie, Ont., Can., June 19, 1914; s. Charles Alexander and Stella Mabel (Watson) W.; grad. high sch.; m. Mildred Frances See, Jan 2, 1936; 1 dau., Mildred Sharon. With Algoma Steel Corp., Ltd., Sault Ste. Marie, Ont., 1937—, mgr. sales, 1948-57, v.p. sales, 1957-73, sr. v.p., 1973—. Bd. dirs. Canadian Steel Industries Constrn. Council. Mem. Am., Internat. iron and steel insts., Internat. Pig Iron Secretariat, Can. Mfrs. Assn. (dir.). Home: 8 Summit Ave Sault Ste Marie ON P6B 2S1 Canada Office: Algoma Steel Corp Ltd Sault Ste Marie ON Canada

WEEKS, DAVID FRANK, found. exec.; b. Salt Lake City, Sept. 9, 1926; s. Frank Harold and Myrtle June (Larsen) W.; student So. Meth. U., 1945, U. Tex., 1946; B.S. (Union Pacific Carl Raymond Gray scholar), U. Idaho, 1949; m. Betty Alice Tellin, Aug. 14, 1949; children—David Rice, Clayton Frank. Pres., Asso. Students U. Idaho, 1948-49; announcer Sta. KBIO, Burley, Idaho, 1949; Idaho rep. Nat. Found. for Infantile Paralysis, Boise, 1949-53, asst. to nat. dir. fund raising, N.Y.C., 1953-57; asst. nat. dir. March of Dimes, N.Y.C., 1957-59; account exec. Kersting, Brown & Co., N.Y.C., 1959-61; exec. dir. Research to Prevent Blindness, Inc., N.Y.C., 1961-70, exec. v.p., 1970—; mem. borough council Borough of Ho-Ho-Kus (N.J.), 1966-68, mayor, 1968-75; consumer rep. subcom. ophthalmic prostheses HEW, 1976—, cons. Bur. Med. Devices, FDA, 1977—. Mem. Ho-Ho-Kus Planning Bd., 1962-65, chmn., 1965; mem. Zoning Bd., 1975—; mem. Bergen County (N.J.) Ethics Bd., 1977—. Served with USN, 1944-46. Recipient Bronze Palm Eagle Scout award Boy Scouts Am.,1941, Distinguished Pub. Service award Am. Acad. Ophthalmology and Otolaryngology, 1976; named Ky. col., 1969. Mem. Assn. Research in Vision and Ophthalmology (hon.), Pan Am. Opthalmol. Assn. (asso.), Am. Soc. Assn. Execs., Bergen County Mayors Assn. (pres. 1975-77), Soc. Valley Hosp., Am. Tentative Soc. (treas. and trustee 1974—). Republican. Club: Met. (N.Y.C.). Home: 8 Brookview Ct Ho-Ho-Kus NJ 07423 Office: 598 Madison Ave New York City NY 10022

WEEKS, DAVID LEE, educator; b. Boone, Iowa, June 24, 1930; s. Leo Elliott and Gretchen Gertrude (Kiefer) W.; B.S., Okla. A. and M. Coll., 1952; M.S., Okla. State U., 1957, Ph.D., 1959; m. Shirley Bea Vaden, June 2, 1957; children—Robert David, Steven Elliott, Jennifer Lea, Derek Clinton. Asst. prof. Okla. State U., Stillwater, 1959-61, asso. prof., 1961-67, prof. statistics, 1967—; cons. Phillips Petroleum Co., 1961—; vis. prof. N.Mex. State U., Las Cruces, 1976-77; gen. engr. U.S. Air Force Armament Lab., Eglin AFB, Fla., summers 1969-73. Served with AUS, 1952-54. NSF faculty fellow, 1967-68. Mem. Am. Statis. Assn., Biometric Soc., Sigma Xi, Phi Kappa Phi. Lutheran (pres. 1964-65, supt. Sunday sch. 1965-67). Home: 71 University Circle Stillwater OK 74074

WEEKS, FRANCIS WILLIAM, educator; b. E. Orange, N.J., Jan. 26, 1916; s. Caleb Ora and Daisy (Tack) W.; B.A. with honors, Swarthmore Coll., 1937; A.M., Columbia, 1939; m. Dorothy Anne Skiles, July 23, 1942; children—Hilda Jean, Alice Anne, Virginia Lueze, Sara Elizabeth, Marjorie Estelle, Cynthia Grace, Janet Christine. Mem. faculty U. Ill., 1939—, prof. bus. and tech. writing, chmn. div., 1963—; vis. prof. bus. communication U. Houston, 1967-68. Fellow Am. Bus. Communication Assn. (exec. dir., treas.); mem. Nat. Council Tchrs. English, Soc. Tech. Communication, Ill. Interfrat. Alumni Assn. (pres. 1967), Am. Soc. Tng. and Devel. (v.p. central Ill. 1975-76), Japan Bus. English Assn. (hon.), Phi Sigma Kappa (dir. Ill. assn. 1962-71, pres. 1964-66, nat. v.p. scholarship 1965-70, nat. chmn. scholarship 1974, trustee Phi Sigma Kappa Found.), Alpha Kappa Psi. Club: Rotary (pres. Urbana 1978). Author: (with C.R. Anderson) Business Reports, 1957; Principles of Business Communication, 1973; (with R.A. Hatch) Business Writing Cases and Problems, 1977. Editor: Readings in Communication from Fortune, 1961; Jour. Bus. Communication, 1963-64. Home: 713 W Washington St Urbana IL 61801

WEEKS, JOHN WINGATE, museum exec.; b. Newton, Mass., June 12, 1920; s. Sinclair and Beatrice (Dowse) W.; grad. Milton (Mass.) Acad., 1939; student Harvard, 1939-42; m. Katharine W. Clafin, July 11, 1942; children—Katharine, Martha, John, David, Sinclair, Stephen, Robert. With First Nat. Bank Boston, 1945-48, dir., 1964-67, president Compania Azucarera Soledad S.A., Cienfuegos, Cuba, 1954-60; vice chmn. bd. Central Aguirre Sugar Co., Boston, 1962-67, pres., 1965-67, also trustee. dep. dir. Museum of Sci., Boston, 1967—; trustee Cambridge Savings Bank, Cambridge, Mass.; dir. Reed & Barton Corp. Sec., treas., trustee Escuela Agricola Pan Americana, Honduras. Treas., exec. com. N. Bennett St. Indsl. Sch., Boston. Trustee Mt. Auburn Hosp. Served with AUS, 1942-45; ETO. Decorated Purple Heart, Bronze Star. Mem. Am. Orchid Soc., Am. Numis. Assn. Home: 595 Concord Ave Belmont MA 02178 Office: Science Park Boston MA 02114

WEEKS, LEROY GILBERT, steel co. exec.; b. Cin., Jan. 27, 1934; s. Warren Warner and Maud (Gilbert) W.; B.B.A., U. Cin., 1957; m. Mary Heathcote, Dec. 20, 1958; children—Ruth Lynn, James Kevin, Harriet Campbell. Staff auditor Haskins & Sells, Cin., 1957-59, sr. auditor, 1960-64; comptroller Begley Drug Co., Richmond, Ky., 1959-60; with Armco Steel Corp., Middletown, Ohio, 1964—, mgr. gen. accounting, 1967-68, asst. to controller, 1968, controller of subsidiary Armco Boothe, 1969, corporate controller, 1969-75, asst. v.p. finance, controller, 1975-77, asst. v.p., treas., 1977-78, group v.p., 1978—. Treas. Mound Builders council Boy Scouts Am., 1970-72, chmn. finance com., 1975; mem. bd. Episcopal Church Found., 1973—; bd. dirs. Middletown-Butler County unit Am. Cancer Soc., 1976—, Middletown YMCA, 1977-78. Served with USAF, 1960-62. C.P.A., Ohio. Mem. Am. Inst. C.P.A.'s, Ohio Soc. C.P.A.'s, Financial Execs. Inst. Episcopalian (vestryman, chmn. finance commn., jr. warden, sr. warden). Clubs: Middletown Tennis, Browns Run Country (Middletown); Wildwood Golf, Shaker Run Golf. Office: 703 Curtis St Middletown OH 45043

WEEKS, RICHARD RALPH, univ. adminstr.; b. Champaign, Ill., Sept. 18, 1932; s. Frank Cook and B. Caroline (Pool) W.; B.S., U. Ill., 1955; M.B.A., Washington U., St. Louis, 1960, D.B.A., 1966; m. Sue Ann Grunwald, Aug. 29, 1953; children—Kimberly Sue, Bret William. Exec. sec., editor bull. Am. Assembly Collegiate Schs. Bus., St. Louis, 1960-64; exec. sec. Beta Gamma Sigma, also editor Beta Gamma Sigma Exchange, 1961-64; 1st ann. A.A.C.B.S. doctoral fellow in bus. adminstrn., 1964-65; dir. MBA program, asst. prof. mktg. Coll. Bus., Okla. State U., 1965-66, asst. dean, dir. MBA program, asso. prof. mktg., 1966-67; dean, prof. mktg. Walter E. Heller Coll. Bus. Adminstrn., Roosevelt U., 1967-70; dean Coll. Bus. Adminstrn. U. R.I., 1970—, acting v.p. bus. and fin., 1976-77, provost for public policy, public service and mgmt., 1979—. Chmn. scholarship selection com. Am. Inst. Real Estate Appraisers', 1962-64. Bd. dirs. Chgo. Econ. Devel. Corp., 1968-70, v.p., 1969-70; bd. dirs. Chgo. Financial Devel. Corp., 1970, Progress Assn. for Econ. Devel., 1972-73; bd. dirs. Council on Postsecondary Accreditation, 1974—, mem. exec. com., 1977—, chmn., 1979—; bd. dirs. Friends of Jamestown Philomenian Library, 1972-77, pres., 1974-76. Served to capt. USAF, 1955-63. Mem. Am. (dir. acad. placement 1966, 68), So. mktg. assns., Am., So. econ. assns., S.W. Social Sci. Assn., Am. Inst. Decision Scis., Eastern Finance Assn. (dir. 1974—), Acad. Mgmt., Council Profl. Edn. Bus. (sec.-treas. 1960-64, exec. com. 1961-64), Am. Assn. U. Adminstrs., Nat. Assn. State Univs. and Land-grant Colls., Commn. on Edn. for Bus. Professions (sec. 1973-76, chmn. 1976-78), Am. Assn. Collegiate Schs. Bus. (various com., bd. dirs. 1976—), Delta Sigma Pi, Alpha Kappa Lambda, Beta Gamma Sigma (various coms., pres. 1978—), Mu Kappa Tau, Pi Sigma Epsilon. Editor: Faculty Personnel, 9th edit., 1965; contbg. editor: Ency. Bus. Information Sources, 1964: editorial adv. bd. Bus. and Soc., 1968-70. Home: 76 Walcott Ave Jamestown RI 02835 Office: Coll of Bus Adminstrn U RI Kingston RI 02881

WEEKS, ROBERT WALKER, mfg. co. exec.; Rock Island, Ill., Aug. 14, 1926; s. Harold Parker and Miriam (Walker) W.; B.S. in Naval Sci., Purdue U., 1947, B.S. in Mech. Engring., 1948; J.D., Northwestern U., 1951; m. Phyllis Anne Grams, July 24, 1948; children—Susan Carol, Katharine Ann, Nancy Jane. Admitted to Ill. bar, 1951; with law dept. Deere & Co., Moline, Ill., 1951—, gen. counsel, 1969—, v.p., 1977—; v.p., dir. John Deere Ins. Co., 1969—; dir. John Deere Credit Co., Iowa-Ill. Gas and Electric Co., Financial Services Co. Midwest, Rock Island Bank, Rock River Ins. Co. Bd. dirs. Chippianock Cemetery Assn., Rock Island, Ill.; trustee Ill. Wesleyan U. Served with USNR, 1944-46. Mem. Am., Ill. bar assns., C. of C. U.S. (dir.). Home: 61 Hawthorne Rd Rock Island IL 61201 Office: John Deere Rd Moline IL 61265

WEEKS, ROLAND, JR., newspaper publisher; b. Knoxville, Tenn., July 8, 1936; B.S., Clemson (S.C.) U., 1958. Sales engr. Metal Products, Inc., Greenville, S.C., 1961-63; mgmt. trainee, then bus. mgr. Columbia Newspapers, Inc., pubs. The State and Columbia (S.C.) Record newspapers, 1963-68; pres., gen. mgr. Gulf Pub. Co., Inc., pubs. Biloxi-Gulfport (Miss.) Daily Herald and S. Miss. Sun, 1968—; dir. Hancock Bank, Gulfport. Pres., Pine Burr area council Boy Scouts Am., 1980, chmn. fin. com., 1979; pres. Gulf Coast Carnival Assn., 1975. Served to 1st lt. USAF, 1958-61. Mem. So. Newspaper Pubs. Assn. (pres. 1981), Young Pres. Orgn. Presbyterian. Home: 28 Church St Gulfport MS 39501 Office: Gulf Publishing Co Inc Gulfport MS 39501

WEEKS, WALTER LEROY, educator; b. Utica, N.Y., Mar. 30, 1923; s. Walter William and Emma (Conley) W.; B.S., U. Mich., 1947; M.S., Mich. State U., 1949; Ph.D., U. Ill., 1958; m. Mary Shirley Wheeler, Dec. 30, 1951; children—Patricia, Walter William, Daniel, Sheryl, Joseph, Kathryn. Instr., Mich. State Coll., 1947-51; asst. prof. N.Mex. State Coll., 1951-54, prof., 1959-60; asso. prof. U. Ill., 1954-59; asst. dir. research and devel. Collins Radio Co., Cedar Rapids, Iowa, Dallas, 1960-63; prof. elec. engring. Purdue U., 1963—; cons. Eli Lilly Co., Collins Radio Co. Served with USAAF, 1942-46. Author: Electromagnetic Theory for Engineering Applications, 1964; Antenna Engineering, 1968. Inventor radiation leak detector, 1975. Home: 2424 Sycamore Ln Box 2162 West Lafayette IN 47906

WEEKS, WILFORD FRANK, glaciologist; b. Champaign, Ill., Jan. 8, 1929; s. Frank Cook and B. Caroline (Pool) W.; B.S., U. Ill., 1951, M.S., 1953; Ph.D. in Geochemistry, U. Chgo., 1955; m. Beverly Jean Weeks, June 8, 1952; children—Ellen Jean, Paul Russell. Glaciologist, Air Force Cambridge Research Center, 1955-57; asst. prof. geology Washington U., 1957-62; glaciologist U.S. Army Cold Regions Research and Engring. Lab., Hanover, N.H., 1962—; adj. prof. earth scis. Dartmouth Coll., 1972—; Japan Soc. for Promotion Sci. prof. Inst. Low Temperature Sci., Hokkaido U., Japan, 1973; Office of Naval Research chair of arctic marine sci. Naval Postgrad. Sch., 1978-79. Bassist, Dartmouth Symphony, Monterey Symphony, Hanover Chamber Orch. Served with USAF, 1955-57. Fellow Geol. Soc. Am., Arctic Inst. N.Am.; mem. Internat. Glaciological Soc. (pres. 1972-75), Am. Geophys. Union, Am. Polar Soc., Nat. Acad. Engring., Phi Beta Kappa, Phi Kappa Phi, Sigma Xi. Contbr. numerous articles to profl. jours. Office: Cold Regions Research and Engring Lab Hanover NH 03755

WEEMS, FRANK TAYLOR, mfg. co. exec.; b. Birmingham, Ala., Dec. 26, 1924; s. Ben Carpenter and Gladys (Taylor) W.; B.S. in Chem. Engring., U. Ala., 1944; S.M. in Chem. Engring. Practice, M.I.T., 1950; m. Kirsten Lee Borgen, Sept. 10, 1949; children—Barbara Lee, William Taylor, Robert Chipley. Sales engr. Dorr Co., 1948-52; tech. dir. Eimco Corp., 1952-55, regional mgr., 1955-67, mktg. dir., 1967-70, pres., 1970-72; exec. v.p., pres. Air Quality Control Group, Envirotech Corp., Menlo Park, Calif., 1972—; dir. Granger Assos., Santa Clara, Calif. Active Little League Baseball, Weston, Conn.; trustee Rowland Hall-St. Marks Sch., Salt Lake City. Served with USNR, 1943-46. NRC fellow. Mem. Am. Inst. Chem. Engrs., Am. Inst. Mining, Metall. and Petroleum Engrs., Tau Beta Pi, Theta Tau. Republican. Episcopalian. Clubs: Mining (N.Y.C.); Alta (Salt Lake City); Los Altos Golf and Country. Home: 610 Nandell Ln Los Altos CA 94022 Office: 3000 Sand Hill Rd Menlo Park CA 94025

WEEMS, KATHARINE LANE, sculptor; b. Boston, Feb. 22, 1899; d. Gardiner Martin and Emma Louise (Gildersleeve) Lane; prep. edn. May Sch., Boston; art edn. Sch. of Museum of Fine Arts, Boston; pupil of Charles Grafly, Anna Hyatt Huntington, George Demetrios and Brenda Putnam; m. F. Carrington Weems, Nov. 15, 1947. Prin. works include Dog Narcisse Noir, Museum Fine Arts, Boston, and Reading (Pa.) Mus., Kanagroo, Pa. Acad. Fine Arts, 12 foot bronze group Dolphins of the Sea Water Plaza, New Eng. Aquarium, Boston; rep. permanent collection: Pigmy African Elephant, Museum Fine Arts, Boston; Circus Horse, Doe and Fawn, Whippet, and Greyhounds Unleashed, also Greyhound, Brookgreen Gardens, S.C.; Greek Horse, Balt. Mus. Art; Bear, Spee Club, Cambridge; Whippet, Glenbow Found. Mus.; Whippet and Fox, Colby Coll. Art Mus., Waterville, Maine; brick carvings and entrance doors, and 2 bronze rhinoceroses, Inst. of Biology, Harvard; sculpture on Lotta Fountain, Boston; small bronzes in pvt. collections; permanent exhbn. Weems Gallery Animal Sculpture, Mus. Sci., Boston; sculptor Goodwin medal Mass. Inst. Tech.; sculptor for U.S. Legion of Merit medal and medal for Merit, also Fincke Meml. medal Groton Sch. Mem. Mass. Art Commission, 1941-47. Decorated chevalier L'Ordre Nat. Merit (France); recipient bronze medal Sesqui-Centennial Exposition, Phila., 1926; Widener Meml. gold medal Pa. Acad. Fine Arts, 1927; honorable mention Paris (France) Salon, 1928; Joan of Arc gold medal Nat. Assn. Women Painters and Sculptors, 1928; hon. mention Grand Central Galleries, N.Y.C., 1929; bronze medal Boston Tercentenary Fine Arts Exhbn., 1930; Anna Hyatt Huntington prize Nat. Assn. Women Painters and Sculptors, 1931; Speyer prize NAD, 1931, 63, 72, Barnet prize, 1932; hon. mention Archtl. League of N.Y., 1942; Anonymous prize Nat. Assn. Women Artists, 1946; Saltus gold medal for merit Nat. Acad. Design, 1960; Lindsey Morris Meml. prize Nat. Sculpture Soc., 1960; gold medal Nat. Arts Club, N.Y.C., 1961. N.A. Mem. Guild Boston Artists, Nat. Assn. Women Artists, Nat. Sculpture Soc. (council 1949), Nat. Inst. Arts and Letters, Grand Central Art Galleries, Archtl. League, Am. Artists Profl. League, N. Shore Arts Assn., Huguenot Soc., Lords of Colonial Manors. Mass. Soc. Colonial Dames Am. Allied Artists Am. Clubs: Chilton (Boston); Cosmopolitan, Pen and Brush (N.Y.C.); Catherine Lorillard Wolfe. Home: PO Box 126 Manchester MA 01944 (winter) 81 Beacon St Boston MA

WEEMS, ROBERT CICERO, JR., economist, educator; b. Meridian, Miss., July 22, 1910; s. Robert Cicero and Susie (Vaughan) W.; B.S. with honors, Miss. State Coll., 1931; M.B.A., Northwestern U., 1934; student Columbia, summers 1935, 37, 39-40; Ph.D. in Econs., Columbia, 1951; m. Frances Dodds, Aug. 13, 1941; 1 dau., Susan. Part-time with Bank of Shubuta, Miss., 1924-33; teaching fellow econs. La. State U., 1933-34; instr. bus. adminstrn. Miss. State Coll., 1934-35, asst. prof. banking and finance, 1935-38, asso. prof., 1938-40, acting dean Sch. Bus. and Industry, 1940-42, dean, 1942-56, asst. dir. Bus. Research Sta. of Coll., 1939-40, dir., 1940-56, asst. dir. engring. sci. and mgmt. War Tng. Program, 1941-43; dean Coll. Bus. Adminstrn., dir. Bur. Research, U. Nev., 1956-77, adviser-cons. U. Nev. Endowment Fund, 1975—. Chmn. Regional (Nev.) Export Expansion Council, 1960-74; mem. Nat. Export Expansion Council, U.S. Dept. Commerce, 1960-74; chmn. adv. council Miss. Employment Security Commn., 1952-56; mem. Western Indsl. Nev.; mem. Nev. Public Employees Retirement Bd., 1963-78, vice chmn., 1975-78; mem. employment security council Nev. Employment Security Dept.; mem. nat. adv. council SBA, 1975-77. Trustee U.S. Travel Data Center, 1973-76; trustee Am. Inst. Econ. Research, chmn. bd., 1972-76. Served to lt. comdr. USN, 1943-46. Mem. Am. Hotel and Motel Assn. (trustee ednl. inst.), Travel Research Assn. (treas.), Western Econ. Assn., Blue Key, Omicron Delta Kappa (hon.), Chi Lambda Rho, Delta Sigma Pi, Beta Gamma Sigma (nat. exec. com. 1970-74), Phi Kappa Phi, Pi Kappa Alpha, Kappa Kappa Psi. Methodist. Club: Rotary (Reno). Home: 1135 Williams Ave Reno NV 89503

WEENING, RICHARD WILLIAM, JR., publishing co. exec.; b. San Bernardino, Calif., Dec. 24, 1945; s. Richard William and Alice Louise (Young) W.; student St. Johns U., 1962-64, U. San Francisco, 1964-66; B.A., U. Wis., 1968; m. Deborah Ann Gardner, Dec. 21, 1976; children—Elicia Louise, Mia Lynn. Legis. asst. U.S. Congressman Henry S. Reuss, Washington, 1968-70; exec. sec., chief of staff Wis. Gov. Patrick J. Lucey, Madison, 1970-72; pres., pub., dir. Raintree Pubs., Ltd., Milw., 1972—; pres., chief exec. officer, dir. Macdonald-Raintree, Inc., George Philip Raintree (Cartographers) Inc., 1978—; v.p., dir. Odyssey Books, Ltd.; chmn., dir. Raintree Pubs. Internat. Ltd., London, 1978—; chmn., dir. Raintree de México Editores, S.A. de C.V., Mexico City. Chmn., Lakefront Devel. Task Force, Milw., 1974; pres. Bd. Harbor Commns., Port of Milw., 1976-78. Mem. Assn. Am. Pubs., Overseas Nat. Press Club, Childrens Book Council, Am. Soc. Curriculum Devel., Nat. Council Tchrs. English, Internat. Reading Assn., Vienna Inst. for Devel., Council for Exceptional Children. Clubs: Milw. Yacht; American, Raffle, White Elephant (London); Exchequer. Home: Northcote North Lake Village of Chenequa WI 53029 Office: 205 W Highland Ave Milwaukee WI 53203

WEENS, HEINZ STEPHEN, educator, physician; b. Berlin, Germany, May 21, 1912; s. Hans and Johanna (Tuerk) Wienskowtiz; M.D., U. Berne (Switzerland), 1937; m. Suzanne Rosenthal, May 29, 1943; 1 dau., Joan Harriet. Came to U.S., 1938, naturalized, 1944. Intern Piedmont Hosp., Atlanta, 1939-40; resident radiology Grady Meml. Hosp., Atlanta, 1940-42; vol. grad. asst. radiology Peter Bent Brigham Hosp., also Mass. Gen. Hosp., Boston, 1942-43; mem. faculty Emory U. Sch. Medicine, 1943—, prof. radiology, 1949—, chmn. dept., 1947—, Charles Howard Candler prof., 1960—. Bd. dirs. Oak Ridge Inst. Nuclear Studies. Fellow Am. Coll. Radiology, mem. Ga. and Atlanta Radiol. Soc. (past pres.), Radiol. Soc. N.Am., Am. Roentgen Ray Soc., AMA, Assn. Univ. Radiologists, So. Soc. Clin. Investigation, Alpha Omega Alpha. Co-author: Radiologic Diagnosis of the Lower Urinary Tract, 1952; The Mediastinum, 1959. Home: 519 Hillside Dr NW Atlanta GA 30342

WEERS, GERD EDUARD, corp. exec.; b. Bockhorn nr. Oldenburg, Germany, Sept. 4, 1927; s. Robert and Agnes Johanne (Janssen) W.; m. Ellen Dodel, Mar. 4, 1966; 1 dau., Doerthe. Formerly overseas sales mgr. Olympia Werke AG; successively mgr. internat. ops., dir. export, gen. mgr. Triumph/Adler Vertriebs GMBH, now chmn. bd., chief exec. officer, Nuernberg, W. Ger.; mem. adv. com. Dresdner Bank AG. Mem. Com. of West German Fgn. Trade. Home: Langenbergweg 16 Langenzenn 8506 Fed Rep Germany Office: Fuerther Strasse 212 Nuernberg 8500 Fed Rep Germany

WEERSING, MARC CALVIN, coll. pres. emeritus; b. Grand Rapids, Mich., Mar. 10, 1914; s. John Jacob and Katherine (Terpstra) W.; B.A., Calvin Coll., 1934; Th.B., Calvin Theol. Sem., 1937; Th.M., Columbia Theol. Sem., 1938; D.D. (hon.), Southwestern at Memphis, 1954; LL.D., The Citadel, 1969; H.H.D., Presbyterian Coll., 1979; m. Jean Barry Adams, Apr. 22, 1939; children—Marcia Marie, James Barry, Ordained to ministry Presbyn. Ch., 1938; pastor in Elberton, Ga., 1938-42, Decatur, Ga., 1942-47, Jackson, Miss., 1947-55, Spartanburg, S.C., 1955-63; pres. Presbyn. Coll., Clinton, S.C., 1963-80, emeritus, 1980—, trustee, 1956-63. Mem. com. evangelism Presbyn. Ch. U.S., 1945-49, mem. gen. council, 1949-56, mem. bd. world missions, 1958-65, chmn. ad interim com. higher edn., 1977, mem. task force higher edn., 1978—, moderator Synod S.C., 1972-73, moderator Synod of S.E., 1979. Chmn. Gov.'s Statewide Rehab. Planning Program, 1966-69; pres. S.C. Found. Ind. Colls., 1969-70. Trustee Columbia Theol. Sem., 1965-72. Mem. S.C. Assn. Colls. Univs. (pres. 1969-70). Kiwanian. Author: Young Peoples Study Book of Presbyterian General Assembly, 1952. Office: Presbyterian Coll Clinton SC 29325

WEERTMAN, JOHANNES, physicist, educator; b. Fairfield Ala., May 11, 1925; s. Roelof and Christina (van Vlaardingen) W.; student Pa. State Coll., 1943-44; B.S., Carnegie Inst. Tech. (now Carnegie Mellon U.), 1948, D.Sc., 1951; postgrad. Ecole Normale Superieure, Paris, France, 1951-52; m. Julia Ann Randall, Feb. 10, 1950; children—Julia Ann, Bruce Randall. Solid State physicist U.S. Naval Research Lab., Washington, 1952-58, cons., 1960-67; sci. liaison officer U.S. Office Naval Research, Am. Embassy, London, Eng., 1958-59; faculty Northwestern U., Evanston, Ill., 1959—, prof. materials sci. dept., 1961-68, chmn. dept., 1964-68, prof. geol. scis. dept., 1963—, Walter P. Murphy prof. materials sci., 1968—; vis. prof. geophysics Calif. Inst. Tech., 1964, Scott Polar Research Inst., Cambridge (Eng.) U., 1970-71. Cons. U.S. Army Cold Regions Research and Engring. Lab., 1960-75, Oak Ridge Nat. Lab., 1963-67, Los Alamos Sci. Lab., 1967—; co-editor materials sci. books MacMillan Co., 1962-76. Honored with naming of Weertman Island in Antarctica. Fulbright fellow, 1951-52; Guggenheim fellow, 1970-71. Fellow Am. Soc. Metals, Am. Phys. Soc., Geol. Soc. Am.; mem. Nat. Acad. Engring., Am. Geophys. Union (Horton award 1962), Am. Inst. Mining, Metall. and Petroleum Engrs. (Mathewson gold medal 1977), Am. Inst. Physics, Internat. Glaciological Soc., AAAS, Arctic Inst., Am. Quaternary Assn., Explorers Club, Sigma Xi, Tau Beta Pi, Phi Kappa Phi, Alpha Sigma Mu, Pi Mu Epsilon. Club: Evanston Running. Author: (with wife) Elementary Dislocation Theory, 1964. Editorial bd. Metal. Trans., 1967-75, Jour. Glaciology, 1972—; asso. editor Jour. Geophys. Research, 1973-75. Contbr. articles to profl. jours. Home: 834 Lincoln St Evanston IL 60201

WEERTS, C. HARRIS, banker; b. Buckley, Ill., Nov. 26, 1920; s. Jake E. and Emma Sofia (Trusheim) W.; M.B.A. in Accounting, U. Chgo., 1949; m. Shirley Sprehe, July 21, 1945; children—Craig, Wendy (Mrs. James Kestner), Terry, Judith. Vice pres., treas., dir. Union Starch & Refining Co., Inc., Columbus, Ind., 1949-67; v.p., treas., then exec. v.p., gen. mgr. Hamilton Cosco, Inc., Columbus, 1967-71; v.p., controller Am. Fletcher Nat. Bank, Indpls., 1971—; v.p., controller Am. Fletcher Corp., 1972—. Served with USAAF, 1943-45. Decorated D.F.C., Air medal with 3 oak leaf clusters. Mem. Financial Execs. Inst., Bank Adminstrn. Inst., Indpls. C. of C. Club: Harrison Lake Country (Columbus). Home: Rural Route 9 Columbus IN 47201 Office: 101 Monument Circle Indianapolis IN 46277

WEESE, BENJAMIN HORACE, architect; b. Evanston, Ill., June 4, 1929; s. Harry Ernest and Marjorie (Mohr) W.; B.Arch., Harvard, 1951, M.Arch., 1957; certificate Ecole des Beaux Arts, Fontainebleau, France, 1956; m. Cynthia Rogers, July 5, 1963; children—Daniel Peter, Catharine Mohr. With Harry Weese & Assos., Architects, Chgo., 1957-77; founder Weese Seegers Hickey Weese Architects Ltd., 1977—; co-founder, pres. Chgo. Sch. Arch. Found., Glessner House, Chgo., 1966—. Fellow AIA, mem. Nat. Council Archtl. Registration Bds. Home: 2133 N Hudson Ave Chicago IL 60614 Office: 230 E Ohio St Chicago IL 60611

WEESE, HARRY M., architect; b. Evanston, Ill., June 30, 1915; s. Harry E. and Marjorie (Mohr) W.; student Yale U., 1936-37; B.Arch., Mass. Inst. Tech., 1938; m. Kate Baldwin, Feb. 8, 1945; children—Shirley, Kate, Marcia. Fellow Cranbrook Acad. Art, 1938-39; prin. firm Baldwin & Weese, Kenilworth, Ill., 1940-42; with firm Skidmore, Owings & Merrill, Chgo., 1946-47; ind. practice as Harry Weese & Assos., Chgo., 1947—; archtl. cons. fgn. bldgs. program Dept. State, 1973-76. Mem. Pres.'s Citizens' Adv. Com. Recreation and Natural Beauty, 1966-69, Pres.'s Citizens' Adv. Com. Environ. Quality, 1969-71, Gov. Ill. Commn. on Orgn. Ill. Dept. Transp., 1972-74; trustee Latin Sch., Chgo. Served to lt. (s.g.) USNR, 1941-45. Fellow AIA (pres. Chgo. chpt. 1975); mem. NAD, Nat. Council on Arts, Art Inst. Chgo. Clubs: Arts, Chgo. Yacht (Chgo.). Principal projects include Am. Embassy, Ghana, Metro Transit System, Washington, Fed. Correctional Center, Chgo., Arena Stage Theatre, Washington, Performing Arts Center, Milw., Time and Life Bldg., Chgo. Home: 314 W Willow St Chicago IL 60610 Office: 10 W Hubbard St Chicago IL 60610

WEG, JOHN GERARD, physician; b. N.Y.C., Feb. 16, 1934; s. Leonard and Pauline M. (Kanzleiter) W.; B.A. cum laude, Coll. Holy Cross, Worcester, Mass., 1955; M.D., N.Y. Med. Coll., 1959; m. Mary Loretta Flynn, June 2, 1956; children—Diane Marie, Kathryn Mary, Carol Ann, Loretta Louise, Veronica Susanne, Michelle Celeste. Commd. 2nd lt. USAF, 1958, advanced through grades to capt., 1967; intern Walter Reed Gen. Hosp., Washington, 1959-60; resident, then chief resident in internal medicine Wilford Hall USAF Hosp., Lackland AFB, Tex., 1960-64, chief pulmonary sect., 1964-66, chief inhalation sect., 1964-66, chief pulmonary and infectious disease service, 1966-67; resigned, 1967; clin. dir. pulmonary disease div. Jefferson Davis Hosp., Houston, 1967-71; from asst. prof. to asso. prof. medicine Baylor U. Coll. Medicine, Houston, 1967-71; asso. prof. medicine U. Mich. Med. Sch. Univ. Hosp., Ann Arbor, 1971-74, prof. 1974—, physician-in-charge pulmonary div., 1971—; cons. Ann Arbor VA, Wayne County Gen. hosps.; advisory bd. Washtenaw County Health Dept., 1973—. Decorated Air Force Commendation medal; travelling fellow Nat. Tb and Respiratory Disease Assn., 1971; recipient Aesculpaius award Tex. Med. Assn., 1971. Diplomate Am. Bd. Internal Medicine. Fellow Am. Coll. Chest Physicians (chmn. bd. govs. Mich. 1976-79, gov. 1975-79, exec. council 1976—, chmn. membership com. 1976-79; prof.-in-residence 1972—, pres.-elect 1979-80), ACP (chmn. Mich. program com. 1974); mem. AAAS, Am. Fedn. Clin. Research, AMA, Am. Thoracic Soc. (sec.-treas. 1974-76), Am. Assn. Inhalation Therapy, Air Force Soc. Internists and Allied Specialists, Soc. Med. Consultants to Armed Forces, Internat. Union Against Tb, Mich. Thoracic Soc. (pres. 1976-78), Mich. Lung Assn. (dir.), Am. Lung Assn., Research Club U. Mich., Assn. Advancement Med. Instrumentation, Central Soc. Clin. Research, Alpha Omega Alpha. Contbr. med. jours., reviewer, mem. editorial bds. Home: 3060

Exmoor St Ann Arbor MI 48104 Office: 1405 E Ann St Ann Arbor MI 48109

WEGENER, CHARLES WILLIAM, educator; b. Oak Park, Ill., July 29, 1921; s. Ernest Henry and Stella (Nagel) W.; A.B., U. Chgo., 1942, Ph.D., 1950; m. Elizabeth Boone Lamb, Sept. 7, 1955; children—Paula C. Schiller, Julie J. Schiller (foster children), Amy Elizabeth. Instr. humanities U. Chgo., 1950-51, asst. prof., 1951-58, asso. prof., 1958-59, prof., 1968—, Howard L. Willett prof. Coll., 1973—, master New Collegiate div., asso. dean Coll., 1970-76. Vis. prof. Williams Coll., Williamstown, Mass., 1959-60. Served to 1st lt., ordnance dept. AUS, 1942-46. Recipient Quantrell prize for excellence in undergrad. teaching U. Chgo., 1955. Mem. Am. Philos. Assn. Author: Liberal Education and the Modern University, 1978. Co-editor Ethics, An. Internat. Jour. of Social, Legal and Polit. Philosophy, 1968-73, cons. editor, 1973—. Home: 5649 Blackstone Ave Chicago IL 60637 Office: U Chgo 5811 Ellis Ave Chicago IL 60637

WEGENER, PETER PAUL, educator; b. Berlin, Aug. 29, 1917; Dr.rer.nat., U. Berlin, 1943; M.A. (priv.), Yale U., 1960; Dr.-Ing. (E.h.), U. Karlsruere, 1979; m. Annette Schleiermacher, Aug. 14, 1961; came to U.S., 1946, naturalized, 1953. Research supersonic wind tunnels, Kochel, Germany, 1943-45, gasdynamics, hypersonic wind tunnels U.S. Naval Ordnance Lab., 1946-53, Jet Propulsion Lab., Calif. Inst. Tech., 1953-60; prof. applied sci. Yale, 1960—, Harold Hodgkinson prof. engring. and applied sci., 1972—, chmn. dept. engring. and applied sci., 1966-71. Fellow Am. Phys. Soc., Conn. Acad. Sci. and Engring. (charter mem.). Asso. editor Am. Scientist. Research and publs. on hypersonics, condensation metastable state, chem. kinetics, flow systems real gases, bubbles. Home: Montgomery Pkwy Branford CT 06405 Office: Yale Univ New Haven CT 06520

WEGMAN, HAROLD HUGH, mgmt. cons.; b. Cin., June 29, 1916; s. Clarence H. and Lillian (de Tellem) W.; B.B.A., U. Cin., 1941; M.B.A., Xavier U., 1954; m. Ruth Ellen Volk, May 1, 1937; children—Susan Ruth (Mrs. Michael Manning), Sally Ann (Mrs. Jerry Fine). Tng. supr., then asst. to v.p. Gruen Watch Co., 1950-55; personnel dir., asst. to pres. Bavarian Brewing Co., Covington, Ky., 1955-59; dir. indsl. relations, asst. to pres. Howard Paper Co., Dayton, Ohio, 1959-62; v.p., gen. mgr. Elano Corp., Xenia, Ohio, 1962-64; v.p., dir. indsl. relations Champion Papers Inc., Hamilton, Ohio, 1964-67; v.p. U.S. Plywood Champion Papers, Inc., 1967-71; v.p. Champion Internat., 1971-72; pres. PEP Group, 1972—; dir. Mgmt. Center, Sacred Heart U., 1974—. Trustee Foreman Found., 1965-71. Served to lt. (j.g.) USNR, 1944-46. Mem. Am. Soc. Personnel Adminstrs. (bd. dirs. 1969—), Am. Soc. for Tng. and Devel., NAM, Am. Paper Inst., Am. Mgmt. Assn., Lambda Chi Alpha. Presbyn. (deacon, elder). Home: 1009 N Ocean Blvd Pompano Beach FL 33062 Office: 160 Southport Woods Dr Southport CT 06490

WEGNER, HELMUTH ADALBERT, lawyer, ret. chem. co. exec.; b. Berlin, Germany, Feb. 5, 1917; s. Leo Michael and Hertha Johanna (Erdmann) W.; came to U.S., 1936, naturalized, 1943; B.S., U. Ill., 1938; postgrad. U. Wis., 1939; J.D., Chgo.-Kent Coll. Law 1950; m. Cordelia Elizabeth Claussen, Aug. 23, 1941; children—Harold C., Ruth Ellen, Linda Ann. Admitted to Ill. bar, 1950, Va. bar, 1979; with G.D. Searle & Co., Skokie, Ill., 1939—, patent dir., 1958-63, gen. counsel, 1963-78, sec., 1972-78, sr. counsel, 1978—; counsel to Stevens, Davis, Miller & Mosher, Arlington, Va. Mem. Am. Bar Assn. (past com. chmn.), Am. Patent Law Assn. (past com. chmn.), Pharm. Mfg. Assn. (past com. chmn.), Am. Chem. Soc. (past dir. Chgo. sect., exec. com.), Va. State Bar, Assn. Internat. Protection Propriété Industrielle, Assn. Corp. Secs., Asociacion Interamericana Propriedad Industrial, Chgo. Chemists Club, Phi Delta Phi. Republican. Mem. United Ch. of Christ. Contbr. articles to profl. jours. Home: 3604 Pinetree Terr Falls Church VA 22041 Office: PO Box 2627 Arlington VA 22202

WEGNER, HERBERT GAIRD, assn. exec.; b. San Francisco, Sept. 20, 1929; s. Armin and Ethel (Slater) W.; B.A. in Polit. Sci., San Francisco State U., 1951; postgrad. U. Cal., 1953, Am. Inst. Fgn. Trade, 1952; m. Susan Aitken, Dec. 28, 1957; children—Steven, Susan, David. Statewide budget officer U. Cal. at Berkeley, 1957-59; internat. relations officer AID, Quito, Ecuador, 1959-61, Washington, 1961-62; spl. projects officer Peace Corps, Washington, 1962-64; Latin Am. dir. Credit Union Nat. Assn., Panama, 1971—, mng. dir. assn., 1973-77, pres., 1977—; dir. CUNADATA Corp., Madison, Wis., 1973-74; pres. CUNA Service Group, Inc., Madison, 1971—; dir. ICU Services Corp., Madison, CUNA Supply Corp., Madison, 1971-75; ex-officio mem. bd. dirs. CUNA Mut. Ins. Soc., CUMIS Ins. Soc.; ex-officio mem. Congress Central Credit Union, 1973—; vice chmn. Nat. Electronic Funds Transfer Commn., 1975—; dir. U.S. Central Credit Union. Trustee Internat. Devel. Conf., CARE, Vol. Devel. Corps. Served to lt. as pilot USNR, 1953-57. Recipient Key Man award Jr. C. of C., Berkeley, 1951. Home: 4230 Waban Hill Madison WI 53711 Office: CUNA 1617 Sherman Ave PO Box 431 Madison WI 53701

WEGNER, KARL HEINRICH, physician, educator; b. Pierre, S.D., Jan. 5, 1930; s. Lester Fred and Nellie (Norbeck) W.; B.A., Yale, 1952; M.D., Harvard, 1959; m. Mary Josephine Waddell, June 15, 1957; children—Madeleine Jean, Peter Norbeck, Mary Nell. Pathologist, Sioux Valley Hosp., Sioux Falls, S.D., 1962—; pathologist dir. Lab. Clin. Medicine, Sioux Falls, 1962—; prof., chmn. dept. pathology U. S.D., 1968-73, v.p. health affairs, dean Sch. Medicine, 1973-79; owner, operator Meadowlark Hereford Farms, Montrose, S.D. Served with USMC. Fellow Coll. Am. Pathologists, Internat. Acad. Pathologists, Am. Soc. Pathologists; mem. Am. Hereford Assn. Home: Sunnymede S Minn Rd Sioux Falls SD 57101 Office: Sch Medicine U SD 2501 W 22d St Sioux Falls SD 57105

WEGNER, PETER, educator; b. Leningrad, Russia, Aug. 20, 1932; s. Leo and Hermine W.; came to U.S., 1964, naturalized, 1971; B.Sc., London U., 1953, Ph.D., 1968; m. Judith Priscilla Romney, July 22, 1956; children—Simon, Mark, Jeremy, Michael. Research asso. M.I.T., 1959-60; research asso. Harvard U., 1960-61; lectr. London U. Sch. Econs., 1961-64; asst. prof. Pa. State U., 1964-66; asso. prof. Cornell U., 1966-69; asso. prof. Brown U., 1969-75, prof. computer sci., 1975—. Mem. Assn. Computing Machinery, Math. Assn. Am., Sigma Xi. Author: Programming Languages, Information Structures and Machine Organization, 1968; Research Directions in Software Technology, 1979; Programming with Ada, 1979. Office: Box 1910 Brown Univ Providence RI 02912

WEGRIA, RENE WILLIAM EDWARD, physician, educator; b. Fumal, Belgium, June 9, 1911; s. Edward and Odile (Vandensteen) W.; M.D. with great distinction, U. Liege, 1936; Laureat du Concours Interuniversitaire de Belgique, 1934-36; D.M.S., Columbia, 1945. Came to U.S., 1937, naturalized, 1947. Fellow Belgian Am. Ednl. Found., Vanderbilt U., Mayo Found. and Western Res. U., 1937-39; fellow, then instr. dept. physiology Western Res. U., 1939-42; asst. resident medicine Cleve. City Hosp., 1942-43; asst. resident cardiology, asst. medicine Presbyn. Hosp. and Columbia Coll. Phys. and Surg., N.Y.C., 1943-46, instr. medicine, 1946-47, asso. medicine, 1947-49, asst. prof. medicine, 1949-58, asso. prof., 1958; cons. medicine St. Barnabas Hosp., 1948-58; vis. prof. Lovanium U., Leopoldville, Belgium Congo, 1958; prof. medicine, dir. dept. St. Louis U., 1958-63, prof. pharmacology, dir. dept. 1963—. Chmn. dean's com. VA Hosp., St. Louis, 1961-62; cons. Food and Drug Adminstrn., Dept. Health, Edn. and Welfare. Fellow AAAS, N.Y. Acad. Scis.; mem. Am. Physiol. Soc., Am. Heart Assn., Soc. Exptl. Biology and Medicine, Am. Soc. Clin. Investigation, Harvey Soc., Am. Pharmacological Soc., N.Y. Heart Assn., N.Y. County, N.Y. State med. assns., A.M.A. (cons. council drugs), Am. Assn. U. Profs., Am. Overseas Educators Assn., Assn. for Med. Sch. Pharmacology, Argentine Soc. Pharmacology and Therapeutics (hon. fgn. mem.). Address: 1402 S Grand Blvd St Louis MO 63104

WEHAUSEN, JOHN VROOMAN, mathematician, educator; b. Duluth, Sept. 23, 1913; s. George W. and Elizabeth (Vroman) W.; B.S., U. Mich., 1934, M.S., 1935, Ph.D., 1938; m. Mary Katherine Wertime, Aug. 19, 1938; children—Sarah, Peter Vrooman, Julia, John David. Instr. math. Brown U., 1937-38, Columbia, 1938-40, U. Mo., 1940-44; mathematician David Taylor Model Basin, Carderock, Md., 1946-49; acting head mechanics br. Office Naval Research, 1949-50; exec. editor Math. Revs., 1950-56; asso. research mathematician Inst. Engring. Research, U. Calif. at Berkeley, 1956-57, research mathematician, 1957—, asso. prof. engring. sci., 1958-59, prof., 1959—; Fulbright lectr. U. Hamburg, 1960-61. Consultant Operations Research Group USN, 1944-46. Mem. Am. Math. Soc., Schiffbautechnische Gesellschaft, Math. Assn. Am., Soc. Naval Architects and Marine Engrs., Soc. Naval Architects of Japan. Home: 15 Hillside Ct Berkeley CA 94704

WEHLE, JOHN LOUIS, brewing co. exec.; b. Rochester, N.Y., Dec. 21, 1916; s. Louis A. and Elizabeth R. (Rabe) W.; ed. U. Rochester, Yale U.; m. Marjorie Strong, Aug. 8, 1942; children—John Louis, Charles S., Henry S. With Genesee Brewing Co., Rochester, 1939—, chmn. bd., 1969—; dir., exec. com. Marine Midland Bank, Rochester. Chmn. bd. Genesee County Mus.; bd. dirs. Rochester Automobile Club; trustee Rochester Mus. and Sci. Center. Recipient Civic Arts award, Rochester, 1977; Bus. Com. Arts award, Indpls., 1977. Mem. Landmark Soc. Western N.Y., Yale U., U. Rochester alumni assns. Club: Genesee Valley. Address: 445 St Paul St Rochester NY 14605

WEHMEYER, WILLIAM ANTHONY, educator; b. Yonkers, N.Y., Nov. 24, 1930; s. William Arthur and Mary Josephine (Egan) W.; A.B., Hamilton Coll., 1952; M.A., Catholic U. Am., 1954; Ph.D., U. Notre Dame, 1962; m. Josephine Ann Marra, Dec. 27, 1965; 1 son, Stephen Connor. Tchr. English and French, Lake Placid (N.Y.) High Sch., 1956-58; asst. prof. English, St. Bonaventure U., 1962-64, asso. prof., 1964-71, prof., 1971—, dean Arts and Scis., 1974—. Served with U.S. Army, 1954-56. Mem. MLA, Nat. Council Tchrs. English, Northeastern MLA (founder), Phi Beta Kappa, Delta Sigma Rho, Delta Epsilon Sigma. Roman Catholic. Home: 944 Prospect Ave Olean NY 14760 Office: PO Box 26 Saint Bonaventure NY 14778*

WEHNER, ALFRED PETER, life scientist; b. Wiesbaden, Germany, Oct. 23, 1926; s. Paul Heinrich and Irma (Schulze) Wl; cand. med. Johannes Gutenberg U., 1949, Zahnarzt, 1951, D.M.D., 1953; m. Ingeborg Hella Miller, Aug. 30, 1955; children—Patricia Ingeborg, Alfred Peter, Jackie Diane, Peter Hermann. Came to U.S., 1953, naturalized, 1958. Individual practice dentistry, Wiesbaden, 1951-53; fellow clin. pedodontia Guggenheim Dental Clinic, N.Y.C., 1953-54; dentist 7100th Hosp., USAF, 1954-56; research asst. Mobil Oil Co., Dallas, 1957-62; sr. research scientist Biometrics Instrument Corp., Plano, Tex., 1962-64; pres. Electro-Aerosol Inst., Plano, Tex., dir. electro-aerosol therapy center, 1964-67; chmn. dept. sci. U. Plano, Tex., 1966-67; sr. research scientist, biology dept. Battelle Pacific Northwest Labs., Richland, Wash., 1967-78, mgr. environ. and indsl. toxicology, 1978—. Cons., VA Hosp., McKinney, Tex., 1963-65; chmn. various internat. sci. congresses and symposia. Fellow Internat. Soc. Med. Hydrology, Tex. Acad. Sci.; mem. Am. Soc. Microbiology, Am. Inst. Med. Climatology (dir. 1972—, sec. 1972—), Internat. Soc. Biometeorology (U.S. rep. 1972—), Sci. Research Soc. Am., Soc. Exptl. Biology and Medicine, Internat. Soc. Aerosols in Medicine (mem. exec. bd. 1970—), Dallas County Dental Soc. (hon.), Am. Physicians Fellowship, N.Y. Acad. Sci., Am. Physiol. Soc. Patentee in field. Author: From Hitler Youth to U.S. Citizenship, 1972. Contbr. to sci. publs. Home: 312 Saint St Richland WA 99352 Office: Battelle Biology Dept PO Box 999 Richland WA 99352

WEHNER, WILLIAM E., finance co. exec.; b. Phila., Dec. 28, 1914; s. Lewis H. and Lillian May (Fisher) W.; ed. Wharton Sch. U. Pa., 1935; m. Ruth May Wagner, May 13, 1938; children—Lewis, William, Ruth, Charlotte, Donna. With Household Finance Corp., Chgo., from 1937, pres. consumer finance div., also dir.; dir. Household Finance Corp. Can., HFC Trust Ltd., London, Eng. Served with USMCR, World War II; PTO. Clubs: Inverness Country; Marco Island (Fla.) Country; Mission Hills Country. Home: 1430 Cayambas Ct Marco Island FL 33937

WEHRLE, LEROY SNYDER, economist, educator; b. St. Louis, Feb. 5, 1932; s. Fred Joseph and Eleanor (Snyder) W.; B.S., Washington U., St. Louis, 1953; M.A. in Econs., Yale, 1956, Ph.D. with honors, 1959; m. JoAnn Griffith, Aug. 29, 1959; children—Chandra Lee, Lon Joseph. Asst. instr. Yale, 1958-59; with econ. sect. AID mission to Laos, 1960-61; sr. staff economist President's Council Econ. Advisers, 1961-62; spl. econ. adviser to U.S. Ambassador Unger, Vientiane, 1962; dep. dir. AID mission to Laos, 1963-64; asst. dir. AID mission, also econ. counsellor to U.S. ambassador, Saigon, 1964-67; asso. dir. AID Mission, Saigon, 1964-67; dept. asst. adminstr. Vietnam, AID, Dept. State, 1967-68; univ. fellow Harvard, 1968-69; sr. fellow Brookings Instn., 1969-70; dir. Ill. Inst. for Social Policy, Springfield, 1970-72; aide to Lt. Gov. Paul Simon, 1972; prof. economics Sangamon State U., 1972—. Mem. spl. study group Alliance Progress, 1962; mem. Rockefeller Latin Am. Mission, 1969; chmn. study team world food and nutrition study Nat. Acad. Sci., 1976-77. Served with AUS, 1953-55. Recipient William A. Jump meml. award, 1966. Mem. Am. Econ. Assn., Council on Fgn. Relations. Home: 2001 Bates Springfield IL 62704 Office: Sangamon State Univ Springfield IL 62708

WEHRLE, RUSSELL SCHILLING, indsl. exec.; b. Charleston, W.Va., Oct. 26, 1926; s. Henry Bernard and Elizabeth (Herscher) W.; B.A. summa cum laude, Princeton, 1947; m. Martha Gaines, Oct. 16, 1954; children—Michael H., Ebersole Gaines, Katherine Schilling, Philip Noyes, Martha Chilton. With McJunkin Corp., Charleston, 1947—, asst. to pres., 1951-64, exec. v.p., dir., 1964—; pres., dir. Hansford Properties, Inc., Charleston, 1965—, McJay Internat. Corp., Charleston, 1977—; dir. Kanawha Banking & Trust Co., Charleston, Teays Valley Nat. Bank, Scott Depot. W.Va., Heck's, Inc. Mem. W.Va. Labor-Mgmt. Adv. Council, 1977—; mem. W.Va. Gov.'s Econ. Adv. Council, 1978—; mem. Kanawha County Bd. Edn., 1966-72; trustee United Fund Kanawha Valley, Inc., 1963-75, pres., 1965-66; trustee Sunrise Found., Inc., 1961-77; trustee Morris Harvey Coll., 1967—, vice chmn. bd., 1976—; past trustee Charleston Area Med Center, YMCA, YWCA. Served with USNR, 1944-46. Mem. Am. Supply Assn. (dir.), Petroleum Equipment Suppliers Assn., N.A.M. (dir.). Home: 1440 Louden Heights Rd Charleston WV 25314 Office: PO Box 513 Charleston WV 25322

WEHRLI, ROBERT LOUIS, mgmt. cons.; b. N.Y.C., Feb. 2, 1922; s. Louis and Lillian C. (Ollendorf) W.; B.S. in Physics, Rensselaer Poly. Inst., 1948, M.S., 1949; m. Margaret E. Wilson, July 22, 1944; children—LuEllen Margaret, Craig John. Physicist, Linde Air Products Co., 1948-49; physicist, chief research Reaction Motors Co., Denville, N.J., 1949-54; with Robertshaw Controls Co., Richmond, Va., 1954-67, mgr. aero. and instrument div., 1955-61, v.p., 1959-64, exec. v.p., 1964-67; mng. dir. Robertshaw Controls, S.A., Geneva, Switzerland, 1960-61; pres. Dresser Systems, Houston, 1967-70; pres. Cybercom Corp., Sunnyvale, Calif., 1970-71; asst. to pres. Varian Assos., Palo Alto, Calif., 1971-72, v.p., gen. mgr., instrument div., 1972-79; mgmt. cons., 1980—. Served as pilot USNR, 1942-45. Mem. Instrument Soc. Am., Sigma Xi. Home: 29700 W Zuma Bay Way Malibu CA 90265

WEHRLY, BEATRICE LORRAINE, educator; b. Madison, Wis., Jan. 30, 1926; d. Bert Haymon and Nettie Dorothea (Peterson) Richards; B.Ed., U. Wis., Whitewater, 1945; M.S., U. Ill., 1948; Ph.D., Tex. A. and M. U., 1969; m. James S. Wehrly, Aug. 25, 1948; children—David James, Donald Richard, Dorothy Lorraine. Tchr. pub. schs., Wis., Ill., Ind., 1945-62; counselor Amarillo (Tex.) Ind. Sch. Dist., 1962-65; asst. prof. counselor edn. Western Ill. U., Macomb, 1969-72, asso. prof., 1972-76, prof., 1976—. Mem. Am. Personnel and Guidance Assn. (internat. relations com.), Ill. Personnel and Guidance Assn. Contbr. articles to profl. jours. Home: 119 Penny Ln Macomb IL 61455 Office: Dept Counselor Education Western Ill U Macomb IL 61455

WEHRWEIN, AUSTIN CARL, newspaperman; b. Austin, Tex., Jan. 12, 1916; s. George S. and Anna (Ruby) W.; A.B., U. Wis., 1937; LL.B., Columbia, 1940; student London Sch. Econs., 1948; m. Judith Oakes, 1950; children—Sven Austin, Paul, Peter, Joanna Judith. Reporter, Washington Bur., United Press, 1941-43, 46-48; information specialist E.C.A., London, Copenhagen, Oslo, Stockholm, 1948-51; financial writer Milw. Jour., 1951-53; staff corr. Time, Inc., Chgo., 1953-55; reporter Chgo. Sun-Times, 1955-56, financial editor, 1956-57; chief Chgo. bur. N.Y. Times, 1957-66; editorial writer Star, Mpls., 1966—; contbr. Washington Post, London Economist, Collier's Year Book; corr. Christian Sci. Monitor, Progressive Chronicle of Higher Edn. Served with USAAF, 1943-45; mem. staff Stars and Stripes, Shanghai, China, 1945-46. Recipient Pulitizer prize for internat. reporting, 1953; Distinguished Journalism award U. Wis., 1963; certificate merit Am. Bar Assn. Gavel competition, 1968, Gavel award, 1969, 71. Home: 2309 Carter Ave St Paul MN 55108 Office: Star Minneapolis MN 55415

WEI, JAMES, educator; b. Macao, China, Aug. 14, 1930; s. Hsiang-chen and Nuen (Kwok) W.; B.S. in Chem. Engring., Ga. Inst. Tech., 1952; M.S., Mass. Inst. Tech., 1954, Sc.D., 1955; grad. Advanced Mgmt. Program Harvard, 1969; m. Virginia Hong, Nov. 4, 1956; children—Alexander, Christina, Natasha, Randolph. Came to U.S., 1949, naturalized, 1960. Research engr. to research asso. Mobil Oil, Paulsboro, N.J., 1956-62; sr. scientist, Princeton, N.J., 1963-68, mgr. analysis, N.Y.C., 1969-70; Allan P. Colburn prof. U. Del., Newark, 1971-77; Sherman Fairchild Distinguished scholar Calif. Inst. Tech., 1977; Warren K. Lewis prof., head. dept. chem. engring. Mass. Inst. Tech., Cambridge, 1977—. Vis. prof. Princeton, 1962-63, Calif. Inst. Tech., 1965; cons. Mobil Oil Corp., Nat. Acad. Sci. on motor vehicle emissions, Battelle Meml. Inst., Minn. Mining & Mfg. Co.; mem. sci. adv. bd. EPA. Recipient Am. Acad. Achievement Golden Plate award, 1966. Mem. Am. Inst. Chem. Engrs. (dir. 1970-72, Inst. lectr. 1968, Profl. Progress award 1970), Am. Chem. Soc. (award in petroleum chemistry 1966), Nat. Acad. Engring., AAAS, Sigma Xi. Bd. editors Chem. Tech. 1971—, Chem. Engring. Communications, 1972—; cons. editor chem. engring. series McGraw-Hill, 1964—. Contbr. papers, monographs to profl. lit. Home: 420 Waverley Ave Newton MA 02158 Office: Chem Engring Dept Mass Inst Tech Cambridge MA 02139

WEICHLEIN, WILLIAM JESSET, educator, assn. exec.; b. Springfield, Mo., May 9, 1917; s. Frank Howard and Lily Ann (Pick) W.; Mus.B., U. Mich., 1949, Mus.M., 1950, Ph.D., 1956; m. Helen Caroline Begley, Sept. 14, 1940; children—Paul I., Frank E. Mem. faculty Sch. Music, U. Mich., 1952—, prof. music history and musicology, 1967—; exec. sec. Music Library Assn., 1965-75, 77—. Served with USAAF, 1943-46. Mem. Am. Musciol. Soc., Coll. Music Soc., Am. Assn. Library Schs., Pi Kappa Lambda (pres. 1970-76). Author: An Alphabetical Index to the Songs of Robert Schumann, 1966; A Check-list of American Music Periodicals, 1850-1900, 1970. Editor: Pi Kappa Lambda Studies in American Music, 1965—. Home: 1309 Culver Rd Ann Arbor MI 48103

WEICHSEL, HANS MILTON, JR., helicopter co. exec.; b. St. Louis, Aug. 25, 1919; s. Hans and Alice (Knapp) W.; B.S., U. Mich., 1943; m. Gillette Spencer, Oct. 15, 1949; children—Hans Bradley, Alice Linda, Herbert Spencer. Flight research engr., pilot Cornell Research Labs., 1943-50; with Bell Helicopter Co., Ft. Worth, 1950—, v.p., 1961-70, v.p. marketing and logistics, 1970-72, sr. v.p., 1972—. Past chmn. bd. trustees, bd. dirs. Selwyn Internat. Coll. Prep. Sch.; bd. dirs. Southwest Outward Bound. Recipient Congl. citation for helicopter contbn. to Vietnam War, 1965. Registered profl. engr., Tex. Fellow Am. Helicopter Soc. (hon., past nat. dir., past nat. sec.); asso. fellow Am. Inst. Aeros. and Astronautics; mem. Assn. U.S. Army (pres. Ft. Worth chpt. 1971-72), Soc. Logistics Engrs. (sr. mem.), Quiet Birdmen, Twirlybirds, U. Mich. Alumni Assn., Army Aviation Assn., Am. Whitewater Assn., Alpha Delta Phi. Clubs: Sierra; Ozark Wilderness Waterway; Ridglea Country (Ft. Worth); University (Washington). Contbr. articles to profl. jours.; also articles on canoeing. Home: 5801 Rockhill Rd Fort Worth TX 76112 Office: PO Box 482 Fort Worth TX 76101

WEICK, PAUL CHARLES, judge; b. Youngstown, Ohio, Aug. 25, 1899; s. Charles J. and Jane (Guttridge) W.; LL.B., U. Cin., 1920, LL.D. (hon.), 1965; m. Hilda Rickard, Sept. 28, 1929 (dec. Aug. 1960); 1 son, Paul A.; m. 2d, Nelle Edwards, Aug. 15, 1963. Admitted to Ohio bar, 1920; practice law, Akron, Ohio, 1920-56; judge U.S. Dist. Ct. No. Dist. Ohio, 1956-59, judge U.S. Ct. Appeals, 6th Circuit, 1959—, chief judge, 1963-69; mem. Jud. Conf. of U.S., 1963-69; mem. bd. bar examiners Supreme Ct. Ohio, 1946-50. Recipient award Fellows of Ohio State Bar Found., 1965; Centennial award U. Akron, 1970. Mem. Am., Ohio (pres. 1950), Akron (pres. 1942) bar assns., Am. Judicature Soc., Am. Law Inst., Inst. Jud. Adminstrn., Am., Ohio State bar founds. Home: 1505 Jefferson Ave Akron OH 44313 Office: 539 Federal Bldg US Court House Akron OH 44308 also 637 US Post Office and Courthouse Bldg Cincinnati OH 45202

WEICKER, LOWELL PALMER, JR., U.S. senator; b. Paris, France, May 16, 1931; s. Lowell Palmer and Mary (Bickford) Paulsen; grad. Lawrenceville Sch., 1949; B.A. in Polit. Sci., Yale, 1953; LL.B., U. Va., 1958; m. Camille DiLorenzo Butler, Nov. 5, 1977; children—Sonny, Lowell Palmer, III; children by previous marriage—Scot, Gray, Brian. Admitted to Conn. bar, 1960; mem. Conn. Gen. Assembly, 1963-69; 1st selectmen Greenwich, Conn., 1964-68; mem. 91st Congress, 4th Dist. Conn., 1969-71; U.S. senator from Conn., 1971—, mem. Com. on Energy and Natural Resources, Com. on Appropriations, Select Com. on Small Bus. Served with AUS,

1953-55. Republican. Episcopalian. Office: Senate Office Bldg Washington DC 20510

WEICKMANN, HELMUT KARL, scientist; b. Munich, Germany, Mar. 10, 1915; s. Ludwig and Therese (Mayer) W.; student U. Leipzig, 1934-36; Ph.D., U. Frankfurt, 1939; Docteur Honoris Causa, Universite Clermont-Ferrand, 1975; m. Ruth Erika Burchardt, Apr. 28, 1945; children—Hans-Joachim, Klaus, Sabine, Peter. Research physicist Deutsche Forschungs Anstalt Fuer Segelflug, 1939-45; dir. Obs. Hohenpeissenberg, Deutscher Wetter-dienst, 1946-50; chief atmospheric physics br. U.S. Army Electronic Labs., Ft. Monmouth, N.J., 1949-65; dir. atmospheric physics and chemistry lab. NOAA, Dept. Commerce, Boulder, Colo., 1965-79; sr. research asso. Coop. Inst. for Research in Environ. Scis., 1979—. Fellow Am. Meteorol. Soc., AAAS; mem. Royal Meteorol. Soc., Am. Geophys. Union, Internat. Commn. for Cloud Physics (pres. 1963-75, hon. mem.). Roman Catholic. Contbr. articles to profl. jours. Home: 603 Wewoka Dr Boulder CO 80303 Office: CIRES Univ Colo Campus Box 449 Boulder CO 80303

WEIDE, WILLIAM WOLFE, housing and recreation vehicles mfr.; b. Toledo, Aug. 19, 1923; s. Samuel and Pearl Celia (Weide) W.; student U. Toledo, 1942, Marquette U., 1943-44; B.S., U. So. Calif., 1949; m. Beatrice Lieberman, June 4, 1950; children—Brian Samuel, Bruce Michael, Robert Benjamin. Asst. controller Eldon Mfg., 1950; mem. Calif. Franchise Tax Bd., 1951; controller Sutone Corp., 1951-53; treas. Descoware Corp., 1953-58; sr. v.p., dir. Fleetwood Enterprises, Inc., Riverside, Calif., 1958-73, pres., chief exec. officer, 1973—; dir. subsidiaries Fleetwood Enterprises, Inc.; treas., So. Eastern Manufactured Housing Inst., Atlanta. Mem. City of Riverside Housing Com.; mem. policy adv. bd. Joint Center for Urban Studies, Harvard-Mass. Inst. Tech., Cambridge; trustee City of Hope Hosp., Duarte, Calif.; mem. pres.'s circle of U. So. Calif. Served with USNR, 1942-46; PTO. Recipient Jack E. Wells Meml. award for service to manufactured housing industry, 1976. Mem. Nat. Assn. Accountants (past v.p., dir. Los Angeles and Orange County chpt.), Manufactured Housing Inst. (chmn.), Trailer Coach Assn., NAM (pub. affairs com.), Riverside C. of C. Home: 2341 Terraza Pl Fullerton CA 92635 Office: PO Box 7638 Riverside CA 92503. *Love your family. Love your job. Give all you can for what you wish to achieve. Be a Johnathan Livingston Seagull.*

WEIDENAAR, REYNOLD HENRY, artist-etcher; b. Grand Rapids, Mich., Nov. 17, 1915; s. Dirk and Effie (Kuiper) W.; Kendall Sch. Design, Grand Rapids, Mich., 1935-36, (scholar, 1938) Kansas City Art Inst., 1938-40; m. Ilse Eerdmans, June 6, 1944; children—Reynold, Carla, Paula. Regular exhibitor N.A.D., U.S. Library of Congress, Detroit Inst. Art, Pa. Acad. Fine Arts, San Francisco Art Mus., Butler Inst., De-Young Meml. Mus.; exhibitor Met. Mus., 1942, Denver Art Mus., 1942; one man shows Nelson Gallery, Kansas City, Arts Club, Washington, Joslyn Meml., Norton Gallery, Fla., 1946, Brooks Meml., Delgado Mus., Norfolk Mus., 1947, Hamline Galleries, 1948, represented in permanent collections Library of Congress, Brooks Meml., Detroit Inst. Arts, Nelson Gallery, Hackley Gallery, Honolulu Acad. Fine Arts. Phila. Mus., Norfolk Mus., Boston Mus. Fine Arts, Conn. Acad., Wadsworth Atheneum, Nat. Gallery South Wales, Liverpool (Eng.) Pub. Library, Carnegie Inst.; instr. Kendall Sch. Design, Grand Rapids, 1956—. Recipient Scholastic mag. awards, 1938; Vander Slice scholar, 1939; Hal H. Smith prize Detroit Inst., 1942; Kate W. Arms prize, Soc. Am. Etchers, 1942, John Taylor Arms prize, 1950; Guggenheim award, 1944; Tiffany scholar, 1948; John Taylor Arms Meml. award N.A.D., 1954, 64; Century Found. award George W. Smith Art Mus., 1956; Gold medal Am. Artists Profl. League, 1958; Purchase prize Gilcrease Inst., 1958; Rothschild prize watercolor Allied Artists Am., 1958; 1st prize graphics Soc. Western Artists, M. H. De Young Mus., 1959; Spl. award Art League L.I., 1959; Bixby award Mich. Fine Arts Ann. Exhbn., 1964; John Taylor Arms prize N.A.D., 1964, others. N.A. Fellow Soc. Western Artists; mem. Am. Watercolor Soc., Soc. Am. Graphic Artists, Mich. Acad. Sci., Arts and Letters, Am. Artists Profl. League, Audubon Artists, Allied Artists Am., Art League of L.I., Watercolor Soc. Ala., Knickerbocker Artists, Silvermine Guild Artists. Clubs: Print, Water Color (Phila.); Arts (Washington); Torch. Author, artist: Our Changing Landscape, 1970. Active in mezzotinting, etching, watercolor, oils, fresco. Address: 4041 Point O'Woods Ct Apt 108 Grand Rapids MI 49508

WEIDENBAUM, MURRAY LEW, educator; b. Bronx, N.Y., Feb. 10, 1927; s. David and Rose (Warshaw) W.; B.B.A., Coll. City N.Y., 1948; M.A., Columbia, 1949; M.P.A. (Banbury fellow), Princeton, 1954, Ph.D., 1958; m. Phyllis Green, June 14, 1954; children—Susan, James, Laurie. Fiscal economist Bur. Budget, Washington, 1949-57; corp. economist Boeing Co., Seattle, 1958-62; sr. economist Stanford Research Inst., Palo Alto, Calif., 1962-63; mem. faculty Washington U., St. Louis, 1964—, prof., chmn. dept. econs., 1966-69, Mallinckrodt prof., 1971—; asst. sec. econ. policy Treasury Dept., Washington, 1969-71. Chmn. research adv. com. St. Louis Regional Indsl. Devel. Corp., 1965-69; exec. sec. Pres.'s Com. Econ. Impact of Def. and Disarmament, 1964; mem. U.S. Financial Investment Adv. Panel, 1970-72; cons. various firms and insts. Served with AUS, 1945. Recipient Alexander Hamilton medal Treasury Dept., 1971, Distinguished Writer award Georgetown U., 1971. Fellow Nat. Assn. Bus. Economists, Am. Inst. Aeros. and Astronautics (asso.); mem. Assn. Evolutionary Econs. (bd. dirs., 1970). City Coll. Alumni Assn. (Townsend Harris medal, 1969), Nat. Economists Club. Club: Cosmos. Author: Federal Budgeting, 1964; Modern Public Sector, 1969; Economics of Peacetime Defense, 1974; Economic Impact of the Vietnam War, 1967; Government-Mandated Price Increases, 1975; Business, Government, and the Public, 1977; The Future of Business Regulation, 1979. Editorial bd. Publius, 1971—, Jour. Econ. Issues, 1972-75, Challenge, 1974—. Home: 1531 Heirloom Ct Creve Coeur MO 63141 Office: Center for Study Am Business Washington U St Louis MO 63130

WEIDENFELD, EDWARD LEE, lawyer; b. Akron, Ohio, July 15, 1943; s. Sam and Beatrice (Cooper) W.; B.S., U. Wis., 1965; J.D., Columbia U., 1968; m. Sheila Rabb, Aug. 11, 1968; 1 son, Nicholas Rabb. Admitted to N.Y. bar, 1968, U.S. Supreme Ct. bar, 1972, D.C. bar, 1973; asso. firm Fried, Frank, Harris, Shriver & Jacobson, N.Y.C., 1968-71, Washington, 1973-74; mem. firm Hall, Estill & Weidenfeld, Washington, 1974-79; partner firm Sellers, Conner & Cuneo, Washington, 1979—; counsel, dir. energy staff Com. on Interior and Insular Affairs, U.S. Ho. of Reps., 1971-73; mem. faculty Am. Law Inst.-Am. Bar Assn. Continuing Legal Edn. Programs; lectr. to profl. groups; spl. cons. N.Y.C. Dept. Bldgs., 1967. Mem. Pres.'s Commn. on White House Fellowships, 1977. Mem. Am., D.C., Fed. Communications bar assns., Am. Law Inst., Assn. Bar City N.Y. Clubs: Met., Federal City (Washington). Editor-in-chief Atomic Energy Law Jour., 1975—; contbr. articles to legal jours. Home: 2903 Q St NW Washington DC 20007

WEIDENTHAL, MAURICE (BUD) DAVID, journalist; b. Cleve., Nov. 26, 1925; s. William and Evelyn (Kolinsky) W.; B.A., U. Mich., 1950; m. Grace Schwartz, Apr. 14, 1957; 1 dau., Susan Elizabeth. Mem. staff Cleve. Press, 1950—, editorial writer, 1950-51, asst. city editor, 1956-58, edn. editor, 1958—; cons. higher edn. Bd. dirs. Cleve. City Club, 1969—; chmn. rev. com. Cleve. Welfare Fedn., 1965—; trustee Hebrew Free Loan Assn., 1975—. Served with AUS, 1944-45. Decorated Air medal. Mem. Edn. Writers Assn., Sigma Delta Chi. Home: 2990 Coleridge Rd Cleveland Heights OH 44118 Office: 901 Lakeside Ave Cleveland OH 44114

WEIDLINGER, PAUL, cons. engr.; b. Budapest, Hungary, Dec. 22, 1914; s. Andrew and Juliete Weidlinger; came to U.S., 1944, naturalized, 1949; M.S., Tech. Inst. Brno, 1929; M.S., Swiss Poly. Inst. Zurich, 1933; m. Solveig Højberg, Dec. 24, 1964; children—Thomas, Pauline, Jonathan. Chief engr. Bur. of Reclamation, La Paz, Bolivia, 1939-42; prof. engring. San Andres U., La Paz, 1939-42; chief engr. Atlas Aircraft, N.Y.C., 1944-46; dir. div. Nat. Housing Agy., Washington, 1946-47; individual practice cons. engring., N.Y.C., 1947—; partner Weidlinger Assos., N.Y.C., 1949—; vis. lectr. Harvard U., M.I.T.; mem. sci. adv. bd. U.S. Air Force; cons. RAND Corp.; fellow Hudson Inst. Fellow ASCE (J.R. Croes medal 1963, Moisseiff award 1975), Am. Concrete Inst., Internat. Assn. Bridge and Structural Engrs., N.Y. Acad. Scis., AIAA. Contbr. articles to profl. and sci. jours. Home: 301 E 47th St New York NY 10017 Office: 110 E 59th St New York NY 10022

WEIDMAN, HAZEL HITSON, anthropologist, educator; b. Taft, Calif., Aug. 3, 1923; d. Frederick Dhu and Estell M. (Griesemer) Hitson; B.S. in Social Anthropology, Northwestern U., 1951; A.M. (Thomas Dana fellow) in Social Anthropology, Radcliffe Coll., 1957, Ph.D. (USPHS fellow), 1959; m. William H. Weidman, Sept. 9, 1960; children—William, Charles. Staff anthropologist Mass. Dept. of Pub. Health, Boston, 1959-60; cons. social sci. USPHS, Washington, 1960, Calif. Dept. Pub. Health, 1964; asst. prof. sociology and anthropology Coll. of William and Mary, Williamsburg, Va., 1964-65; asst. prof. social anthropology dept. psychiatry U. Ala. Med. Center, Birmingham, 1965-67; asso. research fellow Social Sci. Research Inst., U. Hawaii, Honolulu, 1967-68; asso. prof. social anthropology dept. psychiatry U. Miami Sch. Medicine, Miami, 1968-72, prof., 1972—; asso. prof. dept. anthropology U. Miami, Coral Gables, 1968-72, prof., 1972-77. Cons. social sci. U. Ala. Hosps. and Clinics, Birmingham, 1965-67; cons. social anthropology Nat. Center for Health Services Research and Devel., 1970-71; mem. med. adv. bd. Ednl. Film Prodn., Riverside, Calif., 1969—. Am. Philos. Soc. research grantee, 1965; Commonwealth Fund of N.Y. research grantee, 1971-73, Continuation grantee, 1973-75. Fellow Soc. Applied Anthropology, Am. Anthrop. Assn. (chmn. steering com. group for med. anthropology 1967-69, mem. com. on membership 1968-70, chmn. organizing com. 1969-70); mem. So. Anthrop. Soc., Assn. for Behavioral Scis. and Med. Edn., Soc. for Med. Anthropology, Council on Anthropology and Edn., Phi Beta Kappa. Founding editor Med. Anthropology Newsletter, 1968-71. Contbr. articles and book revs. on social anthropology to profl. jours.; contbr. book chpts. on social anthropology. Home: 1133 Placetas Ave Coral Gables FL 33146 Office: Dept of Psychiatry (D8-3) U Miami School Medicine PO Box 016960 Miami FL 33101

WEIDMAN, JEROME, author; b. N.Y.C., Apr. 4, 1913; s. Joseph and Annie (Falkovitz) W.; ed. Coll. City N.Y., 1930-33, Washington Sq. Coll., N.Y.C., 1933-34, N.Y.U. Law Sch., 1934-37; m. Peggy Wright, 1943; children—Jeffrey, John Whitney. Author: I Can Get It for You Wholesale, 1937; What's in It for Me?, 1938; The Horse that Could Whistle Dixie, 1939; Letter of Credit, 1940; I'll Never Go There Any More, 1941; The Lights Around the Shore, 1943; Too Early To Tell, 1946; The Captain's Tiger, 1947; The Price is Right, 1949; The Hand of the Hunter, 1951; The Third Angel, 1953; Traveler's Cheque, 1954; Give Me Your Love, 1954; Your Daughter, Iris, 1955; A Dime A throw, 1957; The Enemy Camp, 1958; (play) Florello!, 1959; Before You Go, 1960; (play) Tenderloin, 1961; My Father Sits In The Dark, 1961; (novel) The Sound of Bow Bells, 1962; (play) I Can Get It For You Wholesale, 1962; Back Talk, 1963; Nine Stories (short stories), 1964; Word Of Mouth, 1964; The Death of Dickie Draper, 1965; Other People's Money, 1968; (novel) The Center of The Action, 1969; (play) Ivory Tower, 1969; (play) Asterisk, 1969; (novel) Fourth Street East, 1971; (novel) Last Respects, 1972; Tiffany Street, 1974; The Temple, 1976; A Family Fortune, 1978. Co-recipient Pulitizer prize in drama for play Fiorello!, 1960; recipient Antoinette Perry award; Drama Critics Circle award. Mem. Authors League Am. (pres. 1969-74). Home: 1390 S Ocean Blvd Pompano Beach FL 33062

WEIDMANN, VICTOR HUGO, civil engr.; b. N.Y.C., Mar. 25, 1926; s. Victor Hugo and Dorothy Gilroe (Caldwell) W.; B.S. in Civil Engring., Northeastern U., 1953; m. Eleanor Janice Porreca, May 27, 1949; children—Donna Lynn, Lisa Marlene, Suzanne V. Safety engr. Am. Associated Ins. Cos., N.Y.C., 1948-49; jr. detailer and cold test engr. Raytheon Mfg. Co., Waltham, Mass., 1949-50; survey party chief Harry Feldman, Boston, 1950-53; engr. U.S. Steel Corp., Pitts., 1953-54, Gary, Ind., 1954-56; asso., br. mgr. Hurst-Rosche & Assos., Gary, 1956-63; owner, mgr. Weidmann Engring., Gary and Hobart, Ind., 1963-73; partner, v.p. James H. Stewart & Assos., Inc., Ft. Collins, Colo., 1973—. Active Community Chest. Served with USCG, 1943-46; CBI, ETO, NATOUSA, MTO, PTO. Registered profl. engr., Colo., Wyo., Ill., Mich., Ind.; registered land surveyor, Colo., Ind.; certified wastewater treatment plant operator, Class IV, Ind.; diplomate Am. Acad. Environ. Engrs. Fellow ASCE (pres. N.W. br. Ind. sect. 1968-69), Am. Cons. Engrs. Council (nat. dir., Colo. chmn. govt. affairs advisory program); mem. Am. Water Works Assn., Ry. Engring. Assn., Nat. Soc. Profl. Engrs., Water Pollution Control Fedn., Inst. Transp. Engrs., Am. Arbitration Assn. (nat. panel), Am., Rocky Mountain quarter horse assns., Metric Assn., Nat. Rifle Assn. Unitarian. Clubs: Shriners, Masons. Engring. works include Oak Knoll Terr. Housing Devel., Gary, 1966, Constrn. Engring. Twin Pipeline Arch Bridge over Ship Canal, Romeoville, Ill., 1971, Central Relief Sewer System, Terre Haute, Ind., 1962. Home: 201 E County Rd 66E Fort Collins CO 80524 Office: 214 N Howes St PO Box 429 Fort Collins CO 80522

WEIDNER, EDWARD WILLIAM, univ. chancellor, polit. scientist; b. Mpls., July 7, 1921; s. Peter Clifford and Lillian (Halbe) W.; B.A. magna cum laude, U. Minn., 1942, M.A., 1943, Ph.D., 1946; postgrad. U. Wis., 1943-45; L.H.D. (hon.), No. Mich. U., 1969; m. Jean Elizabeth Blomquist, Mar. 23, 1944; children—Nancy Louise, Gary Richard, Karen, William. Staff mem. Nat. Municipal League, 1944, research asso., 1944-45; cons. govts. div. U.S. Bur. Census, 1945, statistician, 1946; lectr. U. Wis., 1945; instr. U. Minn., 1945-47, asst. prof., 1947-49, asst. dir. research in inter-govtl. relations, 1946-53; asst. prof. U. Calif. at Los Angeles, 1949-50; faculty Mich. State U., 1950-62, asso. prof., dir. govtl. research bur., prof. polit. sci., 1952-62, head dept., 1952-57, coordinator, chief adviser Vietnam Project, 1955-57, dir. Inst. Research on Overseas Programs, 1957-61; vice chancellor East West Center, 1962-65; prof. polit. sci., dir. Center for Devel. Change, U. Ky., Lexington, 1965-67; chancellor U. Wis., Green Bay, 1966—. Cons. Fgn. Operations Adminstrn., Vietnam, 1954-55, Baltimore County (Md.) Reorgn. Commn., 1953-54, Nat. Assn. Fgn. Student Advisers, 1959-60, Pres.'s Task Force Fgn. Econ. Assistance, 1961, Dept. State, 1962-63, AID, 1964-65; mem. Gov. Mich. Commn. Inter-govtl. Relations, 1954-55; cons. Ford Found., Pakistan, 1956, Lees Coll., 1971-72; mem. UN Univ. Council, 1974—. Bd. dirs. Prairie Sch., 1971—, Inst. for Shipboard Edn., 1976—. Mem. Am. Polit. Sci. Assn. (nat. council 1950-52), Eastern Regional Orgn. Pub. Administrn., Comparative Edn. Soc., Am. Soc. Pub. Adminstrn. (nat. council 1947-50), Am. Council on Edn. (sec. 1971-72, mem. commn. on acad. affairs 1971-74), Assn. Am. Colls. (bd. dirs. 1978—), Nat. Mcpl. League, Nature Conservancy, Audubon Soc., Phi Beta Kappa, Pi Sigma Alpha. Author: (with William Anderson) American City Government, 1950; State and Local Government, 1951; American Government, 1953; (with others) The International Programs of American Universities, 1958; Intergovernmental Relations as Seen by Public Officials, 1960; (with William Anderson, Clara Penniman) Government for the Fifty States, 1960; The World Role of Universities, 1962; Technical Assistance in Public Administration Overseas, 1964. Editor: Development Administration in Asia, 1970. Home: 3015 Bay View Dr Green Bay WI 54301

WEIDNER, RICHARD TILGHMAN, physicist, educator; b. Allentown, Pa., Mar. 31, 1921; s. Miles Percival and Mabel (Aichroth) W.; B.S. summa cum laude, Muhlenberg Coll., 1943; M.S., Yale, 1943, Ph.D., 1948; m. Jean Elizabeth Fritsch, June 28, 1947; children—Christopher, Allegra, Timothy. Instr. physics Yale, 1943-44; instr. Rutgers U., 1947-48, asst. prof., 1948-53, asso. prof., 1953-63, prof. physics, 1963—; asst. dean Rutgers Coll., 1966-69, asso. dean, 1969-77, acting dean, 1977—; physicist U.S. Naval Research Lab., Washington, 1944-46. Mem. Bd. Edn., Bridgewater Twp., N.J., 1957-63. Served as ensign USNR, 1944-45. Fellow Am. Phys. Soc.; mem. Sigma Xi. Lutheran. Author: (with R.L. Sells) Elementary Modern Physics, 2d edit., 1973, Elementary Classical Physics, 2d edit., 1973; (with H.Y. Carr) Physics from the Ground Up, 1971; also many articles in field; contbr. Physics sect. Ency. Brit., 15th edit., 1974. Home: 61 Hillcrest Rd Martinsville NJ 08836 Office: Milledoler Hall Rutgers U New Brunswick NJ 08903

WEIDNER, ROSWELL THEODORE, artist; b. Reading, Pa., Sept. 18, 1911; s. Harry and Amelia (Hughes) W.; student Pa. Acad. Fine Arts, 1932-36, Barnes Found., 1933-35; m. Marilyn Kemp, Dec. 1, 1957; children—Roslyn, Janice. One-man exhbns. include Pa. Acad. Fine Arts, 1940, 60, 65, Reading Mus., 1961, William Penn Meml. Mus., Harrisburg, Pa., 1966, McCleaf Gallery, Phila., 1970, Newman Galleries, Phila., 1978; rep. permanent collections Pa. Acad. Fine Arts, Phila. Mus. Art, Met. Mus. Art, Library of Congress, U. Pa., Conn. State Libraries, others; works exhbt. Kennedy Galleries, N.Y.C., Langman Galleries, Phila.; sr. instr. Pa. Acad. Fine Arts, 1938—. Cresson Fgn. Travelling scholar, 1935-36; recipient Percy Owens award, 1975. Fellow Pa. Acad. Fine Arts (pres. 1955-70); mem. Am. Inst. Conservation Historic and Artistic Works, Nat. Trust Historic Preservation. Clubs: Peal, Society Hill (Phila.). Home: 612 Spruce St Philadelphia PA 19106 Office: Pa Acad Fine Arts Broad and Cherry Sts Philadelphia PA 19102

WEIDNER, STEVEN ARTHUR, lawyer; b. Waterloo, Iowa, Sept. 6, 1940; s. Hamilton D. and Calista S. (Ungs) W.; B.B.A., U. Notre Dame, 1962, J.D., 1965; m. Kathryn M. Della Maria, June 25, 1966; children—Geoffrey Joseph, Maura Susanne, Kenna Elizabeth. Admitted to Iowa bar, 1965; partner firm Swisher & Cohrt, Waterloo, since 1973; formerly corp. sec. Rath Packing Co., Waterloo. Bd. dirs. Iowa div. Am. Cancer Soc., United Way Black Hawk County. Served to lt. USNR, 1965-68. Mem. Iowa, Black Hawk County bar assns. Home: 507 Sunset Rd Waterloo IA 50701 Office: 300 WSB Bldg PO Box 1200 Waterloo IA 50704

WEIGEL, STANLEY ALEXANDER, U.S. judge; b. Helena, Mont., Dec. 9, 1905; s. Louis and Jennie (Hepner) W.; A.B., Stanford, 1926, J.D., 1928; M. Anne Kauffman, Apr. 21, 1940; children—Jane Anne, Susan Mary. Admitted to Calif. bar, 1928; practice in San Francisco, 1928-62; U.S. judge No. Dist. Calif., 1962—. Non resident lectr. Stanford Law Sch., 1952—. Mem. Jud. Panel on Multidist, Litigation, 1968—. Pres. Internat. Hospitality Center Bay Area, 1959-68, Nat. Council for Community Services to Internat. Visitors, 1972-73; adv. gov. Calif. on Automobile Accident Commn., 1959. Chmn. bd. visitors Stanford Law Sch., 1958-63; trustee World Affairs Council No. Calif., 1960—, pres., 1973-74; chmn. Ford Found. vis. com. to study behavioral sci. depts. Stanford, 1956-57. Served to lt. USNR, 1943-45. Decorated chevalier Order Leopold II (Belgium). Mem. Delta Sigma Rho, Phi Alpha Delta, Sigma Delta Chi. Office: US Dist Court San Francisco CA 94102

WEIGEL, WILLIAM FREDERICK, lawyer; b. N.Y.C., Sept. 26, 1923; s. Elmer Peter and Sara Madeline (Westerbeke) W.; grad. Lawrenceville Sch., 1941; student Princeton U., 1941-43; B.S. magna cum laude, Lehigh U., 1949; J.D., N.Y. U., 1951; m. Frances B. Perry, Feb. 14, 1952 (div.); children— Madeleine, Amy, (Mrs. William E. Minor IV), Patricia, William Breck. Admitted to N.Y. State bar, 1951, D.C. bar, 1978; asso. firm Rogers Hoge & Hills, N.Y.C., 1951—, partner, 1959—, sr. partner, 1970—; asso. gen. counsel Proprietary Assn., 1960-71; sec., counsel Am. Found. Pharm. Edn., 1971—; counsel Council Family Health, 1972—; atty. Village of Pelham (N.Y.), 1964-65, trustee, 1965-67, mayor, 1967-70; del. Westchester County Jud. Conf., 1965-71; instr. law Bernard Baruch Sch., CCNY; lectr. N.Y. U. Grad. Sch. Law, Practising Law Inst. Served with USNR, 1942-46. Mem. Am. Bar Assn. N.Y. State Bar Assn. (chmn. food, drug and cosmetic law sect. 1978—; ho. of dels. 1978—), N.Y.C. Bar Assn., Internat. Acad. Law Sci. Republican. Contbr. articles on trademark and food and drug law to profl. jours. Home: 201 E 66th St New York NY 10021 Office: 90 Park Ave New York NY 10016

WEIGEND, GUIDO GUSTAV, educator, geographer; b. Zeltweg, Austria, Jan. 2, 1920; s. Gustav F. and Paula (Sorgo) W.; came to U.S., 1939, naturalized, 1943; B.S., U. Chgo., 1942, M.S., 1946, Ph.D., 1949; m. Areta Kelble, June 26, 1947; children—Nina, Cynthia, Kenneth. With OSS, 1943-45, mil. intelligence War Dept., 1946; instr. geography U. Ill., 1946-47; instr., then asst. prof. geography Beloit Coll., 1947-49; asst. prof. geography Rutgers U., 1949-51, asso. prof., 1951-57, prof., 1957-76, acting chmn. dept., chmn., 1951-67, asso. dean Rutgers Coll., 1972-76; dean Coll. Liberal Arts, prof. geography Ariz. State U., Tempe, 1976—; Fulbright lectr. U. Barcelona, 1960-61; vis. prof. geography Columbia, 1963-67, N.Y. U., 1967, U. Colo., summer 1968, U. Hawaii, summer 1969. Liaison rep. Rutgers U. to UN, 1950-52; mem. U.S. nat. com. Internat. Geog. Union, 1951-58, 61-65; chmn. Conf. on Polit. and Social Geography, 1968-69. Bd. adjustment Franklin Twp., N.J., 1959; mem. Bd. Edn., Highland Park, N.J., 1973-75, v.p., 1975; mem. Ariz. Humanities Council, 1976—; commr. from Ariz. to commn. on instns. of higher edn. North Central Assn. Colls. and Schs., 1976—; mem. exec. com. Fedn. Pub. Programs in Humanities, 1977—. Research for study European ports Office Naval Research, 1952-55; Social Science Research Council grantee, 1956; Ford Found. grantee, 1966; Rutgers Research Council fellow, 1970-71; Fulbright travel grantee, Netherlands, 1970-71; grantee Am. Philos. Soc., 1970-71. Mem. Assn. Am. Geographers (chmn. N.Y. Met. div. 1955-56, editorial bd. 1955-59, mem. council 1965-66; chmn. N.Y.-N.J. div. 1965-66), Assn. Pacific Coast Geographers, Phoenix Com. on Fgn. Relations (vice chmn. 1976-79, chmn. 1979—), Sigma Xi. Author articles profl. jours., also monograph, bulls.; co-author: A Geography of Europe, 4th edit., 1977; geog. editor-in-chief Odyssey World Atlas, 1966. Home: 2094 E Golf Ave Tempe AZ 85282 Office: College of Liberal Arts Ariz State U Tempe AZ 85281

WEIGER, JOHN GEORGE, educator; b. Dresden, Germany, Feb. 6, 1933; s. Willy and Elisabeth (Prinz) W.; came to U.S., 1938, naturalized, 1945; B.A., Middlebury Coll., 1955; M.A., U. Colo., 1957; Ph.D. (NDEA fellow), Ind. U., 1966; m. Leslie Lawrence Carpenter, Dec. 28, 1955; children—Robert Boyden, Mark Owen, Heidi Elaine. Instr., U. Colo., Boulder, 1955-57, Lawrence Coll., Appleton, Wis., 1957-58; instr. Romance langs. U. Vt., Burlington, 1958-62, asst. prof., 1964-67, asso. prof., 1967-73, prof., 1973—, vice chmn. Romance lang. dept., 1964-68, asst. dean Coll. Arts and Scis., 1968-69, asso. dean, 1969-71, dean, 1971-76, instnl. rep. for Rhodes scholarships, Danforth fellowships, Turrell Fund scholarships, 1971-76, program chmn. George Aiken lecture series, 1975; vis. lectr. U. Bologna, 1978. U. Vt. Faculty Research fellow, 1967; Am. Council Learned Socs. grantee, 1978. Mem. Modern Lang. Assn. (chmn. comedia sect. 1970-71), Renaissance Soc. Am., Am. Assn. Tchrs. Spanish and Portuguese, The Comediantes, Council of Colls. of Arts and Scis., Assn. for Gen. and Liberal Studies, Am. Assn. Higher Edn., Internat. Assn. Hispanists, Phi Sigma Iota. Author: Introduction to the Youthful Deeds of the Cid, 1969; The Valencian Dramatists of Spain's Golden Age, 1976; Cristobal de Virues, 1978; Hacia la Comedia, 1978; The Individuated Self: Cervantes and the Emergence of the Individual, 1979; mem. editorial bd. Bull. of Comediantes, 1978—. Contbr. articles to profl. jours., also chpts. to books. Home: Woodbine Rd Shelburne VT 05482 Office: 521 Waterman Bldg U Vt Burlington VT 05405

WEIGER, RALPH JAMES, automotive equipment mfg. co. exec.; b. Hammond, Ind., Jan. 21, 1925; s. Oscar W. and Mabel (Fulton) W.; B.E.E., Purdue U., 1949; student Wis. U., 1943, Ga. U., 1943; m. Eleanor White, Sept. 3, 1949 (div. July 1970); children—Lucy Ellen, Barbara Julia, Ralph James; m. 2d, Katherine C. Chapman, Dec. 30, 1971. Dist. mgr. Square D Co., Cleve., 1949-59; div. mgr. Electronic Fed. Pacific Elec., Newark, 1959-65; pres. Signal-Stat div. Lehigh Valley Industries, N.Y.C., 1965-71, exec. v.p., dir. Lehigh Valley Industries, 1969-71; v.p. Abex Corp., N.Y.C., 1971—; pres., chmn. bd. Signal-Stat Corp. N.Y., 1971-74; pres., chief exec. officer Midas Internat. Corp., Chgo., 1974-78, also dir.; owner W.T. Grimm & Co., Chgo., 1978-79, Authentic Homes Corp N.J., 1973—; pres. Yusaf A. Alganim & Sons, N.Y.C. and Kuwait, 1979—; dir. IC Products Co., Pepsi-Cola Gen. Bottlers, Authentic Homes Corp., N.Y.C. Affiliate Inc.; active numerous civic orgns. Served with USNR, 1943-45. Mem. IEEE, Soc. Automotive Engrs., Automotive Pres.'s Council, Internat. Franchise Assn. (pres.), Motor Equipment Mfrs. Assn., Pres.'s Council Purdue U., Purdue Alumni Assn., Sigma Chi. Clubs: Canoe Brook Country (Summit, N.J.); Morris County Country (Morristown, N.J.); Vail Ski Assn. Home: Sand Spring Rd New Vernon NJ 07976

WEIGER, ROBERT WILLIAM, physician; b. Grantwood, N.J., Nov. 23, 1927; s. Joseph Anthony and Helen Marie (Cochrane) W.; B.S., Northwestern U., 1951, M.D., 1955; m. Nadine Luxmore, Oct. 19, 1957; 1 dau., Wendy Anne. Intern Passavant Meml. Hosp., Chgo., 1955-56; officer USPHS, 1956—, med. dir., 1964; clin. asso. Nat. Cancer Inst., 1956-58; med. clinic physician, Miami, Fla., 1958-59; resident internal medicine USPHS Hosp., Balt., 1959-62; asst. dir. Nat. Cancer Inst., NIH, 1962-65; chief Office of Pesticides USPHS, 1965-66; program coordinator pharmacology and toxicology programs Nat. Inst. of Gen. Medical Scis., Office of Dir., NIH, 1966—; spl. asst. to dir. Nat. Insts. Health, 1964—. Spl. research internal medicine, diabetes melitus, tumor proteins. Mem. A.M.A., Mil Surgeons Assn., Am. Diabetes Assn., Am. Cancer Soc., Am. Diabetes Assn., Am. Pub. Works Assn., Phi Rho Sigma (award 1954). Roman Cath. Author articles in field. Home: 2816 Blazer Ct Wheaton MD 20906 Office: Nat Inst Gen Med Scis Nat Inst Health Bethesda MD 20014

WEIGLE, RICHARD DANIEL, coll. pres.; b. Northfield, Minn., Mar. 9, 1912; s. Luther Allan and Clara Rosetta (Boxrud) W.; A.B., Yale, 1931, A.M., 1937, Ph.D., 1939; student Yale Div. Sch., 1933-34; LL.D., Washington Coll., 1957, LaSalle Coll., 1958, Wabash Coll., 1960, Coll. Notre Dame Md., 1965, Colo. Coll., 1969; L.H.D., Bard Coll., 1970, St. Francis Coll., 1972, St. Mary's Coll. Md., 1975; m. Mary Grace Day, Apr. 4, 1942; children—Mary Martha, Constance Day (Mrs. Thomas W. Mann). Instr. English, Yali Union Middle Sch. (Yale-in-China), Changsha, Hunan, China, 1931-33; instr., then asst. prof. history, econs. and internat. relations Carleton Coll., Northfield, Minn., 1939-42; staff Office Far Eastern Affairs, Dept. State, 1946-49; pres. St. John's Coll., Annapolis, Md., 1949—, also pres. St. John's Coll., Santa Fe, N.Mex., 1961—. Mem. Anne Arundel County School Bd., 1952-64, pres., 1958-63; pres. Md. Assn. Bds. Edn., 1961-62; vice chmn. Ind. Coll. Funds Am., 1967-68; chmn. Md. Commn. on Capital City, 1967-77; vice chmn. Md. Hall of Records Commn., 1949—; cons. Nat. Endowment for Humanities, 1974—. Trustee Yale-China Assn.; trustee Key Sch., Annapolis, chmn., 1972-74, St. Mary's Coll. of Md. Served with USAAF, 1942-45; hdqrs. G-2, G-3, Chinese Army in India; sec. gen. staff Chinese Combat Command. Mem. Annapolis C. of C. (hon. dir.), Newcomen Soc., Am. Hist. Assn., Md. Hist. Soc., Assn. Am. Colls. (chmn. commn. liberal edn. 1955-57, treas. 1963-66, chmn. 1967-68), Phi Beta Kappa. Kiwanian, Rotarian. Clubs: Annapolitan. Contbr. articles to profl. publs. Home: 212 Norwood Rd Annapolis MD 21401 also 1040 Camino San Acacio Santa Fe NM 87501

WEIHAUPT, JOHN GEORGE, scientist, univ. dean; b. La Crosse, Wis., Mar. 5, 1930; s. John George and Gladys Mae (Ash) W.; student St. Norbert Coll., De Pere, Wis., 1948-49; B.S., U. Wis., 1952, M.S., 1953; M.S., U. Wis.-Milw., 1971; Ph.D., U. Wis., 1973; m. Audrey Mae Reis, Jan. 28, 1961. Exploration geologist Am. Smelting & Refining Co., Nfld., 1953, Anaconda Co., Chile, S.Am., 1956-57; seismologist United Geophys. Corp., 1958; geophysicist Arctic Inst. N. Am., Antarctica, 1958-60, Geophys. and Polar Research Center, U. Wis., Antarctica, 1960-63; dir. Participating Coll. and Univ. program, chmn. dept. phys. and biol. sci. U.S. Armed Forces Inst., Dept. Def., 1963-73; dean for acad. affairs Sch. Sci., Ind. U.-Purdue U., Indpls., 1973-78, prof. geology, 1973-78; asst. dean Grad. Sch., prof. geoscis. Purdue U., 1975-78; prof. geology, dean grad. studies and research, v.p. Univ. Research Found., San Jose (Calif.) State U., 1978—. Sci. cons., mem. sci. adv. bd. Holt Reinhart and Winston, Inc., 1967—; sci. editor, cons. McGraw-Hill Co., 1966—; hon. lectr. U. Wis., 1963-73; geol. cons., 1968—; editorial cons. John Wiley & Sons, 1968; editorial adv. bd. Dushkin Pub. Group, 1971—. Mem. Capital Community Citizens Orgn.; mem. Madison Transp. Study Com.; mem. Found. for Internat. Energy Research and Tng., U.S. com. for UN Univ.; mem. sci. council Internat. Center for Interdisciplinary Cycle Research; mem. Internat. Awareness and Leadership Council; mem. governing bd. Moss Landing Marine Labs.; bd. dirs. San Jose State U. Found. Served as 1st lt. AUS, 1953-55, Korea. Mt. Weihaupt in Antarctica named for him, 1966; recipient Madisonian medal for outstanding community service, 1973; Outstanding Cote Meml. award, 1974; Antarctic medal, 1968. Fellow Geol. Soc. Am., Explorers Club; mem. Nat. Sci. Tchrs. Assn., Am. Geophys. Union, Internat. Council Corr. Edu., Soc. Am. Mil. Engrs., Wis. Alumni Assn., Soc. Study Biol. Rhythms, Internat. Soc. for Chronobiology, Marine Tech. Soc., AAAS, Univ. Indsl. Adv. Council, Am. Council on Edn., Expdn. Polaire France (hon.), Found. for Study Cycles, Assn. Am. Geographers, Nat. Council Univ. Research Adminstrs., Soc. Research Adminstrs., Man-Environ. Communication Center, Internat. Union Geol. Scis., Internat. Geog. Union, Internat. Soc. Study Time, Community Council Pub. TV, Internat. Platform Assn., Ind., Midwest assns. grad. schs., Western Assn. Grad. Schs., Council Grad. Schs. in U.S., Wis. Alumni Assn. Indpls., Capital Community Citizens Assn. Clubs: Carmel Racquet, Kiwanis. Author: Oceanography, General Geophysics, Principles of Physical Science, Vol. I and II; Physical Geology, Historical Geology; Exploration of the Oceans: An Introduction to Oceanography; editorial bd. Internat. Jour. Interdisciplinary Cycle Research (Leiden). Co-discoverer USARP Mountain Range (Arctic Inst. Mountain Range), in Victoria Land, Antartica, 1960; co-discoverer Wilkes Land Meteorite Crater, Antarctica. Home: 166 Altura Vista Los Gatos CA 95030 Office: Grad Studies Office San Jose State U Washington Sq San Jose CA 95192. *Each of us as an individual has a responsibility to all other individuals in our world—and responsibility for our own behavior.*

WEIL, FRANK A., lawyer; b. Bedford, N.Y., Feb. 14, 1931; s. Sylvan and Ruth Alice (Norman) W.; B.A. cum laude, Harvard U., 1953, LL.B., 1956; m. Denie Sandison, Feb. 10, 1951; children—Deborah Weil Harrington, Amanda, Sandison, William. Admitted to N.Y. State bar, 1956; practiced in N.Y.C., 1957-60; gen. partner Loeb, Rhoades & Co., N.Y.C., 1960-71; pres. Abacus Fund, Inc., 1968-72; chief fin. officer, dir. Paine, Webber, Jackson & Curtis, N.Y.C., 1972-77; asst. sec. industry and trade Dept. Commerce, Washington, 1977-79; partner firm Ginsburg, Feldman, Weil & Bress, Washington, 1979—; dir. Dorr-Oliver, Inc., Stamford, Conn., 1968-77, Hamburg Savs. Bank, N.Y.C., 1975-77, J.B. Lippincott Co., Phila., 1975-77, Govt. Research Corp., 1975-77, 79—; dir., pres. Norman Found., 1953-77, 79—. Trustee, Tchrs. Coll., Columbia U., 1976-79, Montefiore Hosp., 1960-77; trustee, vice chmn. No. Westchester Hosp., 1971-77; past pres. Ednl. Alliance, trustee, 1957-77; trustee, sec. Fedn. Jewish Philanthropies, N.Y.C., 1965-77; trustee, chmn. Harvey Sch., 1969-76; trustee Hurricane Island Outward Bound Sch., 1974—; bd. dirs., pres. Hickrill Found., Inc., 1953-77, 79—; mem. vis. com. Kennedy Sch. Govt., Harvard U.; chmn. tax com., mem. N.Y. State Econ. Devel. Bd., 1975-77; chmn., mem. N.Y. State Bd. Equalization and Assessment, 1976-77; adv. bd. Sch. Advanced Internat. Studies, Johns Hopkins U., 1979—. Clubs: Century Assn., Harvard, Econ. (N.Y.C.); Met., Fed. City (Washington). Home: 1535 28th St NW Washington DC 20007 Office: 1700 Pennsylvania Ave NW Washington DC 20006

WEIL, GILBERT HARRY, lawyer; b. N.Y.C., Aug. 31, 1912; s. Alexis and Esther (Marks) W.; B.S., N.Y. U., 1933, J.D., 1937; m. Louise Rhoda Cohen, Mar. 14, 1936; children—Allen Charles, Jeffrey Lee. Admitted to N.Y. bar, 1937; law clk. and asso. to Isaac W. Digges, 1935-53; pvt. practice, 1953-65; partner firm Weil and Lee, N.Y.C., 1966-69; partner Weil, Lee & Bergin, N.Y.C., 1969-76, Weil, Guttman & Davis, N.Y.C., 1976—; lectr. in field, 1952—. Served to lt (j.g.) USNR, 1943-45. Contbr. articles to profl. jours. Address: 6910-108th St Forest Hills NY 11375

WEIL, HERMAN, educator; b. Regisheim, Alsace Lorraine, Dec. 15, 1905; Ph.D. in Psychology, U. Marburg (Germany), 1929, state exam. in math., chemistry, physics, 1929, state exam. in edn., Kassel, Germany, 1931; m. Bertha Weiler, July 26, 1931; 1 son, Gunther M. Came to U.S., 1938, naturalized, 1944. Instr., Realgymnasium for Girls, Hersfeld, Germany, 1931-33; instr., studienrat Philanthropin Realgymnasium, Frankfurt on Main, Germany, 1933-38; postdoctoral scholar U. Iowa, 1939; prof. sci. Neb. Central Coll., 1939-40; prof. Milw. Sch. Engring., 1940-43; prof. edn. and psychology, head dept. Wis. State Coll., Milw., 1943-56; prof. psychology U. Wis., Milw., 1956-76, prof. emeritus, 1976—, chmn. dept., 1956-61, chmn. honors program superior students Coll. Letters and Scis., 1960-74, asso. dean, 1967-71, faculty retirement counselor, 1973-75; vis. prof. Northwestern U., summers 1947, 48, 51; cons. Human Relations Workshop, U. Mich., summers 1952-56; dir. Workshops on Human Relations, Wis. State Coll., summers 1952-56; lectr. Milw. Downer Coll., 1943-47; cons. Dept. of State, also U.S. Office Edn., Jugenheim, Germany, 1954; Disting. Service fellow Temple Emanu-El B'ne Jeshurun, 1976-78, 79—, dean adult Jewish Studies, 1978-79; Disting. scholar-in-residence Milw. Jewish Community Center, 1977—. Co-chmn. Wis. region NCCJ, 1952-72, mem. commn. on ednl. orgns., 1955-60, nat. bd. dirs., 1977—; nat. co-chmn. schs. and colls. com. observance of Brotherhood Week, 1957; mem. Gov.'s Commn. on Human Rights, 1953-56; counselor Milw. B'nai B'rith Hillel Found., 1950-60; pres. New Home Club, Inc., 1940-57, hon. pres., 1977—; chmn. Milw. chpt. Am. Jewish Com., 1973-75, mem. nat. exec. com., 1973—. Recipient citation of merit for work in human relations Milw. B'nai B'rith Councils, 1952, Brotherhood award Wis. region NCCJ, 1959, Citation award Internat. Inst. Milw. County, 1960, Disting. Merit citation NCCJ, 1973; Disting. Merit citation Wis. Soc. for Jewish Learning, 1973; Disting. Service award U. Wis.-Milw. chpt. AAUP, 1975; Disting. Merit citation Coll. Letters and Sci., U. Wis.-Milw., 1976; Am. Jewish Com. Inst. Human Relations award, 1978. Mem. A.A.U.P. (pres. Wis. conf. 1973-74), Wis. Soc. for Jewish Learning (past pres.), Wis. (past pres.), Milw. County (past pres.) psychol. assns., Nat. Collegiate Honors Council (mem. exec. com., 1972-73), Ret. Faculty Assn. of U. Wis.-Milw. (pres. 1977-79), Phi Kappa Phi (hon.). Jewish (past v.p., trustee temple). Author: In Quest of Excellence, 1975; University of Wisconsin-Milwaukee Faculty Retirement Guidebook, 1975, 2d edit., 1976. Contbr. chpts. and sects. to books on psychol. subjects. Home: 2027 E Lake Bluff Blvd Milwaukee WI 53211. *The alleviation of prejudice is one of the foremost challenges of our time. To assist in the process of reducing hate between man and man, group and group, nation and nation, requires a life of dedication and earnest commitment. It presents more than the utterances of words and good-will on special occasions of the year; it means the initiation and follow-through of appropriate action patterns in one's smaller and larger environment to bring closer to realization and fruition the ideal of the "Brotherhood of Man under the Fatherhood of God".*

WEIL, IRWIN, educator; b. Cin., Apr. 16, 1928; s. Sidney and Florence (Levy) W.; A.B., U. Chgo., 1948, M.A., 1951; Ph.D., Harvard U., 1960; m. Vivian Weil, Dec. 27, 1950; children—Martin, Alice, Daniel. Sr. social sci. research analyst Library of Congress, 1951-54; teaching fellow Harvard U., 1956-58; mem. faculty Brandeis U., 1958-65; mem. faculty dept. Slavic langs. and lit. Northwestern U., Evanston, Ill., 1966—, chmn. dept., 1976—; vis. prof. U. Moscow, Soviet Acad. Scis. Ford Found. fellow, 1954-55. Mem. Am. Assn. Tchrs. Slavic and East European Langs. (exec. sec. 1962-68), Am. Council Tchrs. Russian (v.p. 1975-79), Internat. Assn. Profs. of Russian (founding U.S. mem.). Jewish. Author books and articles in field. Office: Slavic Dept Northwestern Univ Evanston IL 60201

WEIL, LISL, comml. artist; b. Vienna, Austria. Came to U.S., 1939, naturalized, 1944. Illustrator various mags. and newspapers in Europe; illustrator, author more than 100 children's books; chalk talks for children, schs., libraries, stores, also Book Week for N.Y. Times, N.Y. Herald Tribune; TV show, Children's Sketch Book, NBC; illustrator on stage of music Young Peoples Concerts, Little Orchestra Soc. N.Y. with performances at Carnegie Hall, Avery Fisher Hall, Philharmonic Hall, N.Y.C., New Haven Symphony, Chgo. Symphony, Detroit Symphony Orch., Hartford Symphony Orch., Boston Pops Orch., Indpls. Symphony, Grand Rapids Symphony, Balt. Symphony Orch.; television appearances with Little Orchestra Soc., one hour children's specials on NBC, 1963-64, Boston Pops Orch. Concert spl., NBC-TV, 1967. Address: 25 Central Park W New York City NY 10023. *What blessing to be born with a talent. It means to SEE and FEEL and to EXPRESS it in lines, color and movement to make others see and feel. To me, my art is joy, fulfillment and strength in time of trials. I never stopped working at it since I was three years, and I grow at it and with it with every passing year.*

WEIL, MAX HARRY, physician, educator, med. researcher; b. Baden, Switzerland, Feb. 9, 1927; s. Marcel and Gretchen (Winter) W.; A.B., U. Mich., 1948; M.D., SUNY, 1952; Ph.D., U. Minn., 1957; m. Marianne Judith Posner, Apr. 9, 1955; children—Susan Margot, Carol Juliet. Chief cardiology City Hope Med. Center, Duarte, Calif., 1957-59; mem. faculty U. So. Calif. Med. Sch., 1959—, prof. clin. medicine, 1971—, prof. clin. biomed. engring. Sch. Engring., 1972—, chmn. div. critical care medicine and dir. Inst. Critical Care Medicine, 1978—; vis. prof. anesthesiology, critical care medicine U. Pitts. Med. Sch.; dir. U. So. Calif.-Los Angeles County Med. Center shock research unit, 1961—, sr. attending cardiologist children's div. Los Angeles County Hosp., 1958-65; dir. U. So. Calif. Center for Critically Ill, Hollywood Presbyn. Med. Center, Los Angeles, 1968—; sr. attending physician Los Angeles County-U. So. Calif. Med. Center; cons. physician med. staff Cedars-Sinai Med. Center, Los Angeles, 1965—, Temple Hosp., Midway Hosp.; cons. in acute medicine, physiology, pharmacology and clin. engring. to govt. and industry, mem. coms. Nat. Acad. Sci.-NRC. Chmn. Los Angeles County Com. Emergency Med. Care, 1968-73. Fellow A.C.P., Am. Coll. Cardiology (chmn. emergency room and pre-hosp. care com. 1978—); mem. AAUP, IEEE (sr.), AMA (commn. emergency med. services 1979—), Am. Soc. Pharmacology and Exptl. Therapeutics, Am. Soc. Nephrology, Am. Thoracic Soc., Assn. Computing Machinery, Los Angeles Soc. Internal Medicine, Assn. Univ. Emergency Med. Services, Fed. Soc. Emergency and Critical Care Medicine (pres. 1976-77), Soc. Critical Care Medicine (pres. 1970-72), Am. Physiol. Soc., Am. Fedn. Clin. Research, Western Soc. Clin. Research, Soc. Exptl. Biology and Medicine, Sigma Xi, Alpha Omega Alpha. Co-editor: Diagnosis and Treatment of Shock, 1967; Critical Care Medicine Handbook, 1974; Critical Care Medicine: Current Principles and Practices, 1976; Handbook of Critical Care Medicine, 1978; Manual of Critical Care Medicine, 1978; The Handbook of Critical Care Medicine, 1979; mem. editorial bd. Am. Jour. Medicine, Clin. Engring. Newsletter, Circulatory Shock, Intensive Care Medicine, Critical Care Medicine, Methods of Information in Medicine. Home: 910 N Beverly Dr Beverly Hills CA 90210 Office: U So Calif Sch Medicine 1300 N Vermont Ave Los Angeles CA 90027

WEIL, MYRON, banker; b. Lincoln, Nebr., Apr. 17, 1918; s. Julius and Fannie (Livingston) W.; B.S., Yale, 1939; m. Pauline Clayton, Sept. 26, 1945; children—Michele Susan, Judy Lynn, Layla. Exec. v.p., dir. Nat. Bank Commerce, Lincoln, 1939-67; chmn. bd., dir. First Nat. Bank, Clinton, Iowa, 1967—; exec. v.p. dir., Hawkeye Bancorp., Des Moines, 1967—. Served to maj., Q.M.C., AUS, 1939-45. Decorated Bronze Star. Home: Crescent Dr Clinton IA 52732 Office: 405 S 3d St Clinton IA 52732

WEIL, ROLF ALFRED, economist, univ. pres.; b. Pforzheim, Germany, Oct. 29, 1921; s. Henry and Lina (Landauer) W.; B.A., U. Chgo., 1942, Ph.D., 1950; D. Hebrew Letters, Coll. Jewish Studies, 1967; L.H.D., Loyola U., 1970; m. Leni Metzger, Nov. 3, 1945; children—Susan Linda, Ronald Alan. Came to U.S., 1936, naturalized, 1944. Research asst. Cowles Commn. for Research in Econs., 1942-44; research analyst Ill. Dept. Revenue, 1944-46; mem. faculty Roosevelt U., Chgo., 1946—, prof. finance and econs., also chmn. dept. finance, 1954-65, dean Coll. Bus. Adminstrn., 1957—, acting pres., 1965-66, pres., 1966—. Lectr. Ind. U.; tax cons. Pres., Selfhelp Home for Aged, Chgo.; dir. Edward A. Filene Good Will Fund. Mem. Am. Economic Assn., Investment Analysts Soc. Clubs: Rotary, Cliff Dwellers, Univ., Mid-Am. (Chgo.). Author several articles on finance. Home: 3015 Simpson St Evanston IL 60201 Office: 430 S Michigan Ave Chicago IL 60605

WEIL, ROMAN LEE, accountant, educator; b. Montgomery, Ala., May 22, 1940; s. Roman L. and Charlotte (Alexander) W.; B.A., Yale U., 1962; M.S. in Indsl. Adminstrn., Carnegie-Mellon U., 1965, Ph.D. in Econs., 1966; m. Cherie Buresh, Dec. 28, 1963; children—Alexie Cherie, Charles Alexander, Lacey Lorraine. From instr. to asso. prof. U. Chgo., 1965-74, prof. accounting, 1976—; Mills B. Lane prof. indsl. mgmt. Ga. Inst. Tech., 1974-76; advisory com. replacement cost implementation SEC, 1976-77. NSF grantee, 1967—. C.P.A. Mem. Am. Inst. C.P.A.'s, Ill. Soc. C.P.A.'s, Am. Econ. Assn., Inst. Mgmt. Scis., Nat. Assn. Accountants (certified in mgmt. accounting), Am. Accounting Assn., Inst. Managerial Accounting. Author: Fundamentals of Accounting, 1975; Financial Accounting, 2d edit., 1979; Accounting: The Language of Business, 4th edit., 1979; Inflation Accounting, 1976; Replacement Cost Accounting, 1976; Managerial Accounting, 1979; editor: Handbook of Modern Accounting, 1977; Handbook of Cost Accounting, 1978; Intermediate Accounting, 1980; Accounting Rev., 1974—. Home: 726 Sheridan Rd Evanston IL 60202 Office: Grad Sch Bus U Chgo 1101 E 58 St Chicago IL 60637

WEIL, STEPHEN EDWARD, mus. ofcl.; b. N.Y.C., June 24, 1928; s. Sidney and Beatrice (Sachs) W.; A.B., Brown U., 1949; LL.B., Columbia, 1956; m. Rose Reicherson, Oct. 15, 1950 (div.); children—Rachel J., David N., Michael D.; m. 2d, Elizabeth Carbone, Sept. 7, 1974. Admitted to N.Y. State bar, 1956; asso. firm Rosenman, Colin, Kaye, Petschek & Freund, N.Y.C., 1956-63; v.p., gen. mgr. Marlborough-Gerson Gallery, N.Y.C., 1963-67; adminstr., sec., trustee Whitney Mus. Am. Art, N.Y.C., 1967-74; dep. dir., sec. Hirshhorn Mus. and Sculpture Garden, Smithsonian Instn., Washington, 1974—. Mem. mus. adv. panel N.Y. State Council on Arts, 1974-78; mem. adv. panel Inst. for Mus. Scis. Served with AUS, 1951-52. Mem. Am. Assn. Museums (treas., v.p.). Jewish. Co-author: Art Works-Law, Policy, Practice, 1974. Co-editor: Legal and Business Problems of Artists, Art Galleries and Museums, 1973. Home: 2123 California St NW Washington DC 20008 Office: Hirshhorn Museum Washington DC 20560

WEIL, WILLIAM BACHRACH, JR., physician, educator; b. Mpls., Dec. 3, 1924; s. William Bachrach and Gladys (Moss) W.; B.A., U. Minn., 1945, B.S., 1946, M.B., 1947, M.D., 1948; m. Velma Stehlik, June 5, 1949; children—Susan, Constance. Intern Mpls. Gen. Hosp., 1948-49; resident in pediatrics Children's Hosp. Phila., 1949-51; USPHS fellow Children's Hosp., Boston, 1951-52; practice medicine specializing in pediatrics, Boston, 1951-52, Cleve., 1952-63, Gainesville, Fla., 1963-68, E. Lansing, Mich., 1968—; sr. instr. pediatrics Western Res. U., Cleve., 1952-57, asst. prof., 1957-63; asso. prof. pediatrics U. Fla., Gainesville, 1963-65, A.I. Du Pont prof. handicapped children, 1965-68, acting chmn. dept. pediatrics, 1967-68; chmn. dept. human devel. Mich. State U., East Lansing, 1968-79, prof., 1968—; cons. program Nat. Found., 1964-68; mem. tng. coms. Nat. Inst. Child Health and Human Devel., 1967-71, chmn., 1970-71. Served to capt., M.C., AUS, 1955-57. USPHS spl. postdoctoral fellow Cambridge (Eng.) U., 1960-61. Mem. Am. Acad. Pediatrics (com. children with handicaps 1967-70, com. nutrition 1968-74, com. Indian health 1976—), Soc. Pediatric Research (sec.-treas. 1957-68, pres. elect 1968-69, pres. 1969-70), Assn. Am. Med. Colls., Council of Academic Socs. (adminstrv. bd. 1970-73, sec.

1971-73), Phi Beta Kappa, Alpha Omega Alpha. Contbr. articles to profl. jours. Home: 528 E Oakwood Dr East Lansing MI 48823

WEILBACHER, WILLIAM MANNING, advt. agy. exec.; b. Albany, N.Y., June 23, 1928; s. William Carl and Gladys (Manning) W.; B.S., Yale, 1949; M.S., Columbia, 1951; m. Martha Ethel Meyer, May 19, 1962; children—Barbara Taylor, Elizabeth Manning. supr. product analysis Nat. Biscuit Co., 1951-53; v.p., dir. research Dancer-Fitzgerald-Sample, Inc., 1953-62, sr. v.p., 1971-73, exec. v.p., 1973-74, vice chmn., 1974-79, also dir.; sr. v.p. McCaffrey & McCall, 1962-66; exec. dir. Center for Advanced Practice, partner Jack Tinker and Partners, Interpublic, Inc., 1966-69; v.p., dir. research J. Walter Thompson Co., 1969-70; pres. Master Jazz Recs., Inc., 1967—, D-F-S Realty Inc., 1975-79, D-F-S Holdings Inc., 1974-79; lectr. advt. Grad. Sch. Bus., Columbia, 1956-64, adj. prof. bus., 1976-77; lectr. mktg. Coll. City N.Y., 1955-57; adj. prof. mktg. Grad. Sch. Bus., N.Y. U., 1965-70. Vice chmn. tech. com. Advt. Research Found., 1960-63, chmn., 1963-65, dir., 1965-67. Mem. radio TV Ratings Rev. Com. 1958-65; dir. Audit Bur. Circulation, 1964-71, Broadcast Rating Council, 1963-67. Mem. Am. Assn. Advt. Agys. (past vice chmn. research com.), Copy Research Council, Market Research Council (pres. 1970-71), Am. Mktg. Assn., Alpha Kappa Psi, Beta Gamma Sigma. Club: Yale (N.Y.C.). Author: (with L.O. Brown, R.S. Lessler) Advertising Media, 1957; (with H.C. Barksdale) Marketing Research: Selected Readings and Analytic Commentaries, 1966; (with R.A. Bauer, S.A. Greyser) Advertising in America: The Consumer View, 1968; Marketing Management Cases, 1970, 2d edit., 1975; Advertising, 1979. Contbg. editor: Marketing Handbook, 1965. Home: 955 Lexington Ave New York NY 10021

WEILENMANN, RICHARD ARMIN, musician, condr., educator; b. Queens, N.Y., Mar. 2, 1933; s. Oscar and Louise (Moesch) W.; B.Mus., Rollins Coll., 1955; postgrad. (scholar), Chautauqua, N.Y., summer 1954; M.Mus., Catholic U. Am., 1960; student (scholar) Westport Point (Mass.) Chamber Music Center, 1952-53, Deerwood Adirondack Music Center, 1949, Fred Waring Workshop, 1958; m. Elisabeth Weigelt, Feb. 1, 1963; children—John, Peter. Mem. U.S. Navy Band, 1955-59; music supr. Arlington County (Va.) Dept. Recreation and Parks, 1959-68; chmn. music dept. Landon Sch., Bethesda, Md., 1968—; artistic dir., condr. Washington Civic Opera Assn., Beethoven Soc. Washington; founder, artistic dir., condr. Opera Theatre of No. Va.; co-founder, condr. Beethoven Pops Orchestral Concerts; participant Nat. Symposium, Opera for Youth, J.F. Kennedy Center for Performing Arts; opera lectr. Smithsonian Instn. Served with USN, 1955-59. Mem. Phi Kappa Lambda. Initiated program for student involvement in Washington Civic Opera prodns.; translator operas into English: The Barber of Bagdad, Mignon, Pearl Fishers, Martha. Home: 4910 N 14th St Arlington VA 22205

WEILL, CLAUDIA, film producer and dir., cinematographer. Producer-dir. various documentaries including: Radcliffe Blues: Fran, Metropole, Putney School, Aspen Design Conference, This is the Home of Mrs. Leviant Graham, Joyce at 34, Yoga, Commuters, (with Shirley MacLaine) The Other Half of the Sky: A China Memoir; dir. short films for Sesame St.; owner Cyclops Films, N.Y.C. producer-dir. feature narrative film Girlfriends, 1977; mem. Newsday Films, feminist distbn. coop. Office: Cyclops Films 1697 Broadway New York NY 10019*

WEILL, GEORGES GUSTAVE, educator; b. Strasbourg, France, Apr. 9, 1926; s. Edmond and Germaine (Falck) W.; ed. Ecole Polytechnique, Paris, 1950, E.N.S. Telecom., Paris, 1952; Licence de Mathematiques, U. Paris (France), 1954, D.Sc. in Physics, 1955; Ph.D. in Math., U. Calif. at Los Angeles, 1960. Came to U.S., 1956. Research scientist Compagnie Generale de Telegraphie Sans Fil, France, 1952-56; research fellow dept. elec. engring. Calif. Inst. Tech., Pasadena, 1956-59; teaching asso. math. U. Calif. at Los Angeles, 1959-60; research fellow math. Harvard, 1960-62; lectr., research asso. Yale, 1962-64; vis. asst. prof. Belfer Grad. Sch. Sci., Yeshiva U., 1964-65; asso. prof. math. Poly. Inst. Bklyn., 1964-65, prof., 1966—. Mem. Am. Math. Soc., Societe Mathematique de France, IEEE (sr. mem.), Sigma Xi, Pi Mu Epsilon. Home: 300 E 33d St New York City NY 10016 Office: 333 Jay St Brooklyn NY 11201

WEILL, HAROLD, lawyer; b. N.Y.C., Apr. 30, 1908; s. Isaac and Fannie (Fogler) W.; student Columbia, 1927-31; LL.D. (hon.), Beaver Coll.; m. Lisbeth Goldmann, June 29, 1934; children—Patricia (Mrs. Richard Rosenthal), Judith (Mrs. Louis Levy), Victoria. Admitted to N.Y. bar, 1932, also D.C. bar, U.S. Circuit Ct. of Appeals, Washington, D.C., U.S. Supreme Ct.; practice in N.Y.C., 1932—; partner firm Leon, Weill & Mahony, 1932—; dir., mem. exec. com. Helena Rubinstein, Inc., 1955-73; pres., dir. Brit. Controlled Oil Fields, Inc., 1959-70; treas., dir. World Vets. Fund, 1957-70; dir. London and N.Y. Investments, S.A., Ansbacher & Co. Ltd., Dublin, Ireland. Chmn. bd., Childrens Blood Found.; bd. govs., vice chmn. Third Century Fund; chmn. sub-com. on obstetrics, gynecology and pediatrics, mem. subcoms. on finances, fund raising, investment com., ops. com. Soc. N.Y. Hosp.; bd. govs. Weizmann Inst. Sci.; pres., bd. dirs. Talisman Found.; pres., bd. dirs. Helena Rubinstein Found.; trustee Palm Springs Desert Mus. Decorated Chevalier Order Legion of Honor, Ordre Nat. du Mérite (France). Harold Weill Children's Blood Found. clinic, N.Y. Hosp.-Cornell Med. Center named in his honor, 1975. Hon. fellow Weizmann Inst. Sci., 1972. Mem. Am., Fed. bar assns., N.Y. County Lawyers Assn., Am. Soc. Internat. Law. Clubs: Hillcrest Country (Calif.); City Athletic, Town Tennis Mem. (N.Y.C.). Home: 1185 Park Ave New York NY 10028 Office: 405 Lexington Ave New York NY 10017

WEILL, SANFORD I., banker; b. N.Y.C., Mar. 16, 1933; s. Max and Etta (Kalika) W.; grad. Peekskill Mil. Acad., 1951; B.A., Cornell U., 1955, student Grad. Sch. Bus. and Pub. Adminstrn., 1954-55; m. Joan Mosher, June 20, 1955; children—Marc P., Jessica M. Chmn. bd., chief exec. officer Carter, Berlind & Weill (name changed to CBWL-Hayden, Stone, Inc., 1970, to Hayden Stone, Inc., 1972, to Shearson Hayden Stone 1974), N.Y.C., 1960—, pres., 1978—, also chief exec. officer; dir. Arlen Realty & Devel. Corp.; mem. Midwest Stock Exchange, Ch. Bd. Trade; asso. mem. N.Y. Stock Exchange. Asso. trustee L.I. Jewish Hosp. Mem. N.Y. Soc. Security Analysts, Young Presidents Orgns. Clubs: Cornell, Harmonie (N.Y.C.); Sunningdale Country (Scarsdale, N.Y.). Home: 2 E 67th St New York NY 10021 Office: Shearson Hayden Stone Inc 767 5th Ave New York NY 10022*

WEIMAR, KARL SIEGFRIED, educator; b. Phila., Dec. 1, 1916; s. George John and Florence (Dash) W.; A.B., U. Pa., 1937, A.M., 1938, Ph.D., 1944; m. Florence Wasiliewska, Feb. 26, 1943; children—Eric T., Stephanie A., Gregory G. Real estate salesman, 1940-46; instr. German, U. Del., 1940, U. Ill., 1942-43, Temple U., 1945; mem. faculty Brown U., 1946—, prof. German, 1966—, chmn. dept., 1967-73; editor series of coll. texts for Prentice-Hall, Inc., 1963-77. Mem. N. Kingstown (R.I.) Sch. Com., 1954-60; chmn. Warwick (R.I.) Sch. Com., 1962-66; asst. scoutmaster dist. commnr., chmn. local Boy Scouts Am., 1950-70. Mem. Am. Assn. Tchrs. German (nat. high sch. contest dir. 1962-65), Academy Players, Phi Beta Kappa, Theta Xi, Delta Phi Alpha. Episcopalian (past vestry). Author: Concept of Love in the Works of H. Stehr, 1945; German Language and Literature, 1974; Views and Reviews of Modern German Literature, 1975; also articles, translations, textbooks. Home: 27 Broadview Ave Warwick RI 02889 Office: 190 Hope St Brown Univ Providence RI 02912

WEIMER, ARTHUR MARTIN, economist; b. Rock City, Ill., May 19, 1909; s. Conrad Henry and Anna Louise (Beckmeier) W.; A.B., Beloit (Wis.) Coll., 1929, LL.D., 1953; M.A., U. Chgo., 1931, Ph.D., 1934; LL.D., Am. Grad. Sch. Internat. Mgmt., 1975. Instr. econs. Alma (Mich.) Coll., 1931-33, asst. prof., 1933-34; field research supr. FHA, 1934-35, housing economist, 1936-37; prof., head dept. econs. and social sci. Ga. Sch. Tech., Atlanta, 1935-37; prof. real estate and land econs. Ind. U., 1937-79, dean Sch. Bus., 1939-63, spl. asst. to pres. univ., 1963-79; exec. v.p. Am. Assn. Collegiate Schs. Bus., 1967-71; dir. Railroadmen's Fed. Savs. and Loan Assn.; cons. economist U.S. League Savs. Assns., 1948—; mem. U.S. del. UN Conf. Exploration and Peaceful Uses of Outer Space, Vienna, 1968; chmn. Bus. and Real Estate Trends, Inc., 1949—; pres. Weimer Bus. Adv. Service, Inc., 1953—; dir. Ball Corp., Muncie, Ind. Trustee, Midwest Research Inst. Served to maj. AUS, 1942-45. Mem. Am. Econs. Assn., Am. Fin. Assn., Am. Real Estate and Urban Econs. Assn., Am. Inst. Real Estate Appraisers, Am. Soc. Real Estate Counselors, C. of C. of U.S. (dir.), Phi Beta Kappa, Beta Gamma Sigma, Delta Sigma Rho, Tau Kappa Epsilon. Clubs: Faculty, Country (Bloomington); Tavern (Chgo.); Cosmos (Washington); Columbia Country (Chevy Chase, Md.); Indpls. Athletic. Author: When You Buy or Build a Home (with John J. Rowland), 1937; Principles of Real Estate (with Homer Hoyt and George F. Bloom), 7th edit., 1978; Introduction to Business: A Management Approach (with David Bowen, John Long), 5th edit., 1974. Address: Grad Sch Bus Ind U PO Box 183 Bloomington IN 47402

WEIMER, PAUL K(ESSLER), elec. engr.; b. Wabash, Ind., Nov. 5, 1914; s. Claude W. and Eva V. (Kessler) W.; A.B., Manchester Coll., 1936, D.Sc. (hon.), 1968; M.A. in Physics, U. Kans., 1938; Ph.D. in Physics, Ohio State U., 1942; m. Katherine E. Mounce, July 18, 1942; children—Katherine Weimer Lasslob, Barbara Weimer Blackwell, Patricia. Prof. phys. sci. Tabor Coll., 1937-39; research engr. David Sarnoff Research Center, RCA Labs., Princeton, N.J., 1942—, fellow tech. staff, 1965—. Recipient TV Broadcasters award, 1946; Zworykin TV prize Inst. Radio Engrs., 1959; Sarnoff award in sci. RCA, 1963; Outstanding Paper award Solid State Circuits Conf., 1963, 65. Fellow IEEE (Morris Liebmann prize 1966). Patentee in field; active in initial devel. of TV camera tubes, solid state devices. Home: 112 Random Rd Princeton NJ 08540 Office: RCA David Sarnoff Research Center Princeton NJ 08540

WEIMER, RICHARD GEORGE, architect; b. Thibodaux, La., Feb. 28, 1939; s. Wendeline George and Alice (Richard) W.; student Francis T. Nicholls State Coll., 1957-58; B.Arch., La. State U., 1963; m. Judith Ann Meyn, June 13, 1964; children—Richard George, Stephen Malcolm, Patrick Meyn, Karen Judith, Brian Joseph. Archtl. draftsman F.T. Picou, Thibodaux, 1963-64, architect, 1966-68; partner Picou & Weimer, Thibodaux, 1968—. Past mem. Selective Service Bd., Thibodaux; pres. St. Joseph Sch. Bd., 1974-75; extra-ordinary minister St. Joseph Cath. Ch., Thibodaux, 1974—; mem. LaFourche Parish Bicentennial Com., 1974-76; chmn. housing subcom. Thibodaux Goals Com., 1972-73. Bd. dirs. Thibodaux Playhouse, Laurel Valley Village, 1976—; active Cub Scouts Am. Served with C.E., U.S. Army, 1964-66. Mem. AIA (pres. La. coastal chpt. 1974—, historic resources com. 1977—), La. Architects Assn. (Honor Design award 1968), Nat. Trust for Historic Preservation, Thibodaux Jr. C. of C. (Outstanding Young Man 1969, pres. 1970-71, sec. 1967-68, dir. 1968-69; Spark Plug award 1970), Thibodaux C. of C. (dir. 1977—), LaFourche Historic Preservation Soc. Prin. works include Peltier Municipal Park Facilities, 1968; Activity Bldg., 1968; Thibodaux; S. Lafourche High Sch. Stadium, Galliano, La., 1968; Central Lafourche High Sch. Stadium, Mathews, La., 1968; Thibodaux High Sch. Stadium, 1968; Adminstrn. Bldg., U. New Orleans, 1974. Home: 604 Evergreen St Thibodaux LA 70301 Office: PO Box 229 Thibodaux LA 70301

WEIMER, ROBERT JAY, educator; b. Glendo, Wyo., Sept. 4, 1926; s. John L. and Helen (Mowrey) W.; B.A., U. Wyo., 1948, M.A., 1949; Ph.D., Stanford, 1953; m. Ruth Carol Adams, Sept. 12, 1948; children—Robert Thomas, Loren Edward (dec.), Paul Christner, Carl Scott. Geologist, Union Oil Co. Calif., 1949-54; cons. geologist U.S. and fgn. petroleum exploration, 1954—; Getty prof. geology Colo. Sch. Mines, 1957—; vis. prof. U. Colo., 1961, U. Calgary (Can.), 1970, Inst. Tech., Bandung, Indonesia, 1975; ednl. cons. to petroleum companies, 1964—. Trustee Colo. Sch. Mines Research Found. 1967-70. Served with USNR, 1944-46. Fulbright lectr. U. Adelaide (S. Australia), 1967; Distinguished lectr. and continuing edn. lectr. Am. Assn. Petroleum Geologists (Distinguished Service award). Registered profl. engr., Colo. Mem. Geol. Soc. Am. (chmn. Rocky Mountain sect. 1966-67), Soc. Econ. Paleontologists and Mineralogists (sec.-treas. 1966-67, v.p. 1971, pres. 1972), Colo. Sci. Soc. (hon.), Rocky Mountain Assn. Geologists (pres. 1969, hon. mem.), Wyo. Geol. Assn. (hon.). Clubs: Denver Petroleum; Mt. Vernon Country (bd. dirs. 1956-59) (Golden). Editor: Guide to Geology of Colorado, 1960; Symposium on Cretaceous Rocks of Colorado and Adjacent Area, 1959; Denver Earthquakes, 1968; Fossil Fuel Exploration, 1974; Studies in Colorado Field Geology, 1976. Home: Rural Route 3 25853 Mt Vernon City Club Rd Golden CO 80401

WEIN, GEORGE THEODORE, producer, pianist, singer; b. Boston, Oct. 3, 1925; B.A., Boston U., 1950; hon. doctorate Berklee Coll., 1976. Played with Dixieland combos in Boston, 1940s; producer ann. Newport Jazz Festival, 1954-60, 61—, Ohio Valley Jazz Festival, Cin., 1962—, Down Beat Jazz Festival, Chgo., 1965; created Newport Folk Festival and Found., 1963; founder Newport Jazz Festival-N.Y., 1972, N.Y. Jazz Repertory Co., 1973, Grande Parade Du Jazz Festival, Nice, France, 1974, Memphis Music Heritage Festival, 1976, New Orleans Jazz and Heritage Festival, Hawaii Jazz Fair, 1976, Munich Jazz Festival, 1979, Capital Radio Jazz Festival, London, 1979, Playboy Jazz Festival, Los Angeles, 1979; producer 1st opera festival with Met. Opera, Newport, 1966; producer Kool Super Nights, Kool Country on Tour, throughout U.S., 1979, White House Jazz Festival, 1978; overseas tours gen. festival in Berlin, Germany, other European capitals, U.S. Govt. sponsored presentations; World Jazz Festival, Japan, 1964; jazz festival Hampton Inst.; producer annual Kool Jazz festivals across Am.; rec. artist for Columbia, RCA, Atlantic records. Address: 311 W 74th St New York NY 10023

WEINBAUM, JEAN DAVID, painter, sculptor, stained-glass artist; b. Zurich, Switzerland, Sept. 20, 1926; naturalized Am. citizen, 1974; s. Fritz Ismar and Gisele (Kahn) W.; student Sch. Arts and Crafts, Zurich, 1942-46. Exhibited on one-man shows: Galerie Weiller, Paris, 1955, Galerie Beno, Zurich, 1960, Galerie d'Art du Faubourg, Paris, 1960, 61, U. Calif. Med. Center, San Francisco, 1968, Stanford U., 1968, Triton Museum, Santa Clara, Calif., 1969, Galerie Smith-Andersen, Palo Alto, Calif., 1970, 71, 73, 79, Calif. Palace Legion of Honor, San Francisco, 1971, Musée des Arts Decoratifs, Lausanne, Switzerland, 1972, Bildungszentrum, Gelsenkirchen, Germany, 1972, Humboldt Galleries, San Francisco, 1973, Heimatmuseum, Bottrop, Germany, 1973, Lantern Gallery, Ann Arbor, Mich., 1973, Galerie Numaga, Auvernier, Switzerland, 1974, Linda Farris Gallery, Seattle, 1974, 75, Humboldt Galleries, N.Y.C., 1976, Galerie Smith-Andersen, San Francisco, 1976, Pasquale Iannetti, San Francisco, 1979; exhibited in group shows: Palais de Tokyo, Paris, 1949, Galerie de France, Paris, 1959, Mus. Modern Art, Paris, 1961, 62, 63, 65, Galerie Weiller, Paris, 1961, Gallery Robert Elkon, N.Y.C., 1962, Gallerie Lutece, Paris, 1966, San Francisco Mus., 1971-72, Calif. Palace of Legion of Honor, San Francisco, 1971, and numerous others; represented in permanent collections: Mus. Modern Art, Paris, U. Art Mus. Berkeley, Calif., Nat. Collection Fine Arts, Washington, U. Mich., Ann Arbor, others; works include: stained-glass windows for Chapelle de Mosloy, Ferte Milon, France, 1951, Rosette window for Catholic ch. at Berne Sur Oise, 1955, St. Pieree du Regard Catholic ch., Calvados, France, 1957, Escherange, Moselle, France, 1962, Ailly for Catholic ch., Normandy, France, 1963, Lycee des Jeunes Filles, Bayonne, France, 1966. Home: PO Box 40291 San Francisco CA 94140 Studio: Project Artaud 499 Alabama St San Francisco CA 94110. *The abstract image is a writing which cannot be expressed with words. Light and color are synonyms. Like rhythm is the structure of music, the melody is the color. The rhythm is the expression of Humankind, it is the heartbeat. Painting is light (color), form, rhythm and melody. The enjoyment of a painting has to go through the same channels as the enjoyment of music. A child is able to feel, without understanding. Yet the child's feelings are able to understand things, to "see," when often the adult is "blind."*

WEINBERG, ALVIN MARTIN, physicist; b. Chgo., Apr. 20, 1915; s. J.L. and Emma (Levinson) W.; A.B., U. Chgo., 1935, A.M., 1936, Ph.D., 1939; LL.D., U. Chattanooga, Alfred U.; D.Sc., U. Pacific, Denison U., Kenyon Coll., Worcester Poly. Inst., U. Rochester, Stevens Inst. Tech., Butler U., U. Louisville; m. Margaret Despres, June 14, 1940 (dec. 1969); children—David, Richard; m. 2d, Gene K. DePersio, Sept. 20, 1974. Research asso. math. biophysics U. Chgo., 1939-41, Metall. Lab., 1941-45; joined Oak Ridge Nat. Lab., 1945, dir. physics div., 1947-48, research dir., 1948-55, dir. lab., 1955-74; dir. office Energy Research and Devel., Fed. Energy Office, 1974; dir. Inst. Energy Analysis, Oak Ridge, 1975—; mem. Pres.'s Sci. Adv. Com., 1960-62; mem. Pres.'s Medal of Sci. Com. Recipient Atoms for Peace award, 1960; E.O. Lawrence award, 1960; U. Chgo. Alumni medal, 1966; Heinrich Hertz award, 1975; N.Y. Acad. Scis. award, 1976. Mem. Nat. Acad. Scis. (applied sci. sect.), Am. Nuclear Soc. (pres. 1959-60), Nat. Acad. Engring., Am. Acad. Arts and Scis., Am. Philos. Soc., Royal Netherlands Acad. Sci. (fgn. asso.). Author: Reflections on Big Science, 1967; (with E.P. Wigner) Physical Theory of Neutron Chain Reactors. Home: 111 Moylan Ln Oak Ridge TN 37830 Office: Inst Energy Analysis PO Box 117 Oak Ridge TN 37830

WEINBERG, ARTHUR, journalist; b. Chgo., Dec. 8, 1915; s. Abraham Morris and Anna (Avedon) W.; A.A., YMCA Coll., Chgo., 1935; diploma journalism Northwestern U., 1938, Ph.B., 1941; m. Lila Shaffer, Jan. 25, 1953; children—Hedy Merrill, Anita Michelle, Wendy Clare. With Hart Schaffner & Marx, Chgo., 1935-39; researcher Ill. Writers Project, Chgo., 1939-41; tech. writer Consol. Aircraft Corp., San Diego, 1941-45; editor Ft. Lewis (Wash.) Flame, 1946; reporter Fairchild Publs., Chgo., 1947—; Midwest bureau chief HFD, 1977; lectr. downtown coll. U. Chgo., 1957; moderator radio discussion program Sound-Off, Sta. WXFM, Chgo., 1961; book reviewer Chgo. Daily News, 1962-76, Chgo. Sunday Tribune, 1976—, Women's Wear Daily, Los Angeles Times; faculty Sch. for New Learning, DePaul U., Chgo. Organizer nat. Clarence Darrow Centennial Celebration, 1957, exec. chmn., 1957; chmn. Clarence Darrow Commemorative Com., 1958—; v.p. Clarence Darrow Community Center, Chgo., 1962-64; bd. dirs. Adult Edn. Council Greater Chgo., 1959—, chmn. letters and drama assembly, 1964—. Mem. Soc. Midland Authors (pres. 1967-69), ACLU, Sigma Delta Chi, Press Club, Headline Club (dir.). Editor: Attorney for the Damned, 1957; (with wife) Lila: The Muckrakers, 1961, Verdicts out of Court, 1963, Instead of Violence, 1963; Passport to Utopia, 1968; Some Dissenting Voices, 1970; Clarence Darrow: Sentimental Rebel, 1980. Home: 5421 Cornell Ave Chicago IL 60615 Office: 11 E Adams St Chicago IL 60603

WEINBERG, CHESTER, dress designer; b. N.Y.C., Sept. 23, 1930; s. Irving and Ida Weinberg; student (Nat. Scholastic scholar) Parsons Sch. Design, N.Y.C., 1951, N.Y. U., 1953. Designer, Leonard Arkin, 1951-54, Patullo-Jo Copeland, 1954-56, Herbert Sondheim, 1956-62, Teal Traina, 1962-66; partner Chester Weinberg Ltd., 1966-74; freelance dress designer, 1974—; designer sportswear for Jones Apparel Group, 1979—; designer cashmere sweaters for Ballantyne, Scotland; created costumes for ballet As Time Goes By, 1974; lectr., guest critic Art Inst. Chgo.; bd. overseers Parson Sch. Design. Recipient Coty award, 1970; also designer award from retail stores. Address: 419 E 57th St New York NY 10022

WEINBERG, EDWARD, lawyer; b. Whitewater, Wis., Sept. 5, 1918; s. Bernhard and Molly (Schotzky) W.; B.A., U. Wis.-Madison, 1939, LL.B., 1941; m. Anne Goldsmith, June 10, 1943; children—Mark, Robert. Admitted to Wis. bar, 1941, D.C. bar, 1964, U.S. Supreme Ct. bar, 1965; atty., then asst. chief counsel Bur. Reclamation, 1944-54; asst. solicitor Dept. Interior, 1955-61, asso. solicitor, 1962-63, dep. solicitor, 1963-68, solicitor, 1968-69; practiced in Washington, 1969—; mem. firm Duncan, Weinberg, Palmer & Miller, P.C., 1974—; prin. cons. Nat. Water Commn., 1969-73. Mem. Am., Fed., D.C. bar assns., Order of Coif, Tau Epsilon Rho, Artus. Democrat. Jewish. Author: Intrastate, Interstate and International Problems of Large-scale Water Transfer, 1969; The Colorado River Salinity Dispute, 1973. Home: 540 N St SW Washington DC 20024 Office: 1775 Pennsylvania Ave NW Washington DC 20006

WEINBERG, ELBERT, sculptor; b. Hartford, Conn., May 27, 1928; s. Hyman Philip and Rose May (Apter) W.; B.F.A., R.I. Sch. Design, 1951; M.F.A., Yale U., 1955; m. Joy Earle Davenport, 1958 (div. 1971); 1 dau., Julia Davenport. Instr., Cooper Union Art Sch., 1956-59; vis. prof. sculpture Dartmouth Coll., 1969; vis. asso. prof. Boston U., 1969-70; vis. asso. prof. sculpture Tyler Abroad, Temple U., Rome, Italy, 1974-76; artist-in-residence Union Coll., Schenectady, 1976—; exhbns. include: Borgenicht Gallery, N.Y.C., 1959, 62, 66, 69, 75, Alpha Gallery, Boston, 1966, 69, 71, Mus. Modern Art, N.Y.C., 1959, 75, Guggenheim Mus., 1962; represented in permanent collections: Mus. Modern Art, Whitney Mus., N.Y.C., Bklyn. Mus., Jewish Mus., N.Y.C., Boston Mus. Fine Arts, Hirschhorn Collection, Washington. Recipient Prix de Rome, 1951; sculpture award AAAL, 1968. Mem. Sculptor's Guild N.Y.C. Home: 55 Suellen Rd Schenectady NY 12309 Office: Union Coll Union St Schenectady NY 12308

WEINBERG, EPHRAIM, ednl. adminstr.; b. Phila., Apr. 28, 1938; s. Abraham and Bella (Ciplet) W.; B.F.A., Phila. Coll. Art, 1959; M.S., U. Pa., 1962; m. Sheila Cohen, June 24, 1970; children—Nancy, Benjamin. Lectr., Bournemouth (Eng.) Coll. Art, 1964-65; asst. prof. Phila. Coll. Art, 1969-71, Bucks County Coll., 1971-77; asso. prof., chmn. dept. edn. Sch. Art Inst. Chgo., 1971-77; dean art Pa. Acad. Fine Arts, 1977—. Mem. Assn. Schs. in Arts (dir.), Nat. Assn. Schs. Art, Nat. Art Edn. Assn. Nat. Council Arts Adminstrs., Pa. Art Edn. Assn., AAUP. Home: 828 Youngsford Rd Gladwyne PA 19035 Office: Pa Acad Fine Arts Broad and Cherry Sts Philadelphia PA 19102

WEINBERG, EUGENE DAVID, microbiologist, educator; b. Chgo., Mar. 4, 1922; s. Philip and Lenore (Bergman) W.; B.S., U. Chgo., 1942, M.A., 1948, Ph.D., 1950; m. Frances Murl Izen, Sept. 5, 1949; children—Barbara Ann, Marjorie Jean, Geoffrey Alan, Michael Benjamin. Instr. dept. microbiology Ind. U., Bloomington, 1950-53, asst. prof., 1953-57, asso. prof., 1957-61, prof., 1961—, asso. dean research and grad. devel., 1978—. Served with AUS, 1942-45. Mem. AAAS, Am. Soc. Microbiology, Soc. Geochemistry and Environ. Health. Office: Biology Dept Jordan Hall Indiana University Bloomington IN 47401

WEINBERG, GERHARD LUDWIG, historian; b. Hannover, Ger., Jan. 1, 1928; s. Max Bendix and Kate Sarah (Gruenebaum) W.; came to U.S., 1940, naturalized, 1949; B.A., N.Y. State Coll. Tchrs., Albany, 1948; M.A., U. Chgo., 1949, Ph.D., 1951; m. Wilma Lee Jeffrey, Mar. 29, 1958. Research analyst War Documentation project Columbia U., 1951-54; vis. lectr. history U. Chgo., 1954-55, U. Ky., Lexington, 1955-56; dir. project microfilming captured German documents Am. Hist. Assn., 1956-57; asst. prof. U. Ky., 1957-59; mem. faculty U. Mich., Ann Arbor, 1959-74, prof. history, 1963-74, chmn. dept., 1972-73; William Rand Kenan, Jr. prof. history U. N.C., Chapel Hill, 1974—; bd. dirs. Am. Com. History World War II, 1968—; cons. in field. Chmn. Ann Arbor Democratic Com., 1961-63; mem. Mich. Dem. Central Com., 1963-67. Served with AUS, 1946-47. Fellow Rockefeller Found., Social Sci. Research Council, 1962-63, Am. Council Learned Socs., 1965-66, Guggenheim Found., 1971-72, Nat. Endowment Humanities, 1978-79. Mem. Am. Hist. Assn. (George Louis Baer prize 1971), Conf. Group Central European History, Coordinating Com. Women in Hist. Profession, Phi Beta Kappa. Jewish. Author: Guide to Captured German Documents, 1952; Germany and The Soviet Union, 1939-41, 1954; The Foreign Policy of Hitler's Germany, 1933-1936, 1970; co-author: Soviet Partisans in World War II, 1964. Editor: Hitlers zweites Buch, 1961; Transformation of a Continent, 1975; bd. editors Jour. Modern History, 1970-72, Central European History, 1976—. Home: 331 Azalea Dr Chapel Hill NC 27514 Office: Dept History Univ NC Chapel Hill NC 27514

WEINBERG, HARRY BERNARD, physician; b. Fremont, Nebr., Apr. 29, 1913; s. Ephraim and Goldie (Levynsky) W.; B.S. in Medicine, U. Nebr., 1935, M.D., 1936; m. Evelyn Waxenberg, Mar. 26, 1939; children—Steven M., Gary J. Intern Univ. Hosp., Omaha, 1936-37; resident cardiovascular disease Michael Reese Hosp., Chgo., 1938-40; pvt. practice internal medicine and cardiology, Davenport, Iowa, 1940-69; coordinator Iowa Regional Med. Program, clin. prof. internal medicine U. Iowa Coll. Medicine, 1969-72; dir. med. edn. Meml. Hosp., Hollywood, Fla., 1972-74; pvt. practice medicine specializing in cardiology, Hollywood, 1974—. Bd. dirs. Iowa Heart Assn., 1953-64, pres., 1955-56. Bd. dirs. Davenport C. of C., 1958-61, v.p., 1961. Served to lt. col. AUS, 1940-46. Fellow A.C.P., Am. Coll. Cardiology; mem. A.M.A., Am. Heart Assn. (bd. dirs. 1956-69, fellow council clin. cardiology 1965—), Alpha Omega Alpha. Home: 4925 Washington St Hollywood FL 33021 Office: 921 N 35th Ave Hollywood FL 33021

WEINBERG, HERSCHEL MAYER, lawyer; b. Bklyn., Oct. 13, 1927; s. Jacob and Gertrude (Wernick) W.; B.A., Bklyn. Coll., 1948; LL.B., Harvard, 1952. Admitted to N.Y. State bar, 1952; atty. firm Payne & Steingarten, N.Y.C., 1952-57, Jacobs, Persinger & Parker, N.Y.C., 1957-61; partner firm Rubin, Rubin, Weinberg, & Di Paola, N.Y.C., 1961-78, Pearlman Weinberg Tauber & Bernstein, 1979—; dir. Milgray Electronics, Inc., Vogart Crafts Corp. Served with AUS, 1946-47. Mem. Assn. Bar City N.Y. Club: Harvard (N.Y.C.). Home: 50 Sutton Pl S New York NY 10022 Office: 575 Madison Ave New York NY 10022

WEINBERG, JACK, psychiatrist; b. Kiev, Russia, Jan. 18, 1910; s. Morris M. and Gunia (Geichman) W.; came to U.S., 1924, naturalized, 1937; B.S., U. Ill., 1934, M.D., 1936; m. Ruth S. Skidelsky, Aug. 14, 1935; 1 son, Daniel R. Intern, St. Elizabeth's Hosp., Chgo., 1926-27; resident in psychiatry U. Ill. Med. Sch. and Hosps., 1938-39, Chgo. Inst. Psychoanalysis, 1941-43; asso. dir. residency tng. program Michael Reese Hosp. and Med. Center, Chgo., 1946-50; practice medicine, specializing in psychiatry, Chgo., 1950-64; clin. dir. Ill. State Psychiat. Inst., 1964-75, dir., 1975—; adminstr. Ill. Mental Insts., 1975—; prof. psychiatry Abraham Lincoln Sch. Medicine, U. Ill., Chgo., 1962—, Rush Med. Coll., Chgo., 1972—; vis. prof. Gerontology Inst., U. So. Calif., 1969—; lectr. Indsl. Relations Center, U. Chgo., 1955—; sr. attending psychiatrist Psychosomatic and Psychiat. Inst., Michael Reese Hosp. and Med. Center, 1955—; Disting. sr. scholar Center for Study of Mental Health of the Aging, NIMH, 1978; cons. in field; mem. numerous coms. on aging and elderly. Bd. dir. Council Jewish Elderly, Chgo., 1971—, Jewish Family and Community Services, 1969—. Served to maj. M.C., USAF, 1943-46. Diplomate Am. Bd. Psychiatry and Neurology. Life fellow Am. Psychiat. Assn. (pres. 1977-78), Ill. Psychiat. Soc.; mem. Am. Gerontol. Soc. (Donald P. Kent award 1974), Am. Geriatric Soc., (Edward B. Allen award 1970), AMA, Group Advancement of Psychiatry (pres.-elect 1979—), AAAS, Jewish. Contbr. chpts. to books, articles to med. jour. Home: 434 Greenleaf Ave Glencoe IL 60022 Office: 1601 W Taylor St Chicago IL 60612. *As a psychiatrist, my effort is to make the covert overt, the seemingly bizarre understandable, to point out the order inherent in chaos, and thus make life bearable. One man's suffering, no matter when or where, is the concern of all of us. We are indeed our brother's keeper, and one human's pain is the pain of us all. For all of this, the time is always, the place is everywhere.*

WEINBERG, JOHN LIVINGSTON, investment banker; b. N.Y.C., Jan. 5, 1925; s. Sidney James and Helen (Livingston) W.; student Deerfield Acad., 1943; A.B. cum laude, Princeton, 1948; M.B.A., Harvard, 1950; m. Sue Ann Gotshal, Dec. 6, 1952; children—Ann K. (dec.), John, Jean. With Goldman, Sachs & Co., N.Y.C., 1950—, partner, 1956-76, sr. partner, co-chmn. mgmt. com., 1976; dir. B.F. Goodrich Co., Kraft, Inc., Knight-Ridder Newspapers, Inc., Cluett, Peabody & Co., Inc., Seagram Co. Ltd., Witco Chem. Corp. Bd. govs., v.p. N.Y. Hosp.; trustee Deerfield Acad.; bd. dirs. Josiah Macy, Jr. Found. Served to 2d lt. USMCR, 1942-46, capt., 1951-52. Fellow Inst. Jud. Adminstrn. (chmn. fin. com.); mem. UN Assn. N.Y. (adv. (council). Clubs: Economic, Recess, Princeton, Bond, Harvard Bus. Sch. (N.Y.C.); Blind Brook; Century Country; Lyford Cay. Home: 80 Sherwood Ave Greenwich CT 06830 Office: 55 Broad St New York City NY 10004

WEINBERG, MARTIN HERBERT, psychiatrist; b. Bklyn., Sept. 3, 1923; s. Abe and Ida (Levine) W.; B.S., City Coll. N.Y., 1947; licentiate Royal Coll. Surgeons, Edinburgh, Royal Coll. Physicians, Edinburgh, Royal Faculty Physicians and Surgeons, Glasgow; m. Elizabeth Carwardine, Sept. 20, 1951; children—Mark David, Sheila Ann, Keith Warren. Intern Kings County Med. Center, Bklyn., 1952; resident psychiatry Essex County Overbrook Hosp., Cedar Grove, N.J., 1954-56; staff psychiatrist Ancora State Hosp., Hammonton, N.J., 1956, chief service, 1957, clin. dir., 1958-60, asst. med. dir., 1960-62, dep. med. dir., 1962-67; med. dir. Trenton Psychiat. Hosp., 1967-73; dir. div. mental health and hosps. N.J. Dept. Instns. and Agys., 1973-74; med. dir. Trenton Psychiat. Hosp., 1974-79; surveyor psychiat. programs Joint Commn. Accreditation of Hosps., 1979—. Diplomate Am. Bd. Psychiatry and Neurology; certified mental hosp. adminstr. Fellow Am. Psychiat. Assn., A.A.A.S.; mem. N.J. Psychiat. Assn. (past pres.). Home: 26 Diane Dr West Trenton NJ 08628

WEINBERG, MATTHEW BASIL, lawyer; b. N.Y.C., Jan. 24, 1934; s. Isidore and Blanche Myril (Moskowitz) W.; A.B. cum laude (Class of 1926 fellow), Dartmouth Coll., 1955, postgrad. in Bus. Adminstrn., 1955; J.D., Harvard U., 1960; m. Barbara Diane Kovitz, Dec. 28, 1972; children—Mark Montague, Daniel Justin. Admitted to Calif. bar, 1961; dep. atty. gen. State of Calif., 1960-61; dep. dist. atty. Los Angeles County, 1961; spl. counsel to Gov., spl. asst. commr. of corps. State of Calif., Sacramento, 1962-63; pvt. practice law, San Francisco, 1964—, pres., dir. Matthew B. Weinberg Profl. Corp., 1971—; dir. Aviva Enterprises, Inc., Adam Joseph Industries, Inc., Medicure Leasing Co.; cons. No. Calif. Radiation Therapists and Oncologists, Inc.; counsel to various tax-exempt instns.; guest lectr. Harvard U., 1958-60; coordinator Nat. Conf. Interstate Land Sales, 1962. Trustee West Coast Cancer Found.; mem. exec. com. Nat. Jewish Community Relations Adv. Council, 1978—; chmn. Jewish Community Relations Council San Francisco and Peninsula, 1977—; bd. dirs. San Francisco Jewish Home for the Aged, 1979—; trustee Bd. Rabbis No. Calif. Fund, 1968—; dir. Jewish Welfare Fedn., 1969-75 (mem. social planning and budgeting com. 1979—); dir. State of Israel Bonds Orgn. No. Calif., 1969—, chmn., 1972-74; exec. com. Anti-Defamation League, 1971—; trustee Am. Friends of Hebrew U., exec. com., v.p. No. Calif. chpt., 1973—; mem. Jewish Pub. Affairs Com. Calif., 1977—. Served to lt. USNR, 1956-58. Recipient Daniel Webster Debate award Dartmouth Coll., 1955; Class of 1866 Oratorical prize Dartmouth Coll., 1954; Williston Competition prize Harvard Law Sch., 1960; State of Israel Bonds award, 1974; certified specialist in taxation law Calif. Bd. Legal Specialization. Mem. Am., San Francisco (sec. 1970, chmn. client's relations com. 1971) bar assns., State Bar Calif., Delta Sigma Rho. Clubs: Harvard, Dartmouth of No. Calif. and Nev., Concordia-Argonaut, Commonwealth, Lawyers. Co-author: Trust Deed Securities, 1961; editor: Procs. Nat. Conf. on Interstate Land Sales, 1962. Home: 167 Commonwealth Ave San Francisco CA 94118 Office: Russ Bldg Suite 1642 235 Montgomery St San Francisco CA 94104

WEINBERG, MEYER, educator; b. N.Y.C., Dec. 16, 1920; s. Charles and Anna (Palatnik) W.; B.A., U. Chgo., 1942, M.A., 1945; A.A., Herzl Jr. Coll., 1940; m. Erica C. Mueller, Sept. 5, 1943; children—Rachel (dec.), David, Daniel, Carl, Benjamin. Faculty history Wright br. City Coll. Chgo., 1945-67, coordinator master planning, 1968-69, coordinator innovations center, 1970-71, prof. history Loop br., 1971-78; dir. Center for Equal Edn., Northwestern U., 1972-78; prof. edn., dir. Center for Equal Edn., U. Mass., Amherst, 1978—; chmn. edn. com. Coordinating Council Community Orgns., 1963-67; cons. Howard U., 1964-65, Am. Inst. for Research, 1972, bds. of edn. various cities, univs., 1964-79, Fla. Desegregation Center, U. Miami, 1973, NAACP Legal Def. Fund, 1972, Ford Found., 1978, System Devel. Corp., 1975, Nat. Cath. Conf. on Interracial Justice, 1977-78, Stanford Research Inst., 1976, WTTW-TV, Chgo., 1975-78, Edn. Commn. of States, 1978, Cemrel, Inc., 1977, Rand Corp., 1979, ESSA Human Relations Study, 1977; mem. tech. adv. com. Ill. Bd. Edn., 1971-72. Recipient Center for Human Relations award for creative leadership in edn. NEA, 1971. Mem. Am. Hist. Assn., Soc. for History of Tech., Econ. History Assn., Soc. for Study Social Problems, AAUP, Am. Soc. for Legal History, Council Anthropology and Edn., Nat. Adv. Com. for Evaluation ESSA. Author: (with O. E. Shabat) Society and Man, 1956, 65, TV in America - The Morality of Hard Cash, 1962, Race and Place - A Legal History of the Neighborhood School, 1968, Desegregation Research - An Appraisal, 1968, 70, Minority Students - A Research Appraisal, 1977, A Chance to Learn (A History of the Education of Black, Mexican American, American Indian and Puerto Rican Children), 1977. Editor: Issues in Social Science, 1959, Learning Together, 1964, Integrated Education - A Reader, 1968, Education of the Minority Child - A Comprehensive Bibliography of 10,000 Selected Entries, 1970, W.E.B. DuBois - A Reader, 1970; Integrateducation mag., 1963—, Research Rev. of Edqual Edn., 1977—; contbr. chpts. to books, articles to profl. jours. Home: 7 Winston Ct Amherst MA 01002 Office: Sch Edn U Mass Amherst MA 01003

WEINBERG, MICHAEL, JR., business exec.; b. Chgo., Mar. 19, 1925; s. Michael H. and Leila (Eichberg) W.; B.A., U. Chgo., 1943, student Grad. Sch. Bus., 1946-49; m. Joan F. Rusnak, Feb. 25, 1951; children—Michael Alan, Wendy Lee, Jill Diane. Pres. Great Lakes Pub. Co., Chgo., 1950-53; editor Hyde Park Herald, also Oakland-Kenwood Outlook, Chgo., 1950-53; commodity broker, v.p. Weinberg Bros. & Co., commodity brokers and wholesalers, Chgo., 1953—; exec. dir. Lincoln Park Zool. Soc., 1963—; Chmn. bd. govs., chmn. exec. com. Chgo. Merc. Exchange, 1972-73; dir. Internat. Monetary Market; mem. adv. com. Commodity Futures Trading Commn., Washington, 1975-76. Served with AUS, World War II. Mem. U. Chgo. Alumni Assn., Zeta Beta Tau. Home: 844 Kimballwood Ln Highland Park IL 60035 Office: 222 S Riverside Plaza Chicago IL 60606

WEINBERG, ROBERT LEONARD, lawyer; b. Balt., May 31, 1923; s. Leonard and Beatrice (Lansburgh) W.; student Coll. William and Mary, 1940-43; B.S., Johns Hopkins, 1952; J.D., U. Md., 1949. Admitted to Md. bar, 1948; asso. Weinberg and Green, attys., Balt., 1948-52, partner, 1952—; asst. atty. gen. Md., 1953; instr. labor law and contract law Eastern Coll., 1954-57. Pres. Comprehensive Housing for Aged, Inc., 1969-71, United Way Central Md., 1976-77; v.p. Levindale Hebrew Hosp. and Geriatric Center, 1971-75; bd. dirs. Asso. Jewish Charities Balt., United Way Central Md., Sinai Hosp., Jewish Hist. Soc. Md.; nat. bd. dirs. NCCJ, co-chmn. Md. region, 1968-70. Served with AUS, 1943-46; ETO. Mem. Am. (mem. com. tax. aspects of real estate transactions 1965-68, 72-74), Md. Balt. bar assns., Am. Judicature Soc. (dir.), Md. Hist. Soc. (v.p. 1973-76). Republican. Jewish. Clubs: Suburban of Baltimore County (pres. 1971-74), Center (bd. govs. sec., counsel 1962-72) (Balt.). Office: 10 Light St Baltimore MD 21202

WEINBERG, SIDNEY JAMES, JR., investment banker; b. N.Y.C., Mar. 27, 1923; s. Sidney James and Helen (Livingston) W.; B.A. in Pub. and Internat. Affairs, Princeton, 1945; M.B.A., Harvard, 1949; m. Elizabeth Houghton, June 30, 1951; children—Elizabeth Livingston, Sydney Houghton, Peter Amory. Vice pres. textile div. Owens-Corning Fiberglas Corp., N.Y.C., 1949-65; partner Goldman, Sachs & Co., investment bankers, N.Y.C., 1967—; dir. Corning Internat. Corp., J.P. Stevens & Co., Inc., Tejon Ranch Co., Norris Industries, Inc., Tecumseh Products Co., Sigma-Aldrich Corp., Eagle-Picher Industries Inc. Mem. cons. panel Comptroller Gen. U.S. Trustee Found. Center, 1968-74, Com. Econ. Devel., WNET Ednl. Broadcasting Corp., 1965-79, Carnegie Found. Advancement Teaching, 1965-78, Presbyn. Hosp. City N.Y., Scripps Coll., Claremont, Calif. Served to 1st lt. F.A., AUS, 1944-46; PTO. Clubs: River, Harvard, Recess, Bond, Madison Sq. Garden (N.Y.C.); Century Country (Purchase, N.Y.); Eldorado Country (Indian Wells, Calif.). Home: Greenwich CT Office: 55 Broad St New York NY 10004

WEINBERG, STEVEN, physicist, educator; b. N.Y.C., May 3, 1933; s. Fred and Eva (Israel) W.; B.A., Cornell U., 1954; postgrad. Copenhagen Inst. for Theoretical Physics, 1954-55; Ph.D., Princeton, 1957; A.M. (hon.), for Theoretical Physics, 1954-55; Ph.D., Princeton, 1957; A.M. (hon.), Harvard, 1973; Sc.D. (hon.), Knox Coll., 1978, U. Chgo., 1978, U. Rochester, 1979, Yale U., 1979; m. Louise Goldwasser, July 6, 1954; 1 dau., Elizabeth. Research asso., instr. Columbia, 1957-59; research physicist Lawrence Radiation Lab., Berkeley, Calif., 1959-60; mem. faculty U. Calif. at Berkeley, 1960-69, prof. physics, 1965-69; vis. prof. Mass. Inst. Tech., 1967-69, prof. physics, 1969-73; Higgins Prof. physics, Harvard, 1973—; sr. scientist Smithsonian Astrophys. lab., 1973—; cons. Inst. for Def. Analyses, Washington, 1960-73, ACDA, 1970-73; mem. Pres.'s Com. on Nat. Medal of Sci., 1979-80; vis. prof. Stanford U., 1976-77; Silliman lectr. Yale U., 1977; Lauritsen Meml. lectr. Calif. Inst. Tech., 1979; Bethe lectr. Cornell U., 1979; de Shalit lectr. Weitzman Inst., 1979. Sloan fellow, 1961-65; Loeb lectr. in physics Harvard, 1966-67; recipient J. Robert Oppenheimer meml. prize, 1973; chair in physics, Collège de France, 1971; Richtmeyer Meml. lectr., 1974; Scott lectr. Cavendish Lab., 1975; recipient Dannie Heineman prize in math. physics, 1977; Am. Inst. Physics-U.S. Steel Found. sci. writing award, 1977, Nobel prize in physics, 1979; Elliott Cressin medal Franklin Inst., 1979. Mem. Am. Acad. Arts (past councilor Scis., Am. Phys. Soc. (past councilor at large), Nat. Acad. Sci., Am. Astron. Soc., Council on Fgn. Relations, Am. Mediaeval Acad. Author: Gravitation and Cosmology: Principles and Applications of the General Theory of Relativity, 1972; The First Three Minutes: A Modern View of the Origin of the Universe, 1977; research and publs. on elementary particles, quantum field theory, cosmology. Co-editor Cambridge, U. Press monographs on mathematical physics; mem. editorial bd. Progress in Sci. Culture, Advances in Applied Math. Office: Dept Physics Harvard Univ Cambridge MA 02138

WEINBERG, WILLIAM HENRY, chem. engr., educator; b. Columbia, S.C., Dec. 5, 1944; s. Ulrich Vivian and Ruth Ann (Duncan) W.; B.S., U. S.C., 1966; Ph.D. in Chem. Engring., U. Calif., Berkeley, 1970. NATO postdoctoral fellow in phys. chemistry Cambridge U., Eng., 1971; asst. prof. chem. engring. Calif. Inst. Tech., 1972-74, asso. prof., 1974-77, prof. chem. engring. and chem. physics, 1977—; cons. E.I. DuPont Co. Alfred P. Sloan Found. fellow, 1976-78; NSF fellow, 1966-69; Camille and Henry Dreyfus Found. tchr.-scholar, 1976-81. Recipient Nottingham prize Am. Phys. Soc., 1972; LaMer award Am. Chem. Soc., 1973. Mem. AAAS, Am. Chem. Soc., Am. Inst. Chem. Engrs., Am. Phys. Soc., Am. Vacuum Soc., N. Am. Catalysis Soc., Phi Beta Kappa, Sigma Xi. Editor 4 books in field; contbr. chpts. to books, articles to profl. jours. Mem. editorial bd. Jour. Applications of Surface Sci., 1977—; Handbook of Surfaces and Interfaces, 1978—. Office: Div Chemistry and Chem Engring Calif Inst Tech Pasadena CA 91125

WEINBERGER, CASPAR WILLARD, corp. exec., former govt. ofcl.; b. San Francisco, Aug. 18, 1917; s. Herman and Cerise Carpenter (Hampson) W.; A.B. magna cum laude, Harvard, 1938, LL.B., 1941; m. Jane Dalton, Aug. 16, 1942; children—Arlin Cerise, Caspar Willard. Admitted to Calif. bar; law clk. U.S. Judge William E. Orr, 1945-47; with firm Heller, Ehrman, White & McAuliffe, 1947-69, partner, 1959-69; mem. Calif. Legislature from 21st Dist., 1952-58; vice chmn. Calif. Republican Central Com., 1960-62, chmn. 1962-64; chmn. Com. Cal. Govt. Orgn. and Econs., 1967-68; dir. finance Calif., 1968-69; chmn. FTC, 1970; dep. dir. Office Mgmt. and Budget, 1970-72, dir., 1972-73; counsellor to the Pres., 1973; sec. HEW, 1973-75; gen. counsel, v.p., dir. Bechtel Power Corp., San Francisco, 1975—, Bechtel, Inc., 1975—, Bechtel Corp., 1975—; dir. Pepsi Co, Inc., Quaker Oats Co.; formerly staff book reviewer San Francisco Chronicle; moderator weekly TV program Profile, Bay Area, sta. KQED, San Francisco, 1959-68; Frank Nelson Doubleday lectr., 1974. Chmn., Pres.'s Com. on Mental Retardation, 1973-75; mem. Trilateral Commn.; mem. adv. council Am. Ditchley Found.; bd. dirs. Yosemite Inst.; trustee St. Luke's Hosp., San Francisco, Mechanics Inst., San Francisco; nat. trustee Nat. Symphony, Washington; bd. govs. San Francisco Symphony. Served from pvt. to capt., inf., AUS, 1941-45; PTO. Decorated Bronze Star. Mem. Am. Bar Assn., State Bar Calif. Episcopalian (treas. Diocese of Calif.). Clubs: Century (New York); Bohemian, Pacific Union (San Francisco); Harvard (San Francisco, Washington, D.C.); Burlingame Country. Writer column on Calif. govt., 1959-68. Office: Bechtel Corp 50 Beale St San Francisco CA 94105

WEINBERGER, HANS FELIX, mathematician, educator; b. Vienna, Austria, Sept. 27, 1928; s. Walter and Linda (Haas) W.; came to U.S., 1938, naturalized, 1944; B.S., M.S. in Physics, Carnegie Inst. Tech., 1948, Sc.D. in Math., 1950; m. Laura C. Larrick, Apr. 20, 1957; children—Catherine, Sylvia, Ralph. With Inst. Fluid Dynamics and Applied Math., U. Md., 1950-60, asso. research prof., 1957-60; mem. faculty U. Minn., 1960—, prof. math., 1961—, head Sch. Math., 1967-69. Mem. adv. panel math. scis. NSF, 1969-72; mem. U.S. Nat. Com. for Math.; mem. com. on applications of math. NRC. Mem. Am. Math. Soc., Soc. Indsl. and Applied Math. (asso. editor Jour. Applied Math. 1975—), Soc. Natural Philosophy. Author: A First Course in Partial Differential Equations, 1965; (with M.H. Protter) Maximum Principles in Differential Equations, 1967; Variational Methods for Eigenvalue Approximation, 1974. Asst. editor Proc. Am. Math. Soc., 1968-70; asso. editor Duke Math. Jour., 1970-75, Applicable Analysis, 1970—, Jour. of Math. Physics, 1974-76; Archives for Rational Mechanics, 1978—; editor Bull. Am. Math. Soc., 1972-77. Address: 141 Orlin Ave Minneapolis MN 55414

WEINBERGER, JEROME A., retail drugs co. exec.; b. Cleve., Jan. 20, 1928; s. Adolph and Minnie (Jacobs) W.; B.S., U. Pa., 1950; m. Joy Whitman, Feb. 4, 1956; children—Gail, Ellen, Neil. With Gray Drug Stores, Inc., Cleve., 1952—, v.p., 1959-63, exec. v.p., 1963-66, pres., 1966—, chmn., 1978—, chief exec. officer, 1969—, aldo dir.; dir. Society Nat. Bank Cleve. Div. chmn. Jewish Welfare Fund, 1964-65; asso. chmn. Jewish Welfare Fedn., 1971. Bd. dirs. NCCJ, Am. Friends Hebrew U., Jewish Community Fedn.; bd. dirs., v.p. Jewish Home for Aged; asso. v.p. United Way of Cleve., 1978—, sec., chmn. campaign, 1976—; trustee Univ. Sch. Served with U.S. Army, 1950-52. Recipient Drug and Cosmetic Industries award United Jewish Appeal, N.Y.C., 1963; Torch of Learning award Hebrew U., 1972. Mem. Nat. Assn. Chain Drug Stores (bd. dirs., chmn. bd. 1976-77), Ohio Council Retail Mchts. (chmn. 1977—, dir.). Jewish (mem. bd. temple). Clubs: Rotary, U. Pa. (bd. govs.), Union, Fifty, Oakwood (Cleve.). Home: 23376 Lyman Blvd Shaker Heights OH 44122 Office: 666 Euclid Ave Cleveland OH 44114

WEINBLATT, MYRON BENJAMIN, broadcasting co. exec.; b. Perth Amboy, N.J., June 10, 1929; s. Barney and Renee (Kempner) W.; B.S., Syracuse U., 1951; m. Annie Weitz, Sept. 25, 1956; children—Marc, Richard. Purchasing agt. Kramer-Trenton Co., Trenton, N.J., 1953-56; with NBC, 1957—, dir. participating program sales, N.Y.C., 1964-68, v.p., Eastern sales mgr., 1968-69, v.p. talent and program adminstrn., 1969-73, v.p. sales, 1973-75, sr. v.p. sales, 1975, exec. v.p., 1975—, exec. v.p., gen. mgr., 1977—, pres. Entertainment div., 1978-80, pres. NBC Enterprises, 1980—. Served with CIC, AUS, 1951-53; Japan. Mem. Internat. Radio and TV Soc., Nat. Acad. TV Arts and Scis., Internat. Acad. TV Arts and Scis. (bd.

govs.), Syracuse Alumni Assn. Home: 341 Irving Ave South Orange NJ 07079 Office: 30 Rockefeller Plaza New York NY 10020

WEINER, ARNOLD MURRAY, lawyer; b. Balt., Dec. 27, 1933; s. Benjamin and Matilda (Karlinsky) W.; B.A., U. Md., 1955, LL.B. (Elizabeth Maxwell Carroll Chesnut award 1957), 1957; m. Arleen Waldor, Aug. 25, 1957; children—Ellen, Barry, Deborah. Admitted to Md. bar, 1957; law clk. U.S. Ct. Appeals, 1957-58; asst. U.S. atty. Md. Dist., 1958-61, spl. asst. U.S. atty., 1962-63; partner firm Melnicove, Kaufman & Weiner, Balt., 1962—; instr. U. Md., 1963-65; spl. asst. atty. gen. State of Md., 1966-69; chmn. Md. Adv. Bd. Correction, Parole and Probation, 1970-74. Bd. dirs. Balt. Jewish Council, 1973—. Mem. Am., Fed., Md., Balt. bar assns., Order of Coif. Jewish. Casenote editor Md. Law Rev., 1956-57. Home: 8201 Spring Bottom Way Baltimore MD 21208 Office: 10 Light St Baltimore MD 21202

WEINER, CHARLES, lawyer; b. N.Y.C., Nov. 3, 1931; s. Herman and Pauline (Sonnenschein) W.; A.B., Ind. U., 1953, J.D., 1955; m. Patricia Bartel, June 19, 1955; children—Terry, Ellen, Diane. Admitted to Ind. bar, 1955, Ohio bar, 1957; mem. firm French, Marks, Short, Weiner & Valleau, Cin., 1957—, sr. partner, 1961—. Served with USAF, 1955-57. Mem. Am. Bar Assn., Ohio Bar Assn., Cin. Bar Assn. Office: 700 1st Nat Bank Bldg Cincinnati OH 45202

WEINER, CHARLES, historian, educator; b. Bklyn., Aug. 11, 1931; s. Louis and Minnie (Florman) W.; B.S., Case Inst. Tech., 1960, M.A., 1963, Ph.D., 1965; m. Shirley Marks, Nov. 22, 1956 (div. 1976); 1 dau., Susan. Asst. editor Tooling and Production mag., Cleve., 1958-60, asso. editor, 1961; editor The Explorer, Cleve. Museum of Natural History, 1960-62; dir. Project on History of Recent Physics in the U.S., Am. Inst. Physics, N.Y.C., 1964-65, dir. Center for History of Physics, 1965-74; prof. history of sci. and tech. Mass. Inst. Tech., 1974—, dir. oral history program, 1975—; vis. lectr. Poly. Inst. Bklyn., 1966; dir., lectr. Summer Sch. on History of 20th Century Physics, Italian Phys. Soc., Varenna, Italy, 1972; mem. exec. com. Columbia Seminar on Tech. and Social Change, 1969-75. Mem. com. social orgn. sci. Social Sci. Research Council, 1968-71; adv. com. to Library of Congress on Nat. Union Catalog of Manuscript Collections, 1965-71; mem. editorial adv. bd. Joseph Henry Papers, Smithsonian Instn., 1968—; com. on history of recent biochemistry and molecular biology Am. Acad. Arts and Scis., 1968—, project dir. com. history contemporary physics, 1966-74. Served with U.S. Army, 1951-53. Recipient Distinguished Service citation Am. Assn. Physics Tchrs., 1974. Case fellow, 1961-64; NSF grantee, 1965, 68, 70, 73, 75, 77; Guggenheim fellowship, 1970-71. Fellow AAAS (council 1969-75, com. on meetings, 1969-72), History of Sci. Soc. (council 1968-70, chmn. Met. N.Y. Sect. 1969-70), Am. Hist. Assn., Oral History Assn., Orgn. Am. Historians, Soc. for History of Tech. (adv. council 1977—), Fedn. Am. Scientists. Co-editor: The Legacy of George Ellery Hale, 1972; editor: Exploring the History of Nuclear Physics, 1972; History of 20th Century Physics, 1977. Address: Sch Humanities and Social Sci Mass Inst Tech Cambridge MA 02139*

WEINER, CHARLES R., U.S. judge; b. Phila., June 21, 1922; s. Max and Bessie (Chairney) W.; U. Pa., 1947, M.A., 1967, Ph.D., 1976; LL.B., Temple U., 1950; m. Edna Gerber, Aug. 24, 1947; children—William, Carole, Harvey. Admitted to Pa. bar, 1951; asst. dist. atty., Philadelphia County, 1952-53; mem. Pa. Senate from Phila. County, 1952-67, minority floor leader, 1959-60, 63-64, majority floor leader, 1961-62; U.S. dist. judge Eastern Dist. Pa., 1967—. Mem. Phila. County Bd. Law Examiners, 1959—. Mem. Pres.'s Adv. Commn. Inter-Govtl. Relations, Phila. Pub. Policy Com., Phila. Crime Prevention Assn., Big Bros. Assn.; mem. Pa. Bd. Arts and Scis. Trustee, exec. com. Fedn. Jewish Philanthropies Phila., Allied Jewish Appeal Phila.; bd. dirs. Mental Health Assn. Pa., Phila. Psychiat. Center, Phila. Tribune Charities, Phila. Wharton Center Parkside YMCA, Jewish Publ. Soc. Am., others; chmn. bd. govs. Dropsie U.; mem. nat. bd. advisers Practicing Law Inst. Served as officer USNR, World War II. Recipient Phila. Fellowship award; Founder's Day award Temple U.; Alumni award U. Pa.; Founder's award Berean Inst., others. Mem. Am., Pa., Phila. bar assns., Am. Law Inst. Office: 6613 S US Courthouse Independence Mall West Philadelphia PA 19106

WEINER, DAVID J., food co. exec.; b. Mpls., Mar. 13, 1939; s. Julius and Mabel (Gunderson) W.; B.S. in Bus. Mgmt. and Econs., UCLA; m. Feb. 17, 1962; children—Deborah, Carolyn, Jennifer, Alan. With Marshall Foods, Inc. (Minn.), 1962—, v.p., 1965-69, pres., chief exec. officer, 1969—, chmn. bd., 1976—; bd. dirs. various industry groups. Bd. dirs. Weiner Meml. Med. Center. Served with U.S. Army, 1957-58. Jewish. Clubs: Masons, Shriners. Office: 800 E Southview Dr Marshall MN 56258*

WEINER, EGON, sculptor, educator; b. Vienna, Austria, July 24, 1906; s. Moritz and Elsa (Fischer) W.; student Sch. Arts and Crafts, also Acad. Fine Arts (Vienna); m. Margaret Bass, Nov. 19, 1939; children—Peter, Andrew. Came to U.S., 1938, naturalized, 1944. Prof. sculpture and life drawing Art Inst. Chgo., 1945-71, prof. emeritus, 1971—; vis. prof. art Augustana Coll., 1956-71; exhibited one-man shows Art Inst. Chgo., Renaissance Soc. U. Chgo., Chgo. Pub. Library, Ill. Inst. Tech., U. Ill., Evanston Art Center, Augustana Coll., Kunstneres Hus, Oslo, 1973, 75, 76, Am. Embassy, Oslo, 1974, 75, Am. Center, Stockholm, 1974, Hamburg, Germany, 1977, others; group exhibits Art Inst. Chgo., Pa. Acad. Fine Arts, Oakland Art Gallery, Syracuse Mus. Art, Portland (Oreg.) Art Mus., Asso. Am. Artists Gallery, Chgo., Met. Mus. Art, others; represented permanent collections Syracuse Mus. Fine Arts, Augusburg Coll., Mpls., Augustana Coll., Vatican, pvt. collections; works include Monument of Brotherhood, Chgo., Figure of Christ, Luth. Ch., U. Chgo., Prodigal Son at Salem Ch., Chgo., Monument of St. Paul, Luth. Ch. in Mt. Prospect, Ill., portrait bust Otto Behnke, Midway Airport, Chgo., Senator William Benton for Ency. Brit., Dr. Eric Oldberg for Ill. Research Hosp., Willy Brandt for Harvard U., 1972, Ernest Hemingway for Oak Park (Ill.) Library, 1974; monument for Fire Acad. in Chgo., 1961 (AIA Honor award, 1962), Burning Bush of Knowledge, Gary (Ind.) Library, 1966; bronze figure Am. Ch., Oslo, Norway, 1967, Polyphony, St. Joseph Hosp., Chgo., 1972, portrait bust of Henry Kissinger, 1977, portrait head of dau. of Am. ambassador to Norway, 1977; others; lectr. modern art in Am. Recipient Grand Prix, Paris, 1925; Blumfeld award, Vienna, 1932-34; Municipal Art League prize, 1948, 69; Logan prize Art Inst. Chgo.; Syracuse Mus. Fine Arts prize, 1949; silver and bronze medal Oakland Art Gallery, 1945, 51; honor award Fine Arts, Vienna, 1955; AIA and Brotherhood award in art Roosevelt U., 1956; ann. award for design in hardwood, 1955, 56, 59; Austrian Cross of Honor for Science and Art, 1st Class, 1977. Hon. fellow Am.-Scandinavian Found.; life fellow Internat. Soc. Arts and Letters, Zurich, Switzerland, Mem. Municipal Art League (dir., Gold medal award 1969), Am. Soc. Ch. Architecture, Nat. Soc. Arts and Letters (adv. council Chgo. 1968-70). Author: Art and Human Emotions, 1975. Home: 835 Michigan Ave Evanston IL 60202 Office: Art Inst Chgo Chicago IL 60603

WEINER, IRVING BERNARD, psychologist, univ. adminstr., educator; b. Grand Rapids, Mich., Aug. 16, 1933; s. Jacob H. and Mollie Jean (Laevin) W.; B.A., U. Mich., Ann Arbor, 1955, M.A., 1957, Ph.D., 1959; m. Frances Shair, June 9, 1963; children—Jeremy Harris, Seth Howard. From instr. to prof. psychiatry and pediatrics U. Rochester (N.Y.), 1959-72; head div. psychology U. Rochester Med. Center, 1968-72; prof. psychology, chmn. dept. Case Western Res. U., 1972-77, dean grad. studies, 1976-79; vice chancellor for acad. affairs U. Denver, 1979—; adv. editor John Wiley & Sons, 1967—. Recipient Distinguished Profl. Achievement award Genesee Psychol. Assn., 1974. Diplomate Am. Bd. Profl. Psychology. Fellow Am. Psychol. Assn.; mem. AAAS, N.Y. Acad. Scis., Soc. Adolescent Medicine, Soc. Personality Assessment (pres. 1976-78), Assn. Internship Centers (exec. com. 1971-76), Phi Beta Kappa, Sigma Xi, Phi Kappa Phi. Author: Psychodiagnosis in Schizophrenia, 1966; Psychological Disturbance in Adolescence, 1970; Rorschach Handbook, 1971; Child Development, 1972; Principles of Psychotherapy, 1975; Development of the Child, 1978. Editor: Readings in Child Development, 1972; Clinical Methods in Psychology, 1976. Home: Denver CO Office: Office of Vice Chancellor U Denver Denver CO 80208

WEINER, IRWIN M., pharmacologist, educator; b. N.Y.C., Nov. 5, 1930; s. Samuel and Pearl (Levine) W.; A.B., Syracuse U., 1952; M.D., SUNY, 1956; m. Lois M. Fuxman, Mar. 5, 1961; children—Stephanie, Jeffrey. Postdoctoral fellow pharmacology Johns Hopkins Sch. Medicine, Balt., 1956-58, instr. pharmacology, 1958-60; asst. prof., 1960-66; vis. asst. prof. molecular biology Albert Einstein Coll. Medicine, Bronx, 1964-65; asso. prof. pharmacology Upstate Med. Centre, Syracuse, N.Y., 1966-68, prof., chmn. dept. pharmacology, 1968—; cons., NIH, 1964-68, Am. Heart Assn., 1969-74, Sterling-Winthrop Research Inst., 1969—. Mem. AAAS, Am. Soc. Pharmacology and Exptl. Therapeutics, Soc. Exptl. Biol. Medicine, Soc. Biochem. Pharmacology, Am. Soc. Nephrology. Contbr. numerous articles to profl. jours. Asso. editor: Jour. Pharmocology and Exptl. Therapeutics, 1965-72. Home: 50 Presidential Plaza Syracuse NY 13202 Office: 766 Irving Ave Syracuse NY 13210

WEINER, JEROME HARRIS, educator; b. N.Y.C., Apr. 5, 1923; s. Barnet and Dora (Muchar) W.; B. Mech. Engring., Cooper Union, 1943; A.M., Columbia, 1946, Ph.D., 1952; m. Florence Mensch, June 24, 1950; children—Jonathan David, Eric Daniel. Mem. faculty Columbia, 1952-68, prof. mech. engring. 1960-68, acting chmn. dept., 1961-62; L. Herbert Ballou Univ. prof. Brown U., 1968—. Fulbright research scholar, Rome, Italy, 1958-59, Haifa, Israel, 1965- 66; Guggenheim fellow, 1965-66. Mem. Am. Physical Soc., Am. Mathematical Soc., Am. Soc. M.E. Author: (with B.A. Boley) Theory of Thermal Stresses, 1960. Home: 24 Taber Ave Providence RI 02906

WEINER, MORTON DAVID, banker; b. Balt., Aug. 19, 1922; s. Max and Rose (Wolfe) W.; B.S., Towson State Coll., 1942; grad. exec. program, U. Calif. at Los Angeles, 1959; m. Joan M. Maggin; children—Bruce, Susan, Lori, Julie. Pres., dir., AVNET, Inc., N.Y.C., 1963-69; pres., owner Morton D. Weiner & Co., Inc., N.Y.C., 1969-70; dir. USLIFE Corp., 1968-70; chmn. bd. Nat. Investors Life Ins. Cos., 1970-77; exec. v.p. Norris Grain Co., 1971-78; pres., chief exec. officer Norin Corp., 1971-78; chmn. bd. Maple Leaf Mills, Ltd., Toronto, 1974-78; pres., chief exec. officer, dir. South Atlantic Fin. Corp., 1978—; pres., dir. Atico Fin. Corp., 1979—; dir. Pan Am. Bancshares, Inc., Miami, Fla., Pan Am. Bank, Miami. Served to capt. Signal Corps, U.S. Army, 1942-46; CBI. Office: PO Box 013131 150 SE 3d Ave Miami FL 33101

WEINER, MYRON, educator; b. N.Y.C., Mar. 11, 1931; s. Hyman and Anna (Peretz) W.; B.S.S., City Coll. N.Y., 1951; M.A. in Politics, Princeton, 1953, Ph.D., 1955; m. Sheila Leiman, June 29, 1952; children—Beth, Saul Jeremy. Instr., Princeton, 1951-52; asst. prof. U. Chgo., 1956-61; mem. faculty Mass. Inst. Tech., 1961—, prof. polit. sci., also sr. staff mem. Center Internat. Studies, 1965—, chmn. dept. polit. sci., 1974-77, Ford prof. polit. sci., 1977—; vis. prof. Inst. for Econ. Growth, Delhi (India) U., 1970; vis. scholar U. Paris, 1966-67, Harry S. Truman Inst., Hebrew U., 1979; cons. to govt. and founds. Mem. com. comparative politics Social Sci. Research Council, 1961-71. Fellow Rockefeller-Ford program for population policy, 1975, NSF, 1969, Carnegie Found., 1966, Rockefeller Found., 1961, Guggenheim Found., 1961, Social Sci. Research Council, 1957, Fulbright Found., 1953, Ford Found., 1953. Mem. Assn. Asian Studies (bd. dirs. 1961-69; chmn. adv. com. research and devel. 1966-69; chmn. Indian state politics com. 1960-67), Nat. Acad. Sci. (chmn. project on population policy in less-developed countries 1972-75), Am. Polit. Sci. Assn. (editorial bd. rev. 1966-70), Am. Acad. Arts and Scis., Internat. Union for Sci. Study of Population, Council on Fgn. Relations. Author: Party Politics in India, 1957; Political Change in South Asia, 1963; The Politics of Scarcity, 1962; Party Building in a New Nation: The Indian National Congress, 1967; Sons of the Soil, 1978; India at the Polls, 1978. Co-author: Politics of the Developing Areas, 1960; Rapid Population Growth: Consequences and Policy Implications, 1971; Crises and Sequences in Political Development, 1972; Policy Sciences and Population, 1975. Editor: Modernization: The Dynamics of Growth, 1966; Political Parties and Political Development, 1966; State Politics in India, 1968. Co-editor: Indian Voting Behavior, 1963; Electoral Politics in Indian States, 4 vols., 1974-77. Home: 93 Ivy St Brookline MA 02146 Office: Dept Polit Science Mass Inst Tech Cambridge MA 02139

WEINER, NORMAN, physician, educator; b. Rochester, N.Y., July 13, 1928; s. Samuel and Lillian (Guttenberg) W.; B.S., U. Mich., 1949; M.D., Harvard U., 1953; m. Diana E. Marderosian, Jan. 2, 1955; children—Steven Mark, David Howard, Jeffrey Alan, Gareth Ronald, Eric Adam. Intern, Boston City Hosp., Harvard Med. Service, 1953-54; instr. dept. pharmacology Harvard Med. Sch., 1956-58, asso., 1958-61, asst. prof., 1961-67, dir. neuropharmacology lab. Mass. Mental Health Center, Boston, 1962-67; prof., chmn. dept. pharmacology U. Colo. Sch. Medicine, Denver, 1967—; vis. prof. clin. pharmacology Med. Coll. Ga., 1979; chmn. basic biomed. sci. panel Com. on study of nat. needs for biomed. and behavioral research personnel Nat. Acad. Scis.-NRC, 1979. Nat. Inst. Neurol. Diseases fellow, 1961-62; NIH research career devel. grantee, 1963-67. Mem. Am. Soc. Pharmacology and Exptl. Therapeutics (sec.-treas. 1972-73, chmn. bd. publs. trustees 1978—), Western Pharmacology Soc. (pres. 1978-79), Assn. Med. Sch. Pharmacology (treas. 1978-79), Biochem. Soc., Am. Soc. Neurochemistry, Internat. Soc. Neurochemistry, AAAS, Am. Coll. Neuropsychopharmacology. Co-editor 2 books in field; contbr. articles to profl. jours.; mem. editorial bds. numerous jours. Home: 404 S Niagara St Denver CO 80224 Office: Dept Pharmacology Univ Colo Sch Medicine Denver CO 80262

WEINER, RICHARD, public relations exec.; b. Bklyn., May 10, 1927; s. George M. and Sally (Kosover) W.; B.S., U. Wis., 1949, M.S., 1950; m. Florence Chaiken, Dec. 9, 1956; children—Jessica, Stephanie. Pres., Creative Radio Assos., Madison, Wis., 1951-52, Weiner-Morton Assos., Madison, 1952-53; sr. v.p. Ruder & Finn, Inc., N.Y.C., 1953-68; pres. Richard Weiner, Inc., N.Y.C., 1968—; adj. prof. N.Y. Inst. Tech. Mem. Public Relations Soc. Am. (Silver Anvil award 1965; accredited counselor), Publicity Club N.Y. (lectr.). Jewish. Author: Professional's Guide to Public Relations Services, 1968; News Bureaus in the U.S., 1970; Syndicated Columnists, 1972; Professional's Guide to Publicity, 1979; Military Publications, 1979. Office: 888 Seventh Ave New York NY 10019. *The essence of life is growth, adaptation, change. I hope to continue to succeed in living vigorously.*

WEINER, WALTER HERMAN, lawyer; b. Bklyn., Aug. 29, 1930; s. Harry and Sylvia (Freifeld) W.; B.A., U. Mich., 1952, J.D. (asso. editor Law Rev.), 1953; m. Nina Ester Avidar, Oct. 11, 1966; children—Thomas Field, Jon Michael. Admitted to N.Y. bar, 1953, since practiced in N.Y.C.; of counsel firm Kronish, Lieb, Shainswit, Weiner & Hellman, 1965—; sec., dir. Ad. Press Ltd.; pres. Republic N.Y. Corp., 1980—; dir.; chmn. exec. com., dir. Republic Nat. Bank N.Y.; chief exec. officer, dir. Big V Supermarkets, Inc. Mem. Am., N.Y. State bar assns., Assn. Bar City N.Y. Home: 1025 Fifth Ave New York NY 10028 Office: 1345 Ave of Americas New York NY 10019

WEINER, WARREN, pub. relations cons.; b. Phila., 1936; s. Benjamin and Bella (Tinkleman) W.; B.S., Temple U., 1957; Ph.D. (hon.), U. So. China, Macau, 1971; m. Ethel Z. Scharf, July 28, 1957; children—David B., Mark G. Sportswriter, Phila. Inquirer, 1954-57; news dir. Sta. WITT, Lewisburg, Pa., 1957, St. WRTA, Altoona, Pa., 1958-61; info. officer City of Phila., 1961-62, promotion and publicity mgr., 1962-64, dep. city rep., 1968-69; v.p. pub. relations J.M. Korn & Son. Inc., Phila., 1964-68; dir. pub. relations Franklin Mint, Phila., 1970; pres. Pub. Relations Ltd., Phila., 1971—; v.p. Pa. AP Broadcasters Assn., 1961. Adv. bd. dirs. Friends Ind. Nat. Hist. Park; exec. dir. Phila. Area Council Tourism, 1968-69, Citizens Com. Phila. Improvement Program, 1968-69, Phila. Mayor's Frankford Arsenal Task Force, 1969. Recipient award Am. Film Festival, 1968; Cleaner Air Week award U.S. Air Pollution Control League, 1962; Nat. Noise Abatement Council award, 1962; Outstanding News Operation award Pa. AP Broadcasters Assn., 1960, Outstanding Reporting award, 1960; Best Industry Ann. Report award Fin. World mag., 1974; Silver Anvil award Pub. Relations Soc. Am., 1968, 69. Mem. Am. Philatelic Soc., Soc. Philatelic Americans, Soc. Philaticians. Office: 3 Parkway Philadelphia PA 19102

WEINERT, DONALD G(REGORY), assn. exec., engr.; b. Aberdeen, S.D., Sept. 16, 1930; s. McDonald Donnegan and Susan Mae (Mathis) W.; B.S., U.S. Mil. Acad., 1952; M.S.E., Purdue U., 1958; grad. Northwestern U. Inst. for Mgmt., 1974; grad. Command Staff Gen. Coll., 1965, Armed Forces Staff Coll., 1967, Army War Coll., 1969; commd. 2d lt. U.S. Army C.E., 1952, advanced through grades to brig. gen., 1977; troop comdr., Korea, 1953-54, Ger., 1958-60, 67-68; dist. engr. Little Rock, Ark., 1972-75; staff officer Hdqrs. Dept. Army, Washington, 1970-72; dir. Engr. Study Group, Washington, 1975-77; spl. asst. to Chief Engrs., C.E., Washington, 1978, ret., 1978; exec. dir. Nat. Soc. Profl. Engrs., Washington, 1978—; guest lectr. on personnel mgmt. Dept. of the Army, Ann. Scout show chmn. Quapaw Area council Boy Scouts Am., 1973-75; mem. Keep Am. Beautiful Com., Little Rock, 1972-75. Decorated Legion of Merit (3), Bronze Star medal (2), Army Commendation medal (4); registered profl. engr., Tex. Mem. Soc. Am. Mil. Engrs., Assn. U.S. Army. Republican. Club: Rotary (Washington). Army research study dir.: Real Property Management Activities, 4 vols., 1978. Home: 8121 Dunsinane Ct McLean VA 22101 Office: 2029 K St NW Washington DC 20006

WEINFELD, EDWARD, judge; b. N.Y.C., May 14, 1901; s. Abraham and Fanny (Singer) W.; LL.B., N.Y. U., 1921, LL.M., 1922; m. Lillian Stoll, Dec. 22, 1929; children—Ann, Fern. Admitted to N.Y. bar, 1923; U.S. Dist. judge So. N.Y., 1950—; N.Y. State Commr. Housing, 1939-42; chief counsel N.Y. State Legislative Com. investigating bondholders coms., 1935; del. N.Y. State Constl. Conv., 1938; pres. Nat. Assn. Housing Ofcls., 1941-42, Nat. Housing Conf., 1948-50; v.p., dir. Citizens' Housing and Planning Council N.Y., 1945-50; exec. com. Citizens' Union City N.Y., 1943-50; dir. War Housing N.Y. State War Council, 1940-42; mem. N.Y. State Post War Pub. Works Planning Commn., 1940-42. Chmn. bd. dirs. Citizens' Com. Children N.Y. City, 1950; trustee Fred L. Lavanburg Found. Mem. Phi Sigma Delta. Office: US Court House Foley Sq New York NY 10007*

WEINGARTEN, BERNARD LOUIS, grocery co. exec.; b. Houston, Mar. 25, 1924; s. Joseph and Malvina (Kessler) W.; B.S. in Elec. Engring., U. Tex., 1947; m. Shirley Caplovitz, July 7, 1951; children—Linda, Janet, Susan, Ellen, Eveta. With J. Weingarten, Inc., Houston, 1947—, exec. v.p., 1957-67, pres., 1967—. Mem. Tau Beta Pi. Home: 1 Radney Circle Houston TX 77024 Office: 600 Lockwood Dr Houston TX 77011

WEINGARTEN, HERBERT N., lawyer; b. Detroit, Jan. 5, 1927; s. Harry and Pearl (Kandel) W.; LL.B., U. Mich., 1951; m. Nanci Weisman, Aug. 14, 1953; children—Ann M., James S. Admitted to Mich. bar, 1951, since practiced in Detroit; sr. partner firm Hertzberg Jacob & Weingarten, Detroit, 1957—. Served with USNR, 1945-46. Mem. Am. Bar Assn. (uniform comml. code com. 1963—). Club: Standard (Detroit). Contbr. articles on bankruptcy, comml. law to legal publs. Home: 365 Hamilton Rd Birmingham MI 48010 Office: 1530 Buhl Bldg Detroit MI 48226

WEINGARTEN, HILDE (MRS. ARTHUR KEVESS), artist; b. Berlin, Germany; d. Morris and Clara (Leitner) Weingarten; came to U.S., 1938, naturalized, 1945; student Art Students League, N.Y.C., 1940-41; grad. Cooper Union Art Sch., 1947, B.F.A., 1976; m. Arthur S. Kevess, Jan. 28, 1951 (dec. 1973); children—Ruth, Robert. One man shows include Carlebach Gallery, N.Y.C., 1949, Hicks St. Gallery, Bklyn., 1962, 68, Contemporary Arts Gallery, N.Y.C., 1962, 66, Cadman Plaza Community Hall, Bklyn., 1971; exhbns. include Corcoran Gallery, Seattle Art Mus., Denver Art Mus., Phila. Print Club, Phila. Art Alliance, Bklyn. Mus., N.Y.C., Cleve. Mus. Art, Albright Art Gallery, Rochester Meml. Art Gallery, Dallas Mus. Fine Arts, N.Y. World's Fair, 1965, City Center, A.A.A., A.C.A., other N.Y.C. galleries, Fujikawa Gallery, Osaka, Japan, Palazzo Vecchio, Florence, Italy; represented in permanent collections Israeli Nat. Mus., Jerusalem, Israel, Johnson Mus., Cornell U., Bklyn. Mus., L.I. U., N.Y. Pub. Library, Fogg Art Mus., Cambridge, Mass., Rose Art Mus., Brandeis U., N.Y.C. Community Coll., numerous others; artist Pratt Graphics Center, 1970—. Recipient annual purchase prize Collectors Am. Art, 1947-65; Patrons Art prize (oil) Painters and Sculptors Soc. N.J., 1970, Anonymous prize (graphics), 1973, 1st award (graphics), 1978; Winsor & Newton award (oil) Am. Soc. Contemporary Artists, graphics award, 1976; Watson-Guptill award, 1978; Donna Miller Meml. prize Nat. Assn. Women Artists, 1975, others. Mem. Artists Equity N.Y. (bd. dirs. 1964-72), Nat. Assn. Women Artists, Audubon Artists, Painters and Sculptors Soc. N.J., Am. Soc. Contemporary Artists. Address: 140 Cadman Plaza West Brooklyn NY 11201

WEINGARTEN, MURRAY, engring. co. exec.; b. N.Y.C., Feb. 8, 1925; s. Ellis and Ethel (Gaies) B.E.E., Rensselaer Poly. Inst., 1947; m. Shirley L. Bowersox, Apr. 30, 1955; children—Steven Ellis, Betsy Lori. With J.R. Rider, N.Y.C., 1947-48; engr. Bendix Radio, Towson, Md., 1948-50; with Bendix Field Engring. Corp., Columbia, Md., became v.p., 1963, now chmn. bd., pres., dir.; chmn. bd., pres., dir. Bendix Comml. Services Corp., Columbia; pres. United Geophys. Corp. subs. Bendix Corp., also dir.; pres. Skagit Corp. subs. Bendix Corp., Sedro-Woolley, Wash. Served with USNR, 1943-45. Mem. IEEE (sr.), Armed Forces Communication and Electronics Assn., Soc. Exploration Geophysicists (asso.), Engring. Soc. Balt. Home: 9442 Dunloggin Rd Ellicott City MD 21043 Office: 9250 Rt 108 Columbia MD 21045

WEINGARTNER, H(ANS) MARTIN, educator; b. Heidelberg, Germany, Apr. 4, 1929; s. Jacob and Grete (Kahn) W.; came to U.S., 1939, naturalized, 1944; A.B., S.B., U. Chgo., 1950, A.M., 1951; M.S., Carnegie Mellon U., 1956, Ph.D., 1962; m. Joyce Trellis, June 12, 1955; children—Steven M., Susan C., Eric H., Kenneth L. Economist, Dept. Commerce, 1951-53; instr. Grad. Sch. Indsl. Adminstrn., Carnegie Mellon U., 1956-57; instr., then asst. prof. Grad. Sch. Bus., U. Chgo., 1957-63; asso. prof. fin. Alfred P. Sloan Sch. Mgmt., Mass. Inst. Tech., 1963-66; prof. Grad. Sch. Mgmt., U. Rochester (N.Y.), 1966-77; Brownlee O. Currey prof. fin. Owen Grad. Sch. Mgmt., Vanderbilt U., 1977—; dir. Computer Consoles, Inc., 1974—; cons. to industry. Served with AUS, 1951-53. Mellon fellow, 1954-55; Ford Found. fellow, 1955-56; winner Ford Found. Dissertation competition, 1963. Mem. Inst. Mgmt. Scis. (v.p. fin. 1978—), Am. Economic Assn., Am. Fin. Assn., Beta Gamma Sigma. Author: Mathematical Programming and the Analysis of Capital Budgeting Problems, 3d edit., 1974; (with George Benston and Dan Horsky) An Empirical Study of Redlining, 1978; also articles. Deptl. editor Mgmt. Sci., 1967-73. Home: 1616 Ash Valley Dr Nashville TN 37215 Office: 2505 West End Ave Nashville TN 37203

WEINGARTNER, RUDOLPH HERBERT, educator; b. Heidelberg, Germany, Feb. 12, 1927; s. Jacob and Grete (Kahn) W.; A.B., Columbia, 1950, M.A., 1953, Ph.D., 1959; m. Fannia Goldberg-Rudkowski, Dec. 28, 1952; children—Mark H., Eleanor C. Came to U.S., 1939, naturalized, 1944. Fellow Inst. Philos. Research, San Francisco, 1953-55; instr. philosophy Columbia, 1955-59; from asst. prof. to prof., chmn. dept. philosophy San Francisco State Coll., 1959-68; prof. philosophy Vassar Coll., Poughkeepsie, 1968-74, chmn. dept., 1969-74, Taylor prof. philosophy, 1973-74; dean Coll. Arts and Scis., prof. philosophy Northwestern U., Evanston, Ill., 1974—. Served with USNR, 1945-46. Social Sci. Research Council fellow, 1958-59; Guggenheim fellow, 1965-66; Am. Council of Learned Socs. fellow, 1971-72. Mem. Am. Philos. Assn., Phi Beta Kappa. Author: Experience and Culture: The Philosophy of Georg Simmel, 1962; The Unity of the Platonic Dialogue: The Cratylus, The Protagoras, The Parmenides, 1973; also articles. Editor (with Josef Katz) Philosophy in the West, 1965. Home: 2112 Orrington Ave Evanston IL 60201

WEINGLASS, LEONARD IRVING, lawyer; b. Belleville, N.J., Aug. 27, 1933; s. Sol and Clara (Schwartz) W.; B.A., George Washington U., 1955; LL.B., Yale U., 1958. Individual practice law, Newark, 1961-71, Los Angeles, 1974—; mem. Newark Law Collective, 1971-73; instr. on criminal advocacy U. So. Calif., People's Coll. Law; lectr. on criminal advocacy Practising Law Inst. Served with USAF, 1951-61. Recipient Clarence Darrow Found. award, 1977. Mem. Nat. Lawyer's Guild, Calif. Bar Assn., Calif. Attys. for Criminal Justice (bd. govs. 1976—), Nat. Assn. Criminal Def. Lawyers, Californians for Econ. Democracy. Jewish. Home: 2025 Avon St Los Angeles CA 90026 Office: 304 S Broadway Los Angeles CA 90013

WEINHARDT, CARL J., JR., author, museum dir.; b. Indpls., Sept. 22, 1927; s. Carl J. and Helen Irene (Rost) W.; A.B. magna cum laude, Harvard, 1948, M.A., 1949, M.F.A., 1955; H.H.D., Christian Theol. Sem., 1967; Ph.D., Ind. State U., 1973; m. Annetta E. Hubon, May 1, 1954; children—Carl Rost, Seth Henry, Lucia Rost. Lectr., Boston Archtl. Center, 1954-55; mem. staff Metropolitan Mus., 1955-60, asso. curator, 1958-60; lectr. fine arts Columbia, 1958-60; dir. Mpls. Inst. Arts, 1960-62; dir. Gallery of Modern Art, N.Y.C., 1962-65; dir. Indpls. Mus. Art, 1965-75; supt. mus. div. Dade County Park and Recreation Dept., 1976—; dir. Vizcaya Mus. and Gardens, Miami, Fla., 1976—; coordinator Dade County Center for Fine Arts. Mem. State of Fla. Hist. Preservation Council; v.p. Miami Design Preservation League; cons. Downtown Devel. Authority, Nat. Endowment for Arts. Mem. Coll. Art Assn., Assn. Art Museum Dirs., Soc. Archtl. Historians, Am. Fedn. Arts, Nat. Soc. Arts and Letters, Beacon Hill Assn., Am. Assn. Museums, Festival Music Soc. (founder), Cultural Execs. Council, Fla. Art Mus. Dirs. Assn., Coconut Grove C. of C. (dir.), Phi Beta Kappa. Episcopalian. Clubs: Harvard Musical Assn. (Boston); Portfolio; Literary (Indpls.). Author: Architecture of Beacon Hill, 1957; Newport Preserved, 1965, The Clowes Collection, 1971; The Best of John Held, Jr., 1973; A Village in Miami, 1978, others; also catalogues for spl. exhbns., articles in mus. bulls., Sat. Rev., Art in Am., Muse News, etc. Home: 3725 Frantz Rd Coconut Grove FL 33133 Office: 3251 S Miami Ave Miami FL 33129

WEINHAUER, WILLIAM GILLETTE, bishop; b. N.Y.C., Dec. 3, 1924; s. Nicholas Alfred and Florence Anastacia (Davis) W.; B.S., Trinity Coll., Hartford, Conn., 1948; M.Div., Gen. Theol. Sem., 1951, S.T.M., 1956, Th.D., 1970; m. Jean Roberta Shanks, Mar. 20, 1948; children—Roberta Lynn, Cynthia Anne, Doris Jean. Ordained to ministry Episcopal Ch. U.S.A., 1951; pastor Episcopal parishes Diocese N.Y., 1951-56; prof. N.T., St. Andrews Theol. Sem., Manila, Philippines, 1956-60; asst. prof. N.T., Gen. Theol. Sem., 1961-71; rector Christ Ch., Poughkeepsie, N.Y., 1971-73; bishop Episcopal Diocese of Western N.C., 1973—; chaplain to mil. bases, colls. hosps. Served with USN, 1943-46. Mem. Soc. Bibl. Lit. Home: 9 Beechwood Rd Asheville NC 28805 Office: PO Box 368 Black Mountain NC 28711

WEINIG, ROBERT WALTER, holding co. exec.; b. Columbus, Ohio, Aug. 3, 1930; s. Robert F. and Catherine H. (Walter) W.; B.A., Dartmouth, 1952, M.B.A., Amos Tuck Sch. Bus. Adminstrn., 1955; m. Virginia Doree, Aug. 16, 1958; children—Katrina, Stephen, Cynthia. Engaged in comml. banking, Chgo., 1955-57, in municipal finance, Chgo., 1957-59; asst. v.p. Duff & Phelps, Inc., Chgo., 1959-66; spl. asst. to pres. Eastern Gas & Fuel Assos., Boston, 1966-67, controller, 1967-69, v.p., 1969-70, sr. v.p. fin., 1970-77, sr. v.p. fin. and adminstrn., 1977-79, exec. v.p., chief adminstrv. officer, 1979—. dir. Algonquin Gas Transmission Co. Served to 2d lt. AUS, 1952-54. Chartered fin. analyst. Mem. Fin. Analysts Fedn., Chgo. Soc. Security Analysts. Office: One Beacon St Boston MA 02108

WEINLEIN, ANTHONY GERARD, labor union exec.; b. Milw., June 1, 1913; s. Frank J. and Dorothe (Puerzer) W.; B.A., U. Wis., 1941; M.A., U. Chgo., 1943, Ph.D., 1964; m. Mary Elizabeth Miklesh, Aug. 1, 1949; children—Michael, Kurt, Robert (dec.), Eric, Lisa. Pharmacist with various drugstores, Wis., 1935-43; with Service Employees Internat. Union, Washington, 1943—, exec. asst. to pres., exec. sec., sec.-treas., 1976—. Served with U.S. Army, 1943-45; ETO. Democrat. Unitarian. Home: 6817 Tilden Ln Rockville MD 20852 Office: Service Employees Internat Union 2020 K St NW Washington DC 20006*

WEINMAN, ROBERT ALEXANDER, sculptor; b. N.Y.C., Mar. 19, 1915; s. Adolph Alexander and Margaret Lucille (Landman) W.; student Nat. Acad. Design, 1931-39, Art Students League, N.Y.C., 1939-40; m. Jane Morrison, July 14, 1945; children—Paul Alexander, Christopher Robert. Exhbns. include Nat. Acad. Design, 1937, 38, 49, 53, Pa. Acad. Fine Arts, 1939, N.Y. State Nature Assn., 1939, Nat. Arts Club, 1941, Georg Jensen, Inc., 1941, Allied Artists Am., 1946, 3d Sculpture Internat., Phila., 1949, Nat. Sculpture Soc., 1952, 64, 68, 71, 79, Soc. Animal Artists, 1970, 72; rep. bronze dolphin fountain group S.I. Community Coll., small bronze, Bessie the Belligerent, study of an Indian rhinoceros, and a watercolor, Great Blue Heron, Brookgreen Gardens, Georgetown, S.C., Stations of the Cross, chapel Manhattanville Coll. Sacred Heart, Purchase, N.Y., bronze airman Tulsa Municipal Airport, granite eagle Fed. Res. Bank, Buffalo, rood group and twelve apostles Our Lady of Perpetual Help, Queens, N.Y., others; creator numerous medals for athletic, ednl., bus., mil., religious and cultural orgns. Served with U.S. Army, 1942-45. Recipient Bennett prize Nat. Sculpture Soc., 1952, J. Sanford Saltus medal award Am. Numis. Soc., 1964; Sculptor of Year award Am. Numis. Assn., 1975. Mem. Nat. Sculpture Soc., (pres., 1973-76), N.A.D. Address: Cross River Rd Rural Route 3 Bedford NY 10506

WEINMANN, JOHN GIFFEN, lawyer; b. New Orleans, Aug. 29, 1928; S. Rudolph John and Mary Victoria (Mills) W.; B.A., Tulane U., 1950, LL.B., 1952; m. Virginia Lee Eason, June 11, 1955; children—Winston Eason, Robert St. George Tucker, John Giffen, Mary Virginia Lewis, George Gustaf. Admitted to La. bar, 1952, since practiced in New Orleans; mem. firm Phelps, Dunbar, Marks, Claverie & Sims, 1955—; lectr. bills and notes New Orleans chpt. Am. Inst. Banking, 1958-59; dir. Eason Oil Co., 1961—, chmn., 1977; dir. 1st Nat. Bank of Oklahoma City, Rathborne Land Co. Inc.; asst. sec. Am. Bar Endowment, 1971-76, bd. dirs., sec., 1975—. Bd. govs. Tulane Med. Center; trustee Southwest Legal Found.; trustee Metairie Park Country Day Sch., v.p., 1976-77, pres., 1978—. Mem. Am. (chmn. jr. bar conf. 1963-64, mem. ho. dels. 1964-66, 70, 72-76, sec. com. ethics evaluation 1965, rep. to conv. Nat. des Jeunes Avocats de France 1964, chmn. sect. bar activities, 1969-70), La. (sec.-treas. 1965-67) bar assns., La. Soc. Colonial Wars (gov. 1976), Phi Beta Kappa, Order of Coif, Delta Kappa Epsilon, Omicron Delta Kappa. Episcopalian. Mem. adv. bd. Tulane Law Rev. Home: 611 Hector Ave Metairie LA 70005 Office: Hibernia Bank Bldg New Orleans LA 70112

WEINREB, LLOYD LOBELL, educator; b. N.Y.C., Oct. 9, 1936; s. Victor and Ernestine (Lobell) W.; B.A., Dartmouth, 1957; B.A., U. Oxford, 1959, M.A., 1963; LL.B., Harvard, 1962; m. Ruth Plaut, May 5, 1963; children—Jennifer, Elizabeth, Nicholas. Admitted to N.Y. bar, 1963, Mass. bar, 1969; faculty Harvard Law Sch., Cambridge, Mass., 1965—, prof. law, 1968—. Home: 119 Russell Ave Watertown MA 02172 Office: Harvard Law Sch Cambridge MA 02138

WEINREICH, GABRIEL, physicist, educator; b. Vilnius, Lithuania, Feb. 12, 1928; s. Max and Regina (Szabad) W.; came to U.S., 1941, naturalized, 1949; A.B., Columbia U., 1948, M.A., 1949, Ph.D., 1954; m. Alisa Lourié, Apr. 19, 1951 (dec. 1970); m. 2d, Gerane Siemering Benamou, Oct. 23, 1971; children—Catherine, Marc, Daniel, Rebecca, Natalie. Mem. staff Bell Telephone Labs., Murray Hill, N.J., 1953-60; mem. faculty U. Mich., Ann Arbor, 1960—, prof. physics, 1964—, Collegiate prof., 1974-76. Recipient Distinguished Teaching award U. Mich., 1968. Author: Solids: Elementary Theory for Advanced Students, 1965; Fundamental Thermodynamics, 1968; Notes for General Physics, 1972. Home: 2110 Tuomy Rd Ann Arbor MI 48104 Office: Randall Lab U Mich Ann Arbor MI 48109

WEINRICH, CARL, organist; b. Paterson, N.J., July 2, 1904; s. Charles and Elise (Forrer) W.; A.B., N.Y.U., 1927; student Curtis Inst., Phila., 1927-30; Mus.D. (hon.), Westminster Choir Coll., 1973; m. Edna Tompkins, June 30, 1928; children—Elise, Cynthia; m. 2d, Annette Broderick, May 20, 1978. Organist-choirmaster, Ch. of Holy Communion, N.Y.C., 1930-32; head of organ dept. Westminster Choir Coll., Princeton, 1934-40; instr. in organ Wellesley Coll., 1936-46; tchr. organ Columbia U., 1942-52; dir. music Princeton U. Chapel, 1943-73; Lamb vis. lectr. Harvard, 1950-51. Recital tours, U.S. and Canada, 1934—; recordings of organ music of Bach and forerunners. Fellow Am. Guild of Organists. Protestant. Club: Century. Editor: Variations for Organ (Schönberg). Contbr. articles on Albert Schweitzer's contribution to organ bldg. in Schweitzer Jubilee Book, 1947. Home: 4131 Princeton Pike Princeton NJ 08540

WEINS, LEO MATTHEW, pub. co. exec.; b. Racine, Wis., Sept. 2, 1912; s. Leo Matthew and Lula (Vollman) W.; student Loyola U., Chgo., 1935-36, Northwestern U., 1946-47, U. Chgo., 1937-38; m. Margaret Killion, Oct. 19, 1955. Comptroller, ALA, 1952-57; with H. W. Wilson Co., N.Y.C., 1957—, pres., treas., 1967—; mem. editorial bd. Choice, 1963-70, 77—; mem. govt. advisory com. book and library programs Dept. State, 1973-76; mem. Bronx adv. com. Chase Manhattan Bank, 1968-78; trustee Dollar Savs. Bank N.Y., 1969—; trustee, treas. N.Y. Met. Reference and Research Library Agency, 1979—. Mem. sci. info. council NSF, 1968-72; bd. dirs. Highbridge Conservation Program, Bronx, 1966-69; pres. H.W. Wilson Found., 1967—. Served with AUS, 1943-46. Mem. ALA, Am. Antiquarian Soc. Club: Grolier. Home: 20 Beekman Pl New York NY 10022 Office: 950 University Ave Bronx NY 10452

WEINSCHREIDER, CHARLES JAMES, toy co. exec.; b. Little Falls, N.Y., Nov. 21, 1933; s. Charles James and Julia Elizabeth (Crimmins) W.; B.A., Antioch Coll., 1956; m. Sigrid Schutz, July 15, 1955; children—Kristy, Steven, Carrie Margaret, Charles. Fashion mdse. mgr. Carlisle-Allen Dept. Stores, Ashtabula, Ohio, 1958-64; v.p. mktg. and sales Fisher-Price Toys, East Aurora, N.Y., 1964-77; corp. exec. v.p., pres. toy div. Tonka Corp., Mound, Minn., 1977-79; pres., chief exec. officer Playskool Toys, Chgo., 1979—. Served with U.S. Army, 1956-58. Home: 5522 S Garfield Hinsdale IL 60521 Office: 4501 W Augusta Chicago IL 60651

WEINSTEIN, ALEX, architect; b. Omaha, June 8, 1923; s. Abraham and Soney (Edelman) W.; B.S. in Archtl. Engring., Iowa State U., 1943; M.Arch., Mass. Inst. Tech., 1948; m. Naomi Tamara Blumenthal, Aug. 13, 1968; children—Tracy Renee, Valerie Aviva. Partner, Steele, Weinstein & Assos., architects-engrs., Omaha, 1949-69; prin. Architects Hawaii, Honolulu, 1969—. Mem. Omaha Zoning Bd. Appeals, 1967-69. Served with C.E., AUS, 1941-43; ETO. Mem. A.I.A., Tau Beta Pi, Tau Sigma Delta, Theta Xi. Important works include Behlen Research Lab. of Physics, U. Nebr., 1962, U.S. Post Office and Courthouse, Omaha, 1956, Pacific Trade Center, Honolulu, 1972, Hale Koa Hotel, Honolulu, 1975, Cancer Research Center, Honolulu, 1979. Home: 149 Makaweli St Honolulu HI 96825 Office: 190 S King St Honolulu HI 96813

WEINSTEIN, ALVIN SEYMOUR, educator; b. Lynn, Mass., June 12, 1928; s. Samuel Jacob and Miriam (Levine) W.; B.S. in Mech. Engring., U. Mich., 1951; M.S., Carnegie Inst. Tech., 1955, Ph.D., 1955; m. Helene Zamcheck, Aug. 10, 1952; children—Ruth Caryn, Sandra Beth, Marc Steven. Asst. prof. mech. engring. Carngie Inst. Tech. (now Carnegie-Mellon U.), Pitts., 1955-61, asso. prof., 1961-65, prof., 1965-72, prof. mech. engring. and pub. policy, 1972—; sr. research asso. Max Planck Institut fur Eisenforschung, Dusseldorf, Germany, 1965; vis. prof. U. Bristol (Eng.), 1970; partner Tech. Engring. Consultants; dir. engring. Harvesting Systems, Inc.; mem. evaluation panel Center for Consumer Product Tech., Nat. Bur. Standards, 1976—; cons. J & L Steel Co., Gen. Electric Co., Westinghouse Electric Co., Union Carbide Co., Rockwell Mfg. Co., Joy Mfg. Co. Mem. sch. bd. Chartiers Valley Joint Schs., 1963-66; v.p. Sch. Advanced Jewish Studies, 1974—. Served with AUS, 1946-47. Recipient Research award Am. Soc. for Testing ASTM, 1965, Melville medal ASME, 1972; Western Electric Fund award for outstanding educator Am. Soc. Engring. Edn., 1973. Mem. ASME, Assn. Iron and Steel Engrs., Am. Soc. for Engring. Edn., ASTM, Sigma Xi (v.p. 1971, pres. 1972. Republican. Author: An Introduction to the Art of Engineering, 1970; Product Liability and the Reasonably Safe Product, 1978. Research in metal processing, heat transfer, product liability. Home: 575 Sandrae Dr Pittsburgh PA 15243

WEINSTEIN, BORIS, organic chemist; b. New Orleans, Mar. 31, 1930; s. Israel and Norma Rebecca (Levy) W.; B.S., La. State U., 1951; M.S., Purdue U., 1953; Ph.D., Ohio State U., 1959; postgrad. (Univ. fellow) U. Calif., Berkeley, 1959-60; m. Barbara Joan LeVine, Aug. 16, 1953; children—William Steven, Michael Simon. Chemist, Stanford Research Inst., Menlo Park, Calif., 1960-61; lab. dir. chemistry Stanford U., 1961-67; asso. prof. chemistry U. Wash., 1967-74, prof., 1974—. Served to 1st lt. USAF, 1953-55. Mem. AAAS, AAUP, Am. Chem. Soc., Am. Inst. Chemists, Am. Soc. Neurochemistry, Chem. Soc., N.Y. Acad. Scis., Phytochem. Soc. N. Am. Editor: Peptides: Chemistry and Biochemistry, 1970; Chemistry and Biochemistry of Amino Acids, Peptides, and Proteins, vols. 1-5, 1971—; editor Organic Reactions, 1973—, sec., 1973—. Home: 4410 54th Ave NE Seattle WA 98105 Office: Dept Chemistry BG-10 U Wash Seattle WA 98195

WEINSTEIN, GEORGE, financial cons., accountant; b. N.Y.C., Mar. 20, 1924; s. Morris J. and Sara (Broder) W.; B.S., U. Ill., 1944, student Law Sch., 1944-45; M.B.A., N.Y.U., 1947, student Law Sch., 1947-48; m. Shirley Beatrice Greenberg, Sept. 1, 1945; children—Stanley Howard, Jerrald, Sara Belle. Exec. sec. Ill. Union Bldg. Co., Champaign, Ill., 1944; with Homes & Davis, C.P.A.'s, 1944; with Morris J. Weinstein, Groothuis & Co., C.P.A.'s, N.Y.C., 1944-72, partner, 1945-72, mng. partner, 1962-70; partner Weinstein Assos., fin. cons., N.Y.C. and Milw.; pres. REIT Property Mgrs. Ltd., Milw.; trustee Rainville Trust, N.Y.C., others; pres., trustee Wis. Real Estate Trust; chmn. Ross Devel. and Constrn. Co., Orlando; pres. W-R Inc., Fla. Active various drives United Jewish Appeal, Fedn. Jewish Philanthropies. Chmn. bd. N. Shore Hebrew Acad.; organizer, pres. Great Neck Synagogue; treas. Sarah B. Weinstein Found.; ambassador Yeshivah U.; bd. dirs. Zionist Orgn. Am., Milw., Milw. Old Age Home, Jewish Nat. Fund, Milw. Mem. Am. Inst. Accountants, N.Y. Soc. C.P.A.'s, Hebrew Immigrant Soc., Tau Delta Phi (nat. treas.), Delta Sigma Pi (hon.). Jewish religion (past chmn. bd., hon. pres. synagogue). Mason (past master). Clubs: Engineers (N.Y.C.); Westmoreland (Wilkes Barre, Pa.); Presidents (U. Ill.); Milw. Athletic, Wis. (Milw.); Citrus (Orlando, Fla.). Address: 165 West End Ave New York NY 10023 also 925 E Wells Milwaukee WI 53021

WEINSTEIN, HERBERT, educator; b. Bklyn., Mar. 10, 1933; s. Abraham and Pauline (Feldman) W.; B.Engring. in Chem. Engring., Coll. City N.Y., 1955; M.S. in Chem. Engring., Purdue U., 1957; Ph.D., Case Inst. Tech., 1963; m. Judith Cooper, Apr. 6, 1957; children—Michael Howard, Edward Marc, Ellen Rachel. Staff mem. Los Alamos Sci. Lab., 1956-58; research engr. NASA Lewis Research Center, Cleve., 1959-63; asst. prof. chem. engring. Ill. Inst. Tech., 1963-66, asso. prof., 1966-72, prof., 1972-77, dir. Center for Biomed. Engring., 1973-77; prof. City U. N.Y., 1977—; vis. research asso., mem. Med. Research Inst., Michael Reese Hosp. and Med. Center, Chgo., 1965-77; vis. prof. mech. engring. Technion-Israel Inst. Tech., 1972-73; vis. prof. biomed. engring. Rush Med. Coll., Chgo., 1973-76. Cons. to industry, research labs. Mem. Am. Inst. Chem. Engrs., Sigma Xi, Tau Beta Pi. Jewish. Research and publs. on chem. reactor engring., fluid mechanics, biomed. engring.

WEINSTEIN, I. BERNARD, physician; b. Madison, Wis., Sept. 9, 1930; s. Max and Frieda (Blackman) W.; B.S., U. Wis., 1952, M.D., 1955; m. Joan Anker, Dec. 21, 1952; children—Tamara, Claudia, Matthew. Intern, then resident in medicine Montefiore Hosp., N.Y.C., 1955-57; clin. asso. NIH, 1957-59; research asso. Harvard U. Med. Sch., 1959-60, Mass. Inst. Tech., 1960-71; mem. faculty Columbia U. Coll. Phys. and Surg., 1961—, prof. medicine, 1973—, also dir. div. environ. sci. and coordinator ednl. programs Cancer Research Center; asso. attending physician Presbyn. Hosp., N.Y.C.; bd. dirs. Am. Assn. Cancer Research; cons. Nat. Cancer Inst., Roswell Park Meml. Inst., McArdle Lab. U. Wis., Frederick Cancer Research Center, Nat. Center for Toxicology Research. Served with USPHS, 1957-59. Recipient Meltzer medal Soc. Exptl. Biology and Medicine; European Molecular Biology Orgn. fellow Imperial Cancer Research Fund, London, 1970-71. Mem. Am. Soc. Microbiology, Am. Soc. Clin. Investigation, Am. Soc. Biol. Chemists, Am. Soc. Cell Biology, Internat. Soc. Quantum Biology, Am. Assn. Cancer Research, Inst. Medicine of U.S. Nat. Acad. Scis., Phi Beta Kappa, Sigma Xi, Alpha Omega Alpha. Jewish. Author research papers biochemistry, genetics, cancer biology, chem. carcinogenesis. Home: 249 Chestnut St Englewood NJ 07631 Office: 701 W 168th St New York NY 10032

WEINSTEIN, IRVING BENJAMIN, educator, musician; b. Madison, Wis., July 18, 1929; s. Louis and Anna (Meister) W.; Mus.B., DePauw U., 1951, Mus.M., 1952; artist diploma, Los Angeles Conservatory; postgrad. student U. Calif. at Los Angeles, also U. So. Cal.; m. Natalie Lois Berlin, Dec. 21, 1958; children—Bryan, Mark. Violist, Roth String Quartet, 1958—, Chancellor's Quartet in residence U. Calif. at Los Angeles, 1963—; concert tours U.S., Can. and Eng., 1958—, also radio and TV appearances; rec. artist for Contemporary Records; music tchr. Los Angeles city schs., 1958-68; mem. faculty Los Angeles Conservatory, 1958—; tchr. master class U. Calif. at Los Angeles, 1965 prof. music and humanities Los Angeles Community Coll. Dist., 1968—. Served with USAAF, 1952-56. Mem. Music Educators Nat. Conf., Calif. Music Educators Assn., Am. String Tchrs. Assn., Phi Mu Alpha, Pi Kappa Lambda. Home: 229 Oceano Dr Los Angeles CA 90049

WEINSTEIN, IRWIN MARSHALL, internist, hematologist; b. Denver, Mar. 5, 1926; student Dartmouth Coll., 1943-44, Williams Coll., 1944-45; M.D., U. Colo., Denver, 1949; m. Judith Braun, 1951. Intern, Montefiore Hosp., N.Y.C., 1949-50, jr. asst. resident in medicine, 1950-51; sr. asst. resident in medicine U. Chgo., 1951-52, resident in medicine, 1952-53, instr. in medicine, 1953-54, asst. prof. medicine, 1954-55; vis. asso. prof. medicine U. Calif. Center for Health Scis., Los Angeles, 1955-56, asso. clin. prof., 1957-60, clin. prof., 1970—; sect. chief in medicine, hematology sect. Wadsworth Gen. Hosp., VA Center, Los Angeles, 1956-59; pvt. practice medicine specializing in hematology and internal medicine, Beverly Hills, Calif., 1959—; mem. staff Cedars-Sinai Med. Center, Los Angeles, 1959—, chief of med. staff, 1972-74; mem. staff U. Calif. Center Health Scis., Wadsworth Gen. Hosp., VA Center; vis. prof. Hadassah Med. Center, Jerusalem, 1967; adv. for health affairs to Hon. Alan Cranston, 1971—; mem. com. on space biology and medicine Space Sci. Bd., Nat. Acad. Scis., 1979—. Diplomate Am. Bd. Internal Medicine. Fellow Israel Med. Assn. (hon.), A.C.P.; mem. AAAS, Am. Fedn. Clin. Research, Am. Soc. Hematology (exec. com. 1974-78, chmn. ad hoc com. on practice 1978—, mem. council 1974-78), Am. Soc. Internal Medicine, Assn. Am. Med. Colls., Internat. Soc. Hematology, Internat. Soc. Internal Medicine, Los Angeles Acad. Medicine, Los Angeles Soc. Nuclear Medicine, N.Y. Acad. Sci., Reticulo-Endothelial Soc., Royal Soc. Medicine, Western Soc. Clin. Research, UCLA Comprehensive Cancer Center, Alpha Omega Alpha. Contbr. articles to profl. publs.; editor: (with Ernest Beutler) Mechanisms of Anemia, 1962. Office: 465 N Roxbury Dr Suite 1002 Beverly Hills CA 90210

WEINSTEIN, JACK B., U.S. judge; b. Wichita, Kans., Aug. 10, 1921; s. Harry Louis and Bessie Helen (Brodach) W.; B.A., Bklyn. Coll., 1943; LL.B., Columbia, 1948; m. Evelyn Horowitz, Oct. 10, 1946; children—Seth George, Michael David, Howard Lewis. Admitted to N.Y. bar, 1949; asso. Columbia Law Sch., 1948-49; law clk. N.Y. Ct. Appeals Judge Stanly H. Fuld, 1949-50; partner William Rosenfeld, N.Y.C., 1950-52; mem.faculty Columbia Law Sch., 1952-67, prof. law, 1956-67, adj. prof., 1967—; U.S. judge Eastern Dist. N.Y., 1967—; vis. prof. U. Tex., 1957, U. Colo., 1961, Bklyn. Law Sch., 1977, Hebrew U., 1977. Counsel N.Y. Joint Legislative Com. Motor Vehicle Problems, 1952-54, State Senator Seymour Halpern, 1952-54; reporter adv. com. practice and procedure N.Y. State Temporary Commn. Cts., 1955-58; adv. com. practice N.Y. Judicial Conf., 1963-66; adv. com. rules of evidence Jud. Conf. U.S., 1965-75, mem. com. jurisdiction, 1969-75; mem. N.Y. State Temporary Commn. Revision and Simplification Constn. and to prepare for Constl. Conv., 1966; atty. Nassau County, 1963-65; chmn. Nassau County Law Services Inc., 1966. Chmn. N.Y. Democratic adv. com. on Constl. Conv., 1966. Bd. dirs. N.Y. Civil Liberties Union, 1956-62; nat. adv. bd. Am. Jewish Congress, 1960-67; chmn. lay bd. Riverside Hosp. Adolescent Drug Users, 1954-55. Served to lt. USNR, 1943-46. Mem. Inst. Jud. Adminstrn., AAUP, Am. Law Inst., Am., N.Y. State bar assns., Assn. Bar City N.Y., Soc. Pub. Tchrs. Law (Eng.). Jewish religion. Author: (with Morgan and Maquire) Cases and Materials on Evidence, 4th edit., 1965, (with Maguire, Chadbourne and Mansfield) 5th edit., 1971, 6th edit., 1975; (with Rosenberg) Cases and Materials on Civil Procedure, 1961, rev. edit. (with Smit), 1971, (with Smit, Rosenberg and Korn), 1976; (with Korn and Miller) New York Civil Procedure, 9 vols., rev. edit., 1966; (with Korn and Miller) Manual of New York Civil Procedure, 1967; (with Berger) Weinstein's Evidence, United States Rules, 7 vols., revised annually; Basic Problems of State and Federal Evidence, 1976; Revising Rule Making Procedures, 1977; A New York Constitution Meeting Today's Needs and Tomorrow's Challenges, 1967; also reports, articles. Home: 10 Romola Dr Kings Point NY 11024 Office: 225 Cadman Plaza East Brooklyn NY 11021

WEINSTEIN, LEO, educator; b. N.Y.C., Sept. 22, 1921; s. Max and Rose (Reif) W.; B.A., Bklyn. Coll., 1943; M.A., U. Chgo., 1949, Ph.D., 1958; m. Susanna Berkman, Jan. 3, 1944; children—Robert M., Ruth L. Mem. faculty Smith Coll., 1952—, now Esther Cloudman Dunn prof. polit. sci.; vis. asso. prof. U. Chgo., 1958, Yale, 1961-62. Bd. dirs. Hampshire Interlibrary Conf. Served with AUS, 1943-46. Rockefeller fellow, 1966; William Rainey Harper fellow; Relm Found. fellow, 1966. Mem. Am. Polit. Sci. Assn., AAUP. Contbr. to Essays on the Scientific Study of Politics (editor H. Storing), 1962; also articles polit. jours. Home: 20 Munroe St Northampton MA 01060

WEINSTEIN, LEWIS H., lawyer; b. Vilna, Luthuania, Apr. 10, 1905; s. Jacob Menahem and Kuna (Romanow) W.; brought to U.S., 1906; A.B. magna cum laude, Harvard, 1927, LL.B., 1930; m. Selma Yeslawsky, Sept. 2, 1932; children—David J., Louise. Admitted to Mass. bar, 1930; asso., then partner firm Rome & Weinstein, 1930-45; asst. corp. counsel, Boston, 1934-45; partner firm Foley, Hoag & Eliot, Boston, 1946-79, sr. partner, 1979—; lectr. law Harvard, 1960-75; sr. vis. lectr. dept. city and regional planning Mass. Inst. Tech., 1961-68; occasional lectr. Practising Law Inst., N.Y.C., New Eng. Law Inst., Am. Bar Assn., Am. Law Inst., Mass. Continuing Legal Edn. Sec., Spencer Shoe Corp.; mem. faculty Nat. Inst. Trial Advocacy, Boulder, Colo.; mem. finance com., bd. dirs. B. & M. R.R., 1960-74; trustee Boston 5 Cent Savs. Bank. Cons. U.S. Housing Authority, 1940-42; chmn. Mass. Emergency Housing Commn., 1946-47, Mass. Bd. Housing, 1947-48, Mass. Housing Council, 1948-52; mem. rent control and housing coms. Nat. Def. Commn., 1941-42; past chmn. Nat. Jewish Community Relations Adv. Council; past chmn. Armed Forces Adv. Com. Greater Boston; past pres., gen. campaign chmn., now exec. com. Combined Jewish Philanthropies Greater Boston; mem. adminstrv. com., past pres. Jewish Community Council Met. Boston; nat. council Jewish Welfare Bd.; past. chmn. Conf. Presidents Maj. Am. Jewish Orgns.; past chmn. Nat. Conf. Soviet Jewry; mem. nat. com. Harvard Center for Jewish Studies; past lay rep. Nat. Assembly for Social Policy and Devel.; exec. com. City of Boston Civic Unity Com.; adv. council Mass. Dept. Edn., Mass. Dept. Mental Health; mem. human rights com. also housing and urban renewal com. com. World Peace Through Law Center; formerly adv. com. Mass. Dept. Community Affairs; exec. com., bd. dirs. New Eng. region, nat. bd. dirs. NCCJ; exec. com. Pres.'s Com. Equal Opportunity Housing, 1961-68; past chmn. Gov.'s Task Force to Establish Mass. Dept. Community Affairs; past pres., now mem. exec. com. Council Jewish Fedn. and Welfare Funds; mem. nat. council Am. Jewish Joint Distbn. Com.; past v.p. Nat. Fedn. Jewish Men's Clubs. Trustee United Israel Appeal, Social Law, Ct. House Boston; dir. Am. Jewish League for Israel; past trustee Mass. Fedn. Taxpayer's Assn., Hebrew Rehab. Center Aged, Boston; bd. overseers Hiatt Inst., Lown Inst. Contemporary Jewish Affairs, past mem. bd. overseers Heller Grad. Sch. Pub. Welfare, Brandeis U., also fellow Univ.; past mem. vis. com., bd. overseers Middle Eastern Center and Near Eastern Langs. and Civilizations, Harvard U., mem. nat. com. Center for Jewish Studies, mem. steering com. capital fund campaign, class agt. Law Sch. Class of 1930; trustee Nat. Found. Jewish Culture, Meml. Found. Jewish Culture, Beth Israel Hosp., Boston, Inst. for Jewish Life; pres. Hebrew Coll., Boston, 1946-53, now trustee; mem. assembly Jewish Agy. for Israel; mem. exec. Seminar program Aspen (Colo.) Inst., 1978; mem. Spl. Mass. Commn. To Investigate Corruption and Malfeasance in State and County Constrn., 1978—. Served to col. AUS, World War II. Decorated Legion of Merit, Bronze Star with cluster (U.S.); Legion of Honor, Croix de Guerre with palm (France); nat. citation NCCJ; Heritage award Yeshiva U.; Nat. Community Service award Jewish Theol. Sem. Fellow Am. Coll. Trial Lawyers, Am. Bar Found. Am. Assn. Jewish Edn.; mem. Am. Jewish Hist. Soc. (past mem. exec. council), Assn. U.S. Army (dir. Bay State chpt.), Boston (past mem. council, chmn. eminent domain com.), Mass. (past chmn. grievance com.), Am. (past mem. standing com. fed. judiciary) bar assns., Mil Govt. Assn. (past. pres. Mass. chpt.), Phi Beta Kappa. Jewish religion (former temple trustee). Club: Harvard, Union (Boston). Contbr. articles law and other jours. Home: 56 Varick Rd Waban MA 02168 Office: 10 Post Office Sq Boston MA 02109

WEINSTEIN, LOUIS, physician; b. Bridgeport, Conn., Feb. 26, 1909; s. Harry and Minnie (Rubenstein) W.; B.S., Yale, 1928, M.S., 1930, Ph.D. in Microbiology, 1931; M.D., Boston U., 1943, Sc.D. (hon.), 1974; m. Ethel Raport, Oct. 7, 1934; children—Allan J., Carol F. Research fellow Yale, 1931-37, instr. bacteriology, 1937-39; instr., then asso. prof. medicine Boston U., 1943-57; prof. medicine Tufts U., 1957-75; lectr. medicine Harvard Med. Sch., 1950-75, NIS. prof. medicine, 1975—; chief infectious disease service Univ. Hosp., Boston, 1947-57; chief infectious disease service New Eng. Med. Center Hosp., Boston, 1957-75, asso. physician-in-chief, 1960-71; asso. physician Mass. Gen. Hosp., 1962—; physician med. service, dir. clin. services of infectious disease service Peter Bent Brigham Hosp., Boston, 1975—; chief infectious disease service West Roxbury (Mass.) VA Hosp., 1975-78. Recipient Chapin medal City of Providence; Finland award Infectious Disease Soc. Am., also Bristol award; Presdl. citation and medal Tufts U.; Outstanding Achievement award Am. Soc. for Contemporary Medicine and Surgery; Thorn Teaching award Peter Bent Brigham Hosp. Mem. A.M.A., A.C.P. (master), Am. Soc. Clin. Investigation, Assn. Am. Physicians, Am. Acad. Arts and Scis., Am. Soc. Microbiologists, Am. Acad. Microbiology, Soc. Exptl. Biology and Medicine, Sigma Xi, Alpha Omega Alpha. Home: 26 Greylock Rd Newtonville MA 02160 Office: 721 Huntington Ave Boston MA 02115

WEINSTEIN, MICHAEL ALAN, polit. scientist; b. Bklyn., Aug. 24, 1942; s. Aaron and Grace (Sosin) W.; B.A. summa cum laude, N.Y. U., 1964; M.A. in Polit. Sci., Case Western Res. U., 1965, Ph.D., 1967; m. Deena Schneiweiss, May 31, 1964. Asst. prof. polit. sci. Case Western Res. U., summer 1967, Va. Poly. Inst., 1967-68; asst. prof. Purdue U., 1968-70, asso. prof., 1970-72, prof., 1972—; Milward Simpson disting. prof. polit. sci. U. Wyo., 1979. Recipient Best Paper prize Midwest Polit. Sci. Assn., 1969; Guggenheim fellow, 1974-75; Rockefeller Found. humanities fellow, 1976. Mem. Midwest Polit. Sci. Assn., Phi Beta Kappa. Author: (with Deena Weinstein) Living Sociology, 1974; The Polarity of Mexican Thought, 1976; The Tragic Sense of Political Life, 1977; Meaning and Appreciation, 1978. Home: 800 Princess Dr West Lafayette IN 47906 Office: Dept Polit Sci Purdue U West Lafayette IN 47907. *And which is worse, to be arbitrary or to be contradictory? I have attempted to be the most consistent rationalist of all by refusing to harmonize what is irreconcilable in the name of reason.*

WEINSTEIN, MYRON I., govt. ofcl.; b. Bklyn., Mar. 7, 1930; s. Louis and Augusta (Cohen) W.; B.S. in Police Adminstrn., Mich. State U., 1952; m. Barbara Wendt, May 24, 1953; children—Steven M., Daniel A., Lynn A. With U.S. Secret Service, Washington, 1955—, dep. dir., 1978—. Served with U.S. Army, 1952-54. Mem. Internat. Assn. Chiefs of Police, Southeastern Chiefs of Police Assn. Pa., Pa. Chiefs of Police. Jewish. Office: 1800 G St NW Washington DC 20223

WEINSTEIN, PAUL P., educator; b. Bklyn., Dec. 9, 1919; A.B., Bklyn. Coll., 1941; Sc.D. in Hygiene, Johns Hopkins, 1949; married; 2 children. Jr. parasitologist USPHS, State Bd. Health, Fla., 1942-44, sr. asst. sanitarian, Washington, Ga., P.R., 1944-46; from scientist to scientist dir., chief lab. parasitic diseases NIH, Washington, 1949-69; prof. U. Notre Dame, 1969—, chmn. dept. biology, 1969-75; vis. scientist Nat. Inst. Med. Research, Eng., 1962-63; summer instr. Marine Biol. Lab., Woods Hole, Mass., 1959, 60. Mem., chmn. parasitic diseases panel U.S.-Japan Coop. Med. Sci. Program, 1965-73; mem. internat. centers com. NIH, 1970-73; mem. nat. adv. com. U. Calif. at Davis Primate Research Center, 1973-77; mem. microbiology and infectious diseases adv. com. NIH, 1978—; mem. parasitic diseases com. Walter Reed Army Inst. of Research, 1977—. Adv. sci. bd. Gorgas Meml. Inst. Tropical and Preventive Medicine, 1972—. Recipient award of honor Bklyn. Coll., 1958. Fellow A.A.A.S.; mem. Am. Soc. Tropical Medicine and Hygiene (Ashford award 1957), Am. (v.p. 1969, pres. 1972), Japanese socs. parasitology, Helminth Soc. Washington (v.p. 1953, pres. 1957). Office: Biology Dept U Notre Dame Notre Dame IN 46556

WEINSTEIN, PETER DAVID, lawyer, machinery and constrn. co. exec.; b. N.Y.C., Jan. 24, 1939; s. Joseph Louis and Sylvia (Friedman) W.; B.A., Cornell U., 1960; J.D., Columbia, 1963; m. Laura Gail Goodman, June 30, 1968; children—Alan Martin, Jody Lynn. Admitted to N.Y. bar, 1963; lectr. in law U. Md., European div., 1965; atty. Western Electric Co., N.Y.C., 1966-68; v.p., sec., gen. counsel Parsons & Whittemore, Inc., N.Y.C., 1968—, Hempstead Resources Recovery Corp., 1975—, Alabama River Pulp Co. Inc., 1976—, Resources Recovery (Dade County) Corp., 1976—; gen. counsel Black Clawson Co., 1968—, dir., 1976—; gen. counsel St. Anne-Nackawic Pulp & Paper Co., 1972—, Prince Albert Pulp Co., 1972—, Hydrotile Machinery Co., 1974—, Watervliet Paper Co., 1974—. Served to 1st lt. AUS, 1964-65. Mem. Am. Bar Assn., N.Y. State Bar Assn., Assn. Bar City N.Y. Jewish. Contbr. articles to profl. jours., Ency. Americana. Home: New York NY . *Aim for the impossible. Although your goal will never be reached, so much good will be accomplished along the way.*

WEINSTEIN, ROY, educator, researcher; b. N.Y.C., Apr. 21, 1927; s. Harry and Lillian (Ehrenberg) W.; B.S., Mass. Inst. Tech., 1951, Ph.D., 1954; m. Janet E. Spiller, Mar. 26, 1954; children—Lee Davis, Sara Lynn. Research asst. Mass. Inst. Tech., 1951-54, asst. prof., 1956-59; asst. prof. Brandeis U., Waltham, Mass., 1954-56; asso. prof. Northeastern U., Boston, 1960-63, prof. physics, 1963—, exec. officer, chmn. grad. div. of physics dept., 1967-69, chmn. physics dept., 1974—, vis. scholar and physicist Stanford, 1966-67. dir. Perception Tech., Inc., Winchester, Mass., Omniwave Inc., Gloucester, Mass.; cons. Visidyne Inc., Burlington, Mass., Stanford (Calif.) U., Cambridge Electron Accelerator, Harvard U., Cambridge, Mass., also mem. adv. com., 1967-69; 3d ann. faculty lectr. Northeastern U., 1966; chmn. organizing com. 4th Internat. Conf. on Meson Spectroscopy, 1974, chmn. program com. 5th Conf., 1977. Mem. Lexington (Mass.) Town Meeting, 1973-76, 77—; vice chmn. Lexington Council on Aging, 1977—. Served with USNR, 1945-46. NSF fellow Bohr Inst., Copenhagen, Denmark, 1959-60, Stanford, 1969-70; Guggenheim fellow, Harvard 1970-71; NSF research awards, 1961, 63, 64, 66, 68, 70-80. Fellow Am. Phys. Soc.; mem. Am. Assn. Physics Tchrs., N.Y. Acad. Scis., Sigma Xi, Phi Kappa Phi (pres. chpt. 1977-78), Pi Lambda Phi. Democrat. Unitarian. Mason. Author: Atomic Physics, 1964; Nuclear Physics, 1964; Interactions of Radiation and Matter, 1964; editor: Nuclear Reactor Theory, 1964; Nuclear Materials, 1964. Editor procs. 5th Internat. Conf. on Mesons, 1977. Contbr. articles to profl. jours. Home: 6 Nickerson Rd Lexington MA 02173 Office: Physics Dept Northeastern U Boston MA 02115

WEINSTEIN, SIDNEY, assn. exec.; b. N.Y.C., July 1, 1920; s. Jacob and Yetta W.; B.A., Bklyn. Coll., 1951; M.A., Columbia U., 1955; diploma, Indsl. Coll. Armed Forces, 1964; m. Celia Kahn, Mar. 6, 1943; children—Risa, Jeri. Contract adminstr. U.S. Corps Engrs., 1941-43; mgmt. analyst Dept. Army, N.Y.C., 1946-55; dir. data processing procurement GSA, 1956-68, dep. asst. commr. automated data mgmt. services, Washington, 1968-72, asst. commr. automated data and telecommunications, 1972-75; exec. dir. Assn. Computing Machinery, N.Y.C., 1975—; cons. to chmn. U.S. Civil Service Commn. Served with USAF, 1943-46. Recipient Exceptional service award U.S. Govt., 1975. Mem. Council Engring. and Sci. Soc. Execs., N.Y. Soc. Assn. Execs., Assn. Indsl. Coll. Armed Forces, Assn. Fed. Execs. Inst. Home: 360 E 72d New York NY 10026 Office: 1133 Ave of the Americas New York NY 10036

WEINSTEIN, STEVE, editor; b. N.Y.C., Oct. 6, 1929; s. George D. and Rose (Zuckerman) W.; B.J., U. Mo., 1950; m. Marcia Siskind, Oct. 23, 1951; children—Julie, Joel, John. Asso. editor Drug Trade News, 1951, Food Topics, 1953, Candy Industry, 1953-56; news editor Supermarket News, 1960-67; city editor Women's Wear Daily, 1967-68; editor Footwear News, 1968-71, Supermarket News, 1971—. Pres. Merrick (N.Y.) Youth Council, 1968-69. Bd. dirs. Merrick Brotherhood Council, 1972-74. Served with AUS, 1951-53. Mem. Sigma Delta Chi. Office: 7 E 12th St New York NY 10003

WEINSTOCK, HAROLD, lawyer; b. Stamford, Conn., Nov. 30, 1925; s. Elias and Sarah (Singer) W.; B.S. magna cum laude, N.Y. U., 1947; J.D., Harvard, 1950; m. Barbara Lans, Aug. 27, 1950; children—Nathaniel, Michael, Philip. Admitted to Conn. bar, 1950, Ill. bar, 1950, Calif. bar, 1958; atty. SEC, Washington, 1950-52, IRS, 1952-56; tax atty. Hunt Foods & Industries, Inc., Los Angeles, 1956-58; practiced law, Beverly Hills, Calif., 1958-71, Los Angeles, 1971—; mem. Weinstock, Manion, King, Hardie and Reisman, and predecessor firms, 1958—. Lectr. extension div., estate planning courses U. Calif. at Los Angeles, 1959—, estate planning and taxation courses Calif. Continuing Edn. of the Bar, 1960—. Nat. trustee Union Am. Hebrew Congregations, 1976-79. Served with AUS, 1944-46. Mem. Am., Calif., Beverly Hills (chmn. probate and trusts com. 1967-68), Los Angeles bar assns., Beverly Hills Estate Planning Council (pres. 1968-69), Estate Counselors Forum of Los Angeles (pres. 1963-64). Jewish (pres. temple 1974-76). Author: Planning An Estate, 1977; contbr. articles to profl. publs. Office: 1888 Century Park E Los Angeles CA 90067

WEINSTOCK, HERBERT FRANK, pub. relations exec.; b. Los Angeles, July 26, 1913; s. Frank and Sarah (Mantel) W.; A.A. in Bus. Adminstrn., Los Angeles City Coll., 1933; m. Evelyn June Hanson, July 27, 1940; children—Allan Herbert, William Jay, Joan Louise. With copy desk, financial desk Los Angeles Post-Record, Los Angeles Daily News, 1935-42; financial editor Daily News, 1942-54; pub. relations exec. H. F. Weinstock & Assos., 1954-64, Burton, Booth & Weinstock, Inc., 1964-66; v.p. charge corporate and financial pub. relations Kennett Pub. Relations Assos., 1966-71; pres. Conway/Weinstock/ Assos., Inc., 1971—. Pres. Intercommunity Care Centers, Inc. Served with AUS, 1943-45; with 3d Army, Eng., France, Luxembourg, Belgium and Germany, 1944-45. Clubs: Greater Los Angeles Press (charter mem.), Publicity (Los Angeles). Home: 533 21st St Manhattan Beach CA 90266 Office: 550 N Larchmont Blvd Los Angeles CA 90004

WEINTRAUB, HENRY MORRIS, advt. agy. exec.; b. Bronx, N.Y., July 31, 1937; s. Jack and Sylvia (Fox) W.; B.B.A., CCNY, 1959; m. Janet Eleanor Tomac, May 18, 1969; children—Laura Isabelle, Deborah Beth. Trainee, MacMann John & Adams, N.Y.C., 1960; advt. asst. Knomack, Inc., N.Y.C., 1960-61; traffic mgr. Columbia Records Co., N.Y.C., 1961-62; copywriter Hearst Mags., N.Y.C., 1962-64; asst. advt. mgr. 20th Century Fox, N.Y.C., 1964-66; account exec. Diener Hauser Bates Co. Inc., N.Y.C., 1966-67, 68-77, pres., 1967—; advt. mgr. NBC-TV, N.Y.C., 1967-68. Served with USAR, 1959-60. Democrat. Jewish. Clubs: Variety (dir. local club), B'nai B'rith. Home: 100 Wedgemere Rd Stamford CT 06905 Office: 25 W 43d St New York NY 10036

WEINTRAUB, JOSEPH, lawyer; b. Waynesboro, Ga., Dec. 10, 1904; s. Sigmond and Anne (Goodman) W.; student U. Va., 1922-25, N.Y. U., 1925-26; m. Florence Katz, Jan. 27, 1929; children—Joanne, Michael. Admitted to Fla. bar, 1927, U.S. Dist. Ct., 1927, Supreme Ct. of U.S., 1937; practiced law, Miami, 1972—, head law firm Weintraub, Martin, Schwartz & Spector and predecessor firm, 1943—; also organized Am. Title & Ins. Co., 1936, pres., 1940-56, dir. 1936—, chmn. 1956—; pres. and dir. Gibson Security Corp., 1936—; chmn. Pan. Am. Bancshares, 1969—; Atico Financial Corp., 1962—; dir. Comercial Aseguradora Suizo Americana S.A. of Guatemala, Gulfstream Land & Devel. Co., PanAmerican Bank Miami. Bd. dirs. Miami Heart Inst.; trustee U. Miami, past pres. citizens bd.; trustee Opera Guild Miami. Mem. Miami-Dade C. of C., Dade County (v.p., 1939-40, dir. 1938-41), Fla. and Am. bar assns., Am. Judicature Soc. Jewish religion. Mason (Shriner), Rotarian, Elk. Clubs: Wall Street (N.Y.C.); Westview Country (past pres.), Variety. Home: 108 W Rivo Alto Dr Rivo Alto Island Miami Beach FL 33139 Office: 901 NE 2d Ave Miami FL 33132

WEINTRAUB, KARL JOACHIM, educator; b. Darmstadt, Germany, Dec. 31, 1924; s. Misha and Lisly (Hammel) W.; came to U.S., 1948, naturalized, 1954; B.A., U. Chgo., 1949, M.A., 1952, Ph.D., 1957; m. D. Kathryn Lamphiear, Mar. 16, 1957. Social sci. bibliographer U. Chgo. Libraries, 1954-60; mem. faculty U. Chgo., 1955—, Thomas E. Donnelley Disting. Service prof. history, 1978—, dean div. humanities, 1973—. Trustee Knox Coll., 1978—. Recipient Quantrell Teaching award, 1960; Harbison award distinguished teaching, 1968. Mem. Am. Hist. Assn., Phi Beta Kappa. Club: Quadrangle (pres. 1966) (Chgo.). Author: Visions of Culture, 1966; The Value of the Individual, 1978. Home: 5844 Stony Island Ave Chicago IL 60637

WEINTRAUB, LIONEL, toy mfg. co. exec.; b. 1921. With Ideal Toy Corp., N.Y.C., 1941—, exec. v.p., 1957-62, pres., 1962—, also chmn., chief exec. officer. Address: Ideal Toy Corp 184-10 Jamaica Ave Hollis NY 11423*

WEINTRAUB, MICHAEL IRA, neurologist; b. N.Y.C., Aug. 14, 1940; s. Abraham and Mildred Weintraub (Kuttner) W.; B.A., N.Y. U., 1962; M.D., State U. N.Y., Buffalo, 1966; m. Anita Bellin, Aug. 2, 1964; children—Jeffrey Brian, Lisa Ellen. Intern, E. J. Meyer Hosp., Buffalo, 1966-67; fellow neurology State U. N.Y., Buffalo, 1967-68; fellow neurology Yale U.-New Haven Med. Center, 1968-70, chief resident, 1969-70; instr. neurology Boston U. Sch. Medicine, 1970-72; instr. Albert Einstein Sch. Medicine, Bronx, N.Y., 1972-73; asst. prof. neurology N.Y. Med. Coll., 1974-77, asso. clin. prof., 1977—; chief pediatric neurology Westchester County Med. Center, Valhalla, N.Y., 1974-77; practice medicine specializing in neurology and EEG, Ossining, 1972—; attending neurologist Phelps Meml. Hosp., 1972—; cons. Peekskill Community Hosp., Putnam Community Hosp. Recipient Outstanding Young Men of Am. award U.S. Jr. C. of C., 1971. Diplomate Am. Bd. Psychiatry and Neurology, Am. Bd. EEG. Fellow A.C.P., Am. Coll. Angiology; mem. A.M.A., Am. Acad. Neurology, Westchester County Med. Soc. Contbr. articles to med. jours. Home: 15 Quaker Ln Chappaqua NY 10514 Office: 62 S Highland Ave Ossining NY 10562

WEINTRAUB, MONROE JOSEPH, rubber mfg. co. exec.; b. N.Y.C., Sept. 12, 1922; s. Max and Sarah (Pickman) W.; B.S., U. Pa., 1943; m. Carol Kahn, Oct. 30, 1949; children—James S., William M. With Acme-Hamilton Mfg. Co., Trenton, N.J., 1948—, exec. v.p., 1963-64, pres., 1964-70, chmn. bd., chief exec. officer, 1970—. Active local Boy Scouts Am. Served to 1st lt. Transp. Corps, AUS, 1943-46. Home: 37 N Wood Ln Woodmere NY 11101 Office: Acme-Hamilton Mfg Co E State St Trenton NJ 08603

WEINTRAUB, RUSSELL JAY, lawyer; b. N.Y.C., Dec. 20, 1929; s. Harry and Alice (Lieberman) W.; B.A., N.Y. U., 1950; J.D., Harvard U., 1953; m. Zelda Kresshover, Sept. 6, 1953; children—Sharon Hope, Harry David, Steven Ross. Admitted to N.Y. State bar, 1955, Iowa bar, 1961; teaching fellow Harvard U. Law Sch., 1955-57; asst. prof. law U. Iowa, 1957-61, prof., 1961-65; prof. U. Tex., 1965—, Marrs McLean prof. law, 1970—; vis. prof. law U. Mich., 1965, UCLA, 1967, U. Calif., Berkeley, 1973-74, Inst. Internat. and Comparative Law, Paris, 1975; cons. in field. Trustee, U. Iowa Sch. Religion, 1960-65. Served with U.S. Army, 1953-55. Recipient Disting. Prof. award U. Tex. Sch. Law, 1977, Teaching Excellence award, 1979; cert. of meritorious service Am. Bar Assn., 1977, Tex. Bar Assn., 1978. Jewish. Author: (with Eugene Scoles) Cases and Materials on the Conflict of Laws, 1967, 2d rev. edit., 1972, supplement, 1978; Commentary on the Conflict of Laws, 1971; contbr. numerous articles to profl. jours. Home: 7204 Sungate Dr Austin TX 78731 Office: 2500 Red River St Austin TX 78705. *The only true happiness lies in useful work done to the best of your ability.*

WEINTRAUB, RUTH G., educator; b. N.Y.C., Feb. 15, 1909; d. Morris and Pessa (Noah) Goldstein; A.B., Hunter Coll., 1929; J.D., N.Y. U., 1931; A.M., Columbia U., 1932, Ph.D., 1939; LL.D., Skidmore Coll., 1969; m. Solomon Weintraub, Aug. 26, 1930; 1 son, Jonathan, W. Instr., Hunter Coll., 1929-40, asst. prof., 1940-45, asso. prof. polit. sci., 1946-51, prof., 1951—, coordinator social scis., 1951-56, dean grad. studies arts and sci., 1956-68, dean social scis., 1968-72, dean emeritus, 1972—, chmn. dept. polit. sci., 1956-60; cons. Acad. Ednl. Devel., 1972—, v.p., 1974, sr. v.p., 1977; asso. dean grad. div. City U. N.Y., 1963-68; vis. prof. N.Y. U. Grad. Sch., 1948-49; admitted to N.Y. bar, 1932; chmn. N.Y. State Legis. Internship Program, 1961-72; mem. nat. labor panel Am. Arbitration Assn. Bd. dirs. Asso. YM-YWHA's Greater N.Y., 1968—, v.p., 1974-78, asso. chmn., 1978—. Mem. Am. Polit. Sci. Assn. (nat. com. advancement teaching, 1947-51, nat. council 1956-58, program com. 1960, com. on status of women, 1972-74, chmn. Charles E. Merriam award com. 1976, Am. Soc. Public Adminstrn. (v.p. Met. region 1949-50, sec., 194B-49), Citizens Union (legis. com. 1940-60), ACLU (acad. freedom com. 1947-54), Phi Beta Kappa (com. on qualifications 1973—), Pi Sigma Alpha (pres. 1964-66, exec. council 1964-76). Club: Princeton. Author: Government Corporations and State Law, 1939; How Secure These Rights?, 1949; (with others) Goals for Political Science, 1951, Administrative Questions and Political Answers, 1966; contbr. articles to polit. sci., legal and ednl. publs. Home: 55 Central Park W New York NY 10023

WEINTRAUB, STANLEY, educator, author; b. Phila., Apr. 17, 1929; s. Ben and Ray (Segal) W.; B.S., West Chester (Pa.) State Coll., 1949; M.A., Temple U., 1951; Ph.D., Pa. State U., 1956; m. Rodelle Horwitz, June 6, 1954; children—Mark, David, Erica. Instr. Pa. State U., University Park, 1953-59, asst. prof., 1959-62, asso. prof., 1962-65, prof. English, 1965-70, research prof., 1970—, dir. Inst. for Arts and Humanistic Studies, 1970—. Vis. prof. U. Calif. at Los Angeles, 1963, U. Hawaii, 1973. Pres., Jewish Community Council of Bellefonte (Pa.) State Coll., 1966-67. Served to 1st lt. AUS, 1951-53; Korea. Decorated Bronze Star medal. Guggenheim fellow, 1968-69. Mem. The Authors' Guild. Author: An Unfinished Novel by Bernard Shaw, 1958; C.P. Snow: A Spectrum, 1963; Private Shaw and Public Shaw, 1963; The War in the Wards, 1964; The Yellow Book: Quintessence of the Nineties, 1964; Reggie, 1965; The Art of William Golding, 1965; The Savoy: Nineties Experiment, 1966; The Court Theatre, 1966; Beardlsey, 1967; Biography and Truth, 1967; The Last Great Cause; The Intellectuals and the Spanish Civil War, 1968; Evolution of a Revolt: Early Postwar Writings of T.E. Lawrence, 1968; The Literary Criticism of Oscar Wilde, 1968; Journey to Heartbreak, 1971; Whistler: A Biography, 1974; Lawrence of Arabia: the Literary Impulse, 1975; Four Rossettis, A Victorian Biography, 1977; Aubrey Beardsley: Imp of the Perverse, 1976; The London Yankees: Portraits of American Writers and Artists in England, 1894-1914, 1979. Editor: Shaw: An Autobiography 1856-1898, 1969; Shaw: An Autobiography 1898-1950, 1970: Bernard Shaw's Nondramatic Literary Criticism, 1972; Directions in Literary Criticism, 1973; Saint Joan Fifty Years After: 1923/24-1973/74, The Portable Bernard Shaw, 1977. Home: 840 Outer Dr State College PA 16801 Office: Burrowes Bldg University Park PA 16802. *I subscribe to Bernard Shaw's declaration in the Preface to Man and Superman that "This is the true joy in life, the being used for a purpose recognized by yourself as mighty one; the being thoroughly worn out before you are thrown on the scrap heap; the being a force of Nature instead of a feverish selfish little clod of ailments and grievances complaining that the world will not devote itself to making you happy."*

WEINZWEIG, JOHN JACOB, composer, educator; b. Toronto, Ont., Can., Mar. 11, 1913; s. Joseph and Rose (Burstyn) W.; Mus.B., U. Toronto, 1937; Mus.M., Eastman Sch. Music, U. Rochester, 1938; Mus.D., U. Ottawa, 1969; m. Helen Tenenbaum, July 19, 1940; children—Paul, Daniel. Tchr. theory and composition Royal Conservatory Music, Toronto, 1939-52; prof. composition Faculty Music, U. Toronto, 1952-78, prof. emeritus, 1978—. Composer, condr. films NFB, radio plays CBC, 1943-45. Co-planner, dir. Canadian Music Centre, Toronto, 1959—. Served with RCAF, 1943-45. Recipient Silver medal for music, arts div. Olympiad, London, 1948, Sr. Arts award Can. Council, 1968, 75, Can. Music Council medal, 1978; decorated officer Order of Can., 1974. Mem. Canadian League Composers (co-founder, pres. Toronto 1951, dir.), Composers, Authors and Pubs. Assn. Can. (dir. 1962—, pres. 1973-75). Composer orchestral and piano music, chamber music, choral and vocal works; works include: Red Ear of Corn (ballet), 1948-49; Symphonic Ode, 1958; Concerto for Piano and Orch., 1966; Divertimento No. 4 for Clarinet and Strings, 1968; Dummiyah, 1969; Around the Stage, 1970; Trialogue, 1971; Divertimento for Alto Sax and Strings, 1972; Impromptus, 1973; Riffs, 1974; Contrasts for solo guitar, 1976; commn. for Internat. Guitar Festival, Toronto, 1978; numerous others. Home: 107 Manor Rd E Toronto ON M4S IR3 Canada

WEIR, DONALD CLAIR, physician, educator; b. Grant, Iowa, Mar. 10, 1912; s. Mathew B. and Laura (Liston) W.; B.S., Creighton U., 1934, M.D., 1936. Intern, St. Louis City Hosp., 1936-37, asst. resident internal medicine, 1937-39, resident radiology, 1939-41, dir. radiology, 1946—; dir. X-ray Tech. Sch., William Beaumont Gen. Hosp., 1941-43; dir. radiology 70th Gen. Hosp., 1943-46; dir. radiology St. Marys Hosp., 1960—; prof., chmn. radiology St. Louis U. Med. Sch., 1969—; cons. radiologist VA Hosp., St. Louis, Malcolm Bless and Mo. Pacific Hosp. Served to col. AUS, 1941-46. Diplomate Am. Bd. Radiology. Fellow Am. Coll. Radiology; mem. Radiol. Soc. N.Am., A.M.A., St. Louis Med. Soc. (pres. 1962), Am. Roentgen Ray Soc., Sigma Xi, Alpha Omega Alpha. Home: 625 Sherwood Dr St Louis MO 63119 Office: 6744 Clayton Rd St Louis MO 63117

WEIR, DONALD WILLIAM, gas co. exec.; b. Heavener, Okla., Jan. 23, 1914; s. William and Edith (Converse) W.; B.S., U. Okla., 1935; m. Lola Bennett, Apr. 3, 1940; children—Lola D. Herndon, Donald W. With Ark. Nat. Gas Co., Shreveport, subsidiary Cities Service Co., 1935-53; personnel mgr. Ark. La. Gas Co., Shreveport, 1953-56, asst. to pres., 1956, v.p., dir., 1957-58, exec. v.p., 1958-73, chmn. bd., 1973—; chmn. bd. Arkla Industries, Ark. La. Finance Corp., Arkla Chem. Corp., Arkla Exploration Co., ret., now dir.; dir. Ark. Cement Corp. Past pres. State Fair La. Served to lt. col. F.A., World War II. Recipient Liberty Bell award Shreveport Bar Assn., 1965. Mem. So. Gas Assn. (past pres.), Res. Officers Assn., Mid Continent Oil and Gas Assn. (exec. com.), Shreveport C. of C. (past pres., dir.). Episcopalian. Clubs: Shreveport Country, Shreveport (past pres.), Demoiselle (past pres.) (Shreveport). Home: 6331 E Ridge Dr Shreveport LA 71106 Office: Arkla Bldg Shreveport LA 71101

WEIR, JOHN PAUL, cons. mining engr.; b. Zeigler, Ill., July 14, 1923; s. Paul and Lura Frances (Hickox) W.; B.S. in Chem. Engring., Purdue U., 1944; B.S. in Mining Engring., Pa. State U., 1949; m. Louise Carolyn Carey, Dec. 19, 1950; children—Mary, John, Sally, Tracy. Engring. trainee Dow Chem. Co., Midland, Mich., 1946-47; with Paul Weir Co., cons. mining engrs. and geologists, Chgo., 1949—, v.p., then exec. v.p., 1966, pres., 1970—. Served with USNR, 1943-46. Registered profl. engr., Ill., Ind., Tex. Fellow Am. Cons. Engrs. Council; mem. Am. Inst. Mining, Metall. and Petroleum Engrs., Instn. Mining Engrs., Australasian Inst. Mining and Metallurgy, Ill. Mining Inst. (past pres.), Alpha Tau Omega, Tau Beta Pi, Sigma Gamma Epsilon. Republican. Presbyn. Clubs: Chgo. Athletic Assn., Tower (Chgo.); Skokie Country. Home: 333 Willow Rd Winnetka IL 60093 Office: 20 N Wacker Dr Chicago IL 60606

WEIR, MORTON WEBSTER, univ. adminstr.; b. Canton, Ill., July 18, 1934; s. James and Frances Mary (Johnson) W.; A.B., Knox Coll., 1955; M.A., U. Tex., 1958, Ph.D., 1959; m. Cecelia Ann Rumler, June 23, 1956; children—Deborah, Kevin, Mark. Research asso., asst. prof. U. Minn., Mpls., 1959; asst. prof. U. Ill. at Urbana, 1960-64, asso. prof., 1964-68, prof., 1968-79, head dept. psychology, 1969-71, vice chancellor acad. affairs, 1971-79; dir. Boys Town Center Study Youth Development, 1979—. Served with AUS, 1960. NSF Predoctoral fellow, 1957-59. Fellow Am. Psychol. Assn., A.A.A.S.; mem. Soc. for Research in Child Devel. (chmn. bd. publs. 1971), Sigma Xi. Contbr. numerous articles to profl. jours. Office: Boys Town Center Study Youth Development Boys Town NE 68010

WEIR, STEPHEN JAMES, textile co. exec.; b. Calgary, Alta., Can., Mar. 22, 1940; s. Jack W. and Elizabeth T. (Speirs) W.; M.B.A., U. Western Ont. (Can.), 1967; m. Janet R. Suggitt, July 1963; children—James, Jennifer. Accountant, Winnipeg, Man., 1957-63; mgr. credit and control 3M Co. of Can., London, Ont., 1963-65; asst. credit mgr. corporate credit Bank of Montreal, 1967-72; treas. Dominion Textile Ltd., Montreal, 1972-77, comptroller, 1977—; dir. Canadian Textile Credit Bur., 1975—. Mem. Can. Inst. Chartered Accountants, Financial Execs. Inst.. Office: Dominion Textile Ltd 1950 Sherbrooke St W Montreal PQ H3H 1E7 Canada

WEIS, JOSEPH FRANCIS, JR., fed. judge; b. Pitts., Mar. 12, 1923; s. Joseph Francis and Mary (Flaherty) W.; student Duquesne U., 1941-47; J.D., U. Pitts., 1950; m. Margaret Horne, Dec. 27, 1958; children—Maureen, Joseph Francis, Christine. Admitted to Pa. bar, 1950; individual practice law, Pitts., 1950-68; judge Ct. Common Pleas, Allegheny County, Pa., 1968-70, U.S. Dist. Ct., Western Pa., 1970-73, U.S. Ct. Appeals, 3d Circuit, Pitts., 1973—; lectr. trial procedures, 1965—. Chmn. bd. Grubstake, Inc., 1968-71; mem. Mental Health and Mental Retardation Bd., Allegheny County, 1970-73, Leukemia Soc., Allegheny County, 1970-73; mem. bd. adminstrn. Catholic Diocese Pitts., 1971—; trustee Forbes Hosp. System, Pitts., 1969-74. Served with AUS, 1943-48. Decorated Bronze Star, Purple Heart with oak leaf cluster; recipient St. Thomas More award, 1971. Hon. fellow Internat. Acad. Trial Lawyers; mem. Am., Pa., Allegheny (past v.p.) bar assns., Acad. Trial Lawyers Allegheny County (past pres.). Contbr. articles to legal jours. Home: 225 Hillcrest Rd Pittsburgh PA 15238 Office: US Courthouse Pittsburgh PA 15219

WEIS, KONRAD MAX, chem. co. exec.; b. Leipzig, Germany, Oct. 10, 1928; s. Alfred and Margarete (Leipoldt) W.; came to U.S., 1971; Ph.D., U. Bonn, 1955; m. Gisela Lueg, Aug. 3, 1956; children—Alfred, Bettina. Chemist central sci. lab. Bayer AG, Leverkusen, W.Ger., 1956-61, plant mgr. 1961-65, mem. staff, 1965-71; corp. v.p. Baychem Corp. subs. Bayer AG, N.Y.C., 1971-74; pres., chief exec. officer successor co. Mobay Chem. Corp., Pitts., 1974—; dir. European Am. Bank & Trust Co. Hon. consul Fed. Republic West Germany, Pitts., 1978—. Mem. bus. adv. council Grad. Sch. Adminstrn., Carnegie-Mellon U., 1978—. Mem. German Am. C. of C. (exec. com. 1977-78), Penn's S.W. Assn. (trustee 1976—), Soc. Chem. Industry, Soc. German Chemists. Clubs: Sky (N.Y.C.); Duquesne, St. Clair Country (Pitts.); Houston; RTHC (Leverkusen). Address: Mobay Chem Corp Penn Lincoln Pkwy W Pittsburgh PA 15205

WEISBERGER, BARBARA, tchr., choreographer, artistic dir.; b. Bklyn., Feb. 28, 1926; d. Herman and Sally (Goldstein) Linshes; B.S., Pa. State U., 1945; L.H.D., Swarthmore Coll., 1970; D.F.A., Temple U., 1973; D.F.A. (hon.), Kings Coll., 1978, Villanova U., 1978; m. Sol Spiller, 1945 (div. 1948); m. Ernest Weisberger, Nov. 15, 1949; children—Wendy, Steven. Performed with Met. Opera Ballet, N.Y.C., 1937, 38, Mary Binney Montgomery Co., Phila., 1940-42; tchr., dir. Wilkes-Barre (Pa.) Ballet Theatre, 1953; artistic dir., founder Wilkes-Barre Ballet Guild, 1957; ballet mistress, choreographer Ballet Co. of Phila. Lyric Opera, 1961-62; artistic dir., founder Pa. Ballet Co., 1962—; choreographic works include: Judgment of Paris (Debussy, Griffes); Gingko Tree (Mendtner, Schubert); The Sorceress (Chopin); Quintet in Gay Minor (Gould); The Endless Curve (Debussy); Symphonic Variations (Franck); Italian Concerto, Bach; also operas for Phila. Lyric Opera Co., choreography for contemporary musical theatre. Ford Found. grantee, 1963, 65, 68, 71. Named Distinguished Dau. Pa., 1972; Distinguished Alumna, Pa. State U., 1972. Mem. Psi Chi. Home: 571 Charles Ave Kingston PA 18704 Office: Pennsylvania Ballet 2333 Fairmount Ave Philadelphia PA 19130

WEISBERGER, JOSEPH ROBERT, justice R.I. supreme ct.; b. Providence, Aug. 3, 1920; s. Samuel Joseph and Ann Elizabeth (Meighan) W.; A.B., Brown U., 1942; J.D., Harvard U., 1949; LL.D., R.I. Coll., Suffolk U., Mt. St. Joseph Coll.; D.C.L., Providence Coll.; D.H.L., Bryant Coll.; m. Sylvia Blanche Pigeon, June 9, 1951; children—Joseph Robert, Paula Ann, Judith Marie. Admitted to R.I. bar, 1950; paactice with Quinn & Quinn, Providence, 1951-56; solicitor, Glocester, R.I., 1953-56; judge R.I. Superior Ct., Providence, 1956—, presiding justice, 1972-78; mem. faculty Nat. Jud. Coll.; vis. lectr. Providence Coll., Roger Williams Coll. Chmn. New Eng. Regional Conf. Trial Judges, 1962, 63, 65; chmn. New Eng. Regional Commn. Disorderd Offender, 1968-71, R.I. Com. Adopt on Rules Criminal Procedure, 1968-72, Gov. of R.I. Adv. Com. Corrections, 1973; chmn. elect Nat. Conf. State Trial Judges, 1977-78; exec. com. Appelate Judges Conf., 1979—; bd. dirs. Nat. Center for State Cts., 1975—. Pres. R.I. Health Facilities Planning Council, 1967-70; chmn. Gov. R.I. Council Mental Health, 1968-73; moderator Town of East Providence, 1954-56; mem. R.I. Senate, 1953-56, minority leader, 1955-56; trustee R.I. Hosp., St. Joseph's Hosp. Served to lt. comdr. USNR, 1941-46. Mem. Am. Bar Assn. (mem. ho. of dels., task force on criminal justice standards 1977-79), R.I. Bar Assn., Am. Judges Assn. (gov.), Inst. Jud. Adminstrn., Am. Judicature Soc. Club: K.C. Chmn. editorial bd. Judges Jour., 1973-75. Home: 60 Winthrop St East Providence RI 02905 Office: Supreme Ct of RI Providence County Courthouse Providence RI 02903. *My professional life for the last 23 years has been occupied with judicial duties. I have been blessed with the opportunity to meet ever changing challenges and to attempt to solve a myriad of problems. These opportunities have been rewarding and absorbing. I consider judicial work to be a great privilege.*

WEISBLAT, DAVID IRWIN, pharm. co. exec.; b. Coshocton, Ohio, Aug. 11, 1916; s. Morris and Yetta (Laddin) W.; B.A. summa cum laude, Ohio State U., 1937, Ph.D., 1941, postgrad., 1941-43; m. Edna Christine Hawkinson Weisblat, Apr. 11, 1942; children—Ann Weisblat Ford, Sara Weisblat Shastak, David. With Upjohn Co., Kalamazoo, 1943—, dir. biochem. research, 1962-68, v.p. pharm. research and devel., 1968—, dir., 1973—; mem. chemistry panel Cancer Chemotherapy Nat. Service Center. Chmn. library com. Western Mich. U., 1958-64, mem. chemistry adv. com., 1958-68; mem. sci. adv. com. Pharm. Mfrs. Assn. Found., 1976; pres. Galesburg-Augusta Community Sch. Bd., 1960-62; trustee Charlestown Twp. Bd., 1959-63; trustee Kalamazoo Symphony Soc., Inc., 1968-77, pres., 1971-73; sec. Charleston Twp. Planning Commn., 1979—. Recipient Disting. Service award Western Mich. U., 1968. Fellow AAAS, Intra-Sci. Research Found. (hon.); mem. Am. Chem. Soc. (asso. editor Chem. Revs.), Pharm. Mfrs. Assn., Phi Beta Kappa, Sigma Xi, Phi Lambda Upsilon. Contbr. sci. articles to profl. jours. Patentee in pharm. field. Home: 11185 Hawthorne Dr Galesburg MI 49053 Office: 301 Henrietta St Kalamazoo MI 49001

WEISBORD, SAM, theatrical agt., agy. exec.; b. N.Y.C., Sept. 21, 1911; s. Jacob and Goldie (Kaufman) W.; student public schs., N.Y.C. With William Morris Agy., N.Y.C., 1929-45, Beverly Hills, Calif., 1945—, asst. treas., 1948-65, sr. exec. v.p., 1965-76, pres., 1976—, also dir. Bd. dirs. Menninger Found., Topeka, Cedars-Sinai Hosp., Los Angeles, Motion Picture and TV Fund, Los Angeles. Served with U.S. Army, 1943-45. Office: 151 El Camino Rd Beverly Hills CA 90212

WEISBROD, FRED EDGAR, city mgr.; b. St. Louis, July 26, 1922; s. Fred Edgar and Katherine (Manion) W.; A.A., George Washington U., 1949, B.A. in Bus. Adminstrn., 1951, M.A. in Public Adminstrn., 1953; m. Ann Rossiter, May 25, 1946; children—Fred E., Agnes Marie, Mark Edward, Cecelia Ann, Gary Leo, Patrick Michael. Aid-insp. City Health Dept., Washington, 1947-50; asst. to dir. public works, Montgomery County (Md.), 1950-54; city mgr. City of Oberlin (Ohio), 1954-57, Painesville (Ohio), 1957-59, Oak Ridge (Tenn.), 1959-62, Newport (R.I.), 1962-67, Pueblo (Colo.), 1967—; exec. dir. Council Govts. City-County Pueblo; instr., lectr. Sch. Continuing Edn., Grad. Sch. Public Adminstrn., U. Colo. Mem. Rocky Mountain council Boy Scouts Am., 1968-76; bd. dirs. Pueblo Regional Library, 1967-71, St. Mary Corwin Hosp., 1970-73. Served with USMC, 1942-45. Recipient Outstanding Contbn. award, Disting. Public Service Awards Program, Denver, 1972. Mem. Internat., Colo. city mgmt. assns., Nat. Mcpl. League, Nat. Assn. Council Govts., Pueblo C. of C., Pueblo Crippled Children's Soc., Nat. Assn. Secs. Roman Catholic. Clubs: Rotary, K.C. Home: 505 Starlite Dr Pueblo CO 81005 Office: PO Box 1427 Pueblo CO 81002. *I have always kept in mind my fellow men-whether rich or poor, royalty or commoner - and never let success or failure deter me from the goal of remembering the men who have gone on before and gave me so much, or the ones to come to pass on to them something worthwhile.*

WEISBUCH, JONATHAN BERMAN, physician, govt. ofcl.; b. Boston, Mar. 20, 1937; s. Manuel and Edith (Glodt) W.; B.S., M.I.T., 1959; M.D., N.Y. U., 1963; M.P.H., Harvard U., 1967; m. Kathleen Margaret Sperry, Jan. 15, 1968; children—Joshua, Benjamin. Intern, Kings County Hosp., Seattle, 1963-64; dir. health services Mass. Dept. Correction, Boston, 1974-76; state health officer N.D., Bismarck, 1976—; asst. prof. dept. community medicine U. Ky., Lexington, 1968-69; asso. prof. dept. community medicine Boston U. Sch. Medicine, 1969-76, teaching staff Inst. Law and Health Scis., Sch. Law, 1970-76; asso. prof. dept. community and family medicine U. Mass. Med. Sch., Worcester, 1974-76; clin. prof. community medicine U. N.D., Grand Forks, 1976—; vis. prof. pharmacy Northeastern U., Boston, 1975-76; mem. Mass. Gov.'s Adv. Bd. on Comprehensive Health Planning, 1974—; mem. adv. bd. N.D. State Bd. Embalmers, 1976—, State Bd. Examiners Nursing Home Adminstrn., 1976—; mem. exec. bd. Boston Center for Older Ams., 1972-76; mem. med. adv. com. Fenway Drs. Clinic, Boston, 1972-74; med. cons. Floyd County (Ky.) Comprehensive Health Program, 1967; cons. Family Planning, Inc., New Orleans, 1969, Population/Food Fund, 1976—, ABT Assos., Inc., Cambridge, Mass., 1971-72, others. Mem. adv. bd. N.D. Indian Affairs Commn., 1976—; alumni rep. dean's adv. com. Harvard Sch. Public Health, 1973-76. Served to lt. M.C., USN, 1964-66. Diplomate Am. Bd. Preventive Medicine. Recipient Physicians Recognition award AMA, 1974. Fellow Am. Coll. Preventive Medicine; mem. Assn. State and Territorial Health Ofcls. (Indian health com. 1978-79), Soc. Tchrs. of Family Medicine, Am. Public Health Assn. (manpower and tng. reference com. 1978, program devel. bd. 1978), AAAS, Soc. Epidemioologic Research, Population Assn. Am., Planned Parenthood, N.D. Med. Soc. Contbr. articles to profl. jours. Home: 1019 N Hannifin St Bismarck ND 58501 Office: State Health Dept Bismarck ND 58505. *Regardless of how much we plan for our future and our career, we should never forget the importance of luck, of chance, in shaping our lives. Luck may be good or ill, but usually it is neither, only the exposure to opportunity.*

WEISBURGER, JOHN HANS, med. researcher; b. Stuttgart, Germany, Sept. 15, 1921; s. William and Selma (Barth) W.; came to U.S., 1943, naturalized, 1944; A.B., U. Cin., 1947, M.S., 1948, Ph.D., 1949; children—William, Diane, Andrew. Biochemist, Nat. Cancer Inst., NIH, Bethesda, Md., 1950-61, head carcinogen screening sect., 1961-72, dir. bioassay segment Carcinogenesis Programs, 1971-72; v.p. research Am. Health Found., Valhalla, N.Y., 1972—; research prof. pathology N.Y. Med. Coll., Valhalla, 1974—; mem. biochemistry and nutrition study sect. NIH, 1957-58; mem. interdepartmental panel on carcinogens FDA, Dept. Agr., USPHS, 1962-71; chmn. subcom. Nat. Cancer Program Strategic Plan, 1971-74; chmn. carcinogenesis subcom. Nat. Large Bowel Cancer Project, 1972-75; chmn. subcom. positive controls Nat. Acad. Sci.-NRC Conf. on Carcinogen Testing of New Drugs, 1973; mem. expert panel on nitrites and nitrosamines Dept. Agr., 1973-77; chmn. Workshop Colo-rectal Cancer, Union Internat. Contra Cancrum, Geneva, 1975; mem. Nat. Cancer Inst. Clearinghouse on Environ. Carcinogens, 1976-78; program chmn. Toxicology Forum, 1977. Served with AUS, 1944-46; to col. USPHS, 1950-72. Recipient Def. Service medal, 1964, Meritorious Service medal USPHS, HEW, 1970. Fellow N.Y. Acad. Scis.; mem. Am., European, Japanese (hon.) assns. for cancer research, Am. Chem. Soc., Am. Soc. Biol. Chemists, Am. Soc. Pharmacology and Exptl. Therapeutics, Biochemical Soc. (London), Environ. Mutagen Soc., Soc. Toxicology (chmn. bd. publs. 1968-71, councilor 1972-74), Soc. for Exptl. Biology and Medicine, Japanese Cancer Assn. (hon. life), Sigma Xi, Alpha Chi Sigma (pres. Washington profl. chpt. 1967-68), Phi Lambda Upsilon. Editor: Archives of Toxicology, 1975—; asso. editor Cancer Research, 1969-79, Jour. Nat. Cancer Inst., 1960-62; mem. editorial bd. Chemico-Biological Interactions, 1969-77, Xenobiotica, 1971—; mem. hon. editorial adv. bd. Food and Cosmetic Toxicology, 1967—. Home: 4 Whitewood Rd White Plains NY 10603 Office: Am Health Found Naylor Dana Inst Valhalla NY 10595

WEISE, CHARLES MARTIN, educator; b. Bridgeville, Pa., July 8, 1926; s. Louis August and Alice (Martin) W.; B.S., Ohio U., 1950; M.S., U. Ill., 1951; Ph.D., 1956; m. Joan C. Spencer, July 18, 1951; children—Patricia, Carla, Christopher, Charles, Robert. Asst. prof. biology Fisk U., Nashville, 1953-56; asst. prof. zoology U. Wis. at Milw., 1956-60, asso. prof., 1960-66, prof., 1966—. Served with USMCR, 1945-46. Mem. Am., Brit. ornithologists unions, Wis. Soc. Ornithology, Am. Soc. Zoologists, Phi Beta Kappa. Research physiology of bird migration, population ecology of vertebrates. Home: 2314 E Stratford Ct Shorewood WI 53211 Office: Zoology Dept U Wis Milwaukee WI 53201

WEISE, FRANK EARL, JR., steel co. exec.; b. Allegheny County, Pa., June 25, 1919; s. Frank E. and Caroline S. (Stork) W.; B.S. in Metall. Engring., Lehigh U., 1941; m. Marian M. Hageman, Jan. 17, 1942; children—Frank Earl, III, Pamela D., Kathryn A. With

Bethlehem Steel Co., 1941-49; with Detroit Steel Corp., 1949-64, v.p. ops., 1961-64; with Koppers Co. Inc., Pitts., 1964-69, v.p. engring. and constrn. div., 1966-69; with Fla. Steel Corp., Tampa, since 1969, v.p. mills, 1971, exec. v.p., chief operating officer, dir., 1974—; dir. Bushnell Steel Constrn. Co., Atlanta Constrn. Products Inc. Mem. Am. Iron and Steel Inst., Am. Iron and Steel Engrs., Am. Inst. Steel Constrn., Wire Assn., Asso. Gen. Contractors. Presbyn. Clubs: Belleview Biltmore Country, Carlouel Yacht, Tower, Rotary, Masons. Home: 100 Oakmont Ln Belleair FL 33516 Office: PO Box 23328 Tampa FL 33623

WEISENFLUH, NORMAN DONALD, home furnishings co. exec.; b. Slippery Rock, Pa., Feb. 25, 1932; s. Norman N. and Anna (Shellenberger) W.; B.S., Grove City Coll., 1953; postgrad. Carnegie Inst. Tech., 1954; M.S., U. Pitts., 1962; m. Barbara Ann Bickham, July 12, 1958; children—Wendy Lee, Craig Charles. Supervisory and tech. positions in metal and glass fabricating plants Glass div. P.P.G. Industries, 1954-62; sr. ops. research specialist, corp. data processing staff Dart Industries, Inc., Los Angeles, 1963-66, asso. dir. corporate fin. analysis and rev. dept., 1966-71; dir. corporate devel. Acme Gen. Corp., Pasadena, Calif., 1971; gen. partner Western Resources Co., Los Angeles, 1972-73; v.p., dir. Liken Home Furnishings div. Beatrice Foods Co., Westminster, Calif., 1973-76, pres., Huntington Beach, Calif., 1976-78; pres., dir. Corona Pacific Corp., 1979—. Mem. Am. Statis. Assn., Ops. Research Soc. Am., Inst. Mgmt. Scis. Clubs: Masons; Big Canyon Country (Newport Beach, Calif.). Home: 10 Torrey Pines Ln Newport Beach CA 92660 Office: Corona Pacific Corp 19762 MacArthur Blvd Irvine CA 92715

WEISER, NORMAN SIDNEY, pub. co. exec.; b. Mpls., Oct. 1, 1919; s. Simon and Rosa (Davidson) W.; B.A., Northwestern U., 1939; m. Ruth Miller, Mar. 23, 1943; children—Judith Ann, Richard Alan. Reporter Radio Daily, 1938-42; reporter, editor Billbd. Mag., 1947-52; pub. Down Beat Mag., 1952-59; v.p. United Artists, 1959-62, 64-68, 20th Century Fox, 1962-64; v.p., dir. European ops. Paramount Music Div., 1968-69; v.p., gen. mgr. Chappell Music Co., N.Y.C., 1969-73, pres., 1973-77; sr. v.p., dir. Polygram Corp. U.S.; mem. mgmt. com. Internat. Polygram Pub. Div.; pres. Sesac, Inc., 1978—. Bd. dirs. Parkinson Found.; mem. corp., bd. dirs. UNICEF. Served to capt., USAAF. Decorated Purple Heart, Commendation medal Sec. War; recipient Ben Gurion award 1975. Mem. ASCAP (dir.), Nat. Music Pubs'. Assn. (v.p., dir.), Country Music Assn. (chmn. bd.). Mem. B'nai B'rith. Club: Friars. Author: Writers' Radio Theater, 1940; Writers' Radio-TV Theater, 1942; Under The Big Top, 1947; History AAF, World War II, 1947. Home: 58 W 58th St New York NY 10019 Office: 10 Columbus Circle New York NY 10019

WEISERT, JOHN JACOB, educator; b. Louisville, Dec. 18, 1914; s. John Jacob and Laura (Krug) W.; M.A., Columbia, 1939, Ph.D., 1947; m. Anita Boss, Sept. 7, 1962. Mem. faculty U. Tenn., 1947-48, U. Louisville, 1948-51, Pa. State U., 1951-53; mem. faculty U. Louisville, 1953—, prof. modern langs., 1962—, head dept., 1963-72. Served to capt. AUS, 1942-46. Carl Schurz fellow Columbia, 1939-40; Carnegie fellow gen. edn. U. Chgo., 1955-56. Mem. Modern Lang. Assn., Woodcock Soc., Phi Kappa Phi. Club: Filson (Louisville). Author: The Dream in Gerhart Hauptmann. Home: 1819 Harvard Dr Louisville KY 40205

WEISGALL, HUGO DAVID, composer, condr.; b. Ivancice, Czechoslovakia, Oct. 13, 1912; s. Adolph Joseph and Aranka (Stricker) W.; came to U.S. 1920, naturalized, 1926. student Johns Hopkins, 1929-31, Ph.D., 1940; musical edn. Peabody Conservatory, Baltimore, 1927-30, Curtis Inst., Phila., 1936-39; studied composition with Roger Sessions; m. Nathalie Shulman, Dec. 28, 1942; children—Deborah, Jonathan. Condr. Har Sinai Temple Choir, 1931-42; Y-Alliance Orch., 1935-42; Balt. String Symphony, 1936-38; Md. N.Y.A. Orch., 1940-41. Guest condr. London Symphony, London Philharmonic, BBC Symphony orchs., Orchestre de la Chapelle Musicale de la Reine Elizabeth (Belgium), Radio National Belge; dir. Balt. Inst. Mus. Arts, 1949; instr. composition Cummington Sch. Arts, 1948-51, instr. Julliard Sch. Music Arts, 1957-69; prof. composition Queens Coll., 1960—; Distinguished vis. prof. Penn State U., 1959-60, Peabody Inst., Balt., 1974-75; composer in residence Am. Acad. in Rome, 1966-67. Chmn. faculty Sem. Coll. of Jewish Music, Jewish Theol. Sem. of Am.; pres. Am. Music Center, 1964-73; asso. Lincoln Center Fund, 1965-68; dir. Hilltop Mus. Co., Balt., 1951-54. Composer: Songs, 1929; Quest (ballet), 1937; One Thing Is Certain (ballet), 1939; Hymn for chorus and orch., 1941; Overture in F, 1942; Soldier Songs, 1944-45; Outpost (ballet), 1947; The Tenor (opera), 1949-50; The Stronger (opera), 1952; Three Symphonic Songs for high voice and orch., 1952; Six Characters in Search of an Author (opera), 1956; Purgatory (opera), 1958; Athaliah (opera), 1963; Nine Rivers from Jordan (opera), 1968; Fancies and Inventions (song cycle), 1970; Translations (song cycle), 1971; End of Summer (song cycle), 1974; Song of Celebration (cantata for soprano, tenor, chorus and orch.), 1976; Jenny or the Hundred Nights (opera), 1976. Enlisted as pvt. AUS, 1942; asst. mil. attache to govts. in exile, London, later to Czechoslovakia; cultural attache Am. embassy, Prague, 1946-47. Awarded Bearns prize (Columbia), 1931; traveling fellow Curtis Inst., 1938; Ditson fellow Columbia, 1944; grantee Nat. Inst. Arts and Letters, 1952; Guggenheim fellow, 1955-56, 61-62, 66-67. Mem. Nat. Inst. Arts and Letters. Ditson Opera commn. Columbia, 1952, Koussevitzky commn., 1961. Mem. Phi Beta Kappa. Home: 81 Maple Dr Great Neck NY 11021 Office: 3080 Broadway New York NY 10027

WEISIGER, FELIX MANN, shoe corp. exec.; b. Oklahoma City, July 12, 1912; s. Edward Byron and Florence (Mann) W.; student Andrew Jackson U., 1936; m. Edith Kennedy, Feb. 24, 1939; children—Harry Kennedy, Patricia Mann (Mrs. Mark Morel). With Genesco, Inc., 1930-58, v.p., dir., 1958-62; v.p., gen. mgr., dir. Hanover Shoe Co., Inc., 1962; v.p. retail stores Endicott-Johnson Corp., 1962-63, sr. v.p. sales and marketing, 1963-69, exec. v.p., mem. exec. com., chmn. operating com., 1969—, also dir.; exec. v.p. Haywood div. Genesco, Inc., 1970-73, pres., 1973-74; group pres. Genesco, Inc., 1974—. Home: 366 Elmington Ave Nashville TN 37205 Office: 2300 Elliston Pl Nashville TN 37203

WEISINGER, HERBERT, univ. dean; b. Bklyn., May 19, 1913; s. Joseph and Anna (Schwager) W.; A.B., Bklyn. Coll., 1934; A.M., U. Mich., 1935, Ph.D., 1941; m. Mildred Weinstein, 1938. Instr. English, U. Mich., 1941-42; from instr. to prof. English, Mich. State U., 1942-66; prof. English, SUNY, Stony Brook, 1967-68, 78—, chmn. dept., 1967-68, dean Grad. Sch., 1968-78; vis. prof. U. Calif., Berkeley, 1947, N.Y.U., 1956, Bowling Green U., 1959, U. Ariz., spring 1965; Berg prof. English, N.Y.U., 1965-66; mem. Inst. Advanced Study, Princeton, 1948-49. Examiner, examination English honors Swarthmore Coll., 1960, 61; reader Christian Gauss Awards, 1969-71; trustee Grad. Record Exam., 1970-75, Grad. and Profl. Financial Aid Service, 1972-75. Mem. adv. com. grad. edn. Bd. Regents State N.Y., 1972—; sec.-treas. Northeastern Conf. Grad. Schs., 1975—. Recipient Distinguished Alumnus award Bklyn. Coll., 1964, Distinguished Faculty award Mich. State U., 1965; sr. research fellow Warburg Inst., London, Eng., 1950-52; Howard fellow, 1955-56. Author: Tragedy and the Paradox of the Fortunate Fall, 1953; Readings for Today, 2d edit., 1956; The Agony and the Triumph: Papers on the Use and Abuse of Myth, 1964; also author of numerous articles. Editor: The Laureate Fraternity: An Introduction to Literature, 1960; The Centennial Review of Arts and Science, 1959-66. Home: 24 Crane Neck Rd Setauket NY 11733

WEISKITTEL, RALPH JOSEPH, real estate exec.; b. Covington, Ky., Jan. 1, 1924; s. Nelson I. and Hilda (Nieman) W.; eve. student, Xavier U., Cin., 1946-47; m. Audrey Bushelman, June 19, 1948; children—Thomas, Carol Anne, Barbara Jane. Mem. staff Cin. Enquirer, 1942-43, 45—, home sect. editor, 1958-63, bus. editor, 1963-77; v.p. corporate markets Koetzle Corp. Realtors, 1977-79; v.p. Devitt and Assos., Realtors, 1979—. Mem. city council, Ft. Wright, Ky., 1960-68; mem. St. Agnes Parish Council, 1974-77. Served with AUS, 1943-46. Mem. Nat. Assn. Real Estate Editors, Soc. Am. Bus. Writers. Club: Cincinnati. Home: 1571 St Anthony Dr Fort Wright KY 41011 Office: 3610 Carew Tower Cincinnati OH 45202

WEISKOPF, THOMAS DANIEL, golfer; b. Massilon, Ohio, Nov. 9, 1942; s. Thomas Mannix and Eva Mae (Shorb) W.; student Ohio State U., 1960-62; m. Jeanne Marie Ruth, Oct. 22, 1966; children—Heidi Michelle, Eric Thomas. Won in tournaments, including Buick Open, 1968, Andy Williams San Diego Open, 1968, Kemper Open, 1971, 73, 77, Phila. IVB Golf Classic, 1971, 73, Piccadilly World Match Play, 1972, Jackie Gleason Inverrary Classic, 1972, Colonial Nat. Invitational, 1973, Brit. Open, 1973, South African PGA, 1973, World Series of Golf, 1973, Canadian Open, 1973-75, Greensboro Open, 1975. Served with AUS, 1968-69. Named Player of Year, Golf mag., 1973, Golf Writers Assn. Am., 1973, Golf World mag., 1973. Author: Go for the Flag, 1969. Home: Paradise Valley AZ 85253

WEISL, EDWIN L., JR., lawyer; b. N.Y.C., Oct. 17, 1929; s. Edwin L. and Alice (Todriff) W.; A.B. Yale, 1951; LL.B., Columbia, 1956; m. 2d, Barbara Butler, June 12, 1974; 1 dau. by previous marriage, Angela Jane. Admitted to N.Y. bar, 1956. D.C. bar, 1968; asso. firm Simpson Thacher & Bartlett, N.Y.C., 1956-64, mem. firm, 1964-65, 69-73; adminstr. parks, recreation and cultural affairs, commr. parks City of N.Y., 1973-75. asst. atty. gen. of U.S. in charge of land and natural resources division, 1965-67; asst. atty. gen. in charge civil div., 1967-69. Asst. spl. counsel, preparedness investigating com. U.S. Senate, 1957-58, Dir. N.Y. State Democratic campaign, 1964; Mem. The 1001, World Wildlife Fund; pres. Internat. Found. for Art Research; mem. vis. com. Fogg Art Mus.; mem. vis. com. dept. European paintings Met. Mus. Art; bd. dirs. dirs. N.Y. Hort. Soc., Robert Lehman Found., Washington Internat. Horse Show Assn., Ltd.; mem. corp. Presbyn. Hosp., N.Y.C. Served to lt. (j.g.) USNR, 1951-53. Clubs: Yale (N.Y.C.); Explorers; Warrenton Hunt. Office: 771 Park Ave New York NY 10021

WEISMAN, IRVING, social worker, educator; b. N.Y.C., May 6, 1918; s. Max and Sadie (Berkowitz) W.; B.S., CCNY, 1939; M.S., U. Buffalo, 1942; Ed.D., Columbia U., 1962; m. Cyrille Gold, May 1, 1941; children—Seth, Adam. Caseworker, Nat. Refugee Service, N.Y.C., 1941; warden's asst. Fed. Detention Hdqrs., Bur. Prisons, Dept. Justice, N.Y.C., 1942-43; psychiat. social worker to chief social worker VA, Camden and Union City, N.Y., 1946-49; case supr. Altro Health and Rehab. Service, N.Y., 1949-50; field instr., lectr. Columbia U. Sch. Social Work, 1950-57, asso. prof., 1957-62, prof., 1962—, acting dean, 1964-65, asso. dean, 1967-69; exec. officer doctoral program Hunter Coll. Sch. Social Work, U. City N.Y., 1975-78; clin. practice William Alanson White Inst., 1976-79; UN adv. on social welfare to Ceylon, Sri Lanka, 1963-64; sr. Simon research fellow U. Manchester (Eng.), 1970-71; cons. Office Juvenile Delinquency and Youth Devel., Children's Bur., HEW; cons. N.Y.C. Dept. Personnel, Westchester County (N.Y.) Dept. Mental Health, Community Service Soc., Council Social Work Edn., Moblzn. for Youth; continuing edn. workshops, various locations. Served with USAAF, 1943-46. HEW grantee, 1961-62, 64-76, 77, 79. Cert. social worker N.Y. State. Mem. AAUP, Am. Sociol. Assn., Council on Social Work Edn., Nat. Assn. Social Workers, Nat. Council on Crime and Delinquency, Soc. for Study Addiction to Alcohol and Other Drugs (Eng.). Contbr. articles to profl. jours., also monograph. Home: Alexander Ln Croton-on-Hudson NY 10520 Office: Hunter Coll Sch Social Work 129 E 79th St New York NY 10021

WEISMAN, JOEL DAVID, journalist; b. Chgo., Mar. 20, 1942; s. Maurice and Rose Irene (Harrison) W.; B.S., U. Ill., 1963; J.D., Chgo. Kent Coll. Law, 1969; m. Analee Rudich, Jan. 28, 1965; children—Scott Alan, Mitchell Todd, Matthew Peter. Reporter, City News Bur., Chgo., 1963-65, Gary (Ind.) Post-Tribune, 1965-66; polit. editor, columnist Chgo. Today, 1966-73; polit. columnist Chgo. Sun-Times, 1973-74, met. editor, 1974; chief Midwest bur. Washington Post, Chgo., 1974—; polit. commentator WTTW-TV, Chgo., 1974—; cons. on nat. convs. CBS, 1972; asso. prof. law Kent Coll. Law, Ill. Inst. Tech., Chgo. Bd. dirs. Reporters Com. for Freedom of Press, 1973—. Recipient awards for investigative reporting Atlantic City Press Club, Theta Sigma Phi, Nat. Soc. News Women, 1972; Nat. Polit. Reporting award Edn. Press Assn., 1973; Chgo. Area Emmy award for Polit. Reporting, 1976-77. Mem. Ill., Chgo. Bar Assn., Chgo. Press Club. Author: (with Neal R. Peirce) Great Lake States of America, 1975. Deerfield IL 60015

WEISMAN, MORTON PHILIP, publishing co. exec.; b. Chgo., Dec. 12, 1933; s. Philip and Rose (Beskin) W.; student U. Ill., 1951-53; B.S. in Bus-Adminstrn., Roosevelt U., 1955; m. Judith Rose Ades, Feb. 26, 1956; children—Jordan, Maya. With Allied Radio Corp., Chgo., 1955; with Harrison Corrugated Box Co., Chgo., 1955-61; exec. v.p., sec. A.C. McClurg & Co., Chgo., 1961-68, pres., 1968; pres. Swallow Press, Chgo., 1969—; v.p. Book Supply Co., Chgo. 1961-68, Carl J. Leibel, LaPuente, Calif., 1961-68; pres. Book News Publs. & Promotions, Inc., 1961-68. Treas. Ill. Freedom to Read Com.; bd. dirs. Bus. and Profl. People for Public Interest, 1978-80, Cinema/Chgo. (Chgo. Internat. Film Festival), 1979—, Chgo. Radio Theatre, 1976-78. Served with AUS, 1956-58. Mem. Tau Epsilon Phi. Club: Cliff Dwellers (award of merit for lit. 1971) (Chgo.). Home and office: 811 W Junior Terr Chicago IL 60613

WEISMILLER, EDWARD RONALD, educator, writer; b. Monticello, Wis., Aug. 3, 1915; s. Jacob and Georgia (Wilson) W.; student Swarthmore Coll., 1931-32; B.A., Cornell Coll., 1938, D.Litt., 1953; student Merton Coll., Oxford (Eng.) U., 1938-39, D.Phil., 1950; M.A., Harvard, 1942; m. Frances Merewether Power, June 15, 1941; children—Mariana Weismiller Chaffee, Georgia Louise Weismiller Sargeant, Peter Wilson, Charles Edward, Merie Luverne. Teaching fellow English, Harvard, 1940-43; mem. faculty Pomona Coll., 1950-68, prof. English, 1958-68; prof. English, George Washington U., 1968—; Fulbright prof. U. Leiden (Netherlands), 1957-58; mem. Council for Internat. Exchange of Scholars, 1976-79. Served to 1st lt. USMCR, 1943-46; ETO. Decorated Bronze Star; Medaille de la Reconnaissance Française; Rhodes scholar, 1938-39, 48-50; Guggenheim fellow, 1946-47, 47-48; fellow Fund Advancement Edn., Ford Found., 1953-54; research award Am. Council Learned Socs., 1963, 66, 69, Am. Philos. Soc., 1966, 69; research fellow Folger Library, 1965, 1972-73; spl. research grantee Rockefeller Found., 1965-66; sr. fellow in letters Center Advanced Studies, Wesleyan U., Middletown, Conn., 1967-68; research grantee, Nat. Endowment for Humanities, 1972-73, 77-81. Mem. Phi Beta Kappa. Author: (poems) The Deer Come Down (Yale Series Younger Poets), 1936; (poems) The Faultless Shore, 1946; (novel) The Serpent Sleeping, 1962; also articles. Contbr. The Lyric and Dramatic Milton, 1965. Contbg. editor A Variorum Commentary on the Poems of John Milton, 6 vols., 1970—. Home: 2400 Virginia Ave NW Washington DC 20037

WEISNER, MAURICE FRANKLIN, naval officer; b. Knoxville, Tenn., Nov. 20, 1917; s. Clinton Hall and Adra Inez (Ogg) W.; B.S., U.S. Naval Acad., 1941; aviation tng., 1943; grad. Nat. War Coll., 1959; m. Norma Holland Smith, May 30, 1942; children—Maurice Hall, Franklin Lee, Stewart Holland. Commd. ensign U.S. Navy, 1941, advanced through grades to adm., 1972; assigned U.S.S. Wasp, 1941-42, various aircraft squadrons in PTO, 1942-46, U.S.S. Badoeng Strait, 1947-48; comdr. Patrol Squadron 46, 1949-51; assigned Office Chief Naval Operations, 1951-53; comdr. Fighter Squadron 193, 1954-55; assigned air striking forces study sect. Office Chief Naval Operations, 1955-58; comdr. Fighter Squadron 101, 1959-60, U.S.S. Guadalupe, 1960-61, U.S.S. Coral Sea, 1961-62; assigned Bur. Naval Personnel, 1962-64; dir. air weapons systems analysis staff Office Chief Naval Operations, 1964-65; comdr. Carrier Div. 1, 1965-67; dep. chief naval personnel, 1967-69; comdr. Attack Carrier Striking Force 7th Fleet, 1969-70, 7th Fleet, 1970-71; dep. chief naval operations (air warfare), 1971-72; vice chief of naval operations, 1972-73; comdr. in chief U.S. Pacific Fleet, 1973-76; comdr. in chief, Pacific, 1976—. Decorated D.S.M. with 3 gold stars, Legion of Merit with gold star, D.F.C. with gold star, Air medal with 5 gold stars, Navy Commendation medal. Club: Army-Navy Country (Arlington, Va.). Home: 314 Burwell Ave Knoxville TN 37917 Office: Comdr in Chief Pacific Camp HM Smith HI 96861

WEISS, ANDREW, diversified co. exec.; b. N.Y.C., Aug. 20, 1916; s. Bertram and Emily (Stein) W.; B.B.A., City U. N.Y., 1937; M.B.A., N.Y. U., 1964; m. Ruth Ehrlich, Apr. 4, 1954; 1 son, Harlan Jay. With Louis D. Blum & Co., C.P.A.'s, N.Y.C., 1946-60, partner, 1953-60; treas., sec. Republic Indsl. Corp., N.Y.C., 1960-67; v.p., treas. Vare Corp., N.Y.C., 1967-69; v.p., treas. Microdot, Inc., Darien, Conn., 1969; dir. Microdot subsidiaries. Served with AUS, 1941-46; ETO. Mem. Am. Inst. C.P.A.'s, N.Y. State Soc. C.P.A.'s, Nat. Assn. Accountants, Sigma Beta Alpha. Home: 811 Hillsdale Ave Hillsdale NJ 07642 Office: 23 Old Kings Hwy S Darien CT 06820

WEISS, DAVID, educator; b. Sighet, Rumania, Dec. 21, 1928; s. Callel and Fanny (Weiss) Wiederman; came to U.S., 1947, naturalized, 1953; B.A., Bklyn. Coll., 1953; M.A., N.Y.U., 1956; M.H.L., Jewish Theol. Sem., 1957, D.H.L., 1958; m. Ann Hager, Dec. 9, 1953; children—Bernard, Ephraim, Isaiah. Instr. religion and Talmud, Jewish Theol. Sem., 1957-62, asst. prof. Talmud, 1962-68, asso. prof., 1968—, prof. Rabbinics, 1970—; lectr. religion Columbia, 1961-63, adj. asst. prof., 1963-65, adj. asso. prof. religion, 1965-68, adj. prof. religion, 1968—. Vis. prof. Talmud, Bar-Ilan U., Israel, 1974. Grantee Council Research Humanities Columbia, 1964; Guggenheim fellow, 1970-71; recipient L. Ginzberg award Jewish Theol. Sem., 1971-72. Fellow Am. Acad. Jewish Research (exec. com.). Author (under name Halivni) Sources and Traditions: A Source Ciritical Commentary on The Talmud, Vol. I on Seder Nashim, 1968, Vol. II on Seder Moed, 1974, and others. Mem. editorial bd. Judaism: Quar. Rev., Assn. Jewish Studies Rev., Hadoar, Hebrew weekly. Home: 435 Riverside Dr New York City NY 10025

WEISS, DAVID EDWARD, oboist; b. N.Y.C., Feb. 8, 1947; s. Jerome and Marcia W.; student UCLA, 1965—; U. So. Calif., 1964-65, Duquesne U., 1969-71; m. Connie Goldman, Aug. 28, 1966; children—Jonathan, Benjamin, Jamie. First oboe Met. Opera Nat. Co., 1965-66; asso. 1st oboe Pitts. Symphony, 1969-71; 1st oboe Nat. Symphony, 1971-73; co-prin. oboe Los Angeles Philharmonic, 1973—. Bd. trustees Young Musicians Found., Los Angeles. Served with U.S. Army, 1966-69. Recs. include The Weiss Family Woodwinds. Office: 133 N Grand Ave Los Angeles CA 90012

WEISS, DONALD L(OGAN), sports assn. exec.; b. Aurora, Ill., Aug. 22, 1926; s. Harry H. and Esther (Cook) W.; student Cornell Coll., Mt. Vernon, Iowa, 1943, 46; B.J., U. Mo., 1949; m. Charlene Thomas, Aug. 23, 1947; children—Deborah Lynn, Barbara Jane, Pamela Sue. Sports writer-editor AP, N.Y.C., 1949-63; publs. editor, info. dir. U.S. Golf Assn., N.Y.C., 1963-65; dir. info. Nat. Football League, N.Y.C., 1965-68, dir. public relations, 1968-77, exec. dir., 1977—. Served with USN, 1944-46. Recipient Journalistic Achievement awards Sigma Delta Chi, Kappa Tau Alpha, 1948-49; Trustees' award Ohio U., 1978. Methodist. Contbr. articles on golf and football to profl. publs., 1963—. Office: 410 Park Ave New York NY 10022

WEISS, EDWARD HUHNER, advt. agy. exec.; b. Chgo., Mar. 22, 1901; s. Abraham and Rose (Klapper) W.; Ph.B., U. Chgo., 1922; m. Ruth Wingerhoff, Feb. 12, 1938; 1 son, James, Pres. Edward H. Weiss and Co., advt., Chgo., N.Y.C. and Los Angeles, 1938-62, chmn. bd., chief exec. officer, 1962-67, chmn. bd., 1967—; chmn. bd. Lee King & Partners, 1971—; pioneer motivation research in advt., 1948—. Exhibited one-man and group shows as artist throughout U.S., Europe; one-man shows Art Inst. Chgo., 1949, Kovler Gallery, Chgo., 1963, Martha Jackson Gallery, N.Y.C., 1966, St. Paul (Minn.) Art Center, 1967; portrait exhbn. Main St. Gallery, Chgo., 1958, 71, Main St. Gallery retrospective, Mundelein Coll., 1972; Ill. State Mus., Springfield, 1974; Chgo. Pub. Library Portrait Slide Show, 1974, Chgo. Assn. Commerce and Industry, 1976, 78, Sears Tower, 1976, U. Chgo., 1976, Chgo. Cultural Center, 1977, Time-Life Bldg. Exhibit, 1978. Co-chmn. Chgo. com. Ill. Sesquicentennial Commn., 1968; pres. Friends of Chgo. Pub. Library, 1971-74. Bd. dirs. Tamarind Lithography Workshop, Los Angeles, 1964-76; trustee Chgo. Med. Sch., 1953- 62, gov., 1962—; trustee Inst. for Psychoanalysis, 1950-67, Mus. Contemporary Art, Chgo., 1967—; gov. Menninger Found., 1950-59; governing mem. Orchestral Assn., 1965—; mem. Auditorium Theatre Council, 1961—; pres.'s com., Chgo. Civic Opera, 1969; mem. Chgo. Council on Fine Arts. Clubs: Chgo. Advt., Arts, Standard, Press (Chgo.) Contbr. to periodicals. Home: 1325 N Astor St Chicago IL 60610 Office: 360 N Michigan Ave Chicago IL 60601

WEISS, EDWIN, educator; b. Bklyn., Aug. 23, 1927; s. Paul and Clara Ida (Rodman) W.; B.S., Bklyn. Coll., 1948; Ph.D., Mass. Inst. Tech., 1953; m. Janice S. Gopen, May 25, 1952; children—S. Ariel, Rena R. Instr. U. Mich., 1953-54; mem. Inst. Advanced Study, 1954-55; Benjamin Peirce instr. math. Harvard, 1955-58; asst. prof. U. Calif. at Los Angeles, 1958-59; staff mem. Lincoln Lab., Mass. Inst. Tech., 1959-65; prof. math. Boston U., 1965—. Vis. prof. Weizmann Inst. Sci., 1970-71, summer 1974. Author: Algebraic Number Theory, 1963; Cohomology of Groups, 1969; First Course in Algebra and Number Theory, 1971; co-author: Modern Elementary Mathematics: A Laboratory Approach, 1972. Home: 16 Warwick Rd Brookline MA 02146 Office: Dept Math Boston Univ Boston MA 02215

WEISS, EGON ARTHUR, librarian; b. Vienna, Austria, June 7, 1919; s. Arthur and Martha (Schrecker) W.; came to U.S., 1938, naturalized, 1943; student Berea Coll., 1938-40; A.B. in Econs., Harvard, 1947; M.A. in Germanic Langs. and Lit., Boston U., 1949; M.S. in L.S., Simmons Coll., 1951; m. Renee Hansi, July 11, 1942; children—Helen L., Steven A. Br. dir. Brookline (Mass.) Pub. Library, 1951-58; asst. librarian U.S. Mil. Acad., 1958-63, librarian, archivist, historian, 1963—. Mem. task force on pub. relations Fed. Library

Com., 1969; vice chmn. Citizens Adv. Com., Cornwall, N.Y., 1963—; mem. program adv. com. Office Chief Mil. History, 1963—; adv. com. for librarian career program Dept. of Army, 1965; librarian career program, career planning bd. and screening panel, Dept. of Army, 1969—; mem. study adv. group Study Army Libraries, 1975—. Trustee Mus. Hudson Highlands, 1968—. Served with AUS, 1942-46; ETO; lt. col. Res. Mem. Res. Officers Assn. (sec.-treas. Orange County chpt. 1963-64, pres. 1965), Mil. Govt. Assn. (bd. dirs. N.Y. chpt. 1963-64), A.L.A. (pres. armed forces librarians sect. 1966, mem. John Cotton Dana com. 1975—). Spl. Libraries Assn. (vice chmn., chmn.-elect 1969, chmn. mil. library div. 1970-71), Mil. Libraries Workshop, Southeastern N.Y. Library Resources Council (trustee, vice pres. 1969). Clubs: Newburgh Toastmasters (edn. v.p.); Harvard of Mid Hudson Valley (v.p.). Home: 33 Spruce St Cornwall-on-Hudson NY 12520 Office: US Mil Acad West Point NY 10996. *Fulfillment and happiness! How can we achieve these goals in the face of value systems which equate status and success with accumulated wealth? Let us start on the path of love, compassion and respect for fellow humans—fulfillment and happiness are sure to follow. What greater treasure can there be, except wisdom?*

WEISS, ERIC, chem. co. exec.; b. Erbendorf, Germany, Dec. 30, 1908; s. Solomon and Ada (Reinhold) W.; ed. Humanistisches Gymnasium, Weiden, Germany, 1917-22, Nuremberg, Germany, 1923-24; m. Greta Kobaltzky, Feb. 15, 1934; children—Norman, Fleur Schleifer, Jennifer Robertson, Stephen. Apprentice Fachanstait Füer Neuzeitliches Giesserel-Wesen, Halle Saale, Germany, 1924, moved through ranks to mgr., 1924-31; with Foseco-Minsep Ltd., London, Eng., 1931-78, chmn., 1944-78, pres., 1978—. Trustee Oakham Sch., Rutland, Eng.; bd. govs. United World Coll. of Atlantic. Mem. Inst. Brit. Foundrymen. Home: Manor House Little Marlow Bucks England also 33 Chester Sq London SWI England Office: 36 Queen Anne's Gate London SW 1 England

WEISS, HARRY JOSEPH, educator; b. Pitts., Feb. 15, 1923; s. Ralph and Bessie (Denson) W.; B.S., Carnegie Inst. Tech., 1947, M.S., 1949, D.Sc., 1951; m. Marion Rivkees, May 30, 1947; children—Eric, David, Nancy. Instr. math. Carnegie Inst. Tech., 1947-51; asst. prof. applied math. Brown U., 1951-54; from asst. prof. to prof. math. Iowa State U., 1954-64, prof., head, engring. sci. and mechanics, 1964—; vis. scientist Nat. Bur. Standards, 1961; cons. Gen. Dynamics/Astronautics, 1962-65. Served with AUS, 1943-46; ETO. Decorated Bronze Star medal, Purple Heart. Mem. ASME, Soc. Engring. Sci., Am. Soc. Engring. Edn., Sigma Xi, Phi Kappa Phi. Contbr. to Handbook of Engineering Mechanics, 1962; co-editor: Developments in Mechanics, Vol. 5, 1969. Home: 2529 Northwood Dr Ames IA 50010

WEISS, IRA FRANCIS, ret. banker; b. Providence, Oct. 19, 1909; s. Abraham and Minnie (Chernoff) W.; student Coll. City N.Y., 1926-28; LL.B., St. Lawrence U., 1931; postgrad. Columbia, 1931-33, St. John's Coll. Annapolis, 1975-78, Seminar Coll., New Sch., 1978—; m. Gladys Abbott (div. 1966); children-Abbott, Michael, John. Admitted to N.Y. bar, 1934; pvt. practice, N.Y.C., 1934-37; asst. sec. Credit Utility Co., Inc., N.Y.C., 1937-42; successively asst. sec., asst. v.p., v.p., adminstrv. v.p., sr. v.p. Trade Bank & Trust Co., 1926-33, 45-70; sr. v.p. Nat. Bank N. Am., N.Y.C., 1970-74, sr. cons., 1975. Mem. Jewish Com. on Scouting, N.Y.C., 1950-53; asst. mgr. United Fund, Glen Ridge, N.J., 1959; mem. Civic Conf. Com., 1961-64; mem. Mayor's Transp. Com., 1962-65; mem. Speakers Bur. of United Cerebral Palsy Soc. N.Y.C., 1946-50; adminstrv. asst. to dir. Security and Intelligence Div., Ft. Dix, N.J., 1942-45; treas., exec. bd. nat. exec. council Am. Jewish Com., 1962—. Mem. A.I.M., N.Y. Credit and Financial Mgmt. Assn., Am. Arbitration Assn. (nat. panel), Robert Morris Assos. Home: 300 Mercer St New York NY 10003

WEISS, JAMES MOSES AARON, educator, psychiatrist; b. St. Paul, Oct. 22, 1921; s. Louis Robert and Gertrude (Simon) W.; A.B. summa cum laude, U. Minn., 1941, Sc.B., 1947, M.B., 1949, M.D., 1950; M.P.H. with honors, Yale, 1951; m. Bette Shapera, Apr. 7, 1946; children—Jenny Anne, Jonathan James. Teaching asst. psychology St. Thomas Coll., St. Paul, 1941-42; intern USPHS Hosp., Seattle, 1949-50; resident, fellow psychiatry Yale Med. Sch., 1950-53; from instr. to asst. prof. psychiatry Washington U., St. Louis, 1954-60; mem. faculty U. Mo., 1960—, prof. psychiatry, 1961—, chmn. dept., 1960—, prof. community health, 1971—; vis. prof. Inst. Criminology, Cambridge (Eng.) U., 1968-69; nat. cons. in field, 1958—. Served with Med. Adminstrv. Corps, AUS, 1942-46; PTO; capt. M.C., AUS, 1953-54. Faculty fellow Inter-Univ. Council, 1958; recipient Israeli Bronze medal for leadership, 1963. Diplomate Am. Bd. Psychiatry and Neurology (examiner 1963—). Found. fellow Royal Coll. Psychiatrists; fellow Royal Soc. Medicine, Am. Psychiat. Assn., Am. Orthopsychiat. Assn., Am. Pub. Health Assn., A.A.A.S., Am. Coll. Psychiatrists; mem. Assn. Mil. Surgeons U.S. (hon. life), Assn. Western Profs. Psychiatry (chmn. 1970-71), Mo. Acad. Psychiatry (1st pres. 1966-67), Mil. Order World Wars, Phi Beta Kappa, Sigma Xi, Psi Chi, Alpha Omega Alpha, Gamma Alpha. Clubs: Scholars (Cantab.); Wine Label (London). Author numerous articles in field. Editor, co-author: Nurses, Patients, and Social Systems, 1968. Corr. editor Jour. Geriatric Psychiatry, 1967—; founding editor, chmn. bd. Jour. Operational Psychiatry, 1970—. Research in areas of suicide, homicide, antisocial behavior, aging, social psychiatry. Home: Crow Wing Farm Route 2 Columbia MO 65201

WEISS, JEROME SIDNEY, lawyer; b. Chgo., Feb. 7, 1909; s. Morris Henry and Fannie (Salamson) W.; Ph.B., U. Chgo., 1928, J.D. cum laude, 1930; m. Gertrude Levy, June 20, 1947; children—Marlene Weiss Plotkin, Stanton Henry Berlin. Admitted to Ill. bar, 1930, since practiced in Chgo.; asso. firm Sonnenschein, Carlin, Nath & Rosenthal, 1930-42, sr. mem. firm, 1942—. Asst. sec. Cory Corp.; sec., dir. Unarco Industries, Inc., 1945—; v.p., asst. sec., dir. Don Beachcomber, Inc., 1940-75; sec., dir. Hokin Gallery, Inc.; asst. sec. B. Brody Seating Co.; dir. Goldblatt Bros. Inc. Chmn. character, fitness com. First Ill. Appellate Court Dist., 1956-58, commr., 1951-59; mem. mayor's coms. sch. bd. nominations, 1957-59, youth welfare, 1957-58; past chmn. correctional services advisory bd. Ill. Youth Commn. Past pres. and dir. Juvenile Protective Assn.; dir., past v.p. Welfare Council Met. Chgo. Past dir. Mt. Sinai Hosp.; past pres., hon. dir. Temple Sholom; gov., sec. Sarah Siddons Soc., Inc. Fellow Am. Bar Found.; mem. Am. (del. ho. dels. convs. 1956, 58-59, 69-72), Chgo. (pres. 1958-59, chmn. com. of past presidents 1968—) bar assns., Nat. Conf. Bar Pres., U. Chgo. Law Sch. Alumni Assn. (pres. 1958-61, dir.), Chgo. Law Inst., Order of Coif. Clubs: Standard (pres.), Mid-Day, Metropolitan, Carlton, Nat. Lawyers, Executives, City, Law (v.p. 1978—, exec. com.) (Chgo.). *Died Sept. 11, 1979.*

WEISS, JULIUS SEYMOUR, editor, columnist; b. St. Louis, Apr. 7, 1922; s. Isadore and Bertha (Weisz) W.; student Western Reserve U., 1941-43. Columnist, Linn's Weekly Stamp News, Sidney, Ohio, 1956-63; writer for Airpost Jour. philatelic mag. Am. Airmail Soc., Albion, Pa., 1956-59, Holy Land Philatelist, Israel, 1958-61, Philatelic Trader, Philatelic mag. Harris Publs., London, 1957—, El Eco Filatelico, Pamplona, Spain, 1959—, Filatelia Italiana, Rome, 1962-67; asso. editor Weekly Philatelic Gossip, Holton, Kans., 1958-60; columnist Numis. News, 1965-67, Cleve. Press, 1967-70, Nat. Stamp News, Anderson, S.C.; editor, columnist Weiss Philatelic-Numis. Features; contbr. articles to stamp, hobby, coin mags., newspapers, U.S. and fgn. pubs.; radio broadcaster philatelic and numismatic news. Mgr., Bertha Weisz Philatelic-Numismatic Journalism award; past chmn. amateur radio sect. hobbies div. People-to-People Program. Club: Philatelic Press of N.Y. Address: 16000 Terrace Rd Cleveland OH 44112. *Postage stamps should be made for postal service first; coins struck for trade usage first; those made just for the hobby world will have little value in future years.*

WEISS, LEON P., cell biologist, hematologist; b. Bklyn., Oct. 4, 1925; M.D., L.I. Coll. Medicine, 1948; m. Ellen Fishbein, June 19, 1949; children—Stephen, Philip, Alice, Marisa, Nathaniel, Eve. Intern in medicine Maimonides Hosp., Bklyn., 1948-49, resident, 1949-50; prof. anatomy Johns Hopkins Sch. Medicine, Balt., 1966-76; prof. cell biology, chmn. dept. animal biology U. Pa. Sch. Veterinary Medicine, Phila., 1976—. Mem. corp. Marine Biol. Lab., Woods Hole, Mass. Served to capt. M.C., U.S. Army, 1953-55. Mem. Am. Assn. Anatomists, Am. Soc. Immunology, Am. Soc. for Cell Biology, Soc. for Exptl. Biology and Medicine, Reticuloendothelial Soc. Author: The Blood Cells and Hematopoietic Tissues, 1977; editor: (with R. Greep) Histology, 4th edit., 1977. Office: 3800 Spruce St Philadelphia PA 19104

WEISS, LEONARD, mathematician, engr.; b. N.Y.C., Mar. 14, 1934; s. Max and Sadie (Albert) W.; B.E.E., Coll. City N.Y., 1956; M.S., Columbia, 1959; Ph.D., Johns Hopkins, 1962; m. Sandra Joyce Raynes, June 15, 1958; children—Madelyn, Eugene. Lectr., Coll. City N.Y., 1956-59; staff scientist Research Inst. for Advanced Studies, Balt., 1962-64; asst. prof. Brown U., Providence, 1964-66, asso. prof., 1966-68; prof. U. Md., College Park, 1968-78; legis. asst. to Senator John Glenn of Ohio, 1976-77; cons. Naval Research Lab., Washington, 1970-77; staff dir. Senate Subcom. on Energy, Nuclear Proliferation and Fed. Services, 1977—. Alfred P. Sloan research fellow, 1966-68; IEEE Congl. fellow, 1976. Mem. AAAS, IEEE, Sigma Xi. Editor: Ordinary Differential Equations, 1972. Contbr. articles to profl. jours. Home: 11701 Auth Ln Silver Spring MD 20902 Office: 6206 Dirksen Senate Office Bldg Washington DC 20510

WEISS, LEONARD, internat. econs. cons.; b. Chgo., June 5, 1918; s. Ben and Esther (Tepper) W.; B.A., U. Chgo., 1939,; M.A., Fletcher Sch. Law and Diplomacy, 1941; m. Mary L. Barker, Sept. 21, 1946; children—Susan R., David A. Research asst. Ill. Tax Commn., 1938, Carnegie Endowment for Internat. Peace, 1940; fellow Brookings Instn., 1941-42; economist Office Inter-Am. Affairs, 1942-43, 46; ofcl. Dept. of State, 1946-56, fgn. service officer, 1956-74; asst. chief trade agreements div., alternate chmn. inter-deptl. trade agreements com., until 1957; dep. dir. and acting dir. USOM, Belgrade, Yugoslavia, 1957-60, also 1st sec., 1957-58, then counselor econ. affairs Am. embassy, Belgrade, 1959-60; with Dept. State, Washington, 1960-63, dep. dir., then dir. Office Internat. Trade and Fin., 1960-63; counselor econ. affairs, 1963-65, also minister-counselor polit. and econ. affairs Am. embassy, New Delhi, India, 1965-67; minister econ. and comml. affairs Am. embassy, Bonn, 1968-70; dep. dir. Bur. Intelligence and Research, Dept. State, Washington, 1970-74; chief World Bank mission, Bangladesh, 1974-78; internat. econs. cons., mem. trade policy group U.S. Atlantic Council, 1978—; U.S. del. ECOSOC, 1951, GATT, 1950, 53-54, 55, 61, 62, 63, OEEC Council of Ministers meeting, 1954; vice chmn. U.S. del. to ECAFE, 1965, 66, 67, alt. U.S. rep., 1966-67; spl. rep. for Offset Talks, 1968, mem. U.S. del. to Offset Talks, 1969; mem. Sr. Seminar Fgn. Policy, State Dept., 1967-68; mem. World Bank del. to Bangladesh Aid Group meeting, 1974, 75, 76, 77. Served to lt. (j.g.) USNR, 1943-46. Recipient Superior Service award Dept. State, 1963. Mem. Am. Econ. Assn., Am. Fgn. Service Assn., Diplomatic and Consular Officers Ret., Alumni Assn. Fletcher Sch. Law and Diplomacy, U. Chgo. Alumni Assn., 1819 Soc. (World Bank), Phi Beta Kappa. Home: 4126 N 34th St Arlington VA 22207 Office: 4126 N 34th St Arlington VA 22207

WEISS, LIONEL EDWARD, educator, geologist; b. London, Eng., Dec. 11, 1927; s. S. and E. (Carney) W.; B.Sc. with 1st class honours, U. Birmingham (Eng.), 1949, Ph.D., 1953; Sc.D., U. Edinburgh (Scotland), 1956; m. Liv Mariane Nissen-Sollie Dec. 27, 1964; children—Nicholas Erling, Elin Katrina. Came to U.S., 1956, naturalized, 1972. Commonwealth Fund fellow U. Calif. at Berkeley, 1951-53; sr. research fellow U. Edinburgh, 1953-56; mem. faculty U. Calif. at Berkeley, 1956—, prof. geology, 1964—, Miller research prof., 1965, 66; cons. in field. Guggenheim fellow, 1962, 69; Fulbright scholar, Norway, 1975. Fellow Geol. Soc. Am. Author: (with F.J. Turner) Structural Analysis of Metamorphic Tectonites, 1963; (with others) The Earth, 1970; The Minor Structures of Deformed Rocks, 1972, also articles. Home: 784 Euclid Ave Berkeley CA 94708

WEISS, MELVIN IRVING, engring. exec.; b. Phila., July 19, 1928; s. Jacob and Bertha (Segal) W.; B.S. in M.E., Drexel U., Phila., 1952, M.S. in M.E., 1955; m. Marilyn Marie Calderoni, June 25, 1972; children—Eric, Dana, Karen, Shelah. Analytical engr. P.G.I., Trenton, N.J., 1952-54; analytical engring. supr. Sanders & Thomas, Phila., 1954-55; design engr. Anderson, Greenwood & Co., Houston, 1955-57; chief engr. Gulf and Western Advanced Devel. and Engring. Center, Swarthmore, Pa., 1957—; instr. Spring Garden Inst., Phila., 1958-60. Served with USAAF, 1946-47. Registered profl. engr., Pa., N.J. Mem. Nat. Soc. Profl. Engrs., Franklin Inst., Am. Def. Preparedness Assn., Soc. Automotive Engrs. Jewish. Patentee Aircraft launching and recovery equipment, continuous castings, metal parts mfg. methods. Home: 100 Martins Run Media PA 19063 Office: 101 S Chester Rd Swarthmore PA 19081

WEISS, MILTON, sav. and loan assn. exec., lawyer; b. Bklyn., Feb. 7, 1913; s Jeremiah A. and Rose (Sayetta) W.; LL.B., U. Miami (Fla.), 1935; m. Cecile Alexander, June 8, 1941; children—Kay Esta (Mrs. Neil Harris), Alexa Sara (Mrs. William E. Shockett). Admitted to Fla. bar, 1935; partner firm Meyer, Weiss, Rose Arkin, Sheppard & Shockett, P.A., and predecessor, Miami Beach, Fla., 1937—; pres. Miami Beach Fed. Savs. & Loan Assn. (name changed to Fin. Fed. Savs. and Loan Assn.), 1964—; dir. City Nat. Bank Miami Beach, 1949-57, City Nat. Bank Miami, 1950-57. An organizer Miami Beach Jr. C. of C., 1935; mem. Dade County Sch. Bd., 1940-53, chmn., 1947-49; campaign chmn. Dade County Combined Jewish Appeal, 1967; pres. Greater Miami Jewish Fedn., 1969—. Organizer, 1st pres., sustaining bd. fellow Mt. Sinai Hosp., Miami Beach, 1965, trustee 1968—; trustee Miami U., 1971—. Recipient Silver medallion award Nat. Conf. Christians and Jews; elected to Wisdom Hall Fame, 1970. Mem. Fla. State Bar., Dade County, Miami Beach bar assns., C. of C. Miami Beach (past bd. dirs.). Jewish religion. Kiwanian (past pres. Miami Beach), Elk (past exalted ruler Miami Beach), Mason; mem. B'nai B'rith. Author article. Home: 405 E San Marino Dr Miami Beach FL 33139 Office: 401 Lincoln Rd Miami Beach FL 33139

WEISS, MORTON LOUIS, paper converting co. exec.; b. W. Chester, Pa., Jan. 4, 1918; s. Morris and Anna (Canter) W.; B.S., Harvard, 1939, M.B.A., 1941; m. Julia Meyer, June 10, 1956; children—Kenneth M., Linda Ann, Andrew M., Michael Epstein. Advt. mgr. Montag, Inc., Atlanta, 1945-50, pres., 1950-67; v.p. Westab, Inc., Dayton, Ohio, 1962-67; v.p. Gorham div. Textron, Inc., 1967-69, pres. Eaton Paper div., 1969-73; group v.p. Arvey Corp., Chgo., 1973—, also dir.; dir. Triangle Shoe Co., Narrows Realty Co. (both Kingston, Pa.). Bd. dirs. Atlanta chpt. Nat. Conf. Christians and Jews, 1954-67, Atlanta Jewish Welfare Fund, 1954-67, Atlanta Jewish Community Center, 1952-67, Atlanta Traffic and Safety Council, 1961-67, Community Council Atlanta Area, 1966-67; v.p., dir. Met. Atlanta Community Service, 1962; chmn. Am. Jewish Com., 1956; campaign chmn. Atlanta chpt. ARC, 1957, Atlanta United Fund, 1961; fund council mem. Harvard Bus. Sch., 1960-62; trustee Oglethrope Coll., 1956-67. Served with AUS, 1941- 45. Recipient Distinguished Service award B'nai B'rith Gate City Lodge, 1959; Brotherhood award Nat. Conf. Christians and Jews, 1965. Mem. Paper Stationery and Tablet Mfrs. Assn. (pres. 1961-63, bd. dirs. 1952-66). Clubs: Standard Town and Country (pres. 1959); Commerce (Atlanta). Home: 3180 N Lake Shore Dr Chicago IL 60657 Office: 3450 N Kimball Ave Chicago IL 60618

WEISS, MORTON N., assn. exec.; b. N.Y.C., Aug. 14, 1919; s. Morris and Kate M. (Wellisch) W.; B.S., Coll. City N.Y., 1940; m. Sally R. Sarner, Jan. 17, 1954; children—Ronald, Allison, James. Stock trader Royal Exchange Co., N.Y.C., 1940-43, J. Arthur Warner & Co., N.Y.C., 1946-54; exec. v.p. Singer Mackie & Co., N.Y.C., 1954-69; mng. partner Troster, Singer & Co., N.Y.C., 1969-73; 1st permanent pres. Nat. Security Traders Assn., 1974—; dir. Nat. Over-the-Counter Clearance Corp. Served to lt., inf. AUS, 1943-46. Recipient Over-the-Counter Man of Year award, 1971. Mem. Nat. Assn. Securities Dealers (past chmn. nat. trading com.), Security Traders Assn. N.Y. (past dir., past pres.), Securities Industry Assn. (past chmn. securities trading com.). K.P. Home: 81 Woodhollow Rd Roslyn Heights NY 11577 Office: 55 Broad St New York NY 10004

WEISS, NATHAN, coll. pres.; b. Newark, Dec. 25, 1922; s. Paul and Lena (Berman) W.; A.B., Montclair State Coll., 1948; M.A., Rutgers U., 1949; Ph.D., N.Y. U., 1961; m. Ethel Gelzer, Dec. 25, 1951; children—Paula, Michael. Tchr. Fallsburgh (N.Y.) Central Sch. System, 1949-61; mem. faculty Newark State Coll. (name now Kean Coll. N.J.), 1961—, chmn. dept. history and social sci., 1967-68, prof. polit. sci., 1968—, pres., 1970—, bd. dirs. coll. devel. fund, 1969—; county historian Sullivan County, N.Y.; lectr. Am. Assn. UN. Dir. Title I Program, Hunterdon County, N.Y., 1966; bd. dirs. N.J. Edn. Consortium. Served with USAAF, 1945-48. Recipient Distinguished Alumnus award Montclair State U., 1973. Mem. Am. Assn. State Colls. and Univs., Am. Soc. Pub. Adminstrs., Assn. N.J. State Coll. Pres., Am. Polit. Sci. Assn., World Future Soc., Eastern Union County C. of C., Alpha Sigma Mu. Democrat. Author articles in field. Home: 37 Concord St Cranford NJ 07016 Office: Office of Pres Kean Coll Union NJ 07083*

WEISS, PAUL, philosopher, educator; b. N.Y.C., May 19, 1901; s. Samuel and Emma (Rothschild) W.; B.S.S., Coll. City N.Y., 1927; A.M., Harvard U., 1928, Ph.D. (Sears Travelling fellow), 1929; L.H.D., Grinnell Coll., 1960, Pace Coll., 1969, Bellarmine Coll., 1973, Harverford Coll., 1974; m. Victoria Brodkin, Oct. 27, 1928 (dec. Dec. 1953); children—Judith, Jonathan. Instr., tutor philosphy Harvard U., also instr. Radcliffe Coll., 1930-31; asso. philosophy Bryn Mawr (Pa.) Coll., 1931-33, asso. prof., 1933-40, prof., 1940-46, chmn. dept., 1944-46; Guggenheim fellow, 1938; vis. prof. Yale U., 1945-46, prof. philosophy, 1946-62, Sterling prof. philsophy, 1962-69, emeritus, 1969—, fellow Ezra Stiles Coll.; vis. prof. U. Denver, spring 1969; Heffer prof. philosphy Catholic U. Am., 1969—, lectr., 1975; vis. prof. Philo. Hebrew U., Jerusalem, 1951, Orde Wingate lectr., 1954; Rockefeller-Rabinowitz grantee for study in Israel and India, 1954; lectr. Aspen Inst., 1952, Chancellor's Forum, U. Denver, 1952; Powell lectr. U. Ind., 1958; Gates lectr. Grinnell Coll., 1960; Matchette lectr. Purdue U., 1961, Wesleyan Coll., 1963; Aquinas lectr. Marquette U., 1963; Townsend Harris medalist, 1963; Rhoades lectr. Haverford Coll., 1964; Phi Beta Kappa lectr., 1968-69; resident scholar State U. N.Y., 1969, 70; Eliot lectr. Marquette U., 1970; William De Vane medalist, 1971; Aquinas lectr. St Marys, 1971; medalist City Coll., 1973, Hofstra U., 1973. Bd. govs. Hebrew U., Jerusalem; bd. dirs. Luce Found. Mem. Am. Philos. Assn. (co-pres. 1966), Conf. on Sci. Philos. and Religion (founding mem.), C. S. Peirce Soc. (founding mem., pres.), Metaphys. Soc. Am. (founder, pres. 1951, 52, councillor 1953-58), Philos. Soc. for Study of Sport (founder, pres. 1973), Am. Friends of Hebrew U. (pres. New Haven chpt.), Philos. Edn. Soc., Inc. (founder, v.p.), Société Européenne de Culture, AAUP, Am. Assn. Middle East Studies, Phi Beta Kappa. Clubs: Aurelian, Elizabethan; Washington Philosophic. Author: Reality, 1938; Nature and Man, 1947; Man's Freedom, 1950, Portugese transl., 1960; Modes of Being, 1958; Our Public Life, 1959; World of Art, 1961, Hebrew transl., 1970; Nine Basic Arts, 1961; History: Written and Lived, 1962; Religion and Art, 1963; The God We Seek, 1964; Philosophy in Process, 7 vols., 1955-76; The Making of Men, 1967; Sport: A Philosophic Inquiry, 1969; Beyond All Appearances, 1974; Cinematics, 1975; First Considerations, 1977; You, I and the Others, 1980; co-author: Right and Wrong; A Philosophical Dialogue Between Father and Son, 1967; 7th Internat. Congress of Philosophy, 1930; Am. Philosophy Today and Tomorrow, 1935; Philosophical Essays for A.N. Whitehead, 1936; Approaches to World Peace, 1944; Perspectives on a Troubled Decade, 1950; Moral Principles of Action, 1952; Personal Moments of Discovery, 1953; Perspectives on Peirce, 1965; Dimensions of Job, 1969; Mid-Century American Philosophy, 1974; others; co-editor: Collected Papers of Charles S. Peirce, 6 vols.; founder, editor Rev. of Metaphysics, 1947-63; editorial bd. Judaism; contbr. to profl. periodicals. Address: 2000 N St NW Washington DC 20036

WEISS, PETER JOSEF, govt. ofcl.; b. Vienna, Austria, Nov. 23, 1918; s. George and Margaret (Furst) W.; came to U.S., 1940, naturalized, 1943; B.S., George Washington U., 1951; M.S., Georgetown U., 1953, Ph.D., 1956; m. Lillian Deitch, May 28, 1948; children—Martin H., Irwin E. With FDA, Washington, 1947-79, chief chemistry br., 1957-70, dep. dir., then acting dir. Nat. Center Antibiotic Analysis, Pharm. Research and Testing, Bur. Drugs, 1970-72, dir., 1972-79. Served with AUS, 1943-45. Mem. Am. Chem. Soc., Am. Pharm. Assn., Acad. Pharmacy. Jewish. Club: B'nai B'rith (lodge pres. 1970-72).

WEISS, ROBERT FRANCIS, coll. pres.; b. St. Louis, Aug. 27, 1924; s. Frank L. G. and Helen M. (Beck) W.; B.A., St. Louis U., 1951, Ph.L., 1953, M.A., 1953, S.T.L., 1961; Ph.D., U. Minn., 1964. Joined Soc. of Jesus, 1946; ordained priest Roman Catholic Ch., 1959; tchr. Rockhurst High Sch., Kansas City, Mo., 1953-56; adminstrv. asst. to pres. St. Louis U., 1961-62; asst. dean Rockhurst Coll., Kansas City, Mo., 1964-66, dean, v.p., prof. edn., 1966-72, pres., 1977—; pres. St. Louis U. High Sch., 1973-77. Trustee St. Louis U., 1973—, Loyola U., New Orleans, 1973—, United Student Aid Funds, Inc., 1977—; chmn. bd. dirs. Kansas City Regional Council for Higher Edn., 1978—; bd. dirs. Jesuit Program for Living and Learning, 1977—; nat. chaplain Rainbow Div. Vets Assn. Served with U.S. Army, 1943-46. Decorated Bronze Star, Combat Infantryman's badge. Mem. Am. Assn. Presidents of Ind. Colls. and Univs., Am. Assn. for Higher Edn., Phi Delta Kappa. Contbr. chpts. to books, articles to profl. jours. Home and Office: 5225 Troost Ave Kansas City MO 64110. *The only way for me to look at life is in the light of faith, which I consider one of God's greatest gifts. Life for me is an opportunity to serve God and as many of my neighbors as I can. I am basically an optimist. There is so much beauty around us, so many good people, so many marvels to behold—that I thank the Lord for giving me the ability to know and experience this life and to look forward to eternal life with God, the*

Source of all life. Any success I have had I attribute to taking advantage of the opportunities that God has put in my path.

WEISS, ROBERT JEROME, educator, psychiatrist; b. West New York, N.J., Dec. 9, 1917; s. Harry and Dora (Samuels) W.; student Johns Hopkins, 1937; A.B., George Washington U., 1947; M.D., Columbia, 1951; M.A. (hon.), Dartmouth, 1964; m. Minnie Thompson Moore, Apr. 21, 1945; children—Scott Tillman, James Woodrow, Elizabeth Thompson. Intern Columbia div. Bellevue Hosp., 1951, asst. resident medicine, 1953; resident psychiatry N.Y. Psychiat. Inst., 1954-56; asst. attending Vanderbilt Clinic, 1957-58, Presbyn. Hosp., N.Y.C., 1958-59; chief psychiatry Mary Hitchcock Meml. Hosp., 1959-70; career tchr. trainee Nat. Inst. Mental Health, 1956-58; tchr., research Columbia Coll. Phys. and Surg., 1956-59; prof. psychiatry, chmn. dept. Dartmouth Med. Sch., 1959-70; psychiatrist Beth Israel Hosp., 1970-75; attending physician Presbyn. Hosp., 1975—; vis. prof. community medicine Harvard Med. Sch., 1970-75, also asso. dir. Center for Community Health and Med. Care, 1970-75, asso. dean health care planning, 1970-75; prof. psychiatry and social medicine Columbia Coll. Phys. & Surg., 1975—, also dir. Centers for Community Health, 1975—; cons. N.H. Div. Mental Health, 1959-70, Nat. Center for Health Services Research, 1975—, NIMH, 1977—; cons. psychiatry Mass. Gen. Hosp., 1970-75; chmn. adv. commn. N.H. Dept. Health and Welfare, 1961-65; exec. com. N.H. Mental Health Planning Project, 1964-66; mem. adv. commn. Mental Health Constrn. for N.H. 1965-70; chmn. psychiatry tng. com. NIMH, 1967-68, mem. coordinating panel, 1965-67, ad hoc. com. interdisciplinary tng. program, 1966, mem. agenda com., 1966. Served to maj. AUS, 1941-46. Recipient Bi-Centennial medal Columbia Coll. Phys. and Surg., 1967 Fellow Am. Psychiat. Assn.; mem. N.Y. Soc. Clin. Psychiatry, N.Y. Psychiat. Inst. Alumni Assn. (pres. 1961), Acad. Psychoanalysis, Am. Assn. Med. Colls., AAAS, N.Y. Acad. Sci., N.Y. Acad. Medicine, Herman Biggs Soc., No. New Eng. Psychiat. Soc. (councillor 1969-75), Am. Assn. Chmn. Depts. Psychiatry (pres. 1969-70). Spl. research epidemiology, health care preventive psychiatry. Author articles, chpts. in books. Office: Columbia U Centers for Community Health 21 Audubon Ave New York NY 10032

WEISS, ROBERT ORR, educator; b. Kalamazoo, Apr. 8, 1926; s. Nicholas John and Ruth (Orr) W.; B.A., Albion (Mich.) Coll., 1948; M.A., Northwestern U., 1949, Ph.D., 1954; m. Ann Lenore Lawson, Sept. 16, 1951; children—Elizabeth Ann, John Lawson, James Robert, and Virginia Lenore. Began career as an instr. speech Wayne State U., 1949-51; instr. pub. speaking Northwestern U., 1954-55; mem. faculty DePauw U., 1955—, H.B. Gough prof. speech, 1965—, dir. forensics, head communication arts and scis., 1963-78. Served with AUS, 1945-46. Mem. Speech Communication Assn. (legislative assembly 1966-68), Am. Forensic Assn. (sec.-treas. 1958-59), AAUP (pres. DePauw U. chpt. 1961-62), Central States Speech Assn., Internat. Communication Assn., Phi Beta Kappa, Delta Sigma Rho-Tau Kappa Alpha (regional gov. 1975—), Theta Alpha Phi, Omicron Delta Kappa, Sigma Nu. Editor: Speaker and Gavel, 1968—; co-editor: Current Criticism, 1971. Home: 722 Highridge Ave Greencastle IN 46135

WEISS, ROBERT SAMUEL, ballet dancer; b. N.Y.C., Mar. 1, 1949; s. Jesse Lionel and Sally Ann (Kornfeld) W.; grad. Profl. Children's High Sch., N.Y.C., 1966; m. Kathleen Patricia Haigney, Mar. 10, 1972. Mem. N.Y.C. Ballet, 1966—, prin. dancer, 1977—; choreographer A Promise, Awakening, Leitmotif, Reminiscence, 1979, A Promise and Awakening for Am. Ballet-Theatre, Leitmotif for Ballet 20th Century Belgium; dir., prin. tchr. dance program N.Y. State Summer Sch. Arts, summers 1977-79; created prin. roles in ballets by George Ballanchine, Jerome Robbins; dancer White House for NATO conf., 1978. Nat. Endowment for Arts fellow, 1976. Home: 80 Central Park W New York City NY 10023 Office: NYC Ballet NY State Theatre Lincoln Center New York City NY 10023

WEISS, RUSSELL LEONARD, banker; b. Union City, N.J., Oct. 2, 1930; s. Russell L. and Alice (Bodie) W.; LL.B., St. John's U., 1956; m. Constance P. Pafundi, Sept, 11, 1954; children—Alice Lynn, Karen Ann. Admitted to N.Y. bar 1956; with Bank of Commerce, N.Y.C., 1949—, pres., chief exec. officer, dir., 1965—; dir. Bankers Security Life Ins. Soc., Internat. Intelligence, Inc., Twin Fair, Inc. Bd. dirs., treas. Catholic Big Bros. N.Y.; vice chmn. trustees Mercy Coll. Served to capt. USMCR, 1950-52. Home: 14 Paddington Rd Scarsdale NY 10583 Office: 56 E 42d St New York City NY 10017

WEISS, SAMSON RAPHAEL, clergyman, educator; b. Emden, Germany, Mar. 9, 1910; s. Aron and Judith (Schweiger) W.; student Breslau (Germany) U., 1928, Berlin (Germany) U., 1929, Zurich (Switzerland) U., 1933, Prague (Czechoslovakia) U., 1934, Yeshiva Mir, (Poland), 1934; Ph.D. summa cum laude, U. Dorpat (Estonia), 1938; m. Helene Carlebach, Dec. 27, 1936; children—Yetta (Mrs. Chaim Zelikowitz), Miriam (Mrs. Jonas J. Dissen), Israel Meyer, Devora (Mrs. Chaim Ezriel Kitevitz). Came to U.S., 1938, naturalized, 1944. Ordained rabbi, 1934; dean Hebrew dept. Jewish Tchrs. Coll., Wuerzburg, Germany, 1934-38; prof. codes Ner Israel Rabbinical Coll., Balt., 1938-40; dean Beth Yehuda Talmudical Acad., Detroit, 1940-44; co-founder, nat. dir. Torah Umesorah, Nat. Soc. Hebrew Day Schs., N.Y.C., 1944-45; founder, dean Young Israel Inst. Jewish Studies, N.Y.C., 1945-56; nat. dir. Nat. Council Young Israel, 1947-56; exec. v.p. Union Orthodox Jewish Congregations Am., N.Y.C., 1956-72; prof. of philosophy, chmn. dept. Judaic studies Touro Coll., N.Y.C., 1971—; founder, vis. dean Torah U., Los Angeles, 1961-62; lectr. Jewish Philosophy, Jewish history and contemporary Judaism, U.S., Can., Israel; exec. mem. Jerusalem Inst. for Talmudic Research; chmn. Am. Friends Mirrer Yeshiva in Jerusalem, Inst. Sci. and Malachah, Jerusalem. Recipient Schiller prize City of Breslau, 1928. Mem. Rabbinical Council Am. Contbr. articles, poetry Jewish mags. Home: 1362 E 3d St Brooklyn NY 11230 also 13 Even Hazel St Jerusalem Israel

WEISS, SAMUEL ABBA, educator; b. Rochester, N.Y., Oct. 20, 1922; s. Morris and Celia (Salzberg) W.; B.A., Bklyn. Coll., 1945; M.A., Columbia, 1946, Ph.D., 1953; m. Rana Schima, June 2, 1962. Asst. prof. Knoxville Coll., 1955-57; asst. prof. U. Ill., Chgo., 1957-62, asso. prof., 1962-66, prof. English, 1966—. Recipient Silver Circle awards for excellence in teaching, 1966, 67, U. Ill. Summer fellow, 1962. Mem. AAUP, Nat. Council Tchrs. English. Author: Drama in the Modern World, Vol. I, 1964, Vol. II, 1973; Drama in the Western World, 1968. Contbr. articles profl. jours. Home: 677 Wrightwood St Chicago IL 60614 Office: U Ill Chgo Circle Chicago IL 60680

WEISS, SEYMOUR, educator, ret. fgn. service officer; b. Chgo., May 15, 1925; s. Joseph and Rose (Sogolow) W.; B.A., U. Pa., 1945; M.A. in Internat. Relations, U. Chgo., 1949; m. Deane Griff, Apr. 24, 1949; children—Jay Sheridan, Eric Douglas, Gail Cynthia. Prin. examiner internat. programs Bur. Budget, Washington, 1949-52; dir. mil. assistance coordination Mut. Security Agy., Washington, 1952-55; dir. mil. assistance coordination Dept. State, 1955-60; dir. State Dept. combined policy office Polit. Mil. Affairs, 1960-67; assigned sr. seminar in fgn. policy, 1967-68; dir. Office Strategic Research and Intelligence, State Dept., 1968-69; sr. mem. secretary's planning and coordination staff, 1969-72; dep. dir. State Dept. policy planning staff, 1972-73; dir. State Dept. Bur. Politico-Mil. Affairs, 1973; ambassador to the Bahamas, 1974-76, ret., 1977; research prof. U. Miami Center for Advanced Internat. Studies, 1977—; cons., 1977—; pres. Sy Corp., Bethesda, Md.; v.p. Abington Corp., Washington. Served as officer USNR, 1943-46. Recipient Superior Honor award State Dept., 1965, Outstanding Performance award, 1968, 72, Distinguished Pub. Service medal Dept. Def., 1977. Home: 8905 Transue Dr Bethesda MD 20034 Office: 18th and K Sts NW Washington DC

WEISS, SHIRLEY F., urban and regional planner, economist; b. N.Y.C.; d. Max and Vera (Hendel) Friedlander; B.A., Douglass Coll., Rutgers U., 1942; postgrad. Johns Hopkins, 1948-50; M.Regional Planning, U. N.C., 1958; Ph.D., Duke U., 1973; m. Charles M. Weiss, June 7, 1942. Asso. research dir. Center for Urban and Regional Studies U. N.C., Chapel Hill, 1957—, lectr. planning, 1958-62, asso. prof., 1965-73, prof., 1973—, research asso. Inst. for Research in Social Scis., 1957-73, research prof., 1973—, mem. tech. com. Water Resources Research Inst., 1976—; mem. adv. com. on housing for 1980 census Dept. Commerce, 1976—; cons. Urban Inst., Washington, 1977—; mem. rev. panel Exptl. Housing Allowance Program, HUD, 1977—; Urban Land Inst. research fellow, Washington, 1978—. Fellow Urban Land Inst. (exec. group new communities and large-scale devel. council 1979—); mem. Am. Inst. Cert. Planners, Am. Planning Assn., Am. Econ. Assn., Southern Regional Sci. Assn. (pres. 1977-78), Regional Sci. Assn. (councillor 1971-74, v.p. 1976-77), Interamerican Planning Soc., Internat. Fedn. Housing and Planning, Town and Country Planning Assn. (Eng.), Econometric Soc., Econ. History Assn., Internat. New Towns Assn., History Econs. Soc., Am. Statis. Assn., Am. Real Estate and Urban Econs. Assn. (dir. 1978-80), Royal Econ. Soc. (Eng.), AAUP (chpt. pres. 1976-77, N.C. Conf. pres. 1978-79), Phi Beta Kappa. Author: The Central Business District in Transition, 1957; New Town Development in the United States; Experiment in Private Entrepreneurship, 1973; co-author: A Probabilistic Model for Residential Growth, 1964; Residential Developer Decisions: A Focused View of the Urban Growth Process, 1966; New Communities U.S.A., 1976; co-author, co-editor: Urban Growth Dynamics in a Regional Cluster of Cities, 1962; co-editor: New Community Development: Planning Process, Implementation and Emerging Social Concerns, vols. 1, 2, 1971; City Centers in Transition, 1976; New Communities Research Series, 1976-77; mem. editorial bd. Jour. Am. Inst. Planners, 1963-68, Rev. of Regional Studies, 1969-74, Internat. Regional Sci. Rev., 1975—. Home: 155 Hamilton Rd Chapel Hill NC 27514 Office: Dept City and Regional Planning 207 New East Bldg 033A Univ NC Chapel Hill NC 27514 also Center Urban Regional Studies Evergreen House 051A U NC Chapel Hill NC 27514

WEISS, STANLEY I., govt. adminstr.; b. N.Y.C., Oct. 27, 1925; s. Maurice H. and Malvina (Toffler) W.; B.AeE., Rennsselaer Poly. Inst., 1945, M.S., 1947; Ph.D., U. Ill., 1949; grad. Advanced Mgmt. Program, Harvard U., 1969; m. Catherin Jordan, Oct. 2, 1952; children—Ann Patricia, Audrey Jean, Janet Maura, Marion Gail. Instr., U. Ill., Akron U., 1947-53; supr., dynamics and design devel. engr. Goodyear Aircraft Corp., 1949-55; chief engr. aircraft products div. Kawneer Co., 1955-57; v.p. space systems div. Lockheed Missiles & Space Co., 1957-78; dep. asst. sec. resource applications Dept. Energy, Washington, 1978—; industry adv. San Jose State U. Cybernetic Systems Grad. Program, 1969-75; exec. in residence U. Santa Clara Sch. Bus., 1978-79; bd. dirs. Non-Ferrous Metals Research Council, 1975-78. Mem. statewide edn. com. Calif. C. of C., 1971-77. Served with USN, 1943-46. Fellow AIAA (asso.); mem. No. Calif. World Affairs Council, Sigma Xi, Pi Delta Epsilon. Contbr. articles profl. jours., also reviewer. Office: Fed Bldg 12th and Pennsylvania Ave NW Washington DC 20461

WEISS, STEPHEN JOEL, lawyer; b. N.Y.C., Sept. 12, 1938; s. Morris and Frances (Dinkin) W.; B.S., Queens Coll., 1959; LL.B., Cornell U., 1962; LL.M., Georgetown U., 1966; m. Madeline Adler, Aug. 12, 1962; children—Lowell Andrew, Valerie Elizabeth, Bradley Lawrence. Admitted to N.Y. bar, 1963, D.C. bar, 1966, U.S. Supreme Ct. bar, 1975; atty. SEC, Washington, 1962-65; asso. firm Arent, Fox, Kintner, Plotkin & Kahn, Washington, 1965-70, partner, 1971—; lectr. securities and corporate law Am. Law Inst., Am., Fed. bar assns., Practicing Law Inst., Bur. Nat. Affairs, Exec. Enterprises, Orgn. Mgmt., Inc., confs. Am. Land Devel. Assn. Mem. Am. (fed. regulation securities com. 1970—, chmn. Rule 10b-5 subcom. 1976-78, civil liabilities subcom. 1978—, chmn. ad hoc com. fgn. payments legislation 1976-77), Fed. (chmn. securities law com. 1968-70, chmn. council financing and taxation 1971-72, chmn. publs. bd. 1977-78, nat. council 1972—, Leadership commendation 1973, Distinguished Service award 1970), D.C. bar assns., Am. Law Inst., Cornell Law Club Washington (pres. 1971—). Contbr. articles on securities and corp. law to legal jours. Office: Arent Fox Kintner Plotkin & Kahn 1815 H St NW Washington DC 20006

WEISS, TED, Congressman; b. Hungary, Sept. 17, 1927; s. Joseph and Pearl (Weiss) W.; came to U.S., 1938, naturalized, 1953; B.A., Syracuse U., 1951, LL.B., 1952; children—Thomas D., Stephen R. Admitted to N.Y. bar, 1953; asst. dist. atty. for N.Y. county, 1955-59; mem. 95th-96th Congresses from 20th N.Y. Dist. Mem. N.Y. City Council, 1962-76; del. Dem. Nat. Conv., 1972, Dem. State Conv., 1962. Served with AUS, 1946-47. Mem. New Dem. Coalition, NAACP, N.Y. County Lawyers Assn., Am. Bar Assn., ACLU. Jewish. Office: 37 W 65th St New York NY 10023

WEISS, THEODORE RUSSELL, poet, editor; b. Reading, Pa., Dec. 16, 1916; s. Nathan and Mollie T. (Weinberg) W.; B.A., Muhlenberg Coll., 1938, Litt.D. (hon.), 1968; M.A., Columbia U., 1940, postgrad., 1940-41; Litt.D. (hon.), Bard Coll., 1973; m. Renée Karol, July 6, 1941. Instr. in English, U. Md., 1941, U. N.C., 1942-44, Yale U., 1944-46; prof. English, Bard Coll., 1946-68; vis. prof. poetry Mass. Inst. Tech., 1961-62; resident fellow creative writing Princeton U., 1966-67, prof. English and creative writing, 1968—, William and Annie S. Paton prof. ancient and modern lit., 1977—; Fannie Hurst prof. lit. Washington U., St. Louis, 1978; lectr. New Sch. Social Research, 1955-56, N.Y.C. YMHA, 1965-67; editor pub. Quar. Rev. Lit., 1943—; editor poetry series Princeton U. Press, 1974-78; mem. poetry bd. Wesleyan U. Press, 1964-70; juror in poetry for Bollingen Com., 1965; juror in poetry for Nat. Book Awards, 1967, 77. Recipient Wallace Stevens award, 1956; Ford fellow, 1953-54; hon. fellow Ezra Stiles Coll., Yale; grantee Nat. Found. Arts and Humanities, 1967-68; Ingram Merrill Found. fellow, 1974-75; Creative Arts award Brandeis U., 1977. Author: Selections from the Note-Books of G.M. Hopkins, 1945; The Breath of Clowns and Kings: Shakespeare's Early Comedies and Histories, 1971; (poems) The Catch, 1951, Outlanders, 1960, Gunsight, 1962, The Medium, 1965; The Last Day and the First, 1968, The World Before Us: Poems, 1950-70, 1970; Fireweeds, 1976; Views and Spectacles, Selected Poems, 1978; also articles and recordings. Home: 26 Haslet St Princeton NJ 08540

WEISS, THOMAS MICHAEL, psychologist, author, editor; b. Georgetown, Colo. Apr. 8, 1916; s. Michael Peter and Mary (Horn) W.; student Denver U., 1935-37; B.A., Mich. State U., 1949, M.A. with distinction, 1951, Ph.D. with distinction, 1954; postdoctoral studies Menninger Clinic, 1978, 79; postgrad. in psychiatry U. Pa., 1978. Meteorologist U.S. Weather Bur., 1938-48, climatologist, Colo., 1941-43; instr. natural sci. Mich. State U., East Lansing, 1953-54; guidance and counseling trainer Mich. Dept. Pub. Instrn. and Central Mich. State U., 1954-55; sr. psychologist Gen. Motors, 1955-56; prof. ednl. psychology, head dept. founds. Ariz. State U., 1956-68, dir. lab. and field expts., 1965-68; psychol. tng. specialist RAND Corp., 1957-58; dean Sch. Edn., Calif. State U., Long Beach, 1968-70; head curriculum and instrn. U. Wyo., 1970-80; editor ETC., rev. gen. semantics, 1970-77; staff affiliate Comelback Hosp., Phoenix, 1978—. Mem. Gov. Calif. Com. Ednl. Reform, 1969-70; mem. adv. bds. Wyo. Dept. Environ. Edn., 1970-71, cons. to Desert Center Unified Sch. Dist., 1964-70; summer dir. Am. studies U. Wyo. Inst., 1970-75; rep. to Am. Assn. Colls. Tchr. Edn., 1968—. Served as meteorologist USNR, 1941-42. Recipient certificate outstanding work Calif. Reform Commn., Gov. Cal., 1970; 1st Irving J. Lee award for outstanding research gen. semantics Internat. Soc. Gen. Semantics, 1968; Kenyon Internat. award, 1973; Outstanding Editor award, 1974; Outstanding Professorial award AMACO, 1975. Fellow AAAS, Am. Soc. Clin. Hypnosis; mem. Internat. Soc. Gen. Semantics (bd. dirs. 1965—), Inst. Gen. Sematics, Gen. Semantics Found., Am. Ednl. Research Assn., Am. Psychol. Assn. (div. psychotherapy, counseling and hypnosis), Nat. Assn. Research Sci. Teaching (nat. pub. relations dir. 1960-61, publicity dir. 1961-64), Ariz. Assn. Student Teaching (pres. 1967-68), AAUP, Nat., Wash. edn. assns., Am. Assn. Colls. Tchr. Edn. (instnl. rep. 1968—), N.Y. Acad. Scis., Fellows of Menninger Clinic (charter), Phi Kappa Phi, Kappa Delta Pi. Author: IS of Identity Test, rev. edit., 1971; (with others) Scientific Foundations of Education, 1964; Issues in Teaching, 1964; Psychological Foundation of Education, 1965; Education for Adaptation and Survival, 1975; also numerous articles. Home: 1117 Grand Ave Laramie WY 82070 also 8521 E MacKenzie Dr Scottsdale AZ 85251 Office: 7333 E Monterey Way Suite 12 Scottsdale AZ 85251

WEISS, WALTER STANLEY, lawyer; b. Newark, Mar. 12, 1929; s. Jack and Mollie (Orkin) W.; A.B., Rutgers U., 1949, J.D., 1952; m. Jacqueline Levit, Sept. 3, 1963; children—Jack Stephen, Andrew Scott. Admitted to N.J. bar, 1956, Calif. bar, 1961; trial atty. IRS, Phila., Los Angeles, 1957-62; asst. U.S. atty., chief tax div., Los Angeles, 1962-63; partner firm Goodson & Hannam, Los Angeles, 1963-67; mng. partner firm Long & Levit, Los Angeles, 1967-79; partner firm Greenberg & Glusker, Los Angeles, 1979—. Served to capt. JAGC, USAF, 1953-56. Named Arbitrator Nat. Assn. Securities Dealers, 1974; certified specialist in taxation law Calif. Bd. Legal Specialization. Mem. Am., Los Angeles County, Beverly Hills, Century City bar assns. Clubs: Rotary, Century City. Contbr. articles to legal jours. Home: 611 N Rodeo Dr Beverly Hills CA 90210 Office: Greenberg & Glusker 1900 Ave of Stars Suite 2000 Los Angeles CA 90067

WEISS, WILLIAM LEE, utility co. exec.; b. Big Run, Pa., May 21, 1929; s. Harry W. and Dorothy Jane (McKee) W.; B.S. in Indsl. Engring., Pa. State U., 1951; m. Josephine Elizabeth Berry, June 3, 1951; children—Susan Leigh, David William, Steven Paul. With Bell Telephone Co. of Pa., 1951, 1953-76, v.p. staff, Phila., 1973-74, v.p., gen. mgr. western area, 1974-76; v.p. ops. Wis. Telephone Co., Milw., 1976-78; pres. Ind. Bell Telephone Co., Indpls., 1978—, also dir.; dir. Am. Fletcher Nat. Bank, Indpls., Am. Fletcher Corp., Indpls., Ind. Telephone Assn. Bd. dirs. Ind. State C. of C., United Way of Greater Indpls., Ind. State Symphony Soc., Commn. for Downtown, Inc., Indpls., Crossroads Rehab. Center, Indpls.; bd. govs. Associated Colls. Inds.; chmn. Indpls. area U.S. Indsl. Payroll Savs. Bonds Com., 1979-80. Served with USAF, 1951-53. Mem. Indpls. C. of C. (dir.), Econ. Club Indpls. (dir.), Tau Beta Pi, Alpha Pi Mu, Sigma Tau. Methodist. Clubs: Meridian Hills Country, Columbia, Indpls. Athletic (Indpls.). Office: 240 N Meridian St Indianapolis IN 46204

WEISSBERGER, L. ARNOLD, lawyer; b. N.Y.C., Jan. 16, 1907; s. Harry Arnold and Anna (Lenson) W.; grad. Ethical Cultural Sch., 1923; A.B. magna cum laude, Harvard, 1927, LL.B. cum laude, 1930. Admitted to N.Y. State bar, 1930, since practiced in N.Y.C.; with firms Guggenheimer & Untermeyer, 1930-34, Riegelman, Hess & Hirsch, 1935-39; established own firm, 1939; partner Weissberger & Frosch, 1955-70, Weissberger & Harris, 1972—. Chmn. Friends Theatre and Music Collection, Mus. City N.Y., also trustee mus.; chmn. New Dramatists; v.p., bd. dirs. Bronx House, 1936-50; trustee, chmn. Martha Graham Dance Center Contemporary Dance; trustee Fountain House Found., Am. Inst. Music, John Golden Fund, Inc., Dance Notations Bur., Inc., Actor's Studio, Inc., 1969-72, Fedn. Jewish Philanthropic Socs., 1940-50, Harlem Eye and Ear Hosp., Jose Greco Found. Hispanic Dance, Inc.; adviser Bedside Network; pres. Theatre Hall of Fame, Inc. Served with AUS, 1942-43. Mem. Bar Assn. City N.Y., Phi Beta Kappa. Author: Famous Faces, 1973; also articles in profl. jours. Home: 45 Sutton Pl S New York NY 10022 Office: 120 E 56th St New York NY 10022

WEISSE, PETER DONALD, mfg. co. exec.; b. Winnipeg, Man., Can., Apr. 15, 1929; s. Harry Adam and Olive Mae (Beach) W.; came to U.S., 1930; naturalized, 1960; B.S.M.E., Purdue U., 1951; m. Elizabeth Louise Geurink, June 26, 1954; children—Katherine Elizabeth, James Peter, Patricia Ann, John Patrick, Thomas Robert. Various mktg. and sales positions Kaiser Aluminum & Chem. Corp., Oakland, Calif., Detroit and Hillside, N.J., 1951-66; v.p. mktg. and sales AMAX Aluminum Mill Products, Inc., Riverside, Calif., 1966-68, pres., 1968-71; v.p. mfg. group Cerro Corp., N.Y.C., 1971-75; vice chmn. dir. Internat. Indsl. Service Corp., Lima, Peru, 1974-75; pres. Englehard Industries, Murray Hill, N.J., 1975-76; co-venture with New Ct. Securities Corp., N.Y.C., 1975-79; chmn., chief exec. officer Rome Cable Corp. N.Y.), 1979—; dir. Tubes EuroLens, France; chmn. exec. com. Golconda Corp.; bd. dirs. Am. Bur. Metal Statistics, 1974-75. Bd. advisers Coll. Bus., San Bernardino State Coll., 1969-71. Served with U.S. Army, 1955-57. Mem. Copper Devel. Assn. (operating com. 1971-75, chmn. 1975). Clubs: Copper, Board Room, Econ. (N.Y.C.). Home: 77 Druid Hill Rd Summit NJ 07901 Office: Rome Cable Corp 421 Ridge St Rome NY 13440

WEISSENBERG, ALEXIS, pianist; b. Sofia, Bulgaria, July 26, 1929; student piano and composition with Wladigueroff, also with Olga Samaroff at Julliard Sch. Music. Numerous appearance throughout Europe, S.Am., U.S., Japan; Am. debut with N.Y. Philharmonic; soloist with Berlin, Vienna, Japan, Czech philharmonics, Phila., Cleve., Minn., Royal Danish, Salzburg Festival, Boston orchs., Chgo., Pitts. symphonies, Orchestre de Paris, others; rec. artist RCA, Angel. Recipient 1st prize Internat. Leventritt competition and Phila. Youth competition, 1946. Address: care Columbia Artists Mgmt Inc 165 W 57th St New York NY 10019*

WEISSERT, MARTIN ARTHUR, lawyer; b. South Bend, Ind., Nov. 15, 1933; s. Charles Daniel and Dolly Mabel (Schlosser) W.; B.S. with honors, Ind. U., 1955, LL.B. with honors, 1959; m. Shirley Ann Ferguson, Aug. 15, 1954; children—Teresa Ann, Andrew Martin. Admitted to Ind. bar, 1959; with firm Stevens & Wampler, Plymouth, Ind., 1959-60; with N.Am. Van Lines, Ft. Wayne, Ind., 1960—, v.p., sec., gen. counsel, dir., 1970—. Bd. dirs., v.p. Ft. Wayne United Way. Served with USAF, 1955-57. Edwards fellow, 1958-59. Mem. Am., Ind. bar assns., Motor Carrier Lawyers Assn. Lutheran. Club: Ft. Wayne Country. Home: 5416 Exeter Dr Fort Wayne IN 46815 Office: care North Am Van Lines PO Box 988 Fort Wayne IN 46801

WEISSKOPF, BERNARD, pediatrician, child behavior and devel. specialist, educator; b. Berlin, Dec. 11, 1929; s. Benjamin and Bertha (Loew) W.; came to U.S., 1939, naturalized, 1944; B.A., Syracuse U., 1951; M.D., U. Leiden (Netherlands), 1958; m. Penelope Allderdice, Dec. 26, 1965; children—Matthew David, Stephen Daniel. Intern, Meadowbrook Hosp., East Meadow, N.Y., 1958-59, resident, 1959-60; resident Johns Hopkins Hosp., Balt., 1962-64; fellow child psychiatry Johns Hopkins U. Sch. Medicine, Balt., 1962-64; asst. prof. pediatrics U. Ill. Coll. Medicine, Chgo., 1964-66; faculty U. Louisville, 1966—, prof. pediatrics, 1970—, dir. Child Evaluation Center, 1966—, project dir. Nat. Found.-March of Dimes Birth Defect Center, 1966—. Trustee Jewish Hosp., Louisville, 1974-77. Served to capt. USAF, 1960-62. Fellow Am. Acad. Pediatrics, Am. Assn. Mental Deficiency; mem. Am. Soc. Human Genetics, So. Soc. Pediatric Research. Contbr. articles to profl. jours. Home: 6409 Deep Creek Dr Prospect KY 40059 Office: Child Evaluation Center 334 E Broadway Louisville KY 40202

WEISSKOPF, VICTOR FREDERICK, physicist; b. Vienna, Austria, Sept. 19, 1908; s. Emil and Martha (Gut) W.; Ph.D., U. Goettingen (Germany), 1931; m. Ellen Tvede, Sept. 5, 1934; children—Thomas Emil, Karen Louise; came to U.S., 1937, naturalized, 1942. Research asso. U. Copenhagen (Denmark), 1932-34, Inst. of Tech., Zürich, Switzerland, 1934-37; asst. prof. physics U. Rochester (N.Y.), 1937-43; with Manhattan Project, Los Alamos, N.M., 1943-46; prof. physics Mass. Inst. Tech., 1946-60; dir. gen. European Orgn. for Nuclear Research, Geneva, Switzerland, 1961-65; Inst. prof. Mass. Inst. Tech., 1965—; chmn. high energy physics adv. panel AEC, 1967-73. Recipient Max Planck medal (Germany), 1956, Hi Majorana award, 1970, G. Gamov award, 1971, Boris Pregel award, 1971, Prix Mondial Cino del Duca (France) 1972, L. Boltzmann prize (Austria), 1977. Fellow Am. Phys. Soc. (pres. 1960); mem. Nat. Acad. Scis., Am. Acad. Arts and Scis. (pres. 1975-79), French Academie des Scis. (corr.), Austrian (corr.), Danish (corr.), Bavarian (corr.), Scottish (corr.), Soviet (corr.), Pontifical acads. scis. Author: (with J. Blatt) Theoretical Nuclear Physics, 1952; Knowledge and Wonder, 1962; Physics in the Twentieth Century, 1972. Author articles on nuclear physics, quantum theory, radiation theory, etc. in science jours. Home: 36 Arlington St Cambridge MA 02140

WEISSLER, ARNOLD MERVIN, internist, educator; b. Bklyn., May 13, 1927; s. Solomon F. and Dora (Hocheiser) W.; B.A., N.Y. U., 1948; M.D., SUNY, Bklyn., 1953; m. Gloria Diane Lazarus, June 22, 1952; children—Suzanne Robin, Mark Douglas, Leslie Ann, Jonathan Scott. Intern, Maimonides Hosp., Bklyn., 1953-54; jr. asst. resident Duke Hosp., Durham, N.C., 1954-55, Am. Heart Assn. research fellow, 1955-57, sr. asst. resident, 1957-58, chief resident, 1958-59; chief cardiovascular sect. Durham VA Hosp., 1959-60; asst. prof. medicine U. Tex., Galveston, 1960-61; asst. prof. medicine Ohio State U., Columbus, 1961-63, asso. prof., 1963-67, prof., 1967-71, Gustav Hirsch Meml. prof., 1969-71; prof., chmn. dept. medicine Wayne State U. Sch. Medicine, Detroit, 1971—; chief dept. medicine Harper Hosp., Detroit, 1971—. Served with USNR, 1944-45. Recipient Dudley Meml. medal in surgery; USPHS research career awardee, 1961-68; diplomate Am. Bd. Internal Medicine (chmn. cardiovascular disease subsplty. exam. bd. 1975—). Fellow A.C.P., Am. Coll. Chest Physicians, Am. Clin. and Climatologic Assn., Am. Coll. Cardiology (gov. Mich. sect., chmn. sci. program 1980); mem. Am. Heart Assn. (chmn. council clin. cardiology), Assn. Profs. Medicine, AAUP, Assn. Am. Physicians, Am. Soc. Clin. Investigation, Assn. Univ. Cardiologists, Detroit Heart Club, Central Soc. Clin. Research, AAAS, Am. Soc. Pharmacology and Exptl. Therapeutics, So. Soc. Clin. Investigation, Phi Beta Kappa, Sigma Xi, Alpha Omega Alpha. Author: (with B.H. Marks) Basic and Clinic Pharmacology of Digitalis, 1971; Noninvasive Cardiology, 1974; editor-in-chief Am. Jour. Med. Scis., 1967-70; mem. editorial bd. Am. Jour. Cardiology, Am. Jour. Med. Circulation, Coeur et Med. Interne; contbr. numerous articles to med. jours. Home: 999 Glengarry Circle Birmingham MI 48010 Office: 3990 John R St Detroit MI 48201

WEISSLER, GERHARD LUDWIG, physicist, educator; b. Eilenburg, Germany, Feb. 20, 1918; s. Otto and Margaret (Wendt) W.; B.S., Tech. U., Berlin, Germany, 1938; M.A., U. Calif. at Berkeley, 1941, Ph.D., 1942; m. Claire Markoff, August 15, 1953; children—Roderick A., Robt. E., Mark (dec.). Came to U.S., 1939, naturalized, 1944. Instr. radiol. physics med. center U. Calif., San Francisco, 1942-44; asst. prof. physics U. So. Calif., 1944-48, asso. prof., 1948-52, head dept. physics, 1951-56, prof., 1952—; cons. radiation physics. Certified x-ray, radium physicist Am. Bd. Radiology. Fellow Am. Phys. Soc. (chmn. div. electron physics 1964), Optical Soc. Am.; mem. AAUP, Sigma Xi. Contbr. articles to sci. jours. Home: Encino CA 91436

WEISSMAN, ARTHUR, med. care adminstr.; b. N.Y.C., Mar. 26, 1913; s. Edward and Ray (Greenfield) W.; B.A., Coll. City N.Y., 1934; postgrad. in psychology Columbia, 1935; J.D., George Washington U., 1941; m. Louise Kay, Sept. 14, 1945; children—Ronald, David. Med. care and pub. health adminstrn. and research USPHS, 1937-41, 46-50; admitted to D.C. bar, 1938, Korean bar, 1946; research project dir. Calif. Dept. Pub. Health, 1950-53; dir. med. econs. Kaiser Found. Health Plan, Oakland, Calif., 1953-78, cons., 1978—, sr. v.p. Kaiser Found. Health Plan and Kaiser Found. Hosps., 1971-78, bd. dirs., 1972—; mem. nat. adv. council Leonard Davis Inst. Health Econs., Wharton Sch. Finance, U. Pa., 1967—; panel advisers Nat. Center Health Statistics, HEW, 1969—; mem. State of Calif. Adv. Com. on Health and Med. Care Services, 1977—; mem. tech. cons. panel on statis. systems for nat. health ins. U.S. Nat. Com. on Vital and Health Statistics, 1977—. Trustee Kaiser Community Health Found., Cleve., 1969-78; bd. dirs. Kaiser Found. Health Plan Colo., Denver, 1969—, of Oreg., 1972—, of Ohio, 1978—, Kaiser-Permanente Adv. Service, 1977—. Served from pvt. Q.M.C. to capt. Med. Adminstrv. Corps, AUS, 1942-46. Fellow Am. Pub. Health Assn. Editorial cons. Jour. Med. Care, 1968—; mem. editorial panel Milbank Meml. Fund quar. Health and Society, 1977—. Contbr. articles on med. care adminstrn., statistics and research pub. in med. and pub. health jours. Home: 130 Gellert Dr San Francisco CA 94132 Office: Ordway Bldg One Kaiser Plaza Oakland CA 94612

WEISSMAN, GEORGE, tobacco co. exec.; b. N.Y.C., July 12, 1919; s. Samuel and Rose (Goldberg) W.; student Townsend Harris Prep. Sch., 1933-35; B.B.A., City Coll. N.Y., 1939; postgrad. N.Y.U., U. Ill., 1942; m. Mildred Stregack, June 4, 1944; children—Paul Jonathan, Ellen Victoria, Daniel Mark. Editor, Raritan Valley News, also reporter Newark Star Ledger, Newark Sunday Call, 1939-41; publicist Brit. Am. Ambulance Corps, 1941-42; publicity and advt. Samuel Goldwyn Prodns., N.Y.C., 1946-48; pub. relations account exec. Benjamin Sonnenberg, N.Y.C., 1948-52; asst. to pres. Philip Morris, Inc., N.Y.C., 1952, v.p. 1953-59, dir. marketing, 1957-60, exec. v.p., 1959-66, pres., chief operating officer, 1967-73, vice chmn., 1973-78, chmn. bd., 1978—, dir., 1958—, mem. exec. com., 1964—; chmn. bd., chief exec. officer Philip Morris Internat., 1960-66; dir. Avnet, Inc., Harlem Savs. Bank, Chem. N.Y. Corp. Mem. Bus. Com. for Arts; bd. visitors City Coll. N.Y.; chancellor's adv. com. CUNY; bd. dirs. Bus. Mktg. Corp. for N.Y.C., Lincoln Center Film Soc., dirs., exec. com. Lincoln Center; trustee Lincoln Center Fund, Baruch Coll. Fund, Swarthmore Council, Whitney Mus. Am. Art, Com. Econ. Devel. Served with USNR, 1942-46; comdg. officer subchaser U.S.S. SC 497, exec. officer U.S.S. Horace A. Bass, APD 124. Decorated comdr. Order of Merit (Italy); recipient Exec. of Year award Nat. Assn. Tobacco Distbrs., 1954; award Fedn. Jewish Philanthropies, 1963. Mem. City Coll. N.Y. Alumni Assn. (recipient Townsend Harris medal 1968, medallion 1973), Beta Gamma Sigma. Office: 100 Park Ave New York NY 10017

WEISSMAN, HERMAN BENJAMIN, educator; b. Chgo., May 16, 1920; s. Benjamin Herman and Esther (Siegel) W.; S.B., U. Chgo., 1951; M.S., Ill. Inst. Tech., 1954, Ph.D. in Physics, 1959; m. Marjorie Eads, Dec. 17, 1945; 1 dau., Aerlyn M. Instr., Chgo. Jr. Coll., 1952-54; asst. prof. Elmhurst (Ill.) Coll., 1954-56; prof. physics U. Ill. at Circle Campus, Chgo., 1956—; sr. research scientist Bell & Howell Corp., Charles Bruning Co. Served with AUS, 1943-46. Mem. Am. Assn. Physics Tchrs., Chgo. Art Inst. (life), Field Museum (life), Sigma Xi. Home: 5438 N Wayne Ave Chicago IL 60640

WEISSMAN, JACOB IRA, educator; b. Detroit, Dec. 14, 1913; s. Samuel and Ida (Goldberg) W.; A.B., U. Mich., 1935, J.D., 1936; Ph.D., U. Calif., Berkeley, 1956; 1 son, Stephen. Gen. mgr., N.Y. Bed Spring Co., Detroit, 1937-47; instr. econs. Columbia, 1950-56; research asso. in law and econs. Law Sch., U. Chgo., 1956-58, asso. prof. Grad. Sch. Bus., 1958-63; prof. econs., chmn. econs. dept. Hofstra U., Hempstead, N.Y., 1963—. Bd. dirs. Jewish Community Center, Jewish Social Service Bur. Mem. Am. Econ. Assn., State Bar Mich., Order of Coif, Phi Beta Kappa, Phi Kappa Phi. Author: Law in a Business Society, 1964. Office: Dept Econs Hofstra U Hempstead NY 11550

WEISSMAN, MARVIN, ambassador; b. Cleve., Jan. 25, 1927; s. Joseph and Sarah (Keller) W.; Ph.B., U. Chgo., 1948; M.P.A., Maxwell Grad. Sch., Syracuse U., 1953; grad. student U. Copenhagen (Denmark), 1952-53; m. Maria Elena Sundt, Mar. 28, 1958; children—Warren, Diane, Karen. Examiner, Bur. Budget, Washington, 1950-54 pub. adminstrn. adviser ICA, Dept. of State Mission to Govt. Chile, 1954-56; adminstrv. cons. charge govtl. reorgn. activities Klein and Saks Econ. and Financial Mission to Chile, 1956-58, chief Klein and Saks Mission, reorgn. study Ministry of Health and Social Assistance, Govt. of Venzuela, 1958; chief pub. adminstrn. div. ICA, Dept. of State Mission to Ecuador, 1958-61; regional pub. adminstrn. advisor for Latin Am., 1961-62; dir. office instnl. devel. Alliance for Progress, Dept. State, 1962-63; dir. U.S. AID Mission to Guatemala, 1963-67; dir. U.S. AID Mission to Colombia, 1967-73, to Brazil, 1973-75; dir. Office Central Am. Affairs, Dept. State, 1975-77; ambassador to Costa Rica, 1977—; dir. ICA First Latin American Regional Conf. Adminstrv. Mgmt., 1958; cons. Peruvian Finance Minstry on budgetary adminstrn., 1959. Prof. pub. adminstrn. Cath. U. of Chile, 1955-58; prof. principles and techniques of pub. adminstrn. U. Chile, 1955-58; prof. adminstrv. mgmt. Central U., Ecuador, 1959-60. Served AUS, 1945-46. Fulbright scholar, 1952-53; William A. Jump award, 1961; ICA meritorious service award, 1961; Distinguished Honor award AID, 1973, Distinguished Career Service award, 1977. Address: Am Embassy San Jose Costa Rica

WEISSMAN, MICHAEL LEWIS, lawyer; b. Chgo., Sept. 11, 1934; s. Maurice and Sue (Goldberg) W.; student (White scholar) U. Chgo., 1951-52; B.S. in Econs., Northwestern U., 1954; M.B.A. in Accounting, Wharton Sch. of U. Pa., 1956; J.D., Harvard, 1958; postgrad. (Fulbright scholar), U. Sydney (Australia), 1958-59; m. Joanne Sherwin, Dec. 19, 1961; children—Mark Douglas, Greg Steven, Scott Adam, Brett Anthony. Admitted to D.C. bar, 1958, Ill. bar, 1959; asst. prof. bus. law Roosevelt U., Chgo., 1959-61; practice in Chgo., 1959—; mem. firm Aaron, Aaron, Schimberg & Hess, 1969-78; sr. partner firm Boorstein & Weissman, 1978—. Cons. editor McGraw-Hill Pub. Co., 1970—. Mem. Am., Ill., Chgo. bar assns., Harvard Law Soc. Ill. (gov.), Beta Alpha Psi. Contbr. articles to profl. jours. Home: 2067 Old Briar Rd Highland Park IL 60035 Office: 33 N Dearborn St Chicago IL 60602

WEISSMAN, NORMAN, public relations co. exec.; b. Newark, Apr. 12, 1925; s. Julius and Lenora (Schimmel) W.; B.A. in English, Rutgers U., 1949; M.A. in Journalism, U. Wis., 1951; m. Sheila Holtz, Dec. 12, 1950 (div. Dec. 1973); 1 son, Lee. Asst. editor McGraw Hill Pub. Co., Inc., 1951-54; sec. to dept. Dept. Air Pollution Control, N.Y.C., 1954-56; account exec. Ruder & Finn, N.Y.C., 1956-59, v.p., 1959-62, sr. v.p., 1962-68, pres., 1968—. Served with USN, 1943-46. Mem. Phi Beta Kappa, Sigma Delta Chi. Home: 162 E 93d St New York NY 10028 Office: 110 E 59th St New York NY 10022

WEISSTEIN, ULRICH WERNER, educator; b. Breslau, Germany, Nov. 14, 1925; s. Rudolf and Berta (Wende) W.; came to U.S., 1950, naturalized, 1959; student Goethe-Universitat, Frankfurt, 1947-50, 51-52, U. Iowa, 1950-51; M.A., Ind. U., 1953, Ph.D., 1954; m. Judith Schroeder, May 9, 1964; children—Cristina, Cecily, Eric Wolfgang, Anton Edward. Instr., Lehigh U., Bethlehem, Pa., 1954-58, asst. prof., 1958; asst. prof. English and comparative lit. Ind. U., Bloomington, 1959-62, asso. prof., 1962-66, prof., 1966—, prof. German and comparative lit., 1966—; vis. prof. U. Wis., summer 1966, Middlebury Sch. German, summer 1970, U. Hamburg (Ger.), spring 1971, U. Vienna, 1976, Stanford U., 1979; external examiner comparative lit. U. Hong Kong, 1974-76. MLA grantee, 1958-59; Guggenheim fellow, 1974-75. Mem. MLA, Am. Assn. Tchrs. German, Am., Internat. comparative lit. assns., Internat. Brecht Soc. Author: Heinrich Mann, 1962; The Essence of Opera, 1964, Max Frisch, 1967; Einführung in die Vergleichende Literaturwissenschaft, 1968 (English version: Comparative Literature and Literary Theory, 1973); editor: German sect. Twayne World Authors series, 1964—, Yearbook of Comparative and General Literature, 1960—, Brecht-Jahrbuch, 1970—, Expressionism as an International Literary Phenomenon, 1973; co-editor: Texte und Kontexte: Festschrift für Norbert Fuerst, 1973; translator: The Grotesque in Art and Literature (W. Kayser), 1963. Home: 2204 Queens Way Bloomington IN 47401

WEISZ, PAUL B(URG), scientist; b. Pilsen, Czechoslovakia, July 2, 1919; s. Alexander and Amalia (Sulc) W.; naturalized, 1946; student Tech. U. Berlin, 1938-39; B.S., Auburn U., 1940; Sc.D., Swiss Fed. Inst. Tech., Zurich, 1965; m. Rhoda A.M. Burg, Sept. 4, 1943; children—Ingrid B., P. Randall. Research physicist Bartol Research Found., Swarthmore, Pa., 1940-46, Mobil Oil Corp. (formerly Socony Mobil Oil Corp.), 1958-61, sr. scientist, 1961-69, mgr. process research sect., 1967-69, mgr. Central Research div. Mobil Research & Devel. Corp., Princeton, N.J., 1969—; vis. prof. Princeton U., 1974-76, mem. adv. council dept. chem. engring., 1973-78, mem. adv. and resource council Sch. Engring., 1974—. Recipient ann. award Catalysis Club Phila., 1973. Fellow Am. Phys. Soc., Am. Inst. Chemists (Chem. Pioneer award 1974); mem. Am. Chem. Soc. (sci. award South Jersey sect. 1963, E.V. Murphree award 1972, Leo Friend award 1977), Am. Inst. Chem. Engrs. (R.H. Wilhelm award 1978), Bunsen Soc. Germany, Chem. Soc. U.K., N.Y. Acad. Scis., Nat. Acad. Engring., Assn. Research Dirs. N.Y. Quaker. Club: Nassau (Princeton). Editor: Advances in Catalysis, 1956—; editorial bd. Jour. Catalysis, 1962—, Chem. Engring. Communications, 1972-78. Contbr. articles to sci. jours. Holder 69 U.S. patents. Office: Mobil Research and Devel Corp PO Box 1025 Princeton NJ 08540

WEISZ, WILLIAM JULIUS, electronics co. exec.; b. Chgo., Jan. 8, 1927; B.S. in Elec. Engring., Mass. Inst. Tech., 1948; m. Barbara Becker, Dec. 25, 1947; children—George, Terri, David. With Motorola, Inc., Chgo., 1948—, exec. v.p., 1969-70, pres., 1970—, chief operating officer, 1972—, also dir.; pres. Motorola Communications Internat., 1966-69. Motorola Communications and Electronics, Inc., 1966-69; dir. Motorola Israel. Mem. exec. com. land mobile adv. com. to FCC. Com. chmn. Cub Scout pack Evanston council Boy Scouts Am., 1960-62. Trustee Mass. Inst. Tech., also mem. elec. engring. and computer scis. com., mem. Sloan Sch. vis. com.; mem. devel. com. MIT Corp., 1970—. Served with USNR, 1945-46. Recipient award of merit Nat. Electronics Conf. Fellow I.E.E.E. (past nat. chmn. vehicular communications group); mem. Electronic Industries Assn. (chmn., bd. govs. 1978, past chmn. indsl. elec. div.), Econ. Club Chgo., Sigma Xi, Tau Beta Pi, Eta Kappa Nu, Pi Lambda Phi. Club: Mass. Inst. Tech. (bd. dirs.) (Chgo.).

WEITHORN, STANLEY STEPHEN, lawyer; b. N.Y.C., Aug. 28, 1924; s. Louis W. and Florence O. (Mandel) W.; B.S. in Bus. Adminstrn., Hofstra U., Hempstead, N.Y., 1947; J.D., N.Y. U., 1954, LL.M. in Taxation, 1956; m. Corinne J. Breslow, Dec. 26, 1949; children—Lois Ann, Michael J. Admitted to N.Y. bar, 1955; asso. firm Olwine, Connelly, Chase O'Donnell & Weyher, N.Y.C., 1956-61; partner firm Lewis, McDonald & Varian, N.Y.C., 1961-62; individual practice law, N.Y.C., 1962-63, 67-68; partner firm Wormser, Koch, Keily & Alessandroni, N.Y.C., 1963-66; sr. partner firm Baer Marks & Upham successor to Upham, Meeker & Weithorn, N.Y.C., 1968—. Spl. prof. law Hofstra U., Hempstead, N.Y., 1975—; adj. prof. law U. Miami (Fla.), 1975—, mem. adv. com. Law Center Inst. Estate Planning, 1974—; coordinator fed. budget and tax policy course nat. policy studies program New Sch. Social Research, N.Y.C., 1975, mem. fund raising mgmt. adv. com. Grad. Sch. Mgmt. and Urban professions, New Sch. for Social Research, N.Y.C., 1977—; program chmn. Practising Law Inst. confs. N.Y.C., 1962—; tax cons. Pres's. Council on Environ. Quality, 1970; lectr. fed. taxation to univ. insts., nat. social welfare confs., profl. bus. meetings. Mem. com. tax policy Nat. Assembly Vol. Health, Social Welfare Orgns. Inc., N.Y.C., 1961-73; mem. com. bequests and legacies Nat. Jewish Hosp., Denver, 1965-78, A.R.C. of Greater N.Y., 1970-78; mem. leadership council United Jewish Appeal, N.Y.C., 1966-70; mem. legacy adv. council Am. Jewish Congress, N.Y.C., 1968-72. Co-chmn. Port Washington-Manhasset (N.Y.) unit New Democratic Coalition, 1968-69; tax adviser nat. finance com. McGovern for Pres., 1971-72, mem. N.Y. finance com., 1971-72. Bd. dirs., exec. com. Equal Employment Council Inc., N.Y.C., 1968-71; bd. dirs., sec. New Priorities Edn. Fund, N.Y.C., 1969-70; bd. dirs., exec. com., sec. Fund for New Priorities in Am., 1969—; bd. dirs., treas. Cow Bay Manpower Devel. Corp., Port Washington, 1969-71; bd. dirs., chmn. exec. com., pres. L.I. (N.Y.) Pub. Affairs Council, 1973-78; legacy com. United Cerebral Palsy, N.Y.C., 1975—; bd. dirs. Community Action for Legal Services, N.Y.C., 1976-78; trustee Florence Weithorn Warner Found., N.Y.C., 1967-72; bd. dirs. N.Y. Fedn. Reform Synagogues, 1973-78; mem. Emergency Task Force on Juvenile Delinquency Prevention, 1976—; adv. panel N.Y. chpt. Am. Jewish Com., 1978—; com. on deferred giving Fedn. Jewish Philanthropies N.Y., 1978—. Served with AUS, 1943-46; ETO. Mem. Am. (chmn. subcom. exempt orgns., 1965-69, 71—), N.Y. State (exec. com. 1967-69) bar assns., Assn. Bar City N.Y., Internat. Acad. Estate and Trust Law (exec. council 1974-78), Uptown Tax Discussion Group, Exempt Orgns. Discussion Group (chmn. 1973—), Tax Analysts and Advs. (legal activities policy bd. 1974—), Fresh Meadows Civic Assn. (chmn. 1961-63). Jewish religion (trustee synagogue 1970-74). Club: University (N.Y.C.). Author: Penalty Taxes on Accumulated Earnings and Personal Holding Companies, 1963; Tax Techniques for Foundations and Other Exempt Organizations, 7 vols., 1964; The Accumulated Earnings Tax, 1966. Contbg. editor, mem. adv. bd. Tax Mgmt., 1959-68; feature columnist Nat. Law Jour. Contbr. articles to profl. jours. Home: 144 Woodhill Ln Manhasset NY 11030 Office: 299 Park Ave New York NY 10017

WEITZ, JOHN, fashion designer; b. Berlin, May 25, 1923; s. Robert and Hedy (Jacob) W.; came to U.S., 1940, naturalized, 1943; student Hall Sch., London, 1936, St. Paul's Sch., London, 1936-39; certificate Oxford-Cambridge Sch., 1938; m. Susan Kohner, Aug. 31, 1964; children—Paul John, Christopher John; children by previous marriage—Karen Weitz Curtis, Robert. Designer various cos. until 1954; founder John Weitz Designs, Inc., N.Y.C., 1954—. Served with AUS, 1943-46; ETO. Recipient Sports Illustrated award, 1959, NBC Today award, 1960, Caswell Massey awards, 1963-66, Harpers Bazaar medallion, 1966, Moscow diploma, 1967, Coty award, 1974; named to Internat. Best Dressed List Hall of Fame, 1971. Clubs: Sag Harbor Yacht; East Hampton Yacht; Beach (Palm Beach); Old Pauline (London). Author: Value of Nothing (Best Seller list), 1970; Man in Charge (Best Seller list), 1974. Office: 600 Madison Ave New York NY 10022. *Since my work is done all over the world, I hope to reflect well on my country and myself.*

WEITZEL, EDWIN ANTHONY, newspaper columnist; b. Pitts., Nov. 3, 1905; s. John Howard and Mary Margaret (McGough) W.; student Western Res. U., 1924-28, Cleve. Coll., 1928-29; m. Carmen Whitney Sherman, Aug. 11, 1961; children—Bruce Anthony, Peter Andre, Jon Philip, Jerome Charles (by previous marriage). Reporter, Cleve. News, 1929-32; columnist Scripps-Howard Newspapers, 1932-38, Knight Newspapers, Detroit Free Press, Chgo. Daily News, 1938—, Field Enterprises, Chgo. Daily News, 1958—; travel editor Chgo. Daily News, 1965-71, travel columnist, 1971—; commentator sta. WJR, Detroit, 1941-45, sta. WWJ, Detroit, 1945-48, sta. WBBM, Chgo., 1949-65, sta. WWJ-TV, 1945-48, sta. WMAQ-TV, Chgo., 1951-61, sta. WGN-TV, Chgo., 1961-63; pub. relations dir. U.S. Home, 1971-73. Mem. adv. bd. St. Joseph's Hosp. Mem. Am. Soc. Travel Writers, Navy League, Sigma Delta Chi. Clubs: Marco Country, Marco Island Yacht, Marco Rotary. Author: Chicago, I Will. Home: 848 Fairlawn Ct Circle Marco Island FL 33937 Office: Naples Daily News Naples FL 33940

WEITZEL, JOHN PATTERSON, lawyer; b. Pitts., Aug. 24, 1923; s. Albert Philip and Elizabeth (Patterson) W.; student Deerfield (Mass.) Acad., 1937-40; A.B., Yale, 1946; LL.B., Harvard, 1949; m. Elizabeth Swan, Mar. 20, 1965; children—Mary Middleton, Paul Patterson. Admitted to Mass. bar, 1949; asso. firm Herrick, Smith, Donald, Farley & Ketchum (now Herrick & Smith), Boston, 1949-53, partner, 1961—; spl. asst. to asst. sec. treasury, 1953-55, asst. to under sec. treas, 1955-56, asst. gen. counsel Treasury Dept., 1956-59, dep. to sec. treasury, 1959-60, asst. sec. treasury, 1960-61; U.S. exec. dir. IBRD, 1960-61; dir. Incoterm Corp. Mem. Nat. Security Council Planning Bd., 1959-61; cons. to sec. def., 1973—. Mem. Mass. Council Arts and Humanities, 1966-71. Overseer, dir. sec. Boys Clubs Boston; mem. corp. Mass. Gen. Hosp. Served with USAAF, 1943-45. Mem. Am., Boston bar assns. Clubs: Harvard, Union Boat (Boston). Home: 45 Devon Rd Brookline MA 02167 Office: 100 Federal St Boston MA 02110

WEITZMAN, ELLIOT DAVID, neurologist; b. Newark, Feb. 4, 1929; B.A. cum laude, U. Iowa, 1950; M.D., U. Chgo., 1955. Intern, Kings County Hosp., Bklyn., 1955-56; resident in neurology Presbyn. Hosp., N.Y.C., 1956-58; asst. in neurology Columbia U., 1958-59; asso. in neurology Albert Einstein Coll. Medicine, N.Y.C., 1961-63, asst. prof. neurology, 1963-68, asso. prof., 1968-69, prof., 1969—; chief dept. neurology Montefiore Hosp. and Med. Center, 1969—; chmn. dept. neurology Montefiore div. Albert Einstein Coll. Medicine, 1971—, prof. neurosci., 1974; vis. prof. neurology and psychiatry Stanford (Calif.) U. Sch. Medicine, 1974-75. Adv. bd. Am. Naval Com., 1975, Brain Info. Service, 1977—. Served with M.C., U.S. Army, 1959-61. USPHS grantee, 1969; NASA grantee, 1968; Office Naval Research grantee, 1976-77. Mem. Am. Neurol. Assn., Am. Assn. Univ. Profs. Neurology, Am. Acad. Neurology, Soc. Neurosci., AAAS, Assn. Research in Nervous and Mental Diseases, N.Y. Acad. Sci., Assn. Psychophysiol. Study of Sleep (exec. council 1964-69), N.Y. Neurol. Soc. (pres. 1972-73), Internat. Soc. Chronobiology, Nat. Found. Sudden Infant Death, Assn. Sleep Disorders Clinics (v.p. 1975), Pan Am. Med. Assn. (chmn. N.Am. sect. on neurology). Editorial bd. Jour. Sleep, 1978—. Contbr. articles to med. jours. Home: 2 Verdun Ave New Rochelle NY 10804 Office: 111 E 210th St New York NY 10467

WEITZMANN, KURT, archaeologist, educator; b. Klein Almerode, Germany, Mar. 7, 1904; s. Wilhelm and Antonie (Keiper) W.; student univs. Munster, Wurzburg, Vienna, Berlin, 1923-29; Ph.D., U. Berlin, 1929; Doctor honoris causa U. Heidelberg, 1967; L.H.D., U. Chgo., 1968; m. Josepha Fiedler, Jan. 13, 1932. Came to U.S., 1935, naturalized, 1940. Stipend German Archaeolog. Institut, Greece, 1931; with Archaeol. Institut, Berlin, 1932-34; permanent mem. Inst. Advanced Study, Princeton, 1935-72; asso. prof. art and archaeology Princeton U., 1945-50, prof. art and archaeology, 1950-72, prof. emeritus, 1972—; vis. lectr. Yale, 1954-55, vis. prof. U. Alexandria (Egypt), 1960; guest prof. U. Bonn, 1962. Bd. scholars Dumbarton Oaks Research Library and Collection, Harvard 1949-72; vis. scholar Dumbarton Oaks, 1972-73. Hon. trustee Met. Mus., consultative curator, 1973—. Recipient Prix Schlumberger, Academie des Inscriptions et Belles-Lettres, Paris, 1969. Fellow Medieval Acad. Am. (Haskins medal 1974), Pierpont Morgan Library (hon.); mem. German Archaeol. Institut Berlin, Acad. Scis. Goettingen (corr.), Am. Acad. Arts and Scis., Am. Philos. Soc., Brit. Acad. (corr.), Coll. Art Assn. (Charles Rufus Morey Book award), Archaeolo. Inst. Am., Assn. Internationale des Etudes Byzantines (v.p.), Acad. Scis. Heidelberg (corr.), Pontificia Accedemia Romana di Archeologia (corr.), Am. Acad. Arts and Scis. Author: Die Byzantinischen Elfenbeinskulpturen (with Adolph Goldschmidt), 2 vols., 1930-34; Die Armenische Buchmalerei, 1933; Die Byzantinische Buchmalerei des 9. und 10. Jahrhunderts, 1935; Illustrations in Roll and Codex, 1947; The Joshua Roll, 1948; Greek Mythology in Byzantine Art, 1951; The Fresco Cycle of S. Maria Di Castelseprio, 1951; Ancient Book-illumination (Martin Classical Lectures Volume XVI), 1959; Geistige Grundlagen und Wesen der Makedonischen Renaissance, 1963; Studies in Classical and Byzantine Manuscript Illumination, 1971; (with George H. Forsyth) The Monastery of St. Catherine at Mount Sinai. The Church and Fortress of Justinian: Vol. I: Plates; The Icons. Vol. I: From the Sixth to the Tenth Century, 1976; Late Antique and Early Christian Book Illumination, 1977; The Icon, 1978; The Miniatures of the Sacra Parallela, 1979. Editor: The Illustrations in the Manuscripts of the Septuagint 1941—; Studies in Honor of A.M. Friend, Jr., 1955; Studies in Manuscript Illumination; Age of Sprituality: Catalogue Metropolitan Museum Exhibition, 1979; Expedition Mt. Sinai, 1956, 58, 60, 63, 65. Contbr. articles profl. publs. Home: 30 Nassau St Princeton NJ 08540

WEITZNER, DAVID A., motion picture mktg. exec.; b. N.Y.C., Nov. 13, 1938; s. Fred S. and Evelyn S. Weitzner; B.A. in Advt., Mich. State U., 1960; m. Joan Dayron; children—Dana, Jason, Jonathan. Vice pres. worldwide advt. 20th Century Fox, 1976-79; v.p., gen. mgr. Grey Advt. Co., N.Y.C., 1974-76; v.p., dir. mktg. ABC Pictures Corp., N.Y.C., 1970-74; exec. v.p. Universal Pictures/MCA, Universal City, Calif., 1980—; lectr. on motion picture mktg. Mich. State U., U. So. Calif. Served with inf. U.S. Army, 1961-62. Office: 100 Universal Plaza Universal City CA 91608

WEKSLER, MARC EDWARD, physician; b. N.Y.C., Apr. 16, 1937; s. Jacob J. and Lillian W.; B.A., Swarthmore Coll., 1958; M.D., Columbia U., 1962; m. Babette Barbash; children—David J., Jennifer Lee. Intern, Bronx (N.Y.) Mcpl. Hosp., 1962-63, resident in medicine, 1963-64; asst. prof. medicine Cornell U. Med. Coll., N.Y.C., 1970-75, asso. prof., 1975-78, Wright prof. medicine, 1978—, dir. div. geriatrics and gerontology, 1978—; attending physician N.Y. Hosp., Meml. Hosp., N.Y.C.; cons. NIH. Fellow A.C.P.; mem. Am. Soc. Clin. Investigation, Alpha Omega Alpha. Editorial bd. Jour. Immunology, Proc. Soc. Exptl. Biology and Medicine, Jour. Gerontology. Office: Cornell U Med Coll 1300 York Ave New York NY 10021

WELCH, ARNOLD D(EMERRITT), pharmacologist, biochemist; b. Nottingham, N.H., Nov. 7, 1908; s. Lewis H. and Stella M. (Batchelder) W.; B.S., U. Fla., 1930, M.S., 1931, D.Sc. (hon.), 1973; Ph.D., U. Toronto, 1934; M.D., Washington U., 1939; m. Mary Grace Scott, June 15, 1933; children—Michael Scott, Stephen Anthony, Gwyneth Jeanne; m. 2d, Erika Peter, Mar. 15, 1966. Research asst. U. Fla., 1929-31; fellow pharmacology U. Toronto, 1931-35; asst. pharmacology Washington U., 1935-36, instr., 1936-40; dir. pharmacol. research Sharp and Dohme, Inc., Phila., 1940-44, dir. research, 1943-44; prof. pharmacology, dir. dept. Sch. Medicine, Western Res. U., 1944-53; Fulbright sr. research scholar Oxford U., 1952; prof. pharmacology Sch. Medicine, Yale, 1953-67, chmn. dept., 1953-67, Eugene Higgins prof. pharmacology, 1957-67; dir. Squibb Inst. for Med. Research, 1967-72, pres., 1972-74, chmn. emeritus bd. dirs., 1974—, v.p. E.R. Squibb & Sons, Inc., Princeton, N.J., 1967-74; chmn. dept. biochem. and clin. pharmacology St. Jude Children's Research Hosp., Memphis, 1975—; vol. prof. pharmacology U. Tenn. Sch. Medicine, 1975—. Mem. com. on growth NRC (chmn. panel mech. action 1946-48, chmn. sect. chemotherapy 1948-52, chmn. com., 1952-54); mem. sci. adv. bd. Leonard Wood Meml., 1947-53, Nat. Vitamin Found., 1953-56, St. Jude Children's Research Hosp., Memphis, 1968-71; mem. div. biology and medicine NSF, 1953-55; mem. study sect. pharmacology and exptl. therapeutics USPHS, 1952-56, 1959-63, chmn., 1960-63, chmn. study sect. chemotherapy, 1963-65; chmn. panel pharmacology and biochemistry, mem. coordinating com. cancer chemotherapy Nat. Cancer Service Center, USPHS, 1955-57; mem. research adv. council Am. Cancer Soc., 1956-59; mem. adv. council Biol. sci. Princeton, 1969-74; mem. working cadre Nat. Large Bowel Cancer program Nat. Cancer Inst., 1975—; sci. adv. bd. La Jolla Cancer Research Found., 1979—. Recipient alumni award U. Fla., 1953, Washington U., 1957; Commonwealth fellow U. Frankfurt, also Prague, 1964-65; Torald Sollmann award Am. Soc. Pharmacology and Exptl. Therapeutics, 1966. Mem. Am. Soc. Microbiology, Am. Soc. Pharmacol. and Exptl. Therapeutics, Assn. Am. Physicians, Am. Assn. Cancer Research, A.A.A.S., Am. Soc. Biol. Chemistry, Am. Soc. Clin. Pharmacology and Therapeutics, Am. Soc. Hematology, Am. Chem. Soc., Soc. Exptl. Biology and Medicine, Biochem. Soc. Gt. Britain, Environ. Mutagen Soc., Phi Beta Kappa, Sigma Xi, Phi Kappa Phi, Alpha Omega Alpha, Delta Tau Delta. Asso. editor Cancer Research, 1950-58, Pharm. Revs., 1962-66, Ann. Rev. Pharm., 1965-69; editor for Am. Cont., Biochem. Pharmacology, 1958-62, vice chmn. internat. bd. editors, 1962—; mem. bd. editors Handbuch der experimentellen Pharmakologie, 1966—. Contbr. articles to profl. jours., chpts. to books. Home: 4532 Laurelwood Dr Memphis TN 38117 Office: St Jude Children's Research Hosp Box 318 Memphis TN 38101

WELCH, BERNIE BURNETTE, hosp. system exec.; b. Winston Salem, N.C., Dec. 30, 1930; s. Amery J. and Alma (Wall) W.; A.A., Brevard Coll., 1951; A.B., Duke U., 1953, grad. Grad. Program in Hosp. Adminstrn., 1957; m. Joyce Billings, July 8, 1956; 1 son, Richard. Asst. adminstr. Lakeland (Fla.) Gen. Hosp., 1957-62; adminstr. Broward Gen. Med. Center, Ft. Lauderdale, Fla., 1962-76, exec. dir. North Broward Hosp. Dist., Ft. Lauderdale, 1964—. Dir. Blue Cross, 1970—; preceptor U. Fla. Program in Hosp. Adminstrn. Served with USMC, 1953-55. Fellow Am. Coll. Hosp. Adminstrs.; mem. Am. Hosp. Assn. (del. 1974—), South Fla. Hosp. Assn. (pres. 1973), Fla. Hosp. Assn. (pres. 1973). Methodist. Club: Kiwanis (pres. club 1969) (Ft. Lauderdale). Office: 1625 SE Third Ave Fort Lauderdale FL 33316

WELCH, BYRON EUGENE, cons. co. exec.; b. Kansas City, Mo., Mar. 3, 1928; s. Paul C. and Lucile Irene (Sherman) W.; ed. Swarthmore Coll., Tex. Christian U., U. Tex., Austin; m. Mabel Holmberg, May 18, 1947; 1 son, Byron Eugene, II. Dir. devel. and planning Atlantic Christian Coll., Wilson, N.C., 1956-58; dir. devel. Chapman Coll., Orange, Calif., 1958-59; asst. to pres. Calif. Western U., San Diego, 1959-60, William Woods Coll., Fulton, Mo., 1960-62; pres. Welch Assos., Inc., fund raising and devel. cons., Houston, 1962—; adj. prof. communication U. Tex., Austin, 1968—. Mem. exec. bd. Boy Scouts Am., 1974, chmn. Friends of Scouting, Sam Houston Area council, 1976; exec. bd. Planned Parenthood Houston, 1972—, chmn. planned gifts com.; bd. dirs. Population Program, Baylor U. Coll. Medicine, 1975—; sec., mem. exec. com. U. Ams., Puebla, Mexico, 1978—; chmn. bd. elders, chmn. ch. bd. Bethany Christian Ch., Houston, 1972-79. Served with USNR, 1945-46. Mem. Nat. Soc. Fund Raisers (pres. 1975—, chmn. bd. 1977-78), Tex. Pub. Relations Assn., Southwest Soc. Fund Raisers (pres. 1968-70), U. Tex. Southwest Inst. Fund Raising (dean 1974—). Club: Houston Press. Home: 4515 W Alabama St Houston TX 77027 Office: 3701 Kirby Center Suite 1010 Houston TX 77098. *The supreme satisfaction is to give without counting the cost. I have tried to make it a rule of my life never to remember what I do for others, but never to forget what others do for me.*

WELCH, CLAUDE (RAYMOND), educator; b. Genoa City, Wis., Mar. 10, 1922; s. Virgil Cleon and Deone West (Grenelle) W.; B.A. summa cum laude, Upper Iowa U., 1942; postgrad. Garrett Theol. Sem., 1942-43; B.D. cum laude, (Dwight fellow), Yale, 1945, Ph.D. (Kent fellow), 1950; D.D. (hon.) Ch. Div. Sch. of Pacific, 1972; L.H.D. (hon.), U. Judaism, 1976; m. Eloise Janette Turner, May 31, 1942 (div. 1970); children—Eric, Thomas, Claudia; m. 2d, Theodosia Montigel Blewett, Oct. 5, 1970. Ordained to ministry Methodist Ch., 1947; instr. religion Princeton, 1947-50, asst. prof., 1950-51, vis. prof., 1962; asst. prof. theology Yale Div. Sch., New Haven, 1951-54, asso. prof., 1954-60; Berg prof. religious thought and chmn. dept. U. Pa., Phila., 1960-71, asso. dean Coll. Arts and Scis., 1964-68, acting chmn. dept. philosophy, 1965-66; dean, prof. hist. theology Grad. Theol. Union, Berkeley, Calif., 1971—, pres., 1972—; vis. prof. Garrett Theol. Sem., 1951, Pacific Sch. Religion, 1958, Hartford Sem. Found., 1958-59, Princeton Theol. Sem., 1962-63; Fulbright sr. lectr. U. Mainz (Germany), 1968; Sprunt lectr. Union Theol. Sem., Richmond, Va., 1958; dir. study of grad. edn. in religion Am. Council Learned Socs., 1969-71; del. World Conf. on Faith and Order, 1963. Recipient decennial prize Bross Found., 1970. Guggenheim fellow, 1976. Mem. Am. Acad. Religion (pres. 1969-70), Council on Study of Religion (chmn., 1969-74), Soc. for Values in Higher Edn. (pres. 1967-71), Am. Theol. Soc., Soc. for Sci. Study of Religion, Soc. of Bibl. Lit., Phi Beta Kappa. Author: In This Name: the Doctrine of the Trinity in Contemporary Theology, 1952; (with John Dillenberger) Protestant Christianity, interpreted throughout its Development, 1954; The Reality of the Church, 1958; Graduate Education in Religion: A Critical Appraisal, 1971; Religion in the Undergraduate Curriculum, 1972; Protestant Thought in the 19th Century, vol. 1, 1799-1870, 1972. Editor, translator: God and Incarnation in Mid-19th Century German Theology (Thomasius, Dorner and Biedermann), 1965. Contbr. to publs. in field. Home: 123 Fairlawn Dr Berkeley CA 94708

WELCH, CLAUDE EMERSON, surgeon; b. Stanton, Nebr., Mar. 14, 1906; s. John Hayes and Lettie (Phelan) W.; A.B. summa cum laude, Doane Coll., 1927, D.Sc. (hon.), 1955; A.M. in Chemistry, U. Mo., 1928; M.D. magna cum laude, Harvard, 1932; D.Sc., U. Nebr., 1970; m. Phyllis Heath Paton, Aug. 14, 1937; children—Claude Emerson, John Paton. Asst. instr. organic chemistry U. Mo., 1927-28; surg. resident Mass. Gen. Hosp., Boston, 1932-37, vis. surgeon, 1937—, chief tumor clinic, 1957-63; clin. prof. surgery Harvard Med. Sch., 1964-72, clin. prof. emeritus, 1972—; chmn. Bd. Registration in Medicine, Commonwealth of Mass., 1976—; McLaughlin Gallie vis. prof., hon. fellow Royal Coll. Physicians and Surgeons of Can., 1978—. Served to lt. col. M.C., AUS, 1942-45. Decorated Commendation medal; recipient Distinguished Service award AMA, 1976. Hon. fellow Internat. Soc. Univ. Colon and Rectal Surgeons; mem. A.C.S. (bd. govs. 1960-63, bd. regents 1963-72, pres. 1973-74), Mass. Med. Soc. (pres. 1965), Boston Surg. Soc. (pres. 1965), Internat. Soc. Surgery (pres. U.S. chpt. 1978—), Soc. Surgery Alimentary Tract (pres. 1965), Am. (pres. 1976-77), So., New Eng., Pan Pacific (v.p. 1971—) surg. assns., James IV Assn. Surgeons, N.Y. Soc. Colon and Rectal Surgeons, Alpha Omega Alpha; hon. mem. Coll. Physicians and Surgeons Costa Rica, Los Angeles, Detroit, Kansas City, Portland, Central, N.Y., B.C., St. Paul surg. socs., Am. Soc. Colon and Rectal Surgeons, Harvard Med. Sch. Alumni Assn. (pres. 1972-73). Author: Surgery of the Stomach and Duodenum, 5th edit., 1975; Intestinal Obstruction, 1955; Polypoid Lesions Colon and Rectum, 1964, 2d edit., 1976; Manual of Lower Gastro-Intestinal Tract Surgery, 1979; also numerous articles. Editor: Advances in Surgery, 1964—; editorial bd. Surgery, 1958-70, Am. Jour. Surg., 1979—; mem. com. publs. New Eng. Jour. Medicine, 1962—, chmn., 1969—. Home: 55 Old Concord Rd Belmont MA 02178 Office: 275 Charles St Boston MA 02114

WELCH, CLAUDE EMERSON, JR., educator, univ. ofcl.; b. Boston, June 12, 1939; s. Claude Emerson and Phyllis (Paton) W.; B.A., Harvard, 1961; Ph.D., Oxford U., 1964; m. Nancy Edwards, June 19, 1961 (dec. May 1979); children—Elisabeth Ann, Sarah Jane, Martha Lee, Christopher Claude. Asst. prof. polit. sci. State U. N.Y., Buffalo, 1964-68, asso. prof., 1968-72, prof., 1972—, dean div. undergrad. studies, 1967-70, chmn. African studies faculty com., 1969—, asso. v.p. for acad. affairs, 1976—. Mem. Inter-Univ. Seminar. Fellow African Studies Assn.; mem. Phi Beta Kappa. Author: Dream of Unity, 1966; Political Modernization, 1967; Soldier and State in Africa, 1970; Revolution and Political Change, 1972; Military Role and Rule, 1974; Civilian Control of the Military, 1976; Peasants in Africa, 1978; Anatomy of Rebellion, 1980. Home: 120 Burroughs Dr Buffalo NY 14226 Office: 562 Capen Hall Buffalo NY 14260

WELCH, D. VINCENT, banker; b. New Albany, Ind., Oct. 13, 1915; s. John Arthur and Daisy (McWilliams) W.; student various banking schs.; m. Mary Roberta Biscopink, June 10, 1939; children—Mary Colleen (Mrs. William M. Freeman), D. Michael, Patrick J., Vincent D. With Liberty Nat. Bank, Louisville, 1941—, now exec. v.p.; instr. Am. Inst. Banking, Ky. Sch. Banking. Mem. Am. Inst. Banking. Kiwanian. Clubs: Executive of Louisville, Pendennis. Club. Home: 209 Dunbar St New Albany IN 47150 Office: PO Box 32500 Louisville KY 40232

WELCH, DONALD WILTON, hosp. adminstr.; b. Hastings, Nebr., Oct. 30, 1927; s. Howard Jensen and Ethel May (Long) W.; B.S., Madison Coll., 1950; M.A., Peabody Coll., 1951; m. Loretta Jean Pennington, Aug. 10, 1961; children—Donald Eugene, Melissa Faye. Dept. head Madison (Tenn.) Hosp., 1949-51; adminstr. Hialeah (Fla.) Hosp., 1952-61; adminstr., pres. Fla. Hosp., Orlando, 1961-73; pres. So. Adventist Health and Hosp. System, Inc., Orlando, 1973—; pres., mem. Health Systems Agy. East Central Fla. Mem. exec. com. So. Union Conf. Seventh-day Adventists. Trustee Fla. Conf. Seventh-day Adventists, Forest Lake Acad., So. Missionary Coll., Collegedale, Tenn. Served with AUS, 1946-47. Fellow Am. Coll. Hosp. Adminstrs.; mem. South Fla. (pres. 1961), Central Fla. (pres. 1963) hosp. councils, Fla. (pres. 1971-72), Seventh-day Adventist (pres. 1962) hosp. assns. Home: 2924 Westchester Ave Orlando FL 32803 Office: 601 E Rollins St Orlando FL 32803

WELCH, EDWARD FRANCIS, JR., naval officer; b. Barrington, R.I., Nov. 13, 1924; s. Edward Francis and Nellie Elizabeth (Gauntlett) W.; B.S., U.S. Naval Acad., 1947; M.P.A., Harvard U., 1962; m. Rachael Mary Linehan, Feb. 15, 1950; children—Mary Ellen, James. Commd. ensign U.S. Navy, 1947, advanced through grades to rear adm., 1975; mem. faculty Nat. War Coll., 1966-67, 74-75; pres. U.S. Naval War Coll., Newport, R.I., 1979—; dep. dir. internat. negotiations Joint Staff, 1975-77, 77-79; dep. U.S. commr. U.S.-USSR Standing Consultative Commn., 1977-78. Decorated Legion of Merit (3), Def. Superior Service medal. Mem. U.S. Naval Acad. Alumni Assn., SHAPE Officers Assn., Harvard U. Alumni Assn. Roman Catholic. Address: US Naval War Coll Newport RI 02840

WELCH, FREDRIC BYRON, bottling co. exec.; b. Searcy, Ark., Apr. 5, 1916; s. Fredric Byron and Marguerite J. (Morgan) W.; student Coll. of Ozarks; m. Patricia E. Baker, July 3, 1943; children—Fredric Byron III, Barbara Baker, William Bucklin. With F. S. Yantis & Co., Inc., Chgo., 1935-40, 46-48, pres., dir., 1956-63; v.p., gen. mgr., dir. Pepsi-Cola Bottling Co. Cin., 1963—; v.p. sales, dir. Pepsi-Cola Louisville Bottlers, Inc., 1948-51, pres. and dir., 1951-56; pres. Woodlawn Canners, Inc., 1969-75, chmn. bd., 1975—. Served from pvt. to capt., AUS, 1941-46; maj. Res. Mem. Nat. Pepsi-Cola Bottlers Assn. (dir. 1955-56), Ky. Soft Drink Assn. (pres. 1955-56), Ohio Soft Drink Assn. (pres. 1971-72), Pepsi-Cola Bottlers Assn. of Ohio (pres. 1967-68), Louisville Assn. Mfrs. Reps. (pres. 1955), Greater Cin. C. of C. (dir. 1969-74, v.p. ops. 1973). Clubs: Pendennis (Louisville); Executives (Chgo.); Queen City, Cincinnati, Kenwood Country. Home: 5525 Drake Rd Indian Hill Cincinnati OH 45243 Office: 2121 Sunnybrook Dr Cincinnati OH 45237

WELCH, HARRY SCOVILLE, gas pipeline co. exec.; b. Hugo, Okla., Nov. 14, 1923; s. John Calvin and Gaynell (Potts) W.; B.B.A., U. Tex. at Austin, 1947, LL.B., 1949; m. Peggy Joyce Weis, Dec. 18, 1954; children—Marshall Porter, Gay, Harry Scoville, Mary Margaret, Anne. Admitted to Tex. bar, 1948; atty. Am. Republics Corp., Houston, 1949-51; partner firm Turner, White, Atwood, McLane & Francis, Dallas, 1951-59; exec. asst., then v.p. Tenneco Co., Houston, 1959-73; v.p., gen. counsel Panhandle Eastern Pipe Line Co., Houston, 1973-74, sr. v.p., gen. counsel, 1975—. Mem. bd. adjustment, Hunter's Creek Village, Tex., 1970-77, chmn. 1973-77. Mem. adv. bd. Internat. Oil and Gas Ednl. Center, Southwestern Legal Found., Dallas. Served with USNR, 1943-46. Fellow Tex. Bar Found.; mem. Am., Houston bar assns., State Bar Tex., Phi Kappa Sigma, Phi Alpha Delta. Presbyn. Clubs: Coronado, Forest, Ramada (Houston). Home: 10611 Twelve Oaks St Houston TX 77024 Office: PO Box 1642 Houston TX 77001

WELCH, JAMES S., army officer; b. Floyd Edward and Helen Lois (Huskey) W.; B.A., Stanford U., 1948; M.B.A., Harvard U., 1950; m. Marianne Julianne Freyth, Sept. 23, 1955. Commd. 2d lt. U.S. Army, 1947, advanced through grades to maj. gen., 1979; service in India, Burma, China, Korea, Viet Nam, W. Ger.; comdg. gen. U.S. Army Depot System Command, Chambersburg, Pa., 1978—. Decorated Legion of Merit with oak leaf cluster, Bronze Star, Army Commendation medal, Air Force Commendation medal; C.P.A., Calif. Mem. Assn. U.S. Army, Am. Def. Preparedness Assn., 101 Assn. Republican. Club: Army-Navy Country. Author articles in field. Home: Box 77 Letterkenny Army Depot Chambersburg PA 17201 Office: Hdqrs Depot System Command Chambersburg PA 17201

WELCH, JOHN DAVID, cons. civil engr.; b. Madison, Wis., Dec. 13, 1924; s. John Douglas and Lillian M.A. (Gascoigne) W.; B.S. in Civil Engring., U. Wis., 1947; M.S. in Engring., Princeton U., 1949; m. Jacqueline Watson, Dec. 6, 1975; children by former marriage—John David, Vicki Leigh, Jeffrey Dalton, Leslie Carolyn, James Daniel. Chief soils engr., cons. engr. Howard, Needles, Tammen & Bergendoff, N.Y.C., 1949-60; partner Welch & Malinofsky, Summit, N.J., 1960-67; pres. Eastern Exploration Corp., Summit, 1967-69; prin. Welch & Assos., Summit, 1967-69; partner Joseph S. Ward & Assos., Caldwell, N.J., 1969-72, partner-in-charge, Washington, 1973-76; mktg. devel. cons., pvt. practice geotech. engring., Rockville, Md., 1976-78; v.p. NFS/Nat. Soil Services Inc., Rockville, Md., 1978-79; dir. mktg. Johnson, McCordic & Thompson, P.A., 1979—. Mem. Bernards Twp. (N.J.) Planning Bd., 1958-60; vestryman St. Marks Ch., Basking Ridge, N.J., 1962-65, mem. bldg. com., 1966-69; bd. dirs. Somerset Hills (N.J.) YMCA, 1964-70. Served as ensign USN, World War II. Licensed profl. engr., D.C., Md., N.J., N.Y., W.Va. Fellow Am. Cons. Engrs. Council (dir. 1971-73); mem. ASCE, Internat. Soc. Soil Mechanics and Found. Engring., Soc. for Mktg. Profl. Services, Cons. Engrs. Council N.J. (pres. 1969-70), Cons. Engrs. Council Met. Washington, Sigma Xi. Contbr. articles on soil mechanics to profl. jours. Home: 10942 Wickshire Way Rockville MD 20852

WELCH, JOHN FRANCIS, JR., elec. mfg. co. exec.; b. Peabody, Mass., Nov. 19, 1935; s. John Francis and Grace (Andrews) W.; B.S. in Chem. Engring., U. Mass., 1957; M.S., U. Ill., 1958, Ph.D., 1960; m. Carolyn B. Osburn, Nov. 21, 1959; children—Katherine, John, Anne, Mark. With Gen. Electric Co., Fairfield, Conn., 1960—, v.p., 1972, v.p., group exec. components and materials group, 1973-77, sr. v.p., sector exec., consumer products and services sector, 1977-79, vice chmn., exec. officer, 1979—, also dir.; dir. Gen. Electric Credit Corp. Recipient award U. Mass. Engring. Alumni Assn., 1974. Patentee in field. Office: 3135 Easton Turnpike Fairfield CT 06431

WELCH, LLOYD RICHARD, educator, elec. engr.; b. Detroit, Sept. 28, 1927; s. Richard Clarence and Helen (Felt) W.; B.S., U. Ill., 1951; Ph.D., Calif. Inst. Tech., 1958; m. Irene Althea Main, Sept. 12, 1953; children—Pamela (Mrs. Mark Sanders), Melinda, Diana (Mrs. Delwyn Worthington). Mathematician, Jet Propulsion Lab., Calif. Inst. Tech., Pasadena, 1956-59, Inst. Def. Analyses, Princeton, N.J., 1959-65; mem. faculty U. So. Calif., 1965—, prof. elec. engring., 1968—. Served with USNR, 1945-48, 51-52. Mem. Am. Math. Soc., Math. Assn. Am., Soc. for Indsl. and Applied Math., Nat. Acad. Engrs., Phi Beta Kappa, Sigma Xi, Eta Kappa Nu. Home: 4822 Indianola Way La Canada CA 91001 Office: Powell Hall Univ of So Calif Los Angeles CA 90007

WELCH, LOUIE, assn. exec.; b. Lockney, Tex., Dec. 9, 1918; s. Gilford E. and Nora (Shackelford) W.; B.A. magna cum laude, Abilene Christian U., 1940; m. Iola Faye Cure, Dec. 17, 1940; children—Guy Lynn, Gary Dale, Louie Gilford, Shannon Austin, Tina La Joy. Councilman at large, Houston, 1950-52, 56-62; mayor of Houston, 1964-73, mayor emeritus, 1974—; pres. Houston C. of C., 1974—. Pres., Tex. Municipal League, 1959-60; pres. U.S. Conf. of Mayors, 1972-73. Bd. dirs. Abilene Christian U. Mem. Tex. Mayors and Councilmens Assn. (past pres.), Nat. League Cities (past v.p.). Home: 5013 Happy Hollow Houston TX 77018 Office: 1100 Milam 25th Floor Houston TX 77002

WELCH, NEAL WILLIAM, electric co. exec.; b. North Adams, Mass., Sept. 16, 1908; s. Owen William and Mary Gertrude (McGovern) W.; grad. Bently Coll., 1930; m. Harriet Flood, June 27, 1935; children—Marian, Mary. With Sprague Electric Co., North Adams, 1932—, v.p. sales, 1953-60, sr. v.p. mktg. and sales, 1960-67, exec. v.p., 1967-71, chmn. exec. com., 1968-71, chmn., chief exec. officer, 1971—. Home: Mamahane Farm East Road North Adams MA 01247 Office: Sprague Electric Co North Adams MA 01247

WELCH, PATRICK ERRETT, educator; b. Springfield, Mo., Mar. 10, 1925; s. Errett Lee and Gertrude (Purcell) W.; B.A., U. Tulsa, 1949, M.A., 1950; Ph.D., Ohio State U., 1958; m. Patricia Catherine Cecil, Aug. 7, 1948; children—Michael Errett, Catherine Elizabeth, Jennie Elaine, Margaret Louise. Radio announcer KOME, Tulsa, 1949; television announcer KOTV, Tulsa, 1950; instr. radio-TV, U. Houston, 1950-51, asst. prof., 1951-52, asso. prof., 1952-69, chmn. dept. radio-TV, 1956-63, chmn. dept. communications, 1963-70, prof. communications, 1969-70; prof. radio and television U. Ill., Urbana, 1970—, head dept., 1970-76; instrl. TV utilization coordinator WILL-TV, Urbana, 1978—. Served with USAAF, 1943-45; ETO. Decorated Air medal. Mem. Theta Alpha Phi, Alpha Epsilon Rho (asso.), Kappa Sigma, Omicron Delta Kappa (hon), Kappa Tau Alpha. Home: 711 LaSell St Champaign IL 61820 Office: WILL-TV 1110 W Main St Urbana IL 61801

WELCH, RAQUEL, actress; b. Chgo., Sept. 5, 1942; d. Armand and Josepha (Hall) Tejada; m. James Westley Welch, May 8, 1959 (div.); children—Damon, Tahnee; m. 2d, Patrick Curtis (div.). Former model for Neiman-Marcus stores; films include Fantastic Voyage, 1966, One Million B.C., 1967, The Biggest Bundle of Them All, 1968, Roustabout, 1964, A House is Not a Home, 1964, Swinging Summer, 1965, Shoot Louder...I Don't Understand, 1967, Fathom, 1967, Magic Christian, 1970, Fuzz, 1972, Bluebeard, 1972, Hannie Caulder, 1972, Kansas City Bomber, 1972, Myra Breckinridge, 1970, The Last of Sheila, 1973, The Three Musketeers, 1974, The Wild Party, 1975, The Four Musketeers, 1975, Mother, Jugs and Speed, 1976, Crossed Swords, 1978. Address: care William Morris Agy 151 El Camino Beverly Hills CA 90212*

WELCH, RICHARD EDWIN, JR., educator; b. Newburyport, Mass., June 16, 1924; s. Richard Edwin and Helen (Hale) W.; A.B., Dartmouth, 1948; M.A., Harvard, 1949, Ph.D., 1952; m. Christina S. Marquand, Sept. 4, 1948; children—Catherine Helen, Richard Edwin III, Christina S., Elizabeth M., Margaret Curzon. Instr. history Colgate U., 1952-53; asst. prof. Va. Mil. Inst., 1953-58; asst. prof. Lafayette Coll., Easton, Pa., 1958-62, asso. prof., 1962-70, prof., 1970—, Charles A. Dana prof., 1978—. Served with AUS, 1942-46. Mem. Am. Hist. Assn., Orgn. Am. Historians, Soc. Historians of Am. Fgn. Relations. Author: Theodore Sedgwick, Federalist: A Political Portrait, 1965; George Frisbie Hoar and the Half-Breed Republicans, 1971; Imperialists vs. Anti-imperialists: The Debate Over Expansionism in the 1890s, 1972; Response to Imperialism: The United States and the Philippine-American War, 1899-1902, 1979; also numerous articles. Home: 848 Paxinosa Ave Easton PA 18042

WELCH, ROBERT, publisher, orgn. exec.; b. Chowan County, N.C., Dec. 1, 1899; s. Robert H. W. and Lina (James) W.; A.B. U. N.C., 1916; student U.S. Naval Acad., 1917-19, Harvard Law Sch., 1919-21; m. Marian Lucile Probert, Dec. 2, 1922; children—Robert III, Hillard Walmer. Engaged in candy mfg., 1922-56; pres. Robert Welch, Inc., publishers, 1956—; founder, pres. John Birch Soc., 1958—. Mem. adv. com. candy mfg. bus. OPA, World War II. Mem. Belmont (Mass.) Sch. Com., 1952-55. Candidate for Republican nomination for lt. gov. Mass., 1950. Recipient Candy Industry Man of Year award, 1947. Mem. Nat. Confectioners Assn. (dir. 1945- 49, v.p. 1946-47, chmn. Washington com. 1947-49), United Prison Assn. (dir. 1945-53, treas. 1949), N.A.M. (dir. 1951-57, exec. com., 1953-54, 57, chmn. ednl. adv. com. 1953-54, regional v.p. 1955-57). Clubs: Oakley Country, Harvard (Boston); Harvard (N.Y.C.); Union League (Chgo.). Author: The Road to Salesmanship, 1941; May God Forgive Us, 1952; The Life of John Birch, 1954; Blue Book of the John Birch Society, 1958; The Politician, 1963; The New Americanism, 1966; The Romance of Education, 1973. Editor Am. Opinion, 1956—. Home: 43 Fletcher Rd Belmont MA 02178 Office: 395 Concord Ave Belmont MA 02178

WELCH, ROBERT GIBSON, trade assn. exec.; b. Kewanee, Ill., July 9, 1915; s. Thomas John and Mabel Emily (Bunton) W.; A.B., Stanford, 1937; m. Helen Taylor, Mar. 23, 1940; children—Sherry, Wendy, Taylor. With Dun & Bradstreet, Inc., 1937-42; asst. to treas. Henry J. Kaiser Co., 1942-45; asst. to v.p., gen. mgr. Permanente Cement Co., 1945-46, Permanente Metals Corp., 1946; mgr. distbn. Kaiser Aluminum & Chem. Corp., 1947-54; exec. sec. Steel Service Center Inst. (formerly Am. Steel Warehouse Assn.), 1954-57, exec. v.p., 1957-62, pres., 1962—, also sec.; lectr. indsl. distbn., trade assn. mgmt.; mem. various govt. adv. coms. Bd. dirs. Distbn. Research Edn. Found.; trustee Freedom Found., Valley Forge, Pa. Mem. Am. Iron and Steel Inst., Am. Soc. Assn. Execs. (certified assn. exec., Key award 1970, Key Industry Council), Am. Soc. Assn. Execs. Found. (mem. bd., past chmn.), Nat. Assn. Wholesale Distbrs. (exec. com.), U.S. C. of C. (mem. pub. affairs com.), Cleve. Mus. Art, Mus. Modern Art (Cleve.) (growth bd.), Insts. Orgn. Mgmt. (former chmn. bd. regents, exec. com.), Cleve. Soc. Contemporary Art, Phi Gamma Delta. Clubs: Knollwood, Chicago (Chgo.); Metropolitan (N.Y.C.); Mayfield, Union (Cleve.); Duquesne (Pitts.); Metropolitan (Washington). Author numerous articles. Home: 16800 S Woodland Rd Shaker Heights OH 44120 Office: 1600 Terminal Tower Cleveland OH 44113. *I am very thankful that we live in this great country of ours because of the opportunity America gives to its citizens to grow a bit each day and, in fact, to frequently live and perform "above one's head." That is the inner satisfaction and excitement that enables each of us to very closely approach or reach real happiness.*

WELCH, ROGER, artist; b. Westfield, N.J., Feb. 10, 1946; s. Herbert R. and Yvonne (Miller) W.; B.F.A., Miami U., Oxford, Ohio, 1969; M.F.A., Chgo. Art Inst., 1971. One-man exhbns. include Sonnabend Gallery, Paris and N.Y.C., 1972-73, Milw. Art Center, 1974, Albright-Knox Art Gallery, Buffalo, 1977, Antwerp (Belgium) Gallery, 1979, Museo de Arte Moderno, Mexico City, 1980, numerous others; group exhbns. include Documenta V, Kassel, W. Ger., 1974, Art Now '74, Washington, 1974, Am. Art in Brussels; various multi-media projects include: The Roger Woodward-Niagara Falls Project, 1975, O.J. Simpson Project, 1972, (film) Welch, 1972, Memory Maps series, 1972-76; represented in permanent collections: Ga. Mus. Art, Albright-Knox Art Gallery, Milw. Art Center, Mus. Modern Art, N.Y.C., Palais des Beaux Arts, Brussels; guest vis. instr. U. Calif., Irvine, 1978—; guest lectr. numerous univs., galleries. Grantee, N.Y. State Council Arts, 1973-76, Nat. Endowment Arts, 1974. Mem. Coll. Art Assn., Art Workers Assn. Address: 87 E Houston St New York NY 10012. *A great work of art does not hang on a wall, it is an opening in a wall. That wall exists between what we know and understand and an area that contains all the thoughts, visions, ideas and experiences which have not yet been revealed to us. The artist uses materials such as paint, stone, paper, etc., but an opening in this wall can only be created through imagination, exploration, and an open mind. My goal has been to create works of art which are visual and mental passageways to the other side of that wall, through which we can enter, for awhile, that other land.*

WELCH, SCOTT MEEKS, dentist; b. Cowley, Wyo., Jan. 25, 1925; s. Charles Golden and Ora (Meeks) W.; B.S., U. Wyo., 1948; D.D.S., St. Louis U., 1953; m. Kathleen Peterson, Sept. 4, 1945; children—Chauna Dee, Robert P., Scott P., Bradley P., Gregory P., Barry P., Krystal. Gen. practice dentistry, Lovell, Wyo., 1953—; dental examiner State of Wyo., 1966-73; pres. Wyo. Bd. Dental Examiners, 1966-73. Mem. Lovell Sch. Dist. Bd., 1976—; bd. dirs. North Big Horn Hosp., Lovell, 1956-76; bishop Lovell ward Ch. of Jesus Christ of Latter-day Saints, 1957-66. Served to ensign USNR, World War II. Fellow Am. Coll. Dentists; mem. N.W. Dist. Dental Soc. Wyo., Wyo. Dental Assn. (pres. 1978-79), Am. Assn. Dental Examiners (pres. 1976-77), Pierre Fauchard Acad., ADA. Club: Lions (Lovell). Home: 126 Washakie Ave Lovell WY 82431 Office: 84 Park Ave Lovell WY 82431

WELCH, STUART CARY, mus. curator; b. Buffalo, Apr. 2, 1928; A.B., Harvard U., 1950, postgrad., 1952-54; m. Edith Iselin Gilbert, June 14, 1954; children—Adrienne Edith, Thomas Cary, Samuel Manning, Lucia Cary. Hon. curator manuscripts Harvard Coll. Library; hon. curator, curator Indian and Islamic art Fogg Art Mus., Cambridge, Mass.; sr. lectr. fine arts Harvard U. Author numerous books in field including: Persian Painting, 1976; Indian Drawings and Painted Sketches, 1976; Imperial Mughal Painting, 1978; (with M. B. Dickson) The Houghton Shahnameh, 1979. Office: Islamic Dept Fogg Mus Harvard Univ Cambridge MA 02138

WELCH, VINCENT BOGAN, lawyer; b. Portland, Maine, Oct. 3, 1917; s. Arthur Deehan and Jane Agnes (Bogan) W.; B.A., Bowdoin Coll., 1938, LL.D., 1975; J.D., Harvard, 1941; m. Barbara Gross, Nov. 15, 1941. Admitted to Maine bar, 1941, D.C. bar, 1946; atty. FCC, Washington, 1941-42; sr. partner firm Welch & Morgan, Washington, 1946-77; partner Capital City Oil Co., Washington, 1949—, Dulles Indsl. Center, real estate, Loudoun County, Va., 1969-77; chmn. bd. Conti-Urban TV Corp., San Jose, Calif., 1964—, Warrangal Pty. Ltd., real estate, Sydney, Australia, 1969—; chmn. bd., pres. Linda-Pont Corp., restaurants, Washington, 1966-77; mng. partner Holomua Holdings, real estate, Maui, Hawaii, 1973—, Te Awanui Holdings, real estate, Tauranga, N.Z., 1973—, Rica Cosecha Holdings, real estate, Benidorm, Spain, 1974—; v.p. Rich Hill Corp., real estate, West Bath, Maine, 1973-76; chmn. bd., treas. Des Indes Corp., internat. investments, Washington, 1975-76; mng. partner Pine Tree Holdings, real estate, Maine, 1975—; owner J&P Advt. Agy., Portland, 1977—, Welch Enterprises, Portland, 1977—. Mem. NCCJ, 1955-72; v.p. Ravenwood Citizens Assn., Falls Church, Va., 1954; mem. Fairfax (Va.) Hosp. Assn., 1958-77, Muscular Dystrophy Assn., Washington, 1958-60, Legal Aid Bur., Washington, 1954-60; mem. campaign steering com. Portland Public Library, 1978; corporator, mem. devel. com., ann. fund com. Maine Med. Center, 1978—. Trustee Bowdoin Coll., Brunswick, Maine, 1972—; mem. bd. Washington chpt. Epilepsy Found. Am., 1973-74. Served to lt. (s.g.) USNR, 1942-45; lt. col. USAF Res., ret. Fellow Am. Bar Found.; mem. Am. Legion, AMVETS (comdr. Washington 1948), Harvard Law Sch. Alumni Assn., Am. (ho. dels. 1955), D.C., Fed. Communications (pres. 1954) bar assns., Nat. Conf. Bar Presidents, Portland C. of C., Portland Com. on Fgn. Relations, Portland Soc. Art. Clubs: Cumberland (Portland, Me.). Home: Sunset Chimneys Raymond Cape Rd Raymond ME 04077 Office: 85 Exchange St Portland ME 04101

WELCH, WAYNE WILLARD, educator; b. Clinton, Iowa, May 20, 1934; s. Willard Densmore and Evelyn Louise (Peterson) W.; B.S., U. Wis., 1956, Ph.D., 1966; M.S., U. Pa., 1960, Purdue U., 1963; m. Dorothy Geraldine Dunlap, Sept. 11, 1951; children—William Alan, Jean Carol, Mary Bethania. Research asso. Harvard, 1965-69; prof. ednl. psychology U. Minn., 1969—, asst. dean, 1970-74; vis. prof. NSF, 1972-73; cons. Ford Found., NIE, Nat. Assessment Ednl. Progress, NSF, Minn. Area Health Edn. Center, 1974-77, UNESCO, 1976, Soc. Tchrs. Family Medicine, 1976-77. NSF grantee, 1971-78; Fulbright-Hays lectr., Israel, 1979. Fellow AAAS (councilman 1970-73); mem. Am. Ednl. Research Assn., Nat. Council Measurement in Edn., Nat. Assn. Research in Sci. Teaching (pres. 1973-76). Mem. editorial adv. bd. Sci. Tchr., 1972-77, Jour. Research in Sci. Teaching, 1969-76. Contbr. numerous articles to profl. jours.

WELD, TUESDAY KER (WELD, SUSAN KER), actress; b. N.Y.C., Aug. 27, 1943; d. Lathrop Motley and Aileen (Ker) Weld; attended Hollywood (Calif.) Profl. Sch.; m. Claude Harz, Oct., 1965 (div. 1971); 1 dau., Natasha; m. 2d, Dudley Moore, Sept. 20, 1975 (div.); 1 son, Patrick. Began childhood career as fashion and catalogue model at age of three; by age of twelve appeared regularly on covers of mags. and performed child roles on TV programs, including Playhouse 90, Kraft Theatre, Alcoa Theatre, Climax; later TV appearances include Ozzie and Harriet, The Many Loves of Dobie Gillis, 77 Sunset Strip, The Millionaire, Tab Hunter Show, Zane Grey Theatre, Follow the Sun, Bus Stop, Dick Powell Theatre, Adventures in Paradise, Naked City, Eleventh Hour, Dupont Show of the Month, The Greatest Show on Earth, Mr. Broadway, Fugitive, The Crucible, Cimarron Strip; made movie debut in Rock, Rock, Rock, 1956; other movie appearances include: Rally Round the Flag, Boys!; The Five Pennies; The Private Lives of Adam and Eve; Return to Peyton Place; Wild in the Country; Bachelor Flat; Lord Love A Duck; Pretty Poison; I Walk the Line; A Safe Place; Play It As It Lays; Because They're Young; High Time; Sex Kittens Go to College; The Cincinnati Kid; Soldier in the Rain; I'll Take Sweden; Who'll Stop the Rain; TV movies include Reflections of Murder, 1974, F. Scott Fitzgerald in Hollywood, 1976. Address: care William Morris Agy 151 El Camino Dr Beverly Hills CA 90212*

WELD, WILLIAM FLOYD, lawyer; b. N.Y.C., July 31, 1945; s. David and Mary Blake (Nichols) W.; A.B. summa cum laude, Harvard U., 1966, J.D. cum laude, 1970; diploma with distinction Oxford (Eng.) U., 1967; m. Susan Roosevelt, June 7, 1975; children—David Minot, Ethel Derby, Mary Blake. Admitted to Mass. bar, 1970; law clk. to Hon. R.A. Cutter, Supreme Jud. Ct. Mass., 1970-71; partner firm Hill & Barlow, Boston, 1971—; asso. minority counsel U.S. Ho. of Reps. Judiciary Com. Impeachment Inquiry, 1973-74; trial practice adv. Harvard U. Law Sch. Trustee, Middlesex Sch., Concord, Mass., Trustees of Reservations, conservation found., Milton, Mass.; Republican nominee for atty. gen. Mass., 1978. Mem. Am. Law Inst., Boston Bar Assn., Mass. Bar Assn., Am. Bar Assn., Mass. Acad. Trial Lawyers. Clubs: Tavern, Brookline Country, Harvard, Downtown. Office: 225 Franklin St Boston MA 02110

WELDON, CLARENCE SCHOCK, surgeon, educator; b. Mt. Joy, Pa., Jan. 12, 1929; s. William S. and Lida (Shaeffer) W.; A.B., U. Mich., 1951; M.D., Johns Hopkins, 1955; m. Virginia Ann Verral, Nov. 30, 1963; children—Ann Stuart, Susan Shaeffer. Intern, John Hopkins Hosp., 1955-56; resident surgeon Johns Hopkins Hosp., 1958-63, instr. surgery, 1963-64, asst. prof., 1964-68, asso. prof., 1968; practice medicine specializing in surgery, St. Louis, 1968—; asso. prof., head div. cardiothoracic surgery Washington U. Med. Sch., 1968-70, prof. surgery, head div. cardiothoracic surgery, 1970—; cardiothoracic surgeon-in-chief Barnes and Allied, St. Louis Childrens hosps. John and Mary R. Markle scholar in acad. medicine, 1963-68. Fellow A.C.S., Am. Coll. Cardiology; mem. Am. Assn. Thoracic Surgery, Soc. U. Surgeons, Soc. Thoracic Surgery, Am., So., Central surg. assns., Assn. Acad. Surgery, Internat. Cardiovascular Soc., Soc. Internat. de Chirurgie, So. Thoracic Surg. Assn., Soc. Clin. Surgery, Soc. Vascular Surgery. Home: 4967 Pershing Pl St Louis MO 63108 Office: Suite 3108 Queeny Tower 4989 Barnes Hosp Plaza St Louis MO 63110

WELDON, JAMES ERNEST, microfilm products mfg. co. exec.; b. Jersey Shore, Pa., June 17, 1934; s. Lawrence Marion and Helen (Bitner) W.; B.S.B.A., Drexel U., 1959, postgrad. Drexel U., 1959-61; postgrad. U. Denver, 1961-62; m. Constance Elenor Leeds, Mar. 23, 1963; children—Deborah Kay, Stephen James. Dir. ops. photog. products div. Honeywell, Inc., Littleton, Colo., 1969-76, ops. mgr. internat. div., Mpls., 1976-77; pres. micro design div. Bell & Howell Co., Hartford, Wis., 1977—, group pres. Microfilm Products group, 1978—. Mem. Bd. Adjustment, Littleton, 1964-70, mem. Mayor's Com. on Budget, 1965-68. Served with USNR, 1952-54; ETO. Recipient award of merit City of Littleton, 1970. Mem. Nat. Micrographics Assn., Am. Mgmt. Assn. Presbyterian. Office: 857 W State St Hartford WI 53027

WELDON, NORMAN ROSS, mfg. co. exec.; b. Greencastle, Ind., July 21, 1934; s. David M. and Lenora F. (Evens) W.; B.S., Purdue U., 1956, M.S. in Indsl. Mgmt., 1962, Ph.D., 1964; m. Carol J. Warne, Oct. 2, 1954; children—Thomas D., Cynthia M. With CTS Corp., Elkhart, Ind., 1964-79, exec. v.p., 1970-76, pres., 1976-79, chief exec. officer, 1977-79, also dir.; pres. Cordis Corp., Miami, Fla., 1979—; adv. bd. Investment Co. Am., Inc. Served to capt. USAF, 1956-60. NSF fellow, 1962-63; Ford Found. fellow, 1963-64. Mem. Tau Kappa Epsilon, Phi Eta Sigma, Alpha Zeta. Presbyn. Office: Cordis Corp PO Box 370428 Miami FL 33137

WELDON, ROBERT WILLIAM, fin. and ins. co. exec.; b. Wilmette, Ill., Jan. 30, 1934; s. Clarence William and Irene (LaBerge) W.; B.S. in Animal Husbandry, Colo. State U., 1956; M.B.A., Harvard U., 1960; m. Karla Elaine Hart, Apr. 13, 1958; children—Deborah, Susan, Scott, Cindy. With Internat. Multifood Corp., Mpls., 1960-74, dir. long range planning, 1966-70, dir. fin. planning and asset utilization, 1970-74; v.p. fin., treas. Ill. Agrl. Assn., Bloomington, Ill., 1974—, Country Life Ins. Co., Bloomington, 1974—, Country Mutual Ins. Co., Bloomington, 1974—, County Marine Ins. Co., Bloomington, 1974—, Country Casualty Ins. Co., Bloomington, 1974—, CC Services, Bloomington, 1976—; treas., Country Capital Investment Fund., Bloomington, Country Capital Tax Exempt Bond Fund, 1978—, Country Capital Income Fund, 1978; treas., dir. Country Capital Mgmt. Co., 1974—, Knox Devel. Corp., 1977—, Ill. Agrl. Service Co., 1974—; treas. Ill. Agrl. Auditing Assn., 1974—, IAA Trust Co., 1974—. Served with U.S. Army, 1956-58. Mem. Alpha Zeta, Farm House Fraternity. Home: 1305 Baugh Dr Normal IL 61761 Office: 1701 Towanda Ave Bloomington IL 61701

WELK, LAWRENCE, orchestra leader; b. Strasburg, N.D., Mar. 11, 1903; s. Ludwig and Christine (Schwab) W.; ed. pub. schs.; Mus.D. (hon.), N.D. State U., 1965; L.H.D. (hon.), St. Mary of the Plains Coll., Dodge City, Kans., 1978; m. Fern Renner, Apr. 18, 1931; children—Shirley J. Welk Fredricks, Donna Welk Mack, Larry. Accordionist, 1920; appeared on sta. WNAX, Yankton, S.D.; orch. has appeared throughout U.S., 1927—; appeared on KTLA-TV, Los Angeles, 1950-55, on nat. ABC-TV program, 1955-71, syndicated network, 1971—; rec. artist for Ranwood Records; also appeared at Aragon Ballroom, Chgo., Pacific Ocean Park, 1951-61, Hollywood Palladium, 1961—; has appeared in motion picture musical shorts. Named Top Dance Band of Am., Nat. Ballroom Operators Am., 1955; recipient No. One TV Musical Program award, 1955, TV Radio Mirror award, favorite TV musical program, 1956-57; Am. Legion award, outstanding family TV show, 1957, Horatio Alger award, 1967, Freedom award, 1968, 69, Brotherhood award NCCJ, 1969. Address: care Don Fedderson Prodn Syndication Div 4024 Redford Ave Studio City CA 91604*

WELKER, WALLACE IRVING, neurophysiologist, educator; b. Batavia, N.Y., Dec. 17, 1926; Ph.D. in Psychology, U. Chgo., 1954. Mem. faculty U. Wis. Med. Sch., 1957—, prof. neurophysiology, 1965—. Served with AUS, 1945-47. Sister Kenny Found. scholar, 1957-62; recipient NIH Career Devel. award, 1962-67. Mem. Am. Anat. Soc., Neurosci. Soc. Office: 283 Med Sci Bldg Univ Wis Madison WI 53706. *Know thyself, dare to explore, tolerate uncertainty, employ intuition, aim toward perfection, be satisfied with progress, learn from mistakes, use adversity, know self-limits, treat work as play, live healthily, keep things simple, live one day at a time.*

WELLARD, CARL STANLEY, health services co. exec.; b. Pocatello, Idaho, Oct. 30, 1936; s. Glen Carl and Mable Jane (Rowley) W.; B.A., UCLA, 1958; m. Nancy Tilton Keating, Sept. 4, 1959; children—Wade Wilkinson, Caroline Keating. Mgr. employee relations Xerox Data Systems, El Segundo, Calif., 1965-69; dir. indsl. relations Tridair Industries, Redondo Beach, Calif., 1969-74; exec. v.p. Gen. Health Services, Inc., Culver City, Calif., 1974—; dir. Transequip, Inc., Plowell Assos.; condr. profl. seminars. Bd. dirs. Long Beach (Calif.) Museum Assn., 1965-68, 76-79, Long Beach Symphony Assn., 1967-68; chmn. Dan Beard dist. Long Beach Area council Boy Scouts Am., 1976. Mem. Fedn. Am. Hosps. (dir. 1976-79). Democrat. Methodist. Office: 3828 Delmas Terr Culver City CA 90230

WELLEK, RENÉ, educator, author; b. Vienna, Austria, Aug. 22, 1903; s. Bronislav and Gabriele (von Zelewski) W.; Ph.D., Charles U., Prague, Czechoslovakia, 1926; postgrad. Princeton, 1927-28; L.H.D., Lawrence Coll., 1958; Litt.D., Oxford and Harvard univs., 1960, Rome, 1961; Litt.D., U. Md., 1964, Boston Coll., 1966, Columbia, 1968, U. Montreal, 1970, U. Louvain, 1970, U. Mich., 1972, U. Munich, 1972, U. East Anglia, 1975; m. Olga Brodská, Dec. 23, 1932 (dec. Sept. 1967); 1 son, Alexander Ivan; m. 2d, Nonna D. Shaw, May 21, 1968. Came to U.S., 1939, naturalized, 1946. Instr. Smith Coll., 1928-29, Princeton, 1929-30; privatdocent Charles U., 1930-35; lectr. Sch. Slavonic Studies, U. London (Eng.), 1935-39; mem. faculty U. Iowa, 1939-46, prof. English, 1944-46; prof. Slavic and comparative lit. Yale, 1946-72, dir. grad. studies comparative lit., also chmn. Slavic dept., 1948-59, chmn. dept. comparative lit., 1960-72, fellow Silliman Coll., 1950—, Sterling prof. comparative lit., 1952-72, Sterling prof. emeritus, 1972—; vis. prof. Harvard, 1950, 53-54; lectr. Princeton seminars in lit. criticism, 1950, vis. prof. comparative lit., fall 1973; vis. summer prof. U. Minn., 1947, Columbia, 1948, U. Hawaii, 1961, U. Calif. at Berkeley, 1963; fellow Huntington Library, San Marino, Calif., 1942, Kenyon Sch. English, 1949, Ind. Sch. Letters, 1950-72; vis. Patten prof. comparative lit. Ind. U., Bloomington, spring 1974;

sr. fellow Soc. Humanities Cornell U., 1977. In charge ASTP program on Czechoslovakia, U. Ia., 1943-44; mem. joint com. Am. Council Learned Socs. and Social Sci. Research Council Slavic Studies, 1948-57. Recipient prize for distinguished service to humanities Am. Council Learned Socs., 1959. Guggenheim fellow, 1951-52, 56-57, 1966-67; Fulbright Research scholar, Italy, 1959-60; Fulbright distinguished lectr., Germany, 1969; sr. fellow Nat. Endowment for the Humanities, 1972-73. Mem. Royal Netherlands Acad. (fgn.), Italian Nat. Acad. (fgn.), Am. Acad. of Arts and Scis., Bavarian Acad., Brit. Acad., Internat. Assn. Comparative Lit. (pres. 1961-64), Am. Assn. Comparative Lit. (pres. 1962-65), Czechoslovak Soc. Arts and Scis. Am. (pres. 1962-66), Modern Humanities Research Assn. (pres. 1974), P.E.N. Club N.Y., Modern Lang. Assn. (editorial bd. 1946-50, 53-59, com. research activities 1949-55, exec. council 1959, v.p. 1964), Conn. Acad., Am. Philos. Soc., Linguistic Soc. Author: Immanuel Kant in England, 1931; The Rise of English Literary History, 1941; Literary Scholarship (with Norman Foerster), 1941; Theory of Literature (with Austin Warren). 1949; The English Romantic Poets (with Thomas M. Raysor), 1951; A History of Modern Criticism, Vol. 1 and 2, 1955, 3 and 4, 1965; Dostoevsky, 1962; Concepts of Criticism, 1963; Essays on Czech Literature, 1963; Confrontations, 1965; Discriminations, 1970. Editorial bd. Philological Quar., 1941-46, Comparative Literature, 1949—, Dictionary of the History of Ideas. Home: 45 Fairgrounds Rd Woodbridge CT 06525

WELLENDORF, THEODORE EUGENE, gas co. exec.; b. Youngstown, Ohio, Jan. 28, 1923; s. John T. and May (Casey) W.; B.S., U. Okla., 1949; m. Helen Virginia Miller, Jan. 10, 1946; children—Glen Russell, Donald Rae. Mem. pricing dept. Youngstown Sheet and Tube Co., 1941; asst. supt. stores Western div. Okla. Natural Gas Co., Oklahoma City, 1949-50, asst. supr. gen., statis. accountant, 1950-52, with records sect., Tulsa, 1952-60, supr. budgets and statistics, 1960-62; adminstrv. asst. to treas., 1962-67, asst. treas., 1967-70, treas., 1970—, asst. sec., 1970—, v.p., 1976—. Served with USAAF, 1942-46. Mem. Financial Execs. Inst. Okla. Soc. Financial Analysts, Am. Gas Assn. (financial and adminstrv. mng. com. 1970-73; award accounting merit 1970). Clubs: Tulsa Country, Summit (Tulsa). Home: 4630 S Vandalia St Tulsa OK 74135 Office: 624 S Boston St Tulsa OK 74119

WELLER, GEORGE ANTHONY, fgn. corr.; b. Boston, July 13, 1907; s. George J. and Matilda (McAleer) W.; ed. Roxbury Latin Sch., 1919-25; A.B., Harvard, 1929; student Max Reinhardt Sch., U. Vienna, 1930-31; m. Katherine Deupree, 1932 (div. 1944); 1 dau., Ann; m. 2d, Charlotte Ebener, Jan. 23, 1948. Tchr., Evans Ranch Sch., Tucson, 1929-30; actor Max Reinhardt Theater, Vienna, Austria, 1931; fgn. corr. N.Y. Times, Greece and Balkans, 1932-36; dir. Homeland Found., 1938-40; war corr. Chgo. Daily News in Balkans, Belgian Congo, Abyssinia, Singapore, Java, New Guinea, Solomons, Central Pacific, China, 1940-72; roving corr. Mediterranean, Balkans, Middle East and periodically Southeast Asia and U.N.; now fgn. corr. in Middle East and Mediterranean. Recipient Pulitzer prize for journalism, 1943; Nieman fellow advanced study, Harvard, 1947-48; recipient George Polk Meml. award L.I.U., 1955; Navy Pub. Service pin and citation for ednl. services, 1968. Mem. Phi Beta Kappa (hon.). Author: Not to Eat, Not For Love, 1933; Clutch and Differential, 1936; Singapore is Silent, 1943; Bases Overseas, 1944; The Crack in The Column, 1949; The Paratroops, 1958; Second Saint of Cyprus (play), 1960 (winner internat. drama contest); The Story of Submarines, 1962; Walking Time (play), 1965. Translator (pen-name Michael Wharf) Fontamara (Ignazio Silone), 1934. Lectr., contbr. fiction, articles to nat. mags.; 1st war corr. to qualify as trained paratrooper in Pacific, 1943. Clubs: Overseas Press (N.Y.C.); Stampa Estera (pres. 1954-55, v.p. 1973—) (Rome). Home: Via Meropia 77 Rome Italy also San Felice di Circeo Italy Office: Chicago Daily News Chicago IL 60611 also Stampa Estera Via della Mercede 55 Rome Italy

WELLER, HERMAN GAYLE, lawyer; b. Kenney, Ill., Feb. 13, 1914; s. Herman John and Maude Edith (Darden) W.; A.B., U. Denver, 1936, LL.B. cum laude, 1938; m. Jane Duvall, July 29, 1938; children—Herman Gayle, Melissa, Timothy. Admitted to Colo. bar, 1938, since practiced in Denver; partner firm Weller, Friedrich, Hickisch and Hazlitt and predecessor firms, Denver, 1942-76, counsel to the firm, 1977—. Chmn. Arapahoe County Republican Central Com., 1952-54, Served to lt. (j.g.) USNR, 1944-46. Mem. Am. (chmn. com. on fidelity and surety law 1973-75), Colo., Denver bar assns., Omicron Delta Kappa, Phi Delta Phi. Clubs: Denver, Law, Valley Country (pres. 1958-60), Mile High (Denver). Home: Parker CO 80134 Office: Capitol Life Center Suite 900 Denver CO 80203

WELLER, JOHN MARTIN, physician; b. Ann Arbor, Mich., Mar. 4, 1919; s. Carl V. and Elsie (Huckle) W.; A.B., U. Mich., 1940; M.D., Harvard U., 1943; m. Virginia Brigham, Jan. 10, 1942; children—Wendy J., Mary M.; m. 2d, Jean LesStrang, June 25, 1971; m. 3d, Adelwisa Agas, May 10, 1979. Intern, Peter Bent Brigham Hosp., Boston, 1944; asst. resident medicine Vanderbilt U. Hosp., Nashville, 1944-45; med. resident VA Hosp., Hines, Ill., 1946-48; Alfred Stengel Research fellow A.C.P. and fellow in med. sci. NRC, dept. biol. chemistry, Harvard, 1948-50; asst. medicine Harvard Med. Sch., 1950-52, instr., 1952-53; mem. faculty U. Mich. at Ann Arbor, 1953—, prof. internal medicine, 1963—; practice medicine specializing in internal medicine, Ann Arbor, 1953—; mem. staff Univ. Hosp., Ann Arbor; cons. Ann Arbor VA Hosp., 1957—; mem. sci. adv. bd. Mich. Kidney Found., 1961—. Served to 1st lt. M.C., AUS, 1945-46, to capt., 1953-55. Diplomate Am. Bd. Internal Medicine. Fellow A.C.P.; mem. Soc. Exptl. Biology and Medicine, Am. Physiol. Soc., Am. Fedn. Clin. Research, Central Soc. Clin. Research, Am. Soc. Nephrology. Author (with James A. Greene, Jr.) Examination of the Urine, 1966; editor: Fundamentals of Nephrology, 1979; contbr. chpts. to textbooks, articles to sci. jours. Office: B2954 Univ Hosp Ann Arbor MI 48109

WELLER, RALPH ALBERT, elevator co. exec.; b. Cleve., Sept. 8, 1921; s. Ralph A. and Aileen (Fitzpatrick) W.; B.S., Va. Mil. Inst., 1942; M.B.A., Harvard, 1947; m. Martha Early, Oct. 10, 1950 (div.); children—Michael F., John A., Robert O. With Otis Elevator Co., N.Y.C., 1947—, regional v.p., San Francisco, 1964-66, v.p. engring., prodn. and purchasing, N.Y.C., 1966-68, pres., 1968—, chief exec. officer, 1969—, chmn. bd., 1975—, also dir.; dir. Otis Elevator Internat. Capital Corp., SAXBY (France), Irving Bank Corp.; trustee Harlem Savs. Bank. Served with USMC, 1942-46. Mem. NAM (dir.), U.S. C. of C. Clubs: Olympic (San Francisco); Sky, Economic (N.Y.C.); Blind Brook (Port Chester, N.Y.). Home: 300 E 56th St New York NY 10022 Office: 153 E 53d St New York NY 10022

WELLER, RICHARD IRWIN, coll. dean; b. Newark, Mar. 3, 1921; s. Harry and Nettie (Feinsod) W.; B.Elec. Engring., City U. N.Y., 1944; B.S., Union Coll., 1948; M.S. in Physics, Fordham U., 1950, Ph.D. in Physics, 1953; various postdoctoral courses at colls., univs; children—Rosalyn Eve, Mark David. Electronics engr. N.Am. Philips Co., Mt. Vernon, N.Y., 1944, 45-46; elec. engr. Guy F. Atkinson Co., Aleutian Islands, Alaska, 1944-45; elec. designer Crow, Lewis & Wick, N.Y.C., 1947; elec. designer Edward E. Ashley, cons. engr., N.Y.C., 1948; elec. engr. Allied Processes, N.Y.C., 1950, V.L. Falotico & Asso., Bklyn., 1950-51; elec. designer Singmaster & Breyer, N.Y.C., 1951; instr. Sch. Engring., Manhattan Coll., N.Y.C., 1950; instr. Newark Coll. Engring., 1952-53, City U. N.Y., Bklyn. Coll., 1952-53; asst. prof. State U. N.Y., Maritime Coll., N.Y.C., 1953-54; med. physicist Med. Physics Div. Brookhaven Nat. Lab., Upton, N.Y., 1954-57; prof. physics, chmn. dept. Franklin and Marshall Coll., Lancaster, Pa., 1957-70; dean Sch. Sci. and Math., Edinboro (Pa.) State Coll., also prof. physics, 1970—. Cons., Fairchild Camera & Instrument Corp., 1956, Brookhaven Nat. Lab., 1957-58, Nuclear Sci. & Engring. Corp., 1960. Bd. dirs. nat., state and local vol. health orgns. NSF, USPHS, AEC grantees, 1959-68. Registered profl. engr. Mem. Am. Assn. Physics Tchrs. (past pres. Central Pa. sect.), AAAS, AAUP, Am. Phys. Soc., Am. Soc. Engring. Edn., IEEE, Health Physics Soc., Sigma Xi, Sigma Pi Sigma, Tau Beta Pi. Contbr. articles to sci. jours. Home: 109 Terrace Dr Edinboro PA 16412

WELLER, ROBERT NORMAN, motel exec.; b. Harrisburg, Pa., Feb. 1, 1939; s. Charles Walter and Martha Ann (MacPherson) W.; B.S., Cornell U., 1969; m. Nancy M. Wood, June 21, 1975; children—Wendi Elizabeth, Terrie Lynn, Nikki Ann. Mgr., Hall's Motor Transit Co., Harrisburg, Pa., 1961-65; market research analyst Carrolls Devel. Corp., Syracuse, N.Y., 1970-72; asst. to pres. Econo-Travel Motor Hotel Corp., Norfolk, Va., 1972-74, dir. franchise sales, 1975, pres., dir., 1976—; pres., dir. Econo-Travel Devel. Corp., Norfolk, 1977—; dir. Ins. Mgmt. Corp. Tidewater, Inc. Served in USMC, 1957-60. Mem. Am. Mgmt. Assn. Home: 1348 Whisper Dr Virginia Beach VA 23454 Office: 20 Koger Exec Center Norfolk VA 23502

WELLER, THOMAS HUCKLE, physician, educator; b. Ann Arbor, Mich., June 15, 1915; s. Carl V. and Elsie A. (Huckle) W.; A.B., U. Mich., 1936. M.S., 1937, LL.D. (hon.), 1956; M.D., Harvard, 1940; Sc.D., Gustavus Adolphus U., 1975, L.H.D., Lowell U., 1977; m. Kathleen R. Fahey, Aug. 18, 1945; children—Peter Fahey, Nancy Kathleen, Robert Andrew, Janet Louise. Teaching fellow bacteriology Harvard Med. Sch., 1940-41, research fellow tropical medicine, pediatrics, 1947-48, instr. comparative pathology, tropical medicine, 1948-49, asst. prof. tropical pub. health Sch. Pub. Health, 1949-50, asso. prof., 1950-54, Richard Pearson Strong prof. tropical pub. health, head dept., 1954—; intern bacteriology and pathology Children's Hosp., Boston, 1941, intern medicine, 1942, asst. resident medicine, 1946, asst. dir. research div. infectious diseases, 1949-55; mem. commn. parasitic diseases Armed Forces Epidemiol. Bd., 1953-72, dir., 1953-59. Served to maj. M.C., AUS, 1942-46; charge parasitology, bacteriology, virology sections Antilles Dept. Med. Lab., P.R. Recipient E. Mead Johnson award for devel. tissue culture procedures in study virus diseases, Am. Acad. Pediatrics, 1953; Kimble Methodology award, 1954; Nobel prize in physiology and medicine, 1954; George Ledlie prize, 1963; Weinstein Cerebral Palsy award, 1973; Stern Symposium honoree, 1972. Diplomate Am. Bd. Pediatrics. Fellow Am. Acad. Arts and Scis.; mem. Harvey Soc., AMA, Am. Soc. Parasitologists, Am., Royal socs. tropical medicine and hygiene, Am. Pub. Health Assn., AAAS, Am. Epidemiological Soc., Nat. Acad. Scis., Am. Pediatric Soc., Assn. Am. Physicians, Soc. Exptl. Biology and Medicine, Am. Assn. Immunologists. Soc. Pediatric Research, Phi Beta Kappa. Sigma Xi, Alpha Omega Alpha. Author sci. papers. Home: 56 Winding River Rd Needham MA 02192 Office: 665 Huntington Ave Boston MA 02115

WELLES, EDWARD RANDOLPH, bishop; b. Cin., April 20, 1907; s. Samuel Gardner and Mabel (De Geer) W.; A.B., Princeton, 1928; B.A., Oxford U., 1930, M.A., 1934; S.T.B., Gen. Theol. Sem., 1932, S.T.D., 1950; D.D., Nashotah House, 1950, Missouri Valley Coll., 1950; m. Catharine Van Alstyne, June 2, 1931; children—Katrina (Mrs. G.G. Swanson), Harriet (Mrs. B.C. Foresman), Edward III, Peter. Ordained priest Episcopal Ch., 1931; rector Trinity Church, Woodbridge, N.J., 1931-34; chaplain St. Mark's Sch., Southborough, Mass., 1934-36; dean All Saints Cathedral, Albany, N.Y., 1936-40; rector Christ Ch., Alexandria, Va., 1940-44; dean St. Paul's Cathedral, Buffalo, N.Y., 1944-50; bishop of West Mo. Episcopal Diocese, 1950-72; bishop, Manset, Maine, 1973—; pres. Province of Southwest, 1954-60. Ordained 1st women priests in Episcopal Ch., 1974. Pres. bd. dirs. St. Luke's Hosp., Kansas City, 1950-69, chmn. bd., 1969-72; Episcopal visitor Community of the Transfiguration, Ohio. Author: Ardincaple Castle, 1930; The Christian in World at War, 1940; (autobiography) The Happy Disciple, 1975; columnist Nat. Cath. Reporter, 1978—. Address: Bishop's House Manset ME 04656

WELLES, ORSON, actor, radio and theatrical producer; b. Kenosha, Wis., May 6, 1915; s. Richard Head and Beatrice (Ives) W.; ed. Todd Sch., Woodstock, Ill., 1926-30; m. Virginia Nicholson, Dec. 1934 (div. 1940); 1 son, Christopher; m. 2d, Margarita Cansino (Rita Hayworth), Sept. 7, 1943; 1 dau., Rebecca Welles; m. 3d, Paola Mari, May 8, 1955. Began as actor with Gate Theatre, Dublin, 1931-32; tour with Katharine Cornell, 1933; dir. Woodstock Festival, 1934; played lead in Panic, 1935; dir. Negro Macbeth and Horse Eats Hat, 1936; dir. Dr. Faustus, Cradle Will Rock, 1937; founder Mercury Theatre, dir. Julius Caesar, 1937; dir., producer Shoemakers' Holiday, Heartbreak House, Danton's Death, 1938; writer, dir., artist, radio programs, 1938; including CBS radio series Hello, Americans, in interest of hemispheric relations, 1942-43; v.p. Mercury Theatre, Inc.; made Mercury text records of Shakespeare plays for Columbia Rec. Corp., 1939; producer, writer, dir. R.K.O. Radio pictures, 1939-40; writer, producer, actor, dir. Citizen Kane, 1940; writer, producer, dir. The Magnificient Ambersons, Lady From Shanghai, 1946; Macbeth, 1947; producer Journey Into Fear, 1941-42; producer, star Jane Eyre, 1943; appeared in TV prodn. King Lear, 1952, Fountain of Youth (Peabody award), 1959; now chiefly acting, producing in Europe; among more recent roles has appeared in: Othello, 1952, also Three Cases of Murder, 1955; Moby Dick, 1956; A Royal Affair at Versailles, 1957; Long Hot Summer, Touch of Evil, Roots of Heaven, 1958, Compulsion, 1959; Crack in the Mirror, 1960, The Trial, 1963, play Moby Dick, 1962, A Man for All Seasons, 1966, Kremlin Letter, 1969, Waterloo, Catch 22, 1970, A Safe Place, 1971, Treasure Island, 1972, Necromancy, 1972, Voyage of the Damned, 1976, F for Fake, 1977, Crossed Swords, 1978, The Late Great Planet Earth, 1978, others; narrator documentary film Masters of Congo Jungle (with William Warfield), 1960. Recipient Claire M. Senie award for foremost achievement in Am. Theatre, 1938; Life Achievement award Am. Film Inst., 1975. Mem. AFTRA, Actors Equity Assn. Clubs: Lotos, Advertising (N.Y.C.). Author: Mr. Arkadin, 1957. Editor: Everybody's Shakespeare (with Roger Hill), 1933; Mercury Shakespeare (with Roger Hill), 1939. Traveled in S. and C. Ams. filming Rio Carnival, also own story of Jangadieros (native fishermen), story about Mexico for Office of Coordinator of Inter-Am. Affairs. Office: care L Arnold Weissberger 120 E 56th St New York NY 10022*

WELLFORD, HARRY WALKER, judge; b. Memphis, Aug. 6, 1924; s. Harry Alexander and Roberta Thompson (Prothro) W.; B.A., Washington and Lee U., 1947; student U. N.C., 1943-44; postgrad. U. Mich. Law Sch., 1947-48; LL.D., Vanderbilt U., 1950; m. Katherine E. Potts, Dec. 8, 1951; children—Harry Walker, James B. Buckner P., Katherine T., Allison R. Admitted to Tenn. bar, 1950; atty. McCloy, Myar & Wellford, Memphis, 1950-60, McCloy, Wellford & Clark, Memphis, 1960-70; judge U.S. Dist. Ct., Memphis, 1970—. Mem. Tenn. Republican Exec. Com., 1960-70; del. Rep. Nat. Conv., 1964; campaign chmn. Sen. Howard Baker campaigns, 1964, 66, Gov. Winfield Dunn, 1970; mem. Charter Drafting Com. City of Memphis, 1967; chmn. Shelby County Rep. Party, 1968-69; chmn. Tenn. Hist. Commn.; mem. Tenn. Am. Revolution Bicentennial Commn., 1976; mem. Com. on Adminstrn. of Fed. Magistrates System. Served as ensign USNR, 1944-45; PTO. Recipient Sam A. Myar award for service to profession and community Memphis State Law U., 1963; Tenn. Sr. Tennis Champion, 1974. Mem. Phi Beta Kappa, Omega Delta Kappa. Presbyterian (clk. of session, commr. Gen. Assembly, elder). Club: Memphis Country. Home: 91 N Perkins St Memphis TN 38117

WELLINGTON, GEORGE HARVEY, educator; b. Springport, Mich., Sept. 19, 1915; s. Earl C. and Kate (Griffith) W.; B.S., Mich. State U., 1937, Ph.D., 1954; M.S., Kans. State U., 1940; m. Gladys Ella Brown, Aug. 11, 1939; children—Earl Croby, Mary Wellington Daly) Ann Carol Wellington Marguet. Grad. research asst. Kan. State U., 1938-40; asst. prof. Coll. Agr., Cornell U., Ithaca, N.Y., 1947-49, asso. prof., 1949-57, prof., 1957-78, prof. emeritus, 1978—, also Agrl. Coll. Extension specialist; cons. animal sci. Govt. Syria, 1962, USSR, 1979, Botswana, 1979; Ford Found. vis. prof. U. Aleppo, Syria, 1965. Served to maj. AUS, 1942-46; CBI. Mem. Am. Soc.. Animal Sci. (Distinguished Service award 1975), Inst. Food Technologists, Am. Meat Sci. Assn. (Signal Service award 1966; pres. 1970), Alpha Gamma Rho. Rotarian). Home: 37 Woodlane Ithaca NY 14850

WELLINGTON, HARRY HILLEL, univ. dean; b. New Haven, Aug. 13, 1926; s. Alex M. and Jean (Ripps) W.; A.B., U. Pa., 1947; LL.B., Harvard, 1952; M.A. (hon.), Yale, 1960; m. Sheila Wacks, June 22, 1952; children—John, Thomas. Law clk. to U.S. Judge Magruder, 1953-54, Supreme Ct. Justice Frankfurter, 1955-56; asst. prof. law Stanford, 1954-56; mem. faculty Yale, 1956—, prof. law, 1960—, Edward J. Phelps prof. law, 1967—, dean Law Sch., 1975—. Ford fellow London Sch. Econs., 1965, Guggenheim fellow; sr. fellow Brookings Instn., 1968-71, cons. domestic and fgn. govtl. agys. Admitted to D.C. bar, 1952. Bd. overseers faculty arts and scis. U. Pa. Mem. Am. Bar Assn., Bar Assn. Conn., Am. Law Inst., Am. Arbitration Assn. Author: (with Harold Shepherd) Contracts and Contract Remedies, 1957; Labor and the Legal Process, 1968; (with Clyde Summers) Labor Law, 1968; (with Ralph Winter) The Unions and the Cities, 1971; also articles. Office: Yale Univ Law School New Haven CT 06520

WELLINGTON, JOHN ADAM, educator; b. Chgo., June 12, 1922; s. John and Bernice Johanna (Tertell) W.; student U. Ill., 1946-48; B.S., Northwestern U., 1950, M.A., 1951, Ph.D., 1955; m. Marie Adele Zeilstra, June 19, 1948; 1 dau., Marie Annette. Dean of men, asst. dean students Coe Coll., Cedar Rapids, Iowa, 1951-53; asst. univ. examiner Northwestern U., 1954, counseling psychologist, 1954-57; dir. counselor edn. Loyola U., Chgo., 1957-69, chmn. dept. guidance, counseling and student personnel work in higher edn., 1969-76, prof., 1970—; cons. Ill. Office Supt. Pub. Instrn., 1957-72. Served with AUS, 1942-46; PTO. Mem. Ill. Guidance Personnel Assn. (mem. senate 1970-72, exec. bd. 1971-72), Ill. Counselor Educators and Suprs. (exec. bd. 1963-66, pres. 1971-72), Am. Personnel and Guidance Assn., Am. Assn. Higher Edn., Am. Ednl. Research Assn., Nat. Vocational Guidance Assn., Phi Delta Kappa. Contbr. articles to tech. jours. and textbooks. Home: 130 Cottage Hill Ave Elmhurst IL 60126 Office: 820 N Michigan Ave Chicago IL 60611

WELLINGTON, JOHN STANLEY, zipper co. exec.; b. Pitts., May 20, 1916; s. John Clifford and Mary Simons (Beyer) W.; A.B., Allegheny Coll., Meadville, Pa., 1937; LL.B., U. Pitts., 1940, J.D., 1968; m. Margaret Hawkins Trussell, Oct. 25, 1941; children—John Stanley, Mary Gay, Charles Howard. Admitted to Pa. bar, 1941, U.S. Supreme Ct. bar, 1965; atty. Union Title Guaranty Co., Pitts., 1941-42, 45-48; asso. atty. U.S. Army Engrs., Pitts., 1942-43; asso. atty., asst. sec. Eastern Gas & Fuel Assos., Pitts., 1948-53; div. atty., sec. Talon div. Textron, Inc., Meadville, 1954—; dir. Talon (Hong Kong) Ltd., Talon West Indies Ltd.; sec., dir. Meadville Community Hotel, Inc., 1959—. Bd. dirs. Northwestern Pa. chpt. Am. Heart Assn., 1977—; trustee First Presbyterian Ch., Meadville, 1960-75; mem. Meadville Ins. Com., 1976—; chmn. Airport Commn., 1966-67. Served with inf., AUS, 1943-45. Decorated Purple Heart. Mem. Am., Pa., Crawford County, Allegheny County bar assns., Am. Judicature Soc., Meadville Area C. of C. (dir., sec. 1972-75), Beta Theta Pi, Phi Delta Phi. Republican. Home: Springs Rd Route 7 Box 410 Meadville PA 16335 Office: 626 Arch St Meadville PA 16335

WELLINGTON, ROBERT HALL, mfg. co. exec.; b. Atlanta, July 4, 1922; s. Robert H. and Ernestine V. (Vossbrinck) W.; B.S., Northwestern Tech. Inst., 1943; M.S. in Bus. Adminstrn., U. Chgo., 1958; m. Marjorie Jarchow, Nov. 15, 1947; children—Charles R., Robert H., Christian J., Jeanne L. With Griffin Wheel Co., 1946-61, v.p. parent co. AMSTED, Chgo., 1961-74, exec. v.p., 1974—; dir. L.E. Myers Co., Chgo. Served to lt. USN, 1943-46. Clubs: Chgo., Chgo. Athletic, Econ., Mid-Am. Office: 3700 Prudential Plaza Chicago IL 60601

WELLIVER, NEIL, artist; b. Millville, Pa., July 22, 1929; B.F.A., Phila. Mus. Coll. Art, 1953; M.F.A., Yale U., 1956; m. Norma Cripps, 1953 (div.); children—Silas, Titus; m. 2d, Polly Mudge, 1968 (dec.); children—Eli, Ethan. One-man exhibitions include: N.Y.C., 1962-75; group exhibitions include: Whitney Ann., 1964, 72, 73, Vassar Coll., 1968, Boston Mus. Fine Arts, 1972, Tokyo, Osaka, Japan, 1975, Pa. Acad. Fine Arts, Phila., 1976; represented in permanent collections: Hershorn Mus., Washington, Met. Mus., N.Y.C., Boston Mus. Fine Arts, Whitney Mus., N.Y.C., Mus. Modern Art, N.Y.C., San Francisco Mus. Art, Madison (Wis.) Art Center, Pa. Acad. Fine Arts, N.C. Mus. Art, Raleigh, Houston Mus.; critic U. Pa. Grad. Sch. Fine Arts, 1966-70. Samuel F.B. Morse fellow, 1963. Address: Route 2 Lincolnville ME 04849

WELLIVER, WARREN DEE, lawyer, state supreme ct. justice; b. Butler, Mo., Feb. 24, 1920; s. Carl Winfield and Burdee Marie (Wolfe) W.; B.A., U. Mo., 1945, LL.B., J.D., 1948; m. Ruth Rose Galey, Dec. 25, 1942; children—Gale Dee (Mrs. William B. Stone), Carla Camile (Mrs. Michael Brooks), Christy Marie. Admitted to Mo. bar, 1948; asst. pros. atty. Boone County, Columbia, 1948-54; sr. partner firm Welliver, Atkinson and Eng, Columbia; 1960-74; tchr. law U. Mo. Law Sch., 1948-49; mem. Mo. Senate, 1977-79; justice Supreme Ct. Mo., Jefferson City, 1979—. Mem. Gov. Mo. Adv. Council Alcoholism and Drug Abuse, chmn. drug council, 1970-72; chmn. Task Force Revision Mo. Drug Laws, 1970-71; liaison mem. council Nat. Inst. Alcoholism and Alcohol Abuse, 1972—. Bd. dirs. Nat. Assn. Mental Health, 1970—, regional v.p., 1973-75; pres. Mo. Assn. Mental Health, 1968-69, Stephens Coll. Assos., 1965—; pres. Friends of Library, U. Mo., 1978-79. Democratic county chmn., 1954-64; hon. fellow Harry S. Truman Library Inst., 1979—. Served with USNR, 1941-45. Fellow Am. Coll. Trial Lawyers, Am. Bar Found.; mem. Am., Mo. (pres. 1967-68), Boone County (pres. 1970) bar assns., Am. Judicature Soc., Am. Legion (past post comdr.), Order of Coif. Clubs: Country of Mo., Columbia Country (past pres.). Home: RD 1 Hartsburg MO 65039 Office: Supreme Ct Bldg Jefferson City MO 65101

WELLMAN, ARTHUR OGDEN, textile mfg. co. exec.; b. Brookline, Mass., Oct. 31, 1894; s. Arthur G. and Celia Guinness (McCarthy) W.; student pub. schs., Boston; Dr. Textile Industries, Clemson Coll., 1955; m. Gullan Karlson, Apr. 11, 1969; children—Marjorie (Mrs. George B. Bullock, Jr.), Arthur Ogden, John G. Partner Nichols & Co., 1935—, v.p., 1927-39; pres., dir. Wellman, Inc. (formerly Nichols & Co., Inc.), Boston, 1939-70, chmn. bd., chief exec. officer, dir., 1970-73, hon. chmn., 1973-75; chmn. bd., chief exec. officer, dir. Wellman Industries, Inc., Johnsonville, S.C., 1954-73, hon chmn., 1973-75; treas., chmn. bd., dir. Southwell Combing Co., North Chelmsford, Mass.; dir. Fanny Farmer Candy Shops, Inc., Fieldcrest Mills, Inc.; oil producer. Mem. Wool Assos. N.Y. Cotton Exchange, N.Y. Commodity Exchange. Mason. Clubs: Bath and Tennis, Everglades, Seminole Golf (Palm Beach); Oyster Harbors, Wianno Golf, Wianno Yacht (Osterville). Home: The Villas 425 Worth Ave Palm Beach FL 33480 Office: 1515 S Flagler Dr West Palm Beach FL 33401

WELLMAN, CARL PIERCE, educator; b. Lynn, Mass., Sept. 3, 1926; s. Frank and Carolyn (Heath) W.; B.A., U. Ariz., 1949; M.A., Harvard, 1951, Ph.D., 1954; postgrad. U. Cambridge (Eng.), 1951-52; m. Farnell Parsons, June 20, 1953; children—Timothy, Philip, Lesley, Christopher. Instr. Lawrence U., Appleton, Wis., 1953-57, asst. prof., 1957-62, asso. prof., 1962-66, prof., chmn. dept. philosophy, 1966-68; prof. philosophy Washington U., St. Louis, 1968—. Mem. rev. panel research grants Nat. Endowment Humanities, 1968-71. Recipient Uhrig Distinguished Teaching award Lawrence U., 1968; Am. Council Learned Socs. fellow, 1965-66; Nat. Endowment for Humanities sr. fellow, 1972-73. Mem. Am. Philos. Assn. (exec. com.), Internat. Assn. for Philosophy Law and Social Philosophy (sec. gen.). Author: The Language of Ethics, 1961; Challenge and Response: Justification in Ethics, 1971; Morals and Ethics, 1975. Home: 439 Westgate Ave St Louis MO 63130

WELLMAN, RICHARD HARRISON, plant research co. exec.; b. Mountain View, Alta., Can., May 25, 1914; s. John A. and Eliza W. (Lindsay) W. (parents Am. citizens); came to U.S., 1916; B.S., U. Wash., 1935, Ph.D. in Plant Pathology, 1939; m. Doris Heathman, Nov. 26, 1936; children—William John, James Harrison. Fellow plant pathology Boyce Thompson Inst. for Plant Research, Inc., Yonkers, N.Y., 1939-41, research asso., 1941-44, mng. dir., 1974—; head biol. research div. Union Carbide Corp., 1945-54, mgr. agrl. chem. div., 1954-66, v.p., gen. mgr. agrl. chems., 1966-74; mng. dir. Boyce Thompson Inst., Cornell U., Ithaca, N.Y., 1974—; with OSRD, 1944; mem. Commn. on Edn. in Agr. and Natural Resources, NRC, subcom. on plant pathology, com. on plant and animal pests, 1964-68; mem. agribusiness adv. com. for sec. commerce and agr., 1969; mem. council N.Y. State Coll. Agr. and Life Scis., 1970-73; chmn. study team on world crop prodn. World Food and Nutrition Study, Nat. Acad. Scis., 1975-77, now bd. environ. studies; cons. comml. orgns. Mem. Nat. Agrl. Chems. Assn. (chmn. policy adv. com. 1966-68, chmn. bd. 1969-71), AAAS, Phytopath. Assn., Am. Chem. Soc., N.Y. Acad. Scis. Contbr. sci. articles to profl. jours. Home: 1101 Hector St Ithaca NY 14853 Office: Cornell U Ithaca NY 14853

WELLMAN, RICHARD VANCE, legal educator; b. Worthington, Ohio, Sept. 10, 1922; s. Burton Singley and Blanche (Gardner) W.; A.B., U. Mich., 1947; J.D., 1949; m. Louise Dewey Laylin, Oct. 18, 1944; children—Martha, Anne, Jane, Sarah, Peter Burton, Charles Richard. Admitted to Ohio bar, 1949, Mich. bar, 1960; practice in Cleve., 1949-51, Mt. Vernon, Ohio, 1951-54; mem. faculty U. Mich. Law Sch., 1954-74; Alston prof. law U. Ga. Sch. Law, 1974—. Engaged in nat. effort to encourage state probate code revisions, 1965—; commr. Mich. Uniform State Laws, 1970-73; commr. Ga. Uniform State Laws, 1974—; ednl. dir. Uniform Probate Code, 1971—. Served to 1st lt. AUS, 1943-46. Mem. Am. Bar Assn., Mich. Bar Assn. Home: 190 Tipperary Rd Athens GA 30606

WELLNER, CHARLES JULIUS, ret. editor, writer; b. Phila., Oct. 21, 1909; s. Julius and Maude Marie (May) W.; A.B., Pa. State Coll., 1931; m. Jessica Forman, Nov. 21, 1936. Reporter, Phila. Evening Bull., 1931; asst. sec. Res. Officers Assn., Washington, 1932-33; reporter Honolulu Advertiser, 1933-34; city editor Hilo (Hawaii) Tribune-Herald, 1935-36; editor A.P., Kansas City, Mo., Oklahoma City, Albany and Syracuse, N.Y., also corr.-in-charge, Buffalo, 1937-51; mng. editor Hornell (N.Y.) Evening Tribune, 1951-54; editor, gen. mgr. Auburn (N.Y.) Citizen-Advertiser, 1954-65; editor Lockport (N.Y.) Union-Sun and Jour., 1965-75, editor emeritus, 1975—; free-lance writer, 1975—. Pres., Asso. Dailies of N.Y. State, 1962-63; del. Am. Council on Edn. for Journalism, 1964-68. Bd. dirs. N.Y. State Citizens Council, 1957-58; mem. Cayuga County (N.Y.) Citizens Council, 1957-58; pres. Health Assn. of Niagara County, 1968-70; treas. Lakes Area Regional Med. Program, 1969-71. Served from 2d lt. to 1st lt., AUS, 1942-44. Mem. N.Y. State A.P. Assn. (pres. 1958-59), Am., N.Y. State (pres. 1963-64) socs. newspaper editors, Nat. Conf. Editorial Writers (pres. 1971-72), N.Y. State Pubs. Assn., Asso. Dailies N.Y. State (pres. 1962-63), Lockport C. of C. (dir. 1967-70), Sigma Delta Chi (pres. Greater Buffalo Internat. chpt. 1968). Clubs: Torch (pres. 1957) (Auburn). Author: Challenge and Achievement: A History of the Lakes Area Regional Medical Program, 1975. Home: 4891-B Collwood Blvd San Diego CA 92115. *A constant effort to serve the newspaper readers by enabling them to distinguish clearly the difference between objectivity in reporting the news and subjectivity in commenting upon it, demanding fearlessness and fairness in both.*

WELLS, ALEXANDER FRANK, chemist, educator; b. London, Eng., Sept. 2, 1912; s. Alexander Edward and Emma Isabel (Wilks) W.; M.A., Oxford (Eng.) U., 1937; Ph.D., Cambridge (Eng.) U., 1937, Sc.D., 1956; m. Ada Squires, Dec. 30, 1939; children—Alexander John, Janet (Mrs. John Bray). Came to U.S., 1968. Research univs Cambridge and Birmingham, 1937-44; sr. research asso. Imperial Chem. Industries Ltd., 1944-68; prof. chemistry U. Conn., 1968—; hon. reader chemistry U. Manchester (Eng.), 1966-68; NSF vis. sr. fgn. scientist, 1965-66. Fellow Chem. Soc., Inst. Physics; mem. Am. Chem. Soc. Author: Structural Inorganic Chemistry, 4th edit., 1975; The Third Dimension in Chemistry, 1956; Models in Structural Inorganic Chemistry, 1970; Three-dimensional Nets and Polyhedra, 1977; also articles. Home: 197 Pleasant Valley Rd Willimantic CT 06226 Office: Dept Chemistry Univ Conn Storrs CT 06268

WELLS, BEN HARRIS, beverage co. exec.; b. Saginaw, Mich., June 11, 1906; s. Ben W. and Florence (Harris) W.; student Ind. U., 1922-25; A.B., U. Mich., 1929, M.A., 1931; L.H.D., Westminster Coll., 1979; m. Katherine Gladney, June 17, 1938; children—Katherine Graves, Ben Gladney. Tchr., John Burroughs Sch., St. Louis County, 1929-31, 33-38; critic, tchr. U. Mich. Sch. Edn., 1931-33; with Seven-Up Co., St. Louis, 1938—, pres., 1965-74, chmn., 1974-78; Chmn. Consumer Research Inst., 1970-77. Pres. St. Louis Symphony Soc., 1970-78, chmn., 1978—; bd. dirs. St. Louis council Boy Scouts Am., St. Louis United Way, Civic Progress (emeritus); St. Louis Arts and Humanities Commn., Arts and Edn. Council, Community Found.; chmn. Com. for Arts Mo.; trustee John Burroughs Sch., 1954-61. Mem. Phi Beta Kappa, Sigma Chi. Clubs: Media, St. Louis, Bellerive Country, Bogey, Noonday, Rotary, University, Racquet, (St. Louis). Home: 35 Westmoreland Pl Saint Louis MO 63108 Office: 121 S Meramec Ave Saint Louis MO 63105. *Whatever I have accomplished has been done through people—good people, and expecting good people to do their best.*

WELLS, CHARLES MARION, lawyer; b. Lawrenceburg, Ind., Mar. 15, 1905; s. Charles Lewis and Leona (Rogers) W.; A.B., Butler U., 1927; LL.B., Ind. U., 1929; LL.M., Harvard, 1932; m. Elizabeth Cooper, Oct. 25, 1950; 1 son, John. Admitted to Ind. bar, 1929, U.S. Supreme Ct., 1935; practice in Indpls., 1929—; mem. firm Barnes, Hickam, Pantzer & Boyd, 1940—; spl. counsel Ind. Dept. Financial Instns., 1935-37. Served to lt. col. USAAF, 1943-46. Mem. Am., Ind., Indpls. bar assns., Am. Judicature Soc., Delta Tau Delta, Delta Theta Phi. Republican. Methodist. Mason. Clubs: Indpls. Athletic, Lawyers, Woodstock (Indpls.). Home: 510 Buckingham Dr Indianapolis IN 46208 Office Merchants Bank Bldg Indianapolis IN 46204

WELLS, CHARLES WILLIAM, utility exec.; b. Springfield, Ill., June 25, 1934; s. William Ward and Maxine Deloris (Harris) W.; student Springfield Jr. Coll., 1952-54; B.S. in Elec. Engring., U. Ill., 1956; M.B.A., 1977; m. Lois Vasconcells, Mar. 5, 1954; children—David, Susan, Amy. With Ill. Power Co., 1958—, asst. to service area mgr., Galesburg, 1960-65, supr. residential and comml. sales, Decatur, 1965-70, mgr. sales, 1970-72, v.p., 1972-76, exec. v.p., 1976—, also dir. Served with USN, 1956-58. Mem. Decatur C. of C. Presbyterian. Clubs: South Side Country, Home Park Swimming, Decatur Racquet. Home: 2241 Ravina Park Rd Decatur IL 62526 Office: 500 S 27th St Decatur IL 62525

WELLS, CHARLOTTE GERTRUDE, speech pathologist, educator; b. Omaha, Feb. 10, 1912; d. Charles Fowler and Gertrude (Bethge) Wells: B.F.A. in Edn., U. Nebr., 1931; M.A., U. Wis., 1938, Ph.D., 1941. Tchr. speech N. Platte (Nebr.) High Sch., 1931-37; instr., then asst. prof. Mt. Holyoke Coll., 1941-45; acting asst. prof. Stanford, 1945-46; mem. faculty U. Mo., Columbia, 1946-79, prof. speech, 1953-79, dir. speech and hearing clinic, 1946-79. Mem. Am. Speech-Lang.-Hearing Assn. (life), Am. Cleft Palate Assn. Home: 938 S Kihei Rd Apt 612 Kihei Maui HI 96753

WELLS, DONALD ARTHUR, educator; b. St. Paul, Apr. 17, 1917; s. Harry Edward and Madeline Hammond (Sears) W.; student forestry, U. Minn., 1936-39; B.A. in Philosophy, Hamline U., 1940; S.T.B., Boston U., 1943, Ph.D. in Philosophy, 1946; m. June Elizabeth Mickman, Sept. 7, 1940; children—Miriam June, Michael John. Ordained to ministry Methodist Ch., 1943; pastor in Rice Lake, Minn., 1939-40, Waldoboro Circuit, Me., summer 1942, Allston, Mass., 1942-44, Weston, Mass., 1944-46; therapist Bedford (Mass.) Mental Hosp., 1945-46; lectr. family relations Brown Trust Fund, Portland, Oreg., 1946-48; asst. prof. philosophy and religion Oreg. State Coll., 1946-48; prof. philosophy, chmn. dept. Wash. State U., 1948-69; chmn. dept. philosophy U. Ill., Chgo., 1969-71; prof. philosophy U. Hawaii, 1971—. Democratic precinct committeeman, Pullman, Wash., 1948—; del. Wash. Dem. Conv., 1952, 60. Mem. AAUP (local pres. 1963, state pres. 1963), Am. (exec. com. 1956; div. sec.-treas. 1962-66, v.p. 1967), Northwest (pres. 1950) philos. assns. Author: God, Man and the Thinker: Philosophies of Religion, 1962; The War Myth, 1967. Contbr. articles profl. jours. Office: Dept of Philosophy Univ Hawaii Hilo HI 96720

WELLS, EDWARD CURTIS, cons., ret. engring. exec.; b. Boise, Idaho, Aug. 26, 1910; s. Edward Lansing and Laura Alice (Long) W.; student Willamette U., 1927-29, D.Sc. (hon.), 1963; B.A., with gt. distinction, Stanford, 1931; LL.D., U. Portland, 1946; m. Dorothy Evangeline Ostlund, Aug. 25, 1934; children—Laurie Jo (Mrs. William Tull), Edward Elliott. Draftsman, Boeing Co., Seattle, summer 1930, draftsman, engr., 1931-33, group engr., 1933-34, asst. project engr., 1934-37, chief preliminary design engr., 1937-38, chief project engr., 1938-39, asst. chief engr., 1939-43, chief engr., 1943-47, v.p., chief engr., 1947-48, v.p. engring., 1948-58, 59-61, v.p., gen. mgr. mil. aircraft systems div., 1961-63, v.p. product devel., 1963-65, 66-67, group v.p. airplanes, 1965-66, sr. v.p., 1967-71, ret., 1972; v.p., gen. mgr. Systems Mgmt. Office, 1958-59, dir. in charge preliminary design Boeing Model 299 airplane, prototype of Model B-17, Boeing Flying Fortress following design of model through all phases of devel., 1934; cons., 1972—. State Adv. Council Atomic Energy, 1958-60. Life trustee Willamette U.; mem. adv. bd. Wash. State Inst. Tech., 1957-61; mem. adv. council Stanford Engring. Sch.; pres. bd. Ryther Child Center, 1961-67, now dir.; mem. Def. Sci. Bd., 1969-72. Recipient Lawrence Sperry award Inst. Aero. Scis. for outstanding contbns. to art airplane design with spl. reference to 4-engined aircraft, 1942; Fawcett Aviation award, 1944; Young Man of Year, Seattle, 1943, Fellow Am. Inst. Aeros. and Astronautics (hon.); mem. Am. Soc. Engring. Edn., A.A.A.S., Soc. Automotive Engrs., Nat. Acad. Engring., Phi Beta Kappa Assos., Phi Beta Kappa, Phi Delta Theta, Tau Beta Pi. Clubs: Tennis (Seattle). Office: The Boeing Co PO Box 3707 Seattle WA 98124

WELLS, FRANK G., lawyer, film studio exec.; b. 1932; B.A. summa cum laude, Pomona Coll., 1953; M.A. in Law (Rhodes scholar), Oxford U., (Eng.), 1955; LL.B., Stanford U., 1959. Pres. Warner Bros. Inc. Mem. Phi Beta Kappa. Office: 4000 Warner Blvd Burbank CA 91522*

WELLS, HARRY KENNADY, spice and food processing co. exec.; b. Balt., Sept. 4, 1922; s. Clifton Kennady and Ruth Jones (Coale) W.; B.S. in Mech. Engring., U. Md., 1943; m. Lois Luttrell, Sept. 8, 1946; children—Katherine Anne Wells Witbeck, Robert Grayson, David Kennady. With McCormick & Co., Inc., Balt., 1946—, v.p., gen. mgr. Schilling div., San Francisco, 1966-68, v.p., 1968-69, pres., 1969-77, chmn. bd., pres., chief exec. officer, 1979—, also dir.; chmn. bd. McCormick de Mexico, S.A., Mexico City, McCormick/Lion Ltd., Tokyo; dir. Gilroy Foods, Inc. (Calif.), Md. Properties, Inc., Hunt Valley, McCormick Foods Australia, Pty., Ltd., Cheltenham, Victoria, McCormick Foods (U.K.), Ltd., London, Balt. Gas & Electric Co., Md. Nat. Bank, Balt., Md. Nat. Corp., Balt., PHH Group, Inc., Hunt Valley, Loyola Fed. Savs. & Loan Assn., Balt., Armstrong Cork Co., Lancaster, Pa. Past mem. San Francisco Safety Council; v.p. Hillsborough (Calif.) Bd. Edn., 1965, pres., 1966; mem. Md. sponsoring com. Radio Free Europe Fund, Balt.; bd. dirs. Greater Balt. Com., Mid-Atlantic Legal Found., Phila.; mem. nat. adv. council Salvation Army, N.Y.C.; trustee St. Joseph Hosp., Towson, Md.; former dir. United Fund Central Md., Balt.; past trustee, mem. exec. com. Community Chest Balt. Area; trustee McDonogh (Md.) Sch., Nutrition Found., N.Y.C.; chmn., trustee Food and Drug Law Inst., Washington; chmn. Md. Bd. for Higher Edn., Annapolis. Served to lt. USN, 1943-46. Named Outstanding Engring. Alumnus, U. Md. Sch. Engring., 1976. Mem. Grocery Mfrs. Am. (dir.), NAM (chmn. exec. com.), Pacific Coast Coffee Assn., San Francisco World Trade Club, San Francisco Comml. Club, Nat. Assn. Sport and Phys. Edn. (dir.), Am. Soc. Plant Engrs., Alpha Tau Omega. Methodist. Mason (32 degree, K.T., Shriner). Clubs: Baltimore Country, Center, Maryland (Balt.); Towson; Hunt Valley Golf (Md.); Seaview Country (Absecon, N.J.); Stone Harbor (N.J.) Yacht. Office: 11350 McCormick Rd Hunt Valley MD 21031*

WELLS, HENRY, educator; b. Macomb, Ill., Dec. 15, 1914; s. Maurace Henry and Dorcas (Hart) W.; A.B., U. Ill., 1937; M.A., La. State U., 1939; Ph.D., Yale, 1947; m. Patricia Paul Brown, June 24, 1950; children—Jane Elizabeth Wells Sadtler, Mary Paul, Thomas Gideon, Alexandra, Anthony Morris, Emily Hollingsworth. Instr. polit. sci. Yale, 1947-49, asst. prof., 1949-53; asso. prof., research asso. U. P.R., 1953-56; asso. prof. U. Pa., 1956-69, prof., 1969—, chmn. internat. relations grad. program, 1970-74, dir. Anspach Inst. for Diplomacy and Fgn. Affairs, 1970-74; mem. OAS electoral missions to Dominican Republic, 1961-62, Honduras, 1963, Costa Rica, 1966, Bolivia, 1966, Nicaragua, 1972; Fulbright prof. Sch. Polit. Sci., U. Costa Rica, 1969-70. Mem. bd. aldermen, New Haven, 1950-51, mem. City Plan Commn., 1950-51; judge of elections 36th div. 59th Ward, Phila., 1962-64. Served to lt. USNR, 1942-46. Fellow Social Sci. Research Council, 1946-47, 60-61; Am. Philos. Soc. research grantee, 1977. Mem. Am., Internat. polit. sci. assns., Latin Am. Studies Assn., Caribbean Studies Assn., Am. Peace Soc. (dir. 1970-76, v.p. 1976-78), Phi Beta Kappa. Democrat. Episcopalian (vestryman 1965-69, 78—). Author: The Modernization of Puerto Rico, 1969. Contbr. numerous articles to profl. jours. Home: 8840 Stenton Ave Philadelphia PA 19118

WELLS, HERMAN B, univ. chancellor; b. Jamestown, Ind., June 7, 1902; s. Joseph Granville and Anna (Harting) W.; student U. Ill., 1920-21; B.S., Ind. U., 1924, A.M., 1927, LL.D., 1962; postgrad. U. Wis., 1927-28, LL.D., 1946; LL.D., Butler U., Rose Poly. Inst., DePauw U., 1939, Wabash Coll., 1942, Earlham, 1948, Valparaiso U., 1953, Miami U., Tri-State Coll., 1959, U. Louisville, 1961, Franklin Coll., Anderson Coll., 1962, Ball State Tchrs. Coll., Washington U., 1963, U. Notre Dame, St. Joseph's Coll., U. Calif., Ind. State Coll., 1964, Drury Coll., 1968, Columbia, 1969, Chgo. Circle Campus U. Ill., 1973, Howard U., 1976; L.H.D., Ohio State U., 1963, Marian Coll., 1970; hon. doctorate in edn. Coll. Edn., Bangkok, 1968. Asst. cashier First Nat. Bank, Lebanon, Ind., 1924-26; asst. dept. econs. U. Wis., 1927-28; field sec. Ind. Bankers Assn., 1928-31; sec., research dir. Study Commn. for Ind. Financial Instns., 1931-33; instr. econs. Ind. U., 1930-33, asst. prof., 1933-35; supr. div. of banks and trust cos., div. of research and statistics Ind. Dept. Financial Instns., 1933-35; sec. Commn. for Ind. Financial Instns., 1933-36; prof. adminstrn. Sch. Bus. Adminstrn. Ind. U., 1935-72, dean, 1935-37, acting pres., 1937-1938, pres., 1938-62, univ. chancellor, 1962—, interim pres. Ind. U., 1968; chmn. Ind. U. Found., 1937-62, 69-72, vice chmn., 1975—, pres., 1962-69, chmn. exec. com., 1969—; chmn. Fed. Home Loan Bank of Indpls., 1940-71; dir. Ind. Bell Telephone Co., 1951-72, Chemed Corp., 1970—; dir. Lilly Endowment, Inc., 1973—. Spl. adviser on Liberated Areas, U.S. Dept. State, 1944; cons. U.S. delegation San Francisco Conf. for Am. Council on Edn., 1945. Mem. Allied Missions for Observation Greek elections, rank of Minister, 1946; adviser on cultural affairs to mil. gov., U.S. Zone, Germany, 1947-48; del., 12th Gen. Assembly of UN, 1957; adviser Ministry Edn., Pakistan, 1959; head U.S. delegation SEATO Prep. Commn. on Univ. Problems, Bangkok, 1960; mem. UN com. experts to rev. activities and orgn. UN Secretariat, 1960-61; mem. Nat. Citizen's Commn. Internat. Cooperation; mem. Com. Econ. Devel., 1958-61; chmn. legislature's com. higher edn. State N.Y., 1963-64; mem. Pres.'s Com. U.S. Soviet Trade Relations, 1965; mem. rev. com. on Haile Sellassie I U., Addis Ababa, 1966-75; mem. pres.'s Spl. Com. on Overseas Vol. Activities, 1967; mem. Nat. Commn. on U.S.-China Relation, 1969; tech. adv. bd. Milbanis Meml. Fund, 1973-78. Ex-pres. Nat. Assn. State Univs., State U. Assn.; exec. com. Am. Council on Edn. (chmn. council 1944-45); mem. 1st bd. regents Am. Savs. & Loan Inst. Grad. Sch. Savs. and Loan. Trustee Edn. and World Affairs, 1963-71, chmn. 1963-70; trustee Howard U., 1956-75, Am. U. at Cairo, 1957-75, Ind. Inst. Tech. (emeritus), Earlham Coll. (hon.), Carnegie Found. for Advancement Teaching, 1941-62; former mem. adv. council Am. Sch. of Madrid; mem. nat. com. on govt. fin. Brookings Instn.; bd. visitors Tulane U.; chmn. Aerospace Research Applications Center, Ind. U., 1962-72; nat. bd. dirs. Goodwill Industries Am., 1962-69; bd. dirs. James Whitcomb Riley Meml. Assn. (v.p.), Arthur R. Metz Foundation, Learning Resources Inst., 1959-65, Council on Library Resources, Historic Landmarks Found. Ind., 1974—; chmn. adv. com. Acad. in Pub. Service, 1976—. Recipient Distinguished Service award Ind. Jr. C. of C., 1938; 1st ann. award N.Y. Alumni chpt. Beta Gamma Sigma, 1939; Gold medal award Internat. Benjamin Franklin Soc., 1959; Comdrs. Cross of Order of Merit, Germany, 1960; Radio Sta. WHAS Ind. Man of Year, 1960; Man of Year awards Indpls. Times, 1961, Ind. Optometric Assn., 1961; comdr. Most Exalted Order White Elephant, 1962, knight comdr. 2d class Most Noble Order Crown, 1968 (Thailand); Nat. Interfrat. Conf. award, 1962; Hoosier of Year award Sons of Ind. in N.Y., 1963; Interfrat. Service award Lambda Chi Alpha, 1964; Robins of Am. award, 1964; Distinguished Service Sch. Adminstrn. award Am. Assn. Sch. Adminstrs., 1965; Ind. Arts award, 1977; Liberty Bell award, 1978. Hon. mem. United Steelworkers Am., Dist. 30, Nat. Exchange Clubs, DeMolay Legion of Honor, 1975; hon. v.p. Am. Sunday Sch. Union. Fellow Internat. (hon.), Am. (hon.) colls. dentists, Am. Acad. Arts and Scis.; mem. Am. Philos. Soc., Am. Assn. Sch. Adminstrs., Royal Soc. Art London (Benjamin Franklin fellow), NEA (ex-pres. div. higher edn.), Am. Econ. Assn., Internat. Assn. Univs. (gov., v.p. 1955-60), AAUP, Research Inst. for Arts (chmn. bd. 1975-77), Nat. Commn. on Humanities (vice chmn. 1964-65), Ind. Acad. Social Scis. (past pres.), Ind. Soc. of Chgo., Ind. Soc. Pioneers, Ind. Acad., Ind. Tchrs. Assn., Mortar Bd., Blue Key, Phi Beta Kappa, Phi Mu Alpha, Kappa Delta Pi, Beta Gamma Sigma, Alpha Kappa Psi, Kappa Kappa Psi, Sigma Nu (regent 1968-70). Methodist (trustee). Mason (33 deg.). Kiwanian (hon.), Rotarian (hon.). Clubs: Athenaeum; Columbia, Athletic (Indpls.); Century Assn., University (N.Y.C.); University (Chgo.); Cosmos (Washington). Author: Report of Study Commission for Indiana Financial Institutions (with others), 1932; articles in mags. Home: 1321 E 10th St Bloomington IN 47401 Office: Owen Hall Ind U Bloomington IN 47401

WELLS, HERSCHEL JAMES, physician, hosp. adminstr.; b. Kirkland, Ark., Feb. 23, 1924; s. Alymer James and Martha Thelma (Cross) W.; student Emory U., 1941-42, U. Ark., 1942-43; M.D., U. Tenn., 1946; m. Carmen Ruth Williams, Aug. 5, 1946; children—Judith Alliece (Mrs. W.J. Jarecki), Pamela Elliece (Mrs. G. D. McKinven), Joanne Olivia (Mrs. E.M. Meyer). Rotating intern, then resident internal medicine Wayne County Gen. Hosp. and Infirmary, Eloise, Mich., 1946-50, dir. infirmary div., 1955-65, gen. supt., 1965-74, dir. Walter P. Reuther Meml. Long Term Care Facility, 1974-78; rev. physician DDS, SSA, Traverse City, Mich., 1978—. Served to maj. M.C., AUS, 1948-55. Fellow Am. Coll. Nursing Home Adminstrs.; mem. A. M.A., Mich., Wayne County med. socs., Am. Fedn. Clin. Research, Soc. Nuclear Medicine, Mich. Assn. Professions, Alpha Kappa Kappa, Pi Kappa Alpha. Mason (Shriner, 32 deg.). Home: PO Box 305 Mesick MI 49668 Office: PO Box 712 Traverse City MI 49684

WELLS, JAMES HOWARD, educator; b. Howe, Tex., June 20, 1932; s. Howard Carlock and Vallie Lanier (Duke) W.; B.S., Tex. Tech. Coll., 1952, M.S., 1954; Ph.D., U. Tex., 1958; m. Dorothy Joy Lambert, Sept. 5, 1953; children—Gregory, Valerie. Asst. prof. math. U. N.C., at Chapel Hill, 1958-60, U. Calif. at Berkeley, 1960-62; asso. prof. U. Ky., Lexington, 1962-69, prof., 1969—, chmn. dept., 1969-72. Vis. mem. Inst. Advanced Study, Princeton, N.J., fall 1967; mem. adv. panel math. scis. NSF. Mem. Am. Math. Assn., Am. Math. Soc. Home: 2070 Old Nassau Rd Lexington KY 40504

WELLS, JAMES M., librarian; b. Charleston, W.Va., Nov. 4, 1917; B.S., Northwestern U., 1938; M.A., Columbia, 1939. Instr. English, W.Va. U., Morgantown, 1939-40; Columbia, N.Y.C., 1946-49; custodian John M. Wing Found., Newberry Library, Chgo., 1951—, asso. dir. library, 1965-75, v.p., 1975—; Sandars reader in bibliography U. Cambridge (Eng.), 1977. Served to lt. USNR, 1942-46. Am. Council Learned Socs. fellow, 1941-42, 49-51; Guggenheim fellow, 1978-79. Fellow Soc. Typog. Arts (pres. 1953-54); mem. Renaissance English Text Soc. (sec.-treas. 1965—), Société Typographique de France, Biog. Soc. Am., Am. Antiquarian Soc., Bibliog. Soc., Modern Lang. Assn., Newberry Library Assos. (sec.). Clubs: Caxton (pres. 1968-69), Arts (Chgo.); Rounce and Coffin (Los Angeles); Grolier (N.Y.C.); Pitts. Bibliophiles. Author: Opera di Giovonantonio Tagliente, 1952, The Scholar-Printers, 1964, The Circle of Knowledge, 1968. Contbr. articles to Ency. Brit., Ency. Americana, profl. jours., monographs. Office: 60 W Walton St Chicago IL 60610

WELLS, JOEL FREEMAN, editor, author; b. Evansville, Ind., Mar. 17, 1930; s. William Jackson and Edith (Strasell) W.; A.B. in Journalism, U. Notre Dame, 1952; m. Elizabeth Louise Hein, June 5, 1952; children—William, Eugenia, Susan, Steven, Daniel. Advt. and promotion dir. Thomas More Assocn., Chgo., 1955-64, v.p., 1967—, dir., 1968—; editor The Critic, Chgo., 1964—; lectr. grad. dept. library sci. Rosary Coll., River Forest, Ill., 1964-67. Served to lt. (j.g.) USNR, 1952-55. Author: Grim Fairy Tales for Adults: Parodies of the Literary Lions, 1967; A Funny Thing Happened To The Church, 1969; Under the Spreading Heresy, 1971; The Bad Children's Book, 1972; Second Collection, 1973; (with Elizabeth Wells) Here's to the Family, 1977; also articles. revs. Editor: Pilgrim's Progress, 1979; co-editor: (anthologies) Bodies and Souls, 1961; Blithe Spirits, 1962; Bodies and Spirits, 1964; Through Other Eyes, 1965; Moments of Truth, 1966; Contrasts, 1972. Contbr. to Ann Landers Ency., A to Z, 1978. Home: 827 Colfax St Evanston IL 60201 Office: 180 N Wabash Ave Chicago IL 60601

WELLS, JOEL REAVES, JR., banker; b. Troy, Ala., Nov. 14, 1928; s. Joel Reaves and Julia (Talley) W.; B.S., U. Fla., 1950, J.D., 1951; m. Betty Stratton, June 27, 1953; children—Linda Carol, Martha Sue, Joel Reaves IV. Admitted to Fla. bar, 1951, then practiced in Orlando; partner firm Maguire, Voorhis & Wells, 1956-75; pres., dir. Major Realty Corp., 1972-75; pres. Sun Banks Fla., Inc., Orlando, 1975—, also dir. Pres. United Appeal Orange County, 1960; chmn. Municipal Planning Bd., Orlando, 1962-63; pres. Central Fla. Devel. Com., 1965; trustee Fla. So. Coll. Recipient Distinguished Service award Orlando Jr. C. of C., 1961. Mem. Orlando Area C. of C. (pres. 1970), Fla. Council of 100, Theta Chi (nat. bd. trustees), Phi Delta Phi. Methodist. Mason. Home: 808 Sweetwater Club Blvd Longwood FL 32750 Office: 200 S Orange Ave Orlando FL 32801

WELLS, JOHN ASHLEY, lawyer; b. N.Y.C., Jan. 14, 1908; s. Lucien Roys and Maude (Suckert) W.; B.A. with high honors and high distinction, Wesleyan U., Middletown, Conn., 1932; B.A. Juris (Rhodes scholar), Oxford (Eng.) U., 1934, B.C.L., 1935, M.A., 1953; LL.M., Harvard U., 1936; m. Alicia Kenyon, June 22, 1935 (dec.); children—Michael Coolidge, Meredith Kenyon Wells Brownstein, Sharon Ashley Wells Quick, Jonathan Arnold; m. 2d, Pauline S. Montali, July 5, 1957; children—Antonie Lucienne, Gregory John. Admitted to N.Y. bar, 1937, D.C. bar, 1953, also U.S. Supreme Ct.; with firm Hughes, Schurman & Dwight, N.Y.C., 1936-37, Dwight, Harris, Koegel & Caskey, N.Y.C., 1937-41; A chief counsel OPA, 1942; chief asst. counsel N.Y. State Moreland Commn., 1943; asst. counsel Navy Price Adjustment Bd., 1944-45; partner firm Rogers & Wells, and predecessors, N.Y.C. and Washington, 1947—. Chmn. adv. com. on enforcement policies and practices SEC, 1972; mgr. Republican polit. campaigns, 1948-69. Served to lt. comdr. USNR, 1944-45. Decorated Commendation ribbon; named Distinguished Alumnus Wesleyan U., 1973. Mem. Phi Beta Kappa, Delta Kappa Epsilon. Republican. Episcopalian. Author: The Voter's Presidential Handbook, 1960. Editor: Thomas E. Dewey on the Two-Party System, 1966. Home: 69 Rye Rd Rye NY 10580 Office: 200 Park Ave New York NY 10017

WELLS, JOSEPH MERTON, utility exec.; b. East Chicago, Ind., Jan. 14, 1922; s. Samuel Ralph and Helen Beatrice (Kester) W.; S.B. cum laude, Harvard U., 1943, LL.B., 1952; m. Eileen Agnes Ponsonby; Sept. 1, 1972; children—R. Dodge, David C. Admitted to Ill. bar, 1953; asso., then partner firm Ross, Hardies & O'Keefe, Chgo., 1952-64; mem. corporate staff Peoples Gas Light and Coke Co., also Peoples Gas Co., Chgo., 1962—, v.p., gen. counsel, 1972—. Bd. dirs. Council Community Services Met. Chgo., 1966-77, pres., 1970-72; bd. dirs. United Way Met. Chgo., 1976—. Served with AUS, 1943-49. Mem. Am., Chgo. bar assns. Clubs: University, Econ. (Chgo.). Home: 711 Timber Ln Lake Forest IL 60045 Office: 122 S Michigan Ave Chicago IL 60603

WELLS, KENNETH DALE, economist; b. Akron, Ohio, June 23, 1908; s. Alfred R. and Lonia I. (Dales) W.; B.S., Northwestern U., 1936; grad. student U. So. Calif., Calif. Inst. Tech., U. Akron; LL.D., Fla. So. Coll., 1953, Trinity Coll., 1955, Tex. Christian U., 1959; D.H.L., Temple U.; L.H.D., Salem Coll., 1962; D.B.A., Lincoln Meml. Coll., 1968; Dr. Pub. Service, Brigham Young U., 1969; m. Ruth E. Van Allen, June 9, 1930; children—Kenneth Dale II, Richard James. Reporter, Bradstreet Co., 1931-33; owner fin. reporting orgn. and land-title abstract firm Wells & Bliss, Inc., Akron, 1933-38; tchr. econs. and mgmt. relations U. Akron, U. So. Calif., 1939-44; joined Union Oil Co. of Calif., 1939, safety and tng. exec., 1945-47; v.p., Western mgr. Nat. Assn. Foremen, 1947-48; founder Am. Mgmt. Day at Hollywood Bowl, 1947; dir. ops. joint com. for improvement pub. understanding our econ. system Assn. Nat. Advertisers-Am. Assn. Advt. Agencies, 1947-49; vis. lectr. U. Wash., U. Ala., U. So. Calif., Calif. Inst. Tech., Temple U. Founder, Freedoms Found., Valley Forge, pres., 1949-70; pres. Valley Forge Found., now pres. emeritus, hon. nat. vice chmn., nat. life trustee. Chmn. bd. trustees Family Found. Am., 1977—; candidate for U.S. Congress, 1st Dist. Va., 1972; chmn. bd. trustees Family Found. Am., Williamsburg, Va. Recipient Silver Buffalo and Silver Antelope awards Boy Scouts Am.; Nat. Award for Advancement Mgmt., 1948, Nat. award Mil. Order Purple Heart, 1952; Ann. gold medal VFW, 1953; Nat. award Masonic Shrine, 1956; Magna Charta Day award Baronial Order of Magna Charta, 1960; Citizenship medal Am. Legion, 1963; William Penn medal of Phila., 1962, Nat. award of Ret. Tchrs., 1963; Nat. Ct. Honor, Boy Scouts Am.; Nat. Service citation Congl. Medal Honor Soc., 1966; Patriot Sword, Assn. Colonial Innkeepers, 1966; Silver Helmet award Amvets, 1967; Nat. Service medal Kiwanis Internat., 1968; Nat. Honor medal Nat. Exchange Clubs, 1968; Nat. medal Am. War Mothers, 1968; On Sight degree Knights of Malta, 1970; Honor medal SR, 1971; Distinguished Citizens award United Vets. Council Phila., 1971; Silver medal Union League Phila., 1971; On Sight degree Tall Cedars of Lebanon, 1971; Nat. medal Sertoma Internat., 1971; Freedom Archives at Brigham Young U. dedicated in his name, 1978. Mem. Mil. Order World Wars (nat. hon. mem.), Nat. Assn. Foremen (hon. exec.), N.Y. Advt. Club, Nat. Assn. Bus. Economists, Inst. Polit. Studies (Liechtenstein, Europe), Newcomen Soc. N. Am., Freedom Frat. (pres.), Phi Kappa Tau. Mason (33). Clubs: Penn (Phila.); Capitol Hill (Washington). Home: 1525 S Riverside Dr Edgewater FL 32032. *The most important word in my life is "try." For me success is what you have left, as the Hon. John H. Perry Jr. says, when you have run out of failures.*

WELLS, KITTY (MURIEL DEASON WRIGHT), singer; b. Nashville, Aug. 30, 1919; d. Charles Carey and Murtle Bell (Street) D.; grad. high sch.; m. Johnnie Robert Wright, Oct. 30, 1937; children—Ruby Jean (Mrs. Leo Taylor), Bobby Wright, Carol Sue (Mrs. John Sturdivant). Country music singer; sang gospel in chs. as a child; performed on radio, early 1930's; with John and Jack and the Tenn. Mountain Boys, late 1930's-early 1940's; regular on Grand Ole Opry, from 1952; recs. for Decca. Bd. dirs. Nashville Meml. Hosp. Recipient award as number 1 female singer Cashbox Mag., 1953-62, Billboard, 1954-65; award of yr. for top female country vocalist Record World mag., 1965, award for highest artistic achievement in rec. arts, 1964; various awards Downbeat mag.; award as all-time queen of country music Music Bus. mag., 1964; Woman of Yr. award, 1974; named Top Female Artist of Decade, Record World mag., 1974; named to Country Music Hall of Fame, 1976. Mem. Country Music Assn., Nat. Assn. Rec. Arts and Scis. Mem. Ch. of Christ. Author: Kitty Wells Cookbook, 2 vols. Office: Top Billing Inc 4301 Hillsboro Rd Nashville TN 37215*

WELLS, LEONARD NATHANIEL DAVID, JR., lawyer; b. Akron, Ohio, Aug. 24, 1914; s. Leonard Nathaniel David and Lida Holmes (Carr) W.; B.A., Tex. Christian U., 1934; LL.B., Columbia, 1937; m. Louise Cauker, July 31, 1937; children—Leonard Nathaniel David III, Sarah Ann (Bennett), Lida Louise (Angione), Joe Cauker. Admitted to Tex. bar, 1937; regional atty. for NLRB, St. Louis, 1939-41, sr. atty., Washington, 1941-44, asso. dir. field div., 1944-46; partner firm Mullinax, Wells, Baab, Cloutman & Chapman, and predecessors, Dallas; gen. counsel Tex. State Fedn. Labor, 1947-57; counsel So. Conf. Teamsters, 1956—; monitor Internat. Brotherhood Teamsters, 1958-59. Mem. Am. Bar Assn. (chmn. labor law sect. 1954-55), Tex. State Bar (chmn. labor law sect. 1951-52). Democrat. Home: 7525 Fisher Rd Dallas TX 75214 Office: Elmbrook Gardens 8204 Elmbrook Dr Dallas TX 75247

WELLS, MAXWELL WARNOCK, ret. lawyer; b. Vernon, Fla., Nov. 2, 1901; s. Joel Reaves and Ruth (Warnock) W.; B.S., U.S. Naval Acad., 1922; student U. Fla. Law Sch., 1922-23; m. Lillian Adrea Douglas, Sept. 9, 1924 (dec. Oct. 1977); children—Joel Douglas, Maxwell Warnock, Janis (Mrs. Richard A. Westling). Admitted to Fla. bar, 1924, practiced in Orlando, 1924-75; partner firm Maguire, Voorhis & Wells, and predecessor, 1925-75. Chmn. Orange County chpt. A.R.C., 1947; pres. Fla. Citizens Safety Council, 1950-52. Trustee Masonic Home Fla.; bd. dirs. Boys State Fla. Served as midshipman U.S. Navy, World War I; served to capt. USNR, 1940-45; PTO. Decorated Legion of Merit with combat V; recipient Distinguished Service to Fla. Agr. award Fla. Fruit and Vegetable Assn., 1963; 50 Year certificate Fla. Bar, 1974. Fellow Am. Coll. Trial Lawyers; mem. Am., Fla., Orange County (past pres.) bar assns., Assn. ICC Practitioners, Internat. Assn. Ins. Counsel, Am. Legion (past post and dept. comdr.; past vice chmn. nat. security commn.), Fla., Greater Orlando chambers commerce, Orange Meml. Hosp. Assn., Ret. Officers Assn., U.S. Naval Acad. Alumni Assn. Methodist. Mason. Clubs: Army and Navy (Washington); University (Orlando). Home: 300 E Church St Apt 306 Orlando FL 32801 Office: 135 Wall St Orlando FL 32802

WELLS, MELISSA FOELSCH, fgn. service officer; b. Tallinn, Estonia, Nov. 18, 1932; d. Kuno Georg and Miliza (Korjus) Foelsch; came to U.S., 1936, naturalized, 1941; B.S. in Fgn. Service, Georgetown U., 1956; m. Alfred Washburn Wells, 1960; children—Christopher, Gregory. Consular officer, Trinidad, 1961-64; econ. officer mission OECD, Paris, 1964-66; econ. officer, London, 1966-71; internat. economist Dept. State, Washington, 1971-73; dep. dir. maj. export projects Dept. Commerce, 1973-75; comml. counselor, Brazil, 1975-76; ambassador to Guinea, Bissau and Cape Verde, 1976-77; rep. ECOSOC, UN, N.Y.C., 1977-79; resident rep. UNDP, Kampala, Uganda, 1979—. Mem. Am. Fgn. Service Assn.*

WELLS, PATRICIA ANDREWS, singer; b. Ruston, La.; d. Joseph Michael and Victoria (Andrews) Wells; B.Mus., La. Tech. U., 1963; postgrad. Juilliard Sch. Music, 1965-69. Appeared with N.Y.C. Opera, Chgo. Lyric Opera, Houston Grand Opera, Boston Opera, Opera Soc. Washington, Dallas Civic Opera, Seattle Opera, Omaha Opera, Festival of Two Worlds, Spoleto, Italy, Ravina Festival, Santa Fe Opera, Nat. Arts Centre of Can. Festival, and others; concert appearances with major U.S. symphonies. Winner Munich Competition, 1972. Mem. Am. Guild Musical Artists, Actors Equity. Office: care Columbia Artists Mgmt 165 W 57th St New York NY 10019

WELLS, ROBERT, broadcasting co. exec.; b. Garden City, Kans., Mar. 7, 1919; s. Samuel A. and Donna (Hinshaw) W.; student Garden City Jr. Coll., 1938; m. Katherine Jane Lovitt, Apr. 26, 1947; children—Kim Bradford, Kent Marshall. Gen. mgr. Sta. KIUL, Garden City, 1948-53; pres. KIUL, Inc., Garden City, 1953-69; publisher Garden City Telegram, 1957-61; gen. mgr. Harris Radio Group, Hutchinson, Kans., 1961-69; commr. FCC, Washington, 1969-71; v.p. Harris Enterprises, Garden City, 1971—; group mgr. Sta. WJOL, Joliet, Ill., 1971—, Sta. KBUR, Burlington, Idaho, 1971—, Sta. KTOP, Topeka, Kans., 1971—, Sta. KFKA, Greeley, Colo., 1971—, Sta. KSEL, Lubbock, Tex., 1971—, Sta. KIUL, Garden City, 1971—, Sta. KOZA, Odessa, Tex., 1971—; vice chmn., dir. Microband Corp. Am.; chmn. bd., dir. Broadcast Music Inc.; v.p. Asso. Press Broadcasters. Chmn. Kans. Forestry, Fish, and Game Commn., 1963-67; state chmn. for Senator Dole, 1974. Served with U.S. Army, 1940-46. Republican. Congregationalist. Clubs: Rotary, Burning Tree. Home: 1102 Hackberry St Garden City KS 67846 Office: 308 7th St Box 878 Garden City KS 67846

WELLS, ROBERT LYNN, elec. mfg. co. exec.; b. Evanston, Ill., July 28, 1917; s. Charles Conner and Blanche Agnes (Stephenson) W.; B.S. in Mech. Engring., U. Rochester, 1939; M.S., Calif. Inst. Tech., 1940; m. Anne Wuichet, Jan. 25, 1947; children—Heidi Lamont, Charles Conner II, James Weir, Robert Lynn. With Westinghouse Electric Corp., 1940—, gen. mgr. atomic power div., 1957-60, dir. mgmt. and profl. personnel services, 1960- 64, v.p. engring., 1964-68, v.p., gen mgr. materials divs., 1968-69, v.p. atomic equipment divs., 1969-70; v.p. mgmt. and profl. personnel, 1970-74, v.p. Europe, 1974—; dir. Westinghouse Electric, S.A., Geneva, Westinghouse Electrique France, Paris; pres. Compagnie Dispositif Semiconducteur Westinghouse, Le Mans, Westinghouse Electric Europe. Trustee U. Rochester, 1974—; trustee Am. Sch. Paris, 1975—, pres., 1977-79. Recipient Certificate of Commendation, U.S. Navy, 1947. Mem. ASME, Phi Beta Kappa, Sigma Xi. Presbyterian (trustee). Club: U. Rochester Alumni (pres. Pitts. 1958-61). Home: 14 Rue Laurent Gaudet 78150 Le Chesnay France Office: 41 George V 75008 Paris France

WELLS, TOBIN MICHAEL, magazine publisher; b. Dubuque, Iowa, Jan. 24, 1938; s. Marshall J. and Kathryn A. (Kane) W.; B.A., U. Notre Dame, 1961; J.D., U. Detroit, 1967; m. Paula R. Struck, July 14, 1962; children—Julie, Marshall, Brynn. With Ford Motor Co., 1962-70; chmn. bd., chief exec. officer Sportsman Publs., Farmington Hills, Mich., 1970—; guest lectr. Walsh Coll., Troy, Mich. Mem. Mktg. Communications Execs. Internat. Episcopalian. Home: 555 Fairfax Birmingham MI 48009 Office: 31360 Northwestern Hwy Farmington Hills MI 48018

WELLS, VICTOR HUGH, JR., advt. agy. exec.; b. Bloomington, Ill., Apr. 19, 1924; s. Victor Hugh and Wilma Julia (Codlin) W.; B.S., Bradley U., 1948; m. Jacqueline L. Wade, Nov. 25, 1949; children—Victor Hugh, III, Polly Jo, Ken Douglas. Copywriter, Chgo. Tribune, 1949-54, Earle Ludgin & Co., Chgo., 1954-58, 59-64; group creative dir. Tatham-Larid, Chgo., 1958-59; founder, creative dir., pres. Rink Wells & Assos., advt. agy., Chgo., 1964-72; exec. v.p., dir. creative services N. W. Ayer ABH Internat., Chgo., 1972—, also dir. Served to 2d lt. AC, U.S. Army, 1943-45. Recipient various advt. creative awards, including Clio, Andy awards. Club: Tavern (Chgo.). Office: 111 E Wacker Dr Chicago IL 60601

WELLS, WILLIAM CALVIN, lawyer, ins. co. exec.; b. Staunton, Va., Nov. 1, 1896; s. John Miller and Sarah (Maslin) W.; A.B., Washington and Lee U., 1917; LL.B., Harvard, 1921; m. Pauline Flanery, Feb. 15, 1923; children—Calvin L., Pauline (Mrs. John M. Montgomery, Jr.). Admitted to Miss. bar, 1921; legal dept. A.C.L. R.R., Wilmington, N.C., 1920-21; mem. firm Wells, Stevens & Jones, Jackson, Miss., 1922-30, sr. mem. Wells, Thomas & Wells, Jackson, 1945-68; sr. mem. Wells, Gerald, McLendon, Brand, Watters & Cox, 1968-77, Wells, Downey & Wicker, 1977—; dir., gen. counsel, exec. com. Lamar Life Ins. Co., 1954-67; chmn. exec. com. First Nat. Bank, Jackson, Miss., 1954-67; dir., gen. counsel Downtown Center Corp., Mortgage Bond & Trust Co., Corinth Counce R.R. Co., Miss. Valley Title Ins. Co., Jackson Packing Co.; pres., dir. Fidelity Ins. Co. Am., 1965-73; gen. counsel Hinds-Rankin Met. Water and Sewer Assn., Inc.; div. atty. Gulf, Mobile & Ohio R.R. Co., 1954-73. Served as lt. U.S. Army AC, 1917-19. Mem. Ind. Petroleum Assn. Am., Am. Life Conv., Assn. Ins. Counsel, Internat. Assn. Ins. Counsel, Miss. Colls. Assn., Harvard Law Sch. Assn. Miss. (pres.). Am. Arbitration Assn. (dir.), N.E. Gen. Soc., Am., Miss., Hinds County, Inter-Am., Internat. bar assns., Newcomen Soc. N.Am., Mid-Continent Oil and Gas Assn. (pres. Miss.-Ala. div. 1966-68), Miss. Research and Devel. Council (dir., exec. com.), Jackson C. of C. (dir.), Miss. Bar Found., Nat. Lawyers Club, Am. Judicature Soc., Miss., So. hist. assns., Am. Legion, Kappa Sigma. Presbyn. Mason, Kiwanian (past pres.). Clubs: 100 of Jackson, Knife and Fork, Country of Jackson, Capital City, University, Patio. Home: 3520 Hawthorn Dr Jackson MS 39216 Office: 1100 Deposit Guaranty Bank Bldg PO Box 1970 Jackson MS 39205

WELLS, WILLIAM THOMAS, diversified co. exec.; b. Springfield, Mass., Nov. 26, 1926; s. William Thomas and Minnie Mary (Rogers) W.; A.B. cum laude, U. Mass., 1949; M.B.A., U. Pa., 1950; m. Paulina Fay, Dec. 8, 1945; 1 son, Jeffrey Michael. With Westinghouse Corp., Pitts. and Atlanta, 1950-54; with A.G. Spalding & Bros., Inc., Chicopee, Mass., 1954-58; div. v.p. Ryder System Inc., Miami, Fla., 1958-65, Brunswick Corp., St. Louis, 1965-68; pvt. investments, Miami, 1968-70; pres., chief exec. officer Golden Cycle Corp., Colorado Springs, Colo., 1970—, chmn. bd. dirs., 1975—; chmn., chief exec. officer Smyth Worldwide Movers, Inc., Seattle, 1970-78, Smyth Van Line, Inc., Seattle, 1973-78. Trustee Colorado Springs Fine Arts Center. Served with USAF, 1945-47. Clubs: Cheyenne Mountain Country, Garden of the Gods, Broadmoor Golf, El Paso (Colorado Springs). Home: 6 Gentry Ln Colorado Springs CO 80906 Office: 228 N Cascade Ave Colorado Springs CO 80903

WELMERS, WILLIAM EVERT, educator; b. Orange City, Iowa, Apr. 4, 1916; s. Thomas E. and Jane (Waalkes) W.; B.A., Hope Coll., Holland, Mich., 1936; Litt.D., 1967; Th.B., Westminster Theol. Sem., Phila., 1939, Th.M., 1939; Ph.D., U. Pa., 1943; m. Beatrice Faye Fairbanks, June 21, 1940; children—R. Bruce, Margaret Jean, Richard C. Ordained to ministry Orthodox Presbyn. Ch., 1943; instr. U. Pa., 1943-44, 45-46; missionary Lutheran Mission in Liberia, 1946-48; fellow Am. Council Learned Socs., 1948-50; asst., then asso. prof. linguistics Cornell U., 1950-54; asso. prof. linguistics Hartford (Conn.) Sem. Found., 1955-60; prof. linguistics and African langs. U. Calif. at Los Angeles, 1960—; cons. in field, 1945—. Mem. Linguistic Soc. Am., Internat. African Inst., African Music Soc., African Studies Assn., Linguistic Soc. Liberia, W. African Linguistic Soc. Author: Spoken Kpelle, 1948; Spoken English as a Foreign Language, 1955; (with B. F. Welmers) Igbo: A Learner's Dictionary, 1968; Efik, 1968; Wukari Jukun & Takum Jukun, 1968; African Language Structures, 1973; A Grammar of Vai, 1976; also articles. Home: 2272 Overland Ave Los Angeles CA 90064

WELNA, CECILIA, educator; b. New Britain, Conn., July 15, 1927; d. Joseph and Sophie (Roman) Welna; B.S., St. Joseph Coll., 1949; M.A., U. Conn., 1952, Ph.D., 1960. Instr. Mt. St. Joseph Acad., 1949-50; asst. instr. U. Conn., 1950-55; instr. U. Mass., 1955-56; prof., chmn. dept. math. U. Hartford, 1957—. Mem. Math. Assn. Am., Am. Math. Soc., Nat. Council Tchrs. Math., Research Soc. Am., Assn. Tchrs. Math. New Eng., Sigma Xi. Home: 176 Smith St New Britain CT 06053 Office: University of Hartford West Hartford CT 06117

WELP, THEODORE MARTIN, utility co. exec.; b. San Francisco, June 13, 1934; s. Martin and Paula (Kuper) W.; B.S. in Commerce, U. Santa Clara, 1956; m. D. Elaine Bruno, Oct. 12, 1957; children—Katherine, George, Thomas, Laura. Asst. treas. Pacific Gas and Electric Co., San Francisco, 1967-70, treas., 1970-73; sr. v.p. finance, dir. Tucson Gas & Electric Co., 1974-76, pres., chief exec. officer, 1976—. Served with AUS, 1957-59. Club: Tucson Country. Office: 200 W 6th St Tucson AZ 85715

WELPTON, SHERMAN SEYMOUR, JR., lawyer; b. Omaha, Mar. 21, 1908; s. Sherman Seymour and Jane (Tuttle) W.; LL.B., J.D., U. Nebr., 1931, LL.D., 1978; LL.D., Pepperdine U., 1977; m. Dorothy Virginia Felber, Nov. 7, 1931; children—Sherman Seymour III, Douglas Felber, Virginia Jane (Mrs. William D. Ferguson, Jr.). Admitted to Nebr. bar, 1931, Calif. bar, 1942; partner firm Ramsey & Welpton, Omaha, 1931-38, Ritchie, Swenson & Welpton, Omaha, 1938-42; with firm Gibson, Dunn & Crutcher, Los Angeles, 1942—, sr. partner, 1958—; lectr. U. Calif. at Los Angeles, 1948—. Fellow Am. Coll. Trial Lawyers, Am. Bar Found.; mem. Am., Internat. (del. 1956, 60, 62, 64, 66), Los Angeles County, Calif., Nebr. bar assns., Am. Judicature Soc., World Peace Through Law, Chancery Club, Phi Delta Phi. Clubs: Stock Exchange (pres. 1968-69, bd. dirs. 1958—). Country (Los Angeles); Calif. Club. Home: 407 Robert Ln Beverly Hills CA 90210 Office: 515 S Flower St Los Angeles CA 90071

WELS, PHILIP BERNARD, surgeon; b. N.Y.C., Mar. 24, 1916; s. Harry and Fannie (Weinstein) W.; B.A., U. Buffalo, 1937, M.A., 1939, M.D., 1941; m. Elayne Goldman, Nov. 25, 1948; children—Joan Carol, Robert Allan. Intern, Meyer Meml. Hosp., Buffalo, 1941-42, resident in surgery, 1946-48, now asso. attending staff; exchange teaching resident Millard Fillmore hosp., Buffalo, 1948-49, chmn. dept. surgery, 1968—; exchange teaching resident Roswell Park Meml. Inst., 1949-50, now cons. to clin. staff; practice medicine specializing in surgery, Buffalo, 1941—; asso. attending staff Children's Hosp., Buffalo; cons. in surgery Niagara Falls Meml. Med. Center; asst. clin. prof. surgery State U. N.Y., Buffalo, 1957-68, asso. clin. prof., 1968-70, clin. prof., 1970—, asst. dean, 1964—. Served to capt. U.S. Army, 1942-46. Named to U. Buffalo Athletic Hall of Fame;

recipient Disting. Alumni award SUNY, Buffalo, 1979; diplomate Am. Bd. Surgery, Nat. Bd. Med. Examiners. Mem. A.C.S., Am. Burn Soc., Am. Trauma Soc., N.Y. State, Erie County, Maimonides med. socs., Buffalo, N.Y. State, Roswell Park surg. socs., Buffalo Acad. Medicine, N.Y. State Soc. Surgeons, Am. Coll. Gastroenterology, Soc. Surgery Alimentary Tract, Sigma Xi. Clubs: Erie Downs Country (past pres.), Westwood Country, Buffalo. Contbr. articles to profl. jours. Home: 830 LeBrun Rd Eggertsville NY 14226 Office: 1275 Delaware Ave Buffalo NY 14209

WELS, RICHARD HOFFMAN, lawyer; b. N.Y.C., May 3, 1913; s. Isidor and Belle (Hoffman) W.; A.B., Cornell, 1933; LL.B., J.D., Harvard, 1936; student U. Ariz., 1944; m. Marquerite Samet, Dec. 12, 1954; children—Susan, Amy. Admitted to N.Y. bar, 1936; spl. asst. dist. atty. N.Y. Co., 1936-37; asso. Handel & Panuch, N.Y.C., 1937-38; mem. legal staff, asst. to chmn. Securities and Exchange Commn., Washington, 1938-42; spl. asst. atty. gen. U.S. and spl. asst. U.S. atty., 1941-42; spl. counsel Com. Naval Affairs, U.S. Ho. of Reps., 1943, Sea-Air Commn., Nat. Fedn. Am. Shipping, 1946; trustee, sec. William Alanson White Inst. Psychiatry, N.Y.C., 1946—; vice. chmn., dir. Am. Parents Com.; mem. Moss & Wels, 1946-57, Moss, Wels & Marcus, 1957-68, Sulzberger, Wels & Marcus, 1968-72, Moss, Wels & Marcus, 1972-78, Sperry, Weinberg, Wels, Waldman & Rubenstein, 1979—; gen. counsel Bowling Proprs. Assn. Am., 1956-67; gen. counsel N.Y. State Bowling Proprs. Assn., Am. Acad. Psychoanalysis; commr. Interprofl. Comn. on Marriage and Div.; lectr. Practising Law Inst. Dir. H-R Television, Inc., Broadcast Data Base, Inc. Chmn. bd. govs. Islands Research Found.; bd. govs., chmn., trustee Daytop Village, Inc.; chmn. bd. trustees Bleuler Psychotherapy Center; trustee N.Y. State Sch. Psychiatry, Margaret Chase Smith Library, Skowhegan, Maine. Served from ensign to lt. USNR 1942-46; mem. staff Under Sec. Forrestal, 1943-44; in P.T.O., 1944-46. Vice chmn. Am. Jewish Com., now mem. nat. exec. bd. Mem. Am., N.Y. State (chmn. family law sect.), N.Y. City bar assns., Am. Acad. Matrimonial Lawyers (gov.), Am. Legion, Naval Order U.S., Mil. Order World Wars, Fed. Bar Assn., Res. Officers Assn., Assn. I.C.C. Practitioners, Fed. Communications Bar Assn., Pi Lambda Phi, Sphinx Head. Clubs: Harmonie (gov.), Harvard, Cornell (N.Y.C.); Nat. Lawyers (Washington); Sunningdale Country, Statler (Ithaca, N.Y.). Co-author: Neurotic Interaction in Marriage; Sexual Behavior and the Law. Contbr. articles to profl. jours. Home: 911 Park Ave New York NY 10021 Office: 6 E 43d St New York NY 10017

WELSCH, CHARLES NICHOLAS, JR., trust exec.; b. Mendota, Minn., July 29, 1917; s. Charles Nicholas and Ida (Lau) W.; LL.B., St. Louis U., 1939; m. Margaret E. Williams, Feb. 10, 1945; children—James, Thomas, Joseph, Kathleen, Richard, Michelle, Gregory, Virginia, John. Admitted to Mo. bar, 1939; practice law, St. Louis, 1939-41; with Merc. Trust Co. Nat. Assn., 1945—, trust counsel, 1965—, v.p., 1967—. Served with AUS, 1941-45. Mem. Mo., St. Louis bar assns., Estate Planning Council St. Louis, Corp. Fiduciary Assn. St. Louis. Home: 471 Crabtree Ct Webster Grove MO 63119 Office: 721 Locust St St Louis MO 63101

WELSCH, GLENN ALBERT, educator; b. Woodward, Okla., Apr. 1, 1915; s. George Franklin and Minnie Melissa (Bowers) W.; B.S., Northwestern State Coll., Alva, Okla., 1935; grad. Army Staff and Command Sch., 1943; M.S., Okla. State U., 1949; Ph.D., U. Tex., 1952; m. Irma Richards, Apr. 5, 1942; children—Glenn Andrew, Linden Richards, Mary Ann. Comml. tchr. pub. high sch., Alva, Okla., 1937-40; life ins. salesman Am. Nat. Life Ins. Co., Galveston, Tex., 1946-48; mem. faculty Coll. Bus. Adminstrn., U. Tex., 1952—, prof. accounting, 1956—, chmn. dept., 1959-62, asso. dean grad. studies, 1962-67, John Arch White prof. acctg., 1968-78, Peat, Marwick, Mitchell prof. acctg., 1978—, instr. Exec. Devel. Program, 1956-72; vis. prof., Carman G. Blough Distinguished prof. U. Va., 1970-71; Prickett Distinguished vis. prof. Ind. U., 1975; cons. bus. firms on fin. acctg. and profit planning and control. Served to maj. AUS, 1940-46. C.P.A., Okla., Tex. Mem. Tex. Soc. C.P.A.'s (v.p. 1959-60), Am. Accounting Assn. (pres. 1963), Am. Inst. C.P.A.'s (council 1968-73, accounting prin. bd. 1970-73), Nat. Assn. Accountants, Financial Execs. Inst., Planning Execs. Inst., Beta Alpha Psi, Beta Gamma Sigma. Author: Budgeting: Profit Planning and Control, 4th edit., 1976; (with B.H. Sord) Business Budgeting: A Survey of Management Planning and Control Practices, 1958; (with C.T. Zlatkovich and J.A. White) Intermediate Accounting, 5th edit., 1979; (with C.H. Griffin and T.H. Williams), Advanced Accounting, 1966; (with R.N. Anthony) Fundamentals of Financial Accounting, 1974, rev. edit., 1977; Fundamentals of Management Accounting, 1974, rev. edit., 1977. Home: 3405 Taylors Dr Austin TX 78703

WELSER, JOHN RALPH, veterinarian, univ. dean; b. St. Clair, Mich., June 4, 1936; s. Fred John and Christine Sara (Kennedy) W.; B.S., Mich. State U., 1959, D.V.M., 1961, M.S., 1962; Ph.D., Purdue U., 1966; m. Kathryn L. May, July 6, 1963; children—Jennifer Lynn, Jeffrey John. Pvt. mixed vet. practice, Grand Blanc, Mich., 1961-64; grad. instr. Purdue U., 1964-66, asst. prof., 1966-69, asso. prof., 1969-70; asso. prof. U. Ga., 1970-72, asso. prof. medicine and anatomy, 1972-73, asso. dean Coll. Vet. Medicine, 1973-75; dean Coll. Vet. Medicine, prof. large animal surgery and medicine Mich. State U., 1975—. Elder Presbyterian Ch. Internat. Farm Youth del. to Scotland, 1957; recipient best acad. counselor award Purdue U., 1970. Mem. Am., Mich. vet. med. assns., Assn. Am. Vet. Med. Colls., World, Am. assns. vet. anatomists, Am. Assn. Vet. Clinicians, Sigma Xi, Phi Zeta, Omicron Delta Kappa. Author: (with C.D. Knecht) Fundamentals of Veterinary Surgery, 1975. Contbr. chpts. in books. Office: College of Veterinary Medicine Michigan State University East Lansing MI 48824

WELSH, DAVID JOHN, educator; b. London, Eng., Sept. 15, 1920; s. William and Ada Minnie (Russell) W.; came to U.S., 1961; B.A. (Hons.), U. London, 1954, Ph.D., 1967; M.A., U. Liverpool, 1962. Prof. Slavic langs. and lits. Brit. embassy, Warsaw, Poland, 1951-52; ang. supr. BBC, London, 1956-60; prof. Slavic dept. U. Mich., Ann Arbor, 1961—. Served with Brit. Army, 1939-46. Recipient Jurzykowski Found. award, 1968, Wyspianki award Assn. Polish-Am. Cultural Clubs, 1969; ann. award Polish Writers' Assn., 1971. Author: Russian Comedy, 1765-1823, 1966; Adam Mickiewicz, 1966, Ignacy Krasicki, 1969; Jan Kochanowski, 1974. Translator: Dreambook of Our Time (T. Knowick), 1969, The Doll, 1972, Black Torrent, 1969, Cloak of Illusion, 1969, other; contbr. articles to profl. jours. Office: 3026 Modern Lang Bldg Ann Arbor MI 48109

WELSH, HARRY LAMBERT, physicist; b. Aurora, Ont., Can., Mar. 23, 1910; s. Israel and Harriet Maria (Collingwood) W.; B.A., U. Toronto (Ont.), 1930, M.A., 1931, Ph.D., 1936; postgrad. U. Goettingen (Germany), 1931-33; D.Sc. (hon.), U. Windsor, 1964, Meml. U., 1968; m. Marguerite Hazel Ostrander, June 13, 1942. Demonstrator, U. Toronto, 1936-42, asst. prof. physics, 1942-48, asso. prof., 1948-54, prof., 1954-78, prof. emeritus, 1978—, chmn. research bd., 1971-73. Served to lt. comdr. Royal Can. Naval Vol. Res., 1943-45. Decorated officer Order Can. Fellow Royal Soc. Can. (Tory medal 1963), Royal Soc. London, Am. Phys. Soc., Optical Soc. Am. (Meggers medal 1974); mem. Can. Assn. Physicists (medal 1965, pres. 1973-74). Liberal. Contbr. articles on molecular spectroscopy, physics of high pressure gases, intermolecular forces and other topics to profl. publs. Home: 8 Tally Ln Willowdale ON M2K 1V4 Canada Office: U Toronto Toronto ON M5S 1A4 Canada

WELSH, JOHN FRANCIS, advt. agy. exec.; b. New Haven, May 19, 1916; s. Pierce Jerome and Irene (Kennedy) W.; B.A., Yale, 1937; m. Margaret Burke, Sept. 18, 1947; children—Peter Burke, Diana Margaret. With Warwick & Legler, Inc., N.Y.C, 1946—, exec. v.p., mgmt. supr., mem. mgmt. com.; vice chmn. Warwick, Welsh & Miller, Inc., 1973—. Served with AUS, 1941-45. Decorated Bronze Star, Croix de Guerre (France). Clubs: Yale (N.Y.C.); Tokeneke (Darien). Home: 98 Ridge Acres Rd Darien CT 06820 Office: 375 Park Ave New York City NY 10022

WELSH, LAWRENCE H., bishop. Ordained priest, Roman Cath. Ch., 1962; bishop Archdiocese of Spokane, 1978—. Address: N 709 Cedar St Spokane WA 99210*

WELSH, LESLIE THOMAS, mfr., accountant; b. Bradford, Ill., Nov. 29, 1922; s. Leslie Edward and Anna (Holden) W.; B.S. in Accountancy, U. Ill. at Urbana, 1944; m. Mary Lee Weaver, Aug. 12, 1950; children—Leslie Thomas, Robert Weaver, Barbara Jo Ann, Cynthia Lee. Partner, Arthur Andersen & Co., Chgo., 1944-63; pres. Welsh Sporting Goods Corp., Iowa Falls, Iowa, 1964-72; v.p. finance, chief financial officer Studebaker-Worthington, Inc., 1967-69, sr. v.p., 1969-71, pres., 1971—. Trustee Village of Barrington Hills, Ill., 1963-67. C.P.A. Clubs: Chicago; Barrington Hills Country (dir., pres.). Author film. Contbr. articles to profl. jours. Office: 1300 Grove Ave Barrington IL 60010

WELSH, MATTHEW EMPSON, former gov. of Ind.; b. Detroit, Sept. 15, 1912; s. Matthew and Inez (Empson) W.; B.S., U. Pa., 1934; student U. Ind., 1934-36; J.D., U. Chgo., 1937; m. Virginia Homann, Sept. 25, 1937; children—Katheryn and Janet (twins). Admitted to Ind. bar, 1937, since practiced in Vincennes and Indpls.; U.S. atty. So. dist. Ind., 1950-51; rep. Knox County, Ind. Gen. Assembly, 1941-43; Mem. Ind. Senate from Knox and Daviess counties, 1955-59; Democratic floor leader 1957, 59; gov. Ind., 1961-65; chmn. U.S. sect. Internat. Joint Commn. U.S. and Can., 1966-70; dir. Lincoln Nat. Co., Ft. Wayne, Ind., Variable Annuity Funds. Co-chmn. Ind. Constl. Revision Commn. Democratic Nat. Committeeman from Ind., 1964-68, Democratic nominee Gov. Ind., 1972. Trustee Christian Theol. Sem., Indpls., Vincennes U., Christian Ch. Found., John A. Hartford Found. Served as lt. USNR. Mem. Am., Ind., Knox County bar assns., Phi Delta Phi, Delta Kappa Epsilon. Mem. Christian Ch. (Disciples of Christ). Home: 4546 N Park Indianapolis IN 46205 Office: 1 Indiana Sq Indianapolis IN 46204

WELSH, PETER CORBETT, museum dir., historian; b. Washington, Aug. 28, 1926; s. Arthur Brinkley and Susan Jane (Putney) W.; B.A., Mt. Union Coll., Alliance O., 1950; postgrad. U. Va., 1950-51; M.A. (Hagley fellow), U. Del., 1956; m. Catherine Beatrice Allen, Nov. 27, 1951 (div. 1969); children—Susan Jane, Peter Corbett; m. 2d, Caroline Levert Mastin, Sept. 8, 1970. Research asst., fellowship coordinator Eleutherian Mills-Hagley Found., Wilmington, Del., 1956-59; asso. curator dept. civil history Museum History and Tech., Smithsonian Instn., 1959-61, curator Growth U.S., 1962-64, curator dept. civil history, 1964-69, asst. dir. gen. museums of instn., 1969-70, dir. office Mus. Programs, 1970-71; dir. N.Y. State Hist. Assn., Cooperstown, 1971-74; vis. prof. Cooperstown Grad. Program, N.Y. State Hist. Assn.; dir. Cooperstown Grad. Programs, 1971-74; dir. spl. projects N.Y. State Mus., Albany, 1975-76; dir. Bur. Museums, Pa. Hist. and Mus. Commn., 1976—; adj. prof. State U. N.Y. Cons. FDR Mus. and Little White House, Warm Springs, Ga., 1968-72. Trustee Landon Sch., Bethesda, Md., 1964-70. Served to 1st lt. AUS, 1951-54. Mem. Am. Hist. Assn., Am. Studies Assn., Am. Assn. Museums, N.Y. State Assn. Museums (mem. council 1971-75), Am. Assn. for State and Local History (mem. publ. com.), Soc. History Tech., Sigma Nu. Democrat. Roman Catholic. Club: Cooperstown Country. Author: Tanning in the United States; A Brief History, 1964; American Folk Art: The Art and Spirit of the People, 1967; Track and Road; The American Trotting Horse, 1820-1900, 1968; also articles. Editor: Smithsonian Jour. History, 1967-70. Home: 460 N 25th St Camp Hill PA 17011 Office: Bur Museums Pa Hist and Mus Commn Box 1026 Harrisburg PA 17120

WELSH, ROBERT BERNARD, fin. exec.; b. Pa., May 15, 1926; s. Sylvestor E. and Martha E. (Morris) W.; B.S., U. Calif., Los Angeles, 1949; m. Patricia A. Boncher, Aug. 18, 1956; children—Karen M., Kathleen A., R. Gregory, Eric D. Treas., controller Am. Marc Inc., Inglewood, Calif., 1957-61; gen. mgr. Sheridan Gray, Inc., Torrance, Calif., 1961-65; asst. corporate controller Teledyne, Inc., Los Angeles, 1965-71; pres. Teledyne Acceptance Corp., 1972-73; v.p. fin., treas. Crouse-Hinds Co., Syracuse, N.Y., 1973—. Served with U.S. Army, 1944-45, 50-52. C.P.A., N.Y. Mem. N.Y. Soc. C.P.A.'s. Club: Mapi. Office: PO Box 4999 Wolf and 7th North Sts Syracuse NY 13221

WELSH, ROBERT EDWARD, physicist, educator; b. Pitts., Oct. 1, 1932; s. Maurice Herbert and Mary Regina (Jacob) W.; B.S., Georgetown U., 1954; Ph.D., Pa. State U., 1960; m. Rita R. Varnes, July 7, 1956; children—Patrick R., Richard J., Edward M. Research physicist, asst. dir. Nuclear Research Center, Carnegie Mellon U., 1960-63; mem. faculty Coll. William and Mary, 1963—, prof. physics, 1968—, asst. dir. Space Radiation Effects Lab., 1967-72; vis. research physicist, Rutherford High Energy Lab., Oxon., Eng., 1972-73; cons. in field. Trustee Williamsburg Community Action Agy., 1965-71, H.O.M.E. Inc., 1969-72. Served to 1st lt. USAF, 1955-57. Recipient Kidwell Physics medal Georgetown U., 1954; Gulentz fellow, 1950-54; NSF fellow, 1957-60. Fellow Am. Phys. Soc.; mem. A.A.U.P. Home: 213 Kingswood Dr Williamsburg VA 23185

WELSH, ROBERT JOSEPH, clergyman, educator; b. Phila., July 15, 1921; s. Thomas John and Elizabeth (Walpole) W.; A.B., Villanova Coll., 1943, S.T.L., Gregorian U., Rome, Italy, 1948, S.T.D., 1950; Ph.L., U. St. Monica, Rome, 1950. Joined Order of St. Augustine, 1940, ordained priest Roman Cath. Ch., 1947; prof. dogmatic and moral theology Augustinian Coll., Washington, 1950-56; faculty Villanova U., 1956-71, asso. prof. theology, 1960—, dean liberal arts and scis., 1961—, pres., 1967-71, also trustee univ.; pres. Washington Theol. Coalition, Silver Spring, Md., 1971-75. Mem. Cath. Theol. Soc. Am., Cath. Bibl. Assn., Assn. Higher Edn., Augustinian Ednl. Assn. (dir. 1975—), Delta Epsilon Sigma. Address: Villanova Univ Villanova PA 19085

WELSH, RONALD ARTHUR, physician, educator; b. Houston, Oct. 13, 1926; s. Leo Arthur and Octavia Virginia (Franssen) W.; A.B., U. Tex., 1947, M.D., 1950; m. Mary Jeanne Duncan, June 24, 1950; children—Mary Jeanne, William, James. Intern, USPHS Hosp., New Orleans, 1950-51; resident in pathology USPHS Balt., 1951-55; chief pathology USPHS Hosp., Galveston, Tex., 1955-57; asst. prof. pathology L. Tex. Med. Br., Galveston, 1955-57; asst. prof. pathology La. State U., New Orleans, 1957-59, asso. prof., 1959-61, prof., 1961—; chief surg. pathology Charity Hosp., New Orleans, 1975—; cons. forensic pathology Orleans Parish Coroner, 1961-79, cons. path. Va. Hosp., New Orleans, 1971—. Mem. La. Commn. on Narcotics and Rehab., 1970-72. Bd. dirs. La. div. Am. Cancer Soc., 1960—, nat. div., 1966-68. Served with USNR, 1944-46; USPHS, 1950-57. Recipient Distinguished Prof. award La. State U. Alumni Assn., 1973-74. Mem. Internat. Acad. Pathology, Am. Soc. Exptl. Pathology, Am. Soc. Clin. Pathologists, Coll. Am. Pathologists, Am. Assn. Pathologists, La., Orleans Parish med. socs., Phi Beta Kappa, Alpha Omega Alpha, Nu Sigma Nu. Democrat. Episcopalian. Home: 2429 Octavia St New Orleans LA 70115 Office: 1542 Tulane Ave New Orleans LA 70112

WELSH, THOMAS HAMMOND, JR., savs. and loan assn. exec.; b. Washington, Dec. 11, 1911; s. Thomas Hammond and Rebecca Alexine (Sedwick) W.; B.A., U. Md., 1933, LL.B., 1935; m. Mildred Lowndes Berry, June 30, 1940; children—Mildred B. Welsh Rayhart, Thomas Hammond, III. Admitted to Md. and D.C. bars, 1936; individual practice, 1936-45; mem. firm Welsh and Dyer, 1945-56; sr. partner firm Welsh and Lancaster, Hyattsville, Md., 1970; pres. Md. Fed. Savs. and Loan Assn., Hyattsville, 1963—, chmn. bd., 1977—; chmn. bd. Bldg., Savs. and Loan Assn. Commrs. Md., 1970-75. Chmn. bd. trustees St. Mary's Coll. Md., 1977—. Fellow Am. Coll. Trial Lawyers; mem. Md. Bar Found., Prince George's County Bar Assn. (pres. 1957-58), Md. Bar Assn., Prince George's County C. of C. (pres. 1958-59). Clubs: Annapolis (Md.) Yacht, Columbia Country, Univ. of Washington. Home: 8319 Kerry Rd Chevy Chase MD 20015 Office: 3505 Hamilton St Hyattsville MD 20782

WELSH, THOMAS J., bishop; b. Weatherly, Pa., Dec. 20, 1921; student St. Charles Borromeo Sem., Phila., Cath. U. Am. Ordained priest Roman Cath. Ch., 1946; ordained titular bishop of Scattery Island and aux. bishop of Phila., 1970-74; first bishop of Arlington (Va.), 1974—. Office: 200 N Glebe Rd Arlington VA 22203

WELSH, WILEY ALFRED, clergyman, educator; b. Ft. Worth, June 23, 1917; s. Wiley Alfred and Ann (Couch) W.; B.A., Tex. Christian U., 1938, D.D., 1954; B.D., Brite Div. Sch., Ft. Worth, 1941; doctoral student Columbia, also Union Sem., N.Y.C., 1947-49; D.Litt., Transylvania Coll., Lexington, Ky., 1965; D. Humanities, Lincoln Memorial U., 1971; m. Jennie Ruth Neal, Aug. 7, 1938 (dec. Feb. 1963); children—James Neal, David Lee, Robert Keith; m. 2d, Billie Ruth Cain, Nov. 26, 1964. Prof. N.T., Brite Div. Sch., 1941-42, 45-49; ordained to ministry Christian Ch., 1935; pastor in Tex. chs., 1942-49, E. Dallas Christian Ch., 1949-64; pres. Lexington (Ky.) Theol. Sem., 1965-74; pres. Christian Bd. Publ., St. Louis, 1974—. Bd. dirs. Internat. Conv. Christian Chs., 1963-70, pres., 1963-64; chmn. bd. higher edn. Christian Ch., 1969-71. Named hon. Ky. col., 1965. Rotarian, Mason (33 deg.). Author: Villains on White Horses, 1964. Home: 4400 Lindell Blvd St Louis MO 63108 Office: PO Box 179 St Louis MO 63166

WELSH, WILLIAM BROWNLEE, govt. ofcl.; b. Munfordville, Ky., Sept. 18, 1924; s. Benjamin T. and Mary E. (Cocks) W.; A.B., Berea Coll., 1949; M.A., U. Ky., Lexington, 1950; postgrad. Maxwell Sch., Syracuse U., 1950-52; m. Alice Jean Justice, Jan. 25, 1948; children—Charles B., Mary J., William E. Pres., Nat. Student Assn., Madison, Wis., 1947-48; legis. asst. to Senator Herbert Lehman, Washington, 1952-56; research dir. Democratic Nat. Com., Washington, 1957-59, exec. dir., 1969-72; adminstrv. asst. to Senator Philip A. Hart, Washington, 1959-66; adminstrv. asst. Office V.P., U.S. Senate, 1966-69; exec. dir. govtl. affairs Am. Fedn. State, County and Mcpl. Employees, Washington, 1972-79; asst. sec. for legis. and intergovtl. relations HUD, Washington, 1979; asst. sec. for legis. HEW, Washington, 1979—. Served with U.S. Army, 1943-46.

WELSH, WILLIAM JOSEPH, librarian; b. Weatherly, Pa., Nov. 15, 1919; s. Edward C. and Mary A. (Doheny) W.; A.B. in Philosophy, U. Notre Dame, 1940, student law, 1940- 41; m. Winifred Hatfield, Oct. 21, 1950; children—Douglas B., James F. With Library of Congress, 1947—, dir. processing dept., 1968-76, dep. librarian of Congress, 1976—; cons. in field, 1965—; agy. rep. Assn. Research Libraries, Nat. Commn. Libraries and Info. Sci. Bd. regents Nat. Library Medicine, 1976—, resident adviser and expert on universal bibliog. control. Served to maj. USAAF, 1941-47. Mem. ALA (mem. council 1978—, Melvil Dewey award 1971), Council Library Resources (program mgmt. com.), Internat. Fedn. Library Assns. (chmn. universal bibliog. control steering com., mem. universal availability publs. steering com., profl. bd., sec. sect. nat. libraries). Author articles in field; adv. bd. Scarecrow Press. Home: 4805 Edgefield Rd Bethesda MD 20014 Office: Library of Congress Washington DC 20540

WELTING, RUTH LYNN, singer; b. Memphis, Nov. 5, 1948; d. William Edwin and Mary Francis (Pugh) Welting; student Memphis State U., 1968-71, Juilliard Sch. Music, 1972-73; m. Edo de Waart, Feb. 18, 1976. Mem. N.Y.C. Opera, 1973-76; appeared with Dallas Opera, Chgo. Lyric Opera, Met. Opera, Covent Garden, London, Netherlands Opera, San Francisco Opera; soloist with Chgo. Symphony, Phila. Orch., Memphis Symphony. Rockefeller grantee. Mem. Am. Guild Musical Artists. Home: 1916 Jermyn Cove Memphis TN 38138 Office: care Columbia Artists Mgmt Inc 165 W 57th St New York NY 10019*

WELTMAN, JOSEPH SAMUEL, physician, educator; b. Schenectady, Oct. 17, 1910; s. David and Anna (Hornstein) W.; A.B., Union Coll., Schenectady, 1931; M.D., Albany (N.Y.) Med. Coll., 1935; m. Zelma Ulrich, May 18, 1951; 1 son, James Alan. Intern Ellis Hosp., Schenectady, 1935-36; with VA 1940-72, hosp. dir. VA Center, Togus, Me., 1960-64, VA Hosp., Canandaigua, N.Y., 1964-72; clin. asso. prof. psychiatry Sch. Medicine and Dentistry, U. Rochester, 1965—; sr. asso. psychiatry Strong Meml. Hosp., Rochester, 1965—. Cons. in psychiatry Bath VA Center. Chmn. budget com. Kennebec (Me.) Valley Community Chest, 1964; v.p. Ontario County chpt. A.R.C., 1965-66. Served to maj., M.C., AUS, 1944-46. Recipient certificate of merit V.F.W., 1963. Diplomate Am. Bd. Psychiatry and Neurology. Fellow Am. Psychiat. Assn.; mem. Rochester Acad. Medicine, Central N.Y. State Psychiat. Soc., Ontario County Med. Soc., A.M.A., Am. Legion (certificate most distinguished service 1962). Jewish. Mason; mem. B'nai B'rith (v.p. Lexington, Ky. 1954). Address: 190 Parrish St Canandaigua NY 14424

WELTNER, WILLIAM, JR., educator; b. Balt., Dec. 8, 1922; s. William and Annie (Brown) W.; B.E., Johns Hopkins, 1943; Ph.D., U. Cal. at Berkeley, 1950; m. Catherine Jean Heubeck, June 28, 1947; children—William T., Douglas G., Mark I. Research asst. Manhattan Project, N.Y., 1944-45; instr. Johns Hopkins, 1951-54; group leader Union Carbide Corp., Tarrytown, N.Y., 1956-66; prof. U. Fla., Gainesville, 1966—. Served with AUS, 1945-46. Mem. Am. Chem. Soc., Am. Phys. Soc., Sigma Xi, Alpha Chi Sigma, Delta Upsilon. Address: PO Box 13391 Gainesville FL 32604

WELTON, ARTHUR DORMAN, lawyer; b. Detroit, Jan. 1, 1902; s. Arthur Dorman and Maude (Watton) W.; A.B., Harvard, 1922, LL.B., 1925; m. Juliet Gover Streett Earle, Apr. 29, 1933; children—Richard E., Juliet S. (Mrs. Maurice S. Gulmont). Admitted to Ill. bar, 1926, since practiced in Chgo.; partner firm Winston & Strawn and predecessors, 1942-74, of counsel, 1974-75. Dir. James H. Rhodes & Co., 1940-70, Keokuk Gas Service Co., 1962—; dir. United Furniture Co., 1973—, chmn., 1974—. trustee AMFund, 1958-74. Republican. Clubs: Talbot Country (Easton, Md.); Tred Avon Yacht

(Oxford, Md.); Chicago. Home: Box 310 Oxford MD 21654 Office: 1 First Nat Plaza Chicago IL 60603

WELTON, JAMES RICHARD, mining and constrn. equipment co. exec.; b. Mpls., Sept. 30, 1931; B.B.A., U. Wis., 1955, LL.B., 1957; m. W. Diane Welton, Sept. 30, 1955; children—Timothy, Sarah. Admitted to Wis. bar, 1957, also Mich. bar; with firm Foley & Lardner, Milw., to 1959; with Clark Equipment Co., Buchanan, Mich., 1959—, asst. counsel, 1964-70, asst. sec., 1967-70, sec., 1970-76; gen. atty., asst. sec. Bucyrus-Erie Co., Milw., 1976-77, sec., gen. atty., 1977-78; v.p., asso. gen. counsel Holiday Inns, Inc., Memphis, 1978—. Pres., Berrien County Cancer Service, 1962-67; sec. YMCA, 1965. Mem. Am., Wis. State bar assns., Acacia Frat. Club: Orchard Hills Country (sec. 1965, v.p. 1966). Home: 2221 Thornwood Ln Memphis TN 38138 Office: 3742 Lamar Ave Memphis TN 38118

WELTY, EUDORA, author; b. Jackson, Miss.; d. Christian Webb and Chestina (Andrews) Welty; student Miss. State Coll. for Women; B.A., U. Wis., 1929; postgrad. Columbia Sch. Advt., 1930-31. Author: A Curtain of Green, 1941; The Robber Bridegroom, 1942; The Wide Net, 1943; Delta Wedding, 1946; The Golden Apples, 1949; The Ponder Heart, 1954; The Bride of the Innisfallen, 1955; The Shoe Bird, 1964; Losing Battles, 1970; One Time, One Place, 1971; The Optimist's Daughter, 1972 (Pulitzer prize 1973); The Eye of the Story, 1978; contbr. So. Rev., Atlantic Monthly, Harpers Bazaar, New Yorker. Recipient creative arts medal for fiction Brandeis U., 1966; Nat. Inst. Arts and Letters Gold medal 1972. Mem. Am. Acad. Arts and Letters, Nat. Council on Arts. Home: 1119 Pinehurst St Jackson MS 39202

WELTY, ROBERT WILLIAM, advt. agy. exec.; b. Lodi, Calif., Nov. 4, 1925; s. William O. and Zona (Summers) W.; B.S., U. So. Calif., 1950; m. Marcia Perry Stapp, Nov. 16, 1956; children—Ellen, Matthew. Media buyer Young & Rubicam, Inc., Los Angeles, 1950-56; media supr., San Francisco, 1956-58; v.p., media mgr. J. Walter Thompson Co., N.Y.C., 1958-73; exec. v.p., corp. media dir. Bozell & Jacobs, N.Y.C., 1973—; dir. Bozell & Jacobs, Internat., Inc. Served with U.S. Army, 1943-46. Mem. Inst. Advanced Studies (trustee). Club: Cedar Point Yacht. Office: One Dag Hammarskjold Plaza New York NY 10017

WELZ, CARL JOHN, C.S. practitioner and tchr.; b. San Francisco, Mar. 12, 1913; s. Charles and Henrietta (Groenninger) W.; A.B., San Jose State Coll., 1934; M.A., Columbia, 1939; m. Jerry Beall Hatcher, Dec. 17, 1943; children—Paul Channing, Rebecca Beall; m. 2d, Philadelphia Shideler, Oct. 14, 1979. Tchr. pub. and pvt. schs., Carmichael, Calif., 1935-37, Katonah, N.Y., 1937-39, Montclair, N.J., 1939-40, Avenal, Calif., 1940-41; vice prin. Victory Sch., Stockton, Calif., 1941-42; C.S. practitioner, 1946—; C.S. tchr., 1958—; asso. editor C.S. Jour., C.S. Sentinel, Herald of C.S., Boston, 1961-67, editor, 1970-75. Served to maj. USAAF, 1942-46, chaplain, USAF, 1951-56. Contbr. articles to newspapers. Home: 706 Hillmont St Santa Rosa CA 95405 Office: 2 Embarcadero Center San Francisco CA 94111

WEMPLE, EDWARD LELAND, cons. engr.; b. St. Louis, Oct. 6, 1912; s. Leland Edward and Ona Alice (Hileman) W.; B.S., Mass. Inst. Tech., 1934; m. Ruth Ripley White, Sept. 19, 1942; children—Lynn Wemple Cooley, Richard C. With Remington Arms Co., 1934-49; prodn. mgr. Rem-Cru Titanium Co., 1949-52; partner Coverdale & Colpitts, Inc., N.Y.C., 1952-75, pres., 1970-75; v.p. R. Dixon Speas Assos., Inc., N.Y.C., 1975-79; pres., dir., partner Vollmer-Wemple, Cons. Engrs., 1975—. Fellow Am. Cons. Engrs. Council; mem. Am. Inst. Mining and Metall. Engrs., Inst. Transp. Engrs., Internat. Bridge, Tunnel and Turnpike Assn. Republican. Episcopalian. Clubs: Econ., Wall St., Univ. (N.Y.C.); Wee Burn Country. Home: 12 Hickory Ln Darien CT 06820 Office: 62 Fifth Ave New York NY 10011

WEN, CHIN YUNG, educator; b. Shintzu, Taiwan, Dec. 5, 1928; s. Chi and Yueh Eh (Yu) W.; B.S., Nat. Taiwan U., 1951; M.S. in Chem. Engring., W.Va. U., 1954, Ph.D., 1956; m. Amy Kuo; children—Emily, Edward, Pauline. Came to U.S., 1951. Mem. faculty W.Va. U., Morgantown, 1954—, prof. chem. engring., 1964—, chmn. dept., 1969—. Indsl. and govt. cons. and advisor Grantee NSF, HEW, Dept. of Energy, EPA, NASA, others; ALCOA Found. awards, 1977-79. Fellow Am. Inst. Chem. Engrs.; mem. Am. Chem. Soc., Am. Soc. Engring. Edn., Chem. Engring. Soc. Japan, Chinese Inst. Chem. Engrs., Sigma Xi, Phi Lambda Upsilon, Omega Chi Epsilon. Author books and chpts. on coal conversion tech., fluidization, chem. reaction engring., pneumatic transport and reactor flow models. editor: Energy Technology and Science series Addison-Wesley Pub. Co. Contbr. over 140 articles to profl. jours. Home: 813 Brierwood St Morgantown WV 26505

WENCK, THOMAS LEE, educator; b. Watertown, Wis., June 25, 1931; s. George William and Esther Louise (Vergenz) W.; B.B.A., U. Wis., Madison, 1953, M.B.A., 1959, Ph.D., 1962; m. Beverly Joyce Fiedler, Aug. 29, 1953; children—Sandra Lee, Mark Eric. Underwriter, Continental Casualty Co., Chgo., 1953-54; rep. Aetna Life Ins. Co., Green Bay, Wis., 1956-58; research asso. Wis. Ins. Dept., Madison, 1958-62; prof. ins. Mich. State U., 1962—; treas., dir. Delta Dental Plan of Mich.; pres., dir. MSU Employees Credit Union; profl. ins. cons. Served to lt. AUS, 1954-56. C.L.U., C.P.C.U. Mem. Am. Risk and Ins. Assn., Risk and Ins. Mgmt. Soc., Soc. C.L.U.'s, Soc. C.P.C.U.'s. Contbr. articles profl. jours. Home: 4288 Arbor Dr Okemos MI 48864 Office: Eppley Center Michigan State University East Lansing MI 48824

WENDEBORN, RICHARD DONALD, mfg. co. exec.; b. Winnipeg, Man., Can.; s. Curtis and Rose (Lysecki) W.; came to U.S., 1976; diploma Colo. Sch. Mines, 1952; grad. Advanced Mgmt. Program, Harvard, 1975; mem. Dorothy Ann Munn, Aug. 24, 1957; children—Margaret Gayle, Beverly Jane, Stephen Richard, Peter Donald, Ann Elizabeth. With Canadian Ingersoll-Rand Co., Montreal, 1952—, gen. mgr., v.p., dir., 1968, pres., 1969-74, chmn. bd., 1975—; exec. v.p. Ingersoll-Rand Co., Woodcliff Lake, N.J., 1976—; dir. Can. Machinery Corp., Combustion Engring. Superheater; mem. Can. Govt. Oil and Gas Tech. Exchange Program with USSR, 1972—, Minerals and Metals Mission to Peoples Republic China, 1972—. Mem. Resource Fund Colo. Sch. Mines. Mem. Machinery and Equipment Mfrs. Assn. Can. (dir. 1974—, past chmn.). Home: 34 Grist Mill Ln Upper Saddle River NJ 07458 Office: Ingersoll-Rand Co 200 Chestnut Ridge Rd Woodcliff Lake NJ 07675

WENDEL, RICHARD FREDERICK, educator; b. Chgo., Apr. 29, 1930; s. Elmer Carl and Victoria Matilda (Jeffrey) W.; A.B., Augustana Coll., 1951; M.B.A., U. Pa., 1957, Ph.D. (fellow 1962-64), 1966; m. Leslie Jane Travis, June 15, 1957; children—John Travis, Andrew Stewart. Asst. to pres. Flexonics Corp., Maywood, Ill., 1957-59; sales rep., product mgr. dairy products Kordite Corp. div. Nat. Distillers Corp., Macedon, N.Y., 1959-62; instr. Wharton Sch., U. Pa., 1964-65; asst. prof. mktg. Grad. Sch. Adminstrn., Washington U., St. Louis, 1965-69; asso. prof. U. Conn., 1969-74, prof., 1974—; mem. U.S. Census Field Adv. Commn., 1967-69; mem. acad. adv. commn. Bur. Labor Stats., U.S. Bur. Census Survey of Consumer Expenditures, 1971—; mem. Conn. Export Devel. Council, Dept. Commerce, 1972—. Bd. dirs. Roper Center. Served with USAF, 1951-55. Center for Real Estate and Urban Econs. grantee, 1969-70. Mem. Am. Mktg. Assn., Am. Econs. Assn., N.Y. Acad. Scis., Am. Acad. Social and Polit. Sci. Republican. Episcopalian. Author: (with M.L. Bell) Economic Importance of Highway Advertising, 1966; editor: Readings in Marketing, 1973-74, 75-76, 77-78, 78-79, 79-80; (with C.L. Lapp) Add to Your Selling Know-How, 1968; editorial staff jour. Mktg., 1965-74. Home: Friendship Valley Brooklyn CT 06234 Office: Box U-41M Sch Bus Adminstrn U Conn Storrs CT 06268

WENDEL, WILLIAM H., mfg. exec.; b. Johnstown, Pa., Nov. 15, 1914; s. Daniel Hall and Edna Pearl (Wendell) W.; B.S., U.S. Naval Acad., 1936; M.B.A., Harvard, 1940; m. Louise Davis, June 22, 1940; children—William Hall, Jeffrey Philip, Christine. Asst. to pres. United Engring. Co., 1946; asst. to pres. Carborundum Co., Niagara Falls, N.Y., 1947, mgr. coated products div., 1948-52, v.p. coated products div., 1952-57, group v.p. charge of four divs., 1957-59, exec. v.p., 1959-62, pres., 1962-78, also dir.; pres. Kennecott Copper Corp., N.Y.C., 1978-79, vice-chmn., cons., 1979—; dir. Marine Trust Co. of Western N.Y., N.Y. Telephone Corp., Allegheny Ludlum Industries, Inc., Dunlop Tire & Rubber Corp. Commr. Niagara Frontier Transp. Authority. Served to comdr. USNR, 1940-45. Mem. Niagara Falls C. of C., Am. Soc. Sales Execs. Clubs: Univ. (N.Y.C.); Buffalo; Duquesne (Pitts.); Niagara (Niagara Falls). Office: Kennecott Copper Corp 161 E 42d St New York NY 10017

WENDELKEN, BEN S., lawyer; b. Colorado Springs, Colo., Sept. 10, 1899; s. Martin F. and Harriet (Ewing) W.; A.B., Colo. Coll., 1922; J.D., U. Mich., 1925; m. Mary Louisa Hills, Jan. 8, 1927; children—Robert B., Mary Lou Wendelken Blattenberger. Admitted to Colo. bar, 1925, U.S. Supreme Ct. bar, 1936; asso. firm Chinn and Strickler, Colorado Springs, 1925-36; mem. firm Bennett and Wendelken, Colorado Springs, 1936-37, Murray, Baker & Wendelken, Colorado Springs, 1973—; city atty. City of Colorado Springs, 1928-47; trustee Hester G. and Edwin W. Giddings Found., El Pomar Found.; trustee, v.p. Henry Sachs Found.; dir. Broadmoor Hotel, Inc., El Pomar Investment Co., Westland Theatres, Inc.; pres. Aircadia Investment Corp. Fellow Am. Coll. Trial Lawyers, Am. Coll. Probate Counsel, Am. Bar Found.; mem. Internat. Soc. Barristers, El Paso County (Colo.) (pres. 1939-40), Colo. (v.p. 1952-53, bd. govs. 1956-64) bar assns. Republican. Clubs: Cooking, Cheyenne Mountain Country, Garden of Gods. Home: 220 W Del Norte St Colorado Springs CO 80907 Office: 301 Mining Exchange Bldg Colorado Springs CO 80803

WENDELL, JOHN POTTS, refining co. exec.; b. Pottstown, Pa., Sept. 9, 1919; s. James I. and Marjorie (Potts) W.; grad. The Hill Sch., 1936; A.B. summa cum laude, Princeton, 1940, M.A., 1946, Ph.D., 1947; m. Marian Logan, May 8, 1943; children—John Potts, Stephen L., Julia A. Instr. English, Princeton, 1947-48; with United Refining Co., Warren, Pa., 1948—, exec. v.p., dir., 1957—. Served to lt. comdr. USNR, 1941-45. Woodrow Wilson nat. fellow, 1946-47. Mem. Phi Beta Kappa. Republican. Episcopalian. Home: 1075 Jackson Run Rd Warren PA 16365 Office: United Refining Co Warren PA 16365

WENDELSTEDT, HARRY HUNTER, JR., umpire; b. Balt., July 27, 1938; student Essex Community Coll.; B.S. in Edn., U. Md.; m. Cheryl Maher, Nov. 2, 1970. Profl. baseball umpire, 1962—, with minor leagues, Ga.-Fla., 1962, Northwest, 1963, Tex., 1964, Internat., 1965, with maj. leagues, Nat., 1966—; umpire All-Star Game, 1968, 76, Nat. League championship series, 1970, 72, 77, World Series, 1973; owner, operator Harry Wendelstedt Umpire Sch. Named Top Umpire in Maj. League Baseball, Md. Profl. Baseball Players Assn., 1975. Mem. Major League Umpires Assn. (4 term past pres.). Address: Major League Umpires Assn 88 S St Andrews Dr Ormond Beach FL 32074

WENDEN, HENRY EDWARD, educator; b. N.Y.C., Nov. 24, 1916; s. Henry Edward and Eileen Mary (Crowley) W.; B.S., Yale, 1938; postgrad. U. Ariz., 1946-47, Wash. State Coll., 1940-41; M.A., Harvard, 1950, Ph.D., 1958; m. Beatrice Gertrude Wilson, May 25, 1943; children—Sylvia, Mark, Elaine, Rebecca. Instr. Boston U., 1949-53; asst. prof. Tufts U., Medford, Mass., 1953-57; prof. mineralogy Ohio State U., Columbus, 1957—. Served with USAAF, 1941-45. Recipient Neil Miner award for Distinguished Teaching, 1962, Alumni award for distinguished teaching, 1964, Boyer award for distinguished teaching, 1969. Fellow Mineral. Soc. Am., Ohio Acad. Sci.; mem. Mineral. Soc. Can., Nat. Assn. Geology Tchrs., Internat. Mineral. Assn. (chmn. teaching commn.), Sigma Xi. Club: Rushlight. Author: The Changing Science of Mineralogy, 1962. Patentee in field. Home: 52 E South St Worthington OH 43085 Office: Dept Geology Ohio State U Columbus OH 43210

WENDER, IRA TENSARD, banker; b. Pitts., Jan. 5, 1927; s. Louis and Luba (Kibrick) W.; student Swarthmore Coll., 1942-45; J.D., U. Chgo., 1948; L.L.M., N.Y. U., 1951; m. Phyllis Bellows, June 24, 1966; children—Justin, Sarah; (by previous marriage)—Theodore, Matthew, Abigail, John. Asso. Lord, Day & Lord, N.Y.C., 1950-52, 54-59; asst. dir. internat. program in taxation Harvard Law Sch., 1952-54; lectr. N.Y. U. Sch. Law, 1954-59; partner Baker & McKenzie, Chgo., 1959-61, sr. partner, N.Y.C., 1961-71; partner Wender, Murase & White, N.Y.C., 1971—; chmn. C. Brewer & Co., Ltd., Honolulu, 1969-75; chief exec. officer Warburg Paribas Becker Inc., A.G. Becker, Inc., 1978—; dir. Mercury Securities, Ltd., London, IU Internat., Wilmington, Del.; lectr. numerous law insts. Mem. vis. com. Law Sch., U. Chgo., 1976—; bd. mgrs. Swarthmore (Pa.) Coll., 1978—. Mem. Am., N.Y. State bar assns., Assn. Bar City N.Y. Clubs: Board Room (N.Y.C.); Pacific (Honolulu). Author: (with E. R. Barlow) Foreign Investment and Taxation, 1955. Home: 555 Park Ave New York NY 10021 Office: 55 Water St New York NY 10041 also 400 Park Ave New York NY 10022

WENDER, SIMON HAROLD, biochemist, educator; b. Dalton, Ga., Sept. 4, 1913; s. Louis David and Ella (Mendel) W.; A.B., Emory U., 1934, M.S., 1935; Ph.D., U. Minn., 1938; m. Ruth Wisenberg, Sept. 6, 1942; children—Joseph Harris, Barbara Ray, Sherri Ann. Research chemist Tex. Agrl. Expt. Sta., College Station, 1939-41; faculty U. Ky., 1941-46, U. Okla., Norman, 1946—, prof., 1948-53, research prof. biochemistry, 1953—, George Lynn Cross research prof., 1968—. Vis. research asso. Argonne (Ill.) Nat. Lab., 1954-64; chmn. council Oak Ridge Inst. Nuclear Studies, 1961-64. Bd. dirs. Oak Ridge Asso. Univs., 1961-67. Mem. Phytochem. Soc. N.Am. (1st nat. pres. 1961-62), Am. Soc. Biol. Chemists, Am. Chem. Soc., A.A.A.S., Am. Soc. Plant Physiologists, Soc. for Exptl. Biology and Medicine, Sigma Xi, Phi Beta Kappa, Phi Lambda Upsilon. Contbr. articles to profl. jours. Patentee in field. Home: 2614 Meadowbrook Dr Norman OK 73069

WENDLANDT, WESLEY WILLIAM, educator; b. Galesville, Wis., Nov. 20, 1927; s. William Walter and Bernice (Polzin) W.; B.S., Wis. State U., 1950; M.S., State U. Iowa 1952, Ph.D., 1954; m. Gay McCutchen, Dec. 28, 1968. Research asso. Argonne Nat. Lab. (Ill.), 1954-55; prof. Tex. Tech. Coll., 1954-66; prof., chmn. chemistry dept. U. Houston, 1966—. Vis. prof. N.M. Highlands U., 1961; mem. adv. bd. John Wiley-Intersci. Pub. Co., 1965—; cons. Thiokol, Tech. Equipment Corp. Recipient Mettler award, 1970. Mem. Am. Chem. Soc., Chem. Soc. London, Internat. Confedn. Thermal Analysis, A.A.A.S., Ia., Tex. acads. scis., Sigma Xi, Alpha Chi Sigma, Phi Lambda Upsilon. Author: Thermal Methods of Analysis, 1964; (with H.G. Hecht) Reflectance Spectroscopy, 1966; (with J.P. Smith) Thermal Properties of Transition Metal Complexes, 1967; Modern Aspects of Reflectance Spectroscopy, 1968. Editor-in-chief Thermochimica Acta. Contbr. articles profl. jours. Home: 7818 Sands Point Houston TX 77036

WENDLING, DONALD BRAND, constrn. materials co. exec.; b. Louisville, July 12, 1915; s. George Clifford and Annetta Ethel (Brand) W.; student Auburn (Ala.) U., 1940; m. Ann Marie Snedden, July 12, 1947; children—Donald Brand, Georganne Wendling Wilmot. Asst. to v.p. sales Birmingham Slag Co. (Ala.), 1937-59; v.p. sales Vulcan Materials Co., Chgo., 1959-65; v.p. mktg. cement div. Martin Marietta Corp., N.Y.C., 1965-70; pres. Martin Marietta Aggregates Co., Bethesda, Md., 1971—; v.p. Martin Marietta Corp., 1971—. Mem. Am. Rd. Builders Assn. (dir.), Nat. Limestone Inst. (dir.), Am. Concrete Paving Assn. (dir.), Nat. Crushed Stone Assn. (dir.), Nat. Sand and Gravel Assn., Transp. Research Bd., Sigma Chi. Republican. Presbyterian (elder). Clubs: Bethesda Country, Congl. Country (Bethesda); Vestavia Country (Birmingham); Tamarack Country (Greenwich, Conn.); Sea Pines Country (Hilton Head, S.C.). Home: 12701 Watertown Ct Potomac MD 20854 Office: 6802 Rockledge Dr Bethesda MD 20034

WENDORF, DENVER FRED, JR., educator; b. Terrell, Tex., July 31, 1924; s. Denver Fred and Margaret (Hall) W.; B.A., U. Ariz., 1948; M.A., Harvard, 1950, Ph.D., 1953; m. Angela Elizabeth, Sept. 30, 1976; children—Frederick Carl, Michael Andrew, Gail Susan, Cynthia Ann, Kelly Peta, Scott Frederick. Research asso. Mus. N.Mex., Santa Fe, 1950-56, asso. dir., 1958-64; asso. prof. Tex. Tech. U., Lubbock, 1956-58; prof. anthropology So. Methodist U., Dallas, 1964—, chmn. dept. anthropology, 1968-74, Henderson-Morrison prof. anthropology, 1974—; dir. Ft. Burgwin Research Center, Taos, N.Mex., 1957-76. Chmn. Tex. State Antiquities Com., 1969—. Served with AUS, 1943-47; decorated Purple Heart, Bronze Star. Mem. Soc. for Am. Archaeology (treas. 1974-77, pres. elect 1977). Author numerous books including: The Prehistory of Nubia, 1968; The Midland Discovery, 1955; Paleoecology of the Llano Estacado, 1961; A Guide to Salvage Archaeology; also articles. Home: 10811 Scotspring St Dallas TX 75218

WENDT, FRANK PAUL, investment banker; b. Chgo., Nov. 8, 1925; s. August R. and Mary (Becker) W.; B.S., Northwestern U., 1946; m. Barbara Boothby, Apr. 17, 1948. Chmn., dir. John Nuveen & Co., Inc.; dir. Nuveen Adv. Corp., Nuveen Govt. Securities, Inc., Nuveen Municipal Bond Fund, Inc. Bd. dirs. Mus. Art, Sci. and Industry, Pequot Library. Clubs: World Trade Center, Stock Exchange, Wall Street (N.Y.C.); Pequot Yacht (Conn.); Fairfield (Conn.) Country. Home: 824 Harbor Rd Southport CT 06490 Office: 61 Broadway New York NY 10006

WENDT, KURT FRANK, educator; b. Milw., Jan. 5, 1906; s. Frank J. and Maria (Wendt) W.; B.C.E., U. Wis., 1927, grad. student, 1927-29; D.Sc. (hon.), W. Va. Inst. Tech., 1964; m. Adelaide Roma Jandre, Aug. 24, 1927; children—Jerome David, Richard Kurt, Franklin Jule. Instr. mechanics U. Wis.,1927-36, asst. prof., 1936-41, asso. prof., 1941-46, prof., 1946-71, asso. dir. engring. expt. sta., 1948-53, dean Coll. Engring., 1953-71, spl. asst. to chancellor, 1971-78; cons. U.S. Forest Products Lab., 1941-56, NSF, 1951-56, 59-61; exec. com. engring. and indsl. research NRC, 1961-63. Pres. Univ. Park Corp., 1967—; bd. dirs. Wis. Tchrs. Retirement System, 1970-76; mem. Wis. Investment Bd., 1971-79. Mem. Nat. Transp. Research Bd.; chmn. Wis. Registration Bd. Architects and Profl. Engrs., 1953-71; bd. dirs. Midwest Univs. Consortium for Internat. Activities, 1969-75; chmn. Engineering Coll. Research Council, 1958-60; pres. Assn. NROTC Colls. and Univs., 1958-60. Pres. Madison United Community Chest, 1969-70. Recipient medal Soc. Am. Mil. Engrs., 1959; Engr. of Year award Engrs. Soc. Milw., 1962; Cons. Engrs. Council award outstanding contbrn. engring. profession field edn., 1964; Roy W. Crum award distinguished service Hwy. Research Bd. 1965; Distinguished Service award Wis. Utilities Assn., 1966; Golden Plate award Am. Acad. Achievement, 1966; Distinguished Service award U. Wis. Alumni Assn., 1971; Distinguished Service citation Coll. Engring., U. Wis., 1971; Benjamin S. Reynolds award excellence in teaching U. Wis., 1971; Wason research medal Am. Concrete Inst., 1976. Registered profl. engr. Mem. Am. Soc. Testing Materials, Nat. (nat. bd. ethical rev.), Wis. socs. profl. engrs., Soc. Exptl. Stress Analysis, Am. Soc. Engring. Edn. (pres. 1963-64), Engrs. and Scientists Milw., Sigma Xi, Chi Epsilon, Phi Eta Sigma, Tau Beta Pi, Phi Kappa Phi, Triangle. Methodist. Clubs: Rotary, University. Contbr. articles to profl. publs. Kurt F. Wendt Library at U. Wis. named in his honor, 1976. Home: 110 S Henry St Madison WI 53703

WENDT, LLOYD, writer; b. Spencer, S.D., May 16, 1908; s. Leo L. and Marie (Nylen) W.; student Sioux Falls Coll., 1928-29; S.B., Northwestern U., 1931, S.M., 1934; m. Helen Sigler, June 16, 1932; 1 dau., Bette Joan. Reporter, later columnist, drama reviewer Sioux Falls (S.D.) Press, 1927-28; publicity dir. S.D. Democratic Central Com., 1928; reporter Daily Argus-Leader, 1929, telegraph editor, 1932-33; also tchr. journalism, Sioux Falls Coll.; joined staff Chgo. Tribune, 1934, as reporter, becoming spl. feature writer mag. sect., later editor, Grafic mag., Sunday editor until 1961, asso. Sunday editor, asso. editor, 1975-77; editor Chgo.'s Am. newspaper, 1961-69; pub., editor Chgo. Today, 1969-74, also pres.; free lance writer, 1977—; lectr. fiction writing Northwestern U., 1946; chmn. fiction div. Medill Sch. Journalism, 1950-53. Pres., Soc. Midland Authors, 1947-50. Served to lt. comdr. USNR, 1942-46. Author: Lords of the Levee (with Herman Kogan), 1943; Gunners Get Glory, 1944; Bright Tomorrow, 1945; Bet a Million (with Herman Kogan), 1948; Give the Lady What She Wants (with H. Kogan), 1952; Big Bill of Chicago (with H. Kogan), 1953; Chicago: A Pictorial History (with H. Kogan), 1958; Chicago Tribune, the Rise of a Great American Newspaper, 1979. Home: 1623 Pelican Cove Rd Sarasota FL 33581

WENDT, VERNON EARL, physician; b. Cleve., Mar. 26, 1931; s. Raymond C. and Esther L. (Naujoks) W.; B.S. in Chemistry and Zoology cum laude, Baldwin Wallace Coll., 1952; M.D., Columbia, 1956; m. Hildegard Moeller, Aug. 14, 1953; children—David, Frederick, Kathy, Beth, Doralyn, James, Vernon Earl. Intern Detroit Receiving Hosp., 1956-57, resident, 1957, 59-62, dir. cardiac lab., 1962-65; USPHS postdoctoral fellow cardiology Wayne State U. Sch. Medicine, 1961, instr. medicine, 1961, asst. prof. medicine, 1962-65, asst. clin. prof. medicine, 1965—; dir. research Blodgett Meml. Hosp., Grand Rapids, Mich., 1965-67; practice medicine specializing in internal medicine and cardiology, Grand Rapids, 1967—; chief cardiology service Butterworth Hosp., Grand Rapids; asso. clin. prof. medicine (cardiology) Mich. State U., 1973—. Past pres. regional bd., trustee, pres. Mich. Lung Assn., chmn. state profl. edn. and research com.; elder Hope Luth. Ch., Grand Rapids, now pres. Served as capt. M.C., USAF, 1957-59. Fellow Am. Coll. Cardiology, Am. Coll. Angiology; mem. A.M.A., A.C.P., Mich., Kent County, Christian med. socs., Am., Mich. (trustee, past pres. Kent County chpt.) heart assns., A.A.A.S., Am. Fedn. Clin. Research, Western Acad. Medicine, Detroit Physiol. Soc. Author articles clin. and exptl. cardiovascular diseases. Home: 1620 Andover Rd East Grand Rapids MI 49506 Office: 21 Michigan NE Grand Rapids MI 49503

WENGER, JOHN CHRISTIAN, clergyman, educator; b. Honey Brook, Pa., Dec. 25, 1910; s. Aaron Martin and Martha Anna (Rock) W.; B.A., Goshen Coll., 1934; postgrad. Westminster Theol. Sem., Phila., U. Basle (Switzerland), 1938; M.A., U. Mich., 1942; Th.D., U. Zurich, 1938; m. Ruth Derstine Detweiler, Apr. 3, 1937; children—Daniel, John Paul, Mary, Elizabeth. Faculty Goshen Coll., 1938-70; faculty Bibl. Sem., 1946—, prof. theology, 1945—; ordained to ministry Mennonite Ch. as deacon, 1943, minister, 1944, bishop, 1951—. Mem. Mennonite Bd. Edn., 1935-39; exec. com. Mennonite Publ. Bd., 1946-71; editorial bd. Studies in Anabaptist and Mennonite History, 1946—; asst. editor Mennonite Ency., 1946-59; hist. com. Mennonite Gen. Conf., 1937-73, moderator, 1957-59, moderator Ind.-Mich. Conf., 1954-64; v.p. presidium Mennonite World Conf. 1963-72; exec. council Inst. Mennonite Studies, 1967—. Mem. Am. Theol. Soc., Evang. Theol. Soc., Am. Soc. Ch. History, Am. Soc. Reformation Research, Mennonitischer Geschichtsverein. Author: History of the Mennonites of the Franconia Conference, 1937; Christ the Redeemer and Judge, 1942; Separated Unto God, 1951; Introduction to Theology, 1966; Glimpses of Mennonite History and Doctrine, rev. edit., 1959; The Mennonites in Indiana and Michigan, 1961; Even Unto Death, The Heroic Witness of the 16th Century Anabaptists, 1961; The Church Nurtures Faith, 1963; God's Word Written, 1966; The Mennonite Church in America, 1967; Conrad Grebel's Programmatic Letters of 1524, 1970; The Christian Faith, 1971; Our Christ-Centered Faith, 1973; How Mennonites Came to Be, 1977; What Mennonites Believe, 1977; The Way to a New Life, 1977; The Way of Peace, 1977; Disciples of Jesus, 1977. Editor: The Complete Writings of Menno Simons, 1966; They Met God, 1964; asst. editor Mennonite Quar. Rev. Mem. com. on Bible transl. which prepared the 1978 New Internat. Version, 1965—. Home: 1410 S 8th St Goshen IN 46526

WENGERD, SHERMAN ALEXANDER, ret. educator, geologist; b. Millersburg, Ohio, Feb. 17, 1915; s. Allen Stephen and Elizabeth (Miller) W.; A.B., Coll. of Wooster, 1936; M.A., Harvard, 1938, Ph.D., 1947; m. Florence Margaret Mather, June 12, 1940; children—Anne Marie (Mrs. Michael Riffey), Timothy Mather, Diana Elizabeth (Mrs. Robert Wood), Stephanie Katherine (Mrs. David Allen). Geophysicist, Shell Oil Co., 1937; mining geologist, Ramshorn, Idaho, 1938; Austin teaching fellow Harvard, 1938-40; research petroleum geologist Shell, Mid-continent, 1940-42, 45-47; prof. geology U. N.Mex., 1947-76; ret., 1976; research geologist, 1947—. Served to lt. comdr. USNR, 1942-45; capt. Res., ret. Recipient Disting. Alumnus citation Coll. of Wooster, 1979; registered profl. engr., N.Mex. Fellow Geol. Soc. Am.; hon. life mem. Four Corners (pres. 1953) N.M. geol. socs.; mem. Am. Assn. Petroleum Geologists (nat. editor 1957-59, pres. 1971-72, chmn. adv. council 1972-73, Presdl. award 1948; hon. life mem.), Am. Petroleum Inst. (academic mem., exploration com. 1970-72), Am. Inst. Profl. Geologists, (state sect. pres. 1970, nat. editor 1965-66), Am. Soc. Photogrammetry, Marine Tech. Soc. (charter mem.), Internat. Assn. Sedimentology, Soc. Econ. Paleontologists and Mineralogists (dir. found. 1977), Aircraft Owners and Pilots Assn., Pilots Internat. Assn., Sigma Xi, Sigma Gamma Epsilon, Phi Kappa Phi. Author chpts. in textbooks and encys., articles in geol. bulls., newsletters. Home: 1040 Stanford Dr NE Albuquerque NM 87106

WENGERT, NORMAN IRVING, educator; b. Milw., Nov. 7, 1916; s. Eugene F. and Lydia (Semmann) W.; student Concordia Coll., Milw., 1930-36; B.A., U. Wis., 1938, J.D., 1942, Ph.D., 1947; M.A., Fletcher Sch., 1939; m. Janet Mueller, Oct. 9, 1940; children—Eugene Mark, Christine Ann, Timothy John. With TVA, 1941-48; faculty City Coll. N.Y., 1948-51; mem. program staff Office Sec. Dept. Interior, 1951-52; prof., chmn. social sci. dept. N.D. State U., Fargo, 1952-56; research asso. Resources for Future, Inc., 1956; prof. pub. adminstrn. U. Md., 1956-59; dep. dir. Nat. Outdoor Recreation Resources Rev. Com., 1959-60; prof., chmn. dept. polit. sci. Wayne State U., Detroit, 1960-68; vis. prof. pub. adminstrn. Pa. State U., 1968-69; prof. polit. sci. Colo. State U., Ft. Collins, 1969—; mem. policy analysis staff Office of Chief, U.S. Forest Service, 1978-79; vis. research prof. U.S. Army Engr. Inst. Water resources, 1969-70; research cons. Sch. Natural Resources, U. Mich., 1968-69; Royer lectr. U. Calif., Berkeley, 1975; lectr. U. Sarajevo (Yugoslavia), summer 1978; spl. adviser Govt. of India on food, agr., 1959; cons. U.S. Army Corps Engrs., 1968, Thorne Ecol. Inst., 1972-75, FAA, 1963, Atlantic Richfield Oil Corp., 1973-74, Nat. Water Quality Commn., 1974—, Office Water Resources and Tech., USDI, 1973-75, and states Colo., Md., Ga., Mich., also Western Interstate Nuclear Bd.; summer fellow Fonds für Umweltstudien, Bonn, Germany, 1973. Served as ensign USNR, 1944-45. Mem. Wis. Bar Assn., Western Soc. Sci., Western Polit. Sci. Assn., Am. Forestry Assn., Am. Soc. Pub. Adminstrn., Am. Water Resources Assn. (asso. editor Bull.), Urban Land Inst., Forest Hist. Soc. (bd. dirs.), Soils Conservation Soc. Am., Order of Coif, Sigma Xi, Phi Kappa Phi. Author: Valley of Tomorrow: TVA and Agriculture, 1952; Natural Resources and the Political Struggle, 1955; Adminstration of Natural Resources, 1961; (with George M. Walker, Jr.) Urban Water Policies and Decision Making, 1970; Urban-Metropolitan Institutions for Water Planning, Development and Management, 1972; Impact on the Human Environment of Proposed Oil Shale Development in Garfield County, 1974; Property Rights in Land: A Comparative Exploration of German and American Concepts and Problems, 1974; Public Participation in Water Resources Development, 1974; Land Use Planning and Control in the German Federal Republic, 1975; The Political Allocation of Burdens and Benefits: Externalities and Due Process in Environmental Protection, 1976; (with others) Effects on Local Agricultural Economy of Water Transfer to Cities, 1976, others; also chpts. in other books. Editor: Institutions for Urban-Metropolitan Water Management, 1972; Natural Resources Jour. issue, 1979; co-editor: The Energy Crisis: Reality or Myth, 1973. Home: 1225 Teakwood Dr Fort Collins CO 80525

WENK, EDWARD, JR., civil engr., educator; b. Balt., Jan. 24, 1920; s. Edward and Lillie (Heller) W.; B.E., Johns Hopkins, 1940, D.Eng., 1950; M.Sc., Harvard, 1947; D.Sc. (hon.), U. R.I., 1968; m. Carolyn Frances Lyford, Dec. 21, 1941; children—Lawrence Shelley, Robin Edward Alexander, Terry Allan. Head structures div. USN David Taylor Model Basin, Washington, 1942-56; chmn. dept. engring. mechanics S.W. Research Inst., San Antonio, 1956-59; sr. specialist sci. and tech. Legis. Reference Service, Library of Congress, Washington, 1959-61, chief sci. policy research div., 1964-66; tech. asst. to U.S. President's sci. adviser and exec. sec. Fed. Council for Sci. and Tech., White House, Washington, 1961-64; exec. sec. Nat. Council on Marine Resources and Engring. Devel., Exec. Office of Pres., Washington, 1966-70; prof. engring. and pub. affairs U. Wash., Seattle, 1970—, dir. program in social mgmt. tech., 1973—. Dir. URS Corp. Lectr. U. Md.; cons. in pub. policy for environ. and tech. affairs, ocean engring., Nat. Adv. Com. on Oceans and Atmosphere, 1972-73; vice chmn. U.S. Congress Tech. Assessment Council, 1973—; adviser Congress, U.N. Secretariat, Wash. State, pub. interest groups; vis. scholar Woodrow Wilson Internat. Center for Scholars, 1970-72, Harvard, 1976, Woods Hole Oceanographic Instn., 1976, U. Sussex, 1977. Served as ensign USNR, 1944-45. Recipient Navy Meritorious Civilian Service award, 1946; Ford Found. grantee, 1970; Rockefeller Found. fellow, 1976. Fellow ASME; mem. Soc. Exptl. Stress Analysis (past pres. William M. Murray lectr.), Nat. Acad. Engring. (chmn. com. on pub. policy 1970-75), Am. Soc. for Pub. Adminstrn. (chmn. com. on sci. and tech. in govt. 1974-78), Assembly Engring.-NRC, ASCE, Nat. Soc. Profl. Engrs., Nat. Oceanography Assn. (v.p. pub affairs 1970-72), Cousteau Soc. (chmn. adv. bd.), AAAS, Explorers Club, Sigma Xi (nat. lectr.), Tau Beta Pi, Chi Epsilon. Clubs: Cosmos (Washington). Author: The Politics of the Ocean, 1972; Margins for Survival, 1978. Editor: Engring. Mechanics Jour., 1958-60; Exptl. Mechanics Jour., 1954-56. Contbr. articles to profl. jours. Designer Aluminaut submarine. Home: 15142 Beach Dr NE Seattle WA 98155. *Each of us has the opportunity, indeed responsibility, to contribute to the human experience and to enrich the lives of future generations. In a world of change, cultural diversity and uncertainty, we must be ourselves and not merely slaves of conventional thought. We must act on the basis of what we believe to be right rather in the long run than only from the desire to be loved.*

WENKERT, ERNEST, chemist, educator; b. Vienna, Austria, Oct. 16, 1925; s. Moses and Elcie (Seidmann) W.; came to U.S., 1941, naturalized, 1946; B.S., U. Wash., 1945, M.S., 1947; Ph.D., Harvard, 1951; Dr. honoris causa, U. Paris-Sud, 1978; m. Ann Davis, June 22, 1948; children—Naomi, David, Daniel, Deborah. Faculty, Lower Columbia Jr. Coll., Longview, Wash., 1947-48; faculty Ia. State U., Ames, 1951-61, prof., 1959-61; prof. Ind. U., Bloomington, 1961-69, Herman T. Briscoe prof. chemistry, 1969-73; E.D. Butcher prof. chemistry Rice U., Houston, 1973—, chmn. dept. chemistry, 1976—; cons. chem. industry. Guggenheim fellow, 1965-66. Vis. prof. U. Calif., Berkeley, 1961-62, U. Paris, 1968, 70, U. Calif., Santa Barbara, 1974; Mellor vis. prof. U. Otago, Dunedin, N.Z., 1974; vis. prof. U. Colo., Boulder, 1975, U. Calif., San Diego, 1976, U. Calif., Irvine, 1978; Fulbright lectr. Institut de Chimie des Substances Naturelles, Gif-sur-yvette, France, 1963; prof., acting head dept. organic chemistry Weizmann Inst. Sci., Rehovoth, Israel, 1964-65. Recipient Ernest Guenther award Am. Chem. Soc. Mem. Am. Chem. Soc., Chem. Soc. (London), A.A.U.P., Academia Brasileira de Ciencias, Swiss Chem. Soc., Sigma Xi. Contbr. articles to profl. jours. Office: Dept of Chemistry Rice U Houston TX 77001

WENNER, GENE CHARLES, assn. exec.; b. Catasauqua, Pa., Dec. 21, 1931; s. Clinton G. and Bertha (Taggert) W.; B.S. in Music, W. Chester (Pa.) State Coll., 1953; M.Ed. in Music, Pa. State U., 1954; m. Carole Brunner, Aug. 15, 1953; children—Robert Larren, Laurel Emelie. Tchr. music Phila. public schs., 1945-55, 56-60; asso. prof. Kutztown (Pa.) State Coll., 1960-66, dir. coll. choir, 1960-66; fine arts adv. Pa. Dept. Edn., 1966-69, U.S. Office Edn., 1969-71; asst. dir. arts in edn. program John D. Rockefeller 3d Fund, 1971-78; arts edn. coordinator Office Commr., U.S. Office Edn., 1978-79; pres. Am. Music Conf., Wilmette, Ill., 1979—; mem. bd. Nat. Music Council; guest lectr. Northwestern U.; mus. dir. Allentown (Pa.) Mcpl. Opera, 1962-63, Allentown Civic Little Theatre, 1964, Little Theatre Alexandria (Va.), 1971; dir. Hershey (Pa.) Little Theatre, 1967-68, Hershey Community Chorus, 1967-69; composer I'll Never Forget You, 1968, Chorale of Dedication, 1974, Turn Thou to Me, 1975, Are You Nobody, Too?, 1976, also original music and scripts Robert's Theme and World of Sound for TV series Adventures in the Arts, Hershey, 1968. Served with AUS, 1955-56. Named Best Mus. Dir., Little Theatre Alexandria, 1971. Mem. Music Educators Nat. Conf., Am. Soc. Assn. Execs. Club: Masons. Author papers, reports in field. Office: 1000 Skokie Blvd Wilmette IL 60091

WENNER, HERBERT ALLAN, pediatrician; b. Drums, Pa., Nov. 14, 1912; s. Herbert C. and Verna (Walp) W.; B.S., Bucknell U., 1933; M.D., U. Rochester, 1939; m. Ruth I. Berger, June 27, 1942; children—Peter W., James M., Susan T., Thomas H. Intern in pathology Sch. Medicine, U. Colo., Denver, 1939-40; intern in pediatrics Yale Sch. Medicine, 1940-41, asst. resident and fellow in pediatrics, 1941-43, instr. preventive medicine, 1944-46; NRC fellow Yale U.-Johns Hopkins U., 1943-44; asst. prof. pediatrics and bacteriology Sch. Medicine, U. Kans., Kansas City, 1946-49, asso. prof., 1949-51, research prof. pediatrics, 1951-69, adj. prof., 1975—; Joyce C. Hall Disting. prof. pediatrics, U. Mo. Sch. Med., Kansas City, 1969—, adj. prof. Sch. Dentistry, 1970—; formerly cons. epidemiology Kans. Bd. Health, Mo. Bd. Health. NIH Research Career awardee, 1962. Diplomate Am. Bd. Microbiology, Am. Bd. Pediatrics. Fellow AAAS, Am. Public Health Assn., Am. Acad. Pediatrics; mem. Soc. Pediatric Research, Am. Pediatric Soc., Soc. Exptl. Biology and Medicine, Biometrics Soc., Mo. Med. Assn., AMA, Royal Soc. Health, AAUP, N.Y. Acad. Scis., Am. Epidemiology Soc., Infectious Disease Soc. Am. Episcopalian. Asso. editor Am. Jour. Epidemiology, 1967-79; mem. editorial bd. Intervirology, 1972-79; mem. editorial adv. bd. Archives of Virology, 1975-79; contbr. articles to med. books and jours. Home: 9711 Johnson Dr Merriam KS 66203 Office: Children's Mercy Hosp 24th at Gillham Rd Kansas City MO 64108. *Good parents, a devoted family, superb teachers and hard work have contributed to my career, and the rewards therein.*

WENNER, JANN S., editor, publisher; b. N.Y.C., Jan. 7, 1946; s. Edward and Ruth N. (Simmons) W.; student U. Calif. at Berkeley, 1964-66; m. Jane Ellen Schindelhiem, July 1, 1968. Editor, pub. Rolling Stone mag., San Francisco, 1967—, Look mag., N.Y.C., 1979; editor-in-chief Outside Mag., San Francisco, 1977-78; author: Lennon Remembers, 1971; Garcia, 1972. Recipient Disting. Achievement award U. So. Calif. Sch. Journalism and Alumni Assn., 1976. Office: Rolling Stone 745 Fifth Ave New York NY 10022

WENNER, WILLIAM WATKINS, judge; b. Brunswick, Md., Sept. 24, 1930; s. William B. and Eleanor (Watkins) W.; A.B., Kenyon Coll., 1952; LL.B., U. Md., 1958; m. Lila Ward Chichester, Aug. 20, 1955; children—Peter Wood, Eleanor Ann. Admitted to Md. bar, 1958, practiced in Brunswick and Frederick, 1959-78; dep. state's atty. Frederick County, Md., 1960-64; town atty., Brunswick and Burkittsville, Md., 1961-78; counsel Peoples Bank Office, Farmers & Mechanics Nat. Bank, 1962-78; advisory dir. Farmers & Mechanics Nat. Bank; gen. counsel Bank of Brunswick; partner firm Rollins, Wenner & Price, and predecessor, 1966-78; asso. judge Dist. Ct. Md., 1978—; dir. Md. Blue Cross Inc., 1969-78, exec. com., 1973-78, chmn. bd., 1974-78. Mem. Brunswick Indsl. Devel. Commn., 1959-62; dir. Brunswick Planning Commn., 1963-71, chmn., 1971-73; mem. Advisory Council on Child Welfare, 1966-72; mem. Md. Gov.'s Commn. Children and Youth, 1972-73; Frederick County Advisory Council Mental Health; bd. dirs. Frederick County Heart Assn., Brunswick Pub. Library, 1963-72, treas., 1962-71, pres., 1972; pres. bd. trustees St. James (Md.) Sch., 1975—. Served with C.E., U.S. Army, 1952-54. Fellow Md. Bar Found.; mem. Am., Md. (gov. 1972—), Frederick County (sec. 1961-71, pres. 1972) bar assns., Am. Legion. Democrat. Episcopalian. Clubs: Rotary (pres. 1963), Maryland. Home: 1316 Petersville Rd Brunswick MD 21716 Office: PO Box 596 Frederick MD 21701

WENNERSTROM, JACK ALBERT, bus. services co. exec.; b. Oak Park, Ill., Nov. 11, 1919; s. John Elias and Ethel (Lauerman) W.; B.B.A., Northwestern U., 1943; m. Nancy Church Mossop, Feb. 10, 1974; children—Candace, Jack. Controller, Aurex Corp., Chgo., 1943-47; v.p., treas., chief financial officer A.C. Nielsen Co., Northbrook, Ill., 1947—; treas., dir. Petroleum Info. Corp., Denver, Healthcom, Inc., Phila., A.C. Nielsen (Argentina) S.A., A.C. Nielsen Internat., Inc., Compumark, Inc.; dir. A.C.N. de Mex. Inc., Glenview State Bank (Ill.). Mem. Fin. Execs. Inst. Clubs: Northshore Country, Mission Hills Country. Home: 1650 E Mission Hills Rd Northbrook IL 60062 Office: Nielsen Plaza Northbrook IL 60062

WENSINGER, ARTHUR STEVENS, educator; b. Grosse Pointe, Mich., Mar. 9, 1926; s. Carl Franklin and Suzanne (Stevens) W.; grad. Phillips Andover Acad., 1944; B.A., Dartmouth, 1948; M.A., U. Mich., 1951; postgrad. U. Munich, 1948, 50-51, U. Innsbruck, 1953-54; Ph.D., U. Mich., 1958. Instr., asst. prof., asso. prof. Wesleyan U., Middletown, Conn., 1955-68, prof. German and humanities, 1968—, Marcus Taft prof. German and humanities, 1977—, chmn. dept. German lang. and lit., 1971-74, 78—, also sr. tutor Coll. Letters and Pres. Friends of Davison Art Center. fellow Wesleyan Center for Humanities, 1974. Reynolds fellow, 1950-51; Fulbright fellow, 1954-55; Danforth fellow, 1959; Ford Found. fellow, 1970-71; Inter Nationes grantee, 1978. Mem. Modern Lang. Assn., Am. Assn. Tchrs. German, Heinrich von Kleist Gesellschaft, Internat. Brecht Soc., Kafka Soc. Am., Soc. Preservation New Eng. Antiquities, Conn. Acad. Arts and Scis., Phi Beta Kappa, Phi Kappa Phi, Delta Tau Delta. Author: Hogarth on High Life, 1970. Translator, editor: The Theater of the Bauhaus, 1961; editor: Stone Island (Peter S. Boynton), 1973. Co-editor: Hesse's Siddhartha, 1962. Contbr. articles to profl. jours. Translator in field. Home: Candlewood Hill Higganum CT 06441 Office: Wesleyan U Box 178 Middletown CT 06457

WENTLING, THOMAS LYNCH, banker; b. Greensburg, Pa., Feb. 28, 1916; s. Joseph D. and Mary (Lynch) W.; A.B., Yale, 1938; J.D., Harvard, 1941; m. Elizabeth H. Gregg, June 10, 1950 (dec. Oct. 1970); children—Thomas Lynch, James G., Carolyn J. Partner Tucker, Arensberg & Ferguson (formerly Patterson, Crawford, Arensberg & Dunn), Pitts., 1946-62; pres. S.W. Nat. Bank Pa., Greensburg, Pa., 1962—, also dir.; dir. Westmoreland Computer Services, Inc. Chmn. Greensburg Garden and Civic Commn., 1970—, Greater Greenburg Planning Commn., 1960, Charter Commn. City Greensburg, 1961, Pa. Economy League, 1971—. Trustee Westmoreland Hosp. Assn., Westmoreland Mus. Art, Seton Hill Coll., Greensburg campus U. Pitts., Greensburg Found. Served with USNR, 1942-46. Mem. Am. Law Inst., Pa. Bar Assn., Pa. Bankers Assn. Elk. Clubs: Rolling Rock, Laurel Valley Golf (Ligonier, Pa.); Pitts. Golf. Home: 655 Oak Hill Ln Greensburg PA 15601 Office: 111 S Main St Greensburg PA 15601

WENTORF, ROBERT HENRY, phys. chemist; b. West Bend, Wis., May 28, 1926; s. Robert H. and Sophia (Rusch) W.; B.S. in Chem. Engring., U. Wis., 1948, Ph.D. in Chemistry, 1952; m. Vivian Marty, Aug. 20, 1949; children—Jill, Laine, Rolf. Teaching and research asst. U. Wis., Madison, 1948-52, vis. prof., 1966-67; mem. research and devel. staff Gen. Electric Co., Schenectady, 1952-66, 67—. Served with USN, 1944-45. Recipient New Materials prize Am. Phys. Soc., 1977. Mem. Am. Chem. Soc. (Ipatieff prize 1965), Nat. Acad. Engring., Mohawk Soaring Club (dir., instr. gliding), Sigma Xi, Alpha Chi Sigma, Tau Beta Pi. Editor: Modern Very High Pressure Techniques, 1962; Advances in High Pressure Research, vol. IV, 1974; patentee in field; contbr. articles to sci. jours. Home: RD 2 Valatie NY 12184 Office: Gen Electric Research and Devel Center K-1 Schenectady NY 12345

WENTS, JOHN H(ENRY), JR., geol. and engring. cons.; b. Galva, Iowa, 1905; s. John H. and Julia A. (Hefner) W.; student Stanford U., 1923-27, U. So. Calif., 1934-39, advanced mgmt. program Harvard, 1958; m. Julia Cole Kirkpatrick, Oct. 30, 1940; 1 dau., Doris Roberta; children by previous marriage—Shyrlee (Mrs. Edward Reith), Gwyneth (Mrs. George Stevens). Partner John H. Wents & Son-Cons., Los Angeles, 1938-55; asst. gen. mgr. Central div. Tidewater Oil Co., Tulsa, 1956-59, mgr. prodn. So. div., Houston, 1959-60; exec. asst. prodn. mgr., Los Angeles, 1960-62, adminstrv. asst. to pres. prodn. and exploration, 1964-68, dir., mgr. prodn. and exploration research, 1964-67, dir. univ. relations, 1968-70, ret., 1970; geol. and engring. cons., 1970—; chmn. bd. Vi Roi Drilling Co., 1974—; pres., gen. mgr. Tidewater Canadian Oil Co., Regina, Sask., Can., 1962-64; pres. Key Pipeline Co., 1962-64, No. Light Oil Co., 1962-64. Mem. Canadian Petroleum Assn. (vice chmn. bd. govs. 1963, chmn. bd. dirs. 1963), Am. Assn. Petroleum Geologists, Am. Petroleum Inst., Petroleum Prodn. Pioneers. Republican. Roman Catholic. Club: Petroleum. Home: 6635 Wooster Ave Los Angeles CA 90056

WENTSCH, GEORGE MAURICE, former air force officer, mgmt. cons.; b. Hollywood, Calif., Aug. 13, 1926; s. Harold Earle and Elizabeth (Shulze) W.; B.S., U.S. Mil. Acad., West Point, N.Y., 1949; M.S., Syracuse (N.Y.) U., 1962; grad. Indsl. Coll. of Armed Forces, Washington, 1967; m. Marie Snodgrass, Aug. 5, 1950; children—David, Rhoda, Elizabeth. Commd. 2d lt. U.S. Air Force, 1949, advanced through grades to maj. gen.; various assignments as pilot, 1950-62; research and devel. officer Mil. Air Transport Service, Scott AFB, Ill., 1962; comdr. 357th Tactical Fighter Squadron, Thailand, 1967-69; with Joint Chiefs of Staff, Washington, 1969; comdr. 443d Mil. Airlift Wing, Altus AFB, Okla., 1970-72, 438th Mil. Airlift Wing, McGuire AFB, N.J., 1972-74; vice comdr. 21st AF, 1974-75; vice comdr. Mil. Traffic Mgmt. Command, Washington, 1975-79; ret., 1979; mgmt. cons., 1979—. Decorated D.S.M., Legion of Merit with oak leaf cluster, D.F.C. with 2 oak leaf clusters, Bronze Star, Air Medal with 14 oak leaf clusters, Joint Service Commendation Medal, AF Commendation Medal with oak leaf cluster (U.S.), Presdl. Unit Citation ribbon (Rep. of Korea). Mem. Nat. Def. Transp. Assn., AF Assn., Am. Mgmt. Assn., AF Sgts. Assn. Episcopalian. Club: Order Daedalians. Home: Route 3 Box 224-A Marble Falls TX 78701 Office: Austin TX 78701

WENTWORTH, DAVID FRANK, accountant; b. Fairfield, Iowa, Aug. 7, 1924; s. Harry D. and Eva M. (Anderson) W.; B.S., U. Iowa, 1948; m. Lillian E. Kraemer, June 10, 1944; children—Ellen, Ann, Jill, Karen, Nancy. Staff accountant McGladrey, Hansen, Dunn & Co., Davenport, Iowa, 1948-51, partner, 1951-66, regional adminstrv. partner, 1966-69, exec. partner, 1969-78; regional adminstrv. partner McGladrey Hendrickson & Co., 1978—. Served with AUS, 1943-46. Recipient Sells Silver medal award in C.P.A. exam., 1949. C.P.A., Iowa. Mem. Am. Inst. C.P.A.'s, Iowa Soc. C.P.A.'s (pres. 1977-78), Davenport C. of C. Republican. Methodist. Club: Davenport Optimist (past pres.). Home: 2526 E Columbia St Davenport IA 52803 Office: 908 Davenport Bank Bldg Davenport IA 52801

WENTWORTH, NATHAN HENRY, ins. co. exec.; b. Newton, Mass., Jan. 5, 1911; s. Henry Azor and Edith (Ellis) W.; A.B. magna cum laude, Dartmouth, 1932; m. virginia Willard, Aug. 22, 1936; 1 dau., Linda Monroe (Mrs. Delano C. Cannon, Jr.). Underwriter, Am. Fgn. Ins. Assn., 1933-34, asst. mgr. Paris br., 1934-38, mgr., 1939-41, supt. for Europe and Middle East, 1945-52; Boston mgr. Home Ins. Co., 1941-43; sec. American Fore Ins. Group, 1953-57, v.p., 1957—; v.p. Loyalty Ins. Group, 1958, exec. v.p., dir., 1959; pres. The Continental Ins. Cos. (formerly Am. Fore Loyalty Group cos.), 1959-65, vice chmn., 1965-70, chmn. bd., 1970-76, also dir.; pres., dir. The Continental Corp., 1968-71, chmn. bd., 1970-76; dir. Dominion Ins Corp., Toronto; trustee East River Savs. Bank; dir. Phoenix Assurance Co. N.Y., La Preservatrice, Paris, Nat. Life Assurance Co.

Can. (Toronto), Puerto Rican-American Corp., Continental Reins Corp. Ltd. (Bermuda), Fidelity Union Bancorp., Franklin United Life Ins. Co., Pub. Service Electric and Gas Co. Mem. adv. council Pace Coll. Served from capt. to lt. col. OSS, AUS, 1943-45. Decorated Croix de Guerre (France). Mem. Phi Beta Kappa, Phi Kappa Psi. Clubs: Union League (N.Y.C.); Baltusrol Golf. Home: PO Box 164 Essex CT 06426 Office: 80 Maiden Ln New York NY 10038

WENTWORTH, RICHARD LEIGH, editor; b. Concord, N.H., July 6, 1930; s. Leigh Mayhew and Yvonne Regina (Wilcott) W.; B.A., U. Okla., 1956; m. Marlene McClenning, June 9, 1950; children—Douglas, John, Elizabeth, James. Editorial asst. U. Okla. Press, 1957-58; asst. editor U. Wis. Press, 1958-59; mgr. sales and promotion La. State U. Press, 1959-62, asst. dir., 1962-63, dir., 1963-70; asso. dir., editor U. Ill. Press, Urbana, 1970—. Served with USAF, 1948-52. Mem. Assn. Am. Univ. Presses (dir. 1966, 77-79), Orgn. Am. Historians. Democrat. Elk. Contbr. articles to pub. and sports jours. Home: 808 W Springfield Champaign IL 61820 Office: Univ Illinois Press Urbana IL 61801

WENTZ, FREDERICK KUHLMAN, theol. schs. ofcl.; b. Gettysburg, Pa., Jan. 21, 1921; s. Abdel Ross and Edna (Kuhlman) W.; B.A., Gettysburg Coll., 1942; B.D., Gettysburg Sem., 1945; Ph.D., Yale, 1954; Litt.D., Thiel Coll., Greenville, Pa., 1967; D.D., Hartwick Coll., 1972; m. Marion Jean Benson, Jan. 20, 1951; children—Lisa Jean, Theodore Valentine (dec.), Melanie Kuhlman. Ordained to ministry Lutheran Ch., 1945; pastor in Culver City, Cal., 1945-48; pastor to Luth. students Yale, 1948-49, 50-51; chaplain, asst. prof. religion Hartwick Coll., Oneonta, N.Y., 1951-53; prof. ch. history Luth. So. Sem., Columbia, S.C., 1953-56; prof. hist. theology Gettysburg Sem., 1956-66; pres., Hamma Sch. Theology, Springfield, Ohio, 1966-73, prof. church history, 1966-76; exec. dir. Chgo. Cluster Theol. Schs., 1976—; mem. bd. world missions Luth. Ch. Am., 1966—. Mem. Am. Soc. Ch. History, Phi Beta Kappa. Author: The Times Test the Church, 1956; The Layman's Role Today, 2d edit., 1965; Lutherans and Other Denominations, 1964; The Reaction of the Religious Press in America to the Emergence of Nazism, 1964; Lutherans in Concert, 1968; Set Free For Others, 1969; Getting Into the Act, 1978. Editor (Schmucker) Fraternal Appeal, 1965; My Job and My Faith, 1967; Luth. Quar., 1966-70. Home: 5421 S Cornell Ave Chicago IL 60615

WENTZ, HOWARD BECK, JR., mfg. co. exec.; b. Pitts., Jan. 10, 1930; s. Howard and Emmy Lou W.; B.S.E., Princeton U., 1952; M.B.A., Harvard U., 1957; m. Judith Ann Blough, June, 1958; children—Howard, Roger, Elizabeth. Mfg. exec. TRW Corp., 1957-60; asso. Robert Heller and Assos., Cleve., 1960-63; exec. v.p. Paterson-Leitch Co., Cleve., 1963-69; pres. Duff-Norton subs. Amstar Corp., Charlotte, N.C., 1969-72, corp. v.p. parent co., N.Y.C., 1972-79, exec. v.p., chief operating officer, 1979—, also dir.; dir. Am. European Reins. Co., Skandia Corp., Hudson Ins. Corp. Served with USN, 1952-55. Mem. Am. Mgmt. Assn. (gen. mgmt. council). Office: 1251 Ave of Americas New York NY 10020

WENTZ, ROBERT EARL, supt. schs.; b. Lanark, Ill., Jan. 20, 1933; s. Delbert Earl and Marjorie Irene (Radeke) W.; B.S., Miss. State Coll., 1955; M.A., U. Chgo., 1965, Ph.D., 1970; m. Janice Logue, Sept. 25, 1976; children by previous marriage—Mark, Michael, Murray. Tchr., Sturgis (Miss.) Community High Sch., 1955-56; tchr., prin., asst. supt. Harvey (Ill.) pub. schs., 1956-66; fellow NIMH, U. Chgo., 1966-68; supt. Penn-Harris-Madison (Ind.) Sch. Corp., 1968-71, Pomona (Calif.) Unified Sch. Dist., 1971-75; supt. pub. schs., St. Louis, 1975—. Bd. dirs. Citizenship Edn. Clearing House, 1975-78, St. Louis/St. Louis County Conf. on Edn., 1975-78; adv. council St. Louis Leadership Program, Danforth Found., 1976-78; mem. standing com. communications Council Gt. City Schs., 1976—; chmn. edn. div. Arts and Edn. Fund, 1977, United Way St. Louis, 1976; chmn. sch. adv. com. St. Louis council Boy Scouts Am., also mem.-at-large exec. bd.; trustee ednl. TV sta. KETC, 1975-78; adv. com. Future of St. Louis Award; pres. trustees Parsons Blewett Meml. Fund; mem. scholarship com. Swope Meml. Loan Fund, 1978—; mem. consortium adv. bd. Urban Consumer Edn. Project; mem. adv. com. on edn. and family PET, Inc. Named Outstanding Young Educator, Mishawaka (Ind.) Jaycees, 1969; Outstanding Citizen in St. Joseph County (Ind.), Mishawaka Enterprise-Record, 1969; recipient Hon. Service award Pomona PTA, 1975; also various other service awards; hon. life mem. Ill. PTA. Mem. Am., Mo. assns. sch. adminstrs., Phi Delta Kappa. Home: 4474 Laclede St St Louis MO 63108 Office: 911 Locust St St Louis MO 63101

WENTZ, SIDNEY FREDERICK, ins. co. exec.; b. Dallas, Mar. 27, 1932; s. Howard Beck and Emmy Lou (Cawthon) W.; A.B., Princeton, 1954; LL.B., Harvard, 1960; m. Barbara Strait, Sept. 9, 1961; children—Eric, Jennifer, Robin. Admitted to N.Y. State bar, 1961; atty. firm White & Case, N.Y.C., 1960-65, Western Electric Co., 1965-66, Am. Tel. & Tel. Co., 1966-67; with Crum & Forster Ins. Cos., Morristown, N.J., 1967—, dir., 1968—, sr. v.p., gen. counsel, 1971-73, vice chmn. bd., 1973—; with Crum & Forster, N.Y.C., 1967—, dir., 1969—, exec. v.p., 1972-73, pres., 1973—. Trustee Morristown Meml. Hosp., 1974—. Served to lt. (j.g.) USNR, 1954-57. Clubs: Morris County Golf; Morristown Field; Sakonnet (R.I.) Golf; Baltusrol Golf. Home: 1 White Deer Ln Morristown NJ 07960 Office: 305 Madison Ave Morristown NJ 07960

WENTZ, WALTER JOHN, educator; b. Newburgh, Ohio, June 17, 1928; s. Walter John and Gladys Marjory Wentz; B.A., U. Iowa, 1949, M.A., 1950, Ph.D., 1963; m. Lynne E. Putnam; children—Marcia, Sharon, Diane, Courtney. Pres., Meml. Hosp., Saulte Ste Marie, Mich., 1965-71; asso. prof. Central Mich. U., Mt. Pleasant; prof. health adminstrn. Wichita State U., chmn. dept. health adminstrn. and edn. Coll. Health Related Professions. Served to lt. col., inf. AUS, 1951-56. Decorated Silver Star, Combat Infantryman badge. Fellow Am. Public Health Assn., AAAS, Royal Soc. Health; mem. Sigma Xi, Phi Kappa Phi, Sigma Iota Epsilon, Omicron Delta Kappa, Beta Gamma Sigma. Republican. Methodist. Club: Rotary (dir.). Contbr. articles to profl. jours. Office: Dept Health Adminstrn and Edn Wichita State U Wichita KS 67208

WENTZELL, CECIL RODNEY, business supplies co. exec.; exec.; b. Bethel, Maine, Aug. 10, 1921; s. Stanley H. and Millie (Baker) W.; grad. Bentley Coll., 1947; m. June Elise Little, June 20, 1940; children—Melinda, Stephen. With Gen. Electric Co., 1947-74; treas. gen. Electric Tech. Services Co., Inc., N.Y.C., 1962-72, mgr. Latin Am. fin. planning and analysis, 1972-74; treas. Nashua Corp. (N.H.), 1974—. Served with U.S. Army, 1942-45. Republican. Episcopalian. Home: Mack Hill Rd Amherst NH 03031 Office: 44 Franklin St Nashua NH 03061

WENZEL, ALBIN ROBERT, banker; b. Bklyn., June 30, 1920; s. Albin H. and Marie (Reiblein) W.; B.S. in Banking and Finance, N.Y.U., 1948; grad. Advanced Mgmt. Program, Harvard, 1961; m. Harriet M. Muller, Aug. 4, 1945; children—Karen (Mrs. Ronald Pabian), Wayne. Bank examiner Fed. Res. Bank N.Y., 1938-53; with Bank of N.Y., N.Y.C., 1953—, sr. v.p., 1969-73; pres. Valley-L.I. Region, Bank of N.Y., Valley Stream, 1973—; past chmn., dir. N.Y. Bus. Devel. Corp.; dir. Group Health Ins. Co.; former trustee Richmond Hill Savs. Bank. Trustee Webb Inst. Naval Architecture, Glen Cove, N.Y. Served to maj. USAAF, World War II; ETO. Decorated D.F.C., Air medal with 3 oak leaf clusters, Presdl. citation. Home: 8 Bowden Lane Glen Head NY 11545 Office: 235 Rockaway Ave Valley Stream NY 11582

WENZEL, BERNICE MARTHA, physiologist; b. Bridgeport, Conn., June 22, 1921; d. Edward August and Gertrude (Card) Wenzel; A.B., Beaver Coll., 1942; A.M., Columbia U., 1943, Ph.D., 1948; m. Wendell E. Jeffrey, June 14, 1952. Instr., Newcomb Coll. Tulane, 1945-46; instr. Barnard Coll., 1946-50, asst. prof. psychology, 1950-55; asst. research physiologist U. Calif., Los Angeles Sch. Medicine, 1957-59, asst. prof., 1959-61, asso. prof., 1961-69, prof., 1969—, prof. psychiatry, 1971—, vice chmn. dept. physiology, 1971-73, asst. dean ednl. research, 1974—. Mem. AAAS, Am. Physiol. Soc., Am., Western psychol. assns., Am. Psychosomatic Soc., Internat. Brain Research Orgn., Neurosci. Soc., Internat. Soc. Psychoneuroendocrinology, Soc. Psychophysiol. Research. Contbr. articles to profl. jours. Home: 3334 Scadlock Ln Sherman Oaks CA 91403 Office: Dept Physiology Med Sch Univ Calif Los Angeles CA 90024

WENZEL, LEE BEY, lawyer; b. Edgeley, N.D., July 1, 1930; s. Russell Henry and Dorothy Kay (Greene) W.; B.S. in Bus. Adminstrn., U. Calif., Los Angeles, 1952, LL.B., 1957; m. Barbara Jean Knoll, Apr. 18, 1953; children—Teresa (Mrs. Michael Zinn), Mark D., Neil S., Christine M., Dean J., Julie A., Lisa J., Kent J., Todd J. Admitted to Calif. bar, 1957; dep. city atty., Los Angeles, 1957-59; asso. firm Jarrett & Morgan, 1959-61; partner firm Morgan, Wenzel & McNicholas, Los Angeles, 1961—. Dir., So. Calif. Def. Counsel; regent U. Calif. Served with USNR, 1952-54. Fellow Internat. Assn. Def. Counsel, Internat. Acad. Trial Lawyers; mem. Am. Bd. Trial Advocates (pres. Los Angeles chpt.), U. Calif. at Los Angeles Alumni Assn. (gen. counsel 1971-74, pres. 1978-80). Republican. Roman Catholic. Clubs: Our Lady of Lourdes Mens; Jonathan, Porter Valley Country. Home: 9912 Melvin Ave Northridge CA 91324 Office: 1545 Wilshire Blvd Los Angeles CA 90017

WENZEL, LEONARD ANDREW, chem. engr., educator; b. Palo Alto, Calif., Jan. 21, 1923; s. Robert Nicolas and Frances (Browne) W.; B.S. in Chem. Engring., Pa. State U., 1943; M.S., U. Mich., 1948, Ph.D., 1950; m. Mary Elizabeth Leathers, Oct. 21, 1944; children—Frances Beth, Alma Louise, Jesse Robert, Sara Virginia. Jr. engr. Phillips Petroleum Co., 1943-44; research asst. Mellon Inst., 1944; research asst. Petroleum Refining Lab., Pa. State U., 1946; research asst. U. Mich., 1946-49; sr. research chemist Colgate-Palmolive Co., 1949-51; mem. faculty Lehigh U., 1951—, prof. chem. engring., 1960—, chmn. dept., 1962—; vis. lectr. U. Ala., 1964-66; cons. to industry in cryogenic engring., thermodynamics, and heat transfer; UNESCO expert and project coordinator chem. engring., Bucaramanga, Colombia, 1969-70; UNESCO cons. cryogenic engring., Venezuela, 1974—. Pres. Central Sch. P.T.A., 1953-54, Bethlehem chpt. Am. Field Service, 1965—. Served with AUS, 1944, with USNR, 1944-46. Mem. Am. Inst. Chem. Engrs. (founder Lehigh Valley sect. 1955, chmn. 1960-61), Am. Chem. Soc., Am. Soc. Engring. Edn., Sigma Xi, Tau Beta Pi (faculty adviser 1963—), Sigma Tau, Phi Lambda Upsilon, Pi Mu Epsilon, Theta Xi. Methodist (chmn. commn. on edn. 1965—), Author: (with others) Principles of Unit Operations, 2d edit., 1980; (with L. B. Andersen) Introduction to Chemical Engineering, 1961; also numerous research articles. Home: 517 15th Ave Bethlehem PA 18018

WENZLAU, THOMAS EUGENE, univ. pres.; b. Troy, Ohio, Mar. 31, 1927; s. Charles Norman and Alice (Kessler) W.; B.A., Ohio Wesleyan U., 1950; M.A., Ph.D., U. Ill.; L.H.D., Aoyama Gakuin U., Tokyo, Japan, 1974; m. Nancy Jeanne Allen, Aug. 12, 1950; children—Scott Allen, David Thomas, Katherine Jane, Janet Marie. Instr., then asst. prof. econs. Wesleyan U., Middletown, Conn., 1953-57; asst. prof. econs. Kenyon Coll., Gambier, Ohio, 1957-58; mem. faculty Lawrence U., 1958-69, asso. prof. econs., John McNaughton prof. econs., asso. dean of faculty, 1968-69; pres. Ohio Wesleyan U., Delaware, 1969—. Fulbright lectr. Civil Service Acad., Lahore, Pakistan, 1964-65. Served with USNR, 1945-46. Mem. Am. Econ. Assn., Phi Beta Kappa, Sigma Alpha Epsilon, Omicron Delta Kappa, Omicron Delta Gamma. Home: 135 Oak Hill Ave Delaware OH 43015

WENZLER, WILLIAM PAUL, architect; b. Milw., Feb. 9, 1929; s. Paul C. and Bertha R. (Froemming) W.; student U. Wis., 1947-48; B.S. in Archtl. Engring., U. Ill., 1952; m. Dolores A. Rahn, June 17, 1950; children—Edward, Deborah, John, Joan. Draftsman, H.C. Haeuser, architect, Milw., 1952, A.H. Siewert, architect, Milw., 1952-54; designer Brust and Brust, architects, Milw., 1954-55; pvt. practice, Milw., 1955—; pres. William Wenzler & Assos., Architects, Inc., 1966—; prin. works include Germantown (Wis.) Elementary Sch., 1956, St. Edmunds Episcopal Ch., Elm Grove, Wis., 1957, Zion Evangel. and Reformed Ch., Milw., 1958, 1st Conglist. Ch., Mukwonago, Wis., 1959, Goldendale (Wis.) Elementary Sch., 1959, Bradford Terrace, Milw. Protestant Home for Aged, 1962, Our Shepherd Luth. Ch., Greendale, Wis., 1963, Gerald H. Nickoll residence, Fox Point, Wis., 1963, Inland Steel Co. factory and office bldg., Milw., 1966, Brookfield (Wis.) Evangel. Luth. Ch., 1966, Luth. Social Services Wis. and Upper Mich. hdqrs., Milw., 1967, Lloyd A. Gerlach residence, Elm Grove, 1967, Eden Theol. Sem. Library, Webster Groves, Mo., 1968, Luth. Ch. Living Christ, Germantown, 1969, Grace Episcopal Ch., Galesburg, Ill., 1970, Calvary Baptist Ch., Milw., 1970, Fine Arts Complex, Wis. State U., Stevens Point, 1971, Northridge Lakes Community Devel., Milw., 1971, phys. edn. bldg. Wis. U.-Parkside, 1972; Jewish Vocational Services Milw. (renovation), 1974; theater and anthropology bldg. Beloit Coll., 1975; Elm-Brook Ch., Brookfield, Wis., 1975; Dubuque (Iowa) Theol. Library, 1976; also numerous exhbns. of works. Francis J. Plym fellow U. Ill., 1958; Ford Found. grantee U. Wis., 1961; named one of Wis. 5 Outstanding Young Men, Wis. Jr. C. of C., 1961; recipient Gov. Wis. award for creativity in arts, 1967; various awards for archtl. works. Registered architect, Wis., Ill., Iowa, Mo., Mass., Calif., Tex., Mich., Pa. Fellow AIA; mem. Am. Concrete Inst., Guild Religious Architecture, Gargoyle, Tau Beta Pi. Mem. United Ch. Christ. Home: 2823 N Shepard Ave Milwaukee WI 53211 Office: 205 W Highland Ave Milwaukee WI 53203

WENZLICK, ROY, real estate economist; b. St. Louis, June 13, 1894; s. Albert and Emma (Schall) W.; A.B., Westminster Coll., Fulton, Mo., 1916; student Princeton, 1916-17; Ph.D., St. Louis U., 1942; m. Susan Newsom, June 29, 1918; 1 dau., Jean N. (Mrs. Jean Fullerton). Successively vocational guidance dir. St. Louis YMCA, research dir. St. Louis Post Dispatch, nat. advt. mgr. same, pres. Real Estate Analysts, Inc.; past chmn. bd. Roy Wenzlick Research Corp.; mem. large scale operations com. Hoovers Housing Conf., 1931; econ. cons. capital goods div. Nat. Recovery Act, 1933; econ. cons. industry council O.P.A., 1942; chmn. Census Com. for Greater St. Louis, 1926-53; chmn. research com. Community Council, 1924-32; chmn. research com. Social Planning Council, 1932-38; speaker numerous seminars and profl. groups; chmn. adv. com. on research and record projects for St. Louis dist. WPA: research cons. Nat. Assn. Real Estate Bds., 1934-37; mem. exec. bd. St. Louis council Boy Scouts Am. Recipient distinguished alumni awards Westminster Coll., St. Louis U. Mem. Am. Econ. Assn., Am. Inst. Real Estate Appraisers, St. Louis Real Estate Bd. (life), Urban Land Inst., Am. Soc. Real Estate Counselors. Club: Rotary (Paul Harris fellow). Author: The Federal Census of Metropolitan St. Louis, 1932; The Coming Boom in Real Estate, 1936. Editor, publisher The Real Estate Analyst, 1932-74. Contbr. to nat. mags. Home and office: 301 McDonald Pl Webster Groves MO 63119

WERBOW, STANLEY NEWMAN, educator; b. Phila., Apr. 19, 1922; s. Morris and Sadie (Newman) W.; B.A., George Washington U., 1946; postgrad. Middleburg Coll., 1946-47, U. Mich., 1948; Ph.D., Johns Hopkins, 1953; m. Naomi Esther Ecker, June 1, 1952; children—Susan Linda, Emily Frances, Carol Martha. Tchr., Eastern High Sch., Washington, 1946-47; research analyst specialist U.S. Dept. Def., Washington, 1952-53; faculty U. Tex., Austin, 1953—, prof., 1965-69, 78—, chmn. dept. Germanic langs., 1969-71, dean Coll. Humanities, 1971-78; vis. prof. U. Marburg, 1963. Served with Signal Corps, AUS, 1943-45. Decorated Bronze Star medal; Bundesverdienstkreuz zweiter klasse (W. Ger.); recipient Fulbright award to Netherlands, 1950-51; Guggenheim fellow, 1960; Fulbright research scholar, Germany, 1960-61. Mem. Modern Lang. Assn. (pres. South Central assn. 1976—), Linguistic Soc. Am., Medieval Acad., Internat. Assn. Germanists, Phi Beta Kappa, Phi Kappa Phi, Delta Phi Alpha. Author: Martin von Amberg, 1957; (with Lehmann, Rehder, Shaw) Review and Progress in German, 1959. Editor: Formal Aspects of Medieval German Poetry, 1970. Home: 4205 Prickly Pear Dr Austin TX 78731

WERCHICK, JACK, lawyer; b. Russia, Jan. 14, 1913; s. Leo and Sonia W.; came to U.S., 1915, naturalized, 1934; A.B., San Francisco State Coll., 1936; J.D., U. Calif., San Francisco, 1949; m. Aug. 29, 1936; children—Arne, Susan. Tchr. elementary sch. Vallejo (Calif.) Unified Sch. Dist., 1938-43, prin., 1943-46; admitted to Calif. and Fed. bars, 1950, U.S. Supreme Ct. bar, 1968; asso. firm Elmer P. Delany, San Francisco, 1950-51, partner, 1951-52; individual practice law, San Francisco, 1952-58; individual practice law, San Francisco, 1959-70; partner Werchick & Werchick, San Francisco, 1970—; instr. in law Hastings Coll. Law, U. Calif., 1964-66, asst. prof. law, 1966-68, asso. prof., 1968-70, prof., 1970—; a founder Hastings Coll. Advocacy, 1973, bd. dirs., 1973—; mem. Pres.'s Assos., San Francisco State U.; Named Alumnus of Yr., Hastings Coll. Law, 1975. Mem. Am., Calif. State bar assns., Calif. Trial Lawyers Assn. (life mem., pres. 1964, 65, gov. 1966—), Assn. Trial Lawyers Am. (asso. editor personal injury 1960—, pres. San Francisco chpt. 1962-63), Western Regional Trial Lawyers Assn. (pres. 1963), Am. Bd. Profl. Liability Attys. (a founder, gov.), World Assn. Law Profs. (a founder), San Francisco Lawyers Club, Lawyers Friends of Wine, Am. Arbitration Assn. (nat. panel), AAUP. Democrat. Jewish. Clubs: 1066, Commonwealth of Calif. Author: California Preparation and Trial, 1970, 2d rev. edit., 1974, supplement, 1978. Office: 215 Market St Suite 1500 San Francisco CA 94105

WERKER, HENRY FREDERICK, judge; b. Glendale, N.Y., Apr. 16, 1920; s. August Henry and Celia (Michel) W.; B.A., N.Y.U., 1941, J.D., 1946; m. Virginia Jane Pearson, July 27, 1941; children—Virginia Jane, Henry Frederick. Admitted to N.Y. bar, 1946, U.S. dist. ct. bar So. Dist. N.Y., 1947, U.S. Tax Ct. bar, 1950; asso. firm Abberley Kooiman & Amon, N.Y.C., 1946-51, partner firm, 1957-58; pvt. practice law, Greenville, N.Y., 1958-69; partner firm Fray, Bagley & Chadderdon, Catskill, N.Y., 1961-69; social services atty., asst. county atty., Greene County N.Y., 1967-69; judge Greene County, Surrogate and Family Ct. judge, 1969-74; U.S. Dist. judge So. Dist. of N.Y., N.Y.C., 1974—; past dir. Nat. Bank Coxsackie, Greenville-Norton Hill Lumber, Inc., Stiefel Labs., Inc. Chmn. Greenville Town Republican Com., 1964-68; mem. exec. com. Green County Republicans, 1964-68; pres. Greenville Sch. Bd., 1959-60. Served with USNR, 1942-46. Fellow Am. Bar Found.; mem. Am., N.Y. State, Greene County bar assns., Am. Judicature Soc., Assn Bar of City of N.Y. Office: US Courthouse Foley Sq New York NY 10007

WERLE, IRA CHARLES, ret. mfg. co. exec., lawyer, mgmt. cons.; b. Bklyn., Aug. 6, 1908; s. John Phillip and Charlotte (Williams) W.; B.A., Union Coll., 1930; LL.B., Harvard, 1933; m. Ruth C. Hanrahan, June 9, 1934 (dec. Mar. 1974); children—Susan E. (Mrs. Mark Goddard II), Deborah Ann (Mrs. Richard Emblidge); m. 2d, Herta Ann Leber, Apr. 5, 1975. Admitted to N.Y. State bar, 1934; with firm Root, Clark, Buckner & Ballentine, N.Y.C., 1933-34, Donovan, Leisure, Newton & Lumbard, N.Y.C., 1934-35, 36-49; spl. asst. to atty. gen. State of N.Y., 1935-36; legal dept. Eastman Kodak Co., Rochester, N.Y., 1949-73, asst. sec., asst. gen. counsel, 1957-70, sec., asst. gen. counsel, 1970-73. Trustee Brighton Meml. Library. Mem. Am., N.Y. State bar assns., Assn. Gen. Counsel, Am. Soc. Corp. Secs., Rochester C. of C., Phi Delta Theta, Pi Delta Epsilon. Republican. Presbyn. Clubs: Country of Rochester; Imperial Golf (Naples, Fla.); Delray Beach (Fla.); Boca Del Mar Golf and Tennis (Boca Raton, Fla.); Harvard (N.Y.C.). Address: 400 NW 7th Ave Boca Raton FL 33432

WERMUTH, PAUL CHARLES, educator; b. Phila., Oct. 28, 1925; s. Paul C. and Susan (Manga) W.; A.B., M.A., Boston U., 1951; Ph.D., Pa. State U., 1955; m. Barbara Ethel Braun, Aug. 26, 1951; children—Geoffrey Paul, Paul Charles, Alan John, Stephen Mark. Instr. Clarkson Coll., Potsdam, N.Y., 1951-52; part-time instr., grad. asst. Pa. State U., 1952-55; asst. prof. Coll. William and Mary, 1955-57; mem. faculty Central Conn. State Coll., New Britain, 1957-68, asso. prof. English, 1966-68; prof. English, Northeastern U., 1968—, chmn. dept., 1968-75; vis. prof. Middlebury Coll., 1963-64. Served with USAAF, 1943-46. Danforth summer study grantee, 1961. Mem. Modern Lang. Assn., Coll. English Assn., Nat. Council Tchrs. English, AAUP, Mensa. Author: Modern Essays on Writing and Style, 2d edit., 1969; Essays in English, 1967; Bayard Taylor, 1974; also articles. Home: 73 Mostyn St Swampscott MA 01907 Office: Northeastern Univ Boston MA 02115

WERNER, ALFRED, art critic; b. Vienna, Austria, Mar. 30, 1911; s. Ignatz and Frederika (Silberstein) W.; J.D., U. Vienna, 1934; student Inst. Fine Arts, N.Y. U., 1949-52; m. Lisa Tramm, Mar. 1975. Came to U.S., 1940, naturalized, 1945. Editor, Die Stimme mag., also Gerechtigkeit mag., Vienna, 1935-38; lectr. univ. extension, Vienna, 1935-38; editor Universal Jewish Ency., N.Y.C., 1941-45; cons. Office Jewish Affairs, Am. Jewish Congress, 1946-50; art cons. Theodor Herzl Inst., N.Y.C., 1956-79; contbg. editor Arts mag., 1956-79; U.S. corr. Pantheon Internat. Mag. Art, Munich, Germany, 1960-79; prof. honoris causa Austrian Ministry Edn., 1967; vis. prof. Rutgers U., 1974-79; art editor Ency. Judaica. Author: Modigliani the Sculptor, 1962; Jules Pascin, 1962; Ernst Barlach, 1966; Modigliani, 1967; Chagall, 1968; Degas Pastels, 1968; Inness Landscapes, 1973; Max Weber, 1975; Chaim Soutine, 1977; Edvard Munch, 1978. Home: 453 Hudson St New York NY 10014 Office: 230 W 54th St New York NY 10019 Died July 16, 1979.

WERNER, CHARLES GEORGE, cartoonist; b. Marshfield, Wis., Mar. 23, 1909; s. George J. and Marie (Tippelt) W.; spl. courses at Northwestern U.; student Art Ins. Chgo., 1943; m. Eloise Robertson, Oct. 5, 1935; children—David, Jean, Stephen. Artist, photographer Springfield Leader, 1930-35; mem. art dept. Daily Oklahoma, 1935-37, editorial cartoonist, 1937-41; chief polit. cartoonist Chgo. Sun, 1941-46; cartoonist Indpls. Star, 1946—; instr. cartooning pub.

schs., Oklahoma City, 1939-41; lectr. history polit. cartoons. Recipient Pulitzer prize for cartoon, 1938; honorable mention for cartoon in auto safety contest, 1939, hon. mention Nat. Safety Council cartoons, 1943, Sigma Delta Chi award best cartoon, 1943, Nat. Headliners Club 1st place award, 1951, Freedoms Found. awards, 1951, 52, 53, 55, 56, 58, 62, 63, 1st place award Nat. Found. Hwy. Safety, 1965; winner one of 6 best caricatures Internat. Salon of Cartoons, Montreal, 1969. Hon. lifetime mem. Oklahoma City Jr. C. of C.; mem. Am. Assn. Editorial Cartoonists (pres. 1959-60), Nat. Cartoonists Soc., Sigma Delta Chi (hon.). Episcopalian. Mason (Shriner, Jester). Clubs: Hillcrest Country, Indianapolis Athletic, Columbia (Indpls.). Address: 4445 Brown Rd Indianapolis IN 46226

WERNER, EDWIN ROBERT, health ins. co. exec.; b. N.Y.C., Apr. 1, 1922; s. Edwin and Sidone Frances (Bruilotta) W.; student Pace U., 1940-42; m. Mildred Virginia Gardner, July 3, 1945 (dec. Nov. 1977); children—Helen F. (Mrs. Robert Fuina), Paul J., Joyce A. (Mrs. Kenneth Bergman), Jane T., Karen L. (Mrs. James D'Annibale), Robert M. With Blue Cross/Blue Shield of Greater New York, 1961—, pres., 1972—, also dir.; pres., dir. Health Services Improvement Fund, N.Y.C. Mem. N.Y. State Hosp. Rev. and Planning Council; mem. adv. group, health com. N.Y. State Senate, 1974-75; mem. N.Y. State Council on Health Care Financing, 1978. Served with Transp. Corps, AUS, 1942-45. Decorated D.S.M.; recipient Justin Ford Kimball award, 1978. Mem. Am. Pub. Health Assn., Blue Shield Assn. (dir.), Blue Cross Assn. (gov., chmn. exec. com.), Hosp. Soc. Clubs: Westchester Hills Golf; Sky (N.Y.C.). Home: 51 Soundview Ave White Plains NY 10606 Office: 622 3d Ave New York NY 10017

WERNER, FRITZ, portrait painter; b. Vienna, Austria; s. Louis Stephen and Elisabeth (Klem) W.; ed. Acad. Fine Arts, Vienna, Acad. Fine Arts, Munich, Acad. Fine Arts, Paris; m. Emmy Smetzka. Portrait painter; first one-man show, Munich, later exhibited in Italy; went to Egypt, painted portraits of govt. ofcls. there; then successively in Rumania, Sweden, England, Argentina, finally to U.S. Exhibited at Nat. Acad., Vienna, various other places in Europe, Nat. Acad. Design, N.Y.C., later at Detroit Mus. of Art, Loring Andrews Art Galleries, Cin., Cin. Art Mus. Represented at art museums of Phoenix, Cin., Oklahoma City, Syracuse, N.Y., also Mayo Clinic, Sloan-Kettering Meml. Hosp., also various cts., indsl. concerns and banks. Recipient Gundel Portrait prize and scholarship of Acad. Fine Arts, Vienna. Works include portraits of leading pub., govtl., comml. and indsl. personages in U.S., including Sen. Robert A. Taft, Pres. William H. Taft, Walter R. Bimson, Col. Henry Crown, Col. W.C. Woodward, Woodall Rodgers, F.H. Ecker, Harry A. Bullis, A.O. Smith, Warren Austin, Sewell Avery, John E. Alexander, Pres. Nekoosa-Edwards Paper Co., John L. Burns, pres. RCA N.Y. Col. Harold Byrd, pres. Ling-Temco Aircraft Corp., Princess Youka Troubetzkoy, Robert A. Stranahan, chmn. Champion Spark Plug Corp., Paul W. Goodrich, Pres. Chgo. Title & Trust Co., John Sherman Myers, Dean Am. U., Maurice Pate, dir. UNICEF, Right Rev. Edward R. Welles, bishop W. Mo., Mrs. Hashim S. Hashim, Saudi Arabia, E.K. Gaylord, pub. Daily Oklahoman, Stanley Draper, Pioneer City builder, Robert Hefner, Okla. Heritage Assn. Hall of Fame, Raymond Young, pres. Okla. Heritage Assn. Hall Fame, Dr. Josiah Crudup, pres. Brenau Coll., Dr. Albert Avrack, surgeon, Mrs. A. Avrack, La Jolla, Calif., Mrs. Albert T. Trowbridge, Palomar, Calif., others; also portraits of royalty and govt. ofcls. in Europe, S.A., Egypt. Address: LaJolla Seville 1001 Genter St LaJolla CA 92037. *My great endeavor is to paint life around me, be it a portrait, a bouquet of flowers or a landscape. Art to me is not science, which depends on technique; art is not philosophy, which depends on words to convey it. As religion is aristocracy of behavior, art is aristocracy of feeling. If feeling is achieved, it will show in the work.*

WERNER, GERHARD, pharmacologist, psychoanalyst, educator, univ. ofcl.; b. Vienna, Austria, Sept. 28, 1921; s. Rudolf and Elizabeth (Lukas) W.; M.D., U. Vienna, 1945; m. Marion E. Hollander, July 25, 1958; children—Philip Ralph, Karen Nicole. Came to U.S., 1957, naturalized, 1965. With dept. pharmacology U. Vienna, 1945-50; prof. pharmacology, head dept. U. Calcutta (India) Sch. Tropical Medicine, 1952-54, U. Sao Paulo (Brazil) Med. Sch. of Ribeirao Preto, 1955-57; asso. prof. Cornell U. Med. Sch., 1957-61; asso. prof. pharmacology and physiology Johns Hopkins Med. Sch., 1963-65; prof. pharmacology, head dept. U. Pitts. Med. Sch., 1965-75; dean Sch. Medicine, v.p. profl. affairs Univ. Health Center Pitts., 1975-78, prof. psychiatry, 1978—. Cons. psychobiology program NSF, 1970—, mem. adv. panel regulatory biology, div. biology and med. sci., 1969-70, mem. primate center rev. com., 1973—; mem. chem. biol. info. panel NIH, 1967-70, mem. study sect. pharmacology and exptl. therapeutics, 1964-68; asso. Pitts. Psychoanalytic Inst., 1973—; external examiner for Ph.D. (med. scis.), U. Calcutta, 1953—; adv. bd. Indian Council Med. Research, 1952-54. Mem. Soc. Neurosci., A.A.A.S., Harvey Soc., Am. Soc. Pharmacology and Exptl. Therapeutics, Am. Physiol. Soc., Soc. Gen. Systems Research, Indian Soc. Biochemistry and Physiology, German Pharmacol. Soc., Sigma Xi. Editorial bd. Jour. Neurophysiology, 1970—, Internat. Jour. Neuropharmacology, Jour. Clin. Pharmacology; asso. editor Pharmacol. Revs., 1969-70. Contbr. articles to profl. jours. Home: 1307 Bennington Ave Pittsburgh PA 15217

WERNER, JESSE, chem. co. exec.; b. N.Y.C., Dec. 5, 1916; s. Louis and Clara (Karan) W.; B.S. cum laude, Bklyn. Coll., 1935; M.A., Columbia, 1936, Ph.D., 1938; m. Edna Lesser, Aug. 16, 1943; children—Kenneth Mark, Nancy Ellen. Asst. chemistry Columbia, 1936-38; with GAF Corp. (formerly Gen. Aniline & Film Corp.) N.Y.C., 1938—, v.p., 1959-61, pres., chief exec. officer, 1962—, chmn. bd., 1964—, dir., chmn. subsidiaries; dir. Curtiss-Wright Corp., Kennecott Copper Corp. Mem. Bus. Com. for Arts. Bd. dirs. Film Soc. Lincoln Center. Recipient Alumni Honor award and medal Bklyn. Coll., 1962; Ann. award NCCJ, 1963; trustee Sackler Sch. Medicine. Fellow Am. Inst. Chemists, A.A.A.S., N.Y. Acad. Sci.; mem. Am. Chem. Soc., Am. Inst. Chem. Engrs., Comml. Devel. Assn. (award 1963), Chem. Market Research Assn. (Meml. award 1967), Soc. Chem. Industry (chmn. Am. sect. 1968-69, Chem. Industry medal 1972), Sigma Xi, Pi Mu Epsilon, Phi Lambda Upsilon. Clubs: Economic of New York (pres. 1968—), Hemisphere. Contbr. articles to tech., bus. publs. Patentee field organic chemistry. Office: 140 W 51st St New York NY 10020

WERNER, JOHN BAILEY, banker; b. St. Mary's, Pa., Oct. 13, 1931; s. Leo Anthony and Mary (Bailey) W.; B.A., Randolph-Macon Coll., 1953; postgrad. U. Va., 1953-55, Rutgers U., 1965; m. Anita Paige Swertfeger, June 16, 1961; children—Christopher, Gregory, Timothy. With First & Mchts. Corp., Richmond, Va., 1959—, exec. v.p., 1972-73, vice chmn. bd., 1973—, also dir.; faculty Va.-Md. Bankers Sch., 1972-76; mem. Comptroller of Currency's Nat. Adv. Com., 1975—. Trustee, chmn. exec. com. Randolph-Macon Coll. Served to lt. (j.g.) USNR, 1955-59. Mem. Robert Morris Assos. (nat. policy council 1975-77, pres. Carolina-Virginias chpt. 1977—). Republican. Episcopalian. Clubs: Commonwealth; Downtown. Home: 12 Country Sq Ln Richmond VA 23229 Office: F&M Center PO Box 27025 Richmond VA 23261

WERNER, MORT, TV exec.; b. San Francisco, May 5, 1916; s. Harold John and Carolyn (Abrams) W.; student San Mateo Coll., 1932-34; m. Martha Wilkerson, Mar. 18, 1939; children—Carole, Jill. Radio announcer KJBS, San Francisco, 1934-37; with Phil Harris Orch., Hollywood, 1937-39; free-lance radio producer, 1939-42; co-owner, operator KUEN, Ventura, Cal., 1947-51; producer NBC, N.Y.C., 1951—, v.p. nat. programs, 1956-61, v.p. programs and talent NBC-TV Network, 1961—, sr. v.p. program planning, 1972—; v.p. Kaiser Industries, 1957-60, sr. v.p., 1960-61; v.p., dir. radio-TV dept. Young & Rubicam, Inc., 1959. Dir. programs OWI Pacific Bur., 1942-44. Served with AUS, 1944-47. Mem. Nat. Acad. Television Arts and Scis. (pres. 1963, mem. nat. council; pres. internat. council 1974-76). Home: 280 Aulii Pl Pukalani Maui HI 96788 Office: NBC 30 Rockefeller Plaza New York City NY 10020

WERNER, OSWALD, anthropologist; b. Rimavska Sobota, Czechoslovakia, Feb. 26, 1928; s. Julius Mathew and Bella Lenke (Toth) W.; m. June Leete Travers, Sept. 1, 1957; children—Deborah Jane, Derek Whitney, Richard West. Asst. prof. dept. anthropology Northwestern U., Evanston, Ill., 1963-69; asso. prof., 1969-71, prof., 1971—, chmn. dept., 1978—; Fulbright prof., Chile, 1974. Served with U.S. Army, 1951-53. NSF fellow, 1964; NIMH fellow, 1976; NIMH grantee, 1965—. Mem. Am. Anthrop. Assn. Author works in field. Home: 2609 Ridge Ave Evanston IL 60201 Office: Dept Anthropology Northwestern Univ Evanston IL 60201

WERNER, R(ICHARD) BUDD, corporate fin. exec.; b. Lorain, Ohio, Aug. 27, 1931; s. Paul Henry and Bessie Marie (Budd) W.; B.S. in Commerce, Ohio U., 1953; m. Janet Sue Kelsey, Aug. 28, 1932; children—Richard Budd, David Kelsey, Mary Paula. Sr. auditor Arthur Andersen & Co., Cleve., 1955-59; various fin. positions Glidden Co., Cleve., 1959-65; v.p., asst. treas. Harshaw div. Kewanee Oil Co., Cleve., 1965-72; v.p. finance, treas. Weatherhead Co., Cleve., 1973-77, Hauserman, Inc., Cleve., 1977—; dir., mem. exec. and audit coms. Broadview Fin. Corp. and subs. Broadview Savs. and Loan; dir., mem. audit com. Electric Furnace Co. Mem. Lakewood (Ohio) City Council, 1972-73. Served as lt. Q.M.C. U.S. Army, 1953-55. C.P.A. Mem. Financial Execs. Inst., Ohio Soc. C.P.A.'s, Cleve. Treas.'s Club, Cleve. Met. YMCA, Musical Arts Assn., Cleve. Music Sch. Settlement. Clubs: Cleve. Yachting, Hermit, Clifton, Playhouse. Home: 1218 Overlook Rd Lakewood OH 44107 Office: 5711 Grant Ave Cleveland OH 44105

WERNER, ROBERT JOSEPH, educator; b. Lackawanna, N.Y., Feb. 13, 1932; s. Edward Joseph and Marian L. (Gerringer) W.; B.M.E., Northwestern U., 1953, Mus.M., 1954, Ph.D., 1967; m. Sharon Lynne Mohrfeld, June 22, 1957; children—Mark J., Kurt M., Erik J. Dir. instrumental music Evanston (Ill.) Twp. High Sch., 1956-66; asso. prof. music Harpur Coll., State U. N.Y., Binghamton, 1966-68; dir. contemporary music project Music Educators Nat. Conf., 1968-73; dir. Sch. Music U. Ariz., Tucson, 1973—. Mem. exec. bd. Tucson Symphony Orch., 1974—; mem. bd. Cultural Commn. Tucson, 1974-75. Served with U.S. Army, 1954-56. Mem. Coll. Music Soc. (pres.), Internat. Soc. Music Edn. (v.p.), Music Educators Nat. Conf., Soc. Ethnomusicology, Psi Upsilon, Phi Mu Alpha Sinfonia. Editor: Comprehensive Musicianship: An Anthology of Evolving Thought, 1971. Contbr. articles to profl. jours. Office: Sch Music U Ariz Tucson AZ 85721

WERNER, ROBERT L., lawyer; b. N.Y.C., Feb. 28, 1913; s. Abraham L. and Elsa (Ludwig) W.; A.B., Yale, 1933; L.L.B., Harvard, 1936; m. Raye Davies, Oct. 13th, 1945; children—William, John. Admitted to N.Y. bar, 1936, Supreme Ct. U.S., also various fed. cts. and adminstrv. agys.; spl. asst. to U.S. atty. So. Dist. N.Y., 1936, asst. U.S. atty, 1937-40, confidential asst., 1940-42; 1st asst. civil div. Dept. Justice, Washington, 1946; spl. asst. to Atty. Gen. U.S., 1946-47; mem. law dept. RCA Corp., N.Y.C., 1947, v.p., gen. atty., 1951-62, exec. v.p., gen. atty., 1962-66, exec. v.p., gen. counsel, 1966-78, dir., 1963-79, cons., 1978—; dir. Banquet Foods Corp., 1970-78, Coronet Industries, Inc., 1971-78, Random House, Inc., 1969-78, RCA Alaska Communications, Inc., 1976-78, RCA Am. Communications, Inc., 1976-78, RCA Global Communications, Inc., 1960-78 Hertz Corp., 1967-78. Mem. advisory bd. internat. and comparative law center Southwestern Legal Found., 1973—, treas., 1970-72, vice chmn. 1972-73; chmn. advisory bd., 1974-76, also research fellow, trustee, mem. exec. com.; lectr. Conf. Bd.; lectr. legal topics, mem. nat. advisory council corp. law depts. Practising Law Inst., 1974-78; com. on restrictive bus. practices U.S. council Internat. C. of C., 1973-78; N.Y. Lawyers' Com. for Civil Rights under Law, 1972-78, trustee, 1971—. Chmn. bd. trustees, mem. exec. com. Ithaca Coll., N.Y., 1976—; trustee Salisbury (Conn.) Sch., 1975-77. Served as capt. U.S. Army, 1942-44, to lt. col. USAAF, 1944-46; ETO. Fellow Am. Bar Found.; mem. Internat., Fed., Am., N.Y. State, City N.Y., FCC bar assns., IEEE (sr.), Am. Legion, Harvard Law Sch. Assn., Assn. Gen. Counsel (emeritus), U.S. Naval Inst., Internat. Law Assn. (Am. br.), Nat. Legal Aid and Defender Assn. (dir.), Am. Judicature Soc., Newcomen Soc., N.Y. County Lawyers' Assn., Am. Soc. Internat. Law, Med. Passport Found. (dir.). Clubs: Rockefeller Center Lunch, Yale, Harvard (N.Y.C.); National Lawyers, Army Navy (Washington); Coral Beach (Bermuda). Home: 116 E 68th St New York NY 10021

WERNER, SIDNEY CHARLES, physician, educator; b. N.Y.C., June 29, 1909; s. Max A. and Sadie (Hoffberg) W.; A.B., Columbia, 1928, M.D., 1932, D.Sc. in Medicine, 1937; m. Shirley Benczer, Aug. 18, 1947; children—Pamela Anne, Mady Jo Werner Roberts, Russell Seth, Morgan Simon. Intern medicine Presbyn. Hosp., N.Y.C., 1932-34, mem. staff, 1934—, asst. resident medicine, 1936-38, chief thyroid, 1947-77, chief combined endocrine clinics, 1947-74, cons. in medicine, 1974—; mem. faculty Columbia Coll. Phys. & Surg., 1932—, prof. clin. medicine, 1964-74, prof. emeritus, 1974—; vis. prof. medicine U. Ariz. Med. Center, 1978—; cons. NIH, 1955-63, endocrinology Roosevelt Hosp., N.Y.C., 1954-77, Greenwich (Conn.) Hosp., 1953-77, Grasslands Hosp., Valhalla, N.Y., 1946-77. Jacobaeus lectr. Nordinsulin Found., Sweden, 1968; recipient Thornton Wilson award Eastern Psychiat. Assn., 1960, Stevens Triennial award Columbia Coll. Phys. & Surg., 1966, distinguished thyroid scientist, VII Internat. Thyroid Conf., 1975; gold medal Alumni Assn. Columbia Coll. Phys. and Surg., 1976. Fellow AMA, AAAS, N.Y. Acad. Medicine; mem. Assn. Am. Physicians (emeritus), Am. Soc. Clin. Investigation, Endocrine Soc. (council 1961-65), Am. Thyroid Assn. (1st v.p. 1967, bd. dirs. 1967-74, pres. 1972-73, Distinguished Service award 1969), Soc. Exptl. Biology and Medicine, Harvey Soc., N.Y. Thyroid Club (founder), Phi Beta Kappa, Alpha Omega Alpha; hon. mem. Endocrine Soc. Haiti, Argentine Med. Assn. Soc. Endocrinology and Nutrition, Colombian Soc. Endocrinology, Med. Soc. Finland. Editor: The Thyroid, 4 edits., 1955, 62, 71, 78; Thyrotropin, 1963. Contbr. articles to profl. jours., chpts. to books. Home: 4528 E Calle del Conde Tucson AZ 85718 Office: U Ariz Health Scis Center Tucson AZ 85724

WERNHAM, JAMES CHRYSTALL STEPHEN, educator; b. Kirkcaldy, Scotland, Apr. 14, 1921; s. Archibald Garden and Christina (Noble) W.; M.A., Aberdeen (Scotland) U., 1943; diploma Westminster Coll., Cambridge, Eng., 1946; B.A., St. Johns Coll., Cambridge U., 1945, M.A., 1948; S.T.M., Union Theol. Sem., 1947; m. Rosemary Margaret Soutter, Aug. 9, 1946; children—Christopher, Richard. Lectr. philosophy U. Coll., U. Toronto, 1947-48, 49-54; asst. prof. Carleton U., Ottawa, Ont., Can., 1954-58, asso. prof., 1958-61, prof. philosophy, 1961—, chmn. philosophy dept., 1955-70, clk. of senate, 1962-65. Mills fellow Union Theol. Sem., 1946; grantee in aid of publ. Humanities Research Council of Can., 1968; Can. Council leave fellow, 1971-72. Mem. Can. Philos. Assn., Can. Assn. U. Tchrs. Presbyn. Author: Two Russian Thinkers: An Essay in Berdyaev and Shestov, 1968; contbg. author: Darwin in Retrospect, 1960. Home: Ottawa ON Canada

WERNICK, JACK HARRY, scientist; b. St. Paul, May 19, 1923; s. Joseph and Eva (Legan) W.; B.Met.E., U. Minn, 1947, M.S., 1948; Ph.D., Pa. State U., 1954; m. Sylvia Katz, Dec. 20, 1947; children—Phyllis Roberta Wernick Lauer, Rosanne Pauline. Staff, Manhattan Project, Los Alamos, 1944-46; mem. staff Bell Labs., Murray Hill, N.J., 1954—, head solid state chemistry research dept., 1963—; cons. U.S. Office Sci. and Tech., Nat. Bur. Standards, NSF; mem. steering com. div. nuclear fusion ERDA, 1977-78. Served with U.S. Army, 1944-46. Fellow N.Y. Acad. Scis., Metall. Soc., Am. Phys. Soc.; mem. Nat. Acad. Engrs., Am. Soc. Metals (McFarland award 1969), AAAS, IEEE, AIME, Am. Chem. Soc., Sigma Xi, Phi Lambda Upsilon. Jewish. Author: (with E. A. Nesbitt) Rare Earth Permanent Magnets, 1973; (with J. L. Shay) Chalcopyrite Crystals, 1975; editor: Materials and Energy: Selected Topics, 1977; contbr. articles to profl. jours. Home: 18 Stafford Dr Madison NJ 07940 Office: 600 Mountain Ave Murray Hill NJ 07974

WERNICK, RICHARD FRANK, composer, conductor; b. Boston, Jan. 16, 1934; s. Louis and Irene (Prince) W.; B.A., Brandeis U., 1955; M.A., Mills Coll., 1957; m. Beatrice Messina, July 15, 1956; children—Lewis, Adam, Peter. Music dir. Royal Winnipeg Ballet Can., 1957-58; Ford Found. fellow, 1962-64; instr. music U. Buffalo, 1964-65; asst. prof. music, dir. univ. symphony, U. Chgo., 1965-68; prof. music, dir. Pa. Contemporary Players, U. Pa., 1968—; co-founder Community Youth Orch. of Delaware County; composer: Haiku of Basho, 1967, Moonsongs from the Japanese, 1972, Kaddish Requiem, 1973, String Quartet 2, 1973, Songs of Remembrance, 1974, Visions of Terror and Wonder, 1976, Contemplations of the Tenth Muse, Book I, 1976, Book II, 1978, Introits and Canons, 1977, A Poison Tree, 1979. Recipient Naumburg Recording award, 1976; Music award Nat. Inst. Arts and Letters, 1976, Pulitzer Prize in music, 1977. Nat. Endowment of Arts Grantee, 1975, 79; Guggenheim fellow, 1976. Mem. ASCAP. Democrat. Office: 201 S 34th St Philadelphia PA 19174. *To dwell in a world of art, in general, and music, in particular, is one of the great privileges that life can bestow. We live in a time of enormous artistic change, and it is an honor to be part of that cosmos.*

WERNICK, SIDNEY WILLIAM, judge; b. Phila., Nov. 29, 1913; s. Abraham David and Sadie (Osteicher) W.; B.A., U. Pa., 1934, M.A., 1935; Ph.D. in Philosophy, Harvard, 1937, LL.B., 1940; m. Charlotte Lucille Berman, Aug. 6, 1939; children—Judith Louise (Mrs. Richard Gilmore), Lawrence Bruce. Admitted to Maine bar, 1940; mem. firm Berman, Berman, Wernick & Flaherty, Portland, 1940-69; judge Portland Municipal Ct. 1956-60; justice Superior Ct. Maine, Portland, 1969-70; justice Supreme Jud. Ct. Maine, Portland, 1970—. Dir. Guy Gannett Broadcasting Services, Inc., 1967-69. Trustee U. Maine, 1968-69. Office: Supreme Ct PO Box 25 Downtown Br Portland ME 04112*

WERSON, JAMES BYRD, lawyer; b. Butte, Mont., Dec. 29, 1916; s. Edward L. and Alma (Baker) W.; A.B., U. Calif. at Berkeley, 1938, J.D., 1942; m. Elspeth Lamont Pollard, Feb. 26, 1943; children—Sallie Lamont, Janet Elspeth (Mrs. Michael Garnica), Alice Mary. Admitted to Calif. bar, 1945; spl. agt. FBI, 1942-46; with firm Severson, Werson, Berke & Melchior, San Francisco, 1946—, sr. partner, 1965—. Recipient Distinguished Service award Nat. Consumer Finance Assn., 1968. Mem. Am. Bar Assn. (vice chmn. consumer bankruptcy com. 1960—), Nat. Consumer Finance Assn. (chmn. law com. 1961—), Soc. Former Spl. Agts. FBI. Republican. Episcopalian. Clubs: Merchants Exchange, Bankers (San Francisco); Capitol Hill; Richmond Country (dir.). Mem. Am. swim team touring Europe, 1938. Home: 8615 Thors Bay Rd El Cerrito CA 94530 Office: One Embarcadero Center San Francisco CA 94111

WERT, CHARLES ALLEN, educator; b. Battle Creek, Iowa, Dec. 31, 1919; s. John Henry and Anna (Spotts) W.; B.A., Morningside Coll., Sioux City, 1941; M.S., State U. Iowa, 1943, Ph.D., 1948; m. Lucille Vivian Mathena, Sept. 5, 1943; children—John Arthur, Sara Ann. Mem. staff Radiation Lab., Mass. Inst. Tech., 1943-45; instr. physics U. Chgo., 1948-50; mem. faculty U. Ill. at Urbana, 1950—, prof., 1955, head dept. metall. and mining engring., 1967—; cons. to industry. Fellow Am. Phys. Soc., Am. Inst. Metall. Engrs., Am. Soc. Metals, A.A.A.S., Sigma Xi. Author: Physics of Metals, 1970; Opportunities in Materials Science and Engineering, 1977; also articles. Cons. editor McGraw Hill Book Co. Home: 1708 W Green St Champaign IL 61820 Office: Metallurgy and Mining Bldg Univ Ill Urbana IL 61801

WERT, JAMES EDWARD, educator; b. Clayton, Ohio, Jan. 28, 1923; s. Mark H. and Susan (Reed) W.; B.S., Lebanon Valley Coll., Annville, Pa., 1948; M.B.A., U. Pa., 1951; Ph.D., Ohio State U., 1954; m. Janice F. Brendle, Sept. 14, 1952; children—Nora J., Martin J., Stacia M. Asst. prof. accounting Lehigh U., 1954-57; sr. financial economist Fed. Res. Bank Cleve., 1957-59; prof. finance, chmn. dept. State U. N.Y. at Buffalo, 1959-67; prof. fin. U. Ariz., 1967—, head dept., 1967-78. Served with USAAF, 1942-45. Mem. Am., Western (dir. 1968-70, pres. 1973-74) fin. assns. Fin. Mgmt. Assn. (dir. 1976-78). Author: (with Glenn V. Henderson, Jr.) Financing Business Firms, 6th edit., 1979. Home: 1555 Entrada Segunda Tucson AZ 85718

WERT, JAMES JUNIOR, educator; b. Barron, Wis., Jan. 9, 1933; s. James Lewis and Bernice Janet (Walker) W.; B.S., U. Wis., 1957, M.S., 1958, Ph.D., 1961; postgrad. Carnegie Tech. Inst., 1958-59; m. Jane Alice Thornton, Aug. 14, 1958; children—Thaddeus Thornton, Melissa Jane. Asso. engr. Westinghouse Electric Corp., Pitts., 1958-60; research scientist A.O. Smith Corp., Milw., 1961-62; mem. faculty Vanderbilt U., Nashville, 1962—, prof. material sci. and engring., 1967—, chmn. dept., 1969, chmn. materials, mechanics and structures div., 1969-72, chmn. materials sci. dept., 1975—, chmn. dept. mech. engring. and materials sci., 1976—, George A. Sloan prof. metallurgy, 1968-76; dir. Center for Coatings Sci. and Tech., Nashville; vis. prof. Cambridge U., 1974; cons. Avco, 1964-71, Temco, 1964-71, Arnold Engring. Center, Tullahome, Tenn., 1966-71, Nat. Acad. Scis., 1969-70; pres. Technology Assos., Inc., Nashville, 1975—. Served with AUS, 1953-55. Ampco fellow, 1957-58, Westinghouse-Bettis fellow, 1958-59, Foundary Edn. fellow, 1952-57; recipient Adams award Am. Welding Soc., 1969, Teaching award Tau Beta Pi, 1970. Mem. Am. Inst. Metall. Engrs., Am. Welding Soc., Am. Soc. Metals, Inst. Metals, Am. Soc. Engring. Edn., A.A.U.P., Tau Beta Pi, Phi Eta Sigma, Pi Kappa Alpha. Republican. Methodist. Clubs: Harbor Island Yacht; Sequoia Swimming and Tennis. Contbr. articles to profl. jours. Patentee nuclear fuels and cladding materials. Home: 2510 Ridgewood Dr Nashville TN 37215

WERT, JONATHAN MAXWELL, II, conservation scientist; b. Port Royal, Pa., Nov. 8, 1939; s. Jonathan Maxwell I and Helen Leona (Leonard) W.; B.S. in Biology, Austin Peay State U., 1966, M.S. in Biology, 1968; Ph.D. in Edn. Adminstrn., U. Ala., 1974; children—Jonathan Maxwell III, Kimberly Dee. Park supt., chief interpretive services Bur. State Parks Pa. Dept. Environ. Resources, Harrisburg, 1968-69; chief naturalist Bays Mountain Park Environ. Edn. Center, Kingsport, Tenn., 1969-71; environ. and energy edn. specialist TVA, Knoxville, 1971-75; cons. energy, environment, conservation U. Tenn., Knoxville, 1975; sr. asso.-energy Energy Extension Service, Coop. Extension Service, Pa. State U., 1977—. Counselor Boy Scouts Am., 1975. Served with USMC, 1958-61. Recipient Conservation award Am. Motors Co., 1976. Mem. Am. Soc. Environ. Edn., Conservation Edn. Assn., Phi Delta Kappa. Lutheran. Author: Writing Environmental Education Grant Proposals, 1974; Environmental Education Study Projects for High School Students, 1974; Environmental Education Study Projects for College Students, 1974; Developing Environmental Study Areas, 1974; Developing Environmental Education Curriculum Material, 1974; Finding Solutions to Environmental Problems . . . A Process Guide, 1975; Assessing an Issue in Relation to Environmental, Economic, and Social Impact . . . A Process Guide, 1976; Energy Conservation Measures for Mobile Home Dwellers, 1978; Selected Energy Conservation Options for the Home, 1978; Selected Energy Management Options for Small Business and Local Government, 1978, others. Mem. adv. bd. Environ. Edn. Report, 1974—; cons. editor Jour. Environ. Edn., 1975. Contbr. articles to profl. jours. Home: 42 1st St Port Royal PA 17082 Office: Coop Extension Service Pa State U 336 Agr Adminstrn Bldg University Park PA 16802

WERTHEIM, MITZI MALLINA, govt. ofcl.; b. N.Y.C., Oct. 25, 1937; d. Rudolf and Myrtle B. (McGraw) Mallina; B.A., U. Mich., 1960; m. Ronald P. Wertheim, Feb. 25, 1965; children—Carter, Christiana. Asst. dir. div. research Peace Corps, Washington, 1963-66, 69-70; sr. program officer Cafritz Found., Washington, 1970-76; dep. dir. talent bank Democratic Nat. Com., 1976; prin. personnel officer Carter/Mondale Transition Planning Staff, 1976-77; dep. undersec. navy, 1977—. Chmn. nat. affairs program com. Women's Nat. Dem. Club, 1975-76. Episcopalian. Home: 3230 Highland Pl NW Washington DC 20008 Office: Room 4E725 The Pentagon Washington DC 20350

WERTHEIMER, FREDERICK WILLIAM, dentist, educator; b. Saginaw, Mich., May 21, 1925; s. Frederick and Hazel (Sanor) W.; D.D.S., U. Mich., 1949; M.S. in Periodontics, Northwestern U., 1954; M.S., Georgetown U., 1960; m. Marjorie Ruth Spence, Oct. 19, 1956; children—David, Karen, Eric. Gen. practice dentistry, Lansing, Mich., 1952-53; practice dentistry specializing in periodontics, Lansing, 1954-58; resident in oral pathology NIH, Bethesda, Md., 1958-60; sr. dental surgeon USPHS, NIH, Nat. Inst. Dental Research, 1960-62; sr. asso. dentistry Henry Ford Hosp., Detroit, 1962-68; prof., chmn. dept. pathology Dental Sch., U. Detroit, 1968—; adj. asso. prof. dept. pathology Sch. Medicine, Wayne State U.; cons. oral pathology VA Hosp., Allen Park, Mich., Detroit Gen. Hosp. Served to lt. Dental Corps, USN, 1949-52. Diplomate Am. Bd. Periodontology, Am. Bd. Oral Pathology. Fellow Am. Coll. Dentists, Internat. Coll. Dentists, AAAS, Am. Acad. Oral Pathology; mem. ADA, Mich. Soc. Periodontists (pres. 1971—), Am. Acad. Periodontology, Internat. Assn. Dental Research, Mich. Soc. Pathologists, Sigma Xi. Contbr. articles to profl. jours. Home: 28976 Kendallwood Dr Farmington Hills MI 48018 Office: 2985 E Jefferson St Detroit MI 48207

WERTIMER, SIDNEY, JR., coll. adminstr., economist; b. Buffalo, Oct. 28, 1920; s. Sidney and Florence Belle (Smith) W.; B.S., U. Pa., 1942; M.A., U. Buffalo, 1949; Ph.D., London Sch. Econs., 1952; m. Eleanor M. Walsh, June 21, 1947; instr. U. Buffalo, 1947-50; asst. prof. econs. Hamilton Coll., 1952-56, asso. prof., 1956-64, prof., 1964-67, Leavenworth prof. econs., 1967-79, asso. dean, 1957-65, chmn. dept. econs., 1967-75, provost, 1975—; dir. Otisca Industries, Ltd. Bd. dirs. Adirondack Playhouse, Clinton, N.Y. Served to lt., sr. grade, USN, 1942-46. Mem. Am. Econs. Assn., Mask and Wig, Sadaquada, Delta Kappa Epsilon. Author: (with John S. Gambs) Economics and Man, 1958; contbr. articles to profl. publs. Home: 305 College Hill Rd Clinton NY 13323 Office: Hamilton Coll Clinton NY 13323

WERTMAN, DAN M., journalist; b. Toledo, Nov. 24, 1915; s. Milton Albert and Vernie (Yarger) W.; B.S., Ohio U., 1939; m. Edith Frances Wulf, Mar. 1, 1941; children—Cheryl (Mrs. Robert W. Yoder), Virginia. Successively reporter, asst. city editor, news editor Cleve. News, 1939-60; editor Better Living supplement then asst. city editor Cleve. Plain Dealer, 1960-66, asso. editor, editorial writer, 1966—. Served to lt. USNR, 1942-46. Mem. A.P. Soc. Ohio (pres. 1961), Sigma Delta Chi, Theta Chi. Republican. Conglist. Home: 17302 Riverway Dr Lakewood OH 44107 Office: 1801 Superior Ave Cleveland OH 44114

WERTZ, DAVID FREDERICK, clergyman; b. Lewistown, Pa., Oct. 5, 1916; s. Jesse Price and Ada (Barratt) W.; A.B., Dickinson Coll., 1937, LL.D., 1956; M.A., Boston U., 1939, S.T.B., 1940; D.D., Lycoming (Pa.) Coll., 1969, W.Va. Wesleyan Coll., 1969; m. Betty Jean Rowe, Aug. 25, 1938; children—Robert, Joan, Donna, Elizabeth. Ordained to ministry Methodist Ch., 1940; pastor in Boiling Springs-Hickorytown, Pa., 1934-37, New Bedford, Mass., 1938-40, Doylesburg, Pa., 1940-43, Stewartstown, Pa., 1943-46, Camp Curtin, Harrisburg, Pa., 1946-49, Allison Meml., Carlisle, Pa., 1949-53; supt. Williamsport Dist., 1953- 55; pres. Lycoming Coll., Williamsport, Pa., 1955-68; Resident bishop, United Meth. Ch., Charleston, W.Va. area, 1968—. Mem. N.E. Jurisdictional Conf., Meth. Ch., 1956, 60, 64, 68; mem. Gen. Conf. Meth. Ch., 1964, 68; pres. bd. Global Ministries. Trustee W.Va. Wesleyan Coll. Mem. Phi Kappa Sigma. Republican. Mason (33 deg., K.T.). Home: 1401 Mt Vernon Rd Charleston WV 25314 Office: 900 Washington St E Charleston WV 25301

WERTZ, JOHN EDWARD, educator, phys. chemist; b. Denver, Dec. 4, 1916; s. John and Amalie (Dreuth) W.; B.S. in Chem. Engring., U. Denver, 1937, M.S., 1938; Ph.D., U. Chgo., 1948; m. Florence Marie Carlson, June 5, 1943; children—John A., Byron A., Kristin M. Asst. prof. Augustana Coll., Rock Island, Ill., 1941-44; instr. Gustavus Adolphus Coll., St. Peter, Minn., 1944-45; mem. faculty U. Minn., Mpls., 1945—, prof. phys. chemistry, 1957—. Sr. Fulbright scholar, Guggenheim fellow Clarendon Lab., Oxford, Eng., 1957-58; dir. U.S. Metric conversion study NSF, 1973, made report for Congress, 1976; del. Australian Metric Conversion Bd.-Am. Nat. Metric Council conf., Sydney, 1975. Fellow Am. Phys. Soc., Inst. Physics (London); mem. Am. Chem. Soc. (short-course lectr.), Faraday Soc., N.Y. Acad. Scis. Author: (with J. Bolton) Electron Spin Resonance, 1972, Russian transl., 1975; also articles. Home: 700 Arbogast St St Paul MN 55112 Office: Dept Chemistry U Minn Minneapolis MN 55455

WESBERRY, JAMES PICKETT, clergyman; b. Bishopville, S.C., Apr. 16, 1906; s. William McLeod and Lillian Ione (Galloway) W.; A.B., Mercer U., 1929, M.A., 1930, D.D., 1957; B.D., Newton Theol. Inst., 1931; M. Sacred Theology, Andover Newton Theol. Inst., 1934; postgrad. Harvard, 1931, Union Theol. Sem., N.Y.C., summers 1935, 65, Yale, 1946, So. Bapt. Theol. Sem., 1957; LL.D., Atlanta Law Sch., 1946; L.H.D., LaGrange Coll., 1962; Litt. D., Bolen-Draughan Coll., 1967; m. Ruby Lee Perry, Sept. 5, 1929 (dec. Dec. 1941); children—James Pickett; m. 2d, Mary Sue Latimer, June 1, 1943. Ordained to ministry Bapt. Ch., 1926; pastor, Soperton, Ga., 1928-30, Medford, Mass., 1930-31, Kingstree, S.C., 1931-33, Bamberg, S.C., 1933-44; pastor Morningside Bapt. Ch., Atlanta, 1944-75, pastor emeritus, 1975—; engaged in evangelism, counseling, editing, publishing and chaplaincies, 1975—; mem. exec. com. So. Bapt. Conv., 1959-65, 74—, mem. chaplains commn., 1973—, mem. adminstrv. com., 1974—; pres. Ga. Bapt. Conv., 1956-57, 57-58, rec. sec., 1970—; prof. Mercer U. extension, Atlanta, 1944-53; pres. Highview Nursing Home, Atlanta, 1947-60, chaplain, 1975—; pres. Nat. Youth Courtesy Found., 1971—; staff corr. Christian Century, 1951-58; editor column The People's Pulpit, Atlanta Times, 1964-65; chaplain Yaarab Temple, 15 yrs. Chmn. Ga. Literature Commn., 1953-74; acting chaplain U.S. Ho. Reps., July-Aug., 1949; mem. Gov.'s Citizens Penal Reform Commn., 1968; mem. Fulton County Draft Bd., 1968-71. Bd. dirs. Atlanta Fund Rev. Bd., 1964-70, Grady Met. Girls Club, 1969-72; hon. bd. dirs. Atlanta Union Mission, 1972—, Dogwood Assn. Festival, 1970-71; trustee Mercer U., 1944-49, 54-57, 72-74, mem. pres.'s council, 1974-78, also mem. adv. com. Sch. Pharmacy; trustee Atlanta Bapt. Coll., 1964-72, Truett McConnell Coll., Cleveland, Ga., 1960-65; mem. president's council Tift Coll., Forsyth, Ga., 1976—; bd. mgrs. Lord's Day Alliance Am., 1971—, exec. dir., 1975—. Elected Man of the South, Dixie Bus. mag., 1972; named to South's Hall of Fame, 1972. Mem. Atlanta Area Mil. Chaplains Assn. (hon.). Mason (Shriner), Lion. Clubs: Atlanta Harvard, Atlanta Athletic, Atlanta Amateur Movie. Author: Prayers in Congress, 1949; Every Citizen Has A Right to Know, 1954; Baptists in South Carolina Before the War Between the States, 1966; Rainbow Over Russia, 1962; Meditations for Happy Christians, 1973; Evangelistic Sermons, 1974; When Hell Trembles, 1974; The Morningside Man (Wesberry's biography by James C. Bryant), 1975. Editor: Sunday Mag., 1975—, Basharet, 1976—. Home: 1715 Merton Rd NE Atlanta GA 30306 Office: Suite 107 Baptist Center 2930 Flowers Rd S Atlanta GA 30341. *Life's supreme joy is found in the service of God. Life becomes sublimely beautiful when it is dedicated to something far greater than ourselves. Many years ago The Apostle Paul gave us the secret of his wonderful life and ministry. He said, "I am crucified with Christ; nevertheless I live; yet not I, but Christ liveth in me; and the life I now live in the flesh I live by the faith of the Son of God, who loved me and gave himself for me." This expresses the feeling of my heart and I am forever grateful for the privilege of sharing with him in making this a better world for others.*

WESBURY, STUART ARNOLD, JR., assn. exec.; b. Phila., Dec. 13, 1933; s. Stuart Arnold and Jennie (Glazewska) W.; B.S., Temple U., 1955; M. Hosp. Adminstrn., U. Mich., 1960; Ph.D., U. Fla., 1972; m. June Carol Davis, Feb. 23, 1957; children—Brian, Brent, Bruce, Bradford. Pharmacist, USPHS Hosps., 1955-57; adminstrv. officer, pharmacist USPHS clinic, 1957-58; adminstrv. asst. Del. Hosp., 1960-61; asst. adminstr. Bronson Meth. Hosp., 1961-66; asso. dir., asst. prof. U. Fla. Teaching Hosp., 1966-67, dir., asso. prof., 1967-69; v.p. Computer Mgmt. Corp., Gainesville, Fla., 1969-72; dir., prof. Grad. Studies in Health Services Mgmt., U. Mo.-Columbia, 1972-78; pres. Am. Coll. Hosp. Adminstrs., Chgo., 1979—. Active Boy Scouts Am.; chmn. adminstrv. bd. Meth. Ch.; bd. dirs. Boys Clubs, Gainesville. Served with USPHS, 1955-58. Fellow Am. Coll. Hosp. Adminstrs.; mem. Am. Hosp. Assn., Hosp. Mgmt. Systems Soc., Am. Public Health Assn., Assn. Univ. Programs in Health Adminstrn. (chmn. 1977-78). Club: Rotary (past pres.). Contbr. articles to profl. jours. Home: 140 Briarwood N Oak Brook IL 60521 Office: 840 N Lake Shore Dr Chicago IL 60611

WESCHLER, ANITA, sculptor, painter; b. N.Y.C.; d. J. Charles and Hulda Eva (Mayer) Weschler; married. Exhibited Met. Mus., Modern Mus., Chgo. Art Inst., Pa. Acad., Bklyn. Mus., Carnegie Inst., Whitney Mus., museums and galleries throughout U.S.; represented in permanent collections Syracuse U., Butler Art Inst., Whitney Mus., Norfolk Mus., Brandeis U., Amherst Coll., Yale U., Wichita State Mus., N.Y. State U., others; 12 one-man shows in N.Y.C., 11 group traveling shows, 25 one-man shows nationwide, 1964—, including Birmingham (Ala.) Mus. Art, Main Library, Winston-Salem, N.C., U. Wis., Milw. Awards include commissions for sculpture for U.S. Post Office; del. to U.S. Com. of Internat. Assn. of Art, Fine Arts Fedn. of N.Y. prizes at Corcoran Gallery, San Francisco Mus., Montclair Art Mus., Am. Fedn. Arts Traveling Show; fellow MacDowell Colony, Yaddo. Mem. Archtl. League, Sculptors Guild, Nat. Assn. Women Artists, Internat. Inst. Arts and Letters, Audubon Artists, Fedn. Modern Painters and Sculptors. Author: (poetry book) Nightshade. Address: 136 Waverly Pl New York City NY 10014 also Erwinna Bucks County PA 18920. *An artist's responsibility is not to outer forces. His impulse and diligence must be inner-directed. The blending of aptitude and experience breeds an internal emulsion. Essential in creation is the ability to release this ferment by the power of his will and the method of his need.*

WESCOE, W(ILLIAM) CLARKE, physician, drug co. exec.; b. Allentown, Pa., May 3, 1920; s. Charles H. and Hattie G. (Gilham) W.; B.S., Muhlenberg Coll., 1941; Sc.D., 1957; M.D., Cornell U., 1944; m. Barbara Benton, Apr. 29, 1944; children—Barbara, William, David. Intern N.Y. Hosp., 1944-45, resident, 1945-46; asst. prof. pharmacology Med. Coll., Cornell U., 1949-51; prof. pharmacology and exptl. medicine U. Kans. Med. Center, 1951—, dir., 1953-60, dean Sch. Medicine, 1952-60; chancellor U. Kan., 1960-69; v.p. med. affairs Sterling Drug Inc., N.Y.C., 1969-71, exec. v.p., 1971-72, vice chmn., 1972-74, chmn., 1974—; pres. Winthrop Labs., 1970-73; dir. Phillips Petroleum Co., Hallmark Cards, Inc., Irving Trust Co. Chmn. China Med. Bd. of N.Y., N.Y.C. 1960—. Bd. dirs. Tinker Found.; trustee Samuel Kress Found., Columbia U., Muhlenberg Coll., John Simon Guggenheim Meml. Found. Served as capt., pharmacol. sect., med. div. Army Chem. Center, M.C., AUS, 1946-48. Markle scholar med. scis., 1949-54. Fellow A.C.P.; mem. Am. Soc. Pharmacology and Exptl. Therapeutics, Phi Beta Kappa, Sigma Xi, Alpha Omega Alpha, Alpha Tau Omega, Nu Sigma Nu. Editor: Jour. Pharmacol. and Exptl. Therapeutics, 1953-57. Home: 828 Traylor Dr Allentown PA 18103 Office: 90 Park Ave New York NY 10016

WESCOTT, ROGER WILLIAMS, educator; b. Phila., Apr. 28, 1925; s. Ralph Wesley and Marion (Sturges-Jones) W.; grad. Phillips Exeter Acad., 1942; B.A. summa cum laude, Princeton, 1945, M.A., 1947, Ph.D., 1948; M.Litt., Oxford U., 1952; m. Hilja J. Brigadier, Apr. 11, 1964; children—Walter, Wayne. Asst. prof. history and human relations Boston U. and Mass. Inst. Tech., 1953-57; asso. prof. English and social sci., also dir. African lang. program Mich. State U., 1957-62; prof. anthropology and history So. Conn. State Coll., 1962-66; prof., chmn. anthropology and linguistics Drew U., Madison, N.J., 1966—. Fgn. lang. cons. U.S. Office Edn., 1961. Pres. Sch. Living, Brookville, Ohio, 1962-65; exec. dir. Inst. Exploratory Edn., N.Y.C., 1963-66; Korzybski lectr. Inst. Gen. Semantics, N.Y.C., 1976. Rhodes scholar, 1948-50; Ford fellow, 1955-56; Am. Council Learned Socs. scholar, 1951-52. Fellow Am. Anthrop. Assn., A.A.A.S., African Studies Assn.; mem. New Haven Humanist Assn. (past pres.), Assn. for Poetry Therapy, Internat. Soc. Comparative Study of Civilizations (co-founder), Linguistic Assn. Can. and U.S. (pres. 1976—), Internat. Linguistic Assn., Com. for the Future, Phi Beta Kappa. Author: A Comparative Grammar of Albanian, 1955; Introductory Ibo, 1961; A Bini Grammar, 1963; An Outline of Anthropology, 1965; The Divine Animal, 1969; Language Origins, 1974; Visions, 1975; also poems and articles. Home: 11 Green Hill Rd Madison NJ 07940. *Since our lives are short, it seems appropriate that our reflections on them should be comparably brief. Success is transient and high regard, relative. Though my occupational classification is that of a teacher and administrator, I have rarely been able seriously to picture myself as an educational careerist. I have thought of myself, rather, as an intellectual explorer, perennially fascinated by the unexplained or inadequately explained aspects of man and his world and powerfully impelled to share that sense of fascination with fellow explorers.*

WESELI, ROGER WILLIAM, hosp. adminstr.; b. Cin., Dec. 23, 1932; s. William Henry and Margaret Antoinette (Hoffman) W.; B.A. in Polit. Sci., U. Cin., 1955; M.S. in Hosp. Adminstrn., Northwestern U., 1959; m. Sue Ann Daggett, Sept. 1, 1956; children—Erin, Stacey, Vincent. Adminstrv. asst. Good Samaritan Hosp., Cin., 1959-61, asst. adminstr., 1961-70, asso. adminstr., 1970-75, v.p., adminstr., 1975-78, exec. v.p., adminstr., 1978-79, pres., 1979—; sec. Greater Cin. Hosp. Council, 1978—. Chmn. legislation com. health dept. Ohio Catholic Conf., 1978—; bd. dirs. Friars Boys Club, 1978—. Recipient Alpha Mu Sigma award, 1975; cert. of appreciation Ohio League for Nursing, 1978. Fellow Am. Coll. Hosp. Adminstrs., Am. Mgmt. Assn., Am. Hosp. Assn., Greater Cin. C. of C., Ohio League for Nursing (v.p. 1977-79), Ohio Hosp. Assn. (chmn. govt. liaison com. 1978—). Democrat. Roman Catholic. Home: 3615 Clifton Ave Cincinnati OH 45220 Office: 3217 Clifton Ave Cincinnati OH 45220

WESELY, EDWIN JOSEPH, lawyer, vol. orgn. exec.; b. N.Y.C., May 16, 1929; s. Joseph and Elizabeth (Peles) W.; student Deep Springs Coll., 1945-49; A.B., Cornell U., 1949; J.D., Columbia U., 1954; m. Yolanda Thereza Pyles, July 1, 1950; children—Marissa Celeste, Adrienne Lee. Admitted to N.Y. bar, 1954, U.S. Supreme Ct. bar, 1960, others; law clk. to Judge Sylvester J. Ryan, U.S. Dist. Ct., So. Dist. N.Y., 1954-55; asst. U.S. Atty., So. Dist. N.Y., 1955-57; asso. firm Winthrop, Stimson, Putnum & Roberts, N.Y.C., 1957-63, partner, 1964—; bd. dirs. CARE, 1963—, chmn., 1978—; v.p., bd. dirs. Internat. Rescue Com. Fellow Am. Coll. Trial Lawyers; mem. Am. Bar Assn. (chmn. com. on discovery 1977-78, mem. spl. com. study of discovery abuse 1977—), Assn. Bar City N.Y. (mem. grievance com. 1977—, organizer demonstration observation panel), other bar assns. Clubs: Recess, Club at World Trade Center, Merchants. Home: 12 Brayton Rd Scarsdale NY 10583 Office: 40 Wall St New York NY 10005 also 660 1st Ave New York NY 10016

WESENBERG, JOHN HERMAN, assn. exec.; b. Davenport, Iowa, Jan. 16, 1927; s. Herman B. and Nell (Watterson) W.; student Iowa State U., 1944-45, 47, Amherst Coll., 1946; B.A., U. Iowa, 1951, M.A., 1952; postgrad. Northwestern U., 1952-55, Mich. State U., 1956-67; m. Alice Jane McMahill, Sept. 10, 1949; children—Anne, John, Sue, James. Research asso. Bur. Bus. and Econ. Research, U. Iowa, 1949-52; asst. mgr. Danville (Ill.) C. of C., 1952-54; exec. v.p. Belleville (Ill.) C. of C., 1954-57; sec. Retail Mchts. and Central Dist. Bur., Des Moines, 1957-62; exec. v.p. Greater Des Moines C. of C., 1963—; sec. Greater Des Moines Com., 1963—; lectr. Inst. Orgn. Mgmt., Mich. State U., 1959-67, 69-70, 73, U. Colo., 1970, 75, Syracuse U., 1971, U. Santa Clara (Calif.), 1972, 74-75, Tex. Christian U., 1971, 73, U. Del., 1973-76, U. Ga., 1973, U. Notre Dame, 1975, So. Meth. U., 1975-76, Mills Coll., 1976. Co-chmn. Des Moines Mail Users Council, 1963-68; sec.-treas. Des Moines Housing Corp., Baseball, Inc.; sec. Des Moines Devel. Corp., Des Moines Industries, Inc., Community Improvement, Inc., Greater Des Moines Community Found.; treas. Greater Des Moines Shippers Assn.; trustee Fringe Benefits, Inc., Washington; mem. exec. com. Iowa Council on Econ. Edn., 1978—; mem. planning com. Grand View Coll., 1976—; mem. adv. council, region VIII, SBA, 1973—. Mem. bd. regents Inst. Orgn. Mgmt., Mich. State U., 1962-67, U. Colo., 1977—, chmn., 1965-66; vice chmn. nat. bd. regents Inst. for Orgn. Mgmt., 1978-79, chmn., 1979-80. Served with USAAF, 1944-46. Mem. Am. C. of C. Execs. (dir. 1965-68, pres. 1971-72), Iowa C. of C. Execs. (dir. 1960-66, pres. 1964), Am. Retail Execs. Assn. (dir. 1961-63), Ill. Mfrs. Assn. (exec. com. So. div. 1955-57), St. Louis Indsl. Council (v.p. 1957), Am. Arbitration Assn., Nat. Assn. Housing and Redevel. Ofcls., Internat. Downtown Exec. Assn., Iowa Bd. Internat. Edn., Beta Theta Pi (gen. sec. 1974—, trustee 1974—). Clubs: Des Moines, Wakonda. Home: 1169 Columbine Ct Norwalk IA 50211 Office: 800 High St Des Moines IA 50307

WESLAGER, CLINTON ALFRED, author, historian; b. Pitts., Apr. 30, 1909; s. Fred H. and Alice (Lowe) W.; B.A., U. Pitts., 1933; m. Ruth G. Hurst, June 9, 1934; children—Ruth Ann (Mrs. George G. Tatnall), Clinton Alfred, Thomas Hurst. Vis. prof. Am. history Wesley Coll., 1969, U. Del., 1971-73, Brandywine Coll., 1970-80. Pres. Archeol. Soc. Del., 1942-48, Eastern States Archeol. Fedn., 1954-58. Pres. trustees Richardson Park Sch., 1953-57. Recipient award of merit Am. Assn. State and Local History, 1965, 68; Christian Lindback award for excellence in teaching, 1977; Archibald Crozier award Archeol. Soc. Del., 1978. Fellow Archeol. Soc. N.J.; mem. AAUP, Hist. Soc. Del., Soc. Pa. Archeology, Sigma Delta Chi. Mason. Author: Delaware's Forgotten Folk, 1943; Delaware's Buried Past, 1944; Delaware's Forgotten River, 1947; The Nanticoke Indians, 1948; Brandywine Springs, 1949; Indian Places-Names in Delaware, 1950; Red Men on the Brandywine, 1953; Richardsons of Delaware, 1957; Dutch Explorers, Traders and Settlers, 1961; Garrett Snuff Fortune, 1965; English on the Delaware, 1967; Log Cabin in America, 1969; The Delaware Indians, A History, 1972; Magic Medicines of the Indians, 1973; The Stamp Act Congress, 1976; The Delaware Indian Westward Migration, 1978. Editor: Historic Red Clay Valley, Inc., 1961-69. Home: Old Public Rd Hockessin DE 19707

WESLER, OSCAR, educator, mathematician; b. Bklyn., July 12, 1921; s. Israel Edward and Sarah (Hartman) W.; B.S., Coll. City N.Y., 1942; M.S., N.Y. U., 1943; postgrad. Princeton, 1943-46; Ph.D., Stanford, 1955. Mem. faculty Stanford U., 1952-56, vis. prof. stats., 1978; mem. faculty U. Mich., 1956-64; prof. stats. and math. N.C. State U., Raleigh, 1964—; cons. Inst. Sci. and Tech., U. Mich., 1957-64, IBM, 1966; vis. prof. statistics Stanford, 1962-63, 73, 74, 78, U. Calif., Berkeley, 1972-73; vis. lectr. NSF Program vis. lectrs. in statistics, 1963—. Recipient Outstanding Tchr. award N.C. State U., 1966. Mem. Inst. Math. Statistics, Am. Math. Soc., Sigma Xi, Phi Kappa Phi. Author: Solutions to Problems in Theory of Games and Statistical Decisions, 1954; also articles in profl. jours. Research in statis. decision theory, probability, stochastic processes. Home: 1926 Smallwood Dr Raleigh NC 27605

WESLEY, JAMES WYATT, JR., broadcasting exec.; b. Atlanta, Sept. 5, 1933; s. James Wyatt and Nellie Wesley; B.S., Ga. Inst. Tech., 1955; M.B.A., U. Miami, 1974; m. Era Mary Phillips, Mar. 20, 1954; children—James Alan, David Wyatt. With Sta. WSB, Atlanta, 1955-65, local sales mgr., 1961-65; v.p., gen. mgr. Sta. WIOD/WAIA, Miami, Fla., 1965-73; v.p., gen. mgr. Sta. KFI/KOST, Los Angeles, 1973—; mem. Radio Code Bd., 1975—; pres. Greater Miami Radio Broadcasters Assn., 1968, Fla. Assn. Broadcasters, 1972. Mem. Nat. Assn. Broadcasters (dir. 1973), So. Calif. Broadcasters Assn. (chmn. 1979). Address: 610 S Ardmore Ave Los Angeles CA 90005

WESSEL, CARL JOHN, chemist; b. Pitts., Oct. 5, 1911; s. Reuben and Sarah Veronica (Boyle) W.; student U. Buffalo, 1929-30; B.S., Canisius Coll., 1934; M.S., U. Detroit, 1938; Ph.D., Cath. U. Am., 1941; m. Laura Schell Huntington, Feb. 14, 1942; children—Gretchen Grimm, Gregory Huntington, Colman Langan, Hilary Lindsay, Kenwyn Brennan. Paint, Varnish, lacquer and enamel chemist Pratt & Lambert Co., Buffalo, 1934- 36, charge testing lab., 1935, supr. lacquer formulation, 1936; grad. instr. gen. chemistry U. Detroit, 1936-38, instr. biochemistry, organic chemistry, 1941; microbiologist, chemist Gelatin Products Corp. (now R. P. Scherer Corp.), Detroit, 1941-46, supr. control labs., asso. dir. control, 1942-46; instr. gen. chemistry Wayne State U., 1944-46; biochemist, research asso. prevention of deterioration center div. chemistry-chem. tech., Nat. Acad. Sci.-NRC, 1946-48, asst. dir., 1948-54, asso. dir., 1954, dir., 1955-65, mem. panel on prevention deterioration, materials adv. bd., 1957-58, mem. panel on effects ambient environ. quality, environ. research assessment com., 1975—; treas. The Capital Chemist, Publ. Wash. Chem. Soc., 1951-55; sec. Nat. Fedn. Sci. Abstracting and Indexing Services, 1963-65; sci. info. coordinator FDA, HEW, 1965-66; v.p., chief scientist Tracor Jitco, Inc., Rockville, Md., 1966—, dir. carcinogenesis bioassay program, 1974-76. Fellow Am. Inst. Chemists (pres. Washington chpt. 1957-59), Inst. Environ. Scis., A.A.A.S.; mem. Am. Inst. Biol. Sci., Corrosion Research Council, Seahorse Inst., Am. Chem. Soc., Am. Soc. Info. Scis., Soc. Indsl. Microbiology. Roman Catholic. Clubs: Cosmos, Torch (Washington past dir., pres. 1965) Contbg. author: Chemistry and Chemical Technology of Cotton, 1955, The Encyclopedia of Chemistry, 1957. Editor, contbr. Deterioration of Materials, Causes and Preventive Techniques, 1954. Contbr. articles profl. jours. Home: 5014 Park Pl Brookdale MD 20016 Office: 1776 E Jefferson St Rockville MD 20852

WESSEL, HAROLD COSBY, accountant, business cons.; b. Joplin, Mo., Nov. 28, 1916; s. Harold Owen and Myrtle (Cosby) W.; student U. Mich., 1936-38, Walsh Sch. Bus. Adminstrn., Detroit, 1939-42; m. Geraldine Audrey Ringius, June 28, 1940; children—Alice Merry (Mrs. Bruce Mutchler), Robert William. With Ernst & Ernst, 1941-75, successively accountant, Detroit, Denver, mgr., Colorado Springs, mgr., Denver, partner, Denver, 1941-59, partner, Phila., 1959-75; ret., 1975; treas. Cloverlay, Inc., 1965-68, pres., 1968-70, dir., 1968-70. Bd. dirs. exec. com. Phila. Port Corp., 1970-72; bd. dirs., exec. com. Phila. Indsl. Devel. Corp., 1966—, v.p., 1969-79, treas., 1979—; chmn. Phila. Authority for Indsl. Devel., 1979—; bd. dirs. Pa. Ballet Co., 1965-73, treas., 1965-69; bd. dirs. Spring Garden Coll., 1964-70, Young Men's Inst., 1977-79, Penjerdel Regional Found., 1978—; mem. distbn. com. Phila. Found., 1971—. Mem. C. of C. Greater Phila. (dir. 1961—, pres. 1970-71, chmn. bd. 1971-72), Am. Inst. C.P.A.'s (council 1968-70). Pa. Inst. C.P.A.'s. Clubs: Union League, Midday (mem. bd. 1966-79, pres. 1970-72, treas. 1974-77, v.p. 1977-79), Phila. Country, (Phila.); Merion Golf (treas. 1973-79), Right Angle (mem. bd. 1965-79, v.p. 1970-72, pres. 1973-74). Home and office: Hamilton Dr Valley Forge PA 19481

WESSEL, HERBERT WILLIAM, JR., dairy coop. exec.; b. Balt., May 23, 1928; s. Herbert William and Gertrude (Hines) W.; ed. pub. schs.; m. Mary Fisher, Feb. 24, 1952; children—Joyce E., Thomas W., Phillip R. Dir. Md. Coop. Milk Producers, Inc., Balt., 1961—, v.p., 1966-68, pres., 1969—; dir. Am. Dairy Assn. Atlantic, Inc., Phila., 1967—, v.p., 1968-69, pres., 1970; v.p. Pennmarva Dairymen's Coop. Fedn., Inc., Balt., 1968, pres., 1969; dir. Nat. Milk Producers Fedn., Inc., 1969—; dir. Am. Dairy Assn., Inc., 1969—, sec., 1973-78, v.p., 1978—; dir. United Dairy Industry Assn., 1973—. Named Outstanding Young Farmer in Md., Md. Jaycees, 1960. Mem. Md. Crop Improvement Assn. (pres. 1966-67). Contbr. papers to dairy confs. Home: 2200 Fairmount Rd Hampstead MD 21074 Office: 1717 Gwynn Oak Ave Baltimore MD 21207

WESSEL, RICHARD DEATON, chem. products mfg. co. exec.; b. Greenville, Ohio, July 3, 1924; s. Christian Charles and Blanche (Deaton) W.; B.A., Wittenberg U. Springfield, Ohio, 1947; M.Sc., Ohio State U., 1949, Ph.D. in Entomology and Plant Pathology, 1951; m. Sue Cailor, Apr. 26, 1952; children—Rae Ann, Christian Richard. With Chevron Chem. Co. or affiliates, 1954—, mgr. research and devel. internat., Richmond, Calif., 1965-68, mgr. research and devel. Ortho div., Richmond, 1968-73, pres., dir. gen. Chevron Chm. Co. S.A.F. France, Paris, 1973—. Served to 1st lt. USMCR, 1942-45. Mem. Entomol. Soc. Am., Am. C. of C. in France. Lutheran. Club: Am. of Paris. Home: 9 Rue Avice Sevres 92310 France Office: 12 rue de Penthievre Paris 75008 France

WESSEL, ROBERT HOOVER, economist, educator; b. Cin., Apr. 22, 1921; s. Herman Henry and Bessie (Hoover) W.; student Harvard, 1940, 42; A.B., U. Cin., 1942, M.A., 1946, Ph.D., 1953; m. Helen Ann Mueller, July 26, 1952. With drug products div. Proctor & Gamble Co., 1943-45; mem. faculty U. Cin., 1945-56, 57—, prof. econs., 1960—, David Sinton prof. econs., chmn. dept., 1962-68, vice provost for grad. studies, 1967-73, prof. polit. economy and adminstrn., 1973—; asso. prof. Northeastern U., 1956-57; cons. to industry and govt., 1955—. Mem. Hamilton County Republican Exec. Com.; trustee Ohio Council for Econ. Edn.; bd. dirs. Center for Research Libraries, 1973—, chmn., 1976-77. Mem. Am. Econ. Assn., Am. Fin. Assn., Ohio Assn. Economists and Polit. Scientists (pres. 1969-70), Council Grad. Schs. (grad. cost com. 1967-76), Phi Beta Kappa, Beta Gamma Sigma, Omicron Delta Kappa. Republican. Episcopalian. Author: Statistics Applied to Economics, rev. edit., 1973; Principles of Financial Analysis, 1961; also articles. Home: 2106 Columbia Pkwy Cincinnati OH 45202

WESSELL, NILS YNGVE, educator, found. exec.; b. Warren, Pa., Apr. 14, 1914; s. Rev. Nils Johan and Esther (Wahlquist) W.; B.S., Lafayette Coll., 1934; M.S., Brown U., 1935; Ph.D., U. Rochester, 1938; Sc.Ed. D. (hon.), Lafayette Coll., 1951; L.H.D., Lesley Coll., 1955; LL.D., Boston U., 1956, Boston Coll., 1957, Northeastern U., 1958, Brown U., 1958; L.H.D., Brandeis U., 1961; Jur.D., Portia Law Sch., 1959; Litt.D., Am. Internat. Coll., 1960; LL.D., Tufts U., 1966, Wagner Coll., 1967, Bates Coll., 1968; m. Marian Sigler, Sept. 15, 1938; children—Roberta Sue (Mrs. William A. McCuskey), Nils Hartley. Asst. psychol. Brown U., 1934-36; res. psychologist Bradley Home, 1936-37; fellow U. Rochester, 1937-38; dir. mobile child guidance clinic U. Mich., 1938-39; dean liberal arts Tufts U., 1939-53, asst. prof. psychology, 1939-45, acting chmn. dept., 1943-45, asso. prof., 1945-47, prof., 1947-66, v.p., 1951-53, acting pres., 1953, pres., 1953-66, pres. emeritus, 1977—; pres. Inst. Ednl. Devel., N.Y.C., 1965-68; pres. Alfred P. Sloan Found., N.Y.C., 1968-79; lectr. psychology Harvard, 1943. Pres., N.E. Coll. Fund., 1956-58; dir. Fed. Res. Bank of Boston, 1957-62, chmn. bd., 1961-62; dir. Liberty Mut. Ins. Cos., Liberty Mut. Fire Ins. Co., Polaris Fund Inc. Trustee U. Maine, 1968-78, U. Miami, 1979—, John Fitzgerald Kennedy Library; trustee Scandinavian Seminar, 1960-71, chmn., 1968-71; chmn. Gov.'s Com. Study Mass Correctional System, 1955-56; mem. Rhodes Scholarship Com. (Mass. chmn. 1956-57; mem. Independent Coll. Funds Am., mem. exec. com., 1958-61; mem. corp. Babson Coll., 1978—; rep. Nat. Commn. Accrediting, 1956-60; mem. Bd. Higher Edn., N.Y.C., 1970-73; chmn. edn. div. United Fund Greater N.Y., 1970-71, vice chmn. pub. service div., 1972—; mem. N.Y. Council for Humanities, 1974-77, chmn., 1975—; chmn. N.Y. State Commn. on Future Higher Edn., 1976-77; mem. bd. overseers com. to visit Univ. Extension Program, Summer Sch. Arts and Scis., Edn., Harvard, 1970—; trustee Boston Mus. Fine Arts, 1979; chmn. New Eng. workshop Pres.'s Com. on Edn. Beyond High Sch., 1956; mem. Mass. Council Crime and Delinquency, 1961-66; exec. com. adv. council Mass. Mental Health Planning Project, 1964-66; mem. devel. com. Assn. Am. Colls., 1979—. Decorated knight comdr. Royal Order of North Star (Sweden); Wessell Library named in his honor at Tufts U., 1965; recipient Outstanding Service award Air Force ROTC, 1966; Alexander Meikeljohn award AAUP, 1975; named Swedish Am. of Yr., 1979; Carnegie travel fellow, 1965. Fellow Am. Psychol. Assn., Royal Soc. Arts (Benjamin Franklin fellow); mem. Am. Swedish Hist. Found. (pres., bd. govs.), Swedish Council Am. (chmn. 1973-78, hon. chmn. 1978—), Am. Acad. Arts and Scis. (v.p. 1957-59), Internat. Assn. Univ. Presidents, New Eng. Assn. Colls., and Secondary Schs. (pres. 1960), Assn. Am. Colls. (commn. on adminstrn. 1964-66), Am. Bar Assn. (mem. com. on nat. inst. justice, 1972-73), Am. Edn. Research Assn., Pa. Soc., Council on Fgn. Relations, Nat. Assn. Mental Health (profl. adv. com. 1966-68), Sigma Xi, Phi Beta Kappa (hon.), Alpha Omega Alpha (hon.), Omicron Kappa Upsilon (hon.). Clubs: Commercial (Boston); University (N.Y.C.); Cosmos (Washington). Contbr. to sci. and ednl. jours. Home: Sunset South 6C Sanibel FL 33957

WESSELLS, HELEN E(LIZABETH), librarian; b. Morristown, N.J., June 3, 1903; d. Aldus H. and Marie A. (Shugg) Pierson; grad. Sch. Library Service, Columbia U., 1926; m. Parker F. Wessells, 1927; m. 2d, Herman S. Hettinger, 1952. Asst., Morristown Library, 1922-25; br. librarian N.Y. Pub. Library, 1926-42; dir. Victory Book Campaign, 1942-43; outpost rep., dir. U.S. Info. Library, Melbourne, Australia, O.W.I. overseas br., 1943-45; U.S. Fgn. Service Res., Melbourne, 1945-47; asso. dir. Internat. Relations Office, ALA, Washington, 1948; chief library br., div. libraries and insts. Dept. State, 1949-50; editor Library Jour., 1951-57; librarian Books-Across-the-Sea, English-Speaking Union, N.Y.C., 1972-78, nat. chmn. com., 1967-75, chmn. selection com., 1957-76; cons. Rockefeller Found., Carnegie Corp. N.Y., Conn. Dept. Edn., HEW, others; dir. Wing Prodns., 1966-72; UN nongovtl. rep. Women's Nat. Book Assn., 1957-76; dir. Book Bridges, 1978—. Mem. ALA (editor Leads 1949-73, mem. council, chmn. internat. relations roundtable 1949-50, chmn. numerous coms.), Spl. Libraries Assn. (chmn. pub. div. 1966-67), Am. Inst. Graphic Arts (dir. 1943), D.C. Library Assn. (pres. 1949-51), N.Y. Library Club (pres. 1952-54), Morris Mus. Sci. Club: Dacor (Washington). Author pamphlets; contbr. articles to profl. jours. U.S. and Australia. Home: 433 W 21st St New York NY 10011

WESSELMANN, GLENN ALLEN, hosp. exec.; b. Cleve., Mar. 21, 1932; s. Roy Arthur and Dorothy (Oakes) W.; A.B., Dartmouth, 1954; M.B.A. with distinction, Cornell U., 1959; m. Genevieve De Witt, Sept. 6, 1958; children—Debbie, Scott, Janet. Research aide Cornell U., Ithaca, N.Y., 1958-59; adminstrv. resident Meml. Hosp., N.Y.C., 1957-58, adminstrv. asst., 1959-61, asst. adminstr., 1961-65, asst. v.p., 1965-68; v.p. for adminstrn. Meml. Hosp. for Cancer and Allied Diseases, N.Y.C., 1968-79; exec. v.p., chief operating officer St. John Hosp., Detroit, 1979—. Preceptor Sloan Inst. Hosp. Adminstrn., Cornell U. Co-chmn. Saturday Workshop Program, Demarest, N.J., 1970-72; pack chmn. Cub Scouts Am., 1970-72. Served with MC, AUS, 1955-57. Fellow Am. Coll. Hosp. Adminstrs.; mem. Am. Hosp. Assn., Hosp. Assn. State N.Y. (mem. ad hoc com. malpractice, bylaws and ins.), Am. Public Health Assn., Greater N.Y. Hosp. Assn. (mem. adminstrv. practices com. 1967-70), Medical Group Mgmt. Assn., Sloan Inst. Hosp. Adminstrn. Alumni Assn. (pres. 1970), Soc. Health Service Adminstrs., Hosp. Adminstrn. Discussion Group, Hosp. Adminstrs. Club N.Y., County Med. Soc. (mem. com. hosp.-physician relations), Dartmouth Coll. of Bergen County Assn. (pres. 1966-67), Sigma Phi Epsilon. Home: 56 Lake Shore Ln Grosse Pointe Shores MI 48236 Office: 22101 Moross Rd Detroit MI 48236

WESSELMANN, TOM, painter; b. Cin., Feb. 23, 1931; s. Edwin William and Grace (Duckwall) W.; student Hiram (Ohio) Coll., 1950; B.A., U. Cin., 1956; student Art Acad. Cin., 1954; grad. certificate Cooper Union, 1959; m. Claire Selley, Nov. 27, 1963; 1 dau., Jenny Claire. One-man exhbns.: Tanager Gallery, N.Y.C., 1961, Green Gallery, N.Y.C., 1962, 64, 65, Sidney Janis Gallery, 1966, 68, 70, 72, 74, 76, Gallery Ileana, Sonnabend, Paris, 1967, Mus. Contemporary Art, Chgo., 1968, Calif. State U. at Long Beach, 1974, travelling exhbn. Ohio U., Athens and Nelson Atkins Gallery, Kansas City, 1974, Inst. Contemporary Arts, Boston, 1978. Served with AUS, 1952-54. Address: 231 Bowery St New York City NY 10002

WESSINGER, GEORGE DAVID, pharm. cons.; b. Cherryville, N.C., Sept. 28, 1913; s. Benjamin David and Nancy Virginia (Caughman) W.; B.S. summa cum laude, Fla. So. Coll., 1935; M.S., Northwestern U., 1936, Ph.D., 1939; D.D.S., Loyola U., 1944; m. Ruth Ione Jensen, July 17, 1940; children—David Lee, Mary Louise. Instr. chemistry Northwestern U., Chgo., 1935-39; asso. prof. chemistry Loyola U., Chgo., 1939-44; asst. dir. Sterling-Winthrop Research Inst., Rensselaer, N.Y., 1950-60, asso. dir., 1960-66, dir., 1966-73, cons., 1973—. Trustee, Albany Symphony Orch., 1961-73, pres., 1968-70; trustee Albany Pharmacy Coll., 1970-73. Fellow A.A.A.S.; mem. Am. Chem. Soc., Internat. Assn. for Dental Research, Sigma Xi. Republican. Lutheran. Contbr. articles to profl. jours. Address: RD 2 Brewster MA 02631

WESSLER, STANFORD, physician, educator; b. N.Y.C., Apr. 20, 1917; S. Hugo and Minerva (Miller) W.; grad. Fieldston Sch., N.Y.C., 1934; B.A., Harvard, 1938; M.D., N.Y.U., 1942; m. Margaret Barnet Muhlfelder, Dec. 17, 1942; children—John Stanford, Stephen Lawrence, James Hugh. From fellow to asst. prof. medicine Harvard Med. Sch., 1946-64; from resident to asso. chief med. service Beth Israel Hosp., Boston, 1946-64; prof. medicine Washington U. Sch. Medicine, St. Louis, 1964-74, John L. and Adalaine Simon prof., 1966-74; prof. medicine asso. dean Postgrad. Med. Sch., N.Y.U., 1974—; physician in chief Jewish Hosp., St. Louis, 1964-74; asso. physician Barnes Hosp., St. Louis, 1964-74; attending physician N.Y. U. Med. Center, Univ. Hosp., N.Y.C., 1974—, Bellevue Hosp. Center, N.Y.C., 1974—. Mem. coms. NRC, Nat. Heart Inst.; bd. dirs. N.Y. Heart Assn., 1979—; pres. Council Continuing Med. Edn., N.Y., 1979—. Served with M.C., AUS, 1943-46. Recipient James F. Mitchell award, 1972. Mem. Am. Physiol. Soc., Am. Soc. Clin. Investigation, Assn. Am. Physicians, Am. Heart Assn. (chmn. publs. com. 1972—, chmn. council on thrombosis 1974-76, v.p. for councils 1974-76, award of merit 1978), Alpha Omega Alpha. Author articles vascular disease. Mem. editorial bds. jours. in field. Office: NYU Sch Medicine New York NY 10016

WESSNER, KENNETH THOMAS, mgmt. services exec.; b. Sinking Springs, Pa., May 1, 1922; s. Thomas Benjamin and Carrie Eva (Whitmoyer) W.; B.S., Wheaton (Ill.) Coll., 1947; m. Norma Elaine Cook, Jan. 25, 1945; children—Barbara Wessner Anderson, David Kenneth. Dist. mgr., then sales promotion mgr. Club Aluminum Products Co., 1947-54; with Servicemaster Industries Inc., 1954—, v.p., 1961, pres. Servicemaster Hosp. Corp., 1962, chief operating officer, 1965—, exec. v.p. parent co., Downers Grove, Ill., 1972, pres., 1973—, chief exec. officer, 1976—, also dir.; dir. Bell Fed. Savs. & Loan Assn., Chgo. Vice chmn. bd. trustees Wheaton Coll.; trustee Chgo. Sunday Eve. Club. Served with USAAF, World War II. Mem. Am. Mgmt. Assn., Am., Catholic hosp. assns. Club: Chgo. Golf (Wheaton). Home: 102 E Farnham Ln Wheaton IL 60187 Office: 2300 Warrenville Rd Downers Grove IL 60515

WESSON, ROBERT LAUGHLIN, geophysicist; b. San Francisco, Feb. 26, 1944; s. Robert Henry and Annabel (Laughlin) W.; B.S., M.I.T., 1966; M.S., Stanford U., 1968, Ph.D., 1970; m. Cornelia VanKleeck, June 11, 1966; children—Alexander, Elizabeth. NRC research asso. U.S. Geol. Survey, Menlo Park, Calif., 1970-72, geophysicist, 1972-76, dep. for earthquake mechanics and prediction, Reston, Va., 1976-78, chief Office of Earthquake Studies, 1978—; chmn. U.S.-USSR Working Groups in Earthquake Prediction, 1978—. Pan Am. Petroleum Found. fellow, 1968-69. Mem. Am. Geophys. Union, Seismol. Soc. Am., Geol. Soc. Am., Earthquake Engring. Research Inst., AAAS. Presbyterian. Office: 905 National Center US Geol Survey Reston VA 22092

WEST, A(RNOLD) SUMNER, chem. engr.; b. Phila., Jan. 12, 1922; s. Arnold and Mary (Sumner) W.; B.S. in Chem. Engring., U. Pa., 1943; M.S., Pa. State U., 1946; m. Beverly Helen Lehman, Oct. 5, 1946; children—Barbara Ann, Richard Sumner. With Rohm and Haas Co., Phila., 1946—, research engr., 1946-62, research supr., 1962-72, mgr. research dept., 1972-77, tech. specialist govt. and regulatory affairs, 1978—; cons. dept. chem. engring. U. Pa., 1952-72. Mem. Lower Moreland Twp. (Montgomery County) Authority, 1970, sec., 1971—. Fellow Am. Inst. Chem. Engrs. (dir. 1964-66, treas. 1973-75, v.p. 1976, pres. 1977); mem. Engrs. Joint Council (dir. 1976—), Am. Chem. Soc., Nat. Soc. Profl. Engrs., Soc. Automotive Engrs. Club: The Valley (Huntingdon Valley). Home: 3896 Sidney Rd Huntingdon Valley PA 19006 Office: Rohm and Haas Co Independence Mall W Philadelphia PA 19105

WEST, ANTHONY PANTHER, writer; b. Hunstanton, Norfolk, Eng., Aug. 4, 1914; s. Herbert George Wells; ed. in Eng.; m. Lily Dulany Emmet, Dec. 20, 1952; children by previous marriage—Caroline, Edmund. Came to U.S., 1950. Dairy farmer, breeder registered Guernsey cattle, and occasional contbr. to mags., 1937-43; with Far Eastern desk BBC, 1943-45, Japanese Service, 1945-47; mem. staff New Yorker mag., 1950—. Houghton Mifflin fellow, 1947. Club: Century (N.Y.C.). Author: D.H. Lawrence (critical biography), 1948; The Vintage, 1950; Another Kind, 1952; Heritage, 1955; Principles and Persuasions, 1956; The Trend Is Up, 1960; Mortal Wounds, 1966; (critical biography) John Piper, 1978. Address: care Wallace and Shiel 118 E 61st St New York NY 10021

WEST, ARLEIGH BURTON, consultant; b. Hendricks, Minn., July 18, 1910; s. John Earle and Laura Hannah (Larson) W.; B.A., Hamline U., 1932; grad. student pub. welfare adminstrn., U. Minn., 1933; m. Edith Eleanor Gustad, Feb. 27, 1943; children—John Burton, Richard Allen. With Dept. Pub. Welfare, Mpls., 1933-34, Fed. Emergency Relief Adminstrn., Pierre, S.D., 1935; staff Soil Conservation Service, Tech. Coop. Adminstrn., Bur. Indian Affairs, 1936-40; agrl. economist Dept. Agr., 1940-41; with bur. reclamation Dept. Interior, 1941-71, regional dir., Boulder City, Nev., 1960-70, asst. to commr. program policy, 1970-71; cons. water resources, 1971—; mem. U.S. com. Internat. Commn. on Large Dams, U.S. Nat. Commn. on Irrigation and Drainage; mem. Eldorado Adv. Group, Nev.; chmn., adv. com. on water resources research, Desert Research Inst., U. Nev. Recipient Distinguished Service award Dept. Interior, 1971. Mem. Western Farm Econs. Assn. Rotarian (past pres.). Home: 315 Utah St Boulder City NV 89005

WEST, BARRY GEORGE, lawyer; b. N.Y.C., Feb. 3, 1943; s. Irven M. West and Edith (Eisner) Westermann; B.A., Queens Coll. City U. N.Y., 1959-63; LL.B., St. John's U., 1966; LL.M., Harvard, 1967; m. Sheila Blank, Aug. 6, 1966; children—Stephen Todd, Karen Elyse. Admitted to N.Y. bar, 1967, Calif. bar, 1973; asso. mem. firm Paul, Weiss, Rifkind, Wharton & Garrison, N.Y.C., 1967-69; asst. compliance dir. Smith, Barney & Co. investment bankers, N.Y.C., 1969-70; asso. mem. firm Paul, Weiss, Rifkind, Wharton & Garrison, 1970-72; v.p., gen. counsel Technicolor, Inc., Hollywood, Calif., 1972-73; asso. mem. firm Greenberg & Glusker, Los Angeles, 1973-74, mem. firm, 1975—. Mem. Beverly Hills, Los Angeles County bar assns. Home: 4285 Pasadero Pl Tarzana CA 91356 Office: 1900 Ave of Stars Suite 2000 Los Angeles CA 90067

WEST, BERNIE, producer, writer; b. N.Y.C., May 30, 1918; s. Isidore and Mary (Primakoff) Wessler; B.B.A., City Coll. N.Y., 1940; m. Miriam (Mimi) Berman, Oct. 26, 1947; children—Ellen Paula Wessler Harris, Isabel Lee. Comedian in vaudeville, then supper clubs, 1941-55; Broadway appearances include Bells Are Ringing, 1956-59, All-American, 1962, The Beauty Part, 1963; indsl. show performer, writer M.C.I. Inc., 1964-71; story editor, then producer TV series All In The Family, 1971-75; producer, writer TV series The Jeffersons, 1974—, Three's Company, 1976—. Recipient Emmy award Nat. Acad. TV Arts and Scis. for Bunkers and the Swingers in All in The Family, 1973, Emmy honor as story editor All in The Family, 1972; NAACP Image award for The Jeffersons, best comedy series, 1975, 76. Mem. AFTRA, Screen Actors Guild, Writers Guild West. Democrat. Jewish. Office: 5752 Sunset Blvd Los Angeles CA 90028

WEST, BOBBY BOWLUS, holding co. exec.; b. Big Spring, Tex., June 28, 1934; s. Cecil and Norma Annette (Bowlus) W.; B.B.A., N. Tex. State U., 1956; m. Judy Mathis, July 1, 1955; children—Bobby, Lisa, John Tucker, Lori. Mgr., Haskins & Sells Inc., Dallas, 1965-68; sec.-treas., dir. Gulf United Corp., Dallas, 1968—, sr. v.p., 1976; v.p., treas., dir. Gulf Nat. Land Corp., Dallas, 1973-77, pres., 1977—; pres. Tidal Transmission Co., Dallas, 1977—; v.p., asst. treas., dir. Gulf United Corp. Tex., 1978—; sec.-treas., dir. Sta. WVOJ, Inc., Jacksonville, Fla., 1977—, Gulf Village, Inc., 1978—, WTXQ, Inc., Ft. Worth, 1977—, WGHP-TV, Inc., High Point, N.C., 1977—, WKAP, Inc., Allentown, Pa., 1978—, Rahall Broadcasting Co., Inc., St. Petersburg, Fla., 1978—, Rahall Broadcasting Ind., Inc., Indpls., 1978—, Accent Music Systems, Inc., Indpls., 1978—, WLCY, Inc., St. Petersburg, 1978—, WTSP-TV, Inc., St. Petersburg, 1978—; sec.-treas. Sta. KLBK-TV, Inc., Lubbock, Tex., 1977—; sec., dir. Gulf Life Center Devel. Co., Gulf Master Co., Gulf Regency Co.; dir. Gulf Life Ins. Co., Gulf Life Group Ins. Co., Gulf Group Services Corp., GULFCO Capital Mgmt. Inc., Am.-Amicable Life Ins. Co., Interstate Life & Accident Ins. Co., Gulf Fire and Casualty Co., Fin. Computer Services Inc., Interstate Fire Ins. Co. Served with U.S. Army, 1957-58. Mem. Am. Inst. C.P.A.'s, Tex. Soc. C.P.A.'s, Ins. Accounting and Statis. Assn. Republican. Presbyterian. Home: 13415 Briarbrook St Dallas TX 75234 Office: Suite 600 13101 Preston Rd Dallas TX 75240

WEST, BYRON KENNETH, banker; b. Denver, Sept. 18, 1933; s. Willis Byron and Cecil Bernice (Leathers) W.; A.B., U. Ill., 1955; M.B.A., U. Chgo., 1960; m. Barbara Huth, June 25, 1955. With Harris Bank, Chgo., 1957—, investment analyst, 1957-62, asst. cashier, 1962-63, mem. comml. loan div., 1963, asst. v.p., 1964-66, v.p., 1966-76, asst. div. adminstr. Charge Card div., 1967-68, div. adminstr. Corporate Fin. Services div., 1969-72, dep. group exec. Internat. Banking Group, 1972-74, group exec., 1974-76, head banking dept., exec. v.p., 1976—; dir., Motorola, Inc., Harris Bankcorp, Inc. Mem. Chgo. com. Chgo. Council on Fgn. Relations. Bd. dirs. Rush-Presbyn.-St. Luke's Med Center; governing bd. Chgo.

Orchestral Assn. Served with USNR. Mem. Res. City Bankers Assn., Christian Laymen of Chgo., Phi Beta Kappa. Republican. Clubs: Skokie (Ill.) Country; Univ., Chgo., Commonwealth, Comml. (Chgo.). Home: 200 Forest St Winnetka IL 60093 Office: 111 W Monroe St Chicago IL 60690

WEST, CHARLES ALLEN, biochemist, educator; b. Greencastle, Ind., Nov. 4, 1927; s. Kenneth Elbert and Roxy (Day) W.; A.B., DePauw U., 1949; Ph.D., U. Ill., 1952; m. Carol Venerable, Aug. 3, 1952; children—Jeffrey Allen, David Charles. Instr. chemistry U. Calif. at Los Angeles, 1952, 55-56, asst. prof., 1956-61, asso. prof., 1961-67, prof., 1967—, vice chmn. dept., 1970-75; cons. NIH. Served with AUS, 1953-54. Guggenheim fellow, 1961-62; NIH spl. postdoctoral fellow, 1968-69; NSF faculty sci. fellow, 1976-77. Mem. Am. Chem. Soc., Am. Soc. Plant Physiologists, Am. Soc. Biol. Chemists, Phi Beta Kappa, Sigma Xi, Phi Kappa Psi, Gamma Alpha. Research in biochemistry of plant growth regulation, disease resistance and biosynthesis. Home: 3461 Military Ave Los Angeles CA 90034

WEST, CHARLES CAMERON, mfr.; b. Manitowoc, Wis., Apr. 28, 1938; s. Robert Dunham and Margaret Louise (Korherr) W.; B.A., Cornell U., 1961; M.B.A., U. Chgo., 1977; m. Anne Hougen Murphy, June 29, 1963; children—Margot Helen, Sara Murphy, Catherine Dunham. With The Manitowoc Co., Inc., 1961—, asst. treas., 1969-74, sec., 1972—, treas., 1974—, dir., 1967—. Trustee, Beloit (Wis.) Coll., 1970—, Manitowoc Meml. Hosp., 1972—, Emma Willard Sch., Troy, N.Y., 1979—. Served with AUS, 1962-64. Office: 500 S 16th St Manitowoc WI 54220

WEST, CHARLES CONVERSE, theologian, educator; b. Plainfield, N.J., Feb. 3, 1921; s. George Parsons and Florence (Farish) W.; B.A., Columbia, 1942; B.D., Union Theol. Sem., N.Y.C., 1945; Ph.D., Yale, 1955; m. Ruth Floy Carson, Sept. 6, 1944; children—Russell Arthur, Walter Lawrence, Glenn Andrew. Ordained to ministry U.P. Ch. U.S.A., 1946; missionary, fraternal worker Bd. Fgn. Missions Presbyn. Ch. U.S.A., 1946-56; instr., chaplain Cheeloo U., Hangchow, China, 1948-49; instr. Nanking Theol. Sem., 1949-50; indsl. mission work Gossner Mission, Mainz-Kastel, Germany, 1950-51; lectr. Kirchliche Hochschule, Berlin, 1951-53; Lectr. Hartford Sem. Found., 1955-56; asso. dir. Ecumenical Inst., Bossey, Switzerland under World Council Chs., 1956-61; chargé de cours U. Geneva, 1956-61; instr. Peking Nat. U., 1948; asso. prof. Christian ethics Princeton Theol. Sem., 1961-63, Stephen Colwell prof. Christian ethics, 1963—, acad. dean, 1979—; mem. Commn. to Form Statement Faith U.P. Ch. U.S.A., 1961-67, chmn. internat. affairs adv. com., 1963-66. Chmn. U.S. Com. for Christian Peace Conf., 1965-72; chmn. working com. Dept. Studies in Mission, Evangelism World Council Chs., 1967-68, member Commn. on Internat. Affairs, Nat. Council Chs., 1968-73. Mem. Am. Soc. Christian Ethics (v.p. 1972-73, pres. 1973-74), Am. Theol. Soc., Presbytery N.Y.C., Ams. for Democratic Action. Author: Communism and the Theologians, 1958; Outside the Camp, 1959; Ethics, Violence and Revolution, 1969; The Power to be Human, 1971. Editor: The Sufficiency of God; Essays in Honor of Dr. W. A. Visser't Hooft, 1963. Translator: J. Hamel-A Christian in East Germany, 1960. Home: Mountain Rd Box 173 RD 2 Ringoes NJ 08551 Office: Princeton Theological Seminary Princeton NJ 08540

WEST, CHARLES TYRRELL, cons. engr.; b. Crestline, Ohio, July 1, 1915; s. LaFoy Allen and Mabelle (Hillson) W.; student U.S. Naval Acad., 1934-37; B.C.E., Ohio State U., 1939, M.S., 1946; postgrad., U. Mich., 1948-49; Ph.D., Cornell U., 1951; m. Estella Marie Fahs, Apr. 5, 1947 (dec. July 1973); children—Mary Bronwyn, Charles Tyrrell III. Bridge test analyst Assn. Am. Railroads, 1941-46; instr. engring. mechanics Ohio State U., 1946-53, prof., chmn. dept. engring. mechanics, 1953-72, prof. engring. mechanics, 1973-77, prof. emeritus, 1977—; vis. prof. mech. engring. Indian Inst. of Tech., Kanpur, U.P., India, 1968-70. Cons. Boeing Airplane Co., 1959-60; research scientist Autometric Corp., 1959-63; cons. in dynamics to various corps., 1964—. Served from ensign to lt. comdr., USNR, 1941-46. Fellow ASCE; mem. ASME, Nat. Rifle Assn., Sigma Xi, Tau Beta Pi. Club: Ohio State Faculty. Contbr. articles on vibration and dynamics to profl. jours. Home: 7704 Lincoln Hwy Crestline OH 44827

WEST, DOTTIE (DOROTHY MARIE MARSH), singer; b. McMinnville, Tenn., Oct. 11; d. William and Pelina (Jones) Marsh; B.A. in Music, Tenn. Tech. Coll., 1956; m. William West, 1952 (div. 1972); children—Morris, Kerry, Shelly, Dale; m. 2d, Byron A. Metcalf, Aug. 27, 1973. Singing debut WEWS-TV, Cleve., 1956-60; singer 5-piece band Cross-Country, 1966—; performances include: Grand Ole Opry, 1962—, Memphis Symphony Orch., 1973, Kansas City Symphony, 1961-74; TV appearances include: Eddy Arnold Special, Country Hit Parade, Music Country U.S.A., Hee-Haw, Glen Campbell Show, Jimmy Dean, Mike Douglas, Good Ole Nashville; rec. artist Staeday Records, 1959-61, Atlantic Records, 1962, RCA, 1962—. Recipient Grammy award female artist for Here Comes My Baby, 1965; Named Number One Female Writer in U.S., Billboard Mag., 1974, Number One Female Performer in Eng., 1973, 74; Country Music Artist of Year, British Country Music Assn.; Coca Cola Country Girl, 1972—. Address: Am Mgmt 17337 Ventura Blvd Suite 220 Encino CA 91316*

WEST, EDWIN NELSON, found. exec., lawyer; b. Menominee, Mich., Oct. 21, 1910; s. Ray D. and Eleanor (Nelson) W.; A.B., Lawrence Coll., 1932; LL.B., U. Mich., 1935; m. Ruth Zink, Mar. 4, 1944; 1 son, David L. Admitted to Wis. bar, 1935, Tex. bar, 1961, N.Y. bar, 1965; pvt. practice, Appleton, Wis., 1935-41; asst. gen. atty. Marathon Corp., Menasha, Wis., 1947-51, gen. atty., sec., 1951-57; gen. atty. Marathon div., also asst. sec. parent company Am. Can Co., 1951-61; gen. counsel, sec. Schlumberger Ltd., Houston and N.Y.C., 1961-76, dir., 1970-76; exec. sec., trustee Schlumberger Found., Houston, 1976—. Trustee Lawrence U., Appleton, Wis. Served with USNR, 1941-45. Mem. Phi Beta Kappa. Episcopalian. Mason. Clubs: Houston Country, Houston; University (N.Y.C.). Home: 2828 Bammel Ln Houston TX 77098 Office: Schlumberger Found 2300 West Loop S Houston TX 77027

WEST, ELMER GORDON, U.S. judge; b. Hyde Park, Mass., Nov. 27, 1914; s. William Albert Howard and Edith Louise (Hall) W.; student Northeastern U., 1934-35, Lamar Jr. Coll., Beaumont, Tex., 1935-36; B.S., La. State U., 1941, LL.B., 1942; m. Viola Kay Cayard, Oct. 30, 1942; children—Roger Gordon, Dan Edward. Accountant, Stone & Webster, 1937-42; admitted to La. bar, 1942; mem. firm Long & West, Baton Rouge, 1946-50, Kantrow, Spaht, West & Kleinpeter, and predecessor, Baton Rouge, 1950-61; U.S. dist. judge Eastern Dist. Ct. La., 1961-67; chief judge U.S. Ct., Eastern Dist. La., 1967-72; U.S. dist. judge Middle Dist. La., 1972—. Atty., La. Revenue Dept., 1946-48, La. inheritance tax collector, 1948-52; asst. prof., spl. lectr. La. State U. Law Sch., 1947-48; mem. Jud. Conf. U.S., 1971—, mem. com. on operation jury system, 1972—. Served to lt. USNR, 1942-45. Mem. Am., La., East Baton Rouge bar assns., Am. Judicature Soc., Internat. Assn. Ins. Counsel, Nat. Assn. Compensation Claimants Attys., Alpha Tau Omega, Phi Delta Phi. Episcopalian. Mason. Office: Fed Ct Bldg Room 228 707 Florida Ave Baton Rouge LA 70801*

WEST, ERIC FOWLER, aluminum co. exec.; b. Newton, Mass., Dec. 29, 1923; s. George Saltonstall and Dorothy (Fowler) W.; grad. Groton Sch., 1942; B.S., Harvard, 1946; certificate Centre d'Etudes Industrielles, Geneva, Switzerland, 1947-48; m. Eugenia Lovett, Sept. 21, 1944; children—Eugenia, George, Eric Fowler, Victoria. Salesman, Aluminum Ltd. Sales, Inc., N.Y.C., 1948-52, gen. sales mgr., 1952-54, pres., 1956-70; mgr. U.S. pub. relations and advt. Aluminum Ltd. Inc., 1954-56, pres., 1963-70; pres. Alcan Aluminum Corp., Cleve., 1970-78, also dir.; regional exec. v.p. Alcan Aluminum Ltd., Montreal, Que., Can., 1978—, also dir.; dir. Alcan Aluminum Ltd., U.K., Fiduciary Trust Co. N.Y. Trustee Nat. Recreation Found. Served with USAAF, 1943-45. Clubs: Chagrin Valley Hunt (Cleve.); Westchester Kennel; Links (N.Y.C.). Office: Alcan Aluminum Ltd Inc Sterling City Rd Lyme CT 06371

WEST, FELTON, newspaperman; b. Houston, May 9, 1926; s. Felton Eber and Clara Viola (Ross) W.; student U. N.M., 1943-46; B.S., U. Houston, 1952, M.Litt., 1957; m. Jean Frances Osborn, Oct. 27, 1945; children—Felton Dale, Bruce Eugene, Wade Osborn, Barbara Jean. Mem. staff Houston Post, 1943—, Washington corr., 1961-66, chief Austin (Tex.) capitol bur., 1966—. Served with USNR, World War II. Mem. Phi Kappa Phi, Sigma Delta Chi. Home: 900 Potomac Path Austin TX 78753 Office: Box 12127 Capitol Sta Austin TX 78711

WEST, FREDERIC W., JR., steel co. exec.; b. Phila., Feb. 18, 1919; s. Frederic W. and Marion Etta (Nill) W.; B.S., Cornell U., 1941; grad. Advanced Mgmt. Program, Harvard, 1970; m. Ruth Virginia Landers, July 5, 1947; children—Frederic W., III, Barbara West Connally, John, William. With Bethlehem Steel Corp. (Pa.), 1941—, asst. gen. mgr. sales, 1969-70, v.p. mfg. products sales, 1970-73, exec. v.p., dir., 1973-74, pres., dir., 1974-77, vice chmn., 1977—. Mem. industries advisory com. Advt. Council; mem. Conf. Bd. Mem. advisory council Grad. Sch. Bus. and Pub. Adminstrn., Cornell U., 1975-77. Trustee St. Luke's Hosp., Bethlehem. Served to 1st lt. U.S. Army, 1942-46, 50-52. Decorated Bronze Star. Mem. Am. Iron and Steel Inst. Clubs: Chicago; Saucon Valley Country (Bethlehem); Sky, Economic, Links (N.Y.); Bethlehem; Laurel Valley Golf; Blooming Grove Hunting and Fishing. Home: Saucon Valley Rd RD 4 Bethlehem PA 18015 Office: Martin Tower Bethlehem PA 18016

WEST, GAIL BERRY, lawyer; b. Cin., Sept. 29, 1942; d. Theodore Moody and Johnnie Mae (Newton) B.; B.A., magna cum laude, Fisk U., 1964; M.A., U. Cin., 1965; J.D., Howard U., 1968; m. Togo D. West, Jr., June 18, 1966; children—Tiffany Berry, Hilary Carter. Admitted to D.C. bar, 1969, U.S. Supreme Ct. bar, 1978; staff atty. IBM, 1969-76; spl. asst. to sec. HUD, 1977-78; staff asst. to spl. asst. to Pres., Washington, 1978—. Mem. exec. com. ARC, Washington; bd. dirs. Family and Child Services, Washington. Ford Found. fellow, 1965-68. Mem. Am. Bar Assn., D.C. Bar Assn., Nat. Bar Assn., Unified Bar D.C. Democrat. Episcopalian. Home: 2701 Northampton St NW Washington DC 20015 Office: The White House Washington DC 20500

WEST, HENRY GEORGE, JR., chiropractor; b. Pocatello, Idaho, Apr. 9, 1933; s. Henry George and Helen Constance (Fikstad) W.; A.B. in Chemistry, Brigham Young U., 1958; D.Chiropractic, Western States Chiropractic Coll., 1961; m. Paula Jean Brown, Mar. 6, 1961; children—Janet, Suzanne, Barbara, Jason, Allyson, Nathan. Gen. practice chiropractic medicine, Pocatello, 1961—; mem. grad. sch. faculty Western State Coll. Chiropractic, 1967—, Los Angeles Coll. Chiropractic, 1969—, Texas Chiropractic Coll., 1979—; dir. Nat. Chiropractic Mut. Ins. Co.; mem. ad hoc com. NIH Workshop Spinal Manipulative Therapy, 1974-75; trustee Found. for Chiropractice Edn. and Research, 1979—. Charter mem. Citizens Advisory Com., Pocatello, 1967. Recipient Distinguished Service award Western States Coll. Chiropractic, 1973, Columbia Inst. Chiropractic, 1977, Nat. Coll. Chiropractic, 1977. Diplomate Nat. Council Phys. Therapists, Am. Bd. Chiropractic Orthopedists. Fellow Internat. Coll. Chiropractors; mem. Am. Chiropractic Assn. (pres. 1976-77, mem. council on nutrition, chmn. posture com.), Idaho Assn. Chiropractic Physicians (pres. 1966, 78-79), Found. for Chiropractic Edn. and Research (chmn. com. A for research), Am. Council Chiropractic Orthopedics, Am. Council Chiropractic Physiotherapy, Pocatello C. of C. Republican. Mormon. Clubs: Rotary, Lions (pres. Pocatello 1966-67). Home: 149 S 17th St Pocatello ID 83201 Office: 1355 E Center St Pocatello ID 83201

WEST, HERBERT BUELL, found. exec.; b. Birmingham, Ala., Apr. 19, 1916; s. Edward Hamilton and Clarine (Buell) W.; B.A., Birmingham-So. Coll., 1936; m. Maria Selden McDonald, Nov. 29, 1946; children—Newill, Herbert Buell, William McDonald, Maria Selden, Jane Hamilton. Writer, v.p., account supr. Batten, Barton, Durstine & Osborn, Inc., N.Y.C., 1936-66; dir., mem. distbn. com. N.Y. Community Trust, 1967—; pres. Community Funds, Inc., 1968—, James Found., 1968—. Chmn. bd. trustees, mem. exec. com. The Found. Center, 1975—; bd. dirs. Welfare Research, Inc., 1972-78, chmn. bd. dirs., 1978—; pres., chmn. bd. dirs. Internat. Social Service, Inc., 1966-72, v.p., bd. dirs., 1972—; bd. dirs., mem. exec. com. Nat. Info. Bur., Inc., 1978—; trustee N.Y. U. Med. Center, 1973—; mem. com. on agy. evaluation assistance Greater N.Y. Fund/United Way, 1976—; warden St. Luke's Episcopal Ch., Darien, Conn., 1976—. Served with Maj. Adjt. Gen. Corps, U.S. Army, 1941-46. Decorated Legion of Merit. Clubs: Century Assn., Univ. (N.Y.C.); Tokeneke (Darien). Home: 28 Driftway Ln Darien CT 06820 Office: NY Community Trust 415 Madison Ave New York NY 10017

WEST, HOWARD NORTON, dept. store exec.; b. N.Y.C., May 3, 1919; s. Abraham D. and Flora (Simpson) W.; B.A., Columbia, 1940; m. Caroline E. Dawley, Dec. 15, 1945; 1 son, Andrew D. With Price Waterhouse & Co., C.P.A's, San Francisco, 1945-52; with Carter Hawley Hale Stores, Inc., Los Angeles, 1952—, treas., 1963-73, v.p., treas., 1973-76, sr. v.p.-fin., 1976—; v.p. Carter Hawley Hale Credit Corp., 1971-76, pres., 1976—, also dir. Trustee Palos Verdes Peninsula Unified Sch. Dist., 1961-67, pres., 1964-65; trustee Chadwick Sch. (Roessler-Chadwick Found.), 1967-69, treas., 1967-69; trustee, pres. So. Calif. Regional Occupation Center, 1967-69; commr. Ednl. Research Commn. of Calif. Legislature, 1970-72. Served with USNR 1941-45; PTO. C.P.A., Calif. Mem. Am. Inst. C.P.A.'s, Calif. C. of C. Clubs: Pacific Coast Stock Exchange, Jonathan. Home: 527 17th St Santa Monica CA 90402 Office: 550 S Flower St Los Angeles CA 90071

WEST, JAMES LEROY, leather co. exec.; b. Gravity, Iowa, May 28, 1903; s. Edgar and Anna (Heatherington) W.; student Grinnell Coll., 1919-22, St. Louis U. Sch. Commerce, 1925-26; m. Eunice Pearl East, Jan. 6, 1937. Salesman, Seiberling Rubber Co., Ft. Worth, also Abilene, Tex., 1927-30; mgr. Hinckley-Tandy Leather Co., Houston, 1930-41, partner, 1941-50; dir. Tandy Leather Co., Ft. Worth, 1951-55, v.p., 1955-57, pres., 1957-64, also dir.; pres. Tandy Corp., Wilmington, Del., 1964-74, vice chmn. bd., 1974—; dir. Continental Nat. Bank. Mem. exec. bd. Longhorn council Boy Scouts Am.; bd. dirs. Jr. Achievement of Tarrant County (Tex.), Carter Blood Center, Ft. Worth, Tex. Presbyn. Found., Tex. Wesleyan Found., Ft. Worth, YMCA of Ft. Worth. Mem. Ft. Worth Sales Mgrs. Club, Tex. Asso. Bd. Bus. (state pres. 1968), West Tex. C. of C. (bd. dirs.), Newcomen Soc. N.Am. (honoree 1968). Presbyterian. Club: Masons. Home: 6371 Lansdale Fort Worth TX 76116 Office: 1900 One Tandy Center Fort Worth TX 76102

WEST, JERRY, profl. basketball exec.; b. Chelyan, W.Va., May 28, 1938; grad. W.Va. Coll.; married; two sons. Mem. Los Angeles Lakers Nat. Basketball Assn. team, 1960-74, coach, 1976-79, spl. cons., 1979—; mem. Nat. Basketball Assn. All Star Team, 1961-74, Championship team, 1972. Author: (with William Libby) Mr. Clutch: The Jerry West Story, 1969. Address: Los Angeles Lakers 3900 W Manchester Blvd Los Angeles CA 90306*

WEST, JESSAMYN, novelist; b. Ind., 1902; student Whittier Coll., U. Calif., also studied in Eng.; hon. doctorates Whittier Coll., Mills Coll., Ind. U., Swarthmore Coll., Western Coll. for Women; m. H.M. McPherson. Tchr. at writers confs. Bread Loaf, U. Notre Dame, U. Wash., Ind. U., U. Utah, Stanford, U. Colo., U. Ky.; former writer in residence Wellesley Coll., Mill Coll. Trustee Whittier Coll. Mem. bd. Foster Parents Plan. Mem. Am. Civil Liberties Union, N.A.A.C.P. Mem. Soc. of Freinds. Writer movie scripts The Big Country, Stolen Hours. Author: To See the Dream; Cress Delahanty (also pub. as series in New Yorker mag.); Mirror for the Sky, 1948; The Witch Diggers; The Friendly Persuasion (wrote screenplay for motion picture), 1956; Love, Death and the Ladies Drill Team, 1955; Love Is Not What You Think, 1958; South of the Angels, 1960; The Quaker Reader, 1961; A Matter of Time, 1966; Leafy River, 1967; Except for Me and Thee, 1969; Crimson Ramblers of the World, Farewell, 1970; Hide and Seek, 1973; The Secret Look, 1974; Massacre at Fall Creek, 1975; The Woman Said Yes, 1976; The Life I Really Lived, 1979. Contbr. to mags., including McCalls, Good Housekeeping, Red Book, New Yorker. Home: 2480 3d Ave Napa CA 94558 Office: care Harcourt Brace & Co 757 3d Ave New York NY 10017

WEST, JOHN BURNARD, physician, educator; b. Adelaide, Australia, Dec. 27, 1928; s. Esmond Frank and Meta Pauline (Spehr) W.; M.B.B.S., Adelaide U., 1952, M.D., 1958; Ph.D., London U., 1960; m. Penelope Hall Banks, Oct. 28, 1967; children—Robert Burnard, Joanna Ruth. Came to U.S., 1969. Intern Royal Adelaide Hosp., 1952; resident Hammersmith Hosp., London, Eng., 1953-55; physiologist Sir Edmund Hillary's Himalayan Expdn., 1960-61; dir. respiratory research group Postgrad. Med. Sch., London, 1962-67, reader medicine, 1968; prof. medicine U. Calif. at San Diego, 1969—. Mem. A.A.A.S., Am. Physiol. Soc., Am. Soc. Clin. Investigation, Brit. Physiol. Soc., Am., Brit. thoracic socs., Royal Coll. Physicians (London), Assn. Am. Physicians, Western Assn. Physicians, Western Soc. Clin. Research. Club: Hurlingham. Author: Ventilation/Blood Flow and Gas Exchange, 1965; Respiratory Physiology-The Essentials, 1974; Pulmonary Pathophysiology-The Essentials, 1977; also articles. Home: 9626 Blackgold Rd LaJolla CA 92037

WEST, JOHN CALVIN, bass; b. Cleve., Oct. 25, 1938; s. Howard Kenneth and Marie Hattie (Mullen) W.; student Eastman Sch. Music, 1956-58; grad. diploma Curtis Inst. Music, 1962. Debut, N.Y.C., 1962; orch. and opera appearances include: Phila. Orch., 1961, N.Y. Philharmonic, 1965, Spoleto (Italy) Festival, 1966, Chgo. Symphony, 1967, Cleve. Orch., 1975, Syracuse (N.Y.) Symphony, 1976, Milw. Symphony, 1977, Seattle Symphony, 1978, Dallas Civic Opera, 1977, Chgo. Lyric Opera, 1978, Puebla (Mexico) Festival, 1973; concert singer; mem. faculty Juilliard Sch. Music; pvt. tchr. voice, N.Y.C.; tchr. master classes at various univs. Winner awards Tchaikovsky Internat. Competition, 1970, Munich (W. Ger.) Internat. Competition, 1967, Met. Opera Auditions, 1961, Young Artists, Phila. Orch., 1961; W. M. Sullivan Found. grantee, 1962; Martha Baird Rockefeller Fund for Music grantee, 1970. Mem. Nat. Assn. Tchrs. Singing. Republican. Office: Juilliard Sch Music Lincoln Center New York NY 10023. *I have always believed in honesty and integrity in all facets of my career. Whether performing or teaching, respect for my art has been my overriding principle.*

WEST, JOHN CARL, banker; b. Austin, Tex., Oct. 25, 1940; s. J.S. West; B.B.A., U. Tex., 1962, LL.B., 1963; m. Lynn Painter, July 26, 1974; children—Carrie Lynn and Elizabeth Ann (twins). Accountant, Weller, Hall & Gano, C.P.A.'s, Houston, 1965-67; with Tex. Commerce Bank, Houston, 1968—, exec. v.p., exec. trust officer, 1976—. C.P.A., Tex. Mem. Am. Inst. C.P.A.'s, Tex. Soc. C.P.A.'s, Houston Estate and Fin. Forum, Houston Bus. and Estate Planning Council. Clubs: Houston, Lakeside Country. Office: PO Box 2558 712 Main St Houston TX 77001

WEST, JOHN CARL, ambassador; b. Camden, S.C., Aug. 27, 1922; s. Shelton J. and Mattie (Ratterree) W.; A.B., The Citadel, 1942; LL.B. magna cum laude, U. S.C., 1948; m. Lois Rhame, Aug. 29, 1948; children—John Carl, Douglas Allen, Shelton Anne. Admitted to S.C. bar, 1948; partner firm West, Holland and Furman, Camden, from 1948; mem. S.C. Senate, 1954-66; lt. gov., then gov. State of S.C.; ambassador to Kingdom of Saudi Arabia, 1977—. Served to maj. AUS, 1942-46. Mem. Am. Legion, Kershaw County C. of C. (pres. 1954), Phi Beta Kappa. Democrat. Presbyterian (elder). Club: Kiwanis.

WEST, JOHN DUNHAM, mfg. co. exec.; b. Chgo., May 24, 1906; s. Charles C. and Julia B. (Dunham) W.; student Beloit Coll., 1924-25; M.E., Cornell U., 1932; m. Ruth Cronk St. John, June 28, 1932. Pres. Manitowoc Co., Inc. (Wis.), 1957—; also dir.; pres. Manitowoc Engring. Co., Manitowoc Shipbuilding, Inc.; chief exec. officer Bay Shipbuilding Corp. dir. Manitowoc Savs. Bank; dir. emeritus Employers Ins. of Wausau (Wis.). Mem. Soc. Advancement Mgmt. (Profl. Mgr. citation 1959). Home: 915 Memorial Dr Manitowoc WI 54220 Office: PO Box 66 Manitowoc WI 54220

WEST, JOHN OLIVER, educator; b. El Paso, Tex., Jan. 1, 1925; s. John Milton and Bertha Maxwell (Billingslea) W.; B.A., Miss. Coll., 1948; M.A., Tex. Tech. U., 1951; Ph.D., U. Tex. at Austin, 1964; m. Lucy Lara Fischer, May 29, 1970; 1 dau. by previous marriage—Marianne (Mrs. George B. Raper); 1 son, John Martin. Tchr. English and journalism Central High Sch., Jackson, Miss., 1948-50; teaching asst. English, Tex. Tech. U., 1950-51, 54-55; tchr. history and journalism Gardiner High Sch., Laurel, Miss., 1951-52; asst. prof. English, journalism and pub. relations Miss. Coll., 1952-54; asst. prof. English, W. Tex. State Coll., 1955-56; instr. English and journalism and pub. relations Odessa (Tex.) Coll., 1956-63; mem. faculty U. Tex. at El Paso, 1963—, prof. English, 1966—, head dept., 1965-71; speaker in field. County dir. Ector County (Tex.) chpt. Nat. Found., 1960-62. Served with USNR, 1942, 44-45. Mem. Tex. Folklore Soc. (councillor 1957-60, pres. 1968-69), Westerners. Author: Tom Lea: Artist in Two Mediums, 1967; (introduction) Forty Years A Gambler on the Mississippi, 1967; also articles. Editor Am. Folklore Newsletter, 1970-79. Home: 2308 N Florence El Paso TX 79902

WEST, LEE ROY, lawyer; b. Clayton, Okla., Nov. 26, 1929; s. Calvin and Nicie (Hill) W.; B.A., U. Okla., 1952, J.D., 1956; LL.M. (Ford Found. fellow), Harvard U., 1963; m. MaryAnn Ellis, Aug. 29, 1952; children—Kimberly Ellis, Jennifer Lee. Admitted to Okla. bar, 1956; individual practice law, Ada, Okla., 1956-61, 63-65; faculty U. Okla. Coll. Law, 1961-62; judge 22d Jud. Dist. Okla., Ada, 1965-73; mem. CAB, Washington, 1973-78, acting chmn., 1977; individual practice law, Tulsa, 1978—; spl. justice Okla. Supreme Ct., 1965; U.S. dist. judge Western Dist. Okla., 1979—. Served to capt. USMC, 1952-54.

Mem. U. Okla. Alumni Assn. (dir.), Phi Delta Phi (pres. 1956), Phi Eta Sigma, Order of Coif. Editor Okla. Law Rev. Home: 9803 Hefner Village Pl Oklahoma City OK 73102 Office: 3001 Federal Courthouse Oklahoma City OK 73102

WEST, LEWIS HARMON, corrosion engr.; b. Ridley Park, Pa., Nov. 23, 1924; s. Harmon and Doris H. (Heineman) W.; student Pa. State U., 1942-44; B.S. in Mech. Engring., Cornell U., 1945; m. Agnes D., Apr. 19, 1973; children—James L., Susan L. Engr., Texas Eastern Transp. Corp., Shreveport, La., 1946-49; div. corrosion engr. Standard Oil Co. (Ohio), Cleve., 1949-61; pres., owner Hinchman Co., cons. corrosion engrs., Detroit, 1961-75; cons. corrosion engring., Punta Gorda, Fla., 1975—; gen. chmn. Appalachina Underground Corrosion Short Course, 1964; lectr. corrosion short courses, 1958-75. Served with USNR, 1944-46. Registered profl. engr., 21 states. Fellow Cons. Engrs. Council; mem. Nat. Assn. Corrosion Engrs. (certified, citation of recognition 1973), ASME, Nat. Council State Bds. Engring. Examiners (qualified), U.S. Power Squadrons. Clubs: Isles Yacht, Masons, Elks. Author: The Duriron Iron Manual, 1965; U.S. Air Force Manual on Corrosion and Its Control, 1972-74; contbr. numerous articles on corrosion and its control to profl. jours. Home: 2490 Palm Tree Dr Punta Gorda FL 33950 Office: PO Box 940 Punta Gorda FL 33950

WEST, LOUIS JOLYON, psychiatrist; b. N.Y.C., Oct. 6, 1924; s. Albert Jerome and Anna (Rosenberg) W.; B.S., U. Minn., 1946, M.B., 1948, M.D., 1949; m. Kathryn Louise Hopkirk, Apr. 29, 1944; children—Anne Kathryn, Mary Elizabeth, John Stuart. Mem. faculty Cornell U., 1950-52; chief psychiatry service USAF Hosp., Lackland AFB, San Antonio, 1952-56; prof. psychiatry, head dept. psychiatry, neurology and behavioral scis. U. Okla. Sch. Medicine, 1954-69; chief mental health sect. Okla. Med. Research Found., 1956-69; cons. psychiatry Oklahoma City VA Hosp., Tinker AFB Hosp., 1956-69; prof., chmn. dept. psychiatry and biobehavioral sci. UCLA, 1969—, dir. Neuropsychiat. Inst. at Center for Health Scis., 1969—; psychiatrist-in-chief U. Calif. at Los Angeles Hosp. and Clinics, 1969—; nat. cons. psychiatry Surgeon Gen. USAF, 1957-62; cons. psychiatry Brentwood and Sepulveda VA hosps., 1969—. Mem. nat. adv. coms. NIMH, USAF Office Sci. Research, USPHS, VA, HEW, Nat. Acad. Scis., NRC, Nat. Inst. Medicine, U.S. Army Med. Research and Devel. Panel, A.M.A., White House Conf. Civil Rights; mem. internat. adv. bd. Israeli Center for Psychobiology, Kittay Found., Jerusalem Mental Health Center. Bd. dirs. Brain Research Inst., UCLA Found., Alcoholism Council Calif. Diplomate Nat. Bd. Med. Examiners, Am. Bd. Psychiatry and Neurology. Fellow AAAS, Am. Coll. Neuropsychopharmacology (founding), Am. Coll. Psychiatrists, Am. Psychiat. Assn.; mem. AMA, Am. Acad. Psychiatry and Law, Soc. Biol. Psychiatry, Am. Orthopsychiat. Assn., Acad. Psychoanalysis, Assn. Psychophysiol. Study Sleep, Am. Psychosomatic Soc., Am. Psychopath. Assn., Am. Psychol. Assn., Assn. Research in Nervous and Mental Disease, Assn. Am. Med. Colls., Nat. Acad. Religion and Mental Health (founding), Nat. Council on Alcoholism, Pavlovian Soc. (pres. 1975), Soc. Biol. Psychiatry, Soc. Psychophysiol. Research, So. Profs. Psychiatry (pres. 1963), Soc. Clin. and Exptl. Hypnosis, Alpha Omega Alpha. Author: Explorations in the Physiology of Emotions, 1960; Hallucinations, 1962; Hallucinations: Behavior, Experience, and Theory, 1975; Treatment of Schizophrenia: Progress and Prospects, 1976; Research on Smoking Behavior, 1977; Progress in Behavioral Medicine, 1980. Editorial bd. Med. Aspects of Human Sexuality, Psychiatry Update, Med. Update. Contbr. articles to profl. jours., chpts. in books. Office: U Calif Center for Health Scis Neuropsychiatric Inst 760 Westwood Plaza Los Angeles CA 90024. *When I began my career in psychiatry more than thirty years ago, it was with a great sense of adventure. Psychiatry was a specialty just beginning to fulfill its enormous potentialities. Surely numerous mysteries of human nature, of sanity and madness, of prevention and cure would yield to the onslaughts of modern science and ultra modern technology! Alas, most of the mysteries have not yet yielded. But we are making progress; the joy lies in the search; and the search continues.*

WEST, MAE, actress; b. Bklyn., Aug. 17, 1892; d. John Patrick and Matilda (Delker-Dolger) West; privately tutored; m. Frank Wallace, 1911 (dissolved 1943). Theatrical appearances include Little Nell the Marchioness, 1897, Mrs. Wiggs of The Cabbage Patch, Ten Nights in a Barroom, East Lynne, The Fatal Wedding (all 1897-1903), A la Broadway, 1911, Vera Violetta, 1911, A Winsome Widow, 1912, Such is Life, 1913, Sometime, 1918, Demi-Tasse, 1919, The Mimic World, 1921, Sex, 1926, The Wicked Age, 1927, Diamond Lil, 1928, The Constant Sinner, 1931, Catherine Was Great, 1944; on tour in Vaudeville's Youngest Headliner, 1913-18, Ring Twice Tonight, 1946, Diamond Lil, 1948, 49, 49-50, 1951, Come on Up . . . Ring Twice, 1952, Sextet, 1961; motion picture appearances include Night After Night, 1932, She Done Him Wrong, 1933, I'm No Angel, 1933, Bell of the Nighties, 1934, Goin' to Town, 1935, Klondike Annie, 1936, Go West, Young Man, 1936, Every Day's a Holiday, 1937, My Little Chickadee, 1940, The Heat's On, 1943, Myra Breckenridge, 1969, Sextette, 1978. Author: (play) Pleasure Man, 1928; The Drag, 1927; (autobiography) Goodness Had Nothing to Do With It, 1959; (novels) Diamond Lil, The Constant Sinner. LP rec. The Naked Ape. Address: care William Morris Agy Inc 1740 Broadway New York NY 10019*

WEST, MARY JANE, publisher; b. Winnetka, Ill., July 16, 1942; d. Elmer William and Georgia (Kerr) Glaeser; B.A., Vassar Coll., 1963; m. Charles Peyton West, Feb. 19, 1966; children—Peyton MacLean, Georgia Kerr. Asst. editor Institut fur Erforschung der U.d. S.S.R., Munich, 1963; budget officer L'Organisation Europeene de Recherches Spatiales, Paris, France, 1964-65; sr. editor Clarkson N. Potter, Inc., N.Y.C., 1967-75, exec. editor, 1975-76, editor-in-chief, 1976-77, v.p., pub., 1977—; exec. editor Barre Pub. Co., 1975-76, editor-in-chief, 1976—. Bd. dirs., sec. Virginia Day Nurseries Inc., N.Y.C. Office: One Park Ave S New York NY 10016

WEST, MICHAEL ALAN, hosp. adminstr.; b. Waseca, Minn., Aug. 4, 1938; s. Ralph Leland and Elizabeth Mary (Brann) W.; B.A., U. Minn., 1961, M.H.A., 1963; m. Mary Thissen, Jan. 21, 1961; children—Anne, Nancy, Douglas. Sales corr. Physicians and Hosps. Supply Co., Mpls., 1959-60; adminstrv. resident R.I. Hosp., Providence, 1962-63, adminstrv. asst., 1963-65, asst. dir., 1965-68; exec. asst. dir. Med. Center U. Mo., Columbia, 1968-70, asso. dir., 1970-74, asst. prof. community health and med. practice, 1968-74; v.p. for adminstrn. Luth. Gen. Hosp., Park Ridge, Ill., 1974—. Former vice pres., mem. exec. com., chmn. personnel St. Elizabeth's Home, Providence. Mem. Am., Ill., Chgo. hosp. assns., Am. Coll. Hosp. Adminstrs., N. Suburban Assn. Health Resources (dir.); Park Ridge C. of C. (dir.). Rotarian. Home: 1720 N Beech Rd Mount Prospect IL 60056 Office: 1775 Dempster St Park Ridge IL 60068

WEST, MILLARD FARRAR, JR., banker; b. Washington, Jan. 14, 1910; s. Millard Farrar and Elizabeth (Leech) W.; grad. Blair Acad., Blairstown, N.J., 1928; A.B., Princeton, 1932; LL.B., Nat. U., 1935; m. Emily Stuart Maddox, Oct. 16, 1935, (dec. June 1967); children—Margot West Anderson, Janet Maddox; m. 2d, Doris Aileen Thomas, Oct. 5, 1968. Vice pres. Ferris & Co., Washington, 1933-41; partner Auchincloss, Parker & Redpath, Washington, 1945-70; v.p. Thomson & McKinnon Securities, Inc., Washington, 1970—; dir. Giant Food, Inc., Dist. Photo, Inc., Dewey Electronics Corp., Greater Washington Investors, Inc. Active United Givers Fund; past chmn. Nat. Symphony Sustaining Fund drive; trustee treas. Va. Theol. Sem.; past chmn. finance com. Washington Home for Incurables; mem. finance com., treas. Episcopal Diocese of Washington. Served to lt. col., USAAF, 1941-45. Decorated Legion of Merit. Home: 18 W Kirke St Chevy Chase MD 20015 Office: 1705 H St NW Washington DC 20006

WEST, MORRIS LANGLO, novelist; b. Melbourne, Australia, Apr. 26, 1916; s. Charles Langlo and Florence Guilfoyle (Hanlon) W.; B.A., U. Melbourne, 1937; Litt.D., U. Santa Clara, 1969; m. Joyce Lawford; children—Christopher, Paul, Melanie, Michael. Tchr. modern lang., mathematics, New South Wales, Tasmania, 1933-39; sec. to William Morris Hughes (former prime minister Australia), 1943. Served to lt. Australian Imperial Forces, 1939-43; PTO. Recipient Internat. Dag Hammarskjold prize (grand collar of merit), 1978. Fellow Royal Soc. Lit., World Acad. Arts and Sci. Clubs: Royal Prince Alfred Yacht (Sydney, Australia); Wentworth Golf (Surrey, Eng.). Author: Gallows on the Sand, 1955; Kundu, 1956; Children of the Sun, 1957; The Crooked Road (English title: The Big Story), 1957; The Concubine, 1958; Backlash (English title: The Second Victory), 1958; The Devil's Advocate (Nat. Brotherhood award Nat. Council Christians and Jews 1960, James Tait Black Meml. award 1960, William Hienemann award Royal Soc. 1960, filmed 1977), 1959; The Naked Country, 1960; Daughter of Silence, 1961; Daughter of Silence (play), 1961; The Shoes of the Fisherman, 1963; The Ambassador, 1965; Tower of Babel, 1968; (with R. Francis) Scandal in the Assembly, 1970; The Heretic, A Play in Three Acts, 1970; Summer of the Red Wolf, 1971; the Salamander, 1973; Harlequin, 1974; The Navigator, 1976; Proteus, 1979. Office: care Greenbaum Wolff & Ernst 437 Madison Ave New York NY 10022

WEST, PHILIP WILLIAM, educator; b. Crookston, Minn., Apr. 12, 1913; s. William Leonard and Anne (Thompson) W.; B.S., U. N.D., 1935, M.S., 1936, D.Sc. (hon.), 1958; Ph.D., State U. Iowa, 1939; postgrad., Rio de Janeiro, 1946; m. Tenney Constance Johnson, July 5, 1935 (dec. Feb. 1964); children—Dorothy Anne, Linda West Gueho, Patty West Elstrott; m. 2d, Foymae S. Kelso, July 1, 1964. Chemist, N.D. Geol. Survey, 1935-36; research asst. san. chemistry U. Iowa, 1936-37; asst. chemist Iowa Dept. Health, 1937-40; research microchemist Econ. Lab., Inc., St. Paul, 1940; faculty La. State U., 1940—, prof. chemistry, 1951—, Boyd prof., 1953—, chmn. ann. symposium modern methods of analytical chemistry, 1948-65, dir. Inst. for Environmental Scis., 1967—; O. M. Smith lectr. Okla. State U., 1955; vis. prof. U. Colo. 1963; adj. prof. EPA, 1969—; founder Kem-Tech. Labs., Inc., Baton Rouge, 1954, chmn. bd., 1965-74; co-founder West-Paine Labs., Inc., Baton Rouge, 1978, chmn. bd., 1978—; mem. 1st working party sci. com. on problems of environment, 1971-74. Pres. analytical sect. Internat. Union Pure and Applied Chemistry, 1965-69, mem. sect. indsl. hygiene and toxicology, 1971-73, mem. air quality sect., 1973-75; mem. tech. adv. com. La. Air Pollution Control Com.; cons. WHO. Recipient Charles E. Coates award Am. Inst. Chemistry, 1967, Honor Scroll award La. sect., 1972. Fellow AAAS; mem. Am. Chem. Soc. (Southwest award 1954, Analytical Chemistry award 1974), La. Acad. Sci., Air Pollution Control Assn., Am. Indsl. Hygene Assn., Austrian Microchem. Soc. (hon.), Soc. of Analysts (Hon.), Internat. Union Pure and Applied Chemistry (pres. commn. I), Japan Soc. for Analytical Chemistry (hon.), Sigma Xi, Phi Lambda Upsilon, Phi Kappa Phi, Alpha Epsilon Delta, Alpha Chi Sigma, Tau Kappa Epsilon. Author: Chemical Calculations, 1948; (with Vick) Qualitative Analysis and Analytical Chemical Separations, 2d edit., 1959; (with Bustin) Experience Approach to Experimental Chemistry, 1975. Editor: Science of the Total Environment, 1973-78. Editor Analytica Chimica Acta, 1959-78; Reagents and Reaction for Qualitative Inorganic Analysis; co-editor Analytical Chemistry, 1963; asst. editor Mikrochemica Acta, 1952-78, Michrochem. Jour., 1957-75; advisory bd. Analytical Chemistry, 1959-60; publ. bd. Jour. Chem. Edn., 1954-57. Contbr. articles to profl. jours. Home: 605 Nelson Dr Baton Rouge LA 70808

WEST, QUENTIN MECHAM, govt. ofcl.; b. Morgan, Utah, June 27, 1920; s. Preston D. and Genevieve E. (Mecham) W.; B.S., Utah State U., 1948, M.S., 1949; Ph.D., Cornell U., 1951; m. Ila Lee Martin, Mar. 30, 1944; children—Kenlee, LaQuen, Nuel, Raul. Agrl. economist Inter-Am. Inst. Agrl. Sci., Lima, Peru, 1953-56; asso. prof. Cornell U., Ithaca, N.Y., 1956; chief Far East br., fgn. regional analysis div. ERS, Agr. Dept., Washington, 1958-62, dep. div. dir., 1962-65, dir., 1965-69, adminstr. Fgn. Econ. Devel. Service, 1969-71; adminstr. Econ. Research Service, 1972-77, spl. asst. for internat. sci. and tech. cooperation Office of Sec., 1977-78; dir. Office Internat. Coop. and Devel., 1978—; vice chmn. joint com. U.S./USSR Agrl. Agreement, 1974—; chmn. agrl. com. Joint Commn. Econ. Devel. U.S./Saudi Arabia, U.S./Iran, U.S./Egypt, 1974—; U.S. rep. on bd. dirs. Inter-Am. Inst. Agrl. Scis., 1974—; instr. Agr. Dept. Grad. Sch., 1957—; agrl. econs. Utah State U., 1953. Scoutmaster Boy Scouts Am., 1965-69, regional coordinator, 1969—, mem. council exec. bd., 1976—. Served to 1st lt. AUS, World War II. Recipient Superior Service award Agr. Dept., 1965, Distinguished Service Group award, 1972. Mem. Am. Agrl. Econs. Assn. (Outstanding Thesis award 1952), Internat. Agr. Assn., Alpha Zeta. Mem. Ch. of Jesus Christ of Latter-day Saints (high council 1974-77, stake yM 1977—). Home: 1007 Poplar Dr Falls Church VA 22046 Office: Office Internat Coop and Devel Dept Agr 14th St and Independence Ave SW Washington DC 20250

WEST, RAY BENEDICT, JR., educator, author; b. Logan, Utah, July 30, 1908; s. Ray B. and Mary (Morrell) W.; B.S., Utah State U., 1933; M.A., U. Utah, 1935; Ph.D., U. Iowa, 1945; m. Lucille McMullin, Apr. 28, 1934; children—Lelia West Schoenberg, Julie West Staheli. Asso. prof. English, Utah State U., 1945-46, U. Kans., 1946-49; prof. English, U. Iowa, 1949-59; prof. English, San Francisco State U., 1959—, chmn. creative writing dept., 1968-73; Fulbright prof. U. Innsbruck (Austria), 1951-52; chmn. Am. lit. U. Ankara (Turkey), 1957-58. Mem. Utah Fine Arts Bd., 1976—. Mem. MLA, United Calif. Profs., P.E.N. Club. Author or editor 16 books, including Rocky Mountain Reader, 1946; The Art of Modern Fiction, 1949; The Short Story in America, 1952; Kingdom of the Saints, 1957; The Writer in the Room, 1968; founder, editor Western Rev., 1936-59; poetry editor Contact, 1959-60; editorial com. Studies in Short Fiction, 1963—. Home: Santaquin UT 84655

WEST, RICHARD LUTHER, army officer; b. Ithaca, N.Y., Jan. 8, 1925; s. Luther W. and Beatrice E. (Ryan) W.; student No. Mich. Coll., 1941-42; B.S., U.S. Mil. Acad., 1945; M.S., Princeton U., 1954; M.B.A., George Washington U., 1965; m. June D. Kirby, June 5, 1945; children—John R., Lesley A., Peter L. Commd. 2d lt. U.S. Army, 1945, advanced through grades to lt. gen., 1977; comptroller of the Army, Washington, 1977—. Decorated Legion of Merit with 3 oak leaf clusters, Bronze Star, Air medal with 2 oak leaf clusters, Army Commendation medal with oak leaf cluster. Mem. Assn. U.S. Army, Soc. Am. Mil. Engrs., Am. Soc. Mil. Comptrollers, Am. Preparedness Assn., Sigma Xi. Home: 2 Fort McNair Washington DC 20024 Office: Office Comptroller of Army Dept Army Washington DC 20310

WEST, RICHARD ROLLIN, coll. dean; b. Cleve., Feb. 15, 1938; s. Myron and Lucille Millicent (Shurmer) W.; B.A., Yale, 1960; M.B.A., U. Chgo., 1963, Ph.D., 1964; Joanne Marilyn Lewis, Mar. 22, 1958; children—Michael, Charles, James, Phillip. Mem. faculty Cornell U., 1964-72, prof. bus., 1970-72, asso. dean Sch. Bus., 1968-72; prof. bus., dean Coll. Bus., U. Oreg., Eugene, 1972-76; dean Amos Tuck Sch., Dartmouth Coll., 1976—; cons. in field. Dir. Liberty Communications, Inc., Bohemia, Inc. Mem., chmn. Municipal Securities Rulemaking Bd.; trustee Coll. Retirement Equities Fund. Author: Financial Policy Decisions, 1971; Economics of the Stock Market, 1971. Asso. editor Jour. Fin. and Quantitative Analysis. Contbr. articles to profl. jours. Office: Amos Tuck Sch Dartmouth Coll Hanover NH 03755

WEST, RICHARD VINCENT, museum dir.; b. Prague, Czechoslovakia, Nov. 26, 1934; s. Jan Josef and Katherine Frieda (Mayer) Vyslouzil; came to U.S., 1938, naturalized, 1947; B.A. with highest honors, U. Calif., Santa Barbara, 1961; postgrad. Acad. Fine Arts, Vienna, Austria, 1961-62; M.A., U. Calif., Berkeley, 1965; m. Emilyann Pagenhart, June 26, 1961; 1 dau., Jessica Katherine. Curatorial intern Cleve. Mus. Art, 1965-66, Albright-Knox Art Gallery, Buffalo, 1966-67; curator, dir. Bowdoin Coll. Mus. Art, Brunswick, Maine, 1967-72; dir. Crocker Art Mus., Sacramento, 1973—; mem. Joint Yugoslav-Am. Excavations, Sirmium, 1971; organizer exhbns. Served with USN, 1956-57. Ford Found. fellow, 1965-67; Smithsonian fellow, 1971. Mem. Am., Western (pres. 1975-77) assns. art museums, Assn. Art Mus. Dirs., Internat. Council Museums, Coll. Art Assn. Author: Language of the Print, 1968; Walker Art Building Murals, 1972. Editor: The Pre-Rembrandtists, 1974; Charles Christian Nahl: Artist of the Gold Rush, 1976; Munich and American Realism in the 19th Century, 1978. Office: 216 O St Sacramento CA 95814

WEST, ROBERT COOPER, educator; b. Enid, Okla., June 30, 1913; s. George Washington and Elva A. (Cooper) W.; A.B., U. Calif. at Los Angeles, 1935, M.A., 1938; Ph.D., U. Calif. at Berkeley, 1946; m. Phyllis Devereaux, May 11, 1968. Cartographer OSS, Washington, 1941-45; geographer Smithsonian Instn., Mexico City office, 1946-48; asst. prof. to prof. La. State U. at Baton Rouge, 1948—, Boyd prof., 1970—. Vis. prof. U. Wis. at Madison, 1966, U. Calif. at Los Angeles, 1968, U. Ariz. at Tucson, 1972, 76. Recipient Alumni Faculty award, La. State U., 1965. Guggenheim fellow, 1955. Mem. A.A.A.S., Assn. Am. Geographers (citation for meritorious contbn., 1964, Outstanding Achievement award 1973), Am. Geog. Soc., Latin Am. Studies Assn., Sigma Xi. Author: (with others) Middle America, its lands and peoples, 2d edit., 1976; other books. Vol. editor: Handbook Middle American Indians, vol. 1, Natural Environment and Early Cultures, 1964. Home: 4815 Tulane Dr Baton Rouge LA 70808 Office: Dept Geography and Anthropology La State U Baton Rouge LA 70803

WEST, ROBERT CRAWLEY, engring. co. exec.; b. Keytesville, Mo., Apr. 26, 1920; s. George and Bertie (Taylor) W.; B.C.E., Ga. Inst. Tech., 1949; m. Willie Mae Burgess, June 12, 1946; children—Robert Crawley, Susan. Project mgr. H.K. Ferguson Co., 1950-53; with Sverdrup & Parcel & Assos., Inc., St. Louis, 1953—, exec. v.p., 1969-75, chief operating officer, 1973-75, pres., chief exec. officer, 1975-77, chmn. bd., pres., 1977—; dir. First Nat. Bank, St. Louis, Gen. Steel Industries. Bd. dirs. Mo. Goodwill Industries, Goodwill Industries Am., YMCA Greater St. Louis, Ranken Tech. Inst., Jr. Achievement Mississippi Valley, Inc., St. Louis Symphony Soc.; United Way Greater St. Louis; trustee Drury Coll., Springfield, Mo., Webster Coll., St. Louis; mem. president's council St. Louis U.; exec. bd. St. Louis area council Boy Scouts Am.; bd. dirs. St. Louis Arts and Edn. Council, 1976-77. Served with AUS, 1942-46. Named Engr. of Year, Mo. Soc. Profl. Engrs., 1976; recipient Engring. Achievement award Engrs. Club St. Louis, 1977; named Constrn. Industry Man of Yr., PRIDE/St. Louis, 1978. Registered profl. engr., Mo., 13 other states. Mem. ASCE (pres. St. Louis 1974-75), Am. Cons. Engrs. Council, Nat., Mo. socs. profl. engrs., Soc. Am. Mil. Engrs., ASTM, Brit. Tunnelling Soc., Internat. Assn. Bridge and Structural Engring., Internat. Bridge, Tunnel and Turnpike Assn., Beavers, Moles, Transp. Research Bd., Am. Def. Preparedness Assn. (dir.), St. Louis Regional Commerce and Growth Assn. (dir.), Civic Progress, Municipal Theatre Assn. Clubs: Engineers, Mo. Athletic, Media, St. Louis, Ambassadors, Old Warson Country (St. Louis); Round Table, Bogey Country. Home: 11 Exmoor Dr Saint Louis MO 63124 Office: 800 N 11th St Saint Louis MO 63101

WEST, ROBERT CULBERTSON, chemist, educator; b. Glen Ridge, N.J., Mar. 18, 1928; s. Robert C. and Constance (MacKinnon) W.; B.A., Cornell U., 1950; A.M., Harvard, 1952, Ph.D., 1954; children—David Russell, Arthur Scott. Asst. prof. Lehigh U., 1954-56; mem. faculty U. Wis.-Madison, 1956—, prof. chemistry, 1963—. Indsl. and govt. cons., 1961—; Abbott lectr. U. N.D., 1964; Fulbright lectr. Kyoto U., 1964-65; vis. prof. U. Würzburg, 1968-69, Haile Selassie I U., 1972, U. Calif., Santa Cruz, 1977; Japan Soc. for Promotion Sci. vis. prof. Tohoku U., 1976; Lady Davis vis. prof. Hebrew U., 1979. Pres. Madison Community Sch., 1970-71. Bd. dirs. Women's Med. Fund, 1971—. Recipient F.S. Kipping award, 1970; Amoco Distinguished Teaching award, 1974; Jean Day Meml. lectr. Rutgers U., 1973. Mem. Am. Chem. Soc., Chem. Soc. (London), Japan Chem. Soc., A.A.A.S., Wis. Acad. Sci. Co-editor: Advances in Organometallic Chemistry, Vols. I-XIV, 1964-75. Contbr. articles to profl. jours. Home: 4922 Fond du Lac Trail Madison WI 53705

WEST, ROBERT HARTLEY, mfg. co. exec.; b. Kansas City, Mo., May 9, 1938; s. Elmer Lee and Susan (Sigler) W.; A.B., Princeton U., 1960; m. Sarah Ann Steele, Oct. 1, 1960; children—Elizabeth Atwill, Susan Hartley. With 1st Nat. Bank Kansas City (Mo.), 1962-68, v.p., 1967-68; with Butler Mfg. Co., Kansas City, 1968—, exec. v.p., 1976-78, pres., chief operating officer, 1978—; dir. Commerce Bank Kansas City, ERC Corp. Bd. dirs. Crippled Children's Nursery Sch., St. Luke's Hosp. (both Kansas City). Served as officer U.S. Army, 1960-62. Episcopalian. Home: 6426 Sagamore St Shawnee Mission KS 66208 Office: PO Box 917 Kansas City MO 64141

WEST, ROBERT MACLELLAN, museum curator; b. Appleton, Wis., Sept. 1, 1942; s. Clarence John and Elizabeth Ophelia (Moore) W.; B.A., Lawrence Coll., 1963; M.S., U. Chgo., 1964, Ph.D. (NSF fellow), 1968; m. Jean Mary Sydow, June 19, 1965; 1 son, Christopher. Postdoctoral research asso. Princeton U., 1968-69; asst. prof. biology Adelphi U., Garden City, N.Y., 1969-74; curator geology Milw. Pub. Mus., 1974—; adj. asso. prof. geol. sci. U. Wis., Milw., 1974—; hon. research asso. Vertebrate Fossils Carnegie Mus. Natural History, Pitts., 1977—. NSF research grantee, 1970—, Nat. Geog. Soc. research grantee, 1973, 76, 77, 79. Mem. Soc. Vertebrate Paleontology, Paleontol. Soc., Geol. Soc. Am., Soc. for Study Evolution, Soc. Systematic Zoology, Am. Soc. Mammalogists. Contbr. articles to profl. jours. Office: Milw Pub Mus Milwaukee WI 53233

WEST, ROBERT NIAS, lawyer; b. Newtonville, Mass., Sept. 13, 1898; s. Robert F. and Maude (Nias) W.; A.B., Columbia, 1920, LL.B., 1923; m. Mary F. Sime, Nov. 18, 1927; children—Ruth (Mrs. Amory Houghton, Jr.), Judith (Mrs. David F. Sheldon), Maude (Mrs. John Bigelow). Admitted to N.Y. State bar, 1924, since practiced in

N.Y.C.; mem. firm of Shearman & Sterling, and predecessors, 1937—; dir. Seaboard Oil Corp., Granitevaile Co. Mem. Am., N.Y. State bar assns., Assn. Bar City N.Y., Delta Kappa Epsilon, Phi Delta Phi. Protestant Episcopalian. Clubs: University, Down Town Assn. (N.Y.C.); Bedford (N.Y.) Golf and Tennis. Home: Mt Holly Rd Katonah NY 10536 Office: 53 Wall St New York City NY 10005

WEST, ROBERT SETH, lawyer; b. Bklyn., Aug. 31, 1936; s. Raleigh and Ethel (Singer) W.; B.S., U. Calif. at Los Angeles, 1957; J.D., U. So. Calif., 1962; m. Wende Marts, June 28, 1971; children—Wendy, Randall, Daniel, David. Admitted to Calif. bar, 1962, since practiced in Los Angeles; mem. firm De Castro, West & Chodorow, Inc., 1962—. Trustee City of Hope. C.P.A., Calif. Mem. Am., Los Angeles County, Beverly Hills bar assns., State Bar Calif., Order of Coif. Mem. U. So. Calif. Law Rev. Contbr. articles to profl. publs. Home: Bel Air CA also Point Loma CA Office: 10960 Wilshire Blvd Suite 1800 Los Angeles CA 90024 also San Diego CA

WEST, ROBERT VAN OSDELL, JR., petroleum co. exec.; b. Kansas City, Mo., Apr. 29, 1921; s. Robert Van Osdell and Jacqueline (Quistgaard) W.; B.S., U. Tex., 1942, M.S., 1943, Ph.D., 1949; m. Helen L. West; children—Robert Van Osdell, III, Kathryn Anne, Suzanne Small, Patricia Lynn. Petroleum engr. Slick Urschel Oil Co., 1949-56; pres. Slick Secondary Recovery Corp., 1956-59; v.p. Texstar Corp., also pres. subsidiary Texstar Petroleum Co., 1959-64; founder, 1964, since chmn. bd. Tesoro Petroleum Corp., San Antonio; dir. Commonwealth Oil Refining Co., Inc., Continental Telephone Corp., Cullen/Frost Bankers, Inc., High Stoy Tech. Corp.; Engring. Found. adv. council U. Tex.; adv. council Sch. Bus., St. Mary's U. Past trustee San Antonio City Pub. Service Bd.; chmn. bd. dirs. Tiwanaku Archaeol. Found., Bolivia. Named Distinguished Grad., Coll. Engring., U. Tex., 1973; registered profl engr., Tex. Mem. Am. Petroleum Inst. (dir.), Ind. Petroleum Assn. Am. (dir.), Tex. Ind. Producers and Royalty Owners Assn. (dir.), Mid-Continental Oil and Gas Assn. (dir.), Engring. Found., 25 Year Club Petroleum Industry, Greater San Antonio C. of C. (dir.). Episcopalian. Club: All-Am. Wildcatters. Address: 8700 Tesoro Dr San Antonio TX 78286

WEST, STANLEY LEROY, librarian, lawyer; b. Los Angeles, Jan. 15, 1912; s. Allyn Melville and Maude Ethel (Underwood) W.; A.B., U. Calif., 1933; J.D., U. Fla., 1938; B.S. in L.S., Columbia, 1942; m. Caroline Brevard Cockrell, May 30, 1939; children—Courtney Walker, David Alan. Admitted to Fla. bar; asst. law librarian U. Fla., 1938-40; law librarian U. Pitts., 1940-42; asst. to dir. libraries, Columbia, 1942-43, asso. law librarian, 1946; later dir. libraries, head dept. library sci. U. Fla.; univ. librarian, prof. library studies U. Hawaii, 1968-77; adj. prof. Rutgers U. Grad. Sch. Library Service, spring 1961; partner firm West and West, Gainesville, Fla., 1978—. Fulbright lectr., Italy, 1957. Served with USNR, 1943-45. Mem. ALA, Phi Sigma Kappa, Phi Alpha Delta. Episcopalian. Home: 2604 SW 3d Pl Gainesville FL 32607

WEST, TOGO DENNIS, JR., lawyer, govt. ofcl.; b. Winston-Salem, N.C., June 21, 1942; s. Togo Dennis and Evelyn (Carter) W.; B.S. in E.E., Howard U., 1965, J.D. cum laude, 1968; m. Gail Estelle Berry, June 18, 1966; children—Tiffany Berry, Hilary Carter. Admitted to D.C. bar, 1968, N.Y. bar, 1969, U.S. Ct. Mil. Appeals bar, 1969, U.S. Supreme Ct. bar, 1978; elec. engr. Duquesne Light and Power Co., 1965; patent researcher Sughrue, Rothwell, Mion, Zinn and McPeak, 1966-67; legal intern U.S. Equal Employment Opportunity Commn., 1967; law clk. firm Covington & Burling, Washington, 1967-68, spl. asso., 1968, asso., 1973-75, 76-77; law clk. Honorable Harold R. Tyler Judge U.S. Dist. Ct. for So. Dist. N.Y., 1968-69; asso. dep. atty. gen. U.S. Dept. Justice, Washington, 1975-76; gen. counsel Dept. Navy, Washington, 1977-79; spl. asst. to sec. and dept. sec. Dept. Def., Washington, 1979—. Served to capt. Judge Adv. Gen. Corps, U.S. Army, 1969-73. Decorated Legion of Merit. Mem. Am. Bar Assn., Nat. Bar Assn., Washington Council Lawyers (dir. 1973-75). Democrat. Episcopalian. Mng. editor: Howard Law Jour., 1968. Office: Office of the Secretary of Defense Washington DC 20301

WEST, TOMMY (THOMAS R. PICARDO), rec. co. exec.; b. Jersey City, Aug. 17, 1942; s. Thomas R. and Anna (Neviello) Picardo; B.S. in Social Studies, Villanova (Pa.) U., 1963; m. Ann V. Picardo; children—Brad, Blair. Dir. music Radio WR1B, Long Branch N.J., 1963-66; Staff promotion ABC, ABC Records, N.Y.C., 1966; producer, writer Cashwest Prodns. and Lifesong Records, record, comml. prodn., N.Y.C., 1968—; music pub. Blendingwell Music. Freelance singer radio, TV commls. Served with AUS, 1964. Mem. Nat. Acad. Rec. Arts, Scis., ASCAP, Screen Actors Guild, AFTRA, Nat. Songwriters Assn., Country Music Assn. Composer (with Terry Cashman) American City Suite, 1972; producer of Jim Croce, Dion, Gail Davies, Voltage Bros., Nina Kahle, Ed Bruce, Corbin and Hanner records, including own album Hometown Frolics, 1976. Home: Homestead Rd Pottersville NJ 07979 Office: 488 Madison Ave New York NY 10022

WEST, WARREN REED, educator; b. Washington, Aug. 27, 1894; s. Marion Thomas and Isloy (Redmon) W.; A.B., George Washington U., 1918; Ph.D., Johns Hopkins, 1922; m. Gladys Annie Bush, June 16, 1930; 1 son, Thomas Reed. Instr., George Washington U., 1922-26, asst. prof., 1926-29, asso. prof., 1929-35, prof. polit. sci., 1935-61, prof. emeritus in residence, 1961-66, prof. emeritus, 1966—, asst. dean, Sch. Government, 1934-45, dean div. special students, 1945-62. Served with U.S. Army, 1918. Mem. Am. Polit. Sci. Assn. (chmn. com. on election statistics 1941-47). AAUP, Pi Gamma Mu. Republican. Episcopalian. Mason. Clubs: Cosmos. Author books and articles in field. Contbr. articles to polit. sci. publs. Home: 15101 Glade Dr Apt 307 Silver Spring MD 20906

WEST, WILLIAM BEVERLEY, III, lawyer; b. Ft. Worth, Feb. 5, 1922; s. William Beverley, Jr., and Ella Louise (Moore) W.; B.A., U. Tex., 1942, LL.B., 1948; Indsl. Adminstr., Harvard Grad. Sch. Bus. Adminstrn., 1943; LL.M., Columbia, 1949; grad. Command and Gen. Staff Sch. Admitted to Tex. bar, 1949; practice in Ft. Worth; asst. U.S. atty. No. Dist. Tex., 1953, 1st asst. U.S. atty., 1957-58, U.S. atty., 1958-61; exec. asst. to asst. atty. gen., lands div. Dept. Justice, 1961-63; partner Clark, West Keller, Butler & Ellis, Dallas, 1963—; mem. faculty Acad. Am. and Internat. Law, Southwestern Legal Found., research fellow, 1965; mem. adv. bd. Southwestern Law Enforcement Inst., Dallas, 1959—; mem. adv. com. on criminal rules U.S. Jud. Conf., 1973-77. Served from pvt. to capt. AUS, 1942-46. Decorated Bronze Star. Fellow Tex. Bar Found.; mem. Inst. Jud. Adminstrn. N.Y.C., State Jr. Bar Tex. (dir. 1955-56), Am. (chmn. sect. jud. adminstrn. 1970-71, ho. dels. 1971-74), Fed. bar assns., Am. Judicature Soc., Nat. Inst. for Trial Advocacy (dir. 1970—), Internat. Soc. of Barristers, Delta Tau Delta, Phi Alpha Delta, Pi Sigma Alpha. Episcopalian. Clubs: Fort Worth; Nat. Lawyers (Washington); City (Dallas). Home: 3701 Turtle Creek Dr Dallas TX 75219 Office: 1st Internat Bldg Dallas TX 75270

WEST, WILLIAM LIONEL, educator, pharmacologist; b. Charlotte, N.C., Nov. 30, 1923; s. Lionel Beresford and Cornelia Thedosia (Hairston) W.; B.S., Johnson C. Smith U., Charlotte, 1947; Ph.D., State U. Ia., 1955; m. Edythe Lucy Kearns, Apr. 27, 1972; children—William Lionel II, Edythe Parham. Research asst. zoology State U. Ia., 1949-54, research asso. radiation research dept. Coll. Medicine, 1954-56; mem. faculty Howard U. Coll. Medicine, Washington, 1956—, part-time prof. radiology, 1971—, prof., chmn. dept. pharmacology, 1973—. Served with AUS, 1943-46. Research grantee AEC, 1957, NIH, 1962-64, 72—, Pfieffer Found., 1972, Washington Heart Assn., 1963. Fellow Am. Inst. Chemists, AAAS, Am. Assn. Clin. Chemists; mem. Am. Assn. Cancer Research, Am. Soc. Pharmacology and Exptl. Therapeutics, Internat. Soc. Biochem. Pharmacology, Am. Physiol. Soc., Am. Nuclear Soc., Nat. Med. Assn., Internat. Acad. Law and Sci., Am. Soc. Zoologists, N.Y., Washington acads. scis., D.C. Soc. Exptl. Biology and Medicine, Sigma Xi. Club: Cosmos. Author numerous articles in field. Office: Coll Medicine Dept Phar Room 1414 Preclinical Bldg Howard U 520 W St NW Washington DC 20059

WESTAWAY, JAMES WHITLOCK, ret. ins. co. exec.; b. Regina, Sask., Can., Nov. 21, 1912; s. Charles and Jessie Evelyn (Grobb) W.; B.Comm., U. Toronto (Ont., Can.), 1934; s. Mary Kathryn Ellis, Apr. 3, 1937; children—Mary Lynn, James Glenholm, Peter Whitlock. Group rep. Aetna Life Ins. Co., Los Angeles, Detroit, Toronto, 1934-56, regional mgr. group div., Toronto, 1956-61; with Excelsior Life Ins. Co., Toronto, 1961-77, exec. v.p., 1969-70, pres., 1970-73, chmn., 1973-77, dir. 1970—; dir. Costain Ltd., Aetna Casualty Co. Can.; chmn. Barbecon, Inc. Chmn. Toronto Mendelssohn Choir, 1964-69; pres. Toronto symphony, 1973-75; bd. govs. Massey Hall. Mem. Delta Upsilon. Mem. United Ch. of Can. Clubs: Toronto, Univ., Arts and Letters, Toronto Hunt, Tucson Nat. Golf. Home: 30-A Oriole Rd Toronto ON M4V 2E8 Canada Office: 2300 Yonge St Toronto ON M4P 1E4 Canada

WESTBROOK, JAMES EDWIN, lawyer, univ. dean; b. Camden, Ark., Sept. 7, 1934; s. Loy Edwin and Helen Lucille (Bethea) W.; B.A. with high honors, Hendrix Coll., 1956; J.D. with distinction, Duke, 1959; LL.M., Georgetown U., 1965; m. Elizabeth Kay Farris, Dec. 23, 1956; children—William Michael, Robert Bruce, Matthew David. Admitted to Ark. bar, 1959, Okla. bar, 1977; mem. firm Mehaffy, Smith & Williams, Little Rock, 1959-62; asst. counsel, subcom. of U.S. Senate Jud. Com., Washington, 1963; legis. asst. U.S. Senate, Washington, 1963-65; asst. prof. law U. Mo. at Columbia, 1965-68, asst. dean, 1966-68, asso. prof., 1968-70, prof., 1970-76, James S. Rollins prof. law, 1974-76; dean U. Okla. Coll. Law, Norman, 1976—; arbitrator on nat. labor panel Am. Arbitration Assn. and roster of Fed. Mediation and Conciliation Service, 1974—; reporter Mid-Am. Assembly on Role of State in Urban Crisis, 1970; dir. Summer Internship Program in Local Govt., 1968; cons. various Mo. cities on drafting home-rule charters. Mem. Gov.'s Adv. Council on Local Govt. Law, 1967-68; chmn. Columbia Charter Revision Commn., 1973-74; mem. spl. com. labor relations Mo. Dept. Labor and Indsl. Relations, 1975. Mem. Am. Bar Assn., Assn. Am. Law Schs. (chmn. local govt. law round table council 1972), Order of Coif, Blue Key, Alpha Chi. Episcopalian. Contbr. articles to profl. jours. Home: 2009 Crestmont Norman OK 73069 Office: Dean's Office U Okla Coll Law 300 Timberdell Rd Norman OK 73019

WESTBROOK, JOEL WHITSITT, III, lawyer; b. San Angelo, Tex., June 19, 1916; s. Lawrence Whittington and Minnie Frances (Millspaugh) W.; student U. Va., 1934-35; B.A., U. Tex., 1937, J.D., 1940; m. Elaine Frances Summers, Feb. 13, 1943; 1 son, Jay Lawrence. Admitted to Tex. bar, 1940; 1st asst. U.S. Atty., San Antonio, 1946-51; 1st asst. dist. atty. Bexar County, San Antonio, 1951-52, dist. atty. pro tem, 1956; practice law, San Antonio 1952-54; partner Trueheart, McMillan, Russell & Westbrook San Antonio, 1954-61, Jones, Boyd, Westbrook & Lovelace, Waco, Tex., 1962-68, Sheehy, Cureton, Westbrook, Lovelace & Nielsen, Waco, 1968-74, Trueheart, McMillan, Westbrook & Hoffman, San Antonio, 1974—; vis. lectr. criminal law, legal ethics and evidence St. Mary's Sch. Law, San Antonio, 1957-61, 74-76. Chmn. San Antonio Crime Prevention Com., 1954-56; pres. Action Planning Council, Waco, 1966-68; chmn. Waco-McLennan County Mental Health-Mental Retardation Bd. Trustees, 1967-70; pres. adv. bd. Providence Hosp., Waco, 1969-70; Model City com., Waco, 1969-72, chmn., 1971-72. Served to maj., inf., AUS, 1940-46; ETO, MTO. Decorated Combat Inf. badge, Silver Star, Bronze Star, Purple Heart. Life fellow Tex. Bar Found. (charter); mem. Waco-McLennan County (dir. 1963-66), San Antonio (pres. 1957-58) bar assns., State Bar Tex. (dir. 1965-68), Tex. Assn. Def. Counsel (v.p. 1970-71), U. Tex. Law Sch. Alumni Assn. (dir. 1969-72), Delta Theta Phi, Sigma Alpha Epsilon. Anglican. Clubs: St. Anthony, Four Ten, Fort Sam Houston Officers (San Antonio); Army-Navy (Washington). Contbr. articles to legal and mil. jours. Home: 7709 Broadway Apt 208 San Antonio TX 78209 Office: 1711 Nat Bank of Commerce Bldg San Antonio TX 78205. *I have expected responsibility in others, and I have wanted others to expect responsibility in me.*

WESTBROOKS, LOGAN HART, record co. exec.; b. Memphis, Aug. 28, 1937; s. Alphonso Hart and Erma (Bowen) W.; student Lemoyne Coll., Memphis, 1955-57; B.S., Lincoln U., Jefferson City, Mo., 1961; m. Geraldine Douthet, July 10, 1965; 1 dau., Babette. Mgmt. trainee RCA Victor Distbg. Corp., Des Plaines, Ill., 1965-67; Midwest promotion mgr. Capitol Records, Niles, Ill., 1969-70, adminstrv. asst. to v.p. mktg., Hollywood, Cal., 1970; dir. nat. promotion Mercury Records, Chgo., 1970-71; dir. spl. markets Columbia Records, N.Y.C., 1971-74; dir. spl. markets CBS Internat., N.Y.C., 1974-76; v.p. mktg. Cornelius/Grifter Entertainment Co.-Soul Train TV Prodns., Los Angeles, 1976—; founder, pres. Source Record Co., Los Angeles, 1977—; part-time instr. Calif. State U., Los Angeles; dir. Merit Real Estate Trust, Chgo. Cons., Nat. Med. Assn. Bd. dirs. Continental Inst. Tech. Served with arty. AUS, 1961-63. Recipient awards Los Angeles City Council, 1970, Los Angeles Urban League, 1970, Project 75, Boston, 1973, Mrs. Martin Luther King, Atlanta, 1974. Mem. 100 Black Men, Inc., N.Y.C., Omega Psi Phi. Home: 15223 Rayneta Dr Sherman Oaks CA 91403 Office: 1902 5th Ave Los Angeles CA 90018

WESTBY, GERALD HOLINBECK, geologist; b. Stoughton, Wis., Aug. 4, 1898; s. Julius A. and Harriet (Holinbeck) W.; Ph.B. in Geology, U. Chgo., 1920; student Stanford, 1924, Colo. Sch. Mines, 1926-27; D.Sc. (hon.), U. Tulsa, 1964; LL.D., Okla. Christian Coll., 1973; m. Elaine Carlson, June 5, 1927 (div. Feb. 1942); children—Joan C. (Mrs. John A. Weaver III) (dec.), Dorothy J. (Mrs. Jonathan Westby Campaigne); m. 2d, Kathleen Patton, Feb. 2, 1944; children—Kathleen Harriet, Gerald Holinbeck, John Trygve. Tchr. geology U. Mont., summer 1920; resident geologist in Algeria for S. Pearson & Son, London, Eng., 1920-24; field geologist Empire Oil & Refining Co., 1924-26, chief geophysicist, 1927-33; with Seismograph Service Corp., Tulsa, 1933-70, pres., 1935-67, chmn. bd., chief exec. officer, 1967-68, now hon. chmn. dir.; pres., dir. subsidiaries; dir. Brookside State Bank, 1st Nat. Bank & Trust Co. (both Tulsa). Bd. dirs. Internat. Petroleum Exposition, 1938—, chmn. exposition Hall of Sci., 1953; chmn. bd. Tulsa Psychiatric Found.; bd. govs. Am. Citizenship Center, 1972—. Comdr. N.E. Okla. Group, CAP, 1941-45. Chmn. bd. of trustees U. Tulsa, 1966-69. Served to 2d lt. U.S. Army, World War I. Recipient award for leadership in civic, social and religious activities, U. Chgo. Alumni Assn., 1950. Mem. Am. Assn. Petroleum Geologists, Soc. Exploration Geophysicists (founding com., past officer, hon.), Geophys. Soc. Tulsa (hon. life), Am. Geophys. Union, European Assn. Exploration Geophysicists, Tulsa C. of C. (dir., past pres.), Fgn. Policy Assn., Tulsa (founder), Tulsa Com. Fgn. Relations (charter), Alliance Francaise Tulsa. Clubs: N.Y. Yacht; Cherokee Yacht; So. Hills Country; Tulsa, Tulsa Press (Headliner mem.). Home: 2515 E 28th St Tulsa OK 74114 Office: Suite 428 4815 S Harvard Tower Bldg Tulsa OK 74135

WESTCOTT, RALPH MERRILL, water quality engr.; b. Redlands, Calif., Jan. 7, 1906; s. Clyde Merrill and Effie Rachel (Blodgett) W.; student U. Calif., Los Angeles, 1923-24, 37-39; m. Elizabeth Campbell, June 26, 1926; children—Marilyn Westcott McIntyre, Mila Westcott Moyse. Owner, operator printing bus., Los Angeles, 1926-32; date grower, Coachella Valley, Calif., 1925-47; owner, operator Water Treating Service Co., Los Angeles, 1939-49; cons. engr. Pomeroy & Westcott, Los Angeles, 1949-51; pres. Holladay & Westcott, Los Angeles, 1952-64; cons. water quality, waste disposal, Los Angeles, 1964-73; corrosion specialist Fallbrook, Calif., 1973—; mem. com. on water problems Rainbow Mcpl. Water Dist., Fallbrook, 1975—. Recipient Engr. of Yr. award Cons. Engrs. Assn. Wash., 1960, Actual Specifying Engr. Mag. award, 1965; registered profl. engr., Calif., Nev. Fellow Am. Soc. Heating, Refrigeration, Air Conditioning Engrs. (life, Distinguished Service award 1968), Am. Cons. Engrs. Council (founding mem. 1956, pres. 1959-60); mem. Cons. Engrs. Assn. Calif. (pres. 1956-57), Am. Water Works Assn. (life mem.), Nat. Assn. Corrosion Engrs. (cert. corrosion specialist, chmn. tech. practices com. T-7K non-chem. water treating devices). Clubs: Fallbrook Golf and Country, Men's (pres. 1976). Contbr. numerous articles to trade, tech. jours. Home and Office: 3635 Oak Cliff Dr Fallbrook CA 92028

WESTENBURG, RICHARD, conductor; b. Mpls., Apr. 26, 1932; s. Harry Albin and Frances Bernice (Comstock) W.; B.Mus., Lawrence U., 1954; M.A., U. Minn., 1956; postgrad. Union Theol. Sem. Sch. Sacred Music, 1960-66; student Nadia Boulanger, Jean Langlais, and Pierre Cochereau, Paris, 1959-60; children—Eric Alan, Kirsten Lee. Instr. in music U. Mont., 1956-60; dir. music First Unitarian Ch., Worcester, Mass., 1960-62; organist, choirmaster Central Presbyterian Ch., N.Y.C., 1964-74; music dir. Musica Sacra, N.Y.C., 1968—, Collegiate Chorale, N.Y.C., 1973—; head choral dept. Juilliard Sch. Music, 1977—; dir. music Cathedral St. John The Divine, N.Y.C., 1974—. Mem. Am. Choral Dirs. Assn., Am. Guild Organists, Assn. Profl. Vocal Ensembles. Home: Eaton Rd Monterey MA 01245 Office: 1047 Amsterdam Ave New York NY 10025

WESTER, E. TRUMAN, junior coll. pres.; b. Burneyville, Okla., Jan. 10, 1919; s. Orren N. and Angie B. Wester; B.A. in Edn., Southeastern Okla. State U., 1940; M.A., U. Okla., 1948, Ed.D. (So. Fellowship Fund fellow 1952, Kellogg scholar 1957, NDEA scholar 1961), 1959; m. Edna Earle Roling, Oct. 30, 1937; children—Glenna Kay, Jana Lyn, Nancy Ann. Tchr. math., registrar Central Okla. State U., Edmond, 1948-60; edn. specialist FAA, 1961-65; dir. cons. center U. Okla., 1966-67; v.p. acad. affairs Gray County Coll., Denison, Tex., 1967-72, pres., 1972—. Pres. Texoma Regional Blood Center, 1974-77, Texoma Valley council Boy Scouts Am., 1974-76. Served to lt. comdr. USNR, 1944-46. Mem. Tex. Public Community/Jr. Coll. Assn., Phi Delta Kappa. Democrat. Baptist. Clubs: Kiwanis, Masons (32 deg.). Address: 6101 Hwy 691 Denison TX 75020

WESTER, WILLIAM DANIEL, banker; b. Henderson, N.C., Apr. 4, 1926; s. Alfred B. and Lottie (Daniel) W.; student The Citadel, 1943-44; B.S., U. N.C., 1948; m. Mary Elizabeth Perry, Dec. 13, 1952; children—William Daniel, Susan, Alfred Benjamin III, John Perry, Rebecca. Pres. Wester Investment Co., 1970—, Wester Realty & Ins. Inc., 1953—, Henderson Savs. & Loan Assn., 1953—; chmn. bd. mgrs. Peoples Bank & Trust Co., Henderson, N.C., 1968—; dir. Peoples Bank & Trust Co., Rocky Mount, N.C. Trustee Jubilee Hosp., Henderson; bd. dirs. Kerr Lake Sch., Henderson, 1971-74. Served to ensign USNR, 1945-48. Mem. Inst. Real Estate Mgmt., Nat. Inst. Real Estate Brokers, N.C. Savs. and Loan League (dir. 1977-78). Home: Crestwood Rd Henderson NC 27536 Office: 312 Chestnut St Henderson NC 27536

WESTERFELD, WILFRED WIEDEY, biochemist; b. St. Charles, Mo., Dec. 13, 1913; s. August H. and Caroline (Wiedey) W.; B.S. in Chem. Engring., Mo. Sch. Mines, 1934; Ph.D. in Biochemistry St. Louis U., 1938; postgrad. Oxford U., 1938-39, Columbia U., 1939-40; m. Hannorah McElroy, June 25, 1938; children—Mary, Margaret, William, Noel, John. Instr., asso. Harvard Med. Sch., 1940-45; prof., chmn. dept. biochemistry Syracuse U., 1945-50; prof., chmn. dept. biochemistry SUNY, Upstate Med. Center, 1950-79, Disting. Service prof., 1978, acting dean, 1956, acting pres., 1967. Mem. Am. Soc. Biol. Chemists, Am. Chem. Soc., AAAS, Soc. Exptl. Biol. Medicine, Sigma Xi. Author: Acid-Base Balance, 1972. Contbr. articles to profl. jours. Home: 7607 Hunt Ln Fayetteville NY 13066 Office: 766 Irving Ave Syracuse NY 13210

WESTERFIELD, HOLT BRADFORD, polit. scientist, educator; b. Rome, Italy, Mar. 7, 1928 (parents Am. citizens); s. Ray Bert and Mary Beatrice (Putney) W.; grad. Choate Sch., 1944; B.A., Yale, 1947; M.A., Harvard, 1951, Ph.D., 1952; m. Carolyn Elizabeth Hess, Dec. 17, 1960; children—Pamela Bradford, Leland Avery. Instr. govt. Harvard, 1952-56; asst. prof. polit. sci. U. Chgo., 1956-57; mem. faculty Yale, 1957—, prof. polit. sci., 1965—, chmn. dept., 1970-72; research asso. Washington Center Fgn. Policy Research, Johns Hopkins Sch. Advanced Internat. Studies, 1965-66; vis. prof. Wesleyan U., Middletown, Conn., 1967, 71. Sheldon traveling fellow Harvard, 1951-52; Henry L. Stimson fellow Yale, 1962, 73; sr. Fulbright-Hays scholar, 1973; hon. vis. fellow Australian Nat. U., 1973. Mem. Am. (Congl. fellow 1953-54), Internat. polit. sci. assns., Internat. Studies Assn. Author: Foreign Policy and Party Politics: Pearl Harbor to Korea, 1955; The Instruments of America's Foreign Policy, 1963. Home: 115 Rogers Rd Hamden CT 06517 Office: Dept Polit Sci Yale Univ 3532 Yale Station New Haven CT 06520

WESTERFIELD, PUTNEY, business exec.; b. New Haven, Feb. 9, 1930; s. Ray Bert and Mary Beatrice (Putney) W.; grad. Choate Sch., 1942-47; B.A., Yale, 1951; m. Anne Montgomery, Apr. 17, 1954; children—Bradford, Geoffrey, Clare. Co-founder, v.p. Careers, Inc., N.Y.C., 1950-52; mgr. S.E. Asia Swen Publs., Inc., Manila, Philippines, 1952; mem. joint adv. commn., Korea, 1953-54; polit. officer Am. embassy, Saigon, Vietnam, 1955-57; asst. to pub. Time mag., N.Y.C., 1957-59, asst. circulation dir., N.Y.C., 1959-61, circulation dir., 1961-66, asst. pub., 1966-68; asst. pub. Life mag., N.Y.C., 1968; pub. Fortune mag., N.Y.C., 1969-73; pres. Chase World Information Corp., N.Y.C., 1973-75; v.p. Boyden Assos. Internat., San Francisco, 1976—; dir. Straight Arrow Pubs. Bd. dirs. Urban League, N.Y.C., 1969-71, Children's Village, 1968-71, Mediterranean Sch. Found., 1969-71, Nat. Boys Club, 1970-73, U.S.-S. Africa Leaders Exchange Program, Bus. Council for Internat. Understanding, 1974-76, Yale-China Assn.; trustee Choate Sch., Wallingford, Conn., 1967-76, Westover Sch., Middlebury, Conn., Watch Hill Chapel Soc., 1963-77, Assn. Yale Alumni, 1972-75. Clubs: Links, Yale (N.Y.C.); Burlingame Country (Hillsborough, Calif.); Pacific Union (San Francisco). Home: 360 Robinwood Ln Hillsborough CA 94010 Office: Boyden Assos One Maritime Plaze San Francisco CA 94111

WESTERGAARD, PETER TALBOT, educator, composer; b. Champaign, Ill., May 28, 1931; s. Harald Malcolm and Rachel (Talbot) W.; A.B., Harvard, 1953; M.F.A., Princeton, 1956; m. Barbara Jay, Sept. 11, 1955; children—Elizabeth, Margaret. Fulbright guest lectr. Staatliche Hochschule, Freiburg, Germany, 1957-58; instr. Columbia, 1958-63, asst. prof., 1963-66; vis. lectr. Princeton U., 1966-67; asso. prof. Amherst Coll. (Mass.), 1967-68; asso. prof. music Princeton, 1968-71, prof. music, 1971—, chmn. dept. music, 1974-78, also condr. Princeton U. Orch., 1968-73. Guggenheim fellow, 1964-65. Composer: Cantata I (The Plot against the Giant), 1956; Five Movements for Small Orchestra, 1958; Cantata II (A Refusal to Mourn the Death, by Fire, of a Child in London), 1958; Quartet for Violin, Vibraphone, Clarinet and Violoncello, 1960; Spring and Fall; To a Young Child, 1960, 64; Cantata III (Leda and the Swan), 1961; Trio for Flute, Violoncello and Piano, 1962; Variations for Six Players, 1963; Mr. and Mrs. Discobbolos, 1966; Divertimento on Discobbolic Fragments, 1967; Noises, Sounds and Sweet Airs, 1968; Tuckets and Sennets, 1969; Moto Perpetuo for Six Wind Instruments, 1976; Alonso's Grief, 1977. Author: Introduction to Tonal Theory, 1975. Office: Dept Music Princeton U Princeton NJ 08540

WESTERHOFF, HAROLD E., social agency exec.; b. Hawthorne, N.J., Sept. 14, 1915; s. Jacob J. and Margaret (Laggner) W.; student N.Y.U., U. Pa. Formerly with office comptroller Eclipse-Pioneer div. Bendix Aviation Corp.; mem. Internat. Soc. Christian Endeavor, past pres. N.J. Union, head exec. conf., v.p. charge Middle Atlantic region, also mem. exec. com., former gen. sec. and treas.; trustee, former gen. sec. World's Christian Endeavor Union; leader numerous convs. and confs. of orgn.; v.p. for fiscal affairs Greer-Woodycrest Children's Services, Hope Farm, Dutchess County, N.Y., 1966—; mem. bd. edn. Hope Farm Union Free Sch. Dist. Former mem. hdqrs. com. Ohio Alcohol Edn. Council; former mem. exec. council All-American Conf. to Combat Communism. Pres. bd. edn., Hawthorne, N.J. Served with AUS, World War II. Decorated Bronze Star. Club: Optimist, Lions. Address: Hope Farm Millbrook NY 12545

WESTERHOUT, GART, astronomer; b. The Hague, Netherlands, June 15, 1927; s. Gerrit and Magdalena (Foppe) W.; came to U.S., 1962, naturalized, 1969; Drs., Leiden U., Netherlands, 1954, Ph.D., 1958; m. Judith Mary Monaghan, Nov. 14, 1956; children—Magda C., Gart T., Brigit M., Julian C., Anthony K. Asst., Leiden U. Observatory, 1952-56, sci. officer, 1956-59, chief sci. officer, 1959-62; prof., dir. astronomy U. Md., 1962-73, chmn. div. math. and phys. scis. and engring., 1972-73, prof. astronomy, 1973-77; sci. dir. U.S. Naval Observatory, Washington, 1977—; vis. astronomer Max Planck Inst. Radio Astronomy, Bonn, Germany, 1973-74; Vice chmn. div. phys. sci. NRC, 1969-73; trustee Asso. Univ. Inc., 1971-74; mem. Inter Union Commn. on Allocation of Frequencies, 1974—; mem. sci. council Stellar Data Center, Strasbourg, France, 1978—; chmn. working group on astronomy, astronomy survey com. Nat. Acad. Scis., 1979—; chmn. Arecibo adv. bd. Nat. Astronomy and Ionosphere Center, 1979-80. Recipient citation for teaching excellence Washington Acad. Scis., 1972; U.S. Sr. Scientist award Alexander von Humboldt Stiftung, Ger., 1973; NATO fellow, 1959. Mem. Internat. Astron. Union, Internat. Sci. Radio Union (pres. Commn. on radio astronomy 1975-78), Am. Astron. Soc. (councilor 1975-78), Royal Astron. Soc., Sigma Xi. Roman Catholic. Contbr. articles on radio astronomy and spiral structure of our Galaxy to profl. jours. Office: US Naval Observatory Washington DC 20390

WESTERMAN, JOHN HAROLD, health adminstr.; b. Mpls., July 24, 1933; s. Harold V. and Kay S. Westerman; B.S., U. Minn., 1954, B.B.A., 1958, M.H.A., 1960; m. Mary Julia Snead, Jan. 8, 1977; children by previous marriage—James, Laura (dec.), Eric, Peter. Asst. adminstr., sr. instr. U. Rochester (N.Y.) Med. Center, 1961-64; research asso. Sci. Planning Office, U. Minn., Mpls., 1964-66, asso. prof. pub. health, gen. dir. hosps. and clinics, coordinator health systems research and devel. Office Vice pres., 1967—. Mem. bd. Minn. Blue Cross-Blue Shield, 1972-78; mem. bd. commnrs. Joint Commn. Accreditation Hosps., Chgo., 1976—; pres., mem. bd. Minn. Bd. Health, 1972-78; mem. clin. research adv. com. NIH, 1976-80; accrediting mem. Commn. Edn. for Health Services Adminstrn., 1977. Served with USAF, 1955-58. Recipient Distinguished Service award. Democrat. Episcopalian. Author articles in field. Editorial bd. Jour. Med. Edn., 1972-78, Health Care Mgmt. Rev., 1979—. Home: 303 W Elmwood Pl Minneapolis MN 55419 Office: Box 604 Univ Hosp Minneapolis MN 55455

WESTERMAN, SYLVIA HEWITT, broadcasting exec.; b. Columbus, Ohio, Nov. 14, 1933; d. Harry James and Grace (Doyle) W.; student Bryn Mawr Coll., 1950-51, Ohio State U., 1951-54. With sta. WLW-C, WTVN and WBNS, Columbus, 1954-63; radio producer CBS News, 1963-64, producer Face the Nation, 1967-74, dep. dir. news, 1974-78, v.p. spl. events and polit. coverage, 1978-79; v.p., exec. asst. to pres. NBC News, N.Y.C., 1979—. Recipient Emmy award Nat. Acad. TV Arts and Scis., 1974. Mem. Jr. League Columbus, Sigma Delta Chi, Theta Sigma Pi, Kappa Alpha Theta. Clubs: Washington Press, Deadline. Home: 220 E 63d St Apt 5-A New York NY 10021 Office: 30 Rockefeller Plaza New York NY 10020

WESTERMANN, DAVID, lawyer, electronics co. exec.; b. N.Y.C., Mar. 2, 1920; s. John Jacob and Margaret (Maher) W.; A.B., Columbia U., 1941, LL.B., 1943; LL.D. (hon.), Adelphi U., 1979; m. Edith E. West, Mar. 11, 1972; children by previous marriage—Nancy, John Jacob, David. Admitted to N.Y. bar, 1943; asso. firm Donald A. Gray, N.Y.C., 1947-48, William P. McCool, N.Y.C., 1948-50; atty. Hazeltine Corp., Greenlawn, N.Y., 1950—, v.p., gen. counsel, 1961-66, pres., 1966-77, chief exec. officer, 1966—, chmn., 1977—, dir., 1965—; pres. Hazeltine Research Inc., Chgo., 1963-66, dir., 1963-78; dir. Nat. Bank N.Am.; Bannerman lectr. Naval Postgrad. Sch., 1975. Mem. bd. edn. South Huntington schs., Union Free Sch. Dist. 13, 1956-59, pres., 1959-60; trustee Poly. Inst. N.Y., Electronic Industries Found., Urban League L.I.; mem. N.Y. Gov.'s Adv. Council on High Tech. Opportunity, 1978—; bd. dirs. Action Com. for L.I.; chmn. bd. dirs. Performing Arts Found. L.I. Served to 1st lt. U.S. Army, 1942-46. Mem. Am. Bar Assn., Columbia Coll., Columbia Law Sch. alumni assns., Nat. Security Indsl. Assn. (trustee 1969—, chmn. 1975-76), L.I. Forum for Tech. (chmn. 1977—), Nat. Contract Mgmt. Assn. (bd. advisers 1973—), Am. Legion, Air Force Assn., Delta Psi, Phi Delta Phi. Clubs: Wings, Westhampton Country. Home: 15 Meadow Ln Westhampton Beach NY 11978 also 3050 Palm Aire Dr N Pompano Beach FL 33060 Office: Hazeltine Corp Greenlawn NY 11740

WESTERMANN, FRED ERNST, educator; b. Cin., Mar. 14, 1921; s. Frederick E. and Elizabeth (Hinnenkamp) W.; Ch.E., U. Cin., 1943, M.S., 1947, Ph.D., 1957; m. Margie A. Kopp, July 30, 1949; children—Kathleen M., Paul D., Ann L. Jr. engr. inland mfg. div. Gen. Motors Corp., Dayton, Ohio, 1943-44; instr. U. Cin., 1948-52, asst. prof., 1952-58, asso. prof., 1958-63, prof., 1963—. Served with AUS, 1944-46. Fellow Am. Soc. Metals (past chpt. chmn.); mem. Am. Foundrymens Soc., Am. Soc. Engring. Edn. (past chmn. materials div.), Sigma Xi, Tau Beta Pi, Alpha Sigma Mu, Alpha Chi Sigma. Mem. United Ch. of Christ. Home: 9575 Millbrook Dr Cincinnati OH 45231

WESTERMANN, HORACE CLIFFORD, sculptor; b. Los Angeles, Dec. 11, 1922; s. Horace Clifford and Forita Lynd (Bloom) W.; student Art Inst. Chgo., 1947-53; m. Joanna May Beall, Aug. 31, 1959. Exhibited in one-man shows Corcoran Gallery, Los Angeles, 1974, Assan Frumkin Gallery, 1974, Moore Coll., Phila., 1972, retrospective at Los Angeles County Mus., 1968, Mus. Contemporary Art, Chgo., 1968; exhibited in group shows Made in Chgo. group show Smithsonian Inst., 1974, Guggenheim Mus., N.Y.C., 1970, Carnegie Mus., 1971, Mus. Modern Art, N.Y.C., 1960, Whitney Mus., 1976, Venice Biennale, 1976, others; retrospective exhbn. Whitney Mus. Am. Art, New Orleans Mus. Art, Des Moines Mus. Art, Seattle Mus. Art, San Francisco Mus. Modern Art, 1978; represented in pvt. collections. Served with USMC, 1942-46, 50-52. Recipient Nat. Arts Council award, 1967, Sao Paulo Biennal award, 1972. Mem. Artists Equity Assn. Home and studio: Box 28 Brookfield Center CT 06805

WESTERN, DONALD WARD, mathematician, educator; b. Poland, N.Y., May 7, 1915; s. Erven Byron and Florence (Guller) W.; A.B., Denison U., 1937; M.S., Mich. State Coll., 1939; Ph.D., Brown U., 1946; m. Katherine Ann Jefferis, June 24, 1943; children—Ann, Donald J., Jonathan W., Ruth H., Jean F. Instr. Brown U., Providence 1942-46, asst. prof., 1946-48; asso. prof. Franklin and Marshall Coll., Lancaster, Pa., 1948-53, prof., 1953—, chmn. dept. math. 1952-72. NSF sci. faculty fellow, 1959-60. Mem. Math. Assn. Am. (gov. 1962-67), Am. Math. Soc., Nat. Council Tchrs. Math., NAACP, Urban League, ACLU, Am. Commons Club, Phi Beta Kappa, Sigma Xi. Unitarian. Author: Introduction to Mathematics, 1959; (with Haag) Introduction to College Mathematics, 1968. Home: 38 Girard Ave Lancaster PA 17603

WESTERVELT, PETER JOCELYN, physicist; b. Albany, N.Y., Dec. 16, 1919; s. William Irving and Dorothy (Jocelyn) W.; B.S., Mass. Inst. Tech., 1947, M.S., 1949; Ph.D., 1951; m. Alice Francis Brown, June 2, 1956; children—Dirck Edgell, Abby Brown. Mem. staff radiation lab. Mass. Inst. Tech., 1940-41, underwater sound lab., 1941-45, asst. in physics, 1946-47, research asso., 1948-50; asst. prof. physics Brown U., 1951-58, asso. prof., 1958-63, prof., 1963—; mem. subcom. aircraft noise NASA, 1954-59; mem. com. hearing and bio-acoustics NRC, 1957—, exec. council, 1960-61, 78—, chmn., 1967-68, chmn.-elect, 1979-80; mem. sonic boom com. Nat. Acad. Sci., 1968-71; mem. R.I. Atomic Energy Commn., 1968-73; cons. applied research lab. U. Tex., Austin, 1973—. Fellow Am. Physics Soc., Acoustical Soc. Am. Club: Hope (Providence). Home: 16 John St Providence RI 02906 Office: Brown U Dept Physics Providence RI 02912

WESTFALL, DAVID, educator, lawyer; b. Columbia, Mo., Apr. 16, 1927; s. Wilhelmus David A. and Ruth (Rollins) W.; A.B., U. Mo., 1947; LL.B. magna cum laude, Harvard, 1950; m. Elizabeth Putnam Beatty; children—Elizabeth Stewart, William Beatty, Thomas Curwen, Katharine Putnam. Admitted to Ill. bar, 1950, Mass. bar, 1956; asso. firm Bell, Boyd, Marshall & Lloyd, Chgo. 1950-55; asst. prof. law Harvard Law Sch., 1955-58, prof., 1958—. Served as 1st lt., Judge Adv. Gen. Corps, AUS, 1951-53. Fellow Am. Coll. Probate Counsel (acad.); mem. Am. Bar Assn., Phi Beta Kappa, Phi Delta Theta. Author: Estate Planning Problems, 1973; co-author: (part 21) American Law of Property, 1952; co-editor: Readings in Federal Taxation, 1970. Home: 106 Kendall Rd Lexington MA 02173

WESTFALL, RALPH LIBBY, univ. dean; b. Fort Collins, Colo., Dec. 21, 1917; s. Alfred R. and Dorothy (Towne) W.; B.S., Colo. State U., 1939; M.B.A., Northwestern U., 1940, Ph.D., 1952; m. Charlotte E. Spengler, Feb. 23, 1946; children—Janice L., James S., Teresa A. Comml. analyst Standard Oil Co. (Ind.), 1946; mem. faculty Northwestern U., 1946-75, prof. marketing, 1957-75, asso. dean acad. affairs Sch. Mgmt., 1965-75; dean Coll. Bus. Adminstrn., U. Ill. at Chgo. Circle, 1975—; cons. marketing mgmt. and mktg. research to govt. and industry, 1952—; dir. United Wirecraft, Inc., Mgmt. Planning and Research, Inc. Served to maj. AUS, 1941-46. Decorated Bronze Star with oak leaf cluster, Army Commendation medal. Mem. Am. Econ. Assn., Am. Mktg. Assn. (pres. Chgo. 1957), Beta Gamma Sigma, Phi Kappa Phi, Alpha Tau Omega (Thomas Arkle Clark award 1939). Democrat. Presbyn. (elder 1965—). Co-author: Marketing Research: Text and Cases, 4th edit., 1977; Cases in Marketing Management, 1961; Case in Marketing Strategy, rev. edit., 1964; Cases in Advertising Management, 1964. Co-editor: Contemporary American Marketing, 1957. Home: 2043 Ewing Ave Evanston IL 60201

WESTFALL, RICHARD SAMUEL, historian; b. Fort Collins, Colo., Apr. 22, 1924; s. Alfred Rennselaer and Dorothy (Towne) W.; B.A., Yale U., 1948; M.A., 1949, Ph.D., 1955; postgrad. London U., 1951-52; m. Gloria Marilyn Dunn, Aug. 23, 1952; children—Alfred, Jennifer, Kristin. Instr. history Calif. Inst. Tech., Pasadena, 1952-53; instr., asst. prof. history State U. Iowa, Iowa City, 1953-57; asst. prof. history Grinnell Coll., 1957-60, asso. prof., 1960-63; prof. history of sci. Ind. U., Bloomington, 1963—, prof. history, 1965—, distinguished prof. of history and philosophy of sci., 1976—, chmn. dept., 1967-73. Mem. United Ministry Bd., Bloomington, 1964-73; elder First Presbyterian Ch., Bloomington, Ind. Served with USNR, 1944-46. Mem. Am. Hist. Assn., AAUP, History of Sci. Soc. (Pfizer award 1972, 2d v.p. 1973-74, v.p. 1975-76, pres. 1977-78), Societe internationale d'Histoire des sciences. Author: Science and Religion in Seventeenth Century England, 1958; Force in Newton's Physics, 1971; Construction of Modern Science, 1971. Editor: (with V.E. Thoren) Steps in the Scientific Tradition, 1969. Home: 2222 Browncliff Rd Bloomington IN 47401 Office: Dept of History and Philosophy of Science Indiana University Bloomington IN 47401

WESTFALL, THOMAS DALE, mayor; b. Decatur, Ill., May 14, 1927; s. Ormond Louis and Faye Leota (Vording) W.; B.A., James Millikin U., Decatur, 1948; J.D., U. Ill., 1951; m. Margie Lorraine Peters, Apr. 25, 1951; children—Rebecca D., Kathleen V. Admitted to Ohio bar, 1957; with FBI, 1951-77, asst. spl. agt. charge field offices in Savannah, Ga. and El Paso, Tex., 1965-77; asst. prof. criminal justice Park and Webster colls., El Paso, 1977—; mayor of El Paso, 1979—; dir. Bank of Ysleta (Tex.). Served with USMCR, 1945-46. Mem. Tex. Mcpl. League, W. Tex. Council Govts., Ohio Bar Assn., El Paso Hist. Soc. (pres. 1979), El Paso Archaeol. Soc. (pres. 1973). Democrat. Roman Catholic. Club: El Paso Rotary (past pres.). Author articles on archaeology. Home: 4213 O'Keefe St El Paso TX 79903 Office: City-County Bldg 500 E San Antonio St El Paso TX 79999

WESTFELDT, WALLACE OGDEN, broadcasting exec.; b. New Orleans, Sept. 23, 1923; s. Wallace Ogden and Alice (Vairin) W.; student Emory U., 1943; B.A., U. of South, 1947; postgrad. Columbia Grad. Sch. Polit. Sci. and Internat. Relations, 1948-49; m. Elisabeth Stacy Kauffelt, Oct. 21, 1944; 1 dau., Erica Stacy. Copyboy, then head copyboy, reporter Time mag., Dallas, 1950, reporter, Atlanta, 1951-52; reporter The Nashville Tennessean, 1953-61; editor U.S. Civil Rights Commn., 1961; asso. producer NBC White Paper NBC News, 1961; reporter, field producer Huntley-Brinkley Report NBC News, 1963-67, asso. producer Huntley-Brinkley Report, Washington, 1967-69, exec. producer, 1969-72, exec. producer NBC Reports, now sr. producer Prime Time Saturday. Bd. dirs. Race Relations Info. Center, Nashville; trustee U. of South, 1974-75. Served with USMCR, 1943-46, 50-52; Korea. Recipient 4 Emmy awards for broadcasts on hunger, welfare, drug addiction, fall of Dacca (Bangladesh) 1972-75; exec. producer U.S.A.: People and Politics, CBS, 1976-77, Special Reports, ABC News, 1977-78; Silver Gavel award for broadcast The Meaning of Watergate, Am. Bar Assn.; Peabody award and Ohio Journalism award for U.S.A.: People and Politics; Reid fellow, 1958; Duke U. fellow in communication, 1973-74. Author: (with others) With All Deliberate Speed, 1959; (with others) The First Hundred Days, 1961. Office: care Press Dept NBC News 30 Rockefeller Plaza New York NY 10020

WESTHEIMER, DAVID KAPLAN, novelist; b. Houston, Apr. 11, 1917; s. Adolf and Esther (Kaplan) W.; B.A., Rice Inst., Houston, 1937; m. Doris Gertrude Rothstein, Oct. 9, 1945; children—Fred, Eric. Successively asst. amusement editor, radio editor, mag. editor, TV editor Houston Post, 1939-41, 45-46, 50, 53-60. Served to capt. USAAF, 1941-45, USAF, 1950-53; lt. col. Res. (ret.). Decorated Air medal, D.F.C. Mem. Writer's Guild Am. West, Author's Guild, Ams. for Democratic Action, A.C.L.U. Democrat. Author: Von Ryan's Express, 1964; My Sweet Charlie, 1965; Song of the Young Sentry, 1968; Lighter Than a Feather, 1971; The Avila Gold, 1974; The Olmec Head, 1974; Rider on the Wind, 1979; Von Ryan's Return, 1980; (play) My Sweet Charlie, 1966. Home: 11722 Darlington Ave Apt 2 Los Angeles CA 90049 Office: 407 N Maple Dr Beverly Hills CA 90210

WESTHEIMER, FRANK HENRY, chemist, educator; b. Balt., Jan. 15, 1912; s. Henry Ferdinand and Carrie (Burgunder) W.; A.B., Dartmouth, 1932, Sc.D. (hon.), 1961; M.A., Harvard, 1933, Ph.D., 1935; NRC fellow Columbia, 1935-36; Sc.D. (hon.), U. Chgo., 1973, U. Cin., 1976, Tufts U., 1978; m. Jeanne Friedmann, Aug. 31, 1937; children—Ruth Susan, Ellen. Instr. chemistry U. Chgo., 1936-41, asst. prof., 1941-44, asso. prof., 1946-48, prof. chemistry, 1948-53; vis. prof. Harvard, 1953-54, prof. chemistry, 1954—, chmn. dept., 1959-62; Overseas fellow Churchill Coll., U. Cambridge (Eng.), 1962-63. Mem. President's Sci. Advisory Com., 1967-70; research supr. Explosives Research Lab., Nat. Def. Research Com., 1944-45; chmn. com. survey chemistry Nat. Acad. Scis., 1964-65. Recipient Naval Ordnance Development award, 1946; Army-Navy Certificate of Appreciation, 1948; James Flack Norris award phys.-organic chemistry, 1970; Willard Gibbs medal, 1970; Theodore Richards medal, 1976; Guggenheim fellow, 1962-63; Fulbright-Hays fellow, 1974. Mem. Nat. Acad. Sci. (council 1971-75, 76-79), Am. Philos. Soc., Am. Chem. Soc., Am. Acad. Arts and Scis., Phi Beta Kappa. Asso. editor Jour. Chem. Physics, 1942-44, 52-54; editorial bd. Jour. Am. Chem. Soc., 1960-69. Contbr. articles to profl. jours. Home: 3 Berkeley St Cambridge MA 02138

WESTHEIMER, GERALD, educator, scientist; b. Berlin, Germany, May 13, 1924; s. Isaak and Ilse (Cohn) W.; optometry diploma, Sydney (Australia) Tech. Coll., 1943, fellowship diploma, 1950; B.Sc., U. Sydney, 1947; Ph.D., Ohio State U., 1953. Australian citizen, 1944; came to U.S., 1951. Practice optometry, Sydney, 1945-51; research fellow Ohio State U., 1951-53; prof. physiol. optics U. Houston, 1953-54; asst. prof., then asso. prof. physiol. optics Ohio State U., 1954-60; postdoctoral fellow neurophysiology Marine Biol. Lab., Woods Hole, Mass., 1957; vis. researcher Physiol. Lab., U. Cambridge (Eng.), 1958-59; mem. faculty U. Calif. at Berkeley, 1960—, prof. physiol. optics, 1963-68, chmn. group physiol. optics, 1964-67, prof. physiology, 1968—. Mem. com. vision NRC, 1957-72; mem. visual scis. study sect. NIH, 1966-70, chmn. visual scis. B study sect., 1977-79; mem. vision, research and tng. com. Nat. Eye Inst., NIH, 1970-74; mem. exec. council com. vision Nat. Acad. Sciences-NRC, 1969-72; mem. communicative scis. cluster Pres.'s Biomed. Research Panel, 1975. Fellow AAAS, Optical Soc. Am. (Tillyer medal 1978); mem. Royal Soc. New So. Wales, Soc. Neurosci., Assn. Research in Vision and Ophthalmology (Proctor medal 1979), Internat. Brain Research Orgn., Sigma Xi; asso. mem. Physiol. Soc. Great Britain. Author research papers. Editor Vision Research, 1972—; editorial bd. Investigative Ophthalmology, 1973-77, Exptl. Brain Research, 1973—, Optics Letters, 1977-78. Home: 582 Santa Barbara Rd Berkeley CA 94707

WESTIN, AVRAM ROBERT (AV WESTIN), television news exec.; b. N.Y.C., July 29, 1929; s. Elliot and Harriet (Radin) W.; B.A., N.Y.U., 1949; M.A. in Pub. Law and Govt., Columbia, 1958; m. Kathleen Lingo; 1 son, Mark Eric. Writer for CBS News, 1950-51, reporter, 1951-53, news editor, 1953-55, dir., 1955-58, producer-dir., 1958-67; CBS News producer in Europe, 1961-65; exec. producer CBS News, 1965-67; exec. producer, exec. dir. Columbia Broadcast Lab., 1967; dir. Pub. Broadcast Lab. of NET, Ford Found., 1967-69; exec. producer ABC News, N.Y.C., 1969-76, 77—, v.p. news documentaries, 1973-76, v.p., 1977-79, v.p. for program devel., 1979—; dir. Good Morning with Will Rogers, Jr., 1957; producer The Ruble War (Peabody award), 1958, The Arab Tide (Peabody award), 1958, Jordan: Key to the Middle East, 1958, Integration Battle in the Courts, 1958, Moonshoot, 1958, Big News of '58, 1958, Where We Stand-Part Two (Peabody award) 1959, Hawaii: The 50th State, 1959, Royal Wedding in Japan, 1959, The Geneva Conference, 1959, The Population Explosion (Peabody, George Polk, Ohio State Inst. Radio, TV awards), 1959, President Eisenhower in South Am., 1960, DeGaulle in America, 1960, Hungary 5 Years Later, Germany, Red Spy Target; exec. producer Pres. Nixon's China Trip (Emmy award 1972); producer, writer Heroes and Heroin (Christopher award 1972); exec. producer We Will Freeze in the Dark for Capital Cities Communications. Recipient Emmy award for best documentary writing, 1959, 68, spl. med. journalism award Albert Lasker Found., 1959, Sylvania award, 1959; fellow CBS Found. News and Pub. Affairs, 1957-58; recipient Schoolbell award NEA, 1964; Emmy award as exec. producer Crisis in the Cities, 1968; Peabody award for ABC News Close-Up series, 1973; Alfred I. DuPont-Columbia U. award for ABC News Close-Up series, 1973-74; fellow in communications policy Duke, 1975. Co-author: Heroes and Heroin, 1972. Office: ABC News 7 W 66th St New York NY 10023

WESTING, JOHN HOWARD, educator; b. New Era, Mich., Aug. 5, 1911; s. John and Cora (Haan) W.; B.A., Calvin Coll., 1932; M.B.A., U. Mich., 1935, Ph.D., 1942; m. Margaret Anderson, Sept. 1, 1939; children—Janet Powell, Mary Margaret. Asst. mgr. raw sugar and customs dept. Am. Sugar Refining Co., 1935-38; asso. dir. food rationing div. OPA, 1941-43; chief food allocations div. Fgn. Econ. Adminstrn., 1944-45; chief bus. practices div. Office Internat. Trade Policy, Dept. Commerce, 1945-46; asso. prof. bus. adminstrn. U. Mich., 1947-49; prof., chmn. mktg. dept. Sch. Commerce, U. Wis., 1949-70, asso. dean, 1955-67, prof., 1969-79, emeritus prof., 1979—. Served as lt. (s.g.) USNR, 1943-44. Mem. Am. Mktg. Assn. (named Wis. Marketer of Year 1974), Am. Econs. Assn., Nat. Sales Execs., Nat. Assn. Purchasing Agts. Lutheran. Author: Readings in Marketing, 1953; (with I.V. Fine) Industrial Purchasing, 1955, rev. as Purchasing Management, 4th edit., 1975; (with D.M. Phelps) Marketing Management, 1960, 68; (with G.S. Albaum) Modern Marketing Thought, 1964, 3d edit., 1975. Home: 10826 Amber Train Sun City AZ

WESTLAKE, DONALD WILLIAM SPECK, educator; b. Woodstock, Ont., Can., Feb. 27, 1931; s. Frank and Mary Bel (Yake) S.; B.S., U. B.C., 1953, M.S., 1955; Ph.D., U. Wis., 1958; m. Maureen Elizabeth Walsh, Aug. 28, 1954; children—Douglas MacGregor, Jill

Anne. Asst. research officer bacteriology dept. Prairie Regional Lab., Nat. Research Council Can., 1958-63, asso. research officer mycology dept., 1963-66; sessional lectr. dept. bacteriology faculty medicine U. Sask., 1963-66; asso. prof. dept. microbiology U. Alta., Edmonton, Can., 1966-69, prof., chmn. dept., 1969—; vis. scientist Atlantic Regional Lab., Nat. Research Council Can., 1967—. Mem. Can. Soc. Microbiology (asst. editor Jour. 1972—), Can. Soc. Biochemistry, Chem. Inst. Can., Am. Soc. Microbiology, Soc. Gen. Microbiology, Soc. for Indsl. Microbiology. Home: 12604 62d Ave Edmonton AB T6H 1N5 Canada

WESTLAKE, ROBERT ELMER, physician; b. Jersey City, Oct. 2, 1918; s. Henry Ebenezer and Bertha (Fowle) W.; grad. Lawrenceville Sch., 1936; A.B., Princeton, 1940; M.D., Columbia, 1943; m. Agnes Vivian Kumpf, Oct. 1, 1944; children—Robert Elmer, Barbara Elizabeth, Richard Louis. Intern Englewood (N.J.) Hosp., 1944, 46-47; resident Univ. Hosp., Syracuse, N.Y., 1947-49; instr. medicine State U. N.Y. Med. Center, Syracuse, 1949-50, asst. prof., 1950-52, clin. asso. prof., 1956-67, clin. prof., 1967—; pvt. practice internal medicine, Syracuse, 1952—; mem. staff State Univ., Crouse-Irving-Meml. VA hosps.; dir. profl. services Community Gen. Hosp.; cons. USPHS, 1966-72, Social Security Adminstrn., 1968-71; mem. Com. Rev. Regional Med. Programs, NIH, 1966-67; med. adv. council Dept. Def., 1969-74; pres. Profl. Standards Rev. Orgn. Central N.Y., 1974-77. Pres. Onondaga Found. Med. Care, 1961-68; v.p. Blue Shield Central N.Y., 1965-73, chmn. bd., 1973—. Served to lt. (j.g.) M.C., USNR, 1944-46. Diplomate Am. Bd. Internal Medicine. Fellow A.C.P.; mem. Am. Soc. Internal Medicine (pres. 1965-66), Onondaga County Heart Assn. (pres. 1963-64). Contbr. profl. jours. Home: Reis Circle Fayetteville NY 13066 Office: Community Gen Physicians Office Bldg Broad Rd Syracuse NY 13215

WESTLEY, JOHN LEONARD, educator, biochemist; b. Wilsonville, Nebr., Aug. 29, 1927; s. Charles William and Lois (Noyer) W.; Ph.B., U. Chgo., 1948, Ph.D. in Biochemistry, 1954; m. Aiko Miyake, Dec. 22, 1956; children—Lynn Carol, Laura Kei, Steven Ken. Research fellow Calif. Inst. Tech., 1954-56; mem. faculty U. Chgo., 1956—, prof. biochemistry, 1964—. Mem. adv. panel for molecular biology, div. biol. and med. scis. NSF, 1968-71. Served with AUS, 1946-47. Recipient Research Career Devel. award USPHS, 1962-67, 67-72. Mem. Am. Soc. Biol. Chemists, Phi Beta Kappa, Sigma Xi. Author Enzymic Catalysis, 1969; also papers mechanism of enzyme action, sulfur metabolism, evolutionary origins of biol. catalysis. Office: 920 E 58th St Chicago IL 60637

WESTLEY, RICHARD OWEN, grain mcht.; b. Cooperstown, N.D., July 15, 1912; s. Martin Daniel and Eva (Hutchinson) W.; B.S., U. N.D., 1934; m. Margaret E. Kindschi, June 21, 1937; children—John, Kent, Robert. Various positions including Chgo. br. mgr., Cargill, Inc., 1945-54, mgr. central region, Chgo., 1952-54; mgr. grain dept. Glidden Co., 1955-57, v.p. chemurgy div., 1957-58; v.p. grain merchandising Central Soya Co., Ft. Wayne, Ind., 1958-63; vice chmn., dir. Ferguson Grain Co., Chgo., 1963—; bd. govs. Bd. Trade Clearing Corp., 1965-76, chmn., 1972-73. Mem. Chgo. Bd. Trade (dir. 1967-70), Beta Theta Pi, Beta Gamma Sigma. Clubs: Union League (Chgo.); Skokie Country (Glencoe, Ill.); Turtle Creek (Tequesta, Fla.). Home: 352 Chestnut St Winnetka IL 60093 Office: 141 W Jackson Blvd Chicago IL 60604

WESTMAN, JACK CONRAD, child psychiatrist; b. Cadillac, Mich., Oct. 28, 1927; s. Conrad A. and Alice (Pedersen) W.; M.D., U. Mich., 1952; m. Nancy K. Baehre, July 17, 1953; children—Daniel P., John C., Eric C. Intern, Duke Hosp., Durham, N.C., 1952-53; resident U. Mich. Med. Center, 1955-59, dir. Outpatient Services, Children's Psychiatric Hosp., Ann Arbor, Mich., 1961-65, asso. prof. U. Mich. Med. Sch., 1964-65; coordinator Diagnostic and Treatment Unit, Waisman Center, U. Wis., Madison, 1966-74, prof. psychiatry, 1965—; cons. Joint Commn. on Mental Health of Children, 1967-69, Madison (Wis.) Pub. Schs., 1965-74, Children's Treatment Center, Mendota Mental Health Inst., 1965-69. Vice-pres. Big Bros. of Dane County, 1970-73; v.p. Wis. Assn. Mental Health, 1968-72; co-chmn. Project Understanding, 1968-75. Served with USNR, 1953-55. Diplomate Am. Bd. Psychiatry and Neurology. Fellow Am. Psychiat. Assn., Am. Coll. Psychiatrists, Am. Acad. Child Psychiatry, Am. Orthopsychiat. Assn. (dir. 1973-76); mem. Am. Assn. Psychiat. Services for Children (pres. 1976-80). Author: Individual Differences in Children, 1973; Child Advocacy, 1979; contbr. articles to profl. jours. Home: 1234 Dartmouth Rd Madison WI 53705 Office: 600 Highland Ave Madison WI 53792

WESTMEYER, TROY RUDOLPH, educator, govt. ofcl.; b. Toledo, Oct. 25, 1916; s. Rudolph C. and Eva (Westrup) W.; B.E., U. Toledo, 1940; M.S., Denver U., 1944; Ph.D., N.Y. U., 1963; m. Eleanor J. Dunham, Apr. 4, 1942; children—Wesley R., Lynne. Asso. prof. govt. mgmt. U. Denver, 1946-49; dir. fiscal survey commns. Commonwealth of Mass., Boston, 1949-56; sr. asso. Nat. Mcpl. League, N.Y.C., 1956-58, asso. dir., 1969; asso. dir. Ankara program N.Y. U. Grad. Sch. Public Adminstrn., 1958-60, asso. dean, 1960-67, prof. public adminstrn., 1963—, acting dean, 1968-69; dir. N.Y. State Legis. Commn. on Expenditure Rev., Albany, 1970—. Served with USNR, 1943. Mem. Govtl. Research Assn. (sec.-treas. 1959-74), Am. Soc. Public Adminstrn. (pres. N.Y. met. chpt. 1968). Editor Govtl. Research Assn. Reporter, 1959-74; column editor Nat. Civic Rev., 1962—. Home: 60 Gary Rd Stamford CT 06903 Office: 111 Washington Ave Albany NY 12210 also 4 Washington Sq New York NY 10003

WESTMORE, MICHAEL GEORGE, make-up artist; b. Hollywood, Calif., Mar. 22, 1938; s. Montague George and Edith Adeline (McCarrier) W.; B.A., U. Calif., Santa Barbara, 1961; m. Marion Christine Bergeson, Dec. 4, 1966; children—Michael George, Michelle, McKenzie. Apprentice make-up artist Universal City Studios, Universal City, Calif., 1961-63, staff make-up artist, 1964, asst. head dept. make-up, dir. make-up lab., 1965-71; freelance make-up artist Hollywood studios, 1971—; instr. theatre arts dept. Los Angeles Valley Coll., 1966—; pres. Cosmetic Control Centers, Inc., 1971-76; research cons., lectr. therapeutic cosmetics for med. assns. Served with AUS, 1956. Recipient Emmy for outstanding achievement in makeup for Eleanor and Franklin, Nat. Acad. TV Arts and Scis., 1976. Mem. Internat. Alliance Theatrical Stage Employees, Soc. Make-up Artists, Vikings of Scandia, Gold Pennant Gourmet Soc., Lambda Chi Alpha (life). Author: The Art of Theatrical Makeup for Stage and Screen, 1971; also chpts. in books. Address: 3830 Sunswept Dr Studio City CA 91604

WESTOFF, CHARLES FRANCIS, educator, sociologist; b. N.Y.C., July 23, 1927; s. Frank Barnett and Evelyn (Bales) W.; A.B., Syracuse U., 1949, M.A., 1950; Ph.D., U. Pa., 1953; m. Joan P. Uszynski, Sept. 11, 1948 (div. Jan. 1969); children—David, Carol; m. 2d, Leslie Aldridge, Aug. 1969. Instr. sociology U. Pa., 1950-52; research asso. Milbank Meml. Fund, N.Y.C., 1952-55; research asso. Office Population Research, Princeton, 1955-62, asso. dir., 1962-75, dir., 1976—; prof. sociology at univ., 1962—, Maurice P. During '22 prof. demographic studies and sociology, 1972—, chmn. dept. sociology, 1965-70; asso. prof. sociology N.Y.U., also chmn. dept. sociology Washington Sq. Coll., 1959-62; vis. sr. fellow East-West Population Inst., Honolulu, 1979; Disting. vis. prof. Am. U., Cairo, 1979. Exec. dir. Commn. Population Growth and Am. Future, 1970-72; mem. adv. com. on population studies U.S. Bur. Census, 1973-79; vice chmn. bd. dirs. Alan Guttmacher Inst., 1977—; bd. advisors Population Resources Center, 1976—. Fellow Am. Sociol. Assn., Am. Acad. Arts and Scis.; mem. Planned Parenthood Fedn. Am. (dir. 1978—), Population Assn. Am. (bd. dirs. 1960-62, 68-70, 1st v.p. 1972-73, pres. 1974-75), Internat. Union Sci. Study Population. Author articles demographic and sociol. topics. Co-author: Family Growth in Metropolitan America, 1961; The Third Child, 1963; College Women and Fertility Values, 1967; The Later Years of Childbearing, 1970; From Now to Zero, 1971; Reproduction in the United States: 1965, 1971; Toward the End of Growth: Population in America, 1973; The Contraceptive Revolution, 1976; Demographic Dynamics in America, 1977. Home: 537 Drake's Corner Rd Princeton NJ 08540

WESTON, ARTHUR WALTER, chemist; b. Smith Falls, Ont., Can., Feb. 13, 1914; s. Herbert W. and Alice M. (Houghton) W.; B.A., Queen's U., Kingston, Ont., 1934, M.A., 1935; Ph.D., Northwestern U., 1938; Advanced Mgmt. Program, Harvard, 1958; m. V. Dawn Thompson, Sept. 10, 1940; children—Roger L., Randall K., Cynthia B. Came to U.S., 1935, naturalized, 1952. Research asso. Northwestern U., 1938-40; with Abbott Labs., North Chicago, Ill., 1940—, dir. research and devel., 1959-61, v.p. research and devel., 1961-68, dir. co., 1959-68, v.p. sci. affairs, 1968-77, v.p. corp. licensing, 1977-79; pres. Arthur W. Weston & Assos. Inc., 1979—. Mem. War Manpower Commn. Office Sci. Research and Devel., 1942-45; mem. exec. com. indsl. chemistry, div. chemistry and chem. tech. NRC, 1961-65; mem. indsl. panel on sci. and tech. NSF, 1974—; mem. ad hoc com. chem. agts. Dept. Def., 1961-65. Mem. Research Dirs. Assn. Chgo. (pres. 1965-66), Pharm. Mfrs. Assn., Am. Chem. Soc. (trustee Chgo. 1965—, dir. Chgo. sect. 1952-59, nat. com. corp. assos. 1967-72), Dirs. Indsl. Research, Indsl. Research Inst. (dir. 1970-73), Chem. Inst. Can., Phi Beta Kappa, Sigma Xi, Phi Lambda Upsilon. Contbr. to profl. jours. and books. Patentee in field. Home: 349 E Hilldale Pl Lake Forest IL 60045 Office: Abbott Labs North Chicago IL 60064

WESTON, JOHN FREDERICK, educator; b. Ft. Wayne, Ind., Feb. 6, 1916; s. David Thomas and Bertha (Schwartz) W.; B.A., U. Chgo., 1937, M.B.A., 1942, Ph.D., 1948; m. June Mildred Sherman, May 16, 1942; children—Kenneth F., Byron L., Ellen J. Instr., Sch. Bus., U. Chgo., 1940-42, asst. prof., 1947-48; econ. cons. to pres. Am. Bankers Assn., 1945-46; prof. Grad. Sch. Bus., U. Calif., Los Angeles, 1949—; Distinguished lecture series U. Okla., 1967, U. Miss., 1968, Miami U., 1975, U. Utah, 1972. Bd. dirs. Bunker Hill Fund. Served with Ordnance Dept., AUS, 1943-45. McKinsey Found. grantee, 1965-68, Gen. Electric Co. grantee, 1972. Ford Found. Faculty Research fellow, 1961-62. Mem. Am. Finance Assn. (pres. 1966, adv. bd. 1967-70), Am., Western (pres. 1959-60) econ. assns., Econometric Soc., Am. Statis. Assn., Royal Econ. Soc., Financial Analysts Soc., Financial Mgmt. Assn. Author: Scope and Methodology of Finance, 1968; International Managerial Finance, 1972; Role of Large Firms in U.S. Economy, 1973; Managerial Finance, 6th edit., 1978; asso. editor: Jour. of Finance, 1948-55, mem. editorial bd., 1957-59. Home: 258 Tavistock Ave West Los Angeles CA 90049 Office: Grad Sch Mgmt U Calif Los Angeles CA 90024

WESTON, LEWIS M., securities dealer; b. N.Y.C., Feb. 13, 1926; s. Jacob and Fanny (Feingold) W.; B.B.A., Coll. City N.Y., 1947; m. Beatrice Maidman, June 15, 1947; children—Rosalind (Mrs. John Kinstler), Judy (Mrs. Thomas J. Assad, Jr.), Richard, Joan. Credit analyst Dun & Bradstreet, 1947-49; credit mgr. S. Posner Sons, Inc., paper wholesalers, 1949-51; with Goldman, Sachs & Co., N.Y.C., 1951—. Lectr. econs. dept. Coll. City N.Y.; adj. prof. Hofstra U. Served to lt. (j.g.) USNR, 1942-46. Mem. N.Y. Soc. Security Analysts, Nat. Assn. Securities Dealers (gov.). Clubs: Bond (gov.), Recess (N.Y.C.). Home: 8 Dunster Rd Great Neck NY 11021 Office: 55 Broad St New York NY 10004

WESTON, NORMAN BETTS, banker; b. Wilton, Conn., Dec. 16, 1913; s. George S. and Ethel (Betts) W.; student Rollins Coll., 1932-33, Black Mountain Coll., 1933-35; M.B.A., Harvard, 1940; m. Anne Chapin, Jan. 5, 1935; children—Michael C., Carol B. (Mrs. Robert Klein), John H., Mark S. With Nat. Bank of Detroit, 1941—, v.p., asst. trust officer, 1954-60, v.p., trust officer, 1960-64, sr. v.p., trust officer, 1964-68, exec. v.p., 1968-72, vice chmn. bd., 1972—, also dir.; gen. mgr., dir. Nat. Detroit Corp., Internat. Bank Detroit. Mem. adv. bd. United Found.; mem. bus. and industry com. United Negro Coll. Fund. Bd. dirs. Civic Searchlight; dir. United Community Services; pres., trustee Founders Soc. Detroit Inst. Arts; pres., trustee Oakland U. Found.; trustee Clark Coll., Birmingham Community House, Harvard Bus. Sch. Club Detroit Trust Fund, Met. Fund. Served to lt. USNR, 1942-46. Recipient Outstanding Merit award United Negro Coll. Fund, 1966. Mem. Assn. Res. City Bankers, Am. Bankers Assn., Hundred Club. Clubs: Detroit, Detroit Athletic; Bloomfield Hills (Mich.) Country (gov.); Orchard Lake (Mich.) Country. Office: PO Box 116 Detroit MI 48232

WESTON, RANDY (WESTON, RANDOLPH EDWARD), pianist, composer; b. Bklyn., Apr. 6, 1926; s. Frank Edward and Vivian (Moore) W.; student Parkway Music Inst., Bklyn., 1950-52; children by previous marriage—Cherryl, Pamela, Niles, Kim. Pianist, Am. Soc. African Culture tour, Lagos, Nigeria, 1961, 63; toured with Randy Weston's sextet for State Dept., North and West Africa, 1967; appearances include: Newport Festival, 1958, Monterey Festival, 1966, Carnegie Hall, 1973, Philharm. Hall, N.Y.C., 1973, with Symphony of New Rodl. N.Y.C., 1973, maj. jazz clubs in N.Y.C.; numerous UN concerts, Billie Holiday Theatre, N.Y.C.; European tours, including: Kingsberg Jazz Festival, Oslo, 1974, Montreux (Switzerland) Jazz Festival, 1974, Festival de Costa del Sol, Marbella, Spain, 1974, Ahus Jazz Festival, Kristianstad, Sweden, 1974, Festival at Antibes, 1974; lecture-concerts in Europe, including Bern, Basel, Zurich, Lyons, 1975; rec. artist, including: Blue Moses (number 1 in Record World's jazz chart), 1972; compositions include: Pam's Waltz, 1950, Little Niles, 1950, Hi Fly, 1958, Portrait of Vivian, 1959, Berkshire Blues, 1960, Uhruru Africa suite, 4 movements, 1960, African Cook Book, 1965, The Last Day, 1966, The Ganawa, 1971, Portrait of F.E. Weston, 1974; concert artist for radio-TV and maj. U.S. museums, including Smithsonian Instn.; lectr. on African music UN; performed benefit concerts for anti-apartheid com. at UN through African-Am. Musicians Soc., 1961; appeared in film Jamboree, 1966. Recipient New Star Pianist award Down Beat Internat. Critics Poll, 1955, named Pianist Most Deserving of Wider Recognition, 1972; Broadway award Hollywood Advt. Club, 1965, Premier prix de l'Academie du Jazz, France, 1975; French Office Nationale de Diffusion Artistique grantee, 1976; Nat. Endowment for Arts grantee, 1974. Mem. ASCAP (Composers awards), Am. Fedn. Musicians. Sufi.

WESTON, ROY FRANCIS, environ. cons.; b. Reedsburg, Wis., June 25, 1911; s. Charles Frederick and Hattie (Jensen) W.; B.C.E., U. Wis., 1933; M.C.E., N.Y. U., 1939; m. Madeleen Elizabeth Kellner, Dec. 31, 1934; children—Susan Weston Thompson, Katherine Weston Swoyer. Jr. hwy. engr. Wis. Hwy. Dept., 1934-36; dist. engr. Wis. Dept. Health, 1936-37; san. engring. research fellow N.Y. U., 1937-39; san. engr. Atlantic Refining Co., Phila., 1939-55; pres., chmn. bd. Roy F. Weston, Inc., environ. cons., West Chester, Pa., 1955—; vis. com. dept. civil and urban engring., U. Pa., Phila., also Center for Marine and Environ. Studies, Lehigh U.; mem. Pa. Gov.'s Energy Council; mem. indsl. and profl. adv. com. Pa. State U. Recipient Disting. Service citation U. Wis., 1975; registered profl. engr., 18 states; diplomate Am. Acad. Environ. Engrs. (pres. 1973-74). Fellow ASCE, Am. Pub. Health Assn.; mem. Nat. (Engr. of Year award 1973), Pa. (Engr. of Year award 1970) socs. profl. engrs., Nat. Acad. Engring., Water Pollution Control Fedn. (Arthur Sidney Bedell award 1959, Indsl. Wastes medal 1950), Am. Inst. Chem. Engrs., Am. Chem. Soc., Air Pollution Control Assn., Cons. Engrs. Council, Water Resources Assn. Delaware River (pres. 1976-77), Phila. Engrs. Club (George Washington medal 1973). Club: Overbrook Golf. Contbr. numerous articles on environ. control to profl. publs. Home: 2 Buttonwood Dr Chadds Ford PA 19317 Office: Weston Way West Chester PA 19380

WESTON, STEPHEN BURNS, lawyer; b. Yellow Springs, Ohio, May 4, 1904; s. A.B., Antioch Coll., Yellow Springs, 1925; postgrad. Sorbonne U., Paris, 1925-26; LL.B., Yale U., 1929; LL.D. (hon.), Cleve. Marshall Law Sch., 1969; m. Simonne Humphrey; children—Burns H., Monique W. Clague. Admitted to Ohio bar, 1930, N.Y. State bar, 1976, U.S. Supreme Ct. bar, others; with firm Thompson, Hine & Flory, Cleve., 1929-1935; Ohio adminstr. Nat. Youth Adminstrn., 1935-40, exec. dir., acting chmn. nat. adv. com., Washington, 1940-42; exec. sec. U.S. sect. Anglo-Am. Caribbean Commn., Dept. State, also acting chief Caribbean office, 1942-44; exec. dir. Postwar Planning Council, Met. Cleve. Devel. Council, 1944-46; ret. sr. partner firm Weston, Hurd, Fallon, Paisley & Howley, Cleve.; now individual practice law, Keene, N.Y.; mem. N.Y. State Gov's Exec. Adv. Com. on Sentencing, 1977-79. Mem. citizens adv. com. Justice Center, Cleve., 1970-75; past trustee, chmn. bd. trustees Antioch Coll., mem. interim bd. govs.; past trustee Cleve. Inst. Music; trustee Keene Valley (N.Y.) Neighborhood Services, Inc. Recipient award for outstanding pub. service League Young Democratic Clubs of Ohio, 1936-38, George W. Yancey Meml. award Internat. Assn. Ins. Counsel, 1963, Brother's Keeper award Jewish Community Fedn. Cleve., 1968. Fellow Am. Coll. Trial Lawyers (past com. chmn.), Am., Bar Found.; mem. Bar Assn. Greater Cleve. (Common Pleas Ct., Docket Conf. 1951-53, chmn. jud. candidates and campaign 1955-57, chmn. trial com. for disciplinary action 1956-60, fed. ct. com. 1957-58, 65-66; joint med. and legal com. 1966-67, hdqrs. location com. 1967-68, trustee 1961-64, pres. 1968-69, chmn. com. on sentencing procedures 1975), Am. (past chmn. legis. com., mem. products, gen. liability and consumer law com. sect. of ins., negligence and compensation law), N.Y. State, Ohio (past mem. clients security fund com. 1974-75), Essex County (N.Y.) bar assns., Internat. Assn. Ins. Counsel (past mem. exec. com., com. chmn.), Cleve. Def. Attys. Group (past chmn.), Sixth Circuit Jud. Conf. (life), Essex County Hist. Soc. (trustee, pres. 1976-79), Yale Law Sch. Assn. (alumni exec. com. 1975—). Clubs: Adirondack Mountain; Philos. (past pres.), Rowfant (pres. 1973-74) (Cleve.). Contbr. to Trial Practice Manual of Ohio Legal Center, Ohio Bar Assn., 1965; also articles to profl. jours. Home and Office: West-on-East Keene NY 12942

WESTON, W. DONALD, pediatrician, psychiatrist; b. Pacific Grove, Calif., Dec. 8, 1931, M.D., U. So. Calif., 1958; M.S. in Mgmt. (Sloan fellow), M.I.T., 1976; m. Marcia Ilene, July 19, 1952; children—Donald G., Brian L. Intern in pediatrics Los Angeles Children's Hosp., 1958-59, resident in pediatrics, 1959-60, asst. dir. outpatient clinic, 1961-62, dir. outpatient clinic, 1962-64, chief adolescent unit, 1963-64; fellow in adolescent medicine Boston Children's Hosp.-Harvard Sch. Medicine, 1960-61; resident in psychiatry Los Angeles County-U. So. Calif. Med. Center, 1964-66, career fellow in child psychiatry, 1966-67, chief resident in child psychiatry, 1967-68; instr. U. So. Calif., 1961-63, asst. prof. pediatrics, 1963-64; chief child and adolescent services Community Mental Health Center, St. Lawrence Hosp., Lansing, Mich., 1968-71, med. dir., 1969-71; asst. prof. psychiatry and human devel. Mich. State U., 1968-69, asso. prof., 1969-73, prof., 1973—, asso. dean community and clin. affairs Coll. Human Medicine, 1970-73, asso. dean. 1973-76, dean, 1977—; mem. task force on edn. White House Conf. Aging; chmn. Liaison Com. Mental Health; mem. Com. for Study Internat. Health Care; mem. rev. com. and research task force NIMH; bd. dirs. Grad. Med. Edn., Lansing, Grand Rapids (Mich.) Area Med. Edn. Center, Saginaw (Mich.) Coop. Hosps., Southwestern Mich. Area Health Edn. Corp., Kalamazoo, Flint (Mich.) Med. Edn. Corp. Mem. Ingham County Med. Soc., Mich. Med. Soc., AMA, Mich. Soc. Psychiatry and Neurology, Am. Public Health Assn., Am. Psychiatry Assn. Author: (with others) Community Based Medical Education: An Integrated Modular System of Health Care and Education, 1970; contbr. articles to profl. publs. Home: 3229 Moores River Dr Lansing MI 48910 Office: Mich State U Coll Human Medicine A 116 E Fee Hall East Lansing MI 48824

WESTOVER, HARRY CLAY, judge; b. Williamstown, Ky., May 19, 1894; s. John Homer and Anna R. (Musselman) W.; ed. U. Ariz., 1919; m. Helen E. Equen, Oct. 3, 1919; children—Harry, Dorothy. Mem. Calif. State Senate; judge U.S. Dist. Ct. of So. Calif., Los Angeles, now sr. judge. Served with U.S. Army. Democrat. Methodist. Office: US Courthouse 312 N Spring St Los Angeles CA 90012*

WESTPHAL, PAUL, profl. basketball player; b. Torrance, Calif., Nov. 30, 1950; attended U. So. Calif. With Boston Celtics (Nat. Basketball Assn.), 1972-75, Phoenix Suns (Nat. Basketball Assn.), 1975—. Office: care Phoenix Suns PO Box 1369 Phoenix AZ 85001*

WESTPHAL, ULRICH FRIEDRICH, educator; b. Göttingen, Germany, May 3, 1910; s. Emil and Mathilde (Klingeberg) W.; Ph.D., U. Göttingen, 1933; Dr.phil.habil., U. Berlin (Germany), 1941; m. Ilse Schlegelmilch, Mar. 20, 1940; children—Karin, Antje, Birgit. Came to U.S., 1949, naturalized, 1958. Liebig fellow, mem. staff Inst. Organic Chemistry, Inst. Tech., Free City of Danzig, 1933-36; staff mem., asst. dir. Kaiser Wilhelm Institut für Biochemie, Berlin-Dahlem, 1936-45; chief chem. dept. Medizinische Klinik, U. Tuebingen (Germany), 1945-49; research scientist, chief protein and steroid sect. biochemistry dept. U.S. Army Med. Research Lab., Ft. Knox, Ky., 1949-58, chief biochemistry div., 1959-61; prof. biochemistry dept. U. Louisville Sch. Medicine, 1961—, Career Research prof., 1962—; Rockefeller Found. Research fellow Columbia, 1939. Mem. biochemistry study sect. div. research grants USPHS, 1961-65. Recipient Research Career award USPHS, 1962—. Mem. Am. Soc. Biol. Chemists, Endocrine Soc., Am. Chem. Soc., Soc. Exptl. Biology and Medicine, AAAS, Sigma Xi. Author: Steroid-Protein Interactions, 1971. Research, numerous publs. structure of estrogens; isolation, structure, partial synthesis and excretion of progesterone; steroid interactions with proteins; corticosteroid and progesterone binding globulins. Home: 10217 Hartley Dr Louisville KY 40223

WESTRAN, ROY ALVIN, ins. co. exec.; b. Taft, Oreg., Apr. 30, 1925; s. Carl A. and Mae E. (Barnhardt) W.; B.B.A., Golden Gate Coll., 1955, M.B.A., 1957; m. Dawn M. Oeschger, Oct. 18, 1952; children—Denise, Thomas, Michael, Dawna. Mem. sales staff C.A. Westran Agy., Taft, 1946-49; underwriter Fireman's Fund Group, San Francisco, 1949-52; ins. mgr. Kaiser Aluminum Chem. Co., Oakland, 1952-66; pres., dir. Citizens Ins. Co., Howell, Mich., 1967—; vice chmn. Mich. Catastrophic Claims Assn.; dir. Worcester Mut. Ins. Co.

(Mass.), 1st Nat. Bank, Howell; pres., dir. Am. Select Risk Ins. Co., Columbus, Ohio, 1967—, Beacon Mutual Indemnity Co., Columbus, 1967—; v.p. Hanover Ins. Co.; bd. dirs. Oakland Kaiser Fed. Credit Union, 1957-60. Mem. ins. adv. council Salvation Army, San Francisco, 1957-60; chmn. drive United Fund, Howell, 1970; bd. dirs., mem. exec. com. Portage Trails council Boy Scouts Am., 1970-72; trustee, mem. exec. com. Child and Family Services Mich., 1972-75; bd. dirs. McPherson Health Center, Howell. Served with U.S. Army, 1943-46. Mem. Ins. Inst. Am., Mich. C. of C. (past dir.), Am. Soc. Ins. Mgmt. (past pres.), Soc. C.P.C.U. (nat. pres. 1968-69), Traffic Safety Assn. Detroit (trustee 1967—), Traffic Safety for Mich. Assn. Home: 5835 Griffith Dr Brighton MI 48116 Office: 645 W Grand River Howell MI 48834

WESTROM, FREDERICK NICHOLAS, engring., construction co. exec.; b. Aberdeen, Wash., Mar. 18, 1927; s. W. O. and Rose D. Westrom; B.S.E.E., U. Wash., 1950, B.S.I.E., 1951; m. Martha Ann Brown, June 17, 1950; children—Charles, Clyde. With Ford, Bacon & Davis Constrn. Corp., 1951—, exec. v.p. and resident mgr., 1977-79, pres., N.Y.C., 1979—, also dir. subs. cos.; pres., dir. Bayou Electric, Monroe, La.; v.p., dir. Faberect of La. Inc., Van Duyn Chocolate Shops, Inc. Sr. warden, chmn. St. Christopher's Day Sch. Bd., Grace Episcopal Ch., 1974; chmn. bd. trustees Masur Mus. Art, Twin City Art Found.; mem. Elec. Bd. Monroe; trustee Public Affairs Research Council La. Served with USNR, 1945-46. Mem. La. Engring. Soc., Am. Arbitration Assn. (panel arbitrators). Republican. Clubs: N.Y. Athletic; Bayou DeSiard Country, Lotus. Office: 3901 Jackson St Monroe LA 71202

WESTROPP, THOMAS CHAMPION, savs. and loan exec.; b. Cleve., May 25, 1925; s. Aloysius T. and Martha (Champion) W.; B.A., John Carroll U., 1950; certificate in savs. and loan mgmt. N.Y. U., 1961; m. Mary Ann Braun, June 29, 1950; children—Thomas Champion, Mary Martha, Jo Ann, Clara L., Jordan G., Lillian C., John C., Peter C., Ellen T., Patrick V. With Womens Fed. Savs. & Loan Assn., Cleve., 1949—, exec. v.p., 1958-65, pres., 1965—; dir. Fed. Home Loan Bank Cin.; mem. savs. and loan adv. council Fed Home Loan Bank Bd. Mem. Cleve. Met. Housing Authority, 1968, Cleve. Planning Commn., 1968-70, University Heights Zoning Bd., 1969-72, Gov.'s Housing and Community Devel. Adv. Commn., 1971; pres. Welfare Fedn., 1975, Catholic Charities Corp., 1975-76; treas. Cuyahoga County Democratic Exec. Com., 1970—; bd. dirs. Greater Cleve. Growth Assn., Welfare Fedn., United Torch, Cath. Charities Corp. Served with USMCR, 1943-46, 50-51. Recipient Man of Year awards City of University Heights, Nat. Com. for Civic Responsibility, Cath. Interracial Council, Young Dem. Club, Cleve. Real Estate Bd.; Eleanor Roosevelt Humanities award Israel Bond Orgn., 1975; ann. award Nat. Housing Conf., 1978, Ann. Interfaith Brotherhood award, 1979. Mem. Northeastern Ohio (pres. 1970), Ohio (exec. com.), U.S. savs. and loan leagues. Roman Catholic. Home: 2756 Inverness Rd Shaker Heights OH 44122 Office: 320 Superior Ave Cleveland OH 44114

WESTRUM, EDGAR FRANCIS, JR., educator, chemist; b. Albert Lea, Minn., Mar. 16, 1919; s. Edgar Francis and Nora D. (Kipp) W.; student Hamline U., 1936-38; B.Chemistry, U. Minn., 1940; Ph.D., U. Cal. at Berkeley, 1944; m. Florence Emily Barr, June 13, 1943; children—Ronald Mark, James Scott, Michael Lauren, Margaret Kristin. Scientist, Metall. Lab., U. Chgo., 1944-46, Lawrence Radiation Lab., U. Cal. at Berkeley, 1946; mem. faculty U. Mich., 1947—, prof. chemistry, 1958—; cons. to govt., 1947—. Chmn. U. Mich. Presbyn. Corp., 1962-67. Sec. gen. Internat. Council Sci. Unions Com. on Data for Sci. and Tech., 1974—. Fellow Am. Phys. Soc., AAAS; mem. of the Faraday Society, also a member of the Am. Chem. Soc., Netherlands Phys. Soc., Sigma Xi, Phi Lambda Upsilon, Alpha Chi Sigma. Author: (with others) The Thermodynamics of Organic Compounds, 1967; also articles. Editor Bull. Thermodynamics and Thermochemistry, 1964—, Jour. Chem. Thermodynamics. Home: 2019 Delaware Dr Ann Arbor MI 48103

WESTWATER, JAMES STUART, mining co. exec.; b. Aberdeen, Scotland, Dec. 6, 1912; s. John Taylor and Joan Campbell (Milne) W.; came to U.S., 1920; E.M., Mich. Tech. U., 1934, D.Engring. (hon.), 1975; m. Helen Victoria Antonich, Dec. 5, 1938; children—James Stuart, Mary Joan, Julie Kay, Candace Jane. Drilling and blasting engr. U.S. Engrs., Livingston Channel, Mich., 1935-36, levee constrn. engr., Greenville, Miss., soils lab supr., Vicksburg, Miss., 1936-37; foreman, breaking ground div. Chile Exploration, Chuquicamata, 1937-40; from mining engr., asst. supt., supt. mgr. mines Cleve.-Cliffs Iron Co., Ishpeming, Mich., 1941-58, v.p. mining, 1958-70, sr. v.p., 1970-78; ret., 1978; dir. iron ore div. office asst. adminstr. Metals Emergency Minerals Adminstrn. Dept. Interior, 1959—. Mem. exec. bd. Greater Cleve. council Boy Scouts of Am., 1962-74. Trustee Lakewood Hosp., Mich. Tech. U. Devel. Fund. Recipient Silver Beaver award Boy Scouts Am., 1946; Silver medal bd. control Mich. Technol. U., 1968, Disting. Alumnus award, 1978. Mem. Am. Iron and Steel Inst., Am. Inst. Mining and Metall. Engrs., Mining and Metall. Soc. Am., Canadian Inst. Mining, Newcomen Soc., Tau Beta Pi, Theta Tau. Republican. Presbyn. Clubs: Union, Cleve. Yachting (Cleve.); Westwood Country (Rocky River, Ohio). Home: 3661 N River Canyon Rd Tucson AZ 85715

WESTWATER, JAMES WILLIAM, educator; b. Danville, Ill., Nov. 24, 1919; s. John and Lois (Maxwell) W.; B.S., U. Ill., 1941; Ph.D., U. Del., 1948; m. Elizabeth Jean Keener, June 9, 1942; children—Barbara, Judith, David, Beverly. Mem. faculty U. Ill., Urbana, 1948—, prof., head dept. chem. engring., 1962—; papers chmn. 5th Nat. Heat Transfer Conf., Buffalo, 1960; chmn. 3d Internat. Heat Transfer Conf., Chgo., 1966; Reilly lectr. Notre Dame U., 1958; Donald L. Katz lectr. U. Mich., 1978. Recipient Conf. award 8th Nat. Heat Transfer Conf., 1965; William H. Walker award Am. Inst. Chem. Engrs., 1966; Max Jakob award Am. Inst. Chem. Engrs.-ASME, 1972. Mem. Am. Inst. Chem. Engrs. (dir., past div. chmn., Inst. lectr. 1964), Am. Chem. Soc., ASME, Am. Soc. Engring. Edn. (Vincent Bendix award 1974), Nat. Acad. Engring. Contbr. articles profl. jours. Home: 116 W Iowa St Urbana IL 61801

WESTWOOD, ALBERT RONALD CLIFTON, scientist; b. Birmingham, Eng., June 9, 1932; s. Albert Sydney and Ena Emily (Clifton) W.; came to U.S., 1958, naturalized, 1974; B.S. with honors, U. Birmingham, 1953, Ph.D. in Phys. Metallurgy, 1956, D.Sc. in Materials Sci., 1968; m. Jean Mavis Bullock, 1956; children—Abigail, Andrea. Tech. officer research dept., metals div. Imperial Chem. Industries, Birmingham, 1956-58; scientist and sr. scientist Martin Marietta Labs. (formerly RIAS), Balt., 1958-64, asso. dir., head materials sci. dept., 1964-69, dep. dir., 1969-74, dir., 1974—; Tewksbury lectr. U. Melbourne, 1974; mem. various govt., univ. and editorial coms. Recipient Disting. Young Scientist award Md. Acad. Scis., 1966; Beilby Gold medal Royal Inst. Chemistry, 1970; chartered engr., U.K. Fellow Am. Soc. Metals, Instn. Metallurgists, Inst. Physics; mem. Metall. Soc. AIME (dir.), AAAS, Soc. Advancement Material and Process Engring., Md. Acad. Scis. (mem. council), Md. Inst. Metals. Contbr. numerous articles to profl. jours. Home: 908 E Joppa Rd Towson MD 21204 Office: 1450 S Rolling Rd Baltimore MD 21227

WESWIG, PAUL HENRY, educator; b. St. Paul, July 13, 1913; s. Carl Marcus and Marie Martha (Wing) W.; B.A., St. Olaf Coll.; M.S., Ph.D., U. Minn.; m. Dorothy Eleanor Johnson, Aug. 4, 1940; children—John Marcus, Charles Paul. Prof. agrl. chemistry Oreg. State U., Corvallis, 1941-42, 46—. Nutrition cons. Interdepartmental Com. on Nutrition for Nat. Def., NIH, Bethesda, Md., Ethiopia, 1958, Malaya, 1963, Paraguay, 1965, 72, Sri Lanka, 1978. Co-planner, co-editor Internat. Selenium Symposium. Served to maj. M.SC., AUS, 1942-46. Recipient citation for services Oreg. Acad. Sci., 1976. Mem. Am. Inst. Nutrition, Am. Chem. Soc., Am. Soc. Animal Prodn., Am. Dairy Sci. Assn., AAUP. Contbr. articles on trace element metabolism, inter-relationships including selenium, cadmium, copper. Home: 2112 NW Polk Ave Corvallis OR 97330

WETHERBY, LAWRENCE WINCHESTER, lawyer; b. Middletown, Ky., Jan. 2, 1908; s. Samuel David and Fanny (Yenowine) W.; LL.B., U. Louisville, 1929; m. Helen Dwyer, Apr. 24, 1930; children—Lawrence, Suzanne, Barbara. Admitted to Ky. bar, 1929; practice in Louisville, 1929-50, 56-60; judge Juvenile Ct., Jefferson Co., Ky., 1943-47; lt. gov. Ky., 1947-50; gov. Ky., 1950-55. Vice pres., gen. counsel Bington Engring. Co.; dir. Lincoln Income Ins. Co. Sec. Ky. Dem. Central Exec. Com., 1948-51; sec. Ky. Dem. Central Committee, 1960-67, chmn., 1967-69; candidate U.S. senator, 1956; mem. Ky. Senate from 20th District, 1965—, pres. senate pro tem, 1966-68. Bd. dirs. Big Brothers Frankfort. Mem. Ky., Louisville bar assns., Sigma Nu Phi, Omicron Delta Kappa. Methodist (bd. stewards). Clubs: Country (Frankfort). Home: Wee Hawken Ln Frankfort KY 40601 Office: 415 W Main St Frankfort KY 40601

WETHERILL, EIKINS, stock exchange exec.; b. Phila., Oct. 3, 1919; s. A. Hecksher and Edwina (Brunner) W.; LL.B., U. Pa., 1948; practiced in Phila., 1948-55, Norristown, 1955—; asso. firm Evans, Bayard & Frick, 1948-50; partner firm Reilly, Hepburn, Earle & Wetherill, 1950-55, firm Henderson, Wetherill, O'Hey & Horsey, 1955—; pres. Phila. Stock Exchange, Inc., 1965—; dir. Norfolk So. Ry. Co., Germantown Savs. Bank; fin. commentator CBS-TV News, 1966-68; chmn. bd. Sta. WHYY-TV, 1970-76, dir., 1976—; dir. 1st Pa. Corp., 1st Pa. Bank; solicitor to lt. gov. Pa., 1951-55; asst. U.S. atty. gen., 1953-55; treas. Montgomery County, 1956-59; pres. Montgomery County Bd. Commrs., 1960-63; chmn. Pa. Securities Commn., 1963-65; commr. Delaware Valley Regional Planning Commn., 1965—, chmn., 1968-69, 70-71, 78-79. Mem. Hosp. Services Council; bd. dirs. Greater Phila. Partnership; mem. council Nat. Municipal League; chmn. Phila. Drama Guild, 1975—. Served to capt., cav., Signal Corps, OSS, AUS, 1941-45. Mem. Am., Phila. bar assns., Delta Psi. Episcopalian. Clubs: Phila., Racquet (Phila.). Home: Butler Pike Plymouth Meeting PA 19462 Office: 17th St and Stock Exchange Pl Philadelphia PA 19103

WETHEY, HAROLD EDWIN, educator; b. Port Byron, N.Y., Apr. 10, 1902; s. Charles Edwin and Flora (Keck) W.; A.B., Cornell U., 1923; A.M., Harvard U., 1931, Ph.D., 1934; student U. Paris, summers 1931, 34; m. Alice Luella Sunderland, June 8, 1948; 1 son, David Sunderland. Asst. history of art Harvard U., 1933-34; instr., lectr. then asst. prof. Bryn Mawr (Pa.) Coll., 1934-38; asst. prof. Washington U., St. Louis, 1938-40; asso. prof. U. Mich., Ann Arbor, 1940—, prof. art history, 1946-72, prof. emeritus, 1972—, Henry Russel lectr., 1964-65; vis. prof. U. Tucumán (Argentina), 1943, U. Mex., summer 1960; spl. lectr. Escuela de Estudios Hispano-americanos, La Rabida, Spain, 1948. Recipient Distinguished Faculty Achievement award, 1968; Sheldon fellow Harvard U., 1932-33; Rockefeller fellow, 1944-45; Rackham research grantee, 1948-72; Guggenheim fellow, 1949, 71-72; fellow Am. Council Learned Socs., 1936, 63; Fulbright scholar, Rome, 1958-59; 400th anniversary of death of Titian, speaker U. Venice, 1976. Mem. Hispanic Soc. Am. (Sculpture medal 1962), Coll. Art Assn., Renaissance Soc., Venice Com. Internat. Fund for Monuments, Research Club (U. Mich.), Am. Acad. Franciscan History (corr.), Real Acad. de Bellas Artes de San Fernando (Madrid), Soc. Peruana de Historia, Acad. Nacional de Ciencias de Bolivia, Phi Kappa Phi. Author: Gil Siloe and His School, 1936; The Early Works of Bartolomé Ordóñez and Diego de Siloe, 1943; Colonial Architecture and Sculpture in Peru (award Soc. Archtl. Historians), 1949; Alonso Cano, Painter, Sculptor and Architect, 1955; Alonso Cano, Pintor, 1958; Arquitectura virreinal en Bolivia, 1961; El Greco and His School, 2 vols., 1962, rev. edit. in Spanish, 1967; editor: (Chandler R. Post) History of Spanish Painting, Vol. XIII, The Schools of Aragon and Navarre in the Early Renaissance, Vol. XIV, The School of Castile in the Later Renaissance, 1966; Titian, Vol. I, The Religious Paintings, 1969, Vol. II, The Portraits, 1971, Vol. III, The Mythological and Historical Paintings, 1975; editor bibliography of Spanish Am. art for Handbook Latin-Am. Studies, 1948-59; editorial bd. Art Bull., 1940-44, 64-71; contbr. to art periodicals (complete bibliography in Hortus Imaginum, Essays in Western Art, pub. in his honor 1975). Home: 1510 Cambridge Rd Ann Arbor MI 48104. *As an historian of art I have always sought for accuracy and historical truth. I consult the documentary sources and seek new proofs of fact. Unsupported traditions and sensational theories must be rejected by any serious scholar.*

WETHINGTON, JOHN ABNER, JR., educator; b. Tallahassee, Apr. 18, 1921; s. John Abner and Mary McQueen (Hale) W.; A.B., Emory U., 1942, M.A., 1943; Ph.D., Northwestern U., 1950; m. Kathryn Kemp Greene, Aug. 19, 1943; 1 son, John Abner III. Vis. research asst. Princeton, 1943-44; chemist Fercleve Corp., Oak Ridge, 1944-46; chemist to sr. chemist Oak Ridge Nat. Lab., 1949-53; asst. prof. to prof. nuclear engring. U. Fla., 1953—, on leave as fellow Lawrence Livermore Lab., Calif., 1971-72; vis. scientist P.R. Nuclear Center, 1962-63. U.S. del. to Radiation Congress, Haregate, Eng., 1963, 2d Internat. Conf. Peaceful Uses of Atomic Energy, Switzerland, 1958; faculty participant Oak Ridge Sch. Reactor Tech., 1957-58. Fellow AAAS; mem. Am. Chem. Soc., Am. Nuclear Soc., Phi Beta Kappa, Sigma Xi, Alpha Chi Sigma. Democrat. Methodist. Contbr. articles to profl. jours. Home: 109 NW 22d Dr Gainesville FL 32601

WETLAUFER, DONALD BURTON, biochemist; b. New Berlin, N.Y., Apr. 4, 1925; s, George C. and Olga (Kirckhoff) W.; B.S. in Chemistry, U. Wis., Madison, 1946, M.S. in Biochemistry, 1952, Ph.D., 1954; m. Lucille D. Croce, May 5, 1950; children—Lise, Eric. Chemist, Argonne (Ill.) Nat. Lab., 1944, 46-47, Bjorksten Lab., Madison, 1948-50; Carlsberg Lab., Copenhagen, 1955-56; research asso. Harvard U., 1956-61, tutor biochem. sci., 1958-61; asst. prof. biochemistry Ind. U. Med. Sch., 1961-62; asso. prof., then prof. biochemistry U. Minn. Med. Sch., 1962-75; DuPont prof. chemistry, chmn. dept. U. Del., Newark, 1975—; vis. investigator Max Planck Inst. Ernahrungsphy., 1974-78; mem. fellowship rev. com. NATO, 1970; cons. Nat. Inst. Gen. Med. Sci., 1964—. NSF predoctoral fellow, 1952-54; Nat. Found. Infantile Paralysis postdoctoral fellow, 1955-56; Am. Heart Assn. postdoctoral fellow, 1956-58; grantee USPHS, 1961—, NATO, 1974-77, AEC, 1962; recipient Career Devel. award USPHS, 1961-62. Mem. Am. Chem. Soc. (councilor div. biol. chemistry 1975—), AAAS, Am. Soc. Biol. Chemists, Biophys. Soc., Phi Beta Kappa. Author research papers in field of protein chemistry and biophysics. Office: Dept Chemistry U Del Newark DE 19711

WETMORE, JAMES STUART, bishop; b. Hampton, N.B., Can., Oct. 22, 1915; s. Charles Talbot and Alberta Mae (McCordic) W.; B.A., Kings Coll., Halifax, N.S., 1938, L.Th., 1939, B.S. Lit., 1949, D.D. (hon.), 1960; student Yale U., 1947; m. Frances Howard Robinson, July 4, 1940; children—Nancy Wetmore Faulds, Charles E., Stuart Andrew, Mary, Robin. Came to U.S., 1953. Ordained deacon, 1938, priest, 1939; curate, then rector in N.B., 1947-51 and Eastern field sec. Gen. Bd. Religious Edn., Ch. of Eng. in Can., 1947-51, asst. gen. sec., 1951-53; dir. Christian edn. Episcopal Diocese N.Y., 1953-60, suffragan bishop, 1960—; sec. council Diocese N.Y., 1968—; hon. canon Cathedral St. John the Divine, N.Y.C., 1958—; pres. N.Y.C. Churchman's Clericus, 1960; chaplain Canadian Soc., N.Y.C., 1957—; mem. div. Christian edn. Nat. Council Chs., 1957-61, leadership tng. adv. com. div. Nat. Council P.E. Ch., 1956-62, mem. dept. Christian edn., 1961-65; chmn. Episc. Ch. World Fair Com., 1963-66; dir. N.Y. State Council Chs., 1964-72; mem. N.Am. adminstrv. com. World Council Christian Edn., 1953-65; bd. dirs. Council of Chs., City N.Y., 1960—; rep. N.Y. State to White House Conf., 1960; mem. dept. ch. renewal Nat. Council Chs., 1965-68; sec.-treas. Assn. Christian Mission in N.Y.C., 1968-70; v.p. Ch. Plan Commn. for N.Y. Met. Region, 1966-70; mem. central cons. bd. St. Mary's-in-the-Field, Valhalla, 1973-77; chmn. Ho. of Bishops Christian edn. com.; pres. Good Shepherd on the Island Corp., 1975-78; affiliate mem. Soc. of the Atonement (Graymoor Friars). Vice pres. P.E. City Mission Soc., N.Y.C., Youth Consultation Service; bd. dirs. Met. Urban Service Tng., 1965-75, St. Simeon Found., Westchester Council on Alcoholism, 1970-74; trustee St. Hilda's and St. Hugh's Sch., N.Y.C, 1964-77, Housing Devel. Corp.; bd. govs. King's Coll., Halifax, 1971-73; pres. St. Peter's Sch., Peekskill, 1970—, Anglican Soc., 1970-77; pres. Episc. Housing Corp., 1971—; pres. Friends of Kings Coll., Halifax, Inc., 1958—; sec. House of Bishop, 2d Province, 1961-65, pres., 1972-78; chmn. exec. com. Internat. Council Religions, 1978—. Mem. St. George's Soc., Pilgrims U.S., Atlantic Union. Author: Master, What Shall We Do?, 1952; also chpts. in books. Home: 7 Fox Meadow Rd Scarsdale NY 10583 Office: 1047 Amsterdam Ave New York NY 10025

WETMORE, LOUIS BEMIS, educator; b. Mount Vernon, N.Y., Dec. 3, 1912; s. Louis Leavitt and Laura (Bemis) W.; B.Arch., Mass. Inst. Tech., 1936; grad. fellow Cranbrook Acad. Art, 1936-37; m. Marion Denby, Dec. 18, 1939; children—Edwin Denby, John French, Peter, Daniel. Instr. planning and housing div. Columbia U. Sch. Architecture, 1939-41; asst. dir., later dir. tri-cities planning project TVA, 1941-43; air intelligence specialist Office Asst. Chief Air Staff Intelligence, Washington, 1943-45; sr. planner Providence City Plan Commn., 1945-47; dir. Providence Redevel. Agy., 1947-51; chief planning div. State of R.I. Devel. Council, 1951-52, cons. planning and econ. devel., 1952-55; vis. prof. city planning, dir. urban and regional studies sect. Mass. Inst. Tech., 1952-55; prof. city and regional planning, 1955-76, emeritus, 1976—, head dept. city planning and landscape architecture Coll. Fine and Applied Arts, U. Ill., 1955-65. Mem. rev. panel São Paulo (Brazil) Basic Urban Plan, 1968-70; spl. asst. to mayor Chgo., 1972-75. Mem. exec. com. Council Community Services, Providence, 1949-51; slum clearance adv. com. U.S. HHFA, 1950-53, cons. to adminstr., 1961-64; dep. commnr. dept. devel. and planning City Chgo., 1965-67. Mem. urban research com. Hwy. Research Bd., 1956-60, mem. transp. planning conf. com., 1970-72; mem. Ill. Continuing Edn. Council, 1966-70, Seminar on Regional Planning, Manila, Philippines, 1975. Mem. Am. Inst. Planners (bd. govs. 1949-52, 1956-59, pres. 1957-58, pres. N.E. chpt. 1954-55), Regional Sci. Assn. (counsellor 1957-58), Phi Kappa Phi. Home: 309 W Elm St Urbana IL 61801

WETMORE, THOMAS HALL, educator; b. Kempner, Tex., July 30, 1915; s. Thomas Hall and Mary Sue (Whitcomb) W.; A.B., Lincoln Meml. U., Harrogate, Tenn., 1934; M.A., Duke, 1940; Ph.D. (Horace Rackham fellow), U. Mich., 1956; m. Rosamond Bayne, July 5, 1941; children—Stephen Bayne, Allyn Christophers. Prin., Rehobeth Elementary Sch., Galivants Ferry, S.C., 1934-37; tchr. English, James Gray High Sch., Winston-Salem, N.C., 1937-40; prin. Shelby (N.C.) Jr. High Sch., 1940-42, Shelby Sr. High Sch., 1942-44; faculty Ball State U., Muncie, Ind., 1946-69, prof. English, chmn. dept., 1960-69; chmn. dept. English, Wright State U., Dayton, O., 1969-71, asso. dean grad. studies, 1971-73, prof. English, 1973—. Mem. linguistics com. Conf. Coll. Composition and Communication, 1960-63; English lang. instn. Commn. English, Coll. Entrance Exam. Bd., 1961-62; linguistics cons. Harper-Row, 1965-66; chief area judge Book of Month Club award for coll. writing, 1967-68, 68-69; edn. cons. Coronet Films. Served to lt. (j.g.) USNR, 1944-46. Mem. Modern Lang. Assn. (chmn. present day English sect. 1965-66, mem. adv. com. of sect. 1965-69, chmn. 1969), AAUP (pres. Ind. 1959), Nat. Council Tchrs. English (dir.-at-large 1960-63, mem. commn. English lang. 1960-63), Linguistic Soc. Am., Internat. Reading Assn., Canadian Linguistics Assn., Ind. Council Tchrs. English, Am. Dialect Soc., Midwestern English Conf. (dir., exec. com. 1957-60, 75—), Ind. Tchrs. Assn., NEA, Coll. English Assn. (nat. bd. dirs. 1968-71), Ind. Coll. (pres. 1967), Ohio English assns., Assn. Higher Edn., Speech Assn. Am. Author: The Low-Central and Low-Back Vowels in the English of the Eastern United States, 1959; chpt. on vowel pronunciation in A Various Language, 1971; co-author: New Dimensions in English, 1966; New Approaches to Language and Composition, 1969. Editor Ball State Forum, 1960-61, Midwest English Rev., 1959-60; Twenty-Two Young Indiana Writers, 1962; Indiana Sesquicentennial Poet, 1967; Twenty Four Young Ohio Writers, 1969. Guest editor English jour., 1963; editor: Linguistics in the Classroom, 1964; English editor Elementary English, 1960; editor Pardon's Progeny, 1977—. Home: 1601 Riverside Ave Muncie IN 47303

WETMORE, THOMAS TRASK, III, coast guard officer; b. New London, Conn., Oct. 15, 1925; s. Thomas Trask and Vivian (Brown) W.; student Yale U., 1943-44; B.S. in Marine Engring., U.S. Coast Guard Acad., 1948; postgrad. U.S. Naval Postgrad. Sch., 1951; M.A., N.Y. U., 1973; m. Joan M. Hancock, Feb. 5, 1949; children—Thomas Trask IV, James R., Jennifer W., Daniel H., Judith J. Commd. ensign U.S. Coast Guard, 1948, advanced through grades to rear adm., 1977; instr. profl. studies dept. C. G. Acad., New London, Conn., 1957-61, asst. supt., 1976-77; comdg. officer tender USCGC Papaw, Charleston, S.C., 1961-63; chief communications br. 5th C. G. Dist., Portsmouth, Va., 1963-67, dist. comdr., 1979—; comdg. officer USCGC Chincoteague, Norfolk, Va., 1967-69; communications officer C. G. Atlantic Area, Governors Island, N.Y., 1969-71; chief aids to nav. br. 3d C. G. Dist., Governors Island, 1971-74, chief ops. div., 1974-75, dep. comdr. Atlantic Area, 1975-76; chief Office of Reserve, U.S. C. G. Hdqrs., Washington, 1977-79. Decorated Meritorious Service medal with gold star, C. G. Commendation medal with gold star, C. G. Achievement medal with ops. disting. device. Mem. U.S. C. G. Acad. Alumni Assn., Hampton Roads Maritime Assn., Res. Officers Assn. Home: 301 Sycamore Rd Portsmouth VA 23707 Office: 5th Coast Guard Dist Fed Bldg 431 Crawford St Portsmouth VA 23705

WETTER, EDWARD, broadcasting exec.; b. Hoboken, N.J., Feb. 2, 1919; s. Edward and Ottilie (Steup) W.; B.A., U. Mich., 1939, M.S., 1941; m. Alice Kornat, Nov. 6, 1940 (div. 1946); 1 son, Robert Edward; m. 2d, Ruth Lowenstein, Oct. 26, 1954 (div. 1971); 1 dau., Karen Deborah; m. 3d, Virginia F. Pate, Apr. 7, 1972. Dir. spl. ops.

Office Sec. Def., 1946-57; bus. broker Allen Kander & Co., N.Y.C., 1957-59; pres. Edward Wetter & Co., Inc., Havre de Grace, Md., 1959—, Spectrum Corp., Havre de Grace, 1972-75, Harford Enterprises, Inc., Havre de Grace, 1978—; v.p. Edwin Tornberg and Co., Inc., N.Y.C., 1959-73; sec-treas. Radio One Five Hundred, Inc., Indpls., 1964—, Radio 900, Inc., Louisville, 1966—, Radio 780, Inc., Arlington, Va., 1977—; dir. Multivue Cable Co., Havre de Grace. Served to capt. AUS, 1941-46. Mem. Assn. U.S. Army, Am. Legion, VFW. Clubs: Rotary, Elks. Contbr. to Biol. Scis., Vol. 2, 1955. Home: 1000 Chesapeake Dr Havre de Grace MD 21078 Office: 1000 Chesapeake Dr Havre de Grace MD 21078

WETZEL, CARROLL ROBBINS, lawyer; b. Trenton, N.J., Apr. 5, 1906; s. William and V. Caroline (Wieand) W.; A.B., Wesleyan U., Middletown, Conn., 1927; LL.B., U. Pa., 1930, Gowen fellow, 1931; m. Phoebe Meade Francine, June 21, 1935; children—Anne F., Phoebe Wetzel Griswold, Carroll Robbins. Admitted to Pa. bar, 1931, since practiced in Phila.; partner firm Dechert, Price & Rhoads, 1934-73, counsel, 1973—; mem. adv. com. to Comptroller of Currency, 1962. Bd. dirs. Library Co. Phila., 1952—, pres., 1975—; trustee Phila. Gen. Hosp., 1958-67; bd. dirs. Am. Found., 1962—, Phila. Maritime Mus., 1976—. Served with USAAF, 1942-45; ETO. Mem. Am. Bar Assn. (chmn. sect. corp., banking and bus. law 1966-67; editor Bus. Lawyer 1964-65), Pa. Hort Soc. (pres. 1967-70). Democrat. Episcopalian. Club: Phila. Home: Lewis Ln Ambler PA 19002 Office: 3400 Centre Sq W 1500 Market St Philadelphia PA 19102

WETZEL, FRANK HARRY, petroleum co. exec.; b. Jersey City, Nov. 11, 1921; s. John Adam and Elizabeth (Wellenheider) W.; student Princeton U., 1943, Bates Coll., 1944; B.A., Tufts U., 1947; m. Ramona Schneider, Apr. 4, 1948; children—Anita Louise Zurell, Karen Martha, Laura. Div. comptroller Mobil Oil Corp., Caracas, Venezuela, 1947-56, N.Y.C., 1956-63, Paris, France, 1963-69; fin. officer Union Carbide Petroleum Corp., N.Y.C., 1969-71; comptroller Commonwealth Oil Refining Co., San Juan, P.R., 1971-76, group v.p., 1976—. Dep. town supr., Pound Ridge, N.Y., 1968-72. Served with USNR, 1942-46. Mem. Fin. Execs. Inst., Nat. Assn. Accountants, Am. Petroleum Inst. Clubs: Princeton, Cloud (N.Y.C.); Oak Hills (San Antonio). Home: F&M Ranch Kendalia TX 78027 Office: 8626 Tesoro Dr San Antonio TX 78217

WETZEL, HARRY HERMAN, aerospace co. exec.; b. Howard, Pa., Jan. 27, 1920; s. Harry Herman and Maude Caroline (Thomas) W.; B.S.A.E., Cornell U., 1941; m. Margaret Kirkpatrick, July 23, 1945; children—Sally C., Harry H., Katherine K., John T. With Garrett Corp., 1946—, mgr. Garrett-AiResearch, Los Angeles, 1958-62, exec. v.p., 1962-63, pres., 1963—, chief exec. officer, 1966—; dir. Signal Cos., UOP Inc., Thiokol Corp., Nat. Semicondr. Corp. Mem. bd. govs., vice chmn. exec. council Performing Arts Council Los Angeles Music Center; trustee Donald Douglas Mus. and Library, Calif. Inst. Tech. Served with USAF, 1941-45. Mem. Aerospace Industries Assn. (mem. exec. com., bd. govs.), Los Angeles C. of C., Beta Theta Pi. Home: 401 Via Media Palos Verdes Estates CA 90274 Office: 9851 Sepulveda Blvd Box 248 Los Angeles CA 90009

WETZEL, JAMES LEWIS, corp. exec.; b. Greenfield, Mo., Sept. 23, 1916; s. Lewis A. and Lillian (Lyngar) W.; student U.S. Naval Acad., 1934-36; m. Mary Louise Hill, Dec. 31, 1938; children—James Lewis, John Hill. With Atlas Powder Co., 1937-43, 46-59, Olin Mathieson Chem. corp., 1959-63; pres., dir. A.M. Byers Co., Pitts., 1963-73; group v.p. chems. Gen. Tire & Rubber Co., Akron, Ohio, 1973-77, pres. GTR Chem. Co. subs., 1978—; chmn. bd. Galis Mfg. Co., Fairmont, W.Va., 1964-68; chmn. bd., dir. Mo.-Rogers Corp., Joplin, Mo., 1964-68, Transmission Products, Inc., Columbus, Ohio, 1968-72; dir. Fenix & Scisson, Tulsa, Internat. Synthetic Rubber Producers, Houston. Served to lt. (s.g.) USNR, 1943-46. Clubs: Duquesne (Pitts.); Allegheny Country (Sewickly, Pa.); Sharon Golf (Sharon Center, Ohio). Home: 171 Granger Rd Medina OH 44256 Office: PO Box 1829 Akron OH 44329

WETZEL, ROBERT GEORGE, botanist; b. Ann Arbor, Mich., Aug. 16, 1936; s. Wilhelm and Eugenia (Wagner) W.; B.S., U. Mich., 1958, M.S., 1959; Ph.D., U. Calif. at Davis, 1962; m. Carol Ann Andree, Aug. 9, 1959; children—Paul Robert, Pamela Jeanette, Timothy Mark, Kristina Marie. Research asso. Ind. U., Bloomington, 1962-65; asst. prof. botany Mich. State U., Hickory Corners, 1965-68, asso. prof., 1968-71, prof., 1971—; cons. Internat. Biol. Program, London, 1967-75; chmn. Internat. Seagrass Commn., 1974-75. Served with USNR, 1954-62. AEC grantee, 1965-75, NSF grantee, 1962—, ERDA grantee, 1975-77; Dept. Energy grantee, 1978—. Fellow AAAS; mem. Am. Inst. Biol. Scis., Am. Soc. Limnology and Oceanography (editorial bd. 1971-74, v.p. 1979-80, pres. 1980-81), Aquatic Plant Mgmt. Soc., Ecol. Soc. Am., Internat. Assn. Ecology, Freshwater Biol. Assn. U.K., Internat. Assn. Theoretical and Applied Limnology (gen. sec., treas. 1968—), Internat. Phycological Soc., Mich. Acad. Scis., N. Am. Benthological Soc., Phycological Soc. Am., Internat. Assn. Great Lakes Research, Japanese Soc. Limnology, Mich. Bot. Soc., Internat. Assn. Aquatic Vascular Plant Biologists (founder, pres. 1979—), Sigma Xi, Phi Sigma. Author: Limnology, 1975; Limnological Analyses, 1979; contbr. numerous articles on ecology and freshwater biol. systems to profl. jours.; mem. editorial bd. Aquatic Botany, 1975—. Home: 15216 Marshfield Rd Hickory Corners MI 49060 Office: WK Kellogg Biol Sta Mich State U Hickory Corners MI 49060

WETZEL, WILLIAM JOSEPH, chem. co. exec.; b. Bklyn., Sept. 1, 1931; s. Edward Joseph and Helen Ann (Alter) W.; B.S.M.E., U.S. Merchant Marine Acad., 1955; M.B.A., L.I. U., 1970; m. Martha Ruth Sharpe, Oct. 26, 1955; children—Susan Kay, William Joseph, Sarah Elizabeth. With Hooker Chem. Co., 1971—, asst. gen. mgr. Ruco Div., 1973-76, v.p., gen. mgr., 1976-78, pres. Plastics Group, Houston, 1978—. Mem. Soc. Plastics Engrs., Am. Chem. Soc. Republican. Roman Catholic. Office: 1980 S Post Oak Rd Houston TX 77210

WETZLER, BENJAMIN, stock broker; b. Auburn, N.Y., Jan. 24, 1908; B.S., Syracuse U., 1930; m. Deborah Rabinowitz, Nov. 30, 1946; children—James Warren, Mark, Scott. With Hardy & Co., mem. N.Y. Stock Exchange, N.Y.C., 1957-78, mng. partner, 1968-78; partner Cowen & Co., mem. N.Y. Stock Exchange, N.Y.C., 1978—. Sec. N.Y. State Democratic State Com., 1946-72. Served to col. 18th Airborne Corps, AUS, 1941-46. Decorated Bronze Star medal. Home: 410 E 57th St New York NY 10022 Office: 1 Battery Park Plaza New York NY 10004

WETZLER, ROBERT TAYLOR, ins. co. exec.; b. N.Y.C., July 11, 1918; s. Robert and Anna (Ultzheimer) W.; A.B., Dartmouth, 1940; m. Audrey C. Mayforth, Feb. 27, 1942; children—Anne, Sarah Jane, Robert Taylor. Prodn. control mgr. Grumman Aircraft Co., 1940-43; with Ernst & Ernst, Boston, 1946-50; partner Fairbanks Assos., N.Y.C., 1950-55; v.p. Hanover Life Ins. Co., Boston, 1955-68; sr. v.p. Guardian Life Ins. Co., N.Y.C., 1968-76; v.p. Met. Life Ins. Co., N.Y.C., 1976—; trustee Cohasset Savs. Bank (Mass.), Contemp Guidance Services, N.Y.C., Lifelong Services, N.Y.C.; asso. prof. N.Y. U. Served to lt. USNR, 1943-46. Home: 20 E 9th St New York NY 10003 Office: 1 Madison Ave New York NY 10010

WEXLER, ANNE, govt. ofcl.; b. N.Y.C., Feb. 10, 1930; d. Leon R. and Edith R. (Rau) Levy; B.A., Skidmore Coll., 1951; m. Joseph Duffey, Setp. 17, 1974; children by previous marriage—David Wexler, Daniel Wexler. Mem. Westport (Conn.) Zoning Bd. Appeals, 1966-71; campaign mgr. Joe Duffey for U.S. Senate from Conn., 1969-70; exec. dir. voter rights project Common Cause, 1971-72, Citizens for Muskie, Muskie for Pres., 1972; exec. dir. com. voter registration Democratic Nat. Com., 1972; project dir. telethon, 1974; asso. publisher Rolling Stone mag., 1974-76; mem. Carter-Mondale transition planning group, 1976-77; dep. undersec. Dept. Commerce, 1977-78; asst. to Pres., White House, Washington, 1978—; cons. in field. Mem. nat. steering com. Carter/Mondale, 1976; mem. edn. and tng. council Dem. Nat. Com., 1976. Fellow Inst. Politics, John F. Kennedy Sch. Govt., 1973; named Outstanding Alumna, Skidmore Coll., 1972. Jewish. Home: 2801 New Mexico Ave NW Washington DC 20007 Office: The White House Washington DC 20500

WEXLER, BERNARD CARL, med. researcher, educator; b. Boston, May 1, 1923; s. William and Dora (Gerson) W.; student Dartmouth Coll., 1941; B.A., U. Oreg., 1946; M.A., U. Calif., Berkeley, 1947; Ph.D., Stanford U., 1952; m. Jean Alice Berkel, Sept. 3, 1946; children—Nancy, Helen, William. Responsible investigator AEC, Stanford Research Inst., Menlo Park, Calif., 1952; lectr. Dominican Coll., San Rafael, Calif., 1952; dir. endocrine and pathology dept. Baxter Lab., Morton Grove, Ill., 1953-56; Merrel scholar gerontology, 1956; research asso. May Inst. Med. Research, Jewish Hosp., Cin., 1956-64, dir., 1964—; asst. prof. exptl. medicine and pathology Coll. Medicine, U. Cin., 1956-62, asso. prof., 1962-75, prof., 1975—; mem. med. staff Jewish Hosp.; cons. NSF. Served with U.S. Army, 1942-46. Nat. Heart Inst. Career Devel. awardee, 1962, 72; Am. Heart Assn. fellow, 1960-62. Fellow Gerontol. Soc., Internat. Coll. Angiology; mem. Acad. Medicine Cin., Am. Psychosomatic Soc., AAUP, AAAS, Am. Assn. Lab. Animals Sci., Am. Assn. Pathology and Bacteriology, Am. Diabetes Assn., Biol. Stain Commn., Diabetes Assn. Cin., Internat. Soc. Study Cardiac Metabolism, Internat. Soc. Cardiology, N.Y. Acad. Sci., Am. Soc. Exptl. Pathology, Am. Assn. Med. Colls., Am. Heart Assn., Endocrine Soc., Soc. Exptl. Biology and Medicine, Soc. Sci. Study Reprodn., Sigma Xi. Western hemisphere editor Arterial Wall, 1972—. Home: 7640 DeMar Rd Cincinnati OH 45243 Office: 421 Ridgeway Ave Cincinnati OH 45229

WEXLER, HASKELL, motion picture producer, cameraman; b. Chgo., 1922; s. Simon W.; grad. U. Chgo.; m. Nancy Ashenhurst (div.); two children; m. 2d, Marian Witt; 1 son, Mark. Ednl. documentaries, Chgo., for eleven years; photographer films The Hoodlum Priest; The Best Man; America, America; The Loved One; In The Heat of the Night; Who's Afraid of Virginia Woolf? (Acad. award); The Thomas Crown Affair; American Graffiti; One Flew Over the Cuckoo's Nest, Bound for Glory (Acad. award); Coming Home; (with others) Days of Heaven; producer, writer, dir., photographer Medium Cool, 1969. Address: 6950 Oporto Dr Los Angeles CA 90068

WEXLER, JACQUELINE GRENNAN (MRS. PAUL J. WEXLER), former coll. pres.; b. Sterling, Ill., Aug. 2, 1926; d. Edward W. and Florence (Dawson) Grennan; A.B., Webster Coll., 1948; M.A., U. Notre Dame, 1957; LL.D., Franklin and Marshall Coll., 1968; D.H.L., Brandeis U., 1968; LL.D., Skidmore Coll., 1967, Smith Coll., 1975; D.H.L., Colo. Coll., 1967; Hum.D., U. Mich., 1967, U. Ohio, 1976; D.H.L., Carnegie Inst., 1966; m. Paul J. Wexler, June 12, 1969; stepchildren—Wendy, Wayne. Tchr. English and math. Loretto Acad., El Paso, Tex., 1951-54; tchr. English and math. Nerinx Hall, St. Louis, 1954-59; tchr. English, Webster Coll., 1959-60, asst. to pres., 1959, v.p. devel., 1960, exec. v.p., 1962-65, pres., 1965-69; v.p., dir. internat. univ. studies Acad. for Ednl. Devel., N.Y.C., 1969; pres. Hunter Coll., City U. N.Y., 1969-79; writer, commentator, cons.; mem. Am. Council on Edn., Commn. on Internat. Edn., 1967; mem. adv. com. to dir. NIH, 1978—; mem. exec. panel chief naval ops. U.S. Navy, 1978—; dir. Interpublic Group of Cos., Inc., United Techs. Corp. Mem. Pres.'s Adv. Panel on Research and Devel. in Edn., 1961-65; mem. Pres.'s Task Force on Urban Ednl. Opportunities, 1967. Chmn. bd. dirs. Central Midwestern Regional Ednl. Lab.; bd. dirs. Arts and Edn. Council Greater St. Louis; trustee U. Pa. Recipient N.Y.U. Sch. Edn. Ann. award for creative leadership in edn., 1968; Elizabeth Cutter Morrow award YWCA, 1978; named One of Six Outstanding Women of St. Louis Area, St. Louis chpt. Theta Sigma Phi, 1963, Woman of Achievement in Edn., St. Louis Globe-Democrat, 1964, Woman of Accomplishment, Harpers Bazaar, 1967; Kenyon lectr. Vassar Coll., 1967. Mem. Mo. Acad. Squires, Kappa Gamma Pi. Author: Where I Am Going, 1968. Contbr. articles profl. jours. Address: 222 Park Ave S New York NY 10003

WEXLER, NORMAN, playwright, screenwriter; b. New Bedford, Mass., Aug. 6, 1926; s. Harry and Sophia (Brisson) W.; student Harvard U., 1948; children—Erica, Merin. Screenplays: Joe, 1970, Serpico, 1973, Mandingo, 1975, Drum, 1976, Saturday Night Fever, 1977. Mem. Dramatists Guild, Writers Guild Am. West, Acad. Motion Picture Arts and Scis. Playwright-in-residence Cleve. Playhouse, 1970; NSF grantee.

WEXLER, PETER JOHN, theatrical designer; b. N.Y.C., Oct. 31, 1936; s. S. David and Berda (Sarnoff) W.; B.S. in Design, U. Mich., 1958; student Yale Sch. Drama, 1958; m. Constance Ann Ross, Nov. 30, 1962. Stage designs include White House stage, 1961, War and Peace, 1964, A Joyful Noise, 1966, The White Devils, 1967, In the Matter of J. Robert Oppenheimer, 1968, The Happy Time, 1968, Merv Griffin TV show, 1965; prin. designer Center Theatre Group, Los Angeles, 1967-70; designer N.Y. Philharmonic Promenades, 1965-78; The Trial of the Catonsville 9 (play and film), 1971-72; Leonard Bernstein's Mass, Los Angeles, 1972; N.Y. Philharmonic Rug Concerts, 1973-77; Les Troyens, Met. Opera Co., 1973, Le Prophète, 1976, Terra Nova, 1979, Un Ballo in Maschera, 1980; theatre space Pitts. Pub. Theatre, 1975-77; mem. design team for Frank O. Gehry & Assos. for redesign Hollywood Bowl, 1974—; dir. Cold Storage, Ariz. Theatre Co., 1978. Recipient Internat. Theatre Inst. competition award ANTA, 1965; most imaginative use of scene design award Saturday Rev., 1965; Drama Desk-Joseph Maharan award for The Happy Time as best designer of mus., 1968; Los Angeles Drama Critics Circle award, 1971. Address: 277 West End Ave New York NY 10023

WEXNER, LESLIE HERBERT, retail chain co. exec.; b. Dayton, Ohio, 1937; B.S., Ohio State U., Columbus, 1959, postgrad. Law Sch., 1959-61. Founder, pres., chmn. bd. Limited Stores, Inc., fashion chain, Columbus, 1963—. Mem. bus. adminstrn. adv. council Ohio State U.; founder Orphan's Day at Ohio State Fair; bd. dirs. Hillel Found.; trustee Columbus Jewish Fedn., 1972, Heritage House-Columbus Jewish Home for Aged, 1972, St. Anthony's Hosp., Columbus, 1977, Agudas Achim Synagogue, Columbus. Named Man of Yr., Am. Mktg. Assn., 1974. Mem. Young Pres.'s Orgn., Columbus Area C. of C. (dir.), Sigma Alpha Mu. Club: B'nai B'rith. Office: Limited Stores Inc 1 Limited Pkwy Columbus OH 43216

WEY, HERBERT WALTER, univ chancellor; b. Terre Haute, Ind., June 1, 1914; s. Harry R. and Ruth (Carlisle) W.; B.S., Ind. State Coll., 1937; M.S., U. Ind., 1938, Ed.D., 1950; m. Ruth Jean Jensen, Aug. 22, 1938; children—Buddie Udene (Mrs. Chuck Wetli), Linda Jean (Mrs. Ralph Leach), Mary Jane (Mrs. Roger Cruiser), Brenda Lee (Mrs. Eric Reichard). Instr. mathematics and chemistry Sulphur Springs (Ind.) High Sch., 1937-38; instr. math. Appalachian High Sch., Boone, N.C., 1939-42, prin., 1942-48; dir. tchr. edn., prin. lab. sch. Appalachian State Tchrs. Coll., 1949-52, chmn. dept. edn., 1953; dean grad. studies, 1955-57; mem. faculty U. Miami (Fla.), 1953-55, 58-69, prof. edn., 1958-60, asso. dean Sch. Edn., 1960-69; pres. Appalachian State U., Boone, N.C., 1969-78, chancellor, 1978—. Pres. United Prins. Div. N.C., 1953. Mem. So. Council Tchr. Edn. (editor bull. 1959-61, pres. 1962). So. Assn. Colls. and Schs. (sec. commn. research 1955-56, mem. commn. secondary schs. 1949-55), Assn. Student Teaching, Nat. Assn. Secondary Sch. Prins., Assn. Higher Edn., N.E.A., Phi Delta Kappa (dir. study regional problems and policies relating to desegregation). Presbyn. Author: Action Patterns in School Desegregation—a Guidebook, 1959; Handbook for Principals, 1961; Alternatives in Higher Education: Innovations and Changing Practices Around the World, 1976. Home: Chancellor's Home Appalachian State U Boone NC 28607

WEYAND, ALEXANDER MULQUEEN, army officer; b. Phila., Nov. 11, 1928; s. Alexander Mathias and Marie Walburga (Mulqueen) W.; B.S., U.S. Mil. Acad., 1951; M.A., George Washington U., 1968; postgrad. U. Pitts., 1973; grad. U.S. Air Force Command and Staff Coll., 1963, Armed Forces Staff Coll., 1967, U.S. Army War Coll., 1968; m. Jeanne Coralie Pierce, May 29, 1953; children—Alexander Michael, Julie Kathyleen. Commd. officer, U.S. Army, advanced through grades to maj. gen., 1976; chief vol. army office, Pentagon, 1972-74, dep. comdg. gen. recruiting command, 1974-77; comdr. Allied Command Europe Mobile Force (land), Mannheim-Seckenheim, Fed. Rep. Germany, 1977—. Decorated Legion of Merit with 2 oak leaf clusters, Bronze Star with 2 oak leaf clusters with V, Purple Heart, others. Mem. Assn. of Graduates U.S. Military Acad., Assn. U.S. Army, U.S. Army War Coll. Assn. Roman Catholic. Home: 37 San Jacinto Dr Patrick Henry Village D 6900 Heidelberg Fed Rep Germany Office: Comdr Allied Command Europe Mobile Force Hammonds Barracks D 68 Mannheim-Seckenheim Fed Rep Germany

WEYBREW, JOSEPH ARTHUR, educator, tobacco chemist; b. Wamego, Kans., July 13, 1915; s. Ernest Walter and Sophia Agnes (Hoofset) W.; B.S., Kans. State Coll., 1938, M.S., 1939; student Johns Hopkins, 1938; Ph.D., U. Wis., 1942; m. Lueva Ellinor Alsop, May 27, 1942; children—Thomas Edward, Janis Jean. Asst. nutritionist Kans. State Coll., Manhattan, 1942-43; chief chemist div. indsl. hygiene Kans. Bd. Health, Topeka, 1943; asso prof. nutrition N.C. State U., Raleigh, 1946-49, asso. prof. agronomy, 1949-51, prof., 1951—, William Neal Reynolds Distinguished Prof. agr., 1957—. Served with AUS, 1943- 46. Fellow Am. Inst. Chemists; mem. Am. Chem. Soc., AAAS, N.C. Acad. Sci, Sigma Xi, Phi Kappa Phi, Phi Lambda Upsilon, Pi Mu Epsilon, Phi Sigma. Chmn. editorial bd. Tobacco Sci., 1956-64. Home: 112 Pineland Circle Raleigh NC 27606

WEYERHAEUSER, GEORGE HUNT, forest products co. exec.; b. Seattle, July 8, 1926; s. John Philip and Helen (Walker) W.; B.S. with honors in Indsl. Engring., Yale, 1948; m. Wendy Wagner, July 10, 1948; children—Virginia Lee, George Hunt, Susan W., Phyllis A., David M., Merrill W. With Weyerhaeuser Co., Tacoma, 1949—, successively mill foreman, br. mgr., 1949-56, v.p., 1957-62, exec. v.p., 1962-66, pres., 1966—, also chief exec. officer, dir.; dir. Standard Oil Co. of Calif., Safeco Ins. Co., Boeing Co., Rand Corp. Home: 11801 Gravelly Lake Dr SW Tacoma WA 98499 Office: 2525 S 336th St Tacoma WA 98401

WEYRAUCH, PAUL HUGO, oil co. exec.; b. Sterling, Ill., Oct. 14, 1925; s. Hugo M. and Elizabeth M. (Glafka) W.; B.S., U. Notre Dame, 1948; M.B.A., U. Mich., 1949; m. Marion Palmer, June 19, 1948; children—Elizabeth, Susan, Nancy. With Pitts. Nat. Bank, 1949-53; with Gulf Oil Corp., Pitts., 1953—, asst. treas., 1961-68, fin. rep., 1969-72, treas., 1972—. Trustee Robert Morris Coll., 1973—, Allegheny Gen. Hosp., 1976—. Served with USNR, 1944-47. Lutheran (councilman 1972—). Clubs: Edgeworth, Allegheny Country (Sewickley); Duquesne (Pitts.); University (N.Y.C.). Home: 641 Canterbury Ln Sewickley PA 15143 Office: Gulf Bldg Pittsburgh PA 15219

WEYRAUCH, WALTER OTTO, educator; b. Lindau, Germany, Aug. 27, 1919; s. Hans Ernst Winand and Meta Margarete (Lönholdt) W.; student U. Freiburg, 1937; student U. Frankfurt Main, (Germany), 1940-43, Dr. iur, 1951; LL.B., Georgetown U., 1955; LL.M., Harvard, 1956; J.S.D., Yale, 1962; m. Jill Carolyn White, Mar. 17, 1973; children from previous marriages—Kurt Roman, Corinne Harriet Irene, Bettina Elaine. Came to U.S., 1952. Referendar, Frankfurt, Germany, 1943-48; atty. German cts., U.S. Ct. Appeals, Allied High Commn., Frankfurt, 1949-52; expert on trade regulations, visit in U.S. under auspices Dept. State, 1950; Harvard U. Dumbarton Oaks Library and Collection, Washington, 1953-55; asst. in instrn. Law Sch., Yale, 1956-57; asso. prof. law U. Fla., Gainesville, 1957-60, prof., 1960—. Vis. cons. U. Calif. at Berkeley, Space Scis. Lab., 1965-66; vis. prof. law Rutgers U., 1968; vis. prof. polit. sci. U. Calif. at Berkeley, 1968-69; vis. prof. law U. Frankfurt, 1975; cons. Commn. of Experts on Problems of Succession of the Hague Conf. on Pvt. Internat. Law, U.S. Dept. State, 1968-71. Rockefeller Found. fellow, Europe, 1958-59. Mem. Internat. Assn. Philosophy of Law and Social Philosophy, Law and Soc. Assn., Internat. Soc. on Family Law, AAUP, Assn. Am. Law Schs. (chmn. com. studies beyond 1st degree in law 1965-67) Order of Coif. Author: The Personality of Lawyers, 1964, Zum Gesellschaftsbild des Juristen, 1970; Hierarchie der Ausbildungsstätten, Rechtsstudium und Recht in den Vereinigten Staaten, 1976; contbr. to Clinical Law Training-Interviewing and Counseling, 1972. Home: 2713 SW 5th Pl Gainesville FL 32607 Office: U Fla Coll Law Gainesville FL 32611

WHALE, ARTHUR RICHARD, lawyer, patent adminstr.; b. Detroit, Oct. 28, 1923; s. Arthur B. and Orpha Louella (Doak) W.; B.S. in Chem. Engring., Northwestern U., 1945; LL.B., George Washington U., 1956; m. Roberta Lou Donaldson, Oct. 29, 1949; children—Richard Donaldson, Linda Jean. Chem. engr. Ansul Chem. Co., Marinette, Wis., 1946-47; product devel. Parke, Davis & Co., Detroit, 1947-50, writer med. lit., 1950-52; chem. engr. Bur. Ships, U.S. Dept. Navy, Washington, 1952-54, dep. sect. head, indsl. gas sect., 1954-55; admitted to D.C. bar, 1957, Mich. bar, 1957, Ind. bar, 1977; patent engr. Swift & Co., Washington, 1955-56; patent atty. Upjohn Co., Kalamazoo, 1956-65; asst. mgr. organic chems. sect. patent dept. Dow Chem. Co., Midland, Mich., 1965-66, mgr., 1967-73, mng. counsel, 1973-75; asst. sec., gen. patent counsel Eli Lilly and Co., Indpls., 1975—; lectr. Practicing Law Inst. John Marshall Law Sch. Pres., Nat. Inventors Hall of Fame, Inc., 1978-79. Served to lt. (j.g.) USNR, 1943-46. Mem. State Bar Mich. (chmn. patent trademark copyright sect. 1967-68), Am. Patent Law Assn. (pres. 1974-75), D.C. Bar Assn. (mem. patent trademark copyright div.), Pharm. Mfrs. Assn. (mem. patent trademark copyright com.), Midland County (Mich.) Bar Assn. (pres. 1974-75), Am. Bar Assn. (mem. patent trademark copyright sect.), Assn. Corp. Patent Counsel, Nat. Council Patent Law Assns. (chmn. 1979-80), Club: Masons. Contbr. articles in patent law to profl. jours. Home: 4026 Royal Pine Blvd Indianapolis IN 46250 Office: Eli Lilly and Co Indianapolis IN 46285

WHALEN, CHARLES WILLIAM, JR., business exec.; b. Dayton, Ohio, July 31, 1920; s. Charles William and Colette (Kelleher) W.; B.S., U. Dayton, 1942; M.B.A., Harvard, 1946; postgrad. Ohio State U., 1959-60; LL.D., Central State U. (Ohio), 1966; m. Mary Barbara Gleason, Dec. 27, 1958; children—Charles E., Daniel D., Edward J., Joseph M., Anne E., Mary B. Vice Pres. Dayton Dress Co., 1946-52; faculty U. Dayton, 1952-66, prof. retailing, chmn. dept., 1954-63, prof. econs., chmn. dept.,1963-66; mem. 90th-95th congresses 3d Dist. Ohio; pres. New Directions, Washington, 1978—. Mem. Ohio Ho. of Reps., 1954-60; mem. Ohio Senate, 1960-66; former pres. Dayton Young Republicans. Former trustee Dayton Cerebral Palsy Assn., Dayton Child Guidance Center, Aviation Hall Fame, Grandview Hosp., Dayton Council World Affairs, Dayton Urban League, The Laretto. Served to 1st lt. AUS, 1943-46. Recipient Disting. Alumnus award U. Dayton Alumni Assn., 1975; named One of Top Ten Freshman in Ohio Ho. of Reps., 1955, One of Top Twenty Ohio House Mems., 1957, Outstanding Young Man Dayton Jr. C. of C., 1957, Outstanding Young Man Ohio Jr. C. of C., 1957, One of Top Fifteen Ohio House Mems., 1959, Outstanding Mem. Ohio Senate, 1963. Mem. U. Dayton Alumni Assn., Harvard Bus. Sch. Assn., Am. Legion. Roman Catholic. Clubs: Dayton Agonis, Dayton Nomad, Dayton Bicycle. Office: 305 Massachusetts Ave NE Washington DC 20002

WHALEN, JAMES JOSEPH, coll. pres.; b. Pottsville, Pa., Mar. 6, 1927; s. Frank Leo and Mary M. (McCusker) W.; A.B., Franklin and Marshall Coll., 1950; M.S. (VA fellow), Pa. State U., 1952, Ph.D. in Clin. Psychology (VA fellow), 1955; LL.D., Newton (Mass.) Coll., 1975; m. Gillian Stuart Hamer, Sept. 29, 1956. VA tng. intern clin. psychology Pa. State U., 1951-52, 54-55; clin. psychologist VA Hosp., Pitts., 1955-58; asst. dean, psychologist European div. U. Md., Munich, Germany, 1958-60, asst. dir., prof., Heidelberg, Germany, 1960-64; asso. prof. psychology Ohio U., 1964-66, dir. Psychology Services Center, 1964-65, dean students, 1965-66, prof., 1966-69, adminstrv. v.p., 1966-67, exec. v.p., 1967-69; pres., prof. Newton Coll., 1969-75, also trustee; pres. Ithaca (N.Y.) Coll., 1975—, prof., 1975—; cons. in field; dir., mem. exec. com., vice chmn. trust com. 1st Nat. Bank & Trust Co., Ithaca. Mem. Mayor Newton Com. on Archtl. Planning, 1973-75. Bd. dirs. Ithacare, home for elderly; bd. dirs., chmn. planning and research com., mem. select com. on goals and planning Comm. Ind. Colls. and Univs. N.Y. State. Served with USNR, 1945-46. Pa. State U. scholar, 1950-52; recipient Keiper award Franklin and Marshall Coll., 1948. Licensed psychologist, Mass. Mem. Am., Mass. psychol. assns., Nat. Cath. Edn. Assn. (past pres. coll. and univ. dept. New Eng. unit), N.Y. State C. of C. (edn. com.), Ithaca Garden Club (hon.), Phi Kappa Phi, Phi Delta Kappa, Psi Chi, Phi Kappa Tau. Rotarian (hon.). Clubs: University (N.Y.C.); Royal Auto (London). Contbr. articles on exec. leadership and ednl. adminstrn. to profl. jours. Home: 2 Fountain Pl Ithaca NY 14850 also Jaffrey Center NH

WHALEN, JOSEPH PHILIP, physician, educator; b. Troy, N.Y., June 18, 1933; s. Philip J. and Mary C. (Doyle) W.; A.B., Fordham U., 1955; M.D., SUNY, 1959; m. Elizabeth Varga, July 28, 1972; children—Philip J., Joseph P., Mary P. Intern, SUNY, Syracuse, 1959-60, resident in radiology, 1960-63; practice medicine specializing in radiology, N.Y.C.; instr. radiology Albany (N.Y.) Med. Coll., 1965-66; instr. radiology SUNY, Syracuse, 1963-65, asst. prof., 1966-67, asso. prof., 1967-68; exec. officer dept. radiology N.Y. Hosp., N.Y.C., 1968—; asso. prof. radiology Cornell U. Med. Coll., N.Y.C., 1968-71, prof., chmn. dept. radiology, 1971—; vis. investigator Royal Postgrad. Med. Sch., Hammersmith Hosp., Eng., 1972, Cornell Sch. Veterinary Medicine, 1974; guest lectr. radiology to various univs. in U.S. and Eng., 1972—. Recipient Traveling fellow award Royal Soc. Medicine, 1972; NIH research grantee, 1974—, Winthrope Pharm. Co. grantee, 1973—, Ciba-Ggigy Pharm. Co. grantee, 1974-75, NRC grantee; diplomate Am. Bd. Radiology (guest examiner 1969—). Fellow Royal Coll. Surgeons (Ireland), N.Y. Acad. Medicine; mem. Radiol. Soc. N. Am., Assn. Univ. Radiologists, Am. Roentgen Ray Soc., Internat. Skeletal Soc., Soc. Gastrointestinal Radiologists (founding mem.), Caffey Soc. (hon.). Author: Radiology of the Abdomen, 1976; Radiologic Anatomy of the Colon, 1975. Contbr. chpts. to med. texts, articles to med. jours. Mem. editorial bd. Am. Jour. Roentgenology, Cornell Veterinarian, Investigative Radiology, Skeletal Radiology, Computed Axial Tomography Jour., Radiolog, Jour. Continuing Edn. in Radiology. Office: New York Hosp 525 E 68th St New York NY 10021

WHALEN, KENNETH JOSEPH, telephone co. exec.; b. Whitehall, N.Y., Oct. 16, 1923; s. John B. and Ellen C. (Brown) W.; A.B., Union Coll., Schenectady, 1949; m. Elizabeth R. Horinka, Dec. 27, 1947; children—Jean, Richard, Thomas, Dan. With N.Y. Telephone Co., 1949-68, gen. mgr., Westchester, N.Y., 1959-60, v.p. indsl. relations, N.Y.C., 1960-64, v.p. charge Manhattan-Bronx-Westchester ty., 1964-65, v.p., 1965-68; with ops. and engring. dept. AT&T, 1952; pres. Mich. Bell Telephone Co., 1968-73; v.p. mktg. AT&T, N.Y.C., 1973-78, exec. v.p., 1978—; dir. Am. Motors Corp., Mountain Bell, Warner-Lambert, CORE Industries, Inc. Bd. dirs. Am. Cancer Soc., Hwy. Users Fedn. Mem. Soc. Friendly Sons of St. Patrick. Clubs: Ekwanok Country (Manchester, Vt.); Baltusrol Golf (Springfield, N.J.); Bermuda Dunes Country (Calif.). Home: 15 Kimball Circle Westfield NJ 07090 Office: 295 N Maple Ave Basking Ridge NJ 07920

WHALEN, MYLES VINCENT, JR., lawyer; b. N.Y.C., Feb. 11, 1931; s. Myles Vincent and Julia (Quinn) W.; A.B. magna cum laude, Holy Cross Coll., 1952; LL.B. cum laude, Harvard U., 1955. Admitted to N.Y. bar, 1955; asso. firm Shearman & Sterling & Wright, N.Y.C., 1955-56, 58-62, partner, 1962-68, 70—; v.p., gen. counsel Consol. Edison Co. N.Y., Inc., 1968-70, trustee, 1977—. Mem. N.Y. State Bd. Social Welfare, 1974-76; trustee Coll. New Rochelle, 1971-77, 78—, Presbyn. Hosp. Served with AUS, 1956-58. Roman Catholic. Clubs: Univ., Brook, Links, Down Town Assn. (N.Y.C.); Maidstone (E. Hampton, N.Y.). Home: 3 E 77th St New York NY 10021 Office: 53 Wall St New York NY 10005

WHALEN, PHILIP GLENN, poet, novelist; b. Portland, Oreg., Oct. 20, 1923; s. Glenn Henry and Phyllis Bush W.; B.A., Reed Coll., 1951. Author: (poetry) Three Satires, 1951, Self-Portrait, From Another Direction, 1959, Like I Say, 1960, Memoirs of an Inter-Glacial Age, 1960, Every Day, 1965, Highgrade, 1966, On Bear's Head, 1969, Severance Pay, 1971, Scenes of Life at the Capitol, 1971, The Kindness of Strangers, 1975; (novels) You Didn't Even Try, 1967, Imaginary Speeches for a Brazen Head, 1972; (interviews) Off the Wall, 1978; (juvenile) The Invention of the Letter, 1967; lectr., tchr., 1955—. Served with USAAF, 1943-46. Recipient Poet's Found. award, 1962, V. K. Ratcliff award, 1964; Am. Acad. Arts and Letters grantee-in-aid, 1965; Com. on Poetry grantee, 1968, 70, 71. Office: care Public Relations Harcourt Brace Jovanovich 757 Third Ave New York NY 10017*

WHALEN, RICHARD JAMES, author, consultant; b. N.Y.C., Sept. 23, 1935; s. George C. and Veronica (Southwick) W.; B.A., Queen's Coll., 1957; m. Joan Marie Giuffé, Oct. 19, 1957; children—Richard Christopher, Laura, Michael. Asso. editor Richmond (Va.) News Leader, 1957-59; contbg. editor Time mag., 1959-60; editorial writer Wall St. Jour., 1960-62; asso. editor Fortune mag., 1962-66, sr. editor, 1966; writer-in-residence Center Strategic Studies, Georgetown U., Washington, 1966-70; cons. State Dept., 1970—; chmn. Worldwide Info. Resources, Ltd. Club: Cosmos (Washington). Author: The Founding Father: The Story of Joseph P. Kennedy, 1964; A City Destroying Itself, 1965; Catch the Falling Flag, 1972; Taking Sides, 1974; The Wealth Weapon, 1979. Editor: The Report of The President's Commission on an All-Volunteer Armed Force, 1970; Report of the President's Commission on Financial Structure and Regulation, 1971. Home: 5011 Wyandot Ct Fort Sumner MD 20016 Office: 1101 30th St NW Suite 304 Washington DC 20007

WHALEN, ROBERT PETER, state ofcl.; b. Newburgh, N.Y., Apr. 28, 1925; s. William R. and Mary F. (Barclay) W.; B.S., Mt. St. Mary's Coll., Emmitsburg, Md., 1947; M.D., Albany (N.Y.) Med. Coll., 1951; M.P.H., Harvard U., 1953; m. Jo Ann Martino, Sept. 3, 1949; children—Dennis, Kevin, Brian, Timothy, Robert. Intern, USPHS Hosp., Boston, 1951-52; dep. commr., then med. adminstr. Albany County (N.Y.) Welfare Health, 1953-56; commnr. Albany County Dept. Welfare, 1957-60, Albany County Dept. Health, 1960-63; asso. commr. community health service N.Y. State Dept. Health, Albany, 1963-65, dep. commr. community health and hosp. affairs, 1965-68, 2d dep. commr. exec. office, 1968-75, commr. exec. office, 1975-79; vice chmn. N.Y. State Health Planning Commn., 1979—; prof. community health Albany Med. Coll., 1955; pub. health cons. St. Peter's Hosp., Albany, 1952. Served with M.C., AUS, 1944-46. Diplomate Am. Bd. Preventive Medicine. Mem. Alpha Omega Alpha, Delta Omega. Home: 39 Western Ave Ravena NY 12143 Office: Dept Health Empire State Plaza Tower Bldg Albany NY 12237

WHALEN, WILLIAM JEROME, govt. ofcl.; b. Pitts., July 18, 1940; s. William Jerome and Elizabeth Germaine (Ernzer) W.; B.S., Clarion State Coll., 1960; postgrad. Ind. State U., 1964; m. Mary Chastulik, Mar. 28, 1959; children—William, Dennis, Timothy, Michael. With Nat. Park Service, 1965—, dep. supt. Yosemite Nat. Park, 1971, supt. Golden Gate Nat. Recreation Area, 1972-73, gen. mgr. Calif. Bay Area Nat. Parks, 1974-77, dir. Nat. Park Service, Washington, 1977—. Recipient Arthur S. Flemming award U.S. Jaycees, 1971. Democrat. Roman Catholic. Office: Nat Parks Service 18th and C Sts NW Washington DC 22040

WHALEY, DALLAS F(LAY), JR., assn. exec.; b. San Antonio, Aug. 14, 1934; s. Dallas Flay and Lorene (Tackett) W.; student Tex. Technol. U., 1954-56; B.S., Boston U., 1958; postgrad. Wichita State U., 1960-61, U. Utah, 1968-69; M.B.A., Fla. Atlantic U., 1972; M.H.P.E., U. Ill., 1978; m. Linda L. Woodrum, Mar. 20, 1959 (dec. Aug. 1971); children—Lisa Gaye, Michelle De; m. 2d, Geraldine Pellecer, Jan. 6, 1978. Asst. exec. dir. Kans. Med. Soc., Topeka, 1959-61; exec. dir. Med. Soc. Sedgwick County, Wichita, Kans., 1961-65; field rep. AMA, Chgo., 1965-67; div. chief Intermountain Region Med. Soc., Salt Lake City, 1967-69; exec. v.p. Am. Soc. Plastic and Reconstructive Surgeons, Inc., Chgo., 1970—. Mem. Am. Soc. Assn. Execs. (certified), Am. Med. Writers Assn., AMA, Pub. Relations Soc. Am., Am. Assn. Med. Soc. Execs. Home: 6033 N Sheridan Rd Chicago IL 60660 Office: 29 E Madison St Chicago IL 60602

WHALEY, RANDALL MCVAY, educator; b. Hastings, Nebr., Aug. 21, 1915; s. William Joseph and Kittie (McVay) W.; student Ind. U., 1933-35; B.A., U. Colo., 1938, M.A., 1940; Ph.D., Purdue U., 1947; D.Sc., Phila. Coll. Pharmacy and Sci., 1972; m. Miriam Weckessser, Aug. 25, 1939; children—Suzanne Marie, Lisbeth Ellen, Joseph Randall. Grad. asst. physics U. Colo., 1938-40; grad. research asst. physics Purdue U., 1942- 45, from instr. to prof. physics, 1945-56, exec. asst. head dept., 1956- 59, asso. dean Sch. Sci., Edn. and Humanities, 1959-60; tech. asst. to sales mgr. G-M Labs., Inc., Chgo., 1940-41; v.p. grad. studies and research Wayne State U., 1960-65; chancellor U. Mo. at Kansas City, 1965- 67; spl. cons. Am. Council on Edn., 1967-68; edn. cons. Cresap, McCormick & Paget, N.Y.C., 1968-70; pres. Univ. City Sci. Center, Phila., 1970—; pres. Uni-Coll Corp., Phila., 1971-73, vice chmn., 1973—; acting dir. Purdue Research Found., 1959-60; del. congress Internat. Sci. Film Assn., Moscow, USSR, 1958, Prague, Czechoslovakia, 1960, Paris, 1963, Athens, Greece, 1964; cons. OEEC, summer 1959; mem. State Dept. mission to Baghdad, 1960; participant USIA conf., Cairo, 1960; mem. nat. adv. council on nurse tng. USPHS, 1966—; mem. pub. evaluation com. state tech. services Dept. Commerce, 1966—. Mem. Gov. Ind. Citizens Com. Pub. Schs., 1955-57; exec. dir. adv. bd. edn. Nat. Acad. Scis., 1957-59; trustee Cranbrook Inst. Sci., 1961-65; bd. dirs., exec. com. Met. Fund, Inc., 1963-65; trustee Council Internat. Non-Theatrical Events, 1962-69, Mich. Health and Social Security Research Inst., 1963-65, Midwest Research Inst., Harry S. Truman Library Inst., Kansas City Museum, Met. YMCA Phila., 1975—; mem. John Scott award com. Phila. chpt. Young Audiences, Inc., 1975—, trustee, 1977—; bd. visitors Air U., USAF; bd. dirs. Kansas City Gen. Hosp. and Med. Center, World Affairs Council Phila., West Phila. Corp. Fellow AAAS; mem. Internat. Sci. Film Assn. (pres.), Am. Council Edn. (commn. internat. edn.), Am. Sci. Film Assn. (pres.), Am. Phys. Soc., Am. Assn. Physics Tchrs., AAUP, Am. Soc. Engring. Edn., Nat. Sci. Tchrs. Assn., Engring. Soc. Detroit, Phi Beta Kappa, Sigma Xi (v.p. Purdue 1958-59), Sigma Pi Sigma, Phi Delta Kappa, Phi Eta Sigma. Clubs: Cosmos; Union League (Phila.). Home: 639 Broad Acres Rd Narberth PA 19072 Office: 3624 Market St Philadelphia PA 19104

WHALEY, STORM HAMMOND, govt. ofcl.; b. Sulphur Springs, Ark., Mar. 15, 1916; s. Storm Onus and Mabel Etta (Prater) W.; B.A., John Brown U., 1935; LL.D., 1959; postgrad. Am. U. Law Sch., 1954; m. Jane Florence Bucy, Oct. 6, 1935; children—Carroll Jean Whaley Anderson, Ann Marie Whaley McDonald, Rebecca Glenn Whaley Dyess. Mgr., Sta. KUOA, Siloam Springs, Ark., 1935-53, Sta. KGER, Long Beach, 1948-53, KOME, Tulsa, 1951-53; asst. to Congressman J.W. Trimble, 1953-54; asst. to pres. U. Ark., 1954-59, acting pres., 1959-60, v.p. health scis., 1960-70; asso. dir. communications NIH, Bethesda, Md., 1970—; mem. U.S. del. World Health Assembly, 1962, 63, 64; mem. nat. adv. health council USPHS, 1963-66; chmn. ad hoc com. Report to Pres. and Congress Regional Med. Programs, 1967. Del. Democratic Nat. Conv., 1940, 44, 48, 52. Recipient Superior Service award HEW, 1974. Mem. Broadcast Pioneers, Ark. Broadcasters Assn., Am. Med. Writers Assn., Omicron Delta Kappa, Lambda Chi Alpha. Presbyterian. Clubs: Masons (33 deg.), K.T.; Nat. Press (Washington). Author: They Call It, 1951. Home: 4400 East West Hwy Bethesda MD 20014 Office: 9000 Rockville Pike Bethesda MD 20205

WHALEY, THOMAS GAINES, labor union ofcl.; b. Covington, Ky., May 4, 1930; s. Calloway Bernard and Effie Marie (Furnier) W.; ed. public schs.; m. E. Eileen Hanspire, June 11, 1975; children—Thomas H., Kim B., Karen L., Mark J., James L., Paul M. With Retail Clks. Internat. Union, 1959—, internat. sec.-treas., 1977—; now also exec. v.p. United Food and Comml. Workers Internat. Union. Served iwth U.S. Army, 1948-54. Democrat. Methodist. Clubs: Masons, Shriners. Home: 14723 Wycombe St Centerville VA 22020 Office: 1775 K St NW Washington DC 20006

WHALEY, W(ILLIAM) GORDON, cell biologist; b. N.Y.C., Jan. 16, 1914; s. Frank H. and Mae (Manson) W.; B.S., U. Mass., 1936; Ph.D. (Nathaniel Lord Britton fellow), Columbia U., 1939; m. Clare Youngren, June 19, 1938; 1 dau., Patricia Anne. Lectr., Barnard Coll., 1939-40; instr. Columbia U., 1940-43; asso. geneticist Dept. Agr., 1943-44, sr. geneticist, 1944-46; asso. prof. botany U. Tex., Austin, 1946-48, prof., 1948—, Ashbel Smith prof. cellular biology, 1972—, chmn. dept. botany, 1948-62, dir. Plant Research Inst., 1947-64, dir. Cell Research Inst., 1964-79, asso. dean Grad. Sch., 1957-59, dean Grad. Sch. 1959-72; vis. prof. Rockefeller U., 1964-72, presdl. asso., 1972—; vis. prof. U. Leningrad, 1978; bd. dirs. Austin Diagnostic Clinic Found., 1978-81. Clayton Found. grantee, 1946-56, NSF grantee, 1956-68, NIH grantee, 1958-79, Faith Found. grantee, 1966-78. Mem. Am. Soc. Cell Biology, Bot. Soc. Am. (Merit award 1978), Torrey Bot. Club (hon. life), Soc. Devel. Biology, Internat. Fedn. Cell Biologists, AAAS, Internat. Soc. Study Differentiation, Electron Microscopy Soc. Am., Tex. Soc. Electron Microscopy, Austin Community Assn. (founding), Sigma Xi. Author: Biology for Everyone, 1948; Principles of Biology, 1954, 3d rev. edit., 1964; The Golgi Apparatus, 1975; contbr. numerous articles to profl. jours.; editor Grad. Jour., 1958-75, Jour. Assn. Grad. Schs., 1964-69; editorial bd. Jour. Ultrastructure Research, 1969, Cytobios, 1969, Microbios, 1969. Office: Cell Research Inst U Tex Austin TX 78712

WHALING, ANNE, educator; b. Houston, Mar. 30, 1914; d. Horace Morland and Annie Byrd (Ward) Whaling; B.A., So. Meth. U., 1933, M.A., 1934; Ph.D., Yale U., 1946. Cataloger, specialist in music, fgn. langs., So. Meth. U., 1947-55; tchr. English dept. Arlington State Coll., 1955, instr., 1955-57, asst. prof., 1957-60, asso. prof. English, 1960-67; asso. prof. English, U. Tex., Arlington, 1967-71, prof. English, 1971—. Program annotator for chamber music series Dallas Mus. Fine Arts, 1956-61. Mem. bd. dirs. Dallas Chamber Music Soc., 1954—. Recipient Decima Lantern award So. Meth. U., 1933; Woman of Achievement award So. Meth. U. Alumni Assn., 1968. Mem. Am. Studies Assn. of Tex. (mem. steering com. 1956—, councilor 1961-62), Modern Lang. Assn., Am. Assn. U. Women (chmn. fellowship com. Dallas br. 1959-64), South Central Modern Lang. Assn., The Malone Soc., Phi Beta Kappa. Methodist. Home: 3320 Daniels Ave Dallas TX 75205 Office: U Tex Arlington TX 76010

WHALING, WARD, educator, physicist; b. Dallas, Sept. 29, 1923; s. Horace Morland and Annie Byrd (Ward) W.; B.A., Rice U., 1944, M.A., 1947, Ph.D., 1949; m. Mary Lou Slighter, Sept. 1, 1955; children—Anne Buell, Carol Susan. Mem. faculty Calif. Inst. Tech., 1949—, prof. physics, 1962—. Mem. Am. Phys. Soc. (regional sec. Western states 1964—). Home: 401 S Parkwood Ave Pasadena CA 91107

WHALLEY, EDWARD, chemist; b. Darwen, Eng., June 20, 1925; s. Edward and Doris (Riding) W.; came to Can., 1950; B.Sc., Imperial Coll., London, 1945, Ph.D., 1949, D.Sc., 1964; m. Isabel Elizabeth Gillespie, Aug. 27, 1956; children—Brian, Monica, Kevin. Lectr., Royal Tech. Coll., Salford, Eng., 1948-50; postdoctoral fellow div. chemistry NRC Can., Ottawa, Ont., 1950-52, research officer div. chemistry, 1952-62, head high pressure sect., 1962—; sessional lectr. dept. chem. engring. U. Ottawa, 1954, dept. chemistry, 1967, 69; vis. prof. U. Western Ont., 1967, Kyoto (Japan) U., 1974-75. Fellow Royal Soc. Can. (asso. hon. treas. 1969-71, asso. hon. sec. and chmn. awards com. 1971-74, editor Sect. III 1972-74, hon. sec. 1974-77), Chem. Inst. Can. (chmn. div. phys. chemistry 1971-72); mem. Can. Assn. Physicists, Am. Phys. Soc., Internat. Glaciological Soc., Internat. Assn. High Pressure Sci. and Tech. (treas. 1975—), Internat. Assn. Properties of Steam (chmn. Can. nat. com. 1974—). Club: Alpine of Can. (chmn. Ottawa sect. 1970-74, chmn. safety com. 1975—, eastern v.p. 1978—). Contbr. articles to profl. and mountaineering jours.; co-editor: Physics and Chemistry of Ice, 1974; Can. editor: Accidents in North American Mountaineering, 1976—; leader several Arctic mountaineering expdns. Office: Div Chemistry NRC Can Ottawa ON K1A OR9 Canada

WHALLEY, GEORGE, educator, author; b. Kingston, Ont., Can., July 25, 1915; s. Arthur Francis Cecil and Dorothy (Quirk) W.; B.A., Bishop's U., 1935, M.A., 1948; B.A., Oriel Coll., Oxford U., 1939, M.A., 1945; Ph.D., King's Coll., London, 1950; D.Litt., Carleton Coll., 1977, U. Sask., 1979; D.C.L., Bishop's U., 1979; m. Elizabeth Cecilia Muriel Watts, July 25, 1944; children—Katharine Cecilia Clark, Christopher Gilbert, Emily Elizabeth. Tchr., Rothesay Collegiate Sch., N.B., Can., 1936, 39-40; lectr., asst. prof. English Bishop's U., 1945-48; mem. faculty dept. English Queen's U., Kingston, Ont., Can., 1950—, James Cappon prof., 1962—, head English dept., 1962-67, 77-80; vis. prof. U. Wis., 1962. Pres., Kingston Symphony Assn., 1963-70; mem. adv. com. to Minister of Nat. Def. on Can. Service Colls., 1962-67; bd. dirs. Can. Fedn. for Humanities, 1978—. Served with Royal Can. Navy, 1940-45. Rhodes scholar, 1936-39; Nuffield fellow, 1956-57; Guggenheim Found. fellow, 1967-68; Killam sr. fellow, 1973-75; recipient numerous grants Can. Council. Fellow Royal Soc. Lit., Fellow Royal Soc. Can.; mem. Assn. Can. Univ. Tchrs. English (chmn. 1958-59), Humanities Assn. Can., Charles Lamb Soc. Mem. Ch. of Eng. Author: No Man an Island (poetry), 1948; Poetic Process, 1953, 67, 73; The Legend of John Hornby, 1962, 77; and other books. Contbr. articles to profl. and other jours.; also numerous broadcasts and scripts to radio and TV. Home: Rural Route 1 Hartington ON K0H 1W0 Canada Office: Dept English Queen's Univ Kingston ON K7L 3N6 Canada

WHALLON, EVAN ARTHUR, JR., orch. conductor; b. Akron, Ind., July 24, 1923; s. Evan Arthur and Katharine (Kistler) W.; Mus.B., Eastman Sch. Music, 1948, M.Mus., 1949; Mus.D. (hon.), Denison U., 1963, Otterbein U., 1969, Ohio Dominican U., 1970; m. Jean Borgman, Aug. 28, 1948; children—Paul Evan, Eric Andrew. Debut with Phila. Orch., 1948; condr. opera The Consul, 1950; condr. Springfield (Ohio) Symphony, 1951-56, Columbus (Ohio) Symphony, 1956—; guest conductor Spoleto (Italy) Festival, Phila. Orch., Cleve. Orch., Buffalo Philharmonic, Boston Arts Festival, N.Y.C. Opera, San Francisco Spring Opera, Balt. Symphony, Prague Symphony Orch., Budapest Mav Symphony; condr., mus. dir. Chatauqua (N.Y.) Opera Assn., 1966—. Served to lt. (j.g.) USNR, World War II. Clubs: Torch, Rotary, Kit Kat (Columbus). Home: 2993 Shadywood Rd Columbus OH 43221 Office: 200 E Town St Columbus OH 43215

WHALLON, WILLIAM, educator; b. Richmond, Ind., Sept. 24, 1928; s. Arthur J. and Adelaide (Wheeler) W.; B.A., McGill U., 1950; Ph.D., Yale, 1957; m. Joanne Holland, Aug. 22, 1957; children—Andrew, Nicholas. Faculty, Reed Coll., 1957-62; faculty Mich. State U., East Lansing, 1963—, now prof. comparative lit. Fellow, Center for Hellenic Studies, 1962-63. Author: Formula, Character and Context, 1969. Home: 1532 Parkvale Ave East Lansing MI 48823

WHAM, GEORGE SIMS, mag. exec.; b. Laurens, S.C., Jan. 27, 1920; s. George Sims and Nellie (Melette) W.; B.S., Clemson U., 1941; M.S., U. Tenn., 1947; Ph.D., Pa. State U., 1951; m. Beth Keeler, Sept. 13, 1947; children—Norman Brent, Bonnie Beth, Barry Keeler. Textile technologist USDA, 1947-49; research asso. Sch. Chemistry and Physics, Pa. State U., 1949-51; prof., asst. dean Tex. Women's U., 1951-54; sr. editor Good Housekeeping mag., N.Y.C., 1954-60, v.p., tech. dir., 1961—; dir. research and devel. Phillips Van Heusen, Inc., 1960-61; mem. corporate bd. Underwriters Labs.; dir. BFTB Corp. Guest lectr. Purdue U., U. Md., Ariz. State U., U. Conn., U. Del.,

Clemson U., U. R.I., Mich. State U.; leader U.S. del. Internat. Standards Confs., 1968, 71; pres. Governing Council, Hightstown, N.J., 1960-62; mem. Bd. Edn., Hightstown, 1959-61; bd. dirs. Am. Nat. Standards Inst. Served to maj. AUS, 1941-46. Decorated Silver Star medal, Purple Heart. Mem. Am. Assn. Textile Chemists and Colorists (past pres.), Am. Nat. Standards Inst. (chmn. textile standards bd. 1966-68), Consumer Council (dir.), Sigma Xi, Phi Psi, Omicron Nu. Contbr. articles to profl. jours. Home: 201 E Ward St Hightstown NJ 08520 Office: 959 8th Ave New York NY 10019

WHAM, WILLIAM NEIL, publisher; b. N.Y.C., Dec. 28, 1934; s. William and Jessie (Neill) W.; B.S., Syracuse U., 1956; m. Lynn McCorvie, Mar. 6, 1966; children—McCorvie, Avery. Salesman Mut. N.Y., N.Y.C., 1959-61; regional sales mgr. Doubleday Pub. Co., N.Y.C., 1961-64, Reinhold Pub. Co., N.Y.C., 1964-68; sales mgr. United Bus. Publs., N.Y.C., 1968; pres., pub. Internat. Scientific Communications, Inc., Fairfield, Conn., 1968—. Served with AUS, 1956-58. Founder Am. Lab. (sci. jour.), (with Kenneth S. Halaby) Internat. Lab. Home: 157 Pinewood Trail Trumbull CT 06611 Office: Internat Scientific Communications Inc 808 Kings Hwy Fairfield CT 06430

WHAN, GLENN ALAN, educator; b. North Lima, Ohio, Aug. 8, 1930; s. William H. and Margaret (Roys) W.; B.S., Ind. Inst. Tech., 1951; M.S., Mont. State U., 1953; Ph.D., Carnegie Inst. Tech., 1957; m. Ruth Elaine Fleming, Aug. 13, 1955; children—William, David, Cynthia. Asst. prof. chem. engring. U. N.Mex., 1957-59; staff mem. Los Alamos Sci. Lab., 1959-60; asso. prof. to prof. U. N.Mex., 1961-66, chmn. dept. nuclear engring., 1966-72, chmn. dept. chem. and nuclear engring., 1972-75, asso. dean engring., 1976-79; dir. Los Alamos Grad. Center, 1963-66; tech. cons. Internat. Atomic Energy Agy., Portugal, 1966-67; dir. Western Interstate Energy, Inc.; engring. cons. Fellow Am. Nuclear Soc.; mem. Am. Inst. Chem. Engrs., Am. Soc. Engring. Edn., Nat. Soc. Profl. Engrs., Sigma Xi, Sigma Tau. Home: 925 Truman St NE Albuquerque NM 87110

WHANG, YUN CHOW, educator; b. Foochow, China, Dec. 13, 1931; s. Ta Chun and Wenlun (Lin) W.; came to U.S., 1955; Ph.D., U. Minn., 1961; m. Yeong-Ping Chu, Aug. 29, 1959; children—Ruth, Joyce, Kenneth. Asst. prof. U. Fla., 1961-62; asst. prof. The Cath. U. Am., 1962-63, asso. prof., 1963-67, prof., 1968—, chmn. dept., 1971—; sr. research asso. Nat. Acad. Scis., 1967-68; vis. prof. Royal Inst. Tech., Stockholm, Sweden, 1972-73. Asso. fellow Am. Inst. Aero. and Astronautics; mem. Am. Geophys. Union, ASME. Research solar wind theory, magnetosphere of Mercury, interaction solar wind with moon and planets. Home: 54 Stonegate Dr Silver Spring MD 20904

WHARTON, CLIFTON REGINALD, JR., univ. chancellor; b. Boston, Sept. 13, 1926; B.A., Harvard U., 1947; M.A., Johns Hopkins U., 1948, LL.D., 1970, M.A., U. Chgo., 1956, Ph.D. in Econs., 1958; LL.D., U. Mich., 1970, Wayne State U., 1970, Central Mich. U., 1970, Oakland U., 1971, Georgetown U., 1976, CCNY, 1978, Wright State U., 1979; L.H.D., Columbia U., 1978; m. Dolores Duncan, 1950; children—Clifton, Bruce. Exec. trainee Am. Internat. Assn. Econs. and Social Devel., 1948-49, program analyst, 1949-51, head reports and analysis, 1951-53; research asst. econs. U. Chgo., 1953-56, research asso., 1956- 57; exec. asso. Agrl. Devel. Council, 1957-58, asso. Singapore region, 1958-64, dir. Am. univ. research program, 1964-67, v.p., 1967-69; pres. Mich. State U., 1970-78; chancellor SUNY, 1978—; vis. prof. U. Malaya (Singapore), 1958-60, U. Malaya, 1960-64, Stanford, 1964-65; dir. Ford Motor Co., Equitable Life Assurance Soc.; mem. Presdl. Task Force Agr. in Vietnam, 1966; adv. panel on East Asia and Pacific, State Dept., 1966-69; mem. Presdl. mission to Latin Am., 1969, Presdl. Com. on World Hunger, 1978—; chmn. bd. internat. food and agrl. devel. AID, State Dept., 1976—. Trustee or dir. Rockefeller Found., 1970—, Asia Soc., 1969-77, Overseas Devel. Council, 1969—, Carnegie Found., 1970—, Agrl. Devel. Council, 1973—. Mem. Am. Agrl. Econs. Assn., Am. Econs. Assn., Assn. Asian Studies, Nat. Acad. Edn., Council Fgn. Relations, Internat. Assn. Agrl. Econs. Club: Univ. (N.Y.C.). Co-author: Patterns for Lifelong Learning, 1973; editor: Subsistence Agriculture and Economic Growth, 1968; contbr. articles to profl. jours. Address: Office of Chancellor State U NY State Univ Plaza Albany NY 12246

WHARTON, DON (LACY DONNELL WHARTON, JR.), writer, editor; b. Smithfield, N.C., July 29, 1905; s. Lacy D. and Lilian (Benton) W.; A.B., Davidson Coll., 1927; student Harvard, 1928-29; m. Mary Louise Tilley, Nov. 1, 1930; children—Margaret (Mrs. Hercules A. Segalas), Julia (Mrs. Ralph W. Douglas). Reporter for Greensboro (N.C.) Daily News, 1927-28, New York Herald Tribune, 1929-30; asso. editor Outlook and Independent, 1930-32, The New Yorker, 1932-35; literary editor and staff writer Today Mag., 1935-36; asso. editor Scribner's Mag., 1936-38, exec. editor, 1938-39; roving editor The Reader's Digest, 1958-76. Mem. Phi Delta Theta. Omicron Delta Kappa. Editor: The Roosevelt Omnibus, 1934. Contbr. to Reader's Digest, Saturday Evening Post, New Yorker, Look, Scribner's, McCall's, other mags. Home: 24 Gramercy Park New York NY 10003. *Work. Imagination and luck.*

WHARTON, ELIZABETH AUSTIN, newspaperwoman; b. Laredo, Tex., July 15, 1920; d. Lawrence Hay and Alice (Borchers) W.; B.A., B.J., U. Tex., 1941. Woman's editor Galveston (Tex.) News, 1942; soc. editor Houston Post, 1942-43; mem. staff UPI, 1943—, Congressional corr., Washington, 1945—, week-end editor, 1974-75, overnight editor, 1976—. Mem. Am. Contract Bridge League (life master, life mem.), Washington Press Club, Nat. Press Club, Theta Sigma Phi. Presbyterian. Home: 5 Snow's Ct NW Washington DC 20037 Office: Nat Press Bldg Washington DC 20045

WHARTON, JAMES HENRY, univ. adminstr.; b. Mangum, Okla., July 23, 1937; s. John Henry and Emma Faye (Walling) W.; B.S., N.E. La. Coll., 1959; Ph.D., La. State U., 1962; m. Joan Monette McPherson, Nov. 21, 1956; children—Sherri Shannon, John Scott. Instr. chemistry La. State U., Baton Rouge, 1962, asst. prof., 1965-69, asso. dean chemistry and physics, then dean jr. div., 1969-75, dean Gen. Coll., 1975—, acting chancellor, Alexandria, 1978; scientist Marshall Space Flight Center-NASA, 1963-64. Served with U.S. Army, 1962-65. Mem. Am. Chem. Soc., Phi Kappa Phi, Omicron Delta Kappa. Democrat. Methodist.

WHARTON, TILFORD GIRARD, lawyer; b. Paterson, N.J., June 13, 1904; s. Birdell Lamont and May Stewart (McCollom) W.; B.A., Rutgers U., 1925; LL.B. cum laude, Yale, 1928; m. Isabelle Helen Schillo, Oct. 23, 1931 (dec. Mar. 1964); children—Nancy Jane (Mrs. Alvin E. Duryea, Jr.), Constance Sue (Mrs. Norman D. Nasson), Lucinda Stewart (Mrs. Lucius J. Kellam III). Admitted to N.J. bar, 1928, since practiced in Somerville; sr. partner firm Wharton, Stewart & Davis, 1941—; asst. prosecutor Somerset County, 1931-41, prosecutor, 1946-53. Dir. John A. Roebling's Sons Co., 1936-60; pres., treas., dir. Interam. Mining Corp., N.Y.C., 1959-69; dir. A. Menendez & Co., Miami. Mem. adv. com. profl. ethics Supreme Ct. N.J., 1963—; mem. Gov. N.J. Commn. State Adminstrv. and Profl. Compensation and Commn. on Criminal Law, U.S. Circuit Judge Nominating Commn., 1977—. Gen. chmn. bldg. fund Somerset Valley YMCA; N.J. chmn. Yale Law Sch. capital funds campaign, 1963-64; Eastern regional vice chmn. Yale Law Sch. Fund, 1964-65, nat. chmn., 1965-67, pres., 1967-69, dir., 1967—. Mem. borough council, Somerville, 1947-49; trustee Somerset Med. Center, 1945—; pres., trustee Alpha Rho Meml. Found., 1952—; bd. overseers Rutgers Univ. Found., 1977—. Recipient Herbert Lincoln Harley award Am. Judicature Soc., 1974. Fellow Am. Bar Found., Am. Coll. Probate Counsel; mem. Am. (ho. dels.), N.J. (gen. council 1948-49, trustee 1961-65, 2d v.p. 1965-66, 1st v.p. 1966-67, pres. 1968-69), Somerset County (pres. 1948) bar assns., Assn. Bar City N.Y., Am. Judicature Soc. (dir. 1971-75), N.J. Bar Found. (trustee 1970—), Yale Law Sch. Assn. (nat. v.p. 1967-68, nat. mem. exec. com. 1963-64, pres. N.J. 1964-65; hon. mem. exec. com. 1978—), Phi Beta Kappa, Order of Coif, Chi Psi, Phi Delta Phi. Clubs: Raritan Valley Country (Somerville); Eastern Shore Yacht and Country (Pungoteague, Va.); Lawyers (N.Y.C.); Vesper (Phila.). Home: 1 Prospect St Somerville NJ 08876 Office: 50 W Main St Somerville NJ 08876

WHATLEY, BROWN LEE, mortgage banker, realtor; b. Ashland, Ala., Mar. 19, 1900; s. Madison Hayne and Ola (Northern) W.; student Riverside Mil. Acad., 1917-19, Chgo. Art Inst., 1919-20, Art Students League N.Y., 1920-21, U. Ga., 1922-23; m. Marion Harlan, June 4, 1924; children—Brown L., Marion H. Whatley Law. Mgr., Western Ga. Fair Assn., La Grange, 1919-20; advt. mgr. Southeastern Fair, Atlanta, 1920-21, Fla. State Fair, Jacksonville, 1922-23, Believers in Jacksonville, 1923-24; advt. mgr. Telfair Stockton & Co., Jacksonville, 1925-27, mgr. sales, 1927-29, exec. v.p., 1929-37; pres. Whatley, Davin & Co., St. Nicholas Park Co., San Marco Pl. Co., Southside Properties Inc., 1937-46 (all Jacksonville); pres. Stockton, Whatley, Davin & Co., Jacksonville, 1946-60, chmn. bd., mem. exec. com., 1960—; chmn. pres., mem. exec. com. Arvida Corp., Miami, 1962-72, chmn. bd., mem. exec. com., 1972-77; pres. Arvida Realty Sales Inc., Miami, 1961-72, chmn., 1972-77; vice chmn., dir. Am. Nat. Bank of Jacksonville, 1945-51; dir. Fla. Nat. Bank of Miami, Gen. Am. Oil Co. of Tex. Mem. Duval County (Fla.) Bd. Pub. Instruction, 1933-45; mem. com. govt. expenditures U.S. C. of C., 1958-62; mem. Jacksonville Com. One Hundred, 1961—; mem. Nat. Bd. Fed. City Council, Washington, 1964—; trustee Bapt. Meml. Hosp., Jacksonville, Fla., Grand Central Art Galleries of N.Y.C., Met. Mus. and Art Center Miami. Mem. Jacksonville Bd. Realtors (pres. 1943), Jacksonville (dir.), Fla. chambers commerce, Mortgage Bankers Assn. Am. (pres. 1952-53, life mem. bd. govs.), Mortgage Bankers Legion (life), Sigma Chi (life). Democrat. Baptist (deacon). Clubs: Masons, K.T., Shriners, Rotary; Fla. Yacht, San Jose Country, River, Univ., Ponte Vedra (Jacksonville); Bankers, Miami (Miami); Indian Creek Country, Indian Creek Village, La Gorce Country (Miami Beach); Boca Raton (Fla.) Hotel and Club; Longboat Key Golf (Sarasota, Fla.). Home: 2550 Bay Ave Sunset Island #2 Miami Beach FL 33140 Office: One Biscayne Tower Miami FL 33131 also 100 W Bay St Jacksonville FL 32202

WHATLEY, THOMAS JEWEL, educator, agrl. economist; b. Linville, Ala., Feb. 18, 1918; s. Thomas and Tula (Watts) W.; B.S., Ala. Poly. Inst., 1941; M.S., Purdue U., 1947, Ph.D., 1953; m. Lila Nell Rawlinson, June 18, 1948; children—John Thomas, Beth Anita. County supr. Farm Security Adminstrn., Marion, Ala., 1942-43; asst. agrl. economist, dept. agr. econs. and rural sociology U. Tenn., 1947-53, asso. agr. economist, 1953-56, agr. economist, 1956-58, acting head dept., 1958-59, head dept., 1959—, distinguished service prof., 1964—, asst. dean Tenn. Agrl. Expt. Sta., 1972-76, asso. dean, 1976—. Served to lt. USNR, 1943-46. Mem. Am., So. (pres. 1970) agrl. econ. assns., Am., Tenn. socs. farm mgrs. and rural appraisers, Sigma Xi, Phi Kappa Phi, Gamma Sigma Delta, Alpha Gamma Rho. Contbr. articles profl. jours. Home: 7137 Wellington Dr Knoxville TN 37919

WHATMORE, MARVIN CLEMENT, broadcasting exec.; b. Albia, Iowa, June 22, 1908; s. John and Nora (Evans) W.; A.B., Drake U., 1932, L.H.D., 1966; postgrad. State U. Iowa, 1931-32; Litt.D., St. Bonaventure U., 1964; m. Lois Reynolds, Mar. 3, 1934; children—Sharon Lee, Sue Ann, James Marvin, Linda Reynolds. Asst. auditor Iowa-Des Moines Nat. Bank & Trust Co., 1932-35; accountant Des Moines Register & Tribune Co., 1936; office mgr. Look, Inc., N.Y.C., 1937, asst. treas., 1940, treas., 1941, mem. bd. dirs., bus. mgr. Look mag., 1943, Look, Inc. (became Cowles Mags., Inc., 1943), mem. bd. dirs., 1943, v.p., 1949-64, pres., 1964—, chief exec. officer, 1969-77, chmn. bd., chief exec. officer, 1977— (co. name changed to Cowles Mag. & Broadcasting, Inc., 1961, to Cowles Communications, Inc. 1965); dir. Cavitron Corp. Recipient Distinguished Service award Drake U., 1958. Clubs: Mission Valley Golf and Country, Univ. (N.Y.); Univ. (Sarasota); Oceanside Country (Ormond Beach, Fla.); Halifax (Daytona Beach, Fla.); Oceans Racquet (Daytona Beach Shores, Fla.). Home: 7208 Turnstone Rd Sarasota FL 33581 Office: 444 Seabreeze Blvd Daytona Beach FL 32018. *I believe rewards in life come to the individual with a goal. I know if I am in the process of achieving my goal, I am at that time successful. And I believe self-image sets the boundaries of individual accomplishment. Finally, I believe the reward is equal to the quality of the individual's service performed for others.*

WHAYNE, TOM FRENCH, physician, ret. med. educator; b. Columbus, Ky., Dec. 26, 1905; s. Harry Utterbach and Virginia (French) W.; student Western Ky. State Normal, 1922-23; B.A., U. Ky., 1927; M.D., Washington U., 1931; certificate Med. Field Service Sch., 1935; M.P.H. cum laude, Harvard U., 1949, Dr.P.H., 1950; m. Mary Lutenia Porter, Dec. 21, 1934; children—Thomas French, Mary Patricia. Intern, Mo. Baptist Hosp., St. Louis, 1931-32; house physician Mo. Pacific Hosp., St. Louis; surgeon Civilian Conservation Corps Camp, 1933-34; physician Fitzsimmons Gen. Hosp., Denver, 1934; commd. 1st lt., M.C., U.S. Army, 1934, advanced through grades to col., 1944; assigned U.S., 1934-38, C.Z., 1938-41; chief med. intelligence Surgeon Gen.'s Office, 1941-43, dep. chief preventive medicine div., Washington, 1946-47, chief 1947-48, 51-55; asst. mil. attache for medicine Am. embassy, London, 1943-44; chief preventive medicine sect. 12th Army Group, 1944-45; chief preventive medicine Office Chief Surgeon ETO, 1945-46; mil. adviser U.S. del. 1st World Health Assembly, Geneva, 1948, 6th Assembly, 1953; chief dept. tng. doctrines Army Med. Service Grad. Sch., Walter Reed Army Med. Center, 1950-51; ret., 1955; prof. preventive medicine and pub. health Sch. Medicine, U. Pa., 1955-63, asso. dean Sch. Medicine, 1957-63; asst. v.p. for Med. Center, U. Ky., 1963-67, asso. dean Coll. Medicine, 1963-73, prof. community medicine, 1963-74, prof. emeritus, 1974—, acting dean Coll. Medicine, 1966-67; cons. med. history div. U.S. Army Center Mil. History. Bd. dirs. Gorgas Meml. Inst. Tropical and Preventive Medicine. Decorated Legion of Merit; Croix de Guerre (Belgium and France); Order Couronne de Chene (Luxemburg); recipient Typhus Commn. medal U.S. Diplomate Am. Bd. Preventive Medicine (sec.-treas. 1955-63). Fellow Am. Pub. Health Assn., Coll. Physicians Phila., Am. Coll. Preventive Medicine, N.Y. Acad. Medicine; mem. Am. Soc. Tropical Medicine and Hygiene, Am. Epidemiol. Soc., Assn. Tchrs. Preventive Medicine (pres. 1963), Am. Assn. for History of Medicine, Soc. Med. Consultants to Armed Forces (sec. 1959-62), Mil. Order World Wars, Sigma Xi. Co-author: Global Epidemiology, 3 Vols., 1944, 51, 54; Cold Injury, Ground Type, 1958; asso. editor 12th edit. Control of Communicable Diseases in Man, 1975; adv. editorial bd. History of Preventive Medicine, U.S. Army, World War II. Home: 623 Tateswood Dr Lexington KY 40502

WHEALON, JOHN FRANCIS, clergyman; b. Barberton, Ohio, Jan. 15, 1921; s. John J. and Mary (Zanders) W.; student St. Charles Coll., Catonsville. Md., 1940, St. Mary's Sem., Cleve., 1945; S.T.L., U. Ottawa (Can.), 1946; S.S.L., Pontifical Bib. U., Rome, Italy, 1950; M.A. in Edn., John Carroll U., 1957. Ordained priest Roman Cath. Ch., 1945; asst. pastor Diocese Cleve., 1945-53; founding rector Borromeo Sem., Wickliffe, Ohio, 1953, tchr. Latin, Hebrew, Sacred Scripture, 1953-61; titular bishop Andrapa, 1961—; aux. bishop Cleve., 1961-66; bishop, Erie, Pa., 1967-68; archbishop Hartford, Conn., 1969—. Address: 134 Farmington Ave Hartford CT 06105*

WHEAT, FRANCIS MILLSPAUGH, lawyer; b. Los Angeles, Feb. 4, 1921; s. Carl Irving and Helen (Millspaugh) W.; A.B., Pomona Coll., 1942; LL.B. cum laude, Harvard U., 1948; m. Nancy Loring Warner, Oct. 14, 1944; children—Douglas Loring, Carl Irving, Gordon Warner. Admitted to Calif. bar, 1949; with firm Gibson, Dunn & Crutcher, Los Angeles, 1948-64, partner, 1955-64, 69—; commr. SEC, 1964-69; dir. Phillips Petroleum Co. Trustee S.W. Mus., Los Angeles, 1964, Honnold Library Soc., Claremont, Calif., 1964—; trustee Pomona Coll., 1967—, vice chmn., 1972—; bd. dirs. UN Assn. Los Angeles, 1963-64, Assn. Governing Bds. Univs. and Colls., 1968—, Center for Law in Pub. Interest, 1974—, Sierra Club Legal Def. Fund, 1978—. Served to lt. USNR, 1942-45. Mem. Am. Law Inst., Los Angeles County Bar Assn. (chmn. com. corps. 1963-64, com. juvenile cts. 1957, trustee 1971-76, pres. 1975-76), Alumni Assn. Pomona Coll. (pres. 1964-65), Nat. Assn. Securities Dealers (bd. govs. 1973-76), Phi Beta Kappa. Democrat. Congregationalist (pres. 1961). Contbr. articles to profl. jours. Home: 2130 Lombardy Rd San Marino CA 91108 Office: 515 S Flower St St Los Angeles CA 90017

WHEATCROFT, JOHN STEWART, educator; b. Phila., July 24, 1925; s. Allen Stewart and Laura Irene (Daniel) W.; B.A., Bucknell U., 1949; M.A., Rutgers U., 1950, Ph.D., 1960; m. Joan Mitchell Osborne, Nov. 10, 1950; children—Allen, David, Rachel. Instr., U. Kans., 1950-52; instr. Bucknell U., Lewisburg, Pa., 1952-58, asst. prof., 1958-62, asso. prof., 1962-66, prof. English, 1962—, Presdl. prof., 1979—. Served with USNR, 1943-46. Recipient Lindback award for distinguished teaching, 1964, Alcoa Playwriting award, 1965, Nat. Ednl. TV award, 1967, Phila. Mayors scholarship, 1942. Resident fellow Yaddo, 1972, MacDowell Colony, 1973, Va. Center for Creative Arts, 1978. Mem. Phi Beta Kappa. Author: Death of a Clown, 1964; Prodigal Son, 1967; Edie Tells, 1975; (TV play) OFOTI, 1970; A Voice from the Hump, 1977; Ordering Demons, 1978. Home: 135 S 11th St Lewisburg PA 17837

WHEATLEY, ERNEST HAROLD, newspaper pub.; b. Calgary, Alta., Can., June 2, 1927; s. Ernest Harold and Kathleen May Ellen (Gregory) W.; student U. Alta., 1945-46; m. Vera Isabelle Procter, Sept. 15, 1950; children—Christopher Mark, Patrick Scott. Advt. salesman Calgary Herald, 1945-50; nat. rep. Southam Newspapers, Toronto, 1950-58; nat. advt. mgr. Calgary Herald, 1958-60; advt. dir. Edmonton (Alta.) Jour., 1960-68, mktg. dir., 1968-70, asst. to pub., mktg. dir., 1970-71; pub. Brantford (Ont.) Expositor, 1971-76; pub. Windsor (Ont.) Star, 1976-77; v.p. Southam, Inc., Toronto, 1976; pub. Winnipeg (Man.) Tribune, 1977—. Mem. Canadian Daily Newspaper Pubs. Assn., Commonwealth Press Union, Inter-Am. Press Assn., Audit Bur. Circulations (dir.), C. of C. Presbyterian. Clubs: Man., St. Charles Country, Winnipeg Winter. Home: 301 Boreham Blvd Winnipeg MB Canada Office: 257 Smith St Winnipeg MB R3C 1K9 Canada

WHEATLEY, JOHN CHARLES, physicist; b. Tucson, Feb. 17, 1927; s. Robert C. and Grace (Nowell) W.; B.S. in Elec. Engring., U. Colo., 1947; Ph.D., U. Pitts., 1952; D.Sc. (hon.), Leiden (Netherlands) U., 1975; m. Martha Raup, Jan. 29, 1949; children—William, Benjamin, Jane (dec.). Mem. faculty U. Ill., 1952-67; prof. physics U. Calif., San Diego, 1967—; chmn. S.H.E. Corp. Served with USNR, 1944-46. Guggenheim fellow, 1954-55; Fulbright fellow, Argentina, 1961-62; recipient Simon Meml. prize Low Temperature Group, Inst. Physics and Phys. Soc. (Gt. Britain), 1966; Fritz London award at 14th Internat. Low Temperature Conf., 1975. Mem. Nat. Acad. Scis. Author papers low temperature scis. and tech. Home: RFD Box 138A-2 Del Mar CA 92014 Office: Univ Calif San Diego PO Box 019 La Jolla CA 92093

WHEATLEY, MELVIN ERNEST, JR., bishop; b. Lewisville, Pa., May 7, 1915; s. Melvin Ernest and Gertrude Elizabeth (Mitchell) W.; A.B. magna cum laude, Am. U., 1936; B.D. summa cum laude, Drew U., Madison, N.J., 1939; D.D., Am. U., 1958, U. of Pacific, 1948; m. Lucile Elizabeth Maris, June 15, 1939; children—Paul Melvin, James Maris, John Sherwood. Ordained to ministry Methodist Ch., 1939; pastor, Lincoln, Del., 1939-41; asso. pastor First Meth. Ch., Fresno, Calif., 1941-43; pastor Centenary Meth. Ch., Modesto, Calif., 1943-46, Central Meth. Ch., Stockton, Calif., 1946-54, Westwood Meth. Ch., Los Angeles, 1954-72; bishop Denver Area, 1972—; instr. philosophy Modesto Jr. Coll., 1944; summer session instr. Hebrew-Christian Heritage, U. of Pacific; instr. homiletics U. So. Calif., So. Calif. Sch. Theology, Claremont; St. Luke's lectures, Houston, 1966. Mem. Gen. Council on Ministries, Commn. on Status and Role of Women, United Meth. Ch., 1972—; condr. European Christian Heritage tour, 1961, Alaska and Hawaii Missions, 1952, 54. Chmn., Community Relations Conf. So. Calif., 1966-69. Pres. So. Calif.-Ariz. Conf. Bd. Edn., 1960-68; bd. dirs. Community Justice Center, Inc., Los Angeles; trustee U. Denver, Iliff Sch. Theology, Rocky Mountain Coll., Billings, Mont. Recipient Disting. Alumnus award Am. U., 1979; named Young Man of Year, Stockton Jr. C. of C., 1950, Clergyman of Year, Ch. Fedn. Los Angeles for Westwood Mental Health Clinic, 1958. Author: Going His Way, 1957; Our Man and the Church, 1968; The Power of Worship, 1970; Family Ministries Manual, 1970; Christmas Is for Celebrating, 1977. Contbr. articles to profl. jours. Home: 8705 E Lehigh Ave Denver CO 80237 Office: 2200 S University Blvd Denver CO 80210

WHEATLEY, WILLIAM BACON, chem. co. exec.; b. Penn Yan, N.Y., Feb. 24, 1920; s. William Hiram and Florence Louise (Bacon) W.; A.B., Colgate U., 1942; Ph.D., Ohio State U., 1947; m. Martha Estella McCorkle, Sept. 12, 1942; children—William L., Elizabeth (Mrs. Kenneth M. Kodama), Daniel W., Barbara, Jonathan I. With Bristol Labs., Syracuse, N.Y., 1947—, asst. to sci. dir., 1958-67, dir. library and info. services, 1967-74, dir. chem. documentation, 1974—. Mem. Am. Chem. Soc., Am. Soc. Info. Sci., N.Y. Acad. Sci., AAAS, Sigma Xi, Phi Beta Kappa. Contbr. articles to profl. jours. Patentee in field. Home: 4291 Abbey Rd RD #2 Syracuse NY 13215 Office: PO Box 657 Syracuse NY 13201

WHEATON, PAUL RITCHIE, advt. agy. exec.; b. Kenosha, Wis., June 13, 1928; s. Guy Carl Walter and Velma (Parmelee) W.; B.A. in Bus. Adminstrn., Mich. State U., 1952; M.Bus., Wayne State U., 1965; m. Jo Anne Wonnberger, Aug. 16, 1952; children—Jill, Joyce, Paula Jo. With Ernst & Ernst, C.P.A.'s, Chgo. and Denver, 1952-57; financial supr. Ford Motor Co., 1957-62; treas. Avis, Indsl. Corp., Madison Heights, Mich., 1962-66; controller King-Seeley Thermos Co., Ann Arbor, Mich., 1966-69; v.p. finance Woodall Industries, Inc., 1969-71; dir. owner relations and service adminstrn. Am. Motors Corp., 1971-75; v.p., treas. D'Arcy-MacManus & Masius Advt., Bloomfield Hills, Mich., 1975-78; v.p. fin. and adminstrn. Dore Agy., Detroit, 1978—. Speakers' chmn. Citizens for Birmingham (Mich.)

Schs., 1964-66. Area campaign dir. Republican Party Oakland County, 1960-62. Served with AUS, 1946-48. C.P.A., Colo. Mem. Financial Executive Institute, also mem. of Delta Sigma Pi (pres. 1950-51), Sigma Iota Epsilon (pres. 1964). Republican. Episcopalian. Home: 424 Lakeside St Birmingham MI 48009 Office: Dore Agy Inc 2530 Buhl Bldg Detroit MI 48226

WHEDON, GEORGE DONALD, med. investigator, physiologist; b. Geneva, N.Y., July 4, 1915; s. George Dunton and Elizabeth (Crockett) W.; A.B., Hobart Coll., 1936, Sc.D. (hon.), 1967; M.D., U. Rochester, 1941, Sc.D. (hon.), 1978; m. Margaret Brunssen, May 12, 1942; children—Karen Anne, David Marshall. Intern in medicine Mary Imogene Bassett Hosp., Cooperstown, N.Y., 1941-42; asst. in medicine U. Rochester Sch. Medicine, also asst. resident physician medicine Strong Meml. Hosp., Rochester, 1942-44; instr. medicine Cornell U. Med. Coll., 1944-50, asst. prof. medicine, 1950-52; chief metabolic diseases br. Nat. Inst. Arthritis, Metabolism and Digestive Diseases, NIH, Bethesda, Md., 1952-65, asst. dir., 1956-62, dir., 1962—. Mem. subcom. on calcium, com. dietary allowances Food and Nutrition Bd., NRC, 1959-64; cons. to office manned space flight NASA, 1963—; chmn. Am. Inst. Biol. Scis. med. program adv. panel to NASA, 1971-75; chmn. life scis. com. NASA, 1974-78, mem. space program adv. council, 1974-78. Mem. med. alumni council U. Rochester Sch. Medicine, 1971-76; mem. trustees' council U. Rochester, 1971-76, vice chmn., 1973-74, chmn., 1974-75; trustee Dermatology Found., 1978—. Recipient Superior Service award USPHS, 1967, Alumni citation U. Rochester, 1971; Ayerst award Endocrine Soc., 1974; Exceptional Sci. Achievement medal NASA, 1974. Diplomate Am. Bd. Internal Medicine, Am. Bd. Nutrition. Mem. Am. Fedn. Clin. Research, Assn. Am. Physicians, Pan Am. Med. Assn., Aerospace Med. Assn. (Arnold D. Tuttle meml. award 1978), Am. Rheumatism Assn., Md. Acad. Scis. (mem. sci. council 1964-70), Endocrine Soc., N.Y. Acad. Scis., AAAS, Am. Physiol. Soc., Am. Diabetes Assn., Am. Gasteroenterol. Assn., Gerontol. Soc., Am. Inst. Nutrition, Acad. Orthopaedic Surgeons (hon.), Am. Soc. for Bone and Mineral Research, Orthopaedic Research Soc., Theta Delta Chi. Episcopalian. Editorial bd. Jour. Clin. Endocrinology and Metabolism, 1960-67; adv. editor Calcified Tissue Research, 1967-76. Contbr. articles to profl. publs. Office: Nat Insts Health Bldg 31 Rm 9A52 Bethesda MD 20205

WHEDON, MARGARET BRUNSSEN, producer; b. N.Y.C.; d. Henry and Anna Margaret (Nickel) Brunssen; B.A., U. Rochester, 1938; postgrad. Hunter Coll., 1950; m. G. Donald Whedon, 1942; children—Karen Whedon Green, David Marshall. With ABC-TV and Radio News, asst. producer Coll. News Conf., 1952-60, producer Issues and Answers, 1960—, also producer From the Capitol, ABC Radio, 1962-69, commentator Flair Reports, 1962-64. Recipient NCCJ award, 1968; nominated for Nat. Acad. TV Arts and Scis. award, 1968. Mem. White House Corrs. Assn., Washington Press Club, Am. Newspaper Women's Club, Am. Women in Radio and TV, Radio-TV Corrs. Assn. Home: 5605 Sonoma Rd Bethesda MD 20034 Office: 1124 Connecticut Ave NW Washington DC 20036

WHEELEN, THOMAS LEO, educator; b. Gardner, Mass., May 30, 1935; s. Thomas Leo and Kathryn Elizabeth (McGrath) W.; student Fordham U., 1953-54; B.B.A. cum laude, Boston Coll., 1957; M.B.A., Babson Coll., 1961; D.Bus. Adminstrn., George Washington U., 1969; m. Margaret A. Doyle, June 25, 1966; children—Kathryn, Thomas Leo II, Richard. Grad. teaching asst. Babson Coll., 1960-61; teaching fellow George Washington U., 1965-68; mfg. tng. program Gen. Electric Co., 1961-64, systems programmer, 1964-65; asst. prof. McIntire Sch. of Commerce, U. Va., 1968-71, asso. prof., 1971-74, prof., 1974—. Cons. liaison faculty FBI Acad. Served to lt. USNR, 1957-60. Mem. Am. Mgmt. Assn., So. Mgmt. Assn. (dir. 1978-81), So. Case Research Assn., Acad. Mgmt., Alpha Kappa Psi, Beta Gamma Sigma. Co-editor: Developments in Management Information Systems, 1974; Collective Bargaining in the Public Sector, 1977. Contbr. articles to profl. jours. Home: 1706 Old Forge Rd Charlottesville VA 22901. *The key to success is with and through other individuals.*

WHEELER, BURTON MAYNARD, educator; b. Mullins, S.C., Mar. 12, 1927; s. Paul and Elizabeth (Cleveland) W.; student Yale, 1945-46; A.B., U.S.C., 1948, M.A., 1951; postgrad. So. Baptist Theol. Sem., 1948-49; Ph.D., Harvard, 1961; m. Jacquelyn Mulkey, Aug. 20, 1950; children—Paul Bryan, Geoffrey, Kristin. Asst. dir., dir. U. S.C. YMCA, 1949-51; teaching fellow Harvard, 1953-56; instr., asst. prof., asso. prof., prof. Washington U., St. Louis, 1956—, master Forsyth Houses, 1962-65, dean Coll. Arts and Scis., 1966-78. Pres. University City Residential Service, 1967-71; cons.-evaluator N. Central Assn. Colls. Mem. adv. council Danforth Found. Fellowships, 1968-72, 76—; trustee Coe Coll. Served with AUS, 1945-46. Lilly Found. fellow, 1965-66. Mem. Am. Assn. U. Profs., Modern Lang. Assn., Soc. for Values in Higher Edn., Phi Beta Kappa, Omicron Delta Kappa. Contbr. articles profl. jours. Home: 31 Kingsbury Pl Saint Louis MO 63112 Office: Washington U Saint Louis MO 63130

WHEELER, CHARLES BERTAN, pathologist; b. Kansas City, Mo., Aug. 10, 1926; s. Charles Bertan and Florence (Martin) W.; A.B., U. Louisville, 1946; M.D., U. Kans., 1950; J.D., U. Mo., Kansas City, 1959; m. Marjorie Martin, Aug. 21, 1948; children—Gordon, Mark, Marian, Graham, Nina. Pathologist, dir. labs. Kansas City (Mo.) Gen. Hosp. and Med. Center, 1957-63; asso. pathologist Research Hosp. and Med. Center, Kansas City, Mo., 1963-65, N. Kansas City (Mo.) Meml. Hosp., 1966-68, Independence (Mo.) Sanitarium and Hosp., from 1968; dir. Wheeler Med. Labs., Kansas City, Mo., 1965—; asst. clin. prof. pathology U. Kans. Med. Sch.; coroner Jackson County, Mo., 1967; Western judge Jackson County Ct., 1967-70; mayor of Kansas City, Mo., 1971-79. Served with USNR, 1944-46; to capt. M.C., USAF, 1950-53. Diplomate Am. Bd. Pathology. Fellow Am. Coll. Legal Medicine (chmn. com. constn. and by-laws); mem. Mo. Soc. Pathologists (past pres.), Mo. Med. Assn. (del.), Jackson County Med. Soc. (exec. council), Coll. Am. Pathologists, Am. Soc. Clin. Pathologists, U. Kans. Med. Alumni Assn. (pres. 1969), Sigma Nu, Nu Sigma Nu. Democrat. Episcopalian. Clubs: Zeitgeist, Vanguard, Rotary. Author: Doctor in Politics, 1974. Office: 4320 Wornall Rd Kansas City MO 64111*

WHEELER, CHARLES MERVYN, JR., chemist; b. Moundsville, W.Va., Oct. 29, 1921; s. Charles Mervyn and Olive Ila (Powell) W.; student Kent State U., 1939-40; B.S., W.Va. U., 1947, M.S., 1948, Ph.D., 1950; m. May Kathleen Wickers, Dec. 18, 1943; children—Charles Mervyn, W. Randolph, Jennifer L., N. Kathleen, Timothy A., Anne O. Asst. prof. chemistry U. N.H., 1950-55, asso. prof., 1955-75, prof., 1975—, dean students, 1960-61; cons. chemistry, Lima, Peru, 1957, 59, 60, India, 1965, 67, 68, 69; chmn. grad. chem. dept. Madurai U., 1968-69; panelist UNESCO Internat. Workshop Evaluation in Chemistry, U. Ceylon, 1968. Mem. Durham (N.H.) Zoning Bd. Adjustment, 1961-78, Durham Sch. Bd., 1962-66. Served with inf. AUS, 1942-46; PTO. John Barton Payne scholar, 1941-42; Research Corp. grantee, 1954; AEC grantee, 1955. Mem. Am. Chem. Soc., AAUP, Sigma Xi, Phi Lambda Upsilon, Phi Kappa Phi. Contbr. articles to profl. jours. Home: 47 Mill Rd Durham NH 03824 Office: Parsons Hall Durham NH 03824

WHEELER, CHARLES VAWTER, oil co. exec.; b. Fay, Okla., Nov. 12, 1920; s. Claude A. and Bertha (Cooke) W.; student Harding Coll., Searcy, Ark., 1938-39, U. Okla., 1939-43, U. Tex., 1947; LL.B., U. Okla., 1948; LL.M., N.Y. U., 1973; m. Maryjo Meacham, Jan. 23, 1943; children—Allison Ann, Meacham. Admitted to Okla. bar, 1943; atty. Southwestern Bell Telephone Co., 1948-53; pvt. practice, Oklahoma City, 1953-58; with Cities Service Co., 1958—, gen. counsel, 1969—, also mem. exec. com., dir.; asst. adj. gen. Okla., 1966-68. Trustee, v.p. Cities Service Found. Served with AUS, 1943-47, 50-52. Decorated Legion of Merit. Mem. Am., Okla., N.Y. State bar assns., Am. Petroleum Inst., N.G. Assn., Delta Tau Delta. Presbyterian. Clubs: Metropolitan (N.Y.C.); Tulsa, Southern Hills Country. Home: 2300 Riverside Dr Tulsa OK 74114 Office: 110 W 7th St Box 300 Tulsa OK 74102

WHEELER, CLAYTON EUGENE, JR., dermatologist; b. Viroqua, Wis., June 30, 1917; s. Clayton Eugene and Vista Beulah (Heal) W.; B.A., U. Wis., 1938, M.D., 1941; m. Susie Brooks Overton, Oct. 11, 1952; children—Susan Brooks, Margaret Ann, Elizabeth Clayton. Intern, Cin. Gen. Hosp., 1941-42; resident in internal medicine U. Mich. Hosps., 1942-44, research fellow endocrinology and metabolism, 1947-48, resident in dermatology, 1948-51; from asst. prof. to prof. dermatology U. Va. Med. Sch., 1951-62; prof. dermatology U. N.C. Med. Sch., Chapel Hill, 1962—, chmn. div., 1962-72, chmn. dept., 1972—. Served to maj. M.C., AUS, 1944-47. Diplomate Am. Bd. Internal Medicine, Am. Bd. Dermatology (vice pres. 1977-78, pres. 1978—). Mem. Soc. Investigative Dermatology (pres. 1974-75, Rothman award 1979), Assn. Profs. Dermatology (pres. 1975-76), Am. Acad. Dermatology (past dir.), Phi Beta Kappa, Alpha Omega Alpha. Methodist. Author: Practical Dermatology, 3d edit., 1967; also articles. Home: 2120 N Lakeshore Dr Chapel Hill NC 27514 Office: NC Memorial Hosp Chapel Hill NC 27514

WHEELER, EDWARD KENDALL, lawyer; b. Butte, Mont., Oct. 23, 1913; s. Burton K. and Lulu M. (White) W.; A.B., George Washington U., 1935; LL.B., Harvard U., 1938; m. Charlotte S. Sharp, Apr. 15, 1939; children—Frederica Wheeler Smith, Kendall W. van Orman. Admitted to D.C. bar, 1939; since practiced in Washington, partner Wheeler & Wheeler, 1947—. Served as lt. USNR, 1943-46; mem. Am., Fed. bar assns., ICC Practitioners Assn. Clubs: Chevy Chase; Met., Burning Tree (Washington). Home: 6005 Highland Dr Chevy Chase MD Office: Editors Bldg 1729 H St NW Washington DC 20005

WHEELER, GEORGE WILLIAM, physicist, educator, univ. dean; b. Dedham, Mass., Dec. 23, 1924; s. John Brooks, Jr. and Alice (Chamberlin) W.; B.S. in Physics, Union Coll., Schenectady, 1949; Ph.D., Yale U., 1953; m. Margaret C. Pirie, Oct. 27, 1957; children—William Cameron, Alice Chamberlin. Research asso. Woods Hole (Mass.) Oceanographic Inst., 1953-54; asst. prof. physics, sr. research asso. Yale U., 1954-64; physicist, div. head accelerator dept. Brookhaven Nat. Lab., Upton, N.Y., 1964-72; br. chief high energy physics program, div. phys. research AEC, Washington, 1972-74; dean sci., prof. physics Herbert H. Lehman Coll., City U. N.Y., Bronx, 1974-79; prof. physics Temple U., Phila., 1979—, dean Coll. Liberal Arts, 1979—; cons. in field. Mem. Brandford (Conn.) Bd. Edn., 1961-64; trustee Village of Belle Terre (N.Y.), 1967-69. Served with inf. AUS, 1943-45. Decorated Bronze Star. Mem. IEEE (sr.), Am. Phys. Soc., AAAS, Phi Beta Kappa, Sigma Xi. Author papers on physics, particle accelerators. Office: Coll Liberal Arts Temple U Philadelphia PA 19122

WHEELER, HAROLD ALDEN, radio engr.; b. St. Paul, May, 10, 1903; s. William Archie and Harriet Maria (Alden) W.; B.S., George Washington U., 1925, D.Sc. (hon.), 1972; postgrad. Johns Hopkins, 1926-28; D.Eng. (hon.), Stevens Inst. Tech., 1978; m. Ruth Gregory, Aug. 25, 1926; children—Dorothy, Caroline, Alden Gregory. With Hazeltine Corp., Little Neck, N.Y., 1924—, engr., 1924-39, v.p., chief cons. engr., 1939-45, v.p., dir., 1959-65, chief exec. officer, 1966, chmn. bd., 1965-77, chief scientist, 1971—, dir., chmn. emeritus, 1977—; cons. radio physicist, Great Neck, N.Y., 1946-59; pres. Wheeler Labs., Inc., 1947-68, dir. 1947-70, chief scientist, 1968-70; expert cons. to Office Sec. Def. on guided missiles, 1950-53; mem. Def. Sci. Bd., 1961-64. Recipient medal of Honor IEEE, 1964; Armstrong medal Radio Club of Am., 1964. Fellow IEEE, Radio Club Am.; mem. Inst. E.E. Gt. Britain; mem. Sigma Xi, Gamma Alpha, Tau Beta Pi. Republican. Unitarian. Author: Wheeler Monographs, volume I, 1953; Hazeltine the Professor, 1978; contbr. articles to sci., profl. jours. Holder 180 U.S. patents, including diode automatic volume control. Home: 59 Derby Pl Smithtown NY 11787 Office: Hazeltine Corp Greenlawn NY 11740

WHEELER, HARRY EUGENE, educator; b. Pipestone, Minn., Feb. 1, 1907; s. Benjamin F. and Mary (Denhart) W.; B.S., U. Oreg., 1930; M.A., Stanford, 1932, Ph.D., 1935; m. Loretta Rose Miller, Mar. 21, 1938; children—Eugene, Carolyn, David. Jordan Research fellow Stanford, 1930-33; mem. faculty U. Nev., 1935-48, asso. prof. geology, 1942-48; mem. faculty U. Wash., Seattle, 1948—, prof. geol. scis., 1951-58, emeritus prof., 1958—; geologist Nev. Bur. Mines, 1936-48; vis. prof. Ind. U., 1956-57, U. Tex., 1960, So. Methodist U., Dallas, 1966; conferee Centre Nat. de Resh. Sci., Paris, 1957; cons. Gulf Oil Corp., Western U.S., 1950-58; geol. cons. Mobil Oil Corp., Britain, North Sea and NW Europe, 1973. Mem. Am. Stratigraphic Commn., 1958-60; vis. scientist USSR, Nat. Acad. Sci. and Soviet Acad. Sci., 1963. Fellow Geol. Soc. Am.; mem. Am. Assn. Petroleum Geologists, Soc. Econ. Paleontologists and Mineralogists, Northwest Geol. Soc., Sigma Xi. Research and numerous publs. on stratigraphic principles and concepts and their implications in regional and interregional stratigraphic analysis as bases for hist. interpretation. Home: 5761 60th Ave NE Seattle WA 98105

WHEELER, HENRY CLARK, corp. exec.; b. Bridgeport, Conn., Apr. 27, 1916; s. Dwight Clark and Louise (Carstesen) W.; B.S., Yale U., 1939; m. Phyllis Francis Seeley, Sept. 6, 1940; children—Dwight Clark II, Louise Seeley, Philip Gregory. With Acme Shear Co. (name changed to Acme United Corp., 1971), Bridgeport, 1939—, pres., 1941—, chief exec. officer, 1952—; dir. Conn. Nat. Bank, Bridgeport Metal Goods Co. Served with USNR, 1941. Republican. Congregationalist. Office: 100 Hicks St Bridgeport CT 06609

WHEELER, HEWITT BROWNELL, surgeon; b. Louisville, July 21, 1929; s. Arville and Lois (Vance) W.; student Vanderbilt U., 1945-48; M.D., Harvard U., 1952; m. Elizabeth Jane Maxwell, July 21, 1956; children—Stephen, Elizabeth, Jane, Mary. Cushing fellow Harvard Med. Sch., Boston, 1953, Peters fellow, 1956, research fellow, 1959-60, instr. surgery, 1961-64, clin. asso. surgery, 1964-67, asst. clin. prof. surgery, 1967-70, asso. prof. surgery, 1970-71; asst. in surgery Peter Bent Brigham Hosp., Boston, 1959-60, jr. asso. surgery, 1961-64, asso. surgery, 1964-69, sr. asso. surgery, 1969-71; asst. chief surgery Roxbury VA Hosp., Boston, 1961-62, chief surgery, 1962-71, chief of staff, 1968-71; cons. surgery U. Mass. Med. Sch. at Worcester, 1966-71, prof., chmn. dept. surgery, 1971—, chief staff U. Mass. Hosp., 1974-76; surgeon-in-chief U. Mass. Hosp., 1976—; affiliate prof. biomed. engring. Worcester Poly. Inst., 1974—; lectr. surgery Harvard Med. Sch., 1974—; chief surgery St. Vincent Hosp., Worcester, 1971-75; cons. Meml. Hosp., Worcester City Hosp., 1970—, Worcester Hahnemann Hosp., 1974—, Peter Bent Brigham Hosp., 1973—; chmn. surg. research program com. VA, Washington, 1965-67, nat. participant surg. cons., 1965-69, chmn. ad hoc adv. com. surgery, 1969—. Trustee Central Mass. Health Care Found., 1975-77. Served to 1st lt., M.C., AUS, 1953-55. Mem. Am. Coll. Angiology, A.C.S. (council Mass. chpt. 1973-76, pres. 1980), AAAS, AMA, Am. Surg. Assn., Assn. VA Surgeons, Soc. Univ. Surgeons, Internat. Cardiovascular Soc., Soc. Surg. Chairmen, New Eng. (treas. 1977—), Boston Worcester (pres. 1973-75) surg. socs., Transplantation Soc., Mass., Worcester Dist. med. socs., New Eng. Vascular Soc. Asso. editor Jour. Angiology, Vascular surgery. Research exptl. transplantation, blood vessel surgery, method to detect clinically occult blood clots. Home: 10 Old English Rd Worcester MA 01609

WHEELER, HUGH CALLINGHAM, author; b. London, Eng., Mar. 19, 1912; s. Harold and Florence (Scammell) W.; B.A. in English with honours, U. London, 1932. Recipient Edgar Allen Poe award, 1961, 73; Antoinette Perry award, 1973, 74, 79, Drama Critics Circle award, 1973, 74, 79, Drama Desk award, 1973, 74, 79. Author: (plays) Big Fish, Little Fish, 1961, Look We've Come Through, 1961, We Have Always Lived in the Castle, 1966, (with Stephen Sondheim) A Little Night Music, 1973, Irene, 1973, Sweeney Todd, 1978; (with Leonard Bernstein) Candide, 1974; (with Sondheim and John Weidman) Pacific Overtones, 1976; (novel) The Crippled Muse, 1952; (under pseud. Patrick Quentin) 17 novels latest being Family Skeletons, 1965; (under pseud. Q. Patrick with R. Wilson Webb) 5 novels latest being Return to the Scene, 1952; (under pseud. Jonathan Stagge with R. Wilson Webb) 8 novels latest being The Three Fears, 1953; screenplays Five Miles to Midnight, 1962; Something for Everyone, 1970; Travels with My Aunt, 1973; A Little Night Music, 1977; Nijenski, 1980. Mem. Writers Guild.

WHEELER, JESSE HARRISON, JR., educator; b. Scottsboro, Ala., Nov. 24, 1918; s. Jesse Harrison and Lucy (Enochs) W.; B.S., Auburn U., 1939, M.S., 1941; Ph.D., U. Chgo., 1950; m. Margery Ellen Gray, Oct. 3, 1942; children—Robert Francis, David Russell, Charles Edward. Tchr. English, Boys High Sch., Atlanta, 1940-41; instr. geography U. Mo., Columbia, 1949-50, asst. prof., 1950-55, asso. prof., 1955-64, prof., 1964—, chmn. dept., 1956-70. Served to maj., F.A., AUS, 1941-46. Ford Found. Faculty fellow, 1951-52. Mem. Assn. Am. Geographers (com. chmn.), Nat. Council Geog. Edn., Am. Geog. Soc., Soc. for History of Discoveries, Sigma Xi, Phi Kappa Phi, Kappa Delta Pi. Democrat. Presbyn. Author: Land Use in Greenbrier County, West Virginia, 1950; A Workbook and Study Guide for Regional Geography of the World, 1957; Les États-Unis in Géographie Régionale II, 1979. Author, editor: (with J.T. Kostbade and R.S. Thoman) Regional Geography of the World, 1955. Rev. editor: Annals of the Assn. Am. Geographers, 1961-69. Home: 507 S Glenwood Ave Columbia MO 65201

WHEELER, JOHN ARCHIBALD, scientist; b. Jacksonville, Fla., July 9, 1911; s. Joseph Lewis and Mabel (Archibald) W.; Ph.D., Johns Hopkins U., 1933, LL.D., 1977; Sc.D., Western Res. U., 1958, U. N.C., 1959, U. Pa., 1968, Middlebury Coll., 1969, Rutgers U., 1969, Yeshiva U., 1973, Yale U., 1974, U. Uppsala, 1975, U. Md., 1977; m. Janette Hegner, June 10, 1935; children—Isabel Letitia Wheeler Ufford, James English, Alison Christie Wheeler Ruml. NRC fellow, N.Y., Copenhagen, 1933-35; asst. prof. physics U. N.C., 1935-38; asst. prof. physics Princeton U., 1938-42, asso. prof., 1945-47, prof., 1947-76, Joseph Henry prof. physics, 1966-76, Joseph Henry prof. physics emeritus, 1976—; prof. physics U. Tex., Austin, 1976—, Ashbel Smith prof., 1979—; cons. and physicist on atomic energy projects Princeton U., 1939-42, U. Chgo., 1942, E.I. duPont de Nemours & Co., Wilmington, Del., and Richland, Wash., 1943-45, Los Alamos, 1950-53; dir. project Matterhorn, Princeton U., 1951-53; Guggenheim fellow, Paris and Copenhagen, 1949-50; summer lectr. U. Mich., U. Chgo., Columbia U.; Lorentz prof. U. Leiden, 1956; Fulbright prof. Kyoto U., 1962; 1st vis. fellow Clare Coll. Cambridge U., 1964; Battelle prof. U. Wash., 1975; sci. adviser U.S. Senate del. to 3d ann. conf. NATO Parliamentarians, Paris, 1957; mem. adv. com. Oak Ridge Nat. Lab., 1957-65, U. Calif. (Los Alamos and Livermore), 1972-77; v.p. Internat. Union Physics, 1951-54; chmn. joint com. Am. Phys. Soc. and Am. Philos. Soc. on history theoretical physics in 20th Century, 1960-72; sci. adv. bd. USAF, 1961, 62; chmn. Dept. Def. Advanced Research Projects Agy. Project, 1958; mem. U.S. Gen. Adv. Com. Arms Control and Disarmament, 1969-72, 74-77. Trustee Battelle Meml. Inst., 1959—. Recipient A. Cressy Morrison prize N.Y. Acad. Sci. for work on nuclear physics, 1947; Albert Einstein prize Strauss Found., 1965; Enrico Fermi award AEC, 1968; Franklin medal Franklin Inst., 1969; Nat. medal of Sci., 1971; Herzfeld award, 1975. Fellow AAAS (dir. 1965-68), Am. Phys. Soc. (pres. 1966); mem. Am. Math Soc., Internat. Astron. Union, Am. Acad. Arts and Scis., Nat. Acad. Sci., Am. Philos. Soc. (councillor 1963-66, 76—, v.p. 1971-73), Royal Danish Acad. Scis., Royal Acad. Sci. (Uppsala, Sweden), l'Académie Internationale de Philosophie des Sciences, Internat. Union Physics (v.p. 1951-54), Phi Beta Kappa, Sigma Xi. Unitarian (trustee 1965). Author: Geometrodynamics, 1962; Gravitation Theory and Gravitational Collapse, 1965; Spacetime Physics, 1966; Einstein's Vision, 1968; Gravitation, 1973; Black Holes, Gravitational Radiation and Cosmology, 1974; Frontiers of Time, 1979; contbr. articles to profl. jours. Home: 1410 Wildcat Hollow Austin TX 78746 Office: Physics Dept U Tex Austin TX 78712. *We will first understand how simple the universe is when we recognize how strange it is.*

WHEELER, JOHN HARVEY, polit. scientist; b. Waco, Tex., Oct. 17, 1918; B.A., Ind. U., 1946, M.A., 1947; Ph.D., Harvard U., 1950; m. Norene Burleigh; children—David Carroll, John Harvey, Mark Jefferson. Asst. prof. Johns Hopkins U., 1950-54; asso. prof. Washington and Lee U., 1954-56, prof. polit. sci., 1956-60; fellow in residence Center for Study Democratic Instns., Santa Barbara, Calif., 1960-70, sr. fellow, 1969-75, program dir., 1969-70; chmn., pres. Inst. Higher Studies, Santa Barbara, 1975—; cons. Fund for Republic, 1958-61. Served with AUS, 1941-46. Author: The Conservative Crisis, 1958; (with Eugene Burdick) Fail-Safe, 1962; Democracy in a Revolutionary Era, 1968; The Politics of Revolution, 1971; (with E.M. Nathanson) The Rise of the Elders, 1980; editor (with George Boas) Lattimore, The Scholar, 1953; editor, contbg. author: Beyond Punitive Society, 1973; co-editor Jour. Social and Biol. Structures; contbr. articles to profl. jours. Home: 7200 Casitas Pass Rd Carpinteria CA 93013 Office: Inst Higher Studies Santa Barbara CA 93105

WHEELER, JOHN OLIVER, geologist; b. Mussoorie, India, Dec. 19, 1924; s. Edward Oliver and Dorothea Sophie (Danielsen) W.; B.A.Sc. in Geol. Engring., U. B.C., 1947; Ph.D. in Geology, Columbia U., 1956; m. Nora Jean Hughes, May 17, 1952; children—Kathleen Anna Wheeler Hunter, Jennifer Margaret. Geologist, Geol. Survey Can., Ottawa, Ont., 1951-61, Vancouver, B.C., 1961-65, research scientist, 1965-70, research mgr., Ottawa, 1970—, chief regional and econ. geology div., 1970-73, dep. dir. gen., 1973-79, research scientist Cordilleran div., 1979—. Fellow Royal Soc. Can., Geol. Soc. Can. (pres. 1970-71), Geol. Soc. Am. (councillor 1971-74); mem. Can. Inst. Mining and Metallurgy. Anglican. Club: Alpine, Am. Alpine. Contbr. articles to profl. jours. Home: 3333 Mathers Ave West Vancouver BC V7V 2K6 Canada Office: 100 W Pender St Vancouver BC V6B 1R8 Canada

WHEELER, JOHN PERRY, JR., educator; b. Thomasville, Ga., Apr. 18, 1928; s. John Perry and Addie (Phillips) W.; B.S., Fla. State U., 1950, M.S., 1951; Ph.D., Syracuse U., 1958; m. Edna Gertrude Grubb, June 11, 1950; children—Mary Faran, Dan Grubb, Amy Norwood, John Joshua, Zachariah Phillips. Instr. polit. sci. Middlebury (Vt.) Coll., 1952-55; mem. faculty Hollins (Va.) Coll., 1955—, prof. polit. sci., 1964—, dean coll., 1967-75; researcher U. Cambridge (Eng.), 1975-76; dir. Hollins Abroad, London, 1976-78; dir. state constl. studies project Nat. Municipal League, 1958-61; vis. prof. polit. sci. U. West Indies, 1964-65; cons. in field. Mem. Roanoke City Sch. Bd., 1968—; Democratic candidate for U.S. Congress, 1962. Served with USAAF, 1947-48; capt. USNR Res. Mem. Am., So. polit. sci. assns., Phi Beta Kappa, Omicron Delta Kappa. Author: The Constitutional Convention: A Manual on Its Planning, Organization and Operation, 1961; Magnificent Failure: The Maryland Con-Con of 1967-68, 1969; editor: Salient Issues of Constitutional Revision, 1961. Address: Hollins Coll VA 24020

WHEELER, JOHN ST. CLAIR, bldg. materials co. exec.; b. England, Dec. 18, 1918; s. John St. Clair and Clara Elizabeth (Browne) W.; immigrated to Can., 1919; ed. U. Toronto, 1946; m. Katherine Bothwell, May 26, 1944; children—Peter, Paul, Wendy, James. Founder Ont. Bldg. Materials Ltd., Mississauga, 1945, pres., 1946—. Founding chmn. St. George's Coll., Toronto, 1959. Served with Can. Army, 1940-45. Fellow ASTM (pres. 1976-77). Anglican. Clubs: Lions, Boulevard. Patentee calcium silicates, author articles elec. characteristics of surfaces. Home: 2085 Mississauga Rd Missassuaga ON L5H 2K5 Canada Office: Saxony Court Estates Inc Saxony Court Missassuaga ON L5H 2K5 Canada

WHEELER, KENNETH WILLIAM, univ. adminstr.; b. Amarillo, Tex., Mar. 7, 1929; s. Homer N. and Bertha (Campbell) W.; B.A., U. Tex., 1951; diplome D'etudes Degré Supereur, Sorbonne, Paris, 1956; Ph.D., U. Rochester, 1963; children—Amanda, Philip, David. Lectr., instr. history and city planning, asst. dean Grad. Sch., Ohio State U., 1960-66; asso. dean Met. Coll., acting dean, dir. MetroCenter, asso. prof. history Boston U., 1967-69; prof. history, dean Univ. Coll., Rutgers U., 1969-72, provost, 1972—. Mem. vis. com. Harvard U., 1972—. Trustee, New Brunswick Tomorrow, George Street Theater, All Souls Unitarian Ch., N.Y.C. Served with AUS, 1951-53. Recipient award Am. Philos. Assn., 1966; fellow Am. Council Edn., 1966-67. Mem. Am. Hist. Assn., Orgn. Am. Historians, Soc. des amis de l' Univ. de Paris, Urban League, Phi Kappa Psi, Delta Sigma Pi. Author: To Wear a City's Crown, 1968; editor: For the Union, 1968. Home: 430 Grant Ave Highland Park NJ 08904 Office: Office of Provost Rutgers U New Brunswick NJ 08903

WHEELER, LEONARD, lawyer; b. Worcester, Mass., July 20, 1901; s. Leonard and Elizabeth (Cheever) W.; A.B. magna cum laude, Harvard U., 1922, LL.B., 1925; m. Cornelia Balch, Oct. 5, 1929; children—Cornelia Wheeler Lanou, Leonard, Penelope Wheeler Pi-Sunyer, John B. Admitted to Mass. bar, 1926, since practiced in Boston; asso. firm Goodwin, Procter & Hoar, 1925-72, partner, 1932-72, of counsel, 1972—; dir., clk. Harold Cabot & Co., Inc.; past corporator Cambridge Savs. Bank. Grad. treas. Harvard Law Rev., 1956-71; bd. dirs., past treas., pres. Cambridge Family and Children's Service; past treas., dir. Cambridge council Boy Scouts Am., Internat. Student Assn. Greater Boston; past pres., bd. overseers Shady Hill Sch., Cambridge; past bd. dirs. Boston Legal Aid Soc.; bd. dirs., past v.p. Cambridge Community Services; past bd. dirs., past pres. Chocorua (N.H.) Lake Assn.; trustee Tamworth (N.H.) Found.; past trustee Social Law Library, Boston. Served to col. AUS, 1942-46; mem. pros. staff first Nuremberg War Crimes Trial, 1945-46. Mem. Am., Mass., Cambridge (past pres.) bar assns., Am. Law Inst. Republican. Unitarian-Universalist (standing com. 1st parish, Cambridge). Clubs: Union Boat (past pres.), Union, St. Botolph (Boston); Cambridge (past pres.), Cambridge Boat (past sec.). Home: 123 Coolidge Hill Cambridge MA 02138 Office: 28 State St Boston MA 02109

WHEELER, LINDEN E., retail co. exec.; b. San Antonio; s. Carl Foster and Mary L. W.; student U. Tex.; m. Stella Mae Dukes, Sept. 18, 1939; children—Troyce A., Larry W. With Sears Roebuck & Co., 1941—, asst. treas., Dallas, 1953-57, territorial credit mgr. Midwest, 1958-63, v.p., gen. credit mgr., Chgo., 1963—; dir. Sears Roebuck Acceptance Co.; dir., chmn. Nat. Fedn. Consumer Credit. Bd. dirs., treas. Nat. Com. for Prevention of Child Abuse, 1979; bd. dirs. Nat. Assn. Mental Health, 1969-75, pres., 1974; vice chmn. Nat. Jr. Achievement, 1970-72; trustee Graceland Coll., 1967-79, Park Coll., 1975—. Served with AUS, 1944-45. Mem. Nat. Retail Mchts. Assn. (Silver Plaque award 1972), Internat. Consumer Credit Assn. (dir.). Contbr. articles to jours. Office: Sears Roebuck & Co Sears Tower Chicago IL 60684

WHEELER, MARSHALL RALPH, zoologist; b. Carlinville, Ill., Apr. 7, 1917; s. Ralph Adelbert and Hester Mae (Ward) W.; student Blackburn Coll., 1935-37; B.A., Baylor U., 1939; postgrad. Tex. A. and M. U., 1939-41; Ph.D. (NRC fellow), U. Tex., 1947; m. Linda Carol Lackner, May 10, 1966; children—Sandra Wheeler King, Karen, Carson. Mem. faculty U. Tex., Austin, 1947—, asso. prof. zoology, 1955-61, prof., 1961-78, emeritus prof., 1978—. Gosney fellow Calif. Inst. Tech.; dir. Nat. Drosophila Species Resources Center. Served with USN, 1941-45. NSF grantee; NIH grantee. Mem. Entomol. Soc. Am. (editor Annals 1970-75), Genetic Soc. Am., Soc. Study Evolution, S.W. Assn. Naturalists (pres. 1961), Southwestern Entomol. Soc. (pres. 1978), Am. Soc. Naturalists, Soc. Systematic Zoology, Am. Hemerocallis Soc. Editor: Studies in Genetics, 1960-72. Home: 1313 Ardenwood Rd Austin TX 78722 Office: Dept Zoology U Tex Austin TX 78712

WHEELER, OTIS BULLARD, univ. ofcl.; b. Mansfield, Ark., Feb. 1, 1921; s. Clarence Charles and Georgia Elizabeth (Bullard) W.; B.A., U. Okla., 1942; M.A., U. Tex., 1947; Ph.D., U. Minn., 1951; m. Doris Louise Alexander, Jan. 17, 1943; children—Ann Carolyn, Ross Charles. Faculty, La. State U., Baton Rouge, 1952—, prof. English, 1965—, chmn. dept., 1974, dean grad. sch., 1962-67, vice chancellor for acad. affairs, 1974—; Fulbright-Hayes lectr. U. Innsbruck (Austria), 1968-69. Served with U.S. Army, 1942-46, 51-52. Decorated Bronze Star medal. Mem. AAUP, MLA, S. Atlantic MLA, S. Central MLA, Am. Studies Assn., Phi Kappa Phi. Democrat. Methodist. Author: The Literary Career of Maurice Thompson, 1965. Home: 162 Clara Dr Baton Rouge LA 70808 Office: Office Acad Affairs La State U Baton Rouge LA 70803

WHEELER, RAYMOND MILNER, physician, educator; b. Farmville, N.C., Sept. 30, 1919; s. George Raymond and Sallie Kate (Collins) W.; certificate in medicine, U. N.C., 1941; M.D., Washington U., St. Louis, 1943; m. Mary Lou Browning, June, 1942 (div. 1956); children—Linda Lou, Margaret Browning, David Stewart; m. 2d, Julie Buckner Carr, June 6, 1958. Intern Barnes Hosp., St. Louis, 1943-44; asst. resident medicine N.C. Baptist Hosp., Winston-Salem, N.C., 1946-48; pvt. practice internal medicine, Charlotte, N.C., 1948—; chmn. dept. medicine Charlotte Meml. Hosp., 1961-63; clin. asso. prof. medicine U. N.C. Med. Sch., 1966-70. Mem. Field Found. commn. physicians who studied hunger in Miss., 1967; mem. Citizens Bd. Inquiry into Hunger in U.S., 1968, into Brookside Strike, 1974; cons. prodn. film Hunger in America, 1968. Mem. N.C. Council Human Relations, 1956—, pres., 1957-61; mem. So. Regional Council, 1956—, chmn. exec. com., 1964-69, pres., 1969-74. Chmn. bd. dirs. Children's Found., 1973-74; chmn. exec. com. Nat. Sharecroppers' Fund, 1976-78, pres., 1978—; chmn. exec. com. N.C. Hunger Coalition, 1975-77, pres., 1977-79; bd. dirs. Voter Edn. Project, 1970-75, Southerners for Econ. Justice, 1977—. Served to capt. M.C., AUS, 1944-46. Decorated Silver Star, Purple Heart; recipient Disting. Service award U. N.C. Med. Sch., 1969; Frank Porter Graham award N.C. Civil Liberties Union, 1979. Diplomate Am. Bd. Internal Medicine. Fellow A.C.P.; mem. Am. Pub. Health Assn., Mecklenberg County Med. Soc. Democrat. Unitarian. Author articles. Home: 3724 Warrington Dr Charlotte NC 28211 Office: 2711 Randolph Rd Charlotte NC 28207

WHEELER, RICHARD WARREN, banker; b. Boston, Feb. 8, 1929; s. Wilfrid and Sybil Constance (Leckenby) W.; B.A., Williams Coll., 1952; postgrad. Harvard Bus. Sch., 1962; m. Betty Ann Owens, Sept. 9, 1950; children—Emily, Susan Knight, Thomas Adams, Alice Owens, Sarah Bennett. With 1st Nat. City Bank of N.Y., 1952—, assigned to Hongkong, Manila and Tokyo, 1953-69, v.p., 1967-69, sr. v.p., N.Y.C., 1969—. Bd. dirs., v.p. Am. Australian Assn., Nat. Council U.S.-China Trade; chmn. exec. com. Presiding Bishop's Fund for World Relief, Am. Com. for KEEP; chmn. adv. council Harvard Center for Study World Religions; mem. adv. bd. Georgetown Center for Contemporary Arab Studies; mem. adv. bd. Harvard U. Center for East Asian Studies, Center for Strategic and Internat. Studies; v.p. exec. council Harvard Bus. Sch., 1971-75; trustee Cambridge Sch., Weston, Mass. Served with AUS, 1946-47. Mem. Japan Soc. (chmn. exec. com., dir.), Nat. Planning Assn. (treas.), Australian Am. Soc. (dir.), Nat. Fgn. Trade Council (dir.), Internat. C. of C. (trustee U.S. council), Council on Fgn. Relations. Episcopalian. Clubs: University, Williams (N.Y.C.); Bronxville Field; Manila Polo; Hodegawa Golf, Tokyo Lawn Tennis. Home: 181 Boulder Trail Bronxville NY 10708 Office: 399 Park Ave New York NY 10043

WHEELER, ROBERT FELLOWS, banker; b. Nichols, N.Y., June 6, 1921; s. Ralph Leslie and Grace Elizabeth (Fellows) W.; student Northeastern U., 1939-41, 46, Harvard Sch. Bus., 1970; m. Nathalie Marianne Boulais, Mar. 27, 1944; children—Bonnie Wheeler Dyer, Robert Fellows, Barry J., Belinda Wheeler Liddell, John B. Mgr. fgn. and collection dept. Union Trust Co., Springfield, Mass., 1949-50, mgr. mortgage loan dept., 1951-52, asst. treas., 1952-57, asst. v.p., 1957-59; asst. v.p. New Eng. Mchts. Nat. Bank, 1960-63, v.p., 1963-69, sr. v.p., 1970-74; exec. v.p. Amoskeag Savs. Bank, Manchester, N.H., 1974-75, pres., 1975—; pres. Bass River Savs. Bank, South Yarmouth, Mass., 1977—; activity vector analyst Walter Clarke Assos., Providence. Chmn. small bus. div. United Fund Greater Springfield, 1955, 56; treas., mem. bd. Hampden County Mental Health Clinic, 1957-58. Served to lt. comdr. USNR, 1941-45, 52-54. Clubs: Engrs. (Boston); Scituate (Mass.) Country; Brae Burn Country (Newton, Mass.); Manchester Country. Home: 111 Goose Point Rd Centerville MA 02632 Office: 307 Main St South Yarmouth MA 02664

WHEELER, ROBERT R., ednl. adminstr.; b. Omaha, Apr. 10, 1921; s. Robert Russell and Emma W.; B.S., Lincoln U., 1948; M.S., Columbia U., 1955; m. Sue Elizabeth Anderson, Aug. 7, 1955; children—Robert, Robin. Asst. supt. Sch. Dist. Kansas City (Mo.), 1966-71, supt. schs., 1977—; asso. commr. elem. and secondary edn. U.S. Office of Edn., 1972-74, dep. commr., 1974-77. Bd. dirs. Greater Kansas City Community Found., Sci. Pioneers; trustee Midwest Research Inst.; mem. Civic Council Greater Kansas City; community adv. Jr. League Kansas City. Mem. Internat. Relations Council, Nat. Joint Council on Econ. Edn., C. of C. Club: Rotary. Home: 4604 E 51st St Kansas City MO 64130 Office: 1211 McGee Kansas City MO 64106

WHEELER, ROGER MILTON, corp. exec.; b. Boston, Feb. 27, 1926; s. Sidney S. and Florence W. (Kendall) W.; student Mass. Inst. Tech., 1943-44, Notre Dame U., 1944-45; B.S., Rice U., 1945-46; m. Patricia Jane Wilson, Sept. 6, 1946; children—Roger Milton, Pamela, David, Lawrence, Mark. Engr., Gulf Oil Co., 1946-47, Standard Oil Co. Ohio, 1947-48; pres. Standard Magnesium & Chem. Co., 1949-64; gen. mgr. magnesium projects Kaiser Aluminum & Chem. Co., 1964-65; chmn. bd. Telex, Inc., Tulsa, 1965—, Phoenix Resources Inc., 1973—, Cert. Appliance Distbrs., 1975—; pres. Am. Magnesium Co., 1968—. Served with USNR, 1943-46. Mem. Magnesium Assn. (pres.), Young Pres. Orgn. Author papers in field. Home: 1957 E 41st St Tulsa OK 74105 Office: Telex Inc 41st and Sheridan Sts Tulsa AZ 74105

WHEELER, RURIC E., univ. adminstr.; b. Clarkson, Ky., Nov. 30, 1923; s. Mark H. and Mary (Sullivan) W.; A.B., Western Ky. U., 1947; M.S., U. Ky., 1948, Ph.D., 1952; m. Joyce Ray, May 31, 1946; children—Eddy Ray, Paul Warren. Instr. math. U. Ky., 1948-52; asst. prof. statistics Fla. State U., 1952-53; asso. prof. math. Samford U., 1953-55, prof., head dept., 1955-65, chmn. div. natural scis., 1965-67, asst. to acad. dean, 1967-68; dean Howard Coll. Arts and Scis., 1968-70, v.p. acad. affairs, 1970—; cons. in field; dir. NSF Inst., 1961, Ala. Vis. Scientist Program, 1962-67. Mem. Birmingham Manpower Area Planning Council, 1972-75. Trustee Gorgas Found., 1968—. Served to lt. USAAF, 1943-46. Mem. Am. Edn. Assn., Am. Math. Soc., Am. Math. Assn. (chmn. S.E. sect. 1966-67), Nat. Council Tchrs. Math., Assn. Math. Tchrs. Ala. (pres. 1963), Assn. So. Bapt. Colls. and Schs. (sec. 1973, v.p. 1974, pres. 1975, deans sect.), Ala. Acad. Sci. (pres. 1967-69), Am. Assn. Higher Edn., Assn. Ala. Coll. Adminstrs. (exec. com. 1976—, pres. 1978-79), Am. Assn. U. Adminstrs. (exec. com. Ala. sect. 1972-74, v.p. 1974-76, pres. 1976—), Am. Conf. Acad. Deans. Baptist (deacon). Rotarian. Author: Modern Math, An Elementary Approach, 1966, 4th edit., 1977; Fundamental Concepts of Math, 1968, 2d edit., 1976; Modern Math for Business, 1969, 2d edit., 1975; A Programmed Study of Number Systems, 1972; Finite Mathematics, 1974; Intuitive Geometry, 1975; Mathematics, an Everyday Language, 1979. Home: 1347 Badham Dr Birmingham AL 35216

WHEELER, SESSIONS SAMUEL, found. exec., author; b. Fernley, Nev., Apr. 27, 1911; s. Lister L. and Lythia Marie (Sessions) W.; B.S., U. Nev., 1934, M.S., 1935; m. Nevada Hazel Pedroli, Apr. 24, 1948. Biologist, Fernley High Sch., 1935-36, Reno schs., 1936-66; chmn. sci. dept. Reno High Sch., 1957-66; on leave as exec. dir. Nev. Fish and Game Commn., 1947-50; tchr. conservation edn. U. Nev., summers 1953-72, U. So. Calif., 1961; tchr. conservation natural resources U. Nev., 1966-74; trustee, adminstr. Max C. Fleischmann Found., Reno, 1951—; author: (hist. novel) Paiute, 1965; (non-fiction) The Desert Lake, 1967, The Nevada Desert, 1971, The Black Rock Desert, 1978; also mag. articles; co-author conservation textbooks Conservation and Nevada, 1949, Nevada Conservation Adventure, 1959. Trustee Nev. State Museum, 1955-60; mem. Nev. Indian Affairs Commn., 1965-68. Recipient Distinguished Nevadan award U. Nev., 1963; Conservation Edn. award Nat. Wildlife Fedn.-Sears Roebuck Found., 1965; Fire Prevention award U.S. Forest Service-Nat. Assn. State Foresters, 1965; Bd. Trustees ann. award Nev. Hist. Soc., 1978; named Outstanding Biology Tchr. Nev., Nat. Assn. Biology Tchrs., 1962. Mem. Western Writers Am., Western History Assn., Westeners Internat. (pres. Nev. corral 1977-78), Explorers Club, Phi Kappa Phi, Sigma Nu. Roman Catholic. Home: 25 Moore Ln Reno NV 89509 Office: PO Box 1871 Reno NV 89505

WHEELER, TOWSON AMES, instn. exec.; b. Smithsburg, Md., Oct. 1, 1911; s. Carleton Ames and Elizabeth (Towson) W.; A.B., Harvard, 1932, M.S., 1934; m. Alma Lackey Wilson, Jan. 8, 1937; children—Sue Elizabeth (Mrs. Dwight N. Mason), Sara Ames (Mrs. Dieter Forster), Laurie Wilson (Mrs. Fayette Brown III). Engr., Chrysler Corp., 1934-35; analyst Investment Counsel Inc., Detroit, 1935-38; mem. investment staff Detroit Bank,1939-42; treasury staff U.S. Steel Corp. of Del., Pitts., 1942-46; statistician Allegheny Ludlum Steel Corp., 1946-49, controller, 1949-60, v.p. charge planning, 1960-63, v.p. internat. and affiliated operations, 1963-66, v.p., sec., 1967-68; treas. Smithsonian Instn., Washington, 1968-79. Dir. Nat. Biomed. Research Found., Washington, Center for Natural Areas, South Gardner, Maine. Mem. Phi Beta Kappa, Tau Beta Pi. Clubs: Allegheny Country; Chevy Chase, Metropolitan, Burning Tree (Washington); Mid Ocean (Bermuda). Home: 4645 Hawthorne Ln NW Washington DC 20016

WHEELER, WARREN G(AGE), JR., publishing co. exec.; b. Boston, Dec. 6, 1921; s. Warren Gage and Helen (Hoagland) W.; B.S., Bowdoin Coll., 1943; B.J., U. Mo., 1947, M.A., 1948; m. Jean Frances Moseley, Feb. 22, 1945; children—Richard, Michael, Ann, Duncan. With South Bend (Ind.) Tribune (name changed to Schurz Communications, Inc. 1976), 1948—, gen. mgr., 1964-71, exec. v.p., 1971-75, pres., 1975—; dir. Evergreen Communications, Inc., Bloomington, Ill. Campaign chmn. United Community Services, South Bend, 1960, pres., 1964; treas. South Bend Urban League, 1962-63; trustee St. Joseph's Hosp., South Bend, 1969-77; gen. chmn. St. Joseph County (Ind.) Hosp. Devel., 1969-71; deacon, elder, pres. session First Presbyn. Ch., South Bend. Served with USN, 1943-46. Protestant recipient Brotherhood award South Bend-Mishawaka chpt. NCCJ, 1970. Mem. Am. Newspaper Pubs. Assn., Am. Mgmt. Assn., Newspaper Personnel Relations Assn. (pres. 1955-56), Hoosier State Press Assn. (dir. 1967-70), Inland Daily Press Assn. (pres. 1972, pres. found. 1974-78), Sigma Delta Chi, Kappa Tau Alpha, Kappa Mu. Clubs: South Bend Press, Goose and Duck, Chikaming Country, Summit. Home: 1311 E Woodside St South Bend IN 46614 Office: 225 W Colfax Ave South Bend IN 46626

WHEELER, WILLIAM THORNTON, cons. engr.; b. Okla., Oct. 5, 1911; s. Hugh Luther and Sara Oats (Gallaher) W.; B.C.E., Calif. Inst. Tech., 1933; widower; children—Richard Frederick, Robert W. Structural engr., State of Calif., 1938-41; sr. structural engr. C.E., U.S. Army, 1941-45; asst. chief engr. Summerbell Roof Structures Co., Los Angeles, 1945-46; mem. Wheeler & Gray cons. engrs., Los Angeles, 1946—; rep. UNESCO, Tokyo, 1963. Mem. Calif. Space Shuttle Task Force, 1972. Registered profl. engr., Calif., 9 other states. Fellow ASCE, Earthquake Engring. Research Inst., Inst. Advancement Engring. (Outstanding Engr. merit award, 1974); mem. Structural Engrs. Assn. Calif. (past v.p., dir.; chmn. seismology com. 1957-61) Am. Concrete Inst. (past chpt. pres.), Seismol. Soc. Am., Am. Arbitration Assn. Clubs: Oneonta, Shriners, Rotary, Jonathan (Los Angeles). Contbr. articles to publs. Home: 190 Arroyo Terr 303 Pasadena CA 91103 Office: 7462 N Figueroa St Los Angeles CA 90041

WHEELER, WILMOT FITCH, JR., diversified mfg. co. exec.; b. Southport, Conn., June 5, 1923; s. Wilmot Fitch and Hulda Day (Chapman) W.; B.A., Yale U., 1945; student N.Y. U., 1947-48; m. Barbara Rutherfurd, Sept. 30, 1944 (dec. Sept. 1971); children—Wilmot Fitch III, James Alexander, John R., Susan; m. 2d, Nonnye Landers, Dec. 20, 1973; children—Tracy Lynne, Alexa Margaret. Staff engr. Stevenson, Jordan & Harrison, Inc., mgmt. cons., 1946-51; with Am. Chain & Cable Co., Inc., N.Y.C., 1951-76, chmn., chief exec. officer, 1967-76; chmn., dir. Jelliff Corp., Southport, Conn., 1976—; prin. Case & Co. Inc. mgmt. cons., 1977—; dir. Am. Mut. Liability Ins. Co., Am. Dist. Telegraph Co., Hersey Products, Inc., Manhattan Life Corp., Pratt-Read Corp., Am. Policyholders Ins. Co.; trustee Dollar Savs. Bank, People's Savs. Bank. Bd. dirs. William T. Morris Found., Wilmot Wheeler Found.; trustee U. Bridgeport, Bridgeport Hosp. Served with AUS, 1943-46. Decorated Bronze Star. Episcopalian. Clubs: Yale, Links, Sky (N.Y.C.); County of Fairfield. Home: 328 Sasco Hill Rd Southport CT 06490 Office: Jelliff Corp 354 Pequot Rd Southport CT 06490

WHEELEY, BENTON OTTO, bldg. materials exec.; b. Lafayette, Tenn., July 25, 1921; s. John H. and Georgia (Jenkins) W.; B.S. in Chem. Engring., U. Tenn., 1943; m. Kathleen Wilson, Mar. 12, 1943; children—Nancy, Ben, Stephen, Robert. With H. L. Smith Co., Richmond, Va., 1946-48; with Koppers Co., Inc., Pitts., 1943-46, 48—, v.p., mgr. marketing, 1963-72, sr. v.p., 1972—, dep. chmn. bd., 1978—; dir. U.S. Plastics and Chem. Corp., Koppers Products, Ltd., Bowden & Co. Pub. Affairs fellow Brookings Inst., 1962. Bd. govs. Pa. Baptist Conv.; bd. dirs. Presbyn.-U. Hosp., U.S. Korea Econ. Council, Eastern Coll., Eastern Sem., Am. Bapt. Chs. of Pa. and Del., Salvation Army Western Pa. Named one of outstanding laymen of nation Am. Heritage Found., 1958. Registered profl. engr., Pa. Mem. NAM, Nat. Soc. Profl. Engrs., Alpha Chi Sigma. Home: 116 Sherwood Dr Canonsburg PA 15317 Office: Koppers Bldg Pittsburgh PA 15219

WHEELOCK, ARTHUR KINGSLAND, JR., art historian; b. Worcester, Mass., May 13, 1943; s. Arthur Kingsland and Anne (Kneass) W.; B.A., Williams Coll., 1965; Ph.D., Harvard U., 1973; m. Susan Hoffman, June 13, 1964; children—Arthur Tobey, Laura, Matthew. Instr., Bement Sch., Deerfield, Mass., 1965-66; asst. prof. art history U. Md., College Park, 1974—; David E. Finley fellow Nat. Gallery Art, Washington, 1971-74, research curator, 1974-75, curator Dutch and Flemish painting, 1976—; cons. Central Laboratorium voor Onderzoek van Voorwerpen van Kunst en Wetenschap, Amsterdam, 1969-70. NDEA fellow, 1967-70; Nat. Endowment Arts grantee, 1979-80. Mem. Coll. Art Assn. Democrat. Episcopalian. Author: Perspective; Optics and Delft Artists around 1650, 1977; contbr. articles to profl. jours. and encys. Office: National Gallery Art Washington DC 20565

WHEELOCK, MAJOR WILLIAM, JR., graphics co. exec.; b. Fall River, Mass., Dec. 12, 1936; s. Major William and Mildred Mary (Rogers) W.; B.S., Providence Coll., 1958; m. Rita Pauline Gauthier, Feb. 22, 1962; children—Major William III, Nancy Beth. Budget examiner, spl. asst. to asst. sec. of navy, Washington, 1963-66; legis. analyst, budget examiner Bur. of Budget, Exec. Office of Pres., Washington, 1966-71; exec. asst. to the gov. State of N.H., 1971-73; supt. N.H. Hosp., Concord, 1973-77; preceptor George Washington U. Sch. Hosp. Adminstrn.; exec. dir. N.H. Charitable Fund, Concord, 1977-78; exec. v.p. Rumford Nat. Graphics, Inc., Concord, 1978—. Pres. Young Republican Club, Fall River, Mass., 1957-58. Bd. dirs. N.H. Indsl. Devel. Authority, 1972-75; bd. dirs. Community Health Care Assn., 1974-75, v.p., 1976. Served with U.S. Army, 1959-61. Named N.H. Citizen of Yr., 1977; recipient Bancroft award N.H. Psychiatric Soc., 1977. Mem. N.H. Hosp. Assn., Am. Coll. Hosp. Adminstrs. Roman Catholic. Clubs: Concord Country (pres. 1976-77), Rotary. Home: 14 Shaker Rd Concord NH 03301 Office: 10 Ferry St Concord NH 03301

WHEELON, ALBERT DEWELL, physicist; b. Moline, Ill., Jan. 18, 1929; s. Orville Albert and Alice Geltz (Dewell) W.; B.Sc., Stanford U., 1949; Ph.D., Mass. Inst. Tech., 1952; m. Nancy Helen Hermanson, Feb. 28, 1953; children—Elizabeth Anne, Cynthia Helen. Teaching fellow, then research asso. physics Mass. Inst. Tech., 1949-52; with Douglas Aircraft Co., 1952-53, Ramo-Wooldridge Corp., 1953-62; dep. dir. sci. and tech. CIA, 1962-66; with Hughes Aircraft Co., 1966—, v.p., group exec. space and communications group, El Segundo, Calif., 1970—; mem. Def. Sci. Bd., 1967-77; cons. President's Sci. Adv. Council, 1961-74, NSC, 1974—; Recipient Distinguished Intelligence medal CIA, 1966. Fellow IEEE; mem. Nat. Acad. Engring., Am. Phys. Soc., Internat. Union Radio Sci., Sigma Chi. Republican. Episcopalian. Club: Cosmos (Washington). Author 30 papers on radiowaves propagation and guidance systems. Office: 909 N Sepulveda Blvd El Segundo CA 90245

WHELAN, EUGENE FRANCIS, Canadian politician, farmer; b. Amherstburg, Ont., July 11, 1924; s. Charles B. and Francis L. (Kelly) W.; student Windsor-Walkerville Vocat. and Tech. Sch.; m. Elizabeth Pollinger, Apr. 30, 1960; children—Theresa Ann, Susan Elizabeth, Catherine Frances. Pres. Essex County br. Ont. Fedn. Agr.; an organizer, bd. dirs. Ont. Winter Wheat Prodicers Mktg. Bd., bd. dirs. Harrow Farmer Coop., also pres.; bd. dirs. United Coops. Ont.; an organizer, agt., bd. dirs. Coop. Ins. Assn.; mem. Ho. of Commons for Essex-Windsor, 1962—, chmn. standing com. on agr., forestry and rural devel., 1966; Parliamentary sec. to minister fisheries and forestry, 1968-70; minister of agr., 1972—; del. World Parliamentarians Conf., 1963, 68. Mem. Anderson Twp. Sch. Bd.; reeve of Anderdon Twp.; chmn. Essex County Rd. Com.; warden of Essex County; player Ont. Rural Hockey League. Mem. Harrow Farmers Coop., Ont. Winter Wheat Producers Mktg. Bd. Liberal. Roman Cath. Clubs: Lions, K.C. Office: House of Commons Ottawa ON K1A 0A6 Canada

WHELAN, FRANCIS C., U.S. judge; b. O'Neill, Nebr., Dec. 11, 1907; s. Edward H. and Susan (Quilty) W.; student San Diego State Coll., 1925-28; LL.B., U. Calif., 1932; m. Marian Willette, Feb. 7, 1948 (dec.); stepchildren—Marianne Conway Laub, Francis W. Conway. Admitted to Calif. bar, 1932; pvt. practice, San Diego, 1932-35, Los Angeles, 1948-61; asst. U.S. atty., 1935-39; spl. asst. Dept. Justice, also spl. asst. to U.S. atty. gen., 1939-48; U.S. atty. So. Dist. Calif., 1961-64, U.S. dist. judge, 1964—, now sr. judge. Mem. Am. Bar Assn. Roman Catholic, K.C. Office: US Ct House Los Angeles CA 90012*

WHELAN, GERALD T., lt. gov. Nebr.; b. Hastings, Nebr., May 14, 1925; student Creighton U., U. Colo.; LL.B., U. Nebr.; m. Virginia, Sept. 8, 1948; 4 children. Admitted to Nebr. bar, practiced in Hastings; lt. gov. State of Nebr., Lincoln, 1975—. Sec. Hastings Centennial Commn.; mem. Nebr. State Bd. Edn., 1970-74; bd. dirs. Adams County (Nebr.) ARC, Adams County Fair Assn., Hastings Community Chest. Served in USN, World War II. Mem. Adams County Bar Assn. (past pres.). Democrat. Roman Catholic. Club: Lochland Country. Office: Office Lt Gov State Capitol Lincoln NE 68509*

WHELAN, PAUL AUGUSTINE, univ. pres.; b. Shreveport, July 16, 1928; s. Augustine P. and Margaret C. (Murphy) W.; B.S. in Polit. Sch., Coll. Holy Cross, Worcester, Mass., 1957; M.A. in History, U. Tenn., Knoxville, 1963; Ph.D. in History, St. Louis U., 1967; m. Patricia L. Welsh, Feb. 14, 1950; children—Stephen, Timothy, Michael, Monica, Kevin, Thomas, Patrick, Gregory, Martin, Matthew, Daniel, Moira. Commd. 2d lt. USAF, 1950, advanced through grades to col., 1971; command pilot, service in Europe, Far East, U.S., ret., 1974; acad. dean faculties Spring Hill Coll., Mobile, 1974-76, dean instl. plans and programs, 1976-77; pres. Lewis U., Romeoville, Ill., 1977—; chmn. council liberal arts deans Ala. Council Edn., 1976; chmn. Mobile United Edn. Com., 1976; edn., mgmt. cons. Active local Boy Scouts Am., ARC, YMCA. Decorated D.F.C., Bronze Star, Air Force Meritorious Service medal, Air medal, Air Force Commendation medal. Mem. Am. Assn. Coll. and Univ. Adminstrs., Am. Hist. Assn., Orgn. Am. Historians, Western Hist. Assn., Air Force Assn., Ret. Officers Assn., Daedialians, Catholic Social Justice and Family Life Commn. Roman Catholic. Club: Rotary. Author: The History of the Third Air Division in World War II, 1968; also articles. Home: 908 Buell St Joliet IL 60435 Office: Lewis Univ Route 53 Romeoville IL 60441

WHELAN, ROBERT LOUIS, bishop; b. Wallace, Idaho, Apr. 16, 1912; ed. St. Michael's Coll., Spokane, Wash., Alma (Calif.) Coll. Mem. Soc. of Jesus; ordained priest Roman Cath. Ch., 1944; titular bishop of Sicilibba and coadjutor bishop Fiarbanks, Alaska, 1967-68; bishop of Fairbanks, 1968—. Address: 1316 Peger Rd Fairbanks AK 99701*

WHELAN, THOMAS JOSEPH, ret. army officer, physician; b. Lynn, Mass., June 26, 1921; s. Thomas Joseph and Mildred (Killen) W.; B.A., Yale U., 1943, M.D., 1946; m. Norma Margaret Gianascol, Feb. 19, 1944; children—Sharon Anne Whelan Weiss, Thomas Joseph, Rosemary Whelan Polen, Sally D., Christal K., Michael S. Intern, Strong Meml. Hosp., Rochester, N.Y., 1946-47, resident, 1949-50, 51-54; commd. 1st lt. U.S. Army, 1947, advanced through grades to brig. gen., 1969; chief gen. surgery Valley Forge Army Hosp., 1954-56; chief surgery U.S. Army Hosp., Munich, Germany, 1956-59; asst. chief to chief gen. and vascular surgery Walter Reed Gen. Hosp., Washington, 1959-65; chief dept. surgery Tripler Gen. Hosp., Honolulu, 1965-69; spl. asst. to Surgeon Gen. for Med. Corps Affairs, Washington, 1969-73, ret., 1973; asso. clin prof. surgery George Washington U.; clin. prof. surgery U. Hawaii, now prof., chmn. dept. surgery. Decorated Legion of Merit with oak leaf cluster, Army Commendation medal with 2 oak leaf clusters, D.S.M. Fellow A.C.S., Am. Surg. Assn., Pan-Pacific Surg. Assn., Pacific Coast Surg. Assn., AMA, Southeastern Surg. Congress, Soc. Vascular Surgery, Assn. Mil. Surgeons, Soc. Surgery Chairmen. Contbr. articles to profl. jours. Home: 4395 Aukai Ave Honolulu HI 96816 Office: University Tower 1356 Lusitana St Honolulu HI 96813

WHELAN, WILLIAM ANTHONY, forest products co. exec.; b. Bklyn., Aug. 18, 1921; s. Daniel and Catherine (Pugh) W.; B.S.M.E., U. Calif., Berkeley; m. Marcia M. McCorkle, Nov. 14, 1948; children—Michael, Greer, Danie, Ann. Vice pres. Klamath Machine & Locomotive Works, 1948-58; plant and dist. mgr. U.S. Plywood, 1959-68; v.p. West Coast ops. Champion Internat., 1968-74; v.p. exec. Roseburg Lumber Co., 1975-77; exec. v.p. Pope & Talbot, Inc., Portland, Oreg., 1978, pres., 1979—, also dir. Mem. Western Wood Products Assn. (dir.), Nat. Forest Products Assn. (dir.). Served in U.S. Army, 3 years; Okinawa. Club: Arlington. Office: 1700 SW Fourth Ave Portland OR 97201

WHELAN, WILLIAM JOHN, oil co. exec.; b. Perth, Ont., Can., June 4, 1928; s. Reginald Vincent and Frances M. (Noonan) W.; Chartered Accountant, Queens U.; m. Margaret Elizabeth Harris, Oct. 3, 1952; children—Jerrold Douglas, Blair William, Thomas Richard, Elizabeth Anne. Pub. accountant Eddis & Assos., 1949-54; v.p. Warren Bituminous Paving Co. Ltd., 1954-70; v.p., treas. Ashland Oil Can. Ltd., Calgary, Alta., 1970—; pres. Oily Gas div. Kaiser Resources Ltd., also corporate dir.; pres. Kaiser Oil Ltd. Mem. Fin. Execs. Inst., Inst. Chartered Accts. Mem. Progressive Conservative Party. Clubs: Calgary Golf and Country, Ranchman's. Home: 6913 Livingstone Dr SW Calgary AB Canada Office: 639 5th Ave SW Calgary AB T2P 0N1 Canada

WHELAN, WILLIAM JOSEPH, biochemist; b. Salford, U.K., Nov. 14, 1924; s. William Joseph and Jane Antoinette (Bertram) W.; B.Sc., U. Birmingham, Eng., 1945, Ph.D., 1948, D.Sc., 1955; m. Margaret Miller, Dec. 22, 1951. Asst. lectr. U. Birmingham, 1947-48; sr. lectr. Univ. Coll. of North Wales, 1948-55; sr. mem. Lister Inst., U. London, 1956-64; prof., head dept. Royal Free Hosp. Sch. of Medicine, 1964-67; prof., chmn. dept. biochemistry U. Miami, 1967—. Recipient Ciba medal Brit. Biochem. Soc., 1968; Saare medal Assn. Cereal Research, 1979. Mem. Fedn. European Biochem. Socs. (sec.-gen. 1965-67), Pan Am. Assn. Biochem. Socs. (sec. gen. 1969-71), Internat. Union Biochemistry (gen. sec. 1973—), Am. Soc. Biol. Chemists, Am. Chem. Soc., Biochem. Soc., Sigma Xi. Club: Athenaeum (London). Editor books in field. Home: 1420 S Bayshore Dr Miami FL 33131 Office: PO Box 016129 Miami FL 33101

WHETTEN, JOHN THEODORE, geologist; b. Willimantic, Conn., Mar. 16, 1935; s. Nathan Laselle and Theora Lucille (Johnson) W.; A.B. with high honors, Princeton U., 1957, Ph.D., 1962; M.S., U. Calif., Berkeley, 1959; m. Carol Annette Jacobsen, July 14, 1960; children—Andrea, Krista, Michelle. Mem. faculty U. Wash., Seattle, 1963—, research instr. oceanography, 1963-64, asst. prof., 1964-68, asso. prof., 1968-72, prof. geol. scis. and oceanography, 1972—, chmn. dept. geol. scis., 1969-74, asso. dean Grad. Sch., 1968-69; geologist U.S. Geol. Survey, Seattle, 1975—. Fulbright fellow, 1962-63. Contbr. articles to profl. jours. Home: 6828 51st Ave NE Seattle WA 98115 Office: U Wash Dept Geol Scis Seattle WA 98195

WHETTON, JAMES JUNIOR, businessman; b. Ogden, Utah, Mar. 13, 1921; s. Percy Raynor and Lillian (Edwards) W.; grad. Weber State Coll., 1941, U.S. Naval Acad., 1944; m. Marian Frances Bader, June 8, 1944; children—Frances Louise, James Lovell, Alan Raynor, Leslie Ann, Mark Edward. Adminstrv. asst. to Howard Hughes, 1952-60; owner, operator Jim Whetton Buick, 1960—, Jim Whetton Jeep, 1960—, Jim Whetton AMC, 1960—; gen. mgr. Country Club div. Summa Corp., 1973; asst. gen. mgr. Landmark Hotel, Las Vegas, 1974; gen. mgr. Desert Inn and Country Club, Las Vegas, 1974-78; pres. Inter Mountain Mgmt. Corp., Las Vegas; chmn. Nat. Buick Dealer Council, 1966-67; mem. pres.'s adv. bd. Gen. Motors Corp., 1978—. Pres., McKay Dee Hosp. Found., 1960-70, chmn. bd., 1971—; bd. govs. McKay Dee Hosp. Center, 1971—. Served to comdr. USNR, 1941-47, 51-52. Mem. Nat. Automobile Assn., U.S. Naval Acad. Alumni Assn., Greater Ogden Area C. of C. (pres. 1967). Republican. Mormon. Clubs: Rotary, Ogden Golf and Country (pres. 1966), Desert Inn Country, Elks. Home: 887 N Harrisville Rd Ogden UT 84404 Office: 3520 Wall Ave Ogden UT 84403*

WHICKER, JOHN HAYES CLAYTON, banker; b. London, Apr. 28, 1935; s. Walter George and Marion Farrar (Clayton) W.; came to U.S., 1976; M.A., Oxford (Eng.) U., 1958; m. Lovell, Aug. 8, 1959; children—Sarah, Simon. With Barclays Bank Internat. Ltd., 1958-72, local dir., Nassau, Bahamas, 1971-72; mng. dir. Barclays Bank Zambia, 1972-76; pres. Barclays Bank N.Y., N.Y.C., 1976—. Chmn. Zambia Med. Aid Soc. Fellow Brit. Inst. Bankers; mem. Brit. Inst. Mgmt. Office: Barclays Bank NY 200 Park Ave New York City NY 10017

WHIDDEN, RAY HARVEY, mktg. cons.; b. San Francisco, Sept. 15, 1913; s. Ray Allen and Laura (Harvey) W.; student Northwestern U., 1931-34; m. Agatha Jane Darling, June 6, 1936; children—Wendy, Jane, Peter. With Weco Products Co., 1935-38; v.p. W.A. Sheaffer Pen Co., Ft. Madison, Iowa, 1938-56; sales dir. Bulova Watch Co., Flushing, N.Y., 1956-57, v.p., 1957-60, exec. v.p., 1960-63; pres. R.H. Whidden Assos., Inc., 1964—, Elgin Internat., 1971—; pres., dir. Bulova Internat., Ltd., 1960-63; dir. Eagle Star Ins. Co. Am. Inc., Elgin Internat. (Far East) Ltd., Hong Kong. Mem. council Columbia Coll. Gen. Studies. Served to lt. (s.g.) USNR, 1942-45. Clubs: Greenwich Country; Chgo.; Preston Mountain (Conn.); Ambassadors (London); Sotogrande (Spain). Home: 16 E Lyon Farm Dr Greenwich CT 06830

WHIDDON, FREDERICK PALMER, univ. pres.; b. Newville, Ala., Mar. 2, 1930; s. Samuel Wilson and Mary (Palmer) W.; A.B., Birmingham So. Coll., 1952; B.D. cum laude, Emory U., 1955, Ph.D. in Philosophy, 1963; m. June Marie Ledyard, June 14, 1952; children—Charles Wilson, John Tracy, Karen Marie and Keith Frederick (twins). Grad. asst. Inst. Liberal Arts, Emory U., 1955-56; asst. prof. philosophy, dean students Athens (Ala.) Coll., 1957-59; dir. Mobile Center U. Ala., 1960-63; pres. Univ. S. Ala., Mobile, 1963—; presdl. adv. com. Fed. Home Loan Bank, Atlanta. Chmn., Marine Environ. Scis. Consortium; bd. dirs. Julius T. Wright Sch., Mobile, Mobile Mus. Named Outstanding Young Man in Ala., 1964. Mem. Mobile C. of C. (v.p., dir.). Methodist (steward). Club: Kiwanis (Mobile). Editorial rev. bd. South mag. Home: 2157 Venetia Rd Mobile AL 36605 Office: Univ So Ala Mobile AL 36688

WHIFFEN, JAMES DOUGLAS, surgeon, educator; b. N.Y.C., Jan. 16, 1931; s. John Phillip and Lorna Elizabeth (Douglass) W.; B.S., U. Wis., 1952, M.D., 1955; m. Arlis Edgington, Dec. 30, 1960; 1 son, Gregory James. Intern, Ohio State U. Hosp., 1955-56; resident U. Wis. Hosp., 1956-57, 59-61; instr. dept. surgery U. Wis. Med. Sch., 1962-64, asst. prof., 1964-67, asso. prof., 1967-71, prof., 1971—, vice chmn. dept., 1970-72, acting chmn., 1972-74, asst. dean Med. Sch., 1975—; mem. exam. council State of Wis. Emergency Med. Services, 1974-77. Bd. dirs. Wis. Heart Assn. Served to lt. comdr. USNR, 1957-59. John and Mary R. Markle scholar in acad. medicine, also Research Career Devel. award NIH, 1965-75. Diplomate Am. Bd. Surgery. Fellow A.C.S., Am. Soc. Artificial Internal Organs. Club: Maple Bluff Country. Research, publs. on biomaterials, thrombo-resistant surfaces and the physiology of heart-lung bypass procedures. Home: 17 Cambridge Ct Madison WI 53704 Office: 600 Highland Ave Madison WI 53792

WHILLOCK, CARL SIMPSON, univ. pres.; b. Scotland, Ark., May 7, 1926; s. Joe and Johnnie (Simpson) W.; B.S., U. Ark., 1948, M.A., 1951; J.D., George Washington U., 1960; m. Margaret Moore; children—Timothy, Tom, Sally Haws, Susan Lipe, Sallie Starr, Jenny Carter, Melissa Carter, Larry, Brennam, Benjamin. Exec. asst. to Congressman J.W. Trimble, Berryville, Ark., 1955-63; individual practice law, Clinton, Ark., 1963-66; pros. atty. 14th Jud. Dist., Ark., 1965-66; asst. to pres. U. Ark., 1966-71, instr. polit. sci., 1967, 69, 73, dir. univ. relations, 1971-74, v.p. governmental relations and public affairs, 1975-78; pres. Ark. State U., 1978—; campaign mgr. David Pryor for Gov. Campaign, 1974-75; exec. sec. Gov. of Ark., 1975. Mem. Ark. Legislature; chmn. housing authority City of Fayetteville, Ark.; pres. Sch. Bd., Clinton, Ark.; chmn. water and sewer commn. City of Clinton; bd. dirs. Van Buren County (Ark.) Hosp. Served with U.S. Navy, 1943-46. Democrat. Home: 1503 E Nettleton St Jonesboro AR 72401 Office: PO Drawer A State University AR 72467. *It is my belief that the success of any organization or effort depends on the caliber of the people involved in it. It is important that people be intelligent, imaginative, compassionate, willing to listen to others, courageous, conscientious, honest, and dependable. People who have these qualities have been the greatest inspiration to me.*

WHINNA, WILLIAM, accountant; b. Atlantic City, Feb. 13, 1944; s. William and Jennie Whinna; B.S., Fairleigh Dickinson U., Rutherford, N.J., 1965; m. Linda Haines, June 20, 1964; children—Joni, Jennifer. Audit mgr. Arthur Young & Co., Phila., 1965-72; controller Land Resources Corp., N.Y.C., 1975-76; v.p., treas. Parsons & Whittemore, Inc., N.Y.C., 1976—. C.P.A., Pa. Mem. Am. Inst. C.P.A.'s, Pa. Inst. C.P.A.'s. Office: 200 Park Ave New York NY 10017

WHINNERY, JOHN ROY, educator; b. Read, Colo., July 26, 1916; s. Ralph V. and Edith Mable (Bent) W.; B.S. in Elec. Engring., U. Calif. at Berkeley, 1937, Ph.D., 1948; m. Patricia Barry, Sept. 17, 1944; children—Carol Joanne, Catherine, Barbara. Student engr. Gen. Electric Co., 1937-40, supr. high frequency course advanced engring. program, 1940-42, research engr., 1942-46; part-time lectr. Union Coll., Schenectady, 1945-46; asso. prof. elec. engring. U. Calif. at Berkeley, 1946-52, prof., vice chmn. div. elec. engring., 1952-56, chmn., 1956-59, dean Coll. Engring., 1959-63, prof. elec. engring., 1963—; vis. mem. tech. staff. Bell Telephone Labs., 1963-64; research sci. electron tubes Hughes Aircraft Co., Culver City, 1951-52; bd. editors I.R.E., 1956. Chmn. Commn. Engring. Edn., 1966-68; mem. sci. and tech. com. Manned Space Flight, NASA, 1963-69; mem. Pres.'s Com. on Nat. Sci. Medal, 1970-73, 79-80; standing com. controlled thermonuclear research AEC, 1970-73. Recipient Edn. medal IEEE, 1967; Lamme medal Am. Soc. Engring. Edn., 1975; Microwave Career award IEEE Microwave Theory and Techniques Soc., 1977; Guggenheim fellow, 1959. Fellow I.R.E. (dir. 1956-59), Optical Soc. Am.; mem. Nat. Acad. Engring., Nat. Acad. Scis., IEEE (dir. 1969-71, sec. 1971), Phi Beta Kappa, Sigma Xi, Tau Beta Pi, Eta Kappa Nu. Conglist. Author: (with Simon Ramo) Fields and Waves in Modern Radio, 1944; (with D. O. Pederson and J. J. Studer) Introduction to Electronic Systems, Circuits and Devices; also tech. articles. Home: One Daphne Ct Orinda CA 94563 Office: U Calif Berkeley CA 94720

WHINSTON, ARTHUR LEWIS, lawyer; b. N.Y.C., Feb. 5, 1925; s. Charles Nathaniel and Charlotte (Nalen) W.; B.C.E., Cornell U., 1945; M.S.E., Princeton U., 1947; J.D., N.Y. U., 1957; m. Melicent Ames Kingsbury, Mar. 19, 1949; children—Ann Kingsbury, James Pierce, Melicent Ames, Louise Ellen, Patricia Kingsbury. Engr., Chas. N. & Selig Whinston, N.Y.C., 1947-50; lectr. Coll. City N.Y., 1950-51; structures engr. Republic Aviation Corp., Farmingdale, N.Y., 1951-57; admitted to N.Y. bar, 1957, Oreg. bar, 1964, U.S. Supreme Ct., U.S. Patent Office, Ct. Customs and Patent Appeals; practice in N.Y.C., 1957-64, Portland, Oreg., 1964—; patent lawyer Arthur, Dry & Kalish, 1957-64; partner Klarquist, Sparkman, Campbell, Leigh, Hall & Whinston, 1964—; chmn. Oreg. Bar com. on patent, trademark and copyright law, 1968-69, 77-78, mem. com. unauthorized practice law, 1970-73, chmn., 1972-73, com. on profl. responsibility, 1973-75. Served as ensign, C.E., USNR, 1945-46. Recipient Fuertes medal Cornell U. Sch. Civil Engring., 1945; registered profl. engr., N.Y., Oreg. Mem. Am., Oreg., N.Y., Multnomah County bar assns., Am., N.Y., Oreg. (pres. 1977-78) patent law assns., Profl. Engrs. Oreg. (past state legis. chmn.), Sigma Xi, Chi Epsilon, Phi Kappa Phi. Republican. Unitarian. Club: Multnomah Athletic. Home: 3824 SW 50th Ave Portland OR 97221 Office: 16th Floor Willamette Center Portland OR 97204

WHIPPLE, CHARLES LEWIS, former newspaperman; b. Salem, Mass., May 8, 1914; s. Charles A. and Mary (Lane) W.; A.B., Harvard, 1935; m. Caroline Dalton Drane, Jan. 15, 1946 (dec. 1967); children—Charles A. II, Jonathan L.; m. 2d, Priscilla Preston Cutler, Aug. 16, 1975; stepchildren—Priscilla C. Stiver, Ellen B., James P. and Timothy K. Cutler. With Boston Globe, 1936—, editor editorial page, 1964-75, ombudsman, 1975-79. Organizer Am. Newspaper Guild, 1941-42. Served as field dir. A.R.C., 1942-45. Decorated Purple Heart; recipient various profl. awards. Mem. Nat. Conf. Editorial Writers (exec. bd. 1969-70). Unitarian. Club: St. Botolph (Boston). Contbr. articles to publs. Home: 128 Shutesbury Rd Leverett MA 01054 also East Dover VT 05341 also Holdernes NH 03245

WHIPPLE, FRED LAWRENCE, astronomer; b. Red Oak, Iowa, Nov. 5, 1906; s. Harry Lawrence and Celestia (MacFarland) W.; student Occidental Coll., 1923-24; A.B., U. Calif. at Los Angeles, 1927, Ph.D., at Berkeley, 1931; A.M. (hon.), Harvard, 1945; Sc.D., Am. Internat. Coll., 1958; D.Litt. (hon.), Northeastern U., 1961; D.Sc. (hon.), Temple U., 1961; LL.D., C.W. Post Coll., L.I. U., 1962; m. Dorothy Woods, 1928 (div. 1935); 1 son, Earle Raymond; m. 2d, Babette F. Samelson, Aug. 20, 1946; children—Dorothy Sandra, Laura. Teaching fellow U. Calif. at Berkeley, 1927-29; Lick Obs. fellow, 1930-31; instr. Stanford, summer 1929, U. Calif., summer 1931; staff mem. Harvard Obs., 1931—, instr. Harvard, 1932-38, lectr., 1938-45, asso. prof. astronomy, 1945-50, prof. astronomy, 1950—, chmn. dept., 1949-56, Phillips prof. astronomy, 1968-77; dir. Smithsonian Astrophys. Obs., 1955-73, sr. scientist, 1973—; mem. Research Panel U.S., 1946—, U.S. subcom NASA, 1946-52, U.S. Research and Devel. Bd. Panel, 1947-52; chmn. Tech. Panel on Rocketry, mem. Tech. Panel on Earth Satellite Program, other coms. Internat. Geophys. Year, 1955-59; mem., past officer Internat. Astron. Union; cons. missions to U.K. and MTO, 1944; del. Inter-Am. Astrophys. Congress, Mexico, 1942; active leader project on Upper-Atmospheric Research via Meteor Photog. sponsored by Bur. Ordnance, U.S. Navy, 1946-51, by Office Naval Research, 1951-57, USAF, 1948-62; mem. com. meteorology, space sci. bd., com. on atmospheric sics. Nat. Acad. Scis.-NRC, 1958-65; project dir. Harvard Radio Meteor Project, 1958—; asso. adviser Sci. Advisory Bd., USAF, 1963-67; spl. cons. com. Sci. and Astronautics, U.S. Ho. Reps., 1960-73; chmn. Gordon Research Confs., 1963; dir. Optical Satellite Tracking Project, NASA, 1958-73, project dir. Orbiting Astron. Obs., 1958-72, dir. Meteorite Photography and Recovery Program, 1962-73, cons. planetary atmospheres, 1962-69, mem. space scis. working group on Orbiting Astron. Observatories, 1959-70; chmn. sci. council geodetic uses artifical satellites Com. Space Research, 1965—. Decorated comdr. Order of Merit for research and invention, Esnault-Pelterie award (France); recipient Donohue medals for ind. discovery of 6 new comets; Presdl. Certificate of Merit for sci. work during World War II; J. Lawrence Smith medal Nat. Acad. Scis. for research on meteors, 1949; medal for astron. research U. Liege, 1960; Space Flight award Am. Astronautical Soc., 1961; Distinguished Fed. Civilian Service award, 1963; Space Pioneers medallion for contbns. to fed. space program, 1968, Pub. Service award for contbns. to OAO2 devel. NASA, 1969; Leonard medal Meteoritical Soc., 1970; Kepler medal AAAS, 1971; Career Service award Nat. Civil Service League, 1972; Henry medal Smithsonian Instn., 1973; Alumnus of Year Achievement award U. Calif. at Los Angeles, 1976; Benjamin Franklin fellow Royal Soc. Arts, London, 1968—. Fellow Am. Astron. Soc. (v.p. 1962-64), Am. Rocket Soc., Am. Geophys. Union; asso. Royal Astronomical Soc.; mem. Nat. Acad. Scis., Am. Inst. Aero. and Astronautics (aerospace tech. panel space physics 1960-63), Astronautical Soc. Pacific, Solar Assos.; mem. Internat. Sci. Radio Union (U.S.A. nat. com. 1949-61), Am. Meteoritical Soc., Am. Standards Assn., Am. Acad. Arts and Scis., Am. Philos. Soc. (councillor sect. astronomy and earth scis. 1966—),

Royal Soc. Scis. Belgium (corr.), Internat. Acad. Astronautics (sci. advisory com. 1962—), Internat. Astronautical Fedn., AAAS, Am. Meteorol. Soc., Royal Astron. Soc. (asso.), Phi Beta Kappa, Sigma Xi, Pi Mu Epsilon. Clubs: Examiner (Boston); Cosmos (Washington). Author: Earth, Moon and Planets, rev. edit., 1968. Contbr. sci. papers on astron. and upper atmosphere to Ency. Brit., mags., other publs. Asso. editor Astronomical Jour., 1954-56, 64—; editor: Smithsonian Contributions to Astrophysics, 1956-73; Planetary and Space Science, 1958—, Science Revs., 1961—; editorial bd. Earth and Planetary Sci. Letters. Inventor tanometer, meteor bumper. Home: 35 Elizabeth Rd Belmont MA 02178 Office: 60 Garden St Cambridge MA 02138

WHIPPLE, G(EORGE) HOYT, radiol. health scientist, educator; b. San Francisco, May 4, 1917; s. George Hoyt and Katharine Ball (Waring) W.; B.S., Wesleyan U., Middletown, Conn., 1939; postgrad. Mass. Inst. Tech., 1939-42; Ph.D., U. Rochester (N.Y.), 1953; m. Marta Mrazovic, Aug. 2, 1968; children by previous marriage—Andrew, Dana, Elizabeth, Margaret, Matthew. Mem. staff div. industry cooperation Mass. Inst. Tech., Cambridge, 1942-47; group leader Hanford Works Gen. Electric Co., Richland, Wash., 1947-50; asst. prof. radiation biology U. Rochester, 1950-57; prof. radiol. health U. Mich., Ann Arbor, 1957—; cons. radiation protection for electric utilities AEC, Dept. State. Mem. Am. Bd. Health Physics, Am. Bd. Indsl. Hygiene, AAAS, Am. Indsl. Hygiene Assn., Health Physics. Soc. Contbr. articles in field to sci. jours. Home: 1290 Barrister Rd Ann Arbor MI 48105 Office: Sch Pub Health U Mich Ann Arbor MI 48109

WHIPPLE, LAWRENCE ALOYSIUS, fed. judge; b. N.Y.C., July 26, 1910; s. Earle and Mary E. (Flynn) W.; B.S., Columbia, 1933; LL.B., John Marshall Law Sch., 1939; m. Virginia C. Golden, Apr. 20, 1940; children—Donald, Lawrence, Nancy, Virginia, John. Admitted to N.J. bar, 1941; acting magistrate, Jersey City, 1949-51; law enforcement dir. OPS, 1950; spl. asst. to U.S. atty. Justice Dept., 1951; exec. dir. Jersey City Housing Authority, 1953; dir. pub. safety, Jersey City, 1953-57; county counsel Judson County, 1958-62, prosecutor Hudson County, 1958-63; judge Superior Ct. of N.J., 1963-67; judge U.S. Dist. Ct., Dist. of N.J., Newark, 1967—, now sr. judge. Mem. Fed., N.J., Hudson County (pres. 1957) bar assns., N.Y. Lawyers Assn., Am. Judicature Soc., Catholic Lawyers Guild, Nat. Assn. Pros. Attys., State Prosecutors Assn. N.J. Home: 217 Trenton Blvd Sea Girt NJ 08750 Office: US Post Office and Courthouse Bldg Newark NJ 07102*

WHIPPLE, ROYSON NEWTON, former coll. pres., ednl. cons.; b. Buffalo, May 28, 1912; s. Roy Welles and Amy (Newton) W.; student U. Ala., 1931-32; B.S., U. Mich., 1935; M.S., Cornell U., 1939; student Syracuse U., 1945-52; m. Martha Stevens, July 3, 1935; children—Sharon Lou, Enid Diane. Sci. instr., athletic dir. Webster (N.Y.) High Sch., 1935-45; head food tech. div. State Univ. Tech. Coll., Morrisville, 1945-56, dir., 1957-60, pres., 1960-78; ret., 1978; ednl. cons., 1978—; dir. U.S. Office Edn. Food Tech. Project; cons. on food processing U.S. Office Edn., 1966-68, IBRD. Exec. bd. Boy Scouts Am.; mem. Iranian Found. Recipient Colgate U. award, 1968. Mem. Inst. Food Tech., AAAS, Am. Soc. Engring. Edn., N.Y. Assn. Jr. Colls., N.Y. Hist. Assn., N.Y. Sch. Bds. Assn., Agrl. Soc., Am. Personnel and Guidance Assn., Assn. Higher Edn., Vols. in Tech. Assistance, Internat. Platform Assn., N.Y. Acad. Scis., Assn. Engring. Edn., Phi Delta Kappa. Clubs: Masons, Rotary. Author: History of State University Institute at Morrisville; Curriculum Guide Food Processing Technology; contbr. articles to profl. publs. Home: 330 Bahama Dr Indialantic FL 32903 also Morrisville NY 13408

WHIPPLE, TAGGART, lawyer; b. Manchester, N.H., Oct. 15, 1912; s. Stanley Cornell and Ruth Storey (Taggart) W.; A.B., Harvard U., 1934; J.D., N.Y. U., 1938; m. Katharine G. Brewster, July 10, 1941; children—Christine Whipple Farrington, George S., Hugh W. Admitted to N.Y. bar, 1938; law clk. to v.p., gen. counsel Lehigh Valley R.R. Co., N.Y.C., 1934-38; mem. firm Davis, Polk & Wardwell, and predecessors, N.Y.C., 1938—, partner, 1950—; dir. Distillers Co. Ltd. (Del.), Gordon's Dry Gin Co. Ltd. (Del.). Trustee Hall of Fame for Great Americans, 1974-77, Village of Muttontown (N.Y.), 1956—, N.Y. U., 1970—, N.Y. U. Law Center Found., 1965—, N.Y. U. Inst. Fine Arts, 1970—, Vassar Coll., 1973—, Salisbury Sch., 1968-74, Brit.-Am. Ednl. Found., 1970—, East Woods Sch., 1948-64; bd. dirs. Community Hosp. at Glen Cove, 1948-69, Coral Reef Found., 1978—, Lincoln Center for Performing Arts, Inc., Repertory Theater of Lincoln Center, 1966-73, Theatre, Inc., Phoenix Theatre, 1959-64, Soc. St. Johnsland, 1962-66; mem. corp. Woods Hole Oceanographic Instn. Served with AUS, 1942-45. Fellow Am. Coll. Trial Lawyers, Am. Bar Found.; mem. Am. Law Inst., Am. Judicature Soc., Internat. Bar Assn., Fed. Bar Council, Assn. Bar City N.Y. (chmn. com. trade regulation and trade marks 1953-56), Am. (council sect. antitrust law 1966-70), N.Y. State (chmn. antitrust law sect. 1962-63) bar assns., Council Fgn. Relations, Asso. Harvard Alumni (pres. 1968-69). Episcopalian. Clubs: Century, Union, Down Town Assn., Pilgrims, Piping Rock, Anglers, L.I.; Met. (Washington); Fly Fishers (London). Contbr. articles to profl. jours. Home: Box 694 Muttontown Rd Syosset NY 11791 Office: 1 Chase Manhattan Plaza New York NY 10005

WHISENTON, ANDRE CARL, librarian; b. Durham, N.C., Feb. 4, 1944; s. Andrew C. and Margret Yvonne W.; B.A., Morehouse Coll., 1965; M.S. in Library Sci., Atlanta U., 1966; m. Vera Norman, Aug. 20, 1966; children—Andre Christopher, Courtney Yvonne. Cataloger, Def. Intelligence Agency, Arlington, Va., 1966-68, chief cataloging unit, 1968-71, chief ref. services, 1971-73; library dir. Naval Sea Systems Command, Crystal City, Va., 1973-76, U.S. Dept. Labor Library, Washington, 1976—; lectr. Washington Tech. Inst., 1973, 74. Mem. Spls. Libraries Assn. (com. chmn. sci. and tech. div. 1974-75, rep. to Fed. Library Com. 1975), Met. Washington Council Libraries. Home: 1204 Canyon Rd Silver Spring MD 20904 Office: US Dept Labor Library 200 Constitution Ave NW Washington DC 20210*

WHISLER, THOMAS LEE, educator; b. Dayton, Ohio, Feb. 12, 1920; s. Rolland Foster and Thelma (Wildasin) W.; student U. Cin., 1940; B.S., Miami U., Oxford, Ohio, 1941; M.B.A., U. Chgo., 1947, Ph.D., 1953; m. Ann Elizabeth Wohlen, Feb. 14, 1946; children—John, Barbara. Instr., then asst. prof. bus. mgmt. Sch. Bus., U. Mo., 1947-53; mem. faculty U. Chgo. Grad. Sch. Bus., 1953—, prof. indsl. relations, 1963—, prof. bus. policy, 1975—; vis. prof. Stanford U., summer 1959; instr. Mgmt. Devel. Inst., Cairo, summer, 1960, 61; cons. for Ford Found. to evaluate Nat. Inst. Mgmt. Devel., Cairo, 1963; Ford Found. cons. Center for Productivity Study and Research, State U. Ghent, 1968-69. Served with USNR, 1942-46. Author: (with G. Shultz) Management Organization and the Computer, 1960; Information Technology and Organizational Change, 1970; The Impact of Computers on Organizations, 1970. Home: 9 Wilson Ct Park Forest IL 60466 Office: Univ Chicago Chicago IL 60637

WHISLER, WALTER WILLIAM, neurosurgeon; b. Davenport, Iowa, Feb. 9, 1934; s. Walter William and Dorothy Ruth (Carr) W.; A.B., Augustana Coll., Rock Island, Ill., 1955; M.D., U. Ill., 1959, Ph.D., 1969; m. Jeanette Carol Engelbrecht, June 14, 1959; children—Katharine Jeanne, Laura Caryl. Intern U. Ill., 1959-60, resident in neurosurgery, 1960-64; attending neurosurgeon VA Hosp., Chgo., 1964—; chmn. dept. neurosurgery Rush-Presbyn.-St. Luke's Hosp., Chgo., 1970—; cons. Cook County Hosp., 1972—; clin. asso. prof. U. Ill. Med. Sch., 1970—; prof. biochemistry Rush Med. Coll., chmn. neurosurgery, chmn. dept., 1970—. Mem. Am. Assn. Neurol. Surgeons, A.C.S., AMA, Central, Ill. neurosurg. socs., Congress Neurol. Surgeons, Inst. Medicine Chgo., Internat. Soc. Research in stereoencephalotomy, Research Soc. Neurol. Surgeons, Soc. Neurol. Surgeons. Contbr. articles to med. jours. Home: 1211 Chestnut Ave Wilmette IL 60091 Office: 1725 W Harrison St Chicago IL 60612

WHISNANT, JACK PAGE, neurologist; b. Little Rock, Oct. 26, 1924; s. John Clifton and Zula I. (Page) W.; B.S., U. Ark., 1948, M.D., 1951; M.S., U. Minn., 1955; m. Patricia Anne Rimmey, May 12, 1944; children—Elizabeth Anne, John David, James Michael. Intern, Balt. City Hosp., 1951-52; resident in medicine and neurology Mayo Grad. Sch. Medicine, Rochester, Minn., 1952-55, instr. neurology, 1956-60, asst. prof., 1960-64, asso. prof., 1964-69, prof., 1969—, chmn. dept. neurology Mayo Clinic, yo Med. Sch., Mayo Grad. Sch. Medicine, 1971—; cons. neurology Mayo Clinic, 1955—, head sect. neurology, 1963-71; dir. Mayo Cerebrovascular Clin. Research Center, 1975—. Bd. dirs. YMCA, Rochester. Served with U.S. Army, Air Force 1942-45. Decorated Air medal. NIH grantee, 1958, 76—. Fellow Am. Heart Assn., Fellow Am. Acad. Neurology; mem. Am. Assn. U. Profs. of Neurology, Am. Neurol. Assn., Zumbro Valley Med. Soc., Minn. Med. Assn., Alumni Assn. Mayo Found., Minn. Soc. Neurol. Scis. Central Soc. Neurol. Res. Presbyterian. Contbr. articles on neurology and cerebrovascular disease to med. jours. Home: 1005 7th Ave NE Rochester MN 55901 Office: Dept Neurology Mayo Clinic Rochester MN 55901

WHISTLER, ROY LESTER, educator, chemist; b. Morgantown, W.Va., Mar. 21, 1912; s. Park H. and Cloe (Martin) W.; B.S., Heidelberg Coll., 1934, D.Sc. (hon.), 1957; M.S., Ohio State U., 1935; Ph.D., Iowa State Coll., 1938; m. Leila A.B. Kaufman, Sept. 6, 1935; 1 son, William H. Instr. chemistry Iowa State Coll., 1935-38; research fellow Bur. Standards, 1938-40; chemist, later sect. leader No. Regional Research Lab., Dept. Agr., 1940-46; prof. biochemistry Purdue U., 1946—, now Hillenbrand distinguished prof., asst. dept. head, 1948-60, chmn. Inst. Agrl. Utilization Research, 1961—; vis. lectr. U. Witwatersrand, 1961, 65, 77, Czechoslovakia and Hungary, 1968, Japan, 1969, Taiwan, 1970, Argentina, 1971, New Zealand, Australia, 1967, 74, Acad. Sci., France, 1975, Vladivostock Acad. Sci., 1976, Brazil, 1977, Egypt, 1979; lectr. Bradley Polytech. Inst., 1941-42; indsl. cons. Dir. Allegheny Airlines, Pfanstiehl Lab., Inc., Highland Coal and Chem., Quatrum. Mem. NRC sub-com. nomenclature biochemistry. Recipient Sigma Xi Research award Purdue U., 1953; named one of ten outstanding starch chemists Chgo. sect. Am. Chem. Soc., 1948; recipient Hudson award Am. Chem. Soc., 1960, Anselme Payen award, 1967, Starch award Japanese, 1967, Carl Lucas Alsburg award, 1970; German Saare medal, 1974; Thomas Burr Osborne award, 1974; Spencer award Am. Chem. Soc., 1975. Fellow AAAS; mem. Am. Chem. Soc. (chmn. Purdue sect. 1949-50, carbohydrate div. 1951, cellular div., 1962, nat. councilor 1953—, bd. dirs. 5th dist. 1955-58, chmn. com. edn. and students, chmn. sub-com. polysaccharide nomenclature, symposium dedicated 1979), Am. Assn. Cereal Chemists (pres. 1972-73), Sigma Xi (pres. Purdue sect. 1957-59, nat. exec. com. 1958-62), Internat. Carbohydrate Union (pres. 1972-74), Phi Lambda Upsilon. Club: Rotary (pres. 1966). Author: Polysaccharide Chemistry, 1953; Industrial Gums, 1959, rev. edit., 1973; Methods of Carbohydrate Chemistry, series, 1962—; co-author: Guar, 1979; also numerous sci. papers. Editor: Starch-Chemistry and Technology, 2 vols., 1965, 67. Bd. advisers Advances in Carbohydrate Chemistry, 1950—, Organic Preparations and Procedures Internat., 1970—, Jour. Carbo-Nucleosides-Nucleotides, 1973-77, die Starke, Starch, 1979—. Home: 320 Laurel Dr West Lafayette IN 47906

WHITAKER, BRUCE EZELL, coll. pres.; b. Cleveland County, N.C., June 27, 1921; B.A., Wake Forest U., 1944; B.D., So. Baptist Theol. Sem., 1947, Th.M., 1948, Ph.D., 1950; postgrad. George Peabody Coll., 1952; m. Esther Adams, Aug. 22, 1947; children—Barry Eugene, Garry Bruce. Ordained to ministry Bapt. Ch., 1945; pastor Smithfield, Ky., 1945-49; instr. sociology and philosophy Ind. U., 1947-50; prof. religion Cumberland U., Lebanon, Tenn., 1950-51, Belmont Coll., Nashville, 1951-52; prof. sociology, asst. to pres. Shorter Coll., Rome, Ga., 1952-53; asso. pastor, minister edn., Atlanta, 1953-54; state sec., student dept. Bapt. State Conv., N.C., 1954-57; pres. Chowan Coll., Murfreesboro, N.C., 1957—; mem. adv. com. to Bd. Higher Edn., 1962-66, to N.C. Commn. Higher Edn. Facilities, 1964—; pres. N.C. Conf. Social Service, 1965-67, Assn. So. Baptist Colls. and Schs., 1967-68, Assn. Eastern N.C. Colls., 1968-69; bd. dirs. Regional Edn. Lab. for Carolinas and Va. Pres. bd. trustees N.C. Found. Church-Related Colls., 1970-74; bd. dirs., v.p. Nat. Council Ind. Jr. Colls., 1974-75, pres., 1975-76; mem. advisory council presidents Assn. Governing Bds., 1973—; mem. N.C. Bd. Mental Health, 1966—; bd. dirs. Am. Assn. Community and Jr. Colls., 1976—; pres. N.C. Assn. Colls. and Univs., 1977-78; chmn. N.C. Commn. Mental Health/Mental Retardation Sers., 1978—. Named Tarheel of Week, Raleigh News and Observer, 1962, Boss of Year, N.C. Jaycees, 1972; tribute paid in Congl. Record, 1962; Whitaker Library Chowan Coll. named for him. Mem. N.C. Lit. and Hist. Assn. (pres. 1970-71), Am. Acad. Polit. and Social Scis., NEA, Am. Assn. Community and Jr. Colls. (dir. 1976—), Nat. Assn. Ind. Colls. and Univs. (dir. 1977-78), Am. Assn. Higher Edn., Internat. Platform Assn., Omicron Delta Kappa. Clubs: Rotary (chmn. dist. student exchange com. 1969-72), Optimist; Beechwood Country (Ahoskie, N.C.); Harbor (Norfolk, Va.). Address: Chowan College PO Drawer 37 Murfreesboro NC 27855

WHITAKER, CLEM, JR., advt. and public relations exec.; b. Sacramento, Aug. 30, 1922; s. Clem and Harriett (Reynolds) W.; student Sacramento Jr. Coll., 1942, U. Calif. at Berkeley, 1943; m. Isabel Flood; children—Christina, Isabella Alexandra. Reporter, Sacramento Union, 1938-40; staff mem. Campaigns, Inc.-Whitaker & Baxter, San Francisco, 1946-50, partner, 1950-58, pres., 1958—; partner Whitaker & Baxter Advt. Agy., San Francisco, 1950-58, pres., 1958—; co-pub. Cal. Feature Service, San Francisco, 1950—. Served with USAAF, 1942-46; ETO. Mem. Pub. Relatons Soc. Am., Calif. C. of C. Clubs: Family, Stock Exchange, Press and Union League, Commonwealth of Calif. (San Francisco); Coral Casino and Beach (Santa Barbara); Burlingame Country. Home: 2652 Broadway San Francisco CA 94115 Office: Flood Bldg San Francisco CA 94102

WHITAKER, EILEEN MONAGHAN, artist; b. Holyoke, Mass., Nov. 22, 1911; d. Thomas F. and Mary (Doona) Monaghan; ed. Mass. Coll. Art, Boston; m. Frederic Whitaker. Annual exhibits in nat. and regional watercolor shows; represented in permanent collections Charles and Emma Frye Mus., Seattle, Hispanic Soc., N.Y.C., Atlanta Art Mus., U. Mass., Norfolk (Va.) Mus., Springfield (Mass.) Mus. Art, Reading (Pa.) Art Mus., Okla. Mus. Art, St. Lawrence U., Wichita State U., pvt. collections. Recipient numerous major awards, including several awards Allied Artists Am., Providence Water Color Club, several awards Am. Watercolor Soc., Wong award Calif. Watercolor Soc., De Young Mus. award, Springville (Utah) Mus. Art award, Ranger Fund purchase prize, Orbrig prize NAD, silver medal Am. Watercolor Soc., Watercolor West. Fellow Huntington Hartford Found., 1964. Academician NAD; mem. Am. Watercolor Soc. Providence, Watercolor Club, Soc. Western Artists. Home: 1579 Alta La Jolla Dr La Jolla CA 92037

WHITAKER, GILBERT RILEY, JR., bus. economist, univ. adminstr.; b. Oklahoma City, Oct. 8, 1931; s. Gilbert Riley and Melodese (Kilpatrick) W.; B.A., Rice U., 1953; postgrad. So. Methodist U., 1956-57; M.S. in Econs., U. Wis., Madison, 1958, Ph.D. in Econs. (Ford Found. dissertation fellow), 1961; m. Ruth Pauline Tonn, Dec. 18, 1953; children—Kathleen, David Edward, Thomas Gilbert. Instr., Northwestern U. Sch. Bus., 1960-61, asst. prof. bus. econs., 1961-64, asso. prof., 1964-66, research asso. Transp. Center, 1962-66; asso. prof. Washington U. St. Louis, 1967-68, prof., 1968-76, adj. prof. econs., 1967-76, asso. dean Grad. Sch. Bus. Adminstrn., 1969-76; dean, prof. bus. econs. M. J. Neeley Sch. Bus., Tex. Christian U., 1976-79; dean, prof. Grad. Sch. Bus. Adminstrn., U. Mich., 1979—; dir. La Barge Inc., 1972—, Nat. Bank and Trust of Ann Arbor (Mich.), 1979—, Detroit Bank Corp., 1979—; sr. economist banking and currency com. U.S. Ho. of Reps., 1964; trustee Grad. Mgmt. Admissions Council, 1972-75, chmn., 1974-75. Served with USN, 1953-56. Mem. Am. Econ. Assn., Am. Fin. Assn., Nat. Assn. Bus. Economists. Club: Ft. Worth Boat. Author books, including: (with Marshall Colberg and Dascomb Forbush) Business Economics, 5th edit., 1975; (with Roger Chisholm) Forecasting Methods, 1971. Home: 2360 Londonderry Ann Arbor MI 48104 Office: U Mich Grad Sch Bus Adminstrn Ann Arbor MI 48109

WHITAKER, H. BARON, lab. exec.; B.S. in Elec. Engring., N.C. State Coll., 1936; LL.D., Ill. Inst. Tech., 1968. With Underwriters Labs. Inc., Chgo., 1936-41 46—, exec. engr., 1953-57, asst. to v.p., 1957-63, exec. v.p., 1963-64, pres., 1964-78, cons. to pres., 1978—; mem. Pres.'s Nat. Commn. Fire Prevention and Control, 1970-73; former chmn. Nat. Elec. Code Com. Served to capt. AUS, 1941-45. Registered profl. engr., Ill. Fellow IEEE; mem. Nat. Fire Protection Assn. (dir. 1972—), Am. Nat. Standards Inst. (dir. 1966—), Tau Beta Pi, Eta Kappa Nu. Address: Underwriters Labs 207 E Ohio St Chicago IL 60611

WHITAKER, HENRY PHILIP, educator; b. Penn Yan, N.Y., June 24, 1921; s. Fred C. and Adelia (Hopkins)W.; B.S., Mass. Inst. Tech., 1944, M.S., 1959; m. H. Stephanie Paige, Apr. 5, 1952; children—Robert H., Jonathan P., Charles E. With Consol. Vultee Aircraft Corp., 1944-47; dep. asso. dir. Instrumentation Lab., Mass. Inst. Tech., Cambridge, 1947-59, prof. dept. aeros. and astronautics, 1959—. Trustee Boston Juvenile Ct. Citizenship Tng. Program. Registered profl. engr., Mass. Mem. Am. Inst. Aeros. and Astronautics, Soc. Automotive Engrs., Mas. Jr. C. of C. (past pres.). Home: 19 Coburn Rd Weston MA 02193 Office: Mass Inst Tech Cambridge MA 02139

WHITAKER, JACK, sports broadcaster/commentator; b. May 18, 1924; grad. St. Joseph's Coll., Phila., D.B.A. (hon.); L.H.D. (hon.), U. Scranton, 1978; m. Bertha Raring; children—Mary Beth, Ann, Gerry, Jack, Kewin, Jeff. Radio producer, 1947-50; news and sports broadcaster Sta. WCAU-TV, Phila., 1950-61; with CBS Sports, 1951—, host CBS Sports Spectacular, 1961-67, studio host NFL pre-game, half time and postgame programs, 1964, also play-by-play announcer for soccer, host AAU International Championships, commentator CBS Golf Championship, sports reporter-at-large, 1976—. Recipient Emmy award for Sports Personality of Yr., Nat. Acad. TV Arts and Scis.; Eclipse award for TV achievement. Served with U.S. Army, 1942-45. Office: care CBS Sports 51 W 52d St New York NY 10019*

WHITAKER, JACK FRIEL, cable mfg. co. exec.; b. Kansas City, Mo., Nov. 28, 1914; s. Jack Pendleton and Constance (Friel) W.; B.S. in Elec. Engring., U. Notre Dame, 1936; M.B.A., Harvard, 1938; m. Cosette Routt, Sept. 11, 1937 (dec. 1967); children—Jack H., Jerome R., Mark F., M. Lynn, Christopher G.; m. 2d, Ursula Boland, May 24, 1975; stepchildren—George, Mary, Margaret, James, Elaine. With Whitaker Cable Corp., Kansas City, Mo., 1937—, exec. v.p., 1955-60, pres., 1960—, chmn. bd., chief exec. officer, 1975—, also dir.; pres. Whitaker Cable Can., Whitaker Cable de Mex.; dir. Whitaker Productos, Venezuela, Whitaker Cable Australia, United Mo. Bank, Kansas City, Gas Service Co., Stuart Hall Co. Gen. chmn. Heart Am. United Way, 1967, chmn. bd., 1971-73; co-chmn. fund drive Martin Luther King Hosp., 1968-70, chmn. exec. com., 1970-74. Recipient citation Kansas City chpt. NCCJ. Mem. Motor Equipment Mfrs. Assn. (past pres., chmn. bd.), Asso. Industries Mo. (past pres.), NAM (dir.). Republican. Roman Catholic. Clubs: Kansas City, Indian Hills Country, Serra, K.C. (Kansas City). Home: 476 N Winnebago St Lake Winnebago MO 64034 Office: 2801 Rockcreek Pkwy North Kansas City MO 64116

WHITAKER, JOHN FRANCIS, TV sportscaster; b. Phila., May 18, 1924; s. John Francis and Regina (Herron) W.; B.A., St. Joseph's Coll., Phila., 1947; hon. degree U. Scranton, 1978; m. Bertha Mary Raring, Jan. 31, 1951; children—Mary Beth, Gerard, Ann, John, Kevin, Geoffrey. With Sta. WCAU-TV, Phila., 1950-61; freelance, 1961-64; sportscaster CBS-TV, 1964—. Served with AUS, 1942-45. Decorated Bronze Star, Purple Heart with oak leaf cluster; recipient Charles Englehard award Ky. Breeders Assn., 1974; named Man of Year, N.Y. Athletic Club, 1974; Eclipse award Thoroughbred Racing Assn., 1978. Mem. Alpha Sigma Nu. Roman Catholic. Clubs: N.Y. Athletic; Winged Foot Golf. Home: PO Box 342 Bridgehampton NY 11932 Office: 51 W 52d St New York City NY 10019

WHITAKER, JOSEPH MCSWAIN, ednl. adminstr.; b. Clayton, Tex., Dec. 23, 1914; s. Joseph McSwain and Dena Mae (Davis) W.; B.A., Tex. Am. and M. U., 1937; M.A., Tex. Western Coll., 1948; m. Winnie Alline George, Oct. 11, 1934; children—Donald Kenneth, Barbara June (Mrs. Charles McBryde). Tchr. Longbranch, Tex., 1935-36; tchr., asst. prin. high sch., supr., high sch. prin. El Paso Pub. Schs., 1937-54; registrar, dir. admissions Tex. Western Coll., 1954-64; dir., asst. supt., dep. supt., gen. supt. El Paso Pub. Schs., 1964-79; ret., 1979. Bd. dirs. Wesley Found U. Tex. at El Paso, Mental Health/Mental Retardation El Paso. Mem. Tex. Assn. Collegiate Registrars and Admissions Officers (pres.), 20-30 Club (dist. gov.). Methodist. Lion (pres. East El Paso).

WHITAKER, MEADE, lawyer, automobile co. exec.; b. Washington, Mar. 22, 1919; s. Spier and Haidee (Meade) W.; B.A., Yale U., 1940; LL.B., U. Va., 1948; m. Frances Dunn Baldwin, Feb. 10, 1945; children—Meade, Martin Baldwin, Frances Dunn Whitaker Schoonover; m. 2d, Carol Dekleva, Dec. 26, 1972. Admitted to Ala. bar, 1948; partner Cabaniss, Johnston & Gardner, and predecessor, Birmingham, 1948-69, 70-73; tax legis. counsel Treasury Dept., Washington, 1969-70; asst. gen. counsel Treasury Dept., chief counsel IRS, Washington, 1973-76; partner Arter & Hadden, Cleve., 1977-78; fed. taxes dir. office gen. counsel Ford Motor Co., Dearborn, Mich., 1978—. Served as officer USMCR, 1941-46. Mem. Am., D.C., Ala., Birmingham bar assns., Am. Law Inst. Episcopalian. Office: American Rd Dearborn MI 48121

WHITAKER, ROBERT EARL, SR., publishing co. exec., editor; b. Braddock, Pa., June 29, 1928; s. Earl Edison and Hazel Muriel (Doolittle) W.; student Calif. State Tchrs. Coll., 1946-47; m. Mary Louise, Jan. 6, 1951; children—Lois Jean, Nancy Ann, Robert Earl,

Paul Michael, John David. Mark Edward. Sales engr. Earl E. Whitaker Co., Pitts., 1949-51, 53-55; pres. Whitaker Controls Co., Monroeville, Pa., 1955-70; pres., editor-in-chief Whitaker House, Springdale, Pa., 1970—. Active YMCA Tr. Blazers, 1974—; team mgr. Monroeville (Pa.) Baseball Assn., 1974—. Served with U.S. Army, 1951-53. Recipient Eagle Scout award Boy Scouts Am., 1946, Skipper Sunfish and Flying Jr. award YMCA. Mem. Christian Booksellers Assn. (pres. chpt.). Full Gospel Businessmen's Fellowship Internat. Ind. Assemblies of God—Clergy, YMCA, Am. Automobile Assn. Mem. Christian Fellowship Ch. Club: Toastmasters. Home: 534 Fieldstone Rd Monroeville PA 15146 Office: Whitaker House Pittsburgh and Colfax Sts Springdale PA 15144

WHITAKER, THOMAS WALLACE, botanist; b. Monrovia, Calif., Aug. 13, 1905; s. Walter R. and Mamie (Dunne) W.; B.S., U. Calif., Davis, 1927; M.S., U. Va., 1929, Ph.D., 1931; m. Mary Beverley Somerville, Aug. 15, 1931; children—Thomas Wallace, Beverley W. Rodgers. DuPont fellow U. Va., 1927-31; fellow Arnold Arboretum, Harvard U., 1931-34; asso. prof. biology Agnes Scott Coll., 1934-36; with Dept. Agr., 1936-73, asso. geneticist, sr. geneticist, prin. research geneticist and investigation leader, La Jolla, Calif., collaborator, 1973—; research asso. in marine biology U. Calif., San Diego, 1964-73, in biology, 1973—; Distinguished lectr. in biology Tulane U., 1967; guest lectr. in genetics U. Ariz., 1967; guest lectr. horticulture Purdue U., 1964, U. Calif., Davis, 1967; guest lectr. genetics U. Rajistan and Indian Agrl. Research Inst. Recipient Andrew Flemming prize in biology U. Va., 1931; Merit award Bot. Soc. Am., 1976; Guggenheim Found. fellow, 1946-47, 59-60. Fellow AAAS, San Diego Zool. Soc.; mem. Am. Soc. Naturalists, Torrey Bot. Club, Bot. Soc. Am., Am. Soc. Archeology, Can. Hort. Soc. (hon. life), Am. Soc. Hort. Sci. (pres. 1973-74), Am. Phytopath. Soc., San Diego Natural History Soc., Soc. Study of Evolution, Soc. Econ. Botany (pres. 1969), Am. Inst. Biol. Scis., Am. Genetic Assn., Explorers Club, Am. Soc. Plant Taxonomists, Sigma Xi, Alpha Zeta. Author: (with G. N. Davis) The Cucurbits, 1962; contbr. numerous articles to profl. jours.; developed disease resistant cultivars of lettuce, muskmelons; research on ethnobotany of cucurbits. Home: 2534 Ellentown Rd La Jolla CA 92037 Office: PO Box 150 La Jolla CA 92037

WHITAKER, URBAN GEORGE, JR., ednl. cons., ret. univ. dean; b. Colony, Kans., May 19, 1924; s. Urban George and Flora Gladys (Fackler) W.; A.B., Occidental Coll., 1946; Ph.D., U. Wash., 1954; m. Rebekah Jean Knox, Mar. 18, 1950; children—Susan Whitaker Wittwer, Bruce, Keith. Mem. faculty San Francisco State U., 1954—, prof. internat. relations, dean undergrad. studies, 1969—, dir. all-univ. programs, 1976-78, asso. dean grad. div., 1978-79; vis. research asso. Columbia, 1960-61; vis. prof. U. S.C., 1965-66; radio commentator, UN corr., Pacifica Network, Berkeley, Calif., 1958-65. Mem. exec. com. Commn. to Study Orgn. of Peace, 1963—. Pres. Peninsula Democratic Forum, San Mateo County, 1967-68, 70—; Dem. candidate U.S. Ho. Reps., 1968. Trustee San Bruno (Calif.) Elementary Schs., 1958-60, New Coll. Calif., Sausalito, 1971-76, Council for Advancement for Experiential Living, 1976—; nat. bd. dirs. UN Assn. U.S., 1962-70. Served with USNR, 1943-46, 50-52. Ford Found. fellow, summer 1955; Rockefeller fellow Columbia and UN, 1960-61. Mem. Internat. Studies Assn. (pres. 1966-67). Unitarian. Author: Propaganda and International Relations, 1960; (with Paul Breen and Thomas Donlon) Teaching and Assessing Interpersonal Competence, 1976; Democracies and International Relations, 1960; Politics and Power: A Text in International Law, 1964; (with Bruce Davis) The World and Ridgeway, South Carolina, 1968. Home: 1590 Greenwood Way San Bruno CA 94066. *Law and Order without Justice is tyranny. But Justice without Law and Order is impossible. I try to work for the ideals of world Law and Order, with Justice, by planning all of my projects in three stages: first, taking the time to dream about what is desirable; second, making an estimate of what seems possible; and then setting my course some place in between.*

WHITBREAD, THOMAS BACON, author, educator; b. Bronxville, N.Y., Aug. 22, 1931; s. Thomas Francis and Caroline Nancy (Bacon) W.; B.A., Amherst Coll., 1952; A.M., Harvard U., 1953, Ph.D., 1959. Instr. English, U. Tex. at Austin, 1959-62, asst. prof., 1962-65, asso. prof., 1965-71, prof., 1971—. Vis. asso. prof. Rice U., 1969-70; mem. lit. adv. panel Tex. Commn. on Arts and Humanities, 1972-76. Recipient third Aga Khan prize for fiction Paris Rev., 1960, Lit. Anthology Program award Nat. Endowment for Arts, 1968, Outstanding Freshman Tchr. award Phi Eta Sigma, 1972-73. Mem. Modern Lang. Assn. Am., A.A.U.P., Tex. Inst. Letters (Poetry award 1965), South Central Modern Lang. Assn., Nat., Am. amateur press assns., Phi Beta Kappa. Democrat. Author poetry book: Four Infinitives, 1964; contbg. author: Prize Stories 1962: The O. Henry Awards, 1962. Editor: Seven Contemporary Authors, 1966. Home: 1014 E 38th St Austin TX 78705 Office: Dept of English U of Tex Austin TX 78712

WHITBY, KENNETH THOMAS, mech. engr.; b. Fond du Lac, Wis., Feb. 6, 1925; s. Robert Gerhard and Theresa Mae (Strebe) W.; B.S. in Naval Tech., U. Minn., 1946, B.S.M.E., 1948, Ph.D. in Mech. Engring. (Quaker Oats fellow), 1954; m. Juanita Mae Bergstresser, July 31, 1948; children—Susan Lee, Dean Kenneth, Dale Ross, Evan Robert. Instr., U. Minn., 1946-58, asst. prof. mech. engring., 1958-62, asso. prof., 1962-66, prof., 1966—, dir. particle tech. lab., 1953-72, chief environ. div., dept. mech. engring., 1972—; cons. to industry. Served to lt. (j.g.) USN, 1943-46. USPHS grantee, 1955-65; Nat. Air Pollution Adminstrn. grantee, 1965-70, EPA grantee, 1970—; AEC grantee, 1962-79; U.S. Bur. Mines grantee, 1971—. Mem. ASME, Nat. Acad. Engring., AAAS. Republican. Presbyterian. Contbr. numerous articles to profl. publs.; founder U. Minn. particle tech. lab., 1953; patentee in field. Home: 2943 Quail Ave N Minneapolis MN 55422 Office: Mech Engring Dept U Minn Minneapolis MN 55455

WHITCOMB, BENJAMIN BRADFORD, JR., physician; b. Ellsworth, Maine, Dec. 13, 1908; s. Benjamin Bradford and Katherine Evelyn (Laffin) W.; A.B., Bowdoin Coll., 1930; M.D., C.M., McGill U., Montreal, Que., Can., 1935; m. Margaret Pike, Aug. 1, 1936; children—Stuart Pike, Katherine (Mrs. Paul Joseph Dudzinski), Judith Victoria, Benjamin Bradford III. Intern Hartford (Conn.) Hosp., 1935-37, John A. Wentworth fellow, 1937-38, resident neurosurgery, 1941-42, neurosurgeon, 1942—, dir. dept. neurosurgery, 1968-75; asst. resident in surgery and neurosurgery New Haven Hosp., 1938-41; asst. clin. prof. neurosurgery Yale Med. Sch., 1949-65, asso. clin. prof., 1965-73, clin. prof., 1973-76; clin. prof. neurosurgery dept. surgery U. Conn. Med. Sch., 1973—. Served with AUS, 1943-46. Diplomate Am. Bd. Neurol. Surgery (vice chmn. 1969-70). Mem. Am. Acad. Neurol. Surgery (v.p. 1966-67, pres. 1973-74), A.C.S., A.M.A., Am. Assn. Neurol. Surgeons (v.p. 1971—), Assn. Am. Med. Colls., Assn. for Research Nervous and Mental Diseases, New Eng. Neurosurg. Soc. (pres. 1959-60), New Eng. Surg. Soc., Soc. Brit. Neurol. Surgeons (hon.), Scandanavian Neurosurg. Soc., Soc. Neurol. Surgeons (v.p. 1967-68). Contbg. author: Medical History of World War II. Author articles treatment for spinal disc pathology and various disorders of the brain. Home: 38 High Farms Rd West Hartford CT 06107 Office: 85 Jefferson St Hartford CT 06106. *To have a goal and pursue it with tenacity and patience controls ambition. To admire and commend the good work of others controls pride. To discipline oneself to work more insures growth. To hold each person in genuine affection insures cooperation. To hold honesty paramount controls men.*

WHITCOMB, CLIFFORD HARRY, ins. co. exec.; b. Bklyn., May 31, 1923; s. Roland B. and Lucienne (Gendron) W.; A.B., Cornell U., 1947, M.B.A., 1948; m. Doris Driscoll, Dec. 28, 1946; children—David, Philip, Barbara. With Prudential Ins. Co. Am., Newark, 1948—, asst. comptroller, 1955-62, asso. comptroller, 1962-67, v.p., 1967-70, sr. v.p. and comptroller, 1970—. Served with AUS, 1943-46. Mem. Financial Execs. Inst., Phi Kappa Psi. Home: 7 Dale Dr Chatham NJ 07928 Office: Prudential Plaza Newark NJ 07101

WHITCOMB, EDGAR D., former gov. of Ind., lawyer; b. Hayden, Ind., Nov. 6, 1917; s. John W. and Louise (Doud) W.; LL.B., Ind. U., 1950; m. Patricia Dolfuss, May 20, 1951; children—Patricia, Linda, Shelley, Alice, John. Admitted to Ind. bar, 1952; practice law, N. Vernon, Ind., Seymour, Ind. and Indpls., 1952-66, 73—; mem. Ind. Senate, 1951-54; asst. U.S. atty. So. Dist. Ind., Indpls., 1955-56; sec. state Ind., 1966-68; gov. of Ind., 1969-73. Bd. dirs. U.S. Auto Club. Author: Escape from Corregidor. Home: 636 Popular St Seymour IN 47274 Office: Vehslage Bldg Seymour IN 47274

WHITCOMB, JAMES HOWARD, food co. exec.; b. Lewiston, Maine, June 12, 1927; s. Edwin H. and Alice (McLaughlin) W.; B.A., Bowdoin Coll., 1948; M.B.A., Harvard U., 1951; m. Eleanor Keady, June 7, 1952; children—Susan W., James H., Michael K., Andrew R. Field rep. Aetna Casualty and Surety Co., Boston, 1948-49; retail zone mgr. Time, Inc., N.Y.C., 1951-53; account exec. N.W. Ayer Co., Phila., 1953-57, account supr., N.Y.C., 1957-59; product mgr. Gen. Foods Corp., White Plains, N.Y., 1959-62, mktg. dir., Japan, 1962-64, gen. mgr., Australia, 1964-66, mng. dir., Eng., 1967-69, pres. Gen. Foods Europe, 1969-76, v.p. parent co., 1969-76, 79—, pres. Gen. Foods Latin Am., 1976—. Trustee, Council of the Ams., N.Y.C. Clubs: Harvard Bus. Sch. (N.Y.C); Seaview Country (Absecon, N.J.); New Canaan (Conn.) Country. Home: 170 Bridle Path Ln New Canaan CT 06840 Office: Gen Foods Corp 250 North St White Plains NY 10625

WHITCOMB, LOUIS GORMAN, lawyer; b. Taunton, Mass., July 30, 1903; s. Louis Anceland Mary Elizabeth (Gorman) W.; LL.B., Suffolk Law Sch., Boston, 1929; J.D. (hon.), Suffolk U., 1955; m. Alice Elizabeth Stiles, Aug. 24, 1946; children—Priscilla, Susan. Admitted to Vt. bar, 1929, since practiced in Springfield, 1929; justice of peace, 1932-53; judge Windsor Municipal Ct., 1947-48; exec. clk. Gov. E. W. Gibson, 1947; spl. counsel Vt. Pub. Service Commn., 1949; U.S. atty. Dist. of Vt., 1953-61; sr. mem. Whitcomb, Clark, & Moeser, 1961—. Trustee Claremont Savs. Bank (N.H.). Commr. Springfield Housing Authority. Trustee Springfield Town Library, 1951-75. Served to lt. comdr. aviation br. USNR, 1943-45. Mem. Municipal Judge's Assn. (pres. 1947-48), Am., Vt. (pres. 1966-67), Windsor County bar assns., Am. Legion. Elk. Home: Breezy Hill Rd Springfield VT 05156 Office: Woolson Bldg Springfield VT 05156

WHITCOMBE, JOHN ALFRED, oil co. exec.; b. Moscow, Idaho, May 5, 1927; s. Martin A. and Lillian M. (Davis) Larson; student Bucknell U., 1945, U. Pa., 1945-46; B.S. in Chem. Engring., U. Mich., 1949, M.S. (Teaching fellow), 1950, Ph.D. (Dow Chem. Co. fellow), 1953; m. Julia Beebe, Feb. 7, 1954; children—Nancy, David. Sr. process engr. C. F. Braun & Co., Alhambra, Calif., 1952-57; process devel. engr. Shell Devel. Co., Emeryville, Calif., 1957-63; sr. technologist Shell Chem. Co., N.Y.C., 1963-64; exec. v.p. Tosco Corp., Los Angeles, 1964—, also dir. Served with USNR, 1945-46. Mem. Am. Inst. Chem. Engrs., Alpha Chi Sigma, Tau Beta Pi. Home: 2261 Westridge Rd Los Angeles CA 90049 Office: 10100 Santa Monica Blvd Los Angeles CA 90067

WHITCRAFT, EDWARD C.R., investment banker; b. Lutherville, Md., Oct. 26, 1914; s. Franklin Pierce and Louise Virginia (Regester) W.; B.A., Yale, 1936. With Bank of New York, 1936-58, v.p. investment research, trust investment com., 1952-58; with Clark, Dodge & Co., N.Y.C., 1958-74; v.p. Kidder, Peabody & Co., Inc., 1974—; dir. Lewis Engring. Co., Naugatuck, Conn. Served with USNR, 1944-46. Mem. N.Y. Soc. Security Analysts. Home: Box 194 Locust Valley NY 11560 Office: 460 Park Ave New York NY 10022 also 69 Forest Ave Locust Valley NY 11560

WHITE, ADRIAN MICHAEL STEPHEN, steel co. exec.; b. nr. Kent, Eng., Aug. 15, 1940; s. Malcolm Royston and Joan May (Richards) W.; grad. McGill U., Montreal, 1964; m. Elaine M. Dorion, 1966; children—Malcolm, Catherine. With Coopers & Lybrand, chartered accountants, 1962-66; acting treas. Rothesay Paper Corp., 1965; asst. treas. Genstar Ltd., 1967-71; treas. Brinco Ltd., also Churchill Falls (Labrador) Corp., 1971-75; treas. Algoma Steel Corp., Ltd., Sault Ste. Marie, Ont., 1975—; dir. Hiawathaland Hotels, Sault Ste. Marie, Apieco Assurance Co. Bd. dirs. Art Gallery of Algoma, Sault Ste. Marie. Chartered accountant, Que., Ont. Mem. Fin. Execs. Inst., Internat. Fiscal Assn., Canadian Tax Found., Inst. Chartered Accountants Ont. (council). Mem. editorial adv. bd. Benefius Can. mag. Address: 7 McNeice St Saulte Ste Marie ON Canada

WHITE, ALAN GEORGE CASTLE, educator, biochemist; b. Boston, Eng., Aug. 12, 1916; s. George Alec and Caroline (Castle) W.; came to U.S., 1925, naturalized, 1941; B.S., U. R.I., 1938; M.S., Pa. State U., 1940; Ph.D., Iowa State U., 1947; m. Juliette Marie Perotti, Sept. 13, 1945 (dec. May 1968); children—David Edward, Margaret Marie; m. 2d, Irma M. McGladdery Boesch, July 1968 (dec. Jan. 1979); stepchildren—Carol Ann, Edmond Jules. Research bacteriologist Joseph E. Seagram & Son, Louisville, 1940-41; tech. asst. Rockefeller Inst., N.Y.C., 1941-43; instr. bacteriology Iowa State U., Ames, 1945-47; mem. faculty Tulane U. Sch. Medicine, 1947-67, prof. biochemistry, 1960-67; prof., head dept. biology Va. Mil. Inst., Lexington, 1967—; vis. prof. Osmania Med. Coll., Hyderabad, India, 1961-63. Fellow Ind. Sci. Research Inst., Iowa State U., 1943-45. Mem. Am. Soc. Biol. Chemists, Am. Soc. Microbiologists, Am. Chem. Soc., Soc. Exptl. Biology and Medicine (sec. So. sect. 1965-67), A.A.A.S., Sigma Xi, Phi Sigma, Phi Lambda Upsilon. Research and publs. on carbohydrates metabolism hemolytic streptococci, fatty acid synthesis in yeast; determined arginine requirements streptococci and its metabolism; elucidated path glucose metabolism in entamoeba histolytica. Home: 613 Stonewall St Lexington VA 24450

WHITE, ALLEN INGOLF, ret. coll. dean; b. Silverton, Oreg., July 10, 1914; s. Anders O. and Ingeborg J. (Beaverson) W.; B.S. in Pharmacy, U. Minn., 1937, M.S., 1938, Ph.D., 1940; m. Edith I. Halverson, Sept. 24, 1938; children—Karen S. White Jordan, Connie L. White McNeill, Kathryn A. White DeBrie. Research fellow U. Minn., 1938-40; mem. faculty Wash. State U., Pullman, 1940-79, prof., 1948-79, dean Coll. Pharmacy, 1960-79; mem. pharmacy rev. com. Bur. Health Manpower, NIH, 1968-72. Chmn. Pullman Community Welfare Com., 1948-50; mem. Comprehensive Health Planning Council, Pullman, 1973-76, chmn., 1974-75; mem. governing body Eastern Wash. Health Systems Agy., 1976—; mem. Wash. State Health Coordinating Council, 1978—. Bd. dirs. Lutheran Student Found. Inland Empire, 1952-58, treas., 1953-55, pres., 1955-57; bd. dirs. Am. Found. Pharm. Edn., 1975—, vice chmn., 1977—; trustee Pullman Hosp. Corp., 1972-78, pres., 1974-75. Fellow AAAS, Am. Coll. Apothecaries; mem. Am. Pharm. Assn., Am. Chem. Soc., AAUP, Am. Assn. Colls. Pharmacy (pres. 1974-75), Sigma Xi, Rho Chi, Phi Kappa Phi. Co-author: American Pharmacy, 5th edit., 1960; Textbook of Organic Medicinal and Pharmaceutical Chemistry, 7th edit., 1977. Home: NE 1040 Indiana St Pullman WA 99163

WHITE, ALVIN SWAUGER, aerospace cons.; b. Berkeley, Calif., Dec. 9, 1918; s. Harold Hubbard and Ruth Amelia (Winkleman) W.; student U. Calif. at Davis, 1936-37; student U. Calif. at Berkeley, 1937, 39-41, B.M.E., 1947; m. Mary Lou Kamenzind, May 21, 1942 (div. Oct. 1949); 1 son, Stephen Alan; m. 2d, Virginia M. Lonsdale, June 24, 1950 (div. Aug. 1971); children—Cathie Lee, Leslie Ann; m. 3d, Maureen J. Stoner, Nov. 20, 1971. Engr., test pilot N.Am. Aviation, Inc., Los Angeles, 1954-61, chief test pilot Los Angeles div., 1961-66; mgr. flight ops., research and devel. Trans World Airlines, N.Y.C., 1967-69; aerospace cons. Al White & Assos., Inc., Irvine, Calif., 1969—. Served with USAAF, 1941-46, USAF, 1948-54. Decorated D.F.C., Air medal with 9 oak leaf clusters; recipient Iven C. Kincheloe award Soc. Exptl. Tests Pilots, 1965; Golden Plate award Am. Acad. Achievement, 1966; Octave Chanute award Am. Inst. Aeros. and Astronautics, 1965; Harmon Internat. trophy, 1967; Richard Hansford Burroughs Jr. award Flight Safety Found., 1969. Fellow Soc. Exptl. Test Pilots (pres. 1960-61); asso. fellow Am. Inst. Aeros. and Astronautics; mem. Nat. Aviation Club, Delta Upsilon. Republican. Episcopalian. Club: Masons. Home: 15 Montpellier Newport Beach CA 92660 Office: 2081 Business Center Dr Irvine CA 92715. *As I grow older I look more and more for honesty in my associates. Without it you don't have much. An honest person probably knows better than anyone else how much courage it takes to be honest in some situations; so when you find honesty you find courage and character as well. And since I look for that in other people, I try very hard to be honest myself; I said, "I try very hard!"*

WHITE, AUGUSTUS AARON, III, orthopaedic surgeon; b. Memphis, June 4, 1936; s. Augustus Aaron and Vivian (Dandridge) W.; A.B. cum laude, Brown U., 1957; M.D., Stanford, 1961; Dr. Med. Sci., Karolinska Inst., Sweden, 1969. Intern U. Mich. Hosp., Ann Arbor, 1961-62; asst. resident in gen. surgery Presbyn. Med. Center, San Francisco, 1962-63; asst. resident in orthopaedic surgery Yale Med. Center, New Haven, 1963-65, sr. instr., resident orthopaedic surgery, 1965-66, asst. prof. orthopaedic surgery, 1969-72, asso. prof., 1972-76, prof., 1977-78, dir. biomech. research dept. orthopedics; prof. orthopedic surgery Harvard Med. Sch., Boston and orthopedic surgeon-in-chief Beth Israel Hosp., 1978—; cons. orthopaedic surgery West Haven (Conn.) VA Hosp., 1970—, Hill Health Center, New Haven, 1970—; chief orthopedic surgery Conn. Health Care Plan, 1976—. Mem. admissions com. Yale Med. Sch., 1970-72. Active in New Haven community to improve health care. Trustee emeritus Brown U., Providence; trustee Northfield (Mass.) Mt. Hermon Schs. Served to capt. AUS, 1966-68. Decorated Bronze Star medal; named 1 of 10 Outstanding Young Men, U.S. Jr. C. of C., 1969; recipient Martin Luther King, Jr. Med. Achievement award, 1972, Kappa Delta award, nat. prize for outstanding research in orthopaedics field, 1975. Am.-Brit.-Canadian Travelling fellow Am. Orhopedic Assn., 1975. Fellow Am. Acad. Orthopaedic Surgeons, Scoliosis Research Soc.; mem. Orthopaedic Research Soc., Cervical Spine Research Soc., Internat. Soc. for Study Lumbar Spine, Internat. Soc. Orthopaedic Surgery and Traumatology, Nat. Med. Assn., Sigma Xi. Author: (monograph) Analysis of the Mechanics of the Thoracic Spine in Man, Exhibited Leprosy, The Foot and The Orthopaedic Surgeon at Am. Acad. Orthopaedic Surgeons, 1970; (book) Clinical Biomechanics of the Spine, 1978; contbr. articles to profl. jours., chpts. to sci. books.

WHITE, B. FRANK, ret. govt. ofcl.; b. Memphis, Tex., Oct. 29, 1912; s. John D. and Virgie (Fife) W.; student Tex. Christian U., 1930-33; B.J., U. Tex., 1938; m. Ruthmary Taylor, June 5, 1937; children—Jeanne White Wilson, Gregory, Deborah Gay White-Branning. With U.S. Govt., 1938-71; spl. cons. to commr. IRS, 1953, regional commr., Dallas, 1953-71; tax adv. mission to Turkey, 1963, 65; U.S. del. CENTO Symposium on Tax Adminstrn., Tehran, Iran, 1965; lectr. Dept. Agr. Grad. Sch., 1965-71; mem. faculty Inst. Tax Adminstrn., U. So. Calif., 1971—. Chmn. Dallas-Ft. Worth Fed. Exec. Bd., 1964-65; mem. Dallas Zoning Bd. Adjustment, 1971-75; v.p. Greater Dallas Council Chs., 1973; cons., mem. adv. bd. Southwestern Law Enforcement Inst.; cons., mem. adv. bd. Southwestern Legal Found., Dallas, 1971-77, research fellow, 1978—; vice chmn. Dallas Interfaith Council for Open Housing, 1976-79; 1st v.p. Christian Ch. (Disciples of Christ) in the S.W., 1976-78. Served as communications officer USNR, World War II; mem. staff Comdr. 7th Fleet. Recipient Nat. Civil Service League Career Service award, 1964; Exceptional Service award Treasury Dept., 1971. Mem. Tex., Southwestern (pres. 1970-71) watercolor socs., Pastel Soc. S.W. (v.p. 1979), Soc. Profl. Journalists, Sigma Delta Chi. Club: Press. Home: 627 Monssen Dr Dallas TX 75224

WHITE, BARBARA MCCLURE, coll. pres.; b. Evanston, Ill., July 23, 1920; d. Earl A. and Helen M. (Johnston) W.; A.B., Mt. Holyoke Coll., 1941, LL.D. (hon.), 1972; M.A., Harvard U., 1962. Researcher, Ency. Brit., 1941-42; policy asst. OWI, 1942-43, field rep. in Cairo and Rome, 1944-46; regional specialist State Dept., 1946-47; program sec. internat. affairs, nat. staff LWV, 1947-51; asst. information officer USIS, Rome, 1951-56; pub. affairs officer USIS, Turin, Italy, 1956-58; fgn. affairs officer USIA, Washington, 1958-61; pub. affairs officer Am. embassy, Santiago, Chile, also chmn. Fulbright Commn., Santiago, 1962-65; spl. asst. to dir. USIA, Washington, 1965, 72, asso. dir. policy and research, 1966-70, dep. dir. policy and plans, 1970-71, career minister for info., 1971-76; pres. Mills Coll., Oakland, Calif., 1976—; ambassador, alt. U.S. rep. for spl. polit. affairs U.S. Mission to UN, N.Y.C., 1973-76; alt. U.S. rep. to 6th and 7th spl. sessions and 29th and 30th sessions UN Gen. Assembly, 1973-76; U.S. rep. 16th session Econ. Commn. for Latin Am., 1975; alt. U.S. rep. to Internat. Women's Year Conf. 1975; dir. Am. Council on Edn., 1977—, Bank of Am., Bank Am. Corp. Mem. Am. Council for UN U.; mem. internat. adv. panel East-West Center. Recipient Career Service award Nat. Civil Service League, 1967; Rockefeller Pub. Service award, 1972. Mem. Council on Fgn. Relations, Phi Beta Kappa. Office: Mills College Oakland CA 94613

WHITE, BARCLAY, JR., constrn. co. exec.; b. Phila., Sept. 23, 1922; s. Barclay and Edith (Lewis) W.; B.S. in Civil Engring., Swarthmore Coll., 1943; M.B.A., U. Pa., 1947; m. Margaret W. Harris, Apr. 2, 1949; children—James S., Barbara C., Elizabeth A., Barclay, Stephen C. Staff engr. I. S. Towsley, P.E., 1947-49; v.p. and chief engr. Barclay White & Co., 1949-57, pres., 1957-71; pres. Barclay White Inc., Phila., 1971—; dir. Pocono Hotels Corp. Former mem. bd. dirs. Westtown Sch., Friends Hosp. Served with USNR, 1943. Mem. ASCE, Nat. Soc. Profl. Engrs., Pa. Soc. Profl. Engrs. Republican. Quaker. Clubs: Racquet of Phila., Skytop (dir.), Pine Valley Golf, Radley Run Country, Berwyn Squash Racquets. Office: 400 Market St Philadelphia PA 19106

WHITE, BARRY, singer, rec. artist, record producer; b. Galveston, Tex., Sept. 12, 1944; m. Glodean James, 1974; children—Kevin, Brigette, Barry. With musical group The Upfronts, from 1960; producer singing group Love Unlimited, 1972—, Love Unlimited

Orch., 1973—; solo artist, 1973—; record producer; songs recorded include: I'm Gonna Love You Just A Little Bit More Baby; You're The First, The Last, My Everything; Oh What A Night For Dancing. Recipient numerous Gold Albums for singing and prodn. work. Office: care ICM Artists 8899 Beverly Blvd Los Angeles CA 90048*

WHITE, BETTY, actress, comedienne; b. Oak Park, Ill., Jan. 17; student pub. schs., Beverly Hills, Calif.; m. Allen Ludden, 1963. Appearances on radio shows: Blondie, The Great Gildersleeve, This Is Your FBI; TV series appearances include: Hollywood on Television, The Betty White Show, 1954-58, Life With Elizabeth, 1953-55, A Date With The Angels, 1957-58, The Pet Set, 1971, Mary Tyler Moore Show, 1974-77, The Betty White Show, 1977, also guest appearances on other programs; movie appearance in Advise and Consent, 1962; summer stock appearances: Take Me Along, The King and I, Who Was That Lady?, Critic's Choice, Bells Are Ringing, Guys and Dolls. Recipient Nat. Emmy award Nat. Acad. TV Arts Scis., 1975, 76; Los Angeles Area Emmy award, 1952. Mem. Am. Humane Assn., Greater Los Angeles Zoo Assn. (dir.), AFTRA.*

WHITE, BOB JON, fin. exec.; b. Dallas, June 21, 1933; s. Dillon Elmore and Merrill Rhea (Grainger) W.; B.B.A., U. Tex., 1955; m. Claudia Scherer, Aug. 2, 1978; children—Merrill Allison, Shannon Adele, Heather Adair, Courtney Lester. Mgr. revenue plans and controls IBM, N.Y.C., 1965-67, exec. asst. to pres., 1968; v.p. Greyhound Leasing and Fin. Corp., N.Y.C., 1969; v.p. nat. div. Wachovia Bank and Trust Co., N.A., Winston-Salem, N.C., 1970-71, sr. v.p. and mgr. internat. div., 1971-74; sr. v.p. Wachovia Corp., Winston-Salem, 1975-76; exec. v.p., prin. fin. officer Am. Credit Corp., Charlotte, N.C., 1976-77, pres., mem. exec. com., dir., 1978—. Vice chmn. United Appeal for Mecklenburg/Union Counties, Charlotte, 1977; gen. chmn. Queens Coll. New Horizons Fund Dr., 1979; bd. mgrs. Charlotte Meml. Hosp. and Med. Center, 1978—, mem. various coms. Served to lt. (j.g.) USN, 1955-58. Mem. Nat. Consumer Fin. Assn. (fin. relations com.). Clubs: Twin City (Winston-Salem); Quail Hollow Country, Rotary, Charlotte Athletic (Charlotte). Home: 2011 Forest Dr E Charlotte NC 28211 Office: 201 S Tryon St Charlotte NC 28286

WHITE, BYRON R., asso. justice U.S. Supreme Ct.; b. Ft. Collins, Colo., June 8, 1917; grad. U. Colo., 1938; Rhodes scholar Oxford (Eng.) U.; grad. Yale Law Sch.; m. Marion Stearns; children—Charles, Nancy. Clk. to chief justice U.S. Supreme Ct., 1946-47; atty. firm Lewis, Grant and Davis, Denver, 1947-60; dep. atty. gen. U.S., 1961-62; asso. justice Supreme Ct. U.S., 1962—. Served with USNR, World War II; Pacific. Mem. Phi Beta Kappa, Phi Gamma Delta, Order of Coif. Address: Supreme Ct Bldg 1 First St NE Washington DC 20543

WHITE, CAROLINE TAYLOR, civic worker; b. Wilmette, Ill., Nov. 25, 1893; d. Thomas Herbert and Jettie Edgerton (Hurlbut) Taylor; A.B., Wellesley Coll., 1915, M.Humane Arts (hon.), 1950; m. William Crawford White, June 1, 1917; children—Thomas Taylor, Mary Lavell White Fearey, Norval Crawford. Co-chmn. region 14 Wellesley 75th anniversary drive, 1947-50; v.p. Community Council Greater N.Y. Bd. dirs. Nat. YWCA, 1939-60, sec., 1940-46, chmn. Central br. YWCA of N.Y.C., 1941-47, pres. bd. dirs., 1948-54; trustee Cyrenius Booth Library, Newtown, Conn., 1964-70, Congl. Ch., Newtown, 1965-70, Danbury (Conn.) Hosp., 1967-70. Mem. Wellesley Coll. Alumnae Assn. (v.p. 1946-48, pres. 1949-52), Hist. Soc. Newtown (pres. 1963-66). Democrat. Presbyterian (bd. nat. missions). Clubs: Cosmopolitan, Wellesley (pres. 1928-32) (N.Y.C.). Home: 600 E Cathedral Rd Philadelphia PA 19128

WHITE, CHARLES SAFFORD, distillery exec.; b. Burlington, Vt., Apr. 20, 1903; s. Charles E. and Alice (Roberts) W.; student U. Wis., 1923-26; m. Nan Womelsdorf, Feb. 9, 1939 (dec. Dec. 1962); m. 2d, Sally Shadwick, June 25, 1965. Salesman, U.S. Gypsum Co., Boston, 1927-30; traffic mgr. Am. Airlines, St. Louis, Chgo., 1930-34; v.p. Fleischmann Distilling Corp., N.Y.C., 1945-55, pres., 1956-65, chmn. bd., 1965-67. Served to col. USAAF, 1941-45. Mem. Am. Legion, Air Force Assn., Delta Tau Delta, Skull and Crescent, Haresfoot. Episcopalian. Clubs: Boca Raton, Golden Harbour Yacht. Home: Cloister Del Mar 1180 S Ocean Blvd Boca Raton FL 33432 Office: 625 Madison Ave New York City NY 10022

WHITE, CHRISTIAN SHERWOOD, govt. commn. adminstr., lawyer; b. Washington, Dec. 18, 1945; s. Milton Christian and Jean (Kirkwood) W.; B.A., Williams Coll., 1967; J.D., U. Pa., 1970; m. Judith Walsh, Sept., 1975; children—Melissa, Susannah. Admitted to D.C. bar, 1970; atty. Public Interest Research Group, Washington, 1970-71; atty. advisor to commr. FTC, Washington, 1971-72, atty. div. litigation Bur. Consumer Protection, FTC, 1972, atty. advisor Office of Policy Planning, 1973, asst. to bur. dir., 1973-75, asst. dir. for spl. statutes, 1975-77, asst. to chmn. FTC, 1977-79, exec. dir., 1979—. Mem. D.C. Bar Assn., Am. Bar Assn. Office: Federal Trade Commn Pennsylvania Ave at 6th St NW Washington DC 20580

WHITE, CLIFFORD DALE, bishop; b. Sac City, Iowa, Jan. 20, 1925; s. Daniel Columbus and Anna Frances (Holladay) W.; B.A., Morningside Coll., 1949; S.T.B., Boston U., 1951, Ph.D., 1961; m. Gwendolyn Ruth Horton, Aug. 25, 1946; children—Hazel, Jerry, Rebecca, David, Teresa, Lisa. Ordained to ministry United Methodist Ch.; asso. gen. sec. Gen. Bd. Ch. and Soc., Washington, 1961-68; pastor East Greenwich (R.I.) United Meth. Ch., 1968-71; dist. supt. So. New Eng. Conf. United Meth. Ch., Providence, 1971-76; bishop N.J. area United Meth. Ch., Princeton, 1976—. Recipient Disting. Alumnus award Boston U. Teens columnist Together and United Meth. Today, 1963-70; contbr. numerous articles to various publs.; editor: Dialogue in Medicine and Theology, 1967. Office: Opinion Research Corp Bldg N Harrison St Princeton NJ 08540*

WHITE, CLIFFORD WHITE, bishop; b. Sac City, Iowa, Jan. 20, 1925; s. Daniel Columbus and Anna Frances (Holladay) W.; B.A., Morningside Coll., Sioux City, Iowa, 1949; S.T.B., Boston U., 1951, Ph.D., 1961; m. Gwendolyn Ruth Horton, Aug. 25, 1946; children—Hazel, Jerry, Rebecca, David, Teresa, Lisa. Ordained to ministry United Methodist Ch., 1951; asso. gen. sec. Gen. Bd. Ch. and Society, Washington, 1961-68; pastor E. Greenwich (R.I.) United Meth. Ch., 1968-71; dist. supr. So. New Eng. conf. United Meth. Ch., Providence, 1971-76; bishop N.J. area United Meth. Ch., Princeton, 1976—. Recipient Distinguished Alumnus award Boston U., 1970. Author column Teens in Together and United Meth. Today, 1963-70; also numerous articles. Editor: Dialogue in Medicine and Theology, 1967. Office: ORC Bldg N Harrison St Princeton NJ 08540*

WHITE, DAVID BENJAMIN, philosopher, educator; b. Macon, Mo., Mar. 6, 1917; s. John G. and Louisa Alice (Kirn) W.; B.S., Northeastern State Coll. Okla., 1937; M.A., Okla. State U., 1939; Ph.D., U. Pacific, 1957; m. Beverly Werbes, Dec. 1, 1945. Chmn. dept. English, Friends U., Wichita, Kans., 1946-48; prof. philosophy Macalester Coll., St. Paul, 1948—, chmn. dept., 1972-76, 78—, Elizabeth Sarah Bloedel prof. philosophy, 1974—. Recipient Thomas Jefferson award for teaching and citizenship Robert Earll McConnell Found., 1970. Mem. AAUP, Assn. for Asian Studies, Assn. Asian and Comparative Philosophy, Fellowship of Reconciliation. Mem. Democrat Farmer Labor Party. Quaker. Contbr. articles to profl. jours. Home: 136 Amherst St St Paul MN 55105 Office: Macalester Coll St Paul MN 55105

WHITE, DAVID CALVIN, educator, b. Sunnyside, Wash., Feb. 18, 1922; s. David Calvin and Leafie E. (Scott) W.; B.S., Stanford, 1946, M.S., 1947, Ph.D. (Nat. Canners Assn. fellow 1946-49), 1949; m. Glorianna Giulii, July 30, 1949 (dec. Dec. 1965); 1 dau., Julie Anne Calvin; m. 2d, Margot Ann Fuller, June 4, 1966; 1 dau., Constance Anne. Asso. prof. elec. engring. U. Fla., 1949-52; asst. prof. Mass. Inst. Tech., 1952-54, asso. prof., 1954-58, prof. elec. engring., 1958-62, Ford prof. engring., 1962—, dir. energy lab., 1972—; lectr. U. London, 1961; hon. prof. Inst. Politecnico Nat., Mexico, 1961—; vis. prof. Purdue U., 1963-67; sr. adviser Birla Inst. Tech. and Sci., Pilani, Rajasthan, India, 1968-70. Commr. electric light plant, Concord, Mass., 1959-64, Kalmia Woods Water Dist., Concord, Mass., 1960-63. Fellow Am. Acad. Arts and Scis., IEEE; mem. AAAS, Nat. Acad. Engring., Am. Soc. Engring. Edn. (George Westinghouse award 1961). Author: (with John Wiley) Electromechanical Energy Conversion, 1959. Home: Chart Way New Seabury MA 02649

WHITE, DAVID HYWEL, educator; b. Cardiff, Wales, June 4, 1931; s. William Richard and Bessie (Morgan) W.; B.S., U. Wales, 1953; Ph.D., Birmingham U., 1956; m. Frances Mary Shearman, July 23, 1954; children—Richard Gerwyn, Christopher David. Came to U.S., 1959, naturalized, 1966. Asst. lectr. Birmingham U., 1958-59; asst. prof. U. Pa., 1961-64; asso. prof. Cornell U., Ithaca, N.Y., 1964-69, prof., 1969-78; sr. physicist, head exptl. areas div. Isabelle Project, Brookhaven Nat. Lab., Upton, L.I., N.Y., 1978—, cons., 1967-69, 76-78. NSF sr. postdoctoral fellow, 1970. Fellow Am. Phys. Soc., A.A.A.S. Author: Elementary Electronics, 1967. Editor: Scintillation Counters, 1966. Home: One Dolphin Way Riverhead NY 11901

WHITE, DAVID MANNING, educator; b. Milw., June 28, 1917; s. Max A. and Mary (Kazan) W.; A.B., Cornell Coll., Mt. Vernon, Iowa, 1938, L.H.D., 1964; M.S., Columbia U., 1939; Ph.D., U. Iowa, 1942; m. Catherine Wallerstein, Apr. 20, 1944; children—Steven, Richard, Max. Teaching fellow English, U. Iowa, 1940-42; instr. English, Coll. William and Mary, 1945-46; mem. faculty Bradley U., 1946-49, asso. prof. journalism, chmn. dept., 1947-49; research prof. journalism Boston U., 1949-75, chmn. div. journalism, 1964-72; prof. mass communication Va. Commonwealth U., Richmond, 1975—; vis. prof. Centro Internat. de Estudios Superiores de Periodismo Am. Latina, Quito, Ecuador, Oct. 1970, 71; news commentator Sta. WBZ-TV, Boston, 1949-50; project dir. Center Internat. Studies, Mass. Inst. Tech., 1951, Newspaper Comics Council 3 year study, 1959—; research dir. N.Y. Office Internat. Press Inst., 1952-53; research adviser Sarpay Beikman Inst., Rangoon, Burma, 1957-58; corr. NBC News, Rangoon, 1957-58; supr. Gallup Poll in Boston area, 1952-56; spl. elections editor AP, Boston, 1954-62; mem. UNESCO relations com. State Dept., 1954-56; cons. dept. mass communications UNESCO, Paris, 1954-62; lectr. Burma Sch. Journalism, 1957-58, Centre Internationale d'Enseignement Superieur de Journalisme, U. Strasbourg (France), 1957, 60, 61, 62, Inst. fur Publizistik, Free U., Berlin, 1962, 66; gen. editor Beacon Press contemporary communication series, 1966—; chmn. Gov.'s Com. on Communication, 1965-70. Served to ensign USNR, 1943-44. Decorated chevalier d'Honneur et de Mérite, Ordre Souverain de Saint-Jean de Jerusalem, Chevaliers de Malte, Order of Polonia Restituta; recipient Yankee Quill award, 1970. Mem. Ill. Acad. Sci., Boston Authors Club, Hist. Soc. Iowa, Assn. Edn. Journalism, Council Communications Research (chmn. 1954-57), New Eng. Acad. Journalists (hon.), Phi Beta Kappa, Eta Sigma Phi, Kappa Tau Alpha, Tau Kappa Alpha, Sigma Delta Chi. Democrat. Co-author: Elementary Statistics for Journalists, 1954; Mass Culture: The Popular Arts in America, 1957; (with Al Capp) From Dogpatch to Slobbovia, 1964; Journalism in the Mass Media, 1970; (with Richard Averson) The Celluloid Weapon: Social Comment in the American Film, 1972; editor: Pop Culture in America, 1970; co-editor: Introduction to Mass Communications Research, 1958; Publishing for the New Reading Audience, 1959; Identity and Anxiety: Survival of the Individual in Mass Society, 1960; The Funnies, An American Idiom, 1963; People, Society and Mass Communications, 1964; Sight, Sound and Society, 1968; Electronic Drama: Television Plays of the 1960's, 1971; Mass Culture Revisited, 1971; Popular Culture; Mirror of American Life, 1977; editor TV Quar., 1969-71; commentator Nat. Pub. Radio Network, 1976-78. Home: 4108 Crestwood Rd Richmond VA 23227

WHITE, DAVID MEADE, JR., lawyer; b. Richmond, Va., Mar. 10, 1918; s. David Meade and Bessie (Turner) W.; student McGuire's Univ. Sch., Richmond, 1931-34, Hampden-Sydney Coll., 1934-36; LL.B., U. Richmond, 1939; m. Carolyn McEldowney, Sept. 11, 1942; children—David Meade III, Carolyn McEldowney. Admitted to Va. bar, 1939; sr. partner firm White, Roberts, Cabell and Paris, Richmond, 1939-68, Wicker & White, 1974; sr. partner firm White & Wood, 1975—; judge 12th Va. Jud. Circuit, 1968-74; prof. U. Richmond, 1947; substitute judge Richmond Juvenile Ct., 1952-68; commr. in chancery, 1949—; commr. accounts Chesterfield County, 1957-68; instr. John Tyler Community Coll., 1971-75. Pres. Richmond Jr. C. of C., 1948-49, Va. Jr. C. of C., 1950-51; mem. Chesterfield Bd. Welfare, 1958-68; chmn. Suburban Bank. Trustee Lincoln Meml. U., 1972-74. Named Richmond's Outstanding Young Man of Year, Richmond Jr. C. of C., 1950. Mem. Am., Va. (council 1967-68), Richmond (pres. 1962-63), Chesterfield (pres. 1965-66) bar assns., Phi Gamma Kappa, Beta Gamma Sigma, Sigma Chi, Phi Delta Theta. Episcopalian (sr. warden 1974-75). Clubs: Commonwealth, Country of Va. (Richmond); Princess Anne Country (Virginia Beach, Va.). Home: 8709 Cherokee Rd Richmond VA 23235 Office: 300 W Main St Richmond VA 23220

WHITE, DEREK ALAN, banker; b. Washington, Oct. 28, 1941; s. Paul E.P. and Katherin (McIntosh) W.; B.B.A., Lehigh U., 1964; m. Martha A. Smith, Feb. 13, 1965; children—Andrew Clarke and Philip Alan (twins). Asst. auditing officer Mellon Nat. Bank & Trust Co., Pitts., 1964-69; v.p., auditor N.J. Nat. Bank, Trenton, 1970—. Trustee, treas. Yardley-Makefield Free Library. Served with AUS, 1964. Chartered bank auditor, certified internal auditor. Mem. Trenton C. of C., Bank Adminstrn. Inst., Inst. Internal Auditors. Episcopalian. Home: 359 Ramsey Rd Yardley PA 19067 Office: 1 W State St Trenton NJ 08650

WHITE, DONALD EDWARD, geologist; b. Dinuba, Calif., May 7, 1914; s. Arthur Thomas and Alice Louise (Hughson) W.; A.B., Stanford U., 1936; Ph.D., Princeton U., 1939; m. Helen Beth Severance, Sept. 16, 1941; children—Margaret Anne, Eleanor Louise, Catherine Marie. Mem. staff Nfld. Geol. Survey, 1937-39; with U.S. Geol. Survey, 1939—, asst. chief Mineral Deposits Br., Washington, 1958-60, research geologist Menlo Park, Calif., 1960-71, adviser Geothermal Energy Program, 1971—; adviser geothermal energy, N.Z., Iceland, Japan, Italy, Am. industry; cons. prof. geophysics, Stanford U., 1974; Davidson Meml. lectr. St. Andrews U., Scotland, 1975. Recipient Distinguished Service award Dept. Interior, 1971. Fellow Geol. Soc. Am., Soc. Econ. Geologists (Distinguished Lectr. 1967, 74, v.p. 1977), AAAS; mem. Nat. Acad. Sci., Mineral. Soc. Am. Developer prins. for recognition and evaluation natural geothermal systems for utilizing geothermal energy. Home: 222 Blackburn Ave Menlo Park CA 94025

WHITE, DORIS ANNE, artist; b. Eau Claire, Wis.; d. William I. and Mary (Dietz) White; grad. Art Inst. Chgo., 1950. One woman shows IFA Galleries, Washington, Berestrum Art Center and Museum, Neenah, Wis., Bradley Gallery, Milw.; exhibited in group shows Ill. Mus., Springfield, 1963, Art Alliance, Phila., 1963, Museum Modern Art, N.Y.C., 1967, Pa. Acad. Fine Arts, Phila., 1963, 64, 66, Art Inst. Chgo., 1963, Met. Museum, 1966, N.A.D., N.Y.C., 1962, 63, 64, 65, 67, Butler Inst. Am. Art, Youngtown, Ohio, 1960, 61, 63, 64, 65, Smithsonian Instn., Washington, 1960, Walker Art Center, Mpls., 1963, 64, Madison (Wis.) Salon Art, 1958-63, 64, Spanish Internat. Pavilion, St. Louis, 1969, Utah State U., Logan, 1969, 70, Cleve. Inst. Art, Miami (Fla.) U., Chautauqua (N.Y.) Art Assn., Soc. Four Arts, Palm Beach, Fla., Instituto de arte de Mexico, others; represented in permanent collection Butler Inst. Am. Art, Walker Art Center, Milw. Art Center. Recipient Grand award, 1963, Grumbacker award, 1965, Paul Remmy award, 1964 (all Am. Watercolor Soc.), Ranger Fund Purchase award, Obrig award (both NAD), medal of honor Knickerbocker Artists, 1963; Four Arts award Soc. Four Arts, Palm Beach, 1963; M.L. Jarrot Art scholar Nat. League Am. Pen Women, 1960. Mem. NAD, Am., Calif. watercolor socs., Phila. Watercolor Club. Home: Rt 1 2750 Church Rd Jackson WI 53037

WHITE, ELWYN BROOKS, writer; b. Mount Vernon, N.Y., July 11, 1899; s. Samuel Tilly and Jessie (Hart) W.; A.B., Cornell U., 1921; Litt.D. (hon.), Dartmouth Coll., 1948, U. Maine, 1948, Yale U., 1948, Bowdoin Coll., 1950, Hamilton Coll., 1952, Harvard U., 1954; L.H.D., Colby Coll., 1954; m. Katharine Sergeant Angell, Nov. 13, 1929; 1 son, Joel McCoun. Reporter, 1921; later free lance writer and contbg. editor New Yorker mag.; contbr. monthly dept. to Harper's mag., 1938-43. Served in U.S. Army, 1918. Recipient Gold medal Am. Acad. Arts and Letters; Presdl. medal of Freedom, 1963; Laura Ingalls Wilder award children's books, 1970; Nat. medal for Lit., 1971; Pulitzer Prize spl. citation, 1978. Fellow Am. Acad. Arts and Scis.; mem. Nat. Inst. Arts and Letters, Am. Acad. Arts and Letters, Phi Gamma Delta. Author: The Lady Is Cold (poems), 1929; Is Sex Necessary? (with J. Thurber), 1929; Every Day is Saturday, 1934; Tne Fox of Peapack, 1938; Quo Vadimus, 1939; One Man's Meat, 1942, enlarged edit., 1944; Stuart Little, 1945; The Wild Flag, 1946; Here Is New York, 1949; Charlotte's Web, 1952; The Second Tree from the Corner, 1953; revised William Strunk, Jr.'s The Elements of Style, 1959; The Points of My Compass, 1962; The Trumpet of The Swan, 1970; Letters of E.B. White, 1976; Essays of E.B. White, 1977; editor: Ho Hum, 1931; Another Ho Hum, 1932; A Subtreasury of American Humor (with Katharine S. White), 1941. Office: 25 W 43d St New York NY 10036

WHITE, ERSKINE NORMAN, JR., business exec.; b. N.Y.C., July 21, 1924; s. Erskine Norman and Catharine (Putman) W.; B.E., Yale, 1947; M.S., Mass. Inst. Tech., 1949; m. Eileen E. Lutz, Nov. 5, 1949; children—Erskine Norman III, Carol Putnam, Catharine Lutz. Staff mem. research and devel. bd. Dept. Def., 1949; with methods and research dept. Gorham Mfg. Co. (became Gorham Corp. 1961, Gorham div. Textron Inc. 1968), 1950-51, supr. quality control, 1951-53, asst. plant mgr., Asheville, N.C., 1954-56, plant mgr., 1956-57, asst. to pres., 1958-59, v.p., 1959-64, exec. v.p., 1964-68, pres., 1968-69, dir., 1960-67; group v.p. Textron Inc., Providence, 1969-71, exec. v.p. ops., 1971-75, exec. v.p., 1975-79, exec. v.p. corp. affairs, 1979—); dir. Keystone Provident Life Inst. Co., R.I. Hosp. Trust Co., Leesona Corp., Systems Engring. and Mfg. Corp. Trustee, Women and Infants Hosp. R.I., 1974—; bd. dirs. New Eng. Council, 1979—. Served with USNR, 1954-56; PTO. Mem. Am. Inst. E.E., A.A.A.S., N.A.M. (dir. 1974—, regional v.p. 1975, div. vice chmn. 1978 exec. com.), Am. Mgmt. Assn., Greater Providence C. of C. (dir., pres. 1978), R.I. C. of C. Fedn. (pres. 1979), Sigma Xi, Tau Beta Pi. Home: 216 Nayatt Rd Barrington RI 02806 Office: 40 Westminster Providence RI 02903

WHITE, EUGENE JAMES, technology co. exec.; b. Hartford, Conn., Feb. 28, 1928; s. Mark James and Bernice Katherine (Humphry) W.; B.S. in Finance and Econs., U. Hartford, 1951; m. Vivian Pickral, June 16, 1951; children—Timothy, John, Eugene James. Corp. controller Kaman Corp., Bloomfield, Conn., 1951-60; sr. v.p. fin. EG&G Wellesley, Mass.; treas., dir. Wakefield Engring., Inc.; trustee Boston Five Cents Savs. Bank; dir. E.T. Ryan Iron Works, Inc. Mem. alumni mgmt. group U. Hartford; past mem. Natick Redevel. Commn.; mem. trustee council Leonard Morse Hosp., Natick, Mass.; bd. regents U. Hartford. Served with USCGR, 1945-46. Recipient Distinguished Alumnus award U. Hartford Alumni Assn., 1976. Mem. Am. Mgmt. Assn., Financial Execs. Inst. (pres. N.E. area), Treas.'s Club Boston (past pres.), New Eng. Council (dir.). Roman Catholic. Club: Brae Burn Country (Newton, Mass.). Home: 125 Bacon St Natick MA 01760 Office: EG&G 45 William St Wellesley MA 02181

WHITE, FRANCIS EDWARD, tax cons.; b. Leominster, Mass., Feb. 12, 1915; s. Edward Joseph and Mary Agnes (McDonnell) W.; LL.B. cum laude, Suffolk U., 1938; m. Mary Ellen Hunt, June 6, 1942; children—Marilyn Frances (Mrs. Michael E. Manka), Douglas Edward. Spl. agt. FBI, 1941-49; sales mgr. J.W. Landenberger Co., N.Y.C., 1950-54; sales exec. Alex Lee Wallau, Inc., N.Y.C., 1955-62; v.p. Exeter Hosiery Mills, N.Y.C., 1963-66; Eastern mgr. consumer products div. Glen Raven Mills, N.Y.C., 1966-70; pres. White Tax Services, Waterbury, Conn., 1970—; sr. v.p. Gleason Plant Security, Waterbury, 1973—. Vice chmn. Gov. Conn. Adv. Council Mental Retardation, 1959—; mem. planning com. White House Conf. on Children and Youth, 1970. Past pres., bd. dirs. Nat. Assn. Retarded Citizens; pres. Conn. Assn. Retarded Citizens. Mem. Am. Soc. Indsl. Security. Home: 5 Rushmore Circle Stamford CT 06905 Office: 221 Schraffts Dr Waterbury CT 06705

WHITE, FRANCIS M., banker; b. Waterbury, Conn., May 14, 1927; s. Edmund James and Helen (Nulty) W.; ed. Bentley Coll., 1949; student Stonier Grad. Sch. Banking, Rutgers U., 1953-55; certificate Bank Mgmt. Sch., Columbia, 1962; m. Jean T. Horan, Apr. 19, 1952; children—Sharon Anne, Edmund James, Mary Jean. Pres., chmn. bd., chief exec. officer Colonial Bancorp; chmn. bd. Colonial Bank & Trust Co., Waterbury, 1967—; chmn. bd. Constitution Bank & Trust; dir. Buell Industries, M.J. Daly & Sons, Inc., Reymond Baking Co., MacDermid, Inc., Second New Haven Bank, Plainville Trust; dir., treas. S. Leonard St. Corp. Incorporator Greater Waterbury Easter Seal Soc., Family Service Assn. Treas., bd. dirs. Post Jr. Coll., Naugatuck Valley Indsl. Corp.; bd. dirs. St. Mary's Hosp., Waterbury Non-Profit Devel. Corp.; chmn. Conn. Bus. and Industry Assn. Recipient Community Service award Greater Waterbury C. of C.; named Conn. Man of Yr. New Eng. Council, 1977. Mem. Greater Waterbury C. of C. (past pres.), Am. Inst. Banking (past pres.), Conn. Bankers Assn. (past pres.), Soc. N.Am., Young Pres.'s Orgn. Clubs: Waterbury, Country of Waterbury (past pres.); N.Y.; Cloud; Farmington (N.Y.) Country; Econ. (N.Y.); Highfield (Middlebury, Conn.). Home: Birchwood Terr Middlebury CT 06762 Office: 81 W Main St Waterbury CT 06720

WHITE, FRANK XAVIER, JR., publishing co. exec.; b. Buffalo, Sept. 4, 1919; s. Frank X. and Marie J. (Rafter) W.; A.B. magna cum laude, Harvard, 1941, J.D., 1949; m. Dorothy Louise Gedanic, Sept. 15, 1951; children—Gretchen, Patricia Louise, Frank X. III. Admitted to Mass. bar, 1949, N.Y. bar, 1955; staff Office Mil. Govt.

for Germany, Berlin, 1945-46; atty. Dept. of Army, also CCC, 1949-51; fgn. service officer Am. embassy, Germany, mem. Marshall Plan Mission to Germany, 1951-54; asst. to chmn. American Machine & Foundry Co., 1954-56, charge internat. operations, 1956-64, v.p., 1959-64; pres. AMF Internat., 1961-64; v.p. Am. Metal Climax, Inc., 1964-66; v.p. Joy Mfg. Co., N.Y.C., 1966-73; v.p. Bus. Internat. Corp., Chgo., 1973—; chmn. Aiesec-U.S., 1966-73. Dir. Internat. Inst. Marketing. Bd. dirs. Calvary Hosp., N.Y.C. Served to lt. USNR, 1942-46. Mem. Council Fgn. Relations, Am. Mgmt. Assn. (v.p., dir. 1966—), UN Assn. U.S.A. (vice chmn. 1960-64), Phi Beta Kappa. Clubs: Harvard (N.Y.C.); Chicago. Home: 1435 Sheridan Rd Wilmette IL 60091 Office: One IBM Plaza Chicago IL 60611

WHITE, FRED ROLLIN, JR., mining and shipping co. exec.; b. Cleve., Mar. 23, 1913; s. Fred Rollin and Miriam (Norton) W.; B.A., Yale U., 1935; m. Emma Garretson Raymond, Dec. 21, 1940; children—Emma Stone White Seymour, Carolyn White Barr, Margaret Raymond White Ziering. With Oglebay Norton Co., Cleve., 1935—, successively accountant, in vessel ops., 1935-57, v.p., 1949-57, sr. v.p. transp. and docks, 1957-59, sr. v.p., 1959-78, treas., 1960-63, vice chmn. bd. 1969—, chmn. exec. com., 1978—, dir., 1949—; v.p., dir. Columbia Transp. Co., 1950-57; v.p., trustee Oglebay Norton Found.; treas. Fortune Lake Mining Co., 1950-60, v.p., 1952-60, dir. 1958-60; treas., dir. David Z. Norton Co., 1936—, v.p., 1959-60, pres., 1960—; pres., dir. Internat.-Great Lakes Shipping Co., 1959-61; pres., dir. Toledo Overseas Terminals Co., 1959-72; mem. Lake View Cemetery Assn., 1940—, trustee, 1949-75, pres., 1954-71; v.p. Cleve. Vessel Agy., Inc., 1964-71, dir., 1958-71; v.p., dir. Chillicothe-Center Co., 1960-78; pres., dir. Silloc Ltd., 1966-73; v.p. Can. Ferro Hot Metal Spltys., Ltd., 1971-78; dir. Oglebay Norton Taconite Co., ONCO Eveleth Co., Central Silica Co., T&B Foundry Co., Midwest Forge Corp. (v.p.), ON Coast Petroleum Co., Union Commerce Bank, Union Commerce Corp., Superior Land Co., Licking River Terminal Co., Tex. Mining Co., Saginaw Mining Co. trustee Lake Carriers Assn. Treas. Great Lakes Protective Assn., 1965-76; treas., trustee Home for Aged Women, Cleve.; asst. sec., asst. treas., trustee Horace Kelley Art Found. Served from 1st lt. to lt. col. AUS, 1941-45. Decorated Bronze Star. Mem. Am. Bur. Shipping (bd. mgrs. 1976—), Am. Iron and Steel Inst., Internat. Shipmasters Assn. (hon. life), Soc. Naval Architects and Marine Engrs. First Cleve. Cavalry Assn. (pres. 1967-68), Musical Arts Assn., SAR, Western Res. Hist. Soc. (v.p. 1964-68, trustee), Greater Cleve. Growth Assn., Early Settlers Assn. Western Res., Lake County Hist. Soc. (trustee 1961-79). Republican. Episcopalian. Clubs: Eastern Point Yacht (Gloucester, Mass.); Winous Point Shooting (dir. 1957—, v.p. 1965-69, pres. 1969-77) (Port Clinton, Ohio); Kirtland Country (dir. 1950-59), Union (trustee 1959-70, 1st v.p. 1965-67, pres. 1967-69) (Cleve.). Home: 18900 Shelburne Rd Shaker Heights OH 44118 Office: Hanna Bldg Cleveland OH 44115

WHITE, FREDERIC RANDOLPH, educator; b. Wilkinsburg, Pa., Apr. 13, 1910; s. George Frederic and Edna (Fitz-Randolph) W.; A.B., Oberlin Coll., 1931, M.A., 1932; certificate U. Grenoble, 1932, U. Paris, 1933; Ph.D., (Univ. fellow 1937-41), U. Mich., 1942; Danforth fellow, Columbia, 1955, U. Chgo., 1958, Colo. U., 1961; Ford fellow, Harvard, 1955, U. N.C., 1956; m. Naomi Bossler, May 11, 1935; 1 dau., Anne Randolph. Instr. U. Toledo, 1935-36; asst. prof. Ill. Inst. Tech., 1941-43; asso. prof. Knox Coll., 1943-45; Sage Found. prof. English, Beloit Coll., 1945-60, chmn. dept., 1954-59; prof. comparative lit. and classics Eckerd Coll. 1960—; State Dept. lectr. U. Tehran, Iran, 1956-57. Recipient 1st prize Hopwood Creative Writing Contest, 1940. Mem. Modern Lang. Assn., Internat. Comparative Lit. Assn., Am. Assn. Univ. Profs., Classical Soc., Nat. Council Tchrs. English, Conf. Christianity and Scholarship, North Central Assn. Workshop, Social Action Com., Am. Assn. Comparative Lit. Presbyn. Author: The Development of Homeric Criticism, 1942; Edward Bellamy's Looking Backward, 1946; Famous Utopias of the Renaissance, 1947. Contbr. articles, essays, poems and book reviews various periodicals. Home: 687 Pinellas Point Drive St Petersburg FL 33705

WHITE, FREDERICK ANDREW, educator, physicist; b. Detroit, Mar. 11, 1918; s. Andrew Bracken and Mildred (Witzel) W.; B.S., Wayne State U., 1940; M.S., U. Mich., 1941; postgrad. U. Rochester, 1943-46; Ph.D., U. Wis., 1959; m. Dorothy Janet Sibley, Nov. 7, 1942; children—Wendell William, Lawrence Sibley, Eric Sibley, Roger Randolph. Insp., U.S. Army Ordnance, Rochester, N.Y., 1941-43; research asst. Manhattan project U. Rochester, 1943-45, grad. instr. in research, 1946; research asst., research asso., cons. physicist Gen. Electric Co. Knolls Atomic Power Lab., Schenectady, 1947-62; adj. prof. nuclear sci. Rensselaer Poly. Inst., Troy, N.Y., 1961-62, prof. nuclear engring. and environmental engring., indsl. liaison scientist, 1962—; mem. staff Bell Telephone Labs., 1969; research and liaison scientist Rochester Gas & Electric Co. (N.Y.), 1978—; cons. NASA, 1965—, Niagara Mohawk Power Corp., 1978; organist and acoustic cons., 1952—. Mem. Am. Inst. Aeros. and Astronautics, Am. Nuclear Soc., Am. Phys. Soc., Am. Soc. Engring. Edn., Am. Soc. for Mass Spectrometry, AAAS, IEEE, Optical Soc. Am., Acoustical Soc. Am., Am. Chem. Soc., Am. Guild Organists, Audio Engring. Soc., Sigma Xi. Author: American Industrial Research Laboratories, 1961; Mass Spectrometry in Science and Technology, 1968; Our Acoustic Environment, 1975. Developer mass spectrometric instrumentation and its uses in measurements relating to nuclear and atomic physics. Home: 2456 Hilltop Rd Schenectady NY 12309 Office: Lab for Acoustic Mass Spectrometry and Ion Physics Rensselaer Poly Inst Troy NY 12181

WHITE, GEORGE C., theatre exec.; b. New London, Conn., Aug. 16, 1935; s. Nelson Cooke and Aida (Rovetti) W.; B.A., Yale U., 1957, M.F.A., 1961; student U. Paris, 1956, Shakespeare Inst., 1959; m. Elizabeth Conant Darling, July 5, 1958; children—George Conant, Caleb Ensign, Juliette Darling. Actor on TV series Citizen Soldier, 1959-61; appeared off-Broadway prodn. John Brown's Body; stage mgr. Imperial Japanese Azumakabuki Co., 1955; asst. mgr. Internat. Ballet Festival, Nervi, Italy, 1955; prodn. coordinator Talent Assos., 1961-63; adminstrv. v.p. score prodns. Paramount Pictures, 1963-65; founder, pres. Eugene O'Neill Meml. Theatre Found., 1965—; adviser, dir. Theatre One, Conn. Coll. Women, 1967-70; regional theatre cons. Nat. Ednl. TV Network; guest lectr. Wagner Coll., 1970; acting dir. Hunter Coll. Hunter Arts, 1972-73; adj. prof. U. N.C.; prof. theatre adminstrn. Yale U., 1978-79, co-chmn. theatre adminstrn. program Yale Drama Sch.; mem. exec. com. Theatre Library Assn., 1967; bd. govs. Am. Playwrites Theatre; mem. bd. ANTA, 1967-68; mem. Mayor N.Y.C.'s. Theatre Adv. Com.; advisory bd. Internat. Theatre Inst.; panel mem. Exptl. Theatre; U.S. State Dept. cultural exchange grantee to Australia, guest adminstr. Australian Nat. Playwrights Conf., 1973; U.S. del. Internat. Theatre Inst. Congress, Moscow, 1973; mem. Conn. Commn. on Arts, 1979; co-founder Caribbean-U.S. Theatre Exchange; dir. Actors Theatre St. Paul, 1979, 80, Hartman Repertory Theatre, 1980. Trustee Goodspeed Opera House, 1966-68, Nat. Theatre Conf., 1973-76, Eastern Conn. Symphony, Dance Arts Council, Conn. Opera Assn., Conn. Pub. TV; mem. planning bd. Operation Rescue; bd. dirs. Rehearsal Club, Theater of Latin Am., Manhattan Theatre Club, Performance mag.; exec. com. Yale Drama Alumni, 1963-73; mem. Yale Alumni Bd.; bd. overseers drama dept. Brandeis U.; adv. bd. Am. Musical Theatre Program, Hartford Conservatory; mem. Waterford (Conn.) Rep. Town Meeting, 1975-77. Served with AUS, 1957-59. Recipient spl. citation New Eng. Theatre Conf., 1968; Margo Jones award, 1968; Pub. Service award New London County Bar Assn., 1975; Distinguished Citizen's award Town of Waterford, 1976. Clubs: Yale, Century, Players (N.Y.C.); Cosmos (Washington); Thames (New London); White's Point Yacht. Home: 123 E 80th St New York NY 10021 Office: 1860 Broadway New York NY 10023

WHITE, GEORGE MALCOLM, architect; b. Cleve., Nov. 1, 1920; B.S., Mass. Inst. Tech., 1942, M.S., 1942; M.B.A., Harvard, 1948; LL.B., Case Western Res. U., 1959; m. Susanne Neiley Daniels, Apr. 21, 1973; children—Stephanie, Jocelyn, Geoffrey, Pamela. Design engr. Gen. Electric Co., Schenectady, 1942-47; practice architecture and law, Cleve., 1948-71; Architect of Capitol, Washington, 1971—. Mem. D.C. Zoning Commn.; acting dir. U.S. Bot. Garden; mem. U.S. Capitol Police Bd.; mem. Adv. Council on Hist. Preservation; mem. Internat. Centre Com.; mem. Nat. Conservation Adv. Council, Nat. Capital Meml. Adv. Com.; bd. dirs. Pennsylvania Ave. Devel. Corp.; trustee Freedoms Found. at Valley Forge, Federal City Council; mem. U.S. Capitol Guide Bd.; mem. art adv. com. Washington Met. Area Transit Authority; mem. nat. panel arbitrators Am. Arbitration Assn.; mem. vis. com. dept. architecture and planning M.I.T.; mem. bd. cons.'s Nubian monuments at Philae, Egypt. Recipient Gold medal Archtl. Soc. Ohio, 1971. Fellow AIA; mem. Nat. Soc. Profl. Engrs., Am. Bar Assn., Sigma Xi, Lambda Alpha. Works include First Unitarian Ch., Cleve., 1959, Preformed Line Products Co. Office Bldg., Cleve., 1960, Mentor Harbor Yacht Club, 1968, restoration Old Senate and Supreme Ct. Chambers, U.S. Capitol, 1975, Library of Congress James Madison Meml. Bldg., 1979, U.S. Capitol Power Plant Extension, 1979. Office: Architect of Capitol Washington DC 20515

WHITE, GERALD TAYLOR, educator; b. Seattle, May 14, 1913; s. Loren Festus and Cora Belle (Taylor) W.; A.B., DePauw U., 1934; M.A., U. Calif., Berkeley, 1935, Ph.D., 1938; m. Rita Elizabeth Kuffel, July 15, 1950; children—Kenneth, David, Maria, Steven, Kian. Research asso. U. Calif. at Berkeley, 1938-39; archivist Fireman's Fund Ins. Co., San Francisco, 1939-40; from instr. to prof. history San Francisco State Coll., 1940-68, chmn. dept. history, 1959-64; prof. history U. Calif. at Irvine, 1968—, chmn. dept., 1969-71; historian RFC, 1946-47; lectr. Am. U., 1947. Treas., bd. dirs. Internat. Inst. San Francisco, 1946-53; bd. dirs. San Francisco Met. YMCA, 1963-64. Served with USAAF, 1943-46. Recipient grants Am. Philos. Soc., 1948, 71, Huntington Library, 1963, 66; postdoctoral fellow Grad Sch. Bus. Adminstrn., Harvard U., 1951-52. Mem. Am. Hist. Assn. (council Pacific Coast br. 1964-72, pres. 1968-69, co-chmn. conv. program com. 1973), Orgn. Am. Historians, Econ. Hist. Assn., Lambda Chi Alpha. Democrat. Episcopalian. Author: History of Massachusetts Hospital Life Insurance Company, 1955; Formative Years in the Far West: A History of the Standard Oil Company of California and Predecessors Through 1919, 1962, reprinted 1976; Scientists in Conflict, 1968; Billions for Defense: Government Financing by the Defense Plant Corporation during WWII, 1979; editor The Historian, 1948-53; editorial bd. Pacific Hist. Rev., 1958-61, Bus. Hist. Rev., 1957-58, 70-72. Home: 966 Sandcastle Dr Corona del Mar CA 92625 Office: Dept History U Calif Irvine CA 92717

WHITE, GORDON ELIOT, newspaperman; b. Glen Ridge, N.J., Oct. 25, 1933; s. Maurice Brewster and Sarah Fulilove (Gordon) W.; B.A., Cornell U., 1955; M.S. in Journalism, Columbia U., 1957; m. Nancy Johnson, 1955 (div. 1957); m. 2d, Mary Joan Briggs, Aug. 6, 1960; children—Sarah Elizabeth and Gordon O'Neal Brewster (twins), David McIntyre. Stringer, Nassau Daily Rev.-Star, Rockville Centre, L.I., N.Y., 1948-50, Freeport (N.Y.) Leader, 1949-50; sports writer Morris County (N.J.) Citizen, 1950-51; stringer Ithaca (N.Y.) Evening News, 1951-55; photo editor, editorial writer Cornell Daily Sun, 1951-55; copy editor Am. Banker, N.Y.C., 1958; Washington corr. Chgo. Am., 1958-61; chief Washington bur. Deseret News (Salt Lake City), 1961—; also corr. in Europe, U.S. and Antarctic for WJR, Detroit, KSL-KSL-TV, Salt Lake City, KGMB, Honolulu free lance writer with U.S. Navy, Army and Air Force, 1959. Recipient 1st prize for newsphoto Sigma Delta Chi, 1954; Raymond Clapper Meml. award White House Corrs. Assn., 1978; award for excellence in reporting from Exec. Dept. and White House, Nat. Press Club, 1979; award for investigative reporting Utah-Idaho-Spokane Regional AP. Mem. Sigma Delta Chi, Pi Kappa Phi, Pi Delta Epsilon. Episcopalian. Clubs: Nat. Yacht, Nat. Press (Washington). Covered last atmospheric atomic tests, 1958, Cuban missile crisis, Berlin crisis, U.S. polit convs., 1960-76; exclusive interview Pres. Ford, 1976. Home: 1502 Stonewall Rd Alexandria VA 22302 Office: House Press Gallery Washington DC 20001

WHITE, H. BLAIR, lawyer; b. Burlington, Iowa, Aug. 2, 1927; s. Harold B. and Harriet E. (St. Clair) W.; B.A., U. Iowa, 1950, J.D., 1951; m. Joan Van Alstine, Oct. 2, 1954; children—Blair W., Brian J. Admitted to Ill. bar, 1951; asso. firm Sidley & Austin and predecessor firm, 1951-61, partner, 1962—; dir. DeKalb AgResearch, Inc., 1967—, Kimberly-Clark Corp., 1971—, R.R. Donnelley & Sons Co., 1979—. Pres., bd. dirs. Cook County (Ill.) Sch. Nursing, 1966-71; bd. dirs. Aux. Cook County Hosp., 1971—. Mem. Am. Bar Assn., Ill. Bar Assn., Chgo. Bar Assn., Am. Coll. Trial Lawyers, Bar Assn. 7th Fed. Dits. Clubs: Legal of Chgo., Law of Chgo., Econs. of Chgo.; Skokie Country. Contbr. articles to profl. jours. Home: 1111 Seneca Rd Wilmette IL 60091 Office: Sidley & Austin 1 First National Plaza Chicago IL 60603

WHITE, HARRISON COLYAR, educator, sociologist; b. Washington, Mar. 21, 1930; s. Joel Jesse and Virginia (Armistead) W.; Ph.D. in Physics, Mass. Inst. Tech., 1955; Ph.D. in Sociology, Princeton, 1960; M.A. (hon.), Harvard, 1963; m. Cynthia Alice Johnson, Sept. 10, 1955; children—Elizabeth, John, Benjamin. Ops. analyst Ops. Research Office, Johns Hopkins, 1955-56; fellow Center Advanced Study Behavioral Scis., Stanford, 1956-57; asst. prof. Carnegie Inst. Tech., 1957-59, U. Chgo., 1959-63; mem. faculty Harvard U., 1963—, prof. sociology dept., 1968—, chmn. dept., 1975-78. Dir., chmn. research com. Urban Systems Research and Engring., Inc., 1970—; vis. prof. U. Edinburgh, 1973-74. Guggenheim fellow, 1973. Fellow Am. Sociol. Assn. (Sorokin award 1970, Stouffer award 1975), Ops. Research Soc. Am.; mem. AAAS, Nat. Acad. Scis., Am. Acad. Arts and Scis. Author: An Anatomy of Kinship, 1963; (with Mrs. White) Canvases and Careers, 1965; Opportunity Chains, 1970. Home: 62 Dana St Cambridge MA 02138

WHITE, HARVEY, medical educator; b. Chgo., Sept. 13, 1916; s. Jacob and Tillie (Goldstein) W.; student Loyola U., Chgo., 1933-34, U. Chgo., 1934-36; B.S.M., M.D., U. Ill., 1940; m. Reva Sarah Katz, May 14, 1941; children—Barry, Kenneth, Bonnie. Intern Cook County Hosp., Chgo., 1940-41, vis. attending, 1959—; resident radiology U. Chgo. Clinics, 1946-48; chmn. dept. radiology Children's Meml. Hosp., Chgo., 1949-79, head div. dept. radiology, 1979—; cons. Hines (Ill.) VA Hosp., 1954—, LaRabida Sanitarium, Chgo., 1955-58, Municipal Contagious Hosp., Chgo., 1955-58, Columbus Hosp., Chgo., 1957—; attending VA Research Hosp., Chgo., 1954—; instr. radiology U. Chgo. Med. Sch., 1948-49; mem. faculty Northwestern U. Med. Sch., 1949—, prof. radiology, 1968—, chmn. dept., 1972-73. Co-chmn. advances in pediatric radiology 12th Internat. Congress Radiology, Tokyo, Japan, 1969. Served to maj. M.C., AUS, 1942-46. Decorated Bronze Star; recipient plaque Chgo. Pediatric Soc., 1969, Joseph P. Brenneman award, 1978. Diplomate Am. Bd. Radiology. Fellow Am. Coll. Radiology; mem. Am. Roentgen Ray Soc., Am. Acad. Pediatrics, A.M.A., Radiol. Soc. N.Am., Chgo. Roentgen Ray Soc. (pres. 1965), Soc. Pediatric Radiology. Author articles, chpts. in books. Office: Children's Meml Hosp 2300 Children's Plaza Chicago IL 60614

WHITE, HARVEY ELLIOTT, educator, physicist; b. Parkersburg, W.Va., Jan. 28, 1902; s. Elliott Adam and Elizabeth (Wile) W.; A.B., Occidental Coll., 1925, also Sc.D. (hon.); Ph.D., Cornell U., 1929; m. Adeline Dally, Aug. 10, 1928; children—Donald H., Jerald P., Vernita L. Teaching asst. Cornell U., 1925-26, instr., 1926-29; internat. research fellow Physikalische Techneische Reichsanstalt, Berlin, Germany, 1929-30; asst. prof. U. Calif., 1930-36, asso. prof., 1936-42, prof. 1942-69. prof. emeritus, 1969—; planner, 1st dir. Lawrence Hall Sci., 1960-69; tchr. nationwide NBC-TV broadcast physics course for high sch. tchrs., 1958, Civilian AEC; with OSRD, 1942-45, Guggenheim Fellow, Hawaii, 1948; recipient War Dept. citation, 1947; Thomas Alva Edison TV award, Peabody TV award, Parents mag. medal, Sylvania award, Hans Christian Oersted award Am. Assn. Physics Tchrs., 1968, others. Fellow Am. Phys. Soc.; mem. Optical Soc. Am., Phi Beta Kappa, Sigma Xi, Phi Kappa Phi. Club: Bohemian. Author: Introduction to Atomic Spectra, 1934; Fundamentals of Optics, 4 edits., 1937; Classical and Modern Physics, 1940; Modern College Physics, 6 edits., 1948; Descriptive College Physics, 3 edits., 1955; Atomic and Nuclear Physics, 1964; Introduction to College Physics, 1969; others. Author and lectr. for 1st complete introductory physics course to be put on color film. Home: 543 Spruce St Berkeley CA 94707

WHITE, HERBERT SPENCER, educator; b. Vienna, Austria, Sept. 5, 1927; s. Leon and Ernestine (Lichteneger) Hochweis; came to U.S., 1938, naturalized, 1944; B.S. in Chemistry, Coll. City N.Y., 1949; M.S. in Library Sci., Syracuse U., 1950; m. Mary Virginia Dyer, Feb. 19, 1953; 1 son, Jerome. Intern, Library of Congress, Washington, 1950, mem. tech. information div., 1950-53; tech. librarian AEC, Oak Ridge, 1953-54; organizer, mgr. corporate library Chance Vought Aircraft, Dallas, 1954-59; mgr. engring. library IBM Corp., Kingston, N.Y., 1959-62, mgr. tech. information center, Poughkeepsie, N.Y., 1962-64; exec. dir. NASA Sci. and Tech. Information Facility, College Park, Md., 1964-68; v.p. information mgmt. Leasco Systems & Research Corp., Bethesda, Md., 1968-70; sr. v.p. Inst. Sci. Information, Phila., 1970-74, corporate dir., 1971-74; pres. Stechert-Macmillan, Inc., Pennsaucken, N.J., 1974-75; prof., dir. Research Center, Ind. U. Grad. Library Sch., Bloomington, 1975—. Mem. Pres.'s Adv. Com. for Adminstrn. Title II-B Higher Edn. Act, 1965-68. Served with USAAF, 1946-47. Mem. Am. Soc. Info. Sci. (pres. 1973-74, W. Davis award 1977), Spl. Libraries Assn. (pres. 1969-70), Am. Fedn. Info. Processing Socs. (dir. 1972-78), Federation Internationale de Documentation (Netherlands) (dir. 1976-78, treas. 1978—), Beta Phi Mu. Author books and articles in field. Home: 517 Colony Ct Bloomington IN 47401 Office: Research Center Grad Library Sch Ind U Bloomington IN 47401

WHITE, HOMER, oil co. exec.; b. Weleetka, Okla., Dec. 21, 1917; s. Nealy Homer and Edith I. (Davidson) W.; B.S. in Chem. Engring., U. Okla., 1940; m. Winifred Sprague, Apr. 3, 1940; 1 son, Jerry G. Engr., Gulf Oil Co., Port Arthur, Tex., 1940-42; tech. asst. to v.p. Lion Oil Co., El Dorado, Ark., 1942-46; refinery and tech. supr. Creole Petroleum Corp., Venezuela, 1946-56; mgr. Continental Oil Co., Wrenshall, Minn., supr. Golden Eagle Refinery Co., Nfld., Can.; pres. Nfld. Refining Co., also dir.; exec. v.p. Macmillan Ring-Free Oil Co., Inc., N.Y.C., 1962—, also dir.; dir. Shaheen Natural Resources Inc. Served with USN, 1944-45. Mem. Nat. Petroleum Refiners Assn. (dir.), Soc. Automotive Engrs., Am. Petroleum Inst. Methodist. Clubs: Sky, 60 East, Club Ltd. Office: 90 Park Ave New York NY 10016

WHITE, IAN MCKIBBIN, museum adminstr.; b. Honolulu, May 10, 1929; s. Osborne and Alice Aileen (Dowsett) W.; B.Arch., Harvard U., 1951, postgrad., 1951-52; postgrad. in indsl. design UCLA, 1957-58; m. Florence Hildreth, June 27, 1959; children—Peter, Daniel, Susanna. Adminstrv. asst. Bklyn. Botanic Garden, N.Y.C., 1959-60; supt. Bklyn. Mus., N.Y.C., 1961-63, asst. dir., 1964-67; dir. Calif. Palace of Legion of Honor, San Francisco, 1968—, M.H. de Young Meml. Mus., San Francisco, 1970—; adviser Archives of Am. Art; mem. mus. advisory panel Nat. Endowment for Arts, 1973—. Trustee Louise A. Boyd Natural Sci. Mus., Marin County, Calif., 1969-70, Corning (N.Y.) Mus. of Glass, 1977—. Served with USNR, 1953-56. Decorated Order of Republic of Egypt. Mem. Am. Assn. Museums (advisory council), Am. Fedn. Arts (trustee 1971—), Internat. Council Museums (U.S. nat. com. 1971-73), Am. Assn. Mus. Dirs. (v.p. 1975-76, pres. 1976—), Municipal Art Soc. N.Y.C. (dir. 1966), Victorian Soc. Am. (advisory com. 1970). Clubs: Rembrandt (Bklyn.); Bohemian (San Francisco). Designed Frieda Shiff Warburg Sculpture Garden, Bklyn. Mus., 1966, Peary-MacMillan Arctic Mus. at Bowdoin Coll., Brunswick, Maine, 1967. Asso. editor Am. Art Rev. Home: 2 Lagunitas Rd Ross CA 94957 Office: Calif Palace Legion Honor Lincoln Park San Francisco CA 94121

WHITE, J. DAVID, shipping agy. exec.; b. Anderson, Ind., Apr. 24, 1932; s. Joe and Elizabeth Louise (Zimmerly) W.; B.A., Wabash Coll., 1954; LL.B., J.D., Columbia U., 1959; children—Bradford, Craig, Pamela. Vice-pres. Aeicor, Inc., N.Y.C.; now pres. Sigma Ship Agy., N.Y.C. Home: 5 Windham Loop Staten Island NY 10314 Office: 26 Broadway New York NY 10004

WHITE, JACK EDWARD, banker; b. Shawnee, Okla., Mar. 30, 1936; s. Clifford Lee and Sue Marguerite (Patterson) W.; B.S. in Geology, U. Okla., 1958; postgrad. Grad. Sch. Banking, So. Meth. U., 1970; m. Joan Boxley, July 12, 1958; children—Stephen Boxley, Elizabeth Patterson, Courtney Ann. Geophysicist, Humble Oil and Refining Co., 1958-64; with Liberty Nat. Bank & Trust Co., Oklahoma City, 1964—, exec. v.p. in charge of trust activities, 1977—. Treas., chmn. fin. com. Sunbeam Family Services, 1976—; v.p. lay adv. bd. St. Anthony Hosp., 1979-80; trustee Heritage Hall Sch., 1976-79. Served with USMC, 1957-63. Mem. Am. Bankers Assn., Okla. Bankers Assn., Bank Adminstrn. Inst. Republican. Home: 9600 Lake Ln Oklahoma City OK 73132 Office: PO Box 25848 Oklahoma City OK 73125

WHITE, JAMES BOYD, educator; b. Boston, July 28, 1938; s. Benjamin Vroom and Charlotte Green (Conover) W.; A.B., Amherst Coll., 1960; A.M., Harvard U., 1961, LL.B., 1964; m. Mary Louise Fitch, Jan. 1, 1979; 1 dau., Emma Lillian; children by previous marriage—Catherine Conover, John S. Asso. firm Foley, Hoag & Eliot, Boston, 1964-67; asst. prof. law U. Colo., 1967-69, asso. prof., 1969-73, prof., 1973-75; prof. law U. Chgo., 1975—; vis. asso. prof. Stanford U., 1972. Sinclair Kennedy Traveling fellow, 1964-65; Nat. Endowment for Humanities fellow, 1979—. Mem. Am. Law Inst., Chgo. Council of Lawyers. Author: The Legal Imagination, 1973; (with Scarboro) Constitutional Criminal Procedure, 1976. Office: 1111 E 60th St Chicago IL 60637

WHITE, JAMES DAVID, banker; b. Kannapolis, N.C., Oct. 22, 1922; s. James Alexander and Clifford Mae (Foster) W.; A.B., U. N.C., 1947, J.D., 1954; grad. Advanced Mgmt. Program, Harvard U., 1971; children—David Nash, Mary Kris, James Scott. With Gen. Electric Supply Corp., 1947-51; admitted to N.C. bar, 1955; with N.C. Nat. Bank, Charlotte, 1954-75; exec. v.p. trust Lincoln First Bank, Rochester, N.Y., 1975—. Mem. N.C. State Bar, Sigma Chi, Phi Alpha Delta. Clubs: Country of Rochester, Genesse Valley (Rochester). Home: 32 Berkeley St Rochester NY 14607 Office: One Lincoln First Square Rochester NY 14643

WHITE, JAMES EDWARD, geophysicist; b. Cherokee, Tex., May 10, 1918; s. William Cleburne and Willie (Carter) W.; B.A., U. Tex., 1941, M.A., 1946; Ph.D., Mass. Inst. Tech., 1949; m. Courtenay Brumby, Feb. 1, 1941; children—Rebecca White Vanderslice, Peter McDuffie, Margaret Marie White Curren, Courtenay. Dir., Underwater Sound Lab., Mass. Inst. Tech., Cambridge, 1941-45; scientist Def. Research Lab., Austin, Tex., 1945-46; research asso. Mass. Inst. Tech., 1946-49; group leader, field research lab. Mobil Oil Co., Dallas, 1949-55; mgr. physics dept. Denver Research Center, Marathon Oil Co., 1955-69; v.p. Globe Universal Scis., Midland, Tex., 1969-71; adj. prof. dept. geophysics Colo. Sch. Mines, Golden, 1972-73, C.H. Green prof., 1976—; L.A. Nelson prof. U. Tex., El Paso, 1973-76; Esso vis. prof. U. Sydney (Australia), 1975; del. U.S.-USSR geophysics exchange Dept. State, 1965; mem. bd. Am. Geol. Inst., 1972; mem. space applications bd. Nat. Acad. Engring., 1972-77; exchange scientist Nat. Acad. Sci., 1973-74. Fellow Acoustical Soc. Am.; mem. Soc. Exploration Geophysicists (hon.), Sigma Xi. Club: Cosmos. Unitarian. Author: Seismic Waves: Radiation, Transmission, Attenuation, 1965; editor: Vertical Seismic Profiling (E.I. Galperin), 1974; contbr. articles to profl. jours. Patentee in field. Office: Dept Geophysics Colo Sch Mines Golden CO 80401

WHITE, JAMES H., multi-bank holding co. exec.; b. Jacksonville, Fla., Mar. 25, 1926; s. William Charles and Inez Sarah (Moore) W.; B.S., U.S. S.C., 1947; m. Perilie Hunt, June 13, 1948. Pres., Flagship Banks, Inc., Miami Beach, Fla. Served with USN, 1944-46. Office: Flagship Banks Inc 1111 Lincoln Rd Mall Miami Beach FL 33139

WHITE, JAMES OWEN, lawyer; b. Salt Lake City, May 30, 1920; s. James Owen and Edna Amelia (Hansen) W.; A.B. with distinction, Stanford U., 1942, LL.B., 1948; m. Naomi Ruth Carter, June 1, 1946; children—Carter B., Stewart O. Admitted to Calif. bar, 1948, since practiced in Los Angeles; sr. partner firm Cummins, White, Robinson & Robinson, 1978—. Served with AUS, 1942-46. Decorated Silver Star, Purple Heart. Mem. Am. Coll. Trial Lawyers, Am. Bd. Trial Advocates (exec. com. 1972-73, 77-78), So. Calif. Def. Counsel (pres. 1974-75), Am. Judicature Soc., Am., Los Angeles (jud. evaluation com.) bar assns., Internat. Assn. Ins. Counsel. Republican. Clubs: Jonathan, San Gabriel Country. Home: 1720 Oak Grove Ave San Marino CA 91108 Office: 888 W 6th St Suite 1400 Los Angeles CA 90017

WHITE, JAMES PATRICK, lawyer, educator; b. Iowa City, Sept. 29, 1931; s. Raymond Patrick and Besse (Kanak) W.; B.A., U. Iowa, 1953, J.D., 1956; LL.M., George Washington U., 1959; m. Anna R. Seim, July 2, 1964. Admitted to Iowa bar, 1956, D.C. bar, 1959, U.S. Supreme Ct. bar, 1959; teaching fellow George Washington U. Law Sch., 1958-59; asst. prof. U. N.D. Law Sch., Grand Forks, 1959-62, asso. prof., acting dean, 1962-63, asso. prof., asst. dean, 1963-67, dir. agrl. law research program; prof. law Ind. U. Law Sch., Indpls., 1967—, also dir. urban legal studies program, 1971-74, univ. dean acad. devel. and planning, spl. asst. to the chancellor; cons. on legal edn. Am. Bar Assn., 1974—; commr. Uniform State Laws, N.D., 1961-66; Young Democratic nat. committeeman, Iowa, 1952-54. Served as 1st lt. Judge Adv. Gen., USAF, 1956-58. Carnegie postdoctoral fellow U. Mich. Center for Study Higher Edn., 1964-65. Fellow Am. Bar Found.; mem. Am., Ind., Indpls., N.D., Iowa bar assns., Am. Judicature Soc., Am. Law Inst., Order of Coif. Roman Catholic. Contbr. papers to tech. lit. Home: 7707 N Meridian St Indianapolis IN 46260 Office: Ind Univ 355 N Lansing St Indianapolis IN 46202

WHITE, JAMES PETER, reins. co. exec.; b. Bronx, N.Y., June 29, 1936; s. James M. and Nellie White; grad. All Hallows Inst., N.Y.C., 1954; m. Joan Shanahan, Nov. 22, 1958; children—Robin L., James M., Christopher S. With N.Am. Reins. Corp., 1954-65; with Am. Re-Ins. Co., N.Y.C., 1965—, v.p., then sr. v.p., 1969-75, exec. v.p., 1975—, also dir. Club: City Midday (trustee) (N.Y.C.). Home: 2 Grace Ct Greenlawn NY 11740 Office: 91 Liberty St New York NY 10006

WHITE, JAMES ROBERT, lawyer; b. Balt., Sept. 22, 1929; s. John Joseph and Doretta Isabel (Morrison) W.; A.A., U. Balt., 1957, J.D., 1959; m. Constance Mae Rowland, Dec. 29, 1951; children—Stephanie Ann, James Robert, Paul John. Staff reporter Balt. Evening Sun, 1954-60; admitted to Md. bar, 1959; practiced law, Balt., 1960-65; mem. firm White & Cymek, Balt., 1965-71; partner firm O'Doherty, Gallagher & White, Balt., 1971—. Served to cpl., AUS, 1951-53; Japan, Korea. Fellow Am. Coll. Trial Lawyers; mem. State Bar Md. (bd. govs. 1978-79), Am. (ho. of dels. 1978—), Md., Balt. (pres. 1977-78) bar assns., Md. Criminal Def. Lawyers Assn. (pres. 1972-74), Am. Polygraph Assn. (asso.), Saints and Sinners Clubs Am., Friendly Sons St. Patrick. Democrat. Roman Catholic. Home: 4713 Roundhill Rd Ellicott City MD 21043 Office: 1011 Fidelity Bldg 210 N Charles St Baltimore MD 21201

WHITE, JEAN MARIE, newspaperwoman; b. Williamsport, Pa.; d. Andrew J. and Marie (Wood) White; B.A. summa cum laude, Bucknell U., 1950; M.S. in Journalism, Columbia, 1953. Part-time reporter, editor Grit Pub. Co., Williamsport, Pa., 1943-50; pub. relations work with E.I. duPont de Nemours & Co., Inc., 1950-52; reporter Washington Post, 1953-69, cultural editor, 1969-73, reporter-editor, 1973—. Served with WAVES, 1945-46. Recipient Catherine O'Brien award for journalism Stanley Home Products, 1967; Pulitzer Traveling Journalism scholarship, 1953. Mem. Phi Beta Kappa, Sigma Delta Chi. Club: Press (Washington). Home: 3800 Reno Rd NW Washington DC 20008 Office: 1150 15th St NW Washington DC 20005

WHITE, JERRY MAX, judge; b. Dothan, Ala., Jan. 10, 1941; s. William Calvin and Clyda Mae (Strickland) W.; B.S., U. Ala., 1963, LL.B., 1965; m. Carol Anne Sugg, Aug. 29, 1964; children—Stuart, Jennifer, William. Admitted to Ala. bar; mem. firm, Dothan, 1965-70; dist. atty., 1971-73; judge Circuit Ct., Dothan, 1973—. Mem. Ala. State Bar, Houston County Bar Assn. Baptist. Club: Elks. Home: 1003 Rosebud St Dothan AL 36303

WHITE, JESSE MARC, actor; b. Buffalo, Jan. 3; s. Elias and Freda Weidenfeld; m. Cecelia Kahn, Jan. 18, 1942; children—Carole, Janet. Appeared in 17 Broadway plays including: Harvey, 1944; appeared in 59 movies; appeared in television series: Ann Sothern Show, 1956-62, Danny Thomas' Make Room for Daddy, 1952-58, Marlo Thomas Show, 1969-71; appeared in numerous dramatic and conedy television shows, 1945—; television spokesman Maytag Co., 1967—. Mem. Actors Equity, AFTRA, Screen Actors Guild. Club: Friars of Calif.). Office: care Arnold Soloway Assos 10100 Santa Monica Blvd Century City CA. *At age two I knew what I wanted in life-to bring laughter and joy to the world. I've been blessed twice-to be able to do the thing I know and do best and to make a decent and respectable living at it. I have had a good life in show business and feel sorry for people who are not in it!*

WHITE, JIMM F., lawyer; b. Langley Field, Va., Apr. 30, 1944; s. Robert James and Joyce Jean (Sawyer) W.; A.B., U. Mich., 1966; J.D., Wayne State U., Detroit, 1969; m. Geri R. Rosen, Aug. 15, 1965; children—Deborah Jean, Elizabeth Anne. Admitted to Mich. bar, 1969; practiced in Detroit, 1969-78; partner firm Rollins, White & Rollins, 1973-78, firm Morris, Rowland, Prekel, Paquette, Keidan & White, Troy, Mich., 1978—; asso. dir. Mich. Commn. Housing Law Revision, 1969. Mem. adv. bd. Detroit Area Salvation Army, 1975—. Mem. Am., Detroit bar assns., State Bar Mich. Club: Detroit Yacht. Editor Wayne State U. Law Rev., 1967-69. Home: 3871 Adams Rd Bloomfield Hills MI 48013 Office: 3001 W Big Beaver Rd Suite 504 Troy MI 48084

WHITE, JOHN ARNOLD, educator; b. Chgo., Jan. 30, 1933; s. Maxwell Richard and Dorothy Edith (Arnold) W.; B.A., Oberlin Coll., 1954; M.S., Yale, 1955, Ph.D., 1959; m. Rebecca Anne Cotten, June 20, 1964; children—Lauren, Thomas, Julia. Instr. physics Yale, 1958-59, Harvard, 1959-62; research asso. Yale, 1962-63; research physicist Nat. Bur. Standards, Washington, 1963-64; research asso. U. Md., College Park, 1965-66; asso. prof. Am. U., Washington, 1966-68, prof., 1968—; cons. Nat. Bur. Standards, 1965-72; mem. tech. staff Bell Telephone Labs, summers 1954, 60-62; vis. scientist Mass. Inst. Tech., fall 1972. Honor scholar, 1950-54; Noyes Clark fellow, 1954-57, NSF fellow, 1957-58; recipient grants NSF, 1966, 67, 69, 71, Office Naval Research, 1973, 74. Fellow Am. Phys. Soc.; mem. AAUP, Washington Philos. Soc., Phi Beta Kappa, Sigma Xi. Contbr. sci. papers on atomic structure and fluorescence, magnetism, lasers, speed of light, critical point phenomena. Home: 7107 Fairfax Rd Bethesda MD 20014 Office: Physics Dept American U Washington DC 20016

WHITE, JOHN BARTLETT, glass co. exec.; b. Toledo, Feb. 26, 1924; s. Wilbur McKee and Helen Ruth (Bartlett) W.; B.S. in Mech. Engring., Ohio State U., 1952; m. Helen Florence Collins, Mar. 22, 1952; children—Kenneth M., Ann C., Susan J., David J. With PPG Industries, Inc., 1952—, mgr., Cumberland, Md., 1959-60, mgr., Creighton, Pa., 1960-62, gen. mgr. window glass and plate/float, Pitts., 1962-66, dir. prodn., glass, 1966-67, v.p. mfg., 1967-73, v.p. flat glass group, 1973-77, v.p. primary glass products, 1977. Mem. adv. bd. New Kensington campus Pa. State U., 1970-73, mech. engring. dept. Ohio State U., 1970—; dist. pres. Boy Scouts Am., Cumberland, 1954-55. Served with USAF, 1942-45. Recipient Benjamin G. Lamme award Ohio State U., 1974; registered profl. engr., Ohio, Pa. Mem. ASME, Soc. Automotive Engrs., Nat. Soc. Profl. Engrs., Pitts. C. of C. Clubs: Rotary (v.p. 1960), Masons, Elks. Home: 127 Oak Manor Dr Natrona Heights PA 15065 Office: PPG Industries Inc One Gateway Center Pittsburgh PA 15222

WHITE, JOHN C., polit. party ofcl.; b. Clay County, Tex., Nov. 26, 1924; s. Edward H. and Carrie L. (Campbell) W.; B.S. in Agr., Tex. Tech. U., 1946; m. Wynelle Watson, children—Richard, Edward, Kay Lynn, Russell, Craig Allen. Head agr. dept. Midwestern U., Wichita Falls, Tex., 1948-50; commr. agr. State of Tex., 1950-77; dep. sec. Dept. Agr., 1977-78; chmn. Democratic Nat. Com., Washington, 1978—. Recipient award of Merit for service to internat. agr., Govt. of France, 1968. Democrat. Baptist. Office: Democratic Nat Com 1625 Massachusetts Ave NW Washington DC 20036*

WHITE, JOHN DAVID, composer; b. Rochester, Minn., Nov. 28, 1931; s. Leslie David and Millie (Solum) W.; B.A. magna cum laude, U. Minn., 1953; M.A., U. Rochester, 1954, Ph.D., 1960; m. Marjorie Manuel, Dec. 27, 1952; children—Jeffrey Alan, Michele Kay, David Eliot. Mem. faculty Kent (Ohio) State U., 1956-58, 60-63, 65-73, prof. music, asso. dean Grad. Sch., 1967-73; prin. cellist Eastman Philharmonia, 1959; asst. prof. U. Mich., 1963-65; dean Sch. Music, Ithaca (N.Y.) Coll., 1973-74; vis. prof. U. Wis., 1975-78; compositions performed by major orchs.; cons. Middle States Assn. Served with AUS, 1954-56. Recipient Benjamin award, 1960, Nat. Fedn. Music Clubs award, 1962, ASCAP awards, 1965—, U. Wis.-Oriana Trio Internat. Composition award, 1979, others. Mem. ASCAP, Am. Soc. Univ. Composers, Pi Kappa Lambda, Delta Omicron, Phi Mu Alpha. Author: (with A. Cohen) Anthology of Music for Analysis, 1965; Understanding and Enjoying Music, 1968; Music in Western Culture, 1972; The Analysis of Music, 1976; editor: Music and Man; contbr. articles to profl. jours. Composer: Symphony No. 2, 1960; Blake Songs, 1961; Divertimento for Flute, Violin and Viola, 1961; (opera) The Legend of Sleepy Hollow, 1962; numerous sacred choral works; Three Choruses From Goethe's Faust, 1965; Three Joyce Songs, 1966; Ode to Darkness, 1967; Cantos of the Year, 1969; Variations for Clarinet and Piano, 1971; Whitman Music, 1970; Three Madrigals for Chorus and Orchestra, 1971; Russian Songs for Voices and Winds, 1972; Prayer (Solzhenytsin), 1973; String Quartet 1, 1975; Variations for Piano, 1976; Ode on the Morning of Christ's Nativity (Donne), 1977; Music for Oriana for violin, cello and piano, 1978; Pied Beauty, 1979; Trio Music for Strings, 1980. Home: 6601 Piedmont Rd Madison WI 53711

WHITE, JOHN FRANCIS, ednl. adminstr.; b. Waukegan, Ill., Oct. 11, 1917; s. Edward Sydney and Lilah (McCormick) W.; A.B., Lawrence U., 1941, L.H.D., 1961; A.M., U. Chgo., 1944; LL.D., Cornell Coll., Iowa, 1964, Hamilton Coll., 1967; Litt.D., Temple U., 1968; m. Joan Glasow, May 15, 1943; children—Susan White Lester, Michael, Christopher. Admissions counsellor Lawrence U., 1941-44; dir. admissions Ill. Inst. Tech., 1944-45, asst. dean students, 1945-46, dean students, 1946-48, dean and dir. devel. program, 1948-50; v.p. Western Res. U., 1950-55; gen. mgr. Met. Pitts. Ednl. TV Sta. WQED, 1955-58; pres. Nat. Ednl. TV and Radio Center, 1958-69, Cooper Union, N.Y.C., 1969—; dir. Orange & Rockland Utilities, Inc., Viacom Internat. Inc., Tround Internat. Inc., Old Mchts. House. Pres., Venture Fund Episcopal Diocese of N.Y., co-chmn. Venture in Mission campaign; asso. officer Order of St. John of Jerusalem; trustee Gen. Theol. Sem., Wye Inst., Inst. for Architecture and Urban Studies; mem. devel. com. Chamber Music Soc. Lincoln Center; sr. warden St. Mary's Ch., Tuxedo Park, N.Y. Mem. N.Y. Soc. Architects (hon.). Clubs: Tuxedo, University, Century. Author mag. articles. Home: Turtle Mountain Tuxedo Park NY 10987 Office: Cooper Square New York NY 10003

WHITE, JOHN FRANCIS, food co. exec.; b. Madison, Wis., Dec. 2, 1929; s. Francis Bernard and Helen Margaret (Brown) W.; B.S., U. Wis., 1951; grad. Advanced Mgmt. Program, Harvard U., 1974; m. Arline Marie Keuth, Feb. 19, 1955; 1 dau., Susan Jeanne. With Kraft, Inc., 1954—, v.p., dir. research and devel., Glenview, Ill., 1974—. Served with AUS, 1951-53. Mem. Inst. Food Technologists, Am. Chem. Soc., AAAS. Republican. Roman Catholic. Club: North Shore Country (Glenview). Home: 2643 Oak St Northbrook IL 60062 Office: 801 Waukegan Rd Glenview IL 60025

WHITE, JOHN GORDON, psychiatrist; b. Hamilton, Ont., Can., July 14, 1914; s. Frederick Alfred and Mary (Smith) W.; B.A., McMaster U., 1936; M.D., U. Western Ont., 1950; D.Psych., U. Toronto, 1954; m. Irmgard Anna Maria Kries, July 13, 1957; children—Michael, Peter, Paul, Frederick. Physician Ont. Dept. Health, Hamilton, 1951-52; resident Toronto Psychiat. Hosp., 1952-54; clin. psychiatrist Ont. Hosp., Hamilton, 1954-57, clin. dir., 1957-60, asst. supt., 1960-68; supt. Hamilton Psychiat. Hosp., 1968-70, cons. forensic psychiatry, 1960—, dir. forensic service, 1971—; asst. prof. psychiatry McMaster U., Hamilton. Served with Royal Canadian Army, 1943-46. Mem. Can., Ont. psychiat. assns., Can., Ont. med. assns., Royal Coll. Physicians and Surgeons, Hamilton Acad. Medicine, Hamilton Med-Legal Soc. Home: 142 Judith Crescent Ancaster ON Canada Office: Hamilton Psychiatric Hosp Hamilton ON Canada

WHITE, JOHN JAMIESON, JR., architect; b. Calgary, Alta., Can.; s. John Jamieson and Mary Martha (Walters) W.; B.Arch., U. Mich.; grad. Naval War Coll., 1962; m. Leonore Ruth Snyder; children—Nancy, Alexandra (dec.), John Jamieson III, Alison. Prin. in archtl. and engring. firms Mackenzie Bogert & White, N.Y.C., 1950-54, White Noakes & Neubauer, Washington, 1954-57, John Jamieson White & Assos., Washington, 1957-59, White & Mariani, Washington, 1959-61, White-Greer Assos., Paris, 1961—; archtl. cons. surgeon gen. USAF; chief architect Howard Research Corp.; archtl. adviser Republic Vietnam, 1967-72, Republic Indonesia, 1972-74; prin. works include Naval Air and Communications Complex, Port Lyautey, Morocco, 1950-54, Children's Hosp., San Jose, Costa Rica, 1955, Northwest, Northeast and Braniff air terminal facilities Kennedy Internat. Airport, 1960-61, Orly Hilton Hotel, Paris, 1965. Served to comdr. USN 1940-47, capt. ret., 1969. Decorated Navy Commendation medal; Public Works medal 1st class (Republic Vietnam). Mem. AIA (dir. pub. and profl. relations 1947-50, v.p. Washington Met. chpt. 1943; life), ASCE, Société des Ingenieurs Civils de France. Republican. Clubs: Univ. (N.Y.C.); Army and Navy, Internat. (Washington). Home: 4222 Leland St Chevy Chase MD 20015 Office: 38 rue Croix des Petite Champs 75001 Paris France

WHITE, JOHN PATRICK, govt. ofcl.; b. Syracuse, N.Y., Feb. 27, 1937; s. Walter Thomas and Sara A. W.; B.S., Cornell U., 1959; M.A., Syracuse U., 1964, Ph.D. in Econs., 1969; m. Elizabeth Lucille Michaud, June 20, 1959; children—Ann Marie, Patricia, John, Timothy. Personnel and recruiting specialist Gen. Electric Co., 1959-62; mem. faculty dept. econs. LeMoyne Coll., Syracuse, 1964-68; with Rand Corp., 1968-78, dir. manpower, personnel and tng. research program for Air Force, 1969-71, v.p., 1971-75, sr. v.p., 1975-77, trustee, 1973-77; asst. sec. Def. for manpower res. affairs and logistics, 1977-78; dep. dir. Office Mgmt. and Budget, Exec. Office of Pres., Washington, 1978—. Served to lt. USMC, 1959-61. Democrat. Roman Catholic. Home: 6017 Chesterbrook Rd McLean VA 22101 Office: Room 252 Old Exec Office Bldg Washington DC 20503

WHITE, JOHN PATRICK, educator; b. Cin., Mar. 7, 1924; s. Joseph Harold and Anna Mable (Cummings) W.; student U. Ala., 1942-43, 46-47; A.B., U. Cin., 1949; A.M., U. Chgo., 1952, Ph.D., 1953; m. Mary Louise Stewart, May 1, 1946; children—John Patrick, Karen Ann White Nipper. Mgmt. intern, personnel officer, adminstrv. office Exec. Office Sec. Dept. Navy, Washington, 1953-54; mem. faculty U. Mich., Ann Arbor, 1954-63, successively instr., asst. prof. polit. sci., asso. prof.; prof. polit. sci. Ariz. State U., Tempe, 1963—, chmn. dept., 1964-72. Research cons. Mich. Constl. Conv., 1960-61. Served with AUS, 1943-46. Recipient Distinguished Service award U. Mich., 1962; Ariz. Superior Service award Am. Soc. Pub. Adminstrn., 1972. Social Sci. Research Council fellow, 1954. Mem. Western Polit. Sci. Assn. Republican. Co-author: Apportionment and Representative Institutions, 1963. Home: 1724 N McAllister Ave Tempe AZ 85281

WHITE, JOHN SIMON, opera dir.; b. Vienna, Austria, Mar. 4, 1910; s. Emil and Martha (Pollack) Schwarzkopf; Ph.D., U. Vienna, 1933; student Sorbonne, U. Besançon (France), U. Perugia (Italy). Came to U.S., 1938, naturalized, 1943. Mem. faculty Schotten Realschule, Vienna, 1934, New Sch. Social Research, N.Y.C., Lycée Français, N.Y.C., 1942-43; asst. stage dir. N.Y.C. Opera Assn., 1946-51, asso. dir., 1952-68, mng. dir., 1968—; exec. dir. Vienna Burgtheater guest appearance in N.Y.C., 1968. Cons. Ford Found., 1974—. Co-founder Am. Dressage Inst. for Classical Horsemanship, Saratoga, N.Y., 1967. Bd. dirs. Gert von Gontard Found., 1968—. Served with AUS, 1942-45. Recipient 1st prize, scholarship Italian Cultural Inst., Vienna, 1935. Author: The Renaissance Cavalier, 1959; also research papers. Home: 57 W 58th St New York NY 10019 Office: NY City Opera Lincoln Center Plaza New York NY 10023*

WHITE, JOHN SPENCER, educator; b. River Falls, Wis., Mar. 7, 1926; s. Kenneth S. and Helen D. (Kyle) W.; B.A., U. Minn., 1947, M.A., 1950, Ph.D., 1955; m. Helen M. Peirson, July 7, 1945; children—Jane, Jill. Instr. Wis. State U., Superior, 1947-50; asst. prof. U. Man. (Can.), 1953-56; sr. quality control engr. Honeywell, Inc., 1956-60; sr. research mathematician Gen. Motors Research Labs., 1960-68; prof. mech. engring. U. Minn., 1968—. Served with USNR, 1943-46. Fellow Am. Soc. Quality Control; mem. Inst. Math. Statistics, Am. Statis. Assn., Math. Assn. Am., Operations Research Soc., Am. Inst. Indsl. Engrs. Republican. Episcopalian. Home: 5135 Ranier Pass Columbia Heights MN 55421 Office: Mech Engring Bldg Univ Minn Minneapolis MN 55455

WHITE, JOHN SYLVESTER, actor, author; b. Phila., Oct. 31, 1919; s. John Sylvester and Mary Catherine (O'Neill) W.; A.B. in English, U. Notre Dame, 1941; m. Vasiliki Sarant, 1966. Appeared in Richard III, N.Y.C., 1943-55, 70—; appeared in television films Hustling, The Law, The Gun, The Marcus-Nelson Murders; television programs Kojak, Baretta, as Michael Woodman, the prin. on Welcome Back Kotter. Mem. Dramatists Guild New York, Actors Equity, Screen Actors Guild, AFTRA, Societe des Auteurs Et Compositeurs Dramatiques, Paris. Author: (one act plays) Bugs, 1966, Veronica, 1965; (play) Bananas, 1968. Office: care Greenevine Agy 9021 Milrose Ave Suite 304 Los Angeles CA 90069

WHITE, JOHN VERNON, JR., hosp. adminstr.; b. Sand Springs, Okla., Aug. 22, 1926; s. John Vernon and Carol (Gilmore) W.; B.S., U. Okla., 1954, M.D., 1958; m. Mary Waltina Ledgerwood, Dec. 6, 1961; 1 dau., Debra Lea. Intern, St. John's Hosp., Tulsa, 1958-59, resident in surgery, 1959-60; resident in psychiatry Danville (Pa.) State Hosp., Cherokee (Ia.) Mental Health Inst., 1974-75; gen. practice, Okla., 1960-63; staff physician Hissom Meml. Center Retardation, Sand Springs, 1963-64, Hamburg (Pa.) State Sch. and Hosp. Retarded, 1965; med. dir. Ariz. Children's Colony Retarded, Coolidge, 1966-67; supt. Hosp. Mentally Retarded, Dept. Mental Health, Georgetown, Del., 1967-71, Muscatatuck State Sch. and Tng. Center, Butlerville, Ind., 1971; asst. supt. Rusk (Tex.) State Hosp., 1971-79; med. dir. Benton (Ark.) Services Center, 1979—. Bd. dirs., adv. council Foster Grandparent Program, 1967—; bd. dirs. Del. Wheels for Handicapped, 1968-69. Served with USNR, 1943-46. Mem. Am. Assn. Mental Deficiency, Alpha Epsilon Delta. Republican. Baptist. Contbr. profl. jours. Address: Benton Services Center Benton AR 72015

WHITE, JOHN WARREN, lawyer; b. Wakefield, Mass., Nov. 14, 1912; s. John Francis and Olga (Crowell) W.; A.B., Amherst Coll., 1934; LL.B., Harvard, 1937; m. Katharine Leggett Stone, Dec. 20,

1941; children—Susan Stone West, John Francis, Patience Haydock. Admitted to Mass. bar, 1937; asso. Hurlburt, Jones, Hall & Bickford, Boston, 1937-40, Sawyer, Hardy, Stone & Morrison, 1946-48; partner Parker, Coulter, Daley & White, Boston, 1948-79, of counsel, 1979—. Mem. Republican Town Com., 1953-60; chmn. bd. appeals, Lincoln, 1955-58, town counsel, 1957-66; spl. asst. corp. counsel, Boston, 1965-67. Trustee Robert Breck Brigham Hosp., Boston. Served to lt. col. AUS, 1940-46. Decorated Bronze Star. Fellow Am. Coll. Trial Lawyers; mem. Am., Mass., Boston bar assns., Internat. Assn. Ins. Counsel. Clubs: Oyster Harbors (pres. 1960-65); Somerset (Boston). Home: Old Concord Rd Lincoln MA 01773 Office: One Beacon St Boston MA 02108

WHITE, JOHN WESLEY, JR., coll. pres.; b. Nashville, Oct. 20, 1933; s. John W. and Ernestine (Engle) W.; student Martin Jr. Coll., 1952-54; B.A., Vanderbilt U., 1956, B.D. (Eli Lilly Sr. scholar), 1959; M.A., George Peabody Coll., 1966, Ph.D., 1968; m. Martha Ellen Bragg, June 24, 1956; children—Marcus Wesley, Michelle Suzanne. Dean admissions, dir. student affairs Martin Coll., 1960-65; asst. to acad. v.p. George Peabody Coll., 1965-67; asso. dean for humanities Oklahoma City U., 1968-70, dean Coll. Arts and Scis., 1970-77, asso. prof. English, 1968-73, prof., 1973-77; pres. Nebr. Wesleyan U., 1977—; cons., speaker in field. Head edn. div. United Way of Lincoln (Nebr.), 1979; mem. Nebr. Com. Humanities; bd. dirs. Youth Symphony U.S. Mem. Nebr. Ind. Coll. Found., AAUP, Assn. Colls. and Univs. for Internat.-Intercultural Studies, Blue Key, Kappa Delta Pi, Alpha Mu Gamma. Methodist. Club: Rotary (club pres. 1976) (West Oklahoma City); Lincoln Rotary. Office: Nebr Wesleyan U 50th and Saint Paul Sts Lincoln NE 68504. *Two principles have been paramount in my life: One, related to the attitude toward myself, is that we can help to shape life, not simply endure it. We are "creative" creatures, not just "surviving" creatures. The second principle, related to the attitude toward others, is that communication is essential to coexistence; and only as I make a real effort to hear what is meant, rather than simply what is said or written, am I able to communicate effectively.*

WHITE, JOHN WILLIAM, army officer, physician; b. Washington, June 7, 1920; s. James Todd and Merle Octavius (Turnage) W.; B.S., George Washington U., 1941, M.D., 1944; m. Betty Alden Waitt, Apr. 22, 1944; children—Betty A. White Taylor, Kathryn E. White Seeberg, Margaret M. Intern, Emergency Hosp., Washington, 1944-45; commd. 1st lt. U.S. Army, 1945, advanced through grades to brig. gen., 1974; resident surgery Georgetown U. Hosp. and Children's Hosp., Washington, 1947-50; div. surgeon, med. bn. comdr. 2d Inf. Div., comdg. officer 43d MASH, Korea, 1954; dir. surg. tng. William Beaumont Army Hosp., El Paso, Tex., 1954-59, Europe, 1959-62; dir. surg. tng. Fitzsimons Gen. Hosp., Denver, 1963-66, chief dept. surgery, 1966-68; surg. cons. in Europe, then for Surg. Gen. of Army, 1968-73; comdr. profl. services Brooke Army Med. Center, 1973; comdr. Martin Army Hosp., Ft. Benning, Ga., 1973-74; comdr. Dwight David Eisenhower Army Med. Center, Ft. Gordon, Ga., 1974—; cons. Atomic tests Eniwetok Proving Ground, 1958, Bogota, Colombia, 1964, NRC, 1970-72; asso. prof. clin. surgery U. Colo., 1964-69; asso. prof. surgery Emory U., 1973, Med. Coll. Ga., 1976; liaison mem. Emergency Health Service Adv. Council, Ga. Dept. Human Resources. Mem. exec. com. Augusta chpt. ARC, 1975, Ga.-Carolina council Boy Scouts Am., 1976. Decorated Bronze Star medal, Meritorious Service medal with oak leaf cluster, Army Commendation medal. Diplomate Am. Bd. Surgery. Fellow A.C.S.; mem. Am. Coll. Hosp. Adminstrs., AMA, Am., Ga. hosp. assns., George Washington U. Med. Soc., Am. Med. Soc. in Vienna, Assn. Mil. Surgeons U.S., Assn. U.S. Army, Ga. Heart Assn. Club: Rotary of Augusta. Home: Quarters 4 Boardman Lake Fort Gordon GA 30905 Office: Dwight David Eisenhower Army Med Center Fort Gordon GA 30905

WHITE, JON BURRAN, ins. co. exec.; b. Kilgore, Tex., Jan. 12, 1936; s. Olin W. and Bernice (Burran) W.; A.A. with honors, Kilgore Jr. Coll., 1955; student U. Tex., 1955; B.B.A., Baylor U., 1957; m. Mary Mack Crabb, Oct. 24, 1959; children—Jon Burran, Craig McKinley. Sales promotion asst. Southwestern Life Ins. Co., Dallas, 1957-59, agt., 1959-76, sr. v.p., 1976-78, exec. v.p. ops., 1978—; dir. Park Cities Bank. Mem. adv. bd. Tex. Bd. Ins., 1979—. Coach, Park Cities YMCA, 1970—; chmn. major gift div. So. Meth. U., 1979—; mem. fringe benefits com. City of University Park, Tex., 1976—; mem. steering com. University Park Community League, 1978—; deacon Park Cities Bapt. Ch., 1973—, outreach chmn., 1974—, sec. fellowship of deacons, 1975; bd. dirs. Dallas Family Guidance Center, 1976—, Am. Cancer Soc., Dallas, 1978—, Million Dollar Round Table Found., 1979—, Hankamer Sch. Bus., Baylor U., 1979—, vice chmn., 1979—. Served with U.S. Army, 1959. C.L.U. Mem. Tex. Life Ins. Assn. (dir. 1977—, sec. treas. 1979—), Dallas Central Bus. Dist. Assn. (dir. 1978—), Dallas C. of C. (dir. 1977—), Cotton Bowl Council, All Sports Assn. (dir. 1978—). Home: 3545 Wentwood St Dallas TX 75225 Office: 1807 Ross Dallas TX 75201

WHITE, JOSEPH (JO JO), basketball player; b. St. Louis, Nov. 16, 1946; grad. U. Kans., 1969. Basketball player with Boston Celtics, 1969-79, Golden State Warriors, Oakland, Calif., 1979—. Named to All-Rookie NBA Team, 1970. Office: care Golden State Warriors Oakland Coliseum Oakland CA 94621*

WHITE, JOSEPH ADDISON, JR., educator; b. Mebane, N.C., Feb. 8, 1918; s. Joseph Addison and Lillian May (Barnes) W.; student U. N.C., Chapel Hill, 1935; B.Mus., U. Mich., 1938, M.Mus., 1941, Ph.D., 1958; student Curtis Inst. Music, 1938-40; m. Bertie Elizabeth Taylor, May 16, 1942; children—Joseph A. III, Raymond, Marcia, Carroll. Instr., U. Mich., 1948-50, guest lectr., summer 1953; asst. prof. Fla. State U., 1950-53, asso. prof., 1953-62, prof. music, 1962—; asst. dean Sch. Music, Fla. State U., 1972—. Adjudicator, Fla. and Ga. Music Educators Assn., 1952—; cons. Fla. Dept. Edn., 1965-66, 75—, N.C. Dept. Edn., 1966, Ednl. Testing Service, Princeton, N.J., 1968; del. Gov.'s Conf. on Edn., Fla., 1967. Served to capt., USAAF, 1942-45; MTO. Decorated Brit. Air Force cross. Mem. Music Tchrs. Nat. Assn. (exec. com. theory-composition sect. 1954-56), Music Educators Nat. Assn., Internat. Horn Soc. (adv. bd. 1971—), Phi Mu Alpha. Baptist. Home: 2102 High Rd Tallahassee FL 32303

WHITE, JOSEPH MALLIE, JR., physician, med. sch. pres.; b. Dallas, Dec. 4, 1921; s. Joseph Mallie and Vada (Funderburk) W.; B.S., So. Meth. U., 1944; M.D., U. Tex., Dallas, 1947; M.S. in Pharmacology, U. Iowa, 1950; m. Jane Colleen Dennis, Nov. 26, 1950; children—Cynthia Ann, Jennifer Sue. Intern, Denver Gen. Hosp., 1947-48; resident U. Iowa Hosp., 1948-51; chmn. dept. anesthesiology U. Okla. Med. Sch., 1956-66; asso. dean research affairs U. Okla. Med. Center, 1960-64, asso. dir., asso. dean, 1964-67, dean Med. Faculty, 1967-68; v.p. academic affairs, dean medicine U. Tex. Med. Br., Galveston, 1968-73; provost for health affairs U. Mo.-Columbia, 1973-79; pres. U. Health Scis./Chgo. Med. Sch., 1979—; mem. liaison com. Coordinating Council Med. Edn., 1975-77, chmn., 1979-80. Served with U.S. Army, 1952-54. Decorated Bronze Star; recipient 1st Distinguished Alumnus award U. Tex. Southwestern Med. Sch. at Dallas, 1968. Diplomate Am. Bd. Anesthesiology. Mem. AMA (chmn. council med. edn. 1976-79), Soc. Health and Human Values (pres. 1979-80), Sigma Xi, Alpha Omega Alpha. Editor: Clinical Anesthesiology. Home: 1530 N Dearborn St Chicago IL 60611 Office: Univ Health Scis/Chgo Med Sch 2020 W Ogden Ave Chicago IL 60612

WHITE, JULIUS, educator, chemist; b. Pitts., Mar. 23, 1904; s. Morris and Lena (Garland) W.; A.B., U. Denver, 1925, M.S., 1926; Ph.D., U. Ill., 1931; m. Florence Margaret Roy, Mar. 28, 1932; children—Margaret Jane, Elizabeth Ann, William Jay, Richard Paul. Instr. chemistry U. Ill., 1926-31, research fellow, 1931-32; NRC fellow medicine U. Mich., 1932-34, research asso. biol. chemistry, 1934-38; fellow, research asst. prof. Yale Sch. Medicine, 1938-39; mem. staff Nat. Cancer Inst., 1939-70, head metabolism sect., lab. biophysics, 1952-54, acting chief radiation br., 1954, chief lab. physiology, 1955-70; prof. chemistry Montgomery Coll., Rockville, Md., 1970—. Mem. adv. com. research pathogenesis cancer Am. Cancer Soc., 1961—, chmn., 1962-64. Served to maj. M.C, AUS, 1942-45. Decorated Bronze Star with oak leaf cluster. Mem. Am. Chem. Soc., Am. Assn. Biol. Chemists, Am. Inst. Nutrition, Am. Assn. Cancer Research, Soc. Exptl. Biology and Medicine, Sigma Xi, Phi Lambda Upsilon, Phi Sigma. Author articles field. Home: 24728 Ridge Rd Damascus MD 20750

WHITE, KERR LACHLAN, physician; b. Winnipeg, Man., Can., Jan. 23, 1917; s. John Alexander and Ruth Cecelia (Preston) W.; B.A. with honors (Oliver Gold medal), McGill U., 1940, M.D., C.M., 1949; M.D. (hon.), U. Leuven, 1978; Strathcona fellow Yale Grad. Sch., 1940-41; student London Sch. Hygiene and Tropical Medicine, 1960; m. Isabel Anne Pennefather, Nov. 26, 1943; children—Susan Isabel, Margot Edith. Intern, resident medicine Mary Hitchcock Meml. Hosp., Hanover, N.H., 1949-52; Hosmer fellow McGill U. and Royal Victoria Hosp., Montreal, 1952-53; asst. prof. medicine U. N.C. Sch. Medicine, 1953-57, asso. prof. medicine and preventive medicine, 1957-62; Commonwealth advanced fellow Med. Research Council, Social Medicine Research unit London Hosp., 1959-60; chmn., prof. epidemiology and community medicine U. Vt., 1962-64; prof. Sch. Hygiene and Pub. Health, Johns Hopkins U., 1965-76, chmn. dept. health care orgn., 1965-72; dir. Inst. Health Care Studies, United Hosp. Fund N.Y., 1977-78; dep. dir. health scis. Rockefeller Found., 1978—; chmn. U.S. Nat. Com. Vital and Health Statistics, 1975-79; mem. health adv. panel Office of Tech. Assessment, U.S. Congress, 1975—; cons. Nat. Center for Health Statistics, 1967—, WHO, 1967—. Bd. dirs. Found. for Child Devel., 1969—; trustee Case Western Res. U., 1974-79. Served with Canadian Army, 1942-45. Fellow A.C.P., Am. Pub. Health Assn. (gov. council 1964-68, 71-73, council med. care sect. 1962-65), Am. Acad. Preventive Medicine, Am. Heart Assn., Royal Soc. Medicine, AAAS, Nat. Acad. Sci. (Inst. Medicine; council 1974-76, chmn. membership com. 1975-77); mem. Internat. Epidemiol. Assn. (pres. 1974-77, treas., exec. com. 1964-71, 74-77, council 1971—), Assn. Tchrs. Preventive Medicine (council 1963-68), Am. Hosp. Assn. (adv. council ednl. and research trust 1965-68), AMA, Sigma Xi, Alpha Omega Alpha. Clubs: Cosmos (Washington); Yale, Univ. (N.Y.C.). Contbr. articles to jours., chpts. to books in field; editor: Manual for Examination of Patients, 1960; Medical Care Research, 1965; Health Care: An International Study, 1976; Epidemiology as a Fundamental Science, 1976; editorial bd. Medical Care, 1962-73, Inquiry, 1967-79, Internat. Jour. Epidemiology, 1971—, Internat. Jour. Health Services, 1971-79. Home: Route 1 PO Box 97A Stanardsville VA 22973 Office: Div Health Scis Rockefeller Found 1133 Ave of the Americas New York NY 10036

WHITE, KEVIN HAGAN, mayor of Boston; b. Boston, Sept. 25, 1929; s. Joseph C. and Patricia (Hagan) W.; A.B., Williams Coll., 1952; LL.B., Boston Coll., 1955; m. Kathryn Galvin, June 7, 1956; children—Mark, Caitlin, Elizabeth, Christopher, Patricia Hagan. Admitted to Mass. bar, 1955; asso. firm Cameron & White, Boston, 1955—; corp. counsel Standard Oil of Calif., 1955-56; legal aid to dist. atty. Middlesex County (Mass.), 1956-58; asst. dist. atty. Suffolk County (Mass.), 1958-60; sec. of state Mass., Boston, 1960-67; mayor of Boston, 1967—. Democratic nominee for gov. Mass., 1970. Chmn. Mass. Muscular Dystrophy Assn. drive, 1963, 64, Mass. Heart Assn. drive, 1965. Named One of 10 Outstanding Young Men, Mass. C. of C., 1962. Mem. Am., Mass., Boston bar assns., Nat. Assn. Secs. State, Mass. Trial Lawyers Assn. Democrat. Roman Catholic. Home: 158 Mount Vernon St Boston MA 02108 Office: City Hall Boston MA 02291

WHITE, LARRY LEE, electronics co. exec.; b. Iowa City, Aug. 5, 1937; s. Walter Henry and Dorothy (Stutzman) W.; B.A., Hastings (Nebr.) Coll., 1960; postgrad. in law LaSalle Extension U., 1969; m. Barbara Jean Leonard, Aug. 30, 1959; children—Kari Kay, Tobin Lee. Asst. mgr. credit dept. Inland div. Security First Nat. Bank, Riverside, Calif., 1960-62; mem. pres.'s staff Bourns, Inc., Riverside, 1962-67, spl. asst. to pres., 1967-68, corporate sec., 1968—, v.p. adminstrn., 1970-79, sr. v.p. fin. and adminstrn., 1979—. dir. Bourns D.I.S.C., Inc., BMS Data Handling, Inc., Marlborough Assos., Inc., Ohmic, S.A., Precision Monolithics, Inc., AIM, Inc., Bourns Med. Systems Inc., Bourns Instruments Inc., Wendover Investments Inc. Trustee Bourns Found.; pres. bd. trustees Riverside City Library, 1965; chmn. adv. bd. Riverside Salvation Army, 1966; pres. Riverside Civic League, 1966, Riverside Jr. C. of C., 1964; pres. bd. trustees Calvary Presbyterian Ch., Riverside, 1972; bd. dirs. Riverside United Way, 1975; chmn. Riverside Youth Basketball Assn., 1976-77, Riverside County Swim Conf., 1977-79. Named Outstanding Local Pres., Calif. Jaycees, 1964; recipient Riverside Distinguished Service award, 1965. Mem. Am. Soc. Corporate Secs. Republican. Club: Canyon Crest Country (chmn. bd. govs. 1977). Home: 1591 Country Club Dr Riverside CA 92506 Office: 1200 Columbia Ave Riverside CA 92507

WHITE, LAWRENCE R., television exec.; b. Cohoes, N.Y., July 31, 1926; s. David C. and Frieda O. W.; B.A., Syracuse U., 1948; m. Catherine De Carlo, Sept. 23, 1951; children—Lauren, Carol. Producer, dir. Dumont TV, 1948-51; dir. programming Benton-Bowles, Inc., 1951-59; v.p. daytime programming CBS-TV, 1959-63, v.p. program devel., 1963-65; v.p. daytime programs NBC-TV, 1965-69, v.p. programs East Coast, 1969-72, v.p. programs, 1972-76; exec. v.p. worldwide productions Columbia Pictures Television, 1976-78, pres., 1978—. Served with USNR, 1943-45. Recipient Arents Pioneer medal Syracuse U., Disting. Alumnus award. Mem. Acad. Television Arts and Scis., Hollywood Radio and Television Soc. Office: Columbia Pictures Television Colgems Sq Burbank CA 91505

WHITE, LEE C., lawyer; b. Omaha, Sept. 1, 1923; s. Herman Henry and Ann Ruth (Ackerman) W.; B.S. in Elec. Engring., U. Nebr., 1948, LL.B., 1950; children—Bruce D., Roslyn A., Murray L., Sheldon R., Laura H. Admitted to Nebr. bar, 1950, D.C. bar, 1958; atty. legal div. TVA, 1950-54; legislative asst. to Senator John F. Kennedy, 1954-57; asst. to Joseph P. Kennedy, mem. Hoover Commn., 1954-55; counsel U.S. Senate Small Bus. Com., 1957-58; adminstrv. asst. to Senator John S. Cooper, 1958-61; asst. spl. counsel to Pres. Kennedy, 1961-63; asso. counsel to Pres. Johnson, 1963-65, spl. counsel, 1965-66; chmn. Fed. Power Commn., 1966-69; campaign mgr. R. Sargent Shriver, Democratic candidate v.p. U.S., 1972. Served with AUS, 1943-46. Mem. D.C. Bar (gov. 1977—). Home: 429 N St NW Washington DC 20024 Office: 1156 15th St NW Washington DC 20005

WHITE, LELIA CAYNE, librarian; b. Berkeley, Calif., Feb. 22, 1921; d. James Lloyd and Eulalia Fulton (Douglass) Cayne; B.A., U. Calif., Berkeley, 1943, M.L.S., 1969; children by previous marriage—Douglass Fulton, Cameron Jane. Bibliographer, lectr., asso. U. Calif. at Berkeley Sch. Library and Info. Studies, 1969-72; reference librarian Berkeley-Oakland (Calif.) Service Systems, 1970-76, supervising librarian, 1973-76; dir. Oakland Pub. Library, 1976—; mem. adv. com. U. Calif. at Berkeley Sch. Library Info. Studies, Asian Community Library, Oakland, Mem. Am., Calif. library assns., Pub. Library Execs. Central Calif. (chmn.), League Women Voters. Club: Soroptomists. Home: 1927 Napa Ave Berkeley CA 94707 Office: 125 14th St Oakland CA 94612

WHITE, LEONARD LEROY, found. exec., b. Lansing, Mich., Oct. 31, 1920; s. Earl William and Euphema (Price) W.; B.A., Mich. State U., 1942; children—Jan Gar, Gary Lynn, Sheryl Ann. Receivables clk., accounting office Mich. State U., 1942-43; apprentice personnel and standards depts. Kellogg Co., Battle Creek, Mich., 1945-46; office mgr. W.K. Kellogg Found., Battle Creek, 1946-54, sec., asst. treas., 1954-70, v.p. adminstrn., 1970—; dir., asst. sec.-treas. Atlas Properties, Inc., Battle Creek, 1958-62. Sec. Battle Creek Youth Planning Com., 1956-58; sec. Mayor's Adv. Park Bd., 1958-59; sec. Cacomi Trails Met. Park Dist., 1958-69; chmn. Battle Creek Area Met. Service Agy., 1973-74. Chmn. Conf. Mich. Founds., 1973-75. Served to capt. USAAF, 1943-45. Recipient citations, local press and Nat. Recreation Assn., 1958; merit key award Adminstrv. Mgmt. Soc., 1960, Diamond Merit award, 1966; Bronze Leadership award Jr. Achievement, 1979; spl. recognition award Commn. on Accreditation Rehab. Facilities, 1979. Mem. Adminstrv. Mgmt. Soc., Health and Recreation Assn. (pres. 1957), Battle Creek Area C. of C., Battle Creek Square Dance Assn. (pres. 1957), Mich. State U. Alumni Assn. (past pres., dir.). Home: 15 Hidden Lane Battle Creek MI 49017 Office: 400 North Ave Battle Creek MI 49016

WHITE, LOWELL E., JR., educator, physician; b. Tacoma, Wash., Jan. 16, 1928; s. Lowell E. and Hazel (Conley) W.; B.S., U. Wash., 1951, M.D., 1953; m. Margie Mae Lamb, June 21, 1947; children—Henry, Leanna White Neilson, Inger-britt. Intern. N.C. Meml. Hosp., Chapel Hill, 1953-54; resident neurosurgery, asst. to instr. U. Wash., 1954-60, asst. prof., 1960-64, asso. prof., 1964-70, asso. dean Sch. Medicine, 1965-68; prof., chief div. neurol. surgery U. Fla., 1970-72; prof., chmn. div. neurosci. U. South Ala., 1972—. Chmn. Nat. Advisory Com. Animal Resources, 1966-70; cons. research facilities and resources NIH; cons. div. hosp. and med. facilities USPHS; cons. grants adminstrn. policy Dept. Health, Edn. and Welfare. Bd. dirs. Mobile County Emergency Med. Services Council, 1973—, Mobile chpt. Myesthenia Gravis Found., 1973—, Gulf Coast chpt. Epilepsy Found. Am., 1974—. Served with USNR, 1946-47. Diplomate Am. Bd. Neurol. Surgery. Guggenheim fellow, 1958-59. Mem. Am. Assn. Neurol. Surgeons, Cajal Club, Am. Assn. Neuropathologists, Am. Acad. Neurol. Surgeons, Soc. for Neurosci., Assn. Am. Med. Colls., Am. Assn. Anatomists, Research Soc. Neurol. Surgeons, Neurosurg. Soc. Ala. (pres. 1975), AMA, Sigma Xi. Mason. Contbr. articles profl. jours. Home: 5750 Huffman Dr N Mobile AL 36609

WHITE, MARGITA EKLUND, communications cons.; b. Linköping, Sweden, June 27, 1937; d. Eyvind O. and Ella Maria (Eriksson) Eklund; came to U.S., 1948; B.A. magna cum laude in Govt., U. Redlands, 1959, LL.D. (hon.), 1977; M.A. in Polit. Sci. (Woodrow Wilson fellow), Rutgers U., 1960; m. Stuart Crawford White, June 24, 1961; children—Suzanne Margareta, Stuart Crawford Jr. Asst. to press sec. Richard M. Nixon Presdl. Campaign, Washington, 1960; adminstrv. asst. Whitaker & Baxter Advt. Agy., Honolulu, 1961-62; minority news sec. Hawaii Ho. of Reps., 1963; research asst. to Senator Barry Goldwater and Republican Nat. Com., 1963-64; research asst., writer Free Society Assn., 1965-66; research asst. to syndicated columnist Raymond Moley, 1967; asst. to Herbert G. Klein, White House Dir. Communications, 1969-73; asst. dir. USIA, 1973-75; asst. press sec. to Pres. Gerald R. Ford, 1975; asst. press sec. to Pres., dir. White House Office of Communications, Washington, 1975-76; commr. FCC, 1976-79. Mem. adv. council Women's Inst., Am. U.; bd. dirs. Radio Free Europe-Radio Liberty, Inc.; mem. George Foster Peabody Adv. Bd. Recipient Disting. Service award U. Redlands Alumni Assn., 1974; Superior Honor award USIA, 1975. Mem. Exec. Women in Govt. (founding mem., sec. 1975). Home: 6703 Lupine Ln McLean VA 22101 Office: FCC 1919 M St NW Washington DC 20554

WHITE, MARK WELLS, JR., state ofcl.; b. Henderson, Tex., Mar. 17, 1940; s. Mark Wells and Sarah Elizabeth White; B.B.A., Baylor U., 1962, J.D., 1965; m. Linda Gale Thompson, Oct. 1, 1966; children—Mark Wells III, Andrew, Elizabeth Marie. Admitted to Tex. bar, 1965; asst. atty. gen., ins., banking and securities div. State of Tex., Austin, 1966-69; asso. firm Reynolds, White, Allen & Cook, Houston, 1969-71, partner, 1971-73; sec. of state State of Tex., Austin, 1973-79, atty. gen., 1979—. Bd. dirs. St. David's Hosp., Austin; mem. adv. panel on voter registration Fed. Election Commn.; mem. adv. council Southwestern Baptist Theol. Sem.; mem. Christian Edn. Coordinating Bd. Served with Tex. N.G., 1966-69. Named Lawyer of Year, Baylor U. chpt. Phi Alpha Delta, 1975. Mem. Nat. Assn. Secs. State (pres. 1977—). Democrat. Baptist.*

WHITE, MASTIN GENTRY, lawyer; b. Van Zandt County, Tex., Jan. 1, 1901; s. John Earl and Minnie Lou (Gentry) White; A.B., U. Western N.Mex., LL.B., U. Tex., 1927; LL.M., Columbia U., 1930; S.J.D. (Brandeis research fellow), Harvard U., 1933; m. Marjorie Delight Perry, Mar. 2, 1929. Law clk. Tex. Ct. Criminal Appeals, 1925-27; asst. county atty. Smith County, Tex., 1927-30; asso. prof. law U. Tex., 1930-32; spl. asst. to U.S. atty. gen., 1933-35; solicitor Dept. Agr., 1935-42, Dept. Interior, 1946-53; mem. firm Connally & White, Washington, 1953-55; trial judge U.S. Ct. of Claims, 1955—. Trustee Am. U., Washington. Served to col. AUS, World War II. Decorated Legion of Merit, Commendation medal. Mem. Am., Fed. bar assns., State Bar Tex., D.C. Bar, Bar U.S. Supreme Ct., Order of Coif, Alpha Tau Omega, Phi Delta Phi, Delta Sigma Rho, Alpha Psi Omega. Democrat. Methodist. Club: Cosmos (Washington). Home: 3920 Argyle Terrace NW Washington DC 20011 Office: US Court of Claims 717 Madison Pl NW Washington DC 20005

WHITE, MAURICE, singer, musician; b. Chgo., Dec. 19, 1941; attended Chgo. Conservatory Coll. Drummer, formerly session musician, played in local clubs, also with Ramsey Lewis; founder, percussionist musical group Earth Wind and Fire, 1971—; recorded for Warner Bros., now Columbia Records; soundtracks for movies: Sweet Sweetback's Baaadaaas Song, That's the Way of the World; songs recorded include: Love is Life, Keep Your Head to the Sky, Shining Star, Can't Hide Love, Getaway, Fantasy; albums include: Last Days and Time (Gold Album), Head to the Sky (Gold Album), Open Our Eyes (Gold Album), That's the Way of the World (Gold Album), Gratitude (Gold Album). Office: care Cavallo-Ruffalo Mgmt 9615 Brighton Way Beverly Hills CA 90210*

WHITE, MEREDITH ANN, editor; b. Pensacola, Fla., June 10, 1945; d. Clayton Samuel and Margaret Ann (Reeve) White; B.A., U. Calif., Berkeley, 1967. Editorial asst. Smithsonian mag., Washington, 1971-74, asst. editor, 1974-76, asso. editor, 1976-77; mng. editor Am.

Film, Washington, 1977-78; sr. editor New West mag., Beverly Hills, Calif., 1978-79, mng. editor, 1979—. Office: 9665 Wilshire Blvd Beverly Hills CA 90212

WHITE, MERIT PENNIMAN, engring. educator; b. Whately, Mass., Oct. 25, 1908; s. Henry and Jessie (Penniman) W.; A.B., Dartmouth Coll., 1930, C.E., 1931; M.S., Calif. Inst. Tech., 1932, Ph.D., 1935; m. Jarmila Jaskova, 1965; children—Mary Jessie, Irene Helen, Elisabeth Cecelia, Ellen Patricia. With U.S. Dept. Agr., 1935-37; research asso. Harvard U., 1937-38; research asso. Calif. Inst. Tech., 1938-39; asst. prof. Ill. Inst. Tech., 1939-42; cons. OSRD, 1942-45, War and Navy Depts., 1945-47; prof., head civil engring. dept. U. Mass., 1948—, Commonwealth head of dept., 1961—, Commonwealth prof., 1977—. Recipient Pres.'s certificate of merit, 1948. Fellow Am. Concrete Inst., ASME, Inst. Mech. Engrs.; mem. ASCE (life), Phi Beta Kappa, Sigma Xi, Tau Beta Pi. Contbr. articles to engring. jours. Home: Whately MA 01093 Office: U Mass Amherst MA 01003

WHITE, MORTON GABRIEL, philosopher, author; b. N.Y.C., Apr. 29, 1917; s. Robert and Esther (Levine) Weisberger; B.S., Coll. City N.Y., 1936; L.H.D., City U. N.Y., 1975; A.M., Columbia U., 1938, Ph.D., 1942; m. Lucia Perry, Aug. 29, 1940; children—Nicholas Perry, Stephen Daniel. Instr. philosophy Columbia, 1942-46; instr. physics Coll. City N.Y., 1942-43; asst. prof. philosophy U. Pa., 1946-48; asst. prof. philosophy Harvard, 1948-50, asso. prof., 1950-53, prof., 1953-70, chmn. dept., 1954-57, acting chmn. dept., 1967-69; prof. Inst. Advanced Study, 1970—; Guggenheim research fellow, 1950-51; vis. prof. Tokyo U., 1952, 60, 66, U. Oslo, 1977-78; mem. Inst. Advanced Study, 1953-54, 62-63, 67-68, 68-69; vis. prof. City U. N.Y., 1968-69. Fellow Center Advanced Study Behavioral Scis., 1959-60; fellow Am. Council Learned Socs., 1962-63. Mem. Am. Acad. Arts and Scis., Am. Philos. Soc. Author: The Origin of Dewey's Instrumentalism, 1943; Social Thought in America, 1949; The Age of Analysis, 1955; Toward Reunion in Philosophy, 1956; Religion, Politics, and the Higher Learning, 1959; (with Lucia White) The Intellectual Versus the City, 1962. Editor: (with Arthur M. Schlesinger, Jr.) Paths of American Thought, 1963; Foundations of Historical Knowledge, 1965; Science and Sentiment in America, 1972; Pragmatism and the American Mind, 1973; The Philosophy of the American Revolution, 1978; editor: Documents in the History of American Philosophy, 1972. Office: Inst for Advanced Study Princeton NJ 08540

WHITE, MYRON LESTER, educator; b. Chico, Calif., July 11, 1918; s. Lester Ralph and Edna E. (Shoemaker) W.; A.A., Graceland Coll., 1937; B.A. in English, U. Wash., 1943, Ph.D. in English, 1958; m. Guinevere Evelyn Hussa, Aug. 25, 1943; children—Judith Ann, Michael Steven. Teaching asst. U. Wash., 1947-50, instr. and lectr., 1952-59, asst. prof. lit. and tech. writing, 1959-67, asso. prof., 1967-76, prof., 1976—, chmn. dept. humanistic-social studies Coll. Engring., 1968—; cons. and tchr. tech. communication for bus. and industry, govt. agys., 1956—. Served with USNR, 1943-45, 50-52. Fellow Soc. Tech. Communication; mem. Council for Programs in Tech. and Sci. Communication, AAAS, Am. Soc. Engring. Edn. Author: (with James W. Souther) Technical Report Writing, 2d edit., 1977. Office: 356 Loew Hall FH-40 U Wash Seattle WA 98195

WHITE, NORVAL CRAWFORD, architect; b. N.Y.C., June 12, 1926; s. William Crawford and Caroline Ruth (Taylor) W.; B.S., Mass. Inst. Tech., 1949; student Sch. Fine Arts, Fontainbleau, 1954; M.F.A., Princeton, 1955; m. Joyce Leslie Lee, May 24, 1958 (div.); children—William Crawford, Thomas Taylor, Gordon Crawford, Alistair David. Designer, asso. Lathrop Douglass, Architect, 1955-59; prin. Norval C. White, Architect, N.Y.C., 1959-62, 66-67; partner Rowan & White, Architects, N.Y.C., 1962-66, Gruzen & Partners, N.Y.C., 1967-70; prin. Norval C. White & Assos., N.Y.C., 1970-74; partner Levien, Deliso & White, 1974—; asst. prof. architecture Cooper Union, 1961-67, prof. architecture City Coll., City U. N.Y., 1970—, chmn. dept., 1970-77. Trustee Bklyn. Inst. Arts and Scis.; gov. Bklyn. Mus.; mem. N.Y.C. Art Commn., sec., 1975-77, v.p., 1978—. Served with USNR, 1944-46. Fellow AIA; mem. Soc. Archtl. Historians, N.Y. State Assn. Architects. Democrat. Author: (with E. Willensky) AIA Guide to New York City, 1968, 2d edit., 1978; The Architecture Book, 1976. Prin. works: Seiden House, Tenafly, N.J., 1960; Essex Terrace (housing), 1970; N.Y.C. Police Hdqrs., 1973; Brookhaven Parks (L.I.) San Landfill, 1971; Forsgate Indsl. Park, South Brunswick, N.J., 1978—; Harrison Corp. Park, 1979. Home: 78 State St Brooklyn NY 11201 Office: City Coll Sch Architecture 138th St and Convent Ave New York NY 10031

WHITE, ONNA (MRS. LARRY DOUGLAS), choreographer. b. N.S., Can.; m. Larry Douglas; 1 dau. Profl. debut with San Francisco Opera Ballet Co.; appeared in musicals Finian's Rainbow, 1947, 55; Guys and Dolls, 1950, 55; Silk Stockings, 1955; formerly asst. to Michael Kidd; formerly modern and ballet dancer, asst. choreographer various shows; choreographer N.Y.C. stage shows Music Man, Mame, 1776, London stage Billy, others; choreographer films Music Man, 1962, Bye Bye Birdie, 1963, Oliver, 1968, The Great Waltz, 1973, Mame, 1974, I Love My Wife, Working. Recipient Acad. award for Oliver. Address: Soc Stage Dirs and Choreographers 1501 Broadway New York NY 10036*

WHITE, PAUL A., educator; b. Los Angeles, Aug. 21, 1915; s. Alexander and Eva (Balz) W.; B.A., U. Calif. at Los Angeles, 1937, M.A., 1938; Ph.D., U. Va., 1942; m. Lucille Donovan, Apr. 6, 1939; children—John, Terry, William, Kathleen. Teaching asst. U. Calif. at Los Angeles, 1937-39; instr. U. Va., 1939-42; asst. prof La. State U., 1942-45; mathematician Aberdeen (Md.) Proving Ground, 1945; asst. prof. U. So. Calif., 1945-48, asso. prof., 1948-53, head math. dept., 1950-68, prof., 1953—. Writer, lectr. African Math. Project, 1966-68; NSF cons. India Math. Project, 1967; UNESCO cons. Arab Math. Program, 1969-70. Mem. Am. Math. Soc., Math. Assn. Am., Phi Beta Kappa, Sigma Xi. Author math textbooks. Home: 5330 Weatherford Dr Los Angeles CA 90008

WHITE, PAUL ELLIS, social anthropologist; b. Revere, Mass., Feb. 16, 1931; s. Ellis and Carrie Mae (Grimes) W.; D.H.L. (hon.), Colby Coll., 1974; m. Caroline McCoy, Dec. 30, 1963; children—Lisa, Erik, Sarah. Mem. faculty Johns Hopkins U., 1961—, prof. anthropology, chmn. dept. behaviorial scis., 1972—; adv. Govt. of Pakistan, 1964-67; mem. cancer control intervention programs rev. com. Nat. Cancer Inst., 1977—. Fulbright grantee, 1953. Mem. Acad. Behaviorial Medicine, Am. Anthrop. Assn., Am. Sociol. Assn., Am. Public Health Assn., Soc. Applied Anthropology, Phi Beta Kappa. Contbr. articles to profl. jours. Office: Sch Hygiene and Public Health Johns Hopkins Univ 615 N Wolfe St Baltimore MD 21205*

WHITE, PERRY MERRILL, JR., orthopedic surgeon; b. Texarkana, Ark., Oct. 11, 1925; s. Perry Merrill and Mary Gladys (Shelton) W.; B.S., Baylor U., 1948, M.D., 1953; postgrad. Vanderbilt U., 1948-49; m. Lucy Katherine Freeman, Dec. 23, 1947; children—Perry Merrill III, Georgia Lynette, Katherine Landis White Long, John David. Intern VA Hosp., Houston, 1953-54; gen. practice medicine, Spearman, Tex., 1955-57; resident orthopedic surgery Eugene Talmadge Meml. Hosp., Augusta, Ga., 1957-61; pvt. practice orthopedic surgery, Atlanta, 1961—; chief Ga. Adult Amputee Clinic, 1965-79; active staff Scottish Rite Hosp. for Crippled Children, Decatur, Ga., 1965-73; instr. Ga. Bapt. Hosp. Orthopedic Surgery Residency Program; orthopedic panelist Ga. Dept. Vocational Rehab.; cons. Ga. Crippled Children's Service, 1965-76. Bd. dirs. Haggai Inst., Atlanta, London, Singapore. Served with USNR, 1944-46. Diplomate Am. Bd. Orthopaedic Surgery. Fellow A.C.S., Am. Acad. Orthopedic Surgeons; mem. AMA, So., Ga., Atlanta med. assns., Eastern Orthopaedic Assn., Ga., Atlanta orthopaedic socs., Am. Coll. Sports Medicine, Alpha Kappa Kappa. Republican. Baptist (deacon). Clubs: Cherokee Town and Country, North by Northwest Civic. Home: 1547 Cave Rd NW Atlanta GA 30327 Office: 315 Blvd NE Atlanta GA 30312

WHITE, PETER GEORGE, newspaper exec.; b. Eng., Aug. 1, 1939; s. Cyril Grove and Elizabeth Katherine Mary (Delmore) Costley-White; B.A. in Econs., U. Western Ont., 1966; M.B.A., 1970; m. Martha Grace Blackburn, June 24, 1966; children—Richard, Sarah, Annabelle. With Aluminum Co. of Can. Ltd., 196-68, placement officer, area mgr., 1966-68; mktg. services mgr. London Free Press, 1970-72, planning and devel. mgr., 1972-75, asst. to pres. and pub., 1975-76, pres., gen. mgr., 1976—; dir. London Free Press Holdings Ltd., London Free Press Printing Co. Ltd., CFPL Broadcasting Ltd., Wingham Investments Ltd., Newspaper Mktg. Bur., Inc. Trustee Royal Ont. Mus., Toronto, 1973-79; bd. dirs. Nat. Ballet of Can., United Way of London, London Symphony Orch. Served with Brit. Army, 1958-60. Office: PO Box 2280 London ON N6A 4G1 Canada

WHITE, PHILIP BUTLER, artist; b. Chgo., Jan. 23, 1935; s. Ralph Gerald and Mary (Butler) W.; B.F.A., U. So. Calif., 1957; m. Anita Malisani; children—David, Daniel. One-man show Oehlschlaeger Art Gallery, Chgo., 1976, 78; exhibited in group shows 2d, 3d, ann. nat. art round-ups, Las Vegas, 1957, 58, Union League Club, Chgo., 1959, 63, 65, 67, 69, 72, 74, 76, Ill. State Fair, 1959, 60, 61, 62, 63, 64, 65, 66, 67, 68, Brotherhood Week Art Exhbn., Chgo., 1960, N. Miss. Valley Artists exhibit Ill. State Mus., Springfield, 1961, 63, 65, 67, 69, 70, Magnificent Mile, Chgo., 1961, ann. midyear shows Butler Inst. Am. Art, Youngstown, Ohio, 1962, 63, 64, ann. Chgo. Sun Times exhbns., 1962, 63, 21st ann. exhbn. Audubon Artists, N.Y.C., 1963, ann. exhbns. Nat. Acad. Design, N.Y.C., 1963, 64, 65, 67, 68, 69, 70, 74, 75, 76, Okla. Mus. Art, 1969, 70, Ball State U., 1970, Am. Watercolor Soc. ann., 1970-71; one-man show Oak Park (Ill.) High Sch., 1968; rep. Art Inst. Chgo., Oehlschlaeger Art Gallery, Chgo. Served with AUS, 1958-59. Recipient John Deluca medal Las Vegas, 1957; Henry Ward Ranger Fund Purchase prize Nat. Acad. Design, 1963, Julius Hallgarten award, 1964, 67, 69, Thomas B. Clark award, 1965, 68, 70; Helen H. Chambers Purchase prize Union League Club, 1959; 1st prize in oils Union League Club, 1963, 67, Ill. State Fair, 1960, 65; also numerous other awards, hon. mentions exhbns., various art fairs including Oakbrook, Ill., 1963, Old Capitol at Springfield, 1963, 68, Oak Park, 1963, 78; Emily Goldsmith award, 1971; subject of cover story Am. Artist mag., 1978. Address: 710 Clinton Pl River Forest IL 60305

WHITE, RAE LEO, investment co. exec.; b. Toronto, Ont., Can., Mar. 31, 1938; s. Michael Leo and Ruth Jane (Armstrong) W.; married; children—Christopher, Marc, Gregory. Trainee, Peat, Marwick, Mitchell, C.A.'s, Toronto; controller Gordon & Gotch Ltd., Toronto; now v.p., asst. sec., treas. M. Loeb Ltd., Ottawa. Address: M Loeb Ltd 400 Industrial Ave Ottawa ON K1G 3K8 Canada

WHITE, RALPH PAUL, rubber co. exec.; b. Watertown, Mass., Aug. 1, 1926; s. Irving W. and Margaret (McGowan) W.; B.S. in Indsl. Engring., Columbia U., 1951, postgrad., 1957-58; postgrad. Yale U., 1958-59; m. Shirley I. Christie, Nov. 22, 1947; children—Karen Ann, Eric John. Mgr. product planning and control B.F. Goodrich, Shelton, Conn., 1956-59, mgr. data processing, 1959-61; partner, mgmt. cons. Bavier, Bulger & Goodyear, Naugatuck, Conn., 1961-66; with Davidson Rubber Co., Dover, N.H., 1966—, exec. v.p., 1969, pres., 1969—, corp. v.p. parent co. Ex-Cell-O Corp., 1978—; instr. engring. mechanics U. Conn., 1956-57; dir. Strafford Savs. Bank, Dover, Troy Mills, Inc. (N.H.). Mem. N.H. Indsl. Devel. Authority, 1972-75. Served to 2d lt., inf., AUS, 1944-46; ETO. Registered profl. engr., N.H., Conn. Mem. Am. Inst. Indsl. Engrs., Ops. Research Soc. Am., N.H. Bus. and Industry Assn. (dir.; pres. 1972-73), Soc. Automotive Engrs., Clubs: Abenaqui Country (Rye, N.H.); Recess, Detroit Athletic, Econ. (Detroit). Home: 70 Woodland Rd North Hampton NH 03862 Office: Indsl Park Dover NH 03820

WHITE, RAY EDWARD, JR., fgn. service officer; b. Lewiston, Pa., Mar. 26, 1927; s. Ray Edward and Margaret McKay (McKim) W.; student Lehigh U., 1944-45, Clemson U., 1945; B.S.F.S., Georgetown U., 1954; m. Martha Jane Crabtree, Sept. 16, 1949; children—Ray Edward, III, Margaret Anne, Martha Emmelyn, Rebecca McKim, Elizabeth McKay, John Malcolm. Library clk. D.C. Central Library, 1947-48; statistician div. Tb USPHS, Washington, 1948-50; field rep. Social Security Adminstrn., Washington, 1951; fgn. affairs officer Dept. State, Washington, 1951-54, commd. fgn. service officer, 1955; cultural affairs officer Am. embassy, Helsinki, Finland, 1955-57; acting prin. officer Am. embassy, Basel, Switzerland, 1957-58, U.S. consul, Helsinki, 1958-59; 2d sec. Am. embassy, Bern, Switzerland, 1960-62; 2d sec. Am. embassy, consul, London, 1962-63, acting comml. attache, 1964; chief Spl. Consular Service, London, 1965-67; property and claims officer for Europe, 1967-70; spl. detail officer Czechoslovakia, 1969; U.S. consul, Munich, W.Ger., 1970-73; counselor of embassy Consul Gen., Vienna, Austria, 1973-76; U.S. consul gen. Cape Town, South Africa, 1976-79; counselor of embassy and consul gen. Lagos, Nigeria, 1979—. Served with AC, U.S. Army, 1944-46. Mem. Am. Fgn. Service Assn., Am. Legion, Delta Sigma Pi. Club: Rotary. Home: 4816 Birch Ln Alexandria VA 22312 Office: Am Embassy Lagos Nigeria*

WHITE, RAYMOND PETRIE, JR., dentist; b. N.Y.C., Feb. 13, 1937; s. Raymond Petrie and Mabel Sarah (Shutze) W.; student Washington and Lee U., 1955-58; D.D.S., Med. Coll. Va., 1962, Ph.D., 1967; m. Betty Pritchett, Dec. 27, 1961; children—Karen Elizabeth, Michael Wood. Postdoctoral fellow anatomy Med. Coll. Va., Richmond, 1962-67, resident in oral surgery, 1964-67; asst. prof. U. Ky., Lexington, 1967-70, asso. prof., 1970-71, chmn. dept. oral surgery, 1969-71; prof., asst. dean adminstrn. Va. Commonwealth U., Richmond, 1971-74; prof., dean Sch. Dentistry, U. N.C., Chapel Hill, 1974—; cons. Portsmouth Naval Hosp., Fayetteville VA; mem. staff N.C. Meml. Hosp., mem. exec. com., 1974—, sec., 1977-78; mem. rev. com. health manpower br. USPHS, 1974-76; mem. rev. com. VA Health Manpower Tng. Assistance, 1976—. Recipient A.D. Williams award for highest class standing Med. Coll. Va., 1962, Outstanding Tchr. award U. Ky., 1971. Diplomate Am. Bd. Oral Surgery. Mem. Am. Dental Assn., N.C. Dental Soc., Am. Acad. Oral Pathology, Atwood Wash Oral Surgery Soc., AAAS, Internat. Assn. for Dental Research (pres. Ky. sect. 1970), N.Y. Acad. Scis., Chalmers J. Lyons Acad. Oral Surgery, Am. Assn. Oral and Maxillofacial Surgeons (gen. chmn. 1974-76, Outstanding Service award as committeeman 1976), N.C. Soc. Oral Surgeons, Sigma Xi, Psi Omega, Delta Tau Delta, Alpha Sigma Chi, Sigma Zeta, Psi Omega (Scholarship award 1962), Omicron Kappa Upsilon. Roman Catholic. Author: (with E.R. Costich) Fundamentals of Oral Surgery, 1971. Contbr. sci. articles to profl. jours. Home: 1506 Velma St Chapel Hill NC 27514 Office: 104 Brauer Hall Chapel Hill NC 27514

WHITE, REGINALD PACE, adminstr., educator, physician; b. Lauderdale County, Miss., June 14, 1927; s. David Brett and Allie (Pace) W.; B.A., U. Miss., 1949; M.D., U. Tenn., 1952; m. Mary Jane Madden, Mar. 31, 1951; children—Rebecca Madden, David Madden. Rotating intern St. Joseph Hosp., Memphis, 1953; ward physician Miss. State Hosp., Whitfield, 1954-58, resident psychiatry, 1958-59, sr. psychiatrist, 1961-64; resident psychiatry U. Louisville Hosp., 1959-61; dir. E. Miss. State Hosp., Meridian, 1964-74, 79—; exec. dir. Dept. Mental Health, Jackson, Miss., 1974-75; med. dir. Weems Mental Health Center, Meridian, Miss., 1975-79; clin. asso. prof. psychiatry U. Miss. Sch. Medicine, 1963—. Cons. disability determination unit Vocational Rehab. Div. Miss., 1962-64; chmn. multi-problem family task group Miss. Mental Health Planning Program, 1963—; commnr. Lauderdale County regional commn., region 10, Miss. Interagy. Commn., 1967—; chmn. task force com. mental illness Miss. Planning Study Vocational Rehab. Services, 1967—. Diplomate Am. Bd. Psychiatry and Neurology. Fellow Am., So. psychiat. assns.; mem. Am., Miss., E. Miss., Lauderdale County med. socs., Miss. Psychiat. Soc., Miss. (profl. adv. bd.), Lauderdale County (profl. adv. bd.) mental health assns., Assn. Med. Supts. Mental Hosps., Assn. Community Clinic Psychiatrists, Meridian C. of C. (bd. dirs. 1970-72). Rotarian. Methodist (ofcl. bd.). Author: (with Janet Amendt) Continued Care Services for Mental Patients, 1965; also articles. Home: 1514 52d St Meridian MS 39301 Office: PO Box 4128 Meridian MS 39301

WHITE, RICHARD BOOTH, advt. exec.; b. N.Y.C., Aug. 26, 1930; s. Frank K. and Doris (Booth) W.; B.A., Yale U., 1952; m. Mary Kane Russell, Dec. 9, 1961; children—Katherine Learned, Richard Booth, Anne Tristram, Leslie Russell. Asst. account exec. Batten, Barton, Durstine & Osborn, N.Y.C., 1955, account exec. 1956-58, account supr., 1958-63, v.p., 1959-70, mgmt. supr., 1963-76, sr. v.p., 1970-76, exec. v.p., 1976—, also dir., mem. exec. com.; dir. BBDO Internat. Inc. Bd. dirs. Madison Sq. Boys Club, N.Y.C., Vitam Center, Norwalk, Conn.; trustee New Canaan (Conn.) Country Sch. Served to 1st lt. USMCR, 1952-54. Mem. Beta Theta Pi. Presbyterian. Clubs: Yale, River (N.Y.C.); Country of New Canaan. Home: 108 Logan Rd New Canaan CT 06840 Office: 383 Madison Ave New York NY 10017

WHITE, RICHARD CRAWFORD, congressman; b. El Paso, Tex., Apr. 29, 1923; s. James Crawford and Lela (Mueller) W.; B.A., U. Tex., 1946, LL.B., 1949; m. Katherine Huffman, Dec. 18, 1949 (dec.); children—Rodrick James, Richard Whitman, Raymond Edward; m. 2d, Kathleen F. White; children—Bonnie Kathleen, Sean Carroll, Kenneth Corin, Bryan Fitzgerald. Admitted to Tex. bar, 1949; trial atty., El Paso, 1949-64; mem. Tex. Ho. of Reps. from El Paso County, 1955-58; mem. 89th-96th congresses from 16th Dist. Tex., mem. sci. and tech., armed services, coms. Active civic, vets. orgns.; chmn. El Paso County Democratic Com., 1962-64. Served with USMCR, World War II; PTO. Mem. State Bar Tex., Phi Alpha Delta, Sigma Alpha Epsilon. Episcopalian. Office: 2266 Rayburn House Office Bldg Washington DC 20515

WHITE, RICHARD MANNING, elec. engr.; b. Denver, Apr. 25, 1930; s. Rolland Manning and Freeda Blanche (Behny) W.; A.B., Harvard U., 1951, A.M., 1952, Ph.D., 1956; m. Chissie Chamberlain, Feb. 1, 1964 (div.); children—Rolland Kenneth, William Brendan. Elec. engr. Gen. Electric Microwave Lab., Palo Alto, Calif., 1956-62; vis. prof. U. Calif., Berkeley, 1962-63, asst. prof. elec. engring. and computer scis., 1963-66, asso. prof., 1966-70, prof., 1970—. Guggenheim fellow, 1968-69. Fellow IEEE; mem. Am. Phys. Soc., AAAS. Home: 350 Panoramic Way Berkeley CA 94704 Office: Elec Engring and Computer Scis Dept U Calif Berkeley CA 94720

WHITE, RICHARD STANLEY, coll. pres.; b. Puyallup, Wash., Apr. 22, 1928; s. Wesley Ward and Alberta Norman (Yahn) W.; B.S., Wash. State U., 1951, M.Ed., 1955, Ed.D., 1963; m. Beverly Jean Johnson, Feb. 2, 1951; children—Gary, Steven, Karen. Tchr., adminstr. Mead (Wash.) Sch. Dist., 1951-57; dir. tchr. and adminstrv. placement Wash. State U., 1957-61; dir. personnel Bellevue (Wash.) Pub. Schs., 1961-63; supt. schs. Burlington-Edison (Wash.) Sch. Dist., 1963-65; dean students Shoreline Community Coll., Seattle, 1965-66, pres., 1966—. Dir. Wash. Tchrs. Credit Union, Pemco Ins. Co., Wash. Student Loan Guaranty Assn. Served with USMC, 1946-47. W.K. Kellogg Found. fellow, 1954-55. Mem. Wash. Assn. Community Colls. (chmn. 1971-72), N.W. Assn. Secondary and Higher Schs., Am. Assn. Jr. Colls., Phi Delta Kappa. Home: 440 NW 196th Pl Seattle WA 98177

WHITE, ROBB, author; b. Baquio, Luzon, Philippines, June 20, 1909; s. Robb and Laura Placidia (Bridgers) W.; B.S., U.S. Naval Acad., 1931; m Rosalie Mason, Jan. 24, 1937 (div. 1964); children—Robb IV, Barbara Mason, June; m. 2d, Joan Gibbs, 1964. Active duty as capt. USNR. Author: The Nub, 1935; The Smuggler's Sloop, 1936; Run Masked, 1938; Midshipman Lee, 1938; In Privateer's Bay, 1939; Three Against the Sea, 1940; Sailor in the Sun, 1941; The Lion's Paw, 1946; Secret Sea, 1947; Sail Away, 1948; Candy, 1949; The Haunted Hound, 1950; Deep Danger, 1952; Our Virgin Island, 1953; Misdhipman Lee of the Naval Academy, 1954; Up Periscope, 1956; Flight Deck, 1961; Torpedo Run, 1962; The Survivor, 1964; Surrender, 1966; Silent Ship, Silent Sea (Commonwealth Club medal for best juvenile book), 1967; No Man's Land, 1969; Deathwatch, 1972; The Frogmen, 1973; The Long Way Down, 1977; Fire Storm, 1979; also screen plays. Home: 1780 Glen Oaks Dr Santa Barbara CA 93108

WHITE, ROBERT ALLAN, educator; b. Chgo., Dec. 16, 1934; s. Thomas Arthur and Lillian Frances (Wietzke) W.; B.S., U. Ill., 1957, M.S., 1959, Ph.D., 1963; m. Wilma Ethel Frostenson, Feb. 2, 1957; children—Dawn Roberta, Wendy Linn. Sr. research scientist Aero. Research Inst. of Sweden, Stockholm, 1963-65; asst. prof. dept. mech. engring. U. Ill., 1965-67, asso. prof., 1967-72, prof., 1972—, dir. Automotive Systems Lab., 1979—; cons. Dornier Aircraft, Germany, Aero. Rresearch Inst. Sweden. Fulbright scholar, 1960-61; NATO fellow, 1968, Thord Gray fellow, 1968. Mem. Am. Soc. Engring. Edn., Soc. Automotive Engrs., Sigma Xi, Pi Tau Sigma. Lutheran. Club: Porsche of Am. Contbr. articles in field to profl. jours. Home: 2009 S Cottage Grove St Urbana IL 61801 Office: 127 Mechanical Engineering Bldg University of Illinois Urbana IL 61801

WHITE, ROBERT ARTHUR, lawyer; b. Fort Worth, Sept. 7, 1929; s. Robbie O. and Ethel Lois (Cole) W.; B.S. in Engring., Tex. A. and M. U., 1950; J.D., So. Meth. U., 1956; m. Nancy Elizabeth Whitten, Apr. 25, 1959; children—Kirkwood C., Nancy E., Mark H., John B. Instr. engring. So. Meth. U., 1955-56; admitted to Tex. bar, 1956; with firm Baker & Botts, Houston, 1956-69, firm Arnold, White & Durkee, Houston, 1969-77. Served to capt. C.E., AUS, 1951-53. Registered profl. engr., Tex.; Patent prize Patent Resources Group, 1977. Mem. Am. Bar Assn., State Bar Tex. (chmn. sect. patent, trademark and copyright 1974-75), Am., Houston patent law assns., Tex. Soc. Profl. Engrs. Club: University (Houston). Author: Patent Litigation: Procedure and Tactics, 1971. Home: 12 Memorial Point Houston TX 77024 Died Oct. 26, 1977.

WHITE, ROBERT BENTON, banker; b. Detroit, Aug. 30, 1935; s. Robert B. and Marcena (Thayer) W.; B.S., Ohio State U., 1957; M.B.A., U. Fla., 1958; m. Stella J. Waters, Sept. 19, 1959; children—Michael Lee, Connie Lynn, Barbara Ann, Sandra Elizabeth. With Ford Motor Co., Detroit, 1961-70; with First Nat. City Bank N.Y., N.Y.C., 1970—, exec. v.p., 1974—; dir. Depository Trust Co. N.Y., Consumers Power Co.; mem. industry system and research council Bank Adminstrn. Inst. Mem. adv. council Columbia Grad. Sch. Bus. Served with USAF, 1958-60. Mem. Ohio State U. Alumni Assn. Presbyterian. Clubs: Winged Foot Golf (Mamaroneck, N.Y.); Millbrook (Greenwich, Conn.); Sea Pines (Hilton Head, S.C.). Home: 1 Highgate Rd Riverside CT 06878 Office: 399 Park Ave New York City NY 10022

WHITE, ROBERT EDWARD, educator; b. Jersey City, Aug. 31, 1917; s. Frank Armour and Frances (deGeorge) W.; B.Chem. Engring., Poly. Inst. Bklyn., 1938, M.Chem. Engring, 1940, D.Chem. Engring. (Foster Wheeler grad. fellow), 1942; m. Gloria Elizabeth Ingersoll, June 12, 1943; children—Jeffrey R., Donna L., Barbara J., Linda L., Thomas F. Jr. engr. Vulcan Engring., Cin., 1939, 40; research engr. York Corp. (Pa.), 1942-47; asst. prof. chem. engring. Bucknell U., 1947-49; prof., head dept. chem. engring. Villanova (Pa.) U., 1949—. Cons. chem. engr. petroleum, paper industries, water treatment. Chmn. bd. Newtown (Pa.) Sewer Authority, 1969—; founder, chmn. Citizens for Better Govt., 1966-68. Recipient Centennial Achievement award Poly. Inst. Bklyn., 1956. Fellow Am. Inst. Chem. Engrs. (dir. 1970-72, Disting. award in Chemistry 1979), Am. Soc. for Engring. Edn. (chmn. Middle-Atlantic sect. 1963-64), T.A.P.P.I., Sigma Xi, Tau Beta Pi, Phi Lambda Upsilon, Alpha Chi Sigma. Contbr. articles to profl. jours. Patentee in field. Office: Villanova U Dept Chem Engring Villanova PA 19085

WHITE, ROBERT EDWARD, ambassador; b. Stoneham, Mass., Sept. 21, 1926; s. Edward V. and Emily G. (McGuire) W.; A.B., St. Michael's Coll., 1952, D.H.L., 1978; student Bristol (Eng.) U., 1952-53; M.A., Fletcher Sch. Law and Diplomacy, 1954; m. Mary Anne Cahill, June 4, 1955; children—Christopher, Kevin, Claire, Mary Louise, Laura. Joined U.S. Fgn. Service, 1955; vice consul, Hong Kong, 1958-59; 2d sec., Canada, 1959-61; dep. prin. officer, Ecuador, 1963-65; chief polit. sect., Honduras, 1965-68; Latin Am. dir. Peace Corps, 1968-70; dep. chief mission, Nicaragua, 1970-72, Colombia, 1972-75; dep. U.S. rep. to OAS, 1975-77; ambassador to Paraguay, Asuncion, 1977—. Pres. bd. dirs. Am. Sch., Honduras. Served with USN, 1944-46. Fulbright scholar, 1952-53. Mem. Am. Fgn. Service Assn., Soc. Internat. Devel. Catholic. Office: Am Embassy Mariscal Lopez Ave Asuncion Paraguay

WHITE, ROBERT I., educator; b. Elgin, Ill., Dec. 28, 1908; s. Robert I. and Fannie Temple (Goodenow) W.; Ph.B., U. Chgo., 1929, M.A., 1935, Ph.D., 1945; student Stanford; LL.D., Akron, 1963, Sung Kyun Kwan U., Seoul, 1968, Walsh Coll., 1969; Docteur Humanidades, U. of Ams., Mex., 1968; L.H.D., McKendree Coll., 1969; m. Edna E. McCormick, June 7, 1930; 1 son, Ronald Edward. Tchr. elementary sch., Thornton, Ill., 1929-31; prin. elementary and high sch., Orland Park, Ill., 1931-32; tchr., dir. student activities and asst. prin. Parker High Sch., Chgo., 1932-37; prin. Sr. High Sch. and Jr. Coll., Burlington, Iowa, 1938-46; vis. lectr. U. Chgo., 1946; dean Coll. Edn., Kent (Ohio) State U., 1946-58, v.p., 1958-63, pres., 1963-71, distinguished prof. ednl. adminstrn., 1971—; vis. distinguished prof. Central Mich. U., 1972. Trustee Am. Coll. Testing Program, 1964-71, chmn. bd., 1967-71; exec. com. Nat. Commn. Accrediting; chmn. Ohio Sch. Survey, 1955. Mem. NEA, Am. Assn. Higher Edn., Am. Assn. Sch. Adminstrs., S.E. Iowa Tchrs. Assn. (past pres.), N. Central Assn. (commn. colls. and univs.), Am. Assn. Colls. (State dir. tchr. edn.), Phi Beta Kappa, Sigma Nu, Phi Delta Kappa, Omicron Delta Kappa, Kappa Delta Pi. Conglist. Rotarian. Author: The Feasibility of 6-4-4 Reorganization in School Systems, 1946; American Government: Functions and Structures, 1959; Democracy at Work, 1961. Contbr. jours. and monographs. Home: 227 Overlook Dr Kent OH 44240

WHITE, ROBERT J., educator, neurosurgeon, neuroscientist; b. Duluth, Minn., Jan. 21, 1926; B.S., Coll. St. Thomas, U. Minn., 1951, Ph.D. in Neurosurg. Physiology, 1962; M.D., Harvard, 1953; m. 1950; D.Sc. (hon.), John Carroll U., 1979; children—Robert, Christopher, Patricia, Michael, Daniel, Pamela, James, Richard, Marguerite, Ruth. Intern surgery Peter Bent Brigham Hosp., Boston, 1953-54; resident Boston Children's Hosp. and Peter Bent Brigham Hosp., 1954-55; fellow neurosurgery Mayo Clinic, 1955-58; asst. to staff, 1958-59, research asso. neuro physiol., 1959-61; mem. faculty Case Western Res. U. Sch. Medicine, 1961—, prof. neurosurgery, 1966—, co-dir. neurosurgery, 1972, co-chmn. neurosurgery, 1973—; dir. neurosurg. and brain research lab. Cleve. Met. Gen. Hosp., 1961—; neurosurgeon Univ. Hosps., also sr. attending neurosurgeon VA Hosp., 1961—. Lectr. USSR, 1966, 68, 70, 72, 73, 78, 79. Served with AUS, 1944-46. Recipient Mayo Clinic Research award, 1958; Med. Mut. Honor award, 1975; L.W. Freeman award NPF, 1977. Mem. A.C.S. (com. on trauma task force), Harvey Cushing Soc., Soc. Univ. Surgeons, Am. Physiol. Soc., Soc. Univ. Neurosurgeons (pres. 1978-79), Ohio Neurosurg. Soc. (pres. 1975), Northeast Ohio Neurosurg. Soc. (pres. 1971), Soc. Exptl. Biology, Internat. Soc. Cybernetic Medicine (mem. internat. bd. 1971—), Internat. Soc. Surgery, Soc. Neurol. Surgeons, Neurosurg. Soc. Am., A.C.S., AMA, Acad. Medicine Cleve. (dir., pres. 1978-79). Gen. editor Internat. Soc. Angiol. Jour., 1966; editor Western Hemisphere Jour. Resuscitation, 1971—, Surg. Neurology, Resuscitation, Jour. of Trauma; co-editor Surg. Neurology, 1973—. Contbr. numerous articles to profl. jours.; developed 1st isolated brain models; pioneered brain and cephalon transplant in animals, deep hypothermia techniques in brain and spinal surgery. Address: 3395 Scranton Rd Cleveland OH 44109. *As someone who operates on the human nervous system, particularly the brain, I have always felt that one should bring, not only a scientific, but a moral dedication to his work. One should train oneself to the very limits of operative technology, while at the same time acknowledge the ethical and human limits of medical biology. Throughout my life I have striven to prepare myself scientifically and ethically to carry out these principles.*

WHITE, ROBERT LEE, labor union exec.; b. Jackson, Miss., Mar. 22, 1916; s. Henry and Hattie White; grad. Howard U., 1934; m. Helen Dorothy Harper, Nov. 25, 1939; children—Helen (Mrs. Oladipo), Roberta (Mrs. Slyman Battle), Robert H., Ramon, William, Elizabeth, Dorothy, Mark, Mary, Stephen, Christopher. Employee, U.S. Post Office Dept., 1943—; now mem. Nat. Alliance Postal and Fed. Employees, pres., 1970—. Asso. mem. Democratic Nat. Com. Bd. dirs. Washington chpt. Urban League, NAACP. Recipient Civil Rights award D.C. Civic Assn., 1972. Home: 1814 Jackson St Washington DC 20018 Office: 1644 11th St NW Washington DC 20001*

WHITE, ROBERT LEE, elec. engr., educator; b. Plainfield, N.J., Feb. 14, 1927; s. Claude and Ruby Hemsworth Emerson (Levick) W.; B.A. in Physics, Columbia U., 1949, M.A., 1951, Ph.D., 1954; m. Phyllis Lillian Arlt, June 14, 1952; children—Lauren A., Kimberly A., Christopher L., Matthew P. Asso. head atomic physics dept. Hughes Research Labs., Malibu, Calif., 1954-61; head magnetics dept. Gen. Tel. and Electronics Research Lab., Palo Alto, Calif., 1961-63; prof. elec. engring. Stanford U., Palo Alto, 1963—, vice chmn. elec. engring. dept., 1976—, dir. Inst. for Electronics in Medicine, 1973—; dir. Infomax, Inc., Spectotherm, Inc.; initial ltd. partner Mayfield Fund, Mayfield, II; cons. in field. Served with USN, 1945-46. Guggenheim fellow Oxford U., 1969-70, Kantonsspital Zurich, 1977-78. Fellow Am. Phys. Soc., IEEE; mem. Sigma Xi, Phi Beta Kappa. Author: (with K.A. Wickersheim) Magnetism and Magnetic Materials, 1965; Basic Quantum Mechanics, 1967. Contbr. articles to profl. jours. Home: 23930 Jabil Ln Los Altos Hills CA 94022 Office: Dept Electrical Engineering Stanford U Stanford CA 94305

WHITE, ROBERT M., air force officer; b. N.Y.C., July 6, 1924; s. Michael A. and Helen C. (Butz) W.; B.Elec. Engring., N.Y. U., 1951; M.S. in Bus. Adminstrn., George Washington U., 1966; m. Doris M. Allen, Feb. 6, 1948; children—Gregory, Pamela, Maureen, Dennis. Fighter pilot USAAF, 1942-45; prisoner of war, 1945; rejoined USAF, 1952, now maj. gen.; assigned Japan, 1952-53; test pilot Air Force Flight Test Center, Edwards AFB, Calif., 1955-63; test pilot for X-15 research rocket aircraft; set speed and altitude records, 1961-62; first astronaut so designated in a winged aircraft by flying to 59.6 miles, July 1962; squadron comdr. 36th Tactical Fighter Wing, Germany, 1963-65; student Indsl. Coll. Armed Forces, 1965-66; chief tactical systems office Wright-Patterson AFB, Ohio, 1966-67; stationed Vietnam, 1967-68; dir. F15 System Program Office, Wright-Patterson AFB, 1968-70; comdr. Air Force Flight Test Center, Edwards AFB, Calif., 1970-72; comdt. Air Force ROTC, Maxwell AFB, 1972-75, chief of staff 4th Allied Tactical Air Force, Germany, 1975—. Recipient Harmon Internat. Aviation trophy, 1961, Collier trophy, 1962. Address: Box 6892 APO New York City NY 09012

WHITE, ROBERT M., II, newspaperman; b. Mexico, Mo., Apr. 6, 1915; s. L. Mitchell and Maude (See) W.; grad. Mo. Mil. Acad., 1933; A.B., Washington and Lee U., 1938, LL.B. (hon.), 1972; m. Barbara Whitney Spurgeon, Aug. 19, 1948; children—Barbara Whitney, Jane See, Laura L., Robert M. White. Writer of newspaper articles, Australia, Africa, S.Am., Europe, USSR, 1966—, People's Republic China, 1972, 77; reporter Mexico (Mo.) Eve. Ledger, 1938-39, editor, pub., 1945—; vis. prof. Sch. Journalism, Mo. U., 1968-69; reporter UP Bur., Kansas City, 1939-40; v.p., sec., treas. Ledger Newspapers, Inc., Mexico, Mo., 1947-61, pres., 1961—; spl. cons. to pub. Chgo. Sun-Times, 1956-58; pres. Mark Land Co., Mexico, 1956—, See TV Co., Mexico, 1966—; editor pres., dir. N.Y. Herald Tribune, 1959-61; juror Pulitzer prize journalism, 1964-65; dir. Commerce Bank of Mexico, Commerce Bank of St. Louis, Butler Mfg. Co., Commerce Bancshares, Inc., AP. Bd. dirs. MacArthur Meml. Found.; vice-chmn. Washington Journalism Center; bd. dirs. Mo. Mil. Acad., Stephens Coll. Served to lt. col. AUS, 1940-45. Decorated Bronze Star; recipient nat. distinguished service award for editorials Sigma Delta Chi, 1952, 68; editorial award N.Y. Silurians, 1959; Distinguished Service to Journalism award U. Mo., 1967; Pres. award of merit Nat. Newspapers Assn., 1967; hon. col., Mo. Mem. Nat. Conf. Editorial Writers (past exec. council), Am. Soc. Newspaper Editors (dir. 1968-69, chmn. freedom of info. com. 1970-72), Am. Newspaper Pubs. Assn. (nat. treas. 1963, dir. 1955-63, past dir. research inst.), Inland Daily Press Assn. (chmn. bd. 1958-59, pres., past sec., v.p.), State Hist. Soc. Mo. (dir.), Mo. Press Assn. (dir.), Mo. Press-Bar Commn. (chmn. 1972-74), Sigma Delta Chi (nat. pres. 1967, pres. found. 1968), Beta Theta Pi. Democrat. Methodist. Clubs: Masons; Nat. Press; Rotary; Bohemian (San Francisco); Dutch Treat. Co-author: A Study of the Printing and Publishing Business in the Soviet Union. Home: 3 Park Circle Mexico MO 65265 Office: Ledger Ledger Plaza Mexico MO 65265

WHITE, ROBERT MAYER, scientist; b. Boston, Feb. 13, 1923; s. David and Mary (Winkeller) W.; B.A., Harvard, 1944; M.S., Mass. Inst. Tech., 1949, Sc.D., 1950; D.Sc. (hon.), L.I. U., 1976, Rensselaer Poly. Inst., 1977, U. Wis., Milw., 1978; m. Mavis Seagle, Apr. 18, 1948; children—Richard Harry, Edwina Janet. Project scientist, gen. circulation project Atmospheric Analysis Lab., Air Force Cambridge Research Center, 1950-52, chief large scale processes br., 1952-59, chief meteorol. devel. lab., 1958-59; research asso. Mass. Inst. Tech., 1959; asso. dir. research dept. Travelers Ins. Co., 1959-60; pres. Travelers Research Center, Inc., 1960-63; chief U.S. Weather Bur., 1963-65; adminstr. Environmental Sci. Services Adminstrn., 1965-70, Nat. Oceanic and Atmospheric Adminstrn., 1970-77; pres. Joint Oceanographic Inst., Inc., 1977-79; chmn. Climate Research Bd., Nat. Acad. Scis., 1977-79; adminstr. Nat. Research Council, exec. officer 1979—; permanent U.S. rep., mem. exec. com. World Meteorol. Orgn., 1963-77; U.S. commr. Internat. Whaling Commn., 1973-77; chmn. Marine Fisheries Adv. Com., 1970-77, World Climate Conf., 1979, mem. Nat. Adv. Com. Oceans and Atmosphere, 1979—. Bd. overseers Harvard U., 1977—; vis. com. meteorology and planetary sci. Mass. Inst. Tech.; trustee Univ. Corp. Atmospheric Research, 1977. Served to capt. USAAF, World War II. Recipient Jesse L. Rosenberger medal U. Chgo., 1971; Cleveland Abbe award Am. Meteorol. Soc., 1969; Godfrey L. Cabot award Aero Club Boston, 1966; Rockefeller Pub. Service award, 1974; David B. Stone award New Eng. Aquarium, 1975; Neptune award Am. Oceanic Orgn., 1977; Matthew Fontaine Maury award Smithsonian Instn., 1976; Internat. Conservation award Nat. Wildlife Fedn., 1976. Mem. Am. Meterol. Soc. (council 1965-67, 77—; Charles Franklin Brooks award 1978), Am. Geophys. Union, AAAS (chmn. sect. atmospheric and hydrospheric scis.), Royal Meteorol. Soc., Nat. Acad. Engring. (council 1977), Marine Tech. Soc. Club: Cosmos. Author articles in field. Home: 8306 Melody Ct Bethesda MD 20034 Office: Nat Acad Scis Washington DC 20230

WHITE, ROGER GREENLEES, fiber and licensing co. exec.; b. N.Y.C., Mar. 8, 1927; s. Edwin James and Ada Crawford (Greenlees) W.; B.S., Temple U., 1952, LL.B., 1954; m. Barbara Welsh, Oct. 20, 1953; children—Susan, Edwin, Christopher, Charles. Admitted to Pa. bar, 1955; partner firm Smyth, Straub & Thistle, Phila., 1961-72; gen. counsel Beaunit Corp., N.Y.C., 1972-73, v.p., gen. mgr. fiber div., 1974, exec. v.p., 1974-76, pres., chief operating officer, 1976—; pres. Joseph Bancroft & Sons Co., Wilmington, Del., 1975—; adj. prof. Temple U., 1960-72. Served with USNR, 1945-46. Mem. Am., Pa., Phila. bar assns. Home: Jericho Run Washington Crossing PA 18977 Office: 1000 Wade Ave Raleigh NC 27605 also 140 E State St Doylestown PA 18901

WHITE, RONALD LEON, mfg. co. exec.; b. West York, Pa., July 14, 1930; s. Clarence William and Grace Elizabeth (Gingerich) W.; B.S. in Econs., U. Pa., 1952, M.B.A., 1957; m. Estheranne Wieder, July 31, 1951; children—Bradford William, Clifford Allen, Erick David. Cost analysis supr. Air Products & Chem. Corp., Allentown, Pa., 1957-60; cost control mgr. Mack Trucks, Inc., Allentown, 1960-64; mgmt. cons. Peat, Marwick, Mitchell & Co., Phila., 1964-66; mgr. profit planning Monroe, The Calculator Co. (div. Litton Industries), Orange, N.J., 1966-67, controller, 1967-68, v.p. fin. Bus. Systems and Equipment Group, Beverly Hills, Calif., 1968-70; pres. Royal Typewriter Co. div., Hartford, Conn., 1970-73, exec. v.p., 1973-75, pres., 1975-77; exec. v.p., chief operating officer, treas. Tenna Corp., Cleve., 1973-75, pres., dir., 1975-77; chmn. bd., dir. Tenna, Inc., Delacor Corp., Tenna Dominicana, Inc., Tenna C.B. Inc., Tenna P.M. Inc.; pres., dir. Tenna Mirrors, Inc., Tenna Can. Ltd., Tenna Power Corp., Tenna Industries, Inc.; v.p., rep. dir. Tenna Far East Co., Ltd.; v.p. fin. Arby's, Inc., Youngstown, Ohio, 1978-79; exec. v.p., dir. Roxbury Am., Inc., Jeffran, Inc., Palm-Sunrise, Inc., Uncle John's of Hawaii, Inc., Uncle John's Family Restaurants, Ltd., Beverly Hills, Calif., 1979—; dir. ARCOP, Inc.; instr. accounting Wharton Sch. U. Pa., 1952-53, instr. industry, 1953-54. Bd. dirs. Jr. Achievement Hartford, 1971-73. Served to lt. USNR, 1954-57. Mem. Am. Mgmt. Assn., Nat. Assn. Accountants, Fin. Execs. Inst., Acacia. Mem. United Ch. Christ (deacon). Club: Masons. Home: 10762 Massachusetts Ave Los Angeles CA 90024 Office: 9808 Wilshire Blvd Beverly Hills CA 90212

WHITE, ROY BERNARD, assn. exec.; b. Cin., July 30, 1926; s. Maurice and Anna (Rudin) W.; B.A., U. Cin., 1949; student U. Miami (Fla.), 1946-47; m. Sally Lee Ostrom, June 17, 1951; children—Maurice Ostrom, Barbara Dee, Daniel Robert. Mem. sales staff Twentieth Century Fox Films, Cin., 1949-52; with Mid-States Theatres, Cin., 1952—, pres., 1962—; mem. Nat. Assn. Theatre Owners, N.Y.C., 1962—, dir., 1966-70, nat. pres., 1971-73, exec. com., 1971—, chmn. bd., 1973-75. Mem. film adv. panel Ohio Arts Council, 1974—; bd. dirs. Will Rogers Meml. Fund, Found. Motion Picture Pioneers, Inc.; mem. media arts panel Nat. Endowment for Arts, 1979—. Served with USAAF, 1944-45. Named Exhibitor of Year, Internat. Film Importers and Distbrs. Am., 1973; Ky. col. Mem. Am. Film Inst. (trustee 1972-75, exec. com. 1972-75), Alpha Epsilon Pi, Phi Eta Sigma. Jewish. Clubs: Masons; B'nai B'rith; Cin., Queen City Racquet; Crest Hills Country; Amberley Village Tennis (pres. 1972-73); Bankers. Home: 3140 N Whitetree Circle Cincinnati OH 45236 Office: 120 E 4th St Cincinnati OH 45202

WHITE, RUTH O'BRIEN (MRS. WALLACE B. WHITE), civic worker; b. N.Y.C., Dec. 20, 1909; d. Francis Athos and Caroline Rebecca (Young) O'Brien; student Packer Collegiate Inst., 1921-27, N.Y. Sch. Fine and Applied Art, 1927-30; m. Wallace Beasley White, June 5, 1931; 1 son, John Wallace. Dir.-at-large Nat. Tb Assn., 1949-57, 67—, sec. bd., 1957-60; chmn. med. social service com. United Hosp. Fund Bklyn., 1949-53, chmn. med. social service com. city wide orgn., 1962-66; mem. legis. com. United Hosp. Fund, 1970—, vice chmn. legislative com., 1970—, mem. exec. com., 1972—; del., mem. exec. com. Northeastern Tb Conf., 1960—, pres., 1962-63; dir. Brooklyn Tb and Health Assn., 1946—, v.p., 1957-60, pres., 1960-62, sec. bd. 1966-72, v.p. legis. com., 1978—; advisory com. N.Y. State Bd. Edn., div. vocational rehab., 1954-57. Bd. mgrs., exec. com. Bklyn. Thoracic Hosp., 1940-48, bd. trustees, 1948-57, pres. women's aux., 1956-57; women's exec. bd. Bklyn. Hosp. 1957—, v.p. bd., 1967-72, chmn. med. social service com., 1963—, chmn. com. legislation, 1972—; chmn. ann. meeting program com. Am. Lung Assn., 1973-74; v.p., mem. women's exec. bd. Bklyn. Philharmonic, 1967—; del. Nat. Social Welfare Assembly, 1957-68; mem. social service com. Cancer Care, Inc., 1966—, pub. relations com., 1969, bd. dirs., 1974—, pub. affairs com., 1976—; mem. program and budget com. Nat. Tb and Respiratory Disease Assn., 1967-69; mem. Council Tb and Respiratory Disease Assns. N.Y. State, 1968—; vice chmn. Council Lung Assns. N.Y. State, 1973-75, chmn., 1975—; mem. Action for Clean Air Com., 1965—; mem. housing and community task force Met. Assn., 1978—. Congregationalist (deaconess).

WHITE, SAMUEL, tobacco co. exec.; b. Malden, Mass., Mar. 29, 1919; s. Harry and Fanny (Guteman) W.; student Leland-Powers Coll., Boston; m. Faye Lillian Richardson, Oct. 5, 1942; children—Christopher A., Robert Lee, Sharon A. With Liggett & Myers Tobacco. Co., 1951—, asst. to pres., 1961, v.p. mktg., 1961-69, v.p., dir. corp. mktg., 1969—, also dir; pres. MPI Internat., Inc., MPI Holdings, Inc., N.Y.C.; dir. Paddington Corp., Nat. Oats Co., Brite Mfg. Co., Austin Nichols Co., Perk Foods Co., Pinkerton Tobacco Co., Carillon Corp., Lightolier, Inc. Trustee NCCJ, mem. exec. com., 1965—; co-chmn. tobacco and allied trades div. United Jewish Appeal; com. mem. Fedn. Charities, N.Y.C. Mem. Nat. Assn. Tobacco Distbrs. (mem. bd. young execs. div., dir. exec. mgmt. div.), Sales Execs. Club N.Y.C., Def. Supply Assn., Am. Mktg. Assn., Am. Mgmt. Assn., Grocery Mfrs. Am. Home: Rural Dr New Canaan CT 06840 Office: 770 Lexington Ave New York NY 10021

WHITE, SAMUEL KNOX, oil co. exec., lawyer; b. Narberth, Pa., July 1, 1918; s. Samuel Knox and Gertrude (Bottoms) W.; A.B., U. Pa., 1941, LL.B., 1947; m. Margaret Hough Fisher, May 17, 1949; children—Dana Lynne, Samuel Knox III. Admitted to Pa. bar, 1947; asso. firm Moffet, Frye & Leopold, Phila., 1947-60; partner firm Pepper, Hamilton & Scheetz, Phila., 1960-70; gen. counsel Sun Oil Co., Phila., 1970-72, v.p. legal affairs, 1972—; Treas. Meth. Home for Children, 1957-67, trustee, 1955-69. Served to capt. USAAF, 1942-45. Decorated Bronze Star medal, Belgian Fourragere. Mem. Am., Pa., Phila. bar assns., Phi Beta Kappa, Sigma Alpha Epsilon. Republican. Methodist. Home: 10 Summit Dr Millridge Bryn Mawr PA 19010 Office: 100 Matsonsford Rd Radnor PA 19087

WHITE, SAMUEL WALTER, JR., ret. farm equipment mfg. co. exec.; b. Evanston, Ill., Apr. 23, 1919; s. Samuel Walter and Helen A. (Newell) W.; A.B., Harvard U., 1940, M.B.A., 1942; m. Stephanie Day, July 11, 1942; children—Anne, Helen, Carolyn. With Oliver Corp., Chgo., 1939-68, asst. gen. sales mgr., Western dist. mgr., 1953-56, v.p. industrial sales, 1956-57, pres. Oliver Internat., 1957-60, pres. Oliver Corp., 1960-68; exec. v.p. farm group, dir. White Motor Corp., 1968-70; exec. v.p. Borg-Warner joint venture Aisin-Warner Ltd., Japan, 1971-74; exec. v.p. Kelley Mfg. Co., Tifton, Ga., 1975-76; v.p. mktg. Hesston Corp., 1977-79; dir. Central & S.W. Corp. Served to lt. USNR, World War II. Presbyterian. Home: 2018 Hogback Mountain Rd Tryon NC 28782. *My ideals have been shaped by my association with U.S. rural production agriculture. Farmers form the bulwark of our independent small businessmen. They carry on a proud tradition which founded this country and has sustained its growth. Generalizing their qualities, I see genuine independence, self-reliance, optimism, faith in God and fellow-man, work ethics, pride and success.*

WHITE, SHELDON HAROLD, educator, psychologist; b. N.Y.C., Nov. 30, 1928; s. Edward and Edith (Boorstein) W.; A.B., Harvard, 1951; M.A., Boston U., 1952; Ph.D., State U. Iowa, 1957; m. Barbara Elizabeth Notkin, June 29, 1958; children—Andrew Seth, Gregory Samuel. Instr., then asst. prof. U. Chgo., 1957-65; vis. research fellow, lectr. Harvard, 1963-64, mem. faculty, 1965—, prof. psychology, 1973—; cons. Rand Corp., Huron Inst. Served with AUS, 1952-54. Mem. Am. Psychol. Assn., A.A.A.S., Soc. Research Child Devel., Assn. Advancement Child Psychology and Psychiatry, Soc. Psychophysiol. Research, Sigma Xi. Author: Federal Programs for Young Children: Review and Recommendations. Editor psychol. jours. Contbr. chpts. to books, articles to profl. jours. Home: 214 Upland Rd Newtonville MA 02160 Office: Dept Psychology and Social Relations Harvard Univ Cambridge MA 02138

WHITE, STEPHEN, found. exec.; b. Boston, Nov. 22, 1915; student Harvard U., 1933-34, 37-38; m. Miriam Wheeler, Nov. 19, 1942; children—Lawrence, Geoffrey. Reporter, Boston Herald, 1942-43; mem. staff N.Y. Herald Tribune, 1943-50, roving European corr., 1948-50; European editor Look mag., 1950-51, asst. mng. editor, 1951-54; screen writer Twentieth-Century Fox, 1954-55; dir. film div. Edn. Services, Inc., Cambridge, Mass., 1956-60, dir. spl. projects, 1960-64; producer CBS News, N.Y.C., 1964-65; asst. to chmn. Carnegie Commn. Edl. TV, 1965-67; dir. spl. projects Salk Inst., La Jolla, Calif., 1967-69; program officer Alfred P. Sloan Found., N.Y.C.,

1969-70, v.p., 1970—; cons. in field. Author: Goals for School Mathematics, 1963; Students, Scholars and Parents, 1964; Medical Education Reconsidered, 1965; Public Television, 1967; Should We Now Believe the Warren Report?, 1968; On the Cable, 1972; also articles. Office: Alfred P Sloan Found 630 Fifth Ave New York City NY 10020

WHITE, STEVEN ANGELO, naval officer; b. Los Angeles, Sept. 18, 1928; s. Steven George and Helen Gloria (Blanchard) W.; B.A., U. So. Calif., 1951, student Sch. Law, M.A., 1952; m. Mary Anne Landreau, Jan. 27, 1951; children—Valerie Jeanne, Denise Marie White Walker, Lori Anne White Donlon, Steven Angelo, Kenneth Raymond, Brice Landreau, Mary Elizabeth. Commd. ensign U.S. Navy, 1952, advanced through grades to rear adm., 1974; served aboard U.S.S. Manchester, Korean War; engr. U.S.S. Tang, 1954-56; served aboard U.S.S. Nautilus, 1957-60, including Arctic exploratory ops., 1957, transpolar crossing, 1958; served aboard U.S.S. Ethan Allen, 1960-64, including Christmas Island test, 1962; force nuclear power tng. officer Dep. Comdr. Submarine Force, 1964-65, nuclear power tng. officer comdr. Submarine Force, U.S. Atlantic Fleet, 1965-66; comdg. officer U.S.S. Pargo, 1966-69; comdr. Submarine Div. One Hundred Two, 1969-70, Submarine Div. One Hundred One, 1970; served in Div. Naval Reactors, AEC, 1970-72; comdr. Submarine Squadron Sixteen, Rota, Spain, 1972-74; comdr. Submarine Group Two, New London, Conn., 1974-76; dep. chief naval ops. (ops. and logistics), Washington, 1976-78; asst. dep. chief naval ops. (submarine warfare), Navy Dept., Washington, 1978—. Decorated Navy Commendation medal, Legion of Merit with 2 gold stars, Meritorious Service medal. Office: OPNAV (OP-02B) Washington DC 20350

WHITE, STODDARD, banker; b. Evanston, Ill., Oct. 23, 1923; s. Harry E. and Vance (Heffelfinger) W.; B.S. in Law, Denver U., 1949, J.D, 1950; m. Margaret Mary Meyer, Sept. 6, 1952; children—Marianne, Janet Vance, Stoddard. With Ill.-Calif. Express, Inc., 1949-70, v.p., 1961, pres., 1961-70, also dir.; v.p., dir. Carbon Motorway, Salt Lake City, 1956-59; pres., dir. T O C, Inc., real estate, Denver, 1965-70; dir. Ill.-Calif. Terminals, 1954-63; v.p., dir. Frontier, Inc., 1962-63; admitted to Colo. bar, 1950; v.p., trust officer Mountain States Bank, 1970—, also dir. Served with USNR, 1942-46. Mem. Colo., Denver bar assns., Denver (bd. dirs. 1964-65), Colo. (bd. dirs. 1964-65) chambers commerce, Colo. Assn. Commerce and Industry (chmn. transp. com. 1966), Gyro Internat., Phi Delta Phi. Republican. Episcopalian. Clubs: Denver Country; Grand Lake (Colo.) Yacht (commodore 1973-74). Home: 5221 E 17th Ave Denver CO 80220 Office: 1635 E Colfax Ave Denver CO 80218

WHITE, TERRY ROSS, hosp. adminstr.; b. Athens, Ohio, Nov. 6, 1940; s. Denver L. and Clea (Dusz) W.; B.A., Ohio U., 1962; M.B.A., Xavier U., 1966; m. Cynthia Comerford, May 30, 1966; 1 dau., Stephanie; 1 stepdau., Ann. Adminstrv. asst. Ohio Dept. Health, Columbus, 1963-64; adminstrv. resident Charleston (W. Va.) Gen. Hosp., 1965-66, adminstrv. asst., 1966-67; asst. adminstr. South Side Hosp., Youngstown, Ohio, 1967-68, adminstr., 1968—; pres. Luth. Med. Center, Cleve., 1974—. Bd. dirs. Ohio Hosp. Mgmt. Services, Cleve. Vis. Nurse Assn., Ohio City Redevel. Assn. Served to 1st lt. AUS, 1963-69. Mem. Am., Ohio hosp. assns., Am. Pub. Health Assn., Am. Coll. Hosp. Adminstrs. Club: Clevelander. Home: 575 Crestview Dr Bay Village OH 44140 Office: 2609 Franklin Blvd Cleveland OH 44113

WHITE, THEODORE HAROLD, author; b. Boston, May 6, 1915; s. David and Mary (Winkeller) W.; A.B. summa cum laude, Harvard U., 1938; m. Nancy Ariana Bean, Mar. 29, 1947 (div. 1971); children—Ariana Van Der Heyden, David Fairbank; m. 2d, Beatrice K. Hofstadter, Mar. 1974. Chief of China bur. Time, Inc., 1939-45; covered China war front, Indian Uprising, Honan famine; present at surrender of Japanese aboard U.S.S. Missouri; editor The New Republic, 1947; nat. corr. The Reporter mag.; mem. staff of Colliers, 1955-56; as corr. covered Europe, Marshall Plan, NATO, others, also reported Am. nat. politics, 1955-78; dir. Ency. Brit. Bd. overseers Harvard U., 1968-74; past trustee Asia Soc. Recipient Air medal, 1944; Sidney Hillman award, 1954, Benjamin Franklin award, 1956, Ted V. Rodgers award, 1956; Secondary Sch. Bd. award, 1955, 59, 62; Pulitzer prize, 1962; Sigma Delta Chi award, 1964; Emmy award for best TV show, 1964, for best documentary TV writing, 1967. Mem. Council Fgn. Relations. Clubs: Fgn. Corrs. (pres. 1944-45) (China); Harvard, Century (N.Y.C.). Author: (with Annalee Jacoby) Thunder Out of China (Book of Month Club selection), 1946; The Mountain Road (Book of Month Club selection), 1958; The View from the Fortieth Floor (Lit. Guild selection), 1960; The Making of the President, 1960 (Book of Month Club selection), 1961; The Making of the President, 1964, 1965; Caesar at the Rubicon, 1968; The Making of the President, 1968; The Making of the President, 1972 (Lit. Guild selection), 1973; Breach of Faith (Book of Month Club selection), 1975; In Search of History: A Personal Adventure, 1978; editor: The Stillwell Papers, 1948; Fire in the Ashes (Book of Month Club selection 1953), 1953; contbr. to nat. mags. Home: Old Route 67 Bridgewater CT 06752 Office: 168 E 64th St New York City NY 10021

WHITE, THOMAS, judge; b. Humphrey, Nebr., Oct. 5, 1928; s. John Ambrose and Margaret Elizabeth (Costello) W.; J.D., Creighton U., 1952; m. Joan White, Oct. 9, 1971; children—Michaela, Thomas, Patrick. Admitted to Nebr. bar; county atty. Platte County, Columbus, Nebr., 1955-65; dist. judge 21st Dist. Ct. Nebr., Columbus, 1965-77; judge Nebr. Supreme Ct., Lincoln, 1977—. Served with U.S. Army, 1946-47. Roman Catholic. Clubs: Elks, K.C. Home: 5927 Rolling Hills Lincoln NE 68512 Office: Capitol Bldg Lincoln NE 68509*

WHITE, THOMAS EDWARD, mfg. co. exec., lawyer; b. N.Y.C., July 11, 1933; s. Thomas Aubrey and Gladys Mary (Piper) W.; A.B., Princeton, 1955; LL.B., Columbia, 1960; m. Joan Carolyn Olsen, Dec. 2, 1967; children—Charles Garret, Nancy Carolyn, Linda Marie, Penelope Lindsay, Elizabeth Ann. Admitted to N.Y. bar, 1961; atty. Seward & Kissel, N.Y.C., 1960-69; gen. counsel Howmet Corp., N.Y.C., 1969-70; v.p., gen. counsel, sec. Howmedica, Inc., N.Y.C., 1970-74, sr. v.p., dir., 1974—. Mem. Mamaroneck Town Council, 1971-75. Served as 1st lt. AUS, 1955-57. Republican. Presbyterian (elder 1971-73). Club: Larchmont (N.Y.) Yacht; Princeton (N.Y.C.). Home: 260 Barnard Rd Larchmont NY 10538 Office: 235 E 42d St New York City NY 10017

WHITE, THOMAS JUSTIN, JR., editor; b. Bklyn., May 27, 1919; s. Thomas Justin and Virginia (Gilette) W.; grad. high sch.; m. Sarah Simmons Harris, Aug. 13, 1949; children—Ailla Hugh Harris, Thomas Justin. Reporter, picture editor Balt. News Post, 1945-50; news and publicity dir. Sta. WBAL-TV, Balt., 1950-54; nat. corr. Hearst Washington Bur., 1954-56; publicity dir., city editor, news supr., mng. editor, now sr. editor Balt. News American, 1956—. Served in USN, 1942-45. Recipient Best Story on Horse Racing award Thoroughbred Racing Assn., 1957. Republican. Club: Mchts. (Balt.). Office: Balt News Am 301 E Lombard St PO Box 1795 Baltimore MD 21203*

WHITE, THURMAN JAMES, ret. univ. ofcl.; b. Ponca City, Okla., Nov. 7, 1916; s. Charles L. and Wilnona Faye (Enfield) W.; A.B., Phillips U., 1936; M.S., U. Okla., 1941; Ph.D., U. Chgo., 1950; m. Corrine Laura Hartson, June 13, 1939; children—Sue Ann, Charles Frank. Instr. prison edn. U. Okla., 1937-39, supr. Statewide Mus. Service, 1940-42, dir. audio-visual edn., 1942-46, asst. dir. extension div., 1946-47 (on leave), acting dir., 1947-48, dir., 1949-50, dean extension div., 1950-68, dean coll. continuing edn., 1961-68; v.p. U. Okla., 1968-80, v.p. emeritus, 1980—; fellow Rewley House, lectr., Oxford, Eng., 1967. Mem. Dept. Def. Adv. Com. Edn. Armed Forces, 1957-60, chmn., 1960-61; state chmn. 1960 White House Conf. on Children and Youth; exec. vice chmn. 1961 White House Conf. on Aging; mem. UNESCO, 1963—; mem. Pres.'s Nat. Adv. Council on Extension and Continuing Edn., 1967—; mem. Gov.'s Commn. Econ. Opportunity; bd. dirs. Great Books Found., Center for Study Liberal Edn. for Adults; mem. council higher edn. for adults So. Regional Edn. Bd.; adv. bd. Servicemen's Opportunity Coll., 1978—. Mem. C. of C., Okla. Congress Parents and Tchrs., Okla. Edn. Assn., Okla. Mental Health Assn. (pres. 1960-61), Adult Edn. Assn. U.S.A. (pres. 1965-66), Am. Council Edn. (commn. ednl. credit 1977—), Nat. Univ. Extension Assn. (pes. 1960-61), Southwest Adult Edn. Assn. (exec. com.), Okla. Adult Edn. Assn., Phi Beta Kappa, Phi Delta Kappa, Psi Chi, Pi Kappa Alpha. Clubs: Internat. (Washington); Rotary. Editor: Adult Education. Author articles ednl. jours. Home: 1105 Woodland Dr Norman OK 73069 Office: U Okla 1700 Asp Ave Norman OK 73037

WHITE, WARREN KEITH, telephone co. exec.; b. Johnston County, N.C., Oct. 30, 1935; s. Mervin Lee and Nancy Marie (Peedin) W.; A.B., East Carolina U., 1960; m. Mary Patricia Walters, Aug. 17, 1958; 1 dau., Mary Elizabeth. Coll. trainee Carolina Tel. & Tel. Co., Tarboro, N.C., 1960-62, accountant, 1962-64, disbursement accounting mgr., 1964-65, cost accounting mgr., 1965-75, asst. controller, 1975-76, sec., treas., 1976—. Campaign chmn. Tarboro United Fund, 1971, pres., 1972, bd. dirs., 1968—; mem. Tarboro City Sch. Bd., 1976—; mem. Friends of Edgecombe Library, 1969—; mem. N. Tarboro PTA, 1974-77, pres., 1976-77. Served with U.S. Army, 1954-57. Recipient Distinguished Service award Tarboro Jaycees, 1967. Baptist. Clubs: Tarboro Optimist (charter mem., past lt. gov. N.C. dist.), Hilma Country. Home: 1602 Pine St Tarboro NC 27886 Office: 122 East St James St Tarboro NC 27886

WHITE, WARREN TRAVIS, savs. and loan assn. exec.; b. Bell County, Tex., Dec. 17, 1895; s. Warren W. and Dollie (Plaster) W.; A.B., U. Tex., 1926, A.M., 1931; LL.D., Baylor U., 1952, Tex. Christian U., 1954; m. Leika Clark, May 3, 1917; children—Frances, Naomi (dec.), Warren Travis. Supt., Fairview (Tex.) Schs., 1922-26, Wichita Falls, Tex., 1926-27, Bonham, Tex., 1927-31; prin. Sunset High Sch., Dallas, 1931-41, asst. supt. pub. schs., Dallas, 1941-45, supt., 1945-68; now chmn. bd. Met. Savs. & Loan Assn., Dallas. Mem. Tex. Tchr. Retirement Bd.; pres. Tex. Masonic Sch. Dist. Bd. Served as 1st lt., F.A., U.S. Army, World War I. Mem. NEA (life), Am. Assn. Sch. Adminstrs. (past pres., chmn. yearbook commn.), Tex. Tchrs. Assn., Tex. Secondary Prins. Assn. (past pres.), Phi Beta Kappa, Phi Delta Kappa. Mem. Christian Ch. Clubs: Masons (32 deg.), KCCH, K.T., Shriners, Rotary. Home: 2831 Whitewood Dr Dallas TX 75233 Office: 1401 Main St Dallas TX 75202

WHITE, WARREN WURTELE, retailing corp. exec.; b. McKeesport, Pa., Feb. 29, 1932; s. Jay Leonard and Elizabeth Katherine (Fehr) W.; B.S., Duquesne U., 1954; M.Retailing, U. Pitts., 1957; m. Marjorie Ada Shuman, Mar. 20, 1954; 1 dau., Laura Lynn. With Strawbridge & Clothier, Phila., 1957—, buyer, 1960-67, budget store divisional mdse. mgr., 1968-70, Clover Div. gen. mdse. mgr., 1970-76, v.p. for mdse. and sales promotion, 1977-78, exec. v.p. Strawbridge & Clothier, gen. mgr. Clover Div., 1978—. Bd. dirs. Eastern Star Charity Found. N.J., 1978—. Served to 1st lt. Arty., U.S. Army, 1954-56. Republican. Presbyterian. Clubs: Tavistock (N.J.); Downtown (Phila.), Masons. Home: 1 Heritage Rd Haddonfield NJ 08033 Office: Clover Div Strawbridge & Clothier 801 Market St Philadelphia PA 19105

WHITE, WILLIAM, journalist, editor; b. Paterson, N.J., Sept. 4, 1910; s. Noel D. and Beccia (Firkser) W.; A.B., U. Tenn., Chattanooga, 1933; M.A., U. So. Calif., 1937; student U. Dijon (France), 1951; Ph.D., U. London, 1953; m. Gertrude Mason, June 20, 1951; children—Geoffrey, Roger. Reporter, corr. Chattanooga Times, 1925-34, Hartford Courant, 1931-33, Internat. News Service, 1931, Los Angeles Exam., 1934, Belton Jour., 1946, Detroit Free Press, 1955; editor Four Corners Press, 1954, Rochester Clarion, East Sider, East Side Shopper (all 1955), Wayne Dispatch, 1956, Inkster Jour., Dearborn Press, 1957, Southfield News, 1959, Troy Times, Berkeley Advance, Clawson Times (all 1960), corr., 1961-70, Courier Newspapers, Detroit, 1967; book reviewer Detroit News, 1971-74, Library Jour., 1971—; corr. Dearborn Leader Newspapers, 1972-74, Birmingham Eccentric-Observer, 1974, Pontiac-Waterford Times, 1975—, Oakland Press, 1975—, Book Collector's Market, 1976, Rochester Times, 1978, Oxford-Orion Times, 1978—, Birmingham Patriot, 1978—, Reprint Bull.-Book Revs., 1979—; copy editor Los Angeles Times, 1973; vis. editor Saugatuck Comml. Record, 1978, Whitman Supplement, Long Islander, 1976—; asst. U. So. Calif., 1934-41, UCLA, 1937-40; instr. liberal arts Pacific States U., 1938-41; instr. Whitman Coll., 1941-42; dir. publicity, asst. prof., chmn. dept. journalism Mary Hardin-Baylor Coll., 1946-47, Ohio Wesleyan U., 1947; asst. prof. journalism Wayne State U., 1947-54, asso. prof., 1954-60, prof., 1960-74, acting chmn. dept., 1957, 66-67, dir. Am. studies, 1967-74, vis. prof., 1974-80; prof. communication arts and journalism, dir. journalism program Oakland U., 1974—; vis. prof. U. So. Calif., summer 1962, 79, U. R.I., summer 1966, Calif. State U., Long Beach, 1969, U. Hawaii, summer 1969; vis. prof. U. Fla., 1979; Fulbright prof. Am. lit. Chungang U., Hankuk U. Fgn. Studies, Soong Sil Coll. (all Seoul, Korea), 1963-64. Served with Intelligence Corps, AUS, 1942-45. Recipient Disting. Service award Baylor Sch., 1971; fellow Found. Econ. Edn., 1956, Nat. Endowment Humanities, 1967-68, 70, 72; Am. Philos. Soc. research grantee, 1965; research fellow Oakland U., 1980. Mem. AAUP, MLA, Bibliog. Soc. Am., Am. Assn. History Medicine, Assn. Edn. Journalism, Am. Studies Assn., Modern Humanities Research Assn., Book Club Detroit, Friends Detroit Pub. Library, Pvt. Libraries Assn., Colby Library Assos., Mich. Acad. Sci., Arts and Letters, Thoreau Soc., Australian Med. Congress, Soc. Profl. Journalists, Sigma Delta Chi, Theta Chi, Blue Key, Alpha Scholastic Soc. Author: A Henry David Thoreau Bibliography, 1908-37, 1939; The Parallelogram, The Amphisbaena, The Crocodile by A.E. Housman (edited with intro.), 1941; John Donne Since 1900, 1942; D.H. Lawrence: A Checklist, 1931-50, 1950; This is Detroit 1701-1951 (with M.M. Quaife), 1951; Sir William Osler: Historian and Literary Essayist, 1951; John Ciardi: A Bibliography, 1959; W.D. Snodgrass: A Bibliography, 1960: Karl Shapiro: A Bibliography, 1960; Ernest Hemingway: Guide to a Memorial Exhibition, 1961; Wilfred Owen (1893-1918): A Bibliography, 1967; Walt Whitman's Journalism: A Bibliography, 1969; Guide to Ernest Hemingway, 1969; Checklist of Ernest Hemingway, 1970; Edwin Arlington Robinson: A Supplementary Bibliography, 1971; Nathanael West: A Comprehensive Bibliography, 1975; contbg. editor: Modern Humanities Research Assn. Ann. Bibliography of English Lit., 1949—; Walt Whitman Rev., 1956—, Wayne Journalism Newsletter, 1956-74, Die Casting Engr., 1961-62; (with others) Collected Writings of Walt Whitman, 1961—; Michigan Sportscene, 1967-69; (with H.W. Blodgett) Walt Whitman: An 1855-56 Notebook, 1959; A.E. Housman: A Centennial Memento, 1959; Walt Whitman: The People and John Quincy Adams, 1961, rev. edit., 1962; By-Line: Ernest Hemingway, 1967, London edit., 1968 (transl. 13 langs.); Am. Lit. Scholarship, 1967-71; Studies in The Sun Also Rises, 1969; Walt Whitman in Our Time: Four Essays, 1970; (with R. Asselineau) Walt Whitman in Europe Today, 1972; Ernest Bramah: Kai Lung: Six, 1974; Aphorisms of Kai Lung, 1980; The Bicentennial Walt Whitman, 1976; The SDX Times, 1977; Odyssey: A Journal of the Humanities, 1977—; Jour. of Book Club Detroit, 1978—; Daybooks and Notebooks of Walt Whitman, 1978; (with others) Walt Whitman, Variorum Edition, Leaves of Grass, 1980; gen. editor Serif Series in Bibliography, 1966-75; asso. editor Am. Book Collector, 1965-77; editorial bd. Emily Dickinson Bull., 1972—, U. Miss. Studies in English, 1980—; contbr. New Cambridge Bibliography English Lit., 1968, 72; also articles profl. jours. Home: 25860 W 14 Mile Rd Franklin MI 48025 Office: Oakland U Rochester MI 48063. *Is there a "formula" for success? I doubt it, but a comment may serve. With a certain intelligence, sensitivity (but not too much), an optimistic temperament, experience (what you learn from books and your own coming and going), a sense of humor (so you won't take yourself too seriously), energy, good health, and lots of luck, you may succeed in doing what you set out to do, get a little recognition and some satisfaction; you may even make some money, though that's not important, only pleasant. If you keep busy enough and have the love of one wife and a few good friends, you can find pleasure in life and forget the corruptibility of man.*

WHITE, WILLIAM ALLEN, civil engr.; b. Joliet, Mont., Mar. 27, 1906; s. William McCord (Compton) W.; B.A. in Math., U. Mont., Missoula, 1930, M.A., 1937; m. Lucille Virginia Emmett, Mar. 10, 1934; children—Mack William, Virginia Frances. Tchr. sci. and math. Joliet High Sch., 1932-34; civilian engr. U.S. Corps Engrs., 1934-42, 45-47; statistician Q.M.C., Washington, 1942-45; sec. Calif. Bd. Registration Profl. Engrs., Sacramento, 1948-55; exec. dir. Calif. Council Civil Engrs. and Land Surveyors, 1956-76; panelist Am. Arbitration Assn., 1975—; bd. dirs. Design Professionals Safety Assn., 1976—; trustee, sec. Civil Engrs. and Land Surveyors Trust, 1969—. Recipient Service to Profession award Engring. Council Sacramento Valley, 1968; also various citations, commendations. Life mem. ASCE (Surveying and Mapping award 1976), Am. Congress Surveying and Mapping; mem. Am. Soc. Assn. Execs. Republican. Baptist. Club: Joliet Masons. Author manuals, papers, editor guides. Address: 5505 8th Ave Sacramento CA 95820

WHITE, WILLIAM BLAINE, educator; b. Huntingdon, Pa., Jan. 5, 1934; s. William Bruce and Eleanor Mae (Barr) W.; B.S., Juniata Coll., 1954; Ph.D., Pa. State U., 1962; m. Elizabeth Loczi, Mar. 27, 1959; children—Nikki Elizabeth, William Brion. Research asso. Mellon Inst., Pitts., 1954-58; asst. prof. Pa. State U., University Park, 1963-67, asso. prof., 1967-72, prof. geochemistry, 1972—. Asso. editor The American Mineralogist, 1972-75; earth scis. editor Nat. Speleological Soc. Bull., 1971—. Contbr. articles to profl. jours. Home: 542 Glenn Rd State College PA 16801 Office: Materials Research Lab Pa State U University Park PA 16802

WHITE, WILLIAM D., lawyer; b. Clinton, Miss., Mar. 23, 1909; s. Nola and Elizabeth (Boone) W.; student Miss. State Coll., 1926-27; LL.B., U. Tex., 1931; m. Jean Tullis, June 17, 1929; children—Carolyn (dec.), William D. Admitted to Tex. bar, 1931, since practiced in Dallas; mem. firm White, McElroy & White, 1963—; v.p., gen. counsel Yellow Cab Dallas, Inc.; dir., gen. counsel Dr. Pepper Co., Surtran Taxicabs, Inc. Pres., Young Democratic Club Dallas County, 1934; mem. Camp Bd. Underprivileged Children. Fellow Tex. Bar Found. (life); mem. Am., Tex., Dallas (1st v.p. 1949) bar assns., U. Tex. Law Sch. Alumni Assn. (pres. 1953), Jaycees (state dir.), Salesmanship Club (life). Home: 3421 Villanova St Dallas TX 75225 Office: Republic Nat Bank Tower Dallas TX 75201

WHITE, WILLIAM HENRY, editor, author; b. Glendale, Calif., Sept. 9, 1924; s. William Henry and Esther Ruth (Engel) W.; student U. Mo., 1942; B.A., Columbia, 1948, M.S. in Journalism, 1949; m. Virginia S. Stockton, Jan. 27, 1950; children—Victoria, Deborah. Reporter, N.Y. Times, 1948-49; book editor Look, Quick, Flair mags., Cowles Mags., Inc., 1949-51; med. and sci. editor Look mag., N.Y.C., 1951-54; med. editor Sports Illus., 1954-55; mng. editor Med. News, 1956-59; exec. editor Med. World News, 1959-68; pres., editor Family Health mag., 1969-74; editorial dir. Med. Opinion mag., 1974-77; pres. Newspaperbooks, 1974-78; editor-pub. Cost Containment Newsletter, 1978—; internat. exec. editor World Medicine, Eng. also Medicine Mondiale, France; free-lance writer in field medicine and sci.; writer with 3d Am. Karakoram Expdn., Pakistan, 1953. Asso. Commonwealth Fund, 1955-56. Bd. dirs., v.p. World Rehab. Fund, The Seeing Eye; pres. White Plains Hosp. Med. Center; treas. Royal Soc. Medicine Found. Mem. Nat. Assn. Sci. Writers, Sigma Delta Chi, Phi Kappa Psi. Clubs: Scarsdale Golf (pres.); Oyster Harbor Golf. Home: 23 Oak Ln Scarsdale NY 10583 Office: 322 W 57th St New York NY 10019

WHITE, WILLIAM MATHEWS, JR., investment co. exec.; b. Pueblo, Colo., May 30, 1939; s. William Mathews and Helen (Thatcher) W.; B.A. magna cum laude, Yale, 1961. Vice pres. Allen & Co., Inc., N.Y.C., 1962-66; chmn. bd. Colo. Milling & Elevator Co., Denver, 1966-67; pres., chmn. bd. Gt. Western United Corp., 1968-72; gen. partner Thatcher Partners, 1968-73; prin. William M. White & Assos., N.Y.C., 1973—; owner, dir. The Children's Design Center, Inc., Denver, 1978—; owner, chief exec. officer Saratoga Vichy Spring Co., Saratoga Springs, N.Y., 1978—; pres. Levitt Overseas Exploration Ltd., 1976—. Mem. exec. com. Colo. Environmental Commn., 1970-72; mem. Denver Planning Bd., 1971-73. Trustee Denver Art Mus., 1971—, Whitney Mus. Am. Art, 1969-73, Thatcher Found., 1969-72, Gt. Western United Found., 1969-72, Rocky Mountain Center Environment, 1969-72, Nat. Park Found., 1970—; vis. com. Alfred P. Sloan Sch. Mgmt., M.I.T. Club: Yale (N.Y.C.). Office: care Saratoga Springs Co Inc RD 4 Geyser Rd Saratoga Springs NY 12866

WHITE, WILLIAM NORTH, chemist; b. Walton, N.Y., Sept. 16, 1925; s. George Fitch and Frances (Peck) W.; A.B., Cornell U., 1950; M.A., Harvard U., 1951, Ph.D., 1953; m. Hilda R. Sauter, Sept. 8, 1951; children—Carla Ann, Eric Jeffrey. NRC postdoctoral fellow Calif. Inst. Tech., Pasadena, 1953-54; asst. prof. Ohio State U., Columbus, 1954-59, asso. prof., 1959-63; prof. chemistry U. Vt., Burlington, 1963-76, 77—, chmn. dept., 1963-70, acting chmn. dept., 1975-76; prof. chemistry U. Tex. at Arlington, 1976-77, chmn. dept., 1976-77; NSF sr. postdoctoral fellow Brookhaven Nat. Lab., Upton, N.Y., 1963-64, Harvard U., 1965; vis. scholar Brandeis U., 1974-75; chmn. arrangements com. Nat. Organic Chemistry Symposium, 1965-67. Selectman, Town of Shelburn (Vt.), 1968-74, water commr., 1973-74. Served with AUS, 1943-46. Mem. Am. Chem. Soc. (chmn. Western Vt. sect. 1966-67), Chem. Soc. (Eng.), New Eng. Assn. Chemistry Tchrs., AAAS, N.Y. Acad. Scis., Phi Beta Kappa, Sigma Xi, Phi Kappa Phi, Phi Lambda Upsilon. Contbr. articles on organic chemistry profl. jours. Home: Pierson Dr Shelburne VT 05482 Office: Dept Chemistry U Vt Burlington VT 05401

WHITE, WILLIAM SAMUEL, found. exec.; b. Cin., May 8, 1937; s. Nathaniel Ridgway and Mary (Loundes) W.; B.A., Dartmluth Coll., 1959, M.B.A., Amos Tuck Sch., 1960; H.H.D. (hon.), Eastern Mich. U., 1975; m. Claire Mott, July 1, 1961; 1 dau., Tiffany White Loundes. With Barrett & Williams, N.Y.C., 1961-62; sr. asso. Bruce Payne & Assos., N.Y.C., 1962-71; v.p. C. S. Mott Found., Flint, Mich., 1971-75, pres., 1976—, trustee, 1971—; dir. U.S. Sugar Corp., Continental Water Corp. Mem. exec. com. Daycroft Sch., Greenwich, Conn., 1966-70; bd. dirs. Flint Area Conf., 1971—; mem. citizens adv. task force U. Mich., Flint, 1974—. Served with U.S. Army, 1960-62. Mem. Council Mich. Founds. (chmn. 1978—). Independent Republican. Christian Scientist. Clubs: Flint City, Univ. (Flint); Bath and Tennis (Palm Beach, Fla.). Office: Mott Found Bldg 503 S Saginaw St Flint MI 48502

WHITE, WILLIAM THEODORE, JR., food co. exec.; b. Dayton, Ohio, Nov. 1, 1925; s. William Theodore and Helen (Blackman) W.; student Harvard U., 1943-44; A.B., Dartmouth Coll., 1946; eve. student Northwestern U., 1946-50; C.P.A., Ill., 1950; m. Patrice Elizabeth Duncan, Oct. 10, 1953; children—Melissa Patrice, William Theodore. Staff accountant Arthur Young & Co., 1946-56; controller, asst. sec. Booth Fisheries Corp., 1956-65; asst. treas. Consol. Foods Corp., 1965-66, treas., 1966-68, v.p., treas., 1968—, dir., 1968-75. Served with USNR, 1943-45. Mem. Ill. Soc. C.P.A.'s (dir. 1965-67). Presbyterian (deacon). Clubs: Econ., Univ., Curling (Chgo.); Skokie Country (Glencoe, Ill.). Home: 3005 Iroquois Rd Wilmette IL 60091 Office: 135 S LaSalle St Chicago IL 60603

WHITE, WILLIS SHERIDAN, JR., utilities exec.; b. nr. Portsmouth, Va., Dec. 17, 1926; s. Willis Sheridan and Carrie (Culpepper) W.; B.S., Va. Poly. Inst., 1948; M.S., Mass. Inst. Tech., 1958; m. LaVerne Behrends, Oct. 8, 1949; children—Willis Sheridan, Marguerite Louise White Spangler, Cynthia Diane. With Am. Electric Power Co. System, 1948—, asst. engr. Am. Electric Power Service Corp., N.Y.C., 1948, asst. to pres., 1952-54, office mgr., 1954-57, adminstrv. asst. to operating v.p., 1958-61, div. mgr. Appalachian Power Co., Lynchburg, Va., 1962-66, asst. gen. mgr., Roanoke, Va., 1966-67, asst. v.p., 1967-69, v.p., 1969, exec. v.p., dir., 1969-73, sr. exec. v.p. ops., dir. Am. Electric Power Service Corp., N.Y.C., 1967—, vice chmn. ops., dir., 1975—; dir. Am. Electric Power Co., N.Y.C., 1972—, chmn. bd., chief exec. officer, 1976—; pres., dir. Appalachian Power Co., Ohio Valley Electric Corp., Ind.-Ky. Electric Corp.; dir. Beech Bottom Power Co., Cardinal Operating Co., Castlegate Coal Co., Cedar Coal Co., Central Appalachian Coal Co., Central Coal Co., Central Ohio Coal Co., Central Operating Co., Franklin Real Estate Co., Ind. Franklin Realty Co., Ind. & Mich. Electric Co., Ind. & Mich. Power Co., Kanawha Valley Power Co., Ky. Power Co., Kingsport Power Co., Mich. Gas Exploration Co., Mich. Power Co., Ohio Electric Co., Ohio Power Co., So. Appalachian Coal Co., So. Ohio Coal Co., Twin Br. R.R. Co., W.Va. Power Co., Wheeling Electric Co., Windsor Power House Coal Co.; adv. com. Edison Electric Inst. Trustee Randolph-Macon Woman's Coll.; bd. dirs. Downtown-Lower Manhattan Assn. Served with USNR, 1945-46. Sloan fellow, 1957-58. Mem. Assn. Edison Illuminating Cos. (exec. com.), NAM (dir.), Downtown Lower Manhattan Assn., Eta Kappa Nu. Methodist. Office: 2 Broadway New York NY 10004

WHITE, WILLMON LEE, mag. editor; b. Lamesa, Tex., Mar. 10, 1932; s. Aubrey F. and Jewel (Henderson) W.; B.A., McMurry Coll., Abilene, Tex., 1953; M.A., U. Tex., 1956; m. Carol A. Nelson, Nov. 2, 1957 (div.); children—Tracy, Wrenn, Gehrig, Bob; m. 2d, Barbara K. Kelly, Sept. 16, 1977; 1 dau., Theresa. Reporter, Abilene Reporter-News, 1953-54; public relations writer Tex. Ins. Adv. Assn., Austin, 1955-56; asst. editor Humble Way mag. Humble Oil & Refining Co. (Exxon), Houston, 1956-65; asso. editor, news editor Together mag. Methodist Ch., Park Ridge, Ill., 1965-69; sr. editor World Book Ency., Chgo., 1969-70; asst. editor, then asso. editor The Rotarian mag., publ. Rotary Internat., Evanston, Ill., 1970-74, editor, 1974—, mgr. communications div., under sec., 1979—; intern Newsweek mag., 1954. Mem. Am. Soc. Mag. Editors, Sigma Delta Chi. Club: Evanston Rotary. Office: 1600 Ridge Ave Evanston IL 60201

WHITE, ZEBULON WATERS, forester; b. Balt., Oct. 3, 1915; s. William Zebulon and Madeline Wood (Shepard) W.; A.B., Dartmouth, 1936; M.F., Yale, 1938; m. Marjorie E. Belcher, Aug. 29, 1939; children—Susan, Jonathan, William, Ted. With WPA in Ohio Forest Survey, 1939-40; with Pomeroy & McGowin, cons. foresters, Monticello, Ark., 1940-58, mgr., partner, 1945-58; Clifton R. Musser prof. indsl. forestry Sch. Forestry Yale, 1958-72, asso. dean, 1965-71; cons. forester large indsl. timberland owners, 1972—; pres. Zebulon White & Co., 1972—. Pres., Univ. Research Inst. Conn., 1971. Mem. Soc. Am. Foresters. Home: 114 Arbordale Dr Hammond LA 70401

WHITEFORD, WILLIAM HAMILTON, lawyer; b. Balt., July 28, 1903; s. W. Hamilton and Laura (McCarty) W.; B.S., U. Md., 1926, LL.B., 1930; m. Lydia Burnham, Aug. 12, 1930; children—David H., Richard C., William B. Admitted to Md. bar, 1930, since practiced in Balt.; partner firm Whiteford, Taylor, Preston, Trimble & Johnston, and predecessors, 1940—. Dir. various corps. Chmn. Balt. Mayor's Task Force on Alcoholism. Bd. dirs. Hosp. Cost Analysis Service, Inc. Fellow Am. Coll. Trial Lawyers; mem. Balt. City Bar Assn. (pres. 1965-66). Club: Barristers (past pres.) (Balt.). Home: 201 Kemble Rd Baltimore MD 21218 Office: IBM Bldg Baltimore MD 21202

WHITEHEAD, ALBERT EDWARD, educator; b. Denver, Feb. 28, 1907; s. Albert and Gena (Shaker) W.; B.A., U. Colo., 1929; M.A., U. Wis., 1930, Ph.D., 1944; m. Pauline Lamar, Sept. 8, 1936; 1 son, Albert Edward. Mem. faculty U. Idaho, 1930—, prof. speech, chmn. dept., 1948—. Mem. Am. Assn. U. Profs., Speech Assn. Am., Western Speech Assn. Episcopalian (vestry 1940-55 72-75). Kiwanian. Home: 511 East D St Moscow ID 83843

WHITEHEAD, CHARLES OLIVER, ednl. adminstr.; b. Columbia, Miss., Sept. 16, 1918; s. Charles O. and Bessie (Vining) W.; B.S., Miss. State U., 1940; M.Ed., U. Miss., 1952; m. Rebekah L. Nabors, Feb. 7, 1941; children—Charles, James, Cindy. Tchr., coach Oak Grove (La.) High Sch., 1946-50; supt. Campground (Miss.) Public Schs., 1950-51; dir. tech. tng. Philco Corp., 1952-64; dir. Chattanooga State Tech. Inst., 1964-67; pres. State Tech. Inst., Memphis, 1967—. Served with USNR, 1943-45, 50-51. Recipient Silver Beaver award Boy Scouts Am., 1967. Mem. Am. Vocat. Assn. (past v.p., dir., pres. 1979-80), Am. Tech. Edn. Assn. (trustee), Am. Assn. Community and Jr. Colls., Am. Soc. Engring. Educators. Democrat. Methodist. Office: 5983 Macon Cove Memphis TN 38134*

WHITEHEAD, CLAY THOMAS, cons.; b. Neodesha, Kans., Nov. 13, 1938; s. Clay Bell and Helen (Hinton) W.; B.S., Mass. Inst. Tech., 1960, M.S. in Elec. Engring., 1961, Ph.D. in Mgmt., 1967; m. Margaret Mahon, May 19, 1973; children—Abigail Walton, Clay Cother. Tech. aide Bell Telephone Labs., Murray Hill, N.J., 1958-59, sr. tech. aide, 1960; cons. def. studies RAND Corp., 1961-63, planner, organizer policy research program on health services, 1967-69; teaching asst. Mass. Inst. Tech., 1962-63, lectr., 1966-67; cons. Bur. Budget, 1966-68; mem. Pres.-Elect's Task Force on Budget Policies, 1968-69; spl. asst. to Pres. Nixon, 1969-70; dir. Office Telecommunications Policy, 1970-74; organized Pres. Ford transition, 1974; fellow Harvard Inst. Politics, Mass. Inst. Tech. Center for Internat. Studies, 1974-76; pres. Allison Tech. Services, Santa Monica, Calif., 1976-78; pres. Hughes Communication Services, Inc., Los Angeles, 1979—. Bd. dirs. Keystone Center for Continuing Edn. Served with AUS, 1963-65. Mem. Yosemite Inst. (dir.), Sigma Xi, Tau Beta Pi, Eta Kappa Nu. Office: PO Box 92424 Los Angeles CA 90009

WHITEHEAD, DON, newspaperman; b. Inman, Va., Apr. 8, 1908; s. Harry Ford and Elizabeth (Bond) W.; student U. Ky., 1926-28, LL.D., 1948; m. Marie Patterson, Dec. 20, 1928; 1 dau., Ruth (Mrs. H.E. Graham). City editor Harlan (Ky.) Daily Enterprise, 1930-34; reporter Knoxville (Tenn.) Jour., 1934-35; joined Asso. Press, 1935, feature writer, N.Y.C., 1941-42, war corr., ETO and MTO, 1942-45, bur. chief, Hawaii, 1945-48, spl. corr., polit. reporter, Washington, 1948-56; chief Washington bur. N.Y. Herald Tribune, 1956-57; now columnist Knoxville News-Sentinel; free lance writer. Recipient Medal of Freedom by Army as war corr., World War II; Pulitzer Prize for internat. reporting, 1950, for domestic reporting, 1952. Mem. Sigma Alpha Epsilon. Clubs: Cherokee Country (Knoxville); Gridiron (Washington). Author: The FBI Story, 1956; Journey into Crime, 1960; Border Guard, 1963; The FBI Story for Young Readers, 1964; The Dow Story, 1968; Attack on Terror: The FBI Against the Ku Klux Klan in Mississippi, 1970. Home: 522-3636 Taliluna Ave Knoxville TN 37919 Office: Knoxville News Sentinel 204 W Church Ave Knoxville TN 37901

WHITEHEAD, DONALD FRANCIS, mfg. co. exec.; b. Wilmington, Ohio, June 1, 1916; s. Clarence C. and Florence Audrey (Cocklin) W.; grad. Rutgers U.; m. Carol H. Goodnough, May 4, 1939; children—Leslie, Ellen. With Standard Register Co., 1936—, v.p. ops., then exec. v.p., Dayton, Ohio, 1966-70, pres., chief exec. officer, 1970—. Mem. Internat. Bus. Forms Industry, U.S., Dayton Area (dir.) chambers commerce, NAM. Republican. Lutheran. Clubs: Dayton, Racquet, Moraine Country (Dayton). Office: 626 Albany St Dayton OH 45401*

WHITEHEAD, EDWIN C., analytical instrumentation co. exec.; b. N.Y.C., June 1, 1919; s. Edwin Carl and Lucille (Sternau) W.; student U. Va., 1936-37; m. Elizabeth Augustus, Aug. 1, 1969; children by previous marriage—John, Peter, Susan. With Technicon Corp., Tarrytown, N.Y., 1939—, pres., 1963-68, chmn. bd., 1968—. Founder, trustee Whitehead Inst. for Med. Research; bd. dirs. Inst. Soc., Ethics and Life Scis. (Hastings Inst.); bd. visitors Duke U. Med. Center; trustee Duke U.; trustee, mem. acad. affairs com. N.Y. U.; mem. corp. Greenwich (Conn.) Hosp., Research Triangle Inst.; mem. bd. overseers Harvard Sch. Public Health, bd. dirs. Assn. Handicapped, Rye, N.Y., Coll. Careers Fund Westchester, Nat. Health Council; sponsor Mayo Clinic. Mem. Soc. Analytical Cytology, Sci. Apparatus Makers Assn., Health Industry Mfrs. Assn. (dir.). Patentee in field. Office: 511 Benedict Ave Tarrytown NY 10591

WHITEHEAD, ENNIS CLEMENT, JR., army officer; b. Newton, Kans., June 16, 1926; s. Ennis Clement and Mary Morse (Nicholson) W.; B.S., U.S. Mil. Acad., 1948; M.S. in Engring., U. Ill., 1955; M.S. in Systems Mgmt., George Washington U., 1972; grad. Army Command and Gen. Staff Coll., 1958, Nat. War Coll., 1966; m. Frances Novella Gibson, June 18, 1949; children—Nancy Banks Whitehead Sander, Ennis Clement III. Commd. 2d lt. U.S. Army, 1948, advanced through grades to maj. gen.; Nat. Security Agy. rep. to U.S. Forces in Europe, 1973-75; comdr. 1st Inf. Div. in W. Ger., 1975-76; comdr. U.S. Army Concepts Analysis Agy., Bethesda, Md., 1976—. Decorated Legion of Merit, Bronze Star, Combat Infantryman's badge, Purple Heart. Mem. Assn. U.S. Army, Ops. Research Soc. Am. Office: 8120 Woodmont Ave Bethesda MD 20014

WHITEHEAD, GEORGE WILLIAM, mathematician; b. Bloomington, Ill., Aug. 2, 1918; s. George W. and Mary (Gutschlag) W.; B.S., U. Chgo., 1937, M.S., 1938, Ph.D., 1941; m. Kathleen E. Butcher, June 7, 1947. Instr., Purdue U., 1941-45; mathematician Aberdeen Proving Ground, 1945; instr. Princeton U., 1945-47, vis. prof., 1958-59; asst. prof. Brown U., 1947-48, asso. prof., 1948-49; asst. prof. Mass Inst. Tech., 1949-51, asso. prof., 1951-57, prof. math., 1957—; vis. research fellow Birkbeck Coll., U. London, 1973. Guggenheim fellow, Fulbright research scholar, 1955-56; NSF sr. postdoctoral fellow, 1965-66. Fellow Am. Acad. Arts and Scis.; mem. Am. Math. Soc., Math. Assn. Am., London Math. Soc., Nat. Acad. Scis., Phi Beta Kappa, Sigma Xi. Author: Homotopy Theory, 1965; Recent Advances in Homotopy Theory, 1970; Elements of Homotopy Theory, 1978. Home: 25 Bellevue Rd Arlington MA 02174 Office: Room 2-284 Mass Inst Tech Cambridge MA 02139

WHITEHEAD, JOHN COSTELLO, judge; b. Loup City, Nebr., Mar. 4, 1939; s. Cyrus C. and Regina (Costello) W.; A.B. in History, St. Benedict's Coll., 1961; LL.B., Washburn U., 1964, J.D., 1964; m. Linda L. Lykins, Sept. 11, 1965; children—Sarah, Amy. Admitted to Nebr. bar, 1964, Kans. bar, 1964; mem. firm Snell & Whitehead, Columbus, Nebr., 1965-66, Walker Luckey & Whitehead, Columbus, 1966-71, Walker, Luckey, Whitehead & Sipple, Columbus, 1971-77; judge U.S. Dist. Ct., Columbus, 1977—; dep. county atty. Platte County, 1965-67; atty. Columbus City, 1967-72. Bd. dirs. Lower Loup Natural Resource Dist., 1971-74, vice chmn., 1975-76; bd. dirs. Columbus Family YMCA, 1976—, pres., 1978—; bd. dirs. Platte County Playhouse, 1972—. Mem. Nebr. Bar Assn., Platte County Bar Assn. (pres. 1976-77), Columbus C. of C. (dir. 1977—, pres. 1979). Roman Catholic. Clubs: Elks, K.C., Optimists (pres. 1971-72, lt. gov. Nebr. dist. 1972-73), Toastmasters (pres. 1968) (Columbus). Home: 3069 25th Ave Columbus NE 68601 Office: Platte County Court House Columbus NE 68601. *What bothers me about America today is that we have become a nation of spectators, not just in sports, but in life itself. Life, like sports, provides the most rewards and enjoyment to the participant. The spectators only gain from the association, and when it's over find they have only the memories and no tangible benefits.*

WHITEHEAD, JOHN CUNNINGHAM, investment banker; b. Evanston, Ill., Apr. 2, 1922; s. Eugene C. and Winifred Whitehead; B.A., Haverford Coll., 1943; M.B.A., Harvard, 1947; m. Helene E. Shannon, Sept. 28, 1946 (div. Dec. 1971); children—Anne Elizabeth, John Gregory, Sarah; m. 2d, Jaan W. Chartener, Oct. 22, 1972. With Goldman, Sachs & Co., N.Y.C., 1947—, partner, 1955—; dir. Am. Dist. Telegraph Corp., Crompton Co., Crompton & Knowles Corp., Dillard Dept. Stores, Equitable Life Real Estate Trust, Household Finance Corp., Pillsbury Co. Pres. Internat. Rescue Com.; chmn. trustees Haverford Coll.; trustee Bryn Mawr Coll., Carnegie Corp.; bd. dirs. Assos. of Harvard Bus. Sch., Econ. Devel. Council N.Y., Am. Productivity Center; co-chmn. Rep. Nat. Fin. Com. Served with USNR, 1943-46. Mem. Securities Industry Assn. (past chmn. bd. govs.), N.Y. C. of C. (dir.), Conf. Bd., Georgetown Center for Strategic and Internat. Studies, Council on Fgn. Relations. Clubs: Links, Recess, University (N.Y.C.); Fells Brook. Home: 131 Old Chester Rd Essex Fells NJ 07021 Office: 55 Broad St New York NY 10005

WHITEHEAD, JOHN JED, precision instrument co. exec.; b. N.Y.C., June 1, 1945; s. Edwin Carl and Constance Rosemary (Raywid) W.; B.A., Williams Coll., 1967; postgrad. Case Western Res. U., 1967-68. Dir. chem. marketing, chem. div. Technicon Corp., Tarrytown, N.Y., 1969-70, sr. v.p., gen. mgr. indsl. div., 1970-71, sr. v.p. clin. div., 1971-74, sr. v.p. corporate planning, 1974-75, sr. v.p. research and devel., 1975—, also dir.; v.p., dir. Saint Paul Prodns., Inc., 1978—. Mem. adv. council Nat. Inst. Environmental Health Scis., NIH, 1971-73. Mem. Rockefeller adv. group to President's 1976 Bicentennial Planning Commn., 1971-72. Bd. dirs. Westchester Urban League, 1973-74, Whitehead Research Inst., 1974—. Home: 167 Cantitoe Rd Katonah NY 10536 Office: 511 Benedict Ave Tarrytown NY 10591

WHITEHEAD, MICHAEL ANTHONY, chemist; b. London, June 30, 1935; came to Can., 1962; s. Francis Henry and Edith Downes (Rotherham) W.; B.Sc. in Chemistry with honors, Queen Mary Coll., U. London, 1956, Ph.D., 1960, D.Sc., 1974; m. Karen C. Eliasen, May 28, 1977; 1 son, Christopher Mark Eliasen. Asst. lectr. Queen Mary Coll., U. London, 1958-60; postdoctoral fellow U. Cin., 1960, asst. prof., 1961; asst. prof. theoretical chemistry McGill U., Montreal, Que., Can., 1962-66, asso. prof., 1966-74, prof., 1974—; vis. prof. U. Cambridge (Eng.), 1971-72, U. Oxford (Eng.), 1972-74. Mem. Chem. Soc. (U.K.), Am. Chem. Soc., Am. Phys. Soc., Soc. Magnetic Resonance, Sigma Xi, Phi Lambda Upsilon. Anglican. Research, numerous publs. in field. Office: Chemistry Dept McGill U 801 Sherbrooke St W Montreal PQ A3A 2K6 Canada

WHITEHEAD, RICHARD FRANCIS, ret. naval officer, aviator, mfg. co. exec.; b. Fall River, Mass., Jan. 1, 1894; s. James and Mary Anne (Maher) W.; ed. pub. schs., Fall River; m. Dede Otte Kosche, Aug. 26, 1933; 1 son, Emerson Otte. Enlisted in Naval Militia of Mass., 1912, Commd. ensign, 1916; mobilized into active service, 1917, served in battleships and destroyers, instr. officers materiel sch., Harvard, World War I; trans. to USNR, 1918, commd. in U.S. Navy, 1920, designated naval aviator, 1924, advanced through grades to vice adm., 1956; served in destroyer squadron Eastern Mediterranean and Black Sea, 1921-23; photog. officer Alaskan Aerial Survey Expdn. in survey Southeastern Alaska, 1926, 29; commd., served on U.S.S. Saratoga, 1927-28; comdr. Naval Res. Aviation Base, N.Y.C., 1929-32; sr. aviation U.S.S. Pensylvania, 1932-34; naval attaché and naval attaché for air Am. embassy, Rio de Janeiro, Brazil, 1935-38; comdg. officer aircraft squadron, air group comdr. and air officer U.S.S. Enterprise, 1938-41; aviation aide to comdt. 9th Naval Dist., chief of staff Naval Air Tech. Tng. Command, 1941-42; served with 5th Marine Corps, 2d Marine Div., also as comdr. support aircraft naval amphibious forces Pacific Theatre, participating in capture of Tarawa, Kwajalein, Eniwetok, Saipan, Leyte, Iwo Jima, and Okinawa, 1943-45; comdg. officer U.S.S. Shangri-La, flag-ship comdr. fast carrier task force during final phases of World War II; comdr. naval air bases 14th Naval Dist., 1945-46, Carrier Div. 14, 1946-48; chief Naval Air Res. Tng. Hdqrs., Glenview, Ill., 1948-49; sr. mem. site survey bd., Washington, 1949-50; comdr. Fleet Air Wings Atlantic Fleet, 1950-52; chief U.S. Naval mission to Brazil, 1952-56; ret., 1956; v.p., dir. Am. Gage & Machine Co., 1956-66, vice chmn. bd., dir., 1966—; cons. Katy Industries, Inc. Decorated D.S.M., D.F.C., Legion of Merit with 4 gold stars, Presdl. Unit citation with bronze star, Navy Expeditionary medal; knight Nat. Order So. Cross (Brazil); grand officer Order of Naval Merit (Brazil); named to City of Chgo. Sr. Citizen Hall of Fame. Mem. U.S. Naval Inst. (golden life), Am. Legion. Roman Catholic. Clubs: Mid-Am., Chicago, Executive, Racquet, Tavern, Glen View (Chgo.). Instituted aircraft carrier tng. utilizing merchant ships on Great Lakes, 1942. Office: 135 S LaSalle St Chicago IL 60603

WHITEHEAD, RICHARD LEE, ins. co. exec.; b. Pitts., Feb. 26, 1927; A.B. in Polit. Sci., Otterbein Coll., 1950; student U. Pa. Law Sch., 1950-52; m. Shirley Ann Fritz, Aug. 19, 1950; children—David Lee, Deborah Ann. Claims adjuster Lumberman's Mut. Casualty Ins. Co., Phila., 1951-52; dir. admissions Otterbein Coll., 1952-54; indsl. relations asst. Westinghouse Electric Corp., Pitts., 1954-56; personnel mgr. Home Life Ins. Co., N.Y.C., 1956-63; dir. employee relations, then v.p. personnel and co. relations Berkshire Life Ins. Co., Pittsfield, Mass., 1963-73, sr. v.p., sec., 1973—; dir. Adams Super Markets Corp., Berkshire Bank & Trust; guest speaker mgmt. edn. seminars. Vice pres., dir. Action for Opportunity, 1964-66; pres., dir. Berkshire County Action Council, 1966-68, Berkshire County chpt. United Cerebral Palsy, 1966-67; v.p., bd. dirs. Pittsfield YMCA; bd. dirs., past pres. Pittsfield Urban Coalition; pres. North Adams State Coll. Found.; chmn. Pittsfield Devel. Com., 1976—. Served with USAAF, 1945-47. Mem. Eastern Coll. Personnel Officers (hon.), Life Office Mgmt. Assn. (past dir.), Inst. Life Ins., Life Ins. Assn. Mass. (exec. com.), Berkshire Mgmt. Club (sr. adviser), Soc. Preservation and Encouragement Barbershop Quartet Singing Am. Methodist. Home: 51 Wellesley St Pittsfield MA 02101 Office: 700 South St Pittsfield MA 01201

WHITEHEAD, ROBERT, theatrical producer; b. Montreal, Can., Mar. 3, 1916; s. William Thomas and Lena Mary (Labatt) S.; student Trinity Coll. Sch., Port Hope, Can.; m. Zoe Caldwell, 1968. Comml. photographer, 1936-38; actor, 1938-42; producer, 1946—; plays include Medea (Robinson Jeffers), starring Judith Anderson, 1947, Crime and Punishment, starring John Gielgud, 1947; Member of the Wedding (N.Y. Times Drama Critics Circle award), 1950; Waltz of the Toreadors (N.Y. Times Drama Critics Circle award), 1957; Separate Tables, 1956-57; A Touch of the Poet, 1958; The Visit (N.Y. Times Drama Critics Circle award 1958), 1958; Much Ado About Nothing, 1959; A Man for All Seasons (Tony award 1962, N.Y. Times Drama Critics Circle award 1961), 1961-62; The Physicists, 1964; The Price, 1968; The Prime of Miss Jean Brodie, 1968; Sheep On The Runway, 1970; Bequest to the Nation, 1970; The Creation of the World and Other Business, 1972; Finishing Touches, 1973-74, A Matter of Gravity, 1976; A Texas Trilogy, 1976; No Man's Land, 1976; A Matter of Gravity, 1976; The Prince of Grand Street, 1979. Dir ANTA Am. Shakespeare Festival. Served Am. Field Service, AUS, 1942-45. Recipient Sam S. Shubert Found. award, 1973. Clubs: Centruy, Players (N.Y.C.). Office: Robert Whitehead Prodns 1501 Broadway New York NY 10036*

WHITEHEAD, THOMAS HILLYER, univ. dean; b. Maysville, Ga., Sept. 5, 1904; s. Asa Hillyer and Clara (Comer) W.; B.S., U. Ga., 1925; M.A., Columbia, 1928, Ph.D., 1930; m. Dorothy Lou Simms, Dec. 19, 1931; children—Thomas H., John S. Mem. faculty U. Ga., Athens, 1930—, prof. chemistry, 1946-51, 52—, coordinator instructional instns. Grad. Sch., 1960-68, dean, 1968-72. With Chem. Warfare Service, 1942-46, Army Chem. Center, 1951-52; cons. AEC, 1952—, Wright-Patterson AFB, 1964-68. Decorated Legion of Merit; recipient Distinguished Alumnus award U. Ga., 1973. Fellow Ga. Acad. Sci.; mem. Am. Chem. Soc., A.A.A.S., Sigma Xi, Phi Kappa Phi, Phi Lambda Upsilon. Author: Theory of Elementary Chemical Analysis, 1950. Home: 236 Henderson Ave Athens GA 30605

WHITEHEAD, WALTER DEXTER, JR., educator, physicist; b. San Diego, Nov. 30, 1922; s. Walter Dexter and Lillian (Shepard) W.; B.S., U. Va., 1944, M.S., 1946, Ph.D., 1949; m. Anne Sophie Louise Van Ketel, Apr. 6, 1949; children—Oliver Day, Thomas Kenyon. Research asst. U. Va., Charlottesville, 1943-45, AEC fellow, 1948-49, asst. prof., 1956-57, asso. prof., 1957-61, prof. physics, 1961—, chmn. dept., 1968-69, dir. Center for Advanced Studies, 1965—, dean Grad. Sch. Arts and Scis., 1969—, dean faculty arts and scis., 1971-72; Carnegie Inst. fellow dept. terrestrial magnetism Carnegie Inst., Washington, 1947-48; physicist Bartol Research Found., Swarthmore, Pa., 1949-53; asst. prof. N.C. State Coll., 1953-55, asso. prof., 1955-56; vis. scientist Institut Voor Kern Physisch Onderzoek Amsterdam, The Netherlands, 1959-60; chmn. Gordon Research Conf. on Photonuclear Reactions, 1965. Mem. bd. adminstrs. Va. Inst. Marine Sci., 1971—; mem. Grad. Record Exam. Bd., 1974—; mem. adminstrv. com. Nat. Fellowships Fund, 1973—; mem. bd. adminstrn. Oak Ridge Asso. Univs., 1976—; bd. dirs. Council Grad. Schs., 1978—. Recipient U.S. Naval Ordnance Devel. award, 1946; Thomas Jefferson award U. Va., 1975. Fellow Am. Phys. Soc. (chmn. S.E. sect. 1970-71); mem. Raven Soc. U. Va., A.A.A.S., Am. Assn. U. Profs., Va. Acad. Sci. (chmn. research com. 1970-71, chmn. awards com. 1971—), Am. Assn. Physics Tchrs., So. Assn. Land Grant Colls. and State Univs. (sec. 1974-76), Phi Beta Kappa, Sigma Xi, Sigma Pi Sigma, Alpha Tau Omega, Omicron Delta Kappa. Contbr. articles profl. jours. Home: Box 227 Route 1 Earlysville VA 22936 Office: 438 Cabell Hall U Va Grad Sch Arts and Scis Charlottesville VA 22901

WHITEHEAD, WILLIAM JOHN, organist, condr.; b. Hobbs, N.Mex., June 30, 1938; s. Theodore and Irma A. (Mosley) W.; B.Mus., Okla. U., 1959; artist diploma Curtis Inst. Music, Phila., 1962; M.A., Columbia U., 1970; m. Martha Louise Terry, Dec. 29, 1960; 1 dau., Mary Louise. Organist, Trinity United Ch. Christ, Pottstown, Pa., 1959-60, First Presbyn. Ch., Bethlehem, Pa., 1961-73; mem. faculty Guilmant Organ Sch., N.Y.C., 1965-66, Westminster Choir Coll., Princeton, N.J., 1966-71; festival organist Bethlehem Bach Festival, 1970—; dir. Music Fifth Ave. Presbyn. Ch., N.Y.C., 1973—; mem. faculty Mannes Coll. Music, N.Y.C., 1975—; touring recitalist, 1962—. Recipient Young Artist award Phila. Orch., 1962; U.S. solo rep. Internat. Bach Festival, Berlin, 1976. Mem. Am. Guild Organists, Presbyn. Assn. Musicians (founder), Hymn Soc. Am., Phi Mu Alpha Sinfonia. Presbyterian. Clubs: St. Wilfrid's, University, Bohemians. Author articles. Office: 7 W 55th St New York NY 10019

WHITEHILL, CLIFFORD LANE, food co. exec.; b. Houston, Apr. 14, 1931; s. Clifford Robert and Catalina (Yarza) W.; B.A. in Accounting and Econs., Rice Inst., 1954; LL.B., U. Tex. Law Sch., 1957; LL.M. in Taxation and Internat. Law, Harvard U., 1958; m. Daisy Mae Woodruff, Apr. 19, 1959; children—Scott, Alicia Anne, Stephen. Admitted to Minn. bar, Tex. bar; asso. firm Childress, Port & Crady, Houston, 1957-58, Graves, Dougherty and Greenhill, Austin, Tex., 1958-59; tax auditor Haskins & Sells, 1959; asst. to pres., asst. gen. counsel Tex. Butadiene & Chem. Co., 1959-62; internat. and asst. corp. counsel Gen. Mills, Inc., Mpls., from 1962, now asst. gen. counsel, v.p., gen. counsel. Trustee Meridian House Internat., Washington; bd. dirs., past pres. Minn.-Uruguay Partners of the Alliance; legal adviser UN Assn. Minn. Mem. Tex., Minn., Am. bar assns., Eden Prairie Jaycees (charter mem., legal adviser). Club: Tonka Athletic (dir., pres.). Home: Route 4 Box 495 Excelsior MN 55331 Office: 9200 Wayzata Blvd Minneapolis MN 55426

WHITEHORN, WILLIAM VICTOR, educator, physician; b. Detroit, Oct. 3, 1915; s. David and Rose (Elconin) W.; student Wayne State U., 1932-34; A.B., U. Mich., 1936, M.D., 1939; m. Sarah B. Holland, Aug. 28, 1938; children—David, Gene Allen. Intern, Harper Hosp., Detroit, 1939-40; research asst. physiology U. Mich., 1940-42; research asso. Ohio State U., 1942-44, instr. physiology and medicine, 1944-45, asst. prof., 1945-47; asst. prof. physiology U. Ill., 1947-50, asso. prof., 1950-54, prof., 1954-70, asst. dean for internat. programs, spl. asst. to pres. for med. affairs, dir. div. health scis., prof. health scis. and biol. scis. U. Del., Newark, 1970-74; asst. commr. for profl. and consumer programs FDA, USPHS, HEW, 1974-78, dep. asso. commr. for health affairs, 1978—; chief of party, prof. physiology U. Ill. Chiang Mai Project, Thailand, 1962-64; campus coordinator, 1965-70; cons. West Side VA Hosp., Chgo., 1954-62. Mem. cardiovascular study sect. div. research grants USPHS, 1961-62. Fellow A.A.A.S.; mem. Am. Physiol. Soc., Soc. Exptl. Biology and Medicine (chmn. Ill. sect. 1960-61), Central Soc. Clin. Research, Chgo. Inst. Medicine, Am. Heart Assn., Sigma Xi, Alpha Omega Alpha. Home: 13612 Sherwood Forest Dr Silver Spring MD 20904

WHITEHOUSE, ALTON WINSLOW, JR., oil co. exec.; b. Albany, N.Y., Aug. 1, 1927; s. Alton Winslow and Catherine (Lyda) W.; B.S., U. Va., 1949, LL.B., 1952; m. Helen MacDonald, Nov. 28, 1953; children—Alton, Sarah, Peter. Admitted to Ohio bar, 1953; asso. partner firm McAfree, Hanning, Newcomer, Hazlett & Wheeler, Cleve., 1952-68; v.p., gen. counsel Standard Oil Co. (Ohio), 1968- 69, sr. v.p., 1969-70, pres., chief operating officer, 1970-77, vice chmn. bd., 1977-78, chmn. bd., chief exec. officer, 1978—, also dir., mem. exec. com.; dir. Ferro Corp., Cleve. Trust Co., Midland-Ross Corp., Cleve. Cliffs Iron Co. Trustee Hawken Sch., Cleve. Clinic Found., Case Western Res. U., Cleve. Mus. Art. Mem. Am., Ohio, Cleve. bar assns., Am. Petroleum Inst., Hwy. Users Fedn. Episcopalian. Office: Standard Oil Co 1750 Midland Bldg Cleveland OH 44115

WHITEHOUSE, WALTER MACINTIRE, physician, educator; b. Millersburg, Ohio, Jan. 28, 1916; s. Frank and Maybelle (MacIntire) W.; A.B., Eastern Mich. U., 1936; M.S., U. Mich., 1937, M.D., 1941; m. Barbara N. McIntyre, Jan. 27, 1945 (dec. Mar. 1975); children—Walter MacIntire, Douglas A., Mary B.; m. 2d, Rebecca Sturtevant Marble, July 31, 1976. Staff physician, asst. dir. Mich. State Sanatorium, Howell, 1945-49; resident radiology U. Mich. Med. Sch., Ann Arbor, 1949-52, instr., 1952-54, asst. prof., 1954-57, asso. prof., 1957-63, prof., 1963—, chmn. dept. radiology, 1965-79. Mem. Am. Roentgen Ray Soc., Radiol. Soc. N.Am., Assn. U. Radiologists, Am. Coll. Radiology, A.M.A. Episcopalian. Author: (with F.J. Hodges) The Gastrointestinal Tract: A Handbook of Roentgen Diagnosis, 1965. Editor: (with J.F. Holt and H.B. Latourette) Year Book of Radiology, 1960-70, 71-78. 1150 Heatherway St Ann Arbor MI 48104 Office: 1414 Ann St Ann Arbor MI 48108

WHITEHURST, DANIEL KEENAN, mayor; b. Los Banos, Calif., Oct. 4, 1948; s. William S. and Tarie M. (James) W.; B.A., St. Mary's Coll., 1969; J.D., U. Calif. Hastings Coll. Law, 1972; M.A., Occidental Coll., 1973; m. Kathleen McCann, July 5, 1969; children—Keenan, Jamie. Admitted to Calif. bar, 1972; v.p. Whitehurst Funeral Chapel, Fresno, Calif., 1975—; practiced law, Fresno, 1973-75; mayor City of Fresno, 1977—, councilman, 1975-77. Club: Rotary. Office: 2326 Fresno St Fresno CA 93721

WHITEHURST, GEORGE WILLIAM, congressman; b. Norfolk, Va., Mar. 12, 1925; s. Calvert Stanhope and Laura (Tomlinson) W.; B.A., Washington and Lee U., 1950; M.A., U. Va., 1951; student W.Va. U., 1956-57, Ph.D., 1962; m. Jennette Seymour Franks, Aug. 24, 1946; children—Frances Seymour, Calvert Stanhope. Mem. faculty Old Dominion U., 1950-68, dean students, prof. history, 1963-68; news analyst sta. WTAR-TV, 1962-68; mem. 91st-96th Congresses 2d Dist. Va. Past mem. Mayor Norfolk Commn. Crime and Delinquency, Tidewater Council Health, Recreation and Welfare, Norfolk Council Alcoholism; past pres. Norfolk chpt. Am. Assn. UN, Norfolk Forum; past chmn. Am. Cancer Soc. crusade in Norfolk. Served with USNR, 1943-46. Decorated Air medal with oak leaf cluster. Mem. Am. Hellenic Ednl. and Progressive Assn., V.F.W., Am. Legion, Delta Upsilon. Methodist (past chmn. bd.). Lion. Home: PO Box 685 Sea Pines Sta Virginia Beach VA 23451 Office: Cannon House Office Bldg Washington DC 20515

WHITEHURST, HARRY BERNARD, educator; b. Dallas, Sept. 13, 1922; s. Clement Monroe and Grace Annette (Walton) W.; B.A., Rice U., 1944, M.A., 1948, Ph.D. (Humble Oil fellow), 1950; postdoctoral fellow U. Minn., 1950-51; m. Audry Lucille Hale, June 12, 1948; children—Jonathan Monroe, Katherine Annette. Research chemist Manhatten Project, 1944-46; Owens-Corning Fiberglas Corp., Newark, Ohio, 1951-55, head research dept., 1955-59; research chemist U.S. Naval Radiol. Def. Lab., San Francisco, 1959; prof. chemistry Ariz. State U., Tempe, 1959—. Dir. Ariz. Engr. and Scientist mag., 1964-69. Chmn. univ. United Fund, 1971-72. Served with C.E., AUS, 1944-46. Fellow Am. Inst. Chemists, A.A.A.S., Ariz. Acad. Sci. (pres. 1970-71); mem. Am. Chem. Soc., Am. Def. Preparedness Assn., Sigma Xi, Phi Lambda Upsilon. Baptist. Patentee in field. Home: 630 Concorda St Tempe AZ 85282

WHITEHURST, ROBERT NEAL, educator; b. Edwin, Ala., Oct. 24, 1922; s. Seaborn Bryan and Willie Mae (Brown) W.; B.S. in E.E., U. Ala., 1943, M.S. in Physics, 1948; Ph.D., Stanford, 1958; m. Jane Margaret Elkan, Jan. 20, 1950; children—Thomas Mitchell, Bryan Bennett, Donna Lynn, Kim Margaret. Instr. physics U. Ala., 1948-49, asst. prof., 1954-57, asso. prof., 1957-61, prof., 1961—; teaching research asst. Stanford, 1949-54; cons. Army Missile Commd., 1954-60; vis. scientist Nat. Radio Astronomy Obs., 1970, 76-77. Served to capt. C.E., AUS, 1943-46. Mem. Am. Phys. Soc., Am. Assn. Physics Tchrs., Am. Astronomical Soc. Home: 25 Arcadia Tuscaloosa AL 35404 Office: PO Box 1569 University AL 35486

WHITELAW, JORDAN M., TV and radio producer; b. N.Y.C., Oct. 15, 1920; s. Louis and Dora (Schatzberg) W.; A.B., Harvard U., 1942, M.A. in Am. History, 1948, postgrad. Sch. Arts and Sci., 1948-51. Music producer Sta.-WGBH-FM, Boston, 1951-62, music mgr., producer Boston Symphony Orch. broadcasts, 1953-62, music mgr. and producer Boston Symphony Orch. broadcasts Sta.-WGBH-TV, 1957-62; broadcast producer Boston Symphony Orch., 1970; free-lance TV producer, primarily for Sta.WGBH-FM and its series Evening at Symphony, 1970—; producer Boston Symphony Orch. broadcasts and syndicated tapes Sta.-WCRB, Waltham, Mass., 1971—. Served with OSS, 1944-46; ETO. Author organ transcription: Bach Prelude to Cantata #156, 1966. Home: 295 Marlborough St Boston MA 02116 Office: Symphony Hall Boston MA 02115. *Since music is to be listened to, I demand the highest standards of audio quality. While unashamedly making use of video techniques I insist that the visual product be musically viable and enjoyably instructive. If my pictures get in the way of the music, then I have failed.*

WHITELEY, JOHNNIE B., coll. pres.; b. Batson, Tex., July 8, 1923; s. Johnnie and Francis (Foreman) W.; B.S., Le Tourneau Tech. Inst., East Tex. State Tchrs. Coll.; M.Ed., Tex. A&M U.; m. Paula Laverne, Dec. 15, 1945; children—Johnnie B., III, Mark Wayne, Jennifer Lee. Successively tchr. indsl. arts Amarillo (Tex.) Ind. Sch. Dist., program coordinator, Big Spring, Tex., tchr. trainer Tex. A&M U., supt. occupational and continuing edn. Houston Ind. Sch. Dist.; now pres. Houston Community Coll. System. Mem. various vocat. coms.; lectr. Prairie View A&M U.; vis. prof. U. Ga. Active Boy Scouts Am., Girl Scouts U.S.A. Served with USAAF. Recipient Presdl. award Houston Community Coll. System, Disting. Service award City of Houston, various Outstanding Service awards, including DECA of Am., Vocat. Indsl. Clubs Am. Mem. Am. Vocat. Assn., Tex. Vocat. Assn., Tex. Indsl./Vocat. Assn., Tex. Assn. Sch. Adminstrs., Am. Soc. Tng. and Devel., Houston Assn. Supervision and Curriculum Devel., Tex. State Tchrs. Assn., Nat. Com. Vocat. Edn., Nat. Council Local Adminstrs., Council Chief Execs., Gulf Coast Vocat. Adminstrs., Houston C. of C., Iota Lambda Sigma, Epsilon Pi Tau. Baptist. Clubs: Rotary, Masons. Home: 4310 Dalmatian St Houston TX 77045 Office: 22 Waugh Dr Houston TX 77007

WHITELOCK, ALFRED THEODORE, librarian, clergyman; b. Dorchester, Dorset, Eng., June 5, 1933; s. Frederick Alfred and Kathleen Ann (Whitelock) Woodward; diploma in pianoforte Royal Acad. Music, London, 1950; B.A. in Theology, U. Bristol (Eng.), 1958; diploma (Fulbright scholar) Va. Theol. Sem., 1960; M.L.S., U. Ind., 1970. Ordained priest Ch. of Eng., 1960; curate, priest St. Bartholomew with St. Andrew, Bristol, 1960-62; welfare officer St. Anne's Bd. Mill Co., Bristol, 1962-65; asst. librarian Indpls. Pub. Library, 1965-68; librarian Cath. Sem. Found. Library, Indpls., 1968-71; county librarian Laramie County (Wyo.) Library System, Cheyenne, 1971-77, Park County (Wyo.) Library System, 1977-78; city librarian Roanoke (Va.) City Public Library System, 1978—. Served with RAF, 1952-54. Mem. Wyo. Library Assn. (pres. 1975-76). Home: Route 1 Box 251 Shawsville VA 24162 Office: 706 S Jefferson Roanoke VA 24011

WHITEMAN, HAROLD BARTLETT, JR., coll. pres.; b. Nashville, Apr. 22, 1920; s. Harold Bartlett and Emma Morrow (Anderson) W.; student Montgomery Bell Acad., 1930-34, Taft Sch., 1934-37; A.B., Yale U., 1941, Ph.D., 1958; M.A., Vanderbilt U., 1950; m. Edith Uhler Davis, July 13, 1946; children—Bartlett, Maclin, Priscilla. Adminstrv. asst. Pan Am. Airways Africa, Ltd., 1941-42; instr. Taft Sch., 1946-47, trustee, 1950-55; teaching fellow Vanderbilt U., 1947-48; asst. dean freshmen, dean undergrad. affairs Yale, 1948-54, dean of freshmen, 1954-64, lectr. in history, 1956-64; asst. to pres. N.Y. U., 1964-67; asst. chancellor, 1967-69, vice chancellor, 1969-71, prof. history, 1966-71; pres., prof. history Sweet Briar Coll., 1971—. Bd. dirs. Episcopal Ch. Found.; trustee Chatham Hall, Va. Museum; chmn. bd. trustees Berkeley Div. Sch. Served to maj. USAAF, 1942-46. Mem. Phi Beta Kappa, Delta Kappa Epsilon, Scroll and Key. Author: Neutrality 1941. Editor: Charles Seymour, Letters from the Paris Peace Conf., 1965. Home: Sweet Briar Coll Sweet Briar VA 24595

WHITEMAN, JOSEPH DAVID, fluid power components co. exec.; b. Sioux Falls, S.D., Sept. 12, 1933; s. Samuel D. and Margaret (Wallace) W.; B.A., U. Mich., 1955, J.D., 1960; m. Mary Kelly, Dec. 29, 1962; children—Anne Margaret, Mary Ellen, Joseph David, Sarah Kelly, Jane. Admitted to D.C. bar, 1960; asso. firm Cox, Langford, Stoddard & Cutler, Washington, 1959-64; sec., gen. counsel Studebaker group Studebaker Worthington, Inc., N.Y.C., 1964-71; asst. gen. counsel. United Telecommunications, Inc., Kansas City, Mo., 1971-74; v.p., gen. counsel, sec. Weatherhead Co., Cleve., 1974-77; gen. counsel, sec. Parker Hannifin Corp., Cleve., 1977—; adv. dir. Arkwright-Boston Factory Mut. Ins. Co. Served as lt. USNR, 1955-57. Mem. Am. Bar Assn. Republican. Roman Catholic. Mem. Beta Theta Pi, Phi Delta Phi. Home: 23349 Shaker Blvd Shaker Heights OH 44122 Office: 17325 Euclid Ave Cleveland OH 44112

WHITENACK, CAROLYN IRENE, educator, librarian; b. Harrodsburg, Ky., Apr. 20, 1916; d. John Hughes and Grace (Chilton) Whitenack; A.B., U. Ky., 1948; M.S., U. Ill., 1956. Tchr., Ky. pub. schs., 1934-47; instr. library sci., librarian U. Ky., 1947-50; head cataloger Louisville pub. schs., 1950-53; dir. div. sch. libraries, teaching materials Ind. Dept. Edn., 1953-56; asst. prof. library sci. and audiovisual edn. Purdue U., 1956-60, asso. prof., 1960-67, prof., chmn. media scis., 1967-79; ret., 1979. Mem. N.E.A.-A.L.A. joint com., 1955—, chmn., 1957-58; del. World Confedn. Orgn. Teaching Profession, Stockholm, 1962, Vancouver, 1967, Dublin, 1968, Singapore, 1974; A.L.A. del. Internat. Fedn. Library Assns., Switzerland, 1962, Moscow, 1970; AID cons. Middle East Tech. U., Ankara, Turkey, 1972. Mem. Ednl. Media Council (sec. 1959—), A.L.A. (library edn. div., resources and tech. services div., 2 v.p. 1960-61, councilor 1955-60, chmn. appointment com. 1959, nominating com. 1959-60; Beta Phi Mu award 1976), N.E.A. (and depts.), Am. Assn. Sch. Librarians (joint com. A.A.S.L.-A.C.R.L.-D.A.V.I., chmn. 1959—, pres. 1968), Ind. Sch. Librarians Assn. (pres.), Hoosier Student Librarian Assn., Ind. Library Assn., Ind. Assn. Ednl. Communication and Tech., Assn. Ind. Media Educators, Ind. Assn. Supervision and Curriculum Devel., Ednl. Media Council, Am. Assn. U. Profs., Kappa Delta Pi, Beta Pi Mu. Contbr. articles profl. jours. Home: Route 3 Harrodsburg KY 40330. *(1) Godly parents with goals for their children. (2) Intellectual freedom for myself which required that you give the same to others first. (3) A Christian commitment. (4) A desire for excellence, to be the best in my profession.*

WHITENER, BASIL LEE, lawyer, former congressman; b. York County, S.C., May 14, 1915; s. Levi and Laura (Barrett) W.; grad. Rutherford Jr. Coll., 1933; student U.S.C., 1933-35; LL.B., Duke, 1937; LL.D., Belmont Abbey Coll., 1960, Pfeiffer Coll., 1965; m. Harriet Morgan, Sept. 25, 1942; children—John Morgan, Laura, Basil Lee, Barrett. Admitted to N.C. bar, 1937, since practiced in Gastonia. Mem. N.C. Ho. of Reps., 1941 Session; mem. N.C. Gen Statutes Commn., 1945-46; solicitor 14th Jud. Dist., 1946-56; mem. 85th-87th Congresses, 11th N.C., 88th-90th Congresses, 10th N.C. Dist. Mem. Commn. Improvement of the Adminstrn. of Justice, 1947-49. Del., Democratic Nat. convs., 1948, 60; chmn. bd. trustees Belmont-Abbey Coll., Belmont, N.C.; bd. advs. Sacred Heart Coll., Belmont. Served to lt. USNR, 1942-45. Mem. Am. N.C., Gaston County bar assns., Jr. C. of C. (pres. 1940), N.C. Jr. C. of C. (pres. 1941-42), Am. Legion, V.F.W., 40 and 8, Phi Delta Phi, Omicron Delta Kappa. Methodist (former steward). Mason (32 deg., Shriner), Elk, Kiwanian. Clubs: Young Democrats of N.C. (pres. 1946-47), Young Democratic Clubs AM. (chmn. adv. com. 1950-51, chmn. bd. regional dirs. 1951). Home: 1854 Montclaire Gastonia NC 28052 Office: 129 South St Gastonia NC 28052

WHITESIDE, DANIEL FOWLER, dentist; b. Palatka, Fla., May 1, 1931; s. Leslie Edgar and Mary Elizabeth (Billingsley) W.; student U. Fla., 1949-52; D.D.S., U. Md., 1956; M.P.H., U. N.C., 1961; m. Patricia Dale Littleton, Oct. 3, 1958. Commd. officer USPHS, 1957, asst. surgeon gen., 1971; staff dental officer Sisseton (S.D.) Indian Hosp., 1957-58; chief dental services Pine Ridge (S.D.) Indian Hosp., 1958-60; chief dental aux. utilization and devel. sect., dental health div. USPHS, Washington, 1961-66; dep. dir. health manpower ednl. services div. Health Manpower Bur., NIH, Arlington, Va., 1967-69, dir. health manpower ednl. services, 1969-70; dir. grants and contracts div., 1970-71, asso. dir. bur., 1971-73, asso. adminstr. Health Resources Adminstrn., 1973-74, dir. Bur. Health and Manpower, Health Resources Adminstrn., Hyattsville, Md., 1975—. Diplomate Am. Bd. Dental Pub. Health. Fellow Am. Pub. Health Assn.; mem. Am. Assn. Pub. Health Dentists, Am. Dental Assn., Gorgas Odontological Soc., Delta Omega. Home: 9207 Moultrie Pkwy Potomac MD 20854 Office: 3700 East-West Hwy Hyattsville MD 20782

WHITESIDE, STANSELL EUGENE, lawyer; b. Oklahoma City, June 1, 1927; s. Stansell and Georgia (McMahan) W.; student Amherst Coll., 1946, U.S. Mil. Acad., 1946-47; B.A., U. Okla., 1950, LL.B., 1952; m. Bernice Phillips, Apr. 3, 1964; children—R. Scott, Georgia, John M., Brenda E. Admitted to Okla. bar, 1952, since practiced in Altus; mem. firm Harbison & Whiteside, 1952-62; pvt. practice, 1962-69; mem. firm Whiteside & Bowman, 1969-73, Whiteside & Watt, 1973—. U.S. commr., 1957-71. Partner Pace Constrn. Co.; pres. Western Lease Finance Corp., Golden Triangle Corp.; sec., dir. Tri-W Corp., C & R Constrn. Co.; dir. Metro Airlines, Internat. 2000. Served to 2d lt. AUS, 1945-46. Recipient Outstanding Service award Okla. Bar Assn., 1960; Commendation award Air Force Assn., 1968. Mem. Am., Okla., Jackson County bar assns., Am. Trial Lawyers Assn. (dir.), Okla. Trial Lawyers Assn., Am. Judicature Soc., Air Force Assn. (past chpt. pres.), Phi Alpha Delta, Sigma Alpha Epsilon. Democrat. Mason, Rotarian, Elk. Home: 1601 N Hudson St Altus OK 73521 Office: 217 W Commerce St Altus OK 73521

WHITESIDE, WILLIAM BOLLING, historian, educator; b. Cin., Oct. 17, 1921; s. Samuel Porter and Louise (Weisiger) W.; A.B., Amherst Coll., 1943; Ph.D., Harvard U., 1952; m. Virginia Elizabeth Sandin, May 3, 1944; children—David Sandin, John Porter. From asst. prof. to prof. history Bowdoin Coll., Brunswick, Maine, 1953—, dir. Sr. Center, 1964-71, Frank Munsey prof. history, 1969—; vis. fellow Waikato U., Hamilton, N.Z., summer 1979. Bd. dirs. Maine Lyceum, 1976—, vice chmn., 1977-78. Served with USAAF, 1943-46. Fulbright-Hays lectr., Taipei, Taiwan, 1978-79. Mem. AAUP (pres. chpt. 1977-78), Phi Beta Kappa. Democrat. Home: Orr's Island ME 04066 Office: Bowdoin College Brunswick ME 04011

WHITESIDES, GEORGE MCCLELLAND, chemist; b. Louisville, Aug. 3, 1939; s. George Walter and Sarah Elizabeth (McClelland) W.; B.A., Harvard U., 1960; Ph.D., Calif. Inst. Tech., 1964; m. Barbara Breasted, June 28, 1970; children—George Thomas, Benjamin Hull. With Mass. Inst. Tech., Cambridge, 1963—, prof. chemistry, 1971—, A.C. Cope prof., 1977—. Alfred P. Sloan fellow, 1968. Mem. Nat. Acad. Scis., Am. Acad. Arts and Scis., Am. Chem. Soc. (award in pure chemistry 1975), AAAS. Contbr. articles to profl. jours. Home: 124 Grasmere St Newton MA 02158 Office: Room 18 298 Massachusetts Inst Technology Cambridge MA 02139

WHITE-THOMSON, IAN LEONARD, chem. co. exec.; b. Halstead, Eng., May 3, 1936; s. Walter Norman and Leonore (Turney) W-T.; B.A. with 1st class honors, New Coll., Oxford U., 1960, M.A., 1969; m. Barbara Montgomery, Nov. 24, 1971. Came to U.S., 1969. Mgmt. trainee Borax Consol. Ltd., London, 1960-61, asst. to sales mgr., 1961-64, asst. to sales dir., 1964; comml. dir. Hardman & Holden Ltd., Manchester, Eng., 1965-67, joint mng. dir., 1967-69; v.p. mktg. dept. U.S. Borax & Chem. Corp., Los Angeles, 1969-73, exec. v.p. mktg., 1973—, also dir.; dir. Canpotex Ltd., 1972-76, chmn. bd., 1974-76. Served with Brit. Army, 1954-56. Mem. Canadian Potash Producers Assn. (v.p. 1976-77, dir. 1972-77). Club: Los Angeles. Home: 1234 Wellington St Pasadena CA 91103 Office: 3075 Wilshire Blvd Los Angeles CA 90010

WHITFIELD, ALLEN, lawyer; b. Ruthven, Iowa, Jan. 26, 1904; s. Rev. George and Sarah (Allen) W.; student U. Nebr., 1920-21; B.S., Iowa State U., 1924; LL.B., Harvard, 1927; grad. study Drake U., 1928; D.H.L. (hon.), Morningside Coll., 1978; m. Irma Cowan, Aug. 18, 1927; children—Lura Mae (Mrs. M.K. Johnson), Harley Allen. Admitted to Fla. and Iowa bars, 1928, D.C. bar, 1961; practice in Des Moines, 1928—; partner firm Whitfield, Musgrave, Selvy, Kelly & Eddy. Pres. Des Moines Joint Stock Land Bank, 1936-40; dir. Internat. Bank, Valley Nat. Bank, Fin. Security Group, Inc. Chmn. Vets. Meml. Auditorium Commn., 1946-57; mem. commn. chaplains and related ministries United Methodist Ch., 1968-74, mem. bd. publ., 1965-68; hon. trustee Morningside Coll., Simpson Coll.; bd. govs.

Iowa State U. Found.; trustee U.S. Jaycees Found.; bd. dirs. Greater Des Moines Community Found. Served to lt. col., internat. div. War Dept., AUS, 1942-45. Decorated Legion of Merit. Mem. U.S. Jr. (pres. 1935-36), Iowa Jr. (pres. 1934), Greater Des Moines (pres. 1949), U.S. (dir. 1963-69, 72-78, treas. 1969-72) chambers commerce, Am., Iowa, Polk County bar assns., Internat. Assn. Ins. Counsel, Fedn. Ins. Counsel, Am. Legion, V.F.W., Amvets, Iowa State U. Alumni Assn. (pres. 1942), Kappa Sigma, Sigma Delta Chi, Delta Sigma Rho. Methodist (lay leader Iowa-Des Moines conf., 1951-55). Mason. Home: Park Fleur 3131 Fleur Dr Des Moines IA 50321 Office: Central Nat Bank Bldg Des Moines IA 50309

WHITFIELD, FRANCIS JAMES, educator; b. Springfield, Mass., Mar. 25, 1916; s. Walter Francis and Gertrude (Donnelly) W.; A.B. summa cum laude, Harvard, 1936, A.M., 1937, Ph.D., 1944; student Ecole des Langues Orientales Vivantes, Paris, France, 1937-38; m. Cecylia Stanislawa Rudzka, Apr. 21, 1950. Asst. prof. U. Chgo., 1945-48, acting chmn. linguistics dept., 1947-48; mem. faculty U. Calif. at Berkeley, 1948—, prof. Slavic langs and lit., 1958—, chmn. dept., 1958-64, 69-70, 72-74; vis. asso. prof. Columbia, 1951-52, U. Mich., 1955. Jr. fellow Soc. Fellows, Harvard, 1939-40, 41-45; fellow Library of Congress, 1940-41; Guggenheim fellow, 1964-65; Fulbright-Hays fellow, 1967; recipient Kosciuszko Found. medal, 1962. Mem. Linguistic Soc. Am., Soc. de Linguistique, Lingvistkredsen (Copenhagen), Polish Inst. Arts and Scis., Internat. Linguistic Assn. Author: Beast in View: a Study of the Earl of Rochester's Poetry, 1936; a Russian Reference Grammar, 1944; (with K. Bulas and L.L. Thomas) Kosciuszko Foundation Dictionary, 1959-61. Editor: (D.S. Mirsky) History of Russian Literature, 1949. Translator: (L. Hjelmslev) Prolegomena to a Theory of Language, rev. edit., 1961; Language, 1970; Resume of a Theory of Language, 1975. Home: 506 The Alameda Berkeley CA 94707

WHITFORD, PHILIP BURTON, educator, plant ecologist; b. Argyle, Minn., Jan. 9, 1920; s. Manley C. and Ethel (Cadman) W.; B.E., No. Ill. State Coll., 1941; M.S., U. Ill., 1942; Ph.D., U. Wis., 1948; m. Kathryn Dana Rueber, Feb. 22, 1946; children—Mary Kathryn, Philip Clason. Edn. asst. Md. Bd. Natural Resources, 1948-49; mem. faculty U. Wis.-Milw., 1949—, prof. botany, 1960—, chmn. dept., 1966-69. Fellow A.A.A.S.; mem. Ecol. Soc. Am., Am. Inst. Biol. Scis., Nature Conservancy. Author: (with M. Ackley) Chemistry of Photosynthesis, 1965; also articles. Research on edaphic control along prairie-forest border. Home: 2647 N Booth St Milwaukee WI 53212

WHITHAM, GERALD BERESFORD, educator, mathematician; b. Halifax, Eng., Dec. 13, 1927; s. Harry and Elizabeth (Howarth) W.; B.Sc., Manchester (Eng.) U., 1948, M.Sc., 1949, Ph.D., 1953; m. Nancy Lord, Sept. 1, 1951; children—Ruth H., Michael G., Susan C. Came to U.S., 1956. Lectr., Manchester U., 1953-56; asso. prof. N.Y.U., 1956-59; prof. math. Mass. Inst. Tech., 1959-61; prof. aero. and math. Calif. Inst. Tech., 1961-67, prof. applied math., 1967—. Fellow Royal Soc., Am. Acad. Arts and Scis. Author: Linear and Nonlinear Waves; also research papers applied math., fluid dynamics. Home: 1689 E Altadena Dr Altadena CA 91001 Office: Calif Inst Tech Pasadena CA 91125

WHITHAM, KENNETH, Canadian govt. ofcl.; b. Chesterfield, Derbyshire, Eng., Nov. 6, 1927; s. Joseph and Evelyn (Murphy) W.; came to Can., 1948; B.A. with honors, Cambridge U., Eng., 1948, M.A., 1952; M.A., Toronto U., 1949, Ph.D., 1951; m. Joan Dorothy Glasspool, Nov., 1953; children—Melanie Judith, Katherine Hilary, Stephanie Frances. Research scientist Dominion Observatory, Ottawa, Ont., 1951-59, 60-64; mem. UN Tech. Assistance Adminstrn., Nairobi, Kenya, 1959-60; dir. div. seismology and geothermal studies Earth Physics br. Dept. Energy, Mines and Research, Ottawa, 1964-73, dir. gen., 1973—. Recipient Outstanding Achievement award Public Service of Can., 1970. Fellow Royal Soc. Can.; mem. Can. Geophys. Union, Geol. Assn. Can., Am. Geophys. Union, Seismol. Soc. Am. Anglican. Contbr. articles in field to profl. jours. Home: 1367 Morley Blvd Ottawa ON K2C 1R4 Canada Office: EPB 1 Observatory Crescent Ottawa ON K1A 0Y3 Canada

WHITHAM, (GEORGE) WARREN, JR., lawyer; b. Wichita Falls, Tex., Feb. 1, 1927; s. George Warren and Sarah Edith (VanDeren) W.; B.B.A., U. Tex., Austin, 1947, J.D., 1950; m. Norma Youngblood, Sept. 9, 1950; children—Kimberly Ann, Wayne Bruce. Admitted to Tex. bar, 1950, since practiced in Dallas; partner firm Spafford, Gay & Whitham, 1970—. Bd. dirs. Dallas br. Tex. Soc. Prevention Blindness, 1970-72. Mem. Am., Dallas bar assns., State Bar Tex. (chmn. sch. law sect. 1973-74), Phi Delta Phi. Methodist. Mason. Club: City (Dallas). Home: 6304 Orchid Ln Dallas TX 75230 Office: 210 Adolphus Tower Dallas TX 75202

WHITIN, RICHARD COURTNEY, JR., venture capitalist; b. Worcester, Mass., May 22, 1921; s. Richard Courtney and Ina (Watson) W.; A.B., Williams Coll., 1942; M.B.A., Harvard U., 1946; m. Elizabeth Walsh; children—Susan, Betsy, Leland. Treas., controller, dir. Paul Whitin Mfg. Co., Northbridge, Mass., 1949-54; with Dewey & Almy Chem. Co., Cambridge, Mass., 1955; asso. Booz, Allen & Hamilton, mgmt. cons., Cleve., 1956-60; dir. ops. planning Crowell-Collier Pub. Co., N.Y.C., 1961, v.p. adminstrn. Macmillan Co., N.Y.C., 1962-63; v.p., treas. Boston Capital Corp., 1963-70; pres., chmn. bd., dir. Urban Nat. Corp. 1971-76; mgmt. cons., 1975-77; v.p. Am. Research & Devel., 1977—; dir. Venture Founders, Inc., Mass. Venture Capital Corp., Lekidata Corp. Trustee Boston Urban Found. Served to lt., Supply Corps, USNR, 1943-46. Mem. Kappa Alpha. Club: Country (Brookline, Mass.). Home: 118 Myrtle St Boston MA 02114 Office: One Beacon St Boston MA 02108

WHITING, ALBERT NATHANIEL, univ. chancellor; b. Jersey City, July 3, 1917; s. Hezekiah Oliver and Hildegarde Freida (Lyons) W.; A.B., Amherst Coll., 1938; student Columbia, summer 1938, U. Pitts., 1938-39; M.A. in Sociology, Fisk U., 1941, Ph.D. in Sociology, Am. U., 1952; LL.D., Amherst Coll., 1968, Western Mich. U., 1974, Duke, 1974, Kyung Hee U., Seoul; m. Charlotte Luck, June 10, 1950; 1 dau., Brooke Elizabeth. Research and teaching asst. Fisk U., 1939-41; instr. sociology, dir. rural community study Bennett Coll., Greensboro, N.C., 1941-43, 46-47; asst. prof. sociology Atlanta U., 1948-53; dean coll., prof. sociology Morris Brown Coll., Atlanta, 1953-57; asst. dean coll. Morgan State Coll., Balt., 1957-59, dean of college, 1960-67; pres. N.C. Central U., Durham, 1967-72, chancellor, 1972—. Dir. Gen. Telephone of Southeast. Bd. dirs. Am. Council Edn., Ednl. Testing Service; bd. dirs., past pres. Assn. State Colls. and Univs.; v.p. Internat. Assn. Univ. Pres.; bd. dirs. Research Triangle Inst. N.C. Served to 1st lt. AUS, 1943-46. Episcopalian. Contbr. articles profl. jours. Home: 1108 Chowan Rd Durham NC 27707

WHITING, BASIL JOHN, JR., govt. ofcl.; b. Providence, R.I., Jan. 14, 1938; s. Basil John and Nellie (Woolhouse) W.; B.Sc., Rensselaer Poly. Inst., 1960; M.P.A., Princeton U., 1967; m. Eunice Temple Straight, Dec. 21, 1960; 1 dau., Michaela Temple. Spl. asst. Human Resources Adminstrn., N.Y.C., 1967-68; sr. program officer Ford Found., 1968-77; dep. asst. sec. occupational safety and health adminstr., Dept. Labor, Washington, 1977—. Mem. asso. bd. L.I. Coll. Hosp., 1975-77; bd. dirs. Cobble Hill Assn., Bklyn., 1972-77. Served to capt. U.S. Army, 1960-65. Mem. Indsl. Relations Research Assn., Common Cause. Home: 119 12th St SE Washington DC 20003 Office: Dept Labor 200 Constitution Ave NW Washington DC 20210

WHITING, BEATRICE BLYTH, anthropologist, educator; b. N.Y.C., Apr. 14, 1914; d. Bertram Dukes and Bertha (Reid) Blyth; A.B. in History magna cum laude, Bryn Mawr Coll., 1935; Ph.D. in Anthropology, Yale U., 1943; m. John Wesley Mayhew Whiting, June 8, 1938; children—Susan Blyth, William Bradford (dec.). Lectr. in social relations Brandeis U., 1949-52; mem. research staff Human Relations Service Wellesley U. (Mass.), 1951-53; research asso. lab. human devel. Harvard Grad. Sch. Edn., 1952-63, lectr. social anthropology, 1963-69, lectr. edn., 1969-74, prof. anthropology and edn., 1974—. Bd. dirs. Martha's Vineyard (Mass.) Community Services. NIMH grantee, 1971-73, 73-77; Guggenheim Found. grantee, 1975; Ford Found. grantee, 1976. Mem. Am. Anthrop. Soc., Am. Ethnol. Soc., Soc. Research Child Devel., Soc. Cross Cultural Research, Soc. Psychol. Anthropology, Sigma Xi. Author: (with John W. M. Whiting) Children of Six Cultures: A Psychocultural Analysis, 1975; editor: Six Cultures: Studies of Child Rearing, 1963. Home: 15 Robinson St Cambridge MA 02138 Office: Larsen Hall Appian Way Cambridge MA 02138

WHITING, EDMUND JOHN, heavy machinery co. exec.; b. Detroit, Dec. 10, 1919; s. Charles Birdsill and Florence Ellen (LeBlanc) W.; B.S. in Fgn. Service, Georgetown U., 1946; M.B.A., U. Mich., 1960; m. Mary Alice Mays, May 31, 1947; children—John, Anne Mary, Wanita. Accountant, Gen. Electric Co., Schenectady, 1948-51; accountant Ex-Cell-O Corp., Detroit, 1952-54, benefit adminstr., asst. treas., treas., 1956—; fin. analyst Chrysler Corp., Detroit, 1954-56, v.p., treas., 1978—. Served with USAF, 1943-45. Club: Detroit Athletic. Office: 2855 Coolidge Troy MI 48084

WHITING, FRANK SIMPSON, bus. exec.; b. Somerset, Ky., Dec. 4, 1893; s. Harley Edwin and Ada Augusta (Simpson) W.; student U. Chgo., 1912-16, Queens Coll., Oxford U. (Eng.), 1917; m. Dorothy M. Cooper, May 27, 1919; children—Frank Simpson, Thomas Cooper, Richard Spencer. Partner, dir. Whiting & Co., Chgo., 1921—, pres., 1967—; v.p., dir. Am. Furniture Mart, Chgo., 1922-59, pres., 1959-65, vice chmn., 1965-68, cons., 1968—, dir., 1922—; v.p., treas., dir. Indiana Limestone Co., 1926-45; dir., officer Am. Publs., 1935-59, pres., 1959—; pres. Am. Furniture Mart Club, 1962; Chgo. Order Book and Directory, 1962—; v.p. Wirtz Corp., 1968—; chief furniture and household goods br., consumers durable goods div. WPB, Washington, 1944-45; cons. Dept. Commerce, 1945—. Chmn. numerous charity drives including Community Fund, ARC; chmn. group bldg. Children's and Polio Hosp., Israel; pres. Greater North Michigan Ave. Assn., 1966-67; bd. dirs. Better Bus. Bureau Met. Chgo. Served with Royal Flying Corps, Brit. Army, 1917, USAC, 1917-19. Mem. Am. Legion (post comdr.), U.S. C. of C., Chgo. Assn. Commerce, Phi Kappa Psi. Republican. Presbyterian. Clubs: Masons, Rotary, Univ. (Chgo.); Indian Hill Country (Winnetka, Ill.). Home: 1410 Sheridan Rd Wilmette IL 60091

WHITING, JOHN RANDOLPH, publisher, editor; b. N.Y.C., Apr. 22, 1914; s. John Clapp and Elizabeth Margaret (Zittel) W.; A.B. in Journalism, Ohio U., 1936; m. Helen Louise Gamertsfelder, June 3, 1937; children—Wendy Helen, Merry Natalie, Robin Elizabeth. Reporter newspapers in Ohio and N.Y. State, 1935-36; asso. editor Lit. Digest, 1936-37, True mag., 1937-38; free-lance writer for mags., 1938-40; mng. editor Click mag., 1940-41; mng. editor Popular Photography mag., 1942-46; editor Sci. Illustrated mag., 1947-49; pub., editor Flower Grower mag., 1949-60; exec. v.p. Popular Sci. Pub. Co., 1961-66; pres. Communigraphics Consultants, 1966-67; pub. Motor Boating and Sailing Mag., Hearst Mag. div., 1967-75, mgr. motor boating and sailing books, 1975—; dir. Hastings Fed. Savs. & Loan Assn., Gullers Internat.; lectr. Colonial Williamsburg, Univs., corps, and assns. on photo-journalism, illustrative photography. Recipient Editors' award Am. Seed Trade Assn., 1960. Mem. Am. A.A.S., Internat. Assn. Boating Writers (pres. 1973—), Nat. Assn. Sci. Writers, Garden Writers Assn. (past pres.), Photog. Soc. Am., Phi Delta Theta, Sigma Delta Chi, Kappa Alpha Mu. Presbyn. Clubs: N.Y. Yacht, Overseas Press (N.Y.C.); Cliffdwellers (Chgo.). Author: Photography is a Language, 1946. Editor and co-author books on photography, boating, picture books various subjects. Contbr. mags on photography, scis. Home: 44 Shady Ln Dobbs Ferry NY 10522 Office: 959 8th Ave New York NY 10019

WHITINGER, RALPH JUDSON, accountant; b. Muncie, Ind., Oct. 5, 1908; s. James F. and Emma (Young) W.; B.S., Ball State U., 1929, LL.D., 1969; m. Geraldine E. Geis, Aug. 1, 1952. Practice pub. accounting, Muncie, 1930—; sr. partner R.J. Whitinger & Co., 1943—; dir. Mchts. Nat. Bank Muncie, Maxon Corp., N.G. Gilbert Corp., Muncie Power Products, Inc. Pres. United Fund Delaware County, Ind., 1956; trustee Muncie YMCA; bd. dirs. N.G. Gilbert Found., Margaret Ball Petty Found.; pres. bd. dirs. Ball State U. Found., 1952—. Recipient Silver Beaver award Boy Scouts Am., 1947; Distinguished Service award Muncie Jr. C. of C., 1954; Distinguished Alumni award Ball State U., 1960; Horatio Alger award Boys Club, 1970; named Ky. col. Mem. Am. Inst. C.P.A.'s, Am. Accounting Assn., Ind. Assn. C.P.A.'s (pres. 1948-49), Newcomen Soc., Muncie C. of C. (pres. 1961), Theta Chi. Republican. Presbyterian. Clubs: Columbia (Indpls.); Muncie, Delaware Country (Muncie). Home: 3505 W University Ave Muncie IN 47304 Office: 114 S Franklin St Muncie IN 47305

WHITLATCH, WAYNE EDWARD, air force officer; b. Nebraska City, Nebr., Oct. 9, 1928; s. Harry Harold and Ruth Lewessa (Kirk) W.; B.S. in Mech. Engring., U. Calif., Berkeley, 1950; M.S. in Mech. Engring., Okla. State U., 1963; M.S. in Internat. Affairs, George Washington U., 1970; m. Jenona Lee Morse, Feb. 22, 1955; children—Ann Eileen, Patricia Margaret, Susan Jenona. Enlisted in USAF, 1951, commd. 2d lt., 1953, advanced through grades to maj. gen., 1975; fighter pilot, Eng., Ger. and Vietnam; comdr. 49th Tactical Fighter Wing, Holloman AFB, N. Mex., 1972-73; vice comdr. Tactical Air Warfare Center, Eglin AFB, Fla., 1973-74; asst. dir. tactical systems test and evaluation, prin. asst. dir. test and evaluation Office Sec. Def., Washington, 1974-77; dep. chief of staff for ops. and intelligence Allied Forces Central Europe, 1977—. Decorated Legion of Merit (3), D.F.C. (2), Air medal (8), Joint Commendation medal, Army Commendation medal, Def. Superior Service medal. Mem. Air Force Assn., Air Force Hist. Assn., Order Daedalians. Home and Office: Det 2 1141 USAF SAS Box 1428 APO New York NY 09011

WHITLEY, CHARLES ORVILLE, Congressman; b. Siler City, N.C., Jan. 3, 1927; s. J.B. and Mamie G. (Goodwin) W.; B.A., Wake Forest U., 1948, LL.B., 1950; m. Audrey Kornegay, June 11, 1949; children—Charles Orville, Martha, Sara. Admitted to N.C. bar, 1950; individual practice law, Mt. Olive, 1950-60; town atty. Mt. Olive, 1951-56; adminstrv. asst. to Congressman David Henderson, 1961-76; mem. 95th-96th Congresses from 3d N.C. Dist., mem. Agr. and Armed Services coms. Served with AUS, 1944-46. Democrat. Baptist. Clubs: Masons, Woodmen of World. Home: Smith Chapel Rd Mount Olive NC 28365 Office: 404 Cannon House Office Bldg Washington DC 20515*

WHITLEY, GEORGE EVERETT, finance co. exec.; b. Winnipeg, Man., Can., Feb. 22, 1924; s. Everett Mansfield and Christina (Teskey) W.; B.A., U. Toronto, 1942; Barrister at Law, Osgoode Hall Law Sch., Toronto, 1950; m. Betty Jean Smith, Dec. 28, 1946; 1 son, Everett Michael. Called to Ont. bar, 1950, created queen's counsel, 1975; solicitor Ford Motor Co. Can. Ltd., 1950-59; with Traders Group Ltd., Toronto, 1959—, sec., legal counsel, 1964-72, v.p., sec., gen. counsel, 1972—, also dir.; dir. Trans Can. Credit Corp. Ltd., Traders Homeplan Ltd., Homeplan Realty Ltd., Traders Realty Ltd. Served with RCAF, 1943-45. Mem. Canadian Bar Assn. Conservative. Club: Caledon Mountain Trout (pres.). Home: 37 Munro Blvd Willowdale ON M2P 1C1 Canada Office: 625 Church St Toronto ON M4Y 2G1 Canada

WHITLEY, JOSEPH EFIRD, med. educator; b. Albemarle, N.C., Mar. 22, 1931; s. John Efird and Ola Mae (Huneycutt) W.; B.A. magna cum laude, Wake Forest U., 1951; M.D., Bowman Gray Sch. Medicine, 1955; m. Nancy O'Neil, Dec. 20, 1958; children—John O'Neil, Catherine Anne. Intern, Pennsylvania Hosp., Phila. resident N.C. Babtist Hosp. Winston-Salem: asst. prof. Bowman Gray Sch. Medicine, Winston Salem, N.C., 1962-65, asso. prof., 1965-69, prof. dept. radiology, 1969-78; prof., chmn. dept. diagnostic radiology U. Md. Sch. Medicine, Balt., 1978—. Cons. NIH, Nat. Inst. Neurol. Diseases Stroke, 1969-79. Bd. dirs. James Picker Found., 1974. Fellow Am. Coll. Radiology; mem. Am. Roentgen Ray Soc. Radiologic Soc. N. Am., Assn. Univ. Radiologists, Phi Beta Kappa, Alpha Omega Alpha. Author: (with Nancy O. Whitley) Angiography, Techniques and Procedures, 1971.

WHITLEY, WYATT CARR, educator; b. Salma, N.C., Oct. 17, 1900; s. John Berry and Nancy (Greene) W.; B.S. in Chemistry, Wake Forest Coll., 1928; M.S. in Chemistry, Ga. Inst. Tech., 1933; Ph.D. in Chemistry, U. Wis., 1939; m. Lora Magdeline Dills, Dec. 26, 1934; children—John Bryan, Margaret, Nancy Lucinda. Instr. chemistry George Washington U., 1929; cons. Puritan Chem. Co., Atlanta, 1942-46, Internat. Minerals and Chem. Corp., Atlanta, 1945; faculty Ga. Inst. Tech., 1929—, prof. chemistry, 1944—, chief chem. scis. div., engring. expt. sta., 1956-61, asso. dir. engring. expt. sta., 1962-63, dir. engring. expt. sta., 1963-68, dir. emeritus, 1968—; research participant Oak Ridge Nat. Lab., summers 1951-54; spl. research inorganic and analytical chemistry, radiochemistry, instrumental methods analysis. Mem. Am. Chem. Soc., Ga. Acad. Sci., Ga. Tech. Research Club, Ga. Tech. Athletic Assn. (dir. 1946-58), Sigma Xi, Golden Bough, Alpha Chi Sigma, Phi Lambda Upsilon, Gamma Sigma Epsilon. Democrat. Baptist (deacon). Club: Optimist Internat. (gov. Ga. dist.). Author: (with John L. Daniel) Theory of Analysis, 1939. Home: 1864 Greystone Rd NW Atlanta GA 30318

WHITLOCK, BAIRD WOODRUFF, educator; b. New Brunswick, N.J., June 1, 1924; s. Frank Boudinot and Rosena Craig (Foster) W.; B.A., Rutgers U., 1948; Ph.D., U. Edinburgh (Scotland), 1953; D.Litt., Nasson Coll., 1973; m. Joan Aileen Slinger, Feb. 16, 1953; children—Christopher Austin, Ian Kingsley, Alison L., Erik F. Instr. English, Middlebury (Vt.) Coll., 1948-51, U. Vt., 1953-54; asst. prof. humanities Colby Coll., 1954-56; asso. prof. humanities, 1st holder Kulas chair music Case Inst. Tech., 1956-61; prof. English, chmn. div. humanities, langs. and lit., head English dept. San Francisco State Coll., 1961-64; spl. research 16th and 17th century European arts; vis. prof. U. Hawaii, summer 1964; head dept. English, U. Wyo., 1964-66; prof. English, Elmira (N.Y.) Coll., 1966-72, dir. liberal studies program, 1967-69, course tour dir. in Europe, 1960, 63, 65, 69, 71; pres. Simon's Rock, Great Barrington, Mass., 1972-76; vis. lectr. Phillips Acad., Andover, Mass., 1976-77; dean humanities and social sci. Midwestern State U., Wichita Falls, Tex., 1978—. Bd. dirs. Aston Magna Found., Internat. Chamber Music Festival, So. Berkshire Arts Council; trustee Simon's Rock, Colby-Sawyer Coll.-N.H. Served to 2d lt., pilot, USAAF, 1943-45. Carnegie Corp. and Ford Found. Research grantee, 1976-77. Mem. Intercollegiate Music Council (dir.), Am. Soc. Engring. Edn. (chmn. humanities-social scis. div. 1960) Modern Lang. Assn., N.E. Modern Lang. Assn. (chmn. Renaissance com. 1969, ecology com. 1970), Guild Scholars, Phi Beta Kappa. Episcopalian (choir dir.). Author: Don't Hold Them Back, 1978; also articles, reviews. Address: 3301 Seymour Rd Wichita Falls TX 76309

WHITLOCK, BENNETT CLARKE, JR., assn. exec.; b. Charleston, S.C., June 10, 1927; s. Bennett C. and Isabel Price (Beckman) W.; A.B., Presbyn. Coll., 1946; LL.B., U. S.C., 1949; m. Elizabeth Darley Marshall, July 18, 1959; children—Mary Elizabeth, Bennett C. III. With Am. Trucking Assns., Inc., Washington, 1949—, asst. to mng. dir., 1961-70, asst. to pres., 1970-73, v.p., 1973-75, exec. v.p., chief operating officer, 1975-76, pres., 1976—. Pres., Cove Point Beach Assn.; bd. dirs. Braddock Road Boys Club. Mem. Nat. Def. Transp. Assn. (dir.), Transp. Assn. Am. (dir.), Hwy. Users Fedn. for Safety and Mobility (dir.), Blue Key, Pi Kappa Alpha. Episcopalian. Clubs: Country of Fairfax; Chesapeake Country. Office: Am Trucking Assns Inc 1616 P St NW Washington DC 20036

WHITLOCK, CHARLES PRESTON, univ. dean; b. Highland Park, N.J., June 19, 1919; s. Frank Boudinot and Rosena Craig (Foster) W.; B.A., Rutgers U., 1941; M.A., Harvard, 1947; m. Patricia Hamilton Hoey, Mar. 10, 1960; children—Carol Foster, Adam Hoey, Susan Boudinot, Matthew Fitzsimmons, Beth Brewer. Asso. dir. Bur. Study Counsel, Harvard, 1948-52, Allston Burr sr. tutor, 1952-58, asst. to pres., 1958-70, asso. dean of coll., 1970-72, dean of coll., 1972-76, asso. dean faculty, 1976—, master Dudley House, 1976—. Dir. Cambridgeport Savs. Bank. Mem. Mass. Higher Edn. Facilities Commn. Trustee Charity of Edward Hopkins; bd. corporators New Eng. Deaconess Hosp. Served to col. USAF. Decorated Silver Star, D.F.C., Air medal. Co-author: Harvard University Reading Films. Home: 53 Dunster St Cambridge MA 02138 Office: Harvard College Cambridge MA 02138

WHITLOCK, FOSTER BRAND, pharm. mfg. co. exec.; b. Highland Park, N.J., Oct. 27, 1914; s. Frank Boudinot and Rosena (Foster) W.; student Rutgers U., 1932-33, U. Wis., 1934-36, Columbia, 1954; m. Edna Gertrude Evans, Jan. 26, 1945; children—Charlane (Mrs. Mowery), Frances (Ms. Edmondson), Janet, Brand. Engr., clk. RCA Communications, Inc., 1936-39; salesman Johnson & Johnson, New Brunswick, N.J., 1939-40, pres., dir., 1958-77, mem. exec. com., 1964-77, vice chmn., 1973-77; vice chmn. Johnson & Johnson Internat., 1973; pres. Am. Found. Pharm. Edn., 1972-73; mem. Joint Commn. on Prescription Drug Use, 1976-79; bd. dirs. Project HOPE. Trustee, bd. govs. Rutgers U., 1968-77; chmn. bd. Overlook Hosp., Summit, N.J., 1977-78; trustee Overlook Hosp. Found., 1975—, Robert Wood Johnson Found., 1979—. Served to capt. USAAF, 1942-46. Decorated Bronze Star medal. Mem. Pharm. Mfrs. Assn. (dir., chmn. 1973-74), Internat. Fedn. Pharm. Mfrs. Assns. (pres. 1974-76), S.A.R., Chi Psi. Presbyterian. Clubs: N.Y. Yacht (N.Y.C.); Ocean Reef (Fla.); Baltusrol Golf; Key Largo (Fla.) Anglers. Home: 36 Sunset Cay Rd Key Largo FL 33037 Office: 501 George St New Brunswick NJ 08903

WHITLOCK, JOHN JOSEPH, museum dir.; b. South Bend, Ind., Jan. 7, 1935; s. Joseph Mark and Helen Marcella (Cramer) W.; B.S. in Art, Ball State U., 1957, M.A. in Art, 1963; Ed.D., Ind. U., 1971; m. Sue Ann Kirkman, June 10, 1956; children—Kelly Ann, Michele Lynn, Mark. Tchr. art Union City (Ind.) Pub. Schs., 1957-59; tchr. art,

art dir. Madison (Ind.) City Schs., 1959-64; prof. art, dir. gallery Hanover (Ind.) Coll., 1964-69; dir. Burpee Art Mus., Rockford, Ill., 1970-72; prof. arts and humanities Elgin (Ill.) Community Coll., 1970-72; dir. Brooks Meml. Art Gallery, Memphis, 1972-78; prof. museum studies Southwestern Coll., Memphis, 1973-78; adj. asst. prof. art and museology Memphis State U., 1976-78; dir. Univ. Mus. and Art Galleries So. Ill. U., Carbondale, 1978—, adj. asso. prof. art and anthropology, 1978—. Mem. Human Relations Commn. Rockford, 1971-72; mem. pres.'s council Southwestern Coll., 1973-78. Mem. Am. Assn. Museums, Internat. Council Museums, Midwest Assn. Museums, Assn. Art Mus. Dirs. Office: Univ Mus and Art Galleries So Ill U Carbondale IL 62901

WHITLOW, ROBERT SPENCER, lawyer, energy resources cons.; b. St. Louis, Dec. 21, 1914; s. Joseph Andrew and Mary (Spencer) W.; B.A., U. Chgo., 1936; LL.B., Columbia, 1940; m. Leila Jane Smith, May 23, 1953; children—Robert Spencer, Douglas Andrew, Scott Collister, and Elizabeth Jane Whitlow. Admitted to N.Y. State bar, 1941, D.C. bar, 1962; asso. firm Barry, Wainwright, Thacher & Symmers, N.Y.C., 1941-46; with State Dept., 1946, Treasury Dept., 1946-47; atty., then div. counsel Calif. Tex. Oil Corp., N.Y.C., 1945-61; asst. gen. counsel Gen. Precision Equipment Corp., N.Y.C., 1961-63; gen. counsel, sec. Commonwealth Oil Refining Co., Inc., N.Y.C., 1963-76, v.p., 1970-75, sr. v.p., 1975-76; dir. Eastern regional office U. Chgo., 1976-78; prin. Galaxy Gen. Assos., New Canaan, Conn., 1978—. Mem. bd. finance, New Canaan, Conn., 1962-67. Democratic candidate for town treas., New Canaan, 1963. Served to capt. AUS, 1942-46; ETO. Decorated Bronze Star. Mem. Assn. Bar City N.Y., Am. Fgn. Law Assn., (bd. dirs. 1960-65), Am. Bar Assn., Am. Soc. Internat. Law, Am. Soc. Corp. Secretaries, Alpha Delta Phi (exec. council 1954-69). Baptist. Clubs: Lake (New Canaan); Bankers of Puerto Rico (San Juan); University (N.Y.C.). Home: 191 Brookwood Ln New Canaan CT 06840 Office: PO Box 1321 New Canaan CT 06840

WHITMAN, CHARLES SEYMOUR, III, lawyer; b. N.Y.C., Apr. 19, 1942; s. Charles Seymour and Janet (Russell) W.; A.B., Harvard U., 1964, LL.B., 1967; LL.B., Cambridge (Eng.) U., 1968; m. Christine L. Madden, Oct. 20, 1979. Admitted to N.Y. State bar, 1967, U.S. Supreme Ct. bar, 1971; asso. firm Shearman & Sterling, N.Y.C., 1967; asso. firm Davis Polk & Wardwell, N.Y.C., 1968-71; exec. asst. to chmn. SEC, Washington, 1971-73; gen. counsel Mitchell Hutchins, Inc., N.Y.C., 1974; asso. firm DaVis Polk & Wardwell, N.Y.C., 1974-77, partner, 1977—. Bd. dirs. Brit. Schs. and Univs. Found., N.Y.C., 1969—. Mem. Am. Bar Assn., N.Y.C. Bar Assn., Am. Law Inst. (advisor fed. securities code project). Republican. Presbyterian. Home: 70 E 96th St New York NY 10028 Office: 1 Chase Manhattan Plaza New York NY 10005

WHITMAN, DONALD RAY, univ. adminstr., educator; b. Ft. Wayne, Ind., Nov. 7, 1931; s. John Edward and Martha Lucille (Farmer) W.; B.S., Case Inst. Tech., 1953; Ph.D., Yale, 1957; m. Susan Jane Brott, Feb. 2, 1955 (div.); children—Clifford, Stephen. Asst. prof. chemistry Case Inst. Tech., 1957-63; asso. prof., 1963-70; prof. Case Western Res. U., Cleve., 1970—, asst. to pres., 1971-72, asso. v.p., 1972-74, v.p. for profl. studies and health affairs, 1974—. Mem. Am. Phys. Soc., A.A.A.S. Author: Tables of Quantum Chemistry Integrals. Contbr. articles to profl. jours. Research in theoretical chemistry. Home: 35150 Eddy Rd Willoughby Hills OH 44094 Office: Adelbert Hall Case Western Res U Cleveland OH 44106

WHITMAN, JAMES THOMAS, zoo adminstr.; b. Ft. Worth, Apr. 23, 1943; s. James Price and Nanette Louise (Eager) W.; A.A., Schreiner Inst., 1964; B.S. in Biology and Chemistry, U. Houston, 1968; m. Jeanne Edna Morin, Aug. 11, 1973; children—Brian Thomas, James Ewing, Christine Michele. Curator, Sea Arama, Inc., Galveston, Tex., 1965-69, gen. mgr., 1967-69; aquarium dir. SeaWorld, San Diego, 1969; asst. gen. mgr. A.B.C. Marine World Inc., Redwood City, Calif., 1969-71, oceanarium dir., 1969-71; gen. mgr. Aquarium of Cape Code, West Yarmouth, Mass., 1971-73; zoo dir. Roger Williams Park Zoo, Providence, 1974-75, Buffalo Zool. Gardens, 1975—; bd. dirs. Maude Holms Arboreta, Zool. Soc. Buffalo, Niagara Frontier Underwater Hist. Soc. Mem. Am. Assn. Zool. Parks and Aquariums, Am. Soc. Ichthyologists and Herpetologists, Audubon Soc., Am. Assn. Zoo Veterinarians, Am. Assn. Zoo Keepers, Am. Assn. Museums, Internat. Crane Found., World Pheasant Breeders Assn. Club: Rotary (Buffalo). Home: 243 Greenwood East Aurora NY 14052 Office: Buffalo Zoo Delaware Park Buffalo NY 14214

WHITMAN, MARINA VON NEUMANN, economist; b. N.Y.C., Mar. 6, 1935; d. John and Mariette (Kovesi) von Neumann; B.A. summa cum laude, Radcliffe Coll., 1956; M.A., Columbia U., 1959, Ph.D., 1962; L.H.D., Russell Sage Coll., 1972, U. Mass., 1975, N.Y. Poly Inst., 1975; LL.D., Cedar Crest Coll., 1973, Hobart and William Smith Coll., 1973, Coe Coll., 1975, Marietta Coll., 1976, Rollins Coll., 1976, Wilson Coll., 1977, Allegheny Coll., 1977, Amherst Coll., 1978; m. Robert Freeman Whitman, June 23, 1956; children—Malcolm Russell, Laura Mariette. Mem. faculty U. Pitts., 1962-79, prof. econs., 1971-73, distinguished pub. service prof. econs., 1973-79; v.p., chief economist Gen. Motors Corp., N.Y.C., 1979—; sr. staff economist Council Econ. Advisers, 1970-71; mem. Price Commn., 1971-72; mem. Council Econ. Advisers, Exec. Office of Pres., 1972-73; dir. Mfrs. Hanover Trust Co., Procter & Gamble Co.; mem. Trilateral Commn.; mem. Pres.'s Adv. Group on Contbns. of Tech. to Econ. Strength, 1975-76, mem. Pres.'s Adv. Com. on Tech. and World Trade, 1976—. Bd. overseers Harvard Coll., 1972-78. Recipient Columbia medal for excellence, 1973; George Washington award Am. Hungarian Found., 1975; fellow Earhart Found., 1959-60, AAUW, 1960-61, NSF, 1968-70, also Social Sci. Research Council. Mem. Am. Econ. Assn. (exec. com. 1977—), Commn. on Critical Choices for Ams., Atlantic Council (dir.), Council Fgn. Relations (dir. 1977—), Phi Beta Kappa. Author: Government Risk-Sharing in Foreign Investment, 1965; International and Interregional Payments Adjustment, 1967; Economic Goals and Policy Instruments, 1970; Reflections of Interdependence: Issues for Economic Theory and U.S. Policy; also articles; bd. editors Am. Econ. Rev., 1974-77; mem. editorial bd. Fgn. Policy. Office: Gen Motors Corp 767 Fifth Ave New York NY 10022

WHITMAN, REGINALD NORMAN, railroad ofcl.; b. Jasmin, Sask., Can., Oct. 15, 1909; s. Norman L. and Irene (Haverlock) W.; student St. Joseph Coll., Yorkton, Sask.; grad. Advanced Mgmt. Program, Harvard, 1958; m. Opal Vales, Jan. 31, 1932; children—James, Richard, Donna (Mrs. Ronald Throener). With Great No. Ry., 1929-69; gen. mgr. Alaska R.R., Dept. Interior, 1955-56; fed. railroad adminstr. Dept. Transp., 1969-70; chmn. bd., chief exec. officer M.-K.-T. R.R., 1970—. Mem. Alaska North Commn., 1967-69. Served with AUS, 1943-44. Mem. Nat. Def. Transp. Assn., Am. Legion. Republican. Catholic. Home: 7108 Desco St Dallas TX 75225 Office: 701 Commerce St Dallas TX 75202

WHITMAN, ROBERT, lawyer, educator; b. N.Y.C., May 18, 1936; B.B.A., CCNY, 1956; J.D., Columbia U., 1959; LL.M., N.Y. U., 1970; m. Edith Cybul, June 25, 1961; children—Mara, Miles. Admitted to N.Y. bar, 1959, Conn. bar, 1966; asso. in law Columbia U., N.Y.C., 1959-60; asst. prof. law U. Md., 1960-62; asso. firm Cravath, Swaine and Moore, N.Y.C., 1962-64, Tenzer, Greenblatt, Fallon & Kaplan, N.Y.C., 1964-66; asso. prof. U. Conn., West Hartford, 1966-69, prof., 1969—, also dir. Whitman bar rev. course and continuing edn. estate planning courses; vis. prof. Yale U., U. So. Calif., Brunel U., Uxbridge, Eng., other instns. Bd. dirs. Family Service Soc. Hartford (Conn.). Mem. Am. Bar Assn., Conn. Bar Assn., Am. Law Inst., Am. Judicature Soc., Nat. Conf. Lawyers and C.P.A.'s. Co-author: Accounting and the Law, 1978; reporter Nat. Fiduciary Acctg. study; contbr. articles legal jours. Home: 86 Norwood Rd West Hartford CT 06117 Office: U Conn Law Sch Greater Hartford Campus West Hartford CT 06117

WHITMAN, ROBERT FREEMAN, educator; b. Boston, July 9, 1925; s. Alfred Freeman and Fannie Marie (Whitman) W.; A.B., Cornell U., 1949; M.A., Harvard, 1951, Ph.D., 1956; m. Marina von Neumann, June 23, 1956; children—Malcolm, Laura Mariette. Instr. English, Princeton, 1955-60; asst. prof. U. Pitts., 1960-65, asso. prof., 1965-67, prof., 1967—, chmn. English dept., 1967-72. Served to 2d lt. USAAF, 1943-46. Mem. Modern Lang. Assn., Malone Soc., Am. Assn. Univ. Profs. Democrat. Unitarian. Author: The Play-Reader's Handbook, 1966; Beyond Melancholy, 1973; Shaw and the Play of Ideas, 1977. Home: 5440 Aylesboro Ave Pittsburgh PA 15217

WHITMAN, ROBERT OLIVER, utilities exec.; b. N.Y.C., May 4, 1913; s. Theodore K. and Senja (Salminen) W.; B.S., N.Y.U., 1937; advanced mgmt. program Harvard U., 1956; exec. program Columbia, 1961; m. Sirkka Lindros, Sept. 4, 1937; 1 dau., Pamela. Accountant Elliott Ticket Co., 1932-37; asso. Niles & Niles, C.P.A.'s, N.Y.C., 1937-54; adminstrv. asst. Am. Electric Power Service Corp., N.Y.C., 1954, asst. treas., 1954-55, treas., 1955—, v.p., treas., 1967-73, sr. v.p., treas., 1973-74, exec. v.p., treas., 1974-76, sr. exec. v.p., treas., 1976-79, also dir.; treas., dir. Appalachian Power Co., Mich. Power Co., Central Coal Co., Ind. & Mich. Electric Co., Power Co., Ohio Electric Co., So. Ohio Coal Co., So. Appalachian Coal Co., Ind. & Mich. Power Co., Kingsport Power Company, Twin Br. R.R. Co., Wheeling Electric Co., Central Coal Co., Central Ohio Coal Co., Central Appalachian Coal Co., Windsor Power House Coal Co., Ky. Power Co., Beech Bottom Power Co., Captina Power Co., Kanawha Valley Power Co., Central Operating Co., Franklin Real Estate Co., Indiana Franklin Realty Co., Twin Branch R.R. Co., Cardinal Operating Co., Mich. Gas Exploration Co., South Bend Mfg. Co., W.Va. Power Co.; treas. Am. Electric Power Co. C.P.A., N.Y. Mem. Fin. Execs. Inst., Am. Inst. C.P.A.'s. Clubs: Ardsley Country, Ardsley Curling. Home: 35 Riverview Rd Irvington-on-Hudson NY 10503 Office: 2 Broadway New York NY 10004

WHITMAN, ROBERT VAN DUYNE, civil engr.; b. Pitts., Feb. 2, 1928; s. Edwin A. and Elsie (Van Duyne) W.; B.S., Swarthmore Coll., 1948; S.M., Mass. Inst. Tech., 1949, Sc.D., 1951; m. Elizabeth Cushman, June 19, 1954; children—Jill Martyne, Martha Allerton (dec.), Gweneth Giles. Mem. faculty Mass. Inst. Tech., 1953—, prof. civil engring., 1963—, head structural engring., 1970-74, head soil mechanics div., 1970-72; vis. scholar U. Cambridge (Eng.), 1976-77; cons. to govt. and industry, 1953—. Mem. Town Meeting Lexington (Mass.), 1962-76, mem. permanent bldg. com., 1968-75. Served to lt. (j.g.) USNR, 1954-56. Mem. Am. (Research award 1962), Boston (Structural sect. prize 1963, Desmond Fitzgerald medal 1973, Ralph W. Horne Fund award 1977) socs. civil engrs., Internat. Soc. Soil Mechanics and Found. Engrs., Seismol. Soc. Am., Nat. Acad. Engring., Earthquake Engring. Research Inst. (dir. 1978—). Author: (with T. W. Lambe) Soil Mechanics. Research in soil mechanics, soil dynamics and earthquake engring. Home: 9 Demar Rd Lexington MA 02173 Office: Mass Inst Tech Cambridge MA 02139

WHITMAN, RUTH, poet, educator; b. N.Y.C., May 28, 1922; d. Meyer David and Martha Harriet (Sherman) Bashein; B.A., Radcliffe Coll., 1944; M.A., Harvard, 1947; m. Cedric Whitman, Oct. 13, 1941; children—Rachel Claudia, Leda Miriam; m. 2d, Firman Houghton, July 22, 1959; 1 son, David Will; m. 3d, Morton Sacks, Oct. 6, 1966. Editor, Harvard U. Press, 1947-60; dir. poetry workshop Cambridge Center Adult Edn., 1964-68; fellow poetry and translation Radcliffe Inst., 1968-70; instr. Radcliffe Seminars, 1969—; vis. poet Tufts U., 1972, 73; vis. poet in Israel, 1974; poet-in-residence Hamden Sydney Coll., 1974, Trinity Coll., 1975; founder, pres. Poets Who Teach, Inc., 1974—. Dir. poetry writing program Mass. Council Arts, 1970-73. Recipient Alice Fay di Castagnola award, 1968, Kovner award, 1969, Chanin award, 1972, Guiness Internat. award, 1973; grantee Nat. Found. Jewish Culture, 1968, Nat. Endowment Arts, 1974-75. Mem. Authors League, P.E.N., Poetry Soc. Am., New Eng. Poetry Club, Phi Beta Kappa. Author: Selected Poems of Alain Bosquet, 1963; Anthology of Modern Yiddish Poetry, 1966; Blood and Milk Poems, 1963; Marriage Wig and other poems, 1968; Selected Poems of Jacob Glatstein, 1972; The Passion of Lizzie Borden: New and Selected Poems, 1973. Editor: Poemmaking: Poets in Classrooms, 1975; Tamsen Donner: A Woman's Journey, 1977. Address: 1559 Beacon St Brookline MA 02146

WHITMAN, WILLIAM FIFIELD, JR., investment banker; b. N.Y.C., Feb. 21, 1940; s. William Fifield and Lynn (Forsberg) W.; B.A. with honors, Williams Coll., 1962; M.B.A., Harvard U., 1964; m. Barbara Bowne Kezar, June 20, 1964; children—Laura Bowne, William Fifield. Asso., Blyth & Co., Inc., 1964-67; sr. v.p., dir. corp. fin., dir. Shearson Hayden Stone, Inc., N.Y.C., 1967-70; v.p. Shields & Co., Inc., N.Y.C., 1970-71; exec. v.p., dir. Coenen & Co., N.Y.C., 1971-73; v.p., mgr. corp. fin. Mitchell Hutchins Inc., 1973-77; sr. v.p. Blyth Eastman Paine Webber, N.Y.C., 1977—; chmn., pres., chief exec. officer TMC Industries, Ltd., Rome, Ga., 1978—; dir. Hazeltine Corp. Trustee Eagle Dock Found. Clubs: Bond of N.Y., Recess, Creek, Harvard. Home: 38 Snake Hill Rd Cold Spring Harbor NY 11724 Office: 919 3d Ave New York NY 10022

WHITMAN, WILLIAM TATE, educator, economist; b. Boaz, Ala., Oct. 26, 1909; s. Edward Fenno and Jane Moore (Street) W.; A.B., Duke, 1929, M.A., 1933, Ph.D., 1943, m. Luisita Dye, Aug. 12, 1936; children—Melinda, Ernestine. Asst. prof. bus. adminstrn. The Citadel, 1936-47; instr. econs. Duke, 1939-40; mem. faculty Emory U., 1947—, Charles Howard Candler prof. econs. Sch. Bus., 1960-78, emeritus, 1978—; vis. prof. Davidson Coll., 1979-80. Mem. Am., So. (exec. com. 1959-61, v.p. 1962-63) econ. assns., Indsl. Relations Research Assn., Beta Gamma Sigma, Alpha Kappa Psi, Delta Tau Delta. Co-author: Investment Timing: The Formula Plan Approach, 1953; Corporate Earning Power and Market Valuation: 1935-55, 1959; Marketing Management: A Quantitative Approach. 1964. Co-editor: Essays in Southern Economic Development, 1964. Home: 1533 Emory Rd NE Atlanta GA 30306

WHITMORE, CHARLES HORACE, utility exec., lawyer; b. Atlantic, Iowa, June 29, 1914; s. Tom Cornell and Adda Maria (Baldwin) W.; B.A., Grinnell Coll., 1935; J.D., State U. Iowa, 1940; LL.D., St. Ambrose Coll., 1960; m. Milicent Stahly, May 3, 1935; children—Jacqueline, Tom Cornell. Admitted to Iowa bar, 1937, Ill. bar, 1939; asst. counsel United Light & Power Co., 1937-41, exec. operating asst., 1942-43; asst. to pres. Iowa-Ill. Gas & Electric Co., Davenport, Iowa, 1946-47, gen. counsel, 1948-54, v.p., 1950-54, dir., 1950—, pres., 1954-75, chmn. bd., 1956-79, chmn. exec. com., 1979—; dir. First Nat. Bank Rock Island (Ill.), Equitable Life Ins. Co. Iowa; pres. Quad-City Devel. Group, 1971-73; chmn. Mid-Am. Interpool Network, also mem. Nat. Elec. Reliability Council, 1968-69. Served as lt., aviation supply officer USNR, 1944-45. Mem. Assn. Edison Illuminating Co., Edison Electric Inst., Delta Theta Phi. Presbyterian. Clubs: Crow Valley Golf; Rock Island (Ill.) Arsenal Golf; Univ. (Chgo.); Outing (Davenport). Home: Steepmeadow Rock Island IL 61201 Office: 206 E 2d St Davenport IA 52801

WHITMORE, EDWARD HUGH, mathematician; b. Ottawa, Ill., Feb. 26, 1926; s. Chester Teal and Maude (McCullough) W.; student U. Pa., 1944, U. Notre Dame, 1946; B.S., Ill. State U., 1949, M.S., 1951; Ph.D., Ohio State U., 1956; m. Bertha Harper, June 11, 1949; children—Stephen Harper, Ann Elizabeth. Instr. math. Clinton (Ill.) Community High Sch., 1949-51; grad. asst., asst. instr. math. Ohio State U., 1952-54; asst. prof. math. No. Ill. U., Dekalb, 1955; asst. prof. math. San Francisco State Coll., 1956-59, asso. prof., 1960-65; chmn. dept. math. Central Mich. U., Mt. Pleasant, 1966-74, 76—, prof., 1966—, acting dean Sch. Arts and Scis., 1968-69; cons. sch. systems, Calif., Mich.; mem. Calif. Adv. Com. Math., 1962-64, Mich. Math. Curriculum Com., 1966-67. Served to lt. (j.g.) USNR, 1944-47. Mem. Nat. Council Tchrs. Math. (past com. chmn.), Math. Assn. Am., Kappa Mu Epsilon, Phi Delta Kappa, Phi Eta Sigma. Author: Modern Mathematics, Book 1, 2d edit., 1971, Book 2, 2d edit., 1971; dept. editor The Math. Tchr., 1967-70. Home: 1105 N Fairfield St Mount Pleasant MI 48858

WHITMORE, GEORGE DEWEY, civil engr.; b. Hillman, Mich., Apr. 25, 1898; s. George Edward and Jenny (Ames) W.; student pub. schs., Mich.; m. Helen Fern O'Neill, June 26, 1918; children—Patricia, Richard (dec.), Robert, James, Jane, Margaret. With R.H. Randall & Co., geodetic and topographic engrs., 1917-33, v.p., Toledo, 1926-33; chief surveys, maps and surveys br. TVA, 1933-45; with topographic div. U.S. Geol. Survey, Washington, 1945-68, chief topographic engr., 19S7-68; mem. adv. com. photogrammetry Syracuse (N.Y.) U., 1945-50; adv. com. geodesy, cartography and photogrammetry Ohio State U., 1955-60; chmn. com. topographic maps and aerophotogrammetry, commn. cartography Pan Am. Inst. Geography and History, 1955—; chmn. U.S. Govt. Tech. Adv. Com. Antarctica Mapping, 1957; U.S. Mem. sci. com. Antarctica research Internat. Council Sci. Union, 1959; chmn. com. internat. cartographic matters Nat. Acad. Scis.-NRC, 1960-61; mem. Am. editorial bd. Photogrammetria, 1960-68; chief U.S. rep. UN Tech. Conf. Internat. Map of World, 1962. Recipient Distinguished Service award Dept. Interior, 1958; Carlos Struck award, 1968. Registered profl. engr., N.C., Va., Ind. Fellow ASCE (hon. mem.), Am. Geog. Soc., AAAS; mem. Am. Soc. Photogrammetry (pres. 1952), Am. Congress Surveying and Mapping (pres. 1943-45), Am. Geophys. Union, Soc. Am. Mil. Engrs., Am. Geol. Inst., Internat. Soc. Photogrammetry (gov. council 1960-64), Canadian Inst. Surveying, Wash. Soc. Engrs. Roman Cath. Club: Cosmos (Washington). Author textbooks, chpts. in books, articles. Address: 149 Lawrence Ave Woodstock IL 60098

WHITMORE, JAMES ALLEN, actor; b. White Plains, N.Y., Oct. 1, 1921; s. James Allen and Florence Belle (Crane) W.; B.A., Yale U., 1942; m. Audra Lindley, July 24, 1971; children—James, Steven, Daniel. Appeared in Broadway plays Command Decision, 1947, Winesburg, Ohio, 1956, Inquest, 1970, Will Rogers U.S.A.; appeared in plays Give 'Em Hell Harry, 1974, The Magnificent Yankee, Washington, 1976, nat. town Bully, 1977; appeared in numerous motion pictures, 1948—, including Battleground, 1949, Black Like Me, 1962, Harrad Experiment, 1973, Give 'Em Hell Harry, 1974 (Acad. award nomination 1975), Bully, 1978; TV appearances include My Friend Tony, 1969, Temperature Rising, 1972-73, Will Rogers USA, 1973. Served with USMCR, 1942-46. Recipient Acad. Award nomination, 1949, Antoinette Perry award, 1947; named Most Promising Newcomer, 1947; comedy award Am. Acad. Humor. Malibu CA Office: care Blake Agy Ltd 409 N Camden Dr 202 Beverly Hills CA 90210•

WHITMORE, JOHN EDWIN, banker; b. Tucumcari, N.Mex., Dec. 17, 1907; s. John Elias and Margaret (Neafus) W.; student U. Tex., 1925-26, U. N.Mex., 1926-29; LL.B., Jefferson Law Sch., 1937; m. Clara Bauman, Mar. 28, 1942; children—John Edwin III, Maria, James, Margaret. With Tex. Commerce Bank, Houston, 1945-72, pres., 1965-69, chmn. bd., 1969-72, chief exec. officer, 1966-72; sr. chmn. Tex. Commerce Bancshares, Inc., Houston, 1972—; dir. Tex. Commerce Bank, Tex. Commerce Bankshares, Inc., Gordon Jewelry Corp., Guardian Bank Houston; dir. emeritus Hughes Tool Co. Bd. dirs. Houston Symphony Soc., 1965—; trustee Baylor Coll. Medicine, 1969—. Served to lt. comdr. USNR, 1942-45. Mem. Pi Kappa Alpha. Presbyterian. Clubs: River Oaks, Ramada, Houston, Sugar Creek, Masons. Home: 5555 Del Monte St Houston TX 77056 Office: 712 Main St PO Box 2558 Houston TX 77001

WHITMORE, JOHN ROGERS, banker; b. Columbia, Mo., Nov. 19, 1933; s. Rogers and Catherine (Gray) W.; A.B. in Polit. Sci., U. Mo., 1954, J.D., 1958; m. Suzanne Smith, Dec. 21, 1965; children—Elizabeth Anne, Margaret Penn. Admitted to Ill. bar, 1958, Mo. bar, 1958, D.C. bar, 1967; asst. sec. trust div. Continental Ill. Nat. Bank & Trust Co., Chgo., 1958-66; sr. v.p., trust officer Am. Security and Trust Co., Washington, 1967-75; pres., chief exec. officer Bessemer Trust Co., N.A., N.Y.C., 1975—, Bessemer Trust Co., Newark, 1975—, Bessemer Trust Co. Fla., Palm Beach, 1975—; dir. Bessemer Securities Corp., N.Y.C., Chevy Chase Property Co. Ltd., Bermuda. Chmn. trustees Leonard Wood Meml. Nat. Found. Eradication Leprosy, Washington; trustee Greenwich (Conn.) Acad. Served to lt. comdr. USNR, 1955-57. Mem. Am., Ill., Mo., D.C., Chgo. bar assns., Phi Delta Phi. Mem. Community Ch. Clubs: University, Brook (N.Y.C.); Belle Haven (Greenwich); Metropolitan, Chevy Chase (Washington). Home: 50 Fox Run Ln Greenwich CT 06830 Office: 245 Park Ave New York NY 10017

WHITMORE, RALPH ERVIN, JR., banker; b. Sharon, Pa., Aug. 30, 1932; s. Ralph Ervin and Helen Lucille (Snyder) W.; B.S. in Econs., U. Pa., 1955; m. Nancy Carroll Ward, May 16, 1959; children—Ralph Ervin, III, John Winston. Partner, Whitmore, Bruce & Co., investment bankers, N.Y.C., 1957-61; pres. Whitemore & Co., Inc., investment banking and capital venture, N.Y.C., 1961-68; chmn. bd., chief exec. officer Alaska Bancorp. and Alaska State Bank, Anchorage, 1969—. Office: PO Box 240 Anchorage AK 99510

WHITMORE, SHARP, lawyer; b. Pirce, Utah, Apr. 26, 1918; s. Leland and Anne (Sharp) W.; A.B., Stanford U., 1939; J.D., U. Calif., Berkeley, 1942; m. Frances Dorr, Aug. 15, 1940; children—Richard, William, Ann. Admitted to Calif. bar, 1944; asso. firm Gibson, Dunn & Crutcher, Los Angeles, 1946-50, partner, 1951—; chmn. Calif. Com. Bar Examiners, 1956-58. Pres., Bd. Mcpl. Auditorium Commrs. City of Los Angeles, 1974-75. Served with USNR, 1942-46. Fellow Am. Bar Found.; mem. Los Angeles County Bar Assn. (pres. 1970-71), Nat. Conf. Bar Examiners (chmn. 1957-58), State Bar Calif. (bd. govs. 1962-65, v.p. treas. 1964-65), Am. Bar Assn. (ho. of dels. 1957-58, 68—), Am. Law Inst., Order of Coif (hon.). Republican. Clubs: Bohemian, Sunset, Chancery (pres. 1962-63). Home: 2005 Gird Rd Fallbrook CA 92028 Office: Suite 4000 2029 Century Park E Los Angeles CA 90067

WHITMORE, WILLIAM FRANCIS, missile scientist; b. Boston, Jan. 6, 1917; s. Charles Edward and Elizabeth Manning (Gardiner) W.; S.B., Mass. Inst. Tech., 1938; Ph.D. (Univ. fellow), U. Calif. at Berkeley, 1941; m. Elizabeth Sherman Arnold, Nov. 1, 1946; children—Charles, Edward, Thomas, Peter. Math. physicist Naval Ordnance Lab., 1941-42; instr. physics Mass. Inst. Tech., 1942-46; sr. staff mem. ops. evaluation group U.S. Navy, 1946-57, chief scientist spl. projects office, 1957-59; mem. chief scientist's staff missiles and space div. Lockheed Aircraft Corp., 1959-62, dep. chief scientist Lockheed Missiles & Space Co., Sunnyvale, Calif., 1962-64, asst. to pres., 1964-69, sr. cons. scientist, 1969—; spl. cons. evaluation bd. of USAAF, ETO, 1945; sci. analyst to comdg. gen. 1st Marine Wing, Korea, 1953, to asst. chief naval ops. for guided missiles, 1950-56; cons. adv. panel ordnance, transport and supply Dir. Def. Research and Engring., 1958-62; mem. adv. bd. for Naval Ordnance Labs., 1968-75, chmn., 1968-73; cons. marine bd. NRC, 1973—. Mem. vis. com., math. dept. M.I.T., 1971-78. Recipient Navy Meritorious Pub. Service citation, 1961; Sec. Navy certificate of commendations (3), 1960-66. Asso. fellow Am. Inst. Aeros. and Astronautics; mem. Am. Math. Soc., Math. Assn. Am., Optical Soc. Am., Ops. Research Soc. Am., Nat. Rifle Assn. (life), Phi Beta Kappa, Sigma Xi. Club: Cosmos. Home: 14120 Miranda Ave Los Altos Hills CA 94022 Office: Lockheed Missiles and Space Co Box 504 Sunnyvale CA 94086

WHITMYER, RUSSELL ELIOT, elec. co. exec.; b. Hartford, Conn., Aug. 7, 1915; s. John Erdman and Ruth (O'Connor) W.; B.A., Amherst Coll., 1936; postgrad. Advanced Mgmt. Program, Harvard U., 1953; m. Cecile Bausman Dunlap, Oct. 29, 1960; children—Heather McAlpin (Mrs. C. Charles Richardson), Emily McAlpin Marusi, Elizabeth McAlpin. With Gen. Electric Co., 1936—, treas., mgr. fin. ops. Internat. Gen. Electric Co., 1953-63, v.p., gen. mgr. Latin Am. div., 1964-73, v.p., treas., 1973—. Served to lt. USNR, 1942-46. Mem. Fin. Execs. Inst., Psi Upsilon. Clubs: Lancaster (Pa.) Country; Hamilton (Lancaster); Princess Anne Country (Virginia Beach, Va.); Marco Polo (N.Y.C.). Home: 150 E 77th St New York NY 10021 Office: 570 Lexington Ave New York NY 10022

WHITNAH, DONALD ROBERT, educator; b. Canton, Ill., June 9, 1925; s. Leon Arthur and Anna (Jackley) W.; B.A., U. Ill., 1951, M.A., 1952, Ph.D., 1957; m. Florentine Egger, Aug. 9, 1947; children—Victoria Ann, Tara Beth. Mdse. control mgr. U.S. War Dept. Army Exchange Service, Salzburg, Austria, 1946-47; mem. history faculty Valley City State Coll. (N.D.), 1956-59; asst. prof. history U. No. Iowa, Cedar Falls, 1959-62, asso. prof., 1962-66, prof., 1966—, head dept. history, 1968—. Served with C.E., AUS, 1944-46. Recipient research grants Lincoln Ednl. Found., N.Y.C., 1969-71, U. No. Iowa, 1968. Mem. Am., So. hist. assns., Orgn. Am. Historians, Soc. Historians Am. Fgn. Relations, Am. Com. History World War II, AAUP, Phi Kappa Phi, Phi Alpha Theta. Kiwanian. Author: A History of the United States Weather Bureau, 1961; Safer Skyways: Federal Control of Aviation, 1926-1966, 1967. Home: 1215 Catherine St Cedar Falls IA 50613

WHITNER, GEORGE CRABTREE, banker; b. Jacksonville, Fla., June 27, 1923; s. John Addison and Eleanor Castit (Crabtree) W.; B.S., U. N.C., 1947; grad. Stonier Grad. Sch. Banking, Rutgers U., 1970; m. Virginia Hilyard, Dec. 3, 1955; children—Banta H., Virginia, Eleanor, John A. IV. Field supt. Whitner & Lawrence, Inc., ins., Jacksonville, 1947-57; agt. supt. N.Y. Underwriters Ins. Co., 1957-58; with Fla. First Nat. Bank, Jacksonville, 1958—, pres., 1972—, also dir.; vice chmn. bd. Fla. Bank at Starke; pres. Fla. Bank at Lakeshore. Treas. Jacksonville chpt. Am. Cancer Soc., 1960-63; pres. Speech and Hearing Center Jacksonville, 1966, Fla. Jr. Coll. at Jacksonville Found., 1972-73; v.p. Travelers Aid Soc. Jacksonville, 1973, treas., 1970-72; pres. Travelers Aid Soc. Served to lt. (j.g.) USNR, 1943-46. Mem. Delta Kappa Epsilon. Republican. Presbyn. (elder). Clubs: Meninak (treas. 1968-73), River Timuquana Country (Jacksonville). Home: 3905 Timuquana Rd Jacksonville FL 32210 Office: Fla First Nat Bank West Bay Annex Jacksonville FL 32203

WHITNEY, A(DELBERT) GRANT, mercantile and ins. co. exec.; b. Lowell, Mass., July 25, 1917; s. Adelbert Howard and Julia (Sheehan) W.; B.S. in Bus. Adminstrn., Boston U., 1940; m. Lillian Ritch DeArmon, Nov. 17, 1950; children—Julia Woodley, A. Grant, Frank DeArmon. Asst. to v.p. Belk Stores, Charlotte, N.C., 1946-52, asst. to pres., 1952-55, v.p. sec.-treas. Belk Stores, Inc. Reciprocal, Belk Underwriters, Inc., Charlotte, 1950-58, exec. v.p., sec.-treas., 1958—; sec.-treas. Archdale Mut. Ins. Co., 1962-65, exec. v.p., sec.-treas., 1965—; gen. mgr. ins. dept. Belk Stores Services, Inc., 1951—, sec., mem. exec. com., 1959-68, v.p. 1964-68, employee ins. operating com., 1971, 72; v.p. sec.-treas. Providence Realty Corp., Charlotte, 1950-63, pres., 1959-60, pres., sec.-treas., 1964-75; v.p. Queen City Investors, Inc., Charlotte, 1959-62; sec. Thrifty Investors, Inc., Charlotte, 1961-62, investment chmn., 1964-65, v.p. 1967-68; trustee Elmira (N.Y.) Coll., 1978—. Mem. exec. com. Arthritis and Rheumatism Found., Charlotte, 1959-60, dir., 1959-60; gen. chmn. Billy Graham Appreciation Day, 1968, Billy Graham Birthday Party, 1978; mem. exec. bd. Mecklenburg council Boy Scouts Am., 1949—, v.p., 1962-66, exec. bd. S.E. region, 1973—, mem.-at-large nat. council, 1974—; chmn. N.C. USO, 1959-73; spl. gifts chmn. N.C. div. Am. Cancer Soc., 1967, crusade chmn., 1969, 70, bd. dirs., 1968—, pres., 1972-73; mem. Mayor's Com. Better Charlotte, 1974—; program chmn. Charlotte Bi-Centennial Celebration Com., 1968—, chmn. Charlotte/Mecklenburg Bicentennial Com., 1975, 76; gen. chmn. Mecklenburg Declaration of Independence-Freedom Celebration Day, 1975; industry chmn. laymen's nat. com. Nat. Bible Week, 1967-70, asso. chmn., 1971—; chmn. adv. com. Charlotte Youth for Christ; bd. dirs. Mecklenburg Citizens Better Libraries, 1967-71, Charlotte Council on Alcholism, Contact of Charlotte, Goodwill Industries, Charlotte, Inc., United Arts Council, N.C. Multiple Sclerosis Soc., Charlotte Symphony Soc., 1949-55; creator, dir. Festival in the Park, 1964—; bd. visitors Brevard Music Center; trustee United Community Services; chmn. promotional activities planning com. Downtown Charlotte Assn., 1965-68; bd. govs. Insts. Religion and Health; parents' council Davidson Coll., 1972-73. Served as officer AUS, World War II; col. Res. ret. Recipient Distinguished Service award Jr. C. of C., 1952; named Charlotte Young Man of Year, 1952; recipient Silver Beaver award Boy Scouts Am., 1956, Freedom Found. Bronze medal, Printing Industry of the Carolinas, Franklin Medallion award, 1973, Soldiers medal for Heroism U.S. Army; elected to Exec. and Profl. Hall Fame, 1966 mem. selection com., 1967—; recipient Distinguished Service award Charlotte Rotary Club, 1966, Charlotte Exchange Club, 1967, Jungle Aviation and Radio Service, Inc., 1971; Distinguished Service certificate USO, 1973; Community Bicentennial certificate of commendation U.S. Conf. Mayors, 1976; service to Mankind award Sertoma Clubs of Charlotte, 1977; Distinguished Ser. award Hornets Nest Council Girl Scouts Am., 1976, 77; named Man of Year, Charlotte News, 1975; City proclamation, 1977; Ky. col. Mem. Risk and Ins. Mgmt. Soc. (formerly Am. Soc. Ins. Mgmt. (pres. Va.-Carolinas chpt. 1957-58, Carolinas chpt. 1963-64, nat. v.p. conf. activities 1965-66, 1st v.p. 1966-67, pres., 1967-68, Man of Year award, Pres.'s award 1971), Internat. Ins. Seminars Inc., Am. Mgmt. Assn. (participant confs. seminars), Ins. Hall Fame (internat. bd. electors 1968-70, chamber electors 1972—), Nat. Assn. Ind. Insurers (v.p. 1953-67, dir. 1968—, vice chmn. 1977-78, chmn. 1978-79), Captive Ins. Cos. Assn. v.p. 1973-74, sec. 1974—, U.S. (ins. com. 1967-69), Charlotte chambers commerce, Mil. Order World Wars, Am. Legion, Carolina Carrousel (dir. 1952-57, 70-71, hon. grand marshall parade 1976), Jr. Achievement, Inc., Newcomen Soc. N.Am., Royal Soc. Knights Carrousel (pres. 1955-64, chmn. governing council 1964-68), Soc. 1st Div. Inf. Assn. U.S. Army, Am. Found. Religion and Psychiatry (gov. 1959—), French Fgn. Legion (hon.). Presbyterian (elder). Clubs: Masons (33 deg.), Shriners, Lions; Boston U. Alumni of the Carolinas (pres. 1949-51, nat. alumni council 1962—), Execs. (pres. 1963-64), Myers Park Country, Charlotte City, Goodfellows (Charlotte). Home: 684 Colville Rd Charlotte NC 28207 Office: 308 E 5th St Charlotte NC 28202. *Each of us, endowed with certain talents, has much to do to utilize them to their fullest extent, within the realm of our ability, in order to meet the challenge of life and not let indecision or inaction deter us from accomplishing the meaningful life work of which we are capable.*

WHITNEY, CHARLES ALLEN, astronomer, writer; b. Milw., Jan. 31, 1929; s. Charles Smith and Gertrude (Schuyler) W.; B.S., Mass. Inst. Tech., 1951; A.M., Harvard U., 1953, Ph.D. (Agassiz fellow, NSF fellow), 1955; m. Jane Ann Hall, Jan. 27, 1951; children—Elizabeth Ann, David Hall, Thomas Charles, Peter Schuyler, James Andrew. Physicist, Smithsonian Astrophys. Obs., 1956—; research asso. Harvard Coll. Obs., 1956-62; mem. faculty Harvard, 1958—, asso. prof. astronomy, 1963-68, prof., 1968—. Mem. Am. Astron. Soc., Am. Acad. Arts and Scis., Internat. Astron. Union. Author: The Discovery of Our Galaxy, 1971; Whitney's Star Finder, 1974, rev. edit., 1977; contbr. articles to mags. and profl. jours. Home: 527 Boston Post Rd Weston MA 02193 Office: Harvard Obs Cambridge MA 02138

WHITNEY, CORNELIUS VANDERBILT, corp. exec.; b. N.Y.C., Feb. 20, 1899; B.A., Yale U., 1922; Aero. Sci. (hon.), Embry-Riddle Aero. U., 1978; m. Marie Louise Hosford, Jan. 24, 1958; 5 children. Founder, Pan Am. Airways, 1927, chmn. bd., until 1941; founder Hudson Bay Mining and Smelting Co., 1928, chmn. bd., until 1964, dir., until 1974; pres. Whitney Industries, Inc., 1931—; founder, chmn. bd. Marineland Inc. (Fla.), 1937; co-producer motion pictures A Star is Born, Rebecca, Gone with the Wind, 1930-36; asst. sec. USAAF, 1947-49; undersec. commerce, 1949-50; spl. envoy of Pres. to Eng., Luxemburg, Italy, Spain, 1950. Past trustee Whitney Mus. Am. Art, Am. Mus. Natural History; dir. emeritus Buffalo Bill Hist. Found., Cody, Wyo.; mem. Ky. Gov.'s Econ. Commn. Served to 2d lt., A.C., U.S. Army, World War I; to col. USAAF, 1941-46. Decorated D.S.M., Legion of Merit with 2 battle stars. Clubs: Anglers, River, Brook (N.Y.C.). Author: (autobiography) High Peaks, 1977. Home: 834 Fifth Ave New York NY 10021 Office: 230 Park Ave New York NY 10017

WHITNEY, CRAIG RICHARD, journalist; b. Milford, Mass., Oct. 12, 1943; s. A. Gordon and Carol Alma (Kennison) W.; A.B., Harvard, 1965; m. Heidi Witt, May 11, 1974; children—Alexandra Kennison, Stefan Robert. Reporter New York Times, Washington, 1965-66, N.Y.C., 1969-70, Saigon, Vietnam, 1971-72, Bonn, West Germany, 1973-77, Moscow, USSR, 1977—. Served with USNR, 1966-69. Mem. Fgn. Press Assn. Home and Office: 12-24 Sadovo Samotechnaya Moscow USSR

WHITNEY, DAVID CHARLES, editor, writer; b. Salina, Kans., Mar. 8, 1921; s. William R. and Jerusha F. (McCartney) W.; A.B., U. Kans., 1942; student Columbia, 1946; m. Elizabeth J. West, Jan. 31, 1943; children—Ann G., Katherine W., Jane P., West Martin, Peter A., Lynn McC. Reporter, asst. editor Douglas County (Kans.) Outlook, 1940-41, Topeka Daily Capital, 1942; reporter United Press, 1945-47, asst. copy editor, 1947-49, N.Y.C. overnight bur. mgr. and news editor, 1949-51; asst. to mng. editor World Book Ency., Chgo., 1952-54, mng. editor, 1954-64; v.p., editor-in-chief Ency. Americana, 1964-65; pres., editor Cowies Edn. Corp., N.Y.C., 1965-68; v.p. ednl. systems Universal Edn. Corp., 1969-72; pres., editor David C. Whitney Assos., Inc., 1972—. Pres. Village bd. trustees, mayor Deerfield, Ill., 1961-64; pres. bd. edn. Sch. Dist. 110, Deerfield, Ill., 1956-61; mem. Library bd. trustees, Chappaqua, N.Y., 1975-80, pres., 1978-80. Trustee W. Deerfield Twp. Pub. Library, 1953-59. Served from ensign to lt. USNR, 1942-45. Benjamin Franklin fellow Royal Soc. Arts. Mem. Am. Soc. Curriculum Devel., Soc. Mayflower Descs., Friends of Library, Am. Hist. Soc., Authors Guild, Sigma Delta Chi. Author: Founders of Freedom, Vol. I, 1964, Vol. II, 1965; The American Presidents, 1967, 69, 75, 78; Two Dynamic Decades, 1968; Colonial Spirit of '76, 1974; The American Legacy, 1975, also 20 children's books. Editor: Reader's Digest Almanac, 1974—. Inventor Cycloteacher teaching machine, 1961; created, developed early childhood edn. curriculums: Discovery Program, 1969; Educare System, 1970-72. Address: 291 Roaring Brook Rd Chappaqua NY 10514. *Genuine pleasure can only come from aiding the lives of others.*

WHITNEY, GEORGE HAYWARD, JR., investment banker; b. Boston, May 1, 1927; s. George Hayward and Dorothy A. (Jordan) W.; grad. Milton Acad., 1945; B.S., Harvard, 1950; children—Carol, Anita, George Hayward III; m. 2d, Patricia W. Tailer, Oct. 27, 1970. Trainee, Hathaway Mfg. Co., New Bedford, Mass., 1950-51; broker White, Weld & Co., Boston, 1951-60; v.p. Blyth & Co., Inc., Boston, 1960-72; v.p. nat. sales, dir., mem. exec. com. F.S. Moseley, Estabrook Inc., 1973-74; with H.C. Wainwright & Co., 1975-77, Alex. Brown & Sons, Boston, 1977—; treas. Mass. Venture Capital Corp.; dir. KDOC. Treas., trustee Boston Urban Found. Served with USMCR, 1945-46. Mem. Investment Bankers Assn. (nat. gov.). Home: 49 Moorings Rd Marion MA 02738 Office: Alex Brown & Sons 1 Boston Pl Boston MA 02108

WHITNEY, GEORGE KIRKPATRICK, investment cons.; b. Concord, Mass., Nov. 9, 1907; s. Charles Hayden and Caroline (Patrick) W.; A.B., Harvard U., 1929, M.B.A., 1931; m. Donita Stahl, 1936 (dec.); children—Robert Hayden, Sarah Minot, Faith Thomas Newcomb; m. 2d, Una Rogers King, Sept. 6, 1951. With trust investment div., trust dept. First Nat. Bank Chgo., 1931-34; investment dept. Conn. Bank & Trust Co., 1934-43; investment research dept. Mass. Investors Trust, 1943-47, trustee, 1947-70; dir., mem. investment mgmt. com. Mass. Investors Growth Stock Fund, Inc., 1945-70, v.p., 1963-70; gov. Investment Co. Inst., 1960-63, mem. exec. com., 1960-62; sr. v.p., dir. Mass. Financial Services, 1969-70, cons., 1970-77, ltd. partner, 1977—. Bd. dirs. Big Bros. Assn., Boston; corporator Emerson Hosp., Concord; chmn. Harvard Bus. Sch. Fund, 1963-66; mem. Harvard Overseers Com. to Visit Bus. Sch., 1968-74; bd. dirs. Harvard Bus. Sch. Assos., 1971-74, 75—, mem. adminstrv. bd. Adams Papers. Mem. Mass. Hist. Soc. (v.p., fin. com.), Harvard Bus. Sch. Assn. (exec. council 1966-73, pres. 1967-68; Distinguished Service award 1969), Asso. Harvard Alumni (dir. 1968-70), World Affairs Council Boston (dir., exec. com.), Nat. Trust Historic Preservation (life), Transp. Assn. Am. (dir. 1947—, chmn. 1968-70, hon. chmn. 1970-74, chmn. bd. govs. 1976-77, Seley award 1974), Nat. Assn. Investment Cos. (pres. 1960-61), Am. Hist. Assn. (life), Soc. Preservation of New Eng. Antiquities, Soc. Colonial Wars, New Eng. Historic Geneal. Soc., Bostonian Soc. (life), Am. Forestry Assn. (life), New Eng. Forestry Found. (founder). Republican. Episcopalian. Clubs: Econ., Union (Boston); Harvard (N.Y.C.); Country (Brookline, Mass.); Concord Country; Ekwanok Country (Manchester, Vt.); Harvard Varsity, Speakers' (Cambridge, Mass.); Met. (Washington); Mid-Ocean (Bermuda). Home: 207 Musketaquid Rd Concord MA 01742 Office: 200 Berkeley St Boston MA 02116

WHITNEY, HASSLER, mathematician; b. N.Y.C., Mar. 23, 1907; s. Edward Baldwin and A. Josepha (Newcomb) W.; Ph.B., Yale U., 1928, Mus.B., 1929, Sc.D. (hon.), 1947; Ph.D., Harvard U., 1932; m. Margaret R. Howell, May 30, 1930; children—James Newcomb, Carol, Marian; m. 2d, Mary Barnett Garfield, Jan. 16, 1955; children—Sarah Newcomb, Emily Baldwin. Instr. math. Harvard U., 1930-31, NRC fellow math., 1931-33, instr. math., 1933-35, asst. prof., 1935-40, asso. prof., 1940-46, prof., 1946-52; prof. Inst. Advanced Study, Princeton, N.J., 1952-77, emeritus, 1977—; chmn. math. panel NSF, 1953-56; exchange prof., France, 1951-52; Fulbright exchange prof. Coll. de France, 1957; mem. com. support of research in math. scis. NRC, 1966-67; pres. Internat. Commn. Math. Instrn., 1979—; research math. Nat. Def. Research Com., 1943-45; cons. sch. math. Recipient Nat. medal of Sci., 1976. Mem. Am. Math. Soc. (Colloguium lectr. 1946; v.p. 1948-50; editor Am. Jour. Math. 1944-49, Math. Revs., 1949-54; chmn. com. vis. lectureship 1946-51, com. summer insts. 1953-54), Math. Assn. Am., Nat. Council Tchrs. Math., Swiss Math. Soc. (hon.), Nat. Acad. Scis., Am. Philos. Soc. Club: Am. Alpine (N.Y.C.). Office: Inst Advanced Study Princeton NJ 08540

WHITNEY, JACK MELVILLE, II, lawyer; b. Huntington Beach, Calif., May 16, 1922; s. Jack Melville and Claudia (Chapline) W.; student Millsaps Coll., 1939-41; B.S. in Commerce, Northwestern U., 1943, J.D., 1949. Admitted to Ill. bar, 1949; partner firm Bell, Boyd, Lloyd, Haddad & Burns, Chgo.; mem. SEC, 1961-64; public mem. bus. conduct com. Chgo. Bd. Options Exchange, 1978—. Mem. Am., Ill., Chgo. bar assns., Order of Coif, Beta Gamma Sigma. Clubs: Attic, University, Law (Chgo.); Sheridan Shore Yacht (Wilmette, Ill.). Home: 830 Chestnut Ave Wilmette IL 60091 Office: 135 S LaSalle St Chicago IL 60603

WHITNEY, JOHN CLARENCE, lawyer; b. Green Bay, Wis., Feb. 10, 1915; s. John and May (Salvas) W.; B.A., U. Wis., 1936, LL.B., 1938; m. Helen E. Mayer, May 16, 1942; children—Kathleen A. Whitney Feeney, Robert M., John F. Admitted to Wis. bar, 1938, U.S. dist. ct. bars for Eastern and Western dists. Wis., 1940, 7th Circuit Ct. Appeals bar, 1948; Wis. Public Service Commn., 1938-39; asso. firm Everson, Ryan and Hanaway, Green Bay, Wis., 1939-41; partner firm Everson, Whitney Everson Brehm & Pfankuch and predecessors, Green Bay, 1945—; dir. West Bank & Trust, United Bank Shares, Inc., Green Bay Newspaper Co., Morley-Murphy Co. Mem. Green Bay Bd. Park Commrs., 1946-55; mem. DePere Police and Fire Commn., DePere, Wis., 1956-61; mem. Wis. Gov.'s Jud. Appointment Rev. Commn., 1978-79. Served with U.S. Army, 1941, to lt. comdr. USN, 1941-45. Named Young Man of Yr., Jr. C. of C. of Green Bay, 1949. Mem. Brown County Bar Assn. (pres. 1956), State Bar Wis., (pres. 1961-62), Am. Bar Assn., Am. Bar Found., Am. Law Inst., Am. Coll. Trial Lawyers, Order of Coif. Republican. Roman Catholic. Club: Oneida Golf and Riding. Bd. editors Wis. Law Rev., 1936-38. Home: 100 Rosemont Dr Green Bay WI 54301 Office: PO Box 1263 414 E Walnut St Green Bay WI 54305

WHITNEY, JOHN EDWARD, physiologist, educator; b. Casper, Wyo., July 6, 1926; s. Gary M. and Harriett (Whitney) W.; A.B., U. Calif., Berkeley, 1947, M.A., 1948, Ph.D., 1951; Ph.D., U. Cambridge (Eng.), 1956; m. Barbara Laundrie, June 11, 1949; children—Karen, Kathleen, Eric, Emily, Brian. Research asso. Cedars of Lebanon, Los Angeles, 1951-52, U. Calif., Los Angeles, 1952-54, U. Cambridge (Eng.), 1954-56; mem. faculty U. Ark., Little Rock, 1956—, prof. physiology, head dept., 1962—. Served with USNR, 1944-45. Mem. Am. Physiology, head dept., 1962—. Served with USNR, 1944-45. Mem. Am. Physiology Soc., Soc. Exptl. Biology and Medicine, Endocrine Soc., Am. Diabetes Assn., AAAS, Sigma Xi, Alpha Omega Alpha. Home: 7016 Rockwood St Little Rock AR 72207 Office: University of Arkansas College of Medicine Department of Physiology 4301 W Markham St Little Rock AR 72201

WHITNEY, JOHN HAY, newspaper pub.; Ellsworth, Maine, Aug. 17, 1904; s. Payne and Helen (Hay) W.; student Oxford (Eng.) U., 1926-27, Yale U., 1922-26; L.H.D., Kenyon Coll.; LL.D., Colgate U., Brown U., 1958, Exeter U., 1959, Colby Coll., Columbia U.; M.A. (hon.), Yale U.; m. 2d, Betsey Cushing Roosevelt, Mar. 1, 1942; children—Sara Wilford, Kate. Sr. partner J.H. Whitney & Co., N.Y.C.; chmn. Whitney Communications; U.S. ambassador to Gt. Britain, 1956-61; pub. N.Y. Herald-Tribune and subs.'s, 1957-61, pres., pub., 1961, editor-in-chief, pub., 1961-66; dir., mem. editorial com. World Jour. Tribune, Inc., 1966-67; chmn. Internat. Herald Tribune, Paris; partner Whitcom Investment Co.; John Hay Whitney prof. humanities Yale U., 1977; past dir. Dun & Bradstreet, Inc. Chmn. John Hay Whitney Found.; former mem. N.Y. State Youth Commn., also Pres.'s Com. on Edn. Beyond High Sch.; apptd. spl. adviser and cons. on pub. affairs Dept. State; grad. mem. Bus. Council; past mem. Corp. Pub. Broadcasting; past mem. N.Y. Banking Bd.; mem. Commn. Fgn. Econ. Policy, 1954, Policy Com. on Personnel, 1954; past mem. Saratoga Springs Commn.; trustee emeritus Saratoga Performing Arts Center; hon. mem. bd. govs. N.Y. Hosp.; hon. trustee Mus. Modern Art, N.Y. Racing Assn.; former trustee Nat. Gallery Art (v.p.); co-chmn. emeritus bd. trustees North Shore Hosp.; fellow Yale Corp., 1955-70, sr. fellow, 1970-73; bd. dirs. Ednl. Broadcasting Corp., 1969-70. Served as col. USAAF, World War II. Recipient Yale medal award, 1954; Tuition Plan award, 1954; Hundred Year Assn. gold medal; Albert Einstein Commerative award; Benjamin Franklin medal (Eng.); Elijah Parish Lovejoy award Colby Coll.; decorated Legion of Merit, Bronze Star; chevalier French Légion d'Honneur, La Grande médaille de Vermeil, Paris; knight St. John of Jerusalem; comdr. Order Brit. Empire. Mem. Pilgrims U.S. (hon. v.p.), English-Speaking Union (chmn. nat. bd. 1961-63), Scroll and Key. Clubs: Jockey (steward); Augusta Nat. Golf; N.Y. Yacht, Racquet and Tennis, Scroll and Key (N.Y.C.). Home: Manhasset NY 11030 Office: 110 W 51st St New York NY 10020

WHITNEY, JOHN JOSEPH, lawyer; b. Phila., Mar. 7, 1926; s. Joseph J. and Margaret (Kelly) W.; A.B., Oberlin Coll., 1947; LL.B., Western Res. U., 1950; m. Joan Durand, July 3, 1948; children—Susan E. Whitney Babb, John Joseph, Nancy C., Laura J. Atty., Goodyear Aircraft Corp., 1950-51; practice law, Cleve., 1953—; mem. firm Ford, Whitney, Crump & Schulz; dir. law City of Berea, Ohio, 1966-68, 72. Gen. chmn. Berea chpt. ARC Fund Campaign, 1958; mem. subcom. on water system Berea Civic Com., 1959; mem. Berea Citizens Adv. Com. on Urban Renewal, 1962-65, Berea Bd. Bldg. Code Appeals, 1962-65; chmn. subcom. on profl. personnel Berea City Sch. Dist. Study Com., 1963-64; mem. adv. com. Deaconess Hosp.; trustee Lake Ridge Acad. Served to lt. USNR, 1946-47, 51-53. Mem. Am., Ohio, Cleve. bar assns., Berea, Cleve. chambers commerce. Conglist. Club: Cleve. Rotary. Editor-in-chief: Western Res. U. Law Rev., 1949-50. Home: 445 S Rocky River Dr Berea OH 44017 Office: Williamson Bldg Cleveland OH 44114

WHITNEY, PHYLLIS AYAME, author; b. Yokohama, Japan, Sept. 9, 1903; d. Charles J. and Lillian (Mandeville) Whitney; grad. McKinley High Sch., Chgo., 1924; m. George A. Garner, July 2, 1925; 1 dau., Georgia; m. 2d, Lovell F. Jahnke, 1950 (dec. 1973). Spent first

15 years of life in Japan, China and P.I. (father in shipping and hotel business); instr. dancing, San Antonio, 1 yr.; sold first story to Chgo. Daily News; later wrote for pulp mags.; became specialist in juvenile writing; tchr. juvenile fiction writing Northwestern U., 1945; children's book editor Chgo. Sun, 1942-46, Phila. Inquirer, 1947, 48; instr. juvenile fiction writing N.Y.U., 1947-58; leader juvenile fiction workshop Writers Conf., U. Colo., 1952, 54, 56. Pres. Authors Round Table, 1943, 44; pres. exec. bd. Fifth Annual Writers Conf., Northwestern U., 1944. Recipient Friends of Lit. award contbrs. children's lit., 1943; Reynal and Hitchcock prize ($3000) in Youth Today contest for book, Willow Hill. Mem. Mystery Writers Am. (pres. 1975). Author: A Place for Ann, 1941; A Star for Ginny, 1942; A Window for Julie, 1943; (vocational fiction for teen-age girls); Red Is for Muder (mystery novel for adults), 1943; The Silver Inkwell, 1945; Willow Hill, 1947; Writing Juvenile Fiction, 1947; Ever After, 1948; Mystery of the Gulls, 1949; Linda's Homecoming, 1950; The Island of Dark Woods, 1951; Love Me, Love Me Not, 1952; Step to the Music, 1953; A Long Time Coming, 1954; Mystery of the Black Diamonds, 1954; The Quicksilver Pool, 1955; Mystery on the Isle of Skye, 1955; The Fire and The Gold (Jr. Lit. Guild), 1956; The Highest Dream (Jr. Lit. Guild); The Trembline Hills (Peoples Book Club), 1956; Skye Cameron, 1957; Mystery of the Green Cat, (Jr. Lit. Guild), 1957; Secret of the Samurai Sword (Jr. Lit. Guild), 1958; The Moonflower, 1958; Creole Holiday, 1959; Thunder Heights, 1960; Blue Fire, 1961; Mystery of the Haunted Pool (Edgar award Mystery Writers Am.), 1961; Secret of the Tiger's Eye, 1961; Window on the Square, 1962; Mystery of the Golden Horn, 1962; Seven Tears for Apollo, 1963; Mystery of the Hidden Hand, 1963 (Edgar award Mystery Writers Am. 1964); Black Amber, 1964; Secret of the Emerald Star, 1964; Sea Jade, 1965; Mystery of the Angry Idol, 1965; Columbella, 1966; Secret of the Spotted Shell, 1967; Mystery of the Strange Traveler, 1967; Silverhill, 1967; Hunter's Green, 1968; Secret of Goblin Glen, 1968; Mystery of the Crimson Ghost, 1969; Winter People, 1969; Secret of the Missing Footprint, 1970; Lost Island, 1970; The Vanishing Scarecrow, 1971; Listen for the Whisperer, 1971; Nobody Likes Trina, 1972; Snowfire, 1973; Mystery of the Scowling Boy, 1973; The Turquoise Mask, 1974; Spindrift, 1975; Secret of Haunted Mesa, 1975; The Golden Unicorn, 1976; Secret of the Stone Face, 1977; The Stone Bull, 1977; The Glass Flame, 1978. Address: care McIntosh & Otis 475 Fifth Ave New York NY 10017. *A learning period must be allowed for any talent. The accidental success is unfortunate because the person who achieves it doesn't really know how it happened. This does not mean that it ever becomes easy, even with learning. There is always work involved-long hours and dedication to that work-before a book is ready for publication. Any success demands a price, and the time and effort, and sometimes anguish a successful person gives to his work is that price. For me, the satisfactions have been worth it.*

WHITNEY, ROBERT AVERY, bus. exec.; b. Buffalo, Nov. 7, 1912; s. John Boardman and Cora Edith (Avery) W.; student Berlin (Germany) U., 1931-32, U. Buffalo, 1933; A.B., Hobart Coll., 1935; m. Marie Therese Thone; children—Grace Ann, Marguerite, Barbara Griffith, Robert Avery, John David, Virginia Bradley. Sales rep. Wilson & Co., Stamford, Conn., 1935-37; statistician Francis I. duPont, N.Y., 1937; eastern sales mgr. Simplicity Prevue Mag., N.Y.C., 1937-40; sales promotion and advt. mgr. Corning (N.Y.) Glass Works, 1940-43; chief of controller materials plan div. WPB, 1942-43; promotion dir. McGraw Hill Pub. Co., N.Y., 1943-46; dir. Ency. Brit. Press, Chgo., also N.Y., 1946-47; exec. dir. Nat. Fedn. Sales Execs., N.Y.C., 1947-48; pres. Nat. Sales Execs., Inc., 1948-57; pres. Mgmt. and Mktg. Inst., 1957—, Robert A. Whitney & Co., 1962—. Spl. cons. to dir. RFC, Washington, 1944-45; cons. to dir. Office of War Mblzn. and Reconversion, Washington, 1945-46; adviser to War Assets Adminstrn., Washington, 1944-45; mem. nat. industry advisory council to sec. of treasury; mem. nat. distbn. council to sec. of commerce; mem. industry advisory com. to U.S. Army and Air Force; mem. advisory com. ECA; dir. White House Conf. Distbn. Trustee Hobart Coll., mem. alumni council; trustee Irvington House, N.Y. U. Hosp.; advisory council Sch. Bus. N.Y. U.; bd. dirs. Am. Found. Religion and Psychiatry. Named to Hall of Fame of Distbn., 1953; recipient Outstanding Man in Mgmt. and Mktg. award, 1963. Mem. Nat. Planning Assn. (dir.), N.Y. Bd. Trade, Am. Mgmt. Assn., Internat. C. of C. (chmn. dist. com. U.S. council), Newcomen Soc., Kappa Alpha (nat. pres. 1963-64). Republican. Episcopalian. Clubs: N.Y. Sales Executives, Metropolitan, Canadian (N.Y.C.); Union League (Chgo.); Arts (London). Home: 34 Rock Spring Ave West Orange NJ 07052 also 49 Lennox Gardens SW1 England Office: 1257 Landecy Geneva Switzerland

WHITNEY, ROY POWELL, chem. engr.; b. Milo, Me., May 30, 1913; s. Andrew Donald and Laura Mary (Powell) W.; B.S., Mass. Inst. Tech., 1935, M.S., 1937, Sc.D., 1945; m. Virginia Margaret Gordon, Dec. 27, 1941; children—Patricia Ann, Donald Gordon. Grad. asst. Mass. Inst. Tech., 1935-36, asst. dir., then dir. Bangor Sta. Sch. Chem. Engring. Practice, 1936-42, asst. prof. chem. engring., 1939-45; dir. dept. indsl. cooperation U. Maine, 1945-47, prof. acting head dept. chem. engring., 1946-47; research asso., group leader chem. engring. Inst. Paper Chemistry, 1947-57, dean inst., 1956-76, v.p., 1958-78, asst. to pres., 1977-79; ret., 1979. Mem. bd. edn., Appleton, Wis., 1962-68. Recipient Pro Bono Labore award Finnish Paper Engrs. Assn., 1978. Fellow Am. Inst. Chemists, Am. Inst. Chem. Engrs. (Colburn award 1948), TAPPI (dir. 1969-72; div. award 1969); mem. Am. Chem. Soc. (chmn. cellulose, paper and textiles div. 1978), Am. Soc. Engring. Edn., Sigma Xi, Alpha Chi Sigma, Tau Beta Pi. Author sci., tech. articles. Home: 1709 S Douglas St Appleton WI 54911

WHITNEY, RUTH REINKE, mag. editor; b. Oshkosh, Wis., July 23, 1928; d. Leonard G. and Helen (Diestler) Reinke; B.A., Northwestern U., 1949; m. Daniel A. Whitney, Nov. 19, 1949; 1 son, Philip R. Copy writer edn. dept. of circulation div. Time, Inc., 1949-53; editor-in-chief Better Living mag., 1953-56; asso. editor Seventeen magazine, 1956-62, exec. editor, 1962-67; editor-in-chief Glamour mag., 1967—. Mem. Am. Soc. Mag. Editors (pres. 1975-77), Fashion Group, Alpha Chi Omega. Home: Riverview Rd Irvington-on-Hudson NY 10533 Office: 350 Madison Ave New York NY 10017

WHITNEY, VINCENT HEATH, educator, population and devel. cons.; b. Northwood Ridge, N.H., June 23, 1913; s. Harlan R. and Mary Tarbell (Lowell) W.; Ph.D., U. N.C., 1944; m. Lucy Mansfield, June 14, 1941; children—Caroline Mansfield (Mrs. David Simons), Steven Lowell, Mary Starr. Research asso. N.C. Planning Bd., 1938-39; mem. faculty U. Me., 1939-43, Wesleyan U., Middletown, Conn., 1946; mem. faculty Brown U., 1946-59, prof. sociology, chmn. dept., 1949-59; prof. sociology and demography U. Pa., 1959—, chmn. dept., 1959-69, chmn. grad. group in demography, 1969-70; sr. staff asso. for Asia, Population Council N.Y.C., 1962-76; dir. Population Studies Center, U. Pa., 1961-76; mem. population research and tng. com. NIH, 1969-74. Mem. tech. adv. com. population U.S. Bur. Census, 1966-73, chmn., 1972-73. Mem. Internat. Union Sci. Study Population, Population Assn. Am., Am., Eastern (pres. 1957-58) sociol. socs., Pacific Sci. Assn., Phi Beta Kappa, Alpha Kappa Delta, Chi Phi. Co-author: Atomic Power: An Economic and Social Analysis, 1952; also articles on population, urbanization and devel. Home: 3202 Huey Ave Drexel Hill PA 19026 Office: Depts Sociology and Demography U Pa Philadelphia PA 19104

WHITNEY, WILLIAM CHOWNING, banker; b. Fullerton, Nebr., June 28, 1920; s. Barlow N. and Lena C. (Price) W.; B.S. cum laude, Loyola U., Chgo., 1949; m. Joan F. Whitney; children—William H., David M., Terri Lynn, Sherri Lee, Jonathan P., Laura Louise. Asst. bank examiner Fed. Res. Bank, Chgo., 1938-41; asst. auditor South Side Bank and Trust Co., Chgo., 1946-49; comptroller Peoples Nat. Bank, Bay City, Mich., 1949-52; asst. v.p., comptroller Tex. Bank and Trust Co., Dallas, 1952-54; with Old Kent Bank and Trust Co., Grand Rapids, Mich., 1954—, sr. v.p., cashier, sec. bd., dir., 1965—. Served with AUS, 1941-46. Mem. Financial Execs. Inst., Mich. Banks Assn., Bank Adminstrn. Inst., Grand Rapids C. of C. Mason, Rotarian. Clubs: Peninsular, Cascade Country, University, Athletic (Grand Rapids). Home: 7264 Driftwood Dr SE Grand Rapids MI 49506 Office: 1 Vandenberg Center Grand Rapids MI 49503

WHITNEY, WILLIAM MERRILL, research scientist; b. Coeur d'Alene, Idaho, Dec. 5, 1929; s. Merrill Roderick and Frances Kathryn (Aspinwall) W.; B.S., Calif. Inst. Tech., 1951; Ph.D., Mass. Inst. Tech., 1956; m. Evelyn Diane Moore, Dec. 23, 1950 (div. 1969); children—Steven Scott, Diane Elizabeth; m. 2d, Joyce Jenne Hailey, Dec. 30, 1978. Instr. physics M.I.T., 1956-58, asst. prof., 1958-63; sr. scientist Jet Propulsion Lab., 1963-67, sec. mgr. guidance and control research sect., 1967-70, astrionics research sect., 1970-76, info. systems research sect., 1976—, tech. leader robotics research program, 1972-79. Mem. Am. Inst. Physics. Home: 1161 E Howard St Pasadena CA 91104 Office: Jet Propulsion Lab Bldg 198 Rm 229 4800 Oak Grove Dr Pasadena CA 91103

WHITSEL, ROBERT MALCOLM, ins. co. exec.; b. Lafayette, Ind., Dec. 30, 1929; s. Earl Newton and Elizabeth (Bader) W.; B.S., Ind. U., 1951, M.B.A., 1954; m. Marilyn Katherine House, Oct. 15, 1955; children—Rebecca Sue, Cynthia Ann. With Lafayette Life Ins. Co., 1954—, dir., 1966—, mem. exec. com., 1968—, exec. v.p., 1973, pres., 1973—; dir. Lafayette Nat. Bank. Elder, trustee, deacon Presbyterian Ch., 1965-74; pres. Jr. Achievement Greater Lafayette, Inc., 1976—; pres. Central Presbyn. Found., Edgelea PTA; past pres., bd. dirs. United Way of Greater Lafayette; past v.p., bd. dirs. Wabash Sch. for Mentally Retarded; past treas., bd. dirs. Capital Funds Found. Greater Lafayette; v.p., bd. dirs. Lafayette Home Hosp., 1972—, mem. finance com., 1976—; trustee YWCA Found. Served to 1st lt. USAF, 1951-53. Recipient Nat. Bus. Leadership award, 1977. Mem. Soc. Residential Appraisers, Ind. Mortgage Bankers Assn. (past pres.), Soc. Fin. Analysts, Greater Lafayette C. of C. (past v.p., dir.), Ind. Soc. of Chgo., Beta Gamma Sigma. Republican. Clubs: Masons; Lafayette Country (v.p., dir.); Town and Gown. Home: 541 Old Farm Rd Lafayette IN 47905 Office: 2203 S 18th St PO Box 939 Lafayette IN 47902

WHITSETT, WESLEY GAVIN, r.r. exec.; b. Healing Springs, Ala., Apr. 7, 1906; s. John Allen and Lucy (Winslett) W.; student Duke, 1932-34; m. Nancy Greene, Mar. 18, 1940. Ticket seller, passenger agt., other positions A.C.L. R.R., 1925-32, asst. to gen. passenger agt., 1941-42; with Peninsular & Occidental Steamship Co., Havana, Cuba, 1934-41; gen. passenger agt. L.&N. R.R., New Orleans, 1942-47, asst. to v.p. traffic, 1947-57, asst. to pres., 1957-59, v.p. traffic, 1959-71. Episcopalian. Clubs: Pendennis, River Valley, Louisville Country (Louisville): Chicago; Union League (N.Y.C.). Home: 502 Brandon Rd Louisville KY 40207 Office: 908 W Broadway Louisville KY 40203

WHITSITT, FRANK CASEY, editor; b. Kansas City, Mo., Sept. 22, 1927; s. Garland B. and Mary Catherine (Casey) W.; student Kansas City Jr. Coll., 1945-46, Missouri Valley Coll., 1947; B.J., U. Mo., 1949; m. Helen Virginia Townsend, Nov. 6, 1949; children—Christine Jill, Marsha Dell, Paul Kirk. Reporter, Evansville (Ind.) Courier, 1949-50, Lubbock (Tex.) Avalanche-Jour., 1950-51; reporter, editor Kansas City Star, 1951-65; editor Farmland News, publs. dir. Farmland Industries, Kansas City, 1965—. Dir. newsroom for Billy Graham's World Congress on Evangelism, Berlin, 1966. Served with AUS, 1946. Recipient 1st place writing award Am. Assn. Agrl. Editors, 1974, 75; Klinefelter award, 1977; Common Market Study grantee, 1975. Mem. Coop. Editorial Assn. (pres. 1979), Am. Assn. Agrl. Editors. Republican. Baptist. Home: 3608 NE 49th St Kansas City MO 64118 Office: 3315 N Oak Trafficway Kansas City MO 64116

WHITSON, JAMES NORFLEET, JR., diversified co. exec.; b. Clinton, Okla., Mar. 14, 1935; s. James Norfleet and Georgia (Webb) W.; B.B.A., Tex. Tech. Coll., 1957; m. Lyda Lee Gibson, Apr. 19, 1956; 1 son, James Mark. Field accountant Texfel Petroleum Corp., Monahans, Tex., 1957-59; accountant Wickett Refining Co., Monahans, 1959-60; accounting supr. LTV, Inc., Dallas, 1960-63, asst. to treas., 1963-66, asst. treas., 1966-67, asst. dir. financial plans, 1967-68; v.p. finance LTV Ling Altec, Inc., Dallas, 1968-70; v.p., treas. Omega-Alpha, Inc., 1970-71, v.p. finance, 1971-73; pres. Sammons Communications, Inc., Dallas, 1973—; dir. Sammons Enterprises, Inc. Mem. Alpha Tau Omega. Home: 4312 Mill Creek Rd Dallas TX 75234 Office: PO Box 5728 Dallas TX 75222

WHITT, DAVID VIRGEL, ins. co. exec.; b. N.Y.C., Jan. 17, 1935; s. Virgel E. and Youland (ReDavid) W.; B.S. in Ins./Econs., Butler U., 1957; m. Charlotte Forsyth, Dec. 23, 1961; children—William D., Thomas F. Group rep. Am. United Life Ins. Co., Chgo., 1957-69, coordinator Student Life Plan, Indpls., 1960, regional group mgr., Chgo., 1961-62, Phila., 1963-64, mgr. group sales and adminstrn., Indpls., 1965-69; v.p., dir. group ins. Capitol Life Ins. Co., Denver, 1969-71; sr. v.p. Nat. Investors Life Ins. Co., Little Rock, 1971, exec. v.p., dir., 1972—; v.p., dir. Nat. Investors Fire & Casualty Co., 1971—; sr. v.p., dir. Gt. Atlantic Life Ins. Co., 1971-73; exec. v.p., dir. Mid-West Nat. Life Ins. Co., 1973—; v.p., dir. Nat. Investors Pension Co., 1979—; dir. Nor Securities, Little Rock. Chmn. bd. Westside YMCA, 1973-76. Served with USNR, 1952-60. Mem. Life Office Mgmt. Assn., Little Rock Sales Mktg. Club, Little Rock C. of C. Presbyterian. Clubs: Pleasant Valley Country; Westside Tennis. Home: 6 Cascades Dr Little Rock AR 72212 Office: Second and Broadway Little Rock AR 72201

WHITT, RICHARD ERNEST, journalist; b. Greenup County, Ky., Dec. 15, 1944; s. Walter Charles and Irene (Hayes) W.; student Ashland (Ky.) Community Coll., 1966-68; B.A. in Journalism, U. Ky., 1970; m. Sharon Kay Lyon, June 8, 1968; children—Hayes Chadwick, Emily. Reporter, Middlesboro (Ky.) Daily News, 1970-71; asst. state editor Waterloo (Iowa) Courier, 1971-72; city editor Kingsport (Tenn.) Times, 1972-76; No. Ky. bur. chief Courier-Jour., Louisville, 1977, Frankfort bur. chief, 1977—. Served with USN, 1962-66. Decorated Air medal; recipient Pulitzer prize for coverage of Beverly Hills Supper Club fire, 1978; named Outstanding Ky. Journalist, 1978. Democrat. Office: 614B Shelby St Frankfort KY 40601

WHITTAKER, PHILIP NEWBOLD, corp. exec.; b. Chestnut Hill, Pa., Nov. 7, 1918; s. Frederic S. and Mildred (Thorpe) W.; A.B., U. Pa., 1940; m. Elizabeth Stevenson, Nov. 6, 1948; children—Elizabeth T., Philip Newbold, Stephen A., Nancy C. Bus. mgr. Friends Sch., Wilmington, Del., 1940-41; With IBM Corp., 1946-68, v.p. fed. systems div., Gaithersburg, Md., 1968-69; asst. adminstr. industry affairs NASA, Washington, 1969—; asst. sec. Air Force, The Pentagon, Washington, 1969-72; dir. comml. devel. IBM Corp., Armonk, N.Y., 1973-75; pres. Satellite Bus. Systems, Washington, 1976-79; v.p. Fed. Systems div. IBM, Bethesda, Md., 1979—. Mem. bd. advisers Nat. Contract Mgmt. Assn.; bd. visitors Def. Systems Mgmt. Coll., Fort Belvoir, Va.; trustee Episcopal Div. Sch., Cambridge, Mass. Served to lt. comdr. USNR, 1941-46; PTO. Episcopalian. Clubs: Sandy Bay (Mass.) Yacht; Univ., Congressional Country (Washington). Home: 12305 Beall Spring Rd Potomac MD 20854 Office: Fed Systems Div IBM 10215 Fernwood Rd Bethesda MD 20034

WHITTAKER, ROBERT, congressman; b. Eureka, Kans., Sept. 18, 1939; m. Marlene Arnold; children—Steven, Stephanie, Susan. Practice optometry, Augusta, Kans.; clinic dir. Kans. Low Vision Clinic; mem. Kans. Ho. of Reps., 1975-77; mem. 96th Congress from 5th Kans. Dist. Former chmn. bd. 1st Christian Ch. of Augusta; former v.p. Augusta Med. Complex; former pres. Augusta United Fund; mem. City Planning Commn., Augusta; former project div. Eyeglasses for the Poor, Montemoroles, Mex. Lic. lay minister, Disciples of Christ. Fellow Am. Acad. Optometry; mem. Heart of Am. Contact Lens Soc. (past pres.). Club: Lions (past pres.). Republican. Home: Augusta KS Office: House of Reps B-227 Longworth House Office Bldg Washington DC 20515

WHITTAKER, ROBERT HARDING, educator, ecologist; b. Wichita, Kans., Dec. 27, 1920; s. Clive Charles and Adeline (Harding) W.; A.B., Washburn Municipal U., 1942; Ph.D., U. Ill., 1948; m. Clara Caroline Buehl, Jan. 1, 1953 (dec. Dec. 1976); children—John Charles, Paul Louis, Carl Robert; m. 2d, Linda Susan Olsvig, Dec. 12, 1979. Instr. zoology Wash. State Coll., Pullman, 1948-50, asst. prof., 1950-51; sr. scientist biology Hanford Atomic Products Ops., 1951-54; instr. Bklyn. Coll., City U. N.Y., 1954-58, asst. prof., 1958-62, asso. prof., 1962-64; vis. scientist biology dept. Brookhaven Nat. Lab., Upton, N.Y., 1964-66; prof. biology U. Calif. at Irvine, 1966-68; prof. biology, ecology and systematics Cornell U., Ithaca, N.Y., 1968-76, Charles A. Alexander prof. biology, 1976—. Served with USAAF, 1942-46. Mem. Ecol. Soc. Am. (Mercer award 1966), Am. Soc. Limnology and Oceanography, Brit. Ecol. Soc., Internat. Soc. Tropical Ecology, Internat. Assn. Phytosociology, Am. Soc. Naturalists (pres. 1980), Torrey Bot. Club, Swedish Plant Geographic Soc., AAAS, Am. Soc. Zoologists, Nat. Acad. Scis., Am. Acad. Arts and Scis., Brit. Ecol. Soc. (hon.), Swedish Plant Geog. Soc. (hon.), Phi Beta Kappa, Phi Sigma. Author: Communities and Ecosystems, 2d edit., 1975; Ordination and Classification of Communities, 2d edit., 1978; (with S.A. Levin) Niche: Theory and Application, 1975; (with H. Lieth) Primary Productivity of the Biosphere, 1975. Contbr. articles to profl. jours. Home: 318 Winthrop Dr Ithaca NY 14850

WHITTEMORE, ARTHUR AUSTIN, concert pianist; b. Vermillion, S.D., Oct. 23, 1916; s. Arthur Henry and Helen (Austin) W.; B.F.A., U. S.D., 1935, Mus. D. (hon.), 1965; Mus.M., U. Rochester, 1937. Piano debut with Jack Lowe, N.Y. Town Hall, 1940; recitals throughout Am., Can., and Europe; engagments with major symphonies including Boston, N.Y., Phila., Chgo., San Francisco, and St. Louis; premier performance of contemporary works: Vaughan Williams, Morton Gould, Poulenc, Krenek and others; recording pianist with Mitropoulos, Stokowski and others; regular guest TV Today-Garroway Show, NBC; founder Bravo magainze; co-founder Whit/Lo Singers, nat. tour, 1967; appearing on TV show Personal Touch of Whittemore and Lowe; serious music cons. SESAC, 1978—. Recipient citations U.S. Treasury Dept., U. Rochester. Served with USNR, 1942-46. Mem. Delta Tau Delta. Club: Lotos. Recs. for RCA Victor, Capitol, Angel. Home: Box 476 Quogue NY 11959 Office: CAMI 165 W 57th St New York NY 10019. *I have always believed that my audience must, during a performance, have a new musical experience. This may be by hearing of a new piece of music or by an interpretation of a familiar piece that reveals things the listener has not heard before. Having a real empathy for an audience will not only achieve a success in performance but a real sense of satisfaction in the pursuit of a demanding career.*

WHITTEMORE, EDWARD WILLIAM, diversified mfg. co. exec.; b. N.Y.C., Dec. 25, 1922; s. Harold Clifton and Florence Veronica (Stratton) W.; B.A., Columbia U., 1947; m. Jeanne McConnochie, June 12, 1948; children—Edward William, Jeannette L. With Wilson Jones Co., Chgo., 1947-72, v.p. mktg., 1968-70, exec. v.p., 1970-72; exec. v.p. Swingline Inc., N.Y.C., 1972-75, pres., chief operating officer, 1975-77, pres., chief exec. officer, Long Island City, N.Y., 1977-78; dir., mem. exec. com. Am. Brands, Inc., 1978-79, exec. v.p. operations, 1979—. Served with USAAF, 1943-45. Mem. Bus. Records Mfrs. Assn. (pres. 1971-72), Nat. Office Products Assn. (v.p. 1969-70), Wholesale Stationers Assn. Patentee binder and compression mechanism. Home: 22 Flying Cloud Rd Dolphin Cove Stamford CT 06902 Office: 245 Park Ave New York NY 10017

WHITTEMORE, FREDERICK BREWSTER, investment banker; b. Pembroke, N.H., Nov. 12, 1930; s. Laurence F. and Evelyn (Fulford) W.; A.B., Dartmouth, 1953; M.B.A., Amos Tuck Sch. Bus. Adminstrn., 1954; m. Marion Willi, Sept. 19, 1964; children—Laurence F. III, Edward Brewster. Asso., Morgan Stanley & Co., Inc., N.Y.C., 1958—, partner, 1967—, mng. dir., 1970—; bd. govs. Am. Stock Exchange. Trustee Pembroke (N.H.) Acad.; mem. pres.'s council Mus. City N.Y. Served with USNR, 1954-57. Mem. Securities Industry Assn. (various coms.), Pilgrims U.S., New Eng. Soc. N.Y. (dir.). Clubs: Economic, Brook, Bond, Dartmouth College (N.Y.C.); Misquamicut (Watch Hill, R.I.). Home: 925 Park Ave New York NY 10028 Office: 1251 Ave of Americas New York NY 10020

WHITTEMORE, ROBERT CLIFTON, educator; b. Lockport, N.Y., Feb. 1, 1921; s. Clifton Houghton and Zelia Florence (Duke) W.; B.A., Yale, 1949, M.A., 1951, Ph.D., 1953; m. Dorothy Jane Gordon, June 15, 1959; children—Stanley Allen Lawton, Shirley Anne Lawton. Instr. Yale, 1950-52; mem. faculty Tulane U., 1952—, prof. philosophy, 1963—, dean Univ. Coll., 1968-78. Served with AUS, 1942-45. Mem. Am. Philos. Assn., Metaphys. Soc. Am., So. Soc. Philosophy and Psychology, Southwestern Philos. Conf., Indian Philos. Congress, Episcopalian. Author: Makers of the American Mind, 1964. Home: 7521 Dominican St New Orleans LA 70118

WHITTEMORE, WILLIAM CASSIN, ins. co. exec.; b. Old Saybrook, Conn., Nov. 14, 1912; s. Joseph Butler and Margaret (Cassin) W.; B.S. summa cum laude, Brown U., 1933; certificate in transp. Yale U., 1935; J.D., Boston Coll., 1953; spl. course Harvard U., 1956; m. Constance Irena Sutcliffe, June 24, 1944; 1 dau., Patricia Janet. Clk., United Electric Ry. (R.I.), 1933-34; transp. asst., mech. asst. N.Y., N. H. & H. R.R., 1935-42; investment analyst John Hancock Mut. Life Ins. Co., 1945-49, asst. treas., 1949-59, treas., 1959—, sr. v.p., 1968—; dir. Maritime Life Assurance Co., Hanseco Ins. Co., John Hancock Investors Inc., John Hancock Income Securities Corp., John Hancock Advisors Inc., John Hancock Realty Devel. Corp., John Hancock Bond Fund, Inc., Profl. Econ. Services, Inc. Trustee John Hancock Tax Exempt Income Trust; mem. New Eng. Energy Policy Council; mem. ins. com., com. on corps. and founds. Brown U.; mem. Wellesley Town Meeting; mem. audit com. Town of Wellesley. bd. dirs. New Eng. Council, GEO Transport

Found. New Eng.; bd. vistors U. N.H. Served to lt. USCGR, 1942-45. Mem. Transp. Assn. Am. (dir.), Boston Security Analysts Soc., Sigma Xi, Tau Beta Pi. Republican. Unitarian. Clubs: Wellesley, Appalachian Mountain, Boston Econ. Home: 31 Priscilla Circle Wellesley Hills MA 02181 Office: PO Box 111 Boston MA 02117

WHITTEN, DOLPHUS, JR., former univ. pres., educator; b. Hope, Ark., June 20, 1916; s. Dolphus and Annie Tyree (Logan) W.; B.A., Ouachita Coll., 1936; M.A., U. Tex., 1940, Ph.D., 1961; postgrad. Western Res. U.; LL.D., McMurry Coll., Abilene, Tex., 1964; m. Marie Braden, May 1, 1939; 1 dau., Suzanne (Mrs. H. Robert Guy). High Sch. tchr. and prin., Ark. pub. schs., 1936-42; prin. Hope Jr.-Sr. High Sch., 1945-47; dir. extension and placement services, asso. prof. history Henderson State Tchrs. Coll., Arkadelphia, Ark., 1947-58; adminstrv. dean Oklahoma City U., 1958-61, adminstrv. v.p., 1961-70, acting pres., 1962-63, 69-70, pres., 1970-79, pres. emeritus, 1979—; adj. prof. history Elon Coll., 1979—. Served with USAAF, 1942-45; lt. col. Res. Inducted into Okla. Hall of Fame, 1975. Mem. Assn. Field Services Tchr. Edn. (past pres.), Am. Hist. Assn., UN Assn., Okla. Zool. Soc., Okla. Heritage Assn., Inst. Internat. Edn., Newcomen Soc., Alpha Chi (past pres. region II), Pi Gamma Mu, Phi Alpha Theta, Sigma Alpha Iota. Methodist (gen. council ministries). Rotarian. Home: 635 Country Club Dr Burlington NC 27215

WHITTEN, ERIC HAROLD TIMOTHY, geologist; b. Ilford, Essex, Eng., July 26, 1927; s. Charles Alexander and Muriel Gladys (Smith) W.; came to U.S., 1958; B.Sc. with gen. honors, U. London, 1948, B.Sc. in Geology, 1948, Ph.D. in Geology, 1952, D.Sc. in Geology, 1968; m. Mary Cleopha Staciva, Feb. 28, 1976; children—Catherine, Peter, Jennifer, Adam, James, Joshua. Clk., Rex Thomas (Ins.) Ltd., London, 1943-45; lectr. in geology Queen Mary Coll., London U., 1948-58; asso. prof. geology Northwestern U., 1958-63, prof., 1963—, chmn. dept. geol. scis., 1977—; Geol. Soc. London Daniel Pidgeon Fund grantee, 1954. Fellow Geol. Soc. London, Geol. Soc. Am., AAAS; mem. Internat. Assn. Math. Geology (sec.-gen.), Geologists' Assn. (London), Queen Mary Coll. Student Union Soc. (hon. life), English Speaking Union (life). Club: Hope Town Sailing (Abaco, Bahama Islands). Author: Structural Geology of Folded Rocks, 1966; Quantitative Studies in the Geological Sciences, 1975; editorial bd. Geocom Programs, London, 1971—. Home: 2027 Orrington Ave Evanston IL 60201 Office: Dept Geol Scis Northwestern U Evanston IL 60201

WHITTEN, JAMIE LLOYD, congressman; b. Cascilla, Miss., Apr. 18, 1910; s. Alymer Guy and Nettie (Early) W.; student lit. and law depts., U. of Miss., 1926-31; m. Rebecca Thompson, June 20, 1940; children—James Lloyd, Beverly Rebecca Merritt. Prin. pub. schs., 1931; elected Miss. State Legislature, 1931; elected dist. atty., 17th Dist. of Miss., 1933, reelected, 1935 and 1939; mem. 77th-96th congresses from 1st Miss. Dist., chmn. appropriations com. Mem. Beta Theta Pi, Phi Alpha Delta. Democrat. Mason. Author: That We May Live. Home: Charleston MS 38921 Office: 2314 Rayburn House Office Bldg Washington DC 20515

WHITTEN, LESLIE HUNTER, JR., newspaper reporter, author; b. Jacksonville, Fla., Feb. 21, 1928; s. Leslie Hunter and Linnora (Harvey) W.; B.A. in Journalism and English magna cum laude, Lehigh U., 1950; m. Phyllis Webber, Nov. 11, 1951; children—Leslie Hunter III, Andrew, Daniel. Newsman, Radio Free Europe, 1952-57, I.N.S., 1957-58, U.P.I., 1958, Washington Post, 1958-63; with Hearst Newspapers, 1963-66, asst. bur. chief, Washington, 1966-69; sr. investigator Jack Anderson's Washington Merry-Go-Round, 1969—; vis. asso. prof. Lehigh U., 1967-69. Served with AUS, 1946-48. Recipient hon. mention pub. service Washington Newspaper Guild, 1963, Edgerton award ACLU, 1974. Author: Progeny of the Adder, 1965; Moon of the Wolf, 1967; Pinion, the Golden Eagle, 1968; The Abyss, 1970; F. Lee Bailey, 1971; The Alchemist, 1973; Conflict of Interest, 1976; Sometimes a Hero, 1979; A Washington Cycle, 1979. Home: 114 Eastmoor Dr Silver Spring MD 20901 Office: 1401 16th St NW Washington DC 20036

WHITTENBURG, SAMUEL BENJAMIN, newspaper exec.; b. Plemons, Tex., Aug. 5, 1914; s. George Allen and Lillie Fannie (Archer) W.; student U. Tex., 1932-35; m. Mary Frances Grimes, Dec. 19, 1936; children—Mary Frances, Samuel Benjamin, Thomas Jennings, Bonne Pearl. Gen. mgr. Amarillo (Tex.) Times, 1938-51; pub. Amarillo Globe-Times, 1951-72; pres., gen. mgr. Amarillo Globe-News Pub. Co., Inc., 1955-72; pres. Plains Radio Broadcasting Co., Amarillo, KFYO Inc., Lubbock, Spool Oil Co., Amarillo, Panther Oil Co., Amarillo; dir. Am. Nat. Bank, Amarillo. Bd. dirs. Amarillo Children's Home, 1956-76, Tex. A. and M. U., 1956-76; chmn. bd. regents Tex. State Coll. Women, Denton, 1945-51. Recipient Torch award Tex. Fedn. Bus. and Profl. Women, 1972. Mem. Amarillo C. of C. (past pres.), Tex. Daily Newspaper Pubs. Assn. (pres. 1957-58), Panhandle Press Assn. (pres. 1958), So. Newspaper Pubs. Assn. (dir. 1967-70), Sigma Delta Chi. Presbyterian (elder). Club: Rotary (hon.). Home: Box 12081 Amarillo TX 79101

WHITTIER, CHARLES TAYLOR, educator; b. Chgo., Apr. 15, 1912; s. Charles and Leonore Arlie (Leuckel) W.; A.B., U. Chgo., 1936, M.A., 1938, Ph.D., 1948; m. Sara Jane Leckrone, June 18, 1934; children—Chip, Tim, Cece, Penny Lee. Tchr., Francis W. Parker Sch., Chgo., 1935-38; asst. to supt. Oak Park (Ill.) elementary schs., 1939-40; instr. Iowa State Tchrs. Coll., 1941-43; prin. Monroe Elementary Sch., Davenport, Iowa, 1943-44; asst. prin. Horace Mann Sch., Gary, Ind., 1944-48; prin. Sr. High Sch., St. Petersburg, Fla., 1948-53; dir. instruction Pinellas County (Fla.), 1953-57, asst. supt. for instruction, 1957; supt. schs. Montgomery County (Md.), 1957-64, Phila., 1964-67; exec. dir. Central Atlantic Regional Ednl. Lab., 1967-69; state commr. edn. Kans., Topeka, 1969-75; asso. prof. edn. U. Tex. at San Antonio, 1975—; pres. Research for Better Schs., 1966-67. Mem. NEA, Am. Assn. Sch. Adminstrs., Assn. Ednl. Data Systems (pres. 1965-66), AAUP. Club: Rotary. Author: (with Edward B. Shils) Teachers, Administrators and Collective Bargaining, 1968. Home: 12610 Chateau Forest San Antonio TX 78230. *Year by year it becomes clearer to me that man's relationships to his fellow men are the best indicator of his own relationship to his Supreme Power. My God teaches that as I act toward others I demonstrate how I wish to be treated. While many actions around me seem to show success otherwise, I have tried to evaluate my own actions by this standard.*

WHITTINGHAM, CHARLES ARTHUR, publisher; b. Chgo., Feb. 11, 1930; s. Charles Arthur and Virginia (Hartke) W.; B.S. in English Lit. cum laude, Loyola U., Chgo., 1951; m. Jean Bragger Whittingham, June 4, 1955; children—Mary Elizabeth, Charles Arthur III, Philip Alexander, Leigh Ann. With McCall Corp., Chgo., 1956-59, Time, Inc., Chgo., 1959-62; pub.'s rep. Fortune mag., Time, Inc., N.Y.C., 1962-65, mgr. San Francisco Office, 1965-69; asst. to pub. Fortune, N.Y.C., 1969-70, asst. pub., 1970-78; pub. Life mag., 1978—. Served to lt. (j.g.) USNR, 1951-55. Named to Athletic Hall of Fame, Loyola U. Clubs: University (N.Y.C. and San Francisco); Mt. Kisco (N.Y.) Country. Home: 11 Woodmill Rd Chappaqua NY 10514 Office: Life Mag Time and Life Bldg Rockefeller Center New York NY 10020

WHITTINGHAM, HARRY EDWARD, JR., banker; b. Albany, N.Y., Dec. 25, 1918; s. Harry E. and Mary (Baer) W.; grad. Stonier Grad. Sch. Banking, 1961; m. Gladys D. Willstaedt, Sept. 2, 1942; children—Jeffrey A., Neal E. With Schenectady Trust Co., 1947—, pres., 1974—; pres., chmn. bd. Financial Computer Center Eastern N.Y., Inc., 1969—. Served with AUS, 1941-46. Episcopalian (vestryman). Clubs: Mohawk Golf, Mohawk (Schenectady). Author: (with Purdy, Schneider, Aldom) Automation in Banking, 1962. Home: 2314 Brookshire Dr Schenectady NY 12309 Office: 320 State St Schenectady NY 12305

WHITTINGHILL, GEORGE DAVID, fgn. service officer; b. Rome, Italy, Feb. 17, 1908 (parents Am. citizens); s. Dexter Gooch and Susy Braxton (Taylor) W.; student U. Va., 1926-28; m. Maud Georgina Harris, Apr. 13, 1945; children—Susan Katherine Alexandra, Roderick George, John Dexter. Real estate broker, N.Y.C., 1931-34; Rome corr. Chgo. Daily News and Internat. News Service, 1934-35; editorial staff March of Time, Time mag., N.Y.C., 1936; asst. fgn. news editor Newsweek mag., N.Y.C., 1937; press asst. Am. consulate gen., Milan, Italy, 1937-40; vice consul, prin. officer, Lyon, France, 1940-42; vice consul, Monterrey, Mexico, 1942-43, Le Havre, France, 1946; vice consul, prin. officer, Cherbourg, France, 1946-48; vice consul Am. consulate gen., Genoa, Italy, 1948; consul, prin. officer, Valencia, Spain, 1949-52; consul, attache Am. embassy, Madrid, Spain, 1952-55; consul, prin. officer, Tampico, Mexico, 1955-57; 2d sec., then 1st sec. and consul, Am. embassy, Mexico City, 1958-60; 1st sec., consul Am. embassy, Rome, 1960-62, consul general, 1962-65; consul gen. Am. consulate, Nice, France, 1965—. Acad. overseer Am. Coll. Monaco, 1968-70; bd. dirs. British-Am. Hosp., Nice, 1965—, Anglo-Am. Hosp., Cannes, France, 1967—. Served as capt. Free French Fighting Services, 1940-42; to capt., OSS, AUS, 1943-46. Decorated Presdl. Medal of Freedom; mil. div. Most Excellent Order British Empire; officer Oder St. Charles of Monaco; Croix de Guerre with bronze star, Croix du Combattant Volontaire de la Resistance, Croix du Combattant (France). Mem. Soc. Colonial Wars, Descendents Signers Declaration Independence, S.R., S.A.R., Soc. 2d War with Great Britain. Mem. Am. Ch. Riviera (warden). Home: 3409 Prospect St NW Washington DC 20007 also Kemps House Balcombe Sussex RH17 6JH England

WHITTINGTON, FLOYD LEON, Asian cons., retired oil co. exec., fgn. service officer, economist; b. Fairfield, Iowa, May 27, 1909; s. Thomas Clyde and Ora E. (Trail) W.; A.B., Parsons Coll., 1931; M.A., U. Iowa, 1936; student U. Minn., 1940, Northwestern U., 1941-42; m. Winifred Carol McDonald, July 31, 1933; children—Susan Carol (Mrs. West), Thomas Lee. Econs., speech instr. Fairfield High Sch., 1931-36, Superior (Wis.) High Sch., 1936-40; supr. tchr. tng. Superior State Tchrs. Coll., 1936-40; econs., finance instr. Carroll Coll., Waukesha, Wis., 1940-42; price exec. OPA, Wis. and Iowa, 1942-46; indsl. relations mgr. Armstrong Tire & Rubber Co., Des Moines, 1946-48; dir. price and distbn. div. SCAP, Tokyo, Japan, 1948-51; Far East economist ODM, Washington, 1951-52; asst. adviser to sec. on Japanese financial and econ. problems Dept. State, Washington, 1952-53; chief Far Eastern sect. Internat. Finance div., bd. govs. Fed. Res. System, Washington, 1953-56; officer charge econ. affairs Office Southeast Asian Affairs, Dept. State, 1956-57, dep. dir. Office Southeast Asian Affairs, 1957-58; became counselor of embassy Am. embassy, Bangkok, Thailand, 1958; counselor, polit. officer Am. embassy, Djakarta, Indonesia, 1962-65; counselor of embassy for econ. affairs, Seoul, Korea, 1965-66; v.p. Pacific Gulf Oil, Ltd., Seoul, 1966—; exec. v.p. Southeast Asia Gulf Co., Bangkok, Gulf Oil Co. Siam, Ltd., Bangkok, 1967-72; v.p. Gulf Oil Co.-South Asia, Singapore, 1970-72; now Asian bus. cons. Recipient Meritorious Civilian Service citation Dept. Army, 1950. Mem. Am. Econ. Assn., Am. Acad. Polit. Sci., World Affairs Council Seattle (pres.), Seattle Com. Fgn. Relations, Pi Kappa Delta, Theta Alpha Phi. Presbyn. Mason (Shriner). Clubs: Royal Bangkok (Thailand) Sports; Rainier (Seattle); Everett Yacht. Address: 900 W Rocky Point Dr Camano Island WA 98292

WHITTINGTON, VERLE GLENN, petroleum co. exec.; b. Fairfield, Iowa, Dec. 2, 1929; s. Harold William and Grace Marie (Wilson) W.; B.A., Parsons Coll., Fairfield, 1952; J.D., U. Iowa, 1955; m. Pauline Curran, Oct. 31, 1952; children—Kathleen Ann, James Edd, Mark Steven, Carol Lynn, John Joseph, Michael Aaron. With Shell Oil Co., 1955—, mgr. non-exempt employee relations and indsl. safety, N.Y.C., 1968-70, mgr. indsl. relations, employee relations orgn., Houston, 1970-73, treas., 1973-75, v.p. employee relations, 1975—. Bd. dirs., v.p., exec. com. Jr. Achievement S.E. Tex. Mem. Iowa Bar Assn., Petroleum Club Houston. Roman Catholic. Elk. Club: River Plantation Country (Conroe). Home: 101 Biloxi Ct Conroe TX 77301 Office: One Shell Plaza PO Box 2463 Houston TX 77001

WHITTLE, ALFRED JAMES, JR., naval officer; b. Mt. Vernon, N.Y., Feb. 23, 1924; s. Alfred James and Margaret Mary (Rogers) W.; B.S., U.S. Naval Acad., 1945; grad. Inst. Def. Analysis, 1967; m. Phyllis King Schneible, June 28, 1947; children—Alfred James, III, Jeffrey King. Commd. ensign U.S. Navy, 1942, advanced through grades to adm., 1978; comdr. submarines; comdr. submarine squadron, 1970-71, submarine flotilla, 1972-74; chief of staff to Supreme Allied Comdr. Atlantic, 1976-78; chief naval material, 1978—. Decorated D.S.M. (2), Legion of Merit (3), Meritorious Service medal. Mem. U.S. Naval Inst., U.S. Naval Sailing Assn. (past commodore). Episcopalian. Address: Quarters CC 2300 E St Washington DC 20037

WHITTLE, ROY JOHN, forest products co. exec.; b. London, Jan. 16, 1919; s. John Edward and Elsie May (Lee) W.; m. Gladys Mary Clark, Oct. 11, 1946; children—Ronald, Jacqueline, John, Richard, Patricia. With B.C. Forest Products, Inc., Vancouver, 1952—, exec. v.p., 1977—; dir. Finlay Forest Industries Ltd., Fraser River Pile Driving Co. Ltd., Pinette and Therrien Mills Ltd., Donohue St Felicien, Inc. Alderman, Dist. of North Vancouver, 1958-68. Mem. Council Forest Industries. Clubs: Terminal City, North Shore Winter. Home: 474 Silverdale Pl North Vancouver BC V7N 2Z5 Canada Office: 1050 W Pender St Vancouver BC V6E 2X3 Canada

WHITTUM, CHARLES H., JR., banker; b. Atlanta, Oct. 30, 1929; s. Charles H. and Margaret O. W.; B.A., St. Lawrence U., 1951; postgrad. U. Pa. Stonier Grad. Sch. Banking; m. Juliana Eastwich, May 29, 1954; children—Cabell Eastwich, Leslie West. With First Pa. Bank, Phila., 1954-77, sr. v.p., 1977; exec. v.p. Riggs Nat. Bank, Washington, 1977—. Del., Pa. Constl. Conv., 1967-68; mem. Radnor Twp. (Pa.) Sch. Bd., 1970-76; Radnor Twp. Mcpl. Authority, 1968-76. Served with USMC, 1951-55. Mem. Mortgage Bankers Assn., Robert Morris Assos. Republican. Presbyterian. Home: 1216 Mottram Dr McLean VA 22101 Office: 1503 Pennsylvania Ave NW Washington DC 20074*

WHITWELL, SANFORD MACCALLUM, chem. co. exec.; b. Tacoma, Mar. 25, 1924; s. George Edward and Alice Ruth (MacCallum) W.; B.S., Cornell U., 1944; LL.B., George Washington U., 1949; m. Joan Eicker, July 7, 1951; children—Susan R., George E., John S., Amy J. Admitted to D.C. bar, 1949, N.Y. bar, 1950; engr. Stone & Webster Service Corp., N.Y.C. and Transcontinental Gas Pipeline Co., Houston, 1949-52; with Nat. Distillers & Chem. Corp., N.Y.C., 1952—, asst. sec., 1966-69, v.p., 1969-73, exec. v.p., 1973—; dir. Alta. Distillers, Ltd., John de Kuyper & Son, Inc. Served to lt. (j.g.) USNR, 1944-46. Club: Union League (N.Y.C.). Office: 99 Park Ave New York NY 10016

WHITWORTH, KATHRYNNE ANN, profl. golfer; b. Monahans, Tex., Sept. 27, 1939; d. Morris Clark and Dama Ann (Robinson) Whitworth; student Odessa (Tex.) Jr. Coll., 1958. Winner 80 ofcl. tournaments; 8 times leading money winner; 7 times lowest scoring average; 7 times Player of Year; 2 times A.P. Woman Athlete of Year; joined tour 1959 and Ladies Profl. Golf Assn.; mem. adv. staff Walter Hagen Golf Co., Charles A. Eaton Shoe Co.; rep. Trophy Club, Dallas and Ft. Worth. Mem. Ladies Profl. Golf Assn. (sec. 1962-63, v.p. 1965, 73, pres. 1967, 68, 71, 1st mem. to win over $500,000.00). Home: 10647 Boedeker Dallas TX 75230

WHITWORTH, KERNAN BRADLEY, JR., educator; b. Lakewood, Ohio, Mar. 9, 1923; s. Kernan Bradley and Bernice (Mills) W.; A.B. summa cum laude (Amos C. Miller scholar), Oberlin Coll., 1943; M.A. (Bergen fellow), Princeton, 1947, Ph.D., 1951; postgrad. U. Paris, 1949-50; m. Carolyn Harkins McGill, May 31, 1947; children—Kernan Bradley III, Nancy Lintner. Instr. French, Princeton, 1945-46, Bryn Mawr Coll., 1947-49; lectr. U. Cal. at Los Angeles, 1950-51, instr., 1951-53, asst. prof. French, 1953-57; asst. prof. French, U. Mo.-Columbia, 1957-62, asso. prof., 1962-68, prof., 1968—, asso. chmn. dept. Romance langs., 1965-68, 75-77, chmn., 1968-72. Asso. dir. NDEA Summer Lang. Insts., U. Mo., 1960, 61; Modern Lang. Assn. evaluator NDEA Summer Lang. Insts., 1963; dir. NDEA Summer Inst. for Undergrad. Majors Preparing to Teach French, U. Mo., 1966; field reader U.S. Office Edn. div. grad. programs, Bur. Higher Edn., 1970-72. Served with AUS, 1943-44. Mem. MLA, Am. Assn. Tchrs. French (pres. West Central chpt.), Am. Council Teaching Fgn. Langs., Société Francaise d'Etude du l8e Siecle, Am. Soc. 18th Century Studies, Phi Beta Kappa. Author: (with Herbert A. Gershman) Anthology of Critical Prefaces to the Nineteenth-Century French Novel, 1962. Editor Modern Lang. Forum, 1954-57; mem. editorial com. Literature and Society, 1964. Contbr. articles profl. jours. Home: 210 Tracy Dr Columbia MO 65201

WHORTON, JUDSON SEABORN, life ins. co. exec.; b. Gadsden, Ala., Dec. 26, 1929; s. George Seaborn and Jennie (Griffin) W.; B.S., Jacksonville State U., 1953; m. Carolyn Buckner, Aug. 23, 1953; children—Jane, Elaine, Alan, Bruce. Accountant, Winston, Brooke, C.P.A.'s, Anniston, Ala., 1953-55; chief accountant Atlantic Nat. Life Ins. Co., 1955-57; with Am. Heritage Life Ins. Co., Jacksonville, Fla., 1957—, treas., 1962—, sr. v.p., 1979—; pres., treas., trustee Am. Century Mortgage Investors, 1969—; adv. bd. Atlantic Bancorp., 1978—. Bd. dirs., chmn. fin. com. Baptist Med. Center, Jacksonville, 1968—; trustee U. N. Fla., 1972—. Served with USNR, 1948-49. Mem. Fin. Analysts Soc. Jacksonville, Jacksonville C. of C. Democrat. Baptist. Clubs: River, Ponte Vedra, Univ. Country. Home: 5443 John Reynolds Dr Jacksonville FL 32211 Office: Am Heritage Life Ins Co 11 E Forsyth St Jacksonville FL 32202

WHYBREW, WILLIAM ERNEST, coll. dean; b. Romford, Eng., Mar. 28, 1920; s. Bertie and Elizabeth (Reed) W.; came to U.S., 1924, naturalized, 1941; B.Mus., Eastman Sch. Music, U. Rochester, 1943, M.Mus., 1947, Ph.D., 1953; m. Marguerite Zoppoth, Mar. 3, 1951; 1 son, Stephen William. Mem. Carborundum Band, 1937-39, Rochester Philharmonic, 1941-53, Rochester Civic Orch., 1949-53; mem. faculty Eastman Sch. Music, 1949-53, Ithaca (N.Y.) Coll., 1953-57, Edinboro (Pa.) State Coll., 1957-59; mem. faculty No. Ill. U., DeKalb, 1959-70, dean Coll. Fine and Applied Arts, 1964-70; dean Coll. Creative Arts, No. Ariz. U., Flagstaff, 1970-73; dean Keene (N.H.) State Coll., 1975—. Served with AUS, 1943-46. Mem. Assn. Higher Edn., Coll. Music Soc., Phi Mu Alpha. Author: Measurement and Evaluation in Music, 1962, 71; also articles. Home: 53 Eastview Rd Keene NH 03431

WHYBROW, PETER CHARLES, medical educator; b. Hertforshire, Eng., June 13, 1939; s. Charles Ernest and Doris Beatrice (Abbott) W.; student Univ. Coll., London, 1956-59; M.B., B.S., Univ. Coll. Hosp. Med. Sch., 1962; diploma psychol. medicine Conjoint Bd., London, 1968; M.A. (hon.), Dartmouth Coll., 1974; m. Margaret Ruth Steele, Dec. 11, 1962; children—Katherine, Helen. Came to U.S., 1964, naturalized, 1975. House officer Univ. Coll. Hosp., 1962, sr. house physician psychiatry, 1963-64; house surgeon St. Helier Hosp., Surrey, Eng., 1963; house officer pediatrics Prince of Wales Hosp., London, 1964; resident psychiatry U. N.C. Hosp., 1965-67, instr., research fellow, 1967-68; mem. sci. staff neuropsychiat. research unit Charshalton, Surrey, 1968-69; dir. residency tng. psychiatry Dartmouth Med. Sch., 1969-71, prof. psychiatry, 1970—, chmn. dept., 1970-78; dir. psychiatry Dartmouth Hitchock Affiliated Hosp., 1970-78; vis. scientist NIMH, 1978-79; cons. VA, 1970—; chmn. test com. Nat. Bd. Med. Examiners, 1977—. Recipient Anclote Manor award psychiat. research U. N.C., 1967; Josiah Macy Jr. Found. scholar, 1978-79. Fellow Am. Psychiat. Assn., Royal Coll. Psychiatrists (founding mem.), Am. Coll. Psychiatrists; mem. Assn. Am. Med. Colls., Soc. Psychosomatic Research, Am. Assn. Chmn. Depts. Psychiatry (pres. 1977-78), Royal Soc. Medicine, Sigma Xi, Alpha Omega Alpha. Club: Cosmos (Washington). Contbr. to profl. jours.; editor: Psychosomatic Medicine, 1977. Home: Box 37 Plainfield NH 03781

WHYTE, JAMES PRIMROSE, JR., educator; b. Columbus, Miss., Aug. 25, 1921; s. James P. and Mary (Savage) W.; A.B., Bucknell U., 1943; M.A., Syracuse U., 1948; J.D., U. Colo., 1951; m. Martha Ann Jones, Sept. 11, 1948; children—James Jones, Stuart Ward, Wilson Scott. Admitted to Okla. bar, 1951, Mo. bar, 1957, Va. bar, 1961; with firm Gordon & Whyte, McAlester, Okla., 1951-55; county atty. Pittsburg County, Okla., 1955-56; atty. Great Lakes Pipe Line Co., Kansas City, Mo., 1957; prof. law Coll. William and Mary, 1958, asst. dean, 1958-68, asso. dean, 1969-70, dean, 1970-75. Ad hoc arbitrator Am. Arbitration Assn., Fed. Mediation and Conciliation Service, Va. Dept. Labor, also industry panels. Mem. Bd. Zoning Appeals, Williamsburg, 1971—, chmn., 1977—. Trustee, pres. Williamsburg Regional Library, 1965; trustee Williamsburg Area Meml. Community Center, 1963-68, pres., 1966-67. Served with USNR, 1943-46. Mem. Nat. Acad. Arbitrators, Am., Va. bar assns., Va. State Bar, Phi Beta Kappa, Tau Kappa Alpha, Sigma Tau Delta. Contbr. profl. jours. Mem. editorial adv. bd. John Marshall Papers, 1966-77. Home: 1109 Jamestown Rd Williamsburg VA 23185

WHYTE, JOSEPH LAWRENCE, banker; b. N.Y.C., Nov. 11, 1912; s. Patrick J. and Katherine (Haverty) W.; B.S., N.Y. U., 1936; LL.B., George Washington U., 1944; postgrad. Rutgers U., 1953; m. Charlotte E. Morris, May 8, 1943; children—Barbara E. Whyte Brereton, Diane L. Whyte Warin, J. Lawrence, Robert E. Adminstrv. asst. to v.p., sec. trust dept. Bank of N.Y., 1929-41, 45-46; with Am. Security Bank, N.A., Washington, 1946-78, exec. v.p., officer charge trust dept., vice chmn.; ret., 1978; cons. Wilmington Trust Co. (Del.), 1978—; law clk. James M. Brooks, Esq., 1940-41; lectr. contract and fiduciary law Pace Inst. Accounting, 1945-46; lectr. trust bus. Washington chpt. Am. Inst. Banking, 1951; adj. prof. law on estate planning Georgetown U. Law Center, 1956-78; lectr. C.L.U. Inst., George Washington U., 1958-62; dir. Gen. Services Life Ins. Co., Acacia Investment Mgmt. Co. Bd. dirs., chmn. endowment com. Met.

Police Boys' Club, 1967-78; bd. dirs. Mary and Daniel Loughran Found. Served to lt. comdr. USNR, 1941-45. Mem. Am. (past mem. trust div. exec. com.), D.C. bankers assns., D.C. Bar Assn., Res. Officers Assn. (nat. treas. 1973-78). Clubs: Univ. (past pres., bd. govs.), Met. (Washington); Congressional Country (Bethesda, Md.); Rehoboth Beach (Del.) Country. Home: 28 Tidewaters Henlopen Acres Rehoboth Beach DE 19971

WHYTE, WILLIAM FOOTE, educator; b. Springfield, Mass., June 27, 1914; s. John and Isabel (VanSickle) W.; A.B., Swarthmore Coll., 1936; mem. Soc. of Fellows, Harvard U., 1936-40; Ph.D., U. Chgo., 1943; m. Kathleen King, May 28, 1938; children—Joyce, Martin, Lucy, John. Asst. prof. sociology, acting chmn. dept. anthropology U. Okla., 1942-43; asst., then asso. prof. sociology U. Chgo., 1944-48, exec. sec. Com. Human Relations in Industry, 1946-48; prof. indsl. relations N.Y. State Sch. Indsl. and Labor Relations, Cornell U., 1948—, dir. Social Sci. Research Center, 1956-61. Trustee Found. Research Human Behavior, 1960-67. Fulbright fellow, Peru, 1961-62; recipient Career Research award NIMH. Fellow Am. Anthrop. Assn., Am. Sociol. Assn. (pres. 1980); mem. Am. Acad. Arts and Scis., Soc. Applied Anthropology (pres. 1964), Indsl. Relations Research Assn. (pres. 1963). Author: Street Corner Society, 1943; Human Relations in the Restaurant Industry, 1948; Pattern for Industrial Peace, 1951; Money and Motivation, 1955; Man and Organization, 1959; Men at Work, 1961; Action Research for Management, 1965; Toward an Integrated Theory of Development, 1968; Organizational Behavior, 1969; Dominación y Cambios en el Perú Rural, 1969; Organizing for Agricultural Development, 1975; co-author: Power, Politics, and Progress, 1976; editor: Industry and Society, 1946; Human Organization, 1956-61, 62-63. Home: 1 Sundowns Rd Ithaca NY 14850

WHYTE, WILLIAM GEORGE, ret. steel co. exec.; b. Chgo., Sept. 14, 1915; s. Robert James and Georgia (Kirby) W.; B.S. in Commerce, U. Ill., 1937; postgrad. Journalism Sch., Northwestern U., 1938; m. Margaret Elizabeth Paine, Feb. 6, 1943; children—William Kirby, Roger James. Pub. relations dept. Western Electric Co., Chgo., 1937-41; pub. relations rep. U.S. Steel Corp., Chgo., 1946-49, staff asst. office of chmn., 1949-51, asst. dir. pub. relations, Chgo., 1951-52, asst. to v.p., Washington, 1952-57, asst. v.p., 1957-63, v.p., 1963-77. Chmn. bd. Nat. Capital Area council Boy Scouts Am., mem. exec. bd.; Washington bd. trustees Fed. City Council. Served from 2d lt. to col. AUS, 1941-46. Decorated Legion of Merit, Bronze Star (U.S.); Croix de Guerre (France). Mem. U.S. C. of C. (past vice chmn., dir., chmn. pub. affairs com.), Nat. Security Indsl. Assn. (past pres. Washington), Am. Iron and Steel Inst. (past chmn. govt. relations com.). Republican. Methodist. Clubs: Chevy Chase; Met., Carlton, Burning Tree, 1925 F St. (Washington); Pine Valley Golf (Clementon, N.J.). Home: 491 Sea Oak Dr John's Island Vero Beach FL 32960

WHYTE, WILLIAM HOLLINGSWORTH, writer; b. West Chester, Pa., Oct. 1, 1917; s. William Hollingsworth and Louise (Price) W.; B.A. cum laude, Princeton U., 1939; m. Jenny Bell Bechtel, Oct. 1964; 1 dau., Alexandra. With Vick Chem. Co., 1939-41; writer Fortune mag., N.Y.C., 1946-51, asst. mng. editor, 1951-59; distinguished prof. Hunter Coll., City U. N.Y., 1970-71. Mem. Hudson River Valley Commn., N.Y. State Environ. Bd.; mem. Pres.'s Task Force Natural Beauty, 1964-65; co-dir. White House Conf. Natural Beauty; trustee Episcopal Ch. Sch. Found.; vice chmn. Conservation Found. Am. Conservation Assn.; bd. dirs. N.Y. Landmarks Conservancy. Served to capt. USMCR, 1941-45. Recipient Benjamin Franklin mag. writing award, 1953; Liberty and Justice Book award ALA, 1957. Mem. Soc. of Cin. (Md.). Episcopalian. Clubs: Quadrangle, Century Assn. (N.Y.C.). Author: Is Anybody Listening?, 1952; The Organization Man, 1956; Open Space Action, 1962; Cluster Development, 1964; The Last Landscape, 1968. Home: 175 E 94th St New York NY 10028

WIBBERLEY, LEONARD PATRICK O'CONNOR, author; b. Dublin, Ireland, Apr. 9, 1915; s. Thomas and Sinaid (O'Connor) W.; student Cardinal Vaughan's Sch., London, 1925-30; m. Katherine Hazel Holton, Apr. 10, 1948; children—Kevin, Patricia Wibberley Sheehey, Christopher, Arabella Wibberley Van Hoven, Rory, Cormac. Reporter, London Sunday Dispatch, 1931-32, London Sunday Express, 1932-34, London Daily Mirror, 1935-36; editor Trinidad Evening News (B.W.I.), 1936; oilfield worker, Trinidad, 1936-43; cable editor AP, 1943-44; chief N.Y. bur. London Evening News, 1944-46; editorial writer Los Angeles Times, 1950-54. Served with Trinidad Arty. Vols., 1938-41. Mem. Authors Guild, Dramatists Guild. Author: The Mouse that Roared, 1955; Last Stand of Father Felix, 1974; Meeting with a Great Beast, 1973; 1776 and All That, 1975; One in Four, 1976; Homeward to Ithaka, 1978; The Good-Natured Man—A Portrait of Oliver Goldsmith, 1979; over 90 other books, also 6 plays; contbr. numerous short stories to Sat. Evening Post, articles to N.Y. Times, Los Angeles Times, San Francisco Chronicle, also articles to profl. publs. Home: Box 522 Hermosa Beach CA 90254. *What is hard to do is worth doing. Whether you succeed or not you cannot fail to be benefitted by trying. It follows that by constantly trying to make everything easy for our children in our schools and homes, we are actually handicapping them and depriving them of growth.*

WIBERG, KENNETH BERLE, educator, chemist; b. Bklyn., Sept. 22, 1927; s. Dan and Solveig Berle W.; B.S., Mass. Inst. Tech., 1948; Ph.D., Columbia 1950; m. Marguerite Koch, Mar. 18, 1951; children—Patricia, Robert, William. Mem. faculty U. Wash., 1950-62, prof. chemistry, 1958-62; prof. chemistry Yale, 1962—, Whitehead prof., 1968—, chmn. chem. dept., 1968-71; Boomer lectr. U. Alta. (Can.), 1959. Recipient James Flack Norris award, 1973. Sloan Found. fellow, 1958-62; Guggenheim fellow, 1961-62. Mem. chemistry advisory panel Air Force Office Sci. Research, 1960-66, NSF, 1965-68, chmn., 1967-68. Mem. Nat. Acad. Scis., Am. Acad. Arts and Scis., Am. Chem. Soc. (exec. com. organic div. 1961-63; Calif. sect. award 1963). Author: Laboratory Technique in Organic Chemistry, 1960; Interpretation of NMR Spectra, 1962; Physical Organic Chemistry, 1964; Computer Programming for Chemists, 1966; also articles. Editor: Oxidation in Organic Chemistry, 1966; Sigma M.O. Theory, 1970; mem. editorial bd. Organic Syntheses, 1963-71, Jour. Organic Chemistry, 1968-72; bd. editors Jour. Am. Chem. Soc., 1969-72. Home: 160 Carmalt Rd Hamden CT 06517 Office: Chemistry Dept Yale U New Haven CT 06520

WIBERLEY, STEPHEN EDWARD, tech. inst. vice provost; b. Troy, N.Y., May 31, 1919; s. Irving Charles and Ruth (Stanley) W.; B.A., Williams Coll., 1941; M.S., Rensselaer Poly. Inst., 1948, Ph.D., 1950; m. Mary Elizabeth Bartle, Feb. 21, 1942; children—Stephen Edward, Sharon Elizabeth. Sr. chemist Congoleum Nairn, Inc., Kearny, N.J., 1941-44; prof. chemistry Rensselaer Poly. Inst., Troy, N.Y., 1946-63, dean Grad. Sch., 1964—, vice provost, 1969—; vis. sr. physicist Brookhaven Nat. Lab., Upton, N.Y., 1952; cons. Imperial Paper & Color Corp., Glens Falls, N.Y., 1957—, Socony Mobil Oil Co., Bklyn., 1957—, Huyck Felt Co., Rensselaer, N.Y., 1958—, Schenectady Chems. Inc., 1961—, U.S. Gypsum Co., Buffalo, 1962—. Served with AUS, 1944-46. Mem. Am. Chem. Soc., Am. Assn. U. Profs., Soc. Applied Spectroscopy, Sigma Xi, Phi Lambda Upsilon. Author: Instrumental Analysis, 1954; Laboratory Manual for General Chemistry, 1963; Introduction to Infrared and Raman Spectroscopy, 1964. Home: 1676 Tibbits Ave Troy NY 12180

WIBORG, JAMES HOOKER, corp. exec.; b. Seattle, Aug. 26, 1924; s. John R. and Hazel (Hooker) W.; B.A., U. Wash., 1946; m. Ann Rogers, July 1948; children—Katherine Ann, Mary Ellen, Caroline Joan, John Stewart. Owner Wiborg Mfg. Co., Tacoma, 1946-50; securities analyst Pacific N.W. Co., Seattle, 1950-53; founder Western Plastics Corp., Tacoma, 1953, pres., 1953-55, now chmn. bd., dir.; exec. v.p. Wash. Steel Products Co., Tacoma, 1955-58; mgmt. cons., Tacoma, 1958-60; v.p. United Pacific Corp., Seattle, 1960; pres. Pacific Small Bus. Investment Corp., Seattle, 1961-63; sr. v.p. indsl. div. United Pacific Corp., Seattle, 1963-65, pres., chief exec. officer, dir., 1965; pres., chief exec. officer, dir. Univar Corp. (formerly VWR United Corp.), Seattle, 1966—; dir. Eldec Corp., Seattle, Sea First Corp., PACCAR Inc., Seattle-First Nat. Bank, Gensco/CD Inc., Tacoma, Western Internat. Hotels, Inc., Seattle, Northern Life Ins. Co., Seattle. Trustee U. Puget Sound. Clubs: Tacoma Country and Golf, Tacoma Yacht; Rainier, Harbor (Seattle). Home: 6608 N 46th St Tacoma WA 98407 Office: Norton Bldg Seattle WA 98104

WICE, DAVID HERSCHEL, clergyman; b. Petersburg, Va., Feb. 1, 1908; s. Henry and Rose (Cooper) W.; A.B., Washington and Lee U., 1927, M.A., 1928, D.D., 1948; Rabbi, Hebrew Union Coll., 1933, D.H.L., 1954; m. Sophie Salzer, Feb. 22, 1934; children—Carol Ruth Wice Gross, David Henry. Rabbi, Temple Israel, Omaha, 1933-41, Temple B'nai Jeshurun, Newark, 1941-47, Congregation Rodeph Shalom, Phila., 1947—. Am. dir. World Union for Progressive Judaism, 1945-55, governing bd., exec. com., 1946, later chmn. exec. com., pres., 1974-80; mem. com. Central Conf. Am. Rabbis, 1945-47, 71-72, chmn. com. on structure and orgn., 1956-63, chmn. com. world Jewry, 1965, chmn. com. family, 1967—; pres. Phila. Bd. Rabbis, 1954-56; charter pres. Jewish Community Chaplaincy Service; pres. Marriage Council, 1961-64, also Planned Parenthood; co-chmn. com. on merger Family Service Assn. Am.-Child Welfare League Am.; mem. forum 15, White House Conf. Children and Youth, 1970. Bd. dirs. Family Service Assn. Am., 1959—, v.p., 1963-65, pres., 1965-67; bd. dirs. Union Am. Hebrew Congregations, New Ams., Council Jewish Edn., Fedn. Jewish Agys., Jewish Community Relations Council (all Phila.); co-chmn. bd. overseers Hebrew Union Coll.-Jewish Inst. Religion. Home: 135 S 19th St Apt 1510 Philadelphia PA 19103 Office: 615 N Broad St Philadelphia PA 19123

WICHMANN, EYVIND HUGO, educator, physicist; b. Stockholm, Sweden, May 30, 1928; s. Gertrud Wichmann; A.B., Finland's Inst. Tech., 1950; M.A., Columbia, 1953, Ph.D., 1956; m. Marianne Paischeff, July 26, 1951; children—Mats Daniel, Sonia Martina. Came to U.S., 1951, naturalized, 1961. Mem. Inst. Advanced Study, Princeton, N.J., 1955-57; mem. faculty U. Calif., Berkeley, 1957—, now prof. physics. Served with Finnish Army, 1944. Mem. Am. Phys. Soc., Sigma Xi. Democrat. Home: 2514 Cedar St Berkeley CA 94708

WICHTRICH, ALPHONSE RUDOLPH, assn. exec.; b. Chihuahua, Mex., Oct. 30, 1915; s. Gustav and Fermina (Esparza) W.; B.S., U. Ariz., 1939; m. Rachel Esther Williams, Dec. 23, 1938; children—John, Janet Chave, Ellen Tessada, William, Patricia Barnard. Info. asst. Dept. Agr., Tucson, 1939-41; pres. Royal Crown Cola Co., Panama, 1946-49, dir., Mex. and Central Am., 1949-63; exec. v.p. Am. C. of C. of Mex., 1963-76, pres., 1976—. Student body v.p. U. Ariz., 1937-38, pres., 1938-39; del. at large Nat. Student Fedn. Am., 1938-39. Bd. dirs. Mexico City Conv. Bur., Am. Soc. of Mexico, Fondo Privado de Fomento Turistico, Fomento Educacional, Mexico. Served to lt. col. U.S. Army, 1941-46; CBI. Decorated Legion of Merit, Spl. Breast Order Yun Hiu (Chinese Nat. Govt.); recipient Golden medal Al Merito Turistico, Mexican Nat. Tourism Council, 1971. Mem. U.S.-Mexico C. of C. (dir.). Club: University of Mexico. Office: Lucerna 78 40 Piso Mexico 6 DF Mexico. *Faith in God and in my country and hard work have always been my guiding principles.*

WICK, GIAN CARLO, educator, physicist; b. Torino, Italy, Oct. 15, 1909; s. Federico Carlo and Barbara (Allason) W.; Dr. Physics, U. Turin, Italy, 1930; m. Antonella Civalleri, Dec. 4, 1943; children—Lionel Anthony, Julian Charles; m. 2d, Vanna Chirone. Came to U.S., 1946, naturalized, 1955. Asso. prof. physics U. Palermo, Italy, 1937-38, U. Padova, Italy, 1938-40; prof. physics U. Rome, 1940-45, U. Notre Dame, 1946-48, U. Calif., 1948-50; prof. Carnegie Inst. Tech., 1951-58; sr. physicist Brookhaven Nat. Lab., 1958-65; prof. physics Columbia, 1965—. Mem. Inst. Advanced Study, Princeton, 1953. Fellow Am. Phys. Soc.; mem. Am. Acad. Arts and Scis., Nat. Acad. Scis. Address: Dept Physics Columbia U New York NY 10027*

WICK, HILTON ADDISON, bank exec., lawyer; b. Mt. Pleasant, Pa., Feb. 11, 1920; B.A., Maryville Coll., 1942; LL.B., Harvard, 1948; m. Barbara G. Shaw; children—James H., William S., Mrs. B. Jane Goldstein, Mrs. Ann W. Comstock, Julia A. Admitted to Vt. bar, 1948, since practiced in Burlington, mem. firm Wick, Dinse & Allen, 1949-72; of counsel firm Dinse, Allen & Erdmann, Burlington, 1972—; dir. Chittenden Trust Co., Burlington, 1961—, pres., 1969—; pres. Chittenden Corp., 1973—; dir. Nat. Life Ins. Co. Trustee, vice chmn. bd. Middlebury Coll.; trustee, v.p. Vt. Law Sch., 1975—; trustee Champlain Coll., 1974—. Mem. Chittenden County (pres. 1963-64), Vt. (pres. 1967-68), Am. bar assns., Internat. Soc. Barristers, Am. (dir. 1975—), Vt. (pres. 1973-74) bankers assns., Phi Kappa Delta. Home: Appletree Point Burlington VT 05401 Office: 2 Burlington Sq Burlington VT 05401

WICK, JOHN GERARD, ins. co. exec.; b. Buffalo, Dec. 5, 1924; s. John Kessel and Louise Mary (Schlager) W.; B.A., Canisius Coll., 1949; LL.D., U. Buffalo, 1952; m. Audrey Marie Frieh, July 7, 1951; children—Susan, Barbara, Sharon, Mary Ann, John Gerard. Admitted to N.Y. bar, 1952; partner firm Jaeckle, Fleischmann, Buffalo, 1952-64; adminstrv. v.p. Mchts. Mut. Ins. Co., Buffalo, 1964-68, exec. v.p., 1968-72, pres., chief exec. office, 1972—; dir. Liberty Nat. Bank, Niagara Mohawk Power Corp., United Bank N.Y., S.B. Whistler & Sons; bd. dirs. N.Y. State Auto Club, 1974—, 3d v.p., 1977. Chmn. Cancer Crusade, Buffalo, 1973-74. Served with USN, 1943-46. Decorated knight of St. Gregory, knight of Holy Sepulchre (Vatican). Mem. N.Y. State Bar Assn., C.P.C.U. Republican. Roman Catholic. Clubs: Met., Buffalo, Country of Buffalo K.C. Office: 250 Main St Buffalo NY 14202

WICK, ROBERT HOBBIE, educator; b. Mt. Union, Iowa, Jan. 23, 1913; s. Albert Lincoln and Emma Louise (Hobbie) W.; B.A., U. No. Iowa, 1934; M.A., U. So. Calif., 1940; Ph.D., State U. Iowa, 1955; m. Alice Joan Mead, Apr. 25, 1942; children—Ann Louise (Mrs. Joseph Roettger), Thomas Mead, William Robert. Prin. Andrew (Iowa) High Sch., 1934-36; chmn. dept. speech Newton (Iowa) High Sch., 1936-42; mem. faculty St. Cloud (Minn.) State U., 1948—, dean Sch. Sci., Lit. and Arts, 1962-65, pres. of univ., 1965-71, v.p. univ. relations, 1976-78, disting. service prof., 1971-78; ret., 1978; dir. St. Cloud Nat. Bank and Trust. Pres., St. Cloud Pub. Library, 1960—; mem. Great River Regional Library Bd., 1972, Minn. Manpower Planning Council, 1972; dir. Central Minn. Pub. Service Consortium, 1972; trustee St. Cloud Hosp. Served to capt. AUS, 1942-46. Mem. Assn. Gen. and Liberal Studies, Speech Assn. Am., Central States Speech Assn., Blue Key, Phi Mu Alpha, Phi Delta Kappa, Theta Alpha Phi. Club: Kiwanis (St. Cloud). Home: 1720 N 6th Ave Saint Cloud MN 56301

WICK, ROBERT SENTERS, educator; b. Port Washington, N.Y., Dec. 4, 1925; s. Harold Martin and Irene Marie (Senters) W.; B.S. in Mech. Engring., Rensselaer Poly. Inst., 1946; M.S. in Mech. Engring., Stevens Inst. Tech., 1948; Ph.D., U. Ill., 1952; m. Nancy Bartlett Gallison, June 13, 1947; children—Stephen, Bruce, Carol, James, John. With Standard Oil Devel. Co., 1946-47; with staff Jet Propulsion Lab. Cal. Inst. Tech., 1952-55; with Westinghouse Electric Corp., Pitts., 1955-66; now mem. faculty dept. aerospace and nuclear engring. Tex. A. and M. U. Mem. Whitehall (Pa.) Youth Commn., 1964-66, Friends of Whitehall Library, 1964-66. Served with USN, 1943-46. Recipient faculty distinguished achievement award in teaching Tex. A. and M. U., 1969. Mem. Am. Soc. M.E., Am. Nuclear Soc., Am. Inst. Astronautics and Aeronautics, Am. Soc. Engring. Edn., Sigma Xi, Phi Kappa Phi, Pi Tau Sigma. Episcopalian. Chpt. editor Naval Reactors Physics Handbook, Vol. 1, 1964. Contbr. articles to profl. jours. Home: 1204 Neal Pickett St College Station TX 77840

WICK, WARNER ARMS, ret. educator; b. Youngstown, Ohio, May 19, 1911; s. James Lippincott and Clare (Dryer) W.; B.A., Williams Coll., 1932; B.A., Oxford (Eng.) U., 1934; Ph.D., U. Chgo., 1941; m. Mary Elisabeth Wills, Sept. 12, 1936; children—James Lippincott, Laura Bardsley, John Dryer. Instr. philosophy Central YMCA Coll., Chgo., 1936-37, asst. prof., 1937-43; vis. asst. prof. Dartmouth Coll., 1941-42; asst. supt. Falcon Bronze Co., Youngstown, 1943-44, asst. gen. mgr. prodn., 1944-46, dir., 1946-53; asst. prof. philosophy U. Chgo., 1946-52, asso. prof., 1952-58, prof., 1958—, William Rainey Harper prof. humanities, 1974-79, emeritus, 1979—, dean of students div. humanities, 1950-53, asso. dean coll., chmn. council advanced gen. studies, 1959-63, dean students, 1962-67, master humanities collegiate div., asso. dean div. humanities, 1971-74; vis. research fellow Princeton U., 1956-57. Bd. dirs. Internat. House Assn., 1937-41; bd. govs. Internat. House, Chgo., 1962-75, vice chmn., 1972-74; trustee Art inst. Chgo., 1966—, vice chmn. com. on sch., 1967-75, chmn., 1975—; trustee Beloit Coll., 1960—; bd. dirs. George M. Pullman Ednl. Found., 1965—, sec., 1972—. Mem. Am. Philos. Assn. (exec. com. Western div. 1957-60), Metaphys. Soc. Am., Phi Beta Kappa. Author: Metaphysics and the New Logic, 1942; co-editor Ethics, 1967-73, editor, 1974-79. Home: 5603 Kenwood Ave Chicago IL 60637

WICK, WILLIAM QUENTIN, educator; b. Eau Claire, Wis., Oct. 24, 1927; s. Clarence Johan and Theodora Agnes Marie (Hansen) W.; B.S., Oreg. State U., 1950, M.S., 1952; m. Marie Caroline Stegen, June 20, 1954; children—Rosemary, Susan. Wildlife biologist, Nev. and Wash., 1952-60; extension agt. Oreg. State U., 1960-67, leader marine advisory program, 1968-73, prof. wildlife ecology, 1969—, dir. Sea Grant Coll. Program, 1973—; cons. in field. Served with U.S. Army, 1946-48. Recipient Superior Service medal Dept. Agr., 1971. Mem. Wildlife Soc. (Einarsen award 1972), Marine Tech. Soc. (Compass Disting. Achievement award 1976), Nat. Wildlife Fedn., Izaak Walton League, Pacific N.W. Bird Mammal Soc., Sea Grant Assn. (nat. pres. 1978), Nat. Assn. County Agrl. Agts. Lutheran. Clubs: Rotary, Elks. Contbr. articles to profl. jours. Home: 3740 NW Hayes St Corvallis OR 97330 Office: AdS A 320 Oregon State U Corvallis OR 97331. *To effectively utilize one's talents, a few guidelines seem to help. First, an optimistic outlook on life; second, enthusiasm (It's contagious); third, trying to do everything a bit better than average—not to perfection—but beyond the expectation of oneself and others.*

WICKENS, ARYNESS JOY, economist, statistician; b. Bellingham, Wash., Jan. 5, 1901; d. Oliver Hodgson and Elizabeth (Chapman) Joy; A.B., U. Wash., 1922; A.M., U. Chgo., 1924; m. David Lawrence Wickens, June 29, 1935; children—David Elder (dec.) Donaldson. Instr., then asst. prof. econs. and sociology Mt. Holyoke Coll., 1924-28, research asst. div. research and statistics Fed. Res. Bd., 1928-1933; chief statistician Office Econs. Adviser, Nat. Emergency Council, 1933-35; chief statistician, chief economist U.S. Central Statis. Bd., 1935-37; asst. to commr. Bur. Labor statistics, 1938-40, chief, prices and cost of living br., 1940-45, asst. commr. for program ops., 1945-49, dep. commr. of Bur., 1949-54, acting commr., 1954-55, dep. asst. sec. labor for manpower and employment, 1956-59; econ. adviser to sec. of labor, 1959-62, consumer program adviser, 1962-69, spl. asst. to asst. sec. labor for manpower, 1967-68; dir. Office of Manpower Mgmt. Data Systems, Manpower Adminstrn., 1968-70, cons. to manpower adminstr., 1970-71; pvt. cons., 1971—; statistician Commn. on Fed. Paperwork, 1976-77; mem. adv. bd. Export Import Bank U.S., 1976-77; dir. Washington-Lee Savs. & Loan Assn., McLean, Va., 1965-73, dir. emeritus, 1974—; adviser to U.S. del. 30th and 31st sessions Internat. Labor Conf., 1947, 1948; U.S. del. to 1st gen. assembly Inter-Am. Statis. Inst., 1947; adviser to U.S. del. Econ. and Social Council of UN, 1951, 52, 60, 61. Bd. dirs. Am. Nat. Standards Inst., 1967-69; mem. Consumer Standards Bd., 1963-66; mem. Consumer Council, 1966-69, 70-76. Recipient Distinguished Service award U.S. Dept. Labor, 1955, Fed. Woman's award, 1961. Fellow Am. Statis. Assn. (pres. 1952); mem. Am. Econ. Assn., Nat. Economists Club, Phi Beta Kappa, Kappa Kappa Gamma. Home: 2210 Hunter Mill Rd Vienna VA 22180

WICKER, ELMUS ROGERS, economist; b. Lake Charles, La., Sept. 13, 1926; s. Elmus Rogers Wicker and Georgia Mary (Moss) Wicker Baker; B.A., La. State U., 1945, M.A., 1948; B. Phil. (Rhodes scholar), Oxford (Eng.) U., 1951; Ph.D., Duke U., 1956; m. Carolyn Braswell Winling, Sept. 18, 1948; children—Vanessa Louise, Roger Andrew. Mem. faculty Ind. U., Bloomington, 1955—, prof. econs., 1967—, chmn. econs. dept., 1973-78; cons. to bd. govs. Fed. Res. System, 1963-65. Served with USNR, 1945-46. Ford Found. Faculty Research fellow, 1963. Mem. Am. Econ. Assn., Am. Fin. Assn., Econ. History Assn., AAUP, Lambda Chi Alpha. Democrat. Roman Catholic. Author: Federal Reserve Monetary Policy, 1917-33, 1966; (with James Boughton) Principles of Monetary Economics, 1975. Home: 1315 Nancy St Bloomington IN 47401

WICKER, IREENE, writer, singer, entertainer radio and TV; b. Quincy, Ill.; d. Kenner and Margaret (Hunsaker) Seaton; ed. grade and high schs., Quincy, also U. Ill., 1 yr.; student Goodman Theatre Sch., Art Inst. Chgo., 1927-30; m. Walter C. Wicker; children—Walter Charles, Nancy; m. 2d, Victor Hammer, Jan. 11, 1941. Actress in stock co. at 12; appeared at the Goodman Theatre, Chgo., 1929-30; mem. dramatic staff CBS, 1930-31; played in Today's Children, Song of the City, Judy and Jane, Internat. Radio and TV Soc., Am. Women in Radio and TV, Authors Guild, Broadcast Pioneers, Nat. Acad. TV Arts and Scis. Originated, wrote and performed, Singing Lady radio program; Sunday dramatic program Ireene Wicker's Music Plays, NBC and MBS; co-dir. Merry-Go-Round Children's Theatre; worked with profl. children on ABC-TV, 1951-54; with Shakespearean group Am. Theatre Wing and with Stella Adler and Joseph Kramm, 1955-56; ednl. mus. dramatizations of children's stories, N.Y.C., 1959—. Recipient highest honors 5 years in succession, for children's programs, by radio editors poll, conducted by N. Y. World Telegram; also award for distinguished service to radio, by poll of Radio Star Mag.; recipient award Radio Guide Mag. for leading children's program, 4 yrs. in succession; Peabody award for children's radio programs, 1961; Emmy award Rec. for Record Guild of Am.; Soc. Am. Radio Enthusiasts award, 1975; records made by Decca, Victor, Mercury; song books and plays pub. by Irving Berlin, Inc. Author: The Little Hunchback Horse; Young Music Makers; How the Oscelots Got Their Spots, 1976; Young Master Artists and other books, plays and songs for children; 4 books and albums for Regal and De Luxe rec. Dir. Children's Radio for WNYC-N.Y., C.D.V.O. Presbyn. Made 12 Golden Book Records, Albums of children's stores with songs; rec. cassettes children's books for N.Y. Pub. Library, 1973. Home: 781 Fifth Ave New York NY 10022 Office: 667 Madison Ave New York NY 10021

WICKER, JOHN JORDAN, JR., lawyer; b. Lyndon, Ky., Dec. 31, 1893; s. John Jordan and Elizabeth (Pumphrey) W.; student The Peddie Sch., 1905-09; Furman U., 1909-10; A.B., U. Richmond, 1913, LL.B., 1916, LL.D., 1963; m. Kate Richardson, Sept. 30, 1915 (dec.); children—Katharine Lumpkin Wicker Long, Lila Richardson Wicker Hunt (dec.); m. 2d, Ruby Summers McCarty, July 9, 1962. Admitted to Va. bar, 1915, since practiced in Richmond; sr. partner Wicker, Baker & Shuford, 1950-56, Wicker, Baker & Goddin, 1956-66, Wicker, Goddin & Duling, 1966-69, Wicker, Goddin, Duling & Thurmond, 1969, Wicker, Goddin & Duling, 1970-73, Wicker & White, 1973-74, Wicker, Haskins & Hutchens, 1975—; asso. Sterling H. Moore; pres., gen. counsel Richmond Bridge Corp., 1932-41; state mgr. HOLC, 1933-37; gen. counsel Va. Hotel Assn., 1939-48; v.p., gen. counsel Potomac Pub. Service Corp.; v.p. Richmond Arena Corp., 1965-75; Va. gen. counsel Purolator Courier Corp., 1970—; gen. counsel Va. Trailways Assn. Mem. Va. Bd. Welfare and Instns., 1948-63; founder, hon. chmn., gen. counsel Va. Thanksgiving Festival, Inc., 1958—; chmn. Va. War Meml. Commn., 1950—; Va. chmn. Nat. Football Found. and Hall of Fame, 1961—; mem. Va. Senate, 1932-36; pres. Electoral Coll., 1944; chmn. Constl. Conv. of Va., 1945; pres. Richmond Student Aid Found., 1957—. Decorated officier Légion d'Honneur (France); chevalier Ordre of Leopold Militaire (Belgium); named Hon. Citizen St. Louis, 1964, Paris, 1968; award Congressional Medal of Honor Soc., 1977; named to U. Richmond Hall of Fame, 1976. Fellow Am. Bar Found., Internat. Acad. Trial Lawyers; mem. Fedn. Ins. Counsel, Am. Judicature Soc., Am. (nat. chmn. ins. negligence and compensation law sect. 1959-60), Va. (chmn. judiciary com. 1950-52, chmn. com. on fgn. bar cooperation 1972—), Richmond bar assns., Internat. Assn. Ins. Counsel, Am. Legion (state comdr. Va. 1923-24, nat. exec. com. 1919-21, 25-31, nat. dir. 2d, AEF 1925-27), Army Navy Air Force Vets in Can. (hon), Soc. Am. Legion Founders (nat. pres. 1964-65), Am. Legion Endowment Fund Corp. (dir. 1967—), Omicron Delta Kappa, Phi Kappa Sigma. Democrat. Baptist (hon. bd. mem. various Va. orgns. 1949-73). Clubs: Masons, Shriners, Commonwealth, Downtown, Bull and Bear, Country of Va. (Richmond); Army and Navy (Washington). Home: The Prestwould Richmond VA 23220 Office: Suite 706 Mutual Bldg Richmond VA 23219. *Be cautious about giving your word. Once Given, never break it. If you determine something is truly "Worthwhile"-do everything in your power-no matter how great the obstacles may be-to accomplish it, even though others may declare it to be impossible.*

WICKER, THOMAS GREY, author, journalist; b. Hamlet, N.C., June 18, 1926; s. Delancey David and Esta (Cameron) W.; A.B. in Journalism, U. N.C., 1948; Nieman fellow, Harvard, 1957-58; m. Neva Jewett McLean, Aug. 20, 1949 (div. 1973); children—Cameron McLean, Thomas Grey; m. 2d, Pamela Abel Hill, Mar. 9, 1974. Exec dir. Southern Pines (N.C.) C. of C., 1948-49; editor Sanhill Citizen, Aberdeen, N.C., 1949; mng. editor The Robesonian, Lumberton, N.C., 1949-50; pub. info. dir. N.C. Bd. Pub. Welfare, 1950-51; copy editor Winston-Salem (N.C.) Jour., 1951-52, sports editor, 1954-55, Sunday feature editor, 1955-56, Washington corr., 1957, editorial writer, city hall corr., 1958-59; asso. editor Nashville Tennesseean, 1959-60; mem. staff Washington bur. N.Y. Times, 1960—, chief bur., 1964-68, asso. editor N.Y. Times, 1968—. Served to lt. (j.g.) USNR, 1952-54. Mem. Soc. Nieman Fellows. Author: (pseudonym Paul Connolly) (novels) Get Out of Town, 1951, Tears Are For Angels, 1952, So Fair, So Evil, 1955; (under own name) (novels) The Kingpin, 1953, The Devil Must, 1957, The Judgment, 1961, Facing the Lions, 1973; (non-fiction) Kennedy Without Tears, 1964, JFK and LBJ: The Influence of Personality Upon Politics, 1968, A Time to Die, 1975, On Press, 1978; also contbr. articles to nat. mags., chpts. to books. Office: care NY Times Co 229 W 43d St New York NY 10036

WICKERS, ROGER TRUEMAN, financial exec.; b. E. Orange, N.J., Feb. 7, 1935; s. Arthur Trueman and Cordelia (Smith) W.; B.A., Cornell U., 1957; LL.B., Columbia U., 1960; m. Martie Hubbard, Oct. 1, 1960; children—Mark Trueman, Linda Barrett, Steven Peirce. Admitted to N.Y. bar, 1960; exec. asst. N.Y. Stock Exchange, N.Y.C., 1960-64; sr. v.p., dir. Anchor Corp., Elizabeth, N.J., 1964—, sr. v.p. Anchor Group of Mut. Funds, Elizabeth, 1964—; chmn. money market funds com. Investment Co. Inst., 1974—; chmn. comml. paper com. Penn Central R.R., Phila., 1970-72. Chmn., Mountain Lakes (N.J.) Bd. Adjustments, 1974—; trustee Community Ch. of Mountain Lakes, 1972-73. Mem. Am. Bar Assn., Alpha Delta Phi. Congregationalist. Club: Rockaway River Country (Denville, N.J.). Home: 195 Boulevard Mountain Lakes NJ 07046 Office: Anchor Corp Westminster at Parker Sts Elizabeth NJ 07207

WICKERT, FREDERIC ROBINSON, psychologist, educator; b. Chgo., Mar. 9, 1912; s. Rudolph and Martha H. (Kay) W.; B.A., U. Calif. at Los Angeles, 1933; Ph.D., U. Chgo., 1938; m. Dorothy Ruth Dodge, May 30, 1940; children—Susan, Melissa (Mrs. D. Grostick). Research psychologist Western Electric Co., Hawthorne Sta., Ill., 1936-40, Commonwealth Edison Co., Chgo., 1940-47; asso. prof. psychology Mich. State U., East Lansing, 1947-58, prof. psychology and grad. bus. adminstrn., 1958—, div. chief Vietnam program, 1955-57, asst. dir. Inst. for Overseas Programs, 1958-59. Vis. prof. U. Graz, Austria, 1953-54, U. Toulouse, France, 1960-61, U. Canterbury, New Zealand, 1968, U. Otago, New Zealand, 1968, Monash U., Australia, 1969, Nat. Inst. Adminstrn., S. Viet Nam, 1955-57, U. Chad, 1977, Nat. Sch. Adminstrn., Upper Volta, 1977, Nat. Sch. Adminstrn., Mali, 1977, U. Ivory Coast, 1977; cons., chief of party Ops. Research Office, Johns Hopkins U., 1953; cons. project Spl. Ops. Research Office, Am. U., 1963; cons. to Peace Corps, govts. of Nigeria and Ghana, 1959, to State of Mich., 1960-73, U.S. Army, 1947-54. Served from 2d lt. to lt. col. AUS, 1933-46; col. USAF Res. (ret.). Diplomate Am. Bd. Profl. Psychology. Fellow Am. Psychol. Assn.; mem. Midwestern Psychol. Assn., Internat. Assn. Applied Psychology, Acad. of Mgmt., Am. Mgmt. Assn., Am. Mktg. Assn., Assn. for Consumer Research, Soc. Applied Anthropology, Internat. Assn. Cross Cultural Psychology, Sigma Xi, Phi Beta Kappa, Psi Chi, Sigma Iota Epsilon, Phi Kappa Sigma. Author: (with G. Grimsley) Psychological Techniques in Personnel Research, 1948; (with others) The International Programs of American Universities, 1958; (with D.E. McFarland) Measuring Executive Effectiveness, 1967. Editor: Psychological Research on Problems of Redistribution, 1947; (with H. Meltzer) Humanizing Organizational Behavior, 1976; editor, translator: Readings in African Psychology from French Language Sources, 1967. Contbr. numerous articles on indsl. psychology to profl. jours. Home: 638 Baldwin Ct East Lansing MI 48823 Office: Dept of Psychology Synder Hall Mich State Univ East Lansing MI 48824

WICKESBERG, ALBERT KLUMB, educator; b. Neenah, Wis., Apr. 2, 1921; s. Albert Henry and Lydia (Klumb) W.; B.A., Lawrence Coll., 1943; M.B.A., Stanford U., 1948; Ph.D., Ohio State U., 1955; m. Dorothy Louise Ahrensfeld, Oct. 28, 1944; children—Robert, William, James. Staff accountant S.C. Johnson & Son, Inc., Racine, Wis., 1948-50; asst. prof. Sacramento State Coll., 1950-51; prof. U. Minn., Mpls., 1953—, chmn. dept. bus. adminstrn., 1959-62, dir. grad. studies, 1963-66, chmn. dept. mgmt. and transp., 1971-77. Served with AUS, 1943-46, 51-52. Soc. Advancement Mgmt. fellow, 1972. Mem. Acad. Mgmt., Soc. Advancement Mgmt. (pres. Twin Cities chpt. 1961-62). Congregationalist. Author: Management Organization, 1966. Home: 4501 Roanoke Rd Golden Valley MN 55422 Office: Sch Bus Adminstrn U Minn Minneapolis MN 55455

WICKHAM, JOHN ADAMS, JR., army officer; b. Dobbs Ferry, N.Y., June 25, 1928; s. John Adams and Jean Gordon (Koch) W.; B.S., U.S. Mil. Acad., 1950; M.A., Harvard U., 1955, M.P.A., 1956; grad. Nat. War Coll., 1967; m. Ann Lindsley Prior, June 18, 1955; children—Lindsley, John Adams, Matthew. Commd. 2d lt. U.S. Army, 1950, advanced through grades to gen., 1979; asst. prof. social scis. U.S. Mil. Acad., 1956-60; brigade comdr., chief of staff 3d Inf. Div., Germany, 1969-70; army mem. chmn.'s staff group Office of Chmn. Joint Chiefs of Staff, Washington, 1970-71; dep. chief of staff for econ. affairs Mil. Assistance Command, Vietnam, 1971-73; dep. chief, negotiator U.S. del. Four Party Joint Mil. Commn., Vietnam, 1973; sr. mil. asst. to Sec. Def., Washington, 1973-76; comdr. 101st Airborne Div. (Air Assault), Ft. Campbell, Ky., 1976-78; dir. Joint Staff Orgn., Joint Chiefs Staff, Washington, 1978-79; comdr. in chief UN Command, Korea, 1979—. Decorated Def. and Army D.S.M. (2), Silver Star (2), Legion of Merit (3), Bronze Star for Valor, Air medal (11), Army Commendation medal, Purple Heart. Mem. Assn. U.S. Army, 101st Airborne Assn., Council on Fgn. Relations. Home: Quarters 15-B Fort Meyer KY 22211 Office: Comdr in Chief UN Command APO San Francisco CA 96301

WICKHAM, KENNETH GREGORY, ret. army officer, inst. ofcl.; b. Hayti, Mo., Apr. 8, 1913; s. Charles Lawrence and Nell (Lively) W.; B.S., U.S. Mil. Acad., 1938; M.A., George Washington U., 1963; grad. Armed Forces Staff Coll., 1948, Army War Coll., 1956; m. Helen Wickham, July 12, 1938; 1 dau., Mary Harvey Wickham Anderson. Commd. 2d lt. U.S. Army, 1938, advanced through grades to maj. gen., 1964; assigned arty., U.S. and Hawaii, 1938-42; with inf. in PTO, ETO, 1942-45; various staff and command assignments, 1945-54; assigned Korea, 1954-55; comdt. Adj. Gen.'s Sch., 1959-61; comdg. gen. Combat Service Support Group, Combat Devel. Command, 1964-66; adj. gen. U.S. Army, 1966-71; asst. dir. Bus. Mgmt. Inst., Western Assn. Coll. and Univ. Bus. Officers, Stanford, Calif., 1975—. Area dir. in Korea, ARC campaign, 1955; bd. dirs. Army Emergency Relief Assn., U.S. Olympic Com., Army Mut. Aid Assn., Internat. Mil. Sports Council (pres. 1969-70); mem. exec. com. Council Internat. Mil. Sports, 1967—; pres. Calif. Assn. Mil. Personnel, 1972—. Decorated D.S.M., Legion of Merit with 2 oak leaf clusters, Bronze Star with oak leaf cluster, Purple Heart, Commendation medal; Legion of Honor, Croix de Guerre (France); Cross of Haakon VII (Norway); Ulchi Distinguished Service medal (Korea). Home: 15 Sunkist Ln Los Altos CA 94022

WICKHEM, JOHN CARROLL, lawyer; b. Madison, Wis., Aug. 28, 1921; s. John Dunne and Mary Luella (Carroll) W.; B.A., U. Wis., 1943, J.D., 1949; m. Mary Boyle, Feb. 20, 1944; children—John Boyle, James Dunne, Maryanne, Patty Lu. Admitted to Wis. bar, 1949; partner firm Wickhem & Consigny, Janesville, Wis., 1960-69; pres. Wickhem, Consigny, Andrews & Hemming, S.C., Janesville and Evansville, Wis., 1970—; lectr. U. Wis. Law Sch.; dir. Internat. Crane Found. Chmn. Janesville Police and Fire Commn., 1974-75. Served to 1st lt. U.S. Army, 1942-46; PTO. Recipient Outstanding Young Man of Year award Janesville Jr. C. of C., 1955. Fellow Am. Coll. Trial Lawyers, Am. Bar Found., Wis. Bar Found.; mem. Am. Bar Assn., Wis. Bar Assn. (bd. govs. 1967-71, pres. 1969-70), Rock Country Bar Assn., Bar Assn. 7th Circuit Ct. of Appeals, Am. Law Inst., Fedn. Ins. Counsel, Internat. Assn. Ins. Counsel, Ins. Trial Counsel Wis., Am. Judicature Soc. (dir.), Janesville C. of C. (pres. 1954), Order of Coif, Phi Beta Kappa. Roman Catholic. Office: 303 East Ct Janesville WI 53545

WICKISER, RALPH LEWANDA, painter, author, educator; b. Greenup, Ill., Mar. 20, 1910; s. Herk and Lydia (Denny) W.; student Chgo. Art Inst., 1928-31, Vanderbilt U., 1934-37; B.Ed., Eastern Ill. Coll., 1934, Ph.D. (hon.), 1956; A.M., Peabody Coll., 1935, Ph.D., 1938; m. Jane Bisson, June 1, 1936; children—Eric Lee, Lydia, Walter. Art writer Nashville, also Peabody Reflector, 1934-35; instr. art La. State U., 1937-40, asst. prof., 1940, head fine arts dept., 1941, asso. prof., 1944-49, prof., 1949-56; dir. art edn. div. State U. N.Y. Tchrs. Coll., 1956-59; chmn. art edn. dept. Pratt Inst., 1959-65, dir. grad. programs art and design, 1965-70, acting dean Sch. Art and Design, 1970—, dir. grad. programs in art and design, 1971—; Ford Found. grant advancement edn., 1952-53. Exhibited Grand Central Galleries (N.Y.C.), Tiffany Found. Group, 1934-35, A New So. Group, Gresham Gallery, New Orleans, travelling show, 1937-41, The Arts Club, Washington, Library of Congress Annual Print Exhbn., U. Chattanooga, Asso. Am. Artists Gallery, N.Y.C., Bklyn. Mus., Corcoran Gallery, Washington, Pa. Acad., Phila., Print Club, Phila., San Francisco Mus., Dayton (Ohio) Mus., Dallas Mus., Delgado Mus., Met. Mus., Whitney Mus., New Realism show Suffolk Mus., 1971, Lerner-Miraschi Gallery, N.Y.C., 1972, Pacem in Terris UN, 1976, Lotus Gallery, N.Y.C., 1976; book rev. Sat. Rev., 1952, 53, 54; retrospective exhbn. Eastern Ill. U., 1968; color lithographs for Standard Oil Co., N.J., June 1947; water colors for Ford Motor Co., 1948; creative painting, Woodstock, N.Y., 1948; cons., adv. bd. Unicorn Press for New Standard Ency. of Funk and Wagnalls; lectr. art Vassar Coll., 1949. Mem. council National Com. Art Edn. Served with USNR, 1945-46. Mem. Artists Equity, Am. Soc. Aesthetics, Coll. Art League, Phi Delta Kappa, Kappa Delta Pi. Author: Military Leadership (with Capt. P. E. McDowell), 1944; Introduction to Art Activities, 1947; An Introduction to Art Education, 1957. Editor: Mardi Gras Day (with Caroline Durieux), 1948; contbg. editor: Ency. of the Arts, 1946; contbr. Internat. Ency., Cath. Ency. Home: Box 263 Bearsville NY 12409. *It has been a mystery to me why it takes a lifetime to become fully aware of one's self, one's life. Even for the person who constantly studies there is not enough time to learn all one needs to know, to see all the marvelous things to be seen in nature and fully respond to a falling leaf. It is ironic that we begin to value life when it ebbs. I say all of this because my life has been a search for understanding, to discover the principles behind life and nature and the ideas that defined the principles. Art and education have both offered me a life of activity and quiet contemplation. They have, by diligent pursuit, given me a greater appreciation of things though and seen, felt and intuited.*

WICKLEIN, JOHN FREDERICK, public TV exec., journalist; b. Reading, Pa., July 20, 1924; s. Raymond Roland and Parmilla Catherine (Miller) W.; Litt.B., Rutgers U., 1947; M.S. in Journalism, Columbia, 1948; m. Myra Jane Winchester, July 31, 1948; children—Elizabeth Wicklein Hirsh, Peter, Joanna. Reporter, Newark (N.J.) Evening News, 1947-51; news mng. editor Elec. World (McGraw-Hill weekly), N.Y.C., 1951-54; reporter, editor N.Y. Times, 1954-62; news dir. Sta. WNET-TV, N.Y.C., 1962-64; exec. producer news Sta. WABC-TV, N.Y.C., 1964-67; exec. producer Washington Bur. chief Public Broadcast Lab., Nat. Ednl. TV, 1967-70; mng. news and public affairs broadcasts Sta. WCBS-TV, N.Y.C., 1970-71; gen. mgr. Sta. WRVR, N.Y.C., 1971-74; dean Sch. Public Communication Boston U., 1974-78; sr. asso. Center Internat. Public Issues, 1979—; vis. prof. communication Meth. U., São Paulo, Brazil, 1979; pres., gen. mgr. Sta. WLIW, L.I. Public TV, 1980—; cons. in field; bd. mgrs. Communication Commn. of Nat. Council Chs., 1975—; fellow Inst. Democratic Communication Boston U., 1975--; lectr. journalism Columbia Grad. Sch. Journalism, 1966-67; Danforth lectr. Barnard Coll., 1960-61. Recipient Venice Film Festival Documentary award, 1968; Polk award, 1963. Mem. Nat. Acad. TV Arts and Scis., Assn. Edn. in Journalism, AAUP, Phi Beta Kappa, Sigma Delta Chi. Democrat. Author: (with Monroe Price) Cable Television: A Guide for Citizen Action, 1972, The New Communications and Freedom, 1980; editor: Investigative Reporting: The Lessons of Watergate, 1975; contbg. editor The Washington Monthly, 1969-72; contbr. Atlantic Monthly, 1979—. Home: 26 Shaw Dr Wayland MA 01778

WICKMAN, CLIFFORD WILLIAM, investigative corp. exec.; b. Bklyn., Sept. 10, 1922; s. Joseph Francis and Mary Jane (Long) W.; B.S. in Marine Nav., U.S. Mcht. Marine Acad., 1944; B.S., Fordham U., 1949; m. Virginia E. Ochs, Aug. 31, 1946; children—Richard W., William K., Dennis S. Spl. employee FBI, N.Y.C., 1941-42, spl. agt., Washington, Omaha, Detroit, 1948-51; agt. investigator Thoroughbred Racing Protective Bur., Inc., 1961-70, v.p., 1970-77, pres., Lake Success, N.Y., 1977—. Served to lt. U.S. Merchant Marine, 1942-46, now Res. Mem. Soc. Former Spl. Agts. FBI. Club: West Side Tennis. Home: 1736 Beck Pl North Bellmore NY 11710 Office: 5 Dakota Dr Lake Success NY 11042

WICKMAN, JOHN EDWARD, librarian, historian; b. Villa Park, Ill., May 24, 1929; s. John Edward and Elsie (Voss) W.; A.B., Elmhurst Coll., 1953; A.M., Ind. U., 1958, Ph.D., 1964; LL.D., Lincoln Coll., 1973; m. Shirley Jean Swanson, Mar. 17, 1951; children—Lisa Annette, Eric John. Instr. history Hanover (Ind.) Coll., 1959-62, Southeast Campus, Ind. U., Jeffersonville, 1962; asst. prof. history Northwest Mo. State Coll., Maryville, 1962-64; asst. to Gov. William H. Avery of Kans., Topeka, 1964-65; asst. prof. history Regional Campus, Purdue U., Fort Wayne, Ind., 1965-66; dir. Dwight D. Eisenhower Library, Abilene, Kans., 1966—. Dir. Citizen Bank, Abilene. Served with U.S. Army, 1953-55. Nat. Center for Edn. in Politics faculty fellow, 1964-65; Am. Polit. Sci. Assn. Congl. fellow, 1975-76. Mem. Oral History Assn. (v.p. 1971-72, pres. 1972-73), Western History Assn. (council 1972-75), Kans. Hist. Soc. (2d v.p. 1974-75, pres. 1976-77, dir.). Contbr. articles on Am. West, archival mgmt., adminstrv. history, oral history to profl. publs. Home: Box 325 Enterprise KS 67441 Office: Eisenhower Library Abilene KS 67410

WICKMAN, PAUL EVERETT, public relations exec.; b. Bisbee, Ariz., Aug. 21, 1912; s. Julius and Hilda Wilhelmina (Soderholm) W.; student La Sierra Coll., Arlington, Calif., 1928-30, Pacific Union Coll., Angwin, Cal., 1931-32; spl. student Am. U., 1946; m. Evelyn Gorman, Nov. 22, 1969; children by previous marriage—Robert Bruce, Bette Jane, Marilyn Faye. Internat. traveler, lectr., writer, 1937-44; asso. sec Internat. Religious Liberty Assn., 1944-46; travel lectr. Nat. Lecture Bur., 1944-55; exec. sec., dir. internat. radio and TV prodns. Voice of Prophecy Corp., Faith for Today Corp., 1946-53; v.p. Western Advt. Agy., Los Angeles, 1953-55; dir. devel. Nat. Soc. Crippled Children and Adults, Inc., Chgo., 1955-56; exec. dir. Pub. Relations Soc. Am., Inc., N.Y.C., 1956-57; dir. corp. pub. relations Schering Corps., Bloomfield, N.J., 1957-58; pres. Wickman Pharm. Co., Inc., Calif. Mem. Newport Beach CSC; bd. dirs. U. Calif. at Irvine Found. Mem. Newcomen Soc., Pub. Relations Soc. Am. (accredited), Am. Soc. Assn. Execs., Am., Calif. pharm. assns., Am. Hosp. Assn., Orange County C. of C. (dir.). Clubs: Masons (32 deg.), Shriners, Jesters; Swedish (Los Angeles); Kiwanis (past pres.), Irvine Country (Newport Beach, Calif.); Vikings; 552 Hoag Hospital. Home: 28 Point Loma Dr Corona Del Mar CA 92625 Office: 14451 Franklin Ave Tustin CA 92680

WICKSER, JOHN PHILIP, lawyer; b. Buffalo, Oct. 14, 1922; s. Philip John and Margaretta Melissa (Fryer) W.; B.A., Yale U., 1945; J.D., Columbia U., 1949; m. Frances M. Halsey, July 2, 1949; children—Margaretta Melissa, Philip John, Gaius Halsey. Admitted to N.Y. bar, 1949, since practiced in Buffalo; mem. firm Palmer, Houck & Wickser, 1949-50; now partner firm Palmer, Heffernan Wickser & Beyer; pres. Main-Pearl Corp.; dir. Union-Am. Re-Ins. Co., 1975-77; dir., sec.-treas. Kleinhans Music Hall Mgmt., Inc. Adv. bd. Salvation Army, Internat. Inst., 1951-54; council State Tchrs. Coll., Buffalo, 1954-55; bd. dirs. Greater Buffalo Devel. Found., Grosvenor Soc.; chmn. bd. trustees Buffalo and Erie County Pub. Library; bd. dirs. Buffalo Fine Arts Acad., 1954-77. Served to lt. (j.g.) USNR, World War II. Mem. Buffalo Hist. Soc. (trustee), N.Y. State, Erie County bar assns., Am. Judicature Soc. Republican. Episcopalian. Clubs: Buffalo Country, Pack, Saturn (Buffalo); Yale (N.Y.C.); Elizabethan (New Haven); Pacific, Nantucket Yacht. Home: 22 Oakland Pl Buffalo NY 14222 Office: Rand Bldg Buffalo NY 14203

WICKSTRA, HOWARD EDWARD, med. equipment mfg. exec.; b. New Era, Mich., Sept. 29, 1924; s. John Peter and Jessie (Batten) W.; student Muskegon (Mich.) Sch. Bus., 1945-46; grad. Advanced Mgmt. Program, Harvard, 1972; m. Angeline Hester Brondyke, Apr. 12, 1947; children—Gregg Peter, Donald Jay. With Brunswick Corp., 1947-72, asst. corporate controller, Chgo., 1968-72, v.p., 1977—; pres. Sherwood Med. Industries Inc., St. Louis, 1972—; chmn. bd. Sherwood Med. Industries Ltd., Crawley, Eng., 1972—, Sherwood Med. Industries (Hong Kong) Ltd.; pres., dir. Sherwood Med. Industries (Can.) Ltd.; dir. Nippon-Sherwood Med. Industries Ltd., Tokyo, Japan, Sherwood Med. Industries, S.A., Belgium. Served with USAAF, 1943-45. Clubs: St. Louis, Mo. Athletic, Stadium (St. Louis). Home: 224 Bryn Wyck Pl Saint Louis MO 63141 Office: 1831 Olive St Saint Louis MO 63103

WICKSTROM, JACK KENNETH, educator; b. Omaha, Aug. 7, 1913; s. Albin E. and Agnes B. (Nelson) W.; M.D., U. Nebr., 1939, D.Sc. (hon.), 1979; m. Mary Elizabeth Wilson, Sept. 14, 1940; children—Cynthia (Mrs. Richard E. Wright), Merrilee (Mrs. I. Mims Gage Jr.), Charles Wilson. Med. tng. Charity Hosp., New Orleans, 1939-42; fellow U. Nebr., 1944; fellow Tulane U., 1944-46, instr., 1946-48, asst. prof., 1948-51, asso. prof., 1951-55, prof., 1955-61, Lee C. Schlesinger prof., 1961—; cons. in field. Bd. dirs. La. chpt. Arthritis and Rheumatism Found., Muscular Dystrophy Found. Served with USN, 1942-44. Decorated 2 Purple Hearts, Presdl. citation; recipient Surgeons award Nat. Safety Council, 1975. Diplomate Am. Bd. Orthopedic Surgery; mem. A.M.A., Assn. Bone and Joint Surgeons, Am. Orthopedic Assn. Clubs: Alpine, Round Table, Lamplighter. Asso. editor Jour. Bone and Joint Surgery, 1957-63; Jour. Trauma, 1964; Bull. Am. Acad. Orthopedic Surgeons, 1960-71. Home: 7540 Jeannette St New Orleans LA 70118

WICKSTROM, KARL YOUNGERT, pub. co. exec.; b. Moline, Ill., Sept. 20, 1935; s. George Washington and Harriet L. (Youngert) W.; B.S.J., U. Fla., 1957; m. Patricia Pinkerton, 1959 (div.); children—Eric, Blair, Drew, Holly; m. 2d, Sheila Zehner, June 9, 1979. Writer, editor Orlando (Fla.) Sentinel-Star, 1958-60; writer Miami (Fla.) Herald, 1960-67; adminstrv. asst. Fla. Senate,

Tallahassee, 1968; founder, pres., publisher Wickstrom Pubs. Inc., mags., books, Miami, 1968—. Bd. dirs. Nat. Coalition for Marine Conservation. Served with USAF, 1967-68. Recipient 1st pl. award for pub. service Fla. AP, 1967. Mem. Sigma Delta Chi (nat. 1st pl. award for investigative reporting Miami area crime, corruption 1967). Original pub. Aloft Mag., for Nat. Airlines passengers, 1968—; pub. Fla. Sportsman, 1969—. Home: 8109 SW 81st Ct Miami FL 33143 Office: 2701 S Bayshore Dr Miami FL 33133

WIDASKY, STANLEY WILLIAM, banker; b. Palo Alto, Calif., Dec. 10, 1920; s. Sam and Leah (Zobler) W.; B.A. Stanford U., 1946; m. Ethel Kauffman, Sept. 24, 1968; children—Deborah Widasky Sgambelluri, Gerald W. With Bank of Hawaii, Honolulu, 1946—, v.p. controllers div., 1965-68, v.p., asst. mgr. main office, 1968-69, v.p., cashier, 1969—. Served with AUS, 1942-46. Mem. Fin. Execs. Inst. Jewish. Home: 250 Kawaihae St Honolulu HI 96825 Office: PO Box 2900 Honolulu HI 96846

WIDDER, WILLARD GRAVES, banker; b. Kansas City, Kans., June 21, 1924; s. George A. and Dorothy B. (Graves) W.; B.S. in Mech. Engring., U. Kans., 1946, LL.B., 1949. Admitted to Kans. bar, 1949; since practiced in Kansas City, Kans., 1949-53; with First Nat. Bank Kansas City (Mo.), 1953—, trust officer, 1961-66, v.p., 1966-71, sr. v.p., 1971—. Sec., 1st Nat. Found., Edward F. Swinney Found. Mem. Kansas City Estate Planning Council. Served with USNR, 1943-46. Mem. Phi Alpha Delta. Republican. Methodist. Mason (master 1958—). Home: 6841 Garfield Dr Kansas City KS 66102 Office: 14 W 10th St Kansas City MO 64105

WIDDRINGTON, PETER NIGEL TINLING, brewery, food co. exec.; b. Toronto, Ont., Can., June 2, 1930; s. Gerard and Margery (MacDonald) W.; student Pickering Coll., Newmarket, Ont., 1935-49; B.A. with honors, Queen's U., Kingston, Ont., 1953; M.B.A., Harvard, 1955; m. Betty Ann Lawrence, Oct. 12, 1956; children—Lucinda Ann, Andrea Stacy. Salesman, Labatt's Co., London, Ont., 1955-57, asst. regional mgr. So. Ont. region Labatt's Ont. Breweries Ltd., 1957-58, regional mgr., 1958-61, gen. mgr. Labatt's Man. Breweries Ltd., Winnipeg, Man., 1962-65, Labatt's B.C. Breweries Ltd., Vancouver, B.C., 1965-68; pres. Lucky Breweries Inc., San Francisco, 1968-71; v.p. corp. devel. John Labatt Ltd., 1971-73, sr. v.p., 1973, pres., 1973—; gen. mgr. Kiewel & Pelissiers, Winnipeg, 1961-62; dir. Can. Trust Co., London, B.P. Can. Ltd., Brascon Ltd., John Labatt Ltd. Bd. dirs. The Fraser Inst., Vancouver, Stratford Festival Found. Office: John Labatt Ltd 451 Ridout St London ON N6A 2P6 Canada

WIDENER, HIRAM EMORY, JR., judge; b. Abingdon, Va., Apr. 30, 1923; s. Hiram Emory and Nita Douglas (Peck) W.; student Va. Poly. Inst., 1940-41; B.S. U.S. Naval Acad., 1944; LL.B., Washington and Lee U., 1953, LL.D., 1977; m. Jo Smith O'Donnell; 1 dau., Molly Berentd. Admitted to Va. bar, 1951; individual practice law, Bristol, Va., 1953-69; judge U.S. Dist. Ct., Western Dist. Va., Abingdon, 1969-71, chief judge, 1971-72; judge U.S. Ct. Appeals, 4th Circuit, Abingdon, 1972—. U.S. commr. Western Dist. Va., 1963-66; mem. Va. Election Laws Study Commn., 1968-69, Chmn. Republican party 9th Dist. Va., 1966-69; mem. Va. Republican State Central Com., 1966-69, state exec. com., 1966-69. Served to lt. (j.g.) USN, 1944-49, to lt., USNR, 1951-52. Decorated Bronze Star with combat V. Trustee Va. Intermont Coll.; mem. Am. Law Inst.; mem. Am., Va. bar assns., Va. State bar, Am. Judicature Soc., Inst. Jud. Adminstrs., Am. Legion, Phi Alpha Delta. Republican. Presbyterian. Home: 537 Glenway Ave Bristol VA 24201 Office: PO Box 868 Abingdon VA 24210

WIDENER, WARREN, mayor; J.D., U. Calif., Berkeley, 1967; m. Mary Lee; children—Warren, Michael and Stephen (twins). Admitted to Calif. bar, 1968; atty. Earl Warren Legal Inst., U. Calif., Berkeley, 1970-73; mayor City of Berkeley (Calif.), 1971—; past mem. Berkeley City Council. Past pres. Nat. Black Caucus Local Elected Ofcls., Alameda County Mayor's Conf.; pres. mayor and council dept. League Calif. Cities; adv. bd. U.S. Conf. Mayors; vice chmn. Alameda County Dem. Central Com. Served with USAF, 1960-64. Methodist. Office: Office of Mayor Civic Center Bldg 2180 Milvia St Berkeley CA 94704

WIDETT, HAROLD, lawyer; b. Chelsea, Mass., Sept. 23, 1910; s. Philip and Annie (Taymor) Widetzky; LL.B., Suffolk Law Sch., 1932, D.Jur. (hon.), 1957; m. Edith Richmond, Mar. 8, 1932; children—Joan Louise (Mrs. Karl L. Gollub), Barbara Toby (Mrs. Edward M. Altman). Admitted to Mass. bar, 1933, since practiced in Boston; pres. firm Widett, Slater & Goldman, P.C.; consul gen. of Ecuador in Boston, 1970—. Pres. Mass. Wholesale Food Terminal, Inc., Southampton Wholesale Food Terminal, Inc., New Boston Food Market Devel. Corp. Hon. pres., trustee Brookline Hosp.; hon. pres., mem. exec. bd. Hebrew Rehab. Center for Aged; fellow Brandeis U.; hon. trustee Combined Jewish Philanthropies; trustee, chmn. bd. Eye Research Inst. of Retina Found.; sec., exec. com. Greater Boston Convention and Tourist Bur. Mem. Am., Mass., Boston bar assns. Mason (Shriner), K.P. Club: Greater Boston Brandeis (hon. dir.). Home: 50 Kensington Circle Brookline MA 02167 Office: 100 Federal St Boston MA 02110

WIDMAN, GARY LEE, lawyer, educator; b. Fremont, Nebr., June 1, 1936; s. Benjamin H. and Alice C. (Negley) W.; B.S., U. Nebr., 1957; J.D., Hastings Coll. Law U. Calif., 1962; LL.M., U. Mich., 1966; m. Mary Margaret Donnelly, Mar. 5, 1972; children—Andrew Scott, Natalie Claire. Admitted to Calif. bar, 1962; asso. firm Thelen, Marrin, Johnson & Bridges, San Francisco, 1962-65; asso. prof. law U. Denver, 1966-69; prof., dir. resource and environ. law program Hastings Coll. Law U. Calif., San Francisco, 1969—; gen. counsel Council Environ. Quality, Exec. Office Pres., Washington, 1974-76; lectr. U. Calif. at Davis, 1978, Boalt Hall, 1977-79; trustee Rocky Mountain Mineral Law Found., 1969-74, 77—. Served with U.S. Army, 1957-59. Mem. Am. (council sect. natural resources 1975-77, spl. com. energy law 1977—), Fed. (chmn. com. natural resources 1977), Calif. bar assns., Author and project dir.; Legal Study of Oil Shale on Public Lands, 1969. Home: 131 Taylor Rd Tiburon CA 94920 Office: Hastings Coll Law 198 McAllister St San Francisco CA 94102

WIDMAN, PAUL EDWARD, health care exec.; b. Norwalk, Ohio, Jan. 24, 1918; s. Edward Anthony and Josephine (Brown) W.; B.S., U. Toledo, 1941; m. Rose Hoyt, June 21, 1941; children—Jerry Paul, Kathleen Ann. Asst. dir. purchasing Johns Hopkins Hosp., Balt., 1950-51; dir. purchasing Cleve. Clinic Found., 1951-69, dir. adminstrv. services, 1969-76, dir. opns., 1977—; chmn. bd. dirs. Hosp. Bur. Inc., N.Y.C., 1973—. Served with USNR, 1943. Certified purchasing mgr. Nat. Assn. Purchasing Mgmt. Mem. Am. Hosp. Assn. (George R. Gossett award 1967), Am. Coll. Clinic Mgrs., Am. Coll. Hosp. Adminstrs. Home: 745-26 Windward Dr Aurora OH 44202 Office: 9500 Euclid Ave Cleveland OH 44106. *I have always felt that there are attributes in one's makeup that will automatically guarantee success in whatever field of endeavor a person chooses. Those two attributes are "desire" and the "ability to get along with people". From the very beginning of my career I have believed this to be the reason for success. As each year goes by, it becomes more and more apparent and, indeed, important to ensure success.*

WIDMAN, RICHARD GUSTAVE, engring. and constrn. co. exec.; b. Detroit, Jan. 28, 1922; s. Edward J. and Lena E. (Hurrle) W.; B.C.E., U. Mich., 1947; m. Barbara Jean Roehm, Sept 7, 1946; children—Richard Thomas, Linda Kay Widman Wyer, Jeanne Louise. Various positions Arthur G. McKee & Co., Cleve., 1948-65, gen. mgr. petroleum and chems. div., 1966-68, v.p., 1968-69, exec. v.p., dir., 1969, pres., 1970-71, pres., chief exec. officer, 1971-77, chmn. bd., pres., 1977, also dir.; chmn. bd., pres., chief exec. officer The McKee Corp., 1977-79; dir. Davy Corp. Ltd., London. Vice chmn. bd. dirs. Ohio Motorists Assn. Served with C.E., AUS, 1943-46. Mem. Am. Inst. Chem. Engrs., Am. Petroleum Inst., Cleve. Engring. Soc., Newcomen Soc. N. Am., Tau Beta Pi. Clubs: 50 of Cleve., Rotary, Union (Cleve.); Chagrin Valley Country (Chagrin Falls, Ohio); Jesters. Home: 2901 Gulf Shore Blvd N Naples FL 33940 Office: 6200 Oak Tree Blvd Cleveland OH 44131

WIDMARK, RICHARD, actor; b. Sunrise, Minn., Dec. 26, 1914; s. Carl H. and Ethel Mae (Barr) W.; B.A., Lake Forest (Ill.) Coll., 1936, D.F.A. (hon.), 1973; m. Ora Jane Hazlewood, Apr. 5, 1942; 1 dau., Anne Heath. Instr. drama dept. Lake Forest Coll., 1936-38; actor various radio networks, N.Y.C., 1938-47; Broadway appearances include Kiss and Tell, 1943, Get Away Old Man, 1943, Trio, 1944, Kiss Them for Me, 1944, Dunnigan's Daughter, 1945, Dream Girl, 1946-47; summer stock appearances include The Bo Tree, 1939, Joan of Lorraine, 1947; motion picture appearances include Kiss of Death, 1947, Street with No Name, 1948, Yellow Sky, 1948, Roadhouse, 1948, Down to the Sea in Ships, 1949, Night in the City, 1949, No Way Out, 1949, Panic in the Streets, 1950, Slattery's Hurricane, 1949, Halls of Montezuma, 1950, The Frogman, 1950, Judgement at Nuremberg, 1961, Flight from Ashiya, 1962, How the West Was Won, 1962, The Long Ships, 1963, Cheyenne Autumn, 1963, Bedford Incident, 1964, Alvarez Kelly, 1965, The Way West, 1966, Madigan, 1967, Patch, 1968, Talent for Loving, 1968, The Moonshine War, 1969, When the Legends Die, 1971, Murder on the Orient Express, 1974, The Sellout, 1975, To the Devil, A Daughter, 1975, The Twilight's Last Gleaming, 1976, The Domino Principle, 1976, Roller Coaster, 1976, Coma, 1978, The Swarm, 1977; NBC TV appearance in Vanished, 1970; TV series Madigan, 1972; CBS TV appearance in Benjamin Franklin, 1974. Pres. Heath Prodns., 1955—; v.p. Widmark Cattle Enterprises, 1957—. Bd. dirs. Hope for Hearing. Mem. Phi Pi Epsilon. Clubs: Washington Country (Conn.); Coffee House (N.Y.C.); Valley (Montecito, Calif.). Office: care Internat Creative Mgmt 8899 Beverly Blvd Los Angeles CA 90048*

WIDMER, KEMBLE, geologist; b. New Rochelle, N.Y., Feb. 26, 1913; s. George Ellis and Beth (Kemble) W.; A.B., Lehigh U., 1937; postgrad. Stanford, 1937-39; M.A., Princeton, 1947, Ph.D., 1950; m. Virginia Maiers, Mar. 10, 1939; children—Kemble II, Katharine. Geologist, Newfoundland Geol. Survey, summers 1937-41, 46, 47; asst. prof. geology Rutgers U., 1949-51; asso. prof. geology Chaplain Coll., State U. N.Y., 1951-53; prin. geologist N.J. Bur. Geology, 1953-58; state geologist N.J., 1958—; seminar asso. Columbia U., 1967—; N.J. nuclear indsl. officer, 1964-74; mem. fed. adv. com. on water data for public use U.S. Geol. Survey, 1978—; cons. U.S. Mil. Acad. Served to lt. col. AUS, 1941-46; col. Res. (ret.). Fellow Geol. Soc. Am., N.J. Acad. Sci., AAAS, Company Mil. Historians; mem. Am. Inst. Mining, Metall. and Petroleum Engrs., Sigma Xi. Club: Explorers (N.Y.C.). Home: King George Rd Pennington NJ 08534 Office: 88 E State St Box 1390 Trenton NJ 08625

WIDMER, ROBERT H., corp. exec.; b. Hawthorne, N.J., May 17, 1916; s. Robert and Dora (Buhofer) W.; B.S., Rensselaer Poly. Inst., 1938; M.S., Calif. Inst. Tech., 1939; D.Sc. (hon.), Tex. Christian U., 1967; m. Jeanette Billing, Dec. 22, 1945; children—Robert Lawrence, Gail Widmer Landreth. Draftsman, aerodynamics engr. Consol. Aircraft Corp., San Diego, 1939-42; chief aerodynamics, chief design engr., asst. chief engr. Consol. Vultee Aircraft Corp., Ft. Worth, 1942-54; chief engr., v.p. research and engring. Gen. Dynamics Corp., Ft. Worth div., 1954-71, Convair div., 1971-74, corp. v.p. sci. and engring., St. Louis, 1974—; cons. NSF, OSD-DDR & E, USAF Sci. Adv. Bd., ASD-DAG. Mem. N.Tex. Interuniversity Council; bd. dirs. So. Meth. U. Found. Sci. and Engring., Tex. Christian U. Research Found., U. Tex. Engring. Found. Registered profl. engr., Tex. Recipient Field of Sci. award Air Force Assn., 1949, Spirit of St. Louis medal ASME, 1963. Fellow Am. Inst. Aeros. and Astronautics, Nat. Acad. Engring.; mem. Tex. Soc. Profl. Engrs. (Engr. of Year 1969), Air Force Assn. (hon. life mem.). Mem. Christian Ch. Clubs: Colonial Country (Ft. Worth); Bellerive Country (St. Louis). Home: 22 Bellerive Country Club Grounds Saint Louis MO 63141 Office: Pierre Laclede Center Saint Louis MO 63105

WIDNER, RALPH RANDOLPH, planning exec., pub. adminstr.; b. Phila., Oct. 21, 1930; s. Ralph Litteer and Viola (Cunningham) W.; B.A., Duke U., 1952; student N.Y. U., 1955-57, Georgetown U., 1958; D.H.L. (hon.), Union Coll., Ky., 1970, Capital U., Columbus, Ohio, 1971; m. Joan Sundelius Ziegler, July 9, 1955; children—Jennifer Anne, Wendy Rowe. Journalist, Paterson (N.J.) Evening News, 1955-56, N.Y. Times, 1956-58; Congressional fellow Am. Polit. Sci. Assn., 1958; dir. pub. affairs Pa. Dept. Forests and Waters, 1959-60; asst. dir. Pa. Planning Bd., 1961-62; legis. asst. to U.S. Senator Clark, 1962-65; exec. dir. Appalachian Regional Commn., 1965-71; pres. Acad. for Contemporary Problems, 1971—; adj. prof. pub. adminstrn. and city planning Ohio State U., 1971—; pres. Nat. Tng. and Devel. Service for State and Local Govt., 1979—; mem. urban transp. research com. Nat. Acad. Scis.; mem. adv. com. Nat. Commn. Supplies and Shortages. Bd. dirs. N.E.-Midwest Research Inst., Landscape and Architecture Found., 1977-78. Served to lt. (j.g.) USNR, 1952-55. Urban Land Inst. research fellow. Mem. Am. Forestry Assn. (dir. 1974-77), Am. Pub. Adminstrn. (nat. council), Nat. Acad. Pub. Adminstrn. Democrat. Methodist. Editor: Forests and Forestry in the American States, 1967; Regimal Development in the U.S., 1980; New Directions for Urban Policy, 1980; bd. editors Public Adminstrn. Rev. Home: 2210 Belle Haven Rd Alexandria VA 22306 Office: 1501 Neil Ave Columbus OH 43201 also 400 N Capitol St NW Washington DC. *The opportunities life presents are gifts, but only a fool tries to accept them all. Choice must be limited by one's knowledge of his own skills and limitations and by the life trajectory he wishes to trace during his brief tenure. I believe no man can take credit for the fortune providence has placed at his disposal, but every man must accept responsibility for what he does or does not do with that fortune. There is good luck, but no bad luck.*

WIDULE, CAROL JUNE, educator; b. Chgo., Jan. 4, 1930; d. Walter E. and Pauline (Siegert) W.; B.S., Monmouth Coll., 1952; M.S., MacMurray Coll., 1953; Ph.D., U. Wis., 1966. Asst. prof. Monmouth Coll., 1953-61; research asst., instr. U. Wis., Madison, 1961-65; mem. faculty Purdue U., West Lafayette, Ind., 1965—, asst. prof. phys. edn., 1965-70, asso. prof. phys. edn., 1970-75, prof., 1975—. Mem. Am. Coll. Sports Medicine, AAHPER (editor kinesiology review 1969-73), Am. Ednl. Research Assn., Nat., Midwest assns. phys. edn. coll. women, Ind. Assn. Health, Phys. Edn. and Recreation, ASME (affiliate), Human Factors Soc., AAAS, Am. Assn. Higher Edn., Kappa Delta, Sigma Xi. Contbr. articles to publs. Home: 120 Foster Dr West Lafayette IN 47906

WIEBE, O. ROY, coop. exec.; b. Abedeen, Idaho, June 23, 1920; s. Henry C. and Anna (Funk) W.; A.B., Bethel Coll., N. Newton, Kans., 1942; m. Maryanna Beckenmeyer, Feb. 9, 1952; children—Susan, Richard, Jane, William. Supr. cost accounting, plant auditing U.S. Gypsum Co., 1945-52; v.p., controller Dixie Mills Co., 1952-60; sec.-treas. Airtherm Mfg. Co., 1960-61; sr. v.p. CF Industries, Inc., Chgo., 1961-72; pres. Western Farmers Assn., 1973—; dir. Nat. Council Farmer Coops., Coop. Fertilizers Internat., Agrl. Coop. Devel. Internat.; adv. com. Overseas Coop. Devel. Trustee, exec. com. Seattle Symphony Orch. Office: 201 Elliot Ave W Seattle WA 98119

WIEBEL, ARTHUR VANCE, steel exec.; b. Cumberland, Md., Mar. 26, 1907; s. John Vance and Rachael Louise (Snyder) W.; B.S., Carnegie Inst. Tech., 1928; Ph.D. Science, U. Alabama, 1954; m. Anna Ruth McClelland, May 19, 1934; 1 dau., Gretchen Ann. Designer, squad boss, engring. sec. Koppers Constrn. Co., Pitts., 1928-31; operating engr. Koppers Seaboard Coke Co., Kearney, N.J., 1931-32; instr. math. Carnegie Inst. Tech., 1932-33; estimator Carnegie-Ill. Steel Corp., 1933-37, spl. engr., 1937-38, asst. chief engr., 1938-40, chief engr., 1940; asst. to v.p. in charge engring. and operations U.S. Steel Corp. Del., 1940-46; exec. offices Tenn. Coal, Iron and R.R. Co., Birmingham, Ala., 1946, v.p. in charge operations, 1947-51, pres., dir., 1951-52; pres. Tenn. Coal & Iron div. U.S. Steel Co., 1952-64; dir. U.S. Steel Co., Pitts., 1952-53; adminstrv. v.p. long range planning and new product devel. of U.S. Steel Corp., 1964-66, exec. v.p. engring. and research, 1966—. Trustee So. Research Inst. Exec. cons. to dir. Steel Div. WPB, 1942. Mem. Nat. Soc. Profl. Engrs., Am., Brit. iron and steel insts., Assn. Iron and Steel Engrs., Am. Ordnance Assn., Engrs. Soc. Western Pa., Newcomen Soc. Presbyn. Clubs: Duquesne, Edgeworth (Pitts.); Downtown (Birmingham); Pinnacle (N.Y.C.); Allegheny Country. Home: RD 4 Box 21-B Blackburn Rd Sewickley PA 15143 Office: 600 Grant St Pittsburgh PA 15230

WIEBUSH, JOSEPH ROY, chemist; b. Lancaster, Pa., Oct. 18, 1920; s. Henry William and Catherine May (Hughes) W.; B.S., Franklin and Marshall Coll., 1941; M.S., U. Md., 1951, Ph.D., 1955; m. Dorothy Alice Miller, May 8, 1943; 1 son, James Philip. Chemist, Hercules, Inc., 1941-43, 46-48, Mead Corp., 1955-56; dir. research Nat. Inst. Drycleaning, 1956-61; mem. faculty U.S. Naval Acad., Annapolis, Md., 1961—, now prof. chemistry. Asst. dist. commr. Boy Scouts Am., 1970—; mem. Protestant Com. on Scouting, 1969—; bd. dirs. Lutheran Campus Ministry. Served with USNR, 1943-46, 53-55; capt. Res. ret. Recipient Lamb award Luth. Ch., 1966. Mem. Am. Chem. Soc., Nat. Audubon Soc., Wilderness Soc. Republican. Patentee in field. Home: 1530 Red Oak Dr Silver Spring MD 20910 Office US Naval Acad Chemistry Dept Annapolis MD 21402

WIECKOWSKI, JAN J., banker; b. Warsaw, Poland, July 25, 1923; s. Alexander and Helena Victoria W.; came to U.S., 1948, naturalized, 1956; B.S., Stetson U., 1950; M.A., 1951; m. Joanna Gronkiewicz, June 11, 1965; 1 dau., Maria Alice. Vice pres., mgr. internat. div. Girard Bank, Phila., 1951-67, sr. v.p., 1967—, exec. v.p. internat. banking, 1976—; chmn. bd. Girard Internat. Bank, N.Y.C., Penn Investments (London) Ltd. Bd. dirs. Phila. World Affairs Council. Served with Polish Army, Brit. Army, 1939-48. Mem. Phila. Com. Fgn. Relations. Office: Girard Bank 1 Girard Plaza Philadelphia PA 19101

WIECKOWSKI, JAN J., banker; b. Warsaw, Poland, July 25, 1923; s. Alexander and Helena Victoria W.; came to U.S., 1948, naturalized, 1956; B.S., Stetson U., 1950; M.A., 1951; m. Joanna Gronkiewicz, June 11, 1965. Vice pres., mgr. internat. div. Girard Trust Bank, Phila., 1951-67, sr. v.p., 1967-76, exec. v.p., 1976—; chmn. bd. Girard Internat. Bank, N.Y.C., Penn Investments (London) Ltd., Girard Zurich A.G., Switzerland. Bd. dirs. Phila. World Affairs Council. Served with Polish Army, Brit. Army, 1939-48. Mem. Phila. Com. Fgn. Relations, Bankers Assn. Fgn. Trade. Office: Girard Bank 1 Girard Plaza Philadelphia PA 19101

WIECZYNSKI, FRANK ROBERT, ins. brokerage exec.; b. Balt., Jan. 14, 1939; s. Joseph J. and Margaret A. (Baranowski) W.; B.S. in Accounting, Loyola Coll., Balt., 1961; LL.B., U. Balt., 1968; m. Patricia Lydia Moyer, June 3, 1967; children—Dina M., Steven M. Sr. revenue agt. IRS, Balt., 1961-69; v.p., sec. Alexander & Alexander Services Inc., and subs., Balt., 1969—. Served to 1st lt. U.S. Army, 1962-64. Mem. Am. Soc. Corp. Secs. Home: 4 Bafford Ct Glen Arm MD 21057 Office: 300 E Joppa Rd Baltimore MD 21204

WIED, GEORGE LUDWIG, physician; b. Carlsbad, Czechoslovakia, Feb. 7, 1921; s. Ernst George and Anna (Travnicek) W., M.D., Charles U., Prague, 1945; m. Daga M. Graaz, Mar. 19, 1949 (dec. Aug. 1977). Came to U.S., 1953, naturalized, 1960. Intern, County Hosp., Carlsbad, 1945, U. Chgo. Hosps., 1955; resident obstetrics, gynecology U. Munich (Germany), 1946-48; practice medicine, specializing in obstetrics, gynecology, West Berlin, 1948-53; asst. obstetrics, gynecology Free U., West Berlin, 1948-52; asso. chmn. dept. obstetrics, gynecology Moabit Hosp. Free U., 1953; asst. prof., dir. cytology U. Chgo., 1954-59, asso. prof., 1959-65, prof., 1965—, mem. bd. adult edn., 1964-68, prof. pathology, 1967—, Blum-Riese prof. obstetrics and gynecology, 1968—, acting chmn. dept. obstetrics and gynecology, 1974-75. Hon. dir. Chgo. Cancer Prevention Center, 1959—; chmn. adv. com. cancer control Chgo. Bd. Health, 1961-70; chmn. jury Maurice Goldblatt Cytology award, 1963—. Recipient certificate merit U.S. Surgeon Gen., 1952, Maurice Goldblatt Cytology award, 1961, George N. Papanicolaou Cytology award, 1970. Mem. Am. (pres. 1965-66), Mexican (hon.), Spanish (hon.), Brazilian (fgn. corr.), Latin-Am. (hon.), Japanese (hon.), German (hon.) socs. cytology, Internat. Acad. Cytology (pres. 1977-80), Central Soc. Clin. Research, Chgo. Path. Soc., Chgo. Gynecologic Soc. (hon.), Am. Soc. Cell Biology, German, Bavarian socs. obstetrics and gynecology, German Soc. Endocrinology, Swedish Soc. Medicine (hon.), Sigma Xi. Contbr. articles to profl. jours.; editor-in-chief Acta Cytologica, Clinical Cytology; editor Introduction to Quantitative Cytochemistry, Automated Cell Identification and Cell Sorting, Analytical and Quantitative Cytology; editor-in-chief Jour. Reproductive Medicine. Home: 1640 E 50th St Chicago IL 60615 Office: 5841 S Maryland Ave Chicago IL 60637

WIEDEMAN, GEOFFREY PAUL, physician, air force officer; b. London, Eng., Mar. 9, 1917; s. Julius William Paul and Fanny (Poile) W.; came to U.S., 1934, naturalized, 1942; B.S., U. Vt., 1938, M.D., 1941; m. Carolyn Sterling, Feb. 2, 1947; 1 son, Geoffrey Paul. Commd 1st lt. USAAF, 1942, advanced through grades to brig. gen. USAF, 1970; surgeon Eastern Transport Air Force, McGuire AFB, N.J., 1958-61; comdr. USAF Hosp., Tachikawa, Japan, surgeon 315th Air Div., Japan, also surgeon Kanto Base Command, Japan, 1962-65; comdr. USAF Sch. Health Care Scis., 1965-69; command surgeon Air Tng. Command, Randolph AFB, Tex., 1969-74. Decorated D.S.M., Legion of Merit, Bronze Star, Air medal, Air Force Commendation medal with oak leaf cluster, 1972. Diplomate Am. Bd. Preventive Medicine. Fellow Am. Coll. Preventive Medicine; mem. Aerospace Medicine Assn., Assn. Mil. Surgeons, A.M.A. (Physician's Recognition award in continuing med. edn. 1972, 75), Am. Pub. Health Assn., Air Force Assn. Home: 6134 Windrock San Antonio TX 78239 Office: USAF Clinic Brooks AFB TX 78235

WIEDEMAN, GEORGE HENKINS, physician, educator; b. Moscow, Russia, June 27, 1912; s. Vincent and Helen (Abramovich) W.; student Med. Schs. U. Berlin and Frankfort (Germany), 1931-33; M.D., U. Prague (Czechoslovakia), 1937; m. Rachel Henkins, Apr. 25, 1939; 1 son, Michael. Came to U.S., 1939, naturalized, 1944. Intern Wesson Meml. Hosp., Springfield, Mass., 1939-41; gen. practice medicine, Leominster, Mass., 1941-44; fellow psychiatry, psychiat. resident Menninger Sch. Psychiatry, Topeka, 1946-48; staff psychiatrist VA Mental Hygiene Clinic, Newark, 1949-50; psychoanalytic tng. N.Y. Psychoanalytic Inst., 1949-55; pvt. practice psychiatry and psychoanalysis, N.Y.C., 1950—; lectr. N.Y. Sch. Social Work, Columbia, 1958-62, Marion Kenworthy prof. psychiatry, 1962—; psychiat. cons. Community Service Soc. N.Y., 1952-71; sr. lectr. div. psychiat. edn. dept. psychiatry Downstate Med Center, State U. N.Y., 1972—, tng. and supervising analyst, 1974—. Served to capt. M.C., AUS, 1944-46. Diplomate Am. Bd. Neurology and Psychiatry in psychiatry. Mem. A.M.A., Am. Psychiat. Assn., Am. Psychoanalytic Assn., Am. Orthopsychiat. Assn., A.A.A.S., N.Y. Psychoanalytic Soc., Psychoanalytic Assn. N.Y., Med. Soc. County and State N.Y. Author, editor: Personality Development and Deviation, 1975. Contbr. articles to profl. jours. Home: 300 Central Park W New York City NY 10024

WIEDEMANN, T. J., mfg. co. exec.; b. Phila., Nov. 8, 1935; s. Otto F. and Sarah (Plummer) W.; B.A., Amherst Coll., 1956; postgrad. U. Pa., 1958-60; m. Nancy Maass, Dec. 28, 1957; children—Martha Emily, Amy Lynne, Michael Fredrick. Mgr. data processing Wiedemann Machine Co., Phila., 1962-64; asst. to treas. Warner & Swasey Co., Cleve., 1965-67, treas., 1967-75, sec., 1972-74, v.p. chief financial officer, 1973-76, group v.p., 1977—, dir., 1974—. Served with AUS, 1967. Mem. Phi Alpha Psi. Clubs: Union, University; Cleveland Racquet. Home: 37300 Jackson Rd Moreland Hills OH 44022 Office: 11000 Cedar Ave Cleveland OH 44106

WIEDEN, CLIFFORD OSCAR TITUS, ednl. cons.; b. Wilmington, Del., Aug. 30, 1902; s. Oscar Carl and Selma (Swanson) W.; student Colby Coll., Waterville, Maine, 1919-20; B.S., Acadia U., Wolfville, N.S., 1923; M.Ed., Bates Coll., Lewiston, Maine, 1934; student summer sessions Boston U., 1937-39, 44, Columbia U., 1941; D.Sc. Edn. (hon.), U. Maine, 1958; L.H.D., Aroostook State Coll. of U. Maine, 1970; m. Marguerite Frances Hill, June 1, 1924; children—Carolyn Selma, Carleton Davis (dec.), Clifford Oscar Titus. Sub-prin., Mapleton (Maine) High Sch., 1923-24; tchr. Western State Normal, Gorham, Maine, 1924-40; prin. Aroostook State Normal Sch., Presque Isle, Maine, 1940-43, 46-52, Washington State Normal Sch., Machias, Maine, 1943-46; pres. Aroostook State Coll., U. Maine, 1952-69, emeritus, 1969—; dir. Maine Travel Course, 1947; mem. adv. commn. Maine Higher Edn. Study, 1966-68; chmn. Gov. Maine Task Force to Study Library Services, 1969-71; project dir. A Pilot Study to Improve Ednl. Opportunities in Central Aroostook County, Maine, 1971-72. Pres. A.R. Gould Meml. Hosp., 1971-72; mem. Katahdin Area council Boy Scouts Am.; mem. adv. com. Nat. Assn. Retarded Citizens; bd. dirs. Aroostook Mental Health Assn., 1966-75, Aroostook Health Services, 1973—. Life mem. NEA, Nat. Assn. Study of Edn.; mem. Am. Assn. Sch. Adminstrs., state and county edn. assns., Maine Employees Assn. (pres. 1953-54), Presque Isle C. of C. (pres. 1957-58), New Eng. Tchrs. Coll. Athletics (pres. 1937-38), New Eng. Tchr. Preparation Assn. (pres. 1946-47), Lambda Chi Alpha, others. Congregationalist. Republican. Clubs: Masons, Rotary (dist. gov. 1960-61). Home: 31 Barton St Presque Isle ME 04769

WIEDENBECK, MARCELLUS LEE, educator; b. Lancaster, N.Y., Oct. 11, 1919; s. George and Catherine (Roskey) W.; B.S., Canisius Coll., 1941; M.S., U. Notre Dame, 1942, Ph.D., 1945; m. Jane Kathryn Young, Sept. 14, 1946; children—Mary (Mrs. Emery George), Mark, Susan, Peter, Janice, Michael. Mem. faculty U. Mich., 1946—, prof. physics, 1955—. Fellow Am. Phys. Soc. Research and numerous publs. nuclear physics. Home: 3786 Elizabeth Rd Ann Arbor MI 48103 Office: Dept Physics U Mich Ann Arbor MI 48108

WIEDENSKI, EDWARD FABIAN, pharm. co. exec.; b. Yonkers, N.Y., Aug. 23, 1922; s. Stanley and Antoinette (Witt) W.; grad. Collegiate Inst., N.Y.C., 1949; m. Anna Lillian Posch, July 12, 1947; 1 dau., Regina. With Squibb Corp. and predecessors, 1946—, v.p., treas., 1971—, also dir., officer various subsidiaries. Served with AUS, 1942-46. Home: 36 Clinton Rd Garden City NY 11530 Office: 40 W 57th St New York NY 10019

WIEDERHOLT, WIGBERT C., neurologist; b. Germany, Apr. 22, 1931; s. Carl and Anna-Maria (Hoffmann) W.; came to U.S., 1956, naturalized, 1966; student (Med. Sch. scholar) U. Berlin, 1952-53; M.D., U. Freiburg (Germany), 1955; M.S., U. Minn., 1965; children—Sven, Karen, Kristin. Intern in Ob-Gyn Schleswig (Germany) City Hosp., 1955-56, rotating intern Sacred Heart Hosp., Spokane, Wash., 1956-57; resident in internal medicine Cleve. Clinic, 1957-58, 61-62, U.S. Army Hosp., Frankfurt, Germany, 1958-59, resident in neurology Mayo Clinic, Rochester, Minn., 1962-65; asso. prof. medicine, dir. clin. neuro-physiology Ohio State U., 1965-72; prof. neuroscis., neurologist-in-chief U. Calif., San Diego, 1972—, chmn. dept. and group in Neuroscis., 1978—; chief neurology San Diego VA Hosp., 1972-79. Fulbright scholar, 1956-58. Diplomate Am. Bd. Psychiatry and Neurology. Fellow Am. Acad. Neurology (S. Weir Mitchell award 1965); mem. AAAS, Am. Assn. Electromyography and Electrodiagnosis (sec.-treas. 1971-76, pres. 1977-78), Assn. Univ. Profs. Neurology, Am. EEG Soc., AMA, Am. Neurol. Assn., Calif. Med. Assn., N.Y. Acad. Scis., San Diego County Med. Soc., San Diego Neurol. Soc., Soc. Neurosci., Western EEG Soc., Calif. Neurol. Soc., Internat. Brain Research Orgn. Contbr. numerous articles to profl. publs. Office: Dept Neuroscis (M-008) U Calif at San Diego La Jolla CA 92093

WIEDNER, DONALD LAWRENCE, educator; b. Oceanside, N.Y., Nov. 17, 1930; s. Frank Lawrence and Gladys (Cook) W.; A.B., Colgate U., 1952; A.M., Harvard, 1953, Ph.D., 1958; m. Leslie Ann Williams, Nov. 20, 1976; children—Pamela Jane, David Stephen. Instr. history U. Mich., Ann Arbor, 1958-59, Mt. Holyoke Coll., South Hadley, Mass., 1959-61; asst. prof. U. Alta., Edmonton, Can., 1961-65, asso. prof., head dept. history, 1964-65; prof. African history Temple U., Phila., 1965—, chmn. history dept., 1968-71; cons. Nat. Geog. Soc., 1970—, Sch. Dist. Phila., 1969—. Pres. Com. on African Studies in Can., 1963-65, mem., 1962—. Served to lt. (j.g.), USNR, 1953-55. Fellow African Studies Assn.; mem. Am. Hist. Assn.; Nigerian Hist. Soc. Episcopalian (vestryman 1969-72). Author: A History of Africa South of the Sahara, 1962; also articles. Editor Bull. African Studies in Can., 1962-65; mem. editorial bd. African Studies Bull., 1964-69. Home: 28 W Upsal St Philadelphia PA 19119 Office: Dept History Temple U Philadelphia PA 19122

WIEGANDT, HERBERT FREDERICK, educator; b. Newaygo, Mich., Jan. 4, 1917; s. Otto and Anna (Koch) W.; B.S. in Chem. Engring., Purdue U., 1938, M.S. in Engring., 1939, Ph.D., 1941; m. Jane Scott, Feb. 12, 1944; children—Ellen (Mrs. Urs Luterbacher), Ralph. Chem. engr. Am. Oil Co., 1941-44, Armour Research Found., 1944-47; mem. faculty Cornell U., 1947—, prof. chem. engring., 1960—; tech. adviser Compagnie Francaise de Raffinage, Paris, France, 1972—. Fulbright appointee French Petroleum Inst., 1961-62. Mem. Am. Inst. Chem. Engrs., Am. Chem. Soc. Home: 13 rue de l'Avre 75015 Paris France

WIEGEL, ROBERT LOUIS, cons. engr.; b. San Francisco, Oct. 17, 1922; s. Louis Henry and Antionette L. (Decker) W.; B.S., U. Calif. at Berkeley, 1943, M.S., 1949; m. Anne Pearce, Dec. 10, 1948; children—John M., Carol E., Diana L. Mem. faculty U. Calif. at Berkeley, 1946—, prof. civil engring., 1963—, asst. dean Coll. Engring., 1963-72, acting dean, 1972-73; dir. state tech. services program for Calif., U. Calif., 1965-68; vis. prof. Nat. U. Mexico, summer 1965, Polish Acad. Sci., 1976, U. Cairo, 1978; sr. Queen's fellow in marine sci., Australia, 1977; cons. to govt. and industry, 1946—; chmn. U.S. com. for internat. com. oceanic resources, mem. marine bd. Nat. Acad. Engring.; pres. Internat. Engring. Com. on Oceanic Resources, 1972-75; mem. coastal engring. research bd. Dept. Army; mem. IDOE adv. panel NSF, 1974-77; mem. Gov. Calif. Adv. Commn. Ocean Resources, 1967, Calif. Adv. Commn. on Marine and Coastal Resources, 1967-73; mem. Tsunami Tech. Adv. Council, Hawaii, 1964-66; U.S. del. U.S.-Japan coop. sci. programs, 1964, 65. Served to 1st lt. AUS, 1943-46. Fellow ASCE (chmn. exec. com. waterways, harbors, coastal engring. div. 1974-75, vice chmn. coastal engring. research council 1964-78, chmn., 1978—, chmn. task com. wave forces on structures 1960-67, chmn. com. on coastal engring. 1970-71; Research prize 1962, Moff-att-Nichol Coastal Engring. award 1978); mem. AAAS, Nat. Acad. Engring., Permanent Internat. Assn. Nav. Congresses, Internat. Assn. Hydraulic Research, Sigma Xi. Author, patentee in field. Home: 1030 Keeler Ave Berkeley CA 94708

WIEGERING, WILLIAM HICE, lawyer, banker; b. Youngstown, Ohio, July 31, 1907; s. William Peter and Edith (Hice) W.; student Washington and Lee U., 1926-27; J.D., U. Va., 1931; m. Eleanor Clark, Nov. 4, 1950. Admitted to D.C. bar, 1932; mem. firm Baker, Jackson, Washington, 1932-37; with Riggs Nat. Bank, Washington, 1937-41, 50-72, sr. v.p., trust officer, 1950-72; mem. firm Reasoner, Davis, Vinson Attys., 1972—; dir. Atlantic Creosoting Co., Savannah, Ga., 1960—. Mem. Citizens Traffic Bd. D.C., 1960-74. Served to comdr. USNR, 1941-49. Recipient Meritorious Pub. Service award D.C. Mem. Met. Washington Bd. Trade, D.C. Bankers Assn., D.C., Am. bar assns., Presidents Cup Regatta Assn. (vice chmn. bd.), Sigma Phi Epsilon. Clubs: Corinthian Yacht, Army and Navy (Washington); Cavalier Golf and Yacht (Virginia Beach, Va.). Editor (with Harrison Mann) Pratts Digest Nat. Banking Laws, 1932-41. Home: 2023 Belmont Rd NW Washington DC 20009 Office: 800 17th St NW Washington DC 20013

WIEGERT, HENRY THOMAS, physician; b. Lewistown, Mont., Jan. 5, 1926; s. Henry Charles and Nannie Louise (Peters) W.; student Central Wash. State Coll., 1946-50; M.D., U. Wash., 1955; m. Olga Belzer, Sept. 25, 1949; children—Sheryl, Michael. Intern, State U. N.Y. Upstate Med. Center, Syracuse; pvt. practice medicine, Sunnyside, Wash., 1956-66; joined U.S. Fgn. Service, 1966; med. attache, Rangoon, Burma, 1966-68, New Delhi, India, 1968-72; dep. med. dir. State Dept., 1972-73; asso. prof. family medicine U. Wash., Seattle, 1973-76; asso. dean primary care Coll. Medicine, U. Ky., Lexington, 1976—, chmn. dept. family practice, 1977—. Served with USAAF, 1944-45. Diplomate Am. Bd. Family Practice. Fellow Soc. Advanced Med. Systems; mem. Am. Acad. Gen. Practice, AMA. Address: Chmn Dept Family Practice U Ky Coll Medicine Lexington KY 40506

WIEGHART, JAMES GERARD, journalist; b. Chgo., Aug. 16, 1933; s. Oscar Frederick and Mary Catherine (Rill) W.; B.A. cum laude, U. Wis., 1958; m. Sharon Marie Hulin, Aug. 13, 1955; children—Michelle, Elizabeth, Bridget, Rebecca. Reporter, Milw. Jour., 1958-62, Milw. Sentinel, 1962-64; press sec. U.S. Senator William Proxmire of Wis., 1965; Washington bur. chief Milw. Sentinel, 1966-69; Washington corr. N.Y. New, 1969, Washington bur. chief, 1975—. Served with AUS, 1951-54. Mem. Sigma Delta Chi. Democrat. Roman Catholic. Clubs: Nat. Press (gov. 1970), Gridiron, Fed. City (Washington). Home: 5510 Nevada Ave NW Washington DC 20015 Office: 2101 L St NW Washington DC 20037

WIEGMAN, EUGENE WILLIAM, coll. pres.; b. Fort Wayne, Ind., Oct. 27, 1929; s. A. Henry and E. Catherine (McDonald) W.; B.S., Concordia Coll., 1953; M.S., U. Kans., 1956, Ed.D., 1962; m. Kathleen Wyatt, Apr. 26, 1952; children—Kathryn, Rose Marie, Mark, Jeanine, Gretchen, Matthew. Tchr., coach Trinity Luth. Sch., Atchison, Kans., 1954-58; prin. tchr. St. John's Coll., Winfield, Kans., 1958-61; prof. Concordia Coll., Seward, Nebr., 1961-65; adminstrv. asst. to Rep. Clair Callan, Lincoln, Nebr., 1965-66; asst. to adminstr. fed. extension service Dept. Agr., Washington, 1966-67; dean community edn. Fed. City Coll., Washington, 1967-69; pres. Pacific Luth. U., Tacoma, 1969-75; pres. Independent Colls. Wash., 1975-76; dir. Wash. Office Community Devel., 1977-78; commr. Dept. of Employment Security, 1978—; mem. Wash. State Employment and Tng. Council; mem. cabinet Gov. of Wash., 1977—. Candidate for U.S. Congress from 6th dist. Wash., 1976. Mem. Council on Washington's Future; bd. dirs. Tacoma Area Urban Coalition; chmn. Wash. Friends Higher Edn. Bd. dirs. Tacoma Urban League, Nat. Alliance Businessmen; trustee Tacoma Gen. Hosp., Pacific Sci. Center. Recipient Distinguished Teaching award City Winfield, Kans., 1960, Freedom Found. Teaching award, 1961. Fellow Philosophy of Edn. Soc.; mem. Tacoma, Seattle chambers commerce, Northwest Assn. Pvt. Colls. and Univs., Luth. Acad. for Scholarship, N.E.A., Am. Assn. Higher Edn., Luth. Edn. Assn., Phi Delta Kappa. Club: Kiwanis. Home: 405 N Stadium Way Tacoma WA 98403

WIELAGE, ROBERT CECIL, architect; b. Evanston, Ill., Apr. 28, 1929; s. Marcus Francis and Ada Mary (Bartstra) W.; student U. So. Calif., 1948, U. Miami (Fla.), 1949; B.S., Ga. Inst. Tech., 1953; m. Marian Connelly, Dec. 21, 1952; children—Marcus Francis, Rosemary Wells, Robert Simmons. Practice architecture and master planning, Tampa, Fla., 1954—; prin. works include Fine Arts Bldg., Fla. State U., Fed. Office Bldg., Tampa, Hillsborough Community Coll., Tampa, sci. bldg. F.I.T., Central Hdqrs. and Fire Sta. 1, Tampa, Pinnacle Apts., Tampa., Commodores Cove Apts., Tampa. Bd. govs. Tampa Bay Art Center, 1965-66. Served with AUS, 1946-47, 50-51. Recipient Design citation Progressive Architecture, 1963. Mem. AIA (nat. housing com. 1977-78, honor award 1965, merit award 1957, 64, 66, 73, 76), Soc. Coll. and Univ. Planners, Fla. Assn. Architects, Am. Inst. Planners, Nat. Council Archtl. Registration Bds., Constrn. Specification Inst., Archaeol. Inst. Am., Greater Tampa C. of C., Am. Mensa Soc. Clubs: Palma Ceia Golf and Country, Commerce. Home: 4141 S Bayshore Blvd Tampa FL 33611 Office: 1211 N Westshore Blvd Tampa FL 33607

WIELAND, WILLIAM HENRY, accountant; b. Atlantic City, July 21, 1918; s. William H. and Mary (Malone) W.; A.A., Los Angeles City Coll., 1939; student U. Calif. at Los Angeles, 1946-50, Loyola U., Los Angeles, 1951-54; B.S., Calif. Western U., 1976, M.S., 1977; m. Pauline C. Marsh, June 7, 1941; children—Diana L., Sherilee A. Bank messenger, bookkeeper United Calif. Bank, Los Angeles, 1939-41, with comptroller's dept., 1945-55, head accounting sect., 1955-76, comptroller, 1958—, v.p., 1960-68, sr. v.p., 1968-76; pvt. practice accounting, 1976—; v.p. Ralph C. Sutro Co. (mortgage bankers), 1977—. Served with USAAF, 1941-45. C.P.A. Presbyn. (elder). Home: 740 W Huntington Dr Arcadia CA 91006 Office: 4900 Wilshire Blvd Los Angeles CA 90010

WIELDE, JOHN WILLIAM, heavy equipment mfg. co. exec.; b. Mpls., Aug. 29, 1920; s. Arthur Lawrence and Fannie May (Barlow) W.; student U. Minn., 1938-41; m. Leona Cecellia Bromen, Dec. 13, 1944; children—John Arthur, Mark Anton, Anne Cecellia. With Am. Hoist & Derrick Co., St. Paul, 1946—, asst. controller, then asst. sec., 1955-69, sec., 1969—. Served with AUS, 1941-46. Mem. Nat. Assn. Accountants, Am. Soc. Corporate Secs. Home: 1401 E Ivy Ave Saint Paul MN 55106 Office: 63 S Robert St Saint Paul MN 55107

WIEMER, ROBERT ERNEST, film and television producer; b. Highland Park, Mich., Jan. 30, 1938; s. Carl Ernest and Marion (Israelian) W.; B.A., Ohio Wesleyan U., 1959; m. Rhea Dale McGeath, June 14, 1958; children—Robert Marshall, Rhea Whitney. Child actor Jam Handy Orgn., Detroit, 1946-48; ind. producer, 1956-60; dir. documentary ops. WCBS-TV, N.Y.C., 1964-67; ind. producer of television, theatrical and bus. films, N.Y.C., 1967-72; exec. producer motion pictures and television ITT, N.Y.C., 1973—; pres. subs. Blue Marble Co., Inc., Telemontage, Inc., Alphaventure Music, Inc., Betaventure Music, Inc.; exec. producer Emmy and Peabody award winning children's television show Big Blue Marble. Deacon, Dutch Reform Ch. in Am. Served to capt. USAF, 1960-64. Recipient CINE award, 1974, 76, 77, 79. Mem. Nat. Acad. Television Arts and Scis., Info. Film Producers Assn. (Outstanding Producer award), Nat. Assn. Television Programming Execs., Am. Women in Radio and Television, N.J. Broadcasters Assn. Office: Blue Marble Co Inc 40 W 57th St New York NY 10019

WIEN, LAWRENCE ARTHUR, lawyer, realtor; b. N.Y.C., May 30, 1905; s. Joseph and Bessie (Meyers) W.; A.B., Columbia U., 1925, LL.B., 1927, LL.D., 1974; LL.D., Long Island U., 1962, Brandeis U., 1962; L.H.D., Canisius Coll., 1970; m. Mae Levy, July 21, 1929; children—Enid (Mrs. Lester S. Morse), Isabel (Mrs. Peter L Malkin). Admitted to N.Y. bar, 1928, since practiced in N.Y.C.; sr. mem. firm Wien, Lane & Malkin, and predecessors, 1951—. Mem. Citizens Budget Commn., N.Y.C., 1956—; creator, sponsor Wien Internat. Scholarship Program, Brandeis U., 1957, Nat. Scholarship Program, Columbia Sch. Law, 1959. Officer, N.Y.C. Fusion Party, 1933. Trustee past pres. Fedn. Jewish Philanthropies N.Y.; vice chmn. bd. dirs. Lincoln Center for Performing Arts, N.Y.C.; trustee Citizens Budget Commn., Ednl. Broadcasting Corp., Inst. Internat. Edn., Brandeis U., past trustee Columbia; Recipient first annual award for real estate transaction contbg. most to econ. devel. of N.Y.C., 1958; citation for contbn. towards improvement Fifth Av. and 14th St. area N.Y.C., 1959; Distinguished Classmate award Class 1925 Columbia, 1959. Mem. Assn. Bar City N.Y., N.Y. County Lawyers Assn., Commerce and Industry Assn. N.Y., UN Assn. U.S., Am. Arbitration Assn. (nat. panel arbitrators), Am., N.Y. State bar assns. Clubs: Birchwood Country (founding pres.) (Westport, Conn.); The Golf at Aspetuck (founding pres.) (Easton, Conn.); Palm Beach (Fla.) Country; Ocean Reef (Key Largo, Fla.); Desert Inn Country (Las Vegas); Harmonie, 60 East, Columbia University, 200 500 (N.Y.C.). Home: 785 Fifth Ave New York City NY 10022 Office: 60 60 E 42d St New York NY 10017

WIENANDT, ELWYN ARTHUR, educator; b. Aniwa, Wis., July 23, 1917; s. Charles Herman and Ida (Loehrl) W.; B.Mus. cum laude, Lawrence Coll., 1939; M.Mus., U. Denver, 1948; Ph.D., State U. Iowa, 1951; m. Lois Patricia Trachsel, July 7, 1950; children—Alan Christopher, Linda Beth Wienandt Gandy, Thomas David. Pub. sch. tchr., 1939-49; asst. musicology State U. Iowa, 1950-51, vis. lectr., 1954; asst. prof. music N.Mex. Highlands U., 1951-56; mem. faculty Baylor U., 1956—, prof. music, 1959—, chmn. grad. studies music, 1958—, asso. dean Sch. Music, 1973; dir. choir 1st Presbyn. Ch., Waco, Tex., 1957-72. Served with USNR, 1943-46. Recipient Distinguished Service award Lawrence U. Alumni Assn., 1974. Mem. Music Library Assn., Am. Musicol. Soc. (pres. Tex. 1961-63), Internat. Musicol. Soc., Music Tchrs. Nat. Assn. (vice chmn. musicology com.), Am. Assn. U. Profs. (pres. Baylor chpt. 1975-76), Phi Mu Alpha Sinfonia, Pi Kappa Lambda. Episcopalian. Author: Choral Music of the Church, 1965; (with Robert H. Young) The Anthem in England and America, 1970, Opinions on Church Music, 1974; Bicentennial Collection of American Music, vol. 1, 1974; contbr. to Carl Schalk, Key Words in Church Music, 1978. Composer, editor ch. and chamber music. Home: 1216 Cliffview Rd Waco TX 76710

WIENER, HERMAN, hotel mgr.; b. Krenau, Poland, May 15, 1922; came to U.S., 1959; s. David and Regina (Goldwasser) W.; m. Eva, 1950; children—Regina, Hennie, Ruthie, David. From busboy to gen. mgr. Fairmont Hotel and Tower, San Francisco, until 1974, now gen. mgr. Fairmont Hotel, Phila., since 19—. Club: Rotary. Address: Fairmont Hotel Broad St at Walnut Philadelphia PA 19102

WIENER, HESH (HAROLD FREDERIC), pub., editor, cons.; b. Bklyn., July 20, 1946; s. Jesse Leon and Regina (Rappaport) W.; B.S. in Polit. Sci., Mass. Inst. Tech., 1969. Mem. staff systems devel. Data Gen. Corp., Southboro, Mass., 1969-70; dir. computer edn. project U. Calif. at Berkeley, 1970-72; editor Computer Decisions Mag., Rochelle Park, N.J., 1973-78; editor, pub. Tech. News Am., 1976—; pub. Computer and Communications Buyer Newsletter, 1979—; contbg. editor Bus. and Society Rev., 1978—; cons. Hewlett-Packard Co., 1971-72, Xerox Corp., 1972-73; NSF advisor, 1975—; corr. Computer Weekly (U.K.), 1975—, Computing Can., 1977-78, Computable (Netherlands), 1976—, Ordinateurs, Paris, 1977—, Data News, Brussels, 1979—; contbr. N.Y. Times Syndicate, Los Angeles Times Syndicate, N. Am. Newspaper Alliance Wireservice, Newsday, Rom Mag., Informatique, Paris. Mem. Investigative Reporters and Editors, Overseas Press Club. Home: 246 6th Ave Brooklyn NY 11215 Office: Tech News Am 26 Broadway New York NY 10004

WIENER, LOUISE WEINGARTEN, arts adminstr.; b. Bridgeport, Conn., Oct. 31, 1940; d. Charles and Dorothy M. (Goldstein) Weingarten; B.A., Bryn Mawr Coll., 1962; postgrad. Inst. Fine Arts, N.Y. U., 1964-65; m. Jerry Mortimer Wiener, Apr. 12, 1964; children—Matthew, Ethan, Ross, Aaron. Dir., Associated Am. Artists, publ., N.Y.C., 1962-66; pres. Louise Wiener Arts Promotion, N.Y.C., 1966-71; art critic Atlanta mag., 1972-74; cons. Central Atlanta Progress, 1974-75; curator Homage to Siqueiros exhbn. High Mus. Art, Atlanta, 1974; cons. to HEW, 1976; dep. dir. Washington Issues Office, Carter-Mondale Campaign, 1976; spl. asst. cultural resources U.S. Dept. Commerce, Washington, 1977—; participant White House Conf. on Balanced Growth, 1978. Bd. dirs. Atlanta Arts Festival, 1973-76, Ga. Juvenile Justice and Delinquency Prevention Commn., Atlanta Crime Commn.; pres. bd. assos. Atlanta Coll. Art, 1974-75. Recipient Leadership award City of Atlanta, 1976. Mem. Washington Women's Network, Children's Mus. Washington, Nat. Council Jewish Women (Barbara Lipschutz leadership award), Bryn Mawr Alumnae Assn. Democrat. Jewish.

WIENER, MARVIN S., rabbi, editor, educator; b. N.Y.C., Mar. 16, 1925; s. Max and Rebecca (Dodell) W.; B.S., CCNY, 1944, M.S., 1945; B.H.L., Jewish Theol. Sem. Am., 1947, M.H.L., 1951, D.D. (hon.), 1977; m. Sylvia Bodek, Mar. 2, 1952; children—David Hillel, Judith Rachel. Rabbi, 1951; registrar, sec. faculty Rabbinical Sch.,

Jewish Theol. Sem. Am., 1951-57; cons. Frontiers of Faith TV Series, NBC, 1951-57; dir. Cantors Inst.-Sem. Coll. Jewish Music, Jewish Theol. Sem. Am., 1954-58, faculty coordinator Sem. Sch. and Women's Inst., 1958-64; dir. Nat. Acad. for Adult Jewish Studies, United Synagogue Am., N.Y.C., 1958-78; editor Burning Bush Press, 1958-78, United Synagogue Rev., 1978—; dir. com. congregational standards United Synagogues Am. Sec. joint retirement bd. Jewish Theol. Sem. Am., Rabbinical Assembly and United Synagogue Am., 1968-76, vice chmn., 1976—; co-chmn. Jewish Bible Assn., 1960-64; chmn. bd. rev. Nat. Council Jewish Audio-Visual Materials, 1968-69; mem. exec. com. Nat. Council Adult Jewish Edn., 1966—; mem. exec. bd., editorial adv. bd. Jewish Book Council; chmn. Internat. Conf. Adult Jewish Edn., Jerusalem, Israel, 1972. Mem. Adult Edn. Assn. U.S., Am. Acad. Jewish Research, Assn. Jewish Studies, N.Y. Bd. Rabbis, Rabbinical Assembly. Editor: Adult Jewish Education, also Nat. Acad. Adult Jewish Studies Bull., 1958-78; Past and Present: Selected Essays, 1961; Jewish Tract Series, 1964-78; Talmudic Law and the Modern State, 1973. Home: 67-66 108th St Forest Hills NY 11375 Office: 155 Fifth Ave New York NY 10010

WIENER, PHILIP PAUL, educator, author; b. N.Y.C., July 8, 1905; s. Elias and Sophia (Lorman) W.; B.S., Coll. City N.Y., 1925; M.A., Columbia, 1926; Ph.D., U. So. Calif., 1931; postgrad. U. Paris; D.H.L., Kenyon Coll., 1961; m. Gertrude Schler, Aug. 24, 1934; children—Leonard, Marjorie. Teaching fellow philosophy U. Calif. at Berkeley, 1926-27, U. So. Cal., 1929-31; instr. philosophy City Coll. N.Y., 1933-43, prof., 1953-68, chmn. dept. philosophy, 1959-65, exec. officer Ph.D. program in philosophy, 1966-68; prof. Temple U., 1968—; vis. lectr., prof. Harvard, 1936, Smith Coll., 1943-44, Columbia, 1947, Claremont Grad. Sch., 1950-51, U. Mich., 1954, U. Minn., 1955, U.S. Fla., 1972-73; Fulbright lectr., France, 1953-54; sr. scholar East-West Center, U. Hawaii, 1962-63. Recipient U. Brussels and Liege medal; Inst. Internat. Edn. research fellow, 1931-32; Penrose award Am. Philos. Soc., 1946-47. Fellow A.A.A.S.; mem. Peirce Soc. (pres. 1956-57), Am. Philos. Assn., History Sci. Soc., Internat. Soc. History Ideas (pres. 1971—), Mind Assn., Phi Beta Kappa. Club: Fullerton (pres. 1968-69). Author: Evolution and the Founders of Pragmatism, 1949; Leibniz, 1951; Readings in Philosophy of Science, 1953; (with F. H. Young) Studies in the Philosophy of C. S. Peirce, 1953; Duhem's Aim and Structure of Physical Theory, 1954; C. S. Peirce: Values in a Universe of Chance, 1958; co-author: (with Bronstein and Krikorian) Basic Problems of Philosophy, 4th edit., 1972. Editor: Roots of Scientific Thought, 1957; (with A. Noland) Ideas in Cultural Perspective, 1962; (rev. version) H. Nakamura's Ways of Thinking of Eastern Peoples, 1965; (with P.O. Kristeller) Essays in Renaissance Philosophy, 1969; (with J. Fisher) Aggression and Violence in the History of Ideas, 1974; exec. editor, co-founder Jour. History Ideas, 1940—; editor-in-chief Dictionary History of Ideas, 5 vols., 1967-74; cons. editor Ency. Bioethics, 1975-76. Home: 7608 Louise Ln Wyndmoor PA 19118 Office: Humanities Bldg 749 Temple U Philadelphia PA 19122

WIENER, ROBERT ALVIN, accountant; b. N.Y.C., Jan. 9, 1918; s. George and Rose Vivian (Fink) W.; B.C.S., N.Y. U., 1938; m. Annabelle Kalbfeld, Jan. 1, 1941; children—Marilyn Wiener Grunewald, Marjorie Wiener Petit, Mark. Sr. partner Robert A. Wiener & Co., C.P.A.'s, N.Y.C., 1946-71; partner Alexander Grant & Co., C.P.A.'s, N.Y.C., 1971-73; v.p., gen. auditor Seeburg Industries, Inc., N.Y.C., 1973-77; practice accounting, 1978—; asst. prof. Pace Coll., 1956-77; lectr. Baruch Coll., 1947-77. Served with AUS, 1943-46. Decorated Bronze Star; C.P.A., N.Y., Ill. Mem. Am. Inst. C.P.A.s, N.Y. State Soc. C.P.A.s, Accountants Club Am., Fin. Execs. Inst., Inst. Internal Auditors, Pi Lambda Phi. Clubs: Collectors, N.Y. U. (N.Y.C.). Author: Insolvency Accounting, 1977. Home: 1340 N Astor St Chicago IL 60610 Office: 69 W Washington St Chicago IL 60602

WIENPAHL, PAUL, philosopher, educator; b. Rock Springs, Wyo., Mar. 6, 1916; s. Paul and Constance Mary (DeVelin) W.; B.A., U. Calif. at Los Angeles, 1937, M.A., 1939, Ph.D., 1946; m. Janet Elizabeth Ward, June 9, 1942; children—Mark, Jan. Teaching asst. U. Calif. at Los Angeles, 1937-42, instr. philosophy, 1947; instr. philosophy N.Y.U., 1947-48; asst. prof. U. Calif. at Santa Barbara 1948-54, asso. prof., 1954-62, prof., 1962—, chmn. dept. philosophy, 1960-64. Served with AUS, 1942-46; ETO. Ford Faculty fellow, Paris, France, 1954-55. Mem. Am. Philos Assn., Phi Beta Kappa. Author: The Matter of Zen, 1964; Zen Diary, 1970; The Radical Spinoza, 1979. Contbr. articles to profl. jours. Home: 1489 Tunnel Rd Santa Barbara CA 93105

WIENS, ARTHUR NICHOLAI, educator; b. McPherson, Kans., Sept. 7, 1926; s. Jacob T. and Helen Esau (Kroeker) W.; B.A., U. Kans., 1948, M.A., 1952; Ph.D., U. Portland, 1956; m. Ruth Helen Avery, June 11, 1949; children—Barbara Wiens Sprauer, Bradley, Donald. Clin. psychologist Topeka State Hosp., 1949-53; sr. psychologist outpatient dept. Oreg. State Hosp., Salem, 1954-58, chief psychologist, 1958-61, dir. clin. psychology internship program, 1958-61; clin. instr. U. Oreg. Med. Sch., Portland, 1958-61, asst. prof., 1961-65, asso. prof., 1965-66, prof. med. psychology, 1966—; clin. asso. prof. psychology U. Portland, 1959-61; field assessment officer Peace Corps, 1965; cons. psychologist Portland Center for Hearing and Speech, 1964-67, Dammasch State Hosp., 1967-69, Raleigh Hills Hosp., 1968—; cons. psychologist Oreg. Vocat. Rehab. Div., 1973—, mem. state adv. com., 1976—; cons. William Temple Rehab. House, Episcopal Laymen's Mission Soc., 1968—; chmn. State Oreg. Bd. Social Protection, 1971—; chmn. State Oreg. Bd. Psychologist Examiners, 1974-77; v.p. bd. dirs. Raleigh Hills Research Found., 1974—. Diplomate Am. Bd. Examiners Profl. Psychology. Fellow AAAS, Am. Psychol. Assn. (chmn. com. on vis. psychologist program 1972-76, chmn. accreditation com. 1978); mem. Am. Assn. State Psychology Bds. (pres. 1978-79), Sigma Xi. Contbr. articles to profl. jours. Home: 74 Condolea Way Lake Oswego OR 97034 Office: U Oreg Health Scis Center Portland OR 97201

WIENSHIENK, RALPH, lawyer, accountant; b. Kansas City, Mo., Sept. 27, 1919; s. Charles and Rebecca (Shultz) W.; B.S. in Econs., Northwestern U., 1940; LL.B. cum laude, Yale U., 1947; m. Valy Bloch, June 3, 1945 (div. Feb. 1960); children—Wendy Ann Wienshienk Gilpatric, Joan Wienshienk Whiteman, Mark, John; m. 2d, Rita Cipes, 1966; children—Andrew, David, Nancy. Admitted to N.Y. bar, 1948, Ill. bar, 1948; vis. prof. law Yale, 1947—; lawyer Gen. Counsel's Office, Sec. Air Force, also asso. gen. counsel Small Def. Plants Adminstrn., Washington, 1951-52; practiced in N.Y.C., 1952—; mem. firm Golden, Wienshienk & Mandel, 1952—; chmn. bd. dirs. McCall Pub. Co., 1973-78; pres., chief exec. officer Gt. Adventure Theme Park, 1975-77; dir. Literary Funding Corp. Wormser Sci. Corp. Chmn. urban affairs com., dir. YMCA, Greater N.Y. Served to maj. USAAF, 1942-46. C.P.A. Mem. Bar Assn. City N.Y., Northwestern U., Yale alumni assns., Order of Coif, Phi Epsilon Pi. Clubs: Yale (N.Y.C.); Fenway Country (gov.) (Scarsdale, N.Y.), Jewish (pres., trustee temple). Co-editor: Cases and Materials on Law and Accounting, 1949. Contbr. articles to profl. jours. Home: 3 Kingston Rd Scarsdale NY 10583 Office: 10 E 40th St New York City NY 10016

WIER, PATRICIA ANN, publishing co. exec.; b. Coal Hill, Ark., Nov. 10, 1937; d. Horace L. and Bridget B. (McMahon) Norton; B.A., U. Mo., Kansas City, 1964; M.B.A., U. Chgo., 1978; m. Richard A. Wier, Feb. 24, 1962; 1 dau., Rebecca Ann. Computer programmer AT&T, 1960-62; lead programmer City of Kansas City (Mo.), 1963-65; with Playboy Enterprises, Chgo., 1965-71, mgr. systems and programming, 1971; with Ency. Brit., Inc., Chgo., 1971—, v.p. mgmt. services, 1975-79, exec. v.p. adminstrn., 1979—; mem. dean's adv. council Krannert Grad. Sch. Mgmt., Purdue U., 1977; bd. dirs. Exec. Program Club, U. Chgo., 1978. Mem. Direct Selling Assn. Democrat. Roman Catholic. Office: 425 N Michigan Ave Chicago IL 60611

WIER, RICHARD ROYAL, JR., lawyer; b. Wilmington, Del., May 19, 1941; s. Richard Royal and Anne (Kurtz) W.; B.A. in English, Hamilton Coll., 1963; LL.B., U. Pa., 1963; m. Anne E. Wier, Nov. 25, 1978; children from previous marriage—Richard Royal, III, Mimi Poole. Admitted to D.C. bar, 1967, Del. bar, 1967; asso. firm Connolly, Bove & Lodge, Wilmington, 1966-68; dep. atty. gen. State of Del., 1968-70, atty. gen., 1975-79; state prosecutor Del. Dept. Justice, 1970-74; partner firm Prickett, Sanders, Jones, Elliott & Kristol, Wilmington, 1979—; lectr. criminal law various instns., 1970-75. Active United Way Campaign, 1976, 77; mem. supervisory bd. Gov.'s Commn. on Criminal Justice. Recipient Law Enforcement award Newark Police Dept., 1974; Law Enforcement Commendation medal Nat. Soc. SAR, 1976; Ideal Citizen award Am. Found. for Sci. Creative Intelligence, 1976; commendation Del. Gen. Assembly Senate, 1976, 77, Outstanding Achievement award, 1976. Mem. Nat. Dist. Attys. Assn. (state dir.), Del., D.C. bar assns., Nat. Assn. Attys. Gen. (exec. com.), Am. Judicature Soc., Am., Del. trial lawyers assns., Nat. Assn. Extradition Ofcls. (hon. life mem., regional v.p., exec. dir.), Italian Radio TV Assn. (hon.), Pi Delta Epsilon. Home: 513 Brighton Rd North Hills Wilmington DE 19809 Office: PO Box 1328 Wilmington DE 19899

WIERENGO, JOHN L., JR., lawyer; b. Detroit, 1913; A.B., U. Mich., 1935, J.D., 1937. Admitted to Mich. bar, 1937; mem. firm Varnum Riddering, Wierengo & Christenson, Grand Rapids, Mich. Mem. Am., Grand Rapids (pres. 1957-58) bar assns. State Bar Mich. (commr. 1962-68), Phi Delta Phi. Office: 666 Old Kent Bldg Grand Rapids MI 49503

WIERNIK, PETER HARRIS, physician; b. Crocket, Tex., June 16, 1939; s. Harris and Molly (Emmerman) W.; B.A. with distinction, U. Va., 1961, M.D., 1965; m. Roberta Joan Fuller, Sept. 6, 1961; children—Julie Anne, Lisa Britt, Peter Harrison. Intern, Cleve. Met. Gen. Hosp., 1965-66, resident, 1969-70; resident Osler Service Johns Hopkins Hosp., Balt., 1970-71; sr. asst. surgeon USPHS, 1966, advanced through grades to sr. surgeon, 1971; sr. staff asso. Balt. Cancer Research Center, div. cancer treatment Nat. Cancer Inst., 1966-71, chief sect. med. oncology, 1971-76, chief clin. oncology br., 1976—; dir., 1976—, asso. dir. div. cancer treatment, 1976—; asst. prof. medicine U. Md. Hosp., Balt., 1971-74, asso. prof., 1974-76, prof., 1976—; cons. hematology and med. oncology Union Meml. Hosp., Greater Balt. Med. Center, Franklin Sq. Hosp; bd. dirs. Balt. City unit Am. Cancer Soc., 1971-78, chmn. patient care com., 1972-75; mem. med. adv. com. Nat. Leukemia Assn., 1976—; chmn. adult leukemia com. Cancer and Leukemia Group B, 1976—. Recipient Z Soc. award U. Va., 1961, Byrd S. Leavell Hematology award U. Va. Sch. Medicine, 1965; diplomate Am. Bd. Internal Medicine. Fellow AAAS, Am. Coll. Clin. Pharmacology, Internat. Soc. Hematology, Royal Soc. Medicine (London), A.C.; mem. Am. Soc. Clin. Investigation, Am. Soc. Clin. Oncology (chmn. edn. and tng. com), Am. Assn. Cancer Research, Am. Soc. Hematology, Am. Fedn. Clin. Research, Am. Acad. Clin. Toxicology, Sigma Xi, Phi Beta Kappa, Alpha Omega Alpha, Phi Sigma (award 1961). Mem. editorial bd. Cancer Treatment Reports, 1972-76, Leukemia Research, 1976—, Cancer Clin. Trials, 1977—, Hosp. Practice, 1979—; co-editor Oncology Rounds, Am. Jour. Med. Scis., 1976—; also articles, chpts. in books. Home: 5026 Round Tower Pl Columbia MD 21044 Office: U Md Hosp 22 S Greene St Baltimore MD 21201. *Always remember why you entered a profession in the first place. Leave the politics to those who have forgotten.*

WIERSBE, WARREN WENDELL, clergyman, author; b. East Chicago, Ind., May 16, 1929; s. Fred and Gladys Anna (Forsberg) W.; B.Th., No. Baptist Sem., 1953; D.D. (hon.), Temple Sem., Chattanooga, 1965; m. Betty Lorraine Warren, June 20, 1953; children—David, Carolyn, Robert, Judy. Ordained to ministry Bapt. Ch., 1951; pastor Central Bapt. Ch., East Chicago, 1951-57; editorial dir. Youth for Christ Internat., Wheaton, Ill., 1957-61; pastor Calvary Bapt. Ch., Covington, Ky., 1961-71; sr. minister Moody Ch., Chgo., 1971-78; chmn. bd. Slavic Gospel Assn., Wheaton, 1973—; columnist Moody Monthly, Chgo., 1971-77; author, conf. minister, 1978—; vis. instr. pastoral theology Trinity Div. Sch., Deerfield, Ill. Author numerous books including: William Culbertson, A Man of God, 1974, Live Like a King, 1976, Walking with the Giants, 1976, Be Right, 1977. Home and office: 6400 N Tahoma St Chicago IL 60646

WIERUM, THORNTON BRIGGS, advt. co. exec.; b. N.Y.C., Nov. 24, 1925; s. Thornton Briggs and Charlotte (Provoost) W.; B.A., Dartmouth Coll., 1947; LL.B., Columbia U., 1948; m. Jean E. Hough, Aug. 2, 1947; children—Deborah, Elisabeth, Cynthia. Admitted to N.Y. bar, 1949; mem. legal dept. Home Life Ins. Co., N.Y.C., 1948-53; mem. legal dept. J. Walter Thompson Co., N.Y.C., 1953-65, v.p., adminstr. media dept., 1965-72, sr. v.p., dir. media services, 1972-75, sr. v.p. adminstrn. and fin., Western div., Chgo., 1976—. Bd. dirs. 2440 Lakeview Coop. Served with USMC, 1943-45, 51-53. Episcopalian (vestry). Home: 2440 Lakeview St Chicago IL 60614 Office: 875 N Michigan Ave Chicago IL 60611

WIESE, ALVIN CARL, emeritus educator, chemist; b. Milw., Aug. 13, 1913; s. Alvin John and Clara (Krause) W.; B.S., U. Wis. 1935, M.S., 1937, Ph.D., 1940; m. Hazel Marie Kuntz, Aug. 19, 1944; children—Jon Lee, Ray Alvin. Instr. chemistry Okla. A. and M. Coll., 1940-42; research asso. chemistry U. Ill., also research on chem. warfare agts. Nat. Defense Research Com. at U. Ill., 1942-45. research asst., div. animal nutrition U. Ill., 1945-46; prof., head dept. agrl. chemistry U. Idaho, 1946-63, prof., head agrl. biochemistry and soils, 1963-72, prof. biochemistry, dept. bacteriology and biochemistry, 1972-78, prof. emeritus, 1978—; partner Wiese-Jackson Assos., cons., 1958—. Fellow AAAS, Am. Inst. Chemists; mem. Am. Chem. Soc. (chmn. Wash.-Ida. boarder sect. 1948), Am. Inst. Nutrition, Poultry Sci. Assn., Soc. Exptl.. Biology and Medicine, Sigma Xi, Phi Lambda Upsilon, Phi Sigma, Gamma Alpha. Presbyn. Contbr. articles on nutrition and biochemistry to various sci. jours. Home: 721 S Lynn St Moscow ID 83843

WIESE, ROBERT GEORGE, investment counsel; b. Meriden, Conn., Dec. 26, 1904; s. John and Anne (Nissen) W.; B.A., Yale, 1925, M.A., 1926; m. Esther Wurst, Sept. 29, 1928; children—Robert George, William Hastings. With Scudder, Stevens & Clark, Boston, 1926—, partner, 1936-78; dir. Fiduciary Trust Co. (Boston), corporator Boston Five-Cents Savs. Bank. Trustee emeritus Mt. Holyoke Coll., Boston Hosp. Women, Am. Meml. Hosp., Rheims. Mem. Phi Beta Kappa, Zeta Psi. Clubs: Yale, Somerset (Boston); Country (Brookline, Mass.); Duxbury (Mass.) Yacht. Home: 63 Carisbrooke Rd Wellesley Hills MA 02181 Office: 175 Federal St Boston MA 02110

WIESEL, ELIE, author; b. Sighet, Romania, Sept. 30, 1928; s. Shlomo and Sarah (Feig) W.; student Sorbonne, Paris, France, 1947-50; Litt. D. (hon.), Jewish Theol. Sem., N.Y.C., 1967; Dr. Humane Letters, Hebrew Union Coll., 1968, Manhattanville Coll., 1972, Yeshiva U., 1973, Boston U., 1974; D.H.L., Spertus Coll. of Judaica, Chgo., 1973; Dr. Philosophy (hon.), Bar-Ilan U. (Israel), 1973; LL.D., Hofstra U., 1975; Litt.D., Marquette U., 1975, Simmons Coll., 1976, St. Scholastica Coll., 1978; m. Marion Erster Rose, 1969; 1 son, Shlomo Elisha. Came to U.S., 1956, naturalized, 1963. Distinguished prof. Coll. City N.Y., 1972—; Andrew Mellon prof. in the humanities Boston U., 1976. Recipient Prix Rivarol, 1964, Jewish Heritage award, 1965, Remembrance award, 1965, Prix Medicis, 1968, Prix Bordin, French Acad., 1972, Eleanor Roosevelt Meml. award, 1972, Am. Liberties medallion Am. Jewish Com., 1972, Martin Luther King Jr. award Coll. City N.Y., 1973, Faculty Distinguished Scholar award Hofstra U., 1973-74. Author: Night, 1960; Dawn, 1961; The Accident, 1962; The Town Beyond the Wall, 1964; The Gates of the Forest, 1966; The Jews of Silence, 1966; Legends of Our Time, 1968; A Beggar in Jerusalem, 1970; One Generation After, 1971; Souls on Fire, 1972; The Oath, 1976; Ani Maamin (Cantata), 1974; Zalmen or the Madness of God (play), 1975; Messengers of God, 1976; A Jew Today, 1978; From Hasidic Masters, 1978. Address: care Random House Inc 201 E 50th St New York NY 10022

WIESEL, TORSTEN NILS, neurobiologist; b. Upsala, Sweden, June 3, 1924; came to U.S., 1955; s. Fritz Samuel and Anna-Lisa Elisabet (Bentzer) W.; M.D., Karolinsky Inst., Stockholm, 1954; A.M. (hon.), Harvard U., 1967; m. Ann Grace Yee, Mar. 23, 1973; 1 dau., Sara Elisabet. Instr. in physiology Karolinska Inst., 1954-55; asst. dept. child psychiatry Karolinska Hosp., 1954-55; fellow in ophthalmology Johns Hopkins U., 1955-58, asst. prof. ophthalmic physiology, 1958-59; asso. in neurophysiology and neuropharmacology Harvard U. Med. Sch., Boston, 1959-60, asst. prof. neurophysiology and neuropharmacology, 1960-64, asst. prof. neurophysiology, dept. psychiatry, 1964-67, prof. physiology, 1967-68, prof. neurobiology, 1968-74, Robert Winthrop prof. neurobiology, 1974—, chmn. dept. neurobiology, 1973—; Ferrier lectr. Royal Soc. London, 1972; Grass lectr. Soc. Neurosci., 1976. Recipient Jules Stein award Trustees for Prevention Blindness, 1971, Lewis S. Rosenteil prize Brandeis U., 1972, Friedenwald award Trustees of Assn. for Research in Vision and Ophthalmology, 1975, Karl Spencer Lashley prize Am. Philos. Soc., 1977, Louisa Gross Horwitz prize Columbia U., 1978, Dickson prize U. Pitts., 1979. Mem. Am. Physiol. Soc., AAAS, Am. Acad. Arts and Scis., Swedish Physiol. Soc., Soc. Neurosci. (pres. 1978-79). Contbr. numerous articles to profl. jours. Office: Harvard U Med Sch 25 Shattuck St Boston MA 02115*

WIESEN, DAVID STANLEY, educator; b. N.Y.C., May 27, 1936; s. Seymour and Mae (Halperin) W.; A.B., Harvard, 1957, Ph.D., 1961; m. Ellen Cohen, June 23, 1963; children—Rachel Melanie, Seth Robert, Seymour Jonathan. Instr. classics Cornell U., 1961-63; asst. prof. Swarthmore (Pa.) Coll., 1963-66; prof. classics Brandeis U., 1966-75, U. So. Calif., 1975—. Fellow Nat. Endowment Humanities, 1970-71. Author: St. Jerome as a Satirist, 1964; St. Augustine, City of God, Books 8-11, 1968; contribution of Antiquity to American Racial Thought, 1976; Ancient History in Early American Education. Home: 28520 Seamount Dr Rancho Palos Verdes CA 90274 Office: Univ So Calif Los Angeles CA 90007

WIESER, CHARLES EDWARD, financial cons.; b. St. Marys, Ohio, Apr. 18, 1929; s. Lawrence F. and Rose (Danaher) W.; B.S., Ohio State U., 1951, M.B.A., 1953; m. Anne Esper, Dec. 1, 1962; children—Lawrence, Carolyn, Mark, Charles T. Staff accountant Touche, Ross, Bailey & Smart, C.P.A.'s, 1954-59, supr. audit, 1959-62, mgr. audit, 1962-67, adminstrv. mgr. Detroit office, 1967-68; mgr. corporate finance dept. Manley, Bennett, McDonald & Co., Detroit, 1968-70; v.p. finance Whitehead & Kales Co., Detroit, 1970—; instr. accounting Ohio State U., 1954. Served to 2d lt. AUS, 1951-53. C.P.A., Mich. Mem. Am. Inst. C.P.A.'s, Mich. Assn. C.P.A.'s, Nat. Assn. Accountants, Am. Accounting Assn., Financial Execs. Inst., Ohio State U. Alumni Assn., Beta Alpha Psi. Clubs: State University Alumni Assn., Economic (Detroit). Home: 24525 Emerson St Dearborn MI 48124 Office: 58 Haltiner St River Rouge MI 48218

WIESLER, JAMES BALLARD, banker; b. San Diego, July 25, 1927; s. Harry J. and Della B. (Ballard) W.; B.S., U. Colo., 1949; postgrad. Stonier Sch. Banking, Rutgers U., 1962, Advanced Mgmt. Program, Harvard U., 1973; m. Mary Jane Hall, Oct. 3, 1953; children—Tom, Ann, Larry. With Bank of Am. NT & SA, 1949—, v.p., mgr. San Jose (Calif.) Mian Office, 1964-69, regional v.p. San Jose-Central Coast regional adminstrn., 1969-74, sr. v.p., head No. Europe Area office, Frankfurt, W. Ger., 1974-78, exec. v.p., head Asia div., Tokyo, 1978—, chmn. bd. Bank Am. Asia Ltd., Hong Kong, 1978—, chmn. bd. Asian-Am. Mcht. Bank Ltd., Singapore, 1978—. Pres., Santa Clara County Unit Fund, 1969, 70, San Jose C. of C., 1968; fin. chmn. Santa Clara County Republicans, 1967-74. Served with USNR, 1945-46. Mem. Am. C. of C. in Japan, Internat. House of Japan, ASEAN-U.S. Bus. Council. Presbyterian. Clubs: Bankers of San Francisco; Tokyo American; Sainte Claire (San Jose). Home: 13 Ichigaya Nakano-cho Shinjuku-ku Tokyo Japan 162 Office: Bank of Am 27th floor Toho Seimei Bldg 2-15-1 Shibuya Shibuya-ku Tokyo Japan 150

WIESNER, JEROME BERT, tech. inst. pres.; b. Detroit, May 30, 1915; s. Joseph and Ida (Friedman) W.; B.S., U. Mich., 1937, M.S., 1938, Ph.D., 1950; m. Laya Wainger, Sept. 1, 1940; children—Stephen Jay, Zachary Kurt, Elizabeth Ann, Joshua A. Asso. dir. U. Mich. Broadcasting Service, 1937-40; chief engr. Acoustical Record Lab., Library of Congress, 1940-42; staff Mass. Inst. Tech. Radiation Lab., 1942-45; staff U. of Calif. Los Alamos Lab., 1945-46; mem. faculty Mass. Inst. Tech., 1946-71, dir. research lab. of electronics, 1952-61, head dept. elec. engring., 1959-60, dean of sci., 1964-66, provost, 1966-71, pres., 1971-80, researcher, lectr., 1980—; mem. Army sci. adv. com., 1956-61; spl. asst. to Pres. on sci. and tech., 1961-64; chmn. Pres.'s Sci. Adv. Com., 1961-64; chmn. tech. assessment adv. council Office Tech. Assessment, U.S. Congress, 1976-79. Dir. Celanese Corp., Damon Engring., Schlumberger Ltd. Bd. govs. Weizmann Inst. Sci.; trustee WGBH, Am. Found. for Blind; mem. corp. Mus. of Sci. in Boston. Fellow IEEE, Am. Acad. Arts and Scis.; mem. Am. Philos. Soc., AAUP, Am. Geophys. Union, Am. Soc. Engring. Edn., Acoustical Soc. Am., Nat. Acad. Scis., Sigma Xi, Phi Kappa Phi, Eta Kappa Nu, Tau Beta Pi. Author: Where Science and Politics Meet, 1965. Home: 61 Shattuck Rd Watertown MA 02172 Office: Mass Inst Tech Cambridge MA 02139

WIESNER, KAREL FRANTISEK, chemist; b. Prague, Czechoslovakia, Nov. 25, 1919; came to Can., 1948, naturalized, 1953; s. Karel and Eugenie (Storova) W.; R.N.Dr., Charles U., Prague, 1945; D.Sc. (hon.), U. N.B. (Can.), 1970, U. Western Ont. (Can.), 1972, Universite de Montreal (Que., Can.), 1975; m. Blanka Pevna, June 22, 1942; children—Karel, Blanka (dec.). Asst. dept. phys. chemistry Charles U., 1945-46; postdoctoral fellow ETH, Zürich,

Switzerland, 1946-48; successively asst. prof. organic chemistry U. N.B., Fredericton, then asso. prof., prof., 1948-62, research prof., 1964—, univ. prof., 1976—; asso. dir. research Ayerst Labs. Montreal, 1962-64; cons. in field. Decorated Centennial medal, officer Order Can. Fellow Royal Soc. Can., Royal Soc.; mem. Pontifical Acad. Scis., Chem. Inst. Can. (Palladium medal 1963), Am. Chem. Soc., Chem. Soc. (London) (Centenary lectr. 1977, medal 1977). Research, numerous publs. in field; editor Tetrahedron, 1957—, Tetrahedron Letters, 1959—. Home: 814 Burden St Fredericton NB E3B 4C4 Canada Office: Natural Products Research Centre U NB PO Box 4400 Fredericton NB E3B 5A3 Canada

WIGGERS, HAROLD CARL, physiologist; b. Ann Arbor, Mich., Sept. 1, 1910; s. Carl John and Minerva (Berry) W.; B.A., Wesleyan U., Middletown, Conn., 1932; Ph.D., Western Res. U., 1936; Porter fellow Harvard Med. Sch., 1936-37; Sc.D. (hon.), Union Coll., 1959, Union U., 1975; m. Virginia B. Balay, Nov. 21, 1935; children—Kathrine B., Janet H. Instr. physiology Coll. Physicians and Surgeons, Columbia U., 1937-42; asst. prof. Western Res. U., 1942-43; asso. prof. Coll. Medicine, U. Ill., 1943-47; prof. Albany (N.Y.) Med. Coll., Union U., 1947—, chmn. dept. physiology, 1947-53, dean, 1953-74, exec. v.p., dean, 1966-74, pres. and dean emeritus, 1974—; acting dean and sr. cons. Eastern Carolina U. Sch. Medicine, 1974-77; dir. Bankers Trust Co. Albany; cons. div. physician manpower HEW, 1967-71; cons. to chmn. VA Instl. Research Program, 1968-70; trustee Regional Hosp. Rev. and Planning Council Northeastern N.Y., Inc., 1962-74; mem. adv. council Ednl. TV; mem. adv. staff, senate and assembly coms. health, mental health and retardation N.Y. State Legislature, 1966-67; regents adv. com. Regionalism Northeastern N.Y., 1972-74; adv. council N.Y. State Health Planning Commn., 1968-70, chmn. com. organizational planning coordination, 1969-70; mem. ad hoc panel rev. specialized centers research applications in hypertension Nat. Heart and Lung Inst., 1971. Bd. dirs. Albany County Heart Assn., 1965-66, Albany Blue Cross, 1953-74; adj. trustee Rensselaer Poly. Inst., 1971-74; bd. visitors Capital Dist. Psychiat. Center, 1974—. Mem. AAAS, Am. Heart Assn., Asso. Med. Schs. N.Y. and N.J. (trustee 1973-75), Am. Physiol. Soc., Central Soc. Clin. Research, Assn. Am. Med. Colls. (exec. com. council deans), Nat., N.Y. State socs. med. research, Albany Area C. of C. (dir. 1974—). Unitarian. Clubs: Albany (dir. 1968-74), Greenville Golf and Country, Greenville Rotary, Brook Valley Golf and Country. Home: 711 Iris Ln Vero Beach FL 32960

WIGGINS, CHARLES E., lawyer; b. El Monte, Calif., Dec. 3, 1927; s. Louis J. and Margaret (Fanning) W.; B.S., LL.B., U. So. Calif., m. Yvonne Boots, Dec. 30, 1946 (dec.); children—Steven Louis, Scott Douglas; m. 2d, Betty Burnett, July 12, 1972; stepchildren—Gary, Darla, Craig. Admitted to Calif. bar; partner firm Musick, Peeler and Garrett; mem. 90th-94th congresses 25th Dist. Calif., 95th congress 39th Dist. Calif.; mayor, councilman, El Monte, 1960-66. Served to 1st lt. inf., AUS, 1945-48, 50-52. Republican. Home: 15 Verde Irvine CA 92715 Office: 18662 MacArthur Blvd Suite 325 Irvine CA 92715

WIGGINS, JAMES RUSSELL, editor; b. Luverne, Minn., Dec. 4, 1903; s. James and Edith (Binford) W.; ed. Luverne pub. schs.; LL.D., Colby Coll., 1954, U. Maine, 1967, Bates Coll., 1968; Lit., Annae Mariae Coll., 1976, Clark U., 1977; L.H.D., Husson Coll., Bangor, Maine, 1979; m. Mabel E. Preston, Feb. 8, 1923; children—William James, Geraldine Wiggins Thomssen, Patricia Wiggins Schroth, John Russell. Reporter, Rock County Star, Luverne, 1922-25; editor, pub. Luverne Star, 1925-30; editorial writer Dispatch-Pioneer Press, St. Paul, 1930-33, Washington corr., 1933-38, mng. editor, 1938-45, editor, 1945-46; asst. to pub. N.Y. Times, 1946-47; mng. editor Washington Post, 1947-53, v.p., mng. editor, 1953-55; v.p., exec. editor Washington Post and Times Herald, 1955-60, editor, exec. v.p., 1960-68; U.S. ambassador to UN, 1968-69; editor, pub. Ellsworth (Maine) Am., 1969—. Served to maj. USAAF, 1943-45; air combat intelligence officer, MTO, 1943-44. Mem. Am. Soc. Newspaper Editors (past pres.), Am. Antiquarian Soc. (pres. 1969-77), Sigma Delta Chi. Clubs: Masons; Nat. Press, Cosmos, Gridiron (Washington). Author: Freedom or Secrecy, 1956. Home: Carlton Cove Brooklin ME 04616 Office: Water St Ellsworth ME 04605

WIGGINS, LORIN DEE, advt. exec.; b. Cedar City, Utah, Feb. 17, 1929; s. Eugene Howard and Delores (Hokanson) W.; B.A. in Mktg., U. Utah, 1955, M.B.A., 1957; m. Lou Jean Saunders, Feb. 28, 1951; children—Linda, Kent, Janice, Ted, Ilene. Pres., mgr. Panorama Prodns., Inc., Salt Lake City, 1953-76, dir., 1972-76; prodn. mgr. David W. Evans, Inc., Advt. Agy., Salt Lake City, 1977—. Historian, Sons Utah Pioneers, 1973-74, 1st v.p., 1975-76. Republican. Mormon. Club: Salt Lake Exchange (dir. 1976-77, pres. 1978-79). Home: 3490 S 3570 E Salt Lake City UT 84109 Office: 110 Social Hall Ave Salt Lake City UT 84111

WIGGINS, NORMAN ADRIAN, univ. pres.; b. Burlington, N.C., Feb. 6, 1924; s. Walter James and Margaret Ann (Chason) W.; A.A., Campbell Coll., 1948; B.A., Wake Forest Coll., 1950, LL.B., 1952; LL.M., Columbia U., 1956, J.S.D., 1964; LL.D., Gardner-Webb Coll., 1972; m. Mildred Alice Harmon. Deacon Wake Forest Baptist Ch., Winston-Salem, N.C., 1963-66, Buies Creek (N.C.) Bapt. Ch., 1973—; deacon, tchr. Sunday sch., 1952—; lay preacher, 1953—; pres. N.C. Found. of Ch.-Related Coll., 1969-70; pres. Campbell U., Buies Creek, 1967—, prof. law, 1976—. Chmn. Gov.'s Task Force Com. on Adjudication of the Com. on Law and Order, 1969-71; mem. Com. on Drafting Intestate Succession Act for N.C., 1957-59; mem. Com. for Revision of the Laws Relating to the Adminstrn. of Decedents' Estates, 1959-67, chmn., 1964-67. Trustee Sunday Sch. Bd., So. Bapt. Conv., 1975—, chmn. bd. trustees, 1978—. Mem. Nat. Assn. Coll. and Univ. Attys. (pres. 1972-73), N.C. Assn. Ind. Colls. and Univs. (pres. 1970-72), N.C. Bar Assn., Harnett County Bar Assn., Jay Waugh Evang. Assn. (dir.), Dunn Area C. of C., Wake Forest Alumni Assn., Phi Alpha Delta. Author: Wills and Administration of Estates in North Carolina, 1964—; (with Gilbert T. Stephenson) Estates and Trusts, 1973. Editor: N.C. Will Manual, 1958—; Trust Functions and Services, 1978. Contbr. articles to legal jours. Address: Box 127 Buies Creek NC 27506 Office: Office of President Campbell U Buies Creek NC 27507

WIGGINS, SAMUEL PAUL, educator; b. Salisbury, N.C., Sept. 20, 1919; s. James Andrew and Mollie (Wilhelm) W.; B.S., Ga. Tchrs. Coll., 1940; M.Ed., Duke U., 1942; Ph.D., Peabody Coll., 1952; m. Linda Jean Bessent, June 29, 1947; children—Stanley, David, Timothy, Mark. Teaching prin., Alma, Ga., 1939-40; dir. Lab. Sch., Ga. S.W. Coll., 1940-42; dir. student teaching Emory U., 1947-53; prof., adminstr. Peabody Coll., 1953-67; dean Coll. Edn., Cleve. State U., 1967-75, prof., 1975—; chief adviser Korea Tchr. Edn. Project, 1961-62; Fulbright lectr., Colombia, S.Am., 1966, Lisbon, Portugal, 1978; chmn. nat. adv. council Asso. Orgns. Tchr. Edn., 1972-73; pres. Am. Assn. Colls. Tchr. Edn., 1974-75; mem. forum of leaders Nat. Ednl. Orgns., 1975-77. Served with USNR, 1942-47, Comdr. Res. ret. Author: The Desegregation Era in Higher Education, 1966; Higher Education in the South, 1966; Battlefields in Teacher Education, 1964; editor: Educating Personnel for Urban Schools, 1972; Improving Education for the Youth of Portugal, 1978. Home: 420 Woodlawn Circle Berea OH 44017

WIGGINS, SUSAN RAYE, singer; b. Eugene, Oreg., Oct. 8, 1944; d. Raymond Adams and Thelma Orleans (Burkhart) Aird; grad. high sch.; m. Jerry Wayne Wiggins, Oct. 3, 1971; children—Steven James, Todd Shawn, Scott Kelly, Cale Ryan, Brock Corey. Singer with Buck Owens; rec. artist Capitol Records, now United Artists Records. Recipient various awards, including Female Artist of Year award. Methodist. Office: 17337 Ventura Blvd Suite 220 Encino CA 91316

WIGGINS, THOMAS ARTHUR, educator, physicist; b. Indiana, Pa., Feb. 24, 1921; s. Arthur William and Helen (Simpson) W.; B.S., Pa. State Coll., 1942; M.S., George Washington U., 1949; Ph.D., Pa. State U., 1953; m. Dorothy Blanchard, June 27, 1953; children—Bruce, James. Mem. faculty Pa. State U., University Park, 1953—, prof. physics, 1963—. Fellow Optical Soc. Am., Am. Phys. Soc.; mem. Sigma Xi. Contbr. articles to profl. jours. on light scattering and molecular spectra. Home: 352 Hillcrest Ave State College PA 16801 Office: Dept Physics 104 Davey Lab Pa State U University Park PA 16802

WIGGINTON, MADISON SMARTT, business exec.; b. Evansville, Ind., Oct. 12, 1901; s. Thomas Albert and Belle (Smartt) W.; A.B., Vanderbilt U., 1922, A.M., 1923; m. Georgia Weaver, Sept. 24, 1924; 1 dau., Mrs. Allen Wigginton Bell. Formerly exec. v.p., dir. GENESCO, Inc. (formerly Gen. Shoe Corp.), dir. various subsidiaries; chmn. GENESCO Retirement Trust, 1968—; chmn. Nashville City Bank, 1968-73. Trustee Vanderbilt U. Mem. Phi Beta Kappa, Sigma Chi. Presbyn. Clubs: Belle Meade, Bluegrass, Cumberland. Home: 1211 Chickering Rd Nashville TN 37215

WIGHT, FREDERICK S., artist, dir. art gallery; b. N.Y.C., June 1, 1902; s. Carol Van Buren and Alice (Stallknecht) W.; B.A., U. Va., 1923; student art schs., Paris, Academie Julian, others, 1923-25; M.A., Harvard, 1946; m. Joan Elizabeth Bingham, June 30, 1936; 1 son, George Frederick. Dir. edn. Inst. Contemporary Art, Boston, 1946-50, asso. dir., 1950-53; prof. art, dir. art galleries (named Frederick S. Wight Art Galleries 1972) U. Calif. at Los Angeles, 1953-73, chmn. art dept., 1963-66; one-man shows the Art Center, Marie Sterner Gallery, Kleeman Gallery, New Sch. Social Research, N.Y.C., M. H. deYoung Meml. Mus., San Francisco, 1956, Pasadena Mus., 1956, Fine Arts Gallery of San Diego, 1959, Mus. N.Mex. Art Gallery, 1960, Long Beach Mus., 1961, Stamford Mus., 1978, Palm Desert Mus., 1978, others. Recipient Bronze medal Nat. Gallery Art, 1967. Lt. comdr. USNR, 1942-45. Author: Van Gogh, 1953; Goya, 1954. Co-author: New Art in America, 1957; Looking at Modern Art, 1957; The Potent Image: Art in the Western World from Cave Paintings to the 1970's, 1976. Contbr. articles profl., popular jours. and mags. Home: 456 N Bundy Dr Los Angeles CA 90049

WIGHT, IRA EDWARD, investment banker; b. Paschristian, Miss., Oct. 21, 1900; s. Ira E. and Marie (Ewing) W.; grad. Phillips Acad., Andover, Mass., 1920; student Yale, 1924; m. Elizabeth Bradlee Forrest, Jan 10, 1925; children—Elizabeth (Mrs. Skyler B. Herring), Ira Edward III, John, Nancy; m. 2d, Grace W. Niedringhaus, June 25, 1974. With firm Newhard Cook & Co., St. Louis, 1948—, mng. partner, 1963-70; past dir. St. Louis Union Trust Co. Bd. govs. N.Y. Stock Exchange, 1965-68. Treas. Mo. Republican Finance Com., 1938-40; chmn. Mo. Eisenhower Nomination Finance Co., 1952. Past mem. bd. St. Louis City Art Mus., Barnard Hosp., St. Louis. Served to lt. col. USAAF, 1942-45; ETO. Clubs: St. Louis Country, Log Cabin, Cuivre (St. Louis); Cotton Bay (Eleuthra, Bahamas). Home: 7472 University Dr St Louis MO 63130 Office: 300 S Broadway St St Louis MO 63102. *In these days of more and more inflation, character and training are assets least likely to lose value.*

WIGHTMAN, ARTHUR STRONG, educator, physicist; b. Rochester, N.Y., Mar. 30, 1922; s. Eugene Pinckney and Edith Victoria (Stephenson) W.; B.A., Yale, 1942; Ph.D., Princeton, 1949; D.Sc., Swiss Fed. Inst. Tech., Zurich, 1968; m. Anna-Greta Larsson, Apr. 28, 1945 (dec. Feb. 11, 1976); 1 dau., Robin Letitia; m. 2d, Ludmila Popova, Jan. 14, 1977. Instr. physics Yale, 1943-44; from instr. to asso. prof. physics Princeton, 1949-60, prof. math. physics 1960—, Thomas D. Jones prof. math. physics, 1971—; vis. prof. Sorbonne, 1957. Served to lt. (j.g.) USNR, 1944-46. NRC postdoctoral fellow Inst. Teoretisk Fysik, Copenhagen, Denmark, 1951-52; NSF sr. postdoctoral fellow, 1956-57; recipient Dannie Heineman prize math. physics, 1969. Fellow Am. Acad. Arts and Scis.; mem. Nat. Acad. Scis., Am. Math. Soc., Am. Phys. Soc., AAAS, Fedn. Am. Scientists. Home: 30 The Western Way Princeton NJ 08540

WIGLE, ERNEST DOUGLAS, cardiologist, educator; b. Windsor, Ont., Can., Oct. 30, 1928; s. Douglas St. John and Marjorie Annette (Lyon) W.; M.D., U. Toronto, 1953; m. Mary M. Littlejohn, Dec. 13, 1958; children—Doug, Cam, Mary Lind, Jill, Bruce. Intern, Toronto Gen. Hosp., 1953-54, resident, 1956-58; mem. dept. medicine U. Toronto, 1960—, prof. dept. medicine, 1972—; mem. dept. medicine Toronto Gen. Hosp., 1960—, dir. div. cardiology, 1972—. Fellow Royal Coll. Physicians and Surgeons of Can., A.C.P., Am. Coll. Cardiology; mem. Am. Soc. Clin. Investigation, Assn. Am. Physicians. Home: 127 Roxborough Dr Toronto ON M4W 1X5 Canada Office: 101 College St Toronto ON M5G 1L7 Canada

WIGLEY, WILLARD ROBERT, stock broker; b. Waco, Tex., May 7, 1919; s. Willard Robert and Florence (Patten) W.; A.B., Princeton U., 1942; m. Jerry McDonald, July 20, 1946; children—Sherry Susanne, Karen Grace, Florence Elisa. Supr., Clint W. Murchison, 1945-47; with E.F. Hutton & Co., Inc., Dallas, 1947—, partner, 1953, regional v.p., 1962—, vice chmn. bd., 1967—, also dir., mem. exec. com.; dir. Dallas Bus. Capital Corp., Life Ins. Co. Calif., Energy Resources Corp.; chmn. bd. N.Am. Cattle Co., 1974-77; bd. govs. N.Y. Stock Exchange, 1966-69. Served with USAAF, 1942-45. Mem. Phi Beta Kappa. Episcopalian. Clubs: Brook Hollow Golf; Dallas Petroleum. Home: 5528 Meaders Ln Dallas TX 75229 Office: 2001 Bryan Tower Suite 3308 Dallas TX 75201

WIGNER, EUGENE PAUL, ret. educator; b. Budapest, Hungary, Nov. 17, 1902; s. Anthony and Elisabeth (Einhorn) W.; Chem. Engr. and Dr. Engring., Technische Hochschule, Berlin; hon. D.Sc., U. Wis., 1949, Washington U., 1950, Case Inst. Tech., 1956, U. Chgo., 1957, Colby Coll., 1959, U. Pa., 1961, Thiel Coll., 1964, U. Notre Dame, 1965, Technische Universität Berlin, 1966, Swarthmore Coll., 1966, Université de Louvain (Belgium), 1967; Dr.Jr., U. Alta., 1967; L.H.D., Yeshiva U., 1963; hon. degrees U. Liège, 1967, U. Ill., 1968, Seton Hall U., 1969, Catholic U., 1969, Rockefeller U., 1970, Israel Inst. Tech., 1973, Lowell U., 1976, Princeton U., 1976, U. Tex., 1978, Clarkson Coll., 1979, Allegheny Coll., 1979; m. Amelia Z. Frank, Dec. 23, 1936 (dec. 1937); m. 2d, Mary Annette Wheeler, June 4, 1941 (dec. Nov. 1977); children—David Wheeler, Martha Faith. Came to U.S., 1930, naturalized, 1937. Lectr. Princeton U., 1930, halftime prof. math. physics, 1931-36, Thomas D. Jones prof. theoretical physics, 1938-71; prof. physics U. Wis., 1936-38; on leave of absence, 1942-45 at Metall. Lab., U. Chgo., 1946-47 as dir. research and devel. Clinton Labs.; dir. CD Research Project, Oak Ridge, 1964-65; Lorentz lectr. Inst. Lorentz, Leiden, 1957; cons. prof. La. State U., 1971—; mem. gen. adv. com. AEC, 1952-57, 59-64; mem. math. panel NRC, 1952-54; physics panel NSF, 1953-64; vis. com. Nat. Bur. Standards, 1947-51. Decorated medal of Merit, 1946; recipient Franklin medal Franklin Inst., 1950; citation N.J. Tchrs. Assn., 1951; Enrico Fermi award AEC, 1958; Atoms for Peace award, 1960; Max Planck medal German Phys. Soc., 1961; Nobel prize for physics, 1963; George Washington award Am. Hungarian Studies Found., 1964; Semmelweiss medal Am. Hungarian Med. Assn., 1965; Nat. Sci. medal, 1969; Pfizer award, 1971; Albert Einstein award, 1972; Wigner medal, 1978. Fgn. mem. Royal Soc. Eng.; mem. Royal Netherlands Acad. Sci. and Letters, Am. Nuclear Soc., Am. Phys. Soc. (v.p. 1955, pres. 1956), Am. Math. Soc., Am. Acad. Arts and Scis., Am. Philos. Soc., Nat. Acad. Scis., Austrian Acad. Scis., German Phys. Soc., Franklin Inst., AAAS, Sigma Xi; corr. mem. Acad. Sci., Gottingen, Germany; hon. mem. Hungarian Acad. Sci. Address: 8 Ober Rd Princeton NJ 08540. *As to success, one achieves it best if one does not strive for it too vigorously, has a good deal of luck, does one's duty, follows his inclinations, tries to be understanding and useful. It sounds sanctimonious, and perhaps even boastful, but it is true nevertheless, that being considerate, mindful of the sensitivities of others, gives one more peace of mind, more satisfaction, than success or anything else.*

WIIN-NIELSEN, AKSEL CHRISTOPHER, educator; b. Juelsminde, Denmark, Dec. 17, 1924; s. Aage Nielsen and Marie Christophersen; B.S. in Math., U. Copenhagen (Denmark), 1947, M.S. in Math., 1950; Fil. Lic. in Meteorology, U. Stockholm (Sweden), 1957, Ph.D. in Meteorology, 1960; m. Bente Havsteen Zimsen, Dec. 5, 1953; children—Charlotte, Barbro Marianne, Karen Margrete. Came to U.S., 1959. Staff meteorologist Danish Meteorol. Inst., 1952-55; research meteorologist Internat. Meteorol. Inst., U. Stockholm, 1955-58, asst. prof., 1957-58, exec. editor publ. Tellus, 1957-58; research meteorologist Air Weather Service, USAF, also staff mem. joint numerical weather prediction unit and lectr. George Washington U., 1959-61; research staff mem. Nat. Center Atmospheric Research, 1961-62, asst. dir., 1962-63; prof., chmn. dept. meteorology and oceanography U. Mich., 1963-71; prof. theoretical meteorology U. Bergen (Norway), 1971-72, U. Mich., 1972-74; dir. European Centre for Medium-Range Weather Forecasts, 1974-79; sec. gen. World Meteorol. Orgn., 1980—; pres. Internat. Commn. for Dynamic Meteorology, 1971-79; chmn. working group on numerical experimentation, also mem. joint organizing com. Global Atmospheric Research Program, 1973-79; chmn. working group on earth scis., sci. adv. com. European Space Agy., 1977-79; sci. adv. com. Max Planck Inst. Meteorology, Hamburg, W. Ger. Fellow Am. Meteorol. Soc.; mem. Am. Geophys. Union, Swedish, Norwegian geophys. socs., Royal Soc. (fgn.), Tau Beta Pi. Home: Villa Muskan Ch Des Bosquets 2 Founex Switzerland

WIJSMAN, ROBERT ARTHUR, statistician, educator; b. The Hague, Netherlands, Aug. 20, 1920; s. Johannes and Maria (Alting Mees) W.; Ingenieur in Physics Engring., Delft Inst. Tech., 1945; Ph.D. in Physics, U. Calif. at Berkeley, 1952; m. Gertrud Zierau, June 6, 1953; children—Ellen, Annette, Suzanne. Came to U.S., 1946. Lectr. med. physics, acting asst. prof. statistics U. Calif. at Berkeley, 1952-57; mem. faculty U. Ill. at Urbana, 1957—, prof. math., 1965—. Mem. Inst. Math. Statistics, Am. Math. Soc., Am. Statis. Assn. Asso. editor Annals Math. Statistics, 1964-67. Contbr. articles profl. jours. Home: 507 S Pine St Champaign IL 61820 Office: Dept Math U Ill Urbana IL 61801

WIKSTEN, BARRY FRANK, airline exec.; b. Seattle, June 21, 1935; s. Frank Alfred and Alice Gertrude (Ensor) W.; B.A., Miami U., Oxford, Ohio, 1960; M.A., Fletcher Sch. Law and Diplomacy, 1961; m. Mary Patricia Regan, May 5, 1962; children—Karen Anne, Eric Marshall, Kurt Edward. Dir. econ. programs U.S. Council, Internat. C. of C., N.Y.C., 1962-63; with TWA, N.Y.C., 1964—, dir. fin. relations, 1972, v.p. pub. affairs, 1973, v.p. pub. relations, 1974-75, sr. v.p. pub. affairs, mem. airline policy bd., 1976—. Served with USMC, 1954-57. Mem. Conf. Bd. (pub. affairs research council), Internat. Air Transp. Assn. (pub. relations advisory council), Air Transport Assn. (pub. relations com.). Clubs: Union League (N.Y.); Orange Lawn Tennis (South Orange, N.J.); Univ. (Washington). Office: 605 3d Ave New York NY 10016

WIKTOR, TADEUSZ JAN, virologist; b. Stryj, Poland, Sept. 9, 1920; s. Wincenty W. and Salomea (Soltysik) W.; came to U.S., 1962, naturalized, 1967; Dr.Vet.Med., U. Paris, 1946, Dipl.Trop.Med., 1947; m. Anna Maria Krzyzanowski, Apr. 27, 1948; children—George B.; Stefan Z., Peter J. Virologist charge veterinary research and vaccine prodn., Belgian Congo and Rwanda Urundi, 1948-60; expert FAO in W.Pakistan, 1961; prof. Wistar Inst., Phila., 1962—; asso. prof. Sch. Veterinary Medicine, U. Pa.; mem. WHO Experts Com. for Rabies. Served with Polish Army, 1938-44. Contbr. sci. articles to profl. jours. and chpts. to books. Home: 9 Downs Circle Wynnewood PA 19096 Office: 36th St at Spruce Philadelphia PA 19104

WILBER, CHARLES GRADY, educator, scientist; b. Waukesha, Wis., June 18, 1916; s. Charles Bernard and Charlotte Agnes (Grady) W.; B.Sc., Marquette U., 1938; M.A., Johns Hopkins, 1941, Ph.D., 1942; m. Ruth Mary Bodden, July 12, 1944 (dec. 1950); children—Maureen, Charles Bodden, Michael; m. 2d, Clare Marie O'Keefe, June 14, 1952; children—Thomas Grady (dec.), Kathleen, Aileen, John Joseph. Asst. prof. physiology Fordham U., 1945-49; asso. prof. physiology, dir. biol. labs. St. Louis U., 1949-52; leader Arctic expdns., 1943-44, 48, 50, 51; physiologist Chem. Corps, U.S. Army, 1952-61; asso. physiology and pharmacology U. Pa., 1953-61, chief comparative physiology, 1956-61; profl. lectr. biol. scis. Loyola Coll., Balt., 1957-61, dir. In-Service Inst. Sci. Tchrs., 1958-61; prof. biol. scis., univ. research coordinator, dean Grad. Sch., Kent State U., 1961-64; dir. marine laboratories U. Del., 1964-67; chmn. prof. dept. zoology Colo. State U., 1967-73, prof., 1973—, also dir. forensic sci. lab.; dep. coroner Larimer County (Colo.). Mem. Marine Biol. Lab., Woods Hole, Mass., 1947—; mem. U.S. Army Panel Environ. Physiology, 1952-61; mem. study group Nat. Acad. Scis.-USAF, 1958-61. Served to capt. USAAF, 1942-46; col. USAF Res. ret. Fellow N.Y. Acad. Scis., Am. Acad. Forensic Sci.; mem. Am. Physiol. Soc., Phi Beta Kappa, Sigma Xi, Phi Sigma, Gamma Alpha. Republican. Catholic. Club: Cosmos (Washington). Author: Biological Aspects of Water Pollution, 2d edit., 1971, Japanese edit., 1970; Forensic Biology for the Law Enforcement Officer, 1975; Contemporary Violence, 1975; Ballistic Science for the Law Enforcement Officer, 1977; Medicolegal Investigation of The President John F. Kennedy Murder, 1978; Chemical Trauma from Pesticides, 1979; Forensic Toxicology, 1980; also articles profl. jours. Exec. editor Adaption to the Environment, vol. in series, 1962; editor Am. Lecture Series in Environ. Studies; mem. editorial bd. Am. Jour. Forensic Medicine and Pathology; contbr. Ency. Chemistry, Harper Ency. Nat. vis. lectr. Am. Inst. Biol. Scis., 1957—. Home: 900 Edwards St Fort Collins CO 80524. *My most precious possession has been the right of freedom, and the responsibility for the consequences of my actions. This right of freedom, even to be wrong or stupid, is the essence of mankind. Any abridgement of that freedom, for whatever stated reason is subversive of mankind and dehumanizes the person. Any government that encroaches on that radical freedom in order "to protect me from myself" must be destroyed.*

WILBOURN, HIGH RANDOLPH, JR., telephone co. exec.; b. Little Rock, Sept. 13, 1915; s. Hugh Randolph and Willye May (Bonner) W.; student Ouachita Baptist Coll., 1932-33; m. Edith K.

Morris, June 14, 1936; children—Joe Ellen Wilbourn Ford, Mary Nell Wilbourn Cole, Beverly Anne Wilbourn Pascoe, H.R. Mem. plant dept. Southwestern Bell Telephone Co., 1934-44; sec.-treas. Allied Telephone Co., Little Rock, 1943-62, pres., chmn. bd., 1962-77, chmn. emeritus, chmn. exec. com. of bd. dirs., 1977—. Mem. regional exec. com. Nat. Council Boy Scouts Am., 1968—, pres. Quapaw Area Council, mem. regional adv. council. Recipient Silver Beaver award Boy Scouts Am., 1969. Mem. U.S. Ind. Telephone Assn. (past pres.), Ark. Telephone Assn. (past pres.), Orgn. for Protection and Advancement of Small Telephone Cos. (past pres.), Ark. C. of C. (past dir.). Baptist. Home: PO Box 1576 Little Rock AR 72203 Office: PO Box 2177 Little Rock AR 72203

WILBUR, CORNELIA BURWELL, educator, physician; b. Cleve., Aug. 26, 1908; d. Arthur Warner and Bertha (Schade) Burwell; B.S., U. Mich., 1930, M.S., 1933, M.D., 1939; m. Henry Marsh Wilbur, 1934 (div. 1946); m. 2d, Keith Brown, Aug. 15, 1953 (dec. Oct. 16, 1976). Intern Univ. Hosp., Ann Arbor, Mich., 1939-40, resident neuropsychiatry, 1940-41; asst. physician Pontiac (Mich.) State Hosp., 1941-43; instr. neurology and psychiatry Med. Sch. U. Nebr., 1943-46; pvt. practice medicine specializing in psychiatry and neurology, Omaha, 1942-46, also psychoanalysis, N.Y.C., 1948-65; staff Bishop, Clarkson Meml., Univ. hosps., Omaha, 1943-46, Falkirk Hosp., Central Valley, N.Y., 1959-63, U. W. Va. Hosp., Morgantown, 1965-67, U. Ky. Hosp., Lexington, 1967—; prof. psychiatry U. Ky. Coll. Medicine, 1967-74, prof. emeritus, 1974—, acting chmn. dept., 1969-70; psychoanalyst cons. to book and film Sybil, 1973, 76. Recipient hon. mention sci. exhibit Omaha Mid-West Clin. Soc., 1945, Hofhelmer award hon. mention, 1964; Roy M. Dorcas award, 1972. Diplomate Am. Bd. Neurology and Psychiatry. Charter fellow, founder Am. Coll. Psychiatrists; fellow Am. Psychiat. Assn., Acad. Psychoanalysis; mem. Am., Ky., Fayette (Ky.) County med. assns., Am. Med. Womens Assn., AAAS. Author: (with others) A Psychoanalytic Study of Male Homosexuals, 1962; (movie) Narcosynthesis, 1945. Contbr. articles profl. jours. Home: 408 Bristol Rd Lexington KY 40502

WILBUR, E. PACKER, investment co. exec.; b. Bridgeport, Conn., Sept. 9, 1936; s. E. Packer and Elizabeth (Wells) W.; B.A., Yale U., 1959; M.B.A., Harvard U., 1965; m. Laura Mary Ferrier, Sept. 17, 1965; children—Alison Mary, Andrew Packer, Gillian Elizabeth. Cons., McKinsey & Co. Inc., N.Y.C., 1964-67; dir. corp. planning Am. Express Co., N.Y.C., 1967-69; v.p. Van Alstyne Noel & Co., N.Y.C., 1969-70; exec. v.p., dir., mem. exec. com. Newburger Loeb & Co. Inc., N.Y.C., 1970-73; pres. E.P. Wilbur & Co., Inc., Southport, Conn., 1973—; chmn. bd. Criterion Mgmt., Inc., Lafayette, Ind., Trend Mgmt., Inc., Tampa, Fla., Fairfield Advisors, Inc., Southport, EPW Securities, Inc., Southport; gen. partner Grandland Realty Assos., English Oaks Apts., Pepper Hill Townhouses, Kemar Townhouse Assos., Autumn Woods Assos., Country Villa Assos., others; allied mem. N.Y. Stock Exchange. Bd. dirs. Inst. Govt. Assisted Housing, Washington, Wakeman Meml. Boys' Club, Southport, Greater Bridgeport Jr. Hockey League, Pequot Library, Southport. Served with AUS, 1959-60. Clubs: Pequot Yacht, Pequot Running (chmn.) (Southport); Fairfield County Hunt (Westport, Conn.); Yale (N.Y.C.). Contbr. articles to fin. jours. Home: 181 Taintor Dr Southport CT 06490 Office: 368 Center St Southport CT 06490

WILBUR, JAMES BENJAMIN, III, educator, philosopher; b. Hartford, Conn., Feb. 21, 1924; s. James Benjamin, Jr. and Martha (Shekosky) W.; B.A., U. Ky., 1948; postgrad., Harvard, 1948-50; M.A., Columbia, 1951, Ph.D., 1954; m. Margie Mattmiller, July 9, 1949; children—James Benjamin IV, Ann Elizabeth. Mem. faculty Adelphi U., Garden City, N.Y., 1952-64, chmn. philosphy dept., 1954-64, asst. prof., 1954-59, asso. prof., 1959-64; asso. prof. U. Akron (Ohio), 1964-66, prof., 1966-68, chmn. philosophy dept., 1964-68; chmn. philosophy dept. State U. N.Y. Coll. Arts and Sci., Geneseo, 1966-78, prof. philosophy, 1968—; founder, co-dir. Confs. on Value Inquiry, 1968—; vis. prof. U. Kent, Canterbury, Eng., spring 1971; faculty adviser Empire State Coll., 1972-74. Served with AUS, 1943-45. State U. N.Y. grantee, 1969, 70. Mem. Am. Assn. U. Profs., Am. Metaphys. Soc., L.I. Philos. Soc., (founder 1963), Creighton Club (pres. 1970-72), Rochester Oratorio Soc., Am. Soc. Value Inquiry (sec.-treas. 1971, pres. 1973; founder Jour. Value Inquiry 1968, exec. editor 1968—). Clubs: Hudson (Ohio) Country (founding trustee, hon. life mem.); Equinox Country (Manchester, Vt.). Author: (with H.J. Allen) The Worlds of Hume and Kant, 1967, The Worlds of Plato and Aristotle, 1962, 2d rev. edit., 1979, The Worlds of the Early Greek Philosophers, 1979; editor, contbr. Cartesian Essays (M. Nijhoff), 1969; Spinoza's Metaphysics (Van Gorcum), 1976; co-editor (with E. Laszlo) Human Values and Natural Science, 1970; Values and the Mind of Man, 1971; Value Theory in Philosophy and Social Science 1971; Value and the Arts, 1978; The Dynamics of Value Change, 1978; editor: Human Value and Economic Activity, 1979; The Life Sciences and Human Values, 1979; Human Values and the Law, 1979; Values in the Law, 1980. Home: 22 West View Crescent Geneseo NY 14454

WILBUR, JORDAN ROCKWOOD, pediatrician; b. Rochester, Minn., Apr. 26, 1932; s. Dwight Locke and Ruth Esther (Jordan) W.; A.B. in Psychology, Stanford U., 1953, M.D., 1961; m. Violet Rakich, Aug. 28, 1955; children—Teresa Anne, Bruce Jordan. Asst. dir., then dir. pediatric outpatient dept. Stanford U. Med. Center, 1965-68; asso. pediatrician, head dept. pediatrics M.D. Anderson Hosp. and Tumor Inst., U. Tex., Houston, 1968-72; dir. children's oncology program Children's Hosp., Stanford U., 1972-77, chief staff, 1974-77; chief div. pediatric oncology Presbyn. Hosp. of Pacific Med. Center, San Francisco, 1977—; med. dir. Children's Cancer Research Inst., Pacific Med. Center, 1974—; sci. dir. Nejat Internat. Childhood Cancer Research Soc., Los Angeles, 1977—. Served to lt. (j.g.) USNR, 1953-55. Diplomate Am. Bd. Pediatrics. Fellow Am. Acad. Pediatrics; mem. Ambulatory Pediatric Assn., Leukemia Soc. Am., Internat. Soc. Pediatric Oncology, Am. Soc. Clin. Oncology, Calif., San Francisco med. socs., Theta Delta Chi. Democrat. Contbr. articles to med. jours. Home: 1245 San Mateo Dr Menlo Park CA 94025 Office: Pacific Med Center 2351 Clay St San Francisco CA 94120

WILBUR, LESLIE CLIFFORD, educator; b. Johnston, R.I., May 12, 1924; s. Clifford Elwood and Isabel (Winsor) W.; B.S. in Mech. Engring., U. R.I., 1948; M.S., Stevens Inst. Tech., 1949; m. Gertrude Monica Widmer, Sept. 9, 1950; children—Clifford Leslie, Kenneth Charles, Ted Winsor, Christopher Francis. Instr., then asst. prof. Duke, 1949-57; mem. faculty Worcester Poly. Inst., 1957—, prof. mech. engring., 1961—, dir. nuclear reactor facility, 1959—. Mem. N.E. adv. council Atomic Indsl. Forum, 1972—. Served with AUS, 1943-46; ETO. Registered profl. engr., Mass. Mem. Am. Nuclear Soc. (mem. at large exec. com. Northeastern sect. 1961-62, 66-67, chmn. Northeastern sect. 1968-69), ASME (vice chmn. Eastern N.C. sect. 1956-57), Am. Soc. Engring. Edn., AAAS, Sigma Xi, Tau Beta Pi, Phi Kappa Phi, Pi Tau Sigma. Baptist (deacon 1962-65). Home: 32 Walnut St Berlin MA 01503 Office: Worcester Poly Inst Worcester MA 01609

WILBUR, RALPH EDWIN, printing co. exec.; b. Boston, Mar. 19, 1932; s. Harland Ashley and Helen Dorothy (Miller) W.; B.S. in Bus. and Engring. Adminstrn., Mass. Inst. Tech., 1957; m. Kari Jordbakke, May 28, 1955; children—Randi, Kristi, Siri. Salesman, Tudor Press, Boston, 1957-58, Photocircuits, Glen Cove, N.Y., 1958-59; mgr. High Speed Process Printing, Boston, 1960-67; pres. Graphic Litho, Lawrence, Mass., 1968—; pub. Power Boat Ann., Marine Atlas Series. Bd. dirs. Nat. Council Better Edn., 1976—. Served with Ordnance, U.S. Army, 1956-57. Editor Our Schools Today, 1976; adv. bd. Fundamental Series Books, Edn. Media Press, 1977—. Home: 2 Meadowbrook Dr Andover MA 01810 Office: 130 Shepard St Lawrence MA 01843

WILBUR, RICHARD PURDY, educator, writer; b. N.Y.C., Mar. 1, 1921; s. Lawrence L. and Helen (Purdy) W.; A.B., Amherst Coll., 1942, A.M., 1952, D.Litt., 1967; A.M., Harvard U., 1947; L.H.D., Lawrence Coll., Washington U., Williams Coll., U. Rochester; D.Litt., Clark U., Am. Internat. Coll., Marquette U., Wesleyan U; m. Mary Charlotte Hayes Ward, June 20, 1942; children—Ellen Dickinson, Christopher Hayes, Nathan Lord, Aaron Hammond. Asst. prof. English, Harvard, 1950-54; asso. prof. Wellesley Coll., 1955-57; prof. Wesleyan U., 1957-77; writer in residence Smith Coll., 1977—. Recipient Harriet Monroe prize Poetry mag., 1948; Oscar Blumenthal prize, 1950; Edna St. Vincent Millay Meml. award, 1957; Nat. Book award, 1957; Pulitzer prize, 1957; Prix de Rome, Am. Acad. Arts and Letters, 1954; Sarah Josepha Hale award, 1968; Bollingen prize, 1971; Brandeis U. Creative Arts award, 1971; Prix Henri Desfeuilles, 1971; Shelley Meml. award, 1973; Harriet Monroe Poetry award, 1978. Guggenheim fellow, 1952-53, 63; Ford fellow, 1960-61. Mem. Am. Acad. Arts and Scis., Nat. Inst. Arts and Letters, Am. Acad. Arts and Letters (pres. 1974-76, chancellor 1977-78), Acad. Am. Poets (chancellor). Author: The Beautiful Changes, 1947; Ceremony, 1950; A Bestiary, 1955; Moliere's Misanthrope (translation), 1955; Things of This World, 1956; Poems 1943-56, 1957; Candide (comic opera, with Lillian Hellman), 1957; Advice to a Prophet, 1961; Tartuffe (transl. from Moliere) (co-recipient Bollingen Transl. prize 1963), 1963; Poems of Richard Wilbur, 1963; Loudmouse (juvenile), 1963; Walking to Sleep (poems), 1969; (transl. from Moliere) The School for Wives, 1971; Opposites (juvenile), 1973; The Mind-Reader (poems), 1976; Responses (criticism), 1976; transl. The Learned Ladies (Moliere), 1978. Editor: Complete Poems of Poe, 1959; Poems of Shakespeare, 1966; Selected Poems of Witter Bynner, 1978. Home: Dodwells Rd Cummington MA 01026

WILBUR, RICHARD SLOAN, med. assn. exec.; b. Boston, Apr. 8, 1924; s. Blake Colburn and Mary Caldwell (Sloan) W.; B.A., Stanford, 1943, M.D., 1946; m. Betty Lou Fannin, Jan. 20, 1951; children—Andrew, Peter, Thomas. Intern, San Francisco County Hosp., 1946-47; resident Stanford Hosp., 1949-51, U. Pa. Hosp., 1951-52; postgrad. tng. U. Mich. Hosp., 1957, Karolinska Sjukhuset, Stockholm, 1960; mem. staff Palo Alto (Cal.) Med. Clinic, 1952-69; dep. exec. v.p. A.M.A., Chgo., 1969-71, 73-74; asst. sec. def. for health and environment, 1971-73; sr. v.p. Baxter Labs., Inc., Deerfield, Ill., 1974-76; exec. v.p. Council Med. Splty. Socs., 1976—, sec. liaison com. for continuing med. edn., 1979—; asso. prof. medicine Georgetown U. Med. Sch., 1971—, Stanford Med. Sch., 1952-69. Chmn. Bd. Cal. Med. Assn., 1968-69, Calif. Blue Shield, 1966-68. Vice chmn. Republican Central Com. Santa Clara County (Calif.), 1966-69. Bd. govs. A.R.C.; bd. dirs. Medic Alert Found., Nat. Adv. Cancer Council; bd. visitors Drew U. Postgrad. Med. Sch. Served with USNR, 1942-49. Recipient Distinguished Service medal Dept. Def., 1973; scroll of merit Nat. Med. Assn., 1971; hon. fellow Internat. Coll. Dentistry. Fellow A.C.P.; mem. Inst. Medicine, Am. Assn. Med. Socs. Execs., Ill. Med. Assn., Lake County Med. Soc., Am. Gastroenterol. Assn., Pacific Interurban Clin. Club, Am. Soc. Internal Medicine, Phi Beta Kappa, Alpha Omega Alpha; hon. mem. Santa Clara County Med. Soc. Club: Army and Navy (Washington). Contbr. articles to med. jours. Home: 985 N Hawthorne Pl Lake Forest IL 60045 Office: PO Box 70 Lake Forest IL 60045

WILBUR, WILLIAM HALE, author, ret. army officer; b. Palmer, Mass., Sept. 24, 1888; s. John and Edith B. (Smart) W.; student Haverford Coll., 1907-08; B.S., U.S. Mil. Acad., 1912; grad. Command and Gen. Staff Sch., 1932, Army War Coll., 1935; grad. Ecole Spéc. Militaire, St. Cyr, France, 1919-20, Ecole Superieure de Guerre, Paris, 1922-24; m. Laura Girard Schieffelin, Sept. 8, 1923; children—Mary S. (Mrs. L. H. Cummings), William H. (dec. 1950). Commd. 2d lt. inf. U.S. Army, 1912, advanced through grades to brig. gen., 1942; asst. chief of staff, G-1, personnel officer, Chgo., 1938-40; chief of staff 6th Corps Area, 1940-41; comdg. officer 60th Inf., Ft. Bragg, 1941-42; overseas duty with Allied Landing in N. Africa, 1942; dep. comdr. 36th div., participating in Salerno landing 1944. Apptd. warden Cook County Jail, Chgo., 1950. Mem. of Lake County Crime Commn., 1960—; mem. radio panel, What's Best for America, 1952—; mem. Chicago Crime Commn., 1954—. Trustee Patriotic Edn., Inc., 1965—. Decorated Congl. Medal of Honor by Pres. Roosevelt at Casablanca, Jan. 1943; Ouissam Alaouite medal by Moroccan Govt. (awarded by Sultan of Morocco) Jan. 1943; Legion of Merit with oak leaf cluster, Silver Star, Bronze Star, Combat Inf. badge (U.S.); knight comdr. SS. Maurice and Lazarus (Italy); named Illustrious Grad. U.S. Mil. Acad., 1967; recipient Nat. Collegiate Athletic Assn. award, 1971; Gold medal Nat. SAR, 1976. Mem. Am. Legion, West Point Soc. Chgo. (pres.), V.F.W., Am. Mil. Inst., Lafayette Soc. (dir.), Defenders Am. Liberties (dr.). Kiwanian, (hon.), Rotarian (hon.). Club: Army and Navy (Washington). Author: Koehler Method of Physical Drill, 1918; Guideposts to the Future, 1954; Russian Communism, A Challenge and a Fraud, 1964; Freedom Must Not Perish, 1964; The Making of George Washington, rev. edit., 1973; many articles for profl. jours. Speaker on internat., mil. and ednl. subjects. Home: 922 Shell Point Village Fort Myers FL 33908

WILBURN, ROBERT CHARLES, former univ. pres., govt. official; b. Latrobe, Pa., July 1, 1943; s. Robert C. and Annabel Grace (McWherter) W.; B.S., USAF Acad., 1965; M.P.A., Princeton U., 1967, Ph.D., 1970; m. Patti-Ellen Zuidema, May 18, 1968; children—Jason Robert, Jesse Albert. Commd. 2d lt. USAF, 1965, advanced through grades to capt., 1972; resigned, 1972; v.p. dir. mgmt. sci. div., then v.p., dir. financial planning group Chase Manhattan Bank, N.A., N.Y.C., 1972-75; pres. Indiana (Pa.) U., 1975-79; sec. budget and adminstrn. Commonwealth Pa., 1979—; mem. faculty Trinity Coll., Washington, 1970-71, U. Va., Falls Church, 1971; pub. mem. regional adv. com. Third Nat. Bank Region, 1976-77; cons. in field. Trustee Trinity Coll., 1976—; mem. com. for N.Y. Philharmonic, 1974-75; bd. dirs. Am. Cancer Soc. Indiana County, Bela Bartok Soc. Am., Big Bros./Big Sisters Indiana County, Operation Up-Lift, United Way Indiana County; adv. com. Indiana County Airport. Decorated Air Force Commendation medal, Joint Services Commendation medal; Woodrow Wilson fellow, 1965-67. Mem. Am. Council Edn. (commn. mil.-higher edn. relations), Pa. Commn. State Colls. and Univ. Pres. (vice chmn. 1976, chmn. 1977-79), Am. Econs. Assn., Pa. Council Econ. Edn. (pres. 1978), Assn. State Colls. and Univs., Phi Mu Alpha, Phi Delta Kappa. Author papers. Office: 570 Race St Harrisburg PA 17104

WILCOCK, DONALD FREDERICK, mech. engr.; b. Bklyn., Sept. 24, 1913; s. Frederick and Jennie Marie (Young) W.; B.S. in Civil Engring., Harvard U., 1934; D.Engring. Sci., U. Cin., 1939; m. Marjorie Ellen Ferris, Sept. 3, 1938; 1 son, Donald Everett. Research chemist Sherwin Williams Co., Chgo., 1939-42; with Gen. Electric Co., 1942-65; mgr. tribology dept. Mech. Tech., Inc., Latham, N.Y., 1965-78; pres. Tribolock Inc., Schenectady, 1978—. Fellow ASME (Hersey award), Am. Soc. Lubrication Engrs. Author: Bearing Design and Application, 1957; patentee. Home and Office: 1949 Hexam Rd Schenectady NY 12309*

WILCOCK, JAMES WILLIAM, capital equipment mfg. co. exec.; b. Dayton, Ohio, Sept. 2, 1917; s. Lewis Floyd and Blanche Irene (Conner) W.; B.S., U. Mich., 1938; postgrad. Ohio Wesleyan U., 1938-41; m. Catherine Crosby, July 19, 1941; 1 son, Tod C. With 3M Co., 1948-52, Oliver Iron and Steel Co., 1952-56; mktg. mgr., then mgr. Sturtevant div. Westinghouse Elec. Corp., 1956-62; pvt. cons., 1962-65; with Joy Mfg. Co., Pitts., 1965—, sr. v.p., 1967, pres., chief exec. officer, 1967-76, chmn. bd., chief exec. officer, 1976—; dir. Mellon Bank, N.A., Mellon Nat. Corp., POGO Producing Co., Phoenix Steel Co., H.H. Robertson Co., Wean-United, Inc., Harris Corp. Bd. dirs. Minority Purchasing Council; trustee Sch. Engring., U. Pitts., Outward Bound Schs. Served as officer AUS, 1942-46. Mem. Machinery and Allied Products Inst., Am. Inst. Mining Engrs., Am. Mining Congress. Republican. Episcopalian. Clubs: Duquesne, Allegheny Country, Pine Tree Golf, Laurel Valley Golf, John's Island, Pine Valley Golf, Rolling Rock. Home: Pink House Rd Sewickley PA 15143 Office: 1200 Oliver Bldg Pittsburgh PA 15222

WILCOCK, JOHN, author, journalist; b. Eng. Former staff writer Daily Mirror, London, Eng.; then with UPI, Can.; a founder, organizer underground newspapers The Village Voice, N.Y.C., The East Village Other, N.Y.C., Other Scenes, N.Y.C.; also travel writer formerly with N.Y. Times Travel Sect.; now author numerous $5-a-day guidebooks to countries throughout world; columnist High Times mag. Author: The Autobiography and Sex Life of Andy Warhol, 1971; (with Elizabeth Pepper) The Witch's Almanac, 1970-78; An Occult Guide to South America, 1976; Magical, Mystical Sites, 1977; Traveling in Venezuela, 1979. Address: BCM-Nomad London WC1V England also Box 4137 Grand Central PO New York NY 10017

WILCOX, ARTHUR MANIGAULT, newspaper editor; b. Phila., May 2, 1922; s. John Walter and Caroline (Manigault) W.; B.S., Ga. Inst. Tech., 1943; m. Katherine Moore McMurray, Nov. 25, 1944; children—Margaret Moore, Arthur Manigault, Priscilla McMurray, Robert Manigault. Reporter, Charleston (S.C.) Eve. Post, 1946-52, city editor, 1952-57, editor, 1968-74; asst. editor Charleston News and Courier, 1957-68, editor, 1974—; sec. Evening Post Pub. Co. Curator S.C. Hist. Soc., 1957-60; pres. trustees Charleston Museum, 1971—. Served to lt. (j.g.) USN, 1943-46; rear adm. Res. Mem. Am. Soc. Newspaper Editors, Nat. Conf. Editorial Writers, St. Cecilia Soc., Soc. Colonial Wars, Carolina Art Assn., U.S. Naval Inst., Audubon Soc., Nat. Trust. Mem. P.E. Ch. (vestry 1954-59, 62-66, 68-72, 79—). Clubs: Rotary, Charleston. Carolina Yacht, Tennis (Charleston). Home: 26 St Augustine Dr Charleston SC 29407 Office: 134 Columbus St Charleston SC 29402

WILCOX, CALVIN HAYDEN, educator; b. Cicero, N.Y., Jan. 29, 1924; s. Calvin and Vara (Place) W.; student Syracuse U., 1947-48; A.B. magna cum laude, Harvard, 1951, A.M., 1952, Ph.D., 1955; m. Frances I. Rosekrans, May 29, 1947; children—Annette Faye, Victor Hayden, Christopher Grant. Mem. faculty Cal. Inst. Tech., Pasadena, 1955-61, asst. prof. math., 1957-60, asso. prof., 1960-61; prof. U. Wis.-Madison, 1961-66; prof., head dept. U. Ariz., Tucson, 1966-69; prof. U. Denver, 1969-70, U. Utah, Salt Lake City, 1971—; vis. prof. U. Geneva (Switzerland), 1970-71, U. Liege (Belgium), 1973, U. Stuttgart (West Germany), 1974, 76-77, Kyoto (Japan) U., 1975. Served with AUS, 1945-47. NSF predoctoral fellow, 1952-53; Sr. U.S. Scientist award Alexander von Humboldt Found., W. Ger., 1976-77. Mem. Am. Math. Soc., Math. Assn. Am. Author: Lectures on Scattering Theory for the d'Alembert Wave Equation in Exterior Domains, 1975. Editor: Asymptotic Solutions of Differential Equations and Their Applications, 1964; Perturbation Theory and its Application in Quantum Mechanics, 1966. Office: Dept Math Univ Utah Salt Lake City UT 84112

WILCOX, CAROL ANN, soprano; b. Antioch, Calif., Mar. 9, 1945; d. Frank L. and Bernice G. (Long) W.; B.A., U. Kans., 1969; postgrad. Manhattan Sch. Music, 1969-70; m. Robert Owen Jones, Oct. 5, 1974. Katherine Long scholar Met. Opera, N.Y.C., 1969-70, debut, 1970, with Met. Opera, 1970-72; appeared with numerous U.S. and Can. opera cos., symphonies, including: Berlin Orch. at Kennedy Center for Performing Arts and U.S. Tour, 1973, Houston Grand Opera, 1973, Kansas City Lyric Theatre, 1973-79, Balt. Symphony, 1974, Pitts. Opera, 1974, 75, 77, Portland (Oreg.) Opera, 1975, Can. Opera, 1975, 79, Phila. Opera, 1977, Caracas (Venezuela) Opera, 1977, Greater Miami Opera Guild, 1978, New Orleans Opera, 1978, Santa Fe Opera, 1980; performed in 2 Am. premiers, 2 world premiers; rec. artist, RCA, CRI; recitalist, U.S., 1978-79; affiliate artist Sears & Roebuck and Readers Digest, 1975, 77. Carol Wilcox Day proclaimed in Kansas City, Kans., Feb. 17, 1978. Mem. Am. Guild Mus. Artists, Actors Equity, Can. Equity. Home: New York NY

WILCOX, ELMER DALE, paper co. exec.; b. Glendive, Mont., June 5, 1918; s. Luther Fuller and Alice Drucilla (Bryan) W.; m. Virginia Sue Bailiss, Feb. 11, 1942; children—Gregory Bailiss, Kerry Jane. Salesman Blake, Moffitt & Towne, Spokane, Wash., 1946-57; div. mgr., San Bernardino, Calif., 1957-64, Seattle, 1964-68, pres. Blake, Moffitt & Towne div. Saxon Industries, San Francisco, 1968-74, group v.p., Saxon Industries, Inc., N.Y.C., 1974—. Served with AUS, 1942-46, USAAF, 1951-53. Mem. Nat. Paper Trade Assn. Clubs: Wykagyl Country, N.Y. Athletic Paper, Masons. Home: 200 E 57th St Apt #11D New York NY 10022 Office: 1230 Ave of the Americas New York NY 10020

WILCOX, FRANCIS JOHN, lawyer; b. Eau Claire, Wis., June 28, 1908; s. Roy Porter and Maria Louisa (de Freyre y Santander) W.; B.A., Yale, 1930; LL.B. (editor Law Rev.), U. Wis., 1932; m. Katharine McGiveran, Sept. 1, 1933; children—John F., Roy S., Christopher J., Katharine C. Admitted to Wis. bar, 1932, since practiced in Eau Claire; mem. firm Wilcox and Wilcox, 1932—; lectr. extension div. U. Wis., 1958. Chmn. Wis. Jud. Council, 1956-62. Chmn. appeal bd. SSS Western Dist. Wis., 1955-72; chmn. adv. bd. Sacred Heart Hosp., Eau Claire, 1960-72; sec. bd. Eau Claire Pub. Library, 1967-72; bd. dirs., past chmn. Am. Cancer Soc., also bd. dirs. Wis. div.; exec. com., council Internat. Union Against Cancer, 1970-78. Decorated knight Saint Gregory (papal honor). Mem. Am. Coll. Trial Lawyers, Am. Judicature Soc., Wis. State Bar (pres. 1963-64), Am., Wis. bar. assns., Am. Law Inst. K.C. Home: 132 Marston Ave Eau Claire WI 54701 Office: 131 S Barstow St Eau Claire WI 54701

WILCOX, FRANCIS ORLANDO, educator, govt. ofcl.; b. Columbus Junction, Iowa, Apr. 9, 1908; s. Francis Oliver and Verna (Gray) W.; A.B., U. Iowa, 1930, A.M., 1931, Ph.D., 1933; Dr. ès sciences politiques, U. Geneva, 1935; grad. Inst. Internat. Studies, Geneva (fellow 1934-35), 1933-35; fellow Hague Acad. Internat. Law, 1937; LL.D., U. Louisville, 1960, Hamline U., 1960, Dakota Wesleyan U., 1961; Litt.D., Simpson Coll., 1964; m. Genevieve C. Byrnes, July 23, 1933 (dec. Aug. 1946); 1 dau., Carol Lenore; m. 2d, Virginia Summerlin Sullivan, Aug. 8, 1968; 1 son, Francis Oliver Wilcox. Teaching asst. polit. sci. U. Iowa, 1931-33; fellow Carnegie Endowment Internat. Peace, 1933-34; asst. prof. polit. sci. U. Louisville, 1935-37, asso. prof., 1937-39, chmn. div. social scis.,

1939-42; vis. prof. U. Mich., summer 1941; fellow Gen. Edn. Bd., U. Chgo., 1940; cons. Am. Council Edn., 1941-43; with Office Coordinator Inter-Am. Affairs, Washington, 1942, asso. chief Div. Inter-Am. Activities in U.S.; chief program services sect. Office Civilian Def., 1943; internat. orgn. analyst Bur. of Budget, 1943-44; head internat. relations analyst Library of Congress, 1945-47; chief of staff U.S. Senate Fgn. Relations Com., 1947-55; asst. sec. state, 1955-61; dean Sch. Advanced Internat. Studies, Johns Hopkins, 1961-73; exec. dir. Commn. on Orgn. of Govt. for Conduct of Fgn. Policy, 1973-75; dir.-gen. Atlantic Council of U.S., 1975—; lectr. internat. orgn. George Washington U., 1945-46; lectr. internat. orgn. and fgn. relations Sch. Advanced Internat. Studies, Washington, 1946-52. Dir. Dreyfus Corp. Mem. U.S. del. to UN Conf., San Francisco, 1945, 1st Gen. Assembly UN, London, 1946, 3d Gen. Assembly, Paris, 1948, Japanese Peace Conf., San Francisco, 1951, and subsequent annual meetings of UN Gen. Assembly; U.S. del. World Health Assembly, Geneva, 1956, Mpls., 1958; U.S. del. ILO Conf., Geneva, 1957, 58; U.S. del. 15th UN General Assembly, 1960; mem. President's Commn. on UN, 1971—. Served as 2d lt., O.R.C., 1930-35; lt. (j.g.) USNR, 1944-45. Mem. Am. Soc. Internat. Law (exec. com. 1946-49, 51-54), Am. Polit. Sci. Assn. (exec. council 1948-50; bd. editors Am. Polit. Sci. Rev. 1952-56; v.p. 1957-58; chmn. com. undergrad. instrn. 1946-48, pres. Washington br. 1946-47), Atlantic Council (bd. dirs.), Council Fgn. Relations, Phi Beta Kappa, Phi Kappa Phi, Omicron Delta Kappa, Sigma Chi. Author or co-author books relating to field, also U.S. govt. reports, articles in tech. jours. Home: 2811 McGill Terr NW Washington DC 20008 Office: 1616 H St NW Washington DC 20006

WILCOX, GEORGE LATIMER, elec. mfg. exec.; b. N.Y.C., Jan. 20, 1915; s. Thomas and Louise (Latimer) W.; B.E.E., Poly. Inst. Bklyn., 1939; m. Edith Leah Smallshaw, Sept. 2, 1939; children—Leslie, Holly, George. Elec. engr. Consol. Edison Co., 1930-42; design engr. Westinghouse Electric & Mfg. Co., 1942-43; gen. mgr. Windsor Mfg. & Repair Cor., 1946-50, Westinghouse Internat. Devel. Co., 1950-51; asst. mgr. central sta. dept. Westinghouse Elec. Internat. Co., 1943-46, successively mgr. projects div., gen. sales mgr., v.p. sales, 1951-53, v.p. ops., dir., 1953-56; pres. Westinghouse Can. Ltd., 1956-61; v.p., asst. to pres. Westinghouse Electric Corp., 1961, v.p., dep. exec. v.p., 1962, exec. v.p., 1963-69, vice chmn. corp. affairs, 1969-75, dir.-officer, 1975—; dir. Kaiser Resources Ltd., Kaiser Steel Corp., Pitts. Nat. Corp., Pitts. Nat. Bank. Pres., chmn. Pa. Economy League; bd. dirs. Poly. Inst. N.Y.; trustee Com. for Econ. Devel. Clubs: Duquesne (Pitts.); University (N.Y.C.); Rolling Rock, Laurel Valley (Ligonier, Pa.). Home: Weavers Mill Rd Rector PA 15677 Office: Westinghouse Bldg Gateway Center Pittsburgh PA 15222

WILCOX, HAROLD EDWIN, emeritus educator; b. Sidney, Ohio, June 3, 1913; s. Grover Cleveland and Maude B. (Yantis) W.; B.A., Ohio Wesleyan U., 1934; M.S., Ohio State U., 1937, Ph.D., 1939, postgrad., 1971, 75; postgrad. U. Calif. at Berkeley, 1953-54, Calif. Inst. Tech., 1959-60, 66-67, Stanford U., 1976; m. Ethel Mae Hershey, July 19, 1941; children—Cynthia Jane (Mrs. Denny F. Mince), Carol Ann (Mrs. Larry D. Hare). High sch. tchr., Delaware County, Ohio, 1934-35; chemist Gummed Products Co., Troy, Ohio, 1935-36; mem. faculty Howard Coll., Birmingham, Ala., 1939-46; prof. chemistry Birmingham-So. Coll., 1946-62, head chemistry dept., 1947-62; prof. chemistry Ohio Wesleyan U., Delaware, 1962-78, prof. emeritus, 1978—, acting chmn., 1965-66; vis. prof. Ind. U., Bloomington, 1969; lectr. Capital U., Columbus, Ohio, 1979; cons. chemistry Norwood Clinic, Birmingham, 1952-60, Med. Coll. Ala., 1961-62, Jadavpur U., Calcutta, India, 1966, Barnaras Hindu U., Varanasi, India, 1967. Ford Found. grantee, 1953-54, NSF sci. faculty fellow, 1959-60. Fellow AAAS, Ohio Acad. Sci.; mem. Am. Chem. Soc. (chmn. grad. record exam. com. advanced chemistry test, 1968-72), Am. Assn. Clin. Chemists, Phi Beta Kappa, Sigma Xi, Omicron Delta Kappa, Phi Lambda Upsilon, Sigma Pi Sigma, Sigma Alpha Epsilon. Methodist. Kiwanian. Home: 50 Hillside Dr Delaware OH 43015

WILCOX, HARRY HAMMOND, med. educator; b. Canton, Ohio, May 31, 1918; s. Harry Hammond and Hattie Estelle (Richner) W.; B.S., U. Mich., 1939, M.S., 1940, Ph.D., 1948; m. D. June Freed. June 21, 1941; children—Joyce L. Wilcox Graff, Margaret J. (Mrs. Grayson S. Smith), James Hammond. Asso. prof. biology Morningside Coll., Sioux City, Iowa, 1947-48; asso. in anatomy U. Pa., 1948-52; mem. faculty U. Tenn. Center for Health Scis., 1952—, Goodman prof. anatomy, 1966—. Served with AUS, 1945-46. Mem. Am. Assn. Anatomists, Am. Soc. Zoologists, Am. Acad. Neurology, Biol. Stain Commn., A.A.A.S., Sigma Xi. Asso. editor Anat. Record, 1968—. Home: 1031 Marcia Rd Memphis TN 38117 Office: Dept Anatomy U Tenn Center for Health Scis 800 Madison Ave Memphis TN 38163

WILCOX, HARRY WILBUR, JR., indsl. equipment mfg. exec.; b. Phila., Feb. 13, 1925; s. Harry Wilbur and Justine Elizabeth (Doolittle) W.; B.S., Yale, 1949; m. Colleen Ann Cerra, Apr. 6, 1946; children—Justine (Mrs. Jon J. Hamilton), Harry Wilbur III. With Gen. Electric Co., N.Y.C., 1949-50; mfg. supt. Sylvania Electric Products, 1951-67; v.p., gen. mgr. Granger Assos., electronics, Palo Alto, Calif., 1967-70; gen. mgr. ITT-Cannon Electric Co., Phoenix, 1970-72; pres. Hills McCanna Co., Carpentersville, Ill., 1972-75; group v.p. IU Internat. Corp., 1975-78; exec. v.p. ITT-Grinnell, 1978—. Mem. adv. com. Town of Sherborn, Mass., 1967. Served with U.S. Army, 1943-46. Decorated Bronze star. Patentee in electroluminescence. Office: ITT-Grinnell 260 W Exchange St Providence RI 02901

WILCOX, HARVEY JOHN, govt. ofcl., lawyer; b. Elyria, O., Nov. 1, 1937; s. Hubbard Clyde and Sylvia (Wahter) W.; B.A. cum laude, Amherst Coll., 1959; LL.B., Yale U., 1962; m. Leslie Louise Coleman, Apr. 11, 1970. Admitted to Ohio bar, 1962, since practiced in Elyria; mem. firm Wilcox & Wilcox, 1962-78; with office gen. counsel Dept. Navy, Washington, 1966—, asst. to gen. counsel, 1969-72, counsel Naval Air Systems Command, 1972-76, dep. gen. counsel, 1976—; guest lectr. U.S. Army Logistics Mgmt. Center; mem. Navy contract adjustment bd., 1968-72. Bd. dirs. Navy Fed. Credit Union, 1974-77, sec.-treas., 1974-75, 2d v.p., 1975-77. Served to lt. USNR, 1963-66. Mem. Ohio Bar Assn., Nat. Trust Hist. Preservation. Home: 3800 N 23d St Arlington VA 22207 Office: Office Gen Counsel Dept Navy Washington DC 20360

WILCOX, HOWARD ALBERT, scientist; b. Mpls., Nov. 9, 1920; s. Hugh Brown and Jean (McGilvra) W.; B.A. in Physics magna cum laude, U. Minn., 1943; student Harvard, 1943- 44; M.A., U. Chgo., 1948, Ph.D. in Physics, 1948; m. Evelyn Agnes Johnson, June 15, 1943; children—Carol M., Bruce M., Brian H. Tchr. physics Harvard and Radcliffe Coll., 1943-44; jr. scientist Los Alamos Sci. Lab., 1944-46; research asst. Inst. Nuclear Studies, U. Chgo., 1946-48; instr., then asst. prof. physics, mem. research staff Radiation Lab., U. Calif. at Berkeley, 1948-50; project engr. Sidewinder guided missile, also head missile div. Aviation Ordnance Dept., Naval Ordnance Test Sta., China Lake, Calif., 1950-55, head weapons devel. dept., 1955-57, head research dept., asst. tech. dir. for research, 1957-59; dep. dir. def. research and engring. Office Sec. Def., 1959-60; dir. research and engring., def. systems div. Gen. Motors Corp., 1960-62, dir. research and engring. Def. Research Labs., 1962-66; tech. dir. advanced power systems Research Labs., Gen. Motors Corp., 1966-67; ind. cons., 1967—; prin. scientist Minicars, Inc., 1967-74, v.p., sec., dir., 1969-74; cons. Naval Weapons Center, China Lake, Calif., 1971-74; mgr. ocean food and energy farm project Naval Undersea Center, San Diego, 1974-77; staff scientist Naval Ocean Systems Center, San Diego, 1974-77. Recipient Outstanding Tech. Achievement award IEEE, 1977. Fellow Am. Phys. Soc.; mem. ACLU, AAAS. Home: 882 Golden Park Ave San Diego CA 92106 Office: Code 5304 Naval Ocean Systems Center San Diego CA 92152

WILCOX, JAMES HENRY, univ. dean; b. Bolton, Eng., July 10, 1916; s. John and Henrietta (Vickers) W.; B.S., U. Wis., 1938; M.Mus., Northwestern U., 1941, Eastman Sch. Music, 1953; Ph.D., Fla. State U., 1956; student Pottag, 1937-41, Yegudkin, 1949-53, Dohnanyi, 1954-56; m. Marie Agnes Wiza, Sept. 3, 1940; children—Joan (Mrs. Michael Osborne), Patricia, James Peter, John Christopher, Laurie Ann. Tchr., Hartland (Wis.) High Sch., Carroll Coll., Milw. Pub. Schs., 1938-40; mem. faculty Southeastern La. U., 1946-54, 56—, dir. bands and brass, 1946-54, prof. music theory, 1956-64, head dept. music, 1964-70, dean Coll. Arts and Humanities, 1970—; prin. horn Baton Rouge Symphony, 1946-54, 57-64; teaching asst. Fla. State U., 1954-56; adjudicator music, editor music coll. div. Scott, Foresman Co., Glenview, Ill., 1965-72. Mem. exec. bd. La. Council Music and Performing Arts; bd. dirs. Baton Rouge Symphony Orch. Served with AUS, 1941-46. Mem. Music Educators Nat. Conf., Music Tchrs. Nat. Assn., La. Tchrs. Assn., La. Music Educators Assn. (chmn. coll. div. 1964-66). Methodist (choir dir. 1946-66, mem. adminstrv. bd. 1950—). Publs. for Horn, Boosey-Hawkes, Belwin, Band, G. Schirmer, Programmed Fundamentals of Music Theory. Research in programmed music theory, founder Cantrell Music Press, 1974. Home: 105 College Dr Hammond LA 70401

WILCOX, LARRY DEE, actor; b. San Diego, Aug. 8, 1947; s. John C. and Marion G. Wilcox; student U. Wyo., 1965, Calif. State U., Northridge, 1970-74; m. Mar. 29, 1969 (div.); children—Derek Scott, Heidi Kirsten. Formerly rancher, bartender, laborer, telegrapher; actor on TV series Lassie, 1970-72, Chips, 1977—; dir. TV shows including Ride the Whirlwind, 1979, Tow Truck Lady, 1980. Nat. celebrity chmn. Vets. No Greater Love; nat. safety chmn. Am. Bicycle Assn. Served to sgt. USMC, 1967-70; Vietnam. Decorated Navy Commendation medal; named hon. mem. Calif. Hwy. Patrol, 1979. Mem. Screen Actors Guild, Writers Guild Am., Dirs. Guild Am. Republican. Episcopalian. Clubs: Am. Legion, Demolay. Office: 2040 Ave of Stars 4th Floor Century City Los Angeles CA 90067

WILCOX, MARION WALTER, educator, engr.; b. Broken Arrow, Okla., Aug. 17, 1922; s. Mac and Ollie Mae (Stills) W.; B.S. in Civil Engring., U. Notre Dame, 1948, Sc.D., 1961; M.S. in Civil Engring., Ill. Inst. Tech., 1955; m. Alice Kathryn Lynch, Sept. 11, 1948; children—Barbara Joan, Walter Mark, Sara Kathleen. Asst. stress analyst McDonnell Aircraft Corp., St. Louis, 1948-49; asso. stress engr. Emerson Electric Co., St. Louis, 1949-50; stress analyst Convair, Ft. Worth, 1950-51; asso. research engr. Armour Research Found., Chgo., 1951-55; tech. supr. Bendix Aviation, South Bend, Ind., 1955-58; sr. engr. Convair, Fort Worth, 1958-61; asso. prof. U. Ariz., Tucson, 1961-62; asso. prof. aero. and mech. engring. So. Methodist U., Dallas, 1962-66, prof. solid mechanics, 1966—; exec. v.p. Great Southwest Engring. Cons., Inc., Dallas, 1971—. Served with USN, 1941-46. Registered profl. engr., Tex., Mo. Asso. fellow Am. Inst. Aeronautics and Astronautics; mem. Am. Soc. Engring. Edn., Am. Acad. Mechanics, Am. Soc. Engring. Sci., Tex. Soc. Profl. Engrs., Sigma Xi, Sigma Tau, Club: Statesman (Dallas). Home: 3163 Whirlaway Dallas TX 75229

WILCOX, ROBERT FRASER, univ. dean; b. Ningpo, China, Jan. 15, 1916 (parents Am. citizens); s. Floyd Cleveland and Emily (Carder) W.; B.A., Stanford U., 1937, M.A., 1941, Ph.D., 1950; M.A., Columbia U., 1943; m. Theresa Bardwell, Nov. 25, 1937; children—Kathleen Ann, Robert Fraser. Bur. mgr. United Press, Fresno, Calif., 1937-39; asst. radio and news editor OWI, 1942; sr. research asst. Haynes Found., Los Angeles, 1947-50; mem. faculty San Diego State U., 1950-71, prof. polit. sci., 1956-71, chmn. dept., 1959-63, coordinator pub. adminstrn., 1953-57, dir. pub. adminstrn., 1964-68, dir. Sch. Pub. Adminstrn. and Urban Studies, 1968-71; head Office Pub. Understanding of Sci., NSF, 1971-72; dean Grad. Sch. Pub. Affairs, U. Colo., 1972—; vis. prof. polit. sci. Mich. State U., summer 1953; vis. prof. pub. adminstrn. Thammasat U., Bangkok, Thailand, 1957-58; cons. Fed. Aviation Agy., 1970-71, Office of Pub. Understanding Sci., 1972-75, Denver Urban Obs., 1972-74. Spl. cons. on edn. and tng. Calif. Council Criminal Justice; mem. Calif. Pub. Service Edn. and Tng. Adv. Council, 1968-72; adv. com. Calif. Commn. on Peace Officer Standards and Tng., 1969-72; chmn. charter rev. com. City San Diego, 1968-69. Mem. Democratic County Central Com., 1962-64. Served to lt. (s.g.) USNR, 1942-46. Mem. Am. Soc. Pub. Adminstrn. (nat. council 1961-64, 71-74, chpt. pres. 1974-75), Nat. Acad. Pub. Adminstrn., Nat. Assn. Schs. Pub. Affairs and Adminstrn. (pres. 1970-71), Am., Western, So. Calif. (v.p. 1959-60) polit. sci. assns., Western Govtl. Research Assn. (exec. bd.). Club: Cosmos. Author: Criminal Justice Training by Television: A California Model, 1971; co-author: Metropolitan Los Angeles: Its Governments, 1950; Law Enforcement in Los Angeles, 1952; Highways in Los Angeles, 1953. Bd. editors Western Polit. Quar. Author articles, rev. in field. Home: 73 Wild Horse Circle Boulder CO 80302

WILCOX, THOMAS ROBERT, comml. banker; b. N.Y.C., Aug. 23, 1916; s. Thomas and Louisa (Latimer) W.; student N.Y.U., 1934-38; B.A., Princeton, 1940; m. Jane Collette, Mar. 28, 1943; children—Thomas R., Kirby C., Andrew McK. With First Nat. City Bank, 1934-71, beginning as page, successively asst. cashier, asst. v.p., v.p. charge domestic branches, 1954-57, exec. v.p., 1957-67, vice chmn., 1967-71; vice chmn., dir. Blyth Eastman Dillon & Co., Inc., 1971-73; pres. Crocker Nat. Bank, San Francisco, 1974, chmn., chief exec. officer, 1974—; dir. Colgate-Palmolive Co., Hilton Hotels Corp., Internat. Exec. Service Corps.; trustee Mut. Life Ins. Co. N.Y. Trustee Marine Hist. Assn., Mystic, Conn.; mem. Pan. Am. Internat. Adv. Bd.; mem. adv. council Grad. Sch. Bus., Stanford U.; gov. Performing Arts Council, Los Angeles Music Center. Mem. Conf. Bd., Nat. Golf Links. Clubs: University, Links (N.Y.C.); Bohemian, San Francisco Golf, Pacific Union; Los Angeles Country, Calif. (Los Angeles). Office: One Montgomery St San Francisco CA 94104

WILCOX, VIVIAN MAURINE, fashion editor; b. Aurora, Ont., Can.; d. James Dudley and Vivian (Gardner) W.; B.A., U. Toronto, 1940. Fashion editor Mayfair mag. Maclean-Hunter, Ltd., Toronto, 1943-55, fashion editor Chatelaine mag., 1956-70, Style mag., 1955—. Recipient Woman of Year award Fashion/Can., 1976. Mem. Fashion Group, Inc. Home: 4 Deer Park Crescent Toronto ON M4V 2C3 Canada Office: 481 University Ave Toronto ON M5W 1A7 Canada

WILCOX, WILLIAM HARRY, govt. ofcl.; b. Phila., June 9, 1915; s. Charles Leigh and Myrtle (Kaiser) W.; B.A., U. Conn., 1942; M.P.A., Wayne U., 1947; m. Madeleine Watt, Oct. 5, 1942; children—Gregory, Robin. Govt. researcher, Hartford, Conn., St. Louis, Phila., exec. dir. Civic and Community Devel. Agy., Phila.; sec. community affairs Commonwealth of Pa.; energy cons. HUD, Washington; now adminstr. Fed. Disaster Assistance Adminstrn., Washington; chmn. Pa. Housing Fin. Agy. Mem. N.J. Home Rule Charter Commn., Morristown. Served with USAAF. Decorated D.F.C., Air medal. Democrat. Clubs: Appalachian Mountain, Potomac Appalachian Trial. Home: 9313 Millbranch Dr Fairfax VA 22031 Office: 451 7th St SW Washington DC 20410

WILD, NELSON HOPKINS, lawyer; b. Milw., July 16, 1933; s. Henry Goetseels and Virginia Douglas (Weller) W.; A.B., Princeton U., 1955; LL.B., U. Wis., 1961; m. Joan Ruth Miles, Apr. 12, 1969; children—Mark, Eric. Research asso. Wis. Legis. Council, Madison, 1955-56; admitted to Wis. bar, 1962, Calif. bar, 1967; asso. firm Whyte, Hirschboeck, Minahan, Harding & Harland, Milw., 1961-67, Thelen, Marin, Johnson & Bridges, San Francisco, 1967-70; individual practice law, San Francisco, 1970—. Served with USAF, 1956-58. Bd. dirs. Neighborhood Legal Assistance Found., San Francisco, 1974—, chmn. bd., 1978—. Mem. Am., Calif., San Francisco bar assns. Club: Lawyers of San Francisco (gov. 1975—). Contbr. articles to legal jours. Office: 1929 Union St San Francisco CA 94123

WILD, PETER, educator, poet; b. Northampton, Mass., Apr. 25, 1940; s. Arnold Arthur and Edith Amelia (Mesh) W.; B.A., U. Ariz., 1962, M.A., 1967; M.F.A., U. Calif., Irvine, 1969. Instr. English, U. Ariz., Tuscon, 1971-72, asso. prof., 1972—. Co-chmn. wilderness com. Arizonans for Quality Environment. Author: Cochise, 1973; The Cloning, 1974; Chihuahua, 1976; Pioneer Conservationists of Western America, 1979.

WILD, WILLIAM CHARLES, JR., fgn. service officer; b. Chgo., Sept. 2, 1911; s. William Charles and Julia (Sigmund) W.; m. Marie Angele Ouranis, Apr. 5, 1947; children—William Glen, Judith Anne. Supt. traffic operations Nat. Carloading Corp., C. & N.W. Ry., 1934-44; dir. traffic, chief transp. officer UNRRA, Greece, 1944-48; shipping specialist Dept. of State, Greece, 1948; transp. adviser Greek Govt., 1948-54; 54; chief transp. and commerce div. ICA, Egypt, 1954-56; asst. dir. ICA, East Pakistan, 1956-57; dep. dir. ICA, Pakistan, 1956-59; regional exec. officer Africa and Europe, ICA, Washington, 1959-60; dir. U.S. Operations Mission to Sudan, 1960-61, counselor of embassy for internat. coop., 1961; rep. U.S. AID, Nairobi, Kenya, E. Africa, 1961-63; dir. AID mission to Kenya, 1963-66; regional dir. AID, Vietnam, 1966-70; dir. AID, Liberia, 1970-74; dir. Office of Mgmt. Planning, AID, 1974—. Decorated Giay Ban Khen gold medal, Y-Te-Boi-Tinh gold medal, Kinh-Te Boi-Tinh gold medal (Republic Vietnam); knight comdr. Order Phoenix, 1st class gold medal for Marines (Greece); recipient Distinguished Career Service award AID. Clubs: Mount Kenya Safari, Mnarni Fishing, United Kenya; Propeller; Chicago Transportation; Glyfada Golf; Washington Touchdown. Home: 29 Ipsilantou St Athens Greece Office: Am Embassy APO New York City NY 09253

WILDE, BERTRAM MERBACH, investment banker; b. Phila., Dec. 28, 1898; s. James Taylor and Anna (Pressler) W.; student pub. schs., Pa.; LL.D. (hon.) Gettysburg Coll., 1967; m. Florence Louise Deal, Oct. 5, 1940; 1 dau., Louise P. With Janney Montgomery Scott, Inc., and predecessors, Phila., 1915—, successively office boy, cashier, asst. treas., sec. and treas., v.p., pres., 1943-69, chmn. bd. dirs., 1969—. Past pres. bd. common investing fund Lutheran Ch. Am.; bd. mgrs. Am. Sunday Sch. Union; past bd. govs. Assn. Stock Exchange Firms. Mem. Investment Bankers Assn. Am. (past bd. govs.). Republican. Clubs: Merion Cricket; Union League, Bond (past pres.), Urban (Phila.); Seaview Country (Absecon, N.J.); Rolling Green Golf (Springfield, Pa.); Little Egg Harbor Yacht (Beach Haven, N.J.); Ocean Reef (Key Largo, Fla.); Gulph Mills Golf. Home: 941 Rock Creek Rd Bryn Mawr PA 19010 Office: 5 Penn Center Philadelphia PA 19103

WILDE, CORNEL, actor, producer, director; b. N.Y.C., Oct. 13, 1918; s. Louis Bela and Renee (Vid) W.; student Columbia, 1934-35; B.S., City Coll. N.Y., 1937; student of Lee Strasberg, Leo Bulgakov, Michael Chekhov; m. Patricia Knight, Sept. 3, 1938 (marriage dissolved Sept. 1951); 1 dau.; m. 2d, Jean Wallace, Sept. 4, 1951; 1 son. Theatrical appearances include Moon Over Mulberry Street, Love is Not so Simple, Daughters of Atreus, Having Wonderful Time, Romeo and Juliet; motion pictures include High Sierra, Wintertime, A Song to Remember, The Perfect Snob, A Thousand and One Nights, Leave Her to Heaven, Bandit of Sherwood Forest, Centennial Summer, Forever Amber, The Home Stretch, It Had to be You, Walls of Jerico, Roadhouse, Four Days Leave, Two Flags West, Greatest Show on Earth, At Swords Point, Saadia, Passion, Woman's World, Big Combo, Scarlet Coat, Hot Blood, Star of India, Beyond Mombasa, Omar Khayyam, Edge of Eternity, Constantine the Great, Behind the Iron Mask; actor, producer, dir. Storm Fear, Devil's Hairpin, Maracaibo, The Sword of Lancelot (corride award 1963), The Naked Prey, Beach Red, The Fifth Musketeer, The Norseman; producer, dir., co-screenwriter No Blade of Grass; producer, dir., writer, actor Sharks' Treasure. Recipient Acad. award nomination for best actor in A Song To Remember, 1945, James K. Hackett award, 1974; award Bijou Film Soc., 1975. Address: care Jess Morgan U Co Inc 6300 Wilshire Blvd Los Angeles CA 90048. *I realized long ago that I could not depend on luck to bring me success, and accordingly, I worked hard, extra hard, to improve my chances by increasing my abilities and my experience. It was my goal to accomplish, in my life, something of value, and to do it with self-respect and integrity. I had my share of tough times, and thus I learned that those who succeed owe sympathy and generosity to the less fortunate.*

WILDE, DANIEL UNDERWOOD, educator; b. Wilmington, Ohio, Dec. 27, 1937; s. Arthur John and Ruby Dale (Underwood) W.; B.S. in Elec. Engring., U. Ill., 1960; M.S., M.I.T., 1962, Ph.D., 1966. Research instr. medicine Boston U. Med. Sch., 1964-66; asst. prof. info. adminstrn. U. Conn., 1966-69, asso. prof., 1970-75, prof., 1976—; asso. dir. New Eng. Research Application Center, Storrs, Conn., 1966-72, dir., 1973—; trustee Engring. Index, Inc.; cons. Am. Soc. Metals, 1973—. Served with USAF. Recipient NASA Public Service award, 1975. Mem. Am. Soc. Info. Sci., Assn. Computing Machinery, IEEE, Assn. Info. and Dissemination Centers (sec.-treas. 1976-79, pres. 1979—). Author: Introduction to Computing: Problem Solving, Algorithms and Data Structures, 1973; contbr. articles to profl. jours. Home: 188 Cedar Swamp Rd Storrs CT 06268 Office: NERAC Mansfield Profl Park Storrs CT 06268

WILDE, EDWIN FREDERICK, coll. dean; b. Lombard, Ill., Jan. 14, 1931; s. Edwin Frederick and Carrie Belle (Hammond) W.; B.S., Ill. State U., 1952, M.S., 1953; M.A., U. Ill., 1955, Ph.D., 1959; postgrad. U. Wis., part time, 1955-58, Stanford U., 1964-65; m. Connie Mae Rawlings, Aug. 23, 1952; children—Brad Alan, Bruce Ramon, Elizabeth Lynn. With Beloit (Wis.) Coll., 1955-76, prof. math., dean faculty, 1969-71, v.p. for planning, 1971-75; dean Roger Williams Coll., Bristol, R.I., 1976-80; provost, dean of faculty U. Tampa (Fla.), 1980—; cons. AID insts., India, 1964, Insts. Internat. Edn., East Pakistan, 1969. NSF Sr. Sci. Faculty fellow, 1964-65. Mem. Math. Assn. Am. (bd. govs. 1968-69, 72-75), Sigma Xi. Home: 37 Ferreira Terr Portsmouth RI 02871 Office: U Tampa Tampa FL

WILDE, JOHN, painter, educator; b. Milw., Dec. 12, 1919; s. Emil F. and Mathilda (Lotz) W.; B.S., U. Wis., 1942, M.S., 1948; m. Helen Ashman, July 1943 (dec. Dec. 1966); children—Jonathan, Phoebe; m. 2d, Shirley Miller, 1969. Mem. faculty U. Wis., 1948—, prof. art,

1960—, chmn. dept. art and art edn., 1960-62, Alfred Sessler Distinguished prof. art, 1969—; works exhibited Met. Mus. Art, Mus. Modern Art, Whitney Mus. Am. Art, Corcoran Mus. Art, others; rep. permanent collections Pa. Acad. Art, Detroit Inst. Fine Art, Worcester Art Mus., Wadsworth Atheneum, Whitney Mus. Am. Art, Carnegie Inst., Nat. Collection Art, Smithsonian Instn., Nat. Acad. Design, Butler Inst. Am. Art, others; also extensive exhbns. abroad. Recipient numerous awards for paintings and drawings, regional and nat. exhbns. Home: Evansville WI 53536 Office: 6221 Humanities Bldg Univ Wisconsin Madison WI 53706

WILDE, PATRICIA, ballerina; b. Ottawa, Can., July 16, 1928; d. John Herbert and Eileen Lucy (Simpson) White; student Profl. Children's Sch., N.Y.C.; m. George Bardyguine, Dec. 14, 1953; children—Anya, Youri. Naturalized U.S. citizen, 1957. Soloist, Ballet Russe de Monte Carlo, Marquis de Cuevas Ballet Co., Roland Petit Ballet de Paris, British Met. Ballet; ballerina N.Y.C. Ballet, 1950-65; soloist N.Y. Philharmonic Orch., 1962-65; six European tours, also tour of Orient; numerous TV appearances; toured Russia with N.Y.C. Ballet, 1962; commd. by N.Y. Philharmonic to choreograph ballets Festival, 1964, also for At The Ball, 1965, Viennese Evening, 1966, Petite Suite, 1967; dir. Am. Ballet Theater Sch., 1979—; mem. faculty Dance Educators Am.; tchr., performance coach Am. Ballet Theatre Co., formerly ballet mistress; supr. opening Sch. Ballet of Grand Theatre de Geneve (Switzerland), 1969; tchr., rehearsed Ballet of Royal Opera, Stockholm, Sweden, 1970; now tchr. Met. Opera Ballet, Dance Theatre Harlem, Am. Ballet Theatre Co. and Sch. Adminstr. scholarship fund Sch. Am. Ballet Group; mem. Nat. Bd. Regional Ballet. Mem. Am. Guild Mus. Artists, AFTRA. Office: Am Ballet Theatre 3 W 61st St New York NY 10023

WILDE, WILSON, ins. co. exec.; b. Hartford, Conn., Sept. 24, 1927; s. Philip Alden and Alice Augusta (Wilson) W.; B.A., Williams Coll., 1949; student Swarthmore Coll., 1945-46; m. Joanne Gerta Menzel, June 19, 1953; children—Stephen W., David W., Elizabeth L., Richard A. Sales agt. Conn. Gen. Life Ins. Co., Hartford, 1949-53; with Hartford Steam Boiler Inspection & Ins. Co., 1953—, exec. v.p., 1970-71, pres., chief exec. officer, 1971—, also dir.; dir. Boiler Inspection & Ins. Co. Can., Toronto, Ont., Can., Hartford Nat. Bank & Trust Co., Greater Hartford Corp., Radian Corp., Emhart Corp., Gen. Rad Corp. Corporator Inst. Living, Hartford, now dir.; corporator St. Francis Hosp., Hartford, Hartford Hosp.; bd. dirs. Hartford Stage Co., 1973—, Greater Hartford Arts Council, 1974—, United Way of Greater Hartford, 1974—, Greater Hartford Arts Festival, 1976—, Old State House Assn., 1976—; v.p., bd. dirs. Old State House; trustee Loomis-Chaffee Sch., 1974—. Served with USNR, 1945-47, 51-53. Mem. Am. Ins. Assn. (dir.), Ins. Assn. Conn. (dir.). Club: Hartford (pres. 1974). Office: 56 Prospect St Hartford CT 06102

WILDER, BILLY, motion picture writer, dir., producer; b. Austria, June 22, 1906; m. Audrey Young. Reporter, Berlin; began film writing with People On Sunday, prod. in Berlin, followed by Emil and the Detectives, now in Mus. Modern Art; went to Paris, writer, dir. Mauvaise Graine; came to U.S., 1934; placed under contract as writer Paramount Studios; writer screenplays (in collaboration): Bluebeard's Eighth Wife, 1938, Midnight, 1939, Ninotchka, 1939, Arise My Love, 1940, Hold Back the Dawn, 1941; dir., writer: Five Graves to Cairo, 1943, Double Indemnity, 1944, The Lost Weekend (Acad. award Best Dir., co-award with Charles Brackett for screenplay), 1945, The Emperor Waltz, 1948, A Foreign Affair, 1948, Sunset Boulevard (Acad. award co-award best story, screenplay, 1950; producer, dir., writer (in collaboration): The Big Carnival (Ace in the Hole), 1951, Stalag 17, 1953, Sabrina, 1954, Love in the Afternoon, 1957, Some Like It Hot, 1959, The Apartment (Acad. awards best direction, best picture; co-award best story and screenplay), 1960; co-producer, dir., writer (in collaboration) The Seven Year Itch, 1959; dir., collaborator The Spirit of St. Louis, 1957, Witness for the Prosecution, 1957; producer, dir., writer (in collaboration): One, Two, Three, 1961, Irma La Douce, 1963, Kiss Me, Stupid, 1964, The Fortune Cookie, 1966, The Private Life of Sherlock Holmes, 1970, Avanti, 1972, Fedora, 1979; dir., author screenplay The Front Page, 1974. Head film sect. Psychol. Warfare div. U.S. Army, 1945. Address: Writers and Artists Bldg Beverly Hills CA 90212*

WILDER, BROOKS, pollution control co. exec.; b. Wheaton, Ill., Oct. 4, 1928; s. Almon Brooks and Eloise (Bedlan) W.; A.B., Harvard U., 1950; J.D., U. Ill., 1957; m. Nancy D. Fredricks, Mar. 25, 1952; children—Chip, Martha, Dawn, Todd, Benjamin; m. 2d, Virginia Molenrich, Feb. 25, 1972. Admitted to N.Y. bar, 1958, Ariz. bar, 1960, Calif. bar, 1972; asso. firm Davis, Polk & Wardwell, N.Y.C., 1957-59; asso. Snell & Wilmer, Phoenix, 1959-63, partner, 1963-70; v.p., sec., gen. counsel Envirotech Corp., Menlo Park, Calif., 1970—; sec. Ariz.-Colo. Land & Cattle Co., 1965-70, Bagdad Copper Corp., 1963-70. Bd. dirs. Twelveacres, Inc., 1976—, pres., 1977-78. Served to 1st lt. USAF, 1951-55. Decorated Air medal with 2 oak leaf clusters, D.F.C. Mem. Lawyers Club Phoenix (pres. 1969-70), Am-Soc. Corp. Secs., Am., Ariz. bar assns., State Bar Calif. Club: Harvard (pres. 1969-70) (Phoenix). Home: 1274 Pitman Ave Palo Alto CA 94301 Office: 3000 Sand Hill Rd Menlo Park CA 94025

WILDER, GENE, actor, dir., writer; b. Milw., June 11, 1935; s. William J. and Jeanne (Baer) Silberman; B.A., U. Iowa, 1955; postgrad. Bristol Old Vic Theatre Sch., 1955-56; m. Mary Joan Schutz, Oct. 27, 1967; 1 dau., Katharine Anastasia. Appeared in Broadway play The Complaisant Lover (Clarence Derwent award), 1962; appeared in motion pictures: Bonnie and Clyde, 1967, The Producers (Acad. award nomination), 1968, Start the Revolution Without Me, 1969, Quackser Fortune Has an Uncle in the Bronx, 1970, Willy Wonka and the Chocolate Factory, 1971, Everything You Always Wanted to Know About Sex, 1972, Rhinoceros, 1973, Blazing Saddles, 1973, The Little Prince, 1973, Silver Streak, 1976, The Frisco Kid, 1979; writer screenplay, dir., actor films The Adventures of Sherlock Holmes' Smarter Brother, 1975, The World's Greatest Lover, 1977; TV spl. The Trouble With People, 1973, Marlo Thomas Spl., 1973; TV films: The Scarecrow, 1972, Thursday's Games, 1973; writer screenplay, actor film Young Frankenstein, 1974. Campaigned with Elaine May and Rene Taylor for Eugene McCarthy, Allard Lowenstein and Paul O'Dwyer, 1968. Served with AUS, 1956-58. Office: 9350 Wilshire Blvd Apt 400 Beverly Hills CA 90212*

WILDER, JOHN SHELTON, lt. gov. Tenn.; b. Fayette City, Tenn., June 3, 1921; s. John Chamblee and Martha (Shelton) W.; student U. Tenn.; LL.B., Memphis Law U., 1957; m. Marcelle Morton, Dec. 31, 1941; children—John Shelton, David Morton. Engaged in farming, Longtown, Tenn., 1943—; supr. mgmt. Longtown Supply Co.; admitted to Tenn. bar, 1957, judge Fayette County Ct.; mem. Tenn. Senate, 1959-61, 66-68, 70—; lt. gov. Tenn., 1971-73, past pres. Nat. Assn. Soil Conservation Dists., Tenn. Soil Conservation Assn., Tenn. Agrl. Council; exec. com. So. Legis. Conf.; exec. com. Conf. Lt. Govs.; dir. Oakland Deposit Bank (Tenn.), Somerville Bank and Trust Co. (Tenn.). Served with U.S. Army, 1942-43. Mem. Tenn. Cotton Ginners Assn. (past pres.), Delta Theta Phi. Democrat. Methodist. Club: Shriners. Home: Route 2 Mason TN 38049 Office: Suite 1 Legislative Plaza Nashville TN 37219

WILDER, JOSEPH RICHARD, physician, educator, artist; b. Balt., Oct. 5, 1920; s. David and Dena (Silverston) W.; B.S., Dartmouth U., 1942; M.D., Columbia U., 1945; m. Cynthia K. Fay, June 28, 1960; children—Cathy, Tony, Piper, Alyssa, Nicholas. Intern, St. Lukes Hosp., N.Y.C., 1945-46; instr. pathology Coll. Phys. and Surgs., Columbia, 1946-47; asst. resident, instr. gen. surgery U. Pa. Med. Sch., Phila., 1947-49; asst. resident, instr. gen. surgery Cornell Med. Sch., New York Hosp., 1949-51; chief resident gen. surgery New York Hosp., 1951-52; chief, dir. surg. services Wright Patterson Hosp., Dayton, Ohio, 1952-54; fellow cardiovascular research Karolinska Inst., Stockholm, Sweden, 1954-55; asst. prof. surgery New York Med. Coll., 1955-58; dir. gen. surgery Hosp. for Joint Diseases and Med. Center, N.Y.C., 1964—, also mem. edtoral staff Jour.; prof. surgery Mt. Sinai Sch. Medicine, 1967—, also mem. editorial staff Jour. Represented in permanent collections at Hofstra U. Mus., Dartmouth Coll., David Rockefeller Collection, ABC, John F. Kennedy Airport, Shell Oil Co. Mem. Mayor John F. Lindsay's Hosp. Task Force; mem. adviser N.Y. State Legislature, Office Sen. Robert F. Kennedy; cons. U.S. OEO, N.Y. State Edn. Dept. div. vocational rehab. Served to capt. USAF, 1952-54. Recipient Dazion prize, 1954; John and Mary R. Markle award, 1956. Diplomate Am. Bd. Surgery (examiner). Fellow A.C.S., N.Y. Acad. Medicine (Bowen-Brooke award 1946), Am. Acad. Compensation Medicine; mem. AMA, Med. Soc. State of N.Y., Med. Soc. County of New York, Am., N.Y. heart assns., N.Y. Acad. Scis., N.Y. Soc. for Research, Am. Geriatric Soc. Author: Atlas of General Surgery, 1964. Contbr. chpt. to Cancer in Children, 1959. Contbr. articles to profl. jours. All-Am. La Crosse player, 1941. Home: 151 W 86th St New York NY 10024 Office: 1919 Madison Ave New York NY 10035

WILDER, MICHAEL STEPHEN, ins. co. exec.; b. New Haven, Sept. 8, 1941; s. Harry Walter and Anne (Melin) W.; B.A., Yale U., 1963; J.D. cum laude, Harvard U., 1966; m. Marjorie Levitin, June 13, 1965; children—Kathryn Sara, Amanda Hollis. Admitted to Conn. bar, 1966; law clk. State of Conn., 1966-67; with Hartford Fire Ins. Co. (Conn.), 1967—, asso. gen. counsel, 1971-75, gen. counsel, sec., 1975—; similar positions with affiliated cos. Vice chmn. Greater Hartford Arts Council fund drive, 1977—; bd. corporators Mt. Sinai Hosp. Mem. Am., Conn. bar assns. Clubs: Hartford Yale (v.p. 1976-77, 79—, sec. 1977-79), Hartford. Author legal articles. Home: 11 Fernwood Rd West Hartford CT 06119 Office: Hartford Fire Ins Co Hartford Plaza Hartford CT 06115

WILDER, PELHAM, JR., educator, chemist; b. Americus, Ga., July 20, 1920; s. Pelham and Hattie (Wilder) W.; A.B., Emory U., 1942, M.A., 1943; M.A., Harvard U., 1947, Ph.D., 1950; m. Alma Sterly Lebey, Mar. 20, 1945; children—Alma Ann, Pelham III, Sterly Lebey. Teaching fellow Harvard U., 1943-44, 46-49; instr. chemistry Duke U., 1949-52, asst. prof., 1952-58, asso. prof., 1958-62, prof., 1962-67, prof. chemistry and pharmacology, 1967—; cons. NSF, Washington, 1960-68, Research Triangle Inst., Durham, 1965—, E.I. duPont deNemours & Co., 1966-69. Mem. advanced placement com. Coll. Entrance Exam. Bd., N.Y., 1967-75, chmn. chemistry com., 1969-75, cons., 1975—; mem. exec. com. Gov. N.C. Sci. Advisory Com., 1962-64. Bd. dirs. Durham Acad. (chmn. 1970-72), Exptl. Study of Religion and Soc., Raleigh, N.C., 1966-69. Served with USNR, 1944-46. Recipient 1st annual Alumni Distinguished Undergrad. Teaching award Duke, 1971. Mem. Am. Chem. Soc. (chmn. N.C. sect. 1956), Chem. Soc. London, Phi Beta Kappa (chpt. pres. 1974-75), Sigma Xi, Omicron Delta Kappa. Democrat. Presbyn. (ruling elder; exec. com. Ednl. Instns. Synod of N.C. 1966-72). Rotarian. Club: Torch. Author: (with W.C. Vosburgh) Laboratory Manual of Fundamentals of Analytical Chemistry, 1956; Laboratory Manual of Physical Chemistry of Aqueous Solutions, 2d edit., 1967. Contbr. to articles profl. jours. Home: 2514 Wrightwood Ave Durham NC 27705

WILDER, PHILIP SAWYER, JR., coll. pres.; b. Newton, Mass., July 24, 1924; s. Philip Sawyer and Elisabeth (Clark) W.; B.S., Bowdoin Coll., 1945; M.A., Harvard U., 1948, Ph.D., 1950; m. Barbara Fluker, June 21, 1947; children—Anne, Patricia, Nancy Wilder Watson. From asst. prof. to prof. polit. scis., chmn. social sci. div. Wabash (Ind.) Coll., 1949-67; dean, then acad. v.p. Calif. State Coll., Bakersfield, 1968-77; pres. Hartwick Coll., Oneota, N.Y., 1977—; vis. prof. Pomona Coll., 1963, Ind. U., 1964, U. Ill., 1965, Purdue U., 1967. U.S. senatorial legis. asst., 1953; spl. asst. to chmn. Republican Nat. Com., 1948; chmn. Gov. Ind. Com. Voting Participation, 1964; mem. com. privacy and confidentiality U.S. Census Bur., 1972-74; election analyst on TV, 1964, 66. Served to 1st lt. USAAF, 1943-46. Mem. Am. Polit. Sci. Assn. Presbyterian. Author: Meade Alcorn and the 1958 Election, 1959; co-author: Indiana Government and Politics, 1967. Home: Thornwood Draper Dr Oneonta NY 13820 Office: Hartwick Coll Oneonta NY 13820

WILDER, RAYMOND EDWARD, lawyer; b. Muskegon, Mich., Oct. 7, 1931; s. Raymond Fredrick and Alma Elizabeth (Wenger) W.; B.A. with high honors, Mich. State U., 1957; LL.B., U. Colo., 1960; m. Patricia Ann Erickson, Sept. 10, 1955; children—Ann Marie, John Raymond, Nancy Beth, Janet Lee, Sandra Rochelle, James Richard. Admitted to Colo. bar, 1960; practiced law, Colorado Springs, 1960-63; dep. dist. atty., Colorado Springs, 1961-63; partner firm Quigley, Wilder & Palermo and predecessor, Colorado Springs, 1963-76, Wilder, Wells & Elliott, Colorado Springs, 1976—; state rep. Colo. Gen. Assembly, 1967-69; asst. to Gov. Colo., 1973-75; county atty. El Paso County (Colo.), 1976-77. Served with USMC, 1950-53. Mem. Am., Colo., El Paso County bar assns. Republican. Clubs: El Paso, Cheyenne Mountain Country. Home. 16 Lake Ave Colorado Springs CO 80906 Office: 524 S Cascade Ave Suite 1 Colorado Springs CO 80903

WILDER, RAYMOND LOUIS, science historiographer, mathematician, educator; b. Palmer, Mass., Nov. 3, 1896; s. John Louis and Mary Jane (Shanley) W.; Ph.B., Brown U., 1920, M.S., 1921, D.Sc. (hon.), 1958; Ph.D., U. Tex., 1923; D.Sc. (hon.), Bucknell U., 1955; m. Una Maude Greene, Jan. 1, 1921; children—Mary Jane Wilder Jessop, Sally May Wilder Watkins, Betty Ann Wilder Dillingham, David Elliott. Instr. in math. Brown U., Providence, 1920-21, U. Tex., Austin, 1921-24; asst. prof. math. Ohio State U., Columbus, 1924-26; asst. prof. math. U. Mich., Ann Arbor, 1926-29, asso. prof., 1929-35, prof., 1935-47, research prof., 1947-67, emeritus prof., 1967—; lectr. math. U. Calif., Santa Barbara, 1970-71, research asso., 1971—; vis. research prof. Fla. State U., Tallahassee, 1961-62; mem. staff Inst. Advanced Study, Princeton U., 1933-34; Henry Russel lectr. U. Mich., 1958-59; Josiah Willard Gibbs lectr. Am. Math. Soc., 1969. Served as ensign USN, 1917-19. Guggenheim Meml. Found. fellow, 1940-41; Office Naval Research grantee, 1949-50; NSF grantee; Air Force Office Sci. Research grantee. Mem. Nat. Acad. Scis., Am. Math. Soc. (pres. 1955-56), Math. Assn. Am. (pres. 1965-66, Distinguished Service Math. award 1973), AAAS (v.p. 1948), Assn. Symbolic Logic; fellow Am. Anthropol. Assn. Author: (with W.L. Ayres) Lectures in Topology, 1941; Topology of Manifolds, 1949; Introduction to the Foundations of Mathematics, 1952, rev. edit., 1965; Evolution of Mathematical Concepts, 1968; contbr. articles to profl. jours. Home: 2427 Calle Montilla Santa Barbara CA 93109 Office: Dept Math U Calif Santa Barbara CA 93106

WILDER, ROBERT GEORGE, advt. and pub. relations exec.; b. Hornell, N.Y., Mar. 27, 1920; s. George Reuben and Laura (Nolan) W.; B.A., Coll. Wooster, 1942; m. Annabel D. Heritage, Feb. 21, 1953; children—Loraine A., Gordon Heritage. Propr., Robert G. Wilder & Co., Inc., pub. relations, Phila., 1945-50; dir. pub. relations Lewis & Gilman, advt.-pub. relations, Phila., 1950-55, v.p., 1955-59, exec. v.p., 1959-64, pres., 1964—; dir. Fidelity Mut. Life Ins. Co. Mem. Phila. Adv. Council Naval Affairs. Mem. bd. mgrs. Franklin Inst., Indsl. Adv. Council, Phila. OIC; bd. dirs. Independence Hall Assn., Greater Phila. Partnership, Pa. Ballet Co.; v.p. Union League Phila.; trustee Phila. Coll. Pharmacy and Sci., United Way Phila., Lankenau Hosp., Phila. Served to lt. comdr. USNR, 1942-46. Recipient award Charles M. Price Sch., 1971; Bus. and Industry award Opportunities Industrialization Center, 1971; Distinguished Alumni award Coll. Wooster, 1971. Mem. Pharm. Advt. Club N.Y.C., Res. Officers Assn. (past pres. Pa.), Pa. Acad. Fine Arts (trustee), Greater Phila. C. of C. (vice chmn., dir.). Presbyn. (trustee). Clubs: Union League, Penn, Bachelors Barge (pres.) (Phila.); Philadelphia Country (Gladwyne, Pa.); Merion Cricket (Haverford, Pa.). Home: 900 Bryn Mawr Ave Penn Valley PA 19072 Office: 1700 Market St Philadelphia PA 19103

WILDER, WILLIAM PRICE, gas co. exec.; b. Toronto, Ont., Can., Sept. 26, 1922; s. William Edward and Marjorie M. (Murray) W.; B. Commerce, McGill U., 1946; M.B.A., Harvard, 1950; m. Judith Ryrie Bickle, Sept. 18, 1953; children—Martha H., William E., Thomas B., Andrew M. With Wood Gundy Securities Ltd. (now Wood Gundy Ltd.), Toronto, 1946-72, exec. asst. to dirs., 1958-61, dir., 1961-72, exec. v.p., 1961-67, pres., 1967-72; chmn., chief exec. officer Canadian Arctic Gas Pipeline Ltd., 1972-77; exec. v.p. Gulf Can. Ltd., Toronto, 1977-79; pres., chief exec. officer Consumers Gas Co., Toronto, 1979—; dir. John Labatt Ltd., Maclean-Hunter Ltd., Allstate Ins. Co. Can., Simpsons, Ltd., Lever Bros. Ltd., Simpsons-Sears Ltd., Noranda Mines Ltd. Trustee Hosp. Sick Children, Toronto; mem. exec. com. of adv. com. Sch. Bus. Adminstrn., U. Western Ont. Served to lt. Royal Canadian Navy Vol. Res., 1941-44. Mem. Alpha Delta Phi. Mem. United Ch. Can. Clubs: Badminton and Racquet, Queen's, St. James's (Montreal); Tadenac (Fishing) Toronto, Univ., Toronto Golf, York, Cambridge (Toronto); Brooks's (London, Eng.); Rideau (Ottawa, Ont.); Vancouver (B.C.). Home: 179 Warren Rd Toronto ON M4V 254 Canada Office: Consumers Gas Co 1 First Canadian Pl Toronto ON M5X 1C5 Canada

WILDERMANN, WILLIAM, bass-baritone; b. Stuttgart, Germany, Dec. 2, 1919. Operatic debut with San Carlo Opera Co., N.Y.C., 1940; N.Y.C. Opera debut, 1950; Met. Opera debut, 1957; with Stuttgart Opera, 1963-73; now with Met. Opera, N.Y.C.; appeared in major opera house U.S., Can., Europe, including Chgo. Lyric Opera, San Francisco Opera, Teatro Colon, Buenos Aires, Aregntina; created part of Horace in Regina on Broadway; rec. artist. Office: care Met Opera Guild Inc 1865 Broadway New York NY 10023

WILDHACK, WILLIAM AUGUST, physicist; b. Breckenridge, Colo., Sept. 24, 1908; s. Louis Amandus and Lizzie Frances (Smith) W.; B.S., U. Colo., 1931, M.S., 1932, grad. study, 1932-34; grad. George Washington U., 1936-39; m. Martha Elizabeth Parks, Nov. 26, 1931; children—William August, Michael David. Physicist, Nat. Bur. Standards 1935-69, chief, missile instrument sect., 1948-50, chief Office Basic Instrumentation, 1950-60, spl. asst. to dir., 1960-61, asso. dir. 1961-65, asso. dir. Inst. Basic Standards, 1965-69; tech. cons., 1969—. Chmn. com. sci. equipment NRC, 1947-52; panel aircraft equipment Research and Devel. Bd., 1949-53; cons. sci. equipment for Europe, ECA, 1950; chief U.S. Metrology Delegation to Russia, 1963. Bd. dirs. Nat. Conf. Standards Labs. William A. Wildhack award established by Nat. Conf. Standards Labs., 1970. Fellow Instrument Soc. Am. (hon. mem. 1968, pres. 1954); mem. Am. Assn. Physics Tchrs., Am. Phys. Soc., Inst. Aero. Scis., AAAS, Fedn. Am. Scientists, Washington Acad. Scis., Sigma Xi, Tau Beta Pi, Sigma Pi Sigma. Club: Cosmos (Washington). Inventions, sci. publs. in field. Address: 415 N Oxford St Arlington VA 22203

WILDS, ALFRED LAWRENCE, chemist, educator; b. Kansas City, Mo., Mar. 1, 1915; s. Frank A. and Harriet E. (Hewer) W.; student Kansas City (Mo.) Jr. Coll., 1931-34; B.A., U. Mich., 1936, M.S., 1937, Ph.D., 1939; m. Carolyn A. Simcock, Sept. 4, 1937. Instr. chemistry U. Wis., 1940-42, asst. prof., 1942-45, asso. prof., 1945-46, prof., 1946—, research organic chemistry, 1940—; research organic chemistry U. Mich., 1937-40. Du Pont research fellow U. Mich., 1939-40; co-ofcl. investigator Nat. Def. Research Com., 1942-45. Guggenheim fellow, Zurich, 1957. Mem. Am., London, Swiss chem. socs., Wis. Acad. Scis., Arts and Letters, A.A.A.S., Sigma Xi. Home: 302 Robin Pkwy Madison WI 53705

WILEN, STANLEY HERBERT, lawyer; b. Balt., May 23, 1919; s. Louis Mark and Dora (Schapiro) Wilenzick; Asso. B.A., Balt. Coll. Commerce, 1939; LL.B., U. Balt., 1943; m. Lillian Scheinker, Mar. 20, 1949; children—Samuel A., Deborah R. (Mrs. Howard Schwartz), Judith B. Admitted to Md. bar, 1943, D.C. bar, 1950; sec. Berne Hat, Inc., Balt., 1937-39; controller Aircraft & Marine Splty. Co., Balt., 1940-42; accountant Burke, Landsberg & Gerber, Balt., 1945-50; partner Burke, Gerber & Wilen, Balt., 1951—; instr. taxation Balt. Coll. Commerce, 1948-53, U. Balt., 1950-54. Mem. health and instl. services com. Assoc. Jewish Charities and Welfare Fund, 1966—. Mem. Bd. Jewish Edn., Balt., 1962-68. Bd. dirs. Hebrew Free Loan Assn., 1970—, sec.-treas., 1972-73, v.p., 1973-78, pres., 1978—. Served with USNR, 1942-45. C.P.A., Md. Jewish. Mem. B'nai B'rith. Club: Chestnut Ridge Country. Home: 7937 Long Meadow Rd Baltimore MD 21208 Office: 326 St Paul Pl Baltimore MD 21202

WILENSKY, JULIUS M., pub. co. exec.; b. Stamford, Conn., Oct. 10, 1916; s. Joseph and Mary (Wainstein) W.; student Rensselaer Poly. Inst., 1934-36; m. Dorothy T. Jobrack, July 2, 1939; children—Joseph L. (dec.), Nancy L., Martha J. Methods engr. Yale & Towne Mfg. Co., Stamford, 1939-49, prodn. mgr., 1953-57; dir. purchasing lock and hardware div. Eaton Yale & Towne, Rye, N.Y., 1957-67; mayor of Stamford, 1969-73; dir. materials, arms operations Winchester div. Olin Corp., New Haven, 1973-78; pres. Wescott Cove Pub. Co., 1978—; lectr. in field. First v.p. Met. Regional Council, 1973; mem. Tri-State Regional Planning Commn., 1971-73, Stamford Bd. Finance, 1965-59, Stamford Planning Bd., 1963-65; chmn. Council Republican Clubs, Stamford, 1961-62. Served with USAAF, 1943-46. Named Republican of Yr., Stamford Reps., 1962. Mem. Am. Mgmt. Assn., Stamford Power Squadron, Stamford Good Govt. Assn. (dir., treas. 1949-57), Stamford Chamber Residences (pres. 1953-55). Author guide books on cruising L.I. Sound, Cape Cod, Windward Islands, and Abacos; also articles boating mags., newspapers; contbg. editor Rudder, 1970-77; author cruising columns Eastern and So. edits. Sea Mag. Home: 51 Barrett Ave Stamford CT 06905. *To be productive in fields or enterprises which are useful to other people has been my aspiration, and it's a high one. It's important to set goals early in life, then follow a plan to obtain the education and experience required to achieve these goals. Courage, honesty, objectivity, determination, hard work, and consideration for others will enable one to become outstanding in any field.*

WILES, CHARLES PRESTON, clergyman; b. Frederick, Md., Aug. 5, 1918; s. Charles Wesley and Nellie (Burgess) W.; A.B., Washington Coll., 1939; postgrad. U. Va., 1940; M.A., Duke, 1945, Ph.D. (Univ.

fellow 1947-51, Kearns Honor fellow 1949-50), 1951; B.D., Va. Theol. Sem., 1947; married; children—Charles Preston, Wade Burgess. Tchr. high sch., prin. pub. schs. Va., 1939-44; ordained deacon Episcopal Ch., 1947, priest, 1948; priest-in-charge St. Joseph's Ch., Durham, N.C., 1947-51; rector St. Mary's Episcopal Ch., Burlington, N.J., 1951-64; pres., trustee Burlington Coll., 1951-64, faculty cons., 1956-64; mem. faculty Phila. Div. Sch., 1959-62, lectr. ch. history, 1960-62; dean St. Matthew's Episcopal Cathedral, Dallas, 1964—. Dep. Gen. Conv. from Diocese Dallas, 1967, 69, 70, 73, 76, 79; del. Provincial Synod from Diocese Dallas, 1966, 69, 72, 75, 78; mem. exec. council Diocese Dallas, 1967-77, pres. mem. standing com., 1970-73, pres., 1971-73, mem. bd. missions, 1967-69, chmn. dept. coll. work, 1965-71, mem. bd. examing chaplains, 1965-71, mem. standing liturgical commn.; dean, warden Cathedral Center for Continuing Edn. and Pastoral Concern, 1971—, Commn. Ministry, 1971—; dean Dallas Deanery, 1965-69, Bicentennial preacher, 1975; pres. convocation and clericus Diocese of N.J., 1961-64, examining chaplain, mem. bd. missions, mem. bd. Christina edn., dean Burlington-Trenton convocation; instr., dean Drew Conf. for Adults in N.J., 1952-56; retreat conductor St. Martin's House, Bernardsville, N.J., St. John Bapt. Convent, Mendhan, N.J.; dean Diocesan Sch. Religion N.J., 1962-63; parish life lab. and weekend conductor Nat. Dept. Christian Edn., 1962; co-founder, dean Princeton (N.J.) Conf., 1956-64; mem. Goals for Dallas com. Trustee Gen. Theol. Sem., 1968—; bd. dirs. Evergreen Home for Aging, St. Philip's Community Center, Overseas Mission Soc. Mem. Navy League, Ch. Hist. Soc. (dir. 1960-68, trustee 1970-77). Kiwanian (Distinuished Service award 1951). Clubs: Dallas Athletic; Vesper (Phila.); Burlington County Country. Author: Sacrament and Sacrifice, 2d edit., 1973; Lancelot Andrewes, Caroline Divine, 1951; Lift Up Your Hearts, 1956; A Manual of Prayers, 1975. Home: 4600 St John's Dr Dallas TX 75205 Office: 5100 Ross Ave Dallas TX 75206

WILES, DAVID MCKEEN, chemist; b. Springhill, N.S., Can., Dec. 28, 1932; s. Roy McKeen and Olwen Gertrude (Jones) W.; B.Sc. with honors, McMaster U., 1954, M.Sc., 1955; Ph.D. in Chemistry, McGill U., 1957; m. Valerie Joan Rowlands, June 8, 1957; children—Gordon Stuart, Sandra Lorraine. Research officer chemistry div. Nat. Research Council of Can., Ottawa, 1959-66, head textile chemistry sect. chemistry div., 1966-75, dir. chemistry div., 1975—; chmn. Can. High Polymer Forum, 1967-69; v.p. N.Am. Chem. Congress, Mexico City, 1975. Can. Ramsay Meml. fellow, 1957-59. Fellow Chem. Inst. Can. (chmn. bd. dirs. 1972-74, pres. 1975-76), Textile Inst.; mem. Chem. Soc. London, Am. Chem. Soc., Fiber Soc. Contbr. articles to profl. jours.; mem. editorial adv. bd. numerous profl. jours. Patentee in field. Home: 1927 Fairmeadow Crescent Ottawa ON K1H 7B8 Canada Office: Montreal Rd Ottawa ON K1A 0R6 Canada

WILES, EUGENE F., lawyer; b. Presho, S.D., Dec. 18, 1922; student Boise Jr. Coll., U. Idaho; J.D., U. San Francisco, 1952. Admitted to Oreg. bar, 1952, Alaska bar, 1961, U.S. Dist. Ct. for Alaska, 1961, U.S. Ct. Appeals, 9th Circuit, 1961, U.S. Supreme Ct. bar, 1971; field solicitor Dept. Interior, Anchorage, 1956-59, asst. regional solicitor, 1960-61; mem. Alaska Jud. Council, 1972-75. Mem. Alaska (gov. 1964-67, 1st v.p. 1965-66, pres. 1966-67), Am. bar assns., Oreg. State Bar, Am. Judicature Soc. Home: 6603 Air National Guard Rd Anchorage AK 99502 Office: 1007 W 3d Ave Anchorage AK 99501

WILETS, LAWRENCE, educator; b. Oconomowoc, Wis., Jan. 4, 1927; s. Edward and Sophia (Finger) W.; B.S., U. Wis., 1948; M.A., Princeton, 1950, Ph.D., 1952; m. Dulcy Elaine Margoles, Dec. 21, 1947; children—Ileen Sue, Edward E., James D.; m. 2d, Vivian C. Wolf, Feb. 8, 1976. Research asso. Project Matterhorn, Princeton, N.J., 1951-53, U. Calif. Radiation Lab., Livermore, 1953; NSF postdoctoral fellow Inst. Theoretical Physics, Copenhagen, Denmark, 1953-55; staff mem. Los Alamos Sci. Lab., 1955-58; mem. Inst. Advanced Study, Princeton, 1957-58; mem. faculty U. Wash., Seattle, 1958—, prof. physics, 1962—; cons. to pvt. and govt. labs.; vis. prof. Princeton, 1969, Calif. Inst. Tech., 1971. Del. Dem. Nat. Conv., 1968. NSF Sr. fellow Weizmann Inst. Sci., Rehovot, Israel, 1961-62; Guggenheim fellow Lund (Sweden) U., also Weizmann Inst., 1976—. Fellow Am. Phys. Soc.; mem. Fedn. Am. Scientists, AAUP (pres. chpt. 1969-70, 73-75, pres. state conf. 1975-76), Phi Beta Kappa, Sigma Xi. Club: Explorers. Author: Theories of Nuclear Fission, 1964; also numerous articles. Research in theory of nuclear structure and reactions, nuclear fission, atomic isotope shifts, atomic collisions, many body problems, meson physics.

WILEY, BELL IRVIN, educator, author; b. Halls, Tenn., Jan. 5, 1906; s. Ewing Baxter and Anna (Bass) W.; A.B., Asbury Coll., 1928, Litt.D., 1965; M.A., U. Ky., 1929, LL.D., 1968; Ph.D., Yale, 1933; Litt. D., Lincoln Coll., 1959; L.H.D., Jacksonville U., 1961; LL.D., Tulane U., 1961; M.A. (hon.), Oxford (Eng.) U., 1965; m. Mary Frances Harrison, Dec. 19, 1937; children—George Bell, John Francis. Asst. prof. history and debating Asbury Coll., 1928-31; prof. history, head dept. Miss. So. Coll., 1934-38, U. Miss., 1938-46; Julius Rosenwald fellow, 1941-42; prof. history, head dept. La. State U., 1946-48; prof. history Emory U., 1948-74, prof. emeritus, 1974—; vis. prof. U. S.C., fall 1974; Mellon vis. prof. humanities Tulane U., fall 1975; vis. prof. U. Ky., fall 1977; historian in residence Agnes Scott Coll., 1975-77; vis. lectr. (under State Dept.), Europe, 1964-65, Australia and New Zealand, 1970; Harmsworth prof. Am. history Oxford U., 1965-66; Rockefeller Found. postwar fellow, 1948-49; vis. prof. Peabody Coll., summers 1935-38; lectr. Kyoto (Japan) summer seminar Am. studies, 1970. Served to lt. col., hist. officer, AUS, World War II; wrote preliminary history of 2d Army; asst. hist. officer Army Ground Forces, 1943-46. Decorated Legion of Merit, 1945. Mem. Nat. Civil War Centennial Commn., Am., So. (pres. 1955) hist. assns., Orgn. Am. Historians, Soc. Am. Historians, Nat. Hist. Soc. (chmn. bd. advisers), Phi Beta Kappa. Democrat. Episcopalian. Author: Southern Negroes, 1861-65, 1938; The Life of Johnny Reb: Common Soldier of the Confederacy, 1943; The Plain People of the Confederacy, 1943; The Organization of Ground Combat Troups (with K.R. Greenfield and R.R. Palmer), 1947; The Procurement and Training of Ground Combat Troops (with R.R. Palmer and W. R. Keast), 1948; The Life of Billy Yank: Common Soldier of the Union, 1952; The Road to Appomattox, 1956; (with H.D. Milhollen) They Who Fought Here, 1959. Editor: Sam R. Watkins Co. Aytch, 1953; William A. Fletcher, Rebel Private Front and Rear, 1954; Reminiscence of Big I (by W.N. Wood), 1956: Kentucky Cavaliers in Dixie (by George Dallas Mosgrove), 1957; Recollections of a Confederate Staff Officer (by G.M. Sorrel) 1958; Four Years on The Firing Line (by J.C. Nisbet), 1963; (with H.D. Milhollen) Embattled Confederates: An Illustrated History of Southerners at War, 1964; (with Allan Nevins and James I. Robertson) Civil War Books: A Critical Bibiolgraphy, 2 vols., 1967-69; Confederate Women, 1975; The Common Soldier of the Civil War, 1975. Home: 1636 E Clifton Rd NE Atlanta GA 30307

WILEY, DAVID EARL, educator; b. San Diego, Sept. 4, 1938; s. Harry Vincent and Miriam Esther (Oates) W.; A.B., San Diego State Coll., 1960; M.S., U. Wis., 1963, Ph.D., 1964; m. Annegret Harnischfeger, Aug. 17, 1972; children—David L., Ann M., M. Sachem, Taska M., Kowa A. Asst. prof. edn. UCLA, 1964-65; mem. faculty depts. edn. and behavioral scis. U. Chgo., 1965-79; prof., dean Sch. of Edn., Northwestern U., Evanston, Ill., 1979—; resident advisor Venezuelan Ministry of Edn., Caracas, 1970; fellow Center for Advanced Study, Stanford, Calif., 1971-72; program dir. CEMREL, Inc., St. Louis, 1973-75. Recipient numerous grants NSF, Nat. Inst. Edn., Ford Found., Spencer Found. Mem. Am. Edn. Research Assn., Psychometric Soc., Am. Statis. Assn., Nat. Council of Measurement in Edn., AAAS, Sigma Xi. Democrat. Author: (with A. Harnischfeger) Achievement Test Score Decline: Do We Need to Worry?, 1975; editor: (with M.C. Wittrock) The Evaluation of Instruction: Issues and Problems, 1970. Home: 257 Sheridan Rd Kenilworth IL 60043 Office: Sch of Edn Northwestern U Evanston IL 60201

WILEY, DONOVON LINN, banker; b. Oregon City, Oreg., Oct. 20, 1938; s. Donovan Jean and Thelma Maxine (Linn) W.; B.A. in Econs., U. Calif. at Davis, 1964; M.B.A., Calif. State U. at Long Beach, 1971; grad. Grad. Sch. Credit and Financial Mgmt., Harvard, 1972; grad. Grad. Sch. Sales Mgmt. and Mktg., Syracuse U., 1978; m. Nancy Leigh White, Aug. 22, 1964; children—Jeffrey Richard, Kristen Linn. With First Western Bank & Trust Co., 1964-72, mgr. Santa Ana corp. office, 1969-72; v.p., sr. v.p., dir. Kans. State Bank & Trust Co., Wichita, 1972-73; pres. Ahmanson Bank & Trust Co., Beverly Hills, Calif., 1973-74; v.p. corp. banking div. Lloyds Bank Calif., 1974-75, sr. v.p., dir. mktg., dir. planning, 1975-77, regional v.p., No. Calif., 1977—. Chmn. 3d Annual Wichitennial; bd. dirs. Orange County Heart Assn., Orange County Lung Assn., Calif. Pediatric Center, 1974-78, Los Angeles Central City Assn., 1976; mem. com. for new dimensions Calif. Luth. Coll., 1975—. Served with USMC, 1956-60. Named Boss of Year, Orange County chpt. Am. Inst. Bankers, 1969-70; Mgr. of Year, First Western Bank and Trust Co., 1971. Mem. Robert Morris Assos. Republican. Roman Catholic. Clubs: Round Hill Golf and Country, Family. Home: 202 Las Quebradas Alamo CA 94507 Office: 235 Montgomery St San Francisco CA 94104

WILEY, EDWIN PACKARD, lawyer; b. Chgo., Dec. 10, 1929; s. Edwin Garnet and Marjorie Chastina (Packard) W.; B.A., U. Chgo., 1949, J.D., 1952; m. Barbara Jean Miller, May 21, 1949; children—Edwin Miller, Clayton Alexander, Stephen Packard. Admitted to Ill. bar, 1952, Wis. bar, 1952; asso. firm Foley & Lardner, Milw., 1952-60, partner, 1960—; dir. Badger Meter, Inc., Nat. Rivet & Mfg. Co., Shaler Co., Waukesha Cutting Tools, Inc. Chmn. bd. Blood Center Southwestern Wis., Inc., 1978—; pres. Wis. Conservatory Music, 1968-74; vice chmn. Friends of Schlitz Audubon Center, Inc., 1975—; mem. vis. com. Coll., Law Sch., U. Chgo., 1976—; v.p. Mid. Am. Ballet Co., 1971-73. Mem. Am. Bar Assn., State Bar Wis., State Bar Ill., Milw. Bar Assn., Am. Law Inst., Assn. Bank Holding Cos. (chmn. lawyers com.), Phi Beta Kappa. Unitarian-Universalist. Clubs: Milw., Univ. (Milw.). Author handbooks; contbr. articles to profl. jours. Home: 3017 N Marietta Ave Milwaukee WI 53211 Office: Suite 3800 777 E Wisconsin Ave Milwaukee WI 53202

WILEY, JOHN PRESTON, JR., mag. editor; b. Rahway, N.J., May 22, 1936; s. John Preston and Arabella Mary (Bassett) W.; B.S. in Polit. Sci., Fordham U., 1958; m. Barbara Hick, Aug. 5, 1961; children—John, Peter, Catherine, James. Asso. editor Physics Today, N.Y.C., 1968-69; sr. editor Natural History, N.Y.C., 1969-73; writer, editor FDA, Washington, 1973; asso. editor Smithsonian, Washington, 1973—, bd. editors, 1976—. Mem. Westchester County Democratic com., N.Y., 1970-72, press aide numerous campaigns. Advanced sci. writing program fellow Columbia, 1966-67. Mem. Nat. Assn. Sci. Writers. Home: 12601 Running Brook Dr Clarksburg MD 20734 Office: Smithsonian 900 Jefferson Dr SW Washington DC 20560

WILEY, MARSHALL WAYNE, fgn. service officer; b. Rockford, Ill., Apr. 26, 1925; s. Robert Ernest and Ann (Marshall) W.; Ph.B., U. Chgo., 1943, J.D., 1948, M.B.A., 1949; m. Marjorie Ann Keane, Dec. 30, 1957; children—Cynthia Jeanne, Douglas John, Steven Robert. Staff asst. Ford Found., 1951-52; commd. fgn. service officer Dept. State, 1958; econ. officer, Amman, 1963-64; dep. prin. officer, Cairo, 1969-71, dir. N. African affairs, Washington, 1974; prin. officer, Baghdad, Iraq, 1975; dep. chief of mission Am. embassy, Jidda, Saudi Arabia, 1977-78; ambassador to Sultanate of Oman, Muscat, 1978—. Served with USNR, 1943-45. Unitarian. Address: US Embassy PO Box 966 Muscat Oman

WILEY, RICHARD ARTHUR, banker; b. Bklyn., July 18, 1928; s. Arthur Ross and Anna Thorsen (Holder) W.; A.B., Bowdoin Coll., Brunswick, Maine, 1948; B.C.L. (Rhodes scholar 1949), Oxford (Eng.) U., 1951; LL.M., Harvard U., 1959; m. Carole Jean Smith, Aug. 13, 1955; children—Kandra Elizabeth, Stewart Alan, Garett Smith. Admitted to Mass. bar, 1954; atty. John Hancock Mut. Life Ins. Co., Boston, 1956-58; from atty. to mng. partner firm Bingham, Dana & Gould, Boston, 1959-76; gen. counsel Dept. Def., 1976-77; v.p., counsel First Nat. Bank Boston, 1977-78, exec. v.p., 1978—; dir. First Venture Capital Corp., Boston, Mutron Corp., Nypro, Inc., Term Capital Mgmt. Corp., Univ. Affiliates, Inc.; lectr. Boston U. Law Sch., 1961-64; past chmn. New Eng. Conf. on Doing Bus. Abroad; bd. dirs. New Eng. Legal Found. Bd. overseers Bowdoin Coll., 1966—, pres., 1977—; mem. Wellesley (Mass.) Town Meeting, 1971-75, mem. adv. fin. com., 1973-74; chmn. lawyers div. United Way Mass. Bay, 1975; mem. devel. com., trustees of donations Episcopal Diocese Mass., 1971-75; trustee, exec. com. North Conway Inst.; trustee Greater Boston Fund Internat. Affairs. Served as officer USAF, 1953-56. Decorated Air Force Commendation medal; recipient Disting. Public Service award Dept. Def., 1977. Mem. Am. Bar Assn. (vice chmn. fgn. and internat. bus. law com. 1967-69), Boston Bar Assn. (exec. com., antitrust com. 1965-68), Council on Fgn. Relations, Boston Com. on Fgn. Relations (exec. com.), Phi Beta Kappa. Author: Cases and Materials on Law of International Trade and Investment, 1961; also articles. Office: 100 Federal St Boston MA 02110

WILEY, RICHARD EMERSON, govt. ofcl.; b. Peoria, Ill., July 20, 1934; s. Joseph Henry and Jean W. (Farrell) W.; B.S. with distinction, Northwestern U., 1955, J.D., 1958; LL.M., Georgetown U., 1962; m. Elizabeth J. Edwards, Aug. 6, 1960; children—Douglas S., Pamela L., Kimberly J. Admitted to Ill. bar, 1958, D.C. bar, 1972; mem. law firm Chadwell, Keck, Kayser, Ruggles & McLaren, Chgo., 1962-68; asst. gen. counsel Bell & Howell Co., Chgo., 1968-70; partner law firm Burditt, Calkins & Wiley, Chgo., from 1970; gen. counsel FCC, Washington, 1970-72, mem., 1972-74, chmn., from 1974; now mng. partner firm Kirkland & Ellis, Washington; prof. law John Marshall Law Sch., U. Chgo., 1963-70. Committeeman, Northfield Township Republican Com., 1970. Served to capt., AUS, 1959-62. Mem. Am. (mem. ho. of dels. 1969-71, mem. commn. campus govt. and student dissent 1969-70, chmn. lawyers in govt. com.), Fed. (pres.), Ill., Chgo. bar assns., Phi Delta Phi, Phi Delta Kappa. Methodist. Editor-in-chief Law Notes, 1963-65. Contbr. articles to profl. jours. Home: 3818 N Woodrow St Arlington VA 22207 Office: Kirkland & Ellis Suite 1100 1776 K St NW Washington DC 20006

WILEY, RICHARD HAVEN, chemist, educator; b. Mattoon, Ill., May 10, 1913; s. John Frederick and Mary Frances (Moss) W.; A.B., U. Ill., 1934, M.S., 1935; Ph.D., U. Wis., 1937; LL.B., Temple U., 1943; m. Marybeth Signaigo, Dec. 28, 1940; children—Richard Haven, Frank Edmund. Fellow Wis. Alumni Research Found., 1935-37; research chemist E.I. duPont de Nemours & Co., Wilmington, Del., 1937-45; asso. prof. chemistry U. N.C., 1945-49; prof. chemistry, chmn. dept. U. Louisville, 1949-65; NSF sr. postdoctoral fellow Imperial Coll., London, 1957-58; vis. prof. grad. div. City U. N.Y., 1963-64, exec. officer chemistry, 1965-68; prof. chemistry Hunter Coll., 1965-79; vis. scholar Stanford U., 1978-80. Fellow AAAS, Am. Inst. Chemists, N.Y. Acad. Scis.; mem. Am. Chem. Soc. (Midwest award St. Louis sect. 1965), N.Y. Acad. Scis., Phi Beta Kappa, Sigma Xi, Phi Eta Sigma, Phi Lambda Upsilon, Phi Kappa Psi. Author: (with P.F. Wiley) Pyrazolones, Pyrazolidones and Derivatives, 1963. Editor: Five and Six Membered Compounds with Nitrogen and Oxygen, 1963; Pyrazoles, Pyrazolines, Pyrazolidine and Condensed Ring Systems, 1967; asso. editor Jour. Chem. and Engring. Data, 1966-71; editorial bd. Jour. Macromolecular Chemistry, Jour. Polymer Sci. Contbr. to textbook; articles on organic and polymer chemistry sci. jours. Patentee in field. Home: 8 Roosevelt Circle Palo Alto CA 94306 Office: Dept Chemistry Stanford U Palo Alto CA 94305

WILEY, THOMAS GLEN, investment co. exec.; b. Salt Lake City, Feb. 1, 1928; s. Thomas J. and Juanita (Dean) W.; B.B.A. cum laude, U. Wash., 1951, postgrad., 1954; children by previous marriage—Jana Lynn, Jill, Tina Elizabeth, Tova Suzanne. With Shell Chem. Co., 1954-61, fin. analyst, N.Y.C., 1960-63; mgr. fin. analysis and pricing Lear Siegler, Los Angeles, 1963-72; v.p. finance, treas. Electronic Memories & Magnetics Corp., Los Angeles, 1972—; exec. v.p. Hale Bros. Assos., San Francisco, 1972—. Served to 1st lt. AUS, 1951-53. Home: 1942 Pacific Ave San Francisco CA 94109 Office: 601 California St San Francisco CA 94108

WILEY, THOMAS WRIGHT, lawyer; b. Hutchinson, Kans., Sept. 22, 1931; s. Philip Vernon and Jean (Wright) W.; A.B., Dartmouth Coll., 1953; LL.B., Harvard U., 1959; m. Ann Irwin, Aug. 31, 1954; children—Thomas Merritt, Stephen David, Charles Good, Elizabeth. Admitted to Mass. bar, 1959, Ariz. bar, 1963; asso. firm Bingham, Dana & Gould, Boston, 1959-62; partner firm Fennemore, Craig, von Ammon & Udall, Phoenix, 1962—. Fellow Am. Coll. Probate Counsel; mem. Am. Bar Assn. (council sect. taxation), Am. Law Inst., Phi Beta Kappa. Home: 6225 E Lafayette Blvd Scottsdale AZ 85251 Office: 1700 1st Nat Bank Plaza 100 W Washington St Phoenix AZ 85003

WILEY, WILLIAM BRADFORD, publisher; b. Orange, N.J., Nov. 17, 1910; s. William Carroll and Isabel (LeCato) W.; A.B., Colgate U., 1932, LL.D. (hon.), 1966; m. Esther T. Booth, Jan. 4, 1936; children—William Bradford II, Peter Booth, Deborah Elizabeth Grout. With John Wiley & Sons, Inc., N.Y.C., 1932—, sec., v.p. and sec., exec. v.p., treas., 1938-56, pres., 1956-71, chmn., 1971—, dir., 1942—; chmn., dir. John Wiley & Sons, Can., Wiley Pubs. Can., John Wiley & Sons Ltd., London, Jacaranda-Wiley, Ltd., Brisbane; dir. Wiley Eastern Ltd., India, Limusa, S.A., Mexico. Trustee Drew U. Corder fellow Columbia U. Episcopalian. Clubs: Players, University (N.Y.C.); Sakonnet Golf, Sakonnet Yacht (R.I.); Baltusrol (N.J.) Golf. Home: 57 Prospect Hill Ave Summit NJ 07901 also Bailey's Ledge Little Compton RI 02837 Office: 605 3d Ave New York NY 10016

WILF, MERVIN M., lawyer; b. Phila., Mar. 10, 1926; s. Benjamin and Bessie (Kovalsky) W.; A.B., Pa. State U., 1946; J.D. magna cum laude, U. Pa., 1955; m. Norma Neff, Sept. 11, 1949; children—Michael J., Susan R., Kathy E. Admitted to Pa. bar, 1956; asso., then partner firm White and Williams, Phila., 1955-71; partner firm Townsend, Elliot & Munson, Phila., 1971; partner firm Hudson, Wilf & Kronfeld, Phila., 1972—; lectr. law U. Pa. Law Sch., Rutgers U. Law Sch.; vis. prof. law Temple U. Law Sch. Chmn., pres. Mus. Am. Jewish History, Phila., 1975-78; bd. overseers Gratz Coll., Phila., 1965—. Served with USMC, 1944-45. Mem. Am. Bar Assn. (standing com. on profl. edn. 1978—, mem. council sect. taxation 1977—), Phila. Bar Assn. (mem. council sect. taxation 1976—), Am. Law Inst. Jewish. Club: Union League (Phila.). Articles editor U. Pa. Law Rev., 1954-55; contbr. articles to legal jours. Home: 132 Fairview Rd Narberth PA 19072 Office: 2200 Packard Bldg Philadelphia PA 19102

WILFORD, JOHN NOBLE, JR., editor; b. Murray, Ky., Oct. 4, 1933; s. John Noble and Pauline (Hendricks) W.; student Lambuth Coll., 1951-52; B.S., U. Tenn., 1955; M.A., Syracuse U., 1956; Internat. Reporting fellow Columbia, 1961-62; m. Nancy Everett Watts, Dec. 25, 1966; 1 dau., Nona. Reporter, Comml. Appeal, Memphis, summers 1954-55; reporter Wall St. Jour., N.Y.C., 1956, 59-61; contbg. editor Time mag., N.Y.C., 1962-65; sci. reporter N.Y. Times, 1965-73, asst. nat. editor, 1973-75, dir. sci. news, 1975-79, sci. corr., 1979—. Served with CIC, AUS, 1957-59. Recipient Aviation/Space Writers Book award, 1970; G.M. Loeb Achievement award U. Conn., 1972; Press award Nat. Space Club, 1974. Mem. Aviation/Space Writers Assn., Authors Guild, Sigma Delta Chi, Phi Kappa Phi. Club: Overseas Press (N.Y.C.). Author: We Reach The Moon, 1969. Editor: Scientists at Work, 1979. Home: 232 W 10th St New York NY 10014 Office: 229 W 43d St New York NY 10036

WILFORD, JOSEPH BENJAMIN, ins. co. exec.; b. Ottumwa, Iowa, Aug. 23, 1924; s. Harry L. and May B. (Lewis) W.; student Iowa State Coll., 1946-47; m. Margaret J. Anderson, June 3, 1949; children—Teri L., Jody A., Sheryl J., Cynthia R., Janell A., Belinda M. Chief urban appraiser Doane Agrl. Service, St. Louis, 1950-54; acting dir. Property Tax div. Iowa State Tax Commn., 1955; with N.Y. Life Ins. Co., N.Y.C., 1956—, v.p., 1972-77, sr. v.p., 1977—; chmn. real estate and mortgage loan com. N.Y. State Employees Retirement System; mem. mortgage adv. com. N.Y. U. Real Estate Inst.; mem. adv. bd. N.Y. Real Estate Bd. Served with USMC, 1943-46. Mem. Am. Inst. Real Estate Appraisers (bd. dirs. Kansas City chpt.). Presbyterian. Home: 109 Snowberry Ln New Canaan CT 06840 Office: 51 Madison Ave New York City NY 10010

WILGUS, D.K., educator; b. West Mansfield, Ohio, Dec. 1, 1918; s. Robert Nathaniel and Cora (Knight) W.; B.A., B.Sc., Ohio State U., 1941, M.A., 1947, Ph.D., 1954; m. Evelyn L. Hastings, Nov. 23, 1940; children—Karen (Ms. Abbott), Liscinda (Mrs. Willard Fox). Ednl. adminstr. Purdue U., 1941; instr. English, Ohio State U., 1946-50; prof. English and folklore Western Ky. State. Coll., 1950-62; prof. English and Anglo-Am. folksong U. Calif., Los Angeles, 1962—. Sec. John Edwards Meml. Found., 1962-70, treas., 1971—. Served with AUS, 1942-45. Guggenheim fellow, 1957-58; recipient Chgo. Folklore prize U. Chgo., 1956. Fellow Am. Folklore Soc. (v.p. 1963-64, pres. 1971-72); mem. Ky. Folklore Soc. (pres. 1961-62, dir. 1962—), Modern Lang. Assn., Folklore Soc., Lambda Chi Alpha, Eta Sigma Phi. Author: Anglo-American Folksong Scholarship since 1898, 1959; Folklore International, 1967; Folk-Songs of the Southern United States, 1967; also numerous articles. Editor Ky. Folklore Record, 1955-61, Western Folklore, 1970-75. Home: 1064 Stanford St Santa Monica CA 90403 Office: Folklore and Mythology Program U Calif Los Angeles CA 90024

WILHELM, ALFRED ARNOLD, engring. and constrn. co. exec.; b. Cleve., Dec. 18, 1918; s. Elmer John and Irene (Bissinger) W.; B.A., Heidelberg Coll., 1941; m. Frances Arant, Apr. 12, 1969; children—Keith, Richard. Jr. accountant to mgr. Ernst & Ernst, Cleve., 1941-62; controller Austin Co., Cleve., 1962-64, sec., fin. v.p., 1964—, also dir. subs. Trustee, treas. Fairview (Ohio) Gen. Hosp.; trustee Heidelberg Coll., United Ch. Homes; mem. Rocky River (Ohio) Bd. Edn., 1966-70. Served with AUS, 1942-46. C.P.A., Ohio.

Mem. Ohio Soc. C.P.A.'s. Republican. Mem. United Ch. of Christ. Clubs: Cleve. Yachting, Masons. Home: 20005 Frazier Dr Rocky River OH 44116 Office: 3650 Mayfield Rd Cleveland OH 44121

WILHELM, JOHN REMSEN, univ. dean; b. Billings, Mont., Mar. 5, 1916; s. Charles Cleveland and Marion (Bell) W.; B.A., U. Minn., 1941; m. Margaret Maslin, Jan. 16, 1945; children—Richard Remsen, Lawrence Eppley, Charles Maslin. Martha Marsh. Reporter, Chgo. Tribune, 1941-42; night bur. mgr. United Press, Detroit, 1942, cable desk, N.Y.C., 1943; war corr. Normandy Invasion, Reuters of London, 1944, European corr. Chgo. Sun, London, 1944-47; bur. chief McGraw-Hill World News, Buenos Aires, 1948-49, Mexico, 1949-54, fgn. editor, dir. news bureaus, 1954-67; dir., prof. Sch. Journalism, Ohio Univ., Athens, 1968, now dean Coll. of Communication. Mem. Fgn. Corrs. Assn. Mexico (pres. 1954). Clubs: American of Mexico (sec. 1954); Overseas Press (bd. govs. 1956-58, pres. 1959-60) (N.Y.C.). Author: (with others) Men Who Make Your World, 1949; The Foreign Correspondent, 1951; Guide to All Mexico, 5th edit., 1978; Guide to Caribbean Islands, 1960; Guide to Mexico City, 16th edit., 1974. Home: 190 Longview Heights Athens OH 45701

WILHELM, JOSEPH LAWRENCE, archbishop; b. Walkerton, Ont., Can., Nov. 16, 1909; s. John and Magdalena (Uhrich) W.; J.C.L., Ottawa U., 1948. Ordained priest Roman Cath. Ch., 1934; asst., bishop's sec., Hamilton, Ont., 1934-40; chaplain Canadian Army, 1940-45; pastor St. Peter & Paul Ch., Hamilton, 1946-63; aux. bishop of Calgary, Alta., 1963-67; archbishop of Kingston, Ont., 1967—. Decorated Mil. cross. Address: 279 Johnson St Kingston ON Canada

WILHELM, ROSS JOHNSTON, educator, business economist; b. Arlington, N.J., Jan. 24, 1920; s. Roy Pierre and Annie (Ross) W.; B.B.A., Western Res. U., 1947, M.B.A., 1948; Ph.D., U. Mich., 1963; LL.D. (hon.), Eastern Mich. U., 1977; m. Rowena May, Jan. 4, 1944; 1 son, Peter Bradbury. Mgr., cons. in bus. and govt.; prof. bus. econs. Grad. Sch. Bus., U. Mich., Ann Arbor, 1950-51, 1954—; writer, narrator Business Rev., weekly radio program, 1960—; co-author, narrator Everybody's Business, The Challenge of Change, TV series, 1965; commentator WXYZ-TV, ABC, Detroit, 1969, 70; commentator weekly radio program The Business Roundtable, MBS, 1975-76; dir. Perry Drug Stores, Inc., Plymouth, Mich.; dir. Earhart Condominium, Ann Arbor, 1975-77. Served to 1st lt. U.S. Army, 1942-46. Recipient Distinguished Faculty Service award U. Mich., 1964; Janus award Mortgage Bankers Assn., 1973. Mem. Am. Econ. Assn., Am. Marketing Assn., Mont Pelerin Soc., Sigma Zeta. Author numerous books and articles, weekly newspaper column Inside Business, 1974-77. Home: 710 Greenhills Dr Ann Arbor MI 48105

WILHELM, WILLIAM JEAN, civil engr., educator; b. St. Louis, Oct. 5, 1935; s. Maurice Ferdinand and Eileen Winifred (McClintock) W.; B.M.E., Auburn U., 1958, M.S., 1963; Ph.D., N.C. State U., 1968; m. Patricia Jane Zietz, Aug. 17, 1957; children—William, Robert, Andrew, Mary, David. Structural engr. Palmer & Baker Engrs., Mobile, Ala., 1958-60; instr. engring. graphics Auburn U., 1960-64; asst. prof. civil engring. W.Va. U., Morgantown, 1967-72, asso. prof., 1972-76, prof., 1976-79, chmn., 1974-79; dean engring. Wichita State U., 1979—. Served with C.E., U.S. Army, 1959-62. Fellow Am. Concrete Inst., ASCE; mem. Am. Soc. for Engring. Edn., Nat. Soc. Profl. Engrs., Prestressed Concrete Inst., Sigma Xi, Phi Kappa Phi, Tau Beta Pi, Pi Tau Sigma, Chi Epsilon. man Catholic. Contbr. articles to profl. jours. Home: 2500 Banbury Circle Wichita KS 67226 Office: Coll Engring Wichita State U Wichita KS 67208

WILHELMI, ALFRED ELLIS, biochemist, educator; b. Lakewood, Ohio, Sept. 28, 1910; s. Gustavus Carl and Helena Ethel (Looschen) W.; A.B. summa cum laude, Western Res. U., 1933; B.A. with 1st class honours in Animal Physiology (Rhodes scholar 1933), Oxford U., 1935, D.Phil. in Biochemistry, 1937; m. Jane Anne Russell. Aug. 26, 1940 (dec. Mar. 1967); m. 2d, Mary C. Robertson, June 12, 1973. Alexander Brown Coxe fellow physiol. chemistry Yale, 1939, from instr. to asso. prof., 1940-50; prof., chmn. dept. biochemistry Emory U., 1950-77, Charles Howard Candler prof., 1960-79, prof. emeritus, 1979—. Cons. regulatory biology NSF, 1950-55; cons. endocrinology study sect. NIH, 1954-60, chmn., 1957-60; mem. Nat. Arthritis and Metabolic Diseases Council, 1962. Mem. Nat. Council Humanities, 1967. Fellow A.A.A.S., N.Y. Acad. Sci.; hon. mem. Canadian Physiol. Soc.; mem. Am. Soc. Biol. Chemists, Endocrine Soc. (Upjohn scholar 1960, pres. 1968, Leadership award 1977), Ga. Acad. Sci., Phi Beta Kappa. Sigma Xi, Omicron Delta Kappa. Contbr. articles to profl. jours. Home: 924 Castle Falls Dr NE Atlanta GA 30329

WILHELMY, ROBERT M., pub. co. exec.; b. Marlboro, Mass., July 16, 1924; s. Eudore J. and Georgiana B. (Boudreau) W.; grad. Worcester (Mass.) Acad., 1943; B.A., Tufts U., Medford, Mass., 1949; m. Rita V. Argalli, May 14, 1949; children—Kyle I., Robert M., James F., Virginia B., Bradley E. Bus. trainee Gen. Electric Co., Bridgeport, Conn., 1949-52, supr. gen. accounting and statistics, 1952-54, traveling auditor, Schenectady, 1954-57, mgr. budgets and measurements, Cleve., 1957-60, mgr. gen. and tax accounting, 1960-61; asst. controller McGraw-Hill, Inc., N.Y.C., 1961-63; controller McGraw-Hill Pub. Co., 1963-69, v.p. finance, 1969-72, sr. v.p. corporate financial operations, 1972—; dir. Continuing Edn. Co., Washington, Newton Falls Paper Co. Served with USAAF, 1943-46. Mem. Financial Execs. Inst. (pres., dir. N.Y. chpt.), Worcester Acad. Alumni Council. Home: 1 Melon Patch Ln Westport CT 06880 Office: 1221 Ave of Americas New York NY 10020

WILHITE, JIM, gas co. exec.; b. Greenwood, Ark., Mar. 31, 1938; s. Raymond I. and Margaret E. (Oliver) W.; B.S., Okla. State U., 1960; m. Shirley Parker, June 23, 1963; children—Kimberly Kay, Jeffrey Scott. With Ark. La. Gas Co., Shreveport, La., 1963—, v.p. in charge of employee and indsl. relations, 1972-73, exec. v.p., 1973—. Bd. dirs. Central YMCA, Shreveport, Shreveport Norwella council Boy Scouts Am., Sports Found., Shreveport; campaign chmn. United Way, Shreveport, 1978. Mem. So. Gas Assn., Sales and Mktg. Execs. Shreveport, Mid Continent Oil and Gas, Shreveport C. of C. (dir.), La. Assn. Bus. and Industry (dir.). Methodist. Clubs: Pierremont Oaks Tennis, Shreveport. Home: 582 Janie Ct Shreveport LA 71106 Office: PO Box 21734 Shreveport LA 71106

WILHOIT, JAMES CAMMACK, JR., educator; b. Tulsa, Dec. 22, 1925; s. James Cammack and Lora (Holloway) W.; B.S., Rice U., 1948; M.S., Tex. A. and M. U., 1951; Ph.D., Stanford, 1954; m. Louise LeGros, Jan. 22, 1949; children—James Paul, Ann Holloway, Joan LeGros, John Hiram. Instr. mech. engring. Tex. A. and M. U., 1949-51; asst. prof. mech. engring. Rice U., Houston, 1954-60, asso. prof., 1960-66, prof. 1966—. Mem. exec. com. Harris County Republican Party, 1963-72, 74-78; del. Republican Nat. Conv., 1972. Served with USNR, 1944-46. Registered profl. engr., Tex. Mem. ASME, Sigma Xi, Tau Beta Pi. Presbyn. Contbr. articles profl. jours. Home: 1826 Sunset Blvd Houston TX 77005

WILINSKI, EDWIN ALFRED, constrn. co. exec.; b. N.Y.C., Mar. 15, 1938; s. Edwin Alfred and Kathryn (Rinko) W.; B.S., Ga. Inst. Tech., 1959; J.D., Bklyn. Law Sch., 1970; m. Diane Mary Symkowski, May 5, 1962; children—Eric, Karin, Adrienne, Suzanne, Laura. Agt., IRS, N.Y.C., 1959-66; with Fischbach & Moore, Inc., N.Y.C., 1967—, sec., 1970—, v.p., 1978—. Served with AUS, 1961-62. Home: Massapequa NY 11758 Office: 485 Lexington Ave New York NY 10017

WILINSKY, HARRIET (MRS. SYLVAN GOODMAN), retail exec. b. Boston; d. Charles F. and Jeanette (Isenberg) Wilinsky; grad. Girls' Latin Sch., Boston, 1923; student Wellesley Coll., 1923-24; A.B., Barnard Coll., 1927; m. Sylvan A. Goodman, 1933. Psychologist, Judge Baker Guidance Center, Boston, 1927-29; advt. copywriter R.H. White Co., Boston, 1930-31; advt. mgr. E.T. Slattery Co., Boston, 1931-43; fashion dir. William Filene's Sons Co., 1943-45, sales promotion mgr., 1945-68, v.p. sales promotion div., 1968-72, mem. mgmt. bd., 1945-72; dir. marketing services Wilinsky-Goodman, Boston, 1973—; asso. in retailing Simmons Coll., Boston, 1964. Bd. dirs. Boston Better Bus. Bur., Mass. Advocacy Center, 1976, Young Audiences of Mass., 1966—; trustee Beth Israel Hosp., Boston, 1972—. Named Business Woman Year, Boston, 1952, Boston Advt. Woman of Year, 1961. Mem. Fashion Group Boston (past regional dir.), Fashion Group N.Y., Boston C. of C. (dir.), Retail Trade Bd. Boston, Asso. Merchandising Corp. Publicity Dirs. (chmn. 1954-55), Nat. Retail Mchts. Assn. (dir. 1968—), Business and Profl. Women's Club, Phi Beta Kappa. Clubs: Boston Advertising, Altrusa. Author: Careers in Retailing. Home: 51 Beacon St Boston MA 02108 Office: 151 Tremont St Boston MA 02101

WILKE, ALFRED WALTER, lawyer; b. Detroit, Feb. 16, 1922; s. Alfred Richard and Emma (Schwerkoske) W.; B.S. cum laude, U. Detroit, 1942, J.D. summa cum laude, 1945; m. Marilyn Miller, Apr. 7, 1951; children—Alfred Walter II, Mark C., Lisa Sue. Admitted to Mich. bar, 1945, since practiced in Detroit; asso. firm Lo Cicero & Wilke, 1946-74; partner firm McInally, Brucker, Newcombe, Wilke & DeBona, and predecessor, P.C., 1974—; dir. Plastomer Corp., Chrysler & Koppin Co., Mark Allen Co., Tartan Tool Co., Asso. Mut. Hosp. Service Mich., numerous other corps. in Detroit area. Mem. Am., Mich., Detroit bar assns., Delta Theta Phi. Republican. Lutheran (pres. ch. council). Mason (K.T., Shriner). Clubs: Detroit Athletic, Lochmoor Golf. Home: 171 Merriweather Rd Grosse Pointe Farms MI 48236 Office: 3800 City Nat Bank Bldg Detroit MI 48226 also 17150 Kercheval Ave Grosse Pointe MI 48230

WILKE, CHARLES ROBERT, chem. engr., educator, investment adviser; b. Dayton, Ohio, Feb. 4, 1917; s. Otto Alexander and Stella M. (Dodge) W.; B. Chem. Engring., U. Dayton, 1940; M.S. in Chemistry, State Coll. Wash., 1942; Ph.D. in Chem. Engring., U. Wis., 1944; m. Bernice Lucille Arnett, June 19, 1946. Asso. engr. Union Oil Co. of Calif., 1944-45, cons., 1952—; instr. chem. engring. Wash. State Coll., 1945-46; instr. chem. engring. U. Calif. at Berkeley, 1946-47, asst. prof., 1947-51, asso. prof., 1951-53, prof., 1953—, chmn. dept. chem. engring., 1953-63, asst. to chancellor acad. affairs, 1967-69, prin. investigator Lawrence Berkeley lab., 1950—; indsl. cons., 1952—; chmn. bd. C.R. Wilke Internat. Corp., 1970—; cons. editor Reinhold Pub. Co., 1958-64; mem. Calif. Bd. Registration Civil and Profl. Engrs., 1964-72, pres., 1967-69. Recipient Walker award Am. Inst. Chem. Engrs., 1965, Colburn award, 1951. Fellow Am. Inst. Chem. Engrs. (past chmn. No. Calif. sect.); mem. Soc. Applied Bacteriology, Am. Chem. Soc., Electrochem. Soc., Nat. Acad. Engring., Am. Soc. Engring. Edn. (Chem. Engring. lecture award 1964), Am. Soc. Microbiology, Sigma Xi, Tau Beta Pi. Club: Commonwealth of California, World Trade of San Francisco. Contbr. articles to profl. jours. Home: 1327 Contra Costa Dr El Cerrito CA 94530

WILKENS, HAROLD LOUIS, mgmt. cons., retired chain food store exec.; b. Newport, Ky., July 28, 1906; s. Albert David and Myrtle (Lewis) W.; night student Cin. Law Sch.; m. Ethel May Bowen, Nov. 3, 1923. With Kroger Co., 1930-50, mgr. No. div. produce buying and retail operations, 1951-69; with Nat. Tea Co., Chgo., 1954-69, charge produce operations and procurement, 1954-69, v.p., exec. officer, mgmt. cons., 1969—. Chmn. market research com. Agr. Adv. Bd., Dept. Agr., 1959-69; mem. com. Nat. Assn. Food Chains-United Fruit and Vegetable Growers Assn., 1961-69. Mason. Home: 5574 Pendlewood Ln Fort Myers FL 33907

WILKERSON, JAMES PLATT, advt. exec.; b. Miamisburg, Ohio, Oct. 16, 1914; s. Oscar and Miriam (Wampler) W.; grad. Lawrenceville Sch., 1933; B.A., Amherst Coll., 1937; m. Audrey Olena, Oct. 13, 1939 (div.); children—Ann, Cathlyn, Robin; m. 2d, Audrey Anne Potter, June 21, 1961. With Young & Rubicam, Inc., N.Y.C., 1940-68, sr. v.p., 1959-64, dir. internat. div., 1959-63, dir. client services U.S., 1963—, exec. v.p., 1964-68; pres. Star Stations, Inc., Omaha, 1968-71; vice chmn. Marsteller, Inc., 1968—. Chmn. Amherst Coll. alumni fund com., 1954-55. Recipient Amherst medal for eminent service, 1952. Mem. Internat. Wine and Food Soc. (chmn. 1975—), Royal Agrl. Soc. (gov.). Clubs: N.Y. Yacht; Reform, Anglo-Belgian (London, Eng.). Home: Admington Hall Shipston-on-Stour Warwickshire England Office: Marsteller Inc 866 3d Ave New York NY 10022

WILKERSON, LEO CARL, lawyer; b. Mebane, N.C., Sept. 6, 1933; s. Banks Holt and Cynthia Myrtle (Hinshaw) W.; B.S., U. N.C., 1955; LL.B., U. Va., 1965; m. Patricia R. Crotts, June 18, 1961; children—Carl, Caroline. Supr. cost accounting Thomasville Furniture Industries (N.C.), 1956-61; admitted to Ohio, Va. bars, 1965; asso. counsel Frost & Jacobs, Cin., 1965-69; asso. gen. counsel R.J. Reynolds Industries, Inc., Winston-Salem, N.C., 1970—. Mem. Am., Va. bar assns. Home: 2934 Buena Vista Rd Winston-Salem NC 27106 Office: care RJ Reynolds Industries Inc Winston-Salem NC 27102

WILKES, DONALD FANCHER, electromech. devices co. exec.; b. Portland, Oreg., July 20, 1931; s. Gordon Buell and Catherine (Fancher) W.; B.S. in Mech. Engring., Wash. State U., 1954; M.S., U. N.Mex., 1962; m. Joan Adell Petersen, June 27, 1954; children—Martin Carey, Norma Jean, Roger Alan. Staff mem., mech. engr. Sandia Corp., Albuquerque, 1954-67; sr., v.p., dir., inventor, engr., dir. advanced research and devel. Rolamite Inc. (later Foothill Lab. div. Foothill Group Inc.), Albuquerque, 1968-78; mgr., prin. tech. staff mem. ARDEV-Albuquerque Lab. subs. Atlantic Richfield Co., 1978—. Served with AUS, 1955-57. Mem. ASME. Phi Kappa Phi, Tau Beta Pi, Sigma Tau, Alpha Phi Omega, Pi Tau Sigma (hon.). Presbyn. (elder). Inventor of rolamite. Home: 2816 Charleston St Albuquerque NM 87110 Office: 6139 Edith Rd Albuquerque NM 87107. *As I grow older and my experience base grows, I am coming to realize that everything I have ever done or experienced is synergistically related to everything that I deeply aspire to do, and, more importantly, that I personally have a great deal to contribute to today's situation. I would like to encourage others to use and trust their God-given subconscious minds and try to steer and train our educators toward teaching young people to trust and use their intuitive capabilities.*

WILKES, JAMES OSCROFT, educator; b. Southampton, Eng., Jan. 24, 1932; s. Stephen Robert Colin Meredith and Marion (Oscroft) W.; came to U.S., 1955; B.A., U. Cambridge, 1954, M.A., 1960; M.S., U. Mich., 1956, Ph.D., 1963; m. Mary Ann Gibson, Aug. 18, 1956. Demonstrator dept. chem. engring. U. Cambridge, 1957-60; asst. prof. chem. engring. dept. U. Mich., Ann Arbor, 1963-67, asso. prof., 1967-70, prof., 1970—, chmn. dept., 1971-77. Cons. applied numerical methods. Recipient Distinguished Service awards U. Mich., 1966. Asso., Trinity Coll. Music, London, 1951. English Speaking Union King George VI Meml. fellow, 1955. Mem. Am. Inst. Chem. Engrs., Soc. Petroleum Engrs., Sigma Xi, Tau Beta Pi. Author: (with B. Carnahan and H.A. Luther) Applied Numerical Methods, 1969; (with B. Carnahan) Digital Computing and Numerical Methods, 1973; Pipe Organs of Ann Arbor, 1977. Home: 805 Colliston Rd Ann Arbor MI 48105

WILKES, PAUL, author; b. Cleve., Sept. 12, 1938; s. Paul Thomas and Margaret (Salansky) W.; B.A. in Journalism, Marquette U., 1960; M.A., Columbia, 1967. Free lance writer, 1969—; editor for Harper's Mag. Press, 1970, Harper & Row, publishers, 1969; writer Balt. Sun, 1967-68, Boulder (Colo.) Daily Camera, 1964-66; lectr. feature writing Bklyn. Coll., 1973-75; vis. writer U. Pitts., 1979. Co-founder Christian Help in Park Slope, 1973-75. Served with USNR, 1961-64. Recipient awards Soc. Midland Writers, 1974, Friends of Am. Writers, 1974; By-Line award Marquette U., 1977; Distinguished Alumni award Columbia U. Sch. Journalism, 1978; Julius Ochs Adler fellow, 1966. Author: Fitzgo, The Wild Dog of Central Park, 1973; These Priests Stay, 1974; Trying Out the Dream, 1975; (TV series and book) Six American Families (duPont-Columbia award 1978), 1977; co-writer PBS dramatic film Men of Iron, 1979, The Molders of Troy, 1980. Contbr. articles to profl. jours. and maj. mags. including N.Y. Times Mag., New York, Life, Look, Atlantic, The Nation, Commonweal, GEO. Address: 45 W 10th St New York NY 10011

WILKEY, MALCOLM RICHARD, judge; b. Murfreesboro, Tenn., Dec. 6, 1918; s. Malcolm Newton and Elizabeth (Gilbert) W., A.B., Harvard, 1940, LL.B., 1948; m. Emma Secul Depolo, Dec. 21, 1959. Admitted to Tex. bar, 1948, N.Y. bar, 1963, U.S. Supreme Ct. bar, 1952, Ct. of Appeals, D.C. Circuit, 1958; partner firm Butler Binion Rice & Cook, 1948-54, 61-63; U.S. atty. So. Dist. Tex., 1954-58; asst. atty. gen. U.S., 1958-61; sec., asso. gen. counsel Kennecott Copper Corp. 1963-67, gen. counsel, sec., 1967-70; judge U.S. Ct. Appeals, D.C. Circuit, 1970—. Del. Republican Nat. Conv., 1960. Served from 2d lt. to lt. col. AUS, 1941-45. Fellow Am. Bar Found.; mem. Am. Bar Assn. (commn. on a nat. inst. of justice, chmn. drafting com.), Assn. Bar City N.Y., Am. Law Inst., Jud. Conf. U.S. (com. on standards for admission to fed. cts.), Phi Beta Kappa, Delta Sigma Rho. Club: Metropolitan (Washington). Home: 540 N St SW Washington DC 20024 Office: US Ct Appeals Washington DC 20001

WILKEY, RICHARD AMBROSE, city ofcl.; b. Indpls., Apr. 20, 1940; s. Clarence Ruben and Helen Mary (Spitzer) Frankfurt; B.A., N. Central Coll., 1962; M.A., U. Ill., 1964; m. Joyce Marie Lauck, Aug. 6, 1966; children—Andrew Lawrence, Ryan Richard. Adminstrv. asst., village mgr. Village of Glencoe (Ill.), 1962, Village of Winnetka (Ill.), 1964-66; asst. city mgr. City of Des Moines, 1966-73, acting city mgr., 1973-74, city mgr., 1974—. Mem. bd. dirs. YMCA. Mem. Internat. City Mgmt. Assn., Am. Soc. Pub. Adminstrn., Am. Pub. Works Assn., Iowa City Mgmt. Assn. (pres. 1976-77). Home: 3200 36th St Des Moines IA 50310 Office: City Hall 1st and Locust Sts Des Moines IA 50307

WILKIE, JOHN, utility exec.; b. N.Y.C., Jan. 4, 1904; s. John Lincoln and Edith Blake (Brown) W.; A.B., Harvard, 1923, M.B.A., 1925; student Columbia, 1925-26; m. Dorothea Woodruff Jones, June 29, 1932 (div.); children—Dorothea Rehn (Mrs. D. Lieber), John McNeil, Peter Lex, Edith Blake; m. 2d, Margot Loines Morrow, June 30, 1954; stepchildren—Stephen Morrow, Faith (Mrs. Stephen Williams), Constance (Mrs. Michael Fulenwider). Dir., Central Hudson Gas and Electric Co., Poughkeepsie, N.Y., 1925—, statistician, 1926, successively, asst. treas., treas., v.p., treas., 1936-60, vice chmn. bd., chief financial officer, 1960-64, chmn. bd. and chief financial officer, 1964-68, chmn. bd., chief exec. officer, 1968-75, chmn. fin. com., audit com., 1975—. Sr. mem. Conf. Bd.; past chmn. Hudson River Conservation Soc., Dutchess County War Council; dir. emeritus Regional Plan Assn. (N.Y.). Trustee emeritus, former chmn. bd. Vassar Coll. Mem. Am. Gas Assn., Edison Electric Inst., Newcomen Soc. Eng., Pilgrims of U.S., Delta Psi. Clubs: Downtown Assn., Harvard, Century Assn. (N.Y.C.); Harvard (Boston); Amrita (Poughkeepsie); Bedford (N.Y.) Golf and Tennis; Edgartown (Mass.) Yacht. Home: Mt Holly Rd Katonah NY 10536 Office: One Wall St New York NY 10005

WILKIE, LEIGHTON ALLYN, mfg. exec.; b. Winona, Minn., July 29, 1900; s. Julius C. and Ellen (Leighton) W.; student U. Minn., 1921-22; m. Adele Mearns, Feb. 23, 1935; children—Bonnie A. (Mrs. Jon Henricks), Michael L. Founder, chmn. bd. Continental Machines, Inc., Mpls., 1932—; chmn. Contour Saws, Inc., DoAll Co., Des Plaines, Ill., also 50 DoAll sales store corps., prin. cities, 1942—; dir. First Nat. Bank Des Plaines. Chmn. Wilkie Bros. Found., Des Plaines. Bd. dirs. Santa Barbara Mus. Natural History. Mem. Chevaliers du Tasterein, Newcomen Soc. N.Am., Los Rancheros Visitadores (Santa Barbara), Delta Tau. Clubs: Lake Zurich (Ill.) Golf; Valley, Coral Casino (Santa Barbara, Calif.) Author: Your Life in the Machine World. Home: Apple Orchard Hill Long Grove IL 60047 also 1660 E Valley Rd Santa Barbara CA 93103 also Thunderbird Game Farm Genoa City WI 53128 Office: 254 N Laurel Ave Des Plaines IL 60016

WILKIE, ROBERT JOHN, mfg. co. exec.; b. Winona, Minn., Jan. 18, 1910; s. Julius Christopher and Ellen Marie (Leighton) W.; student U. Minn., 1927-31; m. Bliss Edna Higgins, Mar. 1, 1935 (dec. June 1957); children—Bliss (Mrs. Alan Leroy Bancroft) and Sally (Mrs. David Warren Brown) (twins), Susan (Mrs. John Charles Karrasch), Jonathan Paul; m. 2d, Marjorie Lois Olson, Nov. 13, 1958. Gen. mgr. Continental Machines, Inc., 1932-34, pres., 1934-60, chmn. bd., 1973; vice chmn. bd. Contour Saws, Inc., Des Plaines, Ill., 1941—, DoAll Co., Des Plaines, 1963—, also dir. 60 internat. corps.; dir. Continental Granite Corp., Commander Labs., Inc., Greenlee Tool Co., Inc. Bd. dirs. Wilkie Brothers Found., 1950—. Home: 2660 Hidden Valley Rd La Jolla CA 92037 Office: PO Box D Harmony Grove Rd Escondido CA 92025

WILKIE, VALLEAU, JR., found. exec.; b. Summit, N.J., July 3, 1923; s. Valleau and Amelia Willetts (Parry) W.; A.B., Yale U., 1948; M.A., Harvard U., 1954; m. Marjorie Hankin, Feb. 23, 1946; children—Janice, Robert. Instr. history Phillips Acad., 1948-59; headmaster Governor Dummer Acad., Byfield, Mass., 1959-72, mem. bd. trustees, 1960-72, dir. devel., 1972-73; exec. v.p. Sid W. Richardson Found., Ft. Worth, 1973—. Mem. adv. com. on accreditation and instl. eligibility U.S. Office Edn., 1973-78. Bd. dirs. S.W. Ednl. Devel. Lab., 1976—; bd. dirs. Conf. of S.W. Founds., 1977—, chmn., 1979—. Served to 1st lt. USAAF, 1942-45. Mem. Headmasters Assn., N.E. Assn. Schs. and Colls. (chmn. commn. on ind. secondary schs. 1967-70, pres. 1972-73), Delta Kappa Epsilon. Episcopalian. Address: Fort Worth Nat Bank Bldg Fort Worth TX 76102

WILKIN, ED RAY, JR., advt. agy. exec.; b. Kansas City, Kans., Oct. 20, 1925; s. Ed Ray and Captola Alberta (Lyons) W.; B.J., U. Mo., 1948; m. Jeane Louise Davis, Feb. 6, 1949; children—David, Patricia, Janet. Space salesman Kansas City (Mo.) Star, 1948-49, space salesman, Chgo., 1949-50; advt. mgr. Western div. Foremost Dairies, Appleton, Wis., 1950-56; account exec. Western Advt., Racine, Wis., 1956-57; account exec., v.p., exec. v.p. Byer & Bowman Advt. Agy.,

Columbus, Ohio, 1957-72, pres., 1973—, chmn. bd., 1979—. Vice pres. Berwick Park Civic Assn., 1959-60; pres. Woodlands Civic League, 1970-71. Served with USAAF, World War II. Mem. Mid-Ohio Regional Planning Commn., Columbus Advt. Fedn. (pres. 1972-73, treas. 1974). Republican. Methodist. Club: Little Turtle Country. Home: 5654 Indian Mound Ct Columbus OH 43213 Office: 66 S 6th St Columbus OH 43215

WILKIN, EUGENE WELCH, advt. agy. exec.; b. North Attleborough, Mass., May 14, 1923; s. Laurence Welch and Ruth Marion (Totten) W.; A.B., Dartmouth U., 1948; postgrad. Grad. Sch. Bus. Adminstrn., Harvard, July 1963; m. Anita Drake, Sept. 10, 1949; children—Judith Louise, Lawrence Welch 2d, Diana Lewis, William Alexander. Surety rep. Aetna Casualty Ins. Co., Boston, Providence, 1949-50; asst. to pres., graphic arts salesman J.C. Hall Co., Pawtucket, R.I., 1950-51; copywriter T. Robley Loutit Advt. Agy., Providence, 1951-52; sales rep., local sales mgr. WPRO, Providence, 1952; sales mgr. WPRO-Am-TV, 1953, nat. sales mgr. TV, 1955-61; gen. mgr., WGAN-TV, Portland, Maine, 1961-63; v.p., dir. Guy Gannett Broadcasting Services, Portland, 1963-68, dir. corporate devel., 1966-68; gen. mgr. King Broadcasting Co., Spokane, 1968-73; pres. Wilkin Assos., mgmt. cons., 1974—; chmn. Internat. Mktg. Services, advt. agy., 1979—. Chmn. for Maine, Radio Free Europe Fund, 1963-65; pres. Northeast Hearing and Speech Center, Portland, 1965-68; mem. Gov.'s Com. on Voluntary Programs, 1973-75; chmn. pub. assistance com., citizens adv. bd. Wash. Dept. Social/Health Service; bd. dirs., chmn. 1973 sustaining fund drive Spokane Symphony Soc.; mem. devel. com. Whitworth Coll.; ex-officio mem. devel. com. Mental Health Center; chmn. pub. relations com. United Fund; vice chmn. pub. relations com. Retail Trade Bd.; mem. Am. Com. on E.W. Accord/Communications sub. com.; sec. ad hoc coalition Spokane County Homeowners Assns. Served to capt. C.E., U.S. Army, 1942-46; PTO. Mem. Advt. Fedn. Am., (gov. 1960, bd. dirs. 1966-67), San Juan C. of C., Nat. Assn. Broadcasters, Assn. Profl. Broadcast Edn., Nat. Assn. TV Program Execs., Spokane and Inland Empire Dartmouth Alumni Assn. (pres. 1970-73), Delta Upsilon (life). Author: Where Does Daddy Go, 1962; Broadcasting Directions, 1965. Club: Les Amis du Vin (Washington). Home: 25911 Avenida Cabrillo San Juan Capistrano CA 92675. *My course was set by unique parents and those who cared enough to shake me by the shoulder when there was still time. Being reared somewhat to the left of Jesus Christ and somewhat to the right of Sir Galahad has allowed me to experience modern day crucifixion. It also brought closeness to profoundly influential minds long ago taken by death but who live still in the pages of highly valued books. Were it not for Anita, my wife and dearest friend, I would be a monk.*

WILKIN, RICHARD EDWIN, clergyman, religious orgn. exec.; b. nr. Paulding, Ohio, Nov. 3, 1930; s. Gaylor D. and Beulah E. (Tarlton) W.; student Giffin Jr. Coll., 1948-49; B.S., Findlay Coll., 1952, D.D., 1975; postgrad. Winebrenner Sem., 1952-53, Ind. U., 1959-60; m. Barbara A. Zehender, Aug. 10, 1952; children—Richard Edward, James Lee, Deborah Ann. Ordained to ministry Churches of God in North America, 1953; pastor Neptune Ch. of God, Celina, Ohio, 1952-59, Wharton (Ohio) Ch. of God, 1959-64, Anthony Wayne Ch. of God, Ft. Wayne, Ind., 1964-70; adminstr., chief exec. Chs. of God, Gen. Conf., Findlay, Ohio, 1970—; overseer mission work, India, Bangladesh, Haiti. Dir. summer youth camps, sec., mem. exec. com. Ohio Conf., 1952-59, state clk., pres., 1959-64; chmn. Commn. on Edn., mem. exec. com. Ind. Conf., 1964-70; adv. com. Am. Bible Soc.; steering com. U.S. Ch. Leaders; pres. Ft. Wayne Ministerial Assn.; bd. dirs. Asso. Chs. of Ft. Wayne and Allen County, 1966-70; tchr. Center Twp. Jr. High Sch., Celina, Mendon (Ohio) Union High Sch., Van Del High Sch., Van Wert, Ohio, 1954-59. Vice pres. bd. trustees Winebrenner Haven; mem. adv. com. in race relations regarding sch. reorgn. and busing, Ft. Wayne, 1967-69. Recipient Outstanding Tchr. award, 1958, Disting. Alumnus award Findlay Coll., 1973. Mem. NEA, Ohio Edn. Assn., NAACP, Farm Bur. Club: Lions. Home: 1806 Greendale Ave Findlay OH 45840 Office: Chs of God Gen Conf 2200 Jennifer Ln Findlay OH 45840

WILKINS, (GEORGE) BARRATT, librarian; b. Atlanta, Nov. 6, 1943; s. George Barratt and Mabel Blanche (Brooks) W.; B.A., Emory U., 1965; M.A., Ga. State U., 1968; M.A. (S.C. Library Bd. scholar, Univ. fellow), U. Wis., 1969. Reference librarian S.C. State Library, Columbia, 1969-71; instl. library cons. Mo. State Library, Jefferson City, 1971-73; asst. state librarian State Library Fla., Tallahassee, 1973-77, state librarian, 1977—; abstractor Hist. Abstracts, 1967-71; dir. survey project Nat. Center Edn. Statistics, 1976-77; mem. planning com. Fla. Gov.'s Conf. on Libraries and Info. Services; bd. dirs. Southeastern Library Network, Inc., 1979—; cons. in field. Mem. adv. com. statewide jail project Mo. Assn. Social Welfare, 1971-73, bd. dirs. central div., 1971-73. Mem. Assn. State Library Agys. (pres. 1976-77), Assn. Hosp. Instl. Libraries (dir. 1973-74), Am. Correctional Assn. (instn. library com.), Southeastern Library Assn. (interstate library cooperation com.). Democrat. Episcopalian. Contbr. articles to profl. jours. Home: 280 John Knox Rd Tallahassee FL 32303 Office: State Library of Fla RA Gray Bldg Tallahassee FL 32304

WILKINS, BURLEIGH TAYLOR, educator; b. Bridgetown, Va., July 1, 1932; s. Burleigh and Marie (Taylor) W.; B.A. summa cum laude, Duke, 1952; M.A., Harvard, 1954; M.A., Princeton, 1963, Ph.D., 1965; m. Mary Fisher Cowgill, Aug. 16, 1958; children—Brita Taylor, Carla Cowgill. Asst. prof. history Shorter Coll., Rome, Ga., 1956-57; instr. humanities Mass. Inst. Tech., 1957-60; instr. philosophy Princeton, 1960-61, 63; asst. prof. Rice U., 1965-66, dir. grad. studies in philosophy, 1965-67, asso. prof., 1966-67; asso. prof. U. Calif. at Santa Barbara, 1967-68, prof., 1968—, grad. adviser in philosophy, 1968-70. Mem. Phi Beta Kappa. Author: Carl Becker: A Biographical Study in American Intellectual History, 1961; The Problem of Burke's Political Philosophy, 1967; Hegel's Philosophy of History, 1974. Address: Philosophy Dept Univ Calif Santa Barbara CA 93106

WILKINS, GEORGE THOMAS, ret. educator; b. Anna, Ill., Jan. 16, 1905; s. B. Frank and Nellie Mae (Hileman) W.; B.Ed., So. Ill. Normal, 1937; A.M., U. Ill., 1940; LL.D. (hon.), McKendree Coll., 1959; m. Mary Alice Treece, July 4, 1926; 1 son, George Thomas. Tchr. pub. schs., Anna, 1923-24; tchr., coach pub. sch., Cobden, Ill., 1924-29; prin., coach high sch., Wolf Lake, Ill., 1929-37, supt. pub. schs., 1937-39; supt. pub. schs., Thebes, Ill., 1939-43, Madison, Ill., 1943-47; vis. prof. edn. Shurtleff Coll., Alton, Ill., 1948-56; county supt. schs., Madison County, Ill., 1947-59; ednl. cons., asso. prof. McKendree Coll., Lebanon, Ill., 1956-58; asso. prof. Monticello Coll., Godfrey, Ill., 1955-58; supt. pub. instrn., Ill., 1959-63; asso. prof. edn. So. Ill. U., 1963-69, prof. ednl. adminstrn., 1969-71, prof. emeritus, 1973—. Vice pres. Nathan Hale Life Ins.; dir. Nathan Hale Investment Corp., Vernon Fire and Casualty Ins. Co., Vernon Investment Corp., Colonial Bank of Granite City (Ill.). Mem. bd. So. Ill. U. Found.; mem. Ill. Council on Community Schs., Ill. Sch. Problems Commn., 1959-73. Past pres. Cahokia Mound council Boy Scouts Am. Pres. city planning commn., Madison, Ill. Dir. YMCA, Granite City, Ill. Recipient Silver Beaver award Boy Scouts; Community Leader of America award, 1968; spl. recognition award Belleville Area Coll., 1978; Mentor Graham award. George T. Wilkins Jr. High Sch., Oak Lawn, Ill. named for him. Mem. Ill. Edn. Assn. (past pres. Marquette div.), N.E.A., Ill. Ofcls. Assn., Am., Ill. assns. sch. adminstrs., Madison County Adminstrs. Conf. (past pres.), Central States Chief Sch. Officers (pres.), U. Ill. (life mem.), So. Ill. U. (life mem., pres.) alumni assns., Ill. Assn. County Supts. Schs., Tri-City (past chmn. edn. com.), Ill., chambers commerce, Silver Century Club Found., No. Ill. Round Table Assn., Kappa Phi Kappa, Phi Delta Kappa (past pres. Gateway East chpt.). Democrat. Presbyn. (elder). Mason (Shriner); mem. Order Easter Star. Clubs: Rotary (past pres., past dist. gov.), Tri-City Shrine. Co-author: School Building Construction, 1967; author: The School Law, 1968. Editor S.W. Div. Bull, Ill. Edn. Assn., 1944-48. Home: 2611 Cleveland Blvd Granite City IL 62040. *To everything I do or have done, I apply the Rotary Four Way Test: Is it the truth? Is it fair to all concerned? Will it build good will for the business or profession, and better friendship for our people? Will it be beneficial to all concerned?*

WILKINS, HERBERT PUTNAM, judge; b. Cambridge, Mass., Jan. 10, 1930; s. Raymond Sanger and Mary Louisa (Aldrich) W.; A.B., Harvard U., 1951, LL.B. magna cum laude, 1954; LL.D., Suffolk U., 1976; J.D., New Eng. Sch. Law, 1979; m. Angela Joy Middleton, June 21, 1952; children—Douglas H., Stephen M., Christopher P., Kate T. Admitted to Mass. bar, 1954; asso. firm Palmer & Dodge, Boston, 1954-59, partner, 1960-72; asso. justice Mass. Supreme Jud. Ct., 1972—. Bd. overseers Harvard Coll., 1977—; trustee Milton Acad., 1971-76, Phillips Exeter Acad., 1972-78; mem. Concord (Mass.) Planning Bd., 1957-60; selectman Town of Concord, 1960-66, town counsel, 1969-72; town counsel Town of Acton (Mass.), 1966-72. Mem. Am. Law Inst., Am. Coll. Trial Lawyers (jud. fellow). Republican. Unitarian. Editor Harvard Law Rev., 1953-54. Home: 168 Nashawtuc Rd Concord MA 01742 Office: 1300 Court House Boston MA 02108

WILKINS, J. ERNEST, JR., mathematician, educator; b. Chgo., Nov. 27, 1923; s. J. Ernest and Lucille Beatrice (Robinson) W.; B.S., U. Chgo., 1940, M.S., 1941, Ph.D. in Math., 1942; B.M.E., N.Y. U., 1957, M.M.E., 1960; m. Gloria Louise Stewart, June 22, 1947; children—Sharon Wilkins Hill, J. Ernest. Instr. math. Tuskegee (Ala.) Inst., 1943-44; physicist U. Chgo., 1944-46; mathematician Am. Optical Co., Buffalo, 1946-50; mgr. research and devel. United Nuclear Corp., White Plains, N.Y., 1950-60; asst. lab. dir. Gulf Gen. Atomic, Inc., San Diego, 1960-70; distinguished prof. applied math. and physics Howard U., Washington, 1970-77; asso. gen. mgr. sci. and engring. EG&G Idaho, Inc., Idaho Falls, 1977—. Mem. adv. com. for standard reference materials and methods of measurement AEC, 1964-67, mem. adv. com. nuclear material safeguards, 1967-72; mem. adv. com. for planning and instl. affairs NSF, 1973-74; chmn. Army Sci. Bd., 1978—. Fellow AAAS, Am. Nuclear Soc. (pres. 1975, dir. 1967-77). Office: EG&G Idaho Inc Idaho Falls ID 83401

WILKINS, JAMES RAYMOND, ins. exec.; b. Nipawin, Sask., Can., Nov. 27, 1928; s. Walter Earl and Emma Virginia (DeRosier) W.; grad. Ins. Inst. Am., 1952, Ins. Inst. Can., 1958; m. Frances W. Tait, Oct. 6, 1961; children—James Matthew, Mary Ellen. With Reed Shaw Stenhouse Ltd., and predecessors, 1947—, sr. partner, 1966—, sr. v.p., regional dir., 1968-76, exec. v.p. for Can., Edmonton, 1976—, also dir.; dir., partner Shaunlee Enterprises Ltd., home builders; chmn. bd., dirs. Imperial Lumber Co. Ltd., Imperial Holmes Ltd., York Holdings Ltd., Michelle Bay Lumber Co. Ltd., Demmit Lumber Mills Ltd.; pres. Tara-Tina Investments Ltd., Davray Devels. Ltd., Wilkins Investments Ltd., Lazy J. Ranch Ltd.; sec., dir., past pres. Edmonton Eskimo Football Club. Past pres. Western Football Conf. Mem. Ins. Agts. Assn. Alta. Provincial Conservative. Roman Catholic. Clubs: Mayfair Golf and Country, Royal Glenora (Edmonton); Ironwood Golf and Country (Palm Desert, Calif.). Home: 62 Willow Way Edmonton AB T5T 1C8 Canada Office: 2100 Royal Trust Tower Edmonton Centre Edmonton AB T5J 2Z2 Canada

WILKINS, JOHN WARREN, physicist; b. Des Moines, Mar. 11, 1936; s. Carl Daniel and Ruth Elizabeth (Warren) W.; B.S. in Engring., Northwestern U., 1959; M.S., U. Ill., 1960, Ph.D., 1963. NSF postdoctoral fellow U. Cambridge (Eng.), 1963-64; asst. prof. physics Cornell U., 1964-68, asso. prof., 1968-74, prof., 1974—; vis. prof. H. C. Ørsted Inst., Copenhagen, 1968, Nordita, Copenhagen, 1972-73, 75-76, 79-81. Mem. Am. Phys. Soc., European Phys. Soc. Office: Dept Physics Cornell U Ithaca NY 14853

WILKINS, ROBERT C., banker; b. Columbus, Ohio, May 10, 1938; student Ohio State U., 1956-57; grad. Stonier Grad. Sch. Banking, 1967; m. Christine Webber, Apr. 12, 1969; children—Robert, John, Steven, Scott, Kelly. Asst. v.p. Pompano Beach Bank & Trust Co. (Fla.), 1958-69; exec. v.p. Oceanside Bank, Pompano Beach, 1969-73, Lighthouse Point Bank (Fla.), 1972-73, Fla. Bancorp, Inc., 1972-74; pres. Fla. Coast Bank N.A., Coral Springs, 1974-78, FBC Systems, Inc., Pompano Beach, 1973-76; pres., dir. Fla. Coast Banks, Inc., Pompano Beach, 1974—; chmn. FBC Systems, Inc.; vice chmn., dir. Fla. Coast Bank of Broward County, Fla. Coast Bank Palm Beach County N.A. Served with USCGR. Mem. Fla. (past group chmn.), Broward County (past chmn.) bankers assns., Am. Inst. Banking (past chpt. pres.), Pompano Beach C. of C. (past dir.). Clubs: Pompano Beach Civitan (past pres.), Pompano Beach Rotary; Coral Springs Golf and Tennis. Home: 2381 NW 107th Ave Coral Springs FL 33065 Office: 2850 N Federal Hwy Pompano Beach FL 33064

WILKINS, ROBERT CYRIL, steel co. exec.; b. North Platte, Nebr., Sept. 15, 1929; s. Lester C. and Mamie I. Berridge W.; B.S. in Econs., U. Pa., 1951; m. Mary T. Walters, Aug. 20, 1952; children—Michael, Linda, David, Sheila, Victoria, Charles. With Bethlehem Steel Corp. (Pa.), 1954—, asst. credit mgr., 1961-65, credit mgr., 1965-72, asst. treas., 1972-74, treas., 1974—. Served with USNR, 1951-54. Mem. Am. Iron and Steel Inst., Treas.'s Club, U.S. Naval Res. Assn. Episcopalian (trustee diocese). Club: Saucon Valley Country. Home: RFD 4 Bethlehem PA 18015 Office: Bethlehem Steel Corp Bethlehem PA 18016

WILKINS, ROGER CARSON, ins. co. exec.; b. Houlton, Maine, June 9, 1906; s. George W. and Amanda (Carson) W.; student Ricker Classical Inst., 1919-24; B.A., U. Maine, 1929; LL.D., U. Hartford, 1966, Ricker Coll., 1970, Trinity Coll., 1973; m. Evelyn McFadden, Aug. 23, 1933; 1 dau., Susan J. With Travelers Ins. Companies, Hartford, 1929—, beginning as mgr. mortgage loan dept. for Tex., 1930, successively asst. mgr. home office, mgr., sec. v.p., 1953-65, sr. v.p., 1965-69, pres., 1969-71, chmn. bd., 1971—, also chief exec. officer; chmn. bd. Travelers Corp., 1971-73, chmn. exec. com., 1974—; dir. United Techs. Corp., Allis-Chalmers Corp.; trustee Wells Fargo Mortgage Investor. Bd. dirs. U.S. C. of C. Corporator Hartford Hosp.; pres. Hartford Inst. Living; trustee St. Joseph Coll. Clubs: Hartford, Hartford Golf; Country of Fla.; Gulf Stream Golf (Fla.); Economic (N.Y.C.). Home: 791 Prospect Ave West Hartford CT 06105 Office: 100 Constitution Plaza Hartford CT 06115

WILKINS, ROY, human relations exec.; b. St. Louis, Aug. 30, 1901; s. William D. and Mayfield (Edmondson) W.; A.B., U. Minn., 1923; hon. degreee Lincoln U., 1958, Morgan State Coll., 1963, Central State Coll., 1962, Manhattanville Coll. Sacred Heart, 1964, Oakland U., 1965, Manhattan Coll., 1965, Iona Coll., 1965, Howard U., 1965, Swarthmore Coll., 1965, Notre Dame U., 1965, Middlebury Coll., 1965, Atlanta U., 1965, Fordham U., 1966, Tuskegee Inst., 1966, Oberlin Coll., 1967, Bucknell U., 1968, St. Francis Coll., 1968, C.W. Post Coll., 1968, U. Calif., 1968, Columbia, 1969, St. Peters Coll., 1969, Hebrew Union Coll., 1971, Yeshiva U., 1972, Va. Sem., 1973, Springfield Coll., 1973, Boston U., 1968, Drake U., 1975, Fisk U., 1975, St. John's U., 1975, Temple U., 1977, Villanova, 1977, Niagra U., 1976, Ind. State U., 1977, others; m. Aminda Badeau, Sept. 15, 1929. Mng. editor Kansas City Call, 1923-31; asst. sec. NAACP, 1931-49, acting sec., 1949-50, adminstr., 1950, exec. sec., 1955-64, exec. dir., 1965-77, editor Crisis mag., monthly ofcl. NAACP organ, 1934-49. Pres. Leadership Conf. Civil Rights, 1969; chmn. Am. del. Internat. Conf. Human Rights, Teheran, 1968. Recipient Spingarn medal NAACP, 1964; Freedom award Freedom House, 1967; Theodore Roosevelt Distinguished Service medal. 1968; Presidential Medal Freedom, 1969; Zale award, 1973; Joseph Prize for Human Rights. Hon. fellow Hebrew U., Jerusalem, 1972. Home: 147-15 Village Rd Jamaica NY 11435*

WILKINSON, ALBERT MIMS, JR., lawyer; b. Nashville, June 29, 1925; s. Albert Mims and Mary Nelle (Derryberry) W.; student Emory U., 1942-43; LL.B., U. Ga., 1949; m. Dolores Jean Attard, Oct. 22, 1971; children—William Terry, Elizabeth Ann, David Bush, Mary Dolores. Admitted to Ga. bar, 1948; pvt. practice law, Atlanta, 1950—; hon. legal adviser to Brit. Consul Gen. at Atlanta. Mem. DeKalb County Bd. Elections, 1966-72; chmn. 4th Congl. Dist. Republican Exec. Com., 1968-70, Ga. State Rep. Exec. Com., 1968-74, 1st vice-chmn. Ga. Rep. Party, 1972-74, asst. gen. counsel Ga. Rep. Party, 1974-75; vice-chmn., trustee Atlanta Counseling Center, Inc. Served with USCGR, 1943-46. Fellow Comml. Law Found.; mem. Atlanta, Am. bar assns., State Bar Ga., Ga. Soc. (pres. 1962-63), SAR, Southeastern Members Assn. (pres. 1960-61), comml. Law League Am., St. Andrews Soc., Clan Donald Soc., Old Guard of Gate City Guard. Baptist. Clubs: Commerce, Civitan, Masons. Author: The Winning of the Revolutionary War in the South, 1976; The Rights of Unsecured Creditors-The Law in Georgia, 1979. Home: 1915 Musket Ct Stone Mountain GA 30087 Office: 1069 Spring St NW Atlanta GA 30309

WILKINSON, DAVID TODD, educator; b. Hillsdale, Mich., May 13, 1935; s. Harold Arba and Thelma Ellen (Todd) W.; B.S.E., U. Mich., 1957, M.S.E., 1959, Ph.D., 1962; m. Sharon E. Harper, June 14, 1958 (div. June 1979); children—Wendy, Kenton. Lectr. physics U. Mich., Ann Arbor, 1962-63; instr. Princeton U., 1963-65, asst. prof., 1965-68, asso. prof., 1968-71, prof., 1971—; cons. NASA. Alfred P. Sloane fellow, 1965-67; John Simon Guggenheim fellow, 1977-78. Contbr. articles to profl. jours. Home: 66 The Western Way Princeton NJ 08540

WILKINSON, DONALD ELLSWORTH, govt. agrl. adminstr.; b. Benton, Wis., May 4, 1922; s. Fred William and Edna (Turnbull) W.; student U. Dubuque, 1940-42; B.S., U. Wis.-Madison, 1947; m. Elizabeth Koehler, June 14, 1947; children—David T., Nancy E., Karen E. Tchr. vocat. agr. Waukesha (Wis.) High Sch., 1947-48; info. officer Wis. Dept. Agr., Madison, 1948-51, dir. commodity promotion, 1951-54, chief div. mktg., 1955-64, asst. sec. dept., 1965-69, sec., 1969-75; adminstr. Agrl. Mktg. Service, U.S. Dept. Agr., Washington, 1975-77; gov. Farm Credit Adminstrn., Washington, 1977—. Mem. mktg. advisory com. to U.S. sec. agr., 1964-68; pres. Mid-Am. Internat. Agr. Trade Council, Chgo., 1969-71. Asso. campaign chmn. Madison United Givers, 1968. Pres. bd. dirs. Meth. Hosp., Madison, 1972-75. Served to 1st lt. USAAF, 1942-46. Decorated D.F.C. Mem. Nat. Assn. Mktg. Ofcls. (pres. 1964), Nat. Assn. State Depts. Agr. (pres. 1974). Methodist (del. gen. conf. 1972). Kiwanian. Home: 4116 Sleepy Hollow Rd Annandale VA 22003 Office: Farm Credit Adminstrn 490 L'Enfant Plaza SW Washington DC 20578

WILKINSON, FRANCIS XAVIER, publishing co. exec.; b. Chgo., Sept. 13, 1916; s. Charles Edward and Myrtle Mary (Coan) W.; B.S. in Commerce, DePaul U., 1940; m. Mary E. Sprissler, Oct. 25, 1944; children—Francis, Donald, Dennis, Mary (Mrs. John Payne), Judith (Mrs. Patrick Neary), Philip, Nancy, Joseph, Thomas, Daniel. Account exec. West-Holliday, San Francisco, 1946-48, mgr., Detroit, 1948-53; western mgr. Popular Sci. mag., Chgo., 1953-61, regional v.p., 1961-68, v.p., advt. dir., 1968—, asso. pub., 1976-77, pub., 1977—. Served to maj. USMCR, 1942-46; CBI. Roman Catholic. Clubs: New York Athletic; Lake Shore. Publisher Popular Sci. annuals Boating, Motor Camping, How To, Snowmobiling. Home: 5 April Dr Westport CT 06880 Office: Popular Sci Monthly 380 Madison Ave New York NY 10017

WILKINSON, GLEN ANDERSON, lawyer; b. Ogden, Utah, Apr. 17, 1911; s. Robert Brown and Cecelia (Anderson) W.; B.S., Brigham Young U., 1934; J.D. with honors, George Washington U., 1938; m. Katherine McKinnon, Apr. 26, 1943; children—Frederick McKinnon, Malcolm Glen, Richard Claude, Charles Symmes. Admitted to D.C. bar, 1938; law clk. Bd. Tax Appeals, Washington, 1938-40; asst. corp. counsel D.C., 1940-42; asso. Ernest L. Wilkinson, Washington, 1946-51; partner Wilkinson, Cragun & Barker, Washington, 1951—. Chmn. bd. Piedmont Plush Mills, Greenville, S.C.; dir. Camperdown Co., Greenville, HAR Corp., Washington. Trustee George Washington U., 1975-78, chmn., 1978—. Served to lt. col. AUS, 1942-46. Decorated Legion of Merit. Mem. George Washington U. Law Assn. (pres. 1966), Am., D.C. bar assns., Am. Judicature Soc., George Washington U. Alumni Assn. (trustee, treas. 1969-73). Republican. Mem. Ch. of Jesus Christ of Latter-day Saints. Home: 4308 Forest Ln NW Washington DC 20007 Office: 1735 New York Ave NW Washington DC 20006. *My principal goal has been to contribute, in a broad sense, to improvement of my community, including educational institutions, churches, civic organizations, and the like. This I have endeavored to do by advancing in my chosen profession-the law-and then seeking enough time to contribute financially and in kind to the above enumerated groups and others which, in turn, contribute to improvement of the over-all public welfare.*

WILKINSON, HARRY EDWARD, JR., corp. pres.; b. Richmond Heights, Mo., June 30, 1930; s. Harry Edward and Virginia (Shelton) W.; B.A. in Physics, Princeton U., 1952; M.B.A., Washington U., St. Louis, 1957; D.B.A., Harvard U., 1960; m. Sara Beth Kikendall, Aug. 30, 1958; children—Linda Beth, Cheryl Susan. Staff engr. Southwestern Bell Telephone Co., St. Louis, 1954-57; traffic engr. New Eng. Tel. & Tel. Co., Boston, 1957-60; sr. mgmt. cons. Harbridge House Inc., Boston, 1961-65; dean bus. adminstrn. Northeastern U., 1965-67, dir. Mgmt. Inst., 1965-67; pres., chmn. bd. Univ. Affiliates, Inc., 1967—; pres. Colbridge U., 1970—; cons. to govt. and industry. Served to lt. (j.g.) USNR, 1952-54. Licensed psychologist, Mass. Mem. Acad. Mgmt., Am. Personnel and Guidance Assn., Am. Soc. for Tng. and Devel., Harvard Bus. Sch. Assn. Republican. Clubs: Executives, Harvard (Boston); Harvard Faculty (Cambridge). Home: 8818 Cold Spring Rd Potomac MD 20854 Office: 221 Mt Auburn St Suite 801A Cambridge MA 02138

WILKINSON, HOWARD PRESTON, utility exec.; b. Toano, Va., July 30, 1924; s. Roscoe Franklin and Jessie (Bell) W.; B.S. in Bus. Adminstrn., Va. Poly. Inst. and State U., 1947; m. Jacqueline K. Showalter, Jan. 29, 1948; children—Howard Preston, Brenda (Mrs. George A. Bowling, Jr.), Barbara C., Colin R. Sr. examiner State Corp.

Commn. Va., Richmond, 1947-54; sec., treas. Petersburg & Hopewell Gas Co., Petersburg, Va., 1954-70; sr. v.p. finance, sec. Commonwealth Natural Gas Corp., Richmond, 1970—; v.p., sec. First Mgmt. Corp., Richmond, 1971-75; v.p., treas. Picture Lake Campground, Inc., Petersburg, 1971-75. Mem. Southeastern Gas Assn. (pres. 1967). Baptist (deacon). Clubs: Rotunda (Richmond); Colonial (Petersburg). Home: 1656 Wilton Rd Petersburg VA 23803 Office: 3d and Canal Sts Richmond VA 23219

WILKINSON, JAMES HARVIE, III, editor; b. N.Y.C., Sept. 29, 1944; s. James Harvie and Letitia (Nelson) W.; B.A., Yale U., 1963-67; J.D., U. Va., 1972; m. Lossie Grist Noell, June 30, 1973; 1 son, James Nelson. Admitted to Va. bar, 1972; law clk. to U.S. Supreme Ct. Justice Lewis F. Powell, Jr., Washington, 1972-73; asst. prof. law U. Va., 1973-75, asso. prof., 1975-78; editor Norfolk (Va.) Virginian-Pilot, 1978—; bd. visitors U. Va., 1970-73. Republican candidate for Congress from 3d Dist. Va., 1970. Served with U.S. Army, 1968-69. Mem. Va. State Bar, Va. Bar Assn., Am. Soc. Newspaper Editors. Episcopalian. Author: Harry Byrd and the Changing Face of Virginia Politics, 1968; Serving Justice: A Supreme Court Clerk's View, 1974; From Brown to Bakke: The Supreme Court and School Integration, 1979. Home: 1433 E Bayshore Dr Virginia Beach VA 23451 Office: 150 W Brambleton Ave Norfolk VA 23501

WILKINSON, JAMES RICHARD, architect; b. Washington, Ga., Mar. 21, 1907; s. Thomas Gregg and Mary Agnes (Ezell) W.; B.S. in Architecture, Auburn U., 1928; m. Kathleen Shearer Asher, Mar. 9, 1940; children—James R., Clay Thomas, Thomas Perry. Practiced architecture with various firms, 1928-36; asso. Burge & Stevens, Architects, Atlanta, 1936-45; partner Stevens & Wilkinson, Architects, Engrs., Planners, Inc., Atlanta, 1945-68, pres., 1968-72, chmn. bd., 1972-77, chmn. fin. com., 1977—; profl. advisor Archtl. Sch. Auburn U.; works include: Daniel Bldg., Greenville, S.C., Continuing Edn. Center U. Ga., Athens, Ga. Bapt. Hosp., Atlanta, Sears, Roebuck & Co. stores in SE, Rich's, Inc. stores, Law Sch. Emory U., Atlanta, Hartsfield Internat. Airport, Central Library, Tower Pl., Atlanta, Citgo Hdqrs., Tulsa. Served to 1st lt., constrn. officer USMCR, 1944-45; PTO. Fellow AIA (recipient regional and nat. awards); mem. Phi Delta Theta. Presbyterian. Clubs: Capital City, Piedmont Driving. Home: 1455 W Paces Ferry Rd NW Atlanta GA 30327 Office: 100 Peachtree St NW Atlanta GA 30303

WILKINSON, JOHN BURKE, former govt. ofcl., novelist, biographer; b. N.Y.C., Aug. 24, 1913; s. Henry and Edith (Burke) W.; grad. St. George's Sch., 1931; B.A. magna cum laude, Harvard U., 1935; Lionel Harvard studentship, Cambridge (Eng.) U., 1936; m. Frances I. Proctor, June 11, 1938; children—Eileen B., Charles P. Copy writer Lord & Thomas, advt., 1936-38; asst. advt. mgr. Reynal & Hitchcock, 1938-39; advt. mgr. Little, Brown & Co., 1939-41; free lance writer, 1946-50, 52-54; spl. asst. to asst. sec. state for pub. affairs, 1954-56, dep. asst. sec. state pub. affairs, 1956-58; pub. affairs adviser SHAPE, Paris, 1958-62. Dir. U.S. Nat. Tennis Hall of Fame, v.p., 1962—. Trustee Corcoran Gallery of Art, 1973—. Served from lt. (j.g.) to comdr. USNR, 1941-46, 51-52. Decorated Commendation Ribbon; commendatore Italian Order of Merit. Mem. Phi Beta Kappa; hon. mem. Internat. Lawn Tennis Club France Gt. Britain (chmn. Prentice Cup com. 1956-57). Clubs: Metropolitan, National Press (Washington); Chevy Chase (Md.). Author: Proceed at Will, 1948, Run, Mongoose, 1950, Last Clear Chance, 1954, By Sea and By Stealth, 1956, Night of the Short Knives, 1964, The Helmet of Navarre, 1965, Cardinal in Armor, 1966, The Adventures of Geoffrey Mildmay (trilogy of 1st 3 novels), 1969, Cry Spy! (anthology), 1969, Young Louis XIV, 1970, Francis in All His Glory, 1972; Cry Sabotage!, 1972; The Zeal of the Convert, 1976. Contbr. to N.Y. Times Book Rev., Christian Sci. Monitor, nat. mags. Home: 3210 Scott Pl Washington DC 20007 Office: 1518 K St NW Washington DC 20005. *My life as a writer has been a running battle with the English language. My own 12 books have been in the nature of experimentation in style and language, and this has also held true in doing reviews and magazine articles. Whether novel or article or biography, the purpose has been the same: to try to make the style carry the content as effectively and as clearly as possible. I don't know how well I have succeeded so far, but as Hemingway said authors are apprentices all their lives.*

WILKINSON, JOHN PAUL, JR., banker; b. Bay City, Tex., Nov. 6, 1939; s. John Paul and Lydia (Rasmussen) W.; student U. Tex., 1957-60; B.B.A., Southwestern U., 1966; grad. with honors Sch. Bank Adminstrn., U. Wis., 1974; m. Pamela Fannin, Nov. 14, 1964; children—John Paul III, Damon Everett. With Montgomery Ward & Co., Austin, Tex., 1966-68, controller trainee, 1966, field audit staff, 1967, store controller, Colorado Springs, Colo., 1967-68; with Nat. Bank of Commerce of San Antonio, 1969—, asst. comptroller, 1970-71, auditor, 1971—, v.p., 1975—; gen. auditor Nat. Bancshares Corp. Tex., 1978—. Instr. Inst. Internal Auditors seminars, 1975—, Sch. for Bank Adminstrn., U. Wis., 1979—. Served with AUS, 1960-63. C.P.A. Mem. Am. Inst. C.P.A.'s, Tex. Soc. C.P.A.'s, Inst. Internal Auditors (pres. San Antonio 1974-75), Bank Adminstrn. Inst. (chartered bank auditor; pres. San Antonio 1978-79; asst. state dir. 1978-79), Am. Inst. Banking, Tex. Banking Assn. (adv. council audit/ops. sect. 1975-77), San Antonio Golf Assn. (dir., sec., exec. com. 1978—). Methodist. Clubs: Canyon Creek Country, Fair Oaks Country (San Antonio). Home: 12510 Chateau Forest San Antonio TX 78230 Office: National Bank of Commerce Bldg San Antonio TX 78291

WILKINSON, LAWRENCE, financial cons.; b. Evanston, Ill., Jan. 18, 1905; s. George L. and Adele (Enloe) W.; A.B., Yale, 1926; m. Gertrud Gleich. With N.Y. Trust Co., 1928-30; with Marine Midland Trust Co., 1930-31, 35, v.p., 1938; with Dillon, Read & Co., 1949-50; v.p. Continental Can Co., 1951-57, v.p. finance, 1952-54, group v.p. non-metal divs., 1954-56, exec. v.p., 1956-58, exec. v.p. finance and adminstrn., 1958-65, exec. v.p. internat. operations, dir., 1966-67; cons. Phelps Dodge Corp., 1968—; dir. Phelps Dodge Industries, Pantasote Inc., Naess & Thomas Spl. Fund, Adams Express Co., Consol. Aluminum Corp., Oremet Corp., Corp. Realty Consultants; trustee Corporate Property Investors. Econ. adviser to U.S. Mil. Govt., Berlin, Germany, 1946-49; dir. N.Y. State Civil Def. Commn., 1950-51, chmn., 1950-54. Served to col. Ordnance Dept., AUS, 1941-47. Home: 1125 Fifth Ave New York NY 10028 Office: 300 Park Ave New York NY 10022

WILKINSON, VERNON LEE, lawyer; b. Chelan, Wash., Jan. 31, 1909; s. Joseph Edward and Charlotte (Lee) W.; A.B. magna cum laude, Whitman Coll., 1930; A.M., Am. U., 1931, Ph.D., 1933; Certificat en Droit International, U. Paris, 1932; LL.B., Georgetown U., 1938; m. Dorothy Barbara Lohrman, Sept. 1, 1933; 1 dau., Diane Charlotte; m. 2d, Margery C. Thomas, Dec. 27, 1956. Admitted to D.C. bar, 1937, since practiced in Washington: chief land appeals Dept. Justice, 1942-44, spl. asst. to atty. gen., 1944-45; asst. gen. counsel (broadcasting) FCC, 1945-48; mem. firm Haley, McKenna & Wilkinson, 1948-52; partner McKenna and Wilkinson, Washington, 1952-72, McKenna, Wilkinson & Kittner, 1972—. Mem. bar U.S. Supreme Ct., Ct. Claims, D.C. and 1st-9th Circuits. Mem. Am. Judicature Soc., Am. Bar Assn., Fed. Communications Bar Assn. (exec. com. 1951-54), Phi Beta Kappa, Delta Sigma Rho, Pi Gamma Mu. Asso. editor Georgetown Law Jour., 1937-38. Contbr. articles profl. jours. Home: 3310 Ordway St NW Washington DC 20008 Office: 1150 17th St NW Washington DC 20036

WILKINSON, WARREN SCRIPPS, mfg. co. exec.; b. Detroit, Feb. 2, 1920; s. Almadus DeGrasse and Harriet Gertrude (Whitcomb) W.; grad. Hotchkiss Sch., Lakeville, Conn., 1937; B.S. in Math., Harvard, 1941; student Calif. Inst. Tech., 1941-42; m. Joan Todd, June 14, 1941; m. 2d, Mireille De Bary, Dec. 17, 1966. With U.S. Rubber Co., Detroit, 1942-43; with Hanson Van Winkle-Munning Co., Matavan, N.J., 1946-64, pres., 1961-64; v.p., gen. mgr. Hanson-Van Winkle-Munning div. M & Chems., Inc., 1964-66; chmn. Reinforced Plastic Industry. Marlette, Mich., 1966—; dir. Evening News Assn., Detroit. Bd. dirs. Fedn. French Alliances, 1974—; v.p. Detroit Hist. Soc., 1978—, French Festival of Detroit. Served to lt. (s.g.) USNR, 1943-46. Address: 2 Woodland Pl Grosse Pointe MI 48230

WILKINSON, WILLIAM DURFEE, museum ofcl.; b. Utica, N.Y., Sept. 2, 1924; s. Winfred Durfee and Edith (Lockwood) W.; B.S., Harvard, 1949; postgrad. Munson Inst. Am. Maritime History, Mystic, Conn., 1961-62; m. Dorothy May Spencer, Apr. 2, 1966. Group ins. underwriter Home Life Ins. Co., N.Y.C., 1949-59; adminstr., marine curator Mus. City of New York, 1960-63; registrar Met. Mus. Art, N.Y.C., 1963-71; asso. dir. Mariners Mus., Newport News, Va., 1971-73, dir., 1973—. Bd. dirs. Council Am. Maritime Museums, pres., 1978—; bd. dirs. Peninsula Council of Arts, Mus. Computer Network, Inc.; trustee War Meml. Mus. of Va. Served with C.E., AUS, 1943-45. Mem. Am. Assn. Museums, Soc. for Nautical Research (Gt. Britain), Naval Hist. Found., Nat. Trust Hist. Preservation (maritime preservation com.), Steamship Hist. Soc. Am., Propeller Club of U.S., Explorers Club of N.Y.C., Propeller Club of Port of Newport News (bd. govs.). Club: Hampton Yacht. Home: 101 Museum Pkwy Newport News VA 23606 Office: Museum Dr Newport News VA 23606

WILKINSON, WILLIAM SHERWOOD, lawyer; b. Williston, N.D., Sept. 6, 1933; s. John Thomas and Evelyn (Landon) W.; B.S. in Bus., U. Idaho, 1955; J.D., U. Denver, 1960; m. Carol Ann Burns, Aug. 20, 1960; children—Leslie Ann, Richard Sherwood, Greta Diann. Admitted to Colo. bar, 1960, Mich. bar, 1966; practiced in Canon City, Colo., 1960-66; asst. dist. atty. 11th Jud. Dist., Colo., 1961-65; gen. counsel, sec. Mich. Farm Bur. and affiliate cos., Lansing, 1966—. Lectr., Pre-Parole Release Center, Colo. State Penitentiary, 1961-65; instr. adult edn., Canon City, 1965; counsel Canon City Recreation Dist., 1964-65. Mem. lay adv. bd. St. Thomas More Hosp., Canon City, 1963-66. Del., county, dist. and congl. convs. Republican party, 1964. Served to 1st lt., USAF, 1955-58. Recipient Community Distinguished Service award Canon City Jr. C. of C., 1964. Mem. Am., Colo. bar assns., State Bar Mich., Am. Judicature Soc., Phi Delta Phi, Tau Kappa Epsilon. Methodist (lay leader, mem. ch. ofcl. bd.). Home: 1707 Foxcroft Rd East Lansing MI 48823 Office: 7373 W Saginaw Lansing MI 48917

WILKOWSKI, JEAN MARY, diplomat; b. Wis., Aug. 28; B.A., St. Mary-of-the-Woods Coll.; M.A., U. Wis.; student U. Habana, 1944. Publicity dir. Barry Coll.; reporter on agr. U. Wis.; vice consul, Port-of-Spain; vice consul, Bogota; Milan, Italy; assigned Dept. State, inter-agy. exchange program Dept. Commerce; vice consul, Paris, sec., consul; econs. study U. Calif. at Berkeley; Spanish lang. area tng. Fgn. Service Inst.; 2d sec., Santiago, Chile, 1960; internat. economist Dept. State; sr. seminar fgn. policy Fgn. Service Inst.; 1st sec. Am. embassy, Rome; dep. chief mission Am. Embassy, Tegucigalpa, Honduras; comml. counselor, minister econ. and comml. affairs, Rome, 1970-72; ambassador to Zambia, 1972-76; coordinator U.S. preparations with rank of ambassador UN Conf. Sci. and Tech. for Devel., N.Y.C., 1977—; mem. U.S. del. to 34th UN Gen. Assembly, N.Y.C. Address: Dept State Washington DC 20520

WILKS, ERNEST CRAWFORD, ins. co. exec.; b. Woonsocket, R.I., Jan. 17, 1915; s. Fred and Jennie (Mallows) W.; A.B., Brown U., 1936; m. Lois S. Koerner, Oct. 19, 1946; children—Wade M., Bruce C. With Amica Mut. Ins. Co., Providence, 1937—, successively underwriter, asst. sec., 1937-51, sec., 1951-62, v.p., 1962-68, vice chmn. bd., 1968-71, chmn. bd., 1971—, dir., 1962—; pres., dir. Amica Life Ins. Co., 1969-78, chmn. bd., 1978—; v.p., treas., dir. Amica Services, Inc., 1972—. Mem. Greater Providence C. of C. (dir.). Republican. Episcopalian. Mason. Clubs: Turks Head (Providence); Squantum Assn., University, Agawam. Home: 67 Highland St Woonsocket RI 02895 Office: 10 Weybosset St Providence RI 02940

WILKS, WILLIAM LEE, educator, dean; b. Ft. Wayne, Ind., Nov. 12, 1931; s. Lee and Mildred (Roberts) W.; B.A., Yale U., 1952; J.D., U. Mich., 1955; LL.M., George Washington U., 1973; m. Ellen Hunt, Sept. 5, 1952; children—Sara P., Margaret E., Amy P., David E. Admitted to Ind. bar, 1955, Mich. bar, 1955; with firm Hunt, Suedhoff & Wilks, Ft. Wayne, 1957-70; asst. prof. Dickinson Sch. Law, Carlisle, Pa., 1970-73, asso. prof., 1973-74, prof., asst. dean, 1974-77, prof., dean, 1977—; reporter Commonwealth Ct. of Pa., 1973—; cons. Juvenile Ct. Judges Commn., 1971-75; adv. Motor Vehicle Code Revision, 1973-74; lectr. Pa. Law Enforcement Acad., 1971—, Pa. Bar Inst., 1970—. Bd. dirs. Cumberland-Perry Assn. Retarded Citizens, 1973-76, Legal Services, Inc., 1973-77; bd. advs. Ct. Practice Inst., 1973—, Cumberland County Children's Services, 1975—. Served with U.S. Army, 1955-57. Mem. Am. Trial Lawyers Assn., Def. Research Inst., Ind. Bar Assn., Pa. Bar Assn., Am. Bar Assn. Contbr. articles to legal jours. Home: RD 9 Box 514 Carlisle PA 17013 Office: Dickinson Sch Law 150 S College St Carlisle PA 17013

WILL, FREDERICK LUDWIG, educator; b. Swissvale, Pa., May 8, 1909; s. Frederick Ludwig and Katherine Dora (Graf) W.; A.B., Thiel College, Greenville, Pa., 1929, D.Litt. (hon.), 1965; M.A., Ohio State U., 1931; Ph.D., Cornell U., 1937; m. Louise Hendrickson, June 17, 1932; children—Katherine, George Frederick. Mem. faculty U. Ill., 1938—, prof. philosophy, 1955—, chmn. dept., 1961-63. Guggenheim fellow, 1945-46; sr. Fulbright research scholar U. Oxford (Eng.), 1961; Nat. Endowment for Humanities fellow, 1976. Mem. Am. Philos. Assn. (pres. Western div. 1968-69), A.A.U.P., Phi Kappa Phi. Author: Induction and Justification, 1974. Contbr. articles to profl. jours., chpts. to books. Home: 602 E Harding Dr Urbana IL 61801

WILL, GEORGE F., editor, polit. columnist; b. Champaign, Ill., 1941; attended Trinity Coll., Oxford (Eng.) U., Princeton U., Tchr. politics Mich. State U., U. Ill., U. Toronto (Ont., Can.); congressional aide to Sen. Allott of Colo., Washington, until 1972; became Washington editor Nat. Rev., 1972; polit. columnist Washington Post, Newsweek mag. Recipient Pulitzer prize for Commentary, 1977; named a Young Leader Am., Time mag., 1974. Address: care Washington Post 1150 15th St NW Washington DC 20071*

WILL, HUBERT LOUIS, judge; b. Milw., Apr. 23, 1914; s. Louis E. and Erna (Barthman) W.; A.B., U. Chgo., 1935, J.D., 1937; L.L.D. (hon.), John Marshall Law Sch., 1973; m. Phyllis Nicholson, July 23, 1938; children—Jon Nicholson, Wendy, Nikki, Ami Louise; m. 2d, Jane R. Greene, Dec. 20, 1969. Admitted to Wis. bar, 1937, U.S. Supreme Ct., 1941, Ill. bar, 1946; mem. gen. counsel's staff SEC, Washington, 1937-38; sec. U.S. Senator Robert F. Wagner, 1939; spl. asst. to atty. gen. U.S., 1940-41; asst. to gen. counsel OPA, 1942; tax counsel Alien Property Custodian, 1943; atty. firm Pope & Ballard, Chgo., 1946-48, Nelson, Boodell & Will, Chgo., 1949-61; U.S. dist. judge No. Dist. Ill., 1961—. Mem. Commn. on Bankruptcy Laws of U.S., 1971-73; mem. com. to consider standards for admission to practice in fed. cts. U.S. Jud. Conf., 1976—. Chmn. Chgo. Com. Youth Welfare, 1957-61. Served as capt. OSS, AUS, 1944-45; ETO. Decorated Bronze Star. Mem. Am., Chgo. bar assns., Am. Judicature Soc., Am. Vets Com., World Vets. Fedn. (council U.S.A.). Contbr. articles legal publs. Home: 505 N Lake Shore Dr Chicago IL 60611 Office: 219 S Dearborn St Chicago IL 60604

WILL, JOHN, cons.; b. Cupar Fife, Scotland, Jan. 20, 1917; s. Alexander and Jane (Lindsay) W.; came to U.S., 1924, naturalized, 1940; B.A., U. Redlands, 1938; certificate indsl. relations, U. Cal. at Los Angeles, 1949; m. Marjorie Lois Deuter, Sept. 12, 1941; 1 son, Tom Edward. Supr. employment Am. Can. Co., 1938-42; chief recruitment and placement VA Center, Los Angeles, 1946-50; personnel officer Franklin D. Roosevelt Meml. Hosp., VA, Montrose, N.Y., 1950-51; asst. chief Office Indls. Relations, Bur. Engraving and Printing, Treasury Dept., 1951-54; chief field br., then chief civilian personnel dir. O.M.C., U.S. Army, 1954-59; chief employment mgmt. div., then dept. dir. civilian personnel Hdqrs. U.S. Army, 1959-63; dir. personnel Dept. Commerce, 1963-74; chmn. adminstrn. com. Orange County Grand Jury, 1978-78; cons. on govt. and personnel adminstrn. Mem. fund raising coordinating com. Nat. Capital area United Givers Fund, 1964-74; mem. Pres.' Com. Employment Handicapped, 1963-74; past mem. Health and Welfare Council Nat. Capital Area. Served to lt. USNR, 1942-46. Recipient Meritorious Civilian Service award U.S. Army, 1959: Distinguished Service award U. Redlands Alumni Assn., 1967, Gold medal award for distinguished achievement Dept. Commerce, 1968, others. Mem. Soc. Personnel Adminstrn. (pres. 1963-64), Kappa Sigma Sigma. Presbyn. Home: 301 Calle Pueblo San Clemente CA 92672

WILL, PHILIP, JR., architect; b. Rochester, N.Y., Feb. 15, 1906; s. Philip and Mary Jane (Munro) W.; student Phillips Exeter Acad., 1922-24; B.Arch., Cornell U., 1930; m. Caroline Elizabeth Sinclair, 1933; children—Elizabeth Sinclair, Philip Sinclair. Archtl. draftsman Gordon & Kaelber, Rochester, 1928-29; with Shreve, Lamb & Harmon, N.Y.C., 1930-33; asso. architects South Park Gardens, Chgo., 1934; with Gen. Houses, Inc., Chgo., 1933-34, dir., 1942-48; partner Perkins, Wheeler & Will, Chgo., 1935-46, Perkins & Will, 1946-64, Perkins & Will Partnership, 1964-70; sr. v.p. Perkins & Will, Architects, Inc., 1970-71; vice chmn. Perkins & Will, Inc., 1970-73, dir., 1973—, chmn., 1975—. Mem. Plan Commn., Evanston, Ill., 1959-64, chmn., 1965; chmn. bldg. research advisory bd., com. performance concept in bldg. Northeastern Ill. Plan Commn. Com. Environmental Aspects, 1964—; mem. Governor's Commn. Chgo. World's Fair for 1976; bd. dirs. Higgins Lake Property Owners Assn., 1978—. Trustee Cornell U., 1963-73, trustee emeritus, 1973—. Fellow AIA (dir. Chgo. chpt. 1946-50, pres. 1952-54; nat. pres. 1960-62; recipient special citation of merit 1968), Royal Archtl. Inst. Can. (hon.), Philippine Inst. Architects (hon.); mem. Alumni Cornell U. Coll. Architecture (pres. 1955-57), Am. Inst. Planners (affiliate), Gargoyle Soc., Sigma Phi, Tau Beta Pi, Lambda Alpha; hon. mem. Sociedad de Architectos Mexicanos, Sociedad de Architectos del Peru, Cruceiro Sul de Brasil. Unitarian. Home: 2949 Harrison St Evanston IL 60201 Office: 2 N LaSalle St Chicago IL 60602. *The appetite for innovation and the stomach for leadership.*

WILL, ROBERT ERWIN, educator; b. Dousman, Wis., Mar. 8, 1928; s. Erwin and Gena (Luedtke) W.; B.A. cum magna laude, Carleton Coll., 1950; M.A., Yale, 1951, Ph.D., 1965; m. Barbara Anne Couture, Dec. 22, 1956; children—Jonathan, Leslie Anne, Jennifer. Mem. faculty Yale, 1951-54, U. Mass., 1954-57; mem. faculty econs. Carleton Coll., Northfield, Minn., 1957—, prof., 1968-73, W.A. Williams prof., 1973—, chmn. dept. econs., dir. execs. seminars, 1971—; vis. prof. U. Minn., 1965; vis. fellow Inst. Devel. Studies, U. Sussex (Eng.), 1970-71; John de Quedville Briggs lectr. St. Paul Acad., 1966-70. Mem. Minn. Dept. Manpower Services Advisory Council, 1966—; mem. Wilton Park, Brit. Fgn. Office Study Center, 1970—. Dir. Community Electronics Corp., Mpls., Minn. World Affairs Center, 1972—, Minn. World Trade Week, 1978—. Mem. policy com. United Shareowners Am., 1960—. Served with USNR, 1945-46. Ford Found. Faculty fellow, 1962-63; NSF Faculty fellow, 1970-71; Mellon grantee, Mex., 1976, Interuniv. Centre for European Studies fellow, 1975—. Mem. Am. Econ. Assn., Indsl. Relations Research Assn., World Future Soc., Soc. for Internat. Devel., Bus. and Econ. History Soc., Assn. Cultural Economics, Am. Friends Wilton Park, Assn. Evolutionary Econs., History Econ. Assn., N.Am. Economic Studies Assn., Minn., Midwest econ. assns., Phi Beta Kappa. Democrat. Episcopalian. Club: Chactonbury Ring (Sussex). Author: Poverty in Affluence: The Social, Political and Economic Dimensions of Poverty in the United States, 1965; Scalar Economies and Urban Service Requirements, 1965; also articles and research on manpower, tourism, and devel. Home: 708 E 3d St Northfield MN 55057

WILLARD, DONALD SMITH, ins. co. exec.; b. Hartford, Conn., Mar. 31, 1924; s. Everett C. and Sarah Esther (Northrop) W.; student U. N.C., 1941-44; M.B.A., Harvard U., 1947; m. Alison Johnston Rice, Oct. 28, 1944; children—Scott, Malcolm, Laura. Purchasing agt. to comptroller Mt. Holyoke Coll., 1947-54; with Tchrs. Ins. & Annuity Assn. Am., N.Y.C., 1954—, v.p., 1960-70, exec. v.p. 1970—; mem. faculty U. Nebr. at Omaha, 1956-74; cons. Acad. Ednl. Devel., 1964-68. Deacon United Ch. of Christ, Westport, Conn., 1965-68, trustee, 1971-74. Served to lt. (j.g.) USNR, 1943-46. C.L.U. Mem. Am. Soc. C.L.U.'s, Harvard Bus. Sch. Club N.Y., Delta Sigma Pi. Home: 58 Maple Ave S Westport CT 06880 Office: 730 3d Ave New York City NY 10017

WILLARD, EDWARD WARREN, investment banker; b. Galveston, July 27, 1896; s. Frank and Margaret (Warren) W.; student pub. schs. of Denver; LL.D., Colo. Coll., 1970; m. Muriel L. McLagan, Sept. 15, 1926 (dec.); children—Jean, Robert, Ann; m. 2d, Katherine Kenny, Mar. 4, 1972. Statis. clk. D.& R. G.W. R.R., 1913-17; credit mgr. B.K. Sweeney Electric Co., Denber, 1917-18; municipal bond buyer Keeler Bros., investment bankers, Denver, 1919-21; municipal buyer, treas. Boettcher, Porter & Co., 1921-29; mgr. municipal, trading depts. Boettcher-Newton & Co., 1929-33; v.p. Boettcher & Co., Denver, 1933-37, partner, 1937-38, mng. partner, 1938-70, exec. partner, 1971—; dir. Brown Palace Hotel Co. Gov. N.Y. Stock Exchange, 1955-57. Hon. trustee Kent Sch.; trustee Children's Hosp. Assn., YMCA, State Hist. Found; trustee, pres. Boettcher Found.; trust fund com. Mile High United Fund Denver, mem. exec. com. Denver area, also hon. v.p.; dir., Mem. fin. com. Iliff Sch. Theology; bd. dirs. Boys Clubs of Denver; hon. life trustee U. Denver. Recipient Distinguished Service award U. Colo., 1970. Served as radio technician USN, 1918-19. Recipient honors Nat. Jewish Hosp., 1976, Children's Hosp., 1978—. Mem. Investment Bankers Assn. (gov. 1934-37), Nat. Assn. Security Dealers (gov. 1942-45), Assn. Stock Exchange Firms (past gov.), Colo. Hist. Soc. (pres. 1974—, trustee). Clubs: Cherry Hills Country, Denver, Brown Palace, Denver Country, Mile High, Tower Wigwam, One Hundred (Denver); Flat Irons, Masons. Home: 2901 E Floyd Dr Denver CO 80210 Office: 828 17th St Denver CO 80202

WILLARD, FREDERIC CHARLES, actor; b. Cleve., Sept. 18, s. Fred Charles and Ruth Beatrice (Weinman) W.; B.A., Va. Mil. Inst.; m. Mary Elizabeth Lovell, Dec, 20, 1968; 1 dau., Hope Christina.

Mem. Greco & Willard, comedy team, 1962-65; appeared off-Broadway in Little Murders, N.Y. Circle in the Square, 1969; appeared on TV series Sirota's Court, 1976, Fernwood 2 Night, 1977, America 2 Night, 1978, Real People, 1979—. Served with arty. U.S. Army. Mem. Screen Actors Guild, AFTRA. Episcopalian. Office: care Compass Mgmt Inc 211 S Beverly Dr Beverly Hills CA 90212

WILLARD, HARVEY BRADFORD, physicist, educator; b. Worcester, Mass., Aug. 9, 1925; s. George H. and Virginia (Wohlbruck) W.; B.S., Mass. Inst. Tech., 1948, Ph.D., 1950; m. Isabella V. Rallis, Nov. 2, 1950; children—Karl Philip, Karen Elizabeth. Group leader 5.5 mV Van de Graaff, Oak Ridge Nat. Lab., 1951-57, co-dir. high voltage accelerator lab., 1957-63, asso. dir. physics div., 1963-67; Ford Found. prof. physics U. Tenn., Knoxville, 1963-67; chmn. physics dept. Case Western Res. U., Cleve., 1967-71, prof. physics, 1967—, vice provost sci. and tech., dean sci., 1970-76; mem. nuclear cross sect. adv. group AEC, 1962-64; chmn. Los Alamos Meson Physics Facility Users Group, 1977. Mem. bd. Argonne Asso. Univs., 1976—. Served with AUS, 1944-46. Fellow Am. Phys. Soc., AAAS, Sigma Xi. Contbr. articles to profl. jours. Home: 15 N Strawberry Ln Moreland Hills OH 44022 Office: Dept Physics Case Western Res U Cleveland OH 44106

WILLARD, JOHN ELA, educator; b. Oak Park, Ill., Oct. 31, 1908; s. Wallace Watson and Mary (Ela) W.; S.B., Harvard, 1930; Ph.D., U. Wis., 1935; m. Adelaide Ela, June 12, 1937; children—Ann, Mark, David, Robert. Instr. Avon (Conn.) Old Farms Sch., 1930-32, Haverford Coll., 1935-37; mem. faculty U. Wis., 1937—, prof. chemistry, 1947-79, emeritus prof. chemistry, 1979—, chmn. dept., 1970-72, dean Grad. Sch., 1958-63, Vilas prof. chemistry, 1963-79; with metall. lab. U. Chgo., 1942-44, 45-46, div. dir., 1945-46; area supr. Hanford works E.I. duPont de Nemours & Co., 1944-45; vis. prof., Japan, 1977. Mem. phys. chemistry panel Office Naval Research, 1948-50; plutonium prodn. survey com. AEC, 1949, isotope distbn. adv. com., 1953-57; exec. bd. participating instns. Argonne Nat. Lab., 1950-53, chmn. bd., 1952-53, mem. div. chemistry vis. com., 1958-64; adv. bd. Gordon Research Confs., 1955-61, chmn. Conf. Radiation Chemistry, 1968; mem. panel basic research and nat. goals Nat. Acad. Sci., 1964-65; chmn. panel adv. to physical chemistry div. Nat. Bur. Standards, 1968-70; chem. div. vis. com. Brookhaven Nat. Lab., 1956-59; panel basic research and grad. edn. President's Sci. Adv. Com., 1959-60. Mem. Am. Chem. Soc. (council policy com. 1957, chmn. div. phys. chemistry 1957; award nuclear applications in chemistry 1959), Am. Phys. Soc., Soc. Radiation Research. Author research publs. chem. effects nuclear transformation, radiation chemistry, photochemistry. Asso. editor Chem. Revs., 1955-58, Radiation Research, 1965-68. Home: 2306 Hollister Ave Madison WI 53705

WILLARD, LOUIS CHARLES, librarian; b. Tallahassee, Fla., Sept. 28, 1937; s. Bert and Rose (De Milly) W.; B.A., U. Fla., 1959; B.D., Yale, 1965, M.A., 1967, Ph.D., 1970; m. Nancy Booth, June 22, 1963. Tchr., Tripoli (Lebanon) Boys' Sch., 1959-62; ordained to ministry Presbyn. Ch., 1965; acting librarian Princeton Theol. Sem., 1968-69, librarian, 1970—. Mem. A.L.A., Theol. Library Assn., Soc. Bibl. Lit., Phi Beta Kappa, Chi Phi. Home: 205 State Rd Princeton NJ 08540

WILLARD, RALPH LAWRENCE, physician; b. Manchester, Iowa, Apr. 6, 1922; s. Hosea B. and Ruth A. (Hazelrigg) W.; student Cornell Coll., 1940-42, Coe Coll., 1945; D.O., Kirksville Coll. Osteo. Medicine, 1949; m. Margaret Dyer Dennis, Sept. 26, 1969; children—Laurie, Jane, Ann, H. Thomas. Intern, Kirksville Osteo. Hosp., 1949-50, resident in surgery, 1954-57; chmn. dept. surgery Davenport Osteo. Hosp., 1957-68; dean, prof. surgery Kirksville Coll. Osteo. Medicine, 1969-73; asso. dean acad. affairs, prof. surgery Mich. State U. Coll. Osteo. Medicine, 1974-75; dean Tex. Coll. Osteopathic Medicine, 1975—; v.p. med. affairs N. Tex. State U., Denton, 1976—; mem. Nat. Adv. Council Edn. for Health Professions, 1971-73; mem. Iowa Gov.'s Council Hosps. and Health Related Facilities, 1965-68; chmn. council deans Am. Assn. Colls. Osteo. Medicine, 1970-73, pres., 1979-80. Served with USAAF, 1942-45, USAF, 1952-53; col. USAFR. Decorated D.F.C., Air medal with 4 oak leaf clusters. Fellow Am. Coll. Osteo. Surgeons; mem. Am., Tex. osteo. assns., Am. Acad. Osteopathy, Assn. Hosp. Med. Edn., Acad. Osteo. Dirs. Med. Edn., Aerospace Med. Assn. Democrat. Episcopalian. Clubs: Fort Worth, Carswell Officers, Century II, Colonial Country, Rotary, Masons (Shriner). Home: PO Box 9074 Fort Worth TX 76107 Office: Camp Bowie at Montgomery Fort Worth TX 76107

WILLARD, ROBERT EDGAR, lawyer; b. Bronxville, N.Y., Dec. 13, 1929; s. William Edgar and Ethel Marie (Van Ness) W.; B.A. in Econs., Wash. State U., 1954; J.D., Harvard, 1958; m. Shirley Fay Cooper, May 29, 1954; children—Laura Marie, Linda Ann, John Judson. Admitted to Calif. bar, 1959; law clk. to U.S. dist. judge, 1958-59; practiced in Los Angeles, 1959—; asso. firm Flint & Mackay, 1959-61; individual practice, 1962-64; mem. firm Willard & Baltaxe, 1964-65, Baird, Holley, Baird & Galen, 1966-69, Baird, Holley, Galen & Willard, 1970-74, Holley, Galen & Willard, 1975—. Dir. various corps. Served with AUS, 1946-48, 50-51. Mem. Am., Los Angeles County bar assns., State Bar Calif., Assn. Trial Lawyers Am., Am. Judicature Soc., Acacia Frat. Democrat. Conglist. Club: Calcutta Saddle and Cycle. Home: 8434 Enramada St Whittier CA 90605 Office: 611 W 6th St Suite 2400 Los Angeles CA 90017

WILLAUER, WHITING RUSSELL, systems engring. and systems integration co. exec.; b. Boston, May 24, 1931; s. Whiting and Louise Knapp (Russell) W.; B.S., Princeton U., 1955, M.S., 1959; Ph.D., Georgetown U., 1964; m. Julie Matheson Arnold, July 11, 1959 (div.); children—Whiting Russell, Jr., William Arnold. Research asso. joint research com. Dept. Def., 1951-52; ops. mgr. Civil Air Transport Taiwan, 1952-53; scientist Analytic Services, Inc., 1958-61; asst. prof. astronomy Georgetown U., 1965-68; mgr. TRW Systems Group support to chief ops., McLean, Va., 1968-73; mgr. TRW Spl. Antisubmarine projects, 1973-79; mgr. TRW Amphibious Ship Acquisition project, 1978—; cons. Nat. Geog. Soc., 1961-65, U. Tex., 1962, NSF, 1963, Booz-Allen Applied Research, Inc., 1966-67. Research fellow Georgetown U., 1961-65. Fellow AAAS (council); mem. Am. Astronautical Soc. (v.p. fin.), Blue Ridge Ski Council (pres. 1976-78), U.S. Ski Assn. (Eastern div., bd. dirs.), Sigma Xi. Clubs: Chevy Chase (Md.); Nantucket (Mass.) Yacht (vice commodore). Mng. editor Jour. Astronautical Scis., 1969-71. Designer, Orrery (planetarium) on permanent exhibit New Explorers Hall, Nat. Geog. Soc. Home: 4201 Cathedral Ave NW Washington DC 20016 Office: TRW Defense and Space Systems Group 7600 Colshire Dr McLean VA 22102

WILLBERN, YORK, educator; b. Runge, Tex., Dec. 29, 1915; s. David York and Berta (Young) W.; A.B., Southwest Tex. State Coll., 1934; A.M., U. Tex., 1938; Ph.D., 1943; m. Johnne Bryant, Dec. 25, 1937; children—Cynthia, Ann Bryant. Tchr. high schs. of Tex., 1934-39; asst., tutor, instr. U. Tex., 1939-43; asst. prof. govt. North Tex. State Coll., 1942-43; asst. prof. pub. adminstrn., asst. dir. bur. pub. adminstrn. U. Ala., 1946, asso. prof., asst. dir., 1947-49, prof., acting dir., 1949-50, prof. polit. sci., head dept. polit. sci., dir. bur. pub. adminstrn., 1950-56, prof., head dept. polit. sci., coodinator Univ., Study and Planning Program, 1956-57; prof. govt., dir. bur. govt. research Ind. U., 1957-63, Univ. prof. polit. sci., 1965—, dir. Inst. Pub. Adminstrn., 1963-66, prof. pub. and environmental affairs, 1972—; vis. prof. Duke, 1956, Columbia, 1957, Syracuse U., 1968, U. Tex., 1971, Lewis and Clark Coll., 1979, Portland State U., 1979; lectr. pub. adminstrn. Victoria U., New Zealand, 1954; vis. prof. pub. adminstrn. Am. U. of Beirut, 1967. Chmn. adminstrv. com. So. Regional Tng. Program Pub. Adminstrn., 1949-57; dir. urban obs. project Nat. League Cities, 1968-74; chmn. Ind. Housing Bd., 1975-77. Served to 1st lt. USAAF, 1943-46. Mem. Am. Polit. Sci. Assn. (council 1956-58, exec. com. 1957-58), Am. Soc. Pub. Adminstrn. (v.p. 1958-59, council 1959-67, pres. 1963-64), AAUP (pres. Ala. conf. 1955-56; council, nat. 2d v.p. 1966-68), Am. Soc. Planning Ofcls. (bd. dirs. 1963-66), Internat. Assn. U. Profs. and Lecturers (exec. com. 1966-68), Nat. Acad. Pub. Adminstrn. (exec. com. 1967-70, trustee 1970-73), So. Polit. Sci. Assn. (past council mem.), Phi Beta Kappa. Club: Cosmos (Washington). Author: Cities and Riverfront Lands, 1947; The Withering Away of the City, 1963. Editor-in-chief Public Administration Review, 1956-58; compiler Technical Assistance to Alabama Governments: A Directory, 1949. Contbr. articles to profl. jours. Home: 1404 Longwood Dr Bloomington IN 47401

WILLCOX, WILLIAM BRADFORD, historian, educator; b. Ithaca, N.Y., Oct. 29, 1907; s. Walter Francis and Alice Elouise (Work) W.; student Cambridge (Eng.) U., 1926-27; A.B., Cornell U., 1928; B.F.A. (architecture), Yale, 1932, Ph.D., 1936; m. Faith Mellen, Oct. 31, 1936; children—Alanson Francis, Ellen Seymour, Faith Marian. Instr. history Williams Coll., 1936-41; asst. prof. U. Mich., 1941-46, asso. prof., 1946-50, prof. history, 1950-69, acting chmn. dept., 1958-60, 63-64, chmn., 1965-69, Hudson research prof., 1962-63; prof. history Yale, 1970—; mem. Inst. Advanced Study, 1946. Mem. council Inst. Early Am. History and Culture, 1955-58; chmn. Midwest Conf. Brit. Hist. Studies, 1959-61. Recipient Porter prize Yale, 1936; Russel award U. Mich., 1945; Bancroft prize Columbia, 1965; Fulbright lectr. Oxford (Eng.) U., 1957-58. Mem. Am. Hist. Assn. (council 1966-70, exec. com. 1967), Conf. Brit. Studies (exec. com. 1965-67), Internat. Soc. for 18th Century Studies (exec. com. 1975), Phi Beta Kappa (vis. scholar 1975-76, 77-78), Psi Upsilon. Clubs: Elizabethan, Century. Author: Gloucestershire: A Study in Local Government, 1590-1640, 1940; Star of Empire: a Study of Britain as a World Power, 1485-1945, 1950; Portrait of a General: Sir Henry Clinton in the War of Independence, 1964; The Age of Aristocracy, 1688-1830, 1966. Editor: The American Rebellion: Sir Henry Clinton's Narrative of His Campaigns, 1775-1782, 3d edit., 1976; The Papers of Benjamin Franklin, 1970—. Contbr. articles to hist. jours. Address: 1603 A Yale Sta New Haven CT 06520

WILLE, FRANK, lawyer, former govt. ofcl.; b. N.Y.C., Feb. 27, 1931; s. Frank Joseph and Alma (Schutt) W.; grad. Phillips Acad., Andover, Mass., 1947; A.B. cum laude, Harvard, 1950, LL.B. cum laude, 1956; LL.M. in Taxation, N.Y. U., 1960; m. Barbara Bowen, July 2, 1969; children—Serena, Alison. Admitted to bar; asso. firm Davis Polk & Wardwell, 1956-60; asst. counsel Gov. N.Y., Albany, 1960-62, 1st asst. counsel, 1962-64; supt. banks State N.Y., 1964-70; chmn. bd. dirs. FDIC, Washington, 1970-76; mem. firm Calwalader Wickersham & Taft, 1976—; mem. Com. on Interest and Dividends, 1971-73. Former mem. N.Y. Job Devel. Authority; former dir. N.Y. State Urban Devel. Corp. Served with USNR, 1951-54. Independent. Clubs: Metropolitan (Washington); Down Town Assn. (N.Y.C.); Chevy Chase. Home: 4733 Berkeley Terr Washington DC 20007 Office: One Wall St New York NY 10005 also 1333 New Hampshire Ave NW Washington DC 20036

WILLE, WAYNE MARTIN, editor; b. Des Plaines, Ill., Nov. 17, 1930; s. Clarence Louis and Lois Naomi (Martin) W.; B.S.J., Northwestern U., 1952, M.S.J., 1953; m. Lois Jean Kroeber, June 6, 1954. Reporter, Chgo. Sun Times, 1956-57; dir. press info. WBBM-TV and CBS-TV, Chgo., 1957-58; feature editor Sci. and Mechanics mag., 1958-60, mng. editor, 1960-62; news editor Nat. Safety Council, Chgo., 1962-64, asst. dir. pub. information, 1964-67; mng. editor World Book Year Book, Chgo., 1967-69, exec. editor, 1969—; asst. v.p. World Book-Childcraft Internat., Inc., Chgo., 1972—. Served with AUS, 1953-55. Mem. Chgo. Headline Club (pres. 1967-68), Soc. Profl. Journalists, Sigma Delta Chi. Club: Chgo. Press. Home: 902 S Laflin Chicago IL 60607 Office: Merchandise Mart Plaza Chicago IL 60654

WILLEMIN, ROBERT BEN, mfg. co. exec., lawyer; b. Ionia, Mich., Sept. 29, 1918; s. Ernest G. (Briggs) W.; B.S. in Mech. Engring., U. Mich., 1940, J.D., 1950; m. Velva O. Long, Sept. 1948; children—Diane V., David R. Mech. engr. Phila. Naval Shipyard, 1940-46; admitted to Mich. bar, 1951, U.S. Patent Office, 1952; spl. asst. Master in Chancery, Fed. Dist. Ct., Toledo, 1950; atty. Gibson Refrigerator Co., Greenville, Mich., 1951-53; atty. Whirlpool Corp., St. Joseph, Mich., 1953—, sec., 1957-73, v.p., 1959-66, group v.p., 1966-77, exec. v.p., 1977—, also chief fin. officer, gen. counsel, dir.; dir. Malleys Ltd., Sydney, Australia; chmn., dir. Appliance Buyers' Credit Corp., Inglis Ltd. (Can.). Bd. dirs. Greater Mich. Found.; vice chmn. bd. trustees Southwestern Mich. Health Care Assn., St. Joseph. Registered profl. mech. engr., Pa. Mem. Am. Bar Assn., State Bar Mich., ASME, Am. Patent Law Assn. Mason. Club: Union League (Chgo.). Home: 1110 Sylvan Dr Benton Harbor MI 49022 Office: Whirlpool Corp Administrative Center Benton Harbor MI 49022

WILLEN, JOSEPH, social welfare cons.; b. Kushnitza, Russia, June 22, 1897; s. Barnet and Sarah (Katch) Willencheck; brought to U.S., 1905, naturalized, 1918; B.A., Coll. City N.Y., 1919; H.H.D. (hon.), Boston U., 1963; LL.D. (honoris causa), Jewish Theol. Sem. Am., 1964; children—Paul, Deborah (Mrs. Frederic C. Meier); m. 2d, Janet Younker Sonnenthal, Dec. 1970. Pioneer devel. techniques community orgn., fund-raising; asso. Fedn. Jewish Philanthropies of N.Y., 1919—, exec. v.p., 1941-67, exec. cons., 1967—. Dir. Greater N.Y. Community Council, Inc., Council Jewish Fedns. and Welfare Funds, Nat. Jewish Welfare Bd. (exec. com. 1962); bd. dirs. United Neighborhood Houses; past cons. Am. Red Cross, Greater N.Y. Fund. Chmn. coordinating com. Documentary History of Am. Jews; bd. advisers Vocational Adv. Service; nat. council Am.-Jewish Joint Distbn. Com.; vice pres., chmn. 54th ann. meeting Am. Jewish Com.; mem. exec. council Am. Jewish Hist. Soc.; trustee National Found. Jewish Culture; mem. India Famine Emergency Commn., 1947, Citizens Budget Commn. of N.Y.C., Mayor's Com. on Unity; bd. dirs. Fountain House, 1965-70, Stockbridge Sch., 1965-70, Technion U., N.Y. Urban League, Pro Deo U. Rome; bd. overseers Florence Heller Grad. Sch. Advanced Studies in Social Welfare, Brandies U., 1962-71, fellow Brandies U., 1963; exec. com. Jewish Theol. Sem. 1966-72; bd. overseers N.Y.U. Grad. Sch. Social Work; mem. bd. Community Council. Served as pvt., inf., U.S. Army, World War I. Mem. Navy League. Home: 125 E 72d St New York NY 10021

WILLENBECHER, JOHN, artist; b. Macungie, Pa., May 5, 1936; s. John George and Geneva (Bacon) W.; B.A., Brown U., 1958, postgrad. N.Y. U., Inst. Fine Arts, 1958-61. Exhibited in one-man shows, including: Hamilton Gallery Contemporary Art, N.Y.C., 1977, U. Mass. Art Gallery, Amherst, 1977, Wright State U. Art Gallery, Dayton, Ohio, 1977, Jaffe-Friede Gallery, Dartmouth Coll., Hanover, N.H., 1977, Fine Arts Center, U. R.I., Kingston, 1978, Neuberger Mus., SUNY at Purchase, 1979, Allentown (Pa.) Art Mus., 1979; exhibited in numerous group shows, including: Albright-Knox Art Gallery, Buffalo, 1963, Whitney Mus. Am. Art, N.Y.C., 1964, 65, 66, 67, 68; represented in permanent collections, including: Solomon R. Guggenheim Mus., N.Y.C., Met. Mus., N.Y.C., Whitney Mus. Am. Art, N.Y.C., Albright-Knox Art Gallery, Phila. Mus. Art, Centre d'Art et Culture Georges Pompidou, Paris, Hirshhorn Mus. and Sculpture Garden, Washington, Chgo. Art Inst. Nat. Endowment for Arts grantee, 1977. Subject of profl. articles and catalogues.

WILLENBROCK, FREDERICK KARL, engr., educator, univ. dean; b. N.Y.C., July 19, 1920; s. Berthold Daniel and Anna Marie (Koniger) W.; B.S., Brown U., 1942; M.A., Harvard U., 1947, Ph.D., 1950; m. Mildred G. White, Dec. 20, 1944. Lectr., research fellow Harvard, 1950-55, lectr., asso. dir. labs., div. engring. and applied physics, 1955-60, dir. labs., 1960-63, asso. dean, 1960-67; provost Faculty Engring. and Applied Scis., prof. engring. and applied scis. SUNY, Buffalo, 1967-70; dir. Inst. Applied Tech., Nat. Bur. Standards, 1970-76; Green prof. engring. So. Meth. U., Dallas, 1976—, dean Sch. Engring. and Applied Sci., 1976—; indsl., ednl. and govt. cons. Served to lt. USNR, 1943-46. Recipient Distinguished Engring. Service award Brown U., 1962. Fellow IEEE (dir. 1962-71, editor 1965-66, v.p. publs. activities 1966-68, pres. 1969), AAAS; mem. Am. Phys. Soc., Am. Soc. Engring. Edn., ASTM, Sigma Xi, Tau Beta Pi. Home: 5645 Stonegate Dallas TX 75209 Office: Sch Engring and Applied Science So Methodist U Dallas TX 75275

WILLENS, DORIS, pub. relations exec.; b. N.Y.C.; d. Sam and Bertha (Heskin) Willens; B.A., UCLA, 1945; M.S., Columbia U., 1947; m. Milton Lewis Kaplan, May 26, 1949 (dec.); children—Jeffrey M., Andrew L., Dan H. Reporter, Mpls. Tribune, 1948-49, Editor and Pub. mag., N.Y.C., 1949-50; freelance writer, London, 1950-55; columnist N.Y. Jour.-Am., 1957-61; pub. relations exec. Grey Advt., N.Y.C., 1961-63; reporter, copy editor Washington Post, 1963-66; dir. pub. relations Doyle Dane Bernbach, Inc., N.Y.C., 1966—, v.p., 1974—. Mem. Pub. Pub. Relations Soc. Am., Broadcast Music, Inc. Mem. Babysitters, performer-songwriting group, recs. for Vanguard, 1958, 60, 64, 68; lyricist Piano Bar, off Broadway, 1978; also numerous children's songs. Home: 5355 Henry Hudson Pkwy Riverdale NY 10471 Office: 437 Madison Ave New York NY 10022

WILLENS, HAROLD, bus. exec.; b. Chernigov, Russia, Apr. 26, 1914; s. Sam and Bertha (Heskin) W.; naturalized U.S. citizen, 1924; B.A., U. Calif. at Los Angeles, 1944; m. Grace Silverman, Nov. 30, 1935; children—Lawrence, Ronald, Michele. Self employed 1935-49; founder, 1949, now chmn. bd. Factory Equipment Corp., Los Angeles; Nat. co-chmn. Bus. Execs. Move for Vietnam Peace, 1967-69; bd. dirs. Fund for Peace, Center for Def. Info., Common Cause, 1972-78; nat. chmn. Businessmen's Ednl. Fund, 1969-78; mem. Pres.'s Commn. on White House Fellowships, 1977—; U.S. del. UN Spl. Session on Disarmament, 1978. Served to capt. USMCR, 1944-46. Mem. Phi Beta Kappa. Author articles. Home: 321 S Bristol Ave Los Angeles CA 90049 Office: 1122 Maple Ave Los Angeles CA 90015. *The most valuable lesson life has taught me is the need for balance between extremes of all kinds. To accumulate wealth obsessively "for the benefit of loved ones" is to sacrifice meaningful relationships with them and possibly even their love. To concentrate on economic achievement to the exclusion of physical, social, cultural and other activities ("I'll do those things when I retire") is a sure prescription for failure. Since democracy assures no more than that its citizens get exactly what they deserve, political involvement - no matter how limited at any given point - is a must. Here, too, balance is essential to prevent political arteriosclerosis (hardening of the attitudes) and to keep open pipelines of communication with persons who can teach us useful things if we do not excommunicate them with ideological labels.*

WILLENS, RITA JACOBS, broadcasting co. exec.; b. Chgo., June 13, 1927; d. Bernard M. and Ruth L. (Kaplan) Smith; B.A., Roosevelt U., Chgo., 1948; m. Bernard Jacobs, June 25, 1950; 1 son, Noah Ben Jacobs-Willens; m. 2d, David L. Willens, July 17, 1966. Co-founder Fine Arts Sta. WFMT, Chgo., 1951, v.p., 1951-68, editor, asso. pub. sta. mag. Perspective on Ideas and the Arts, 1961-64; cons. fine arts broadcasting, 1968-74; pres., producer fine arts programs for nat. syndication Gamut Prodns., Inc., Barrington, Ill., 1974—; alternate host weekly program Saturday Night Midnight Spl., WFMT, 1977—; media adviser Nat. Endowment for the Humanities. Co-recipient Friends of Lit. award, 1953, George Foster Peabody award, 1961, Alfred I. duPont award, 1957, 60, Ohio State U. award, 1959, Thomas Alva Edison award, 1959; recipient Ohio State U. and 1st place Maj. Armstrong award for Gamut: The Great Idea of Man, 1975 and The Follies of '52 or Were Those Really the Days, 1977; Maj. Armstrong awards, Gabriel award, 1978, Ohio State award, 1979 for Rozhinkes mit Mandlin (Raisins with Almonds). Mem. Art Inst. Chgo., Smithsonian Instn. Clubs: Hadassah, ORT, B'nai B'rith. Address: Route 2 Box 61A Barrington IL 60010

WILLERDING, MARGARET FRANCES, mathematician; b. St. Louis, Apr. 26, 1919; d. Herman J. and Mildred F. (Icenhower) Willerding; A.B., Harris Tchrs. Coll., 1940; M.A., St. Louis U., 1943, Ph.D., 1947. Tchr. pub. schs. St. Louis, 1940-46; instr. math. Washington U., St. Louis, 1947-48; asst. prof. Harris Tchrs. Coll., St. Louis, 1948-56; mem. faculty San Diego State Coll., 1956—, asso. prof., 1959-65, prof. math., 1966-76, prof. emeritus, 1976—. Mem. Nat. Council Tchrs. Math., Assn. Tchrs. Sci. and Math., Am. Math. Soc., Math. Assn. Am., Greater San Diego Math. Council (dir. 1963-65), Sigma Xi, Pi Mu Epsilon. Author: Intermediate Algebra, 1969; Elementary Mathematics, 1971; College Algebra, 1971; College Algebra and Trigonometry, 1971; Arithmetic, 1968; Probability: The Science of Chance, 1969; Mathematics Around the Clock, 1969; Mathematical Concepts, 1967; From Fingers to Computers, 1969; Probability Primer, 1968; Mathematics: The Alphabet of Science, 1972, 74, 77, A First Course in College Mathematics, 1973, 77, Mathematics Worktext, 1973, 77, Business and Consumer Mathematics for College Students, 1976, The Numbers Game, 1977. Home: 10241 Vivera Dr La Mesa CA 92041 Office: Dept Math San Diego State Coll San Diego CA 92041

WILLES, MARK HINCKLEY, banker; b. Salt Lake City, July 16, 1941; s. Joseph Simmons and Ruth (Hinckley) W.; A.B., Columbia U., 1963; Ph.D., 1967; m. Laura Fayone, June 7, 1961; children—Wendy Anne, Susan Kay, Keith Mark, Stephen Joseph, Matthew Bryant. Mem. com. staff banking and currency com. Ho. of Reps., Washington, 1966-67; asst. prof. fin. U. Pa., 1967-69; economist Fed. Res. Bank, Phila., 1967, sr. economist, 1969-70, dir. research, 1970-71, v.p., dir. research, 1971, 1st v.p., 1971-77; pres. Fed. Res. Bank of Mpls., 1977—. Home: 555 Pineview Ln N Plymouth MN 55441 Office: 250 Marquette Ave Minneapolis MN 55480. *My success is based on adherence to principles I learned in the home, which is the most basic and important organizational unit in the world. Three of those principles stand out in my mind: -Be just, honest and moral—do things not only because they are required, but because they are right. -Have mercy—care enough about others to be fair and kind. -Be humble—you can get more done effectively with the help of others than you can do on your own.*

WILLET, HENRY LEE, stained glass artist; b. Pitts., Dec. 7, 1899; s. William and Anne (Lee) W.; student Princeton, 1918-20, Wharton Sch. of U. Pa., 1920-21; study and research in Europe, 1924-27; Art D. (hon.), Lafayette Coll., 1951; L.H.D. (hon.), Geneva Coll., 1966;

L.H.D. (hon.), Ursinus Coll., 1967; D.F.A. (hon.), St. Lawrence U., 1972; m. Muriel Crosby, Oct. 22, 1927; children—E. Crosby, Ann (Mrs. John M. Kellogg, Jr.), Zoe (Mrs. William C. Cotton). Creator of stained glass, 1920—; chmn. bd. Willet Stained Glass Studios. Represented by windows in Washington Cathedral, Cadet Chapel, U.S. Mil. Acad., many others in chs., chapels throughout U.S., 50 States, 11 fgn. countries, latest Covenant Presbyn. Ch., Charlotte, N.C., St. Thomas Episcopalian Ch., N.Y.C., 1973, Princeton U. Chapel, Cathedral of St. John the Divine, N.Y.C. all glass Nat. Presbyn. Ch., Washington, also in St. Mary's Roman Cath. Cathedral, San Francisco, 6 Bays Grace Cathedral, San Francisco; sculpture and glass facade Ch. Center at UN, 1963; 5400 glass panels Hall of Sci., N.Y. World's Fair, 1964, Mormon Temple, Washington, 1973, St. Anselm Ch., Tokyo, Japan, Coral Ridge Presbyn. Ch., Fort Lauderdale. Pres. bd. commrs. Upper Dublin Twp., 1946-59; dir. bd. Christian edn. Presbyn. Ch. U.S.A., 1948-60, mem. spl. com. arts, 1968—, commr. to Gen. Assembly, 1936, 43; pres. 22 Found., Princeton U. Recipient Craft award Archtl. League N.Y., 1956; citation Religious Heritage Am., 1971; Brown medal Franklin Inst., 1972. Fellow Stained Glass Assn. Am. (pres. 1942-44); Benjamin Franklin fellow Royal Soc. Arts; fellow London, Am. Soc. Ch. Arch.; mem. A.I.A. (hon.), Guild Religious Architecture (dir.; Conover award 1963), Archtl. League N.Y., Fairmont Park Art Assn., Phila. Art Alliance (dir.; medal achievement, 1952), Pa. Mus. Art, Pa. Acad. Fine Arts. Am. Fedn. Art, T Square (Phila.), Woodmere Art Gallery Phila. (hon.), Smithsonian Instn. Club: Union League (Phila.). Exhibited leading art galleries; lectr. art and craft of stained glass. Presbyn. Home: 8005 Douglas Rd Wyndmoor PA 19118 Office: 10 E Moreland Ave Philadelphia PA 19118. *In our apprentice school I teach a course entitled "The Three 'L's" - The lure, the lust, and the love of stained glass. With this type of dedication and devotion to your chosen field, you undoubtedly will achieve success. At least you will be assured of a happy and worthwhile life.*

WILLEY, CALVERT LIVINGSTON, assn. exec.; b. Cambridge, Md., Dec. 11, 1920; s. Henry Calvert and Virginia Mae (Mills) W.; B.S., U. Md., 1949. Research dir. Clifton Corp., Washington, 1952-53; asst. to exec. dir. Nat. Soc. Profl., Engrs., 1953-56; exec. sec. Am. Soc. Lubrication Engrs., Chgo., 1957-61; exec. sec. Inst. Food Technologists, Chgo., 1961-66, exec. dir., 1966—. Served with the USNR, 1942-45, 49-52; lt. Res. Fellow AAAS; mem. Am. Soc. Assn. Execs., Council Engring. Soc. Execs. Home: 3950 Lake Shore Dr B-2010 Chicago IL 60613 Office: 221 N LaSalle St Chicago IL 60601

WILLEY, GORDON RANDOLPH, anthropologist, archaeologist, educator; b. Chariton, Ia., Mar. 7, 1913; s. Frank and Agnes Caroline (Wilson) W.; A.B., U. Ariz., 1935, A.M., 1936; Ph.D., Columbia U., 1942; A.M. honoris causa, Harvard U., 1950; Litt.D. honoris causa, Cambridge U., 1977; m. Katharine W. Whaley, Sept. 17, 1938; children—Alexandra, Winston. Archaeol. asst. Nat. Park Service, Macon, Ga., 1936-38; archaeologist La. State U., 1938-39; archaeol. field supr., Peru, 1941-42; instr. anthropology Columbia, 1942-43; anthropologist Bur. Am. Ethnology, Smithsonian Instn., 1943-50; Bowditch prof. archaeology Harvard, 1950—, chmn. dept. anthropology, 1954-57; vis. prof. Am. archaeology Cambridge (Eng.) U., 1962-63; mem. expdns. to Peru, Panama, 1941-52, Brit. Honduras, 1953-56, Guatemala, 1958, 60, 62, 64, 65, 66, 67, 68, Nicaragua, 1959, 61, Honduras, 1973, 75-77. Overseas fellow Churchill Coll., Cambridge U., 1968-69; decorated Order of Quetzal (Guatemala); recipient Viking Fund medal, 1953; Gold medal Archaeol. Inst. Am., 1973, Alfred V. Kidder medal for achievement in Am. Archaeology, 1974; Huxley medal Royal Anthrop. Inst., London, 1979. Fellow Am. Anthrop. Assn. (pres. 1961), Am. Acad. Sci., London Soc. Antiquaries, Soc. Am. Archaeology (pres. 1968); mem. Nat. Acad. Sci., Royal Anthrop. Inst. Great Britain and Ireland; corr. mem. Brit. Acad. Clubs: Cosmos (Washington); Tavern (Boston). Author: Excavations in the Chancay Valley, Peru, 1943; Archaeology of the Florida Gulf Coast, 1949; Prehistoric Settlement Patterns in the Viru Valley, Peru, 1953; Introduction to American Archaeology, 2 vols., 1966-71; The Artifacts of Altar de Sacrificios, 1972; Excavations of Altarde Sacrificious, Guatemala, 1973; Das Alte Amerika, 1974; The Artifacts of Seibal, Guatemala, 1978; co-author: Early Ancon and Early Supe Cultures, 1954; The Monagrillo Culture of Panama, 1954; Method and Theory in American Archaelogy, 1958; Prehistoric Maya Settlements in the Belize Valley, 1965; The Ruins of Altar de Sacrificios, Department of Peten, Guatemala: An Introduction, 1969; the Maya Collapse: An Appraisal, 1973; A History of American Archaeology, 1974; The Origins of Maya Civilization, 1977. Co-editor: Courses Toward Urban Life, 1962; editor: Prehistoric Settlement Patterns of the New World, 1956; Archaeological Researches in Retrospect, 1974. Home: 25 Gray Gardens E Cambridge MA 02138

WILLEY, JOHN COFFIN, book publisher; b. Cherryfield, Maine, Dec. 28, 1914; s. Kilburn Holt and Mertie Alta (Grant); grad. Cherryfield Acad., 1931; A.B., U. Maine, 1935; M.A., Harvard U., 1940, M.B.A. (Baker scholar), 1943; m. Fern Audrey Morrison, Oct. 23, 1943. Instr. English, Coburn Classical Inst., Waterville, Maine, 1935-39, submaster, 1937-39; instr. English, U. Mo., 1940-42; asst. to pres. William Morrow & Co., Inc., 1946-52, treas., 1952-60, editor, 1957-77, cons. editor, 1977—, v.p., 1965-77; sec. William Sloane Assos., Inc., 1952-57, v.p., editor, 1957-60, also dir.; editor Sloane Assos. div. William Morrow & Co., 1960-66; sec. M.S. Mill Co., 1949-51, treas., 1949-52, editor, 1949-68, pres., 1951-68. Served to capt. Transp. Corps, AUS, 1943-46. Mem. Phi Beta Kappa, Phi Kappa Phi, Sigma Chi. Club: The Players (N.Y.C.). Home: 3 Midrocks Dr Norwalk CT 06851 Office: 105 Madison Ave New York NY 10016

WILLEY, JOHN DOUGLAS, newspaper exec.; b. Melrose, Mass., June 4, 1917; s. Arthur Peach and Lillian (Holden) W.; LL.D. (hon.), U. Toledo, 1972; m. Marilynn Miller, July 3, 1943; children—Margery Lynn (Mrs. James Marshall), John Douglas, James Campbell, David Spencer, Peter Whitney, Sec., Boston & Maine R.R., Boston, 1935-40; sec. Jones & Lamson Machine Co., Springfield, Vt., 1940-41; reporter The Blade, Toledo, 1946-49, asst. to pub., 1949-51, 58-65, city editor, 1952-54, asst. mng. editor, 1954-56, dir. pub. relations, 1956-58, treas., 1962-69, asso. pub., 1965—; pres. Toledo Blade Co., 1969—, dir., 1964—; pres. Clear Water, Inc., 1966—; dir. Buckeye Cablevision, Inc., 1965—; v.p., dir. Lima Communications Corp., 1971—; v.p., dir. Monterey Peninsula Herald, 1967—, Register Pub. Co., 1965—; mem. Ohio advisory bd. Liberty Mut. Ins. Co., 1976—. Mem. exec. com. of bd. trustees, treas. Toledo Area Med. Coll. and Edn. Found. 1960-75, hon. trustee, 1975—; mem. adv. bd. St. Vincent Hosp., 1961-75; trustee Maumee Valley Country Day Sch., 1974-77; treas. Amateur Athletic Union Task Force Com., 1976—. Served to capt. A.C., U.S. Army, 1942-46. Mem. Sigma Delta Chi. Club: Belmont Country. Home: 3534 River Rd Toledo OH 43614 Office: 541 Superior St Toledo OH 43660

WILLEY, RICHARD LEE, univ. dean; b. Walnut Grove, Mo., Dec. 30, 1928; s. Cash W. and Faye (Jones) W.; B.S. in Edn., S.W. Mo. State U., Springfield, 1950; M.S. in Edn., Drury Coll., Springfield, 1956; Ed.D. in Adminstrn., U. Mo., 1962; m. Elsie Colene Miller, June 2, 1957; children—Robyn Lea, Teri Francis, Jean Ellen, Richard Lee, Jonathon Allen. Tchr. in Ellington, Union and DeSoto, Mo., 1950-53; tchr.-prin., Waynesville, Mo., 1953-55; prin. jr.-sr. high sch., Vandalia, Mo., 1955-59, Marshall, Mo., 1959-61; instr. U. Mo., 1961-62; asso. prof. U. Wyo., 1962-66; dean Coll. Edn., Idaho State U., 1966-78; dean Coll. Edn. Ind. State U., 1978—; vis. prof. S.W. Mo. State Coll., summer 1962, U. Nev., summer 1970. Bd. dirs. Rocky Mountain Ednl. Lab., 1965—, North Central chmn. Wyo., 1964-65, Idaho Council on Econ. Devel., 1972—, Fedn. Rocky Mountain States, Human Resource Council, 1973-75; bd. dirs., exec. com. N.W. Regional 1965—, Lab., 1970—; mem. exec. bd. Diagnostic and Learning Lab., Pocatello, Ida., 1966-74. Gregory fellow, 1961-62. Mem. Asso. Orgns. Tchr. Edn., NEA, Idaho Edn. Assn., Am. Assn. Coll. Tchr. Edn., Tchr. Ednl. and Profl. Standards, Pocatello C. of C., Phi Kappa Phi, Phi Delta Kappa. Methodist (Sunday sch. supt., ofcl. bd.). Mason, Kiwanian, Rotarian. Contbr. articles to prof. jours. Home: 1070 Castle Dr Terre Haute IN 47802

WILLEY, RUSSELL WILLIAM, bus. exec.; b. Bridgeville, Del., Feb. 11, 1916; s. Ira and Fannie L. (Short) W.; B.S., U. Del., 1947; M.A., U. Pa., 1950; student Atlanta Law Sch., 1944-45; C.P.A., 1947; m. Hattie T. Robinson, Mar. 15, 1945. Agt., Internal Revenue Service, 1940-42; instr. U. Del., 1947-50; accountant-economist E.I. duPont de Nemours & Co., Inc., 1950-56; with Beneficial Corp., Wilmington, Del., 1956—, v.p., controller, 1969—. Served to capt. U.S. Army, 1942-46. Mem. Financial Analysts Fedn. Methodist. Author: Foreign Exchange: The Accounting, Economics and Control, 1977. Home: 1 Wellington Rd Welshire Wilmington DE 19803 Office: 1300 Market St Wilmington DE 19899

WILLI, GEORGE, judge; b. N.Y.C., May 1, 1924; s. George and Helen (Bour) W.; B.B.A., LL.B., Univ. of Wis., 1950; m. Hazel Sellers, July 5, 1969; children—George John, Jean, Brian. Admitted to Wis. bar, 1950, D.C. bar, 1964, also U.S. Ct. Claims; carriers atty. Nat. R.R. Adjustment Bd., 1950-51; trial atty., tax div. Dept. Justice, 1951-63; partner firm Haynes & Miller, Washington, 1964; trial judge U.S. Ct. of Claims, 1965—. Served to capt. USAAF, 1943-46. Decorated D.F.C., Air medal with oak leaf clusters; Superior Performance award Dept. Justice, 1963. Mem. Phi Delta Theta (pres. U. Wis. chpt. 1949), Phi Delta Phi. Home: 3915 N Woodstock St Arlington VA 22207 Office: 717 Madison Pl NW Washington DC 20005

WILLIAMS, ALAN DAVISON, pub. co. exec.; b. Duluth, Minn., Oct. 25, 1925; s. Curtis Gilbert and Marjorie Barton (Townsend) W.; grad. Phillips Exeter Acad., 1944; B.A., Yale, 1949; m. Beverly Alexander, Apr. 1, 1951; children—Elizabeth Wistar Williams Rawls, Anne Alexander, Marjorie Curtis. Advt. mgr. McGraw-Hill Book Co., 1949-53; publicity mgr., editor J.B. Lippincott Co., 1953-58; N.Y. editor Little, Brown & Co., 1959-65; mng. editor, editorial dir., v.p. Viking Press, Inc., N.Y.C., 1965—; v.p. editorial Viking-Penguin Inc., 1975—. Mem. adv. council English dept. Princeton, 1972—. Trustee Episcopalian Mag., 1966-74, Mercer County Community Guidance Center, 1967-73. Mem. P.E.N. Club: Century Assn. (N.Y.C.). Home: 19 Maple St Princeton NJ 08540 Office: 625 Madison Ave New York NY 10022

WILLIAMS, ANDY, entertainer; b. Wall Lake, Iowa, Dec. 3, 1930; s. Jay Emerson and Florence (Finley) W.; m. Claudine Longet, Dec. 15, 1961; children—Noelle, Christian, Robert. Worked with 3 brothers as Williams Brothers Quartet on radio stations, Des Moines, Chgo., Cin. and Los Angeles, 1938-47; Williams Brothers teamed with Kay Thompson in night clubs, U.S. and Europe, 1947-52; regular performer Steve Allen Tonight TV show, 1953-55; star Andy Williams TV Show; night club and concert entertainer; rec. artist for Columbia Records; recordings include Love Story, Hawaiian Wedding Song, Canadian Sunset, Happy Heart, Moon River, Born Free, The Days of Wine and Roses, Dear Heart, Can't Get Used to Losing You; appeared in motion picture I'd Rather Be Rich; pres. Barnaby Records, Barnaby Prodns., Barnaby Sports; maj. stockholder Phoenix Suns Basketball Team; host Andy Williams San Diego Golf Open. Named number 1 male vocalist Top Artist on Campus Poll, 1968; awarded 17 gold albums; recipient 2 Emmy awards. Home: Beverly Hills CA Office: 816 N LaCienega Blvd Los Angeles CA 90069

WILLIAMS, ARTHUR, engring. cons.; b. Swindon, Eng., July 29, 1904; s. Joseph and Emily (Chirgwin) W.; student Swindon Coll. Engring. Sch., 1921-26, Harvard Bus. Sch., 1955; m. Ellen M.I. Cullingford, Apr. 8, 1929; children—Valerie (Mrs. Robert C. Norcross), Brian R. Came to U.S., 1926, naturalized, 1942. Chief engr. Superheater Co., East Chicago, Ind., 1927-42, v.p., 1946; v.p. Combustion Engring., Inc., 1949-58; v.p., sec. Submerged Combustion, Inc., 1958-65; cons. Selas Corp. Am., 1965-66; cons. engr., 1966—. Episcopalian. Address: 1145 Ludlam Dr Miami Springs FL 33166

WILLIAMS, ARTHUR MIDDLETON, JR., elec. utility exec.; b. Charleston, S.C., Sept. 16, 1914; s. Arthur Middleton and Katherine (Ward) W.; B.S. in Textile Chemistry, Clemson U., 1936; J.D., magna cum laude, U. S.C., 1942; m. Katherine Murphy, Nov. 4, 1943; children—Katherine Elizabeth (Mrs. Mahon), Patricia LaBruce (Mrs. Boykin), Elizabeth Middleton. Joined U.S. Army, 1936, served in cav. until 1938; transferred to inactive duty, 1938-42; active duty with armored forces, 1942-43; ret., 1943; admitted to S.C. bar, 1942, U.S. Supreme Ct.; practice in Columbia, S.C., 1943-44; with S.C. Electric & Gas Co., Columbia, 1944—, sr. v.p., 1961-66, pres., 1966-77, chief exec. officer, 1967-79, chmn. bd., 1977—, also dir.; tchr. law U.S.C. Law Sch., 1947-50; dir. Liberty Corp., S.C. Nat. Corp.; dir. emeritus S.C. Nat. Bank, Columbia. Chmn. S.C. Employment Security Commn. Merit System Council, 1950-56; mem. Gov. S.C. Fiscal Survey Commn., 1955, S.C. Commn. Human Affairs, 1971-75; mem. So. Govs.' Conf. Peacetime Uses Nuclear Energy, 1955-59; mem. exec. com. So. Interstate Nuclear Bd., 1959-63; sec. S.C. Nuclear Energy and Space Commn., 1962-63. Mem. bd. sch. commrs. Dist. 1, Richland County, S.C., 1958-71; mem. U. S.C. Bus. Partnership Found., pres., 1969-71. Bd. dirs. United Fund Community Services, Columbia and Richland County, 1955-58, pres., 1956; bd. dirs. Richland County chpt. A.R.C., 1945-48, Family Welfare Assn. Richland County, 1950-55, Columbia U.S.O., 1948-51; bd. dirs. Carolinas United, 1959-62, exec. com., 1959-62; trustee Porter Gaud Sch., Charleston, 1966-68, Converse Coll., 1971-75, Benedict Coll., 1979—. Recipient Freedoms Found. award, 1950; Algernon Sydney Sullivan award U. S.C., 1972, Distinguished Alumni award, 1975. Mem. S.C. (v.p. 5th jud. circuit 1954), Am., Richland County bar assns., Columbia C. of C. (bd. dirs. 1951-57, 61-64, pres. 1955, nat. counselor 1956), S.C. C. of C. (bd. dirs. 1963-66, pres. 1968, chmn. bd. 1969), Edison Electric Inst. (bd. dirs. 1973-76, 78—), Southeastern Electric Exchange (pres. 1970-71, bd. dirs. 1966-79), NAM (dir. 1970-73), Phi Beta Kappa, Scabbard and Blade, Blue Key, Phi Psi, Beta Gamma Sigma, Sigma Nu (Centennial award 1969). Episcopalian (past vestryman). Clubs: Palmetto (pres. 1967-71, bd. govs. 1959—), Cotillion, Quadrille, Pine Tree Hunt, Centurian, Forest Lake, Summit, Columbia Sailing (Columbia); Winyah Indigo Soc. (Georgetown); Carolina Yacht (Charleston). Office: 328 Main St Columbia SC 29201 also PO Box 764 Columbia SC 29218

WILLIAMS, ARVIN SAMUEL, educator; b. Appalachia, Va., Nov. 7, 1920; s. Irvin Patrick and Cleo (Blankenship) W.; B.S., Milligan Coll., 1942; postgrad. Johns Hopkins, 1947, U. Md., 1948, Madison Coll., 1965-66; M.A., George Washington U., 1967, postgrad., 1967—; m. Emma Keren Mauck, Aug. 13, 1949; 1 dau., Lucy Ellen. Tchr., coach Norton (Va.) High Sch., 1942-43; math. instr., coach Randolph-Macon Acad., Front Royal, Va., 1947-55, registrar, 1949-55, athletic dir., 1955-65, exec. v.p., 1965-69, pres., 1969—. Democratic committeeman Warren County, Va., 1968—. Served with USAAF, 1944-47; ETO; col. USAF ret. Mem. Nat. Assn. Secondary Sch. Prins., Front Royal Jr. C. of C. (sec., bd. dirs. 1950-55), C. of C. (bd. dirs. 1969—, pres. 1973). Methodist (chmn. adminstrv. bd. 1971, pres. assn. ednl. instns. Va. conf. 1969-70, 74-75). Kiwanian (pres. 1971—). Address: Randolph-Macon Academy Front Royal VA 22630

WILLIAMS, BARBARA JEAN MAY, state librarian; b. Alphoretta, Ky., June 5, 1927; d. Andrew Jackson and Bess (Salisbury) May; A.B. in Spanish, Centre Coll., 1949; postgrad. Columbia U., 1957; M.S. in Library Sci., U. Ky., 1963. Librarian, Midway Jr. Coll., 1960-62, Ky. Dept. Libraries, Frankfort, 1965-68; planning librarian Ky. Program Devel. Office, Frankfort, 1968-71, Ky. Exec. Dept. for Fin. and Adminstrn., Frankfort, 1972-76; asst. state librarian Ky. Dept. Libraries and Archives, Frankfort, 1976, state librarian, 1977—; mem. dean's adv. council U.K. Coll. Library Sci.; mem. Depository Library Council to Public Printer. Mem. ALA, Southeastern Library Assn., Ky. Library Assn. (sec. spl. library sect. 1976, then chmn. sect. 1976, Chief Officers State Library Agys. (liaison com. office Edn. 1979-80), Assn. State Library Agys. (Index State Library Activities 1979-80), Council Planning Librarian (treas.), Ky. Council Archivists, Ky. Hist. Soc., J. B. Speed Museum Guild. Presbyterian. Clubs: Democratic Woman's, Filson. Office: Ky Dept Library and Archives PO Box 537 Frankfort KY 40602

WILLIAMS, BARRY, actor; b. Santa Monica, Calif., Sept. 30, 1954; s. Frank Millar and Doris May (Moore) Blenkhorn. Actor, appearing in free-lance TV and commls., 1966-69; actor in series Brady Bunch, 1969-74; singer and rec. artist, 1971—; voice on cartoon show Brady Kids, 1972; stage entertainer; appeared in Pippin, nat. tour, 1974-75, N.Y.C., 1976. Mem. Screen Actors Guild, AFTRA, Am. Guild Variety Artists. Composer song Till I Met You (performed on Brady Bunch TV show), 1971. Office: Internat Creative Management 8899 Beverly Blvd Los Angeles CA 90048

WILLIAMS, BEN AMES, JR., ret. banker; b. Waltham, Mass., Oct. 25, 1915; s. Ben Ames and Florence (Talpey) W.; A.B., Dartmouth U., 1938; m. Jessie Ames Marshall, Nov. 30, 1940; children—Jessie M. (Mrs. Llewellyn Howland III), Ann C. (Mrs. Edward Woll, Jr.), Susan A. (Mrs. Michael Moser). With First Nat. Bank Boston, 1940-79, exec. v.p., 1971-79, also dir.; dir. Arthur D. Little, Inc., 1969—, chmn. exec. com., 1975—. Chmn., trustee Thompson Acad., Boston, 1968—; trustee Children's Hosp. Boston, New Eng. Coll. Fund, Museum Sci.; bd. dirs. Boston council Boy Scouts Am., Mass. Fund Children and Youth; bd. overseers Boys Clubs Boston. Served as lt. (j.g.) USNR, 1943-46. Author: Mr. Secretary, 1940. Home: 98 Rockwood St Jamaica Plain MA 02130

WILLIAMS, BEN FRANKLIN, JR., lawyer; b. El Paso, Tex., Aug. 12, 1929; s. Ben Franklin and Dorothy (Whitaker) W.; B.A., U. Ariz., 1951, LL.B., 1956; m. Daisy Federighi, June 2, 1951; children—Elizabeth Lee, Diane Marie, Katherine Ann, Benjamin Franklin III. Admitted to Ariz. bar, 1956; with Bd. Immigration Appeals, Dept. Justice, 1957, ICC, 1959; practice in Douglas, Ariz., 1956—; city atty., Douglas and Tombstone, 1962; atty. Mexican consul, 1960. Dir. Fidelity Fed. Savs. & Loan Assn., Ariz. Pub. Service Co. Pres. Douglas Sch. Bd., 1963, 69, 70; mem. bd. Ariz. Dept. Econ. Planning and Devel. Ward committeeman Douglas Republican Com., 1962. Served to 1st lt. AUS, 1951-53. Mem. Am., Internat., Ariz. (treas. 1963), Cochise County (pres. 1959) bar assns., Am. Judicature Soc., Ariz. Hist. Soc. (dir.), Sigma Nu, Phi Delta Phi, Blue Key. Episcopalian. Elk. Home: 2100 9th St Douglas AZ 85607 Office: 1930 11th St Douglas AZ 85608

WILLIAMS, BEN T., state judge; b. 1911; LL.B., U. Okla. Admitted to Okla. bar, 1933; practiced in Pauls Valley; chief justice Supreme Ct. Okla. Office: Supreme Ct State Capitol Bldg Oklahoma City OK 73105*

WILLIAMS, BENJAMIN DAVIS, III, ednl. adminstr.; b. N.Y.C., Mar. 8, 1936; s. Benjamin Davis and Isobel (Pirie) W.; grad. St. Paul's Sch., Concord, N.H., 1953; A.B., Princeton U., 1957; M.A., U. Conn., 1969; m. Nancy Nielsen, Nov. 25, 1961; children—Benjamin, Frederick, Joseph. Trainee, W.E. Hutton Co., investment brokers, N.Y.C., 1961-62; faculty Pomfret Sch. (Conn.), 1962-69; headmaster Lawrence Acad., Groton, Mass., 1969—; dir. Carson Pirie Scott & Co., Chgo. Hunter safety instr., Pomfret, 1965-69. Mem. Pomfret Town Planning Bd., 1968-69; v.p. Ind. Schs. Found. Mass., 1970-72. Bd. dirs. Applewild Sch., 1974—; v.p. Nashua River Watershed Assn., 1975-77, pres., 1977—. Served to capt. USMCR, 1957-61. Mem. Lepidopterist's Soc., Ind. Schs. Assn. Mass. (dir. 1973—, v.p. 1974—). Home and office: Lawrence Acad Powderhouse Rd Groton MA 01450

WILLIAMS, BEVERLY CHAN, librarian; b. Ancon, C.Z., Dec. 5, 1927; d. Harry Yee and Rosa (Luthas) C.; A.A., C.Z. Coll., 1947; B.S., Syracuse U., 1949, M.A., 1951; M.S., Columbia U., 1958; m. Charles Joseph Williams, Apr. 14, 1956; children—Patrick Charles, Paul Martin. Reference librarian C.Z. Library-Museum, Balboa Heights, 1955-63, chief readers service, 1963-77, librarian-curator, 1978—. Vice chmn. C.Z. chpt. ARC, 1978-79. Roman Catholic. Home: PSC Box 564 APO Miami FL 34002 Office: Panama Canal Commn Library-Museum APO Miami FL 34011

WILLIAMS, BILLY DEE, actor; b. N.Y.C., Apr. 6, 1937; student (Hallgarten scholar) Nat. Acad. Fine Arts and Design; student acting Paul Mann and Sidney Poitier, Actor's Workshop in Harlem. Child actor; Broadway adult debut The Cool World, 1961; other stage appearances include: A Taste of Honey, 1961, I Have a Dream, 1976, Hallelujah, Baby; films: The Last Angry Man, 1959, The Out-of-Towners, 1970, The Final Comedown, Lady Sings the Blues, 1972, Hit!, 1973, Mahogany, 1975, The Bingo Long Travelling All-Stars and Motor Kings, 1976, Scott Joplin, 1977; TV films: Brian's Song, 1971, The Glass House (Emmy nomination); guest appearances TV series: The Interns, The FBI, Mission: Impossible, Mod Squad, Police Woman, The Jeffersons; appeared in TV movie Scott Joplin: King of Ragtime, 1978. Office: care Internat Creative Mgmt 40 W 57 St New York NY 10019*

WILLIAMS, BRUCE DAVID, corp. exec.; b. Washington, June 15, 1932; s. Leo Nicholas and Ruth (Hager) W.; A.B. cum laude, Harvard, 1954; M.B.A., Stanford, 1956; m. Deirdre O'Brien, Feb. 20, 1960; children—Katherine Colwell, Nicole Hager. With Standard Oil Co. (N.J.), 1956-61; with Ingersoll Rand Co., Woodcliff Lake, N.J., 1961—, treas., 1969-74, v.p., treas., 1974—. Trustee N.J. Coll. Fund Assn., Englewood Hosp. Clubs: Knickerbocker Country (Tenafly, N.J.); Englewood Field (N.J.). Home: 391 Johnson Ave Englewood NJ 07631 Office: Woodcliff Lake NJ 07675

WILLIAMS, BRYAN, univ. dean; b. Longview, Tex., July 28; s. Lewis Bryan and Margaret Louise (Smart) W.; M.D., Southwestern Med. Sch., Dallas, 1947; m. Frances Montgomery, Mar. 31, 1950; children—Harrison, Amy, Philip, Nickolas, Margaret, Lincoln. Practice medicine specializing in internal medicine, Dallas, 1957-70;

asso. dean student affairs Southwestern Med. Sch., 1970—. Bd. dirs. Dallas Mus. Fine Arts, Dallas Symphony Orch., Dallas Civic Music Assn., St. Mark's Sch., Dallas Grand Opera Assn. Diplomate Am. Bd. Internal Medicine. Fellow A.C.P. (regent); mem. Inst. Medicine Nat. Acad. Scis. (charter). Home: 3712 Beverly Dr Dallas TX 75205 Office: 5323 Harry Hines Blvd Dallas TX 75235

WILLIAMS, C. DICKERMAN, lawyer; b. Milton, Pa., Oct. 1, 1900; s. Howard Hunter and Adelia Margaret (Dickerman) W.; A.B., Yale U., 1922, LL.B. magna cum laude, 1924; m. Virginia Fain, Sept. 6, 1930; children—Joan (Mrs. George Farr III), Honor Adele (Mrs. Hisato Ishida), Stephen Fain. Admitted to N.Y. bar, 1926; law clk. to chief justice William H. Taft, 1924-25; asst. U.S. atty., 1925-27; asso. spl. counsel N.Y. Transit Commn., 1928-31, to City N.Y. in rapid transit matters, 1934-37; engaged in gen. practice, 1927—; mem. firm Breed, Abbot & Morgan, 1948-51; v.p., gen. counsel Am. Locomotive Co., N.Y., 1944-48, gen. counsel 1948-50, ret. 1950; gen. counsel Dept. Commerce, 1951-53; mem. Maclay, Morgan & Williams 1954-62; mem. firm Baker, Nelson, Williams & Mitchell, 1962-74, counsel, 1974—; vis. Sterling lectr. law Yale, 1946. Bd. dirs. Concern for Dying, 1976—, Cancer Research Inst., Inc., 1956-77, pres., 1960-66, hon. trustee, 1966—; bd. dirs. Berkshire Farm Center, Canaan, N.Y., 1936-71, treas., 1939-48; trustee Fed. Bar Council, 1972—. Mem. Am. Bar Assn., Bar Assn. City N.Y. Republican. Presbyn. Club: Century (N.Y.C.). Home: 1133 Park Ave New York NY 10028 Office: Baker Nelson & Williams 444 Madison Ave New York NY 10022

WILLIAMS, C(HARLES) K(ENNETH), poet, educator; b. Newark, Nov. 4, 1936; s. Paul B. and Dossie Williams; student Bucknell U., 1954-55; B.A., U. Pa., 1959; m. Catherine Mauger, Apr. 18, 1975; children—Jessica Anne, Jed Mauger. Tchr. Poetry Center, Phila., 1973, 75; prof. Beaver Coll., 1975—, Drexel U., 1977; writer in residence Franklin and Marshall Coll., 1977. Sponsor People's Fund, Phila., 1970-75; vis. prof. U. Calif., Irvine, 1978, Boston U., 1979-80. John Simon Guggenheim Found. fellow, 1974-75. Recipient hon. mention Melville Cane prize, 1978. Author: A Day for Anne Frank, 1968; Lies, 1969; I Am the Bitter Name, 1972; With Ignorance, 1978; (poetry) (with Gregory Dickerson) Women of Trachis (transl. from Sophocles), 1978. Contbg. editor Am. Poetry Rev., 1973—; lit. editor Phila. Arts Exchange. Home: 173 Newbury St Boston MA 02116

WILLIAMS, CAMILLA, operatic soprano; b. Danville, Va.; d. Booker and Fannie (Cary) Williams; B.S., Va. State Coll., 1941; student langs. U. Pa., 1942; student Mme. Marian Szekely-Freschl, 1943-44, 1952, Berkowitz and Cesare Sodero, 1944-46, Rose Dirman, 1948-52, Sergius Kagen, 1958-62; m. Chas. T. Beavers, Aug. 28, 1950. Engaged as music instr. pub. schs., Danville, 1941-42; contract with RCA Victor as exclusive Victor Red Seal recording artist, 1944—; also concert and opera engagements including role of Nedda in Pagliacci, Mimi in La Boheme, Aida, Marguerite in Faust, others; as winner 1st prize Phila. Orch. Youth Concert audition appeared with Phila. Symphony Orch., 1944; first Negro to sing Madame Butterfly with maj. opera co., N.Y.C. Center, under direction of Laszlo Halasz, Vienna Volksoper, Anina, St. of Bleeker St., Vienna Premier; contract Columbia Records, 1951, MGM Records, 1952; tours in Europe (12th tour 1960), New Zealand and Australia, 1955, Africa (auspices State Dept.), 1958, Africa, Japan, Korea, Hong Kong, Viet Nam, Laos and Philippines, 1961; command performance White House, 1960; past prof. voice Ind. U. Sch. Music. Recipient Marian Anderson award, 1943-44; named to Hall of Fame, Danville, Va., 1974; award for contbn. to music Sta. WLIB; gold medal Emperor of Ethiopia; Keys to city of Danville, Taiwan; named Distinguished Virginian Gov. of Va. Mem. N.A.A.C.P. (hon. life), Internat. Platform Assn., Alpha Kappa Alpha. Camilla Williams Park, Danville, named in her honor. Home: 309 W 104th St New York NY 10025 Office: care Pacific World Artists 250 W 57th St New York NY 10019

WILLIAMS, CARL HARWELL, utilities exec.; b. Mansfield, Ga., Oct. 22, 1915; s. John Horace and Mary Ruby (Harwell) W.; student U. Fla., 1934-35; B.S., Ga. Sch. Tech., 1939; postgrad. Harvard Advanced Mgmt. Program, U. Hawaii, 1956; m. Diane Barnes, June 25, 1967; children—Edward Vincent, Lesa Anne. Engr., Fla. Power & Light Co., Miami, 1939-41; with Hawaiian Electric Co., Inc., Honolulu, 1945—, mgr. engring., 1955-62, v.p., 1962-71, exec. v.p., 1971-72, pres., 1972—, also dir.; chmn. bd., dir., Maui Electric Co. (subsidiary), 1972—, chmn. bd., dir. Hawaii Electric Light Co. (subsidiary), 1972—; dir. Bank of Hawaii. Bd. dirs. Aloha United Way, Oahu Devel. Conf., chmn., 1979—; bd. visitors Coll. Bus. Adminstrn., Hawaii, also mem. adv. com. advanced mgmt. program, also mem. adv. com. Hawaii geothermal project; mem. State Energy Policy Task Force; mem. Hawaii Energy Conservation Council; mem. Gov.'s Com. Alt. Energy Devel. Served to lt. col., Signal Corps, AUS, 1941-45. Decorated Legion of Merit. Registered profl. engr., Hawaii. Fellow IEEE; mem. Hawaii C. of C., Engring. Assn. Hawaii, Nat. (past dir.), Hawaii (past dir., pres.) socs. profl. engrs., Pacific Coast Elec. Assn. (v.p., dir.), AIEE, (past chmn. Hawaii sect.). Clubs: Pacific, Outrigger Canoe. Home: 2969 Kalakaua Ave Honolulu HI 96815 Office: PO Box 2750 Honolulu HI 96840

WILLIAMS, CARLTON HINKLE, dentist; b. St. Louis, Sept. 16, 1914; s. Thomas A. and Lillian (Hinkle) W.; student Calif. State U., 1932-33; D.D.S., U. So. Calif., 1937; m. Evelyn Stewart, Dec. 31, 1934; children—Lynn (Mrs. Bernard J. Martin), Gayle (Mrs. David Landin). Pvt. practice dentistry, San Diego, 1937—. Chmn. med. instns. commn. for San Diego County, 1949-70. Served to maj. AUS, 1953-55. Fellow Am. Coll. Dentists, Internat. Coll. Dentists, Am. Inst. Oral Biology; mem. Am. Acad. Restorative Dentistry, Am. Acad. Periodontology, Acad. Gen. Dentistry, San Diego County Dental Soc. (pres. 1946), So. Calif. (pres. 1959), Am. (pres. 1973-74) dental assns., Calif. Dental Service (pres. 1961-62), Federation Dentaire Internationale (speaker gen. assembly 1975—). Kiwanian (hon.). Home: 10840 Melva Rd La Mesa CA 92041 Office: 2654 4th Ave San Diego CA 92103. *I have always felt confident that I could accomplish whatever goals I set for myself, and I have always set goals. I have always felt it was foolhardy to deceive oneself.*

WILLIAMS, CARROLL MILTON, biologist, educator; b. Richmond, Va., Dec. 2, 1916; s. George Leslie and Jessie Ann (Hendricks) W.; S.B., U. Richmond, 1937, D.Sc. (hon.), 1960; A.M., Harvard, 1938, Ph.D., 1941, M.D. summa cum laude, 1946; m. Muriel Anne Voter, June 26, 1941; children—John Leslie (dec.), Wesley Conant, Peter Glenn (dec.), Roger Lee. Asst. prof. Harvard 1946-48, asso. prof. zoology, 1948-53, prof., 1953-66, Benjamin Bussey prof. biology, 1966—, chmn. dept., 1959-62; chief scientist phase C of Alpha Helix Expdn. to Upper Amazon, 1967. Trustee Radcliffe Coll., 1961-64. Mem. Internat. Center for Insect Physiology and Ecology, Nairobi, Kenya, 1970—. Recipient Newcomb Cleveland prize A.A.A.S., 1950, Boylston prize and medal Harvard Med. Sch., 1961, George Ledlie prize Harvard, 1967, Howard Taylor Ricketts award U. Chgo., 1969. Guggenheim fellow 1955-56. Fellow Am. Acad. Arts and Scis. (council 1954-57, 1973-77), Entomol. Soc. Am., AAAS (council 1952-54); mem. Nat. Acad. Sci. (chmn. sect. zoology 1970-73 (council 1973-76), Inst. Medicine, Am. Soc. Zoologists, Am. Physiol. Soc., Soc. Gen. Physiologists, Am. Philos. Soc., Soc. Devel. Biology, Harvey Soc., Lepidopterists Soc., Phi Beta Kappa, Sigma Xi. Research on juvenile hormones in insects. Home: 27 Eliot Rd Lexington MA 02173

WILLIAMS, CHARLES DAVID, barrister; b. Toronto, Ont., Can., June 28, 1916; s. David Selkirk and Clara Floss (Jewel) W.; B.A., U. Alta., 1938, LL.B., 1940; m. Georgie MacBraire Smith, May 12, 1945; children—Frederick Charles, Elizabeth Jane. Called to bar, Alta., 1947, B.C., 1967; apptd. Queen's counsel, 1962; Can. counsel Can. Seaboard Oil Co., 1949-58, Tenn. Gas Transmission Co., 1958-66; v.p., sec. Tenneco Oil & Minerals, Ltd., 1964-66; gen. counsel Westcoast Transmission Co. Ltd., Vancouver, B.C., 1973—, sec., 1975—, v.p., 1976—. Served with Can. Army, World War II. Mem. law socs. Alta., B.C., Can., Vancouver bar assns., Delta Upsilon. Clubs: Calgary Golf and Country, Calgary Petroleum, Terminal City. Contbr. articles to profl. jours. Home: 10854 Madreno Dr Rural Route 1 Sidney VI

WILLIAMS, CHARLES LAVAL, JR., physician, internat. orgn. ofcl.; b. New Orleans, Jan. 19, 1916; s. Charles Laval and Lewise (McLaurine) W.; student U. Va., 1933-35; M.D., Tulane U., 1940; M.P.H., U. Mich., 1945; m. Ellen Clendenin Ustick, Dec. 14, 1946; children—Ellen Clendenin, Katherine McLaurine. Intern U.S. Marine Hosp., New Orleans, 1941; with USPHS, 1941-67, assigned N.C. State Health Dept., 1941-44, States Relations div., 1944, U. Mich., 1944-45, Am. Acad. Pediatrics Nat. Study Child Health Services, 1945-47, chief planning unit, asst. chief div. commd. officers, 1947-51; with US/AID Div. Pub. Health, 1951-62, chief pub. health adviser AID Mission to Peru, 1959-62; asso. dir. internat. relations Office Internat. Health, 1962-64; chief Office Internat. Research, NIH, Bethesda, Md., 1965-66; dep. dir., then dir. Office Internat. Health, Office Surgeon General, USPHS, Washington, 1966-67; dep. dir. Pan Am. Health Orgn., 1967—. Diplomate Am. Bd. Preventive Medicine and Pub. Health. Fellow Am. Pub. Health Assn.; mem. Am. Soc. Tropical Medicine and Hygiene, U.S.-Mexico Border Pub. Health Assn., Phi Kappa Phi, Delta Omega. Home: 2726 Unicorn Ln NW Washington DC 20015 Office: 525 23d St Washington DC 20037

WILLIAMS, CHARLES MARVIN, educator; b. Romney, W. Va., Apr. 20, 1917; s. W. Marvin and Lula H. (Taylor) W.; A.B., Washington and Lee U., 1937; M.B.A., Harvard, 1939, D.C.S., 1951; LL.D., Washington and Lee U., 1966; m. Elizabeth Huffman, Oct. 19, 1946; children—Holland H., Andrea L. Credit trainee Mfrs. Trust Co., N.Y.C., 1939-41; asst. prof. finance Harvard Grad. Sch. Bus. Adminstrn., 1947-51, asso. prof., 1951-56, prof. bus. adminstrn., 1956-60, Edmund Cogswell Converse prof. banking and finance, 1960-66, George Gund prof. comml. banking, 1966—; dir. U.S. Leasing Internat., Inc., So. Natural Gas Co., Fort Dearborn Income Securities, Inc., Mass. Co., Hammermill Paper Co., Nat. Life Ins. Co., Inst. Fin. Mgmt., So. Natural Resources, Inc., Merrill Lynch Instl. Fund, Inc.; trustee San Francisco Real Estate Investors; propr. Charles M. Williams Assos. Served to lt. comdr., Supply Corps, USNR, 1941-47. Mem. Am. Fin. Assn., Phi Beta Kappa, Kappa Alpha. Club: Harvard (N.Y.C.) Author: Cumulative Voting for Directors, 1951; (P. Hunt) Case Problems in Finance, 1949; (with P. Hunt and G. Donaldson) Basic Business Finance, 1958. Home: 50 Cherry Brook Rd Weston MA 02193 Office: Soldiers Field Boston MA 02163

WILLIAMS, CHARLES MATTHEW, ins. co. exec.; b. Cin., Aug. 21, 1912; s. Charles Finn and Elizabeth Mary (Ryan) W.; A.B., Georgetown U., 1934; m. Elizabeth Hilborg Sigfried, Sept. 10, 1940; children—Elizabeth, Stella, Charles. With Western & So. Life Ins. Co., Cin., since 1931, pres., 1951-66, chmn. bd., 1967-74, chmn. exec. com., 1974—, also dir. Republican. Roman Cath. Clubs: Queen City, Bankers, University, Cin. Country, Camargo (Cin.). Home: 4325 Drake Rd Cincinnati OH 45243 Office: 400 Broadway Cincinnati OH 45202

WILLIAMS, CHARLES STANLEY, JR., univ. dean, former naval officer; b. San Pedro, Calif., Nov. 18, 1921; s. Charles Stanley and Lillian Mabel (Odell) W.; B.S., U.S. Naval Acad., 1945; M.A. in Edn., Stanford U., 1959; m. Elizabeth Bleecker Henry, June 10, 1945; children—Elizabeth Seton Williams Garry, Alison Lee Williams Marquart. Enlisted in U.S. Navy, 1940, commd. ensign, 1945, designated naval aviator, 1949, advanced through grades to rear adm., 1973; service in China, Japan, Trinidad, Philippines, Italy, Spain; comdr. Fleet Air Mediterranean, 1974-76, Task Force 67, 1974-76, Maritime Air Forces, Mediterranean, 1974-76; dir. aviation manpower and tng. Office Chief Naval Ops., 1976-78; acad. dean Embry-Riddle Aero. U., Daytona Beach, Fla., 1978—. Chmn. Mediterranean dist. Boy Scouts Am., 1974-76; pres. exec. bd. Naples (Italy) USO, 1974-76. Decorated Legion of Merit, Bronze Star, Meritorious Service medal; named Distinguished Eagle in Europe, Boy Scouts Am., 1976. Republican. Presbyterian. Home: 235 Pine Cone Trail Ormond Beach FL 32074 Office: Embry-Riddle Aero U Daytona Beach FL 32014. *I have never been satisfied that my performance in any undertaking has been completely the quality that I aspire to.*

WILLIAMS, CHARLES THOMAS, distillery exec.; b. Nogales, Ariz., Jan. 25, 1916; s. James Harrington and Zellee (Jones) W.; student Los Angeles City Coll., 1943, U. So. Calif., 1946; L.H.D. (hon.), King Meml. Coll., 1977; m. Brenda Smith, Dec. 13, 1947; children—Charles Thomas II, Kirk G., Rhoda Jo. With U.S. Post Office, Los Angeles, 1938-43, 1947-51; sales rep. Schenley Industries Inc., N.Y.C., 1951-53, nat. brand devel. mgr., 1953-58, asst. nat. sales mgr., 1959-61, asst. divl. mgr., 1961-63, v.p. Schenley Distiller Co., N.Y.C., 1963—, Schenley Affiliated Brands Corp., 1976—; dir. Merchant Prince Corp., Nat. Bus. Corp. Nassau County chmn. Economic Opportunity Commn., 1966-73; vice-chmn. bd. Roslyn Non Profit Corp., 1968-73; mem. Nassau County Health & Welfare Council, 1966-72; bd. dirs. Nat. Fedn. Settlements and Neighborhood Centers, sec., 1976—, now pres.; trustee Interracial Council Business Opportunity, L.I. Fund., Booker T. Washington Found. Served with USAAF, 1943-46. Decorated Air medal, Purple Heart. Mem. Nat. Bus. League (chmn. bd. 1968—). Home: 40 Hickory Dr Roslyn NY 11576 Office: 888 7th Ave New York NY 10019

WILLIAMS, CHARLES WILEY, educator; b. Augusta, Ky., Mar. 24, 1912; s. Thomas Sanford and Effie (Nickel) W.; A.B., Harvard, 1933; M.A., U. Md., 1936; Ph.D., U. Va., 1949; m. Margaret Bliss Ashby, June 6, 1945; children—Jane, Thomas, Elizabeth, Margaret, Kathryn. Instr. math. Washington and Lee U., 1937-39, Armstrong Jr. Coll., Savannah, Ga., 1939-42, U. N.C. at Chapel Hill, 1943-45, N.C. State Coll., 1945-46; mem. faculty Washington and Lee U., Lexington, Va., 1948—, prof. math., 1964—; vis. prof. U. Va., summers 1960-71; vis. fellow Dartmouth, 1969-70. Mem. Am. Math. Soc., Math. Assn. Am., Sigma Xi. Home: RFD 2 Lexington VA 24450

WILLIAMS, CHESTER ARTHUR, JR., educator; b. Blakely, Pa., Mar. 6, 1924; s. C. Arthur and Alice (Robinson) W.; A.B., Columbia U., 1947; A.M., 1949, Ph.D., 1952; m. Roberta Riegel, Sept. 1, 1951; children—Robert Arthur, Bruce Allan. Lectr. ins. U. Buffalo (N.Y.), 1950-52; asst. prof. U. Minn., 1952-55, asso. prof., 1955-58, Ford Found. faculty fellow, 1957-58, prof., 1958—, acting dean, 1970-71, asso. dean, 1971-72, dean, 1972-78. Dir. St. Paul Cos., Inc. Bd. dirs. State Bd. Credit Union, 1965-68, pres., 1967-68; bd. dirs. Consumers Union, 1972-75; bd. dirs. Minn. State Council on Econ. Edn., 1973-78, chmn., 1975-77. Served to 1st lt., USAF, 1943-46. Mem. Am. Risk Ins. Assn. (dir. 1960-65, pres. 1965), Am. Acad. Actuaries, Am. Inst. Decision Sci., Am. Statis. Assn., Am. Finance Assn., AAUP, Phi Beta Kappa, Beta Gamma Sigma. Episcopalian. Author: Price Discrimination in Property and Liability Insurance, 1959; Economic and Social Security, 1957; Risk Management and Insurance, 1964; Insurance Arrangements under Workmen's Compensation, 1969; Insurance Principles and Practices: Property and Liability, 1976; Principles of Risk Management and Insurance, 1978. Contbr. articles to profl. jours. Home: 1984 Shryer Ave W Roseville MN 55113 Office: College Business Administration Univ Minnesota Minneapolis MN 55455

WILLIAMS, CLARKE, sci. adminstr., nuclear engr., physicist; b. N.Y.C., May 4, 1902; s. William Robert and Flora (Nabersberg) W.; A.B., Williams Coll., 1922, Sc.D. (hon.), 1964; B.C.E., Mass. Inst. Tech., 1924; Ph.D. in Physics, Columbia U., 1935; m. Lindsay Clement Field, June 30, 1927 (div. Apr. 1933); 1 son, David Field Williams South; m. 2d, Margaret Stevens Button, Aug. 12, 1933; children—Evan Thomas, Thomas Button Williams. Rodman, Duke Price Power Co., 1924-25; asst. engr. N.Y. Central R.R., 1925-26; asst. physics Columbia U., 1926-30, research, devel. gaseous diffusion project Div. War Research, 1941-46; tutor, instr., asst. prof. physics Coll. City N.Y., 1930-49; sr. physicist Brookhaven Nat. Lab., 1946—, chmn. nuclear engring. dept., 1952-62, dep. dir., 1962-67, dep. dir. emeritus, 1967—; research adminstr. Marine Resources Council, L.I. Regional Planning Bd., Hauppauge, N.Y., 1967—; mem. N.Y. State Atomic Energy Adv. Com., 1956-59, 66, chmn. 1960 Nuclear Congress; mem. atomic safety and licensing bd. panel AEC, 1966-74; tech. adviser, paper coordinator 2d Internat. Conf. Peaceful Uses Atomic Energy, 1958; adviser U.S. del. 3d Geneva Conf., 1964. Mem. exec. council Suffolk County council Boy Scouts Am., 1966-76; mem. Brookhaven Town Indsl. Commn. 1962—; bd. dirs. Skills Unltd., 1962—, v.p. 1968, pres., 1971-78; bd. dirs. Suffolk County Community Council, v.p., 1968-70; trustee United Fund L.I.; trustee emeritus Williams Coll. Fellow Am. Nuclear Soc. (dir. 1957-60, pres. 1963), AAAS; mem. Am. Phys. Soc., N.Y. Acad. Sci., Fedn. Am. Scientists, U.S. Power Squadron, Phi Beta Kappa, Epsilon Chi, Sigma Psi. Club: Williams (N.Y.C.). Home: 200 South Country Rd PO Box W Bellport NY 11713 Office: Marine Resources Council Hauppauge NY 11787

WILLIAMS, CLIFFORD DAVID, cons. engr.; b. Clark, S.D., July 8, 1900; s. Albert William and Hattie Alice (Smith) W.; B.S.C.E., Cleve. State U., 1937; C.E., Iowa State U., 1950; m. Myrtle Mannie, Nov. 8, 1922; children—Doris Williams Morejohn, Kenneth A., Victor L. Engr., S.D. Hwy Commn., 1920-23; owner Mobridge (S.D.) Engring. Co., 1923-25; structural engr., City of Pasadena, Calif., 1926-27, So. Calif. Edison Co., 1927-28, N.Y.C. R.R., Cleve., 1928-37; head prof. civil engring. Fenn Coll., Cleve., 1937-42; supr. stress engrs. Fisher Body Aircraft, Cleve., 1943-44; asst. supr. engr. J.E. Greiner Co., Balt., 1944-45; head prof. civil engring. U. Fla., 1945-52; chief engr. Patchen and Zimmerman, Augusta, Ga., 1952-58; partner, dir. engring. Patchen, Mingeldorff & Williams, Augusta, 1958-61; pres., chmn. bd. Williams, Nelson & Assos., P.C., Augusta, 1961—; pres., chmn. bd. Southeastern Architects and Engrs., Inc., Augusta, 1964—. Fellow ASCE (pres. Fla. sect. 1951, dir. dist. 1964-66, v.p. Zone II 1967-68, pres. S.C. sect. 1973), Am. Cons. Engrs. Council; mem. Am. Railway Engring. Assn. (life), Ga. Cons. Engrs. Council, Fla. Engring. Soc., Nat. Soc. Profl. Engrs., Am. Concrete Inst., ASTM. Methodist. Clubs: Pinnacle, Exchange (Augusta). Author: Analysis of Statically Indeterminate Structures, 1943; (with E.C. Harris) Structural Design in Metals, 1949; (with C.E. Cutts) Structural Design in Reinforced Concrete, 1954. Home: 1021 Hampton Terr North Augusta SC 29841 Office: 1331 Greene St Augusta GA 30901

WILLIAMS, CLYDE MICHAEL, JR., radiologist; b. Marlow, Okla., Oct. 8, 1928; s. Clyde Michael and Betty Howard (Black) W.; B.A., Rice U., 1948; M.D., Baylor U., 1952; D.Phil. (Rhodes Scholar), Oxford U., 1954; m. Martha Adelaide Smither, Jan. 29, 1953; children—Edith, Michael, Kathleen, John. Intern, Royal Victoria Hosp., Montreal, P.Q., Can., 1954-55; tech. dir. radioisotope lab. VA Hosp., Pitts., 1958-60; resident in radiology U. Fla. Coll. Medicine, Gainesville, 1960-63, asst. prof. radiology, 1963-64, asso. prof., 1964-65, prof., chmn. radiology, 1965—; radiologist Shands Teaching Hosp. Served as capt. USAF, 1955-58. Mem. Am. Coll. Radiology, Am. Roentgen Ray Soc., Am. Physiol. Soc., Fla. Med. Assn., Soc. Nuclear Medicine, Radiol. Soc. N.Am., Fla. Radiology Soc. Contbr. articles to med. jours. Office: Dept Radiology Box J-374 JHMHC U Fla Gainesville FL 32610*

WILLIAMS, CRATIS DEARL, univ. dean; b. Blaine, Ky., Apr. 5, 1911; s. Curtis and Mona (Whitt) W.; B.A., U. Ky., 1933, M.A., 1937; Ph.D., N.Y.U., 1961; m. Sylvia Graham, Aug. 7, 1937 (dec. Dec. 1942); m. 2d, Elizabeth Lingerfelt, July 31, 1949; children—Sophie, David Cratis. Tchr. rural schs. Eastern Ky., 1929-33; tchr. English, prin. Blaine (Ky.) High Sch., 1933-38; prin. Louisa (Ky.) High Sch., 1938-41; instr. Apprentice Sch. of Internat. Nickel Co., Huntington, W.Va., 1942; critic tchr., asst. prin., guidance dir. Appalachian Demonstration High Sch., Boone, N.C., 1942-46; asst. prof. English and speech Appalachian State U., Boone, 1946-49, prof. English, 1952—, dean Grad. Sch., 1958-74, acting vice chancellor, 1974, acting chancellor, 1975; part time instr. English Washington Sq. Coll., 1949-50. Recipient Founders Day award N.Y.U., 1962, O. Max Gardner award, 1973, Brown Hudson award, 1975, So. Found. fellow, 1954. Mem. Modern Lang. Assn., Am., N.C. (past pres.) folklore socs., Appalachian Consortium (dir.), So. hist. assns., N.C. Hist. Soc., Western N.C. Hist. Assn. Mason. Author: Mountain Speech, 1960; Southern Mountaineer in Fact and Fiction, 1975. Contbr. articles to ednl. jours. Address: Appalachian State U Boone NC 28608. *The more I learn about Appalachian Mountain folk, the better pleased I am about who I am. Son of poor mountain farm folk who taught me how to love work, to speak truth, and to hold myself responsible for my own actions.*

WILLIAMS, CYNTHIA JANE, actress; b. Van Nuys, Calif., Aug. 22, 1947; d. Beachard J. and Frances Marie (Bellini) Williams; student Los Angeles City Coll., 1965-68. Acting debut on TV series Room 222, 1970; film debut in Gass-s, 1970; appeared in numerous motion pictures, including Drive He Said, 1971, Travels With My Aunt, 1972, Beware The Blob, 1972, The Killing Kind, 1973, American Grafitti, 1973, The Conversation, 1974, Mr. Ricco, 1974, The First Nudie Musical, More American Graffiti, 1979; appeared on TV series The Funny Side, NBC, 1970-71; co-star on TV series Laverne and Shirley, ABC, 1975—; appeared in TV movie The Migrants, 1974. Active in saving endangered species of animals. Nominated Best Supporting Actress (Brit.), 1974. Mem. Screen Actors Guild, AFTRA, Equity Guild. Democrat. Office: care Paul Kohner-Michael Levy Agy 9169 Sunset Blvd Los Angeles CA 90069*

WILLIAMS, DAN C., ins. co. exec.; b. Brenham, Tex., Feb. 22, 1913; s. Dan C. and Harriet (Wilkin) W.; B.S. in Petroleum Engring., U. Tex., Austin, 1935; m. Ellen Carolyn Carpenter, June 18, 1936; children—Carolyn Williams Marks, Harriet Williams Peavy, Suzanne William Nash. Petroleum engr. Magnolia Petroleum Co., Dallas,

1935-49; pres., dir. Southland Life Ins. Co., Dallas, 1952-69; chmn. bd., dir. Southland Fin. Corp., Dallas, 1969—. Bd. dirs. Dallas chpt. ARC, Dallas County United Way, State Fair Tex.; bd. regents U. Tex. System, 1968-81, chmn., 1979-81; mem. coordinating bd. Tex. Colls. and Univs., 1965-71; elder Highland Park Presbyn. Ch., Dallas. Recipient Linz award, 1961; Disting. Alumnus award U. Tex. Sch. Engring., 1962. Clubs: Dallas Country, Las Colinas Country, Dallas Petroleum, City, Dallas, Chapparral. Home: 3711 Lexington Ave Dallas TX 75205 Office: PO Box 61208 Dallas TX 75261

WILLIAMS, DAVID ALAN, historian, educator; b. Columbus, Ohio, June 14, 1928; s. David and Clarice Irene (Stevens) W.; B.A., Westminster Coll., New Wilmington, Pa., 1952; M.A., Northwestern U., 1954, Ph.D. (William Randolph Hearst fellow, Colonial Williamsburg fellow), 1957; m. Llwanda Marie Knepshield, Aug. 9, 1952; children—Scott, Todd, Kevin. Asst. prof. history, chmn. history and polit. sci. Queens Coll., Charlotte, N.C., 1956-57; instr. history U. Va., 1957-59, asst. prof., 1959-65, asso. prof., 1965—, asst. dean, 1963-66, asst. provost, 1966-68, dean student affairs, 1968-69, v.p. student affairs, 1970-74. Mem. exec. com. Atlantic Coast Conf., 1971-75, 78—, pres., 1973-74, 79-80; cons. panel Nat. Endowment Arts Humanities, 1974-78. Served with USN, 1946-48. Mem. Am., Va. hist. socs., Orgn. Am. Historians, Sigma Nu. Democrat. Presbyn. Author: Colonial Virginia, 1959; Road to Independence: Virginia, 1763-1783, 1975. Home: 1412 Lester Dr Charlottesville VA 22901

WILLIAMS, DAVID BENTON, advt. agy. exec.; b. Chgo., May 18, 1920; s. Howard D. and Margaret (Clark) W.; A.B. magna cum laude, Harvard U., 1942; m. Edith Chapin Huntington, Aug. 24, 1943; children—David Huntington, Deborah Benton, Howard Chapin. Service detail, media, prodn. Erwin Wasey, Chgo., 1946-47, copy contact, Los Angeles, 1947-48, account exec., v.p., Los Angeles, 1948-49, v.p. mgmt., N.Y.C., 1949-54, exec. v.p., gen. mgr., 1954-56, pres. 1956; pres. Erwin Wasey, Ruthrauff & Ryan (merger of Erwin Wasey & Co. and Ruthrauff & Ryan), N.Y.C., 1957-65; sr. v.p. Interpub. Group of Cos., Inc., 1965-68, former dir.; exec. v.p. Interpub. S.A., 1966-68; sr. v.p. Wilson Haight & Welch, advt., Hartford, Boston, Greenwich, N.Y.C., Phila., Tampa and Houston, 1969-72, exec. v.p., dir., 1972—, pres., dir., 1974-78; advt. dir., 1978—; pres., dir. 1035 5th Ave. Corp. Bd. dirs. Point O'Woods Assn., Community Council Greater N.Y. Served with CIC, U.S. Army, Mem. Phi Beta Kappa. Clubs: University, Union (N.Y.C.); Harvard (Boston); Preston Mountain (Kent, Conn.); American (London). Home: 1035 Fifth Ave New York NY 10028. *Always hire people as able, or better yet, more able than yourself. Trust them. Support them. Their success will be your own. Take intelligent risks. Always bet on people - as the right ones are the magic that makes business work.*

WILLIAMS, DAVID BRYAN, editor; b. Bloomington, Ill., Apr. 12, 1945; s. Merle and Norma Marie (Lauher) W.; student Ill. Wesleyan U., 1963-67. Asst. editor Rev. of Popular Astronomy, Sky Map Publs., St. Louis, 1967-70; asst. editor Kiwanis mag., Kiwanis Internat., Chgo., 1970-72, asso. editor, 1972-74, exec. editor, 1974—. Sec. bd. trustees Ill. Wesleyan U. Acacia Corp., Bloomington, 1967-77. Recipient Award of Merit, Acacia Frat., 1976. Mem. Coll. Frat. Editors Assn. Clubs: Kiwanis (Chgo.); Masons (Bloomington, Ill.). Editor Jour. of Acacia Frat., 1974—. Home: 605 E Prospect St Apt 1E Mount Prospect IL 60056 Office: 101 E Erie St Chicago IL 60611

WILLIAMS, DAVID GARDNER, educator; b. Platteville, Wis., Nov. 1, 1907; s. William Hill and Bertha Lucile (Gardner) W.; student Platteville State Normal Sch., 1924-26, (scholar) Juilliard Sch. Music Extension, 1929-31; A.B., U. Wis., 1930, Mus.B., 1931, A.M., 1932; A.M., Harvard, 1939, Ph.D., 1946; m. Mildred Johnson Bickford, June 15, 1941; children—Kirsten Elizabeth, David Henry, William Gardner. Tchr. jr. high sch., Western Springs, Ill., 1926-28; asst. dept. English, U. Wis., 1931-32; tchr. English and music Hotchkiss Sch., 1932-37; teaching fellow, tutor Harvard, 1939-43; asst. prof. English, Amherst Coll., 1943-45; from instr. to asso. prof. humanities U. Chgo., 1945-56, prof., 1956-73, prof. emeritus, 1973—, chmn. coll. humanities staff, 1957-60, coll. examiner, 1960-63, asst. dean undergrad. students, 1977—. Recipient Quantrell award for excellent undergrad. teaching U. Chgo., 1960. Mem. Modern Lang. Assn., Amateur Chamber Music Players, Phi Beta Kappa, Phi Mu Alpha Sinfonia, Sigma Alpha Epsilon. Club: Quadrangle (U. Chgo.). Home: 5427 S Hyde Park Blvd Chicago IL 60615

WILLIAMS, DAVID PERRY, mfg. co. exec.; b. Detroit, Nov. 16, 1934; s. M.S. Perry and Virginia (Hayes) W.; B.A., Mich. State U., 1956, M.B.A., 1964; m. Jill Schneider, July 27, 1972; children—Tracy, Perry, David. Vice pres. sales Automotive div. Kelsey Hayes Co., Romulus, Mich., 1958-71; v.p., automotive product line mgr. ITT, N.Y.C., 1971-76; v.p., dir. Budd Co., Troy, Mich., 1976—. Served to 1st lt. USAF, 1956-58. Mem. Soc. Automotive Engrs., Engring. Soc. Detroit, Beta Gamma Sigma. Republican. Episcopalian. Clubs: Bloomfield Hills Country; Country of Detroit; Recess; Yondotega; Detroit Athletic; Internat. Golf. Home: 333 Lincoln St Grosse Pointe MI 48230 Office: 3155 Big Beaver Rd Troy MI 48084

WILLIAMS, DAVID WELFORD, judge; b. Atlanta, Mar. 20, 1910; s. William W. and Maude (Lee) W.; A.A., Los Angeles Jr. Coll., 1932; A.B., U. Calif. at Los Angeles, 1934; LL.B., U. So. Calif., 1937; m. Ouida Maie White, June 11, 1939; children—David Welford, Vaughn Charles. Admitted to Calif. bar, 1937, since practiced in Los Angeles; judge Municipal Ct., Los Angeles, 1956-62, Superior Ct., Los Angeles, 1962-69, U.S. Dist. Ct., Central Dist. Calif., Los Angeles, 1969—; judge Los Angeles County Grand Jury, 1965. Recipient Russwurm award Nat. Assn. Newspapers, 1958; Profl. Achievement award UCLA Alumni Assn., 1966. Office: US District Court 312 N Spring St Los Angeles CA 90012

WILLIAMS, DELWYN CHARLES, telephone co. exec.; b. Idaho Falls, Idaho, Apr. 27, 1936; s. Charles H. and Vonda (Wood) W.; B.S. in Bus., U. Idaho, 1959, m. Marlene Grace Nordland, Feb. 29, 1964; children—Stephen, Kirstin, Nicole. Accountant, Peat, Marwick, Mitchell & Co., C.P.A.'s, San Francisco, 1960-65; treas. Dohrmann Instruments Co., Mountain View, Calif., 1965-68; with Continental Telephone Co. of Calif., Bakersfield, 1968—, controller, 1969-70, v.p., treas., 1970-77, v.p., gen. mgr., 1977-79, pres., 1979—, also dir.; dir., officer affiliate cos. Continental Telephone Co. C.P.A., Calif. Mem. Am. Inst. C.P.A.'s, Calif. Soc. C.P.A.'s. Home: 13145 Waco Rd Apple Valley CA 92307 Office: Mojave Dr Victorville CA 92392

WILLIAMS, DON R., singer, songwriter; b. Floydada, Tex., May 27, 1939; s. James and Loveta M. W.; grad. high sch.; m. Joy Bucher, Apr. 10, 1960; children—Gary, Timmy. Played guitar and sang with group in high sch. years; formed trio Pozo Seco Singers, 1964-71; entered bus., Tex.; wrote country songs for Jack Clemens Pub.; rec. artist, formerly with JIM and ABC, now with MCA; albums include: Your're My Best Friend (Brit. Country Music Assn. Album of Year 1975), Visions (Brit. Country Music Assn. Album of Year and Best Mktg. award 1977), Images (Brit. Phonographic Inst. Double Platinum award 1979), 20 Of My Best (K-Tel Internat., Ltd. Platinum award 1979), also 6 gold albums in Britain; singles include: I Recall A Gypsy Woman (Brit. Country Music Assn. Single of Year 1976), You're My Best Friend (Country Music People Mag. and BBC Radio-2 Country Club program All-Time Favorite Country Record 1977), Tulsa Time (Acad. Country Music Single of Year 1979); numerous concert appearances; appeared in film W.W. and The Dixie Dance Kings, 20th Century Fox; TV appearances include Tonight Show and NBC telecast of 14th Acad. of Country Music Awards; mem. Grand Ole Opry. Served with Security Agy., U.S. Army, 4 years. Named Male Vocalist of Year, Brit. Country Music Assn., 1975, N.Y. Sta. WHN spl. poll. and Radio & Records poll; named Internat. Male Volcalist of Year, U.K. Internat. Country Music Awards, 1977; recipient Top Male Records Sales award Music Week mag., Britain, 1978. Mem. Country Music Assn. (Male Vocalist of Year 1978). Mem. Christian Ch. (Disciples of Christ). Office: care Brokaw-Gangwisch 207 Westport Rd Kansas City MO 64111

WILLIAMS, DON STEWART, ins. co. exec.; b. St. Paul, Feb. 12, 1920; s. Leslie and Maude (Wainman) W.; B.A., Macalester Coll., 1942; M.B.A., Harvard U., 1950; m. Ellen Fuller, Feb. 28, 1943; children—Kimberly, Laurie, Judd, Donna. Securities analyst First Bank Stock Corp., St. Paul, 1946-48; investment officer Employers Reins. Co., Kansas City, Mo., 1951-61; sr. v.p. Waddell & Reed, Kansas City, 1961-73; v.p.-fin. and treas. ERC Corp., Kansas City, 1974—; dir. Employers Reins. Corp., Nat. Fidelity Life Ins. Co., Centennial Life Ins. Co., First Fidelity Equity Corp. Served to capt. USAF, 1942-45. Clubs: Univ., Milburn Country. Home: 4302 W 66 Terr Prairie Village KS 66208 Office: ERC Corp 21 W 10th St Kansas City MO 64105

WILLIAMS, DONALD CLYDE, lawyer; b. Oxnard, Calif., Oct. 12, 1939; s. Leslie Allen and Elizabeth Esther (Orton) W.; B.A. in Gen. Bus., Fresno State Coll., 1963; J.D., Willamette U., 1967; m. Miriam Arline, Oct. 5, 1966; children—Erin K., Nikki Dawn. Admitted to Oreg. bar, 1967; practice in Grants Pass, 1967-70; partner Myrick, Seagraves, Williams & Nealy, 1968-70; asst. atty. gen. Am. Samoa, 1970-71, atty. gen., 1971-75; asso. justice High Ct. Trust Territory of the Pacific Islands, 1975-77; partner Carlsmith, Carlsmith, Wichman & Case, 1977—. Served with USCGR, 1958-59. Mem. Am., Oreg., Am. Samoa, Guam, Hawaii bar assns. Address: PO Box 2263 Agana GU 96910

WILLIAMS, DONALD JOHN, research physicist; b. Fitchburg, Mass., Dec. 25, 1933; s. Toivo John and Ina (Kokkinen) W.; B.S., Yale U., 1955, M.S., 1958, Ph.D., 1962; m. Priscilla Mary Gagnon, July 4, 1953; children—Steven John, Craig Mitchell, Eino Stenroos. Sr. staff physicist Applied Physics Lab., Johns Hopkins U., 1961-65; head particle physics br. Goddard Space Flight Center, NASA, 1965-70; dir. Space Environ. Lab., NOAA, Boulder, Colo., 1970—, Sci. Research award, 1974, Disting. Authorship award, 1976; prin. investigator Energetic Particles expt. NASA Jupiter Orbiter Mission, 1977—. Mem. nat. and internat. sci. planning coms. Served to lt. USAF, 1955-57. Mem. AAAS, Am. Geophys. Soc., Am. Phys. Soc. Asso. editor Jour. Geophys. Research, 1967-69; editor (with G.D. Mead) Physics of the Magnetosphere, 1969; Physics of Solar-Planetary Environments, 1976; mem. editorial bd. Space Sci. Revs., 1975—; contbr. articles to profl. jours. Home: 4949 Twin Lakes Way Boulder CO 80301 Office: Space Environment Lab Nat Oceanic and Atmospheric Adminstrn Boulder CO 80302

WILLIAMS, DOUGLAS GEORGE, computer scientist, educator; b. Edinburgh, Scotland, Oct. 11, 1932, (came to U.S. 1961); s. John Walters and Mary (Wallace) W.; M.A. with 1st class honors, U. Edinburgh, 1954; m. Kathleen Dorothy Mills, Mar. 28, 1959; children—Neil Douglas, Susan Mary. Sci. officer Royal Aircraft Establishment, Farnborough U.K., 1954-58; lectr. computer lab. U. Glasgow (Scotland), 1958-61; mem. faculty Naval Postgrad. Sch., 1961—, prof. math., dir. computer center, 1962—. Fellow British Computer Soc.; mem. Assn. Computing Machinery. 1059 Indian Village Rd Pebble Beach CA 93953

WILLIAMS, DOUGLAS LEE, constrn. co. exec.; b. Scottsburg, Ind., Nov. 2, 1934; s. Theodore Roosevelt and Wilma Helena (Hauer) W.; B.S.C.E., Purdue U., 1956; m. Nancy Ann Butcher, June 10, 1956; children—Janice, Julie, David. Structural engr. N.Y. Central R.R., Indpls., 1956-57; estimator M&D Builders, Inc., Indpls., 1958; exec. v.p. Huber, Hunt & Nichols, Inc., Indpls., 1959—. Served to 2d lt., C.E., U.S. Army, 1958. Clubs: Indpls. Athletic, Elks. Office: PO Box 128 Indianapolis IN 46206

WILLIAMS, DUDLEY, physicist; b. Covington, Ga., Apr. 12, 1912; s. Arthur Dudley and Ethel (Turner) W.; A.B., U. N.C., Chapel Hill, 1933, M.A., 1934, Ph.D., 1936; m. Loraine Decherd, June 12, 1937; children—Francis Dudley, Harriet Thomson. Instr., then asst. prof. physics U. Fla., Gainesville, 1936-41; mem. staff Radiation Lab., Mass. Inst. Tech., 1942-43; asst. prof. U. Okla., 1943-44; mem. staff Manhattan Atomic Bomb project Los Alamos Lab., 1944-46; asso. prof., then prof. physics Ohio State U., 1946-63, chmn. dept., 1952-53, 59-60; prof., head dept. physics N.C. State U., Raleigh, 1963-64; Regents distinguished prof. physics Kans. State U., 1964—; cons. NSF, NASA. Guggenheim fellow, 1956; NSF sr. postdoctoral fellow, 1962-63. Fellow Am. Phys. Soc., Optical Soc. Am. (pres. 1979, asso. editor jour. 1958—); mem. Am. Assn. Physics Tchrs., Phi Beta Kappa (past chpt. pres.), Sigma Xi (past chpt. pres.). Clubs: Cosmos, Rotary. Co-author: Elements of Physics, 5th edit., 1971; editor, contbr. Molecular Physics, 2d edit., 1974; Spectroscopy, 1976. Contbr. numerous papers profl. jours. Address: Dept Physics Kans State Univ Manhattan KS 66506

WILLIAMS, DUDLEY EUGENE, dancer; b. N.Y.C., Aug. 18, 1938; s. Ivan and Austa (Beckles) W.; student Juilliard Sch. Music, 1959-61. Dancer, Eleo Pomare Dance Co., 1958, May O'Donnell Dance Co., 1959, Donald McKayle Dance Co., 1960, Talley Beatty Dance Co., 1961; soloist Martha Graham Dance Co., 1962-65; prin. dancer Alvin Ailey Am. Dance Theater, N.Y.C., 1964—; various world tours under auspices Dept. State; appeared in inaugural of Kennedy Center and Carter Inauguration Gala; tchr. Martha Graham Sch. of Dance, Am. Dance Center, George Faison Dance Co. Scholar, Met. Opera Ballet Sch., 1959-62, Juilliard Sch. Music, 1959-61, Martha Graham Sch. of Dance, 1959-65. Mem. Am. Guild Musical Artists, AFTRA. Office: care Alvin Ailey City Center Dance Theatre Office 229 E 59th St New York NY 10022*

WILLIAMS, E. VIRGINIA, artistic dir., choreographer; b. Melrose, Mass.; d. Charles F. and Mary Virginia (Evitts) W.; trained in Boston, N.Y.C.; also student piano, drama and art; 3 hon. doctorates in the arts; married; 1 child. Profl. dancer in concert cos. and opera ballet; tchr. ballet; choreographer; dir. New England Civic Ballet Co., 1958-62; founder, artistic dir. Boston Ballet, 1962—. Adv. council Jacob's Pillow Dance Festival; artistic adviser Lyric Opera of Chgo. Ballet, 1971-73. Recipient Dance Mag. award, 1976; Disting. Woman of Yr. award Boston chpt. Sigma Alpha Iota; regional citation NE Theater Conf.; named An Outstanding Woman of Mass., Internat. Women's Yr., 1975. Mem. Dance Teacher's Club Boston (past pres.; hon. citation). Office Boston Ballet 19 Clarendon St Boston MA 02116

WILLIAMS, EDDIE NATHAN, assn. exec.; b. Memphis, Aug. 18, 1932; s. Ed and Georgia Lee (Barr) W.; B.S., U. Ill., 1954; postgrad. Atlanta U., 1957; Am. Polit. Sci. Assn. fellow, 1958; postgrad. Howard U., 1960; m. Sallie Elizabeth Smart, June 8, 1958; children—Traci Lynne, Edward Lawrence. Reporter, Atlanta Daily World Newspaper, 1957-58; staff asst. U.S. Senate Com. on Fgn. Relations, Washington, 1959-60; fgn. service res. officer U.S. Dept. State, Washington, 1961-68; v.p., U. Chgo., 1968-72; pres. Joint Center for Polit. Studies, Washington, 1972—. Advisor, Am. Polit. Sci. Assn., 1973—; chmn. adv. com. on black population 1980 census U.S. Census Bur., 1975—. Bd. visitors Afro-Am. Studies Program, Harvard, 1973—; vice chmn. bd. dirs. Children's TV Workshop, 1970—; bd. dirs. Drug Abuse Council, 1972—, Nat. Center Community Action, 1975—. Served to lt. AUS, 1955-57. Mem. Kappa Tau Alpha. Editor Delivery Systems for Model Cities, 1969. Editorial columnist Chgo. Sun Times, 1970-72. Office: 1426 H St NW Washington DC 20005*

WILLIAMS, EDGAR GENE, univ. adminstr.; b. Posey County, Ind., May 4, 1922; s. Noley Wesley and Anna Lena (Wilsey) W.; A.B., Evansville Coll., 1947; M.B.A., Ind. U., 1948, D.B.A., 1952; m. Joyce Ellen Grigsby, May 7, 1944; children—Cynthia Ellen Williams Mahigian, Thomas Gene. Instr., Ind. U., Bloomington, 1948-52, asst. prof., 1952-55, asso. prof., 1955-58, prof. bus. adminstrn., 1958—, asso. dean, 1965-69, v.p., 1974—. Bd. dirs. Found. for Sch. of Bus., Ind. U., Bloomington, 1966—. Served with U.S. Army, 1943-46. Mem. Am. Soc. for Personnel Adminstrn., Am. Mgmt. Assn., Beta Gamma Sigma. Democrat. Methodist. Clubs: Masons; Indpls. Athletic; Bloomington Country. Home: 1126 E 1st St Bloomington IN 47401

WILLIAMS, EDSON POE, automotive co. exec.; b. Mpls., July 31, 1923; s. Homer A. and Florence C. W.; B.S.M.E. cum laude, U. Minn., 1950; m. Irene Mae Streed, June 16, 1950; children—Thomas, Louise, Steven, Linnea, Elisa. Pvt. practice operation spl. purpose machinery, 1946-50; mfg. mgr., project engr. Crestliner div. Bigelow Sanford Inc., 1950-53, v.p., mgr. mfg. and engring., 1953-58, pres., 1958-63; with Ford Motor Co., 1963—, service mgr. customer service div., 1973, gen. mgr. Ford Mexico, 1973-75, pres. Ford Mid-East & Africa, 1975-78, pres. Ford Asia-Pacific Inc., 1979—, v.p. Ford Motor Co., 1975—; dir. Ford-Asia-Pacific Inc., Ford Products Co., Ford Motor Co. Australia Ltd., Ford Sales Co. Australia Ltd., Japan Automatic Transmission Co. Ltd., Ford Industries Ltd. (Japan), Ford Motor Co. Malaysia Sdn. Bhd., Ford Motor Co. N.Z. Ltd., Ford Philippines Inc., Ford Motor Co. Pvt. Ltd. (Singapore), Ford Lio Ho (Taiwan) Ltd. Served with USAAF, 1942-46. Club: Renaissance (Detroit). Home: 1875 Chipping Way Bloomfield Hills MI Office: 33 Albert Rd Melbournce Victoria Australia

WILLIAMS, EDWARD BENNETT, lawyer; b. Hartford, Conn., May 31, 1920; s. Joseph Barnard and Mary (Bennett) W.; A.B. summa cum laude, Coll. Holy Cross, 1941, S.J.D., 1963; LL.B., Georgetown U., 1945, LL.D., 1968; LL.D., Loyola Coll., 1967, Fairfield U., 1968, Loyola U., Chgo., 1970, Albert Magnus Coll., 1971, St. Joseph's Coll., Phila., 1971, Lincoln (Ill.) Coll., 1972, Suffolk U., 1974, U. Detroit Sch. Law, 1976, Mount St. Mary's Coll., 1977; m. Dorothy Adair Guider, May 3, 1946 (dec. 1959); children—Joseph Barnard, Ellen Adair, Peter Bennett; m. 2d, Agnes Anne Neill, June 11, 1960; children—Edward Neill, Dana Bennett, Anthony Tyler, Kimberly Anne. Admitted to D.C. bar, 1944, since practiced in Washington; sr. partner firm Williams & Connolly and predecessor firms, 1967—; prof. criminal law and evidence Georgetown U. Law Sch., 1946-58, gen. counsel univ., 1949—; guest prof. U. Frankfurt (Germany), 1954; vis. lectr. Yale Law Sch., 1971; pres., dir. Washington Redskins Football Club; chmn. bd., owner Balt. Orioles Baseball Club. Mem. U.S. Jud. Conf. Adv. Com. on Fed. Rules of Evidence, 1965-74, Chief Justice's Com. on Court Facilities and Design, 1971-74; chmn. Md. Judicial Nominating Commn. 6th Judicial Dist., 1971-78; mem. President's Fgn. Intelligence Adv. Bd., 1976-77. Treas. Dem. Nat. Com., 1974-77; trustee Coll. Holy Cross, 1976—. Served with USAAF, 1941-43. Mem. Am. Bar Assn. (com. minimum standards for adminstrn. criminal justice 1965-67, chmn. spl. com. crime prevention and control 1970-72), D.C. Bar, Bar Assn. D.C. (v.p. 1950, 55-56, Lawyer of Year award 1966), Am. Coll. Trial Lawyers (bd. regents 1968-72), Internat. Acad. Trial Lawyers (bd. dirs.). Democrat. Roman Catholic. Clubs: University, Federal City, Vinson, Nat. Lawyers, Metropolitan, Barristers, Alfalfa, Nat. Press (Washington). Author: One Man's Freedom, 1962. Contbr. articles to profl. publs. Home: 8901 Durham Dr Potomac MD 20854 Office: Hill Bldg Washington DC 20006

WILLIAMS, EDWARD GILMAN, banker; b. Ware, Mass., Apr. 11, 1926; s. Carl Emmons and Susan Helen (Gilman) W.; B.A., Trinity Coll. (Conn.), 1950; m. Barbara Thompson Russell, June 19, 1959; children—Thomas Clarke, Susan Gilman. With Union Trust Co., New Haven, 1951—, asst. trust officer, 1956-59, trust officer, 1959-64, v.p., 1964-65, v.p., sr. adminstrv. officer, 1965-69, sr. v.p., 1969-72, exec. v.p., 1972—; v.p. Northeast Bancorp., Inc., 1972—; dir. Elm City Photo Co., New Haven. Mem. finance com. Yale-New Haven Hosp.; former treas. Leila Day Nurseries, Inc., New Haven; pres. bd. dirs. Vis. Nurse Assn. New Haven, 1970-75; trustee Williams Coll. Sch. Banking, 1971-74. Served with USNR, 1944-46. Mem. Conn. Bankers Assn. (chmn. trust div. 1968-70), Am. Inst. Banking, Soc. Colonial Wars. Mason. Clubs: New Haven Lawn, Quinnipiack (New Haven). Home: 38 Garfield Ave North Haven CT 06517 Office: PO Box 404 New Haven CT 06502

WILLIAMS, EDWARD JOSEPH, mfg. co. exec.; b. St. Louis, Aug. 3, 1922; s. Edward J. and Bertha Louise (Gerberding) W.; certificate accountancy, Washington U., St. Louis, 1952; m. Mary Ellen Justice, June 7, 1952; children—Linda Kay, Karen Ann, Mark Edward, David Justice. With Price Waterhouse & Co., C.P.A.'s, St. Louis, 1947-50; controller, sec., treas. Laclede Christy Co., St. Louis, 1951-54; controller, asst. sec. Magic Chef, Inc., St. Louis, 1955-56; with Gen. Aniline & Film Corp., N.Y.C., 1957-61, v.p. financial planning and control, 1960-61; v.p. finance, treas. Interlake, Inc., Chgo., 1962-63, exec. v.p., chief operating officer, 1963-64, also dir.; exec. v.p., chief operating officer Jos. Schlitz Brewing Co., Milw., 1964-69; exec. v.p., mem. mgmt. com. dir. GAF Corp., N.Y.C., 1969-72; pres., dir. McGraw-Edison Co., Elgin, Ill., 1972-73, chmn. bd., pres., chief exec. officer, dir., 1973—; dir., chmn. audit com. Interlake Steel Corp., Chgo.; dir. L.E. Myers Co., L.E. Myers Co. Internat. Ltd., Dukane Corp. Chmn., Jr. Achievement Chgo.; trustee Thomas Alva Edison Found. Served with U.S. Army, 1942-46. C.P.A., Mo. Mem. Am. Inst. C.P.A.'s, NAM (dir.), Ill. Mfrs. Assn. (dir.). Clubs: Mid-America, Economic, Chicago, Executives (Chgo.); Barrington Hills Country (Barrington); Butler Nat. Golf. Office: 333 W River Rd Elgin IL 60120*

WILLIAMS, EDWIN GANTT, ret. physician, radiobiologist; b. Monticello, Fla., Nov. 13, 1902; s. John Franklin and Mary Lizzie (Bearden) W.; M.D., Emory U., 1926; D.T.M., Liverpool Sch. Tropical Medicine, 1932, D.T.H., 1933; m. Walter Harnesberger Dallas, Mar. 1, 1929; children—Edwin Gantt, Kate Weaver, Mary Bearden, Stephen Harnesberger. Instr. first aid Am. Tel. & Tel. Co., 1926; instr. physiology Emory U. Sch. Medicine, 1926-29; commd. asst. surgeon USPHS, 1929, advanced through grades to med. dir.,

1949; on hosp. duty, 1929-31, immigration and fgn. quarantine duty, 1931-34, research in physiologic aspects drug addiction, Lexington, Ky., 1935-45, research, field work, adminstrn., radiobiology, 1945-59; research and supervision radiation protection NIH, 1945-48, chief radiol. health br., 1948-51; atomic medicine cons. Fed. Civil Def. Adminstrn., 1951-57; chief spl. weapons protection br. USPHS Hdqrs., 1957-59; dir. div. radiol. and occupational health Fla. Bd. Health, Jacksonville, 1959-69. Mem. Nat. Com. Radiation Protection, 1946-71. Commd. O.R.C., U.S. Army, 1923-29; spl. assignment U.S. Army, 1946. Recipient citation for meritorious conduct in the performance of outstanding service, 1946. Mem. Am. Bd. Indsl. Hygiene, AMA, Phi Beta Pi, Phi Sigma. Democrat. Methodist. Contbr. articles to med. jours., other periodicals. Home: 6560 Colgate Rd Jacksonville FL 32217. *Standards of conduct: Do you like the person you are with when no one else is there? I have often not been satisfied with me.*

WILLIAMS, EDWIN WILLIAM, publisher; b. N.Y.C., May 3, 1912; s. William and Amelia (Koch) W.; student Columbia U., 1930; m. Doris O. Smith, June 3, 1953; children—Edwina, Andrew. Publisher Quick Frozen Foods Internat. mag., N.Y.C., 1938—, Pvt. Label mag., 1979—; pres. Pioneer Assos., Inc., North Bergen, N.J., 1972—, E.W. Publns. Co., N.Y.C., 1940—, Williams Electric Co., Charlotte, N.C., 1970—; dir. Avi Pub. Co., Westport, Conn.; organizer frozen food industry directories and convs., speaker in field; chmn. Dept. Commerce mission to Eastern countries. Recipient award ICA, 1956, Internat. Assn. Refrigerated Warehouses, 1960, Presdl. E award 1962. Mem. Advt. Club N.Y.C., Am. Frozen Food Inst. Republican. Clubs: Overseas Press, Engrs. (N.Y.C.). Author: Frozen Foods, Biography of an Industry, 1969. Home: 8200 Blvd East North Bergen NJ 07047 Office: 370 Lexington Ave New York NY 10017. *If a man early in his career carves his dream like a sculptor on the unyielding stone of life, with many a sharp incision, he is bound to reach his goal; he has caught the angel vision.*

WILLIAMS, EMLYN, playwright, actor; b. Mostyn, North Wales, Nov. 26, 1905; s. Richard and Mary Williams; M.A., Christ Church, Oxford (Eng.) U., also LL.D., 1949; m. Molly O'Shann (dec. 1970); children—Alan Emlyn, Brook Richard. Began as an actor and has appeared in Wild Decembers, Richard III, On the Spot, The Frightened Lady, The Winslow Boy, Othello, Measure for Measure, The Merchant of Venice, As Charles Dickens, As Dylan Thomas, Montserrat, The Wild Duck, A Man For All Seasons, The Deputy, Forty Years On, others; also appeared films Wreck of The Mary Deare, 1961, The L-Shaped Room, Major Barbara, The Stars Look Down, Hatters Castle, Eye of The Devil, The Walking Stick, David Copperfield, The Deep Blue Sea; author plays: Full Moon, 1927; Glamour, 1928; A Murder Has Been Arranged, 1929; Night Must Fall, 1935; He Was Born Gay, 1937; The Corn Is Green, 1938; The Light of Heart, 1940; The Morning Star, 1941; The Druid's Rest, 1943; The Wind of Heaven, 1945; Trespass, 1947, 48-49; Accolade, 1950; Someone Waiting, 1953 (also starred in prodn. at Cambridge Theatre, London 1965); A Month in the Country, 1965, numerous others; writer, dir. film The Last Days of Dolwyn; also writer TV plays. Decorated comdr. Order Brit. Empire. Author books: George: An Early Autobiography, 1962; Beyond Belief, 1967; Emlyn, 1973. Address: 123 Dovehouse St London SW3 England*

WILLIAMS, EMORY, retail co. exec., banker; b. Falco, Ala., Oct. 26, 1911; s. William Emory and Nelle (Turner) W.; A.B., Emory U., 1932; m. Janet Hatcher Allcorn, May 15, 1943; children—Nelle (Mrs. Frederick Temple), Janet (Mrs. Lawrence MacNamara), Bliss (Mrs. Howell Browne), Carol (Mrs. James Schroeder), Emory. With Sears, Roebuck & Co., 1933-75, pres. Sears, Roebuck, S.A. (Brazil), 1958-60, pres. Homart Devel. Co., 1960-67, treas. parent co., 1962-64, v.p., treas., 1964-75; chmn. bd., chief exec. officer Sears Bank & Trust Co., 1975—, also dir.; dir. Armstrong Rubber Co., Ft. Dearborn Income Securities Inc., Bobbie Brooks, Inc., Chgo. Milw. Corp., Foote Cone Belding Communications, Sears Investment Mgmt. Co., VSI Corp. Div. chmn. Chgo. Crusade of Mercy, 1962-64, gen. chmn., 1966, pres., 1976-78; chmn. Ill. Health Edn. Commn., 1968-70; pres. Adler Planetarium, 1972-75, Ravinia Festival Assn., 1972-78; pres. bd. dirs. Community Fund, 1970-73. Trustee, Emory U., Chgo. Community Trust, Northwestern Meml. Hosps. Served to lt. col. C.E. U.S. Army, World War II; CBI. Clubs: Piedmont Driving (Atlanta); Chicago, Old Elm, Commercial (Chgo.); Indian Hill (Winnetka, Ill.); Everglades (Palm Beach). Home: 1420 Sheridan Rd Wilmette IL 60091 Office: Sears Tower Chicago IL 60606

WILLIAMS, ERNEST EDEN, editor; b. Logansport, Ind., Oct. 21, 1916; s. Chester Warren and Anna (Krueger) W.; A.B., Ind. U., 1939; m. Hildreth Ellen Elliott, Aug. 24, 1941; children—Ellen Anne Williams Blais, Timothy Royse, Mark Elliott, John Krueger, Elizabeth Eden. With Fort Wayne (Ind.) News-Sentinel, 1945—, editor, 1966—; v.p., dir. News Pub. Co.; dir. Fort Wayne Newspapers, Inc. Bd. dirs., v.p. Foellinger Found., Fort Wayne. Clubs: Quest, Fortnightly (Fort Wayne). Home: 436 Englewood Ct Fort Wayne IN 46807 Office: 600 W Main St Fort Wayne IN 46802

WILLIAMS, ERNEST EDWARD, zoologist, museum curator; b. Easton, Pa., Jan. 7, 1914; s. Edward and Alma Laura (Miller) W.; B.S., Lafayette Coll., 1933; Ph.D., Columbia U., 1949. Instr., Harvard U., 1949-52; asst. prof. zoology, 1952-57, prof. biology, 1970—, Alexander Azassiz prof. zoology, 1972—; curator reptiles and amphibians Mus. Comparative Zoology, Harvard U., 1957—. Served with U.S. Army, 1942-45. Decorated Purple Heart. Mem. Nat. Acad. Arts and Scis., Brasilian Acad. Sci. Office: 26 Oxford St Cambridge MA 02138

WILLIAMS, ERNEST GOING, paper co. exec.; b. Macon, Miss., Sept. 24, 1915; s. Augustus Gaines and Mary (Sanford) W.; B.S. in Commerce and Bus. Adminstrn., U. Ala., 1938; m. Cecil Louise Butler, Aug. 18, 1951; children—Ernest Sanford, Turner Butler, Elizabeth Cecil. Asst. to treas. U. Ala., 1938-42, 45-48, treas., 1948-56; v.p. First Nat. Bank Tuscaloosa (Ala.), 1956-58, dir., 1956—; v.p., dir. Gulf States Paper Corp., Tuscaloosa, 1958-77; chmn. bd., dir. Affiliated Paper Cos., Inc., Tuscaloosa, 1977—; dir. Tuscaloosa Fed. Savs. and Loan Assn., Peninsular Paper Co. Trustee U. Ala., David Warner Found., Asso. Industries Ala. Group Trust. Served with USNR, 1942-45. Named Tuscaloosa Citizen of Year, Civitan Club, 1974. Mem. Asso. Industries Ala., Greater Tuscaloosa C. of C., Newcomen Soc. N.Am., Kappa Alpha, Omicron Delta Kappa. Presbyterian. Clubs: University, River (Jacksonville, Fla.); Indian Hills Country; University, Exchange (Tuscaloosa); North River Yacht (dir.). Home: 156 The Highlands Tuscaloosa AL 35401 Office: PO Drawer 31 Tuscaloosa AL 35401

WILLIAMS, ERNEST WILLIAM, JR., economist, educator; b. Scranton, Pa., Oct. 27, 1916; s. Ernest William and Kathryn (Winterstein) W.; B.S., Columbia, 1938, M.S., 1939, Ph.D., 1951; m. Thelma Foxwell Klohr, Dec. 7, 1957. Economist, Nat. Resources Planning Bd., 1940-42, WPB, 1942-44; chief transp. div. U.S. Strategic Bombing Survey, 1944-45; fiscal analyst U.S. Bur. Budget, 1945-46; lectr. transp. Grad. Sch. Bus. Columbia, 1947-52, asso. prof., 1952-58, prof. transp., 1958—, vice dean, 1977-79; vis. prof. mgmt. U. Ariz., 1972, 74; cons. ODM, 1951-60; dir. transp. study Dept. Commerce, 1959-60. Dir. ACF Industries, Inc., N.Y.C., 1960—. Mem. N.Y.-N.J. Met. Rapid Transit Commn., 1955-58; mem. task force Pres.'s Adv. Com. Transp. Policy and Orgn., 1954-55; mem. task force on regulatory agencies First Hoover Commn., 1948. Trustee TAA Research Fund, 1962-65; bd. visitors U.S. Army Transp. Sch., 1963-66. Recipient Medal for Freedom. Fellow Am. Geog. Soc.; mem. Am. Econ. Assn., Am. Soc. Traffic and Transp., Acad. Polit. Sci. Author: (with Marvin L. Fair) Economics of Transportation, rev. edit., 1959; The Regulation of Rail-Motor Rate Competition, 1958; Freight Transportation in the Soviet Union, 1962; The Future of American Transportation, 1971; (with Marvin L. Fair) Economics of Transportation and Logistics, 1974. Contbr. articles to profl. publs. Office: Columbia U 116th St and Broadway New York NY 10027

WILLIAMS, EUGENE FLEWELLYN, JR., banker; b. St. Louis, July 24, 1923; s. Eugene Flewellyn and Marie (Wight) W.; B.A., Yale U., 1947; m. Evelyn N. Niedringhaus, June 11, 1947; children—Rebecca Williams deKertanguy), Eugene Flewellyn, III, John H., Evelyn E., Edward W. With St. Louis Union Trust Co., 1947—, pres., 1967-75, chief exec. officer, 1970—, chmn. bd., 1975—, also dir.; vice chmn. bd. dirs., First Union Bancorp.; dir. Emerson Electric Co., First Nat. Bank St. Louis, First Union Trust Co., Kansas City, Mo., Clin Corp., Pitchford Land & Cattle Co., Squibb Corp. Bd. dirs. Arts and Edn. Council Greater St. Louis, Central Inst. Deaf, Civic Progress, Inc., St. Louis Area council Boy Scouts Am., St. Louis Municipal Opera, St. Louis Symphony Soc.; trustee St. Louis U. Clubs: Augusta (Ga.) Nat. Golf; Lyford Cay, Maidstone; St. Louis Country. Home: 701 Barnes Rd St Louis MO 63124 Office: 510 Locust St St Louis MO 63101

WILLIAMS, FERD ELTON, physicist, educator; b. Erie, Pa., June 9, 1920; s. Earl V. and Osa M. (Riddle) W.; B.S., U. Pitts., 1942; M.A., Princeton, 1945, Ph.D., 1946; m. Anne Lindberg, Nov. 25, 1948; children—Karen, Gareth, Geoffrey, Kevin, Quentin. Research engr. RCA, 1942-46; asst. prof. chemistry U. N.C., 1946-49; mgr. light generation research Gen. Electric Research Lab., 1949-61; H. Fletcher Brown prof. physics U. Del., Newark, 1962—, chmn. dept., 1961-77; vis. prof. univs. Liège, Nijmegen and Paris, 1975-76, univs. Tokyo and Paris, 1978; prin. investigator basic luminescence program sponsored by Army Research Office, 1962—; indsl. and govt. cons. solid-state and chem. physics. Mem. adv. com. solid state Oak Ridge Nat. Lab., 1963-67; chmn. Com. for Internat. Confs. on Luminescence. Named Outstanding Educator of Year, 1974. Fellow Am. Phys. Soc., A.A.A.S.; mem. Am. Chem. Soc., Optical Soc. Am., A.A.U.P. (pres. Del. chpt. 1968-69), Am. Inst. Physics (regional councilor Del. 1964—), Am. Assn. Physics Tchrs. (pres. Chesapeake sect. 1966-67), Sigma Xi. Editor-in-chief Jour. Luminescence, 1970—. Contbr. articles to profl. jours. Patentee in field. Home: Dixon Dr Christine Manor Newark DE 19711 Office: Physics Dept U Delaware Newark DE 19711

WILLIAMS, FIELDING LEWIS, lawyer; b. Richmond, Va., June 22, 1906; s. Lewis Catlett and Maria Ward (Williams) W.; grad. Woodberry Forest Sch., 1924; B.A., U. Va., 1928, LL.B., 1930; m. Susan Roy Carter, Nov. 18, 1939; children—Fielding Lewis, Susan Carter Williams Turrell. Admitted to Va. bar, 1929; since practiced in Richmond; asso., then partner Williams, Mullen, Christian, Pollard and Gray and predecessor firms, 1930—; dir. emeritus Universal Leaf Tobacco Co. Mem. Va. Commn. for Visually Handicapped, 1960-75. Trustee Woodberry Forest Sch., 1953-59; chmn. bd. govs. Greater Richmond Commn. Found., 1969-78. Served as lt. USNR, 1942-44. Fellow Am. Bar Found.; mem. Am., Va., Richmond (pres. 1966) bar assns., Raven Soc., Phi Beta Kappa, Omicron Delta Kappa, Phi Delta Phi, Delta Psi. Clubs: Country of Virginia (pres. 1965-67), German (emeritus). Home: 65 Westham Green Richmond VA 23229 Office: United Virginia Bank Bldg Richmond VA 23219

WILLIAMS, FRANCIS S., investment co. exec.; b. Boston, 1901; B.A., Harvard, 1922, M.B.A., 1925; m. Elsie de Forest Wheeler, Apr. 15, 1936; 1 dau., Harriett de Forest (Mrs. William I. Procter). Vice chmn. F. Eberstadt & Co., Inc., N.Y.C., until 1976; ret., 1976; hon. chmn. Chem Fund, Inc., Surveyor Fund, Inc.; mem. fin. com. Research Corp. Mem. N.Y. Soc. Security Analysts. Clubs: Harvard, Recess (N.Y.C.); Riverside Yacht (past commodore). Home: Marks Rd Riverside CT 06878 Office: 61 Broadway New York NY 10006

WILLIAMS, FRANKLIN HALL, found. exec., lawyer, govt. ofcl.; b. Flushing, N.Y., Oct. 22, 1917; s. Arthur Lee and Alinda (Lowry) W.; A.B., Lincoln U., 1941; J.D., Fordham U., 1945; m. Shirley Broyard, May 27, 1944; children—Franklin Hall, Paul Anatole. Admitted to N.Y. bar, 1945, Calif. bar, 1951; also U.S. Supreme Ct.; asst. spl. counsel nat. office NAACP, 1945-50, West coast regional dir., 1950-59; asst. atty. gen. Calif., 1959-61; dir. univ., pvt. and internat. orgn. div. Peace Corps, 1961-62, dir. African Regional Office, 1963; U.S. rep. ECOSOC of UN, 1964-65; U.S. ambassador to Ghana, 1965-68; dir. Urban Center, Columbia, 1968-70. Dir. Chem. Bank N.Y., U.R.S. Inc., Consol. Edison, Inc., Borden, Inc. Chmn. N.Y. State adv. com. to U.S. Civil Rights Commn. Bd. dirs. Spencer Found., N.Y. City Opera, Council Fgn. Relations, Nat. Newspaper Council, Resources for Future, Lincoln U. Mem. Fordham Law Alumni Assn., Century Assn. Home: 52 W 89th St New York NY 10024

WILLIAMS, FREDERICK, educator; b. Middlesbrough, Eng., Feb. 9, 1922; s. Frederick William and Violet (Taylor) W.; came to U.S., 1926; B.S.E., U. Mich., 1947, M.B.A. with distinction, 1948; Ph.D., Northwestern U., 1958; m. Frances Marian Sacks, July 7, 1945. Teaching asst. statistics U. Mich., 1947-48; instr. statistics Northwestern U., 1948-54; instr., then asst. prof. statistics U. Ill., 1954-58; asso. prof. statistics U. Mo., 1958-61, prof., 1961—, chmn. dept. 1966-71, 1973-76, tchr. exec. devel. program, 1959-65, dir. grad. studies statistics, 1971-72; cons., lectr. in field. Served with USNR, 1943-46. Mem. Am. Statis. Assn., Operations Research Soc. Am., AAUP, Beta Gamma Sigma, Phi Kappa Phi. Co-author: An Introduction to Probability, 1965. Home: 213 Ruby Ln Columbia MO 65201

WILLIAMS, G. MENNEN, state justice; b. Detroit, Feb. 23, 1911; s. Henry Phillips and Elma Christina (Mennen) W.; student Detroit Univ. Sch., 1919-25, Salisbury Sch., 1925-29; A.B. cum laude, Princeton, 1933; J.D. cum laude, Mich. Law Sch., 1936; LL.D., Wilberforce U., Mich. State U., U. Liberia, U. Mich., Aquinas Coll., St. Augustine's Coll., 1961, Ferris Inst., 1961, Western Mich. U., 1963; D.C.L., Lincoln U., 1964; H.H.D., Lawrence Inst. Tech.; m. Nancy Lace Quirk, June 26, 1937; children—Gerhard Mennen, Nancy Quirk (Mrs. Ketterer), Wendy (Mrs. Burns). Admitted to Mich. bar, 1936; asso. Griffiths, Williams & Griffiths, Detroit, 1947-48; atty., Social Security Bd., 1936-38; asst. atty. gen. Mich., 1938-39; exec. asst. to U.S. atty. gen., 1939-40; with criminal div. Dept. Justice, 1940-41; dep. dir. Mich. OPA, 1946-47; liquor control commr. Mich., 1948; gov. of Mich., 1949-60; asst. sec. state for African affairs, 1961-66; U.S. ambassador to Republic of Philippines, 1968-69; justice Mich. Supreme Ct., 1971—. Served to lt. comdr. USNR, 1942-46. Decorated Legion of Merit with combat V, Presdl. Unit Citation with three stars; grand officer Order of Orange Nassau (Netherlands); grand comdr. Royal Order of Phoenix (Greece); Humane Band of African Redemption (Liberia); grand officer Order of Niger; comdr. Order Ivory Coast; pro merito (Latvia); Polonia Restituta (Polish Govt. in Exile); datu Order of Sikatuna (Philippines). Mem. Nat. Grange, Amvets, Am. Legion, V.F.W., Res. Officers Assn., SAR, Abepa, Steuben Soc., Edelweiss, Order of Coif, Phi Beta Kappa, Phi Gamma Delta, Phi Delta Phi. Democrat. Episcopalian. Mason (33 deg.), Eagle, Elk, Moose. Club: Detroit Country. Home: 25 Tonnancour Pl Grosse Pointe Farms MI 48236

WILLIAMS, GARTH MONTGOMERY, illustrator; b. N.Y.C., Apr. 16, 1912; studied Westminster Sch. Art, Royal Coll. Art, London; married; 6 children. Illustrator numerous children's books, among them Stuart Little, Little Fur Family, Tall Book of Make Believe, Three Little Animals, Cricket in Times Square, Sailor Dog, Miss Bianca, Charlotte's Web, The Rescuers, The Turret, Amigo, The Books of Laura Ingalls Wilder, Animal ABC, Push Kitty, Tuckers Countryside; also wrote Adventures of Benjamin Pink, The Rabbit's Wedding; Chicken Book. Recipient Brit. Prix de Rome for sculpture, 1936. Address: Apartado Postal 123 Guanajuato Guanajuato Mexico

WILLIAMS, GEORGE ABIAH, educator; b. Bklyn., Apr. 1, 1931; s. George A. and Helen (Burchard) W.; B.A., Colgate U., 1952; Ph.D., U. Ill., 1956; divorced; children—Robin, Scott, Brian. Research asso. physics Stanford, 1956-59; mem. tech. staff Bell Tel. Labs., Murray Hill, N.J., 1959-63; vis. asst. prof. physics Cornell U., 1963-64; asso. prof. physics U. Utah, Salt Lake City, 1964-69, prof. physics, 1969—. Mem. Am. Phys. Soc., Phi Beta Kappa. Author: Elementary Physics: Atoms, Waves, Particles, 1969, 2d edit., 1976; (with R. Doerhoff and M. Bolen) Challenges to Science: Physical Science, 1973, 2d edit. (with R. Barnes, R. Doerhoff and M. Bolen), 1979. Home: 1898 S 1300 E Salt Lake City UT 84105

WILLIAMS, GEORGE ARTHUR, educator; b. Willcox, Ariz., Jan. 14, 1918; s. James Arthur and Leone (George) W.; student Sul Ross State Tchrs. Coll., 1935-37; B.S. in Mining Engring., Tex. Coll. Mines and Metallurgy, 1943; Ph.D. in Geology, U. Ariz., 1951; m. Agatha Bervette, June 16, 1943; children—James Oliver, George Clay, Margaret Irene. Engr., ASARCO Mining Co., Inc., Mexico, 1946; geologist Peru Mining Co., 1946-48; supt. Kearney Mine, 1948; geologist U.S. Geol. Survey, 1951-54; exploration geologist Union Carbide Corp., 1954-57, mgmt. cons., 1957; mem. faculty U. Idaho, Moscow, 1957—, prof. geology, 1964—, head dept. geology and geography, 1964-70, head dept. geology, 1970—. Mem. control bd. Ida. Bur. Mines and Geology, 1969—. Committeeman Boy Scouts Am., Moscow, 1959-67. Precinct committeeman Republican Party, Moscow, 1962-68. Served to lt. USNR, 1943-45. Fellow AAAS, Geol. Soc. Am., Explorers Club; mem. Idaho N.W. mining assns., N.W. Sci. Assn., Am. Assn. Petroleum Geologists, Ida. Assn. Profl. Geologists (chmn. membership com. 1972-74, pres. 1976), Idaho Acad. Sci., Soc. Econ. Mineralogists and Paleontologists, Soc. Econ. Geologists. Presbyterian (elder). Elk. Home: 1105 Orchard Ave Moscow ID 83843

WILLIAMS, GEORGE CHARLES, lawyer; b. Wellsboro, Pa., May 10, 1916; s. Joseph Horton and Sarah (Lebling) W.; grad. Phillips Exeter Acad., 1935; A.B., Williams Coll., 1939; LL.B., U. Pa., 1942; m. Nancy L. Chisler, Dec. 20, 1941; children—Joseph C., Amy Tabor, Caleb. Admitted to Pa. bar, 1942, N.Y. and D.C. bars, 1956, Ohio bar, 1959; pvt. practice in Williamsport and Wellsboro, 1942-51, 67—; with Consol. Natural Gas System Companies, 1951-67, sec. Consol. Natural Gas Co., N.Y.C., 1965-67. Served with USNR, 1942-45. Decorated Navy Commendation medal. Mem. Am., Pa., Ohio bar assns., Assn. Bar City N.Y. Home: 68 Waln St Wellsboro PA 16901 Office: 33 Pearl St Wellsboro PA 16901

WILLIAMS, GEORGE EARNEST, indsl. co. exec.; b. Bartow, Fla., Nov. 27, 1923; s. Earnest Roscoe and Ruby Barnett (Mathews) W.; B.S. in Engring. with honors, U.S. Coast Guard Acad., 1944; postgrad. Harvard U., 1945-46; S.M. in Mgmt., Mass. Inst. Tech., 1949; m. Muriel Theodorsen, June 9, 1949. Asst. to pres. Indsl. Nucleonics Corp., Columbus, Ohio; project engr., bus. cons. Ebasco, N.Y.C.; design engr., prodn. supr. Minute Maid Corp., Orlando, Fla.; asst. controller, div. controller, group controller, corp. dir. fin. planning and analysis United Technologies Corp., Hartford, 1957-76, v.p., 1977—; sr. v.p. fin. Otis Elevator Co., N.Y.C., 1976-77. Mem. exec. com. Conn. Commn. Services and Expenditures, 1971. Served with USCG, 1941-47. Mem. Fin. Execs. Inst., Am. Inst. Aeros. and Astronautics, Am. Mgmt. Assn. Methodist. Clubs: Farmington Country; Army and Navy (Washington); Board Room (N.Y.C.). Originator pricing system purchase of Fla. oranges for concentrate mfg.; contbr. articles to fin. jours. and handbooks. Office: United Technologies Bldg Hartford CT 06101

WILLIAMS, GEORGE HOWARD, lawyer, assn. exec.; b. Hempstead, N.Y., Feb. 12, 1918; s. George R. and Marcella (Hogan) W.; A.B., Hofstra Coll., 1939, LL.D. (hon.), 1969; J.D., N.Y. U., 1946, LL.D. (hon.), 1969; postgrad. Inst. Advanced Legal Studies, U. London, 1959; m. Mary Celeste Madden, Nov. 23, 1946; children—Mary Beth Williams Barritt, Stephen, Kevin, Jeanne Marie. Admitted to N.Y. bar, 1946; adminstrv. asst. to dean N.Y. U. Law Sch., N.Y.C., 1946-48, instr. law, 1948-50, asst. prof., 1950-52, asso. prof., 1952-55, prof., 1956-62, v.p. univ. devel., 1962-66, exec. v.p. planning and devel., 1966-68; pres. Am. U., Washington, 1968-75; exec. v.p., dir. Am. Judicature Soc., Chgo., 1976—. Bd. dirs. Nat. Center Edn. Politics, 1948-58, trustee, 1958-65; trustee Hofstra U., 1961-64; chmn. bd. trustees Trinity Coll., Vt., 1978—. Served to lt. col., inf., AUS, World War II. Decorated Legion of Merit, Silver Star. Mem. Am. Polit. Sci. Assn., Am. Bar Assn., Assn. Bar City N.Y., Alpha Kappa Delta, Phi Delta Phi. Clubs: N.Y. U. (N.Y.C.); Nat. Lawyers (Washington). Author: (with A.T. Vanderbilt and L.L. Pelletier) Report on Liberal Adult Education, 1955. Home: 1322 Judson Ave Evanston IL 60201 Office: Am Judicature Soc 200 W Monroe St Chicago IL 60606

WILLIAMS, GEORGE HUNTSTON, ch. historian, educator; b. Huntsburg, Ohio, Apr. 7, 1914; s. David Rhys and Lucy Adams (Pease) W.; student U. Munich (Germany), 1934-35; A.B., St. Lawrence U., 1936; B.D., Meadville Theol. Sch., U. Chgo., 1939; postgrad. (Cruft traveling fellow), U. Strasbourg, 1939-40, U. Calif., 1942-44; Th.D., Union Theol. Sem., 1946; m. Marjorie Louise Derr, July 27, 1941; children—Portia, Jeremy, Jonathan, Roger. Ordained to ministry Unitarian and Congl. Chs., 1940; asst. minister Ch. of Christian Union, Rockford, Ill., 1940-41; mem. faculty Starr King Sch. for Ministry, Pacific Sch. Religion, Berkeley, Calif., 1941-47, asso. prof. ch. history, 1946-47; lectr. ch. history, head dept. Harvard Div. Sch., 1947-53, asso. prof., acting dean, 1953-55, prof., 1955—, Winn prof. ecclesiastical history, 1956, Hollis prof. div., 1963—; Fulbright lectr. U. Strasbourg, 1960-61; vis. prof. Union Theol. Sem., 1967, 68. Chmn. com. ch. and state Mass. Council Chs.; chmn. N.Am. Com. for Documentation Free-Ch. Origins; Protestant observer II Vatican Council, 1962-65; chmn. Governor's Com. Birth Control. Decorated knight Order of St. Gregory the Great (John Paul II); Guggenheim fellow and IREX scholar U. Lublin (Poland), 1972-73; Nat. Endowment for Humanities grantee, 1980. Mem. Am. Soc. Reformation Research (pres. 1967), Patristic Soc., Am. Acad. Arts and Scis., Mediaeval Acad. Am., Am. Soc. Ch. History (pres. 1958), Société Europeénede Culture, Civil Liberties Union Mass. (adv. com.), Americans United for Life (pres. 1971-77). Author: The Church and the Democratic State and the Crisis in Religious

Education, 1948; An Examination of the Thought of Frederic Henry Hedge, 1949; The Norman Anonymous of ca. 1100, 1951; Public Aid to Parochial Education, 1951; Christology and ChurchState Relations in the Fourth Century, 1951; Church History in the U.S., 1900-1950, 1951. Editor, contbr.: Harvard Divinity School History, 1954; Ministry in the Patristic Period, 1956; Golden Priesthood and the Leaden State, 1957; Anabaptist and Spiritual Writers, 1957; Anselm, 1960; The Radical Reformation, 1962 (enlarged Spanish edit. 1980); Wilderness and Paradise, 1962; Camillo Renato, 1965; Georges Florovsky, 1965; Sacred Condominium in American Debate on Abortion, 1970; The Last Catholic Modernist, 1973; Two Social Strands Italian Anabaptism, 1973; The Stancarist Schism, 1980; co-editor Harry A. Wolfson, Studies, also Writings of Thomas Hooker before 1633, 1976; Polish Brethren, 1601-85, 1978; Protestantism in The Ukraine, 1550-1701, 1978; Philosophy of John Paul II, 1978; mem. editorial bd. or co-editor: Harvard Theol. Rev. and Studies, Church History, Greek, Roman and Byzantine Studies, Studies in Romanticism, Mennonite Quar. Rev., Reflections; honored by jubilee vol. Continuity in Church History, 1979. Home: 58 Pinehurst Rd Belmont MA 02178 Office: Widener Library K Cambridge MA 02138

WILLIAMS, GEORGE JAMES, chem. co. exec.; b. Wolverine, Mich., Oct. 31, 1920; s. Donald and Marjorie Alberta (Gunn) W.; B.A. in Econs., Williams Coll., 1942; J.D., U. Mich., 1948; m. Lyla Katherine Landis, June 6, 1942; children—Schuyler Landis, Patricia Ann Williams Sessler, George James. Admitted to Mich. bar, 1948; with Dow Chem. Co., Midland, Mich., 1948—, comml. dir. U.S. area, 1968-75, fin. v.p., 1975—, also dir.; dir. Dow Corning Corp. Bd. dirs. Nat. Legal Center for Pub. Interest. Served with USAAF, 1943-45. Mem. Mich. Bar Assn., NAM (dir.). Episcopalian. Clubs: Rotary; Bohemian. Home: 13 Snowfield Ct Midland MI 48640 Office: 2030 Dow Center Midland MI 48640

WILLIAMS, GEORGE MIDDLETON, ry. co. exec.; b. Daphne, Ga., June 11, 1919; s. James Robert and Pauline Leslie (Thistlewood) W.; student Middle Ga. Coll., 1935-37; B.S., Clemson U., 1939; M.B.A., Harvard U., 1951; m. Ernestine Barnes, Dec. 29, 1942; children—George Middleton, Marsha Emily (Mrs. Jacques Mouyal), Leslie Barnes. With S.C. Expt. Sta., Clemson, 1939-40, Am. Nat. Red Cross, Columbia, S.C., 1945-49, Gulf Oil Corp., Pitts., 1951-53, Royal Globe Ins. Group, 1953-57; with So. Ry. Co., Washington, 1957—, treas., 1972—, asst. v.p., 1961—; mem. adv. bd. Am. Security & Trust Co., Washington. Mem. treasury div. Assn. Am. Railroads; mem. finance com. Alexandria Hosp. Served with USNR, 1940-45. Republican. Methodist. Club: Army Navy Country (Arlington, Va.). Home: 507 Canterbury Ln Alexandria VA 22314 Office: PO Box 1808 Washington DC 20013

WILLIAMS, GEORGE RAINEY, surgeon, educator; b. Atlanta, Oct. 25, 1926; s. George Rainey and Hildred (Russell) W.; student U. Tex., 1944-46; B.S., Northwestern U., 1948; M.B., 1950, M.D., 1950; m. Martha Vose, June 16, 1950; children—Bruce, Alden, Margaret, Rainey. Intern Johns Hopkins Hosp., 1950-51, William Stewart Halsted fellow surgery, 1951-52, asst. resident surgery, 1952-53, asst. resident surgeon, 1955-57, resident surgeon, 1957-58; practice medicine specializing in gen. and thoracic surgery, Oklahoma City, 1958—; asst. prof. surgery U. Okla. Health Scis. Center, Oklahoma City, 1958-61, asso. prof., 1961-63, prof. surgery School of Medicine, 1963—, chmn. dept. surgery, 1974—. Dir. Okla. Natural Gas Co., The Village Bank. Bd. dirs. Am. Bd. Surgery. Markle scholar in med. sci., 1960. Served lt., MC, 3d Inf. Div., AUS, 1953-55. Mem. Am. Coll. Surgeons, Soc. U. Surgeons, Am. Assn. Thoracic Surgery, So. Surg. Assn., Am. Surg. Assn., Phi Beta Kappa, Delta Kappa Epsilon, Phi Beta Pi, Alpha Epsilon Delta, Alpha Omega Alpha, Pi Kappa Epsilon. Contbr. articles on cardiovascular surgery to profl. jours. Home: 6512 Hillcrest Oklahoma City OK 73116 Office: U Okla Health Sciences Center Oklahoma City OK 73190

WILLIAMS, GEORGE ZUR, physician; b. Inchun, Korea, Apr. 7, 1907; s. Franklin Earl Cranston and Alice Lavinia (Barton) W.; came to U.S., 1921; student U. Denver, 1924-27; M.D., U. Colo., 1931, D.Sc. (hon.), 1968; m. Hulda Michael, 1927 (dec. 1933); children—Kenneth DeLee, Jeannine Alyse; m. 2d, Julienne Erlene Talpas, May 10, 1935. Intern St. Anthony Hosp., Denver, 1931-32; pathologist U. Colo. Sch. Medicine, 1931-36, Nat. Jewish Hosp., Denver, 1933-36; asso. prof. pathology Med. Coll. Va., Richmond, 1936-46; prof. pathology, 1946-53, dir. dept. oncology, 1946-53, dir. dept. clin. pathology, 1946-53, dir. cancer research and teaching Med. and Dental Schs., 1947-53, dir. dept. clin. pathol., hosp. labs., blood bank, 1946-53; chief dept. clin. pathology, research in cytology Lab. Automation and radiation affects Nat. Cancer Inst., NIH, 1953-69; dir. Inst. Health Research, San Francisco, 1970—, Inst. Med. Scis., Pacific Med. Center; cons. pathology, oncology VA Hosp., Richmond, Va., 1946-53; cons. pathology med. div. AEC, Oak Ridge. Chmn. expert panel on hosp. labs. WHO; cons. clin. pathology surgeon gen. Dept. Air Force, 1959—. Served to comdr. M.C., USNR, 1940-46; CBI, PTO, Korea. Decorated Bronze Star; recipient Ward Burdick award Am. Soc. Clin. Pathologists, 1961; Distinguished Service award sec. health, edn. and welfare for contbns. to pathology. Diplomate Am. Bd. Pathologists. Founding fellow Coll. Am. Pathologists (gov.); mem. Am. Soc. Clin. Pathology, Am. Cancer Soc. (certificate for 10 yrs. service on bd. trustees Va. div. 1948), Sigma Xi. Author chpt. on pneumonoconiosis Textbook of Industrial Medicine (Wampler), 1942, also chpts. in Tech. and Health Care Systems in the 1980's, 1972, others. Clubs: San Francisco Yacht; Chesapeake Bay. Home: 1915 Straits View Dr Tiburon CA 94920 Office: Inst Med Scis 2200 Webster St San Francisco CA 94115

WILLIAMS, GERALD ALBERT, physician, educator; b. Plankinton, S.D., Apr. 1, 1921; s. Albert T. and Leila (Morehead) W.; B.S., S.D. State Coll., 1945; M.D., George Washington U., 1949; m. Dorothy Jayne Burks, Aug. 12, 1950; children—Jeffrey B., Douglas A., Jonathan G. Intern, U.S. Naval Hosp., Phila., 1949-50; resident medicine VA Hosp., Washington, 1950-55; practice medicine specializing in endocrinology, Charlottesville, Va., 1955-59, Chgo., 1959—; fellow metabolic diseases U. Va. Sch. Medicine, 1955-57, instr. medicine, 1957-59; asst. prof. medicine U. Ill. Coll. Medicine, Chgo., 1959-64, asso. prof., 1964-69, prof. medicine, 1969—; attending physician, chief endocrinology U. Ill. Hosp., Chgo., 1959—; chief nuclear medicine service and endocrinology sect. VA West Side Hosp., 1959—. Served with AUS, 1942-45, USNR, 1949-50. Mem. Am. Fedn. for Clin. Research, A.C.P., Endocrine Soc., Central Soc. for Clin. Research, Soc. for Exptl. Biology and Medicine. Contbr. chpts. to books, articles to profl. jours. Home: 734 N Elmwood Ave Oak Park IL 60302 Office: 820 S Damen Ave Chicago IL 60612

WILLIAMS, GERALD ALVIN, architect; b. Seattle, Oct. 10, 1932; s. Morley Lawrence and Kathryn Janet (Higbie) W.; B.Arch., U. Wash., 1956; M.F.A., U. Pa., 1962; m. Karin Alice Estey, Sept. 19, 1959; children—Blake Evan, Colin Stuart. Draftsman, Young, Richardson, Carleton & Deltie, 1955-56, draftsman, designer, 1958-68; asso. The Richardson Assos., Seattle, 1968-75, partner, 1975-77; partner TRA, Seattle, 1978—; lectr. in field. Served with U.S. Army, 1956-58. Fellow AIA (pres. Seattle 1972, pres. Wash. State council 1977), Wash. State Bd. Registration for Landscape Architects, Phi Beta Kappa, Tau Sigma Delta. Home: 4720 NE 36th St Seattle WA 98105 Office: 215 Columbia St Seattle WA 98104

WILLIAMS, GERALD HALIBURTON, elec. equipment mfg. co. exec.; b. Chatham, Ont., Can., Nov. 8, 1925; s. William Henry and Margaret (Patterson) W.; student public schs.; m. Ruth Lorraine Leard, Apr. 6, 1946; children—Richard, Karen, Jeffrey. With DeVilbiss (Can.) Ltd., exec. v.p., 1967-68, pres., chmn. bd., 1968-76, pres. DeVilbiss Co. div. Champion Spark Plug Co., Toledo, 1976—, dir. parent co., 1977—. Alderman, City of Barrie, Ont., 1967-68, Twp. of Sandwich West, 1958-59; bd. dirs. Jr. Achievement, Toledo, Toledo Community Chest. Served with Royal Can. Navy, 1944-46. Mem. Am. Mgmt. Assn., NAM, Toledo C. of C. (dir.). Clubs: Inverness Country; Rotary. Home: 5063 Chatham Valley Dr Toledo OH 43615 Office: DeVilbiss Co div Champion Spark Plug Co 300 Phillips Ave Toledo OH 43612

WILLIAMS, GLEN MORGAN, fed. judge; b. Jonesville, Va., Feb. 17, 1920; s. Hughy May and Hattie Mae W.; A.B. magna cum laude, Milligan Coll., 1940; J.D., U. Va., 1948; m. Jane Slemp, Nov. 18, 1961; children—Susan, Judy, Rebecca, Melinda. Admitted to Va. Bar, 1947; practiced law, Jonesville, 1948-76; judge U.S. Dist. Ct. for Western Va., 1976—; commonwealth's atty. Lee County, Va., 1948-51. Mem. Va. Senate, 1953-55; mem. Lee County Sch. Bd., 1972-76; trustee, elder First Christian Ch., Pennington Gap, Va. Served to lt., sr. grade, USN, 1942-46; MTO. Mem. Va. State Bar, Va., Am., Fed. bar assns., Am. Legion, 40 & 8. Republican. Clubs: Lions, Lee Players, Masons, Shriners. Editorial bd. Va. Law Rev., 1946-47. Home: Jonesville VA 24263 Office: Fed Bldg Abingdon VA 24210

WILLIAMS, GLENN CARBER, chem. engr., educator; b. Princeton, Iowa, Oct. 9, 1914; s. H. Lurie and Jessie Elizabeth (Hire) W.; B.S., U. Ill., 1937, M.S., 1938; Sc.D., Mass. Inst. Tech., 1942; m. Dorothy Cleo Bryan, Aug. 27, 1939; children—Glenn Lurie, Cheryl. Research engr., engring. expt. sta. U. Ill., 1937-38; asst. Mass. Inst. Tech., 1938-40, instr., 1940-42, asst. prof., 1942-46, asso. prof., 1946-54, prof., 1954—; pres., dir. Combustion Inst., Nat. Def. Research Com., 1942-45; mem. sub-com. on combustion NACA, 1946-59, com. on chem. energy conversion, 1960-63; mem. panel on heat div. Nat. Bur. Standards, 1959-63; panel on propulsion NRC, 1949-50; adv. com. Army Ordnance Research and Devel.; mem. com. on motor vehicle emissions Nat. Acad. Scis., 1971-74. Recipient Naval Ordnance Devel. Award. Mem. Am. Chem. Soc., Am. Inst. Chem. Engrs., Combustion Inst. (pres.), Inst. Aero Scis., Am. Acad. Arts and Scis., Sigma Xi, Alpha Chi Sigma, Omega Chi Epsilon, Kappa Kappa Sigma, Delta Sigma Phi, Tau Beta Pi. Unitarian. Author: Thermodynamics of Combustion Processes (with H. C. Hottel, C. N. Satterfield), 1949. Home: 20 Barberry Rd Lexington MA 02173 Office: 77 Massachusetts Ave Cambridge MA 02139

WILLIAMS, GODWIN, JR., cons., ret. govt. ofcl., b. Dyersburg, Tenn., Nov. 15, 1913; s. Godwin and Ethel (Robinson) W.; student Cumberland U., 1932-33; B.S. in Elec. Engring., U. Tenn., 1936; m. Etta Culbertson, Aug. 22, 1958; 1 dau. by previous marriage, Margot (Mrs. Bosko Milosavljevic); 1 stepdau., Evelyn Kennedy. With Tenn. Electric Power Co., 1936-39; with TVA, 1939-78, asst. mgr. power, Chattanooga, 1971-76, mgr. power, 1976-78; cons., 1978—; mem. adv. com. Electric Power Research Inst.; vice chmn. Southeastern Electric Reliability Council; trustee Nat. Electric Reliability Council. Mem. Nat., Tenn. (pres. Chattanooga 1958) socs. profl. engrs., IEEE, U. Tenn. Alumni Assn. (pres. Hamilton County 1968), Order of the Engr., Sigma Alpha Epsilon. Democrat. Episcopalian. Clubs: Chattanooga Engineers; Signal Mountain Golf and Country. Home and Office: 201 Arrow Dr Signal Mountain TN 37377

WILLIAMS, GORDON BRETNELL, constrn. co. exec.; b. Phila., Apr. 3, 1929; s. Thomas W. and Helen (Berryman) W.; B.S., Yale, 1951; m. Susan M. Cunningham, June 20, 1953; children—Lucy Chase, Marcus Bretnell. Chief indsl. engr. Chrysler Corp., Detroit, 1954-57; pres., dir. Cunningham-Limp Co., Birmingham, Mich., 1957-76; v.p.-mktg. H.K. Ferguson Co., Cleve., 1976-78, pres., 1979—. Trustee, Cranbrook Ednl. Community Retirement Plan, Bloomfield Hills, Mich. Served as ensign, ordnance, USNR, 1952-54. Registered profl. engr., Mich., Ohio, Tex. Mem. Phi Gamma Delta. Clubs: Union (Cleve.); Yale of Ohio. Home: 2761 Sherbrooke Shaker Heights OH 44122 Office: HK Ferguson Co One Erieview Plaza Cleveland OH 44114

WILLIAMS, GORDON ROLAND, librarian; b. Ontario, Oreg., July 26, 1914; s. Herbert Harrison and George Lola (Davis) W.; A.B., Stanford, 1936; M.A., U. Chgo., 1952; m. Jane Margaret Smith, Apr. 25, 1942; 1 dau., Megan Davis. Vice pres. Brentano's Inc., Calif., 1945-49; chief asst. librarian U. Calif. at Los Angeles, 1952-59; dir. Center for Research Libraries, Chgo., 1959—. Mem. 1st Japan-U.S. Conf. on Libraries in Higher Edn., Tokyo, 1969, 2d Japan-U.S. Conf. on Libraries in Higher Edn., Wingspread, 1972, Internat. Conf. on Library Automation, Brasenose Coll., Oxford U., 1966; mem. archives and library com. Nat. Conservation Advisory Council, 1973—. Trustee, Biosis. Info. of Biol. Abstracts, 1977—; chmn. Conf. Cataloging and Info. Sers. for Machine-Readable Data Files, 1978; mem. Study Com. Libraries and Archives Nat. Conservation Advisory Council, 1973—. Served with USNR, 1942-45. Decorated Commendation medal. Mem. A.L.A. (chmn. com. nat. union catalogue 1960—), Internat. Inst. Conservation Historic and Artistic Works, Assn. Research Libraries (com. on preservation of research library materials 1960-68, dir. 1964-67), Soc. Am. Archivists (chmn. com. on paper preservation 1970—). Clubs: Caxton, Quadrangle (Chgo.); Rounce and Coffin (Los Angeles). Author: Ravens and Crows, 1966; Bewick to Dovaston, Letters 1824-1828, 1968; Cost of Owning vs. Borrowing Serials, 1969; hon. editorial adv. Interlending Rev., Eng. Home: 2118 Vardon Ln Flossmoor IL 60422 Office: 5721 Cottage Grove Ave Chicago IL 60637

WILLIAMS, HAL, actor; b. Columbus, Ohio, Dec. 14, 1940; student Ohio State U. Starred in On The Rocks series, ABC-TV, 1975-76; appeared in various comedy shows including Good Times, 1975, Temperatures Rising, 1974, The New Dick Van Dyke Show, 1973; continuing roles on TV shows That Girl, 1971-73, The Waltons, 1973—, Kung-Fu Series, 1973-74; appeared on Gunsmoke, 1974, The Magician, 1974, Cannon, 1973, 1976; appeared in Hard Core, Columbia Pictures, 1979; appeared as Officer Smitty in Sanford and Son, Tandem Prodns., 1971-76; appeared as Paul in Rose's Park, Rose's Park Prodns., 1978; appeared as guest star in School for Killers, ABC-TV, 1974; featured role as Marshall W. Rhodus in Police Story, NBC Movie of the Week, 1973; leading role as Aleck Haley in Roots II-The Next Generations, ABC-TV, 1978-79. Mem. AFTRA, Screen Actors Guild, Actors Equity Assn., Acad. of TV Arts and Scis., NAACP, Far West Ski Assn. Club: Four Seasons West Ski. Home: PO Box 90525 Worldway Center Los Angeles CA 90009 Office: Allen Goldstein & Assos Ltd 9000 Sunset Blvd Los Angeles CA 90069

WILLIAMS, HAROLD ELLIS, ret. textile co. exec.; b. Wilkes-Barre, Pa., Apr. 21, 1914; s. Watkin and Erma (Catley) W.; B.S.C., Drexel U., 1936, D.Sc. and Commerce (hon.), 1976; postgrad. N.Y.U. Grad. Sch. Bus., 1939-40; m. Beatrice Hamil, June 4, 1938; children—Heather Ellen (Mrs. Heather W. Bunnell), Robert Watkin. With Haskins & Sells, C.P.A.'s, N.Y.C., 1936-43; asst. controller Deering-Milliken & Co., Inc., N.Y.C., 1943-55; with Am. Thread Co., N.Y.C., 1955-78, sec., 1960-78, treas., 1962-71, 75-78, v.p., 1960-78, also dir.; ret., 1978; v.p., sec., treas., dir. Conmar-Am., Inc., 1960-73, Atcot Corp., 1965-78, Calico Compress & Warehouse Co., Inc., 1966-74, Calico Printers, Ltd., 1970-78. Mem. dist. com. Monmouth council Boy Scouts Am., 1959-70, mem. exec. bd., 1962-70, mem. Pomperaug and exec. com., 1971-73, mem. exec. com. Fairfield County council, 1973-79; mem. Red Bank (N.J.) Recreation Com. Mem. borough council, Red Bank, 1950-57, 64-67. Mem. deans visitation com. Drexel U., 1965—, asso. trustee, 1975. Recipient Outstanding Alumni award Drexel U., 1961, 78. C.P.A., N.Y., N.J. Mem. Fin. Execs. Inst. (dir., sec. chpt., pres. chpt. 1976), Am. Inst. C.P.A.'s, N.J. Soc. C.P.A.'s, Am. Mgmt. Assn., Am. Textile Mfrs. Assn. Methodist. Mason (Shriner). Clubs: Patterson (Fairfield); Palmetto-Pine Country (Cape Carol, Fla.). Home: 4828 Golf Club Ct Apt 6 Bldg B North Fort Myers FL 33903

WILLIAMS, HAROLD LEWIS, lawyer; b. Homerville, Ohio, Jan. 26, 1907; s. Ira Flay and Mary (Fenstermaker) W.; B.A., Western Res. U., 1929, LL.B., 1931; m. Mary Streett, Mar. 5, 1935; children—Nancy (Mrs. George Hamilton Fisk), Carol (Mrs. Robert Kornegay), John Streett. Admitted to Ohio bar, 1932, also U.S. Dist. Ct. Cleve.; since practiced in Medina; asso. John A. Weber, 1932-58; partner Williams & Batchelder, 1958—; spl. counsel apptd. by Comptroller of Currency, 1935-37. Dir. Seville Centrifugal Bronze, Inc. Mem. Medina Bd. Edn., 1940-50. Trustee Medina Community Hosp., 1942-50. Mem. Ohio Gen. Assembly, 1937-38, Ohio Democratic Exec. Com., 1937-38. Mem. Am., Ohio, Medina County bar assns., Internat. Assn. Ins. Counsel, Phi Gamma Delta, Delta Theta Phi. Conglist. Home: 950 Hickory Grove Medina OH 44256 Office: 105 W Liberty St Medina OH 44256

WILLIAMS, HAROLD MARVIN, govt. ofcl., former univ. dean; b. Phila., Jan. 5, 1928; s. Louis W. and Sophie (Fox) W.; A.B., U. Calif. at Los Angeles, 1946; LL.B., Harvard, 1949; postgrad. U. So. Calif. Grad. Sch. Law, 1955-56; m. Estelle Feinstein, Sept. 24, 1950; children—Ralph A., Susan J. Admitted to Calif. bar, 1950; practiced in Los Angeles, 1950, 53-55; with Hunt Foods and Industries, Inc., Los Angeles, 1955-68, v.p. 1958-60, exec. v.p., 1960-68, pres., 1968; gen., mgr. Hunt-Wesson Foods, 1964-66, pres., 1966-68; chmn. finance com. Norton Simon, Inc., 1968-70, chmn. bd., 1969-70, dir., 1959-77; prof. mgmt., dean Grad. Sch. Mgmt., U. Calif. at Los Angeles, 1970-77; pres., dir. Special Investments & Securities Inc., 1961-66; chmn. SEC, Washington, 1977—. Mem. Commn. for Econ. Devel. State of Calif., 1973-77; energy coordinator City of Los Angeles, 1973-74; pub. mem. Nat. Advt. Review Bd., 1971-75; co-chmn. Pub. Commn. on Los Angeles County Govt. Served as 1st lt. AUS, 1950- 53. Mem. State Bar Calif. Office: 500 N Capitol St Washington DC 20549*

WILLIAMS, HAROLD MILTON, trade assn. exec.; b. Lemmon, S.D., Oct. 10, 1907; s. William Daniel and Lillian (Jackson) W.; B.A., U. Wis., 1929; M.B.A., U. Chgo., 1947; m. Alice Rosamond Fox, Jan. 20, 1931; children—Rosemary M. (Mrs. James E. DeMore), Martha E., Maudie (Mrs. Robert J. Bremer), David H., Daniel J. With Swift & Co., Chgo., 1929-31, Williams Packing Co., Chgo., 1931-43; plant mgr. Hofhers Meat Co., Chgo., 1943-44; v.p. Fox De Luxe Foods, Inc., Chgo., 1944-57; pres., dir. Inst. Am. Poultry Industries, Chgo., 1958-75, con., 1975—; dir. Poultry and Egg Nat. Bd., 1959—; pres. Poultry and Egg Inst. of Am., Inc., 1971—; asso. W.T. Grimm & Co. Mem. U.S. Pres.'s Food for Peace Com., 1962—; adminstr. coop. program between Fgn. Agr. Service of U.S. Dept. Agr. and Inst. Am. Poultry Industries, 1958; del. European Am. Symposium on Agr. Trade, Amsterdam, Holland, 1963; mem. Am. Freedom from Hunger Found.; tech. poultry adviser Kennedy Round Table. Named hon. citizen Kansas City, Mo., 1963, New Orleans, 1969. Mem. U.S. Livestock San. Assn., Inst. Food Technologists, Assn. Food and Drug Ofcls., Am. Security Council, U.S. Food Packaging Council (gov.), Chgo. Assn. Commerce and Industry, Phi Kappa Phi. Clubs: Serra of North Shore, Executive, Lake Shore (Chgo.); University (Washington); Executive Program (U. Chgo.). Home: 2842 W Chase St Chicago IL 60645 Office: 135 S LaSalle St Chicago IL 60603. *As president of a national nonprofit trade association, my purpose is to encourage businessmen to think as philosophers as well as businessmen, and to put into perspective the ultimate of purpose of business: to serve people as human beings. The last hope for our free-enterprise system lies in demonstrating that this is the system that can serve their interests best. It is the only economic system that lets people develop as free, well-rounded individuals. We face a moral crisis. And, as Joseph Schumpeter said, "The stock market is a poor substitute for the Holy Grail."*

WILLIAMS, HARRISON ARLINGTON, JR., U.S. senator; b. Plainfield, N.J., Dec. 10, 1919; s. Harrison A. and Isabel (Lamson) W.; B.A., Oberlin Coll., 1941; LL.B., Columbia, 1948; student Georgetown U. Fgn. Service Sch.; LL.D. (hon.), Rutgers U., Rider Coll., Seton Hall U., Princeton U., Suffolk U. Law Sch.; L.H.D. (hon.), Glassboro State Coll., D. Civil Laws (hon.), Bloomfield Coll.; D. Sc., (hon.), M.J. Lewis Coll.; m. Jeanette Richardson Smith, Aug. 24, 1974; children—Peter, Wendy, Jonathan, Nina. Admitted N.H. bar, 1948, N.J. bar, 1951; practice in N.J., 1951—; mem. 83d-84th Congresses, 6th Dist. N.J.; U.S. Senator from N.J., 1958—, chmn. com. labor and human resources, subcom. securities housing and urban affairs, com. on banking; mem. Senate democratic steering com. Named Man of Year Am. Transit Assn., 1969; recipient Gerry award Nat. Geriatrics Soc., 1972, Conservation and Animal Welfare award Internat. Fund for Animal Welfare, 1977; Trumpeter award Nat. Consumers League. Home: Bedminster NJ 07921 Office: Senate Office Bldg Washington DC 20510

WILLIAMS, HARRY JOHN, accountant; b. West Frankfort, Ill., June 21, 1900; s. George Harry and Lydia (Morgan) W.; student U. Ill., 1920-22; m. Helita Eubanks Durham, Oct. 24, 1922; children—Harry John, Patricia (Mrs. Reynold Hobson Richaud). With Peat, Marwick, Mitchell & Co., C.P.A.'s, 1922-63, mng. partner, New Orleans, 1943-63, ltd. partner, 1963—; accounting adviser Internat. Finance Corp., Washington, 1963-67, accounting cons., 1967—; instr. City Coll. Law and Finance, St. Louis, 1927, Loyola U. of South, New Orleans, 1935. Chmn. Sea Transp. Industry Com., 1952-63; mem. Petroleum Industry Com., 1948-63, chmn. subcom. accounting procedures, 1955-63; mem. trade mission to Orient, 1961, mem. Internat. Com. on Accounting Coop., 1966-73, treas., 1966-67. Bd. dirs. Internat. House, New Orleans, 1958-63. C.P.A., Mo., La. Mem. Am. Inst. C.P.A.'s, Soc. La. C.P.A.'s (pres. 1941-42), Nat. Assn. Accountants (pres. New Orleans 1942-43). Republican. Presbyn. Mason (K.T.). Clubs: Pickwick, Southern Yacht, Country (New Orleans). Author pamphets in field. Home: New Orleans LA . *I have always tried to act with truthfulness, with independence of thought and judgment, and with honesty and fairness to all.*

WILLIAMS, HARRY LEVERNE, chem. engr.; b. Watford, Ont., Can., Nov. 16, 1916; s. Harry Young and Rosa Malinda (Brown) W.; B.A., U. Western Ont., 1939, M.Sc., 1940; Ph.D., McGill U., Montreal, 1943; m. Mary Eileen Cawson, Aug. 31, 1946; children—Harvey Thomas Leverne, Jai Joan Mary Williams Field. From research chemist to prin. scientist research and devel. div. Polysar Ltd., Sarnia, Ont., 1946-67; prof. chem. engring. and applied chemistry U. Toronto, 1967—; dir. Chem. Engring. Research Cons. Ltd.; cons. in field. Research grantee Nat. Research Council Can., Def. Research Bd. Can., Imperial Oil Enterprises Ltd., Polysar Ltd.

Registered profl. engr., Ont. Fellow Chem. Inst. Can. (Dunlop lectr. macromolecular scis. div. 1977), Royal Inst. Chemistry, Plastics and Rubber Inst., AAAS, N.Y. Acad. Scis.; mem. Am. Chem. Soc., Soc. Plastics Engrs. (sr.), Soc. Plastics Industry, Soc. Chem. Industry, Sigma Xi. Author, patentee in field. Home: 255 Glenlake Ave Toronto ON M6P 1G2 Canada Office: Dept Chem Engring Univ Toronto Toronto ON M5S 1A4 Canada

WILLIAMS, HARVEY LADEW, internat. mgmt. cons.; b. Stamford, Conn., July 10, 1900; s. Harvey Ladew and Hannah Haydock (Willis) W.; grad. Harvard, 1920, Mass. Inst. Tech., 1922; m. Gertrude E. Hoxie, Feb. 28, 1927 (div. 1942); children—Eleanor Ladew, Sheila, Hannah Hooker, Harvey Ladew; m. 2d, Brenda Hedstrom Boocock, Sept. 18, 1943. With Stone & Webster, Inc., 1922-27; pres., dir. Air Investors, Inc., 1927-32; mem. exec. com., dir. Aviation Corp., 1928-32, Am. Airways, Inc., 1928-32; pres., dir. United Aviation Corp., 1930-32; sr. partner, mgmt. cons. Harvey Williams & Assos., Delray Beach, Fla., 1931—; v.p. charge overseas operations, dir., mem. exec. com. H.J. Heinz Co., 1946-53; v.p. Avco Mfg. Corp., N.Y., also gen. mgr. internat. div., 1953-56; pres., dir. Philco Internat. Corp., N.Y.C., Phila., 1956-63, Philco Corp. Can., Ltd., 1956-63; chmn., dir. Philco. Italiana S.p.A., Milano; dir. Philco Internat., Ltd., London, Philco Corp. S.A., Fribourg, Switzerland, Cia Mexicana Electromercantil, Mexico City, Philco S.A. de C.V., Mexico City, Philco Argentina, S.A., Buenos Aires, Bendix Home Appliances do Brazil, Sao Paulo; pres., dir. The Co. for Investing Abroad, Phila., 1963-66; trustee U.S. council Internat. C. of C., 1962—, sr. trustee, 1966—, pres., 1973-77, hon. pres., 1977—; chmn. com. expansion internat. trade, 1961-66; sec.-treas. U.S.A. bus. and industry adv. com. to OECD, Paris, 1973-77. Chmn. northeastern div. Air Def. League, 1935-38, N.E. Aviation Conf., 1940, Conn. Aero. Devel. Commn., 1939-41; tech. cons. devel. div. Army Ground Forces Hdqrs., Washington, 1942-45. Vice pres. and life trustee Tabor Acad., Marion, Mass. Life fellow Inst. Dirs. (London); mem. Internat. House Phila. (dir. 1963-69), Nat. Aviation Assn. (nat. councillor 1939-41), Aero. C. of C. Am. (gov. 1929-31), Internat. Mgmt. Assn. (chmn. planning council 1958-60), Am. Mgmt. Assn. (v.p. 1958-60), Am. Australian Assn. (dir. 1948—), Inst. Aero. Scis., Army Ordnance Assn. (life), U.S. Naval Inst. (life), Electronics Industries Assn. (chmn. exec. com. internat. div. 1958-60), English Speaking Union (life), Newcomen Soc., Fgn. Policy Assn., Pres.'s Assn., Soc. Colonial Wars, Am. Soc. Legion d'Honneur, Am. Soc. in London, Am. Legion. Clubs: Harvard, Wings, University (N.Y.C.); Lake Placid (Essex County, N.Y.); Melbourne (Australia); St. Andrews, Delray Beach Yacht, Seagate (Delray Beach, Fla.); Beverly Yacht, Kittansett (Marion, Mass.); Buck's (London); Steward's Enclosure (Henley, Eng.); The Travellers (Paris); Athenaeum, Racquet (Phila.). Home: 220 MacFarlane Dr Delray Beach FL 33444. *Look upon crises as opportunities; upon difficulties as challenges. Defeat commences within oneself. Confidence is based on that which is sound and fair. Tenacity of purpose and effort often win through what others regard as impossible.*

WILLIAMS, HIBBARD EARL, physician; b. Utica, N.Y., Sept. 28, 1932; s. Hibbard G. and Beatrice M. W.; A.B., Cornell U., 1954, M.D., 1958; m. Karin Roser, Aug. 12, 1952; children—Robin, Hans. Intern in medicine Mass. Gen. Hosp., Boston, 1958-59, asst. resident in medicine, 1959-60, resident in medicine, 1962-63, chief resident in medicine, 1963-64, asst. physician, 1964-65; clin. asso. Nat. Inst. Arthritis and Metabolic Diseases, NIH, Bethesda, Md., 1960-62; instr. medicine Harvard U., Boston, 1964-65; asst. prof. medicine U. Calif., San Francisco, 1965-68, asso. prof., 1968-72, prof., 1972-78, chief div. med. genetics, 1968-70, vice chmn. dept. medicine, 1970-78; prof., chmn. dept. medicine Cornell U., 1978—; physician-in-chief N.Y. Hosp.-Cornell Med. Center, N.Y.C., 1978—; mem. program project com. NIH Nat. Inst. Arthritis and Metabolic Diseases, 1971-73. Served with USPHS, 1960-62. Recipient Career Devel. award USPHS, 1968, award for excellence in teaching Kaiser Found., 1970, Disting. Faculty award U. Calif. Alumni-Faculty Assn., 1978; John and Mary R. Markle scholar in medicine, 1968. Diplomate Am. Bd. Internal Medicine. Fellow A.C.P.; mem. AAAS, Am. Fedn. Clin. Research, Am. Soc. Clin. Investigation (sec.-treas. 1974-77), Am. Soc. Human Genetics, Assn. Am. Physicians, Calif. Acad. Medicine (sec.-treas. 1971-78), San Francisco Diabetes Assn. (dir. 1971-72), Western Assn. Physicians (v.p. 1977-78), Western Soc. Clin. Research, Am. Clin. and Climatol. Soc., Alpha Omega Alpha. Clubs: N.Y. Yacht, St. Francis Yacht, Larchmont Yacht. Contbr. numerous articles to profl. publs.; editor med. staff confs. Calif. Medicine, 1966-70; editorial bd. Clin. Research, 1968-71; asso. editor Metabolism, 1970—; mem. adv. bd. physiology in medicine New Eng. Jour. Medicine, 1970—. Office: 525 E 68th St New York NY 10021

WILLIAMS, HIRAM DRAPER, painter, educator; b. Indpls., Feb. 11, 1917; s. Earl Boring and Inez Mary (Draper) W.; B.S., Pa. State U., 1950, M.Ed., 1951; m. Avonell Baumunk, July 7, 1941; children—Curtis Earl, Kim Avonell. Tchr. art U. So. Calif., 1953-54, UCLA, summer 1959, U. Tex., 1954-60; mem. faculty U. Fla., Gainesville, 1960—, now prof. of art paintings; exhibited Pa. Acad. Fine Arts anns., Whitney Mus. Am. Art bi-anns., Corcoran Gallery Bi-anns., U. Ill. bi-anns., Mus. Modern Art exhbns., also Nordness Gallery, N.Y.C.; represented in permanent exhbns. Mus. Modern Art, Wilmington Art Center, Whitney Mus. of Am. Art, N.Y.C., Sheldon Meml. Art Mus., Milw. Art Center, also pvt. collections. Mem. chancellor's council U. Tex. System. Served to capt. C.E., U.S. Army, World War II; ETO. Tex. Research grantee, 1958; Guggenheim fellow, 1962-63. Author: Notes for a Young Painter, 1963. Contbr. articles to mags. Address: 2804 NW 30th Terr Gainesville FL 32605. *My desire as a painter is to animate material with imagery that strikes conjunctions of art and life.*

WILLIAMS, HOWARD RUSSELL, lawyer, educator; b. Evansville, Ind., Sept. 26, 1915; s. Clyde Alfred and Grace (Preston) W.; A.B., Washington U., St. Louis, 1937; LL.B., Columbia, 1940; m. Virginia Merle Thompson, Nov. 3, 1942; 1 son, Frederick S.T. Admitted to N.Y. bar, 1941; with firm Root, Clark, Buckner & Ballantine, N.Y.C., 1940-41; prof. law, asst. dean U. Tex. Law Sch., Austin, 1946-51; prof. law Columbia Law Sch., N.Y.C., 1951-63, Dwight prof., 1959-63; prof. law Stanford Law Sch., 1963—, Stella W. and Ira S. Lillick prof., 1968—. Oil and gas cons. President's Materials Policy Commn., 1951; mem. Calif. Law Revision Commn., 1971—, vice chmn., 1976-77, chmn., 1978-79. Bd. regents Berkeley Baptist Div. Sch., 1966-67; trustee Rocky Mountain Mineral Law Found., 1964-66, 68—. Served to maj. U.S. Army, 1941-46. Mem. Phi Beta Kappa. Democrat. Author: Cases on Property, 1954; Cases on Oil and Gas, 4th edit., 1979; Decedents' Estates and Trusts, 1968; Future Interests, 1970; Oil and Gas Law, 7 vols., 1959-64, abridged edit., 1973. Home: 811 Mayfield Ave Stanford CA 94305

WILLIAMS, HULEN BROWN, univ. dean; b. Lauratown, Ark., Oct. 8, 1920; s. Ernest Burdett and Ann Jeanette (Miller) W.; B.A., Hendrix Coll., 1941; M.S., La. State U., 1943, Ph.D., 1948; postgrad. Cornell U., summer 1950, U. Calif. at Berkely, 1953; m. Virginia Anne Rice, June 20, 1942 (dec. June 1970); children—James Browning, Virginia Jean; m. 2d, Michaela Galasso, Mar. 20, 1971. Instr. through asso. prof. La. State U., Baton Rouge, 1947-56, prof., head chemistry dept., 1956-68, dean Coll. Chemistry and Physics, 1968—. Cons. to chem. and legal professions. Served to lt. (j.g.) USNR, 1944-46. Mem. Am. Chem. Soc., Am. Inst. Chemists, Sigma Xi, Sigma Pi Sigma, Phi Lambda Upsilon, Phi Kappa Phi, Omicron Delta Kappa. Co-author books on chemistry. Contbr. articles to profl. jours. Home: 470 Castle Kirk Dr Baton Rouge LA 70808

WILLIAMS, J. HAROLD, lawyer; b. Waterbury, Conn., Dec. 23, 1893; s. John Ellis and Geneva Louise (Porter) W.; A.B., Yale U., 1917, LL.B., 1920; m. Martha Schultz, June 5, 1926 (div. 1943); children—Marcia, John H. Admitted to Conn. bar, 1920, since practiced in Hartford; sr. mem. firm Gross, Hyde & Williams. Former dir. Heublein, Inc. Mem. City Plan Commn., Hartford, 1947-56; pres. Ch. Council Found.; bd. dirs. Am. Heart Assn. Greater Hartford, Inc., Ch. Homes, Inc.; trustee Hartford Sem. Found. Served with U.S. Army, World War I. Mem. Am., Conn., Hartford County bar assns., Am. Judicature Soc., Christian Activities Council (life). Conglist. Mason. Home: 806 Prospect Ave Hartford CT 06105 Office: 799 Main St Hartford CT 06103

WILLIAMS, J(OHN) TILMAN, real estate and ins. broker, mayor; b. Detroit, Feb. 26, 1925; s. Aubrey and Martha Lou W.; B.S. in Agr., Mich. State U., 1951; m. Sally Jane Robinson, Aug. 22, 1947; children—Leslie Ann, Martha Lou. Pres., Satellite Ins. Brokerage, Garden Grove, Calif., 1959—; pres. Satellite Real Estate, Satellite Mortgage & Loan Co.; mayor, Garden Grove, 1976—. Mem. Ad Hoc Com. on Property Tax to Limit Govt. Spending with Spirit of 13 Initiative; past pres. Garden Grove High Sch. Band Boosters. Served with USAAF, World War II; PTO. Mem. Bd. Realtors, Ind. Ins. Agts. Assn., Am. Legion, VFW. Democrat. Methodist. Clubs: Lions; Elks; Toastmasters (Anaheim, Calif.). Home: 11241 Chapman Ave Garden Grove CA 92640 Office: 12311 Harbor Blvd Garden Grove CA 92640

WILLIAMS, J. VERNON, lawyer; b. Honolulu, Apr. 26, 1921; s. Urban and W. Amelia (Olson) W.; student Phillips Andover Acad., 1937-39; B.A. cum laude, Amherst Coll., 1943; LL.B., Yale, 1948; m. Malvina H. Hitchcock, Oct. 4, 1947 (dec. May 1970); children—Carl H., Karin, Frances E., Scott S.; m. 2d, JoAnn Isaacson Fray, Aug. 25, 1972 (div. Sept. 1975). Admitted to Wash. bar, 1948; since practiced in Seattle; asso. Riddell, Riddell & Hemphill, 1948-50; partner Riddell, Williams, Ivie, Bullitt & Walkinshaw and predecessor firms, 1950—; lectr. Wash. Bar Rev. Assos., 1949-63. Sec., dir. Airborne Freight Corp., 1968-79, gen. counsel, 1968—. Chmn. March of Dimes, Seattle, 1954-55. Mem. Mayor's City Charter Rev. Com., 1968-69; chmn. Seattle Bd. Park Commrs., 1966-68; co-chmn. parks and open space com. Forward Thrust, 1966-69; dir. bd. and commrs. br. Nat. Recreation and Parks Assn., 1968-69; chmn. Gov.'s adv. com. Social and Health Services, 1972-75. Bd. dirs. Seattle Met. YMCA, pres., 1976-79; trustee Lakeside Sch., 1971-79; mem. alumni council Phillips Andover Acad., 1970-73, Yale Law Sch., 1969-77; chancellor St. Mark's Cathedral, Seattle, 1964—. Served with USAAF, 1943-45. Republican. Episcopalian. Clubs: University, Seattle Tennis, Washington Athletic (Seattle); Bainbridge Racquet. Home: One NE Williams Ln Bainbridge Island WA 98110 Office: 4300 Seattle First Nat Bank Bldg Seattle WA 98154

WILLIAMS, JACK KENNY, med. center adminstr.; b. Galax, Va., Apr. 5, 1920; s. Floyd Winfield and Mary Josephine (Vass) W.; B.A., Emory and Henry Coll., 1940; M.A., Emory U., 1947, Ph.D., 1953; summer student U. Va., 1948, U. Ky., 1949; m. Emma Margaret Pierce, June 10, 1943; children—Katherine Winfield, Mary Kenny. High sch. tchr., Va., 1940-42; mem. faculty Clemson (S.C.) U., 1947-66, dean Grad. Sch., 1957-60, dean univ., 1960-66, v.p. acad. affairs, 1963-66; commr. coordinating bd. Tex. Colls. and Univs., 1966-68; v.p. U. Tenn. System, Knoxville, 1968-70; chancellor U. Tenn. Med. Sch., 1969-70; pres. Tex. A. and M. U. and Univ. System, College Station, 1970-77, chancellor, 1977-79; exec. v.p. Tex. Med. Center, Houston, 1980—; mem. Coll. Entrance Exam. Bd. 1974-76; dir. Frozen Food Express, Inc., Anderson-Clayton Co., Diamond Shamrock Co., Campbell-Taggert Co., Gifford-Hill Co. Bd. dirs. Nat. Merit Scholarship Corp.; Mem. Sam Houston Council Boy Scouts Am.; U.S. nat. com. World Energy Conf., 1976-77; chmn. Tex. Natural Fibers and Food Protein Commn., 1978. Mem. civilian adv. com. U.S. Army Command and Gen. Staff Coll., 1966-70. Served as officer USMCR, 1942-46. Memd So. Assn. Colls. and Schs. (chmn. commn. colls. 1968-76), Assn. Tex. Colls. and Univs. (pres. 1978-79), USMCR Officers Assn., Phi Beta Kappa, Phi Kappa Phi. Methodist. Author: Vogues in Villiany, 1958; Dueling in the Old South, 1980. Contbr. articles to profl. jours. Home: 2318 Carter Creek Bryan TX 77840

WILLIAMS, JAMES ALEXANDER, lawyer; b. Pine Bluff, Ark., Oct. 30, 1929; s. Absalom Alexander and Kyle (Baggarly) W.; student U. Ark., 1948; B.A., So. Methodist U., 1951, J.D., 1952, M.L.A., 1971; m. Janet L. Bray, Nov. 27, 1953; children—Laura Kay, Victoria Lynn, Diana Leigh. Admitted to Tex. bar, 1952, since practiced in Dallas; mem. firm Touchstone, Bernays & Johnston, 1955-57; partner firm Bailey, Williams, Westfall, Lee and Fowler, 1957—. Bd. dirs. Spl. Care Sch.; bd. mgmt. YMCA; chmn. adminstrv. bd. Univ. Park United Meth. Ch., 1973. Served to lt. USNR, 1952-55. Mem. Am., Dallas bar assns., State Bar Tex., Dallas, Tex. assns. def. counsel, Internat. Assn. Ins. Counsel, Fedn. Ins. Counsel, Am. Bd. Trial Advocates, Soc. Hosp. Attys., Trial Attys. Am., So. Meth. U. Law Alumni Assn. (pres. 1970-72), Lambda Chi Alpha, Phi Alpha Delta. Democrat. Clubs: Exchange (pres. 1967); Dallas; Brookhaven Country. Home: 4630 Northaven Rd Dallas TX 75229 Office: Suite 2150 One Dallas Centre Dallas TX 75201

WILLIAMS, JAMES EARL, economist, univ. adminstr.; b. Fonde, Ky., July 16, 1922; s. Hobart Lee and Beatrice (Seal) W.; B.A., Carson-Newman Coll., 1949; M.A., U. Tenn., 1950; Ph.D., U. Wis., 1961; m. Marjorie Marie Hybarger, June 16, 1951. Instr. econs. U. Tenn., 1949-50, asst. prof., asso. prof., 1958-65; instr. industry Wharton Sch., U. Pa., 1950-51; dir. econs. program Austin Peay State Coll., 1954-56; teaching asst. labor econs. U. Wis., 1956-57, vis. prof. econs., 1963; dir. div. employment programs OEO, Office of Pres., 1965-66; prof. econs. and mgmt., dir. Inst. Labor and Indsl. Relations, U. Houston, 1966-78; prof. econs., mgmt., indsl. relations, urban life, dir. Center Indsl. Relations, Ga. State U., Atlanta, 1978—; exec. sec. Southwestern Regional Manpower Adv. Com., 1966-74; chmn. Manpower Devel. Tng. Act Adv. Com., Houston-Galveston Area, 1971-72; mem. Nat. Task Force on Unemployment Ins. and Manpower, 1972-73; mem. task force Harris County Community Action Assn., 1973-75; chmn. Tex. Employment Commn. Adv. Council, 1978; adminstrv. dir. manpower studies S.W. Africa, AID, State Dept., 1976—; dir. Houston br. Fed. Res. Bank of Dallas. Served with USMC, 1942-45. Recipient Disting. Service award Postal, Telephone and Telegraph Internat., Lima, Peru, 1966; Communication Workers Am. and Annie Gorham U. Scholarship research grantee U. Wis., 1956-58. Mem. Univ. and Coll. Labor Edn. Assn., Indsl. Relations Research Assn., Am. Acad. Polit. and Social Sci., AAUP, Am. Arbitration Assn., Nat. Acad. Arbitrators, Soc. for Profls. in Dispute Resolution, Adult Edn. Assn. U.S.A., Southwestern Council for Latin Am. Studies, Midwestern Assn. for Latin Am. Studies, Phi Kappa Phi, Delta Sigma Pi. Author: Labor Economics, 1972; Plantation Politics: The Southern Economic Heritage, 1972; Agriculture to Automation: History of the American Labor Movement, 1974. Contbr. articles to profl. jours. Home: 3370 Habersham Rd NW Atlanta GA 30305 Office: Center Indsl Relations Ga State U Univ Plaza Atlanta GA 30303

WILLIAMS, JAMES EDWARD, JR., textile mfg. co. exec.; b. Lexington, N.C., Sept. 16, 1917; s. James Edward and Pattie Sue (Smith) W.; B.S. in Commerce, U. N.C., 1940, Advanced Mgmt. Program in Bus. Adminstrn., 1965-66; m. Eleanor Larue Edwards, Dec. 31, 1941; children—Nancy Ellis (Mrs. Hersy G. Basham, III), James Hugh. Bookkeeper, clk. R.J. Reynolds Tobacco Co., Winston-Salem, N.C., 1940; salesman trainee Burroughs Adding Machine Co., Winston-Salem, 1940-41; sr. accountant Williams & Wall, C.P.A.'s, Raleigh, N.C., 1946-48; sr. accountant W.M. Russ & Co., C.P.A.'s, Raleigh, Winston-Salem, 1948-54; chief cost accountant Fieldcrest Mills, Inc., Eden, N.C., 1954-58, mgr. cost accounting, 1958-63, mgr. budgets and cost accounting, 1963-65, mgr. budgets and mill accounting, 1966-70, corporate controller, 1970—. Cubmaster, Boy Scouts Am., 1956-59; pres. Jr. High Sch. P.T.A., 1962-64. Served to maj. AUS, 1941-46. Named Boss of Year, Eden Jr. C. of C., 1969. Mem. N.C. Assn. C.P.A.'s, Financial Execs. Inst., Nat. Assn. Accountants, Eden C. of C., S.A.R., Phi Beta Kappa, Beta Gamma Sigma, Delta Sigma Pi. Presbyn. (elder, deacon, chmn. bd. deacons 1962, 66). Rotarian. Home: 335 Monticello St Eden NC 27288 Office: Fieldcrest Mills Inc Eden NC 27288

WILLIAMS, JAMES ELMO, film corp. exec.; b. Lone Wolf, Okla., Apr. 30, 1913; s. Oscar P. and Audra Odessa (Etter) W.; student public schs.; m. Lois Lorraine Cunningham, Dec. 23, 1940; children—Stacy Audra, Toby Dieter, Jody Hester. Film editor Brit. Dominions Films, Wilcox Prodns., Imperator Prodns., Imperadio Prodns., all London, 1933-38; film editor RKO Pictures, Hollywood, Calif., 1938-40, editor, 1945-47; editor-dir. Signal Corps, Wright Field, Dayton, Ohio, 1941-43, Spl. Services, L.I., N.Y. and Los Angeles, 1943-44; dir.-editor Dunn-Williams Prodns., producer-pres. Impact, TV, Inc., 1947-48; dir. TV Capitol Records, Hollywood, 1949-51; editor, Acad. award winner High Noon, 1952; dir. Lippert Films, 1953-55; dir.-editor Disney Prodns., United Artists, DFZ Prodsn., 1956-59; asso. producer The Longest Day, 20th Century Fox Corp, 1960, mng. dir. European prodn., 1961-67, producer Tora! Tora! Tora!, 1967-69, v.p. worldwide prodn., 1971-73; pres. Ibex Films, Inc., Los Angeles, 1974—, producer Sidewinder One, 1976, Caravans, 1977; guest lectr. U. So. Calif., 1956, UCLA, 1957, Orange Coast Coll., 1958, Pasadena City Coll., 1958; advisor Motion Picture Acad. Arts and Scis., 1947—. Recipient Gold Scissors award, 1952. Mem. Acad. Motion Picture Arts and Scis., Am. Cinema Editors (Spl. award 1971), Screen Dirs. Guild, Motion Picture Producers Assn. Republican. Presbyterian. Home: 956 Corsica Dr Pacific Palisades CA 90272

WILLIAMS, JAMES H., II, govt. ofcl.; b. Ocala, Fla., June 17, 1926; B.A., U. Fla., 1966; m. Louise, 1 son, 2 daus. Citrus grower, cattle rancher; mem. Fla. Senate, 1968-74; lt. gov. Fla., Tallahassee, 1975-79; dep. sec. U.S. Dept. Agr., Washington, 1979—. Served with USAAF, World War II. Recipient Allen Morris award for legis. leadership, 1973. Mem. Marion County Cattlemen's Assn. Democrat. Methodist. Office: Dept Agr 14th and Independence Ave SW Washington DC 20250*

WILLIAMS, JAMES KELLEY, fertilizer co. exec.; b. Bentonia, Miss., Mar. 29, 1934; s. James C. and Kathryn (Kelley) W.; B.S. in Chem. Engring., Ga. Inst. Tech., 1956; M.B.A., Harvard U., 1962; m. Jean Pittman, June 16, 1956; children—James Kelley, George P., Clifford C. With Continental Oil Co., Ponca City, Okla., 1956-57, Tyrone Hydraulics Co., Corinth, Miss. and Portland, Oreg., 1962-65, Independent Stave Co., Lebanon, Mo., 1966; mgr. corporate planning and devel. First Miss. Corp., Jackson, 1967-69, v.p., 1969-71, pres., 1971—; dir. Deposit Guaranty Corp., W.E. Walker Stores, Inc.; adv. bd. Deposit Guaranty Nat. Bank. Bd. dirs. United Way, Com. for Econ. Devel., Jackson; trustee Piney Woods Country Life Sch.; nat. adv. bd. Ga. Inst. Tech.; deacon Northminster Baptist Ch. Served with USAF, 1957-60. Mem. Fertilizer Inst., Young Pres.'s Orgn., Newcomen Soc., Mfg. Chemists Assn., Jackson C. of C. (dir.). Clubs: Jackson Country, River Hills, Hundred of Jackson. Home: 3830 Greentree Pl Jackson MS 39211 Office: PO Box 1249 Jackson MS 39205

WILLIAMS, JERRE STOCKTON, lawyer, educator; b. Denver, Aug. 21, 1916; s. Wayne Cullen and Lena (Day) W.; A.B., U. Denver, 1938; J.D., Columbia, 1941; m. Mary Pearl Hall, May 28, 1950; children-Jerre Stockton, Shelley Hall, Stephanie Kethley. Admitted to Colo. bar, 1941, Tex. bar, 1950, U.S. Supreme Ct. bar, 1944; instr. U. Iowa Law Sch., 1941-42; asst. prof. U. Denver Law Sch., 1946; mem. faculty U. Tex. Law Sch., Austin, 1946—, John B. Connally prof. civil jurisprudence, 1970—; mem. faculty Inst. Internat. and Comparative Law San Diego U.; mem. faculty Merton Coll. Oxford (Eng.) U., 1977, Magdalen Coll., 1979; chmn. Adminstrv. Conf. U.S., 1967-70, pub. mem., 1972-78. Labor arbitrator, bd. govs. Nat. Acad. Arbitrators, 1964-67, v.p., 1974-75; chmn. Southwestern Regional Manpower Adv. Com., 1964-66; cons. Bur. Budget, 1966-67. Served to capt. USAF, 1942-46. Mem. Internat. Soc. Labor Law and Social Legis., Am. (winner Ross Essay contest 1963, chmn. sect. adminstrv. law 1975-76), Fed., Tex. bar assns., Assn. Am. Law Schs. (pres. elect 1979). Democrat. Methodist. Author: Cases and Materials on Employees Rights, 1952; The Supreme Court Speaks, 1956. Editor-in-chief: Labor Relations and the Law, 3d edit., 1965; Constitutional Analysis, 1979. Home: 3503 Mt Barker Dr Austin TX 78731 Office: 2500 Red River St Austin TX 78705

WILLIAMS, JIM R., credit union exec.; b. Magic City, Tex., Oct. 24, 1934; s. Talmadge Monroe and Hattie E. Lois (Montgomery) W.; B.B.A. in Economics, W. Tex. State U., M.B.A., 1959; m. Ann I. Jennings, Aug. 2, 1972; children—Ronald, Denny, Stephen, Jason, Tiffini. With SBA, 1959-60; mgr. Amarillo (Tex.) AFB Credit Union, 1960-63, Govt. Employees Credit Union, San Antonio, 1963-66; asst. mgr. Tex. Central Credit Union, Dallas, 1966-68; pres., chief exec. officer Govt. Employees Credit Union, San Antonio, 1968-79; pres. Credit Union Nat. Assn., Madison, Wis., 1979—, GECU Services Corp., San Antonio Area Central Credit Union; chmn. Financial Data Services Corp.; vice chmn. Tex. Share Guaranty Credit Union; dir. CUNA Service Group, CU Bank Shares, Inc., CU Trust Co.; mem. Tex. Credit Union Commn., 1971-77. Bd. dirs. Beautify San Antonio Assn., 1974-76. Served with AUS, 1953-55. Recipient letter appreciation Office Sec. Def., 1974. Mem. Am. Mgmt. Assn., Adminstrv. Mgmt. Soc. (chpt. dir.), Credit Union Execs. Mgrs. Soc. (charter), Credit Union Nat. Assn. and Affiliates (chmn. 1976-78), Tex. Credit Union League (chmn. 1974-75), Air Force Assn. (exec. com., v.p. awards com. San Antonio chpt. 1974; Orgn. of Year award Alamo chpt. 1973, 77), Greater San Antonio C. of C. (chmn. sub-com., mil. affairs council 1972-75), Assn. U.S. Army (chpt. dir. 1976-77). Home: 7016 Applewood Dr Madison WI 53711 Office: PO Box 431 Madison WI 53701

WILLIAMS, JOAN LEE, educator; b. Clifford, Ill., Sept. 24, 1930; d. Lawrence Singleton and Mabel Marie (Nance) Williams; B.S., So. Ill. U., 1954, M.S., 1960, Ph.D., 1963; postgrad. Ind. U., 1961-62. Tchr., North Bend Sch., Carterville, Ill., 1948-50, Colp (Ill.) Standard Sch., 1950-53, Herrin (Ill.) City Schs., 1954-60; instr. edn. So. Ill. U., Carbondale, 1960-63; asst. prof. edn. U. Conn., Storrs, 1963-64; faculty Ball State U., Muncie, Ind., 1964—, prof. elementary edn., 1975—; lectr., cons. in field. Normal Sch. scholar, 1947-54, NDEA fellow, 1960-62; faculty research grantee Ball State U., 1970-71. Mem.

Internat. Reading Assn., NEA, Nat. Council Tchrs. English, Ind. Tchrs. Assn., Assn. Supervision and Curriculum Devel., AAUP, Ind. Reading Profs., Pi Lambda Theta, Kappa Delta Pi. Home: 2020 N Ball Ave Muncie IN 47304 Office: Ball State U McKinley Ave Muncie IN 47306

WILLIAMS, JOHN, guitarist; b. Melbourne, Australia, Apr. 24, 1941; studied with Andre Segovia at Accademia Musicale Chigiana, Siena, Italy; attended Royal Coll. Music, London. London debut, 1958; Am. debut, 1963; has since toured widely in N. Am., Europe, Japan and Soviet Union; numerous recs. as solo Guitarist and with Phila. and English chamber orchs., as well as duets with Julian Bream; premiered guitar concertos by Andre Previn, Stephen Dodgson and Torroda; tchr. master classes in Spain and Eng. Recipient Grammy award, 1973. Office: care Shaw Concerts Inc 1995 Broadway New York NY 10023*

WILLIAMS, JOHN A., author; b. Jackson, Miss., 1925; grad. Syracuse U.; LL.D., Southeastern Mass. U., 1978; m. Lorrain Isaac; 1 son, Adam; children by previous marriage—Gregory, Dennis. Started writing poetry during World War II in Pacific; later employed by Vanity Pub. House, advt. agy., Am. Com. on Africa (all N.Y.C.). Lectr., Coll. City N.Y.; guest writer Sarah Lawrence Coll.; distinguished prof. English La Guardia Community Coll., 1973-74, 74-75; regents lectr. U. Calif., Santa Barbara, 1972; vis. prof. Boston U., 1978-79. Recipient Centennial medal for outstanding achievement Syracuse U., 1970. Author: (novels) The Angry Ones, 1960; Night Song, 1961; Sissie, 1963; The Man Who Cried I Am, 1967; Sons of Darkness, Sons of Light, 1969; Captain Blackman, 1972; Mothersill and the Foxes, 1975; The Junior Bachelor Society, 1976, also 7 vols. of non-fiction, vol. of poems, 2 anthologies. Home: 693 Forest Ave Teaneck NJ 07666

WILLIAMS, JOHN CLIFTON, educator; b. June 19, 1928; B.A., Baylor U., 1952, M.P.S., U. Colo., 1954; Ph.D., Purdue U., 1958. Asso., Shepherd Assos., 1955-58, staff psychologist, 1958-59; instr. Baylor U., Waco, Tex., 1954-56, asst. prof., 1957-58, asso. prof., 1959-62, prof., 1962-67, chmn. dept., 1962-64, dean of grad. sch., 1967-69, adminstrv. v.p., 1968-69, prof. mgmt., 1972—, H.R. Gibson prof. mgmt. devel., 1975—; indsl. psychologist, 1969-72. Address: Route 1 Box 53 McGregor TX 76657

WILLIAMS, JOHN CORNELIUS, lawyer; b. Lee Valley, Tenn., Jan. 24, 1903; s. Hugh and Kitty (Lawrence) W.; A.B., Wofford Coll., 1927; LL.B., U. S.C., 1931; 1 son by former marriage, John Cornelius; m. 2d, Darthey I. Black, Aug. 12, 1954; 1 dau., Kitty. Prin. Campobello High Sch., Spartanburg County, S.C., 1927-28; admitted to S.C. bar, 1931; practiced in Spartanburg, 1931-61; U.S. atty. Western Dist. S.C., 1951-54, 61-68; partner law firm Williams and Williams, Spartanburg, 1968—. Mem. S. C. Legislature, 1931-32, 49-50. Served to col. U.S. Army, 1940-46. Mem. S.C., Spartanburg County (past pres.) bar assns., 4th U.S. Jud. Conf., V.F.W. (past comdr. S.C.), Am. Legion, 40 and 8, Blue Key, Pi Kappa Delta, Phi Kappa Sigma, Phi Alpha Delta. Democrat. Baptist. Club: Masons (32 deg.). Home: 318 S Park Dr Spartanburg SC 29302 Office: 186 W Main St Spartanburg SC 29301

WILLIAMS, JOHN GILMORE, lawyer; b. N.Y.C., Mar. 12, 1914; s. Andrew M. and Helen (Ogden) W.; grad. St. Paul's Sch., Concord, N.H., 1932; A.B. magna cum laude, Princeton, 1936; LL.B. cum laude, Harvard, 1940; m. Phyllis Gerry, July 8, 1939; children—John Gilmore, Eve Williams Puloka, Jessie Williams Gilbert. Admitted to Pa. bar, 1940, since practiced in Phila.; partner firm Drinker, Biddle & Reath, 1948—. Trustee Phila. Sav. Fund Soc.; dir. Pitcairn Co. Bd. dirs. Phila. Hosp. Survey Com., 1964-67, pres., 1968-71. Mem. Pa. Hort. Soc. (pres. 1965-68), Zool. Soc. Phila. (pres. 1971-76). Served to lt. comdr. USNR, 1942-47. Mem. Phi Beta Kappa. Home: 831 Black Rock Rd Gladwyne PA 19035 Office: 1100 Phila Nat Bank Bldg Philadelphia PA 19107

WILLIAMS, JOHN GROUILLE, JR., naval officer; b. Portland, Oreg., July 24, 1924; s. John Grouille and Julia Alice (Hoare) W.; B.S., U.S. Naval Acad., 1946; m. Dorothy Marie Trondsen, June 6, 1946; children—John G., Curtis B., Trond R., Barbara C., Brongwyn K. Commd. ensign U.S. Navy, 1946, advanced through grades to rear adm., 1972; submarine officer, 1949—, comdg. officer U.S.S. Sterlet, 1960-61, U.S.S. Haddo, 1962-66, U.S.S. Daniel Webster, 1966-68; logistics dep. submarine force Atlantic staff, 1968-71; comdr. Submarine Squardron 16, Spain, 1971-72; chief Navy sect. Joint U.S. Mil. Mission for Aid to Turkey, Ankara, 1972-74; comdr. submarine group 5, 1974-77; asst. dept. chief naval ops. for submarine warfare, Dept. Navy, Washington, 1977-78, dir. gen. planning and programming div., 1978—. Decorated Legion of Merit. Presbyterian. Home: 2322 Fort Scott Dr Arlington VA 22202 also Ilwaco Washington DC Office: OP 90 Navy Dept Washington DC 20350

WILLIAMS, JOHN HORTER, civil engr., diversified co. exec.; b. Havana, Cuba, Aug. 17, 1918; s. Charles P. and Alice Magruder (Dyer) W.; B.S., Yale, 1940; m. Emily Alice Ijams, June 6, 1942 (dec.); children—John H., Burch I., S. Miller; m. 2d, Joanne Harwell Simpson. With Williams Companies, Tulsa, 1940-42, 46-50, pres., dir., 1950-70, chmn., chief exec. officer, 1971-78, now dir.; dir. Bank of Okla., Crutcher Resources Corp., N.Y. Stock Exchange, Penn Central Corp., Central & S.W. Corp. Served with USNR, 1942-46. Decorated Order of Condor of Andes (Bolivia); named to Okla. Hall of Fame, 1977. Registered profl. engr., Okla., Minn. Mem. ASCE, Yale Engring. Assn. Office: 1 Williams Center Tulsa OK 74103

WILLIAMS, JOHN RODNEY, polit. scientist, educator; b. Detroit, Nov. 21, 1919; s. Ralph Hill and Myrtle Anna (Ryan) W.; A.B. summa cum laude, Lawrence Coll., 1944; M.A., Johns Hopkins, 1947; Ph.D., Duke, 1951; postgrad. (Haynes fellow) London (Eng.) Sch. Econs. and Polit. Sci., 1951-52; m. Madeleine Louise Josephine Cremilliac, Aug. 28, 1952; children—Jacques Ralph Andre, Mark Thinh Tien. Instr. polit. sci. Wellesley Coll., spring 1947, 48-49; mem. faculty W.Va. U., Morgantown, 1949—, prof. polit. sci., 1961—, chmn. dept., 1961-72, coordinator honors program, 1972—, mem. univ. senate, 1974—; columnist Morgantown Dominion Post; Fulbright research fellow Australian Nat. U., Canberra, 1958-60; vis. prof. polit. sci. Waynesburg Coll., 1963-64, Fayette Campus of Pa. State U., part time, 1967-68; lectr. polit. sci. Pa. State U., summer 1966; acad. vis. London Sch. Econs. and Polit. Sci., 1972. Mem. Monongalia County Com. UN. Vice pres. Suncrest Lake Assn. Mem. Am. W.V.A. (v.p. 1967-68, pres. 1968-69), Canadian polit. sci. assns., Internat. Platform Assn., Australasian Polit. Studies Assn., Conservative and Unionist Assn., Am. Acad. Polit. and Social Sci., AAUP, Australian Inst. Polit. Sci., Univ. Profs. for Acad. Order, Nat. Coll. Honors Council, Am. Friends London Sch. Econs., Phi Beta Kappa, Pi Sigma Alpha, Delta Tau Delta. Episcopalian. Author: The Conservative Party of Canada, 1920-1949, 1956; John Latham and the Conservative Recovery from Defeat, 1969. Contbr. articles to profl. publs. Home: 1498 Eastern Ave Morgantown WV 26505 Office: Dept Polit Sci WVa U Morgantown WV 26506. *One of the most important contributions to my life and philosophy came from Elias Michael School, in St. Louis, where, in addition to learning from dedicated teachers in an atmosphere of encouragement, I started in a wheelchair, moved through crutches, and finally walked unaided. The positive spirit of the teachers and therapists has frequently been an inspiration, and the school motto of Elias Michael "Service, Sportsmanship, Courage" has remained my guide through the years.*

WILLIAMS, JOHN T., composer, condr.; b. Flushing, N.Y., Feb. 8, 1932; attended Juilliard Sch. Composer film scores: The Secret Ways, 1961, Diamond Head, 1962, None But the Brave, 1965, How to Steal a Million, 1966, Valley of the Dolls, 1967, The Cowboys, 1972, The Poseidon Adventure, 1972, Tom Sawyer, 1973, Earthquake, 1974, The Towering Inferno, 1974, Jaws, 1975, The Eiger Sanction, 1975, Family Plot, 1976, Midway, 1976, The Missouri Breaks, 1976, Raggedy Ann and Andy, 1977, Black Sunday, 1977, Star Wars, 1977, Close Encounters of the 3d Kind, 1977, The Fury, 1978, Jaws 2, 1976, Superman, 1978, Dracula, 1979; condr. Boston Pops Orch., 1980—. Recipient Emmy award for outstanding achievement in music composition for a spl. program Jane Eyre, 1972, Grammy award best original score for motion picture or TV spl. Jaws, 1976, Grammy awards for Star Wars: best instrumental composition, best pop instrumental recording, best original score written for motion picture or TV spl., 1978, Golden Globe award, 1978. Address: care Boston Symphony Orch 301 Massachusetts Ave Boston MA 02115*

WILLIAMS, JOSEPH DALTON, pharm. mfg. co. exec.; b. Washington, Pa., Aug. 15, 1926; s. Joseph Dalton and Jane (Day) W.; B.Sc. in Pharmacy, U. Nebr., 1950, D.Pharmacy (hon.), 1978; m. Mildred E. Bellaire, June 28, 1973; children—Terri Williams, Daniel Williams. Pres., Parke-Davis Co., Detroit, 1973-76; pres. pharm. group Warner-Lambert Co., Morris Plains, N.J., 1976-77, pres. Internat. Group, 1977-79, pres., dir. Warner-Lambert Corp., 1979—; dir. Fidelity Union Bank. Served with USNR, 1943-46. Mem. Pharm. Mfrs. Assn., Am. Pharm. Assn., N.J. Pharm. Assn., Am. Soc. Hosp. Pharmacists Research and Edn. Found. Clubs: Met. (N.Y.C.); Baltusrol Golf (Springfield, N.J.). Office: 201 Tabor Rd Morris Plains NJ 07950

WILLIAMS, JOSEPH HILL, diversified industry exec.; b. Tulsa, June 2, 1933; s. David Rogerson and Martha Reynolds (Hill) W.; diploma St. Paul's Sch., 1952; B.A., Yale, 1956, M.A. (hon.), 1977; postgrad. Sch. Pipeline Tech. U. Tex., 1960; children—Joseph Hill Jr., Peter B., James C.; m. Terese T. Ross, May. 7, 1977; stepchildren—Margot Ross, Jennifer Ross. Field employee domestic constrn. div. Williams Cos., Tulsa, 1958-60, project coordinator engring. div., 1960-61, project supt., Iran, 1961-62, asst. resident mgr., Iran, 1962-64, project mgr., 1964-65, resident mgr., 1965-67, exec. v.p., 1968—, pres., chief operating officer, 1971-78, chmn., chief exec. officer, 1979—; dir., dep. chmn. Fed. Res. Bank of Kansas City; dir. Parker Drilling Co. Bd. dirs. Industries for Tulsa, Tulsa Area United Way, Okla. C. of C.; mem. adv. com. Jr. Achievement; fellow, trustee Yale Corp. Served with AUS, 1956-58. Mem. Am. Petroleum Inst. (dir.), Young President's Orgn., Council on Fgn. Relations, Nat. Petroleum Council, Conf. Met. Tulsa C. of C. (dir.). Episcopalian. Clubs: Southern Hills Country, Summit, Tulsa, Yale sec.) (Tulsa); Springdale Hall (Camden, S.C.); Augusta (Ga.) Nat. Golf; Links (N.Y.); Grandfather Golf and Country (Linville, N.C.). Office: One Williams Center PO Box 2400 Tulsa OK 74103

WILLIAMS, JOSEPH LEON, utility exec.; b. Omaha, Jan. 2, 1921; s. Joseph Leon and Eva Lorraine (Helms) W.; B.S. in Elec. Engring., Oreg. State U., 1948; grad. Exec. Devel. Program, Stanford U., 1963; m. Patricia Ann Eng, Dec. 21, 1978. With Portland Gen. Electric Co. (Oreg.), 1948—, v.p. engring. and constrn., 1971, exec. v.p., 1977—. Past chmn. bd. Jr. Achievement Columbia Empire; pres. Pacific Internat. Livestock Exposition, 1969-70. Served with AUS, 1942-46. Registered profl. engr., Oreg. Mem. Nat. Mgmt. Assn. (nat. dir., past chpt. pres.; Silver Knight Mgmt. award 1978), Nat. Soc. Profl. Engrs., N.W. Electric Light and Power Assn., Electric Club Oreg., Portland C. of C. Republican. Methodist. Clubs: Aero of Oreg., Masons, Order Demolay (hon. Legion of Honor). Office: 121 SW Salmon St Portland OR 97204

WILLIAMS, JOSEPH RICHARD, hotel and motel exec.; b. Salt Lake City, Nov. 5, 1924; Central Wash. Coll.; postgrad. U. Utah, 1945-47; m. Lucille Timms; children—Susan, Steven, Summer, Stace. Builder Holiday Motel, Salt Lake City, 1948, Town House Motel, Salt Lake City, 1961: founder Friendship Inns Internat., Salt Lake City, 1963, pres., 1963—. Served with USAAF, 1943-44. Named to Hospitality Hall of Fame, 1972; recipient award Motel Assn. Am., 1975, Motel-Hotel Women Am., 1973. Mem. Nat. Innkeeping Assn. (v.p. 1974), Utah-Nev. Hotel-Motel Assn. (pres. 1968, 77). Mormon. Author: World of Friendship, 1976. Home: 2662 Comanche Dr Salt Lake City UT 84108 Office: 739 S 4th West Salt Lake City UT 84101

WILLIAMS, JUDSON FINLON, savs. and loan assn. exec.; b. Fort Worth, Tex., June 19, 1913; s. Samuel Jones Tilden and Emily Beaty (Clugston) W.; B.A., Hardin Simmons U., 1934; B.Journalism, M.A., U. Mo., 1940; Ph.D., U. Tex., 1952; m. Jackie Roe, June 25, 1941; children—Judith (Mrs. Michael Ridley), Jeanne (Mrs. William G. Fowler), Jerith (Mrs. Victor P. Clarence, Jr.), Judson Charles. High sch. prin., coach, Rochester, Tex., 1935-36, Grandfalls, Tex., 1936-39; dir. pub. relations, instr. journalism Tex. Coll. Mines, 1940-52; dean students, prof., chmn. dept. journalism-radio-TV, Tex. Western Coll., 1942-56; v.p., dir. White House Dept. Stores, El Paso, Tex., 1956—; v.p., dir. First Savs. & Loan Assn., El Paso, 1957—; pres. Uptrends, Inc., 1969—; chmn. bd. So. Union Prodn. Co., Inc., 1979—; dir. Ark. Western Gas Co., So. Union Gas Co., Bus. Products and Services, State Nat. Bank El Paso, Pan Nat. Group, Inc., Mountain Bell Telephone Co., Aero Systems Inc., Farah Mfg. Internat. Inc., Energy Found. of Tex. Inc.; bd. advisers Mountain States Telephone Co., 1958-63, 71—. Cons. Hogg Found., 1946—, U. Tex.; v.p., dir. S.W. Sun Country Assn., 1960-63; bd. dirs., mem. exec. com. Tex. Municipal League Cities, 1963, pres., 1967-69; exec. com. urban affairs So. Conf. Council State Govts., 1967—; pres. Southwestern Sun Carnival Assn., 1957, El Paso County Bd. Devel., 1960-62, El Paso Indsl. Devel. Corp., 1964, United Fund El Paso, 1961. Mayor of El Paso, 1963-69. Bd. dirs. Lee Moore Children's Home; bd. regents Tex. Tech. U. Named El Paso's Young Man of Year, 1946, El Paso's Outstanding Citizen, 1966; recipient Medallion of Merit, U. Tex., 1967, Headliner of Year award by Press, 1967, Outstanding Citizen award Tex. Inst. Traffic Engrs.; elected to El Paso Hall of Fame El Paso County Hist. Soc., 1973; named Outstanding Citizen Mil. Orders World Wars, 1975. Mem. Acad. Polit. Sci., Nat. League Cities, El Paso Rancheros (past pres.), El Paso C. of C. (pres. 1962), Sigma Delta Chi, Phi Delta Kappa, Kappa Tau Alpha, Alpha Phi Gamma, Alpha Epsilon Rho. Presbyn. (trustee). Clubs: Touchdown (past pres.), El Paso, El Paso Country, Coronado Country (El Paso). Kiwanian. Home: 4200 O'Keefe Dr El Paso TX 79902 Office: 506 N Mesa El Paso TX 79901

WILLIAMS, KARL C., lawyer; b. Egan, Ill., Oct. 2, 1902; s. Aaron Otis and Alma (Glynn) W.; A.B., Dartmouth, 1923; LL.B., Harvard, 1926; LL.D. (hon.), Rockford Coll., 1959, Coll. Gt. Falls, 1966; m. Mary E. Commons, May 10, 1934; children—Judith Glynn, Meredith. Admitted Mass. bar, 1926, Ill. bar, 1927; asst. states atty. Winnebago County, Ill., 1927-32; master in chancery Winnebago County, 1940-42; spl. asst. atty. gen. Ill., 1943-49; mem. law firm Williams, McCarthy, Kinley, Rudy & Picha and predecessor firm. Trustee Rockford Coll., 1939—, chmn., 1949-70. Fellow Am. Bar Found. (chmn. fellows 1969-70, treas. 1972-75), Am. Coll. Trial Lawyers; mem. Bar Assn. 7th Fed. Circuit (dir. 1967-76, 78—), Am. (ho. of dels. 1949-51, 54-56, 60-77; bd. govs. 1968-72; treas. 1972-75; chmn. com. jurisprudence and law reform 1958-59, 62; chmn. com. clients security fund 1961-68, chmn. com. on scope and correlation 1963-64, chmn. consortium on legal services and the pub. 1975-76), Ill. (bd. govs. 1944-51, pres. 1954-55), Winnebago County (pres. 1954-55) bar assns., Am. Judicature Soc. (dir. 1953-56), Nat. Conf. of Bar. Pres. (mem. exec. council 1954-, chmn. 1958-59), Ill. Soc. Trial Lawyers. Republican. Methodist. Rotarian. Clubs: Union League, University (Chgo.); Country, University (Rockford). Home: 2449 Clinton Rd Rockford IL 61103 Office: Talcott Bldg Rockford IL 61101

WILLIAMS, KENNETH RAYNOR, univ. pres.; b. Norfolk, Va., Aug. 16, 1912; s. Kenneth Raynor and Vandelia (Perry) W.; A.B., Morehouse Coll., 1933, D.H.L.; M.A., Boston U., 1936, S.T.B., 1952, Ph.D., 1962; LL.D. (hon.), Wake Forest Coll., 1963; LL.D., So. Ill. U.; m. Edythe Williams, June 7, 1938; children—Kenneth Raynor III, Ronald, Norman. Ordained to ministry Baptist Ch., 1936; pastor, Winston-Salem, N.C., 1936-64; instr. history and religion Winston-Salem State U., 1936-61, pres., 1961—, chancellor, 1972-77. Former mem. bd. Citizens Coalition; mem. Winston-Salem Bd. Aldermen. Bd. dirs. Forsyth County A.R.C., Gallaudet Coll.; mem. council Winston-Salem/Forsyth County Am. Revolution Bicentennial Commn. Served as chaplain AUS, 1942-46. Mem. Am. Assn. Colls. Tchr. Edn. (rep. 1964-66, dir.), Nat. Council for Tchr. Edn. (dir. 1968—), Winston-Salem C. of C. (dir.). Rotarian. Home: 1015 Rich Ave Winston Salem NC 27101

WILLIAMS, LANGBOURNE MEADE, trustee; b. Richmond, Va., Feb. 5, 1903; s. Langbourne Meade and Susanne Catherine (Nolting) W.; A.B., U. Va., 1924; M.B.A., Grad. Sch. Bus. Adminstrn. Harvard, 1926; m. Elizabeth Goodrich Stillman, 1930 (dec. 1956); m. 2d, Frances Pinckney Breckinridge, 1959. With Lee, Higginson & Co., N.Y.C., 1926-27; asso. John L. Williams & Sons, Richmond, 1927-30; v.p., treas. Freeport Minerals Co., 1930-33, pres. 1933-58, chmn., 1957-69, chmn. exec. com., 1969-73; dir. Texaco, Inc., 1958-74, B.F. Goodrich Co., 1938-60, So. Railway, 1957-65; trustee Bank of N.Y., 1941-57. First dir. industry div. ECA (Marshall Plan), Paris, France, 1948; councillor, former chmn. The Conf. Bd. Mem. vis. com. Harvard Bus. Sch., 1933-64; hon. mem. Bus. Council. Hon. mem. bd. govs. Soc. N.Y. Hosp.; trustee George C. Marshall Research Found.; Am. Ch. Inst. for Negroes, 1936-57, Va. Inst. Sci. Research, 1959-69; mem. bd. visitors U. Va., 1963-68, Tulane U., 1954-61. Mem. Harvard Alumni Assn. (past dir.), Va. Hist. Soc. (trustee), Soc. of Cincinnati, Assn. Preservation Va. Antiquities, Phi Beta Kappa, Omicron Delta Kappa, Delta Psi. Episcopalian. Clubs: Century, Union (N.Y.C.); Metropolitan (Washington); Commonwealth (Richmond). Home: Retreat Rapidan VA 22733 Office: Rapidan VA 22733

WILLIAMS, LAUREN S., brewing co. exec.; b. Milford, Conn., Aug. 17, 1937; s. Gordon Spencer and Sylvia (Lerner) W.; B.S. in Indsl. Adminstrn., Yale U., 1959; M.B.A., U. Chgo., 1961; m. Judith Krysto, Apr. 25, 1965; children—Andrew, Scott, Jeffrey. Successively corp. planner, asst. brand mgr., brand mgr. new products, asst. to dir. packaging services, mgr. fin. relations, asst. to pres. Philip Morris Inc., 1964-71, v.p., 1978—; v.p. corp. planning Miller Brewing Co., Milw., 1971, v.p. sales, 1972, v.p. mktg., 1973-78, exec. v.p., 1978—, also dir. Bd. dirs. Milw. Children's Hosp., Wis. Soc. Prevention Blindness. Served with USAR, 1961-67. Named Outstanding Corp. Mktg. Exec., Gallagher Report, 1977. Clubs: Milw. Athletic, Milw. Country. Office: 3939 W Highland Blvd Milwaukee WI 53201

WILLIAMS, LAWRENCE EUGENE, songwriter; b. Riverside, Calif., Aug. 17, 1949; s. Charles Wafford and Myra Evalena (A'neals) W.; student Pasadena City Coll., 1968-70; m. Bobbi Jean Becerra, Aug. 2, 1969; children—Justin Charles, Evin Andres. Vocalist and lead guitar The Second Helping, 1965-68, Gold, 1968-71; equipment mgr. Neil Diamond, 1973-77; songwriter Bicycle Music Co., Hollywood, Calif., 1974—; composer, lyricist: Let Your Love Flow, 1976 (Broadcast Music Inc. award for most performed song of yr. 1976), Gentle To Your Senses, 1977. Mem. Broadcast Music Inc. Home: 306 N St Crispen Brea CA 92621 Office: 8756 Holloway Dr Los Angeles CA 90069

WILLIAMS, LAWRENCE HARVEY, army officer; b. Salem, Mass., May 20, 1922; s. Harry and Irene (Morrison) W.; B.S. Law, U. Minn., 1947; J.D., U. Colo., 1948; grad. Indsl. Coll. Armed Forces; m. Margaret J. Anderson, May 7, 1949; 1 dau., Susan E. Commd. 2d lt. U.S. Army, advanced through grades to maj. gen., 1975; admitted to Colo. bar, 1948, U.S. Supreme Ct. bar, 1953; staff judge adv. 3d Armored Div., 1961, III Corps, 1967, Mil. Assistance command, Vietnam, 1969; asst. judge adv. gen. for mil. law Army Dept., Washington, 1971-75, asst. judge adv. gen. Army Dept., 1975-79; ret., 1979. Decorated D.S.M., Legion of Merit with 2 oak leaf clusters, Bronze Star, Air medal with 4 oak leaf clusters. Mem. Am., Fed. bar assns., Judge Advs. Assn. Home: 2425 N Woodrow St Arlington VA 22207

WILLIAMS, LEA EVERARD, educator; b. Milw., July 25, 1924; s. William Everard and Paula Herndon (Pratt) W.; B.A., Cornell U., 1950; M.A., Harvard U., 1952, Ph.D., 1956; m. Daisy Shen, Sept. 15, 1949; children—Adrienne Paula, William Herndon. With U.S. Fgn. Service, Chungking, China, 1944-45, Am. vice consul, Shanghai, 1945-48; with Brown U., 1956—, prof. Asian history, 1969-76, prof. history, 1976—, dir. East Asia Lang. and Area Center, 1969—; vis. prof. history U. Singapore, 1961-63; vis. prof. Asian affairs Fletcher Sch., 1964-65; lectr. fgn. service U.S. Dept. State. Served with U.S. Army, 1943. Social Sci. Research fellow, 1957; Fulbright-Hays fellow, 1966-67; Am. Council Learned Socs. fellow, 1969. Mem. The South Seas Soc., Assn. Asian Studies, Royal Asiatic Soc. (Malayan br.), Koninklijk Instiuut voor Taal, Land-en Volkenkunde, Phi Beta Kappa. Clubs: Bristol Yacht (R.I.), Catboat Assn., Am. Club (Singapore), Royal Singapore Yacht, S.A.R. Author: Overseas Chinese Nationalism, 1960; The Future of the Overseas Chinese in Southeast Asia, 1966; Southeast Asia: A History, 1976; Editor, transl.: The Origins of the Modern Chinese Movement in Indonesia, 1969. Home: 73 Transit St Providence RI 02906 Office: East Asia Language and Area Center Box 1850 Brown University Providence RI 02912

WILLIAMS, LESLIE HOWARD, JR., lawyer; b. Lamesa, Tex., Oct. 2, 1942; s. Leslie Howard and Irene Hester W.; B.B.A., Tex. Tech. U., 1966; J.D., St. Mary's U., 1969; m. Linda McCall, May 5, 1965; children—Reagan Marshall, Ryan Dylan. Admitted to Tex. bar, 1969, Kans. bar, 1975; mem. firm Culton, Morgan, Britain & White, Amarillo, Tex., 1969-74; corp. counsel Mo. Beef Packers, Inc., Amarillo, 1974-75; v.p., sec., gen. counsel MBPXL Corp., Wichita, Kans., 1975—; dir. Marcom, Inc., Williams Farms, Inc. Bd. dirs. YMCA, Wichita. Mem. Am. Bar Assn., Tex. Bar Assn., Kans. Bar Assn., Amarillo Jr. Bar Assn. (past pres.), Kappa Sigma, Delta Theta Phi. Republican. Presbyterian. Office: 2901 N Mead Wichita KS 67201

WILLIAMS, LESLIE PEARCE, educator; b. Harmon-on Hudson, N.Y., Sept. 8, 1927; s. George and Addie Adelia (Williams) Greenberg; B.A., Cornell U., 1949, Ph.D., 1952; m. Sylvia Irene

Alessandrini, Sept. 4, 1949; children—David Rhys, Alison Ruth, Adam Jonathan, Sarah Lucille. Instr. history Yale U., 1952-56; asso. historian Nat. Found. for Infantile Paralysis, N.Y.C., 1956-57; asst. prof. U. Del., 1956-59; asst. prof. history Cornell U., 1960-62, asso. prof., 1962-65, prof., 1965-71, John Stambaugh prof. history of sci., 1971—, chmn. dept. history, 1969-74. Served with USNR, 1945-46. NSF fellow, 1959-60. Mem. Am. Hist. Assn., History Sci. Soc., Royal Institution of Great Britain, Academie internationale d'histoire des sciences. Democrat. Author: Michael Faraday, A Biography, 1965; The Origins of Field Theory, 1967; Album of Science: The Nineteenth Century, 1978; (with Henry John Steffens) A History of Science in Western Civilization, 3 vols., 1978. Editor: The Selected Correspondence of Michael Faraday, 2 vols., 1972; Relativity Theory: Its Origin and Impact on Modern Thought, 1968; (with B. Tierney and D. Kagan) Great Issues in Western Civilization, 2 vols., 1968. Home: 218 Iradell Rd Ithaca NY 14850 Office: Department of History Cornell University Ithaca NY 14853

WILLIAMS, LEWIS CROXTON, investment banker; b. Cleve., Oct. 26, 1912; s. Lewis Blair and Helen (Croxton) W.; B.S., Yale, 1934; M.B.A., Harvard, 1936; m. Lydia Field Emmet, Sept. 18, 1937; children—Lewis Scott, Philip Hone, Temple Emmet, Helen Croxton II. Vice pres. Nat. City Bank of Cleve., 1942-51; exec. v.p., dir. Merrill, Turben & Co., Inc., Cleve., 1951-63, pres., 1963-65; gen. partner Prescott & Co., Cleve., 1965-68; gen. partner Prescott, Merrill, Turben & Co. (merger Prescott & Co. and Merrill, Turben & Co., Inc.), 1968-69; with Goodbody & Co., Cleve., 1969-71, Merrill Lynch Pierce Fenner & Smith, 1971-77, Smith Barney Harris Upham & Co., 1977—. Trustee Univ. Hosp., Cleve., John Huntington Poly. Trust, John Huntington Fund for Edn.; pres. Cleve. Mus. Art. 1971—. Home: 14000 County Line Rd Chagrin Falls OH 44022 Office: Bond Ct 1300 E 9th St Cleveland OH 44113

WILLIAMS, LINWOOD ROGER, financial and investment co. exec.; b. Balt., Apr. 3, 1918; s. Linwood Robert and Mabel (Binnix) W.; B.A., Duke U., 1940; B.A., Columbus Sch. Law, 1942; m. Jeanette Harris, Dec. 25, 1941; children—Randolph, Carole Williams Segal. With Treasury Dept., 1941-46, Dept. State, 1946-51, Exec. Office of President, 1951-56, Export Import Bank, 1956-61, Interam. Devel. Bank, 1961-62; v.p. GTE Internat. Co., 1962-65, Beloit Internat. Corp., 1964-68; v.p., treas. Gen. Telephone & Electronics Internat. Inc., Stamford, Conn., 1968-76; pres. Gen. Energy Corp., 1977—, Internat. Investment and Fin. Advisors, 1977—; mem. internat. adv. bd. dirs. Nat. Export Council. Clubs: Congl. Country (Washington); Siwanoy Country (Bronxville); Indian Creek Yacht and Country (Kilmarnock, Va.). Address: Return Bend Weems VA 22576

WILLIAMS, LLOYD PYRON, educator; b. Dallas, Sept. 1, 1918; s. Samuel Alfred and Leda (Nash) W.; B.S. in History, North Tex. State Coll., 1940, M.S. in Philosophy of Edn., 1941; Ph.D. in History and Philosophy of Edn., U. Tex., 1951; m. Louise Scott Mackenzie, Apr. 11, 1942; children—David Nash, Douglas Stuart, Chesley Llewellyn, Lloyd Prescott. Faculty, Ohio State U., Columbus, 1948-54, Muskingum (Ohio) Coll., 1954-56, U. Okla., Norman, 1956—, David Ross Boyd prof. history and philosophy of edn., 1968—. Vis. prof. Mich. State U., U. Mo., U. Ill., U. Ariz. Recipient Distinguished Teaching award U. Okla., 1966. Ford Found. fellow Harvard, 1953-54. Mem. Southwestern Philosophy of Edn. Soc., Okla. Edn. Assn., Phi Delta Kappa. Review editor Jour. of Thought, 1969—. Contbr. articles to profl. jours. Home: PO Box 266 Washington OK 73093

WILLIAMS, LOIS VIRGINIA, ret. educator; b. Phila., June 29, 1913; d. John L. and Estelle (Bohanan) Williams; A.B. summa cum laude, Beaver Coll., 1935; M.A., U. Pa., 1939; Ph.D., Johns Hopkins, 1946; postgrad. Am. Acad. in Rome, 1947-48. Tchr. Latin and French, Montrose Sch. for Girls, 1942-43; instr. classics Juniata Coll., Huntingdon, Pa., 1943-47; faculty State U. N.Y., Albany, 1948-79, prof. classics, 1964-79. Fellow Am. Acad. in Rome, 1947-48. Mem. Am. Philol. Assn., Archael. Inst. Am., Am. Classical League, Classical Assn. N.Y., AAUP, Home: 48 Providence McKownville NY 12203

WILLIAMS, LOUIS ALVIN, naval officer; b. Ypsilanti, Mich., Aug. 26, 1931; s. Elijah Mac and Iva Lee (Clinkscales) W.; B.S. in Bus. Adminstrn., U.S. Naval Post Grad. Sch., 1975; m. Faye Williams, Sept. 3, 1955; children—Ivan, Kirk (dec.). Enlisted in U.S. Navy, 1952, commd. naval aviator, 1954, advanced through grades to rear adm., 1979; assigned various squadrons and aircraft carriers, 1954-75; comdr. officer Naval Air Sta., Agana, Guam, 1975-77; dep. dir. aviation programs Navy Dept., Washington, 1977-78; comdr. tng. command U.S. Atlantic Fleet, Norfolk, Va., 1978—. Decorated Air medal (2), Navy Commendation medal (2), Joint Service Commendation medal (2). Home and Office: 838 Harriet St Ypsilanti MI 48197

WILLIAMS, LOUIS GRESSETT, educator, biologist; b. Owensboro, Ky., Oct. 28, 1913; s. Walter Wiatt and Ella Mae (Lohrfink) W.; A.B., Marshall U., 1937; M.A., Duke, 1940, Ph.D., 1948; m. Dorothy Belle Huntley. Asst. prof. botany U. N.C., Chapell Hill, 1948; asso. prof. biology Furman U., Greenville, S.C., 1948-57; in charge aquatic biology program Nat. Water Quality Network, Taft San. Engring. Center, Cin., 1957-65; in charge plankton biology program Nat. Water Quality Lab., Duluth, Minn., 1965-67; prof. biology U. Ala., University, 1967—. Cons. water pollution, radionuclide contamination. Served to lt. USNR, 1941-45. Carnegie grantee, 1947-48; Ford Found. fellow, 1952. Fellow AAAS, Ecol. Soc. Am., Assn. Southeastern Biologists; mem. Bot. Soc. Am., Phycol. Soc. Am., Internat. Phycol. Soc., Soc. Limnology and Oceanography. Contbr. articles to profl. publs. Home: 1246 Northwood Lake St Northport AL 35476 Office: Dept of Biology PO Box 1927 University AL 35486

WILLIAMS, LOUIS STANTON, glass and chem. mfg. co. exec.; b. Honolulu, Oct. 7, 1919; s. Urban and Amelia (Olson) W.; A.B., Amherst Coll., 1941; M.B.A., Harvard, 1943; m. Dorothy Webster Reed, June 12, 1943; children—Eric Reed, Timothy Howell, Steven Neil, Deborah Reed Sawin. With PPG Industries (formerly Pitts. Plate Glass Co.), 1946—, chief accountant Creighton factory, 1948-50, div. accountant glass div., 1950-53, mgr. cost planning, glass accounting, 1953-56, asst. controller, 1956, became controller, 1956, v.p. finance, 1963-75, dir., 1975—, exec. v.p., 1975-76, vice chmn., 1976-78, chmn., chief exec. officer, 1979—; chmn. Fed. Home Loan Bank, Pitts., 1971-73; dir. Pitts.-Corning Corp., PPG Industries Can. Ltd., Duplate Can. Ltd., Dravo Corp., Rubbermaid Inc. Trustee Family and Children's Service, Pitts., 1955-61; treas. YMCA, Pitts., 1959-65, dir., 1959—, v.p., 1966-75, pres., 1975-77, mem. nat. council, 1967—, mem. nat. bd., 1973—; mem. exec. com. Allegheny Conf. on Community Devel., 1978—; bd. dirs. Community Chest Allegheny County, 1961-67, St. Margaret's Meml. Hosp., Pitts., 1969—, Pitts. Symphony Soc., 1978—; div. chmn. United Way Campaign of Allegheny County, 1975-77, bd. dirs., 1978—; trustee Carnegie-Mellon U., Carnegie Inst. Served to lt. USNR, 1943-46. Mem. Financial Execs. Inst. (pres. Pitts. 1965-66, nat. dir. 1968-73, nat. v.p. 1972-73), Phi Beta Kappa. Presbyn. Clubs: Duquesne, Fox Chapel Golf, Harvard-Yale-Princeton (Pitts.); Laurel Valley Golf, Rolling Rock (Ligonier, Pa.); Iron City Fishing (Can.). Home: 108 Hawthorne Rd Pittsburgh PA 15238 Office: 1 Gateway Center Pittsburgh PA 15222

WILLIAMS, LUKE GLADSTONE, visual info. systems mfg. co. exec.; b. Spokane, Wash., Oct. 4, 1923; s. Luke Campbell and Grace Colby (Murray) W.; grad. Eastern Wash. State Coll., Cheney; m. Beuletta M. Nordby, Oct. 16, 1947; children—Brenda Louise, Mark Edward. Partner Williams Bros. Neon Products, Spokane, 1946-48; pres. Williams Bros. Inc., Spokane, from 1948; co-founder, v.p. Am. Sign and Indicator Corp., Spokane, to 1963, pres., chief exec. officer, 1963—; dir. Seattle-First Nat. Bank. Past chmn. Spokane Sports, Entertainment, Arts and Conv. Adv. Bd.; mem. Spokane City Council, 1962-66; chmn., mem. exec. com. Wash. Commn. EXPO 1974; founder Am. economy program Pacific Lutheran U., United for Wash.; bd. dirs. Wash. Council Econ. Edn. Served with USN, 1942-46. Recipient various commendation awards, certs. appreciation. Mem. NAM (state dir.). Republican. Presbyterian. Club: Shriners. Home: 931 Comstock Ct Spokane WA 99203 Office: 2310 N Fancher Way Spokane WA 99206

WILLIAMS, LYLE, congressman; b. Phillippi, W.Va., Aug. 23, 1942; s. Dale and Frankie Williams; m. Nancie Lee Peterson, Oct. 20, 1964; children—Vikki, Diane, Debra, Jason. Employed as barber; mem. Trumbull County Bd. Commrs., Warren, Ohio, 1972-79; mem. 96th Congress from 19th Ohio Dist. Republican. Home: 2061 Lyntz Rd Warren OH 44483 Office: Rm 1004 Longworth House Office Bldg Washington DC 20515

WILLIAMS, MARJORIE J. (MRS. BILL H. WILLIAMS), physician; b. Calcutta, India; degrees in medicine and surgery U. Bristol (Eng.), 1944; m. Bill H. Williams; 1 son. Successively asst. pathology U. Bristol, also Tulane U. Med. Sch., then pathologist St. John's Hosp., Joplin, Mo., 1944-48; with VA, Washington, 1949—, dep. dir. pathology and allied scis. services, 1962-63, dir., 1963—; prof. George Washington U. Med. Sch., 1979. Organizer, chmn. Interagy. Com. Lab. Medicine; mem. com. on pathology NRC-Nat. Acad. Scis. Bd. dirs. Am. Blood Commn. Recipient Nat. Civil Service award, 1967, Fed. Woman's award, 1967, Stitt award Assn. Mil. Surgeons, 1972. Fellow Coll. Am. Pathologists (bd. govs., chmn. com. mgmt. planning, chmn. internat. affairs com., Pathologist of Yr award 1978), Am. Soc. Clin. Pathologists, Royal Soc. Medicine; mem. Royal Coll. Surgeons, Internat. Acad. Pathology, Am. Assn. Pathologists, Path. Soc. Gt. Britain and Ireland, AMA, AAUW, Editorial bd. Jour. Med. Edn. Address: 1225 4th St SW Washington DC 20024

WILLIAMS, MARSHALL HENRY, JR., physician, educator; b. New Haven, July 15, 1924; s. Marshall Henry and Henrietta (English) W.; grad. Pomfret Sch., 1942; B.S., Yale, 1945, M.D., 1947; m. Mary Butler, Aug. 27, 1948; children—Stuart, Patricia, Marshall, Frances, Richard. Intern, Presbyn. Hosp., N.Y.C., 1947-48, asst. resident medicine, 1948-49; asst. resident medicine New Haven Hosp., 1949-50, asst. in medicine, 1950; trainee Nat. Heart Inst., 1950; practice medicine, specializing in internal medicine, Bronx, N.Y.; chief respiratory sect., dept. cardiorespiratory diseases Army Med. Service Grad. Sch., Walter Reed Army Med. Center, 1953-55; dir. cardiorespiratory lab. Grasslands Hosp., Valhalla, N.Y., 1955-59; dir. chest service Bronx Municipal Hosp. Center, 1959; vis. asst. prof. physiologyy Albert Einstein Coll. Medicine, Bronx, N.Y., 1955-59, asso. prof. medicine and physiology, 1959-66, prof. medicine, 1966—. Served from 1st lt. to capt., U.S. Army, 1950-52. Diplomate Nat. Bd. Med. Examiners, Am. Bd. Internal Medicine. Mem. Am. Physiol. Soc., A.A.A.S., Am., Westchester (dir., past pres.) heart assns., Am. Thoracic Soc., Am. Fedn. Clin. Research, N.Y. Acad. Sci., N.Y. Trudeau Soc. (past pres.), Am. Soc. Clin. Investigation, Soc. Urban Physicians (past pres.), N.Y. Tb. and Health Assn. (past dir.), Alpha Omega Alpha. Author: Clinical Applications of Cardiopulmonary Physiology, 1960. Contbr. articles to profl. jours. Home: 13 Colvin Rd Scarsdale NY 10583 Office: Albert Einstein Coll Medicine Bronx NY 10461

WILLIAMS, MARTHA ETHELYN, educator; b. Chgo., Sept. 21, 1934; d. Harold Milton and Alice Rosemond (Fox) Williams; B.A., Barat Coll., 1955; M.A., Loyola U., 1957. With IIT Research Inst., Chgo., 1957-72, mgr. info. scis., 1962-72, mgr. computer search center, 1968-72; adj. asso. prof. sci. info. Ill. Inst. Tech., Chgo., 1965-73, lectr. chemistry dept., 1968-70; research prof. info. sci., coordinated sci. lab. Coll. Engring., also dir. info. retrieval research lab., affiliate computer sci. dept. U. Ill., Urbana, 1972—; chmn. large data base conf. Nat. Acad. Sci./NRC, 1974, mem. ad hoc panel on info. storage and retrieval, 1977; numerical data adv. bd. Nat. Acad. Sci., 1979; mem. task force on sci. info. activities NSF, 1977; U.S. rep. review com. for project on broad system of ordering UNESCO, Hague, Netherlands, 1974; cons. to numerous cos. and research founds. Bd. dirs. Engring. Index, 1976—, v.p., 1978-79; regent Nat. Library Medicine, 1978-81. Recipient best paper of year award H. W. Wilson Co., 1975; NSF travel grantee, Luxembourg, 1972, Honolulu, 1973, Tokyo, 1973, Mexico City, 1975, Scotland, 1976. Mem. AAAS, Am. Chem. Soc., Am. Soc. Info. Sci. (councilor 1971-72), Assn. for Computing Machinery (pub. bd. 1972-76), Assn. Sci. Info. Dissemination Centers (pres. 1975-77), Nat. Acad. Sci., U.S. Nat. Com. for Internat. Fedn. for Documentation. Contbr. articles to profl. jours.; editor Ann. Rev. Info. Sci. and Tech., On-Line Rev.; contbg. editor column on Data Bases to Bull. Am. Soc. Info. Sci., 1974—. Home: Route 1 Monticello IL 61856 Office: Univ of Ill CSL 5-135 Urbana IL 61801

WILLIAMS, MARTIN, mus. ofcl., critic; b. Richmond, Va., Aug. 9, 1924; B.A., U. Va.; M.A., U. Pa.; grad. student, Columbia; 3 sons. Formerly instr. English, Columbia also editor various pub. houses; former jazz critic Saturday Rev., Evergreen Rev., N.Y. Times, Down Beat; dir. jazz and Am. culture programs div. performing arts Smithsonian Instn., Washington, 1970—. Recipient Deems Taylor award in music criticism ASCAP, 1971. Author: Where's the Melody? A Listener's Introduction to Jazz; Jazz Masters of New Orleans; The Jazz Tradition; Jazz Masters in Transition, 1957-69. Editor: (anthologies) The Art of Jazz, Jazz Panorama; co-editor: Smithsonian Collection of Newspaper Comics; also articles on children's lit., films, radio, TV. Address: 2101 Shenandoah Rd Alexandria VA 22308

WILLIAMS, MARY PEARL, lawyer, judge; b. Brownsville, Tex., Jan. 12, 1928; d. Marvin Redman and Theo Mae (Kethley) Hall; B.A., U. Tex., 1948, J.D., 1949; m. Jerre Stockton Williams, May 28, 1950; chidlren—Jerre Stockton, Shelley Hall, Stephanie Kethley. Admitted to Tex. bar, 1949, U.S. Supreme Ct. bar, 1955; asst. atty. gen. State of Tex., Austin, 1949-50; relief judge Municipal Ct., Austin, 1964; asst. instr. dept. govt. U. Tex., Austin, 1966-67; atty. Office of Emergency Preparedness, Exec. Office of Pres., Washington, 1968-70; labor arbitrator, mem. arbitration panel Am. Arbitration Assn., 1972-73; judge County Ct. at Law 2, Travis County, Tex., 1973—, pres. judge, 1976—; cons. Dept. HEW, 1966-67. Mem. adv. com. Juvenile Bd. of Travis County, 1964-67; trustee United Way, 1974-78. Named Outstanding Woman, Austin Am.-Statesman, 1974, Austin Citizen, 1978; named Woman of Yr., Austin dist. Bus. and Profl. Women, 1977. Mem. State Bar Tex., Travis County Bar Assn., Am. Bar Assn., Am. Law Inst., Am. Judicature Soc., Inst. Jud. Adminstrn., AAUW, Bus. and Profl. Women, Jr. League of Austin, Kappa Alpha Theta, Delta Kappa Gamma (hon.). Democrat. Methodist. Home: 3503 Mt Barker Dr Austin TX 78731 Office: County Courthouse Austin TX 78701

WILLIAMS, MASON, author, composer, writer, performer; b. Abilene, Tex., 1938; student Oklahoma City U. Guitarist, composer Classical Gas; former writer Smothers Brothers TV Show, also Andy Williams, Roger Miller, Petula Clark, Glen Campbell, Pat Paulsen. Recipient Emmy award for Smothers Bros. TV Shows, 1968, Grammy award (2), 1968. Author books including: Bus; Mason Williams Reading Matter; Flavors; FCC Rapport; recs. include Mason Williams Phonograph Record; Ear Show; Music; Hand Made; Share Pickers; Them Poems; Fresh Fish; orchestral compositions Train Ride in 6; Gypsy Noodle; symphony concert program Bluegrass on the Green; art concepts Bus; Sunflower. Address: PO Box 25 Oakridge OR 97463

WILLIAMS, MAURICE JACOUTOT, internat. orgn. exec.; b. New Brunswick, Can., Nov. 13, 1920 (parents American citizens); s. Alfred Jacoutot and Yvonne (Theberge) W.; student Northwestern U., 1940-42, U. Manchester, Eng., 1945; M.A., U. Chgo., 1949; research fellow London Sch. Econs., summer 1948; m. Betty Jane Bath, Dec. 18, 1943; children—Jon, Peter, Stephen. Dir. U.S. student program U. Fribourg, Switzerland, 1946; prin. examiner Chgo. Civil Service Commn., 1949; economist Office Internat. Trade Policy, Dept. State, Washington, 1950-53; econ. officer Am. embassy, London, 1953-55; chief Econ. Def. Coordination, 1955-58; asst. dir. U.S. Operations Mission to Iran, ICA, 1958-60, dep. dir., 1961-63; dep. dir. USAID/Pakistan, 1963-65, dir., 1965-67; chief program div. Near East-South Asia, 1961; asst. adminstr. Nr. East-South Asia, AID/W, 1967-70, dep. adminstr. AID, 1970-74; chmn. Devel. Assistance Com. OECD, Paris, 1974-78; exec. dir. UN World Food Council, 1978—. Presdl. coordinator Fgn. Disaster Relief, Bangladesh, Peru, Philippines, Managua, Sahel, 1971-74; chief U.S. del. U.S.-N. Vietnam Joint Econ. Commn., 1974—. Recipient Nat. Civil Service award, 1971, AID Distinguished Honor award, 1974, Rockefeller Pub. Service award, 1974. Club: Cosmos. Address: World Food Council Via delle Terme di Caracalla Rome Italy

WILLIAMS, MAX LEA, JR., engr., educator; b. Aspinwall, Pa., Feb. 22, 1922; s. Max Lea and Marguerite (Scott) W.; B.S. in Mech. Engring., Carnegie Inst. Tech., 1942; M.S., Calif. Inst. Tech., then Aero. Engr. and Ph.D. in Aeronautics, 1946-50; m. Melba Cameron, July 26, 1967; children—Gregory S., Christine C. Williams Mann, Richard L. Mem. faculty, successively lectr., asst. prof., asso. prof., prof. aeronautics Calif. Inst. Tech., 1948-66; dean, prof. engring. U. Utah, 1965-73, distinguished prof. engring., 1973; dean, prof. engring. U. Pitts., 1973—; mem. exec. com. Internat. Congress Fracture, 1965—; sci. dir. NATO Advisory Study Inst., Italy, 1967; mem. biomaterials advisory commn. Nat. Inst. Dental Research, 1967-70; mem. chem. rocket advisory com. NASA, 1968-73; mem. engring. advisory com. NSF, 1969-72; mem. nat. materials advisory bd. Nat. Research Council, and chmn. Council on Materials Structures and Design, 1975-77; asso. mem. Def. Sci. Bd., 1975-76; cons., lectr. in field. Dir. MPC Corp., Pitts., U.S. World Energy Conf., Washington, 1977—. Pres. Utah Engring. Devel. Fedn., 1969-79; adviser Regional Indsl. Devel. Corp., Pitts., 1973—, Ams. for Energy Independence, Washington, 1976—. Served to capt. USAAF, 1943-46. Registered profl. engr. Calif., Pa., Utah. NSF sr. postdoctoral fellow Imperial Coll., London, 1971-72; recipient Adhesion Research award ASTM, 1975. Mem. AAAS, Utah Acad. Scis., N.Y. Acad. Scis., Am. Soc. Engring. Edn., Am. Chem. Soc., Am. Inst. Aeros. and Astronautics, Soc. Rheology, Soc. Exptl. Stress Analysis, Sigma Xi (nat. lectr. 1972), Theta Tau, Tau Beta Pi. Club: Cosmos (Washington); University (Pitts.). Editor in chief Internat. Jour. Fracture, Leiden, Netherlands, 1965—; cons. editor Ency. Solid State, 1969—. Contbr. numerous articles to profl. jours. Home: 1236 Murrayhill Ave Pittsburgh PA 15217

WILLIAMS, MELVIN JOHN, sociologist, educator; b. Stovall, N.C., Feb. 13, 1915; s. John Presley and Mary Jenera (Wilkerson) W.; A.B., Duke, 1936, B.D., 1939; Ph.D., 1941; m. Frances Clark, Oct. 15, 1936; children—Kay Frances (Mrs. Bradley Yount), Dorothy Virginia (dec.), Melvin John, Deborah Susan (Mrs. Monte F. Little), Steven Clark, Eric Stanton. From instr. to asst. prof. sociology Albion (Mich.) Coll., 1941-44; prof. sociology, head dept. Wesleyan Coll., Macon, Ga., 1944-47; asso. prof. sociology Fla. State U., Tallahassee, 1947-52; prof. sociology, head dept. Stetson U., De Land, Fla., 1952-60, prof. sociology, chmn. social work, 1960-63; prof. sociology. East Carolina U., Greenville, 1963—, chmn. dept. sociology, 1963-71; vis. prof. summers Mich. State Normal Coll., 1943, Whittier Coll., 1957, U. N.C., 1970. With Duke Found., summer 1936; co-dir. Addison project Kresge Found., 1942-44; dir. YWCA Community Survey, Macon, Ga., 1944; dir., family counselor Children's Center, Macon, 1946-47; dir. Adolescent Research project Wesleyan Coll., 1944-46, East Carolina U., 1963; research and sociol. cons., 1946—; dir. NSF Inst. in Sociology, 1967. Fellow Am. Sociol. Assn.; mem. AAAS, AAUP, Am. Acad. Polit. and Social Sci., So. Sociol. Soc. (sec. treas. 1953-55, 1st v.p. 1955-56), Groves Conf., Nat. Council Family Relations, S.A.R., Omicron Delta Kappa, Alpha Kappa Delta, Pi Gamma Mu. Methodist. Lion (pres. DeLand, Fla. 1960). Author: (with others) Contemporary Social Theory, 1940; Catholic Social Thought, Its Approach to Contemporary Problems, 1950; Social Norms of Adolescents, A Study in Social Guidance, 1959; Moral and Spiritual Values in Education, 1955; Contbr. articles to profl. publs. Home: 2010 Pinecrest Dr Greenville NC 27834

WILLIAMS, MILLER, poet, translator; b. Hoxie, Ark., Apr. 8, 1930; s. Ernest Burdette and Ann Jeanette (Miller) W.; B.S., Ark. State Coll., 1951; M.S., U. Ark., 1952; postgrad. La. State U., 1951, U. Miss., 1957; m. Lucille Day, Dec. 29, 1951 (div.); m. 2d, Rebecca Jordan Hall, Apr. 11, 1969; children—Lucinda, Robert, Karyn. Instr. in English, La. State U., 1962-63, asst. prof., 1964-66; vis. prof. U. Chile, Santiago, 1963-64; asso. prof. Loyola U., New Orleans, 1966-70; Fulbright prof. Nat. U. Mexico, Mexico City, 1970; co-dir. grad. program in creative writing U. Ark., 1970—, asso. prof., 1971-73, prof. English and fgn. langs., dir. program in transl., 1973—, dir. poetry-in-the prisons programs div. continuing edn., 1974-79, chmn. program in comparative lit., 1978—; fellow Am. Acad. in Rome, 1976—; first U.S. del. Pan Am. Conf. Univ. Artists and Writers, Concepcion, Chile, 1964; mem. poetry staff Bread Loaf Writers Conf., 1967-72; founder, exec. dir. Ark. Poetry Circuit, 1975. Recipient Henry Bellaman Poetry award, 1957, award in Poetry, Arts Fund, 1973; Prix de Rome Am. Acad. Arts and Letters, 1976; Bread Loaf fellow in poetry, 1961; Amy Lowell Travelling scholar in poetry, 1963. Mem. S. Central Modern Lang. Assn., Modern Lang. Assn., Am. Lit. Translators Assn. (v.p. 1978-79, pres. 1979—), ACLU, AAUP. Author: (poems) A Circle of Stone, 1964; (peoms) Recital, 1965; (poems) So Long At the Fair, 1968; The Achievement of John Ciardi, 1968; (poems) The Only World There Is, 1971; The Poetry of John Crowe Ransom, 1971; Contemporary Poetry in America, 1972; Halfway From Hoxie: New & Selected Poems, 1973; (with John Ciardi) How Does a Poem Mean?, 1974; Why God Permits Evil (poems), 1977; translator: Poems & Antipoems, 1967, Emergency Poems, 1972 (Nicanor Parra); Giuseppe Gioachino Belli/Some of the Sonnets, 1980; editor: 19 Poetas de Hoy en Los Estados Unidos, 1966; (with John William Corrington) Southern Writing in the Sixties: Poetry, 1967, Southern Writing in the Sixties: Fiction, 1966; Chile: An Anthology of New Writing, 1968; (with James A. McPherson)

Railroad: Trains and Train People in American Culture, 1976; A Roman Collection: An Anthology of Writing about Rome and Italy, 1980; poetry editor La. State U. Press, 1966-68; founding editor New Orleans Rev., 1968-69; contbg. editor Translation Rev., 1978—; contbr. articles to profl. publs. Home: 1111 Valley View Dr Fayetteville AR 72701 Office: Dept English U Ark Fayetteville AR 72701

WILLIAMS, MURAT WILLIS, ret. govt. ofcl.; b. Richmond, Va., June 11, 1914; s. Lewis Catlett and Maria Ward (Williams) W.; student Woodberry Forest Sch., 1928-31; A.B., U. Va., 1935; B.A., Oxford U. (Rhodes Scholar, 1936-39), 1938, M.A., 1943; m. Eda Louise Burke, May 2, 1942 (dec. July 29, 1944); m. 2d, Joan Cunningham, Jan. 24, 1946; children—Kathleen, Brigid, Nicholas, Michael. Reporter, Richmond News Leader, 1935-36, asst. to editor, 1940; asst., Dept. of State, 1946-47; pvt. sec. to U.S. ambassador to Spain, 1939-40; apptd. fgn. service officer, 1947, 1st sec., San Salvador, 1947-49, 1st sec. and sometime charge d'affaires, Bucharest, 1949-51, asst. to dep. undersec. of state, 1951-53; student Nat. War Coll., 1953-54; consul gen., Salonika, 1954-55; fgn. service insp., 1955-56, dep. dir. Office of Greek, Turkish, Iranian Affairs, Dept. State, 1956-59, counselor of embassy, Tel Aviv, Israel, 1959-61, ambassador to San Salvador, 1961-64, dep. dir. coordination Bur. Intelligence and Research, Washington, 1964-65; vis. scholar Mary Washington Coll. Chmn. Va. State Com. for McCarthy for Pres., 1968; Democratic nominee for U.S. Ho. of Reps. from 7th Dist. Va., 1970, 72; mem. Dem. State Central Com.; pres. Va. center for Creative Arts, 1974-75; bd. dirs. Pub. Welfare Found., Piedmont Environ. Council, Nat. Assn. for So. Poor; chmn. adv. bd. Sch. Internat. Service, Am. U. Served to lt. comdr. USNR, 1940-45. Decorated Sec. of Navy's Commendation ribbon. Mem. Phi Beta Kappa, Delta Psi. Episcopalian. Clubs: Metropolitan (Washington); Genesee Valley (Rochester, N.Y.); St. Anthony. Contbr. to Ency. Brit. Yearbooks, Grolier's Ency., Chronicle of Higher Edn., Va. Quar. Rev. Address: Edgewood Farm Madison Mills VA 22953

WILLIAMS, NEWELL FRANKLIN, cons.; b. Bogotá, Colombia, Aug. 28, 1908 (parents Am. citizens); s. Charles Spencer and Maude (Newell) W.; B.A., State U. Ia., 1929, M.A., 1933; m. Grace Lowene Barger, July 25, 1931; 1 son, Charles Spencer; adopted children—Roderick Jose Alexis, Meredith Grace. Plant mgmt. trainee Fisher Body div. Gen. Motors Corp., Detroit, 1929-30; instr. Romance langs. and swimming Western Mil. Acad., Alton, Ill., 1930-42; spl. agt. FBI, San Diego, 1942-43, Washington, 1943-45, Paraguay, 1945-46; exploration staff Union Oil Co. of Calif., 1946, charge govt. relations and personnel, Paraguay, 1947-50, contract negotiations, govt. relations and mgr., Costa Rica, 1951-53, Peru, 1953-54, Guatemala, 1955-58, mgr. negotiations, relations, personnel, Latin Am., Europe, Africa, Australia and Indonesia, 1958-61; dir. U.S. AID Mission to Dominican Republic, 1962-63; dir. U.S. AID Mission to Honduras, C.Am., 1964-67; regional devel. officer pvt. enterprise Central Am. and Panama, AID, 1967; asst. dir., regional AID ops. mgr., 1967-72; cons., 1972—; pres. TICASA Shipping and industry devel., 1973—; dir. Internat. Wood Products S.A. Director Domingo Soldati (Boys' Town), Costa Rica; a founder Albergue Juvenil (Boys' Shelter), Guatemala. Served as capt. Ill. N.G. Res., 1936-40. Decorated for inter-country services, Paraguay; recipient award Regional Central Am. Tourist Assn., Coop. Assn. Honduras; named hon. citizen Honduras. Mem. North Central Pvt. Schs. Tchrs. Assn., Soc. Ex-Spl. Agts. FBI, Phi Kappa Sigma. Clubs: Internat. (Washington); Rotary (Paraguary, Tegucigalpa); Costa Rica Yacht, Union, Cariari, Tennis. Home: Los Yoses Apartado 5292 San Jose Costa Rica Central America

WILLIAMS, OLIVER JOSEPH, JR., ins. co. exec.; b. Jacksonville, Fla., Aug. 13, 1928; s. Oliver J. and Neville Claire (Moncrief) W.; B.B.A. in Accounting, U. Ga., 1950; m. Eileen Donnelly, May 24, 1958; children—Mark, Stephen, Christine. With group div. Aetna Life & Casualty Co., 1950—, regional dir. Pacific region, 1973-74, v.p. Pacific region, San Francisco, 1974—, v.p. Western region, 1978—; v.p. Pacific region Aetna Casualty & Surety Co. Am., 1974—, v.p. Western region, 1978—. Mem. Grosse Pointe Park (Mich.) City Council, 1971-73. Clubs: Orinda Country, Lafayette Tennis. Office: Aetna Life & Casualty Group Div One Post St Suite 1970 San Francisco CA 94106

WILLIAMS, OLIVER PERRY, educator; b. McPherson, Kans., Mar. 14, 1925 s. Oliver Perry and Lucy (Sell) W.; B.A., Reed Coll., 1951; M.A., U. Chgo., 1954, Ph.D., 1955; children—Ruth, Jessica. Asst. prof. govt. Wesleyan U., Middletown, Conn., 1955-57; asst. prof. polit. sci. Mich. State U., 1957-60; asst. prof. U. Pa., Phila., 1960-65, asso. prof., 1965-68, prof. polit. sci., 1968—, chmn. dept., 1967-75, dir. M. Pub. Adminstrn. program, 1971-73; vis. prof. Harvard, 1970; scholar in residence Bellagio Study Center, Rockefeller Found., 1977, Netherlands Inst. Advanced Study, 1977. Ford faculty fellow Centre Environmental Studies, London, 1970-71. Mem. Am. Polit. Sci. Assn., AAUP, Am. Soc. Pub. Adminstrn. Editor: (with Charles Press) Democracy in Urban America, 1961; (with Charles Adrian) Four Cities, 1963; (with others) Suburban Differences and Metropolitan Policies, 1965; Metropolitan Political Analysis, 1971. Home: 501 Carpenter Ln Philadelphia PA 19119

WILLIAMS, OWEN WINGATE, govt. ofcl.; b. Trouville, France, Aug. 24, 1924; s. Maynard Owen and Daisy Martha (Woods) W.; A.B., Kalamazoo Coll., 1948; postgrad. George Washington U. Grad. Sch., 1948-50, Fed. Exec. Inst., Charlottesville, Va., 1970; m. Betty Lou Trowbridge, June 15, 1946; children—Janet, John, Marlene, Todd, Daniel. Geodesist, Army Map. Service, 1948-55; phys. scientist Aero. Chart and Information Center, Washington, 1955-57; dir. Terrestrial Scis. Labs., Air Force Cambridge Research Labs., Hanscom Field, Bedford, Mass., 1957-72; asst. dep. dir. plans, requirements and tech. Hdqrs. Def. Mapping Agy., Washington, 1972-76, dep. dir. for systems and techniques, 1976—; vis. lectr. earth scis. U.S., Europe, USSR. Mem. adv. bd., Southborough, Mass., 1971. Served with USNR, 1943-46. Recipient award Instrument Soc. Am., 1965, award Air Force Cambridge Research Labs., 1961, Air Force Meritorious Civilian award, 1973. Fellow AAAS; mem. Earth Sci. Technologies Assn. (pres. 1963-65, award 1969), Am. Geophys. Union (pres. geodesy sect. 1976-78), Am. Congress Surveying and Mapping, Armed Forces Mgmt. Assn. (pres. Boston area 1966-68). Conglist. Contbr. articles to profl. jours. Home: 4703 Ponderosa Dr Annandale VA 22003 Office: Bldg 56 US Naval Obs Washington DC 20305

WILLIAMS, PARHAM HENRY, JR., univ. dean; b. Lexington, Miss., June 8, 1931; B.A., U. Miss., 1953, J.D., 1954; LL.M. (Sterling fellow), Yale U., 1965. Admitted to Miss. bar, 1954, U.S. Supreme Ct. bar, 1966; dist. atty. 4th Jud. Dist. Miss., 1957-63; asso. prof. law U. Miss., University, 1963-65, prof., 1966—, dean Sch. of Law, 1971—; fellow in law adminstrn. N.Y. U., 1968; mem. Nat. Conf. Commn. on Uniform State Laws, 1972. Mem. Am., Miss. bar assns. Home: 919 Hayes St Oxford MS 38655 Office: Sch Law U Miss University MS 38677

WILLIAMS, PAT, congressman; b. Helena, Mont., Oct. 30, 1937; student U. Mont., 1956-57; B.A., U. Denver, 1961; m. Carol Griffith, 1965; children—Griff, Erin, Whitney. Mem. Mont. Ho. of Reps., 1967, 69; exec. dir. Hubert Humphrey Presdl. campaign, Mont., 1968; exec. asst. to U.S. Rep. John Melcher, 1969-71; mem. Gov.'s Employment and Tng. Council, 1972-78; mem. Mont. Legis. Reapportionment Commn., 1973; co-chmn. Jimmy Carter Presdl. campaign, Mont., 1976; mem. 96th Congress from 1st Mont. dist.; coordinator Mont. Family Edn. Program, 1971-78; mem. Mont. Manpower Council, 1973-78. Served with U.S. Army, 1960-61, Army N.G., 1962-69. Mem. Mont. Fedn. Tchrs. Democrat. Club: Elks. Office: 1233 Longworth House Office Bldg Washington DC 20515*

WILLIAMS, PAUL HAMILTON, singer, composer; b. Omaha, Sept. 19, 1940; s. Paul Hamilton and Bertha Mae (Burnside) W.; grad. high sch. Film appearances include: The Loved One, 1964; The Chase, 1966; Watermelon Man, 1971; Planet of the Apes; The Cheap Detective, 1978; Smokey and the Bandit, 1977; wrote scores for A Star is Born, 1976, One on One, 1977, The Phantom of the Paradise, 1977, The End, 1978, The Muppet Movie, 1979; numerous TV appearances including 4 NBC Midnight spls., co-host on Mike Douglas show, appearances with Merv Griffin, Jonathan Winters, others; asso. A & M Records, 1970—; pres. Hobbitron Enterprises, 1973—. Co-recipient Grammy award for best songwriter, 1978. Mem. ASCAP, Nat. Acad. Rec. Arts and Scis. (trustee). Composer: We've Only Just Begun, 1970; Rainy Days and Mondays, 1971; An Old Fashioned Love Song, 1972; Family of Man, 1972; Let Me Be the One, 1972; Evergreen (Acad. award), 1976. Office: care Denny Bond 1888 Century Park E Suite 1500 Los Angeles CA 90067*

WILLIAMS, PAUL LEON, educator; b. Friendly, W.Va., Feb. 12, 1929; s. James Blaine and Kathryn (Tennant) W.; B.S., Northwestern U., 1951; M.S., Ill. Inst. Tech., 1953, Ph.D. in Psychology, 1966; m. Maryalice Walsh, Aug. 21, 1948; children—Patricia Mary, Robert James, Paul Leon, Aaron Blaine. Staff psychologist Personnel Lab., Chgo., 1951-54; test adminstr. R.R. Donnelly & Sons, Chgo., 1954-56; staff psychologist, cons. Booz, Allen & Hamilton, Chgo., 1956-58; dir. indsl. relations Chgo. Aerial Industries, 1958-60; orgn. planning asso. Mead Johnson & Co., Evansville, Ind., 1961-62; asst. prof. S.D. State U., Brookings, 1962-66, asso. prof., head dept. psychology, 1966-67; prof. psychology Yankton (S.D.) Coll., 1967-70, asso. dean of coll., 1967-68, dean, 1968, exec. v.p., 1970; v.p. Vernon Psychol. Lab., 1971—, partner, dir., 1973—, pres., 1978—; cons. Brookings Area Guidance Center, 1963-67; vis. lectr. U. Wis., Milw., Marquette U., Cardinal Stritch Coll. Served with USN, 1946-48. Mem. Am., Midwest, Wis. psychol. assns., Sigma Xi, Pi Gamma Mu, Psi Chi. Author: (with Dr. Kenneth Krause) Personality Characteristics Related to Managerial Success of Eastern South Dakota Farm Couples, 1968. Home: 12505 Center St Brookfield WI 53005 Office: 2600 N Mayfair Rd Milwaukee WI 53202

WILLIAMS, PAUL WHITCOMB, lawyer; b. Rochester, N.Y., July 12, 1903; s. Henry B. and Lillian Gray (White) W.; A.B. magna cum laude, Harvard, 1925, LL.B., 1929; student Emmanuel Coll., Cambridge (Eng.) U., 1925-26; LL.D., New Bedford Inst. Tech., 1958, Southeastern Mass. U., North Dartmouth, 1975; L.H.D., Bard Coll., 1975; m. Minerva Fedyn Sawdon, Aug. 10, 1956. Admitted to N.Y. bar, 1931; asso. Cravath, de Gersdorf, Swaine & Wood, 1929-31; asso. Cahill Gordon & Reindel, N.Y.C., 1933-39, partner, 1939-42, 45-54, 58-77; asst. U.S. atty. So. Dist. N.Y., 1931-33, U.S. atty., 1955-58; spl. counsel to Ins. Dept. State N.Y., 1951-52; spl. asst. atty. gen. State of N.Y. charge investigations in Saratoga and Columbia counties, 1952-54; justice Supreme Ct. State of N.Y., 1954. Dir. Sterling Bancorp., Standard Financial Corp., Sterling Nat. Bank & Trust Co. (N.Y.); mem. advisory bd. Internat. and Comparative Law Center, Southwestern Legal Found. Chmn. minimum wage bd. Confectionery Industry, N.Y., 1947. Pres. Manhattan council Boy Scouts Am., 1952-56, mem. exec. bd. of Greater New York councils, 1956—, pres., 1962-65, chmn. bd., 1965-67, hon. chmn. chmn., 1967-77; chmn. bd. Am. Cancer Soc., N.Y.C. div., 1965-74, chmn. exec. com. nat. orgn., 1977-78, vice chmn. bd., 1978—; chmn. bd. trustees Bard Coll., 1964-74, life trustee, 1974—. N.Y.C. Republican candidate for Congress, 8th N.Y. Dist., 1946. Served as. lt. comdr. USNR, 1942-45; comdr. Res (ret.). Decorated officer Order of Merit (France). Mem. Assn. Bar City N.Y. (chmn. sect. on trials, appeals, 1949-51, 58-59, v.p. 1958-59), Harvard Law Sch. Assn. N.Y. (v.p. 1958-59), Pilgrims of U.S., Soc. Colonial Wars (gov. 1975-77, dep. gov. gen. 1978-79), N.Y. County Lawyers Assn., Am. Law Inst., Am. Judicature Soc., Inst. Jud. Adminstrn., Am. Bar Found., Am. Coll. Trial Lawyers, Am., Fed. (pres. Empire chpt. 1956-58), New York State bar assns., V.F.W., S.R. (pres. 1962-64), Mil. Order World Wars, Am. Legion, Phi Beta Kappa. Episcopalian. Mason. Clubs: Brook, River, New York Young Republican (pres. 1936), Harvard, Angler's University (N.Y.C.); Southampton, Shinnecock Hills Golf (Southampton, L.I.); L.I. Wyandach (pres. 1974-77) (Eastport); Quantuck Beach (L.I.); Bathing Corp of Southampton (L.I.); Bath and Tennis, Seminole Golf, Everglades (Palm Beach, Fla.). Home: 12445 Plantation Ln North Palm Beach FL 33408 summers Homans Ave Westhampton Beach NY 11978

WILLIAMS, PAUL X., judge; b. Booneville, Ark., Feb. 19, 1908; s. Charles X. and Salley Ethel (Cruce) W.; B.A., U. Ark., 1928, J.D., 1930; m. Elizabeth Hays, May 16, 1935; children—Paul X., Charles David, Elizabeth Williams Danielson, Sara Virginia, John Roger. Admitted to Ark. bar, 1931; individual practice law, Ark., 1931-47; chancery judge, Ark., 1948-67; judge U.S. Dist. Ct., Western Dist. Ark., Fort Smith, 1967—, chief judge, 1976—. Served with USNR, 1942-45. Office: PO Box 1623 Fort Smith AR 72901*

WILLIAMS, PERCY DON, lawyer; b. Dallas, Sept. 19, 1922; s. Percy Don and Frances (Worrill) W.; B.A. with honors, So. Methodist U., 1942, M.A., 1943; LL.B. magna cum laude, Harvard U., 1946; m. Helen Lucille Brunsdale, Aug. 4, 1955; children—Anne Lucy, Margaret Frances, Elizabeth Helen. Admitted to Tex. bar, 1951; instr. So. Meth. U. Law Sch., 1946-47; asst. prof., then asso. prof. U. Tex. Law Sch., Austin, 1947-49; lectr. U. Va. Law Sch., 1951; law clk. to U.S. Supreme Ct. Justice Tom C. Clark, 1949-51; pvt. practice, Houston, 1952—; sr. partner firm Williams & Shanks, 1975—. Mem. Am. Bar Assn., Am. Law Inst., Am. Judicature Soc., Fed. Bar Assn., State Bar Tex., Houston Bar. Assn., Phi Beta Kappa, Order of Coif, Pi Sigma Alpha, Tau Kappa Alpha, Kappa Sigma. Clubs: Houston, Forest, Plaza (Houston). Contbr. articles to legal jours. Home: 31 Briar Hollow Ln Houston TX 77027 Office: 1609 First City Nat Bank Bldg Houston TX 77002

WILLIAMS, PRESTON CLARK, JR., food co. exec.; b. Griffin, Ga., Feb. 23, 1925; s. Preston Clark and Sarah Luline (Lofton) W.; student Mercer U., 1943-44, U. Miami (Fla.), 1944-45; m. Sara Margaret Penn, Dec. 6, 1946; children—Preston Clark III, William K. Wholesale grocery salesman service Wholesale Co., Griffin, 1946-61; v.p. sales So. Frozen Foods, Montezuma, Ga., 1961-64, pres., 1966—; sales mgr. So. div. Doug Milne Co., Jacksonville, Fla., 1964-66; pres. Seabrook Foods Co., Montezuma, 1974—, dir., 1974—; dir. Montezuma Banking Co. Mem. Macon County (Ga.) Bd. Edn., 1971—; mem. Macon County Democratic Exec. Com., 1970—. Served with USN, 1943-46, 51-52. Mem. Montezuma C. of C. Baptist. Clubs: Masons, McKenzie Meml. (Montezuma). Home: 100 Marshall St Montezuma GA 31063 Office: 321 Plant St Montezuma GA 31063

WILLIAMS, PRESTON NOAH, educator; b. Alcolu, S.C., May 23, 1926; s. Anderson James and Bertha Bell (McRae) W.; A.B., Washington and Jefferson Coll., 1947, M.A., 1948; B.D., Johnson C. Smith U., 1950; S.T.M., Yale, 1954; Ph.D., Harvard, 1967; m. Constance Marie Williard, June 4, 1956; children—Mark Gordon, David Bruce. Ordained to ministry Presbyn. Ch., 1950; Martin Luther King. Jr. prof. social ethics, Boston U. Sch. Theology, 1970-71; Houghton prof. theology and contemporary change Div. Sch., Harvard, Cambridge, Mass., 1971—, acting dean Div. Sch.. 1974-75; acting dir. W.E.B. DuBois Inst., 1975-77. Mem. Am. Acad. Religion (pres. 1975—), Am. Soc. Christian Ethics (dir., pres. 1974-75), Phi Beta Kappa. Club: Harvard (Boston). Editor-at-large: Christian Century, 1972—. Contbr. articles to profl. jours. Home: 36 Fairmont St Belmont MA 02178 Office: 45 Francis Ave Cambridge MA 02138

WILLIAMS, RALPH CHESTER, JR., physician, educator; b. Washington, Feb. 17, 1928; s. Ralph Chester and Annie (Perry) W.; A.B. with distinction, Cornell U., 1950, M.D., 1954; m. Mary Elizabeth Adams, June 23, 1951; children—Cathy, Frederick, John (dec.), Michael, Ann. Intern Mass. Gen. Hosp., Boston, 1954-55, asst. resident internal medicine, 1955-56; resident internal medicine N.Y. Hosp., 1956-57; chief resident Mass. Gen. Hosp., Boston, 1959-60; guest investigator Rockefeller Inst., N.Y.C., 1961-63; practice medicine specializing in internal medicine (subspecialty rheumatology), 1963—; asso. prof. U. Minn. at Mpls., 1963-68, prof., 1968-69; prof., chmn. dept. medicine U. N.Mex., Albuquerque, 1969—. Mem. study sect. allergy and immunology NIH. Served to capt. USAF, 1957-59. Diplomate Am. Bd. Medicine. Fellow A.C.P.; mem. Am. Assn. Immunology, Am. Rheumatism Assn., Assn. Am. Physicians, Am. Fedn. Clin. Research, Am. Soc. Clin. Investigation, Central Soc. Clin. Research, Western Soc. Clin. Research, Am. Thoracic Soc., Alpha Omega Alpha, Phi Beta Kappa. Asso. editor Jour. Lab. and Clin. Medicine, 1966-69; editorial bd. Arthritis and Rheumatism, 1968—. Contbr. numerous articles to profl. jours. Research in immunologic processes and connective tissue diseases. Home: 3408 La Sala Del Oeste NE Albuquerque NM 87111

WILLIAMS, RALPH WATSON, JR., securities co. exec.; b. Atlanta, July 2, 1933; s. Ralph Watson and Minnie Covington (Hicks) W.; student Davidson Coll., 1951; B.B.A., U. Ga., 1955; m. Nancy Jo Morgan, Mar. 19, 1955; children—Ralph Watson III, Nancy Jane, John Martin Hicks. Trainee banking Trust Co. Ga., Atlanta, 1955; municipal sales staff Courts & Co., Atlanta, 1955-57; v.p., salesman securities First Southeastern Corp., Atlanta, 1957-60; br. mgr. Francis I. duPont & Co., 1960-69, spl. partner duPont Glore Forgan Inc., N.Y.C., 1969-70, gen. partner, 1970, exec. v.p., 1971—, sr. v.p., 1972—, also dir.; sr. v.p., dir., mem. exec. com. duPont-Walston Inc., 1973-74; sr. v.p. E.F. Hutton & Co. Inc., 1974—. Mem. Nat. Assn. Security Dealers (chmn. dist. com. 7), Benedicts Atlanta, Phi Delta Theta. Methodist. Clubs: Commerce, Capital City, Piedmont Driving (Atlanta). Home: 4740 Millbrook Dr NW Atlanta GA 30327 Office: Tower Place Mall Level 3340 Peachtree Rd NE Atlanta GA 30326

WILLIAMS, RANDALL LEE, judge; b. Pleasant Hill, La., June 7, 1924; s. Jim J. and Thelma Catherine (Barnhill) W.; student A. and M. Coll., Monticello, Ark., 1942-44; LL.B., U. Ark., 1950; grad. Nat. Coll. State Trial Judges, 1971; m. Willie Merle Hankins, June 3, 1956; 1 dau., Julie Camille. Admitted to Ak. bar, 1950; practicing atty., Monticello, 1950-60; dep. pros. atty. Drew County, Ark., 1951-55, 57-59; municipal judge, Monticello, 1958-60; with Regional Attys. Office of U.S. Dept. Agr., Little Rock, 1960; practicing atty., Pine Bluff, Ark., 1961-71; dep. pros. atty. Jefferson County, Ark., 1965-71; circuit judge 11th Jud. Circuit Ark., Pine Bluff, 1971—. Mem. Ark. Ho. of Reps., 1955-56. Served with AUS, 1947-48. Mem. Am., Ark. bar assns., Am. Judicature Soc., Am. Legion. Mason (Shriner), Lion (pres. 1970-71). Home: 235 Linden Hts Pine Bluff AR 71601 Office: Courthouse Pine Bluff AR 71601

WILLIAMS, RAY W., mfg. co. exec.; b. Cleve., June 30, 1932; s. Ray W. and Alma Rose (Son) W.; student Kent State U., 1954-56, Fenn Coll., 1956-57; m. Sept. 1, 1955; children—Mark, David, Christine, Nancy. Vice pres. McGregor-Doniger, N.Y.C., 1965-68; v.p. V.F. Corp., Reading, Pa., 1968-70; exec. v.p., dir. H.D. Lee Co., Kansas City, Kans., 1970-78; pres., dir. Farah Mfg. Co., El Paso, Tex., 1978—. Served as capt. USMC, 1950. Office: PO Box 9519 El Paso TX 79985

WILLIAMS, REGINALD LAMAR, lawyer; b. Jacksonville, Fla., Sept. 22, 1912; s. Benjamin D. and Lily (Skeels) W.; J.D., U. Fla., 1934; m. Helen M. Werner, Apr. 10, 1942; 1 son, Richard Lamar. Admitted to Fla. bar, 1934; practiced in Tampa, 1934-38, Miami, 1938-78; of counsel firm Bradford, Williams, McKay, Kimbrell, Hamann, Jennings & Kniskern, P.A., Miami, Fla., 1950-79, of counsel, 1979—. Mem. joint com. continuing legal edn. Am. Bar Assn.-Am. Law Inst., 1963-67; mem. Fla. Bd. Bar Examiners, 1965-70, chmn., 1970. Served from 1st lt. to lt. col., U.S. Army, 1940-45. Decorated Bronze Star medal, officer Order Brit. Empire; cavalier officer Order Sts. Maurice and Lazarus (Italy); recipient Distinguished Service award Stetson U., 1963. Fellow Am. Coll. Trial Lawyers, Am. Bar Found.; mem. Am. (ho. dels. rep. Dade County Bar Assn. 1958-62, rep. Fla. bar and state del. 1962-68, assembly del. 1970-78, mem. scope and correlation of work com., chmn. 1977-78), Dade County (pres. 1956-57) bar assns., Fla. Bar (bd. govs. 1957-60, pres. 1962-63), Internat. Assn. Ins. Counsel, Fedn. Ins. Counsel, Am. Judicature Soc., Beta Theta Pi, Phi Alpha Delta. Methodist. Clubs: Miami; Key Biscayne Yacht, Riviera Country. Contbr. to legal jours. Home: Island House 200 Ocean Lane Dr Key Biscayne FL 33149 Office: 101 E Flagler St Miami FL 33131

WILLIAMS, RICHARD BLONDELL, petroleum and petroleum services co. exec.; b. Balt., Aug. 26, 1932; s. E.J. and Margaret B. (Blondell) W.; A.B., Georgetown U., 1954; postgrad. U. Tex., 1956-58; J.D., So. Meth. U., 1959; grad. Advanced Mgmt. Program, Harvard, 1971; m. Julia Sauer, June 26, 1959; children—Christopher, Sarah, E. James, Michael, Mary. Admitted to Tex. bar, 1959; practiced law, Dallas, 1959-71; with legal dept. Lone Star Gas Co., Dallas, 1962—, v.p., gen. counsel, 1970-71, sr. v.p. non-utility operations, 1971-74; pres., chief operating dir. Enserch Exploration, Inc. and Enserch Energy, Inc.; vice chmn., chief operating officer, dir. Pool Co., 1975-78; chmn., chief exec. officer Enserch Exploration, Inc., Nipak, Oiltools Internat., Ltd., Solus Schall Internat., Ltd., Samson Ocean systems; sr. v.p. Enserch Corp. Served with USAF, 1954-56. Mem. Tex. State Bar, Am. Petroleum Inst., Ind. Petroleum Assn. Am., Mid-Continent Oil & Gas Assn. (dir.). Home: 12243 Treeview Ln Dallas TX 75234 Office: 1817 Wood St Dallas TX 75201

WILLIAMS, RICHARD EDMUND, animated film producer, dir., writer; b. Toronto, Ont., Can., Mar. 19, 1933; s. Kenneth D.C. and Kathleen (Bell) W.; came to U.S., 1975; student Royal Ont. Coll. Art, 1949-53; m. Margaret French, Jan. 17, 1976; children—Timothy Michael, Holly Rebekah; children by previous marriage—Alexander Steuart, Virginia Claire. Founder, 1956, since owner Richard Williams Animation Ltd., London and Richard Williams Animation Inc., Hollywood, Calif., 1977; producer, dir. The Little Island, 1958, Love Me, Love Me, Love Me, 1962, A Christmas Carol, 1973; designer film sequences and titles for What's New Pussycat, 1965, A Funny Thing Happened On The Way to The Forum, 1966, Casino Royale, 1975, The Charge of The Light Brigade, 1967, The Return of The Pink

Panther, 1975, The Pink Panther Strikes Again, 1976; designer prologue for Murder on The Orient Express, 1976; dir., supr. Raggedy Ann and Andy, 1977. Recipient numerous awards including Brit. Acad. award for best animated film The Little Island, 1958; Oscar Acad. award for best animated short subject A Christmas Carol, 1973. Mem. Acad. Motion Picture Arts and Scis., Dirs. Guild Am., Assn. Cinematograph and TV Technicians, Screen Actors Guild. Office: 5631 Hollywood Blvd Hollywood CA 90028

WILLIAMS, RICHARD HIRSCHFELD, baseball mgr.; b. St. Louis, May 7, 1929; s. Harvey Grote and Kathryn Louise (Rohde) W.; student Pasadena City Coll., 1946-47; m. Norma Marie Mussato, Oct. 23, 1954; children—Kathi, Richard Anthony, Marc Edmund. Profl. baseball player, 1947-64, mem. Bklyn. Dodgers, 1951-56, Balt. Orioles, 1956-58, 61-62, Cleve. Indians, 1957, Kansas City Athletics, 1959-60, Boston Red Sox, 1963-64; baseball mgr. Toronto Maple Leafs, 1965-66, Boston Red Sox, 1967-69, Oakland A's, 1971-73, Calif. Angels, 1974-76, Montreal Expos, 1977—. Served in U.S. Army, 1951. Played in World Series, 1952-53, managed teams in World Series, 1967, 72-73; named All Star Mgr., 1968, 73-74; Nat. League Mgr. of Yr., AP, 1979. Mem. Baseball Players Assn. Am. Roman Catholic. Office: care Montreal Expos PO Box 500 Station M Montreal PQ H1V 3P2 Canada*

WILLIAMS, RICHARD LIPPINCOTT, writer, editor; b. Seattle, Nov. 28, 1910; s. Charles Richard and Dolly DeMaris (White) W.; B.A., U. Wash., 1933; m. Dorothy Mahone (dec. 1957); children—Diane Louise, Julie Demaris; m 2d, Maria Teresa McGee; children—Richard, David, Robert, Mary, Virginia. With Seattle Times, 1933-41, Wash. State Def. Council, 1941-44, Boeing Aircraft Co., 1944-45; corr., writer Time, Inc., 1945-52; editor Dell Pub. Co., 1953-60; series editor Time-Life Books, Foods of the World, Life Library of Photography, others, 1962-73; freelance editor, 1973-75; bd. editors Smithsonian mag., 1975—. Mem. Alpha Delta Sigma, Sigma Delta Chi, Tau Kappa Epsilon. Club: Overseas Press (N.Y.C.). Author: Family Doctor; The Northwest Coast; The Cascades; The Loggers. Home: Route 2 Unadilla NY 13849 also 5918 Chesterbrook Rd McLean VA 22101

WILLIAMS, RICHARD RHYS, priest; b. Bethlehem, Pa., Apr. 21, 1923; s. Loren Edward and Margaret Eleanor (Rees) W.; B.A., Lehigh U., 1944; M.A., Columbia, 1950; M. Div., Gen. Theol. Sem., 1947, Th.D., 1960; m. Mary Barton, June 14, 1947; children—Michael, Margaret, Gertrude, Jane. Ordained priest Episcopal Ch., 1947; pastor curate chs., Ill., 1947-49, Conn., 1949-53; instr. Old Testament, Gen. Theol. Sem., N.Y.C., 1950-53; rector Northeast Harbor, Maine, 1953-58, Christ Ch., Poughkeepsie, N.Y., 1961-70, St. Peters' Ch., Lithgow, N.Y., 1970—; asso. prof. Old Testament, Nashotah (Wis.) Ho., 1958-61; asso. prof. religion Marist Coll., Poughkeepsie, 1970—; examining chaplain Maine, 1954-58, N.Y., 1963-70; chaplain Vassar Coll., 1961-70. Mem. drafting com. The Psalter, 1968-76; trustee Gen. Theol. Sem., 1968-77; headmaster St. George's Sch., Poughkeepsie, 1963-70. Mem. Am. Acad. Religion, Soc. Bibl. Lit., Am. Schs. Oriental Research, Phi Beta Kappa. Home: RD 1 Millbrook NY 12545 Office: Marist Coll Poughkeepsie NY 12601

WILLIAMS, ROBERT DRAYTON, banker; b. Los Angeles, Sept. 23, 1912; s. Stanley W. and Isabel (Robbins) W.; B.A., Pomona Coll., 1934; grad. Pacific Coast Banking Sch., 1959; m. Flora Sands, Dec. 26, 1945; children—Kathleen Sands, Marilyn Frances. Br. mgr. Bank of Am., Los Angeles, 1936-55; with First Nat. Bank Ariz., Phoenix, 1955-77, exec. v.p., 1964-65, pres., 1965-77, chief exec. officer, 1972-77, ret., 1977, also dir.; dir. Western Bancorp. L.A., 1975-77. Mem. regional comptrollers adv. com. on banking policies and practices 12th Nat. Bank Region, 1966-68. Bd. dirs. United Fund Phoenix, 1965-70, Community Council, 1971—; Phoenix Fine Arts Assn., 1967-69; adv. bd. Central Phoenix Bus. and Profl. Assn., 1970—, Phoenix Salvation Army, 1966—, treas., 1967-68, chmn., 1969-70; mem. nat. council Pomona Coll., 1965—. Served to lt. col AUS, 1940-46. Mem. Am. (v.p. Ariz. 1966-68, nat bank div. exec. com. 1969-70, govt. relations council 1971, dir. 1974-75), Ariz. (exec. council 1964-71, 1st v.p. 1968-69, pres. 1969-70) bankers assns., Ariz. Council Econ. Edn., Phoenix Met. C. of C. (past pres.). Republican. Espicopalian. Kiwanian (dir. local chpt. 1969-70). Clubs: Arizona (Phoenix); Paradise Valley Country (Scottsdale, Ariz). Office: First Nat Bank Plaza Phoenix AZ 85003

WILLIAMS, ROBERT EDMOND, mgmt. cons., former steel co. exec.; b. San Francisco, Feb. 7, 1913; s. George A. and Ynez (Smith) W.; B.S., U. Calif. at Berkeley, 1935; m. Ellen Reinecke, Aug. 12, 1936; children—Robert Edmond, Richard. With U.S. Steel Corp., 1935-60, v.p. sales Nat. Tube div., 1960-61; v.p. sales Youngstown Sheet and Tube Co., (Ohio), 1961-63, exec. v.p., 1963-65, pres., 1965, chief exec. officer, 1966-70, dir., 1964-70, also mem. exec. com.; vice chmn., chief adminstrv. officer, dir. Lykes-Youngstown Corp., 1969-70; pres., chief exec. officer GF Bus. Equipment Inc., Youngstown, 1973-76, also dir.; chmn., dir. Pinole Point Steel Co. (Calif.); dir. Pitts. Nat. Bank, Dollar Savs. & Trust Co., Wean United Corp., Comml. Shearing & Stamping Co., A.Y. McDonald Mfg. Co. Bd. dirs. Youngstown Hosp. Assn. Mem. Am. Iron and Steel Inst. (dir.). Clubs: Duquesne (Pitts.); Rolling Rock (Ligonier, Pa.); Youngstown, Youngstown Country. Home: 1359 Virginia Trail Youngstown OH 44505

WILLIAMS, ROBERT EDWIN, lawyer; b. Los Angeles, June 16, 1917; s. Donald Sheridan and Flavia (Sodergren) W.; A.B., U. So. Calif., 1939, LL.B., 1941; m. Sheila Frances Hopkins, Aug. 1, 1964; children—Stanley H., Bradley B., Andrew R., Laurie A., Samuel S., Jennifer, Kathleen. Admitted to Calif. bar, 1941, U.S. Supreme Ct. bar, 1941; mem. firm Newlin & Ashburn, 1941-50, Swanwick, Donnelly & Proudfit, 1950-56; with United Calif. Bank, Los Angeles, 1956—, exec. v.p., gen. counsel, 1968—. Bd. dirs. Braille Inst. Served with USNR, 1943-45. Mem. Los Angeles County Bar Assn., Calif. State Bar Assn., Am. Bar Assn. Republican. Episcopalian. Clubs: Calif., Newport Harbor Yacht. Office: 707 Wilshire Blvd Los Angeles CA 90017

WILLIAMS, ROBERT GAINSFORD WYNNE, JR., ret. naval med. officer; b. Woodbury, N.J., June 10, 1921; s. Robert Gainsford Wynne and Alice McNeil (Moffet) W.; B.S. in Biology, Rutgers U., 1943; M.D., Hahnemann Med. Coll., Phila., 1946; m. D. Jeanne Myers, Sept. 9, 1944; children—Robert Gainsford Wynne, David Lawrence, Barbara Jeanne. Intern, U.S. Naval Hosp., Phila., 1946-47; commd. lt. (j.g.) M.C., U.S. Navy, 1946, advanced through grades to rear adm., 1973; various assignments in U.S., 1947-72; comdg. officer Naval Regional Med. Center, Newport, R.I., 1972-73, Nat. Naval Med. Center, Bethesda, Md., 1973-75; staff med. officer to comdr.-in-chief Pacific and comdr.-in-chief Pacific Fleet, 1975-77; dep. surgeon gen. Dept. Navy, Washington, 1977-78; ret., 1978. Decorated Legion of Merit, Navy and Marine Corps medal, Meritorious Service medal with gold star, Joint Service Commendation medal. Mem. A.C.P., Assn. Mil. Surgeons U.S., Am. Heart Assn., Soc. Med. Cons. Armed Forces. Home: 3801 Old Gun Rd E Midlothian VA 23113. *Honesty and fairness in dealing with others. Courtesy. Hard work. Maintain a sense of humor in business and social endeavors. Integrity, empathy in relationships with others. Avoidance of all prejudices. Neatness in dress and appearance.*

WILLIAMS, ROBERT GORDON, banker; b. Mimico, Ont., Can., Nov. 27, 1934 (parents Am. citizens); s. Robert James and Blanche Ruth (Riblin) W.; B.S., Babson Coll., Wellesley, Mass., 1956; student advanced mgmt., Wharton Sch., U. Pa., 1965; grad. Advanced Mgmt. Program, Harvard, 1970; m. Rosalind White, July 30, 1957; children—Linda, Gail, Louise. With Girard Trust Bank, Phila., 1958—, sr. v.p., 1970-73, head trust dept., 1972-75, exec. v.p., 1973-75, vice chmn. bd., dir., 1975—; dir. Old Phila. Devel. Corp., Penn's Landing Corp., NARCO Sci. Industries, Inc. Bd. dirs. World Affairs Council Phila. Served with AUS, 1956-58. Mem. Assn. fin. City Bankers. Republican. Quaker. Clubs: Pine Valley Golf, Tavistock Country. Address: 1 Girard Plaza Philadelphia PA 19101

WILLIAMS, ROBERT HOPE, JR., lawyer; b. Balt., June 28, 1910; s. Robert Hope and Jennie (Homan) W.; student Johns Hopkins, 1929-31, St. John's Coll., Annapolis, Md., 1932-33; LL.B., U. Md., 1937; m. Louise Winslow, April 15, 1950. Admitted to Md. bar, 1938, practiced law, 1938-39, admiralty practice, 1939-41, 46-57; partner firm Niles, Barton, Yost & Dankmeyer, Balt., 1957-61; partner Niles, Barton, Gans & Markell, Balt., 1961-67; partner Niles, Barton & Wilmer, Balt., 1968—. Served to maj., Judge Adv. Gen. Dept., AUS, 1941-46. Mem. Barristers' Club Balt. (pres. 1967), Am., Md. bar assns., Maritime Law Assn. U.S., Bar Assn. Balt. City, Judge Advs. Assn., Am. Judicature Soc., Md. Hist. Soc., Star-Spangled Banner Flag House Assn., Balt. Mus. Art, Newcomen Soc. N.Am., So. Md. Soc., Sigma Alpha Epsilon (alumni pres. 1953). Democrat. Episcopalian. Rotarian. Clubs: Maryland (Balt.), Johns Hopkins (N.Y.C.). Home: 309 Suffolk Rd Baltimore MD 21218 Office: 929 N Howard St Baltimore MD 21201

WILLIAMS, ROBERT JENE, leasing co. exec.; b. Darby, Pa., Oct. 30, 1931; s. Joslyn Justus and Dolores Marie (Dugan) W.; B.S., Ursinus Coll., 1953; J.D., U. Pa., 1956; m. Shirley Geraldine Fiedler, Aug. 8, 1953; children—Robin Jeanne, Sara Ann. Admitted to N.J. bar, 1957, Pa. bar, 1959, Ill. bar, 1973; asso. firm Bleakly, Stockwell & Zink, Camden, N.J., 1956-58; atty., asst. gen. atty. Reading Co., 1958-69; gen. counsel, sec. Trailer Train Co., Phila., 1969-71, Chgo., 1971—, v.p., 1975—. Mem. Am., Pa., Phila., Ill., Chgo. bar assns., ICC Practitioners Assn., S.A.R., Nat. Social Scis. Honors Soc., Mayflower Soc., Soc. of Friends. Club: Metropolitan (Chgo.). Home: 1349 Woodland Dr Deerfield IL 60015 Office: 300 S Wacker Dr Chicago IL 60606

WILLIAMS, ROBERT LEON, psychiatrist, neurologist, educator; b. Buffalo, July 22, 1922; s. Leon R. and L. Paulyne (Ingraham) W.; B.A., Alfred U., 1944; M.D., Albany Med. Coll., Union U., 1946; m. Shirley Glynn Miller, Feb. 5, 1949; children—Karen, Kevin. Chief neurology and psychiatry Lackland AFB Hosp., USAF, San Antonio, 1952-55; cons. neurology and psychiatry to USAF Surgeon Gen., 1955-58; faculty Coll. Medicine, U. Fla., Gainesville, 1958-72, prof., chmn. dept. psychiatry, 1964-72; prof., chmn. dept. psychiatry Baylor Coll. Medicine, Houston, 1972—, prof. neurology, 1976—; mem. faculty various univs., part time 1949-58 including Albany Med. Coll. at Union U., Columbia Coll. Phys. and Surg., Boston U., U. Tex., Georgetown U. Served from 1st lt. to lt. col., USAF, 1948-58; col. Res., ret. Recipient USAF Certificate Profl. Achievement, USAF Surgeon Gen., 1967. Mem. Am. Psychiat. Assn., Am. Electroencephalographic Soc., Am. Coll. Psychiatrists, Am. Acad. Neurology, A.M.A., Group for Advancement of Psychiatry, Alpha Omega Alpha. Author: (with W.B. Webb) Sleep Therapy: A. Bibliography and Commentary, 1966; (with others) EEG of Human Sleep: Clinical Applications, 1974. Editor: (with Ismet Karacan) Psychopharmacology of Sleep, 1976; Sleep Disorders: Diagnosis and Treatment, 1978. Research and publs. on basic psychophysiology of human sleep. Home: 1744 South Blvd Houston TX 77098 Office: Baylor Coll Medicine Texas Med Center Houston TX 77030

WILLIAMS, ROBERT LUTHER, city planning cons.; b. Porterville, Calif., June 24, 1923; s. Luther Esco and Mary (Lyon) W.; student Utah State Coll., 1944; A.B., U. Calif. at Berkeley, 1949, M.C.P., 1951; children—Jeffrey Robert, Derrick Paul, Gail Diane. Asst. planning dir., Stockton, Calif., 1951-54; planning dir., Alameda, Calif., 1954-57, Alameda County, 1957-63; exec. dir. Am. Inst. Planners, 1963-69; v.p. Hill Devel. Corp., Middletown, Conn., 1969-71; dir. land mgmt. dept. Gulf Oil Corp., Reston, Va., 1971-74; pres. Coleman-Williams, Inc., Greenbrae, Calif., 1975-78; pres. Robert Williams Assos., Inc., Larkspur, Calif., 1978—; lectr. U. Calif. at Berkeley extension, 1956-59; tech. adviser regional planning Assn. Bay Area Govts., Cal., 1961-63; vis. prof. U. R.I., 1969-71. Bd. dirs. Planning Found. Am., 1965-70, communities Found., Inc., 1973—. Served to 1st lt. AUS, 1943-46, 52. ETO. Named Young Man of Year, Alameda, 1956. Mem. Am. Inst. Cert. Planners (pres. Calif. chpt. 1960), Am. Planning Assn., World Future Soc., Lambda Alpha, Lambda Chi Alpha. Democrat. Presbyn. Home: 127 Sylvia Way San Rafael CA 94903 Office: 700 Larkspur Landing Circle Suite 199 Larkspur CA 94939

WILLIAMS, ROBERT MARTIN, educator; b. N.Y.C., May 4, 1913; s. Joseph Tuttle and Mary Adeline (Johnson) W.; B.A., Pomona Coll., 1934; M.A., UCLA, 1942; Ph.D., Harvard U., 1950; m. Vera Jean Bobsene, July 31, 1956; 1 son, Kenneth Martin. Teaching fellow physics Dartmouth, 1935-36; mgmt. trainee Western Electric Co., Inc., Los Angeles, 1936-40, lectr., 1947-51, asst. prof., 1951-56, asso. prof., 1956-63, prof. bus. econs. and statis. Grad. Sch. Mgmt., UCLA, 1963—, vice chmn. dept. mgmt., 1961-67, dir. bus. forecasting project, 1952—. Dir. Imperial Corp. Am.; mem. exec. com., dir. Imperial Savs. and Loan Assn., 1978—; econ. cons. Fed. Res. Bank Kansas City, Lockheed Aircraft Corp., others, also state and fed. agys. Served to lt. comdr. USNR, 1942-46. Resources for Future, Inc. Research grantee, 1962; NSF grantee, 1965. Mem. Am. Econ. Assn., Am. Statis. Assn., Nat. Assn. Bus. Economists, World Future Soc., Centre for Internat. Research on Econ. Tendency Surveys. Editor, contbr. The UCLA Business Forecast for the Nation and California, 1961—. Contbr. numerous articles on bus. forecasting and regional econ. devel. Home: 750 Enchanted Way Pacific Palisades CA 90272

WILLIAMS, ROBERT RAY, bus. exec., ret. army officer; b. Evanston, Wyo., June 30, 1918; s. Henry Long and Flora (Morrison) W.; B.S., U.S. Mil. Acad., 1940; grad. Armed Forces Staff Coll., 1955, Army War Coll., 1959; m. Alice Jean Blair, Feb. 14, 1941; children—Robert Blair, Kathleen Rae, Keith Morrison. Commd. 2d lt., arty., U.S. Army, 1940, advanced through grades to lt. gen., 1970; designated first master aviator, 1957; mem. test group for organic army aviation, 1942; chief flight div. Dept. Air Tng., 1942-44; staff officer Hdqrs. USAAF, 1944-45; air officer U.S. Constabulary, Europe, 1946-49; chief army aviation br. Dept. Army, 1951-55; pres. U.S. Army Aviation Bd., 1955-58; chief aviation div. Office Chief Research and Devel., Dept. Army, 1958-60; assigned Office Sec. Def., 1961; comdg. gen. U.S. Army Aviation Center, 1962-63, Test, Evaluation and Control Group, Fort Benning, Ga., 1963-65; asst. div. comdr. 2d Inf. Div., 1965-66; dir. army aviation Dept. Army, Washington, 1966-67; aviation officer U.S. Army Vietnam and comdg. gen. First Aviation Brigade, 1967-69; asst. chief staff force devel. Dept. of Army, 1969-72; dep. comdr.-in-chief U.S. Army Pacific, 1972-74, ret.; pres. Bell Helicopter Internat. Inc., 1975—. Recipient Alexander Klemin award for achievement advancement rotary wing aircraft, 1962. Asso. fellow Inst. Aerospace Scis.; hon. fellow Am. Helicopter Soc.; mem. Army Aviation Assn. Am. (pres.), Nat. Aeros. Assn., Daedalians, Quiet Birdmen, Kappa Sigma. Mason (32 deg.). Home: 5825 Jacqueline Rd Fort Worth TX 76112 Office: 1901 Central Dr Bedford TX 76021

WILLIAMS, ROBERT TOWNSEND, city ofcl.; b. Fauquier County, Va., Aug. 7, 1936; s. Andrew J. and Pearl M. W.; B.A. in Econs., U. Va., 1959; m. Ann Kirby, Aug. 10, 1957; children—Steven, Cynthia. Asst. dir. fin. and aux. services City of Portsmouth (Va.), fin. dir., 1971-74, asst. city mgr., 1974-75, city mgr., 1975—. Bd. dirs. Portsmouth United Fund. Served with U.S. Army, 1959-60. Mem. Internat. City Mgrs. Assn., Nat. Mcpl. Fin. Officers Assn. (chmn. dataprocessing com. 1971), S.E. Va. Planning Dist. Com., Va. Mcpl. League, Am. Mgmt. Assn., Portsmouth Indsl. Found., Tidewater Data Processing Mgmt. Assn. (past pres.), Portsmouth C. of C. Home: 2913 Tanbark Ln Portsmouth VA 23703 Office: #1 High St Portsmouth VA 23704*

WILLIAMS, ROBERT WALTER, educator; b. Palo Alto, Calif., June 3, 1920; s. Philip S. and Louise (Brown) W.; A.B., Stanford, 1941; M.A., Princeton, 1943; Ph.D., Mass. Inst. Tech., 1948; m. Erica Lehman, Sept. 23, 1969; children—Paul, David, Eric. Asso. physicist Los Alamos Lab., 1943-46; research asso. Mass. Inst. Tech., 1946-48, asst. prof., 1948-52, asso. prof., 1952-59; prof. physics U. Wash., Seattle, 1959—. Cons., Boeing Co., Seattle, 1961—. Fellow Am. Phys. Soc., Am. Acad. Arts and Scis. Research and publs. on cosmic-ray air showers and cosmicradiation, analysis of nuclear radii, measurement of properties of fundamental particles. Home: 3845 49th Ave NE Seattle WA 98105 Office: Dept Physics U Wash Seattle WA 98105

WILLIAMS, ROBIN, actor, comedian; b. Chgo., July 21, 1952; s. Mr. and Mrs. Robert W.; attended Claremont (Calif.) Men's Coll., Marin Coll., Kentfield, Calif., Juilliard Sch., N.Y.C.; m. Valerie Velardi, June 4, 1978. Started as stand-up comedian in San Francisco clubs, including Holy City Zoo, Intersection, Great Am. Music Hall, The Boardinghouse; later became regular at Comedy Store, Los Angeles; appeared in TV series: Laugh-In, The Richard Pryor Show, America 2-Night, Happy Days; star of TV series Mork and Mindy, 1978—; performs regularly at Comedy Store, Improvisation and with group Off The Wall, Los Angeles; appears in coast-to-coast nightclub act; rec. album: Reality, What a Concept, 1979. Recipient Golden Apple award Hollywood Women's Press Club, Golden Globe award, People's Choice award.*

WILLIAMS, ROBIN MURPHY, JR., educator; b. Hillsborough, N.C., Oct. 11, 1914; s. Robin Murphy and Mabel Claire (Strayhorn) W.; B.S., N.C. State Coll., 1933, M.S., 1935; postgrad. Cornell U., 1935-36; Ph.D. (Austin fellow, 1938-39), Harvard U., 1943; m. Marguerite York, July 29, 1939; children—Robin Murphy III, Nancy, Susan. Various research positions govtl. agys., 1933-37; asst. rural sociologist N.C. Agrl. Expt. Sta., 1936-38; instr., research asst. U. Ky., 1939-42; research analyst and statistician, research br. U.S. War Dept., 1942-45; prof. sociology Cornell U., Ithaca, N.Y., 1946—, Henry Scarborough prof. social sci., 1967—, chmn. dept. sociology and anthropology, 1956-61, dir. Soc. Sci. Research Center, 1949-54; vis. prof. sociology U. Hawaii, 1958. Cons. Nat. Inst. Mental Health, 1949-67; mem. sci. adv. bd. USAF, 1950-54; adv. com. for social scis. NSF, 1967-69; com. on life sci. and social policy NRC, 1968-74; vis. scholar Russell Sage Found., 1968-69; vis. fellow Center for Creative Leadership, 1974-75; Center for Advance Study Behavioral Scis. fellow, 1961-62; NSF Sr. postdoctoral fellow. Mem. Am. (council, 1st v.p. 1956, pres. 1958, sec. 1965-68), Eastern (pres. 1966) sociol. socs., Am. Philos. Soc., Am. Acad. Arts Scis., Sociol. Research Assn. (pres. 1958), Soc. Study Social Problems, Rural Sociol. Soc. Am., Phi Kappa Phi, Alpha Zeta. Author: The Reduction of Intergroup Tension, 1947; (with others) The American Soldier, Vols. I and II, 1949; American Society, 1951, 60, 70; (with others) What College Students Think, 1960; Strangers Next Door, 1964; Mutual Accommodation, 1977. Editor: (with Margaret W. Ryan) Schools in Transition, 1954. Office: 342 Uris Hall Cornell U Ithaca NY 14853

WILLIAMS, ROBLEY COOK, molecular biologist; b. Santa Rosa, Calif., Oct. 13, 1908; s. William C. and Anna Mae (Cook) W.; A.B., Cornell U., 1931, Ph.D., 1935; m. Margery Ufford, June 20, 1931; children—Robley Cook, Grace Elizabeth. Instr. astronomy U. Mich., 1935-40, asst. prof. 1940-45, asso. prof. physics, 1945-48, prof., 1948-50; prof. biophysics dept. biochemistry, biophysicist virus lab. U. Calif. at Berkeley, 1950-59, prof. virology, 1959-64, prof. molecular biology, 1964-76, emeritus, 1976—, chmn. dept., 1964-69, research biophysicist, asso. dir. virus lab., 1959-76; research asso. OSRD, Washington, 1941-42; research staff U. Cambridge (Eng.), 1956-57; founder Evaporated Metal Films Corp., Ithaca, N.Y., 1935, dir., v.p., 1935-50. Mem. council, pres. commn. molecular biophysics Internat. Union Pure and Applied Biophysics, 1961-69; mem. U.S. Nat. Commn. UNESCO, 1963-69. Trustee Telluride Assn., 1929-49, Deep Springs (Cal.) Coll., 1968-76. Guggenheim fellow, 1966; recipient Longstreth medal Franklin Inst., 1939; John Scott award, 1954. Mem. Electron Microscopy Soc. Am. (pres. 1951), Nat. Acad. Scis. (council 1960-63), Am. Acad. Arts and Scis., Biophys. Soc. (pres. 1958), Phi Beta Kappa, Sigma Xi. Contbr. articles profl. jours. Home: 1 Arlington Ct Berkeley CA 94707

WILLIAMS, ROGER, lawyer; b. Milw., Feb. 26, 1924; s. Clifton and Jessie Isabelle (Conger) W.; A.B., U. Calif., Los Angeles, 1947; J.D., U. Mich., Ann Arbor, 1949; m. Helen E. Gherardini, Sept. 9, 1948; children—Patricia Carol, Margaret Callie, Roger Lockwood, Polly Caitlin. Admitted to Calif. bar, 1950; asso. Macdonald & Pettit, Los Angeles, 1949-50, O'Melveny & Myers, Los Angeles, 1952-56; atty. Western Gulf Oil Co., Los Angeles, 1956-60; asst. chief counsel, mng. dir. Lockheed Aircraft Internat., A.G. Geneva, pres. Lockheed Western Export Co., Lockheed Aircraft Corp., 1960-71; exec. v.p., gen. counsel Great Western Fin. Corp., Beverly Hills, Calif., 1971-78; sr. v.p., gen. counsel, sec. Ticor Title Insurers, Los Angeles, 1978—. Served with AUS, 1943-46, 50-52; ETO, Korea. Decorated Bronze Star with V, Purple Heart, Army Commendation medal. Mem. Am. Bar Assn., State Bar Calif., Los Angeles County Bar Assn. Republican. Club: Oneonta Men's (South Pasadena, Calif.). Home: 1610 Marengo Ave South Pasadena CA 91030 Office: 6300 Wilshire Blvd 8th Floor Los Angeles Hills CA 90048

WILLIAMS, ROGER JOHN, ret. chemist, educator; b. Octacumund, India, Aug. 14, 1893 (parents Am. citizens); s. Robert Runnels and Alice Evelyn (Mills) W.; student U. Calif., 1914-15; B.S., U. Redlands (Calif.), 1914, D.Sc. (hon.), 1934; M.S., U. Chgo., 1918, Ph.D., 1919; D.Sc. (hon.), Columbia, 1942, Oreg. State Coll., 1956; m. Hazel Elizabeth Wood, Aug. 1, 1916 (dec. 1952); children—Roger John, Janet, Arnold; m. 2d, Mabel Phyllis Hobson, May 9, 1953; 1 stepson, John W. Hobson. Research chemist Fleischmann Co., Chgo., 1919-20; asst. prof. chemistry U. Oreg., Eugene, 1920-21, asso. prof., 1921-28, prof., 1928-32; prof. chemistry Oreg. State Coll., Corvallis, 1932-39; prof. chemistry U. Tex., Austin, 1939-71, emeritus, 1971—; research scientist Clayton Found. Biochem. Inst. Tex., Austin, 1971—, dir., 1941-63. Mem. Pres.'s Adv. Panel on Heart Disease, 1972. Recipient Mead-Johnson award Am. Inst. Nutrition, 1941; Chandler medal Columbia, 1942; S.W. Region award Am. Chem. Soc., 1950. Fellow AAAS; mem. Am. Chem. Soc. (pres. 1957), Am. Soc. Biol. Chemists, Am. Assn. Cancer Research, Soc. Exptl. Biology and Medicine, Nat. Acad. Scis., N.Y. Acad. Sci., Biochem. Soc. London, Phi Beta Kappa, Sigma Xi, Phi Kappa Phi, Phi Sigma, Pi Kappa Delta, Phi Lambda Upsilon. Methodist. Author or co-author books relating to chemistry; latest: (with R.E. Eakin, E. Beerstecher, W. Shive) The Biochemistry of B Vitamins, 1950; Nutrition and Alcoholism, 1951; Free and Unequal, 1953; Biochemical Individuality, 1956; Alcoholism: The Nutritional Approach, 1959; Nutrition in a Nutshell, 1962; You Are Extraordinary, 1967; Nutrition Against Disease: Environmental Prevention, 1971; Physicians' Handbook of Nutritional Science, 1975; The Wonderful World Within You: Your Inner Nutritional Environment, 1977. Discoverer pantothenic acid; concentrated and named folic acid; also made microbiol. study of vitamins, individual metabolic patterns. Home: 1604 Gaston Ave Austin TX 78703 Office: U Tex Austin TX 78712

WILLIAMS, ROGER LEWIS, ret. newspaper editor; b. Oakland, Calif., Sept. 4, 1913; s. Alexander Edmund and Alice (Dithridge) W.; student Coll. San Mateo, 1932-33, Mich. State U., 1942; m. Jean Turner, June 14, 1936; children—Gary, Joan (Mrs. Mark C. Coleman). Sports editor San Mateo (Calif.) Times, 1934-37; sports columnist San Francisco News, 1937-58, sports editor, 1958-59, San Francisco News-Call Bull., 1959-66; sports editor San Francisco Examiner, 1966-79. Served to 1st lt., pilot, USAAF, World War II. Mem. Am. Aviation Writers Assn. (past v.p.), Am. Football Writers Assn., Am. Baseball Writers Assn. Clubs: Press, Union League, Olympic (editor Olympian) (San Francisco). Home: 964 Corbett Ave San Francisco CA 94131

WILLIAMS, ROGER MILLER, journalist; b. N.Y.C., Feb. 21, 1934; s. Arden C. and Margaret (Vervaet) W.; B.A. cum laude, Amherst Coll., 1956; m. Connie Louise Young, Apr. 20, 1974; 1 dau., Cristina; children by previous marriage—Christopher, Diana. Staff writer Sports Illustrated mag., 1959-62; corr. Time mag., 1962-72; sr. editor World, now Saturday Rev. mag., N.Y.C., 1972-75, 77—, contbg. editor, 1975-77; dir. So. Investigative Research Project, So. Regional Council, Atlanta, 1975-76; free lance writer, N.Y.C., 1977—. Served with AUS, 1956-58. Mem. PEN. Fellow in pub. affairs reporting Am. Polit. Sci. Assn., 1970-71. Author: Sing a Sad Song: The Life of Hank Williams, 1970; The Bonds: An American Family, 1971. Editor: The Super Crooks, 1973. Office: Saturday Review 1290 Ave of Americas New York NY 10019

WILLIAMS, ROGER WRIGHT, educator; b. Great Falls, Mont., Jan. 24, 1918; s. Elmer Howard and Mary (Stuart-Davidson) W.; B.S., U. Ill., 1939, M.S., 1941; postgrad. Cornell U., U. N.C. Sch. Pub. Health; Ph.D., Columbia Sch. Pub. Health, 1947; m. Marjorie Madeline Jones, May 9, 1943; children—Barbara, Stuart Roger. Mem. faculty Columbia Sch. Pub. Health, N.Y.C., 1944—, prof. med. entomology, 1966—, acting head div. tropical medicine, 1970. Cons. USPHS, Alaska, 1949, Newton, Ga., 1952, Therapeutic Research Found., 1949; cons. Jackson Hole Preserve, Govt. V.I., U.S. Nat. Park Service, 1959-61, cons. Rockefeller Found., Trinidad, W.I. and Brazil, 1963; filariasis research project WHO, Rangoon, Burma, 1966-70; mem. arbovirus field staff Rockefeller Found., Nigeria, 1964-65. Rockefeller traveling fellow, 1947, Childs Frick fellow, Bermuda, 1955, 57; NSF sr. postdoctoral fellow U. London (Eng.) Sch. Hygiene and Tropical Medicine, 1956-57; La. State U. Sch. Medicine fellow in tropical medicine Central Am., 1957. Mem. Tenafly (N.J.) Community Orch., 1960-63; mem. Tenafly Town-Wide Com., 1970, mem. Boys Activities Com., 1968-72, trustee, 1969-72, pres., 1970-72; chmn. troop 140 Boy Scouts Am., Tenafly, 1968-69, merit badge councilor, 1965—, Trustee Tenafly Nature Center, 1967-71, v.p., 1968-71; adv. bd. Am. Christian Coll., 1972-78. Fellow AAAS; mem. Internat. Coll. Tropical Medicine, Internat. Filariasis Assn., Am., Wash. entomol. socs., Am. Mosquito Control Assn., Am. Soc. Parasitologists, Am. Royal socs. tropical medicine and hygiene, Elisha Mitchel Sci. Soc., N.Y. Soc. Tropical Medicine (pres. 1969-70) Corp. Bermuda Biol. Sta. for Research, Phi Sigma. Presbyn. (deacon 1968-74, elder 1974—). Club: Tenafly Swim (trustee 1972-74, v.p. 1973, Pres. 1974). Contbr. articles on arthropods of med. importance and diseases they transmit to profl. jours. and books. Co-discoverer West African Arbovirus, Dugbe virus. Home: 16 Virginia St Tenafly NJ 07670 Office: 630 W 168th St New York City NJ 10032. *Success is living in peace and contentment with one's self. I have attempted to achieve this by leading what I consider to be a Christian Life and helping others to do the same; by giving some of my time to help improve the world around us for others; and by giving a little more effort to a task than the minimum necessary to just get it done.*

WILLIAMS, RONALD, univ. pres.; b. Cleve., June 17, 1927; s. Wilbert and Mary (Malone) W.; B.A. in Speech and Hearing, Western Res. U., 1954, M.A. in Speech Pathology, 1960; Ph.D. in Phonetics and Psycholinguistics, Ohio State U., 1969; m. Arlene Harris, Oct. 31, 1952; children—Robert, Rhonda. Coordinator speech therapy services Cleve. pub. schs., 1958-62; lectr., dir. Speech Clinic, Oberlin (Ohio) Coll., also cons. Oberlin city schs., 1962-64; mem. faculty Ohio U., 1964-69, asst. prof., 1967-69, acting exec. dean Afro-Am. affairs, asso. prof., 1969, dir. Summer Inst. Speech and Lang., 1969; prof. speech, dean Coll. Ethnic Studies, Western Wash. State Coll., Bellingham, 1969-71; prof., chmn. dept. communication scis. Federal City Coll., Washington, 1971-72, provost, v.p. acad. affairs, 1972-76; pres., prof. psychology Northeastern Ill. U., Chgo., 1976—; adj. prof. U. Pitts., 1973; mem. Ill. Jud. Inquiry Bd., 1979—; mem. nat. adv. bd. Inst. for Acad. Improvement, Center for Study Higher Edn., Memphis State U., 1978—; trustee Washington Center Met. Studies, 1973-76; site visitor Am. Bd. Examiners Speech Pathology and Audiology, 1975—; chmn. Chgo. Met. Higher Edn. Council, 1978—; bd. advisors Coop. Computer Center, 1978—; mem. Urban Health Program Community Adv. Council, 1978—. Bd. dirs. Cinema/Chgo., 1979—. Served with AUS, 1945-48. Danforth Tchr. grantee, 1967-69. Fellow Am. Speech and Hearing Assn.; mem. Am. Assn. State Colls. and Univs. (dir. 1979—), Am. Assn. Higher Edn., Soc. for Coll. and Univ. Planning (internat. adv. com. 1978—), Am. Council Edn. (govtl. relations com. 1978—, Ill. panel for nat. identification program for advancement women in higher edn. adminstrn. 1979—), Nat. Black Assn. for Speech, Lang. and Hearing (chmn. bd. dirs. 1978—), Phi Kappa Phi (E.J. Taylor award 1967). Author articles, revs. Cons. editor Acta-Symbolica, 1969, Jour. Speech and Hearing Disorders, 1975. Office: 5500 N St Louis Ave Chicago IL 60625

WILLIAMS, RONALD JAMES, educator; b. Dublin, Ireland, May 9, 1917; s. James and Florence (Roberts) W.; B.A., U. Toronto, 1940, M.A., 1943, B.D., 1943; Ph.D., U. Chgo., 1948; postgrad. (Nuffield Found. fellow) Oxford (Eng.) U., 1953-54; m. Vivien Tremain, Aug. 20, 1940; children—Madlwyn, Gwethalyn. Ordained to ministry United Ch. of Canada, 1943; lectr. U. Toronto (Ont.), 1944-47, asst. prof., 1947-55, asso. prof., 1955-57, prof. Egyptology, dept. Nr. Eastern studies, 1957—, chmn. dept. Nr. Eastern studies, 1967-72. Commr., Greater Toronto region Boy Scouts of Can., 1963-69, provincial commr. for Ont., 1969-72. Recipient Can. medal, 1967. Fellow Royal Soc. Can.; mem. Internat. Orgn. for Study Old Testament, Soc. for Study Egyptian Antiquities, Am. Schs. Oriental Research, Egypt Exploration Soc., Internat. Assn. Egyptologists, Soc. for Old Testment Study, Soc. Bibl. Lit. Mem. United Ch. of Canada. Author: Hebrew Syntax: an Outline, 1967, rev. edit., 1976. Office: Dept Nr Eastern Studies U Toronto ON M5S 1A1 Canada*

WILLIAMS, RONALD LORAINNE, assn. exec.; b. Akron, Ohio, July 30, 1935; s. Reuben and Thelma W.; B.S. in Pharmacy, Ohio No. U., 1957. Pharmacist, pharmacy owner, Akron, 1957-66; exec. sec. Student Am. Pharm. Assn., Washington, 1968-71, 77—; asst. exec. sec. Am. Pharm. Assn. Acad. Pharm. Practice, Washington, 1971-72, exec. sec., 1972—. Mem. nat. high blood pressure coordinating com. Interdisciplinary Task Force on Provider Roles, U.S. Drug Enforcement Adminstrn./Pharmacy Working Com.; co-chmn. Nat. Conf. on High Blood Pressure Control, 1979-80. Mem. Am. Pharm. Assn., Acad. Pharm. Sci. (exec. sec. 1978—), AMA (affiliate), Am. Pub. Health Assn., Friendship Neighborhood Coalition. Democrat. Methodist. Club: Masons. Editor Pharmacy Practice, 1971—, Pharmacy Student, 1977—; Acad. Reporter, 1978. Home: 4401 Harrison St NW Washington DC 20015 Office: 2215 Constitution Ave NW Washington DC 20037

WILLIAMS, ROSS NORMAN, naval officer; b. N.Y.C., May 13, 1927; s. Harry Howard and Ruth Marie (Hanson) W.; B.S., U.S. Naval Acad., 1951; postgrad. oceanography, U. Wash., Seattle, 1957-58; m. Helen June Willis, Feb. 11, 1955; children—Paul Norman. Commd. ensign U.S. Navy, 1951, advanced through grades to rear adm., 1975; navigator, engr. and comdg. officer ships based U.S. and Hawaii; program coordinator undersea long range missile system, head Trident program coordination br. Office Chief Naval Ops., 1969-73; comdg. officer U.S.S. L.Y. Spear, Norfolk, Va., 1973-75; mil. asst. to dep. undersec. def. for research and engring., strategic and space systems Office Sec. Def., 1975-79; oceanographer U.S. Navy, also dir. Naval Oceanographic div. OPNAV, 1979—. Decorated Def. Superior Service Medal, Legion of Merit with gold star, Meritorious Service medal, Navy Commendation medal. Methodist. Home: 600 E Broad St Falls Church VA 22046 Office: Room 4E482 The Pentagon Washington DC 20350

WILLIAMS, SAM B., mech. engr., jet engine co. exec.; b. Seattle, May 7, 1921; s. Clyde E. and Martha Pugsley (Barlow) W.; B.S. in Mech. Engring., Purdue U., 1942; m. Barbara Moore Gibson, 1955; children—Margo, Gregg, Scott. Project engr. Chrysler Corp., Detroit, 1943-54; pres., chmn. bd. Williams Research Corp., Walled Lake, Mich., 1954—; v.p. Williams Investment Co.; dir. Mich. Nat. Bank West Metro. Trustee Detroit Sci. Center, Mich. Opera Theatre; mem. vis. com. div. phys. scis. U. Chgo. Recipient Collier trophy, 1978, R. Tom Sawyer award, 1979. Fellow ASME; mem. Assn. Unmanned Vehicle Systems (hon. trustee), Soc. Automotive Engrs., Am. Helicopter Soc., Assn. U.S. Army, AIAA. Club: Bloomfield Hills Country. Patentee in field. Office: 2280 W Maple Rd Walled Lake MI 48088*

WILLIAMS, SAMUEL WESLEY, JR., cons. engr.; b. Southbridge, Mass., Nov. 28, 1920; s. Samuel Wesley and Louise (Locke) W.; B.C.E., Worcester (Mass.) Poly. Inst., 1942; M.S. in San. Engring., Harvard U., 1947; m. Lila Louise Waring, May 17, 1952; children—Samuel Robert, Elizabeth Louise. Project engr. Greeley & Hansen, cons. engrs., Chgo., 1947-56; asso., then partner O'Brien & Gere Engrs., Inc., Syracuse, N.Y., 1956-66, mng. partner, 1966-71, pres., 1971—; chmn. bd. O'Brien & Gere, Inc., Charlotte, N.C.; dir. Phillips & Assos., Surveyors, Syracuse; trustee Onondaga Savs. Bank. Bd. dirs. Met. Devel. Assn., Onondaga Indsl. Devel. Corp.; trustee Rescue Mission Alliance Syracuse, 1969—, pres., 1974-76. Served with USNR, 1943-46. Registered profl. engr., N.Y. Mem. N.Y. Water Pollution Control Assn. (pres. 1962-63), Am. Water Works Assn., Am. Cons. Engrs. Council, Nat. Soc. Profl. Engrs., New Eng. Water Works Assn., Syracuse C. of C. (dir., exec. com.). Episcopalian. Clubs: Century, Univ. (N.Y.C.). Contbr. articles to profl. jours. Home: 211 Sherbrooke Rd Manlius NY 13104 Office: 1304 Buckley Rd Syracuse NY 13221

WILLIAMS, SHIRLEY, journalist; b. Frew, Ky., Feb. 18, 1935; d. Norman Allen and Mollie (Hamilton) Stamper; A.B. in Art, Berea Coll., 1957; m. Owen Dale Williams, Sept. 13, 1954; 1 son, Stephen. Asst. book editor Courier-Jour., Louisville, 1961-71; book editor Courier-Jour. & Times, Louisville, 1971—, column Bookends, 1970—; Ky. corr. Newsweek Mag., 1968—. Mem. Ky. Arts Commn. literary evaluation panel, 1973—, judging com. Weatherford award, 1973—. Nat. Endowment Humanities journalism fellow Stanford, 1973-74. Mem. Louisville Writers Club, Louisville Classic Guitar Soc., Sigma Delta Chi. Democrat. Home: 1299 Willow Ave Louisville KY 40204 Office: 525 W Broadway Louisville KY 40202

WILLIAMS, SPENCER M., dist. judge; b. Reading, Mass., Feb. 24, 1922; s. Theodore Ryder and Anabel (Hutchison) W.; A.B., U. Calif. at Los Angeles, 1943; postgrad. Hastings Coll. Law, 1946; J.D., U. Calif. at Berkeley, 1948; m. Kathryn Bramlage, Aug. 20, 1943; children—Carol Marcia (Mrs. James B. Garvey), Peter, Spencer, Clark, Janice, Diane. Admitted to Calif. bar, 1949, U.S. Supreme Ct. bar, 1952; asso. firm Beresford & Adams, San Jose, Calif., 1949, Rankin, O'Neal, Center, Luckhardt, Bonney, Marlais & Lund, San Jose, Evans, Jackson & Kennedy, Sacramento; atty. office county counsel Santa Clara County, 1949-50, 52-55, county counsel, 1955-67; adminstr. Calif. Health and Welfare Agy., Sacramento, 1967-69; judge U.S. Dist. Ct. No. Dist. Calif., San Francisco, 1969—. County exec. pro tem Santa Clara County; adminstr. Calif. Youth and Adult Corrections Agy., Sacramento; sec. Calif. Human Relations Agy., Sacramento, 1967-70. Chmn. San Jose Christmas Seals Drive, 1953, San Jose Muscular Dystrophy Drive, 1953, 54; team capt. fund raising drive San Jose YMCA, 1960; co-chmn. indsl. sect. fund raising drive Alexian Bros. Hosp., San Jose, 1964; team capt. fund raising drive San Jose Hosp.; mem. com. on youth and govt. YMCA, 1967-68. Candidate for Calif. Assembly, 1954, Calif. Atty. Gen., 1966, 70. Bd. dirs. San Jose Better Bus. Bur., 1955-66, Boys City Boys' Club, San Jose, 1965-67; pres. trustees Santa Clara County Law Library, 1955-66. Served with USNR, 1943-46, to lt. comdr. JAG Corps, USNR, 1950-52; PTO. Named San Jose Man of Year, 1954. Mem. Am., Calif. (vice chmn. com. on publicly employed attys. 1962-63), Santa Clara County, Sacramento bar assns., Calif. Dist. Attys. Assn. (pres. 1963-64), Nat. Assn. County Civil Attys. (pres. 1963-64), Theta Delta Chi. Kiwanian. Office: Fed Bldg 450 Golden Gate Ave San Francisco CA 94102

WILLIAMS, STEPHEN, educator, anthropologist; b. Mpls., Aug. 28, 1926; s. Clyde Garfield and Lois (Simmons) W.; B.A., Yale, 1949, Ph.D., 1954; M.A., U. Mich., 1950; M.A. (hon.), Harvard, 1962; m. Eunice Ford, Jan. 6, 1962; children—Stephen John, Timothy. Asst. anthropology Peabody Museum, Yale, 1950-52; mem. faculty Harvard, Cambridge, Mass., 1958—, prof. anthropology, 1967-72, Peabody prof., 1972—, chmn. dept., 1967-69; research fellow Peabody Mus., Harvard, 1954-57, mem. staff, 1954—, dir., 1967-77; leader expdns. to ancient Indian village sites Mo., La. and Miss.; dir. excavations Peabody Museum's Lower Miss. Survey, Holly Bluff, Miss., 1958-60; cond. survey and excavations Upper Tensas Basin in La., 1963-64. Contbr. articles to profl. jours. Home: 103 Old Colony Rd Wellesley Hills MA 02181 Office: Peabody Museum Harvard Univ Cambridge MA 02138

WILLIAMS, STEPHEN FAIN, lawyer; b. N.Y.C., Sept. 23, 1936; s. Charles Dickerman and Virginia (Fain) W.; B.A., Yale U., 1958; J.D., Harvard U., 1961; m. Faith Morrow, June 11, 1966; children—Susan, Geoffrey Fain, Sarah Margot Nu, Timothy Dwight. Admitted to N.Y. State bar, 1962, Colo. bar, 1977; asso. firm Debevoise, Plimpton, Lyons & Gates, N.Y.C., 1962-66; asst. U.S. atty. So. Dist. N.Y., 1966-69; asst. prof. law U. Colo., Boulder, 1969-77, prof., 1977—; vis. prof. UCLA, 1975-76; vis. prof., fellow in law and econs. U. Chgo., 1979-80; cons. Adminstrv. Conf. U.S., 1974-76. Mem. Boulder Area Growth Study Commn., 1972-73. Served with U.S. Army, 1961-62. Mem. Am. Law Inst., Am. Bar Assn. Libertarian. Quaker. Contbr. articles to law revs., mags. Home: 1001 10th St Boulder CO 80302 Office: U Colo Sch Law Boulder CO 80309

WILLIAMS, SUMNER HENRY, chem. co. exec.; b. Lowell, Mass., Nov. 13, 1901; s. Sumner Wheeler and Louise Mary (Shephard) W.; student Lowell Tech. Inst.; m. Ruth Grace Hudnall, June 12, 1931; children—Sumner Henry, Edward Bernard, Patricia Anne (Mrs. W.R. Chisholm), Peggy Jane (Mrs. R.P. Roy). Overseer dyeing and finishing Houston Textile Mills, 1924-28; asst. mgr. Gen. Dye Stuff Corp., Charlotte, N.C., 1933-43, mgr., 1943-52, v.p., gen. sales mgr., dir., 1952-54; integrated with Gen. Aniline & Film Corp., 1954, v.p. Gen. Aniline & Film Corp., N.Y.C., 1954-65, sr. v.p., 1965—; v.p. GAF Internat. Operations, 1962—, dir., 1964—; dir. Morrison Machine Co., Morrison Textile Machine Co. Mem. Am. Assn. Textile Chemists and Colorists, Acad. Sci., Phi Psi. Club: Governor's Island (Laconia, N.H.). Contbr. papers on dyeing techniques and processes; inventor textile machinery, textile dyeing processes. Home: 65 Joanna Way Short Hills NJ 07078 also Governor's Island Laconia NH 03246

WILLIAMS, SUSAN J., govt. ofcl.; b. Phila., July 31, 1940; B.A., Upsala Coll. Editor, Center for Applied Linguistics, 1962-65; spl. edn. cons. HEW, 1965-73; spl. asst. to D.C. del. Walter Fauntroy, Washington, 1973-77; with Dept. Transp., 1977—, dep. asst. sec., govtl. and public affairs, then acting asst. sec., 1979—, asst. sec., 1979—. Founder, vice chmn. No. Va. Democratic Women's Polit. Caucus; vice chmn. Fairfax County (Va.) Commn. for Children. Address: Office Govtl and Public Affairs Dept Transp 400 7th St SW Washington DC 20590*

WILLIAMS, TED (THEODORE SAMUEL), former baseball player, mgr.; b. San Diego, Aug. 30, 1918; s. Samuel Steward and May W.; m. Doris Soule; 3 children. Played with Boston Red Sox, 1939-42, 46-60; mgr. Washington Senators, 1969-71, Tex. Rangers, 1972; sports cons. Sears, Roebuck & Co. Served to 2d lt. USMCR, 1942-45. Named to Am. League All-Star Team, 1940-42, 46-51, 54-60; named Sporting News Player of Year, 1941, 42, 47, 49, 57, Am. League Most Valuable Player, 1946, 49, Am. League Mgr. of Year, 1969; elected to Baseball Hall of Fame, 1966. Author: (with John Underwood) My Turn at Bat: The Story of My Life, 1968; The Science of Hitting, 1972. Office: PO Box 481 Islamorada FL 33036

WILLIAMS, TENNESSEE THOMAS LANIER, playwright; b. Columbus, Miss., Mar. 26, 1911; s. Cornelius and Edwina (Dakin) W.; student U. Mo., 1931-33, Washington U., St. Louis, 1936-37; A.B., U. Iowa, 1938; hon. L.H.D., H.H.D. Author: (plays) Battle of Angels, 1940; The Glass Menagerie (N.Y. Drama Critics Circle award), 1944; You Touched Me, 1946; A Streetcar Named Desire (Pultizer prize, Drama Critics Circle award), 1947; Summer and Smoke, 1948; Rose Tattoo, 1950; Roman Spring of Mrs. Stone, 1950; Camino Real, 1953; Cat on a Hot Tin Roof (N.Y. Drama Critics Circle award, Pulitzer prize for drama), 1954; Orpheus Descending, 1957; Garden District, 1958; Sweet Bird of Youth, 1959; Period of Adjustment, 1950; The Night of the Iguana (Drama Critics award, Tony award), 1962; The Milk Train Doesn't Stop Here Anymore, 1963; Slapstick Tragedy, 1966; In the Bar of Tokyo Hotel and Other Plays, 1969; Small Craft Warnings, 1973; Outcry, 1974; Red Devil Battery Sign, 1976; This is an Entertainment, 1976; Vieux Carre, 1977; A Lovely Sunday for Creve Coeur, 1979, Clothes for a Summer Hotel, 1980, others; (screenplays) Suddenly Last Summer, 1959, The Fugitive Kind; (book) 27 Wagonsfull of Cotton, 1946; (short play collection) Dragon Country, 1970; (short story collections) One Arm, Hard Candy, The Knightly Quest, Eight Mortal Ladies Possessed; (novel) Noise and the World of Reason; Memoirs, 1975; (TV play) I Can't Imagine Tomorrow, 1970; (poems) In the Winter of Cities, 1956, Androgyne, Mon Amour; (essays) Where I Live, 1979. Recipient Brandeis U. Creative Arts medal in theater, 1965; Rockefeller fellow, 1940; Nat. Inst. Arts and Letters grantee, 1943, Gold medal for drama, 1969, Theatre Hall of Fame, 1979, Kennedy Honors award, 1979. Mem. Am. Automatic Control Council (pres. 1965-67), Alpha Tau Omega. Address: care Mitch Douglas ICM 40 W 57th St New York NY 10019

WILLIAMS, THEODORE EARLE, diversified mfg. co. exec.; b. Cleve., May 9, 1920; s. Stanley S. and Blanche (Albaum) W.; student Wayne U., 1937-38; B.S. in Engring., U. Mich., 1942, postgrad. in bus. adminstrn., 1942; m. Rita Cohen, Aug. 28, 1952; children—Lezlie, Richard Atlas, Shelley, William Atlas, Wayne, Patti. Pres., Wayne Products Co., Detroit, 1942-43, Los Angeles, 1947-49; pres. Williams Metal Products Co., Inglewood, Calif., 1950-69; chmn. bd., pres., chief exec. officer Bell Industries, Los Angeles, 1970—; instr. U. Mich., 1942. Served to 1st lt. AUS, 1943-46. Mem. Am. Soc. Mfg. Engrs. Democrat. Patentee in field. Home: 435 N Layton Way Los Angeles CA 90049 Office: 1880 Century Park E Los Angeles CA 90067. *It seems to me that many of our current problems in this world originate from the drift away from concern for other people to the emphasis on self. We are reluctant to get involved, and as this spaceship gets smaller, we become more interdependent all the time. If we don't learn to live together, I'm afraid we may all perish together.*

WILLIAMS, THEODORE JOSEPH, educator; b. Black Lick, Pa., Sept. 2, 1923; s. Theodore Finley and Mary Ellen (Shields) W.; B.S., Pa. State U., 1949, M.S., 1950, Ph.D., 1955; M.S. in Elec. Engring., Ohio State U., 1956; m. Isabel Annette McAnulty, July 18, 1946; children—Theodore Joseph, Mary Margaret, Charles Augustus, Elizabeth Ann. Research fellow Pa. State U., University Park, 1947-51; asst. prof. Air Force Inst. Tech., 1953-56; technologist Monsanto Co., 1956-57, sr. engring. supr., 1957-65; vis. prof. Washington U., St. Louis, 1962-65; prof engring., dir. control and information systems lab. Purdue U., Lafayette, Ind., 1965—, dir. Purdue Lab. Applied Indsl. Control, 1966—. Served to capt. USAAF, 1942-45, USAF, 1951-56. Decorated Air medal with 3 oak leaf clusters. Fellow Instrument Soc. America (president 1968-69), Am. Inst. Chemists; sr. mem. I.E.E.E.; mem. Am. Chem. Soc. Am. Inst. Chem . Engrs., A.A.A.S., Am. Automatic Control Council (pres. 1965-67), Am. Fedn. Info. Processing Socs. (pres. 1976-78), Sigma Xi, Tau Beta Pi, Phi Kappa Phi, Phi Lambda Upsilon. Author: Systems Engineering for the Process Industries, 1961; Automatic Control of Chemical and Petroleum Processes, 1961; Progress in Direct Digital Control, 1969; Interfaces with the Process Control Computer, 1971; Modeling and Control of Kraft Production Systems, 1975; editor: Computer Applications in Shipping and Shipbuilding, 6 vols., 1973-79. Home: 208 Chippewa St West Lafayette IN 47906 Office: Purdue Lab for Applied Indsl Control M Golden Engring Lab Purdue Univ Lafayette IN 47907

WILLIAMS, THOMAS (ALONZO), author, educator; b. Duluth, Minn., Nov. 15, 1926; s. Thomas Alonzo and Charlotte Clara (Marvin) W.; student U. Chgo., 1945, 48-49; B.A., U. N.H., 1950, M.A., 1958; postgrad U. Paris, 1950-51, U. Ia., 1956-58; m. Elizabeth Mae Blood, May 26, 1951; children—Peter Alonzo, Ann Joslin. Prof.

English, U. N.H., Durham, 1958—. Served to cpl. U.S. Army, 1944-46. Guggenheim fellow, 1963, Dial fellow Fiction, 1963; recipient Roos/Atkins Literary award, 1963, Rockefeller grantee Fiction, 1969, Nat. Book award fiction, 1975. Mem. Authors Guild, AAUP. Democrat. Author: Ceremony of Love, 1955; Town Burning, 1959; The Night of Trees, 1961; A High New House, 1963; Whipple's Castle, 1969; The Hair of Harold Roux, 1974; Tsuga's Children, 1977; The Followed Man, 1978. Home: 13 Orchard Dr Durham NH 03824

WILLIAMS, THOMAS FFRANCON, chemist, educator; b. Colwyn Bay, Wales, Jan. 30, 1928; s. David and Margaret (Williams) W.; came to U.S., 1961; B.Sc., Univ. Coll., London, Eng., 1949; Ph.D., U. London, 1960; m. Astra Silvia Birins, Jan. 31, 1959; children—Ifor Rainis, Gwyn David. Sci. officer U.K. Atomic Energy Authority, Harwell, Eng., 1949-55, sr. sci. officer, 1955-61, prin. sci. officer, 1961; research scientist Ill. Inst. Tech. Research Inst., Chgo., 1961; asst. prof. chemistry U. Tenn., Knoxville, 1961-63, asso. prof., 1963-67, prof., 1967—, Alumni Distinguished Service prof., 1974—. Teaching, research asso. Northwestern U., Evanston, Ill., 1957-58; NSF vis. scientist Kyoto (Japan) U., 1965-66; coordinator U.S.-Japan Sci. Sem., Hakone, Japan, 1969; chmn. Gordon Research Conf. on Radiation Chemistry, New Hampton, N.H., 1971; John Simon Guggenheim Meml. Found. fellow Swedish Research Councils' Lab., Studsvik, Nykoping, 1972-73, vis. scientist Royal Inst. Tech., Stockholm, Sweden, 1972-73; Chmn. 10th Southeastern Magnetic Resonance Conf., 1978. AEC, ERDA, Dept. Energy grantee, 1962-79. Mem. Am. Chem. Soc. (program chmn. sect. 1968-69), Brit. Chem. Soc., Nat. Geog. Soc., Knoxville Welsh Soc., Phi Beta Kappa (hon.), Sigma Xi. Contbg. author: Fundamental Processes in Radiation Chemistry, 1968; Radiation Chemistry of Macromolecules, 1972. Contbr. numerous articles on chem. effects of high energy radiation to profl. jours. Home: 3117 Montlake Dr Knoxville TN 37920 Office: Dept of Chemistry U of Tenn Knoxville TN 37916

WILLIAMS, THOMAS FRANKLIN, physician, educator; b. Belmont, N.C., Nov. 26, 1921; s. T.F. and Mary L. (Deaton) W.; B.S., U. N.C., 1942; M.A., Columbia, 1943; M.D., Harvard, 1950; m. Catharine Carter Catlett, Dec. 15, 1951; children—Mary Wright, Thomas Nelson. Intern, Johns Hopkins, Balt., 1950-51, asst. resident physician, 1951-53; resident physician Boston VA Hosp., 1953-54; research fellow U. N.C., Chapel Hill, 1954-56; instr. dept. medicine and preventive medicine U. N.C., 1956-57, asst. prof., 1957-61, asso. prof., 1961-68, prof., 1968; attending physician Strong Meml. Hosp., Rochester, N.Y., 1968—; cons. physician Genesee Hosp., 1973—, St. Mary's Hosp., 1974—, Highland Hosp., 1973— (all Rochester); prof. medicine, preventive medicine and community health U. Rochester, 1968—, also prof. radiation biology and biophysics, 1968—, mem. adv. bd. Sch. Medicine and Dentistry, 1968—; med. dir. Monroe Community Hosp., Rochester, 1968—. Mem. rev. coms. Nat. Center for Health Services Research. Mem. adv. bd. St. Ann's Home. Served with USNR, 1943-46. Diplomate Am. Bd. Internal Medicine. USPHS fellow, 1966-67. Markle scholar, 1957-61. Fellow Am. Pub. Health Assn., A.C.P.; mem. N.Y. State, Monroe County med. socs., Inst. Medicine, Nat. Acad. Scis., Am. Diabetes Assn. (dir. 1974—), A.A.A.S., Am. Fedn. Clin. Research, Soc. Exptl. Biology and Medicine, Rochester Regional Diabetes Assn. (pres. 1977-79), N.C. Council for Human Relations (chmn. 1963-66), Episcopalian. Contbr. articles on endocrine disorders, diabetes, health care delivery in chronic illness and aging to profl. publs. Home: 287 Dartmouth St Rochester NY 14607 Office: Monroe Community Hosp 435 E Henrietta Rd Rochester NY 14603

WILLIAMS, THOMAS RHYS, univ. dean, anthropologist; b. Martins Ferry, Ohio, June 13, 1928; s. Harold K. and Dorothy (Lehew) W.; B.A., Miami U., Oxford, O., 1951; M.A., U. Ariz., 1956; Ph.D., Syracuse U., 1956; m. Margaret Martin, July 12, 1952; children—Rhys M., Ian T., Tom R. Asst. prof., asso. prof. anthropology Calif. State U., Sacramento, 1956-65; vis. asso. prof. anthropology U. Calif. Berkeley, 1962; vis. prof. anthropology Stanford U., 1976; prof. anthropology Ohio State U., Columbus, 1965-78, chmn. dept, 1967-71, mem. Grad. Council, 1969-72; mem. Univ. Athletic Council, 1968-74, chmn., 1973-74, exec. com. Coll. Social and Behavior Scis., 1967-71; dean Grad. Sch., George Mason U., Fairfax, Va., 1978—. Mem. United Democrats for Humphrey, 1968, Citizens for Humphrey, 1968. Served with USN, 1946-48. NSF basic research grant, 1958, 62; Am. Council Learned Socs.-Soc. Sci. Research Council basic research grant, 1959, 63, Ford Found. S.E. Asia basic research grant, 1974, 76. Fellow Am. Anthrop. Assn., Royal Anthrop. Inst. Gt. Britain; asso. Current Anthropology; mem. AAAS, Sigma Xi. Author: The Dusun: A North Borneo Society, 1965; Field Methods in the Study of Culture, 1967; A Borneo Childhood: Enculturation in Dusun Society, 1969; Introduction to Socialization: Human Culture Transmitted, 1972. Editor, contbr. Psychological Anthropology, 1975, Socialization and Communication in Primary Groups, 1975; contbr. articles to profl. jours. Office: Grad Sch 2204 Robinson Hall George Mason U 4400 University Dr Fairfax VA 22030

WILLIAMS, THOMAS RICE, banker; b. Atlanta, Sept. 14, 1928; s. George K. and Isabel (Rice) W.; B.S. in Indsl. Engring., Ga. Inst. Tech., 1950; M.S. in Indsl. Mgmt., Mass. Inst. Tech., 1954; m. Loraine Plant, Mar. 18, 1950; children—Janet, Susan, Thomas Rice. Indsl. engr. Dan River Mills, Danville, Va., 1950-53; dir. indsl. engring. Riegel Textile Corp., Ware Shoals, S.C., 1954-59; v.p. Bruce Payne & Assos., Inc., N.Y.C., 1959-64; asst. to pres. Patchogue-Plymouth Co., N.Y.C., 1964-65; from v.p. to exec. v.p. Nat. City Bank, Cleve., 1965-72; pres. First Nat. Bank Atlanta, 1972-76, chief exec. officer, 1976—, chmn. bd., 1977—; pres. First Nat. Holding Corp. (now First Atlanta Corp.), 1974—, chmn. bd., 1977—; dir., chmn. audit com. Nat. Service Industries, Inc.; dir. Nat. Life Ins. Co., Equifax, Inc.; dir.-at-large VISA U.S.A. Inc. Trustee Atlanta U. Center, 1977—, Alexander-Tharpe Scholarship Fund, 1975-76, Ga. Tech. Found., 1975—, Agnes Scott Coll., 1975—, Westminster Schs., 1976—, Atlanta Arts Alliance, 1976—, Wesley Homes, 1974—; bd. dirs. Fulton County unit Am. Cancer Soc., 1973—; bd. dirs. Atlanta Area council Boy Scouts Am., 1973-75, adv. bd. mem., 1975—; co-chmn. new membership and rates com. Central Atlanta Progress, 1973—, treas., 1975—; treas. United Way Met. Atlanta, 1975-77, Concerned Businessmen's Congl. Forum, 1977—; trustee YMCA Met. Atlanta, 1974—, treas. bd. trustees, 1976—; adv. bd. Christian Council Met. Atlanta, 1977—. Mem. Conf. Bd., Assn. Res. City Bankers, Am. Bankers Assn., Am. Inst. Banking, Assn. Bank Holding Cos., Atlanta (dir., chmn. econ. devel. com. 1973-76), Ga. (vice chmn. fgn. trade zone task force 1974—, dir. 1975—) chambers commerce, Gridiron Soc., Sigma Alpha Epsilon. Episcopalian. Clubs: Rotary (dir. 1976—), Capital City (gov. 1977—), Piedmont Driving, Commerce (dir. 1976—), (Atlanta); Union (Cleve.). Office: PO Box 4148 Atlanta GA 30302*

WILLIAMS, TIMOTHY GLYNE, psychiatrist; b. nr. Winchester, Tenn., May 16, 1916; s. Timothy M. and Maude (Reynolds) W.; B.S., U. of South, 1939; M.D., Vanderbilt U., 1943; m. Christine E. Beazley, Dec. 13, 1941; children—Timothy Walden, Thomas Clinton, Marjorie Candace. Intern Baroness Erlanger Hosp., Chattanooga, 1943; resident St. Elizabeth's Hosp., Washington, also U.S. Naval Hosp., Norman, Okla., 1944-45; psychotherapist VA Mental Hygiene Clinic, Balt., 1946-50; mem. staff Spring Grove State Hosp., Catonsville, Md., 1950-53, clin. dir., 1953-56; dir. pilot study for psychiat. adminstrn. Yale, 1956-60; dir. Okla. Dept. Mental Health and Mental Retardation, 1960-63; asst. commr. Md. Dept. Mental Hygiene, 1963-69; supt. Rosewood State Hosp., Owings Mills, Md., 1964-72; asso. dir. Md. Psychiatric Research Center, Catonsville, 1972-75; dir. Central Clin. Services Spring Grove State Hosp., Catonsville, 1975—; lectr. Cath. U. Am., 1947-48; instr. U. Md., 1953-56; asst. prof. psychiatry and pub. health Yale, 1956-60; asso. prof. psychiatry and preventive medicine U. Okla. 1961-63. Served to lt. M.C., USNR, 1944-46. Diplomate Am. Bd. Psychiatry and Neurology. Fellow Am. Psychiat. Assn. (chmn. mental hosp. sect. 1963, liaison to Social Security Adminstrn. 1966-68), Am. Orthopsychiat. Assn.; mem. A.A.A.S. Home: 3414 Pierce Dr Ellicott City MD 21043 Office: Box 3235 Catonsville MD 21228

WILLIAMS, TIMOTHY SHALER, mfg. co. exec.; b. Bklyn., July 2, 1928; s. Herbert Howard and Marion (Reese) W.; B.A., Cornell U., 1951; LL.B. cum laude, Harvard U., 1957; postgrad. Kyoto (Japan) U., 1959; m. Rosemary Beeching Turvey, Apr. 26, 1968; children—Mari, Samuel, Keiko, Jonathan, James, Timothy Shaler, Carolyn. Admitted to D.C. bar, 1957, N.Y. bar, 1962; grad. fellow Japanese-Am. Program cooperation in Legal Studies, 1957-61; asso. firm Nattier & Anderson, N.Y.C., 1961-63; partner James B. Anderson, N.Y.C., 1963-68; Sr. Counsel Far East, ITT Corp., 1969-70; Sec., Gen. Counsel ITT Rayonier Inc., N.Y.C., 1971—, v.p., 1976—; research fellow Parker Sch. Comparative Law, Columbia U., 1962-63, lectr. law Columbia Law Sch., 1963-68. Bd. dirs. Staten Island Mental Health Soc., 1964-69. Served with AUS, 1951-53. Fulbright fellow, 1957-60. Mem. N.Y. State Bar Assn., Assn. Bar City N.Y., N.W. Pulp and Paper Assn. (trustee 1975-79, pres. 1977-79). Democrat. Clubs: Milford; Harvard (N.Y.C.). Editorial bd. Law in Japan, 1966-69. Address: 167 Fairview Ave Stamford CT 05902

WILLIAMS, TROY DAVIS, judge; b. Gary, Tex., June 23, 1915; s. Joe Hooker and Clara May (Davis) W.; B.B.A., Angelo State Coll. (now Angelo State U.), 1967; J.D., U. Tex., 1970; m. Estelle V. Reid, Feb. 3, 1935; children—Jacquelyn (Mrs. P.H. Shacklette), Bill T., Larry R., Kathryn (Mrs. Richard Mayfield). Partner J.H. Williams & Sons Grocery, Ozona, Tex., 1931-46; rancher Crockett County, 1938—; owner, mgr. Troy Williams Motor Co., Ozona, 1951-61; ind. contractor builder, Ozona, 1954-63; admitted to Tex. bar, 1969, since practiced in Ozona; county judge Crockett County, 1971-77; judge 112th Jud. Dist., Ozona, Tex., 1977—. Ex-officio county sch. supt. Crockett County, 1971-77; supr. Crockett County Soil Conservation Dist., 1950-55; county chmn. Planning Com., 1966-70. Bd. dirs. Baptist Memls. Center, San Angelo, Tex. Mem. Concho Hereford Assn. (pres. 1960-62), Am., Tex., Trans-Pecos bar assns., Nat. Assn. Probate Judges, Ozona C. of C. (pres. 1964-65), Phi Alpha Delta, Delta Sigma Pi. Baptist (trustee 1949—). Lion. Home: 407 Rugged Rd Ozona TX 76943 Office: Ave D 11th St Ozona TX 76943

WILLIAMS, WALKER ALONZO, ret. automobile co. exec.; b. Wellington, Mo., June 8, 1901; s. Henry A. and Helen (Walker) W.; student U. Ill., 1922-23, Kansas City Sch. Law, evenings 1921, Kansas City Jr. Coll., evenings 1921; m. Evelyn Forrester, Sept. 25, 1926; children—Walker Forrester, John Haviland. With traffic dept. Armour Grain Co., Kansas City, Mo., 1920-22; with accounting dept. Am. Can Co., Kansas City, Mo., 1924-25; various positions up to wholesale mgr. Ford Motor Co., Kansas City, Mo., 1925-34, asst. br. mgr., Omaha, 1934-39, Kansas City, Mo., 1939-41, br. mgr., Salt Lake City, 1941-42, 44-45, Somerville, Mass., 1945-46, Ford sales mgr., Dearborn, Mich., 1946-48, gen. sales mgr. Ford div., 1948-50, v.p. sales and advt. for co., 1950-56, v.p., also vice chmn. dealer policy bd. for co., 1956- 58, v.p., asst. gen. mgr. Lincoln-Mercury div., 1958-61, ret., 1961; bus. mgr. Kalunite Inc., Salt Lake City, 1942-44. Charter mem. Detroit Symphony Orch.; mem. Detroit Grand Opera Assn.; gen. chmn., bd. dirs. United Found. Detroit, 1958; chmn. Crusade for Freedom, State Mich., 1951-52; past bd. dirs. Automobile Safety Found., Washington; founder mem. Soc. Performing Arts, Boca Raton, Fla. Past mem. Rapid Transit Commn., Detroit. Mem. Automotive Old Timers (life), DeMolay Legion of Honor, Fla. Atlantic Music Guild, Opera Soc. Ft. Lauderdale, English Speaking Union, Founders Soc. of Detroit Inst. Arts, Phi Gamma Delta. Clubs: Detroit Athletic; Boca Raton (Fla.), Boca Raton Hotel and Club, Royal Palm Yacht and Country; Vermilion Fairways Golf (Cook, Minn.). Home: 1355 Fan Palm Rd Boca Raton FL 33432

WILLIAMS, WALLACE CECIL, state ofcl.; b. Kannapolis, N.C., Sept. 23, 1921; s. Willie and Mary (Ware) W.; student Pace Coll., 1947-48, Columbia U., 1948-50, Detroit Inst. Tech., 1957-58, Wayne State U., 1969-70, U. Detroit, 1971—; children—Joyce, Wallace J. Asst. interviewer N.Y. State Employment Service, N.Y.C., 1947-53; prison fiscal officer U.S. Bureau of Prisons, Washington, Dansbury, Conn. and Milan, Mich., 1953-58; employment and claims interviewer Mich. Employment Security Commn., 1958-65, employment security exec., 1965-69; econ. devel. exec. Mich. Dept. Commerce, Detroit, 1969—. Chmn. Minority Bus. Opportunity Com., Detroit, 1972-75, editor, pub. Minority Bus. Newsletter, 1971—; trustee, mem. exec. council Trade Union Leadership Council, 1972-74; bd. dirs., mem. exec. bd. Inner City Bus. Improvement Forum, 1972-74, dir. constrn. contractors assistance program; bd. dirs. People's Community Civic League, 1971-73, HOPE, Inc., 1974—; trustee Orchestra Hall Found., 1972—; bd. dirs. Lewis Bus. Coll., 1973—, Highland Park YMCA. Served with AUS, 1942-46. Recipient Layman of the Year award United Christian Ch., 1961, Outstanding and Dedicated Service award Contacts, Inc., 1971, Valuable Service to Bus. Community award City of Detroit, 1974; Spirit of Detroit award City of Detroit; Testimonial resolution Ho. of Reps.; certificate appreciation U.S. Dept. Commerce; Outstanding Contbn. award Detroit Fed. Exec. Bd. Mem. Nat. Bus. League, NAACP, VFW, Detroit C. of C. (mem. adv. com. 1972—), Nat. Assn. Accountants, New Detroit, Am. Mgmt. Assn. Mem. Christian Ch. (deacon). Clubs: Cotillion, Detroit Press. Home: 9000 E Jefferson Detroit MI 48214. *Whatever success I have achieved is due to hard work, belief in God and self, and treating others fair.*

WILLIAMS, WALTER CHARLES, JR., aero. research exec.; b. New Orleans, July 30, 1919; s. Walter Charles and Emilia A. (Brunnier) W.; B.S. in Aero. Engring., La. State U. 1939, Dr. Engring. (hon.), 1963; m. Helen E. Manning, Dec. 16, 1939; children—Charles M., Howard L., Elizabeth A. With NACA, Langley Field, 1940-46, asst. head stability and control br. flight research div., 1944-46, flight research project engr. XS-1 (supersonic research airplane), 1945-47, charge all NACA-NASA flight test activities Muroc AFB, later Edward AFB, 1946-59, including 1st manned supersonic flight, flight beyond M-2.0, operations dir. Project Mercury, NASA; asso. dir. NASA Manned Spacecraft Center; v.p. Aerospace Corp., gen. mgr. vehicle systems div., El Segundo, Cal., 1964-75; chief engr. NASA, Washington, 1975—. Mem. subcom. high speed aerodynamics, also high-speed flight sta. rep. com. aerodynamics of missiles and spacecraft NASA; mem. flight test and instrumentation techniques panel, adv. group for aero. research and devel. NATO; chmn. X-15 flight test steering com. Joint USAF-NASA Com., 1956-59. Recipient Astronautics award Am. Inst. Aeros. and Astronautics, 1964; Distinguished Service medal NASA, 1962; Sylvanus Albert Reed award, 1963. Fellow Am. Astronautical Soc., Am. Inst. Aeros. and Astronautics; mem. Tau Beta Pi, Omicron Delta Kappa. Mason. Home: 8011 Ferncliff Ct Springfield VA 22153

WILLIAMS, WALTER FRED, steel co. exec.; b. Upland, Pa., Feb. 7, 1929; s. Walter James and Florence Missouri (Stott) W.; B.Civil Engring. summa cum laude, U. Del., 1951; m. Joan Bernice Carey, Aug. 26, 1950; children—Jeffrey F., Richard C., Douglas E. With Bethlehem Steel Corp. (Pa.), 1951—, asst. chief engr. on staff v.p. operations, 1965-66, chief engr. constrn., Burns Harbor (Ind.) plant, 1966-67, chief engr. projects group engring. dept., Bethlehem, then mgr. engring. in charge projects, design and constrn., 1967-68, asst. to v.p. engring., 1968, asst. v.p. shipbldg., 1968-70, v.p. shipbldg., 1970-75, v.p. steel operations, 1975-77, sr. v.p. steel operations, 1978—, also dir. Served to 1st lt. U.S. Army, 1951-53. Mem. Am. Iron and Steel Inst. Methodist. Club: Saucon Valley Country (Bethlehem). Home: Saucon Valley Rd 4 Bethlehem PA 18015 Office: Bethlehem Steel Corp Bethlehem PA 18016

WILLIAMS, WALTER JACKSON, JR., engr.; b. Elkhart, Ind., Jan. 17, 1925; s. Walter Jackson and Mary (Delcamp) W.; B.S. in Elec. Engring., Purdue U., 1948, M.S., 1950; Ph.D., 1954; m. Helen L. Evans, July 20, 1944; children—David, Eileen, Valerie. From grad. asst. to instr. Purdue U., Layfayette, Ind., 1948-54; jr. engr. Argonne Nat. Lab., 1950, Naval Ordnance Plant, Indpls., 1951; engr. Internat. Tel. & Tel. Co., Ft. Wayne, Ind., 1954-60, cons., 1961-63, sr. tech. advisor Aerospace Optical div., 1975—; chmn. dept. elec. engring. Ind. Inst. Tech., Ft. Wayne, 1961-65, dean engring., 1963-67, v.p., acad. dean, 1967-75, interim pres., 1970-72; cons. in field, 1960—. Bd. dirs. Asso. Chs., Ft. Wayne, 1965-67. Served with AUS, 1943-46. Mem. IEEE, Am. Soc. Engring. Edn., Nat., Ind. (dir. Ft. Wayne 1968-70) socs. profl. engrs., Ft. Wayne Engrs. Club (pres. 1967-68, dir. 1969-71), Sigma Xi, Tau Beta Pi, Eta Kappa Nu. Patentee in field. Home: 6710 S Calhoun St Fort Wayne IN 46807

WILLIAMS, WALTER JOSEPH, lawyer; b. Detroit, Oct. 5, 1918; s. Joseph Louis and Emma Geraldine (Hewitt) W.; student Bowling Green State U., 1935-36; B.S.B.A., Ohio State U., 1940; J.D., LL.B., U. Detroit, 1942; m. Maureen June Kay, Jan. 15, 1944; 1 son, John Bryan. Admitted to Mich. bar, 1942; title atty. Abstract & Title Guaranty Co., 1946-47; corp. atty. Ford Motor Co., 1947-51, Studebaker-Packard Corp., 1951-56; asst. sec., house counsel Am. Motors Corp., Am. Motors Sales Corp., Am. Motors Pan-Am. Corp., Evart Products Co., Ltd., 1956-65, corp. sec. house counsel, 1965-72; asst. corp. sec., dir. Am. Motors (Can.) Ltd.; dir. Evart Products Co., 1959-72; dir., corporate sec., house counsel Jeep Corp., Jeep Sales Corp., Jeep Internat. Corp., 1968-72; partner Gilman and Williams, Southfield, Mich., 1972-74; atty. Detroit Edison Co., 1974-75; asst. sec., sr. staff atty. Burroughs Corp. and subsidiaries, 1975—. Charter commr. city of Dearborn Heights, Mich., 1960-63; dir. Detroit Met. Indsl. Devel. Corp., 1962-72, also asst. sec. Served to capt. U.S. Army, 1942-46. Mem. Am., Detroit (chmn. corp. gen. counsel com. 1965-68), Fed. bar assns., State Bar Mich., Ohio State U. Alumni Assn. (pres. Detroit 1961-63), U. Detroit Law Alumni, Delta Theta Phi. Club: Oakland Hills Country. Home: 3644 Darcy Dr Birmingham MI 48010 Office: Burroughs Pl Detroit MI 48232

WILLIAMS, WALTER WAYLON, lawyer, pecan grower; b. Gause, Tex., Nov. 12, 1933; s. Jesse Nathaniel and Lola Fay (Matthews) W.; B.B.A. with honors, U. Tex., 1959, J.D. with honors, 1960; m. Velmalene Von Gonten, Mar. 6, 1953; children—Diana Lee, Virginia Marie. Admitted to Tex. bar, 1960; since practiced in Houston; mem. firm Fulbright, Crooker, Freeman, Bates & Jaworski, 1960-63, Bates & Brock, 1964-66, Brock, Williams & Boyd, 1966—. Pres. Tex. Pecan Growers Assn., Federated Pecan Growers Assn., 1976—. Served with AUS, 1953-55. Named Outstanding Soldier of Second Army, 1955. Mem. Am., Houston bar assns., State Bar Tex., Tex. (dir. 1972-76), Houston (dir. 1969) trial lawyers assns., Assn. Trial Lawyers Am., Chancellors, Beta Gamma Sigma, Phi Delta Phi. Home: 9607 Meadowglen St Houston TX 77063 Office: 1212 Main St Houston TX 77002

WILLIAMS, WAYNE DEARMOND, lawyer; b. Denver, Sept. 24, 1914; s. Wayne Cullen and Lena Belle (Day) W.; A.B., U. Denver, 1936; J.D., Columbia U., 1938; m. Virginia Brinton Deal, Sept. 9, 1937; children—Marcia Lee, Daniel Deal. Admitted to Colo. bar, 1938; individual practice law, Denver, 1938-43, 46-58; partner firm Williams & Erickson, and predecessors, Denver, 1958-77; gen. counsel Denver Water Dept., 1977—; asst. city atty. Denver, 1939-43; spl. asst. atty., Denver, 1946-49; chmn. Denver County Ct. Nominating Commn., 1968-69; mem. Denver Dist. Ct. Nominating Commn., 1969-75; lectr. in field U. Denver, 1947-60. Chmn., Denver Municipal Airport Adv. Commn., 1963-65. Served to capt. JAGC, U.S. Army, 1943-46. Mem. Am. (Ross Essay prize 1944), Colo. (gov. 1974-77), Denver (pres. 1974-75), Fed., Inter-Am. bar assns., Am. Soc. Internat. Law, Sigma Alpha Epsilon, Phi Delta Phi, Omicron Delta Kappa. Democrat. Methodist. Clubs: Lions, Masons. Contbr. articles to legal jours. Home: 3340 E Kentucky Ave Denver CO 80209 Office: Denver Water Dept 1600 W 12th Ave Denver CO 80254

WILLIAMS, WENDELL STERLING, educator, physicist; b. Lake Forest, Ill., Oct. 27, 1928; s. Sterling Price and Mary Eleanor (Myers) W.; student Deep Springs Jr. Coll.; B.A. in Physics, Swarthmore Coll., 1951; Ph.D. in Physics, Cornell U., 1956; m. Dorothy Ellen Watt, June 28, 1952; children—Jennifer Anne, Laura Kathleen. Research physicist Leeds & Northrup Co., Phila., 1951; research physicist Union Carbide Corp., Parma, O., 1956-65, 66-67; sr. research visitor Cambridge (Eng.) U., 1965-66; prin. investigator Materials Research Lab. U. Ill., Urbana-Champaign, 1967—, asso. prof., 1967-69, prof. physics and ceramic engring., 1969—, prof. bioengring., 1973—, dir. program on ancient technologies and archeol. materials, 1979—; cons. in field. Mem. adv. com. metals and ceramics div. Oak Ridge Nat. Lab., 1972-74; mem. materials sci. com. Argonne Center for Ednl. Affairs, chmn. 1972-73; guest worker Nat. Bur. Standards, 1972; with div. materials research Nat. Sci. Found., Washington, 1974-75, head metallurgy and materials sect., 1977-78. Founder, conductor S.W. Messiah Chorale, Cleve., 1960-67, Unitarian-Universalist Church Choir, Urbana, Ill., 1968-73. Trustee Telluride Assn., 1949-59, v.p., 1953. Fellow Am. Phys. Soc.; mem. AAAS, Am. Ceramic Soc., AIME, Fedn. Am. Scientists, Materials Research Soc. (councillor), Sigma Xi. Unitarian-Universalist. Club: Cosmos (Washington). Editorial adv. bd. Jour. of Non-Metals, 1972—. Contbr. articles on physics of refractory materials and biological materials to profl. jours. Home: 501 E Mumford Dr Urbana IL 61801

WILLIAMS, WILEY HERBERT, constrn., real estate fin. exex.; b. Brunswick, Ga., Mar. 4, 1929; s. Wiley Patrick and Era B. (Cain) W.; B.B.A. in Accounting, Lamar Tech. Coll., Beaumont, Tex., 1957; children—Virginia, Sandra, Dolly. Accountant, Port Arthur (Tex.) News, 1952-57; mem. staff to sr. auditor Arthur Young & Co., C.P.A.'s, Ft. Worth, 1957-59; from controller to sec.-treas. Ben Hogan Co., Ft. Worth, 1959-63; from controller to v.p., treas. Profl. Golf Co., Chattanooga, 1963-71, also dir.; controller Titan Group, Inc., Paramus, N.J., 1972-73, v.p. finance, 1975-79; with the Mack Cos., Rochelle Park, N.J., 1979—. Served with U.S. Army, 1950-52. C.P.A., Tex., Tenn. Mem. Am. Inst. C.P.A.'s, Tex., Tenn. socs. C.P.A.'s. Home: 770 Anderson Ave Cliffside Park NJ 07010 Office: Mack Cos 370 W Passaic St Rochelle Park NJ 07662

WILLIAMS, WILLIAM APPLEMAN, educator, author; b. Atlantic, Iowa, June 12, 1921; s. William Carleton and Mildrede (Appleman) W.; B.S., U.S. Naval Acad., 1944; student U. Leeds (Eng.), 1948; M.A., U. Wis., 1948, Ph.D., 1950. Commd. ensign U.S. Navy, 1944; served in PTO, 1944-46; retired, 1947; joined faculty U. Wis., Madison, 1957, became prof. history, 1960; now prof. history Oreg. State U., Corvallis; Fulbright scholar U. Melbourne, 1977; James Pinckney Harrison prof. history Coll. William and Mary, 1980. Active Civil Rights Movement, 1946-47, socialist politics. Mem. Orgn. Am. Historians (pres. 1980-81). Author: American-Russian Relations, 1784-1947, 1950; The Shaping of American Diplomacy, 1763-1970, 1970; The Tragedy of American Diplomacy, 1960; The Contours of American History, 1961; The United States, Cuba and Castro, 1962; The Great Evasion, 1964; The Roots of the Modern American Empire, 1969; Some Presidents: From Wilson to Nixon, 1972; History As A Way of Learning, 1975; America Confronts a Revolutionary World: 1776-1976, 1976; Americans In a Changing World, 1978; Empire As a Way of Life, 1980; contbr. articles to mags. and newspapers. Office: History Dept Oreg State U Corvallis OR 97331

WILLIAMS, WILLIAM HARRISON, librarian; b. Seattle, Apr. 18, 1924; s. William E. and Letah M. (Hollenback) W.; B.S., Brigham Young U., 1969, M.L.S., 1970; m. Mary Helen Sims, Apr. 19, 1945; children—Linda Lee, Dee Ann (Mrs. Larry H. Crismon). Dir. Provo (Utah) Pub. Library, 1969-70; Wyo. State Librarian, 1970—; dir. Wyo. state Archives and Hist. dept., 1971—; exec. sec. Wyo. Hist. Soc., 1971—. Served to lt. col. USAF, 1943-64. Decorated USAF commendation with oak leaf cluster. Mem. Am., Mountain Plains, Wyo. library assns., Western Hist. Soc., Am. Assn. State and Local History, Beta Phi Mu, Phi Alpha Theta. Rotarian, Kiwanian. Home: Box 2637 Airport Sta Cheyenne WY 82001 Office: Barrett Bldg Cheyenne WY 82002

WILLIAMS, WILLIAM HENRY, justice Wash. State Supreme Ct.; b. Spokane, Wash., Apr. 27, 1922; s. Ralph David and Ruth Grace W.; B.A. in Polit. Sci., U. Idaho, 1948; J.D., Gonzaga U., 1951; m. Ruth Bernice Bevers, May 28, 1955. Admitted to Wash. bar, 1951; dep. pros. atty. Spokane County, 1951-54; practiced law, Spokane, 1954-58; judge Wash. State Superior Ct., Spokane, 1958-78; justice Wash. State Supreme Ct., 1979—. Served with USAAF, 1943-45. Office: Supreme Ct Wash Temple of Justice Olympia WA 98504

WILLIAMS, WILLIAM IVOR, editor; b. Easton, Pa., Aug. 31, 1923; s. William A. and Annie (Jones) W.; student pub. schs.; m. Dulcie Lorraine Williamson, Sept. 1. 1943; children—S. Garry, Judie Williams Wheaton. Reporter, London Free Press, 1945-50, city editor, news editor, mng. editor, 1950-73; editor Regina (Sask.) Leader-Post, 1973—; pres. Canadian Mng. Editors Conf., 1968-70. Served with RCAF, 1941-45, Aux., 1946-67. Decorated Can. decoration. Mem. Canadian Daily Newspaper Pubs. Assn. (chmn. editorial div. 1975-76), Am. Soc. Newspaper Editors, Can. Fighter Pilots Assn., Royal United Services Inst., London City Press Club. Presbyterian. Clubs: Assiniboia, Regina Golf and Country (Regina). Home: 4011 Gordon Rd Regina SK S4S 6G6 Canada Office: 1964 Park St Regina SK S4P 3G4 Canada. *A man's character is what he is when by himself.*

WILLIAMS, WILLIAM JOHN, steel co. exec.; b. Penn Yan, N.Y., Aug. 10, 1928; s. Freeburn and Josephine Charlotte (O'Keefe) W.; J.D., U. Richmond, 1955; m. Sara Jane Washeim, Sept. 2, 1950; children—William John, Anne Ross, David Blakley, Robert Freeburn. Admitted to Ohio bar, Va. bar; mem. firm Hunton, Williams, Gay, Powell & Gibson, 1957-63; with Republic Steel Corp., Cleve., 1963—, exec. v.p., 1977—, also dir.; dir. Liberia Mining Co., Inc., Res. Mining Co., Mooney Aircraft Corp., Beatrice Pocahontas Co., and Republic Steel Corp. subsidiaries. Trustee Cleve. Play House; chmn. bd. Marymount Hosp.; vice chmn. Keuka Coll. Mem. Am. Bar Assn., Cleve. Bar Assn., Ohio Bar Assn., Va. Bar Assn., Ohio C. of C., Cleve. Growth Assn., Govt. Research Inst., Am. Iron and Steel Inst. Clubs: Mayfield Country, Pepper Pike, Union, Met. Office: 1705 Republic Bldg Cleveland OH 44115

WILLIAMS, WILLIAM JOSEPH, physician, educator; b. Bridgeton, N.J., Dec. 8, 1926; s. Edward Carlaw and Mary Hood (English) W.; student Bucknell U., 1943-45; M.D., U. Pa., 1949; m. Margaret Myrick Lyman, Aug. 12, 1950; children—Susan Lyman, William Prescott, Sarah Robb. Intern U. Pa., 1949-50, Am. Cancer Soc. research fellow in Biochemistry, 1950-52, resident medicine, 1954-55, asso. to asst. prof. medicine, 1955-58, asso. prof. to prof. medicine, chief hematology, 1961-69; sr. instr. microbiology Western Res. U., 1952; asst. prof. medicine Washington U., St. Louis, 1959-60; research fellow Oxford U. (Eng.), 1960-61; mem. hematology tng. com. Nat. Inst. Arthritis and Metabolic Disease, 1964-68, research career program com., 1968-72; prof., chmn. dept. medicine Upstate Med. Center, State U. N.Y., Syracuse, 1969—. Mem. thrombosis adv. com. Nat. Heart and Lung Inst., 1969-73, chmn., 1971-73; adv. council Nat. Arthritis, Metabolism and Digestive Diseases, 1975-79; mem. hematology com. Am. Bd. Internal Medicine, 1976—. Trustee Everson Mus. Art. Served with USNR, 1944-46, 52-54. Recipient Research Career Devel. award Nat. Heart Inst., 1963-68; Daland fellow Am. Philos. Soc., 1955-57; Markle scholar, 1957-62; diplomate Am. Bd. Internal Medicine. Mem. Am. Soc. Biol. Chemists, Am. Soc. Clin. Investigation, Assn. Am. Physicians, Am. Clin. and Climatol. Assn., A.C.P. (gov. Upstate N.Y. 1976), Am. Heart Assn. (council on thrombosis exec. com. 1977—), Internat. Soc. Thrombosis and Haemostasis, Assn. Profs. Medicine, Am. Soc. Hematology, AMA, Interurban Clin. Club (sec. 1964-70), Internat. Hematology Soc., Alpha Omega Alpha. Mem. Soc. Friends. Editor-in-chief Hematology, 1972, 2d edit., 1977; contbr. articles to med. lit. Home: 3 Standish Terr Syracuse NY 13224 Office: 750 E Adams St Syracuse NY 13210

WILLIAMS, WILLIAM LANE, univ. adminstr., anatomist; b. Rock Hill, S.C., Dec. 23, 1914; s. Oscar Kell and Cora Robertson (Mobley) W.; B.S., Wofford Coll., 1935; M.A., Duke U., 1939; Ph.D., Yale U., 1941. Instr. anatomy U. Rochester (N.Y.), 1941-42, Yale U., 1942-43; asst. prof. anatomy La. State U., Baton Rouge, 1943-45; asst. prof. U. Minn., Mpls., 1945-49, asso. prof., 1949-58; prof. U. Miss. Med. Center, Jackson, 1958—, chmn. dept. anatomy, 1958—, asst. vice chancellor, 1975—. Donner Found. fellow, 1942-43; NIH grantee, 1949-73. Mem. Am. Assn. Pathologists, Am. Physiol. Soc., Endocrine Soc., Histochem. Soc., Soc. Exptl. Biology and Medicine, Inst. Nutrition, Am. Assn. Anatomists. Presbyterian. Asso. editor Anat. Record, 1959-75. Office: 2500 N State St Jackson MS 39216

WILLIAMS, WILLIAM LAWRENCE, educator, biochemist; b. St. Cloud, Minn., June 14, 1919; s. Will L. and Edith (Mottram) W.; B.S., U. Minn., 1942; M.S., U. Wis., 1947, Ph.D., 1949; m. Opal Fay Romedy, Apr. 4, 1946; children—Lawrence K., Jan R. Biochemist, Fleischmann Lab., Stamford, Conn., 1942-44, Naval Med. Research Inst., Bethesda, Md., 1945-56; mem. faculty N.C. State Coll., Raleigh, 1949-50; group leader Lederle Labs., Pearl River, N.Y., 1950-59; research prof. biochemistry U. Ga., Athens, 1959—. Recipient Career Research award NIH, 1962-72; named Ga. Scientist of Year, 1969. Mem. Soc. for Study Reprodn. (dir.), Am. Soc. Biol. Chemists, Am. Physiol. Soc., Mark L. Morris Animal Found. (hon. dir. research), Am. Inst. Nutrition, Sigma Xi. Contbr. articles to profl. jours. Home: 3755 Barnett Shoals Rd Athens GA 30601

WILLIAMS, WILLIAM RALSTON, bank and trust co. exec.; b. Hattiesburg, Miss., Jan. 20, 1910; s. William Ralston and Beulah (Smith) W.; student Central State Coll., Edmond, Okla., 1929-32, Okla. State U., 1933; m. Mary E. Marsh, May 8, 1936; chiildren—Mary J. (Mrs. Charles W. Cargill, Jr.), Julie D. Dist. mgr. Oklahoma City area Internat. Harvester Co., 1935-43; owner Stipes-Williams Co., Altus, Okla., 1943-55, Williams Investment and Ins. Co., Altus, 1955-69; sr. v.p. Fidelity Nat. Bank & Trust Co., Oklahoma City, 1968—. Regent A. and M. Colls. Okla., 1952-69, chmn., 1957-64; v.p. Am. Assn. Gov. Bds. Colls. and Univs. Am., 1958. Mem. Altus City Council, 1948-52. Served to lt. USNR, 1944-46. Mem. Oklahoma City C. of C., Am. Legion, Beta Theta Pi. Democrat. Episcopalian. Kiwanian (pres. Altus 1947, lt. gov. 1952), Mason (32, K.T., Jester), Elk. Club: Quail Creek Country (Oklahoma City). Home: 3012 Thorn Ridge Rd Oklahoma City OK 73120 Office: Harvey at Park Ave Oklahoma City OK 73124

WILLIAMS, WILLIAM REGINALD, ins. co. exec.; b. Los Angeles, Sept. 13, 1927; s. William Reginald and Kathryn (Bell) W.; B.A., Occidental Coll., 1951, certificate in applied policies and econs., 1951; m. Joan Martin, Aug. 13, 1954; children—William Reginald III, Julie Ann, Travis Martin. With Occidental Life Ins. Co., 1949-66, 2d v.p., 1964-65, mgr., Houston, 1961-64; with Gt. So. Life Ins. Co., Houston, 1966-75, dir., 1968-75, mem. exec. com., 1971-75, exec. v.p., 1972-75; pres., chief operating officer Calif. Life Ins. Co., Los Angeles, 1975-76; exec. v.p. Southland Life Ins. Co., Dallas, 1976-79, agency sales mgr., 1979—; asso. dir. Calif. Life Ins. Co., Calif. Life Corp.; dir. Gt. So. Corp., Southland Life Ins. Served with USNR, 1945-46. C.L.U. Mem. Tex. Life Conv. (chmn. agy. sect. 1973—), Austin Assn. Life Underwriters, Austin C. of C., Phi Gamma Delta. Methodist. Club: Onion Creek (Austin). Home: 11246 Pinehurst Dr Austin TX 78747 Office: Southland Life Ins 1016 La Posada Dr Suite 156 Austin TX 78752

WILLIAMS, WILLIAM THOMAS, JR., exec.; b. Angleton, Tex., June 3, 1908; s. William Thomas and Nannie (Borum) W.; LL.B., U. Tex., 1930; m. Valerie Clotilde Mansbendel, Feb. 14, 1933 (dec.); children—William Thomas III, Valerie Clotilde (Mrs. Sidney C. Brown); m. Helen Steck Malone, Jan. 1, 1977. Admitted to Tex. bar, 1930; practiced in Austin, 1930-40; asst. city atty., Austin, 1940-42, 46-47, 1949-51, city atty., 1951-55; tax assessor-collector, Austin, 1947-49; city mgr., Austin, 1955-67; exec. v.p. Walter Carrington Enterprises, 1967-69; v.p. Nash Phillips-Copus Co., 1969—. Pres. McCallum High School P.T.A., 1956-57. Former mem. dist. bd. dirs. Am. Cancer Soc. Served to capt. AUS, 1942-46; ETO; col. Res. ret. Decorated Bronze Star Medal. Mem. Austin C. of C. (dir. 1971-74), Internat. City Mgrs. Assn., Am., Tex. bar assns., Res. Officers Assn. (pres. Austin 1946-47), Assn. U.S. Army, Ret. Officers Assn., Am. Judicature Soc., Delta Theta Phi. Episcopalian (exec. bd. diocese Tex. 1972-74). Lion (pres. North Austin 1948-49). Club: Headliners (Austin). Home: 3820 Ave F Austin TX 78751 Office: Hwy 290 at IH 35 Austin TX

WILLIAMS, WILMER LAMAR, investment co. exec.; b. Tampa, Fla., Mar. 25, 1924; s. Gearry Wootson and Sophronia (Airline) W.; B.S. in Bus. Adminstrn., U. Ala., 1948; postgrad. Columbia U., 1951-52; m. Adele Catherine Binger, July 1, 1951; children—Gary Douglas, Patricia Jean. Staff accountant Price Waterhouse & Co., 1948-51; with Lehman Corp., N.Y.C., 1951—, v.p., treas., 1973—; sr. v.p., treas., dir. Lehman Mgmt. Co., N.Y.C., 1975—; treas., dir. Gas Properties Inc., N.Y.C., 1955—; v.p., One William St. Fund, N.Y.C., 1975—. Served with U.S. Army, 1943-45. C.P.A. N.Y. Home: 550 Elm Ave River Edge NJ 07661 Office: 55 Water St New York NY 10004

WILLIAMS-ASHMAN, HOWARD GUY, educator, scientist; b. London, Eng., Sept. 3, 1925; s. Edward Harold and Violet Rosamund (Sturge) Williams-A.; B.A., U. Cambridge, 1946; Ph.D., U. London, 1949; m. Elisabeth Bächli, Jan. 25, 1959; children—Anne Clare, Christian, Charlotte, Geraldine. Came to U.S., 1950, naturalized, 1962. From asst. prof. to prof. biochemistry U. Chgo., 1953-64; prof. pharmacology and exptl. therapeutics, also prof. reproductive biology Johns Hopkins Sch. Medicine, 1964-69; prof. biochemistry Ben May Lab. for Cancer Research, U. Chgo., 1969—, Maurice Goldblatt prof., 1973—. Recipient Research Career award USPHS, 1962-64. Fellow Am. Acad. Arts and Scis. (Amory prize 1975); mem. Am. Soc. Biol. Chemists, Am. Soc. for Pharmacology and Exptl. Therapeutics, Soc. Study Reprodn. Contbr. numerous articles in field to publs. Home: 5421 S Cornell Ave Chicago IL 60615 Office: Ben May Lab for Cancer Research U Chgo Chicago IL 60637

WILLIAMSON, BURKE, lawyer; b. Leesville, La., Mar. 30, 1906; s. William Burke and Hazel (Allis) W.; A.B., Washington and Lee U., 1926; J.D., Northwestern U., 1930; m. Elise Hamill Clow, Sept. 9, 1939; children—Eleanor Hamill (Mrs. Frederic Fischer, Jr.), Rosalie Allis. Admitted to Ill. bar, 1930, N.C. bar, 1974; since practiced in Chgo.; mem. firm Gordon, Adams & Pierce, 1930-34; partner Adams, Williamson & Turney, 1934-72; partner Adams & Williamson, 1972—. Pres. bd. trustees Hull House Assn., 1957-60. Served from pvt. to capt. inf. U.S. Army, 1942-46. Mem. Chgo. (bd. of mgrs. 1963-65) Bar Assn., U.S. Army Res., Kappa Sigma, Phi Delta Phi, Phi Beta Kappa. Episcopalian. Clubs: Law, Legal, Chicago (Chgo.); Biltmore Forest Country (N.C.); Mountain City (Asheville, N.C.). Home: 18 Cedarcliff Rd Asheville NC 28803 Office: 11 S LaSalle St Chicago IL 60603

WILLIAMSON, CLARENCE KELLY, coll. dean, microbiologist, b. McKeesport, Pa., Jan. 19, 1924; s. James Frederick and Loretta (McDermott) W.; B.S., U. Pitts., 1949, M.S., 1951, Ph.D., 1955; m. Dorothy Birgit Ohlsson, Aug. 18, 1951; children—Lisa Ann, Erik James. Bacteriologist, E.S. Magee Hosp., Pitts., 1951; instr. pharmacognosy and bacteriology U. Pitts., 1951-55; instr. bacteriology Pa. State U., summer 1953; mem. faculty Miami U., Oxford, O., 1955—, chmn. dept. microbiology, 1962-72, prof., 1963—, dean Coll. Arts and Sci., 1971—; cons. Warren-Teed Products Co., Columbus, O., 1953-62; cons. editor microbiology World Pub. Co., Cleve., 1965-68. Sec.-treas. McCullough-Hyde Meml. Hosp., 1968-70, trustee, bd. dirs., 1967-77, vice chmn., 1970-71, 72-74, chmn., 1974-76. Mem. commn. on arts and scis. Nat. Assn. State Univs. and Land-Grant Colls., 1974—; bd. govs. Am. Inst. Biol. Scis., 1977—; bd. dirs. Council Colls. of Arts and Scis., 1975—, pres., 1977-78. Served with USNR, 1943-46. Fellow Am. Acad. Microbiology, Ohio Acad. Sci. (v.p. med. sci. sect. 1970-71); mem. Am. Soc. Microbiology, Sigma Xi, Rho Chi, Phi Sigma (nat. v.p. 1975-77, pres. 1977—). Clubs: Rotary (pres. Oxford 1967-68); Torch (pres. Butler County 1969-70). Spl. research poststreptococcal glomerulonephritis, classification of viridans streptococci, dissociation of Pseudomonas aeruginosa. Home: 104 McKee Ave Oxford OH 45056

WILLIAMSON, DANIEL LESTER, JR., govt. ofcl.; b. Wilmington, N.C., Nov. 29, 1924; s. Daniel Lester and Margaret Myrtle (Patterson) W.; A.A., George Washington U., 1948; m. Catherine Bryan, Aug. 14, 1945; children—Michael, Anne (Mrs. Larry Blackburn), Patricia, Lynn. Joined Dept. State, 1946; adminstrv. officer, Jidda, Saudi Arabia, 1966-69; dep. exec. dir. Bur. Near East and South Asia Affairs, Washington, 1969-70, exec. dir., 1974—; counselor adminstrv. affairs, Tokyo, 1971-74; exec. dir. Near East and South Asia Bur., Washington, 1974-75, dep. asst. sec. for budget and fin. Adminstrn. Bur., 1975-78, sr. insp. Office of Insp. Gen., 1978, counselor adminstrv. affairs, London, 1979—. Served to lt. (j.g.) USNR, 1943-46, 51-53. Recipient Dept. State Meritorious Honor award, 1969. Mem. Am. Fgn. Service Assn. Club: Royal Calcutta Golf (Calcutta, India). Home: Am Embassy Box 40 FPO New York NY 09510 Office: Am Embassy London England

WILLIAMSON, DONALD JAMES, lawyer, educator; b. Hoboken, N.J., May 12, 1936; s. Oswald J. and Rose Agnes (Zimmerman) W.; B.S., St. Peter's Coll., Jersey City, 1958; J.D. (Arthur Garfield Hays fellow), N.Y. U., 1961; m. Barbara Lee Cochran, June 4, 1960; children—Gregory, Glenn Robert, Laura Anne. Admitted to N.Y. bar, 1961; U.S. Supreme Ct. bar, 1965, N.J. bar, 1970; trial atty. div. antitrust U.S. Dept. Justice, Washington, 1961-65; asso. firm Shearman & Sterling, N.Y.C., 1965-68; asso. firm Weil Gotshal & Manges, N.Y.C., 1968-70; Chief Asst. U.S. Atty. N.J., Newark, 1970-71; partner firm Burgoyne, Rose & Williamson, N.Y.C., 1971-77; of counsel firm Gibney, Anthony & Flaherty, N.Y.C.; prof. antitrust law Seton Hall U., Newark, 1972-73. Spl. counsel, Jersey City, 1972-77, Twp. of Dover (N.J.), 1975-78. Sec. bd. dirs. youth dept. Archdiocese of Newark, 1976—; trustee Bede Sch. Roman Catholic. Recipient Internat. Humanitarian award B'nai B'rith, 1978. Home: 1066 Wildwood Rd Oradell NJ 07649 Office: 420 Lexington Ave New York NY 10017 also Gateway I Newark NJ 07102

WILLIAMSON, ERNEST LAVONE, petroleum co. exec.; b. Perryton, Tex., Sept. 10, 1924; s. Ernest and Mabel Robert (Donnell) W.; B.S. in E.E., U. Okla., 1950; student Hill's Bus. Coll., 1943; m. Gertrude Florence Watkins, Dec. 2, 1950; children—Richard Dean, Judith Watkins, Mary Nan, David Ernest. Sales and service rep. Hughes Tool Co., 1950-52; with land dept. Phillips Petroleum Co., 1952-54; with La. Land & Exploration Co., New Orleans, 1954—, exec. v.p., 1967-74, pres., 1974—, also dir.; chmn. bd. LL & E Can. Ltd., LL&E Indonesia, LL&E Netherlands; pres. La. Land Offshore Exploration Co.; dir. Hibernia Nat. Bank, New Orleans. Mem. adv. bd. Salvation Army, 1971—; bd. dirs. Internat. House, New Orleans; trustee Children's Hosp., New Orleans. Served with U.S. Army, 1943-46; PTO. Mem. Am. Assn. Petroleum Landmen, Ind. Petroleum Assn. Am., Mid-Continent Oil and Gas Assn., Am. Petroleum Inst. Presbyn. Clubs: Bienville, Plimsol, Petroleum, Internat. House, New Orleans Country (New Orleans); Metaire Country; Denver. Home: 83 Dogwood Dr Covington LA 70433 Office: 225 Baronne St New Orleans LA 70112

WILLIAMSON, FREDERICK BEASLEY, III, rubber co. exec.; b. Balt., June 21, 1918; s. Frederick Beasley and Virginia Ogden (Ranson) W.; student Princeton, 1937-40; m. Katherine Stryker, Apr. 19, 1941; children—Katherine L., Frederick Beasley IV, Marsha R. With Goodall Rubber Co., Trenton, N.J., 1940-41, 46—, pres., dir., 1957—; dir. Dixon Valve & Coupling Co., N.J. Nat. Bank, N.J. Nat. Corp. Bd. dirs. Mercer Med. Center, Trenton, N.J. Served to capt., 5th Armored Div., U.S. Army, 1942-46. Mem. Rubber Mfrs. Assn. (dir.), N.J. Bus. and Industry Assn. (dir., chmn), N.J. Mfrs. Ins. Co. (chmn., dir.). Clubs: Princeton (N.Y.C.); Trenton Country; Hartwood (Port Jervis, N.Y.); Pine Valley Golf. Home: RD 2 New Hope PA 18938 Office: PO Box 8237 Trenton NJ 08650

WILLIAMSON, JAMES LAWRENCE, animal research exec.; b. Rebecca, Ga., Feb. 28, 1929; s. George and Clarice (Livingston) W.; B.S., U. Ga., 1951; M.S., U. Ill., 1952, Ph.D., 1957; m. Renee Lucille Johnson, Dec. 4, 1949; children—Renee Elizabeth, Lisa Melinda, Rise Marie. Grad. asst. U. Ill., 1955-57; mgr. beef cattle, sheep research Ralston-Purina Co., St. Louis, 1957-63, mgr. livestock research div., 1963-64, dir. research Chow div., 1964-65, v.p. research Chow div., 1965—. Served with USAF, 1952-55. Mem. Agrl. Research Inst., Nutrition Council, Am. Feed Mfg. Assn., Animal Sci. Assn., Dairy Sci. Assn., Poultry Sci. Assn., Am. Registry Cert. Animal Scientists. Home: 6 Fox Meadows Saint Louis MO 63127 Office: Ralston-Purina Co Checkerboard Sq Saint Louis MO 63188

WILLIAMSON, JOHN GARRETT, utility exec.; b. Muskogee, Okla., Sept. 8, 1915; s. John Ira and Dorothy (Garrett) W.; B.Sc., U. Tulsa, 1936; m. Sara Hosack Stauffer, Sept. 16, 1944; children—Peggy (Mrs. Frank Roth), Philip, Deborah (Mrs. Neil Mikel), With So. Calif. Gas Co., Los Angeles, 1936-47, Seattle Gas Co., 1947-49, Tex. Gas Transmission Co., Monroe, La., 1949-52; gen. supt. Western Ky. Gas Co., Owensboro, 1952-56; exec. v.p., dir. Kans. Power & Light Co., Salina, 1956—; dir. Nat. Bank of Am. Mem. Central Kans. council Girl Scouts, 1957-62. Mem. Salina Library Bd., 1961-65. Trustee St. John's Mil. Sch., 1958-61, St. Francis Boys' Homes, 1957-60. Mem. Am. Gas Assn., Pacific Coast Gas Assn., Midwest Gas Assn. (dir.), Newcomen Soc., Salina C. of C. (dir. 1958-61). Episcopalian. (vestryman, sr. warden). Club: Salina Rotary (pres. 1967). Home: 909 Millwood Dr Salina KS 67401 Office: 818 Kansas Ave Topeka KS 66601

WILLIAMSON, JOHN HERBERT, publishing co. exec.; b. Belfast, N. Ireland, Jan. 20, 1923; s. Herbert and Annie (Geddes) W.; came to U.S., 1929, naturalized, 1935; B.S., So. Conn. State Coll., 1943; M.A. Columbia, 1948; m. Rosemarie Gay, Sept. 9, 1950; children—Valerie, Lisa, John Herbert, Jacquelne. Asst. prin. Acad. Profl. Children, N.Y.C., 1946-49; asst. editor Silver Burdett Co., N.Y.C., 1949-51; dir. speaker's bur. Nat. Coal Assn., Washington, 1951-54; asst. mng. editor Silver Burdett, Morristown, N.J., 1954-66; chief elementary editor, exec. editor for elementary/high sch. publs. Harcourt, Brace & World (now Harcourt Brace Jovanovich), N.Y.C., 1966-68; exec. v.p. Silver Burdett div. Gen. Learning Corp., 1968-70, pres., 1970-74; v.p. Gen. Learning Corp., 1970-74; pres., dir. Silver Burdett Co. subs. Scott, Foresman & Co., Morristown, N.J., 1974—; dir. Scott, Foresman & Co., Glenview, Ill., GLC Pubs. Ltd., Can., Judy Co., Minn. Active United Way Morris County (N.J.), Nat. Assn. Retarded Children. Served with USAAF, 1942-45. Mem. Assn. Supervision and Curriculum Devel., Internat. Reading Assn. Episcopalian. Office: Silver Burdett Co 250 James St Morristown NJ 07960*

WILLIAMSON, JOHN PRITCHARD, utility exec.; b. Cleve., Feb. 22, 1922; s. John and Jane (Pritchard) W.; B.S. in Bus. Adminstrn., Kent State U., 1945; postgrad. U. Toledo, 1953-56, U. Mich., 1956; m. Helen Morgan, Aug. 3, 1945; children—John Morgan, James Russell, Wayne Arthur. Sr. accountant Arthur Andersen & Co., Detroit and Cleve., 1945-51; dir. methods and procs. Toledo Edison Co., 1951-59, asst. treas., 1959-60, sec., 1960-62, sec.-treas., 1962-65, v.p. finance, 1965-68, sr. v.p., 1968-72, pres., chief exec. officer, 1972—, dir., 1962—; dir. emeritus 1st Nat. Bank, Toledo, chmn., 1975-76; dir. Toledo Trust Co., Ohio Valley Electric Co. Bd. dirs. Nat. Electric Reliability Council, Ohio Electric Utility Inst., Toledo Area Govt. Research Assn.; chmn. Toledo Devel. Com., 1974-75, CAPCO Power Pool; vice chmn. East Central Area Power Coordination Pool; trustee Greater Toledo Corp., Toledo Orch., Toledo Hosp., Toledo Mus. Art. C.P.A., Ohio. Mem. Am. Inst. C.P.A.'s, Financial Analysts Soc. Toledo (pres. 1968-69), Systems and Procs. Assn. (internat. treas.

1960), Inst. Pub. Utilities (chmn. exec. com. 1969-70), Toledo C. of C. (pres. 1970), Ohio C. of C. (1st v.p.; Toledo's Outstanding Citizen 1976), Toledo Boys Club (Echo award 1974), Kent State U. Alumni Assn. (pres. 1971-72, outstanding alumnus 1974), Blue Key, Delta Sigma Pi, Beta Alpha Psi, Delta Upsilon. Republican. Methodist. Clubs: Toledo, Tower, Press, Inverness (bd. govs.); Rockwell Springs. Kiwanian (past pres. Toledo). Home: 4517 Brittany Rd Toledo OH 43615 Office: 300 Madison Ave Toledo OH 43652

WILLIAMSON, KENNETH LEE, educator; b. Tarentum, Pa., Apr. 13, 1934; s. James D. and Mary June (Becker) W.; B.A. cum laude (Nat. scholar) Harvard, 1956; Ph.D. (Allied Chem. and Dye Co. fellow), U. Wis., 1960; m. Mary Louise Hoerner, Sept. 15, 1956; children—Christopher Lee, Tania Louise, Kevin Keith. Mem. faculty Mt. Holyoke Coll., 1961—, prof. chemistry, 1969—. mem. Grad. Faculty, U. Mass., 1965—; vis. prof. Cornell U., 1966. NIH postdoctoral fellow Stanford, 1960-61; NSF sci. faculty fellow U. Liverpool (Eng.), also fellow of univ., 1968-69; Guggenheim fellow 1975-76, Oxford (Eng.) U. fellow of univ., 1976. Mem. Am. Chem. Soc., A.A.A.S., Sigma Xi. Author papers and book in field. Home: 43 Woodbridge St South Hadley MA 01075

WILLIAMSON, MERRITT ALVIN, educator, engr.; b. Littleton, N.H., Apr. 1, 1916; s. Berton Alexander and Nellie E. (Cross) W.; grad. Phillips Exeter Acad.; B.E., Yale, 1938, M.S., 1940, Ph.D., 1946; M.S., Calif. Inst. Tech., 1945; M.B.A., U. Chgo., 1953; m. Jean E. Goodrich, July 3, 1943; children—Janet, Marilyn, Linda, Roxanne Williamson Leonard, Karen Williamson Wilson, Valerie Williamson Jakes. Metallurgist, Scovill Mfg. Co., Waterbury, Conn., 1937-42, Remington Arms Co., Bridgeport, Conn., 1942-44; dir. tech. research Solar Aircraft Co., San Diego, 1946-48; asso. dir. devel. Pullman Standard Car Mfg. Co., Hammond, Ind., 1948-52; mgr. research div. Burroughs Corp., Paoli, Pa., 1952-56; spl. lectr. U. Pa., 1954-56; dean Coll. Engring. and Architecture, Pa. State U., 1956-66. prof. engring., 1959-66, Orrin Henry Ingram distinguished prof. engring. mgmt., dir. engring. mgmt. program Sch. Engring., Vanderbilt U., Nashville, 1966—, prof. mgmt. Grad. Sch. Mgmt., 1969-77; tech. mgmt. cons., 1956—. Commr., vice chmn., acting chmn. Pa. Turnpike Commn., 1957. Served from ensign to lt. (j.g.), USNR, 1944-46. Registered profl. engr., Tenn. Fellow AAAS, Yale Engring. Assn. (past pres.); mem. Am. Inst. Mining and Metall. Engrs., Am. Soc. Engring. Edn. (past pres.), Nat. Conf. Adminstrn. Research (past chmn.), Am. Inst. Indsl. Engrs., Academy Mgmt., Pa. Engring. Soc. (hon.), Tenn., Nat. socs. profl. engrs. Conn. Acad. Arts and Scis., Inst. Certification Engring. Technicians (past chmn.), Order of Engr., Yale Metall. Alumni (past chmn.), Internat. Soc. Gen. Semantics, Inst. Gen. Semantics, Calif. Inst. Tech. Alumni Assn., U. Chgo. Exec. Program Club, Triangle, Sigma Xi, Tau Beta Pi, Phi Kappa Phi, Phi Eta Sigma, Sigma Tau, Gamma Alpha, Alpha Chi Sigma, Pi Tau Sigma, Eta Kappa Nu, Omicron Delta Kappa, Alpha Pi Mu, Beta Gamma Sigma. Clubs: University (Nashville); Cosmos (Washington). Editor, Engring. Mgmt. Internat., 1979—; contbg. editor Research and Engring., 1956-57, Ind. Laboratories, 1958-59, Ind. Sci. and Engring., 1958-59, Research and Devel., 1959—. Home: 6605 Rolling Fork Dr Nashville TN 37205 Office: Box 1576 Station B Nashville TN 37235

WILLIAMSON, MONCRIEFF (GRAHAME), museum ofcl.; b. E. Linton, Scotland, Nov. 23, 1915; s. James Watt and Gwendoline Pilkington (Jackson) W.; LL.D. (hon.), Edinburgh Coll. Art; m. Pamela Upton Fanshawe, Sept. 28, 1948; 1 son, Timothy Malcolm. Curator, Art Gallery Greater Victoria, 1957-59, 63-64; dir. art dept. Glenbow Found., Calgary, Alta., 1960-63; dir. Confedn. Art Gallery, Charlottetown, P.E.I., 1964—. Recipient Centennial medal, 1967; Diplome d'Honneur gold medal Royal Canadian Acad., 1975; mem. Order of Can. Fellow Royal Soc. Arts; mem. Am. Art Museum Dirs., Canadian Museum Dirs. Assn., Canadian Museums Assn., Commonwealth Assn. Museums, Canadian Conf. of Arts, Museum Dirs. Assn. Can. Mem. Anglican Ch. Club: Masons. Author: Canadian Fine Crafts, 1967; Robert Harris, an unconventional biography, 1971; Robert Harris Portraits, 1973; Through Canadian Eyes, 1976. Home: 14 Churchill Ave Charlottetown PE C1A 1Y8 Canada Office: Confederation Art Gallery Museum Charlottetown PE C1A 7L9 Canada

WILLIAMSON, NICOL, actor; b. Hamilton, Scotland, Sept. 14, 1938; s. Hugh and Mary (Storrie) W.; student Central Grammar Sch., Birmingham, Eng.; m. K. Jill Townsend, July 17, 1971 (div. 1977); 1 son. Appeared with Dundee Repertory Theatre, 1960-61; joined Royal Shakespeare Co., 1962; appeared in plays: Ginger Man, London, 1963, Waiting for Godot, London, 1964, Inadmissible Evidence (N.Y. Drama Critics award), London, N.Y.C., 1965-66, Diary of a Madman, London, 1967, Hamlet, London, N.Y.C., 1968-69, Uncle Vanya, 1973, Corialanus, 1973, Nicol Williamson's Late Show, 1973, Midwinter Spring, 1973-74, Twelfth Night, 1974, Macbeth, 1974, Rex, 1976; motion pictures include: Inadmissible Evidence, 1967, The Bofors Gun, 1967, Laughter in the Dark, 1968, The Reckoning, 1968, Hamlet, 1969, Jerusalem File, 1972, I Know What I Meant (TV), 1974, Robin and Marion, 1976, The Seven-Per-Cent-Solution, 1976, The Goodbye Girl, 1977, The Cheap Detective, 1978. Office: care Chasin-Park-Citron Agy 9255 Sunset Blvd Los Angeles CA 90069*

WILLIAMSON, OLIVER EATON, economist; b. Superior, Wis., Sept. 27, 1932; s. Scott Gilbert and Lucille S. (Dunn) W.; S.B., Mass. Inst. Tech., 1955; M.B.A., Stanford U., 1960; Ph.D., Carnegie-Mellon U., 1963; m. Dolores Jean Celeni, Sept. 28, 1957; children—Scott, Tamara, Karen, Oliver, Dean. Project. engr. U.S. Govt., 1955-58; asst. prof. econs. U. Calif., Berkeley, 1963-65; asso. prof. U. Pa., Phila., 1965-68, prof., 1968—, Charles and William L. Day prof. econs. and social sci., 1977—; spl. econ. asst. to asst. atty. gen. for antitrust Dept. Justice, 1966-67; dir. Center for Study of Organizational Innovation, U. Pa., 1976—; cons. in field. Fellow Center for Advanced Study in Behavioral Scis., 1977-78; Guggenheim fellow, 1977-78. Recipient Alexander Henderson award Carnegie-Mellon U., 1962. Fellow Econometric Soc.; mem. Am. Econ. Assn. Author: The Economics of Discretionary Behavior, 1964; Corporate Control and Business Behavior, 1970; Markets and Hierarchies, 1975. Asso. editor Bell Jour. Econs., 1973-74, editor, 1975—. Office: Dept Econs U Pa Philadelphia PA 19104

WILLIAMSON, PETER DAVID, lawyer; b. Houston, Oct. 13, 1944; s. Sam and Sophie Ann (Kaplan) W.; B.A., U. Ill., 1966; J.D., U. Tex., 1969; m. Carol Jane Ivy, Aug. 1, 1972; children—Heather, Amber, Asia. Admitted to Tex. bar, 1969; atty. United Farm Workers, AFL-CIO in Tex., McAllen, 1969-70; pvt. practice law, Houston, 1971—. Bd. dirs. Immigration Counseling Center, Houston, 1977-79, Centro para Immigrantes, Houston, 1978-79. Mem. Gen. Aviation Pilots Assn. (dir.), Assn. Immigration and Nationality Lawyers (v.p. Tex. chpt. 1978-79, pres. 1979-80). Home: 4130 Martinshire Houston TX 77025 Office: 821 Americana Bldg Houston TX 77002

WILLIAMSON, RENE DE VISME, educator; b. Chgo., May 28, 1908; s. Hiram Parker and Alice (de Visme) W.; A.B., Rutgers U., 1931; A.M., Harvard U., 1932, Ph.D., 1935; student U. Munich, summer 1932, U. Berlin, summer 1933; m. Virginia Hardgrove Sutherland, Sept. 12, 1936; children—Parker Trevilian, Warren Ligon, Roger Leigh. Mem. facutly Princeton, 1935-37, Davidson Coll., 1937-44, Beloit Coll., 1944-45, U. Tenn., 1945-54; mem. faculty La. State U., 1954—, now prof., past chmn. dept. govt.; mem. summer faculty U. Mich., 1949, Western Res. U., 1950, U. Neb., 1957; vis. prof. bd. edn. Presbyn. Ch. in U.S. to colls. and univs. in the South, 1953, to univs. S.A., including Peru, Chile, Argentina, Uruguay, Brazil; vis. prof. U. Natal (S. Africa), Spring 1969. Mem. Christian edn. com. Synod of La., Presbyn. Ch. U.S., 1956—, chmn. Adv. Council on Higher Edn., 1961-65. Bd. dirs. Southwestern U. Memphis, 1968-72. Mem. Presbyn. Ednl. Assn. of South (chmn. profs. sect. 1953-55), Nat. Council Chs. (exec. com. faculty Christian fellowship 1953-57), Am. Polit. Sci. Assn. (exec. council 1959-61), So. Polit. Sci. Assn. (pres. 1959-60), AAUP, Phi Beta Kappa. Democrat. Author: The Politics of Planning in the Oil Industry under the Code, 1936; Culture and Policy: The U.S. and the Hispanic World, 1949; Independence and Involvement: A Christian-Re-prientation in Political Science, 1964; Politics and Protestant Theology: An Interpretation of Tillich, Barth, Bonhoeffer and Brunner, 1976; The Integrity of the Gospel: A Critique of Liberation Theology, 1979. Editor: (with L.S. Greene) Five Years of British Labour: 1945-50, 1950. Contbr. articles profl. publs. Home: 3234 Fritchie Dr Baton Rouge LA 70809

WILLIAMSON, RICHARD EDMUND, educator; b. Chgo., May 23, 1927; s. Richard E. and Josephine (Hahn) W.; A.B., Dartmouth, 1950; Ph.D., U. Pa., 1955; m. Genevieve M. Belcher, Aug. 19, 1950. Research asso. U. Pa., 1956; with math. dept. Dartmouth, Hanover, N.H., 1957—. Research asso. Harvard, 1961, Stanford, 1965, Cornell U., 1970; cons. Cowles Found. for Econ. Research, 1962. Served with USNR, 1945-46. Mem. Am. Math. Soc., Math. Assn. Am. Author: (with R.H. Crowell and H.F. Trotter) Calculus of Vector Functions, rev. 1972; (with H.F. Trotter) Mutivariable Mathematics, 1974. Home: Elm St Norwich VT 05055 Office: Math Dept Dartmouth Coll Hanover NH 03755

WILLIAMSON, RICHARD LAVERNE, univ. dean; b. Corning, N.Y., Apr. 15, 1916; s. Linn Robert and Ellen Anis (Church) W.; B.A., Cornell U., 1938. M.B.A., Northwestern U., 1951; D.B.A., Ind. U., 1956; m. Edith Julia Cunningham, Oct. 23, 1938; children—Richard Laverne, Linn Douglas, Keith Allen, Lee Ann. Asst. instr. accounting Cornell U., 1938-39; group leader material control dept., traveling auditor contract terminations Bell Aircraft Corp., 1942-45; staff accountant Colo. Fuel & Iron Corp., 1945-46; instr. econs. U. Buffalo, 1946; instr. to asst. prof. econs. and bus. adminstrn., dir. dept. Wheaton Coll., 1946-53; teaching asso. Ind. U. Sch. Bus., 1953-55; asst. prof. accounting Bowling Green State U., 1955-56; mem. faculty U. So. Calif., Los Angeles, 1956-67, prof. accounting, asso. dean Grad. Sch. Bus. Adminstrn., 1959-67, chmn. faculty adv. com. Computer Scis. Lab., 1960-66; dean Coll. of Bus. Adminstrn., Loyola U. of Los Angeles, 1967—. C.P.A., Ind. Mem. Am. Inst. C.P.A.'s (council 1971-74), Calif. Soc. C.P.A.'s (dir. 1967-69, exec. com. 1968-69), Am. Soc. for Pub. Adminstrn., Acad. of Mgmt., NEA, Am. Assn. for Higher Edn., Fin. Execs. Inst., Am. Assn. Collegiate Schs. Bus. Assembly (planning com. 1969-71), Am. (dir.), Western (exec. com. 1968, pres. 1970-71) assns. collegiate schs. bus., Conf. Jesuit Colls. Bus. Adminstrn. (chmn. 1970-71), Am., Western econ. assns., Am. Assn. U. Adminstrs., Town Hall Calif., Los Angeles Area C. of C., Nat. Assn. Accountants, Am. Accounting Assn., Beta Gamma Sigma (pres. Beta of Calif. chpt. 1963-65), Beta Alpha Psi, Pi Gamma Mu, Alpha Sigma Nu, Phi Kappa Phi. Author: Salesmanship for the Christian Bookstore, 1954; Suggested Guidelines for the Formation and Operation of an Advisory Council for the Business School, 1970. Home: 7543 McConnell Ave Los Angeles CA 90045

WILLIAMSON, SAM, lawyer; b. Detroit, Aug. 15, 1910; s. Solomon and Minnie (Nichamin) W.; B.A., U. Ill., 1937, J.D., 1940; m. Sophie Ann Kaplan, May 6, 1943; children—Peter D., Jane Williamson Kessler, Marianne Williamson McGinty. Admitted to Ill. bar, 1940, Tex. bar, 1946, since practiced in Houston. Served with AUS, 1942-46. Mem. Am., Fed. (pres. Houston chpt. 1952), Houston bar assns., Assn. Immigration and Nationality Lawyers (past chmn. Tex., nat. gov.), Am. Soc. Internat. Law. Home: 3616 Tartan Ln Houston TX 77025 Office: 1320 Americana Bldg Houston TX 77002

WILLIAMSON, SAMUEL RUTHVEN, JR., historian, univ. adminstr.; b. Bogalusa, La., Nov. 10, 1935; s. Samuel Ruthven and Frances Mitchell (Page) W.; B.A., Tulane U., 1958; postgrad. (Fulbright scholar) U. Edinburgh, 1958-59; A.M., Harvard U., 1960, Ph.D., 1966; m. Joan Chaffe Andress, Dec. 30, 1961; children—George Samuel, Treeby Andress, Thaddeus Miller. Asst. prof. U.S. Mil. Acad., 1963-66; instr. history Harvard U., 1966-68, asst. prof., 1968-72, Allston Burr sr. tutor, 1968-72, asst. to dean of Harvard Coll., 1969-70; research asso. Inst. Politics, faculty asso. Center for Internat. Affairs, 1971-72; mem. faculty J.F. Kennedy Sch. Govt., 1971-72; asso. prof. history U. N.C., Chapel Hill, 1972-74, prof., 1974—, now dean Coll. Arts and Scis.; cons. Historian's Office, Office of Sec. of Def., 1974-76; vis. fellow Churchill Coll., 1976-77; mem. adv. com. U.S. Army Hist. Collection, 1974-76; cons. Stanford U. Arms Control Textbook, 1974. Served to capt. U.S. Army, 1963-66. Woodrow Wilson fellow, 1958-63; Danforth fellow, 1958-63; Nat. Endowment Humanities fellow, 1976-77; Ford Found. grantee, 1976. Recipient George Louis Beer prize for best book on internat. history Am. Hist. Assn., 1970. Mem. Am. Hist. Assn., Internat. Inst. Strategic Studies, Inter-Univ. Seminar on War and Soc. Democrat. Episcopalian. Author: The Politics of Grand Strategy: Britain and France Prepare for War, 1904-1914, 1969. Editor: The Origins of a Tragedy, July 1914, 1980. Am. editor War and Soc. Newsletter, 1973—. Home: 18 Kendall Dr Chapel Hill NC 27514 Office: Dept History Univ of NC Chapel Hill NC 27514

WILLIAMSON, THOMAS ARNOLD, publishing co. exec.; b. Sagamore, Pa., Oct. 4, 1939; s. Thomas and Mabel (Kennedy) W.; grad. Phillips Exeter Acad., 1957; A.B., Harvard, 1961; m. Kathryn Steiner White, Mar. 1, 1980. With Harcourt Brace Jovanovich, Inc., N.Y.C., 1962—, editor-in-chief coll. dept., 1971-76, dep. dir. coll. dept., 1976-77; sr. v.p. Academic Press, Inc., N.Y.C., 1977—; dir. Continuing Profl. Edn. Group; vice chmn. Coll. Pubs. Group, N.Y.C., 1974-75, chmn., 1975-76; v.p. Health Careers Acad.; dir. Harcourt Brace Jovanovich Ltd. Can. Mem. Japan Soc., Am. Hist. Soc. Clubs: Harvard, N.Y. Badminton (N.Y.C.). Home: 709 Howell Dr Brielle NJ 08730 Office: 111 Fifth Ave New York NY 10003

WILLIAMSON, WARREN PYATT, JR., broadcasting co. exec.; b. Youngstown, Ohio, May 10, 1900; s. Warren Pyatt and Mary (Thompson) W.; student U. Mich., 1920-23; m. Isabel DeNio, Feb. 6, 1924; children—Barbara (Mrs. David Stewart) (dec.), Warren Pyatt III, Joseph Dallas II. Founder, WKBN Broadcasting Corp., Youngstown, 1926, pres., 1926—, operating radio stas. WKBN, 1926—, WKBN-FM, 1947—, TV sta. WKBN-TV, 1953—; dir. Mahoning Nat. Bank. Mem., pres. Youngstown Bd. Edn., 1940-67. Bd. dirs. Regional Growth Found.; pres. Mahoning Valley Hist. Soc.; trustee C. C. Choffin Estate Trust. Served with U.S. Army, 1918-19. Recipient Man of Year award Ohio Assn. Broadcasters, 1969, Frank Purnell Meml. award, 1973. Mem. Nat., Ohio (past pres.) assn. broadcasters, Radio Pioneers, Youngstown C. of C. (dir. 1946-68, award for civic leadership 1978). Clubs: Masons, Shriners, Elks; Youngstown, Youngstown Country; Duquesne Hunting and Fishing (Britt, Ont., Can.); Spring Creek Hunting and Fishing (Kane, Pa.); Rockwell Springs Trout (Castalia, Ohio). Home: 4500 Rush Blvd Youngstown OH 44512 Office: 3930 Sunset Blvd Youngstown OH 44501

WILLIAMSON, WILLIAM LANDRAM, educator; b. Lexington, Ky., Aug. 13, 1920; s. Clarence Linden and Eugenia Potts (Dunlap) W.; student U. Ky., 1937; B.A., U. Wis., 1941; B.A. in L.S., Emory U., 1942; M.S., Columbia, 1949; Ph.D., U. Chgo., 1959; m. Daisy Levy, Aug. 18, 1962; 1 dau., Andrea J. (Mrs. Elvin Irizarry). Reference librarian Atlanta Pub. Library, 1942, 46; asst., asso. and acting librarian Baylor U., 1947-48, 49-51; Butler Librarian Columbia, 1954-64, sr. lectr., 1964; chief librarian Montclair (N.J.) State Coll., 1964-66; prof. library sci. U. Wis., Madison, 1966—; vis. lectr. U. Chgo., summer, 1966, 76; library cons. Ford Indonesia Project, 1960-62, Md. State Colls., 1966, Indonesian Ministry Edn., summer 1970; vis. prof. U. Hawaii, summer 1970; research leave Cambridge U., summer, 1973, 77. Served to 1st lt. U.S. Army, 1942-46. Mem. A.L.A., Am. Assn. U. Profs. (pres. chpt. 1966), Archons of Colophon. Author: William Frederick Poole and the Modern Library Movement, 1963. Editor: The Impact of the Public Law 480 Program on Overseas Acquisitions by American Libraries, 1967; Assistance to Libraries in Developing Nations: Papers on Comparative Studies, 1971; A Search for New Insights in Librarianship: A Day of Comparative Studies, 1976. Contbr. articles to profl. publs. Home: 5105 Tomahawk Trail Madison WI 53705

WILLIE, CHARLES VERT, educator; b. Dallas, Oct. 8, 1927; s. Louis James and Carrie (Sykes) W.; B.A., Morehouse Coll., 1948; M.A., Atlanta U., 1949; Ph.D., Syracuse U., 1957; D.D. (hon.), Gen. Sem., 1974; D.H.L. (hon.), Berkeley Div. Sch., Yale, 1972; M.A. (hon.), Harvard, 1974; m. Mary Susannah Conklin, Mar. 31, 1962; children—Sarah Susannah, Martin Charles, James Theodore. Instr. dept. preventive medicine State U. N.Y., Upstate Med. Center, Syracuse, 1955-60; research dir. delinquency prevention project Pres.' Com. on Juvenile Delinquency and Youth Crime, Washington, 1962-64; vis. lectr. sociology Lab. Community Psychiatry Harvard Med. Sch., Boston, Mass., 1966-67; instr. to asst. prof. sociology Syracuse (N.Y.) U., 1952-63, asso. prof., 1964-67, prof., 1968-74, chmn. dept. sociology, 1967-71, v.p. Syracuse U., 1972-74; prof. edn. and urban studies Grad. Sch. Edn. Harvard, 1974—; vis. lectr. ch. and soc. Episcopal Theol. Sch., Cambridge, Mass., 1966-67. Commr. Pres.'s Commn. on Mental Health, 1977-78. Mem. tech. adv. bd. Maurice Falk Med. Fund, 1968—; bd. dirs. Social Sci. Research Council, 1969-75; mem. Behavioral and Social Scis. Assembly Nat. Research Council, 1973-78; master Boston Sch. Desegregation case, Fed. Dist. Ct., 1975. Bd. trustees Episcopal Div. Sch., Cambridge, Mass. Recipient Faculty Service award Nat. Univ. Extension Assn., 1969, 50th Anniversary Distinguished Alumnus award Maxwell Sch. Syracuse U., 1974. Fellow Am. Sociol. Assn.; mem. Eastern Sociol. Soc. (pres. 1974-75), Sociol. Research Assn., Urban League (bd. dirs. Eastern Mass. 1975-77), Phi Beta Kappa, Alpha Phi Alpha. Episcopalian (mem. nat. exec. council 1967-74, v.p. gen. conv. 1970-74). Author: Church Action in the World, 1969; Black Students at White Colleges, 1972; Race Mixing in the Public Schools, 1973; Oreo, 1975; A New Look at Black Families, 1976; The Sociology of Urban Education, 1978; The Caste and Class Controversy, 1979; editor: The Family Life of Black People, 1970; Racism and Mental Health, 1973; Black/Brown/White Relations, 1977; Black Colleges in America, 1978; Community Politics and Educational Change, 1980. Home: 41 Hillcrest Rd Concord MA 01742 Office: 457 Gutman Library Harvard Grad Sch of Education 6 Appian Way Cambridge MA 02138

WILLIFORD, DONALD BRATTON, accountant; b. York, S.C., Sept. 20, 1936; s. Thomas Leslie and Odessa (Brown) W.; B.S. in Bus. Adminstrn., U. S.C., 1958; m. Linda Craven, June 12, 1959; 1 dau., Sharon. With Haskins & Sells, C.P.A.'s, Charlotte, N.C., 1959-62; with auditing dept. Belk Stores Services, Inc., Charlotte, 1962-69; corporate sec., asst. treas. Ruddick Corp., Charlotte, N.C., 1969—. Served with U.S. Army, 1958-59. Mem. Am. Inst. C.P.A.'s, N.C. Assn. C.P.A.'s, Am. Soc. Corporate Secs. Club: River Hills Country. Home: 16 Hamiltons Ferry Rd Clover SC 29710 Office: 2000 First Union Plaza Charlotte NC 28282

WILLIFORD, JOHN HUGO, pharm. co. exec.; b. Sarasota, Fla., July 20, 1930; s. Henry Lee and Marjorie (Hugo) W.; B.S. in Journalism, U. Fla., 1951; m. Thomasine Orr, July 23, 1955; children—John Hugo, Jamie Anne, Lee Scott. Successively v.p. and group product dir., group v.p. Vick Chem. Co., 1951-69; pres., chief operating officer USV Pharm. Corp., Tuckahoe, N.Y., 1969-72, chmn. bd., chief exec. officer, 1972—; dir. Revlon Inc., 1972, v.p., 1976—. Mem. Proprietary Assn. (dir.), Fla. Blue Key Leadership, Pi Kappa Alpha. Clubs: Westchester Country, Whippoorwill Country. Home: 5 Deer Trail Armonk NY 10504 Office: 1 Scarsdale Rd Tuckahoe NY 10707

WILLIG, KARL VICTOR, restaurant chain exec.; b. Idaho Falls, Idaho, June 4, 1944; s. Louis Victor and Ethel (McCarty) W.; B.A., Coll. of Idaho, 1968; M.B.A. (Dean Donald Kirk David fellow), Harvard U., 1970; m. Julianne Erickson, June 10, 1972; 1 son, Ray. Pres., Ariz. Beef, Inc., Phoenix, 1971-73; group v.p. Ariz.-Colo. Land & Cattle Co., Phoenix, 1973-76; v.p. Rufenacht, Bromagen & Hertz, Inc., Chgo., 1976-77; pres. Sambo's Restaurants, Inc., Santa Barbara, Calif., 1977—. Home: 405 Via Hierba Santa Barbara CA 93110 Office: 3760 State St Santa Barbara CA 93162

WILLIG, ROBERT DANIEL, economist; b. Bklyn., Jan. 16, 1947; s. Jack David and Meg Willig; B.A., Harvard U., 1967; M.S. in Ops. Research, Stanford U., 1968, Ph.D. in Econs., 1973; m. Virginia Mason, July 8, 1973; 1 son, Jared Mason. Lectr., Stanford U., Palo Alto, Calif., 1971-73; mem. tech. staff Bell Labs., Holmdel, N.J., 1973-77, supr. dept. econs. research, 1977-78; prof. econs. and public affairs Princeton U., 1978—; cons. in field; research fellow U. Warwick (Eng.), 1977. Mem. organizing com. Telecommunications Policy Research Conf., 1977-78; mem. Aspen Inst. Task Force on Future of Postal Service, 1978—; mem. adv. bd. B'nai B'rith Hillel Found., Princeton U., 1978—. NSF grantee, 1979—. Mem. Am. Econ. Assn., Econometric Soc. (program com. World Congress 1978—). Author: Welfare Analysis of Policies Affecting Prices and Products, 1973; mem. editorial bd. M.I.T. Press Series on Govt. Regulation, 1978—; contbr. articles to Am. Econ. Rev., Bell Jour. Econs., other profl. jours. Office: Woodrow Wilson Sch Princeton U Princeton NJ 08540

WILLIG, WINSTON ARMIN, ret. towing co. exec., assn. ofcl.; b. Louisville, Oct. 19, 1912; s. Frederick William and Elsa (Peklenk) W.; B.A., U. Louisville, 1934; m. Mona Tate Russell, July 10, 1937; children—Mona Tate Russell, Caldwell Russell. Report writer Dun & Bradstreet, Inc., 1934-37; with sales dept. Jefferson Island Salt Co., 1937-42; advt. mgr., indsl. relations dir. Girdler Corp., 1942-52; v.p. charge sales, dir. Am. Comml. Lines, 1952-63; pres., dir. Ohio Falls, Inc., Louisville, 1963-68, Harvest Towing Co., 1963-72, Gulf Transp. Co., 1963-65; dir. First State Bank Lyon County, 1962-63, Leisure Industries, Inc., 1969-78, pres. W & R Investments, Inc., 1975—; chmn. bd. Dixie Beer Distbrs., Inc., 1975—. Bd. dirs. Am. Cancer Soc., 1962—, vice chmn. nat. bd., 1971-73, chmn. bd., 1973-75, pres. Ky. div., 1959, bd. dirs., 1945-79; bd. overseers U. Louisville, 1956—, Ohio Valley Improvement Assn., 1954-63, Am. Automobile Assn.,

1962-71; bd. dirs. La. Indsl. Found., 1976—, Regional Cancer Center Ky., 1978—, Louisville Indsl. Found., 1975—; mem. citizens adv. council Bellarmine Coll., 1960-69; pres., dir. Louisville Museum Natural History, 1963-79, Louisville Zool. Commn., 1971-74; bd. dirs. Louisville Automobile Club, 1954—, pres., 1963-66; campaign chmn. Louisville United Appeal, 1959—; mem. Louisville and Jefferson County Crime Commn., 1968-69; chmn. finance com. Internat. Union Against Cancer, 1974-78; bd. dirs. Council on Pub. Higher Edn., 1970-73; chmn. Louisville Devel. Com., 1970-72, Jefferson County Improvement Dist.; judge Jefferson County, 1969-70; chmn. bd. Historic Homes Found. Bd. dirs. Norton Meml. Hosp., Louisville River Fields Found., U. Louisville Med. Center: bd. dirs., pres. Bernheim Found., 1969—. Recipient Distinguished Service medal Am. Cancer Soc., 1957; named Citizen Laureate, 1971. Mem. Louisville C. of C. (pres. dir.), Louisville Audubon Soc. (dir. 1970-71). Clubs: Louisville Country, Jefferson, Old Kentucky Home Country, Pendennis, Filson (bd. dirs. 1970—) (Louisville); Harmony Landing Country. Home: 1810 Mayo Ln Prospect KY 40059

WILLING, RICHARD THOMAS, JR., journalist; b. Oak Park, Ill., Mar. 6, 1949; s. Richard Thomas and Mary Anne (Fortin) W.; B.A. cum laude, Yale U., 1971; M.A. with high honors (Kiplinger fellow in public affairs reporting), Ohio State U., 1975; postgrad. Fordham U. Law Sch., 1975. Reporter, Rockland (N.Y.) Jour.-News, 1972-74; teaching fellow Ohio State U. Sch. Journalism, 1974-75; asst. editor MacMillan, Inc., N.Y.C., 1975; Mich. politics reporter Detroit News, 1975—; mem. Ford Found. Panel on Law and Media, Ann Arbor, Mich., 1978. Recipient Nat. Student award More mag., 1975. Mem. Yale Alumni Assn. (schs. com. 1975-79). Club: Yale of Mich. Home: 1321 Orleans Detroit MI 48207 Office: 615 W Lafayette St Detroit MI 48231

WILLINGHAM, CALDER BAYNARD, JR., novelist, playwright, screen writer; b. Atlanta, Dec. 23, 1922; s. Calder Baynard and Eleanor (Willcox) W.; ed. The Citadel, 1940-41, U. Va., 1941-43; m. Helene Rothenberg; m. 2d, Jane Marie Bennett, 1953; 4 sons, 2 daus. Author: End as a Man, 1947; Geraldine Bradshaw, 1950; Reach to the Stars, 1951; The Gates of Hell, 1951; Natural Child, 1952; To Eat a Peach, 1955; Eternal Fire, 1963; Providence Island, 1969; Rambling Rose, 1972; The Big Nickel, 1975; The Building of Venus Four, 1977; movies: End as a Man, Paths of Glory, The Vikings, One Eyed Jacks, Little Big Man, The Graduate, Thieves Like Us; play: End as a Man. Address: care Manor Books Inc 432 Park Ave S New York NY 10016*

WILLINGHAM, CLARK SUTTLES, lawyer; b. Houston, Nov. 29, 1944; s. Paul Suttles and Elsie Dell (Clark) W.; B.B.A., Tex. Tech. U., 1967; J.D., So. Methodist U., 1971; m. Jane Joyce Hitch, Aug. 16, 1969; children—Meredith Moores, James Barrett. Accountant Peat, Marwick, Mitchell & Co., Dallas, 1967-68; admitted to Tex. bar, 1971; since practiced in Dallas; partner firm Kasmir, Willingham & Krage, Dallas, 1972—; partner Western Trio Cattle Co., 1972—; dir. Tex. Commerce Bank-Campbell Centre, Master Feeders, Inc., Master Feeders II, Inc., Booker Custom Packing Co., Five Flags Cattle Co. Underwriter, dir. Dallas Summer Musicals, 1975—; dir. Dallas Theatre Center, 1978—. Mem. Am., Dallas bar assns., State Bar Tex., Am., Nat., Tex., Okla., Kan., Colo. cattlemen's assns. Republican. Episcopalian. Kiwanian. Contbr. articles to profl. jours. Home: 3824 Shenandoah Dallas TX 75205 Office: 2001 Bryan St Dallas TX 75201

WILLINGHAM, WARREN WILLCOX, psychologist, testing service exec.; b. Rome, Ga., Mar. 1, 1930; s. Calder Baynard and Eleanor (Willcox) W.; student Ga. Inst. Tech., 1952; Ph.D., U. Tenn., 1955; m. Anna Michal, Mar. 17, 1954; children—Sherry, Judith, Daniel. Research asso. World Book Co., N.Y.C., 1959-60; dir. evaluation studies Ga. Inst. Tech., Atlanta, 1960-64; dir. research Coll. Bd., N.Y.C., 1964-68; dir. access research office Coll. Bd., Palo Alto, Calif., 1968-72; asst. v.p., disting. research scientist Ednl. Testing Service, Princeton, N.J., 1972—; mem. advisory bd. on ednl. requirements Sec. Navy, 1968; cons. to numerous schs., colls., U.S. Office Edn. Served to lt. USNR, 1955-59. Recipient Ann. award So. Soc. Philosophy and Psychology, 1958. Fellow Am. Psychol. Assn., AAAS; mem. Nat. Council on Measurement in Edn. (dir.), Am. Ednl. Research Assn., Sigma Xi. Author: Free Access Higher Education, 1970; Source Book for Higher Education, 1973; College Placement and Exemption, 1974; Assessing Experiential Learning, 1977; Selective Admissions in Higher Education, 1977; also various monographs; editor: Measurement in Education, 1969-72; editorial bds. Jour. Ednl. Measurement, 1971—, Alternate Higher Education, 1976—, Am. Ednl. Research Jour., 1968-71; contbr. articles, tech. reports to profl. jours. Office: Educational Testing Service Princeton NJ 08540

WILLIS, ARTHUR BURGESS, lawyer; b. Washington, May 22, 1914; s. Robert Chadwick and Mary Ermine (Burgess) W.; B.C.S., Benjamin Franklin U., Washington, 1933, M.C.S., 1935; postgrad. George Washington U., 1935-38, George Washington U. Sch. Law, 1938-39, Loyola U. Sch. Law, Chgo., 1939-41; J.D., Loyola U., Los Angeles, 1942; m. Evelyn Marjorie Davis, Aug. 11, 1939; children—Jean Louise, Allen Lloyd. Mgr. tax dept. Arthur Andersen & Co., 1936-45; admitted to Calif. bar, 1943; practiced in Los Angeles, 1945—; partner Dempsey, Thayer, Deibert & Kumler, 1945-47, Willis, Butler, Scheifly, Leydorf & Grant and predecessors, 1947—. Instr., U. So. Calif. Law Sch., 1951-60; vis. lectr. U. Calif., Berkeley, 1964—; mem. planning com. Inst. Fed. Taxation, 1954-69; mem. adv. com. N.Y. U. Inst. Fed. Taxation, 1962-66; chmn. adv. group to Mills Subcom., Ways and Means Com., U.S. Ho. of Reps., 1956-61; chmn. Ann. Tax and Probate Forum, Title Ins. & Trust Co., Los Angeles, 1966—; chmn. Commn. to Revise Tax Structure, 1969—. Trustee, exec. com. bd. trustees, investment and student life coms. U. Redlands, 1964-76; trustee J.W. and Ida M. Jameson Found. Recipient Dana Latham award for outstanding services to tax law profession, 1976. Fellow Am. Bar Found.; mem. Am. Judicature Soc., Am. Law Inst., Am., Calif., Los Angeles County bar assns., Phi Alpha Delta. Republican. Presbyn. (elder). Club: California (Los Angeles). Author: Handbook of Partnership Taxation, 1957; Willis on Partnership Taxation, 1971; Partnership Taxation, 1976. Editor: Studies in Substantive Tax Reform, 1969. Contbr. articles profl. jours. Home: 1406 La Plaza Dr Lake San Marcus CA 92069 Office: 606 S Olive St Los Angeles CA 90014

WILLIS, BENJAMIN COPPAGE, ret. ednl. adminstr.; b. Balt., Dec. 23, 1901; s. Clarence Milton and Elizabeth Estelle (Coppage) W.; student St. John's Coll., Annapolis, Md., 1918-19; A.B., George Washington U., 1922, Dr. Pub. Service (hon.), 1964; A.M., U. Md., 1926; student Johns Hopkins, 1933; Ed.D., Columbia U., 1950; LL.D. (hon.), Northwestern U., 1955, Bradley U., 1960, Harvard U., 1960; L.H.D., Central Mich. Coll., 1959, Nat. Coll. Edn., 1961, Am. Internat. Coll., 1965; m. Rachel Davis Webster, Jan. 24, 1925; 1 dau., Margaret Rachel (Mrs. Henry H. Bischoff). Prin., Henderson (Md.) Elementary and High Sch., 1922-23, Federalsburg (Md.) Elementary and High Sch., 1923-27, Caroline High Sch., Denton, Md., 1927-31, Sparrows Point High Sch., 1931-32, Catonsville (Md.) High Sch., 1932-34; supt. schs. Caroline County, Denton, 1934-40, Washington County, Hagerstown, Md., 1940-47, Yonkers, N.Y., 1947-50, Buffalo, 1950-53; supt. schs. Chgo., 1953-66; owner Benjamin C. Willis Ednl. Asso., Inc., Chgo.; supt. schs. Broward County, Fort Lauderdale, 1969-72. Exec. dir. Mass. Edn. Survey, 1963-65; former cons. Peace Corps; mem. Pres.'s Sci. Adv. Com., 1962-66 chmn. bd. Ednl. Planning Assos., Inc., 1969—; dir. Ednl. Facilities Labs., Inc.; former dir. Northwestern Mut. Life Ins. Co. Chmn. Ednl. Policies Commn., President's Panel of Cons. on Vocational Edn., 1962-63; mem. adv. com. Edn. in Ill. Bd. dirs. Chgo. Boys Clubs, Jr. Achievement Chgo., mem. exec. bd. Chgo. council Boy Scouts Am.; nat. adv. com. Girls Scouts U.S.A.; mem. Chgo. YMCA; mem. citizens bd. U. Chgo.; citizens com. U. Ill.; citizen fellowship Inst. Medicine Chgo.; trustee Chgo. Planetarium Soc., Chgo. Ednl. TV Assn., Stanford. Mem. U.S. C. of C. (edn. com.), Ill. Assn. Sch. Adminstrs., Ill. Edn. Assn., Ill State C. of C. (edn. com.). Chgo. Assn. Commerce and Industry, N.E.A. (life), Am. Assn. Sch. Adminstrs. (chmn. yearbook commn. 1954, pres. 1961), Kappa Delta Pi, Phi Delta Kappa. Clubs: Economic, Executives, Rotary (Chgo.). Contbr. articles to ednl. jours. and bus. revs. Address: 5555 N Sheridan Rd Chicago IL 60640. *Prepare myself, work hard, select excellent associates, and try to help children, youth, and adults.*

WILLIS, BETTY JO, inland waterway transp. exec.; b. Elkins, W.Va., Mar. 26, 1926; d. Parker Davis and Elsie (Durrett) Fink; student U. Cin.; m. Ronald Dewitt Willis, June 5, 1954 (dec.), 1 dau., Vickie D. Stearns. With Midland Enterprises Inc./Ohio River Co., and predecessor, Cin., 1950—, corp. sec., asst. treas., 1970—. Mem. Am. Soc. Corp. Secs. Republican. Presbyterian. Club: Cin. Zonta (pres. 1979-81). Home: 3182 Portsmouth Ave Cincinnati OH 45208 Office: 1400 580 Bldg Cincinnati OH 45202

WILLIS, BEVERLY A., architect; b. Tulsa, Feb. 17, 1928; d. Ralph William and Margaret (Porter) W.; B.A., U. Hawaii, 1954; student U. So. Calif., 1956, Oreg. State U., 1956-58. Exhibited in one man show at Maxwell Art Gallery, San Francisco, 1952; executed murals Palama Music Settlement, 1955, United Chinese Soc., 1956; pres. Willis & Assos., Inc., San Francisco, 1956—; dir. Manulytics, Inc. Mem. bldg. research advisory bd. Nat. Acad. Scis.; chmn. Fed. Constrn. Council. Bd. dirs. Calif. Heritage Council. Recipient Excellence in Design award Honolulu Art and Artist Club, 1958, Nat. award for remodeling of Campbell-Ewald Bldg., San Francisco, 1965, Significant Achievement in Beautification citation Bldgs. Mag., 1966, A.I.A. Bay Area award for Union St. Store Devel., 1967, award of exceptional distinction for environmental design for work on Union St., Gov. Calif., 1967; named Outstanding Woman in San Francisco Bay Area, Bay Area Bus. and Profl. Womens Club, 1958, One of San Francisco Distinguished Citizens, Hearst Newspapers, 1969. Mem. AIA (Home and Home Merit award 1976, pres. Calif. council), Lambda Alpha, Alpha Phi. Important works include rehab. Union St. stores, Campbell-Ewald Bldg., Nob Hill Ct. Home: 3977 Clay St San Francisco CA 94118 Office: 545 Mission St San Francisco CA 94105

WILLIS, CLAYTON, govt. ofcl., oilman, educator, publisher, writer, cons., lectr.; b. Washington, Aug. 11, 1933; s. William H. and Elizabeth (Keferstein) W.; B.A., George Washington U., 1957; student The Sorbonne, Paris, 1953-54, U. Oslo, summer 1953; grad. N.Y. Inst. Finance, 1966, Assn. Commodities Exchange Firms Sch., Am. U., 1972, George Washington U., 1973. Spl. assignment U.S. embassy, London, Eng., 1957; writer NBC radio show Tex and Jinx, 1958, spl. corr. NBC News, 1959; contbr., corr. Newsweek mag., Christian Sci. Monitor, Chattanooga Times, The Washington Daily News, Washington Post, Cape Argus of Capetown (South Africa), Bangkok Post, Irish Times, Dublin; reporter, movie, art critic Albuquerque Tribune, 1959-61; asst. editor Newsweek Mag., N.Y.C., 1961-62; TV broadcaster-writer U.P.I. Newsfilm, N.Y.C., 1962; White House, Washington corr. World Radio News, Houston, WAVA Radio Sta., Washington, 1963-65; editorial writer, corr. Hearst Newspaper, N.Y.C., 1965; press officer UN, N.Y.C., 1965-66; spl. assignment Am. embassy, Reykjavik, Iceland, 1967; editorial writer, critic, reporter N.Y. Amsterdam News, N.Y.C., 1967-68; cons. Ford Found., N.Y.C., 1968-69; dir. pub. affairs U.S. Equal Employment Opportunity Commn., Washington, 1969-70; cons. Office Econ. Opportunity, Washington, 1970, Pres.'s Nat. Council on Indian Opportunity, Washington, 1970-71, Community Relations Service, U.S. Dept. Justice, Washington, 1970-73, Cabinet Com. on Opportunities for Spanish Speaking People, 1971-72, Pres.'s Commn. on Fed. Statistics, Fed. Energy Adminstrn., Washington, 1973-74; dir. pub. affairs Office Petroleum Allocation U.S. Dept. Interior, 1973-74; dir. congl. relations, dir. public affairs Pres.'s Commn. on Fire Prevention and Control, 1971-73; pub., editor Four Corners Chieftain, Ignacio, Colo., 1972-73; lectr. U. of D.C., Washington, 1973-74; owner Willis News Service, Palm Beach, Fla., 1974—; adviser to Fernando E.C. de Baca spl. asst. to the Pres., White House, 1974-76. lectr. nat., internat. affairs, energy. Dir. pub. affairs Vets. Inaugural Com., Washington, 1976-77. Recipient Outstanding Service award Harlem Prep. Sch.; Letter of Commendation Pres. Mem. Overseas Press Club Am. Contbg. author: Capital Fare; contbr. articles to Palm Beacher, Lake Worth (Fla.) Herald, Palm Beach Evening News, Umtali Post, Zimbabwe, Gwelo (Zimbabwe) Times, To the Point, news mag., Johannesburg, The Citizen, Johannesburg, Hartford Courant, Sacramento Union, other mags. and newspapers; visited 150 countries; specialist South African goldmines. Address: Willis News Service 205 Worth Ave Suite 210 Palm Beach FL 33480

WILLIS, DAVID EDWIN, geophysicist; b. Cleve., Mar. 13, 1926; s. Russell E. and Eleanor Marie (Himebaugh) W.; B.S., Case Western Res. U., 1950; M.S. (U. Mich. Engring. Research Inst. fellow), U. Mich., 1957, Ph.D., 1968; m. Martha Louise Mumma, Jan. 3, 1948; children—Karen, Mark, Marta, Seth. Party chief, asst. supr. Keystone Exploration Co., Houston, 1950-55; research geophysicist, geophysics lab. head U. Mich., Ann Arbor, 1955-70, asso. prof., 1968-70; prof. dept. geol. scis. U. Wis., Milw., 1970—, chmn. dept., 1972-76; v.p. Geo-Aid Corp., 1975—. Served with USNR, 1944-46. NSF grantee, 1964-79; Air Force Office Sci. Research grantee, 1958-76; AEC grantee, 1971-74; ERDA grantee, 1974-77. Mem. Seismol. Soc. Am., Geol. Soc. Am., Am. Geophys. Union, Soc. Exploration Geophysicists, Phi Beta Kappa, Sigma Xi, Phi Kappa Phi. Contbr. articles to profl. jours. Home: 4958 N Cumberland Blvd Whitefish Bay WI 53217 Office: Dept Geol Scis U Wis Milwaukee WI 53201

WILLIS, DAVID LEE, radiation biologist; b. Pasadena, Calif., Mar. 15, 1927; s. Olan Garnet and Ida May (Lott) W.; B.Th., Biola Sem., Los Angeles, 1949; B.A., Biola Coll., 1951; B.S., Wheaton (Ill.) Coll., 1952; M.A., Calif. State U., Long Beach, 1954; Ph.D., Oreg. State U., 1963; m. Earline L. Fleischman, Dec. 26, 1950; children—David Lee, Paul J., Daniel N. Tchr. sci. high schs. in Calif., 1952-57; instr. biology Fullerton (Calif.) Jr. Coll., 1957-61; mem. faculty Oreg. State U., 1962—, prof. radiation biology, 1971—, chmn. dept. gen. sci., 1969—; cons. in radioecology. Mem. AAAS, Am. Sci. Affiliation (pres. 1975), Health Physics Soc., Radiation Research Soc. Republican. Baptist. Co-author: Radiotracer Methodology in Biological Science, 1965, Life in the Laboratory, 1965, Radiotracer Methodology in the Biological, Environmental and Physical Sciences, 1975. Home: 3135 NW McKinley Dr Corvallis OR 97330 Office: Gen Sci Dept Oreg State Univ Corvallis OR 97331

WILLIS, DONALD SIGURDSON, educator; b. Astoria, Oreg., June 16, 1917; s. Arza McCellen and Anna (Sigurdson) W.; student U.S. Naval Japanese Lang. Sch., U. Colo., 1942-43; B.A., U. Wash., 1943, Ph.D., 1951; m. Mary Jean Kerr, Dec. 24, 1942; children—Carol (Mrs. Michael Fetterman), Richard, Randall. Teaching, research asst. U. Wash., 1942, 46-48; asst. prof., asso. prof. Oriental langs. U. Oreg., Eugene, 1948-62; prof. Chinese and Japanese, chmn. dept. Slavic, Eastern langs. U. Colo., Boulder, 1962-65, chmn. dept. Oriental langs. and lits., 1965-77, chmn. dept. Oriental and Slavic langs. and lit., 1977—, also dir. Center East Asian Studies, 1966-70, 72-75; prof., head dept. Asian langs. U. Canterbury, Christchurch, New Zealand, 1970-71. Cons. Asian langs. New Zealand Ministry Edn., 1970-71. Served with U.S. Army, 1935-38, USN, 1942-45. Chinese Ministry Edn. fellow, 1947-48; Ford Found. fellow, 1955-56. Mem. Assn. Asian Studies, Assn. Tchrs. Japanese, Chinese Lang. Tchrs. Assn. Contbr. articles to profl. jours. Home: 980 6th St Boulder CO 80302

WILLIS, EDGAR ERNEST, educator; b. Calgary, Alta., Can., July 12, 1913; s. Samuel Ernest and Ethel Annie (Fairbourn) W.; brought to U.S., 1920, naturalized, 1931; B.A., Wayne State U., 1935, M.A., 1936; Ph.D., U. Wis., 1940; m. Zella Carine Nobles, Sept. 16, 1938; children—Richard, Franklin, Andrea, (Mrs. Richard Lee Weaver II). Producer radio dept. Detroit pub. schs., 1935-43; asst. prof. speech Wayne State U., 1946; asso. prof. San Jose (Calif.) State Coll., 1946-51, prof., 1951-52; asso. prof. U. Mich., Ann Arbor, 1952-57, prof., 1957—, chmn. dept. speech communication and theatre, 1969-79; news analyst WWJ-TV, Detroit, 1953-54; program asso. Nat. Ednl. TV, 1958-59; Fulbright lectr. in TV, Gt. Britain, 1963-64; cons. in TV, Cyprus Broadcasting Corp., 1963. Bd. dirs. Family Service Assn., Ann Arbor, 1959-61. Served from ensign to lt. (j.g.) USNR, 1943-46; PTO. Mem. Speech Communication Assn. (adminstrv. council 1954-56, 67-69, chmn. radio-TV film div. 1957), Central States, Mich. speech assns., Phi Beta Kappa, Delta Sigma Rho. Baptist. Author: Foundations in Broadcasting, 1951; A Radio Director's Manual, 1961; Writing Television and Radio Programs, 1967; (with others) Television and Radio, 1978; also articles. Home: 1112 Clair Circle Ann Arbor MI 48103

WILLIS, ELLEN JANE, journalist; b. N.Y.C., Dec. 14, 1941; d. Melvin H. and Miriam F. (Weinberger) Willis; A.B., Barnard Coll., 1962; postgrad. U. Calif. at Berkeley, 1962-63. Free-lance writer, 1966—; asso. editor Cheetah mag., 1967-68; staff writer New Yorker mag., 1968—; asso. editor US mag., 1969; contbg. editor MS mag., 1972-75, Rolling Stone mag., 1976-78; staff writer Village Voice, 1979—. Co-founder, RedStockings, 1969; mem. staff Home Front, center for anti-war soldiers, Colorado Springs, Colo., 1969-70. Office: New Yorker Magazine 25 W 43d St New York City NY 10036

WILLIS, EVERETT IRVING, lawyer; b. Canadian, Tex., Oct. 28, 1908; s. Newton Percy and Lena (Powers) W.; student Austin Coll., Sherman, Tex., 1924-26. A.B., U. Mo., 1928; LL.B. magna cum laude, Harvard, 1932; m. Margaret Virginia Wilson, Dec. 25, 1935; children—Everett Irving, Robert Frampton. Admitted to N.Y. bar, 1932, since practiced in N.Y.C.; with firm Dewey, Ballantine, Bushby, Palmer & Wood, and predecessors, 1932—, partner, 1944—. Mem. Bd. of Edn., Rye, N.Y., 1946-52, pres. 1951-52. Recipient drug industry Man of Year award, 1964. Mem. Am. (council pub. utilities sect. 1966-69), Fed. Energy, N.Y. State, Internat. bar assns., Assn. Bar City N.Y., N.Y. County Lawyers Assn., Phi Beta Kappa, Sigma Nu, Alpha Pi Zeta. Republican. Presbyterian. Clubs: Univ., City Midday (N.Y.C.); Coral Beach and Tennis (Bermuda); Manursing Island, Apawamis (Rye, N.Y.). Home: Hillandale Rd Port Chester NY 10573 Office: 140 Broadway New York NY 10005

WILLIS, GEORGE EDMUND, chem. processing and elec. mfg. co. exec.; b. Newmarket, Ont., Can., July 16, 1920; (came to U.S., 1925, naturalized, 1937); s. George Clarence and Marion Romer (Gillespie) W.; B.S. in Chem. Engring. cum laude, Mich. State Coll., 1942; M.B.A., Harvard U., 1947; m. Dorothy Anne Rice, June 7, 1943; children—Dorothy Anne, Jacqueline Pamela, Marion Jean, George Patterson Rice, James Edmund, Lorna Isabel. Engr. Lincoln Electric Co., Cleve., 1947-51, supt. electrode div., 1951-59, v.p., 1959-69, exec. v.p., 1969-72, pres., 1972—, also dir. 1959; dir. Lincoln Big Three, Inc., Big Three Lincoln Alaska, Inc. Founder Health Fund of Greater Cleve., 1958, pres., 1969-72, vice chmn. bd., 1972—; trustee; pres., treas., trustee, chmn. bd. Camp Ho Mita Koda, Newbury, Ohio, 1959—; trustee Lake Erie Coll., Painesville; mem. corp. Euclid (Ohio) Gen. Hosp., 1961—; bd. govs. Geauga County YMCA. Served from 2d lt. to maj., AUS, 1942-46; ETO, PTO. Decorated Bronze Star with oak leaf cluster. Mem. Wire Assn., Am. Welding Soc., Greater Cleve. Growth Assn., Cleve. Com. on Fgn. Relations, Amateur Fencers League Am. (exec. com., trustee No. Ohio div.), Alpha Chi Sigma, Phi Kappa Phi, Tau Beta Pi. Presbyn. (elder). Clubs: Harvard Business School, 50 of Cleveland (Cleve.). Home: 11661 Sperry Rd Chesterland OH 44026 Office: Lincoln Electric Co 22801 St Clair Ave Cleveland OH 44117

WILLIS, GLEN O., oil co. exec.; b. Tulsa, Oct. 27, 1933; s. E. C. and Madeline (Boyd) W.; B.B.A., U. Tulsa, 1960; m. Betty L. Smith, Aug. 30, 1957; children—Glenda Kaye, Janet Lynn, Beth Renee. Budget analyst Tenneco Inc., Houston, 1960-66; fin. and budget analyst Skelly Oil Co., Tulsa, 1966-70; fin. and budget analyst Tenneco Oil Co., Houston, 1970-76, treas., 1976—. Served with U.S. Army, 1954-56. Mem. U. Tulsa Alumni Assn. (dir.). Home: 12907 Indian Wells Houston TX 77066 Office: PO Box 2511 Houston TX 77001

WILLIS, HENRY STUART KENDALL, physician, educator; b. High Point, N.C., July 19, 1891; s. Samuel Edward and Cora (Stuart) W.; A.B., U. N.C., 1914; M.D., Johns Hopkins, 1919, M.A., 1920; m. Jeannette Pearce, Sept. 22, 1917 (dec.); children—Henry Stuart Kendall, David Pearce; m. 2d, Gertrude F. Mitchell, Sept. 10, 1955. Intern Johns Hopkins Hosp., 1919-20; asst. in medicine Johns Hopkins U., 1919-20, instr., 1920-22, asso., 1922-28, lectr. in medicine, 1928-30; dispensary physician Johns Hopkins Hosp., 1927-30, vis. physician, 1928-30; practice medicine specializing in tuberculosis and diseases of chest, Balt., 1928-30; summer lectr. U. La., 1925, U. Kans., 1928 pathologist Dept. Health, Detroit, 1930-33; pathologist Maybury Sanatorium, Northville, Mich., 1930-33, supt. and med. dir., 1933-47; supt., med. dir. N.C. Sanatorium System, McCain, 1947-53, Chapel Hill, 1953-68, ret.; asso. clin. prof. medicine U. N.C., 1954-59, clin. prof. medicine, 1959-69. Chmn. Tb study sect. USPHS, 1946-48. Bd. dirs. Carolina Friends Sch., 1965—, chmn., 1966-73, 77—; bd. dirs. Haitian Am. Tb Inst., 1962—. Served as pvt. U.S. Army, 1918. Recipient So. Tb Conf. award, 1956, Bruce Douglas award, 1960, Distinguished Alumni award U. N.C., 1970, Trudeau medal Am. Lung Assn., 1976. Fellow A.C.P.; mem. Assn. Am. Pathologists and Bacteriologists, Am. Soc. Clin. Investigation, Am. Pub. Health Assn., Am. Clin. and Climatol. Assn., Nat. Tb Assn. (dir. 1938-70, mem. exec. com., sec. 1947-51, v.p. 1946, pres. 1961), Am. Thoracic Soc. (mem. council, exec. com., pres. 1955-56), Soc. Exptl. Biology and Medicine, So. Tb Conf. (pres. 1963-64), N.C. Tb Assn. (pres. 1960), Sigma Xi. Mem. Soc. of Friends. Author: Laboratory Diagnosis and Experimental Methods in Tb, 1928; Studies on Tuberculosis Infection (with A.K. Krause and W.S. Miller) (printed privately), 1928; (monograph) Pneumonoconiosis and Tuberculosis (Medicine), 1930; Diagnostic and Experimental Methods in Tuberculosis (with M.M. Cummings), 1950; numerous scientific papers on diseases of chest. Home: 155 Carol Woods Chapel Hill NC 27514

WILLIS, JOHN FRISTOE, optometrist; b. St. Louis, Jan. 27, 1910; s. Prior Fristoe and Elva Cora (Moss) W.; A.B., Washington U., St. Louis, 1932, postgrad., 1934; postgrad. U. So. Calif., 1938, Am. Conservatory Music, Chgo., 1952-55; Dr. Optometry, No. Ill. Coll. Optometry, 1948; m. Alice Alvana Overbay, Aug. 31, 1943; 1 son, John Thomas. Violinist-soloist, stations KWK, WIL, KSD, KMOX, St. Louis, 1927-32; supr. music Prosser (Wash.) Pub. Schs., 1935-36; prof. violin Fla. State Sch. for Deaf and Blind, 1937; violin soloist So. Calif. Symphony Orch., 1939, concertmaster, 1939-41; concertmaster Albert Coates Grand Opera Symphony, Los Angeles, 1939; pvt. practice optometry, Villa Park, Ill., 1955—. Violin soloist Chgo. Bus. Men's Symphony, 1956-61, 71-72, concertmaster, 1956—. Chmn. Save Our Sight program Lions Club, Villa Park, 1971, 75. Bd. dirs. Chgo. Bus. Men's Orch., 1972. Served with USNR, 1942-45. Recipient Albert Coates Masterly Violinist award, 1939. Mem. Am., Ill. optometric assns., VFW, SAR, Tau Kappa Epsilon. Lion. Home: 106 E Kenilworth St Villa Park IL 60181 Office: 4 W Central St Villa Park IL 60181

WILLIS, JOHN STEELE, physiologist; b. Long Beach, Calif., Jan. 19, 1935; s. William Washington and Ada Beatrice (Rivers) W.; B.A., U. Calif., Berkeley, 1956; M.A., Harvard, 1957, Ph.D., 1961; m. Judith Horwitz, Sept. 28, 1958. Research fellow biochemistry Oxford (Eng.) U., 1961-62; mem. faculty U. Ill., Urbana, 1962—, prof. physiology, 1972—; past cons. physiology study sect. NIH, merit rev. bd. VA. NSF predoctoral fellow, 1956-59; predoctoral fellow NIH, 1959-60, postdoctoral fellow, 1961-62; exchange fellow Nat. Acad. Scis.-Czechoslovakia Acad. Scis., 1975. Mem. Soc. Exptl. Biology (Gt. Britain), Am. Physiol. Soc., Am. Soc. Zoologists, Soc. Gen. Physiologists, Soc. Cryobiology, Phi Beta Kappa, Sigma Xi. Club: Halifax House (Oxford). Author research papers. Co-editor: Hibernation-Hypothermia, Perspectives and Challenges, 1972; asso. editor Am. Jour. Physiology; editorial bd. Crybiology. Home: 611 W Indiana Ave Urbana IL 61801 Office: 524 Burrill Hall Univ Ill Urbana IL 61801

WILLIS, KENNETH REED, ins. co. exec.; b. Milw., Mar. 21, 1932; s. Maurice R. and Ruth (Priebe) W.; B.B.A., U. Wis., 1953, M.B.A., 1960; m. Elaine Kusta, Nov. 27, 1954; children—David, Barbara, Mark, Patricia. Salesman, Mut. of N.Y., 1957; with Time Ins. Co., Milw., 1957—, asst. to pres., 1963-64, asst. v.p., 1964-68, v.p., 1968-69, sr. v.p., 1969—, sec., 1968—, also dir.; pres. Time Holdings Founds., Inc.; pres., dir. Time Equities, Inc., Milw. 1968—. Pres. Elm Grove Lutheran Sch. P.T.A., Brookfield, Wis., 1969; chmn. Cub Scouts Am., 1965; chmn. Bd. Edn., Elm Grove Luth. Schs., 1970—. Served to comdr. USCGR, 1953-57. C.L.U. Fellow Life Mgmt. Inst. Home: 16040 Gebhardt Rd Brookfield WI 53205 Office: 515 W Wells St Milwaukee WI 53203

WILLIS, PAUL ALLEN, librarian; b. Floyd County, Ind., Oct. 1, 1941; s. Clarence Charles and Dorothy Jane (Harritt) W.; A.B., U. Ky., 1963, J.D., 1969; M.L.S., U. Md., 1966; m. Barbara Marcum, June 15, 1963; children—Mark, Sally. Cataloger, Library of Congress, Washington, 1963; head descriptive cataloging br. Sci. and Tech. Information Facility, NASA, College Park, Md., 1963-66; law librarian, prof. law U. Ky., Lexington, 1966-73, dir. libraries, 1973—, acting dean Coll. Library Sci., 1975-76; exec. sec. Ky. Jud. Retirement and Removal Commn., 1977—; mem. adv. com. Center for Jud. Conduct Orgns., Am. Judicature Soc., Chgo., 1979—. Home: 2055 Bridgeport Dr Lexington KY 40502 Office: Director's Office U Ky Library Lexington KY 40506

WILLIS, PAUL GENE, educator, polit. scientist; b. Ashland, Ky., Feb. 27, 1916; s. Otis and Sara M. (Kelley) W.; B.A., Marshall U., 1937; A.M., La. State U., 1939; Ph.D., Ind. U., 1949; m. Ann Smith Hardie, Sept. 21, 1940. Instr., then asst. prof. polit. sci. Ind. U., 1946-57; asst. to chmn. Democratic Nat. Com., 1955-57; pres. Holiday Homes, Inc., El Paso, Tex., 1957-61; adminstrv. asst. to Congressman Jim Wright, 1961-63; prof. polit. sci. Drake U., Des Moines, 1963—, chmn. dept., 1963-78. Chmn. El Paso County Planning Commn., 1960-61; mem. Gov. Ia. Commn. Intergovtl. Relations, 1966-68. Served to lt. USNR, 1942-46. Mem. Am. Polit. Sic. Assn., Am. Acad. Polit. and Social Scis., Sigma Delta Chi. Author: Juries and Judicial Review, 1950; (with Dr. G.L. Willis) Politics of the 22d Amendment, 1952; Election '64 and Now What?; 1964; (film) Voting Procedures, 1955. Home: 5421 Aurora Apt 196 Des Moines IA 50310

WILLIS, THORNTON WILSON, artist; b. Pensacola, Fla., May 25, 1936; s. Willard Wilson and Edna Mae (Hall) W.; B.S., U. So. Miss., 1962; M.A., U. Ala., 1966; m. Peggy Jean Whisenhant, June, 1960; 1 son, David Shaw. One-man exhbns. include: Henri Gallery, Washington, 1968, Paley and Lowe, N.Y.C., 1970, New Orleans Mus. Art, 1972; group exhbns. include: Phila. Civic Center, 1970, Whitney Mus., 1971; represented in permanent collections: Whitney Mus., N.Y.C., New Orleans Mus. Art, Rochester Meml. Gallery, Chase Manhattan Collection, William Paley Collection, CBS; vis. artist in residence La. State U., New Orleans, 1971-72. Served with USMC, 1954-57. John Simon Guggenheim fellow, 1978-79. Asso. editor Re-View, 1978—. Home: 85 Mercer St New York NY 10012 Office: 87 Mercer St New York NY 10012

WILLIS, WILLIAM DARRELL, JR., neurophysiologist, educator; b. Dallas, July 19, 1934; s. William Darrell and Dorcas (Chamberlain) W.; B.S., B.A., Tex. A. and M. U., 1956; M.D., U. Tex. Southwestern Med. Sch., 1960; Ph.D., Australian Nat. U., 1963; m. Jean Colette Schini, May 28, 1960; 1 son, Thomas Darrell. Postdoctoral research fellow Nat. Inst. Neurol. Diseases and Blindness, Australian Nat. U., 1960-62, Istituto di Fisiologia, U. Pisa (Italy), 1962-63; from asst. prof. to prof. anatomy, chmn. dept. U. Tex. Southwestern Med. Sch., Dallas, 1963-70; chief lab. comparative neurobiology Marine Biomed. Inst., prof. anatomy and physiology U. Tex. Med. Br., Galveston, 1970—, dir. Marine Biomed. Inst., 1978—. Mem. neurology B. study sect. NIH, 1968-70, chmn., 1970-72, mem. neurol. disorders Program Project rev. com., 1972-76. Mem. A.A.A.S., Am. Assn. Anatomists, Am. Physiol. Soc., Soc. Exptl. Biol. Medicine, Soc. Neurosci., Sigma Xi, Alpha Omega Alpha. Mem. editorial bd. Exptl. Neurology, Jour. Neurophysiology and Neurosci.; chief editor Jour. Neurophysiology, 1978—. Home: 4608 Ave O Galveston TX 77550

WILLIS, WILLIAM ERVIN, lawyer; b. Huntington, W.Va., Oct. 11, 1926; s. Asa Hannon and Mae (Davis) W.; student Ind. U., 1944, N.Y. U., 1945; A.B., Marshall U., 1948; J.D., Harvard U., 1951; m. Joyce Litteral, Sept. 1, 1949; children—Kathryn Cunningham, Anne Dresser, William. Admitted to N.Y. State bar, 1952; practiced law, N.Y.C., 1951—; mem. firm Sullivan & Cromwell, 1951—; lectr. Practising Law Inst., 1963—; trustee Fed. Bar Council, 1968-72; mem. 2d Circuit Commn. on Reduction Burdens and Costs Civil Litigation, 1977—. Served with AUS, 1944-46. Fellow Am. Coll. Trial Lawyers, Am. Bar Found.; mem. Am. Bar Assn., N.Y. State Bar Assn. (chmn. antitrust sect. 1976-77, exec. com. 1976—), Assn. Bar City N.Y., Am. Judicature Soc., Am. Arbitration Assn. (panel arbitrators), N.Y. Law Inst., N.Y. County Lawyers. Clubs: Broad St.; Internat. (Washington). Contbr. articles to legal jours. Home: Dogwood Ln Alpine NJ 07620 also Otterhole Rd West Milford NJ 07480 Office: 125 Broad St New York NY 10004

WILLIS, WILLIAM HILLMAN, educator; b. Trenton, Tenn., Oct. 28, 1908; s. William David and Maud (Hillman) W.; A.B., Union U., 1930; M.S., Ia. State U., 1931, Ph.D., 1933; m. Travis McDonald, Nov. 1, 1934; children—William David II, Travis H. Asso. soil scientist U.S. Dept. Agr., Ft. Worth, 1934-42; faculty La. State U., Baton Rouge, 1942—, prof. agronomy, 1948-79, head dept. agronomy, 1966-79, prof. emeritus, dept. head emeritus, 1979—; chmn. So. Regional Soil Research Com., 1972-75. Recipient Distinguished Teaching award Gamma Sigma Delta, 1961, Outstanding Prof. Coll. Agr., 1975-76; La. State U. Alumni faculty fellow, 1976-77. Mem. Am. Soc. Agronomy (pres. So. br. 1972), Soil Sci. Soc. Am., Sigma Xi, Gamma Sigma Delta, Alpha Zeta, Sigma Alpha Epsilon, Omicron Delta Kappa. Mason (33 deg.). Home: 1505 Stuart Ave Baton Rouge LA 70808 Office: Agronomy Dept La State Univ Baton Rouge LA 70803

WILLIS, WILLIAM SCOTT, univ. adminstr.; b. Gordonsville, Va., Nov. 29, 1921; s. Harry Sydnor and Jennie Carter (Dettor) W.; B.A. with honors (Dupont scholar), U. Va., 1942, M.A., 1947; postgrad. Lafayette Coll., 1943-44; Doctorat de l'Universite (Am. Field Service fellow 1947-49, Bennett Wood Green travel fellow 1948-50), U. Paris, 1951; m. Hester Fleming Williams, May 2, 1953; children—Julia, Spitz, Scott. Adminstrv. asst. UN, N.Y.C., 1951-52; dir. coll. dept. Coop. Bur. for Tchrs., N.Y.C., 1952-53; asst. to dean Washington Sq. Coll., N.Y. U., 1953-57, univ. dir. spl. projects, 1957-61, asst. dean Grad. Sch. Arts and Scis., 1961-65, dir. Internat. Student Center, 1965-68, instr. in French, 1953-55, asst. prof. French, 1955-68; dir. Sesquicentennial, U. Va., 1968-69, asst. dean Coll. Arts and Scis., 1969-72, asso. prof., 1968-72; dean Grad. Sch., George Mason U., Fairfax, Va., 1972-78, prof., 1972—. Trustee, The Tandem Sch., Charlottesville, Va., 1970-73; mem. Albermarle-Charlottesville Am. Independence Bicentennial Commn., 1971-76. Served with U.S. Army, 1942-45. Decorated chevalier de l'Ordre des Palmes Academiques (France); recipient Grande Médaille Alliance Francaise, Paris, 1958; recipient certificate of merit Orgn. Arab Students in U.S., 1967; N.Y. U. Grad. Arts, Scis. Research Fund grantee, 1964-65; Am. Philos. Soc. grantee, 1964-65. Mem. Conf. So. Grad. Schs. (exec. com. 1976—), Alliance Francaise (sec. gen. Fedn. French Alliances in U.S. 1954-57, editor L'Echo 1955-57, v.p. N.Y.C. chpt. 1960-68, pres. Charlottesville chpt. 1969-71), Am. Assn. Tchrs. French, Modern Lang. Assn., Nat. Assn. Fgn. Student Affairs, Am. Assn. Collegiate Registrars and Admissions Officers, Higher Edn. Assn. Washington. Episcopalian. Author: (with Haac and Strozier) Points de Vue, 1959; Foreign Student Credentials Guide, 1968; editor: Women and Education: A Mutual Responsibility, 1959. Home: 5913 One Penny Dr Fairfax Station VA 22039 Office: 4400 University Dr Fairfax VA 22030

WILLITS, WILLIAM COOPER, chems., health products and specialized equipment co. exec.; b. Phila., June 11, 1914; s. Merritt N., Jr. and Louretta (Cooper) W.; student U. Pa., 1933-35; grad. Babson Coll., 1937; m. Marjorie Huber, July 12, 1941; children—Christopher N., William Cooper, Jordan H. Trust investment analyst Fidelity-Phila. Trust Co., 1938-48; mgr. statis., research dept. Kidder, Peabody & Co., Phila., 1948-56; asst. to pres., treas., v.p., treas. Pennsalt Chems. Corp., Phila., 1956-67; pres. S.S. White Co. div. Pennwalt Corp., also v.p. dental health operations, 1967-70, sr. v.p., treas., chief financial officer parent co., 1974—; mng. dir. Pennwalt Overseas Finance N.V. Chmn. Paoli Area Sch. Authority, 1965—; chmn. zoning bd. Willistown Twp., Pa., 1962—. Served to 2d lt., inf. AUS, 1943-46. Republican. Episcopalian. Clubs: Union League (Phila.); Corinthian Yacht of Philadelphia. Home: 340 S Valley Rd Paoli PA 19301 Office: Pennwalt Bldg Philadelphia PA 19102

WILLKE, THOMAS ALOYS, univ. adminstr.; b. Rome City, Ind., Apr. 22, 1932; s. Gerard Thomas and Marie Margaret (Wuennemann) W.; A.B., Xavier U., 1954; M.S., Ohio State U., 1956, Ph.D., 1960; m. Geraldine Ann Page, Dec. 28, 1954; children—Richard, Susan, Donald, Jeanne, Mary, Kathleen. Sr. engr. N.Am. Aviation, Columbus, Ohio, 1959-60; instr. math. Ohio State U., 1960-61; research mathematician U.S. Nat. Bur. Standards, Washington, 1961-66; asst. prof. math. U. Md., College Park, 1963-66; asso. prof. Ohio State U., 1966-70, asso. prof. statistics, 1970-72, prof., 1972—, dir. statistics lab., 1970-73, vice provost Arts and Scis., 1973—. Mem. Inst. Math. Statistics, Council Ohio Deans, Am. Conf. Acad. Deans, Council Colls. Arts and Scis., Am. Statis. Assn., Math. Assn. Am. Roman Catholic. Contbr. articles on statis. non parametric methods and robustness to profl. jours. Home: 4375 Mumford Dr Columbus OH 43220 Office: Ohio State U 121 Denney Hall 164 W 17th Ave Columbus OH 43210

WILLMAN, JOHN NORMAN, hosp. and med. equipment mfr.; b. St. Joseph, Mo., Jan. 19, 1915; s. John N. and Frances (Potter) W.; student St. Benedict's Coll., 1936; m. Victoria King, May 9, 1941; 1 dau., Victoria. With Am. Hosp. Supply Corp., 1940-59, v.p., 1954-59; with Brunswick Corp., St. Louis, 1959-68, v.p., 1961-68, pres. Health and Sci. div., 1961-68; v.p. Sherwood Med. Industries, Inc., St. Louis, 1961-67, pres., 1967-72, vice chmn. bd., 1972-73, also dir.; pres., chief exec. officer, dir. IPCO Hosp. Supply Corp., Valhalla, N.Y., 1973-78. Clubs: Old Warson Country, Noonday (St. Louis); St. Joseph (Mo.) Country. Home: 530 N Spoede Rd Creve Coeur MO 63141

WILLMAN, MARILYN DAWN, ednl. adminstr.; b. Hancock, Mich., Dec. 31, 1928; d. Carl Donald and Myrtle J. (Hoyem) Willman; B.S. in Nursing, U. Mich., 1952; M.S. in Nursing, U. Tex., 1959, Ph.D., 1961. Staff nurse Wis. Gen. Hosp., Madison, 1952-53, instr. Madison Gen. Hosp. Sch. Nursing, 1953-57; asso. prof., asst. and asso. dean U. Tex. Nursing Sch., Austin, 1961-67, dean, prof., 1967-72, pres., 1972-76; dir. Sch. Nursing U. British Columbia, 1977—; mem. research in nursing in patient care review com. div. nursing USPHS, 1967-69, USPHS Profl. Nurse Traineeship, 1957-58; mem. Health Services Research Tng. Com. Bur. Health Services Research, 1974-77. USPHS Spl. Research fellow, 1958-61. Mem. Am. Nurses Assn., Am. Psychol. Assn., Am. Acad. Nursing (charter), Pi Lambda Theta. Sigma Theta Tau. Contbr. articles to profl. jours. Home: 4755 Lancelot Ct Richmond BC V7C 4S2 Canada

WILLMAN, VALLEE LOUIS, educator, surgeon; b. Greenville, Ill., May 4, 1925; s. Philip Louis and Marie Anna (Doll) W.; student U. Ill., 1941-43, 45-47; M.D., St. Louis U., 1951; m. Melba Lorraine Carr, Feb. 2, 1952; children—Philip, Elizabeth, Susan, Stephen, Mark, Timothy, Jane, Sarah, Vallee. Intern Phila. Gen. Hosp., 1951-52, asst. resident surgery, 1952-55; resident surgery St. Louis U. Sch. Medicine, 1955-56, Ellen McBridge fellow, 1956-57, mem. faculty, 1957—, prof. surgery, 1963—, chmn. dept., 1969—; cons. artificial heart program Nat. Heart and Lung Inst., NIH, 1968-76. Mem. surgery study sect. NIH, 1969-75; mem. Nat. Heart, Lung and Blood Adv. Council, 1978—. Served to ensign USNR, 1943-45. Diplomate Am. Bd. Surgery (dir.), Am. Bd. Thoracic Surgery. Fellow A.C.S.; mem. Am. Surg. Assn., Am. Assn. Thoracic Surgery, Am. Physiol. Soc., Soc. Univ. Surgeons, Internat. Cardiovascular Soc., Am. Soc. Artificial Internal Organs (council 1969), Central Surg. Assn. (sec. 1967-70, pres. 1971), Soc. Vascular Surgery, Phi Beta Kappa, Alpha Omega Alpha. Roman Catholic. Author articles in field. Home: 450 Sherwood Dr Webster Groves MO 63119 Office: 1325 S Grand Blvd St Louis MO 63104

WILLMARTH, WILLIAM WALTER, educator; b. Highland Park, Ill., Mar. 25, 1924; s. Sinclair Anson and Dorothy (Cox) W.; B.S. in Mech. Engring., Purdue U., 1949; M.S. in Aero. Engring., Calif. Inst. Tech., 1950, Ph.D., 1954; m. Nancy Robinson, Nov. 20, 1959; children—Robert, Deborah, Elizabeth, Kathleen. Research fellow, then sr. research fellow Calif. Inst. Tech., 1954-58; mem. faculty U. Mich., Ann Arbor, 1958—, prof. aerospace engring., 1961—; cons. to industry, 1952—. Served with AUS, 1943-46. Vis. fellow Joint Inst. Lab. Astrophysics, Boulder, Colo., 1963-64; fellow Max Planck Inst. für Stromungsforschung, Göttingen, West Germany, summer 1975. Mem. Am. Inst. Aeros. and Astronautics, Am. Phys. Soc., AAUP, Sigma Xi, Tau Beta Pi, Tau Sigma. Author papers, reports. Home: 765 Country Club Rd Ann Arbor MI 48105

WILLMORE, BERT LEROY, mfg. co. exec.; b. Rexburg, Idaho, Jan. 29, 1915; s. Herbert J. and Drucilla (Parker) W.; B.S. in Agr., U. Idaho, 1937; grad. Advanced Mgmt. Program, Harvard, 1959; m. Kathryn Adams, Jan. 29, 1938; children—James A., Kathryn E., Dena G., Margaret D. With Bur. Agrl. Econs., Dept. Agr., Berkeley, Calif., 1938-41, OPA, Washington, 1941-46; with Bemis Co., Inc., Mpls., 1946—, v.p., 1960—, also dir.; dir. Morgan Adhesive. Home: 6509 Navaho Trail Minneapolis MN 55435 Office: 800 North Star Center Minneapolis MN 55402

WILLMOT, DONALD GILPIN, brewing co. exec.; b. Toronto, Ont., Can., Mar. 7, 1916; s. Harold Edward and Florence (Gilpin) W.; B.A.Sc., U. Toronto, 1937; m. Ivy Vivian Sutcliffe, Nov. 18, 1939; children—Michael, Wendy, David. Engr., Canadian SKF Co. Ltd., Toronto, 1937-38; plant supt. Anthes Imperial Ltd., St. Catharines, Ont., 1939-41, pres., dir., 1948-68; successively supt., mgr. personnel and pub. relations, asst. to v.p., gen. mgr. Atlas Steels Ltd., Welland, Ont., 1942-48; pres., dir. Molson Industries Ltd., 1968-73; dep. chmn. bd. Molson Cos. Ltd., 1973-74, chmn. bd., 1974—; pres., dir. Rende Hall Investments Ltd.; v.p., dir. Bank N.S.; dir. Molson Breweries Can. Ltd., The Ontario Jockey Club, Internat. Nickel Co. Can. Ltd., Petro-Can. Ltd., Crown Life Ins. Co., Hayes-Dana Ltd., Jannock Corp. Ltd.; past chmn. bd. govs. Brock U., St. Catharines. Mem. Canadian Mfrs. Assn. (exec. council). Home: Kinghaven Farms Rural Route 2 King City ON L0G 1K0 Canada Office: PO Box 6015 Toronto AMF ON L5P 1B8 Canada

WILLMOTT, PETER S., bus. exec.; b. 1937; B.A., Williams Coll., 1959; M.B.A., Harvard, 1961; m. Sr. analyst Am. Airlines, 1961-63; cons. Booz Allen & Hamilton, 1964-66; asst. treas. Continental Baking Co., 1966, treas., 1969, v.p.; exec. v.p. finance and adminstrn. Fed. Express Corp., Memphis, 1974—. Address: Fed Express Corp Memphis Airport Memphis TN 38130

WILLNER, SIDNEY HAROLD, lawyer, hotel chain exec.; b. Union Hill, N.J., May 16, 1916; s. Max and Mary W.; A.B., Columbia U., 1935; LL.B. magna cum laude, Harvard U., 1938; m. Dorothy; children—Karen Willner Ferguson, Denise. Admitted to N.Y. bar, 1940, D.C. bar, 1946, U.S. Supreme Ct. bar, 1946; law clk. to Judge Learned Hand, U.S. Ct. Appeals 2d Circuit, 1938-39; asso. solicitor, asso. dir. div. pub. utilities and corporate regulations SEC, Washington, 1941-50; chief decartelization and deconcentration div. U.S. High Commn. for Germany, 1950-53; spl. adviser U.S. Del. to European Coal and Steel Community, 1952-53; pvt. practice law, Washington, 1953-58; gen. counsel, exec. v.p. fin. and corporate devel. Hilton Internat. Co., N.Y.C., 1958—. Chmn. exec. com. World Fedn. UN Assns.; bd. dirs. UN Assn. U.S., Internat. Voluntary Services Inc. Served to capt., JAGC, AUS, 1945-46. Mem. Am. Bar Assn., Bar Assn. City N.Y. Home: 1 Sutton Pl S New York City NY 10022 Office: 301 Park Ave New York City NY 10022

WILLOCKS, ROBERT MAX, librarian; b. Maryville, Tenn., Oct. 1, 1924; s. Willis Lemuel and Hannah (Emert) W.; B.A., Maryville Coll., 1949; B.D., Golden Gate Bapt. Theol. Sem., 1951, Th.M., 1962; M.A. in Library Sci., Peabody Coll., 1962; m. Neysa Nerene Ferguson, May 23, 1947; children—Margret Sharon, Samuel David, Mark Timothy, Robert Daniel, Kent Max. Ordained to ministry Bapt. Ch., 1950; pastor in Calif., 1950-56; missionary to Korea, So. Bapt. Fgn. Mission Bd., Taejon, 1956- 65; asso. dir. library Heidelberg Coll., Tiffin, Ohio, 1965-67, dir. library Columbia (S.C.) Coll., 1967-70; asst. dir. libraries Syracuse (N.Y.) U., 1970-76; asso. dir. libraries U. Fla., Gainesville, 1976—. Cons. Choong Chung Nam Province Library Assn., Korea, 1962-65; dir. Korea Bapt. Press, 1959-61; prof. ch. history Korea Bapt. Sem., 1957-65, acting pres., 1958-59, librarian, 1959-65; Vice chmn. Korea Bapt. Mission, 1962-64; del. Fla. Gov.'s Conf. on Libraries, 1978. Chmn. trustees Wallace Meml. Bapt. Hosp., Pusan, Korea, 1964-65. Served with USNR, 1943-46. Mem. Am. (chmn. telefacsimile com. 1976-78), Fla., Southeastern library assns., Am. Assn. U. Profs., Peabody Coll. Alumni Assn. (pres. S.C. 1968-69). Editor: (Korean translations) Thus it is Written, 1963; The Progress of Worldwide Missions, 1965. Home: 1930 NW 12th Rd Gainesville FL 32605

WILLOUGHBY, KEITH GODWIN, banker; b. Milw., Feb. 5, 1927; s. Geoffrey and Marion Van Arsdale (Helliwell) W.; B.A., U. Wis., 1950, M.A., 1951; grad. Stonier Grad. Sch. Banking, 1966; m. Lieselotte Luise Haack, July 8, 1954; children—Geoffrey A., Gregory J. With Dun & Bradstreet, N.Y.C., 1955-59, Wm. E. Pollock & Co., N.Y.C., 1959-61, Chase Manhattan Bank, N.Y.C., 1961-68; with Mut. Bank for Savs. (formerly Newton Savs. Bank), Newton, Mass., 1968—, pres., 1973—; mem. Savs. Bank Economic Forum. Trustee Lasell Jr. Coll. Mem. Nat. Assn. Mut. Savs. Banks (fed. legis. com.). Episcopalian. Author: Objective Aspects of Bank Investments, 1966. Home: 32 Nehoiden Rd Waban MA 02168 Office: 1188 Centre St Newton MA 02159

WILLOUGHBY, RODNEY ERWIN, oil co. exec.; b. Dallas, July 24, 1925; s. Charles V. and Juanita (Jones) W.; B.B.A., Tulane U., 1945; M.B.A., Harvard U., 1947; m. Marie J. Johnston, Feb. 27, 1954; five children. Mem. dean's staff Harvard Bus. Sch., 1947-48; with ECA, Paris, France, 1948-49; petroleum attache Am. embassy, London, Eng., 1949-52; concession mgr. Gulf Oil Corp., N.Y.C., 1952-55; mem. fgn. staff Standard Oil Co. Cal., San Francisco, 1955-65; pres. Refineria Conchan Chevron, Peru, 1965-69; pres. Chevron Oil Co. Latin Am., 1969-71; treas. Standard Oil Co. Calif., San Francisco, 1971—. Bd. dirs. Mills Meml. Hosp., Am. Council on Ger.; trustee Sta. Catalina Sch. Served to lt. (j.g.) USNR, 1943-46. Clubs: Pacific Union, Burlingame Country; Bankers. Office: 225 Bush St San Francisco CA 94104

WILLOUGHBY, STEPHEN SCHUYLER, educator; b. Madison, Wis., Sept. 27, 1932; s. Alfred and Elizabeth Frances (Cassell) W.; A.B. (scholar), Harvard, 1953, A.M. in Teaching, 1955; Ed.D. (Clifford Brewster Upton fellow), Columbia, 1961; m. Helen Sali Shapiro, Aug. 29, 1954; children—Wendy Valentine, Todd Alan. Tchr., Newton (Mass.) Pub. Schs., 1954-57, Greenwich (Conn.) Pub. Schs., 1957-59; instr. U. Wis., Madison, 1960-61, asst. prof., 1961-65; prof. math. edn. and math. N.Y. U., N.Y.C., 1965—, chmn. math. edn. dept., 1967—, head div. sci. and math. edn., 1970-76, chmn. math. sci. and ednl. statistics dept., 1976—. Adv. bd. ERIC Center for Math., 1969—. Mem. Nat. Council Tchrs. Math. (dir. 1968-71, chmn. com. to prepare guidelines for preservice prep. tchrs. math). Author: Contemporary Teaching of Secondary School Mathematics, 1967;

Probability and Statistics, 1973; also chpts. in year-books, anthologies. Contbr. articles to encys., profl. jours. Home: 13 Dingletown Rd Greenwich CT 06830 Office: 23 Press Bldg 32 Washington Pl New York U New York City NY 10003

WILLOUGHBY, WILLIAM FRANCIS, journalist; b. Dayton, Ohio, Nov. 26, 1928; s. Herbert and Marjorie (Hall) W.; student Sinclair Coll., 1947-48, Columbia Bible Coll., 1948-50; B.S., Nyack Coll., 1952; postgrad. Okla. U., 1954-55, Internat. Sch. Law, 1974—; m. Evangeline Pax Farah, Sept. 5, 1952; children—Brenda Lynn, Duane Lewis, Kent Lee, Michelle Mildred. Editor-in-chief Pittsfield (Maine) Advertiser, 1952-53; reporter Cape Cod (Mass.) Standard-Times, 1955-58, news editor, 1959-61; exec. sec. Buzzards Bay (Mass.) Area C. of C., 1958-59; publs. dir. Internat. Students, Inc., Washington, 1961-62; news editor Manassas (Va.) Jour. Messenger, 1963-64; Washington corr. Religious News Service, 1964-69; religious news editor, editorial writer Washington Star, 1969-79; pres. Wm. Willoughby Pubs., Inc., Washington, 1979—; Washington corr. Nat. Courier, 1975—; news commentator Bill Willoughby on Religion WCTN, Potomac, Md. Founder, Bourne (Mass.) Arts and Crafts Soc., 1959; founder, pres. Cape Cod Writers Guild, 1959. Candidate Va. State Senate, 1964; candidate for mayor, Fairfax, Va., 1968, candidate for City Council, 1979; chmn. Fairfax Park Commn., 1968-70. Trustee Religious Heritage of Am., Audrey McDaniel Faith and Hope Found. Recipient Faith and Freedom award for religious journalism, 1971, merit award Religious Pub. Relations Council, 1973; Freedom award, 1976. Fellow Religious Pub. Relations Council; mem. Summer Inst. Linguistics, Nat. Press Club, Washington Star Speakers Bur. Rotarian, Kiwanian. Club: Cosmos (Washington). Writer column Washington Perspective, 1969—, Logos Jour., 1971—, Moody Monthly mag., 1977—. Contbg. editor Baker's Dictionary Christian Ethics, 1973. Office: Wm Willoughby Pubs Inc 600 Pennsylvania Ave SE Washington DC 20003

WILLS, GARRY, journalist; b. Atlanta, May 22, 1934; s. John and Mayno (Collins) W.; B.A., St. Louis U., 1957; M.A., Xavier U., Cin., 1958; M.A., Yale U., 1959, Ph.D., 1961; m. Natalie Cavallo, May 30, 1959; children—John, Garry, Lydia. Fellow Center Hellenic Studies, 1961-62; asso. prof. classics Johns Hopkins U., 1961-67, adj. prof. 1968-69, 73—; Washington Irving prof. modern history and lit. Union Coll., Schenectady, 1976-77; contbg. editor Esquire mag., 1967-70; newspaper columnist Universal Press Syndicate, 1970—; author: Chesterton, 1961; Politics and Catholic Freedom, 1964; Roman Culture, 1966; Jack Ruby, 1967; Second Civil War, 1968; Nixon Agonistes, 1970; Bare Ruined Choirs, 1972; Inventing America, 1978; At Button's, 1979; Confessions of a Conservative, 1979; Explaining America, 1980. Mem. The Johnsonians. Roman Catholic. Address: Humanities Dept Johns Hopkins Univ Baltimore MD 21218

WILLS, JOHN GORDON, physicist; b. Greeley, Colo., Feb. 4, 1931; s. Robert William and Ruth (Stepp) W.; A.B., San Diego State U., 1953; M.S., U. Wash., 1956, Ph.D., 1963; m. Beverly Elaine Howerton, June 18, 1954; children—Debra Louise, Mechele Elaine, Kristine Marie, Joanne Carole, Michael Robert. Staff mem. Los Alamos Sci. Lab., 195660; faculty Ind. U., Bloomington, 1964—, prof. physics, 1976—. Mem. Am. Phys. Soc. Home: 3624 Morningside Dr Bloomington IN 47401 Office: Ind U Bloomington IN 47401

WILLS, JOHN HARVEY, banker; b. Elgin, Ill., Sept. 12, 1905; s. John Valentine and Anna (Grimm) W.; S.B., Mass. Inst. Tech., 1926; grad. student, Harvard U., 1926-27, 30-31; A.M., Princeton U., 1940; m. Gertrude Ellen Pitney, June 21, 1928; children—Virginia, Caroline Ellen. With econ. dept. First Nat. Bank of Boston, 1930-34, Moody's Investors Service, 1935-38; v.p. No. Trust Co., Chgo., 1943-64, sr. v.p., 1964-70; cons., 1970—; lectr. Rutgers U. Coll., 1935-43; mem. faculty Princeton, 1940-43, Grad. Sch. Banking, U. Wis., 1947—. Bd. dirs. Family Service of Evanston, Ill. Hon. sec. Mass. Inst. Tech. Mem. Am. Econ. Assn., Am. Statis. Assn., Conf. Bus. Economists, Tau Beta Pi. Presbyn. Clubs: University, Economic, Bankers (Chgo.); Westmoreland Country (Wilmette, Ill.). Home: 2425 Central St Evanston IL 60201 Office: 50 S La Salle St Chicago IL 60690

WILLS, RILEY JAMES, banker; b. Humphrey, Ark., Aug. 26, 1928; s. Riley Oliver and Nettie (Ables) W.; B.S., U. Ark., 1960; student U. Va., 1960-63; m. Mary Janelle Kemp, Feb. 11, 1949; 1 dau., Pamela Janelle. With Worthen Bank & Trust Co., Little Rock, 1947—, mgr. installment loan dept., 1964-66, mgr. correspondent bank div., 1967-69, sr. v.p., mgr. comml. div., 1969—. Served with U.S. Army, World War II, Korean Conflict. Mem. Little Rock C. of C., Nat. Assn. Accountants (pres. Central Ark. chpt. 1967-68, nat. dir. 1970-72), Stuart Cameron McLeod Soc. Club: Pleasant Valley Country (Little Rock). Home: 14 Cimarron Valley Circle Little Rock AR 72207 Office: PO Box 1681 Little Rock AR 72203

WILLS, ROBERT HAMILTON, editor; b. Colfax, Ill., June 21, 1926; s. Robert Orson and Ressie May (Hamilton) W.; B.S., M.S., Northwestern U., 1950; m. Sherilyn Lou Nierstheimer, Jan. 16, 1949; children—Robert L., Michael H., Kendall J. Reporter, Duluth (Minn.) Herald & News-Tribune, 1950-51; reporter Milw. Jour., 1951-59, asst. city editor, 1959-62; city editor Milw. Sentinel, 1962-75, editor, 1975—; v.p., dir. The Jour. Co.; sr. v.p., dir. Newspapers, Inc. Pres., Wis. Freedom of Info. Council, 1979-80; mem. media-law relations com. State Bar Wis. Served with USNR, 1944-46. Named Wis. Newsman of the Year, Milw. chpt. Sigma Delta Chi, 1973. Mem. Wis. Newspaper Assn. (dir.), Am. Soc. Newspaper Editors, Internat. Press Inst., Milw. Press Club, Sigma Delta Chi (pres. Milw. chpt. 1979-80). Unitarian. Home: 17965 Maple Tree Ln Brookfield WI 53005 Office: Milwaukee Sentinel 918 N 4th Milwaukee MI 53201

WILLS, SIDNEY HAYWARD, real estate exec.; b. Balt., July 8, 1926; s. F. Reed and Madeline (Hayward) W.; B.S., Syracuse U., 1949; div.; children—Sidney Hayward, Lila Gantt, Benjamin Reed, John Bowling. Buyer, R.H. Macy & Co., 1949-51; former pres., chmn. bd., GAC Corp.; dir. Pa. Power & Light Co., Eastern Industries, Inc., Barnett Banks of Fla. Bd. dirs. United Fund Dade County; trustee Fla. Internat. U. Served to lt. AUS, 1944-46. Club: Union League (N.Y.C.). *

WILLS, WALTER JOE, educator; b. Beecher City, Ill., Oct. 8, 1915; s. Joe J. and Lillian L. (Buzzard) W.; student Blackburn Coll., Carlinville, Ill., 1934; B.S. in Agr. U. Ill., 1936, M.S. in Agrl. Econs., 1937, Ph.D., 1952; m. Mary E. Triffet, May 22, 1942. Credit examiner Prodn. Credit Corp., St. Louis, 1937-47; asst. prof. U. Ill., 1947-52; dir. farm relations Am. Trucking Assn., 1953-54; extension marketing specialist Wash. State Coll., 1954-56; prof. agrl. marketing So. Ill. U., Carbondale, 1956—, chmn. agrl. industries dept., 1957-72. Fulbright lectr. Ege U., Izmir, Turkey, 1969-70. Mem. Ill. Sci. Advisory Council. Served to capt., ordnance dept., U.S. Army, 1941-46. Recipient Outstanding Coop. Educator award Am. Inst. Cooperation, 1978. Mem. Am. Econs. Assn., Am. Farm Econs. Assn., Internat. Assn. Agrl. Economists, Nat. Agr. Mktg. Assn., Phi Kappa Phi, Gamma Sigma Delta, Alpha Zeta. Rotarian. Author: Introduction to Grain Marketing, 1972; Introduction to Agribusiness Management, 1973. Home: 904 Valley Rd Carbondale IL 62901

WILLSON, FRED E., advt. exec.; b. Kansas City, Mo., Oct. 22, 1917; s. Fred E. and Hazel Inez (Tarter) W.; B.S., U. Ill., 1940; m. Pat Mary Draper, July 12, 1946; children—Michael, Haley, Jill, Laurie, Peter, Mark. Writer, salesman Sta. WDWS, Champaign, Ill., 1940-42; program dir. Sta. WIND, Chgo., 1942-45; account exec. Ivan Hill, Inc., Chgo., 1945-50; art and prodn. mgr. Post-Keyes-Gardner, Inc., Chgo., 1950-51, account exec., 1951-55, account supr., 1955-64, mgmt. supr., 1964-70, sr. v.p., gen. mgr., 1970—, also dir. Bd. dirs. Kidney Found. Ill., 1976—; mem. End Stage Renal Disease Network 15. Episcopalian. Club: Lake Shore. Home: 838 S Garfield St Hinsdale IL 60521 Office: 875 N Michigan Ave Chicago IL 60611

WILLSON, JAMES DOUGLAS, aerospace co. exec.; b. Edinburgh, Scotland, May 24, 1915 (came to U.S. 1921); s. George William and Margaret (Douglas) W.; B.S. with honors, Ohio State U., 1937, M.B.A., 1938; m. Genevieve Best, Nov. 11, 1939; children—James Douglas, Stephen J., Wendy. Sr. auditor Arthur Andersen & Co., C.P.A.'s, N.Y.C., 1938-42; controller Stinson div. Consol. Vultee Aircraft Corp., 1946-48, Plaskon div. Libbey-Ownes-Ford Glass Co., 1948-53; treas. Affiliated Gas Equipment Co., Cleve., 1953; v.p. finance, treas. Norris-Thermador Corp., Los Angeles, 1957-59; controller, mgr. finance Tidewater Oil Co., Los Angeles, 1959-60, v.p. finance, 1960-66; v.p. finance Northrop Corp., Los Angeles, 1966-70, sr. v.p. finance, treas., 1970—, also dir.; dir. Bunker Hill Income Securities, Page Communication Engrs., Inc. Served to lt. comdr. USNR, 1942-46. C.P.A., N.Y. Mem. Nat. Assn. Accountants (Lybrand Gold medal 1960), Am. Inst. C.P.A.'s, Controllers Inst. Am. Author: (with J. Brooks Heckert) Controllership, 1952, 63; Business Budgeting and Control, 1956, 57. Home: 1715 Chevy Chase Dr Beverly Hills CA 90210 Office: 1800 Century Park East Los Angeles CA 90266

WILLSON, JAMES HARDIN, farm equipment co. exec.; b. Athens, Tenn., Sept. 27, 1907; s. Elbert Lane and Lucy Mable (Smith) W.; student Carson-Newman Coll., 1924-26, U. Chattanooga, 1927, Tenn. Wesleyan Coll., 1928; m. Doris A. Davis, Nov. 8, 1939; children—Doris (Mrs. Kenneth Kirkpatrick), Elaine (Mrs. Fred Wynn), Rebecca Ann Willson Milne. Mary (Mrs. Lee Mixson), James Hardin. Asst. gen. mgr. Athens Plow Co., 1929-31, sec.-treas., 1931-43, gen. mgr.; 1943-49, pres., 1949-65, chmn. bd., 1965—, also dir.; dir., mem. exec. com. First Nat. Bank McMinn County; dir. Austin Industries, Dallas. Mem. Civil Service Commn. Tenn., 1962—, chmn., 1968—; chmn. McMinn County Council, 1949-55. Past pres., bd. dirs. United Community Fund; past dir., v.p. So. States Indsl. Council; past trustee Tenn. Wesleyan Coll., E. Tenn. Baptist Hosp.; trustee Harrison-Chilhowee Acad, Mem. Tenn. Mfrs. Assn. (past pres., dir.), So. Farm Equipment Mfrs. (past pres.), N.A.M. (dir.), Farm and Indsl. Equipment Inst. (pres. 1964-65). Mason (Shriner), Elk. Clubs: Springbrook Golf and Country (Athens); Chattanooga Golf and Country; Atlanta Country; Johns Island (Vero Beach); Pine Valley Golf (Clementon); Union League (Chgo.). Home and Office: 433 Forrest Park Circle Athens TN 37303

WILLSON, MEREDITH, flutist, composer, condr., author, lyricist; b. Mason City, Iowa, May 18, 1902; s. John David and Rosalie (Reiniger) W.; ed. Damrosch Inst. Mus. Art; hon. doctorates Coe Coll., Cedar Rapids, Iowa, Parsons Coll., Fairfield, Iowa, Ind. Inst. Tech., Ft. Wayne, Regis Coll., Denver; m. Elizabeth Wilson, Aug. 29, 1920 (div. Mar. 1948); m. 2d, Ralina Zarova, Mar. 13, 1948 (dec. Dec. 1966); m. 3d, Rosemary Sullivan, Feb. 14, 1968. Formerly solo flutist with John Philip Sousa, also flutist N.Y. Philharmonic Orch.; later mus. dir. Western div. NBC; composer, lyricist, also librettist The Music Man (N.Y. Critics award best musical; Perry award; Grammy award for album Nat. Acad. Rec. Arts and Scis.), 1958; composer and lyricist The Unsinkable Molly Brown, Here's Love, also 1491; composer score The Great Dictator (film), The Little Foxes (film); author-composer You and I, May the Good Lord Bless and Keep You, 76 Trombones, other songs; composer Symphony of San Francisco, Missions of California Suite, The Jervis Bay, O.O. MacIntyre Suite; composer for chorus Mass of the Bells. Served to maj. AUS, 1942-45. Recipient Big Bro. of Year award, 1962; Edwin Franko Goldman citation Am. Bandmasters Assn., 1964; Carbon Mike award Pacific Pioneer Broadcasters, 1976. Mem. ASCAP, Am. Guild Composers and Authors, AFTRA. Club: Family (San Francisco). Author: The Music Man; And There I Stood with My Piccolo; But He Doesn't Know the Territory; Who Did What to Fedalia?; Eggs I Have Laid. Office: 151 El Camino Dr Beverly Hills CA 90212*

WILLSON, PHILIP JAMES, lawyer; b. Morning Sun, Iowa, Sept. 30, 1923; B.A., Parsons Coll., 1946; LL.B., Yale U., 1949. Admitted to Iowa bar, 1949; mem. firm Smith, Peterson, Beckman & Willson, Council Bluffs, Iowa, 1949, partner, 1951—. Past pres. Council Bluffs Pub. Library, Council Bluffs YMCA. Mem. Am., Iowa (pres. 1977-78), S.W. Iowa, Pottawattamie bar assns., Council Bluffs C. of C. (past pres.). Author: (with Allan D. Vestal) Iowa Practice, 1974. Home: 548 Cogleywood Ln Council Bluffs IA 51501 Office: 370 Midlands Mall PO Box 249 Council Bluffs IA 51502

WILLY, ROY EARLE, lawyer; b. Chgo., Dec. 2, 1889; s. Milo Ambrose and Mary Lincoln (Early) W.; LL.B., U. Mich., 1912, J.D., 1968; m. Josephine Amelia Lien, Jan. 11, 1920. Admitted to bars of Mich. and S.D., 1912; practiced at Platte, S.D., 1912-25, state's atty., Charles Mix County, 1919-24; spl. counsel State Banking Dept. of S.D., 1925-28; gen. practice, Sioux Falls, S.D., 1928—; partner Willy, Pruitt, Matthews & Jorgensen and predecessor firms; referee in bankruptcy for S.D., 1948-69; dir. Union Security Co., United Nat. Bank Sioux Falls. Mem. exec. bd. Sioux council Boy Scouts Am., 1928-54, commr. 1930-34; nat. council mem., 1935-50, v.p. 1939, pres. 1940-45; chief of civilian def., Sioux Falls, 1942-45, dir., 1950-58; civilian aide sec. Army, 1947-62. Served with inf. U.S. Army, 1918; 2d lt. inf., O.R.C., 1921. Recipient Silver Beaver award Boy Scouts Am., 1932, Outstanding Civilian Service medal Army, 1963. Pres. El Riad Trustees, Inc., 1951—. Fellow Am. Bar Found. (life mem.; recipient Disting. Service award 1968); mem. Am. Inst. of Jud. Adminstn. Am. Bar Assn. (state del. 1939-64, chmn. Ho. of Dels. 1950-52, chmn. state legislation com., 1955-56, mem. fed. judiciary com. 1957-68, mem. com. on expansion facilities 1962-69), Am. Law Inst. (life), State Bar S.D. (pres. 1939), Minnehaha County Bar Assn. (pres. 1950), Am. Legion, S.A.R. Presbyn. Mason (32 deg., Shriner, Jester), Elk. Club: Minnehaha Country. Mem. bd. editors Am. Bar Assn. Jours., 1950-67; chmn. editorial bd. S.D. Bar Jour., 1947-67. Home: 105 E 34th St Sioux Falls SD 57104 Died Dec. 2, 1978. *I have tried to guide my operations by being as honest with myself as with others and have endeavored at all times to live up to my obligations without procrastination. I have endeavored throughout my active career to devote a substantial portion of my time to the welfare of the profession of which I am a member, as well as to my community, my state, and my nation, feeling that this was a part of the obligation which I owe as a citizen.*

WILMARTH, CHRISTOPHER MALLORY, sculptor; b. Sonoma, Calif., 1943; B.F.A., Cooper Union, 1965. Prof. sculpture and drawing Cooper Union, N.Y.C., 1969—; vis. artist Yale U., 1971-72, Columbia U., 1976, 78, U. Calif., Berkeley, 1979; exhibited in one man shows at Graham Gallery, N.Y.C., 1968, Paula Cooper Gallery, N.Y.C., 1971, 72, Janie C. Lee Gallery, Dallas, 1971, Galleria dell'Arieta, Milan, 1973, Rosa Esman Gallery, N.Y.C., 1974, Daniel Weinberg Gallery, San Francisco, 1974, Wadsworth Atheneum, Hartford and St. Louis Mus. Art, 1974, 75, Galleris Aronowitsch, Stockholm, 1975, Grey Art Gallery, N.Y. U., 1978, Studio for the First Amendment, N.Y.C., 1978, Seattle Mus., 1979; exhibited in group shows at Park Pl. Gallery, N.Y.C., 1966, Whitney Mus. Am. Art, 1966, 68, 70, 73, 76, 79, Found. Maeght, France, 1970, Mus. Modern Art, 1971, 79, Indpls. Mus. Art, 1972, 74, Art Inst. Chgo., 1972, Met. Mus., 1974, 79, I.C.A., Chgo., 1977, Phila. Mus., 1978, Albright Knox Gallery, 1979; represented in permanent collections at Mus. Modern Art, Art Inst. Chgo., Phila. Mus. Art, R.I. Sch. Design Mus. Art, Woodward Found., Met. Mus. Art, Fogg Art Mus., Des Moines Art Center, Walker Art Center, St. Louis Mus., Wadsworth Atheneum, Dallas Mus. Fine Art, Wichita Mus., Yale Art Mus., San Francisco Mus., Whitney Mus. Am. Art. Recipient Norman Wait Harris award Art Inst. Chgo., 1972. Nat. Endowment for Arts grantee, 1969, 77; Guggenheim fellow, 1970, Howard Found. fellow Brown U., 1972. Contbr. articles on sculpture to profl. publs. Address: PO Box 203 Canal St Station New York NY 10013

WILMER, RICHARD HOOKER, JR., educator; b. Ancon, C.Z., Apr. 13, 1918; s. Richard Hooker and Margaret (Van Dyke Grant) W.; grad. Taft Sch., 1935; B.A., Yale, 1939, M.Div., Gen. Theol. Sem., 1942, S.T.D. (hon.), 1958; D.Phil., Oxford U. (Eng.), 1948; D.D. (hon.), Berkeley Div. Sch., 1970; m. Elisabeth F. Green, June 6, 1942; children—Richard, Margaret, Stephen, Natalie, Rebecca (dec.), Christine; m. 2d, Sarah King, Aug. 2, 1969. Ordained deacon Episcopal Ch., 1942, priest, 1942; deacon-in-charge, vicar and rector St. John's Ch., Mt. Rainier, Md., 1942-45; chaplain U. of South, 1948-53; minister to Episcopal students Yale, 1953-57, prof. theology, dean Berkeley Div. Sch., 1957-69; vis. prof. religious studies U. Pitts., 1970-72; prof. religious studies, 1972—, chmn. dept. religious studies, U. Pitts., 1972-78. Served as chaplain USNR, 1945-46. Author: The Doctrine of the Church in the English Reformation, 1952. Home: 1128 Heberton St Pittsburgh PA 15206

WILMERDING, JOHN, curator, educator; b. Boston, Apr. 28, 1938; s. John Currie and Lila Vanderbilt (Webb) W.; A.B., Harvard, 1960, A.M., 1961, Ph.D., 1965. Asst. prof. art Dartmouth, 1965-68, asso. prof., 1968-73, Leon E. Williams prof., 1973-77, chmn. dept. art, 1968-72, chmn. humanities div., 1971-72; sr. curator Am. art Nat. Gallery of Art, 1977—; vis. lectr. history of art Yale, 1972; vis. prof. fine arts Harvard, 1976; vis. prof. art U. Md., 1979. Hon. curator painting Peabody Mus., Salem, Mass.; adv. bd. Dunlap Soc., Washington, IRS; vis. com. Inst. Contemporary Art, Boston; mem. fine arts com. State Dept. Trustee Found. for Art Edn., N.Y., Shelburne Mus., Vt., St. Gaudens Nat. Historic Site, Cornish, N.H., Groton (Mass.) Sch., Joslin Diabetes Found., Boston, Lewis Walpole Library, Hartford. Guggenheim fellow, 1973-74. Mem. Coll. Art Assn., Am. Studies Assn. Author: Fitz Hugh Lane, American Marine Painter, 1964; A History of American Marine Painting, 1968; Pittura Americana dell' Ottocento, 1969; Robert Salmon, Painter of Ship and Shore, 1971; Fitz Hugh Lane, 1971; Winslow Homer, 1972; Audubon, Homer, Whistler and 19th Century America, 1972; The Genius of American Painting, 1973; American Art, 1976; Painting in America, 1977. Mem. editorial bd. Am. Art Rev., Art Bull., Am. Art Jour. Office: Dept Am Art Nat Gallery Art Washington DC 20565

WILMOT, IRVIN GORSAGE, hosp. adminstr., educator; b. Nanking, Chine, June 30, 1922 (parents U.S. citizens); s. Frank Alonzo and Ethel (Ranney) W.; B.S., Northwestern U., 1955; M.B.A., U. Chgo., 1957; m. Dorothy Agnes Mohlfeld, Feb. 6, 1943; children—Marcia Beth, David Michael. With Internat. Register Co., Chgo., 1946-47; buyer U. Chgo., 1947-49; adminstrv. asst., then asst. supt. U. Chgo. Clinics, 1949-61; adminstr. N.Y. U. Med. Center-Univ. Hosp., 1961-68, exec. v.p., 1973—; instr. then asst. prof. U. Chgo., 1957-61; asso. prof. N.Y. U., 1961-68, prof., asso. dir. hosp. and health services, 1968-73; asso. dir. U. Chgo. Grad. Program Hosp. Adminstrn., 1959-61; mem. Regional Adv. Bd. II; dir. Blue Cross/Blue Shield of Greater N.Y.; mem. hosp. rev. and planning council State of N.Y., 1979—. Bd. dirs. N.Y. Blood Center, 1978—. Served with USN, 1940-46. Fellow Am. Coll. Hosp. Adminstrs. (chmn. central. com. insts. 1959-65, regent N.Y. State and P.R., 1974—); mem. Assn. U. Programs Hosp. Adminstrs. (exec. sec. 1959-61), Am. Hosp. Assn. (mem. council research and planning 1965-68, council on mgmt. and planning 1979—), Assn. Am. Med. Colls. (chmn. council teaching hosps. 1970-71), Greater N.Y. Hosp. Assn. (bd. govs., pres. 1973-74), Hosp. Assn. N.Y. State (trustee, chmn. 1976-77). Home: 34 Helen Ave Rye NY 10580 Office: 550 1st Ave New York NY 10016

WILMOT, WILLIAM VERNON, JR., educator; b. Newark, Sept. 15, 1916; s. William Vernon and Agnes (Reed) W.; A.B., Syracuse U., 1937, A.M., 1939; Ph.D., U. Wis., 1954; m. Clarice Mary King, Sept. 2, 1941; children—Barbara Mary, William Vernon III. Resident adviser Syracuse U., 1937-39, grad. asst. econs., 1939-40; instr., then asst. prof. U. Wis., 1947-57; mem. faculty U. Fla., 1957-74, prof. mgmt. and bus. law, chmn. dept., 1959-71; prof. bus. and econs. St. Andrews Presbyn. Coll., 1972-75; prof. indsl. mgmt. Clemson U., 1975—; asso. economist Office Def. Transp., Office Emergency Mgmt., 1942-43; sec., treas., dir. Order Assos., Inc., 1965—. Served to lt. USNR, 1943-46. Mem. Acad. Mgmt., Inst. Mgmt. Scis., Econometric Soc., Am. Econ. Assn., So. Mgmt. Assn., Sigma Phi Epsilon, Beta Gamma Sigma, Chi Eta Sigma, Alpha Kappa Psi (Distinguished Service award 1962). Presbyn. Author: (with John Bangs) Plant Management, 1963. Home: 4918 NW 39th Terrace Gainesville FL 32601

WILMOUTH, ROBERT K., commodities exec.; b. Worcester, Mass., Nov. 9, 1928; s. Alfred F. and Aileen E. (Kearney) W.; B.A., Holy Cross Coll., 1949; M.A., U. Notre Dame, 1950; m. Ellen M. Boyle, Sept. 10, 1955; children—Robert J., John J., James P., Thomas G., Anne Marie. Exec. v.p., dir. 1st Nat. Bank Chgo., 1972-75; pres., chief adminstrv. officer Crocker Nat. Bank, San Francisco, 1975-77; pres., chief exec. officer Chgo. Bd. Trade, 1977—; dir. Victoria Station, LaSalle Bank, Chgo. Trustee, U. Notre Dame. Served to 2d lt. USAF, 1951-53. Clubs: Chgo., Barrington Hill Scountry. Home: Rural Route 4 Caesar Dr Barrington IL 60010 Office: 141 W Jackson Blvd Chicago IL 60604

WILMSEN, HARRY ROBERT, architect; b. McIntosh, S.D., Jan. 14, 1918; s. Harry Robert and Almeda (Senn) W.; B.Arch., U. Oreg., 1941; m. Winifred June Miller, June 21, 1942; children—Susan Joy Wilmsen Setziol, Sherry Lynn. Propr., Robert Wilmsen, Architect, Eugene, Oreg., 1946-48; partner Wilmsen & Endicott, Eugene, 1948-60, Wilmsen, Endicott & Unthank, Eugene and Portland, 1960-68, Wilmsen, Endicott, Greene & Bernhard, Eugene and Portland, 1968-73; pres. Wegroup P.C., Eugene and Portland, 1973—; mem. Oreg. Bd. Archtl. Examiners, 1959-64. Bd. dirs. Oreg. Art Museum, 1960-62; mem. Eugene (Oreg.) Bd. Appeals, 1949-52. Fellow AIA (pres. S.W. Oreg. chpt. 1952, Portland chpt. 1968, Oreg. council 1969). Club: Multnomah Athletic (Portland). Editorial adviser Symposia mag., 1970—. Home: 2190 SW King Ct Portland OR 97205 Office: 812 SW Washington St Suite 1200 Portland OR 97205

WILNER, DANIEL MURRAY, educator; b. Gostynin, Poland, July 17, 1918; s. Samuel and Florence (Saxe) W.; came to U.S., 1923, naturalized, 1934; B.A., UCLA, 1946, Ph.D., 1951; m. Lucile Jones, Dec. 27, 1942; children—Olivia (Mrs. Benson Schaeffer), David, Justin, Adam. Asst. prof. psychology N.Y. U., 1950-54; asso. prof. biostatistics Johns Hopkins, 1954-60; mem. faculty U. Calif., Los Angeles, 1960—, prof. pub. health, preventive, social medicine, 1962—, chmn., asso. dean Sch. Pub. Health, 1969-71. Mem. nat. advisory com. housing sr. citizens Dept. HUD, 1964-66; chmn. epidemiologic studies rev. com. Nat. Inst. Mental Health, 1968-69. Served with AUS, 1943-46. Fellow Am. Pub. Health Assn. (gov. council 1970-72); mem. Western Gerontol. Soc. (pres. 1966-67), Am. Psychol. Assn., Gerontol. Soc. Author: (with Walkley, Cook) Human Relations in Interracial Housing, 1955; (with Walkley, Tayback) The Housing Environment and Family Life, 1962: (with Kassebaum) Narcotics, 1965; (with Walkley, Sherman) Retirement Housing in California, 1966; (with Kassebaum, Ward) Prison Treatment and Parole Survival, 1971; Evaluation: The State of the Technical Art, 1975; (with Walkley, O'Neill), Introduction to Public Health, 7th edit., 1978. Office: School Public Health U Calif 405 Hilgard Ave Los Angeles CA 90024

WILNER, MARIE, artist; b. Paris, France, July 24, 1910; d. Joseph and Helene Spring; B.A., Hunter Coll., 1927; student Art Students League, 1929-32; m. Joseph Walter Wilner, Sept. 4, 1927; children—Harvey Ira, Helen (Mrs. Harold Cornell), George D. Exhibited in group shows at Knickerbocker Artists, Catherine Lorrilard Group, Irvington Mus., Ross Gallery, Newark, Pa. Acad. Fine Arts. Phila., Contemporary Arts Gallery, Barzansky Gallery, Collectors of Am., Village Art Center, Raymond Duncan Gallery, Paris, France, Athens, Brussels World Far, Tokyo, Butler Art Inst., N.Y. U. Mus., Evansville, Ind. Mus., Joe and Emily Lowe Mus., Fla., Birmingham Mus., Norfolk Mus., Ga. Mus., Nat. Mus. Art and Sport, Bronx Mus. Art, Academia Internationale de Lutece, Met. Mus. Art, N.Y.C., 1979, Salamgundi Club, 1979, various galleries; traveling show of Nat. Assn. of Women Artists covering various museums in U.S. and abroad; one man shows Gallery 721, N.Y.C., 1959, Bodley Gallery, N.Y.C., 1960, 61, Galerie Renoir, Brussels, 1961, Galerie Raymond Duncan, 1962, Revel Gallery, N.Y.C., 1963, Evansville (Ind.) Mus. Art, 1963, Irving Gallery, Milw., 1964, Pietrantonio Westhampton Beach Gallery, 1964, Musee d' Art Moderne, Paris, Club International Feminin, Paris, 1964, Sheldon Swope Mus., 1964, 68, N.Y. U. Mus., 1965, Dickson Gallery, Washington, 1968, 69, LaSalle Coll., 1968, Bohman's Gallery, Stockholm, Sweden, 1968, Tweed Mus., 1968, 69, Rioboo Neuva Gallery, Buenos Aires, Argentina, 1969, Bridgeport (Conn.) Mus., 1969, Galerie Diana de Renucy, N.Y., 1970, Bohman's Gallery, Stockholm, Galerie Fur Zeitgenossische Kunst, Hamburg, Germany, 1975, others; represented in permanent collection museums of Angouleme and Cognac, France, Tweed Mus. U. Minn., Community Coll. N.Y., Safad Bat Yam, Israel, Ga. Mus. Art, Mus. of Ala., S.I. Mus., Musée de Monbart, France, Musée de Lyons, France, Butler Art Inst., Mus. Isadora and Raymond Duncan, French Mus., Met. Mus., N.Y.C. Recipient first prize N.J. Mus., 1957; Grumbacher-purchase award, Nat. Assn. Women Artists, 1962; gold medal American Artists Profl. League, 1963; Talens prize Artist and Sculptors of New Jersey, 1963; Bronze medal Internat. Art Exhbn., Charleroi, Belgium, 1972; Gold medal Academia de Ciencias, 1977; decorated chevalier 4th class then 3d class (Belgium); named Laureate de Paris-Critique with Palme d'Or, 1975, Laureate of the Grand Prix Humanitaire de France with silver medal, 1975; others. Work recorded in the Library of Congress, Washington. Mem. Nat. Assn. of Women Artists (chmn. jury awards 1963, dir.), Am. Artists Profl. League, Soc. Am. Artists and Sculptors, League of Present Day Artists (pres. 1976-79), Royal Soc. Arts of London (life), Arts Found. of Caravan (chmn.), Internat. Arts Guild Monaco, Haute Academie Litteraire et Artistique de France, Artists Equity (dir.), Internat. Platform Assn., Alumni Assn. Hunter Coll., Internat. Arts Guild, Artists and Sculptors N.J., Kappa Pi. Address: 77 7th Ave New York NY 10011

WILNER, MORTON HARRISON, lawyer; b. Balt., May 28, 1908; s. Joseph A. and Ida (Berkow) W.; B.S. in Econs., U. Pa., 1930; J.D., Georgetown U., 1934; m. Zelda Dunkelman, Nov. 3, 1940; children—James D., Thomas B., Lawrence J., Theodora. Admitted to D.C. bar, 1933; mem. firm Wilner & Scheiner, and predecessors, Washington, 1946—; sec., treas. Joseph A. Wilner & Co.; dir. Security Nat. Bank, Giant Food, Inc.; gen. counsel Armed Forces Relief and Benefit Assn., Aerospace Industries Assn. Chmn. Combined Benefit Appeal, 1961; past pres. Jewish Community Center of Greater Washington. Emeritus life trustee U. Pa.; trustee Jewish Publ. Soc. Am.; past pres. Nat. Child Research Center; bd. govs. St. Albans Sch., 1968-72. Served to maj. USAAF, dep. dir. aircraft div. WPB, 1942-45. Decorated Legion of Merit; recipient Ourisman Meml. award for civic achievement, 1970; Ben Franklin award U. Pa. Alumni, 1973, award of merit, 1975, Friar of Yr. award U. Pa., 1976. Mem. Fed., Am. (ho. dels. 1971-73), D.C., Internat. bar assns., Fed. Communications Bar Assn. (pres. 1969-70). Clubs: Army and Navy; Touchdown; National Lawyers; Woodmont Country; City Tavern. Home: 2701 Chesapeake St Washington DC 20008 Office: 2021 L St NW Washington DC 20036

WILSON, ALEXANDER ERWIN, JR., lawyer; b. East Point, Ga., Aug. 26, 1910; s. Alexander Erwin and Evelyn (Smith) W.; A.B., Emory U., 1930, A.M., 1932; m. Constance Dinkler, June 10, 1932; children—Constance Dinkler (Mrs. E. Ralph Paris, Jr.), Alexander Erwin III. Admitted to Ga. bar, 1931; practiced in Clarkesville, 1930-34; atty. HOLC, 1934-37; regional atty. NLRB, 1937-42; practiced law, Atlanta, 1942—; partner Wilson & Wilson and predecessor firm, 1947-76, Jones, Bird & Howell, 1976—. Mem. Sigma Pi (nat. pres. 1956-58). Episcopalian. Clubs: Atlanta Athletic, Capital City, Commerce, Peachtree Golf, Piedmont Driving, (Atlanta). Home: 358 King Rd NW Atlanta GA 30342 Office: HAAS-Howell Bldg 75 Poplar St Atlanta GA 30303

WILSON, ALEXANDER MURRAY, mining co. exec.; b. Tulare, Calif., May 17, 1922; s. Alexander Murray and Grace Ethel (Creech) W.; B.S. in Metall. Engring., U. Calif. at Berkeley, 1948; m. Beverlee Elaine Forsblad, Jan. 4, 1948; children—Shelley Blaine, Kristin Holly, Alexis Elayne. With Bradley Mining Co., Stibnite, Idaho, 1948-51, Molybdenum Corp. Am., Nipton, Calif., 1951-54; with Utah Internat. Inc. subs. Gen. Electric Co. (formerly Utah Constrn. & Mining Co.), San Francisco, 1954—, successively metall. engr., asst. mgr. mining, mgr. dept. uranium ops., mgr. mining ops., v.p., mgr. mining div., sr. v.p., exec. v.p., 1954-71, pres., 1971-79, chief exec. officer, 1978—, chmn., 1979—, also dir.; dir. First Security Corp., Fireman's Fund Ins. Co., Cyprus-Pima Mining Co.; chmn., dir. Utah Devel. Co. Served with U.S. Army, 1944-46; CBI. Mem. Am. Mining Congress, (dir.), Nat. Coal Assn. (dir.), Mining and Metall. Soc. Am., Soc. Mining Engrs., Pacific Basin Econ. Council. Office: 550 California St San Francisco CA 94104

WILSON, ALLEN BARNUM, inventor, artist; b. Chgo., Apr. 8, 1898; s. Samuel Allen and Florence (Barnum) W.; student U. Wis., 1915-17, Sorbonne, Paris, France, 1919; Chgo. Acad. Fine Arts 1923-24; student of Frederic Tellander, 1935-39; m. Marion Gahan, Sept. 12, 1925; 1 son, Gahan. Dir. art gallery Carson Pirie Scott & Co., Chgo., 1923-26; exhibitor paintings galleries in U.S., 1926-27; with Acme Steel Co., Chgo., 1927-62, v.p., 1945-62, dir., ret. 1962; pres., chmn. bd. Breakwaters, Inc., Chgo., 1957-68; currently practicing artist. Inventor fibre drums, paper ice cream can, metal venetian blinds, breakwaters, wave diverting and dissipating means, bldg. materials. Address: 2920 NE 19th St Pompano Beach FL 33062

WILSON, ALMA DOROTHY BELL (MRS. WILLIAM A. WILSON), judge; b. Pauls Valley, Okla., May 25, 1917; d. William R. and Anna L. (Schuppert) Bell; student Principia Coll., 1935-36, Oklahoma City U., 1936-37; A.B., Okla. U., 1939, J.D., 1941; m. William Allan Wilson, May 29, 1948; 1 dau., Lee Anne. Admitted to Okla. bar, 1941; law clk. U.S. Dist. Judge, Muskogee, Okla., 1941; investigator O.P.A., 1943; asso. Campbell, Randolph, Mosteller & McElroy, 1944-45; Speck & Howell, 1945-46, Howard K. Berry 1946-48; partner Wilson & Wilson, 1948-67; municipal judge City of Pauls Valley, 1967-68; spl. dist. judge, Pauls Valley and Purcaell, Okla., 1969-75, dist. judge Cleveland County, 1975—. Mem. Okla. Assn. Women Lawyers (past pres.), Am. Assn. U. Women (past chpt. pres.), Am. Legion Aux. (past chpt. pres.), Chi Omega. Christian Scientist. Home: 300 S Hall Muldrow Dr Norman OK 73069 Office: Courthouse Norman OK 73069

WILSON, ALMON CHAPMAN, physician, naval officer; b. Hudson Falls, N.Y., July 13, 1924; s. Almon Chapman and Edith May (Truesdale) W.; B.A., Union Coll., Schenectady, 1946; M.D., Albany Med. Coll., 1952; M.S., George Washington U., 1969; student Naval War Coll., Newport, R.I., 1968-69; m. Sofia M. Bogdons, Jan. 24, 1945; 1 son, Geoffrey Peter. Served as enlisted man U.S. Navy, 1943-46; commd. lt. j.g., M.C., U.S. Navy, 1952, advanced through grades to rear adm., 1976; intern U.S. Naval Hosp., Bremerton, Wash., 1952-53; resident VA Hosp., Salt Lake City, 1954-58; chief of surgery Sta. Hosp., Naval Sta., Subic Bay, Philippines, 1959-61; staff surgeon Naval Hosp., San Diego, 1961-64; asst. chief surgery Naval Hosp., Chelsea, Mass., 1964-65; comdg. officer 3d Med. Bn., 3d Marine Div. Fleet Marine Force, Pacific, Vietnam, 1965-66; chief surgery Naval Hosp., Yososuka, Japan, 1966-68; assigned Naval War Coll., 1968-69; fleet med. officer, comdr. in chief U.S. Naval Forces, Europe and sr. med. officer Naval Activities, London, 1969-71; dep. dir. planning div. Bur. Medicine and Surgery, Navy Dept., Washington, 1971-72, dir. div., 1972-74, with additional duty as med. adv. to dep. chief naval ops. (logistics) and personal physician to chmn. Joint Chiefs of Staff, 1972-74; comdg. officer Naval Hosp., Gt. Lakes, Ill., 1974-76; asst. chief for material resources Bur. Medicine and Surgery, Navy Dept., Washington, 1976-79; comdg. officer Navy Health Scis. Edn. and Tng. Command, 1979—; mem. grad. med. edn. adv. com. Dept. Def. Decorated Legion of Merit with gold V, Meritorious Service medal, Joint Service Commendation medal, Presdl. Unit Citation, Navy Unit Commendation with 1 gold star (U.S.); Meritorious Unit Citation with Gallantry Cross Color, Campaign Ribbon with clasp (Republic Vietnam). Diplomate Am. Bd. Surgery. Fellow A.C.S. (gov.); mem. Assn. Mil. Surgeons U.S. Office: Naval Health Scis Edn and Tng Command Bethesda MD 20014

WILSON, ANDREW WILKINS, geographer; b. Santa Ana, Calif., Aug. 13, 1913; s. James Dick and Clara (Wagner) W.; A.B., Pomona Coll., 1935; M.B.A., Stanford U., 1937, postgrad., 1939; postgrad. U. So. Calif., 1946, U. Calif., Los Angeles, 1947; Ph.D., U. Syracuse, 1955; m. Loramay Roose, July 15, 1946; children—Andrew Wilkins, Wendy Jean. Salesman, Pacific Mut. Life Ins. Co., Santa Ana, 1938-39; bursar Mills Coll., 1940-42; instr. State Coll., Fresno, Calif., 1946-48; grad. asst. U. Syracuse, 1949-50; instr. bus. adminstrn. U. Ariz., 1950-56, asst. prof., 1956-58, asso. prof., 1958-61, prof. geography, regional devel. and urban planning, 1961-78, prof. emeritus, 1978—, dir. Ariz. basic indsl. devel. course, 1969-76. Pres. San Xavier Non-profit Devel. Corp., Tucson, 1962-72; sec. Tucson Com. on Community Goals, 1965-67; mem. Citizen's Com. on Municipal Blight, Tucson. Mem. AAAS, Assn. Am. Geographers, AAUP (pres. chpt. 1957-59, chmn. Ariz. conf. 1962-63), Assn. Pacific Coast Geographers, Nat. Council Geog. Edn., NEA, ACLU, Internat. Geog. Union (vice chmn. working group on desertification 1972-80, arrangements chmn. intercongress meeting Tucson 1979), Sigma Xi (pres. chpt. 1966-67, pres.-elect 1979-80), Beta Gamma Sigma (pres. Alpha of Ariz. chpt. 1960-61). Editor: (with David H.K. Amiran) Coastal Deserts, 1973; contbr. articles to profl. publs. Home: 4435 E Timrod St Tucson AZ 85711

WILSON, ARLENE MAY, univ. adminstr.; b. Leonardville, Kans., Mar. 25, 1924; d. Roy E. and Agnes (Nyberg) Wilson; B.S., Kans. State U., 1946; M.S., Purdue U., 1957. Intern dietetics Colo. State Hosp., Pueblo, 1947; chief dietitian Larned (Kans.) State Hosp., 1949-51; mem. faculty, staff Med. Center, Ind. U., Indpls., 1951—, dir. dept. nutrition and dietetics, also prof. Med. Sch., 1961—. Mem. Ind. Nutrition Council, 1960—. Recipient Distinguished Alumna award Kan. State U., 1973, Distinguished Alumna award Purdue U., 1974, Honored Dietitian of Ind., 1973. Mem. Am. (pres. 1973), Ind. (pres. 1966), Central Ind. (pres. 1967) dietetic assns., Internat. Soc. Food Service Consultants, Sigma Xi, Omicron Mu. Club: Zonta Internat. (Indpls.). Home: 4218 Springwood Trail Indianapolis IN 46208 Office: 1100 W Michigan St Indianapolis IN 46202

WILSON, ASHER BOLDON, educator; b. Long Beach, Calif., July 7, 1920; s. Asher Boldon and Harriet Amanda (Smith) W.; B.A., Stanford U., 1942, M.A., 1952, Ph.D., 1962; m. Marcia Mae Shaughnessy, Apr. 3, 1943; children—Asher Boldon, III, Clark Shaughnessy, James Edward, Mark Leonard. Instr., Coll. Idaho, 1950-53; asst. prof. U. Nev., Reno, 1955-59; asso. prof. Portland (Oreg.), State U., 1959-62, prof. theater arts, 1962—, chm. dept., 1959-77. Served from ensign to lt. USNR, 1943-46. Mem. Sigma Alpha Epsilon. Club: University (Portland). Author: John Galsworthy's Letters to Leon Lion, 1965. Home: 916 SW Davenport St Portland OR 97201

WILSON, BARBARA LYNN, corp. exec.; b. South Bend, Ind., Oct. 29, 1936; d. John Homer and Madelyn Virginia (Copp) Wilson; student Ind. U., South Bend, 1956-58, U. Hawaii, 1977—. Sec., bookkeeper Copp Music Center, South Bend, 1954-56; sec., legal sec., office mgr. Pfaff, Ettl & Mills, Mills & Rowe, attys., South Bend, 1956-65; exec. sec., Communications Center supr., adminstrv. asst. to corporate sec., asst. corporate sec., asst. v.p., asst. sec., sec. subs. Amfac, Inc., Honolulu, 1966—. Mem. Hawaii Soc. Corporate Secs. Home: 6570 Hawaii Kai Dr Honolulu HI 96825 Office: 700 Bishop St PO Box 3230 Honolulu HI 96801

WILSON, BERNARD EDGAR, ins. co. exec.; b. Chattanooga, Feb. 23, 1912; s. Bernard E. and Lillian (Ledford) W.; B.S., Eastern Ky. State U., 1936; M.A., U. Ky., 1938; m. Elizabeth Irene Howard, Apr. 20, 1942; children—Bernard E., William Gerald. High sch. coach, Harlan, Ky., 1936-39; athletic dir. Union Coll., 1939-46; head basketball coach Coll. William and Mary, 1946-51; with Commonwealth Life Ins. Co., 1951-59, br. mgr., 1959; v.p. dir. agys. Appalachian Nat. Life Ins. Co., 1959-61, dir., 1960-61; v.p., dir. agys. Am. Gen. Life Ins. Co. of Del., from 1962, sr. v.p., until 1969; exec. v.p., dir. Life & Casualty Ins. Co., Am. Gen. Life Ins. Co. of Ohio, from 1969; now exec. v.p. sales and mktg. Life & Casualty Ins. Co. of Tenn., Nashville; dir. Am. Gen. Life of Tex. Served to maj. USAAF, 1942-46. Mem. Nat., Nashville assns. life underwriters, Newcomen Soc., Nashville Area C. of C., Sales and Mktg. Execs. Assn., Gen. Agts. and Mfrs. Assn. Methodist. Clubs: Hillwood Country, Exchange, Nashville City, Duquesne. Home: 1104 Stonewall Jackson Ct Nashville TN 37220 Office: Life and Casualty Tower Nashville TN 37219

WILSON, BOB (ROBERT C.), congressman; b. Calexico, Calif., Apr. 5, 1916; s. George Wellington and Olive (Richardson) W.; student San Diego State Coll., 1933-35; m. Shirley Haughey Sarrett, May 16, 1974; children by previous marriage—Frances (Mrs. James Wilson), Mary Ann (Mrs. Michael W. Chapple), Bryant. Mem. 83d-96th Congresses, now dean Calif. del. Chmn. Nat. Republican Congl. Com., 1961-73. Served with inf. AUS, World War II. Named Minute Man of 1976 Res. Officers Assn. Mem. San Diego Jr. C. of C. (past pres.), Navy League, Am. Legion, Fleet Res. Assn., SAR. Presbyn. Elk, Rotarian, Kiwanian. Office: Fed Bldg Room 6(S)15 880 Front St San Diego CA 92188 also 2307 Rayburn Bldg Washington DC 20515

WILSON, BRIAN DOUGLAS, recording artist, composer, record producer; b. Inglewood, Calif., June 20, 1942; s. Murry Gage and Audree Neva (Korthof) W.; student El Camino Coll.; m. Marilyn Sandra Rovell, Dec. 7, 1964; children—Carnie, Wendy. Mem. musical group The Beach Boys, 1961—; composer Surfer Girl, Be True to Your School, I Get Around, Fun Fun Fun, Don't Worry Baby, Help Me Rhonda, Good Vibrations, others. Address: care Brother Records 10880 Wilshire Blvd Los Angeles CA 90024*

WILSON, BRUCE PAGE, banker; b. Binghamton, N.Y., Jan. 12, 1920; s. Thomas A. and Gertrude (Page) W.; grad. Princeton U., 1942; m. Laura Dell Meacham, June 1, 1946; children—Jay MacLean, Barbara Wilson Schweizer, Katharine Wilson Denby, Laura Campbell. With Balt. and Annapolis Railroad Co., Balt., 1949-61, pres., to 1961; regional v.p., divisional v.p. Carling Brewing Co., 1961-70; exec. v.p. Mercantile Bankshares Corp., Balt., 1970-76; chmn. exec. com. Mercantile Safe Deposit and Trust Co., Balt., 1970-76, pres., 1976—; dir. Balt. and Annapolis Railroad Co., Nat. Distributing Properties, Inc., Walker-Wilson Travel, Ltd., Ward Machinery Co., Sta. WMAR-TV, Inc., Steeltin Can Corp. Bd. dirs. United Way of Central Md. Served to maj., U.S. Army, 1946. Clubs: Maryland, Elkridge. Home: Hillside Rd Brooklandville MD 21022 Office: 2 Hopkins Plaza Baltimore MD 21201

WILSON, CARL DEAN, singer; b. Los Angeles, Dec. 21, 1946; s. Murry Gage and Audree Neva W.; grad. high sch.; m. Annie C. Hinsche, Feb. 3, 1966; children—Jonah, Justyn. Mem. singing group The Beach Boys, 1961—; rec. artist for Candix, Capitol, Reprise, CBS records. Address: care Brother Records 10880 Wilshire Blvd Los Angeles CA 90024*

WILSON, CARROLL LOUIS, engring. adminstr.; b. Rochester, N.Y., Sept. 21, 1910; s. Louis William and Edna (Carroll) W.; B.S., Mass. Inst. Tech., 1932; Sc.D. (hon.), Williams Coll., 1947; Eng. D. (hon.), Worcester Polytech. Inst., 1976; m. Mary Bischoff, Apr. 1, 1937; children—Paul, Diana (Mrs. Paul B. Hoven, Jr.), Rosemary, Barbara. Asst. to pres. Mass. Inst. Tech., 1932-36, adviser to v.p. and dean engring., 1936-37; with Research Corp. of N.Y., 1937-40; exec. asst. to dir. OSRD, 1940-46; sec. to bd. of cons. to State Dept. for preparation report on plan for internat. control atomic energy, 1946; v.p. Nat. Research Corp. of Boston, 1946-47; gen. mgr. U.S. AEC, 1947-51; with Climax Molybdenum Co., 1951-54; pres. Climax Uranium Co., 1951-54; v.p., gen. mgr. Metals & Controls Corp., Attleboro, Mass. 1954-56, pres., gen. mgr., 1956-58; dir. Millipore Corp., Hitchener Mfg. Corp., Procor Corp.; prof. Mass. Inst. Tech., 1959—, Mitsui Prof. emeritus problems contemporary tech., 1974—, dir. workshop Alternative Energy Strategies, 1974—; dir. World Coal Study, 1977—. Mem. Rockefeller Bros. Fund panel on internat. security, 1957-58; governing bd. Internat. Centre Insect Physiology and Ecology (Nairobi), 1969-74. Dir. study on critical global environ. problems, 1970, man's impact on climate, 1971; trustee Woods Hole Oceanographic Instn.; dir. MIT fellows in Africa, 1960-67; Hon. dir. R.I. Hosp., R.I. Hosp. Trust Co.; trustee, chmn. World Peace Found. of Boston; trustee Internat. Fedn. Inst. Advanced Study, Stockholm; U.S. mem. com. sci. research OECD, 1961-70; mem. adv. com. on application sci. and tech. to devel. ECOSOC, UN, 1964-70; sr. adviser UN Conf. on Human Environ., mem. Trilateral Commn., Commn. on Critical Choices for Ams.; mem. energy prize selection com. Krupp Found., Essen, W. Ger. Decorated Officer Order Brit. Empire. Mem. Am. Inst. Mining, Metall. and Petroleum Engrs., Council Fgn. Relations (dir., Elihu Root lectr. 1973), Am. Acad. Arts and Scis., Royal Swedish Acad. Engring. Scis., Pilgrim Soc. Am. Clubs: Century Association (N.Y.C.); Cosmos (Washington); Club of Rome. Home: 130 Jacob St Seekonk MA 02771 Office: Sch Engring Mass Inst Tech Cambridge MA 02139

WILSON, CHARLES, congressman; b. Trinity, Tex., June 1, 1933; student Sam Houston State U., Huntsville, Tex., 1951-52; B.S., U.S. Naval Acad., 1956; m. Jerry Carter, 1963. Commd. ensign U.S. Navy, 1956, advanced through grades to lt.; ret., 1960; mem. Tex. Ho. of Reps., 1960-66; mem. Tex. Senate, 1966-72; mem. 93d-96th congresses from 2d Dist. Tex. Mgr. lumber yard, 1962-72. Democrat. Office: 1214 Longworth House Office Bldg Washington DC 20515

WILSON, CHARLES BANKS, artist; b. Springdale, Ark., Aug. 6, 1918; s. Charles Bertram and Bertha Juanita (Banks) W.; student Art Inst. Chgo., 1936-41; m. Edna Frances McKibben, Oct. 10, 1941; children—Geoffrey Banks, Carrie Vee. Mag. and book illustrator, 1943-60; head art dept. N.E. Okla. A. & M. Coll., Miami, Okla., 1947-61; now painter, printmaker; executed mural Okla. State Capitol; represented in permanent collections: Met. Mus., N.Y.C., Library of Congress, Washington, U.S. Capitol Bldg., D.C. Corcoran Gallery, Smithsonian Inst., Philbrook Art Center, Tulsa, Nat. Cowbow Hall of Fame, Oklahoma City. Bd. dirs. Thomas Gilcrease Mus. History and Art, Tulsa, 1957-61; chmn. Pub. Library Bd., Miami, Okla., 1954-59. Named to Okla. Hall of Fame. Mem. Internat. Inst. Arts and Letters (Geneva, Switzerland). Democrat. Presbyterian. Illustrator numerous books. Home: 110 B St NE Miami OK 74354 Office: 100 1/2 N Main Miami OK 74354

WILSON, CHARLES BRYON, educator, physician; b. Neosho, Mo., Aug. 31, 1929; s. Byron Sanders and Margaret (Polson) W.; B.S., Tulane U., 1951, M.D., 1954; children—Rebecca, Robert Craig, Byron. Intern Charity Hosp., New Orleans, 1954-1955; resident pathology Tulane U., New Orleans, 1955-56, instr., 1960-61; resident in neurosurgery Ochsner Clinic, 1956-60; instr. La. State U., New Orleans, 1961-63; asst. prof., U. Ky., Lexington, 1963-68; prof., chmn. dept. neurol. surgery U. Calif., San Francisco, 1968—. Mem. Am. Acad. Neurol. Surgery, Soc. Neurol. Surgery, Neurosurg. Soc. Am., Am. Assn. Neuropathologists. Research brain tumors, brain tumor chemotherapy. Home: 16 Old Landing Rd Tiburon CA 94920 Office: Dept Neurosurgery U Calif Med Center San Francisco CA 94143

WILSON, CHARLES GLEN, zoo adminstr.; b. Clinton, Okla., Aug. 24, 1948; s. Claude Lee and Alva Dean (Gaskins) W.; B.S., Okla. State U., 1972, postgrad., 1972-74; m. Susan Elizabeth Mosher, Nov. 21, 1975; 1 dau., Erica Dean. Research asst. Oklahoma City (Okla.) Zool. Gardens, 1972-73, zool. curator, 1973-75; dir. Little Rock Zool. Gardens, 1975-76; dir. Memphis Zool. Gardens, 1976—. Served with

U.S. Army, 1968-70. Recipient Ark. Traveler award, 1977. Fellow Am. Assn. Zool. Parks and Aquariums (profl., chmn. plan center 1977—); mem. Am. Soc. Mammalogists. Contbr. articles in field to profl. jours. Office: 2000 Galloway St Memphis TN 38112

WILSON, CHARLES H., congressman; b. Magna, Utah, Feb. 15, 1917; s. Charles H. and Janet Chalmers (Hunter) W.; ed. pub. schs., m. Betty Gibbel, Mar. 23, 1947 (dec. July 5, 1974); children—Stephen C., Donald H., Kenneth A., William J.; m. 2d, Hyun Ju Chang. With Security First Nat. Bank; propr. Charles H. Wilson Ins. Agy., Los Angeles, 1945—; mem. Calif. Assembly, 1954-62, chmn. com. on revenue and taxation; mem. 88th-96th Congresses, 31st Calif. Dist., mem. coms. on armed services, post office, civil service. Served with AUS, 1942-45. Mem. Am. Legion. Democrat. Clubs: Masons, Shriners, Elks, Kiwanis. Office: Rayburn House Office Bldg Washington DC 20515*

WILSON, CHARLES LOWRY, air force officer; b. Paris, Tex., June 15, 1924; s. Frank and Vera (Gaches) W.; student Tex. A. and M. U., 1942-43; B.S., B.B.A., So. Meth. U., 1950; M.S., Mass. Inst. Tech., 1963; student Army War Coll., 1965-66; m. Suzanne Sadler, Jan. 21, 1950; children—Howard, Barry, Rebecca. Commd. 2d lt. USAAF, 1944, advanced through grades to maj. gen. USAF, 1975; plans officer Hdqrs. 1st Missile Div., SAC, Vandenberg AFB, Cal., 1958-61; astronaut. engr., plans officer Directorate Plans, Hdqrs. SAC, Offutt AFB, Nebr., 1963-65; chief strategic and def. br. Directorate Command Control and Communications, Hdqrs. USAF, Washington, 1966-68; chief systems div., joint command control requirements group Orgn. Joint Chiefs Staff, 1968-70; dep. comdr. Air Force Satellite Control Facility, Space and Missile Systems Orgn., Los Angeles, 1970-71; vice-comdr. electronic systems div. L.G. Hanscom Field, Bedford, Mass., 1971-72, insp. gen. Air Force Systems Command, Andrews AFB, Md., 1972, dep. chief staff procurement and prodn., 1972-74; spl. asst. to chief of staff SHAPE (NATO), 1974-78; vice comdr. acquisition logistics div. Air Force Logistics Command, Wright-Patterson AFB, Ohio, 1978—. Decorated D.S.M. with oak leaf cluster, Meritorious Service medal, Joint Service Commendation medal, Air Force Commendation medal with 2 oak leaf clusters, Army Commendation medal with 1 oak leaf cluster, Missileman and Command Pilot badges. Home: 420 Metzger Dr Wright-Patterson AFB OH 45433 Office: Air Force Logistics Command Wright-Patterson AFB OH 45433

WILSON, CHARLES MAYE, educator; b. Mt. Olive, N.C., Oct. 16, 1916; s. Joseph Earl and Bertha (Flowers) W.; student Coll. William and Mary, 1937-39; B.Sc., U. Va., 1941, M.A., 1942; Ph.D., Harvard, 1950. NRC postdoctoral fellow U. Calif., 1950-51; instr. biology Harvard, 1951-53; prof. biology McGill U., Montreal, Que., Can., 1953—, chmn. dept., 1962-70. Served to lt. USNR, 1942-46. Mem. Bot. Soc. Am., Mycological Soc. Am., Am. Inst. Biol. Scis., Raven Soc. Research on meiosis and polyploidy in the Phycomycetes. Home: 3460 Simpson St Montreal PQ H3G 2J4 Canada

WILSON, CHARLES PEAIRS, coll. dean; b. Meade, Kans., July 28, 1916; s. Robert William and Helen Cordelia (Peairs) W.; student U. Wichita, 1933-34; B.S., Kans. State Coll., 1938, M.S., 1940; Ph.D., U. Calif. at Berkeley, 1958; m. Doris Smith, Nov. 20, 1941; children—Susan, Kathleen, Carver. Successively instr., asst. prof., asso. prof. agrl. econs. Kans. State Coll., 1938-52, prof., asst. dir. Kans. Agr. Expt. Sta., 1952-62, dir., resident instrn. Coll. Agr., 1955-62, asso. dean Coll. Agr., dir. Kans. Agr. Expt. Sta., 1962-65; dean Coll. Tropical Agr., U. Hawaii, Honolulu, 1965-75, prof. agrl. econs., 1975—; mem. adv. com. Census Agr., 1959; chmn. Expt. Sta. mktg. research adv. com., 1961-64; chmn. com. of nine, also chmn. Western Agrl. Expt. Sta. Dirs., 1972; cons. Ford Found., Rural U., Minas Gerais, Brazil, 1963, Nairobi, Kenya, 1972; cons. to sec. agr. U.S. Dept. Agr., 1963. Recipient Distinguished Service award Kans. State U., 1971. Served with USAAF, 1942-46. Mem. Am., Western agrl. econ. assns., AAAS, Farm House (past nat. dir.; Master Builder of Men award), Alpha Zeta, Phi Kappa Phi, Gamma Sigma Delta. Presbyn. Contbr. articles to profl. jours. Home: 1610 Ihiloa Loop Honolulu HI 96821

WILSON, CHARLES REGINALD, real estate exec.; b. Bear Lake, Pa., Nov. 7, 1904; s. Earl Ayling and Edith (Finch) W.; student U. Pitts., 1927; m. Josephine Harrison, Sept. 8, 1927; children—Charles Reginald, Jacquelyn Ann. Asst. dean men U. Pitts., 1927-29; bus. promotion mgr. Hotel Schenley, Pitts., 1929-35; sales mgr. William Penn Hotel, Pitts., 1935-39, v.p., gen. mgr., 1952; mgr. Roosevelt Hotel, Pitts., 1939-52; sr. v.p. Union Nat. Bank of Pitts. (formerly Commonwealth Bank & Trust Company), 1952-71; sr. v.p. Realty Growth Corp., Pitts., 1972—; pres. Commonwealth Real Estate Co., 1957-64; dir. Glenshaw Glass Co., Homestead Industries, Inc., Hankison Corp. Pres., Panther Found., U. Pitts.; exec. com. Pitts. Conv. and Visitors Bur. Trustee Allegheny County Med. Soc. Found. Mem. Pitts. Athletic Assn., Soc. Indsl. Realtors, Delta Tau Delta, Omicron Delta Kappa. Mason. Clubs: Pittsburgh Field, Duquesne. Home: 4601 Fifth Ave Pittsburgh PA 15213 Office: Roosevelt Bldg Sixth St and Penn Ave Pittsburgh PA 15222

WILSON, CHARLES WILLIAM, lawyer; b. Walls, La., Feb. 22, 1910; s. Charles William and Elizabeth (Slaughter) W.; B.A., La. State U., 1931, J.D., 1933; m. Claire Prince, Jan. 2, 1933; children—Linda (Mrs. Thomas P. Landry), Claire (Mrs. Harold I. Bahlinger), Rebecca, Mary Scott (Mrs. L. J. Fergesen), Charles William III, Alonzo Prince, Alexander Jerome. Admitted to La. bar, 1933, since practiced in Baton Rouge; mem. firm Watson, Blanche, Wilson, & Posner and predecessor firms, 1940—; chmn. bd., pres. State Nat. Life Ins. Co.; dir. Air Waves, Inc., Baton Rouge Motor Lodge Corp. Trustee, v.p. Womans Hosp. Found. Fellow Am. Coll. Trial Lawyers; mem. Am., La. (dir. 1966-67), Baton Rouge (pres. 1956), Internat., Fed., Inter-Am. bar assns., Internat. Assn. Ins. Counsel, Def. Research Inst., Ins. Club New Orleans, Nat. Rifle Assn., Amateur Trap Shooting Assn., Nat. Skeet Shooting Assn., Baton Rouge Assembly, Baton Rouge C. of C., Phi Delta Phi, Sigma Chi. Democrat. Roman Catholic. Kiwanian. Clubs: Serra, Baton Rouge Country, City, Camelot (Baton Rouge). Home: 938 Steele Blvd Baton Rouge LA 70806 Office: 505 North Blvd PO Box 2995 Baton Rouge LA 70821

WILSON, CHARLES WILLIAM, psychiatrist, parapsychologist, lectr., author, publisher; b. St. Joseph, Mo., Aug. 12, 1916; s. Jacob Resor and Estella (Cherrie) W.; B.A., Wichita U., 1938; M.D., U. Kans., 1942; m. Frances Preshia Stephenson, June 20, 1942; children—Charles William II, Walter Stephen, Cherrie, James Robin. Intern, Harper Hosp., Detroit, 1942-43; resident neurology Univ. Hosps., Iowa City, Ia., 1946-47; resident psychiatry Griffin Meml. Central State Hosp., Norman, Okla., 1964-67; gen. practice medicine and surgery, St. Francis, Kans., 1947-62, LaCrosse, Kans., 1962-64; staff psychiatrist Bi-State Mental Health Found., Ponca City, Okla., 1967-71; dir. Bi-State Mental Health Clinic, Okla. State U., Stillwater, 1968-71; staff psychiatrist Santa Barbara County Mental Health Services, Santa Maria, Calif., 1971-72, San Luis Obispo (Calif.) Community Mental Health Services, 1973-75; practice medicine, specializing in psychiatry and hypnosis, Santa Maria, 1971—; staff psychiatrist Atascadero (Calif.) State Hosp., M.C. 1975-79. Mem. Elementary Sch. Bd., St. Francis, 1959-62. Served to lt. M.C. USNR, 1943-46. NIMH grantee, 1964-67. Fellow Internat. Platform Assn.; mem. Am. Soc. Clin. Hypnosis (charter), So. Calif. Psychiat. Soc., Am. Psychiat. Assn., Acad. Parapsychology and Medicine, Phi Beta Pi, Delta Upsilon. Mason. Author: Stop Bedwetting, 1979; Help Your Child—Love Therapy, 1980; developer body image therapy-programmed personality integration, reality insight therapy, sleep-teach therapy, indirect remote psychotherapy. Address: 4655 Basque Dr Santa Maria CA 93454. *Human mental suffering inspired me to create four systems of rapid psychotherapy. The patient I am working with is the most important person in the world at that time. I have had the good fortune of being God's channel to help many people find better mental health. The love and encouragement of Frances and the family were with me. They believed in what I was doing.*

WILSON, CHARLES ZACHARY, JR., univ. adminstr.; b. Greenwood, Miss., Apr. 21, 1929; s. Charles Zachary and Ora Lee (Means) W.; B.S., U. Ill., 1952, Ph.D., 1956; postgrad. Carnegie-Mellon U., Pitts.; m. Julia Ann Newman, Aug. 29, 1975; 1 son, Jonathan Keith; children by previous marriage—Charles Zachary III, Joyce Lynne, Joanne Catherine, Gary Thomas. Lectr. econs. State U. N.Y. at Binghamton, 1957-59, asso. prof. econs., 1962-68; spl. asst., adminstrv. vice chancellor U. Calif. at Los Angeles, 1967-68, asst. vice chancellor ednl. planning and programs, 1968-70, vice chancellor acad. programs, prof. edn., 1970—; dir. Mercury Savs. & Loan. Cons. project devel. Tratec Corp.; cons. Nat. Inst. Edn. HEW, 1973—. Mem. Presdl. Adv. Council Minority Bus. Enterprise, 1972-74. Bd. dirs., treas. Los Angeles County Mus. Art; chmn. bd. trustees Joint Center for Community Studies, Los Angeles, TIAA-CREF. State U. N.Y. Summer fellow, 1963; vis. research assn. Carnegie-Mellon U., 1965; Am. Council on Edn. fellow, 1967-68. Mem. Am. Ednl. Research Assn., Inst. Mgmt. Scis., Am. Econ. Assn., AAUP. Author: Organizational Decision-Making, 1967. Home: 1053 Tellem Dr Pacific Palisades CA 90272 Office: 405 Hilgard Ave Los Angeles CA 90024

WILSON, CHRISTOPHER WILLIAM, lawyer; b. Bklyn., Apr. 27, 1910; s. Christopher W. and Marion A. (Smith) W.; A.B. Cornell U., 1931; LL.B., Harvard, 1934; LL.D., Blackburn Coll., 1967; m. Margaret Ella Pettengill, June 5, 1948; children—Anthony P., Nancy F., Priscilla P. (Mrs. Wells), Christopher William, III. Admitted to N.Y. bar, 1934, Ill. bar, 1951; with firm White & Case, N.Y.C. and Paris, 1934-51; atty. First Nat. Bank Chgo., 1952-56, v.p., gen. counsel, 1956-62, sr. vice pres., gen. counsel, 1962-63, exec. v.p., 1963-67, exec. v.p., cashier, 1967-70, exec. v.p., gen. counsel, 1970-72; counsel Hopkins, Sutter, Mulroy, Davis & Cromartie and predecessor firm, Chgo., 1972—; dir. Scott, Foresman & Co. Bd. dirs. Children's Meml. Hosp.; trustee Blackburn Coll., U. Chgo. Served as lt. USNR, 1944-46. Mem. Am., Ill. Chgo. bar assns., Delta Upsilon. Clubs: Mid-Day, Chicago, Commonwealth, Commercial, (Chgo.); Indian Hill (Winnetka, Ill.); Old Elm (Fort Sheridan, Ill.); Mission Valley (Laurel, Fla.). Home: 714 Rosewood Ave Winnetka IL 60093 Office: One First Nat Plaza Chicago IL 60603

WILSON, CLAUDE RAYMOND, JR., lawyer; b. Dallas, Feb. 22, 1933; s. Claude Raymond and Lottie (Watts) W.; B.B.A., So. Meth. U., 1954, LL.B., 1956, LL.M. in Taxation, 1958; m. Barbara Jean Cowherd, Apr. 30, 1960; 1 dau., Deidra Nicole. Asso. firm Cervin & Melton, Dallas, 1956-58; atty. Tex. & Pacific R.R. Co., Dallas, 1958-60; atty. office regional counsel IRS, San Francisco, 1960-63, sr. trial atty. Office Chief Counsel, Washington, 1963-65; partner firm Golden, Potts, Boeckman & Wilson, Dallas, 1965—. C.P.A., Calif., Tex. Mem. Dallas, Am. bar assns., State Bar Tex., Dallas Soc. C.P.A.'s, Tex. Soc. C.P.A.'s (dir. 1973—, sec. 1978-79), Delta Sigma Phi, Delta Theta Phi. Republican. Episcopalian. Mason (Shriner, Jester). Clubs: Dallas Gun, Willow Bend Hunt and Polo, Chaparral. Home: 4069 Hanover St Dallas TX 75225 Office: 2300 Republic Bank Tower Dallas TX 75201

WILSON, COLON HAYES, physician, educator; b. Marshallberg, N.C., Apr. 10, 1932; s. Colon Hayes and Ethel P. (Nelson) W.; B.A., Duke U., 1952, M.D., 1956; m. Patricia Webb, June 23, 1956; children—Susan, W. Hayes, Patricia. Intern, U. Va. Hosp., Charlottesville, 1956-57, asst. resident medicine, 1957-58; resident Edward J. Meyer Hosp., Buffalo, 1961-63; fellow rheumatic diseases SUNY, Buffalo, Buffalo Gen. Hosp. and E.J. Meyer Meml. Hosp., 1963-66; asst. prof. medicine (rheumatology) Emory U. Sch. Medicine, Atlanta, 1966-69, asso. prof., 1969-74, prof., 1974—. Bd. dirs. Arthritis Found. N.Y., 1971-72, 74—, acting med. dir., 1977—; bd. dirs. Ga. chpt. Arthritis Found., 1966—, Breakthru House, 1970—. Served to capt. U.S. Army, 1958-61. Fellow A.C.P.; mem. Nat. Soc. Clin. Rheumatologists, AMA, Am. Rheumatism Assn., Ga. Rheumatism Soc. (pres. 1969-70), Fulton County Med. Soc., Med. Assn. Ga., Reticuloendothelial Soc., Am. Fedn. for Clin. Research. Methodist (mem. adminstr. bd. 1970—). Home: 32 Huntington Rd Atlanta GA 30309 Office: 69 Butler St SE Atlanta GA 30303

WILSON, COYT TAYLOR, ret. ednl. adminstr.; b. Fulton, Miss., July 27, 1913; s. Sumpter A. and Bertha (Davis) W.; B.S., Ala. Poly. Inst., 1938, M.S., 1941; Ph.D., U. Minn., 1946; m. Alma Inez Brackeen, Aug. 29, 1936; children—Patricia, Kenneth. With Auburn U. (formerly Ala. Poly. Inst.), 1940-41, 44-64, successively instr. botany, asst. plant pathologist agrl. expt. sta., prof. plant pathology, asst. dean and dir. Sch. Agr. and agrl. expt. sta., asst. dean Sch. of Agr. and asso. dir. Agrl. exptl. sta., 1955-64; asso. dir. Va. Agrl. Expt. Sta., Va. Poly. Inst., Blacksburg, 1964-65, dir., 1966-79, asso. dean research div., 1966-70, exec. asso. dean research div., 1970-79; instr. plant pathology U. Minn., 1941-43; agrl. research cons. Ministry Agr. of Iran, Turkey and Pakistan, 1961. Mem. Sigma Xi, Gamma Sigma Delta. Lion. Asso. editor Phythopathology, 1951. Contbr. chpts. in yearbooks. Address: 2010 Linwood Ln NW Blacksburg VA 24060

WILSON, DARCY BENOIT, immunologist; b. Rhinebeck, N.Y., May 14, 1936; s. William Darcy and Rosamonde (Cyr) W.; B.A., Harvard Coll., 1958; Ph.D., U. Pa., 1962; m. Dianne Haley Wilson, Dec. 24, 1973; children—Kathryn, Rebecca, Amy, Jessica. Postdoctoral research fellow Wistar Inst., 1962-63, asso., 1963-65; research fellow dept. med. genetics U. Pa., Phila., 1965-66, asst. prof., 1966-69, asso. prof., 1969-74, prof. depts. pathology and med. genetics, 1974—, head div. research immunology dept. pathology, 1978—; prof. Wistar Inst., 1977—; mem. corp. Marine Biol. Lab., Woods Hole, Mass.; mem. com. on cancer immunology USPHS/Nat. Cancer Inst.; mem. exec. com. U. Pa. Cancer Center, 1974—. Mem. Am. Assn. Immunologists. Mem. editorial bd. Jour. Exptl. Medicine, 1977—, Jour. Reticuloendothelial Soc., 1974-75, Immunogenetics, 1973, Transplantation, 1972-75, Jour. Immunology, 1972-76. Office: Dept Pathology Univ of Pa Med Sch 36th and Hamilton Walk Philadelphia PA 19104

WILSON, DAVE, television dir. Dir. Miss America Pageant; dir. TV series NBC's Saturday Night Live, 1975—; other direction includes: 4 Alan King TV spls., Festival of Country Music, The Corner Bar, College Girl of the Year, David Frost Presents the Best, Really Raquel, Three by Martha Graham, Wrinkles, Birthdays and Other Fables, Feeling Good, The Friars Roast Don Rickles. Recipient Emmy award Nat. Acad. TV Arts and Scis., 1976. *

WILSON, DAVID BRUCE, journalist; b. Bklyn., Dec. 31, 1927; s. William Wallace and Alice Elizabeth (Corl) W.; A.B., Harvard Coll., 1948; m. Constance Gay Bauman, May 29, 1954; children—Laura Hope Wilson Sirrico, Barbara Bauman, Sarah Louise. With Grand Rapids (Mich.) Press, 1949-52, Boston Herald, 1953-65, Boston Globe, 1965—. Served with U.S. Army, 1946-47. Republican. Episcopalian. Office: Boston Globe Boston MA 02107

WILSON, DAVID JAMES, educator, chemist; b. Ames, Ia., June 25, 1930; s. James Calmar and Alice Winona (Olmsted) W.; B.S. in Chemistry, Stanford U., 1952; postgrad., 1952-53, 55-57; Ph.D., Calif. Inst. Tech., 1958; m. Martha Carolyn Mayers, Sept. 6, 1952; children—John Wesley, Charles Steven, William David, Andrew Lyman, Joyce Ballin. Faculty, U. Rochester (N.Y.), 1957-69, asso. prof., 1963-67, prof. phys. chemistry, 1967-69; prof. Vanderbilt U., Nashville, 1969—, prof. chemistry and environ. engring., 1977—. Vis. sr. lectr. chemistry U. Ife (Nigeria), 1964-65. Mem. Rochester Com. for Sci. Info., 1960-69, v.p., 1966-69; chmn. Nashville Com. for Sci. Info., 1971-74. Served with AUS, 1953-55. Recipient award Monroe County Conservation Council, 1967, Tenn. Conservation League, 1971. Alfred P. Sloan Found. fellow, 1964-66. Mem. Am. Chem. Soc., Am. Phys. Soc., AAAS, Phi Beta Kappa, Sigma Xi. Home: 3600 Wilbur Pl Nashville TN 37204

WILSON, DONALD EDWARD, physician, educator; b. Worcester, Mass., Aug. 28, 1936; s. Rivers Rivo and Licine (Bradshaw) W.; A.B., Harvard U., 1958; M.D., Tufts U., 1962; m. Patricia C. Littell, Aug. 27, 1977; children—Jeffrey D.E., Sean D. Intern, St. Elizabeth Hosp., Boston, 1962-63; resident in medicine, research fellow in medicine VA Hosp. and Lemuel Shattuck Hosp., Boston, 1963-66; asso. chief gastroenterology Bklyn. Hosp., 1968-71; instr. medicine SUNY Downstate Med. Center, Bklyn., 1968-71; asst. prof. medicine U. Ill., Chgo., 1971-73, asso. prof., 1973-75, prof., 1975-80, acting head dept. medicine, 1976-77; dir. div. gastroenterology U. Ill. Hosp., Chgo., 1971-80, chief of gastroenterology, 1973-80, physician-in-chief, 1976-77; prof., chmn. dept. medicine SUNY Downstate Med. Center, Bklyn., 1980—; vis. prof. medicine U. London, Kings Coll. Med. Sch., 1977-78. Active mem. Art Inst., Chgo., Chgo. Zool. Soc. Served to capt. M.C., USAF, 1966-68. Recipient Research award HEW, 1971, 74, John A. Hartford Found., Inc., 1972-79, Distilled Spirits Council U.S., 1972-74, VA, 1974. Diplomate Am. Bd. Internal Medicine. Fellow A.C.P.; mem. Am. Gastroent. Assn., Am. Fedn. Clin. Research, Central Soc. Clin. Research, Central Research Club, Am. Assn. Study Liver Disease, Chgo. Soc. Gastroenterology (pres. 1978-79), Digestive Disease Found. Clubs: Harvard (Chgo.); Midwest Gut, Soc. for Exptl. Biology and Medicine, AAAS, Chgo. Soc. Gastrointestinal Endoscopy (pres. 1979-80). Contbr. articles to med. jours. Office: 450 Clarkson Ave Brooklyn NY 11203. *By respecting the rights and desires of others, one can achieve a high sense of self-respect and pride. Pride and self-respect have been important goals for me; without these qualities no amount of work or accumulation of tangibles would be satisfying.*

WILSON, DONALD GREY, minerals co. exec.; b. Bridgeport, Conn., Sept. 20, 1917; s. William Gray and Jeannetta Gardner (Kerr) W.; B.S. in Elec. Engring., Rensselaer Poly. Inst., 1938; S.M., Harvard U., 1939, M.E.S., 1947, Ph.D., 1948; m. Elizabeth Jean Lanning, Apr. 24, 1943 (div. Mar. 1971); children—Kirk Lanning, William Grey, Craig Gardner. Mgr. automatic fire alarm div. Sealand Corp., Bridgeport, Conn., 1939-40; instr. elec. engring. Rensselaer Poly. Inst., 1940-42; staff mem. Radiation Lab. Mass. Inst. Tech., 1942-45; with dept. elec. engring. U. Kan., Lawrence, 1947-55, prof., 1950-55, chmn. dept., 1948-55; cons. U.S. Naval Ordnance Test Sta., China Lake, Calif., 1953-54, asso. dir. research dept. Stromberg-Carlson Co., San Diego, 1955-59, gen. mgr., 1959; asst. v.p., 1959-60; v.p. research P.R. Mallory & Co., Indpls., 1960, v.p. research and engring., 1961-71, v.p. research, engring. and environ. affairs, 1971-75; pres. Contemporary Custom Cabinets, San Diego, 1975-76; mgmt. cons., 1976-78; v.p. Continental Resources and Minerals Corp., Dayton, Ohio, 1978—; alt. dir. Mallory Metall. Products (Eng.), 1967-69. Sr. lectr. U. Rochester, 1956-57. Bd. dirs. Speech and Hearing Clinic, Indpls., 1960-66, Washington Twp. Sch. Dist., 1964-68, pres., 1966-67. Mem. IEEE, AAAS, Sigma Xi, Sigma Phi Epsilon, Tau Beta Pi, Eta Kappa Nu. Contbr. articles to profl. jours. Home: 3110 Levante Carlsbad CA 92008 Office: 4140 Linden Ave Suite 200 Dayton OH 45432

WILSON, DONALD HURST, JR., ins. co. exec.; b. Balt., Mar. 29, 1920; s. Donald Hurst and Flora (Winkelman) W.; B.S. cum laude, Johns Hopkins, 1942; m. Winifred Arnold Leist, June 12, 1943; children—Donald Hurst III, David Alexander, Laura Ellen. Chief plant accountant Rheem Mfg. Co., Sparrows Point, Md., 1945-47; security analyst Monumental Life Ins. Co., Balt., 1947-50, asst. v.p., 1950-59, v.p., 1959-62, sr. v.p., dir., 1962-67, pres., 1967-78, also dir.; dir. Momumental Corp., Balt., 1968-78, sr. v.p., 1977—; dir. Hartford Mutual Ins. Co., Merc. Bankshares Corp.; mem. exec. com., dir. Merc. Safe Deposit & Trust. Mem. exec. com. Greater Balt. Com., 1970-78, chmn., 1973-74. Trustee, Goucher Coll., 1968-74, chmn. Human Resources Program, 1971-73; trustee Maryland Realty Trust, 1973—, chmn., 1977—; met. chmn. Nat. Alliance Bus., 1979. Recipient Distinguished Alumnus award Johns Hopkins. Mem. Johns Hopkins Alumni Assn. (pres. 1972), Phi Gamma Delta, Omicron Delta Kappa. Episcopalian. Home: 1408 Margarette Ave Towson MD 21204 Office: Monumental Life Ins Co 2 E Chase St Baltimore MD 21202

WILSON, DONALD LAURENCE, physician; b. Hamilton, Ont., Can., Oct. 2, 1921; s. Donald Alexander and Laura Louise (Dressel) W.; M.A., U. Toronto, 1948; M.D., C.M., Queen's U., 1944; m. Mary Isobel Pierce, Jan. 6, 1945; children—Mary Barbara, Judith Isobel, John Alexander, Peter Pierce, Helen Elizabeth, Donald Bruce. Intern, Hamilton (Ont.) Gen. Hosp., 1944-45; research fellow biochemistry U. Toronto, 1946-48; sr. intern medicine Kingston Gen. Hosp., 1948-49, attending physician, 1951—, pres. med. staff, 1956, chmn. med. adv. com., 1964-65; fellow medicine Harvard Med. Sch., also asst. medicine Peter Bent Brigham Hosp., 1949-51; Schering fellow endocrinology, 1949-51; asst. prof. medicine Queen's U., Kingston, Ont., 1951-59, asso. prof., 1960-68, prof., 1968—, chmn. dept. medicine, 1976—. Served with M.C., Royal Canadian Army, 1945-46. Fellow Royal Coll. Physicians (Can.), A.C.P.; mem. Can. (dir. 1972-75, chmn. bd. 1976-78, pres. 1979-80), Ont. (pres. 1973-74) med. assns., Canadian Physiol. Soc., Canadian Soc. Clin. Investigation, Am. Diabetes Assn., Endocrine Soc., Coll. Physicians and Surgeons Ont. (univ. rep. on council 1960-67, pres. 1964-65). Mem. United Ch. Can. Contbr. articles to profl. jours. Home: Rural Route 1 Kingston ON Canada Office: Etherington Hall Stuart St Kingston ON Canada

WILSON, DONALD MALCOLM, publishing exec.; b. Glen Ridge, N.J., June 27, 1925; s. Robert and Adelaide (Streubel) W.; grad. Deerfield (Mass.) Acad., 1943; B.A., Yale U., 1948; m. Susan M. Neuberger, Apr. 6, 1957; children—Dwight Malcolm, Katherine Loudon, Penelope. Reporter, Life mag., 1949-53, chief Far Eastern corr., 1953-56, chief Washington corr., 1956-60; dep. dir. USIA, 1961-65; gen. mgr. Time- Life Internat., 1965-68; asso. pub. Life mag., N.Y.C., 1968-69, v.p. corporate and pub. affairs Time, Inc., 1969—. Adv. council Edward R. Murrow Center, Tufts U.; mem. Pub. Broadcasting Authority of N.J., 1969-73, 76—. Trustee Vassar Coll.,

The Brearley Sch.; bd. dirs. Nat. Corp. Fund for Dance, Inc. Served to 2d lt. USAAF, 1943-45; ETO. Decorated Air medal. Mem. Council on Fgn. Relations. Clubs: Federal City (Washington); Century Assn. (N.Y.C.). Home: 4574 Province Line Rd Princeton NJ 08540 Office: Time-Life Bldg Rockefeller Center New York NY 10020

WILSON, DOROTHY CLARKE, author; b. Gardiner, Maine, May 9, 1904; d. Lewis Herbert and Flora Eva (Cross) Clarke; A.B., Bates Coll., 1925, Litt.D., 1947; m. Elwin L. Wilson, Aug. 31, 1925; adopted children—Joan S. (Mrs. George V. Wilson), Harold Elwin. Author of about seventy religious plays, including The Brother, The Carpenter, Simon the Leper, The Other Shepherd, No Room in the Hotel, others, vol. religious plays Twelve Months of Drama for the Average Church, 1934; (novels) The Brother, 1944; The Herdsman, 1946; Prince of Egypt (winner Westminster $7500 award for best religious novel), 1949; House of Earth, 1952; Fly With Me to India, 1954; Jezebel, 1955; The Gifts, 1957; Dr. Ida (a biography Dr. Ida S. Scudder of India), 1959; The Journey, 1962; Take My Hands (biography Dr. Mary Verghese), 1963; The Three Gifts, 1963; Ten Fingers for God (biography Dr. Paul Brand), 1965; Handicap Race, the story of Roger Arnett, 1967; Palace of Healing, The Story of Dr. Clara Swain, 1968; Lone Woman (biography Dr. Elizabeth Blackwell), 1970; The Big-Little World of Doc Pritham, 1971; Hilary, The Brave World of Hilary Pole, 1973; Bright Eyes, the Story of Susette La Flesche-an Omaha Indian, 1974; Stranger and Traveler, The Story of Dorothea Dix, American Reformer, 1975; Climb Every Mountain, 1976; Granny Brand, Her Story, 1976; Twelve Who Cared, My Adventures with Christian Courage, 1977. Trustee Bates Coll. Recipient Woman of Distinction award Alpha Delta Courage, 1977. Kappa, 1971, New Eng. United Meth. award, 1975, Distinguished Achievement award U. Maine, 1977. Lectr. on India, Middle East. Mem. Phi Beta Kappa. Home: 114 Forest Ave Orono ME 04473

WILSON, DRAKE, army officer; b. Ft. Sill, Okla., Aug. 17, 1930; s. Leroy Clark and Dorothy Wainwright (Ross) W.; B.S., U.S. Mil. Acad., 1952; M.S. in Engring., Princeton U., 1957; m. Ann Franklin Hofford, Oct. 20, 1952; children—Mark, Christopher, Elizabeth, Jean. Commd. 2d lt. U.S. Army, 1952, advanced through grades to maj. gen., 1979; asst. prof. U.S. Mil. Acad., 1961-64; dist. engr., Mobile, Ala., 1973-76; dep. dir. civil works C.E., 1976-78; div. engr. U.S. Army Engr. Div., Europe, 1978—. Bd. dirs. Boy Scouts Am., Mobile, Ala., 1973-76, YMCA, Mobile, United Fund, Mobile; pres. Fed. Execs. Bd., Mobile, 1975-76; dist. commr. Boy Scouts Am., Frankfurt, Ger., 1978-80. Decorated Bronze Star, Air medal, Legion of Merit; named Maritime Man of the Year, Port of Mobile, 1975. Mem. Soc. Am. Mil. Engrs., ASCE, Assn. U.S. Army. Club: Army-Navy Country (Washington). Office: US Army Engr Div Europe APO New York NY 09757

WILSON, EARL, columnist, radio commentator, editor; b. Rockford, Ohio, May 3, 1907; s. Arthur Earl and Cloe (Huffman) W.; student Heidelberg Coll.; B.S., Ohio State U., 1931; m. Rosemary Lyons, Jan. 10, 1936; 1 son, Earl Lyons. Newspaper mag. writer, 1923; columnist It Happened Last Night, N.Y. Post, 1942—, syndicated by Hall Syndicate; radio commentator WOR-Mut., 1945. Mem. Sigma Delta Chi, Alpha Tau Omega. Methodist. Club: Lambs. Author: Jungle Performers, 1941; I Am Gazing Into My 8-Ball, 1945; Pike's Peek or Bust, 1947; Let Em Eat Cheese Cake, 1949; Look Who's Abroad Now, 1953; Earl Wilson's New York, 1964; The Show Business Nobody Knows, 1971; Show Business Laid Bare, 1974; Sinatra, 1976; contbr. Sat. Eve. Post, Liberty, Esquire mags. Office: Field Newspaper Syndicate 401 N Wabash Ave Chicago IL 60611*

WILSON, EARL STEVENSON, SR., lawyer; b. Jackson County, Ky., Apr. 23, 1906; s. Phillip and Lucienda Catherine (Dees) W.; student Cumberland Coll., 1927-28; B.S., U. Ky., 1930, LL.B., 1936; m. Mary Elizabeth McNabb, Sept. 2, 1940; children—Philip Erwin, Earl Stevenson. Admitted to Ky. bar, 1940; tchr., basketball coach pub. high schs., Livingston, Ky., 1931-33; atty. Ky. Dept. Revenue, Frankfort, 1937-40; asst. atty. gen. State of Ky., Frankfort, 1940-43; mem. firms Ogden, Tarrant, Galphin & Street, Louisville, 1944-48, Bullitt, Dawson & Tarrant, Louisville, 1948-63, Kincaid, Wilson, Schaeffer & Hembree, Lexington, Ky., 1963—; chmn. bd. Ky. Central Life Ins. Co., 1976—, Central Bank & Trust Co., 1976—, Ky. Central TV Inc., 1976—, Dania Bank (Fla.), 1976—, Marathon Bank (Fla.), 1976—. Bd. dirs. Lexington Center Corp., 1976—. Mem. Ky., Am. bar assns. Democrat. Baptist. Home: 713 Brookhill Dr Lexington KY 40502 Office: 500 Central Bank Bldg Lexington KY 40507

WILSON, EDGAR BRIGHT, educator; b. Gallatin, Tenn., Dec. 18, 1908; s. Edgar Bright and Alma (Lackey) W.; B.S., Princeton U., 1930, A.M., 1931; Ph.D., Calif. Inst. Tech., 1933; A.M., Harvard, 1942; D. honoris causa, U. Brussels, 1975; D.Sc., Dickinson Coll., 1976, Columbia U., 1979; Dr. Chem., U. Bologna, 1976; m. Emily Buckingham, June 15, 1935 (dec. 1954); children—Kenneth, David, Nina (Nina W. Cornell); m. 2d, Therese Bremer, July 25, 1955; children—Anne, Paul, Steven. Research fellow Cal. Inst. Tech., 1933-34; jr. fellow Soc. of Fellows, Harvard, 1934-36, asst. prof. chemistry, 1936-39, asso. prof., 1939-46, prof., 1946-79, Theodore William Richards prof. chemistry, 1947-79, prof. emeritus, 1979—; research dir. Underwater Explosives Research Lab., 1942-44; chief div. 2, Nat. Def. Research Com., 1944-46; research dir., weapons systems evaluation group Dept. Def., 1952-53. Recipient Am. Chem. Soc. award, 1937, medal for Merit U.S. govt., 1948, Debye award, 1962; Distinguished Service award Calif. Inst. Tech., 1966; Pauling award; 1972, Rumford medal, 1973, Nat. Medal Sci., 1976, Feltrinelli award, 1976, Ferst award Sigma Xi, 1977; Pitts. Spectroscopy award, 1978; Robert A. Welch award, 1978; Willard Gibbs award, 1979; Guggenheim fellow, 1949-50, 70-71; Fulbright grantee Queen's Coll., Oxford, Eng., 1949-50. Mem. Am. Chem. Soc. (Norris award N.E. sect. 1966, Lewis award Calif. sect. 1969, T.W. Richards medal N.E. sect. 1978), Am. Phys. Soc. (Plyler award 1978), Am. Philos. Soc., Am. Acad. Arts and Scis., Internat. Acad. Quantum Molecular Scis., Nat. Acad. Scis., Phi Beta Kappa. Author: (with Linus Pauling) Introduction to Quantum Mechanics, 1935; Introduction to Scientific Research, 1952; (with P.C. Cross, J.C. Decius) Molecular Vibrations, 1955. Home: 52 Martha's Point Rd Concord MA 01742 Office: 12 Oxford St Cambridge MA 02138

WILSON, EDGAR HUNTER, educator; b. Asheville, N.C., Feb. 2, 1923; s. Edgar Hunter and Ethel Lee (Lunsford) W.; student Wake Forest U., 1940-41, Biltmore Coll., 1941-42, George Washington U., 1942-43; LL.B., Duke, 1948, LL.M., 1948, S.J.D., 1954; m. Carolyn Eskridge Gibbs, Sept. 10, 1946; 1 dau., Dorothy D. Admitted to N.C. bar, 1948, Ga. bar, 1955, Okla. bar, 1970; prof. law Mercer U., Macon, Ga., 1948-68, dean Sch. Law, 1972-77, Macon prof. law, 1977—; exec. dir. Fla. Law Revision Commn., Gainesville, 1968-69; prof. law U. Fla., 1968-69; dean Coll. Law, U. Tulsa, 1969-72. Rep., Ga. Gen. Assembly, 1956-60; mayor, Macon, 1960-64. Mem. Bibb County Bd. Edn., 1959-63; mem. Macon Hosp. Commn., 1960-64; v.p. Ga. Municipal Assn., 1962-63; vice chmn. Middle Ga. Goliseum Authority, 1962-66; spl. hearing officer Dept. Justice, 1965-67. Chmn. Macon-Bibb County Water and Sewer Authority, 1974—. Bd. dirs. Macon-Bibb County Indsl. Authority, 1959-63. Served with USAAF, 1943-46. Mem. Order of Coif, Phi Delta Phi. Co-author: Georgia Insurance Code, 1960; Georgia Criminal Code, 1968; Florida Criminal Procedure Code, 1970. Home: 4931 Rivoli Dr Macon GA 31210 Office: Mercer University Macon GA 31207

WILSON, EDWARD CONVERSE, JR., oil and natural gas prodn. co. exec.; b. Cambridge, Mass., Jan. 1, 1928; s. Edward Converse and Jean (McLean) W.; A.B., Harvard U., 1949; m. Patricia Ann Cairns, Sept. 10, 1953; children—Amy Cairns, Sarah Converse. Brokerage trainee Estabrook & Co., Boston, 1951; Midwest Stock Exchange clk. Paul H. Davis & Co., Chgo., 1951-52; mem. Chgo. Bd. Trade, 1952-78, dir., 1966-67, chmn., 1970-71; partner Nolan & Wilson Co., specialists on Midwest Stock Exchange, 1965-72; sr. partner Wilson Prodn. Co., Ft. Smith, Ark., 1972-74; dir. Rutledge Assos., Wakefield, Mass., 1965-74, Paul H. Robinson Inc., Chgo., 1972—. Mem. devel. com. Chgo. chpt. Nat. Multiple Sclerosis Soc., 1970; mem. vis. com. on univ. resources Harvard, 1971-74, 76—. Bd. dirs. Franklin Blvd. Community Hosp., 1970-74. Served with USAAF, 1946-47. Clubs: Harvard (dir.), Racquet (Chgo.); Harvard (Boston); Shore Acres (Lake Bluff, Ill.). Home: 11114 Wickwood Dr Houston TX 77024 Office: 1717 St James Pl Houston TX 77056

WILSON, EDWARD DOBBINS, banker; b. Maplewood, N.J., Apr. 1, 1917; s. George William and Jane (Dobbins) W.; B.S., N.Y.U., 1942; m. Marian P. Brokaw, June 3, 1939 (dec. 1979); children—Edward B., M. Kathleen. With Mut. Benefit Life Ins. Co., Newark, 1934-53, Irving Trust Co., N.Y.C., 1953-74, v.p., 1958-64, sr. v.p., 1964-69, exec. v.p., 1969-74; exec. v.p. Charter N.Y. Corp., 1974-78, sr. exec. v.p., 1978; sr. exec. v.p. Irving Trust Co., N.Y.C., 1979—; dir. Charter N.Y. Leasing Corp., 1974-79, Charter credit corp., Central Trust Co., Rochester, Mchts. Nat. Bank & Trust, Syracuse. Mem. men's com. Greater N.Y. council Girl Scouts U.S.A., 1964-74, chmn., 1965-67; banking com. Greater N.Y. council Boy Scout's Am., 1962-64. Sec. bd. assessors, Chatham, N.J., 1951-55. Served to lt. (j.g.) USNR, 1943-46. Mem. Am. Inst. Real Estate Appraisers, Nat. Assn. Real Estate Bds., Real Estate Bd. N.Y., Brantingham Lake Assn. Clubs: Sky, Economic (N.Y.C.). Home: 2 Fifth Ave New York NY 10011 Office: 1 Wall St New York NY 10005

WILSON, EDWARD GEORGE, lawyer; b. Richmond, Ind. Mar. 23, 1909; s. Harvey T. and Ruth (Wiggins) W.; A.B., Earlham Coll., 1930; J.D., N.Y. U., 1934; LL.D., Earlham Coll., 1976; m. Jane Hunt Johnson, Nov. 19, 1932; 1 son, Edward Folger. With J. Walter Thompson Co., N.Y.C., 1930-36, 38-71, gen. counsel 1946-61, treas., 1959-62, v.p., 1954-62, exec. v.p., 1962-71, sec., 1965-71, dir., 1957-72; admitted to N.Y. bar, 1935; asso. Donovan, Leisure, Newton & Lumbard, 1936-38. Life trustee Earlham Coll.; bd. dirs., sec. Assn. Governing Bds. Univs. and Colls.; trustee Common Fund, 1973-77. Served as lt. USNR, 1943-45. Decorated Legion of Merit. Trustee, AFTRA Pension and Welfare Funds, 1954-62. Mem. Mil. Order Fgn. Wars, Assn. Bar City N.Y., Am. Bar Assn., Internat C. of C. (trustee and chmn. advt. com. U.S. council, vice chmn. advt. comm. 1964-71), Am. Soc. Corporate Secs. (asso.). Episcopalian. Clubs: Pilgrims, University (N.Y.C.); Metropolitan (Washington). Address: Fairchild Rd Sharon CT 06069

WILSON, EDWARD NICHOLAS, electronics co. exec., lawyer; b. Bklyn., July 31, 1936; s. Elmer Newton and Dorothy Rosalie W.; A.B., Coll. Holy Cross, 1958; LL.B., Columbia U., 1963; m. Isis Maria Rivero, Apr. 24, 1965; children—Maria Teresa, Alicia Marie. Mem. firm Wilkie Farr & Gallagher, N.Y.C., 1963-72; v.p., sec. Loral Corp., N.Y.C., 1972—. Served with USNR, 1958-60. Mem. Am. Bar Assn., N.Y. State Bar Assn., Assn. Bar City N.Y., Am. Soc. Corp. Secs. Democrat. Roman Catholic. Clubs: Heights Casino (Bklyn.); Millbrook (N.Y.) Golf and Country. *

WILSON, EDWARD OSBORNE, educator; b. Birmingham, Ala., June 10, 1929; s. Edward Osborne and Inez (Freeman) W.; B.S., U. Ala., 1949, M.S., 1950; Ph.D., Harvard U., 1955; m. Irene Kelley, Oct. 30, 1955; 1 dau., Catherine Irene. Jr. fellow Soc. Fellows, Harvard, 1953-56, mem. faculty, 1956—, Baird prof. sci., 1976—, curator entomology, 1971—. Recipient Nat. Medal Sci., 1976; Pulitzer prize for nonfiction, 1979; Leidy medal Acad. Natural Sci., Phila., 1979; Disting. Service award Am. Inst. Biol. Scis., 1976. Fellow Am. Acad. Arts and Scis., Am. Phil. Soc.; mem. Nat. Acad. Sci. Home: 9 Foster Rd Lexington MA 02173 Office: Mus Comparative Zoology Harvard Univ Cambridge MA 02138

WILSON, ELMER DEE, geophys. co. exec.; b. Joplin, Mo., July 23, 1921; s. John Elmer and Verda Bess (Douse) W.; student Tex. A. and M. U., Tulsa U.; m. Betty Jean McGhee, Dec. 6, 1944; children—Paula Jo, Dee Anne. With Seismograph Service Corp., Tulsa, 1946—, treas., then fin. v.p., 1961, pres., 1966, chief exec. officer, 1969—, also chmn. bd., chmn. fin. com. Chmn. Tulsa Met. Crime Commn., 1971-73; trustee Tulsa Psychiat. Center; coordinating chmn. Energy Advocates. Served with USAAF, 1942-45. Decorated D.F.C., Air medal with 4 oak leaf clusters. Mem. Tulsa C. of C., Soc. Exploration Geophysicists, Inst. Internal Auditors. Fin. Execs. Inst., Nat. Assn. Accountants. Republican. Clubs: Cedar Ridge Country, Tulsa, Petroleum, Summit, Elks. Office: Seismograph Service Corp 6200 E 41st St Tulsa OK 74102*

WILSON, ERNEST RAYMOND, ret. banker; b. Arlington, Va., Mar. 10, 1916; s. Edward Everett and Maude (King) W.; certificate Am. Inst. Banking, 1940; B.C.S., Southeastern U., 1945; m. Frances J. Simpson, May 15, 1948; 1 son, Thomas E. Auditor, comptroller, cashier, v.p., sr. v.p. Bank of Commerce, Washington, 1935-66; exec. v.p. Nat. Savs. & Trust Co., Washington, 1966-76, ret. Asst. treas. Community Chest Fedn., Washington, 1953-55; pres. Calvary Found., 1972-73. Mem. Am., D.C. bankers assns., Bank Adminstrn. Inst., Met. Washington Bd. Trade. Methodist. Rotarian. Home: 2300 S Inge St Arlington VA 22202

WILSON, EVERETT DALE, coll. dean; b. Covington, Ind., July 13, 1928; s. Clarence and Maxine (Perry) W.; B.S (Acad. scholar), Ind. U., 1950; M.S., Ind. State U., 1951; Ph.D., Purdue U., 1960; m. Delores Ann Dare, Oct. 29, 1952; children—Denise, Dale, Deonne, Di Anne. Tchr., Rabb Grace Sch., Covington, Ind., 1948-50; tchr. sci., coach basketball Perrysville (Ind.) High Sch., 1955-56; supr. process control Olin-Mathieson Chem. Corp., Covington, 1956-57; grad. teaching asst. biology Purdue U., Lafayette, Ind., 1957-58, grad. research asst., 1958-60; asst. prof. biology So. Ill. U., Carbondale, 1960-61; asso. prof. biology Sam Houston State Tchrs. Coll., Huntsville, Tex., 1962-64, prof. biology, 1964-65, dean Coll. Sci., 1965—. Research fellow R.B. Jackson Meml. Lab., Bar Harbor, Me., 1959; chief population reprodn. grants bd. Nat. Inst. Child Health, Washington, 1972-73; adviser, cons. Oak Ridge Population Research Center, Oak Ridge, 1971; chief population and reprodn. grants br. Inst. Child Health and Human Devel., NIH, 1971—; cons., NIH, 1971—. Mem. Tex. Bd. Examiners in the Basic Scis., 1966-69, 69—; speaker sch. activities, civic organs. and service clubs, 1952-55. Bd. dirs. Tex. System Natural Labs. Served with USNR, 1952-55. Lalor Found. research fellow, 1961; U.S. State Dept. postdoctoral fellow Cambridge (Eng.) U., 1962; AEC research fellow Oak Ridge Inst. Nuclear Studies, 1963, Oak Ridge Asso. Univs. grantee, 1968. Mem. Am. Assn. Basic Sci. Bds. (v.p. 1970, pres. 1971), Am. Inst. Biol. Scis., Tex. Acad. Sci. (vis. scientist Tex. jr., sr. high schs. 1964-67), Tex. Water Conservation Assn., Am. Soc. Zoologists, Endocrine Soc., Am. Soc. Animal Sci., Wildlife Soc., Soc. Study of Reproduction (constn. com.), English Soc. Study Fertility, Italian Soc. Progress of Zootechnic (corr.), So. Assn. Colls. and Schs. (vis. com. mem., chmn. com.), Huntsville C. of C., V.F.W., Am. Legion, Sigma Xi. Methodist. Mason. Contbr. numerous articles to profl. jours. Home: Elkins Lake Box 38 Huntsville TX 77340

WILSON, FLIP, comedian; b. Jersey City, Dec. 8, 1933; divorced; 4 children. Appeared on Tonight Show, Ed Sullivan Show, Rowan and Martin's Laugh-In; star Flip Wilson Show, 1970-74; star TV spls., 1974-76; appeared TV spl. Pinocchio, 1976; comedy recs. include Cowboys and Colored People, 1967, Flippin', 1968, Flip Wilson, You Devil You, 1968; appeared in films Uptown Saturday Night, 1974, Skatetown U.S.A., 1979. Served with USAF, 1950-54. Recipient Grammy award for best comedy rec., 1971. Address: care William Morris Agy 1350 Ave of Americas New York NY 10019*

WILSON, FRANK BOYD, univ. adminstr., speech pathologist; b. Detroit, Jan. 8, 1929; s. Harry O'Brian and Norah Kathaleen (Welham) W.; came to Can., 1972; B.Sc., Bowling Green State U., 1950; Ph.D., Northwestern U., 1956; m. Ann J. Callewaert, Aug. 12, 1950; children—Joseph B., Kathaleen J., Madeline R., Erick J., Harry Christopher, Frank Bradford, Rebecca Ann. Coordinator speech and hearing services St. Louis County Spl. Edn. Program, 1959-65, dir. research, 1972-74; dir. speech pathology Jewish Hosp. St. Louis, 1965-72; asso. prof. Washington U., St. Louis, 1964-74; dean Faculty Rehab. Medicine, prof. speech pathology U. Alta. (Can.), Edmonton, 1974—. Fellow Am. Speech and Hearing Assn.; mem. Am. Cleft Palate Assn. Author: Voice Disorders, 1977; editor Jour. Human Communications, 1975—. Office: Faculty Rehab Medicine U Alta Edmonton AB T6G 2E1 Canada

WILSON, FRANK WILEY, U.S. judge; b. Knoxville, Tenn., June 21, 1917; s. Frank Caldwell and Mary Elizabeth (Wiley) W.; B.A., U. Tenn., 1939, LL.B., 1941; m. Helen Elizabeth Warwick, Apr. 6, 1942; children—Frank Carl, William Randall. Admitted to Tenn. bar, 1941; with firm Poore, Kramer & Cox, Knoxville, 1941-42, Wilson & Joyce, Oak Ridge, 1946-61; county atty. Anderson County, 1948-50; city atty., Norris, 1950-61; U.S. dist. judge Eastern Dist. Tenn., Chattanooga, 1961—, chief judge, 1969—. Vice pres., dir. Bank of Oak Ridge, 1953-61. Trustee Siskin Meml. Found. Democratic candidate for Congress, 1950. Served with USAAF, 1942-46. Mem. Am. Bar Assn., Am. Judicature Soc., Am. Legion (past post comdr.), Order of Coif, Scabbard and Blade, Phi Kappa Phi, Phi Delta Kappa. Rotarian (past pres. Oak Ridge). Home: 103 Stratford Rd Signal Mountain TN 37377 Office: US Dist Ct Chattanooga TN 37402

WILSON, FRED MADISON, ophthalmologist; b. Chgo., Mar. 19, 1914; s. Charles Benjamin and Gayle (Neill) W.; A.B., Ind. U., 1936, M.D., 1939; m. Betty Fredrick, Oct. 14, 1938; children—Fred Monroe, Carol, Marcia. Intern, St. Vincent's Hosp., Indpls., 1939-40; gen. practice medicine, Kokomo, Ind., 1940-42; grad. study ophthalmology Bellevue Med. Center, N.Y. U., 1945-46; asst. resident, resident ophthalmology Ind. U. Med. Center, Indpls., 1946-48, asst. prof., 1951, prof. ophthalmology, chmn. dept., 1954-79, prof. emeritus, 1979—; instr. U. Ill. Coll. Medicine, Chgo., 1948-49; staff Ill. Eye and Ear Infirmary, Chgo., 1948-49; practice of ophthalmology, Austin, Tex., 1949-51; asso. R.J. Masters, 1951-52; cons. ophthalmology VA Hosp., Indpls. Mem. ophthalmology tng. com. USPHS, 1956-59; mem. Ind. Adv. Com. for Blind, 1959—; mem. Ind. Spl. Edn. Com. Visual Handicapped, 1959—; med. dir. Ind. Lions Eye Bank, 1966—. Served to capt. M.C. USAAF, 1942-45. Diplomate Am. Bd. Ophthalmology (dir. 1960-68, vice chmn. 1967, cons. 1969-77). Fellow A.C.S.; mem. Nat. Soc. Prevention Blindness (chmn. Ind. com. 1953-56), A.M.A., Retina Soc. (charter), Am. Ophthal. Soc., Am. Acad. Ophthalmology, Assn. Research Ophthalmology, Phi Beta Kappa, Phi Kappa Psi, Nu Sigma Nu. Contbr. articles to profl. publs. Home: Route 2 Box 296 Carmel IN 46032 Office: 1100 W Michigan St Indianapolis IN 46223

WILSON, FRED TALBOTT, architect; b. Houston, Oct. 2, 1912; s. Fred Taylor and Irene (Davis) W.; student Vanderbilt U.; B.A., Rice Inst., 1934, B.S., 1936; m. Irene Lee, Nov. 27, 1945; children—Elizabeth Valentine, Michael Talbott. Jr. partner of Claude Hooton, 1934-37; designer draftsman N.Y.C., 1935-36; formed archtl. firm Wilson & Morris, Houston, 1938, became Wilson, Morris, Crain & Anderson, 1958, Wilson, Crain, Anderson, 1972-74, Wilson/Crain/Anderson/Reynolds, 1974—, W/C/A Inc., Talbott Wilson/Assos., 1979—. Mem. nat. archtl. adv. bd. Gen. Services Adminstrn., 1971-73; regional chmn. Internat. Design Conf., Aspen, Colo., 1964-68; chmn. Houston Com. Fgn. Relations, 1961-62, sec.-rapporteur, 1968—. Bd. dirs. Brazos Presbyn. Homes., 1966-70, pres., 1970, adviser, 1971—; bd. dirs Am. Cancer Soc., crusade chmn. Harris County unit, 1969, chmn. bd. 1973-74; bd. dirs. Nat. Com. on U.S. China Relations, 1968-72, Rice Center For Community Design and Research, 1972-75. Bd. govs. Rice U., 1970—. Served as lt. col. Arty., AUS, 1941-46. Decorated Bronze Star. Recipient Cloud and Banner with 2 personal citations (China); 1st honor award Tex. Architecture 1954, award of merit, 1963, award of honor, 1967, 68, 11 awards of merit for design Houston chpt. A.I.A.; Sr. certificate Nat. Council Archtl. Registration Bds. Fellow A.I.A. (pres. Houston chpt. 1951), Internat. Inst. Arts and Letters; mem. Tex. Soc. Architects (dir. 1954), Friends of Fondren Library (past pres.), Houston C. of C. (chmn. com. on community improvement 1964), Houston Mus. Fine Arts, Houston Contemporary Arts Mus., Rice U. Assos., UN Assn., Alumni Assn. of Rice Univ. (pres. 1968-69), Delta Kappa Epsilon. Presbyn. (ruling elder). Author series editorial page columns on world affairs Houston Post, 1975. Home: 2 Briartrail Houston TX 77027 Office: 2223 West Loop S Suite 515 Houston TX 77027

WILSON, GABRIEL HENRY, radiologist; b. Caruthersville, Mo., Jan. 30, 1929; s. Michael Earl and Alma Alberta (Cecil) W.; student St. Mary's Coll., 1946-48, U. Calif. at Los Angeles, 1952-53; B.S., Loyola U., Chgo., 1955; M.D., Creighton U., 1959. Rotating intern Los Angeles County Harbor Gen. Hosp., Torrance, Calif., 1959-60, resident in radiology, 1960-63, staff radiologist, 1963-64, 65-66, vis. physician in neuroradiology, 1964-67, instr. in radiology, 1963-64, asst. prof., 1964-66; asst. prof. radiology U. Calif. at Los Angeles, 1966-70, asso. prof., 1970-74, prof., 1974—, chmn. dept. radiol. scis., 1973—; cons. neuroradiology VA Hosp., Long Beach, Calif., 1965-66; cons. VA Hosp., Los Angeles, 1965—. Served with USNR, 1948-52. Diplomate Nat. Bd. Med. Examiners, Am. Bd. Radiology. Fellow Am. Coll. Radiology (councilor 1976—); mem. AMA, Calif. Med. Assn. (asst. sec. sect. on radiology 1970-71, sec. 1971-72, chmn. 1972-74, chmn. adv. panel radiology, 1972-73, 76—), Calif. (exec. com. 1976—, pres.-elect 1979-80), Los Angeles (exec. com. 1971—, treas. 1971-72, sec. 1972-73, pres. 1974-75), radiol. socs., Japan Radiol. Soc., Radiol. Soc. So. Calif. (bd. dirs. 1976—, sec.-treas. 1979-80), Radiol. Soc. N.Am. (councilor 1976—), Am. Soc. Neuroradiology (v.p. 1979-80), Western Neuroradiol. Soc. (pres. 1968-70, chmn. nominating com. 1971-72, chmn. membership com. 1974), Fedn. Western Socs. Neurol. Sci. (bd. dirs. 1968-76, chmn. nominating com. 1968-69, chmn. auditing com. 1969-70, sec.-treas. 1971-73, chmn. 1973-75), Inter-Am. Fedn. Neuroradiology, Los Angeles Soc. Neurology and Psychiatry, Soc. Chairmen of Acad. Radiology Depts., Am. Roentgen Ray Soc., Alpha Omega Alpha. Home: 4009 Ocean Front Walk Venice CA 90291 Office: U California Dept of

Radiological Sciences Center for Health Sciences Los Angeles CA 90024

WILSON, GAHAN, cartoonist, author; b. Evanston, Ill., Feb. 18, 1930; s. Allen Barnum and Marion (Gahan) W.; student Art Inst. Chgo., 1948-52; m. Nancy Dee Midyette (Nancy Winters), Dec. 30, 1966; stepchildren—Randy Winters, Paul Winters. Collections include: Gahan Wilson's Graveyard Manner, 1965; The Man In the Cannibal Pot, 1967; I Paint What I See, 1971; Weird World of Gahan Wilson, 1975; Gahan Wilson's Cracked Cosmos, 1975; First World Fantasy Collection Anthology, 1977; Gahan Wilson's Favorite Tales of Horror, 1977; And Then We'll Get Him, 1978; Nuts, 1979; Short Story Collection, 1980; Novel, 1979; juvenile works include: Harry, The Fat Bear Spy, 1973; The Bang Bang Family, 1974; Harry and the Sea Serpent, 1976; Harry and the Snow Melting Ray, 1980; contbr. to New Yorker, Collier's, Look, Playboy, Punch, Esquire, Fantasy and Sci. Fiction, Paris Match, Pardon, Nat. Lampoon. Mem. Mystery Writers Am., Sci. Fiction Writers Am., Soc. Illustrators, Wolfe Pack, Cartoonists Guild (pres.). Commentator, Nat. Public Radio. Office: 1345 3d Ave New York NY 10021

WILSON, GARFF BELL, educator; b. Ogden, Utah, Jan. 9, 1909; s. Robert Emmett and Alva (Garff) W.; A.B., U. Calif. at Berkeley, 1931, M.A., 1933; Ph.D., Cornell U., 1940. Dir. drama, dean men Humboldt State Coll., 1933-38; dir. staff Cornell U. Theatre, 1938-40; mem. faculty U. Calif. at Berkeley, 1941-42, 46—, prof. speech and dramatic art, 1958—, spl. asst. to chancellor, 1966—, chmn. pub. ceremonies, 1948—, dir. Centennial Celebration, 1967-68. Served to capt. U.S. Army, 1942-46; ETO, PTO. Recipient Centennial citation U. Calif. at Berkeley, 1968, service award Calif. Alumni Assn., 1968, elected Berkeley fellow, 1977. Mem. Speech Assn. Am. (prize for best book in field 1966, mem. legislative council 1956-57, legislative assembly 1962-65), Ednl. Theatre Assn., Western Speech Assn. (nat. chmn. oral interpretation interest group 1955). Democrat. Author: History of American Acting, 1966; Three Hundred Years of American Drama and Theatre, 1973. Asso. editor Ednl. Theatre Jour., 1963-65. Contbr. articles to profl. publs. Home: 45 Vicente Rd Berkeley CA 94705

WILSON, GARLAND, JR., meat packing co. exec.; b. Bethany, Mo., Sept. 18, 1916; s. Garland and Harriett (Darr) W.; student Ga. Inst. Tech., 1934-35; A.B., U. Mo., 1937; m. Jane A. Alford, Sept. 17, 1938; children—Garland III, Theodore A. Pres., Featherstone Corp., 1976—, also dir.; dir. First Stock Yards Bank, Sterling Colo. Beef Co., Circle C Beef Co., St. Joseph Light and Power Co. Vice-chmn. Region VIII, Boy Scouts Am., 1966-68, mem. exec. bd., 1962-73; bd. dirs. United Fund, 1959-66, 68, chmn. drive, 1967. Served to maj. AUS, 1942-46. Decorated Bronze Star medal, Air medal; recipient Boy Scouts Am. Silver Antelope award. Mem. St. Joseph C. of C., Alpha Tau Omega, Alpha Chi Sigma. Clubs: Benton. Home: Frederick Towers Saint Joseph MO 64506 Office: 2400 Frederick Ave Saint Joseph MO 64506

WILSON, GARY LEE, hotel and motel co. exec.; b. Alliance, Ohio, Jan. 16, 1940; s. Elvin John and Fern Helen (Donaldson) W.; B.A., Duke U., 1962; M.B.A., Wharton Sch., U. Pa., 1963; m. Susan Browne Moody, Aug. 11, 1962; children—Derek, Christopher. Vice pres. fin., dir. Trans-Philippines Investment Co., Manila, 1964-70; exec. v.p., dir. Checchi & Co., Washington, 1971-73; sr. v.p. fin. and devel. Marriott Corp., Washington, 1973—; dir. Enstrom Helicopter Co., Menominee, Mich. Home: 11329 Willowbrook Dr Potomac MD 20854 Office: Marriott Dr Washington DC 20058

WILSON, GEORGE ANDREW, broadcasting exec.; b. Raymond, Wash., Mar. 29, 1925; s. Jack and Catherine (Arakcheev) Veteff; B.A., U. Wash., 1947; m. Marion Ellen Maloney, May 29, 1948; children—Laura, Michael, Nancy. Publisher, Sunset Jour., Santa Monica, Calif., 1949-51; sales mgr. KBLE AM-FM Radio, Seattle, 1952, gen. mgr., 1952-71, pres., 1971—; pres. KARI Radio, Blaine, Wash., 1960—; gen. mgr. KASA Radio, Phoenix, 1967-73, pres., 1973—. Served with U.S. Army, 1943-45. Mem. Am. Legion, Sigma Chi. Clubs: Rainier, Wash. Athletic. Office: 114 Lakeside Ave Seattle WA 98122

WILSON, GEORGE ANGUS, metals co. exec., lawyer; b. Mansfield, La., Feb. 1, 1910; s. George and Elizabeth (Pitts) W.; A.B., Centenary Coll., 1930, LL.D. (hon.), 1979; LL.B., Tulane U., 1933; m. Lola Nelson, Dec. 27, 1963. Admitted to La. bar, 1933, practiced New Orleans, 1933-41; faculty law sch. Tulane U., 1933-40; gen. counsel La. Dept. Conservation, 1940-41, Standard Oil Co. N.J., 1941-46; pres., dir. Interstate Natural Gas Co., Inc., 1946-53, Interstate Oil Pipe Line Co., 1954-55; pres. TXL Oil Corp., Dallas, 1955-62; pres., dir., chief exec. officer Lone Star Steel Co., 1962-77, chmn. bd., 1963—; dir. Phila. & Reading Corp., Tex.-Pacific Land Trust, N.W. Industries, Inc., Am. Petrofina, Inc., Employers Ins. Co. of Tex. Mem. Mil. Petroleum Adv. Bd., 1946-50; dir. petroleum supply, transp. Petroleum Adminstrn. for War, 1942-45. Bd. administrs. Tulane U. Mem. Mid-Continent Oil and Gas Assn., Ind. Petroleum Assn. Am. (dir.), N.A.M., Tex. Mfrs. Assn. (pres. 1967-68, dir.), Am. Iron and Steel Inst. (dir. 1962-77), Am. Petroleum Inst., La. Bar Assn., Order of Coif. Clubs: Brook Hollow, Dallas, Dallas Gun, Petroleum (Dallas); Boston, Petroleum, Round Table (New Orleans); University (N.Y.C.). Home: 5141 Meaders Ln Dallas TX 75229 Office: PO Box 35888 Dallas TX 75235

WILSON, GEORGE BALCH, educator, composer; b. Grand Island, Neb., Jan. 28, 1927; s. George B. and Helen (Hart) W.; B.Mus., U. Mich., 1951, M.Mus., 1953, D.Mus. Arts, 1962; student Conservatoire Royal de Musique, Brussels, 1953-54; pvt. student Ross Lee Finney, Jean Absil, Nadia Boulanger, Roger Sessions; children—Brian Lewis, James Hugh. Faculty, U. Mich. Sch. Music, Ann Arbor, 1961—, dir. Electronic Music Studio, 1964—; founder, 1966, since mus. dir. Contemporary Directions. Served with USAAF, 1945-46. Recipient Publ. award for String Quartet, Am. Soc. Publ. Am. Music, 1952, Rome prize Am. Acad. Rome, 1958, 59, 60, award and citation Nat. Inst. Arts and Letters, 1970, Walter Hinrichsen award for composers, 1973. Fulbright scholar, Belgium, 1953. Mem. Am. Soc. U. Composers, Phi Kappa Phi, Pi Kappa Lambda, Phi Mu Alpha. Composer: String Quartet, 1950; Sonata for Viola and Piano, 1951; Adagio for Strings and Horns, 1951; Sonata for Cello and Piano, 1952; Overture for Orchestra, 1954; Fantasy for Violin and Piano, 1957; String Trio, 1949, 59; Six Pieces for Piano, 1959; Six Pieces for Orchestra, 1960; Fragments (electronic sound), 1964; incidental electronic music for Sartre's The Flies, 1966; Exigencies (electronic sound), 1968; Concatenations for 12 Instruments, 1969; Polarity for Solo percussion and Electronic Sounds, 1975. Address: Sch Music U Mich Ann Arbor MI 48105

WILSON, GEORGE HOWARD, judge; b. Mattoon, Ill., Aug. 21, 1905; s. George Duncan and Helen Maude (Bresee) W.; A.B., Phillips U., 1926, LL.D., 1975; student U. Mich. Law Sch., 1926-27; LL.B., U. Okla., 1929, J.D., 1970; grad. Nat. Coll. State Trial Judges, U. Nev., 1970; m. Myrna Kathryn Reams, June 26, 1929; children—Jane Kathryn, Sandra Kay, Myrna Lee, George Howard, II. Admitted to Okla. bar, 1928, U.S. Supreme Ct., 1934, U.S. Dist. Ct. of Western Okla., 1930, Supreme Ct. of Neb., 1935, U.S. Dist. Ct. of No. Ill., 1936; practiced in Enid, Okla., 1929—; spl. agt. FBI., U.S. Dept. Justice, 1934-38; city atty., Enid, 1939-42; mem. 81st Congress (1949-51), 8th Dist. of Okla.; dir. Okla. State Crime Bur., 1951-52; judge Superior Ct. Garfield County (Okla.), 1952-69; presiding dist. judge div. 1, 4th Jud. Dist., 1969-77; mem. div. 10, div. 21 Okla. Ct. Appeals, 1969-70; presiding judge Appeal Ct. of Bank Review, 1971-74; chief judge Okla. Administrv. Zone Number 1, 1967. Past pres. bd. dirs. YMCA, Enid; v.p. Great Salt Plains council Boy Scouts of Am.; pres. Enid Community Chest; chmn. adv. bd. St. Mary's Hosp. Served to col., judge adv. gen.'s dept. AUS, 1942-46. Commd. commodore by Okla. gov., 1954; recipient Legionnaire of Honor DeMolay, 1951; Distinguished Alumnus award Phillips U., 1972. Mem. Am., Garfield County, Okla. bar assns., Am. Legion, Okla. Jud. Conf. All State Judges (pres. 1968), Acacia, Phi Delta Phi, Delta Sigma Rho, Order of Coif. Democrat. Presbyn. (elder). Mason (K.T.), Kiwanian (dist. lt. gov. 1961). Home: 1724 West Cherokee Enid OK 73701

WILSON, GEORGE HUGH, educator; b. Circleville, O., July 5, 1922; s. Austin J. and Jessie Mae (Conaway) W.; B.S. in Music Edn., Ohio State U., 1947, Ph.D., 1958; Mus.M., U. Mich., 1950; m. Jean F. Jackson, June 22, 1947; children—Jane L., James W., Judy L. Tchr. pub. schs., Ohio, 1947-53; mem. faculty Bowling Green (O.) State U., 1947-48, Ohio State U., Columbus, 1953-69; bassoonist Ohio State U. woodwind quintet; prof., head music edn. dept. Chgo. Mus. Coll., Roosevelt U., 1969—; 1st bassoonist Columbus Symphony Orch., 1953-61. Condr. Columbus (O.) Youth Symphony, 1955-69. Trustee, Roosevelt U., 1974—. Mem. Music Educators Nat. Conf. (pres. north central div. 1970-72), Ohio Music Edn. Assn. (pres. 1964-66), Pi Kappa Lambda, Phi Mu Alpha, Kappa Kappa Psi, Phi Delta Kappa. Author: (with others) Secondary School Music: Philosophy, Theory, Practice, 1970. Home: 522 Park Ave Elmhurst IL 60126

WILSON, GEORGE WHARTON, newspaperman; b. Phila., Feb. 22, 1923; s. Joshua Wharton and Eva (Frear) W.; B.A., Western Md. Coll., 1947; postgrad. U. Pa., 1948; m. Neva Jean Gossett, Nov. 18, 1950; children-Guy Richard, Lee Robert. Reporter, city editor News-Chronicle, Shippensburg, Pa., 1945-46; asst. news dir. radio sta. WILM, Wilmington, Del., 1947-48; sports editor Evening Chronicle, Uhrichsville, O., 1948-49, editor, 1949-50; editor Daily Record, Morristown, N.J., 1950-54; chief editorial writer Standard-Times, New Bedford, Mass., 1954-59; editorial writer Phila. Inquirer, 1959-64, chief editorial writer, 1964—. Served with USAAF, 1942-45. Recipient George Washington honor medal Freedoms Found., 1961, 67, 72; Phila. Press Assn. award editorial writing, 1967, 68, award for editorial writing Pa. Press Assn., 1972, 79; award for editorial writing U.S. Indsl. Council, 1975, 77, Distinguished Service award Sigma Delta Chi, 1977; Disting. Journalism award Citizens Com. on Public Edn. in Phila., 1978. Mem. Am. Acad. Polit. and Social Sci., Phila. Zool. Soc., Pa. Soc., Franklin Inst., Acad. Natural Sci., Hist. Soc. Pa., Soc. Profl. Journalists, Phila. Mus. Art, Friends of Independence Nat. Hist. Park, Huguenot Hist. Soc. Republican. Conglist. Elk. Club: Pen and Pencil (Phila.). Author: Yesterday's Philadelphia, 1975. Home: Wildman Arms Apartment 530 Swarthmore PA 19081 Office: 400 N Broad St Philadelphia PA 19101

WILSON, GEORGE WILTON, economist, b. Winnipeg, Man., Can., Feb. 15, 1928 (came to U.S. 1952, naturalized 1970); s. Walter and Ida (Wilton) W.; B.Commerce, Carleton U., Ottawa, Can., 1947-50; M.A., U. Ky., 1951; Ph.D., Cornell U., 1955; m. I. Marie McKinney, Sept. 6, 1952; children—Ronald Leslie, Douglas Scott, Suzanne Rita. Economist, Bd. Transp. Commrs., Ottawa, 1951-52; teaching fellow Cornell U., 1952-55; asst. prof. econs. Middlebury (Vt.) Coll., 1955-57; prof. transp. Ind. U., Bloomington, 1957-66, prof. econs., chmn. dept., 1966-70, dean Coll. Arts and Scis., 1970-73. Collaborator study South Asia, 20th Century Fund, 1962-65, dir. research Can.'s needs and resources, 1964-65; dir. case studies role transp. in econ. devel. Brookings Instn., 1964, study transport and econ. devel. of Indochina, 1974; mem. Presdl. Task Force Transp., 1964, 68. Mem. Am. Econ. Assn., Transp. Research Forum (pres. 1969), Gamma Sigma. Author: Essays on Some Unsettled Questions in the Economics of Transportation, 1962; co-author: Mathematical Models and Methods in Marketing, 1961; Canada: An Appraisal of Its Needs and Resources, 1965, The Impact of Highway Investment on Development, 1966; Growth and Change at Indiana U., 1966; Transportation on the Prairies, 1968; Asian Drama, 1968; Essays in Economic Analysis and Policy, 1970; Southeast Asian Regional Transport Survey, 1972. Editor: Classics of Economic Theory, 1964; Technological Development and Economic Growth, 1971. Home: 2325 Woodstock Pl Bloomington IN 47401

WILSON, GERALD LOOMIS, elec. engr., educator; b. Springfield, Mass., Apr. 29, 1939; s. Benjamin J. and Theresa W.; B.S., M.I.T., 1961, M.S., 1963, Sc.D., 1965; m. Marian Saunders Wilson, June 11, 1958; children—Daniel Scott, Karen Elizabeth, Marjorie Ruth, David Owen. Asst. prof. M.I.T., Cambridge, Mass., 1965-70, asso. prof., 1970-76, dir. electric power systems engring. lab., 1971—, Philip Sporn prof. energy processing, 1973—, prof., 1976—, head dept. elec. engring. and computer sci., 1978—; cons. in field. Ford Found. fellow, 1965-67. Fellow IEEE (Hickernell award 1971); mem. Am. Nat. Standards Inst., Am. Phys. Soc., Sigma Xi. Home: 29 Highgate Rd Wayland MA 02139 Office: Rm 38-401 77 Massachusetts Ave Cambridge MA 02139

WILSON, GERALD STANLEY, trumpeter, composer, arranger; b. Shelby, Miss., Sept. 4, 1918; s. Shelby James and Lillian (Nelson) W.; grad. high sch.; m. Josefina Villasenor, Sept. 1, 1950; children—Geraldine, Lillian, Nancy Jo. Trumpeter, composer and arranger for orchs. of Jimmie Lunceford, 1939-42, Count Basie, 1947-49, Duke Ellington, 1947-66; music performed at Carnegie Hall, 1948, 66 Music Center Los Angeles, 1968, Hollywood Bowl, 1967; condr. own orch., 1944—; has arranged and orchestrated for Nancy Wilson, Ray Charles, Al Hibler, Bobby Darin, Julie London, Al Hirt; mus. dir. Redd Foxx TV Show, ABC-TV, 1977-78; contb. orchestrations to library of Ella Fitzgerald; movie credits include Where The Boys Are, Love Has Many Faces, Ken Murray's Hollywood My Home Town. faculty, music dept. San Fernando Valley State Coll., 1969—, Calif. State U. Northridge. Participant Kongsberg (Norway) Jazz Festival, 1973. Served with USNR, 1943-44. Recipient awards Downbeat mag., 1963-64, nominations Nat. Acad. Recording Arts and Scis., 1963, 64. Composer: Royal Suite, 1948; Josefina, 1950; Blues for Yna Yna, 1962; Viva Tirado, 1963; Paco, 1964; El Viti, 1965; Carlos, 1966; Teotihuacan Suite, 1966; Collage, 1968; Debut 52172 (performed Los Angeles Philharmonic Orch.). Home: 4625 Brynhurst Ave Los Angeles CA 90043

WILSON, H. CLIFTON, utilities co. exec.; b. Madison, Ill., Feb. 14, 1924; s. H. Clifton and Frances (Ulffers) W.; B.S., Miss. State U., 1948; postgrad. U. Ida., 1958; m. Joyce Bending, Oct. 3, 1948; children—H. Clifton III, Richard Bending, Elizabeth Anne (Mrs. John P. Buchanan), Frances Patricia, Charles Allen. Dist. and student engr. Miss. Power & Light Co., 1948-50; dist. engr. Cia. Elec. Mexicana del Norte-Torreon, Mexico, 1950-53; power engr. Guanajuato (Mexico) Power & Light Co., 1953-59; asst. mgr. Empresa Electrica de Guatemala-Guatemala, 1959-62, pres., gen. mgr., 1962-64; pres., gen. mgr. Panama Power & Light Co., 1964-68; pres. Ebasco Internat. Corp., N.Y.C., 1968-72; v.p. Central Hudson Gas & Electric Corp., Poughkeepsie, N.Y., 1972-73, sr. v.p., 1973-74, exec. v.p., 1974-75, pres., dir., 1975—; v.p., dir. Empire State Electric Energy Research Corp. Trustee Poughkeepsie Savs. Bank, St. Francis Hosp.; chmn. bd. trustees Marist Coll. Served to lt. USNR, 1942-45. Mem. I.E.E.E., Am. Soc. Guatemala (pres. 1963-64), Am. Soc. Panama (pres. 1968), Kappa Sigma, Tau Beta Pi. Mem. Reformed Ch. Clubs: Metropolitan (N.Y.C.); Dutchess Golf and Country (Poughkeepsie). Home: 19 Carriage Hill Ln Poughkeepsie NY 12603 Office: 284 South Ave Poughkeepsie NY 12601

WILSON, HAROLD GRAHAM, steel co. exec., accountant; b. Dartmouth, N.S., Can., July 21, 1931; s. George Weston and Margaret Agnes W.; B.Commerce, Dalhousie U., Halifax, N.S., 1953; Chartered Accountant, U. Western Ont., 1971; m. Marjorie, May 4, 1957; children—Heather Ann, Karen Margaret. Auditor and accountant Lee & Martin, Halifax, 1953-58; chief fin. officer UN-Middle East, Lebanon and Jordan, 1958-62; chief accountant Dominion Foundries and Steel, Ltd., Hamilton, Ont., 1963-68, asst. sec., 1968-75, corp. sec., 1975—. Mem. Inst. Chartered Accountants Ont., Am. Soc. Corporate Secs., Inst. Chartered Secs. and Adminstrs., Ont. C. of C. (chmn. bd.), Assn. Can. Clubs (chmn.). Anglican. Clubs: Hamilton, Canadian of Hamilton (pres. 1974-75). Home: 3040 First St Burlington ON L7N 1C3 Canada Office: 1330 Burlington St E Hamilton ON Canada

WILSON, HAROLD WOODROW, educator; b. Alcester, S.D., Oct. 21, 1913; s. Gust William and Hilma Christine (Johnson) W.; student Sioux Falls Coll., 1933-34; B.A., S.D. State U., 1942; M.A., U. Kan., 1947; m. Victoria Pollard, July 21, 1956; children—Sharon, Beth. Printer, U. Kan. Press, Lawrence, 1942-43; asst. instr. U. Kans., 1946-47; instr. U. Minn., Mpls., 1947-52, asst. prof., 1952-56, asso. prof., 1956-66, prof. journalism, 1966—; cons. newspapers and mags. Mem. Ayer Award Com. for Selecting Best Typography and Makeup of U.S. Newspapers, 1959. Served with AUS, 1943-46. Internat. Advt. Exec. Assn. Summer fellow Milw. Jour., 1950, N.C. Charlotte Observer, 1953. Mem. Mpls. Advt. Club, Internat. Assn. Bus. Communicators (pres. North Star chpt. 1970), Internat. Graphic Arts Edn. Assn., Assn. for Edn. in Journalism, (bus. mgr. publs., treas. 1966—). Producer filmstrip series on publ. makeup for journalism edn., 1966-68, graphic processes for graphic arts edn., 1965-71. Home: 4459 Benjamin St NE Minneapolis MN 55421

WILSON, HARRIS WARD, educator; b. Frederick, Okla., Sept. 8, 1919; s. John Benjamin and Anna (Harris) W.; A.B., U. Mo., 1941; A.M., U. Chgo., 1947; Ph.D. in English, U. Ill., 1953; children—Golder North, John Robert. Instr., Auburn U., 1947-49; instr. U. Ill., Urbana, 1953-55, asst. prof., 1955-57, asso. prof., 1957-60, prof. English, 1960—. Served to capt. AUS, 1941-46. Decorated Air medal; Guggenheim fellow, 1960-61. Mem. Modern Lang. Assn., Nat. Council Tchrs. English, Am. Assn. U. Profs. Author: Correspondence H.G. Wells-Arnold Bennett, 1960; University Handbook of English, 1960; University Readings, 1962. Editor: The Wealth of Mr. Waddy (H.G. Wells). Contbr. articles to publs. Home: 2015 Vawter Urbana IL 61801

WILSON, HARRY B., pub. relations co. exec.; b. St. Louis, May 17, 1917; s. H. Burgoyne and Margaret (Drew) W.; Ph.B., St. Louis U., 1938; m. Helen Cain, July 27, 1940; children—Margaret Wilson Pennington, Harry B., Andrew B., Daniel B., Josephine Wilson Havlak, Julie, Ellen. Mng. editor Sedalia (Mo.) Capital, 1939-40; reporter Kansas City Star, also state capital bur. chief St. Louis Globe-Democrat, 1940-42; polit. writer, columnist, St. Louis Globe-Democrat, 1946-52; corr. Business Week mag., 1948-52; with Fleishman-Hillard Inc., St. Louis, 1953, sr. partner, 1964-70, pres., 1970-74, chmn. bd., 1974—. Bd. dirs. Laumeier Sculpture Park, St. Louis Symphony Soc. Served with USNR, 1942-46. Home: 5240 Westminster Pl Saint Louis MO 63108 Office: 1 Memorial Dr Saint Louis MO 63102

WILSON, HILLSMAN VAUGHAN, food co. exec.; b. Crewe, Va., Dec. 29, 1928; s. Joseph Henry and Lucy (Vaughan) W.; B.A., Coll. William and Mary, 1951; B.C.L., Marshall Wythe Law Sch., 1953; m. Anne Steuart Gantt, May 15, 1965; children—Pamela H. Wilson Greaves, Richard Hillsman, Daniel Vaughan, Robert Vaughan. Admitted to Va. bar, 1952, Md. bar, 1956; practiced law, Crewe, 1955; with McCormick & Co., Inc., 1955—, v.p. fin., 1973-77, exec. v.p., 1977-79, pres., chief operating officer, 1979—, mem. exec. com., sec., 1969—, also dir.; dir., chmn. bd. McCormick Properties, Inc.; dir. various divs., subs's. McCormick & Co. Inc.; dir. Union Trust Bancorp., Balt. Life Ins.; corporator Savs. Bank of Balt. Bd. dirs. Assn. Ind. Colls. in Md., Greater Balt. chpt. Nat. Found. March of Dimes; trustee endowment assn. Coll. William and Mary. Served to 2d lt. F.A., U.S. Army, 1953, to 1st lt. JAGC, U.S. Army, 1953-55. Mem. Am. Bar Assn., Sigma Nu. Methodist. Clubs: Hunt Valley Golf, Seaview Country, Center. Office: 11350 McCormick Rd Hunt Valley MD 21031

WILSON, HOWARD BAGBY, JR., educator; b. Vicksburg, Miss., Sept. 2, 1935; s. Howard Bagby and Selma Alice (Green) W.; B.S. in Civil Engring., U. Ala., 1957, M.A. in Math., 1959; Ph.D. in Theoretical and Applied Mechanics, U. Ill., 1963; m. Emma Garland Smith, Nov. 13, 1954; children—Robert Louis, Laura Leigh. Instr. engring. mechanics U. Ala., University, 1957-59, asso. prof., 1963-67, prof. mechanics and math., 1963-67, 68—; research engr. Rohm and Haas Co., Huntsville, Ala., 1959-60; research asso. U. Ill., 1960-63; vis. asso. engring. Cal. Inst. Tech., 1967-68; cons. in field. NSF postdoctoral fellow 1967-68. Mem. Am. Soc. Engring. Edn., Sigma Xi, Tau Beta Pi, Pi Mu Epsilon, Chi Epsilon. Contbr. articles to profl. jours. Home: 35 Vestavia Hills Northport AL 35476 Office: PO Box 2908 University AL 35486

WILSON, HUGH HAMILTON, JR., writer, dir., television producer; b. Miami, Fla., Aug. 21, 1943; s. Hugh Hamilton and Frances Xavier (Nugent) W.; B.A., U. Fla., 1965; m. Charters Irwin Smith, Feb. 1, 1978; 1 dau. by previous marriage, Julia Cannon. Pres., Burton Campbell Advt. Agy., Atlanta, 1973-74; free lance writer, dir.; producer Tony Randall Show, 1976-77; creator, exec. producer television series WKRP in Cin., 1978—. Democrat. Roman Catholic. Office: CBS Studio City 4024 Radford Ave Studio City CA 91604

WILSON, HUGH SHANNON, bus. exec.; b. Bklyn., July 1, 1926; s. Matthew and Margaret (Shannon) W.; B.Ch.E., Pratt Inst., 1951; m. Rita Vigliarolo, Feb. 14, 1953; children—Noel C. Wilson Fillers, Hugh V., Hugh S., Hugh T. With Moore Products Co., 1951—, br. mgr., Chgo., 1953-55, Wilmington, Del., 1955-62, mgr. chem. internat., 1966-72, internat. sales mgr., 1972-78, v.p. internat. ops., 1979—. Served with USAAF, 1945. Fellow Instrument Soc. Am. (pres. 1978-79), Inst. Measurement Control. Clubs: Univ., Whist (Wilmington). Home: 2616 Pennington Dr Wilmington DE 19810 Office: Sumneytown Pike Spring House PA

WILSON, IAN ROBERT, soft drink co. exec.; b. Pietermaritzburg, South Africa, Sept. 22, 1929; s. Brian J. and Edna C. Wilson; Canadian citizen; B.Commerce, U. Natal (South Africa), 1952; postgrad. Harvard U. Bus. Sch., 1968; m. Susan Diana Lasch, Jan. 14, 1970; children—Timothy Robert, Christopher James, Diana Louise, Jason Luke. With Coca-Cola Export Corp., Johannesburg, South Africa, 1956-74, mgr. South African region, 1969-72, v.p., regional mgr.,

1972-73, area mgr. So. Africa area, 1973; pres., chief exec. officer Coca-Cola Ltd., Toronto, Ont., Can., 1974-76, chmn. bd., dir., 1976—; exec. v.p. Coca-Cola Co., Atlanta, 1976-79, vice chmn., 1979—; pres. Pacific group, dir. Coca-Cola Export Corp., Atlanta, 1976—. Mem. Church of Eng. Clubs: Durban (South Africa) Country; Inada Hunt and Polo, River (Johannesburg); Granite, Lambton Golf and Country, Griffiths Island Atlantic Salmon (Toronto); Capital City, Commerce (Atlanta). Home: 505 Argonne Dr NW Atlanta GA 30305 Office: PO Drawer 1734 Atlanta GA 30301

WILSON, J. ROBERT, utility co. exec.; b. Meade, Kans., Dec. 3, 1927; s. Robert J. and Bess O. (Osborne) W.; B.A., Kan. U., 1950, LL.B., 1953; m. Marguerite Jean Reiter, Nov. 27, 1960; 1 son, John Ramsey. Admitted to Kans. bar, 1953, Neb. bar, 1961; practiced in Meade, 1953-57; county atty. Meade County, Kans., 1954, 56; city atty., Meade, 1954-57; asst. gen. counsel Kans. Corp. Commn., 1957-59, gen. counsel, 1959-61, mem., 1961; atty. Kans.-Nebr. Natural Gas Co., Inc., Hastings, Nebr., 1961-75, personnel dir., 1964-67, v.p., treas., 1968-75, exec. v.p., 1975-78, pres., 1978—. with USNR, 1945-46. Mem. Phi Kappa Sigma. Democrat. Presbyn. Home: 1327 Heritage Dr Hastings NE 68901 Office: 300 N St Joseph St Hastings NE 68901

WILSON, J. TYLEE, business exec.; b. Teaneck, N.J., June 18, 1931; s. Eric J. and Florence Q. Wilson; A.B., Lafayette Coll., 1953; m. Patricia F. Harrington, July 17, 1970; children—Jeffrey J., Debra L., Christopher F. Group v.p., dir. Chesebrough-Pond's Inc., 1960-74; pres., chief exec. officer, dir. RJR Foods, Inc., 1974-76; chmn. chief exec. officer, dir. R.J. Reynolds Tobacco Internat., Inc., Winston-Salem, N.C., from 1976, exec. v.p., dir. R.J. Reynolds Industries Co. Inc., Winston-Salem, from 1976; now pres., dir. R.J. Reynolds Industries Co., Inc., Winston-Salem. Bd. visitors Wake Forest Coll.; trustee Lafayette Coll. Served with U.S. Army, 1954-56. Clubs: Old Town, Twin City (Winston-Salem); Apawamis Club (Rye, N.Y.); Ocean Reef (Key Largo, Fla.); Ponte Vedra (Fla.). Home: 2585 Club Park Rd Winston-Salem NC 27104 Office: care RJ Reynolds Industries Inc 401 N Main St Winston-Salem NC 27102*

WILSON, JAMES CALDWELL, civil engr.; b. Paris, Tenn., Aug. 18, 1908; s. Quitman L. and Harriett (Tyler) W.; B.S., U. N.Mex., 1935; m. Ruth M. McCarty, Oct. 1, 1937; 1 dau., Rebecca L. Engr., Mountain Bell Telephone Co., Albuquerque, 1935-40, engr., El Paso, Tex., 1940-52, dist. engr., Roswell, N.M., 1952-62, staff engr., Albuquerque, 1962-66, project engr., 1966-73; cons. Limbaugh Engring. Inc., Albuquerque, 1973-74, pres., 1974—; v.p. Bovay Engrs., Inc., 1975—. Named Engr. of Year, N.Mex. Soc. Profl. Engrs., 1963. Registered profl. engr., N.Mex. Mem. Nat. (pres. 1971-72), N.Mex. (past pres.) socs. profl. engrs., Albuquerque C. of C. (past com. chmn.). Episcopalian (pres. Mens Club 1964-65). Kiwanian. Home: 7508 Pickard St NE Albuquerque NM 87110 Office: 3125 Carlisle Blvd NE Albuquerque NM 87110

WILSON, JAMES GRAVES, educator; b. Clarksdale, Miss., Apr. 2, 1915; s. James Preston and Lula Clyde (Pittman) W.; B.A., Miss. Coll., 1936; M.A., U. Richmond, 1938; postgrad. Brown U., 1938-39; Ph.D., Yale, 1942; m. Harriet Chamberlain, Sept. 6, 1941; children—Mary Pittman, James Chamberlain, Arthur Sydney. Instr. in anatomy U. Rochester, 1942-46, asst. prof., 1946-50, sect. head embryology AEC project, 1948-50; asso. prof. anatomy U. Cin., 1950-54, prof., 1954-55; prof., head dept. anatomy U. Fla., Gainsville, 1955-66; prof. research pediatrics and anatomy Children's Hosp. Research Found. Cin., 1966—; designed, prepared originals Wilson-Ward embryology models. Mem. com. on post-doctoral fellowships NSF, 1958-62, human embryology and devel. study sect. NIH, 1962-66, mem. anatomical scis. tng. com., 1966-70; gen. chmn. 2d Teratology Conf., Bethesda, Md., 1957; mem. panel on herbicides Office Sci. and Tech., Exec. Office of Pres., 1969-70; chmn. adv. com. on 2,4,5-T, Environmental Protection Agy., 1970—. Mem. Am. Assn. Anatomists, Soc. Exptl. Biology and Medicine, Teratology Soc. (pres. 1961-62), Toxicology Soc., European Teratology Soc., AAAS, Am. Inst. Biol. Sci., So. Soc. Anatomists (pres. 1963-64), Soc. Developmental Biology, Sigma Xi. Asso. editor Teratology, 1968—, Anatomical Record, 1965—, Teratology and Mammalian Reprodn. Author, editor books, articles to nat. sci. jours. Home: 3223 Hardisty Ave Cincinnati OH 45208

WILSON, JAMES HARGROVE, JR., lawyer; b. Oliver, Ga., Nov. 26, 1920; s. James Hargrove and Louise (Sealy) W.; A.B. with honors, Emory U., 1940; LL.B. summa cum laude, Harvard U., 1947; m. Frances Audra Schaffer, Dec. 24, 1942; children—Susan Frances, James Hargrove. Admitted to Ga. bar, 1947, D.C. bar, 1951; asso. firm Sutherland, Tuttle & Brennan (now Sutherland, Asbill & Brennan), Atlanta and Washington, 1947-53, partner, 1953—; lectr. Emory U., 1959, chmn. bd. visitors, 1967-68; trustee The Northwestern Mut. Life Ins. Co., Milw., 1972—; mem. advisory group Commr. of Internal Revenue, 1963-64. Chmn. bd. trustees Met. Atlanta Crime Commn., 1970-71; mem. Harvard U. Overseers Com. to Visit Law Sch., 1959-65. Served to lt. comdr. USNR, 1942-46. Fellow Am. Bar Found.; Mem. Am. Law Inst. (council 1974—), Am. Bar Assn., State Bar Ga., D.C. Bar, Atlanta Bar Assn., Lawyers Club Atlanta (pres. 1960-61), Am. Judicature Soc., Harvard Law Sch. Assn., Emory U. Alumni Assn. (pres. 1966-67), Phi Beta Kappa, Omicron Delta Kappa, Kappa Alpha Order. Methodist. Clubs: Capital City, Piedmont Driving, Commerce (Atlanta); Harvard of Atlanta, Harvard of N.Y.C. Pres. Harvard Law Review, 1946-47. Home: 3171 Marne Dr NW Atlanta GA 30305 Office: 3100 First National Bank Tower Atlanta GA 30303

WILSON, JAMES LAWRENCE, chem. co. exec.; b. Rosedale, Miss., Mar. 2, 1936; s. James Lawrence and Mary Margaret (Klingman) W.; B.Mech. Engring., Vanderbilt U., 1958; M.B.A., Harvard, 1963; m. Barbara Louise Burroughs, Aug. 30, 1958; children—Lawrence Burroughs, Alexander Elliott. Vice pres. Nyala Properties, Inc., Phila., 1963-65; staff asso. Rohm & Haas Co., Phila., 1965-67, exec. asst. to pres., 1971-72, treas., 1972-74, regional dir. Europe, 1974-77, dir., group v.p. fin. and adminstrn., 1977—; treas. Warren-Teed Pharms., Inc., Columbus, Ohio, 1967-68, v.p., 1969; pres. Consol. Biomed. Labs., Inc., Dublin, Ohio, 1970-71; dir. Rohm and Haas Co. Bd. dirs. Area Council for Econ. Edn., 1977—; bd. mgrs. St. Christopher's Hosp. for Children, 1978—. Served with C.E.C., U.S. Navy, 1958-61. Mem. Pa. Economy League (gov., exec. com. 1977—). Co-author: Creative Collective Bargaining, 1964. Home: 209 Wakefield Rd Rosemont PA 19010 Office: Rohm & Haas Co Independence Mall W Philadelphia PA 19105

WILSON, JAMES Q., educator; m.; 2 children. Henry Lee Shattuck prof. govt. Harvard U., also chmn. task force on core curriculum; former mem. bd. syndics Harvard U. Press. Former chmn., Nat. Adv. Council for Drug Abuse Prevention. Vice chmn. Police Found.; former mem. Commn. on Presdl. Scholars, Sloan Commn. on Cable Communications. Former dir. Joint Center for Urban Studies Mass. Inst. Tech. and Harvard. Author: Negro Politics; Amateur Democrat; City Politics; Varieties of Police Behavior; Political Organizations; Thinking About Crime; The Investigators: Managing FBI and Narcotics Agents; American Government: Institutions and Policies. Address: Littauer Center Harvard Univ Cambridge MA 02138

WILSON, JAMES WARNER, educator; b. Schenectady, Apr. 27, 1923; s. Benjamin Warner and Bessie May (Davis) W.; B.S. in Psychology, St. Lawrence U., 1944; M.A. in Psychology, U. Rochester, 1947; Ph.D. in Edn., U. Chgo., 1954; m. Sally Anne Beck, July 14, 1945; children—Debra JoAnne, Jeffrey James, Rebecca Jane. Mem. faculty Rochester Inst. Tech., 1946-68, vocat. counselor, 1947-54, coordinator Ednl. Research Office, 1954-59, dean Coll. Gen. Studies, 1959-66, dir. Center for Ednl. and Instnl. Research, 1966-68; research prof. coop. edn. Northeastern U., Boston, 1968-75, Asa S. Knowles prof., 1975—, dir. Coop. Edn. Research Center, 1973—; exec. dir. Study of Coop. Edn., 1958-59; dir. research Nat. Commn. for Coop. Edn., 1965—. Vis. fellow Swinburne Coll. Tech., Hawthorn, Victoria, Australia, 1975-76. Mem. Nat. Soc. Study Edn., Am. Ednl. Research Assn., Coop. Edn. Assn. Presbyn. Author: Work-Study College Programs, 1961. Home: 249 Harris Ave Needham MA 02192 Office: Coop Edn Research Center Northeastern U Boston MA 02115

WILSON, JAMES WILLIAM, lawyer; b. Spartanburg, S.C., June 19, 1928; s. James William and Ruth (Greenwaldt) W.; student Tulane U., 1945-46; B.A., U. Tex., Austin, 1950, LL.B., 1951; m. Elizabeth Clair Pickett, May 23, 1952; children—Susan Alexandra, James William. Admitted to Tex. bar, 1951, since practiced in Austin; partner McGinnis, Lochridge & Kilgore, and predecessors, 1960-76; counsel Stubbeman, McRae, Sealy, Laughlin & Browder, 1976—; asst. atty. gen. Tex., 1957-58; counsel Senate Democratic Policy Com., legis. asst. to senate majority leader Lyndon B. Johnson, 1959-60; lectr. U. Tex. Law Sch., 1962-63; dir. Tex. Internat. Airlines, Inc. Served from ensign to lt. (j.g.), USNR, 1952-55. Fellow Tex. Bar Found.; mem. Am., Tex., Travis County bar assns., Am. Law Inst., Order of Coif, Phi Beta Kappa. Home: 2705 Wooldridge Dr Austin TX 78703 Office: 18th Floor Am Bank Tower Austin TX 78701

WILSON, JANE, artist; b. Seymour, Iowa, Apr. 29, 1924; d. Wayne and Cleone (Marquis) Wilson; B.A., U. Ia., 1945, M.A., 1947; m. John Gruen, Mar. 28, 1948; 1 dau., Julia. Exhibited one-man shows include Hansa Gallery, N.Y.C., 1953, 55, 57, Stuttman Gallery, N.Y.C., 1958, 59, Tibor de Nagy Gallery, N.Y.C., 1960-66, Graham Gallery, N.Y.C., 1968, 69, 71, 73, 75, Fischbach Gallery, N.Y.C., 1978; represented in permanent collections Met. Mus., N.Y.C., Mus. Modern Art, Whitney Mus., Wadsworth Atheneum, Heron Art Mus., N.Y. U., Rockefeller Inst., Pa. Acad. Fine Arts, Hirschorn Mus. Washington. Mem. fine arts faculty Parsons Sch. Design, 1973-79; vis. artist U. Iowa, 1974; adj. asso. prof. painting and sculpture Columbia U., 1975-79; Andrew Mellon vis. prof. painting Cooper Union, 1977-78. Ingram-Merrill grantee, 1963; Louis Comfort Tiffany grantee, 1967. Recipient Purchase prize Childe Hassam Fund, 1971, 73, Ranger Fund Purchase prize, 1977. Mem. Phi Beta Kappa. Address: 317 W 83d St New York NY 10024

WILSON, JEAN DONALD, physician; b. Wellington, Tex., Aug. 26, 1932; s. J. D. and Maggie E. (Hill) W.; B.A. in Chemistry, U. Tex., 1951, M.D., 1955. Intern, then resident in internal medicine Parkland Meml. Hosp., Dallas, 1955-58; clin. asso. Nat. Heart Inst., Bethesda, Md., 1958-60; instr. internal medicine U. Tex. Southwestern Med. Sch., Dallas, 1960-61, prof., 1968—. Served as sr. asst. surgeon USPHS, 1958-60. Recipient Oppenheimer award Endocrine Soc., 1972; Amory prize Am. Acad. Arts and Scis., 1977. Diplomate Am. Bd. Internal Medicine. Mem. Am. Fedn. Clin. Research, Am. Soc. Clin. Investigation, Soc. Exptl. Biology and Medicine, Am. Soc. Biol. Chemists, Endocrine Soc., Assn. Am. Physicians. Editor Jour. Clin. Investigation, 1972-77. Home: 4517 Watauga Rd Dallas TX 75209 Office: Dept Internal Medicine U Tex Health Sci Center Dallas TX 75235

WILSON, JOE BRANSFORD, educator, microbiologist; b. Dallas, June 29, 1914; s. William Ringgold and Kate (Bransford) W.; B.A., U. Tex., 1939; M.S., U. Wis., 1941, Ph.D., 1947; m. Dorothy Louise Simmons, Oct. 16, 1944; children—Joe Bransford, Kathleen Scott. Instr. U. Tex., 1939; mem. faculty U. Wis. Madison, 1939-42, 46—, prof. bacteriology, 1947—, chmn. dept. bacteriology, 1968-74, asso. dean Grad. Sch., 1965-69, prof., chmn. dept. med. microbiology, 1976—. Mem. adv. council Chem. Corps, 1955-65; mem. tech. adv. com. Office Sec. Def., 1954-63; mem. bacteriology and mycology study sect. NIH, USPHS, 1965-69. Diplomate Am. Bd. Microbiology. Fellow A.A.A.S., Am. Acad. Microbiology (bd. govs. 1969-75); mem. Am. Soc. Microbiology (council 1970-73), Am. Assn. Immunologists, Soc. Exptl. Biology and Medicine, Soc. Gen. Microbiology (Gt. Britain), Phi Kappa Psi. Author: (with others) Microbiology, 1951; also articles. Editorial bd. Jour. Bacteriology, 1963-69. Home: 3427 Sunset Dr Madison WI 53705

WILSON, JOHN, artist; b. Boston, Apr. 14, 1922; s. Reginald and Violet (Caesar) W.; diploma with highest honors Boston Mus. Sch. (Paige fellow for European study), 1944; B.S. in Edn., Tufts U., 1947; student Fernand Leger's Sch., Paris, France, 1948-49; student (John Hay Whitney fellow) Esmeralda Sch. of Art, Mex.; m. Julia Kowitch, June 25, 1950; children—Rebecca, Roy, Erica. Instr. Boston Mus. Sch., 1949-50, Bd. Edn., N.Y.C., 1959-64; prof. Boston U., 1964—; exhibited at Atlanta U., Smith Coll., Carnegie Inst. Annual Art Show, Library of Congress Print Nationals, Mus. Modern Art, at N.Y.C. Met. Mus. Art, N.Y.C., Rose Art Mus., Brandeis U., Detroit Inst. Arts, Mus. Fine Arts, Boston; represented in permanent collections Boston Pub. Library, Smith Coll., Mus. Modern Art, Atlanta U., Carnegie Inst., Bezalel Mus., Jerusalem, Rose Art Mus., Brandeis U., Howard U., Tufts U., Dept. Fine Arts, French govt. Sculpture fellow Mass. Arts and Humanities Found., 1976. Bd. dirs. Elma Lewis Sch. Fine Arts, Boston, 1970-75. Illustrator children's books: Spring Comes to the Ocean (Jean Craighead George), 1965; Becky (Julia Wilson), 1970; Striped Ice Cream (Joan Lexau), 1968; Malcolm X (Arnold Adoff), 1970. Home: 44 Harris St Brookline MA 02146 Office: 855 Commonwealth Ave Boston MA 02215

WILSON, JOHN ALAN, chem. co. exec., lawyer; b. Glen Ridge, N.J., Sept. 1, 1917; s. Robert and Adelaide Anna (Streubel) W.; grad. Deerfield (Mass.) Acad., 1935, A.B., Princeton U., 1939; LL.B., Yale U., 1942; m. Dorothy Francisco, Aug. 9, 1947; children—Robert Alan, Anne Elizabeth. Admitted to Ohio bar, 1950; house counsel Dresser Industries, Inc., 1949-50; sec. Affiliated Gas Equipment, Inc., 1950-55; dir. law Diamond Shamrock Corp. (formerly Diamond Alkali Co.), Cleve., 1956-61, sec., 1961-79, gen. counsel, 1964—, v.p., 1967—. Legislative asst. to Senator Robert Taft, 1946-49. Mem. St. Luke's Hosp. Assn., also mem. trustees devel. council Served with AUS, 1942-45. Mem. Am., Fed. bar assns., Am. Soc. Corp. Secs. Clubs: Cleveland Skating, Clevelander; Union, Princeton (N.Y.C.); Sea Pines (Hilton Head Island, S.C.). Home: 2684 Leighton Rd Shaker Heights OH 44120 Office: Diamond Shamrock Bldg 1100 Superior Ave Cleveland OH 44114

WILSON, JOHN COWLES, export trading co. exec.; b. Spartanburg, S.C., Sept. 16, 1921; s. Charles Berkeley and Laura Shorter (Cowles) W.; A.B., Emory U., 1942; M.B.A. magna cum laude, Harvard, 1943; m. Margaret Eugenia Creekmore, June 5, 1948; children—Caroline C. (Mrs. Scott Spansenberg), Charles Berkeley II, Laura R. With Horne-Wilson, Inc., Atlanta, distbr. heating, air conditioning, plumbing, metal and appliances, 1947—, pres., 1962-75, vice chmn., 1975—, pres. Multimart Corp., 1975—; chmn. bd. Fed. Res. Bank Atlanta, 1972-73; dir. Haverty Furniture Cos. Inc., Fulton Nat. Bank. Chmn. bd. Met. Atlanta United Appeal, 1966; trustee Beck Emory Fund, 1970—, Agnes Scott Coll., 1972—. Served to 1st lt. U.S. Army, 1943-46. Named Corp. Wholesaler of Yr., Supply House Times mag., 1965; recipient award outstanding contbns. internat. understanding Consular Corps Atlanta, 1970, Citizen of Yr. in Internat. Trade award World Trade Council Atlanta, 1971. Mem. Am. Supply Assn. (pres. 1969), Atlanta C. of C. (pres. 1970, dir. 1968—), Ga. C. of C. (chmn. export com. 1977—), Phi Beta Kappa, Chi Phi, Alpha Kappa Psi. Clubs: Capital City (gov. bd. 1971-73), Commerce (gov. bd. 1970-74), Piedmont Driving (governing bd. 1975—, v.p. 1978—) (Atlanta). Home: 2898 Habersham Rd NW Atlanta GA 30305 Office: 1800 Peachtree Center Bldg 230 Peachtree St NW Atlanta GA 30303

WILSON, JOHN D., univ. adminstr.; b. Lapeer, Mich., Aug. 17, 1931; s. Myron John and Helen (O'Conner) W.; B.A., Mich. State U., 1953, Ph.D., 1965; M.A., Oxford (Eng.) U., 1955; m. Anne Veronica Yeomans, Sept. 21, 1957; children—Stephen, Anthony, Patrick, Sara. Asst. to v.p. acad. affairs Mich. State U., East Lansing, 1958-59, asso. dir. Honors Coll., 1963-65, dir., 1965-67, dir. undergrad. edn., 1967-68; asst. to pres. State U. N.Y., 1959-63; pres. Wells Coll., Aurora, N.Y., 1969-75; v.p. acad. affairs Va. Poly. Inst. and State U., Blacksburg, 1975—, univ. provost, 1976—. Served with USAF, 1955-57. Mem. Assn. Am. Rhodes Scholars, Phi Beta Kappa, Phi Kappa Phi. Home: RFD 1 Box 232 B Blacksburg VA 24060

WILSON, JOHN DENNISTON, investment co. pres.; b. Scranton, Pa., Nov. 9, 1917; s. John D. and Helen (Mott) W.; grad. Lawrenceville Sch., 1937; Asso. Bus. Adminstrn., Nichols Coll., 1940; m. Shirley Jane Mansfield, Sept. 5, 1943; children—Wendy S., John Denniston, Amelia Jane. Salesman, Vick Chem. Co., N.Y.C., 1940-41, Alfred D. McKelvy Co., N.Y.C., 1946-49, Distbrs. Group, Cleve., 1952-55; with Vance, Sanders & Co., Inc., Cleve., 1952-63, Boston, 1963—, v.p., 1962-69, exec. v.p., 1969-73, pres., 1973—, also dir. Served with AUS, 1941-46, 49-52. Methodist. Clubs: Weston (Mass.) Golf; Down Town (Boston). Home: 60 Bullard Rd Weston MA 02193 Office: One Beacon St Boston MA 02108

WILSON, JOHN DONALD, banker, economist; b. McKeesport, Pa., Feb. 8, 1913; s. John Johnston and Katherine A. (Hollerman) W.; B.A. magna cum laude, U. Colo., 1935; M.A. in Econs. (Braker teaching fellow), Tufts Coll., 1937; M.A. in Econs., Harvard, 1940; m. Myriam Rohr, Mar. 10, 1942 (div. Feb. 18, 1950); 1 dau., Nina Marie; m. 2d, Danesi Matthews Hilton, Nov. 3, 1951; children—John Douglas, David Matthews, Mary Danesi. Instr. econs. Harvard, 1937-40; editor Survey of Current Bus., U.S. Dept. Commerce, 1940-42; economist Editor and Publisher, McGraw-Hill Pub. Co., 1946-50, established McGraw-Hill Am. Letter; mem. research and devel. staff N.Y. Life Ins. Co., 1950-51; v.p. charge operations Inst. Internat. Edn., 1951-53; with Chase Manhattan Bank, 1953—, successively bus. cons., v.p. and dir. econ. research, group exec. econ. research, pub. relations and market research, 1961-63, sr. v.p., dir. bank's corp. plans, 1963-69, sr. v.p., dir. econ. group, 1969—; dir. Chase Econometric Assos., 1971—, chmn., 1971-75. Bd. dirs. United Neighborhood Houses, N.Y.C., 1955-78; treas., organizing trustee Found. Library Center, N.Y.C., 1956-63; dir. Asso. Alumni U. Colo., 1959-63; trustee Inst. Internat. Edn., N.Y.C. Served to lt. (j.g.) USNR, 1943-46; OSS. Mem. Council Fgn. Relations, Am. Econ. Assn., Am. Mgmt. Assn. (dir. 1965-68, president's council 1969—), Internat. C. of C. (exec. com. U.S. council 1969—), Am. Statis. Assn., Am. Finance Assn., Phi Beta Kappa, Sigma Chi. Presbyn. Clubs: Economic, Harvard (N.Y.C.). Home: 6 Sunset Ave Bronxville NY 10708 Office: 1 Chase Manhattan Plaza New York NY 10081

WILSON, JOHN ERIC, biochemist; b. Champaign, Ill., Dec. 13, 1919; s. William Courtney and Marie Wynette (Lytle) W.; S.B., U. Chgo., 1941; M.S., U. Ill., Urbana, 1944; Ph.D., Cornell U., 1948; m. Marion Ruth Heaton, June 7, 1947; children—Kenneth Heaton, Douglas Courtney, Richard Mosher. Research asst. Proxylin Products, Inc., Chgo., summers 1941-42, Gen. Foods Corp., Hoboken, N.J., summer, 1943; asst. in chemistry U. Ill., 1941-44; asst. in biochemistry Cornell U. Med. Coll., N.Y.C., 1944-48, research asso., 1948-50; asst. prof. biochemistry U. N.C., Chapel Hill, 1950-60, asso. prof., 1960-65, prof., 1970—, dir. grad. studies, dept. biochemistry, 1965-71, acting dir. neurobiology program, 1968-69, asso. dir. 1969-72, dir., 1972-73; Kenan prof. U. Utrecht (Netherlands), 1978. Scoutmaster Occoneechee council Boy Scouts Am., 1959-66; mem. Chapel Hill Twp. Adv. Council, 1978—; mem. Orange County (N.C.) Planning Bd., 1979—. Fellow AAAS; mem. Am. Chem. Soc., Am. Soc. Biol. Chemists, Am. Soc. Neurochemistry, Soc. Neurosci. (council 1969-70, chmn. fin. com. 1973-78, organizer and mem. exec. com. N.C. chpt. 1974-75) Harvey Soc., N.Y. Acad. Sci., N.C. Acad. Sci., Sigma Xi, Phi Lambda Upsilon, Alpha Chi Sigma, Beta Theta Pi. Contbr. numerous articles on biochemistry and neurochemistry to profl. publs. Home: Route 3 Box 144 Hillsborough NC 27278 Office: U NC Sch Medicine Dept Biochemistry and Nutrition Chapel Hill NC 27514

WILSON, JOHN FREDERICK, educator; b. Ipswich, Mass., Apr. 1, 1933; s. Frederick Colburn and Esther Ryerson (Gregory) W.; A.B., Harvard U., 1954; M.Div., Union Theol. Sem., N.Y.C., 1957, Ph.D., 1962; postgrad. Inst. for Hist. Research, London, 1958-59; m. Ruth Alden Cooke, June 8, 1954; children—Abigail Mira, Nathaniel Carl, Johanna Margaret, Jeremy Stuart. Asst. in instrn., lectr. dept. religion Barnard Coll., Columbia, 1956-58; instr., asst. prof., asso. prof., prof., Collord prof., chmn. dept. religion Princeton, 1960—, asst. dean of Coll., 1965-72. Mem. Am. Soc. Ch. History (pres. 1976), Am. Hist. Assn., Soc. for Values in Higher Edn. Author: Pulpit in Parliament, 1969; Public Religion in American Culture, 1979; editor, contbr.: Church and State in American History, 1965; contbr. articles to profl. jours. Home: 820 Kingston Rd Princeton NJ 08540

WILSON, JOHN JOHNSTON, lawyer; b. Washington, July 25, 1901; s. John Henry and Mattie Belle (Coursey) W.; LL.B., George Washington U., 1921, LL.D. (hon.), 1978; m. Alice Adelaide Grant, Sept. 25, 1923 (dec. Apr. 1978); m. 2d, Betty M. Rawlings, Aug. 18, 1979. Admitted to D.C. bar, 1922, since practiced in Washington; mem. Whiteford, Hart, Carmody & Wilson 1940-76, formerly sr. partner, now of counsel; asst. U.S. atty. D.C., 1931-40, chief asst., 1938-40; mem. com. on admissions and grievances U.S. Dist. Ct., D.C. 1945-58, vice chmn. commn. Jud. Disabilities and Tenure, 1971-73; mem., then chmn. personnel security rev. bd. AEC, 1957-71. Hon. trustee George Washington U. (charter trustee 1962-77). Recipient alumni achievement award George Washington U., 1965. Fellow Am. Coll. Trial Lawyers; mem. Am., D.C. (Lawyer of Year 1962) bar assns., D.C. Bar, Kappa Alpha, Phi Delta Phi. Republican. Baptist. Clubs: Barristers (past pres.), Lawyers, Metropolitan. Home: 3900 Watson Pl NW Washington DC 20016 Office: 1050 17th St NW Washington DC 20036

WILSON, JOHN LONG, educator, physician; b. Sturgis, Ky., Feb. 9, 1914; s. Clarence Herbert and Anna Opie (Long) W.; B.A., Vanderbilt U., 1935; M.D., Harvard, 1939; m. Janice Lee Schwensen, July 10, 1944; children—Rosser Schwensen, John Randolph, Wyndham Hopkins, Burgess Christiansen, Damaris Ann. Intern, resident Mass. Gen. Hosp., 1939-42, 46-49; resident U.S. Naval Hosp., Chelsea, Mass., 1945-46; clin. instr. surgery Stanford Med.

Sch., 1949-52; asst. prof. surgery Washington U. Sch. Medicine (posted to med. schs. in Bangkok, Thailand), 1952-53; prof. surgery Am. U., Beirut, Lebanon, 1953-68, dean faculties med. scis., 1966-68; asso. clin. prof. surgery U. Cal. Sch. Medicine, San Francisco, 1958-60; chief surgery Ft. Miley VA Hosp., San Francisco, 1958-60; prof. surgery, asso. dean Stanford Sch. Medicine, 1968-70, 71—, acting dean, 1970-71. Served from lt. (j.g.) to lt. comdr. M.C., USNR, 1942-46. Diplomate Am. Bd. Surgery, Bd. Thoracic Surgery. Mem. A.M.A., A.C.S., Am. Assn. Thoracic Surgery, Internat. Soc. Surgery. Author: Handbook of Surgery, 5th edit., 1973. Home: 87 Crescent Dr Palo Alto CA 94301 Office: Deans Office Sch Medicine Stanford CA 94305

WILSON, JOHN RIGBY, mech. engr.; b. Wake Forest, W.Va., Sept. 26, 1924; s. John Rigby and Julia (Gardiner) W.; B.Mech. Engring., Gen. Motors Inst., 1950; M.S., U. Mich., 1961; m. Mary Ellen McBee, June 5, 1945; children—Douglas, Beth. With AC Spark Plug div. Gen. Motors Corp., 1961—, works mgr., 1967, gen. mgr., Flint, Mich., 1976—. Bd. regents Gen. Motors Inst.; regional v.p. for adminstrn. Boy Scouts Am., 1979-80; v.p. bd. dirs. Urban Coalition. Served with USAAF, 1943-46. Mem. Soc. Automotive Engrs., Mfrs. Assn. Flint (pres.), Flint C. of C. (chmn. pvt. industry council), Tau Beta Pi, Beta Gamma Sigma. Office: 1300 N Dort Hwy Flint MI 48556*

WILSON, JOHN STEUART, author; b. Elizabeth, N.J., Jan. 6, 1913; s. Wylie G. and Alice (Niven) W.; A.B., Wesleyan U., Middletown, Conn., 1935; M.S., Columbia Sch. Journalism, 1942; m. Susan Barnes, Jan. 2, 1950; children—Gordon Barnes, Duncan Hoke. Promotion, product devel. Vick Chem. Co., N.Y.C., 1935-41; entertainment editor, sports editor, columnist PM, N.Y.C., 1942-49; New York editor Down Beat mag., N.Y.C., 1948-50; editor Common Council for Am. Unity, N.Y.C., 1951-52; jazz critic N.Y. Times, also High Fidelity Mag., 1952—. Author: The Collector's Jazz: Traditional and Swing, 1958; The Collector's Jazz: Modern, 1959; Jazz: The Transition Years, 1966. Producer, commentator: The World of Jazz, radio sta. WQXR, N.Y.C., 1954-70, Jazz Today, Voice of America, 1971—. Address: RD 1 Princeton NJ 08540

WILSON, JOHN TODD, educator; b. Punxsutawney, Pa., Mar. 7, 1914; s. Clark Hayes and Alice (Haire) W.; A.B. with distinction, George Washington U., 1941; M.A., State U. Iowa, 1942; Ph.D., Stanford U., 1948; m. Ann B. Camilli, Nov. 23, 1939. Asst. exec. sec. Am. Psychol. Assn., 1948-49; asst. prof. psychology George Washington U., 1949; head personnel and tng. res. br. Office Naval Research, 1949-52; program dir. for psychology NSF, 1952-55, asst. dir. for biol. and med. sci., 1955-61; prof. psychology U. Chgo., 1961—, spl. asst. to pres., 1961-63, v.p., dean faculties, 1968-69, provost, 1969-75, provost, acting pres., 1975, pres., 1975-78, prof. higher edn., 1978—. Served from ensign to lt. comdr. USNR, 1942-46. Mem. AAAS, Am. Acad. Arts and Scis., Phi Beta Kappa, Sigma Xi. Home: 5555 S Everett Ave Chicago IL 60637

WILSON, JOHN TUZO, geologist; b. Ottawa, Ont., Can., Oct. 24, 1908; s. John Armitstead and Henrietta Loetitia (Tuzo) W.; student Ashbury Coll., Ottawa, 1919-25; B.A., Trinity Coll., U. Toronto, 1930; M.A., U. Cambridge, 1940; Sc.D., 1958; Ph.D., Princeton, 1936; LL.D., Carleton U., 1958, Simon Fraser U., 1978; D.Sc., U. Western Ont., 1958, Acadia U., Meml. U. Nfld., 1968, Franklin and Marshall Coll., 1969, McGill U., 1973, U. Toronto, 1977, Laurentian U., 1978; D.Univ., U. Calgary, 1972; m. Isabel Jean Dickson, Oct. 29, 1938; children—Patricia Isabel, Susan Loetitia Clark. Staff, Geol. Survey of Can., 1936-39; prof. geophysics U. Toronto, 1946-74, also prin. Erindale Coll.; dir. gen. Ont. Sci. Centre, 1974—; flight over North Pole, May 1946, 1st ascent of Mt. Hague, Mont., 1935. Served as 2d lt. to col., Canadian Army, 1939-46, 4 yrs. overseas; dept. dir. Exercise Musk-ox. Decorated companion Order of Can.; officer Order of Brit. Empire; recipient Vetlesen prize Columbia U., 1978. Fellow Royal Soc. Can., Geol. Soc. Am., Royal Soc. London; mem. Nat. Acad. Scis. (fgn. asso.), Arctic Inst. N.Am. (pres. 1947-48), Internat. Union Geodesy and Geophysics (pres. 1957-60), Am. Acad. Arts and Scis., Royal Canadian Geographic Soc. (v.p.), Am. Philos. Soc. (hon.). Anglican. Author: One Chinese Moon, 1959; (with J.A. Jacobs, R.D. Russell) Physics and Geology, 1959, 2d edit., 1973; IGY: Year of the New Moons, 1961; Unglazed China, 1973; editor: Continents Adrift, 1972; Continents Adrift and Continents Aground, 1976. Home: 27 Pricefield Rd Toronto ON M4W 1Z8 Canada

WILSON, KEITH LEROY, educator, musician; b. Garden City, Kans., Aug. 15, 1916; s. John William and Mary Ena (Patrie) W.; B.S. in Music Edn., U. Ill., 1938, Mus.B., 1939, Mus.M., 1942; m. Rachel Louise Smith, June 11, 1939; children—Joem Christy, Laura Beth, Holly Marie, Heidi Louise. Instr. woodwind instruments, theory, also asst. condr. bands U. Ill., 1938-46; mem. faculty Yale, 1946—, prof. music, 1960—, also dir. Summer Sch. Music and Art, asso. dean, 1973. Served with USAAF, 1943-45. Mem. Coll. Band Dirs. Nat. Assn. (pres. 1962), Am. Bandmasters Assn. Arranger: (concert band) Le Journal du Printemps, 1951; Three Contemporaries (Douglas Moore), 1959; Symphonic Metamorphosis on Themes by Carl M. von Weber (Hindemith), 1962. Home: 38 Giles St Hamden CT 06517 Office: Yale Univ Sch Music New Haven CT 06520

WILSON, KEMMONS, realtor, motel co. exec.; b. Osceola, Ark., Jan. 5 1913; s. Charles Kemmons and Ruby (Hall) W.; ed. pub. schs.; m. Dorothy Lee, Dec. 2, 1941; children—Spence, Robert, Kemmons, Betty, Carol. Builder, realtor, Memphis, 1945—; founder, owner first Holiday Inn, Memphis, 1952; Holiday Inns of Am., Inc., formed 1953, now chmn. bd. co. operating 1,708 inns in U.S., Can., P.R., Bahamas, Hawaii, Europe, Asia, South Africa; pres. Kemmons Wilson, Inc., 1946—, Kemmons Wilson Realty Co. 1948—. Exec. com. bd. govs. Am. Acad. Achievement; adv. com. U. Tenn. Devel. Council. Trustee Lambuth Coll.; bd. dirs. Memphis State U.; bd. mgrs. Meth. Hosp. Served as flight officer Air Transport Command, 1942-45. Recipient Horatio Alger award, 1970. Mem. Home Builders Assn. Memphis (past pres.), Chief Execs. Forum, Memphis C. of C. (past chmn.), Sportsman Pilot Assn. Methodist (steward). Mason (Shriner, Jester). Clubs: University, Variety, Memphis Country. Home: 3615 S Galloway Dr Memphis TN 38111 Office: 3742 Lamar Ave Memphis TN 38118

WILSON, KENNETH, coll. dean; b. Pasadena, Calif., Jan. 9, 1911; s. Ben and Jennie (McIlrath) W.; B.S.C., State U. Iowa, 1931, M.A., 1939, Ph.D., 1949; m. Edith Akery, June 15, 1934 (dec.); children—Terry Lane, Sherry Lee; m. 2d, Leone Shallow, Apr. 19, 1972. Prin. high sch., Alburnett, Iowa, 1932-38; chmn. retailing, salesmanship program East High Sch., Des Moines, Iowa, 1938-43; instr. Iowa State Coll., 1946- 47; instr. State U. Iowa, 1947-48, asso. prof., chmn. marketing, 1948-50, 50-53, prof., dir. curriculum in food distbn., 1953-56, dir. div. bus. and head dept. gen. bus. Coll. Bus. and Pub. Service, 1956-58, asst. dean Coll. Bus. and Pub. Service, in charge div. bus. and econs., head dept. gen. bus., 1958, asst. dean grad. studies Coll. Bus. and Pub. Service, Mich. State U., 1958; dean Coll. Bus. Adminstrn., U. Cin., 1958-72, prof. bus. adminstrn., 1972—. Dir. Sheridan Assos., Inc., Sheridan Sales Co., Standard Fed. Savs. & Loan Assn., Cin., C.E.T., Inc. Dep. chmn. Cin. Regional Postmaster's Selection Bd.; past dir. Nat. Inst. Orgn. Mgmt.; past pres. Cin. Sales Execs. Council; dir. Jr. Achievement Greater Cin., Citizens School Com.; dir. George A. Ramlose Found. Served from lt. (j.g.) to lt. comdr. USNR, 1943-46. Mem. Am. Marketing Assn. (dir.), Sales and Marketing Execs. Internat. (past dir.), Midwest Econs. Assn., Soc. Advancement Mgmt., Acad. Mgmt., Financial Execs. Inst., Alpha Kappa Psi, Beta Gamma Sigma. Beta Alpha Psi. Order of Artus. Clubs: Sales Executives (past dir., v.p.) (Lansing); Sales Executives Council (dir.) (Cin.). Contbr. articles profl. jours. Home: 6689 Apache Circle Cincinnati OH 45243

WILSON, LANFORD, playwright; b. Lebanon, Mo., Apr. 13, 1937; s. Ralph E(ugene) and Violetta (Tate) W.; student San Diego State Coll., 1955-56. Playwright, 1962—; resident playwright, dir. Circle Repertory Co., N.Y.C., 1969—. Recipient Vernon Rice award, 1966-67, Obie award, 1972, 75, Outer Critics Circle, Drama Critics Circle awards, 1973; Rockefeller grantee, 1967, 73; ABC Yale fellow, 1969; Guggenheim grantee, 1970. Author plays including: So Long at the Fair, 1963, Home Free, No Trespassing, The Madness of Lady Bright, 1964, Ludlow Fair, Balm in Gilead, This is the Rill Speaking, 1965, The Gingham Dog, The Rimers of Eldritch, 1966, Wandering, Days Ahead, 1967, Lemon Sky, 1969, Serenading Louie, The Great Nebula in Orion, 1970, The Hot L Baltimore, The Family Continues, 1972; The Mound Builders, 1975; 5th of July, 1978; Talley's Folly, 1979; author books: Balm in Gilead and Other Plays, 1966, The Rimers of Eldritch and Other Plays, 1968, The Gingham Dog, 1969, Lemon Sky, 1970, The Hot L Baltimore, 1973, The Mound Builders, 1976; 5th of July, 1979.

WILSON, LAUREN ROSS, univ. dean; b. Yates Center, Kans., May 4, 1936; s. Roscoe C. and Margaret D. Wilson; B.S., Baker U., Baldwin, Kans., 1958; Ph.D., U. Kans., 1963; m. Janie Haskin, Jan. 25, 1959; children—Lance Kevin, Keela Lynn. Mem. faculty Ohio Wesleyan U., Delaware, 1963—, prof. chemistry, 1971—, dean acad. affairs, 1978—; vis. prof. Ohio State U., 1968, 74; vis. research asso. Oak Ridge Nat. Lab., 1972-73. Recipient Outstanding Tchr. award Ohio Wesleyan U., 1968. Mem. Am. Chem. Soc., AAAS, AAUP, Chem. Soc. London, Ohio Acad. Sci., Sigma Xi. Office: Ohio Wesleyan Univ S Sandusky St Delaware OH 43015

WILSON, LELAND LESLIE, ret. educator; b. Williamsburg, Ky., June 13, 1914; s. Albert and Susan (Stinson) W.; B.S., Eastern Ky. U., 1934; M.S., U. Ky., 1941; Ph.D., George Peabody Coll., 1951; postgrad. Vanderbilt U., 1949-50; m. Margaret Harvin, June 4, 1938; children—Nancy Elizabeth (Mrs. Gerald Ashbach), Mary Sue (Mrs. Kenneth Coleman), Rebecca Wilson (Mrs. Robert Brunswig, Jr.). Tchr. high sch., 1933-42; asst. prof. Eastern Ky. U., 1951-52; faculty Ga. Tchrs. Coll., Statesboro, 1952-55, prof., 1953-55; prof. chemistry U. No. Iowa, Cedar Falls, 1955-79. NSF Sci. Faculty fellow chemistry dept. U. Wis., 1959. Mem. Am. Chem. Soc., A.A.A.S., Ia. Acad. Sci., Nat. Sci. Tchrs. Assn. Author: (with Willard Poppy) Exploring the Physical Sciences, 1965, 2d edit., 1973; (with W. Poppy) The Physical Sciences, 1970. Home: 349 Colony Blvd Lexington KY 40502

WILSON, LEWIS KENNETH, librarian; b. Lamar, Colo., Mar. 15, 1925; s. Ben R. and Effie B. (Kenner) W.; A.A., Colo. Coll., 1947; B.A., UCLA, 1949; M.S. in L.S., U. So. Calif., 1952; m. Wilma D. Fledderman, Sept. 6, 1956; 1 dau., Heidi C. Geology librarian, asst. head dept. circulation UCLA, 1947-55; bus. and tech. librarian, acting city/county librarian Santa Barbara (Calif.) Public Library, 1957-59; librarian Palo Alto City (Calif.) Library, 1959-68; mgr. dir. dept. community services City of Palo Alto, 1968-73; librarian Burbank (Calif.) Public Library, 1973-78; librarian San Diego Public Library, 1978—. Sec., bd. dirs. YMCA, Palo Alto, 1963-73, Burbank, 1972-73; bd. dirs. Palo Alto/Stanford United Way, 1968-73; pres. Burbank chpt. ARC, 1972-73; bd. dirs. Burbank Hist. Commn., 1970-73; pres. Burbank Sister City Commn., 1972; bd. dirs. San Diego-Tema Sister City Soc., 1978—. Served with U.S. Army, 1943-46. Mem. ALA, Calif. Library Assn., Beta Theta Pi. Democrat. Editor, compiler Know Your Geology Library, 1954, Know Your Geologic Literature, 1955. Home: 5415 Mantua Ct San Diego CA 92124 Office: 202 C St San Diego CA 92101

WILSON, LIONEL J., mayor Oakland (Calif.); b. 1915; A.B., J.D., U. Calif. Judge, Superior Ct. Calif., to 1977; mayor of Oakland, 1977—. Office: City Hall 14th and Washington Sts Oakland CA 94612

WILSON, LOUIS HUGH, marine corps officer; b. Brandon, Miss., Feb. 11, 1920; s. Louis and Bertha (Buchanan) W.; B.A., Millsaps Coll., 1941, LL.D. (hon.), 1976; H.H.D. (hon.), Rollins Coll., 1978; m. Jane Clark, Nov. 14, 1944; 1 dau., Janet. Commd. 2d lt. USMC, 1941, advanced through grades to gen., 1975; co. officer 9th Marine Regt., Guadalcanal, Bougainville, Guam, 1942-44; detachment comdr. Marine Barracks, Washington, 1944-46; aide-de-camp to comdg. gen. Fleet Marine Force, Pacific, 1946-48; recruiting officer, N.Y.C., 1949-51; comdg. officer 1st Tng. Bn., also various staff assignments Marine Corps Edn. Center, Quantico, Va., 1951-54; asst. G-3, asst. chief staff G-3, also bn. comdr. 1st Marine Div., 1954-56; staff officer G-3 div. Hdqrs. U.S. Marine Corps, 1956-58; comdg. officer Tng. and Test Regt., Quantico, 1958-60, Basic Sch., Quantico, 1960-61; staff officer Hdqrs. USMC, 1962-64; asst. chief staff G-3, 1st Marine Div., 1964-66; dir. 6th MarCorDist, Atlanta, 1966-67; legislative asst. to commandant MarCor, Hdqrs. USMC, 1967-68; chief staff Fleet Marine Force, Pacific, 1968-70; comdg. gen. I MAF/3d Marine Div., 1970-71; dir. Edn. Center, Quantico, 1971-72; comdg. gen. Fleet Marine Force, Pacific, 1972-75; comdt. Marine Corps, Washington, 1975—; mem. Joint Chiefs Staff, 1978—; mem. Am. Battle Monuments Commn., 1978—; dir. Unifirst Fed. Savs. and Loan Assn. Chmn. bd. mgrs. Navy Relief Soc., 1978—. Decorated Medal of Honor, Def. D.S.M., Legion of Merit with combat V and 2 gold stars, Purple Heart with 2 stars; recipient Golden Plate award Am. Acad. Achievement, Gold medal Nat. Football Found. and Hall of Fame, 1977; Spl. Timmie Americanism award Touchdown Club, Washington, 1978. Mem. Congl. Medal of Honor Soc., Marine Corps Assn., 3d Marine Div. Assn. Presbyn. Club: Army Navy Country. Office: Comdt USMC HQ MC Washington DC 20380. *I feel that the primary influences upon my life were the principles, ideas, goals, and standards of conduct assimilated in a family environment and from religious and educational institutions. These influences served, throughout my life, as a frame of reference in making individual or collective judgements and decisions of social, economic and professional import.*

WILSON, LUTHER, editor; b. Pineville, Ky., Feb. 2, 1944; s. Luther and Lillian R. (Lee) W.; B.A., Oakland U., 1964; 1 son, Eric Thomas. Vol., Peace Corps, Dominican Republic, 1965-66; salesman Holt, Rinehart & Winston, Ind., 1967-68; salesman Harper & Row, Pubs., Chgo., 1969, editor sociology and polit. sci., N.Y.C., 1970-72; editor Cambridge U. Press, N.Y.C., 1972-76, editor-in-chief U. Okla. Press, 1976—. Mem. Am. Anthropol. Assn. Home: 1530 Briar Meadow Norman OK 73071 Office: 1005 Asp Norman OK 73019

WILSON, M(ATHEW) KENT, educator; b. Salt Lake City, Dec. 22, 1920; s. Mathew Bytheway and Helen Marie (Marsh) W.; B.S., U. Utah, 1943; Ph.D., Calif. Inst. Tech., 1949; m. Gladys E. Acevedo, Oct. 25, 1944; 1 son, Mathew K. Instr. Harvard, 1948- 51, asst. prof., 1951-56; prof. chemistry, chmn. Tufts U., 1956-66, Robinson prof., 1957-66; head chemistry sect. Nat. Sci. Found. 1966-74, head office Energy Related Gen. Research, 1974-75, dep. asst. dir. math. and phys. scis. and engring. directorate, 1975-77, sr. sci. asso. office of the dir., 1977, dir. office of planning and resource mgmt., 1977—. Fulbright research scholar, 1954-55, Guggenheim fellow, 1954-55. Fellow Am. Acad. Arts and Scis.; mem. Am. Chem. Soc., Sigma Xi. Author: General Chemistry: A Topical Introduction, 1954. Contbr. articles profl. jours. Office: 1800 G St Washington DC 20550

WILSON, MALCOLM, lawyer, banker, former gov. N.Y. State; b. N.Y.C., Feb. 26, 1914; s. Charles H. and Agnes (Egan) W.; B.A., Fordham U., 1933, LL.B., 1936, LL.D., 1959; LL.D., Siena Coll., 1959, Pace Coll., 1959, St. Bonaventure Coll., 1960, SUNY, 1978, Bklyn. Law Sch., 1962, Canisius Coll., 1963, Le Moyne Coll., 1964, St. John Fisher Coll., 1964, Manhattan Coll., 1964, Columbia U., 1974; L.H.D., Alfred U., 1961; m. Katharine McCloskey, Sept. 6, 1941; children—Kathy, Anne. Admitted to N.Y. State bar, 1936, since practiced in White Plains; partner firm Kent, Hazzard, Jaeger, Wilson, Freeman & Greer, 1946-77; chmn. bd., chief exec. officer Manhattan Savs. Bank, 1977—; mem. N.Y. State Assembly from 1st Westchester Dist., 1939-58; lt. gov. N.Y. State., 1959-73, gov., 1974; dir. Shearson Hayden Stone Inc., Colin Service Systems, Inc., Levin Fixture Corp.; trustee Manhattan Savs. Bank. Bd. dirs. Catholic Youth Orgn., Archdiocese N.Y., Farmers Mus., N.Y. State Hist. Assn.; trustee NCCJ. Served with USNR, 1943-45. Recipient John Peter Zenger award N.Y. State Soc. Newspaper Editors, 1957. Mem. Am. Bar Assn., N.Y. State Bar Assn., Westchester County Bar Assn., Ancient Order Hibernians, Soc. Friendly Sons St. Patrick, N.Y. Farm Bur. Club: K.C. Home: 24 Windsor Rd Scarsdale NY 10583 Office: 385 Madison Ave New York NY 10017

WILSON, MARGARET BUSH, lawyer, civil rights leader; b. St. Louis, Jan. 30, 1919; B.A. cum laude, Talladega Coll., 1940; LL.B., Lincoln U., 1943; 1 son, Robert Edmund. Individual practice law, St. Louis, 1947-65; now with firm Wilson, Smith & Smith; asst. dir. St. Louis Lawyers for Housing, 1969-72; dep. dir./acting dir. St. Louis Model City Agency, 1968-69; adminstr. Mo. Commn. Service and Continuing Edn., 1967-68; asst. atty. gen. Mo., 1961-62; atty. Rural Electrification Adminstrn., Dept. Agr., St. Louis, 1943-45; instr. civil procedure St. Louis U. Sch. Law, 1971; chmn. St. Louis Land Reutilization Authority, 1975-76; mem. Mo. Council Criminal Justice, 1972—; treas. NAACP Nat. Housing Corp., 1971, chmn. nat. bd., 1975; dir. Monsanto Co. Mem. gen. adv. com. U.S. Arms Control and Disarmament Agy., 1978—; trustee Washington U., St. Louis; nat. bd. dirs. ARC, United Way, Police Found. Mem. St. Louis Arts and Edn. Council, Am., Nat., Mo., Mound City, St. Louis bar assns., Alpha Kappa Alpha. Recipient Bishop's award Episcopal Diocese Mo., 1962; Juliette Derricotte fellow, 1939-40. Office: care NAACP 1790 Broadway New York NY 10019 also Wilson Smith & Smith 4054 Lindell Blvd Saint Louis MO 63108

WILSON, MARJORIE PRICE, physician, assn. exec.; b. Pitts., Sept. 25, 1924; d. Robert John and Grace Alma (McMillen) Price; student Bryn Mawr Coll., 1942-45; M.D., U. Pitts., 1949; m. Lynn Minford Wilson, Sept. 15, 1951; children—Lynn Deyo, Liza Price. Intern, U. Pitts. Med. Center Hosps., 1949-50; resident Children's Hosp. U. Pitts., 1950-51, Jackson Meml. Hosp., U. Miami Sch. Medicine, 1954-56; chief residency and internship div. edn. service Office of Research and Edn., VA, Washington, 1956, chief profl. tng. div., 1956-60, asst. dir. edn. service, 1960; chief tng. br. Nat. Inst. Arthritis and Metabolic Disease, NIH, 1960-63, asst. to asso. dir. for tng. Office of Dir., NIH, 1963-64; asso. dir. extramural programs Nat. Library Medicine, 1964-67; asso. dir. program devel. OPPD, NIH, 1967-69, asst. dir. program planning and evaluation, Bethesda, Md., 1969-70; dir. dept. instl. devel. Assn. Am. Med. Colls., Washington, 1970—; mem. Inst. Medicine, Nat. Acad. Scis., 1974—; bd. visitors U. Pitts. Sch. Medicine, 1974—; mem. governing bd. Robert Wood Johnson Health Policy Fellowships, 1975—; trustee Analytic Services, Inc., Falls Church, Va., 1976—. Mem. Assn. Am. Med. Colls., Am. Fedn. Clin. Research, Am. Med. Women's Assn., AAAS, IEEE. Episcopalian. Contbr. articles to profl. jours. Home: 6913 Bradley Blvd Bethesda MD 20034 Office: Assn Am Med Colls One DuPont Circle Washington DC 20034

WILSON, MARK CURTIS, entomologist; b. Ware, Mass., Sept. 19, 1921; s. Lyndon Benjamin and Clara Belle (Richardson) W.; B.S., U. Mass., 1944; M.S., Ohio State U., 1946, postgrad., 1946-47. Grad. asst. Ohio State U., 1944-47; entomologist Purdue U. Agrl. Expt. Sta., 1947—, asst. prof. entomology, Sch. Agr., 1955-64, asso. prof., 1964-72, prof., 1972—. Fellow Ind. Acad. Sci.; mem. Am. Registry Profl. Entomologists, Entomol. Soc. Am. Clubs: Masons, K.T. Author: (with others) Practical Insect Pest Management, 6 mans., 1977-78; contbr. numerous articles on cereal and forage crop pest mgmt. to profl. jours. Home: 2236 Miami Tr West Lafayette IN 47906 Office: Dept Entomology Purdue U West Lafayette IN 47907

WILSON, SISTER MARY LAWRENCE, clergywoman, educator; b. Toledo, June 6, 1907; d. Frank Dean and Margaret Agnes (Casey) Wilson; student Mary Manse Coll., 1927-30; B.S. in Edn., DeSales Coll., 1936; M.A., Fordham U., 1946, Ph.D., 1948. Elementary sch. tchr., 1927-41; elementary sch. supr. gen. edn., 1947-48; dean Mary Manse Coll., Toledo, 1949-64, pres., 1964-68, prof. edn., 1968—; curriculum dir. Toledo Diocesan Schs., 1971—; prin. St. Angela Hall, 1977-79. Mem. Mayor's Dist. Council for Urban Renewal, Toledo. Trustee Med. Coll. Ohio, Toledo, 1964—, Med. Coll. of Ohio at Toledo Found., Inc. Recipient Stella Maris medal Mary Manse Coll., Mother Adelaide award Lourdes Coll. Mem. Phi Kappa Phi. Club: Zonta Internat. Roman Catholic. Home: 2413 Collingwood Blvd Toledo OH 43620

WILSON, MARY LOUISE, educator; b. Chgo., June 29, 1940; d. John Baptiste and Marion Margaret (Coveney) Sweig; student U. Toronto, 1960-61; B.A., Smith Coll., 1962; M.A., Emerson Coll., 1965; Ph.D., Northwestern U., 1968; m. John Paul Wilson, June 7, 1969; 1 son, Devin Sweig. Asso. prof. speech pathology California (Pa.) State Coll., 1968-69; prof. communication scis. and disorders U. Vt., 1969—, dir. program in communication sci. and disorders, 1971—, acting chmn., 1977—, dir. E. M. Luse Center for Communication Disorders, 1971—; cons. Head Start, South Burlington (Vt.) Pub. Schs.; mem. Vt. State Adv. Com. on Spl. Edn., 1974; project dir. Bur. Edn. of Handicapped, 1971—. Dir., Hinesburg Sch. Bd. Mem. AAUP, Am. Speech and Hearing Assn., Am. Assn. Mental Deficiency, Linguistic Soc. Am., Vt. Speech and Hearing Assn. Author: Wilson Initial Syntax Program, 1972; Wilson Expanded Syntax Program, 1976; Syntax Remediation: A Generative Grammar Approach to Language Development, 1977; Prescriptive Analysis of Language Disorders: Receptive Syntax Assessment, 1979; Expressive Syntax Assessment, 1979. Home: Rural Free 1 Box 468 Hinesburg VT 05461 Office: Allen House U Vt Burlington VT 05405

WILSON, MAURICE JULIUS, lawyer; b. New Orleans, Aug. 16, 1909; s. Maurice Cannon and Katherine (Thompson) W.; student Va. Mil. Inst., 1928-29; B.A., La. State U., 1931, J.D., 1933; m. Nita Sims Breazeale, Oct. 28, 1938; children—Nita Sims (Mrs. Stephen Bishop Street), Maurice Julius. Admitted to La. bar, 1933; practice in Baton Rouge, 1940—; commd. as spl. asst. to atty. gen. La., 1934; with law dept. Standard Oil Co. of La., 1937-39; with Am. Petroleum Inst., 1939-40; partner Breazeale, Sachse & Wilson, 1940-79, of counsel, 1979—. Bd. dirs. Cancer Soc. Greater Baton Rouge, Cancer Radiation and Research Found. Baton Rouge, Our Lady of Lake Hosp. Served with USNR, 1942-45. Fellow Am. Coll. Trial Lawyers; mem. Internat. Assn. Ins. Counsel, Am., La. (past ins. sect. chmn., ho. of dels., bd. govs.), Baton Rouge (past pres.) bar assns., Phi Delta Phi, Sigma Chi. Episcopalian. Clubs: Baton Rouge Country, City (Baton Rouge). Home: 3384 PP6100 Belmont Ave Baton Rouge LA 70808 Office: 7th Floor Fidelity Nat Bank Bldg 440 N Riverside Mall Baton Rouge LA 70801

WILSON, MICHAEL HOLCOMBE, Can. govt. ofcl., mem. Can. Ho. of Commons; b. Toronto, Ont., Can., Nov. 4, 1937; s. Harry Holcombe and Constance L. (Davies) W.; student Upper Can. Coll.; B. Comm., U. Toronto, 1959; m. Margaret Catherine Smellie, Oct. 17, 1964; children—Cameron, Geoffrey, Lara. With Harris & Partners Ltd., Toronto, 1961-63, 65-79, v.p., 1972; exec. v.p. Dominion Securities Corp., 1973-79; mem. Can. Ho. of Commons, Ottawa, 1979—; minister of state for internat. trade Govt. Can., Ottawa, 1979—. Campaign chmn. Can. Cancer Soc., 1972-75, pres., 1977-78; bd. dirs. Dellcrest Children's Home. Mem. Investment Dealers Assn. (chmn. Ont. dist. 1975-76), Kappa Alpha. Progressive Conservative. Anglican. Clubs: Toronto, Toronto Golf, Badminton and Racquet, Osler Bluff Ski, Can. of Toronto (dir. 1972-78, v.p. 1976-78). Office: House of Commons Ottawa ON K1A 0A6 Canada

WILSON, MILNER BRADLEY, III, banker; b. Spartanburg, S.C., Nov. 17, 1933; s. Milner Bradley and Margaret (Nash) W.; A.B., Duke, 1955; LL.B., U. S.C., 1961; A.M.P., Harvard, 1973; m. Nancy Brock, Aug. 18, 1956; children—Margaret, Julia, Bradley. With Citizens & So. Nat. Bank S.C., Charleston, 1961—, gen. trust officer, 1971—, exec. v.p., 1972—. Served with USMCR, 1955-58. C.L.U. Mem. Am., S.C. bar assns. Clubs: Palmetto (Columbia). Home: 304 Crown Point Rd Columbia SC 29209 Office: PO Box 727 Columbia SC 29202

WILSON, MILTON, univ. dean; b. Paducah, Ky., July 20, 1915; s. Jesse and Rhea (Day) W.; B.S. in Bus., W.Va. State Coll., 1937; M.C.S., Ind. U., 1945, D.B.A., 1951; student behavioral scis., U. Chgo., 1959-60; m. Zelda Summers, May 29, 1941; children—Zelda C. (Mrs. Wendel F. Mosley), Milton James, Rhea Ann. Head dept. bus., also bus. mgr. St. Philip's Jr. Coll., San Antonio, 1940-41; chief accountant Samuel Plato, gen. contractor, Louisville, 1941-43; chief cost accountant Office Emergency Mgmt., Washington, 1943-44; head accounting dept. Hampton (Va.) Inst., 1944-46; head bus. dept. Dillard U., 1946-49; mem. faculty Tex. So. U., 1949-70, dean Sch. Bus., 1955-70; dean Sch. Bus. and Pub. Adminstrn., Howard U., Washington, 1970—; vis. prof. bus. Harvard, 1957-58; certified pub. accountant, Houston, 1952-56; sr. partner Wilson & Cooke, C.P.A.'s, Houston, 1957—; cons. in field, 1952—; ednl. cons. Gen. Accounting Office, 1971—; dir. Gt. Western Fin. Corp. Gen. Edn. Bd. fellow, 1949-51; Found. Econ. Edn. fellow, 1956; Relm Found. Fellow, 1959-60. C.P.A., Ind., Tex., La. Mem. Am. Assn. C.P.A.'s, Am. Accounting Assn. Lutheran. Home: 14124 North Gate Dr Silver Spring MD 20906 Office: 2345 Sherman Ave NW Washington DC 20001

WILSON, MILTON THOMAS, educator; b. Toronto, Ont., Can., Feb. 23, 1923; s. Garnet Stanley and Myrtle Adele (Cork) W.; B.A., U. Toronto, 1945, M.A., 1946; Ph.D., Columbia U., 1957; m. Joanna Crawford, Sept. 6, 1947; children—Barbara, Katharine, Gregory, Victoria, Timothy, Antony. Mem. faculty dept. English Trinity Coll., U. Toronto, 1949—, prof. English, 1966—, chmn. dept., 1975—. Served with Royal Can. Navy, 1943-45. Fellow Royal Soc. Can.; mem. Assn. Can. Univ. Tchrs. English. Author: Shelley's Later Poetry, 1959; E. J. Pratt, 1969; editor: Poetry of Mid-Century, 1964; Poets Between the Wars, 1967; mng. editor Can. Forum, 1959-68. Home: 17 Alexandra Wood Toronto ON M5N 2S2 Canada Office: Trinity Coll U Toronto Toronto ON Canada

WILSON, NANCY, singer; b. Chillicothe, Ohio, Feb. 20, 1937; d. Olden and Lillian (Ryan) W.; ed. Columbus (Ohio) schs.; m. Kenneth C. Dennis (div. 1969); 1 son, Kenneth C.; m. 2d, Wiley Burton, 1974. Began career as singer with local groups, then joined Rusty Bryant band, 1956, and toured Midwest and Can. until 1958; singing independently, 1959—; rec. artist Capitol Records; recs. include But Beautiful; Can't Take My Eyes Off You; Close-Up; For Once in My Life/Who Can I Turn To; How Glad I Am; Hurt So Bad; Now I'm a Woman; Right to Love; Son of a Preacher Man; Come Get To; TV appearances include Bob Hope Show, Danny Kaye Show, Hollywood Palace Show, Carol Burnett Show, Glen Campbell Goodtime Hour, Hawaii Five-O, Flip Wilson Show, Dean Martin Show, The FBI, Police Story, others; hostess TV series KNBC, Los Angeles, 1974-75. Office: care John Levy Enterprises Inc 109 N Almont Dr Los Angeles CA 90048*

WILSON, NEIL LESLIE, educator; b. Vancouver, B.C., Can., Jan. 30, 1922; s. John Shaw and Effie May (Murdoch) W.; B.A., U. B.C., 1947; M.A., U. Toronto, 1948; Ph.D., Yale U., 1951. Lectr. in philosophy U. Western Ont., London, 1951-52; lectr. Bishop's U., Lennoxville, Que., 1952-54, asst. prof., 1954-57; instr. Duke U., Durham, N.C., 1957-58, asst. prof., 1958-60, asso. prof., 1961-64, prof. philosophy, 1964-69; prof. philosophy McMaster U., Hamilton, Ont., Can., 1969—; asst. vis. prof. Harvard, 1960-61. Chmn. Guelph-McMaster Ph.D. Programme in Philosophy, 1970-72, 78—. Served with RCAF, 1941-45. NSF grantee, 1963-66. Mem. Am. (exec. com. Eastern div. 1961-64), Canadian (dir. 1974-76) philos. assns. Author: The Concept of Language, 1959. Home: Rural Route 2 Lynden ON Canada Office: Dept Philosophy McMaster U Hamilton ON Canada

WILSON, NEWTON KENNEDY, food and hotel co. exec.; b. New London, Iowa, Jan. 15, 1908; s. James Clyde and Bertha Jane (Waters) W.; B.S. in Bus. Adminstrn., Monmouth (Ill.) Coll., 1929; M.B.A. in Finance, Northwestern U., 1935; m. Esther Marie Benefiel, June 20, 1942; 1 son, Bruce B. Tchr., prin., athletic coach Pawnee City (Nebr.) High Sch., 1929-33; bus. mgr. traveling univ. Omnibus Coll., summers 1930-34; with Am. Airlines, Inc., 1935-42, supt. passenger service, 1938-42; pres. Sky Chefs, Inc., N.Y.C., 1942-70, dir., cons., now ret. Recipient Distinguished Alumni award Monmouth Coll., 1960. Mem. Theta Chi. Clubs: Wings (N.Y.C.). Home: 18 Linda Rd Port Washington NY 11050

WILSON, ORME, JR., fgn. service officer; b. N.Y.C., July 3, 1920; s. Orme and Alice (Borland) W.; student St. Alban's Sch., Washington, 1929-33, St. Mark's Sch., Southborough, Mass., 1933-38; S.B. cum laude, Harvard, 1942; M.A., George Washington U., 1951; diploma USAF War Coll., 1965; m. Mildred Eddy Dunn, Feb. 16, 1950; children—Marshall, Elsie Dunn, Orme III. Jr. pilot Pan Am. World Airways, 1946-47, U.S. Army Map Service, 1950; joined Fgn. Service, 1950; vice consul Frankfurt/am/Main, Germany, 1951-53; vice consul, Southampton, Eng., 1953-54; 2d sec., Belgrade, Yugoslavia, 1958-61; 2d then 1st sec., Athens, Greece, 1961-64; assigned, Washington, 1965-70; consul gen., Zagreb, Yugoslavia, 1970-74; adviser U.S. Mission to U.N., 1974-77; polit. counselor U.S. Mission to NATO, 1977—. Bd. dirs. Laurel Race Course, Laurel, Md. Trustee Bishop Rhineland Found. for Episcopal Chaplaincy Harvard and Radcliffe, 1967-71, 76—. Served to lt. USNR, 1942-46. Fellow Am. Geog. Soc.; mem. U.S. Tennis Assn. (Prentice Cup Com.), Thoroughbred Club Am., Am. Horse Council. Episcopalian. Mason. Clubs: Internat. Lawn Tennis of U.S.A., Harvard, Racquet and Tennis (N.Y.C.); Metropolitan, Chevy Chase (Washington). Contbr. to Eastern Europe: Essays in Geographical Problems, 1970. Home: White Post VA 22663 Office: U S Mission to NATO Brussels Belgium

WILSON, PAUL EDWIN, educator; b. Quenemo, Kans., Nov. 2, 1913; s. Dale Edwin and Clara (Jacobs) W.; B.A., U. Kans., 1937, M.A., 1938; LL.B., Washburn U., 1940; m. Harriet Eileen Stephens, June 16, 1941; children—Elizabeth, Mary Paulette, Eileen, David. Admitted to Kans. bar, 1940, U.S. Supreme Ct. bar, 1952, U.S. Ct. Appeals, 1950; individual practice law, Ashland, Kans., 1941-42, Lyndon, Kans., 1946-50; atty. County of Osage, Kans., 1947-50; gen. counsel dept. social welfare State of Kans., 1950-51, asst. atty. gen., 1951-53, 1st asst. atty. gen., 1953-57; asso. prof. law U. of Kans., 1957-62, prof., 1962-68, Kane prof., 1968—; asso. dir. Inst. Judicial Adminstrn., 1964-65; vis. prof. The Menninger Found., 1972; cons. in field. Mem. Lawrence (Kans.) Planning Commn., 1962-65; chmn. Bd. Zoning Appeals, Lawrence, 1966-67; mem. Kans. Historic Sites Bd. Rev., 1973-77; trustee Ft. Burgwin (N.Mex.) Research Center, 1977—. Served with U.S. Army, 1942-46. Mem. Am. Bar Assn., Kans. Bar Assn. (chmn. com. criminal law 1960-68), Am. Law Inst., Am. Bar Found., Selden Soc., Nat. Trust Historic Preservation (bd. advisors 1972-78), Order of Coif, Phi Alpha Delta. Republican. Methodist. Author: (with Reams) Segregation and the Fourteenth Amendment in the States, 1975; Pattern Rules of Court and Code Provisions, 1975; Judicial Education in the United States, 1965. Editor: American Criminal Law Quarterly, 1963-70. Contbr. articles in field to profl. jours. Home: 2622 W 24th Terr Lawrence KS 66044 Office: 315C New Green Hall University of Kansas Lawrence KS 66045. *Few things in my life have happened according to a preconceived plan. My admonition to the young is "Don't plan, just live." Perhaps I should add "also let live," by which I mean a concern for humanity, contemporary and prospective.*

WILSON, PETE, mayor San Diego; b. Lake Forest, Ill., Aug. 23, 1933; s. James Boone and Margaret (Callahan) W.; B.A., Yale, 1955; LL.B., U. Calif., 1962; m. Betty Weedn Robertson, July 14, 1968. Admitted to Calif. bar; mayor San Diego, 1971—. Mem. Presdl. Adv. Com. Environ. Quality, Task Force Land Use and Urban Growth Policy; asst. exec. dir. Republican Assos. San Diego County, 1963-64; exec. dir. San Diego County Rep. Central Com., 1964-65; legal service officer Calif. State Rep. Central Com., 1965—; mem. Calif. Assembly, 1967-71. Bd. dirs. San Diego region Nat. Council Christians and Jews, Big Bros. Inc., Clairemont Boys Club, City of Hope Med. Center. Served with USMC, 1955-58. Named Outstanding Young Man of Year San Diego Jaycees, 1969, One of 200 Young Leaders, Time mag., 1976. Fellow AIA (hon.); mem. Calif., Fla., San Diego County bar assns., San Diego C. of C., Navy League, League Calif. Cities (dir., past pres.), Phi Delta Phi, Zeta Psi. Episcopalian. Kiwanian. Club: Commonwealth. Home: 4146 Genesee Ave San Diego CA 92111 Office: 202 C St San Diego CA 92101

WILSON, PETER CECIL, auctioneer; b. Eshton Hall, Yorkshire, Eng., Mar. 8, 1913; s. Mathew and Barbara (Lister) W.; student New Coll., Oxford U.; m. Grace Helen Ranken, 1935 (div.). Formerly with Reuters, also Connoisseur mag.; dir. Sotheby's London, 1938—, chmn., 1958—, chmn. Parke-Bernet Galleries, Inc., N.Y.C. (now Sotheby Parke Bernet, Inc.). Vice chmn., trustee Leeds Cante Found., Maidstone, Kent. Decorated comdr. Brit. Empire; recipient Benjamin Franklin medal, 1968. Home: 4 Green St London W1 England Office: Sotheby Parke Bernet & Co 34-35 New Bond St London W1 A 2AA England also 980 Madison Ave New York NY 10021

WILSON, PHILLIPS ELDER, JR. (PHIL WILSON), composer, musician, musical dir., publishing co. exec., ednl. adminstr.; b. Belmont, Mass., Jan. 19, 1937; s. Phillips Elder and Susan (Howe) W.; student Phillips Exeter Acad., 1951-55, New Eng. Conservatory, 1955-58; m. Patricia Ann Ferry, Sept. 8, 1968; children—Paul William, Marian Margaret. Trombonist Woody Herman Band, Clark Terry Band, Louis Armstrong Band, Herbie Hancock Band, Marian McPartland Band, Bobby Hackett Band, Dorsey Bros. Orch.; instr. arranging and composition, chmn. dept. trombone, founder, dir. Thursday Night Dues Band and Jazz Trombone Choir Berklee Coll., 1965-74; chmn. Afro-Am. dept. New Eng. Conservatory, 1974-77; mus. dir. Big Money, weekly TV game show; founder, Phil Wilson Music div. Outrageous Mother Inc., pub. jazz ensemble charts. Clinician, Conn. Band Instrument Co., 1965-79, Yamaha Internat. Corp., 1979—; mem. faculty Nat. Stage Band Camps, 1965—; dir. dept. music Summer Sch., Phillips Exeter (N.H.) Acad., 1967-71; dir. Four Weeks with Phil Wilson, jazz-rock summer program Choate Sch., Wallingford, Conn., 1972-74; co-founder, dir. Boston Sackbut Week, 1973—; arranger, composer Woody Herman, Buddy Rich, Clark Terry, Doc Severinsen, Marian McPartland; rec. artist. Mem. Internat. Trombone Assn. (dir.). Co-author: Chord Studies for Trombone. Composer numerous works including: The Left and the Right (condr. Westchester (N.Y.) Symphony Orch. and Marian McPartland Trio 1971); The Earth's Children, (condr. Boston Symphony Orch. 1972); arranger numerous compositions, including Mercy, Mercy, Mercy (Grammy nominee for Buddy Rich rec. 1969); rec. artist on albums: Live & Cookin'; Getting It All Together, Wilson, That's All, The Sound of the Wasp, Fiedler in Rags, Thurs. Night Dues, Serenade in Blue, The Prodigal Son, My Kind of Broadway, Woody's Goodies, Recorded Live, Woody Herman, 1964, Woody Herman 40th Anniversary, Encore Woody Herman, 1963, Woody Herman, 1963, The New World of Woody Herman, Music from Norad; arrangements and compositions on albums: Buddy Rich Plays and Plays and Plays, The Sound of the Wasp, Thurs Night Dues, Serenade in Blue, A Different Drummer, The Best of Buddy Rich, Mercy, Mercy, Buddy Rich Swingin' New Big Band, Woody Herman Recorded Live, The New World of Woody Herman, Music from Norad, The Big Sound. Home: 8 Hammond Rd Belmont MA 02178 Office: Berklee Coll Music 1140 Boylston St Boston MA 02215

WILSON, RALPH COOKERLY, JR., corp. exec.; b. Columbus, Ohio, Oct. 17, 1918; s. Ralph Cookerly and Edith (Cole) W.; A.B., U. Va., 1940; student U. Mich. Law Sch., 1940-41; m. Jane Evans, Aug. 30, 1973; children—Christy Cole, Linda Brown, Edith Denise. Pres. Ralph C. Wilson Industries, Inc., ins., trucking, mfg., broadcasting and photog. ops., Detroit, 1946—; pres., owner Buffalo Bills Profl. Football Club, 1959—. Served with USNR, 1941-46. Decorated Commendation medal. Presbyn. Clubs: Country of Detroit; Grosse Pointe (Mich.); Bloomfield Hills (Mich.) Country; Buffalo Country; Shriners. Home: 824 Lake Shore Rd Grosse Pointe Shores MI 48236 Office: 400 Renaissance Center Suite 2250 Detroit MI 48243

WILSON, RALPH EDWIN, lawyer; b. Osceola, Ark., Sept. 28, 1921; s. Emmett A. and Lillie (Simmons) W.; student U.S. Naval Acad., 1943; A.B., Union U., 1946; J.D., Vanderbilt U., 1949; m. Mary Ann Murray, Apr. 23, 1949; children—Ralph Edwin, Teresa Ann, Don Alan. Admitted to Tenn. bar, 1948, Ark. bar, 1948; pvt. practice in Osceola, 1949—; city atty., Osceola, 1949; dep. pros. atty. 2d Jud. Dist. Ark., 1950-53; spl. asst. to atty. gen. Ark., 1956-60. Pres. Liberal State Bank, Gt. Eastern Assurance Co., North Little Rock; v.p., dir. Cook Enterprises, Ltd., Memphis, sec., dir. Fitzpatrick Jewelers, Inc.; dir. Allied Cos., Inc., Does-More Products Corp, Allied Real Estate Investment Trust, Osceola Land Devel. Co. Mem. adv. council Nat. Pub. Works Week, 1964. Alderman, Osceola City Council, 1958-61. Served as lt. U.S. Mcht. Marines, USNR, 1943-45. Recipient Ark. House and Senate Concurrent Resolutions Commendation, 1971. Mem. Ark. (past mem. exec. com.), Osceola (pres.) bar assns., Am. Trial Lawyers Assn., U.S. Bar (Supreme Ct.), Am. Legion, Phi Alpha Delta, Alpha Tau Omega, Tau Kappa Alpha. Democrat. Methodist. Kiwanian (internat. v.p. 1970-71, trustee 1966-70, life fellow internat. found.). Home: 903 W Hale St Osceola AR 72370 Office: 318 W Hale St Osceola AR 72370

WILSON, RALPH ERDMAN, JR., C.P.A.; b. Phila., Sept. 17, 1927; s. Ralph Erdman and Elizabeth Jane (Oakley) W.; B.S. in Bus. Adminstrn., U. Fla., 1953; m. Linda Lee Cleveland, Sept. 17, 1960; children—Lee Erdman, Elizabeth Pearson. Pub. accountant Hall & Fisher, Jacksonville, Fla., 1953-61; sec.-treas., dir. Pierce, Wulbern, Murphey Corp., Jacksonville, 1961-75; pub. accounting, 1975—. C.P.A., Fla. Mem. Am., Fla. insts. C.P.A.'s, Blue Key, Beta Theta Pi. Republican. Presbyn. (treas.). Home: 4627 Wadham Lane Jacksonville FL 32210 Office: 2111 Smith St Orange Park FL 32073

WILSON, RAMON B., agrl. economist, educator; b. Ogden, Utah, Sept. 22, 1922; s. Benjamin Andrew and Hannah Josephine (Browning) W.; B.S., Utah State U., 1947; M.S., Purdue U., 1948, Ph.D., 1950; postgrad. U. Calif., Berkeley, 1972, Georgetown U., 1976; m. Ruth G. Worlton, July 27, 1945; children—Lynn, William Scott, Bruce Ramon, JoAnne, Kathleen. Extension economist Utah State U., Logan, 1950-53; mktg. economist Calif. Dept. Agr., Sacramento, 1953-55; asst. prof. Purdue U., West Lafayette, Ind., 1955-57, asso. prof., 1957-63, prof. agrl. econs., 1963-78, prof. emeritus, 1978—, market service dir., 1960-68, asst. dir. Ind. Coop. Extension Service, 1963-74, asso. dir. agrl. expt. sta., asst. to dean agr., 1968-74; asst. dir. research Benson Agrl. Food Inst., Brigham Young U., Provo, Utah, 1979—; asst. to sec. U.S. Dept. Agr., Washington, 1974-76; agrl. advisor, asst. to lt. govs. Ind., 1961-74; head office intergovtl. affairs U.S. Dept. Agr., 1974-76; mem. faculty Acad. in Pub. Service, Georgetown U., 1976—; pres. Nat. Assn. State Depts. Agr., 1966; bd. dirs. Mid-Am. Internat. Agri-Trade Council, 1970-74; cons., lectr. in field. Bd. dirs. People to People Travel Program, 1961—. Served with U.S. Army, 1943-46. Recipient citations for service to agr. Nat. Assn. State Depts. Agr., 1966, Ill. Dept. Agr., 1968, Ky. Dept. Agr., 1967, Ind. Soil and Water Conservation Com., 1973, Hoosier Coop. Clinic, 1964. Republican. Mem. Ch. Jesus Christ of Latter-day Saints. Contbr. articles to profl. jours. Home: 435 E 2200 North Provo UT 84601 Office: Benson Agrl Food Inst 392 Widtsoe Brigham Young Univ Provo UT 84602

WILSON, RAPHAEL, univ. pres.; b. Trenton, Apr. 25, 1925; s. Edward and Sarah Elisabeth (Lyden) W.; B.S., U. Notre Dame, 1948; M.A., U. Tex., Austin, 1951; Ph.D., U. Tex., Galveston, 1954. Joined Congregation of Holy Cross, Roman Catholic Ch., 1944; instr., St. Edward's U., 1948-51, asst. prof. biology, 1951-55, asso. prof., 1955-58, prof., 1958-59, dean, 1951-59; asst. prof. microbiology U. Notre Dame, 1959-64, asso. prof., 1964-70, dir. admissions, 1965-69; prof. exptl. biology Baylor Coll. Medicine, Houston, 1970-76; prof. biology U. Portland, 1976-78, pres., 1978—; mem. Oreg. Energy Facility Siting Council, 1979—. Trustee Stonehill Coll., 1977—; bd. dirs. Hospice of Oreg., Inc., 1979; mem. med. adv. com. Tri-County March of Dimes, Oreg., 1979. Am. Soc. Microbiology pres.'s fellow, 1960; Office Naval Research grantee, 1963-65; NIH grantee, 1963-71; AEC grantee, 1964-65; Hartford Found. grantee, 1965-70. Mem. Radiation Research Soc., Transplantation Soc., Am. Soc. Microbiology, Gerontol. Soc., Soc. Exptl. Biology and Medicine, Internat. Soc. Exptl. Hematology, Assn. Gnotobiotics, Tex. Acad. Sci. Contbr. numerous articles to sci., ednl. jours.; research in germ-free life sci. Home: Holy Cross Ct 5 5410 N Strong St Portland OR 97203 Office: U Portland 5000 N Willamette Blvd Portland OR 97203

WILSON, RAYMOND CLARK, hosp. exec.; b. Birmingham, Ala., July 8, 1915; s. Raymond Clyde and Lida (Gay) W.; student Oglethorpe U., 1933-34; student U. Ga., 1934-37, Tulane U., 1948; D.Bus. Adminstrn. (hon.), William Carey Coll.; m. Sara Elizabeth Paris, Feb. 17, 1940; children—Margery Jo, Richard Clark, Sara Elizabeth, Raymond Paul. Office mgr. firm C.R. Justi, contractor, Atlanta, 1933-42; paymaster J.A. Jones Constrn. Co., Brunswick, Ga., 1942-45; asst. supt. So. Bapt. Hosp., New Orleans, 1946-53, adminstr., 1953-68, exec. dir., 1969-77; pres. Affiliated Bapt. Hosps., Inc., 1977—, Health Care Cons. & Mgmt. Services, Inc., 1977—; exec. dir. Bapt. Meml. Hosp., Jacksonville, Fla., 1973-77; dir., treas. La. Health and Indemnity Co.; dir. New Orleans Area Health Planning Council, 1969-74. Bd. dirs. Bapt. Hosp. Found., 1970-78. Served with USAAF, 1945-46. Fellow Am. Coll. Hosp. Adminstrs. (bd. regents 1972-75); mem. Hosp. Service Assn. (bd. dirs., treas. 1953-74), Am. (ho. dels. 1972-75), La. (pres. 1956) hosp. assns., New Orleans Hosp. Council (pres. 1954-55), Southeastern Hosp. Conf. (pres. 1963), Bapt. Hosp. Assn. (pres. 1964-65), New Orleans C. of C. Baptist (trustee, deacon). Rotarian. Home: Box 1456 HW W Sunnybrook Rd Carriere MS 39426 Office: 135 St Charles Ave Suite 402 New Orleans LA 70130

WILSON, REGINALD, ednl. adminstr.; b. Detroit, Feb. 24, 1927; s. Oliver Leon and Nancy McCrimmon (Golden) W.; B.S., Wayne State U., 1950, M.A., 1958, Ph.D., 1971; m. Dolores Stewart, Apr. 2, 1960; children—Adam, Kafi. With Detroit Pub. Schs., 1950-65, chief psychologist, 1960-65; asso. dir. upward bound Oakland U., 1965-67; asso. dean testing, dir. research Oakland Community Coll., 1967-70; dir. Center for Black Studies, U. Detroit, 1970-71; pres. Wayne County Community Coll., Detroit, 1971—; adj. instr. psychology U. Mich., 1974—; v.p. CRW Assos., Ann Arbor, Mich., 1976—. Chmn. bd. Your Heritage House, Detroit, 1975—; vice chmn. United Negro Coll. Fund, Detroit campaign, 1975—; bd. dirs. Detroit Ednl. TV, Sta. WTVS-TV, 1976-78. Served with USAAF, 1945-46. Named Distinguished Alumnus Wayne State U., 1974, Outstanding Citizen Detroit PTA, 1971; recipient distinguished service award City of Detroit, 1976, 77. Mem. Am. Psychol. Assn., Nat. Assn. Black Psychologists, Mich. Assn. Black Psychologists (past pres.), Met. Fund. Detroit, New Detroit Inc., Phi Delta Kappa. Club: Jim Dandy Ski (past pres., instr.). Author: (with Jonas Chenault and Charles Green) Human Development in the Urban Community, 1967. Home: 20189 Warrington Dr Detroit MI 48221 Office: 4612 Woodward Ave Detroit MI 48201

WILSON, RICHARD, physicist, educator; b. London, Eng., Apr., 29, 1926; s. Percy and Dorothy (Kingston) W.; B.A., Christ Church, Oxford U., 1946, M.A., D.Phil., 1949. M.A., Harvard, 1957; m. Andrée Desirée DuMond, Jan. 6, 1952; children—Arthur Christopher, Michael Thomas, Nicholas Graham, Elaine Susan, Annette Adele, Peter James. Came to U.S., 1950. Research lectr. Christ Ch., Oxford, 1948-53, research officer Dept. Sci. and Indsl. Research, 1953-55; research asso. U. Rochester, 1950-51, Stanford, 1951-52; asst. prof. Harvard, 1955-57, asso. prof., 1957-61, prof., 1961—, asso. Adams House, 1971—; cons. NRC. Guggenheim fellow, 1961, 69; Fulbright fellow, 1959, 69. Fellow Am. Phys. Soc.; mem. Am. Acad. Arts and Scis., N.Y. Acad. Scis., Soc. Psychical Research (London). Asst. editor Annals of Physics, 1956—; contbr. articles to sci. jours. Home: 15 Bracebridge Rd Newton MA 02159 Office: Lyman Lab Harvard University Cambridge MA 02138

WILSON, RICHARD CHRISTIAN, educator; b. Bethlehem, Pa., July 17, 1921; s. Christian and Laura Barrows (Langham) W.; B.S., Carnegie-Mellon U., 1943; M.S., Lehigh U., 1947; Ph.D., U. Mich., 1961; m. Jean M. Avis, July 16, 1949; children—Richard A., Christy. Mfg. engr. Westinghouse Electric Corp., East Pittsburgh, 1943; instr. mech. engring. Carnegie-Mellon U., Pitts., 1943-44; vacuum test engr. Kellex Corp., N.Y.C., 1944; area supr. Carbide & Carbon Chem. Co., Oak Ridge, 1945-46; apparatus engr. Westinghouse Electric Corp., Jackson, Mich., 1947-55; instr. indsl. and operation engring. U. Mich., 1955-61, asst. prof., 1961-63, asso. prof., 1963-66, prof., 1966—, chmn. dept., 1973-77, asso. dean Coll. Engring., 1968-72; dir. Cascade Data Corp., 1969-72. Bd. dirs. Ecumenical Assn. Internat. Understanding, 1970—, pres., 1975-76. Mem. IEEE, Inst. Mgmt. Sci., Am. Inst. Indsl. Engrs., Ops. Research Soc. Am., Sigma Xi, Beta Theta Pi, Phi Kappa Phi. Club: Rotary. Contbr. articles to profl. jours. Home: 805 Mount Pleasant Ann Arbor MI 48103 Office: Dept Indsl Engring U Mich Ann Arbor MI 48109

WILSON, RICHARD HAROLD, govt. ofcl.; b. Waterloo, Iowa, July 15, 1930; s. Clarence Hough and Mary (Dillon) W.; B.A., U. Ill., 1952; M.P.A., U. Kans., 1958; Fulbright fellow Leiden (The Netherlands) U., 1959-60; m. Elaine Elizabeth Aniol. June 14, 1957; children—Elizabeth Aniol, Andrew Edward. Adminstrv. asst. to city mgr., San Antonio, 1956-58; budget analyst, Kansas City, Mo., 1959; research asso. Internat. Union Local Authorities. The Hague, 1959-60; city mgr., Nevada, Mo., 1960-65; asst. to city mgr., Ft. Worth, 1965-67; asst. city mgr., Albuquerque, 1967-68, city mgr., 1968-72; dir. housing and urban rehab. Dallas, 1972—. Bd. dirs. Neighborhood Housing Services of Am., Inc.; chmn. Housing Task Force of North Central Tex. Council Govts., also mem. human resources com.; active Boy Scouts Am. Served to lt. (j.g.) USN, 1952-55; comdr. Res. Mem. Nat. Assn. Housing and Redevel. Ofcls. (v.p. Tex. chpt., mem. S.W. regional council), Internat., Tex. city mgmt. assns., Am. Soc. Pub. Adminstrn. (pres. N.Mex. 1968-69, v.p. N. Tex. 1976-77, pres. N. Tex. 1977-78), Naval Res. Assn., Phi Gamma Delta. Pi Sigma Alpha. Episcopalian. Club: Rotary (Dallas). Home: 5320 Meadow Crest Dr Dallas TX 75229 Office: City Hall 1500 Marilla St Dallas TX 75201

WILSON, ROBERT ALEXANDER, lawyer; b. Waco, Tex., May 31, 1905; s. Robert Alexander and Sadye (Grace) W.; A.B., Baylor U., 1924, LL.B., 1927; m. Blanche Erdman, Mar. 2, 1929 (dec. Aug. 1978); children—Robert A. Molly Lou (Mrs. Allan R. Reko); m. 2d, Margo Stone, Jan. 5, 1980. Admitted to Tex. bar, 1927, since practiced in Amarillo; partner firm Underwood, Wilson, Sutton, Berry, Stein & Johnson predecessors, 1938—. Trustee Amarillo Ind. Sch. Dist., 1948-54, pres., 1951-52. Mem. Am., Amarillo (pres. 1941) bar assns., State Bar Tex., Am. Judicature Soc., Internat. Assn. Ins. Counsel, Tex. Bar Found., Tex. Assn. Def. Counsel, Am. Coll. Trial Lawyers. Methodist (chmn. ofcl. bd. 1950-52, pres. trustees 1962-66). Clubs: Amarillo, Amarillo Country; Palo Duro (Randall County). Home: 3203 Parker St Amarillo TX 79109 Office: Plaza One Amarillo TX 79101

WILSON, ROBERT ANDREW, television exec.; b. Boston, July 3, 1941; s. Joseph Murray and Elizabeth (McGrail) W.; B.A., Dartmouth, 1963; grad. Program for Mgmt. Devel., Harvard U., 1974; m. Laura Cunningham, Sept. 7, 1963; children—Andrew, Owen, Luke. Asst. to chmn. Tex. Industries, 1967-68; exec. v.p., gen. mgr. Channel 13, KERA TV, Dallas, 1968-73, pres., 1973-76; founder Robert A. Wilson Assos., Inc., 1976—. Home: 5422 Farquhar St Dallas TX 75209 Office: 2530 Cedar Springs Dallas TX 75201

WILSON, ROBERT BECKER, forest products co. exec.; b. Spokane, Wash., July 16, 1915; s. Ray L. and Genevieve (Becker) W.; B.A., Yale, 1938; postgrad. Harvard, 1939; m. Constance Hoyt, Aug. 26, 1939; children—Judith B., Hoyt F., Gregg S., Katharine B. (dec.), Genevieve A., Martha C.; m. 2d, Barbara P. Kerr, Mar. 10, 1970. Vice pres., logging mgr. Warm Springs Lumber Co. (Oreg.), 1941-51, former pres., dir.; former v.p., dir. Jefferson Plywood Co., Madras; v.p., dir. Equity Mgmt. Co., Portland, Oreg., 1958-67, pres., 1967—; pres. U.S. Bancorp., 1969-73, now dir.; exec. v.p. U.S. Nat. Bank Oreg., 1969-71; chmn. bd., dir. Weyerhaeuser Co.; dir. Burlington No., Inc., U.S. Nat. Bank, Portland. Commr., Port of Portland, 1961-73. Served to lt. USNR, 1942-45. Clubs: Arlington, Waverley Country, Multnomah Athletic (Portland). Home: 1100 SW Skyline Blvd Portland OR 97221 Office: 621 SW Harrison St Portland OR 97205

WILSON, ROBERT C., (see Wilson, Bob)

WILSON, ROBERT CHARLES, computer peripherals co. exec.; b. Hazelton, Ida., Jan. 9, 1920; s. John Willard and Daisy Irene (Sothern) W.; B.S. in Mech. Engring., U. Calif. at Berkeley, 1941; m. Frances Barbara Miller, Feb. 1, 1947; children—Eleanor, Kathleen, Deborah. With Gen. Electric Co., 1941-43, 46-69, v.p., 1966-69; corp. v.p., pres. comml. products group N.Am. Rockwell, 1969-71, exec. v.p. indsl. products and electronics, 1971, also dir., mem. exec. com.; pres., chief exec. officer Collins Radio Co., 1971-74, also dir., mem. exec. com.; pres., chmn. bd. Memorex Corp., Santa Clara, Calif., 1974—. Served to lt. USNR, 1943-46. Co-author: Capacitors for Industry, 1950. Home: 274 Catalpa Dr Atherton CA 94025 Office: Memorex Corp San Tomas at Central Expressway Santa Clara CA 95052

WILSON, ROBERT EUGENE, ret. educator; b. Ada, O., Mar. 1, 1915; s. William Birch and Elma (Creighton) W.; B.S., Ohio No. U., 1939; B.S., Ohio State U., 1938, M.A., 1946, Ph.D., 1949; m. Louise Rosalie Taylor, Dec. 30, 1948; children—Roberta, Jennifer, Jeffrey. Asst. supt. schs., Elyria, O., 1949-51, Canton, O., 1951-54; supt. schs., Gambier, O., 1948-49, Mansfield, O., 1954-58; asso. prof. Temple U., 1959-62; chmn. dept. ednl. adminstrn. Kent (O.) State U., 1962-76, ret., 1976, prof. emeritus, 1977—; Fulbright grantee U.S. and Cyprus Commn. for Ednl. Exchange; cons. bds. edn. Served to capt., CIC, AUS, 1941-45; PTO. Mem. Am. Assn. Sch. Adminstrs., Phi Delta Kappa. Author: Accounting and Budgeting for Schools, 1959; The Modern School Superintendent, 1960; How to Guide Your Child's Education, 1961; The Superintendency Team, 1964; Educational Adminstration, 1966; School Board Policies, 1968. Home: 1273 Lake Martin Dr Kent OH 44240

WILSON, ROBERT HENRY, educator; b. Gary, Ind., Apr. 5, 1909; s. Joseph Henry and Nell (Cox) W.; student Kenyon Coll., 1924-25; A.B., Stanford U., 1928, M.A., 1929; Ph.D., U. Chgo., 1932; m. Lucille Bridgers, May 28, 1936; 1 dau., Edith Margaret Wilson Miles. Instr. English, U. Tex., Austin, 1934-36, 37-38, asst. prof. 1947-52, asso. prof., 1952-63, prof., 1963—; instr. La. State U., 1944-47. Mem. MLA, Modern Humanities Research Assn., Internat. Arthurian Soc., Phi Beta Kappa. Episcopalian. Contbr. to A Manual of the Writings in Middle English, 1972. Contbr. articles in field to profl. jours. Home: 4201 Shoal Creek Blvd Austin TX 78756 Office: English Department University of Texas Austin TX 78712

WILSON, ROBERT JAMES, airline exec.; b. Grand Rapids, Mich., June 15, 1902; s. James Alexander and Annie E. (McAlpine) W.; A.B., U. Mich., 1925, LL.B., 1929; m. Alice Beckham, May 29, 1935 (div., Aug. 1955); m. 2d. Marilyn Jones, Dec. 26, 1956 (dec. 1958); m. 3d, Helen Gillespie, Aug. 22, 1959. Admitted Mich. bar, 1929; partner Warner, Norcross & Judd, Grand Rapids, 1936-42; v.p. Capital Airlines, Inc., Washington, 1942-61, also dir.; mem. firm Patterson, Belknap & Webb, 1963—; chmn. bd. Airlines Nat. Service Co.; pres. Zantop Air Transport, Inc., 1966—, also dir.; pres., dir. Universal Airlines, Inc., 1966-67, chmn. bd., 1967—; pres., dir. Universal Aircraft Service; dir. Airlines Personnel Relations Conference, Airlines Terminal Corp., Airlines Nat. Terminal Service Co., Inc. City commissioner of East Grand Rapids, Mich., 1936-42; chmn. Indsl. Adv. com. Loudoun County, Va. Recipient Presdl. commendation, 1972, Presdl. citation, 1976, 78. Mem. Am., Mich. State bar assns., Nat. Alliance Businessmen (exec. v.p., sec.-treas. 1969—), Sigma Phi, Phi Delta Phi. Episcopalian (sr. warden 1972—). Home: Route 2 Box 39 4 Leesburg VA 22075 Office: Nat Alliance Bus Adminstrn 1730 K St Washington DC

WILSON, ROBERT LEE, educator, mathematician; b. Champaign, Ill., Mar. 7, 1917; s. William Harold and Esther (Barney) W.; B.A., U. Fla., 1938; M.A., U. Wis., 1940, Ph.D., 1947; m. Anna Katherine Fulton, Sept. 11, 1940; children—Robert Lee, William F., Anna Katherine, Steven K. Acting instr. U. Wis., 1947, instr., 1947-48; asst. prof. U. Tenn., 1948-56; sr. aerophys. engr. Convair Ft. Worth Gen. Dynamics, 1956-58; adj. prof. math. Tex. Christian U., 1956-58; prof., chmn. dept. math. Ohio Wesleyan U., 1958-66, asst. to pres., 1962-63, prof., 1966-79, prof. emeritus, 1979—. Vis. prof., dir. computing centre U. Ibadan, Nigeria, 1966-68; cons. Rockefeller Found., 1968-73, 77—, Buckeye Computing Services, 1978—. Served to 2d lt. F.A., U.S. Army, 1938-39, to lt. col., 1941-46; ETO. Decorated Bronze Star; Croix de Guerre with silver star (France). Mem. Am. Math. Soc., Math. Assn. Am. (bd. govs. 1976—), Assn. Computing Machinery, Australian Math. Soc., Nat. Council Tchrs. Math., AAAS, Alpha Tau Omega, Mu Alpha Theta (pres. 1969-71). Presbyn. Author: (with E.D. Eaves) Introductory Mathematical Analysis, 1958; Much Ado About Calculus, 1974, 79. Home: Route 1 Box 57-L Lexington VA 24450

WILSON, ROBERT M., theatrical performer, artist; b. Waco, Tex., Oct. 4, 1944; s. D.M. and Loree Velma (Hamilton) W.; student U. Tex., 1962; B.F.A., Pratt Inst., 1965. Theatrical performances U.S. and Europe include: Byrdwoman, The King of Spain, The Life and Times of Sigmund Freud, Deafman Glance, Ka Mountain and Guardenia Terrace, King Lyre and Lady in the Wasteland, The Life and Times of Joseph Stalin, A Mad Man A Mad Giant A Mad Dog A Mad Urge A Mad Face, The Life and Times of Dave Clark, A Letter for Queen Victoria, The $ Value of Man, Dialog, Spaceman and Einstein on the Beach, I Was Sitting on my Patio This Guy Appeared I Thought I Was Hallucinating, 1977, Death, Destruction, and Detroit, 1979, Edison, 1979; exhibited drawings and sculpture, Willard Gallery, N.Y.C., 1971; one man shows Iolas Gallery, N.Y.C., Palazzdi Gallery, Milan, Galeric Fred Lanzenberg, Brussels, Paula Cooper Gallery, N.Y.C.; one-man show Musee Galliera, Paris, 1972, group show, 1974; works represented in permanent collections Mus. Modern Art, N.Y.C., Mus. Modern Art, Paris, The French Govt., Paris; films include The House, Slant, Overture for a Deafman, Murder; condr. seminars U. Calif. at Berkeley, 1970, George Sch., New Hope, Pa., 1970, U. Ia., 1970, Newark State Coll., 1971; lectr. Internat. Sch., Paris, 1971, Atelje Festival, Belgrade, Yugoslavia, Internat. Theater Inst. of UNESCO, Durdan, France, 1971, Skowhegan Art Sch., Maine, 1977; condr. workshops, Royaumont, France, 1972, Boulder, Colo., 1973, Ohio State U., 1975, Centre de Development du Potential Humain, Paris, 1973, 74. Recipient Best Fgn. Play award Le Syndicat de la Critique Dramatique et Musicale, Paris, 1970; Drama Desk award for direction, 1971; Obie Spl. Citation award for direction, 1974; nominated for Tony award for best score and libretto for A Letter for Queen Victoria, 1975; Maharam Found. award for scenic design, 1975, Best Lyric Theater Le Syndicat de la Critique Dramatique et Musicale, Paris, 1976; best play award for Einstein on the Beach, Theatre of Nation, Belgrade, Yugoslavia, 1976; Most Outstanding Theater Designer of the Seventies U.S. Inst. Theater Tech., Washington, 1977; Lumen award for Einstein on the Beach, 1977; Rockefeller grantee, 1970; Guggenheim fellow, 1971. Mem. Societe des Auteurs et Compositeurs Dramatiques. Author: Two Conversations with Edwin Denby, 1973; A Letter for Queen Victoria, 1974; contbg. author anthology New American Plays Vol. III, 1970. Address: 147 Spring St New York NY 10012

WILSON, ROBERT RATHBUN, univ. prof.; b. Frontier, Wyo., Mar. 4, 1914; s. Platt Elvin and Edith (Rathbun) W.; A.B., U. of Calif., 1936, Ph.D., 1940; hon. degree Notre Dame U., U. Bonn; m. Jane Inez Scheyer. Aug. 20, 1940; children—Daniel, Jonathan, and Rand. Instr. Princeton U., 1940-42, asst. prof., 1942-45; head exptl. nuclear physics div. Los Alamos Lab., Atomic Bomb Project, 1944-46; asso. prof. physics Harvard, 1946-47; prof. physics and dir. Lab Nuclear Studies, Cornell U., 1947-75; prof. physics U. Chgo., 1967—, Peter B. Ritzma prof.; dir. Nat. Accelerator Lab., Batavia, Ill., 1967-78. Recipient Elliott Cresson medal Franklin Inst., 1964; Nat. medal sci., 1973. Fellow Am. Phys. Soc.; mem. Am. Philos. Soc., Am. Acad. Arts and Scis.; Fedn. Am. Scientists (chmn. 1946), Nat. Acad. Sci., Sigma Xi. Contbr. articles to Physics Rev. Home: 5825 Dorchester Ave Chicago IL 60637

WILSON, ROBERT THOMPSON, publisher; b. Chgo., June 19, 1918; s. Robert T. and Anna M. (Schalk) W.; B.A. in Econs., Lawrence Coll., Appleton, Wis., 1940; m. Doris Jane Quant, Feb. 19, 1943; children—Robin Jane, Scott Alan. Profl. musician with dance orchs., 1934-42; life ins. underwriter, 1940-42; advt. space salesman, then gen. sales mgr. Gillette Publishing Co., Chgo., 1946-60; sales mgr. Dun-Donnelley Pub. Corp., Chgo., 1960-70, publisher, 1970—; dir. The Road Info. Program. Served with AUS, 1942-46. Mem. Bus.-Profl. Advertisers Assn., Chgo. Bus. Pubs. Assn., Am. Bus. Press, Constrn. Industries Mfg. Assn. (bd. dirs.), Asso. Gen. Contractors Am., Am. Rd. and Transp. Builders Assn., Asso. Equipment Distbrs., Nat. Sand and Gravel Assn. Home: 23 Kyle Ct Clarendon Hills IL 60514 Office: 1301 Grove Ave Barrington IL 60010

WILSON, ROBERT WOODROW, radio astronomer; b. Houston, Jan. 10, 1936; s. Ralph Woodrow and Fannie May (Willis) W.; B.A. with honors in Physics, Rice U., 1957; Ph.D., Calif. Inst. Tech., 1962; m. Elizabeth Rhoads Sawin, Sept. 4, 1958; children—Philip Garrett, Suzanne Katherine, Randal Woodrow. Research fellow Calif. Inst. Tech., Pasadena, 1962-63; mem. tech. staff Bell Labs., Holmdel, N.J., 1963-76, head radio physics research dept., 1976—. Recipient Henry Draper medal Royal Astron. Soc., London, 1977, Herschel medal Nat. Acad. Scis., 1977; Nobel prize in physics, 1978; NSF fellow, 1958-61; Cole fellow, 1957-58. Mem. Am. Astron. Soc., Internat. Astron. Union, Am. Phys. Soc., Internat. Sci. Radio Union, Phi Beta Kappa, Sigma Xi. Discoverer of 3 deg. k Microwave Backgraound Radiation, 1965; discoverer of CO and other molecules in interstellar space using their millimeter wavelength radiation. Home: 20 Spring Valley Dr Holmdel NJ 07733 Office: Bell Labs HOH L239 Holmdel NJ 07733

WILSON, ROWLAND BRAGG, cartoonist; b. Dallas, Aug. 3, 1930; s. Elford Foman and Thelma (Bragg) W.; B.F.A., U. Tex., 1952; postgrad. Columbia, 1952-54; m. Elaine Libman, Nov. 21, 1953 (div.); children—Amanda, Reed Elizabeth, Kendra Page and Megan Blair (twins). Freelance cartoonist, N.Y.C., 1952-54; animation cartoonist Keitz & Herndon, Dallas, 1954; art dir. Young & Rubicam, N.Y.C., 1957-64; freelance, N.Y.C., 1957—; daily comic strip Noon, 1967—; resident designer Richard Williams Animation Ltd., London, Eng., 1973-75. Served with AUS, 1954-56. Recipient Clio award for film design of comml. Trans-Siberian Express, 1975, 1st prize comml. 3d Internat. Animation Festival, N.Y.C., 1975, Bronze Lion award Venice Animation Festival, 1975, Grand Prix, Irish Animation Festival, 1975. Methodist. Author: (cartoons) The White of Their Eyes, 1963. Illustrator: Bigger Than a Breadbox, 1967; (children's books) Tubby and the Lantern, 1972, Tubby and the Poobah, 1972. Rep. anthologies. Address: 21 N Turkey Hill Westport CT 06880

WILSON, ROY KENNETH, ret. educator; b. Charleston, Ill., July 9, 1913; s. George William and Ruth (Woody) W.; B.Ed., Eastern Ill. State Coll., 1936; A.M., U. Ill., 1943; Litt. D., Glassboro (N.J.) State Coll., 1959; m. Ruth June Royce, Aug. 19, 1939; 1 son, Robert Royce. Asso. editor Nat. Printer Journalist, The Printing Industry, Springfield, Ill., 1935-37; dir. pub. relations Eastern Ill. U., Charleston, 1937-42; asst. dir. div. press and radio relations N.E.A., Washington, 1946-57, dir. div. press, radio and TV relations, 1957-68; sec-treas., staff dir. Nat. Sch. Pub. Relations Assn., 1950-68, exec. dir., 1968-76; cons. Ednl. Research Service, 1977—; guest lectr. San Francisco State Coll., George Peabody Coll., U. So. Calif.; editorial dir. Edn. U.S.A., 1958-76. Mem. NEA, Pub. Relations Soc. Am., Am. Soc. Assn. Execs., Nat. Sch. Pub. Relations Assn., Am. Assn. Sch. Adminstrs., Phi Delta Kappa. Methodist. Clubs: Nat. Press; Springfield (Va.) Golf and Country. Home: 8252 Toll House Rd Annandale VA 22003 Office: 1800 N Kent St Suite 1020 Arlington VA 22209

WILSON, RUBY LELIA, nurse, educator; b. Punxsutawney, Pa., May 29, 1929; d. Clark H. and Alda E. (Armstrong) W.; B.S. in Nursing Edn., U. Pitts., 1954; M.S.N., Case Western Res. U., 1959; Ed.D., Duke U., 1969. Staff nurse, asst. head nurse Allegheny Gen. Hosp., Pitts., 1951-52, night clin. instr., adminstrv. supr., 1951-55; staff nurse, asst. head nurse Fort Miley VA Hosp., San Francisco, 1957-58; instr. nursing Duke U. Sch. Nursing, Durham, N.C., 1955-57, asst. prof. med. surg. nursing, 1959-66, asso. in medicine, 1963-66, prof. nursing, 1971—, dean Sch. Nursing, 1971—, asst. prof. dept. community and family medicine Inst. Medicine, Duke U. Sch. Medicine, 1971—. Fellow Am. Acad. Nursing; mem. Am. Assn. Colls. Nursing, Am. Assn. Higher Edn., Am. Nurses Assn., Nat. League Nursing, N.C. Med. Care Commn., Inst. Planning Com. Assn. for Acad. Health Centers. Club: Torch. Contbr. articles to profl. jours. Office: Sch Nursing Duke Univ Durham NC 27710

WILSON, RUFUS HAROLD, govt. ofcl; b. Sweetwater, Tenn., Sept. 14, 1925; s. James Samuel and Jessie Mae (Marshall) W.; student Wayne U., 1945-46; spl. degree Am. U., 1946; student Washington Coll. Law, 1950; LL.B., U. Balt., 1969; m. Florence Carol Mieczkowski, Nov. 26, 1949; children—Douglas Harold, Michael, Laureen. Mich. state service dir. AMVETS, 1947. asst. nat. service dir., 1948, chmn. nat. savs. bond com., 1948, nat. service and legislative dir., 1952, nat. comdr., 1954-55; asst. dir. field service VA, 1955-56, dir. Congressional Liason Service, 1956-58, mgr. regional office, St. Petersburg, Fla., 1958-65, mgr. regional office, Lincoln, Nebr., 1965, Balt., 1965-69, chief benefits dir. central office, 1969-70, asso. dep. adminstr., 1970-75, dir. Nat. Cemetery Service, 1975-76, chief benefits dir., 1975-77, dep. adminstr. VA, 1977—. Mem. Gov.'s Com. Employment of Handicapped, Md.; chmn. Civil Servant of Yr. Com.; profl. adviser Fla. Com Employment Handicapped; chmn. rehab. com. World Vets. Fedn., Gen. Assembly, Vienna, 1954, mem. council, 1954—; chmn. Am. del. Brussels, 1956; mem. Pres.'s Com. on Employ the Physically Handicapped, 1948, 76, Fed. Adv. Council, 1953. Vice pres. United Fund, St. Petersburg, Fla., 1965. Served with USMC, 1943-45. Decorated Purple Heart, Presdl. Unit Citation; recipient fellowship Georgetown U., 1959-60; Nat. citation for DAV and Mil. Order Purple Heart; Nat. Civil Service League award, 1975; Exceptional Service award VA, 1977; cited bd. Md. depts. of Am. Legion, VFW, Jewish War Vets, also Md. Vets. Comm., 1969; named Md. Vet. of Yr., Joint Vets. Council of Md., 1970. Mem. DAV (cited by Md. dept. 1969), Mil. Order Purple Heart, Am. Legion, VFW, Fed. Exec. Assn. Md. (pres. 1968-69). Address: 5165 Evangeline Way Columbia MD 21044

WILSON, RUSSELL HOWARD, physician; b. Eldorado, Okla., Oct. 31, 1912; s. Carl Arthur and Elizabeth (Settliff) W.; B.S., U. Okla., 1938, M.D., 1940; M.S., U. Minn., 1951, Ph.D., 1953; m. Elizabeth Johnson, July 27, 1951; children—Mary Elizabeth, John B., Anne B. Intern, USPHS Hosp., Seattle 1940-41; surgeon USPHS for UN in Greece, 1941-46; fellow, instr. medicine U. Minn., 1946-53; asso. prof. medicine U. Tex. Southwestern Med. Sch., 1954-65; prof., chmn. dept. physiology pharmacology U. N.D. Sch. Medicine, 1965-72, prof. physiology pharmacology, 1972-73; internist Wysong Clinic, McKinney, Tex., 1972-73; asso. prof. medicine S.W. Med. Sch., 1972—; spl. lectr. Tex. Women's U., 1973—; mem. Kaiser Prudential Med. Staff, 1979—. Bd. dirs. Am. Cancer Soc., 1970-72. Served with USNR, 1943-45. Diplomate Am. Bd. Internal Medicine (also recertified). Fellow A.C.P., Am. Coll. Chest Physicians; mem. A.M.A., Am. Physiol. Soc., Am. Assn. for Cancer Research, Central Soc. Clin. Research, Am. Cancer Soc. Baptist. Home: 6218 Walnut Hill Lane Dallas TX 75230. *My philosophy: Be happy with each day; love one's family, friends and business associates. Discipline one's self for one's chosen profession to excel with optimism. Be guided by the Ten Commandments.*

WILSON, SALLIE, ballerina; b. Fort Worth, Apr. 18, 1932; d. Edward Lawrence and Sybil (Mahler) W.; student of Margaret Craske and Antony Tudor; m. Ali Pourfarrakh, Mar. 11, 1960. Soloist, Met. Opera Ballet, 1950-55, Am. Ballet Theatre, 1955-58, N.Y.C. Ballet, 1959; ballerina Am. Ballet Theatre, 1960—; guest appearances with civic ballet cos. in Balt., Denver, Bloomington, Ind., also Jacob's Pillow Dance Festival, Martha Graham & Co.; TV appearance on World of Music with Agnes DeMille and Morton Gould; leading roles in Pillar of Fire, Fall River Legend, The Moor's Pavane, Les Sylphides. Address: care Am Ballet Theatre 888 7th Ave New York NY 10019*

WILSON, SAMUEL, JR., architect; b. New Orleans, Aug. 6, 1911; s. Samuel and Stella (Poupeney) W.; B.Arch., Tulane U., 1931; m. Ellen Elizabeth Latrobe, Oct. 20, 1951. Architect office Moise H. Goldstein, 1930-33, Historic Am. Bldgs. Survey in La., 1934-35; architect office Richard Koch, 1935-42, asso., 1945-55, partner Richard Koch & Samuel Wilson Jr., New Orleans, 1955-72, Koch and Wilson Architects, 1972—; lectr. La. architecture Tulane U. Mem. adv. bd. area council Boy Scouts Am.; bd. dirs. Maison Hospitaliere, Friends of Cabildo. Served with USCGR, 1942-45. Recipient Edward Langley scholarship AIA, 1938; citation Nat. Trust for Historic Preservation, 1968; Merit award Am. Assn. State and Local History, 1977. Fellow AIA; mem. Soc. Archtl. Historians, La. Landmarks Soc. (pres. 1950-56; bd.). Roman Catholic. Clubs: Boston (New Orleans). Author: A Guide to Architecture of New Orleans, 1699-1959; other publs. in field. Editor: Impressions Respecting New Orleans (by B. H. B. Latrobe), 1951. Contbr. articles profl. publs. Home: 1121 Washington Ave New Orleans LA 70130 Office: 1100 Jackson Ave New Orleans LA 70130

WILSON, SAMUEL MACK, univ. dean, educator; b. Newport, Tenn., Feb. 25, 1921; s. Ronald Earl and Virgie (Murr) W.; B.A., Maryville Coll., 1946; M.B.A., U. Pa., 1948, Ph.D., 1955; m. Lois Elisabeth Graf, July 1, 1944; 1 son, Samuel Mayhew. From instr. to prof. bus. adminstrn. Temple U., 1948—, chmn. mgmt. dept., 1969-71, asso. dean Sch. Bus. Adminstrn., 1970-73; cons. to bus. and industry. Served from lt. to col. USMC Res., 1944—. Mem. Soc. Advancement of Mgmt. (pres. Phila. chpt., also gov. regional v.p. 1975, nat. fin. v.p. 1979-80), Delaware Valley Maryville Coll. Alumni Club (pres.), AAUP (pres. Temple U. chpt. 1979), Delta Sigma Pi, Beta Gamma Sigma. Presbyn. (ruling elder). Contbr. articles profl. jours. Home: Thurwood 1730 Susquehanna Rd Abington PA 19001 Office: Speakman Hall 13th and Montgomery Av Philadelphia PA 19121. *In a democratic society, human development requires some balance between equal opportunities and freedom of choice with more emphasis on freedom of the individual. Opportunities are sources of hope, motivation and accomplishments while freedom is the basis for individual fulfillment.*

WILSON, SAMUEL SMITH, lawyer, educator; b. Cin., Aug. 11, 1924; A.B., Princeton U., 1947; LL.B., U. Cin., 1961. Admitted to Ohio bar, 1961; asso. firm Nieman, Aug, Elder & Jacobs, Cin., 1961-65; asso. prof. U. Cin. Coll. Law, 1965-68, prof., 1968-74, 78—, Nippert prof., dean, 1974-78; reporter Cin. Times Star, 1947-53, Washington corr., 1953-56, editorial writer, 1956-58; actor Juvenile Ct. program WCPO-TV, Cin., 1975—; chmn. Cin-Hamilton County Criminal Justice Supervisory Commn.; pres. Cin. Legal Aid Soc., 1977—. Mem. Am., Ohio, Cin. bar assns., Am. Law Inst. Author: (with Phillips) Bicentennial History of U.S. Sixth Court of Appeals, 1977; (with Beirne, Harper and Young) Ohio Civil Practice, 1973; editor-in-chief Law Rev. U. Cin. Coll. Law, 1960-61; contbr. articles to profl. jours. Home: 1278 Dillon Ave Cincinnati OH 45226 Office: U Cin College Law Cincinnati OH 45221

WILSON, SLOAN, writer, lectr.; b. Norwalk, Conn., May 8, 1920; s. Albert F. and Ruth (Danenhower) W.; grad. Fla. Adirondack Sch. 1938; A.B., Harvard, 1942; m. Elise Pickhardt, Feb. 4, 1941 (div.); children—Lisa, Rebecca, David Sloan; m. 2d, Betty Stephens; 1 dau., Jessica. Writer, contbr. New Yorker and other mags.; with Providence Jour., 1946-47, Time, Inc., 1947-49, Nat. Citizens Commn. for Pub. Schs., 1949-53; dir. information services, asst. prof. English, Buffalo U., 1953-55; asst. dir. White House Conf. on Edn., 1955-56. Served to lt. USCGR, World War II. Author: Voyage to Somewhere, 1946; The Man in the Gray Flannel Suit, 1955; A Summer Place, 1958; A Sense of Values, 1960; Georgie Winthrop, 1962; Janius Island, 1966; Away From It All, 1969; All The Best People, 1970; What Shall We Wear to This Party, 1976; Small Town, 1978; Ice Brothers, 1979. Address: . *Although some of my books have been widely read, I of course am not as successful as a writer as I would like to be. Almost all writers, after all, must, if they are honest, suspect that their triumps are temporary. This is no cause for lament, for the same happens to almost everybody in all walks of life. I am lucky to have a wife who makes my private life a joy and three daughters and a son who with my grandchildren give me a kind of immortality. Much like the characters in most of my books, I find my family the only part of my life which does not disappoint. My children and my wife always give me excellent reviews which never yellow in a scrapbook. I sometimes lecture on the topic of "Success." Nowadays that word seems to be to be much more complex than it did when I was young.*

WILSON, SLOAN JACOB, physician, educator; b. Dallas, Jan. 22, 1910; s. Jacob Resor and Estella (Cherrie) W.; A.B., U. Wichita, 1931, M.S., 1932; B.S. in Medicine, U. Kans., 1934, M.D., 1936; m. M. June Bowles, June 14, 1959; children—Sloan Richard, Charles Rook, Nancy Joan, Mark Samuel. Intern, Ohio State U. Hosp., Columbus, 1936-37, resident, 1937-40; instr. U. Wichita, 1933-34, Ohio State U., 1940; asst. prof. medicine U. Kans., Kansas City, 1946-53, asso. prof., 1954-61, prof., 1962—, chief exec. officer dept. medicine, 1962-76; treas. Med. Assn. Chartered, 1962-76, cons., 1976—. Bd. dirs. Community Blood Bank Greater Kansas City, 1956-59; active Friends of Art, Nelson Gallery of Art, Kansas City. Served to lt. col. M.C., U.S. Army, 1940-46. Recipient Disting. Service award dept. medicine U. Kans., 1976, Spl. Services award U. Kans. Med. Alumni Assn., 1978; named hon. curator Japanese art U. Kans., 1962. Diplomate Am. Bd. Internal Medicine. Fellow A.C.P. (gov. Kans. 1964-70, nat. gov. 1964-70), Fin. Analysts Fedn.; mem. Central Soc. Clin. Research, N.Y. Acad. Scis., Kansas City Soc. Fin. Analysts, Japan Am. Soc., SAR, Delta Tau Delta, Phi Beta Pi. Presbyterian. Clubs: Homestead Country, Masons. Author: Public Participation in the Stock Market, 1962; The Speculator and the Stock Market, 1962; Introduction to Stock Market Credit Analysis, 1965; Borrowed Money and Stock Market Trends, 1975; Hematology, Basic Course, 1975; Hematology, Advanced Course, 1975; Hematology, Pediatric Course, 1975; contbr. chpt. to New Ency. of Stock Market Techniques, 1977-78; also articles to med. jours. Home: 5618 W 62d St Shawnee Mission KS 66202 Office: 39th and Rainbow Blvd Kansas City KS 66103. *As an educator and physician, it is my fond hope and wish that all students maintain open, receptive minds. May they continue to follow the principles and compassion of our great leaders who have gone before them. The greatness of our nation is based on the individual's realization of his inherent worth and responsibility.*

WILSON, TED LEWIS, mayor; b. Salt Lake City, May 18, 1939; s. Robert L. and Eva (Simpson) W.; B.S., U. Utah, 1964; M.Ed. (NSF fellow), U. Wash., 1969; m. Kathryn Carling, June 10, 1963; children—Benjamin, Jennifer, Melissa, Jessica. Tchr., Granite Sch. Dist., Salt Lake City, 1966-73; adminstrv. asst. to a congressman, 1973-75; social services dir. Salt Lake County, Utah, 1975-76; mayor of Salt Lake City, 1976—. Bd. dirs. Intermountain Health Care, Inc. Served with U.S. Army, 1961-62. Recipient Valor award Dept. of Interior, 1968. Mem. U.S. Conf. of Mayors (adv. bd.), Nat. League of Cities and Towns, Am. Soc. Pub. Adminstrs., Common Cause. Democrat. Mormon. Contbr. articles to profl. jours. Office: Room 300 City and County Bldg Salt Lake City UT 84111

WILSON, THEODORE ALLEN, educator; b. Evansville, Ind., Sept. 27, 1940; s. Benjamin Harrison and Anna Lee (Basham) W.; A.B., Ind. U., 1962, M.A. (Ford Found. fellow), 1963, Ph.D., 1966; m. Judith Kay Juncker, Sept. 5, 1962; children—Laura Marie, Andrew Allen. Asst. prof. history U. Kans., Lawrence, 1965-69, asso. prof., 1969-73, prof., 1973—, asso. dean, 1976-78, chmn., 1978—; sr. research asso. Harry S. Truman Library Inst., Independence, Mo., 1969-72; vis. prof. Univ. Coll., Dublin, 1975-76. Recipient Francis Parkman prize Soc. Am. Historians, 1969; Nat. Endowment for Humanities fellow, 1971-72; Guggenheim fellow, 1972-73. Mem. Soc. Am. Historians, Orgn. Am. Historians, Soc. Historians Am. Fgn. Relations, Phi Beta Kappa. Author: The First Summit: Roosevelt and Churchill at Placentia Bay, 1941, 1969; Three Generations in Twentieth Century America, 1976. Editor: World War II: Critical Issues, 1974; (with others) The Makers of American Diplomacy, 1974; The Marshall Plan, 1977. Home: 2925 Topeka Ln Lawrence KS 66044

WILSON, THOMAS HASTINGS, educator, physiologist; b. Phila., Jan. 31, 1925; s. David Wright and Helene (Connet) W.; student Oberlin Coll.; M.D., U. Pa., 1948; Ph.D. (Am. Cancer Soc. exchange student), U. Sheffield (Eng.), 1953; m. Dorothy Marguerite Blanchard, Dec. 27, 1952; children—Katherine, Peter, Susan, Elizabeth. Intern, U. Pa. Hosp., Phila., 1948-49; mem. faculty U. Pa., 1949-50, Washington U., St. Louis, 1956-57; mem. faculty Harvard Med. Sch., 1957—, prof. physiology, 1966—. Author: Intestinal Absorption, 1962. Home: 21 Hillside Terr Belmont MA 02178 Office: 15 Shattuck St Boston MA 02115

WILSON, THORNTON ARNOLD, airplane co. exec.; b. Sikeston, Mo., Feb. 8, 1921; s. Thornton Arnold and Daffodil (Allen) W.; student Jefferson City (Mo.) Jr. Coll., 1938- 40; B.S., Iowa State Coll., 1943; M.S., Calif. Inst. Tech., 1948; Sloan fellow Mass. Inst. Tech., 1952-53; m. Grace Miller, Aug. 5, 1944; children—Thornton Arnold III, Daniel Allen, Sarah Louise. With Boeing Co., Seattle, 1943—, asst. chief tech. staff, project engring. mgr., 1957-58, v.p., mgr. Minuteman br. aerospace div., 1962-64, v.p. operations and planning, 1964-66, exec. v.p., dir., 1966-68, pres., 1968—, chief exec. officer, chmn. bd., 1972—. Bd. govs. Ia. State U. Found.; mem. Bus. Council. Fellow Am. Inst. Aeros. and Astronautics; mem. Beta Theta Pi. Club: Seattle Golf. Home: 126 S W 171st Seattle WA 98166 Office: The Boeing Co PO Box 3707 Seattle WA 98124

WILSON, TIMOTHY WATSON BURR, photographer; b. Hollywood, Calif., Nov. 12, 1948; s. George Penrose and Barbara Jean (McCabe) W.; student U. Calif. at San Diego, 1969-70, San Diego State U., 1970-72. From clk. to photographer San Diego Union and Evening Tribune newspapers, from 1968, photography editor Evening Tribune, 1975-77; now freelance; partner Mime Ltd., graphics and pub.; owner Zygote, design studio. Recipient 1st place award in fashion Nat. Press Photographers Assn., 1974, 1st place in feature category A.P. News Execs. Council, 1975, numerous others; named Outstanding News Photographer, Copley newspapers, 1972. Mem. Calif. Press Photographers Assn. (v.p. 1973-74, 1st place award in creative color 1973, 1st place award in portrait 1975). Home: 4680 Santa Monica Ave San Diego CA 92107

WILSON, TOM, cartoonist, greeting card co. exec.; b. Grant Town, W.Va., Aug. 1, 1931; s. Charles Albert and Hazel Marie W.; grad. Art Inst. Pitts. Advt. layout man Uniontown (Pa.) Newspapers Inc., 1950-53; designer Am. Greetings Corp., Cleve., 1955-56, creative dir., 1957-78, v.p. creative devel., 1978—; cartoonist: The Ziggy Treasury, Never Get Too Personally Involved in Your Own Life, Encore, Encore, It's A Ziggy World, Life is Just A Bunch of Ziggy's; former mem. faculty Cooper Sch. Art. Served with U.S. Army, 1953-55. Recipient Purchase award Butler Museum Nat. Painting Competition. Developer Soft Touch line of greeting cards. Office: 12120 Elmwood Ave Cleveland OH 44111

WILSON, VERNON EARL, educator; b. Kingsley, Iowa, Feb. 16, 1915; s. Willie Earl and Elizabeth Pearl (Kinney) W.; B.S., U. Ill., 1950, M.S. in Pharmacology, M.D., 1952; m. Ula R. Rhone, July 1, 1947; children—William Earl, Carla Jean. Asst. pharmacology U. Ill. Sch. Medicine, 1950-52; asst. prof. pharmacology, asst., then asso. dean U. Kans., 1953-59; prof. pharmacology, dean Sch. Medicine, dir. Med. Center, U. Mo., 1959-67, exec. dir. health affairs, 1967-68, v.p. acad. affairs, 1968-70; adminstr. health services and mental health adminstrn. USPHS, Dept. Health, Edn. and Welfare, 1970-73; prof. pharmacology, community health U. Mo., Columbia, 1973-74; vice pres. med. affairs, prof. med. adminstrn. Vanderbilt U., Nashville, 1974—. Cons. health edn. and constrn. USPHS, 1964-67, coordinator Mo. Regional Med. Program, 1966-68; bd. dirs. United Health Found.; trustee Midwest Research Inst.; mem. Adv. Council on Health Research Facilities, NIH, 1965-69; edni. adv. com. VA, 1968-73; mem. Gov.'s Adv. Council on Comprehensive Health Planning, 1967-73. Bd. dirs. Am. Bd. Family Practice. Served with USNR, 1943-46. Mem. Assn. Am. Med. Colls. (exec. council 1961-67, steering com. council on fed. relations 1968—), Am. Assn. History Médicine, A.M.A. (council on med. edn. 1967-75), Am. Acad. Family Practice, Nat. Assn. State Univs. and Land Grant Colls. (mem. commn. on health professions 1966-70, chmn. 1966-68), Mid-Am. State Univs. Assn. (council, exec. com. 1968-73), Sigma Xi, Alpha Kappa, Phi Mu Phi, Alpha Omega Alpha, Pi Kappa Epsilon. Rotarian. Home: 1912 Cromwell Dr Nashville TN 37215 Office: Vanderbilt U 21st and Garland Nashville TN 37232

WILSON, VERNON KEITH, banker; b. Providence, Nov. 30, 1930; s. Vernon Keith and Elizabeth Mae (Colburn) W.; A.B., Harvard U., 1952, J.D., 1959; m. Margaret Elizabeth Mullen, July 29, 1967; children—Elizabeth Parks, Kathryn Margaret, Emily Drake. Admitted to Maine bar, 1959; With Maine Nat. Bank, Portland, 1959—, sr. v.p., head trust div., 1972—, exec. v.p., 1974—; mem. faculty Colby tax Inst., U. So. Maine. Bd. dirs. Maine div. Am. Cancer Soc.; mem. deferred gifts com. Maine Med. Center. Served with USNR, 1952-56. Mem. Maine Bar Assn., Maine Estate Planning Council, Cumberland County Bar Assn. Clubs: Cumberland, Rotary. Home: 98 Carroll St Portland ME 04102 Office: 400 Congress St Portland ME 04104

WILSON, VICTOR JOSEPH, educator; b. Berlin, Germany, Dec. 24, 1928; s. Andrew A. and Lydia (Yampolsky) W.; B.S., Tufts Coll., 1948, M.S., 1949; research student U. Cambridge (Eng.), 1949-50; Ph.D., U. Ill., 1953; m. Isa Hermer, June 7, 1953; children—Janet, Denise. Research asso. Rockefeller U., N.Y.C., 1953-58, asst. prof., 1958-62, asso. prof., 1962-69, prof. physiology, 1969—. Served to 1st lt. U.S. Army, 1954-56. Mem. Am. Physiol. Soc., Soc. Neurosci., Harvey Soc., Sigma Xi, Phi Beta Kappa. Research physiology central nervous system. Home: 4525 Henry Hudson Pkwy New York City NY 10471

WILSON, WADE, coll. pres.; b. July 29, 1914; s. Blaine and Rosa (Ragland) W.; B.S., Cheyney State Coll., 1936; M.Ed., Pa. State U., 1937; Ed.D., N.Y. U., 1954; LL.D., Hahnemann Med. Coll., 1969; m. Naomi A. Sewell; 1 son, Glenn A. Asso. prof. indsl. edn. Md. State Coll., 1937-39, 46-47; chmn. dept. Savannah State Coll., 1939-40, Tenn. Agrl. and Indsl. State Coll., 1940-42; instr. Cheyney State Coll., 1947-52, asso. prof., 1952-57, prof. indsl. edn., dir., 1957-67, dir. devel., 1967-68, pres., 1968—. Mem. exec. com. Assn. Pa. State Coll. Faculties, 1957-65, mem. legis. com., 1959-65, pres., 1962-65; chmn. credit com. Delaware County Fed. Tchrs. Credit Union, 1960-64; mem. Nat. Council Accreditation Tchr. Edn. Visitation and Appraisal Team, 1961; mem. adv. com. tchr. edn. and certification Pa. Dept. Pub. Instrn., Harrisburg, 1962-63; cons. in field. Mem. Delaware County Authority. Bd. dirs. Research Better Schs., Clara Baldwin House, Delaware County Econ. Devel. Center; bd. visitors Sch. Edn. U. Pitts., Haverford Twp. Sch. Dist., 1975, Afro-Am. Hist. and Cultural Mus. Mem. N.E.A., (chmn. task force human rights 1967-68, mem. human rights council, exec. com. 1968-74, Pa. State Edn. Assn. (pres. 1967). Pa. Indsl. Arts Assn. (pres. 1962), Epsilon Pi Tau (laureate mem.), Phi Delta Kappa, Kappa Delta Pi, Omega Psi Phi, Sigma Pi Phi. Co-author Workbook for the Maintenance Engineering Student, 1943. Contbr. articles to profl. jours. Address: Cheyney State Coll Cheyney PA 19319

WILSON, WALTER WILLIAM, investment banker; b. Washington, Kans., Dec. 19, 1905; s. Walter E. Wilson; B.S., U. Pa., 1925; M.B.A., Harvard U., 1927; m. Helen Scudder, Aug. 16, 1933; 1 dau., Sandra W. With Continental Ill. Nat. Bank & Trust Co. of Chgo., 1927-37; with Morgan Stanley & Co., Inc., 1937—, gen. partner, 1945—. Life trustee Com. Econ. Devel. Clubs: Apawamis, Manursing Island (Rye); Links, Harvard (N.Y.C.). Home: 33 Mohawk St Rye NY 10580 Office: 1251 Ave of Americas New York City NY 10005

WILSON, WARNER RUSHING, educator; b. Jackson, Miss., July 27, 1935; s. William Enouch and Ruby (Goyne) W.; A.B., U. Chgo., 1956; M.A., U. Ark., 1958; Ph.D., Northwestern U., 1960. Teaching asst. Northwestern U., 1957-60; research psychologist E.I. duPont de Nemours & Co., Wilmington, Del., 1960; asst. prof. U. Hawaii, 1960-65; asso. prof. U. Ala., 1965-73; prof. Wright State U., Dayton, Ohio, 1973—. Cons., Bryce State Hosp., Tuscaloosa, Ala., 1966, Ednl. Testing Service, 1968, Tuscaloosa VA Hosp., 1968-74, H.R.B. Singer Co., 1972. Trainee Downey (Ill.) VA Hosp., summer 1959; spl. summer fellow in evaluation research Northwestern U., 1973-74. Research grantee DuPont Co., 1961-62, NIMH, 1965, 68-70, NSF, 1966-68. Named Outstanding Psychology student U. Ark., 1956-57. Mem. Am., Midwestern, Southeastern psychol. assns., AAUP, NAACP, ACLU, Psychonomic Soc., Soc. Exptl. Social Psychology, Sigma Xi, Psi Chi. Contbr. articles to profl. jours. Home: 854 Edinboro Ct Dayton OH 45431 Office: Dept Psychology Wright State U Dayton OH 45431

WILSON, WILBURN LEROY, assn. exec.; b. Plain Dealing, La., July 2, 1913; s. James Dave and Rosa (Wallace) W.; grad. Chillicothe (Mo.) Bus. Coll., 1931; m. Jeanne Marion Clohesey, Oct. 15, 1964; children—Susan Jeanne, Linda, John. With Lions Internat., Oak Brook, Ill., 1932—, asst. treas., 1942-43, treas., 1944-69, exec. adminstr., 1970—. Named Ambassador of Good Will award Lions Internat.; recipient numerous Presdl. awards. Mem. Central Lions Club Chgo. Lutheran. Home: 825 N Merrill St Park Ridge IL 60068

WILSON, WILLIAM DANIEL, architect; b. Louisville, Mar. 11, 1919; s. Jesse Rodman and Louise Kemper (Perkins) W.; A.B., Princeton U., 1941, M.F.A. (Woodrow Wilson fellow), Sch. Architecture, 1949; m. Margaret Halstead Corry, Apr. 29, 1972; children by previous marriage—Peter Langston, Rodman Phair, Christopher Pierce. Partner, Holden Egan Wilson & Corser, Architects, N.Y.C., 1953-67, Gruzen & Partners, Architects & Planners, N.Y.C., Newark, 1967—; vis. lectr. structural design Princeton Sch. Architecture; bd. govs. Clinton Housing Devel. Co.; trustee Citizens Housing and Planning Council, N.Y.C.; mem. housing urban devel. com. Community Service Soc., N.Y.C.; chmn. Bldg. Bd. Appeals, Darien, Conn., 1953-55, vice chmn. Planning Zoning Commn., 1956-62; architect Police Hdqrs., N.Y.C., 1974, Schomburg Plaza, N.Y.C., 1975. Fellow AIA (pres. N.Y. chpt. 1965-65); mem. Phi Beta Kappa. Office: Gruzen & Partners 1700 Broadway New York NY 10019

WILSON, WILLIAM JEWELL, educator, physician; b. St. Joseph, Mo., Dec. 14, 1932; s. Truman Jewell and C. Bernice (Reardon) W.; A.B., William Jewell Coll., 1954; M.D., U. Mo., 1958; m. Mildred Jane Brown, June 4, 1957; children—Susan Kay, Christopher Leighton, Nancy Patricia, William Jewell, Alice Ann. Intern, U.S. Naval Hosp., St. Albans, N.Y., 1958-59; resident radiology U. Mo., 1962-65; fellow in cardiovascular radiology U. Minn., Mpls., 1965-66; asst. prof. radiology U. Va., 1966-68; Found. prof., chmn. radiology U. Nebr. Coll. Medicine, Omaha, 1968-74; dir. radiology Long Beach Meml. Hosp. Med. Center, 1974—. Chmn. urban crisis task force First United Meth. Ch., Omaha, 1968-70; Cub Scouts den father, adult counselor Boy Scouts Am., 1968—. Served to lt. M.C., USNR, 1958-62. Markle scholar in acad. medicine, 1967. Fellow Am. Coll. Cardiology, Am. Coll. Radiology (com. chmn., mem. Commn. on Diagnosis); mem. Calif. Med. Assn., AMA (vice chmn. radiology residency rev. com. 1972-78), Soc. Chairmen Acad. Radiology Depts., Assn. U. Radiologists, Alpha Omega Alpha. Author: Computer Analysis of Gastric Ulcers, 1965; Prosthetic Cardiac Valve Motion, 1966; Coronary Arteriography and Cesium Myocardial Scanning, 1968; Computer Radiology Information Storage and Retrieval, 1969; Remote Radiographic Image Transmission, 1973; A Clinically Useful Microfocal Spot X-Ray Tube, 1975; Computerized Axial Tomography, 1977. Editor: Computers in Radiology, 1975; Cardiac Radiology, 1979; editorial cons. Continuing Education in Family Practice, 1973. Home: 2801 Atlantic Ave Long Beach CA 90801

WILSON, WILLIAM JULIUS, sociologist; b. Derry Twp., Pa., Dec. 20, 1935; s. Esco and Pauline (Bracy) W.; B.A., Wilberforce U., 1958; M.A., Bowling Green State U., 1961; Ph.D., Wash. State U., 1966; m. Mildred Marie Hood, Aug. 31, 1957; children—Colleen, Lisa; m. 2d, Beverly Ann Huebner, Aug. 30, 1970; children—Carter, Paula. Asst. prof. U. Mass., Amherst, 1965-69, asso. prof., 1969-71; vis. asso. prof. U. Chgo., 1971-72, asso. prof. dept. sociology, 1972-75, prof., 1975—, chmn. dept. sociology, 1978—; mem. bd. univ. publs. U. Chgo. Press, 1975-79. Bd. dirs. Social Sci. Research Council, 1979—. Served with U.S. Army, 1958-60. Recipient Disting. Tchr. of Year award U. Mass., Amherst, 1970. Mem. Am. Sociol. Assn. (Sydney M. Spivack award 1977), Sociol. Research Assn., Internat. Sociol. Assn., Chgo. Urban League (Beautiful People award 1979). Democrat. Author: Power, Racism and Privilege, 1973; Through Different Eyes, 1973; The Declining Significance of Race, 1978. Home: 5228 S Greenwood Ave Chicago IL 60615 Office: Dept Sociology U Chgo 1126 E 59th St Chicago IL 60637

WILSON, WILLIAM PRESTON, psychiatrist; b. Fayetteville, N.C., Nov. 6, 1922; s. Preston Puckett and Rosa Mae (VanHook) W.; B.S., Duke U., 1943, M.D., 1947; m. Dorothy Elizabeth Taylor, Aug. 21, 1950; children—William Preston, Benjamin V., Karen E., Tammy E., Robert E. Intern, Gorgas Hosp., Ancon, C.Z., then resident psychiatry Duke U. Med. Center, later resident neurology, 1949-54; asst. prof. psychiatry Duke U. Med. Sch., 1955-58; asso. prof. psychiatry, dir. psychiat. research U. Tex. Med. Br., Galveston, 1958-60; asso. prof. psychiatry Duke U. Med. Center, 1961-64, head div. clin. neurophysiology, 1961-76, prof. psychiatry, head div. biol. psychiatry, 1964—; chief neurophysiol. labs. VA Hosp., Durham, N.C., 1961-76; sec. Am. Bd. Qualification in Electroencephalography, 1971—; mem. Gov. N.C. Task Force Diagnosis and Treatment; med. adv. com. N.C. Found. Mental Health Research; bd. dirs. nat. div. Contact Teleministry USA, also mem. internat. commn. healing; cons. numerous area hosps. Mem. ofcl. bd. Asbury United Methodist Ch., Durham; mem. program and curriculum com. United Meth. Ch., 1973—; trustee Meth. Retirement Home, Durham, N.C.; pres. United Meth. Renewal Services, Inc., 1978—. Served with AUS, 1943-46. Fellow EEG, Montreal Neurol. Inst., 1954-55; NIMH postdoctoral fellow; Finch lectr. Fuller Theol. Sem., Pasadena, Calif., 1974. Diplomate Am. Bd. Psychiatry and Neurology (examiner). Mem. Am., So. (pres. 1977-78) psychiat. assns., Am., So. (chmn. sect. neurology and psychiatry 1970) med. assns., Med. Soc. N.C., Durham-Orange County Med. Soc. (chmn. student recruitment com. 1965) med. assns., Soc. Biol. Psychiatry, Am. (councillor), So. (pres. 1964) EEG socs., Assn. Research Nervous and Mental Diseases, Am. Epilepsy Soc., AAAS, Am. Acad. Neurology, Sigma Xi, Alpha Omega Alpha. Republican. Club: U.S. Power Squadron (comdr. Durham 1971). Editor: Applications of Electroencephalography in Psychiatry. Contbr. med. jours. Home: 1209 Virginia Ave Durham NC 27705 Office: PO Box 3838 Duke Medical Center Durham NC 27710

WILT, JAMES WILLIAM, educator, chemist; b. Chgo., Aug. 28, 1930; s. Edward Frank and Mary (Manarik) W.; A.B., U. Chgo., 1949, M.Sc., 1953, Ph.D. (NSF fellow), 1954; m. Catherine R. McAndrews, Jan. 10, 1953; children—Donna M., Susan A., Gregory E., Catherine M., Maureen T. Instr. U. Conn., 1955; mem. faculty Loyola U., Chgo., 1955—, prof. chemistry, 1966—, chmn. dept. chemistry, 1970-77. Mem. Am. Chem. Soc., Phi Beta Kappa, Sigma Xi. Contbr. articles to profl. jours. Home: 2745 Pauline Ave Glenview IL 60025 Office: Dept Chemistry Loyola U 6525 N Sheridan Rd Chicago IL 60626

WILT, MATTHEW RICHARD, library assn. exec.; b. Hollidaysburg, Pa., Apr. 14, 1924; s. Howard Matthew and Leta (mcFadden) W.; B.A., Coll. San Luis Rey, 1946; M.A., Cath. U. Am., 1949; M.L.S., Columbia U., 1955. Tchr. high sch. and jr. coll. Franciscan Sem., Hollidaysburg, 1949-54; fgn. book buyer Sidney Kramer Books, Washington, 1956-57; acquisitions librarian Georgetown U., 1957-60; exec. sec. Cath. Library Assn., 1960-64, exec. dir., 1964—; instr. Sch. Library Sci., Villanova U., 1968—; faculty Sch. Library Sci., Drexel Inst. Tech. Mem. ALA, Cath. Press Assn., Pa. Library Assn., Council Nat. Library Assns., Library Pub. Relations Assn. Phila., Booksellers Phila. Editor Cath. Library World, 1961-64, mng. editor, 1964—. Home: 421 E Durham St Philadelphia PA 19119 Office: 461 W Lancaster Ave Haverford PA 19041

WILTON, (JAMES) ANDREW (RUTLEY), museum curator; b. Farnham, Surrey, Eng., Feb. 7, 1942; came to U.S., 1976; s. Herbert Rutley and Mary Cecilia (Buckerfield) W.; B.A., Trinity Coll., Cambridge U., 1964, M.A., 1966; m. Christina Frances Benn, Sept. 7, 1976. Asst. keeper Walker Art Gallery, Liverpool, Eng., 1965-67; asst. keeper dept. prints and drawings Brit. Mus., London, 1967-76; curator prints and drawings Yale Center for Brit. Art, New Haven, 1976—; lectr. history of art Yale U. Fellow Royal Soc. Arts. Author: Turner in Switzerland, 1976; British Watercolours, 1750-1850, 1977; J.M.W. Turner: His Art and Life, 1979; Williams Yars: Journey through the Alps, 1979. Office: Yale Center for British Art Chapel St New Haven CT 06520

WILTON, WILLIAM EVERETT, tel. and tel. co. exec.; b. East St. Louis, Ill., May 23, 1916; s. Lane E. and Nettie May (Lukey) W.; A.B. in Econs., Ill. Coll., 1939; m. Ruth Jean Campbell, June 4, 1966; children—Douglas H., Kent R. Mfg. technician Jasper Blackburn Corp., St. Louis, 1939-47, works mgr., 1947-53, v.p. engring. and mfg., 1953-61, exec. v.p., 1961-67, pres., 1967—; pres. ITT Blackburn Co. subs. ITT, St. Louis, 1968—; gen. mgr. Utility Products ITT, 1972—; dir. DeBron Corp., St. Louis, Boatmen's Nat. Bank, St. Louis, Fin. Data Systems, Inc., St. Louis. Chmn. bd. mgrs. YMCA, Webster Groves, Mo.; trustee Ill. Coll., Jacksonville, Deaconess Hosp.; bd. dirs. Jr. Achievement of Mississippi Valley, Inc. Mem. St. Louis Electric Bd. Trade, Am. Electric Mfg. Corp. (pres. 1969-71), Pres.'s Assn. of Am. Mgmt. Assn. Congregationalist (chmn. endowment trust 1971-75, chmn. bd. trustees 1966-70). Club: Engineers (St. Louis). Home: 321 Planthurst Rd Webster Groves MO 63119 Office: 1525 Woodson Rd Saint Louis MO 63114

WILTSE, CHARLES MAURICE, historian; b. San Francisco, Apr. 4, 1907; s. Herbert Alphonso and Mary Eastman (Blake) W.; A.B., W.Va. U., 1929; Ph.D., Cornell U., 1932; Litt.D., Marshall Coll., 1952; m. Kelly Tollolah Tooks, Dec. 24, 1952. Mem. staff Nat. Resources Com., 1934-38; asst. to dir. edn. NYA, 1938- 40; spl. asst. to exec. sec. WPB, 1943-46; cons. Nat. Security Resources Bd., 1948-49; dep. exec. sec., dir. secretariat Nat. Prodn. Authority and Def. Prodn. Adminstrn., 1951-53; historian Army Med. Service, 1954-60, chief historian, 1960-67; editor Papers of Daniel Webster; prof. history Dartmouth Coll., Hanover, N.H., 1967—. Mem. Nat. Hist. Publs. Commn., 1970-74. Served with U.S. Army, 1943. Guggenheim fellow, 1949-51. Mem. Soc. Am. Archivists, Orgn. Am. Historians, Western History Assn., Am. Hist. Assn., Soc. Am. Historians. Unitarian. Author: The Jeffersonian Tradition in American Democracy, 1935; Life of John C. Calhoun, 3 vols., 1944-51; Industrial Mobilization for War (with J. W. Fesler, others), 1947; The New Nation, 1800-1845, 1961; Medical Service in the Mediterranean and Minor Theatres in World War II, 1965; also numerous govt. publs., essays, reviews, articles. Home: 17 Haskins Rd Hanover NH 03755 Office Baker Library Dartmouth Coll Hanover NH 03755

WILTSHIRE, RAYMOND STANLEY, elec. engr.; b. West Portsmouth, Ohio, Dec. 17, 1929; s. Arley Hayes and Elizabeth Jane (Redden) W.; B.E.E., Ohio State U., 1952; M.B.A., Denver U., 1976; m. Mary Louise Mahan, Oct. 10, 1954; children—Blaine J., Brenda Jane. Sr. field engr. Nat. Cash Register Co., 1952-55; nuclear project engr. White Sands Missile Range, 1955-57; systems test engr. RCA, 1957-58; with Martin Marietta Corp., Denver, 1958—, mgr. Viking systems integration, 1969-71, dir. research and tech. programs, 1973—. Bd. dirs. Castlewood Fire Dept., 1968-70; troop chmn. local Boy Scouts Am., 1968-73; mem. Greenwood Greenbelt Commn., 1973-75, Gov. Colo. Com. to obtain Solar Energy Research Inst., 1975—; mem. tech. com. Denver Urban Obs., 1976—; adv. panel Denver Research Inst.; adv. bd. exec. M.B.A. program U. Denver. Served with AUS, 1955-57. Registered profl. engr., Ohio, Colo. Asso. fellow Am. Inst. Aeros. and Astronautics; mem. Am. Astron. Soc. (charter chmn. Rocky Mountain sect.), Am. Radio Relay League. Author publs. in field. Home: 8302 Riding Ridge Pl McLean VA 22102 Office: Martin Marietta-Aerospace 6801 Rockledge Dr Bethesda MD 20034

WILTSHIRE, RICHARD WATKINS, ins. co. exec.; b. Richmond, Va., July 17, 1921; s. William Ernest and Essie (Watkins) W.; B.A., U. Va., 1943; m. Jean Watkins Betts, Sept. 5, 1942; children—Mrs. Henry M. Massie, Jr., Richard Watkins, Jr., William Betts, Virginia Betts. With Home Beneficial Life Ins. Co., Richmond, Va., 1946—, dir. agy. tng., 1947, asst. supr. agys., 1947-50, asst. v.p., 1950-52, dir., 1949—, v.p., 1952-66, exec. v.p., gen. mgr., 1966-68, pres., 1968—; dir. First & Merchants Corp. Trustee The Collegiate Schs., Richmond Meml. Hosp., Crippled Childrens Hosp. Served with USMCR, 1942-45. Presbyterian (elder). Home: 8916 Tolman Rd PO Box 27572 Richmond VA 23261 Office: 3901 W Broad St Richmond VA 23230

WILZIG, SIGGI BERT, banker; b. Krojanke, Germany, Mar. 11, 1926; s. Isidor and Sophie (Sommerfeld) W.; came to U.S., 1947, naturalized, 1956; student high sch., Berlin; m. Naomi Barbara Sisselman, Dec. 31, 1953; children—Ivan, Sherry, Alan. Unskilled worker, salesman, 1947-54; gen. mgr. Nieswand & Son, Newark, 1954-58; dir., exec. v.p. Bronze & Granite Memorials, Inc., Clifton, N.J., 1958—; pres., chief exec. officer Wilshire Oil Co. Tex., N.Y.C., 1965—; dir. Trust Co. N.J., Jersey City, 1968—, vice chmn., 1970-71, chmn. bd., chief exec. officer, 1971—, pres., 1974—; pres., chief exec. officer Wilshire Electronics Group, Wilshire Oil Can., Calgary, Alta.; lectr. U.S. Mil. Acad., 1975. Mem. Jersey City Fiscal Adv. Bd., 1974. Mem. nat. campaign cabinet State of Israel Bonds, chmn. banking div. No. N.J. region; trustee Daus. of Miriam Center for Aged, Clifton; dir. trustees, fellow N. Cordozo Sch. Law Yeshiva U.; bd. dirs. Jewish Hosp. and Rehab. Center of N.J., N.J. Banking Adv. Bd., Passaic County Econ. Devel. Commn.; mem. adv. bd. President's Commn. on Holocaust, 1978. Recipient Prime Minister's medal State of Israel, 1975, Distinguished Service award Yeshive U., 1977. Nazi forced laborer 1941-42; in Auschwitz concentration camp, 1943-45, Mauthausen concentration camp, 1945. Mem. Passaic (dir.), Jersey City (dir.) chambers commerce. Jewish (trustee congregation). Mem. B'nai B'rith. Odd Fellow. Club: Marco Polo (N.Y.C.). Home: 340 Dwas Line Rd Clifton NJ 07012 Office: 250 Park Ave New York NY 10017. *Free men do not deserve a bright future if they forget their bitter past.*

WIMAN, DAVID WAYNE, clergyman; b. Oblong, Ill., Aug. 31, 1910; s. George Everett and Cora (Hamilton) W.; A.B., Bethel Coll., 1935; B.D., Cumberland Presbyn. Theol. Sem., 1936, D.D., 1951; m. Helen Bright, May 27, 1941 (dec. 1954); children—David, Vicki Lynn; m. 2d, Louise Long, Nov. 17, 1957. Ordained to ministry Cumberland Presbyterian Ch., 1932; pastorates, Ill., Ky., Tenn., 1932-38; field rep. Gen. Assembly Bd. Tithing and Budget, Assembly, Cumberland Presbyn. Ch.; sec.-treas., office exec., Memphis, 1939-45, clk., treas. Gen. Assembly, financial agt., gen. traveling sec., supt. transportation, 1945-55; pastor Second Cumberland Presbyn. Ch., Chattanooga. Trustee Gen. Assembly, Cumberland Presbyn. Ch.; sec.-treas., office exec., Commn. on Evangelism, 1945—; pastor Margaret Hank Meml. Presbyn. Ch., Paducah, Ky. Mem. Bd. Missions and Ch. Erection, 1937-39, chmn. com. lit. and theology, 1938-46. Mem. Bethel Coll. Alumni Assn. (pres. 1946-47), Phi Delta Sigma. Mason (Shriner), Kiwanian. Author: History of the Colored Cumberland Presbyterian Church, 1936. Home: 3632 Brighton Cove Paducah KY 42001

WIMBERG, JAMES JOHN, savs. assn. exec.; b. Cin., June 26, 1931; s. Leo Joseph and Julia (Cunningham) W.; A.B., Xavier U., 1952; LL.B., Chase Coll., 1960; m. Carol Joering, June 1, 1957; children—Theresa Anne, Steven Joseph, Christine Anne. Bldg. and loan examiner Ohio Commerce Dept., 1954-60; v.p., treas. Hunter Savs. Assn., Cin., 1960-67; exec. v.p., dir. Eagle Savs. Assn., Cin., 1967-70, pres., 1970—, dir., chief exec. officer, 1971—; chief exec. officer Eagle Investment Co., Cin.; dir., sec.-treas. Swissco Inc., Cin. Mem. City-County Planning Commn., Cin., 1973—; mem. OKI Housing Policy Commn., Cin., 1973—. Trustee Cin. Rehab. Fin. Corp., Summit Country Day Sch., 1979-80. Pres., bd. dirs. Neighborhood Housing Services Cin.; mem. alumni council Xavier U., Cin., investment adv. council, 1978-79. Served with U.S. Army, 1952-54. Mem. Ohio Bar Assn., U.S. (mem. legis. com., funds transfer services com. 1978-79), Ohio (mem. legis. com. 1971-75, mem. exec. com. 1975, trustee 1978-79) leagues savs. assns., Savs. and Loan League Southwestern Ohio (pres. 1979, trustee 1979). Roman Catholic. Clubs: Kenwood Country, Queen City, Bankers (Cin.). Home: 2 Grandin Farm Lane St Cincinnati OH 45208 Office: 580 Walnut St Cincinnati OH 45202

WIMBERLY, GEORGE JAMES, architect; b. Ellensburg, Wash., Jan. 16, 1915; s. George Welch and Eurma (Bezdechek) W.; B.Arch., U. Wash., 1937; student in Mex., 1938; m. Janet Harrietta Brebner, July 7, 1939 (div. Sept. 1969); 1 dau., Heather Mary; m. 2d, Walton Jeffords, Dec. 12, 1969. Draftsman, designer, Seattle, Los Angeles, Phoenix, 1938-40; architect U.S. Civil Service, Pearl Harbor, 1940-45; practice architecture, Honolulu, 1945—; partner Wimberly & Cook, 1945-59; pres., dir. Wimberly, Whisenand, Allison, Tong & Goo, Architects, Ltd., 1959—; prin. works include Keelikolani State Bldg., Honolulu, 1950, Canlis Restaurant, Seattle, 1951, Coco Palms Hotel, Kauai, Hawaii, 1952, First Nat. Bank, Waikiki, 1953, Canlis Restaurant, Honolulu, 1954, Honolulu Gas Co. Bldg., 1955, Hawaiian Trust Co. Bldg., Honolulu, 1956, Windward City Shopping Center, Kaneohe, Hawaii, 1957, First Nat. Bank, Kapiolani br., Honolulu, 1958, Finance Factors home office bldg., Honolulu, 1958, Home Ins. Bldg., Honolulu, 1959, Princess Kaiulani Hotel Waikiki, 1960, Hotel Tahiti, 1960, 3019 Kalakaua Ave Apt., 1961; Sheraton Maui Hotel, 1962, Civic Auditorium, American Samoa, 1963, Pago Pago Intercontinental Hotel, American Samoa, 1965, Bank of Hawaii Bldg., Waikiki, 1967, Visitor Center Mt. Rainier Nat. Park, 1967, Kona-Hilton Hotel, 1968, Taharaa's Intercontinental Hotel, Tahiti, 1968, Fijian Hotel, Nadi, Fiji, 1968, Sheraton Kauai Hotel, Kauai, 1968, Mauna Kea Beach Hotel South Wing, Kamuela, Hawaii, 1968; New Surfrider Hotel, Waikiki, 1969, Royal Hawaiian Diamond Head Wing, Waikiki, 1969, Tokyu Djakarta Hotel, Indonesia, 1971, Sheraton Waikiki Hotel, Honolulu, 1971, Hawaiian Telephone Office Bldg., Honolulu, 1972, Ibusuki Kanko Hotel, Tokyo, 1972, Maui Land and Pineapple Co. Bldg., 1972, Mauna Kea Beach Hotel Addition, Kamuela, 1972, First Hawaiian Bank, Waianae, Oahu, 1972, Hayashida Onsen Hotel, Japan, 1973, Iwasaki Hotel, Japan, 1973, Wailea Golf Clubhouse, Maui, 1973, Hanalei Beach and Racquet Club, 1975, Hyatt Regency at Hemmeter Center, Waikiki, 1976. Cons. for tourist facilities, Western Samoa, 1967-69, Ceylon, 1968, New Zealand, 1968, Australia, 1969, Singapore, 1970, Taiwan, 1971, Malaysia, 1971, Fiji, 1972, India, 1972, Nepal, 1975. Mem. Hawaii Bd. Registration Profl. Architects and Engrs., 1959-67. Pres., Waikiki Assn., 1951-53. Bd. dirs. Honolulu Community Theatre, 1961-64, Honolulu Theatre for Youth, 1960-63; mem. Honolulu Visitors Bur., 1952—, bd. dirs., 1973-77. Recipient Institutions Mag. Design awards; Holiday Mag. Design award; White Cement award of excellence Portland Cement Assn., 1972. Fellow AIA (pres. Hawaii 1953, hon. awards Hawaii chpt. 1955, 60 (3), 1962, 64, 66, 68 (2), 1972, 73-75); mem. Pacific Area Travel Assn. (contbg. mem., alt. dir. 1972—), Honolulu C. of C., Waikiki Improvement Assn., Tau Sigma Delta (pres. 1936). Clubs: Sports Car Club Am.; Les Chevaliers du Deuxième Hemisiècle; Le Grand Chevalier Intérimaire; Pacific, Outrigger Canoe (Waikiki). Office: 2222 Kalakaua Ave Honolulu HI 96815

WIMBERLY, JOHN HARRY, gas co. exec.; b. Houston, Dec. 6, 1904; s. Stonewall Jackson and Hallie (Holland) W.; student Rice Inst., 1922; B.B.A., U. Tex., 1927; m. Edith Cooney, Oct. 15, 1931; children—Bryan Holland, Lane Mayfield, Thomas Allan. Auditor, Houston Natural Gas Corp., 1931-40, treas., 1940-45, v.p., treas., 1945-47, exec. v.p., 1947-55, pres. corp. and subsidiaries, 1955-67, chmn. bd. corp. and subsidiaries, 1967-73, sr. chmn. bd. corp. and subsidiaries, 1973-75, hon. chmn., 1975—, dir., 1940—; dir. Port City State Bank, Houston. Pres., Houston Jr. C. of C., 1936. Trustee S.W. Research Inst., St. Luke's Episcopal Hosp. Mem. Am. (past dir., past pres.), So. (pres. 1952) gas assns., Tex. Bur. Econ. Understanding (past dir. v.p.), Tex. Research League (dir.), Tex. Mid-Continent Oil and Gas Assn (past dir.). Episcopalian (pres. churchmen's assns. 1949). Clubs: Houston Country (past pres.), Tejas (Houston). Home: 5421 Sturbridge Dr Houston TX 77027 Office: Houston Natural Gas Bldg PO Box 1188 Houston TX 77001

WIMBERLY, W. CARL, univ. adminstr.; b. Granite City, Ill., June 28, 1924; s. William and Ola (Marler) W.; B.S., M.A., So. Ill. U., 1949; Ph.D., U. Ill., 1957; m. Barbara Ann Haroldson, Feb. 4, 1950; children—Scott, Neil, Gail, Brian. Faculty, U. Wis., La Crosse, 1953—, prof. polit. sci., dean Coll. Letters and Sci., 1957-73, vice chancellor, 1973—. Chmn., United Ministries in Higher Edn. Wis., 1967. Served with AUS, 1943-45. Mem. Am., Midwest polit. sci. assns., Eta Phi Alpha. Presbyterian. Home: 3103 Glendale St La Crosse WI 54601

WIMPFHEIMER, CHARLES ANTHONY, publishing co. exec.; b. N.Y.C., Apr. 20, 1928; s. Harold David and Pat (Selwyn) W.; grad. Deerfield (Mass.) Acad., 1945; B.A., Williams Coll., 1949; m. Ann Rosenfeld, July 28, 1950; children—Kate, Andrew T. With Rutgers U. Press, 1949-51; with Random House, Inc., N.Y.C., 1951—, v.p., mng. editor adult trade div., 1966—. Trustee, treas. Town Sch., N.Y.C., 1960-73; trustee, chmn. health communications and community relations Lenox Hill Hosp., N.Y.C., 1970—; trustee Taft Sch., Watertown, Conn., 1974—. Clubs: Sunningdale Country (Scarsdale, N.Y.); Taconic (Williamstown, Mass.). Home: 911 Park Ave New York City NY 10021 Office: Random House 201 E 50th St New York City NY 10022

WIMSATT, WILLIAM ABELL, educator; b. Washington, July 28, 1917; s. William Church and Alma Engelbretson (Cheyney) W.; student George Washington U., 1935-36, Cath. U. Am., 1936-38; A.B., Cornell U., 1939, Ph.D., 1943; m. Ruth Claire Peterson, June 18, 1940; children—William C., Michael H., Mary S., John L., Jeffrey H., Ruth A. Instr. anatomy Harvard Med. Sch., 1943-45; faculty zoology Cornell U., 1940-43, 45—, prof., 1951—, chmn. dept., 1959-64. Research collaborator Brookhaven Nat. lab. 1954-59. Trustee Cornell U., 1960-65. Guggenheim fellow, 1962-63. Fellow AAAS; mem. Am. Assn. Anatomists, Am. Soc. Zoologists, Soc. Mammalogists, Histo-chem. Soc., Soc. for Study Reproduction, Sigma Xi, Phi Zeta, Phi Kappa Phi, Phi Gamma Mu. Home: 121 Cayuga Park Rd Ithaca NY 14850

WINANDY, JOHN PIERRE, chem. co. exec.; b. Luxembourg, July 28, 1926; s. Pierre and Catherine (Boever) W.; B.S., Purdue U., 1956; M.B.A., Harvard, 1958; m. Helen E. Magee, July 3, 1952; children—Catherine, John. Came to U.S., 1953, naturalized, 1957. Mgr. accounting and budgets W.R. Grace Overseas Chem. div., Cambridge, Mass., 1958-63; mgr. fgn. financial analysis Celanese Corp., N.Y.C., 1963-64; internat. controller Atlas Chem. Industries, Wilmington, Del., 1964-68; v.p. finance Internat. Flavors & Fragrances, Inc., N.Y.C., 1968—. Home: 17 Birch Rd Briarcliff Manor NY 10510 Office: 521 W 57th St New York City NY 10019

WINCENC, CAROL, flautist; b. Buffalo, June 29, 1949; d. Joseph Frank and Margaret (Miller) W.; Diploma, Santa Cecilia Acad. Music, Rome, 1967; Diploma d'Honore, Chigiana Acad. Music, Siena, Italy, 1968; student Oberlin Conservatory Music, 1967-69; Mus.B., Manhattan Sch. Music, 1971; Mus. M., Juilliard Sch. Music, 1972; m. Ronald J. Dennis, May 23, 1976. Prin. and solo flutist St. Paul Chamber Orch., 1972-77; solo flute recitalist, soloist with orch. and chamber music groups, 1978—; prin. flutist Aspen (Colo.) Chamber Symphony, Aspen Festival, summers 1970-72, Claremont (Calif.) Music Festival, 1973, Grand Teton (Wyo.) Music Festival, 1974-77; prin. and solo flutist in residence Marlboro (Vt.) Music Festival, 1978, 79; solo flutist Spoleto (Italy) Festival, in U.S. and Italy, 1977; flute tchr. and coach. Recipient Solo Debut Recital award Concert Artists Guild N.Y., 1972, Solo. Recital award Met. Museum N.Y. Introductions Series, 1977, 1st prize Walter W. Naumburg Solo Flute Competition, 1978, citation for bringing world outstanding recognition to Buffalo, Buffalo Area C. of C., 1978; Fulbright-Hayes French Govt. grantee. Mem. Asso. Musicians Greater N.Y., Nat. Flute Assn. Recorded with St. Paul Chamber Orch., Tashi Chamber Ensemble. Home and Office: 875 West End Ave New York NY 10025

WINCH, DAVID MONK, educator; b. London, July 22, 1933; s. Alexander and Lily Ruth (Monk) W.; came to Canada, 1957; B.Sc. in Econs., London Sch. Econs., 1954, Ph.D., 1957; postgrad. Yale U., 1955-56; M.A., St. John's Coll., Cambridge, Eng., 1970; m. Mary Elizabeth Scadding, July 6, 1957; children—Elizabeth Ann, Alexander David. Research asso. U. Toronto, 1957-58, vis. prof., 1965-66; spl. lectr. U. Sask., 1958-60; asst. prof. Econs. U. Albt., 1960-63, asso. prof., 1963-66; prof. econs. McMaster U., Hamilton, Ont., 1966—, chmn. dept. econs., 1971-77; mem. Ont. Economic Council, 1973—. Recipient Can. Council Killam award, 1970-71. Fellow St. John's Coll., Cambridge, 1970-71. Fellow Royal Soc. Can.; mem. Canadian Econs. Assn., Am. Econs. Assn. Author: The Economics of Highway Planning, 1963; Analytical Welfare Economics, 1971. Contbr. articles in field to profl. jours. Home: 661 Holt Dr Burlington ON L7T 3N4 Canada Office: Department of Economics McMaster University Hamilton ON L8S 4M4 Canada

WINCH, RALPH PHILIP, ret. educator; b. Milton Junction, Wis., Oct. 19, 1905; s. Philip George and Eva Leonore (Thompson) W.; A.B., Milton Coll., 1927; M.A., U. Wis. (scholar), 1929, Ph.D., 1931; m. Mary Elizabeth Johnson, June 8, 1930; children—Martha Elizabeth, Roger Holmes, Katherine Jean. Asst. physics Milton (Wis.) Coll., 1926-27, U. Wis., 1928-31, asst. astronomy, 1930-31; vis. asst. prof. physics Princeton, 1942; instr. Williams Coll., 1931-36, asst. prof., 1936-42, asso. prof., 1942-45, acting chmn. dept. physics, 1943-45, 53-54, chmn., 1960-70, prof., 1945-71, Barclay Jermain prof. natural philosophy, 1950-71, emeritus, 1971—; vis. prof. Brown U., 1953, Wesleyan U., Middletown, Conn., summer 1959-65, 68-71. Liaison officer Williams Coll.-Mass. Inst. Tech. Combined Plan, 1936-62. Fellow AAAS; mem. Am. Phys. Soc. (chmn. N.E. sect. 1957-58), Am. Assn. Physics Tchrs. (sec. 1961-66), Am. Inst. Physics, AAUP. Clubs: Williams College Faculty (past pres.) (Williamstown); Williams (N.Y.C.). Author textbook, also articles sci. jours. Home: 27 Bingham St Williamstown MA 01267

WINCHELL, FRANK JENNINGS, automobile co. exec.; b. Evansville, Ind., Jan. 15, 1918; s. Frank and Florence Lily (Jennings) W.; student Purdue U., 1936-39, D.Engring. (hon.), 1974; m. Margaret Nora Shaughnessy, Aug. 5, 1941; children—Judy Winchell Gigante, Quanah Winchell Holland. With Gen. Motors Corp., 1941—, mgr. planning Chevrolet Motor div., 1969-70, spl. asst. to pres. for engring. product, 1970-71, v.p. engring. staff, 1971—, also chmn. gen. tech. com. Trustee, Gen. Motors Inst.; mem. bd. visitors Sch. Engring., Oakland U. Fellow Engring. Soc. Detroit, Soc. Automotive Engrs. (tech. bd. 1975-78); mem. Mich. Acad. Sci., Arts and Letters (hon.), Purdue Alumni Assn., Tau Beta Pi, Beta Theta Pi. Clubs: Orchard Lake Country; Birmingham Athletic; Tequesta (Fla.) Country. Patentee in field. Home: 3463 W Shore Dr Orchard Lake MI 48033 Office: Engring Staff Gen Motors Tech Center Warren MI 48090

WINCHELL, PAUL, actor; b. N.Y.C., Dec. 21, 1922; s. Sol and Clara (Fuchs) W.; student Columbia U., 1958-59; grad. Acupuncture Research Inst. Coll., 1974; D.Sc., Nat. Christian U., Richardson, 1975; children—Stephanie, Stacy Paul. Appeared on own radio show, 1943—; created Jerry Mahoney, 1936, Knucklehead Smiff, 1950; ventriloquist, star Winchell and Mahoney show NBC-TV, 1947, Dunninger and Winchell, 1948-49, The Paul Winchell and Jerry Mahoney Speidel Show, 1950-53, Paul Winchell and Jerry Mahoney's What's My Name, 1952-54, Toy Land Express, 1955, Circus Time, 1956-57, The Paul Winchell Show, 1957-60, Cartoonsville, 1963, Winchell and Mahoney Time, 1965, Runaround, 1972-73; provides voices for numerous TV cartoon shows; appeared in Stop, Look and Laugh, 1959; Which Way to The Front?, 1970; The Aristocats, 1971; Winnie the Pooh and the Blustery Day (Acad. award), 1971; The Man from Clover Grove, 1973; Winnie the Pooh and Tigger Too, 1974; played in theatres, night clubs; dir., producer numerous TV shows and programs; appeared TV movie The Treasure Chest Murder, 1975. Recipient 1st prize Maj. Bowes Original Amateur Hour, 1936; TV's Most Versatile Performer award Look mag., 1952, 53; grammy for Best Children's Record Album, 1974. Author: Ventriloquism for Fun and Profit, 1954; (with Dr. Keith E. Kenyon) Pressure Points, 1974.

Inventor, patentee artificial heart, donated to U. Utah. *When I get a good idea, I recognize the value of it, and I do not underestimate it because it is mine. When I decide to pursue the idea and accomplish it, I do not let it go for a moment until I achieve it.*

WINCHELL, RICHARD PAUL, chem. co. exec.; b. Arlington, Mass., Feb. 16, 1922; s. Guilbert and Evelyn Sue (Saylor) W.; B.S. magna cum laude in Mech. Engring., Tufts U., 1943; m. Martha Field Smith, Jan. 29, 1944; children—David, Stephen, Peter, Linda. Engr., Liquid Carbonic Corp., 1946-47, gen. mgr. Liquido Carbonico Colombiana, S.A., Bogota, Colombia, 1947-56, gen. mgr. internat. ops. Liquid Carbonic div. Gen. Dynamics Corp., 1956-60, v.p. internat. ops., 1961-68, exec. v.p. Liquid Carbonic Corp. subs. Houston Natural Gas Corp., Chgo., 1969—, dir. co., internat. subs. cos. Trustee Gloria Dei Luth Ch., Silvanus Pakard Soc. Tufts U. Served to lt. USNR, 1943-46. Mem. Chgo. Council Fgn. Relations, Tau Beta Pi, Theta Delta Chi. Republican. Clubs: Union League, Ruth Lake Country. Office: 135 S LaSalle St Chicago IL 60603

WINCHESTER, ALBERT MCCOMBS, educator, author; b. Waco, Tex., Apr. 20, 1908; s. Robert Stevenson and Mamie Katherine (Moore) W.; A.B., Baylor U., 1929; A.M., U. Tex., 1931, Ph.D., 1934; postgrad. U. Chgo., 1940, Harvard, 1952, U. Mich., 1959, U. Munich, 1960; m. Josephine Milam Walker, Dec. 23, 1934; 1 dau., Betty Jo. Head biol. dept. Okla. Bapt. U., Shawnee, Okla., 1935-42; prof. biology Baylor U., 1942-46; head biology dept. Stetson U., DeLand, Fla., 1946-61; prof. biology U. No. Colo., Greeley, 1962—, specialist in human heredity and biol. photography. Mem. Colo. Bd. Examiners in Basic Scis. Named Outstanding Scholar of Year U. No. Colo., 1972. Fellow AAAS; mem. Am. Soc. Human Genetics, Genetics Soc. Am., Eugenics Soc. Am., Sigma Xi. Elk, Lion. Author: Zoology-the Science of Animal Life, 1947, rev. 1961; Biology and its Relation to Mankind, 1949. rev. 1957, 69, 75; Genetics, A Survey of the Principles of Heredity, 1951, rev. 1958, 71, 76, Hebrew transl., 1974, Spanish transl., 1977, Chinese transl., 1977; Heredity and Your Life, 1957, rev. 1960, 1966, Spanish transl., 1974; Genetics Laboratory Manual, 1958, 77; Heredity, 1962, rev., 1975; Modern Biological Principles, 1965, rev. edit., 1970, Russian transl., 1976; Human Development and Inheritance, 1968; Concepts of Zoology, 1970; Human Heredity, 1971, rev., 1975, 78; The Nature of Human Sexuality, 1973; Heredity, Evolution and Humankind, 1975. Author sects. on biology Am. People's Ency. and Yearbooks, World Book, Ency. Brit., Ency. Sci. Home: 2316 15th St Apt 411 Greeley CO 80631

WINCHESTER, JAMES HUGH, writer; b. Midlothian, Tex., June 27, 1917; s. James Hugh and Mary (Adams) W.; ed. pub. schs., Calif.; m. Josephine Mary Nowodzinski, Feb. 12, 1948; children—Kenneth, Nancy. Reporter, Stockton (Calif.) Independent, also Stockton Record, 1933-35, N.Y. Morning Telegraph, 1935-38; pub. relations with Am. Airlines, also CBS, 1938-42; feature writer King Features Syndicate, 1946-61; free-lance writer, 1961—; staff writer Reader's Digest, 1967-74, roving editor, 1974—; regular contbr. nat. mags., also author syndicated column, TV documentaries. Served with USAAF, 1942-45. Decorated Army Commendation ribbon; recipient 1st prize annual TWA Aviation Writing award, 1950, 51, 52, 53, 61, 64, 65; Streibig award Aviation Space Writers Assn., 1967; Med. Writing award Am. Acad. Family Physicians, 1978. Mem. Am. Soc. Travel Writers (bd. dirs. 1961-64; 1st prize journalism award 1949), N.Y. Soc. Travel Writers, Aviation/Space Writers Assn. (Mag. Writing award 1974), Internat. Soc. Aviation Writers, Soc. Mag. Writers, Writers Guild Am., Screen Actors Guild, Am. Assn. Sci. Writers, Med. Writer's Assn., Sigma Delta Chi (Deadline Club award 1974). Democrat. Club: Overseas Press (N.Y.C.). Author: Wonders of Water, 1964; Hurricanes, Storms, Tornadoes, 1966. Contributing editor: Hit Parade of Flying Stories, 1965. Home: 5B Heritage Circle Southbury CT 06488

WINCKLER, CHARLES EDWIN, ret. aluminum co. exec.; b. Bklyn., Nov. 15, 1916; s. Lucien and Elvira (Stromberg) W.; B.S., N.Y. U., 1943; student Am. Inst. Banking, 1934-37, U. Houston, 1956-57; m. Helen Margaret Schwaner, June 15, 1940; children—Edwin A., Caryl E. (Mrs. Robert E. Terrell), Lois J. (Mrs. Robert E. Paul). With Aluminum Co. Am., 1937-79, v.p., controller, 1971-77, v.p. taxes and internal auditing, 1977-79. Recipient award N.Y. Soc. Pub. Accountants, 1943. Mem. Tax Execs. Inst. (bd. dirs. 1968-70), Financial Execs. Inst., U.S. C. of C., N.A.M., Am. Mining Congress, Machinery and Allied Products Inst., Beta Gamma Sigma. Home: Route 4 93 Skysail Rd Salisbury NC 28144

WIND, HERBERT WARREN, writer; b. Brockton, Mass., Aug. 11, 1916; s. Max E. and Dora W.; B.A., Yale U., 1937; M.A., Cambridge (Eng.) U., 1939. Staff writer New Yorker mag., N.Y.C., 1947-54, 62—, staff writer The Sporting Scene; editor, writer Sports Illustrated mag., N.Y.C., 1954-60; cons., writer, asso. producer Shell's Wonderful World of Golf, TV series, 1961-62; author: (with Jack Nicklaus) The Greatest Game of All—My Life in Golf, 1969, (with Ben Hogan) The Modern Fundamentals of Golf, 1957, The Story of American Golf, 1948; contbr. articles to various mags.; tchr. seminar on lit. of sports Yale U., 1973. Served with USAAF, 1942-46; PTO. Mem. Oxford and Cambridge Golfing Soc., Yale Golf Assn. Clubs: Royal and Ancienc Golf of St. Andrews, Jesters. Editor books, including: The Complete Golfer, 1954; The Realm of Sport, 1966; Game, Set and Match, 1979. Home: 301 E 66th St New York NY 10021 Office: 25 W 43d St New York NY 10036

WINDAL, FLOYD WESLEY, educator; b. Bradley, Ill., Sept. 23, 1930; s. Floyd and Marguerite (Meyer) W.; B.S. in Accounting, U. Ill., 1952, M.S., 1955, Ph.D., 1959; m. Vicky Lou Seeley, June 27, 1964; children—Jodie Lynn, Blake Elliott. Mem. audit staff Arthur Andersen & Co., Chgo., 1952, Los Angeles, 1958-59; grad. asst., instr. U. Ill., 1954-58; mem. faculty Mich. State U., East Lansing, 1959-72, prof. accounting and financial adminstrn., 1969-72; prof. accounting and bus. law, head dept. U. Ga., Athens, 1972-77, prof., dir. Sch. Acctg., 1977-78, prof., 1978—. Served to 1st lt. AUS, 1952-54. Postdoctoral fellow Price-Waterhouse Found., 1966-67. C.P.A., Ill. Mem. Am. Inst. C.P.A.'s, Ga. Soc. C.P.A.'s, Am. Acctg. Assn. (sec.-treas. 1975-77, S.E. regional v.p. 1977-78), Nat. Assn. Accountants, Fin. Execs. Inst., Alpha Kappa Lambda. Christian Scientist (1st reader 1973-75). Mason. Author: (with Robert N. Corley) The Professional Accountant: Ethics, Responsibility, and Liability, 1980; contbr. articles to profl. jours. Home: 305 St George Dr Athens GA 30606

WINDELS, PAUL, JR., lawyer; b. Bklyn., Nov. 13, 1921; s. Paul and Louise E. (Gross) W. A.B., Princeton, 1943; LL.B., Harvard U., 1948; m. Patricia Ripley, Sept. 10, 1955; children—Paul III, Mary H., James H.R., Patrick D. Admitted to N.Y. State bar, 1949; spl asst. counsel N.Y. State Crime Commn., 1951; asst. U.S. atty. Eastern Dist. N.Y., 1953-56; N.Y. regional adminstr. SEC, 1956-61, also spl. asst, U.S. atty. for prosecution securities frauds, 1956-58; lectr. law Am. Inst. Banking, 1950-57; partner Windels, Marx, Davies & Ives and predecessor firms, 1961—; dir. Security Traders Assn. N.Y. Trustee, v.p. Bklyn. Law Sch.; trustee, chmn. Lycée Francais de N.Y.; trustee Fed. Bar Council, French Inst./Alliance Francais, Fedn. French Alliances in U.S. Served from pvt. to capt. F.A., AUS, 1943-46; ETO; maj. Arty. Res. Recipient Flemming award for fed. service; decorated chevalier Order French Acad. Palms, officer Nat. Order Merit France. Mem. Am., N.Y. State bar assns., Assn. Bar City N.Y., N.Y. County Lawyers Assn., Harvard Law Sch. Assn. N.Y.C. (v.p.). Republican. Presbyterian. Author: Our Securities Markets-Some SEC Problems and Techniques, 1962. Home: 1220 Park Ave New York City NY 10028 Office: 51 W 51st St New York City NY 10019

WINDER, CLARENCE LELAND, educator, psychologist; b. Osborne County, Kans., June 16, 1921; s. Clarence McKinley and Edna (Ikenberry) W.; student Santa Barbara State Coll., 1941; A.B. with honors, U. Calif. at Los Angeles, 1943; M.A., Stanford U., 1946, Ph.D., 1949; m. Elizabeth Jane Jacobs, Aug. 14, 1943; children—David William, Christina Louise. From instr. to asso. prof. Stanford, 1949-61, dir. Psychol. Clinic, 1953-61; prof., dir. Psychol. Clinic, Mich. State U., 1961-62, prof. psychology, 1961—, chmn. dept., 1963-67, dean Coll. Social Sci., 1967-74, asso. provost, 1974-77, provost, 1977—; prof., dir. Psychol. Services Center, U. So. Calif., 1962-63; cons. V.A., Mich. Dept. Mental Health; spl. research psychol. aspects schizophrenia, parent-child relations and personality devel. Served to 1st lt. USAAF, 1943-45. Decorated Air medal with 7 clusters, D.F.C. Fellow Am. Psychol. Assn.; mem. Mich. Psychol. Assn., AAAS, Sigma Xi. Home: 1776 Hitching Post Rd East Lansing MI 48823

WINDER, RICHARD BAYLY, educator; b. Greensboro, N.C., Sept. 11, 1920; s. Richard Bayly and Julia (Purnell) W.; A.B., Haverford Coll., 1946; A.M., Princeton, 1947, Ph.D., 1949; m. Viola Hitti, Oct. 12, 1946; 1 son, Bayly Philip. Mem. staff Am. U. Beirut (Lebanon), 1947-49; from instr. to asso. prof. and asst. dean coll. Princeton, 1947-64; prof. history and Near Eastern langs. and lit. N.Y. U., 1966—, chmn. dept. Near Eastern langs. and lit. Washington Sq. Coll., 1966-68, dir. Center for Near Eastern Studies, 1966-76, acting dean Washington Sq. Coll., 1968-69, dean of coll., 1969-71, dean faculty of arts and sci., 1970-77. Summer tchr. U. Mich., 1951, U. So. Calif., 1957, Harvard, 1963, U. Utah, 1964, U. Pa., 1969; cons. to industry, 1951—. Cons. Ford. Found. on Edn. Egypt, 1960-61, HEW, 1967-72, Dept. State, 1979; mem. nat. screening com. Asia and Near East, Fgn. Area Fellowship Program, 1964-67, chmn. 1965-67; mem. nat. screening com. Near East, Fulbright Hays, 1963-67; advisory com. Cons. Service U.S. Undergrad. Study Abroad, 1962-65; dir. Nat. Undergrad. Program Overseas Studies Arabic, 1961-66; mem. UNESCO Internat. Commn. Textbooks for Arab Refugees, 1968-69; chmn. grants com. Am. Research Center in Egypt, 1971-76, treas., mem. exec. com., bd. govs., 1972-79. Treas., Princeton chpt. Am. Field Service, 1951-60, nat. bd. dirs., mem. exec. com., 1961-68; bd. dirs. Am. Middle East Rehab, 1968-73, East West Group, Ltd., 1973—, Amideast, 1974—; trustee Am. U. in Cairo, Am. Sch. Oriental Research. With Am. Field Service, 1942-45. Decorated Purple Heart; mentioned in despatches (Brit.). Ford Found. fgn. area tng. fellow, Damascus, Syria, 1955-56; Princeton African travel grantee, 1959. Mem. Am. Oriental Soc., Middle East Inst., Am. Hist. Assn., Royal Central Asian Soc. (local hon. sec. U.S.), Royal Asiatic Soc., Middle East Studies Assn. (dir. 1966-71, pres. 1968-69), Brit. Soc. for Middle Eastern Studies, Oriental Club N.Y., Am. Assn. Tchrs. Arabic, Cum Laude Soc., Council Fgn. Relations, Phi Beta Kappa. Clubs: Century, Nassau, 200; Travellers' (London). Author: (with F.J. Ziadeh) An Introduction to Modern Arabic, 6th edit., 1957; Saudi Arabia in the Nineteenth Century, 1965. Collaborator (with Edward J. Jurji) Saudi Arabia, 3d rev. edit., 1958. Editor: (with J. Kritzeck) The World of Islam; Studies in Honour of Philip K. Hitti, 3d edit., 1960; Current Problems in North Africa, 1960; Near Eastern Round Table 1967-68, 1969. Translator: (Tewfik El Hakim) Bird of the East, 1966; (Constantine Zuraik) The Meaning of The Disaster, 1956. Home: 86 Castle Howard Ct Princeton NJ 08540 Office: Center for Near Eastern Studies New York U New York NY 10003

WINDHAGER, ERICH ERNST, physiologist; b. Vienna, Austria, Nov. 4, 1928; came to U.S., 1954, naturalized, 1969; s. Maximilian and Berta Elisabeth (Feitzinger) W.; M.D., U. Vienna, 1954; m. Helga Rapant, June 19, 1956; children—Evelyn Ann, Karen Alice. Research fellow Harvard Med. Sch., 1956-58; instr. physiology Cornell U. Med. Coll., N.Y.C., 1958-61, asst. prof., then asso. prof., 1961-69, prof., 1969—, chmn. dept. physiology, 1973—, Maxwell M. Upson prof., 1978—; vis. scientist U. Copenhagen, 1961-63. Recipient Homer W. Smith award N.Y. Heart Assn., 1978. Mem. Am. Physiol. Soc., Biophysical Soc., Am. Soc. Nephrology, N.Y. Acad. Sci., Internat. Soc. Nephrology, Gesellschaft fur Nephrologie. Office: Dept Physiology Cornell Univ Med Coll 1300 York Ave New York NY 10021

WINDHAM, CHARLES WYATT, shopping center exec., investor; b. Burkeville, Tex., Mar. 7, 1901; s. Thomas J. and Elizabeth P. (Harrell) W.; student Alford Acad., 1918; grad. Dallas Inst. Tech. Law, 1926; m. Gladys Mae Patman, Dec. 20, 1919; children—Donald Kinard, Muriel Esther. Personnel dir. City of Dallas, 1939-41; chmn. Dallas Civil Service Bd., 1935-39; exec. v.p. Western States Life Ins. Co., 1939-65; pres. Guardian Internat. Life Ins. Co., 1941-65, Guardian Underwriters Ins. Co., Guardian Life Ins. Co., Dallas, 1952-65; mgr. Central Park Shopping Center, San Antonio; dir. Exchange Bank & Trust Co., Dallas; pres. Exchange Park Co., 1956-65; owner of various bus. enterprises. Served as sp. investigator for congl. com. of Ho. of Reps., 1942-46. Mem. Dallas YMCA, Nat., Tex., Dallas bldg. owners and mgrs. assns., Life Ins. Assn. Am., Life Ins. Inst. Am., Life Mgrs. Assn. Dallas, Dallas St. and Newspaper Boys (chmn. com. mgmt.). Mem. Christian Ch. (elder). Mason (32, Shriner), Lion. Clubs: Dallas County Democratic Womens, Athletic, Cipango, Executive (Dallas); Brook Hollow Country. Home: 818 Wedgwood Apts San Antonio TX 78230 Office: 243 Central Park San Antonio TX 78216

WINDHAM, EDWIN OTIS, computer co. exec.; b. Hartford, Conn., Apr. 27, 1930; s. Edwin Otis and Edlie Bernice (McCraw) W.; B.S. in Bus. Adminstrn., U. Denver, 1952; postgrad. U. Calif. at Berkeley, 1954-55; m. Joyce Lois Hansen, Jan. 26, 1953; children—Gayle Claire, Jeffrey Lind, Glenn Kirby. Mgr. Arthur Andersen & Co., San Francisco, 1955-59, San Juan, P.R., 1959-64, San Jose, Calif., 1964-68; controller Arcata Nat. Corp., Menlo Park, Calif., 1968-73; asst. controller Rohr Industries, Inc., San Diego, 1973-74; v.p. finance Commodore Bus. Machines, Palo Alto, Calif., 1974-76; dir. fin. NRC Micrographic Systems, Mountain View, Calif., 1976—. Served with AUS, 1952-54. C.P.A., Calif. Mem. Am. Inst. C.P.A.'s, Calif. Soc. C.P.A.'s, Financial Execs. Inst., Pi Kappa Alpha, Beta Alpha Psi. Republican. Lutheran. Club: Clear Lake Riviera Yacht and Golf (Lakeport, Calif.). Home: 3473 Woodstock Ln Mountain View CA 94040 Office: NCR Micrographic Systems Mountain View CA 94040

WINDLE, JOSEPH RAYMOND, bishop; b. Ashdad, Ont., Can., Aug. 28, 1917; s. James David and Bridget (Scollard) W.; student St. Alexander's Coll., Limbour, Que., 1936-39; D.D., Grand Sem., Montreal, 1943; D.C.L., Lateran U., Rome, 1953. Ordained priest Roman Catholic Ch., 1943; asst. priest, later parish priest and vice-chancellor Pembroke Diocese, 1943-61; aux. bishop Ottawa, 1961-69; coadjutor bishop Pembroke, 1969-75, bishop, 1975—. Clubs: K.C. Home: 188 Remfrew St Pembroke ON K8A 6X1 Canada*

WINDLE, WILLIAM FREDERICK, educator; b. Huntington, Ind., Oct. 10, 1898; s. William C. and Georgia (Kimball) W.; B.S., Denison U., 1921, D.Sc. (hon.), 1947; postgrad. U. Mich., 1923, U. Chgo., 1924, U. Wis., 1925; M.S., Northwestern U. Med. Sch., 1923, Ph.D., 1926; m. Ella Grace Howell, June 14, 1923; children—Mary (Mrs. R.A. Skyer), William. Asst. in anatomy Northwestern U. Med. Sch., 1922, instr., 1923-26, asst. prof., 1926-29, asso. prof., 1929-35, prof. microscopic anatomy, 1935-42; prof. neurology, dir. Inst. Neurology, 1942-46; prof. anatomy, dir. dept. U. Wash. Med. Sch., Seattle, 1946-47; prof. anatomy, chmn. dept. U. Pa. 1947-51, research prof. 1951; sci. dir. Baxter Labs., Inc., Morton Grove, Ill., 1951-53; chief lab. neuroanat. scis. Nat. Inst. Neurol. Diseases and Blindness, NIH, 1953-60, asst. dir., 1960-61, chief lab. perinatal physiology, San Juan, P.R., 1960; research prof. rehab. medicine, also dir. research Inst. Rehab. Medicine, N.Y. U. Med. Center, N.Y.C., 1964-71, emeritus, 1971—; research prof. Denison U., Granville, Ohio, 1971—. Vis. instr. U. Colo. Med. Sch., 1926; lab. guest physiology Cambridge U., 1935-36; Commonwealth prof., Louisville, 1944, professorial lectr. Emory U., 1948; miembro honorario facultad de medicina U. Chile, 1961—; prof. ad-honorem U. P.R., 1962-64; vis. prof. U. Cal. at Los Angeles, 1970, 72, 74, 76; Robert Zeit Meml. lectr. Northwestern U., 1963, Ranson Meml. lectr., 1964; Distinguished Scientist lectr. Tulane U., 1970; guest lectr. Orbeli Inst. Physiology, Yerevan, USSR, 1974. Trustee, v.p. Biol. Stain Commn., 1943-46. Mem. research adv. bd. United Cerebral Palsy Assn.; mem. Human Embryology and Devel. Study Sect., div. research grants NIH, 1954-60, mem. anat. scis. tng. com., 1958-60; mem. sci. adv. com. Div. Research Facilities and Resources, NIH, 1964-67; chmn. sci. adv. com. Nat. Paraplegic Found., 1970-74. Served as pvt. U.S. Army, World War I. Recipient War-Navy award, 1948; Max Weinstein award United Cerebral Palsy, 1957; Albert Lasker Med. Sci. award, 1968; William Thomson Wakeman award, 1972; Paralyzed Vets. Am. award, 1972, Henry Gray award, 1977. Fellow AAAS; mem. Am. Acad. Neurology, Assn. for Research Nervous and Mental Diseases (award 1971), Soc. Exptl. Biology and Medicine (chmn. Ill. sect. 1945-46), Am., Phila., Chgo., Seattle (pres. 1950-51) neurol. assns., Nat. Acad. Medicine Buenos Aires (corr.), Harvey Soc. (hon.), Am. Assn. Anatomists (exec. com. 1957-61, 1st v.p. 1966-67), Am. Physiol. Soc., Soc. Obstetrics and Gynecology Chile (hon.), Soc. Pediatrics Brazil (hon.), Alpha Kappa Kappa, Sigma Chi, Sigma Xi. Club: Cosmos (Washington). Author: Physiology of the Fetus, 1940; Textbook of Histology, 1949, 5th edit., 1976; Asphyxia Neonatorium, 1950; Fetal Physiology, 1971. Editor: NINDB Symposia in Neuranatomical Sciences 1954-64; founder Experimental Neurology, 1959, editor, 1959-75, chmn. editorial bd., 1975—. Home: 229 Cherry St Granville OH 43023

WINDMAN, ARNOLD LEWIS, mech. engr.; b. N.Y.C., Oct. 17, 1926; s. Raphael and Anna (Wexler) W.; B.M.E., Coll. City N.Y., 1947; m. Patricia Foley, Dec. 13, 1967; children—Richard, Marjorie, Kevin, Colleen, Sean, JoAnn, Brian, William. Project engr. F.E. Sutton, N.Y.C., 1947-50; with Syska & Hennessy, Inc., N.Y.C., 1950—, pres., 1976—, also dir. Bd. dirs. Phelps Meml. Hosp., Tarrytown, N.Y., 1974—. Registered profl. engr., N.Y., 13 other states. Mem. Am. Soc. Heating, Refrigerating and Air Conditioning Engrs. (chpt. pres. 1965), N.Y. Assn. Cons. Engrs. (v.p., dir. 1977), ASME, Tau Beta Pi, Pi Tau Sigma. Democrat. Jewish. Home: 182 Locust Rd Briarcliff Manor NY 10510 Office: 11 W 42d St New York NY 10036. *Professional integrity, enthusiasm, and a continuing effort to train younger people for advancement are three key ingredients of a successful career.*

WINDOM, WILLIAM, actor; b. N.Y.C., Sept. 28, 1923; s. Paul and Isobel Wells (Peckham) W.; student Williams Coll., 1942, The Citadel, 1943, Antioch Coll., 1943, U. Ky., 1943, Biarritz Am. U., 1945, Fordham U., 1946, Columbia U., 1946; m. Patricia Veronica Tunder, Dec. 31, 1975; children—Rachel, Heather Juliet, Hope, Rebel Russell. Actor, N.Y.C., 1946-61, Los Angeles, 1961—; mem. Am. Reperatory Theatre, 1946-47; plays include Mlle. Colombe, 1954, Fallen Angels, 1956, USA, 1958; films include: To Kill a Mockingbird, 1962, For Love or Money, 1963, Cattle King, 1963, One Man's Way, 1964, The Americanization of Emily, 1964, Hour of the Gun, 1967, The Detective, 1968, The Angry Breed, 1969, The Gypsy Moths, 1969, Brewster McCloud, 1970, Echoes of a Summer, 1974; leading role comedy series The Farmer's Daughter, 1962-65, My World and Welcome to It, 1969-70; one-man theatrical presentation Thurber I, 1972, Thurber II, 1975, Ernie Pyle I, 1976, Ernie Pyle II, 1979. Served with 508th parachute inf. AUS, 1943-46. Recipient Emmy award, 1969-70. Mem. The Players, Catboat Assn., Actors Equity Assn. Address: care Creative Artists Agy 1888 Century Park E Suite 1400 Los Angeles CA 90067

WINDSOR, DUCHESS OF (BESSIE WALLIS WARFIELD SIMPSON); b. Blue Ridge Summit, Pa., June 19, 1896; d. Teackle Wallis and Alice (Montague) W.; attended Oldfields pvt. sch., Cockeysville, Md.; m. Earl Winfield Spencer, Jr. (div.); m. 2d, Ernest Aldrich Simpson, 1928 (div. 1936); m. 3d, Albert Edward, Duke of Windsor, (became King Edward VIII, Jan. 20, 1936, abdicated, Dec. 11, 1936), June 3, 1937 (dec. May 1972). Made debut in Balt., 1914; presented at English Ct., June, 1931; resided French Riviera, beginning 1938, Cannes, France, 1940, Bahama Islands, 1940-45, where the Duchess supervised the renovation of Govt. House and actively participated in Red Cross and other civic work; now lives in Paris, France. Author: The Heart Has Its Reasons, 1956. *

WINDSOR, LAURENCE CHARLES, JR., communications and public affairs exec., author, lectr.; b. Bronxville, N.Y., July 4, 1935; s. Laurence Charles and Margaret (Phalen) W.; distinguished grad. St. John's Mil. Acad., 1953; student Grinnel Coll., 1953-55 (distinguished AFROTC cadet), U.S. Mil. Acad., 1957-58 (disting. plebe); m. Frances P. Seelinger, Apr. 3, 1959 (div. 1976); children—Patience Wells, Laurence Edward; m. 2d, Ruth Ester Lindstrom, 1977. Circulation adminstrn. staff Hearst Mags., N.Y.C., 1959-62; promotion dir. Medalist Publs., Chgo., 1962-64, Mill & Factory Mag., N.Y.C., 1964-66, True Mag., N.Y.C., 1966-67, Purchasing Mag., N.Y.C., 1967-69; asso. promotion dir. Life mag., N.Y.C., 1969-70, merchandising dir., 1970—; v.p., dir. advt. and pub. relations Sterling Communications subsidiary Time-Life; spl. asst. to postmaster gen. U.S., 1972-74; exec. v.p. Calderhead, Jackson, Inc., 1974-76; promotion dir. Family Weekly Mag., 1977-79; account mgr. Young & Rubicam Inc., N.Y.C., 1979—; appeared in motion picture The D.I., 1957. Pub. relations cons. Penobscot Charitable Trust, 1966. Mem. pub. edn. com. N.Y. Gov.'s Conf. on Alcohol Problems. Served with USMC, 1955-57. Decorated Commemorative War Cross (Royal Yugoslav Army); recipient Am. Spirit Honor medal as expert rifleman, outstanding marine of yr., 1955; Citation of Merit, Wis. Res. Officers Assn. Mem. U.S. Sales Promotion Exec. Assn. (dir., named Promotion Man of Year 1969), Marine Corps Combat Corr. Assn. (sec.), West Point Soc. N.Y. (gov. 1967—), Publicity Club N.Y., Publicity Club Chgo., Nat. Acad. TV Arts and Scis., Internat. Radio and TV Soc., Am. Inst. Plant Engrs., Order Vet. Corps Arty. (aide-de-camp, comdg. gen., Distinguished Expert pistol award, 1st Provincial Regtl. medal, Order Centennial Legion), 7th Regt. Rifle Club, Marine Corps Pub. Affairs Unit, U.S. Darting Assn., Nat. Sci. Tchrs. Assn., Assn. U.S. Army, Am. Def. Preparedness Assn., Kosciuszko Assn., Marine Corps League, Nat. Rifle Assn., Met. Squash Racquets Assn., Conn. Amateur Athletic Union U.S., Nat. Jogging Assn., New Eng. Soc., Ends of Earth Assn., Ch. Club of N.Y.,

Soverign Mil. Order of the Temple of Jerusalem, Time-Life Alumni Soc., Nat. Com. for Responsible Patriotism, St. Georges Soc., Nat. Eagle Scout Assn., Old Boys Assn., Nat. Fedn. Flemish Giant Rabbit Breeders, Soc. Colonial Wars, Soc. Colonial Clergy, Alpha Phi Omega, Republican. Episcopalian (vestryman, lay reader). Clubs: Union League, Manhattan (N.Y.C.); Bedford Bicycle Polo, Bombay Bicycle, Squadron A, Road Runners. Home: PO Box 219 Katonah NY 10536

WINE, DONALD ARTHUR, lawyer; b. Oelwein, Iowa, Oct. 8, 1922; s. George A. and Gladys E. (Lisle) W.; B.A., Drake U., 1946; LL.D., State U. Iowa, 1949; m. Mary L. Schneider, Dec. 27, 1947; children—Mark, Marcia, James. Admitted to Iowa bar, 1949, D.C. bar, 1968; pvt. practice in Newport and Wine, 1949-61; U.S. atty. So. Dist. Iowa, 1961-65; now partner firm Davis, Hockenberg, Wine, Brown & Koehn. Bd. dirs. Des Moines YMCA, 1963-75; bd. dirs. Salvation Army, chmn. advisory bd., 1971; bd. dirs. Davenport YMCA, 1961; bd. dirs. Internat. Assn. Y's Mens, 1957-59, area v.p., 1961. Mem. internat. com. YMCA's U.S. and Can., 1961-75; v.p. Iowa Council Chs.; pres. Des Moines Area Religious Council, 1975; chmn. bd. trustees First Bapt. Ch., 1975. Organizer, Young Democrats, Iowa, 1946; co-chmn. Scott County Citizens for Kennedy, 1960. Served to capt., navigator USAAF, 1943-45. Decorated D.F.C. Mem. Am. (chmn. com. jud. adminstrn. jr. bar sect. 1958), Iowa (pres. jr. bar sect. 1957), Polk County (sec. 1973-74) bar assns., Des Moines C. of C. (chmn. city-state tax com. 1978—, Order of Coif, Sigma Alpha Epsilon. Clubs: Masons, Kiwanis (pres. Downtown club 1969), Des Moines, Wakonda. Home: 3124 Park Plaza Dr Des Moines IA 50311 Office: Financial Center Bldg Des Moines IA 50309

WINE, JAMES WILMER, lawyer; b. Cabell County, W.Va., Oct. 1, 1918; s. James Wilmer and Marie (Sturgill) W.; A.B., U. Ky., 1940, LL.B., 1942; m. Emmy Lou Turck, Feb. 7, 1942; children—Vi, Lisbeth, Charles Edwin, James Michael. Admitted to Ky. bar, 1942, D.C. bar, 1968; gen. practice in Pikeville, 1945-57; county judge protem Pike County, 1949; U.S. commr. Eastern Dist. Ky., 1950-52; spl. circuit judge Ky., 1956; v.p. Park Coll., Parkville, Mo., 1957-58; asso. gen. sec. Nat. Council Chs., 1959-60; U.S. ambassador to Luxembourg, 1961-62; U.S. ambassador, Republic Ivory Coast, 1962-67; spl. asst. to sec. state for refugee and migration affairs, 1967-68; counsel Internat. Bank Washington, 1968—. Mem. Jud. Reform Commn. Ky., 1956-57. Democratic candidate Congress 7th Dist. Ky., 1954; spl. asst. John F. Kennedy presdl. campaign, 1960. Served to maj., inf. U.S. Army, World War II; lt. col. Res. Decorated Bronze Star medal. Mem. Am., D.C., Ky. bar assns., Phi Delta Phi, Sigma Chi, Omicron Delta Kappa. Presbyn. (elder). Author: Manual for Jurors, 1950. Home: 3342 Prospect St NW Washington DC 20007 Office: Suite 1100 1701 Pennsylvania Ave NW Washington DC 20006

WINE, SHERWIN T., rabbi; b. Detroit, Jan. 25, 1928; s. William Harry and Tillie (Israel) W.; B.A., U. Mich., 1950, A.M., 1952; B.H.L., Hebrew Union Coll., Cin., M.H.L., 1956, rabbi, 1956. Rabbi, Temple Beth El, Detroit, 1956-60, Temple Beth El, Windsor, Ont., Can., 1960-64, Birmingham (Mich.) Temple, 1964—; cons. editor Humanistic Judaism, 1966—. Bd. dirs. Center for New Thinking, Birmingham, 1977—. Served as chaplain AUS, 1956-58. Author: A Philosophy of Humanistic Judaism, 1965; Meditation Services for Humanistic Judaism, 1977; Humanistic Judaism-What Is It?, 1977. Home: 555 S Woodward Birmingham MI 48011 Office: 28611 W Twelve Mile Rd Farmington MI 48024

WINEGARDNER, ROY EUGENE, hotel exec.; b. Springfield, Mo., Nov. 15, 1920; s. Sam J. and Frona (Day) W.; m. Alicia Pardo, Dec. 19, 1974; children—Jane Kay, Jill, Nicky, Diego. Contractor, 1945-59; owner Holiday Inn franchise, 1959—; 1st vice chmn. bd. Holiday Inns, Inc., Memphis, 1974-79, pres., chmn. bd., chief exec. officer, 1979—; dir. 1st Tenn. Banking Corp. Bd. dirs. Nat. Jr. Achievement. Served with U.S. Merchant Marines, 1943-45. Office: Holiday Inns Inc 3742 Lamar Ave Memphis TN 38195

WINELAND, FRED L., sec. state Md.; b. Washington, Aug. 16, 1926; s. Lloyd and Elsie L. (Pezold) W.; student Am. U.; B.C.S., Southeastern U.; m. Mary K. Flack, Nov. 3, 1948; children—David, Gail, William, Kirwan. Vice pres., treas. Wineland Enterprises, Prince George's County, Md.; mem. Md. Ho. of Dels., 1963-64, Md. Senate, 1965-71; sec. state Md., 1971—. Mem. S.E. Hosp. Action Com.; area chmn. United Givers Fund; ann. fundraising chmn. Prince George's County Cancer Crusade, 1972; active PTA; bd. dirs. German Orphan Home; del. Dem. Nat. Conv., 1976. Served in USN, World War II. Named State Legislator of Year, Md. Assn. Citizens, Sportsman; Hon. Distinguished Italian Am., Columbus Citizen's Nat. League; recipient Outstanding Service award Iverson Mall Mchts. Assn.; Man of Year award Md. VFW. Mem. So. Md. Bd. Trade, Aircraft Owners and Pilots Assn., Farm Bur., Am. Legion, VFW, Prince George's County C. of C., Nat. Assn. Secs. of State (pres. 1978). Democrat. Methodist. Clubs: Masons, Shriners, Elks, Lions, Nat. Press. Home: 1100 W River Rd Silesia MD 20022 Office: Office Sec State State House Annapolis MD 21404*

WINER, HAROLD, ret. educator; b. S.I., N.Y., Mar. 31, 1910; s. Leonard and Lillian (Block) W.; B.S., Cornell U., 1932, student summers, 1933-36; student Sch. Advanced Internat. Studies, Johns Hopkins, 1958; m. Elizabeth G. Jensen, Apr. 21, 1934; children—Peter D., Susan A., Jane L. Tchr. vocational agr., Richmondville, N.Y., 1933-39; tchr. vocational agr., farm mgr., Canaan, N.Y., 1939-41; chief edn. and tng. sect. VA, Albany, 1946-53; chief vocational adviser Govt. of Iran, U.S. Operations Mission, Tehran, 1953-55, dep. chief edn. adviser, 1955-58; chief edn. adviser Govt. of Nepal, U.S. Operations Mission, Kathmandu, Nepal, 1959- 64; chief Instnl. Devel. div. Bur. Near East and So. Asia, AID, Dept. State, Washington, 1964-65; chief edn. adviser to Govt. South Vietnam, U.S. AID, Saigon, 1965-69; ret. Dept. State, 1970. Served from 2d lt. to maj., inf. AUS, 1941-46. Decorated Legion of Merit, Silver Star, Bronze Star; conspicuous service medal State of N.Y.; Ministry Edn. medal of Culture and Edn., Medal of Merit, Ministry of Vets. Affairs medal 1st class (Vietnam); U.S. medal for Civilan Service in Vietnam. Mem. Am. Fgn. Service Assn., Diplomatic and Consular Officers Ret., Marines Meml. Assn., Am.-Nepal Soc., 77th Div., Assn., Am. Legion, Disabled Officers Assn., Ret. Officers Assn., Cornell U. Alumni Assn. Jewish. Clubs: Masons, Officers, Cornell (Washington). Home: 500 Roosevelt Blvd 421 Falls Church VA 22044

WINER, LINDA, journalist; b. Chgo., May 6, 1946; d. Irving and Marjorie (Novak) Winer; B.A. magna cum laude, Northeastern Ill. U., 1968; postgrad. U. So. Calif., 1968-69; m. Conrad Pitcher II, Dec. 30, 1968. Dance critic, theater critic, Chgo. Tribune, 1969—. Arts critic WTTW-TV, 1976-77; Chgo. corr. N.Y. Theater Review, 1977—; asso. Writing in Chgo. Program, 1978. Rockefeller Found. grantee tng. music critics, 1968; Conn. Coll. Am. Dance Festival Dance Critics fellow, summer 1969. Mem. Music Critics Assn., Dance Critics Assn., Theater Critics Assn. Office: 435 N Michigan Ave Chicago IL 60611

WINER, LOUIS HARRY, physician; b. Superior, Wis., Mar. 19, 1903; s. Israel Henry and Celia (Milavetz) W.; B.S., U. Minn., 1922, M.B., 1924, M.D., 1925; postgrad. U. Vienna Allegemeine Kranken Haus; m. Helen Mae Grouse, Dec. 28, 1930; children—Barbara Fraida (Mrs. Gerald H. Levin), Marylee (Mrs. Alvin Silverman). Intern, Mpls. Gen. Hosp., 1925-26, resident, 1926-28; asst. to clin. asso. prof. dermatology U. Minn., 1926-45; clin. asso. prof. dermatology U. So. Calif. Med Sch., 1945-50; clin. prof. dermatology U. Calif. at Los Angeles Med. Sch., 1950—; sr. attending physician Los Angeles County Hosp., 1945—; mem. staff Cedars-Sinai, Brotman Meml. Hosp., St. Johns Hosp., Midway Hosp., Temple Hosp., Hollywood Community Hosp.; cons. VA Hosp., Los Angeles. Diplomate Am. Bd. Dermatology. Mem. AMA, Am. Dermatol. Assn. (v.p. 1968), Am. Soc. Dermatopathology (pres. 1972), Am. Acad. Dermatology (v.p. 1962), Calif. Med. Assn. (pres. sect. dermatology 1956), Chgo. (hon.), Minn., Pacific (hon.) dermatol. assns., Los Angeles Acad. Medicine, Internat. Soc. Derm. Surgery, Dermatol. Research Assn. (pres.), Internat. Soc. Tropical Dermatology, Los Angeles (pres. 1962—, hon.), Austrian (hon.), Israeli (hon.), Danish (hon.), French (corr.), Ibero-Latino Am., Brazilian (corr.), Austral-Asian (corr.), Sonoran dermatol. socs. Contbr. articles to profl. jours. Home: 1036 Corsica Dr Pacific Palisades CA 90272 Office: 9915 Santa Monica Blvd Beverly Hills CA 90212

WINER, WARD OTIS, mech. engr., educator; b. Grand Rapids, Mich., June 27, 1936; s. Mervin Augustus and Ina Katherine (Wood) W.; Asso., Grand Rapids Jr. Coll., 1956; B.S., U. Mich., 1958, M.S., 1959, Ph.D., 1961; Ph.D. (Cavendish Lab. fellow), Cambridge (Eng.) U., 1961-63; m. Mary Jo Wielinga, June 15, 1957; children—Mathew Owen, James Edward, Paul Andrew, Mary Margaret. Asst. prof. dept. mech. engring. U. Mich., Ann Arbor, 1963-66, asso. prof., 1966-69; asso. prof. mech. engring. Ga. Inst. Tech., 1969-71, prof., 1971—; chmn. Gordon Research Conf. on Friction, Lubrication and Wear, 1980. Democratic precinct chmn., 1967-68. Mem. exec. bd. Horace H. Rackham Sch. Grad. Studies, U. Mich., 1968. Recipient Distinguished Faculty Service award Coll. Engring., U. Mich., 1967; certificate of recognition NASA, 1977; Clarence E. Earle Meml. award Nat. Grease Lubricating Inst., 1979. Mem. ASME (mem. exec. com. lubrication div. 1972-78, Melville Medal 1975), Am. Soc. Lubrication Engrs., Am. Acad. Mechanics, AAAS, Soc. Rheology, Soc. Engring. Sci. (dir. 1980-82), AAUP (pres. Ga. Tech. chpt. 1972-74, v.p. state conf. 1973-75), Sigma Xi (Sustained Research in Engring. award 1975), Tau Beta Pi, Pi Tau Sigma, Phi Kappa Phi. Contbr. articles to profl. jours. Home: 1025 Mountain Creek Trail Atlanta GA 30328

WINES, JAMES N., architect, sculptor; b. Oak Park, Ill., June 27, 1932; s. William Bradford and Irene (Forgy) W.; B.A., Syracuse U., 1955; 1 dau., Suzan. One man sculpture shows include: Balt. Mus. Art, 1958. Silvan Simone Gallery, Los Angeles, 1958, 59, Galleria Trastevere, Rome, Fine Arts Assos., N.Y.C., 1961, Walker Art Center, Mpls., 1964; group shows include: Art Inst. Chgo., 1959, Oberlin Coll. Mus., 1962, Whitney Mus., N.Y.C., 1962, 65, 73, Tate Gallery, London, 1965, Mus. Modern Art, N.Y.C., 1975, Pompidou Center, Paris, 1975; represented in permanent collections: Cleve. Mus. Art, Los Angeles County Mus., N.Y. U. Art Collection, Stedelijk Mus. Amsterdam, Walker Art Center, Mpls., Whitney Mus. Am. Art; recent archtl. designs include showrooms for Best Products Co., Houston, 1975, Sacramento, 1977, parking lot Hamden Plaza Shopping Center, Hamden, Conn., 1977; pres., prin. in charge Site, Inc., N.Y.C., 1970—; instr. art Sch. Visual Arts, N.Y.C., 1965-71; prof. environ. design N.Y. U., 1965—; prof. architecture N.J. Sch. Architecture, 1975—. Ford Found. grantee, 1964, Guggenheim fellow, 1962, Nat. Endowment for the Arts grantee, 1973, 75. Home: 60 Greene St New York City NY 10012

WINESANKER, MICHAEL MAX, educator, musicologist; b. Toronto, Ont., Can., Aug. 7, 1913; s. Samuel and Ida (English) W.; student composition with Healey Willan, 1931-36; B.Mus., U. Toronto, 1933; M.A., U. Mich., 1941; L.Mus., Trinity Coll., London, Eng., 1940; Ph.D., Cornell U., 1944; m. Esther Frumhartz, Dec. 12, 1937; children—Miriam Ruth, Rebecca Ann. Came to U.S., 1945, naturalized, 1951. Debut as concert pianist performing own composition, Eaton Auditorium, Toronto, 1937; pvt. tchr. piano and theory, Toronto, 1933-39; tchr. piano and theory Hambourg Conservatory, Toronto, 1940-42; prof. music history and theory Bayview (Mich.) Summer Coll., 1945; prof. musicology U. Tex., 1945-46, summer 1946; mem. faculty Tex. Christian U., 1946—, prof. musicology, 1949—, Piper prof., 1976—, chmn. dept. music, 1956—. Bd. dirs. Van Cliburn Internat. Piano Competition (v.p.), Fort Worth Symphony Assn. (v.p.). Past pres. Fort Worth Youth Symphony Orch. Grantee Am. Council Learned Socs., 1943, Tex. Christian U.-Carnegie Found., 1948, Tex. Christian U. Research Com., 1953. Mem. Am. Musicological Soc. (pres. Tex. chpt. 1950-52, 56-58, council 1958-60), Music Tchrs. Nat. Assn. (chmn. editorial and publs. com. 1961-65, chmn. musicology com. 1968—), Tex. Assn. Music Schs. (pres. 1960-61), Fort Worth Music Tchrs. Assn. (pres. 1963-65), Nat. Assn. Schs. Music (chmn. library com.), Pi Kappa Lambda, Phi Mu Alpha. Author: A List of Books on Music, 1977; Books on Music, A Classified List, 1979. Contbr. articles profl. jours. Home: 3613 Park Ridge Blvd Fort Worth TX 76109

WINFIELD, JOHN ALLEN, glass container mfg. co. exec.; b. Girard, Ohio, Apr. 30, 1922; s. Harry H. and Flora (Jagger) W.; B.S. in Commerce, Ohio U., 1944; C.P.A., Mich., 1947; m. Virginia M. Cekuta, Sept. 20, 1944; 1 dau., Sherilyn Lee. With Arthur Andersen & Co., C.P.A.'s, Detroit, 1944-48; asst. treas. Electromaster, Inc., Mt. Clemens, Mich., 1948-49; with Philco Corp., 1949-62, mgr. spl. markets consumer products, 1961-62; exec. v.p. Knox Glass, Inc. (Pa.), 1963-65, pres., chief operating officer, dir., 1965-68; exec. v.p. Brockway Glass Co., Inc. (Pa.), 1968-74, pres., chief operating officer, 1974-77, pres., chief exec. officer, 1977-78, chmn., pres., chief exec. officer, 1978—, also dir. Mem. Beta Theta Pi. Home: 950 Walnut Ave DuBois PA 15801 Office: Brockway Glass Co Inc Brockway PA 15824

WINFIELD, PAUL EDWARD, actor; b. Los Angeles, May 22, 1941; s. Clarence and Lois Beatrice (Edwards) W.; student U. Portland, 1957-59, Stanford U., 1959, Los Angeles City Coll., 1959-63, U. Calif., Los Angeles, 1962-64. Films include: Gordons War, 1973, Huckleberry Finn, 1974, Conrack, 1974, Guess Who's Minding the Mint, 1969, Sounder (Acad. Award nomination 1973), 1972, Hustle, 1975, Twilights Last Gleaming, 1976, A Hero Ain't Nothing But A Sandwich, 1978; TV appearances include Green Eyes, 1976, All Deliberate Speed, 1976, King, 1978 (Emmy nomination); guest star Room 222, High Chaparral, Julia, Ironside, Nichols, Young Rebels, Perry Mason, Young Rebels, Name of the Game, Roots II (Emmy nomination); artist in residence Stanford U., 1964-65, U. Hawaii, 1965, U. Calif., Santa Barbara, 1970-71. Home: 74 Mountain Spring St San Francisco CA 94114 Office: 6420 Wilshire Blvd 19th Floor Los Angeles CA 90048

WINFIELD, RODNEY M., artist; b. N.Y.C., Feb. 6, 1925; s. Benjamin Lionel and Helen (Oscar) W.; student U. Miami, 1943, Cooper Union, N.Y.C., 1944-45; m. Margaret Elizabeth McKenzie, Sept. 7, 1946; children—Christopher John, David Peel, Robin Lizabeth, Nancy Carol. One man shows include Galerie Creuze, Paris, 1950, Martin Schweig Gallery, St. Louis, Pope Pius Library at St. Louis U.; Pallette Blea, Paris; exhibited group shows City Art Mus., St. Louis; represented permanent collections Steinberg Gallery, Washington U., St. Louis, also pvt. collections; executed 3 dimensional windows Shaare Zedec, St. Louis, 1958, bronze and steel Ark Wall, Temple Israel, St. Louis, 1962, doors, interior artifacts Good Samaritan Hosp. Chapel, Mount Vernon, Ill., 1968; Space Window, Washington Cathedral, 1973; designer Apostle Spoons, Franklin Mint; designer Emil Frei Assos., St. Louis; prof. art Maryville Coll., St. Louis, 1976—. Home and Office: 4444 Laclede Pl St Louis MO 63108

WINFIELD, WILLIAM HOOD, chem. co. exec.; b. Clarksburg, W.Va., Oct. 10, 1907; s. John Buckner and Frances (McKee) W.; A.B., W.Va. U., 1930; M.B.A., Harvard, 1934; m. Alice M. Turner, Apr. 15, 1939; children—Mary, Frances, William, Alice. Asst. to gen. mgr. TVA, 1934-37; dir. indsl. research Weyerhaeuser Co., 1937-43; cons. McKinsey & Co., 1946-48; dir. marketing research Monsanto Chem. Co., 1948-55; pres. Allied Chem. Internat. Corp., 1955—. Served to commdr. USNR, 1943-46. Home: 21 Owenoke Way Riverside CT 06878

WINFREY, DORMAN HAYWARD, state librarian; b. Henderson, Tex., Sept. 4, 1924; s. Luke Abel and Linnie (Fears) W.; B.A., U. Tex., 1950, M.A., 1951, Ph.D., 1962; m. Ruth Carolyn Byrd, June 12, 1954; children—Laura Madge, Jennifer Ruth. Social sci. research asso. research in Tex. history Tex. State Hist. Assn. at U. Tex., 1946-58, archivist, 1960-61; state archivist Tex., 1958-60; librarian, dir. Tex. State Library, 1962—; chmn. State Bd. Library Examiners, 1962—, State Records Preservation Adv. Com., 1965—; mem. Tex. Travel Trails Com.; mem. adv. bd. Nat. Archives, 1975—. Bd. dirs. James Dick Found. for Performing Arts. Served with Armed Forces, 1943-46. Clara Driscoll scholar for research in Tex. history, 1952-54. Fellow Soc. Am. Archivists (internat. archival affairs com., council), Tex. Hist. Assn. (pres., mem. council); mem. ALA, Tex., Southwestern library assns., E. Tex. Hist. Assn., Am. Assn. State and Local History (council), Austin Com. Fgn. Relations, Philos. Soc. Tex. (sec.), Tex. Inst. Letters, Bicentennial Assn. Tex., Sons of Republic of Tex. (hon.), Phi Alpha Theta, Pi Sigma Alpha. Mem. Disciples of Christ Ch. (mem. bd.). Author: Arturo Toscanini in Texas; The 1950 NBC Symphony Orchestra Tour, 1967; also articles; editor: Texas Indian Papers, 1825-43, 1959; Texas Indian Papers, 1844-45, 1960; Texas Indian Papers, 1846-1859, 1960; A History of Rusk County, Texas (award of merit Am. Assn. State and Local History), 1961; Julien Sidney Devereux and His Monte Verdi Plantation (award merit Am. Assn. State and Local History), 1964; hist. coordinator: Six Missions of Texas, 1965; editor: Indian Papers of Texas and the Southwest, 1825-1916, 5 vols., 1966; Seventy-Five Years of Texas History: The Texas State Historical Association, 1897-1972, 1974; staff writer: Handbook of Texas, 1952; asso. editor Jr. Historian of the Texas State Hist. Assn., 1951-58; spl. editor for Tex., Ency. for Young People, 1962. Home: 6503 Willamette Dr Austin TX 78723 Office: Tex State Library Box 12927 Capitol Station Austin TX 78711

WING, GEORGE MILTON, educator, mathematician; b. Rochester, N.Y., Jan. 21, 1923; s. George O. and Louise (Weiss) W.; B.A., U. Rochester, 1944, M.S., 1947; Ph.D., Cornell U., 1949; m. Nina A. John, June 7, 1958 (div. Nov. 1970); m. 2d, Janet Sweedyk Bendt, Aug. 26, 1972. Staff mem. Los Alamos Sci. Lab., 1945-46, 51-58, Sandia Lab., Albuquerque, 1959-64; faculty U. Calif. at Los Angeles, 1949-52, U. N.Mex., 1958-59; prof. applied math. U. Colo., Boulder, 1964-66; prof. math. U. N.Mex., Albuquerque. 1966-73; chmn. dept. math. So. Methodist U., Dallas, 1977-78, prof., 1978—; cons. Rand Corp., 1958-65, Sandia Corp., 1958-59, E.H. Plesset & Assos., 1958-59, 64-67, Los Alamos Sci. Lab., 1958-59, 64—, U. So. Calif. Project on Applications Math. to Medicine, 1970—; vis. prof. Tex. Tech. U., Lubbock, 1975-76. Mem. Am. Math. Soc., Math. Assn. Am., Soc. Indsl. and Applied Math. (vis. lectr. 1961-62, 64-66), Phi Beta Kappa, Sigma Xi. Author: An Introduction to Transport Theory, 1962; (with R.C. Allen, Jr.) Problems for a Computer-Oriented Calculus Course, 1973; (with Richard Bellman) An Introduction to Invariant Imbedding, 1975. Asso. editor Jour. Math. Analysis and Applications, 1969—. Research on transport theory, radiative transfer, applied math. Home: 107 Tunyo Los Alamos NM 87544

WING, IVAN WILFORD, investment banker; b. Seattle, Jan. 25, 1907; s. Arthur Wilford and Grace (Dow) W.; A.B., U. Wash., 1929; m. Virginia Elizabeth Barnett, Jan. 9, 1935; children—Grace, Christopher Barnett. With Nat. City Co., Harriman Ripley & Co., 1929-37; with Weeden & Co., San Franisco, 1938—, v.p., 1952—. Mem. Municipal Forum N.Y. Mem. Investment Bankers Assn. Am. (govs. 1964-67), San Francisco Bond Club (past pres.), Municipal Bond Club San Francisco (past pres.), Delta Kappa Epsilon. Clubs: Merchants Exchange (San Francisco); Sharon Hts. Golf-Country (Menlo Park, Calif.). Home: 300 Sand Hill Circle Apt 202 Menlo Park CA 94025 Office: 601 Montgomery St San Francisco CA 94111

WING, JOHN ADAMS, fin. services co. exec.; b. Elmira, N.Y., Nov. 9, 1935; s. Herbert Charles and Clara Louise (Stewart) W.; B.A. in Econs., Union Coll., 1958; LL.B., George Washington U., 1963; m. Joan Cook Montgomery, June 19, 1964; children—Lloyd Montgomery, Elizabeth Montgomery, Mary Ellen. Admitted to Va. bar, 1963, D.C. bar, 1965, Ill. bar, 1968; fin. analyst Securities & Exchange Commn., Washington, 1960-63, trial atty., 1963-66; asst. to pres. Investors Diversified Services, Inc., Mpls., 1966-67; v.p., gen. counsel A.G. Becker & Co., Chgo., 1968-71, sr. v.p., 1971-74, pres., 1974—, also dir.; dir. Becker Warburg Paribas Group, Midwest Stock Exchange, Chgo. Bd. Options Exchange. Bd. dir. Allendale Sch., Villa Park, Ill. Served with U.S. Army, 1958-60. Mem. Ill. Bar Assn., Va. Bar Assn., Fed. Bar Assn., Nat. Assn. Securities Dealers (vice chmn. bd. govs. 1979—). Episcopalian. Clubs: Chgo., Mid-Day, Bond. Office: 2 First National Plaza Chicago IL 60603

WING, MAURICE J., journalist; b. Beatrice, Nebr., Aug. 31, 1904; s. Henry J. and Kate (Faxon) W.; student U. Nebr., 1922-24; m. Frances Elliott, Aug. 29, 1931; children—Susan, John, Thomas, Edward. Worked on various newspapers in Lincoln (Nebr.), Omaha, Denver, Phila. and Atlantic City, 1922-29; joined Asso. Press, Lincoln, 1929, trans. to N.Y.C. 1934, feature editor, 1938-69, started ecology column, nationally syndicated, 1970. Home: 15 Briarcliff Dr Port Washington NY 11050

WINGATE, ARLINE, sculptor; b. N.Y.C., Oct. 18, 1906; d. Benjamin Shapiro and Isabel (Roth) Shapiro; student, Smith Coll., 1924-25, with Archipenko, 1929-31, European mus., 1933; m. Clifford Hollander; 1 son, Richard Clifford. Tchr. sculpture YMHA, 1942; lectr. modern sculpture, N.E.; held 6 one man shows, N.Y.; exhibited in Whitney Mus., Wadsworth Athaeneum, Balt. and Riverside museums, Pa. Acad., Art Inst. Chgo., Bklyn. Mus., San Francisco Golden Gate Expn., N.Y. World's Fair, Birmingham (Ala.) Mus., Syracuse U. Mus., Norfolk Mus., Petit Palais, Paris, France, Met. Mus., N.Y.C., Farnsworth Mus., Maine, Burlington Galleries, London, Museo des Belles Artes, Buenos Aires; represented in permanent collections Farnsworth Mus., Maine, Parish Mus., South Hampton, N.Y., Guild Hall Mus., East Hampton, N.Y., St. Lawrence U., Newark Mus., Nat. Mus., Stockholm, Sweden, Mus. Ghent (Belgium), Mus. Syracuse U., Norwalk (Va.) Mus. Arts and Scis., Purdue U. Mus., Heckesher Mus., L.I., Hobart U. Mus., N.Y., Archives of Am. Art, also pvt. collections. Mem. Sculptors Guild,

Fedn. Modern Painters and Sculptors, Nat. Assn. Women Artists. Home: Baiting Hollow Rd East Hampton NY 11937

WINGATE, HENRY SMITH, business exec.; b. Talas, Turkey, Oct. 8, 1905; s. Henry Knowles and Jane Caroline (Smith) W.; B.A., Carleton Coll., 1927, L.H.D., 1973; J.D., U. Mich., 1929; LL.D., U. Man., 1957, Marshall U., York U., 1967, Laurentian U., 1968, Colby Coll., 1970; m. Ardis Adeline Swenson, Sept. 11, 1929; children—Henry Knowles, William Peter. Admitted to N.Y. bar, 1931; asso. Sullivan & Cromwell, N.Y.C., 1929-35; asst. sec. Internat. Nickel Co. of Can., Ltd., 1935-39, sec., 1939-52, dir., 1952-75, v.p., 1949-54, pres., 1954-60, chmn. bd., chmn. exec. com., 1960-72, chmn. adv. com. dir., 1972-75, mem. adv. com., 1978—; former dir. Am. Standard, Inc., U.S. Steel Corp., J.P. Morgan & Co., Morgan Guaranty Trust Co., Bank of Montreal; trustee Seamen's Bank for Savs., N.Y.; mem. adv. council Morgan Guaranty Trust Co. N.Y. Hon. mem. Bus. Council Washington; mem. council Found. for Child Devel.; mem. Can.-Am. com. sponsored by Nat. Planning Assn. and C.D. Howe Research Inst. Can.; bd. dirs. People's Symphony Concerts, Societe De Chimie Industrielle, Paris; v.p., bd. dirs. Am. Friends Can. Com.; sr. mem. Conf. Bd. N.Y.C. Recipient Sesquicentennial award U. Mich., 1967. Mem. Canadian Inst. Mining and Metallurgy, Mining and Metall. Soc. Am., Council Fgn. Relations, Pilgrims U.S., Canadian Soc. N.Y., Order of Coif, Delta Sigma Rho. Clubs: Lloyd Harbor Bath; Huntington Country; Union, Univ., Recess (N.Y.C.). Home: 520 E 86th St New York NY 10028 Office: 1 New York Plaza New York NY 10004

WINGER, HOWARD WOODROW, educator; b. Marion, Ind., Oct. 29, 1914; s. Joseph Pendleton and Amanda Ellen (Shoemaker) W.; A.B. with high distinction, Manchester Coll., 1936, LL.D., 1975; B.S., George Peabody Coll., 1945; M.S., U. Ill., 1948, Ph.D., 1953; m. Helen Margaret Gray, Dec. 25, 1941; children—John, Michael, Philip, Elizabeth, Robert. Tchr. Swayzee (Ind.) High Sch., 1936-37; copy writer Crowell Pub. Co., Springfield, Ohio, 1937-38; tchr. Jefferson Twp. High Sch., Warren, Ind., 1940-42; asst. librarian U. Ill. at Urbana, 1945-50; asst. prof. U. Wis.-Madison, 1950-53; asst. prof. Grad. Library Sch., U. Chgo., 1953-59, asso. prof., 59-68, prof., 1968—, dean, 1972-77. Bd. library dirs. Park Forest (Ill.) Pub. Library, 1955-61. Served with U.S. Army, 1942-44. Mem. ALA (mem. council 1956-60), Assn. of Am. Library Schs. (sec. 1953-56), Beta Phi Mu (internat. pres. 1977), Tau Kappa Alpha. Mem. United Protestant Ch. (chmn. bd. elders 1966-68). Clubs: Quadrangle (Chgo.). Author: Iron Curtains and Scholarship, 1959; Seven Questions About the Profession' of Librarianship, 1962; The Medium Sized Public Library, 1964; Area Studies and the Library, 1966; Deterioration and Preservation of Library Materials, 1970; Printers and Publishers Devices, 1976; American Library History: 1876-1976, 1976; At This Point in Time (verse), 1976; mng. editor Library Quar., 1961-72, 79—. Home: 121 Walnut St Park Forest IL 60466 Office: 1100 E 57th St Chicago IL 60637

WINGER, MAURICE H., JR., business exec.; b. Kansas City, Dec. 28, 1917; s. Maurice H.; B.A., William Jewel Coll., 1939; LL.B., Duke U., 1942; m. Virginia McNabb, 1940; children—Eric, Stephen. Admitted to N.Y. bar, 1942, D.C. bar, 1946; asso. firm Sullivan & Cromwell, N.Y.C., 1942, Douglas, Proctor,, MacIntyre & Gates, Washington, 1946-48, Debevoise, Plimpton & McLean, N.Y.C., 1948-50; with Export-Import Bank, Washington, 1943-44; sec., asst. gen. counsel Am. Enka Corp. (name changed to Am. Enka Co. div. Akzona, Inc., 1970) (N.C.), 1950-60, gen. mgr. Brand-Rex, 1960-64, gen. mgr. Nylon div., 1964—, v.p., 1966-70, pres., 1970-78, vice chmn. corp., 1979—; dir. Piedmont Aviation, Inc. Past chmn. Better Bus. Bur., Asheville; chmn. Man-Made Fiber Producers Assn. Trustee U. N.C., Asheville. Served to 1st lt. USMCR, 1944-46. Recipient Disting. Service award; named Man of Year, Asheville Jr. C. of C., 1953. Office: Akzona Inc PO Box 2930 Asheville NC 28802

WINGERTER, ROBERT GEORGE, corp. exec.; b. Detroit, Oct. 5, 1916; s. Hugh and Bertha (Seeger) W.; B.S. in Mech. Engring., Wayne State U., 1938; grad. Advanced Mgmt. Program Columbia, 1955; m. Dorothy E. Dipman, Aug. 5, 1939; children—Gail E. (Mrs. Edward Sponseller), Janice R. (Mrs. Janice Dixon), Robert H. With Timken Roller Bearing Co., Canton, O., 1938-63, asst. chief engr. indsl. div., 1941-45, sales engr. automotive div., 1945-50, asst. gen. mgr. automotive div., 1950-55, gen. mgr. 1955-59, dir. sales, 1959-63; exec. v.p., dir. Rockwell-Standard Corp., Detroit, 1963-67, pres. automotive div., 1964-67; with Libbey-Owens-Ford Co., 1967—, exec., v.p. corp. planning, 1967, pres., chief exec. officer, 1967-76, chmn., chief exec. officer, 1976—; dir. Timken Co., Toledo Trust Co., LOF Plastics, Inc., N.W. Ohio Bancshares, Inc., Toledo Edison Co., Marathon Oil Co., Greater Toledo Corp. Bd. dirs. Toledo Area Community Chest; trustee Am. Enterprise Inst., Toledo Mus. Art (also treas.), Toledo Hosp., Symphony Orch. Assn., Devel. Council, Med. Coll. Ohio; bd. dirs. Better Bus. Bur. Toledo. Mem. Am. Def. Preparedness Assn., Am. Mgmt. Assn., NAM (dir.), Bus. Roundtable, Assn. U.S. Army, Soc. Automotive Engrs., Hwy. Users Fedn. (dir.), Automotive Old Timers, Newcomen Soc. N.Am., Tau Beta Pi. Clubs: Bloomfield Hills (Mich.) Country; Detroit, Detroit Athletic, Economic of Detroit; Toledo; Belmont; Ocean Reef of Key Largo (Fla.); Answer, Tower (Toledo). Office: 811 Madison Ave Toledo OH 43695

WINGFIELD, CLYDE JOYE, univ. ofcl.; b. Arkadelphia, Ark., Mar. 13, 1931; s. Clyde W. and Thelma (Bledsoe) W.; B.A., East Tex. State U., 1952, M.A., 1956; Ph.D., Syracuse U., 1960; Claire Wengrove, May 14, 1977; children—Wesley Hughes, Stephanie Jill. Asst. prof. polit. sci. and adminstrn. Pa. State U., State College, 1959-62; asso. prof., dir. pub. adminstrn. program No. Ill. U., 1962-64; prof. polit. sci., head dept. U. Tex., El Paso, 1964-67, exec. v.p. univ., 1967-69; McElvaney prof. polit. sci., dir. grad. program pub. adminstrn. So. Meth. U., Dallas, 1969-71; pres. Baruch Coll., City U. N.Y., 1971-76; exec. v.p., provost U. Miami, Coral Gables, Fla., 1976—; cons. to regional dir. U.S. Civil Service Commn., Dallas, 1969, to Ambassador Raymond Telles, 1967-68; cons. planning and mgmt., municipal govts., 1959-65. Served with USAF, 1953-56. Ford Found. faculty research fellow, 1964-65. Mem. Nat. Assn. Schs. Pub. Affairs and Adminstrn. (pres. 1973-74), Am. Soc. Pub. Adminstrn. (council 1973-74), Am., Western polit. sci. assns., AAUP, Southwestern Social Sci. Assn., AAAS. Author (with others) and editor: The American University: A Public Administration Perspective, author with others: Managing the Modern City, 1971, Decisions in Syracuse, 1961, 65. Editor: Political Science: Some New Perspectives, 1966; Urbanization in the Southwest, 1968. Contbr. articles to profl. jours. Home: 177 Ocean Lane Dr Key Biscayne FL 33149 Office: Univ of Miami Coral Gables FL 33124

WINHOLD, DUNCAN RAMSAY, ins. co. exec.; b. Brantford, Ont., Can., Nov. 2, 1932; B.A. in Math. and Physics; m. Harriet L. James; 2 children. With Mut. Life Assurance Co. of Can., Waterloo, Ont., 1953—, asso. treas., 1966-69, treas., 1969-70, v.p., treas., from 1970, now sr. v.p., treas. Fellow Soc. Actuaries, Canadian Inst. Actuaries. Home: 19 Pittsford Close Waterloo ON N2K 1V5 Canada Office: 227 King St S Waterloo ON N2J 4C5 Canada

WINHOLTZ, HOWARD MESSICK, hosp. adminstr.; b. Omaha, Oct. 6, 1918; s. Messick Ernest and Selma Ruth (Ericson) W.; B.S. in Bus. Adminstrn., U. Omaha, 1940; M.A. in Bus. Adminstrn., U. Minn., 1948, M.H.A., 1951; m. Dorothy Elizabeth Peterson, Dec. 21, 1946; children—Linda Christine, Mary Elizabeth, Mark Howard, Thomas James, Susan Louise. From instr. to asso. prof. bus. adminstrn. Augsburg Coll., Mpls., 1946-49; mgr. Worthington (Minn.) Clinic, 1951-57; mem. adminstrv. staff Rochester (Minn.) Methodist Hosp., 1957—, adminstr., 1965-72, exec. dir., 1972—. Served with inf. AUS, 1941-46; ETO. Decorated Purple Heart. Fellow Am. Coll. Hosp. Adminstrs. (regent); mem. Am., Minn. (pres. 1977) hosp. assns., Rochester Area C. of C. (pres. 1976). Republican. Lutheran. Address: 201 W Center St Rochester MN 55901. *There are many ways to approach "Thoughts on my Life." The limited space requires a succinct and fundamental statement. At this point I feel that I have had maximum opportunity for the education I have and background from which I come. The really important things have come to me although I didn't always recognize them or for what I was struggling. I attribute all or most of this success to acceptance and communication with a force or power greater than myself. This has kept my perspective fresh, my attitudes flexible and given me a faith that sustains through all problems and difficulties.*

WINICK, CHARLES, educator, sociologist; b. N.Y.C., Aug. 4, 1922; s. David and Sadie (Brussel) W.; B.A., City Coll. N.Y., 1941; M.A., N.Y.U., 1949; Ph.D., 1950; m. Mariann Pezzella, July 2, 1961; children—Elizabeth, Laura, Raphael. Asst. prof. U. Rochester, 1951-53; research dir. Anti- Defamation League, 1953-55; lectr. Queens Coll., 1953-56; vis. prof. Mass. Inst. Tech., 1956-57, Columbia, 1957-58, 61-63, 75-77, N.Y. U., 1975-76, New Sch., 1974-76; dir. basic research J. Walter Thompson Co., 1959-61; research dir. N.Y. State Narcotics Commn., 1957-59; cons. Am. Social Health Assn., 1961-73; research dir. Postgrad. Center Mental Health, 1957-66; cons. Central Labor Rehab. Council N.Y., 1977—; prof. sociology City Coll. and grad. center of City U. N.Y., 1966—; asso. univ. seminar Columbia, 1963—. Sec., dir. Nat. Adv. Council Narcotics, 1949—; cons. subcom. juvenile delinquency U.S. Senate, 1955-57, Joint Commn. Mental Health Children, 1968-69, Commn. on Obscenity and Pornography, 1969-70, Commn. on Marihuana and Drug Abuse, 1972-73. Served with AUS, 1942-46. Recipient Flowerman award Postgrad. Center Mental Health 1960; Edn. Press award Ednl. Press Assn., 1963; Peabody award, 1964; Progressive Architecture award, 1979. Mem. Am. Sociol. Assn., Am. Psychol. Assn., Brit. Soc. Study Addiction, Am. Assn. Pub. Opinion Research, Soc. Study Social Problems, Soc. Psychol. Study Social Issues. Author: Trends in Human Relation Research, 1955; Dictionary of Anthropology, 1956; Taste and Censor, 1959; Insights into Pricing from Behavioral Science and Operations Research, 1961; For the Young Viewer, 1962; Practicum of Group Psychotherapy, 1963, 2d edit., 1974; Outer Space Humor, 1963; U.S.S.R. Humor, 1964; Group Psychotherapy Today, 1965; The New People, 1968; The Narcotic Addiction Problem, 1968; The Glue Sniffing Problem, 1968; The Lively Commerce, 1971; Children's Television Commercials, 1973; Sociological Aspects of Drug Dependence, 1974; Deviance and Mass Communications, 1978; The Television Experience, 1979. Editor, Yearbook of Drug Dependence, 1978—, Annual Rev. of Research in Deviance, 1978—. Office: City Coll Convent Ave and 138th St New York NY 10031

WINICK, MARVIN, lawyer; b. Des Moines, Mar. 7, 1933; s. Louis and Sarah (Korn) W.; B.S.C. in Accounting, State U. Iowa, 1955, J.D., 1959; m. Marilyn Robinow, Aug. 29, 1954; children—Laura, Ellen, Steven. Staff accountant Peat, Marwick, Mitchell & Co., C.P.A.'s, Des Moines, 1959-60; admitted to Iowa bar, 1959; partner firm Swift, Brown, Winick & Graves and predecessor firm, Des Moines, 1960—. Instr. accounting State U. Iowa, 1957-59; mem. Iowa Bd. Tax Rev., 1969-71; mem. Midwest regional liaison com. IRS, 1971-74. Vice pres., trustee Jewish Welfare Fedn. Des Moines; pres. Tifereth Israel Synagogue, 1975-77; adv. bd. Mercy Hosp., 1977—. Served to capt. USAF, 1955-57. C.P.A., Iowa. Mem. Am., Iowa (chmn. tax com. 1970-73), Polk County bar assns., Iowa Soc. C.P.A.'s. Mem. B'nai B'rith. Home: 1912 76th St Des Moines IA 50322 Office: Register and Tribune Bldg Suite 1200 Des Moines IA 50309

WINICK, MYRON, educator, physician; b. N.Y.C., May 4, 1929; s. Charles B. and Ruth E. (Gesser) W.; A.B., Columbia, 1951; M.S., U. Ill., 1952; M.D., State U. N.Y., 1956; m. Elaine L. Lasky, Sept. 19, 1964; children—Jonathan, Stephen. Intern, U. Pa., Phila., 1956-57; asst. resident pediatrics Cornell U. Med. Coll., N.Y.C., 1957-59, chief resident, 1959-60; attending pediatrician Stanford U. Hosp., 1963-64; asst. prof. pediatrics Cornell U. Med. Coll., N.Y.C., 1964-68, asso. prof. pediatrics and nutrition, 1968-70, prof., 1970-71; prof. pediatrics, dir. Inst. Human Nutrition, Columbia, 1972—, R.R. Williams prof. nutrition, 1973—, dir. Center for Nutrition, Genetics and Human Devel., 1975—. Vis. prof. pediatrics U. Chile, Santiago, 1967; asst. attending pediatrician N.Y. Hosp., N.Y.C., 1964-68, asso. attending pediatrician, 1968-70, attending pediatrician, 1970-71; attending pediatrician Presbyn. Hosp., N.Y.C., 1972—; cons. Pan Am. Health Orgn., 1966—. Trustee Found. for Internat. Child Health; mem. nutrition interdisciplinary cluster Pres.' Biomed. Research Panel, 1975; mem. panel on infants and children Pres.' Commn. on Mental Health, 1977; cons. Office of Tech. Assessment, U.S. Congress, 1976-78. Served with USNR, 1960-62. Bank of Am.-Gianini Found. fellow, Stanford, 1962; NIH Spl. fellow, 1963; recipient NIH Career Devel. award, 1968-71; E. Mead Johnson award pediatric research, 1970; Osborne and Mendel award Am. Inst. Nutrition, 1976. Fellow Royal Soc. Health, Am. Acad. Pediatrics; mem. AAAS, Am. Soc. Cell Biology, Soc. Developmental Biology, Harvey Soc., Soc. Pediatric Research, Brit. Nutrition Soc., Am. Inst. Nutrition, Am. Soc. Clin. Nutrition, N.Y. Acad. Scis., N.Y. Acad. Medicine, Soc. for Exptl. Biology and Medicine, Soc. for Neurosci. Author: Malnutrition and Brain Development, 1976; (textbook) Nutrition in Health and Disease, 1980. Editor: Current Concepts in Nutrition, 1972—; Nutrition: Pre- and Postnatal Development, Vol. I; Human Nutrition: A Comprehensive Treatise, 1979; contbg. editor Nutrition Revs., 1969-76; editorial bd. Jour. Nutrition, 1972-76, The Year in Metabolism (now Contemporary Metabolism), 1975—. Office: Inst Human Nutrition Columbia U 701 W 168th St New York NY 10032

WINIKATES, CHARLES JOHN, lawyer; b. Chgo., July 21, 1927; s. Henry James and Catherine Therese (O'Reilly) W.; B.S., U. Ill., 1950; J.D., So. Meth. U., 1950; m. Bonnie Mary Eichorn, Dec. 29, 1956; children—Charles John, Bonnie Mary, Catherine Leslie, Regina Mary, Mary Elizabeth. Admitted to Tex. bar, 1950, since practiced in Dallas; partner firm Winikates & Curtis; dir. Prosper State Bank (Tex.), 1965, vice chmn. bd., 1971—; chmn. bd. B/D, 1976; pres., gen. counsel, dir. Temxo Corp., Dallas, 1957—. Served with U.S. Army. Mem. Am., Dallas bar assns., State Bar Tex., Am., Tex., Dallas trial lawyers assns., Delta Theta Pi. K.C. Clubs: Dallas Athletic; Serra. Home: 5948 Melshire St Dallas TX 75230 Office: 2535 Republic Bank Tower Dallas TX 75201

WINKEL, ADRIAN P., ter. ofcl.; b. Breckenridge, Minn., Apr. 15, 1915; B.A., St. John's U., Minn., 1937; postgrad. U. Minn., U. Notre Dame; m. Isabel Frances Browne; 6 children. Instr., Marquette U., Milw., 1943-47, Coll. St. Thomas, Minn., 1947-49; staff asst. to Congressman Eugene J. McCarthy, 1949-55; asst. to commr. taxation City of St. Paul, 1955-57; commr. pub. works St. Paul, 1957-60; chmn. Minn. Democratic Party Central Com., 1960-61; regional dir. U.S. Post Office, Mpls., 1961-69, dep. regional dir., 1969-70; staff asst. to Rep. Phillip Burton, 1971-73; staff cons. on ters. House Com. on Interior and Insular Affairs, 1973-77; high commr. of U.S. Trust Ter. of Pacific Islands, 1977—. Office: Office of High Commr Saipan Mariana Islands 96950

WINKEL, NINA (CATHERINE MARIA JOHANNA), sculptor; b. Borken, Germany, May 21, 1905; d. Ernest Joseph and Augustine (Bauer) Koch; student sculpture Staedel Mus. Sch., Frankfurt/Main, Germany, also Paris, France; m. George Joseph Winkel, Dec. 15, 1934. Came to U.S., 1942, naturalized, 1945. One-man shows include Sculpture Center, N.Y., 1944, 47, 58, 72 (retrospective), U. Notre Dame, 1954; exhbns. include N.A.D., Pa. Acad. Fine Arts, Met. Mus., Whitney Mus., San Francisco Mus., Am. Acad. Arts and Letters, others; sculptor monuments, human figures and horses; pub. monument for Wiesbaden, W. Ger., 1964; installed hist. panels in copper Hanes Corp., N.Y.; lectr. art treasures and antiquities in Europe. Trustee Keene Valley (N.Y.) Pub. Library, Adirondack Mus., Elizabethtown, N.Y. Pres., Sculpture Center, Inc., 1970-73, emeritus, 1973—; juror for monuments competition Olympics, 1980. Recipient E. Watrous gold medal N.A.D., 1945, 78; Samuel F.B. Morse medal, 1964; hon. mention Avery award Archtl. League, N.Y.C., 1958-59; bronze medal Nat. Sculpture Soc., 1967, 71. Academician, N.A.D. Fellow Nat. Sculpture Soc. (sec. 1965-68); mem. Sculptor's Guild, Internat. Platform Assn. Home: Keene Valley NY 12943 Office: Sculpture Center 167 E 69th St New York City NY 10021. *For a creative artist a philosophy of life is more important than a theory of art. I believe that creation is not an intellectual process. Art grows like a plant in the humus of a personality and of life with its pains and joys. A positive acceptance of life and particularly of its sorrows and difficulties can make a human being strong to transmit lasting values to others through his work; not so much by a reasoned program, but by the natural and spontaneous productiveness of a loving nature. The ideal artist is like a fruit tree, bringing forth its fruit regardless of gatherers or markets. Art is love, transformed into work.*

WINKELMAN, JOHN, educator; b. N.Y.C., May 8, 1911; s. William and Marie (Asendorf) W.; B.A., Coll. City N.Y., 1933, M.S., 1938; Ph.D., U. Mich., 1952; m. Phyllis V. Higley, Sept. 9, 1939; children—John Higley, Alice Marie (Mrs. Harold Berberick), William Brewster. Instr. Massanutten Acad., Woodstock, Va., 1935-38; instr. Montclair (N.J.) Acad., 1938-40; teaching fellow U. Mich., 1940-45; instr. U. Mo., 1945-53; asst. prof. U. Neb., 1953-58, asso. prof., 1958-63; prof. German, U. Waterloo (Ont., Can.), 1963-66; prof., chmn. German dept. State U. N.Y. at Albany, 1966-70, prof., 1970-80, prof. emeritus, 1980—. Civilian lang. expert U.S. Strategic Bombing Survey, Germany, 1945. Mem. Modern Lang. Assn. Am., Am. Assn. Tchrs. German, AAUP. Author: Social Criticism in the Early Works of Erich Kästner, 1953; The Poetic Style of Erich Kästner, 1957; Kafka's Forschungen eines Hundes, 1967; An Interpretation of Kafka's "Das Schloss", 1972; Felice Bauer and Kafka's "Der Prozess," 1977. Contbr. articles to profl. jours. Home: 33 Broadleaf Dr Clifton Park NY 12065 Office: State U NY Albany NY 12222

WINKELMAN, STANLEY JAY, clothing store exec.; b. Saulte Sainte Marie, Mich., Sept. 23, 1922; s. Leon George and Josephine (Rosenblum) W.; B.S. in Chemistry, U. Mich., 1943; m. Margaret Jayne Wallace, Mar. 27, 1943; children— Andra Wallace (Mrs. Lewis Barr), Marjory Beth (Mrs. Donald Epstein), Roger Edward. Research chemist OSRD projects Calif. Inst. Tech., also U. Calif., 1943-44; with Winkelman Stores, Inc., Detroit, 1946—, mdse. adminstr., 1948-51, sr. v.p., dir. 1957-60, exec. v.p., 1960-65, pres., 1965—, chmn. bd., chief exec. officer, 1976—; corporate mem. Merrill-Palmer Corp. Bd. dirs. New Detroit, Inc., 1967—, chmn., 1971; bd. advs. Wayne State U. Press, 1955—; adv. com. Archives Labor History and Urban Affairs, Wayne State U., 1973—; mem. Econ. Devel. Corp., 1968-71; mem. Mich. Fair Campaign Practices Commn., 1966-68, Mich. Gov.'s Ethical and Moral Panel, 1963-67; v.p. Detroit Conv. Bur., 1966, bd. dirs., 1959-70; mem. Mich. Welfare League; co-chmn. citizens' edn. task force Detroit Bd. Edn., 1972-76, now mem. monitoring commn.; mem. exec. com. Jewish Community Council, 1956—, pres., 1960-63; exec. com. Jewish Welfare Fedn., 1965-77, v.p., 1969-74, bd. govs., 1956—; mem. Detroit High Sch. Study Commn., 1966-68; co-chmn. expenditures task force Econ. Growth Council Detroit, 1976-78, bd. dirs. Econ. Growth Corp., 1978—; hon. chmn. adv. com. Mayor's Supported Work Program, 1976—; v.p. Wayne State Fund, 1975, bd. dirs., 1976—; mem. U. Mich. campaign com. East Asian Capital Fund, 1977—; citizen's adv. com. U. Mich., Dearborn, 1970—; past bd. dirs. Council Jewish Fedns. and Welfare Funds; bd. dirs. Wayne State U. Health Care Inst., 1977—, exec. com., 1978—; trustee, exec. com. Met. Fund Detroit, 1968-76, v.p., 1974, chmn., 1976—; bd. dirs. United Found., 1955—, exec. com., 1969—; trustee Met. N.W. Detroit Hosps. Corp., 1972—, United Community Services, 1970—76; nat. adv. com. Nat. Urban Coalition, 1973—. Served to lt. (j.g.) USNR, 1944-46. Recipient St. Cyprian award, 1965, Am. Jewish Congress Amity award, 1968, Detroit Bar Assn. Liberty Bell award, 1968, U. Detroit Human Relations award, 1968, Wayne State U. Builder of Detroit award, 1975. Mem. Nat. Retail Mchts. Assn. (dir. 1966—, exec. com. 1974, consumer affairs chmn. 1976—, v.p. 1978—), Detroit Round Table Christians and Jews (dir. 1963—), Nat. Mcpl. League (council 1977—). Democrat. Jewish (1st v.p., trustee temple 1966). Clubs: Economic of Detroit (dir. 1963—), Franklin Hills Country, Standard, Circumnavigators, U. Mich.'s Pres.'s, Renaissance. Home: 1921 Pine Ridge Ln Bloomfield Hills MI 48013 Office: 25 Parsons St Detroit MI 48201

WINKELSTEIN, WARREN, JR., educator, physician; b. Syracuse, N.Y., July 1, 1922; s. Warren and Evelyn (Neiman) W.; B.A., U. N.C., 1942; M.D. cum laude, Syracuse U., 1947; M.P.H., Columbia, 1950; m. Veva Kerrigan, Feb. 14, 1976; children by previous marriage—Rebecca (Mrs. Peter Yamin), Joshua, Shoshana. Intern Charity Hosp., New Orleans, 1947-48; with I.C.A., Vietnam, 1951-53; dir. div. communicable disease control to 1st dep. commr. local and environmental health services Erie County Health Dept., 1953-62; asso. prof. to prof. State U. N.Y. at Buffalo, 1962-68; prof. epidemiology, dean pub. health U. Calif., 1972—. Served with AUS, 1944-46. Diplomate Am. Bd. Preventive Medicine (trustee). Mem. Am. Pub. Health Assn., AAAS, Assn. Tchrs. Preventive Medicine, Internat., Am. epidemiol. socs., Am. Heart Assn. Author: Basic Readings in Epidemiology, 1972. Contbr. articles profl. jours. Home: 560 Washington Ave Point Richmond CA 94801

WINKLER, ELMER LOUIS, petroleum co. exec.; b. Wichita, Kans., Sept. 12, 1930; s. Louis Emil and Clara (Roeder) W.; B.S., Swarthmore Coll., 1952; m. Norma Jean Lenhart, Nov. 10, 1966; children—Michael, Philip, Eric, Holly. Engr., Westinghouse Elec. Corp., Balt., 1952-54; controller, asst. to treas. Rock Island Refining Corp., Indpls., 1956-62, asst. to pres., 1962-66, v.p., 1966-70, pres., dir., 1970—; pres. Progressive Oil Co. Inc., Ft. Wayne, Ind., 1963-76, Hartley Oil Co., Muncie, Ind., 1962-72; dir. Hoosier Coal & Oil Co. Inc., 1966—, Am. Fletcher Nat. Bank, Indpls., 1973—, Am. Fletcher Corp., Indpls., 1975—. Served with AUS, 1954-56. Mem. Nat. Petroleum Refiners Assn. (exec. com. 1972—), ASME. Kiwanian.

Home: 7415 Colony Circle Indianapolis IN 46260 Office: PO Box 68007 Indianapolis IN 46268

WINKLER, HENRY FRANKLIN, actor; b. N.Y.C., Oct. 30, 1945; s. Harry Irving and Ilse Anna Maria (Hadra) W.; student Emerson Coll., 1963-67, D.H.L., 1978; student Yale Sch. Drama, 1967-70; m. Stacey Weitzman, May 5, 1978. With Yale Repertory Theatre, 1970-71, off-Broadway shows, 1972-73, Cin. Playhouse, 1973; films include: The Lords of Flatbush, 1972; Heroes, 1977; The One and Only, 1977; starred TV series Happy Days, 1973—; appeared on ABC-TV movie An American Christmas Carol, 1979; exec. producer TV program Who Are the Debolts and Where Did They Get Nineteen Kids; pres. Fair Dinkum Prodns., Hollywood, Calif., 1979—; founder New Haven Free Theatre, 1968, Off The Wall N.Y., improvisation co., 1972; tchr. drama U. Calif. at Los Angeles Adult Extension. Named hon. youth chmn. Epilepsy Found.; chmn. Toys for Tots, 1977; lifetime patron Variety Club. Named Best Actor in Comedy Series, Photoplay mag., 1976-77, also Golden Globe award, 1976, 77, 78; named King of Baccus, Mardi Gras, New Orleans, 1977; Emmy nominee, 1975, 76, 77. Mem. AFTRA, Screen Actors Guild, Actors Equity. Contbr. article My Turn to Newsweek mag., 1976. Office: care Paramount Pictures 5451 Marathon St Hollywood CA 90038

WINKLER, HENRY RALPH, educator, historian; b. Waterbury, Conn., Oct. 27, 1916; s. Jacob and Ethel (Rieger) W.; A.B., U. Cin., 1938, M.A. 1940; Ph.D., U. Chgo., 1947; hon. degrees Lehigh U., 1974, Rutgers U., 1977, No. Ky. U., 1978, St. Thomas Inst., 1979; m. Clare Sapadin, Aug. 18, 1940; children—Allan Michael, Karen Jean; m. 2d, Beatrice Ross, Jan. 28, 1973. Instr., U. Cin., 1939-40; asst. prof. Roosevelt Coll., 1946-47; mem. faculty Rutgers U., 1947-77, prof. history, 1958-77, chmn. dept., 1960-64, dean Faculty Liberal Arts, 1967, vice provost, 1968-70, acting provost, 1970, v.p. for acad. affairs, 1970-72, sr. v.p. for acad. affairs, 1972-76, exec. v.p., 1976-77; exec. v.p. U. Cin., 1977, pres., 1977—; mng. editor Am. Hist. Rev., 1964-68. Vis. prof. Bryn Mawr Coll., 1959-60, Harvard, summer 1964, Columbia, summer 1967; faculty John Hay Fellows Inst. Humanities, 1960-65. Nat. chmn. European history advanced placement com. Coll. Entrance Exam. Bd., 1960-64; mem. Nat. Commn. on Humanities in Schs., 1967-68; Am. specialist Eastern Asia, 1968; exec. com. Conf. on Brit. Studies, 1968-75; chmn. bd. Nat. Humanities Faculty, 1970-73; chmn. adv. com. on history Coll. Entrance Exam. Bd., 1977—, mem. council on acad. affairs, mem. bd. trustees. Pres., Highland Park (N.J.) Bd. Edn., 1962-63; mem. exec. com. Nat. Assn. State Univs. and Land-Grant Colls.; bd. dirs. Am. Council on Edn. Served with USNR, 1943-46. Mem. Am. Hist. Assn., Phi Beta Kappa, Tau Kappa Alpha, Phi Alpha Theta. Clubs: Century Assn., Queen City, Bankers, Cin. Author: The League of Nations Movement in Great Britain, 1914-19, 1952; Great Britain in the Twentieth Century, 1960, 2d edit., 1966. Editor: (with K.M. Setton) Great Problems in European Civilization, 1954, 2d edit., 1966; Twentieth-Century Britain, 1977. Editorial bd. Historian, 1958-64; adv. bd. Partisan Rev., 1972-79. Contbr. articles to jours., revs. Office: U of Cincinnati Cincinnati OH 45221

WINKLER, IRWIN, motion picture producer; b. N.Y.C., May 28, 1931; s. Sol and Anna W.; B.A., N.Y. U., 1955. Mailroom messenger William Morris Agy., N.Y.C., 1955-62; co-founder Chartoff-Winkler Prodns., Culver City, Calif., 1964; producer Rocky (10 Acad. award nominations, winner 3 including best picture), 1976, They Shoot Horses Don't They (9 Acad. award nominations), 1969, Nickelodeon, 1976, The Gambler, 1974, Up the Sandbox, 1972, The New Centurions, 1972, Point Blank, 1967, Double Trouble, 1967, Leo the Last (Best Dir. award Cannes Film Festival 1970, Belgrade Film Festival 1970), The Strawberry Statement (Jury prize Cannes Film Festival 1970), The Split, 1968, Breakout, 1975, Believe in Me, 1971, The Gang That Couldn't Shoot Straight, 1971, The Mechanic, 1972, Busting, 1974, SPYS, 1974, Peeper, 1975, New York, New York, 1977, Valentino, 1977, Uncle Joe Shannon, 1978, Comes A Horseman, 1978, Rocky II, 1979, Raging Bull, 1980. Served with U.S. Army, 1951-53. Office: 10125 W Washington Blvd Culver City CA 90230

WINKLER, JOSEPH CONRAD, recreational products mfg. co. exec.; b. Newark, May 20, 1916; s. Charles and Mollie (Abrams) W.; B.S., N.Y. U., 1941; m. Geraldine M. Borok, Sept. 20, 1953; children—Charles H., David J. Gen. mgr. Indsl. Washing Machine Corp., New Brunswick, N.J., 1941-48; controller Mojud Corp., N.Y.C., 1948-52; controller, asst. treas. Barbizon Corp., N.Y.C., 1952-57; controller Ideal Toy Corp., N.Y.C., 1957-58, dir. fin. and adminstrn., 1960-62, v.p. fin., 1962-68, sr. v.p. fin., 1968-78, exec. v.p., chief operating officer, dir., 1978—; controller McGregor-Doniger, Inc., N.Y.C., 1958-59; dir. Ideal Toy Co. Ltd., Wokingham, Eng., Ideal Toy Corp. Australia Ltd., Melbourne, ITC Industries Ltd., Hong Kong, Ideal Toy K.K., Tokyo, Ideal Toy Corp. Can., Ltd., Toronto, Ont., Arxon Spiel & Freizeit, Rodgau W. Ger. Committeeman, troop treas. Boy Scouts Am., Tenafly, N.J., 1965-71. Served with Office Statis. Control, USAAF, 1945. Mem. Fin. Execs. Inst. Home: 96 Buckingham Rd Tenafly NJ 07670 Office: 184-10 Jamaica Ave Hollis NY 11423

WINKLER, LEE B., bus. mgmt. cons. firm exec.; b. Buffalo, Dec. 31, 1925; s. Jack W. and Caroline (Marienthal) W.; B.S. cum laude, N.Y. U., 1945, M.S. cum laude, 1947; children—James, Stewart Gilbert, Nicole Borgenicht. Mgr. Equitable Life Assurance Soc., N.Y.C., 1948-58; pres. Winkler Assos. Ltd., Beverly Hills, Calif., and N.Y.C., 1958—, Global Bus. Mgmt. Inc., Beverly Hills, 1967—; v.p. Bayly Martin & Fay Inc., N.Y.C., 1965-68, John C. Paige & Co., N.Y.C., 1968-71; cons. Albert G. Ruben Co., Beverly Hills, 1971—. Served with AUS, 1943-45. Decorated chevalier comdr. Order Holy Cross Jerusalem, also spl. exec. asst., charge d'affaires, 1970; chevalier comdr. Sovereign Order Cyprus, 1970. Mem. Nat. Acad. TV Arts and Scis., Nat. Acad. Recording Arts and Scis., Beverly Hills C. of C., Phi Beta Kappa, Beta Gamma Sigma, Mu Gamma Tau, Psi Chi Omega. Home: Beverly Hills CA 90210 Office: 9601 Wilshire Blvd Beverly Hills CA 90210. *In the final analysis The bottom line, if you will—the only thing that truly matters in life are those friends and family that hold you dear to them. Sucess, and its attendant monies, rise and fall like the tides, and even vanish at times, but earned love is as constant as the earth's rotation is independent of the tides.*

WINKLES, BOBBY BROOKS, profl. baseball coach; b. Tuckerman, Ark., Mar. 11, 1930; B.S., Ill. Wesleyan U., 1952; M.S., U. Colo., 1956; m. Ellie Hoemann, Feb. 28, 1953; children—Kelly Jaime, Kristi. Infielder Chgo. White Sox Farm Club System, 1951-58; baseball coach Ariz. State U., Tempe, 1958-71; mem. staff Cal. Angels Am. League baseball team, Anaheim, 1971-74, first base coach, 1972, mgr., 1973-74; coach Oakland Athletics, 1974-75, San Francisco Giants, 1976-77; mgr. Oakland Athletics, 1977-78; coach Chgo. White Sox, 1979—. Served with AUS, 1952-54. Office: care Comiskey Park Dan Ryan at 35th St Chicago IL 60616

WINN, ALBERT CURRY, clergyman; b. Ocala, Fla., Aug. 16, 1921; s. James Anderson and Elizabeth (Curry) W.; A.B., Davidson Coll., 1942, LL.D., 1968; B.D., Union Theol. Sem., Va., 1945, Th.D., 1956; Th.M., Princeton Theol. Sem., 1949; LL.D., Stillman Coll., 1975; m. Grace Neely Walker, Aug. 29, 1944; children—Grace Walker (Mrs. Stewart E. Ellis), James Anderson, Albert Bruce Curry, Randolph Axson. Ordained to ministry Presbyn. Ch., 1945; asst. prof. Davidson Coll., 1946-47; pastor Potomac Rural Parish, Va., 1948-53; prof. Bible, Stillman Coll., 1953-60; prof. theology Louisville Presbyn. Theol. Sem., 1960-73, pres., 1966-73; pastor 2d Presbyn. Ch., Richmond, Va., 1974—. Moderator, Presbyn. Synod Ala., 1958, Presbyn. Synod Ky., 1969, Gen. Assembly, Presbyn. Ch. in U.S., 1979. Chmn. trustees Stillman Coll., 1965-70. Served as chaplain USNR, 1945-46. Mem. Am. Theol. Assn., Phi Beta Kappa, Beta Theta Pi, Omicron Delta Kappa. Author: Layman's Bible Commentary on Acts, 1960; The Worry and Wonder of Being Human, 1966; Where Do I Go From Here, 1972. Office: 13 N 5th St Richmond VA 23219

WINN, EDWARD BURTON, lawyer; b. Dallas, Sept. 23, 1920; s. Edward Frost and Verdie Catherine (Robbins) W.; B.A., U. Tex., 1942; LL.B., Yale, 1948; m. Conchita Elisa Hassell, June 1, 1945; children—Edward Arthur, David Burton, William Hassell, Richard Wellington, Alan Randolph. Admitted to Tex. bar, 1948, since practiced in Dallas; partner firm Lane, Savage, Counts & Winn. 1958—. Pres., Dallas Jr. Bar Assn., 1951, Jr. Bar Tex., 1953, Dallas Estate Council, 1954-55; adv. council Dallas Community Chest Trust Fund, 1965-68; mem. staff armed forces preparedness subcom U.S. Senate, 1951; chmn. Inst. on Wills and Probate, Southwestern Legal Found., 1966—. Chmn. Dallas County Profl. and Bus. Men for Kennedy-Johnson, 1960; vice chmn. Dallas County Democratic Exec. Com., 1964-66. Bd. dirs. Operation LIFT, 1962—; trustee Nat. Pollution Control Found. Served to lt. USNR, 1942-46; ETO. Decorated with the Admirals' Commendations, 1943. Fellow Am. Coll. Probate Counsel (pres. 1974-75); mem. Am. (chmn. com. fiduciary law and procedure 1952-53, com. improvement probate procedure 1953-54, council 1955—, sect. chmn. 1963-64, sect. real property probate and trust law, ho. of dels. 1965-66, 78—), Dallas (dir. 1959-61) bar assns., Dallas UN Assn. (pres.), U N Assn. of U.S. (exec. com. dir., pres. Tex. div. 1967-71), State Bar Tex. (chmn. sect. real estate, probate and trust law 1962-63), Am. Bar Found., Dallas Council World Affairs (pres. young execs. group 1959-60, bd. dirs. 1958-73), Yale Law Sch. Alumni Assn. N. Tex. (pres. 1962-66; regional rep. 1966—), U. Tex. Ex-Students Assn. Dallas (pres. 1963-64), Phi Kappa Sigma (pres. Sigma chpt. 1941-42), Phi Eta Sigma. Club: Calyx (Dallas). Co-author: How to Live and Die with Texas Probate; Texas Estate Administration. Contbr. articles to profl. jours. Home: 6712 Prestonshire Ln Dallas TX 75225 Office: Republic Nat Bank Bldg Dallas TX 75201

WINN, EDWARD LAWRENCE, JR. (LARRY), congressman; b. Kansas City, Mo., Aug. 22, 1919; S. Edward Lawrence and Gertrude (Shepherd) W.; B.A., U. Kans., 1941; m. Joan Elliott, May 5, 1942; children—Edward Lawrence III, Robert Elliott, Douglas Shepherd, Janet Gay (Mrs. Donald A. Payne), Cynthia Joan (Mrs. Gary Burr). Sports announcer radio sta. WHB, Kansas City, 1941-42; asst. recreation dir. N.Am. Aviation Co., Kansas City, 1943-44; pub. relations dir. A.R.C., Kansas City, 1944-45; pvt. builder, Johnson County, Kans., 1946-47; salesman Hamilton-Crawford Realty Co., Johnson County, 1948-49; v.p. Winn-Rau Corp., Overland Park, Kans.; mem. 90th-96th Congresses 3d Dist. Kans. Dir. Southgate State Bank, Prairie Village, Kans. Vice pres. Kaw council Boy Scouts Am., 1966, nat. council rep., 1958—; mem. steering com. Johnson County Health, Edn. and Recreation Council; mem. U. Kans. Devel. Com. Republican dist. chmn., 1964-66; mem. Rep. Exec. Com. Kans., 1964-66. Bd. dirs. Community Chest Greater Kansas City, Johnson County United Funds Council; mem. adv. bd. Shawnee Mission Hosp., Jr. Achievement Greater Kansas City, Linwood Sch. Bd. Dist. No. 1, People to People. Recipient Silver Beaver award Boy Scouts Am. Mem. Nat. Assn. Home Builders (nat. dir.), Home Builders Assn. Greater Kansas City (past pres.), Home Builders Assn. Kans. (past v.p.), Kans. Farm Bur., Sigma Delta Chi, Phi Kappa Psi. Mem. Christian Ch. Club: Rotary. Office: 2416 Rayburn House Office Bldg Washington DC 20515

WINN, ELLENE, lawyer; b. Clayton, Ala.; B.A. magna cum laude, Agnes Scott Coll., 1931; M.A., Radcliffe Coll., 1932; LL.B., Birmingham (Ala.) Sch. Law, 1941. Admitted to Ala. bar, 1941; asso. firm Bradley, Arant, Rose & White, Birmingham, 1942-57, partner, 1957—. Trustee Birmingham Civic Opera Assn., 1955—, Birmingham Music Club, 1969—; mem. senate U. Ala., Birmingham, 1978—. Mem. Am., Ala., Birmingham bar assns., Ala. State Bar. Clubs: Birmingham Country, Relay House. Home: 715 Fairway Dr Birmingham AL 35213 Office: Brown-Marx Bldg Birmingham AL 35203

WINN, WILLIS JAY, banker; b. Plattsburg, Mo., Apr. 26, 1917; s. Sam J.and Emma (Sell) W.; A.B., Central Coll., 1939, LL.D., 1959; M.A., U. Pa., 1940, Ph.D., 1951; m. Lois Gengelbach, Nov. 25, 1942; children—Judith Ann, Steven Jay. Research asso. Nat. Bur. Econ. Research, N.Y.C., 1942-46; with U. Pa., 1946-71, beginning as instr. finance, successively asst. prof., asso. prof., 1946-57, prof. finance, 1957-71, vice dean Wharton Sch. Finance and Commerce, 1955-57, acting dean, 1957-58, dean, 1958-71, vice provost univ., 1958-71; pres. Fed. Res. Bank, Cleve., 1971—. Chmn. Fed. Res. Bank of Phila. Dir. Nat. Bureau Econ. Research, Inc., 1959—. Mem. Am. Finance Soc., Am., Royal econ. socs. Home: 3075 Lander Rd Pepper Pike OH 44124 Office: Federal Reserve Bank Cleveland OH 44101

WINNEFELD, JAMES ALEXANDER, naval officer; b. Paterson, N.J., Jan. 1, 1929; s. Carl Herbert and Helen Dorothy (Renecker) W.; student Drew U., 1946-47; B.S., U.S. Naval Acad., 1951; M.A. in Internat. Affairs, Stanford U., 1960; m. Fredda Coupland, Mar. 15, 1952; children—Lea Winnefeld Sandman, James Alexander. Commd. ensign U.S. Navy, 1951, advanced through grades to rear adm., 1977; ops. officer for comdr. Carrier Div. Six, 1971-72; exec. asst. and sr. aide to Chief Naval Personnel, 1972-74; comdg. officer U.S.S. Trenton, 1974-75; comdr. Amphibious Squadron Two, 1975-76; comdt. of midshipmen U.S. Naval Acad., 1976-78; dir. Total Force Programming div. Office Chief Naval Ops, 1978—. Decorated Bronze medal with Combat V, Meritorious Service medal (3), Air medal (2), Navy Commendation medal (2). Mem. U.S. Naval Inst. (dir.). Presbyterian. Clubs: Naval Acad. Sailing Assn., Athletic Assn. Contbr. articles to jours. Home: 4000 Belle Rive Terr Alexandria VA 22309 Office: Office of CNO (Op-12) Dept of Navy Washington DC 20350

WINNER, FRED M., judge; b. Denver, Apr. 8, 1912; s. Frank N. and Clara (Morse) W.; B.A., U. Colo., 1933, B.S., 1933, LL.B., 1936; m. Frankie R., Sept. 2, 1933; children—Claire Winner March, Margi Winner Raley. Admitted to Colo. bar; practiced in Denver, 1936-70; U.S. dist. judge, Denver, 1970—, now chief judge; instr. Westminister Law Sch., 1951-54; mem. jud. selection commn. Colo. Supreme Ct. Served with USNR, 1942-46. Mem. Am. Coll. Trial Lawyers, Internat. Acad. Trial Lawyers. Office: US Courthouse 1929 Stout St Room C-224 Denver CO 80294*

WINNER, MICHAEL ROBERT, film dir., writer, producer; b. London, Oct. 30, 1935; s. George Joseph and Helen (Zloty) W.; degree in law and econs. with honors, Downing Coll., Cambridge (Eng.) U., 1956. Writer, Fleet St. newspapers, London, 1956-58; engaged in film prodn., 1956—; dir. films Play it Cool, 1962, The Cool Mikado, 1962, West II, 1963, The Girl Getters, 1964, You Must be Joking, 1965, The Jokers, 1966, I'll Never Forget What's 'is name, 1967, Hannibal Brooks, 1968, The Games, 1970, Lawman, 1970, The Nightcomers, 1971, Chato's Land, 1971, The Mechanic, 1972, Scorpio, 1972, The Stone Killer, 1973, Death Wish, 1974, Won Ton Ton The Dog Who Saved Hollywood, 1975, The Sentinel, 1976, The Big Sleep, 1977, Firepower, 1978. Office: 6-8 Sackville St Piccadilly London W1X 1DD England

WINNER, THOMAS G., educator; b. Prague, Czechoslovakia, May 4, 1917; s. Julius and Franziska (Grünhutová) Wiener; came to U.S. 1939, naturalized, 1950; student U. Prague, 1936-38, U. Lille (France), 1936; B.A., Harvard 1942, M.A., 1943; Ph.D., Columbia, 1950; M.A. (hon.), Brown U., 1966; m. Irene Portis, Sept. 25, 1942; children—Ellen, Lucy Franziska. With OWI, 1943-46; vis. fellow Johns Hopkins, 1947-48; from instr. Russian to asso. prof. Duke, 1948-58; asso. prof., then prof. Slavic langs. and lits. U. Mich., 1958-65; prof. Slavic langs. and comparative lit. Brown U., 1965—, chmn. dept. Slavic langs., 1968-72, dir. Center for Research in Semiotics, 1977—; Fulbright lectr. Sorbonne, Paris, 1956-57; exchange prof. U. Warsaw, 1972-73, U. Zagreb, spring 1973; mem. seminar theory lit. Columbia, 1968—. Nat. Endowment Humanities sr. fellow, 1972, Rockefeller grantee, 1977. Mem. Am. Com. Slavists, Modern Lang. Assn., Internat. Assn. for Semiotic Studies, Semiotics Soc. Am. pres. 1977-78), Assn. Am. Tchrs. Slavic and East European Langs., Comparative Lit. Assn., Internat. Assn. Slavists, Am. Assn. for Advancement Slavic Studies. Author: Oral Art and Literature of the Kazakhs of Russian Central Asia, 1958; Chekhov and his Prose, 1965. Editor: Brown U. Slavic Reprints, 1966—, Russian Literature, Czech Literature, Semiotics and Poetics. Address: Box E Brown U Providence RI 02912

WINNERT, FRANKLIN ROY, bldg. materials mfg. co. exec.; b. Buffalo, Sept. 28, 1932; s. Franklin R. and Verna W.; B.Sc., Cornell U., 1954, M.B.A., 1955; m. Carol Elaine Cochran, Sept. 10, 1955; children—Laurie Ellen, Deborah Kim. Corporate merchandising v.p. Owens-Corning, 1964-67, v.p. decorating and home furnishings div., 1967-69; exec. v.p. Peckham Industries, Inc., White Plains, N.Y., 1969-70; with CertainTeed Corp., Valley Forge, Pa., 1970—, exec. v.p., 1978, chief operating officer, 1979—; dir. Safeguard Industries, Inc. Mem. Harvard-M.I.T. Policy advisory bd.; co-chmn. business and industry campaign Heart Fund, Phila., 1979; dir. Pa. Ballet, Phila. Served with USNR, 8 ears. Mem. Asphalt Roofing Mfrs. Assn., Nat. Housing Center Council, U.S. Pro Indoor Tennis Assn., Cornell Alumni Assn. (pres. 1978-80). Presbyterian. Club: Aronimink Golf. Home: 7 Fenimore Ln Saint Davids PA 19087 Office: PO Box 860 Valley Forge PA 19482

WINNET, NOCHEM SAMUEL, lawyer; b. Russia, Aug. 6, 1898; s. Charles and Rose (Metzger) W.; A.B., Harvard, 1920. LL.B., 1923; LL.D., Antioch, 1967, Pa. Coll. Optometry, 1976; m. Alma Goldstein, Mar. 10, 1929; children—Martha, Donald. Admitted to Pa. bar, 1923; practice law, 1923-40; asst. dir. pub. safety, Phila., 1940; judge County Ct., 1940-50; partner firm Fox, Rothschild, O'Brien & Frankel, Phila., 1950—. Hon. pres. Crime Prevention Assn. (pres. 1940-60), campaign chmn. Citizens Com. for Home Rule Charter, 1951; pres. Fedn. Jewish Agys. Greater Phila., 1962-65, trustee, 1950—; mem. exec. com. United Fund (v.p. 1961-65); dir. Greater Phila. Movement, 1951-69, Phila. Housing Assn., Jr. Achievement Del. Valley, Inc., Assn. for Jewish Children; v.p. Am. Joint Distbn. Com.; dir. Council Jewish Fedns.; mem. exec. com. Blue Cross Greater Phila.; mem. Jewish Agy. Assembly, Israel, 1972. Exec. vice-chmn. Eisenhower-Nixon Campaign for S.E. Pa., 1952. Pres. Samuel S. Fels Fund; trustee White-Williams Found.; chmn. bd. trustees Beaver Coll.; asso. trustee U. Pa., 1964-67, chmn. adv. bd. Pa. Sch. Social Work, 1959-62. Served with U.S. Army, 1918. Recipient Famous Fifty Philadelphians award, 1959; Citizens award United Fund, 1975; Golden medallion B'nai B'rith, 1975. Mem. Am., Pa. (spl. achievement award 1978), Phila. (Fidelity Bank award 1977) bar assns., Am. Coll. Trial Lawyers. Am. Law Inst., World Affairs Council Phila. (v.p. 1963-69), Lawyers Club Phila. (pres. 1965-67, dir.). Contbr. articles in field to law jours., newspapers, popular mags. Office: 2000 Market St Philadelphia PA 19103

WINNETT, FREDERICK VICTOR, educator; b. Oil Springs, Ont., Can., May 25, 1903; s. Frederick Walter and Sarah Jane (Blain) W.; B.A., U. Toronto (Ont.), 1923, M.A., 1924, Ph.D., 1928; m. Margaret Johnston Taylor, Sept. 15, 1928; children—William, Marilyn. Lectr., U. Toronto, 1929-35, asst. prof., 1935-44, asso. prof., 1944-52, prof. Nr. East studies, 1952-71, head dept. Nr. East studies, 1952-67, vice prin. Univ. Coll., 1966-69, prof. emeritus, 1971—; dir. Am. Sch. Oriental Research, Jerusalem, 1950-51, 58-59. Fellow Royal Soc. Can.; mem. Am. Oriental Soc., Am. Schs. Oriental Research, Soc. Bibl. Lit., Toronto Oriental Club. Mem. United Ch. of Canada. Author: A Study of the Lihyanite and Thamudic Inscriptions, 1938; (with W.L. Reed) Ancient Records from North Arabia, 1970; (with G.L. Harding) Inscriptions from 50 Safaitic Cairns, 1978. Home: 56 Otter Crescent Toronto ON M5N 2W5 Canada Office: Room 185 Univ Coll U Toronto Toronto ON M5S 1A1 Canada

WINNETT, WILLIAM LEONAL, educator; b. Greenup, Ill., Jan. 31, 1922; s. Benjamin Lee and Isa (Spesard) W.; B.S., Eastern Ill. U., 1947; M.S., U. Ill., 1950, Ed.D., 1957; m. Julia Lucille Parker, Jan. 18, 1941; children—Barbara Anne, William Lee. Lay-out technician Allison div. Gen. Motors Corp., Indpls., 1941-44; tchr. Hume (Ill.) High Sch., 1947-48; instr. U. Ill., 1948-52, supr. student teaching, 1952-53; tchr. Toledo (Oreg.) High Sch., 1953-54; supr. student teaching San Francisco State U., 1954-63; vocational edn. specialist, acting chief party Ednl. Devel. Project, Liberia, W. Africa, 1963-65; prof. bus. San Francisco State U., 1965—, chmn. dept., 1969, dir. grad. studies in bus., 1972-78, prof. edn., 1978—. Cons. govt. schs., Monrovia, Liberia, also schs., businesses, vocational edn. centers, consumer insts.; mem. Calif. Commn. Teacher Preparation and Licensing, 1971. Served with AUS, 1944-45. Mem. Nat. Research Evaluation Program (dir. 1967-74), Calif., Nat. bus. edn. assns., Phi Delta Kappa, Delta Pi Epsilon. Author: Cross-Cultural Values in Office Education, 1968. Editor: Calif. Bus. Edn. Jour., 1966-68; co-editor Nat. Bus. Edn. Assn. Yearbook, 1973. Home: 1080 Crestview Dr Millbrae CA 94030 Office: Sch Edn San Francisco State U San Francisco CA 94132

WINOGRAD, ARTHUR, symphony conductor; b. N.Y.C., Apr. 22, 1920; s. Elias and Mildred (Shapiro) W.; student New Eng. Conservatory Music, 1937-40, Curtis Inst. Music, 1940-41; m. Winifred Schaefer, July 4, 1941; 1 son, Nicholas; m. 2d, Elizabeth Olsen, May 4, 1950; children—Wendy, Peter. Cellist Boston Symphony Orch., 1940, NBC Symphony, 1942-43; founder-mem. Julliard String Quartet, also mem. chamber music faculty, 1946-55; staff condr. MGM Records, 1954-58, Audio Fidelity Records, 1958-60; condr., music dir. Birmingham (Ala.) Symphony Orch., 1960-64, Hartford Symphony, 1964—. Address: 31 Stratford Rd West Hartford CT 06007

WINOGRAD, DONALD SEYMOUR, lawyer; b. N.Y.C., Nov. 28, 1930; s. Abraham and Anne E. (Kaiserman) W.; student Boston U., 1947-49, U. Chgo., 1949-50; LL.B., Columbia U., 1953; m. Marilyn J. Hammett, Jan. 31, 1953; children—Audrey Beth, Richard Cole. Admitted to N.Y. State bar, 1953; asso. firm Cohen & Weiss, N.Y.C., 1955-59, Cooper, Ostrin & Devarco, N.Y.C., 1960; asst. sec., counsel

Foster Grant Co., Leominster, Mass., 1960-69; sec., counsel Franklin Mint Corp., Franklin Center, Pa., 1969—. Served with AUS, 1953-55. Mem. Am. Soc. Corporate Secs. Home: 2107 Coventry Dr Wilmington DE 19810 Office: Franklin Mint Corp Franklin Center PA 19091

WINOGRAD, SHMUEL, mathematician; b. Tel Aviv, Jan. 4, 1936; came to U.S., 1956, naturalized, 1965; s. Pinchas Mordecai and Rachel W.; B.S. in Elec. Engring., M.I.T., M.S. in Elec. Engring.; Ph.D. in Math., N.Y. U., 1968; m. Elaine Ruth Tates, Jan. 5, 1959; children—Danny H., Sharon A. Mem. research staff IBM, Yorktown Heights, N.Y., 1961-70, dir. math. sci. dept., 1970-74, IBM fellow, 1972—; permanent vis. prof. Technion, Israel. Fellow IEEE (W. Wallace McDowell award 1974); mem. Am. Math. Soc., Math. Assn. Am., Assn. Computing Machines, Nat. Acad. Scis., Soc. Indsl. and Applied Math. Author: (with J.D. Cowan) Reliable Computations in the Presence of Noise; research on complexity of computations. Home: 235 Glendale Rd Scarsdale NY 10483 Office: IBM Research PO Box 218 Yorktown Heights NY 10598*

WINOKUR, ROBERT M., lawyer; b. N.Y.C., Oct. 28, 1924; s. Harry S. and Katherine S. W.; B.S., City U. N.Y., 1947; S.J.D., Columbia U., 1949; m. Diane R. Kramer, June 21, 1953; children—Hugh R., Andrew S., Douglas B. Admitted to Calif. bar, N.Y. bar, U.S. Supreme Ct. bar; sr. partner firm Winokur, Schoenberg, Maier & Zang, and predecessors, San Francisco, 1954—; dir. Redwood Bank; guest lectr. U. Calif., Berkeley, N.Y. U. Tax Inst., U. So. Calif. Tax Inst., Practising Law Inst.; mem. adv. group to U.S. Commr. Internal Revenue, 1967-68. Served to lt. U.S. Army, 1943-46. Decorated Bronze Star. Mem. Am., Calif., San Francisco bar assns., Am. Law Inst. Democrat. Clubs: Bankers, San Francisco Tax, Silverado Country. Contbr. articles to legal jours. Home: 3921 Clay St San Francisco CA 94118 Office: 1 California St San Francisco CA 94111

WINOLD, CHARLES ALLEN, musician, educator; b. Cleve., May 7, 1929; s. Earl Albert and Gladys Marie (Riddell) W.; B.Mus., Coll. Music Cin., 1950, Mus.M., 1951; Ph.D., Ind. U., 1963; m. Helga Ulsamer, Dec. 17, 1963; children—Claire Elisabeth, Erika Marie, Bettina Julia, Hans Peter. Asso. concertmaster N.C. Symphony, 1950-51, later condr.; with Cin. Symphony, 1951; mem. faculty Wilmington (Ohio) Coll., 1952-54; music therapist Columbus (Ohio) State Hosp., 1953-55; prof. music theory, Ind. U., Bloomington, 1956—; guest prof. Vienna Acad. Music, 1972-73; condr. Alta. (Can.) Province Orch., summers 1968, 69, 70, 76. Named Outstanding Tchr., Ind. U. Sr. Class, 1975. Mem. Coll. Music. Soc., Pi Kappa Lambda. Quaker. Author: Elements of Musical Understanding, 1966; Music Reading: An Ensemble Approach, 1971; Introduction to Music Theory, 1971; Aspects of Contemporary Music, 1975; Involvement with Music, 1975; How to Read Music, 1975; The Open Court Music Program, 1975; (with Ray Robinson) The Choral Experience, 1975; Excerpts for Study, 1977; Basic Principles of Music Theory, 1979. Home: 2233 Moore's Pike Bloomington IN 47401 Office: School of Music Indiana U Bloomington IN 47401

WINPISINGER, WILLIAM P., labor union ofcl.; b. Cleve., Dec. 10, 1924; ed. pub. schs., Cleve.; married; 5 children. Automotive mechanic, 1942-51; with Internat. Assn. Machinists and Aerospace Workers, 1947—, grand lodge rep., 1951-58, air transp. dept., 1958-64, automotive coordinator, 1965-67, gen. v.p., 1967, now pres., also co-chmn. and union trustee pension fund; mem. exec. council AFL-CIO; mem. Fed. Com. on Apprenticeship. Co-chmn. Machinists Non-Partisan Polit. League; council N.Y. State Sch. Indsl. and Labor Relations, Cornell U. Served in USN, 1942-45. Mem. Nat. Planning Assn. (planning com.). Office: Machinists Bldg 1300 Connecticut Ave Washington DC 20036*

WINSHIP, CHARLES THIOT, indsl. distbg. co. exec.; b. Atlanta, Nov. 13, 1903; s. George and Elizabeth (Thiot) W.; student Emory U., 1926, LL.D., 1970; m. Juliet Leach Crenshaw, May 12, 1926 (dec. Nov. 1976). Read law in offices King, Caldwell and Partridge, Atlanta, 1931-32; admitted to Ga. bar, 1932; practice in Atlanta, 1932-57; with Fulton Supply Co., Atlanta, 1932—, pres., 1956-62, chmn. bd., 1962-70, chmn. exec. com., 1970—, also dir.; dir. Atlantic Realty Co. Bd. trustees Emory U., 1962—, past sec. bd.; bd. trustees Young Harris Coll., 1926—, chmn. bd., 1938-48; chmn. bd. Lewis H. Beck Found., 1957-77; chmn. finance com. Methodist Found. Ret. Ministers, Atlanta, 1946. Mem. Am., Ga., Atlanta bar assns., Chi Phi (nat. treas. 1935-37, grand chancellor 1946-51). Methodist (past chmn. trustees). Kiwanian. Clubs: Commerce, Lawyers, Piedmont Driving (Atlanta). Home: 40 Montclair Dr NE Atlanta GA 30309 Office: 1013 Hurt Bldg Atlanta GA 30303

WINSHIP, FREDERICK MOERY, journalist; b. Franklin, Ohio, Sept. 24, 1924; s. Wilbur William and Edna B. (Moery) W.; A.B., DePauw U., 1945; M.S., Columbia, 1946; m. Joanne Tree Thompson, Aug. 29, 1967. Corr., U.P.I., 1946—, assigned UN, 1947-49, editorial staff, N.Y.C., 1950-60, cultural affairs editor, 1960-72, sr. editor, 1972-75, asst. mng. editor, 1975—. Pres., Letters Abroad, Inc., 1962—; chmn. Easter Seal Soc., N.Y.C., 1964-73, Oratorio Soc. N.Y., 1965-75, N.Y. Conf. Patriotic Socs., 1967-72. Bd. dirs. Museum of City of N.Y., 1974—, Odell House-Rochambeau Hdgrs., 1965-75, N.Y. State Easter Seal Soc., 1969-72, Recipient Am. Legion Journalism award, 1955; Whitelaw Reid Journalism fellow, India, 1958; Creative Club Journalism award, 1962. Mem. S.A.R. (sec. N.Y. chpt. 1963-68), St. Nicholas, Founders and Patriots, Mayflower Descs., Soc. Colonial Wars (bd. dirs.), S.R., Soc. Cincinnati, Sigma Delta Chi. Republican. Episcopalian. Contbr. articles mags. Home: 417 Park Ave New York City NY 10022 Office: 220 E 42d St New York City NY 10017

WINSHIP, THOMAS, newspaperman; b. Cambridge, Mass., July 1, 1920; s. Laurence L. and Ruth (Spindler) W.; A.B., Harvard, 1942; m. Elizabeth S. Coolidge, Sept. 15, 1942; children—Margaret S., Laurence P., Joanna S., Benjamin W. Served with USCGR, ETO, 1942-45; reporter 1945-56; Washington corr. Boston Globe 1956, editor Globe, 1965—. Clubs: Tavern, Drifter's, Union (Boston); Federal City (Washington). Home: Old Concord Rd South Lincoln MA 01773 Office: Boston Globe 135 Morrissey Blvd Boston MA 02107*

WINSLOW, ROBERT ALBERT, petroleum industry exec.; b. Carthage, Ind., Feb. 5, 1922; s. William Howard and Ione (Morris) W.; B.S. in Chem. Engring., Purdue U., 1943; m. Totsye Harper, June 14, 1944; children—A. Robert, M. Craig, Judith Winslow Huchton. Various engring. and managerial positions Exxon Co., USA, 1946-66; sr. v.p. Esso Chemicals Europe, 1966-68, pres., 1968-70; pres. Exxon Chemicals USA, 1970-74; exec. v.p. Exxon Chemicals, Inc. and v.p. Exxon Corp., 1974-79; pres. Exxon Enterprises, Inc., N.Y.C., 1979—. Served with USN, 1943-46. Mem. Soc. Chem. Industry, Mfg. Chemists Assn. Presbyterian. Clubs: Stanwich (Greenwich, Conn.); Riverhill (Kerrville, TeX.); Italian (Stamford, Conn.). Home 305 Laurel Rd Stamford CT 06903 Office: 1251 Ave of the Americas New York NY 10020

WINSLOW, SAMUEL RINN, investment banker; b. Punxsutawney, Pa., Sept. 14, 1909; s. Eugene Hale and Margaret Salome (Rinn) W.; student Hill Sch., Chestnut Hill Acad., Yale, 1927-29; m. Elizabeth Nickerson, 1927 (div. 1941); 1 dau., Elizabeth M.; m. 2d, Jean Martin Munroe, May 12, 1949. Partner Dyer Hudson & Co., 1928-37, Winslow, Douglas & McEvoy, 1937-56; partner Winslow, Cohu & Stetson, 1956-59; pres. Winslow, Cohu & Stetson, Inc., 1959—; exec. v.p. Weis, Voisin & Co., Inc., N.Y.C., 1969-73, Smith Barney, Harris Upham & Co., 1973-79; dir. 49 E. 79th St. Corp., Bd. dirs. Hewitt Sch. Served to lt. comdr. USNR, 1942-45. Mem. Soc. Colonial Wars. Clubs: Brook, Links (N.Y.C.); Southampton (v.p., bd. govs.), National Golf Links (gov. Southampton, L.I.). Home: 39 E 79th St New York City NY 10021 Office: Wertheim & Co 200 Park Ave New York City NY 10017

WINSOR, KATHLEEN, writer; b. Olivia, Minn.; d. Harold Lee and Myrtle Belle (Crowder) Winsor; A.B., U. Calif., 1938; m. Robert J. Herwig (div.); m. 2d, Paul A. Porter, June 26, 1956 (dec. Nov. 1975). Author: (hist. novel) Forever Amber, 1944; Star Money, 1950; The Lovers, 1952; America, with Love, 1957; (hist. novel) Wanderers Eastward, Wanderers West, 1965; Calais, 1979. Address: care Arthur Abelman 1271 Ave of Americas New York NY 10020

WINSOR, ROY WILLIAM, author; b. Chgo., Apr. 13, 1912; s. Edward Arthur and Florence Louise (Williams) W.; A.B. cum laude, Harvard U., 1936; m. Martha March Ricker, Oct. 22, 1938; children—Ann March, Mary Wilcox, Ricker Edward, Catherine Louise. Apprentice-in-tng. CBS, N.Y.C., 1936-37; asst. program-prodn. mgr. WCCO, Mpls., 1937-38; dir. Vic and Sade, NBC, Chgo., 1938-39; radio dir. Leo Burnett Co., Chgo., 1939-40; supr. P & G Radio, Blackett-Sample Hummert, Inc., Chgo., 1940-46, radio dir., 1943; free lance dir.-writer, Chgo., 1946-50; v.p. TV-radio Biow Co., N.Y.C., 1950-55; creator, producer first daytime TV serial Search For Tomorrow, 1951; pres. Roy Winsor Prodns., Inc., N.Y.C., 1955-69; freelance TV serial cons. CBS-TV and P & G Prodns., Inc., 1969-73; head writer serial Somerset, NBC, 1974; tchr. TV serial writing New Sch., 1974-75; writer CBS Radio Mystery Theatre, 1974—; freelance instr. Famous Writers Sch., Westport, Conn., 1974—. Mem. Mystery Writers Am. (Edgar award for best paperbound mystery of year 1975). Author: The Corpse That Walked, 1974; Three Motives for Murder, 1976; Always Lock Your Bedroom Door, 1976. Address: 1007 Prospect Ave Pelham Manor NY 10803

WINSTANLEY, PETER FRANCIS, food and beverage co. exec.; b. Boston, June 13, 1944; s. Peter Francis and Gertrude Louise (Tierney) W.; B.A. Colby Coll., 1966; M.B.A., Boston U., 1968; m. Melissa Conkling, Dec. 28, 1974. Trainee 1st Nat. Bank Boston, 1968; fin. analyst Trans World Airlines, N.Y.C., 1969-70; Eng. mgr. Treasury Internat., London, 1971, Paris mgr., 1972-73; mgr. internat. fin. Standard Brands Inc., N.Y.C., 1973-75; treas. Standard Brands Ltd., Toronto, 1975—. Mem. Am. Mgmt. Assn., Assn. Pension Fund Mgmt. Canada, Conf. Bd. Clubs: Royal St. Lawrence Yacht, Montreal Amateur Athletic, Yale; Cambridge. Home: 79 Maclean Ave Toronto ON M4E 2Z8 Canada Office: Standard Brands Ltd 1 Dundas St W Toronto ON M5G 2A9 Canada

WINSTEAD, MELDRUM BARNETT, educator; b. Lincolnton, N.C., Oct. 19, 1926; s. Meldrum Barnett and Annie Elizabeth (Heim) W.; B.S., Davidson Coll., 1946; M.A., U. N.C., 1949, Ph.D., 1952; m. Merle Luise Holden, Mar. 21, 1959; children—Deborah Anne, Charles Holden, Ellen Matilda. Instr., Davidson Coll., 1946-47, U. N.C., 1947-51; asst. prof. chemistry Bucknell U., 1952-56, asso. prof., 1956-69, prof., 1969—, faculty research fellow, 1970-71, 78-79. Research asso. Lawrence Berkeley Lab., U. Calif. at Berkeley, 1968-69; vis. asso. Calif. Inst. Tech., 1967-68; cons., tchr. Sadtler Research Labs., Phila., 1959-70; cons. Glyco Chem. Corp., 1958; vis. research scientist Medi-Physics, Inc., 1972-78. Research grantee PRF, 1961-62, AAAS, 1959-60, Research Corp., 1954-56; NSF grantee, 1962-64, 72-73; USPHS fellow, 1967-68; DuPont research fellow, 1951-52; NIH grantee, 1965, 74-77. Mem. Am. Chem. Soc., Susquehanna Valley Chorale, Soc. for Preservation Barbershop Quartet Singing in Am., Phi Beta Kappa, Sigma Xi, Phi Sigma, Phi Mu Alpha, Gamma Sigma Epsilon, Delta Phi Alpha, Pi Kappa Phi, Omicron Delta Kappa, Alpha Chi Sigma. Democrat. Methodist. Author: Organic Chemistry Structural Problems, 1968; contbr. chpt. to book, articles to profl. jours. Home: RD 1 Box 395 Lewisburg PA 17837

WINSTEAD, NASH NICKS, phytopathologist, univ. adminstr.; b. Durham, N.C., June 12, 1925; s. Nash L. and Lizzy (Featherston) W.; B.S., N.C. State U., 1948, M.S., 1951; Ph.D., U. Wis., 1953; m. Geraldine Larkin Kelly, Sept. 17, 1949; 1 dau., Karen Jewell. Asst. prof. plant pathology, Raleigh, 1953-58; asso. prof. N.C. State U., Raleigh, 1958-61, prof., 1961—, dir. inst. biol. scis., 1965-67, asst. dir. agrl. exptl. sta., 1965-67, asst. provost, 1967-73, asso. provost, 1973-74, provost, 1974—. Phillip Found. intern acad. adminstrn. Ind. U., 1965-66. Mem. N.C. Council on Higher Edn. for Adults, 1967-75; inst. rep. So. Assn. for Colls. and Schs., 1967-74; chmn. interaction between protoplasm and toxicants com. So. Regional Edn. Bd., 1964-65. Bd. dirs. N.C. State U. YMCA, 1963-65. Served with USAAF, 1943-46. Recipient Sigma Xi research award, 1960. Mem. Am. Phytopath. Soc. (chmn. disease, pathogen physiology com.), Am. Inst. Biol. Scis., N.C. Acad. Sci., N.C. Assn. Colls. and Univs. (exec. com. 1974—, pres. 1979), Acad. Deans for So. States, AAAS, Sigma Xi, Phi Kappa Phi, Omicron Delta Kappa. Club: Torch Internat. (sec.). Contbr. articles profl. jours. Home: 1109 Glendale Dr Raleigh NC 27612

WINSTEAD, RAYMOND LANDON, banker; b. nr. Fayetteville, Ark., May 15, 1909; s. George Marion and Alice (West) W.; student U. Ark., 1927-29, Grad. Sch. Banking, Rutgers U., 1946; m. Elizabeth O'Bannon, Jan. 25, 1930; children—Raymond Landon, Jane Elizabeth (Mrs. Timothy Lee Wilson). Asst. cashier San Angelo Nat. Bank (Tex.) until 1946; asst. v.p. 1st Nat. Bank, Houston, 1946-47; v.p., dir. 1st Nat. Bank, Wichita Falls, Tex., 1947-61; sr. v.p. Tex. Nat. Bank Commerce, Houston, 1961-66, adv. dir., 1965—, gen. v.p., 1966—; vice chmn. bd. Tex. Commerce Bank. Nat. Assn., 1970-74. Mem. planning, curriculum com. Southwestern Grad. Sch. Banking, So. Meth. U., 1964-67. Trustee S. Tex. Jr. Coll., Houston, 1964-74, mem. finance com., 1970-74. Mem. Sigma Phi Epsilon. Episcopalian. Clubs: Houston Country, Houston. Home: 5803 Bayou Glen Rd Houston TX 77057 Office: 712 Main St Houston TX 77002

WINSTEN, ARCHER, newspaper and movie critic; b. Seattle, Sept. 18, 1904; s. Harry Jerome and Nell (Archer) W.; student Augusta Mil. Acad., 1916-18, Univ. Sch., Cleve., 1918-22; A.B., Princeton, 1926; m. Sheila Raleigh, Feb. 6, 1931 (div.); children—Kezia, Stephen, Martha. Reporter, Phila. Evening Pub. Ledger, 1928-30, New Yorker mag., 1930; columnist (In the Wake of the News), New York Post, 1933-35, motion picture critic, 1936—, also ski editor, 1947—; motion picture documentary script writer Princeton Film Center, 1944-48, for R.K.O. Pathe, 1946; lectr., asso. in journalism Columbia U., 1946, 47. Recipient 1st prize, Harper's 1st Intercollegiate Short Story prize contest, 1926. Mem. Am. Newspaper guild. Episcopalian. Home: 425 W Broadway New York City NY 10012 Office: New York Post 210 South St New York City NY 10002. *Having learned in the course of almost seven decades of varied living that I am neither a physical marvel nor a mental giant, I have adjusted to my limitations but have resisted complete rejection of either competition in sports, which I enjoy, or independent thinking, which keeps my mind out of total desuetude. I try to do unto others as I would be done by, at the same time resisting the temptation to control others (for their good) or be controlled (for my good). This has enabled me to regard life, in success or failure, as rather fascinating. The past is remembered, the future a suspense story proceeding to a known destination. I am moderately content.*

WINSTON, CAREY, mortgage banker; b. Seattle, May 5, 1901; s. James Richmond and Emma Jane (Williams) W.; student U. Wash., 1920-24; m. Evelyn Cram, Sept. 3, 1927; children—Jane (Mrs. Richard D. Hall), James Michael. Vice pres. Continental Mortgage Co., Seattle, 1928-33; asst. gen. mgr. HOLC, Washington, 1934-38; dep. Fed. Home Loan Bank Bd., Washington, 1938-40; chmn. Carey Winston Co., Washington, 1941—; chmn. trustees Capital Mortgage Investments (REIT); dir. Metropolis Bldg. Assn., Dist. Realty Title Ins. Co., Nat. Savs. & Trust Co. Mem. P.E. Found., also chmn. finance com. Washington Cathedral. Pres. Anson Mills Found. Bd. dirs. Travelers Aid Soc., United Community Services. Mem. Inst. Real Estate Mgmt. (pres. 1950), Mortgage Bankers Assn. Am. (pres. 1963-64), Washington Bd. Realtors (pres. 1955), Sigma Chi. Episcopalian (jr. warden). Clubs: Kiwanis (pres. 1960), Nat. Press, Metropolitan (Washington); Capital Hill. Home: 4100 Cathedral Ave NW Washington DC 20016 Office: 4350 East-West Hwy Bethesda MD 20014

WINSTON, CLARA BRUSSEL, writer, translator; b. N.Y.C., Dec. 6, 1921; m. Richard Winston, Sept. 12, 1941; children—Krishna, Justina. Translator numerous books (with Richard Winston), including: A Part of Myself (Carl Zuckmayer), 1967, Hope and History (Joseph Pieper), 1969, The Glass Bead Game (Herman Hesse), 1969, The Letters of Thomas Mann, 1971, The Inward Turn of Narrative (Erich Kahler), 1973, memoirs (Joseph Cardinal Mindszerty), 1974, Letters to Family, Friends and Editors (Franz Kafka), 1977, Winterspell (Alfred Andersch), 1978, The Magic Stone (Leonie Kooiker), 1978, numerous others; also translator articles, lit.; novels: The Closest Kin There Is, 1952, The Hours Together, 1961, Painting for the Show, 1969; history books: (with Richard Winston) Notre-Dame de Paris, 1971, Daily Life in the Middle Ages, 1975 (Nat. Book award 1978). Mem. Am. Translators' Assn., PEN. Home: Duino Farm via Jacksonville Stage Brattleboro VT 05301

WINSTON, GORDON CHESTER, economist, educator; b. San Francisco, Feb. 9, 1929; s. Chester Parker and Lois Genevieve (Warner) W.; A.B., Whitman Coll., Walla Walla, Wash., 1950; postgrad. U. Wash., 1950-51; M.A., Stanford U., 1961, Ph.D., 1964; m. Mary Primrose Wales, June 13, 1953 (div. 1975); children—Victoria, Gordon Parker, Pamela. Salesman, Internat. Paper Co., 1953-56, W.Va. Pulp and Paper Co., 1956-60; instr. Stanford U., 1962-63; asst. prof. econs. William Coll., Williamstown, Mass., 1963-67; sr. research advisor Yale U. Pakistan Project, Karachi, Pakistan, 1966-67, 70-71; fellow Nuffield Coll. and Queen Elizabeth House Oxford U., 1971; prof. econs. Williams Coll., 1967-73, Orin Sage prof. polit. economy, 1974—; mem. Sch. Social Sci. Inst. Advanced Study, Princeton, N.J., 1978-79; vis. scholar Inst. for Internat. Econ. Studies, Stockholm U., 1979-80; cons. in field. Served with C.E., U.S. Army, 1951-53. Ford Found. grantee, 1971-73, Edna McConnell Clark Found. grantee, 1977-78; grantee Inst. Internat. Economic Studies, Stockholm, 1979-80. Mem. Am. Econ. Assn., Royal Econ. Soc., Western Econ. Assn. Contbr. articles in field to profl. jours. Home: 4 Greylock Village Condominiums Williamstown MA 01267 Office: Dept Econs Williams Coll Williamstown MA 01267

WINSTON, MORTON MANUEL, oil co. exec.; b. N.Y.C., Dec. 9, 1930; s. Myron Hugh and Minna (Schneller) W.; A.B., U. Vt., 1951; M.A., U. Conn., 1953; LL.B. magna cum laude, Harvard U., 1958; m. Katherine Tupper Winn, Feb. 3, 1979; children by previous marriages—Gregory Winston, Livia Winston; stepchildren—Wesley Hudson, Laura Hudson. Admitted to D.C. bar, 1961; law clk. to Justice Frankfurter, Supreme Ct. U.S., 1959-60; asso. firm Cleary, Gottlieb, Steen & Hamilton, N.Y.C., Washington, 1960-67; v.p. Tosco Corp., N.Y.C., 1964-67, exec. v.p., 1967-71, pres., 1971—, chief exec. officer, 1976—; dir. Baker Internat. Corp., 1976—. Chmn. bd. trustees Craft and Folk Art Mus., Los Angeles, 1976—; trustee City of Hope, Los Angeles, 1977—; bd. govs. Performing Arts Council, Los Angeles. Served to lt. (j.g.) USCGR, 1953-55. Office: 10100 Santa Monica Blvd Los Angeles CA 90067

WINSTON, RICHARD, writer, translator; b. N.Y.C., July 21, 1917; s. Robert and Etta Winston; B.A., Bklyn. Coll., 1939; m. Clara Brussel Sept. 12, 1941; children—Krishna, Justina. Books include: Charlemagne: From the Hammer to the Cross, 1954; Thomas Becket, 1967; (with Clara Winston) Notre-Dame de Paris 1971, Daily Life in the Middle Ages, 1975; translator: (with Clara Winston) The Demons (Heimito von Doderer), 1961, Memories, Dreams, Reflections (C.G. Jung), 1963, A Part of Myself (Carl Zuckmayer), 1967, The Glass Bead Game (Hermann Hesse), 1969, Inside the Third Reich: Memoirs (Albert Speer), 1970, The Letters of Thomas Mann, 1971, The Inward Turn of Narrative (Erich Kahler), 1973, Letters to Family, Friends and Editors (Franz Kafka), 1977, Winterspelt (Alfred Andersch), 1978, numerous others; reviewer N.Y. Herald Tribune Book Week, 1955-63; adviser in field. Trustee public funds Town of Halifax (Vt.), 1975—. Guggenheim fellow, 1971-72; recipient Alexander Gode medal Am. Translators Assn., 1966; PEN Transl. prize, 1971; Nat. Book award, 1978. Mem. PEN, Am. Translators Assn.

WINSTON, ROLAND, physicist, educator; b. Moscow, USSR, Feb. 12, 1936 (parents Am. citizens); s. Joseph and Claudia (Goretskaya) W.; A.B., Shimer Coll., 1953; B.S., U. Chgo., 1956, M.S., 1957, Ph.D., 1963; m. Patricia Louise LeGette, June 10, 1957; children—Joseph, John, Gregory. Asst. prof. physics U. Pa., 1963-64; mem. faculty U. Chgo., 1964—, prof. physics, 1975—; physicist Argonne (Ill.) Nat. Lab., since 1974. Sloan fellow, 1968-70; Guggenheim fellow, 1977-78. Fellow Am. Phys. Soc.; mem. Am. Optical Soc. Patentee ideal light collector for solar concentrators. Home: 5217 C South University Ave Chicago IL 60615 Office: 5630 S Ellis Ave Chicago IL 60637

WINTER, ARCH REESE, architect, city planner; b. Mobile, Ala., Sept. 13, 1913; s. Augustus Reese and Winona (Battson) W.; B.Arch., Auburn U., 1935; M.Arch., Catholic U. Am., 1937; postgrad. Cranbrook Acad. Art, 1939-41. Cons. Nat. Resources Planning Bd., 1941-43; practice architecture, city planning firm as Arch R. Winter, Mobile, 1946—. Cons. Mobile Planning Commn., Mobile Housing Bd., 1946—. Mem. Medalist Selection Com. Thomas Jefferson Meml. Found. U. Va., 1975—. Served to lt. USNR, 1943-46. Fellow AIA (chmn. environment commn. 1970-71, del. Commn. d'Urbanisme Athens, Greece 1962, recipient Gulf States Honor award 1957, citation for excellence in community architecture for Shreveport downtown plan 1965); mem. Am. Inst. Planners. City plans include Natchez and Gulfport, Miss., Shreveport and Monroe, La., Old Louisville restoration area; archtl. projects have included Isle Dauphine Club, Dauphin Island, Ala. Home: 9 Bienville Ave Mobile AL 36606 Office: Van Antwerp Bldg Mobile AL 36602

WINTER, CHARLES ERNEST, educator; b. Colorado Springs, Colo., Sept. 9, 1914; s. Ernest E. and Christina (Senning) W.; B.A., Colo. Coll., 1936, M.A., 1938; M.S., U. Md., 1945, Ph.D., 1947; m.

Betty L. Schaefer, June 15, 1937; children—Robin Louise, Christie Ann. Bacteriologist, U.S. Fish and Wildlife Service, 1945-47; prof. biology Columbia Union Coll., Takoma Park, Md., 1943-45, China Tng. Inst., Kiang Su, China, 1947-50; mem. faculty Loma Linda (Calif.) U. Sch. Medicine, 1950—, prof. microbiology, 1960—. Vol. Hong Kong Def. Command, 1941. Decorated Def. medal (Hong Kong). Mem. AAAS, Am. Soc. Microbiology, Am. Pub. Health Assn., AMA, Am. Assn. Dental Schs., Am. Assn. Med. Colls., Sigma Xi. Republican. Seventh-day Adventist. Club: Rotary. Home: 24476 University Ave Loma Linda CA 92354

WINTER, CHESTER CALDWELL, educator, physician; b. Cazenovia, N.Y., June 2, 1922; s. Chester Caldwell and Cora Evelyn (Martin) W.; B.A., U. Iowa, 1943, M.D., 1946; m. Cary Margaret Jones, June 18, 1945; children—Paul, Ann, Jane. Intern, Meth. Hosp., Indpls., 1946-47; med. resident St. Luke's Hosp., Cedar Rapids, Iowa, 1947; resident gen. surgery VA Hosp., Los Angeles, 1952-53; resident urology VA Hosp.-U. Calif. at Los Angeles Med. Center, 1953-57; physician, Mentone, Calif., 1950-51; clin. asst. surgery U. Calif. at Los Angeles, 1954-57, instr. surgery and urology, 1957-58, asst. prof. surgery and urology, 1958-59, asst. prof. Step II, 1959-60; prof. surgery and urology Ohio State U., 1960—; dir. urology Univ., Childrens' hosps., Columbus, 1960-78; cons. urology VA, Air Force hosps., Dayton. Served to capt. M.C., U.S. Army, 1943-46, 48-49. Diplomate Am. Bd. Urology. Fellow A.C.S., Am. Acad. Pediatricians; mem. Am. Assn. Genitourinary Surgeons, Am. Urol. Assn., Soc. Univ. Surgeons, Soc. Pediatric Urology, Soc. Univ. Urologists, Internat. Soc. Urology, AMA, Urol. Investigators Forum, Ohio State Med. Assn., Columbus Surg. Soc., Central Ohio Urology Soc., Columbus Acad. Medicine, Ohio State U. Med. Soc., Am., Central Ohio heart assns., Sigma Xi. Club: York Country (Worthington, Ohio). Author: Radioisotope Renography, 1963; Correctable Renal Hypertension, 1964; Nursing Care of Patients with Urologic Diseases, 4th edit., 1977; Practical Urology, 1969; Vesicoureteral Reflux, 1969. Editorial cons. Exerpta Medica: Nuclear Medicine; editorial bd. Urol. Survey. Contbr. articles to med. jours. Home: 6425 Evening St Worthington OH 43085 Office: 456 Clinic Dr Columbus OH 43210

WINTER, DAVID JOHN, mathematician; b. Painesville, Ohio, May 2, 1939; s. John Willis and Verna Mae (Young) W.; B.A., Antioch Coll., 1961; postgrad. Tuebingen (Germany) U., 1959-60, (NSF grantee) U. Bonn (Germany), 1967-68; M.A., Yale U., 1963, Ph.D., 1965; m. Linda Patriarca, July 23, 1977; 1 dau., Alison. Asst. prof. math. U. Mich., 1968-69, asso. prof., 1969-74, prof., 1974—; vis. prof. Calif. Inst. Tech., 1972-73. Mem. Am. Math. Soc. Author: Abstract Lie Algebras, 1972; Structure of Fields, 1974.

WINTER, DAVID LEON, physician, ofcl. NASA; b. N.Y.C., Nov. 10, 1933; s. Clement and Margaret (Ternamian) W.; A.B., Columbia U., 1955; M.D., Washington U., St. Louis, 1959; children—David, Lisanne, Alaric, Lorianne, Jonathan. Intern, Barnes Hosp., St. Louis, 1955-60; fellow physiology Baylor Sch. Medicine, Houston, 1960-62; research physician USPHS, NIH, Bethesda, Md., 1962-64, Walter Reed Army Inst. Research, Washington, 1964-67, chief dept. neurophysiology, 1967-71; dep. dir. life scis. Ames Research Center NASA, Moffett Field, Calif., 1971-74, dir. for life scis. Hdqrs. NASA, Washington, 1974—. Served with USPHS, 1962-64. Mem. Am. Physiol. Soc., AAAS, Soc. Neurosci., Aerospace Med. Assn. Internat. Astronaut. Acad. Address: NASA Washington DC 20546

WINTER, DONALD FERGUSON, applied mathematician, oceanographer; b. Buffalo, Oct. 6, 1931; s. Charles Allen and Janet Elizabeth (Ferguson) W.; B.A. summa cum laude, Amherst Coll., 1954; M.A. (Amherst Coll. Rufus B. Kellogg fellow), Harvard U., 1959, Ph.D. (Kellogg fellow), 1962; children—Timothy, Geoffrey, Rebecca. Engring. specialist Sylvania Electronics Systems, Waltham, Mass., 1956-58, 62-63; research scientist Boeing Sci. Research Labs., Boeing Co., Seattle, 1963-70; sr. research asso. U. Wash., 1970-72, asso. prof., 1972-75, prof. oceanography and applied math., 1975—; vis. lectr. U. Manchester (Eng.), 1966-67; cons. to engring. firms. Bd. dirs. Population Dynamics, Seattle, 1972-74, Classical Music Supporters, Seattle, 1978—; co-founder, pres. Friends of Phila. String Quartet, 1977—. Served to lt. USAF, 1954-56. Mem. AAAS, Am. Geophys. Union, Soc. Harvard Engrs. and Scientists, Soc. Indsl. and Applied Math., Phi Beta Kappa, Sigma Xi. Contbr. numerous articles on various fields to profl. publs., including electromagnetic wave propagation, lunar and planetary physics, heat and mass transfer, geophys. fluid dynamics. Office: Dept Oceanography U Wash Seattle WA 98195

WINTER, EDGAR HOLLAND, entertainer; b. Beaumont, Tex., Dec. 28, 1946; s. John Dawson and Edwina (Holland) W.; grad. high sch.; m. Roma Caroline Zurga, June 28, 1975. Proficient numerous instruments; concert tours, N. Am., Europe, 1969—; TV appearances include In Concert, Rock Concert, Midnight Special, Mike Douglas Show; rec. artist CBS Records, Inc., 1969—; albums include: Entrance, Edgar Winter's White Trash, Roadwork, They Only Come Out At Night, Shock Treatment, Jasmine Nightdreams, Edgar Winter Group with Rick Derringer. Recipient Platinum album awards for "They Only Came Out at Night," Gold album awardee "Roadwork and Shock Treatment," Gold record "Frankenstein," Playboy Jazz and Pop Poll award, 1972, 73, 74, 75, Grammy nomination as composer, 1974, as performer, 1974. Mem. Houston Profl. Musicians Assn., Broadcast Music, Inc. Address: Blue Sky Records 745 Fifth Ave New York NY 10022*

WINTER, ELMER LOUIS, corp. ofcl.; b. Milw., Mar. 6, 1912; s. Sigmund and May (Kraus) W.; B.A., U. Wis., 1933, LL.B., 1935, LL.D., 1970; m. Nannette Rosenberg, Sept. 11, 1936; children—Susan, Lynn, Martha. Tax editor Commerce Clearing House, 1935; admitted to Wis. bar, 1935, Ill., bar 1942; partner Scheinfeld & Winter, Milw., 1936-42, Chgo. and Milw., 1944-48; co-founder Manpower, Inc., 1948, pres. Manpower, Inc. and affiliated firms, 1948-76, chmn. adv. bd., 1976—. Chief price atty. for Wis., OPA, 1942-44. Mem. White House Task Force on Employment and Economy of Youth; mem. exec. com. Nat. Alliance to Save Energy, 1977-80; chmn. Milw. Alliance to Save Energy, 1978; Hon. nat. pres. Am. Jewish Com. Bd. govs. U. Haifa (Israel); chmn. Com. for Econ. Growth of Israel. Recipient various awards, including Horatic Alger award, 1967, Boston Coll. Hall of Fame in Franchising award. Mem. Internat. Franchise Assn. (past pres.). Author: Women at Work, 1967; Your Future in Jobs Abroad, 1968; A Complete Guide to Making a Public Stock Offering, 1973; The Successful Manager/Secretary Team, 1974. Home: 8014 N Lake Dr Milwaukee WI 53217 Office: 5301 Ironwood Rd Milwaukee WI 53217

WINTER, FREDERICK ELLIOT, educator; b. Barbados, W.I., June 19, 1922; s. Edward Elliot and Constance Mabel (Gill) W.; B.A., McGill U., 1945; Ph.D., U. Toronto, 1957; m. Joan Elizabeth Hay, June 9, 1951; children—Elizabeth, Penelope, Mary, Michael. Instr. U. Toronto, 1947-49, 50-51, lectr., 1951-57, asst. prof., 1957-61, asso. prof., 1961-68, prof., 1968, chmn. dept. fine art, 1971-77; chmn. U. Toronto Assn. Teaching Staff, 1968-69. Mem. mng. com. Am. Sch. Classical Studies, Athens, Greece. Recipient Gold medal in classics McGill U., 1945; Flavelle fellow U. Toronto, 1947-48; White fellow Am. Sch., Athens, 1949-50, spl. research fellow, 1978-79; Am. Philos. Soc. grantee, 1957. Mem. Classical Assn. Can., Archeol. Inst. Am. Author: (with G.S. Vickers, P.H. Brieger) Art and Man, Vol. I, 1963; Greek Fortifications, 1971. Home: 164 Highgate Ave Willowdale ON M2N 5G8 Canada Office: Dept Fine Art U Toronto Toronto ON Canada

WINTER, FREDERICK HERBERT, JR., advt. agy. exec.; b. Chgo., Sept. 7, 1919; s. Frederick H. and Margaret H. (Proctor) W.; B.A., Northwestern U., 1948; m. Shirley M. Beucus, July 4, 1927; children—Kenneth, Diane. Mgr. prodn. and quality control Wilson & Co., Chgo., 1940-48; financial v.p., mng. partner Tatham-Laird & Kudner, Chgo., 1949—. Dir. Sparkle Plenty, Inc. Served with USNR, 1943-46. C.P.A., Ill. Home: 1238 Strieff Ln Flossmoor IL 60422 Office: 625 N Michigan Ave Chicago IL 60611

WINTER, GEORGE, engr., educator; b. Vienna, Austria, Apr. 1, 1907; s. Morris and Hedwig (Fleischer) W.; Dipl. Ing., Technische Hochschule, Munich, 1930; Ph.D., Cornell U., 1940; student Technische Hochscule, Vienna, 1926-27, at Stuttgart, 1927-28; Dr. Ing. (hon.) Technische U. Munich, 1969; m. Anne Singer, July 4, 1931; 1 son, Peter Michael. Came to U.S., 1938, naturalized, 1943. Structural designer, Vienna, 1930-32; fgn. cons. Sverdlovsc, USSR, 1932-38; charge structural design large indsl. plants, and part-time lectr. Mining Inst. and Indsl. Inst., 1934-38; Cornell U., 1938—, as research investigator, instr., asst. and asso. prof., prof., 1948-63, Class of 1912 prof. engring., 1963-75, emeritus, 1975—, chmn. dept. structural engring., 1948-70, dir. research cold-formed steel structures Cornell U. for Am. Iron and Steel Inst., 1939—, dir. other research projects at univ. sponsored by industry and govt. Vis. prof. Calif. Inst. Tech., 1950, U. Calif. at Berkeley, 1969; vis. lectr. U. Liege, Belgium, 1957; vis. scholar U. Cambridge, 1956-57; cons. to Am. Iron and Steel Inst., others. Recipient Moisseiff award, 1948, J.J. Croes medal, 1961 (both Am. Soc. C.E.); Wason Research medal, 1965, Turner medal, 1972, Kelly award, 1979 (all Am. Concrete Inst.); Guggenheim Meml. fellow. Mem. Am. Concrete Inst. (hon. mem.; com. bldg. code), Am. Acad. Arts and Scis., Nat. Acad. Engring., Structural Stability Research Council (chmn. 1974-78), ASCE (hon. mem.; mem. several tech. coms.), Internat. Assn. Bridge and Structural Engring. (mem. permanent com., chmn. com. on stabilty of joint com. on tall bldgs.), Archaeol. Inst. Am., Sigma Xi, Tau Beta Pi, Chi Epsilon. Author: Design of Concrete Structures, 9th edit. (with A.H. Nilson), 1979. Contributed numerous research papers on structural mechanics, steel and concrete structures profl. periodicals U.S., abroad; contbr. Ency. Britannica, Am. Civil Engring., Structural Engring. Handbook. Home: 1010 Highland Rd Ithaca NY 14850 also West Tremont ME 04690

WINTER, GIBSON, clergyman, educator; b. Boston, Oct. 6, 1916; s. Howard and Cecilia (Gibson) W.; A.B., Harvard U., 1938, M.A., 1951, Ph.D., 1952; B.D., Episcopal Theol. Sch., 1941; m. Sara B.H. Ballard, Apr. 11, 1942; children—Marcus Cole, Sara B.C., Anne Gibson, Jacqueline B. Ordained priest Episcopal Church, 1941; curate St. John's Ch., Waterbury, Conn., 1941-43; rector All Saints Ch., Belmont, Mass., 1943-44; rector St. Mark's Ch., Foxboro, Mass., 1946-49; mem. Parishfield Community, Brighton, Mich., 1949-56; asst. prof. ethics and soc. Fed. Theol. Faculty U. Chgo., 1956-63, prof. Div. Sch., 1964-75; prof. Christianity and soc. Princeton Theol. Sem., 1976—. Served as lt. (j.g.) USNR, 1944-46. Mem. Soc. for Sci. Study Religion, Religious Research Assn., Am. Soc. Social Ethics, Am. Acad. Religion. Author: Love and Conflict: New Patterns in Family Life, 1958; The Suburban Captivity of the Churches, 1961; The New Creation as Metropolis, 1963; Elements For A Social Ethic, 1966; Being Free, 1970. Home: 111 N Main St Pennington NJ 08534

WINTER, GORDON ARNAUD, lt. gov. Nfld.; b. St. Johns, Nfld., Can., Oct. 6, 1912; s. Robert Gordon and Ethel Phyllis (Arnaud) W.; student Bishop Feild Coll., St. Johns, 1922-26; LL.D., Meml. U. Nfld., 1970; m. Millicent Anderson, Sept. 2, 1937; children—Linda, Valda. Pres., Nfld. Bd. Trade, 1946; chmn. St. Johns Housing Corp., 1949-50; gov. Canadian Broadcasting Corp., 1952-58; mem. advisory bd. Nfld. Savs. Bank, 1959-62; chmn. T & M Winter, Ltd., Standard Mfg. Co., Ltd.; lt. gov. Nfld., 1974—. Mem. Nfld. Del. that negotiated and signed terms of Union between Nfld. and Can., 1948; minister fin. First Provincial Govt. Nfld., 1949; chmn. bd. regents Meml. U. Nfld., 1968-74. Decorated knight St. John, Officer of the order of Can. Anglican. Clubs: Bally Haly Golf and Country; Murrays Pond Fishing, Coral Beach and Tennis, Bermuda. Address: Govt House Saint Johns NF A1C 5W4 Canada*

WINTER, HARRISON L., judge; b. Balt., Apr. 18, 1921; s. J. George and Bessie (Biden) W.; A.B., Johns Hopkins U., 1942; LL.B., U. Md., 1944; m. Gladys Woolford, June 28, 1947; children—Barbara B., Anne B. Admitted to Md. bar, 1945; asso. firm Miles, Walsh, O'Brien & Morris, 1946-51, partner, 1951-53; partner Miles & Stockbridge, 1953-59; asst. atty. gen. Md., 1948-51; dep. atty. gen. Md., 1954-55; city solicitor Balt., 1959-61; judge U.S. Dist. Ct. of Md., Balt., 1961-66; U.S. circuit judge U.S. Ct. of Appeals, 4th Circuit, Richmond, Va., 1966—. Trustee Johns Hopkins U., also vice chmn. bd.; bd. dirs. Peabody Inst. (chmn. bd. 1967-77), Evergreen House Found. Fellow Am. Bar Found.; mem. Am. Law Inst., Inst. Jud. Adminstrn., Am., Md., bar assns., Am. Coll. Trial Lawyers, Order of Coif, Omicron Delta Kappa. Episcopalian. Clubs: Md., 14 W. Hamilton St., Elkridge, Center (Balt.). Home: 16 Roland Mews Baltimore MD 21210 Office: 101 W Lombard St Baltimore MD 21201

WINTER, HARVEY JOHN, govt. ofcl.; b. New Albion, N.Y., Apr. 6, 1915; s. George J. and Irene (Harvey) W.; B.A. magna cum laude, U. Buffalo, 1938, M.A., 1939; teaching fellow George Washington U., 1939-40; m. Virginia M. Shaw, Sept. 2, 1939; 1 son, Jeffrey S. Historian, U.S. Nat. Park Service, 1940-42; archivist U.S. Nat. Archives, 1942-43; with U.S. Office Alien Property Custodian, 1943-51, chief reports and statistics sect., 1948- 51; with State Dept., 1951—, chief internat. bus. practices div., 1959- 61, asst. chief, 1961-70, chief bus. practices div., 1970-71, dir. office bus. protection, 1971-73, dir. office bus. practices, 1973—. U.S. del. European Productivity Agy. cartel meetings, Paris, France, 1958-60; mem. U.S. delegation diplomatic conf. Internat. Design Agreement, The Hague, 1960, 17th session GATT, Geneva, Switzerland, 1960; U.S. alternate rep. 5th session Intergovtl. Copyright Com., London, Eng., 1960, 6th session, Madrid, Spain, 1961, 7th session, New Delhi, India, 1963; U.S. alternate rep. Interunion Coordinating Com., Geneva, 1963-69; U.S. observer African Seminar on Indsl. Property, Brazzaville, Congo, 1963; U.S. alternate observer Latin Am. Indsl. Property Seminar, Bogota, Colombia, 1964, Asian Indsl. Property Seminar, Colombo, Ceylon, 1966; U.S. alternate rep. Com. of Experts on Inventors' Certificates, Geneva, 1965, Com. of Experts on Adminstrv. Agreement, Geneva, 1965, Intellectual Property Diplomatic Conf., Stockholm, Sweden, 1967, Diplomatic Conf. on Agreement for Classification of Indsl. Designs, Locarno, Switzerland, 1968, Diplomatic Conf. on Patent Cooperation Treaty, Washington, 1970, Diplomatic Conf. on Agreement for Internat. Patent Classification, Strasbourg, 1971, Diplomatic Conf. on Universal Copyright Conv., Paris, 1971, Diplomatic Conf. on Phonogram Conv., Geneva, 1971, Diplomatic Conf. on Indsl. Property, Vienna, 1973; U.S. rep. Com. Experts on Type Face Agreement, Geneva, 1972, Com. Experts on Communications Satellites Problems, Nairobi, Kenya, 1973; U.S. del. Diplomatic Conf. on Communications Satellites Conv., Brussels, Belgium, 1974, Diplomatic Conf. on Treaty for Deposit Microorganisms, Budapest, Hungary, 1977, Diplomatic Conf. on Plant Protection Conv., Geneva, 1978. Recipient Superior Honor award Dept. State, 1971, 76. Mem. Phi Beta Kappa. Episcopalian (vestry). Home: 1019 S 22d St Arlington VA 22202 Office: Dept of State Washington DC 20520

WINTER, JOHN DAWSON, III, performer, songwriter; b. Beaumont, Tex., Feb. 23, 1944; s. John Dawson II and Edwina (Holland) W.; grad. high sch. Organizer, performer numerous rock and blues bands; rec. artist CBS Records, Inc., 1969—; TV and concert appearances through U.S. and Europe, 1969—; albums include Johnny Winter, 1969, Second Winter, 1969, Johnny Winter-And, 1970, Live (Gold Record award 1974), 1971, Still Alive and Well, 1973, Saints and Sinners, 1974, John Dawson Winter III, 1974, Nothin' But the Blues, White Hot and Blue. Named Artist of Year, Rolling Stone mag., 1969. Mem. Broadcast Music Inc., Musicians Union. Office: care Blue Sky Records 745 Fifth Ave New York NY 10022*

WINTER, JOHN RINN, JR., ednl. adminstr.; b. Syracuse, N.Y., Sept. 18, 1925; s. John Rinn and Katharine Tallman (Wheatley) W.; B.A. cum laude, Amherst Coll., 1950; M.A., Boston U., 1952; m. Susan Jane Lowry, Mar. 29, 1947 (div. May 1968); children—Margaret Wheatley, Katharine Stafford; m. 2d, Marilyn Jean Osgood, June 25, 1971. Adminstrv. asst. to headmaster, bus. mgr. Suffield (Conn.) Acad., 1952-70, dir. finance, 1970-77, sec. corp., 1969-77, asst. treas., 1972-77; founder, gen. mgr. Bus. Advisory Service for Individuals and Schs. (BASIS), New Hartford, N.Y., 1977—. Bd. dirs. Utica Symphony Orch. Served with USNR, 1943-46; PTO. Mem. Nat. (dir. 1973-76), Conn. (dir. 1967-76, treas. 1972-76, chmn. bus. officers council 1969-72) assns. ind. schs., Phi Alpha Theta, Pi Gamma Mu, Cum Laude Soc. Clubs: Ft. Schuyler, Hartford. Home and Office: 9 Darby Ct New Hartford NY 13413

WINTER, LUMEN MARTIN, painter, sculptor, designer; b. Elerie, Ill., Dec. 12, 1908; s. William Grant and Mary Blanche (Nicholson) W.; hon. deg., Grand Rapids Jr. Coll., 1928; grad. Cleve. Sch. Art, 1929; student N.A.D., 1929-30, pvt. class Walter Biggs, 1934; m. Grace Harmon, Mar. 13, 1948; children—Thomas Martin, William Grant, II, Susan Anne. Began painting, 1923; asst. to Ezra Augustus Winter in execution of Radio City murals, George Rogers Clark Meml. murals, Vincennes, Ind.; murals and sculpture executed several pub. and pvt. bldgs., including: space mural AFL-CIO new addition, Washington, Refectory at University Notre Dame, Ch. St. Paul, The Apostle, N.Y.C., New Penn Sheraton Bldg., Phila., Murray Bldg., Internat. Union Elec., Radio and Machine Workers, Bklyn. Savs. Bank, Apollo mural St. Regis Hotel, J.F.K. Meml. Inc., Washington, Gerald R. Ford Center, Grand Rapids, Mich., Titans Mural Gen. Assembly, UN, Dove of Peace at City Hall Plaza, Poughkeepsie; mosaic Pub. Sch. 60, Staten Island, sculpture for library Fairfield U., U.S. Air Force Acad., Astor Home for Children, Rhinebeck, N.Y., South Shore High Sch., N.Y., Cathedral Coll. Immaculate Conception, Shrine of Our Lady, Haverstraw, N.Y.; Thornton Donovan Sch., New Rochelle, N.Y.; designed ofcl. medallion for Apollo XIII flight. Mural awards Nat. Competitions for Senate Chamber, Wash. State Capitol Bldg., 1948, Va. State Library, 1950, Rotunda murals Kans. State Capitol, Topeka, 1976; Gold medal exhbns. Archtl. League N.Y., 1951-52; Ranger Fund Purchase, N.A.O.; 1st prize New Rochelle Art Assn.; Petersen award Salmagundi Club, many others. Exhibited pvt., pub. galleries U.S. and abroad including: Modern Mus., Whitney Mus., Topeka Art Guild, Nat. Acad. Design, Penn Acad. Internat.; one-man shows numerous galleries including: Grand Rapids Art Mus., Galerie Internationale, N.Y.C.; represented Artists for Victory, Library of Congress, many pvt. and pub. collections including Art Inst. Chgo., U. Israel, Vatican. Mem. New Rochelle (N.Y.) Art Commn., 1975-76. Served as artist World War II. Mem. Nat. Soc. Mural Painters (1st v.p., adviser), Archtl. League of N.Y. (past v.p.), Am. Watercolor Soc., New Rochelle Art Assn. (past pres.), Artists Equity, Soc. Illustrators. Club: Salmagundi. Illustrator numerous publs. and books; co-author (with Harrison Kinney) and illustrator: The Last Supper of Leonardo Da Vinci. Address: 144 Overlook Circle New Rochelle NY 10804 also 1600 Old Pecos Trail Santa Fe NM 87501 . *The artist is born with an initial ability to serve mankind by helping to make the world a better place in which to live through dedicated effort and reverence for nature and the divine intelligence which created it.* ☆

WINTER, MAX, profl. football team exec.; b. Ostrava, Austria, June 29, 1904; s. Jacob and Bertha (Kuker) W.; came to U.S., 1913, naturalized, 1920; student Hamline U., 1925-26, U. Chgo., 1927; m. Helen Horovitz, Dec. 5, 1939; children—Susan (Mrs. Robert Diamond), Nancy (Mrs. Dennis Ditlove), Diane (Mrs. Richard Cohen). Co-owner, gen. mgr. Mpls. Lakers Basketball Team, 1947-56; originator Minn. Vikings (Nat. Football League), Mpls., 1960, pres., 1960—; pres. Max Winter Enterprises, Max Winter Enterprises, Hawaii; v.p. Income Guarantee, Aloha C.A.T.V.; dir. Downtown Bank of St. Paul, Bank of Mpls., Viking Enterprise Mpls., Mpls. Bank and Trust Co., Gambles Continental Bank, Mem. County Park Bd., 1959-64; chmn. Muscular Dystrophy, 1961; mem. Gov.'s Bus. Adv. Com., 1965; chmn. Nat. Govs. Conf., 1965. Recipient Hon. Scout award, 1946, 47, 48. Mem. Mpls. C. of C. (pres. 1969). Jewish religion. Rotarian. Clubs: Optimist; Minneapolis Athletic; Oak Ridge Country; Waialae Country, Outrigger (Honolulu). Author: Sports Books for Children, 1957. Office: 7110 France Ave S Edina MN 55435*

WINTER, MORICE FREDERICK, athletic adminstr.; b. Wellington, Tex., Feb. 25, 1922; s. Marion Ernest and Thesera Osela (Rodgers) W.; A.S., Compton Jr. Coll., 1946; student Ore. State U., 1943; B.S., U. So. Cal., 1947; m. Nancy Chase Bohnenkamp, July 11, 1946; children—Russell Fredrick, Christopher Chase, Brian Ernest. Asst. basketball coach Kan. State Coll., 1947-51; head basketball coach Marquette U., 1951-53, Kan. State U., 1953-68, U. Wash., 1968-71, Houston Rockets, 1971-73, Northwestern U., Evanston, Ill., 1973-78, Calif. State U., Long Beach, 1978—. Served with USNR. Named U.P.I. Coach of Year, 1958, Big 8 Coach of Year, 1964-68. Mem. Nat. Assn. Basketball Coaches (3d v.p.). Author: Triple Post Offense. Home: 2403 Petaluma Long Beach CA 90815 Office: 1250 Bellflower Blvd Los Angeles CA 90840

WINTER, PAUL THEODORE, musician; b. Altoona, Pa., Aug. 31, 1939; s. Paul Theodore and Beaulah (Harnish) W.; B.A., Northwestern U., 1961. Leader, Paul Winter Sextet, 1961-65, Winter Consort, 1967—; performed concerts in 26 countries and throughout U.S.; recorded numerous albums; founder Living Music Found., 1976—. Fellow Lindisfarne Assn., 1977. Address: Box 68 Litchfield CT 06759

WINTER, PAULA CECELIA, artist; b. N.Y.C., Oct. 26, 1929; d. Henry and Marie (Heynen) Winter; student Cooper Union Night Sch., 1952-55; m. Harold Berson, July 2, 1958. Group shows: Eggleston Gallery, N.Y.C., 1951, Leonard Hutton Gallery, N.Y.C., 1960; illustrator: The Bear and the Fly, 1976 (Am. Library Assn. Notable Children's Book, 1976, Children's Book Show Case, 1977, N.Y. Times Best Illustrated Children's Books of Yr., 1976, Saturday Rev. Children's Book Best of Season, 1976). Home: 172 Stanton St New York NY 10002 Office: care Crown Pubs 1 Park Ave New York NY 10016

WINTER, ROBERT ALFRED, diversified industry exec.; b. N.Y.C., Oct. 28, 1919; s. Robert A. and Minnie (Eder) W.; B.S., City Coll. N.Y., 1939; M.B.A., Harvard, 1940; J.D., St. John's U., 1944; m. Winifred G. Wike, Aug. 16, 1946; children—Deborah G. (Mrs. Bruce C. Davidson), Robert A., Richard W. Admitted to N.Y. State bar, 1945; adviser dist. contracting officer Eastern Procurement Dist., USAAF Material Command, N.Y.C., 1942-44; chief financial officer, gen. counsel Gen. Aircraft Corp., N.Y.C., 1945; tax counsel W.R. Grace Co., N.Y.C., 1945-49; planning asst. to v.p. internat. Ford Motor Co., Dearborn, Mich., 1949-66; v.p. Bell & Howell Co., Chgo., 1966—. Trustee Village of Riverwoods (Ill.), 1969-77. Club: Harvard Bus. Sch. Chgo. (dir. 1974-77). Home: 2620 Crestwood Ln Deerfield IL 60015 Office: 7100 McCormick Rd Chicago IL 60645

WINTER, ROLF GERHARD, physicist, educator; b. Dusseldorf, Germany, June 30, 1928; s. Julius and Erika (Wolff) W.; came to U.S., 1938, naturalized, 1944; B.S., Carnegie Inst. Tech., 1948, M.S., 1951, D.Sc., 1952; m. Patricia Mae Saibel, Jan. 31, 1951; children—Erika Louise, Edward Paul Merritt, James Frederick. Instr., then asst. prof. Western Res. U., 1951-54; asst. prof., then asso. prof. Pa. State U., 1954-64; prof. physics Coll. William and Mary, 1964, chmn. dept., 1966-72; vis. physicist, vis. lectr. Carnegie Inst. Tech., 1955-56, Oxford (Eng.) U., 1961-62, U. Wis., summer 1963, U. Sask., summer 1976; cons. in field, 1955—. Recipient Phi Beta Kappa chpt. faculty award for advancement scholarship, 1967; Knight of Mark Twain award, 1972. Fellow Am. Phys. Soc.; mem. AAUP (chpt. pres. 1975-76), Va. Acad. Sci. Author: Quantum Physics, 1979; contbr. articles to profl. jours. Home: 609 Indian Springs Ct Williamsburg VA 23185 Office: Dept Physics Coll William and Mary Williamsburg VA 23185

WINTER, RUTH GROSMAN (MRS. ARTHUR WINTER), journalist; b. Newark, May 29, 1930; d. Robert Delmas and Rose (Rich) Grosman; B.A., Upsala Coll., 1951; m. Arthur Winter, June 16, 1955; children—Robin, Craig, Grant. With Houston Press, 1955-56; gen. assignment Newark Star Ledger, 1951-55, sci. editor, 1956-69; columnist Los Angeles Times Syndicate, 1973-78; contbr. to N.Y. Times Spl. Features, Enterprise Sci. Service, Consumer Mags.; instr. St. Peters Coll., Jersey City. Recipient award of merit Am. Dental Assn., 1966, Cecil award Arthritis Found., 1967, Am. Soc. Anesthesiologists award, 1969, Arthritis Found. award, 1978; named Alumnus of Year, Upsala Coll., 1971, Woman of Year, N.J. Daily Newspaper Women, 1971. Mem. Soc. Mag. Writers, Authors League, Nat. Assn. Sci. Writers, Am. Med. Writers Assn., Overseas Press Club, N.J. Daily Newspaper Women (awards news series 1958, 70, named Woman of Achievement 1971), Am. Soc. Journalists and Authors (pres. 1977-78). Author: Poisons in Your Food, rev. edit., 1971; How to Reduce Your Medical Bills, 1970; A Consumers Dictionary of Food Additives, 1972; Vitamin E: The Miracle Worker, 1972; So You Have Sinus Trouble, 1973; Ageless Aging, 1973; So You Have a Pain in the Neck, 1974; A Consumers Dictionary of Cosmetic Ingredients, 1974, rev. edit., 1976; Don't Panic, 1975; The Fragile Bond: Marriage in the '70's, 1976; Triumph Over Tension, 1976; The Smell Book: Scent, Sex and Society (N.J. Press Women's Book award), 1976; Scent Talk Among Animals, 1977; A Cancer Causing Agents: A Preventive Guide, 1979; The Great Self-Improvement Sourcebook, 1980. Home and office: 44 Holly Dr Short Hills NJ 07078

WINTER, SIDNEY GRAHAM, JR., educator; b. Iowa City, Ia., Apr. 20, 1935; s. Sidney Graham and Eva Madge (Threlkeld) W.; student U. Iowa, 1953-54; B.A. with highest honors, Swarthmore (Pa.) Coll., 1956; M.A., Yale, 1957, Ph.D., 1964; m. Georgie Ann Paltnavich, Mar. 2, 1963; children—Jeffrey Graham, Sidney Christopher. Research economist Rand Corp., Santa Monica, Calif., 1959-61, 1966-68; mem. staff Council Econ. Advisers, Washington, 1961-62; asst. prof. econs. U. Calif. at Berkeley, 1963-66; prof., research scientist U. Mich., Ann Arbor, 1968— prof. econs., prof. Sch. Orgn. and Mgmt., Yale, New Haven, 1976—; cons. Office Sec. Def., 1962-63, Nat. Acad. Scis., 1963, 67, NSF, 1975. Mem. Ann Arbor Cablecasting Commn., 1971-72, chmn., 1972. Fellow Econometric Soc.; mem. Am. Econ. Assn., AAAS, Phi Beta Kappa. Asso. editor Jour. Econ. Theory, 1969-71, Adminstrv. Sci. Quar., 1969-72, Behavioral Sci., 1969-79; contbr. articles, revs. to profl. jours. Home: 31 Alston Ave New Haven CT 06515

WINTER, TED, publishing co. exec.; b. Chgo., May 9, 1919; s. Irving E. and Florence (Regensteiner) W.; student U. Mich., 1937-40, Loyola U., Chgo., 1940-41; m. Joan Lee, July 1, 1941; children—John L., Thomas. Gen. mgr. Children's Press, Chgo., 1946-50, pres., 1950—; pres. Regensteiner Pub. Enterprises, Inc., Chgo., 1961—, chmn. bd., 1972—; del. White House Conf. on Edn., 1960. Mem. Bd. Edn. Dist. 113, Highland Park, Ill., 1964-70; vice chmn. bd. dirs. Am. Jewish Com., 1960-64; bd. dirs. Duncan YMCA, 1971-79, West Central Assn., 1966-79, Bur. Jewish Employment Problems, 1968-79; bd. assos. Nat. Coll. Edn., 1964-79. Served to 1st lt. Signal Corps, AUS, 1941-46. Mem. Assn. Am. Pubs., Printing Industries Am., Zeta Beta Tau. Jewish. Clubs: Northmoor Country, Standard. Home: 223 Linden Park Pl Highland Park IL 60035 Office: 1224 W Van Buren St Chicago IL 60607

WINTER, WILLIAM BERGFORD, mfg. co. exec.; b. LaCrosse, Wis., July 16, 1928; s. Gustav J. and Bergliot H. W.; B.S. in Civil Engring., U. Wis.-Madison, 1951; m. Marie Ann; children—Jonathan, Jennifer. With Bucyrus-Erie Co., South Milwaukee, Wis., 1953—, gen. mgr. constrn. machinery div., 1963-65, v.p. mfg. and fgn. ops., 1965-71, mng. dir. Ruston-Bucyrus Ltd., Lincoln, Eng., 1971-77, dir., 1975—, pres. Bucyrus-Eris Co., 1978—, chmn. bd. Ruston-Bucyrus, Ltd., 1978—; dir. Wis. Gas Co. Mem. exec. bd. dirs. YMCA Met. Milw. Served with C.E., U.S. Army, 1951-53. Clubs: Western Racquet, Univ., Milw. Country. Office: 1100 Milwaukee Ave South Milwaukee WI 53172

WINTER, WILLIAM EARL, soft drink co. exec.; b. Granite, City, Ill., Sept. 21, 1920; s. William Martin and Ada Maude (Compton) W.; A.B., U. Ill., 1942; m. Dorothy E. (dec. 1976); children—William C., Douglas E.; m. 2d Mildred E. Stiebel, Mar. 18, 1977. With Seven-Up Co., St. Louis, 1946—, mktg. dir., 1965-70, exec. v.p., 1970-75, pres., chief exec. officer, 1975-79, chmn. bd., 1979—; v.p. Philip Morris, Inc., N.Y.C.; dir. Miller Brewing Co., Mission Viejo Co., First Nat. Bank of St. Louis, Bank Bldg. & Equipment Co. Bd. dirs. YMCA of Greater St. Louis, St. Louis Area council Boy Scouts Am., Deaconess Hosp., St. Louis, Cardinal Ritter Inst., St. Louis. Served with USAF, 1942-46. Named to Promotion Mktg. Assn. Am. Hall of Fame. Mem. Am. Mktg. Assn., Sales and Mktg. Execs. Baptist. Clubs: St. Louis, Masons. Office: 121 S Meromec St Saint Louis MO 63105

WINTER, WILLIAM EARL, beverage co. exec.; b. Granite City, Ill., Sept. 21, 1920; s. William Martin and Ada (Compton) W.; A.B., U. Ill., 1942; m. Dorothy Eve Schuster, Feb. 20, 1944 (dec. May 1976); children—William Craig, Douglas Earl; m. 2d, Mildred E. Stiebel, Mar. 18, 1977. With The Seven-Up Co., St. Louis, 1946—, exec. v.p., 1972-74, pres., 1974—, chief exec. officer, 1976—, chmn., 1979—, also dir.; dir. Miller Brewing Co., Mission Viejo Co., Oreg. Freeze Dry Foods, Bank Bldg. & Equipment Co., St. Louis, First Nat. Bank in St. Louis. Nat. v.p. Muscular Dystrophy Assn. Am.; bd. dirs., vice chmn. Met. St. Louis YMCA; bd. dirs. St. Louis Area council Boy Scouts Am., Cardinal Ritter Inst.; trustee Deaconess Hosp. Served to capt. USAAF, World War II. Named to Hall of Fame, Promotion Mktg. Assn. Am., 1979. Mem. Premium Advt. Assn. Am. (chmn. 1971-72), Am. Marketing Assn., Sales and Marketing Execs., Phi Beta Kappa, Omicron Delta Gamma. Baptist. Mason. Home: 12310 Boothbay Ct Creve Coeur MO 63141 Office: 121 S Meramec St Saint Louis MO 63105

WINTER, WILLIAM FORREST, gov. Miss., lawyer; b. Grenada, Miss., Feb. 21, 1923; s. William Aylmer and Inez (Parker) W.; B.A., U. Miss., 1943, LL.B., 1949; m. Elise Varner, Oct. 10, 1950; children—Anne, Elise, Eleanor. Admitted to Miss. bar, 1949; practice in Grenada, 1949-58, Jackson, Miss., 1968—; partner Watkins, Pyle, Ludlam, Winter and Stennis, 1968-80; mem. Miss. Ho. of Reps., 1948-56; state tax collector, 1956-64; state treas., 1964-68; lt. gov. State of Miss., 1972-76, gov., 1980—. Pres. bd. trustees Miss. Dept. Archives and History; trustee Belhaven Coll., Columbia Sem.; bd. dirs. Lamar Soc., Miss. Found. Ind. Colls. Served with AUS, 1943-46, 51. Recipient Margaret Dixon Freedom of Info. award AP, 1972. Mem. Am., Miss., Hinds County bar assns., Phi Delta Phi, Omicron Delta Kappa (Outstanding Alumnus U. Miss. 1975), Phi Delta Theta. Democrat. Presbyterian. Club: Univ. (Jackson). Home: Governors Mansion Jackson MS 39201 Office: Sillers State Office Bldg Jackson MS 39201

WINTERER, PHILIP STEELE, lawyer; b. San Francisco, July 8, 1931; s. Steele Leland and Esther Pomeroy (Hardy) W.; B.A., Amherst Coll., 1953; LL.B., Harvard U., 1956; m. Patricia Dowling, June 15, 1955; children—Edward Jernigan, Amey Cutler. Admitted to N.Y. bar, 1957, Republic of Korea bar, 1958; asso. firm Debevoise, Plimpton, Lyons & Gates, N.Y.C., 1956-65, partner, 1965; trustee Empire Savs. Bank, N.Y.C. Bd. dirs. Brookwood Child Care, 1962-65, Sch. Am. Ballet, 1974—; exec. com. alumni council Amherst Coll., chmn., 1977—. Mem. Am., N.Y. State bar assns., Assn. Bar City N.Y., Am.-Italy Soc. (sec., dir. 1966—), Am. Law Inst., Council Fgn. Relations. Home: 1165 Fifth Ave New York NY 10029 Office: 299 Park Ave New York NY 10017

WINTERNITZ, FRITZ ALFRED, bus. products co. exec.; b. Vienna, Austria, Apr. 2, 1922; s. Mario Dubini and Sophie S. (Bruckner) W.; came to U.S., 1975; Dipl. Ing. E.T.H., Fed. Inst. Tech., Zürich, Switzerland, 1947; Doctorate in Engring. with spl. distinction, Vienna Tech. U., 1959; m. Anne Sutherland Fulton, June 30, 1949; children—Robert, Peter, Ingrid, Joanna. Research engr. Escher WYSS AG, Zürich, 1947-50; with Nat. Engring. Lab., U.K., East Kilbride, Scotland, 1951-62, sr. prin. sci. officer dept. sci. and indsl. research, 1951-59, head div. fluid dynamics, 1959-62; tech. dir. SPP Ltd., Gateshead, U.K., 1962-65; group dir. engring., Asso. Engring. Ltd., Leamington, U.K., 1965-73; group dir. engring. Rank Xerox, Eng., London, 1973-75, corporate v.p. research and devel. Xerox Corp., Stamford, Conn., 1973-79; corp. v.p., dir. spl. projects Rank Xerox Ltd., London, also dir.; dir. Fuji Xerox. Fellow Inst. Mech. Engrs., Royal Aero. Soc. (asso.); mem. Instn. German Engrs. Presbyterian. Club: Wee Burn Country (Darien, Conn.). Contbr. over 20 articles to profl. jours., 1955-65. Home: 26 Prides Crossing New Canaan CT 06840 Office: Rank Xerox Ltd 338 Euston Rd London NW1 3BH England

WINTERS, BARBARA JO, musician; b. Salt Lake City; d. Louis McClain and Gwendolyn (Bradley) Winters; A.B. cum laude, U. Calif. at Los Angeles, 1960, postgrad., 1961; postgrad. Yale, 1960. Mem. oboe sect. Pasadena (Calif.) Symphony, 1958-60; mem. oboe sect. Los Angeles Philharmonic, 1961—, now co.-prin. oboist. Recs. movie, TV sound tracks. Home: 3529 Coldwater Canyon Studio City CA 91604 Office: 135 N Grand Ave Los Angeles CA 90012

WINTERS, DAVID, dir., producer, choreographer; b. London, Apr. 5, 1939; s. Samuel and Sadie Weizer; came to U.S., 1953, naturalized, 1956; student (scholar) Lodge Profl. Sch., N.Y.C.; m. Jilen Splawn, Dec. 31, 1977. Dir., producer films including A Star is Born, 1978, Racquet, 1979, Roller Boogie, 1980; producer, dir. TV movie Doctor Jekyl & Mr. Hyde, 1973; producer, dir. TV spls. including: Raquel, 1970, Ann-Margaret, 1968, 69, Lucy in London, 1968, Star Wars, 1978; producer, choreographer Hot Stuff 1979; producer, dir. stage prodn. Diana Ross, 1979, 80; tchr. dancing Carnegie Hall, 1956-57; owner, mgr. Dance Center, Los Angeles, 1963-67. Recipient Peabody award, 1971, Christopher award, 1971, World TV awards, 1970, 71, 72. Mem. Dirs. Guild Am., Motion Picture Assn. Am. Home: 13160 Mulhulland Dr Beverly Hills CA 90210 Office: 1900 Ave of Stars Los Angeles CA 90067

WINTERS, DENNY, artist; b. Grand Rapids, Mich., 1909; d. James Henry Sonke and Eva May (Taylor) Sonke; student Chgo. Acad. Fine Arts, Chgo. Art Inst.; m. Herman Joseph Cherry, Sept. 20, 1940; m. 2d, Lew Dietz, 1951. Work exhibited Mus. Modern Art, Carnegie Mus., Pa. Acad. Fine Arts, Chgo. Art Inst., San Francisco (Calif.) Mus., Nat. Acad. show, 1968, Nat. Acad. Art, 1970-72; one-man shows Los Angeles Mus., San Francisco Mus., Mortimer Levitt Gallery, N.Y.C., Wiscasset (Maine) Mus., 1961, Rehn Art Gallery, N.Y.C., 1953, 57, 63, 72, 76, U. Maine, 1959, 65, 78, C. of C. Northeast Harbor, Maine, 1960, 62, Phila. Art Alliance, 1964, Bowdoin Coll., 1968, Grand Rapids (Mich.) Art Mus., 1972, Kalamazoo Inst. Fine Arts, 1972, Talent Tree Gallery, Augusta, Maine, Bates Coll., Lewiston, Maine, 1975, U.S. Ct. House, Phila., 1976, Unity (Maine) Coll., 1976, Barridoff Gallery, Portland, Maine, 1978, Payson Mus., Westbrook Coll., Portland, 1978. Tchr., Camden (Maine) Extension; traveled, painted in France, Italy, 1949. Mem. Maine Visual Arts Com. for Arts and Humanities Commn. Recipient first prize for prints San Francisco Mus., 1941, 1st prize for oils Denver Mus., 1940; Purchase prize Butler Inst. Am. Art, 1964; Skowhegan Art award, 1973. Guggenheim fellow, 1948. Mem. Me. Coast Artists (exhibitor 1951—), Maine Hist. Soc. Illustrator: Full Fathom Five (Lew Dietz), Wilderness River (Lew Dietz). Address: Rockport ME 04856

WINTERS, J. OTIS, banker; b. Tulsa, Nov. 6, 1932; s. John McAfee, Jr. and Marian Dunn (McClintock) W.; M.S. in Petroleum Engring., Stanford U., 1955; M.B.A., Harvard U., 1962; m. Ann Allene Varnadow, Oct. 18, 1958; children—John, Richard, David, Paul. Vice pres. Warren Am. Oil Co., Tulsa, 1962-65; pres. Ednl. Devel. Corp., Tulsa, 1965-73; exec. v.p., dir. Williams Cos., Tulsa, 1973-77; pres. Zephyr Corp., Tulsa, 1977—; exec. v.p. First Nat. Bank of Tulsa, also dir.; chmn. Am. Magnesium Co.; dir. Hydratane Gas Co., Miss Jackson's Inc. Vice chmn. bd. First United Meth. Ch., 1977—; pres. Downtown Tulsa Unltd., 1977; former vice chmn. bd. Oral Roberts U.; bd. dirs. Jr. Achievement; commr. Tulsa Urban Renewal Authority; 1st v.p. Ark. Basin Devel. Assn. Served as 1st lt., C.E., U.S. Army, 1955-57. Recipient various pub. service awards. Registered profl. engr., Okla. Mem. Tulsa C. of C. (dir.). Clubs: So. Hills (Tulsa); Pine Valley; Augusta; Cypress Point. Home: 3303 S Florence St Tulsa OK 74105 Office: Box 1 1st Nat Tower Tulsa OK 74193

WINTERS, J(OHN) SAM, lawyer; b. Amarillo, Tex., July 7, 1922; s. John Howard and Guydelle (Vineyard) W.; B.A., U. Tex., 1944, LL.B., 1948; m. Dorothy Jean Rushing, Dec. 21, 1947; 1 dau., Leila. Admitted to Tex. bar, 1948; briefing atty. Supreme Ct. Tex., 1948-49; chief corp. sect. Tex. Dept. State, 1949-50; mem. firm Bagby & Winters, Austin, 1950-57, Clark, Thomas, Winters & Shapiro, Austin, 1957—; chmn. bd. dirs. Nat. Bank of Commerce, Austin. Mem. Nat. Hwy. Safety Adv. Com., 1967-70; bd. dirs. Tex. Research League, 1976—, Jr. Achievement. Served with USNR, World War II. Fellow Am., Tex. (charter) bar founds.; mem. Am. Judicature Soc., State Bar Tex. (chmn. adminstrv. law com. 1963-67, 75-77, uniform laws com. 1967-70, vice chmn., 1970-71, chmn. resolutions com. 1975-76). Am. Bar Assn. (council, sect. public utility law), Travis County Bar Assn. (pres. 1961-62), Internat. Assn. Ins. Counsel, Fedn. Ins. Counsel, Assn. Ins. Atty., Tex. Assn. Def. Counsel, Am. Law Inst., Philos. Soc. Tex., Panhandle-Plains, Tex. hist. assns., Phi Alpha Delta, Phi Kappa Psi. Episcopalian. Home: 1708 Windsor Rd Austin TX 78703 Office: Capital Nat Bank Bldg PO Box 1148 Austin TX 78767

WINTERS, JOHN WESLEY, real estate exec., state senator; b. Raleigh, N.C., Jan. 21, 1920; s. Charlie and Lillie (Summerville) W.; student Va. State Coll., 1939-40; student Shaw U., 1940-41, LL.D., 1968; m. Marie Montague, Feb. 3, 1941; children—John, Frances Winters Davis, Donna Winters LaRoche, Naomi Regina, Rebecca Joyce, Roland Edward, Seanne Marie. Started constrn. bus., 1950; former John W. Winters & Co., Raleigh, 1957, now also real estate broker, land developer; mem. N.C. Senate, 1975-77. Dir. Raleigh Mchts. Bur., Mechanics and Farmers Bank; mem. N.C. Utilities Commn. Mem. Raleigh City Council, 1961-67; vice chmn. Wake County (N.C.) Democratic exec. com., 1964-70; del. Dem. Nat. Conv., Miami, Fla., 1972; mem. Gov.'s Commn. on Internat. Relations, 1962; mem. N.C. Good Neighbor Council, 1963—. Bd. dirs. N.C. Housing Corp.; trustee Shaw U.; bd. govs. Univ. System N.C. Mem. Home Builders Assn. Raleigh (dir. 1970-75), Nat. Assn. Home Builders (nat. dir. 1972-75), Raleigh C. of C., N.A.A.C.P. (life), Omega Psi Phi. Roman Catholic. Home: 8001 Caddy Rd Raleigh NC 27603 Office: 507 E Martin St Raleigh NC 26601

WINTERS, JONATHAN, actor; b. Dayton, Ohio, Nov. 11, 1925; s. Jonathan H. and Alice Kilgore (Rodgers) W.; student Kenyon Coll., 1946; B.F.A., Dayton Art Inst., 1950; m. Eileen Ann Schauder, Sept. 11, 1948; children—Jonathan IV, Lucinda Kelley. With radio sta. WING, Dayton, 1949; disc jockey sta. WBNS-TV, Columbus, Ohio, 1950-53; appeared on Garry Moore Show, 1954-63, Steve Allen Show, 1954-61, Omnibus, 1954, NBC Comedy Hour, 1956, Jonathan Winters Show, 1956-57, Jack Paar Show, 1963-64, Andy Williams Show, 1966-67, Dean Martin Show, 1966-67, Jonathan Winters Show, CBS-TV, 1968-69, Wacky World of Jonathan Winters, 1972-73; numerous appearances NBC Monitor show, 1963—, Hollywood Squares, 1975—; night club appearances, 1953-60; motion picture appearances: It's a Mad, Mad, Mad World, 1963, The Loved One, 1964, The Russians Are Coming, The Russians Are Coming, 1966, Penelope, 1967, The Midnight Oil, 1967, 8 On the Lam, 1967, Oh Dad, Poor Dad, 1968, Viva Max, 1969, The Fish That Saved Pittsburgh, 1979; rec. artist Columbia Records. Served with USMCR, 1943-46; PTO. Author: Mouse Breath, Conformity and Other Social Ills, 1965. Office: George Spota 9000 Sunset Blvd Suite 510 Los Angeles CA 90069

WINTERS, LEO, treas. Okla.; b. Hooker, Okla., Nov. 7, 1922; s. David and Gertrude (Strochin) W.; A.B., Panhandle A and M Coll., Goodwell, Okla., 1950; LL.B. U. Okla., 1957. Admitted to Okla. bar, 1957, since practiced in Oklahoma City; lt. gov. Okla., 1963-67, treas., 1967—. Served as pilot USAAF, World War II. Mem. Am. Quarter Horse Assn. Democrat. Mason (32 deg.). Office: PO Box 53411 Oklahoma City OK 73152

WINTERS, ROBERT WAYNE, educator, physician; b. Evansville, Ind., May 23, 1926; s. Frank and Clara (Flentke) W.; A.B. summa cum laude, Ind. U., 1948; M.D. cum laude, Yale U., 1952; m. Agnete Thomsen, Feb. 11, 1976; children by previous marriage—Henry N., R. George. Intern, also Bank of Am.-Giannini Found. research fellow U. Calif. at San Francisco, 1952-54; asst. chief resident, also Nat. Found. fellow U. N.C. Sch. Medicine, 1954-58; asst. prof. physiology, dir. med. student research tng. program U. Pa. Sch. Medicine, 1958-61; mem. faculty Columbia Coll. Physicians and Surgeons, 1961—, prof. pediatrics, 1962—. Mem. sci. adv. bd. Blythedale Children's Hosp., Valhalla, N.Y., 1965; mem., chmn. growth and tng. com. Nat. Inst. Child Health and Human Devel., 1969-73; sci. adv. bd. Nat. and N.Y. Kidney Found.; career scientist Health Research Council, City N.Y., 1963—. Served to 2d lt. U.S. Army, 1944-46. Recipient E. Mead Johnson award research pediatrics, 1966; Borden award Am. Acad. Pediatrics, 1974. Mem. Am. Soc. Clin. Investigation, Am. Pediatric Soc., Soc. Pediatric Research, Am. Physiol. Soc., Assn. Am. Physicians, Harvey Soc., Marine Biol. Lab., Phi Beta Kappa, Sigma Xi, Alpha Omega Alpha. Contbr. articles to profl. jours. Home: 10 Isabella Way Demarest NJ 07627

WINTERS, SHELLEY, motion picture actress; b. St. Louis, Aug. 18, 1922; student Wayne U.; m. Vittorio Gassman (div.); 1 child, Vittoria; m. 3d, Anthony Franciosa, 1957 (div.). Began acting career in vaudeville, later played roles on legitimate stage; motion pictures include: A Thousand and One Nights, A Double Life, Take One False Step, South Sea Singer, A Place in the Sun, He Ran All the Way, Playgirl, Executive Suite, Night of the Hunter, C.O.D., Jagged Edge, The Diary of Anne Frank (Acad. award best supporting actress), 1958; Odds Against Tomorrow, Let No Man Write My Epitaph, Matter of Convictions, Lolita, 1962, Wives and Lovers, 1963, The Balcony, 1964, A House Is Not a Home, 1964, Patch of Blue, Time of Indifference, 1965, Alfie, 1965, The Moving Target, 1965, How Do I Love Thee, 1971, What's the Matter with Helen, 1971, The Poseidon Adventure, 1972, Blume in Love, 1973, Cleopatra Jones, 1973, Something to Hide, 1973, Diamonds, 1975, Next Stop Greenwich Village, 1976, The Tenant, 1976, Pete's Dragon, 1977, King of the Gypsies, 1978; appeared in TV films Revenge!, 1971; The Devil's Daughter, 1973; Double Indemnity, 1974; The Sex Symbol, 1974; appeared in plays: A Hatfull of Rain, 1955, Girls of Summer, 1957, Night of the Iguana, Cages, Who's Afraid of Virginia Wolf?, Minnie's Boys; appeared in TV miniseries The French Atlantic Affair, 1979. Recipient Emmy award Best Actress, 1964; Monte Carlo Golden Nymph award, 1964; Internat. TV award as best actress Cannes Festival, 1965. Author: (play) One Night Stands of a Noisy Passenger, 1971. Address: care Internat Creative Mgmt 8899 Beverly Blvd Los Angeles CA 90048*

WINTERSON, HOWARD MARTIN, steam generating equipment mfg. co. exec.; b. Salt Lake City, June 11, 1916; s. Warren Scott and Florence Vera (Hansen) W.; B.A. in Econs., Duke U., 1939; m. Arlene De Mots, Feb. 20, 1944; children—Christine, John, Warren, Howard Martin. Indsl. engr. Lukens Steel Co., Coatesville, Pa., 1940-52; with Blaw Knox Co., Pitts., 1953-65, exec. v.p., 1963-65; exec. v.p. Lummus Co., N.Y.C., 1965-67; corp. v.p., dir., pres. power systems group Combustion Engring., Inc., Windsor, Conn., 1967—; dir. Combustion Engring. Can., Cyclops Corp., Uddcomb-Sweden, A.B.; bd. dirs. Atomic Indsl. Forum, Am. Nuclear Energy Council, Slurry Transp. Assn. Mem. president's assos. Duke U., also bd. visitors Sch. Engring.; bd. visitors Sch. Bus. Adminstrn., U. Conn.; trustee Hartford Grad. Center. Served to lt. USN, 1942-46. Mem. Am. Nuclear Soc. Home: South Rd Harwinton CT 06790 Office: 1000 Prospect Hill Rd Windsor CT 06095

WINTERSTEEN, BERNICE MCILHENNY, civic worker; b. Phila., June 16, 1903; d. John D. and Frances (Plumer) McIlhenny; B.A. with Honors in History, Smith Coll., 1925; L.H.D. (hon.), Ursinus Coll., 1965, Villanova U., 1967, Hahnemann Med. Coll. and Hosp., 1967; hon. degree Moore Coll. Art, Wilson Coll.; m. John Wintersteen, Oct. 30, 1929 (dec. Oct. 1952); children—John, James McI., H. Jeremy, George F. Trustee Phila. Mus. Art, 1942, gov., 1937-64, chmn. bd. govs., 1959-64, pres. Mus., 1964-68, mem. women's com. 1928, now mem. bd.; chmn. bd. mgrs. Moore Coll. Art, 1968-71; past mem. Phila. Art Commn.; past vis. com. dept. visual art Harvard, 1963-68; vis. com. Princeton U. Art Mus.; mem., 1st chmn. vis. com. Smith Coll. Mus. Art; co-chmn. Phila. Art Festival, 1962, chmn., 1967; vice chmn. Pa. Council Arts, pres., dir. Friends of the Wissahickon, 1953-56; mem. bd. counselors Smith Coll., 1951-57, mem. Am. civilization adv. council U. Pa., also mem. com. for devel. research in sci.; past trustee Drexel Inst. Tech.; trustee Pa. Acad. Fine Arts; hon. trustee Phila. Coll. Art, Maxwell Mansion Com.; former bd. dirs. Montgomery County Soc. for Prevention Cruelty to Animals; former bd. govs. Atheneium Library. Recipient Phila. Woman of Year Gimble award, 1966; Woman of Year award Am. Friends Hebrew U., 1966; Art Alliance award, 1974. Mem. Distinguished Daus. Pa., Phi Beta Kappa Assos. (bd. dirs.), Phi Beta Kappa. Republican. Presbyn. Clubs: Acorn, Print (pres. 1952-55), Gulph Mills Golf, Planters Garden (Phila.); Prouts Neck (Maine) Country (dir.); Merion Country. Lectr. art and travel. Home: 100 Grays Ln Haverford PA 19041

WINTHROP, JOHN, investment co. exec.; b. Boston, June 22, 1936; s. Nathaniel Thayer and Serita Bartlett (Harwood) W.; grad. with distinction, St. Mark's Sch., 1954; B.A., Harvard, 1958; M.B.A., Columbia, 1962; children—John, H. Grenville, Bayard. With Wood, Struthers & Winthrop, N.Y.C., 1964—, Mgmt. Co. (subsidiary DJL), now chmn.; dir. Donaldson, Lufkin, Jenrette; pres., dir. de Vegh Fund, 1973—. Chmn. Red Cross Drive, Greenwich. Past bd. dirs. Greenwich Country Day Sch., Ednl. Policy Center, N.Y.C.; bd. dirs. Fresh Air Fund, N.Y.C., Nat. Audubon Soc.; mem. vis. coms. history dept. Harvard; bd. govs. Investment Co. Inst., Washington. Served with USNR, 1958-60. Mem. N.Y. Soc. Security Analysts, Bond Club N.Y. Republican. Clubs: Harvard, Knickerbocker (N.Y.C.). Author: Book of Bad Verse, 1972; also articles for Atlantic Community News, Boston Globe, Barrons, Financial Analysts Jour., Wall St. Jour. Home: John St Greenwich CT 06830 Office: 14 Wall St New York NY 10005

WINTHROP, ROBERT, banker; b. Boston, Jan. 21, 1904; s. Frederic and Dorothy (Amory) W.; A.B., Harvard, 1926; postgrad. Trinity Coll., Cambridge, Eng., 1926-27; Harvard Bus. Sch., 1927-28; m. Theodora Ayer, Apr. 9, 1928; children—Theodora (Mrs. T.L. Higginson), Elizabeth Amory (Mrs. Malcolm Ripley), Cornelia (Mrs. Edward S. Bonnie); m. 2d, Margaret Stone, Apr. 25, 1942. Clk., Nat. City Bank of N.Y., 1928-29; clk. Wood, Struthers & Winthrop, Inc. (formerly Robert Winthrop & Co., 1929-31, partner, 1931-69, hon. chmn., 1969— (ret. 1972); dir. Citibank, 1939-64; former trustee Seamans Bank Savs. Former mem. L.I. State Park Commn.; trustee Presbyn. Hosp., N.Y.C.; bd. Nassau Hosp., Mineola, N.Y.; pres. N. Am. Wildlife Found. Served as 1st lt. F.A., Res., 1926-39; lt. comdr. USNR, World War II, 1942-45. Clubs: Brook, Piping Rock, Meadowbrook, DTA, Sommerset, Boston. Home: Village of Old Westbury Nassau County NY 11568 Office: 14 Wall St New York NY 10005

WINTMAN, MELVIN ROBERT, theatre co. exec.; b. Chelsea, Mass., June 28, 1918; s. Hyman A. and Annie (Chansky) W.; student U. Mass., 1935-36; J.D., Northeastern U., 1940; m. Audrey E. Levine, Nov. 21, 1959; children—Alison H., Bruce I. Admitted to Mass. bar, 1940; practiced law, Boston, 1947-48; with Gen. Cinema Corp., 1949—, exec. v.p., 1963—, also dir.; pres. GCC Theatres, Inc., Chestnut Hill, Mass., 1975—; bd. dirs. Will Rogers Meml. Fund. Bd. dirs. NATO, 1969-70. Served as maj., inf., AUS, 1941-46. Decorated Bronze Star with oak leaf cluster. Clubs: Pine Brook Country, Masons. Home: 56 Sevland Rd Newton Centre MA 02159 Office: Box 1000 27 Boylston St Chestnut Hill MA 02167

WINTROBE, MAXWELL MYER, med. educator; b. Halifax, N.S., Can., Oct. 27, 1901; s. Herman and Ethel (Swerling) W.; B.A., U. Man. (Can.), Winnipeg, 1921, M.D., 1926, B.Sc. in Medicine, 1927, D.Sc., 1958; Ph.D., Tulane U., 1929; D.Sc., U. Utah, 1967, Med. Coll. Wis., Milw., 1974; m. Becky Zanphir, Jan. 1, 1928; children—Susan Hope, Paul William H. (dec.). Came to U.S., 1927, naturalized, 1933. Gordon Bell fellow, Manitoba, 1926-27, instr. in medicine Tulane U., 1927-30, also asst. vis. physician Charity Hosp., New Orleans; instr. medicine Johns Hopkins, 1930-35, asso. in medicine, 1935-43, also asso. physician, 1935-43; physician in charge, clinic for nutritional, gastro-intestinal and hemopoietic disorders Johns Hopkins Hosp., 1941-43; prof. medicine U. Utah, 1943-70, Distinguished prof. internal medicine, 1970—, head dept. medicine, 1943-67, dir. cardiovascular research and tng. inst., 1969-73; physician in chief Salt Lake Gen. Hosp., 1943-65, U. Utah Med. Center, 1965-67; cons. to surgeon-gen. U.S. Army; chief cons. Va Hosp., Salt Lake City; dir. lab. for study of hereditary and metabolic disorders U. Utah, 1945-73; spl. cons. nutritional anemias WHO, UN. Council mem. Nat. Adv. Arthritis and Metabolic Diseases Council, USPHS, 1950-54, chmn. hematology study sect., 1956-59, council mem. Nat. Allergy and Infectious Disease Council, 1967-70; mem. com. research in life scis. Nat. Acad. Sci., 1966-69; chmn. sci. adv. bd. Scripps Clinic and Research Found., 1964-74; med. cons. AEC; mem., then chmn. adv. council Life Ins. Med. Research Fund, 1949-53; dir. Am. Soc. Human Genetics, 1948; chmn. hematology com. Research and Devel. Command Surg. Gen.'s U.S. Army; cons. FDA, Dept. Health, Edn. and Welfare; vis. prof. many univs. including Rochester, Vanderbilt, Marquette, N.Y., Tufts, Johns Hopkins, Tulane, U. Calif. at San Diego, Brown U., N.C., Emory, U. Fla., Gainesville, Ala., Southwestern at Dallas, Harvard, UCLA, U. Toronto, McGill U.; Bd. dirs., v.p. Salt Lake Chamber Music Soc.; nat. adv. bd. Utah Symphony Orch., bd. dirs. Pro-Utah. Recipient gold medals, polit. econ. and French, 1921, Isbister prizes, 1920-25 (all U. Man.). Mem. Anti-Anemia Preparations adv. bd., U.S. Pharmacopeia, 1941-49, com. revision, 1950-60. Diplomate Am. Bd. Internal Medicine. Fellow A.C.P. (John Philips Meml. award 1967, master 1973); corr. mem. Italian, Swiss, Brit. Assn. Clin. Pathology, German Soc. for Hematology; mem. Am. Soc. Hematology (pres. 1971-72), AMA (vice chmn. council on drugs, 1964-68, chmn. sect. on adverse reactions), Assn. Am. Physicians (Kober medal 1974, councillor 1957-63, pres. 1964-65), Assn. Profs. Medicine (Robert H. Williams award 1973, councillor 1962-63, pres. 1965-66), Western Assn. Physicians (pres. 1956-57), Am. Soc. Exptl. Pathology, AAAS, Nat. Acad. Scis. (com. on sci. and public policy), Soc. Exptl. Biology and Medicine, Leukemia Soc. (chmn. nat. med. adv. bd.), Pacific Interurban Clin. Club, Western Soc. Clin. Research (Mayo Soley award 1970), European (corr.), Internat. (councillor-at-large 1972-74, pres. 1976-78, Ferrata award Rome 1958) socs. hematology, Harvey Soc. (hon.), Assn. Clin. Pathologists (Eng.) (corr.), Am. Fedn. Clin. Research, Phi Beta Kappa (hon.), Sigma Xi, Sigma Alpha Mu. Mng. editor Bull. Johns Hopkins Hosp., 1942-43; asso. editor Nutrition Revs., Boston, 1943-49; adv. editor Tice Practice of Medicine, 1943-76; asso. editor Internat. Med. Digest, 1944- 58, Blood, 1945-75, Am. Jour. Medicine, 1946-56, Medicine, Cancer, Jour. Clin. Pathology; editorial bd. Jour. Clin. Investigation, 1948-49, Gen. Practitioner 1949-59, Jour. Clin. Nutrition, 1952-65, Jour. Chronic Diseases, 1955—. Author: Clinical Hematology, 1942, 7th edit., 1974; also numerous sci. articles. Editor: Harrison's Principles of Internal Medicine, 1950, editor-in-chief, 6th edit., 1970, 7th edit., 1974. Home: 5882 Brentwood Dr Salt Lake City UT 84121 Office: U Utah Med Center Salt Lake City UT 84132. *Never guess, secure the facts; measure rather than estimate; differentiate fact from hypothesis. Whatever one undertakes should receive one's best efforts, without consideration of reward other than the satisfaction of a job well done.*

WINWAR, FRANCES (FRANCESCA VINCIGUERRA), novelist, literary critic; b. Taormina, Sicily, May 3, 1900; d. Domenico and Giovanna (Sciglio) Vinciguerra; brought to U.S., 1907, naturalized, 1929; ed. Hunter Coll., New York, Coll. City of N.Y., and Columbia U.; m. Bernard D.N. Grebanier, Sept. 22, 1925 (div.); 1 son, Francis Grebanier. Contbr. The Freeman, 1923; book reviewer for Laurence Stallings in The World, 1923-25; co-founder Leonardo da Vinci Art Sch., New York, 1923, exec. sec., 1923-30; lectured on Victorian lit. figures, 1934-36; novelist and biographer since 1927. Visiting prof. U. of Kansas City (Mo.), 1942. Awarded Atlantic Monthly $5,000 nonfiction prize for biography, "Poor Splendid Wings," 1933. Mem. Poetry Soc. Am. Democrat. Author, 1927—; (biography) The Immortal Lovers; Elizabeth Barrett and Robert Browning, 1950; The Eagle and The Rook, 1953; The Last Love of Camille, 1954; Wingless Victory, 1956; The Haunted Palace; Edgar Allan Poe, 1959; Jean Jacquès Rouseau; Conscience of an Era, 1961; Up from Caesar, 1965. Translator: Don Carlo, Lucia di Lammermoor, LaTraviata, 1950; Boccoccio's Decameron, 1930, Modern Library edit., 1956. Contbr. to nat. mags. Home: PO Box 1267 Jensen Beach FL 33457 Office: Harper & Bros 10 E 53d St New York City NY 10022

WINZENRIED, JESSE DAVID, petroleum co. exec.; b. Byron, Wyo., June 13, 1922; s. Fritz and Margaret Ann (Smith) W.; B.S., U. Wyo., 1945; M.S., U. Denver, 1946; Ph.D., N.Y. U., N.Y.C., 1955; m. Marion Suzan Jacobson, Mar. 15, 1945; children—Suzan (Mrs. Richard Glen Carlston), Jay Albert, Keith Frederic. Dir. research Tax Found., N.Y.C., 1947-56; sr. v.p. Husky Oil Ltd., Cody, Wyo., 1956-65, Calgary, Alta., Can., 1965-67; v.p. firm Booz, Allen & Hamilton, Cleve., 1968-69; v.p. Coastal States Gas Corp., Houston, 1969-74; group v.p. Crown Central Petroleum Corp., Balt., 1974—. Lectr. mgmt. N.Y. U., 1955-56. Served with USAAF, 1942-43. Republican. Mem. Ch. of Jesus Christ of Latter-day Saints. Contbr. articles to profl. jours. Office: 1 N Charles St Baltimore MD 21203

WIOT, JEROME FRANCIS, radiologist; b. Cin., Aug. 24, 1927; s. Daniel and Elvera (Weisgerber) W.; M.D., U. Cin., 1953; m. Andrea Kockritz, July 29, 1972; children—J. Geoffrey, Jason. Intern, Cin. Gen. Hosp., 1953-54, resident, 1954-55, 58-59; gen. practice medicine, Wyoming, Ohio, 1955-57; mem. faculty U. Cin., 1959-67, 68—, prof., chmn. radiology, 1973—; practice medicine specializing in radiology, Tampa, Fla., 1967-68. Served with USN, 1945-46. Diplomate Am. Bd. Radiology (trustee, treas.). Fellow Am. Coll. Radiology (chmn. commn. on diagnostic radiology); mem. Radiol. Soc. N.Am., Am. Roentgen Ray Soc., Ohio Med. Assn., Cin. Acad. Medicine, Radiol. Soc. Greater Cin., Ohio Radiol. Soc., Ohio Thoracic Soc., Fleischner Soc., Soc. Gastrointestinal Radiologists. Contbr. articles to med. jours. Home: 7900 Indian Hill Rd Cincinnati OH 45243 Office: U Cin 234 Goodman St Cincinnati OH 45267

WIRE, WILLIAM SHIDAKER, II, apparel co. exec.; b. Cin., Jan. 5, 1932; s. William Shidaker and Gladys (Buckmaster) W.; student U. of South, 1950; A.B., U. Ala., 1954, J.D., 1956; LL.M., N.Y. U., 1957; m. Alice Dumas Jones, Aug. 31, 1957; children—Alice Jones, Deborah Buckmaster. Admitted to Ala. bar, 1956; atty. Hamilton, Denniston, Butler & Riddick, Mobile, 1959-60; with Talladega Ins. Agy. (Ala.), 1961-62; with Genesco, Inc., Nashville, 1962—, now v.p. fin., chief fin. officer. Served with USAF, 1957-59. Mem. Fin. Execs. Inst., Nashville Com. on Fgn. Relations, Kappa Alpha. Presbyterian. Clubs: Belle Meade Country, Hillwood Country (Nashville); Cumberland. Home: 6119 Stonehaven Dr Nashville TN 37215 Office: Geneseo Park Nashville TN 37202

WIRGES, MANFORD FRANK, energy resource co. exec.; b. Beatrice, Nebr., Jan. 18, 1925; s. Frank Jessie and Leta Irene (Coon) W.; B.S. in Chem. Engring., U. Okla., 1943, M.S., 1945; m. Joan Audrey Kelly, Sept. 3, 1949; 1 dau., Kelly Marie. With Cities Service Co., 1946—, mgr. corporate planning, then v.p. research and corporate planning, Tulsa, 1965-72, v.p. research and tech. div., 1972—; pres. Cities Service Research & Devel. Co.; adv. bd. Coll. Engring., U. Tulsa. Adv. bd. St. John Med. Center, Tulsa. Standard Oil Devel. Co. fellow, 1944-45. Mem. Am. Inst. Chem. Engrs., Am. Petroleum Inst., Inst. Mgmt. Scis., 25 Year Club Petroleum Industry. Club: Summit. Home: 3208 E 69th St Tulsa OK 74136 Office: Box 300 Tulsa OK 74102

WIRSIG, WOODROW, bus. exec.; b. Spokane, Wash., June 28, 1916; s. Otto Alan and Beulah Juliet (Marohn) W.; student Kearney (Nebr.) State Tchrs. Coll., Los Angeles City Coll., UCLA, 1933-39; B.A., Occidental Coll., 1941; M.S., Columbia, 1942; m. Jane Barbara Dealy, Dec. 11, 1942; children—Alan Robert, Guy Rodney, Paul Harold. Dir. Occidental Coll. News Bur., 1939-41; radio newswriter WQXR, N.Y.C., 1941-42, news writer, propaganda analyst CBS, 1942-43; rewrite man Los Angeles Times, 1943-44; asst. editor This Week mag., 1944-45; staff writer Look mag., 1946, asst. mng. editor, 1946-49, exec. editor, 1950-52; mng. editor Quick mag., 1949-50; asso. editor Newsweek mag., Ladies' Home Jour., 1952; editor Woman's Home Companion, 1952-56; editorial cons. Ednl. Testing Service, Princeton, 1957-67; television cons. NBC-TV, ABC-TV; creator Nat. Daytime Radio Programs, 1957-60, radio documentary Companion; pres. communications firm Wirsig, Gordon and O'Connor, Inc., 1956-58; editor Printers' Ink mag., N.Y.C., 1958-65, Salesweek mag., 1959-60; editorial dir. Overseas Press Club ann. mag. Dateline, 1961, 62; creator, editorial dir. Calif. Life mag.; pres. Better Bus. Bur. Met. N.Y., Inc., 1966-77, also pres. Edn. Research Found.; pres. Bus. Advocacy Center, Inc., 1977—. Cons. to Office Sec. HEW, 1965-66. Recipient gold medal Benjamin Franklin Mag. Awards, 1956. Mem. Soc. Consumer Affairs Profls. (v.p.), Newcomen Soc., Sigma Delta Chi, Phi Gamma Delta, Gamma Delta Upsilon, Archons. Democrat. Presbyterian. Clubs: Players; Overseas Press; Nat. Press; N.Y. Advt.; City (N.Y.C.); Springdale Country (Princeton); University. Editor, contbr. Your Diabetes (Dr. Herbert Pollack), 1951. Editor: Advertising: Today-Yesterday-Tomorrow; New Products Marketing. Cons. editor: Principles of Advertising. Contbr. nat. mags.; lectr.; syndicated columnist Los Angeles Times, other newspapers, 1964-65. Home: 25 Gordon Way Queenston Common Princeton NJ 08540 Office: 404 Park Ave S New York NY 10016

WIRSZUP, IZAAK, educator, mathematician; b. Wilno, Poland, Jan. 5, 1915; s. Samuel and Pera (Golomb) W.; came to U.S., 1949, naturalized, 1955; Magister of Philosophy in Math., U. Wilno, 1939; Ph.D. in Math., U. Chgo., 1955; m. Pera Poswianska, Apr. 23, 1949; 1 dau. Marina (Mrs. Arnold M. Tatar). Lectr. math. Tech. Inst. Wilno, 1939-41; dir. Bur. d'Études et de Statistiques Spéciales, Société Centrale d'Achat-Société Anonyme des Monoprix, Paris, France, 1946-49; mem. faculty U. Chgo., 1949—, prof. math., 1965—. Cons. Ford Found., Colombia, Peru, 1965, 66, Sch. Math. Study Group, 1960, 61, 66-68; participant, writer tchr. tng. material African Math. Program, Entebbe, Uganda, summer 1964, Mombasa, Kenya, summers 1965, 66; asso. dir. Survey Recent E. European Math. Lit., 1956-68, dir., 1968—, dir. NSF program application computers to mgmt., 1976—. Cons. NSF-AID Sci. Edn. Program, India, 1969; mem. U.S. Commn. on Math. Instn., 1969-73. Recipient Lewellyn John and Harriet Manchester Quantrell award U. Chgo., 1958; resident master Woodward Ct., U. Chgo., 1971—. Mem. N.Y. Acad. Scis., Am. Math. Soc., Math. Assn. Am., Nat. Council Tchrs. Math. (chmn. com. internat. math. edn. 1967-69). Contbr. articles to profl. jours. Editor math. books, transls., adaptions from Russian. Adviser math. Ency. Brit., 1971—. Home: 5825 Woodlawn Ave Chicago IL 60637 Office: Dept Math U Chgo 5734 University Ave Chicago IL 60637

WIRT, FREDERICK MARSHALL, polit. scientist; b. Radford, Va., July 27, 1924; s. Harry Johnson, Sr., and Goldie (Turpin) W.; B.A., DePauw U., 1948; M.A., Ohio State U., 1949, Ph.D., 1956; m. Elizabeth Cook, Sept. 5, 1947; children—Leslie Lee, Sandra Sue, Wendy Ann. Instr. to prof. polit. sci. Denison U., Granville, Ohio, 1952-66; vis. prof., lectr. U. Calif., Berkeley, 1966-68, 69-72; dir. policy scis. grad. program U. Md. Balt. County, 1972-75; prof. polit. sci. U. Ill., Urbana, 1975—; dir. Inst. for Desegregation Problems, U. Calif., Berkeley, 1970-72; cons. Motion Picture Assn. Am., Rand Corp., Stanford Research Inst., Ill. Office Edn., State U. N.Y. Sch. Edn. Albany; vis. prof. U. Rochester, U. Calif. Berkeley, Nova U. Mem. Granville City Charter Commn., 1964. Grantee Am. Philos. Soc., Denison Research Assn., U. Ill. Research Bd., Nat. Endowment Humanities, Ford Found. Mem. Am. Polit. Sci. Assn. (nat. council), Midwestern Polit. Sci. Assn., Am. Ednl. Research Assn., Policy Studies Orgn., Law and Soc. Assn. Author: Politics of Southern Equality, 1970 (hon. mention for best book 1972); Power in the City, 1974; (with others) Political Web of American Schools, 1972, On the CitV's Rim, 1972. Editor: The Polity of the School, 1975; (with others) Political Science and School Politics, 1977. Home: 2018 Zuppke Circle Urbana IL 61801 Office: Dept of Political Science University of Illinois Urbana IL 61801

WIRT, ROBERT DUANE, educator; b. Whittier, Calif., Apr. 28, 1924; s. Duane Arthur and Helen (Brennan) W.; A.A., Los Angeles City Coll., 1942; B.A., U. Calif., Berkeley, 1948; M.A., Stanford U., 1951, Ph.D., 1952; m. Anne Louise Antelman, Feb. 19, 1955 (div. May 1972); 1 dau., Elizabeth Anne. Asst. dir., instr. psychol. clinic, Stanford U., Palo Alto, Calif., 1952-53; asst. prof. psychology, child devel., psychiatry U. Minn., Mpls., 1954-58; asso. prof., 1958-61, prof., 1961—, dir. tng. clin. child psychology, 1954-71, dir. clin. psychology tng. program, 1962-71, dir. div. health care psychology, 1971—, coordinator edn. in psychiatry Health Scis. Center, 1971—; chief psychologist Twin Cities Psychiat. and Psychol. Services, Mpls., 1958—; cons. Minn. Dept. Corrections, St. Paul, Minn. Dept. Edn., Minn. Dept. Pub. Welfare, Minn. VA, Mpls., Mpls. pub. schs. Chmn. Minn. Mental Health Advisory Council, 1964—; mem. Gov.'s Crime Commn., 1967—. Served to capt. USMCR, 1942-47, 51-52. Diplomate Bd. Examiners in Profl. Psychology. Fellow Am. Psychol. Assn., AAAS; mem. Minn. Psychol. Assn., Soc. for Research in Child Devel., Sigma Xi. Author: (with W.E. Broen) Personality Inventory for Children, 1958; (with W.Simon) Differential Treatment and Prognosis in Schizophrenia, 1959; (with James L. Jacobson) The Men in Prison in Minnesota, 1966; con[: tbr. articles to profl. jours. Home: 2615 Irving Ave S Minneapolis MN 55408 Office: Health Scis Center U Minn Minneapolis MN 55455

WIRTH, JOHN D(AVIS), historian; b. Dawson, N.Mex., June 17, 1936; B.A. magna cum laude, Harvard Coll., 1958; spl. student for inter-disciplinary subjects Columbia U. Latin Am. Center, 1963-64; Ph.D. in Latin Am. History (Ella Moore Shiel fellow 1962-63, Fgn. Area fellow 1963-65), Stanford U., 1966; m. Nancy Meem; 3 sons. Tchr. history Putney (Vt.) Sch., 1959-61; asst. prof. history Stanford U., 1965-72, asso. prof., 1972-78, prof., 1978—, vice chmn. dept. history, 1972-74, dir. Center Latin Am. Studies, 1975—; mem. screening com. Fulbright-Hayes Program, Office Edn., 1976; chmn. coordinating com. Intercollegiate Study Program in Brazil, 1978—; Albert Bildner grantee, lectr. Am. Schs. in South Am., 1978. Bd. dirs. Pan Am. Soc. San Francisco, 1979—. Served with U.S. Army, 1958-59. HEW Center-Faculty (Fulbright) fellow, 1967; Social Sci. Research Council grantee, 1968-70, summer 1972; Center for Research in Internat. Studies at Stanford U. grantee, 1969-70. Mem. Conf. Latin Am. History (sec. com. Brazilian history 1975, chmn. com. Brazilian history 1975), Latin Am. Studies Assn. (exec. council 1979-80). Author: The Politics of Brazilian Development, 1930-1954, 1970 (Conf. Latin Am. History Bolton Meml. prize 1971, Pacific Coast Council on Latin Am. Studies prize 1971); Minas Gerais in the Brazilian Federation, 1889-1937, 1977 (Bolton Meml. prize hon. mention 1978); editor: (with Robert L. Jones) Manchester and Sao Paulo: Problems of Rapid Urban Growth, 1978. Bd. editors Hispanic Am. Hist. Rev. Home: 37 Park Dr Atherton CA 94025 Office: Center Latin Am Studies Bolivar House Stanford U Stanford CA 94305

WIRTH, THEODORE JULIAN, landscape architect; b. New Orleans, July 8, 1927; s. Conrad Louis and Helen Agustus (Olson) W.; B.S. in Landscape Architecture, Iowa State U., 1950; m. Glorianne Swanson, Aug. 28, 1954; children—Cheryl Anne, Theodore Jay. Park planner Ky. Park Div., Frankfort, 1950-51; landscape architect Midwest region U.S. Nat. Park Service, Omaha, 1951-54, Grand Teton Nat. Park, Wyo., 1954-58, Yellowstone Nat. Park, Wyo, 1959-61; pres. Wirth Assos., Planning Design Cons., Billings, Mont., 1961—; pres.-elect Council of Park and Recreation Consultants. Registered landscape architect. Fellow Am. Soc. Landscape Architects (v.p.); mem. Nat. Recreation and Park Assn. Episcopalian. Home: 2445 Teton Ave Billings MT 59102 Office: 1739 Grand Ave Billings MT 59102

WIRTH, TIMOTHY ENDICOTT, Congressman; b. Santa Fe, Sept. 22, 1939; s. Cecil and Virginia Maude (Davis) W.; B.A., Harvard U., 1961, M.Ed., 1964; Ph.D., Stanford U., 1973; m. Wren Winslow, Nov. 26, 1965; children—Christopher, Kelsey. White House fellow, spl. asst. to sec. HEW, Washington, 1967; asst. to chmn. Nat. Urban Coalition, Washington, 1968; dep. asst. sec. for edn. HEW, Washington, 1969; v.p. Great Western United Corp., Denver, 1970; mgr. Rocky Mountain office Arthur D. Little, Inc., cons. firm, Denver, 1971-73; mem. 94th-96th congresses from 2d Dist. Colo., mem. interstate and fgn. commerce com., sci. and tech. com., budget com. Mem. Gov.'s Task Force on Returned Vietnam Vets., 1970-73; trustee Planned Parenthood, Denver Head Start. Ford Found. fellow, 1964-66. Mem. White House Fellows Assn. (pres. 1968-69), Denver Council Fgn. Relations (exec. com. 1974-75). Home: 3215 35th St NW Washington DC 20016 Office: 312 Cannon House Office Bldg Washington DC 20515

WIRTH, WILLARD RALPH, JR., advt. exec.; b. New Orleans, July 9, 1930; s. Willard Ralph and Ethel (Kehoe) W.; B.A., Yale, 1952; M.B.A., Harvard, 1956; m. Marnee Van Vlaanderen, Oct. 19, 1962; children—Thomas Ewing, Marnee Wendel. With McCann-Erickson Advt., N.Y.C., 1956-59; with Foote, Cone & Belding Advt., Inc., N.Y.C., 1960—, sr. v.p., gen. mgr., after 1969, now exec. v.p. Served to lt. USNR, 1952-54. Clubs: Sky (N.Y.C.); Racquet, Saddle and Cycle (Chgo.); Glen View (Ill.). Home: 1555 Astor St Chicago IL 60610 Office: 401 N Michigan Ave Chicago IL 60611

WIRTH, WILLIAM COLLINS, ins. co. exec.; b. Elmira, N.Y., Mar. 10, 1923; s. Chauncey Martin and Winifred (Collins) W.; A.B., Syracuse U., 1947; m. Constance Crowe, Dec. 21, 1946; 1 dau., Judith Ann Williams. Actuarial asst. Conn. Gen. Life Ins. Co., 1947-53; asst. actuary Life Ins. Co. of Va., Richmond, 1953-55, asso. actuary, 1955-56, mgr. pension div., 1956, 2d v.p. group ins. and pension dept., 1956-66, v.p. group ins. and pension dept., 1966-72, sr. v.p., 1972-79; exec. v.p. Continental Fin. Services Co., Richmond, 1980—. Served with USAAF, 1943-46. C.L.U. Fellow Soc. Actuaries; mem. Am. Acad. Actuaries, Va., Richmond chambers commerce. Presbyterian. Club: Willow Oaks Country (Richmond). Home: 206 Seneca Rd Richmond VA 23226 Office: 6610 W Broad St Richmond VA 23230

WIRTHLIN, DAVID BITNER, hosp. adminstr.; b. Salt Lake City, Sept. 19, 1935; s. Joseph L. and Madeline (Bitner) W.; B.S. in Bus. Adminstrn. cum laude, U. Utah, 1960; M.H.A., U. Minn., 1963; m. Anne Goalen, Apr. 26, 1961; children—Kimberly, Jennifer, David, Deborah, John, Marianne. Asst. adminstr. Idaho Falls (Idaho) Latter Day Saints Hosp., 1963-66; asst. to adminstr. Latter Day Saints Hosp., Salt Lake City, 1966-67, 1st asst. adminstr., 1967-70, asso. adminstr., 1970-73, adminstr., 1973—, adminstr. Primary Children's Med. Center, 1973-75; trustee Utah State Hosps.; mem. rev. com. Great Salt Lake Health Planning Agy., 1974; mem. Comprehensive Health Planning Rev. Com., 1975; chmn. Met. Hosp. Council, 1975; mem. bd. Utah Profl. Rev., 1975-77. Fellow Am. Coll. Hosp. Adminstrs.; mem. Am., Utah (past pres.) hosp. assns., Western Assn. Hosps., Council Teaching Hosps. Republican. Mormon. Clubs: Kiwanis, Timpanogos. Home: 2757 Saint Marys Way Salt Lake City UT 84108 Office: 325 8th Ave Salt Lake City UT 84143

WIRTHS, THEODORE WILLIAM, govt. ofcl.; b. Ansonia, Conn., June 23, 1924; s. Theodore Eugene and Elizabeth (McLean) W.; B.A., Yale, 1947; M.A., U. Ky., 1949; postgrad. U. N.C., 1948-51; m. Claudine Turner Gibson, Dec. 28, 1945; children—William M., David G. Teaching fellow U. N.C., 1949-50, field dir. urban studies, 1951-53; with AEC, 1953-66, chief reports and emergency planning Savannah River Ops., Aiken, S.C., 1960-62, real estate officer, Washington, 1962-64, planning officer, 1964-65; Congl. fellow, 1965-66; congl. liaison officer NSF, Washington, 1966-70, dep. for govt. liaison, 1970-73, dir. Office of Govt. and Pub. Programs, 1973-76, dir. Office Small Bus. Research and Devel., 1976—. Chmn. Aiken Zoning Bd. Adjustment, 1956-62. Served with AUS, 1943-45. Recipient Meritorious Service award NSF, 1970. Mem. AAAS, Am. Acad. Polit. and Social Sci. Episcopalian. Author: (with Chapin, Gould and Denton) In the Shadow of a Defense Plant, 1954. Home: 1715 Wilmart St Rockville MD 20852 Office: 1800 G St NW Washington DC 20550

WIRTS, CHARLES WILMER, JR., physician; b. Pitts., June 12, 1907; s. Charles Wilmer and Marie Fredericka (Kimmel) W.; grad. Mercersburg (Pa.) Acad., 1926; B.S., Lafayette Coll., 1930; M.D., Jefferson Med. Coll., 1934; m. Jessie G. Bayliss, May 5, 1938; children—Leslie G., Steven B. Intern St. Johns Hosp., Pitts., 1934-35; resident St. Francis Hosp., Pitts., 1934-35; resident St. Francis Hosp., Pitts., 1935-36, Am. Hosp., Paris, France, 1937-38; Ross V. Patterson fellow gastroenterology Jefferson Med. Coll., 1940-42; asso. prof. medicine Jefferson Med. Coll. and Hosp., 1932-62, prof. medicine, 1970—, head div. gastroenterology, 1946-71; attending physician Jefferson Hosp., Phila., 1939—; cons. gastroenterology USAH Hosp., Ft. Dix, N.J., VA Hosp., Phila. Mem. examing bd. Subspeciality Bd. Gastroenterology, 1956-62. Served from capt. to lt. col. M.C., AUS, World War II. Diplomate Am. Bd. Internal Medicine and Gastroenterology. Fellow A.C.P.; mem. Phila. Med. Soc. (dir. Postgrad. Inst. 1957-59), AMA, Phila. Coll. Physicians, Am. Fedn. Clin. Investigation, Am. Gastroent. Assn., Am. Gastroscopic Soc. (pres. 1959), Am. Coll. Gastroenterology (pres. 1957-58, chmn. bd. 1958), N.Y. Acad. Sci., Alpha Omega Alpha. Mem. Evang. Luth. Ch. (council holy communion 1950-52, 55-57, 60-63). Contbr. articles to profl. jours., textbooks. Home: 2017 Delancey St Philadelphia PA 19103

WIRTZ, ARTHUR MICHAEL, corp. ofcl., bus. exec.; b. Chgo., Jan. 23, 1901; s. Frederick C. and Leona (Miller) W.; B.A., U. Mich., 1922; m. Virginia Wadsworth, Mar. 1, 1926; children—Cynthia, William, Arthur Michael, Elizabeth V. Founder, chmn., chief exec. officer Wirtz Corp., realtors, Chgo.; founder, chmn., chief exec. officer Consol. Enterprises, Inc., Chgo., also an officer, dir. controlled and affiliated cos.; chmn., chief exec. officer Chgo. Milw. Corp.; chmn. Griggs-Cooper & Co., Inc., St. Paul, Rathjen, San Francisco, 1st Nat. Bank of South Miami (Fla.), Chgo. Stadium Corp., Chgo. Blackhawk Hockey Team, Inc.; founder, chmn. bd., chief exec. officer Wirtz Prodns. Inc., internat. ice shows; chmn. Standard Theatres, Inc., Milw.; dir. Longhorn Liquors, Inc., Arlington, Tex. Mem. bd. Met. Fair and Expn. Authority, operators McCormick Pl. Chgo.; trustee, pres. Chgo. Urban Transp. Dist. Mem. Hockey Hall of Fame; recipient Man of Year award Chgo. Boys' Clubs, 1977. Clubs: Knollwood Country; Racquet, Chgo. Athletic, Saddle and Cycle, Tavern, Chgo. Yacht (Chgo.). Home: 1420 Lake Shore Dr Chicago IL 60610 Office: 666 Lake Shore Dr Chicago IL 60611

WIRTZ, CABLE AMBROSE, former lawyer; b. Honolulu, May 9, 1910; s. Ambrose J. and Mary Emma (Meyer) W.; A.B., Santa Clara U., 1932; LL.B., Harvard U., 1935, J.D., 1970; m. Margaret Virginia Hughes, June 17, 1937; children—Richard Paul, Sheila Marie. Admitted to Hawaii bar, 1935; with firm Smith, Wild, Beebe & Cades, Honolulu, 1935-39; dep. city and county atty., Honolulu, 1939-42, city and county atty., 1942-44; judge Circuit Ct. 2d Jud. Circuit, 1944-51, 56-59; dist. magistrate Hana, Maui, 1954-56; asso. justice Supreme Ct. of Hawaii, 1959-67; pvt. practice law, Wailuku, Maui, 1951-56, 68-79, Honolulu, 1968-73; mem. firm Wooddell Mukai, Wirtz Ichiki & Whitfield, 1968-73; of counsel to Mukai, Ichiki, Raffeto & MacMillan, 1974-79. Mem. Territorial Commn. on Children and Youth, 1949-54, Maui Commn. on Children and Youth, 1949-54, Territorial Loyalty Bd., 1951-57, Hawaii Aero. Commn., 1953-56; chmn. Maui Cath. Bd. Edn., 1968-69; arbitrator labor disputes. Del. Constl. Conv., 1950. Bd. dirs. Ka Lima O'Maui (Rehab. Center). Mem. Am. Judicature Soc., Inst. Jud. Adminstrn., Am., Hawaii, Maui County (pres. 1970-71, bd. ethics) bar assns., Maui C. of C. (dir. 1971-74), Harvard Law Sch. Assn., Santa Clara Alumni Assn., Maui County Fair and Racing Assn., Maui Hist. Soc., Polynesian Voyaging Soc., Hawaiian Ry. Soc. Clubs: Harvard (Hawaii); Maui Rotary. Home: 446 S Alu Rd PO Box 1013 Wailuku HI 96793

WIRTZ, WILLEM KINDLER, garden and lighting designer, pub. relations counsel; b. N.Y.C., Jan. 8, 1912; s.. Carel Augustus Marie and Wilhelmina Johanetta (Kindler) W.; ed. Ethical Culture Sch., N.Y.C., also Inst. Musical Art, N.Y.C. Dir. exhibits service Pa. Art Program, 1937-42, pub. relations dir., 1937-42; partner Campbell-Wirtz Assos., Phila., 1942-51; pres. Willem Wirtz Assos., Phila., 1952—; founder, 1961, since pres. Willem Wirtz Garden Assos., Inc., also subsidiary div. Contemporary Plantings Unltd.; design asso. Am. Soc. Interior Decorators; dir. Am. Jour. Nursing Co., also chmn. Pa. bull. award com., 1964; guest lectr. Charles Morris Price Sch., Phila.; pres. Phila. chpt. Am. Pub. Relations Assn., 1954-56, nat. sec., 1955-57, Eastern v.p., 1960. Mem. Nat. Assn. Pub. Relations Counsel (dir.), Pub. Relations Soc. Am. (v.p. 1961, assembly del. 1961-63). Pa. Hort. Soc., Phila. Art Alliance, Zool. Soc. Palm Beaches (sec. 1971), Netherlands-Am. Soc., Soc. of Four Arts. Club: Pen and Pencil (Phila.). Home: 2405 Panama Ct Philadelphia PA 19103 Office: 228 Phipps Plaza Palm Beach FL 33480 Office: 326 S 24th St Philadelphia PA 19103

WIRTZ, WILLIAM WADSWORTH, corp. exec.; b. Chgo., Oct. 5, 1929; s. Arthur Michael and Virginia (Wadsworth) W.; A.B., Brown U., 1950; m. Joan Roney, Dec. 15, 1950; children—William R., Gail W., Karen K., Peter R., Alison M. Pres. Am. Furniture Mart, Chgo., 1965—, Chgo. Blackhawk Hockey Team, Inc., 1966—, Chgo. Stadium Corp., 1966—, Consol. Enterprises, Inc., Chgo., 1966—. First Security Trust and Savs. Bank, Elmwood Park, Ill., 1960—, Forman Realty Corp., Chgo., 1965—, 333 Building Corp., Chgo., 1966—, Wirtz Corp., Chgo., 1964—. Clubs: Saddle and Cycle, Racquet, Mid-America (Chgo.); Fin and Feather (Elgin, Ill.). Home: Winnetka IL Office: 666 Lake Shore Dr Chicago IL 60611*

WIRTZ, WILLIAM WILLARD, lawyer; b. DeKalb, Ill., Mar. 14, 1912; s. William Wilbur and Alpha Belle (White) W.; ed. No. Ill. State Teachers Coll., DeKalb, Ill., 1928-30, U. Calif. at Berkeley, 1930-31; A.B., Beloit Coll., 1933; LL.B., Harvard 1937; m. Mary Jane Quisenberry, Sept. 8, 1936; children—Richard, Philip. Instr., Kewanee (Ill.) High Sch., 1933-34, U. Iowa, 1937-39; asst. prof. Sch. Law, Northwestern U., 1939-42; asst. gen. counsel Bd. Econ. Warfare, 1942-43; with War Labor Bd., 1943-45, gen. counsel and pub. mem., 1945; chmn. Nat. Wage Stblzn. Bd., 1946; prof. law Northwestern U., 1946-54; engaged law practice, 1955-61; sec. of labor Dept. Labor, 1962-69; now partner Wirtz and Lapointe, Washington. Mem. Ill. Liquor Control Commn., 1950-56. Mem. Nat. Acad. Arbitrators, Am., Ill. bar assns., Phi Beta Kappa, Beta Theta Pi, Delta Sigma Rho. Office: 1211 Connecticut Ave NW Washington DC 20036

WISBAUM, WAYNE DAVID, lawyer; b. Niagara Falls, N.Y., May 29, 1935; s. Franklin C. and Elizabeth (Boff) W.; B.A., Cornell U., 1956; LL.B., Harvard U., 1959; m. Janet Katz, July 3, 1960; children—Karen, Wendy, Deborah. Admitted to N.Y. bar, 1960; asso. firm Kavinoky, Cook, Hepp, Sandler, Gardner & Wisbaum, Buffalo, 1960-66, partner, 1966—; of counsel firm Smith, Mandler, Spivak, Parker & Werner, Miami Beach, Fla., mem. adv. com. Abstract Title div. Title Guarantee Co.; dir. Kleinhans Music Hall Mgmt. Inc. Pres., Buffalo Council on World Affairs, 1968-70; mem. Young Leadership Cabinet Nat. United Jewish Appeal, 1967-73; mem. com. on leadership devel. Nat. Council Jewish Fedn. and Welfare Funds, 1967—; mem. Mayor's Com. on Youth Opportunity; bd. dirs. Anti-Defamation League; mem. Council Internat. Studies, SUNY, Buffalo; chmn. Buffalo chpt. Am. Jewish Com.; treas. Buffalo Fedn. Jewish Philanthropies; bd. govs. United Jewish Fedn., Buffalo; bd. dirs., v.p. Buffalo Philharm. Orch. Soc.; bd. dirs., pres.-elect Jewish Family Service of Erie County. Served to capt. U.S. Army, 1964. Recipient United Jewish Fedn. Buffalo Leadership award, 1967. Mem. Am. Bar Assn., N.Y. State Bar Assn. (chmn. com. lawyers title guaranty funds), Erie County Bar Assn., Am. Law Inst., Harvard Law Sch. Assn. Western N.Y. (sec.), Zool. Soc. Buffalo (dir., mem. exec. com.), Zeta Beta Tau. Club: Harvard (pres.)(Buffalo). Home: 180 Greenaway Rd Eggertsville NY 14226 Office: 120 Delaware Ave Buffalo NY 14202

WISCHNER, GEORGE JOSEPH, educator, psychologist; b. N.Y.C., Apr. 14, 1914; s. Morris L. and Esther (Goldfarb) W.; B.A. cum Laude, Bklyn. Coll., 1938; M.A., State U. Iowa, 1941, Ph.D., 1947; m. Sary Kadis, Sept. 16, 1947 (div. 1965); children—Cathy Evian, Claudia March, m. 2d, Mary Ellen Gerlach-Carder, 1972. Area supr., state supr. Iowa Remedial Edn. Survey, 1940-42; asst. prof., psychologist student health service U. Mo., 1947-48; asst. prof. child psychology Iowa Child Welfare Research Sta., State U. Iowa, 1948-49; asst. prof. psychology, speech U. Ill., 1949-52; project leader tng. methods div. Human Resources Research Office, George Washington U., 1952-53, dir. research, 1953-55; prof. psychology U. Pitts., 1955-72; prof., chmn. Cleve. State U., 1972-79, prof. emeritus, 1979—, interim dir. Office of Research Services, 1979—; psychol. cons. VA, 1955—. Served with USAAF, 1942-46. Fellow Am. Speech and Hearing Assn. (councilor 1966-68, exec. com. 1968), Am. (mem. council of reps. 1967—), Pa. (pres. 1964-65) psychol. assns., AAAS; mem. Midwestern, Eastern psychol. assns., Psychonomic Soc., Sigma Xi. Adv. editor Jour. Cons. Psychology, 1955-58; asso. editor Perceptual Motor Skills, 1959—; editorial cons. Jour. Speech and Hearing Disorders, 1962—. Contbr. to books, and profl. jours. Home: 6280-301 Greenwood Pkwy Sagamore Hills OH 44067

WISDOM, JOHN MINOR, judge; b. New Orleans, May 17, 1905; s. Mortimer Norton and Adelaide (Labatt) W.; A.B., Washington and Lee U., 1925; LL.B., Tulane U., 1929, LL.D., 1976; LL.D., Oberlin U., 1963, San Diego U., 1979; m. Bonnie Stewart Mathews, Oct. 24, 1931; children—John Minor, Kathleen Mathews, Penelope Stewart Wisdom Tase. Admitted to La. bar, 1929; mem. firm Wisdom, Stone, Pigman & Benjamin, New Orleans, 1929-57; judge U.S. Ct. of Appeals, 5th Circuit, 1957—, mem. Multi-Dist. Litigation Panel, 1968-79, chmn., 1975-79, mem. Spl. Ct. Regional Reorgn. of R.R.'s, 1975—. Adj. prof. law Tulane U., 1938-57. Mem. Pres.'s Com. on Govt. Contracts, 1953-57; past pres. New Orleans Council Social Agys. Republican nat. committeeman for La., 1952-57, mem. exec. com. Trustee Washington and Lee U., 1953—. Served from capt. to lt. col. USAAF, 1942-46. Decorated Legion of Merit; Army Commendation medal. Mem. Am. Acad. Arts and Scis., Am. (chmn. appellate judges conf.), La., New Orleans bar assns., Am. Law Inst. (mem. council), La. Law Inst., Order of Coif, Delta Kappa Epsilon, Phi Alpha Delta, Omicron Delta Kappa. Episcopalian. Clubs: Boston, Louisiana (New Orleans); Metropolitan (Washington). Office: 600 Camp St New Orleans LA 70130

WISE, BILL MCFARLAND, govt. ofcl.; b. Shawnee, Okla., Nov. 1, 1936; s. William R. and Inez (McFarland) W.; B.Journalism, U. Okla., 1958; m. Gail-Joy Alexander, July 7, 1977; 1 child, Lindsay; children by previous marriage—Anne, Eric. Mng. editor, editor Okla. Daily, Norman, 1957-58; reporter Tulsa Tribune, Tulsa Okla., 1960; edn. editor Tulsa Tribune, 1961; corr. Life mag., 1961-68, bur. chief, Beirut, Lebanon, 1968-69; press sec. Sen. Birch Bayh, 1969-76, dir. communications Com. for Birch Bayh, 1976; press sec. Sen. Birch Bayh, 1976-77; asst. to sec. for public affairs HUD, Washington, 1977-79; asst. sec. for public affairs HEW, Washington, 1979—. Democrat. Author: The Wisdom of Sam Ervin, 1973. Office: 200 Independence Ave SW Washington DC 20201

WISE, CHARLES CONRAD, JR., former govt. ofcl., author; b. Washington, Apr. 1, 1913; s. Charles Conrad and Lorena May (Sweeney) W.; A.B., George Washington U., 1938, J.D., 1936; M. Fiscal Adminstrn., Columbus, 1943; m. Ruth Miles Baxter, Nov. 19, 1938; children—Gregory Baxter, Charles Conrad III, Jenifer. Admitted to D.C. bar, 1935, clk. U.S. Dept. Agr., 1933-36; adminstrv. asst. Bur. Accounts, Treasury Dept., 1936-39; atty. R.R. Retirement Bd., 1939-41; claims atty. Q.M.C., C.E., U.S. War Dept., 1941-43; asst. counsel Office Gen. Counsel, U.S. Navy Dept., 1946-47; gen. counsel War Contracts Price Adjustment Bd., 1948-51, mem., 1950-51; legislative counsel R.F.C., 1951-53; exec. sec. Subversive Activities Control Bd., 1953-61; dept. counsel indsl. personnel security Dept. Def., 1962-71, chief dept. counsel, 1971-73; asso. English dept. George Washington U., 1960, Am. U., 1961; instr. thanatology, religion and philosophy Blue Ridge Community Coll., 1973—. Served as lt. USNR, 1944-46. Mem. Fed. Bar Assn., Delta Theta Phi, Phi Beta Kappa. Author: Windows on the Passion, 1967; Windows on the Master, 1968; Ruth and Naomi, 1971; Mind Is It: Meditation, Prayer, Healing and the Psychic, 1978; Picture Windows on the Christ, 1979; The Magian Gospel, 1979; various articles for mags. Home: Solon-Lair Penn Laird VA 22846

WISE, DAVID, author, journalist; b. N.Y.C., May 10, 1930; s. Raymond L. and Karena (Post) W.; B.A., Columbia, 1951; m. Joan Sylvester, Dec. 16, 1962; children—Christopher James, Jonathan William. Reporter, N.Y. Herald Tribune, 1951-66, chief bur., Albany, N.Y., 1956-57, mem. Washington bur., 1958-66, chief bur., 1963-66; fellow Woodrow Wilson Internat. Center for Scholars, 1970-71; lectr. in polit. sci. U. Calif. at Santa Barbara, 1977-79. Recipient George Polk Meml. award, 1974; Page One award Newspaper Guild N.Y., 1969. Mem. Washington Ind. Writers, White House Corrs. Assn., Am. Polit. Sci. Assn. Clubs: Federal City, Gridiron (Washington). Author: The Politics of Lying: Government Deception, Secrecy, and Power, 1973; The American Police State: The Government Against the People, 1976; (with Thomas B. Ross) The U-2 Affair, 1962; The Invisible Government, 1964; The Espionage Establishment, 1967; (with Milton C. Cummings, Jr.) Democracy Under Pressure: An Introduction to the American Political System, 1971, 3d edit., 1977; contbg. author: The Kennedy Circle, 1961; None of Your Business: Government Secrecy in America, 1974; The CIA File, 1976. Contbr. articles to nat. mags. Address: care Sterling Lord Agy 660 Madison Ave New York NY 10021

WISE, EDMUND N., lawyer; b. Columbus, Ohio, Mar. 27, 1931; s. Herbert and Frieda (Neustadt) W.; B.A., Yale U., 1953; LL.B., Harvard U., 1956; m. Susan Sweeney, June 27, 1969; children—Elicia, Stephen, Jennifer. Admitted to Ohio bar, 1959, D.C. bar, 1964; atty. Devel. Loan Fund, Washington, 1959-61, AID, 1961-63; pvt. practice, Washington, 1963—; partner firm Dutton, Zumas & Wise, 1967—. Served with AUS, 1956-58. Mem. D.C. Bar Assn. Office: 1140 Connecticut Ave Washington DC 20036

WISE, ERBON WILBUR, publisher; b. Leesville, La., Aug. 14, 1920; s. Edmond Wesley and Eula E. (Bridwell) W.; B.S., Northwestern State U., 1941; m. Willie Marie Norris, July 7, 1942; children—Bonnie Marie (Mrs. Jimmie Everett), Edmond Wesley, Edna Ann, Larry Hunt. Pres. Wise Publs., Inc., Sulphur, La., 1946—; pres. Southwest Builder, Inc., 1959—; pres. Leesville Leader, Inc., 1968—; chmn. Community Media, Inc., 1979—. Mem. La. N.G., 1964—, maj. gen., 1964, adj. gen. La., 1964-68; dir. La. SSS, 1964-69; state dir. La. CD, 1969. Served with USAAF, 1941-46; ETO. Recipient La. Distinguished Service medal; Outstanding Civilian Service award Dept. of Army. Democrat. Baptist. Author: Wise Family of Louisiana, 1960; Bob, 1965; The Bridwell Family of America, 1968; Tall Pines, The Story of Vernon Parish, 1971; '29 Was a Good Year In Vernon Parish, 1975; '30 Was A Good Year in Vernon Parish, 1976; '31 Was A Good Year in Vernon Parish, 1977; "Bold As A Lion" Country Journalism, 1977; Huey P. Long and Vernon Parish, 1977. Home: Sam Dunham Rd Sulphur LA 70663 Office: PO Box 99 Sulphur LA 70663

WISE, GENE, educator; b. Willard, Ohio, Apr. 13, 1922; s. Pearl Ellsworth and Marvel Henrietta (Voight) W.; B.S., Capital U., 1947; Ph.D. (Standard Oil Ohio fellow) Western Res. U., 1950; m. Helen Joanna Giddings, June 13, 1964; children—Kathryn Ann, Jennifer Carol. Faculty, Va. Mil. Inst., Lexington, 1950—, prof. chemistry, 1960—, head dept., 1977—. Cons. chem. div. Gen. Tire & Rubber Co., Akron, Ohio, 1957-63; research asso. Northwestern U., summers 1953-54. Chmn. ARC, 1964—. Served with USNR, 1943-46, 51-52. Mem. Am. Chem. Soc. (sect. chmn. 1963, sect. councillor 1974—), Sigma Xi. Home: 302 Letcher Ave Lexington VA 24450

WISE, GEORGE EDWARD, lawyer; b. Chgo., Feb. 26, 1924; s. George E. and Helen L. (Gray) W.; m. Patricia E. Finn, Aug. 3, 1945; children—Erich, Peter, Abbe, Raoul, John. Admitted to Calif. bar, 1949; law clk. Calif. Supreme Ct., 1948-49; practice law, Los Angeles and Long Beach, Calif., 1949—; partner firm Wise & Nelson, Long Beach, 1950. Served with USNR, 1943-45. Fellow Am. Coll. Trial Lawyers; mem. Mem. Am., Los Angeles County, Long Beach (past pres.) bar assns., Calif. State Bar. Home: 5401 El Cedral St Long Beach CA 90815 Office: 400 Oceangate St Suite 1310 Long Beach CA 90802

WISE, GEORGE SCHNEIWEIS, univ. chancellor; b. Pinsk, Poland, Apr. 7, 1906; s. Noah and Chaya (Rabinowitz) Schneiweis; came to U.S., 1926, naturalized, 1939; B.S. summa cum laude, Furman U., 1928, LL.D., 1973; M.A., Columbia, 1930, Ph.D., 1950; Ph.D. (hon.), Hebrew U., 1957, Tel Aviv U., 1972, Bar Ilan U., 1976; LL.D., U. Miami, 1977; H.L.D., U. Fla., 1977; m. Florence Rosenberg, Dec. 8, 1933. Asso. dir. Bur. Applied Social Research, Columbia, 1949-52, lectr. sociology, 1950-52; vis. prof. U. Mexico, 1956; pres. Tel-Aviv U., 1963-71, Chancellor for life, 1971—; dir. Center for Advanced Internat. Studies, U. Miami, Coral Gables, Fla.; pres. Mt. Sinai Center for Med. Edn., Miami Beach, Fla. Pres., Inter-Am. Paper Corp., Fabricas de Papel Tuxtepec, Mex., 1955-63; pres., chmn. Clal Israel Latin Am. Devel. Co., 1962-69; dir., exec. Israel Corp., Ltd.; dir. Indsl. Devel. Bank Israel, Israeli Paper Mills (Hadera). Chmn. bd. govs. Hebrew U., 1953-62; chmn. Jewish Telegraphic Agy., 1951-55; trustee Mount Sinai Med. Center, Miami, 1977—. Decorated Order Aguila Azteca Govt. Mex., 1946. Fellow Am. Sociol. Soc.; mem. Israel Am. Soc. (pres.), Israel Am. C. of C. Clubs: Yale, Columbia U. (N.Y.C.); Univ. (Mex.); Bankers, Standard (Miami). Author: Caudillo, 1951; Mexico de Aleman, 1952. Home: 5500 Collins Ave Miami Beach FL 33140 Office: 1531 Brescia Coral Gables FL 33124 also Mt Sinai Center for Med Edn Miami Beach FL 33140

WISE, HAROLD L., psychologist; M.A., U. Iowa, 1958, Ph.D., 1960. Instr., State U. Iowa, 1960; asst.-asso. prof. Case-Western Res. U., 1960-65; editorial test cons., test dir. Am. Edn. Publs., Middletown, Conn., 1965-67, Harcourt, Brace, Jovanovich, N.Y.C., 1968-69; editorial dir. Nelson-Hall Pub. Co., Chgo., 1971—; dir. evaluation for reimbursable programs Dist. 14, Bklyn., 1972—; pres. Wise Ednl. Programs, Inc., Woodstock, N.Y., 1973—; mem. staff Ulster County Community Services, N.Y. Dept. Mental Health, 1976-78. U.S. Office Edn. grantee, 1962. Mem. Am. Psychol. Assn., Am. Ednl. Research Assn., AAAS, Internat. Soc. Gen. Semantics. Contbr. articles to profl. jours. Address: 21 Old Wagon Rd Woodstock NY 12498

WISE, HENRY ERLE, lawyer; b. Henryetta, Okla., Jan. 16, 1925; s. Henry Erle and Chloe Wise (Tolerton) W.; LL.B., So. Methodist U., 1952; m. Arlene James, Sept. 5, 1958; children—James Michael, Margie Ann. Admitted to Tex. bar, 1952; asst. U.S. atty., Fort Worth, 1953-58; atty. Continental Emsco Co. div. Youngstown Sheet & Tube Co., Dallas, 1959-73; practiced in Dallas, 1973—. Served with AUS, 1943-47. Home: Route 1 Box 54D Grapevine TX 76051 Office: Suite 602 3131 Turtle Creek Blvd Dallas TX 75219

WISE, HENRY SEILER, U.S. judge; b. Mt. Carmel, Ill., July 16, 1909; A.B., LL.B., Washington U., St. Louis, 1933; m. G. Louise Hawkins, Dec. 10, 1938; children—H. Michael, Patricia (Mrs.

Stephen Satre), N. Susanne (Mrs. Robert Lang), Marilyn (Mrs. Gerald L. Furnish), David. Admitted to Mo. bar, 1933, Ill. bar, 1934; practice in Danville, Ill., 1934—; mem. firms Jinkins & Jinkins, 1934-37, Meeks & Lowenstein, 1937-42, Meeks & Wise, 1942-51, Graham, Wise, Meyer, Young & Welsch, 1951-66; judge U.S. Dist. Ct., Eastern Dist. Ill., Danville, 1966—; sr. U.S. dist. judge Central Dist. Ill., 1978—. Commr., Ill. Ct. of Claims, 1949-53; mem. Ill. Parole and Pardon Bd., 1961-66. County chmn. Democratic party, 1948-54; del. Dem. nat. conv., 1952, 56, 60, 64. Mem. Am., Ill., Vermilion (Ill.) County bar assns., Am. Judicature Soc. K.C. (4), Elk. Club: Danville Country. Home: 507 Chester Ave Danville IL 61832 Office: US Dist Ct Danville IL 61832

WISE, HERBERT HERSCHEL, publisher; b. Bklyn., July 3, 1928; s. Alexander and Dorothy (Bilt) W.; B.A., U. Calif. at Los Angeles, 1950; Mus.M. In Theory and Composition, Syracuse U., 1952. Pres., pub. Music Sales Corp., N.Y.C., 1969—, also pres., pub. Quick Fox trade book div.; photographer, designer, 1965—. Served with AUS, 1952-54. Author: Made with Oak, Living Places, Good Lives, Rooms With A View, Attention to Detail. Office: 33 W 60th St New York NY 10023

WISE, JOHN, Canadian govt. ofcl.; b. St. Thomas, Ont., Can., Dec. 12, 1935; s. Clayton Wesley and Mary Louise (White) W.; ed. U. Guelph; m. Ann Dimora Richardson, Oct. 18, 1958; children—Elizabeth Ann, Susan Marie. Engaged in dairy farming, St. Thomas; former chmn. Elgin Coop. Services, Elgin Planning Bd., 1971-72; reeve Yarmouth Twp., 1968-69; warden Elgin County, 1969; mem. Can. Ho. of Commons 1972—; now Can. minister of agr., Ottawa, Ont. Progressive Conservative. Anglican. Club: Masons. Office: Dept Agr Sir John Carling Bldg 930 Carling Ave Ottawa ON K1A 0C5 Canada

WISE, JOHN AUGUSTUS, JR., lawyer; b. Detroit, Mar. 30, 1938; s. John Augustus and Mary Blanche (Parent) W.; A.B. cum laude, Coll. Holy Cross, 1959; student U. Vienna, 1957-58; J.D., U. Mich., 1962; postgrad. (Ford Found. grantee), U. Munich, 1962-63; m. Helga M. Bessin, Nov. 27, 1965; children—Monique Elizabeth, John Eric. Admitted to Mich. bar, 1963, D.C. bar, 1966; asso. firm Dykema, Wheat, Spencer, Goodnow & Trigg, Detroit, 1962-64; asst. to pres. Internat. Econ. Policy Assn., Washington, 1964-66; practiced in Detroit, 1967-70; partner Ziegler, Dykhouse & Wise, Detroit, 1970—; dir. Peltzer & Ehlers Am. Corp., Columbian Am. Friends Inc. Bd. dirs. Hyde Park Coop., 1974-77; trustee Friends Sch., Detroit, 1977—. Mem. Am., Mich., Detroit bar assns. Roman Catholic. Clubs: Detroit Athletic, Detroit Economic. Home: 1221 Yorkshire St Grosse Pointe MI 48230 Office: 3000 Book Bldg Detroit MI 48226

WISE, JOHN HICE, educator; b. Marysville, Pa., Nov. 6, 1920; s. Mervin Lamb and Sara (Eppley) W.; S.B., Haverford Coll., 1942; Ph.D., Brown, 1947; m. Yvette Georgette Pusey, Apr. 3, 1943; children—Susan Leigh, John Christopher, Judith Marie. Chemist, Manhattan project Brown U., 1943-46; instr., then asst. prof. Stanford, 1947-53; mem. faculty Washington and Lee U., 1953—, prof. chemistry, 1961—, head dept. chemistry, 1970—; vis. asso. prof. Brown U., 1959-60; part-time vis. prof. Hollins Coll., 1963-64; summer tchr. U. Va., also Stanford; research participant Argonne Nat. Lab., 1972-73; cons. Oak Ridge Nat. Lab. Mem. Am. Chem. Soc. (chmn. Blue Ridge sect. 1968-69), Am. Phys. Soc., Va. Acad. Sci. (chmn. chemistry sect. 1968), Sigma Xi. Home: 606 Marshall St Lexington VA 24450 Office: Dept Chemistry Washington and Lee U Lexington VA 24450

WISE, LOUIS NEAL, coll. adminstr.; b. Slagle, La., Jan. 27, 1921; s. Louis Harold and Wilhemena (McCausland) W.; B.S. in Sci. and Edn., Northwestern State Coll., Natchitoches, La., 1941; B.S. in Gen. Agr., La. State U., 1946, M.S. in Agronomy, 1947; Ph.D. in Agronomy, Purdue U., 1950; m. Doris Johns, Nov. 16, 1944; children—Michael Louis, Richard William. Mem. faculty Miss. State U., 1950—, prof. agronomy, 1953—, former dean Coll. Agr., 1961, v.p. Coll. Agr. and Sch. Forestry and Vet. Medicine 1966—; asst. agronomist Miss. Agrl. Expt. Sta., 1950-61; dir. Miss. Seed Tech. Lab., 1952-61; crop improvement cons. Tech. Assisstance programs, 1958-60; campus coordinator Miss. State U. AID/Brazil, 1964—. Served as pilot USAAF, 1941-46; lt. col. Res. Named Man of Year in So. Agr., So. Seedsmens Assn., 1958; named Man of Year in Miss. Agr., 1973. Mem. Sigma Xi, Sigma Chi, Alpha Zeta, Gamma Sigma Delta, Phi Kappa Phi, Omicron Delta Kappa, Blue Key. Presbyn. Author: The Lawn Book, 1961. Home: 903 S Montgomery Starkville MS 39759 Office: PO Box 5386 State College MS 39762*

WISE, MARVIN JAY, lawyer; b. San Antonio, Apr. 6, 1926; s. Philip and Anna Edith (Corman) W.; B.A. magna cum laude, U. Tex., 1945; LL.B. cum laude, Harvard, 1949; diploma comparative legal studies, U. Cambridge (Eng.), 1950; m. Gloria Marian Johnston, Sept. 19, 1954; children—Philip Johnston, Jennifer Lea, Amelia Ann. Admitted to Tex. bar, 1949; asso. firm Thompson, Knight, Simmons & Bullion, Dallas, 1950-57; partner firm Wise and Stuhl, Dallas, 1957—. Bd. dirs. Dallas Assn. Mental Health, Dallas Home Jewish Aged, Dallas Civic Ballet Soc. Served with AUS, 1945-46. Fulbright scholar, 1949-50. Mem. Am., Tex., Dallas bar assns., UN Assn. (dir. Dallas chpt.), Phi Beta Kappa, Alpha Phi Omega, Phi Eta Sigma, Pi Sigma Alpha. Jewish. Club: Dallas. Home: 3444 University Dallas TX 75205 Office: 2520 Republic National Bank Tower Dallas TX 75201

WISE, MILTON B., educator; b. Newland, N.C., July 17, 1929; s. Otis C. and Ellen (Ford) W.; B.S., Berea Coll., 1951; M.S., N.C. State U., 1953; Ph.D., Cornell U., 1957; m. Elenita Ruth Ellison, Sept. 30, 1951; children—Milton B., Timothy Lee, Rebecca Ellen. Grad. asst. N.C. State U., 1951-53, research asso., 1953-54; grad. asst. Cornell U., 1954-55, instr. animal husbandry, 1955-57; asst. prof. ruminant nutrition N.C. State U., 1957-61, asso. prof., 1961-64, prof., 1964-70; prof., head dept. Va. Poly. Inst., 1970-79, asso. dean Coll. Agr. and Life Sci., 1979—. Recipient Outstanding Tchr. award N.C. State U., 1966, 69. Mem. Am. Soc. Animal Sci. (pres.-elect 1979), Am. Inst. Nutrition, AAAS, Sigma Xi, Alpha Zeta, Gamma Sigma Delta, Phi Kappa Phi, Epsilon Sigma Phi. Contbr. articles to sci. jours. Home: 610 Country Club Dr SE Blacksburg VA 24060

WISE, PATRICIA ANN, lyric-coloratura; b. Wichita, Kans., July 31, 1944; d. Melvin R. and Genevieve (Dotson) W.; B. Music Edn., U. Kans., Lawrence, 1966. Debut as Susanna in Marriage of Figaro, Kansas City, 1966; appeared with leading Am. opera cos., including Chgo. Opera, Santa Fe Opera, N.Y.C. Opera; European appearances, 1971-76: London Royal Opera, Glyndebourne Festival, Vienna Volksoper; guest artist with Vienna, Hamburg and Munich (W.Ger.) staatsopers and Rome Opera, 1976-81; appeared with orchs.: Chgo. Symphony Orch., Los Angeles Symphony Orch., N.Y. Handel Soc., Israel Philharmonic Orch., Vienna Philharmonic Orch. Recipient Morton Baum award N.Y.C. Center, 1971, Dealey Meml. award Dallas Symphony, Dallas, 1966, Naftzger Young Artist award Wichita Symphony, 1966, Midland Young Artist award Midland Symphony Orch., Tex., 1966; M. B. Rockefeller Fund grantee, 1967-70; Sullivan Found. grantee, 1967-68.

WISE, ROBERT, producer, dir.; b. Winchester, Ind., Sept. 10, 1914; student Franklin Coll.; Dr. Fine Arts (hon.), Franklin Coll., 1968. Staff cutting dept. R.K.O., 1933, became sound cutter, asst. editor, film editor, 1939-43, dir., 1943-49; with 20th Century-Fox, 1949-52, M.G.M., 1954-57; free-lance, 1958-73; independent producer dir. various studios; motion pictures include The Body Snatcher, The Set Up, Day the Earth Stood Still, Executive Suite, Helen of Troy, Tribute to a Bad Man, Somebody Up There Likes Me, Until They Sail, Run Silent Run Deep, I Want to Live, Odds Againt Tomorrow, West Side Story, Two for the Seesaw, The Haunting, The Sound of Music, The Sand Pebbles, The Andromeda Strain, The Hindenburg, Audrey Rose, Star Trek-The Motion Picture; partner in ind. film co., 1970—. Past mem. Nat. Council of Arts. Mem. Dirs. Guild (pres. 1971). Address: Paramount Pictures Bldg E Hollywood CA 90038

WISE, ROBERT EDWARD, radiologist; b. Pitts., May 21, 1918; s. Joseph Frank and Victoria Rose (Conley) W.; B.S., U. Pitts., 1941; M.D., U. Md., 1943; m. Yvonne Burkhard, Mar. 27, 1943; children—Lynne Dailey, Robert Edward, John Burkhard. Intern, U.S. Naval Hosp., Phila., 1943-44; fellow in radiology Cleve. Clin. Found., 1947-49; radiologist Cleve. Clinic, 1949-52; practice medicine specializing in radiology, Pitts., 1952-53; radiologist Lahey Clinic Found., Boston, 1953—, chief exec. officer, chmn. bd. govs., 1975—; clin. prof. radiology Sch. Medicine, Boston U. Trustee Boston Ballet Co; mem. corp. New Eng. Bapt. Hosp. Served in M.C., USN, 1943-47. Mem. Am. Coll. Radiology (pres. 1975), Radiol. Soc. N.Am. (pres. 1974), AMA, Mass. Med. Soc. Mass. Radiol. Soc. (pres. 1973), Eastern Radiol. Soc. (pres. 1965). Roman Catholic. Clubs: Algonquin (Boston); Brae Burn Country (West Newton, Mass.). Author: Intravenous Cholangiography, 1962; Accessory Digestive Organs, 1973. Home: 155 Cliff Rd Wellesley Hills MA 02181 Office: 605 Commonwealth Ave Boston MA 02215

WISE, ROBERT IRBY, physician, educator; b. Barstow, Tex., May 19, 1915; s. Jess P. and Louise (Irby) W.; B.A., U. Tex., 1937, M.D., 1950; M.S., U. Ill., 1938, Ph.D., 1942; m. Mary Catherine Dosterschill, June 11, 1940; children—Robert Irby, Joyce Lynn (Mrs. Joyce Beene), John Karl. Research asst. div. animal genetics, then asst. instr. bacteriology U. Ill., 1938-42; asst. prof., then asso. prof. bacteriology U. Tex. Med. Sch., 1943-46; research asso. medicine, then asst. prof. medicine and bacteriology U. Minn. Med. Sch., 1951-55; mem. faculty Jefferson Med. Coll., Phila., 1955—, Magee prof. medicine, head dept., 1959-75, emeritus Magee prof. medicine, 1975—; asst. chief of staff VA Center, Togus, Maine, 1975-77, chief of staff, 1977—. Mem. adv. com. Inter-Soc. Commn. for Heart Disease Resources, 1967-71; exec. com. XII Internat. Congress Internal Medicine, 1971-72; mem. adv. com. for registry of tissue reactions to drugs Univs. Asso. for Research and Edn. in Pathology, 1970—; mem. Brucella tech. com. Dept. Agr., 1976—. Trustee Magee Meml. Hosp., Phila., 1959-75, Drexel U., 1966-75. Diplomate Am. Bd. Internal Medicine. Fellow A.C.P. (mem. com. internat. med. activities); Philadelphia County Med. Soc., Med. Soc. Pa., AMA (v.p. internal medicine sect. 1966-67, pres. internal medicine sect. 1976-77), Am. Fedn. Clin. Research, Pa. Soc. Bacteriologists, Assn. Am. Physicians, Infectious Disease Soc., Coll. Physicians Phila. (councillor 1970-72), Sigma Xi. Alpha Omega Alpha, Phi Sigma (pres. U. Ill. chpt. 1941), Phi Eta (pres. U. Ill. chpt. 1940-41), Nu Sigma Nu (pres. U. Tex. chpt. 1949-50). Mem. med. adv. bd. Med. Letter, 1959—; editorial bd. Annals Internal Medicine, 1961-68. Home: Mountain Rd Jefferson ME 04348 Office: VA Center Togus ME 04330

WISE, SHERWOOD WILLING, lawyer; b. Hazelhurst, Miss., Aug. 13, 1910; s. Joseph Sherwood and Myra (Willing) W.; B.A., Washington and Lee U., 1932, J.D., 1934; m. Elizabeth Carter Powell, July 28, 1937; children—Elizabeth (Mrs. Clyde X. Copeland, Jr.), Sherwood Willing, Joseph Powell, Robert and Louise (twins). Admitted to Miss. bar, 1934, since practiced in Jackson; partner firm Wise Carter Child Steen & Caraway, 1941—; commr. Miss. Bar, 1958-60; gen. counsel Miss. Power & Light Co., 1961—. Pres., Jackson Community Chest, 1950; Miss. chmn. Ducks Unlimited, Inc., 1961-71; mem. exec. com. Episcopal Diocese Miss., 1941, past mem. dept. missions and standing com., also trustee, 1959—; del. Episcopal Gen. Conv., 1952, 64, 67, 69, 70, 79; mem. joint commn. ecumenical relations Episcopal Ch., 1967-73; a founder, organizer St. Andrews Day Sch., Jackson, 1947, trustee, 1947-72, 78—; trustee Nat. Cathedral Assn., 1975-77. Del., Democratic Nat. Conv., 1940. Bd. dirs. State Dept. Archives and History, 1964—. Served to lt. comdr. USNR, 1942-46. Fellow Am. Coll. Trial Lawyers, Am. Coll. Probate Counsel; mem. Am. (standing com. fed. judiciary 1969-75, chmn. Nat. Conf. Lawyers and Design Profls. 1979—), Miss. (pres. 1961-62), Hinds County (pres. 1958-59) bar assns., Edison Electric Inst. (legal com.), Nat. Assn. R.R. Trial Counsel, Am. Judicature Soc., Scribes, Jackson C. of C. (past v.p., dir.), Newcomen Soc., Kappa Sigma, Omicron Delta Kappa, Phi Delta Phi. Rotarian (past dir.). Clubs: Jackson Country (past bd. govs.), Capital City Petroleum, Jackson Yacht (past gov.). Home: 3839 Eastover Dr Jackson MS 39211 Office: PO Box 651 Jackson MS 39205

WISE, WATSON WILLIAM, petroleum co. exec.; b. Findlay, Ohio; s. William Alfred and Nella Jane (Watson) W.; Ph.B., Yale; D.Letters, Ambassador Coll.; m. Emma Foote. Dir., Peoples Nat. Bank, Tyler, Tex., Tex. Research League, Austin, Ark. Best Corp., Ft. Smith, Nat. Civil Service League, Washington, Lone Star Steel Co., Dallas; prof. Salzburg Seminar in Am. Studies, Austria, 1963. Chmn., Good Neighbor Commn. of Tex., 1957-63; spl. counsel Schuman Plan, NATO; U.S. del. Atlantic Congress, London, 1962, North Atlantic Alliance, Luxembourg, Lisbon, 1968, The Hague, 1970; U.S. del. Session UN, Trustee, George Washington U., 1958, Briarcliff Coll., Briarcliff Manor, N.Y., 1961-70, Southwestern Med. Found., Dallas, 1964, Tyler Jr. Coll., 1950-70, Atlantic Council U.S., 1977—; mem. coordinating bd. Tex. Coll. and U. Systems, Austin. Recipient T.B. Butler award as outstanding citizen of Tyler. Hon. mem. Acad. Econ. and Social Soc., Trieste, Italy. Clubs: Metropolitan (Washington); Dallas Petroleum; Yale, Explorers (N.Y.C.); Rolling Rock (Ligonier, Pa.). Author: Siberia, Fewer Bears, Less Cavier, 1973, Tumasik and the Spicy Islands, 1978. Donor dialysis units to 7 hosps. in S.W. Address: PO Box 297 Tyler TX 75701

WISE, WILLIAM JERRARD, lawyer; b. Chgo., May 27, 1934; s. Gerald Paul and Harriet Muriel (Rosenblum) W.; B.B.A., U. Mich., 1955, M.B.A., 1958, J.D. with distinction, 1958; m. Peggy Spero, Sept. 3, 1959; children—Deborah, Stephen, Betsy, Lynne. Admitted to Ill. bar, 1959; spl. atty. Office Regional Counsel, IRS, Milw., 1959-63; with firm McDermott, Will & Emery, Chgo., 1963-70, Coles & Wise, Ltd., 1971—. Lectr., contbr. Ill. Inst. Continuing Legal Edn. Mem. Village of Winnetka (Ill.) Caucus, 1974-75. Bd. dirs. Blind Service Assn., Chgo., 1964-74. Served with AUS, 1958-59. Mem. Chgo. Bar Assn. Club: Old Willow (Northfield, Ill.). Home: 1401 Tower Rd Winnetka IL 60093 Office: One IBM Plaza Suite 4501 Chicago IL 60611

WISEHART, ARTHUR MCKEE, business exec., lawyer; b. Evanston, Ill., July 3, 1928; s. Arthur J. and Dorothy H. (Rice) W.; B.A., Miami U., Oxford, Ohio, 1950; M.P.A., Wayne State U., 1953; J.D., U. Mich., 1954; m. Mary Elizabeth Dodson, 1953; children—William, Ellen, Arthur, Charles. Admitted to N.Y. bar, 1955; with firm Chadbourne, Parke, Whiteside & Wolff, N.Y.C., 1954-59; with Am. Airlines, Inc., 1959-69, corp. sec., asst. gen. counsel, 1968-69; sr. v.p., gen. counsel, sec. REA Express, 1969-74; dir., sec. REA Holding Corp., 1969-74; sr. partner Law Offices of Arthur M. Wisehart, 1974-75; sr. partner Wisehart, Friou & Koch, 1975—; dir. Hoover Co., 1975-76. Mem. Am. Bar Assn., Assn. Bar City N.Y., Order of Coif, Delta Chi. Presbyn. Clubs: Pinnacle (N.Y.C.); Lawyers, University (Washington). Author articles. Office: 36 W 44th St New York City NY 10036

WISEMAN, GORDON GRAY, educator, physicist; b. Livingston, Wis., Feb. 24, 1917; s. Clinton Raymond and Pearl (Gray) W.; B.S. in Elec. Engring., S.D. State U., 1938; M.S., U. Kans., 1941, M.A., 1947, Ph.D., 1950; m. Mavis Lucille Paterson, Apr. 5, 1942; children—William Clinton, Alan Gray. Instr. physics Culver-Stockton Coll., Canton, Mo., 1941-43; faculty physics U. Kans., Lawrence, 1943—, prof., 1964—. Cons. USN, Midwest Research Inst., Kansas City, Mo., Raven Industries, Sioux Falls, S.D. Mem. AAAS, Am. Assn. Physics Tchrs., AAUP, Am. Phys. Soc., Kans. Acad. Sci., Sigma Xi, Phi Delta Kappa. Presbyterian. Research in solid state physics. Home: 1661 Stratford Rd Lawrence KS 66044

WISEMAN, JAMES RICHARD, classicist, archaeologist, educator; b. North Little Rock, Ark., Aug. 29, 1934; s. James Morgan and Bertie Lou (Sullivan) W.; B.A., U. Mo., Columbia, 1957; M.A., U. Chgo., 1960, Ph.D., 1966; postgrad. Am. Sch. Classical Studies, Athens, Greece, 1959-60; m. Margaret Lucille Mayhue, Aug. 20, 1954; children—James Alexander, Stephen Michael. Instr., U. Tex., Austin, 1960-64, asst. prof. classics, 1964-66, asso. prof., 1966-70, prof., 1970-73, dir. archaeol. excavations at Ancient Corinth, Greece, 1965-72, chmn. archaeol. studies program, 1969-73; prof. classics Boston U., 1973—, prof. art history, 1975—, chmn. dept. classical studies, 1974—, dir. archaeol. studies program, 1975-76, 79—, dir. summer program in Greece, 1976-77; vis. asso. prof. classics U. Colo., Boulder, 1970; Am. prin. investigator, co-dir. Am.-Yugoslav Archaeol. Excavations at Stobi, Yugoslavia, 1970-80; project supr. Boston U. Archaeol. Excavations in Temple, N.H., 1975-76; vis. research prof. Am. Sch. Classical Studies, Athens, 1978-79; cons. archaeology. Served with USN, 1952-55. Recipient Bromberg award U. Tex., 1964, Bronze Plaque award City of Titov Veles, SR Makedonija, Yugoslavia; Am. Council Learned Socs. fellow; Guggenheim fellow, 1971-72; U. Tex. Research Inst. grantee, summers 1961, 66, 67, and 1967-68, 71-72; Nat. Endowment for Humanities grantee, 1968, 69, 76-80; Ford Found. grantee, 1968-72; Smithsonian Instn. grantee, 1970-75, 79-80. Mem. Archaeol. Inst. Am. (exec. com. 1973-77, pres. Central Tex. Soc. 1962-64, pres. Boston Soc. 1979-81), Am. Philol. Assn., Am. Sch. Classical Studies at Athens (exec. com. 1973-76), Am. Acad. at Rome, Assn. Ancient Historians, Assn. Field Archaeology (exec. com. 1970—), Am. Inst. Nautical Archaeology, Internat. Assn. Archaeology, Center Materials Research in Archaeology and Ethnology (exec. com. 1975-78), Soc. Hist. Archaeology. Democrat. Author: Stobi, A Guide to the Excavations, 1973; The Land of the Ancient Corinthians, 1978; contbr. numerous articles on ancient history, epigraphy, classical studies, archaeology to profl. jours.; editor, contbg. author: Studies in the Antiquities of Stobi I, 1973, II, 1975, III, 1980; founding editor Jour. Field Archaeology, 1974—. Home: 60 Browne St Apt 4 Brookline MA 02146 Office: Boston U Dept Classical Studies 745 Commonwealth Ave Boston MA 02215

WISEMAN, THOMAS ANDERTON, JR., judge; b. Tullahoma, Tenn., Nov. 3, 1930; s. Thomas Anderson and Vera Seleta (Poe) W.; B.A., Vanderbilt U., 1952, LL.B., 1954; m. Emily Barbara Matlack, Mar. 30, 1957; children—Thomas Anderton III, Mary Alice, Sarah Emily. Admitted to Tenn. bar; practice law, Tullahoma, 1956-71, partner firm Haynes, Wiseman & Hull, Tullahoma and Winchester, Tenn., 1963-71; state treas. State of Tenn., 1971-74; partner firm Chambers & Wiseman, 1974-78; judge U.S. Dist. Ct., Middle Dist. of Tenn., Nashville, 1978—; mem. Tenn. Ho. of Reps., 1964-68; Democratic candidate of gov., Tenn., 1974. Chmn. Tenn. Heart Fund, 1973; chmn. Middle Tenn. Heart Fund, 1972. Served with U.S. Army, 1954-56. Mem. Am. Bar Assn., Tenn. Bar Assn. Presbyterian. Clubs: Amateur Chefs Am., Masons, Shriners. Asso. editor Vanderbilt Law Rev., 1953-54. Office: 824 US Courthouse Nashville TN 37203

WISENER, ROBERT ATLEE, investment dealer; b. Toronto, Ont., Can., Feb. 8, 1927; s. Philip Atlee and Margaret Jeanne (McLaughlin) W.; B.Sc., U. Toronto, 1950; m. Patricia King, Feb. 29, 1976; children—Cynthia, Philip, Lee, Robin, Susan, Joanne, James, Timothy. With Pacific Petroleums Ltd., 1950-52, Tanner Bros. Ltd., Calgary, 1952-54, Dawson, Hannaford Ltd., Toronto, 1954-56, Wisener & Co. Ltd., Toronto, 1956-61; with Wisener, MacKeller & Co. Ltd., Toronto, 1961-66; with Wisener & Partners Co. Ltd., Toronto, 1967-74, chmn. bd., 1972-74; vice chmn. Cochran Murray & Wisner, Toronto, from 1975; now vice chmn. Walway Stodgell Cochran Murray Ltd., Calgary, Alta.; dir. Northway-Gestalt Corp., EEE Gesellschaft Explor. Von Erdal und Ergas, Taro Industries Ltd., Patrician Land Devel. Corp. Ltd., Bluesky Oil & Gas Ltd.; bd. govs. Toronto Stock Exchange, 1967-69; mem. Businessmen's Adv. Bd. Industry Trade and Commerce, Nat. Adv. Com. Conservation and Renewable Energy. Clubs: Royal Can. Yacht, Badminton and Racquet (Toronto); National. Home: Site 19 Box 36 SS 1 Calgary AB T2M 4N3 Canada Office: 680 401 9th Ave SW Calgary AB T2P 3C5 Canada

WISHAM, LAWRENCE HERMAN, physician; b. N.Y.C., Jan. 17, 1918; s. William and Sarah (Kagan) W.; B.S., N.Y. U., 1938; M.D., Chgo. Med. Sch., 1943; m. Shirley D. Schatz, Sept. 24, 1942; 1 dau., Elizabeth. Resident, Bronx VA Hosp. Phys. Medicine and Rehab., 1948-50; fellow Inst. Rehab. Medicine, 1950-51; dir. dept. phys. medicine and rehab. Brookdale Hosp., Bklyn., 1951-54; asso. dir. dept. rehab. medicine Mt. Sinai Hosp., N.Y.C., 1954-58, dir., 1958—; asst. clin. prof. rehab. medicine Columbia Coll. Phys. and Surg., 1956-66; prof. rehab. medicine, chmn. dept. Mt. Sinai Sch. Medicine, 1966—; sr. cons. dept. rehab. medicine Bronx VA Hosp.; spl. research blood flow. Served to capt. M.C., AUS, 1944-46; PTO. Fellow Am. Acad. Phys. Medicine and Rehab., N.Y. Acad. Medicine; mem. N.Y. Soc. Phys. Medicine and Rehab. (pres. 1964-65). Contbr. articles to profl. jours. Home: 640 W 231st St New York City NY 10463 Office: 1176 Fifth Ave New York City NY 10029

WISHART, ALFRED WILBUR, JR., found. exec.; b. Pitts., Dec. 21, 1931; s. Alfred Wilbur and Corrine Gunnison (Bell) W.; B.A., Coll. Wooster, 1953; M.Div., Union Theol. Sem., 1956; L.H.D., Waynesburg Coll., 1976; m. Barbara Joan Scott, June 4, 1956; children—Scott Sheridan, Kathryn Ann, Craig Gunnison. Ordained to ministry Presbyterian Ch., 1956; asst. pastor Shadyside Presbyn. Ch., Pitts., 1956-61; pastor Arlington Ave. Presbyn. Ch., East Orange, N.J., 1961-70; dir., sec. Pitts. Found., 1970—; exec. dir. Howard Heinz Endowment, Pitts., 1970—; exec. sec. Pitcairn-Crabbe Found., Pitts., 1970—; trustee, sec. H. J. Heinz II Charitable and Family Trust. Bd. dirs. Pitts. Theol. Sem., World Affairs Council Pitts., Pitts. History and Landmarks Found.; trustee United Presbyn. Found., Carnegie Hero Fund, Pitts., Citizens' Sponsoring Com. of Allegheny Conf. Community Devel., Pitts. Named Man of Yr. for Howard Heinz Endowment, Pitts. Jaycees, 1972. Mem. Council on Founds., Nat. Council Philanthropy, Greater Pitts. C. of C. Allegheny Conf.

Community Devel. Clubs: Duquesne, Longue Vue, Fox Chapel Racquet. Home: 408 Buckingham Rd Pittsburgh PA 15215 Office: 301 Fifth Ave Suite 1417 Pittsburgh PA 15222

WISHENGRAD, HYMAN, editor, writer; b. Brest-Litovsk, Russia, Aug. 28, 1903; s. Samuel and Augusta (Naidus) W.; came to U.S., 1907, naturalized, 1916; Litt.B. in journalism, Columbia, 1926; m. Ruth S. Goldman, Oct. 15, 1926 (dec. 1964); children—Paul Francis, Kay Susan, Bette Ann; m. 2d, Eleanor S. Eisnitz, 1965. Reporter, N.Y. Times, 1926-27; editor-in-chief Jewish Telegraphic Agy., 1935-41; co-founder editor Overseas News Agy., 1940-52, fgn. corr., 1946; founder, editor Press Freatures, Inc., 1947-52; owner, editor Editor Syndicate, 1952-59; exec. editor Bridgeport (Conn.) Sunday Herald; 1959-61; owner, editor Page One Syndicate, N.Y.C., 1961—; mng. editor Scarsdale (N.Y.) Inquirer; editor Washington Star Syndicate, 1968-79. Home: 630 W 246th St New York NY 10471 Office: 444 Madison Ave New York NY 10022

WISHNER, MAYNARD IRA, finance co. exec.; b. Chgo., Sept. 17, 1923; s. Hyman L. and Frances (Fisher) W.; B.A., U. Chgo., 1944, J.D., 1947; m. Elaine Loewenberg, July 4, 1954; children—Ellen (Mrs. Tom Kenemore), Jane, Miriam. Admitted to Ill. bar, 1947; exec. dir. Chgo. Commn. on Human Relations, 1947-52; chief ordinance enforcement div. Law Dept., City of Chgo., 1952-55; mem. law firm Cole, Wishner, Epstein & Manilow, Chgo., 1955-63; with Walter E. Heller & Co., Chgo., 1963—, pres., 1974—; dir. Walter E. Heller Internat. Corp., Am. Nat. Bank & Trust Co., Chgo., Goldblatt Bros. Dept. Stores, Inc. Vice pres. Jewish Fedn. Met. Chgo., 1969-70; chmn. nat. exec. council Am. Jewish Com., 1973—, chmn. bd. govs., 1977—, recipient Human Rights medallion, 1975. Bd. dirs. Nat. Found. for Jewish Culture, Nat. Council Jewish Fedns.; mem. exec. com. Nat. Jewish Community Relations Adv. Council; commr. Nat. Hillel Found.; mem. vis. com. U. Chgo. Sch. Social Service Adminstrn. Served with AUS, 1943. Home: 1131 Sheridan Rd Evanston IL 60202 Office: Walter E Heller & Co 105 W Adams St Chicago IL 60690*

WISHNICK, WILLIAM, chem. co. exec.; b. Bklyn., Nov. 9, 1924; s. Robert I. and Freda M. (Frankel) W.; student Carnegie Inst. Tech., 1942, 45-47; B.B.A., U. Tex., 1949; m. Dion Imerman, June 16, 1949 (div. 1969); children—Elizabeth Anne (dec.), Gina I., Amy Jo, Kendall Freda; m. 2d, Lisa Fluet, July 12, 1975. With Witco Chem. Co., Inc., N.Y.C., 1949—, v.p., 1954-56, treas., 1956—, exec. v.p. 1957-64, chmn. bd., 1964—, chief exec. officer, 1971—, also dir.; pres., dir. Witco Chem. Co., Can., Ltd., 1958-62, vice chmn. bd., 1962-64, chmn. bd., 1964—; pres. Sonneborn Chem. & Refining Corp.; treas., dir. Ultra Chem. Works, Inc., 1956—; dir. Witco Chem. Co. Ltd. (Eng.), Golden Bear Oil Co., Los Angeles, Continental Carbon Co., Houston, Witco Chem. (France) S.A.R.L. Trustee Mt. Sinai Hosp., N.Y.C. Mem. Am. Chem. Soc., Am. Petroleum Inst., N.Y. Rubber Group, Salesmens Assn. Am. Chem. Industry, Young Pres.'s Orgn., Tau Delta Phi. Republican. Clubs: Chemists (past trustee, jr. v.p.), Harmonie (N.Y.C.); Standard (Chgo.). Office: 277 Park Ave New York NY 10017

WISHNOW, EMANUEL, musical educator; b. London, Eng., June 25, 1910; s. Hyman and Sarah (Jacobson) W.; came to U.S., 1920, naturalized, 1936; B.F.A. U., Nebr., 1932; M.A., N.Y. U., 1939; m. Kitty Bendeth, Apr. 11, 1957. Faculty, U. Nebr., 1933—, prof. violin, 1951—, U. Nebr. Found. prof., 1966-70, George Holmes prof. music, 1970—, condr. univ. symphony orch., 1941—, chmn. dept. music, 1958-67, dir. Sch. Music, 1968-72. Appearances with Jacques Gordon String Quartet, Music Mountain, Conn., 1935, 38, 40, 49, Library of Congress, 1938; dir., 1st violinist Fine Arts Ensemble, Joslyn Art Mus., Omaha, 1948-70, condr. Omaha Symphony, 1951, 52; mem. Lincoln Symphony Orch., 1928-50, concertmaster, 1936-50, bd. dirs., 1976—. Bd. dirs. Lincoln Community Art Council. Served with AUS, 1942-45; mem. Glenn Miller Air Force Band, overseas 1944-45. Mem. Nebr. Arts Council, Phi Beta Kappa (hon.). Producer ednl. filmstrips for string instruments. Research string music 17th and 18th centuries in Eng. and Italy. Home: 1200 S 49th St Lincoln NE 68510

WISLAR, GEORGE GARSED, ins. co. exec.; b. Bucks County, Pa., Jan. 24, 1901; s. George Brouse and Mary Benton (Garsed) W.; student Drexel Inst.; m. Marian B. Wakefield, Dec. 8, 1923; children—Edwin Wakefield, George Rowland. With Raymond Concrete Pile Co., 1919-20, John W. Ferguson Co., 1920-23; with N.J. Mfrs. Ins. Co., 1923—, pres., 1957-66, ret. Mem. S.R. Republican. Episcopalian. Club: Bedens Brook. Address: Rt 1 Lambertville NJ 08530

WISLOCKI, FLORENCE. see Clothier, Florence.

WISOTZKY, JOEL, educator; b. Chgo., Feb. 17, 1923; s. Isadore Hersch and Rose (Sheveloff) W.; B.S., Central YMCA Coll., Chgo., 1945; D.D.S., Loyola U. Chgo., 1947; Ph.D., U. Rochester, 1956; m. Eleanor Annette Pinsky, Feb. 16, 1949; children—Sharen Rose, Philip Joseph, Ira Harold. Pvt. practice dentistry, Chgo., 1947-48; asst. dental surgeon, then sr. asst. dental surgeon USPHS, 1949-51; with div. dental medicine Colgate-Palmolive Co., hon. asso. research specialist Rutgers U. Bur. Biol. Research, 1956-59; prof. oral biology and medicine Case Western Res. U. Sch. Dentistry, 1959—, dir. grad. tng. and research, 1969-77, dir. dental research, 1961-77. Served with AUS, 1942-45. Mem. Internat. Assn. Dental Research, AAAS, Am. Assn. Dental Schs., Sigma Xi, Omicron Kappa Upsilon. Contbr. articles to profl. jours., chpts. in books. Home: 3407 Blanche Ave Cleveland Heights OH 44118 Office: 2123 Abington St Cleveland OH 44106

WISSLER, JOHN GEORGE, naval officer; b. Chgo., Mar. 12, 1927; s. John Albert and Hermine L. Wissler; student Coll. St. Thomas, 1944-46; B.S.C.E., Marquette U., 1948; M.S. in Bus. Adminstrn., Indsl. Coll. Armed Forces and George Washington U., 1968; m. Elizabeth Brooke Mordecai, June 20, 1957; children—John Brooke, Susan, Cecelia. Commd. ensign U.S. Navy, 1948, advanced through grades to rear adm., 1978; comdg. officer carrier fighter squadron, 1965-66; comdr. carrier air wing, 1966-67; mgr. attack aircraft test program, 1968-69; dir. Test Directorate, 1969-71; aviation plans officer, 1971-72; comdg. officer Naval Air Station, Cubic Point, Philippines, 1972-74; comdg. officer Human Resource Center, Pearl Harbor, Hawaii, 1974-76; dep. comdr. Naval Air Test Center, Patuxent River, Md., 1976-78, comdr., 1979—; insp. gen. U.S. Atlantic Fleet, 1978-79. Decorated Legion of Merit with gold star, Meritorious Service medal with gold star. Mem. Soc. Exptl. Test Pilots, AIAA. Episcopalian. Office: Naval Air Test Center Patuxent River MD 20670

WISWALL, FRANK LAWRENCE, JR., admiralty lawyer; b. Albany, N.Y., Sept. 21, 1939; s. Frank Lawrence and Clara Elizabeth (Chapman) W.; B.A., Colby Coll., 1962; J.D., Cornell U., 1965; Ph.D. in Jurisprudence, Cambridge U., 1967; m. Elizabeth Curtiss Nelson, Aug. 9, 1975; children by previous marriage—Anne Chapman, Frank Lawrence. Admitted to Maine bar, 1965, N.Y. bar, 1968, U.S. Supreme Ct. bar, 1968, D.C. bar, 1975, Va. bar, 1978; mem. firm Wiswall & Wiswall, Castine, Maine, 1965-72; atty. Burlingham, Underwood, Barron, Wright & White, N.Y.C., 1967-73; maritime legal adviser Republic of Liberia, 1968—, admiralty counsel, 1974—; gen. counsel Liberian Services, Inc., N.Y.C. and Reston, Va., 1973-77, pres., 1974—; partner firm Martin, Whitfield, Smith & Bebchick, Washington, 1975-78, counsel, 1979—; mem. legal com. Internat. Maritime Orgn., London, 1972—, vice chmn., 1974—; vis. faculty U. Va. Law Sch., UN Center for Oceans Law and Policy, 1978—; vis. lectr. Cornell Law Sch., 1969-76; tutorial supr. internat. law Clare Coll., Cambridge, Eng., 1966, 67; del. Internat. Conf. Marine Pollution, London, 1973; del. Internat. Conf. Carriage of Passengers and Luggage by Sea, Athens, 1974, Internat. Conf. on Safety of Life at Sea, London, 1974, 3d UN Conf. on Law of Sea, Caracas, Venezuela, 1974, all subsequent sessions; del., chmn. com. final clauses Internat. Conf. on Limitation of Liability for Maritime Claims, London, 1976; del. UN Conf. Carriage of Goods by Sea, Hamburg, 1978; counsel various marine casualty bds. of investigation, 1970—; harbormaster Port of Castine, 1960-62; lic. master small passenger vessels. Recipient Yorke prize U. Cambridge, 1968-69. Fellow Royal Hist. Soc.; mem. Maritime Law Assn. U.S., Selden Soc., Am. Socs. Legal History and Internat. Law, U.K., U.S. assns. average adjusters, Am., Maine, Va., D.C., City N.Y. (admiralty com. 1971-78) bar assns., Alpha Delta Phi, Phi Delta Phi. Club: United Oxford and Cambridge U. (London). Author: The Development of Admiralty Jurisdiction and Practice Since 1800, 1970; contbr. articles to profl. jours. Office: Reston Internat Center Reston VA 22091 also 548 Fifth Ave New York NY 10036

WIT, DANIEL, educator; b. N.Y.C., June 8, 1923; s. Benjamin and Stella (Bloom) W.; A.B., Union Coll., N.Y., 1943; postgrad. Institut d'Etudes Politiques (Paris), 1945-46; A.M., Princeton, 1948, Ph.D., 1950; m. Phyllis J. Citron, June 15, 1947; children—Pamela S., Frederick W. Mem. dept. polit. sci. Ohio State U., 1948-50, U. Cin., 1950-54, U. Mich., 1954-56, Ind. U., 1956-58, George Washington U., 1959-61; head dept. polit. sci. No. Ill. U., Dekalb, 1961-69, dir. internat. programs, 1969-77, dean internat. and spl. programs, 1977—; co-dir. Center S.E. Asian Studies and Tng., 1962-69. Fulbright prof. Inst. Social Studies, The Hague, Netherlands, 1966-67; vis. prof. pub. adminstrn. adviser Ind. U.-ICA program in Thailand, 1956-58; dir. internat. studies Govtl. Affairs Inst., Washington, 1959-61, project dir. Brazilian Labor-A Mgmt. Survey, 1960, Indonesian Labor-A Mgmt. Survey, 1961; cons. Peace Corps tng. programs S.E. Asia, Thai labor Dept. Labor; faculty Nat. War Coll., 1963-64. Mem. Am. Polit. Sci. Assn. (nat. council 1967-69), Am. Soc. Pub. Adminstrn., Internat. Studies Assn., Midwest Polit. Sci. Conf., Phi Beta Kappa. Author: Comparative Political Institutions, 1953; A Comparative Survey of Local Government and Administration, 1958; Local Government in Thailand, 1958; Manpower Problems in Southeast Asia, 1960; Labor Conditions in Thailand, 1960; Labor Law and Practice in Thailand, 1964; Thailand: Another Vietnam, 1968; (co-author) Our American Government and Political System, 1972. Contbr. articles to profl. jours. Home: 222 Fairmont Dr DeKalb IL 60115

WIT, HAROLD MAURICE, investment banker, lawyer, investor; b. Boston, Sept. 6, 1928; s. Maurice and Martha (Bassist) W.; A.B. magna cum laude, Harvard, 1949; J.D. (editor law jour.), Yale, 1954; m. Louise Untermyer, 1949 (div.); m. 2d, Joan Rosenthal, Apr. 6, 1960 (div.); children—David Edmund, Hannah Edna. Admitted to N.Y. bar, 1954; asso. Cravath, Swaine & Moore, N.Y.C., 1954-58; asst. sec. One William St. Fund, Inc., N.Y.C., 1958-59, v.p., sec., 1959-60; asso. Allen & Co., Inc., 1960—, v.p., 1965-70, exec. v.p., 1970—, chief operating officer, also dir., mem. exec. com.; pres., dir. Wit Securities Corp.; mem. exec. com., dir. DPF, Inc.; dir. Toys-R-Us, Inc., Grey Advt. Inc., Allegheny & Western Energy Corp., Interstate Brands Corp., MCI Communications Corp. Bd. dirs., mem. exec. com. Group for America's South Fork; bd. dirs. South Fork Land Found., Inc., Dolly Madison Found.; bd. advs. Nat. Taxpayers Union; mem. Panel on Future of Govt. in N.Y. Served with Mass. N.G., 1947-50, lt. (j.g.) USNR, 1951-53. Mem. Phi Beta Kappa, Phi Delta Phi. Clubs: University, Yale, Harvard (N.Y.); Harvard (Boston). Home: 160 E 65th St New York NY 10021 also Cross Hwy East Hampton NY 11937 Office: 711 Fifth Ave New York NY 10022

WITCHER, ROBERT CAMPBELL, bishop; b. New Orleans, Oct. 5, 1926; s. Charles Swanson and Lily Sebastian (Campbell) W.; B.A., Tulane U., 1949; M.Div., Seabury-Western Theol. Sem., 1952; M.A., La. State U., 1960, Ph.D., 1968; m. Elisabeth Alice Cole, June 4, 1957; 2 children. Ordained priest Episcopal Ch., 1953; consecrated bishop, 1975; priest-in-charge St. Andrew Ch., Linton, La. and St. Patrick Ch., Zachary, La., 1953-56; priest-in-charge St. Augustine Ch., Baton Rouge, La., 1953-54, rector, 1954-61; canon pastor Christ Ch. Cathedral, New Orleans, 1961-62; rector St. James Ch., Baton Rouge, 1962-75; coadjutor bishop L.I., 1975-77, bishop, 1977—; dir. numerous camps, confs. and retreats, 1953-75. Trustee U. of South, 1963-69, Seabury-Western Theol. Sem., 1963—, Gen. Theol. Sem., 1979—; pres. trustees estate belonging to Diocese of L.I.; pres. Ch. Charity Found., Mercer Sch. Theology; v.p. Anglican Soc. N.Am.; del. Nat. Council Chs. Governing Body, 1978. Capt. USNR. Author: The Founding of the Episcopal Church in Louisiana, 1805-38. Office: 36 Cathedral Ave Garden City NY 11530

WITCOFF, SHELDON WILLIAM, lawyer; b. Washington, July 10, 1925; s. Joseph and Zina (Ceppos) W.; B.S. in Elec. Engring., U. Md., 1949; J.D., George Washington U., 1953; m. Margot Gail Hoffner, Sept. 6, 1953; children—Lauren Jill, David Lawrence, Lisa Ann, Julie Beth. Admitted to D.C. bar, 1953, N.Y. bar, 1955, Ill. bar, 1956; patent examiner Patent Office, Dept. Commerce, 1949-53; patent lawyer Bell Telephone Labs., Murray Hill, N.J., 1953-55; partner firm Bair, Freeman & Molinare, Chgo., 1955-69; partner firm Molinare, Allegretti, Newitt & Witcoff, Chgo., 1970—. Chmn. bd., v.p. Art Splty. Co., Chgo., 1967—; v.p. Caspian Fur Trading Co., N.Y.C. Fire and police commnr. Skokie, Ill., 1960-63. Served with USNR, 1943-46. Mem. Bar Assn. 7th Circuit, Chgo. Patent Law Assn., Order of Coif, Tau Epsilon Phi, Phi Delta Phi. Mem. B'nai B'rith. Home: 235 Maple Hill Rd Glencoe IL 60022 Office: 125 S Wacker Dr Chicago IL 60606

WITEK, JAMES EUGENE, army officer; b. LaPorte, Ind., Sept. 14, 1932; s. Stanley and Victoria (Peret) W.; A.B., Ind. U., 1954; M.A., U. Mo., 1970; m. Mary Carolyn Hood, June 18, 1955; children—James Jay, Janet Marie, Jeffrey Patrick, Jean Theresa. Joined U.S. Army, 1954, commd. 2d lt., 1954, advanced through grades to lt. col., 1968, editor, pub. Infantry Mag., Fort Benning, Ga., 1968-70, advisor to Vietnamese Mil. Region IV Ranger Comdr., 1970-71, plans officer CINCPAC, Hawaii, 1971-75, exec. editor Soldiers, Washington, 1975-77, editor in chief, 1977-79; dir. public affairs Nat. Com. for Employer Support Guard and Res., Arlington, Va., 1979—. Decorated Legion of Merit, Bronze Star, Air Medal, Purple Heart, Vietnamese Cross of Gallantry with Silver Star. Mem. Assn. U.S. Army, Ret. Officers Assn., Airborne Assn., VFW, Phi Beta Kappa, Tau Kappa Alpha, Pi Kappa Phi. Roman Catholic. Home: 3240 Atlanta St Fairfax VA 22030 Office: NCE SGR 1117 N 19th St Arlington VA 22209

WITHAM, BERTRAM HIGH, JR., data processing co. exec.; b. Woodland, Calif., Nov. 13, 1918; s. Bertram High and Mary A. (Gray) W.; B.S. in Bus. Adminstrn., U. Calif. at Berkeley, 1948; M.Letters, U. Pitts., 1950; m. Patricia Swallum, Sept. 4, 1942; children—Jana, Brenda (Mrs. Russell Jones), Marsha (Mrs. Frank Whitman), Patricia. Commd. cadet USAAF, 1939, advanced through grades to col., 1951, ret., 1961; adminstrn. asst. to v.p. finance IBM World Trade Corp., N.Y.C., 1961-62, controller, 1962-63, treas., 1963-65, v.p., 1965-74, now dir.; controller IBM Europe, Paris, France, 1962; treas. IBM Corp., Armonk, N.Y., 1974—; dir. IBM World Trade Americas/Far East Corp., Adela Investment Co. S.A., Fidelity Group. Bd. dirs. Nat. Fgn. Trade Council, Am. Grad. Sch. Internat. Mgmt.; trustee William Jewell Coll. Decorated Legion of Merit, D.F.C. Baptist. Mason (Shriner). Clubs: Tamarack Country, Army/Navy Country, University. Home: 89 Fox Hill Rd Stamford CT 06903 Office: Old Orchard Rd Armonk NY 10504

WITHAM, PETER MARTIN, transp. co. exec.; b. Knoxville, Tenn., Mar. 16, 1933; s. Henry B. and Elsa A. (Dethlas) W.; B.S., Ind. U., 1955, J.D., 1958; m. Chantal De La Fosse, Jan. 21, 1962; children—Marc, Eric. Admitted to Ind. bar, 1958, U.S. Supreme Ct. bar, 1975; dep. atty. gen. State of Ind., 1961-65; corporate sec. Eastern Express, Inc., Terre Haute, 1965-78; mem. corp. atty. Am. Freight System, Inc., 1978—; sec. Eastern Properties, Inc.; asst. sec. R-C Motor Lines, Inc. Jacksonville, Fla. Served from 1st lt. to maj. Judge Adv. Gen. Corps, AUS, 1959-61. Mem. Am., Ind. bar assns., Kappa Sigma, Phi Delta Phi. Clubs: Marketing, Management, Sailing, Law. Home: 8300 W 97th Terr Overland Park KS 66212

WITHERELL, NORMAN HERBERT, mining co. exec.; b. Bentley, Alta., Can., Mar. 24, 1933; s. Maurice Sheldon and Ida Mildred (Roberts) W.; B. Commerce, U. Alta., 1958. Audit mgr. Arthur Young, Clarkson Gordon & Co., Rio de Janeiro, Brazil, 1966-68; financial cons. Rio Tinto Patino S.A., Madrid, Spain, 1968-69; asst. v.p. finance, treas. Falconbridge Dominicana C por A, Toronto, Ont. and Santo Domingo, 1969-73; treas. Falconbridge Nickel Mines Ltd., Toronto, 1973—. Chartered accountant, Ont. Home: 190 St George St Apt 1104 Toronto ON M5R 2N4 Canada Office: PO Box 40 Commerce Ct W Toronto ON M5L 1B4 Canada

WITHERS, ORVAL RAYMOND, ret. physician; b. Medicine Lodge, Kans., Dec. 19, 1898; s. Frank A. and Katherine (Cunningham) W.; student Leland Stanford U., 1918-20, U. Kans., 1920-21; A.B., Northwestern U., 1924, M.D., 1926; m. Mary Louise Holdman, 1926; children—H. Theodore, William F.; m. 2d, Kathleen Goggan, 1952. Intern, Charity Hosp., New Orleans, 1926-28; established 1st free Allergy Clinic, in Greater Kansas City area, 1931; head allergy dept. Outpatient Clinic, U. Kans. Med. Center, 1931-56; asso. clin. prof. medicine Kans. U. Med. Sch., 1947-61, clin. prof., 1961-71, emeritus, 1972—; former staff U. Kans. Med. Center, Bapt. Meml. Hosp., St. Mary's Hosp., Kansas City, Mo.; regional cons. Children's Asthma Research Inst. and Hosp., Denver; cons. in medicine VA Hosp., Kansas City, Mo., 1954-61; bd. dirs. Nat. Asthmatic Children's Found., 1973-74. Recipient Selective Service medal U.S. Congress; cited by Pres. Franklin D. Roosevelt and Harry S. Truman, 1940-47. Fellow AMA, World Med. Assn., Am. Coll. Allergists (founder group, bd. regents 1951-55, v.p. 1944-45, pres. 1957-58), Internat. Assn. Allergolists (founder group, v.p. 1958-61), A.C.P., Am. Acad. Allergy, Am. Coll. Chest Physicians; mem. Am., Mo. socs. internal medicine, Am. Med. Assn. Vienna (life), West Coast Allergy Soc., S.W. Allergy Forum (founder group, pres. 1953), Royal Soc. Medicine London, Am. Assn. Micrological Investigations (founders group), Mexican Assn. Allergy, So., Mo. allergy assns., Jackson County Med. Soc. (treas. 1944-45), Nat. Cowboy Hall Fame and Western Heritage Center (life), SAR, Am. Legion, Phi Beta Pi, Alpha Omega Alpha. Clubs: Westerners, Carriage, Rotary; Last Man's (Kansas City, Mo.). Contbg. author: Allergy—Methods of Treatment, 6th-7th edits., 1956, 58; Current Therapy, 1953-58. Mem. editorial bd. Annals of Allergy, 1943-58. Contbr. articles to profl. jours. Home: 114 Cypress Lee's Summit MO 64063

WITHERS, ROY JOSEPH, constrn. co. exec.; b. Lancashire, Eng., June 18, 1924; s. Joseph and Irene Ada (Jones) W.; grad. in Mech. Scis. with 1st class honours (Yates prize, sr. scholar), Trinity Coll., Cambridge U., 1944; m. Pauline M.G. Johnston, Dec. 20, 1947; children—Christopher, Stephen, Paul, Robert. Sr. engr. I.C.I. Inc., 1948-55; tech. dir. Humphreys & Glasgow Ltd., 1955-63; engring. dir., then mng. dir. Power Gas, 1963-72; chief exec. officer Davy Power Gas Ltd., 1972-73; mng. dir. Davy Corp. Ltd. (UK), 1974—, also dir.; chmn. Davy Inc. (U.S.), 1979—; dir. Transmark Ltd.; mem. Overseas Project Bd. Fellow Inst. Mech. Engrs., Brit. Inst. Mgmt.; mem. Inst. Gas Engrs. Conservative. Mem. Ch. of Eng. Clubs: Charlton, Hampstead Golf. Office: 15 Portland Pl London W1 England

WITHERS, W. RUSSELL, JR., broadcasting exec.; b. Cape Girardeau, Mo., Dec. 10, 1936; s. Waldo Russell and Dorothy Ruth (Harrelson) W.; B.A., S.E. Mo. State U., 1958; 1 dau., Dana Ruth. Disc jockey KGMO Radio, Cape Girardeau, 1955-58; account exec. WGGH Radio, Marion, Ill., 1961-62; v.p. LIN Broadcasting Corp., Nashville, 1962-69; exec. v.p., dir. Laser Link Corp., Woodbury, N.Y., 1970-72; owner Withers Broadcasting Cos., Minn., Hawaii, Mo., Ill., and W.Va., 1972—; chmn. bd., chief exec. officer Withers Beverage Corp., Mobile, Ala., 1973—; dir. Ina (Ill.) State Bank, Theatrevision, Inc., Turnerfe Island Lodge, Ltd., Belize, Central Am. Served in U.S. Army, 1957-58. Mem. Mt. Vernon C. of C. (dir.), Nat. Assn. Broadcasters, Ill. Broadcasters Assn. (dir.), Mut. Radio Network Affiliates (adv. bd.), Sigma Chi. Christian Scientist. Clubs: Monroe (Chgo.); Stadium, Mo. Athletic (St. Louis); Elks. Home: 1 Sleepy Hollow Mount Vernon IL 62864 Office: PO Box 1238 Mount Vernon IL 62864

WITHERS, WILLIAM, educator, economist; b. St. Louis, Dec. 21, 1905; s. John W. and Margaret (Mathews) W.; A.B., Columbia, 1926, A.M., 1928, PH.D., 1932; m. Irma Rittenhouse, May 29, 1931. Instr. econs. Lehigh U., 1927-29, N.Y. U., 1929-31; research asso. Tchrs. Coll. Columbia, 1931-32, chmn. social sci. dept. New Coll., 1932-37, asst. prof. edn. Tchrs. Coll., 1935-37; prin. research supr. WPA, 1937; asst. prof. econ. Queens Coll., 1937-40, asso. prof., 1940-51, prof., 1951-74, prof. emeritus, 1974—, chmn. econs. dept. and div. social scis., 1937-42, chmn. div. contemporary civilization, 1950, chmn. econ. dept., 1959; dir. N.Y. U. Farm Labor Study, 1960; chief pub. requirements br. WPB, 1942-43. Vice pres. N.Y. Tchrs. Guild, 1943-46; vice chmn. Liberal party N.Y. State, 1945-46. Mem. Ricardo Assn. (pres. 1974—), N.Y. Tchrs. Pension Assn. (pres. 1976—), Am. Econ. Assn., Latin Am. Study Assn., Phi Beta Kappa. Author: The Retirement of National Debts, 1932; Current Social Problems, 1936; Financing Economic Security, 1939; The Public Debt, 1945; Public Finance, 1948; Social Foundations of Education, 1955; Economic Crisis in Latin America, 1964; Freedom Through Power, 1965; Business in Society, 1966; The Corporations and Social Change, 1972; The Crisis in Old Age Finance, 1979. Contbr. to Ency. Social Scis., Am. Econ. Rev., Latin Am. Hist. Rev., Indsl. Gerontology, others. Home: RD 1 Box 40A Eatontown NJ 07724 Office: 500 Fifth Ave Suite 1423 New York NY 10036

WITHERSPOON, GIBSON BOUDINOT, lawyer; b. Lexington, Va., Aug. 7, 1903; s. Elias Boudinot and Magdalene Moore (Gibson) W.; A.B., Washington and Lee U., 1925, J.D., 1927; m. Jewel Cook, Apr. 25, 1940; children—Mary Elizabeth (Mrs. J. George Smith), Jane May (Mrs. Harold Pagan Hope). Admitted to Va. bar, 1926, Miss. bar, 1927, U.S. Supreme Ct. bar; practiced in Meridian, Miss., 1927—; mem. firm Witherspoon, Compton & Mason and predecessor firm. Commr. uniform state laws Miss., 1945—. Pres., Scribes, 1955; dir. Miss. Econ. Council, 1962—. Del., Democratic Nat. Conv., Los Angeles, 1960. Fellow Am. Bar Found.; mem. Am. Bar Assn. (chmn. state legislation com. 1962-63, mem. bd. govs. 1970-72, mem. ho. of dels. 1955-75, Nat. Inst. Justice 1977—), Probate Counsel, Fedn. Ins. Counsel, Internat. Assn. Ins. Counsel, Internat. Trial Counsel, Miss. Bar Assn. (past pres.), Miss. (dir.), Meridian (dir.) chambers commerce. Presbyterian (elder). Clubs: Northwood Country, Downtown, Meridian Kiwanis (past pres., bd. govs.). Contbr. articles to legal jours. Asso. editor Comml. Law Jour., 1945—, bd. govs., 1962-72. Home: 2698 23d Ave Meridian MS 39301 Office: Citizens Nat Bank Bldg Meridian MS 39301

WITHEY, ROBERT ARTHUR, state ofcl.; b. Long Branch, N.J., Dec. 21, 1929; s. Clarence Waldo and Mary Josephine (White) W.; B.A., Rutgers U., 1952, M.A., 1957, postgrad., 1957-59; m. Maria Ann Foderaro, Aug. 16, 1952; children—Robert J., Kimberly S., Theodore P. Tchr., counselor, coach, adminstr. pub. schs., Metuchen, N.J., 1952-59; cons. N.J. Dept. Edn., 1959-60, asst. dir., 1960-70, chief, 1970-72; dep. commr. Vt. Dept. Edn., Montpelier, 1972, commr., 1972—. Mem. Vt. Gov.'s Cabinet, Vt.-1202 Commn., Bicentennial Commn., Tchr. Retirement Commn., Ednl. TV Commn.; exec. sec. N.J. Assn. High Sch. Councils, 1961-68; mem. steering com. Ednl. Commn. of States. Mem. Nat., Vt. edn. assns., New Eng., Vt. supts. assns., Am. Assn. Sch. Adminstrs., Vt. Sch. Dirs. Assn. Rotarian. Club: Exchange. Author transparencies. Home: Mt Philo Rd Shelburne VT 05482 Office: Vermont Dept Edn State St Montpelier VT 05602

WITHROW, FRANK BURDON, JR., educator; b. Dallas, Feb. 9, 1926; s. Frank Burdon and Desdie (Thomas) W.; B.S., Washington U., St. Louis, 1951, M.S., 1953, Ph.D., 1963; m. Margaret Ellen Schram, July 28, 1950; children—David, Desdie, Ellen, Kirti. Tchr., supr., research asst. Central Inst. for Deaf, St. Louis, 1952-61; dir. research and clin. services Ill. Sch. for Deaf, Jacksonville, 1961-67; acting dir. div. tng. programs Bur. Edn. for Handicapped, U.S. Office Edn., Washington, 1967, dir. div. edn. services, 1967-72, chief ednl. tech. devel. programs Office of Libraries and Learning Resources, 1978—; exec. sec. nat. adv. com. on handicapped children, nat. adv. com. on edn. of deaf HEW, 1972-73, exec. sec. nat. adv. com. on handicapped, 1973—. Battelle Meml. Inst. fellow, Columbus, Ohio, 1974-75; spl. asst. Bur. Edn. for Handicapped, U.S. Office of Edn., 1975. Scoutmaster, neighborhood commr. Boy Scouts Am., 1952-67. Served with USMCR, 1943-45, 51-52. Mem. Am. Speech and Hearing Assn., Council Exceptional Children. Home: 232 E St NE Washington DC 20002 Office: Dept Edn 400 Maryland Ave SW Washington DC 20202

WITHROW, RICHARD MARSHALL, stockbroker; b. Duluth, Minn., Mar. 4, 1917; s. Atkinson Wray and Willena (Marshall) W.; B.S., Northwestern U., 1938; m. Helen Bull, July 12, 1947; children—Richard Marshall, John Howells, David Bull. Trader, Hulburd, Warren & Chandler, Chgo., 1938-42, office mgr., Dixon, Ill. br., 1947-50; mng. partner Lamson Bros. & Co., Chgo., 1950—; exec. v.p., dir. Shearson Hayden Stone, Inc., 1976—. Tchr., Grain Exchange Inst., 1953-54, dir., 1955-70, pres., 1970; dir. Chgo. Bd. Trade, 1963-64, 2d vice-chmn., 1965. Campaign chmn. Crusade of Mercy, 1959-60. Served with USNR, 1942-46; PTO. Mem. Assn. Commodity Commn. Mchts. (pres. 1970-71), N.Y. Stock Exchange (asso.), Commodity Club Chgo., Chgo. Merc. Exchange, Chgo., Mpls., Kansas City bds. trade, Sigma Chi. Clubs: Chgo. Econ., Chgo. Yacht. Contbr. articles to yachting mags. Home: 822 Dundee Ave Barrington IL 60010 Office: 111 W Jackson St Chicago IL 60604

WITHROW, WILLIAM JOHN, museum dir.; b. Toronto, Ont., Can., Sept. 30, 1926; s. Wilfred Forbes and Evelyn W.; B.A., U. Toronto, 1950, B.Ed., 1955, M.Ed., 1958, M.A., 1961; m. June Roselea Van Ostrom, 1948; children—John, Stephen, Ann, David. Head dept. art Earl Haig Collegiate, North York, Ont., 1951-59; dir. Art Gallery Ont., Toronto, 1961—. Served to capt. Canadian Army, 1945-47. Recipient Centennial medal Govt. Can., 1967. Mem. Canadian Museums Assn., Assn. Art Mus. Dirs., Canadian Art Mus. Dirs. Orgn. Club: Univ. (Toronto). Author: Sorel Etrog Sculpture, 1967; Contemporary Canadian Painting, 1972. Office: 317 Dundas St W Toronto ON M5T 1G4 Canada

WITKE, EDWARD CHARLES, educator; b. Los Angeles, Sept. 22, 1931; s. Emil Ernst and Ethel Ann (Martin) W.; A.B., UCLA, 1953; A.M., Harvard, 1957, Ph.D., 1960; m. Aileen Patricia Gatten, Oct. 10, 1975; 1 dau., Alexandra Astra. Asst. prof. classics U. Chgo., 1962-63; asst. prof., asso. prof. classics U. Calif. at Berkeley, 1963-70; prof. classics State U. N.Y., Binghamton, 1970-71; prof. Greek and Latin, U. Mich., Ann Arbor, 1971—, asso. dean Coll. Lit., Sci and Arts, 1971-74, dir. Program in Comparative Lit., 1971-78; prof. in charge archaeol. summer sch. Am. Acad. in Rome, 1967; lectr. Kyoto U., 1966-67, Columbia U. Seminar on Classical Civilization, 1971—; coordinator Nat. Endowment for Humanities curricular innovation seminar Heidelberg Coll., summer 1973. Served with AUS, 1953-56. Recipient Prix de Rome in classics Am. Acad. in Rome, 1960-62. Fulbright fellow, Italy, 1960-61. Mem. Am. Philol. Assn., Dante Soc. Am., Mediaeval Assn. of Pacific States (pres. 1970), Mediaeval Acad. Am. (councillor 1971-74), Soc. for Promotion Roman Studies (Britain), Phi Beta Kappa. Democrat. Anglican. Club: University (Ann Arbor). Author: Enarratio Catulliana, 1968; Latin Satire: The Structure of Persuasion, 1970; Numen Litterarum: The Old and the New in Latin Poetry from Constantine to Gregory the Great, 1971; articles and revs. in numerous profl. jours. Mem. editorial bd. Medievalia et Humanistica, 1970—, Mich. Quarterly Review, 1977—. Home: 1224 Olivia Ave Ann Arbor MI 48104. *In my work, the world of late antiquity and early Christianity offers many parallels startlingly familiar to modern history and the society of our times, patterns and parallels invisible without an awareness of what came before.*

WITKIN, EVELYN MAISEL, geneticist; b. N.Y.C., Mar. 9, 1921; d. Joseph and Mary (Levin) Maisel; A.B., N.Y. U., 1941; M.A., Columbia U., 1943, Ph.D., 1947; D.Sc. honoris causa N.Y. Med. Coll., 1978; m. Herman A. Witkin, July 9, 1943 (dec. July 1979); children—Joseph, Andrew. Mem. staff genetics dept. Carnegie Inst., Washington, 1954-55; mem. faculty State U. N.Y. Downstate Med. Center, Bklyn., 1955-71, prof. medicine, 1968-71; prof. biol. scis. Douglass Coll., Rutgers U., 1971-79, Barbara McClintock prof. genetics, 1979—. Postdoctoral fellow Am. Cancer Soc., 1947-49; fellow Carnegie Instn., 1957; Selman A. Waksman lectr., 1960; grantee NIH, 1956—; recipient Prix Charles Leopold Mayer, French Acad. Scis., 1977, Lindback award, 1979. Mem. Nat. Acad. Scis., AAAS, Am. Acad. Arts and Scis., Am. Genetics Soc., Am. Soc. Microbiology, Radiation Research Soc. Author articles; mem. editorial bds. profl. jours. Home: 88 Balcort Dr Princeton NJ 08540 Office: Douglass Coll Rutgers Univ New Brunswick NJ 08903

WITKIN, ISAAC, internat. mcht.; b. N.Y.C., Feb. 3, 1892; s. Myer and Rachel (Smerling) W.; A.B., Harvard, 1914; m. Miriam N. Newman, Dec. 23, 1915; children—Richard, William Isaac. With J. Aron & Co., Inc., coffee importers, N.Y.C., 1914-26, mgr. export dept., 1918-19, dir., 1918- 26, v.p., 1926-38; engaged principally in importation of cocoa beans and commodity futures on Commodity Exchange and N.Y. Cocoa Exchange, 1938-75; sr. partner Gen. Cocoa Co.; mng. dir. Gen. Cocoa Co. Holland B.V., Amsterdam, 1962—; cons. Otto Gerdau & Co., N.Y.C., 1977—. A founder, mem. N.Y. Cocoa Exchange, Inc. 1925, 1st pres., 1925-26, mem. bd. mgrs., 1925-51; pres., 1944-47 pres. emeritus, 1975—. Mem. N.Y. State Guard, 1940-43. Mem. Phi Beta Kappa. Jewish. Club: Harvard (N.Y.C.). Lectr., contbr. articles on world cocoa trade and econ. and polit. subjects to trade, fin. and other periodicals. Home: 1 Fifth Ave New York NY 10003 also Bridgewater CT 06752 Office: 82 Wall St New York NY 10005

WITKOP, BERNHARD, chemist; b. Freiburg, Baden, Germany, May 9, 1917; s. Philipp W. and Hedwig M. (Hirschhorn) W.; diploma U. Munich, 1938, Ph.D., 1940, Sc.D., 1945, Privat-Dozent, 1947; m. Marlene Prinz, Aug. 8, 1945; children—Cornelia Johanna, Phyllis, Thomas. Came to U.S., 1947, naturalized, 1953. Matthew T. Mellon research fellow Harvard, 1947-48, mem. faculty, 1948-50; spl. USPHS fellow NIH Nat. Heart Inst., 1950-52; vis. sci. Nat. Inst. Arthritis and Metabolic Diseases, 1953, chemist, 1954-55, chief sect. metabolities, 1956—, chief lab. chemistry, 1957—. Vis. prof. U. Kyoto (Japan), 1961, U. Freiburg (Germany), 1962. Mem. bd. Internat. Sci. Exchange, 1974, mem. exec. Com. NRC, 1975, mem. Com. Internat. Exchange, 1977. Recipient Superior Service award USPHS, 1967; Paul Karrer gold medal U. Zurich, 1971; Kun-ni-to (medal of sci. and culture 2d class) Emperor of Japan, 1975; Alexander von Humboldt award for sr. U.S. scientists, 1978. Mem. Am. Chem. Soc. (Hillebrand award 1958), Nat. Acad. Scis., Acad. Leopoldina (fgn.), Pharm. Soc. Japan (hon.). Home: 3807 Montrose Dr Chevy Chase MD 20015 Office: Nat Insts Health Bethesda MD 20014

WITKOP, CARL JACOB, educator, geneticist; b. East Grand Rapids, Mich., Dec. 27, 1920; s. Carl J. and Frances (Miller) W.; B.S., Mich. State Coll., 1944; D.D.S., U. Mich., 1949, M.S., 1954; m. Mary Worcester, Sept. 3, 1946; children—Carl Gray, Mary Margaret, Martha Frances; m. 2d, Mary Ann Jacobson, Oct. 6, 1966; children—Andrea Jean, Steven Carl, Annake Karin. Commd. asst. dental surgeon USPHS, 1949, advanced through grades to dental dir., 1961; dental officer Nat. Inst. Dental Research, 1950-54, chief human genetic br., Bethesda, Md., 1954-66; instr. med. genetics Georgetown U., 1959-65; chmn. div. genetics, prof. U. Minn. Dental Sch., 1966—, prof. dermatology, 1971—. Cons. Childrens Hosp., Washington, 1955—, Nat. Found., NIH. Diplomate Am. Bd. Oral Pathology. Fellow Am. Acad. Oral Pathology (pres. 1974), AAAS (chmn. sect. on dentistry); mem. Am. Dental Assn., Am. Soc. Human Genetics (sec. 1968-70), Am. Soc. Dermatopathology, Am. Soc. Dermatogenetics, Sigma Xi. Author: Genetics and Dental Health, 1962; Albinism, 1971; (with J.J. Sauk, Jr.) Dental and Oral Manifestations of Hereditary Diseases, 1971. Home: 9 Manitoba Rd Hopkins MN 55343 Office: Sch Dentistry U Minn Minneapolis MN 55455. *For true progress to occur in science, original observations must be made. Therefore it is as important to know what is not known about a field of science as it is to know what is known.*

WITMER, GEORGE ROBERT, state justice; b. Webster, N.Y., Dec. 26, 1904; s. George H. and Lillian (Woodhull) W.; A.B., U. Rochester (N.Y.), 1926; LL.B., Harvard U., 1929; m. Marian P. Costello, June 27, 1936; children—George Robert, John R., Thomas W., Sylvia Witmer Bissell. Admitted to N.Y. bar, 1929; pvt. practice, Rochester, 1929-45; partner firm Easton & Witmer, 1931-45; surrogate, Monroe County, 1946-53; justice N.Y. State Supreme Ct., 1954—, asso. justice appellate div., 1st dept., 1963-67, appellate div., 4th dept., 1968—, adminstrv. judge 7th Jud. Dist., 1962-68; town atty., Webster, 1934-35. Supr., Town of Webster and County of Monroe, 1936-45; chmn. Webster Republican Com., 1933-45, mem. exec. com., 1933-45. Mem. Am., N.Y. State, Monroe County bar assns., Am. Law Inst., Webster Grange, Webster C. of C., Theta Chi. Club: Masons. Co-author: N.Y. Pattern Jury Instructions-Civil, Vol. 1, 1965, Vol. 11, 1968. Home: 45 Corning Park Webster NY 14580 Office: Hall of Justice Exchange St Rochester NY 14614

WITMER, GEORGE ROBERT, JR., lawyer; b. Rochester, N.Y., Mar. 23, 1937; s. George Robert and Marian Pauline (Costello) W.; A.B., U. Rochester, 1959; LL.B., Harvard U., 1962; m. Nancy Rosetta Wenner, Dec. 28, 1968; children—Wendy Lynn, Heidi Dawn, George Robert, III, Frank David. Admitted to N.Y. State bar, 1962; asso. firm Nixon, Hargrave, Devans & Doyle, Rochester, 1962-70, partner, 1970—; instr. in bus. law U. Rochester, 1965-66; mem. com. to advise and cons. Jud. Conf. State N.Y. on Civil Practice Law and Rules, 1970-77. Mem. N.Y. State Republican Com., 1976—; trustee Eastman Dental Center, Rochester, 1977—, U. Rochester, 1979—; chmn. trustees' council U. Rochester, 1977-78. Mem. Am. law Inst., Monroe County (N.Y.) Bar Assn., N.Y. State Bar Assn. (ho. of dels. 1978—), Am. Bar Assn., Phi Beta Kappa. Clubs: Rotary (dir. local club 1977-79) (Rochester); Masons. Home: 756 John Glenn Blvd Webster NY 14580 Office: Lincoln First Tower Rochester NY 14604

WITMER, GLENN EDWARD, publisher; b. Kitchener, Ont., Can., Oct. 15, 1942; s. Vernon Hallman and Vinetta Rose (Shantz) W.; B.A., York U., Toronto. Tchr., Scarborough Bd. Edn., Toronto, 1962-65; dir. Canadian Acad. Langs., Toronto, 1965-66; v.p. Burns & MacEachern Pub. Ltd., Toronto, 1966-71; gen. sales mgr. McClelland & Stewart Pubs., Toronto, 1971-73; mng. dir. Pagurian Press Ltd., Toronto, 1973-75; exec. dir. Can. Book Pubs. Council, Toronto, 1975-78; pres. Personal Library Pubs. div. Bestsellers Inc., Toronto, 1978—; pub. The Can. Report: The Internat. Newsletter of the Publishing Industry in Can., 1978—. Author: Protecting Your Home and Property, 1979. Home: 145 Marlee Ave Toronto ON M6B 3H3 Canada Office: Personal Library Publishers Suite 439 17 Queen St E Toronto ON M5C 1P9 Canada

WITMER, JOHN ALBERT, librarian; b. Lancaster, Pa., Nov. 29, 1920; s. Albert Franklin and Mary Esther (Conrad) W.; A.B., Wheaton Coll., 1942, A.M., 1946; Th.M., Dallas Theol. Sem., 1946, Th.D., 1953; M.S. in L.S., E. Tex. State U., 1969; m. Doris May Ferry, June 10, 1943; children—Marilyn May (Mrs. John Marc Custis), John Richard, Deborah Carol (Mrs. Richard Allan Redd). Mng. editor Child Evanglism mag., Dallas, 1944-46; instr. systematic theology Dallas Theol. Sem., 1947-54, asst. prof., 1954—, librarian Mosher Library, 1964—; certified instr. Dale Carnegie Course, 1956—. Treas., Evang. Communications Research Found., 1970-73. Bd. dirs. Dallas Bible Coll., chmn., 1974-77; bd. dirs. Evangelical Projects, 1975—. Mem. ALA, S.W., Tex. (publs. com. 1979—), Dallas County (pres. 1969-70), Am. Theol. library assns., Christian Librarians Fellowship (chmn. 1970-71), Evang. Theol. Soc. Contbr. articles to profl. jours., essays; editor The Christian Librarian, 1972-74. Home: 6630 Westlake Ave Dallas TX 75214

WITMER, WILLIAM KERN, petroleum exec.; b. Bartlesville, Okla., June 16, 1926; s. Russell Rudolph and Crystal Orien (Kern) W.; B.S., Okla. State U., 1949; grad. Advanced Mgmt. Program, Harvard, 1973; m. Joan Curtis, Nov. 17, 1950; children—Diane (Mrs. Charles Carselowey), Joanne, Marianne, Robert. With Cities Service Oil Co., Bartlesville, Okla., 1949-58, mgr. budget dept., 1956-58; with Cities Service Co., N.Y.C., 1958-71, mgr. investor relations, 1964-66, staff v.p., 1964-66, gen. mgr. real estate, 1968-71, treas., Tulsa, 1975—; v.p. finance, treas. Cities Service Gas Co., Oklahoma City, 1971-75. Served with USNR, 1944-46. Mem. Financial Execs. Inst. (dir. Okla. chpt.), Newcomen Soc., Am. Petroleum Inst., Beta Alpha Psi, Kappa Sigma. Mason. Club: Summit. Home: 4304 E 76th St Tulsa OK 74136 Office: Box 300 Tulsa OK 74102

WITMEYER, STANLEY HERBERT, educator, artist; b. Palmyra, Pa., Feb. 14, 1913; s. Harry George and Carrie (Himmelberger) W.; Asso. in Arts and Sci., Rochester (N.Y.) Inst. Tech., 1936; B.S., State U. N.Y. at Buffalo, 1939; M.F.A., Syracuse U., 1946; m. Marian Hebing, June 22, 1940 (dec. May 1977); children—Gail, Donald, Robert, Anne, Paul; m. 2d, Helen, Jan. 13, 1979. Designer, Eastman Kodak Co., Rochester, 1936; designer Giant Enterprises, Harrisburg, Pa., summers 1937-38; free lance designer, Rochester, Buffalo, Harrisburg, 1936—; art supr. Cuba (N.Y.) Pub. Schs., 1939-43; dir. Sch. Art and Design Rochester Inst. Tech., 1952-78, asso. dean Coll. Fine and Applied Arts, 1970-78, ret., 1978—. Exhibited in group shows Rochester, Buffalo, Syracuse, Olean, N.Y., Honolulu; permanent and pvt. collections. Mem. Art Commn. Rochester. Served with C.E., AUS, 1943-46. Recipient Distinguished Alumni award State U. Coll. N.Y., Buffalo, 1968; Distinguished Alumni award Rochester Inst. Tech., 1971, Distinguished teacher award State of N.Y. Art Teachers, 1978, named to Athletic Hall of Fame, 1971. Mem. N.Y. Tchrs. Art Assn., Nat. Art Edn. Assn., Nat. Assn. Schs. Schs. Art (chmn. program com. 1972—). Presbyn. Club: Rochester Art, Rochester Torch (dir.). Home: 300 Sunnyside Dr Rochester NY 14623

WITSCHI, MARTIN BERCHTOLD, banker; b. Basel, Switzerland, Aug. 12, 1929; s. Hermann and Rosa (Gerber) W.; m. Jolanda M. Wyssling, Mar. 27, 1954; children—Franziska, Mark, Thomas. With J. Henry Schroder Bank & Trust Co., N.Y.C., 1952—, sr. v.p., 1971-73, exec. v.p., 1973-76, pres., 1976—, also dir., dir. Schroders Inc., 1975—. Office: 1 State St New York City NY 10015

WITT, CHARLES E., coal co. exec.; b. Jenkins, Ky., Sept. 24, 1917; s. L. L. and Dez (Litton) W.; A.B., W.Va. U., 1939; m. Jane Reed, Sept. 11, 1940; children—Cordella Witt Carrico, Susan Witt Beam, Amy. Purchasing agt. Fairmont Supply Co. (subs. Consolidation Coal Co.), Washington, Pa., 1946-57, br. mgr., 1956-57, dir. purchases parent co., Pitts., 1957-62, v.p. purchasing, 1962-72, chmn. bd. Fairmont Supply Co., 1972-77, sr. v.p. Consolidation Coal Co., 1972-77; dir. Nat. Mine Service Co., 1977—. Home: 118 Lebanon Hills Dr Pittsburgh PA 15228 Office: 600 Grant St Suite 4975 Pittsburgh PA 15219

WITT, NORBERT ALBERT, chem. co. exec.; b. Muskegon, Mich., Oct. 5, 1908; s. Anthony and Anna (Bethke) W.; ed. pvt. schs.; m. Cecil Ray Porter, July 28, 1935; children—Barbara Ann (Mrs. James Ryon), Carol Ann (Mrs. Leeland Stanford Macphail III). With Procter & Gamble Co., 1928-32; with Lever Bros. Co., 1933-55, dist. mgr. nat. sales, 1946-55; with Noxzema Chem. Co. (now Noxell Corp.), Balt., 1955—, exec. v.p., 1960-63, pres., 1963-73, chief exec. officer, 1970-73, vice chmn. bd., 1973—, also dir.; dir. Noxzema Chem. Co. Can., Md. Nat. Bank, Provident Savs. Bank, U.S. Fidelity & Guarantee, Proprietary Assn. Served with AUS, 1944-46; ETO. Mem. N.A.M. (dir.). Office: Noxell Corp 11050 York Rd Baltimore MD 21203*

WITT, RAYMOND BUCKNER, JR., lawyer; b. Lenoir City, Tenn., Apr. 20, 1915; s. Raymond Buckner and Gertrude (Jackson) W.; A.B., U. Chattanooga, 1937; LL.B., U. N.C., 1939; m. Florence Elder Bagley, Sept. 14, 1943; children—Florence Elder, Mary Alice, George Evans. Admitted to Tenn. bar, 1939, since practiced in Chattanooga; with Witt, Gaither, Whitaker and predecessor firms, 1945—, partner, 1946—. Dir., gen. counsel Dixie Yarns, Inc., 1947—. Pres., Met. Council Community Services, 1966-68; mem. Chattanooga Bd. Edn., 1953-65, vice chmn., 1963-65; chmn. Chattanooga Bicentennial Religious Com., 1976; chmn. bd. Chattanooga-Hamilton County Bicentennial Library. Trustee Westend Found.; trustee, sec., gen. counsel U. Chattanooga Found. Served to lt. comdr. USNR, 1942-45; PTO. Recipient Distinguished Service award Chattanooga Kiwanis, 1963, Tenn. Sch. Bds. Assn., 1963. Methodist (chmn. commn. on Christian edn. 1953-55, ch. sch. supt. 1955-60). Home: 1615 Minnekahda Rd Chattanooga TN 37405 Office: American Nat Bank Bldg Chattanooga TN 37402

WITT, ROBERT J., advt. agy. exec.; b. Chgo., Apr. 21, 1928; s. Henry F. and Fannie (Greenberg) W.; B.S., U. Ill., 1949; m. Diane J. Glassman, May 23, 1953; children—Gregg, Steven, Teri Ann. Mgr. sales, advt. Sterling Furniture Corp., Chgo., 1949-50; advt. dir. Nat. Appliance Radio/TV Dealers Assn., Chgo., 1950; account exec. Garfield-Linn & Co., Chgo., 1950-53, v.p., 1953-57, exec. v.p., 1957-70, pres., 1971—. Chmn. communications div. Jewish United Fund, 1973-74, cabinet mem., 1975, 76-78. Mem. Chgo. Advt. Club, Indsl. Advertisers Assn., Am. Assn. Advt. Agys. (bd. govs.), Western Advt. Golf Assn., Old Elm Civic Assn., Alpha Delta Sigma. Mem. B'nai B'rith. Club: Briarwood Country (Deerfield). Home: 2931 Twin Oaks Dr Highland Park IL 60035 Office: 875 N Michigan Ave Chicago IL 60611

WITT, ROBERT JOHN, retailer; b. Detroit, July 8, 1925; s. Vernon and Anastasia (Kruszewski) Witkowski; B.B.A., U. Mich., 1946; M.B.A., Harvard, 1948; m. Janice T. Kelly, June 24, 1950; children—Robert John, Wendy Ann, Geoffrey Rowen, Douglas Edward. With R. H. Macy Co., N.Y.C., 1948-51; mdse. mgr. Wallachs Inc., 1951-61, pres., 1965-70; pres. Baskin Clothing Co., Chgo., 1961-65; pres. Hart Schaffner & Marx Retail Stores div. Hart Shaffner & Marx, Chgo., 1967—, chmn., chief exec. officer, 1972—, exec. v.p. parent co., 1972—, also dir. parent co.; pres. Retail Stores div. Cluett, Peabody & Co., Inc., Chgo., 1979—, pres. Lytton's, Chgo., 1979—. Chmn. men's wear industry div. Lighthouse for Blind, N.Y.C., 1965, Greater N.Y. Fund, 1966; active local Boy Scouts Am., 1956—. Served to lt. (j.g.) USNR, 1943-46. Mem. World Bus. Council, Chgo. Presidents Orgn. Clubs: N.Y. Athletic, Harvard, Union League (N.Y.C.); Indian Hill Country (Winnetka, Ill.). Home: 29 Indian Hill Rd Winnetka IL 60093 Office: 14 E Jackson Blvd Chicago IL 60604

WITT, ROBERT R., lawyer; b. Newark, Nov. 17, 1921; grad. Seton Hall Coll.; LL.B., Fordham U., 1948; m. Mary Witt; children—Patricia, Robert R., Gregory, Pamela. Admitted to N.J. bar, 1948; mem. firm Carton, Nary, Witt & Arvantis, Asbury Park, N.J. Trustee, v.p. Jersey Shore Med. Center. Fellow Am. Coll. Trial Lawyers, Internat. Acad. Trial Lawyers; mem. Trial Attys. N.J. (chmn. bd., past pres.), Def. Research Inst., Am., N.J. State, Monmouth County (past pres.) bar assns., Am. Arbitration Assn., Fedn. Ins. Counsel. Office: Route 66 at Garden State Pkwy PO Box 1229 Asbury Park NJ 07712

WITTBRODT, EDWIN STANLEY, bank exec., former air force officer; b. Flint, Mich., Aug. 13, 1918; s. Stanley Frank and Marie (Ross) W.; student Gen. Motors Inst. Tech., 1936-38, Grad. Sch. Dept. Agr., 1950-51, Indsl. Coll. Armed Forces, 1961-62, George Washington U., 1962, U. So. Calif., 1963-64; m. Joan Helen Miller, Apr. 22, 1950; children—Stephanie Rita, Candace Lee, Edwin Stanley. Joined U.S. Army, 1941, commd. 2d lt., 1942, advanced through grades to brig. gen. USAF, 1968; various assignments, U.S., 1941-49; budget officer Hdqrs. USAF, 1949-53, 56-61; dir. budget and accounting Hdqrs. N.E. Air Command, Nfld., 1953-56; comptroller space systems div., Los Angeles, 1962-64, aero. systems div.,

Wright-Patterson AFB, 1964-66; asst. comptroller USAF, 1966-67; dir. accounting and finance Hdqrs. USAF, 1967-68; asst. comptroller air force for accounting and finance, comdr. Air Force Accounting and Finance Center, Denver, 1968-71, v.p. systems Central Bank Denver, 1971—; dir. Computer Congenerics Corp. Colo., Hasa Corp. Co-chmn. Combined Fed. Campaign, Denver, 1968-69. Hon. dir. USO, Denver, 1968—, mem. council, 1971—. Decorated Legion of Merit, D.S.M., Soldier's medal, Air Force Commendation medal with oak leaf cluster. Mem. Am. Soc. Mil. Comptrollers (past pres. Washington chpt., nat. v.p. 1968-70, pres. Denver chpt. 1971-72), Assn. Govt. Accountants, Assn. Mil. Banks (dir. 1974—), Am. Inst. Banking, Denver C. of C. (chmn. mil. affairs com. 1979—), Air Force Assn. (v.p. N. Colo. 1971-72, pres. Silver and Gold chpt. 1972-73, state treas. 1976—). Home: 10 Niblick Ln Littleton CO 80123 Office: Two Park Central PO Box 5548 TA Denver CO 80217. *I have adopted two attitudes that I believe assisted me in all of my undertakings: (1)—that of being what I call a "responsible non-conformist" and (2)—"no problems—just opportunities."*

WITTCOFF, HAROLD AARON, chem. co. exec.; b. Marion, Ind., July 3, 1918; s. Morris and Bessie (Pruss) W.; A.B. magna cum laude, DePauw U., 1940; Ph.D., Northwestern U., 1943; grad. Advanced Mgmt. Program, Harvard U., 1964; m. Dorothy Brochin Glance, Mar. 31, 1946; children—Ralph, Theodore A. With Gen. Mills, Inc., Mpls., 1943-79, head chem. research dept., 1952-56, dir. chem. research, 1956-67, v.p., dir. chem. research and devel., 1967-69, v.p., dir. corp. research, 1969-79; dir. research and devel. Kour Chems., Beer Sheva, Israel, 1979—; adj. prof. chemistry U. Minn., 1973—. Recipient Minn. award Am. Chem. Soc., 1976. Mem. Phi Beta Kappa, Sigma Xi, Phi Eta Sigma. Author: The Phosphatides, 1951; Industrial Organic Chemistry: A Perspective, 1979. Contbr. articles to profl. jours. Patentee in field. Office: PO Box 60 Beer Sheva Israel

WITTE, MERLIN MICHAEL, oil co. exec.; b. Los Angeles, Mar. 28, 1926; s. Anthony A. and Julia (Mackey) W.; B.A., Loyola U., Los Angeles, 1949; m. Donna Patricia Hurth, Jan. 22, 1949; children—James Anthony, Daniel Michael, Catherine Ann, Michael Leon, Robert Joseph, Joseph William, Anne Marie, William Benson, Janet Mary. With IRS, U.S. Treasury Dept., 1949-51; investment, tax mgr. McCulloch Motors Corp., also Robert P. McCulloch, 1951-55; pres., gen. mgr., dir. McCulloch Oil Corp., Los Angeles, 1956—. Served with USAAF, 1944-45. Mem. Ind. Oil and Gas Producers Assn., Ind. Petroleum Assn., Western, W. Central Tex. oil and gas assns., Petroleum Club Los Angeles, Town Hall. Clubs: Bel-Air Country (Los Angeles); La Quinta (Calif.) Country. Home: 565 Moreno Ave Los Angeles CA 90049 Office: 10880 Wilshire Blvd Los Angeles CA 90024

WITTEN, DAVID MELVIN, radiologist; b. Trenton, Mo., Aug. 16, 1926; s. Buford Isom and Mary Louise (Melvin) W.; student Trenton Jr. Coll., 1943-44, 46-47; A.B., Washington U., St. Louis, 1950, M.D., 1954; M.S., in Radiology, Mayo Grad. Sch. Medicine, U. Minn., 1960; m. Netta Lee Watkins, Dec. 23, 1950; children—David Melvin, II, Michael Lee. Intern, Virginia Mason Hosp., Seattle, 1954-55; practice medicine specializing in family medicine, Trenton, Mo., 1955-57; fellow in radiology Mayo Clinic/Mayo Found., Rochester, Minn., 1957-60, cons. in diagnostic roentgenology Mayo Clinic, 1960-70; instr. Mayo Grad. Sch. Medicine, Rochester, 1960-66, asst. prof. radiology, 1966-70; pvt. practice medicine specializing in radiology, Aberdeen, Wash., 1970-71; prof. diagnostic radiology, chmn. dept. diagnostic radiology U. Ala., Birmingham, 1971—; diagnostic radiologist in chief Univ. Hosp., Birmingham, 1971—; pres. U. Ala. Health Services Found., 1973-75. Served with USNR, 1944-46. Diplomate Am. Bd. Radiology. Fellow Am. Coll. Radiology; mem. Radiologic Soc. N. Am., Am. Roentgen Ray Soc., AAAS, Soc. Genitourinary Radiology, Assn. Univ. Radiologists, AMA, Ala. Acad. Radiology, Izaak Walton League, Nat. Audubon Soc. Author: Atlas of Tumor Radiolo - The Breast, 1969; Clinical Urography, 1977; contbr. numerous articles on radiology of breast cancer, urologic and gastrointestinal disease to profl. jours.; editorial bd. Am. Jour. Roentgenology, 1976—, Applied Radiology, 1978—, Urologic Radiology, 1979—. Home: 3516 Old Leeds Ct Birmingham AL 35213 Office: 619 S 19th St Birmingham AL 35233

WITTEN, LOUIS, educator; b. Balt., Apr. 13, 1921; s. Abraham and Bessie (Perman) W.; B.E., Johns Hopkins, 1941, Ph.D., 1951; B.S., N.Y. U., 1944; m. Lorraine Wollach, Mar. 27, 1949; children—Edward, Celia, Matthew, Jesse. Research asso. Princeton, 1951-53, U. Md., 1953-54; staff scientist Lincoln Lab. Mass. Inst. Tech., 1954-55; asso. dir., head physics dept. RIAS, Martin-Marietta Corp., Balt., 1955-68; adj. prof. physics Drexel Inst. Tech., 1956-68; prof. physics, head dept. physics U. Cin., 1968—. Fulbright lectr. Weizmann Inst. Sci., Rehovot, Israel, 1963-64. Trustee, v.p. Gravity Research Found., 1967—, Balt. Hebrew Coll., 1965-68. Served to 1st lt. USAAF, 1942-46. Mem. Am. Assn. Physics Tchrs., AAAS, AAUP, Am. Math. Soc., Am. Astron. Soc., Am. Phys. Soc., Sigma Xi, Tau Beta Pi. Editor: Gravitation: An Introduction to Current Research, 1962; Relativity: Proceedings of the Relativity Conference in the Midwest, 1969; Asymptotic Structure of Space-Time, 1977. Contbr. articles to profl. jours. Patentee in field. Home: 7920 Rollingknolls Dr Cincinnati OH 45237

WITTENBERG, JAMES KEECH, lawyer; b. Mpls., Oct. 11, 1930; s. Wilber W. and Josephine (Keech) W.; A.B., Dartmouth, 1952; LL.B., Harvard, 1955; m. Alice Hamlin Edge, Dec. 30, 1960; children—Anne Hamlin, Charles Keech, Katherine Glessner. Admitted to Minn. bar, 1955, Calif. bar, 1957; practiced in San Francisco, 1957-63, Mpls., 1963—; asso. firm Brobeck, Phleger & Harrison, 1957-63; atty. Internat. Multifoods Corp., 1963—, gen. counsel, sec., 1967—, v.p., then corporate devel., 1969—; partner firm Doherty, Rumble & Butler, 1973—. Bd. dirs. Minn. Fgn. Policy Assn. St. Paul Chamber Orch.; trustee The Blake Schs., 1971—. Mem. Am., Minn., Calif. bar assns., Com. on Fgn. Relations. Clubs: Minneapolis, Minikakda. Home: 2305 Oliver Ave S Minneapolis MN 55405 Office: 3750 IDS Tower Minneapolis MN 55402

WITTENMEYER, CHARLES E., lawyer; b. Centerville, Iowa, Sept. 3, 1903; s. Thomas William and Maggie E. (Lantz) W.; LL.B., Drake U., 1928, J.D.; m. Dorothy P. Proctor, Mar. 4, 1931; 1 dau., Sheila JoAnn (Mrs. Floyd Darrell Goar). Admitted to Iowa bar, 1928, U.S. Supreme Ct.; practiced in Mapleton, 1928-33, Davenport, 1933—; city atty. Davenport, 1944-54; dir. Brenton First Nat. Bank, Davenport. Trustee Fejervary Home. Chmn., Scott County Young Republicans, 1934-36, 2d Dist. Young Reps., 1936-38; chmn. Scott County Rep. Central Com., 1938-56, Rep. City Central Com., 1944-57, 1st Dist. chmn., 1952-56; Rep. nat. committeeman from Iowa, 1956-75; del. Rep. Nat. Conv., 1944, 56, 60, 64, 68, 72, chmn. credentials com., 1964, chmn. com. rules and order bus., 1968. Mem. Am., Iowa (life), Scott County bar assns., Iowa Hist. Soc. (life), Davenport C. of C. (past pres., past dir.), Iowa Farm Bur. Assn., S.A.R., Gen. Soc. War 1812, Phi Alpha Delta, Phi Gamma Lambda, Theta Nu Epsilon, Helmet and Spurs. Methodist (past trustee ch.). Mason (Shriner). Clubs: Davenport; Hi-12. Home: 301 Forest Rd Davenport IA 52803 Office: Davenport Bank Bldg Davenport IA 52801

WITTER, THOMAS WINSHIP, investment banker, broker; b. Oakland, Calif., Nov. 12, 1928; s. Jean C. and Catherine (Maurer) W.; B.A., U. Calif. at Berkeley, 1951; m. Barbara Rogers, June 22, 1951; children—Jane, Susan, Nancy, Barbara, Thomas. Exec. v.p., dir. Dean Witter Orgn., Dean Witter & Co., Inc. Hon. dir. Samuel Merritt Hosp., Oakland; regent U. Pacific. Served to 1st lt. USMC, 1951-53. Mem. Bond Club San Francisco, Guardsmen. Clubs: Pacific-Union, Olympic, Bohemian (San Francisco); Claremont Country (Oakland). Home: 125 Wildwood Gardens Piedmont CA 94611 Office: 45 Montgomery St San Francisco CA 94106

WITTER, WENDELL WINSHIP, investment banker; b. Berkeley, Calif., Oct. 16, 1910; s. George Franklin, Jr., and Mary Ann (Carter) W.; A.B., U. Calif. at Berkeley, 1932; m. Florence Corder, Oct. 18, 1935 (div. 1973); 1 dau., Wendelyn (Mrs. J. Philip Kistler); m. 2d, Janet Hutchinson Alexander, Dec. 11, 1973 (dec. July 1977); m. 3d, Evelyn Grinter Hankins Gooding, Mar. 26, 1978. Salesman, Dean Witter & Co., San Francisco, 1933-50, partner, 1950-68; exec. v.p., dir. Dean Witter & Co., Inc., 1968-75; cons. Dean Witter Reynolds Inc., 1975-78. Trustee Calif. State Univs. and Colls., 1971-79. Mem. Coordinating Council on Higher Edn., 1970-71. Regent ex-officio U. Calif., 1969-70; trustee San Francisco Bay Area Council; bd. dirs. Golden Gate chpt. A.R.C., San Francisco Symphony Assn.; bd. govs. Assn. Stock Exchange Firms, 1958-62, pres., 1961. Served to lt. col. USAAF, 1941-46. Mem. Investment Bankers Assn., Am. (gov. 1964-66, pres. 1965), Calif. Taxpayers Assn. (dir. 1966-75), Calif. Alumni Assn. (pres. 1968-70), Zeta Psi. Clubs: San Francisco Bond (pres. 1956-57), San Francisco Golf, Pacific-Union, Bohemian, Commonwealth of Calif. Home: 303 Deer Hollow Napa CA 94558 Office: 45 Montgomery St San Francisco CA 94104

WITTER, WILLIAM MAURER, investment banker; b. San Francisco, Feb. 18, 1923; s. Jean Carter and Catharine (Maurer) W.; B.A., U. Calif. at Berkeley, 1947; m. Christene Allen, Aug. 20, 1953. Partner, Dean Witter Reynolds Orgn. (formerly Dean Witter & Co.), 1949-54, mng. partner Midwest div., Chgo., 1953-68, exec. v.p., dir. Dean Witter & Co., Inc., 1968-69, pres., 1969-70, chmn., chief exec. officer, 1970--. Gov., Midwest Stock Exchange, 1964-67, chmn., 1968-69; chmn. Chgo. Assn. Stock Exchange Firms, 1963-64. Trustee Ill. Children's Home and Aid Soc. Mem. Investment Bankers Am. (chmn. central states group 1966-67, gov. 1967-69), Nat. Assn. Security Dealers (gov. 1969), San Francisco C. of C. (pres. 1974, chmn. bd. dirs. 1975). Clubs: Chicago; Links (N.Y.C.); Pacific Union, Bohemian (San Francisco). Home: 1000 Mason St San Francisco CA 94108 Office: 45 Montgomery St San Francisco CA 94106

WITTICH, JOHN JACOB, coll. pres.; b. Huntley, Ill., Nov. 13, 1921; s. John and Eva (Karl) W.; B.A., DePauw U., 1943, LL.D., 1971; M.A., U. N.Mex., 1949; Ph.D., Stanford U., 1952; L.H.D. (hon.), Ill. Coll., 1979; m. Leah Glynn, Apr. 2, 1944; children—Karen Ann, Jane Ellen, John Elliott. Grad. asst. U. N.M., Albuquerque, 1947-48; tchr. Albuquerque High Sch., 1948-49; teaching asst. Stanford, 1949-51; asst. prof. psychology Coll. of Pacific, Stockton, Cal., 1951-52; dean of admissions, dir. scholarships, asso. prof. DePauw U., Greencastle, Ind., 1952-61; dir. Coll. Center of Finger Lakes, Corning, N.Y., 1961-63; exec. dir. Coll. Student Personnel Inst., Claremont, Calif., 1963-68; vis. lectr. Claremont Grad. Sch., 1963-68; pres. MacMurray Coll., Jacksonville, Ill., 1968—. Mem. exec. com. Div. Higher Edn., Central Ill. Conf. of United Meth. Ch., 1968—; mem. exec. com. Fedn. Independent Ill. Colls. and Univs. and Asso. Colls. Ill.; mem. non-pub. adv. com. Ill. Bd. Higher Edn., 1972-78; mem. Nat. Merit Scholarship Selection Com., 1956, 61; cons. Calif. Gov.'s Conf. on Edn., 1965, on Youth, 1966. Served with USMCR, 1943-46. Rockefeller fellow Aspen Inst. for Humanistic Studies, 1979. Mem. Am. Coll. Personnel Assn., Nat. Assn. Coll. Admissions Counselors, AAUP, Am. Psychol. Assn., Central States Coll. Assn. (exec. com. 1969-77, treas. 1970, sec.-treas. 1971-77), DePauw U. So. Calif. Alumni Assn. (pres. 1966-68). Republican. Rotarian. Contbr. articles to popular and profl. jours. Home: 339 E State St Jacksonville IL 62650 Office: MacMurray Coll Jacksonville IL 62650

WITTING, CHRIS J., elec. mfg. exec.; b. Cranford, N.J., Apr. 7, 1915; s. Nicholas and Anne (Begasse) W.; B.S., N.Y. U., 1941; grad. Am. Inst. Banking; student Fordham Law Sch.; D.Eng. (hon.), Clarkson Coll. Tech.; m. Grace Orrok, Oct. 8, 1938; children—Leland James, Anne Kristin, Nancy Jane, Chris J. Exec. asst. Guaranty Trust Co., 1933-36, N.Y. Trust Co., 1936-39; mgr. Price Waterhouse & Co., 1939-41; comptroller, treas. U.S.O. Camp Shows, Inc., 1941-46; mng. dir. Allen B. DuMont Labs., Inc., 1946-53; pres. Westinghouse Broadcasting Co., 1953-54, group v.p. and gen. mgr. consumer products group, Westinghouse Electric Corp., 1954-64; v.p. exec. asst. to chmn. and pres. Internat. Tel.& Tel. Corp., 1964-65; chmn., chief exec. officer, dir. Crouse-Hinds Co., Syracuse, N.Y., 1965—; dir. 1st Trust & Deposit Co., Carrier Corp., Syracuse, Belden Corp., Chgo., Arkwright-Boston Mfrs. Mut. Ins. Co., Mut. Boiler and Machinery Ins. Co., Boston, 1st Comml. Bank Corp., Albany, N.Y. Pres., Crouse-Hinds Found.; chmn. Pub. Auditorium Authority of Pitts. and Allegheny County, 1963-64. Bd. dirs. Mem. Nat. Electric Mfrs. Assn. (chmn. bd. govs., bd. dirs.), Electronic Industries Assn. (bd. govs. 1961-62, dir. 1960-63), Nat. Planning Assn. (nat. council), Am. Mgmt. Assn. (mem. marketing planning council), Elec. Mfrs. Club, Mfrs. Assn. of Syracuse (dir.), Met. Devel. Assn. of Syracuse and Onondaga County, N.Y. (dir.). Clubs: Wall Street, Athletic, Union League, Pinnacle (N.Y.); Duquesne (Pitts.); Lambs; Seaview Country (Absecon, N.J.); Century, Onondaga Country (Syracuse, N.Y.). Office: Crouse-Hinds Co PO Box 4999 Syracuse NY 13221*

WITTLAKE, JESSE CLARKE, ins. co. exec.; b. McCook, Nebr., Sept. 15, 1910; s. Charles and Effie Maude (McCain) W.; student Rutgers U., 1929-30; B.S., U. Nebr., 1935; M.S., U. Iowa, 1936; m. Jamie Jewell Lewis, Aug. 20, 1935; 1 dau., Linda. With Bus. Men's Assurance Co., Kansas City, Mo., 1936—, asst. actuary, 1946-47, asst. to pres., 1947-56, v.p. adminstrn., 1956-64, exec. v.p., 1964-71, exec. v.p., chief adminstr. officer, 1971-73, pres., 1973-77, ret., also dir. Vice pres., bd. dirs. United Campaign; bd. dirs. Kansas City Mus., United Community Services, Greater Kansas City Sports Commn., Civic Council; chmn. corp. div. United Way Campaign; bd. dirs. Community Service Broadcasting of Mid-Am., Inc. Served to maj. AUS, 1942-46. Mem. Casualty Actuarial Soc., Am. Acad. Actuaries, Am. Legion, Pi Mu Epsilon, Beta Gamma Sigma. Presbyterian. Clubs: Kansas City; Mission Hills. Home: 10008 Howe Dr Leawood KS 66206

WITTMAIER, HERBERT DIEMER, clergyman; b. Phila., Dec. 20, 1908; s. Frederick Jacob, Jr. and Lillian Rose (Diemer) W.; Ph.B., Muhlenberg Coll., 1937; B.D., Moravian Sem., 1940; Th.M., Princeton Sem., 1945; m. Miriam Amelia Nixon, June 16, 1932; children—Herbert Nixon, Bruce Charles, Jack Frederick. Ordained to ministry Evang. Congl. Ch., 1937; pastor various chs. in Eastern Conf., Reamstown, Williams Twp., Allentown, Reading and Plymouth Meeting, Pa., 1931-66; instr. Evang. Congl. Sch. Theology, 1953-60; dist. supt. Evang. Congl. Ch., Sinking Spring, Pa., 1966-73, bishop, 1973-78; ret., 1979. Trustee, Evang. Sch. Theology, Myerstown, Pa., Evang. Congl. Ch. Retirement Village. Mem. Nat. Assn. Evangs. Address: 159 Beacon Rd Route 5 Sinking Spring PA 19608

WITTMANN, OTTO, art museum exec.; b. Kansas City, Mo., Sept. 1, 1911; s. Otto and Beatrice Knox (Billingsley) W.; student Country Day Sch., Kansas City; A.B., Harvard, 1933; postgrad., 1937-38, Carnegie scholar, summer 1937; LL.D., U. Toledo; D.F.A., Hillsdale Coll., Bowling Green State U., U. Mich., Kenyon Coll.; m. Margaret Carlisle Hill, June 9, 1945; children—William Hill, John Carlisle. Curator prints Nelson Gallery Art, Kansas City, 1933-37; instr. history of art Emerson Sch., Boston, 1937-38; curator Hyde Collection, Glens Falls, N.Y., 1938-41; instr. history of art Skidmore Coll., Saratoga Springs, N.Y., 1938-41; asst. dir. Portland (Oreg.) Mus. Art, 1941; asso. dir. Toledo Mus. Art, 1946-59, trustee, 1958—, dir., 1959-76, dir. emeritus, 1977—; v.p., cons., art advisor, 1977—; trustee, cons. Los Angeles County Mus. Art, 1977—; cons. J. Paul Getty Mus., 1977—. Organizer exhbns. art activities Am. museums USIA, 1953-55; editorial cons. Gazette des Beaux Arts; vice chmn. Nat. Collection Fine Arts Commn. Dir. Toeldo Trust Co. Mem. mus. advisory panel Nat. Council Arts, Nat. Endowment for Humanities; chmn. advisory panel Nat. Found. Arts and Humanities; mem. art advisory panel IRS; mem. nat. arts accessions com. U.S. embassies; mem. U.S.-ICOM Nat. Com.; former sec. gen. com. pour Musées du Verre, ICOM; founding mem. Ohio Arts Council; sponsor Nat. Trust Sch., Attingham, Shropshire, Eng. Served to maj. AUS, USAAF, OSS, 1941-46. Decorated officer Legion of Honor (France), Order Orange Nassau (Netherlands), Order Arts and Letters (France); comdr. Order of Merit (Italy). Fellow Museums Assn. (Eng.); mem. Intermus. Conservation Assn. (pres. 1955-56, trustee), Harvard Soc. Contemporary Art (co-dir. 1931-33), Assn. Art Mus. Dirs. (pres. 1961-62, 71-72), Am. Assn. Museums (former v.p.), Coll. Art Assn., Archeol. Inst. Am., Internat. Inst. for Conservation of Hist. and Artistic Works, Soc. Archtl. Historians, Verien der Feurnde Antiker Kunst, Am. Soc. French Legion Honneur, Alliance Francaise de Toledo (trustee), Phi Kappa Phi. Episcopalian (vestryman). Clubs: Traveller's (London); Century Assn. (N.Y.C.); Toledo, Harvard (pres. 1956-57); Rotary (pres. 1963-64). Editorial chmn. Toledo Mus. Catalogue of European Paintings and Guide to Collections. Writer numerous museum catalogues, profl. articles. Home: 2516 Underhill Rd Toledo OH 43615 Office: Toledo Mus Art Box 1013 Toledo OH 43697

WITTREICH, JOSEPH ANTHONY, JR., educator; b. Cleve., July 23, 1939; s. Joseph Anthony and Mamie (Pucel) W.; B.A., U. Louisville, 1960, M.A., 1961; Ph.D., Western Res. U., 1966. Faculty, U. Wis., 1966-78; prof. English, U. Md., 1978—; vis. prof. Calif. State U., Los Angeles, 1972, U. Md., 1977, Brown U., 1978, Inst. Renaissance and Eighteenth-Century Studies, Folger Shakespeare Library, 1979. Nat. Endowment for Humanities grantee, 1974; Nat. Endowment for Humanities-Huntington Library grantee, 1976; Guggenheim fellow, 1978. Mem. Renaissance Soc. Am., Blake Found. Am., Milton Soc. Am. (pres. 1979), MLA, Internat. Assn. Profs. English. Democrat. Roman Catholic. Author: The Romantics on Milton, 1970; Calm of Mind, 1971; Milton and the Line of Vision, 1975; Angel of Apocalypse, 1975; Visionary Poetics, 1979. Home: 320 S 16th St Philadelphia PA 19102 Office: Taliaferro Hall U Md College Park MD 20742

WITTROCK, MERLIN C., ednl. psychologist, educator; b. Twin Falls, Idaho, Jan. 3, 1931; s. Herman C. and Mary Ellen (Baumann) W.; B.S. in Biology, U. Mo., Columbia, 1953, M.S. in Ednl. Psychology, 1956; Ph.D. in Ednl. Psychology, U. Ill., Urbana, 1960; m. Nancy McNulty, Apr. 3, 1953; children—Steven, Catherine, Rebecca. Prof., Grad. Sch. Edn., UCLA, 1960—, founder Center for Study Evaluation, 1966, chmn. Grad. Sch. Edn.; fellow Center for Advanced Study in Behavioral Scis., 1967-68; vis. prof. U. Wis., U. Ill., Ind. U.; cons. to Sec. HEW. Served to capt. USAF. Ford Found. grantee. Fellow Am. Psychol. Assn., AAAS, Am. Ednl. Research Assn. (chmn. ann. conv.), Phi Delta Kappa. Author or editor: The Evaluation of Instruction, 1970; Changing Education, 1973; Learning and Instruction, 1977; The Human Brain, 1977; The Brain and Psychology, 1979; Instructional Psychology: Education and Cognitive Processes of the Brain. Editor-in-chief: Readings in Educational Research, 7 vols., 1977; asso. editor Ednl. Psychologist; contbr. articles to profl. jours. Office: 321 Moore Hall U of Calif Los Angeles CA 90024

WITWER, SAMUEL WEILER, lawyer; b. Pueblo, Colo., July 1, 1908; s. Samuel W. and Lulu (Richmond) W.; Ph.B., Dickinson Coll., 1930, LL.D., 1970; J.D., Harvard, 1933; LL.D., Simpson Coll., 1955, U. Ill., 1971, John Marshall Law Sch., 1976; L.H.D., DePaul U., 1971; D.Jur. Sci., Lake Forest Coll., 1971; m. Ethyl L. Wilkins, Aug. 14, 1937; children—Samuel Weiler III, Michael Wilkins, Carole Ann Witwer Dalton, David R. Admitted to Ill. bar, 1933, since practiced in Chgo.; now mem. firm Witwer, Moran, Burlage and Atkinson; spl. asst. Ill. Atty. Gen., 1971—. Ill. chmn. U.S.O., 1958-63; citizens com. U. Ill.; mem. Bd. Social and Econ. Relations, Methodist Ch., 1954-60, mem. Council World Service and Finance, 1960-64; mem. jud. council Supreme Ct. of Methodism, 1964-72. Chmn., Ill. Com. Constl. Revision, 1950-55; pres. 6th Ill. Constnl. Conv., 1969-70. State chmn. Ill. Citizens for Eisenhower-Nixon, 1956; v.p. United Republican Fund of Ill., Rep. candidate U.S. senate (Ill.), 1960. Pres. bd. trustees Dickinson Coll.; trustee Northwestern Meml. Hosp.; regent Lincoln Acad. Ill.; v.p. Chgo. Women's Hosp. and Maternity Center. Recipient 1st Distinguished Service medal of Ill., 1970; named A Chicagoan of Year, 1954, 68, The Chicagoan of Year, 1970, Chgo. Jr. C. of C.; Chicagoan of Year, Chgo. Press Club, 1971; Ill. Man of Year, Ill. News Broadcasters, 1970; Citizen Fellow award Inst. Medicine Chgo., 1973; Ill. laureate Lincoln Acad. Ill., 1974. Mem. Am. Law Inst. (dir.), Am., Ill. (citation civic service 1972), Chgo. (bd. mgrs. 1944-46) bar assns., Chgo. Council on Fgn. Relations (past dir.), Chgo. Urban League (past dir.), Chgo. Sunday Evening Club (trustee), Omicron Delta Kappa, Sigma Chi. Republican. Methodist. Clubs: Legal, Union League, Commercial, Law (Chgo.); Exmoor Country. Contbr. articles on constl. law and govt. to legal publs. Home: 111 Abingdon Rd Kenilworth IL 60043 Office: 125 S Wacker Dr Suite 2700 Chicago IL 60606

WITZIG, WARREN FRANK, educator, nuclear engr.; b. Detroit, Mar. 26, 1921; s. Arthur Judson and Mary (Bender) W.; B.E.E., Rensselaer Poly. Inst., 1942; M.S., U. Pitts., 1944, Ph.D., 1952; m. Bernadette Sullivan, Mar. 31, 1942; children—Eric, Leah Witzig Curling, Marc, Lisa Witzig Coleman. Research engr. Westinghouse Research, Pitts., 1942-48; mgr. reactor physics, engr. Bettis Atomic, Pitts., 1948-60; co-founder, sr. v.p., dir. NUS Corp., Washington, 1960-67; head dept. nuclear engring. Pa. State U., 1967—. Cons. nuclear engr. utilities, industry; chmn. Gov. of Pa. Com. Atomic Energy Devel., 1970—; mem. waste com. Nat. Acad. Scis., 1971-73; mem. uranium enrichment com. Atomic Indsl. Forum, 1971-73. Mem. bd. mgmt. YMCA, 1955-64. Registered prof. engr. Fellow Am. Nuclear Soc. (mem. exec. com. edn. div., past chmn. nat. com. on pub. info.); mem. Am. Phys. Soc., IEEE (past chmn. nuclear eng. and plasma div.), Sigma Xi, Eta Kappa Nu, Pi Kappa Alpha, Sigma Pi Sigma. Presbyterian (elder). Designer: S5W submarine reactor, 1956-60. Home: 1330 Park Hills Ave State College PA 16801 Office: Sackett Bldg University Park PA 16802

WIXON, RUFUS, educator; b. Cherokee County, Iowa, Nov. 27, 1911; s. Rufus and Stella Maude (Mathews) W.; B.S.C., U. Iowa, 1933, M.A., 1935; Ph.D., U. Mich., 1945; m. Doris Elizabeth Hunter, Oct.

28, 1939; children—Marjorie Jeanne, Joanne Elizabeth, Kathryn Ann. Staff accountant I.B. McGladrey & Co., Cedar Rapids, Iowa, 1933-34; instr. accounting U. N.D., 1935-36; staff accountant Edward Gore & Co., Chgo., 1936-37; instr. accounting Wayne U., 1937-41; lectr. econs. U. Mich., 1941-45, asst. prof. econs., 1945-47; prof. accounting, chmn. dept. U. Buffalo, 1947-49, U. Pa., 1949-65; prof. accounting Fla. Inst. chair accountancy U. Fla., Gainesville, 1965-66; prof. accounting U. Pa., Phila., 1966—, asso. chief, specialist accounting U. Pa.-U. Karachi Project, Karachi, Pakistan, 1955-57. Cons. Office Asst. Sec. Def. (comptroller), 1958-60; prof. IMEDE, Mgmt. Devel. Inst., Lausanne, Switzerland, 1961-62; accounting editorial bd. Found. Press. Mem. Am. Acad. Polit. and Social Sci., Am. Accounting Assn. (chmn. com. standards accounting instrn., v.p. 1959), Am. Econ. Assn., Controllers Inst. Am., Order of Artus, Beta Gamma Sigma, Beta Alpha Psi. Phi Kappa Phi, Alpha Kappa Psi, Alpha Tau Omega. Author: Problems and Practise Sets for Essentials of Accounting (with W.A. Paton, R.L. Dixon), 1949; Budgetary Control, 1952, rev., 1961; Principles of Accounting (with R.G. Cox), 1961, 2nd edit., 1969. Editor: Accountant's Handbook, 5th edit., 1970. Home: 504 Oak Crest Ln Wallingford PA 19086 Office: Wharton Sch U Pa Philadelphia PA 19104

WLEUGEL, JOHAN PETER, mfg. co. exec.; b. Hoyanger, Sogn, Norway, July 1, 1929; s. Johan and Helga (Faye) W.; B.A., U. Copenhagen, 1953; M.B.A., U. Toronto, 1957; m. Leonor Abaroa, Dec. 1959; children—Jan Andrew, Cecilia Maria. With Belgium Machine Tool Assn., 1953-54; with Massey-Ferguson Ltd., Toronto, 1954-71, treas., 1968-71, also dir. several subsidiaries; sr. v.p. Bata Ltd., Toronto; dir., officer several subsidiaries Bata Shoe Orgn., Don Mills, Ont., Can., 1972—. Mem. Financial Execs. Inst. Club: University (Toronto). Home: 5 Campbell Crescent Willowdale ON Canada Office: Bata Ltd 59 Wynford Dr Don Mills Toronto ON Canada

WOBST, FRANK GEORG, banker; b. Dresden, Germany, Nov. 14, 1933; s. Robert Georg and Marianne (Salewsky) W.; student U. Erlangen, 1952-54, U. Goettingen, 1954-58, Rutgers U., 1964; m. Joan Shuey Firkins, Aug. 24, 1957; children—Franck Georg, Ingrid, Andrea. Came to U.S., 1958, naturalized, 1963. With Fidelity American Bankshares, Inc., Lynchburg, Va., 1958-74, exec. v.p., dir., 1973-74; pres., chief exec. officer, dir. Huntington Nat. Bank, 1974—; exec. v.p., dir. Huntington Bancshares, Inc., 1974—. Mem. Greater Columbus C. of C., Am. Inst. Banking, Robert Morris Assos., Newcomen Soc. Club: Scioto Country. Home: 129 N Columbia Ave Columbus OH 43209 Office: 17 S High St Columbus OH 43215

WODLINGER, MARK L., broadcasting co. exec.; b. Jacksonville, Fla., July 13, 1922; s. Mark H. and Beatrice Mae (Boney) W.; B.S., U. Fla., 1943; m. Connie Jean Bates, May 3, 1974; children—Mark, Jacqueline, Steve, Mike, Kevin. Salesman, Sta. WQUA, Moline, Ill., 1948; mgr. Sta. WOC-AM-FM-TV, Davenport, Iowa, 1949-58; v.p. Sta. WMBD-TV, Peoria, Ill., 1959-61; v.p., gen. mgr. Sta. WZZM-TV, Grand Rapids, Mich., 1962-63; v.p., gen. mgr. Sta. KMBC-TV, Kansas City, Mo., 1963-69; pres. Intermedia, Kansas City, 1969-73; builder, owner comml. radio stas., Swaziland, Africa, operator Radio Malawi, Blantyre, and Marknews TV and Radio News Bur., Nairobe, Kenya, 1971-74; owner, pres. Sta. KBEQ, Kansas City, 1973— dir. Sta. KCPT-TV, Kansas City. Bd. dirs. Kansas City Philharmonic, Kansas City Civic Council, Naples (Fla.) YMCA. Served to lt. U.S. Navy, 1941-45. Mem. Nat., Mo. assns. broadcasters, Broadcast Pioneers. Republican. Episcopalian. Clubs: Kansas City, Univ., Carriage, Rotary, Port Royal.

WOEHLE, FRITZ, architect; b. Harrisburg, Pa., Mar. 23, 1929; s. Max and Alma Elizabeth (Kimmel) W.; B.Arch., U. Fla., 1952; m. Lynn Ludington, Mar. 16, 1956; children—Lee, Fritz, Katharyn Lynn. Pvt. archtl. practice, Birmingham, Ala., 1958—; chmn. Sidewalk Art, Birmingham, 1960—; prin. works include Woehle house, Birmingham, 1964, Pilgrim Congl. Ch., Birmingham, 1960. Served with USMCR, 1952-54. Recipient Garage Restoration award, 1975. Fellow AIA (pres. Birmingham chpt. 1966; honor awards for design); mem. Birmingham Art Assn. Republican. Clubs: Birmingham Country, Relay. Home: 4212 Old Brook Trail Birmingham AL 35243 Office: 2304 10th Terrace S Birmingham AL 35205

WOELFFER, EMERSON SEVILLE, artist; b. Chgo., July 27, 1914; s. George K. and Marguerite (Seville) W.; student Art Inst. Chgo., 1935-38; B.F.A., Inst. Design, Chgo., 1949; m. Diane Anderson, Dec. 7, 1945. One-man shows: Paul Kantor Gallery, Beverly Hills, Calif., 1953, 60, Poindexter Gallery, N.Y.C., 1958, 61, Primus-Stuart Gallery, Los Angeles, 1961, Santa Barbara (Calif.) Mus. Art, 1964, Quay Gallery, San Francisco, 1967, Jodi Scully Gallery, Los Angeles, 1972, 73, Newport Harbour Art Mus., Newport Beach, Calif., 1974, Phillips Collection, Washington, 1975, Gruenebaum Gallery, N.Y.C., 1978; represented in permanent collections: Art Inst. Chgo., Whitney Mus. Am. Art, Mus. Modern Art, N.Y.C., Los Angeles County Mus. Art, Washington Gallery Modern Art, Wight Galleries of UCLA, San Francisco Mus. Art, Bauhaus Archives, Berlin, Smithsonian Archives Am. Art, Washington, numerous others; head painting dept. Otis Art Inst., Los Angeles, 1974—; artist in residence, one-man show Honolulu Acad. Arts, 1970. Guggenheim grantee, 1968-69; NEA grantee, 1974. Home: 475 Dustin Dr Los Angeles CA 90065

WOELFLE, ARTHUR WILLIAM, food co. exec.; b. Dunkirk, N.Y., Mar. 8, 1920; s. Arthur and Agnes (Johnson) W.; B.S., U. Buffalo, 1943; postgrad. U. Lucerne, Switzerland, 1966, 70, Northwestern U., 1972; m. Ruth G. Godden, Dec. 29, 1943; children—Gretchen, Christine, Ann. Sec.-treas. Bedford Products Co., Dunkirk, 1946-55; sr. v.p. Bedford Products div. Kraft Foods, Dunkirk, 1955-59; div. product mgr. Kraft Foods, 1959-66, chief exec. officer Kraft Foods W.Germany, 1966-69; chmn., mng. dir. Kraft Foods Ltd. in U.K. and Scandinavia, 1969-73; pres., chief operating officer Kraft Inc., Glenview, Ill., 1973—; dir. Santa Fe Industries, Inc., First Nat. Bank of Chgo., First Chgo. Corp. Served to lt. USMCR. Mem. Inst. of Dirs. (London, Eng.). Clubs: Chicago; Union League (N.Y.C.); Glenview Golf. Office: Kraft Inc Kraft Court Glenview IL 60025*

WOERTHWEIN, ARTHUR THEODORE, communications co. exec.; b. Chgo., May 21, 1915; s. Fred Eugene and Viola Myrtle (Longwell) W.; B.A., Northwestern U., 1938; M.B.A., U. Chgo., 1955; m. Alice Luella Boyd, Oct. 4, 1947; children—Theodore, William Pegausch. With Bell and Gossett (acquired by ITT 1963), Morton Grove, Ill., 1941-63, successively cost accountant, comptroller, v.p., exec. v.p.; v.p., group exec. Tech. Indsl. Products Group, ITT, N.Y.C., 1963—, also spl. rep., office of chief exec. Mem. council Grad. Sch. Bus. U. Chgo. Mem. Gas Appliance Mfrs. Assn. (pres. 1972-73). Clubs: N.Y. Athletic (N.Y.C.); Union League (Chgo.); Boca Raton (Fla.). Home: 875 E Camino Real Boca Raton FL 33432 Office: 320 Park Ave New York NY 10022*

WOFFORD, HARRIS LLEWELLYN, JR., lawyer; b. N.Y.C., Apr. 9, 1926; s. Harris Llewellyn and Estelle (Gardner) W.; B.A., U. Chgo., 1948; study fellow, India, 1949, Israel, 1950; LL.B., Yale, 1954, Howard U., 1954; m. Emmy Lou Clare Lindgren, Aug. 14, 1948; children—Susanne, Daniel, David. Admitted to D.C. bar, 1954, U.S. Supreme Ct. bar, 1958, Pa. bar, 1978; asst. to Chester Bowles, 1953-54; law asso. Covington & Burling, Washington, 1954-58; legal asst. to Rev. Theodore Hesburgh, Commn. on Civil Rights, 1958-59; asso. prof. Notre Dame Law Sch., 1959-60, on leave, 1961-66; asst. to Sen. Kennedy, 1960; spl. asst. to Pres. Kennedy, 1961-62; spl. rep. for Africa, dir. Ethiopian program U.S. Peace Corps, 1962-64; asso. dir. Peace Corps, Washington, 1964-66; pres. Coll. at Old Westbury, State U. N.Y., 1966-70, Bryn Mawr (Pa.) Coll., 1970-78; of counsel firm Schnader, Harrison, Segal and Lewis, Phila. vis. lectr. Howard Law Sch., 1956. Mem. Commn. to Study Orgn. of Peace, 1957—; co-chmn. Com. for Study of Nat. Service, 1977—; trustee The Am. Coll., Bryn Mawr, 1975—; v.p. Internat. League for Human Rights; bd. dirs. Public Interest Law Center Phila. Served with USAAF, 1944-45. Mem. Am. Bar Assn., Council on Fgn. Relations. Episcopalian. Author: It's Up to Us, 1946; (with Clare Wofford) India Afire, 1951; Of Kennedys and Kings, 1980; editor: Embers of the World, 1970. Co-editor: Report of the U.S. Commission on Civil Rights, 1959. Home: 407 Old Gulph Rd Bryn Mawr PA 19010 Office: 1719 Packard Bldg Philadelphia PA 19102

WOFSY, LEON, educator, biochemist; b. Stamford, Conn., Nov. 21, 1921; s. Isadore and Rose (Gordon) W.; B.S., Coll. City N.Y., 1942; M.S., Yale, 1960, Ph.D., 1961; m. Rosalind Taub, Nov. 25, 1942; children—Carla, David. Chmn., Labor Youth League 1949-56; postdoctoral fellow U. Calif. at San Diego, 1961-64; faculty U. Calif. at Berkeley, 1964—, prof. immunology, 1964—, chmn dept. bacteriology and immunology, 1967-72. Served with AUS, 1943. Research on molecules and cells of immune system. Home: 7030 Westmoorland Dr Berkeley CA 94705

WOGAN, GERALD NORMAN, educator; b. Altoona, Pa., Jan. 11, 1930; s. Thomas B. and Florence E. (Corl) W.; B.S., Juniata Coll., 1951; M.S., U. Ill., 1953, Ph.D., 1957; m. Henrietta E. Hoenicke, Aug. 24, 1957; children—Christine F., Eugene E. Asst. prof. physiology Rutgers U., New Brunswick, N.J., 1957-61; asst. prof. toxicology Mass. Inst. Tech., Cambridge, 1962-65, asso. prof., 1965-69, prof., 1969—, head dept. nutrition and food sci., 1979—; cons. to nat. and internat. govt. agys., industries. NIH grantee, 1963-76; NSF grantee, 1965-68. Mem. Am. Assn. Cancer Research, Am. Soc. Pharmacology and Exptl. Therapeutics, Am. Soc. Microbiology, Soc. Toxicology, Am. Inst. Nutrition, AAAS, Sigma Xi. Mem. editorial bd. Cancer Research, 1971—, Applied Microbiology, 1971—, Chem.-Biol. Interactions, 1975—, Toxicology, Environ. Health, 1974—. Contbr. articles and revs. to profl. jours. Home: 125 Claflin St Belmont MA 02178 Office: Dept Nutrition Food Sci Mass Inst Tech Cambridge MA 02139

WOGAN, ROBERT, broadcasting co. exec.; b. N.Y.C., Oct. 13, 1925; s. Robert and Johanna (Hilderbrandt) W.; grad. pub. schs.; m. Phyllis Jayn Volz, Nov. 21, 1965; children—Robert, Stephen. Page NBC, 1943, asst. mgr. guest relations, 1945-46, night announcer, sec., 1946, asst. supr. announcing, 1946-47, prodn. div., 1947-48, night adminstrv. asst., 1948-50, supr. network program operations, 1950-55, Eastern radio program and prodn. mgr., 1955-63, v.p. radio network programs, 1963-73, exec. producer spl. programs NBC Radio Network, 1973-75, regional mgr. affiliate relations, 1975—. Mem. Nat. council Boy Scouts Am., 1970—; chmn. Radio com. United Hosp. Fund, 1972. Served with AUS, 1944-45. Recipient Radio-TV All-Am. of Year award for Experiment in Drama, 1963, Gabriel award for pub. service programming, 1967, Freedoms Found. award, 1972, Peabody awards, 1972, 73. Mem. Broadcast Pioneers, Internat. Radio and TV Soc. Home: 410 W 24th St New York NY 10011 Office: 30 Rockefeller Plaza New York NY 10020

WOGSLAND, JAMES WILLARD, mfg. co. exec.; b. Devils Lake, N.D., Apr. 17, 1931; s. Melvin Leroy and Mable Bertina (Paulson) W.; B.A. in Econs., U. Minn., 1957; m. Marlene Claudia Clark, June 22, 1957; children—Karen Lynn, Steven James. Various positions Caterpillar Tractor Co., Peoria, Ill., 1957-64, treas., 1976—; with Caterpillar Overseas S.A., Geneva, 1965-76, sec.-treas., 1970-76. Mem. dist. com. Boy Scouts Am., 1976—. Served with USAF, 1951-55. Mem. U.S. C. of C. (monetary and fiscal affairs com., export policy task force), Ill. Econ. Assn., U. Minn. Alumni Club, Alpha Delta Phi Alumni. Republican. Presbyterian. Club: Mount Hawley Country, Phoenix, Lincoln. Home: 1029 W Burnside Peoria IL 61614

WOHL, JOSEPH GENE, research co. exec.; b. Chgo., May 8, 1927; s. Max and Frieda (Friedman) W.; B.S. in Physics and Math., U. Wis., 1949; postgrad. U. Md., George Washington U., Mass. Inst. Tech.; m. Carol Weiss, June 26, 1949; children—David, Michael, Nancy, Betsy. Scientist, U.S. Naval Research Lab., 1948-52, Office Naval Research, 1952-54; sr. engr. Sperry Gyroscope Co., 1954-57; v.p. Dunlap & Assos. Inc., cons., Darien, Conn., 1957-69, Infoton, Inc., mfr. electronics, Burlington, Mass., 1969-71; dir. systems analysis Addressograph Data Systems Tech. Center, Cambridge, Mass., 1971-72; head dept. advanced planning Mitre Corp., Bedford, Mass., 1972—; adj. asso. prof. Columbia U., 1958-66; program chmn. NATO Agard Simulation Symposium, Paris, 1979. Mem. fin. com. Plainview (N.Y.) Sch. Bd., 1955-56. Served with USNR, 1945-46. Fellow AAAS (gov. council 1971); sr. mem. IEEE (chmn. man-machine systems group 1969-71, program chmn. Man-Machine Systems Symposium, Cambridge, Eng. 1969); mem. Systems, Man and Cybernetics Soc. (v.p. 1980), Sigma Xi. Editorial bd. Ergonomic Abstracts, 1971—. Patentee in field.

WOHL, MARTIN, educator; b. Greensboro, N.C., July 13, 1930; s. Stanley Siedenbach and Helen (Robertson) W.; student U.S. Mil. Acad., 1948-50; B.S., M.I.T., 1956, M.S. 1960; D.Eng., U. Calif., Berkeley, 1966; m. Ann Hedges Findley, Dec. 20, 1958 (div.); children—Charles Martin, Richard Thomas. Mem. staff, asst. prof. M.I.T., 1957-62; cons. to asst. sec. Dept. Commerce, Washington, 1962-63; lectr. econs. Harvard U., 1963-65; acting asso. prof. U. Calif., Berkeley, 1967; sr. staff mem. Rand Corp., 1967-68; mgr. transp. analysis dept., corp. planning staff Ford Motor Co., Dearborn, Mich., 1968-69; dir. transp. studies Urban Inst., Washington, 1969-72; prof. Carnegie-Mellon U., 1972—; cons. various govt. agys., cos. Bd. dirs. Cambridge (Mass.) Civic Assn., 1958-62. Served to 1st lt. U.S. Army, 1953-55. Recipient Past Pres.'s award Inst. Traffic Engrs., 1958; NSF faculty fellow, 1965-66. Mem. Inst. Traffic Engrs., Regional Sci. Assn., Transp. Research Bd., Sigma Xi, Chi Epsilon. Author: (with John R. Meyer, John F. Kain) The Urban Transportation Problem, 1965; (with Brian Martin) Traffic System Analysis, 1967; Transportation Investment Planning, 1972; (with R. Kirby, K. Bhatt, M. Kemp and R. McGillivray) Para-Transit: Neglected Options for Urban Mobility, 1975. Home: 7520 Carriage Ln Pittsburgh PA 15221

WOHL, ROBERT ALLEN, lawyer, aerospace exec.; b. Chgo., June 21, 1931; s. Max and Frieda (Friedmann) W.; student U. Wis., 1948-50; B.A., San Diego State U., 1952; postgrad. U. Calif., Berkeley, 1954-56; J.D., U. San Diego, 1960; m. Christine Allison, 1974; children—Melissa, Suzanne. Admitted to Calif. bar, 1961; mgr. contracts Gen. Dynamics Corp., San Diego, 1956-62, mgr. program control, space programs, 1962-63, asst. to v.p., N.Y.C., 1963-68, corp. dir. contracts, 1968-70; v.p. adminstrn., sec. Canadair Ltd., Montreal, Que., Can., 1970-79, sr. v.p. adminstrn. and legal, 1979—. Served with USAF, 1952-54; 1st lt. Res. Mem. Am. Bar Assn., Am. Soc. Internat. Law, Union Internationale des Avocats, Nat. Mgmt. Assn. (chpt. 1st v.p. 1962), Blue Key, Phi Alpha Delta (chpt. pres. 1956), Zeta Beta Tau. Club: Wings of N.Y. Home: 21 Pacific Ave Senneville PQ H9X 1A2 Canada Office: 1800 Laurentian Blvd Saint Laurent PQ H3C 3G9 Canada

WOHLSCHLAG, DONALD EUGENE, zoologist, marine ecologist; b. Bucyrus, Ohio, Nov. 6, 1918; s. Herman Albert and Agnes Mae (Canode) W.; B.S., Heidelberg Coll., 1940; Ph.D., Ind. U., 1949; m. Elsie Marjorie Baker, June 5, 1943; children—William Eugene, Nancy Sue, Sarah Ann. Research asso. in zoology U. Wis., 1948-49; asst. prof. biol. scis. Stanford U., 1949-56, asso. prof., 1956-64, prof., 1964-65; prof. zoology and marine scis. U. Tex., 1965—, dir. Marine Sci. Inst., 1965-70; mem. U.S. Marine Subcom. for Internat. Biol. Program, 1966-71; mem. com. on ecol. research interocean-canal Nat. Acad. Scis., 1969-70; mem. Tundra Biome Panel, NSF, 1971-74; mem. water ecosystems com. Inst. Ecology, 1974-76. Served to 1st lt. USAAF, 1942-46. Recipient Antarctic medal NSF, 1965; NSF grantee, 1955-70; NOAA grantee, 1976-79; Office Naval Research grantee, 1952-54; Tex. Dept. Water Resources grantee, 1975-79. Fellow AAAS, Am. Inst. Fisheries Research Biologists, Arctic Inst. N. Am., Explorers Club; mem. Am. Fisheries Soc., Am. Soc. Limnology and Oceanography, Am. Soc. Zoologists, Am. Soc. Ichthyology and Herpetology, Ecol. Soc. Am. (pres. Western sect. 1965), Estuarine Research Fedn. (dir. 1976-78), Gulf Estuarine Research Soc. (pres. 1976-78), Sigma Xi. Contbr. numerous articles on arctic, antarctic and Gulf Coast fish ecol. research to profl. publs.; editor Contbns. in Marine Sci., 1974—. Home: 615 Ave C Port Aransas TX 78373 Office: U Tex Port Aransas Marine Lab Port Aransas TX 78373

WOHLSTETTER, CHARLES, telephone co. exec.; b. 1910. With Charles R. Hammerslough & Co., N.Y.C., 1929-32, Theodore Prince Co., N.Y.C., 1932-33; partner Rubinger, Wohlstetter & Co., 1933-38; investment dept. Allen & Co., 1938-40; pres. Cyclohm Motor Corp., 1940-48; partner Seskis & Wohlstetter, 1950-71; chmn. bd. Continental Telephone Corp., 1960-71, chmn. bd., chief exec. officer, 1971—, also dir.; chmn. bd. IMC Magnetics Corp.; partner J.F. Nick & Co.; dir. Tesoro Petroleum Corp. Chmn. Billy Rose Found.; trustee Nat. Symphony, Kennedy Center; bd. dirs. Inst. for Ednl. Affairs, Bus. Com. for the Arts. Office: Continental Telephone Corp 405 Park Ave New York NY 10004

WOIT, ERIK PETER, corp. exec.; b. Riga, Latvia, Mar. 10, 1931; s. Walter E. and Sigrid (Radzins) W.; A.B., Allegheny Coll., 1953; J.D., Harvard, 1956; m. Bonnie Jean Ford, June 16, 1953; children—Peter Gordon, Steven Ford. Admitted to N.Y. bar, 1959; asso. Mudge, Stern, Baldwin & Todd, N.Y.C., 1956-57, 60-62; asst. sec., internat. counsel Richardson-Merrell, Inc., 1962-71; sec., gen. counsel Amerace Corp., N.Y.C., 1971-73; v.p., group exec. Amerace Corp., 1973-74, v.p., 1974—, pres. ESNA div., 1974-77, v.p. adminstrn., 1977-79; sr. v.p. adminstrn., 1979—; dir. Simmonds S.A., Paris, Fujimold Ltd., Tokyo. Served to capt. USMCR, 1957-60. Mem. Assn. Bar City N.Y., Am. Bar Assn., Fin. Execs. Inst., Sigma Alpha Epsilon. Clubs: Landmark (Stamford, Conn.); Harvard, Board Room (N.Y.C.). Home: 559 West Rd New Canaan CT 06840 Office: 555 Fifth Ave New York NY 10017

WOITACH, RICHARD, condr., pianist; b. Binghamton, N.Y., July 27, 1935; s. Peter T. and Ester L. (Karkula) W.; B.M., Eastman Sch. Music, 1956; m. Theresa Ballester, June 29, 1957 (div.); children—Paul, Karl: m. 2d, Jeryl E. Metz, Apr. 16, 1976. Asst. condr. Met. Opera, N.Y.C., 1959-68; music dir. Western Opera Theatre of San Francisco Opera, 1968-72; guest lectr. in music Ind. U., 1972; condr. Met. Opera, 1973—; guest tchr. Tanglewood Inst., 1965-66; artistic cons. Syracuse Research Corp., 1978. Mem. Am. Fedn. Musicians. Solo piano recs. on Opus One Label, 1967, 71. Home: 697 West End Ave New York NY 10025 Office: care Metropolitan Opera Lincoln Center New York NY 10023. *As a dealer in sound and time, I as a musician view my life as a constant search for balance and the tempo giusto, that which the Italians view as a pace at which all moves fluidly and yet with deliberation enough so that all sounds are clear—in other words, the "golden mean."*

WOIWODE, LARRY ALFRED, author; b. Carrington, N.D., Oct. 30, 1941; s. Everett Carl and Audrey Leone (Johnston) W.; A.A., U. Ill., 1964; D.Litt., N.D. State U., 1977. m. Carole Ann Peterson, May 21, 1965; children—Newlyn Smith, Joseph William Thiel. Free-lance writer, 1964—; writer in residence U. Wis., Madison, 1973-74. Judge, Nat. Book awards, 1972. Guggenheim fellow, 1971-72. Mem. P.E.N. (exec. bd. 1972). Author: What I'm Going To Do, I Think (William Faulkner award for best 1st novel), 1969; Beyond The Bedroom Wall (Friends of Am. Writers award), 1975; Even Tide, 1977. Contbr. to New Yorker, N.Y. Times, Audience, Atlantic Monthly, Esquire, Harper's, Mademoiselle, McCalls, New Am. Rev., Partisan Rev., Poetry North: Five North Dakota Poets, Transatlantic Rev., Works in Progress. Address: care Farrar Straus & Giroux 19 Union Sq W New York City NY 10003

WOJCICKI, ANDREW ADALBERT, educator; b. Warsaw, Poland, May 5, 1935; s. Franciszek and Janina (Kozlowa) W.; B.S., Brown U., 1956; Ph.D., Northwestern U., 1960; postdoctoral fellow U. Nottingham (Eng.), 1960-61; m. Marba L. Hart, Dec. 21, 1968; children—Katherine, Christina. Mem. faculty Ohio State U., Columbus, 1961—, asso. prof. chemistry, 1966-69, prof., 1969—. Cons. Owens-Ill., 1967; vis. prof. Case Western Reserve U., 1967; vis. researcher Univ. Coll. London, 1969; sr. U.S. scientist Alexander von Humboldt Found., Mülheim/Ruhr, West Germany, 1975-76; Guggenheim fellow U. Cambridge (Eng.), 1976. Recipient Alumni award for distinguished teaching Ohio State U., 1968. Mem. Am. Chem. Soc., Chem. Soc. (London), AAAS, Sigma Xi, Phi Lambda Upsilon. Contbr. to profl. jours. Home: 825 Greenridge Rd Worthington OH 43085

WOJCICKI, STANLEY GEORGE, physicist; b. Warsaw, Poland, Mar. 30, 1937; s. Franciszek and Janina (Kozlow) W.; A.B., Harvard U., 1957; Ph.D., U. Calif., Berkeley, 1962; m. Esther Denise Hochman, Nov. 17, 1961; children—Susan Diane, Janet Maia, Anne Elizabeth. Physicist, Lawrence Radiation Lab., Berkeley, 1961-66; asst. prof. physics Stanford U., 1966-68, asso. prof., 1968-74, prof., 1974—, chmn. Stanford Linear Accelerator Center Exptl. Program Adv. Com. NSF fellow, 1964-65; Sloan Found. fellow, 1968-72; Guggenheim fellow, 1973-74. Mem. Am. Phys. Soc. Asso. editor Phys. Rev. Letters for Exptl. High Energy Physics, 1978—. Home: 825 Tolman Dr Stanford CA 94305 Office: Physics Dept Stanford U Stanford CA 94305

WOJCIECHOWSKI, JERZY ANTONI, philosopher, educator; b. Brzesc, Poland, June 20, 1925; s. Roman and Antonina (Widawska) W.; came to Can., 1949, naturalized, 1955; student in mech. engring. Warsaw Tech. U., 1942-44; B.Ph. (Centre des Hautes Etudes Polonaises en Belgique scholar), Universite de Louvain, 1949; Ph.L. (Ministere de la jeunesse du Quebec scholar), Laval, 1951, Ph.D. magna cum laude, 1953; m. Cecile Cloutier, Dec. 27, 1966; children—Maria, Ewa. Tchr., Seminaire de Philosophie, Montreal, Que., Can., 1952-53; asst. prof. St. Francis Xavier U., Antigonish, N.S., Can., 1953-54; asst. prof. philosophy U. Ottawa (Ont., Can.), 1954-59, asso. prof., 1959-65, prof., 1965—; lectr. in field; cons. U. Victoria, Moncton, Conf. Rectors and Prins. of Que. Univs. Served with Polish Underground Army, 1942-45. Humanities Research

Council Can.-Can. Council grantee, 1955, 60, 67-68, 73-74. Mem. Can. Philos. Assn. (1st hon. life mem.; v.p., acting pres. 1968-69, pres. 1969-70), Am. Philos. Assn., Am. Catholic Philos. Assn. (exec. council 1966-69), Polish Soc. Arts and Scis. Abroad (London), Polish Inst. Arts and Scis. in Am., Inter-Univ. Com. on Can. Slavs (pres. 1967-69), Polish Can. Congress (v.p. 1968-74, 76-78), Humanities Research Council of Can. (exec. com. 1970-72, chmn. com. external relations 1972-74), Can. Council (selection com. for spl. M.A. scholarships 1973), Metaphys. Soc. Am., Societe Francaise de Philosophie. Author: Survey on the Status of Philosophy in Canada, 1970; editor: Conceptual Basis of the Classification of Knowledge, 1974; co-editor: Polonia of Tomorrow, 1977; contbr. articles to profl. jours. Home: 80 Pleasant Park Rd Ottawa ON K1H 5L9 Canada Office: Dept Philosophy U Ottawa Ottawa ON K1N 6N5 Canada. *The longer I live the more wondrous the world appears to me and the more complex the adventure of life. The older I grow the more I am preoccupied with the future and the less with the past, and the more I desire to contribute to the shaping of the future.*

WOLAS, HERBERT, lawyer; b. Bronx, N.Y., June 27, 1933; s. Irving and Mary (Kessner) W.; A.A., U. Calif. at Los Angeles, 1953, B.A., 1954, J.D., 1960; m. Annette Rudolph, Aug. 20, 1957; children—Cherise, Collette, Claudine. Admitted to Calif. bar, 1961, since practiced in Los Angeles; prin. firm Robinson, Wolas & Diamant P.C., Los Angeles, 1963—. Served with F.A., AUS, 1955-56. Office: Robinson Wolas & Diamant 1888 Century Park E Suite 900 Los Angeles CA 90067

WOLBACH, WILLIAM WELLINGTON, bus. exec.; b. Boston, May 9, 1915; s. S. Burt and Anna (Wellington) W.; student Milton Acad., 1928-34, Harvard, 1934-36; m. Josephine Neilson Harmar, Apr. 15, 1944; children—William Wellington, Josephine Harmar Devlin. Pres., chief exec. officer South Eleuthera Properties; dir., mem. exec. com. Boston Co., Boston Safe Deposit & Trust Co., Seaboard Industries; trustee Suffolk-Franklin Savs. Bank; dir. Stop & Shop, Inc., Boston Profl. Hockey Assn., Inc., New Boston Garden Corp.; hon. dir. West Point-Pepperell, Inc. Mem., v.p. Com. of Permanent Charity Fund; chmn. Children's Hosp. Med. Center; trustee New Eng. Aquarium. Clubs: The Country (Brookline); Harvard Varsity (Cambridge); Myopia Hunt (Hamilton); Golf Society Great Britain (Kent, Eng.); Essex County (Manchester); Cotton Bay (Eleuthera-Bahamas); Harvard, Bay, Madison Square (Boston). Home: 185 Sargent Rd Brookline MA 02146 also 160 Western Ave Gloucester MA 01930 Office: 1 Boston Pl Suite 923 Boston MA 02108

WOLBERG, LEWIS ROBERT, physician, psychiatrist; b. Russia, July 4, 1905; s. Max and Anna (Hurwitz) W.; A.B., U. Rochester, 1927; M.D., Tufts Coll., 1930; m. Arlene Robbins, 1931; children—Barbara Jane, Ellen May. Asst. exec. officer Boston Psychopathic Hosp. (name now Mass. Mental Health Center), 1932; supervising psychiatrist Kings Park State Hosp., 1932-45; clin. prof. psychiatry N.Y. Med. Coll., 1946-70, faculty postgrad. psychoanalytic div., 1946-70; founder, med. dir., dean Postgrad. Center for Mental Health, 1945-72, now chmn. bd. trustees; clin. prof. psychiatry N.Y. U. Med. Sch., 1970—, attending psychiatrist Med. Center, 1970—; psychiatrist Flower-Fifth Ave. Hosp., 1938-70; neuropsychiatrist Univ., Bellevue hosps. Fellow Am. Psychiat. Assn. (life mem.), N.Y. County Med. Soc., Acad. Psychoanalysis (founding), Am. Acad. Psychiatry; mem. A.M.A., N.Y. Soc. Clin. Psychiatry, Am. Psychosomatic Soc., Am. Group Therapy Assn., Assn. Advancement Psychotherapy, Soc. Med. Psychoanalysts. Author: Psychology of Eating, 1936; Hypnoanalysis, 1945, 2d edit., 1967; Medical Hypnosis, 1948; The Technique of Psychotherapy, 1954, 3d edit., 1977; Short-term Psychotherapy, 1965; Psychotherapy and Behavioral Sciences, 1966; The Dynamics of Personality, 1969; Handbook of Short-term Therapy, 1969; Micro-art: Art Images in a Hidden World, 1970; Hypnosis: Is It for You, 1972; Group Therapy, 1974, 75, 76, 77, 78, 79; Zooming In: Photographic Discoveries under the Microscope, 1974; Art Forms from Photomicrography, 1975. Mem. editorial bd. Jour. Am. Acad. Psychoanalysis, Am. Jour. Clin. Hypnosis; contbr. articles to sci. jours., Funk & Wagnalls Ency. Home: Roaring Brook Lake Rural Route 1 Putnam Valley NY 10579 Office: 124 E 28th St New York NY 10016

WOLBRECHT, WALTER FREDERICK, clergyman; b. St. Louis, Sept. 11, 1915; s. Arthur and Emille (Brandt) W.; student Concordia Coll., Milw., 1934; theol. diploma Concordia Sem., St. Louis, 1948; M.A., U. Neb.; grad. student U. Chgo., Marquette U., Municipal U. Omaha; D.D., Concordia Sem., Springfield, Ill.; LL.D., Augustana Lutheran Coll., Rock Island Ill., 1962; m. Marie Helen Suedekum, Apr. 20, 1941; children—William, Thomas, Timothy. Ordained to ministry Luth. Ch.; instr. Concordia Coll., Milw., 1938-40; pastor, Missoula, Mont., also part-time instr. Mont. State U., 1940-45; prof. religion and social sci. Concordia Tchrs. Coll., Seward, Neb., 1945-51; pres. St. Paul's Coll., Concordia, Mo., 1951-54; asst. exec. sec. bd. higher edn. Luth. Ch. Mo. Synod, 1954-55, exec. sec. bd., 1955-61, exec. dir. synod, 1961-71; pres. Luth. Sch. Theology, Chgo., 1972-76. Pres. Ministry Studies Bd.; mem. bd. pensions Lutheran Ch. Am., 1974—; mem. bd. Ch. Exec. Devel. Bd., Lutheran Benevolent Assn. Mem. Am. Soc. Ch. History, Luth. Acad. Scholarship, Assn. Sch. Bus. Ofcls., Soc. Sci. Study Religion, Phi Delta Kappa. Home: 3500 Milam P-201 Shreveport LA 71109

WOLBRINK, JAMES FRANCIS, assn. exec.; b. Charles City, Iowa, Sept. 8, 1942; s. Richard William and Anna (Butt) W.; B.S. in Indsl. Engring., Iowa State U., 1966, postgrad., 1968-72; m. Karen Ann Dunkerly, June 18, 1966. Tech. writer/editor Lawrence Radiation Lab., Livermore, Calif., 1966-67; editor, head engring. publs. Engring. Research Inst., Iowa State U., Ames, 1967-70; mng. dir., publisher, editor-in-chief Am. Inst. Indsl. Engrs., Norcross, Ga., 1971—; lectr., tchr., cons. in field. Mem. com. for fund drive Northside Hosp., Atlanta, 1974. Recipient Outstanding Man award Active 20-30 Internat., 1967; named Outstanding Young Alumnus, Iowa State U., 1977; cert. assn. exec.; Sr. mem. Am. Inst. Indsl. Engrs.; mem. Am. Soc. Assn. Execs., Am. Soc. Engring. Edn., Am. Soc. Info. Scis., Delta Chi. Contbr. profl. jours. Home: 4520 Northside Dr NW Atlanta GA 30327 Office: 25 Technology Park Norcross GA 30092

WOLCOTT, ALAN THANE, auditing assn. exec.; b. Hebron, Nebr., Sept. 17, 1916; s. Arthur Ernest and Cora (Olmstead) W.; B.S. in Bus. Adminstrn., U. Nebr., 1937; m. Margaret G. Cumming, Aug. 17, 1968; children by previous marriage—Mark Alan, Wendi Thane. Advt. exec. Gen. Electric Co., 1937-42, 45-54; with Audit Bur. of Circulations, Chgo., 1954—, pres., mng. dir., 1960—; sec.-gen. Internat. Fedn. Audit Burs. Circulations, 1964-66. Public mem. com. on allied health edn. and accreditation AMA, 1978-79. Served to lt. USNR, 1942-45. Mem. Soc. Assn. Execs., Theta Chi. Clubs: Executives, Advertising (Chgo.). Home: 505 N Lake Shore Dr Chicago IL 60611 Office: 123 N Wacker Dr Chicago IL 60606

WOLCOTT, ARTHUR STANTON, food co. exec.; b. Corning, N.Y., Jan. 1, 1926; s. Samuel K. and Fanny S. Wolcott; A.B., Cornell U., 1949; m. Audrey Strude, Aug. 28, 1949; children—Bruce S., Susan B., Mark S., Grace G. Founder Senaca Foods (now S.S. Pierce Co.), Dundee, N.Y., 1949, chmn., chief exec. officer, 1949—; dir. Moog Inc., A.T.I. Inc. Served with AUS, 1944-46. Mem. Nat. Canners Assn. (dir.), Chief Execs. Forum. Republican. Presbyn. Clubs: Rotary, Rochester (N.Y.) Country, Masons. Home: 311 E Lake Rd Penn Yan NY 14527 Office: 74 Seneca St Dundee NY 14837

WOLCOTT, CHARLES, composer, assn. exec.; b. Flint, Mich., Sept. 29, 1906; s. Frederick Charles and Frances Mae (Terwilliger) W.; B.A., U. Mich., 1927; m. Harriett Louise Marshall, Aug. 30, 1928; children—Sheila Joan Wolcott Banani, Marsha Jean Wolcott Gilpatrick. Leader own orch., 1925; pianist, arranger Jean Goldkette Orgn., Detroit, including Casa Loma Orch.; composer, arranger, condr. Paul Whiteman Orch., 1931; on radio with Andre Kostelanetz, Arnold Johnson, others, 1933-37; with Walt Disney, Hollywood, Calif., 1938-48, gen. mus. dir., 1944-48; with Metro-Goldwyn-Mayer, 1950-60, gen. mus. dir., 1958-60; vice chmn. Nat. Spiritual Assembly of Baha'is of U.S., 1953-59, sec., 1960-61, sec.-gen. Internat. Baha'i Council, Haifa, 1961-63; elected mem. Baha'i Universal House of Justice, 1963, 78—; head (with 8 others) of Baha'i religion. Mem. ASCAP, Acad. Motion Picture Arts and Scis., Screen Composers Assn., Am. Guild Authors and Composers, Sigma Chi. Rotarian. Composer: Reluctant Dragon, 1941, Saludos Amigos, 1942, Sailors of the Air, 1942, Mexico, 1944, Two Silhouettes, 1945, Sooner or Later, 1946, From The Sweet-Scented Streams, 1948, Julie, 1953, Oh Thou, By Whose Name, Llama Serenade, Inca Princess, Blessed Is the Spot, 1955, Ruby Duby Du, 1960; (music for motion pictures) Three Caballeros, Make Mine Music, Song of South, Blackboard Jungle, Key Witness. Address: Baha'i World Center PO Box 155 Haifa Israel. *Some fifty years or more have passed since my undergraduate days, but I remember clearly the endless discussions about God and man's purpose in life. Then during the depths of the Great Depression I found these grains of truth for which we had so ardently sought—that there is but one God; that from time immemorial this Supreme Unknowable Essence has guided mankind by a succession of divinely-inspired human beings; and that all mankind belongs to one family whose members have but one purpose—to carry forward an ever-advancing civilization united under one God.*

WOLCOTT, JOHN WINTHROP, III, bus. exec.; b. Balt., Dec. 3, 1924; s. John Winthrop, Jr. and Dorothy C. (Fraser) W.; B.Indsl. Engring., Gen. Motors Inst., 1951; m. Elizabeth Thelin Hooper, Apr. 24, 1948; children—John Winthrop IV, Elizabeth T., Katherine C. With Gen. Motors Corp., 1946-53, Weatherhead Co., Cleve., 1957-60; v.p. H.K. Porter Co., Inc., Pitts., 1960-64; pres. Ametek, Inc., N.Y.C., 1964-66; v.p. Am. Machine & Foundry Co., 1966—, group exec. process equipment group, 1967-70, exec. v.p. ops. AMF, Inc., 1970-77, also dir.; pres., chief exec. officer, dir. Transway Internat. Corp., N.Y.C., 1978—; dir. Waterman S.S. Corp., N.Y.C. Served with USCGR, 1943-46. Registered profl. engr., Ohio. Mem. Soc. Automotive Engrs., Soc. Colonial Wars, Newcomen Soc., Pa. Soc. Episcopalian. Clubs: Mount Kisco Country, Maryland (Balt.); Union League (N.Y.C.). Home: 14 Wolf Hill Rd Chappaqua NY 10514 Office: 747 3d Ave New York NY 10017

WOLCOTT, MERLIN DEWEY, librarian; b. Sandusky, Ohio, Oct. 22, 1920; s. Melvin Clary and Adella (Winklea) W.; student Bowling Green State U., 1950, Kent State U., 1953, Western Res. U., 1953-54. Asst. sci. and tech. div. Cleve. Pub. Library, 1952-53; head librarian Avon Lake (Ohio) Pub. Library, 1955-56, Elyria (Ohio) Pub. Library, 1957-62, Stark County Dist. Library, 1962—. Adviser, Council Protestant Youth, Elyria, 1958-60. Bd. dirs. Welfare Council, Council Chs. (both Elyria), 1958-60. Served with AUS, 1942-45. Mem. Am., Ohio library assns., Mayflower Soc., Soc. Descs. Henry Wolcott, Greater Canton Econ. Council, Nat. Microfilm Assn., Nat. Assn. Accountants, Beta Phi Mu. Mason, Rotarian. Clubs: Service, Library. Contbr. articles to profl., hist. publs. Home: 506 Aultman Ave NW Canton OH 44708 Office: 236 3d St SW Canton OH 44702

WOLCOTT, OLIVER DWIGHT, internat. trading co. exec.; b. Marshfield, Oreg., Oct. 17, 1918; s. Dwight Oliver and Agnes Beatrice (Kunkel) W.; B.S., U. Calif., 1940; M.B.A., Stanford U., 1942; m. Valborg K. Rasmussen, Mar. 22, 1942; 1 son, John Oliver. With Chemurgic Corp., 1943-50, pres., 1947-50; with subs. W.R. Grace & Co., 1950-60, v.p., 1958-60; with Balfour Guthrie & Co., San Francisco, 1961-77, v.p., 1964-65, exec. v.p., 1966, pres., 1967-77; dir. Barclays Bank Calif., 1974—, chmn., 1979—; dir. United Leighton Ltd., Adpac Corp.; dir. Bd. Trade San Francisco, 1969-77. Club: Pacific-Union. Address: 840 Powell St San Francisco CA 94108

WOLCOTT, ROBERT BOYNTON, JR., pub. relations co. exec.; b. San Francisco, Sept. 24, 1920; s. Robert Boynton and Carrie (Rommel) W.; B.A., U. Calif. at Los Angeles, 1942; m. Ruth Denas, Oct. 8, 1949; children—Robin Laurine Fayette, Denis McKennett, Stephen Randall. Pub. relations rep. Time Inc. So. Calif., 1944-46; asst. to pub. Time mag., 1946-47, Life mag., 1947-48; dir. pub. relations Calif. Loan and Finance Assn., 1949-50; founder Robert B. Wolcott Assos., Inc., Los Angeles, 1950, pres., 1950-67; chmn. Wolcott, Carlson & Co., Inc., 1967-73, (merged with Burson-Marsteller 1973) exec. v.p., 1973-77; prin. Robert B. Wolcott-Pub. Relations Cons., 1977—. Mem. Pub. Relations Soc. Am. (bd. dirs., v.p. 1965-66, pres. 1966, chmn. pub. service council 1969-72, Presdl. citation for Meritorious Service 1959, 60, 67, 69, 72), Internat. Pub. Relations Assn., Nat. Investor Relations Inst. (v.p., dir.), Alpha Tau Omega. Clubs: California, Oakmont Country. Home: 1536 Glenmont Dr Glendale CA 91207 Office: 505 E Wilson Ave Glendale CA 91206

WOLCOTT, SAMUEL HUNTINGTON, JR., investment trust co. exec.; b. Milton, Mass., Aug. 31, 1910; s. Samuel Huntington and Hannah (Stevenson) W.; grad. St. Paul's Sch., Concord, N.H., 1929; A.B., Harvard, 1933; m. Mary Elizabeth Weld, Sept. 8, 1934; children—Samuel H. III, Philip W., Pamela, William Prescott. With First Nat. Bank of Boston, 1933-37; profl. trustee, financial adviser, 1937—; v.p., trustee Consol. Investment Trust, 1950, treas. 1951, pres., 1952—; dir. Big Sandy Co., Essex Co.; trustee Penn Mut. Life Ins. Co., Mt. Auburn Cemetery; dir., mem. exec. com. State Street Bank & Trust Co., State Street Boston Financial Corp. Trustee Harvard Mut. Found., Sailors Snug Harbor. Served from ensign to lt. comdr., USNR, 1942-45. Clubs: Country (Brookline, Mass.); City (Boston); Mid-Ocean (Bermuda). Home: 1726 Canton Ave Milton MA 02186 Office: 35 Congress St Boston MA 02109

WOLD, FINN, biochemist, educator; b. Stavanger, Norway, Feb. 3, 1928; s. Sverre and Herdis (Rasmussen) W.; came to U.S., 1950, naturalized, 1957; student U. Oslo, 1946-50; M.S., Okla. State U., 1953; Ph.D., U. Calif. at Berkeley, 1956; m. Bernadine Moe, June 13, 1953; children—Eric Robert, Marc Sverre. Research asso. U. Calif. at Berkeley, 1956-57; asst. prof. biochemistry, U. Ill., Urbana, 1957-62, asso. prof., 1962-66; prof. biochemistry U. Minn. Med. Sch., Mpls., 1966-74, St. Paul, 1974—, head dept., 1974—; vis. prof. Nat. Taiwan U., 1971, Rice U., 1974; cons. in field. Fulbright fellow, 1950, John Simon Guggenheim fellow, 1960-61; recipient Lalor Found. Research award, 1958, NIH research career devel. award, 1961-66. Mem. Am. Soc. Biol. Chemists (councilor 1978—), Am. Chem. Soc., Biochem. Soc. (London), A.A.A.S. Author, contbg. author books, contbr. articles profl. publs. Mem. editorial bd. Jour. Biol. Chemistry and Biochemistry, 1974—. Home: 2161 Folwell St St Paul MN 55108

WOLD, JOHN SCHILLER, geologist, former congressman; b. East Orange, N.J., Aug. 31, 1916; s. Peter Irving and Mary (Helff) W.; A.B., St. Andrews U., Scotland and Union Coll., Schenectady, 1938; M.S., Cornell U., 1939; m. Jane Adele Pearson, Sept. 28, 1946; children—Peter Irving, Priscilla Adele, John Pearson. Dir. Fedn. Rocky Mountain States, 1966-68; v.p. Rocky Mountain Oil and Gas Assn., 1967, 68; mem. Wyo. Ho. of Reps., 1957-59; Republican candidate for U.S. Senate, 1964, 70; mem. 91st Congress at large from Wyo.; pres. BTU, Inc., J & P Corp., Nuclear Exploration & Devel. Co., Lander, Wyo.; pres. Wold Nuclear Co., Wold Mineral Exploration Co., Casper, Wyo.; founding pres. Central Wyo. Ski Corp.; dir. 1st Nat. Bank, Casper, Kans.-Nebr. Natural Gas Co. Chmn. Wyo. Rep. Com., 1960-64, Western State Rep. Chmns. Assn., 1963-64; mem. exec. com. Rep. Nat. Com., 1962-64; chmn. Wyo. Rep. State Fin. Com. Active Little League Baseball, Boy Scouts Am., United Fund, YMCA, Boys Clubs Am.; pres. bd. trustees Casper Coll. Served to lt. USNR, World War II. Named Wyo. Mineral Man of Yr., 1979. Mem. Wyo. Geol. Assn. (pres. 1956), Am. Assn. Petroleum Geologists, Ind. Petroleum Assn. Am., AAAS, Wyo. Mining Assn., Sigma Xi, Alpha Delta Phi. Espicopalian (past vestryman, warden). Contbr. articles to profl. jours. Home: 1231 W 30th Casper WY 82601 Office: Suite 200 Mineral Resource Centre Casper WY 82601

WOLEK, FRANCIS WILLIAM, govt. ofcl.; b. Bklyn., Feb. 15, 1935; s. Francis Joseph and Louisa (Bittman) W.; B.Geol. Eng., Colo. Sch. Mines, 1957; M.B.A., Harvard U., 1962, D.B.A., 1968; m. Gloria Gore Peez, Dec. 29, 1956; children—Linda Ann, Michael Edward, William Charles, Terese Elizabeth. Research geologist Sinclair Research Labs., 1957-60; asst. prof. U. Pa., 1965-75; dir. Knowledge Utilization Center, University City Sci. Center, 1975-77; dep. asst. sec. for sci. and tech. Dept. Commerce, Washington, 1977—. Author: Administering Research and Development, 1964; Technology and Information Transfer, 1970; contbr. articles to profl. jours. Office: Dept Commerce 14th between East and Constitution Ave NW Washington DC 20230

WOLF, ALFRED, clergyman; b. Eberbach, Germany, Oct. 7, 1915; s. Hermann and Regina (Levy) W.; B.A., U. Cin., 1937; M.H.L., Hebrew Union Coll., 1941; D.D., 1966; Ph.D., U. So. Calif., 1961; m. Miriam Jean Office, June 16, 1940; children—David B., Judith C., Dan L. Came to U.S., 1935, naturalized, 1941. Rabbi, 1941; rabbi Temple Emanuel, Dothan, Ala., 1941-46; S.E. regional dir. Union Am. Hebrew Congregations, 1944-46, Western regional dir., Los Angeles, 1946-49; rabbi Wilshire Blvd. Temple Los Angeles, 1949—. Lectr., U. So. Calif., 1955-69, Hebrew Union Coll., Jewish Inst. Religion, Calif., 1963-65, 74—; lectr. religion Seven Seas div. Chapman Coll., 1967; adj. prof. theology Loyola U. Los Angeles, 1967-74; lectr. sociology Calif. State U., Los Angeles, 1977—. Mem. camp commn. adminstv. com. Camp. Hess Kramer, 1951—; mem. Los Angeles Com. on Human Relations, 1956-72, mem. exec. bd., 1960—, chmn., 1964-66, hon. mem., 1972—; pres. Anytown U.S.A., 1964-66; mem. community relations com. Jewish Fedn. Council, 1966—; mem. United Way Planning Council Bd., chmn., 1974—; mem. youth adv. com. NCCJ, 1968—, exec. bd., 1972—; founding pres. Interreligious Council So. Calif., 1970-72; chmn. clergy adv. com. Los Angeles Sch. Dist., 1971—; chmn. Nat. Workshop on Christian-Jewish Relations, 1978; bd. govs. Hebrew Union Coll., bd. alumni overseers, 1972—; bd. dirs. Jewish Fedn. Council, 1978—; bd. dirs. Jewish Family Service Los Angeles, sec., 1978—. Recipient Samuel Kaminker award as Jewish educator of year Western Assn. Temple Educators, 1965; John Anson Ford Human Relations award County Commn. on Human Relations, 1972; Harry Hollzer Meml. award Los Angeles Jewish Fedn. Council, 1978. Mem. Bd. Rabbis So. Calif. (pres.), Am. Jewish Com. (exec. com. Los Angeles chpt.), Nathan Stauss Israel Soc. (dir.), Central Conf. Am. Rabbis (exec. bd., mem. commn. on Jewish edn. 1970-72, treas. 1975—, chmn. interreligious activities com. 1975—), Pacific Assn. Reform Rabbis (pres.), So. Calif. Assn. Liberal Rabbis (pres.), Synagogue Council Am. (mem. com. interreligious affairs), Alumni Assn. Hebrew Union Coll., Jewish Inst. Religion, Town Hall, Los Angeles World Affairs Council, U. So. Calif. Alumni Assn. Author: (with Joseph Gaer) Our Jewish Heritage. 1957. Home: 3389 Ley Dr Los Angeles CA 90027 Office: 3663 Wilshire Blvd Los Angeles CA 90010

WOLF, ALFRED LOEB, lawyer; b. Atlantic City, July 29, 1904; s. Albert and Minnie (Loeb) W.; student Friends Sch., Phila.; B.S., Princeton, 1924; M.A. in Juris (hon.), Oxford (Eng.) U., 1926; grad. civil and mil. airplane, mil. jet, helicopter pilot schs.; m. Constance Cann, Nov. 17, 1931. Admitted to Pa. bar, 1928; partner Wolf, Block, Schorr & Solis Cohen, Phila., 1928—; nat. counsel Airplane Mechanics Sch., 1930-40; a founder, trustee, gen. counsel Aircraft Owners and Pilots Assn.; gen. counsel Am. Helicopter Soc., 1950-77; columnist Legally Speaking, The AOPA Pilot, 1939—. City aviation dir., Phila., 1936-39, chmn. airport zoning bd. Phila. and Delaware County; examiner CAB, 1939—; U.S. adviser ICAO in Paris, 1951-52, Air Coordinating Com. for West Germany, 1952; del. Fedn. Aeronautique Internat. Ann. Conf., Paris, Cleve., Stockholm, Brussels, Madrid 1948-52, FAO in Thailand, Pakistan Iran, 1955. Trustee Vertical Flight Found. Brig. gen. USAF Ret. Fellow Am. Helicopter Soc.; mem. Am., Pa. (chmn. aero. law and space sect. 1933-75), Phila. bar assns. Club: Philadelphia Aviation Country; Racquet; Explorers, Wings (N.Y.C.). Contbr. numerous articles to profl. jours. Civil pilot certificates, U.S., U.K., Austria, France, South Africa, Sweden. Home: Blue Bell PA 19422 Office: Packard Bldg Philadelphia PA 19102. *You have to start by having friendly parents with no financial problems and, at appropriate times, receive from sundry sources, in appropriate amounts, an inheritance substantial enough to make possible the continuance of avoidance of financial problems. Then delegate the shepherding of this wealth to worthy fiduciaries. Then comes the most difficult thing: Try to find out what you want to do. If you, at any time, are lucky enough to discover this, do it. It is the failure to indulge your every whim that makes for less than total happiness. Then, avoid mating unless and until you are more than ready. You may, in this way, find marriage a plus. Jog, swim, and keep healthy, hoping for longevity. If you do all these things carefully you may avoid the need for religion, and possibly for doctors. There you have it in a nutshell.*

WOLF, CLARENCE, JR., stock broker; b. Phila., May 11, 1908; s. Clarence and Nan (Hogan) W.; student Pa. Mil. Prep. Sch., Chester, Pa., 1921; grad. Swarthmore (Pa.) Prep. Sch., 1923; m. Alma C. Backhus, Sept. 11, 1942; founder French-Wolf Paint Products Corp., Phila., 1926, pres. until 1943; admitted to Phila.-Balt. Stock Exchange, 1937; asso. Reynolds Securities, Inc. (now Dean Witter Reynolds Inc.), 1944—, spl. rep. Miami Beach, Fla., 1946—, now v.p. investments; dir. Superior Zinc Co., 1938-44, Hercules Cement Co., 1937-57, George S. MacManus Co., 1948—, Rand Broadcasting Co., owners radio and television stas., also hotels, 1946-68; dir. Amcord, Inc., 1958—, vice chmn., mem. exec. com., 1970—. Pres. Normandy Isles Improvement Assn., Miami Beach, 1952-53; mem. Presidents Council Miami Beach, 1952—. Mem. Alumnus Assn. Pa. Mil. Coll. (dir. Fla. chpt. 1961-64). Clubs: Jockey, Standard, Miami Shores Country, Variety (Miami, Fla.); Clermont (London). Home: Jockey Club 11111 Biscayne Blvd Apt 901 Miami FL 33161 Office: care Dean Witter Reynolds Inc 700 Brickell Ave Sixth Floor Miami FL 33131

WOLF, DALE JOSEPH, utilities co. exec.; b. Hays, Kans., Aug. 21, 1939; s. Henry and Irene W.; B.S., Ft. Hays (Kans.) State U., 1961; M.B.A., U. Mo., 1970; m. Patricia Ceule, May 28, 1966. With Mo. Public Service Co., Kansas City, 1962—, asst. treas., 1972-76, treas., 1976—. Pres., Jackson County United Way, 1978—. Mem. Mo.-Ark. Assn. Tax Reps., Planning Execs. Inst., Mo. Valley Electric Assn. Club: Kiwanis (pres. Raytown, Mo.). Office: 10700 E 350 Hwy Kansas City MO 64138*

WOLF, DALLAS RICHARD, oil co. exec.; b. Chgo., July 4, 1930; s. Chris Albert and Esther Christina (Garbe) W.; student U. Ill., 1947; B.S. in Bus. Adminstrn., U. S.W. La., 1955; m. Rae Catherine Crittenden, Aug. 23, 1952; children—Deborah Lynn Wolf Joiner, Patricia Gail Wolf Burton. With Shell Oil Co., 1955—, mgr. credit card center, 1973-74, gen. mgr. Info. and Computer Services, Houston, 1975-76, treas., 1977—. Bd. dirs. Tulsa Jr. Achievement, 1974-75; trustee Hilcrest Hosp., Tulsa, 1974. Served with USAF, 1948-52. Certified data processor. Recipient Certificate of Appreciation, Okla. Petroleum Council, 1974. Mem. Fin. Execs. Inst., Blue Key. Lutheran. Clubs: Lakeside Country, Houston, Rotary. Home: 11010 Ella Lee Houston TX 77042 Office: 1 Shell Plaza PO Box 2463 Houston TX 77001

WOLF, DON ALLEN, hardware wholesaler exec.; b. Allen County, Ind., June 18, 1929; s. Ellis Adolphus and Bessie Ruth (Fortman) W.; student exec. course Ind. U., 1969; m. Virginia Ann Lunz, Oct. 8, 1949; children—Rebecca, Donna, Richard, Lisa. With Hardware Wholesalers Inc., Fort Wayne, Ind., 1947—, purchasing mgr., 1957—, v.p., gen. mgr., 1967—; dir. Lyal Electric Co. Pres., bd. dirs. Big Brothers, Fort Wayne, 1973-74; nat. pres. Big Brothers Soc. Am., 1977—; active Jr. Achievement, Fort Wayne, 1977; bd. dirs. Russell Mueller Research Found., 1970—. Mem. Nat. Wholesale Hardware Assn. (bd. dirs. 1977—, named Hardware Wholesaler of Year 1973), Fort Wayne C. of C. (bd. dirs. 1973-74, 78). Republican. Lutheran. Office: PO Box 868 Nelson Rd Fort Wayne IN 46801

WOLF, EDWIN, II, librarian; b. Phila., Dec. 6, 1911; s. Morris and Pauline (Binswanger) W.; grad. William Penn Charter Sch., Phila., 1927, Bedales Sch., Eng., 1930; D.H.L. (hon.), Coll. Jewish Studies, Chgo., 1965; m. Margaret Gimbel Dannenbaum, July 2, 1934 (dec. June 1964); children—Ellen R. (Mrs. Schrecker), Anthony E., Mary (Mrs. Hurtig); m. 2d, Mary Paxson Matthews, Nov. 16, 1965; stepchildren—Sandra M., Barbara M., Ann M. Cataloger, bibliographer, mgr. Rosenbach Co., rare books and manuscripts, 1930-52; lectr. bibliography Bryn Mawr Coll., 1941-42; curator Library Co. of Phila, 1953-55, librarian, 1955—; Rosenbach fellow in bibliography U. Pa., 1964. Pres., Fedn. Jewish Charities Greater Phila., 1959-62; pres. Nat. Found. Jewish Culture, 1960-65, Jewish Exponent, 1966-68; pres. Greater Phila. Cultural Alliance, 1977-78; pres. Fellows in Am. Studies, 1976-77. Served with AUS, 1943-45; M.I. Corps., French mil. intelligence interpreter in Belgium, spl. agt. C.I.C., Germany. Guggenheim fellow, 1961. Recipient Athenaeum Lit. award, 1961, Penn Club award, 1979. Mem. Am. Philos. Soc., Am. Antiquarian Soc., Hist. Soc. Pa., Bibliog. Soc. Am. (past pres.), Inst. Early Am. History and Culture (past mem. council), Mass. Hist. Soc., Modern Lang. Assn., Jewish Publ. Soc. Am. (past pres.), Friends U. Pa. Library (past pres.), Athenaeum of Phila. Jewish. Clubs: Philadelphia, Franklin Inn (past pres.) (Phila.); Grolier (N.Y.C.). Author: Descriptive Catalogue of the Lewis College of European Manuscripts, 1937; William Blake, A Descriptive Catalogue of an Exhibition (with Elizabeth Mongan), 1939; Doctrina Christiana, the First Book Printed in the Philippines, 1947; Franklin's Way to Wealth as a Printer, 1951; William Blake's Illuminated Books (with Geoffrey L. Keynes), 1953; History of the Jews of Philadelphia (with Maxwell Whiteman), 1956; Rosenbach: A Biography (with John F. Fleming), 1960; American Song Sheets, 1950-1870, 1963; Negro History: 1553-1903, An Exhibition, 1969; James Logan, 1674-1751, Bookman Extraordinary, an Exhibition, 1971; The Library of James Logan of Philadelphia, 1974; Philadelphia: A Portrait of an American City, 1975; At the Instance of Benjamin Franklin, 1976; A Flock of Beautiful Birds, 1977. Contbr. articles to profl. jours. Office: 1314 Locust St Philadelphia PA 19107

WOLF, EMANUEL L., corp. exec.; b. Bklyn., Mar. 27, 1927; s. Morris and Rose (Hausknecht) W.; A.B., Syracuse, U., 1950, A.M. (Maxwell scholar), 1952; m. Judith E. Levine, July 15, 1964; children—Elissa Lee, Alexander. Mgmt. cons. Exec. Office Sec. Navy, Dept. Interior, Washington, 1952-55; nat. dir. program, adminstrn. VA, 1956; pres. E.L. Wolf Assos., Inc., Washington, 1957-61; treas. Kalvex, Inc., N.Y.C., 1961-65, pres., 1965—, chmn. bd., 1966—; chmn. Allied Artists Industries; pres., chmn. bd. Allied Artist Pictures Corp., 1968—. Mem. corp. adv. council Syracuse U.; mem. nat. adv. council Weizmann Inst. Sci. Served with M.C., AUS, 1946-47. Named Man of Year, Drug and Cosmetic Industry, 1967. Mem. Chi Eta Sigma. Office: care Allied Artists Industries Inc 15 Columbus Circle New York NY 10019*

WOLF, EMIL, educator, physicist; b. Prague, Czechoslovakia, July 30, 1922; B.Sc., U. Bristol (Eng.), 1945, Ph.D., 1948; D.Sc., U. Edinburgh (Scotland), 1955. Research asst. optics Cambridge (Eng.) U., 1948-51; research asst., lectr. math. and physics U. Edinburgh, 1951-54; research fellow theoretical physics U. Manchester (Eng.), 1954-59; asso. prof. optics U. Rochester (N.Y.), 1959-61, prof. physics, 1961—, prof. optics, 1978—; Guggenheim fellow, vis. prof. U. Calif. at Berkeley, 1966-67; vis. prof. U. Toronto, 1974-75. Fellow Optical Soc. Am. (Frederic Ives medal 1977, dir.-at-large 1972-74, v.p. 1976, pres. 1978), Am. Phys. Soc., Brit. Inst. Physics and Phys. Soc., Am. Inst. Physics (governing bd. 1977-78). Author: (with M. Born) Principles of Optics, 1959. Editor: Progress in Optics, Vol. I-XV 1961-77; (with L. Mandel) Selected Papers on Coherence and Fluctuations of Light, 1970, Coherence and Quantum Optics, 2d edit., 1978. Contbr. articles to profl. jours. Address: Dept Physics and Astronomy U Rochester Rochester NY 14627

WOLF, ERIC ROBERT, anthropologist, educator; b. Vienna, Austria, Feb. 1, 1923; s. Arthur George and Maria (Ossinovski) W.; came to U.S., 1940, naturalized, 1943; B.A., Queens Coll., 1946; Ph.D. (Viking Fund fellow), Columbia, 1951; m. Kathleen Bakeman, Sept. 24, 1943; children—John David, Daniel Jacob; m. 2d, Sydel Finfer Silverman, Mar. 18, 1972. Asst. prof. U. Ill., 1952-55, U. Va., 1955-58; vis. asst. prof. Yale, 1958-59; asso. prof. U. Chgo., 1959-61; prof. U. Mich., Ann Arbor, 1965-71, chmn. dept. anthropology, 1970-71; Distinguished prof. Herbert H. Lehman Coll. City U. N.Y., 1971—. Field work P.R., 1948-49, Mexico, 1951-52, Italy, 1960-61. Bd. dirs. Inter U. Com. for Debate on Fgn. Policy. Served with AUS, 1943-45. Decorated Silver Star; Guggenheim fellow, 1960-61; recipient Career award NIH, 1964-69; sr. fellow NEH, 1973-74. Mem. Am. Anthrop. Assn., Royal Anthrop. Inst. Author: Sons of the Shaking Earth, 1958; Anthropology, 1964; Peasants, 1968; Peasant Wars of the Twentieth Century, 1969. Home: Taxter Rd Elmsford NY 10523 Office: Herbert H Lehman Coll City U NY Bronx NY 10468

WOLF, FRANK GERALD, mag. publisher; b. Omaha, Nov. 12, 1922; s. Joseph Louis and Anna (Wirthsafter) W.; B.A., Pomona Coll., 1944; m. Judith Hermine Cohn, Jan. 8, 1944; children—Jeffrey L., Wendy C. With TV Guide mag., 1954-72, nat. advt. mgr., 1962-72; pub. Good Food mag., 1973-74, Seventeen mag., N.Y.C., 1974—, Panorama mag., 1980—. Served with AUS, 1943-46. Decorated Army Commendation ribbon. Office: 850 3d Ave New York NY 10022

WOLF, FREDERIC EASTMAN, lawyer; b. Wauseon, Ohio, Apr. 10, 1909; s. Fred H. and Lillian (Eastman) W.; B.A., U. Mich., 1930, J.D., 1932; m. Elaine Merrifield Huffman, Mar. 9, 1934 (dec. 1954); children-Mary Lynn (Mrs. Richard A. Thompson), Myrna Elizabeth (Mrs. Paul Malec), Michael A.; stepchildren—G. Scott Huffmann, B. Bruce Huffmann; m. 2d, Gertrude Powell Treece, Dec. 4, 1954 (dec. 1969); 1 dau., Jill Joanne; 1 stepson, Ian E. Treece; m. 3d, Frances Clock Brown, Jan. 19, 1973; 1 stepson, David. Admitted to Ohio bar, 1932; with firm Smith, Beckwith, Ohlinger & Froelich, Toledo, 1932-38; partner firm Beckwith, Ohlinger, Koles & Wolf, Toledo, 1939, Ohlinger, Koles, Wolf & Flues, Toledo, 1940-42; chief rent atty. Toledo rent area OPA, 1942-46; partner firm Ohlinger, Koles & Wolf, Toledo, 1946-62, Eastman, Stichter, Smith & Bergman, Toledo, 1963—. Mem. Am., Ohio, Mich., Toledo bar assns., Barristers, Phi Beta Kappa, Order of Coif, Phi Eta Sigma, Phi Kappa Phi, Delta Theta Phi. Mason. Contbr. articles to profl. jours. Bd. editors U. Mich. Law Rev., 1931-32. Home: 4411 Bowen Rd Toledo OH 43613 Office: United Savs Bldg 240 Huron St Toledo OH 43604

WOLF, FREDERICK BARTON, bishop; b. Cedar Rapids, Iowa, Apr. 12, 1922; s. Frederick Barton and Julietta (Reynolds) W.; B.A., Grinnell Coll., 1946; B.D., Seabury-Western Theol. Sem., 1945, D.D., 1969; LL.D., St. Frances Coll., 1969; J.U.D., Nasson Coll., 1969; S.T.D., Gen. Theol. Sem., 1974; m. Barbara Buckley, Oct. 5, 1946; children—Mary Julietta Wolf, Martha Clare, Jane Margaret. Ordained priest Episcopal Ch., 1946; priest-in-charge, then rector Trinity Ch., Belvidere, Ill., 1946-50; rector St. Christopher's Ch., Oak Park, Ill., 1950-54; dean Cathedral Ch. St. John, Quincy, Ill., 1954-58; asso. sec. dept. Christian edn. Nat. Council Episc. Ch., 1958-59; rector St. Peter's Ch., Bennington, Vt., 1959-68; bishop of Maine, 1968—; dep. Episc. Gen. Conv., 1964, 67; pres. standing com. Diocese Vt., 1964-68; chmn. gen. bd. exam. chaplains Episc. Ch., 1973-74; pres. Province of New Eng., 1974—, Convenor Council Advice to Presiding Bishop, 1974—. Chmn. bd. trustees Gen. Theol. Sem., N.Y.C., 1974—. Author: (with Barbara B. Wolf) Christian Forgiveness, 1957, Journey in Faith, 1959, Exploring Faith and Life, 1965. Home: 88 Park St Portland ME 04101 Office: 143 State St Portland ME 04101

WOLF, GEORGE ANTHONY, JR., physician, educator; b. East Orange, N.J., Apr. 20, 1914; s. George Anton and Jane Agnes (Devine) W.; B.S., N.Y. U., 1936; M.D., Cornell U., 1941; D.Sc. (hon.), Union U., m. Marguerite Girton Hurrey, Aug. 2, 1939; children—Patricia, Deborah. Teaching fellow biology N.Y. U., 1935-36; intern N.Y. Hosp., 1941-42, asst. resident, 1942-43, resident physician, 1943-44, physician out-patient dept., 1944-49, asst. attending physician, 1949-52, dir. personnel health services, 1948-50; asst. anatomy Cornell U. Med. Coll., 1939-41, asst. medicine, 1942-43, instr., 1944-49, Com. Med. Research research fellow, 1944-46, asst. prof. clin. medicine, 1949-52, asst. prof. pub. health and preventive medicine, 1948-50; prof. clin. medicine U. Vt. Coll. Medicine, 1952-61, also dean Coll.; v.p. for med. and dental affairs, prof. medicine Tufts U., 1961-66, exec. dir. Tufts New Eng. Med. Center, 1961-66; dean, provost, prof. medicine U. Kans. Med. Center, 1966-70; prof. medicine U. Vt., Burlington, 1970-79, prof. emeritus medicine, 1979—, prof. nursing, 1978—. Diplomate Am. Bd. Internal Medicine. Fellow A.C.P.; mem. Vt., Chittenden County med. socs., N.Y. Acad. Medicine, AAAS, Harvey Soc., Assn. Am. Med. Colls. (pres.), Phi Beta Kappa, Sigma Xi, Zeta Psi, Alpha Omega Alpha, Phi Chi. Author: Collecting Data from Patients, 1977; also articles in med. jours. Home: Box 96 Jericho Center VT 05465 Office: U Vt Coll Medicine Burlington VT 05401. *In the fields of teaching, patient care, adminstrn. and research, identification of the problem is of prime importance. Too often thinking is directed toward solutions of imprecisely defined problems.*

WOLF, GEORGE VAN VELSOR, lawyer; b. Balt., Aug. 10, 1908; s. Stewart George and Angeline Perkins (Griffing) W.; student Ecole Alsacienne, Paris, France, 1925, Andover Acad., 1926; A.B., Yale, 1930; LL.B., Harvard, 1933; m. Alice Roberts Kimberly, Feb. 3, 1940; children—Constance, Van Velsor, Timothy. Admitted to Md. bar, 1933; with Piper & Marbury and predecessor firms, Balt., 1933—, partner, 1940-76, counsel, 1976—; asst. atty. gen. Md., 1944-45. Mem. character com. Md. Ct. of Appeals, 1949-56; mem. Pub. Service Law Revision Commn., 1951-53, Commn. to Study and Revise Testamentary Laws Md., 1965-70. Dir. Title Guarantee Co. Trustee Children's Hosp., Balt., v.p. 1962-71; trustee Kent and Queen Anne's Hosp., Chestertown; mem. bd. Salvation Army, pres. 1947-49. Fellow Am., Md. bar founds., Am. Coll. Probate Counsel (regent 1972-78); mem. Md. Soc. Med. Research (pres. 1951-53), Am. Law Inst., Am. (chmn. real property, probate and trust law sect. 1970-71), Md. (chmn. estate and trust law sect. 1961-65), Baltimore City (exec. com. 1956-59) bar assns. Clubs: Merchants, 14 W. Hamilton St. (Balt.). Author, lectr. on estate planning. Home: Kentfields Quaker Neck Chestertown MD 21620 Office: First Md Bldg 25 S Charles St Baltimore MD 21201

WOLF, GORDON JOSEPH, lawyer, indsl. co. exec.; b. Cin., Jan. 6, 1905; s. Joseph and Hanna (von Epstein) W.; Ph.B. summa cum laude, Yale, 1926; J.D. cum laude, Harvard, 1930; m. Evelyn M. Best, Aug. 2, 1948; children-Joseph G., Alice Margaret, Robert Houston. Admitted to Ohio bar, 1930, Calif. bar, 1973; practice in Cin. as partner Cohen & Wolf, 1933-68; v.p., Aeronca, Inc., Torrance, Calif., 1969-73, sec., 1969—, also dir.; partner law firm Jones, Day, Cockley & Reavis, Los Angeles, 1973-76; dir. Aeronca Indsl. Products, Inc., Cleve. Machine Tool Co., Mercury Aerostructures, Inc. Trustee, sec. Aeronca Found.; bd. dirs. Cin. Charter Com., 1947-48; trustee Jewish Hosp. Cin., 1956-68, Adler Found., 1964-69, Lauer Found., 1966-69. Served to col., arty. AUS, 1941-46; ETO. Decorated Legion of Merit. Mem. Am., Ohio, Cin., Calif. bar assns., Am. Soc. Corp. Secs., Res. Officers Assn. (pres. Cin. chpt. 1937-39), Mil. Order World Wars, Am. Arbitration Assn., Army Aviation Assn., Mensa, Phi Beta Kappa. Republican. Mason (Shriner). Clubs: Army and Navy (Washington); Calif. Yacht (Los Angeles). Home: 7100 Spurlock Dr Austin TX 78731 Office: 200 Rodney St Pineville NC 28134

WOLF, HANS ABRAHAM, pharm. co. exec.; b. Frankfurt, Germany, June 27, 1928; s. Franz Benjamin and Ilse (Nathan) W.; came to U.S., 1936, naturalized, 1944; A.B. magna cum laude, Harvard, 1949, M.B.A., 1955; B.Ph., Trinity Coll., 1951; m. Elizabeth J. Bassett, Aug. 2, 1958; children—Heidi Elizabeth, Rebecca Anne, Deborah Ellen, Andrew Robert. Math. instr. Tutoring Sch., 1946-47; statis. research Nat. Bur. Econ. Research, N.Y.C., 1948-49; research Georgetown U., 1951-52; confidential aide Office Dir. Mut. Security, Washington, 1952; analyst Ford div. Ford Motor Co., Dearborn, Mich., summer 1954; foreman prodn. M & C Nuclear Inc., Attleboro, Mass., 1955-57; asst. supt. prodn. Metals & Controls Corp., Attleboro, 1957-59, mgr. product dept., 1959-62, controller, 1962-67; asst. v.p., controller materials and services group Tex. Instruments Inc., Dallas, 1967-69, treas., v.p., 1969-75; v.p. finance, chief fin. officer Syntex Corp., Palo Alto, Calif., 1975-78, exec. v.p., 1978—. Mem. Norton (Mass.) Sch. Bd., 1959-62, chmn., 1961-62. Pres., bd. dirs. Urban League of Greater Dallas, 1971-74; bd. dirs. Dallas Health Planning Council, mem. community adv. com., 1973-75; bd. dirs. Children's Health Council of the Mid Peninsula; cubmaster Boy Scouts Am., 1976-78. Served with USAF, 1952-53. Mem. Am. Mgmt. Assn. (planning council finance div. 1970—), Phi Beta Kappa. Mem. United Ch. Christ (elder 1970-73, vice-chmn. gen. bd. 1970-71, moderator 1978—). Author: Motivation Research—A New Aid to Understanding your Markets, 1955. Home: 895 Mockingbird Ln Palo Alto CA 94306 Office: Stanford Indsl Park Palo Alto CA 94304

WOLF, HAROLD ARTHUR, educator; b. Lind, Wash., Feb. 10, 1923; s. Edward and Olga (Limert) W.; B.A., U. Oreg., 1951; M.A., U. Mich., 1952, Ph.D., 1958; m. March 23, 1961; children—Mark, Suellen. Economist Prudential Life Ins. Co., Newark, 1957-58; asst. prof. fin., money, banking U. Colo., 1958-67, prof., 1967-68; prof. fin. U. Tex., Austin, 1969—; pvt. practice consulting for fin. instns., 1960—. Served with U.S. Navy, 1941-47. Mem. Am. Economic Assn., Am. Fin. Assn., So. Fin. Assn. Author: Personal Finance, 1978; Managing Your Money, 1977; Economics: Principles and Practices, 1979. Home: 7004 Edgefield St Austin TX 78731 Office: Dept Finance University of Texas Austin TX 78712

WOLF, HAROLD HERBERT, univ. adminstr.; b. Quincy, Mass., Dec. 19, 1934; s. John I. and Bertha F. (Sussman) W.; B.S., Mass. Coll. Pharmacy, 1956; Ph.D., U. Utah, 1961; m. Joan Z. Silverman, Aug. 11, 1957; children—Gary Jerome, David Neal. Asst. prof. pharmacology Coll. Pharmacy Ohio State U., 1961-64, asso. prof., 1964-69, prof., 1969-76, chmn. div. pharmacology, 1973-76; dean Coll. of Pharmacy, U. Utah, Salt Lake City, 1976—; vis. prof. U. Sains Malaysia, 1973-74; mem. Nat. Joint Commn. on Prescription Drug Use, 1976-80; mem. NIH rev. com. Biomed. Research Devel. Grant Program, 1978-79; external examiner U. Malaya, 1978, U. Sains Malaysia, 1980. Fellow Acad. Pharmaceutical Scis.; mem. Am. Soc. Pharmacology and Explt. Therapeutics, Am. Pharma. Assn., AAAS, Am. Assn. Colls. of Pharmacy (pres. 1977), Sigma Xi. Jewish. Contbr. articles in field of central nervous system pharmacology and field of pharm. edn. Home: 4512 Bruce Salt Lake City UT 84117 Office: Coll Pharmacy U Utah Salt Lake City UT 84112

WOLF, HARRY CHARLES, III, architect; b. Charlotte, N.C., June 28, 1935; s. Harry Charles, Jr. and Harriet Aubrey (Howard) W.; B.S., Ga. Inst. Tech., 1958; B. Arch., Mass. Inst. Tech., 1960; m. Janice Grigg, Nov. 13, 1966; children—Harry Charles IV, Harriet Craig. Pres. Wolf Assos., Architects and Planners, Charlotte, 1965—. Mem. Charlotte-Mecklenburg Environ. Council, 1973—, phys. environment subcom. Charlotte-Mecklenburg Citizens Com. Urban Living, 1969; chmn. Joint Coordinating Com. Urban Affairs and Environment, Charlotte, 1969-71. Bd. dirs. Charlotte Nature Museum, 1968-73, pres., 1970-71; bd. dirs. Charlotte Nature Mus. Found., 1969-71, chmn., 1973-77; bd. dirs. Mint Mus. Art, 1975—, Central Charlotte Assn., 1970—. Served with USAF, 1961-62. Recipient Archtl. Record awards, 1970, 72; Bartlett award Pres.'s Com. Employment Handicapped, 1971, 74; Nat. Plywood Assn. Design citation, 1973. Fellow AIA (nat. honor awards jury 1972; chmn. nat. design com. 1974; chmn. nat. task force Design by Creative Pub. Adminstrn. 1973; pres. Charlotte sect. 1973-74; dir. N.C. chpt. 1973-74, chpt. v.p. 1977; nat., regional, state awards 1966, 68, 73-74, 76-79); mem. Am. Inst. Planners (asso.), Newcomen Soc. N.Am., Phi Delta Theta. Democrat. Episcopalian. Clubs: Charlotte City, Charlotte Country. Important works include N.C. Nat. Banks, Beatties Ford and Park Rd., Latta Arcade restoration, Charlotte, Bank of Okla. Williams Cos., Tulsa, Ponte Travers Wolf Devel. plan, Charlotte, Mecklenburg Hall Justice, Charlotte, Sch. Design wing N.C. State U., Raleigh, Bank of Okla., Tulsa, Classroom and Office Bldg., U.N.C.-Charlotte. Contbr. articles, archtl. works to profl. jours. Home: 501 Hermitage Ct Charlotte NC 28207 Office: 213 Latta Arcade 322 S Tryon St Charlotte NC 28202

WOLF, HENRY, art dir.; b. Vienna, Austria, May 23, 1925; s. Stephen Armin and Lili Rona; came to U.S., 1941, naturalized, 1943; studies art with Hermann Kosel, design and photography with Alexey Brodovitch, painting with Stuart Davis; student N.Y. Sch. Indsl. Arts, 1941-42; m. Renate Vogel, Dec. 30, 1951 (div. Apr. 1956); m. 2d, Macha Gagarine, May 19, 1960. Designer, Arnold Studios, 1946-47; art dir. Geer, duBois & Co., Inc., 1947-51, U.S. Dept. State, N.Y., 1951-52, Esquire mag., 1952-58, Harper's Bazaar, 1958-61; art dir. Show mag., N.Y.C., 1961-64, Jack Tinker & Partners, 1964-66; exec. v.p., creative dir. Trahey Advt., Inc., N.Y.C., 1966; exec. v.p., partner Trahey-Wolf Advt., Inc., 1967-72; pres. Henry Wolf Prodns., Inc., N.Y.C., 1972—. Instr. design Cooper Union, N.Y.C., Sch. Visual Arts, N.Y.C. Recipient gold medal for mag. design Art Dirs. Club N.Y., 1956, 57, 59, 61, 63; gold medal Am. Inst. Graphic Arts, 1976; Ben Franklin fellow Royal Soc. Arts. (London). Mem. Am. Inst. Graphic Arts (pres.), Alliance Graphique Internat., Internat. Design Conf. (v.p.). Contbr. articles to trade mags. Address: 167 E 73d St New York City NY 10021

WOLF, HERBERT CHRISTIAN, educator; b. Balt., Apr. 6, 1923; s. Carl George and Margaret (Umhau) W.; A.B., Johns Hopkins, 1943; B.D., Luth. Theol. Sem., 1947; M.A., U. Chgo., 1959; Th.D., Harvard, 1968; m. Margaret Schroder, June 18, 1947; children—Gretchen, Gary, Martin, Allen, Miriam. Instr. religion Capital U., Columbus, Ohio, 1945-47; ordained to ministry Luth. Ch., 1948; pastor Univ. Luth. Ch., Nat. Luth. Council, campus pastor, lectr. religion Mich. State U., 1948-57; prof. religion Wittenberg U., Springfield, Ohio, 1957—, chmn. dept. 1969—; vis. prof. United Theol. Coll., Bangalore, India, 1974. Participant faculty study seminar in India of Kansas City Council Higher Edn. and Nat. Council Assos. Internat. Studies, 1971; vis. prof. Hood Coll., Frederick, Md., 1971-72. Mem. Clark County Democratic exec. com., 1960—, chmn., 1966-72; chmn. Clark County Dem. Central Com., 1966-72; sec. Ohio Dem. County Chmns. 1966-72. Danforth tchr. study grantee, 1961-62, 64-65. Mem. AAUP, Am. Acad. Religion, Am. Theol. Soc. Author: Kierkegaard and Bultmann: The Quest of the Historical Jesus, 1965. Contbr. articles to profl. jours. Home: 1126 N Fountain St Springfield OH 45504

WOLF, JACK KEIL, educator, elec. engr.; b. Newark, Mar. 14, 1935; s. Joseph and Rosaline Miriam (Keil) W.; B.S., U. Pa., 1956; M.S.E., Princeton, 1957, M.A., 1958, Ph.D., 1960; m. Toby Katz, Sept. 10, 1955; children—Joseph Martin, Jay Steven, Sarah Keil. With R.C.A., Princeton, N.J., 1959-60; asso. prof. N.Y. U., 1963-65; from asso. prof. to prof. elec. engring. Poly. Inst. Bklyn., 1965-73; prof. dept. elec. and computer engring. U. Mass., Amherst, 1973—, chmn. dept., 1973-75. Mem. tech. staff Bell Telephone Labs., Murray Hill, N.J., 1968-69; cons. to industry, State N.J., fed. agys. Served with USAF, 1960-63. NSF sr. postdoctoral fellow, 1971-72. Fellow I.E.E.E. (pres. info. theory group 1974, co-recipient info. theory group prize paper award 1975); mem. AAAS, Sigma Xi, Sigma Tau, Eta Kappa Nu, Pi Mu Epsilon, Tau Beta Pi. Editor for coding I.E.E.E. Transactions on Information Theory, 1969-72. Research on information theory and communication theory. Home: 108 Lessey St Amherst MA 01002

WOLF, JOHN BAPTISTE, educator; b. Ouray, Colo., July 16, 1907; s. John B. M. and Anna Mae (Stader) W.; A.B., U. Colo., 1929, M.A., 1930; postgrad. Northwestern U., 1930-31; Ph.D., U. Minn., 1933; m. Theta Holmes, June 17, 1933; 1 son, John K.F. From instr. to asst. prof. U. Mo., 1934-43; asso. prof. U. Minn., 1943-49, prof. history, 1949-66; prof. history U. Ill., Chgo. Circle, 1966-74, emeritus, 1974—; professorial lectr. U. Chgo., 1967-72, Folger Library Seminar, 1974.

Tchr. summers Colo. State Coll., 1940, U. Neb., 1941; hon. mem. U.S. Commn. on Mil. History; Fulbright research prof. Sorbonne, U. Paris, 1951-52. Guggenheim fellow, Paris, 1959-60, Paris, Madrid, 1967-68. Decorated chevalier des Palmes Academiques. Mem. Am. Hist. Assn. (chmn. European sect. 1964), Upper Midwest Hist. Assn., Soc. Franc d'Archeologie, Soc. d'hist. Modern, Soc. XVII Siecle, Soc. French Hist. Studies (pres. 1968-69), History Sci. Soc. Author: The Diplomatic History of the Bagdad Railroad, 1936; France 1815 to the Present, 1940; A History of Civilization (with others), 1946; The Emergence of the Great Powers 1685-1715, 1951; The Emergence of Modern Europe, 1962; Louis XIV, 1968; Toward a European Balance of Power, 1640-1720, 1969; Early Modern Europe, 1972; Louis XIV, a Profile, 1972; also chpts. in books. Editorial bd. Jour. Modern History, Annales Canadiennes, War and Society, A Journal of Military History. Home: 173 Beacon Ln Jupiter Inlet Colony FL 33458 also RFD 2 Luck WI 54853

WOLF, JOHN CLEMENT, editor, writer; b. N.Y.C., Dec. 4, 1940; s. Bernard and Emma Nanette (Mayer) W.; A.B., N.Y. U., 1962; postgrad. Yale Law Sch., 1962, Columbia, 1963-64; m. Susan Barbara Anderson, May 30, 1969; children—Alexandra Constance, Benjamin David. Editor, Prentice-Hall, Inc., Englewood Cliffs, N.J., 1964; asst. editor Am. Photog. Book Pub. Co., Inc., N.Y.C., Garden City, N.Y., 1965-66, mng. editor, 1966-67, editor-in-chief, 1967-76; partner Cook and Wolf, 1977—. Editor, pub. community newspaper Inwood Adv., 1971-73; mem. Friends of Inwood Hill Park, 1971—; mem. exec. bd. Park Terrace Gardens Tenants' Assn., 1970-74. Mem. County Democratic Com., 1972—, Dem. dist. leader, 1975-77; Dem. jud. del., 1977, 78, 79. Jewish. Author, illustrator: Miranda Sensorex Guide, 1971; Minolta SR-T Guide, 1972; Minolta Reflex Photography, 1977; Nikon Guide, 1978; Minolta Guide, 1979; Vivitar Guide, 1980. Home: 25 Indian Rd New York NY 10034

WOLF, JOHN MARTIN, furniture co. exec.; b. Mishawaka, Ind., June 25, 1917; s. Arthur Francis and Elizabeth (Cunniff) W.; B.S.C. in Accounting magna cum laude, U. Notre Dame, 1941; certificate advanced mgmt. U. Chgo., 1957; m. Mary Louise Pfaff, Dec. 27, 1947; children—Christopher F., John Martin, Gregory J., Michael J., Stephen P., Mary C., Andrew L. Jr. accountant Willet & Wharton, C.P.A.'s, South Bend, Ind., 1941-42; asst. prof. accounting U. Notre Dame, 1940-47; asst. sec.-treas. Steel-Shot Products, Butler, Pa., 1948-52; internal auditor Wheelabrator Corp., Mishawaka, 1943-45, controller, 1952-60; controller Bell Intercontinental Corp., 1960, treas., 1960-61; v.p., gen. mgr. Lake Erie Machinery Corp., Buffalo, 1961-63; v.p. accounting and controls Mueller Brass Co., Port Huron, Mich., 1963-65; treas. Lab. for Electronics, Inc., Waltham, 1966-68; v.p. finance Steelcase Inc., Grand Rapids, 1968—. C.P.A., Ind. Mem. Financial Execs. Inst. (1st pres. Michiana chpt. 1958), Am. Inst. C.P.A.'s, Ind. Assn. C.P.A.'s (past chmn. com. indsl. accounting). Home: 707 Plymouth Rd SE Grand Rapids MI 49506 Office: 1120 36th St SE Grand Rapids MI 49501

WOLF, JOSEPH ALBERT, educator, mathematician; b. Chgo., Oct. 18, 1936; s. Albert M. and Goldie (Wykoff) W.; B.S., U. Chgo., 1956, M.S., 1957, Ph.D., 1959. Vis. mem. Inst. for Advanced Study, Princeton, 1960-62, 65-66; asst. prof. U. Calif. at Berkeley, 1962-64, asso. prof., 1964-66, prof., 1966—, vice chmn. for instrn., dept. math., 1968-69, Miller research prof., 1972-73; vis. prof. Rutgers U., 1969-70, Hebrew U., Jerusalem, 1974-76, Tel Aviv U., 1974-76; Alfred P. Sloan research fellow, 1965-67; NSF fellow, 1959-62. Mem. Am. (mng. editor Proc.), French, Swiss math. socs. Author: Spaces of Constant Curvature, 1967, 72, 77; Unitary Representations on Partially Holomorphic Cohomology Spaces, 1974; Unitary Representations of Maximal Parabolic Subgroups of the Classical Groups, 1976. Editor: Geometriae Dedicata. Contbr. articles to profl. jours. Office: Dept Math U Calif Berkeley CA 94720

WOLF, JULIUS, med. educator; b. Boston, Aug. 15, 1918; s. Herman and Rose (Kurgan) W.; S.B., Boston U., 1940, M.D., 1943; m. Irene H. Bechtloff, May 4, 1945; children—Maritja Ann, Miriam Jeanne, Brenda Joyce. Intern, L.I. Coll. Hosp., 1943-44, resident, 1944-45; resident Bronx VA Hosp., 1947-48, sect. chief medicine, chief gastroenterology sec., chief med. service, 1948-72, chief of staff, 1972—; asso. prof. medicine Columbia Coll. Phys. and Surg., 1961-67; prof. clin. medicine Mt. Sinai Sch. Medicine, 1968—, asso. dean for VA programs, 1972—; chmn. VA Lung Cancer Group, 1962—. Served to capt. AUS, 1943-45. Fellow A.C.P.; mem. Am. Soc. Clin. Endoscopy, Harvey Soc., Am. Soc. Clin. Oncology. Home: 315 Covert Ave New Hyde Park NY 11040 Office: 130 W Kingsbridge Rd Bronx NY 10468

WOLF, LARRY M., lawyer; b. Balt., July 11, 1937; s. William W. and Mildred Cecil (Livingston) W.; A.B., Johns Hopkins, 1958; LL.B., Yale, 1961; m. Lois Twersky, Aug. 23, 1960; children—Jill Tara, Wendy Lynn, Rachel Millicent. Admitted to Md. bar, 1961, since practiced in Balt.; partner firm Wolf, Pokempner & Hillman, 1972—; instr. labor law U. Balt. Law Sch., 1965-70, 72—. Bd. dirs. Balt. Bd. Jewish Edn., Asso. Placement and Guidance Bur. Recipient Philip Wainer Meml. award Asso. Placement and Guidance Bur., 1973. Mem. Am., Md. bar assns., Bar Assn. Balt. City, Phi Beta Kappa, Omicron Delta Kappa, Pi Sigma Alpha, Alpha Epsilon Pi. Jewish (officer congregation). Mason. Contbr. articles to legal jours. Home: 8 Burr Oak Ct Randallstown MD 21133 Office: 810 WR Grace Bldg Baltimore MD 21202

WOLF, LEONARD NICHOLAS, health orgn. exec.; b. McKeesport, Pa., Jan. 3, 1911; s. Leonard and Elizabeth (Kronenberger) W.; B.Sc., St. Vincent Coll., Latrobe, Pa., 1933, D.Sc., 1971; M.S., U. Pitts., 1934, Ph.D., 1939; m. Anne Marie Breslin, May 1, 1943; children—Gregory T., Leonarda (Mrs. James J. Dolan), Elizabeth J. (Mrs. John Connolly), Maria I. (Mrs. Pierre Hennequin), John P., Andrea T., Anitra C. Asst. prof. biology St. Thomas Coll., Scranton, Pa., 1937-40; prof. biology, chmn. dept. U. Scranton, 1940-74, v.p. for planning, 1969-74; exec. dir. Greater Delaware Valley Regional Med. Program, 1974-76, Pa. Indsl. Rehab. Center, Inc., 1976—; dir. Health Care Mgmt. Corp. Mem. Pa. Council Higher Edn., 1963-73, Pa. Bd. Edn., 1963-73, Pa. Bd. Vocat. Edn., 1963-73; chmn. Pa. Commn. Acad. Facilities, 1966-72; chmn. regional adv. group. Greater Delaware Valley Regional Med. Program, 1970-74; mem. Gov.'s Adv. Council on Comprehensive Health Planning, 1970-76. Recipient Pro Deo et Universitatae medal U. Scranton, 1960; Benjamin Rush award, 1970. Mem. Am. Soc. Zoologists, Nat. Assn. Biology Tchrs., Am. Inst. Biol. Scis., AAAS, N.Y., Pa. acads. sci., AAUP, Am., Pa. pub. health assns., Sigma Xi, Phi Sigma, Alpha Sigma Nu. Founder, 1941, since editor Best Sellers, nat. bi-weekly book rev. Home: 1502 N Washington Ave Scranton PA 18509

WOLF, MILTON ALBERT, Am. Ambassador, economist; b. Cleve., May 29, 1924; s. Sam and Sylvia (Davis) W.; B.A. in Chemistry and Biology, Ohio State U., 1948; B.S. in Civil Engring. summa cum laude, Case Inst. Tech., 1953; M.A. in Western Res. U., 1973, postgrad. in econs., 1973-76, L.H.D., 1980; m. Roslyn C. Zehman, June 23, 1949; children—Leslie Eric, Caryn Sue, Nancy Gail, Sherri Hope. Pres., Zehman-Wolf Constrn. Co., Cleve., 1948-76; econ. adv. Ohio Savs. Assn., 1975-77; U.S. ambassador to Austria, 1977—; U.S. del. UN Conf. on Sci. and Tech. for Devel., 1979; U.S. rep. dedication of UN City, Vienna, 1979. Chmn. Fulbright Commn. for Austria, 1977-80; trustee, past treas., v.p. Mt. Sinai Hosp., Cleve.; mem. econ. adv. task force Carter Presdl. Campaign, 1976; mem. Carter Inauguration Com.; trustee Hathaway Brown Sch., Cleve.; past trustee Menorah Park Home for Aged, Bellefaire Children's Home; v.p., life trustee Park Synagogue, Cleve.; v.p. trustee Jewish Community Fedn., Cleve.; mem. various coms. Case Western Res. U., Case Inst. Tech., Case Western Res. Med. Sch. Served with USAAF, 1943-46. Recipient Great Golden medal for improving Austro-Am. relations Province of Salzburg, 1979. Mem. Am. Econ. Assn., Cleve. Engring. Soc., Cleve. Builders Assn. (past pres., life trustee), Nat. Assn. Home Builders (life dir.), Case Inst. Tech. Alumni Assn. (officer, life trustee), Builders Econ. Council, Ohio State U. Alumni Assn. (life), Tau Beta Pi. Office: Am Embassy Boltzmanngasse 16 1091 Vienna Austria

WOLF, RICHARD CHARLES, educator, ch. historian; b. Dayton, Ohio, Aug. 2, 1912; s. Norman Samuel and M. Estella (Tawney) W.; A.B., Gettysburg (Pa.) Coll., 1934; B.D., Luth. Theol. Sem., Gettysburg, 1937; postgrad. Oberlin Coll. Grad. Sch. Theology, 1937-41; Ph.D., Yale Div. Sch., 1947; m. Marjorie Edith Gongwer, Nov. 25, 1944; 1 son, Norman Tracy. Ordained to ministry Luth. Ch., 1937; pastor, Plymouth, Ohio, 1937-41; from teaching fellow to asst. prof. ch. history and adminstrv. asst. to pres. Luth. Theol. Sem., 1942-49; lectr. history Gettysburg Coll., 1943-45; asst. prof. Am. ch. history Yale Div. Sch., 1949-52; from asso. prof. to prof. Oberlin Coll. Grad. Sch. Theology, 1952-66; Charles Grandison Finney prof. ch. history Vanderbilt U. Div. Sch., 1966-78, emeritus, 1978—; pastor emeritus First Luth. Ch., Nashville, 1978—. Mem. bd. theol. edn. Luth. Ch. Am., 1964-70. Pres., Oberlin chpt. Am. Field Service, 1964-65; mem. Oberlin Health and Welfare Commn., 1963-66, Oberlin Fair Housing Com., 1962-63. Mem. Am. Hist. Assn., Am. Soc. Ch. History, Luth. Hist. Conf., Am. Acad. Polit. and Social Sci., Am. Soc. Reformation Research, Miss. Valley Hist. Soc., Phi Beta Kappa, Phi Alpha Theta, Tau Kappa Alpha, Phi Sigma Iota. Author: History of First Lutheran Church, Plymouth, Ohio, 1940; Our Protestant Heritage, 1956; The Americanization of the German Lutherans, 1683-1829, 1964; Lutherans in North America, 1965; Documents of Lutheran Unity, 2d edit., 1978. Editor: American Church, Facet Books hist. series. Contbr. articles to profl. jours. Home: 6694 Clearbrook Dr Nashville TN 37205

WOLF, RICHARD CLARENCE, educator; b. Lancaster, Pa., Nov. 28, 1926; s. Clarence Lester and Bertha Mae (Felker) W.; B.S., Franklin and Marshall Coll., 1950; Ph.D., Rutgers U., 1954; m. Marilyn Jean Miller, Aug. 23, 1952; children—Mark, Eric. Faculty dept. physiology U. Wis.-Madison, 1957—, prof., 1966—, chmn., 1971—, mem. endocrinology-reproductive physiology program, 1963—, co-dir., 1968-70, dir., 1970—. Cons. NIH, Ford Found.; mem. sci. bd. Yerkes Regional Primate Center, Emory U., 1972—. Served with AUS, 1945-46. Waksman-Merck fellow Rutgers U., 1954-55; Milton fellow Harvard, 1955-56, USPHS fellow, 1956-57. Mem. A.A.A.S., N.Y. Acad. Scis., Endocrine Soc., Am. Soc. Zoologists, Am. Physiol. Soc., Soc. for Endocrinology (Gt. Britain), Soc. Exptl. Biology and Medicine (sec. Wis.), Soc. Study Fertility, Internat. Soc. for Research in Biology of Reproduction, Soc. for Study Reproduction, Sigma Xi. Phi Beta Pi. Lutheran. Mason. Contbr. articles to profl. jours. Home: 4205 Manitou Way Madison WI 53711

WOLF, ROBERT ALBAN, ret. aero. engr.; b. Appleton, Wis., Sept. 4, 1907; s. Jacob Lawrence and Elizabeth Marie (Weiland) W.; student Lawrence U., 1926-28; B.Sc. in Aero. Engring., U. Mich., 1931, M.S. in Aero. Engring., 1932; m. Alice Wilkinson Hannel, Aug. 25, 1934; children—Virginia (Mrs. Warner L. Peticolas), Martha Jane Carter. Aerodynamics, structures analyst Consol. Aircraft Corp., Buffalo, 1932-36; asst. chief aircraft and helicopter design and devel. Bell Aircraft Corp., Buffalo, 1936-51; ops. research Cornell Aero. Lab. (now Calspan Corp.), Buffalo, 1951-60, head transp. research dept., 1962-72, dir. automotive crash injury research project, 1960-68. Engring. rep. for helicopters CAA, 1947-49; mem. pub. adv. bd. automotive safety standards U.S. Gen. Services Adminstrn., 1965-66. Mem. East Aurora (N.Y.) Sch. Bd., 1956-59, Com. Needs Aurora, 1970—. Bd. dirs. Human Dimensions Inst., Buffalo. Recipient Elmer A. Sperry award advancing art transp. safety, 1967. Asso. fellow Am. Inst. Aeros. and Astronautics (Aerospace Pioneer award 1973); mem. Soc. Automotive Engrs., ops. Research Soc. Am., Jet Pioneers, Sigma Xi. Episcopalian. Patentee in field. Home: 2705 Blakeley Rd South Wales NY 14139

WOLF, ROBERT B., lawyer; b. Phila., Aug. 18, 1914; s. Morris and Pauline (Binswanger) W.; B.A., Haverford Coll., 1936; LL.B., Harvard, 1939; children—Edwin David, Virginia. Admitted to Pa. bar, 1939; partner Wolf, Block, Schorr & Solis-Cohen, 1940-43, 46-56, 57—; gen. counsel FHA, Washington, 1956-57. Instr. humanities Haverford Coll., 1948-49, 71-72; chmn. audit com., dir. Seagrave Corp.; dir. Commonwealth Land Title Ins. Co. Chmn. mayor's coordinated housing improvement program, Phila., 1951; past chmn. Pa. Com. Crime and Delinquency; chmn. Phila. Youth Services Coordinating Com., 1978—; mem. juvenile adv. com. Pa. Commn. on Crime and Delinquency, 1976—. Trustee Benjamin Franklin Found., Berlin, Germany, 1955-56. Served to 1st lt. inf. AUS, 1943-45; office Asst. Sec. War, 1945-46. Mem. Am., Pa., Phila., Fed., Inter-Am. bar assns., Phi Beta Kappa. Home: 2101 Hart's Ln Miquon Conshohocken PA 19428 Office: Packard Bldg Philadelphia PA 19102

WOLF, STEWART GEORGE, JR., physician, educator; b. Balt., Jan. 12, 1914; s. Stewart George and Angeline (Griffing) W.; student Phillips Acad., 1927-31, Yale, 1931-33; A.B., Johns Hopkins, 1934, M.D., 1938; M.D. (hon.), U. Göteborg (Sweden), 1968; m. Virginia Danforth, Aug. 1, 1942; children—Stewart George III, Angeline Griffing, Thomas Danforth. Intern, N.Y. Hosp., 1938-39, resident medicine, 1939-42, NRC fellow, 1941-42; research fellow Bellevue Hosp., 1939-42, clin. asso. vis. neuropsychiatrist, 1946-52; research head injury and motion sickness Harvard neurol. unit Boston City Hosp., 1942-43; asst., then asso. prof. medicine Cornell U., 1946-52; prof., head dept. medicine U. Okla., 1952- 67, Regents prof. medicine, psychiatry and behavioral scis., 1967—, prof. physiology, 1967-69; dir. Marine Biomed. Inst., U. Tex. Med. Br., Galveston, 1968-77, dir. emeritus, 1977—, prof. medicine univ., also prof. internal medicine and physiology med. br., 1970-77; prof. medicine Temple U., Phila., 1977—; v.p. med. affairs St. Luke's Hosp., Bethlehem, Pa.; dir. Totts Gap Inst., Bangor, Pa., 1958—; supr. clin. activities Okla. Med. Research Found., 1953-55, head psychosomatic and neuromuscular sect., 1952-67, head neuroscis. sect., 1967-69; adv. com. Space Medicine and Behav. Scis., NASA, 1960-61; cons. internal medicine VA Hosp., Oklahoma City, 1952-69; cons. European Office (Paris), Office Internat. Research, NIH, 1963-64; mem. edn. and supply panel Nat. Adv. Commn. on Health Manpower, 1966-67; mem. Nat. Adv. Heart Council, 1961-65, U.S. Phamacopeia Scope Panel on Gastroenterology, Regent Nat. Library Medicine (chmn. 1968-69); mem. Nat. Adv. Environ. Health Scis. Council, 1978—; exec. v.p. Frontiers Sci. Found., 1967-69; mem. sci. adv. bd. Muscular Dystrophy Assns. Am., Inc.; mem. gastrointestinal drug adv. com. HEW; bd. Internat. Cardiology Fedn.; mem. bd. visitors dept. biology Boston U., 1978—. Served as maj. M.C., AUS, World War II. Recipient Disting. Service citation U. Okla., 1968. Mem. Am. Soc. Clin. Investigation, Am. Clin. and Climatol. Assn. (pres. 1975-76), Assn. Am. Physicians, Am. Psychosomatic Soc. (pres. 1961-62), A.M.A. (council mental health 1960-64), Am. Gastroent. Assn. (award 1943, Hofheimer prize for research 1952, pres. 1969-70), Am. Heart Assn. (award merit 1965, citation internat. achievement 1977, chmn. com. on internat. program), Coll. Physicians Phila., Philos. Soc. Tex., Okla. City Symphony Soc. (pres. 1956-61). Club: Cosmos (Washington); Bethlehem (Pa.). Author: Human Gastric Functon, 1943; The Stomach, 1965; others. Adv. editor Internat. Dictionary Biology and Medicine, 1978—. Home: Route 1 Box 1262 Bangor PA 18013 Office: St Luke's Hosp Bethlehem PA 18015

WOLF, WERNER PAUL, educator, physicist; b. Vienna, Austria, Apr. 22, 1930; s. Paul and Wilhelmina (Wagner) W.; B.A., Oxford (Eng.) U., 1951, D.Phil, 1954, M.A., 1954; M.A. (hon.), Yale, 1965; m. Elizabeth Eliot, Sept. 23, 1954; children—Peter Paul, Mary-Anne Githa. Came to U.S., 1963, naturalized, 1977. Research fellow Harvard, 1956-57; Fulbright travelling fellow, 1956-57; Imperial Chem. Industries research fellow Oxford U., 1957-59, univ. demonstrator, lectr., 1959-63, lectr. New Coll., 1957-63; faculty Yale, 1963—, prof. physics and applied sci., 1965—, dir. grad. studies dept. engring. and applied sci., 1973-76, Becton prof., chmn. dept. engring. and applied sci., 1976—; cons. to industry, 1957—; vis. prof. Technische Hochschule, Munich, Germany, 1969. Mem. program com. Conf. Magnetism and Magnetic Materials, 1963, 65, chmn., 1968, mem. adv. com., 1964-65, 70-76, steering com., 1970-71, conf. gen. chmn., 1971; mem. organizing, program coms. Internat. Congress on Magnetism, 1967; vis. physicist Brookhaven Nat. Lab., 1966, 68, vis. sr. physicist, 1970, research collaborator, 1972, 74, 75, 77. Fellow Am. Phys. Soc. (edn. com. 1977—, program dir. Indsl. Grad. Intern Program 1978—); sr. mem. IEEE; mem. Am. Assn. Crystal Growers. Contbr. papers on solid state and low temperature physics. Home: Apple Tree Ln Woodbridge CT 06525 Office: Becton Center Yale U New Haven CT 06520

WOLF, WILLIAM CHESTER, hotel exec.; b. Chgo., Mar. 13, 1917; s. Charles F. and Henrietta (Hagen) W.; student Herzl Coll., 1936, U. Ill., 1937-38; m. Adeline A. Loughlin. Feb. 14, 1940; children—William Chester, John Charles, Lizbeth Clarke, Patricia Loughlin. Asst. mgr. Stevens Hotel, Chgo., 1938-42; asst. mgr. Hotel Duluth (Minn.), 1942-43, mgr. 1946-53; mgr. Lowry Hotel, St. Paul, 1953-58; gen. mgr. Hotel St. Paul, 1958-66, Astor Tower Hotel, Chgo., 1966-80; gen. mgr. Park Regency-on-the-Lake, Milw., 1980—. Pres., St. Paul Winter Carnival, 1960, St. Paul Conv. Bur., 1962-63; mem. Gov. Minn. Tourist Adv. Council, 1955-62; bd. dirs. Chgo. Conv. and Tourism Bur. Served with AUS, 1943-46. Mem. Am. Hotel and Motel Assn. (nat. dir. 1965-66), Greater Chgo. Hotel-Motel Assn. (pres.), Minn. Hotel Assn. (pres. 1958). Clubs: St. Paul Yacht (commodore 1963-65), Masons, Shriners, Jesters, El Hajj, Lions. Address: 1626 N Prospect Ave Milwaukee WI 53202

WOLF, WILLIAM JOHN, educator, clergyman; b. Hartford, Conn., Jan. 17, 1918; s. William Henry and Mabel Bodine (Griggs) W.; A.B., Trinity Coll., 1940; B.D., Episcopal Theol. Sch., 1943; S.T.M., Union Theol. Sem., N.Y.C., 1944, Ph.D., 1945; D.S.T., Kenyon Coll., 1959, Trinity Coll., 1960; D.D., Gen. Theol. Sem., 1973; m. Eleanor Hale Dun, Aug. 10, 1946; children—Edwin Mershon, John de Nervaud, Stephen Hale. Ordained to ministry P.E. Ch., 1943; asst. minister Grace Ch., N.Y.C., 1943-45; faculty Episcopal Div. Sch., 1945—, prof. theology Howard Chandler Robbins chair, 1951—; pastor St. Elizabeth's Ch., Sudbury, 1947-51. Acting dir. laymen's inst. World Council Chs., Switzerland, 1952; rep. P.E. Ch., Faith and Order Commn., Evanston assembly World Council Chs.; del. observer of Episcopal Ch. to 2d Vatican Council; rep. P.E. Ch. Joint Commn. on Ecumenical Relations, Consultation on Ch. Union; mem. Interorthodox and Pan-Anglican Joint Doctrinal Commn.; mem. Anglican-Roman Cath. Commn. Mem. Am. Theol. Soc., Soc. Theol. Discussion. Author: Man's Knowledge of God, 1955; No Cross, No Crown, 1957; The Almost Chosen People, 1959; The Religion of Abraham Lincoln, 1963; The Thought of Frederick Maurice, 1963; A Plan of Church Union; Catholic, Evangelical and Reformed, 1965; Thoreau: Mystic, Prophet, Ecologist, 1974; Freedom's Holy Light, 1977. Editor: Protestant Churches and Reform Today, 1964; The Spirit of Anglicanism, 1979. Contbr. to The Theology of Reinhold Niebuhr, 1955; Calvinism and Political Order, 1965; The Second Vatican Council, 1967; Church Union at Midpoint, 1972. Home: 9 Phillips Pl Cambridge MA 02138 Office: 99 Brattle St Cambridge MA 02138

WOLF, WILLIAM MILTON, advt. exec.; b. N.Y.C., July 4, 1923; s. Saul and Bertha (Dryer) W.; B.A., Coll. City N.Y., 1946; postgrad. N.Y. U., 1947-49; m. Norma Miller, July 7, 1956; children—Adam, Leonard. Vice pres. Leonard Wolf & Assos., N.Y.C., 1949-61; copy chief Fairfax, Inc., N.Y.C., 1962-63; exec. v.p. William Douglas McAdams, Inc., N.Y.C., 1963—. Served with USAAF, 1942-45; ETO. Mem. Pharm. Advt. Club, Midwest Pharm. Advt. Club, Jewish War Vets. Contbr. short stories and poetry to lit. mags. Home: 489 Grenville Ave Teaneck NJ 07666 Office: 110 E 59th St New York City NY 10022

WOLFBEIN, SEYMOUR LOUIS, economist, educator; b. Bklyn., Nov. 8, 1915; s. Samuel and Fanny (Katz) W.; B.A., Bklyn. Coll., 1936; M.A., Columbia, 1937, Ph.D., 1941; m. Mae Lachterman, Mar. 1, 1941; children—Susan Lois, Deeva Irene. Research asso. U.S. Senate Com. on Unemployment and Relief, 1938; economist, div. research WPA, 1939-42; economist Bur. Labor Statistics, Dept. Labor, 1942-45, chief occupational outlook div., 1946-49, chief div. manpower and productivity, 1949-50, chief div. manpower and employment, 1950-59, dep. asst. sec. labor, 1959-67, dir. Office Manpower, Automation and Tng., 1962-67, spl. asst. to sec. labor for econ. affairs, 1965-67; dean Sch. Bus. Adminstrn., Temple U., Phila., 1967-78, Joseph A. Boettner prof. bus. adminstrn., 1978—; prof. econs. Am. U., Washington; vis. prof. edn. U. Mich., 1950. Dir. Lincoln Bank of Phila. Chmn., U.S. Manpower Com. for Middle Atlantic Region; mem. commn. on human resources Nat. Acad. Scis.; mem. adv. com. NSF. Served with U.S. Army, 1944-45. Recipient alumni award of honor Bklyn. Coll., 1954; Distinguished Service award Dept. Labor, 1955, 61. Fellow Am. Statis. Assn., AAAS; mem. Md. Civic Assn. (pres. Bannockburn 1957-59), Washington Statis. Soc. (pres.), Data Mgmt. Processing Assn. (hon. life), Am. Statis. Assn. (chmn. social statistics sect. 1956-57), Nat. Vocational Guidance Assn. (Eminent Career award 1970, chmn. occupational research com.), D.C. Guidance and Personnel Assn. (trustee). Author: Decline of a Cotton Textile City, 1942; The World of Work, 1951; Employment and Unemployment in the U.S.—A Study of American Labor Force, 1964; Employment, Unemployment and Public Policy, 1965; Education and Training for Full Employment, 1967; Occupational Information: A Career Guidance View, 1968; Emerging Sectors of Collective Bargaining, 1970; Work in American Society, 1971; Manpower Policy: Perspectives and Prospects, 1973; Labor Market Information for Youth, 1975; Men in the Pre-Retirement Years, 1977; Establishment Reporting in the U.S., 1978; contbr. articles to tech. and profl. jours. Home: E 706 Parktowne 2200 Benjamin Franklin Pkwy Philadelphia PA 19130

WOLFE, ALBERT BLAKESLEE, lawyer; b. Parkersburg, W.Va., Apr. 6, 1909; s. William Henry and Katharine (White) W.; grad. Hill Sch., 1927; A.B., Princeton, 1931; LL.B., Harvard, 1934; m. Beatrice Ewan, Oct. 23, 1942; children—Katharine Ward (Mrs. Carl H. Winder), Diana Ewan. Admitted to Mass., W.Va., bars, 1934, since practiced in Boston with firm Rackemann, Sawyer & Brewster, partner, 1940-74. Pres., Parkersburg Property Mgmt. Co., 1956—. Chmn., Cambridge Hist. Commn., 1963-73; mem. Mass. Hist. Commn., 1963-73; pres. Keystone Fund (W.Va.) 1951—. Trustee Marietta Coll., 1961-74, life asso., 1974—; trustee Nat. Trust for Historic Preservation, 1970-79; bd. dirs. N.H. Preservation Action. Served to lt. comdr. USNR, 1942-45. Fellow Am. Bar Found. (life), Mass. Bar Found. (life); mem. Am. (chmn. real property, probate and trust law sect. 1968-69, mem. council 1957-70), Mass., W.Va., Boston bar assns., Am. Law Inst., Soc. Colonial Wars. Clubs: Princeton (N.Y.C.); Harvard, Abstract (pres. 1965-73) (Boston); Harvard Faculty (Cambridge). Home: Old Harrisville Rd Box 97 Dublin NH 03444 also 28 Bradbury St Cambridge MA 02138 Office: 28 State St Boston MA 02109

WOLFE, ALEXANDER MCWHORTER, JR., banker; b. Balt., May 31, 1926; s. Alexander McWhorter and Sarah C. Wolfe; B.A., Bowdoin Coll., 1950; m. Diana Alys Paterson, July 16, 1954; children—Diane Elizabeth, Robert McWhorter. With First Nat. Bank of Boston, 1952-76, v.p., div. head internat. dept., 1970-72, sr. v.p., 1972-76; chmn. bd., chief exec. officer S.E. First Nat. Bank of Miami (Fla.) 1976—; pres. banking group, chief operating officer S.E. Banking Corp. Bd. dirs. United Way of Dade County, 1977—; trustee, vice chmn. bd. Council of the Americas, 1977—; bd. dirs. Greater Miami Opera Assn., 1977—, pres., 1978-79. Served to lt. USN, 1946-52. Mem. Bankers Assn. Fgn. Trade (past pres.), Assn. Res. City Bankers, Am. Inst. Banking (mem. internat. banking exec. com.). Clubs: Bankers, Miami, Key Biscayne Yacht; Union League (N.Y.C.). Office: 100 S Biscayne Blvd Miami FL 33131

WOLFE, BERTRAM, physicist; b. Bronx, N.Y., June 26, 1927; s. Paul and Sally (Greenberg) W.; A.B., Princeton U., 1950; Ph.D. in Nuclear Physics, Cornell U., 1954; m. Leila Ann Katz, Dec. 23, 1950; children—Sarah Elizabeth, Donald Stewart, William Allen. Physicist, Eastman Kodak Co., Rochester, N.Y., 1954-55; with Gen. Electric Co., 1955-69, 71—, gen. mgr. breeder reactor dept., San Jose, Calif., 1971-74, gen. mgr. fuel recovery and irradiation products dept., San Jose, 1974-77, gen. mgr. nuclear energy programs ops., 1977-78, v.p., gen. mgr. nuclear energy programs div., San Jose, 1978-79, v.p., gen. mgr. nuclear fuels and services div., 1979—; asso. dir. Battelle Northwest Lab., Richland, Wash., 1969-70; v.p., tech. dir. WADCO, Richland, 1970-71. Served with USNR, 1945-46. NSF predoctoral fellow, 1952-53; registered profl. engr., Calif. Fellow Am. Nuclear Soc. (pres. No. Calif. 1966, nat. dir. 1974-77); mem. Am. Phys. Soc., AAAS, Atomic Indsl. Forum (nat. dir. 1977—), Am. Nuclear Energy Council (nat. dir. 1977—), Sigma Xi, Phi Beta Kappa. Phi Kappa Phi. Jewish. Author, patentee nuclear energy, nuclear reactor projects. Home: 15453 Via Vaquero Monte Sereno CA 95030 Office: 175 Curtner Ave San Jose CA 95125

WOLFE, CHARLES JORDAN, ret. supt. schs.; b. Hudson, Mich., Mar. 19, 1910; s. Otto Charles and Margaret Marian (Jordan) W.; A.B., Wayne State U., 1932, M.A., 1938, Ed.D., 1954, LL.D., 1975; LL.D., Central Mich. U., 1966; m. Margaret Darnell, Nov. 3, 1933; children—Nancy (Mrs. Charles E. Humphrey, Jr.), Susan (Mrs. Dennis Miller). Tchr., Angell Sch., Berkeley, Mich., 1936-37, Tappan Jr. High Sch., Detroit, 1937-43, Southwestern High Sch., Detroit, 1946-50; counselor Mumford High Sch., Detroit, 1950-52; asst. prin. Northwestern High Sch., Detroit, 1952-54, Mumford High Sch., 1954-57; prin. Redford High Sch., Detroit, 1957-58; dist. adminstr. S.E. dist. Detroit Pub. Schs., 1958-60, East dist., 1960-61, asst. supt. for adminstrn. schs., 1961-67, exec. dept. supt., 1967-71, acting gen. supt., 1971, gen. supt., 1971-75. Chmn. commn. large urban dists., mem. adminstrv. com. N. Central Assn. Colls. and Schs.; mem. edn. and adv. com. Sales-Mktg. Execs., Inc. Bd. dirs. YMCA, Jr. Achievement Mich., Close-Up, Detroit Ednl. TV Found.; trustee Inst. Econ. Edn.; steering com. Detroit area council Boy Scouts Am.; adv. bd. Mich. Arthritis Found. Served with USNR, World War II; capt. Res. (ret.). Mem. Am., Mich. assns. sch. adminstrs., Detroit Schoolmen's Club, Detroit Schoolmen's Ex-Service Club, Gt. City Schs. Research Council (chmn. needs assessment com.), Detroit, Detroit, Mich. hist. socs., Wayne State U. (pres. 1968, distinguished alumnus award 1971), Wayne State U. Coll. Edn. (pres. 1963-64) alumni assns., Mackenzie Honor Soc., Engring. Soc. Detroit (asso.), Beta Sigma Phi. Clubs: Economic, Torch, Detroit Press (asso.), Rotary. Home: 1810 New Palm Way Boynton Beach FL 33435

WOLFE, CLIFFORD HENRY, mktg. cons.; b. Kasota, Minn., Mar. 25, 1904; s. Jacob Albert and Caroline Marie (Gilbertson) W.; B.S., Iowa State U., 1927; m. Nell Mabel Taylor, Feb. 25, 1933; children—Jon T., Linda (Mrs. Rodger A. Salman). Marketing exec. Ralston Purina Co., St. Louis, 1927-32; sales promotion mgr. Swift & Co., Chgo., 1932-40; advt. and sales promotion mgr. Pabst Brewing Co., Chgo., 1940-42; account exec., v.p. Biow Co., advt. agy., N.Y.C., 1942-49; sr. v.p. Dancer-Fitzgerald-Sample, Inc., advt. agy., N.Y.C., 1949-72; mktg. cons. Wolfe Assos., Inc., Larchmont, N.Y., 1972—. Bd. govs. New Rochelle Hosp. and Med. Center, 1956—, pres., 1968-71; bd. govs. Iowa State U. Found., 1958—; bd. dirs. Asso. Vis. Nurses Service Westchester, 1976—, pres., 1979. Mem. Cardinal Key, Sigma Delta Chi, Alpha Zeta. Presbyterian. Clubs: Larchmont Yacht, Royal Norwegian Yacht, Saratoga Reading Rooms. Address: 40 Ocean Dr Larchmont NY 10538

WOLFE, CLYDE ALAN, advt. exec.; b. Wyo., May 3, 1932; s. Clyde Allison and Margaret Virginia (Joyce) W.; B.A. in Psychology, U. Wyo., 1958; m. F. Carilouise Wood, Dec. 6, 1957; children—Kirk, Kelley, Alison. Asst. product mgr. to merchandising mgr. Gen. Mills Inc., Mpls., 1958-62; from asst. mktg. dir. to v.p., account supr. Compton Advt. Inc., Chgo. and N.Y.C., 1963-66; from v.p., account supr. to exec. v.p., gen. mgr. Wells, Rich, Greene, Inc., N.Y.C., 1967-76; exec. v.p., dir. N.W. Ayer A.B.H. Internat., N.Y.C., 1976—. Served with USN, 1951-55. Home: 149 Wexford Way Basking Ridge NJ 07920 Office: 1345 Ave Americas New York NY 10019

WOLFE, DAVID K., lawyer; b. Lafayette, Ind., Feb. 6, 1922; s. Simon and Nora (Connaroe) W.; J.D., U. Ariz., 1950; m. Charity Phillips, Aug. 19, 1958. Admitted to Ariz. bar, 1950, since practiced in Tucson; now engaged in individual practice law. Served with USAAF, 1943-45, USAF, 1950-52, maj. USAF Res. ret. Decorated D.F.C. with 1 oak leaf cluster, Air medal with 4 oak leaf clusters. Mem. State Bar Ariz., Order of Coif, Phi Kappa Phi, Theta Xi. Home: 3407 Arroyo Chico Tucson AZ 85716 Office: Pima Bldg 149 N Stone Ave Tucson AZ 85701

WOLFE, DEBORAH CANNON PARTRIDGE, govt. edn. cons.; b. Cranford, N.J.; d. David Wadsworth and Gertrude (Moody) Cannon; B.S., N.J. State Coll.; M.A., Ed.D., Tchrs. Coll. Columbia; postgrad. Vassar Coll., U. Pa., Union Theol. Sem., Jewish Sem. Am.; hon. doctorates Seton Hall U., Coll. New Rochelle, Morris Brown U.; 1 son, Roy. Former prin., tchr. pub. schs., Cranford, also Tuskegee, Ala.; faculty Tuskegee Inst., Grambling Coll., N.Y. U., Fordham U., U. Mich., Tex. Coll., Columbia; supervision and adminstrn. curriculum devel., social studies U. Ill., summers; prof. edn., affirmative action officer Queens Coll.; prof. edn. and children's lit. Wayne State U., summer; now edn. chief U.S. Ho. of Reps. Com. on Edn. and Labor, 1962—; Princeton, 1957-58; Fulbright prof. Am. lit. N.Y. U. Editorial cons. Macmillan Pub. Co.; cons. Ency. Brit.; adv. bd. Ednl. Testing Service; asso. minister First Bapt. Ch., Cranford, N.J. Mem. State Bd. Edn., 1964—, N.J. Bd. Higher Edn., 1967—; mem. nat. adv. panel on vocat. edn. HEW; mem. citizen's adv. com. to Bd. Edn., Cranford; mem. Citizen's Adv. Com. on Youth Fitness; mem. Pres.'s Adv. Com. on Youth Fitness; mem. White House Conf. Children and Youth, 1950, 60, White House Conf. Edn., 1955, White House Conf. Aging, 1960, White House Conf. Civil Rights, 1966, White House Conf. on Children, 1970; mem. Adv. Council for Innovations in Edn.; v.p. Nat. Alliance for Safer Cities; cons. Vista Corps, OEO. Bd. dirs. Cranford Welfare Assn., Community Center, 1st Bapt. Ch., Cranford, Community Center Migratory Laborers, Hurlock, Md.; trustee Sci. Service, Seton Hall U. Recipient Nat. Achievement award Nat. Assn. Negro Bus. and Profl. Women's Clubs, 1958; Woman of Year award Delta Beta Zeta, Morgan State Coll., Achievement award Atlantic region Zeta Phi Beta. Mem. Council Nat. Orgns. Children and Youth, Am. Council Human Rights (v.p.), NCCJ, Nat. Panhellenic Council (bd. dirs.), Nat. Assn. Negro Bus. and Profl. Women (chmn. speaker's bur.), Nat. Assn. Black Educators (pres.). NEA (life), League Women Voters, N.Y. Tchrs. Assn., Am. Tchrs. Assn., Fellowship So. Churchmen, AAUW (nat. edn. chmn.), AAUP, Internat. Reading Assn., Comparative Edn. Soc., Am. Acad. Polit. and Social Sci., Internat. Assn. Childhood Edn., Nat. Soc. Study Edn., Am. Council Edn. (commn. fed. relations), Assn. Supervision and Curriculum Devel. (rev. council), AAAS (chmn. tchr. edn. com.), Nat. Alliance Black Educators (pres.), NAACP, Internat. Platform Assn., Ch. Women United (UN rep., mem. exec. com.), Delta Kappa Gamma Edn. Soc. (chmn. world fellowship com.), Kappa Delta Pi (chmn. ritual com.), Pi Lambda Theta, Zeta Phi Beta (internat. pres. 1954, chmn. edn. found. 1974—). Contbr. articles to ednl. publs. Home: 62 S Union Ave Cranford NJ 07016 Office: Queens Coll City U NY New York NY. *I am most grateful to my parents for the two most important influences in my life: commitment to education and spiritual development. I have found that with "God power" and "brain power" all things are possible. I have, therefore, dedicated my life to people and in so doing have found joy.*

WOLFE, DOUGLAS ARTHUR, pollution ecologist; b. Dayton, Ohio, July 6, 1939; s. Ranald Milton and Julia Marie (Good) W.; B.Sc., Ohio State U., 1959, M.Sc., 1961, Ph.D. (NIH fellow), 1964; m. Nancy Suzanne Meeker, June 13, 1959; children—Cynthia Marie, Nicholas Arden, Catherine Ann. Grad. teaching asst. physiol. chemistry Ohio State U., 1959-62, research asst., 1962-63; chief program biogeochemistry Bur. Comml. Fisheries Radiobiol. Lab., Beaufort, N.C., 1964-69; chief scientist I program marine biology div. radioecology P.R. Nuclear Center, Mayaguez, 1969-70; leader program elemental cycling Nat. Marine Fisheries Service Center for Estuarine and Menhaden Research, Beaufort, 1969-72; dir. div. ecology Atlantic Estuarine Fisheries Center, Beaufort, 1972-75; liaisson scientist Nat. Marine Fisheries Service, 1975-77; dep. dir. Nat. Oceanic and Atmospheric Adminstrn. Outer Continental Shelf Environ. Assessment Program, Boulder, Colo., 1977—. Adj. asso. prof. zoology N.C. State U., 1966-75; cons. Nat. Acad. Scis. Recipient Superior Performance award Nat. Marine Fisheries Service, 1974. Mem. Am. Littoral Soc., Atlantic Estuarine Research Soc., Estuarine Research Fedn., Am. Chem. Soc., Am. Soc. Limnology Oceanography, Cave Research Found., Ecol. Soc. Am., Am. Malacological Union, N.C. Shell Club (v.p. 1971, pres. 1972, 73), Sigma Xi, Phi Eta Sigma Phi Lambda Upsilon. Contbg. author: Handbook of Biochemistry and Biophysics, 1966; Impingement of Man on the Ocean, 1971; Coastal Ecological Systems of the U.S., 1974; Estuarine Research, 1975. Editor: Fate and Effects of Petroleum Hydrocarbons in Marine Ecosystems and Organisms, 1977. Research, publs. on trace metals, radioactivity, pesticides in marine organisms and ecosystems, and on biology of molluscs. Home: 68A Wild Horse Circle Boulder CO 80302 Office: Nat Oceanic and Atmospheric Adminstrn Outer Continental Shelf Program RB3 East Campus Boulder CO 80303

WOLFE, ETHYLE RENEE (MRS. COLEMAN HAMILTON BENEDICT), educator; b. Burlington, Vt., Mar. 14, 1919; d. Max M. and Rose (Saiger) Wolfe; B.A., U. Vt., 1940, M.A., 1942; postgrad. Bryn Mawr Coll., 1942-43; Ph.D., N.Y. U., 1950; m. Coleman Hamilton Benedict, Dec. 4, 1954. Teaching fellow U. Vt., 1940-42; research fellow Latin, Bryn Mawr (Pa.) Coll., 1942-43; instr. classics Bklyn. Coll., 1947-49, instr. classical langs., 1949-54, asst. prof., 1954-59, asso. prof., 1960-68, prof., 1968—, acting chmn. dept. classics and comparative lit., 1962-63, chmn. dept., 1967-72, dean sch. Humanities, 1971-78; mem. exec. com., chmn. com. on undergrad. affairs City U. N.Y. faculty senate. Mem. Columbia U. Seminar in Classical Civilization. Recipient Kirby Flower Smith award, 1939; Goethe prize U. Vt., 1940. Mem. Am. Philol. Assn., Archeol. Inst. Am., Vergilian Soc. Am., Classical Assn. Atlantic States (exec. com.), Am. Soc. Papyrologists, N.Y. Classical Club (past pres.), Phi Beta Kappa (past pres. Rho chpt.). Asso. editor Classical World, 1965-71; co-editor The American Classical Review, 1971—. Home: 360 W 22d St New York City NY 10011 Office: Bklyn Coll Bedford Ave and Ave H Brooklyn NY 11210. *I have worked so hard on each task at hand all through my long career that I have never had time to think about achieving success. Unconscious of self-interest, I have always served when called upon to assume large or small responsibilities, with intellectual honesty and humanity as my guiding principles. But, as I look back over three decades the keynote of my endeavors is best summed up in Horace's Nil sine magna labore.*

WOLFE, GREGORY BAKER, univ. pres.; b. Los Angeles, Jan. 27, 1922; s. Harry Norton and Laura May (Baker) W.; A.B., Reed Coll., 1943; M.A., Fletcher Sch. Law and Diplomacy, 1947, Ph.D., 1961; m. Mary Ann Nelson, June 15, 1946; children—Gregory Nelson, Laura Ann, Melissa Helene. With internat. div. Arthur D. Little, Inc., Cambridge, Mass., 1951-57; dir. Greater Boston Econ. Study Com., 1957-61; dir. Latin Am. program Com. Econ. Devel., 1961-64; dir. intelligence and research for Am. republics State Dept., 1964-69; pres. Portland (Oreg.) State U., 1968-74; dean Sch. Internat. Service, Am. U., Washington, 1975-79; pres. Fla. Internat. U., Miami, 1979—. Fed. negotiator Joint Transp. Com., Washington, 1962-66. Chmn., Sch. Com. Wayland, Mass., 1959-61; mem. Gov. Md. Sci. Resources Adv. Bd., 1962-68, Oreg. Symphony Bd., 1972-75, Urban Redevel. Council, Urban Land Inst., 1972-75. Mem. Internat. Studies Assn., Am. Fgn. Service Assn., Washington Inst. for Fgn. Affiars. Contbr. articles to profl. jours. Home: 5709 Riviera Dr Coral Gables FL 33146 Office: Office of Pres Fla Internat U Tamiani Trail Miami FL 33199

WOLFE, HUGH CAMPBELL, physicist; b. Parkville, Mo., Dec. 18, 1905; s. Arthur Lester and Gertrude Remington (Snow) W.; A.B., Park Coll., 1926, Sc.D. (hon.), 1962; M.S., U. Mich., 1927, Ph.D., 1929; m. Ithmer M. Coffman, Sept. 3, 1929; children—Arthur, Elizabeth, James, Helen. Nat. Research fellow Calif. Tech., U. Calif., 1929-31; fellow Lorentz Found., Utrecht, Holland, and Heckscher research asst. Cornell U., 1931-32; instr. Ohio State, 1932-33; instr. Coll. City N.Y., 1934-42, asst. prof. physics, 1942-48, asso. prof. physics, 1949; prof., head dept. physics Cooper Union Sch. Engring., N.Y.C., 1949-60; dir. publs. Am. Inst. Physics, 1960-70, tech. asst. pub. and info., 1971-72, cons., 1973—; dir., chmn. bd.'s mgmt. com. Eastern Coops., Inc., 1949-51, dir., 1952-59; pres. Mid-Eastern Coops., Inc., 1952-59; dir. Cognitronics Corp., 1967—. Tech. aide OSRD, NDRC, 1944-46; exec. com. Nat. Com. for Sane Nuclear Policy, 1958-62; chmn. interdivisional com. on symbols units and terminology Nat. Acad. Scis.-NRC, 1962-73; mem. metric practice com. Am. Nat. Metric Council, 1973—. Recipient Naval Ordnance Award, 1945. Fellow Am. Phys. Soc.; mem. Internat. Union Pure and Applied Physics (pres. commn. on publ. 1966-72), Fedn. Am. Scientists (chmn. 1949, vice chmn. 1950), Am. Assn. Physics Tchrs., Am. Nat. Standards Inst. (mem. metric adv. com. 1970-76, graphics standards bd. 1968-72), Internat. Orgn. for Standarization (mem. adv. panel 1963—). Presbyterian. Home: 30 Lawrence Pkwy Tenafly NJ 07670 Office: 335 E 45th St New York NY 10017

WOLFE, JAMES DIGBY, author, producer, dir.; b. Harrow, Eng., June 4, 1931; s. Leslie Julian and Winifred (Withers) W.; student Thurlestone Coll., Dartmouth, Eng., 1948. Came to U.S., 1964. Writer, leading roles prodns. Chelsea at Nine, Wolfe at the Door, Wolfe in Sheep's Clothing, Juke-Box Jury (Eng., 1958-59), also Curtain Call, Revue '61, Revue '62, Australia, 1960-62; TV writer That Was the Week that Was, 1963, Ernie Ford spls., 1967, Jonathan Winters show, 1967, Wayne Newton spl., 1967, Soul, 1968, Colgate Comedy Hour, 1968, Leslie Uggams spl., 1967, Shirley McLaine spl., 1971, Doris Day Today, 1975, Cher spl., 1975, John Denver and Friend, 1976, The New Bill Cosby Show, Cher, Goldie Hawn spl., 1977, Laugh-In, 1977; co-creator Laugh-In, 1967-73; producer, dir., writer Opryland-U.S.A., 1972; producer, writer Li'l Abner, 1978. Recipient Emmy award outstanding writing achievement for Laugh-In, 1968. Office: care Adams Ray & Rosenberg 9220 Sunset Blvd Los Angeles CA 90069*

WOLFE, JAMES RICHARD, lawyer, r.r. exec.; b. Hannibal, Mo., Nov. 7, 1929; s. James Edward and Grace (Kirn) W.; student Georgetown U., 1947-49; B.S., Loyola U., 1951; J.D., DePaul U., 1953; m. Helene Lorraine Rosedale, Dec. 29, 1951; children—Yvonne Bazar, Mary Viano, Theresa, James E., Michaela, Kathleen, Lorraine. Admitted to Ill. bar, 1953, U.S. Supreme Ct. bar, 1961; atty. Burlington R.R., Chgo., 1953-55, 58-59; mem. Nat. R.R. Adjustment Bd., Chgo., 1959-63; counsel Southeastern Carriers Conf. Com., 1959-65; gen. atty. Nat. Ry. Labor Conf., 1965-67, gen. counsel, 1967-68; v.p. labor relations Chgo. and Northwestern Transp. Co., 1968-73, v.p. ops., 1973-76, pres., 1976—, also chief exec. officer, trustee, dir., also dir. C&NW subs., Western Ry. Coal Properties and NICOR, No. Ill. Gas Co.; mem. Nat. Adv. Transp. Task Force. Mem. pres.'s council Trinity Coll., Washington; vice chmn. bd. trustees De Paul U., Chgo.; trustee, mem. exec. com. Fenwick High Sch., Oak Park, Ill. Served to capt. U.S. Army, 1955-58. Mem. Assn. Am. Railroads (dir.), Western Ry. Assn. (dir.), Nat. Ry. Labor Conf. (dir.). Clubs: Hinsdale (Ill.) Golf; Sombero Country (Marathon, Fla.); Chicago, Mid-Am., Carlton, Internat. Wine and Food Soc. Chgo. Home: 422 S Oak St Hinsdale IL 60521 Office: 400 W Madison St Chicago IL 60606

WOLFE, JOHN WALTON, investment banker; b. Columbus, Ohio, Sept. 4, 1928; s. Edgar T. and Alice (Alcorn) W.; student Miami U., Oxford, Ohio, 1946-47; m. Norina V. Lovelace, July 20, 1978; children by previous marriage—Ann M., Robert F., Victoria G., Douglas B. With Ohio Nat. Bank of Columbus, 1948-57; v.p. BancOhio Corp., bank holding co., Columbus, 1957-74, also dir.; chmn. bd. Ohio Co., Columbus, 1974—, Dispatch Printing Co.; dir. RadiOhio Inc., WBNS-TV, Inc., VideoIndiana, Inc., Ohio Equities, Inc., Golden Bear Muirfield, Inc. Bd. dirs. Columbus Cancer Clinic; bd. govs. Aviation Safety Inst., Columbus; trustee Central Ohio Heart Assn., Columbus Mus. Fine Arts, More Bus. for Columbus Inc., Columbus Zoo Assn.; pres. Wolfe Assos. Inc., charitable found., Columbus. Mem. Nat. Assn. Security Dealers, Nat. Council on Humanities. Clubs: Athletic of Columbus, Buckeye Lake Yacht, Columbus, Columbus Country, Columbus Maennerchor, Muirfield Village Golf, Nat. Press, Press of Columbus, Masons, Shriners. Office: 155 E Broad St Columbus OH 43215

WOLFE, KENNETH GILBERT, oil co. exec.; b. Kalispell, Mont., Aug. 7, 1920; s. Kenneth and Isabel (Gilbert) W.; B.S. in Civil Engring., U. Calif., Berkeley, 1942; m. Madelynne J. Hatch, July 16, 1944; children—David K., Steven L., Bruce H. Various positions Bechtel Corp., San Francisco, 1949-67, mgr. constrn., power and indsl. div., 1969-72, project mgr. refinery and chem. div., 1972-74; v.p., mgr. ops. Wellman Lord, Lakeland, Fla., 1968; v.p. engring. and constrn. Occidental Petroleum Corp., Los Angeles, 1974—. Served with U.S. Army, 1942-46. Mem. ASCE. Club: Commonwealth of Calif. Home: 11814 Bel Terrace Los Angeles CA 90049 Office: 10889 Wilshire Blvd Los Angeles CA 90024

WOLFE, LEONHARD SCOTT, neurochemist; b. Auckland, N.Z., Mar. 25, 1926; s. Paul George and May (Kelsall) W.; B.Sc., Canterbury U., Christchurch, N.Z., 1947, M.Sc., 1949; sr. scholar U. N.Z., 1951; Ph.D., Cambridge U., Eng., 1952, Sc.D., 1976; M.D., U. Western Ont., 1958; m. Jeanne Mary Saunders, Aug. 5, 1959; children—Elizabeth Anne, Alexander Paul. Jr. lectr. Canterbury U., 1949; insect toxicologist Pesticide Research Lab., London, Ont., 1952-54; sr. biologist Fed. Dept. Agr., Ottawa, Ont., 1954-57; intern Royal Victoria Hosp., Montreal, Que., 1958-59; Med. Research Council Can. fellow, Inst. Psychiatry, Maudsley Hosp., U.K., 1960; asst. prof. McGill U., Montreal, 1961-64, asso. prof., 1964-70, prof., 1970—; asso. Med. Research Council Can., Montreal, 1963—; dir. Donner Lab., Montreal Neurol. Inst., 1964—; cons. Royal Victoria Hosp., Montreal. Fellow Royal Coll. Physicians (Can.); mem. Am. Soc. Biol. Chemists, Brit., Canadian biochem. socs., Canadian Physiol. Soc., Internat., Am. socs. neurochemistry, Internat. Brain Research Orgn. Dep. chief editor Jour. Neurochemistry, 1973—; editor: Prostaglandins, 1976; editorial bd. Canadian Jour. Neurol. Sci., 1975—; contbr. articles to profl. jours. Research in insect physiology and biology of biting flies, in neurochemistry, neurol. diseases, and prostaglandins. Home: 4700 Westmount Ave Montreal PQ H3Y 1X4 Canada Office: 3801 University St Montreal PQ H3A 2B4 Canada

WOLFE, LOUIS, publisher; b. N.Y.C., Mar. 2, 1935; s. Nathan and Goldie (Cohen) W.; B.A., CCNY, 1956; m. Emily Gordon, Sept. 16, 1957; children—Barbara, Debra. Vice pres., gen. sales mgr. New Am. Library, N.Y.C., 1959-70; dir. Australasia, Times Mirror Co., Sydney, Australia, 1970-72; gen. mgr. Gordon & Breach, N.Y.C., 1972-75; mktg. dir. Ballantine Books, N.Y.C., 1975-76; sr. v.p., gen. mgr. Avon Books, N.Y.C., 1976—; cons. Franklin Book programs, 1973. Mem. U.S. Book Assn., Assn. Am. Publishers. Office: 959 8th Ave New York NY 10019

WOLFE, RAPHAEL DAVID, bus. exec.; b. Toronto, Ont., Can., Aug. 3, 1917; s. Maurice and Tillie (Manovitz) W.; B.A., U. Toronto, 1939; m. Rose Senderowitz; children—Jonathan, Elizabeth. Chmn., pres. Oshawa Group Ltd., Toronto, 1958—; chmn. IGA Can Ltd., Can. Jewish News; dir. Bank N.S., Consumers Distbg. Co. Ltd., Confedn. Life Ins. Cos., Can.-Israel Devel. Ltd., Can. Pacific Ltd., Supersol, Ltd., Food Mktg. Inst.; chmn. Can. Jewish News. Bd. dirs. Can. Council Christians and Jews, Retail Council Can., Internat. Assn. Chain Stores, Baycrest Center for Geriatric Care; bd. govs. Mt. Sinai Hosp.; mem. advisory bd. U. Western Ont. Sch. Bus. Adminstrn.; mem. council of trustees Inst. for Research on Public Policy. Served with RCAF, 1943-46. Recipient Human Relations award Can. Council Christians and Jews, 1958; Ben Sadowski Award of Merit, 1975; hon. fellow U. Haifa, 1978. Mem. Can.-Israel C. of C. (chmn.). Clubs: Montefiore; Oakdale; Primrose. Home: 89 Bayview

Ridge Willowdale ON M2L 1E3 Canada Office: 302 The East Mall Islington ON M9B 6B8 Canada

WOLFE, RAYMOND GROVER, JR., educator, chemist; b. Oakland, Calif., June 1, 1920; s. Raymond Grover and Grace Caroline (McCombie) W.; A.B., U. Calif., Berkeley, 1942, Ph.D., 1955; m. Barbara Anne Knuth, Jan. 25, 1946; children—Gordon, Katherine, Donald. Biochemist, Donner Lab., 1948-55; research asso. chemistry U. Wis., Madison, 1955-56; prof. chemistry U. Oreg., Eugene, 1956—. Biochem. research Biochemistry Inst., U. Vienna, 1963-64; vis. prof. U. Bristol (Eng.), 1970-71, Cornell U., 1978-79. Served to lt. USNR, 1943-45. Decorated D.F.C., Air medal. Nat. Found. Infantile Paralysis fellow, 1955-56, Guggenheim fellow, 1963-64. Mem. Am. Chem. Soc., Am. Soc. Biol. Chemists, AAAS. Home: 1926 Potter St Eugene OR 97405

WOLFE, ROBERT RICHARD, agrl. engr., educator; b. Chippewa Falls, Wis., Nov. 9, 1937; s. Lewis Samuel and Bernice (Quale) W.; B.S., U. Wis., 1960, M.S., 1961; Ph.D., Purdue U., 1964; m. Carol Abrams, June 23, 1974; 1 dau., Laura Allene. Research engr. A. O. Smith Corp., Milw., 1961; research asst. Purdue U., Lafayette, Ind., 1963; asst. prof. agrl. engring. U. Wis., Madison, 1964-70; asso. prof. Rutgers U., New Brunswick, N.J., 1970-77, prof., 1977—. NSF grad. fellow, 1962. Mem. Am. Soc. Engring. Edn., Am. Soc. Agrl. Engrs. (Outstanding Paper award 1973, 77), Inst. Food Technologists, Instrument Soc. Am., AAUP, Sigma Xi. Tau Beta Pi, Phi Kappa Phi, Alpha Epsilon, Alpha Zeta, Delta Theta Sigma. Contbr. numerous articles to profl. jours. Home: 1759 Sandhill Rd Monmouth NJ 08852 Office: Biol and Agrl Engring Dept Rutgers U New Brunswick NJ 08903

WOLFE, ROLLAND EMERSON, educator; b. Hartville, Ohio, Feb. 25, 1902; s. Edson Weaver and Elta (Henney) W.; A.B., Manchester Coll., Ind., 1924, D.D. (hon.), 1952; B.D., Oberlin Grad. Sch. Theology (Monroe award for advanced study 1928), 1928, S.T.M., 1929; Ph.D., Harvard, 1933; m. Esther Hoff, Sept. 3, 1925; children—Frank Emerson, Homer George. Ordained to ministry Ch. of Brethren, 1929-38, Congl. Christian Ch., 1938-57, United Ch. Christ, 1957—; pastor Congl. Chs., Greenwich and Ripley, Ohio, 1926, Pilgrim Community Ch., Elyria, Ohio, 1927-29, 1st Congl. Ch., Boxford, Mass., 1929-39; instr. O.T. lit., Semitic langs. Crane Theol. Sch., Tufts U., Medford, Mass., 1934-35, asst. prof., 1935-46, acting dean, 1944, 46; Harkness prof. Bibl. lit. Case Western Res. U., 1946-71, emeritus, 1971—, chmn. dept. religion, 1956-67; adj. prof. Cleve. State U., 1971-74. Lectr., Bibl. subjects, archaelolgy; excavation at Moabite Dibon, 1953, Bibl, Bethel, 1960. Mem. Nat. Assn. Standard Med. Vocabulary (spl. cons. on Bibl. med. terms), Am. Acad. Religion (pres. 1947), Soc. Bibl. Lit., Am. Schs. Oriental Research, Archaeol. Inst. Am. Author: The Editing of the Book of the Twelve, 1933 (German monograph 1935); Tufts Papers on Religion (with Skinner), 1938; Meet Amos and Hosea, 1945; Men of Prophetic Fire, 1951. Contbr. to Ency. Religion, 1945. Home: 69-D Yorktowne Pkwy Whiting NJ 08759

WOLFE, STANLEY, composer, coll. adminstr.; b. N.Y.C., Feb. 7, 1924; s. Bert S. and Dorothy (Sanders) W.; student Stetson U., 1946-47, Henry St. Music Sch., 1947-48; B.S. in Composition, Juilliard Sch. Music, 1952, M.S. in Composition, 1955; m. Marguerite Wiberg, Aug. 10, 1960; children—Jeffrey, Madeleine. Faculty, Juilliard Sch., N.Y.C., 1955—, dir. extension div., 1963—; adj. prof. music Lincoln Center campus Fordham U., 1969-73. Served with AUS, 1943-46. Guggenheim fellow in composition, 1957; Nat. Endowment for Arts grantee, 1969, 70, 77. Mem. ASCAP, Am. Music Center, Am. Symphony Orch. League (Alice Ditson award 1961), Nat. Assn. Am. Composers and Condrs., U.S. Chess Fedn. Prin. compositions include; King's Heart (dance score), 1956; Canticle for Strings, 1957; Lincoln Square Overture, 1958; Symphony Number 3, 1959; String Quartet, 1961, Symphony Number 4, 1965; Symphony Number 5 (Lincoln Center Commn.), 1970. Home: 32 Ferndale Dr Hastings-on-Hudson NY 10706

WOLFE, THOMAS KENNERLY, JR., author, journalist; b. Richmond, Va., Mar. 2, 1931; s. Thomas Kennerly and Helen (Hughes) W.; A.B., Washington and Lee U., 1951, Litt.D. (hon.), 1974; Ph.D. in Am. Studies, Yale, 1957; D.F.A. (hon.), Mpls. Coll. Art, 1971. Reporter, Springfield (Mass.) Union, 1956-59; reporter, Latin Am. corr. Washington Post, 1959-62; reporter, mag. writer N.Y. Herald Tribune, 1962-66; mag. writer N.Y. World Jour. Tribune, 1966-67; contbg. editor New York mag., 1968-76, Esquire Mag., 1977—; contbg. artist Harper's Mag., 1978—; exhibited one-man show of drawings Maynard Walker Gallery, N.Y.C., 1965, Tunnel Gallery, N.Y.C., 1974. Recipient Front Page awards for humor and fgn. news reporting Washington Newspaper Guild, 1961; award of excellence Soc. Mag. Writers, 1970; Frank Luther Mott Research award, 1973; Va. laureate for lit., 1977. Author: The Kandy-Kolored Tangerine-Flake Streamline Baby, 1965; The Electric Kool-Aid Acid Test, 1968; The Pump House Gang, 1968; Radical Chic and Mau-mauing the Flak Catchers, 1970; The New Journalism, 1973; The Painted Word, 1975; Mauve Gloves and Madmen, Clutter and Vine, 1976; The Right Staff, 1979; contbr. articles to Esquire, Harpers Mag., others. Address: Care Farrar Straus & Giroux Inc 19 Union Sq W New York NY 10003

WOLFE, TOWNSEND DURANT, III, arts center adminstr.; b. Hartsville, S.C., Aug. 15, 1935; s. Christian Townsend and Elizabeth Seignious (Bryant) W.; student Ga. Inst. Tech., 1954-56; B.F.A., Atlanta Art Inst., 1958; M.F.A., Cranbrook Acad. Art, 1959; certificate Inst. for Art Adminstrn., Harvard U., 1970; m. Jane Rightor Lee, Aug. 28, 1968; children—Juliette Fielding, Mary Bryan, Townsend Durant, Zibilla Lee. Instr. Memphis Acad. of Art, 1959-64, Scarsdale Studio Workshop, 1964-65; dir. Wooster Community Art Center, Danbury, Conn., 1965-68; art dir. Upward Bound Project, Danbury, summers 1966-68; exec. dir. Ark. Arts Center, Little Rock, 1968—; exhibited one-man shows including Madison Gallery, N.Y.C., 1961, U. Miss., 1963, Southwestern U., Memphis, 1964, Ark. State U., Jonesboro, 1964, 70; exhibited group shows including Ball State Tchrs. Coll., Muncie, Ind., 1959, 63, 65, 67, Ann. New Eng. Exhbn., 1966-67, Wadsworth Atheneum, Hartford, Conn., 1967, Audubon Artists, N.Y.C., 1968; mem. adv. council Contemporary Art/Southeast, 1976—; sec. Ark. Arts Center Found.; cons. in field; bd. dirs. Arts in Edn., 1975; represented in permanent collections including Ark. State U., Union Planters Nat. Bank, Memphis, Mint Mus. Art, Charlotte, N.C., E. Tenn. State U. Mem. Southeastern Mus. Conf. (mem. council 1973-77, pres. 1978-80), Am. Assn. Museums, Asso. Council on the Arts. Episcopalian. Home: 2102 S Louisiana St Little Rock AR 72206 Office: PO Box 2137 Little Rock AR 72201

WOLFE, WILLIAM GERALD, educator; b. Clarksburg, W.Va., June 23, 1917; s. William Granison and Olive Grace (Holbert) W.; B.A., W.Va. U., 1940; M.A., U. Iowa, 1942, Ph.D., 1947; m. Mayrel R. Stalnaker, Mar. 25, 1942; 1 son, William Gregory. Instr. dept. speech W.Va. U., 1940-41, instr., dir. speech clinic, 1942-43; personnel dept. Goodyear Aircraft Corp., Akron, Ohio, also Ariz., 1943-44; personnel mgr. Wingfoot Homes subsidiary Goodyear Tire & Rubber Co., Litchfield Park, Ariz., 1944-45; vis. prof. edn., dir. spl. edn. U. N.C, 1947-49; prof. ednl. psychology, dir. program spl. edn. U. Tex., Austin, chmn. dept. ednl. psychology, 1961-65, chmn. dept. spl. edn., until 1969, prof. spl. edn., 1969—; project dir. spl. edn. Instructional Materials Center, 1966-74; dir. Austin Cerebral Palsy Center, Austin, 1949-58; research cerebral palsy, dir. W.K. Shepperd project utilizing psychogalvanic skin response techniques. Mem. com. Mid-Century White House Conf. on Exceptional Children; mem. commn. on tng. tchrs. exceptional children So. Regional Edn. Bd. Mem. nat. exec. com., nat. v.p., S.W. region United Cerebral Palsy Assn.; pres. United Cerebral Palsy of Tex. Fellow Am. Speech and Hearing Assn., Am. Acad. Cerebral Palsy; mem. Am., Tex., Southwestern psychol. assns., AAAS, Internat. Council Exceptional Children (chmn. nat. council tchr. edn.), NEA, Coll. Classroom Tchrs. Assn., Sigma Xi, Phi Kappa Phi, Phi Delta Kappa. Democrat. Baptist. Author: X-Ray Study of Certain Structures and Movements Involved in Naso-pharyngeal Closure, 1942; A Comprehensive Study of Fifty Cases of Cerebral Palsy, 1950; A Survey of Cerebral Palsy in Texas; Education of the Cerebral Palsied in the South, 1960; An Annotated Bibliography of Selected References in Cerebral Palsy. Contbr. articles to ednl. publs. Home: 5508 Exeter Austin TX 78723. *I believe that a difference isn't a difference unless it makes a difference-too many times we allow something to make a difference when, in reality, there is no difference.*

WOLFE, WILLIAM ROY, JR., army officer; b. Honolulu, June 13, 1924; s. William Roy and Anita (McCormick) W.; B.S., U.S. Mil. Acad., 1945; M.A., Vanderbilt U., 1950; postgrad. Command and Gen. Staff Coll., 1955-56, Armed Forces Staff Coll., 1960, Army War Coll., 1965-66; m. Sarah Frances Herbers, June 14, 1947; children—Anita Clare (Mrs. John Alfred Knabb), Mary Lee (Mrs. Keith T. Kornelis), William Roy III, Barbara Emily. Commd. 2d lt. U.S. Army, 1945, advanced through grades to maj. gen., 1972; staff and faculty Army Gen. Sch., 1950-52, U.S. Mil. Acad., 1956-60; staff officer Hdqrs. Allied Forces So. Europe, 1961-64; comdg. officer 2d Bn. 33d Arty., 1964-65; Army gen. staff, 1966-68; comdg. officer 1st Cav. Div. Arty., Vietnam, 1968-69; with Joint Chiefs of Staff, 1969; dep. comdg. gen. U.S. Army Alaska, 1970; chief of staff Alaskan Command, 1970-72; dep. dir. operations U.S. Mil. Asst. Command Vietnam, 1972-73; dep. dir. operations Office Joint Chiefs Staff, Washington, 1973-74; dep. comdr. Combined Arms Combat Devel. Activity, Ft. Leavenworth, Kan., 1974-75; chief Joint U.S. Mil. Mission to Turkey, Ankara, 1975-77; comdr. U.S. Army So. European Task Force, 1977-79; chief staff 5th U.S. Army, Ft. Sam Houston, Tex., 1979—. Decorated Legion of Merit, Bronze Star medal, Air medal, Joint Services Commendation medal, Army Commendation medal; Cross of Gallantry (Vietnam). Mem. Assn. Grads. U.S. Mil. Acad., Assn. U.S. Army, 1st Cav. Div. Assn., Assn. Grads Army War Coll. Presbyn. Office: Chief Staff 5th US Army Fort Sam Houston TX 78234

WOLFENSOHN, JAMES DAVID, banker; b. Sydney, Australia, Dec. 1, 1933; s. Hyman and Dora (Weinbaum) W.; B.A., U. Sydney, 1954, LL.B., 1957; M.B.A., Harvard, 1959; m. Elaine Ruth Botwinick, Nov. 26, 1961; children—Sara, Naomi, Adam. Admitted to bar Supreme Ct. Australia, 1957; partner Ord Minnett, brokers, Australia, 1963-65; mng. dir. Darling & Co., bankers, Australia, 1965-67; mng. dir. J. Henry Schroder Wagg, London, 1967-69; pres. J. Henry Schroder Banking Corp., N.Y.C., 1970-76; exec. dep. chmn., dir. Schroders Ltd., London; prin. exec. officer Schroder Group, 1974-77; gen. partner Salomon Bros., N.Y.C., 1977—; chmn. Salomon Bros. Internat., London. Vis. lectr. finance U. New South Wales, 1963-66. Mem. Australian Olympic Team, 1956. Bd. dirs. Carnegie Hall Corp., N.Y.C., Met. Opera Assn., Joint Center for Polit. Studies; trustee Population Council, Inst. for Advanced Study, Princeton, N.J., N.Y. Landmarks Conservancy; pres. Internat. Fedn. Multiple Sclerosis Socs. Served as flying officer Royal Australian Air Force, 1954-60. Clubs: Century Assn., Harvard (N.Y.C.). Contbr. articles to profl. jours. Home: 1010 Fifth Ave New York City NY 10028 Office: One New York Plaza New York City NY 10004

WOLFENSTEIN, LINCOLN, physicist; b. Cleve., Feb. 10, 1923; s. Leo and Anna (Koppel) W.; S.B., U. Chgo., 1943, S.M., 1944, Ph.D., 1949; m. Wilma Caplin, Feb. 3, 1957; children—Frances, Leonard, Miriam. Physicist, Nat. Adv. Com. Aeros., 1944-46; mem. faculty dept. physics Carnegie-Mellon U., Pitts., 1948—, asso. prof., 1957-60, prof., 1960-78, Univ. prof., 1978—. Guggenheim fellow, 1973. Mem. Am. Phys. Soc., Fedn. Am. Scientists, AAAS, Nat. Acad. Sci. Contbr. articles to profl. jours. Home: 5853 Marlborough Ave Pittsburgh PA 15217 Office: Carnegie Mellon U Pittsburgh PA 15213

WOLFERT, RICHARD JEROME, state ofcl.; b. Chgo., Oct. 18, 1929; s. Jerome and Emma (Awe) W.; M.L.S., U. Chgo., 1959; m. Ann Zaslavsky, Feb. 11, 1953; children—Jenny, Emily. Tech. services librarian Chgo. Municipal Reference Library, 1957-60; head tech. services dept. Racine (Wis.) Pub. Library, 1960-64; dir. state reference and loan library, div. library services Wis. Dept. Pub. Instruction, Madison, 1965-67; city librarian Bismarck (N.D.) Pub. Library, 1967-69; state librarian N.D. State Library Commn., Bismarck, 1969—. Bd. dirs. N.D. Hist. Soc., 1969—, N.D. Com. for Humanities and Public Issues, 1973-74; mem. citizens adv. com. Centennial Heritage Series, 1978—; mem. adv. council Biomed. Communications System, Sch. Med., U. N.D., Grand Forks, 1974-75; mem. N.D. Hist. Records Adv. Bd., 1977—. Author: North Dakota Constitutional Convention, 1971-72; A Newspaper Account, 1974; editor N.D. Library Notes, 1970—, Flickertale Newsletter, 1970—; contbr. articles to profl. jours. Home: 523 Ave A W Bismarck ND 58501 Office: State Library Hwy 83 N Bismarck ND 58501. *Every person needs a sense of balance and a sense of movement in his life. The sense of balance is satisfied by a feeling of well-being in health, economic and social security, mental alertness, physical comfort, and spiritual wholeness. The sense of movement is satisfied by an intuitive knowing of personal growth toward God.*

WOLFF, AARON SIDNEY, lawyer, labor arbitrator; b. Chgo., May 9, 1930; s. Joseph S. and Esther (Nadell) W.; B.S., Northwestern U., 1951, J.D., 1954; m. Arlene Gottlieb, Aug. 10, 1952; children—Elizabeth, Peter. Admitted to Ill. bar, 1955; asso. Alex Elson and Elson & Lassers, Chgo., 1955-63; partner Elson, Lassers & Wolff, Chgo., 1963-78, Elson & Wolff, Chgo., 1978-79; counsel firm Rosenthal & Schanfield, P.C., Chgo., 1979—; spl. arbitrator bd. arbitration U.S. Steel and United Steelworkers, 1969—. Mem. Am., Ill., Chgo. bar assns., Chgo. Council Lawyers, Am. Arbitration Assn. Author: (with others) Illinois and Federal Civil Practice Forms, 1965. Home: 591 Broadview Highland Park IL 60035 Office: 55 E Monroe St Chicago IL 60603

WOLFF, BEVERLY, dramatic mezzo-soprano; b. Atlanta, Nov. 6, 1928; studied with Gertrude McFarland; student Acad. Vocal Arts, Phila.; studied with Boris Goldovsky, Tanglewood, Mass. Opera debut as Cherubino in Nozze di Figaro, N.Y.C. Opera, 1960; appearances with maj. opera cos. in Europe and N.Am., including: Opera Co. Boston, Houston Grand Opera, Milw. Florentine Opera, Phila. Grand Opera, San Francisco Opera, Santa Fe Opera; appearances with symphony orchs. and in recital; repertoire coach. Office: care Columbia Artists Mgmt Inc 165 W 57th St New York NY 10019*

WOLFF, BRUCE WALTER, advt. agy. exec.; b. Berlin, Germany, Mar. 30, 1927; s. Felix and Margaret (Wolitzer) W.; came to U.S., 1946, naturalized, 1950; student CCNY, 1947-51; m. Anne Irmgard Lieb, Sept. 15, 1948 (div. 1979); children—Nina Joan, Eric Roger, Amy Margaret. Market research analyst Netherlands C. of C., N.Y.C., 1947-50; internat. sales corr. Hygrade Food Products Corp., Newark, 1950-52; asst. to pres. Cosmos Chem. Corp., N.Y.C., 1953-57; group v.p., mem. exec. com. Frohlich/Intercon Internat., Inc., N.Y.C., 1957-72; chmn. bd. Lavey/Wolff/Swift, Inc., N.Y.C., 1972—. Pres., Riverdale-Yonkers Ethical Culture Soc., 1967-69. Mem. Assn. for Advancement Med. Instrumentation, Am. Med. Writers Assn., Biomed. Mktg. Assn. (bd. dirs., past pres.), Pharm. Advt. Club, Midwest Pharm. Advt. Club. Office: 488 Madison Ave New York NY 10022

WOLFF, CHRISTOPH JOHANNES, music historian; b. Solingen, Germany, May 24, 1940; came to U.S., 1970; s. Hans Walter and Annemarie (Halstenbach) W.; ed. U. Berlin, 1960-63, U. Freiburg (Germany), 1963-65; Dr. Phil., U. Erlangen (Germany), 1966; m. Barbara Mahrenholz, Aug. 28, 1964; children—Katharina, Dorothea, Stephanie. Lectr., U. Erlangen, 1966-69; vis. asst. prof. U. Toronto (Ont., Can.), 1968-69; asso. prof. musicology Columbia U., 1970-73, prof., 1973-76; prof. musicology Harvard U., 1976—; vis. prof. Princeton U., 1973, 75. Recipient Dent medal Royal Mus. Assn., London, 1978. Mem. Internat. Musicol. Soc., Am. Musicol. Soc., Gesellschaft fuer Musikforschung. Author: Der Stile Antico in der Musik J.S. Bachs, 1968; contbr. numerous articles, especially on Bach and Mozart, to profl. jours.; editor Bach-Jahrbuch, 1974—; editor critical edits. of music by Scheidt, Bach, Mozart, Hindemith. Office: Dept Music Harvard U Cambridge MA 02138

WOLFF, DERISH MICHAEL, fin. cons.; b. Boston, May 14, 1935; s. Nathan and Ruth Mae (Derish) W.; B.A., U. Pa., 1957; M.B.A., Harvard U., 1959; children—Jeffrey Scott, Hayley Beth. Adminstrv. asst. Sigmund Werner, Inc., Belleville, N.J., 1959-61; devel. economist Louis Berger, Inc., East Orange, N.J., 1961-65, chief economist, 1965-67, v.p., 1968-74, exec. v.p., 1975—; dir. Louis Berger Internat., Inc., Internat. Ventures Corp.; lectr. Fgn. Service Inst. Mem. vis. com. N.Y. Poly. Inst.; class chmn. U. Pa. Ann. Giving, 1975-79. Mem. Am. Econs. Assn., Soc. Internat. Devel. Jewish. Club: Harvard (N.Y.C.). Mem. editorial bd. Modern Engring. Tech., 1978-79, Modern Govt. and Nat. Devel. mag., 1972-79. Home: 320 S Harrison St East Orange NJ 07019 Office: 100 Halsted St East Orange NJ 07019

WOLFF, GEOFFREY ANSELL, novelist, critic, educator; b. Los Angeles, Nov. 5, 1937; s. Arthur Saunders III, and Rosemary (Loftus) W.; grad. cum laude, Choate Sch., 1955; student Eastbourne (Eng.) Coll., 1955-56; B.A. summa cum laude, Princeton, 1961; student Churchill Coll., Cambridge (Eng.) U., 1963-64; m. Priscilla Bradley Porter, Aug. 21, 1965; children—Nicholas Hinckley, Justin Porter. Lectr. in comparative literature Robert Coll., Istanbul, Turkey, 1961-63; lectr. in Am. civilization Istanbul U., 1962-63; book editor Washington Post, 1964-69; book editor Newsweek mag., 1969-71; book editor New Times mag., 1974-79; book critic Esquire mag., 1979—; lectr. aesthetics Md. Inst. Coll. Art, 1965-69; vis. lectr. creative arts Princeton U., 1970-71, 72-74; lectr. English lit. Middlebury Coll., 1976, 78; vis. lectr. Columbia U., 1979; founder Golden Horn, lit. mag., 1962; contbr. to New Leader, New Republic, Book Week, London Times, Cambridge Forward, Am. Scholar, Atlantic Monthly, More, Esquire, others. Woodrow Wilson fellow, 1961-62, 63-64; Fulbright fellow, 1963-64; Guggenheim Fellow, 1972-73, 77-78; Nat. Endowment for Humanities sr. fellow, 1974-75; Nat. Endowment for Arts fellow, 1979-80. Mem. P.E.N. Clubs: Princeton (New York); Colonial (Princeton, N.J.); Coffee House (N.Y.C.). Author: Bad Debts, 1969; The Sightseer, 1974; Black Sun, 1976; Inklings, 1978; The Duke of Deception, 1979. Home: Prickly Mountain Warren VT 05674

WOLFF, HERBERT ERIC, army officer; b. Cologne, Ger., May 24, 1925; s. Hugo and Juanna Anna (Van Dam) W.; B.A., Rutgers U., 1953; B.S., U. Md., 1957; M.A., George Washington U., 1962; grad. U.S. Army War Coll., 1962, Command and Gen. Staff Coll., 1958; postgrad. Kennedy Sch., Harvard U., 1979; m. Billy Rafael, Nov. 13, 1946; children—Karen, Herbert E., Allen R. Drafted into AUS, 1943, commd. on battlefield as 2d lt., 1945, advanced through grades to maj. gen. U.S. Army; service in PTO, W.Ger., Greece, Iran and Vietnam; dep. dir. ops. NSA/CSS, 1973-75; dep. corps comdr. V Corps, Frankfurt, W.Ger., 1975-78; comdr. gen. U.S. Army Western Command, Hawaii, 1978—. Decorated D.S.M., Silver Star with oak leaf cluster, Legion of Merit with 2 oak clusters, D.F.C., Bronze Star with V and 3 oak leaf clusters, Air medal (24), Joint Services Commendation medal, Army Commendation medal, Combat Inf. badge, Purple Heart; Gallantry Cross with 2 palms, Gallantry Cross with silver star, Nat. Order 5th class (S. Vietnam); Order Nat. Security Merit Choen-Su (S. Korea). Mem. Assn. U.S. Army, 1st Inf. Div. Assn., 1st Cav. Div. Assn., U.S. Army Museum Soc., Phi Kappa Phi. Clubs: Plaza, Outrigger Canoe, Rotary. Author: The Man on Horseback, 1962; The Tenth Principle of War, 1964; Public Support, 1964; The Military Instructor, 1968. Office: US Army Western Command Fort Shafter HI 96858

WOLFF, JANET LOEB, advt. agy. exec.; b. San Francisco; d. Albert I. and Aurene (Goddard) Loeb; student U. Paris; grad. Finch Coll.; m. James A. Wolff, June 24, 1946; children—James Alexander, John, Barbara Ann, Timothy Grant. Copywriter, J. Walter Thompson Co., N.Y.C., Crompton Co., N.Y.C.; now exec. v.p. William Esty Co. Inc., N.Y.C.; mem. Fashion Group, N.Y.C. Mem. Bus. Council, N.Y.C. Named Advt. Woman of Yr., Advt. Women of N.Y., 1968. Author: What Makes Women Buy, 1958; Let's Imagine series, 1960. Office: 100 E 42d St New York NY 10017

WOLFF, KURT H(EINRICH), educator, sociologist; b. Darmstadt, Germany, May 20, 1912; s. Oscar Louis and Ida (Kohn) W.; student univs. Frankfurt, Munich, 1930-33; Laurea, U. Florence, 1935; postgrad. U. Chgo., 1943-44, Harvard, 1955-56; m. Carla Elizabeth Bruck, June 11, 1936; 1 son, Carlo Thomas. Came to U.S., 1939, naturalized, 1945. Tchr., Schule am Mittelmeer, Recco, Italy, 1934-36, Istituti Mare-Monte, Ruta, Italy, 1936-38; research asst. So. Meth. U., Dallas, 1939-43; asst. prof. sociology Earlham Coll., Richmond, Ind., 1944-45; asst. prof. sociology Ohio State U., 1945-52, asso. prof., 1952-59; prof. sociology, chmn. Brandeis U., 1959-62, prof. sociology, 1962—, Yellen prof. social relations, 1969—. Grantee Wenner-Gren Found. for anthrop. research, 1947, 49; mem. Inter-Univ. Social Sci. Research Council summer inst. Northwestern U., 1952; U.S. specialist Dept. State, Frankfurt Inst. Social Research, 1952, 53; faculty fellow Fund for Advancement Edn., Harvard, 1955-56; sr. Fulbright lectr. U. Rome, 1963-64; vis. prof. Coll. Pacific, 1948, New Sch. Social Research, 1950, Sir George Williams U., 1965, U. Freiburg, 1966, U. Frankfurt, 1966-67, U. Paris-Nanterre, 1967, York U., 1971. Fellow Am. Sociol. Assn.; mem. Internat. Social Assn. (chmn. research com. sociology knowledge 1966-72), Internat. Soc. for Sociology Knowledge (pres. 1972—), ACLU, AAUP. Author: Versuch zu einer Wissenssoziologie, 1968; Hingebung und Begriff, 1968; Von Einhorn zu Einhorn, 1972; Trying Sociology, 1974; Surrender and Catch: Experience and Inquiry Today, 1976; Vorgang und immerwährende Revolution, 1978. Editor, translator books; contbr. to symposiums. Contbr. articles to profl. jours. Home: 58 Lombard St Newton MA 02158 Office: Brandeis U Dept Sociology Waltham MA 02154

WOLFF, LEO THOMAS, physician; b. Suffern, N.Y., Mar. 26, 1942; s. Leo and Ruth W.; B.S. cum laude, Siena Coll., 1964; M.D., Albany Med. Coll., 1968; m. Carol C. Corey, June 12, 1965; children—Kathleen, Deborah, Patricia, Kimberley. Intern, St. Joseph Hosp. Health Center, Syracuse, N.Y., 1968-69, resident in family practice, 1969-71; clin. asst. instr. medicine SUNY Upstate Med. Center, Syracuse, 1970-71; asst. dir. family practice, ambulatory care cons. Surgeon Gen.'s Office, Washington, 1971-73; instr. family medicine Med. Coll. Va., 1972-73; chmn. dept. family practice Upstate Med. Center, Syracuse, 1973—, asso. prof., 1973-75, prof., 1975—; dir. med. edn. St. Joseph's Hosp. Health Center, 1973—; cons. in field. Bd. dirs. Vis. Nurse Assn. Central N.Y. State. Served to maj. M.C., U.S. Army, 1971-73. Recipient Mead Johnson award, 1970; diplomate Am. Bd. Family Practice. Fellow Am. Acad. Family Physicians (charter); mem. Soc. Tchrs. Family Medicine (dir. 1976-78), N.Y. Acad. Family Physicians (dir. research and edn. found. 1977—), N.Y. State Acad. Family Physicians, Assn. Am. Med. Colls., Assn. Chmn. Depts. Family Medicine, N.Y. State Med. Soc., Onondaga County Med. Soc. Office: 301 Prospect Ave Syracuse NY 13203

WOLFF, LESTER LIONEL, congressman; b. N.Y.C., Jan. 4, 1919; s. Samuel and Hannah (Bartman) W.; student N.Y. U., 1935-39; m. Blanche Silver, Mar. 31, 1940; children—Bruce Stuart, Diane Hope. Lectr., N.Y. U., 1939-41; head mktg. dept. Collegiate Inst., N.Y.C., 1945-49; pres. Co-ordinated Marketing Agy., N.Y.C., 1948-65; moderator, producer Between the Lines, weekly polit. affairs TV program, 1948-60; producer TV shows Showcase, 1958-60, Wendy Barrie Show, 1955-58, others; mem. 89th-96th Congresses, 6th Dist. N.Y.; mem. com. on internat. relations, chmn. subcom. on Asian and Pacific affairs; chmn. select com. on narcotics abuse and control, 1972-74; mem. U.S. Trade Mission to Malaysia and Hong Kong, 1963, Philippines, 1962; chmn. adv. com. to subcom. consumers study Ho. of Reps., 1957. Food industry chmn. Fedn. Jewish Philanthropies, 1954-63, United Jewish Appeal, 1958-63; food div. chmn. Boys Town Italy, 1955; mem. dinner bd. Italian Bd. Guardians dinner, 1962-63; speakers com. Fedn. Jewish Philanthropies, 1962-64; chmn. dinner com. Cath. Interracial Council, 1959; chmn. food div. NCCJ, 1960; chmn. Mayor N.Y.C. Com. Interfaith Days, 1950-51; trustee Nat. Jewish Hosp., Denver, Deborah Hosp., Denver; bd. visitors U.S. Mcht. Marine Acad. Served to maj. USAAF, World War II. Recipient Distinguished Service award Nat. Citizens Affairs Com., 1956; named Man of Year, Food Industry Sq. Club, 1962; Guest of Honor award United Jewish Appeal, 1961, Denver Jewish Hosp., 1962, Deborah Hosp., 1961; Great Neck (L.I.) Hadassah award, 1961; Golden Dozen award Printers Ink mag., 1962; Coronet medal St. Edwards U., 1964; Captive Nations medal, 1966; Friend of Irish award Internat. Hall of Fame, 1974. Hon. life mem. Order of Hibernians; mem. Air Force Aux. (comdr. congl. squadron) Democrat. Jewish (trustee temple). Office: Rayburn Office Bldg Washington DC 20515*

WOLFF, MANFRED ERNST, medicinal chemist, educator; b. Berlin, Germany, Feb. 14, 1930; s. Adolph Abraham and Kate (Fraenkel) W.; B.S., U. Calif. at Berkeley, 1951, M.S., 1953, Ph.D., 1955; m. Helen S. Scandalis, Aug. 1, 1953 (div. 1971); children—Stephen Andrew, David James, Edward Allen; m. 2d, Susan E. Hurbert, Jan. 19, 1973 (div. 1975). Research fellow U. Va., 1955-57; sr. medicinal chemist Smith, Kline & French Labs., Phila., 1957-60; mem. faculty U. Calif. at San Francisco, 1960—, prof. medicinal chemistry, 1965—, chmn. dept. pharm. chemistry, 1970—. Fellow Acad. Pharm. Scis.; mem. Am. Chem. Soc., Am. Pharm. Assn., AAAS, Sigma Xi. Editor: Burger's Medicinal Chemistry, 4th edit., 1978; asst. editor Jour. Medicinal Chemistry, 1968-71. Contbr. articles to profl. jours. Patentee in field. Office: Sch Pharmacy U Calif Med Center San Francisco CA 94143

WOLFF, PETER ADALBERT, physicist; b. Oakland, Calif., Nov. 15, 1923; s. Adalbert and Ruth Margaret W.; A.B. in Physics, U. Calif., Berkeley, 1945, Ph.D. in Physics, 1951; m. Catherine C. Carroll, Sept. 11, 1948; children—Catherine Mia, Peter Whitney. Research scientist Lawrence Radiation Lab., 1951-52; staff scientist Bell Telephone Lab., Murray Hill, N.J., 1952-63, dept. head, dir. electronic research lab., 1964-70; prof. physics U. Calif., San Diego, 1963-64; prof. physics, head solid state and atomic physics div., asso. dir. material sci. center M.I.T., Cambridge, 1970-76, prof. physics, dir. research lab. of electronics, 1976—; dir. Draper Lab. Served with C.E., U.S. Army, 1945-46. Mem. Am. Phys. Soc. Contbr. articles to profl. jours. Home: 17 Brewster St Cambridge MA 02138 Office: MIT 77 Massachusetts St Cambridge MA 02139

WOLFF, ROBERT LEE, educator, historian; b. N.Y.C., Dec. 22, 1915; s. Samuel Lee and Mathilde (Abraham) W.; A.B., Harvard, 1936, A.M., 1937, Ph.D., 1947; Litt.D., Williams Coll., 1961; m. Mary Andrews, Nov. 24, 1937; children—Rosamond Capen (Mrs. Dennis W. Purcell), Katharine, Robert Lee, James A. Teaching fellow history Harvard, 1937-41, asso. prof., 1950-55, prof., 1955—, Coolidge prof. history, 1965—, chmn. dept. history, 1960-63; asst. to dir., chief Balkan sect. Research and Analysis br. OSS, 1942-46; asst. prof., then asso. prof. history U. Wis., 1947-50. Harvard lectr. Yale, 1961; lectr. École Universitaire des Hautes Études Internationales, Geneva, 1957. Trustee Brooks Sch., Radcliffe Coll. Fellow Am. Philos. Soc., Am. Acad. Arts and Scis.; mem. Am. Hist. Assn., Mediaeval Acad. Am. Clubs: Knickerbocker (N.Y.C.); Somerset, Tavern (Boston). Author: The Balkans in Our Time, 2d edit., 1974; The Golden Key, 1961; Strange Stories, 1971; Studies in the Latin Empire of Constantinople, 1976; Gains and Losses: Novels of Faith and Doubt in Victorian England, 1977; Sensational Victorian: The Life and Fiction of Mary Elizabeth Braddon, 1979; William Carlton, Irish Peasant Novelist: A Preface to his Fiction, 1980; co-author: A History of Civilization, 1955, 5th edit., 1975; History of the Crusades II, 1962, 2d edit., 1969. Home: 10 Follen St Cambridge MA 02138

WOLFF, ROBERT PAUL, educator; b. N.Y.C., Dec. 27, 1933; s. Walter Harold and Charlotte (Ornstein) W.; A.B., Harvard, 1953, M.A. in Philosophy, 1954, Ph.D., 1957; m. Cynthia Griffin, June 9, 1962; children—Patrick Gideon, Tobias Barrington. Instr., Harvard, 1958-61; asst. prof. philosophy U. Chgo., 1961-63; vis. lectr. Wellesley Coll., 1963-64; asso. prof. philosophy Columbia, 1964-69, prof. 1969-71; prof. philosophy U. Mass., 1971—. Author: Kant's Theory of Mental Activity, 1963; A Critique of Pure Tolerance, 1965; Political Man and Social Man, 1966; Kant: A Collection of Critical Essays, 1967; Poverty of Liberalism, 1968; The Ideal of the University, 1969; In Defense of Anarchism, 1970; Philosophy: A Modern Encounter, 1971; The Autonomy of Reason, 1973; About Philosophy, 1975; Understanding Rawls, 1977. Home: 26 Barrett Pl Northampton MA 01060

WOLFF, SANFORD IRVING, lawyer, union exec.; b. Chgo., Apr. 13, 1915; s. Herbert Barron and Libby (Levey) W.; B.A., Knox Coll., 1936; grad. John Marshall and U. Chgo. law schs., 1940; m. Ann Barry, Mar. 21, 1970; children—Paul, David, Laura. Admitted to Ill. bar, 1940, N.Y. bar, 1973; practice in Chgo., 1945—; chief exec. AFTRA, AFL-CIO, N.Y.C., 1968—. Trustee Harris Sch., Chgo. Served with AUS, 1940-45. Decorated Combat Inf. badge, Purple Heart, Bronze Star with cluster, Silver Star. Mem. Am., N.Y., Chgo. bar assns. Office: 1350 Ave of Americas New York City NY 10019

WOLFF, SHELDON, educator; b. Peabody, Mass., Sept. 22, 1928; s. Henry Herman and Goldie (Lipchitz) W.; B.S. magna cum laude, Tufts U., 1950; M.A., Harvard, 1951, Ph.D., 1953; m. Frances Faye Farbstein, Oct. 23, 1954; children—Victor Charles, Roger Kenneth, Jessica Raye. Teaching fellow Harvard, 1951-52; sr. research staff biology div. Oak Ridge Nat. Lab., 1953-66; prof. cytogenetics U. Calif., San Francisco, 1966—. Vis. prof. radiation biology U. Tenn., 1962, lectr., 1953-65; cons. several fed. sci. agys. Recipient E.O. Lawrence meml. award U.S. AEC, 1973. Mem. Genetics Soc. Am., Radiation Research Soc. (counselor for biology 1968-72), Am. Soc. Naturalists, Am. Soc. Cell Biology, Environmental Mutagenesis Soc. (council 1972—, pres.-elect 1979), Sigma Xi. Democrat. Editorial bd. Radiation Research, 1968-72, Photochemistry and Photobiology, 1962-72, Radiation Botany, 1964—, Mutation Research, 1964—, Caryologia, 1967—, Radiation Effects, 1969—, Genetics, 1972—. Contbr. articles to sci. jours. Home: 41 Eugene St Mill Valley CA 94941 Office: Lab Radiobiology U Calif San Francisco CA 94143

WOLFF, SHELDON MALCOLM, physician; b. Newark, Aug. 19, 1930; s. Harold D. and Margaret (Turen) W.; B.S., U. Ga., 1952; M.D., Vanderbilt U., 1957; D. honoris causa, Fed. U., Rio de Janeiro, 1976; m. Lila Leff, May 30, 1956; children—Steven B., Suzanne M., Daniel S. Clin. asso. Lab. Clin. Investigation, Nat. Inst. Allergy and Infectious Diseases, NIH, Bethesda, Md., 1960-62, sr. investigator, 1963-64, head clin. physiology, 1964-68, clin. dir. and chief, 1968-77; Endicott prof., chmn. dept. medicine Tufts U. Sch. Medicine, Boston, 1977—; physician-in-chief New Eng. Med. Center Hosp., 1977—; adj. prof. internat. health Fletcher Sch. Law and Diplomacy, Tufts U., 1977—; mem. exec. com. gt. neglected disease program Rockefeller Found., 1978—. Served with USPHS, 1960-64, 75-77. Recipient Squibb award, 1976; Superior Service award NIH, 1971. Diplomate Am. Bd. Internal Medicine (asso. mem. bd. 1976—). Mem. Infectious Disease Soc. Am. (pres.-elect 1979), Assn. Am. Physicians, Am. Soc. for Clin. Investigation, A.C.P., Am. Fedn. Clin. Research, Am. Clin. and Climatol. Assn., Am. Assn. Immunologists, AAAS, Am. Soc. for Microgiology, Assn. Profs. Medicine, Reticulo-Endothelial Soc., Soc. for Exptl. Biology and Medicine, Soc. for Health and Human Values. Contbr. chpts. to textbooks, articles to profl. jours. Office: 171 Harrison Ave Boston MA 02111

WOLFFER, WILLIAM AUBREY, govt. ofcl.; b. Arlington, Mass., May 6, 1917; s. Cyrus William and Marion Louise (Brown) W.; B.Ed., Keene (N.H.) State Coll., 1940; M.Ed., Boston U., 1948, D.Ed., 1952; LL.D., N.H. U., 1970; m. Leona Martha Ott, Mar. 28, 1943; 1 dau., Lynne Lee Perrone. Tchr., prin. pub. schs., Piermont, N.H., 1940-41; prin. Lab. Sch., Keene State Coll., 1948, asso. prof., 1949-51; vis. prof. Boston U., 1950-52, 54, teaching fellow, 1951-52; prof. U. N.H., Keene, 1952-55; tchr. edn. adviser USOM, Jordan, 1955-57, chief edn. div., 1957-58; dep. dir. Office Ednl. Services ICA, Washington, 1958-61; chief Instl. Devel. Div. Bur., Near East and South Asia AID, Washington, 1962-64, dep. dir. mission, Jordan, 1964-67, Afghanistan, 1967-69, AID affairs officer Fletcher Sch. Law and Diplomacy, 1969-70, asso. dir. mission, Pakistan, 1970-72, provincial dir., East Pakistan, 1971, dep. dir. mission, Pakistan, 1972-77, dir., 1978-79. Chmn. youth com. Waynewood Citizens Assn., Fairfax, Va., 1959-62. Served with USCG, 1942-46. Recipient Superior Honor award AID, 1974, others. Mem. Nat. Council Social Studies, Nat., N.H. edn. assns., Sigma Tau Gamma, Kappa Delta Phi, Phi Delta Kappa. Home: 874 Cal Cove Dr Fort Myers FL 33907 Office: AID Islamabad (ID) Dept State Washington DC 20520

WOLFGANG, MARVIN EUGENE, sociologist, criminologist, educator; b. Millersburg, Pa., Nov. 14, 1924; s. Charles T. and Pauline (Sweigard) W.; B.A., Dickinson Coll., Carlisle, Pa., 1948; M.A., U. Pa., 1950, Ph.D., 1955; m. Lenora D. Poden, June 1, 1957; children—Karen Eleanor, Nina Victoria. Instr., asst. prof. Lebanon Valley Coll., 1948-52; instr. to prof. sociology U. Pa., Phila., 1952—, chmn. dept., 1968-72, prof. sociology and law, 1972—, also dir. Center for Studies in Criminology and Criminal Law; vis. prof., fellow Churchill Coll., U. Cambridge (Eng.), 1968-69; cons. Rand Corp. Chmn. rev. com. on crime and delinquency NIMH, 1971-73; research dir. Nat. Commn. on Causes and Prevention of Violence, 1968-69; commr. Nat. Commn. on Obscenity and Pornography, 1968-70. Bd. dirs. Thomas Skelton Harrison Found. Served with AUS, 1943-45; ETO. Recipient Fulbright Research award, 1957-58, Research award Am. Soc. Criminology, 1960. Guggenheim fellow, 1957-58, 68-69. Mem. Am. Philos. Soc., Am. Acad. Arts and Scis., Internat., Am. (past pres.) socs. criminology, Am. Acad. Polit. and Social Sci. (pres.), Pa. Prison Soc. (dir., past pres.). Author: Patterns in Criminal Homicide, 1958; Crime and Race, 1964; (with T. Sellin) The Measurement of Delinquency, 1964; (with F. Ferracuti) The Subculture of Violence, 1967; Crime and Culture, 1968; (with L. Radzinowicz) Crime and Justice, 3 vols., 1971, rev. edit., 1977; (with T. Sellin, R. Figlio) Delinquency in a Birth Cohort, 1972; (with R. Figlio, T. Thornberry) Criminology Index, 2 vols., 1975; Evaluating Criminology, 1978. Home: 4106 Locust St Philadelphia PA 19104

WOLFHAGEN, JAMES LANGDON, chemist, educator; b. Portland, Oreg., Dec. 9, 1920; s. Carl and Gladys (Burr) W.; A.B., Linfield Coll., McMinnville, Oreg., 1946; Ph.D., U. Calif., Berkeley, 1951; m. Helen Jane Acheson, Jan. 23, 1948; children—Carl Frederick, Margaret Jo, Roger Charles. Analytical chemist N.W. Testing Labs., Portland, 1941-42; asst. prof. Whitworth Coll., Spokane, Wash., 1949-51; asst. prof. U. Maine, Orono, 1952-58, asso. prof., 1958-64, prof., 1964—, chmn. dept. chemistry, 1967-75; research scientist dept. forest sci. Tex. A & M U., 1976-77. Served to 1st lt. USAAF, 1943-46; ETO, PTO. Mem. Am. Chem. Soc., AAUP, AAAS, Sigma Xi. Home: 18 Grove St Orono ME 04473

WOLFLE, DAEL LEE, educator; b. Puyallup, Wash., Mar. 5, 1906; s. David H. and Elizabeth (Pauly) W.; B.S. U. Wash., 1927, M.S., 1928; postgrad. U. Chgo., summers 1929, 30; Ph.D., Ohio State U., 1931, D.Sc., 1957; D.Sc., Drexel U., 1956, Western Mich. U., 1960; m. Helen Morrill, Dec. 28, 1929; children—Janet Helen (Mrs. Wilhelm G. Christophersen), Lee Morrill, John Morrill. Instr. psychology Ohio State U., 1929-32; prof. psychology U. Miss., 1932-36; examiner in biol. scis. U. Chgo., 1936-39, asst. prof. psychology, 1938-43, asso. prof., 1943-45, on leave for war work with Signal Corps, 1941-43, with OSRD, 1944-45; exec. sec. Am. Psychol. Assn., 1946-50; dir. commn. on human resources and advanced tng. Asso. Research Councils, 1950-54; exec. officer AAAS, 1954-70, editor Sci., 1955, pub., 1955-70; prof. pub. affairs U. Wash., Seattle, 1970-76, prof. emeritus, 1976—. Mem. sci. adv. bd. USAF, 1953-57; mem. def. sci. bd. Dept. Def., 1957-61; mem. adv. council on mental health NIMH, 1960-64; mem. nat. adv. health council USPHS, 1965-66; mem. commn. on human resources NRC, 1974-78; chmn. adv. bd. Geophys. Inst., Fairbanks, Alaska. Trustee Russell Sage Found., 1961-78, Pacific Sci. Cent. Found.; chmn. bd. J. McK. Cattell Fund. Named Alumnus Summa Laude Dignatus, U. Wash., 1979. Mem. Am. Psychol. Assn., AAAS, AAUP, Sigma Xi. Author: Factor Analysis to 1940, 1941; Science and Public Policy, 1959; The Uses of Talent, 1971; The Home of Science, 1972. Editor: America's Resources of Specialized Talent, 1954; Symposium on Basic Research, 1959. Home: 4545 Sand Point Way NE Seattle WA 98105 Office: Grad Sch Pub Affairs U Wash Seattle WA 98195

WOLFLEY, ALAN, coal co. exec.; b. Rockford, Ill., Dec. 23, 1923; s. Chester E. and Lois (Karlson) W.; B.A. cum laude, Middlebury (Vt.) Coll., 1947; M.B.A., Harvard, 1949; m. Joanne Higgins, Jan. 6, 1945; children—C. Alan, Susan (Mrs. Peter M. Baumgartner), E. William. Budget supr. Merck & Co., Rahway, N.J., 1949-52; asst. to treas. Standard Vacuum Oil Co., 1952-59; asst. treas. Parke-Davis & Co., 1959-64; v.p. finance Cardorundum Co., 1964-68; v.p. finance, dir. Scovill Mfg. Co., 1968-71; exec. v.p., mem. exec. com., dir. Cerro Marmon Corp., Chgo., 1971-76; dir. Marmon Group, Inc., 1977—; chmn. bd., dir. Incontrade, Inc., 1972—; pres., dir. Inconcoal Corp., 1976—, Greenley Energy Corp., 1978—; dir. Am. Coal Industries, Inc. Bd. dirs. Salk Inst., 1979—. Served to capt. USAAF, World War II. Decorated Silver Star, D.F.C., Air medal, Purple Heart. Mem. Chi Psi. Republican. Methodist. Clubs: Racquet and Tennis, Harvard (N.Y.C.); Wee Burn Country (Darien, Conn.); Pine Valley Golf (Clementon, N.J.). Home: 22 Canaan Close New Canaan CT 06840 Office: 123 Main St PO Box 218 New Canaan CT 06840

WOLFMAN, BERNARD, lawyer, educator; b. Phila., July 8, 1924; s. Nathan and Elizabeth (Coff) W.; A.B., U. Pa., 1946, J.D., 1948; LL.D. (hon.), Jewish Theol. Sem., 1971; m. Zelda Bernstein, Dec. 25, 1948 (dec. Oct. 1973); children—Jonathan L., Brian S., Dina A.; m. 2d, Toni A. Grotta, June 12, 1977. Admitted to Pa. bar, 1949, Mass. bar, 1976; with firm Wolf, Block, Schorr & Solis-Cohen, Phila., 1948-63; prof. law U. Pa. Law Sch., 1963-76, dean, 1970-75, Kenneth W. Gemmill prof. tax law and tax policy, 1973-76, chmn. Faculty Senate, 1969-70; Fessenden prof. law Harvard U., 1976—. Vis. prof. Stanford Law Sch., summer 1966; mem. editorial bds. law div. Little, Brown & Co., Jour. Corp. Taxation; gen. counsel AAUP, 1966-68, mem. council, 1979—. Mem. adv. group to commr. internal revenue, 1966-67; cons. tax policy U.S. Treasury Dept., 1963-68, 77—; chmn. Task Force Univ. Governance, U. Pa., 1968-70; mem. steering com. IRS project Adminstrv. Conf. U.S., 1973—; mem. legal activities policy bd. Taxation with Representation Fund, 1974—; exec. com. Fed. Tax Inst. New Eng., 1976—; adv. com. Commn. Philanthropy and Pub. Needs, 1973-75; mem. Phila. regional council Pa. Gov.'s Justice Commn., 1973-75; trustee Found. Center, N.Y.C., 1970-76, Fedn. Jewish Agys. Greater Phila., 1968-74, Phila. Lawyer's Com. Civil Rights Under Law, 1970-74, Phila. Defender Assn., 1955-69; mem. Nat. Lawyers Adv. Council of Earl Warren Legal Tng. Program. Served with AUS, 1943-45. Fellow Center Advanced Study in Behavioral Scis., 1975-76. Mem. Am. (chmn. com. on taxation and relation to human rights, council sect. individual rights and responsibilities), Am. Law Inst. (cons. fed. income tax project 1974—), ACLU (nat. dir. 1973-75, dir. Phila. chpt. 1964-76, pres. 1972-75), Phi Beta Kappa, Order of Coif. Author: Federal Income Taxation of Business Enterprise, 1971, supplement, 1979; (with J. and M. Silver) Dissent Without Opinion: The Behavior of Justice William O. Douglas in Federal Tax Cases, 1975. Contbr. articles to profl. jours. Home: 229 Brattle St Cambridge MA 02138 Office: Harvard Law Sch Cambridge MA 02138

WOLFMAN, EARL FRANK, JR., physician, uniV. dean; b. Buffalo, Sept. 14, 1926; s. Earl Frank and Alfreda (Peterson) W.; B.S. cum laude, Harvard U., 1946; M.D. cum laude, U. Mich., 1950; m. Lois Jeannette Walker, Dec. 28, 1946; children—Nancy Jeannette, David Earl, Carol Anne. Intern, U. Mich., 1950-51, asst. resident in surgery, 1951-52, resident in surgery, 1954-55, jr. clin. instr. surgery, 1955-56, sr. clin. instr., 1956-57, instr., 1957-60, asst. prof., 1960-63, asso. prof., 1963-66, asst. to dean, 1960-61, asst. dean, 1961-64; pvt. practice medicine specializing in surgery, 1957—, Sacramento, 1966—; prof., chmn. dept. surgery Sch. Medicine, U. Calif., Davis, 1966—, asso. dean, 1966—; mem. staff, chief surg. services Sacramento Med. Center, 1966—; cons. surgery David Grant Hosp., Travis AFB, 1966—, USPHS Hosp., San Francisco, 1966—. Served to lt. M.C., USNR, 1952-54. Diplomate Am. Bd. Surgery. Fellow A.C.S.; mem. AMA, Central, West, Sacramento, Pacific Coast surg. socs., Calif. Acad. Medicine, Frederick A. Coller Surg. Soc., Aerospace Med. Assn., Pan Am. Med. Assn., Soc. Surgery Alimentary Tract, Soc. Surg. Chairmen, Sacramento, Yolo med. socs., Calif. Med. Assn. Methodist. Clubs: Commonwealth (San Francisco); Comstock (Sacramento). Contbr. articles to profl. jours. Home: 2928 N El Macero Dr El Macero CA 95618 Office: U Calif Sch Medicine Dept Surgery 4301 X St Sacramento CA 95817

WOLFMAN JACK, SEE - Smith, Robert W

WOLFOWITZ, JACOB, mathematician, educator; b. Warsaw, Poland, Mar. 19, 1910; s. Samuel and Helen (Pearlman) W.; B.S., Coll. City N.Y., 1931; M.A., Columbia, 1933; Ph.D., N.Y. U., 1942; m. Lillian Dundes, Mar. 3, 1934; children—Laura M. (Mrs. Tsvi Sachs), Paul D. Asso. dir. statis. research group Columbia, 1942-45, asso. prof., 1946-49, prof., 1949-51; asso. prof. math. stats. U. N.C., 1945-46; disting. prof. math. Cornell U., Ithaca, N.Y., 1951-70, U. Ill. at Urbana, 1970-78; prof. math. U. South Fla., Tampa, 1978—; vis. prof. U. Calif. at Los Angeles, 1952-53, U. Ill., 1953, Israel Inst. Tech., Haifa, 1957-58, U. Paris, 1967, U. Heidelberg (Germany), 1969; mem. Nat. Acad. Scis. Fellow Am. Acad. Arts and Scis., Inst. Math. Stats. (past pres., Rietz lectr., Wald lectr.), Econometric Soc.; mem. Am. Math. Soc., IEEE (Shannon lectr. 1979), Internat. Statis. Inst. Author monographs on sci. subjects. Asso. editor Annals Math. Stats., 1953-57, Jour. Statis. Planning and Inference, Jour. Combinatorics, Info. and Systems Scis., Am. Jour. Math. and Mgmt. Scis. Contbr. articles to profl. jours. Office: Dept of Math University of South Fla Tampa FL 33620

WOLFOWITZ, PAUL DUNDES, govt. ofcl.; b. N.Y.C., Dec. 22, 1943; s. Jacob and Lillian (Dundes) W.; B.A. in Math., Cornell U., 1965; M.A., U. Chgo., 1967, Ph.D. in Polit. Sci., 1972; m. Clare Selgin, Nov. 25, 1968; 1 dau., Sara Elizabeth. Lectr., asst. prof. Yale U., 1970-73; spl. asst. to dir. ACDA, 1974-75, dep. asst. dir., 1976, spl. asst. for SALT, 1976-77; with Dept. Def., Washington, 1977—, dep. asst. Sec. of Def., regional programs, program analysis and evaluation, Office of Sec. of Def., 1977—. NSF fellow, 1965-68. Mem. Internat. Inst. Strategic Studies, Am. Polit. Sci. Assn., Inter-Univ. Consortium on Armed Forces and Soc. Home: 5444 Nevada Ave NW Washington DC 20015 Office: Pentagon Washington DC 20301

WOLFSIE, JACK HAROLD, physician; b. N.Y.C., Jan. 7, 1916; s. Maurice and Dorothy (Bazaar) W.; B.A. magna cum laude, N.Y. U., 1935, M.D., 1939; m. Beulah Shirley Simon, Jan. 19, 1941; children—Douglas Lewis, Andrea. Rotating intern N.Y.C. Hosp., 1939-41; asst. to med. dir. Am. Cyanamid Co., Bound Brook, N.J., then dir. med. services, Linden, N.J., 1945-64; corp. med. dir. Uniroyal, Inc., N.Y.C., 1964-71; v.p., med. dir. Equitable Life Assurance Soc. U.S., N.Y.C., 1971—. Served to capt. M.C., AUS, 1941-44. Diplomate Am. Bd. Preventive Medicine (occupational medicine), Am. Bd. Indsl. Hygiene. Mem. Am. Occupational Med. Assn., Am. Acad. Occupational Medicine, Am. Indsl. Hygiene Assn., Assn. Life Ins. Med. Dirs. Am., Am. Pub. Health Assn., Am. Acad. Indsl. Hygiene, N.Y. Acad. Scis., N.J., Union County (N.J.) med. socs., N.Y. State Soc. Indsl. Medicine, Am. Acad. Clin. Toxicology, Soc. Occupational and Environ. Health. Contbr. articles to profl. jours. Home: 810 Nancy Way Westfield NJ 07090 Office: 1285 Ave of Americas New York NY 10019

WOLFSON, ALBERT, educator, biologist; b. N.Y.C., Feb. 3, 1917; s. Sigmund and Pauline (Segall) W.; B.S., Cornell U., 1937; Ph.D. (Abraham Rosenberg research fellow zoology), U. Calif. at Berkeley, 1942; m. Dorothy Duke, June 19, 1937 (dec. Mar. 1971); children—Linda Jean Rostrom, Robert Neal; m. 2d, Sylvia Holland Mayer, Dec. 19, 1971; children—Jan Alynn (Mrs. Robert L. Walker), Diane Lee (Mrs. Laurence Istvan), Gary Arthur. Instr., U. Calif. at Berkeley, 1942-44; faculty Northwestern U., 1944—, prof., 1957. Lectr., Am. Inst. Biol. Scis., 1959-61; Alumni Fund lectr. Northwestern U., 1964. Mem. Biol. Scis. Curriculum Study Com., 1961-65; cons. div. biol. and medical scis. NSF, 1965-67; research asso. Field Mus., Chgo.; mem. adv. com. for biotron U. Wis., 1975-78. Active Evanston council Boy Scouts Am., 1957-67. Recipient Phi Sigma medal in biology U. Cal., 1941. Sr. postdoctoral fellow NSF of Zool. Inst. Tokyo, 1961-62. Fellow AAAS, Am. Ornithologists Union (Brewster Meml. medal, award 1962, sec. 1951-53); mem. Am. Soc. Naturalists, Am. Soc. Zoologists, Chgo. Acad. Scis. (1st v.p. 1975—), Endocrine Soc., Brit. Ornithologists Union, Phi Beta Kappa, Sigma Xi, Phi Kappa Phi. Author: The Human, The Earthworm, The Frog (all 1955). Editor: Avian Biology, 1955. Contbr. articles to profl. jours., books, encys. Research on migration and breeding cycles in birds, biogeography, reproductive physiology and neuroendocrinology. Home: 1260 Sherwood Rd Highland Park IL 60035

WOLFSON, EDWARD ALBERT, physician; b. N.Y.C., Feb. 4, 1926; s. David Louis and Lillian (Sklar) W.; A.B., Cornell U., 1948; M. Nutrition Sci., 1949, M.D., 1953; M.P.H., Columbia U., 1971; m. Barbara A. Freedman, Dec. 4, 1955; children—Michael Jay, Andrew Alan, Nancy Louise. Intern, resident N.Y. Hosp., Cornell Med. Center, 1953-57; practice medicine specializing in internal medicine, Paterson, N.J., 1957-69; sr. cons. in community medicine St. Joseph's Hosp.; physician to out-patients N.Y. Hosp.; instr. medicine Cornell U. Med. Coll., 1957-67; asso. prof. medicine N.J. Med. Sch., 1969, prof. com., health and preventive medicine, 1969, dir. div. drug abuse, 1969-73, asso. dean for health care, 1972, asso. dean for affiliations, 1974; now prof. health care adminstrn. and medicine, dean clin. campus at Binghamton State U. N.Y., Upstate Med. Center, Syracuse; mem. N.Y. Bd. for Medicine. Served with Inf. AUS, 1943-46. Decorated Purple Heart. Diplomate Am. Bd. Internal Medicine. Fellow A.C.P., Am. Coll. Preventive Medicine; mem. Am., N.J. socs. internal medicine, Am. Pub. Health Assn., AMA, N.J. State (chmn. credentials com. 1957, council pub. relations 1966-68, cons. com. med. edn.), N.Y. State (ref. com. on med edn.), Passaic County (pres.) med. socs., N.J. Gastroent. Soc., N.J. Heart Assn. (trustee 1966-68), Passaic County Heart Assn. (dir., pres.), Sigma Alpha Mu, Phi Delta Epsilon, Alpha Omega Alpha, Phi Kappa Phi. Office: State U of NY Upstate Med Center Clinical Campus State U New York Binghamton Binghamton NY 13901

WOLFSON, IRVING S., ins. co. exec.; married; 2 children. Exec. v.p. Phoenix Mut. Life Ins. Co.; pres., dir. Phoenix Fund, Inc., Phoenix Capital Fund, Inc.; v.p., dir. Phoenix Gen. Ins. Co., Phoenix Life Ins. Co.; dir. Phoenix Equity Planning Corp., Phoenix Investment Counsel of Boston, Inc.; asso. dir. Conn. Bank & Trust Co. Fellow Soc. Actuaries; mem. Phi Beta Kappa. Address: 1 American Row Hartford CT 06115

WOLFSON, JOSEPH LAURENCE, univ. dean; b. Winnipeg, Man., Can., July 22, 1917; s. Samuel and Diana (Dell) W.; B.S. with honours, U. Man., 1942, M.S., 1943; Ph.D., McGill U., 1948; m. Beatrice Heifetz, Aug. 6, 1944; children—Diana Dell, Jon Gordon. Asst. research officer Atomic Energy of Can., Chalk River, Ont., 1948-55; radiation physicist Jewish Gen. Hosp., Montreal, Que., 1955-58; asso. research officer Nat. Research Council, Ottawa, Ont., 1958-64; prof., asso. dean Faculty Arts and Sci., U. Sask., Regina, 1964-74; dean Faculty of Sci., Carleton U., Ottawa, 1974—. Mem. Canadian Assn. Physicists, Am. Phys. Soc. Home: 951 Blythdale Rd Ottawa ON K2A 3N9 Canada

WOLFSON, LESTER MARVIN, univ. chancellor; b. Evansville, Ind., Sept. 13, 1923; s. William and Bess (Silverman) W.; A.B., U. Mich., 1945, A.M., 1946, Ph.D. (Horace H. Rackham fellow), 1954; m. Esther Evans, July 3, 1949; children—Alice Jeanette, Margaret Gail, George Stephen. Teaching fellow in English, U. Mich., 1945-47; instr. English, Wayne State U., 1950-53; asst. prof. English and speech U. Houston, 1953-55; asst. prof. English, Ind. U. N.W., Gary, 1955-61, asso. prof., 1961-64; asso. prof. English, Ind. U., South Bend, 1964-67, prof. English, 1967—, dir., asst. dean, 1964-66, dean, 1966-68, dean, acting chancellor, 1968-69, chancellor, 1969—. Vis. asst. prof. English, U. Calif. at Santa Barbara, 1958-59. Bd. dirs. Michiana Pub. Broadcasting Corp., Michiana Arts and Scis. Council, Stanley Clark Sch., Meml. Hosp. South Bend, Civic Center Found. Mem. Nat. Council Tchrs. English, Coll. English Assn., Modern Lang. Assn., AAUP, South Bend-Mishawaka Area C. of C. (dir.), Phi Beta Kappa, Phi Kappa Phi, Phi Eta Sigma. Contbr. articles to profl. jours. Home: 17350 Darden Rd South Bend IN 46635

WOLFSON, MITCHELL, bus. exec.; b. Key West, Fla., Sept. 13, 1900; s. Louis and Rosa (Gruner) W.; student Erasmus Hall, 1914-18, Columbia; LL.D., U. Miami, 1955; m. Frances Cohen, Jan. 27, 1926; children—Louis, Frances Louise, Mitchell. Pres., chmn. bd. Wometco Enterprises, Inc.; chmn. bd. Financial Fed. Savs. & Loan Assn.; founder, operator 1st television sta. WTVJ, Miami, Fla., 1949. Mayor, mem. council Miami Beach, 1939-43; mem. Met. Charter Bd. Dade County, Orange Bowl Com; mem. South Fla. council Boy Scouts Am., hon. chmn. Frontiers '74 Scout Show, Miami, 1974; chmn. Miami Off-St. Parking Bd.; trustee Miami-Dade Community Coll.; mem. Nat. Trust for Historic Preservation; past chmn. Dade County Devel. Com.; founder, Audubon House, Key West; trustee Mt. Sinai Hosp., Fla. House, Sheriff's Boys Ranch; chmn. ann. brotherhood dinner Nat. Conf. Christians and Jews, 1975. Served to lt. col. AUS, World War II. Decorated Bronze Star medal (U.S.); Croix de Guerre (France); recipient Good Samaritan award Variety Club, 1954; Silver medallion NCCJ, 1962; Outstanding Citizen award City Miami Beach, 1965, also Mitchell Wolfson Park named in his honor, 1977; Walt Disney Humanitarian award Nat. Assn. Theater Owners, 1972, Spl. award of merit, 1974; Alfred I. Dupont Broadcast Journalism award Columbia U., 1972; Leonard L. Abess Human Relations award Anti-Defamation League of B'nai B'rith, 1975; Humanitarian award Miami Heart Inst., 1976; Gov.'s award Miami chpt. Nat. Acad. TV Arts and Scis., 1978; named Businessman of Yr. in Dade County, Miami News, 1975; Fla. Patriot, Bicentennial Commn. Fla., 1976; st. in Key West renamed Mitchell Wolfson Pl.; learning resources center Miami-Dade Community Coll. named in his honor; Mitchell Wolfson Plaza named in his honor City of Miami, 1975. Mem. Miami Jaycees (hon. life), Theatre Owners Am., Inc. (pres. 1950-51, chmn. bd. 1951-52), English Speaking Union Miami, Nat. Assn. Theatre Owners (dir. exec. bd.), Newcomen Soc., Motion Picture Exhibitors of Fla. (dir.), Nat. Assn. Mus. Elk. Mason (Shriner, 32 deg.), Rotarian. Clubs: Variety, Westview Golf and Country, Miami (Miami); Two Hundred; Thoroughbred; Vizcayans; Asheville (N.C.) Country; Harmonie (N.Y.C.). Home: 5030 N Bay Rd Miami Beach FL 33140 Office: 306 N Miami Ave Miami FL 33128

WOLFSON, RICHARD FREDERICK, broadcasting co. exec.; b. N.Y.C., Jan. 7, 1923; s. William Leon and Gertrude (Quitman) W.; B.S., Harvard, 1942; LL.B., Yale, 1944; m. Elaine Cecile Reinherz, June 6, 1954; children—Lisa Reinherz (Mrs. Clement Biddle Wood III), Paul Reinherz Quitman. Admitted to N.Y. bar, 1945, Fla. bar, 1956; law clk. to judge U.S. Ct. of Appeals, 2d Circuit, 1944-45, Justice Wiley Rutledge, U.S. Supreme Ct., 1945-47; mem. firm Kurland & Wolfson, N.Y.C., 1947-52; asst. to pres. Wometco Enterprises, Inc., Miami, Fla., 1952-59, v.p., dir., 1959-62, sr. v.p., dir., 1962-72, exec. v.p., gen. counsel, 1973—, chmn. exec. com., 1976—. Mem. adv. com. Law and Econs. Center, U. Miami Law Sch.; past pres. Ransom-Everglades Sch.; bd. dirs. Met. Mus. Miami, Miami Philharmonic Soc. (past pres.), Opera Guild Greater Miami, Friends of Art, Lowe Art Mus., Greater Miami chpt. Am. Jewish Com.; mem. exec. com. Fla. region NCCJ; trustee Fla. Internat. U. Found. Guggenheim fellow, 1949-50. Mem. Fla., N.Y. State bar assns., Nat. Assn. Theater Owners. Clubs: Standard, Palm Bay, Westview, Harvard, Miami (Miami); Harvard (N.Y.C.); Standard. Author: (with Kurland) Jurisdiction of the Supreme Court of the United States, 1951; also articles in profl. jours., poetry. Home: 630 University Dr Coral Gables FL 33134 Office: 306 N Miami Ave Miami FL 33128. *Passion, Power are different ways: which to follow wastes my days.*

WOLFSON, ROBERT LOWELL, business exec.; b. Mpls., Mar. 24, 1918; s. Abraham Samuel and Sarah Ruth (Weisberg) W.; student U. Minn., 1935-37; m. Suzanne Feld, June 7, 1947 (div. Jan. 1962); children—Andrew Scott, Anne Feld, Robert Lowell; m. 2d, Ethel Coopersmith, Nov. 14, 1963. Chmn. bd. Feld Chevrolet, Inc., St. Louis, Manchester Lease Corp., Brentwood Volvo, Ltd.; chmn. bd. Progress Bank, St. Louis; organizer, 1957, Gem Internat. (and predecessor companies), St. Louis, chmn. bd., 1957-65, chmn. exec. com. Parkview-Gem, 1965-67; pres. Dubob Realty, St. Louis; treas., v.p. St. Louis Arena Corp., St. Louis Blues Nat. Hockey League Team, 1967-77. Chmn. bd. Jewish Community Centers Assn., St. Louis; bd. dirs. Jewish Hosp., St. Louis; trustee Brandeis U. Served to capt. AUS, 1943-46; CBI. Recipient Nat. Leadership award Boys Town of Italy, 1961. Jewish. Club: Westwood Country. Home: 816 S Hanley St Apt 7B Saint Louis MO 63105 Office: 14 S Bemiston Ave Saint Louis MO 63105

WOLGA, GEORGE JACOB, educator; b. N.Y.C., Apr. 2, 1931; s. Samuel and Irene Wolga; B.Engring. Physics with distinction, Cornell U., 1953; Ph.D., Mass. Inst. Tech., 1957; m. Martha Ann Wright, Jan. 31, 1960; children—Andrea Emily, Kenneth Martin, Sarah Anne. Instr. physics Mass. Inst. Tech., 1957-60, asst. prof., 1960-61; asst. prof. elec. engring. Cornell U., 1961-64, asso. prof. elec. engring. and applied physics, 1964-68, prof., 1968—; co-founder, v.p. Lansing Research Corp., Ithaca, 1964—; dir. Edmac Assos. Inc., Rochester, N.Y. Mem. Am. Phys. Soc., IEEE, AAUP, Sigma Xi, Tau Beta Pi. Research in atomic and molecular physics, lasers and quantum electronics, optical instrumentation. Home: 324 Snyder Hill Rd Ithaca NY 14850

WOLINS, JOSEPH, painter; b. Atlantic City, Mar. 26, 1915; s. Morris and Rebecca (Vullinska) W.; student Nat. Acad. Design, 1931-35; m. Selma Polikoff Lazaar, Dec. 7, 1957; children—Richard Lazaar, David Lazaar, John Wolins, Sarah Wolins. Painter with WPA arts projects, 1934-41; tchr. South Shore Art Sch., Rockville Center, N.Y., 1950-55, Westchester Workshop, White Plains, N.Y., 1954-55, 92d St. YMHA, N.Y.C., 1960, Bklyn. Mus. Art Sch., 1961-62, Long Beach (N.Y.) High Sch., 1962-68; pvt. classes, 1961—; one-man exhbns. include Contemporary Arts Gallery, N.Y.C., Bodley Gallery, N.Y.C., Silvermine Guild, Norwalk, Conn., Agra Gallery, Washington; group exhbns. include World's Fair, N.Y.C., 1939, J.B. Neumann Gallery, N.Y.C., Toledo Mus., Corcoran Art Gallery, U. Ill. Mus., Pa. Acad. Fine Art, Whitney Mus., Sao Paolo Mus. Modern Art, Norfolk (Va.) Mus., Smithsonian Instn., Butler Art Inst., Youngstown, Ohio; rep. permanent collections Met. Mus. Art, Norfolk Mus., Albert Gallery at St. Joseph's (Mo.) U., Fiske U. Art Gallery, Mobile, Mus. in Ein Horod, Israel, Butler Art Inst., also pvt. collections. Grantee Mark Rothko Found., 1971; recipient Painting award Audubon Artists, 1976, Nat. Inst. Arts and Letters, 1976, Am. Soc. Contemporary Artists, 1976. Mem. Audubon Artists, Am. Soc. Contemporary Artists. Address: 463 West St New York City NY 10014

WOLINSKY, EMANUEL, educator, physician; b. N.Y.C., Sept. 23, 1917; s. Jacob and Bertha (Siegel) W.; B.A., Cornell U., 1938, M.D., 1941; m. Marjorie Claster, Nov. 15, 1946; children—Douglas, Peter. Intern, resident medicine N.Y. Hosp., 1943-45; bacteriologist Trudeau Lab., Saranac Lake, N.Y., 1947-56; faculty Case Western Res. U. Sch. Medicine, 1956—, prof. medicine, 1968—; dir. microbiology Cleve. Met. Gen. Hosp., 1959—. Mem. Tb panel U.S.-Japan Co-op. Med. Sci. Program, 1969-75. Diplomate Am. Bd. Microbiology. Mem. Am. Soc. Microbiology, Am. Thoracic Soc., Infectious Diseases Soc. Am., Phi Beta Kappa, Alpha Omega Alpha. Contbr. articles to profl. jours., textbooks. Asso. editor Am. Rev. Respiratory Diseases. Home: 24761 S Woodland Rd Beachwood OH 44122 Office: 3395 Scranton Rd Cleveland OH 44109

WOLINSKY, JOSEPH, educator, organic chemist; b. Chgo., Dec. 3, 1930; s. Gershon and Rose (Tefsky) W.; B.S., U. Ill., 1952; Ph.D., Cornell U., 1956; m. Sheila L. Rubin, July 15, 1951; children—Debra Sue, Kharry Beth, Rebecca Ellen, Michael R., Julie Berna. Project asso. U. Wis., 1956-58; asst. prof. Purdue U., 1958-62, asso. prof., 1962-67, prof. chemistry, 1967—. Mem. Am. Chem. Soc., Alpha Chi Sigma, Phi Lambda Upsilon Research on chemistry of terpenes, alkaloids and related natural products. Home: 823 Elmwood Dr West Lafayette IN 47906

WOLK, ELLIOT SAMUEL, educator; b. Springfield, Mass., Aug. 5, 1919; s. Max and Jennie (Robinson) W.; A.B., Clark U., 1940; Sc.M., Brown U., 1947, Ph.D., 1954; m. Eleanor F. Lisniansky, Dec. 24, 1950; children—Joel L., Daniel P., Sara F. Faculty, U. Conn., Storrs, 1950—, prof. math., 1964—, head dept. math., 1967-73. Cons. Electric Boat div. Gen. Dynamics Corp., 1957-58. Mem. Am. Math. Soc., Math. Assn. Am. Author math. textbooks; contbr. articles to profl. jours. Home: Birchwood Heights Storrs CT 06268

WOLKE, ROBERT LESLIE, scientist, educator, writer; b. Bklyn., Apr. 2, 1928; s. Harry Louis and Sophia (Norma) W.; B.S., Poly. Inst. Bklyn., 1949; Ph.D., Cornell U., 1953; m. Elizabeth Ann Maruca, Dec. 25, 1964; 1 dau., Leslie Ann. Research asso. Enrico Fermi Inst. U. Chgo., 1953-56; nuclear chemist Gen. Atomic, San Diego, 1957; asst. prof. to asso. prof. chemistry U. Fla., Gainesville, 1957-58, asso. prof., 1958-60; asso. prof. U. Pitts., 1960-67, prof., 1967—, dir. univ. office faculty devel., 1977—. Researcher Oak Ridge Nat. Lab., 1957-60; vis. prof. U. P.R., 1970; mem. AID mission, Venezuela, 1973. Mem. Am. Chem. Soc., Am. Phys. Soc., AAAS, Profl. and Orgnl. Devel. Network, Phi Beta Kappa, Sigma Xi. Editor: Impact: Science on Society. Author: Chemistry Explained. Contbr. to profl. jours. Research on nuclear chemistry and radiochemistry. Home: 615 Maple Ln Edgeworth Sewickley PA 15143 Office: Office of Faculty Devel 3600-CL U Pittsburgh Pittsburgh PA 15260

WOLKEN, A. JONATHAN, choreographer, dancer; b. Pitts., July 12, 1949; s. Jerome J. and Dorothy Olive (Malinger) W.; B.S. in Philosophy, Dartmouth Coll., 1971. Founding mem. Pilobus Dance Theatre, Washington, Conn., 1970—; participant documentary for Dance in Am. Series, 1977. Recipient Edinburgh Festival award, 1974, Herman Critics prize, 1976, Brandeis award, 1978; Guggenheim fellow, 1976; grantee Nat. Endowment Arts, Am. Dance Festival. Home: Tophet Rd Roxbury CT 06783 Office: Box 233 Washington CT 06793

WOLKEN, JEROME JAY, educator, biophysicist; b. Pitts., Mar. 28, 1917; s. Abraham I. and Dina (Lando) W.; student Pa. State U., 1935-36, Duquesne U., 1937-39; B.S., U. Pitts., 1946, M.S., 1948, Ph.D., 1949; m. Dorothy O. Mallinger, June 19, 1945 (dec. 1954); children—Ann Alex, A. Jonathan; m. 2d, Tobey J. Holstein, Jan. 26, 1956; children—H. Johanna, Erik Andrew. Research fellow Mellon Inst., 1943-47, Rockefeller Inst., 1950-52; asst. prof. U. Pitts. Sch. Medicine, 1953-57, asso. prof., 1957-61, prof. biophysics physiology, 1962-66; head dept. biophysics Carnegie Inst. Tech., Pitts., 1964-67, prof. biophysics, 1964—; head biophys. research lab. Carnegie-Mellon U., 1964—, Eye and Ear Hosp., Pitts., 1953-64. Research asso. Carnegie Mus.; guest prof. Pa. State U., 1963, U. Paris, 1967-68, Inst. Theoretical Studies, Miami, Fla., 1966, Univ. Coll., London, 1971, Pasteur Inst., Paris, 1972; research fellow Princeton U., 1978. Served with USNR, 1941-43. Recipient Career award USPHS, 1962-65. Fellow N.Y. Acad. Scis., AAAS, Optical Soc. Am. (pres. Pitts. sect. 1964-65), Am. Inst. Chemists, Explorers Club; mem. Am. Chem. Soc., Am. Soc. Plant Physiologists, Chemistry Club N.Y., Am. Inst. Biol. Sci., Biophysics Soc., Soc. Gen. Physiologists, Am. Soc. Protozoologists, Pa. Acad. Scis., Am. Soc. Cell Biology, Soc. Neurosci., Sigma Xi, Phi Sigma. Author 7 books; editor 2 books; contbr. articles to profl. jours. Home: 5817 Elmer St Pittsburgh PA 15232

WOLKIN, PAUL ALEXANDER, lawyer, inst. exec.; b. Phila., Oct. 14, 1917; s. Alex and Rebecca (LiKalter) W.; B.A., U. Pa., 1937, M.A., 1938, J.D., 1941; m. Martha Kessler, June 25, 1944; children—Rachel, Adam. Admitted to Pa. bar, 1942, U.S. Supreme Ct. bar, 1947; clerk to judge U.S. Circuit Ct. Appeals, Phila., 1942-44; atty. Fgn. Econ. Adminstrn., Washington, 1944-45; asso. gen. counsel French Supply Council, Washington, 1945-46; asst. legal adviser Dept. State, 1946-47; legal draftsman Phila. Charter Commn., 1948-51; spl. asst. to Phila. Solicitor, 1951; partner firm Wolkin, Sarner & Cooper, Phila., 1951-66; counsel Sarner, Cooper & Stein, Phila., 1966-69, firm Hudson, Wilf & Kronfeld, Phila., 1971-78, firm Rawle & Henderson, 1980—; asst. dir. Am. Law Inst., Phila., 1947-77, exec. v.p., 1977—, sec., 1979—; exec. dir. Am. Law Inst.—Am. Bar Assn. Com. on Continuing Profl. Edn., 1963—; sec. permanent editorial bd. Uniform Comml. Code, 1962—; mem. com. specialized personnel Dept. Labor, 1964-69. Pres. Phila. Child Guidance Center, 1966-72. Fellow Am. Bar Found.; mem. Am. Law Inst., Am. (spl. com. on standards and codes 1974—), Pa., Phila. bar assns., Pa. Bar Inst. (bd. dirs. 1967-75), Am. Judicature Soc., Order of Coif, Lawyers Club, Sociolegal Club, Scribes (past pres.). Editor: The Practical Lawyer, 1955—; contbr. articles to profl. jours. Home: 1610 N 72d St Philadelphia PA 19151 Office: Am Law Inst 4025 Chestnut St Philadelphia PA 19104

WOLKING, JOSEPH ANTHONY, pub. co. exec.; b. Morris, Minn., May 7, 1934; s. Lawrence William and Tecla Catherine (Loegering) W.; student Fordham U., 1952-54; B.A., U. Minn., 1957; m. Kathleen Marie Poehling, Apr. 18, 1959; children—Christopher, Lisbeth, Gregory, Rebecca, Eric. With Ojibway Press Inc., Duluth, Minn., 1958-69; asst. to pres. Petroleum Pub. Co., Tulsa, 1969, pub. Dental Econs., 1972-75, v.p., group pub., 1975—, dir., 1977—. Home: 3775 S Canton St Tulsa OK 74135 Office: 1421 S Sheridan St Tulsa OK 74112

WOLKOFF, EUGENE ARNOLD, lawyer; b. N.Y.C., June 9, 1932; s. Oscar and Jean (Zablow) W.; A.B., Bklyn. Coll., 1953; LL.B., St. John's U., 1961; m. Judith Gail Edwards, Oct. 15, 1967; children—Mandy, Elana, Alexa, Justine. Admitted to N.Y. State bar, 1962, since practiced in N.Y.C.; mem. firm Callahan & Wolkoff, 1965—. Dir. IHS Enterprises, Inc., Municipal Street Sign Co., Inc., Traffic Sign Materials, Inc., Prodn. Spraying and Mfg. Corp. Mem. nat. panel arbitrators Am. Arbitration Assn. Served to lt. col. USAFR, 1953-75. Mem. N.Y. State Bar Assn., Pi Beta Gamma. Office: 67 Wall St New York NY 10005

WOLKOMIR, NATHAN TULLY, ret. labor union ofcl.; b. Baku, Russia, Oct. 12, 1909; s. Boris and Rose (Silver) W.; came to U.S., 1912, naturalized, 1917; B.S., N.Y. U., 1929, St. John's U., 1930, St. Francis Coll., N.Y.C., 1930; M.Ed., St. John's U., 1940; D.Ed., U. Ill., 1960; m. Louise Orthelia Schimmen, Mar. 10, 1944; 1 dau., Rhya Natalia. Tchr., N.Y.C., 1940-42; ednl. specialist, tng. command USAAF and USAF, 1942-64; mem. Nat. Fedn. Fed. Employees, 1942-76, pres. Ill., 1950-52, nat. pres., 1964-76. Chmn., Community Concerts, Rantoul, Ill., 1960, Rantoul Recreation Bd., 1961; pres. Chanute AFB Recreation and Welfare Orgn., 1962; mem. Pres.'s Com. on Hiring Handicapped, 1965, Eligibility Bd. for Administering Fed. Fund Raising Program, Employee Advisory Com. on Fed. Employers Health Benefits Program; mem. advisory council Nat. Wage Bd.; mem. Nat. Job Evaluation and Pay Rev. Task Force; mem. Wm. A. Jump award and selection com. Dept. Agr., 1978—; mem. Nat. Council on Aging. Police commr., Rantoul, 1962. Mem. Soc. Personnel Adminstrn., Soc. Programmed Instruction, Am. Soc. Pub. Adminstrn., Pub. Personnel Assn., Am. Acad. Polit. and Social Scis., Nat. Civil Service League, Air Force Assn. Clubs: Masons (32 deg.), Shriners, Odd Fellows, Moose. Author: (with others), Modern Airmanship, 1957; editor Federal Employee, Report from Washington. Home: 1001 Lamberton Dr Silver Spring MD 20902 Died Aug. 29, 1979. *Communication is the art of understanding and being understood.*

WOLL, JOSEPH ALBERT, lawyer; b. Chgo., Feb. 16, 1904; s. Matthew and Irene (Kerwin) W.; J.D., U. Ill., 1927; m. Genevieve Carey, May 15, 1930; children—Mary Cynthia Geddes, Phyllis Irene (Mrs. Paul Stokes, Jr.), David Carey. Admitted to Ill. bar, 1927; Chgo.'s asst. state's atty. for Cook County, 1930-34; trial work and preparation briefs before Ill. Supreme Ct.; in charge preparation all indictments, 1932-34; apptd. spl. asst. to atty. gen. U.S., 1934; head comml. frauds sect. U.S. Dept. Justice, 1939-40; apptd. U.S. atty. No. Dist. Ill., by Pres. Roosevelt, 1940-47; individual pvt. practice, 1947—. Gen. counsel AFL-CIO, Internat. Union Operating Engrs., labor orgns., Com. on Polit. Edn. Div.; mem. exec. com. Union Labor Life Ins. Co., now chmn. bd. Former mem. exec. com., chmn. adv. com. Fed. Bus. Assn. Chgo. area. commr., mem. exec. bd. Chgo. council Boy Scouts Am., 1942-47, mem. Nat. council; mem. exec. com., bd. dirs. Soldiers and Sailors Service Council Ill., 1941-45; past bd. dirs. Cath. Charities D.C., Cath. Youth Orgn., Washington, D.C. Tb Assn.; bd. dirs. Nat. Legal Aid and Defender Assn.; bd. dirs., treas. Nat. Conf. on Citizenship; mem. Pres.' Conf. on Adminstrv. Procedure, Pres.' White House Conf. to Fulfill These Rights; bd. dirs. Nat. Council on Crime and Delinquency; trustee Supreme Ct. Hist. Soc. Mem. Am., D.C., Md., Fed. bar assns., Am. Arbitration Assn. (dir. N.Y.C.), Am. Judicature Soc., Selden Soc., John Carroll Soc., Friendly Sons St. Patrick, Phi Kappa, Phi Alpha Delta. Roman

Catholic. Club: University. Office: 736 Bowen Bldg 815 15th St NW Washington DC 20005

WOLLAEGER, ERIC EDWIN, ret. educator, physician; b. Milw., Mar. 6, 1910; s. Edwin and Frieda (Schucht) W.; A.B. summa cum laude, Dartmouth Coll., 1931, postgrad. Med. Sch., 1931-32; M.D., Harvard, 1934; M.S. in Medicine (fellow medicine Mayo Found.), U. Minn., 1941; m. Lieselotte Ann Hager, Sept. 20, 1938; children—Andrea Marie, Sarah Louise and Wendy Ann (twins), Lucy Jane. Intern, Roosevelt Hosp., N.Y.C., 1935-36; asso. medicine Mayo Clinic, Rochester, Minn., 1941-77, head sect. medicine, 1955-67, sr. cons. medicine, 1967-77, pres. staff, 1962, asso. editor Mayo Clinic Proc., 1965-77; attending physician St. Mary's and Rochester Methodist hosps., 1941-77; faculty Mayo Found. Grad. Sch., U. Minn., 1941—, prof. medicine, 1956-77, dir. tng. program gastroenterology, 1960-65. Diplomate Am. Bd. Internal Medicine (mem. sub.-splty. bd. gastroenterology 1955-61). Mem. AMA, Minn. Soc. Internal Medicine (pres. 1971), Central Clin. Research Club, Central Soc. Clin. Research, Am. Soc. Clin. Investigation, Am. Gastroenterologic Assn. (com. edn. and tng. 1959-61), Phi Beta Kappa, Sigma Xi (chpt. pres. 1970-71). Presbyn. Mem. editorial bd. Am. Jour. Digestive Diseases, 1967-68. Contbr. articles to profl. jours. Home: 1026 Plummer Circle Rochester MN 55901

WOLLE, WILLIAM DOWN, fgn. ser. officer; b. Sioux City, Iowa, Mar. 11, 1928; s. William Carl and Vivian Lucille (Down) W.; B.A., Morningside Coll., 1949; M.Internat. Affairs, Columbia, 1951; m. Mimmi Torlen, May 21, 1955; children—Laila Jean, William Nicholas. Joined U.S. Fgn. Service, 1951; consular officer, Baghdad, Iraq, 1951-52, econ. officer, 1952-53; consular officer, Manchester, Eng., 1954-57; trainee Arab lang. and area, Beirut, Lebanon, 1957-58; fgn. service officer gen., Aden, So. Yemen, 1958-59; econ. officer, Jidda, Saudi Arabia, 1959-62; internat. economist, Washington, 1962-64, internat. relations officer, 1964-65, officer in charge Arab-Israeli affairs, 1965-67, detailed Nat. War Coll., 1967-68; counselor polit. affairs, Kuwait City, Kuwait, 1968-70; econ. officer, dir. AID, Amman, Jordan, 1970-73; econ. officer Nairobi, 1973-74; ambassador to Oman, Muscat, 1974-78; dir. Middle Eastern/South Asian Research Office, Dept. State, 1978-79; ambassador to United Arab Emirates, 1979—. Served with AUS, 1946-47. Recipient Superior Service award Dept. State, 1974. Address: Abu Dhabi Dept State Washington DC 20520

WOLLEMBORG, LEO JOSEPH, newspaperman; b. Loreggia, Italy, Aug. 30, 1912; s. Leone and Alina (Fano) W.; Ph.D. in Litt. (History), U. Rome (Italy), 1933, Ph.D. in Law, 1936; m. Mafalda Cusi, Mar. 27, 1962; 1 son, Leo R. Came to U.S., 1939, naturalized, 1943. Lectr. internat. relations Columbia Grad Sch., 1940-42; script writer, news editor Italian sect. OWI, 1942-43; Rome corr. Washington Post, 1953-70, Italian and Vatican corr. Los Angeles Times-Washington Post News Service, 1962-70; Rome corr. Phila. Bull., 1970-72, 78—; asso. pub., polit. commentator Daily Am., Rome, 1972-76. Participant round table debates internat. affairs Italian television 1961—. Served with AUS, 1943-47; ETO. Mem. Fgn. Press Assn. Rome. Author: Tra Washingtone Roma, 1959; Italia al Rallentatore, 1966. Contbr. numerous articles to nat. mags., jours. Address: 373 Via Nomentana Rome Italy

WOLLENBERG, ALBERT CHARLES, U.S. dist. judge; b. San Francisco, June 13, 1900; s. Charles M. and Romilda (Judell) W.; A.B., U. Calif. at Berkeley, 1922, J.D., 1924; m. Velma Bercovich, Sept. 5, 1925; children—Jean (Mrs. M.J. Waldman), Albert Charles. Admitted to Calif. bar, 1925; gen. practice law, San Francisco, 1925-28, 34-47; asst. U.S. atty. No. Dist. Calif., 1928-34; judge Superior Ct., City and County of San Francisco, 1947-58; U.S. dist. judge No. Dist. Calif., 1958—. Pres., Conf. Calif. Judges, 1956-57; mem. Jud. Council Calif., 1957—. Mem. Calif. Legislature from 21st dist., 1939-47. Served with USN, 1918. Jewish (past pres. temple). Club: Masons. Office: US Courthouse PO Box 36060 San Francisco CA 94102*

WOLLENBERG, J. ROGER, lawyer; b. N.Y.C., May 1, 1919; s. Harry Lincoln and Gertrude (Arnstein) W.; B.A., U. Calif. at Berkeley, 1939, LL.B., 1942; m. Patricia S. Albright, Jan. 2, 1948; children—Christopher, Meredith, Pamela, Peter, Edward. Admitted to Calif. bar, 1946, D.C. bar, 1954; law clk. U.S. Supreme Ct. Justice William O. Douglas, 1946; with Dept. Justice, 1947-52; asst. gen. counsel FCC, 1952-54; pvt. practice, 1954—; partner firm Wilmer & Pickering, Washington, 1962—. Mem. Falls Church (Va.) Sch. Bd., 1960-71, chmn., 1962-70. Served to lt. USNR, 1942-46. Mem. FCC Bar Assn. (pres. 1965-66), Am. Bar Assn. (ho. of dels. 1967-71). Home: 508 Lincoln Ave Falls Church VA 22046 Office: 1666 K St NW Washington DC 20006

WOLLENBERG, RICHARD PETER, paper mfr.; b. Juneau, Alaska, Aug. 1, 1915; s. Harry L. and Gertrude (Arnstein) W.; B.S. in Mech. Engring., U. Calif. at Berkeley, 1936; M.B.A., Harvard U., 1938; grad. Army Indsl. Coll., 1941; D.Pub. Affairs (hon.), U. Puget Sound, 1977; m. Leone Bonney, Dec. 22, 1940; children—Kenneth Roger, David Arthur, Keith Kermit, Richard Harry, Carol Lynne. Prodn. control Bethlehem Ship, Quincy, Mass., 1938-39; with Longview Fibre Co. (Wash.), 1939—, safety engr., asst. chief engr., chief engr., mgr. container operations, 1951-57, v.p., 1953-57, v.p. operations, 1957-60, exec. v.p., 1960-69, pres., 1969-78, pres., chief exec. officer, 1978—, also dir. Mem. Wash. State Council for Postsecondary Edn., 1969-79, chmn., 1970-73. Bassoonist S.W. Washington Symphony. Trustee Reed Coll., Portland. Served from 2d lt. to lt. col. USAAF, 1941-45. Home: 1632 Kessler Blvd Longview WA 98632

WOLLER, OLGA, author; b. Zidani Most, Yugoslavia; d. Ivan and Josephine V. (Stockel) Malgaj; student Acad. Fine Arts, Vienna, Austria; m. Rudolph Weigner, 1918; children—Raoul M., Madeleine R. (Mrs. John T. Taeni); m. 2d, Franz H. Woller, Apr. 14, 1934. Author: Sex Alarm, 1946; Strange Conflict, 1955; The Heartbeat of Rome (hist. novel), 1957; Foolish, But Oh So Sweet, 1963; The Eccentric Loves of Elagabal, 1964; (poetry) Book of Golden Verse, 1974. Composer songs: There Will Be Sunday; No, No Johnny, Let It Be. Home: 101 Greenway N Forest Hills NY 11375 also Pinehurst NC 28374

WOLLHEIM, DONALD ALLEN, publisher, author; b. N.Y.C., Oct. 1, 1914; s. Jacob Lewis and Rose (Grinnell) W.; B.A., N.Y. U., 1935; m. Elsie Balter, June 25, 1943; 1 dau., Elizabeth Rosalind. Editor, Ace mags., 1942-47, Avon Books, 1947-52; editorial v.p. Ace Books, 1952-71; pres., publisher DAW Books, Inc., N.Y.C., 1971—; author Mike Mars series, 1961-65; Biography of Lee deForest, 1962; (lit. criticism) The Universe Makers, 1971; pub. over 35 anthologies including 1st sci. fiction anthology The Pocket Book of Science Fiction, 1943. Named to 1st Fandom Hall of Fame, 1975; recipient Com. award Melbourne Sci. Fiction Conv., 1975, Fritz Leiber award for contbn. to adult fantasy, 1978. Mem. Sci. Fiction Writers Am., Mystery Writers Am., Western Writers Am., Am. Booksellers Assn., Order St. Fantony, Count Dracula Soc. (hon. nat. chmn. 1972; Ann Radcliffe award 1975), Brit. Sci. Fiction Assn. (dir. 1977—). Clubs: Overseas Press (life), Hydra. Home: 66-17 Clyde St Rego Park NY 11374 Office: 1633 Broadway New York NY 10019

WOLLMAN, HARRY, medical educator; b. Bklyn., Sept. 26, 1932; s. Jacob and Florence Roslyn (Hoffman) W.; A.B. summa cum laude (hon. John Harvard scholar 1950-53, hon. Harvard Coll. scholar 1953-54, Detur award 1951), Harvard, 1954, M.D., 1958; m. Anne Carolyn Hamel, Feb. 16, 1957; children—Julie Ellen, Emily Jane, Diana Leigh. Intern U. Chgo. Clinics, 1958-59; resident U. Pa., 1959-63, asso. in anesthesia, 1963-65, mem. faculty, 1965—, prof. anesthesia, 1970—, prof. pharmacology, 1971—, Robert Dunning Dripps prof., chmn. dept. anesthesia, 1972—, prin. investigator Anesthesia Research Center, 1972-78, program dir. Anesthesia Research Tng. Grant, 1972—. Mem. anesthesia drug panel, drug efficacy study, com. on anesthesia Nat. Acad. Scis.-NRC, 1970-71, com. on adverse reactions to anesthesia drugs, 1971-72; mem. pharm. and toxicology tng. grants com. NIH, 1966-68, anesthesia tng. grants com., 1971-73, surgery, anesthesia and trauma study sect., 1974-78; chmn. com. on studies involving human beings U. Pa., 1972-76, chmn. clin. practice exec. com., 1976—. NIH research traineeship fellow, 1959-63; Pharm. Mfg. Assn. fellow, 1960-61. Diplomate Am. Bd. Anesthesiology. Mem. Pa. Soc. Anesthesiologists (pres. 1972-73), Am. Physiol. Soc., Assn. U. Anesthetists (exec. council 1971-74, chmn. sci. adv. bd. 1975-77), Soc. Acad. Anesthesia Chairmen (chmn. com. on financial resources 1973-77, pres.-elect 1976-77, pres., 1977-78), Am. Soc. Anesthesiologists, Phila. Soc. Anesthesiologists, AMA, Pa. Med. Soc., Phila. County Med. Soc., John Morgan Soc., Coll. Physicians Phila., Phi Beta Kappa, Sigma Xi. Republican. Unitarian. Asso. editor for revs. Anesthesiology, 1970-75. Contbr. and editor books. Home: 2203 Delaney Pl Philadelphia PA 19103 Office: Dept Anesthesia Hosp University Pa 3400 Spruce St Philadelphia PA 19104

WOLLMAN, LEO, physician; b. N.Y.C., Mar. 14, 1914; s. Joseph and Sara (Samrick) W.; B.S., Columbia, 1934; M.S., N.Y. U., 1938; M.D., Royal Coll. Edinburgh, 1942; Ph.D., Rochdale, 1972; D.Sc. (hon.), U. Mich.; m. Eleanor Rakow, Aug. 16, 1936 (dec. Sept. 1953); children—Arthur Lee, Bryant Lee; m. 2d, Charlotte Kornberg Seidman, Oct. 6, 1954 (div. Jan. 1969). Intern Cumberland Hosp., Bklyn., 1942-43; resident Leith Gen. Hosp., 1942; practice medicine specializing in obstetrics and gynecology, Bklyn., 1944—, in psychiatry, 1961—; mem. staff Maimonides, Coney Island, Caledonian hosps., Bklyn., Park East, Mt. Sinai hosps., N.Y.C. Recipient Jules Weinstein Ann. Pioneer in Modern Hypnosis award, 1964. Diplomate Am. Bd. Obstetrics and Gynecology, Nat. Bd. Acupuncture Medicine, Am. Bd. Psychiatry and Neurology. Fellow Am. Geriatrics Soc., N.Y. Acad. Scis. (life), Acad. Psychosomatic Medicine (sec. 1965), Soc. Clin. and Exptl. Hypnosis, Am. Soc. Clin. Hypnosis, Soc. Sci. Study Sex (pres. Eastern region 1979—), Am. Soc. Psychical Research (life), Am. Med. Writers Assn. (life), Internat. Soc. Comprehensive Medicine, Am. Acad. Psychiatry and Neurology; mem. Nat. Geog. Soc. (life), AAAS (council 1971—), Am. Assn. Social Psychiatry, Am. Soc. Abdominal Surgeons, Internat. Soc. Nonverbal Psychotherapy, N.Y. State Soc. Med. Research, Royal Medico-Psychol. Assn. (Eng.), N.Y. Soc. for Gen. Semantics, Nat. Assn. on Standard Med. Vocabulary (sec. 1964—), Am. Assn. History Medicine, Am. Assn. Study Headache, Am. Acad. Dental Medicine, Am. Assn. Marriage Counselors, Soc. Med. Jurisprudence, Bklyn. Psychol. Assn., Canadian Soc. for Study Fertility, Am. Fertility Soc., Internat. Fertility Assn., Internat. Soc. for Clin. and Exptl. Hypnosis, Am. Soc. Psychosomatic Dentistry and Medicine (pres. 1969), Assn. Advancement Psychotherapy, Pan-Am., Brit. med. assns., Bklyn. Acad. Medicine, Internat. Soc. Psychoneuroendocrinology, L.I. Hist. Soc., numerous others, also hon. mem. numerous fgn. orgns. Author: Write Yourself Slim, 1976; also numerous articles in profl. jours. Editor-in-chief Jour. Am. Soc. Psychosomatic Dentistry and Medicine, 1968—; editor newsletter Soc. Sci. Study Sex; asso. editor Jour. Sex Research; internat. editor Latin Am. Jour. Clin. Hypnosis, others; films I Am Not This Body, 1970, Strange Her, 1971, Let Me Die a Woman, 1978. Address: 2802 Mermaid Ave Brooklyn NY 11224. *I have learned that to be busily occupied doing the work I like is to be happy. Doing what you like to do usually results in a job well done. To take pride in one's work is a virtue.*

WOLLMAN, NATHANIEL, educator, economist; b. Phila., May 15, 1915; s. Leon and Rose (Schimmel) W.; A.B., Pa. State U., 1936; Ph.D., Princeton U., 1940; LL.D., Colo. Coll., 1972; m. Lenora Levin, Dec. 25, 1939; children—Stephen, Eric. Instr., asst. prof. Colo. Coll., 1939-48; asso. prof., prof. U. N.Mex., 1948—, chmn. dept. econs., 1960—, dean Coll. Arts and Scis., 1969—. Economist, Resources for the Future, 1959-60, 64-65. Chmn. Internat. Environ. Programs Com. Served with USNR, World War II. Mem. Am. Econs. Assn. Author: (with others) Alternative Uses of Water, 1960; Water Supply and Demand, 1960; Water Resources of Chile, 1968; (with Gilbert Bonem) The Outlook for Water: Quality, Quantity and National Growth, 1971; (with others) Man, Materials and Environment, 1973. Home: Box 358 Corrales NM 87048

WOLLMAN, ROGER LELAND, judge; b. Frankfort, S.D., May 29, 1934; s. Edwin and Katherine (Kleinsasser) W.; B.A., Tabor Coll., 1957; J.D., U. S.D., 1962; LL.M., Harvard U., 1964; m. Diane Schroeder, June 21, 1959; children—Steven James, John Mark, Thomas Roger. Admitted to S.D. bar, 1962; individual practice law, Aberdeen, S.D., 1964-71; state's atty., Brown County, S.D., 1967-71; asso. judge Supreme Ct. of S.D., 1971-78, chief justice Supreme Ct. of S.D., 1978—. Served with U.S. Army, 1957-59. Mem. Mennonite Brethren Ch. Home: 1516 E Sunset Dr Pierre SD 57501 Office: State Capitol Pierre SD 57501

WOLLSTADT, PAUL, petroleum cons.; b. Rockford, Ill., July 28, 1910; s. John and Hilda (Ekstrom) W.; A.B., U. Ill., 1932; m. Elzada Elizabeth Rogers, June 19, 1934 (dec. Apr. 1974); children—Roger Davis, David Carl, Loyd James; m. Elizabeth Peters, Apr. 25, 1975. Reporter, editorial writer, editor editorial page Rockford Register-Republic, 1932-45; mng. editor Nat. Petroleum News and Platt's Oilgram, 1945-51; asso. mgr. pub. relations dept. Mobil Oil Corp., 1951-58, asst. to chmn. 1958-59, v.p., 1959-62, sr. v.p., 1962-69; dep. asst. sec. def., 1969-71; petroleum industry cons., 1971—. Mem. Am. Petroleum Inst. Republican. Presbyn. Clubs: Internat., Nat. Press (Washington); Maplewood Country. Home: 77 Slope Dr Short Hills NJ 07078 Office: Suite 700 2101 L St Washington DC 20037. *Tell your boss and other business associates what you believe—not what you think they want to hear. Try to deal with each of the people with whom you work directly as an individual who is different from all other individuals in ability, energy, and career goals. Try to anticipate next year's problems and opportunities while working on this year's.*

WOLMA, FRED JOHN, JR., medical educator; b. Albuquerque, Dec. 10, 1916; s. Fred John and Marion Gertrude (Kittermann) W.; B.A., U. Tex., 1940, M.D., 1943; m. Dorothy Jean Egert, Nov. 19, 1943; children—Fred John III, Cynthia Ann. Intern, Med. Coll. Va., 1943-44, resident in surgery, 1947-48; resident U. Tex. Med. Branch, Galveston, 1948-51, faculty, 1951—, asso. prof., 1968-69, prof. surgery, 1969—, chief div. gen. surgery, 1968-70; cons. vascular surgery U.S. Pub. Health Hosp., Galveston, 1967—, St. Marys Hosp., Galveston, 1951—; attending surgeon U. Tex. Med. Branch Hosps., 1951—. Served to lt. comdr. USNR, 1944-46. Mem. A.C.S., Am. Assn. for Surgery of Trauma, Southwestern Surg. Congress, Tex., So., Western surg. socs., A.M.A., Soc. Surgery Alimentary Tract, Tex. Med. Assn., Sigma Xi, Alpha Omega Alpha. Episcopalian. Author: Intravenous Abdominal Aertography and Placentography, 1967; also films, articles. Home: 4404 Sherman St Galveston TX 77550

WOLMAN, ABEL, san. engr.; b. Balt., June 10, 1892; s. Morris and Rose (Wachsman) W.; A.B., Johns Hopkins, 1913, B.S. in Engring., 1915; D.Engring., 1937; m. Anne Gordon, June 10, 1919; 1 son, Markley Gordon. Began as asst. engr. USPHS, 1914; chief engr. Dept. Health, 1922-39; lectr., prof. san. engring. Johns Hopkins Sch. Engring. and Sch. Hygiene and Pub. Health, also Harvard, Princeton, U. Chgo., other univs.; cons. engr. City Balt., Baltimore County, USPHS, TVA, U.S. Army, Seattle, Jacksonville, Fla.; cons., mem. adv. com. on reactor safety AEC. Chmn. permanent com. on san. engrs. Pan Am. San. Bur.; chmn. san. engring. com. Div. Med. Scis., NRC; cons. Assn. Am. R.R.'s, Bethlehem Steel Co., Detroit Met. Area, Miami Conservancy Dist.; adviser ARC; chmn. bd. tech. advisors Internat. Boundary and Water Commn. U.S. and Mex., 1976; chmn. Task Force on Population Migration City of Balt., 1977; mem. com. internat. health Inst. Medicine NIH, 1978. Recipient Lasker award, 1960, Nat. medal Sci., 1975; Tyler Ecology award, 1976. Mem. ASCE, Am. Water Works Assn. (pres. 1942), Am. Pub. Health Assn. (pres. 1939), AAAS, Faraday Soc. (Eng.), Royal Inst. Pub. Health (Eng.), Nat. Acad. Scis., Nat. Acad. Engring. Home: 3213 N Charles St Baltimore MD 21218 Address: Johns Hopkins U 209 Ames Hall Baltimore MD 21218

WOLMAN, J. MARTIN, newspaper publisher; b. Elizabeth, N.J., Mar. 8, 1919; s. Joseph D. and Dora (Baum) W.; student U. Wis., 1937-42; m. Anne Paley, Sept. 12, 1943; children—Natalie, Jonathan, Ruth Ellen, Lewis Joel. With Wis. State Jour., Madison, 1936—, pub., 1968—; pres., gen. mgr., dir. Madison Newspaper, Inc., 1969—; dir. Lee Enterprises, Inc., 1971-74; sec.-treas. Madison Improvement Corp., 1958-62. Treas., Wis. State Jour. Empty Stocking Club, 1948, Children and Youth Services Inc., 1962—; mem. Mayor Madison Adv. Com., 1965; bd. dirs. United Givers Fund, 1960-64; ex-officio Roy L. Matson Scholarship Fund, 1961, Central Madison Com., Madison Art Assn.; trustee Edgewood Coll., Madison, Univ. Hosp., Madison; bd. dirs. Univ. Health Sci. Center, Madison, 1975. Served with AUS, 1942-46. Named Advt. Man of Year, Madison Advt. Club, 1969, Madison Man of Achievement, 1976. Mem. Madison C. of C. (dir. 1966-70, 74—), Inland Daily Press Assn. (dir. 1961-65), Wis. Daily Newspaper League (pres. 1961-65), Wis. Newspaper Assn. (dir. 1977). Clubs: B'nai B'rith, Madison. Office: 1901 Fish Hatchery Rd Madison WI 53708

WOLMAN, M. GORDON, educator; b. Balt., Aug. 16, 1924; s. Abel and Anna (Gordon) W.; student Haverford Coll.; A.B. in Geology, Johns Hopkins, 1949; M.A. in Geology, Harvard, 1951, Ph.D., 1953; m. Elaine Mielke, June 20, 1951; children—Elsa Anne, Abel Gordon, Abby Lucille, Fredericka Jeannette. Geologist, U.S. Geol. Survey, 1951-58, part-time, 1958—; asso. prof. geography Johns Hopkins, Balt., 1958-62, prof., 1962—, chmn. dept. geography and environ. engring., 1958—. Mem. adv. com. geography U.S. Office Naval Research; mem. exec. com. Div. Earth Sci., NRC, mem. com. internat. environ. programs, mem. environ. studies bd.; mem. com. water Nat. Acad. Sci.; mem. exec. com. Earth Sci. div., Nat. Acad. Scis., mem. com. mineral resources and environment, chmn. nat. commn. water quality policy; cons. in field to City of Balt., Balt. County, State of Md. Mem. Balt. City Charter Revision Commn.; mem. Community Action Com., Balt. Trustee Park Sch., Balt., Sinai Hosp., Balt.; pres. bd. Resources for Future. Served with USNR, 1943-46. Recipient Meritorious Contribution award Assn. Am. Geographers, 1972. Mem. Am. Geophys. Union (chmn. subcom. sedimentation, pres. hydrol. sect.), Geol. Soc. Am. (councilor 1976-79), Washington Geol. Soc., ASCE, Am. Hist. Soc., Am. Geog. Soc. (councilor 1965-70), Assn. Am. Geographers, Phi Beta Kappa, Sigma Xi, Md. Acad. Scis. (mem. exec. com.). Author: Fluvial Processes in Geomorphology, 1964. Editorial bd. Science mag. Home: 2104 W Rogers Ave Baltimore MD 21209

WOLOHAN, RICHARD VINCENT, lumber co. exec.; b. Saginaw, Mich., Oct. 9, 1915; s. Charles John and Anna (O'Brien) W.; ed. pvt. sch., Birch Run, Mich.; m. Angela Marie Phoenix, Feb. 3, 1942; children—Richard P., Mary K., Patricia A., Sharon L., James L., Christine M., Michael J. Br. mgr., treas. Charles Wolohan, Inc., 1932-50, mgr. Wickes Corp., Saginaw, 1950-52 div. pres., gen. mgr. Wickes Lumber Co., Saginaw, 1952-64; pres. Wolohan Lumber Co., Saginaw, 1964-77, chmn. bd., 1977—; dir. 2d Nat. Corp., 2d Nat. Bank, A.C.E. Corp., Redford, Mich. Bd. dirs. Profit Sharing Council Am., Chgo.; trustee Profit Sharing Research Found. Served with U.S. Army, 1942-43. Mem. Pres's. Assn. Clubs: Serra, Saginaw Country, Saginaw, Hidden Valley. Office: 1740 Midland Rd Saginaw MI 48603

WOLPE, HOWARD ELIOT, congressman; b. Los Angeles, Nov. 2, 1939; s. Leon Zachariah and Zelda Harriett (Shapiro) W.; B.A., Reed Coll., 1960; Ph.D., M.I.T., 1967; m. Celia Jeanene Taylor, Feb. 9, 1963; 1 son, Michael Stevenson. Asso. prof. polit. sci. Western Mich. U., 1967-72; mem. Kalamazoo City Commn., 1969-72; mem. Mich. State Legislature, 1973-76; regional rep. to U.S. Senator Donald Riegle of Mich., 1977-78; mem. 96th Congress from 3d dist. Mich. Office: 416 Cannon Bldg Washington DC 20515

WOLPER, DAVID LLOYD, motion picture and TV exec.; b. N.Y.C., Jan. 11, 1928; s. Irving S. and Anna (Fass) W.; student Drake U., 1946, U. So. Calif., 1949; m. Margaret Dawn Richard, May 11, 1958; children—Mark, Michael, Leslie; m. 2d, Gloria Hill, June 11, 1974. Vice pres., treas. Flamingo Films, TV sales co., 1948-50, v.p., 1954-58; v.p. charge West coast ops. Motion Pictures for TV, 1950-54; chmn. bd., pres. Wolper Prodns., Los Angeles, 1958—; pres. Fountainhead Internat., 1960—, Wolper TV Sales Co., 1964—; v.p., chmn. bd. Metromedia, Inc., 1965-68; pres., chmn. bd. Wolper Pictures, Ltd., 1968—, Wolper Prodns., Inc., 1968—; cons. Warner Bros., Inc.; TV prodns. include Biography, The Story of, Hollywood and the Stars, Men in Crisis, Race for Space, Project: Man in Space, The Rafer Johnson Story, Biography of a Rookie, Hollywood: The Golden Years, Hollywood: The Fabulous Era, Hollywood: The Great Stars, D-Day, Escape to Freedom, The Making of the President 1960, 1964, 68, The Yanks Are Coming, Berlin: Kaiser to Khrushchev, December 7: Day of Infamy, The American Woman in the 20th Century, The Rise and Fall of American Communism, Legend of Marilyn Monroe, Four Days in November, Krebiozen and Cancer, Nat. Geog. Series, Undersea World of Jacques Cousteau Series, China: Roots of Madness, The Journey of Robert F. Kennedy, Say Goodbye, George Plimpton series, Appointment with Destiny, American Heritage, Smithsonian Spls., They've Killed President Lincoln, Sandburg's Lincoln, Primal Man, The First Woman President, Chico and the Man, Get Christie Love, Welcome Back, Kotter, Collision Course, Roots; Roots: The Next Generations; feature films include: The Devil's Brigade, The Bridge at Remagen, If It's Tuesday, This Must be Belgium, I Love My Wife, Wattstax, Visions of Eight, Birds Do It, Bees Do It, Willy Wonka and the Chocolate Factory, The Hellstrom Chronicle; TV movies include the Morning After, Unwed Father, Men of the Dragon. Chmn. bd. dirs. Los Angeles Dodger Baseball Museum; bd. dirs. Cedars of Lebanon-Mt. Sinai Hosp., Thalina Clinic Emotionally Disturbed Children; founder-mem. Hollywood Mus.; chmn. Pres.'s Advisory Council to Am. Revolution Bicentennial

Adminstrn.; mem. Los Angeles Olympic Organizing Com. Recipient award for documentaries San Francisco Internat. Film Festival, 1960, Golden Mike award Am. Legion, 1963, George Foster Peabody award, 1963, Distinguished Service award U.S. Jr. C. of C., 1963, 28 Emmy awards, 93 nominations Nat. Acad. TV Arts and Scis., award Monte Carlo Internat. Film Festival, 1964, Grand Prix for TV program Cannes Film Festival, 1964, 71, Oscar award, 11 nominations Acad. Motion Picture Arts and Scis. Mem. Nat. Acad. TV Arts and Scis., Screen Producers Guild, Am. Rocket Soc., Writers Guild Am., Manuscript Soc. Am. Home: 10847 Bellagio Rd Los Angeles CA 90024 Office: care Warner Bros Inc 4000 Warner Blvd Burbank CA 91522

WOLPER, MARSHALL, ins. cons.; b. Chgo., Nov. 19, 1922; s. Harry B. and Bessie (Steiner) W.; B.A. in Polit. Sci. and Econs., U. Ill., 1942; m. Thelma R. Freedman, April 15, 1957 (div. Oct. 1968); m. 2d, Jacqueline N. Miller, Sept. 19, 1969 (div. Jan. 1976). With Kent Products, Chgo., 1946; pres. Marshall Industries, Chgo., 1947-52; with Equitable Life Assurance Soc., 1953—, nat. honor agt., 1966, nat. sales cons. 1967—; sr. partner Wolper & Katz, 1958—; partner Wolper and Katz Thoroughbred Racing Stable, 1977—; instr. life underwriting and pensions U. Miami, 1959—; pres. Marshall Wolper Co., 1963—; chmn. bd. M.W. Computer Systems, Inc., 1971—; pres. Marshall Wolper Pension Sers. Inc., 1978—; lectr. life ins., employee benefit plans, pensions, estate planning to various univs. and spl. meetings; pres. Greater Miami Tax Inst., 1963, Estate Planning Council Greater Miami, 1969-70; faculty Practicing Law Inst., 1967—; mem. adv. com., lectr. Inst. on Estate Planning. Bd. dirs. Dade County chpt. A.R.C., Profl. Selling Inst. Served to 1st lt. AUS, World War II; ETO. Decorated Bronze Star medal, Purple Heart; recipient Paragon award Equitable Life Assurance Soc., 1972; C.L.U. Mem. Am. Soc. C.L.U.'s (pres. Miami chpt. 1963, inst. faculty 1963-65, dir. 1966-67, regional v.p. 1968), Am. Coll. Life Underwriters (joint com. on continuing edn. 1965—), Nat. Assn. Life Underwriters (lectr. 1963-66), Million Dollar Round Table (life, speaker 1962, 64, 65, 69, exec. com., pres. 1977), Assn. Advanced Life Underwriting (lectr. 1966, pres. 1972), Am. Soc. Pension Actuaries (dir.), Nat. Assn. Pension Consultants and Adminstrs. (treas.). Author: Medical Entities Taxed as Corporations, 1961; Tax and Business Aspects of Professional Corporations and Associations, 1968. Contbr. articles to profl. jours. Home: 714 W DiLido Dr Miami Beach FL 33139 Office: 444 Brickell Ave Miami FL 33131

WOLPERT, EDWARD ALAN, psychiatrist; b. Chgo., Apr. 22, 1930; s. Sol and Dorothy (Greenwald) W.; B.A., U. Chgo., 1950, M.A., 1954, Ph.D., 1959, M.D., 1960; m. Gloria Adele Yanoff, Mar. 23, 1958; children—Seth Isaac, Andrew Oxman, Edward Greenwald. Intern medicine U. Ill. Research Hosp., 1960-61; resident psychiatry Michael Reese Hosp., 1961-64, dir. clin. services Psychosomatic and Psychiat. Inst., 1966-79, dir. of hosp., 1979—; clin. asso. prof. psychiatry Pritzker Sch. Medicine, U. Chgo., 1972-76, clin. prof. psychiatry, 1976—; cons. Sonia Shankman Orthogenic Sch., 1973—. Diplomate Am. Bd. Neurology and Psychiatry. Fellow Am. Psychiat. Assn.; mem. AMA, Ill., Chgo. med. socs., Ill. Psychiat. Soc. (exec. council, AAAS, Am. Psychoanalytic Assn. (certified in psychoanalysis), Assn. for Psychophysiol. Study of Sleep, Am. Psychol. Assn., N.Y. Acad. Scis., George S. Klein Meml. Psychoanalytic Research Forum, Am. Soc. for Clin. Pharmacology and Therapeutics, Chgo. Psychoanalytic Soc. Asso., Inst. Medicine Chgo., Wis. Acad. Arts, Letters and Scis. (asso.). Editor: Internat. Jour. of Psychoanalytic Psychotherapy, 1974-79; contbr. articles to profl. jours. Home: 727 Elmwood Wilmette IL 60091 Office: Michael Reese Hosp and Med Center 2959 S Ellis Ave Chicago IL 60616

WOLPERT, JULIAN, univ. adminstr., geographer; b. N.Y.C., Dec. 26, 1932; s. Harry and Rose W.; A.B., Columbia Coll., 1953; M.S. in Geography, U. Wis., 1954, Ph.D., 1963; m. Eileen R. Selig, Sept. 11, 1955; children—Seth, Jesse, Joshua, Rebekah. Asst. prof. geography and regional sci. U. Pa., 1963-65, asso. prof., 1966-68, prof., 1969-73; Henry G. Bryant prof. geography, public affairs and urban planning Woodrow Wilson Sch. and Sch. Architecture and Urban Planning, Princeton U., 1973—, dir. undergrad. program Woodrow Wilson Sch., 1977-79, dir. urban planning program, 1979—; cons. in field. Served with USN, 1955-59. Mem. Assn. Am. Geographers (pres. 1973-74), Am. Geog. Soc. (v.p. 1977-79), Nat. Acad. Scis. Office: Woodrow Wilson Sch Princeton U Princeton NJ 08540

WOLPERT, STANLEY ALBERT, educator, historian, author; b. Bklyn., Dec. 23, 1927; s. Nathan and Frances (Gittelson) W.; A.M., U. Pa., 1955, Ph.D., 1959; B.A., Coll. City N.Y., 1953; m. Dorothy Guberman, June 12, 1953; children—Daniel, Adam. Mem. faculty U. Calif. at Los Angeles, 1958—, prof. history, 1967—, chmn. dept., 1967-70; vis. asso. prof. U. Pa., summers 1964, 65. Recipient Pell medal Coll. City N.Y., 1953; Watumull prize Am. Hist. Assn., 1963; Ford Found. overseas tng. and research fellow, 1953-55, 57-58; Am. Council Learned Socs.-Social Sci. Research Council S. Asia area fellow, 1962-63. Mem. Am. Hist. Assn., Assn. Asian Studies, Am. Oriental Soc., Phi Beta Kappa, Phi Alpha Theta. Author: (fiction) Aboard the Flying Swan, 1954; Nine Hours to Rama, 1962; The Expedition, 1968; An Error of Judgement, 1970; (non-fiction) Tilak and Gokhale, 1962; Morley and India, 1906-1910, 1967; India, 1965; A New History of India, 1977.

WOLTER, ALLAN BERNARD, educator; b. Peoria, Ill., Nov. 24, 1913; s. Bernard Gregory and Marianne (Strub) W.; B.A., Our Lady of Angels Franciscan Sem., 1937; M.A., Cath. U. Am., 1942, Ph.D., 1947; Lector Generalis Franciscan Inst. St. Bonaventure U., 1952; D.Sc., Quincy Coll., 1967. Ordained priest Roman Cath. Ch., 1940; asst. prof. chemistry, biology, philosophy Our Lady of Angels Franciscan Sem., Cleve., 1943-45; asso. prof. philosophy Franciscan Inst. St. Bonaventure U., 1946-52, prof., 1952-62; vis. prof. Cath. U. Am., 1962-63, prof., 1963—; research asso. Center Medieval and Renaissance Studies, UCLA, 1978-80. Editor, Franciscan Inst. Publs., Philosophy Series, 1946-62, Franciscan Studies, 1949-52, Quincy Coll. Publs., 1964—; vis. lectr. Princeton U., 1965; vis. prof. U. Mich., 1967, N.Y. U., 1969, UCLA, 1978; exchange prof. Am. U., 1970. Sr. fellow Nat. Endowment for Humanities, 1973-74. Mem. Am., Am. Cath. philos. assns., Philosophy Sci. Assn., Metaphys. Soc. Am., Mind Assn., AAAS. Author: The Transcendentals and Their Function in the Metaphysics of Duns Scotus, 1946; Book of Life, 1954; Summula Metaphysicae, 1958; Life in God's Love, 1958; Duns Scotus: Philosophical Writings, 1960; John Duns Scotus: A Treatise on God as First Principle, 1966; (with J.F. Wippel Medieval Philosophy: From Augustine to Ockham, 1969; (with F. Alluntis) John Duns Scotus: God and Creatures, 1975. Office: Sch Philosophy Catholic U Am Washington DC 20064

WOLTER, JURGEN REIMER, physician, educator; b. Halstenbek, Germany, May 9, 1924; s. Claus Henry and Wiebke Maria (Peters) W.; M.D., U. Hamburg (Germany), 1949; m. Lieselotte Schlote, Oct. 19, 1952; children—Klaus H., W. Maria, Jan D., Niels R. Came to U.S., 1953, naturalized, 1959. Intern, resident U. Hamburg Med. Sch.; faculty U. Mich. Med. Sch., 1956—, prof. ophthalmology, 1964—; chief, eye service VA Hosp., Ann Arbor, Mich., 1962—. Mem. AMA, Assn. Research Ophthalmology, Mich. Med. Soc., Am. Ophthal. Soc., Sigma Xi. Editor: Jour. Pediatric Ophthalmology, 1967—; editorial bd. Graefe's Archiv Ophthal., 1976. Contbr. articles to profl. jours. Home: 2565 Bedford St Ann Arbor MI 48104

WOLTERINK, LESTER FLOYD, biophysicist, educator; b. Marion, N.Y., July 28, 1915; s. John and Ruth Lavina (Voorhorst) W.; A.B., Hope Coll., 1936; M.A., U. Minn., 1940, Ph.D., 1943; m. Lillian Ruth Nichols, June 30, 1938; children—Charles Paul, Timothy John. Faculty Mich. State U., East Lansing, 1941—, prof. physiology, 1952—; asso. scientist AEC, Argonne Nat. Lab., 1948; cons., then biosatellit project scientist Ames Research Center, NASA, 1963-66. Mem. various coms. AEC Conf. on Isotopes in Plant and Animal Research, 1952-59; mem. NASA Manned Space Sta. Commn., 1966; cons. NSF, 1967-70; mem. panel on nitrogen oxides Nat. Acad. Sci./NRC, 1973-75. Mem. Mich. Nucleonic Soc. (pres. 1961), Soc. Exptl. Biology and Medicine (sec. Mich. sect. 1961-63), Am. Astronautic Soc. (chmn. San Francisco sect. 1966), Am. Acad. Mechanics, AAUP, Am. Inst. Biol. Scis., Am. Physiol. Soc., Am. Soc. Zoologists, IEEE, Biomed. Engring. Soc., Biophys. Soc., Ecol. Soc. Am., Explorers Club, Sigma Xi (jr. scientist Mich. State U. 1954). Club: Torch. Contbr. articles to profl. publs., reports to govt. agys. Home: 221 Spartan Ave East Lansing MI 48823 Office: Dept Physiology Mich State U East Lansing MI 48824

WOLTERSTORFF, ROBERT MUNRO, bishop; b. St. Paul, Aug. 29, 1914; s. Frederick William and Genevieve Parker (Munro) W.; B.A., St. Ambrose Coll., 1937; Th.L., Seabury-Western Theol. Sem., 1940, D.D., 1966, Ch. Div. Sch. of the Pacific, 1978; m. Helen Elvida Seeger Fellows, Jan. 4, 1947; 4 children. Ordained priest Episcopal Ch., 1941; deacon-in-charge Messiah Ch., St. Paul, 1940-41, rector, 1941-55; asso. rector St. James Ch., La Jolla, Calif., 1955-57; rector St. James-by-the-Sea Ch., La Jolla, 1957-74; first bishop of San Diego, 1974—; chaplain/instr. Breck Sch., Minn., 1942-49; chaplain Macalester Coll., St. Paul, 1948-51; youth adviser Diocese of Minn., 1949-52; mem. nat. youth commn., 1950-53. Exec. Council Episcopal Ch., 1979—; v.p. community service com. Diocese of San Diego, 1957-61, chmn. bd., 1969—; chaplain Scripps Meml. Hosp., 1967-70; mem. Joint Com. on Constn. and Canons of Gen. Conv., 1976—. Bd. dirs. Episc. Theol. Sem., Claremont, Calif., 1974—, Seabury-Western Theol. Sem., 1953-55, 73—; bd. dirs. Bishops Sch., 1959—, chmn. bd., 1974—; v.p. bd. dirs. Scripps Meml. Hosp., 1968-73. Office: 2728 6th Ave San Diego CA 92103

WOLTZ, CHARLES KILLIAN, educator; b. Salem, Va., July 10, 1914; s. Maxwell Farrar and Irma (Killian) W.; B.A., U. Va., 1934, LL.B., 1937; m. Dawn Rosalie Daniel, Nov. 27, 1942; children—Robin Barclay, Dabney Killian, Charlotte Farrar. Admitted to Va. bar, 1937; practice in Richmond, 1937-47; asso. Christian, Barton & Parker, 1937-41, partner, 1946-47; asso. prof. law U. Va., Charlottesville, 1947-52, prof., 1952—, asst. dean Law Sch., 1949-52, Doherty prof., 1967—; reporter Va. Supreme Ct. Appeals, 1953-67. Mem. Albemarle County Sch. Bd., 1952-56; pres. Va. Sch. Bd. Assn., 1955. Mem. gen. assembly Nat. Council Chs. Christ U.S.A., 1955-56. Trustee Marion Coll. Served to capt. AUS, 1941-46. Decorated Bronze Star medal. Mem. Va. Bar Assn. (exec. com. 1965-68), Va. Hist. Soc., Am. Boxwood Soc., Albemarle County Hist. Soc. (pres. 1972-74), Order of Coif, Phi Beta Kappa, Omega Delta Kappa, Phi Delta Phi, Raven Soc. Democrat. Lutheran (exec. council Luth. Ch. Am. 1968-70). Home: 1645 Keith Valley Rd Charlottesville VA 22901

WOLVERTON, ROBERT EARL, univ. adminstr.; b. Indpls., Aug. 4, 1925; s. Robert N. and Vivian (Lefflar) W.; A.B., Hanover Coll., 1948; M.A., U. Mich., 1949; Ph.D., U. N.C., 1954; Litt.D., Coll. Mt. St. Joseph on the Ohio, 1977; m. Margaret Jester, Sept. 13, 1952; children—Robert Earl, Laurie Ann, Edwin J., Gary A. Asst. prof. classics U. Ga., 1954-59; asst. prof. classics, history Tufts U., 1959-62; asst. prof., asso. prof. classics, dir. honors program Fla. State U., 1962-67; asso. prof. classics, asso. dean U. Ill. Grad. Coll., 1967-69; dean Grad. Sch. and Research, prof. classics Miami U., Oxford, Oxford, 1969-72; pres., prof. classics Coll. Mt. St. Joseph on Ohio, Cin., 1972-77; v.p. for academic affairs, prof. classics Miss. State U., 1977—. Fellow Acad. Adminstrn. Internship Program, 1965-66; field reader U.S. Office Edn.; cons., reviewer N.Central Assn. Colls. and Schs. Mem. exec. com. Council Grad. Schs. U.S., 1970-73; chmn. Midwest Conf. Grad. Study and Research, 1971; mem. Regents Adv. Com. Grad. Edn. Ohio, 1969—, chmn., 1971-72; mem. Medford (Mass.) Edn. Council, 1961-62; pres. Council of Laity, St. Marys of Oxford, 1969-70; v.p. Starkville Community Theatre, 1978-79; pres. St. Joseph Ch. Parish Council, 1979. Trustee, v.p. Greater Cin. Consortium Colls. and Univs., St. Francis Hosp., Ohio, Cin. councils on econ. edn. Mem. Am. Classical League (pres. 1972-76), Am. Philol. Assn., Classical Assn. Middle West and South, Vergilian Soc., Am. Assn. Higher Edn., Assn. Ind. Colls. and Univs. Ohio (sec. 1973-75, vice chmn. 1975-77), Council Basic Edn., Acad. Polit. Sci., Ohio Program in Humanities, Sigma Chi, Omicron Delta Kappa, Eta Sigma Phi, Phi Kappa Phi. Author: Classical Elements in English Words, 1965; An Outline of Classical Mythology, 1966; contbg. translator A Life of George Washington in Latin Prose (Francis Glass), 1976. Editor: (with others) Graduate Programs and Admissions Manual, 1971, 72. Contbr. articles to profl. jours. Home: 108 Edinburgh Dr Starkville MS 39759

WOLVINGTON, WINSTON WARREN, judge; b. Denver, July 10, 1923; s. William T. and Bessie (Roberts) W.; A.B., Oberlin Coll., 1949; J.D., U. Mich., 1948; m. Shirley Anne Vail, Sept. 9, 1944; children—Gloria Jean (Mrs. James Hurdle), Judith Kay (Mrs. Richard Hampleman), Donald Edward, Glenn Winston. Admitted to Colo. bar, 1949; practiced in Denver, 1949-72; partner firm Wolvington, Dosh, Demoulin, Anderson & Campbell until 1973; judge 1st Jud. Dist., Golden, Colo., 1973—. Treas., Central Jeffco Democratic Club, 1968-71. Bd. dirs. Jefferson County Legal Aid Soc. Served to lt. (j.g.) USNR, 1943-46. Mem. Am. Judicature Soc., Am., Colo., Denver, 1st Jud. (trustee. v.p. 1968-69) bar assns. Mason. Home: 1391 S Winston Dr Golden CO 80401 Office: Hall of Justice Golden CO 80401

WOLZ, HENRY GEORGE, educator; b. Kornwestheim, Germany, Sept. 10, 1905; s. John and Catherin (Pflueger) W.; came to U.S., 1930; B.S., Fordham U., 1936, M.A., 1938, Ph.D., 1946; m. Barbara L. Dertwinkel, Mar. 20, 1955; 1 dau., Ursula. Columbia Coll., 1947, Tutor, Bklyn. Coll., 1947, Hunter Coll., 1947-49; asst. prof. Wagner Coll., 1947-51; asst. prof. Queens Coll., City U. N.Y., 1951-56, asso. prof., 1956-64, prof., 1964—. Served with AUS, 1942-45. Mem. Am. Philos. Assn., Metaphys. Soc. Am. Contbr. numerous articles to profl. jours. Home: 25 Ryan St Syosset NY 11791 Office: 65-30 Kissena Blvd Flushing NY 11367

WOMACH, EMILY HITCH, banker; b. Laurel, Del., Jan. 27, 1927; d. Elon G. and Jennie (Neal) Hitch; student Salisbury (Md.) Bus. Inst., 1948; grad. Sch. Financial Pub. Relations Northwestern U., 1957, Am. Inst. Banking, 1958, Stonier Grad. Sch. Banking, Rutgers U., 1968; m. William S. Womach, Mar. 13, 1943; 1 son, William Richard. With Sussex Trust Co., Laurel, 1945-68, sec., asst., cashier, 1956-62, asst. v.p., sec., 1962-67, v.p., sec. 1967-68; adminstrv. asst. to gov. Del., 1968-69; sales rep. Robinson Real Estate, 1969-71; treas. State of Del., 1971-73, also dir. div. treasury dept. finance; v.p., mem. sr. mgmt. Farmers Bank State Del., Wilmington, 1973-76; chmn. bd., pres., chief exec. officer Women's Nat. Bank, Washington, 1976—; mem. adv. bd. Weal Fund, 1978—; dir. Penjerdel Corp. Lectr. in field, 1958—; econ. commentator Spectrum on Economy, WCAV Radio, 1975-76; fin. cons. Past mem. nat. adv. council Small Bus. Adminstrn.; mem. Del. Bank Adv. Bd., 1963-71. Chmn. budget com., auditor Laurel League Women Voters, 1959-71; bd. dirs. Music at Noon, D.C. Performing Arts Soc., 1978—; mem. edn. com., also fund drive com. Delmarva Poultry Industry, 1963-66; mem. fin. com. Women's Nat. Democratic Club, 1977—; sec.-treas. Overall Econ. Devel. Program Com., 1967-71; mem. Del. State Small Bus. Adv. Council, 1965-71, Laurel Planning Commn., 1965-68; mem. D.C. Employment Security Bd., 1978—; v.p. Del. div. Am. Cancer Soc., 1964-68, mem. Del. exec. com. and bd., 1957-71, mem. Sussex County unit bd., 1957-71; bd. dirs. Nat. Capital Area region NCCJ, 1978—; chmn. Del. Heart Fund, 1972; bd. dirs., treas. Community Found. Greater Washington, 1978—; mem. adv. council The Women's Inst./Am. U., 1978—; trustee Wesley Coll., 1973—, Peninsula Ann. conf. United Meth. Ch., Peninsula United Homes and Hosps., Inc. Recipient Outstanding Woman Who Works award Downtown Assn. Memphis, 1964; named Outstanding Citizen of Laurel, 1965, award of merit Del. Fed. Bus. and Profl. Women's Club, 1966, others. Mem. Nat. Assn. Bank Women (v.p. Middle Atlantic div. 1960-61, nat. v.p. 1962-63, nat. pres. 1963-64), Am. Inst. Banking (pres. Sussex chpt. 1958-59), Am. (exec. com. savs. div. 1966-67, communication com. mktg. div. 1974-75, mem. adminstrv. com. govtl. relations council 1975-76), Del. (chmn. pub. relations com. 1959-63, vice chmn. legis. com.) bankers assns., Am. Newspaper Women's Club (asso.), Del. C. of C. (dir. 1974-76, Josiah Marvel cup award 1967), D.C. C. of C. (dir.), Bus. and Profl. Women's Club (pres. Laurel 1951), Soc. Internat. Devel., Internat. Platform Assn., Am. Acad. Polit. and Social Sci., Rehoboth Art League, Delta Kappa Gamma (hon.). Democrat. Methodist.

WOMACK, JOHN, JR., historian; b. Norman, Okla., Aug. 14, 1937; B.A., Harvard Coll., 1959, Ph.D. Harvard, 1965; Rhodes Scholar Oxford (Eng.) U., 1959-61; divorced; 1 dau., Liza Kathryn; m. 2d, Andrea M. Petersen, Oct. 25, 1969. Instr. history Harvard, 1965-68, asst. prof., 1968- 70, prof., 1970—; mag. reporter on Latin Am., 1968—. Nat. scholar Harvard, 1955-59, Bliss fellow, 1961-65. Mem. Phi Beta Kappa. Author: Zapata and the Mexican Revolution, 1969. Home: 22 Hancock St Cambridge MA 02139

WOMBLE, GEORGE MORGAN, life ins. co. exec.; b. Raleigh, N.C., Oct. 9, 1926; s. George Morgan and Dorothy Hempstead (Price) W.; J.D., Wake Forest U., 1950; grad. Advanced Mgmt. Program, Harvard U., 1975; m. Mary Phyllis Cowdery, Aug. 8, 1946; children—George M. III, Robert Byron, Elizabeth Vaughn. Admitted to N.C. bar, 1950; individual practice law Elizabeth City, N.C., 1950; with Durham Life Ins. Co., Raleigh, 1950—, gen. counsel, 1965-67, exec. v.p. adminstrn., 1967-75, sr. exec. v.p. ops., 1976-78; pres., chief exec. officer, 1978—, also dir.; dir. State Capital Ins. Co., Durham Life Broadcasting Service Inc. Chmn. admission and planning United Way Wake County, 1976-79, v.p., 1979—; bd. visitors Wake Forest U. Sch. Law, 1974—; elder, trustee W. Raleigh Presbyterian Ch., 1977—. Served with USAAF, 1945-46. Mem. N.C., Wake County bar assns., Raleigh C. of C. (dir. 1978—). Clubs: MacGregor Downs Country, Civitan (dir. local chpt.). Home: 2129 Coley Forest Pl Raleigh NC 27607 Office: 2610 Wycliff Rd Raleigh NC 27607

WOMBLE, WILLIAM FLETCHER, lawyer; b. Winston-Salem, N.C., Oct. 29, 1916; s. Bunyan Snipes and Edith (Willingham) W.; A.B., Duke, 1937, J.D., 1939; m. Jane Payne Gilbert, Oct. 11, 1941; children—William Fletcher, Jane (Mrs. Donald G. Haver), Russell G., Ann P. Admitted to N.C. bar, 1939; asso. firm Womble, Carlyle, Sandridge & Rice, and predecessors, 1939-47, partner, 1947—. Dir., Integon Corp. Mem. N.C. Gen. Statutes Commn., 1953-55, N.C. Bd. Higher Edn., 1955-57, 60-63, N.C. Adv. Budget Commn., 1957-58; campaign chmn. Forsyth County Community Chest, 1948. Mem. N.C. Ho. of Reps., 1953-58, chmn. com. on higher edn., 1957, vice chmn. finance com., 1957. Trustee, past chmn. High Point (N.C.) Coll., Winston-Salem Tchrs. Coll., 1953-55; past trustee, past pres. Children's Home; chmn. council for higher edn. Western N.C. Conf. United Methodist Ch., 1975-77; bd. dirs., treas. Triad United Meth. Home, 1975—. Served to maj. USAAF, 1941-46. Mem. Am. (del.), N.C. (pres. 1966-67), Forsyth County (pres. 1962) bar assns., Winston-Salem C. of C. (pres. 1960-61). Democrat. Methodist (steward, chmn. bd. 1961-63). Rotarian (pres. 1964). Clubs: Old Town, Twin City. Home: 2027 Virginia Rd Winston-Salem NC 27104 Office: Wachovia Bldg Winston-Salem NC 27101

WOMER, CHARLES BERRY, hosp. exec.; b. Cleve., Mar. 30, 1926; s. Porter Blake and Margaret (Berry) W.; M.S. in Hosp. Adminstrn., Columbia, 1953; B.S. in Mech. Engring., Case Inst. Tech., 1949; m. Elizabeth Benson, Oct. 7, 1950; children—Richard B., Carol E., John C. Asst. dir. Univ. Hosps., Cleve., 1957-61, asso. dir., 1961-65, pres., 1976—; adminstr. Yale-New Haven Hosp., 1965-67, dir., 1968-76, pres., 1976; lectr. Yale. Mem. Conn. Commn. on Hosps. and Health Care, 1973-76. Bd. govs. U. New Haven, 1972-76. Served with AUS, 1944-46. Fellow Am. Coll. Hosp. Adminstrs.; mem. Am. (chmn. council on mgmt. and planning, 1977—, Conn. (trustee 1970-74, pres. 1972-73, Distinguished Service award 1976) hosp. assns., Assn. Am. Med. Colls. (exec. council 1974-77, treas. 1975-76, chmn. 1979-80, adminstrv. bd. council teaching hosps. 1972-77, chmn. 1975-76). Home: 195 Aspenwood Dr Moreland Hills OH 44022 Office: 2065 Adelbert Rd Cleveland OH 44106

WOMMACK, WILLIAM WALTON, mfg. co. exec.; b. Winston-Salem, N.C., Dec. 12, 1922; s. Sidney LaMar and Ada (Culler) W.; B.Chem. Engring, N.C. State Coll., 1943; M.B.A., Harvard U., 1948; m. Jean Emery, Sept. 14, 1951; children—Judith J., Kent W., Lynne E., Mary E. Engr. thru div. controller Libbey-Owens-Ford, Toledo, 1948; treas., controller Ottawa River Paper Co., Toledo, 1955-58; asst. gen. mgr. Mead. Corp., Cin., 1958-64, v.p. bd., Dayton, Ohio, 1964-65, group v.p. bd., 1965-69, exec. v.p., 1969-72, vice chmn. bd., 1972—, also dir.; dir. 1st Nat. Bank Cin., Robbins & Myers, Inc., Clark Equipment Co. Served to lt. USNR, 1943-46. Office: Mead World Hdqrs Courthouse Plaza NE Dayton OH 45463

WONDER, JOHN PAUL, educator; b. Long Beach, Calif., July 29, 1921; s. John Paul and Etta (Jones) W.; A.B., Stanford, 1943, A.M., 1948, Ph.D., 1952; Exchange scholar Universidad Central, Madrid, 1950-51; m. Jane Josephine Walder, Dec. 22, 1946; children—John Walder, Peter Charles. Grad. fellow Stanford, 1946-50; instr., asst. prof. Spanish, U. Ariz., 1951-56; dir. Binational Center, Belo Horizonte, Brazil with USIA, also Rio de Janeiro and Port-au-Prince, Haiti, 1956-62; asst. prof. Los Angeles State Coll., 1962-63; prof. Spanish, U. Pacific, Stockton, Calif., 1963—, chmn. dept. modern langs., 1964-75. Served as 1st lt., arty. M.I., AUS, 1943-46; ETO. Mem. Alpha Tau Omega. Author: (with Aurelio M. Espinosa, Jr.) Gramática Analítica, 1976. Home: 660 W Euclid St Stockton CA 95204

WONDER, STEVIE (STEVLAND MORRIS), singer, musician, composer; b. Saginaw, Mich., May 13, 1950; student pub. schs. in Detroit until age 12, then transferred to Mich. Sch. for Blind; m. Syreeta Wright, 1971 (div. 1972); m. 2d, Yolanda Simmons; children—Aisha, Keita. Solo singer Whitestone Bapt. Ch., Detroit,

1959; rec. artist with Motown Records, Detroit, 1963-70; founder, pres. music pub. co. Black Bull Music, Inc., 1970—; recs. include Fingertips, 1963, Uptight/Purple Raindrops, 1965, Someday At Christmas/The Miracles of Christmas, 1966, I'm Wondering/Everytime I See You I Go Wild, 1966, I Was Made To Love Her/Hold Me, 1967, Shoo-Be-Doo-Be-Doo-Da-Day/Why Don't You Lead Me To Love, 1968, You Met Your Match/My Girl, 1968, For Once In My Life, I Don't Know Why, My Cherie Amour, Yester-Me, Yester-You, Yesterday, Never Had a Dream Come True, Signed, Sealed, Delivered I'm Yours, Heaven Help Us All, I Wish (Grammy award 1977), Don't You Worry 'Bout a Thing, You Haven't Done Nothin', Boogie on Reggae Woman (Grammy award 1975), Isn't She Lovely, Sir Duke, Another Star, As, You Are The Sunshine of My Life (Grammy award 1974), Superstition (Grammy award 1974), Higher Ground, Living For the City (Grammy award 1975); albums recorded include 12 Year Old Genius, Tribute To Uncle Ray, Jazz Soul, With A Song In My Heart, Signed Sealed & Delivered, My Cherie Amour, At The Beach, Uptight, 1966, Down To Earth, 1966, I Was Made To Love Her, 1967, Someday At Christmas, 1967, Stevie Wonder's Greatest Hits, 1968, Music of My Mind, 1972, Innervisions (Grammy award 1974), 1973, Fulfillingness' First Finale (Grammy award 1975), Songs In the Key of Life (Grammy award 1977), 1976, Stevie Wonder Live, Where I'm Coming From, 1972, Talking Book, 1972, Journey Through the Secret Life of Plants, 1979; appeared films: Bikini Beach, 1964, Muscle Beach Party, 1964; frequent TV appearances include: Ed Sullivan Show, American Band Stand, Shivaree, Flip Wilson Show, Symphonic Soul, Mike Douglas Show, others. Named Musician of Year, Down Beat mag. Rock/Blues Poll, 1973-75, 77-78; Best Selling Male Soul Artist of Year, Nat. Assn. Rec. Merchandisers, 1974; recipient numerous Grammy awards also numerous awards for best singer/songwriter; Rock Music award, 1977, Am. Music award, 1978. Address: care Keith Harris 6255 Sunset Blvd Suite 1700 Los Angeles CA 90028

WONDER, STEVIE (STEVLAND MORRIS), singer, musician, composer; b. Saginaw, Mich., May 13, 1950; student pub. schs. in Detroit until age 12, then transferred to Mich. Sch. for Blind; m. Syreeta Wright, 1971 (div. 1972); m. 2d, Yolanda Simmons; 1 dau., Aisha Zakia. Solo singer Whitestone Bapt. Ch., Detroit, 1959; rec. artist with Motown Records, Detroit, 1963-70; founder music pub. co. Black Bull, 1970; recs. include Fingertips, 1963, Uptight/Purple Raindrops, 1965, Someday At Christmas/The Miracles of Christmas, 1966, I'm Wondering/Everytime I See You I Go Wild, 1966, I Was Made To Love Her/Hold Me, 1967, Shoo-Be-Doo-Be-Doo-Da-Day/Why Don't You Lead Me To Love, 1968, You Met Your Match/My Girl, 1968, For Once in My Life, I Don't Know Why, My Cherie Amour, Yester-Me, Yester-You, Yesterday, Never Had a Dream Come True, Signed, Sealed, Delivered I'm Yours, Heaven Help Us All, I Wish (Grammy award 1977), Don't You Worry 'Bout a Thing, You Haven't Done Nothin', Boogie on Reggae Woman (Grammy award 1975), Isn't She Lovely, Sir Duke, Another Star, As, You Are The Sunshine of My Life (Grammy award 1974), Superstition (Grammy award 1974), Higher Ground, Living For the City (Grammy award 1975); albums recorded include 12 Year Old Genius, Tribute To Uncle Ray, Jazz Soul, With A Song In My Heart, Signed Sealed & Delivered, My Cherie Amour, At The Beach, Uptight, 1966, Down To Earth, 1966, I Was Made To Love Her, 1967, Someday At Christmas, 1967, Stevie Wonder's Greatest Hits, 1968, Music of My Mind, 1972, Innervisions (Grammy award 1974), 1973, Fulfillingness' First Finale (Grammy award 1975), Songs in the Key of Life (Grammy award 1977), 1976, Stevie Wonder Live, Where I'm Coming From, 1972, Talking Book, 1972, Journey Through the Secret Life of Plants, 1979; appeared films: Bikini Beach, 1964, Muscle Beach Party, 1964; frequent TV appearances include: Ed Sullivan Show, American Band Stand, Shivaree, Flip Wilson Show, Symphonic Soul, Mike Douglas Show, others. Named Musician of Year, Down Beat mag. Rock/Blues Poll, 1973-75, 77-78; Best Selling Male Soul Artist of Year, Nat. Assn. Rec. Merchandisers, 1974; recipient numerous Grammy awards also numerous awards for best singer/songwriter; Rock Music award, 1977, Am. Music award, 1978. Address: care Chris Jonz 6255 Sunset Blvd 17th Floor Los Angeles CA 90028

WONG, CURTIS F., editor, publisher; b. Los Angeles, Nov. 21, 1949; s. Bing and Mary (Chinn) W.; student Woodbury Coll., 1968-71, Los Angeles Art Center Coll. Design, 1971. Owner, founder Sil Lum Kung-Fu Schs., Panorama City, Calif., 1972—, Inside Kung-Fu mag., Hollywood, Calif., 1972—, Mantis Supplies Co., Hollywood, 1972—; owner, pub. Racquetball Illus. mag., Hollywood, 1978—. Mem. Am. Athletic Union, Screen Actors Guild, Chinese C. of C. Office: 7011 Sunset Blvd Hollywood CA 90028

WONG, EDWIN SAU NIN, business exec.; b. Honolulu, Aug. 26, 1929; s. A.F. and Helen A.H. (Tom) W.; B.A., U. Hawaii, 1951; M.P.A., Syracuse U., 1956; m. Sheila Sumiko Sonoda, June 16, 1951; children—Michael Allen, Patrick Scott, Carrie Jean, Maureen Ellen. Labor relations negotiator Hawaii Employers Council, Honolulu, 1961-63; indsl. relations mgr. Matson Nav. Co., Honolulu, 1963-66, v.p. indsl. relations, from 1966, later v.p. mktg., sales, v.p. Hawaiian Freight Service, San Francisco, to 1970; v.p. indsl. relations Alexander & Baldwin, Inc., Honolulu, 1970-74, sr. v.p. adminstrn., 1974—; dir. Waterhouse Properties, Inc., Imua Builders, Inc., Kahului Trucking & Storage, Inc., McBryde Sugar Co., Ltd., Wailea Land Corp. Trustee Blood Bank of Hawaii, 1975—, pres., 1979; bd. dirs. Hawaii Med. Service Assn., 1979—, Rehab. Hosp. of Pacific; active Boy Scouts Am. Served with Airborne Inf., U.S. Army, 1951-55. Mem. Hawaii Ednl. Council, Hawaii Employers Council, Hawaii Joint Council for Econ. Edn., Hawaiian Sugar Planters Assn., Indsl. Relations Research Assn., Hawaii C. of C. (dir., chmn. 1978). Episcopalian. Clubs: Oahu Country, Waialae Country, Plaza. Office: Alexander & Baldwin Inc 822 Bishop St Honolulu HI 96813

WONG, KUANG CHUNG, anesthesiologist, educator; b. Chungking, China, Nov. 12, 1936; s. Yeu Wah and Lily (Chang) W.; B.S. in Chemistry, Iowa State U., 1959; M.S. In Pharmacology, State U. Iowa, 1962; Ph.D. in Pharmacology (Dr. Ernest Tibbets Manning Meml. scholar), U. Nebr., 1966, M.D., 1968; m. Cherry Eula Buffington, July 9, 1961; children—Jade, Shale, Amber. Instr. pharmacology U. Nebr., Omaha, 1965-67, asst. prof., 1967-68, asso. grad. faculty, 1968-69, vis. prof., 1971; intern Bishop Clarkson Hosp., Omaha, 1968; intern U. Nebr. Coll. Medicine Hosp., 1968, resident, 1968-69; resident in anesthesiology U. Wash., Seattle, 1969-70, asst. prof. anesthesiology and pharmacology, 1970-74; attending anesthesiologist U. Wash. Med. Center and Affiliated Hosps., 1970-74; attending staff anesthesiologist U. Utah, Salt Lake City, 1974—, asso. prof. anesthesiology and pharmacology, 1974-76, prof., chmn. anesthesiology, 1976—, prof. pharmacology, 1980—. NIH grantee, 1969-72; Wash. State Heart Assn. grantee, 1972-74; Utah Heart Assn. grantee, 1975-79. Mem. Am. Soc. Anesthesiologists, Am. Soc. Clin. Pharmacology and Chemotherapy, Am. Soc. Pharmacology and Exptl. Therapeutics, AMA, Internat. Anesthesia Research Soc., Utah, Salt Lake County med. socs., Utah Soc. Anesthesiologists, Sigma Xi. Contbr. numerous articles to profl. jours. Home: 2740 Comanche Dr Salt Lake City UT 84108

WONG, WARREN JAMES, educator, mathematician; b. Masterton, New Zealand, Oct. 16, 1934; s. Ken and Jessie (Ng) W.; B.Sc., U. Otago, 1955, M.Sc., 1956; Ph.D., Harvard, 1959; m. Nellie Gee, May 12, 1962; children—Carole, Frances, Andrea. Lectr. math. U. Otago, Dunedin, New Zealand, 1960-64; asso. prof. math. U. Notre Dame, 1964-68, prof. math., 1968—. Mem. Am., Australian math. socs., Math. Assn. Am., Sigma Xi. Anglican. Contbr. articles to profl. jours. Office: PO Box 398 Notre Dame IN 46556

WONG, YAU CHUN, architect; b. Canton, China, Apr. 4, 1921; s. Gee Shun and Su (Lai) W.; came to U.S., 1948, naturalized, 1956; M.Arch., Ill. Inst. Tech., 1951; m. Ruth Hung-Fong Lau, Sept. 27, 1952; children—Phillip, Vera, Ernest, Sophia. With Mies Van der Rohe, Chgo., 1950-51, 52, 53-57, Skidmore, Owings & Merrill, Chgo., 1951-52, Archie Davis, Durham, N.C., 1953-53, C.F. Murphy Assos., Chgo., 1957-59; prin. Y.C. Wong & Assos., Chgo., 1959-63; partner Y.C. Wong, R. Ogden Hannaford & Assos., Chgo., 1963-67. Bd. dirs. First Unitarian Ch., Chgo., 1973-75; bd. dirs. S.E. Chgo. Commn. Recipient 1st honor awards Homes For Better Living AIA, House and Home, 1963, others. Fellow AIA (honor award for excellence in architecture Chgo. chpt. 1962, 65, 66, 69, dir. Chgo. chpt. 1976-78); mem. Soc. Coll. and Univ. Planning. Home: 1241 E Madison Park Chicago IL 60615 Office: 116 S Michigan Ave Chicago IL 60603

WONHAM, FREDERICK STAPLEY, investment banker; b. N.Y.C., Apr. 8, 1931; s. Wilson Stapley and Mary Knight (Lincoln) W.; B.A., Princeton U., 1953; postgrad. N.Y. U., 1955-59; m. Ann Hayden Brunie, June 18, 1953; children—Stapley, Henry, Lincoln. Various positions G.H. Walker & Co., investment bankers, N.Y.C., 1955-71, pres., 1971-74; with White, Weld & Co. Inc., N.Y.C., 1974-78, pres., chief operating officer, dir., 1975-78; sr. v.p. U.S. Trust Co. N.Y., 1978—; dir. Conrac Corp.; chmn. Provident Loan Soc., N.Y.C., 1974—. Trustee Community Service Soc., Brunswick Sch. Served to 1st. lt. AUS, 1953-55. Mem. Investment Assn. N.Y. (pres. 1961). Clubs: Bond N.Y. (gov. 1974—), (N.Y.C.); Roundhill (Greenwich, Conn.). Home: 238 June Rd Cos Cob CT 06807 Office: 1 Liberty Plaza New York NY 10006

WONNACOTT, RONALD JOHNSTON, educator; b. London, Ont., Can., Sept. 11, 1930; s. Gordon and Muriel (Johnston) W.; B.A., U. Western Ont., 1955; A.M., Harvard U., 1957, Ph.D., 1959; m. Eloise Howlett, Sept. 11, 1954; children—Douglas, Robert, Cathy Anne. Mem. faculty U. Western Ont., London, 1958—, prof. econs., 1964—, chmn. dept., 1969-72. Vis. asso. prof. U. Minn., Mpls., 1961-62; cons. Stanford Research Inst., Resources for the Future, Econ. Council Can. Mem. Canadian, Am., econ. assns. Clubs: London Hunt, Sunningdale Golf. Author: Canadian-American Dependence: An Interindustry Analysis of Production and Prices, 1961; (with Paul Wonnacott) Free Trade Between the U.S. and Canada, 1967; (with Thomas H. Wonnacott) Introductory Statistics, 1969; (with Thomas H. Wonnacott) Econometrics, 1970; Canada's Trade Options, 1975; (with Paul Wonnacott) Economics, 1979. and others. Contbr. to profl. jours. Home: 171 Wychwood Park London ON N6G 1S1 Canada

WOO, CHIA-WEI, physicist, educator, univ. provost; b. Shanghai, China, Nov. 13, 1937; s. Chih-Ming and Janet (Hsia) W.; came to U.S., 1955; naturalized, 1972; B.S., Georgetown Coll., Ky., 1956; M.A., Washington U., 1961, Ph.D., 1966; m. Yvonne Lo, Jan. 23, 1960; children—De-Kai J., De-Yi Y., De-Hwei M. Applied mathematician Monsanto Co., St. Louis, 1959-62; research asso., Washington U., St. Louis, 1966; asst. research physicist U. Calif. at San Diego, La Jolla 1966-68, provost Revelle Coll., prof., 1979—; asst. prof. physics Northwestern U., Evanston, Ill., 1968-70, asso. prof., 1971-73, prof., 1973-79, chmn. dept. physics and astronomy, 1974—. Vis. asso. prof. U. Ill., Urbana, 1970-71; cons. Argonne Nat. Lab., 1967—, NSF, 1977—. Alfred P. Sloan Research fellow, 1971-73. Fellow Am. Phys. Soc. Home: 8725 Nottingham Pl La Jolla CA 92037 Office: Provosts Office Revelle Coll U Calif at San Diego La Jolla CA 92093

WOO, WILLIAM FRANKLIN, journalist; b. Shanghai, China, Oct. 4, 1936 (mother Am. citizen); s. Kyatang and Elizabeth Louise (Hart) W.; came to U.S., 1946; B.A., U. Kans., 1959; m. Patricia Ernst, Dec. 18, 1964. Reporter, Kansas City Star, 1957-62; feature writer St. Louis Post-Dispatch, 1962-69, editorial writer, 1969-74, editor of editorial page, 1974—; Nieman fellow Harvard U., 1966-67. Served with USAF, 1962. Brookings Instn. journalism fellow, 1978. Office: St Louis Post-Dispatch 900 N 12th Blvd Saint Louis MO 63101

WOOD, ARTHUR MACDOUGALL, corp. exec.; b. Chicago, Ill., Jan. 27, 1913; s. R. Arthur and Emily (Smith) W.; A.B., Princeton U., 1934, LL.D., 1976; LL.B., Harvard U., 1937; m. Pauline Palmer, Nov. 17, 1945; children—Pauline, Arthur MacDougall. Admitted to Ill. bar, 1937; atty. Bell, Boyd & Marshall, Chgo., 1937-41; atty. Sears, Roebuck & Co., 1946-52, sec., 1952-56, v.p., 1956-68, dir., 1959—, comptroller, 1960-62, v.p. charge Pacific Coast ter., 1962-67, v.p. midwestern ter., 1967, pres. 1968-72, chmn., chief exec. officer, 1973-77; dir. Quaker Oats, Continental Ill. Corp., Simpsons-Sears, Ltd., Homart Devel. Co., Allstate Ins. Co. Ill. Tool Works, G.D. Searle & Co., Santa Fe Industries Inc. Chmn. bd. trustees Art Inst. Chgo.; trustee Rush-Presbyn.-St Luke's Med. Center; mem. public oversight bd. Am. Inst. C.P.A.'s. Served from pvt. F.A., AUS to lt. col. USAAF, 1941-45. Decorated Legion of Merit. Mem. Bus. Council. Office: Sears Tower Chicago IL 60684

WOOD, BENJAMIN OLANDO, JR., banker; b. Washington, May 19, 1936; s. Benjamin Olando and Evely Brown (Mayhugh) W.; B.C.S. in Accounting, Strayer Coll., 1957; postgrad. Georgetown U., 1959-62; diploma Bank Adminstrn. Sch. U. Wis., 1966; postgrad. Stonier Grad. Sch. Banking, Rutgers State U., 1967-69; m. Jeanette Warren, Mar. 16, 1957; children—Bruce, Dennis, Jay. Asst. auditor Nat. Savs. and Trust Co., Washington, 1963-70, controller, 1970-74, v.p., cashier, 1974-77, sr. v.p., cashier, 1977—. Mem. D.C. Bankers Assn. (sec. audit, control and operations sect. 1973, treas. 1974, vice chmn. 1974-75, pres. 1975-76, state dir. 1976-80). Home: 5813 Shalott Ct Alexandria VA 22310 Office: 15th and New York Ave NW Washington DC 20005

WOOD, BRIAN, fin. corp. exec.; b. Stretford, U.K., Sept. 29, 1920; s. James William and Constance (Medcalf) W.; came to U.S., 1947, naturalized, 1957; student Manchester U., 1935-38, Royal Coll. Tech., Manchester, 1946; m. Carolyn Elizabeth Wilber, May 31, 1945; children—Christine Elizabeth, Robin Ann Wood Pohlman. Salesman export div. J.P. Stevens & Co., Inc., 1947-54; v.p. Walker Bros. Inc., 1954-62; export sales mgr. Warner Bros. Corp., 1962-63; exec. v.p., dir. Fenchurch Corp., N.Y.C., 1964-77; exec. v.p., dir., S.H. Lock, Inc., N.Y.C., 1964-74, pres., 1975—; exec. v.p., dir. Tozer Kemsley & Milbourn (Can.) Ltd., 1966-73, TKM Pacific Ltd., 1972-74; joint mng. dir. Fenchurch NV, Curacao, 1972-77. Served to lt. comdr. air br. Royal Navy, 1940-45. Mem. Trinidad and Tobago C. of C. N.Y. (founding dir., pres. 1975). Republican. Clubs: Patterson (Fairfield, Conn.); Jamaica (Kingston); Union (Port of Spain, Trinidad). Home: 109 Mill River Rd Fairfield CT 06430 Office: 535 Fifth Ave Room 903 New York NY 10017. *Success in life is relative, not only to the achievements of others but also to your own aspirations. It cannot be measured by material possessions but only by the inner gratification which comes from acceptance by your peers and the knowledge that you have, at least, tried to contribute as much to your community and fellow men as they have given to you.*

WOOD, CHALMERS BENEDICT, cons., ret. fgn. service officer; b. N.Y.C., Dec. 9, 1917; s. Chalmers and Katherine Benedict (Turnbull) W.; grad. St. Mark's Sch. 1936; A.B., Harvard, 1940; m. Barbara Lindner, 1942 (div. 1967); children—Ramsay, Chalmers Benedict; m. Patricia Houghton, July 12, 1969; children—Felicity, Penelope. Admitted to D.C. bar, 1947; entered U.S. Fgn. Service, 1947; 3d sec. Am. embassy, Brussels, Belgium, 1948-52, 2d sec., Manila, 1952; assigned Dept. State, Washington, 1952, officer charge Greek affairs, 1954-57; 2d sec. Am. embassy, Saigon, 1957-59; officer charge Vietnamese affairs Dept. State, 1959-63, sr. seminar Dept. State, 1963-64; 1st sec. Am. embassy, London, 1964-66; office dir. Cyprus, Dept. State, 1966-67; sr. province adviser, Binh Dinh, Viet Nam, 1967-69; with Philippine affairs State Dept., 1970; counselor Am. embassy, Wellington, New Zealand, 1971-72, chargé, 1971-74; cons. ERDA, Washington, 1976-77. Served from pvt. to capt. USAAF, 1940-45. Clubs: Metropolitan (Washington); Brook (N.Y.C). Address: 45 Cleveland Ln Princeton NJ 08540

WOOD, CHARLES, educator, physicist; b. Ilford, Eng., Nov. 6, 1924; s. Charles and Matilda (Thomas) W.; B.Sc., Sir John Cass Coll., London U., 1951; M.Sc., Chelsea Poly., London U., 1955; Ph.D., London U., 1962; m. Pamela L. Wood, Apr. 8, 1950; children—Clare E., Wendy L., Malcolm C. Came to U.S., 1956, naturalized, 1963. Asso. physicist research lab. Gen. Electric Co., Wembly, Eng., 1951-53; physicist Electronic Tubes Ltd., 1953-54; dep. group leader Caswell Research Lab., Plessey Co., Eng., 1954-56; group supr. research div. Philco Corp., 1956-60; sect. head Kearfott div. Gen. Precision Instruments Co., 1960-61; dir. Intermetallic Products, 1961-63; mgr. research div. Xerox Corp., 1963-67; prof. physics No. Ill. U., DeKalb, 1967—, head dept., 1968-70. Served with Brit. Navy, 1942-46. Mem. Am. Phys. Soc., Am. Assn. Physics Tchrs., Sigma Xi. Contbr. papers to profl. lit. Home: 14 Cari Ct DeKalb IL 60115 Office: Dept Physics No Ill Univ DeKalb IL 60115

WOOD, CHARLES TUTTLE, educator; b. St. Paul, Oct. 29, 1933; s. Harold Eaton and Margaret (Frisbie) W.; A.B., Harvard, 1955, A.M., 1957, Ph.D., 1962; m. Susan Danielson, July 9, 1955; children—Lucy Eaton, Timothy Walker, Martha Augusta, Mary Frisbie. Investment analyst, trader Harold E. Wood & Co., St. Paul, 1955-56; trader First Boston Corp., 1957; teaching fellow gen. edn. Harvard, 1959-61, instr. history, 1961-64; mem. faculty Dartmouth, 1964—, prof. history, 1971—, acad. dir. Dartmouth Alumni Coll., 1972-75, chmn. dept. history, 1976-79, chmn. dept. comparative lit., 1977. Chmn. Dresden Bd. Sch. Dirs., 1972-74. Recipient Distinguished Service award N.H. Sch. Bds. Assn., 1975. Mem. Mediaeval Acad. Am., Am. Hist. Assn. (chmn. nominating com. 1977, Adams prize com. 1976-78), Conf. Brit. Studies, N.H. Sch. Bds. Assn. (2d v.p. 1974-75), New Eng. Medieval Conf. (pres. 1978-79), Am. Soc. Legal History, Phi Beta Kappa. Club: St. Botolph (Boston). Author: The French Apanages and the Capetian Monarchy, 1224-1328, 1966; Philip the Fair and Boniface VIII, 2d edit., 1971, reprint, 1976; Felipe el Hermoso y Bonifacio VIII: Mexico: UTEHA, 1968; The Age of Chivalry: Manners and Morals 1000-1450, 1970; The Deposition of Edward V, Traditio, 1975; also articles. Home: 7 N Balch St Hanover NH 03755

WOOD, CLIFF CALVIN, banker; b. Harrison, Ark., Oct. 1, 1903; s. Walker Lee and Emma (Johnson) W.; grad. high sch.; m. Sarah Mildred Wood, Dec. 18, 1938; children—Mary Jeanette (Mrs. Stanley Wood, Jr.), Cynthia Taylor (Mrs. Peter Grant Marston). Asst. cashier People's State Bank, Berryville, Ark., 1925-27; cashier First Nat. Bank, Batesville, Arks., 1928-29; nat. bank examiner Office Comptroller of Currency, St. Louis, Little Rock, 1930-41; v.p. First Nat. Bank, Memphis, 1941-47; v.p., sr. loan officer Republic Nat. Bank, Dallas, 1948-68; cons. to chmn. bd. Union Nat. Bank, Little Rock, 1970—, also dir. Bd. dirs. Southwestern Hist. Wax Mus., Dallas. Mem. Little Rock C. of C. Republican. Methodist. Mason. Clubs: Little Rock, Country (Little Rock); Admiral's (N.Y.C.). Home: 8580 Cantrell Rd Little Rock AR 72207

WOOD, DAVID ALVRA, educator, pathologist; b. Flora Vista, N.Mex., Dec. 21, 1904; s. Evans and Blanche D. (Wormell) W.; A.B., Stanford U., 1926, M.D., 1930; m. Ora Belle Bomberger, May 15, 1937; children—Kate Douglas (Mrs. K.J. Bossart, Jr.), David A., John Archer, William Allen, Charles Evans. Faculty, Stanford, 1930-51; prof. pathology (oncology) U. Calif. Sch. Medicine, 1951-72, dir. Cancer Research Inst., 1951-72, cons., 1974—, dir., prof. emeritus, 1972—, research oncologist, 1972-74. Cons. pathology San Francisco area VA, 1954-66, cons. Nat. Cancer Inst., USPHS, 1956-70, participant Nat. Cancer Program Plan, chmn. screening population groups, 1971-74; spl. cons., co-chmn. adv. com. cancer control program Bur. State Services USPHS, 1959-64; mem. cancer adv. council Calif., 1959—, chmn., 1966-71; mem. U.S. nat. com. Nat. Acad. Scis. to Internat. Union Against Cancer, 1961-63, U.S. nat. organizing com. to 10th Internat. Cancer Congress, 1967-70; vice chmn. Am. Joint Com. on Clin. Staging and End Results Reporting, 1959-69; research collaborator, med. dept Brookhaven Nat. Lab., Upton, N.Y., 1963-71; mem. fellowships selection com. Internat Agy. Research on Cancer, WHO, Lyon, France, 1970-73, Internat. Reference Center (stomach, esophagus) WHO, Tokyo, 1968-74; rep. Internat. Socs. Pathology meeting in Turku, Finland, 1974; mem. cadre and chmn. subcom. Pathology Nat. Large Bowel Cancer Project, U. Tex., Houston, 1973-75. Served to capt. M.C., USNR, World War II. Recipient award and medal Am. Joint Com. Cancer Staging and End Result Reporting, 1969; Meritorious Service award SSS, 1972. Fellow Am. Coll. Radiology (hon.), Am. Geog. Soc.; mem. Calif. Med. Assn. (chmn. cancer commn. 1958-60, vice chmn. 1960-63, sci. bd. 1963-71, chmn. cancer com. 1963-67), Am. Cancer Soc. (Bronze medal 1950, Nat. Service award 1972, pres. 1956-57, hon. life.), Armed Forces Inst. Pathology (sci. adv. bd. 1956-61, hon. cons. 1969), Internat. Acad. Pathology, Am. Soc. Cytology (hon.; chmn. awards com. 1958-65), Assn. Clin. Pathologists Gt. Britain (corr.), Royal Soc. Medicine (London), Coll. Am. Pathologists (pres. 1952-55, Sci. Products Found award 1958), Calif. Acad. Sci., James Ewing Soc. (Lucy Wortham James award 1970), Am. Assn. Cancer Insts. (pres. 1970-72), Am. Assn. Cancer Edn. (Samuel C. Harvey lectr. 1973), Calif. Acad. Medicine, AMA (council vol. health agys. 1952-63, chmn. com. on continuing profl. edn. program of vol. health agys.), Am. Assn. Pathologists and Bacteriologists, Am. Assn. Cancer Reearch, Fedn. Am. Soc. Exptl. Biology, Stanford Med. Alumni Assn. (pres. 1947), S.A.R., Sigma Xi, Phi Lambda Upsilon. Clubs: Commonwealth of Calif., Pacific Union (San Francisco). Editorial bd. Excerpta Medica (Cancer), Amsterdam, Netherlands. Author profl. articles on dual pulmonary circulation of lungs, neoplastic diseases, med. edn., acute virus hepatitis. Home: 54 Commonwealth Ave San Francisco CA 94118

WOOD, DAVID KENNEDY CORNELL, choreographer, educator; b. Fresno, Calif., Feb. 24, 1925; s. Earl Warner and Elsie Bliss (Kennedy) W.; B.A., U. Calif., 1945; student Neighborhood Playhouse, N.Y.C., 1947-48, also other theatre and dance schs.; m. Marni Pope Thomas, Dec. 28, 1958; children—Marina, Raegan, Ellis. Choreographer, Broadway musicals, TV, N.Y.C. Opera Ballet, Met. Opera Ballet, 1950-58; soloist Hanya Holm Co., 1948-50; soloist, rehearsal dir. Martha Graham Co., 1953-68; prof. dance U. Calif., 1968—; artistic dir. Bay Area Repertory Dance Co.; guest soloist Belles Artes of Mexico, 1958-59, Sweden Ballet Akademien, 1960-61. Served with USNR, 1943-46. Recipient choreographic award Nat. Endowment for Arts, 1973-74, 77-78. Mem. Am. Guild Musican Artists, Actors Equity, AFTRA, Calif. Dance Educators Assn., Am. Assn. Dance Cos. Choreographer: Pre-Amble, 1971; Post Script, 1974; Cassandra, 1974; Changelings, 1970; The Immigrant, 1974; In the Glade, 1977; Jeux, 1978. Home: 3090 Buena Vista Way Berkeley CA 94708

WOOD, DAVID SHOTWELL, engr., educator; b. Akron, Ohio, May 21, 1920; s. Henry Randolph and Janet Elizabeth (Stevenson) W.; B.S., Calif. Inst. Tech., 1941, M.S., 1946, Ph.D., 1949; m. Constance Loret Simonsen, Jan. 20, 1945; 1 dau., Alison J. Research engr. Calif. Inst. Tech., Pasadena, 1941-44; staff engr. U. Calif., Los Alamos, N.Mex., 1944-45; mem. faculty Calif. Inst. Tech., 1949—, prof. materials sci., 1961—; cons. in field. Councilman, City of Sierra Madre, Calif., 1954-58; dir. San Gabriel Valley Mcpl. Water Dist., Alhambra, Calif., 1959-66. Recipient Templin award ASTM, 1950. Mem. ASME, Am. Inst. Mining and Metall. Engrs., Am. Soc. Metals, AAAS, AAUP. Contbr. articles to profl. jours. Home: 590 Elm Ave Sierra Madre CA 91024 Office: 1201 E California Blvd Pasadena CA 91125

WOOD, DAVID THOMAS, U.S. atty.; b. Deadwood, S.D., Oct. 23, 1941; s. Clarence Arthur and Agnes Anna (Ringlbauer) W.; B.A. in English, Walla Walla (Wash.) Coll., 1963; J.D., Willamette U., 1969; m. Ellen Faye Perrine, June 17, 1962; children—Amanda Leigh, Jason Thomas. Tchr. English, Columbia Acad., Battleground, Wash., 1963-66; admitted to Wash. bar, Guam bar; jr. partner firm Jones & Wood, Walla Walla, 1969-70; dep. pros. atty. Spokane County, 1971-74; asst. atty. gen. Guam, 1974-75; dep. pub. defender Guam, 1976; asst. U.S. atty., Guam, 1976-77, U.S. atty., 1977—; U.S. atty. Commonwealth of No. Mariana Islands, 1978—. Mem. Fed., Guam, Wash. bar assns. Democrat. Office: PO Box Z Agana GU 96910

WOOD, DON JAMES, civil engr., educator; b. Northeast, Pa., July 28, 1936; s. Glenn Norman and Elizabeth (Biel) W.; B.S., Carnegie Mellon U., 1958, M.S., 1959, Ph.D., 1961; m. Joan Bernice Palmer, Sept. 5, 1959; children—Wendy, Doug, Jana. Asst. prof. civil engring. Clemson (S.C.) U., 1961-62, Duke U., 1962-66; prof. civil engring., asso. dean U. Ky., Lexington, 1966—; cons. in field. NSF fellow, 1958-61; recipient Gt. Tchr. award U. Ky., 1971, Outstanding Engring. Educator award Southeastern U.S.A. sect. Am. Soc. Engring. Edn., 1975. Mem. ASCE (Huber Research prize 1975), ASME, AAUP, Sigma Xi. Author papers on hydraulics; developer computer program water distbn. systems. Home: 2622 Westmoreland Rd Lexington KY 40511 Office: Dept Civil Engring Univ Ky Lexington KY 40506

WOOD, DONALD EURIAH, lawyer; b. Guymon, Okla., May 27, 1935; s. Theodore and Lula Elizabeth (Rider) W.; B.A., Panhandle A. and M. Coll., 1958; LL.B., Okla. U., 1964, J.D., 1970; m. Lynda Sharon Harris, Sept. 30, 1960; children—Donald Craig, Tana Dawn, Kristen Lynn. Admitted to Okla. bar, 1964; asst. county atty. Texas County, 1964, county atty., 1965-67; dist. atty. Okla. 1st Jud. Dist. Guymon, 1967—. Mem. adv. com. Okla. Commn. Criminal and Traffic Enforcement Systems, 1972; mem. Gov.'s Commn. Community Affairs and Planning, 1972-75 mem. faculty Panhandle State Coll., 1974—; mem. Okla. Dist. Atty. Tng. Council, 1976—. Served with inf., AUS, 1958-60. Mem. Okla. (legal ethics com. 1971—), Texas County (pres. 1966, 1970-71) bar assns., Nat., Okla. (pres. 1972, exec. com. 1971—) dist. attys. assns., Phi Alpha Delta. Presbyn. Elk, Rotarian. Home: 605 Hillcrest Dr Guymon OK 73942 Office: 319 N Main St Guymon OK 73942

WOOD, EARL HOWARD, educator, physiologist; b. Mankato, Minn., Jan. 1, 1912; s. William Clark and Inez (Goff) W.; B.A., Macalester Coll., 1934, D.Sc., 1950; B.S., U. Minn., 1939, M.S., M.B., Ph.D., 1941; M.D., 1942; m. Ada C. Peterson, Dec. 20, 1936; children—Phoebe, Mark Goff, Guy Harland, Earl Andrew. Teaching fellow physiology U. Minn., 1936-39, instr., 1940; NRC fellow med. scis., dept. pharmacology U. Pa., 1941; instr. pharmacology Harvard Med. Sch., 1942, research asst. acceleration lab. Mayo Aero Med. Unit, 1943; asst. prof. physiology Mayo Found., U. Minn. Grad. Sch., 1944, prof. physiology and medicine, 1950—; staff mem. sect. physiology Mayo Clinic, 1947—; chmn. biophys. scis. unit Mayo Med. Sch.; career investigator Am. Heart Assn., 1961—. Sci. cons. air surgeon USAF Aero Med. Center, Heidelberg, Germany, 1946; vis. prof. U. Bern, 1965-66; vis. scientist dept. physiology Univ. Coll., London, 1972-73. Recipient Presdl. certificate of merit, Distinguished Lectr. award Am. Coll. Chest Physicians, 1974. Fellow Aerospace Med. Assn.; mem. Am. Physiol. Soc. (past chmn. circulation group), Am. Soc. Pharmacology and Exptl. Therapeutics, Am., Central socs. clin. investigation, Soc. Exptl. Biology and Medicine, Am. Heart Assn. (Research Achievement award 1973, past chmn. basic sci. sect.), AAAS, Nat. Acad. Medicine Mex., Nat. Acad. Arts and Scis. (Netherlands), Phi Beta Kappa, Sigma Xi, Alpha Omega Alpha. Contbr. articles to profl. jours., chpts. to books; research, numerous publs. on devel. instrumental techniques and procedures for study heart and circulation in health and diesease; applications of these procedures to detection and quantitation of various types of acquired and congenital heart disease, study of effects and compensatory reaction of heart and circulation to various types of circulatory stress. Home: 1147 2d St NW Rochester MN 55901

WOOD, EDMUND REYNOLDS, lawyer; b. Dallas, May 26, 1943; s. Harold Edmund and Ruth Kathryn (Reynolds) W.; B.B.A., So. Methodist U., 1965; J.D., U. Houston, 1968; m. Linda Rebecca Sharrock, Oct. 30, 1965; children—Barry Burke, Mark Sharrock. Admitted to Tex. bar, 1968; practice law, Dallas, 1968—, partner Chancellor & Wood, 1973—; dir. Sharrock Brothers Electric Co., Inc.; mem. Tex. Gov.'s Commn. Uniform State Laws. Del. Republican State Conv., Tex., 1970; campaign dir. state senate campaign, 1976. Mem. Am., Tex., Dallas (chmn. advt. com.) bar assns., Am., Tex. trial lawyers assns., Dallas Young Lawyers Assn. Republican. Methodist. Clubs: Dallas Dervish, Lakewood Country, Mustang Athletic. Home: 3832 Colgate Dallas TX 75225 Office: Stewart Title Bldg 5728 LB Johnson Freeway Suite 200 Dallas TX 75240

WOOD, ERSKINE BIDDLE, lawyer; b. Portland, Oreg., June 21, 1911; s. Erskine and Rebecca Baird (Biddle) W.; A.B., Harvard, 1933, LL.B. magna cum laude, 1936; m. Elizabeth Hoffman, 1935 (div. 1959); children—Mardi, Spencer, Erskine II; m. 2d, Virginia Tooze, Dec. 4, 1959 (div. 1968); children—Rebecca, Mary; m. 3d, Ronnie Fenton, Sept. 1978. Admitted to Oreg. bar, 1936, U.S. Supreme Ct. bar; practice in Portland, 1936—; sr. partner firm Wood, Tatum, Mosser, Brooke & Holden. Dir. small vessel procurement War Shipping Adminstrn., 1942-44, chmn. com. just compensation, 1944-45; chmn. Citizens Conservation Com. Portland, Past pres., Catlin-Hillside Sch., Portland; past v.p. Oreg. Mus. Sci. and Industry. Served as lt. USNR, 1944-45. Mem. Am. Bar Assn., Maritime Law Assn. (past mem. exec. com.), Izaak Walton League (v.p. Portland). Clubs: University; Multnomah; Oreg. Flyfishers; Associated Harvard (past regional v.p.). Asso. editor Am. Maritime Cases. Home: 13125 SE Evergreen Hwy Vancouver WA 98664 Office: Standard Plaza Portland OR 97204

WOOD, EVELYN NIELSEN, educator; b. Logan, Utah, Jan. 8, 1909; d. Elias and Rose (Stirland) Nielsen; B.A., U. Utah, 1929, M.A., 1947; postgrad. Columbia, 1956-57; m. Myron Douglas Wood, June 12, 1929; 1 dau., Carolyn (Mrs. Ray J. Davis). Tchr., Weber Coll., Ogden, Utah, 1931-32; girls counselor Jordan High Sch., Sandy, Utah, 1948-57; tchr. jr. and sr. high schs., 1948-59, U. Utah, 1957-59; founder, originator Evelyn Wood Reading Dynamics, 1959—; now cons.; tchr. rapid reading U. Del., 1961; author, conductor radio programs, 1947; guest lectr. NEA, 1961, Internat. Reading Assn., Tex. Christian U., 1962; faculty Brigham Young U., research specialist for reading, 1973-74. Author: (with Marjory Barrows) Reading Skills, 1958; A Breakthrough in Reading, 1961; A New Approach to Speed Reading, 1962; Speed Reading for Comprehension, 1962; also articles. *

WOOD, FRANK BRADSHAW, astronomer, educator; b. Jackson, Tenn., Dec. 21, 1915; s. Thomas Frank and Mary (Bradshaw) W.; B.S., U. Fla., 1936; postgrad. U. Ariz., 1938-39; A.M., Princeton, 1940, Ph.D., 1941; m. Elizabeth Hoar Pepper, Oct. 5, 1945; children—Ellen, Eunice, Mary, Stephen. Research asso. Princeton, 1946; NRC fellow Steward Obs., U. Ariz., also Lick Obs., U. Calif., 1946-47; asst. prof. U. Ariz., 1947-50; asso. prof. U. Pa., 1950, prof. astronomy, 1954-68, chmn. dept., 1954-57, 58-68; exec. dir. Flower and Cook Obs., 1950-54, dir., 1954-68, Flower prof. 1958-68; prof. astronomy, dir. optical astron. observatories U. Fla., Gainesville, 1968—, asso. chmn. dept., 1971-77. Served with USNR, 1941-46. Fulbright fellow Australian Nat. U., 1957-58; NATO sr. fellow in sci. U. Canterbury, Christchurch, New Zealand, 1973; Fulbright fellow Instituto de Astronomia y Fisica del Espacio, Buenos Aires, 1977. Mem. Am. Astron. Soc. (council 1958-61), Royal Astron. Soc. New Zealand (hon.), Internat. Astron. Union (pres. commn. 42 1967-70, v.p. commn. 38, 1979—), Royal Astron. Soc., Fla. Acad. Sci. (chmn. phys. scis. sect. 1974-75), Astron. Soc. Can., Explorers Club, Ret. Officers Assn., Navy League. Episcopalian. Clubs: Torch, Kiwanis, Troa. Author: (with J. Samade) Interacting Binary Stars, 1978. Editor: Astronomical Photoelectric Photometry, 1953; Present and Future of Telescope of Moderate Size, 1958; Photoelectric Astronomy for Amateurs, 1963. Contbr. articles to profl. jours. Home: 714 NW 89th St Gainesville FL 32601

WOOD, FRANK PREUIT, educator, former air force officer; b. Greenville, Tex., Feb. 28, 1916; s. William L. and Ethel (Preuit) W.; B.S. in Elec. Engring., U. Tex., 1939; grad. USAF pilot tng. schs., 1941; m. Harriet Louise Brawner, Oct. 25, 1941; 1 son, Frank M. Commd. 2d lt. USAAF, 1941, advanced through grades to brig. gen. USAF, 1964; dep. chief staff personnel Air Tng. Command, Randolph AFB, Tex., 1962-66; comdr. Lackland Mil. Tng. Center, San Antonio, 1966-67; chief Mil. Assistance Adv. Group, Italy, 1967-69; dep. chief staff for personnel Tactical Air Command, Langley AFB, Va., 1969-70; ret., 1970; apptd. asso. dir. Bur. Engring. Research, U. Tex. Coll. Engring., Austin, 1970, now dir. Decorated Legion of Merit with 4 oak leaf clusters; named Distinguished Grad., U. Tex. Coll. Engring., 1968. Mem. Christian Ch. (elder 1975—, chmn. ofcl. bd. 1977). Home: 3416 Mt Bonnell Circle Austin TX 78731

WOOD, FRANKLIN SECOR, lawyer; b. Hopewell Center, N.Y., Aug. 3, 1901; s. Albert Frank and Elizabeth (Ketcham) W.; A.B., Cornell U., 1923, LL.B., 1925; m. Kate Visscher, Dec. 28, 1931; children—Franklin Secor, Harmin Visscher, Mary Visscher. Admitted to N.Y. bar, 1925; with firm Cotton & Franklin, N.Y.C., 1925-29, Prosser, Anderson & Marx, Honolulu, 1930, Robb, Clark & Bennitt, N.Y.C., 1933-34; pvt. practice, N.Y.C., 1934-45, mem. firm Hawkins, Delafield & Wood, 1945-70, counsel 1971-74. Mem. council Cornell U. Mem. Assn. Bar City N.Y., Am., N.Y. State bar assns., Phi Delta Phi. Clubs: Downtown Execs., University (N.Y.C.); Siwanoy Country; Wadawanuck Yacht (Stonington, Conn.). Home: 6 Northern Ave Bronxville NY 10708 also RD 1 Stonington CT 06378

WOOD, GEORGE F., lawyer; b. Frankville, Ala., Dec. 11, 1916; s. Andrew J. and Minnie (Granade) W.; B.S., Spring Hill Coll., Mobile, Ala., 1937; LL.B., U. Ala., 1940; m. Helen E. Fletcher, Sept. 4, 1940; children—Marcus A., Judith. Admitted to Ala. bar, 1940; practice in Prichard, 1940-41, Mobile, 1947—; personnel asst. Ala. Drydock & Shipbldg. Co., 1941; asst. personnel dir. City of Mobile and Mobile County, 1941-42, 46-47; partner firm Reams, Tappan, Wood, Vollmer, Philips & Killion, and predecessor, 1947—. Trustee Mobile Coll. Served from ensign to lt. comdr. USNR, 1942-46: PTO. Decorated Bronze Star medal. Mem. Ala., Mobile County (past pres.) bar assns., Maritime Law Assn., Phi Alpha Delta. Baptist (deacon). Home: 51 W Ridgelawn Dr Mobile AL 36608 Office: 3662 Dauphin St Mobile AL 36608

WOOD, GORDON STEWART, educator, historian; b. Concord, Mass., Nov. 27, 1933; s. Herbert G. and Marion (Friberg) W.; A.B., Tufts U., 1955; A.M., Harvard, 1959, Ph.D., 1964; m. Louise Goss, Apr. 30, 1956; children—Christopher, Elizabeth, Amy. Fellow, Inst. Early Am. History and Culture, Williamsburg, Va., 1964-66; asst. prof. Harvard, 1966-67; asso. prof. U. Mich., Ann Arbor, 1967-69; prof. history Brown U., Providence, 1969—. Served with USAF, 1955-58. Recipient Bancroft prize Columbia, 1970. Mem. Am. Hist. Assn. (John Dunning prize), Orgn. Am. Historians, Am. Studies Assn. Author: The Creation of the American Republic, 1776-1787, 1969; The Rising Glory of America, 1760-1820, 1971; co-author: The Great Republic, 1977. Home: 258 Nayatt Rd Barrington RI 02806 Office: 142 Angell St Providence RI 02912

WOOD, HARLAND GOFF, educator, biochemist; b. Delavan, Minn., Sept. 2, 1907; s. William C. and Inez (Goff) W.; A.B., Macalester Coll., 1931, D.Sc. (hon.), 1946; Ph.D., Iowa State Coll., 1935; D.Sc., Northwestern U., 1972; m. Mildred Lenora Davis, Sept. 14, 1929; children—Donna, Beverly, Louise. Fellow NRC, biochem. dept. U. Wis., 1935-36; asst. prof. bacteriol. dept. Iowa State Coll., 1936-43; asso. prof. physiol. chem. dept. U. Minn., 1943-46; prof., dir. biochemistry dept. Case Western Res. U., Cleve., 1946-65, prof. biochemistry, 1965—, dean scis., 1967-69, Univ. prof., 1970—. Chmn. isotope panel NRC com. on growth, 1947-48; adv. council Life Ins. Med. Research Fund, 1957-62; mem. tng. grant com. NIH, 1965-69; advisory bd. Case Inst. Tech., 1971-78; advisory com. div. biology and medicine U.S. AEC, 1957-62; mem. Presdl. Sci. Advisory Com., Washington, 1968-72, mem. physiol. chemistry study sect., 1973-77. Recipient Eli Lilly research award in bacteriology, 1942, Carl Neuberg award, 1952, Nat. Acad. Scis., 1953, Glycerine award, 1954, Modern Med. award Distinguished Achievement, 1968; Lynen lectr. and medal, 1972; Humbolt prize, sr. U.S. scientist, W. Ger., 1979; Fulbright fellow, 1955; Guggenheim fellow, 1962. Mem. Am. Acad. Arts and Scis., Am. Heart Assn. (research com. 1949), Am. Am. Chem. Soc., Am. Soc. Biol. Chemists (pres.), Biochem. Soc. Gt. Britain, N.Y. Acad. Scis., Am. Cancer Soc. (advisory bd. 1965-69), Internat. Union Biochemistry (mem. council 1967-76, sec. gen. 1970-73, pres. elect 1979), Soc. Am. Bacteriologists, Sigma Xi; corr. mem. Der Bayerischen Akademie der Wissenschaften. Methodist. Office: 2109 Adelbert Rd Cleveland OH 44106

WOOD, HARLESTON READ, mfg. exec.; b. Phila., Oct. 18, 1913; s. Alan and Elizabeth Frances (Read) W.; student Haverford Sch., 1929-31; A.B., Princeton, 1936; LL.D., Hobart and William Smith Colls., 1959; m. Emily Newbold Campbell, June 21, 1942; children—Harleston R., Alan IV, Ross G., Morrow, Anthony. Various positions Alan Wood Steel Co. (name changed to Vesper Corp. 1979), 1938-42, sales devel. engr., dir., 1946-50, mgr. planning and devel., 1950-52, asst. v.p., 1952-54, v.p., 1954, pres., 1955-72, chmn., 1962—; dir. Fidelity Mut. Ins. Co., Frederick Co., Penco Products Inc. Gen. chmn. Phila. United Fund Torch drive, 1972; bd. dirs. Ursinus Coll. Del. Rep. Nat. Conv., 1972. Mem. Am. Iron and Steel Inst. Episcopalian. Clubs: Racquet, Phila. Country. Home: 641 Righters Mill Rd Narberth PA 19072 Office: Vesper Corp 301 City Line Ave Bala Cynwyd PA 19004

WOOD, HARLINGTON, JR., judge; b. Springfield, Ill., Apr. 17, 1920; s. Harlington and Marie (Green) W.; A.B., U. Ill., 1942, J.D., 1948. Admitted to Ill. bar, 1948, practiced in Springfield, 1948-69; U.S. atty. So. Dist. Ill., 1958-61; partner firm Wood & Wood, 1961-69; asso. dep. atty. gen. for U.S. attys. U.S. dept. Justice, 1969-70; asso. dep. atty. gen. Justice Dept., Washington, 1970-72, asst. atty. gen. civil div., 1972-73; U.S. dist. judge So. Dist. Ill., Springfield, 1973-76; judge U.S. Ct. Appeals for 7th Circuit, 1976—. Mem. Am., Ill. bar assns., Abraham Lincoln Assn. (v.p.). Address: 219 S Dearborn St Chicago IL 60604

WOOD, HAROLD SAMUEL, educator; b. Long Beach, Calif., Mar. 8, 1913; s. Samuel Bury and Helen Imogene (Hawkins) W.; A.B., U. Redlands, 1942; M.B.A., U. So. Calif., 1947; M.A., Columbia, 1952. With Trans World Airlines, Inc., Los Angeles, 1946-49; faculty St. Louis U.-Parks Coll. Aero Tech., Cahokia, Ill., 1949—, prof. aero. adminstrn., 1964—, chmn. dept., 1957—. Served with AUS, 1940-46. Recipient William A. Wheatley award, 1961; FAA award, 1966. Mem. Am. Soc. Engring. Edn., Univ. Aviation Assn. (exec. sec.), Nat. Intercollegiate Flying Assn. (exec. dir.), Nat. Aviation Edn. Council, Nat. Aero. Assn. (Frank G. Brewer trophy 1972), Am. Soc. Aerospace Edn. (v.p.), Alpha Eta Rho (nat. sec.-treas.), Alpha Phi Omega, Phi Delta Kappa, Delta Nu Alpha, Alpha Beta Gamma, Alpha Gamma Nu. Baptist. Home: 402 Mildred Ave Cahokia IL 62206

WOOD, HARRY EMSLEY, JR., artist, educator; b. Indpls., Dec. 10, 1910; s. Harry Emsley and Bessie Moore (Houser) W.; B.A., U. Wis., 1932, M.A., 1933; M.A., Ohio State U., 1938, Ph.D., 1941; student Accademia di Belle Arti, Florence, Italy, 1949-50, Bisttram Sch. Art, Taos, N.Mex., summer 1939; m. Antoinette Claypoole, July 8, 1938; children—Nancy Ann (Mrs. Keith Leafdale), Sarah (Mrs. Tom Freese), Lucy (Mrs. Jack Barcelo), David. Instr. English and journalism Ohio Wesleyan U., 1934, asst. prof., 1935-42; prof. art, head dept. Ill. Wesleyan U., 1942-44; dean Coll. Fine Arts, Bradley U., 1944-50; chmn. art dept. Ariz. State U., 1954-66, prof. art, 1966—, emeritus, 1976—; exhibited in one man shows at Florence, Italy, Columbus, Ohio, Beloit, Wis., Peoria, Ill., Ill. State Mus. at Springfield, Decatur, Ill., Galesburg, Ill., Phoenix Art Mus., Ariz. State U., Gallery Wall, Phoenix, Garelick Gallery, Scottsdale; represented in permanent collections Nat. Portrait Gallery, Smithsonian Instn., others in Japan, Can., Italy, Mex., U.S.; muralist; portrait painter of various persons including Robert Frost, George Santayana, Adlai Stevenson, Yehudi Menuhin, Frank Lloyd Wright, James Caesar Petrillo, Sen. Paul Douglas, Sen. Everett Dirksen, Ambassador James Clement Dunn, Clare Booth Luce, Max Ernst, René Magritte, Igor Stravinsky, Senator Carl Hayden, Gov. Ernest MacFarland; bassoonist Indpls. Symphony, 1933, Phoenix Symphony, 1954-55; film commentator TV Channel 8, Phoenix, 1972-76; profl. lectr. Recipient Ariz. Artist Guild purchase prize sculpture Ariz. State Fair, 1958; Murphy award sculpture, 1959. Mem. Nat. Art Edn. Assn. (nat. council 1959-62), Pacific Arts Assn. (pres. 1958-60), Ariz. Art Edn. Assn., Phoenix Art Mus., Phi Beta Kappa, Phi Kappa Psi, Phi Eta Sigma, Sigma Delta Chi, Phi Mu Alpha Sinfonia. Author: Lew Davis, 25 Years of Painting in Arizona, 1961; Soul, 1970; The Faces of Abraham Lincoln, 1970. Playwright: Rich Man, Poor Man, 1933; Hands of God, 1933. Art critic, illustrator Scottsdale Progress, 1974-77, Lincoln Herald, 1976-77. Contbr. articles profl. jours. Art critic Arizona Republic 1959-62. Home: 104 Vista del Cerro Tempe AZ 85281. *Drawing, painting, writing poetry, and learning to respond in depth to the design, the expressiveness and the symbolism of works of art — in other words learning to SEE, outwardly and inwardly — offer, I believe, the most effective pathway to satisfying creative participation in the human adventure.*

WOOD, HARRY EUGENE, judge; b. Spartanburg, S.C., May 31, 1926; s. Boyce Eugene and Jane (Gurley) W.; student Wofford Coll., 1942-43; A.A., George Washington U., 1949, J.D., 1952; m. I. Katherine Terrell, Aug. 23, 1947. Admitted to Fed. bar, 1952, D.C. bar, 1952; law clk. U.S. Ct. Claims, Washington, 1952-54; asso. firm Ansell and Ansell, Washington, 1954-57; partner firm Emery and Wood, Washington, 1958-69; commr., now trial judge U.S. Ct. Claims, Washington, 1969—. Served with AUS, 1944-46. Mem. Am., Fed., D.C. bar assns., Bar Assn. D.C., Order of Coif. Methodist. Club: Masons. Home: 628 S Wakefield St Arlington VA 22204 Office: US Ct Claims 717 Madison Pl NW Washington DC 20005

WOOD, HOWARD GRAHAM, banker; b. Balt., July 27, 1910; s. Howard and Etta (Graham) W.; B.A., Johns Hopkins, 1932; LL.B., U. Md., 1936; m. Florence Tottle, Apr. 2, 1977; children by previous marriage—Robert Graham, Virginia Beecher. Admitted to Md. bar, 1936; with First Nat. Bank Md., 1932—, now chmn. trust adminstrn. com.; dir. Balt. Equitable Soc. Mem. Commn. on Revision Balt. City Charter, 1965; treas. S.S. Hist. Soc. Am. Bd. dirs. Presbyn. Home Md. Served to maj. Intelligence Div., AUS, 1942-46. Mem. Phi Beta Kappa, Phi Gamma Delta. Clubs: Mchts., Elkridge, Johns Hopkins (Balt.). Author: (with Robert H. Burgess) Steamboats Out of Baltimore, 1969. Home: 919 Bellemore Rd Baltimore MD 21210 Office: First Md Bldg Baltimore MD 21202

WOOD, J. FRANK, lawyer; b. Chester, Pa., Aug. 1, 1908; s. J. William and Sarah (Black) W.; A.B., Harvard, 1930, Sheldon travelling fellow, 1930-31, J.D., 1934; m. Ann Budd, Feb. 4, 1939; children—John Frank, Lydia A. Wood Sargent, Susannah Wood Tavernier, Sarah Morton Wood Lewis, William Howard. Admitted to N.Y. bar, 1935; asso. atty. Barry, Wainwright, Thacher & Symmers, N.Y.C., 1934-37; trust rep., trust officer Chem. Bank & Trust Co., N.Y.C., 1937-43; dep. supt., counsel N.Y. State Banking Dept., 1943-44, 45-50; sr. v.p., trustee Dollar Savs. Bank, N.Y.C., 1951-54; partner firm Thacher, Proffitt & Wood, and predecessor firm, N.Y.C., 1954-74, counsel, 1974—; trustee Savs. Banks Life Ins. Fund, N.Y.C., 1953-54; dir., mem. exec. com. Instl. Investors Mut. Fund, Inc., N.Y.C., 1953-54; trustee Franklin Savs. Bank, N.Y.C., 1956-78. Mem. N.Y. State Pension Commn., 1954-60; mem. adv. council pensions N.Y. State Civil Service Dept., 1960-69, chmn., 1967-69. Bd. dirs., mem. exec. com. Allergy Found. Am., 1956-72. Mem. N.Y. N.G., 1935-38. Served to capt. USMCR, 1944-46. Mem. Am. Bar Assn., Assn. Ex-Mems. Squadron A., Descs. Signers Declaration Independence, Phi Beta Kappa. Republican. Presbyterian. Clubs: Down Town Assn., Harvard, Union (N.Y.C.); St. Andrews Golf (Hastings, N.Y.). Home: 133 E 80th St New York NY 10021 Office: 40 Wall St New York NY 10005

WOOD, JACK CALVIN, cons. health care industry; b. Greenwood, Ind., Jan. 9, 1933; s. Earl Leon and Gertrude Ruby (Stott) W.; A.B., DePauw U., Greencastle, Ind., 1954; J.D., Harvard U., 1961. Admitted to Ill. bar, 1961, Tex. bar, 1965, D.C. bar, 1978; asso. firm Hopkins-Sutter, Chgo., 1961-65; gen. counsel Sisters of Charity Health Care System, Houston, 1965-73; sr. partner firm Wood, Lucksinger & Epstein, Houston, 1973—; editor-in-chief Topics In Health Care Financing, 1974—; clin. prof. law St. Louis U. Med. Sch., 1976—; adj. prof. health care adminstrn. Tex. Women's U., 1977—. Pres. St. Joseph Hosp. Found., Houston, 1966-68, bd. dirs., 1966—. Served to lt. comdr. USNR, 1954-65. Mem. Am. Soc. Hosp. Attys. (pres. 1974-75). Author: Financial Management, 1973; Medicare Reimbursement, 1974; Private Third Party Reimbursement, 1975. Home: 2203 Dunraven St Houston TX 77019 Office: 1600 One Houston Center Bldg Houston TX 77002

WOOD, JAMES, banker; b. Mt. Kisco, N.Y., May 2, 1927; s. L. Hollingsworth and Martha (Speakman) W.; grad. Deerfield (Mass.) Acad., 1945; ed. Haverford Coll., 1950; m. Frances Randall, May 2, 1953; children—Emily Morris, Stephen H. Mfrs. rep. distbn. fertilizers, 1950-54; with Bank of N.Y., 1954—, asst. v.p., 1960-61, v.p., 1961—. Trustee Bryn Mawr Coll.; v.p., trustee Jewish Found. for Edn. Women; pres., bd. dirs. Oakwood Cemetery, Mt. Kisco; bd. mgrs. Am. Bible Soc.; v.p., bd. dirs. Howard Meml. Fund; dir. Investor Responsibility Research Center. Served with USNR, 1945-46. Home: Braewold Rt 1 Box 142 Mount Kisco NY 10549 Office: Bank of NY 48 Wall St New York NY 10015

WOOD, JAMES ALLEN, lawyer; b. McMinnville, Tenn., Jan. 14, 1906; s. Ira and Emma (Calhoun) W.; A.B., U. Tenn., 1929; LL.B., U. Tex., 1934; m. Eva Beth Sellers, Dec. 28, 1941; 1 son, Eben Calhoun. Tchr., Bolton High Sch., Alexandria, La., 1929-32; admitted to Tex. bar, 1934, since practiced in Corpus Christi; mem. firm Wood & Burney, 1971—; state dist. judge, Corpus Christi, 1941-43; dir. Gulfway Nat. Bank, Corpus Christi. Mem. rules adv. com. Supreme Ct. Tex. Bd. dirs. Nueces River Authority. Served to lt. USNR, 1943-45. Fellow Am. Coll. Trial Lawyers; mem. Am., Tex., Nueces County (pres. 1941) bar assns. Contbr. articles to profl. jours. Home: 458 Doplhin St Corpus Christi TX 78411 Office: Petroleum Tower Corpus Christi TX 78401

WOOD, JAMES NOWELL, museum ofcl.; b. Boston, Mar. 20, 1941; s. Charles H. and Helen N. (Nowell) W.; diploma Universita per Stranieri, Perugia, Italy, 1962; B.A., Williams Coll., Williamstown, Mass., 1963; M.A. (Ford Mus. Tng. fellow), N.Y. U., 1966; m. Emese Forizs, Dec. 30, 1966; children—Lenke Hancock, Rebecca Noel. Asst. to dir. Met. Mus., N.Y.C., 1967-68, asst. curator dept. 20th Century art, 1968-70; curator Albright-Knox Art Gallery, Buffalo, 1970-73, asso. dir., 1973-75; dir. St. Louis Art Mus., 1975-80, Art Inst. Chgo., 1980—; adj. prof. dept. art history State U. N.Y., 1972—; dir. St. Louis Art Mus., 1975—. Mem. Intermuseum Conservation Assn. (pres.). Office: Art Inst of Chgo Michigan Ave at Adams St Chicago IL 60603

WOOD, JAMES PLAYSTED, author; b. N.Y.C., Dec. 11, 1905; s. William Thomas and Olive Padbury (Hicks) W.; A.B., Columbia, 1927, M.A., 1932; m. E.S. Elizabeth Craig, Aug. 14, 1943. Editorial library N.Y. Tribune, 1922-24; advt. copywriter McGraw-Hill Book Co., N.Y.C., 1927-29; tchr. English, Dalton (Mass.) High Sch., 1929-30, duPont Manual High Sch., Louisville, 1930-37, Tabor Acad., summer 1936; instr. English, Amherst, 1937-42, asst. prof., 1942-46; with Curtis Pub. Co., Phila, 1946-66. Served from 2d lt. to maj. USAAF, 1943-46. Mem. Holly Soc. Am. Author: The Presence of Everett Marsh, 1937; Magazines in the United States, 1949; Selling Forces, 1953, German edit. 1955; The Beckoning Hill, 1954; An Elephant in the Family, 1957; The Story of Advertising, 1958; Of Lasting Interest, 1958; Advertising and the Soul's Belly, 1960; The Queen's Most Honorable Pirate, 1961; The Elephant in the Barn, 1961; A Hound, A Bay Horse, and a Turtle Dove, 1963; Trust Thyself, 1964; The Life and Words of John F. Kennedy, 1964; The Lantern Bearer, 1965; Very Wild Animal Stories, 1965; Elephant on Ice, 1965; The Snark Was a Boojum, 1966; What's the Market?, 1966; When I was Jersey, 1967; Alaska, The Great Land, 1967; Spunkwater, Spunkwater, 1968; Mr. Jonathan Edwards 1968; I Told You So, 1969, The Mammoth Parade, 1969; Scotland Yard, 1970; The Unpardonable Sin, 1970; This Little Pig, 1971; The Curtis Magazines, 1971; Emily Elizabeth Dickinson, 1972; Poetry Is, 1972; The Great Glut, 1973; Kentucky Time, 1977, others. Editor: American Literature of 1847, 1947; American Literature of 1848, 1948; text editor, contbr. to Marketing Research Practice, 1950. Contbg. editor Limited Editions Club, 1974-76. Home: 103 Atwater Rd Springfield MA 01107. *Perhaps because essentially I understand and care about little but work, I have seldom been unduly conscious of goals, standards of conduct, or over-riding ideas. I like skilled men-whether they are farmers, scholars, firemen or carpenters-and try to be as good at my job, which happens to be writing, as a sound nurseryman is at his. I value what seems to me excellence and have a corresponding dislike of bombast and fakery.*

WOOD, JAMES RALPH, JR., ins. co. exec., lawyer; b. Sherman, Tex., Sept. 16, 1926; s. James Ralph and Kathleen (Cook) W.; B.A., So. Meth. U., 1949; LL.B., U. Tex., 1951; m. Sarah Muire, Mar. 11, 1955; children—James Ralph, III, Dorothy Lee, Clinton Hiram. Admitted to Tex. bar, 1951; partner firm Scurry, Scurry, Pace & Wood, Dallas, 1951-62; with Southwestern Life Ins. Co., Dallas, 1962—, v.p., gen. counsel, 1974-77, v.p., spl. counsel, 1977—. Bd. dirs. Shakespeare Festival of Dallas, Dallas Theater Center, Dallas Legal Services Project; pres. elect Vis. Nurses Assn., Dallas, 1978; deacon, elder Highland Park Presbyn. Ch., Dallas. Served with USN, 1944-46. Mem. Dallas, Am. bar assns., State Bar Tex. (chmn. sect. corporate counsel), Assn. Life Ins. Counsel. Club: City. Home: 3406 Princeton Ave Dallas TX 75205 Office: PO Box 2699 Dallas TX 75221

WOOD, JEANNE CLARKE, charitable orgn. exec.; b. Pitts., Dec. 21, 1916; d. Joseph Calvitt and Helen Caroline (Mattson) Clarke; student Collegiate Sch. for Girls, Richmond, Va., 1932-33; m. Herman Eugene Wood, Jr., May 6, 1936 (dec.); children—Helen Hamilton (Mrs. John Harry Mortenson), Herman Eugene III. Asst. to Dr. and Mrs. J. Calvitt Clarke, Christian Children's Fund, Inc., Richmond, 1938-64; founder Children, Inc., Richmond, 1964, pres., internat. dir., 1964—. Recipient citation Eastern Council Navajo Tribe, 1970, citations Mayor of Pusan, Korea, 1971, Mayor of Seoul, Korea, 1971, Gov. of Kanagawa Prefecture, Japan, 1972, commendation Pres. of U.S., 1972, citation Stephen Philibosian Found., 1975. Author: (with Helen C. Clarke) In Appreciation: A Story in Pictures of the World-Wide Family of Christian Children's Fund, Inc., 1958, Children's Christmastime Around the World, 1962, Children's Games Around the World, 1962, Children-Hope of the World-Their Needs, 1965, Children-Hope of the World-Their Friends, 1966. Editor: CI News, 1964. Address: 1000 Westover Rd PO Box 5381 Richmond VA 23220. *While there are many things about which we can make no choice in this volatile world where change is constant and sometimes disastrous, it has seemed to me that one can make the choice between accepting things positively or negatively. I have chosen to accept them positively.*

WOOD, JOHN, actor; attended Bedford Sch., Jesus Coll., Oxford U. (Eng.); m. Gillian Neason (div.); 1 son, Sebastian; m. 2d, Sylvia Vaughan; children—Sibylla, Ghislaine Rufus. Stage appearances at Old Vic Co., 1954-56; appeared in plays: Camino Real, 1957, The Making Of Moo, 1957, Brouhaha, 1958, The Fantasticks, 1961, Rosencrantz and Guildenstern are Dead, 1967, Exiles, 1970, Enemies, 1971, The Man of Mode, 1971, Exiles, 1971, The Balcony, 1971, The Comedy of Errors, 1972, 73, Collaborators, 1973, A Lesson in Blood and Roses, 1973, Sherlock Holmes, Travesties (Evening Standard Best Actor award 1974, Tony award 1976), 1974, The Devil's Disciple, 1976, Ivanov, 1976, Death Trap, 1978; joined Royal Shakespeare Co., 1971; TV appearances: A Tale of Two Cities, Barnaby Rudge, 1964-65, The Victorians, 1965, The Duel, 1966; films: Nicholas and Alexandra, 1971, Slaughterhouse Five, 1972, Somebody Killed Her Husband, 1978. Office: care Agy for Performing Arts Inc 9000 Sunset Blvd Suite 315 Los Angeles CA 90069*

WOOD, JOHN ARMSTEAD, geochemist; b. Roanoke, Va., July 28, 1932; s. John Armstead and Lillian Cary (Hall) W.; B.S. in Geology, Va. Polytech. Inst., 1954; Ph.D. in Geology, Mass. Inst. Tech., 1958; post-doctoral study U. Cambridge, Eng., 1959-60; m. Elisabeth Mathilde Heuser, June 12, 1958 (div.); children—Crispin S., Georgia K. Staff scientist Smithsonian Astrophys. Obs., Cambridge, Mass., 1959, 61-62, 65—; research asso. Enrico Fermi Inst. U. Chgo., 1962-65; lectr. Harvard dept. geol. scis., 1973—. Vice chmn. Lunar Sample Analysis Planning Team, 1971-72. Recipient NASA medal for exceptional sci. achievement, 1973; J.L. Smith medal Nat. Acad. Scis., 1976. Fellow Am. Geophys. Union, Meteoritical Soc. (pres. 1971-72. Leonard medal, AAAS; mem. Internat. Astron. Union. Author: Meteorites and the Origin of Planets, 1968; The Solar System, 1979. Home: 29 Concord Ave Cambridge MA 02138 Office: 60 Garden St Cambridge MA 02138

WOOD, JOHN EDWARD, III, chem. co. exec.; b. Lynchburg, Va., May 20, 1916; s. John Edward and Louise (Walker) W.; B.A., Lynchburg Coll., 1936; Ph.D., Mass. Inst. Tech., 1939; m. Morrill Macleod, Dec. 27, 1946; 1 dau., Nancy W. Jackson; stepsons—Edward G. Tyree, Walter P. Tyree. Research chemist Esso Research & Engring. Co., Linden, N.J., 1939-40; mfg. supr. Esso Standard Oil Co., Baton Rouge, 1941-52, mgr. mfg., 1953-55, gen. mgr. chems., N.Y.C., 1955-58; pres. Enjay Chem. Co., N.Y.C. (div. Humble Oil & Refining Co.), 1959-65; chmn. bd. Nat. Plastics Products Co., 1962-65; exec. v.p., dir. Vulcan Materials Co., 1965-72, v.p. oil and gas, 1973—, pres. chems. div., 1965-69. Mem. chemistry departmental vis. com. Coll. William and Mary; mem. corp. devel. com. Mass. Inst. Tech.; bd. dirs. Ala. affiliate Am. Heart Assn., Big Bros. Greater Birmingham; mem. exec. bd., v.p. Birmingham area council, 2d v.p. area IV, Boy Scouts Am. Mem. Am. Chem. Soc., Am. Inst. Chem. Engrs., Am. Inst. Chemists, Mfg. Chemists Assn. (dir., mem. exec. com., 1965-68), Nat. Planning Assn. (trustee, mem. finance com.), Soc. Chem. Industry, Ala. C. of C. (dir., pres.), Newcomen Soc. Episcopalian. Rotarian (dir. Birmingham). Clubs: Econ. of N.Y., N.Y. Yacht (N.Y.C.); Mountain Brook. Home: 1120 Beacon Pkwy E Birmingham AL 35205 Office: Vulcan Materials Co PO Box 7497 Birmingham AL 35223

WOOD, JOHN KARL, JR., physicist, educator; b. Logan, Utah, July 8, 1919; s. John Karl and Phebe (Ricks) W.; B.S., Utah State U., 1941; M.S., Pa. State U., 1942, Ph.D., 1946; m. Margaret Wilson, Mar. 15, 1947; children—James, Robert, Donald, Elizabeth. Optical engr. Bausch & Lomb Optical Co., 1946-48; prof. physics U. Wyo., 1948-56; prof. physics Utah State U., 1956—, head dept., 1956-66. Mem. Am. Phys. Soc., Acoustical Soc. Am., Am. Assn. Physics Tchrs., Sigma Xi. Contbr. articles to profl. jours. Home: 1359 Juniper Dr Logan UT 84321

WOOD, JOHN LEWIS, biochemist, educator; b. Homer, Ill., Aug. 7, 1912; s. Walter Horton and Ellen (Palmer) W.; student Blackburn Coll., 1930-32, D.Sc., 1955; B.S., U. Ill., 1934; Ph.D., U. Va, 1937; m. Amy Josephine Berks, Oct. 4, 1941; children—Linda Ellen, Philip Berks. With George Washington U. Med. Sch., 1937-38; research asso. Cornell U. Med. Sch., 1938-39; Finney-Howell fellow Harvard, 1940-41; asso. chemist U.S. Dept. Agr., Phila., 1941-42; research asso. Cornell U., 1942-44, asst. prof., 1944-46; mem. faculty U. Tenn., Memphis, 1946—, prof. biochemistry, 1950—, chmn. dept. biochemistry, 1954-68, Distinguished Service prof., 1972—, asso. dean Grad. Sch. Med. Scis., 1978—. Nat. Acad. Sci.-Polish Acad. Scis. exchange visitor, 1970. Oak Ridge Inst. fellow, 1949; Guggenheim fellow, 1954; USPHS Spl. Research fellow, 1965. Fellow Tenn. Acad. Scis.; mem. Am. Chem. Soc., Assn. Cancer Research, AAUP, Soc. Exptl. Biology and Medicine, AAAS, Soc. Biol. Chemists, Sigma Xi, Alpha Chi Sigma, Phi Lambda Upsilon. Research and publs. on organic and biochemistry. Home: 49 Sevier St Memphis TN 38111

WOOD, JOHN WAYNE HEADLEE, educator; b. Greene County, Mo., Aug. 1, 1929; s. John Roscoe and Midge Naydeen (Headlee) W.; B.A., S.W. Mo. State Coll., 1950; M.A., State U. Iowa, 1952, Ph.D., 1956. Research asst. Inst. Pub. Affairs, State U. Iowa, 1954-56; asst. prof. polit. sci., asst. dir. Bur. Govt. Research, U. Okla., 1956-58, 60-62; vis. asst. prof. U. Conn., 1958-59; faculty U. Okla., Norman, 1956—, prof. polit. sci., 1967—, chmn. dept., 1967-74, asst. dean Grad. Coll., 1974-76, dir. advanced programs (Europe), 1974-76. Cons. in field, 1957—. Tech. dir. Okla. Conf. State Govt. 1957; del. So. Assembly State Legislatures, 1967. Served with AUS, 1952-54. Mem. Am. Polit. Sci. Assn., Am. Soc. Pub. Adminstrn., AAUP, Pi Sigma Alpha. Author: (with H.V. Thronton) Problems in Oklahoma State Government, 1957. Home: 1415 Sycamore St Norman OK 73069

WOOD, JOSHUA WARREN, III, found. exec., lawyer; b. Portsmouth, Va., Aug. 31, 1941; s. Joshua Warren and Mary Evelyn (Carter) W.; A.B., Princeton U., 1963; J.D., U. Va., 1971; m. Marcia Neal Ramsey, Feb. 29, 1964; children—Lauren Elaine, Joshua Warren, IV. Comml. banking asst. Bankers Trust Co., N.Y.C., 1967-68; admitted to Va. bar, 1971, N.J. bar, 1976, U.S. Supreme Ct. bar, 1977; asso. firm McGuire, Woods & Battle, Richmond, Va., 1971-75; sec. Robert Wood Johnson Found., Princeton, N.J., 1975-77, sec., gen. counsel, 1977—. Bd. dirs. Princeton Area United Way, 1979—. Served to capt. arty. U.S. Army, 1963-67. Decorated Army Commendation medal. Mem. Am. Bar Assn., Princeton Bar Assn., Nat. Health Lawyers Assn., Order of Coif. Club: Princeton of N.Y. Editorial bd. Va. Law Rev., 1969-71. Office: PO Box 2316 Princeton NJ 08540

WOOD, LARRY (MARYLAIRD WOOD), journalist; b. Sandpoint, Idaho; d. Edward Hayes and Alice (McNeel) Small; B.A. magna cum laude, U. Wash., Seattle, 1938; M.A., 1940; postgrad. Stanford U., 1941-42; postgrad. U. Calif., Berkeley, 1943-44, certificate in photography, 1971; postgrad. journalism U. Wis., 1971-72, U. Minn., 1971-72, U. Ga., 1972-73; postgrad. in Art, Architecture and Biology, U. Calif., Santa Cruz, 1974-76; m. W. Byron Wood, Jan. 30, 1942 (div. May 1975); children—Mary, Marcia, Barry. By-line columnist Oakland (Calif.) Tribune, San Francisco Chronicle, 1946—; feature writer Western region Christian Sci. Monitor, CSM Radio Syndicate and Internat. News, 1973—, Register and Tribune Syndicate, Des Moines, 1975—, Calif. Today mag.; stringer Travelday mag., 1976—; No. Calif. contbg. editor Fashion Showcase, Dallas; regional corr. Spokane mag.; feature writer travel sect. San Jose Mercury-News; photographer/feature writer Scholastic Publs., 1974—; Calif. corr. Seattle Times Sunday mag.; freelance writer mag. including Parents', Sports Illus., Family Circle, Mechanix Illus., Oceans, Sea Frontiers, House Beautiful, Am. Home, Off-Duty, other nat. mags., 1946—; feature writer Donnelley Publs., Oak Brook, Ill.; dir. pub. relations No. Calif. Assn. Phi Beta Kappa, 1969—; cons., feature writer Met. Transp. Commn. No. Calif., 1970—; asst. prof. journalism San Diego State U., 1975—; prof. journalism San Jose State U., spring 1976; asst. prof. journalism Calif. State U., Hayward; prof. environ./sci. journalism U. Calif. Journalism Extension, 1979; prof. journalism U. of Pacific, spring 1979; keynote speaker Calif. State U. Women in Communications Conf., 1979, Nat. Assn. Edn. Journalism/Soc. Profl. Journalism Conf., 1979, Soc. Am. Travel Writers Conv., 1979; chmn. nat. travel writing contest for U.S. univ. journalism students Assn. for Edn. in Journalism/Soc. Am. Travel Writers, 1979-80; dir. public relations/cons. in field of sci., environ. affairs and recreation to numerous, firms, instns., assns.; del. Nat. Press Photographers Flying Short Course, 1979. Public Pub. relations dir. YWCA, YM-YW USO, Seattle, 1942-46, YWCA, Oakland, Calif., 1946-56, Children's Home Soc. Calif., 1946-56, Children's Med. Center No. Calif., 1946-70, Eastbay Regional Park Dist., 1946-58, Calif. Spring Garden Shows, 1946-58, Girl Scouts U.S.A., Oakland, 1948-56; speaker for ednl. insts., profl. groups, 1946—; sec. Jr. center of Arts, Oakland, 1952—; vol. pub. relations Am. Cancer Soc., YMCA, Oakland, 1946-52; pub. relations writer ARC, 1946-56; cons. Oakland Park Dept., YMCA, Seattle, Oakland. Bd. dirs. Camp Fire Girls, Oakland, Joaquin Miller PTA, Oakland. Trustee Calif. State Parks Found., 1976—. Recipient citations U.S. Forest Service, 1975, Nat. Park Service, 1976, Oakland Mus. Assn., 1978-79; named Calif. Woman of Achievement, 1979. Mem. Pub. Relations Soc. Am., Nat. Sch. Public Relations Assn., Environ. Cons. N.Am., Internat. Environ. Cons., Oceanic Soc., Internat. Oceanographic Soc., Am. Assn. Edn. in Journalism (exec. bd. nat. mag. div. 1978—, newspaper div. 1974-77), U. Wash. Ocean Scis. Alumni Assn. (charter), Investigative Reporters and Editors, Soc. Travel Writers Am., Soc. Profl. Journalists, Women in Communications, Calif. Acad. Environ. News Writers, Nat. Press Photographers Assn., San Francisco Press Club, Eastbay Women's Press Club, Calif. Writers Club, Sigma Delta Chi, Theta Sigma Phi. Home: 6161 Castle Dr Oakland CA 94611. *A creed I follow is Ralph Waldo Emerson's statement: "nothing great was ever achieved without enthusiasm." Living life creatively seems to require plenty of self-discipline, faith, focusing on goals and keeping a sense of wonderment.*

WOOD, LEE BLAIR, business exec.; b. Corry, Pa., Mar. 7, 1893; s. Perrie Grant and Mary Lavinia (Laing) W.; A.B., Amherst Coll., 1916; m. Mildred Louise Rody, June 26, 1924. Reporter, Cleve. Leader, 1916-17; telegraph editor Cleve. Press, 1920-22, night editor, 1923-24, news editor, 1924-25; mng. editor Okla. News, 1925-27; news editor York Telegram (later World Jour. Tribune), 1927-28, mng. editor, 1929-30, exec. editor, 1931-60, editor, 1960-62, pres., 1962-65; pres. Scripps-Howard Investment Co., N.Y.C., 1965—. Served as pvt. French Army, 1917; 2d lt. Motor Transport, U.S. Army, 1917-19. Mem. Phi Kappa Psi. Presbyterian. Mason. Home: 2021 King James Pkwy Apt 108B Westlake OH 44145 Office: Scripps-Howard Newspapers 200 Park Ave New York NY 10017

WOOD, MILTON LEGRAND, bishop; b. Selma, Ala., Aug. 21, 1922; s. Milton LeGrand and Roberta (Hawkins) W.; B.A., U. of South, 1943, B.D., 1945, D.D., 1967; clin. tng. Norristown (Pa.) State Hosp., 1945-46; m. Ann Scott, May 3, 1949; children—Leigh, Ann, Milton, Roberta. Ordained priest Episcopal Ch., 1946; rector in Mobile, 1946-52, Atlanta, 1952-60; dir. Appleton Ch. Home, also archdeacon, Macon, Ga., 1960-63; canon to bishop of Atlanta, 1963-67; suffragan bishop of Atlanta, 1967-74; exec. for adminstrn. Episcopal Ch. U.S.A., N.Y.C., 1974—. Home: 157 Old Church Rd Greenwich CT 06830 Office: 815 2d Ave New York NY 10017

WOOD, NATALIE (NATASHA GURDIN), actress; b. San Francisco, 1938; d. Nicholas and Marci (Kuleff) Gurdin; m. Robert Wagner, 1957 (div. 1962); m. 2d, Richard Gregson, May 31, 1969 (div.); 1 dau.; m. 3d, Robert Wagner, July 16, 1972; 1 dau., Courtney. First motion picture performance at age 4 in Happy Land, 1943; appeared in Tomorrow is Forever, 1946; other motion pictures include: The Bride Wore Boots, 1946, Miracle on 34th St., 1947, No Sad Songs for Me, 1950, Our Very Own, 1950, The Star, 1953, Rebel Without a Cause, 1955, The Searchers, Burning Hills, Girl He Left Behind, 1956, Marjorie Morningstar, 1957, Kings Go Forth, 1958, Cash McCall, 1959, All the Fine Young Cannibals, 1960, West Side Story, 1961, Splendor in the Grass, 1961, Gypsy, 1963, Sex and the Single Girl, 1964, The Great Race, 1965, Inside Daisy Clover, 1966, Penelope, 1966, Love with the Proper Stranger, 1964, This Property is Condemned, 1966, Bob and Carol and Ted and Alice, 1969, Peeper, 1975, Meteor, 1979; appeared on TV in Cat on a Hot Tin Roof, From Here to Eternity. Address: care Internat Creative Mgmt 8899 Beverly Blvd Los Angeles CA 90048*

WOOD, PERCY ADDISON, airline exec.; b. Oakland, Calif., June 7, 1920; s. Percy Addison and Eliza Raphelea (Baum) W.; student Stanford U., 1938-40, Boeing Sch. Aeros., 1940-42; m. Mary Josephine Sherwood, Sept. 24, 1942; children—Andrew P., Robert W., Richard H., Kenneth A. With United Air Lines, Inc., Chgo., 1941—, sr. v.p., gen. mgr. Eastern div., 1971-74, group v.p. ops. services, 1974-75, exec. v.p., 1975-78, chief operating officer, 1975—, pres., 1978—; pres. Peninsula Mfrs. Assn., San Mateo, Calif., 1968, named Industry Man of Year, 1968. Mem. San Francisco Air Pollution Control Bd., 1966-68; pres. Jr. Achievement of San Francisco, 1967, Jr. Achievement of Northwestern Suburbs, Chgo., 1969; dir. Nat. Jr. Achievement Program, 1967, Transp. Research Bd., 1974-75. Mem. Soc. Automotive Engrs., Max McGraw Wildlife Found. Clubs: Internat. (Washington); Wings (N.Y.C.); Chgo. Yacht; Knollwood. Home: 887 Forest Hill Lake Forest IL 60045 Office: PO Box 66100 Chicago IL 60666

WOOD, PETER LAWRENCE, theatrical and TV dir.; b. Colyton. Devonshire, Eng., Oct. 8, 1927; s. Frank and Lucy Eleanor (Meeson) W.; student Downing Coll., Cambridge U. Directorial debut Moment of Truth, Arts Theatre Club, Cambridge, 1954; dir. Worthing Repertory Theatre; resident dir. Oxford Playhouse, 1955-56, Arts Theatre, London, 1956-57; dir.: The Iceman Cometh, 1958; The Birthday Party, 1958; Mary Stuart, 1958; As You Like It (Shakespeare Festival, Ont.), 1959; The Winter's Tale, 1961; The Devils, 1961; Hamlet, 1961; The Private Ear and the Private Eye, Eng., 1962, N.Y.C., 1963; The Beggar's Opera, 1963; The Master Builder, 1964; Carving a Statue, 1964; Poor Richard, 1964; touring prodn. of Loot, 1965; Love for Love, Eng., 1965, Can., 1967; Incident at Vichy, 1966; The Prime of Miss Jean Brodie, 1966; Design for Living, Los Angeles, 1971; Rosencrantz and Guildenstern are Dead, 1971; Jumpers, Eng., 1972, Vienna, 1973, Washington and N.Y.C., 1974; Macbeth, Los Angeles, 1975; Travesties, Eng., 1974, N.Y.C., 1975; dir. film In Search of Gregory, 1970; dir. numerous plays and dramatic programs on Brit. and Am. TV, including Hamlet, 1970, Long Day's Journey into Night, 1973, Dear Love, 1976, Flint, 1977; dir. Caedmon Records and RCA; dir. opera The Mother of Us All, Santa Fe, summer 1976, The Guardsman, 1977, Cosi Fan Tutte, Santa

Fe, 1977, Betrayal, Vienna, 1978, The Guardsman, The Double Dealer, London, 1978, Night and Day, London, 1979. Served with RAF, 1946-48.

WOOD, PHILIP W., bus. exec.; b. Chatham, N.J., Dec. 29, 1924; s. Ernest Bowker and Sara Frances (Cook) W.; A.B., Princeton U., 1948; m. Emily Churchill, June 22, 1946; children—Martha, Arthur, Benjamin, Warren. Tech. rep. Union Carbide Corp., St. Louis, 1948-51; v.p. sales KSH Plastics, High Ridge, Mo., 1951-53; region mgr., dept. mgr. Union Carbide Corp., Chgo., N.Y.C., 1953-66; v.p. plastics div. Cities Service Co., N.Y.C., 1966-72, v.p. plastics and spl. products div., 1972-76, v.p. planning and econ. div., Tulsa, 1976-78, exec. v.p. planning and tech. div., 1978—. Vice-pres. Arts and Humanities Council of Tulsa, 1979-80; bd. dirs. Tulsa Opera, Inc., 1979-80. Served with AUS, 1943-46. Mem. Nat. Assn. Bus. Economists. Clubs: Petroleum, Summit (Tulsa); Princeton Colonial (N.Y.C.). Home: 3622 S Yorktown Pl Tulsa OK 74105 Office: PO Box 300 Tulsa OK 74102

WOOD, QUENTIN EUGENE, oil co. exec.; b. Mechanicsburg, Pa., Mar. 5, 1923; s. Lloyd Paul and Greta (Myers) W.; B.S., Pa. State U., 1948; m. Louise Lowe, Apr. 14, 1958. Petroleum engr. Quaker State Oil Refining Corp., Parkersburg, W.Va., 1948-52, chief engr., Bradford, Pa., 1952-55, mgr. prodn., 1955-68, v.p. prodn., Oil City, Pa., 1968-70, exec. v.p., Oil City, 1970-73, pres., chief operations officer, Oil City, 1973-75, pres., chief exec. officer, 1975—. Chmn. industry tech. advisory com. U.S. Bur. Mines, 1960—, Penn Grade Tech. Advisory Com., 1955-69, Pa. Oil and Gas Conservation Commn., 1961—. Trustee Pa. State U. Served to 1st lt. USAAF, 1943-46. Mem. Am. Inst. Metall. Engrs., Pa. Grade Crude Oil Assn. (dir.), Pa. Oil Producers Assn. (past pres., dir. Bradford dist.), Am. Petroleum Inst. (dir.), Nat. Petroleum Refiners Assn. Home: 5 Crestview Dr Oil City PA 16301 Office: 11 Center St Oil City PA 16301

WOOD, RAWSON LYMAN, ret. foundry exec.; b. N.Y.C., Sept. 16, 1908; s. Rawson Lyman and Teresa (Schwab) W.; A.B., Harvard, 1930; LL.D., Seton Hall U., St. John's U., Xavier U.; m. Elizabeth F. Ford, Oct. 10, 1931; children—Sheila (Mrs. Walter G. Langlois), Ellen (Mrs. Gunther Barth), Rawson Lyman, Carolyn (Mrs. Dudley Moorhead), Hilary. Chmn. bd. J.R. Wood & Sons, N.Y.C., 1930-70, Arwood Corp., Rockleigh, N.J., 1943-76; dir. Lenox Corp., 1970—. Mem. North Hempstead Housing Authority, 1946-53, chmn., 1951-53; chmn. Nassau County Commn. on Human Rights, 1965-68. Bd. dirs. Council Profit Sharing Industries, 1945-65, chmn. bd., 1960-62; chmn. bd. Africa Service Inst., N.Y.C., 1960-67; v.p. N.Y. Urban League, 1968-72; trustee Xavier U., 1971-76, Marlboro Sch. Music, Profit Sharing Research Found.; treas. Forum on Future N.H., 1978—; mem. Lakes Region Planning Commn., 1979—. Mem. Nat. Audubon Soc. (dir. 1967-73), Audubon Soc. N.H. (trustee). Author: (with Davidlee Von Ludwig) Investment Casting for Engineers, 1952. Home: High Haith Rd Center Harbor NH 03226

WOOD, RAYMOND HARLAND, coast guard officer; b. Concord, N.H., June 24, 1927; s. Ariel Remington and Ruth (Kibby) W.; B.S. in Engring., U.S. Coast Guard Acad., 1950; grad. U.S. Naval War Coll., 1970; M.S. in Internat. Affairs, George Washington U., 1970; m. Marjorie Stearns, June 4, 1950; children—Janet Louise Wood Bilodeau, Stephen Allan. Commd. ensign U.S. Coast Guard, 1950, advanced through grades to rear adm., 1977; served on various ships, 1950-57; officer-in-charge Officer Candidate Sch., 1959-61; comdr. USCGC Blackhaw, 1961-63; mem. staff USCG, Boston, 1963-66, Washington, 1966-69, chief congressional affairs, 1972-76; chief of staff 5th Coast Guard Dist., Portsmouth, Va., 1976-77; chief Office Public and Internat. Affairs, USCG Hdqrs., Washington, 1977-79; maritime policy adv. to Sec. Transp., Washington, 1979—. Decorated Coast Guard Commendation medal, Meritorious Service medal with gold star. Mem. U.S. Naval Inst., Nat. Geog. Soc., U.S. Coast Guard Acad. Alumni Assn. Office: 400 7th St SW Washington DC 20590

WOOD, REUBEN ESSELSTYN, educator, chemist; b. Lansing, Mich., Apr. 1, 1915; s. Frank Esler and Helen (Esselstyn) W.; B.S., Calif. Inst. Tech., 1936, Ph.D., 1939, postdoctoral fellow, 1939-43; M.S., U. Chgo., 1937; sr. research fellow Md. Research Labs., 1943-45; asst. prof. chemistry George Washington U., 1945-51, asso. prof., 1952-57, prof., 1958—. Cons. Office of Saline Water, 1955-65; chemist Nat. Bur. Standards, 1955-70; pres. Med. & Tech. Summaries, Inc. Mem. Am. Chem. Soc., Electrochem. Soc., AAUP, AAAS, Washington, N.Y. acads. scis., Am. Inst. Chemists. Club: Cosmos (Washington). Author: (with Walter Hamer) Electrolytic Conductivity and Electrode Processes, rev. edit., 1967; Introduction to Chemical Thermodynamics, 1970. Contbr. articles to tech. jours. Research in electrochemistry, thermodynamics. Home: 3120 N Pershing Dr Arlington VA 22201 Office: George Washington Univ Washington DC 20052

WOOD, RICHARD DONALD, pharm. co. exec.; b. Brazil, Ind., Oct. 22, 1926; s. Howard T. and Dorothy F. (Norfolk) W.; B.S., Purdue U., 1948, LL.D., 1973; M.B.A., U. Pa., 1950; LL.D., DePauw U., 1972, LL.D., Phila. Coll. Pharmacy and Sci.; D.Sc., Butler U., 1974; m. Billie Lou Carpenter, Dec. 29, 1951; children—Catherine Ann, Marjorie Elizabeth. Gen. mgr. ops. in Argentina, Eli Lilly & Co., 1961, dir. ops. Mex. and Central Am., 1962-70; pres. Eli Lilly Internat. Corp., 1970-72; pres. Eli Lilly & Co., Indpls., 1972-73, chmn. bd., chief exec. officer, dir., 1973—; dir. N.Y. Chem. Corp., Chem. Bank, Elizabeth Arden, Inc., Standard Oil Co. (Ind.), Dow Jones & Co., Eli Lilly Internat., Elanco Products Co., IVAC Corp. Bd. dirs. Lilly Endowment, Inc.; trustee Am. Enterprise Inst., Park-Tudor Sch., DePauw U.; bd. govs. Asso. Colls. of Ind. Mem. Internat. C. of C. (trustee U.S. council), Com. for Econ. Devel., Conf. Bd., Council Fgn. Relations, Indpls. Mus. Art (dir.), Pharm. Mfrs. Assn. (dir.), Ind. State Symphony Soc. (dir.). Presbyterian. Clubs: Links (N.Y.C.); Indpls. Athletic, Meridian Hills Country (Indpls.). Home: 5715 Sunset Ln Indianapolis IN 46208 Office: 307 E McCarty St Indianapolis IN 46206

WOOD, ROBERT COLDWELL, supt. schs.; b. St. Louis, Sept. 16, 1923; s. Thomas Frank and Mary (Bradshaw) W.; A.B., Princeton U., 1946; M.A., Harvard U., 1947, M.P.A., 1948, Ph.D., 1950; m. Margaret Byers, Mar. 22, 1952; children—Frances, Margaret, Frank Randolph. Asso. dir. Fla. Legis. Reference Bur., Tallahassee, 1949-51; mgmt. orgn. expert U.S. Bur. Budget, Washington, 1951-54; lectr. govt. Harvard U., 1954-55, asst. prof., 1955-57; asst. prof. polit. sci. M.I.T., 1957-59, asso. prof., 1959-62, prof., 1962-66, head dept., 1965-66, 69-70; undersec. HUD, Washington, 1966-68, sec., 1969; chmn. Mass. Bay Transp. Authority, Boston, 1969-70; dir. Harvard U.-M.I.T. Joint Center for Urban Studies, Cambridge, 1969-70; pres. U. Mass., 1970-77; now supt. Boston Pub. Schs. Trustee Mus. Sci. Boston. Served with inf. AUS, World War II. Decorated Bronze Star. Mem. Am. Acad. Arts and Scis., Am. Soc. Pub. Adminstrn., Council on Fgn. Relations, Phi Beta Kappa. Clubs: Cosmos (Washington); Tavern (Boston); University (N.Y.C.). Author: Suburbia, Its People and Their Politics, 1958; Metropolis Against Itself, 1959; 1400 Governments, The Political Economy of the New York Region, 1960; The Necessary Majority, Middle America and Urban Crisis, 1972; (with others) Schoolmen and Politics, 1962, Government and Politics of the U.S., 1965.

WOOD, ROBERT EDWARD, newspaper exec.; b. Libertyville, Ill., Dec. 30, 1941; s. John Howard and Ruth (Hendrickson) W.; A.B. cum laude, Princeton, 1963; M.B.A., Harvard, 1968; m. Beth Henryta Oakes, Aug. 10, 1968; children—David Charles, John Robert. Financial writer Los Angeles Times, 1968-72, financial editor, 1972-75, editorial writer, 1975-78; asst. v.p. Mpls. Star and Tribune Co., 1978—. Served with USNR, 1963-66. Decorated Purple Heart, Vietnamese medal of honor 1st Class; recipient Sec. Navy commendation for achievement. Home: 1809 James Ave S Minneapolis MN 55403 Office: Mpls Star and Tribune Co IDS Tower 6th Floor Minneapolis MN 55402

WOOD, ROBERT ELKINGTON, II, retail co. exec.; b. Houston, May 7, 1938; s. Robert Whitney and Elizabeth Cushing (Neville) W.; B.A., Princeton U., 1960; m. Susan Mayer, Jan. 5, 1963; children—Katherine, Elizabeth. With Sears, Roebuck & Co., 1960—, v.p., Chgo., 1970—; dir. Standard Havens, Inc., Kansas City, Mo. Trustee Hull House Assn., 1970—, pres., 1974-75; bd. dirs. Urban Ventures, Inc., 1971-76. Republican. Episcopalian. Office: Sears Roebuck & Co Sears Tower Chicago IL 60684

WOOD, ROBERT HART, cons. civil engr.; b. Columbus, Miss., Dec. 9, 1910; s. Charles Lyon and Lena (Roden) W.; B.C.E., Miss. State Coll., 1932; M.S., Purdue U., 1933; m. Esther Louise Drake, Sept. 21, 1940; children—Robert Hart, Charles Drake, Sarah Esther. With Miss. Hwy. Dept., 1933-37, 38-40, 46; structural designer Va. Bridge Co., Birmingham, Ala., 1937-38; asst. chief engr., then asso. Hazelet & Erdal, cons. engrs., Louisville, 1946-56, partner, 1956—. Trustee Ridgewood Assn., 1954-58; mem. Louisville and Jefferson County Planning and Zoning Commn., 1954-57. Served to lt. col. AUS, 1940-46. Registered profl. engr., Ky., Miss., Ind., Mich., Tenn., Ark., Ga., La. Fellow, life mem. ASCE; fellow Am. Cons. Engrs. Council, Am. Concrete Inst.; mem. Ky. Soc. Profl. Engrs. (Outstanding Engr. in Pvt. Practice award 1975-76), Cons. Engrs. Council Ky. (dir., past pres.), Internat. Assn. Bridge and Structural Engrs., Transp. Research Bd., ASTM, Louisville Area C. of C. (charter), Hon. Order Ky. Cols., Sigma Xi, Tau Beta Pi, Phi Kappa Phi. Democrat. Presbyterian. Clubs: Pendennis, Big Spring Country (Louisville). Author articles in field. Home: 502 Ridgewood Rd Louisville KY 40207 Office: 304 W Liberty St Louisville KY 40202

WOOD, ROBERT HEMSLEY, educator; b. Bklyn., May 8, 1932; s. Alexander Hemsley and Mildred Irene (Cuthbert) W.; B.S. in Chemistry, Calif. Inst. Tech., 1953; Ph.D., U. Cal., Berkeley, 1957; m. Peggy Ann Jackson, July 13, 1956; children—Michael Hemsley, Mark Lynn. Instr. chemistry U. Del., Newark, 1957-58, asst. prof., 1958-63, asso. prof., 1963-70, chmn. dept., 1969-71, prof., 1970—. Vis. prof. U. Newcastle Upon Tyne, Eng., 1966. Mem. Am. Chem. Soc., Del. Acad. Sci., Sigma Xi. Research in phys.-inorganic chemistry. Home: 206 Grantham Pl Newark DE 19711

WOOD, ROBERT JAMES, pub. relations exec.; b. Syracuse, N.Y., Nov. 27, 1918; s. John Marshall and Anna Mae (Wood) W.; student U. Toronto, 1936-37, Syracuse U., 1937-38; postgrad. Columbia U. Grad. Sch. Bus., 1953; m. Jean K. Buchanan, Feb. 22, 1945; children—Judith Ann, Robert James, Maureen Elizabeth. Reporter, Syracuse (N.Y.) Herald Jour. and Central N.Y. corr. AP, 1939-43; v.p. Carl Byoir & Assos., Inc., N.Y.C., 1951-61, exec. v.p., 1961-65, pres., 1965—, chief exec. officer, 1976—. Vice pres. Found. Public Relations Research and Edn., 1975—; trustee Ill. Coll., JacksonVille, 1967—; chmn. pub. relations com. Community Fund Scarsdale (N.Y.), 1955-56. Served as officer USAF, 1943-46. Mem. Pub. Relations Soc. Am. Republican. Roman Catholic. Clubs: Winged Foot Golf (Mamaroneck, N.Y.); Pinnacle, Board Room (N.Y.C.). Home: 45 Drake Rd Scarsdale NY 10583 Office: Carl Byoir & Assos 380 Madison Ave New York NY 10017

WOOD, RONALD, musician; b. London, June 1, 1947. Guitarist and bassist with Jeff Beck Group, 1966-69, Faces, 1969-75, Rolling Stones, 1975—, New Barbarians, 1979; solo recs. include: I've Got My Own Album to Do, New Look, Gimme Some Neck. Office: Rolling Stones Records 75 Rockefeller Plaza New York NY 10019*

WOOD, ROY VAUGHN, educator; b. Salida, Colo., Sept. 18, 1939; s. Dwight Maynard and Allene (Swafford) W.; B.A., U. Denver, 1961, M.A., 1962, Ph.D., 1965; m. Mary Alice Tudor, Aug. 28, 1960; children—Shelley Lynne, Angela Jane. Asst. prof. and dir. forensics U. Denver, Denver, 1965-67; asst. prof. speech Northwestern U., Evanston, Ill., 1967-68, asst. dean, 1968-69, asso. prof. and asso. dean, 1969-72, prof. and dean Sch. Speech, 1972—. Cons. Sears, Roebuck & Co., 1969—, A.C. Nielsen & Co., 1969—; cons. N. Central Assn., 1973—. Bd. dirs. Evanston Theatre Co., 1975—. Mem. Advanced Mgmt. Inst. (dir. 1973—), Internat. Communication Assn., Speech Communication Assn., Assn. Communication Adminstrs. Author: Strategic Debate, 1968, and others. Contbr. articles to profl. jours. Office: 1905 Sheridan Rd Evanston IL 60201

WOOD, SARAH CATHERINE. see Marshall, Sarah Catherine Wood

WOOD, STANLEY GEORGE, cons. co. exec.; b. Taunton, Mass., Aug. 6, 1919; s. George H. and Anna G. (Melia) W.; B.S. in Chem. Engring., Northeastern U., 1942; M.S. in Meteorology, Calif. Inst. Tech., 1943; m. Shirley C. Douglas, Mar. 15, 1943; children—Sally L., Douglas A., Donald S. Supt., Fall River Gas Co. (Mass.), 1946-53; exec. asst. to pres. Atlanta Gas Light Co., 1954-60; cons. Stone & Webster, N.Y.C., 1960-63, sr. v.p. Wash. Natural Gas Co., Seattle, 1963-73; exec. v.p., dir. Cascade Natural Gas Corp., Seattle, 1973-76; v.p. Stone & Webster Mgmt. Consultants, Inc., N.Y.C., 1976—. Served with USAAF, 1942-46. Mem. Am., New Eng. gas assns. Republican. Methodist. Home: 275 Lake St Upper Saddle River NJ 07458 Office: 90 Broad St New York City NY 10004

WOOD, STEVEN PIERPONT JEFFRIS, mfg. co. exec.; b. Forsythe, Mont., 1917; s. Pierpont J.E. and Helen (Jeffris) W.; grad. Phillips Exeter Acad., 1935; student Princeton U., Ill. Inst. Tech.; m. Colette Blitz, Apr. 11, 1962; children—Paula, Susan B. With Warner Electric Brake & Clutch Co., Beloit, Wis., 1946—, chmn. bd., dir., 1953—, pres., 1953-67; dir. Warner Electric, Inc., Lausanne, Warner France, LeMans, Warner GmbH, Stuttgart, Warner Electric Ltd., Durham, Eng., Beaver Precision Products, Inc., Troy, Mich. Mem. Wis. Republican. Finance Com. Pres. stateline United Givers Fund, 1966; adv. com. Wis. Found. for Ind. Colls. Served from pvt. to maj. F.A., AUS, 1941-46. Mem. Ill. C. of C., Wis. Hist. Soc. (bd. curators), Delta Kappa Epsilon. Clubs: University (Chgo.); Princeton (Milw.); Canon (Princeton U.). Office: Warner Electric Brake & Clutch Co 449 Gardner St South Beloit IL 61080

WOOD, THOMAS HAMIL, educator; b. Atlanta, June 22, 1923; s. Edwin McEuin and Abbie Sherman (Huckaby) W.; B.S., U. Fla., 1946; Ph.D., U. Chgo., 1953; m. Mary Lucy Mendenhall, Mar. 17, 1951; children—David, Robert, Scott. Asst. prof. U. Pa., Phila., 1953-57, asso. prof., 1957-63, prof. physics, 1963—. Vis. scientist Institut du Radium, Paris, 1961-62; vis. prof. U. Leicester (Eng.), 1967-68. Served with USNR, 1944-46. NSF Sr. Faculty fellow, 1961-62; NIH Spl. fellow, 1967-68. Mem. Biophys. Soc., Radiation Research Soc., Genetics Soc., Microbiol. Soc., Phi Beta Kappa. Home: 375 Baird Rd Merion PA 19066 Office: Dept Physics U Pa Philadelphia PA 19104

WOOD, THOMAS HERMON, newspaper exec.; b. Knoxville, Tenn., Nov. 3, 1939; s. Jesse Hermon and Lena (Lovett) W.; B.S., U. Tenn., 1961; m. Evelyn Frances Martin, June 4, 1960; children—Jennifer Carol, Karen Patricia. With Haskins & Sells, C.P.A.'s, Atlanta, 1961-66; controller Atlanta Newspapers, Inc., 1966-68, sec., treas., 1968-70, bus. mgr., treas., 1970-75, exec. v.p., gen. mgr., 1975-76, pres., 1976—; sec. Cox Enterprises, Inc. Sec., trustee James M. Cox Found. of Ga. C.P.A., Ga. Mem. Am. Newspaper Pubs. Assn., Newspaper Advisory Bur. (dir.), Atlanta C. of C. (dir.). Home: 3559 Castlehill Way Tucker GA 30084 Office: 72 Marietta St Atlanta GA 30303

WOOD, WILLIAM BARRY, III, biologist, educator; b. Balt., Feb. 19, 1938; s. William Barry, Jr. and Mary Lee (Hutchins) W.; A.B., Harvard, 1959; Ph.D., Stanford, 1963; m. Marie-Elisabeth Renate Hartisch, June 30, 1961; children—Oliver Hartisch, Christopher Barry. Asst. prof. biology Calif. Inst. Tech., Pasadena, 1965-68, asso. prof., 1968-69, prof. biology, 1970-77; prof. molecular, cellular and developmental biology U. Colo., Boulder, 1977—; chmn. dept., 1978—; mem. panel for developmental biology NSF, 1970-72, physiol. chemistry study sect. NIH, 1974-78; mem. com. on sci. and public policy Nat. Acad. Scis., 1979—. Recipient U.S. Steel Molecular Biology award, 1969; NIH research grantee, 1965—; Guggenheim fellow, 1975-76. Mem. Nat. Acad. Scis., Am. Acad. Arts and Scis., Am. Soc. Biol. Chemists, Soc. for Developmental Biology, AAAS. Author: (with J.H. Wilson, R.M. Benbow, L.E. Hood) Biochemistry: A Problems Approach, 1974; (with L.E. Hood and J.H. Wilson) Molecular Biology of Eucaryotic Cells, 1975; (with L.E. Hood and I.L. Weissman) Immunology, 1978; Concepts in Immunology, 1978. Contbr. articles to profl. jours. Office: Dept MCD Biology U Colorado Boulder CO 80309

WOOD, WILLIAM JEROME, lawyer; b. Indpls., Feb. 14, 1928; s. Joseph Gilmore and Anne Cecelia (Morris) W.; student Butler U., 1945-46; A.B. with honors, Ind. U., 1950, J.D. with distinction, 1952; m. Joann Janet Jones, Jan. 23, 1954; children—Steven, Matthew, Kathleen, Michael, Joseph, James, Julie, David. Admitted to Ind. bar, 1952; mem. firm Wood, Tuohy, Gleason & Mercer, and predecessor, Indpls., 1952—; dir. Am. Income Life Ins. Co., Waco, Tex., Grain Dealers Mut. Ins. Co., Indpls., gen. counsel Ind. Realtors Assn., Ind., Cath. Conf., Ind. Assn. Osteo. Physicians and Surgeons; city atty. Indpls., part-time, 1959-60; instr. Ind. U. Sch. Law, part-time, 1960-62. Mem. Ind. Corp. Survey Commn., 1963—, chmn., 1977—. Past bd. dirs. Alcoholic Rehab. Center, Indpls., Indpls. Lawyers' Commn., Community Service Council Indpls., Indpls. Bar Found. Served with AUS, 1946-48. Recipient Brotherhood award Ind. region NCCJ, 1973. Mem. Am., Ind. (award 1968, sec. 1977-78), Indpls. (pres. 1972-73) bar assns., St. Thomas More Legal Soc. (pres. 1970), Nat. Audubon Soc. Democrat. Roman Catholic. Clubs: Indianapolis Literary (pres. 1973-74), K.C., Indianapolis Athletic. Home: 7265 Merriam Rd Indianapolis IN 46240 Office: 19th Floor Indiana Tower 1 Indiana Sq Indianapolis IN 46204

WOOD, WILLIAM RANSOM, univ. pres.; b. nr. Jacksonville, Ill., Feb. 3, 1907; s. William James and Elizabeth Ransom) W.; A.B., Ill. Coll., 1927, LL.D., 1960; A.M., U. Iowa, 1936, Ph.D., 1939; m. Margaret Osborne, 1930 (dec. 1942); 1 son, William Osborne (dec. 1978); m. 2d, Dorothy Jane Irving, Mar. 18, 1944; children—Mark Irving, Karen Jane Parrish. Tchr. and coach pub. schs., Mich., Iowa, Ill., 1928-46; asst. supt. Evanston (Ill.) Twp. Schs., 1948-50; specialist jr. colls. and lower divs. U.S. Office Edn., 1950-53, program planning officer, 1953; dean statewide devel. higher edn. U. Nev., 1954-55, acting chmn. dept. English, 1955-56, acad. v.p., 1955-60, acting pres., 1958-60; pres. U. Alaska, 1960-73; mayor, Fairbanks, Alaska, 1978—. Pres. Pacific Alaska Assos., Ltd., 1971—; exec. v.p. Fairbanks Indsl. Devel. Corp. Mem. staff study needs and resources higher edn. FAO, Libya, 1955; study group off-duty ednl. program armed forces in Europe, Dept. Def., 1955; del. Am. Assembly Fgn. Relations, 1957-58; chmn. Nev. com. Fulbright Scholarships, 1957, 58; mem. chancellor's panel State U. N.Y.; mem. sci. group traveling to Antarctica, New Zealand, Australia. Chmn. for Alaska Am. Cancer Soc.; v.p. Alaska council Boy Scouts Am.; mem. bd. Rampart Dam Advisory Com.; mem. Gen. Med. Scis. Nat. Advisory Council; mem. Alaska Higher Edn. Facilites Commn., 1967, Alaska Small Bus. Advisory Council, 1968, Satellite Communications Task Force; chmn. Greater Fairbanks Community Hosp. Found.; mem. White House Fellows Selection Panel, 1975—; mem. Nat. Adv. Council on Edn. Professions Devel.; chmn. Alaska Heart Assn. Served to lt. USNR, 1943-46. Fellow Arctic Inst. N. Am.; mem. Am. Geog. Soc., Assn. Higher Edn. (exec. com.), Nat. Univ. Extension Assn., N.W. Assn. Secondary and Higher Schs., Western Assn. Colls., Navy League, AAAS, Assn. Applied Solar Energy (advisory council 1959), Am. Assn. Land-grant Colls. and State Univs., Internat. Assn. Univ. Presidents (exec. com.). Methodist. Rotarian. Clubs: Explorers; Fairbanks Petroleum; Washington Athletic. Editor: Looking Around, 1953; From Here On, 1954; All Around the Land, 1954; Youth and the World, 1955; To Be An American, 1957; editor, author: On Your Own, 1953. Co-editor; Short Stories as You Like Them, 1940; Youth Thinks it Through, 1941; Just for Sport, 1943; Fact and Opinion, 1945; Short, Short Stories, 1951; Study of Financing of Higher Education in Asia, 1968. Address: 665 10th Ave Fairbanks AK 99701. *On her 100th birthday, my mother—now past 103—gave me this good counsel: "Son, if there is ever anything to be done that is really important to you, do it yourself. Don't ask others or the government to do it for you; rely upon yourself to accomplish whatever is necessary and right."*

WOODALL, NORMAN EUGENE, banker; b. Miss., June 10, 1916; s. Albert Edward and Annie (Smith) W.; B.S. in Bus. Adminstrn., Miss. State U., 1939; postgrad. Am. Inst. Banking, 1962; grad. Sch. Banking of South, La. State U., 1964, Advanced Inf. Sch., 1959, Command and Gen. Staff Coll., 1965, Indsl. Coll. Armed Forces, 1970; m. Virginia Dale Willard, Aug. 12, 1967. Adjuster Comml. Credit Co., Jackson, Miss., 1939-41; loan examiner RFC, Birmingham, Ala., 1946-55; sr. v.p. First Nat. Bank Birmingham, 1955—. Bd. dirs. Birmingham chpt. ARC, 1974-78. Served with AUS, 1941-46. Decorated Bronze Star with V devise, Legion of Merit. Mem. Res. Officers Assn., Assn. U.S. Army, Am. Inst. Banking, Miss. State U. Alumni Assn., Birmingham C. of C., Birmingham Exchange Club (gov. 1960-62, 71-72, 75-76, v.p. 73-74, pres. 1974-75), Newcomer Soc. N.Am., Sigma Chi. Clubs: Vestavia Country (Vestavia Hills, Ala.); The Club Birmingham. Home: 3422 Loch Ridge Trail Birmingham AL 35216 Office: 1900 5th Ave N Birmingham AL 35203

WOODALL, WILLIAM CLEMENTS, JR., broadcasting co. exec.; b. Columbus, Ga., Oct. 2, 1916; s. William C. and Virginia Ethel (McGehee) W.; A.B., U. Ga., 1940; m. Margaret Anne Swindle, June 29, 1940; children—Dorothy, Orson, Hardy. Founder, mgr., owner Sta. WDWD, Dawson, Ga., 1948—; owner, mgr. Sta. WGRA, Cairo, Ga., 1950—, Sta. WFPM, Fort Valley, Ga., 1952—, Sta. WIMO, Winder, Ga., 1954—, Sta. WGSW, Greenwood, S.C., 1955—, Sta. WBBK, Blakeley, Ga., 1956—, Sta. WDSR, Lake City, Fla., 1968—, WTLD-FM, Lake City, 1968—, WMEN, Tallahassee, Fla., 1971—,

Sta. WPFA, Pensacola, Fla., 1971—, Sta. WWNS, Statesboro, Ga., 1975—. Sta. WMCD, Statesboro, 1975—; dir. Bank of Terrell, Dawson; chmn. Ga. Radio Inst., U. Ga., Athens, 1955. Served with USN, 1942-45. Mem. Nat., Ga. (award 1955) assns. broadcasters, Nat. Radio Broadcasters Assn. Republican. Methodist. Club: Rotary. Home: 410 Johnson St Dawson GA 31742 Office: 110 N Main St Dawson GA 31742

WOODARD, CHARLES CLIFTON, JR., cable TV cons.; b. Los Angeles, Aug. 11, 1923; s. Charles Clifton and Lois (McClure) W.; A.B., U. Calif. at Los Angeles, 1946; J.D. Stanford, 1949; m. Margaret Evalyn McHaffie, June 20, 1944; children—Charles Clifton III, Kathryn Ann, Melissa Sue, Deborah Jean. Admitted to Calif. bar, 1950, N.Y. bar, 1955; atty. legal dept. CBS, Los Angeles, 1950-53, sr. TV atty., also asst. gen. atty., N.Y.C., 1953-57; v.p. Westinghouse Broadcasting Co., N.Y.C., 1957-63, 65-70; v.p. Teleprompter Corp., 1970-72; asso. dir. Peace Corps, 1963-65; pres. Clearview of Ga., 1965-70, Micro-Relay, Inc., 1965-70, Theta Cable of Calif., 1971-72, Covenant Cable, Inc., 1972-74; v.p. Broad Street Communications, 1972-74; pres. Charles Woodard Assos., Inc., 1974—. Mayor, Hastings-on-Hudson, 1959-61, mem. Bd. Edn., 1968-71. Served to 1st lt., inf. AUS, 1943-46. Decorated Bronze Star, Purple Heart. Mem. State Bar Calif. Unitarian. Address: 60 Edgars Ln Hastings-on-Hudson NY 10706

WOODARD, CLARENCE JAMES, mfg. co. exec.; b. Conde, S.D., May 8, 1923; s. Wayne W. and Sarah (Halley) W.; student Stanford, 1941-43; B.S. in Mech. Engring., Calif. Inst. Tech., 1944; m. Patricia Ann Roberts, Jan. 12, 1946; children—Charles D., Sarah H., Scott D., Thomas J. Div. gen. mgr. Baldwin-Lima-Hamilton Co., 1946-53; with Rucker Co., Oakland, Calif., 1953-77, chmn. bd., chief exec. officer, 1965-77; cons. to bd. dirs., dir., mem. operating and fin. coms. NL Industries, Inc., 1977—; dir., chmn. audit and nominating coms. Delta Calif. Industries, Oakland. Past chmn., mem. West Coast exec. council Nat. Indsl. Conf. Bd. Bd. dirs., adv. bd. U. Calif. Schs. Bus. Adminstrn.; bd. dirs. Boys Clubs Am., Alameda County YMCA; past chmn. San Francisco Bay Area council Boys Club Am.; bd. dirs., past pres. Oakland Boys Clubs; past bd. dirs. Childrens Hosp. Found. Oakland; mem. nat. council Salk Inst.; trustee Orinda Found.; past bd. dirs., vice chmn. gen. budget com. United Way of Bay Area. Served to lt. (j.g.) USNR, 1943-46. Mem. ASME, Inst. Environ. Scis., Tau Beta Pi. Clubs: St. Francis Yacht, World Trade, Commonwealth (San Francisco); Athenian Nile (Oakland); Orinda (Calif.) Country; Les Ambassadeurs (London). Office: PO Box 23230 Oakland CA 94623

WOODARD, GEORGE HATFIELD, mgmt. cons.; b. Schenectady, Mar. 4, 1906; s. William E. and Phebe A. (Hatfield) W.; M.E., Cornell U., 1928; m. Anita Synnestvedt, Dec. 8, 1934 (dec. 1945); children—Anna (Mrs. Dandridge Pendleton,), David W., Kim; m. 2d, Nancy C. Horigan, Feb. 23, 1946; children—Dan H., Matthew. Devel. engr. Ingersoll-Rand Co., 1928-36; mgr. new products div., mgr. aviation gas turbine div. Westinghouse Electric Corp., 1936-47; mgmt. cons., 1947—; partner Welling & Woodard, Inc., Jenkintown, Pa., 1953-59, pres., 1959-69, chmn. 1969—; dir. Am. Brands, Inc. Trustee Acad. New Church, Bryn Athyn, Pa. Club: N.Y. Yacht (N.Y.C.); Edgartown (Mass.) Yacht. Home: 2732 Alnwick Rd Bryn Athyn PA 19009 Office: Valley Forge Plaza Suite 690 King of Prussia PA 19406

WOODARD, GEORGE SAWYER, JR., physician, ret. army officer; b. N.Y.C., June 16, 1924; s. George Sawyer and Mildred Allice (Eckels) W.; B.S. in Medicine, U. Mo., 1947; M.D., Washington U., St. Louis, 1949; m. Anita Alvera Harper, May 31, 1952; children—Anita Alvera Woodard Martinez, Mildred Allice, George Sawyer III. Commd. 1st lt. M.C., U.S. Army, 1949, advanced through grades to brig. gen., 1973; intern Letterman Gen. Hosp., San Francisco, 1949-50; resident in orthopaedics Walter Reed Army Med. Center, Washington, 1951-53; service in U.S., Hawaii, France, Korea and C.Z., 1943-78; chief dept. surgery, dep. comdr. Brooke Army Med. Cnter, Ft. Sam Houston, Tex., 1970-73; comdr. Martin Army Hosp., Ft. Benning, Ga., 1973, Letterman Army Med. Center, 1973-78; chief orthopedic service Maricopa County Gen. Hosp., Phoenix, 1978—; pres. Med. Soc. Isthmian C.Z., 1971-72. Decorated Army Commendation medal with 2 oak leaf clusters, Legion of Merit with oak leaf cluster, D.S.M. Diplomate Am. Bd. Orthopedic Surgery. Fellow Am. Acad. Orthopaedic Surgeons; mem. AMA, Pan Am. Med. Assn., Maricopa County Med. Soc., Assn. Mil. Surgeons U.S., Soc. Mil. Orthopaedic Surgeons, Alpha Omega Alpha, Phi Beta Pi. Democrat. Episcopalian. Clubs: Bohemian (San Francisco); Shriners (Washington). Home: 7418 E Kalil Dr Scottsdale AZ 85260 Office: 2601 E Roosevelt Phoenix AZ 85008

WOODARD, HAROLD RAYMOND, patent lawyer; b. Orient, Iowa, Mar. 13, 1911; s. Abram Sylvanus and Grace Lenora (Brown) W.; B.S., Harvard U., 1933, LL.B., 1936; children—Walter J., Turner J., Laurel C. Admitted to Ind. bar, 1936, since practiced in Indpls.; mem. firm Woodard, Weikart, Emhardt & Naughton. Adj. prof. patent law Ind. U. Sch. Law, Indpls. Served as lt. USNR, 1942-46. Fellow Internat. Acad. Law and Sci., Am. Coll. Trial Lawyers; mem. Am., Ind. 7th Circuit (pres.) bar assns., Am. Patent Law Assn., Lawyers Assn. Indpls. (past pres.). Methodist. Clubs: Columbia (past pres.), Woodstock (past pres.), University (past pres.). Home: Columbia Club 121 Monument Circle Indianapolis IN 46204 Office: One Indiana Sq Suite 2670 Indianapolis IN 46204

WOODBERRY, ROBERT LEONARD, securities exec.; b. Boston, Apr. 16, 1933; s. Ronald S. and Elsie E. (Carney) W.; B.A., Dartmouth Coll., 1954; M.B.A., Amos Tuck Sch., 1955; m. Marlinda Mason, Dec. 30, 1961; children—John Parker, Sarah Warren, Peter Sturgis, Paul Thomas. Salesman, First Boston Corp., N.Y.C., 1957-59; account exec. Merrill Lynch Pierce Fenner & Smith, Denver, 1959-66; mgr. Dean Witter & Co., Denver, 1966-69, div. sales mgr., San Francisco, 1969-72, nat. sales mgr., 1972—, exec. v.p., 1977—, also dir. Served with AC, U.S. Army, 1955-57. Clubs: Olympic, Mchts. Exchange (San Francisco); Orinda (Calif.) Country. Home: 11 El Sueno Orinda CA 94563 Office: 45 Montgomery St San Francisco CA 94104

WOODBRIDGE, HENRY SEWALL, cons., bus. exec.; b. N.Y.C. Sept. 20, 1906; s. George and Harriet (Manley) W.; student Rivers Sch., Middlesex Sch., Harvard, 1923-26; m. Dorothy Steese White, Jan. 8, 1928; children—Henry Sewall, Anne Sidney (Mrs. William Pickford), Victoria (Mrs. Richard G. Hall). With Stone & Webster, Inc., 1926-27; gen. mgr., dir. Raymond Whitcomb, Inc., 1927-40; bus. mgr., asst. to pub. Boston Evening Transcript, 1940-41; former v.p. Am. Optical Co., Southbridge, Mass., dir., 1941-77; pres. Todd-AO Corp., N.Y.C., 1954-58; financial and mgmt. cons., 1958—; chmn. bd. True Temper Corp., 1960-66, pres., 1964-65; cons. Editoria Guias LTB SA, Rio de Janeiro and Sao Paulo, Brazil, 1966—, Internat. Horizons, Inc., 1975—; pres., mng. dir. Hillwood Corp., 1966—, also dir.; dir. Internat. Horizons, Inc., Metritape, Inc., Union Labor Life Ins. Co. Chmn., Sch. Bldg. Com. Pomfret (Conn.), 1943-47, 58-60; mem. Finance Com. Brookline, Mass., 1936-39, chmn. Fire, Safety, Pub. Welfare Sub-Com., 1938-39; mem. Conn. Devel. Commn., 1948-55; industry rep. Nat. War Labor Bd., 1942-45; mem. safety equipment adv. com. WPB, 1942-46. Trustee Old Sturbridge Village, 1941—, chmn., 1965-66; trustee Middlesex Sch., Day-Kimball Hosp. Mem. Indsl. Relations Research Assn., Spl. Devices Assn. (hon.), New Eng. Soc. N.Y. (pres. 1962-65). Episcopalian. Clubs: India House, Coffee House, Harvard, Union (N.Y.C.); Harvard (Boston); Metropolitan, Cosmos (Washington). Home: Drumlin-Ho Pomfret CT 06258 Office: PO Box 156 Pomfret CT 06258

WOODBRIDGE, HENRY SEWALL, JR., banker; b. Boston, Dec. 11, 1928; s. Henry Sewall and Dorothy (White) W.; B.A., Yale U., 1951; M.B.A., Harvard U., 1955; m. Rosamond Logan, June 6, 1951; children—Rosamond deW., Dorothy M., Lisa K., Henry S. III. With R.I. Hosp. Trust Nat. Bank, 1955—, v.p., 1966-68, sr. v.p. adminstrv. div., 1968-71, exec. v.p. comml. banking ops., chief adminstrv. officer, 1971, pres., 1971—, chief exec. officer, 1974—; dir. Hosp. Trust Corp., Hosp. Trust Leasing Corp., Washington Row Co., Amica Mut. Life Ins. Co., New Eng. Automated Clearinghouse, Providence Gas Co., Bus. Devel. Co. of R.I., Providence Indsl. Devel. Corp.; fed. adv. council Fed. Res. Bd. Vice-pres., bd. dirs. Jr. Achievement R.I.; trustee Middlesex Sch., Concord, Mass.; vice chmn. bd. NCCJ; mem. exec. com., trustee R.I. Council Econ. Edn.; dir., treas. R.I. Urban Project; R.I. chmn. U.S. Savs. Bonds; dir., chmn. long-range planning com. United Way; bd. dirs. Ocean State Performing Arts Center, R.I. Public Expenditure Council; trustee Three Seas Found.; treas. Hart's Neck, Inc. Served with USMCR, 1951-53. Mem. Greater Providence C. of C. (dir., chmn. fin. com.). Clubs: Agawam Hunt, Anawan, Hope, Squantum Assn. Office: 1 Hospital Trust Plaza Providence RI 02903

WOODBRIDGE, HENSLEY CHARLES, librarian, educator; b. Champaign, Ill., Feb. 6, 1923; s. Dudley Warner and Ruby Belle (Mendenhall) W.; A.B., Coll. William and Mary, 1943; M.A., Harvard, 1946; Ph.D., U. Ill., 1950, M.S. in L.S., 1951; student U. Nacional de Mexico, summer 1941, 45; D.Arts, Lincoln Meml. U., 1976; m. Annie Emma Smith, Aug. 28, 1953; 1 dau., Ruby Susan. Corr., Worldover Press, Mexico, 1945; instr. French and Spanish, U. Richmond, 1946-47; teaching asst. U. Ill., 1948-50; reference librarian Ala. Poly. Inst., 1951-53; librarian Murray (Ky.) State Coll., 1953-65; Latin-Am. bibliographer, asso. prof. modern langs. So. Ill. U., Carbondale, 1965-71, prof., 1971—. Mem. Ky. Folklore Soc., Medieval Soc. Am., Modern Lang. Assn., Am. Assn. Tchrs. Spanish and Portuguese, Bibiog. Soc. Am., Instituto de estudios madrilenos. Author: (with Paul Olson) Tentative Bibliography of Ibero-Romance Linguistics, 1952; Jesse Stuart: a bibliography, 1960; (with Gerald Moser) Ruben Dario y el Cojo ilustrado, 1964; (with John London, George Tweney) Jack London: a bibliography, 1966, rev. edit., 1973; Jesse Stuart and Jane Stuart: a bibliography, 1969, rev. edit., 1979; Rubén Darío: A selective critical bibliography, 1975; Rubén Darío: una bibliografía selectiva, clasificada y anotada, 1975; Benito Pérez Galdós: A selective annotated bibliography, 1975; (with L.S. Thompson) Printing in Colonial Spanish America, 1976. Editor: Ky. Library Assn. Bull., 1959-60, Ky. Folklore Record, 1963-64, Am. Assn. Tchrs. Spanish and Portuguese-Scarecrow Press Bibliographical Series; contbg. editor Am. Book Collector, 1965—; asso. editor Hispania, 1967—; editor, pub. Jack London Newsletter, 1967—; mem. editorial bd. Modern Lang. Jour. 1971-73; co-editor Basic List of Latin American Materials in Spanish, Portuguese and French, 1975. Home: 1804 W Freeman Carbondale IL 62901

WOODBRIDGE, JOHN MARSHALL, architect, urban planner; b. N.Y.C., Jan. 26, 1929; s. Frederick James and Catherine (Baldwin) W.; B.A. magna cum laude, Amherst Coll., 1951; M.F.A. in Architecture, Princeton U., 1956; m. Sally Byrne, Aug. 14, 1954; children—Lawrence F., Pamela B., Diana B.; m. 2d, Carolyn Kizer, Apr. 8, 1975. Designer, John Funk, Architect, San Francisco, 1957-58; designer, asso. partner Skidmore, Owings & Merrill, San Francisco, 1959-73; staff dir. Pres.'s Adv. Council and Pres.'s Temporary Commn. on Pennsylvania Ave., Washington, 1963-65; exec. dir. Pennsylvania Ave. Devel. Corp., Washington, 1973-77; prin. Braccia, Joe & Woodbridge, San Francisco, 1977-79; lectr. architecture U. Calif., Berkeley; vis. prof. U. Oreg., Washington U., St. Louis; mem. council architecture Episcopal Ch. Fulbright scholar to France, 1951-52. Fellow AIA; mem. Nat. Trust Historic Preservation, Phi Beta Kappa. Democrat. Episcopalian. Co-author: Buildings of the Bay Area, 1960; A Guide to Architecture in San Francisco and Northern California, 1973. Home and office: 1401 Le Roy Ave Berkeley CA 94708

WOODBURN, WILLIAM KERVIN, lawyer; b. Reno, July 1, 1910; s. William and Mary (Kervin) W.; A.B., U. Nev., 1931; LL.B., Georgetown U., 1936; m. Betty Howell, Sept. 18, 1937; children—Patricia Woodburn Cobb, Mary Elizabeth Woodburn Zideck, Sarah Woodburn Holmes. Admitted to Nev. bar, 1936, since practiced in Reno; mem. firm Woodburn, Wedge, Blakey & Jeppson; dir. Sierra Pacific Power Co., Reno. Democratic nat. committeeman for Nev., 1956-60. Mem. State Bar Nev. (pres. 1955), Am. Bar Assn. (ho. of dels. 1955-56), Sigma Alpha Epsilon. Phi Alpha Delta. Club: Prospectors Hidden Valley Country. Home: 835 Arlington Ave Reno NV 89501 Office: 1 E 1st St Reno NV 89505

WOODBURY, LAEL JAY, univ. dean; b. Fairview, Idaho, July 3, 1927; s. Raymond A. and Wanda (Dawson) W.; B.S., Utah State U., 1952; M.A., Brigham Young U., 1953; Ph.D. (Univ. fellow), U. Ill., 1954; m. Margaret Lillian Swenson, Dec. 19, 1949; children—Carolyn Inez (Mrs. Donald Hancock), Shannon Margaret (Mrs. Michael J. Busenbark), Jordan Ray, Lexon Dan. Teaching asst. U. Ill., 1953; asso. prof. Brigham Young U., 1954-61; guest prof. Colo. State Coll., summer 1962; asst. prof. Bowling Green State U., 1961-62; asso. prof. U. Iowa, 1962-65; producer Ledges Playhouse, Lansing, Mich., 1963-65; prof. speech and dramatics, chmn. dept. Brigham Young U., 1966-70, asso. dean Coll. Fine Arts and Communications, 1969-73, dean, 1973—; dir. Eagle Mktg. Corp. Chmn. gen. bd. drama com. Young Men's Mut. Improvement Assn., 1958-61; v.p. Arts Council Central Utah. Bd. dirs. Repertory Dance Theatre; vice chmn. Utah Alliance for Arts Edn.; mem. advisory council Utah Arts Festival. Served with USNR, 1942-46. Recipient Creative Arts award Brigham Young U., 1971, Distinguished Alumni award, 1975. Mem. Rocky Mountain Theatre Conf. (past pres.), Am. Theatre Assn. (chmn. nat. com. royalties 1972—), Soc. Stage Dirs. and Choreographers, Theta Alpha Phi. Author: Play Production Handbook, 1959; Mormon Arts, vol. 1, 1972; Mosaic Theatre, 1976; also articles, original dramas. Home: 1303 Locust Ln Provo UT 84601

WOODBURY, LEONARD, educator; b. Regina, Sask., Can., Aug. 30, 1918; s. Ernest F. and Florence L. (Crisp) W.; B.A. with honors, U. Man., 1940; M.A., Harvard U., 1942, Ph.D., 1944; m. Marjorie R. Bell, May 13, 1944 (dec. 1977); children—Christopher Dawson, Alison Bell. With dept. classics Univ. Coll., U. Toronto, 1945—, prof., 1959—, head dept., 1958-66. Fellow Royal Soc. Can.; mem. Soc. Ancient Greek Philosophy (pres. 1965-66), Classical Assn. Can. (pres. 1974-76), Am. Philological Assn. (chmn. com. on award of merit 1966-67, 76-78). Contbr. articles to profl. jours. Office: Univ College U Toronto Toronto ON M5S 1A1 Canada

WOODBURY, MARION A., ins. co. exec.; b. Wilmington, N.C., 1923; ed. U. N.C., 1949; law Woodrow Wilson Coll., 1954; m. Alice Battey Bryson; children—Sheldon, Marion A., Frank, Spencer, Alice. Former exec. v.p., now pres. Reins. Corp. N.Y., also chmn. bd., chief exec. officer United Reins. Corp. N.Y.; pres. N.Y. Reins. Corp. S.A., Brussels. Home: 30 Hawthorne Pl Summit NJ 07901 Office: 99 John St New York NY 10038

WOODBURY, MAX ATKIN, educator, biomathematician; b. St. George, Utah, Apr. 30, 1917; s. Angus Munn and Grace (Atkin) W.; B.S., U. Utah, 1939; M.S., U. Mich., 1941, Ph.D., 1948; M.P.A., U. N.C., Chapel Hill, 1977; m. Lida Gottsch, May 30, 1947; children—Carolyn, Max Ten Eyck, Christopher, Gregory. Faculty, U. Mich., 1947-49, Princeton, 1950-52, U. Pa., 1952-54; mem. Inst. Advanced Study, Princeton, 1949-50; prin. investigator logistics research project Office Naval Research, George Washington U., 1954-56; faculty N.Y. U., 1956-65; prof. computer sci. Duke, prof. biomath. Duke Med. Center, 1966—; sr. fellow Center for Study of Aging and Human Devel., Duke, 1975—. Pres., Biomed. Information-processing Orgn., 1961-62, Inst. for Biomed. Computer Research, 1961-71; cons. WHO, UNIVAC, CBS on computer election forecasts, 1952-62, sci. orgns., univs., govt. agys., corps. Served with USAAF, 1941-46; MTO. USPHS, NIH grantee, also other govt. agys., 1947—. Fellow AAAS, Am. Statis. Assn., Inst. Math. Statistics; mem. numerous sci., profl. socs., Phi Beta Kappa, Sigma Xi, Phi Kappa Phi. Contbr. articles to profl. jours. Address: PO Box 3200 Duke U Med Center Durham NC 27710

WOODBURY, RICHARD BENJAMIN, anthropologist, educator; b. West Lafayette, Ind., May 16, 1917; s. Charles G. and Marion (Benjamin) W.; student Oberlin Coll., 1934-36; B.S., Harvard, 1939, M.A., 1942, Ph.D., 1949; postgrad. Columbia, 1939-40; m. Nathalie Ferris Sampson, Sept. 18, 1948. Archeol. research, Ariz., 1938, 39, Fla., 1940, Guatemala, 1947-49, El Morro Nat. Monument, N.Mex., 1953-56, Tehuacan, Mex., 1964; archaeologist United Fruit Co. Zaculeu Project, Guatemala, 1947-50; asso. prof. anthropology U. Ky., 1950-52, Columbia, 1952-58, U. Ariz., 1959-63; curator archeology U.S. Nat. Mus., Washington, 1963-65; head Smithsonian Office Anthropology, asst. dir. U.S. Nat. Mus., Washington, 1965-67, curator anthropology, 1967-69; chmn. dept. anthropology U. Mass., Amherst, 1969-73, prof., 1973—, acting asso. provost, dean grad. sch., 1973-74. Mem. div. anthropology and psychology NRC, 1954-57. Fellow Am. Anthrop. Assn. (exec. bd. 1963-66); mem. Archaeol. Inst. Am. (exec. com. 1965-67), AAAS (council 1961-63, com. arid lands 1969-74), Soc. Am. Archeology (treas. 1953-54, pres. 1958-59), Sigma Xi. Author: (with A.S. Trik) The Ruins of Zaculeu, Guatemala, 2 vols., 1953; Prehistoric Stone Implements of Northeastern Arizona, 1954. Editor: (with I.A. Sanders) Societies Around the World (2 vols.), 1953; (with others) The Excavation of Hawikuh, 1966; Alfred V. Kidder, 1973. Editor: Am. Antiquity, 1954-58; Abstracts of New World Archaeology; editor-in-chief Am. Anthropologist, 1975-78. Editorial bd. Am. Jour. Archeology, 1957-72. Office: Dept Anthropology Machmer Hall U Mass Amherst MA 01003

WOODBURY, ROLLIN EDWIN, utility exec. b. Redfield, S.D., Aug. 20, 1913; s. Claire E. and Helen (Rollins) W.; A.B. (Joffre medal 1934), Stanford, 1934; LL.B., Harvard, 1939; m. Ruth L. Armitage, June 22, 1940; children—Richard Barnum, Roger Edwin, Russell Thomson. Admitted to Calif. bar, 1939; with So. Calif. Edison Co., Los Angeles, 1940—, asst. gen. counsel, 1948-57, gen. counsel, 1957—, v.p. 1967-78; of counsel firm Chase, Rotchford, Drukler & Bogust, Los Angeles, 1978—. Mem. Am., Calif., Los Angeles bar assns., Los Angeles C. of C., Pacific Coast Elec. Assn., Harvard Law Sch. Assn., Phi Beta Kappa, Delta Sigma Rho. Republican. Clubs: University, Downtown Optimist (past pres.) (Los Angeles); Annandale Golf. Home: 1520 Pegfair Estates Dr Pasadena CA 91103 Office: 2244 Walnut Grove Ave Rosemead CA 91770

WOODBURY, WENDELL WILFRED, fgn. service officer; b. Crocker, S.D., Apr. 29, 1920; s. Wallace Charles and Inga Otilda (Skavang) W.; B.A., State U. Iowa, 1942; student U. Chgo., 1946; A.M., Harvard, 1949; m. Elizabeth Delano, Oct. 9, 1950; children—Alden Nicholas, Jonathan Wendell. Joined U.S. Fgn. Service, 1949; 3d sec., Tokyo, Japan, 1949-50; vice consul, Yokohama, Japan, 1950-52; 2d sec., Ciudad Trujillo, Dominican Republic, 1952-54; consul, Algiers, Algeria, 1955-57; intelligence research specialist Bur. Intelligence Research and Analysis, State Dept., 1957-61; 1st sec., Tokyo, 1961-64; officer in charge NE Asian econ. affairs, Dept. State, 1964-66, spl. asst. to asst. sec. for East Asia, 1966-68, 72-73, chief div. econ. policy Bur. Internat. Orgn. Affairs, 1974—; counselor Am. embassy, Copenhagen, Denmark, 1968-71; detailed Sr. Seminar on Fgn. Policy, 1973-74. Served to capt. AUS, 1943-46; PTO. Mem. Am. Econ. Assn., Am. Fgn. Service Assn., Phi Beta Kappa. Order Artus. Episcopalian (mem. ch. council). Home: 315 S Pitt St Alexandria VA 22314 Office: Dept of State Washington DC 20521

WOODCOCK, GEORGE, author; b. Winnipeg, Man., Can., May 8, 1912; s. Samuel Arthur and Margaret Gertrude (Lewis) W.; student Morley Coll., London, Eng.; LL.D., U. Victoria, U. Winnipeg; D.Litt., Sir George Williams U., U. Ottawa, U. B.C.; m. Ingeborg Hedwig Elisabeth Linzer, Feb. 10, 1949. Broadcaster contbg. several hundred talks and scripts of plays and documentaries to CBC programs; editor of Now, 1940-47; profl. writer, 1946—, first in Eng. to 1949 and afterwards in Can.; faculty U. Wash., 1954-55; asso. prof. English, U. B.C., Vancouver, 1956-63, lectr. Asian studies, 1963—; editor Canadian Lit. Recipient Gov. Gen.'s award, 1966, Molson prize, 1973. Can. Council Travel grantee, 1961, 63, 65; Guggenheim fellow, 1951-52, Canadian Govt. Overseas fellow, 1957-58, Can. Council Killam fellow, 1970-71, Can. Council Sr. Arts fellow, 1975, 78. Author: The White Island, 1940; The Centre Cannot Hold, 1943; William Godwin, A Biography, 1946; The Incomparable Aphra: A Life of Mrs. Aphra Behn, 1948; The Writer and Politics, 1948; Imagine the South, 1947; The Paradox of Oscar Wilde, 1950; A Hundred Years of Revolution: 1848 and After, 1948; The Letters of Charles Lamb, 1950; The Anarchist Prince, 1950 (later trans. into French); Ravens and Prophets: Travels in Western Canada, 1952; Pierre-Joseph Proudhon, 1956; To the City of the Dead: Travels in Mexico, 1956; Incas and Other Men: Travels in Peru, 1959; Anarchism, 1962; Faces of India, 1964; Asia, Gods and Cities, 1966; The Greeks in India, 1966; A Choice of Critics, 1966; The Crystal Spirit, 1966 (Gov. Gen. award for Eng. Non-fiction); Kerala, 1967; Selected Poems, 1967; The Doukhobors, 1968; Canada and the Canadians, 1969; The Hudson's Bay Company, 1970; Odysseus Ever Returning, 1970; Gandhi, 1971; Dawn and the Darkest Hour: A Study of Aldous Huxley, 1972; Herbert Read, The Stream and the Source, 1972; The Rejection of Politics, 1972; Who Killed the British Empire?, 1974; Amor de Cosmos, 1975; Gabriel Dumonis, 1975; Notes on Visitations, 1976; South Sea Journey, 1976; Peoples of the Coast, 1977; Thomas Merton, Monk and Poet, 1978; Faces from History, 1978; The Kestrel and Other Poems, 1978; The Canadians, 1979. Home: 6429 McCleery St Vancouver BC V6N 1G5 Canada

WOODCOCK, LEONARD, ambassador, labor union ofcl.; b. Providence, Feb. 15, 1911; s. Ernest and Margaret (Freel) W.; ed. St. Wilfred's Coll.; student Wayne State U., 1928-30, Walsh Inst. Accountancy, Detroit, 1928-30; numerous hon. degrees; m. Sharon Lee Tuohy, Apr. 14, 1978; children—Leslie, Janet, John. Staff rep. internat. union UAW, 1940-46, adminstrv. asst. to pres., 1946-47, regional dir., 1947-55, internat. v.p., 1955-70, pres., 1970-77, pres. emeritus, 1977—; chief of mission with rank of ambassador U.S. Liaison Office, Peking, 1977-78, ambassador to China, 1978—;

dynomometer operator Continental Aviation & Engring. Co., 1947. Bd. govs. emeritus Wayne State U., 1970; Mem. NAACP (life). Office: PO Box 15145 Detroit MI 48215

WOODD-CAHUSAC, SYDNEY ANGLIN, univ. ofcl.; b. N.Y.C., Apr. 2, 1918; s. Kenneth Anglin and Beatrice Maude (Barry) Woodd-C.; A.B., Princeton, 1940; J.D., Yale, 1947; m. Jean Elizabeth Fleming, Dec. 1, 1951; children—Katherine Lee Woodd-Cahusac Cowans, Ann Blythe Woodd-Cahusac Augenthaler, Kenneth Anglin. Admitted to N.Y. bar, 1948; with firm Simpson Thacher & Bartlett, N.Y.C., 1947-52, Wickes, Riddell, Bloomer, Jacobi & McGuire, N.Y.C., 1952-54; with Am. Standard, Inc., N.Y.C., 1954-67, treas., 1962-67; sec., gen. counsel Perkin-Elmer Corp., Norwalk, Conn., 1967-69; asso. treas. Rockefeller U., N.Y.C., 1969-71, treas., 1971—; spl. asst. gen. N.Y. State, 1951. Mem. Bd. Tax Rev. Greenwich, Conn., 1958-60, Bd. Estimate and Taxation, 1964-71; mem. com. to nominate trustees Princeton, 1967-70; past v.p., dir. YMCA Greater N.Y.; trustee Interch. Center, N.Y.C., 1973—, N.Y. Law Sch., N.Y.C., 1975; bd. dirs. Cultural Council Found., N.Y.C., 1975—; vestryman Christ Ch., Greenwich, Conn., 1975-79. Served with USMCR, 1942-46. Episcopalian. Clubs: Field (Greenwich); Century (N.Y.C.). Home: 121 Clapboard Ridge Rd Greenwich CT 06830

WOODEN, HOWARD EDMUND, museum dir.; b. Balt., Oct. 10, 1919; s. Howard Edmund and Maria (Barth) W.; B.S., Johns Hopkins, 1946, M.A., 1948; m. Virginia Irene Burkert, Oct. 18, 1941; children—Virginia Lee (Mrs. Gary R. Beaulieu), Howard Edmund III. Fulbright instr. Athens (Greece) Coll., 1951-52; lectr. U. Evansville (Ind.), 1956-63; asso. prof. U. Fla., 1963-66; dir. Sheldon Swope Art Gallery, Terre Haute, Ind., 1966-75; dir. Wichita (Kans.) Art Mus., 1975—; adj. asso. prof. art history Ind. State U., 1967-75. Lectr., cons. in field. Grantee NIH, 1956-66. Mem. Coll. Art Assn., Soc. Archtl. Historians, Archaeol. Inst. Am., Am. Assn. Museums, Am. Assn. Mus. Dirs., Internat. Council Museums, Sigma Phi Epsilon. Author: Architectural Heritage of Evansville, 1963; The Rose Polytechnic Collection of British Watercolors, 1969; The Sheldon Swope Art Gallery-Fifty Paintings and Sculptures, 1972; also numerous exhbn. brochures and catalogues, articles in profl. jours. Home: 1828 W 18th St Wichita KS 67203 Office: 619 Stackman Dr Wichita KS 67203

WOODEN, JOHN ROBERT, former basketball coach; b. Martinsville, Ind., Oct. 14, 1910; s. Joshua Hugh and Roxie (Rothrock) W.; B.S., Purdue U., 1932; M.S., Ind. State U., 1947; m. Nellie C. Riley, Aug. 8, 1932; children—Nancy Anne (Mrs. Mel Nethery), James Hugh. Athletic dir., basketball and baseball coach Ind. State Tchrs. Coll., 1946-48; head basketball coach UCLA, 1948-75; lectr. to colls., coaches, business. Served to lt. USNR, 1943-46. Named All-Am. basketball player Purdue U., 1930-32, Coll. Basketball Player of Yr., 1932, to All-Time All-Am. Team, Helms Athletic Found., 1943, Nat. Basketball Hall of Fame, Springfield (Mass.) Coll., as player 1960, as coach, 1970, Ind. State Basketball Hall of Fame, 1962, Calif. Father of Yr., 1964, Coach of Yr., U.S. Basketball Writers Assn., 1964, 67, 69, 70, 72, 73, Sportsman of Yr., Sports Illustrated, 1973; recipient Whitney Young award Urban League, 1973, 1st ann. Velvet Covered Brick award Layman's Leadership Inst., 1974; 1st ann. Dr. James Naismith Peachbasket award, 1974. Author: Practical Modern Basketball, 1966; They Call Me Coach, 1972. Contbr. articles to profl. jours. . *I have tried to live the philosophy of my personal definition of success which I formulated in the middle thirties shortly after I entered the teaching profession. Not being satisfied that success was merely the accumulation of material possessions or the attainment of a position of power or prestige, I chose to define success as "peace of mind which can be attained only through the self-satisfaction that comes from knowing you did your best to become the best that you are capable of becoming."*

WOODFILL, WILLIAM STEWART, hotel operator; b. Greensburg, Ind., Aug. 19, 1896; s. William Cones and Elizabeth (Donnell) W.; student Bowdoin Coll.; LL.D. (hon.), Western Mich. U., 1966; m. Elizabeth Apple, Oct. 27, 1927 (div. 1954). Engaged in lumber bus., Ind., 1919-22; mgr. hotels, Fla., Mich., 1923-25; pres., part owner Grand Hotel, Mackinac Island, Mich., 1925-28, owner, operator, 1933—; hon. dir. Zenith Radio Corp. Served as ensign A.C., USN, World War I. Recipient Merit award Am. Assn. State and Local History, 1961; cert. of recognition Mackinac Bridge Authority, 1978, Mackinac Island State Park Commn., 1978. Mem. Theta Delta Chi. Presbyterian. Club: University (Chgo.). Home: (winter) Scottsdale AZ (summer) Mackinac Island MI 49757 Office: 222 Wisconsin Ave Lake Forest IL 60045

WOODFIN, GENE MACK, marine constrn. and heavy fabrication co. exec.; b. Paris, Tex., Feb. 7, 1919; s. John Elmer and Alma Kathryn (Smiley) W.; grad. U. Tex. Law Sch., 1940; m. Jane Gentry, May 7, 1941 (dec.); children—William S., Kathryn J.; m. Jerry Ann Young, Mar. 24, 1979. Admitted to Tex. bar, 1940; lawyer firm Vinson, Elkins, Weems & Searls, Houston, 1940-42, partner, 1946-59; sr. partner firm Loeb, Rhoades & Co., N.Y.C., 1959-73; chmn., chief exec. officer, dir. Marathon Mfg. Co., Houston, 1973—; dir. Studebaker-Worthington Inc., Jim Walter Corp., Fed. Res. Bank of Dallas (Houston br.). Former pres., U. Tex. Found.. 1973-74, mem. chancellors counsel. Trustee Akin Hall Assn., Pawling. N.Y. Served to lt. USNR, 1942-46. Mem. Am. Bar Assn., State Bar of Tex., Acad. Polit. Sci., Econ. Club N.Y.. Newcomen Soc. Clubs: Houston Country; Ramada; Petroleum; Coronado; Links; Nat. Golf Links Am. Home: 506 Shadywood St Houston TX 77057 Office: 1900 Marathon Bldg 600 Jefferson St Houston TX 77002

WOODFORD, CHARLES DAY, architect; b. Laramie, Wyo., May 21, 1910; s. Everett Luther and June Pauline (Johnson) W.; student U. Wyo., 1928-31; B.Arch., U. Minn., 1934; m. Helen Shattuck Hammond, Sept. 28, 1935; children—Wendy Jacklyn (Mrs. James Franklyn DePaolo), Pamala Lyn, Ted Shattuck. Archtl. designer Nat. Park Service, 1935-36; archtl. draftsman Richard D. Neutra, 1936-40, John Parkinson & Donald B. Parkinson, 1940-46; partner Parkinson, Powelson, Briney, Bernard & Woodford, Los Angeles, 1946-52; sr. partner in charge Woodford & Bernard, Los Angeles, 1952—. Recipient awards for excellence in architecture City of Santa Barbara, 1954, 56, Am. Tel.&Tel. Co., N.Y., 1960, 62, 64, 68. Fellow A.I.A. (pres. So. Calif. chpt. 1961, dir. Cal. council exec. com. 1961-66, nat. dir. Calif. region 1963-66, Architects Distinguished Service award Calif. Council 1972); mem. Sigma Nu. Republican. Episcopalian. Clubs: California (Los Angeles); Pauma Valley (Cal.) Country. Prin. works include: Telephone Accounting Centers, 1958, 66; Jr. High Sch., Glendale, 1962; Calif. State Coll. Gymnasium, Fullerton, 1967; Microwave Tower and Telephone Equipment Bldg., Los Angeles, 1968; Hoover High Sch., Glendale, 1969; Telephone Equipment Bldgs., Gardena, 1971, Anaheim, 1976, San Diego, 1977. Home: 32166 Atosana Dr Pauma Valley CA 92061 Office: 410 N La Brea Los Angeles CA 90036 also 530 Broadway Suite 1038 San Diego CA 92102

WOODHAMS, BERTHOLD, ins. exec.; b. Aurora, Ill., Feb. 28, 1894; s. Herbert and Amelia (Degenhardt) W.; student pub. schs.; LL.D. (hon.), Ferris Inst., Big Rapids, Mich. m. Florence M. Legg, June 29, 1921; children—Carolyn W. (Mrs. Arthur L. Jones, Jr.), Frederick B. Claims adjuster Citizens' Mut. Automobile Ins. Co., Howell, Mich., 1920-26, v.p., 1926-50, dir., pres., 1950-63, chmn. bd., 1963-65, hon. chmn. bd., 1965—; chmn. bd. First Nat. Bank, Howell, 1966—, also dir. Pres., Conf. Mut. Casualty Cos., 1955. Past mem. Bd. Edn. Howell; mayor City of Howell, 1943-49. Gov., Mich. Ins. Info. Ser. Mason (past master, K.T., past comdr.), Rotarian (past pres.). Author: Man-to-Man and Dad-to-Daughter good driving agreements distributed by safety orgns., automobile clubs. Home: 1108 Burns Dr Howell MI 48843 Office: Citizens' Mut Automobile Ins Co 1180 Burns Dr Howell MI 48843

WOODHEAD, ROBERT KENNETH, constrn. co. exec.; b. Wendell, Idaho, Feb. 11, 1925; s. Albert Arthur and Clara (Larson) V.; B.A., U. Idaho, 1948; m. Dolores Lucille Calvert, Apr. 29, 1951; 1 dau., Linda D. With Morrison-Knudsen Co. Inc., Boise, Idaho, 1948—, treas., 1968—, v.p. adminstrn., 1969-72, v.p. corp. affairs, 1972-73, sr. v.p. corp. affairs, 1973—; also dir.; dir. Nat. Steel and Shipbuilding, H.K. Ferguson Co., Emkay Devel., Broadway Ins. Co. Bd. dirs. U. Idaho Found. Served with USAF, World War II. Mem. Delta Chi. Elk. Home: 3509 Woodacres Dr Boise ID 83705 Office: PO Box 7808 Boise ID 83729

WOODHOUSE, JOHN FREDERICK, food distbn. co. exec.; b. Wilmington, Del., Nov. 30, 1930; s. John Crawford and Anna (Houth) W.; B.A., Wesleyan U., 1953; M.B.A., Harvard, 1955; m. Marilyn Ruth Morrow, June 18, 1955; children—John Crawford II, Marjorie Ann. Bus. devel. officer Canadian Imperial Bank of Commerce, Toronto, Ont., 1955-59; various fin. positions Ford Motor Co., Dearborn, Mich., 1959-64; various fin. positions Copper Industries, Inc., Mount Vernon, Ohio, 1964-67, treas., Houston, 1967-69; treas. Crescent-Niagara Corp., Buffalo, 1968-69; fin. v.p. Sysco Corp., Houston, 1969-72, pres., 1972—, also dir., mem. exec. com.; dir. Houston Nat. Bank. Chmn., Mich. 16th dist. Republican Club, 1962-64. Treas., Cooper Industries Found., 1967-69; trustee Wesleyan U. Mem. Houston Soc. Fin. Analysts, Fin. Execs. Inst., Sigma Chi. Presbyn. (ruling elder). Clubs: Houston, West Side Tennis, Houstonian. Home: 650 Ramblewood Rd Houston TX 77079 Office: 1177 West Loops Houston TX 77027

WOODIN, HOWARD EUGENE, educator; b. Schenectady, July 2, 1924; s. Howard Eugene and Florence (Hayner) W.; B.S., Union Coll., N.Y., 1948, M.S., 1950; Ph.D. in Plant Ecology, Purdue U., 1953; m. Beverly A. Huber, Sept. 10, 1949; children—David Eugene, Christopher Lee. Asst., Union Coll., 1948-50; instr. biology Purdue U., Lafayette, Ind., 1951, asst., 1951-52; instr. Middlebury (Vt.) Coll., 1953-56, asst. prof., 1956, asso. prof., 1959-67, prof., 1967—, coordinator environmental studies, 1967—, Old Dominion prof., 1970—. Dir. Middlebury Savs. & Loan Bank. Mem. exec. bd. Green Mountain council Boy Scouts Am. Trustee, research dir. Vt. Wild Land Found., Means Meml. Woods Res. Served with AUS, 1942-46. Home: Quarry Rd RD 3 Middlebury VT 05753

WOODIN, MARTIN DWIGHT, ednl. adminstr.; b. Sicily Island, La., July 7, 1915; s. Dwight E. and Gladys Ann (Martin) W.; B.S., La. State U., 1936; M.S., Cornell U., 1939, Ph.D., 1941; m. Virginia Johnson, Sept. 7, 1939 (dec.); children—Rebecca Woodin Johnson, Pamela Woodin Nelson, Linda Woodin Middleton; m. 2d, Elisabeth Wachalik, Oct. 8, 1968. Faculty, La. State U., 1941—, prof. agrl. econs., head dept., 1957-59, dir. resident instrn. Coll. Agr., 1959-60, dean La. State U. at Alexandria, 1960-62, exec. v.p. La. State U. System, Baton Rouge, 1962-72, pres., 1972—. Cons. agr. and planning, Nicaragua, Taiwan, Thailand. Dep. dir. La. Civil Def. Agy., 1961-72; v.p., exec. com. United Givers Baton Rouge; sec. La. State U. Found.; mem. La. Constn. Revision Commn.; mem. Arts and Humanities Council of Greater Baton Rouge, 1974—; mem. pres.'s council Nat. Assn. State Univs., 1972—; mem. council of trustees Gulf South Research Inst., 1972—; pres. Council So. Univs., 1975-76. Served with USNR, 1942-46; PTO. Mem. Am. Agrl. Econ. Assn., Am. Marketing Assn., Am. Legion (post comdr.), Internat. House, So. Assn. Land Grant Colls. and State Univs. (pres. 1977-78), Sigma Xi, Omicron Delta Kappa, Phi Kappa Phi (pres.), Beta Gamma Sigma, Phi Eta Sigma, Gamma Sigma Delta, Alpha Zeta, Pi Gamma Mu. Presbyn. Elk, Rotarian. Contbr. articles to profl. jours. Home: 2959 E Lakeshore Dr Baton Rouge LA 70808

WOODIWISS, KATHLEEN ERIN, author; b. Alexandria, La., June 3, 1939; d. Charles Wingrove, Sr. and Gladys (Coker) Hogg; student pub. schs., La.; m. Ross Eugene Woodiwiss, July 20, 1956; children—Sean Alan, Dorren James, Heath Alexander. Author: The Flame and the Flower, 1972; The Wolf and the Dove, 1974; Shanna, 1977. Republican. Office: care Avon Books 959 8th Ave New York NY 10019*

WOODKA, S. JOSEPH, univ. dean; b. South Bend, Ind., June 3, 1923; s. Stephen and Josephine (Pawlok) W.; B.S., Ball State U., 1948; M.A., U. Mich., 1949, Ph.D., 1959; m. Patricia Berry, May 15, 1954; children—Carole Elaine, Janice Marie, Mark Joseph. Instr. polit. sci. Central Mich. U., Mt. Pleasant, 1950-52, asso. prof., 1955-66; instr. polit. sci. U. Detroit, 1954-55; chmn., prof. polit. sci. U. Wis.-Stevens Point, 1966-70, dean Coll. Letters and Sci., 1970—. Exec. sec. Gov.'s Study Commn. on Elections, 1954; mem. Gov.'s Constl. Conv. Citizens' Adv. Com. on State Exec. Dept., 1961. Chmn., Mt. Pleasant Zoning Bd. of Appeals, 1962-64; mem. City Commn., Mt. Pleasant, 1964-66, mayor pro tem, 1966. Served with AUS, 1943-46. Mem. Am., Midwest, Wis. (pres. 1967-68) polit. sci. assns., Midwest Conf. Acad. Affairs Adminstrs., Am. Conf. Acad. Deans, Council Colls. Arts and Scis. Home: 2825 Simonis St Stevens Point WI 55481

WOODLAND, DON L., educator; b. Ballinger, Tex., Sept. 3, 1936; s. Tom B. and Rena E. (Grant) W.; B.B.A., U. Tex., 1958, M.B.A., 1959, Ph.D., 1962; m. Molly Howell, June 3, 1960; children—Wendy Kay, Leigh Anne. Fin. economist Fed. Res. Bank, Dallas, 1962-65; asst. prof. Okla. State U., 1965-66; prof. banking La. State U., Baton Rouge, 1966-76, dean Sch. Bus., 1976—; v.p. Sch. of Banking of the South; pres. Central Am. Banking Sch. Mem. Fin. Mgmt. Assn., Am. Fin. Assn., Southwestern Fin. Assn., So. Fin. Assn., Delta Sigma Pi, Beta Gamma Sigma. Democrat. Methodist. Clubs: City of Baton Rouge, Bocage Racquet. Author: (with Peter Rose and Edward Reed) Cases in Commercial Banking, 1970. Home: 774 Castle Kirk Baton Rouge LA 70808 Office: 3304 Coll Bus Adminstrn La State Univ Baton Rouge LA 70803

WOODLEY, KENNETH HAROLD, communications co. exec.; b. Belleville, Ont., Can., June 14, 1929; s. Harold George and Helen (Green) W.; certified gen. accountant, 1953; m. Joyce Markle, May 23, 1949; children—David, Susan, Steven. With No. Telecom Ltd., Montreal, Que., Can., 1948—, corporate v.p. adminstrn., 1972-73, exec. v.p. staff, 1973-74, group v.p., 1974—, dir. Cook Electric Ltd., No. Telecom Can. Ltd., Boise Cascade Can. Ltd., Teledirect Ltd. Pres. So. Dist. council Boy Scouts Can., 1963. Mem. Canadian Export Assn. (vice chmn. 1974), Can. Elec. Assn. (dir. 1971), Can. C. of C. (mem. exec. council 1973). Club: Lambton Golf and Country (Toronto, Ont.). Home: 63 Farningham Crescent Islington ON Canada Office: 304 The East Mall Islington ON Canada

WOODLIEF, JOSEPH BENJAMIN, metal co. exec.; b. Ottawa, Kan., Feb. 9, 1920; s. Harold B. and Geraldine (Russell) W.; student U. Mo., 1939; Ph.B., U. Wis., 1943; LL.B., U. Mont., 1948; m. Jean M. Hample, Jan. 1, 1944; children—Pamela (Mrs. Kerwin Shedd Webster), John Boyd, Philip. Admitted to Mont. bar, 1948; practice in Butte, 1948-52; with Anaconda Co., 1952-66, counsel, 1958-64, v.p. indsl. relations, 1964-66; pres., chief exec. officer Anaconda Aluminum Co., Louisville, 1966-74, v.p. Anaconda Co., 1972-74; chmn. bd., pres. Anaconda Jamaica, 1972-74; pres., chief exec. officer Diversified Industries, St. Louis, 1975-79, now dir.; dir. 1st Nat. Bank Louisville, Ky. Trust Co., 1st Ky. Co., Reliance Universal Co., Glenmore Distilleries Co., Anaconda Co. Bd. dirs. Inf. Mus. Assn., Columbus, Ga. Served to capt., inf. AUS, 1943-46. Mem. Am., Mont. bar assns., Am. Judicature Soc., Am. Inst. Mining, Metall. and Petroleum Engrs. Clubs: Mining (N.Y.C.); Nat. Lawyers (Washington); Pendennis, Louisville Country; St. Louis. Office: 1034 S Brentwood Blvd Richmond Heights MO 63117*

WOODLIFF, GEORGE FRANKLIN, lawyer, ins. co. exec.; b. Athens, Ga., Jan. 10, 1914; s. George A. and Amelia (Beck) W.; student Millsaps Coll., 1933-34; B.A., U. Miss., 1936; LL.B., 1938; m. Ann Morse, June 6, 1946; children—George Franklin III, Daniel Morse, Ann, Ruth. Admitted to Miss. bar, 1938; partner Heidelberg, Woodliff & Franks, Jackson. Gen counsel So. Farm Casualty Ins. Co., So. Farm Bur. Life Ins. Co., Miss. Farm Bur. Mut. Ins. Co. Mem. Miss. Legislature, 1939-42. Mem. Miss. Bd. Bar Admissions, 1948-50; former vice chmn. Miss. Ins. Commn. Trustee St. Andrew's Episcopal Day Sch. Served to lt. USNR, 1942-45. Fellow Am. Coll. Trial Lawyers; mem. Fedn. Ins. Counsel (pres., chmn. bd. govs. 1959-60), Miss. Def. Lawyers Assn. (pres. 1968), Am., Miss., Hinds County bar assns., Omicron Delta Kappa, Phi Delta Phi, Sigma Alpha Epsilon. Blue Key. Episcopalian (vestryman). Clubs: University, Petroleum, River Hills, Capital City, Jackson Country, Kiwanis. Home: 1334 Belvior Pl Jackson MS 39202 Office: Capitol Towers Jackson MS 39205

WOODMAN, HAROLD DAVID, historian; b. Chgo., Apr. 21, 1928; s. Joseph Benjamin and Helen Ruth (Sollo) W.; B.A., Roosevelt U., 1957; M.A., U. Chgo., 1959, Ph.D., 1964; m. Leonora Becker; children—Allan James, David Edward. Lectr., Roosevelt U., 1962-63; asst. prof. history U. Mo., Columbia, 1963-66, asso. prof., 1966-69, prof., 1969-71; prof. Purdue U., West Lafayette, Ind., 1971—. Served with U.S. Army, 1950-52. Recipient Everett E. Edwards award Agrl. History Soc., 1963, Ramsdell award So. Hist. Assn., 1965; Woodrow Wilson Internat. Center for Scholars fellow, 1977; Social Sci. Research Council faculty grantee, 1969-70. Mem. Am. Hist. Assn., Orgn. Am. Historians, Econ. History Assn., Agrl. History Soc., Bus. History Conf. (pres. elect). Author: (with Allen F. Davis) Conflict and Consensus in American History, 1966; Slavery and The Southern Economy, 1966; King Cotton and His Retainers, 1968; Legacy of the American Civil War, 1973; editorial bd. Jour. So. History, 1972-75, Wis. Hist. Soc., 1972-76, Bus. History Rev., 1971-77, Agrl. History, 1976—. Home: 1100 N Grant St West Lafayette IN 47906 Office: Dept History Purdue U West Lafayette IN 47907

WOODMAN, HARRY ANDREWS, JR., life ins. co. exec.; b. Orange, N.J., June 15, 1928; s. Harry Andrews and Mildred Amelia (Woods) W.; B.A., Amherst Coll., 1950; m. Betty Jo Pulsford, July 1, 1950; children—Richard Cushman, Andrea Ellen, Lynn Adele, Thomas Gordon. With N.Y. Life Ins. Co., N.Y.C., 1950—, 2d v.p., 1968-71, v.p., 1971—. Served with USN. 1952-53. Mem. Soc. Actuaries, Home Office Life Underwriters Assn. Home: 58 Old Stone Bridge Rd Cos Cob CT 06807 Office: 51 Madison Ave New York NY 10010

WOODMAN, ROY HARPER, corp. exec., mgmt. cons.; b. Winnipeg, Man., Can., June 4, 1922; s. Alonzo Edwin and Flora McIntosh (Harper) W.; B.A., U. B.C., 1949, B.Comm., 1950; M.B.A., Harvard 1952; m. Marcia M. Carmichael, June 14, 1947 (div. June 1974); m. 2d, Irene Bolshakov, Sept. 1974; children—Roderick Earl, Cameron Roy, Neil Elliot, Kimberly Paige. With John Labatt Ltd., London, Ont., 1952-62, v.p., regional gen. mgr., pres., 1959-62; pres. Lucky Lager Breweries, San Francisco, 1963-65; cons. to industry, U.S., Can., 1966—; exec. v.p., treas. Saga Adminstrv. Corp., Menlo Park, Calif., 1967-73; exec. v.p., dir. Video Logic Corp., 1974-75, pres., dir., chief exec. officer, 1976—; pres., dir., chief exec. officer Internat. Video Corp., 1977-79; chmn. Internat. Video, 1978—. Bd. dirs. La Salle Gen. Hosp. Served with RCAF, 1941-45. Club: St. James's (Montreal). Home: 1214 Gronwall Ln Los Altos CA 94022 Office: 597 N Mathilda Ave Sunnyvale CA 94086 also 453 W Maude Ave Sunnyvale CA 94086

WOODRESS, JAMES LESLIE, JR., educator; b. Webster Groves, Mo., July 7, 1916; s. James Leslie and Jessie (Smith) W.; A.B., Amherst Coll., 1938; A.M., N.Y. U., 1943; Ph.D., Duke, 1950; m. Roberta Wilson, Sept. 28, 1940. News editor radio sta. KWK, St. Louis, 1939-40; rewriteman, editor U.P.I., N.Y.C., 1940-43; instr. English, Grinnell (Iowa) Coll., 1949-50; asst. prof. English, Butler U., Indpls., 1950-53, asso. prof., 1953-58; asso. prof. English, San Fernando Valley (Calif.) State Coll., 1958-61, prof., 1961-66, chmn. dept., 1959-63, dean letters and scis., 1963-65; prof. English, U. Calif. at Davis, 1966—, chmn. dept., 1970-74; vis. prof. Sorbonne, Paris, France, 1974-75. Served to lt. AUS, 1943-46. Ford Fund for Advancement Edn. fellow, 1952-53; Guggenheim fellow, 1957-58; Fulbright lectr. France, 1962-63, Italy, 1965-66. Mem. Modern Lang. Assn. (sec. Am. Lit. group 1962-63), AAUP, Phi Beta Kappa. Author: Howells and Italy, 1952; Booth Tarkington; Gentleman from Indiana, 1955; A Yankee's Odyssey; The Life of Joel Barlow, 1958; Dissertations in American Literature, 1957, 62, 68; Willa Cather: Her Life and Art, 1970, 75; American Fiction 1900-50, 1974. Editor: Eight American Authors, 1971; American Literary Scholarship: An Annual, 1965-69, 75—; (with Richard Morris) Voices from America's Past, anthology, 1961-62, 75. Office: Dept English U Calif Davis CA 95616

WOODRING, CARL, educator; b. Terrell, Tex., Aug. 29, 1919; s. Felix Jessie and Naomi (Cole) W.; B.A., Rice U., 1940, M.A., 1942; A.M., Harvard, 1947, Ph.D. (Bowdoin prize, Dexter Traveling scholar) 1949; m. Mary Frances Ellis, Dec. 24, 1942. Instr. English, U. Wis., 1948-51, asst. prof., 1951-54, asso. prof., 1954-58, prof., 1958-61; prof. English, Columbia, 1961—, George Edward Woodberry prof. lit., 1976—, chmn. dept., 1968-71. Mem. English dissertation selection com. Woodrow Wilson Nat. Fellowship Found., 1962-66; Phi Beta Kappa vis. scholar, 1974-75. Served with USNR, 1942-45. Fund for Advancement Edn. fellow, 1955; Guggenheim fellow, 1955; Am. Council Learned Socs. fellow, 1965. Mem. Modern Lang. Assn. (exec. council 1965-68), Internat. Assn. U. Profs. English, Keats-Shelley Assn. Am. (dir.), Am. Acad. Arts and Scis., Acad. Lit. Studies, Assn. Depts. English (pres. 1971), Grolier Club. Author: Victorian Samplers-William and Mary Howitt, 1952; Politics in the Poetry of Coleridge, 1961; Wordsworth, 1965; Virginia Woolf, 1966; Politics in English Romantic Poetry (Van Am award, Christian Gauss prize 1971), 1970. Editor: Prose of the Romantic Period, 1961; editorial bd. Studies in English Literature, 1961—; Research in the Humanities, 1977—; editorial adviser Wordsworth Circle, 1970—, Essays in Literature, 1973—. Home: 404 Riverside Dr New York City NY 10025

WOODRING, DEWAYNE STANLEY, clergyman, ch. ofcl.; b. Gary, Ind., Nov. 10, 1931; s. J. Stanley and Vera Luella (Brown) W.; B.S. in Speech with distinction, Northwestern U., 1954, postgrad.

studies in pub. and community relations, 1954-57; M.Div., Garrett Theol. Sem., 1957; L.H.D., Mt. Union Coll., Alliance, Ohio, 1967; D.D., Salem (W.Va.) Coll., 1970; m. Donna Jean Wishart, June 15, 1957; children—Judith Lynn, Beth Ellen. Asso. youth dir. Gary YMCA, 1950-55; ordained to ministry United Methodist Ch., 1955; minister of edn. Griffith (Ind.) Meth. Ch., 1955-57; minister adminstrn. and program 1st Meth. Ch., Eugene, Oreg., 1957-59; dir. pub. relations Dakotas area Meth. Ch., 1959-60, Ohio area, 1960-64; adminstrv. exec. to bishop Ohio East area United Meth. Ch., Canton, 1964-77; asst. gen. sec. Gen. Council on Fin. and Adminstrn., United Meth. Ch., Evanston, Ill., 1977-79, asso. gen. sec., 1979—; mem. staff, dept. radio services 2d assembly World Council Chs., Evanston, 1954; mem. commn. on entertainment and program North Central Jurisdictional Conf., 1968—, chmn., 1972-76; mem. commn. on gen. conf. United Meth. Ch., 1972—, bus. mgr., 1976—, mem. div. interpretation, 1969-72; creator nationally distbd. radio series The Word and Music; writer, dir. television series Parables in Miniature, 1957-59; chmn. communications commn. Ohio Council Chs., 1961-65; mem. exec. com. Nat. Assn. United Meth. Founds., 1968-72; del. World Meth. Conf., London, Eng., 1966, Dublin, Ireland, 1976; bd. dirs. Ohio East Area United Meth. Found., 1967—, v.p., 1967-76; chmn. bd. mgrs. United Meth. Bldg., Evanston, 1977—; lectr., cons. on fgn. travel. Adviser, East Ohio Conf. Communications Commn., 1968-76; pres. Guild Travel Assos., 1971—. Trustee, 1st v.p. Copeland Oaks Retirement Center, Sebring, Ohio, 1969-76. Mem. Am. Soc. Assn. Execs., Meeting Planners Internat. Pub. Relations Soc. Am., Religious Conv. Mgrs. Assn., Def. Orientation Conf. Assn. (dir.). Contbr. articles to religious publs. Home: 205 Enid Ln Northfield IL 60093 Office: 1200 Davis St Evanston IL 60201

WOODRING, PAUL, educator, psychologist; b. Delta, Ohio, July 16, 1907; s. Peter David and Ethel (Gormley) W.; B.S. in Edn., Bowling Green U., 1930, L.H.D., 1965; M.A., Ohio State U., 1934, Ph.D. in Psychology, 1938; L.H.D., Kalamazoo Coll., 1959; Pd.D., Coe Coll., 1960; Litt.D., Ripon Coll., 1963; LL.D., U. Portland, 1966; m. Jeannette McGraw, Sept. 19, 1938. Pub. sch. tchr., Ohio, 1927-33; instr. Ohio State U., 1935-37; clin. psychologist Detroit Criminal Cts., 1937-39; faculty Western Wash. U., Bellingham, 1939—, Distinguished Service prof., 1962—, interim pres., 1964-65. Ednl. adviser Ford Found.; cons. Fund for Advancement Edn., 1956-62; edn. editor Saturday Rev., 1960-66, editor at large, 1966-70. Served to lt. col. AUS, 1942-46; PTO. Recipient Tuition Plan award, 1958; Distinguished Alumnus award Bowling Green State U., 1960; Sch. Bell award N.E.A., 1962, 63; Ednl. Press Assn. award, 1963, 64, 66; Edn. Writers Assn. award, 1965. Diplomate clin. psychology Am. Bd. Examiners Profl. Psychology. Fellow Am. Psychol. Assn.; mem. AAAS, Psychol. Assn. Wash. (past pres.). Author: Let's Talk Sense About Our Schools, 1953; A Fourth of a Nation, 1957; New Directions in Teacher Education, 1957; Introduction to Education, 1965; also articles. Editor: The Professional Education for Teachers Series, 1965; American Education Today, 1963; The Higher Learning in America: A Reassessment, 1968; Investment in Innovation, 1970. Home: 1512 Knox Ave Bellingham WA 98225

WOODROE, WILLIAM MAY, lawyer; b. Charleston, W.Va., Jan. 21, 1906; s. James David and Jane Welles (May) W.; LL.B., W.Va. U., 1927; m. Isabel Tomasa Clark, Dec. 21, 1929; children—Stephen Clark, James Thaddeus (dec.). Admitted to W.Va. bar, 1927; with firm Love, Wise, Robinson & Woodroe, and predecessor firms. Pres., Buckskin council Boy Scouts Am., 1948. Mem. Am., W.Va., Kanawha County (past pres.) bar assns., W.Va. State Bar (past pres.), Charleston Area C. of C. (pres. 1964), Sigma Chi, Phi Delta Phi. Democrat. Episcopalian. Clubs: Charleston Tennis; Edgewood Country. 513 Linden Rd Charleston WV 25314 Office: Charleston Nat Plaza Charleston WV 25301

WOODROW, ROBERT HENRY, JR., banker, lawyer; b. Birmingham, Ala., Nov. 24, 1920; s. Robert Henry and Carrie (Shaw) W.; A.B., U. of South, 1941; J.D., U. Va., 1947; postgrad. Rutgers U. Stonier Grad. Sch. Banking, 1955; m. Martha Glaze, Mar. 31, 1944; children—Robert Henry III, John P., Catherine, Philip. With First Nat. Bank Birmingham, 1947—, asst. trust officer, 1950-53, trust officer, 1953-57, v.p., trust officer, 1957-61, sr. v.p., 1962-67, exec. v.p., trust officer 1967-70, exec. v.p. comml. loan, 1971, chmn. bd., chief exec. officer, 1972-76, vice chmn. bd. Ala. Bancorp., 1976—; admitted to Ala. bar, 1948. Served with AUS, 1942-46. Home: 3308 Hermitage Rd Birmingham AL 35223 Office: Alabama Bancorporation PO Box 11007 Birmingham AL 35288

WOODRUFF, ARCHIBALD MULFORD, JR., former univ. pres.; b. Newark, July 30, 1912; s. Archibald M. and Eleanor B. (Van Etten) W.; B.A., Williams Coll., 1933, LL.D. (hon.); postgrad. U. Berlin, 1935; Ph.D., Princeton, 1936; L.H.D. (hon.), Trinity Coll.; LL.D. (hon.), Tarkio Coll., U. Hartford, Annhurst Coll.; m. Barbara Jane Bestor, July 13, 1940; children—Archibald Mulford III, Paul B., Nathan V.E., Timothy R. Mortgage dept. Prudential Ins. Co., 1936-42, 44-50; Kelly Meml. prof. urban land studies U. Pitts., 1950-59, dir. Bur. Bus. Research, 1954-59; dean Sch. Govt. George Washington U., Washington, 1959-64; provost U. Hartford (Conn.), 1964-67, chancellor, 1967-70, pres., 1970-77. Dir. Soc. for Savs., Hartford, C.G. Fund, Inc., Hartford; past adv. dir. Western Pa. Nat. Bank. Past chmn. Nat. Capital Planning Commn.; past pres., Conn. Conf. Ind. Colls. Past chmn. bd. dirs. Tarkio (Mo.) Coll.; bd. dirs. Wadsworth Atheneum, Watkinson Sch.; trustee Mark Twain Meml., YMCA; mem. Bd. Higher Edn., Hartford bd. dirs. Land Reform Tng. Inst., Taoyuan, Taiwan, Republic of China, E.B. Found., Simsbury; v.p. Lincoln Found., 1965—. Recipient medal Ministry Edn., Republic of China. Mem. Am. Econ. Assn., Phi Beta Kappa. Universalist. Clubs: Hartford Golf, Hartford (Conn.); Cosmos (Washington). Author: books, monographs and articles on land econs., especially taxation. Home: PO Box 582 Simsbury CT 06070 Office: 1040 Prospect Ave Hartford CT 06105

WOODRUFF, ARNOLD BOND, psychologist, educator; b. Columbus, Ohio, Sept. 15, 1920; s. Arnold and Gladys Ruth (Bond) W.; A.B., Olivet Nazarene Coll., 1941, Th.B., 1942; M.A., Ohio State U., 1948, Ph.D., 1951; m. Margaret May Flint, Sept. 6, 1941; children—Arnold F., Margaret M., Lawrence T., Emily Ruth, Martin R., Kenneth J. Ordained to ministry Ch. of Nazarene, 1942-59, pastor in Ind., 1942-45, Ohio 1947-49; asst. instr. Ohio State U., 1948-50; from asst. prof. to prof. psychology Olivet Nazarene Coll., 1950-57, head dept., 1950-57, chmn. div. edn. and psychology, 1951-57; research scientist Human Resources Research Office, George Washington U., Ft. Knox (Ky.) Unit, 1957-59; lectr. U. Louisville, 1957-59; prof. psychology No. Ill. U., 1959—, head dept., 1959-69; Fulbright-Hays prof. psychology U. Ghana, Legon, 1970-72. Served as chaplain U.S. Army, 1945-47. Mem. Am., Midwestern, Ill. psychol. assns., AAUP (pres. No. Ill. U. chpt. 1961-62), Sigma Xi. Home: 1810 Raintree Ct Sycamore IL 60178

WOODRUFF, ASAHEL DAVIS, educator; b. Salt Lake City, Oct. 21, 1904; s. Elias Smith and Nellie Maria (Davis) W.; student U. Utah, 1927-29, Denver U., 1929-31; B.S., Brigham Young U., 1936, M.S., 1937; Ph.D., U. Chgo., 1941; m. Eva Mildred Stock, Apr. 14, 1930 (dec. 1969); children—Gaile (Mrs. D. Cecil Clark), Carolyn (Mrs. Russell L. Sutherland); m. 2d, Dorothy N. Candland, Mar. 13, 1972. Prin. various Latter-day Saints sems., 1935-39; dir. Latter-day Saints Inst. Religion, Ogden, Utah, 1941-42; instr. ednl. psychology Cornell U., 1942-44, asst. prof., 1944-46, asso. prof., 1946-47, prof., 1947-49; dean grad. sch., prof. psychology, edn., Brigham Young U., 1949, dean coll. edn., 1954-60; dean U. Utah Coll. Edn., 1960-66, prof. ednl. psychology emeritus, 1973—, campus coordinator Ethiopian Tchr. Edn. project, 1960-68; pres. Ednl. Devel., Inc., 1973—; asso. dir. human resources research office George Washington U., Washington until 1954. Vis. prof. summer ednl. psychology Utah State Agrl. Coll., 1947, U. Ill., 1950, U. Calif., 1955, 59, State U. Coll. Geneseo, N.Y., 1967, 68. Mem. Am., Utah psychol. assns., Am. Ednl. Research Assn., NEA, Utah Edn. Assn., Utah Conf. on Higher Edn. (pres. 1951-52), Sigma Xi, Phi Kappa Phi, Phi Delta Kappa, Sigma Chi. Mem. Ch. of Jesus Christ of Latter-day Saints. Author: The Psychology of Teaching, 1946; Parent and Youth, 1952; Education for Democracy, Productiveness and Character, 1957; Principles of Curriculum and Teaching, 1957; Teaching the Gospel, 1958; Basic Concepts of Teaching, 1961; Cognitive Models of Instruction, 1967; A Teaching Behavior Code. 1968; The Life-Involvement Model of Education, 1973. Contbr. articles, reasearch reports to psychol. lit. Home: 485 N Hill Dr Salt Lake City UT 84103

WOODRUFF, CALVIN WATTS, pediatrician; b. New Haven, July 16, 1920; s. William W. and Myra (Kilborn) W.; B.A., Yale, 1941, M.D., 1944; m. Betty Carter Perry, June 17, 1950; children—Virginia, Carl, William. Intern, Babies and Childrens Hosp., Cleve., 1944-45; asst. resident, then asso. prof. pediatrics Vanderbilt U. Med. Sch., 1947-60; prof. pediatrics Am. U., Beirut, Lebanon, 1960-63, U. Mo. Med. Sch., 1965—. Served with USNR, 1945-46, 52-53. Markle scholar med. sci., 1952-58. Mem. Am. Pediatrics Soc., Am. Inst. Nutrition, Soc. Pediatric Research, Am. Gastroenterol. Soc., Sigma Xi, Alpha Omega Alpha. Contbr. articles to profl. jours. Home: 910 Wayne Rd Columbia MO 65201

WOODRUFF, FRANK GEORGE, chem. co. exec.; b. Newark, Dec. 29, 1916; s. Frank Wilson and Fannie Margaret (Radcliffe) W.; student Essex County (N.J.) Jr. Coll., 1935; B.S. in Mining Engring., Mich. Technol. U., 1939, B.S. in Geology, 1940; m. Mary Catherine Banks, Nov. 25, 1939; children—Patricia (Mrs. Gordon L. Bergthold), Susan Parsons, Jane (Mrs. Ronald Thorp), Barbara (Mrs. Bryan Bartlett), F. James, Michael R., R. Bruce. Insp. core-boring U.S. Army C.E., Mo., also Ark., 1939-40; mine capt. Pickands-Mather & Co., Caspian, Mich., 1940-46; gen. mgr. Warren Foundry & Pipe Corp., Mount Hope, N.J., 1946-54, Kennecott Copper Corp., Hurley, N.M., 1962-70; pres. Gulf Resources & Chem. Corp., Houston, 1974—, Reeves MacDonald Inc., 1971—. Mem. Am. Inst. Mining, Metall. and Petroleum Engrs., Am. Mining Congress. Republican. Episcopalian. Clubs: Champions Golf, Hayden Lake Country, Athletic of Houston, Spokane Country; Mining (N.Y.C.). Office: 1100 Milam Bldg 47th Floor Houston TX 77002*

WOODRUFF, GEORGE ROBERT, univ. athletics adminstr.; b. Athens, Ga., Mar. 14, 1916; s. Joe G. and Mary L. (Phillips) W.; B.S. Engring., U. Tenn.; m. Margaret Artley, Sept. 3, 1942 (dec. Feb. 1977); children—William Robert, Joe G., Mark A., Margaret E. Asst. coach U. Tenn., 1939, 41, 61, 62, athletic dir., 1963—; asst. coach Ga. Inst. Tech., 1946; head coach Baylor U., 1947-50; head coach, athletic dir. U. Fla, 1950-60; mem. U.S. Olympic Com. Served to maj. U.S. Army, 1942-46. Named to Savannah (Ga.) Hall of Fame, Tenn. Hall of Fame. Mem. NACDA, SEC, Nat. Coll. Athletic Assn. Democrat. Baptist. Clubs: Rotary, ATO.

WOODRUFF, HALE ASPACIO, artist, educator; b. Cairo, Ill., Aug. 26, 1900; student John Herron Art Inst., Indpls., Fogg Art Museum, Harvard, Academie Scandinave, Academie Moderne, Paris, France; studied fresco painting under Diego Rivera, Mexico; D.F.A., Morgan State Coll., 1968, Ind. U., 1978; L.H.D., Atlanta U., 1972; m. Theres A. Barker, June 14, 1934; 1 son, Roy H. One-man shows at Internat. Print Soc., N.Y.C., 1943, Bertha Schaefer Gallery, N.Y.C., State Mus. N.C., Raleigh, U. N.C., Chapel Hill, Greensboro, Eastern Mich. State Tchrs. Coll., U. So. Ill., Hampton (Va.) Inst., High Mus. Art, Atlanta, N.Y. U., N.Y.C., U. Mich., Tuskegee Inst.; exhibited in numerous group shows including Tex. Centennial Celebration, Dallas, Detroit Inst. Art, Los Angeles County Mus., Boston Mus., Kansas City (Mo.) Art Inst., Whitney Mus., N.Y.C., Va. Mus., Richmond, Balt. Mus., Raleigh Mus., Newark Mus., Grace Horne Gallery, Boston, Pyramid Club, Phila., Riverside Mus., N.Y.C., Bklyn. Mus.; represented in permanent collections including: Newark Mus., IBM Collection, Atlanta U., Howard U., Washington, Met. Mus. Art, N.Y.C., N.Y. U., Library of Congress, Lincoln U., Harmon Found., N.Y.C., Smithsonian Instn., Washington, Jackson Coll., Spelman Coll., Johnson Pub. Co., Chgo., Indpls. Mus. Art, Detroit Inst. Art; important works include murals: The Amistad Mutiny and Founding of Talladega, both at Talladega Coll., 1938-39, History of California for Golden State Mut. Life Ins. Co., Los Angeles, 1948-49, The Art of the Negro, at Atlanta U., 1950-51; dir. art Atlanta U.; asso. prof. art edn. to prof. N.Y. U., to 1968, prof. emeritus, 1968—; lectr. in field. Mem. com. on art edn. Mus. Modern Art, N.Y.C.; mem. Art Commn. City N.Y., N.Y. State Council on Arts; lectr. Assn. Am. Colls.; U.S. rep. at 1st Internat. Festival of Negro Arts, Dakar, Senegal, 1966. Recipient Bronze award Harmon Found., First award High Mus. Art, Second and Third awards Diamond Jubilee Expn., Chgo., Atlanta U. award, medal of Honor N.J. Soc. Artists, Great Tchr. award N.Y. U., 1966; Julius Rosenwald fellow, 1943-45. Address: 22-26 E 8th St New York NY 10003

WOODRUFF, JAMES ARTHUR, food retail chain exec.; b. Greenville, Tex., May 1, 1943; s. James Thurman and Mildred (Proctor) W.; B.B.A., N. Tex. State U., 1965; m. Rosemary Boggess, Sept. 6, 1962; children—Misty, James, Melanie, Jason. Owner, sec., treas. Woody's Superettes, Inc., Woody's Discount Food & Family Center, Inc., Greenville, 1965—; dir., treas. Affiliated Food Stores, Inc., Dallas, 1970-73; dir. First Greenville Nat. Bank. Vice pres. Big Bros. Greenville, 1972; pres. Greenville Ambassadors, 1973. Bd. dirs. fund drives United Fund, Am. Cancer Soc., Am. Heart Assn., Easter Seal Soc., YMCA, Greenville. Named Jaycee of Year, Greenville Jaycees, 1970, recipient Presdl. Award of Honor, 1972. Mem. Greenville Jaycees (pres. 1970), Greenville C. of C. (dir. 1969-71, 75-77), N. Tex. Grocers Assn. (adv. bd. 1970), Tex. Retail Grocers Assn. (dir. 1978-80), Nat. Assn. Convenience Stores. Methodist (trustee, chmn. fin. com., chmn. council ministries). Rotarian. Home: 6306 Villa Fontana Greenville TX 75401 Office: 4808 S Wesley St Greenville TX 75401

WOODRUFF, JAMES DONALD, physician; b. Balt., June 20, 1912; s. Trowbridge Blanchard and Luella Lloyd (Redding) W.; B.S., Dickinson Coll., 1933; M.D., Johns Hopkins Hosp., 1937; m. Bettye Muriel Gardner, Apr. 15, 1939; children—J. Donald, David Crane, Gary Blanchard Moore. Intern Johns Hopkins Hosp., Balt., 1937-38, resident in gynecology, 1938-42; asso. prof. gynecology and obstetrics Johns Hopkins U. Sch. Medicine, from 1960, asso. prof. pathology, from 1961, prof., from 1968, Richard W. TeLinde prof. gynecologic pathology, 1975—. Chmn. health and safety com. Balt. Area Boy Scouts Am., 1959-70; vestryman Ch. of the Redeemer, Balt., 1958-61. Served with M.C., AUS, 1943-45. Mem. Internat. Soc. for Study of Vulvar Disease (pres. 1974), Am. Assn. Obstetricians and Gynecologists (pres. 1977), Johns Hopkins Med. and Surg. Assn. (pres. 1977), Soc. Gynecologic Oncologists. Episcopalian. Clubs: Johns Hopkins, Elkridge. Co-author 2 med. textbooks; contbr. chpts. to textbooks, articles to profl. jours. Office: Johns Hopkins U Sch of Medicine Baltimore MD 21205

WOODRUFF, JOHN ROWLAND, educator; b. Akron Ohio, June 14, 1909; s. Clarence Merle and Althea (Rowland) W.; A.B., Oberlin Coll., 1933; M.A., Western Res. U., 1936; Ph.D., Cornell U., 1949; m. Frances Siddall, Aug. 29, 1933; children—Susan (Mrs. James Price), Janet (Mrs. David Neal Hopkins); m. 2d, Evelyn Barrille, Oct. 8, 1959; children—Steven Dana, Douglas Michael. Teaching asst. Mt. Holyoke Coll., 1933-35; guest dir. Wells Coll., 1936-40; dir. Montgomery (Ala.) Little Theater, 1937; instr. Tufts U., 1940-49, asst. prof., 1949-54, asso. prof., 1954-57; asso. prof. Carleton Coll., Northfield, Minn., 1957-60, prof., 1960-74; vis. prof. La Verne (Calif.) Coll., 1974—, founder Entr'acte; founder Prologue, Tufts U.; founder Padua Hills Writer's Workshops for Playwrights, For Critics. Founder, Northfield Arts Guild, 1959; dir. Guthrie Theater. Mem. New Eng. Theater Assn. (past pres.), Am. Theater Assn., Nat. Theater Conf. Am. Nat. Theater and Acad., Eugene O'Neill Meml. Found. Author: (play) Welcome, Stranger, 1940. Contbr. articles to profl. jours. Home: PO Box 184 La Verne CA 91750 Office: Dailey Theater La Verne CA 91750

WOODRUFF, JUDSON SAGE, lawyer; b. Birmingham, Ala., May 18, 1925; s. Ernest Wrigley and Margaret (Martin) W.; B.S. in Physics, U. Okla., 1948, LL.B., 1950; Sterling fellow in grad. law Yale, 1950-51; m. Ruth Eleanor Dick, June 16, 1949 (div.); 1 dau., Jennifer; m. 2d, Millicent Imel Coats, Oct. 25, 1974. Admitted to Okla. bar, 1950, Ohio bar, 1960; with CIA, Washington, 1951-52; asst. econ. attache Fgn. Service, State Dept., Washington, 1951-52, Tokyo, Japan, 1952-54, Seoul, Korea, 1955; law clk. U.S. Dist. Ct., Eastern Dist. Okla., Muskogee, 1955-56; atty. Marathon Oil Co., Tulsa, 1956-60, Findlay, Ohio, 1960-62, Geneva, Switzerland, 1962-63, London, Eng., 1962-63, Tripoli, Libya, 1962-63; partner firm McAfee, Taft, Mark, Bond, Rucks & Woodruff, Oklahoma City, 1964—. Instr., Tulsa U. Law Sch., 1958-60. Asso. bar examiner State of Okla., 1967-69. Chmn., Gov.'s Com. Ad Valorem Taxation, 1967-68; mem. Okla. Alcoholic Beverage Control Bd., 1968-69, Okla. Hwy. Commn., 1969-71. Served as lt. (j.g.) USNR, 1942-46. Mem. Sigma Pi Sigma, Phi Delta Phi, Order of Coif. Republican. Episcopalian (sr. warden 1968-70). Okla. editor Oil & Gas Reporter, Southwestern Legal Found., 1964—. Home: 3110 Harvey Pkwy Oklahoma City OK 73118 Office: 100 Park Ave Oklahoma City OK 73102

WOODRUFF, JUDY CARLINE, broadcast journalist; b. Tulsa, Nov. 20, 1946; d. William Henry and Anna Lee (Payne) W.; student Meredith Coll., 1964-66; B.A., Duke U., 1968. News announcer, reporter Sta.-WAGA-TV, Atlanta, 1970-75; news corr. NBC News, Atlanta, 1975-76, White House corr., Washington, 1977—; mem. bd. advs. U. Ga. Henry Grady Sch. Journalism, 1979. Bd. dirs. Atlanta chpt. Camp Fire Girls, 1973-75. Recipient award Leadership Atlanta, Class of 1974, Atlanta chpt. Women in Communications, 1975. Mem. Nat. Acad. TV Arts and Scis. (charter mem. Atlanta chpt.; Atlanta chpt. Emmy award 1975). Office: 4001 Nebraska Ave NW Washington DC 20016

WOODRUFF, NEAL, JR., educator; b. Kansas City, Mo., Apr. 16, 1925; s. Neal and Lulu Mae (Hazard) W.; student U. Ill., 1942-43; B.A., U. Kans., 1946; M.A., Yale, 1947, Ph.D., 1955; m. Christine Louise Lipps, Aug. 30, 1952; children—Susan Barnes, David Presley. Instr., Carnegie Inst. Tech. (now Carnegie-Mellon U.), Pitts., 1952-54, asst. prof., 1954-60, asso. prof. English, 1960-68; prof. English, Coe Coll., Cedar Rapids, Iowa, 1968-78, Howard Hall prof English, 1978—, chmn. dept. English, speech and theater, 1968-74. Mem. exec. com. Assn. Depts. English, 1971-73, pres., 1973. Cons. communications, coll. curriculum. Mem. Modern Lang. Assn. (chmn. adv. com. on job market 1975-77), Nat. Council Tchrs. English, AAUP, Phi Kappa Phi. Democrat. Co-editor English and Foreign Languages: Employment and the Profession, 1976. Home: 218 15th St NE Cedar Rapids IA 52402

WOODRUFF, NEIL PARKER, agrl. engr.; b. Clyde, Kans., July 25, 1919; s. Charles Scott and Myra (Christian) W.; B.S., Kans. State U., 1949, M.S., 1953; postgrad. Iowa State U., 1959; m. Dorothy Adele Russ, June 15, 1952; children—Timothy C., Thomas S. Agrl. engr. Agrl. Research Service, Dept. Agr., Manhattan, Kans., 1949-63, research leader, 1963-75; cons., Manhattan, 1975-77; civil engr. Kans. Dept. Transp., Topeka, 1977-79; prof., mem. grad. faculty Kans. State U., civil engr. planning, 1979—; mem. sci. exchange team to Soviet Union, 1974. Fellow Am. Soc. Agrl. Engrs. (Hancor Soil Water Engring. award 1975); mem. Soil Conservation Soc. Am., Sigma Xi, Gamma Sigma Delta. Contbr. articles to tech. jours. and books. Home: 2315 Timberlane St Manhattan KS 66502 Office: Dykstra Hall Kans State U Manhattan KS 66506

WOODRUFF, ROBERT PAUL, lawyer; b. Houston, June 23, 1925; s. Matthew Franklin and Arvie Elizabeth (Weaver) W.; LL.B., U. Tex., Austin, 1949. Admitted to Tex. bar, 1949; practice in Houston, 1949-51, Dallas, 1951—; partner firm Woodruff & Ellis, 1957—. Served to 2d lt. USAAF, 1943-45. Fellow Am. Coll. Trial Lawyers, Am. Bd. Trial Advocates, Tex. Bar Found.; mem. Am., Dallas (chmn. bd. dirs. 1967) bar assns., State Bar Tex., Assn. Trial Lawyers Am., Tex. Trial Lawyers Assn., Dallas Assn. Trial Lawyers (pres. 1974). Home: Rt 2 Kemp TX 75143 Office: 2322 Republic Nat Bank Tower Dallas TX 75201

WOODRUFF, TRUMAN OWEN, educator; b. Salt Lake City, May 26, 1925; s. Wilford Owen and Evelyn (Ballif) W.; A.B., Harvard, 1947; B.A., Oxford (Eng.) U., 1950; Ph.D., Calif. Inst. Tech., 1955; m. Ambrosina Lydia Solaroli, Sept. 14, 1948. Nat. scholar Harvard, 1942-44, 46-47, Sheldon traveling fellow, 1947-48; Rhodes scholar Oxford U., 1948-50; Dow Chem. Co. fellow, Howard Hughes fellow Calif. Inst. Tech., 1950-54; research asso. physics U. Ill., 1954-55; physicist Gen. Elec. Research Lab., 1955-62; prof. physics Mich. State U., 1962—, chmn. dept., 1972-75. Cons. physics to indsl. research orgns. Served with USNR, 1944-46. Fulbright fellow U. Pisa, 1968-69. Fellow Am. Phys. Soc.; mem. Assn. Harvard Chemists, Phi Beta Kappa, Sigma Xi. Contbr. articles to sci. jours. Office: Mich State U Dept Physics East Lansing MI 48824

WOODRUM, PATRICIA ANN, librarian; b. Hutchinson, Kans., Oct. 11, 1941; d. Donald Jewell and Ruby Pauline (Shuman) Hoffman; B.A., Kans. State Coll., Pittsburg, 1963; M.L.S., U. Okla., 1966; m. Clayton Eugene Woodrum, Mar. 31, 1962; 1 son, Clayton Eugene, II. Br. librarian Tulsa City-County Library System, 1964-65, head brs., 1965-66, head reference dept., 1966-67, chief extension, chief pub. service, 1967-73, asst. dir., 1973-76, dir., 1976—; adv. com. U. Okla. Sch. Library Sci.; community adv. council Tulsa Jr. League; mem. Tulsa Arts and Humanities Council, Tulsa Area Council on Aging, Downtown Tulsa Unltd.; mem. exec. com. Friends of Tulsa Library; bd. dirs. Friends of Okla. Libraries, Leadership Tulsa; del. White House Conf. on Libraries; mem. Okla. Health Systems Agy. Council. Mem. ALA (council, dir. public libraries div., com. on orgns.), Southwestern (exec. bd.) Okla. (pres. 1977) library assns., Met. C. of C., LWV (exec. com.). Republican. Mem. Christian Ch. (Disciples of Christ). Home: 214 E 24th Pl Tulsa OK 74114 Office: 400 Civic Center Tulsa OK 74103

WOODS, CHARLES ELLERBE, air force officer; b. Milwaukee, N.C., Nov. 25, 1927; s. John and Elizabeth Terry (Ellerbe) W.; B.S., East Carolina U., 1950; M.B.A., Golden Gate U., 1953; grad. diploma Indsl. Coll. Armed Forces, 1970; m. Ruby Lee Bordeaux, Aug. 20, 1949; children—John Shockley, David Owen. Served as enlisted man AC, U.S. Army, Shanghai, China, 1945-47; commd. 2d lt. U.S. Air Force, 1950, advanced through grades to maj. gen., 1978; served as student pilot, fighter pilot, aircraft maintenance officer, 1950-57, as aide de camp, 1957-60; ops. staff officer and air ops. officer, Norton AFB, Calif., 1960-63; flight tng. instr., ops. officer 3525th Pilot Tng. Wing, Williams AFB, Ariz., 1963-65; protocol officer Hdqrs. Air Tng. Command, Randolph AFB, Tex., 1965; ops. officer 433d Tactical Fighter Squadron of 8th Tactical Fighter Wing, Thailand, 1967; congressional liaison officer Directorate of Legis. Liaison, Office Sec. of Air Force, 1967-70; dep. comdr. for ops. 3575th Pilot Tng. Wing, Vance AFB, Okla., 1970, comdr., 1971; comdr. 47th Flying Tng. Wing, Laughlin AFB, Tex., 1972; vice comdr. 13th Air Force Advanced Echelon, Udorn Royal Thai AFB, 1973; comdr. 56th Spl. Ops. Wing, Nakhon Phanon Royal Thai AFB, 1973; chief resources div. Directorate of Programs, Hdqrs. U.S. Air Force, Washington, 1974-77, dep. dir. programs, 1977; comdr. Air Force Commissary Service, Kelly AFB, Tex., 1978—; bd. dirs. Air Force Commissary. Mem. Gt. Salt Plains Area council Boy Scouts Am., 1971-72. Decorated D.S.M., Legion of Merit with oak leaf cluster, D.F.C., Meritorious Service medal with oak leaf cluster, Air medal with 11 oak leaf clusters, Air Force Commendation medal with oak leaf cluster. Mem. Air Force Assn., Order Daedalians. Methodist. Clubs: Masons, Shriners. Home: 2531 Turkey Oak St San Antonio TX 78232 Office: Comdr Air Force Commissary Service Kelly AFB TX 78241

WOODS, FRANK HENRY, business exec.; b. Lincoln, Nebr., May 2, 1905; s. Frank H. and Nelle S. (Cochrane) W., A.B., Yale, 1928; D.H.L., Lake Forest Coll., 1970; LL.D., U. Neb., 1975; m. Louise Hamilton Brewer, Feb. 16, 1935; children—Louise (Mrs. Benkert), Lucia (Mrs. Lindley), Brewer (dec. 1976), Amy (Mrs. Nelson Gore). Asso., Harris Trust & Savs. Bank, Chgo., 1928-33; asst. to pres. Sahara Coal Co., Chgo., 1933-38, sec.-treas., 1938-44, pres., treas., 1944—, chmn. bd., 1978—; dir. Lincoln Tel. & Tel. Co. (Nebr.), 1937-79, exec. com., 1942—, chmn. bd. dirs., 1958-79; dir., exec. com. Addressograph Multigraph Corp. (Cleve.), 1946, chmn. bd., 1958-76; dir. Harris Trust & Savs. Bank, Chgo., 1954-75. Chmn., Gov.'s Com. for Ill., Midcentury White House Conf. on Children and Youth 1949-51; mem. City of Lake Forest Plan Commn., 1954-58; mem. corp., gifts chmn. Community Fund of Chgo., 1947, dir., 1954-67, pres., 1957-59; pres. A.R.C. Joint Appeal of Chgo., 1957-58, North Side Boys' Clubs, 1940-47. Bd. dirs. United Community Funds and Councils Am., N.Y., 1958-64, v.p., 1960-61; pres. Welfare Council Met. Chgo., 1953-57, bd. dirs., 1947-66; treas., trustee Woods Charitable Fund, Chgo., 1941; life trustee, gov. mem. Chgo. Zool. Soc.; bd. dirs. Council on Founds., 1960-76, pres., 1964-65; bd. dirs. Hosp. Planning Council for Met. Chgo., 1957-66; trustee, life mem. gov. bd. Art Inst. Chgo., 1955-75, pres. 1966-70; life trustee U. Chgo., 1962—. Mem. Ill. Mfrs. Assn. (dir. 1955-58), Nat. Soc. Prevention Blindness Inc. (dir. 1948-60), Ill. Soc. Prevention Blindness (pres. 1947-57, dir. 1946-62), Chgo. Hort. Soc. (trustee 1962, v.p. 1965, life trustee 1976—), Taxpayers Fedn. Ill. (trustee 1948-58). Episcopalian. Clubs: Chicago, Comml., Casino, Onwentsia. Home: 550 E Deer Path Lake Forest IL 60045 Office: 332 S Michigan Ave Chicago IL 60604

WOODS, GEORGE W., corp. exec.; b. Montreal, Que., Can., 1921; ed. McGill U., 1947. Vice chmn., chief operating officer TransCan. PipeLines; dir. Gt. Lakes Gas Transmission Co. Office: PO Box 54 Commerce Ct W Toronto ON M5L 1C2 Canada

WOODS, GURDON GRANT, sculptor; b. Savannah, Ga., Apr. 15, 1915; s. Frederick L. and Marion (Skinner) W.; student Copley Soc., Boston, 1934-35, Art Student's League N.Y.C., 1936-39, Bklyn. Mus. Sch., 1945-46; Ph.D. (hon.), Coll. San Francisco Art Inst., 1966; m. Judith Colman, Aug. 27, 1976. Exhibited Pa. Acad., 1941, Allied Am. Artists, 1945, N.A.D., 1948, 49, San Francisco Art Assn. anns., 1952-54, Denver Mus. Anns. 1952, 53, Whitney Mus. Ann., 1953, Sao Paulo Biennial, 1955, Bolles Gallery San Francisco, 1969, 70, 72, So. Sculptors ann., 1970, Janus Gallery, Los Angeles, 1976, Los Angeles Municipal Gallery, 1977; tchr. Riverdale Country Sch., N.Y.C. 1947-49, Town Sch. for Boys, San Francisco, 1949-55; organizer, head art dept. Lick-Wilmerding, exec. dir. San Francisco Art Inst., 1955-64, dir. Calif. Sch. Fine Arts, 1955-65; prof. Adlai E. Stevenson Coll., U. Cal. at Santa Cruz, 1966-74; dir. Otis Art Inst., Los Angeles, 1974-77; asst. dir. Los Angeles County Mus. Natural History, 1977—. Commns. include cast concrete reliefs and steel fountain IBM Center, San Jose, Calif., fountain Paul Masson Winery, Saratoga, Calif., McGraw Hill Pubs., Novato, Calif. Sculptor mem. San Francisco Art Commn., 1954-56; mem. Santa Cruz County Art Commn., Regional Arts Council of Bay Area. Recipient citation N.Y.C., 1948; prize N.A.D., 1949; purchase prize for sculpture San Francisco Art Festival, 1950, 61; sculpture prize San Francisco Art Assn. anns., 1952, 54, Richmond Art Center, 1953; Chapelbrook Found. research grantee, 1965-66; Sequoia Fund grantee, 1967; Research grantee Creative Arts Inst., U. Calif., 1968; grantee Carnegie Corp., 1968-69. Mem. Artists Equity Assn (pres. No. Calif. chpt. 1950-52, nat. dir. 1952-55). Address: 3109 Coolidge Ave Los Angeles CA 90066

WOODS, HENRY, lawyer; b. Abbeville, Miss., Mar. 17, 1918; s. Joseph Neal and Mary Jett (Wooldridge) W.; B.A., U. Ark., 1938, J.D. cum laude, 1940; m. Kathleen Mary McCaffrey, Jan. 1, 1943; children—Mary Sue, Thomas Henry, Eileen Anne, James Michael. Admitted to Ark. bar, 1940; spl. agt. FBI, 1941-46; mem. firm Alston & Woods, Texarkana, Ark., 1946-48; exec. sec. to Gov. Ark., 1949-53; mem. firm McMath, Leatherman & Woods, Little Rock, 1953—; referee in bankruptcy U.S. Dist. Ct., Texarkana, 1947-48; spl. asso. justice Ark. Supreme Ct., 1967-74, chmn. com. model jury instrns., 1973—; chmn. bd. Center Trial and Appellate Advocacy, Hastings Coll. Law, San Francisco, 1975-76; mem. joint conf. com. Am. Bar Assn.-AMA, 1973—, Ark. Constl. Revision Study Commn., 1967-68. Pres. Young Democrats Ark., 1946-48; mem. Gubernatorial Com. Study Death Penalty, 1971-73. Mem. Am., Ark. (pres. 1972-73; Outstanding Lawyer award 1975), Pulaski County bar assns., Assn. Trial Lawyers Am. (gov. 1965-67), Ark. Trial Lawyers Assn. (pres. 1965-67), Internat. Acad. Trial Lawyers, Internat. Soc. Barristers, Am. Coll. Trial Lawyers, Am. Bd. Trial Advocates, Phi Alpha Delta. Methodist. Author treatise comparative fault. Contbr. articles to legal jours. Home: 42 Wingate Dr Little Rock AR 72205 Office: 711 W 3d St Little Rock AR 72201

WOODS, JAMES DUDLEY, mfg. co. exec.; b. Falmouth, Ky., July 24, 1931; s. Alva L. and Mabel L. (Miller) W.; A.A., Long Beach City Coll., 1958; B.A., Calif. State U., Fullerton, 1967, postgrad., 1968-70; m. Darlene Mae Petersen, Nov. 8, 1962; children—Linda, Debbie, Jeffrey, Jamie. Mgr. planning and control Baker Internat., Los Angeles, 1965-68, v.p. fin. and adminstrn. Baker div., 1968-73, corp. v.p., group fin. officer Baker Internat., 1973-76, pres. Baker Packers, Houston, 1976-77, corp. v.p. Baker Internat., pres. Baker Oil Toos, Orange, Calif., 1977—. Served with USAF, 1951-55. Republican. Lutheran. Office: 500 City Parkway W Orange CA 92668

WOODS, JOE DARST, educator, chemist; b. Knoxville, Iowa, Jan. 2, 1923; s. James Isaac and Mary (Darst) W.; B.S. cum laude, Central Coll. Iowa, 1947; M.S., Iowa State U., 1950, Ph.D., 1954; m. Nadine Reed, Nov. 14, 1945; children—Miriam, John. Sci. tchr. Albia High Sch., 1947-48; faculty Drake U., Des Moines, 1952—, prof. chemistry, 1964—, chmn. dept., 1969—. Fulbright lectr. St. Louis U., Baguio City, Phillipines, 1967-68. Mem. AAAS, Iowa Acad. Sci. (chmn. sci. talent search 1960-67, co-chmn. chem. edn. sect. 1974-76), Midwest Assn. Chemistry Tchrs. in Liberal Arts Colls. (pres. 1977-78), Am. Chem. Soc., AAUP, Sigma Xi, Phi Lambda Upsilon. Research, publs. on oxidation of metals, isotropic tracer reaction mechanisms. Home: 4107 Ardmore Rd Des Moines IA 50310

WOODS, JOHN DOWS, banker; b. Oak Park, Ill., Dec. 6, 1929; s. Donald Carmel and Helen (Dows) W.; B.A., U. Colo., 1956; grad. Sch. Banking U. Wis., 1967; m. Marion Heidenreich, May 6, 1953; children—John, Donald, Susan, Charles, Lisen. Asst. cashier No. Trust Co., Chgo., 1956-64; with Winters Nat. Bank & Trust Co., Dayton, Ohio, 1964-75, sr. v.p., 1969-71, exec. v.p., 1971-72, pres., chief operating officer, dir., 1972-75; pres., chief exec. officer Omaha Nat. Bank, 1975-78, chmn., chief exec. officer, 1978—; pres., chief exec. officer Omaha Nat. Corp., 1975—, also chmn., 1976—; dir. Fed. Res. Bank, Kansas City, United Benefit Life Ins. Co., Omaha, Orange Co., Columbus, Ohio, Orr Felt Co., Piqua, Ohio. Trustee USAF Mus., Dayton, Creighton U., Omaha, U. Nebr. Med. Sch., Omaha; bd. dirs. Bishop Clarkson Meml. Hosp.; mem. consultation staff SAC Hdqrs., Omaha. Served with USAF, 1949-54. Mem. Res. City Bankers. Clubs: Omaha, Omaha Country, Ak Sar Ben (bd. govs.) (Omaha); Univ. (N.Y.C.).

WOODS, JOHN HAYDEN, univ. pres.; b. Barrie, Ont., Can., Mar. 16, 1937; s. John Frederick and Gertrude Mary (Hayden) W.; B.A., U. Toronto, 1958, M.A., 1959; Ph.D., U. Mich., 1965; m. Carol Gwendolyn Arnold, July 13, 1957; children—Catherine Lynn, Kelly Ann, Michael John. From lectr. to asso. prof. U. Toronto, 1962-71; asso. prof. Linguistics Soc. Am., Ann Arbor, Mich., 1967; vis. prof. Stanford U., 1971; prof. philosophy U. Victoria (B.C., Can.), 1971-76, asso. dean arts and scis., 1975-76; asst. prof. Inst. Philosophy, U. Calgary (Alta., Can.), 1965, prof. philosophy, dean humanities, 1976-79; prof. philosophy, pres., vice chancellor U. Lethbridge (Alta.), 1979—. Mem. Com. for Ind. Can., 1971; mem. exec. com. Univs. Coordinating Council Alta., 1977—; Can. Council research fellow, 1968-69, 71; Humanities Research Council Can. grantee, 1974, 76. Mem. Can. Philos. Assn. (exec. com.), Am. Philos. Assn. (exec. com. 1971-74), Soc. Exact Philosophy, Humanities Assn. Can., Can. Fedn. for Humanities (exec. com. 1978—), Phi Beta Kappa. Author: Proof and Truth, 1974; The Logic of Fiction, 1974; Engineered Death, 1978; editor: (with L. W. Sumner) Necessary Truth, 1969; (with H.G. Coward) Humanities in the Present Day, 1979; (with T. Pavel) Formal Semantics and Literature, 1979; Dialogue: Canadian Philos. Rev., 1974—. Home: 1410 20th Ave S Lethbridge AB Canada Office: Office of Pres U Lethbridge 4401 University Dr Lethbridge AB T1K 3M4 Canada

WOODS, JOHN LUCIUS, mgmt. cons.; b. Oxford, Ohio, Feb. 18, 1912; s. George B. and Helen (Smith) W.; student Am. U., 1929-31; B.S., Northwestern U., 1933; m. Mary Torkilson, Apr. 2, 1938; children—Thomas George, Judith Ann, Jean Katharine, John Franklin. Asst. cashier Mackubin, Legg & Co., 1933-34; accountant Arthur Andersen & Co., 1934-42; office mgr. Bauer & Black, 1942-44; controller Amphenol Corp., Broadview, Ill., 1944-55, v.p. finance and adminstrn., dir., mem. exec. com., 1955-68; v.p. finance Bunker Ramo Corp. (combination Amphenol Corp. and Bunker Ramo Corp.), 1968-71; mgmt. cons., Chgo., 1971—; dir. Tower Products Inc., Valuation Counselors, Inc.; dir., treas. Power Packaging, Inc., 1971-74; pub., dir. Northview (Ill.) Pub. Co., 1950-53; pres., dir. Borg Investment Co., 1964-71. Mem. Glenview Sch. Bd., 1945-51; commr., v.p. Glenview Park Bd., 1953-60; pres. Northfield Twp. High Sch. Bd. Edn., 1947-51; pres. Glen Oak Acres Community Assn., 1947-48. C.P.A., Ill., Wash., D.C. Mem. Financial Execs. Inst., Am. Inst. Accountants, Ill. Soc. C.P.A.'s, Am. Mgmt. Assn., Newcomen Soc. N.Am., Chgo. Dist. Golf Assn. (dir. 1971—). Republican. Clubs: Mid-Day, Executives, Union League, Economic (Chgo.); Knollwood (pres. 1970-73 Lake Forest); Wall Street (N.Y.C.). Home: 5 Ct of Bucks County Lincolnshire IL 60015 Office: 230 W Monroe St Chicago IL 60606

WOODS, JOHN WILLIAM, lawyer; b. Ft. Worth, Dec. 10, 1912; s. John George and Eugenia (Smith) W.; B.S., North Tex. State U., 1951, M.Ed., 1952; J.D., St. Mary's U., San Antonio, 1967; postgrad. Fresno State Coll., 1952, West Tex. State U., 1959; m. Gertie Leona Parker, Apr. 15, 1954. Tchr., Corcoran, Calif., 1952-53, Pampa, Tex., 1953-63, Harlandale Sch. Dist., San Antonio, 1963-67; admitted to Tex. bar, 1966; practicing atty., Amarillo, Tex., 1967-68; county atty., Sherman County, Tex., 1969-72, justice of peace, 1975—; pvt. practice law, Stratford, Tex., 1968—. Served to ensign USN, 1930-47; ETO. Mem. Tex., 69th Jud. bar assns., Am. Legion. Democrat. Mem. Disciples of Christ. Mason (Shriner). Home: 1115 Putnam St Stratford TX 79084 Office: 220 N Main St Stratford TX 79084

WOODS, JOHN WITHERSPOON, banker; b. Evanston, Ill., Aug. 18, 1931; s. J. Albert and Cornelia (Witherspoon) W.; B.A., U. of South, 1954; m. Loti Moultrie Chisolm, Sept. 5, 1953; children—Loti, Cindy, Corrie. With Chem. Bank, N.Y.C., 1954-69, v.p., head So. div., 1965-69; chmn., pres., dir. Ala. Bancorp., 1972—; vice chmn., dir. First Nat. Bank Birmingham, 1969—; dir. Avondale Mills, Inc., Sylacauga, Ala., Protective Life Ins. Co., Birmingham, Engel Mortgage Co., Birmingham, Ala. Power Co. Birmingham. Treas., trustee Children's Hosp.; trustee, So. Research Inst., Miles Coll., Birmingham; bd. dirs. Met. Devel. Bd. Birmingham; chmn. bd. Greater Birmingham Conv. and Visitors Bur. Served to 1st lt. USAF, 1955-57. Mem. Birmingham Area C. of C. (chmn. bd.; pres. 1978, dir., exec. com.), Assn. Res. City Bankers, Young Presidents Orgn. Home: 4516 Old Leeds Rd Birmingham AL 35213 Office: 1900 5th Ave N PO Box 11007 Birmingham AL 35288

WOODS, LAWRENCE MILTON, petroleum co. exec.; b. Manderson, Wyo., Apr. 14, 1932; s. Ben Ray and Katherine (Youngman) W.; B.Sc. with honors, U. Wyo., 1953; M.A., N.Y. U., 1973, Ph.D., 1975; LL.D., Wagner Coll., 1973; m. Joan Frances Van Patten, June 10, 1952; 1 dau., Laurie. Admitted to Mont. bar, 1957; accountant firm Peat, Marwick, Mitchell & Co., C.P.A.'s, Billings, Mont., 1953; supervisory auditor Army Audit Agy., Denver, 1954-56; accountant Mobil Producing Co., Billings, Mont., 1956-59; planning analyst Socony Mobil Oil Co., N.Y.C., 1959-63, planning mgr., 1963-65, v.p. North Am. div. Mobil Oil Corp., N.Y.C., 1966-67, gen. mgr. planning and econs., 1967-69, v.p., 1969-77, exec. v.p., 1977—, also dir.; dir. Marcor, Inc., Montgomery Ward & Co., Mobil Corp., Container Corp., W.F. Hall Printing Co.; trustee Greenburgh Savs. Bank. Am. Trustee Wagner Coll. C.P.A., Colo., Mont. Served with AUS, 1953-55. Mem. Am., Mont. bar assns., Am. Inst. C.P.A.'s. Republican. Lutheran (treas. Lutheran Ch. Am. 1972—, mem. exec. council 1972—). Club: Pinnacle (N.Y.C.). Author: Accounting for Capital, Construction and Maintenance Expenditures, 1967; The Wyoming Country Before Statehood, 1971; co-author: Takeover, 1980; contbr. Accountants' Encyclopedia, 1962. Home: 84 Hickory Rd Briarcliff Manor NY 10510 Office: 150 E 42d St New York NY 10017

WOODS, MARK WINTON, ret. educator, biologist; b. Takoma Park, D.C., Oct. 15, 1908; s. Albert Frederick and Bertha Gerneaux (Davis) W.; B.S., U. Md., 1931, M.S., 1933, Ph.D., 1936; m. Vera Lorraine Klein, Dec. 23, 1933; children—Judith Patricia, Mark Alvin. From instr. plant pathology to asso. prof. U. Md., 1936-47; biologist Nat. Cancer Inst., 1947-73, ret., 1973, spl. research metabolism cancer, hereditary properties mitochondria, cell responses to plant viruses. Served with USNR, 1942-45. Fellow AAAS; mem. Phytopathol. Soc. Am., Am. Assn. Cancer Research, Am. Soc. Biol. Chemists, Washington, N.Y. acads. scis., Sigma Xi, Phi Kappa Phi, Alpha Zeta, Alpha Tau Omega. Presbyterian (elder). Home: 10718 Brookside Dr Sun City AZ 85351. *It seems to me that the basic criterion as to whether a thing is worth doing or not should be decided on the basis of whether it can help to advance the quality of life on this earth.*

WOODS, PAUL HARLOW, banker; b. Kingman, Kans., July 9, 1906; s. Paul S. and Grace (Harlow) W.; B.S., U. Kans., 1928; m. Wilda Cline, May 24, 1930; children—Harlow Verne, Paula, Michael. Teller, First Nat. Bank, Wichita, Kans., 1928-29, asst. v.p., 1938-42, 44-48, v.p., 1948-55, exec. v.p., 1955-58, pres., 1958-71, now dir.; chmn. bd. dirs. Energy Reserves Group, Inc., 1973—; dir. Beech Acceptance Corp., Misco Industries, Central Nat. Bankshares, Inc.; asst. cashier First Nat. Bank, Kingman, Kans., 1929-34; sec. Fed. Intermediate Credit Bank, Wichita, 1934-38. Pres. bd. edn., Wichita, 1951-52, mem., 1950-61. Pres. United Fund Wichita and Sedgewick County, 1968; chmn. bd. St. Joseph Hosp. and Med. Center, 1976-78. Served to maj. AUS, 1942-44. Mem. Delta Tau Delta. Mem. Christian Ch. Club: Wichita. Home: 324 S Fountain St Wichita KS 67218 Office: First Nat Bank Bldg Wichita KS 67202

WOODS, PHILIP SARGENT, educator, biologist; b. Concord, N.H., Nov. 25, 1921; s. Arthur Page and Beulah (Sargent) W.; B.S., Mich. State U., 1947; Ph.D., U. Wis., 1952; m. Dorothy Barrett, Mar. 15, 1946; children—Thomas B., Karen L. Radiobiologist, Army Med. Research Lab., Ft. Knox, Ky., 1952-53; USPHS fellow Columbia, 1953-55; cytologist Brookhaven Nat. Lab., Upton, N.Y., 1955-62; asso. prof. dept. biol. sci. U. Del., Newark, 1962-67; prof. dept. biology Queens Coll. of City U N.Y., Flushing, 1967—. Mem. Am. Soc. Cell. Biology, Electron Microscopy Soc. Am., Sigma Xi. Office: Dept Biology Queens Coll Flushing NY 11367

WOODS, PHILIP WELLS (PHIL), jazz musician; b. Culpepper, Va., Nov. 2, 1933. Alto saxophone and clarinet with Dizzy Gillespie, Quincy Jones, Benny Goodman; now leads own group. Winner Downbeat Readers Poll, 1975, 76, 77. Office: care Norman Schwartz Gryphon Prodns 157 W 57 St New York City NY 10036

WOODS, RICHARD SEAVEY, accountant, educator; b. Albion, N.Y., Mar. 1, 1919; s. Stanley Taylor and Helen Saxe (Seavey) W.; A.B., U. Rochester, 1941; M.B.A., U. Pa., 1947, Ph.D., 1957; m. Dorothy Signor Blake, Dec. 19, 1945; children—David Blake, Michael Signor, Martha Seavey, Catherine Hardie. Tchr. English pub. schs., Shortsville N.Y., 1941-42; instr. accounting U. Pa. Wharton Sch., Phila., 1947-52, asst. prof., 1952-58, asso. prof., 1958-64, prof., 1964—, asso. chmn. dept., 1961-63, acting chmn., 1961-62, 75-76, chmn., 1963-69. Served to lt. USNR, 1942-46. C.P.A., Pa. Mem. Am. Accounting Assn., Am. Inst. C.P.A.'s. Author: (with O.S. Nelson) Accounting Systems and Data Processing, 1961. Cons. editor Accountant's Handbook, 1970; editor, contbr. Audit Decisions in Accounting Practice, 1973; Audit Decision Cases, 1973. Home: 62 Snyder Ln Springfield PA 19064 Office: Dietrich Hall University of Pa Philadelphia PA 19104

WOODS, ROBERT ARCHER, investment counsel; b. Princeton, Ind., Dec. 28, 1920; s. John Hall and Rose Erskine Heilman W.; A.B., U. Rochester, 1942; M.B.A., Harvard, 1946; m. Ruth Henrietta Diller, May 27, 1944; children—Robert Archer III, Barbara Diller (Mrs. Gregory Alan Klein), Katherine Heilman, James Diller. Account exec. Stein Roe & Farnham, investment counsel, Chgo., 1946-53, partner, 1954—; pres., dir. Stein Roe & Farnham Balanced Fund, Chgo., 1971, Stein Roe & Farnham Stock Fund, Chgo., 1971; dir. Stein Roe & Farnham, Capital Opportunities Fund; Gov. Investment Co. Inst. Trustee U. Rochester; bd. dirs. Chgo. Juvenile Protective Assn., Chgo. Infant Welfare Soc. Served to lt. (s.g.), USNR, 1943-46. Mem. Am. Mgmt. Assn. (trustee 1973), Harvard Bus. Sch. Club Chgo. (pres. 1961), Phi Beta Kappa, Delta Upsilon. Clubs: Univ. Chgo., Chicago, Metropolitan, Tower. Home: 470 Orchard Ln Winnetka IL 60093 Office: 150 S Wacker Dr Chicago IL 60606

WOODS, ROBERT CLAUDE, chemist, educator; b. Atlanta, Mar. 24, 1940; s. Robert Claude and Thelma (Powell) W.; B.S., Ga. Inst. Tech., 1961; A.M. in Chemistry, Harvard U., 1962, Ph.D., 1965; m. Charlotte Elizabeth O'Kelley, June 29, 1963; children—Kenneth, Cynthia. Instr. chemistry U.S. Naval Acad., 1965-67; asst. prof. chemistry U. Wis., Madison, 1967-73, asso. prof., 1973-77, prof., 1977—. Served with USNR, 1965-67. Mem. Am. Phys. Soc., Am. Chem. Soc., AAAS, Sigma Xi. Home: 10 Regis Circle Madison WI 53711 Office: Dept Chemistry Univ of Wis 1101 University Ave Madison WI 53706

WOODS, RONALD JOHN, shelter related products retailing exec.; b. Buffalo, Nov. 22, 1933; s. Glenn Woods and Mildred (Maleck) W.; B.A., Mich. State U., 1958; m. Joanne Rose Marble, June 20, 1959; children—Juliet K., Lisa J., Anthony J., Nicholas J., Jennifer L. Mgmt. cons. to bus. firm Lybrand Ross Bros. & Montgomery, C.P.A.'s, Detroit, 1960-66; with The Wickes Corp., 1966—, dir. planning and analysis, 1966-69, exec. v.p., gen. mgr. Colonial Products Co. subsidiary, 1970, exec. v.p., corp. planning and services, 1971, sr. v.p., head office of the pres., 1972-73, sr. v.p. mobile home and recreational vehicles group, San Diego, 1973-75, sr. v.p. corp. devel., 1975—. Treas. Saginaw Twp. Bd. Edn., 1969-70, trustee, 1970-71, pres., 1971-72. Served with AUS, 1954-56. C.P.A., Mich. Mem. Am., Mich. assns. C.P.A.'s. Republican. Office: Wickes Corp 110 West A St San Diego CA 92101

WOODS, ROSE MARY, consultant; b. Sebring, Ohio, Dec. 26, 1917; d. Thomas M. and Mary (Maley) Woods; ed. high sch.; L.D.H., Pfeiffer Coll., 1971. With Royal China, Inc., Sebring, 1935-43, Office Censorship, 1943-45, Internat. Tng. Adminstrn., 1945-47, Herter Com. Fgn. Aid, 1947, Fgn. Service Ednl. Found., 1947-51; sec. to senator, then v.p. Nixon, 1951-61; asst. Mr. Nixon with firm Adams, Duque & Hazeltine, Los Angeles, 1961-63, firm Nixon, Mudge, Rose, Guthrie, Alexander & Mitchell, N.Y.C., 1963-68; exec. asst. to former Pres. Nixon, 1969-75; now consultant. Named 1 of 10 Women of Year Los Angeles Times, 1961, 1 of 75 Most Important Women in Am., Ladies Home Jour., 1971. Home and Office: 2500 Virginia Ave NW Washington DC 20037

WOODS, SAMUEL HUBERT, JR., educator; b. Ardmore, Okla., Mar. 10, 1926; s. Samuel Hubert and May (Wilson) W.; student U. Okla., 1943-45; A.B. cum laude, Harvard, 1947, M.A., 1949; Ph.D., Yale, 1956; m. Clara Belle Brown, Aug. 21, 1962. Instr., English U. Colo., Boulder, 1949-51; instr. Duke U., Durham, N.C., 1954-55,

Rutgers U., New Brunswick, N. J., 1955-56; faculty Okla. State U., Stillwater, 1956—, instr., 1956-57, asst. prof., 1957-61, asso. prof., 1961-65, prof., 1965. Mem. Modern Lang. Assn., S. Central Modern Lang. Assn., Am. Soc. 18th Century Studies, South Central Soc. 18th Century Studies, Okla. Council Tchrs. English, AAUP, Sigma Alpha Epsilon. Democrat. Episcopalian. Author: (with others) Introduction to Literature, 1968; (with Mary Rohrberger) Reading and Writing about Literature, 1971. Cons. editor Cimarron Rev., 1968-74. Contbr. articles to profl. jours. Home: 1709 W 3d Ave Stillwater OK 74074

WOODS, THOMAS COCHRANE, JR., communications co. exec.; b. Lincoln, Nebr., May 4, 1920; s. Thomas Cochrane and Sarah (Ladd) W.; B.A., U. Nebr., 1943; m. Marjorie Jane Jones, June 1, 1943; children—Thomas Cochrane, Avery Ladd. Asst. advt. mgr. Addressograph-Multigraph Corp., Cleve., 1947-58; pres., chmn. exec. com. Lincoln Tel.-Tel. Co. (Nebr.), 1958—; pres. Nellewood Corp., Lincoln, 1961—, T-V Transmission, Inc., Lincoln, 1966-75; v.p. Lincoln Devel. Co., 1958—, W.K. Realty Co., Lincoln, 1958—; dir. Sahara Coal Co., Chgo., Woodmen Accident & Life Co., Lincoln; dir., mem. exec. and trust coms. 1st Nat. Bank & Trust Co., Lincoln. Pres. Woods Charitable Fund, Inc., Chgo., 1968—; mem. State Bldg. Commn., Lincoln, 1966—; mem. exec. com. Bryan Meml. Hosp., 1962-66; mem. Lincoln City Park and Recreation Adv. Bd., 1962-72, Lincoln Center Devel. Assn., 1967—; trustee Nebr. Human Resources Research Found., 1968—, U. Nebr. Found., 1961—, Joslyn Liberal Arts Soc., Omaha, 1964—, Nebr. Ind. Coll. Found., 1965-73. Served to 1st lt. AUS, 1943-46. Mem. U.S., Lincoln chambers commerce, SAR. Congregationalist. Clubs: Lincoln Univ., Lincoln Country, Nebr. (Lincoln). Home: 2540 Woodscrest Ave Lincoln NE 68502 Office: 1440 M St PO Box 81309 Lincoln NE 68501

WOODS, THOMAS G., JR., utility co. exec.; b. Mobile, Ala., July 30, 1926; s. Thomas G. and Maude Irene (Rhyther) W.; B.S. in Elec. Engring., U. Ariz., 1950; m. Sally Lota Sanders, Aug. 22, 1949; children—Robert Milton, William Delaney, Cynthia Marie, Thomas Michael. With Allison Steel Co., Phoenix, 1945-50; with Ariz. Public Service Co., Phoenix, 1950—, exec. v.p. ops., 1976—, also dir. Mem. Am. Soc. Metals, Nat. Reclamation Assn., Ariz. Wildlife Fedn., Pacific Coast Gas Assn., IEEE, Pacific Coast Elec. Assn. Republican. Roman Catholic. Office: PO Box 21666 #1910 Phoenix AZ 85036

WOODS, WILFRED RUFUS, newspaper publisher; b. Wenatchee, Wash., Sept. 30, 1919; s. Rufus and Mary Marcia (Greenslit) W.; B.A., U. Wash., 1947; postgrad. Institut Brittannique, Paris, 1948; m. Kathleen Marie Kingman, Dec. 1, 1951; children—Kara, Rufus, Gretchen. Printer apprentice Wenatchee World, 1937-38, sterotyper-pressman, 1940-41, news reporter, 1947-48, 49-50, editor, pub., 1950—; dir. 1st Mut. Savs. Bank, Wenatchee Mountain, Inc. Bd. dirs. Wenatchee Valley YMCA (Man of Year 1967-68, Golden Triangle award 1970); mem. Wash. Parks and Recreation Commn., 1967, Citizens Adv. Com. on Hwy. Safety, 1960—; mem. bd. curators Wash. Hist. Soc., 1973—; mem. vis. com. Grad. Sch. Pub. Affairs, U. Wash., 1967-76; mem. White House Conf. on Natural Beauty, 1965; mem. numerous environ. and devel. bds. State of Wash. Served with U.S. Army, 1942-45. Recipient Nat. Grange award, 1951; Good News award Pacific N.W. Ann. Conf., Methodist Ch., 1967; Merit citation Wash. Recreation and Park Soc., 1971; Spl. Service award for soil and water conservation State of Wash., 1972; other citations and service awards. Mem. Am. Forestry Assn. (dir., pres. 1976-77), Allied Daily Newspapers Wash. (pres. 1961), Okanogan Cariboo Trail Assn. (pres. 1960), Sigma Delta Chi. Author: Europe in Transition, 1949; From Germany to the Jordan, 1954; Up the Columbia, 1957; Middle East Turmoil, 1959. Home: 1107 Orchard Ave Wenatchee WA 98801 Office: 14 N Mission St Wenatchee WA 98801

WOODS, WILLIAM PEACOCK, utility exec.; b. Selma, Ala., Feb. 23, 1907; s. Marion Thomas Byers and Anabel (McIlwain) W.; B.S., Ala. Polytech. Inst., 1930; m. Caroline Oliver, June 22, 1940; children—William Peacock, Caroline Lucile (dec.), Katherine Louise. With Ala. Pub. Utility Service Corp., 1930-31, Ga. PUb. Utility Co., 1932-34, Ga. Natural Gas Corp., 1935-36; gen. supt. Fla. Pub. Utility Co., West Palm Beach, 1936-42; gas. engr. Atlanta Gas Light Co., 1942-44; gen. supt. Tex. Pub. Utility Co., Galveston, 1944-46; v.p., then pres. Conversions & Surveys, Inc., N.Y.C., 1946-60; v.p. Stone & Webster Service Corp., N.Y.C., 1954-60; chmn. bd., dir. Wash. Natural Gas Co., Seattle, 1960—. Regent, Seattle U. Mem. Am. (past chmn.), Pacific Coast (past pres.) gas assns. Clubs: Washington Athletic; Rainier; Seattle Golf; Overlake Golf. Home: 1501 86th Ave NE Bellevue WA 98004 Office: Washington Natural Gas Co 815 Mercer St Seattle WA 98111

WOODS, WILLIAM SLEDGE, educator; b. Chester, S.C., July 14, 1910; s. Harper Robert and Clara (Sledge) W.; A.B., U. S.C., 1931, M.A., 1932; postgrad. Johns Hopkins, 1934-35, Sorbonne, 1936; Ph.D., U. N.C., 1947. Instr. romance langs. U. S.C., 1935-40, asso. prof., 1947-48; instr. romance langs. U. N.C., 1946- 47; asso. prof. Tulane U., 1948-51, prof., 1951-77, prof. emeritus, 1977—; chmn. French and Italian, 1957-69. Served from pvt. to 2d lt., Signal Corps, AUS, 1942-45. Decorated Palmes Academiques (France). Mem. S. Central Modern Lang. Assn., Medieval Acad. Am., Renaissance Soc. Am., Modern Lang. Assn. Am., Phi Beta Kappa, Phi Sigma Iota, Omicron Delta Kappa. Address: 4222 Baronne St New Orleans LA 70115

WOODS, WILLIAM SPROUL, JR., oil co. exec.; b. Wildwood, N.J., July 3, 1920; s. William Sproul and Jane Alna (Rakestraw) W.; B.S., U. Pa., 1941, M.B.A., 1947; m. Johnina Clapperton, Sept. 13, 1952; children—Barbara J. Woods Gonsar, Betsy Anne, Bonnie Susan. Instr. acctg. U. Pa., Phila., 1945-47; with Sun Oil Co., 1947—, v.p. investments and financing Radnor, Pa., 1979—; dir. Claymont Investment Co., Sperry-Sun Inc., Totem Ocean Trailer Express. Trustee Am. Oncologic Hosp., 1960—, Phila. Coll. Bible, 1978—. Served to capt. AUS, 1942-45. Decorated Bronze Star medal. Mem. Am., Pa. insts. C.P.A.'s, Am. Petroleum Inst. Republican. Baptist. Clubs: Riverton Country, Union League. Home: 35 Colwick Rd Cherry Hill NJ 08002 Office: 100 Matsonford Rd Radnor PA 19087

WOODSIDE, DONALD GARTH, orthodontist; b. Pitts., Apr. 28, 1927; s. Marshall Leslie and Eleanor (Murchison) W.; B.Sc., (Kellogg scholar) Dalhousie U., 1948; D.D.S., 1952; M.Sc., U. Toronto, 1956; m. Sheila Margaret McDonald, Aug. 8, 1953; children—Donald Blake, Thane Paul, Scott McDonald. Practice dentistry for children N.S. Govt. Dept. Pub. Health, 1952-53; mem. faculty U. Toronto, 1955—, prof., head dept. orthodontics, 1962—; pvt. practice orthodontics, Toronto, 1955—; mem. faculty Tweed Found. Orthodontic Research Centre, Tucson, 1963—; cons. Burlington Orthodontic Research Centre, 1963. Diplomate Am. Bd. Orthodontics (Milo Hellman Research award 1970). Fellow Royal Coll. Dentists Can.; mem. Am. Assn. Orthodontists, Canadian Soc. Orthodontists, Edward H. Angle Soc. Orthdontia (asso.), European Orthodontic Soc., Omicron Kappa Upsilon. Home: 6 May Tree Rd Willowdale ON Canada Office: Dept Orthodontics U Toronto 124 Edwards St Toronto 101 ON Canada also 185 St Clair Ave W Toronto 7 ON Canada

WOODSIDE, GILBERT LLEWELLYN, ret. sci. adminstr.; b. Curwensville, Pa., Feb. 9, 1909; s. William W. and Minnie (Kester) W.; A.B., De Pauw U., 1932; A.M., Harvard, 1933, Ph.D., 1936; D.Sc., U. Mass., 1965; m. Mary Calhoun Livingston, Sept. 1, 1934; children—Kenneth Hall, Richard Livingston. Asst. prof. biology U. Mass., 1936-46, prof. biology, 1946-64, head dept. zoology, 1948-61, dean Grad. Sch., 1950-61, provost, 1961-63; asst. to dir. for sci. program planning and devel. Nat. Inst. Child Health and Human Devel., Bethesda, Md., 1964-65, asst. sci. dir. for extramural programs, 1965-67, asso. dir. for extramural programs, 1967-73, acting dir., 1973-75, dep. dir., 1975-79. Mem. Am. Soc. Zoologists, Soc. Cell Biology, Soc. Developmental Biology, Phi Beta Kappa, Sigma Xi, Phi Kappa Phi. Author articles on exptl. embryology and cancer research. Home: 9706 Parkwood Dr Bethesda MD 20014

WOODSIDE, HOWARD BUSH, ins. co. exec.; b. Pitts., Aug. 14, 1921; s. Hugh Nevin and Kathryn (Smith) W.; B.A., U. Wis., 1943, J.D., 1948; m. EmmaLine Gray Smith, Jan. 1, 1944; children—Lucille S., Paisley Anne. Admitted to Wis. bar, 1948; practice in Marshfield, 1948-51, 54-56; with Sentry Ins. Co., Stevens Point, Wis., 1956—, asst. gen. counsel, asst. sec., 1963-78, v.p. govtl. affairs, 1978—; dir. Sentry Life Ins. Co., Bank of Plover (Wis.). Chmn. indsl. adv. com. Wis. Ins. Laws Revision Com., 1969-78; mem. Marshfield Bd. Edn., 1950-51, Plover Zoning Bd., 1967-69. Vice chmn. Wood County Republican Com., 1955-56; chmn. 7th Rep. Dist. Wis., 1961-69; del. Nat. Rep. Conv., 1964, 68. Served to capt. AUS, 1943-46, 51-54. Decorated Commendation ribbon with medal pendant. Mem. Portage County Bar Assn. (pres. 1962), Am., Wis. bar assns., Order of Coif, Beta Theta Pi, Pi Alpha Delta, Phi Eta Sigma, Phi Kappa Phi. Presbyn. Mason, Elk, Kiwanian (charter pres. Marshfield 1955). Club: Stevens Point Curling (founder 1956). Home: 2603 Plover Rd Plover WI 54467 Office: 1800 N Point Dr Stevens Point WI 54481

WOODSIDE, ROBERT ELMER, lawyer, past judge; b. Millersburg, Pa., June 4, 1904; s. Robert E. and Ella (Neitz) W.; A.B., Dickinson Coll., 1926, LL.B., 1928, LL.D. (hon.), 1951; m. F. Fairlee Habbart, July 11, 1931; children—William Edward, Robert James, Jane Fairlee. Admitted to Pa. bar, 1928; practiced in Millersburg and Harrisburg, Pa., 1928-42; judge Ct. Common Pleas, Dauphin Co., 1942-51; became atty. gen. Commonwealth of Pa., 1951; judge Superior Court Pa., 1953-65; now partner law firm Shearer, Mette & Woodside, Harrisburg. Adj. prof. Dickinson Sch. Law, Carlisle, Pa., 1969—. Legislator Pa. State House of Reps., 1932-42, Rep. house leader, 1939, 41; mem. Joint State Govt. Commn., 1939-42; del. 16th congl. dist. Rep. Nat. Conv., 1952; chmn. Pa. Little Hoover Comm. Chmn. Pa. Council Juvenile Ct. Judges, 1947-49. Pres. bd. trustees Pa. Industrial Sch., White Hill, Pa., 1945-55; chmn. on Commn. on Constl. Revision; mem. Pa. Constl. Conv., 1967-68. Mem. Omicron Delta Kappa, Phi Kappa Sigma, Tau Kappa Alpha. Methodist. Mason (33 deg., Shriner), Red Man, Royal Arcanum. Home: 276 North St Millersburg PA 17061 Office: 1801 N Front St Harrisburg PA 17101

WOODSIDE, ROBERT HANKS, banker; b. Perryville, Md., Apr. 8, 1923; s. Amos Harris and Minnie (Milly) Woodside; B.S., Temple U., 1947; grad. Stonier Grad. Sch. Banking, 1958; m. Gloria D. Nicholson, Sept. 3, 1949; children—Robert H., J. Stephen, John T., Christine G., Anne E. Sr. v.p. Am. Nat. Bank & Trust N.J., Morristown, N.J., 1971—; past dir. Nat. Comml. Finance Conf. Inc.; past instr. Rider Coll. Evening Eve. Sch. Served as ensign USNR, World War II. Mem. Robert Morris Assos., Sigma Phi Epsilon. Episcopalian. Club: Springdale Golf (Princeton). Home: 143 Riverside Dr Princeton NJ 08540 Office: 225 South St Morristown NJ 07960

WOODSIDE, WILLIAM STEWART, mfg. co. exec.; b. Columbus, Ohio, Jan. 31, 1922; s. William Stewart and Frances (Moorman) W.; B.S. in Bus. Adminstrn., Lehigh U., 1947; M.A. in Econs., Harvard, 1950. With Am. Can Co., 1950—, asst. to v.p., gen. mgr. Dixie Cup div., Easton, Pa., 1962-64, adminstrv. asst. to chmn. bd., 1964-66, v.p., 1966-69, sr. v.p. packaging, 1969-74, exec. v.p. operations, 1974-75, pres., chief operating officer, 1975—. Office: American Ln Greenwich CT 06830

WOODSON, HERBERT HORACE, engring. educator; b. Stamford, Tex., Apr. 5, 1925; s. Herbert Viven and Floy (Tunnell) W.; S.B., S.M., M.I.T., 1952, Sc.D. in Elec. Engring., 1956; m. Blanche Elizabeth Sears, Aug. 17, 1951; children—William Sears, Robert Sears, Bradford Sears. Instr. elec. engring., also project leader magnetics div. Naval Ordnance Lab., 1952-54; mem. faculty M.I.T., 1956-71, prof. elec. engring., 1965-71, Philip Sporn prof. energy processing, 1967-71; prof. elec. engring., chmn. dept. U. Tex. at Austin, 1971—, Alcoa Found. prof., 1972-75, dir. Center for Energy Studies, 1973—; staff engr. elec. engring. div. AEP Service Corp., N.Y.C., 1965-66; cons. to industry, 1956—. Served with USNR, 1943-46. Registered profl. engr., Tex., Mass. Fellow IEEE (pres. Power Engring. Soc. 1978-80); mem. Am. Soc. Engring. Edn., Nat. Acad. Engring., AAAS. Author: (with others) Electromechanical Dynamics, parts I, II, III. Patentee in field. Home: 7603 Rustling Rd Austin TX 78731

WOODSON, RILEY D., cons. engr.; b. Penalosa, Kans., Nov. 29, 1908; s. Guy Malcolm and Grace Greenwood (Ogle) W.; B.S.M.E. cum laude, U. Kans., 1935; m. Virginia Marie Anderson, May 31, 1947; children—R. Donald, Marjorie Gayl Woodson Brownlee. With Black and Veatch Cons. Engrs., 1935—, partner, head power div., 1958-78, prin. engr., cons. power div., 1979—. Fellow ASME, Am. Inst. Cons. Engrs.; mem. IEEE, Am. Nuclear Soc., Nat. Soc. Profl. Engrs., Tau Beta Pi, Sigma Tau. Republican. Methodist. Club: Indian Hills Country. Patentee in field. Home: 2012 W 50th Terr Shawnee Mission KS 66205 Office: 11401 Lamar Overland Park KS 66211 also PO Box 8405 Kansas City MO 64114

WOODSON, WARREN BROOKS, athletic dir.; b. Ft. Worth, Feb. 24, 1903; s. William Warren and Jeanette (Brooks) W.; A.B., Baylor U., 1924; B.Phys. Edn., Springfield (Mass.) Coll., 1926; m. Muriel Young, Dec. 23, 1928; 1 dau., Dawn. Dir. phys. edn. San Marcos (Tex.) Acad., 1926-27; dir. phys. edn., head football coach Texarkana (Tex.) Coll., 1927-35, Ark. State Tchrs. Coll., 1935-41; athletic dir., head football coach Hardin-Simmons U., 1941-42, 46-52; head football coach U. Ariz., 1952-56; athletic dir., head football coach N.Mex. State U., 1958-68; athletic dir. Trinity U., 1968-74, head football coach, 1969-73. Bd. dirs. Tucson YMCA, 1953-58. Served to lt. comdr. USNR, 1942-45. Named Football Coach of Yr., Coll. Coaches Am., 1960; named to Helms Athletic Hall Fame, 1959; Warren Woodson Day in N.Mex. celebrated, 1961; recipient citation of honor for contbns. to coll. football Football Writers Assn. Am., 1965; named Christian Football Coach Century, also elected mem. Churchman's Sports Hall Fame, Tullahoma, Tenn., 1973; named to Texarkana Sports Hall of Fame, 1976, Tex. Sports Hall of Fame, 1977, Ark. Sports Hall of Fame, 1979, Hardin-Simmons U. Athletic Hall of Fame, 1979. Mem. Am. Football Coaches Assn. (football rules com. 1962-64). Rotarian. Baptist. Author football textbook, Victory Offense, 1977; originator Wing-T offensive, 1941, Space-T offensive, 1964. Home: 7076 Briarmeadow Dr Dallas TX 75230

WOODWARD, ALBERT YOUNG, ret. airline exec.; b. Miss., Aug. 27, 1909; s. Albert Y. and Ellen Bailey (Sullivan) W.; B.A., U. Miss., 1932; m. Felicia DeLao, July 31, 1943. With Signal Oil & Gas Co., Los Angeles, 1935-74, v.p., 1959-74; founder, pres. Finish Fedder Co., Alexandria, Va., 1950-75; v.p. Signal Cos., Inc., 1968-74; v.p. Burmah Oil and Gas Co., 1974; v.p. fed. affairs Flying Tiger Line, Inc., Washington, 1974-76. Staff, Petroleum Adminstrn. for War, 1942-43. Bd. dirs. Animal Welfare League, Arlington, Va. Served to capt. AUS, 1943-46. Mem. Am. Legion (post comdr. 1960-61), Sigma Alpha Epsilon. Home: 1205 N Nash St Arlington VA 22209

WOODWARD, C(OMER) VANN, historian; b. Vanndale, Ark., Nov. 13, 1908; s. Hugh Allison and Bess (Vann) W.; Ph.B., Emory U., 1930; M.A., Columbia U., 1932; Ph.D., U. N.C., 1937, LL.D., 1959; LL.D., U. Mich., 1971; D.Litt., Princeton U., 1971; L.H.D., Columbia U., 1972, Northwestern U., 1977; Litt. D., Cambridge U., 1975; m. Glenn Boyd MacLeod, Dec. 21, 1937; 1 son, Peter Vincent (dec.). Instr. English, Ga. Sch. Tech., 1930-31, 1932-33; asst. prof. history U. Fla., 1937-39; vis. asst. prof. history U. Va., 1939-40; asso. prof. history Scripps Colls., 1940-43; asso. prof. history Johns Hopkins U., 1946, prof., 1947-61; Commonwealth lectr. U. London, 1954; Harmsworth prof. Am. history Oxford U., 1954-55; Sterling prof. history Yale U., 1961-77, emeritus, 1977—, Jefferson lectr. in humanities, 1978. Served as lt. USNR, 1943-46. Recipient Nat. Inst. Arts and Letters Lit. award, 1954; Am. Council Learned Socs. prize, 1962; Guggenheim Found. fellow 1946-47, 60-61. Mem. Am. Philos. Soc., Nat. Inst. Arts and Letters, Am. (pres. 1968-69), So. (pres. 1952) hist. assns., Orgn. Am. Historians (pres. 1968-69), Am. Acad. Arts and Scis., Brit. Academy, Royal Hist. Soc., Phi Beta Kappa. Author: Tom Watson: Agrarian Rebel, 1938; The Battle for Leyte Gulf, 1947; Origins of the New South (1877-1913) (Bancroft prize), 1951; Reunion and Reaction, 1951; The Strange Career of Jim Crow, 1955; The Burden of Southern History, 1960; American Counterpoint, 1971; editor: The Comparative Approach to American History, 1968; Responses of the Presidents to Charges of Misconduct, 1974. Home: 83 Rogers Rd Hamden CT 06517 Office: Hall of Grad Studies Yale U New Haven CT 06520

WOODWARD, CHARLES NAMBY WYNN, merchandising exec.; b. Vancouver, B.C., Can., Mar. 23, 1924; s. William Culham and Ruth Wynn (Johnson) W.; student St. George's Sch., Vancouver U., B.C., 1940-42; m. Rosemary Jukes, Jan 7, 1947; children—Wynn, John, Robyn, Christpher. With mdse. dept. Woodward Stores (Capilano), Ltd., 1945- 50, store mgr., 1950-54, store mgr. Woodward Stores (Westminster), Ltd., 1954-55, gen. mgr. Woodward Stores, Ltd., 1955-57, now chmn., chief exec. officer, dir.; pres. Woodward Stores (Edmonton), Ltd., Woodward Stores (Port Alberni), Ltd., Woodward Stores (Capilano), Ltd., Woodward Stores (Victoria), Ltd., Woodward Stores (Westminster), Ltd.; pres., dir. Douglas Lake Cattle Co., Ltd., 1959—; dir. Montreal Trust Co. Bd. dirs. Salvation Army, Boy Scouts, Girl Guides, G. F. Strong Rehab. Centre. Served as lt. B.C. Regt., Canadian Army, 1942-45. Clubs: University (Vancouver); Capilano Golf and Country; Shaughnessy Golf and Country. Office: 101 W Hastings St Vancouver BC V6B 1H4 Canada*

WOODWARD, CLEVELAND LANDON, artist; b. Glendale, Ohio, June 25, 1900; s. Henry L. and Eloise (Cleveland) W.; student Cin. Art Acad., 1923-26, Charles Hawthorne's Cape Cod Sch. Art, summer 1924, Brit. Art Acad., Rome, Italy, 1928-29; m. Emily Crosby, Dec. 20, 1919; children—Cleveland Crosby, Eloise Cleveland (Mrs. Frank H. Gardner), Ralph Crosby. One-man shows at Traxel Art Gallery, Cin., 1929, Fine Arts Mus. of South at Mobile, 1968, 72, 77, Percy Whiting Mus., Fairhope, Ala., 1969, 71; exhibited in group shows at Cin. Art Mus. Spring Exhbn., 1925, 26; represented in permanent collections at Fine Arts Mus. of South at Mobile, Provincetown (Mass.) Art Assn., Arctic Mus., Brunswick, Maine, Boardman Press, Nashville, United Lutheran Pub. House, Phila., Providence Lithograph Co., Stanard Pub. Co., Cin., Christian Bd. Publ., St. Louis, others; commns. include Samuel and Eli mural 7th Presbyn. Ch., Cin., 1949, painting for Donald B. MacMillan of Arctic Mus., 1952, 16 watercolor illustrations for World Bible, World Pub. Co., 1962, Peter and John mural, West End Baptist Ch., Mobile, 1972, portrait Martin Luther, United Lutheran Pub. House, Phila., hist. paintings for Proctor & Gamble Co., Cin., numerous others; instr. oil painting Eastern Shore Acad. Fine Arts, 1972-73; lectr. Bibl. art. Cleveland Woodward Foundation established Fine Arts Mus. of the South, Mobile. Mem. Cape Cod (1st bd. dirs.), Eastern Shore (dir. 1966-69, 71-74) art assns. Illustrator: By An Unknown Disciple; The Other Wise Man; Painting Christ Head; also for other pubs., mags. and corps.; work subject article Am. Artist mag., 1973. Address: 354 Boone Ln Fairhope AL 36532. *An artist must do his best to master the technical side of his profession! He must draw well and understand the uses of his chosen medium. This supplies him with the language to speak when inspiration comes.*

WOODWARD, DANIEL HOLT, librarian; b. Ft. Worth, Oct. 17, 1931; s. Enos Paul and Jessie Grider (Butts) W.; B.A., U. Colo., 1951, M.A., 1955; Ph.D., Yale, 1958; M.S. in L.S., Cath. U. Am., 1969; m. Mary Jane Gerra, Aug. 27, 1954; children—Jeffrey, Peter. Mem. faculty Mary Washington Coll. of U. Va., 1957-72, prof. English, 1966-72, librarian, 1969-72; librarian Huntington Library, Art Gallery and Bot. Gardens, San Marino, Calif., 1972—. Served with AUS, 1952-54. Mem. Renaissance Soc. Am., Bibliog. Soc. Am., Phi Beta Kappa, Beta Phi Mu. Editor: The Poems and Translations of Robert Fletcher, 1970. Home: 1540 San Pasqual St Pasadena CA 91106 Office: 1151 Oxford Rd San Marino CA 91108

WOODWARD, DON ADCOOK, wheat farmer; b. Walla Walla, Wash., Jan. 24, 1915; s. George Benjamin and Lucy Isora (Lieuallen) W.; B.A. in Math., Whitman Coll., Walla Walla, 1937; m. Ethel Brown, Apr. 9, 1937; children—Sharon Woodward Lenhart, James Jerrod, Diane Woodward Nelson. Engaged in wheat farming in Oreg., 1938—; life mem. Oreg. Wheat Growers League, 1945—, pres., 1965-66; pres. Western Wheat Assn., USA, Inc., Portland, Oreg., 1970-71; pres. Nat. Assn. Wheat Growers, 1975-76, internat. trade affairs rep., 1977-79; mem. White House Conf. Food, Nutrition and Health, 1969-70, Presdl. Advisory Com. Trade Negotiations, 1975-76, 77-79, Can. Am. Com., 1977-79; wheat producer advisor to U.S. negotiating team Internat. Wheat Council meeting, London and Geneva, 1975-79; bd. dirs. East West Trade Council, 1977-79, Fed. Land Bank Assn., 1973-75; past dir. Farmers Mut. Warehouse, Helix, Oreg., Pendleton Grain Growers, Inc. (Oreg.); mem. Agri-Bus. Council Oreg.; mem. steering com. World Affairs Council Oreg., 1978-79. Bd. dirs. Greasewood Sch. Bd., 1950; past elder, trustee First Presbyterian Ch., Pendleton. Republican. Clubs: Pendleton Country, Elks. Home: 811 NW 4th St Pendleton OR 97801 Office: 1030 15th St NW Suite 1030 Washington DC 20005

WOODWARD, EDWARD ROY, surgeon, educator; b. Chgo., Sept. 6, 1916; s. Lee Roy and Lynne Adelia (Webster) W.; B.A., Grinnell Coll., 1938; M.D., U. Chgo., 1942; m. Dorothy Furry, Sept. 9, 1939; children—James Roy, Suzanne Louise. Intern, research fellow, asst. resident, then chief resident U. Chgo. Clinic, 1942-43, 46-51, instr. surgery, 1949-53; asst. to asso. prof. surgery U. Calif. at Los Angeles, 1953-57; prof., head dept. surgery U. Fla. Coll. Medicine, 1957—. Served from lt. (j.g.) to comdr. M.C., USNR, 1943-46, 50-51. Recipient Distinguished Service award U. Chgo., 1968. Diplomate Bd. Surgery, Fellow A.C.S.; mem. Soc. Clin. Surgery, Am., So. surg. assns., Am. Physiol. Soc., Am. Gastroent. Assn., Halsted Soc., Alpha Omega Alpha. Home: 601 NW 23d St Gainesville FL 32607

WOODWARD, HALBERT OWEN, fed. judge; b. Coleman, Tex., Apr. 8, 1918; s. Garland A. and Helen (Halbert) W.; B.B.A., U. Tex., LL.B., 1940; m. Dawn Blair, Sept. 28, 1940; children—Halbert Owen, Garland Benton. Admitted to Tex. bar, 1941; practice in Coleman, 1949-68; chmn. Tex. Hwy. Commn., 1959-68; U.S. dist. judge No. Dist. Tex., 1968—, now chief judge; dir. S.W. State Bank, Brownwood, Tex. Bd. dirs. Overall Meml. Hosp., Coleman. Served with USNR, 1942-45. Mem. Am., Tex. bar assns., Am. Judicature Soc., Beta Theta Pi. Office: 1205 Texas Ave Lubbock TX 79401*

WOODWARD, HARMAN, wholesale trade co. exec.; b. Bluefield, W.Va., Jan. 9, 1916; s. Harman and Fox H. (Brown) W.; B.S., Davidson Coll., 1937; m. June W. Rish, Nov. 25, 1939; children—Harman Rish, Thomas Hale, Crissie Jane, John William, David Wesley, Anne Houston. Statistician bituminous coal div. Dept. Interior, Washington, 1937-38; sales rep. Sovereign Pocahontas Coal Co., Detroit, 1939-40; accountant Bluefield Supply Co. (W.Va.), 1940-41, asst. comptroller, 1942-52, asst. sec., 1953-55, sec., 1956-79, dir., 1969—; ret., 1979; dir., former sec. Dixie Appliance Co., Rish Equipment Co., Crawford Equipment Co. Treas. Appalachian council Boy Scouts Am., 1951-52, v.p., 1971-72, pres., 1973-78; treas. United Fund, 1962. Served to capt., inf., AUS, 1941-45; lt. col. Res. (ret.). Decorated Bronze Star, Purple Heart; recipient Silver Beaver award Boy Scouts Am., 1962. Mem. Res. Officers Assn. (past chpt. pres.), Phi Beta Kappa, Pi Kappa Phi. Mason. Clubs: Clover (past treas., past pres.), Bluefield Country (past pres. and dir.) (Bluefield). Home: 1301 Liberty St Bluefield WV 24701 Office: 100 Bluefield Ave Bluefield WV 24701

WOODWARD, HARPER, lawyer; b. Rochester, N.Y., Nov. 26, 1909; s. Roland B. and Anne (Murray) W.; grad. St. Paul's Sch., Concord, N.H., 1927; A.B., Harvard, 1931, LL.B., 1934; m. Ruth Keller, Aug. 1, 1942 (dec. July 1966); m. 2d, Edith M. Laird, Mar. 18, 1967; children—Bruce A., Belinda B. (Mrs. Glen R. Kendall), Edwin C. Laird III, Bonnie B. (Mrs. Stephane Y. Christen). Sec. to pres. Harvard U., 1934-35; admitted to N.Y. bar, 1936; mem. firm Barry, Wainwright, Thacher & Symmers, 1935-37, Woodward & Woodward, 1937-38, Spence, Windels, Walser, Hotchkiss & Angell, 1938-42, Spence, Hotchkiss, Parker & Duryee, 1946; asso. Laurance S. Rockefeller, N.Y.C., 1946-66; asso. Rockefeller Family & Assos., 1966-76, cons., 1976—; dir., mem. exec. com., fin. and audit com. Eastern Air Lines; dir. Rockresorts, Inc., Caneel Bay Plantation, Wayfarer Ketch Corp. Trustee Meml. Sloan-Kettering Cancer Center; v.p., vice chmn. bd. mgrs. Meml. Hosp. Cancer and Allied Diseases, N.Y.C. Served with USAAF, 1942-45. Mem. Harvard Law Sch. Assn. Clubs: Wings (N.Y.C.); Am. Yacht. Home: Watrous Point Rd Essex CT 06426 Office: 30 Rockefeller Plaza New York NY 10020

WOODWARD, HERBERT NORTON, indsl. co. exec.; b. Altadena, Calif., Dec. 26, 1911; s. Arthur H. and Edith May (Norton) W.; grad. Choate Sch., Wallingford, Conn.; A.B., Cornell U., 1933; J.D., U. Chgo., 1936; D.C.L., Blackburn Coll., 1972; m. Nancy Thomas, Oct. 2, 1948; children—Cynthia (Mrs. Gerould P. King), James, Deborah (Mrs. Edwin F. Leach II). Admitted to Ill. bar, 1937; practice in Chgo., 1937-41; asst. to pres. Intermatic, Inc. (formerly Internat. Register Co.), 1941-43, dir., 1946—, vice chmn. bd., 1968-73, chmn. bd., 1973—; with D.K. Mfg. Co., Batavia, Ill., 1946-68, chmn. bd., 1958-68; chmn. bd. Dunbar Kapple, Inc., Batavia, 1968-71, Printing Plate Supply Co., Chgo., 1968-75; pres. Monroe Industries (formerly Internat. Sci. Industries), 1969-75, chmn. bd., 1975—; dir. Vaughan-Jacklin Corp., Programming Technologies, Inc., Ideal Roller & Graphics Co. Chmn. bd. trustees Blackburn Coll. Served to lt. USNR, 1943-45. Mem. Chgo. Bar Assn., Delta Phi. Clubs: University, Literary (Chgo.); Indian Hill (past pres.) (Winnetka). Author: The Human Dilemma, 1971; Capitalism Can Survive in a No-Growth Economy, 1976; also articles. Home: 4 Golf Ln Winnetka IL 60093 Office: 100 W Monroe St Chicago IL 60606. *Environmental, energy, resource and population constraints will modify all our lives in future years. The painful transition to an eventual no-growth society may be immensely disruptive. We must maintain human values through this period to insure that civilization will continue and that quality of life will benefit. I believe that, in thinking about the future, we must remember that, without a deep concern for individual freedom and rights, we will be less than human. At the same time, we must be hardheaded in discarding sentimental palliatives which only make long-term solutions more difficult. Broad education, keen intelligence and immense goodwill will all be necessary more than ever in the decades to come.*

WOODWARD, JOANNE GIGNILLIAT, actress; b. Thomasville, Ga., Feb. 27, 1930; d. Wade and Elinor (Trimmier) W.; student La. State U., 1947-49; grad. Neighborhood Playhouse Dramatic Sch., N.Y.C.; m. Paul Newman, Jan. 29, 1958; children—Elinor Terese, Melissa Stewart, Clea Olivia. First TV appearance in Penny, Robert Montgomery Presents, 1952; understudy broadway play Picnic, 1953; appeared in play Baby Want a Kiss, 1964; motion pictures include Three Faces of Eve (Acad. award Best Actress, Nat. Bd. Rev. award, Fgn. Press award), 1957, Count Three and Pray, 1955, Long Hot Summer, 1958, No Down Payment, 1957, Sound and the Fury, 1959, A Kiss Before Dying, 1956, Rally Round the Flag Boys, 1958, The Fugitive Kind, 1960, Paris Blues, 1961, The Stripper, 1963, A New Kind of Love, 1963, A Big Hand for the Little Lady, 1965, A Fine Madness, 1965, Rachel, Rachel, 1968, They Might Be Giants, 1971, The Effect of Gamma Rays on Man-in-the-Moon Marigolds (Cannes Film Festival award), 1972, Summer Wishes, Winter Dreams (N.Y. Film Critics award), 1973, The Drowning Pool, 1975, The End, 1978; TV appearances include All the Way Home; tv-film appearances in Sybil, 1976, Come Back, Little Sheba, 1977, See How She Runs, 1978. See How She Runs, 1978, Streets of L.A., 1979. Democrat. Episcopalian. Office: care Creative Artists Agy 1888 Century Park E Suite 1400 Los Angeles CA 90067*

WOODWARD, LEWIS KLAIR, JR., physician, govt. ofcl.; b. Westminster, Md., Dec. 8, 1906; s. Lewis Klair and Phoebe (Neidig) W.; A.B., Western Md. Coll., 1927; M.D., U. Md., 1935; m. Fannie Mae Mundy, Sept. 11, 1933; 1 dau., Martha Frances (Mrs. Richard G. Davis). Intern U. Hosp., Balt., 1935-36, Holston Valley Hosp., Kingsport, Tenn., 1936-37; resident surgery Balt. City Hosp., 1937-40; pvt. practice surgery, Front Royal, Va., 1940-43, Woodstock, Va., 1946-56; with State Dept. and U.S. Fgn. Service, 1956—, dep. med. dir., 1956-62, med. dir., 1962-67, spl. asst. to med. dir., 1967-69, cons. to med. dirs., 1969—; internat. med. dir. Project Concern, San Diego, 1972—; asso. staff surgeon Shenandoah County Meml. Hosp., Woodstock, 1946-63, Warren Meml. Hosp., Front Royal, 1946-69. Mem. bd. Shenandoah County (Va.) Sch., 1951-55, pres., 1954-55. Bd. dirs. Project Concern, 1971. Served to lt. comdr. USNR, 1942-46; comdr. Res. Fellow Am., Internat. colls. surgeons, Southeastern Surg. Congress; mem. Am. Med. Assn., med. socs. Va., D.C., Med. Assn. Valley Va. (pres. 1952), Council Fed. Med. Dirs. for Occupational Health (pres. 1966-67). Presbyn. (chmn. bd. deacons 1966-67, elder 1967—). Clubs: Rotary (pres. Woodstock 1950). Home: Box 112 Woodstock VA 22664

WOODWARD, M. IRENE, coll. pres., nun; b. Laramie, Wyo., Apr. 18, 1933; d. Richard Joseph and Mary Irene (Campbell) Woodward; B.A., U. So. Calif., 1961; M.A. with distinction, Cath. U. Am., 1963, Ph.D. with distinction, 1966; L.H.D., Dominican Sch. Philosophy and Theology, Berkeley, Calif., 1978. Joined Sisters of Holy Names, 1951; music tchr. St. Elizabeth Sch., Altadena, Calif., 1954-58, Ramona Convent High Sch., Alhambra, Calif., 1958-61; asso. prof. philosophy Holy Names Coll., Oakland, Calif., 1963-72, pres., 1972—. Bd. dirs. Oakland Symphony Assn., 1975—, Jesuit Sch. Theology at Berkeley, 1975—; mem. nat. adv. council Danforth Found. Asso. Program, 1973-76, Danforth asso., 1968—; Inst. Ednl. Mgmt. Harvard Bus. Sch. grantee, 1973. Mem. Am. Cath. Philos. Soc., Metaphys. Soc. Am., Assn. Ind. Calif. Colls. and Univs. (trustee, exec. com. 1978—), Oakland Mus. Assn., Assn. Cath. Colls. and Univs. (dir.), Oakland C. of C. Editor: The Catholic Church: The U.S. Experience, 1978. Address: Holy Names Coll Oakland CA 94619

WOODWARD, MADISON TRUMAN, JR., lawyer; b. New Orleans, Feb. 15, 1908; s. Madison Truman and Maude (Weill) W.; LL.B., Tulane U., 1927; postgrad., U. Mich., 1927-28; m. Elvina Bernard, June 30, 1937 (dec. Sept. 26, 1964); children—Anne Carol Woodward Baker, Elizabeth H. Woodward Ryan, Lucie B. Woodward Cavaroc, Margaret E., Madison Truman III; m. 2d, Ethel Dameron, June 24, 1977. Admitted to La. bar, 1929, since practiced in New Orleans; asso. firm Milling, Benson, Woodward, Hillyer, Pierson & Miller and predecessors, 1929-36, mem. firm, 1937—. Trustee Trinity Episcopal Sch., New Orleans, 1965-71. Fellow Am. Bar Found., Am. Coll. Trial Lawyers, Am. Coll. Probate Counsel; mem. Am. (ho. of dels. 1979—), La. (pres. 1973-74), New Orleans (exec. com. 1964-67) bar assns., Am., La. (council 1957—, v.p. 1969-80, pres. 1980—) law insts., Nat. Conf. Bar Presidents (exec. council 1973-75), 5th Circuit Jud. Conf. (del. 1966—), Jud. Council Supreme Ct. La., Am. Judicature Soc. (dir. 1973-76), Notaries Assn. New Orleans (pres. 1961-63), Valencia Inc. (gov. 1960—, pres. 1963-64), New Orleans C. of C., Garden Dist. Assn. (pres. 1964-65), Soc. Colonial Wars in La. (council 1973—, lt. gov. 1979—), Pi Kappa Phi. Clubs: Pickwick, New Orleans Country, Plimsoll, Stratford, Petroleum, International House (New Orleans); City (Baton Rouge). Author: Louisiana Notarial Manual, 1952, 2d edit., 1962, Supplement, 1973; contbr. articles to legal jours. Home: 1234 6th St New Orleans LA 70115 Office: Whitney Bldg New Orleans LA 70130

WOODWARD, RALPH LEE, JR., historian, educator; b. New London, Conn., Dec. 2, 1934; s. Ralph Lee and Beaulah Mae (Suter) W.; A.B. cum laude, Central Coll., Mo., 1955; M.A., Tulane U., 1959, Ph.D. (Henry L. and Grace Doherty Found. fellow), 1962; m. Sue Dawn McGrady, Dec. 30, 1958; children—Mark Lee, Laura Lynn, Matthew McGrady. Asst. prof. history Wichita (Kans.) U., 1961-62, U. S.W. La., Lafayette, 1962-63; asst. prof. history U. N.C., Chapel Hill, 1963-70, asso. prof., 1967-70; prof. history Tulane U., New Orleans, 1970—, head dept. history, 1973-75, dir. Tulane Summer in C. Am., 1975-78, prof. in charge Tulane Jr. Year Abroad, Paris, 1975-76; Fulbright lectr. Universidad de Chile and Universidad Catolica de Valparaiso, Chile, 1965-66, Universidad del Salvador and Universidad Nacional, Buenos Aires, Argentina, 1968. Regional liaison officer Emergency Com. to Aid Latin Am. Scholars, 1974. Served to capt. USMC, 1955-58. Mem. Am. Hist. Assn. (mem. cons. Latin Am. history, mem. gen. council 1974-76), Southeastern Conf. Latin Am. Studies (program chmn. 1975, pres. 1975-76), Latin Am. Studies Assn., Com. on Andean Studies (chmn. 1972-73). Author: Class Privilege and Economic Development, 1966; Robinson Crusoe's Island, 1969; Positivism in Latin America, 1850-1900, 1971; Central America: A Nation Divided, 1976; contbr. articles to profl. jours. Office: Dept History Tulane U New Orleans LA 70118

WOODWARD, RICHARD JOSEPH, JR., geotechnical engr.; b. Pueblo, Colo., Dec. 16, 1907; s. Richard Joseph and Anna Catherine (Earley) W.; B.S., Colo. Coll., 1930; M.S., U. Calif., Berkeley, 1947; m. Mary Irene Campbell, Aug. 29, 1932 (dec.); children—Rita Ann, Sue Marie, Richard Joseph, Patricia Irene. Naval architect U.S. Navy, 1941-45; lectr. civil engring. U. Calif., Berkeley, 1946-50; partner Woodward-Clyde Cons.'s and predecessor firms, San Francisco, 1950-73, chmn. bd., 1954-73, chmn. emeritus, 1973—; founding pres. Design Profl.'s Ins. Co., until 1972. Mem. Mayor's Com. for Equal Opportunity, Oakland, Calif., 1958-64; bd. regents Holy Names Coll., Oakland, 1964-72. Decorated knight magistral grace Sovereign Mil. Order Malta, Western Assn. Fellow ASCE (life mem., chmn. exec. com. soil mechanics and founds. div. 1966-70, Middlebrooks award 1964), Am. Cons. Engrs. Council (Past Pres.'s award for outstanding contbns. 1972); mem. Internat. Fedn. Cons. Engrs. (chmn. standing com. profl. liability 1971-76), Structural Engrs. Assn. No. Calif. (dir. 1958-60), Sigma Xi, Chi Epsilon, Delta Epsilon. Democrat. Roman Catholic. Clubs: Serra (Berkeley); Athens (Oakland); Commonwealth (San Francisco). Co-author: Earth and Earth-Rock Dams, 1963; Drilled Pier Foundations, 1972. Contbr. tech. articles to profl. jours. Home and office: 689 Terra California Dr #2 Walnut Creek CA 94595

WOODWARD, RICHARD LEWIS, cons. engr.; b. Kansas City, Mo., Dec. 11, 1913; s. John Bennett and Grace (Baker) W.; B.S. in Civil Engring., Washington U., 1935; M.S. in San Engring., Harvard U., 1949; Ph.D., Ohio State U., 1952; m. Hele Beal, June 17, 1939; children—Brenda, Melinda, Richard, Amy. Engr., Horner and ShiFrin, St. Louis, 1935-36; san. engr. USPHS, Washington, Atlanta, Cin., 1937-63; sr. research asso. Harvard U., Boston, 1963-66; process cons., v.p. Camp Dresser & McKee, Inc., Boston, 1966—; lectr. Harvard U., 1965-67; cons. in field. Served to capt. USPHS. Recipient Meritorious Service medal USPHS, 1963; T.R. Camp award Water Pollution Control Assn., 1975; Research award Am. Water Works Assn., 1977. Mem. Nat. Acad. Engring., ASCE, Brit. Assn. Water Engring. and Scientists, Internat. Assn. Water Pollution, Water Pollution Control Fedn., Am. Water Works Assn., Am. Geophysical Union, Am. Acad. Environ. Engrs. Contbr. articles to profl. jours. Home: 18 BelAir Rd Hingham MA 02043 Office: 1 Center Plaza Boston MA 02108

WOODWARD, ROBERT FORBES, ret. govt. ofcl., cons.; b. Mpls., Oct. 1, 1908; s. Charles Emerson and Ella (Robertson) W.; A.B., U. of Minn., 1930; student George Washington U., 1941; LL.D., U. of Pacific, 1962; m. Virginia Parker Cooke, Feb. 20, 1943; children—Robert Forbes, Mary Cooke. Joined U.S. Fgn. Service, 1931; vice consul at Winnipeg, Man., Can., 1932-33; student Fgn. Service Tng. Sch., Dept. of State, Washington, 1933; vice consul, Buenos Aires, 1933-36; temp. vice council Asuncion, Paraguay, 1935; 3d sec. legation and vice consul, Bogota, Colombia, 1936-37; vice consul, Rio de Janeiro, Brazil, 1937-38; assigned div. Latin Am. Affairs, Dept. State, Washington, 1938-42, 44; 2d sec. of embassy and consul, La Paz, Bolivia, 1942-44; dep. chief mission, La Paz, Bolivia, 1942-44, Guatemala, 1944-46, Habana, 1946-47; dep. dir. Inter-Am. Affairs, Dept. State, Washington, 1947-49; assigned Nat. War Coll., 1949-50; deputy chief mission, Stockholm, Sweden, 1950-52; chief fgn. service personnel Dept. State, 1952-53; dep. asst. sec. state for Inter-Am. Affairs, 1953-54; ambassador to Costa Rica, 1954-58, to Uruguay, 1958-61, to Chile, 1961, to Spain, 1962-65; asst. sec. state for Inter-Am. affairs, 1961-62; adviser to spl. negotiators Canal Treaties with Panama, 1965-67; interim dir. Office of Water for Peace, 1967; ret., 1968; acting provost Elbert Covell Coll., U. of Pacific, Stockton, Calif., 1970; cons. Dept. State, 1968—, Research Analysis Corp., 1969—, Youth for Understanding, 1972—. Chmn. U.S. del. Econ. Commn. Latin Am., Santiago, Chile, 1961; vice chmn. U.S. del. Alliance for Progress Conf., Punta del Este, 1961; vice chmn. U.S. del. Fgn. Ministers meeting, Punta del Este, 1962; chmn. U.S. del. Internat. Red Cross Conf., Vienna, 1965; chmn. U.S. del. Conf. for Revision of OAS Charter, Panama, 1966; conducted study on Panama Canal for Dept. Army, Research Analysis Corp., 1971; conducted study on usefulness of UNESCO to U.S. for Dept. State, 1972; coordinator, chief U.S. del. to Working Group with Latin Am. and Caribbean Govts. on transnat. enterprises, 1974-75. Mem. Inter-Am. Commn. on Human Rights, 1972-76. Recipient Distinguished Service award U. Minn., 1963. Clubs: Metropolitan, Chevy Chase (Washington). Home: 1642 Avon Pl NW Washington DC 20007

WOODWARD, ROBERT UPSHUR, newspaperman; b. Geneva, Ill., Mar. 26, 1943; s. Alfred E. and Jane (Upshur) W.; B.A., Yale U., 1965. Reporter Montgomery County (Md.) Sentinel, 1970-71; reporter Washington Post, 1971-78, met. editor, 1979—. Served with USNR, 1965-70. Decorated Navy Commendation medal; recipient George Polk Meml. award, 1972, Drew Pearson Found. award, 1973, Heywood Broun award, 1973, Sidney Hillman award, 1973, Sigma Delta Chi award, 1973. Author: (with Carl Bernstein) All the President's Men, 1974; The Final Days, 1976; (with Scott Armstrong) The Brethren, 1979. Office: 1150 15th St NW Washington DC 20005

WOODWARD, THEODORE ENGLAR, physician; b. Westminster, Md., Mar. 22, 1914; s. Lewis Klair and Phoebe H. (Neidig) W.; B.S., Franklin and Marshall Coll., 1934, D.Sc. (hon.), 1954; M.D., U. Md., 1938; D.Sc. (hon.), Western Md. Coll., 1950; m. Celeste Constance Lauve, June 24, 1938; children—William Englar, Lewis Omer (dec.), Randolph Craig, Celeste Lauve. Intern Univ. Hosp., Balt., 1938-40; asst. resident medicine Henry Ford Hosp., Detroit, 1940-41; practice medicine, 1946-48; mem. faculty U. Md. Sch. Medicine, 1948—, prof. medicine, head dept., 1954—; physician-in-chief U. Md. Hosp., 1954—; instr. preventive medicine Johns Hopkins Sch. Medicine, 1946-48; mem. U.S. Typhus Mission, Malaya, 1948, Plague Mission, Africa, Madagascar, 1952; vis. prof., lectr.; asso. mem. commn. immunization Armed Forces Epidemiol. Bd., 1950-63, asso. mem. commn. hemorrhagic fever, 1952-55, mem. commn. Rickettsial diseases, 1954-73, dir. commn. epidemiol. survey, 1959-74; chmn. bd. sci. counselors Nat. Inst. Allergy and Infectious Diseases, 1962-63; adv. com. cholera NIH, 1960-68, mem. com. internat. centers med. research and tng., 1961-62; ad hoc com., panel weapons tech. for chem. and biol. warfare Office Sci. and Tech., 1965-67; U.S. adv. com. U.S.-Japan Coop. Med. Sci. Program, 1965—; mem. Armed Forces Epidemiological Bd., 1968, pres., 1976. Trustee Gilman Sch. Served to lt. col., M.C., AUS, 1941-46. Recipient U.S.A. Typhus Commn. medal, Pasteur medal; diplomate Am. Bd. Internal Medicine (also recert.). Fellow A.C.P. (Bruce award 1970); mem. Balt. Med. Soc., Md. Med. and Chirurgical Faculty, AMA, Am. Soc. Clin. Investigation, Am. Clin. and Climatol. Assn. (pres. 1970), Md. Arthritis and Rheumatism Assn., N.Y. Acad. Medicine, Assn. Am. Physicians, Interurban Clin. Club (pres. 1968), Infectious Diseases Soc. Am. (pres. 1977), Soc. Med. Co. Armed Forces, U. Md. Hosp. Med. Assn., Johns Hopkins Med. and Surg. Assn. Author: (with C. L. Wisseman, Jr.) Chloromycetin, 1958; also numerous articles, chpts. in books. Home: 1 Merrymount Rd Baltimore MD 21210 Office: Univ Maryland Hosp Baltimore MD 21201

WOODWARD, THOMAS MORGAN, actor; b. Ft. Worth, Sept. 16, 1925; s. Valin Ridge and Francis Louise (McKinley) W.; A.A., Arlington State Coll., 1948; B.B.A., U. Tex., 1951; m. Enid Anne Loftis, Nov. 18, 1950; 1 dau., Enid Anne. Motion picture and TV actor, 1955—; numerous TV appearances include: Wyatt Earp, Star Trek, Gunsmoke, The F.B.I., Wagon Train, Bonanza, I Love Lucy, Walt Disney Presents, All in the Family; motion pictures include: The Great Locomotive Chase, 1955, Slaughter on 10th Ave., 1957, The Gun Hawk, 1962, Cool Hand Luke, 1966, The Wild Country, 1973, Which Way Is Up, 1977, Speed Trap, 1978. Served to capt. USAAF, 1944-45, USAF, 1951-53. Named Disting. Alumnus of Arts, U. Tex., 1969. Mem. Acad. Motion Picture Arts and Scis., SAR, Pi Kappa Alpha. Office: care Charter Mgmt 9000 Sunset Blvd Los Angeles CA 90069

WOODWELL, GEORGE MASTERS, ecologist, educator; b. Cambridge, Mass., Oct. 23, 1928; s. Philip McIntire and Virginia (Sellers) W.; A.B., Dartmouth Coll., 1950; A.M., Duke U., 1956, Ph.D., 1958; D.Sc. (hon.), Williams Coll., 1977; m. Alice Katharine Rondthaler, June 23, 1955; children—Caroline Alice, Marjorie Virginia, Jane Katharine, John Christopher. Mem. faculty U. Maine, 1957-61, asso. prof. botany, 1960-61; vis. asst. ecologist, biology dept. Brookhaven Nat. Lab., Upton, N.Y., 1961-62, ecologist, 1965-67, sr. ecologist, 1967-75; dir. Ecosystems Center, 1975—; dep. and asst. dir. Marine Biol. Lab., Woods Hole, Mass., 1975-76. Lectr., Yale Sch. Forestry, 1967—. Founding trustee Environ. Def. Fund, 1967; founding trustee Natural Resources Def. Council, 1970—, vice chmn., 1974; bd. dirs. World Wildlife Fund, 1970—, Conservation Found., 1975-77. Fellow AAAS; mem. Brit. Ecol. Soc., Ecol. Soc. Am. (v.p. 1966-67, pres. 1977-78), Sigma Xi. Editor: Ecological Effects of Nuclear War, 1965; Diversity and Stability in Ecological Systems, 1969; (with E.V. Pecan) Carbon and the Biosphere, 1973. Research, pub. in structure and function of natural communities, especially ecol. effects of ionizing radiation, effects of persistent toxins, world carbon cycle. Home: 64 Church St Woods Hole MA 02543 Office: Marine Biological Lab Woods Hole MA 02543

WOODWORTH, ALFRED SKINNER, banker; b. Framingham, Mass., Aug. 10, 1907; s. Arthur V. and Margaret (Kennard) W.; A.B., Harvard, 1929, M.B.A., 1931; m. Beatrice H. Gelatt, May 17, 1947; children—Alfred Skinner, Virginia, Charles. Credit dept. 2d Nat. Bank, Boston, 1931-37, asst. v.p., 1937-45, v.p., 1945-50; sr. v.p. State Street Bank & Trust Co., 1950-61, 1st v.p., 1961-65, chmn. exec. com., 1965-72, now dir.; chmn. bd. dirs. Federal Street Capital Corp.; dir. Codex Book Co., White Consol. Industries, Inc., Albert Trostel & Sons Co. Served as lt. comdr. USN, 1941-45. Club: Country. Home: 85 Essex Rd Chestnut Hill MA 02167 Office: 225 Franklin St Boston MA 02110

WOODWORTH, JAMES RICHARD, coll. dean; b. Ohio, Nov. 18, 1918; s. George W. and Ida (Holcker) W.; A.B., Western Res. U., 1940; M.A., Harvard, 1948, Ph.D., 1956; m. Virginia B. Roper, May 13, 1942; children—Deborah Lyn, Victoria Lorraine. Mem. faculty Miami U., Oxford, Ohio, 1948—, prof. polit. sci., 1963—, chmn. dept., 1963-70, asso. registrar, 1952-56, dir. honors program, 1961-63, acting asso. dean Coll. Arts and Sci., 1971-72, asso. dean, 1972—. Mem. ednl. adv. com. Ohio Civil Rights Commn., 1969-76. Chmn. Oxford Charter Commn., 1960-61; councilman, Village of Oxford, 1961-63. Trustee McCullough-Hyde Meml. Hosp., 1967-69. Served with USAAF 1941-45. Hon. fellow U. Minn., 1970-71. Mem. Am., Midwest polit. sci. assns., Ohio Assn. Economists and Polit. Scientists. Episcopalian. Author: Revue of Parliamentary Procedure, 1963; (with E. F. Rickets) Report of Public Adminstration Service on Study of State and Local Food and Drug Programs, 1965; (with others) Camelot: An Urban Politics Simulation Handbook, 1978; also articles. Home: 116 E Central Ave Oxford OH 45056

WOODWORTH, ROBERT HUGO, educator, biologist; b. Boston, Feb. 24, 1902; s. Charles Hugo and Elizabeth (Ball) W.; B.S., Mass. Agrl. Coll., 1924; M.A., Harvard, 1927, Ph.D., 1928; m. Helen L. Cummings, June 4, 1927; children—Robert C., Ronald S., Barry B.

Instr. biology, then asst. prof. Harvard, 1928-35, curator bot. garden, 1930-35; prof. biol. scis. Bennington Coll., 1935—, also coordinator new sci. facility, 1966—, coordinator new art center, 1974—, acting pres., 1976—; vis. prof. Hiram (Ohio) Coll., 1955-56, Williams Coll., 1964, U. Fla., 1963-64, 64-68, Southwestern U. at Memphis, 1970-71. Trustee Village of North Bennington, 1936-46, police chief civil def., 1944-46. Mem. AAAS, No. New Eng. Acad. Sci., Sigma Xi. Author articles in field, also producer films. Address: Bennington Coll Bennington VT 05201

WOODY, KENNERLY, cemetery exec.; b. Moberly, Mo., Nov. 12, 1902; s. John Henry and Virginia Elizabeth (Christian) W.; A.B., Central Coll., Fayette, Mo., 1924; m. Elizabeth Romans, Oct. 17, 1928 (dec. June 1959); children—Kennerly Merritt, John Melvin; m. 2d, Dorothy Moore Burnham, Sept. 16, 1961. Tchr., Moberly High Sch., 1924-25; editor Courier, Centralia, Mo., 1925-26; pub. relations Southwestern Bell Telephone Co., St. Louis, 1926-47; asst. v.p. advt. Am. Tel. & Tel. Co., N.Y.C., 1947-50; v.p. pub. relations N.Y. Telephone Co., 1950-62, v.p., sec., 1962-65; pres., trustee Woodlawn Cemetery, N.Y.C., 1965—; dir. Guardian Life Ins. Co. Am. Mem. N.Y.C. C. of C., 23d Street Assn. (dir.). Clubs: Country of New Canaan (Conn.); Century Assn., 200 Fifth Ave., N.Y. U. Faculty (N.Y.C.). Office: Woodlawn Cemetery 20 E 23d St New York NY 10010

WOOL, IRA GOODWIN, biochemist, educator; b. Newark, Aug. 22, 1925; s. Abraham Herman and Edith (Jacobs) W.; A.B., Syracuse U., 1949; M.D., U. Chgo., 1953, Ph.D., 1954; m. Glorye Needlman, Sept. 14, 1950; children—Christopher Douglas, Jonathan Andrew. USPHS postdoctoral fellow in physiology U. Chgo., 1953-54, Commonwealth fellow dept. physiology, 1956-57, asst. prof. physiology, 1957-62, asso. prof., 1962-65, prof. depts. physiology, biochemistry, 1965-73, A.J. Carlson prof. biol. scis., dept. biochemistry, 1973—; intern Beth Israel Hosp., Boston, 1954-55, asst. resident in internal medicine, 1955-56; teaching fellow in physiology Harvard, 1955-56. Mem. molecular biology study sect. NIH, 1974. Served with AUS, 1943-46. Mem. Am. Physiol. Soc., Biochem Soc. (Eng.), AAAS (council), Am. Soc. Biol. Chemists, Phi Beta Kappa, Sigma Xi, Alpha Omega Alpha. Editor: Vitamins and Hormones: Endocrinology, 1963-68. Overseas adv. bd. Biochem. Jour., 1973—, Jour. Biol. Chemistry, 1975—, Archives Biochem. Biophys., 1976—. Contbr. articles sci. jours. Home: 5811 Dorchester Ave Chicago IL 60637

WOOLAM, GERALD LYNN, surgeon; b. Lubbock, Tex., Apr. 16, 1937; s. Rawson Harp and Christine Leta (Rampy) W.; B.A., Tex. Tech. U., 1958; M.D., Baylor U., 1962; m. Nan Kelly, Feb. 28, 1959; children—Kelly Ann, Gerald Lynn, Gregory Alan. Rotating intern Parkland Meml. Hosp., Dallas, 1962-63; resident gen. surgery Mayo Clinic and Mayo Grad. Sch. Medicine, U. Minn., Rochester, 1963-67, chief resident asso. in surgery, 1967-68; practice medicine specializing in surgery, Lubbock, 1968—; chief of surgery St. Mary of the Plains Hosp., 1970, 73; pres. med. staff Highland Hosp., 1971-72, chief of surgery, 1969—; asso. clin. prof. surgery Tex. Tech. U. Sch. Medicine, 1972-74, clin. prof., 1975—; mem. med. adv. bd. W. Tex. Home Health Agy., 1971—. Chmn. med. fund drive United Fund of Lubbock, 1970; bd. dirs. Community Concert Assn. of Lubbock, 1968-71, First United Meth. Ch., Lubbock, 1970-75, 76—; trustee W. Tex. Found., 1971-74. Served with USNR, 1954-62. Recipient Outstanding Clin. Prof. award Tex. Tech. U., 1977. Diplomate Am. Bd. Surgery. Fellow A.C.S.; mem. AAAS, Priestley Soc. (dir. 1970-73), Lubbock Surg. Soc. (pres. 1972), AMA, Lubbock-Crosby-Garza County Med. Soc. (treas., exec. com. 1971—), Osler Soc., Am. Cancer Soc. (pres. Lubbock unit 1972-73, pres. Tex. div. 1978-79), Am. Heart Assn. (pres. Lubbock County div. 1973-74), Tex. Surg. Soc., Soc. Surgery Alimentary Tract, Central Assn. Dentists and Physicians, Sigma Xi, Phi Chi, Alpha Omega Alpha, Phi Kappa Phi, Phi Eta Sigma, Alpha Epsilon Delta. Contbr. articles to profl. jours. Home: 4007 69th St Lubbock TX 79413 Office: 4809 University Ave Lubbock TX 79413

WOOLDREDGE, WILLIAM DUNBAR, rubber products co. exec.; b. Salem, Mass., Oct. 27, 1937; s. John and Louise (Sigourney) W.; student Milton Acad., 1949-55, Yale, 1955-56; B.A., Colby Coll., 1961; M.B.A., Harvard, 1964; m. Brenda Lenore Lewison, June 23, 1962; children—John, Rebecca Wistar. With Sun Oil Co., Phila., 1964-67; treas. Ins. Co. N.Am., Phila., 1967-72; treas. B.F. Goodrich Co., Akron, Ohio, 1972-76, v.p., 1975-76, v.p. fin. and planning, 1977-78, sr. v.p., 1978-79, exec. v.p., 1979—; dir. Transohio Fin. Corp., Cleve. Bd. dirs. Salvation Army, Akron Child Guidance Center. Served with AUS, 1956-58. Mem. Fin. Execs. Inst. (chpt. dir.), Alpha Delta Phi, Sigma Theta Psi. Episcopalian. Clubs: Portage Country, Hudson Country, University (Akron). Home: 7330 Valley View Dr Hudson OH 44236 Office: 500 S Main St Akron OH 44318

WOOLDRIDGE, CHARLES WILLIAM, electric utility exec.; b. Ft. Worth, Jan. 14, 1908; s. Clarence Enos and Bulah (Miller) W.; B.S. in Textile Engring., Tex. Tech. U., 1930; m. Evelyn Allred, Aug. 24, 1934; children—Charles William, Robert Allred, John Claren. With Tex. Power & Light Co., 1930-77, v.p. engring., purchasing and transp., 1964-67, exec. v.p., dir., 1967—, chmn. bd., 1973-75, cons., 1975-77; dir. Met. Savs. and Loan Assn., 1965—. Pres., chmn. bd. Cotton Bowl Athletic Assn., 1963-66, bd. dirs., 1958—; founder, charter pres. Tex. Dogwood Trails, Inc., 1938-40; co-chmn. campaign Dallas County chpt. A.R.C., 1957. Bd. dirs. Dallas Summer Musicals, 1960-75; bd. regents Tex. Tech. Coll., 1947-53, Dallas YMCA, 1947-57, Dallas County A.R.C., 1954-58, Family Service Bur., 1942-46; bd. dirs. Trinity River Authority, 1971—. Named to Tex. Tech. Athletic Hall of Honor, 1964; named Tex. Tech. U. Distinguished Engr., 1968, Distinguished Alumnus, 1973. Registered profl. engr., Tex. Mem. Nat., Tex. (Engr. of Yr. award Dallas chpt. 1973) socs. profl. engrs. Mem. Ch. of Christ (elder, Bible tchr.). Rotarian (pres. Dalls 1947-48, dist. gov. 1939-40). Clubs: Northwood, Dallas (Dallas). Home: 5712 Ridgetown Circle Dallas TX 75230 Office: 1511 Bryan St Dallas TX 75201

WOOLDRIDGE, DEAN EVERETT, scientist, exec.; b. Chickasha, Okla., May 30, 1913; s. Auttie Noonan and Irene Amanda (Kerr) W.; A.B., U. Okla., 1932, M.S., 1933; Ph.D., Calif. Inst. Tech., 1936; m. M. Helene Detweiler, Sept. 1936; children—Dean Edgar, Anna Lou, James Allan. Mem. tech. staff Bell Telephone Labs., N.Y.C., 1936-46; co-dir. research and devel. labs Hughes Aircraft Co., Culver City, Calif., 1946-51, dir., 1951-52, v.p. research and devel., 1952-53; pres., dir. Ramo-Wooldridge Corp., Los Angeles, 1953-58, Thompson Ramo Wooldridge, Inc., Los Angeles, also Cleve., 1958-62; research asso. Calif. Inst. Tech., 1962—. Inst. Tech. Recipient citation of Honor Air Force Assn., 1950, Raymond E. Hackett award, 1955, Westinghouse Sci. Writing award AAAS, 1963. Fellow Am. Acad. Arts and Sci., Am. Phys. Soc., IEEE, Am. Inst. Aeros. and Astronautics; mem. Nat. Acad. Scis., Nat. Acad. Engring.; Calif. Inst. Assos., Am. Inst. Physics, AAAS, Phi Beta Kappa, Sigma Xi, Tau Beta Pi, Phi Eta Sigma, Eta Kappa Nu. Author: The Machinery of the Brain, 1963; The Machinery of Life, 1966; Mechanical Man, 1968, Sensory Processing in the Brain, 1979; also articles. Address: 4545 Via Esperanza Santa Barbara CA 93110

WOOLF, HARRY, educator; b. N.Y.C., Aug. 12, 1923; s. Abraham and Anna (Frankman) W.; B.S., U. Chgo., 1948, M.A., 1949; Ph.D., Cornell U., 1955; D.Sc. (hon.), Whitman Coll., 1979; m. Patricia A. Kelsh; children—Susan Deborah, Alan, Aaron, Sara Anna. Instr. physics Boston U., 1953-55; instr. history Brandeis U., 1954-55; asst. prof. history U. Wash., 1955-58, asso. prof., 1958-59, prof. history of science, 1959-61; Willis K. Shepard prof. history of sci. Johns Hopkins, 1961-76, provost, 1972-76; pres., chmn. bd. Johns Hopkins Program for Internat. Edn. in Gynecology and Obstetrics, Inc., 1973-76, trustee, 1976—; dir. Inst. for Advanced Study, Princeton, N.J., 1976—. Mem. adv. council Sch. Advanced Internat. Studies, Washington, 1973-76; adv. bd. Smithsonian Research awards, 1975-79; trustee Asso. Univs., Inc., Brookhaven Nat. Labs., 1972—; mem. vis. com. student affairs Mass. Inst. Tech., 1973-77, mem. corp. vis. com. dept. linguistics and philosophy, 1977-79, mem. corp. vis. com. dept. physics, 1979—; mem. joint com. health policy Nat. Assn. State Univs. and Land Grant Colls./Am. Assn. Univs., 1976—; mem. Nat. Advisory Child Health and Human Devel. Council NIH, 1977—; mem. vis. com. Research Center for Language Scis., Ind. U., 1977—; com. visitors Vanderbilt Grad. Sch., Nashville, Tenn., 1977—; trustee Hampshire Coll., Amherst, Mass., 1977-79; bd. govs. Tel-Aviv U., 1977-79; trustee-at-large Univs. Research Assn., Inc., 1978—, chmn. bd., 1979—. Served with AUS, 1943-46. NSF sr. postdoctoral fellow, Europe, 1961-62. Fellow AAAS (v.p.); mem. History of Sci. Soc. (council), Acad. Internat. d'Histoire des Sciences, Am. Philos. Soc., Council on Fgn. Relations, Phi Beta Kappa, Sigma Xi (Bicentennial lectr. 1976), Phi Alpha Theta. Author: Transits of Venus, 1959; Quantification, 1961; Science as a Cultural Force, 1964. Contbr. articles, revs. to profl. publs. Editor: Isis Internat., rev. devoted to history of sci. and its cultural influences, 1958-64; series editor The Sources of Science, 1964—. Asso. editor Dictionary of Scientific Biography. Editorial bd. Interdisciplinary Sci. Revs., 1975—; editorial adv. bd. The Writings of Albert Einstein, 1977—. Address: Inst for Advanced Study Olden Ln Princeton NJ 08540

WOOLF, HENRY BOSLEY, ret. editor; b. Roanoke, Va., June 30, 1910; s. Ernest Lee and Anna Laura (Bond) W.; B.A. summa cum laude, Emory and Henry Coll., 1931, Litt.D., 1971; Ph.D., Johns Hopkins, 1936. Mem. faculty La. State U., 1936-55, prof. English, 1948-55; with G. & C. Merriam Co., Springfield, Mass., 1955-75, editorial dir. dictionaries, 1971-75; vis. prof. U. N.C., summer 1947, U. Va., summers 1949, 54. Served with USAAF, 1942-45. Recipient Alumni award for distinguished achievement Emory and Henry Coll., 1976. Mem. Modern Lang. Assn. Am., Linguistic Soc. Am., Mediaeval Acad. Am., Modern Humanities Research Assn., Am. Dialect Soc., Phi Beta Kappa. Club: Tudor and Stuart (Balt.). Author: The Old Germanic Principles of Name-Giving, 1939; also articles. Co-editor: Philologica, 1949; editor-in-chief Webster's Intermediate Dictionary, 1972, Webster's New Collegiate Dictionary, 1973, The Merriam-Webster Dictionary, 1974; Webster's Concise Family Dictionary, 1975. Home: 248 Union St Springfield MA 01105

WOOLF, NEVILLE JOHN, educator, astrophysicist; b. London, Eng., Sept. 15, 1932; s. Henry Robert and Lily (Diminsky) W.; B.Sc., Manchester (Eng.) U., 1956, Ph.D., 1959; m. Suzanne Hoff, Dec. 22, 1966 (dec. July 1969); 1 son, David; m. Patricia Martin, Sept. 2, 1972; 1 son, Martin. Came to U.S., 1959. Radcliffe student Radcliffe Obs., 1959; research asso. Lick Obs., 1959-61, Princeton Obs., 1962-65; asso. prof. U. Tex., 1965-67; adj. asso. prof. Columbia, N.Y.C., 1965-67; prof. astrophysics, dir. U. Minn. Obs., Mpls., 1968-74; prof. U. Ariz., Tucson, 1974—, acting dir. Multiple Mirror Telescope Obs., 1978-79. Served with Brit. Army, 1952-53. Sr. postdoctoral fellow Nat. Acad Scis., 1965-67; Sloan fellow, 1967. Fellow Royal Astron. Soc.; mem. Internat. Astron. Union, Am. Astron. Soc. Research on astrophysics. Home: 4318 E Whitman St Tucson AZ 85711

WOOLF, ROBERT GARY, lawyer; b. South Portland, Maine, Feb. 15, 1928; s. Joseph Rubin and Anna Rose (Glovsky) W.; A.B., Boston Coll., 1949; LL.B., J.D., Boston U., 1952; m. Anne Joy Passman, June 2, 1963; children—Stacey Lee, Gary Evan, Tiffany Jill. Admitted to bar; practice law specializing in representation of profl. athletes, Boston. Mem. exec. com. Boston council Boy Scouts Am.; dir. Am. Cancer Soc. Boston. Bd. dirs. Mass. Repertory Co.; mem. pres.' council Franklin Pierce Coll.; bd. dirs. St. Jude's Hosp. Found. Served with AUS, 1952-54. Recipient Citation of Merit for contribution to sports, Commonwealth of Mass., 1974; Masada award, State of Israel, 1974. Mem. Am., Mass. bar assns., Mass. Trial Lawyers' Assn. Mason (Shriner). Author: Behind Closed Doors, 1976. Home: 6 Nelson Dr Chestnut Hill MA 02167 Office: 4575 Prudential Tower Boston MA 02199. *Having negotiated over 1,000 contracts for professional athletes, I have found that it is important to establish a base of mutual trust and respect. One does not have to be disagreeable in order to disagree. If you have the courage to do the right thing, even though it may appear to be disadvantageous to you, economically or otherwise, somehow or other, it always seems to turn out well. Athletes and general managers alike still can appreciate honesty and straightforwardness, and despite today's newspaper headlines, integrity is not corny or outdated.*

WOOLF, WILLIAM BLAUVELT, editor; b. New Rochelle, N.Y., Sept. 18, 1932; s. Douglas Gordon and Katharine Hutton (Blauvelt) W.; A.A., John Muir Jr. Coll., 1951; student U. Calif. at Berkeley, 1951; B.A., Pomona Coll., 1953; M.A., Claremont (Calif.) Grad. Sch., 1955; Ph.D., U. Mich., 1960. Instr., asst. prof., asso. prof. U. Wash., Seattle, 1959-68; asso. sec., dir. adminstrn. AAUP, Washington, 1968-79; mng. editor Math. Revs., Am. Math. Soc., Ann Arbor, Mich., 1979—. Bd. dirs. Nat. Child Research Center, Washington, 1975-77. Fulbright Research fellow U. Helsinki, Finland, 1963-64. Fellow AAAS; mem. Am. Math. Soc., Math. Assn. Am., ACLU (treas. Washington 1966-68). Home: 1600 South Blvd Ann Arbor MI 48104 Office: 611 Church St Ann Arbor MI 48109

WOOLFENDEN, WILLIAM EDWARD, museum ofcl.; b. Detroit, June 27, 1918; s. Frederick and Clara Mae (Mackie) W.; M.A., Wayne-State U., 1942. Asst. curator Am. art Detroit Inst. Arts, 1945-49, dir. edn., 1949-60; asst. dir. Archives Am. Art, Detroit, 1960-62, dir., 1962-69; dir. Archives Am. Art, Smithsonian Instn., N.Y.C., 1970—; mem. spl. faculty Wayne State U., 1945-60; cons. Minn. Mus. Art; mem. vis. com. dept. am. paintings Met. Mus. Art. Mem. Am. Assn. Museums, Coll. Art Assn., Soc. Archtl. Historians. Office: Smithsonian Instn Archives Am Art 41 E 65th St New York NY 10021

WOOLFORD, ROBERT GRAHAM, educator; b. London, Ont., Can., Apr. 14, 1933; s. Robert George and Edythe May (Shouldice) W.; B.Sc., U. Western Ont., 1955, M.Sc., 1956; Ph.D., U. Ill., 1959; m. Lillian Alma Ellis, Aug. 20, 1955; children—David Grant, Kenneth Graham. With chemistry dept. U. Waterloo (Can.), 1959—, asso. dean sci., 1967-75, asso. chmn. dept. chemistry, 1977—. Fellow Chem. Inst. Can. Contbr. articles to profl. jours. Home: 276 Rosemount Dr Kitchener ON Canada Office: University of Waterloo Waterloo ON Canada

WOOLHEATER, ROBERT LEROY, electronics co. exec.; b. Sioux Falls, S.D., May 17, 1930; s. Bernard Leroy and Adeline Agnes (Lass) W.; B.S., U. Calif., Los Angeles, 1952; m. Lorna Colquhoun, Feb. 11, 1956; children—Richard, Carol, Dale, Robert. Controller, Vernitron Corp., Torrance, Calif., 1960-64; mgr. fin. FMA Inc., Los Angeles, 1964-68; treas. Anthony Industries, South Gate, Calif., 1968-69; v.p., treas., controller Craig Corp., Los Angeles, 1969—; advisor accounting curriculum Calif. Colls., 1974. Served with U.S. Army, 1952-54. Mem. Nat. Assn. Accountants, Fin. Execs. Inst., Assn. Gen. Importers, Assn. Electronic Importers, Fgn. Trade Assn. Los Angeles. Home: 3821 Heather St Seal Beach CA 90740 Office: 921 W Artesia Blvd Compton CA 90220

WOOLLEN, CHARLES RUSSELL, composer, keyboard musician, educator; b. Hartford, Conn., Jan. 7, 1923; s. Ernest and Esther Agnes (Gallivan) W.; B.A., St. Mary's U., Balt., 1944; M.A. in Theology and Romance Langs., Catholic U. Am., 1948; M.A. in Music (Univ. fellow), Harvard U., 1954, postgrad. in music, 1954-56; m. Carolyn Jane Fox, Dec. 23, 1971 (dec.); m. 2d, Margaret Joanne Crotchett, June 4, 1977; 1 dau., Christina. Mem. music faculty Cath. U. Am., 1948-62, Howard U., 1969, 74; piano soloist Nat. Ballet Co., on tour, 1963-68; staff keyboard artist Nat. Symphony Orch., Washington and on tours, 1956—; tchr. theory, composition and vocal coaching, Washington, 1963—; compositions include: Symphony No. I, 1961, Cantata, In Martyrum Memoriam for Mixed Chorus, Soloists, & Orchestra, 1969, Cantata, The Pasch for Mixed Voices, Soloists, & Orchestra, 1974, Monadnock, on sketches of Robert Evett (Nat. Symphony Bicentennial Commn.), 1976, Symphony No. II, 1979; freelance recital and chamber music accompanist. Recipient George Arthur Knight prize in chamber music Harvard U., 1954, Ernst Bloch Choral award, 1962. Mem. Am. Composers Alliance, Broadcast Music Inc. Democrat. Roman Catholic. Home and Office: 4747 Berkeley Terr NW Washington DC 20007

WOOLLETT, WILLIAM, architect; b. Albany, N.Y., Feb. 20, 1901; s. William Lee and Louise May (Briggs) W.; B.A., U. Minn., 1930; postgrad. Columbia U., 1924, Ecole d'Beaux Arts, N.Y.C., 1925; m. Sarah M. Sharp, Oct. 26, 1927; children—William, James, Joseph, Morgan; m. 2d, Ruth Robertson, Nov. 30, 1944. Apprentice, trainee James Garable Rogers and Alexander Trowbridge, architects, N.Y.C., 1924-25, William Lee Woollett, Los Angeles, 1925-32; practice architecture, Los Angeles, 1932-65; cons. architect Westmont Coll., Santa Barbara, Calif.; adv. La Purisima Mission, Calif. hist. monument; mem. Calif. Bd. Examiners Historic Preservation, 1965; founder Calif. Recreation Council, 1965-68; founder, mem. Los Angeles City Cultural Heritage Bd., 1962-72; one-man exhbns. of lithographs, 1935—, latest bring Am. Public Works Assn. conv., 1976, Kaiser Center, Oakland, Calif., 1967; executed numerous drawings and lithographs for public records. Recipient various public service awards. Fellow AIA; mem. Nat. Trust Historic Preservation, Calif. Etchers Soc., Santa Barbara Art Assn., Alpha Delta Phi. Republican. Club: Toastmasters. Author articles in field. Office: 955 La Paz Rd Santa Barbara CA 93108*

WOOLLEY, CATHERINE (JANE THAYER), author; b. Chgo., Aug. 11, 1904; d. Edward Mott and Anna L. (Thayer) Woolley; A.B., UCLA, 1927. Advt. copywriter Am. Radiator Co., N.Y.C., 1927-31; free-lance writer, 1931-33; copywriter, editor house organ Am. Radiator & Standard San. Corp., N.Y.C., 1933-40; desk editor Archtl. Record, 1940-42; prodn. editor SAE Jour., N.Y.C., 1942-43; pub. relations writer NAM, N.Y.C., 1943-47; condr. workshop in juvenile writing Truro Center for Arts, 1977, 78; instr. juvenile writing Cape Cod Writers Conf., 1965, 66. Trustee Truro Pub. Libraries, 1974—. Mem. Passaic (N.J.) Bd. Edn., 1953-56, Passaic Redevel. Agy., 1952-53; pres. Passaic LWV, 1949-52. Mem. Authors League Am., Friends of Truro Libraries, Truro Hist. Soc., Vols. for A.I.M. Amnesty Internat. U.S.A., Kenilworth Soc. Democrat. Author juvenile books (under name Catherine Woolley); I Like Trains, 1944, rev., 1965; Two Hundred Pennies, 1947; Ginnie and Geneva, 1948; David's Railroad, 1949; Schoolroom Zoo, 1950; Railroad Cowboy, 1951; Ginnie Joins In, 1951; David's Hundred Dollars, 1952; Lunch for Lennie, 1952 (pub. as L'Incontentabile Gigi in Italy); The Little Car That Wanted a Garage, 1952; The Animal Train and Other Stories, 1953; Holiday on Wheels, 1953; Ginnie and the New Girl, 1954; Ellie's Problem Dog, 1955; A Room for Cathy, 1956; Ginnie and the Mystery House, 1957; Miss Cathy Leonard, 1958; David's Campaign Buttons, 1959; Ginnie and the Mystery Doll, 1960; Cathy Leonard Calling, 1961; Look Alive, Libby!, 1962; Ginnie and Her Juniors, 1963; Cathy's Little Sister, 1964; Libby Looks for a Spy, 1965; The Shiny Red Rubber Boots, 1965; Ginnie and the Cooking Contest, 1966 (paperback 1979); Ginnie and the Wedding Bells, 1967; Chris in Trouble, 1968; Ginnie and the Mystery Cat, 1969; Libby's Uninvited Guest, 1970; Cathy and the Beautiful People, 1971; Cathy Uncovers a Secret, 1972; Ginnie and the Mystery Light, 1973; Libby Shadows a Lady, 1974; Ginnie and Geneva Cookbook, 1975; (under name Jane Thayer) The Horse with the Easter Bonnet, 1953; The Popcorn Dragon, 1953; Where's Andy?, 1954; Mrs. Perrywinkle's Pets, 1955; Sandy and the Seventeen Balloons, 1955; The Chicken in the Tunnel, 1956; The Outside Cat, 1957 (English edit. 1958); Charley and the New Car, 1957; Funny Stories To Read Aloud, 1958; Andy Wouldn't Talk, 1958; The Puppy Who Wanted a Boy, 1958; The Second-Story Giraffe, 1959; Little Monkey, 1959; Andy and His Fine Friends, 1960; The Pussy Who Went To the Moon, 1960 (English edit. 1961); A Little Dog Called Kitty, 1961 (English edit. 1962, 75); The Blueberry Pie Elf, 1961 (English edit. 1962); Andy's Square Blue Animal, 1962; Gus Was a Friendly Ghost, 1962 (English edit., 1971); A Drink for Little Red Diker, 1963; Andy and the Runaway Horse, 1963; A House for Mrs. Hopper; the Cat that Wanted to Go Home, 1963; Quiet on Account of Dinosaur, 1964 (English edit. 1965, 74); Emerald Enjoyed the Moonlight, 1964 (English edition, 1965); The Bunny in the Honeysuckle Patch, 1965 (English edit. 1966); Part-Time Dog, 1965 (English edit. 1966); The Light Hearted Wolf, 1966; What's a Ghost Going to Do?, 1966 (English edit. 1972); The Cat that Joined the Club, 1967 (English edit. 1968); Rockets Don't Go To Chicago, Andy, 1967; A Contrary Little Quail, 1968; Little Mr. Greenthumb, 1968 (English edit. 1969); Andy and Mr. Cunningham, 1969; Curious, Furious Chipmunk, 1969; I'm Not a Cat, Said Emerald, 1970 (English edit. 1971); Gus Was A Christmas Ghost, 1970 (English edit. 1973); Mr. Turtle's Magic Glasses, 1971; Timothy And Madam Mouse, 1971 (English edit. 1972); Gus And The Baby Ghost, 1972 (English edit. 1973); The Little House, 1972; Andy and the Wild Worm, 1973; Gus Was a Mexican Ghost, 1974 (English edit. 1975); I Don't Believe in Elves, 1975; The Mouse on the Fourteenth Floor, 1977; Gus Was a Gorgeous Ghost, 1978, English edit., 1979; Where Is Squirrel?, 1979; Try Your Hand, 1980; contbr. stories to juvenile anthologies, sch. readers, juvenile mags. Home: Higgins Hollow Rd Truro MA 02666

WOOLLEY, EUGENE ELLSWORTH, food co. exec.; b. Osborne, Kans., Apr. 2, 1919; s. Samuel Wesley and Frances Irene (Woodward) W.; student Washburn U., 1937-38; B.S., Kans. State U., 1941; student Harvard Grad. Sch. Bus. Adminstrn., 1944-45; m. Frances Odell Paschal, July 26, 1941; children—Steven Eugene, Linda Frances, Carol Sue. Chemist, USDA, 1939-40; with Gen. Mills, Inc., 1941-43, 47—, v.p., gen. mgt. feed div., 1960-62, v.p. employee relations, 1963-71, v.p. purchasing and transp., 1966-69, v.p. chem., furniture and restaurants, 1969-71, exec. v.p., 1971—. Vice pres., mem. bd. Mpls. Aquatennial Assn., 1964, commodore, 1971; mem. Citizens League Mpls.; active fund raising Mpls. YMCA. Del. Minn. Republican Party Conv., 1952. Mem. adv. com. Kans. State U., 1956—. Served with AUS, 1944; to lt. (j.g.) USNR, 1945-46. Mem. Am. Feed Mfg. Assn. (dir.), Assn. Operative Millers, Millers Nat.

Fedn., U.S. C. of C., Phi Kappa Phi, Alpha Zeta, Alpha Mu. Lutheran. Clubs: Minneapolis; Lafayette Country; Interlachen Country (Edina, Minn.); Wilderness Country (Naples, Fla.). Home: 3220 Bohns Point Ln Wayzata MN 55391 Office: 9200 Wayzata Blvd Minneapolis MN 55426

WOOLLEY, GEORGE WALTER, biologist; b. Osborne, Kans., Nov. 9, 1904; s. George Aitcheson and Nora Belle (Jackson) W.; B.S., Iowa State U., 1930; M.S., U. Wis., 1931, Ph.D., 1935; m. Anne Geneva Collins, Nov. 2, 1936; children—George Aitcheson, Margaret Anne, Lawrence Jackson. Fellow U. Wis., 1935-36; mem. staff Jackson Meml. Lab., Bar Harbor, Maine, 1936-49, bd. dirs., 1937-49, v.p. bd. 1943-47, asst. dir. and sci. adminstr., 1947-49, vis. research asso., 1949—; mem. chief div. steroid biology Sloan-Kettering Inst., N.Y.C., 1949-58, prof. biology, 1949-58; prof. biology Sloan-Kettering div. Cornell U. Med. Coll., 1951—, chief div. human tumor exptl. chemotherapy, 1958-61, chief div. tumor biology, 1961-66; asso. scientist Sloan-Kettering Inst. Cancer Research, 1966—; health sci. adminstr., program coordinator, head biol. scis. sect. Nat. Inst. Gen. Medical Scis., NIH, 1966—; cons. Nat. Edn. Service U.S., Washington, 1961—; spl. cons. to Nat. Cancer Inst., NIH, 1956—. Mem. Expert Panel on Carcinogenicity, unio intern. contra cancerum, 1962—; mem. panel com. on growth NRC, 1945-51; mem. several internat. med. congresses. Trustee Dalton Schs. Fellow AAAS, N.Y. Acad. Sci.; mem. Am. Mus. Natural History, Nat. Sci. Tchrs. Assn. (cons. 1961—), Am. Assn. Cancer Research (dir. 1951-54), Am. Soc. Human Genetics, Mt. Desert Island Biol. Lab., Soc. Exptl. Biology and Medicine, Am. Inst. Biol. Scis., Am. Assn. Anatomists, Am. Genetic Assn., Wis. Acad. Arts Sci. and Letters, Jackson Lab. Assn., Genetics Soc. Am., Environ. Mutagen Soc., Sigma Xi. Clubs: Bar Harbor, Bar Harbor (Maine) Yacht. Author chpts. in med. books. Mem. editorial bd. Jour. Nat. Cancer Inst., 1947-50. Home: Apt 336 Kenwood Pl 5301 Westbard Circle Bethesda MD 20016 Office: 5333 Westbard Ave Bethesda MD 20014

WOOLMAN, MYRON, psychologist; b. Phila., Jan. 18, 1917; s. Irvin and Rose (Goldberg) W.; B.S. magna cum laude, Columbia, 1950, M.A. (Pres.'s scholar), 1951, Ph.D. in Psychology, 1955; m. Eugenia Marr Johnston, Nov. 1, 1941; children—Marcia Isabel, Bruce Douglas, Diana Eugenia. Chief proficiency measurements McConnell AFB, Kans., 1952-56; sr. scientist Human Resources Office, George Washington U., 1956-61; dir., prin. investigator Inst. Ednl. Research, 1961—; cons., prin. investigator for major projects U.S. Dept. Labor, NIMH, OEO, Office Child Devel., govts. Nigeria and Ghana, 1961—; pres. Myron Woolman, Inc., 1969—; William H. Robinson lectr. Hampton (Va.) Coll., 1978; systems cons. Nat. Urban League, 1979, U.S. Dept. Agr./AID, 1979. Adviser to mayor of Detroit in riot prevention, 1967; prin. investigator, designer manpower devel. and learning systems for edn., govt. and industry in U.S. and abroad, 1967—. Bd. dirs. James Farmer Center Community Action, 1964-65; mem. Consortium Developmental Continuity Coll. Human Ecology, Cornell U. Served with USAAF, 1942-46. Mem. Am. Psychol. Assn., AAAS, Am. Assn. Mental Deficiency, AAUP, Council Exceptional Children, Kappa Delta Pi, Phi Delta Kappa. Author numerous papers in field. Office: 4828 16th St NW Washington DC 20011

WOOLSEY, CLARENCE OLIN, lawyer; b. Chillicothe, Mo., June 20, 1911; s. Olin Moore and Emma Ethel (Robertson) W.; A.B., Northwest Mo. State Coll., 1933, B.S. in Edn., 1933; LL.B., Missouri U., 1936; m. Mary Jane Smedley, May 1, 1941; children—William Tinker, Nancy Jane, Christopher Olin. Admitted to Mo. bar, 1936, since practiced in Springfield; with firm Woolsey, Fisher, Whiteaker, McDonald & Ansley, and predecessors, 194—. Mem. Mo. Gov.'s Crime Commn., Mo. Gov.'s Edn. Commn. Pres., U. Mo. Law Sch. Found. Served with U.S. Army, 1941; from ensign to lt., USNR, 1942-45. Recipient commendations Admiral Halsey, Nimitz, Denfeld; citation of merit in law U. of Missouri, 1968. Fellow Am. Bar Found.; mem. Am. Bar Assn. (ho. dels. 1959-60), Mo. Bar (bd. govs. 1953-60, pres. 1958-59, award of merit 1959), Internat. Assn. Ins. Counsel, Fedn. Ins. Counsel, Phi Delta Phi. Presbyn. Home: 2307 Fritts Ln Springfield MO 65804 Office: Bank of Springfield Office Center Suite 600 Springfield MO 65806

WOOLSEY, FREDERICK WILLIAM, journalist; b. Miles City, Mont., Oct. 7, 1919; s. Fred W. and Louise (Gaylord) W.; B.J., U. Mo., 1943; m. Mary Lou Hubbard, Apr. 27, 1957 (dec. June 1976). Radio news writer Sta. KXOK, St. Louis, 1943; telegraph desk The Times, Shreveport, La., 1946; reporter, features writer Nashville Tennessean, 1947-55, night city editor, 1955; reporter, rewrite desk Louisville Times, 1956-65, music critic, 1960—; feature writer Courier-Jour. Sunday mag., 1965—; author radio series Tall Tales of Tenn., folklore, Sta. WSM, Nashville, 1954-55. Mem. Louisville Human Rights Com., 1960; chmn. pub. relations com. City-County Human Relations Commn., 1961-62; mem. Ky. Civil Liberties Union, 1956—. Bd. dirs. Louisville Urban League, 1958-68, Widowed Persons Ser., 1978—. Served with USAF, 1943-46. Recipient certificate of merit for mag. writing Am. Bar Assn., 1974. Democrat. Episcopalian. Contbr. articles to journalism anthologies. Home: 2416 Dundee Rd Louisville KY 40205 Office: 525 W Broadway Louisville KY 40202

WOOLSEY, ROBERT JAMES, JR., govt. ofcl.; b. Tulsa, Sept. 21, 1941; s. Robert James and Clyde (Kirby) W.; B.A. with great distinction, Stanford U., 1963; M.A. (Rhodes scholar), Oxford (Eng.) U., 1965; LL.B., Yale U., 1968; m. Suzanne Haley, Aug. 15, 1965; children—Robert Nathaniel, Daniel James, Benjamin Haley. Admitted to Calif. bar, 1969, D.C. bar, 1970; atty. firm O'Melveny & Myers, Los Angeles, 1968; program analyst Office Sec. Def., Washington, 1968-70, NSC, Washington, 1970; gen. counsel Com. Armed Services, U.S. Senate, 1970-73; mem. firm Shea & Gardner, Washington, 1973-77; undersec. of navy, after 1977; advisor U.S. del. SALT, Helsinki and Vienna, 1969-70. Trustee Stanford U., 1972-74. Served with U.S. Army, 1968-70. Danforth scholar, 1963; Woodrow Wilson fellow, 1963. Mem. Council Fgn. Relations, Stanford Assos., Phi Beta Kappa. Presbyn. Club: Metropolitan (Washington). Home: 6808 Florida St Chevy Chase MD 20015 Office: Room 4E714 The Pentagon Washington DC 20350

WOOLSEY, SAMUEL MITCHELL, educator; b. Leander, Tex., Jan. 18, 1911; s. Arthur Mitchell and Anna (Kerr) W.; B.A., U. Tex., 1931, M.B.A., 1933; Ph.D., 1954; M.B.A., Harvard, 1935, m. Louise Ankersheil, June 17, 1936; children—Samuel Mitchell, Catherine Louise. Accountant, Schuhmacher Co., Austin, Tex., 1933-34, Peat, Marwick, Mitchell & Co., New Orleans, 1935-36, Shell Petroleum Co., New Orleans, 1936-37; instr. Bowling Green (Ky.) Coll. Commerce, 1937-42; asst. prof. Bowling Green State U., 1942-44; asso. prof. Butler U., 1944-46; prof. Baylor U., 1946-47, asst. prof. U. Tex., 1947-54; asso. prof. Pa. State U., 1954-57; chmn. accounting dept. U. Houston, 1960-63, prof. accounting, 1957—; owner, mgr. Personal Investment Adv. Service, Houston, 1958—. C.P.A., Tenn. Mem. Am. Inst. C.P.A.'s, Am. Accounting Assn., S.W. Social Sci. Assn., Tex. Soc. C.P.A.'s, Beta Gamma Sigma, Beta Alpha Psi, Alpha Kappa Psi. Democrat. Presbyn. Contbr. articles profl. pubs. Home: 4367 Graduate Circle Houston TX 77004

WOOLSON, JAMES EDWARD, diversified mfg. co. exec.; b. Detroit, Oct. 5, 1929; s. Lawrence Irving and Helen L. (Chappell) W.; B.A., Mich. State U., 1954; m. Beverly Helen DeJong, July 14, 1951; children—Dana S., Lawrence W., Matthew S. Controller, Gen. Time Corp., Phoenix, 1970-78, now v.p.; v.p., gen. mgr. Westclox Mil. Products, LaSalle, Ill., 1978—. Served with U.S. Army, 1951-53. Mem. Fin. Execs. Inst., Am. Ordnance Assn., Nat. Security Indsl. Assn. Home: Rural Route 1 Oglesby IL 61348

WOOLVERTON, JOHN JACOBS, JR., mfg. co. exec.; b. South Bend, Ind., Oct. 10, 1905; s. John J. and Lillian (Ware) W.; B.S. in Mech. Engring., U. Wis., 1927; m. Jean Christman, Jan. 20, 1934; children—Jean (Mrs. Robert G. Yale), Anne (Mrs. Robert E. Oswald). With South Bend Range Corp. (Ind.), 1929—, asst. sec. treas., 1940-45, v.p., 1945-53, asst. to pres., 1953-56, pres., 1956-72, chmn. bd., 1972—, also dir.; dir. St. Joseph Bank Trust Co. Active United Fund. Bd. dirs. South Bend Meml. Hosp. Mem. Psi Upsilon. Mason (32 deg., Shriner), Rotarian. Presbyn. (trustee). Clubs: South Bend Country, Indiana (South Bend); Country Fla. and Yacht (Pelray Beach). Office: 201 S Cherry St South Bend IN 46627*

WOOLVERTON, WILLIAM HENDERSON, JR., mgmt. cons.; b. Boston, Apr. 21, 1920; s. William Henderson and Frances (Curtis) W.; grad. Choate Sch., 1937; B.A., Yale, 1941; div.; children—William Henderson III, Frederick C., Benjamin N., Celia L.; m. 2d, Ethel Manville Handy, Jan. 6, 1968. Asso. with Frederick H. Cone & Co., Inc., N.Y.C., 1945—, v.p., 1950-55, pres., 1955—; v.p. Rhodia, Inc., N.Y.C., 1972-75; mgmt. cons., 1975—; partner, dir. Alicanto S.A., Buenos Aires; dir. Nat. Ry. Publs. Co. Served to capt. OSS, AUS, 1941-45. Mem. Am. Importers Assn. (dir.), Am. Asiatic Assn. (dir.). Clubs: University, India House, Church (N.Y.C.); Piping Rock (Locust Valley, L.I.). Home: 87 Cove Rd Oyster Bay NY 11771 Office: 100 William St New York NY 10038

WOOLWORTH, ALAN ROLAND, archeologist, museum curator; b. Clear Lake, S.D., Aug. 19, 1924; s. William Doring and Alice L. (Rose) W.; student S.D. State Coll., 1946-48; A.B., U. Nebr., 1950; M.A., U. Minn., 1956; m. Nancy Louise Kubanek, Sept. 2, 1960; children—Kathryn Ann, Marian Alicia. Archeologist, N.D. Hist. Soc., Bismarck, 1953-57; curator exhibits, curator research Dearborn (Mich.) Hist. Mus., 1957-60; mus. curator Minn. Hist. Soc., St. Paul, 1960-67, chief mus.-historic sites depts., 1967-68, chief archeologist, 1969—. Cons., U.S. Dept. Justice, Indian Claims, 1965-77, Nat. Park Service, 1961—, U.S. Fish and Wildlife Service, 1970—; cons., contractor archeol. and hist. research to govt. and pvt. firms; chmn. N.Am. Fur Trade Conf., St. Paul, 1965; program chmn. Soc. Hist. Archaeology Conf., 1972; chmn. 34th Plains Conf., 1976; mem. Minn. rev. com. Nat. Register Hist. Places. Served with inf. AUS, 1943-45. Decorated Purple Heart with oak leaf cluster, Bronze Star, Combat Inf. Badge. Mem. Soc. Am. Archeology, Soc. Profl. Archeologists, Plains Conf. for Anthropology, Soc. for Hist. Archeology (dir. 1973-76), Minn. Archeol. Soc. (pres. 1977, 78, editor 1976—). Presbyterian (elder). Club: Masons. Contbr. articles to profl. jours. Home: 3719 Sun Terr White Bear Lake MN 55110 Office: Minn Hist Soc Fort Snelling Br Bldg 27 Fort Snelling St Paul MN 55111

WOOSTER, WARREN S(CRIVER), educator; b. Westfield, Mass., Feb. 20, 1921; s. Harold Abbott and Violet (Scriver) W.; Sc.B., Brown U., 1943; M.S., Calif. Inst. Tech., 1947; Ph.D., UCLA, 1953; m. Clarissa Pickles, Sept. 13, 1948; children—Susan (Mrs. Tim Allen), Daniel, Dana. From research asst. to prof. Scripps Instn. Oceanography, U. Calif., 1948-73; dir. UNESCO Office Oceanography, 1961-63; dean Rosenstiel Sch. Marine Atmospheric Sci., U. Miami, 1973-76; prof. marine studies, fisheries and oceanography U. Wash., Seattle, 1976—. Chmn. ocean scis. bd. NRC. Served with USNR, 1943-46. Fellow Am. Geophys. Union, Am. Meterol Soc.; mem. Sci. Com. Oceanic Research, Sigma Xi. Contbr. to books, profl. jours. Office: U Wash Inst for Marine Studies Seattle WA 98105

WOOTEN, LOUIS ERNEST, cons. engr.; b. Edgecombe County, N.C., Jan. 22, 1894; s. Amos Monroe and Amanda Millicent (Lewis) W.; B.S. in Engring., N.C. State U., 1917, M.S., 1931; m. Edith Rembert Williamson, Aug. 24, 1918; children—Louis Ernest, Edith Wooten Padgette, Sarah Wooten Little, Robert Edward. Hwy. engr. N.C. Hwy. Commn., 1919-20; instr., then asso. prof. N.C. State U., Raleigh, 1920-35; regional engr. Farm Security Adminstrn., 1935-36; owner L.E. Wooten, cons. engr., Raleigh, 1936-48; pres. L.E. Wooten & Co., cons. engrs., Raleigh, 1949-73, chmn. bd., 1949—; dir. Cape Fear Feed Products, 1957-58; instr. Yale U., summer 1929. Served to 2d lt., C.E., U.S. Army, 1918-19. Registered profl. engr., N.C. Fellow Am. Cons. Engrs. Council (pres. N.C. chpt., nat. dir. 1967-68), ASCE; mem. N.C. Soc. Professions, SAR. Episcopalian. Club: Raleigh Kiwanis. Home: 1031 Harvey St Raleigh NC 27608 Office: 120 N Boylan Ave Raleigh NC 27602

WOOTEN, OSCAR SMITH, utility exec.; b. Camden, S.C., Aug. 26, 1923; s. Ernest L. and Carrie (Durrette) W.; B.S. in Bus. Adminstrn., U. Richmond, 1948; m. Helen Lawson, Apr. 15, 1950; children—Oscar, Charles, Catherine, Richard. Acct. firm Derrick, Stubbs & Stith, Columbia, S.C., 1948-51; audit supr. AEC, Aiken, S.C., 1951-54; with S.C. Electric & Gas Co., Columbia, 1954—, v.p., mem. exec. com., 1967-68, sr. v.p., 1968-77, exec. v.p. finance, 1977—, also dir.; dir., mem. adv. bd. Citizens & So. Nat. Bank, Columbia, 1967-72, chmn., 1972—; dir., mem. exec. com. 1st Bankshares Corp.; dir. 1st Nat. Bank S.C. Bd. dirs. United Community Services; trustee Palmer Coll. Served to 1st lt. USAAF, 1943-46. C.P.A., S.C. Mem. S.C. Assn. C.P.A.'s, Am. Inst. C.P.A.'s, Southeastern Electric Exchange (chmn. accounting div.), Edison Electric Inst., Columbia C. of C. (dir.), Kappa Alpha. Presbyterian (elder). Clubs: Palmetto, Forest Lake (Columbia), Rotary. Home: 7604 York House Rd Columbia SC 29206 Office: 328 Main St PO Box 764 Columbia SC 29218

WOOTTON, CHARLES GREENWOOD, fgn. service officer; b. Elizabethtown, Ill., Aug. 8, 1924; s. Estel Charles and Bertha (Greenwood) W.; B.A., Columbia, 1947; M.A., Stanford, 1959; student U. Ky., 1942-43, U. Conn., 1943-44, Yale, 1944-45, N.Y.U. Med. Coll., 1945-46; m. Elizabeth Grechko, Oct. 21, 1944; children—Cheryl, Laurel, Cynthia, Emily and Virginia (twins), Charles. With U.S. Fgn. Service, 1949—; vice consul, Stuttgart, Germany, 1949-51; 2d sec., Manila, Philippines, 1952-54; vice consul, then consul, Bordeaux, France, 1954-56; desk officer for Viet-Nam, Cambodia and Laos, Dept. Commerce, 1956-58; attache, 2d sec., then 1st sec. U.S. Mission to European Com., Brussels, Belgium, 1959-64; rep. U.S. State Dept. at Canadian Nat. Def. Coll., 1964-65; econ. counselor Am. embassy, Ottawa, Ont., Can., 1965-70; counselor for econ. and comml. affiars Am. embassy, Bonn, Bad Godesberg, Germany, 1970-71, minister econ. and comml. affairs, 1971-74; dep. sec. gen. OECD, Paris, France, 1974—; chmn. Standing Con. of Secs. Gen. of Coordinated Orgns., 1974—; chmn. OECD Ad Hoc Group on Steel Industry, 1977-78. Recipient Superior Honor award State Dept., 1964; German Gold Sports medal, 1973. Mem. Am. Fgn. Service Assn. Presbyn. (elder). Rotarian (mem. crippled children's com. Ottawa). Office: OECD Chateau de la Muette 2 rue André-Pascal 75775 Paris 16 CEDEX France

WOOTTON, JOHN FRANCIS, educator; b. Penn Yan, N.Y., May 31, 1929; s. John Edenden and Margaret Eliza (Smith) W.; B.S., Cornell U., 1951, M.S., 1953, Ph.D., 1960; m. Joyce Albertine MacMullen, Aug. 29, 1959; children—John Timothy, David MacMullen, Barbara Helen, Bruce Christopher. Postdoctoral fellow Nat. Found., U. London (Eng.), 1960-62; asst. prof. Cornell U. N.Y. State Vet. Coll., 1962-64, asso. prof., 1964-70, prof. biochemistry, 1970—; hon. research asst. U. London, 1962; vis. scientist Lab. Molecular Biology, Med. Research Council, Postgrad. Med. Sch., Cambridge (Eng.) U., 1969-70; vis. scientist Stanford U. Med. Sch., 1977-78. Served to lt. U.S. Army, 1954-56. Mem. Am. Chem. Soc., Am. Soc. Biol. Chemists, Sigma Xi, Phi Kappa Phi, Phi Zeta, Gamma Alpha, Omega Tau Sigma. Episcopalian. Contbr. articles enzyme and protein chemistry to tech. jours. Home: 83 Garrett Rd Ithaca NY 14850

WOOTTON, PETER, physicist; b. Peterborough, Northampton, Eng., Apr. 30, 1924; s. Sidney William and Daisy Bella (Broomhead) W.; came to U.S., 1951; B.Sc. with honors, Birmingham (Eng.) U., 1944; m. Jean Margaret Galbraith Bell, Aug. 2, 1947; children—Hamish Tarlton, Francesca St. Clair, Katrina McAllister. Radiation physicist Royal Infirmary, Glasgow, Scotland, 1948-51; research physicist Reckitt and Colman, 1947-48; instr. M.D. Anderson Hosp., U. Tex., Houston, 1951-53; radiation physicist Tumor Inst. Swedish Hosp., Seattle, 1953-64; asst. prof. U. Wash., Seattle, 1964-67, head div. med. radiation physics, 1964—, asso. prof., 1967-72, prof., 1972—; chmn. bd. N.W. Med. Physics Center; cons. in field. Served with Brit. Navy, 1943-47. Fellow Am. Coll. Radiology, Inst. Physics (London); mem. Am. Assn. Physicists in Medicine (pres. N.W. chpt. 1977, nat. pres. 1978, exec. com. 1976-79), Am. Soc. Therapeutic Radiologists, Soc. Nuclear Medicine. Contbr. articles to profl. jours. Office: Univ Hosp RC-08 Seattle WA 98195

WOOZLEY, ANTHONY DOUGLAS, educator; b. Beaconsfield, Eng., Aug. 14, 1912; s. David A. and Kathleen (Moore) W.; B.A., Oxford (Eng.) U., 1935, M.A., 1938; m. Thelma S. Townshend, June 26, 1937 (div. Mar. 1978); 1 dau., Jane (Mrs. Brian Gunton). Fellow All Souls Coll., Oxford (Eng.) U., 1935-37, fellow, tutor philosophy Queen's Coll., 1937-54; prof. moral philosophy St. Andrews (Scotland) U., 1954-67; prof. philosophy U. Va., Charlottesville, 1966-77, Commonwealth prof. philosophy, 1974—, Univ. prof. philosophy and law, 1977—; vis. prof. U. Rochester (N.Y.) 1965, U. Ariz., 1972. Served to maj. Brit. Army, 1940-45. Mem. Am., Va. philos. assns., Mind Assn., Aristotelian Soc. Author: Thomas Reid's Essays on the Intellectual Powers of Man, 1941; Theory of Knowledge, 1949; (with R.C. Cross) Plato's Republic, 1964; John Locke's Essay Concerning Human Understanding, 1964; Law and Obedience, 1979; also articles in encys. and philos. jours. Editor: Philos. Quar., 1957-62, Oxford Univ. Paperbacks Series, 1959-68, Philosophers in Perspective, 1966—. Home: 655 Kearsage Circle Charlottesville VA 22901

WOPAT, ROBERT MACKAY, telecommunications co. exec.; b. Kansas City, Mo., July 17, 1915; s. John William and Anna Elizabeth (MacKay) W.; B.S. in Engring., U. Mich., 1936; m. Dorothy Marie Clark, Aug. 5, 1940. Operating v.p. Gen. Telephone Co. Ohio, 1952-54; pres. Gen. Telephone Co. Upstate N.Y., 1954-56; v.p. Automatic Electric Co., Chgo., 1956-60; pres. Gen. Telephone Labs., 1956-60; pres. Gen. Telephone Co. Ill., 1960-62, dir., 1960—; exec. v.p. Gen. Telephone & Electronics Co., 1962-64, v.p. planning and devel., 1964; pres. Gen. Telephone Co. of Ohio, Marion, 1965—; pres. No. Ohio Telephone Com., 1968—; dir. Nat. City Bank of Marion (Ohio), Celina Fin. Corp. Past pres. Marion County Child Services Bd.; chmn. Ohio Med. Center Found.; bd. govs., past pres. Community Hosp. Served to lt. (s.g.) USNR, 1943-45. Registered profl. engr., Ohio, Ind., Tex. Mem. IEEE, Ohio Ind. Telephone Assn. (dir., past pres.), Sigma Alpha Epsilon. Rotarian (past local pres.), Mason (Shriner). Home: 931 Yorkshire Dr Marion OH 43302 Office: 100 Executive Dr Marion OH 43302

WORCEL, ABRAHAM, biochemist; b. Buenos Aires, Argentina, Jan. 14, 1938; s. Pedro and Esther (Szafir) W.; came to U.S., 1960, naturalized, 1978; B.A., Nacional Mitre, Buenos Aires, 1954; M.D., U. Buenos Aires, 1960; m. Linda Durkin, Aug. 12, 1966; 1 dau., Sonia. Postdoctoral fellow dept. physiol. chemistry U. Wis., Madison, 1962-63, research asso. Inst. Enzyme Research, 1963-68; vis. Helen Hay Whitney fellow Institut Pasteur, Paris, 1968-71; asst. prof. biochem. scis. Princeton U., 1971-74, asso. prof., 1974-78, prof., 1978—. Recipient Career Devel. award USPHS, 1975-80. Mem. Am. Soc. Biol. Chemists. Research, publs. on structure of bacterial and eucaryotic chromosomes, 1970-78. Home: 261 Hawthorne Ave Princeton NJ 08540 Office: Princeton U Princeton NJ 08540

WORCESTER, DONALD EMMET, educator; b. Tempe, Ariz., Apr. 29, 1915; s. Thomas Emmet and Maud (Worcester) Makemson; A.B., Bard Coll., 1939; M.A., U. Calif., 1940, Ph.D., 1947; m. Barbara Livingston Peck, July 5, 1941; children—Barbara Livingston and Elizabeth Stuart (twins), Harris Eugene. Lectr. Calif. Coll. Agr., Davis, 1946, U. Calif., 1947; asst. prof. U. Fla., 1947-51, asso. prof., 1951-55, head dept., 1955-59, prof. history, 1955-63; chmn. dept. history Tex. Christian U., 1963-72, Lorin A. Boswell prof. history, 1971—; vis. prof. U. Madrid, 1956-57. Chmn. bd. Univ. Press Mgrs., 1961-63. Served from ensign to lt. comdr., USNR, 1941-45. Recipient Golden Spur award Western Writers Am., 1975. Mem. Authors League Am., Am., So., Western (v.p. 1973-74, pres. 1974-75) hist. assns., Western Writers Am. (v.p. 1972-73, pres. 1973-74), N.Mex. Hist. Soc., Westerners Internat. (dir. 1975—, pres. 1978, 79), Tex. Inst. Letters, Phi Beta Kappa, Phi Alpha Theta (pres. 1960-62). Author: The Interior Provinces of New Spain, 1786, 1951; (with Wendell G. Schaeffer) The Growth and Culture of Latin America, 1956, 2d edit., 1971; Sea Power and Chilean Independence, 1962, Spanish edit., 1971; The Three Worlds of Latin America, 1963; (with Maurice Boyd) American Civilization, 1964; (with Robert and Kent Forster) Man and Civilization, 1965; Makers of Latin America, 1966; (with Maurice Boyd) Contemporary America: Issues and Problems; Brazil: From Colony to World Power, 1973; also children's books. Editor: Forked Tongues and Broken Treaties, 1975; Bolivar, 1977; mng. editor Hispanic Am. Hist. Rev., 1960-65; editor TCU Monographs in History and Culture, 1966—. Home: Route 2 Box 61 Aledo TX 76008 Office: Texas Christian U Ft Worth TX 76129

WORDEN, ALFRED MERRILL, former astronaut; b. Jackson, Mich., Feb. 7, 1932; s. Merrill Bangs and Helen (Crowell) W.; B.S., U.S. Mil Acad., 1955; M.S. in Engring., U. Mich., 1963; m. Pamela Ellen Vander Beek, June 9, 1955 (div. Dec. 1969); children—Merrill Ellen, Alison Pamela; m. 2d, Sandra Lee Landry, Sept. 1974. Commd. 2d lt. USAF 1955, advanced through grades to lt. col., 1971; stationed at Andrews AFB, Md., 1956-61, U. Mich., 1961-63, Farnborough, Eng., with RAF, 1963-65; instr. Aerospace Research Pilots Sch., Edwards AFB, Calif., 1965-66; astronaut Manned Spacecraft Center, NASA, Houston, 1966-72, command module pilot Apollo XV, 1971, sr. aerospace engr., test pilot, dir. systems studies div. Ames Research Center, Moffett Field, Calif., 1972-75; ret., 1975; v.p. High Flight Found., Colorado Springs, Colo., 1975—; dir. energy systems mgmt. program Northwood Inst., Midland, Mich., 1975—; pres. Alfred M. Worden Inc. subs. Bowmar Instrument Corp., energy mgmt. service co., 1977—. Bd. dirs. Boys' Clubs Am., Palm Beach County, Salvation Army. Mem. Soc. Exptl. Pilots, AIAA, Am. Astron. Soc., Assn. Energy Engrs., Explorers Club, ASHRAE, Nat. Assn. Corp. Real Estate Execs., Sports Car Club Am. Episcopalian (sr. warden

1969-71). Club: Circumnavigators. Author: (poetry) Hello Earth-Greetings from Endeavour, 1974; (children's book) A Flight to the Moon, 1974. Office: 340 Royal Palm Way Palm Beach FL 33480

WORDEN, FREDERIC GARFIELD, neuroscientist; b. Syracuse, N.Y., Mar. 22, 1918; s. Vivien S. and Alice Garfield (Davis) W.; A.B., Dartmouth Coll., 1939; M.D., U. Chgo., 1942; m. Katharine Cole, Jan. 8, 1944; children—Frederic, Dwight, Philip, Barbara, Katharine. Intern, Osler Med. Clinic, Johns Hopkins Hosp., Balt., 1942-43, house officer Henry Phipps Psychiat. Clinic, 1943, house officer to chief resident, 1946-50; asst. in psychiatry, Commonwealth Found. fellow Johns Hopkins Med. Sch., 1946-48; instr. psychiatry, 1949-52; tng. Balt. Psychoanalytic Inst., 1947-53; clin. dir. Sheppard and Enoch Pratt Hosp., Towson, Md., 1950-52, supr. therapy, 1952-53; research psychiatrist, prof. psychiatry Med. Sch., U. Calif. at Los Angeles, 1953-69, head div. adult psychiatry, 1968-69; prof. psychiatry, dir. neuroscis. research program Mass. Inst. Tech., 1969—; mem. research scientist devel. rev. com. NIMH, mem. bd. sci. counselors, 1975—; mem. com. on brain scis. NRC. Bd. dirs. Founds. Fund for Research in Psychiatry; bd. overseers Dartmouth Med. Sch., 1979—. Served to maj. AUS, 1943-46. Diplomate Am. Bd. Psychiatry and Neurology, Nat. Bd. Med. Examiners. Fellow Am. Acad. Arts and Scis.; mem. Am. Psychiat. Assn. (chmn. task force on research tng. council on med. edn. and devel.), Soc. for Neurosci. (chmn. program com. 1972), Acoustical Soc. Am., AAAS, Am. Psychoanalytic Assn., Brain Research Inst., Psychiat. Research Soc., N.Y. Acad. Scis., Los Angeles Psychoanalytic Inst., Los Angeles Psychoanalytic Soc. Clubs: St. Botolph (Boston). Author: (with R. Galambos) Auditory Processing of Biologically Significant Sounds, 1972; (with F.O. Schmitt) The Neurosciences: Third Study Program, 1974; (with J.P. Swazey and G. Adelman) The Neurosciences: Paths of Discovery, 1975; also numerous research publs. in psychiatry, neurophysiology. Home: 45 Hilltop Rd Weston MA 02193 Office: 165 Allandale St Jamaica Plain Sta Boston MA 02130

WORDEN, HELEN (MRS. W. H. H. CRANMER), author; b. Denver, July 12, 1896; d. Charles George and Wilbertine (Teters) W.; student Hamilton Inst. for Girls, 1904-06; pvt. tutors, 1906-15; student U. Colo., 1915-19; spl. student under Dean J. Raymond Brackett; student art Académie Julien, Paris, 1925-26; also Andre Lhote's Atelier; m. John Erskine, July 3, 1945 (dec. June 1951); m. 2d, William Henry H. Cranmer, Jan. 1959 (dec. May 1967). Feature writer N.Y. Sunday World, 1926, soc. editor N.Y. Evening World, 1927-31; writer Morning World; mem. staff N.Y. World-Telegram, 1931-44; columnist Scripps Howard Syndicate, 1935-44; spl. assignment writer Reader's Digest and Liberty Mag., 1944-47; columnist N.Y. Herald Tribune, 1947-49; asso. editor Collier's mag., 1951-56; writer Dorothy Dix Syndicated newspaper column, 1960-64. Recipient award for best news feature N.Y. Newspaper Women's Club; Spl. medal U. Dijon. Mem. Met. Opera Guild, French Inst. (life), N.Y. Geneal. and Biog. Soc., Smithsonian Instn., Authors League Am., Dramatists Guild, Nat. Hist. Soc., N.Y. Bot. Gardens, Friends Columbia U. Libraries. Republican. Episcopalian. Author: The Real New York, 1932; Round Manhattan's Rim, 1934; Society Circus, 1937; Here is New York, 1939; The Boudoir Companion (contbr.), 1938; (with Mrs. Oliver Harriman) Etiquette, 1942; Discover New York (guide book for Am. Women's Vol. Services), 1943; Out of This World, 1953; Many Sinners and a Few Saints, 1977; High Chair at Rector's 1977. Contbr. to nat. mags.

WORDEN, PENN WILLIAM, JR., assn. exec.; b. Knoxville, Tenn., May 18, 1919; s. Penn William and LaVerne (Penland) W.; B.A., U. Tenn., 1941; m. Wilhelmina Blair Durham, Oct. 11, 1947; children—Frances Stuart, Penn William, III, Anne Blair. Communications mgr. Office of Emergency Mgmt., Central Adminstrv. Services, Atlanta, 1943-45; pub. relations dir. Atlanta C. of C., 1945-47; exec. sec. Johnson City (Tenn.) C. of C., 1947-52; projects mgr. Ga. C. of C., Atlanta, 1952-58, indsl. mgr., 1958-74, exec. v.p., 1974-78, indsl. devel. dir., 1978—. Treas. Ga. Adv. Council on Vocat. Edn., 1976-77; mem. Ga. 4-H Club Adv. Com. 1963-77; bd. dirs. Spl. Audiences, Inc., 1977—; trustee Ga. Ind. Coll. Found., 1979—. Mem. Tenn. (past pres.), Ga. (past pres.) chambers commerce execs. assns., So. Indsl. Devel. Council, Ga. Soc. Assn. Execs. Republican. Methodist. Clubs: Commerce, Druid Hills Golf. Home: 2159 Superior Pl Decatur GA 30033 Office: 1200 Commerce Bldg Atlanta GA 30303

WORDEN, RALPH EDWIN, physician, educator; b. Berwyn, Nebr., Dec. 23, 1917; s. Floyd Otis and Willie (Smith) W.; B.S., U. Nebr., 1941, M.D., 1944; M.S. (fellow), Mayo Found., 1949; m. Eileen Kealy, Dec. 23, 1943; children—Kathleen, Daniel, Lawrence, Peter, Mark, Kevin, Timothy, Brian, Karen. Instr. phys. medicine and rehab. U. Minn. Coll. Medicine, 1949-51; from asst. prof. to prof. phys. medicine and rehab. Ohio State U. Coll. Medicine, 1951-58; prof. phys. medicine and rehab., chmn. dept. UCLA Sch. Medicine, 1958-67, prof. medicine (rehab.), 1967—, prof. psychiatry, 1972—, dir. alcoholism program, 1977, 80. Served to lt. M.C., USNR, 1945-46. Mem. Am. Med. Soc. on Alcoholism, So. Calif. Bioenergetic Soc., Alpha Tau Omega, Nu Sigma Nu. Home: 341 S Bristol Ave Los Angeles CA 90049 Office: 1000 Veteran Ave Los Angeles CA 90024

WORK, HENRY HARCUS, physician, assn. exec.; b. Buffalo, Nov. 11, 1911; s. Henry Harcus and Jeannette (Harcus) W.; A.B., Hamilton Coll., Clinton, N.Y., 1933; M.D., Harvard, 1937; m. Virginia Codington, Oct. 20, 1945; children—Henry Harcus III, David Codington, William Bruce, Stuart Runyon. Intern, resident Boston Children's Hosp., 1937-40, Emma P. Bradley Home Providence, 1940, Buffalo Children's Hosp., 1940-42, N.Y. Hosp., 1945-47; psychiat. services adviser, chief U.S. Children's Bur., Washington, 1948-49; asso. prof. pediatrics U. Louisville, 1949-55; mem. faculty U. Calif. at Los Angeles, 1955-72, prof. psychiatry and pub. health, 1966-72; chief profl. services Am. Psychiat. Assn., Washington, 1972—; clin. prof. George Washington, Georgetown univs., 1973—. Served to capt. AUS, 1942-45. Mem. So. Calif. Psychiat. Assn. (pres. 1966-67), Am. Orthopsychiat. Assn. (v.p. 1968-69). Author: A Guide to Preventive Child Psychiatry, 1965; Minimal Brain Dysfunction: A Medical Challenge, 1967; Psychiatric Emergencies in Childhood, 1967; Crisis in Child Psychiatry, 1975; also articles. Home: 7001 Glenbrook Rd Bethesda MD 20014 Office: 1700 18th St NW Washington DC 20009

WORK, JAMES, coll. adminstr.; b. Phila., Mar. 4, 1893; s. Robert Dickson and Elizabeth (Berry) W.; grad. Nat. Farm Sch., 1913; student Franklin Inst., 1916-18; D.Sc. (hon.), Delaware Valley Coll. Sci. and Agr., 1963, LL.D., 1971; m. Bertie Bishop, Sept. 22, 1921; children—Elizabeth Emilie (Mrs. Donald Meyer), Mary Louise (Mrs. Peter Glick, Jr.); m. 2d, Elizabeth Young, Sept. 9, 1936; 1 dau., Elizabeth Virginia Evans; m. 3d, Jean Hafley, Oct. 19, 1967. Farmer, 1913-16; supervising draftsman Navy Dept., 1917-21; asst. chief engr., chief draftsman U.S. Naval Air Sta., Lakehurst, N.J., 1921-26; asst. to mgr., aero. engr. U.S. Naval Aircraft Factory, 1926-28; v.p., gen. mgr. Detroit Aircraft Corp. and Lockheed Aircraft Co., 1928-32; pres., chmn. bd. Brewster Aero. Corp., 1932-46; pres. Work Engring. Corp., 1932-40; pres. Delaware Valley Coll. Sci. and Agr., Doylestown, Pa., 1946-73, chancellor, 1974—. Head football coach Nat. Farm Sch., 1913-21, Naval Air Sta., Lakehurst, 1922-28. Served to lt., Aviation Corps, USNR, 1927-35. Republican. Episcopalian. Mason (32 deg.). Address: Doylestown PA 18901 Died Nov. 6, 1977.

WORK, JOHN DAVID, investment banker; b. Parkersburg, W.Va., Aug. 26, 1933; s. Howard Clifford and Nancy Francis (Keenan) W.; grad. Phillips Andover Acad., 1951; B.A., Yale, 1956; M.B.A., Harvard, 1962; m. Carole Marchand, Aug. 3, 1957; children—Christine K., Jeanne D., Suzanne L., J. David. Exec. v.p. Shearson Hayden Stone Inc., N.Y.C., 1962-77, also dir.; now chmn. bd., chief exec. officer, dir. Johnson Steel & Wire Corp., Worcester, Mass.; chmn. bd. Delta Wire Corp.; mng. dir. J.D. Work & Co.; dir. Ehrenreich Photo-Optical Industries, Famolare, Inc.; adviser March Co. Served to lt. USNR, 1957-60. Home: 41 Whittredge Rd Summit NJ 07901 Office: 53 Wiser Ave Worcester MA 01607

WORK, MARTIN HAVERTY, cons.; b. San Francisco, May 5, 1915; s. Carl Zenas and Annie Madeline (Haverty) W.; A.B. cum laude, Loyola U., Los Angeles, 1937; postgrad. U. Calif. at Los Angeles, 1939; A.M. magna cum laude, U. So. Calif., 1940; m. Maria Cespedes, Apr. 17, 1948; children—Juliana, Christopher, Kathleen. Dir. radio dept. Loyola U., Los Angeles, 1937; free lance writer NBC and CBS, 1937-41; radio cons. U.S.O. Nat. Catholic Community Service, 1941-42, program dir., 1949-50; expert cons. to sec. of war, 1942-43; prodn. supr. Young & Rubicam, Inc., advt., N.Y.C., 1946-48; advt. and sales mgr. Repcal Mfg. Co., Los Angeles, 1948-49; exec. dir. Nat. Council Catholic Men, 1950-70; mem. Pontificial Council of Laity, 1967—; dir. adminstrn. and planning Archdiocese Denver, 1970—. Expert cons. Nat. Security Resources Bd. and Civil Def. Adminstrn., 1950-51; bd. dirs. World Congress Lay Apostolate, 1951. Served to col. Armed Forces Radio Service, AUS, 1942-46. Decorated knight of St. Gregory. Mem. Phi Kappa (hon.). Roman Catholic. Club: University (Washington). Home: 22 Club Ln Littleton CO 80123 Office: 200 Josephine Denver CO 80204

WORK, RICHARD NICHOLAS, educator; b. Ithaca, N.Y., Aug. 7, 1921; s. Paul and Helen Grace (Nicholas) W.; student Oberlin Coll., 1938-39; B.A., Cornell, 1942, M.S. (John C. McMullen scholar), 1944, Ph.D., 1949; m. Catherine Verwoert, July 17, 1948; children—Barbara Jane, Douglas Richard, Sarah Grace. Physicist Nat. Bur. Standards, Washington, 1949-51; research asso. Princeton, 1951-56; asst. prof. Pa. State U., 1956-61, asso. prof., 1961-65; prof. physics Ariz. State U., Tempe, 1965—, asst. dean Coll. Liberal Arts, 1965-68, asso. dean, 1969-73, chmn. dept. physics, 1977—. Cons., White Sands Missile Range, 1953-65, Sandia Corp., Albuquerque, 1964-68, Acushnet Co., New Bedford, Mass., 1973—. Mem. State College (Pa.) Housing Code Commn., 1964-65, Bldg. Code Commn., 1964-65, Bldg. Bd. Appeals, 1964-65. NSF research grantee, 1965-74. Fellow Am. Phys. Soc., AAAS; mem. Am. Assn. Physics Tchrs., Sigma Xi. Research on polymer physics and dielectric theory and measurements; contbr. to Dielectric Properties of Polymers (F.E. Karasz), 1972; also articles to profl. jours. Home: 413 E Geneva Dr Tempe AZ 85282

WORK, WALTER PAXTON, otolaryngologist; b. Cannsburg, Pa., Sept. 4, 1909; s. James Milligan and Alice Helen (Closson) W.; A.B., U. Mich., 1931, M.D., 1935; m. Alice Elizabeth Tyler, July 29, 1939; children—Walter Paxton, James C., Mary Alice, Martha A. Intern U. Hosp., Ann Arbor, Mich., 1935-36, resident in Surgery, 1936-37, resident in otolaryngology, 1937-41; clin. prof. Stanford Med. Sch., 1941-57, U. Calif. Med. Sch., San Francisco, 1957-61; prof., chmn. dept. otorhinolaryngology U. Mich., Ann Arbor, 1961-78; sec.-treas. Am. Bd. Otolaryngology, 1971—; lectr. sect. otolaryngology dept. surgery U. Ariz., 1979—; cons. VA Hosps., 1946—. Served to maj. M.C., U.S. Army, 1942-46. Decorated Legion of Merit; diplomate Am. Bd. Otolaryngology. Mem. AMA, Am. Laryngol. Assn., Am. Otological Soc., Am. Council Otolaryngology, Am. Head and Neck Soc., Soc. Univ. Otolaryngologists, Am. Acad. Otolaryngology, Am. Assn. Facial Plastic and Reconstructive Surgery, Otosclerosis Study Group. Club: Rotary. Contbr. chpts. to books, articles to profl. jours. Office: 220 Collingwood Ann Arbor MI 48103

WORK, WILLIAM, assn. exec.; b. Ithaca, N.Y., Aug. 10, 1923; s. Paul and Helen Grace (Nicholas) W.; A.B., Cornell U., 1946. M.A., U. Wis., 1948, Ph.D., 1954; m. Jane Noel Magruder, Nov. 26, 1960; children—Paul Magregor, Jeffrey William. Instr., asso. dir theatre Purdue U., 1948-50; from instr. to prof., dir. theatre Eastern Mich. U., 1951-63; exec. sec. Speech Communication Assn., Falls Church, Va., 1963—; mem. faculty U. Wis., 1950-51, So. Ill. U., 1959; cons., reader, review panelist U.S. Office Edn., 1966-71; del. White House Conf. Children, 1970. Mem. Mich. Cultural Commn., 1959-60; mem. Hastings-on-Hudson (N.Y.) Bd. Edn., 1972-75. Recipient Alex Drier award, 1962. Mem. Alliance Assn. Advancement Edn. (pres. 1977), Council Communication Socs. (pres. 1974-77), AAAS, Am. Theatre Assn., Internat. Communication Assn., Internat. Inst. Communications, Phi Kappa Phi. Democrat. Presbyterian. Contbr. articles, revs. profl. jours. Office: 5205 Leesburg Pike Falls Church VA 20041. *If, as George Santayana wisely noted, those who cannot remember the past are condemned to repeat it, then it must be equally true that those who fail to prepare for the future are condemned to endure it.*

WORKMAN, DONALD HAMILTON, trade assn. exec.; b. Lakewood, Ohio, Feb. 3, 1916; s. James Clark and Effie (Roosa) W.; B.S., U. Pa., 1938; m. Florence May Emhardt, Aug. 24, 1940; 1 son, James Clark. Trainee Philadelphia Electric Co., 1938-40, personnel asst. personnel and pub. relations dept., 1940-42, 1945-48; promotion mgr. Iron Castings Soc., Inc. (formerly Gray & Ductile Iron Founders Soc. Inc.), Cleve., 1948-50, exec. v.p., 1950—; also mng. editor Ironcaster (formerly Gray and Ductile Iron News); lectr. Nat. Inst. Orgn. Mgmt., 1957-59. Served as lt. (s.g.), USNR, 1942-45. Mem. Am. Soc. Assn. Execs. (treas., dir., Mgmt. Achievement award 1964), Cast Metals Fedn. (exec. sec. of adminstrv. com.), Cleve. Soc. Assn. Execs. (dir., pres.), C. of C., Am. Foundrymens Soc., Sigma Chi. Episcopalian (vestryman). Clubs: U. of Pa. Varsity; Westwood Country (Rocky River, Ohio). Home: 2965 Macbeth Dr Rocky River OH 44116 Office: Cast Metals Fedn Bldg 20611 Center Ridge Rd Rocky River OH 44116

WORKMAN, JAMES CLARK, mfg. co. exec.; b. Phila., Nov. 20, 1942; s. Donald H. and Florence M. (Emhardt) W.; B.A. in Econs., Wesleyan U., Middletown, Conn., 1964; J.D., Harvard, 1967; m. Jane Greenlee Henry, June 21, 1969; children—Gillian Clark, James Henry. Admitted to Ohio, Wis. bars; with firm Baker, Hostetler & Patterson, Cleve., 1967-72; asst. gen. counsel Trane Co., La Crosse, Wis., 1972-75, gen. counsel, sec., 1975—, v.p., 1979—. Bd. adviser Viterbo Coll., La Crosse; chmn. United Way of La Crosse, 1977-78. Mem. Phi Beta Kappa. Conglist. Club: La Crosse Country. Home: 2404 Vine St La Crosse WI 54601 Office: 3600 Pammel Creek Rd La Crosse WI 54601

WORKMAN, JOHN ROWE, classical philologist; b. Lancaster, Pa., June 3, 1918; s. Charles Emery and Mary Dorothy (Rowe) W.; A.B., Princeton U., 1940, M.A., 1942, Ph.D. (Page fellow), 1944; M.A. ad eundem Brown U., 1957. Instr. classics Princeton U., 1943; master Latin, St. Mark's Sch., 1945-47; faculty Brown U., Providence, 1947—, prof. classics, 1966—, chmn. dept. classics, 1959-66, asst. dean coll., 1950-52; mem. mng. com. Am. Sch. Classics Studies, Athens; mem. adv. council Am. Acad. Romé. Fulbright fellow Edinburgh U., 1953-54; Carnegie intern and asst. prof. Columbia Coll., 1952-53. Mem. Am. Philol. Assn., Classics Assn. New Eng. Mem. Reformed Ch. Clubs: Nassau, Providence Art, Masons. Author: A Term of College Latin, 1952; New Horizons of Higher Education, 1959; editor: Arx Antiqua, 1948; N. Am. editor Latomus. Home: 79 Williams St Providence RI 02906 Office: Dept Classics Brown U Providence RI 02912

WORKMAN, WILLIAM DOUGLAS, JR., journalist; b. Greenwood, S.C., Aug. 10, 1914; s. William Douglas and Vivian (Watkins) W.; A.B., The Citadel, 1935, Litt.D., 1969; grad student Law Sch., George Washington U., 1935-36; Litt.D., Newberry Coll., 1969; m. Rhea Thomas, June 10, 1939; children—William Douglas III, Dee. Reporter, News and Courier, Charleston, S.C., 1936-39; mgr. sta. WTMA, Charleston, 1939-40; capital corr. News and Courier, 1946-61, Greenville (S.C.) News, 1956-62; columnist Hall Syndicate, N.Y.C., 1960-62; asso. editor The State, Columbia, S.C., 1963-66, editor, 1966-73, editorial analyst, 1973—. News analyst sta. WIS, Columbia, 1950-62; news analyst, panelist sta. WIS TV, 1953-62. Republican nominee U.S. Senate, 1962. Bd. dirs. James F. Byrnes Found., pres., 1973—. Served with AUS, 1940-45, col., ret. Decorated Legion of Merit. Mem. Assn. Citadel Men (pres. 1952-53), S.C. Press Assn. (pres. 1971), Univ. South Caroliniana Soc. (pres. 1974-78). Author: The Case for the South, 1960; The Bishop from Barnwell, 1963; (with others) This is the South, 1959, With all Deliberate Speed, 1957, Southern Schools, Progress and Problems, 1959. Home: 915 Belt Line Blvd Columbia SC 29205 Office: care The State Box 1333 Columbia SC 29202

WORKMAN, WILLIAM GATEWOOD, ret. educator; b. Camden, S.C., May 29, 1909; s. John James and Martha Rives (Boykin) W.; B.Ph., Emory U., 1929, M.A., 1931, B.D., 1942; Ph.D., U. Chgo., 1951; m. Mildred Matthews Turnbull, June 22, 1938; children—William Workman, Eleanor Turnbull (Mrs. Thomas W. Payne, Jr.). Instr. psychology and Bible, Emory U., 1937-39, asst. prof. psychology and Bible, 1939-43, asso. prof. psychology, 1943-51; prof. psychology Davidson (N.C.) Coll., 1951-67, Richardson prof. psychology, 1967-77, prof. emeritus, 1977—; interim dir. Behavioral Enrichment unit Broughton Hosp., Morganton, N.C., 1978—; vis. prof. psychology Trinity Coll., Hartford, Conn., summers 1960, 62; originator, dir. spl. summer program in abnormal psychology Broughton Hosp., Morganton, N.C. Served as chaplain USNR, 1944-46. Recipient Thomas Jefferson award Robert Earll McConnell Found. and Davidson Coll., 1967. Mem. Am., N.C. (sec.-treas. 1954-57, pres. 1957-58), Southeastern psychol. assns., So. Soc. Philosophy and Psychology, AAUP, AAAS, Sigma Xi, Sigma Chi, Omicron Delta Kappa, Psi Chi. Democrat. Presbyterian. Home: 209 Lorimer Rd Davidson NC 28036. *Nothing enriches life more than the knowledge that one is loved and commitment to a task that one feels is worth doing.*

WORLEY, BLAND WALLACE, banker; b. Kinston, N.C., Aug. 14, 1917; s. Bland W. and Ida Ruth (Gooding) W.; B.S., U. N.C., 1938; grad. exec. program, 1955; grad. Grad. Sch. Banking, Rutgers U., 1954; m. Ada Harvey, June 28, 1941; children—Anne, Ada, Bland W. Insp., Hooper Holmes Bur., Greensboro, N.C., 1938-39; mgr. CIT Corp., Salisbury, N.C., 1939-42; mgr. time payment dept. Wachovia Bank & Trust Co., High Point, N.C., 1946-50, v.p., also High Point office exec., 1951-56, sr. v.p. charge Greensboro operations, 1956-69, exec. v.p. charge statewide banking div., Winston-Salem, N.C., 1969-70, also dir.; vice-chmn., dir. Wachovia Corp., Winston-Salem, 1970-75; trustee Wachovia Realty Investments; chmn., chief exec. officer, dir. Am. Credit Corp.; dir. Adams-Millis Corp., Blue Bell, Inc. Vol. chmn. for N.C., U.S. Savs. Bond Program, chmn. nat. exec. com. for vol. state chairmen, 1969-77; pres. Greater Greensboro United Fund, 1975-77; treas., mem. nat. exec. bd. Boy Scouts Am. Bd. dirs. N.C. Citizens Assn.; bd. dirs., past pres. Bus. Found. of N.C.; chmn. bd. trustees Greensboro Coll.; trustee Atlantic Christian Coll., Wilson, N.C.; bd. visitors Guilford Coll., Greensboro; past chmn. adminstrv. bd. Methodist Ch., 1974-76. Named High Point Young Man of Year, 1953, Outstanding Young Businessman N.C., 1958; recipient Silver Beaver, Silver Antelope, Silver Buffalo awards Boy Scouts Am. Mem. Am., N.C. (past pres.) bankers assns., Nat. Consumer Fin. Assn. (exec. com., dir.), Greensboro C. of C. (past pres., distinguished citizen award 1968), Greater Charlotte C. of C. (vice-chmn.). Clubs: Country of N.C.; Old Town Country; Quail Hollow Country; Charlotte City; Collins Creek Gun. Home: 310 Arbor Rd Winston-Salem NC 27104 Office: PO Box 2665 Charlotte NC 28234

WORLEY, EVELYN L., banker, assn. ofcl.; b. Monroe, Ga.; d. W. Pierce and Ann (Brewer) Landers; m. Brooke F. Worley, Apr. 1, 1933. With Citizens & So. Nat. Bank, Atlanta, 1942—, v.p. charge staff tng. program, 1964—. Named Atlanta Woman of Year in Bus., 1964. Mem. Nat. Assn. Bank Women (pres. 1964-65), Am. Inst. Banking, Financial Pub. Relations Assn., Bus. and Profl. Women's Club, Women's C. of C. Atlanta. Home: 2965 Pharr Ct NW Atlanta GA 30305 Office: Citizens and So Nat Bank Atlanta GA 30303

WORLEY, GORDON ROGER, retail chain fin. exec.; b. Arlington, Nebr., Oct. 13, 1919; s. Carl H. and Zella E. (Ludwig) W.; B.S., U. Nebr., 1945; M.B.A., Northwestern U., 1956; With Aldens, Inc., Chgo., 1940-67, asst. treas., 1956-57, v.p., treas., 1957-67; v.p., controller Gamble-Skogmo, Inc., Mpls., 1967; v.p. fin. Montgomery Ward & Co., Inc., 1967-68, exec. v.p. fin., Chgo., 1975—, also dir.; v.p. fin. Marcor Inc., Chgo., 1968-75, also dir.; dir. Container Corp. Am., Montgomery Ward Credit Corp., Signature Fin./Mktg. Inc., Standard T Chem. Co., Montgomery Ward Ins. Group, Marinco Ins. Internat., Ltd., Bliss & Laughlin Industries, Oak Brook, Ill., Ill. Power Co., Decatur; mem. adv. bd. to fin. com. Northwestern U; Bd. dirs. Northwestern Meml. Hosp.; trustee Garrett-Evang. Theol. Sem.; mem. and vice chmn. Ill. Capital Devel. Bd., 1973-77; mem. Nat. Commn. on Electronic Fund Transfers. Served with USAAF, 1943-46. C.P.A., Ill. Mem. Conf. Bd. Council of Fin. Execs., Fin. Execs. Inst., Nat. Retail Mchts. Assn., Fin. Acctg. Standards Bd. Methodist. Clubs: Chgo., Execs. Chgo., Econ. Chgo., Mid-Am., Oak Park Country. Office: Montgomery Ward Plaza Chicago IL 60671

WORLEY, JAMES CLARK, bus. pub. relations exec.; b. Springfield, Ohio, Jan. 12, 1927; s. Joseph Cuyler and Aleta Grace (Jones) W.; student Harvard U., 1947-48; A.B. in English Lit., Principia Coll., Elsah, Ill., 1948-50; postgrad. Sch. Journalism Boston U., 1951; grad. Inst. Orgn. Mgmt., Yale, 1960; m. Chloe Marguerite Schmidt, June 12, 1950; children—David Clark, Sharon Joy. Mem. editorial staff Christian Sci. Monitor, 1950-52; asst. pub. information officer Ohio Mil. Dist., 1952-53; mem. pub. relations staff Nationwide Ins. Co., Columbus, Ohio, 1953-56; pres. James C. Worley Assos., pub. relations, Columbus, 1953—; founder, pres. Riverside Inst. History and Current Affairs, 1968—; exec. sec. Am. Cemetery Assn., Columbus, 1956-59, exec. v.p., 1959-68, also editor assn. bulls., others in field; founder, mgr. Cemetery Mgmt. Inst., 1961-68. Founder, 1941, Boys Navy Club Am., and predecessor, pres. until 1945. Served with inf. AUS, 1945-47. Hon. lt. col. Ala. Militia. Mem. Pub. Relations Soc. Am., Am. Soc. Assn. Execs. Christian Scientist (Sunday sch. supt., pres. ch., chmn. bd. trustees). Mason (32 deg.). Address: 6853 McVey Blvd Worthington OH 43085

WORLEY, JAMES SAMUEL, economist, educator; b. Birmingham, Ala., Apr. 16, 1926; s. Arthur R. and Katherine (Gill) W.; B.A., Vanderbilt U., 1949, M.A., 1950; Ph.D., Princeton, 1959; m. Rosemary Nichols, Dec. 19, 1947; children—Paul N., Marian G., Susan P., James Samuel. Instr., Wofford Coll., 1950-51, asst. prof., 1951-53; instr. Princeton, 1955-57; asst. prof. econs. Vanderbilt U., Nashville, 1958-62, asso. prof., 1962-67, prof. econs. and bus. adminstrn., 1967—, dir. grad. program in econ. devel., 1964—, asso. provost of univ., 1968-71, chmn. dept. econs. and bus. adminstrn., 1971-74. Served with AUS, 1944-46; ETO. Mem. Am., So. econ. assns., Phi Beta Kappa. Office: Box 1608 Sta B Vanderbilt U Nashville TN 37235

WORLEY, WILL J., mech. engr., educator; b. Gibson City, Ill., Aug. 2, 1919; s. William Carlton and Anna (Osborn) W.; B.S., U. Ill., 1943, M.S., 1945, Ph.D., 1952; m. Carolyn Suzanne Juergensmeyer, Aug. 22, 1954; children—James Logan, Thomas Richard, Fred Burton, Mem. faculty U. Ill at Urbana, 1943—, prof. theoretical and applied mechanics, 1960—; cons., tchr. acoustics lab. IBM Corp., Endicott, N.Y., 1960, mech. analysis dept., San Jose, Calif., 1961, cons. acoustics lab., Poughkeepsie, N.Y., 1963; pres. Worley Systems; Inc., Urbana; cons. systems approach to prevention and analysis system failure, also cons. to lawyers on hwy. and indsl. accident investigation. Registered profl. engr., Ill. Mem. Acoustical Soc. Am., Am. Inst. Physics, ASME (past com. chmn.), Sigma Xi, Pi Tau Sigma, Pi Mu Epsilon. Editor: Shock and Vibration Symposium, 1962. Contbr. articles to profl. jours. Patentee in field. Home: 2106 Zuppke Urbana IL 61801

WORMSER, RENÉ ALBERT, lawyer, author, lectr. estate planning, internat. law, taxes, pub. affairs; b. Santa Barbara, Cal., July 17, 1896; s. David and Angeline Louise (Boeseke) W.; B.S., Columbia, 1917, LL.B., 1920; LL.D., Valparaiso U., 1964, U. Miami, 1976; m. Ella Madge Ward, Aug. 7, 1945; children—Angela Boeseke, Elissa Ward. Admitted to N.Y. State bar, 1920, and practiced as asso. Hornblower, Miller, Garrison & Potter, 1920-22, Bate, Boyd, & Swinnerton, 1923; individual practice, 1924-30; partner Wormser & Kemp, 1930-35, Wormser, Morris & Kemp, 1935-37, Folger, Rockwood, Wormser & Kemp, 1937-39, Delaney, Myles & Wormser, 1939-40, Haggerty, Myles & Wormser, 1941-50, Myles, Wormser & Koch 1950-60, Wormser, Koch, Kiely and Alessandroni, 1960-71, Wormser, Kiely, Alessandroni & McCann, 1972-77; firm Wormser, Kiely, Alessandroni, Hyde & McCann, 1978—; lectr. estate planning N.Y. U., 1948-55; mem. faculty and planning com. N.Y. U. Fed. Tax Inst., 1945-55; vis. adj. prof. Law Sch., U. Miami, 1973—. Gen. counsel Ho. of Reps. Spl. Com. to Investigate Tax Exempt Founds., 1953-54; chmn. advanced estate planning panels Practising Law Inst., 1956-68; chmn. adv. com. Miami U. Estate Planning Inst., 1967—; mem. advisory com. on tax-exempt orgns. Commr. Internal Revenue. Served with USN, World War I. Mem. Am., N.Y. State bar assns., Assn. Bar City N.Y., Delta Upsilon. Clubs: Belle Haven (Greenwich); Union League (N.Y.C.). Author: Your Will and What Not to do about It, 1937; Personal Estate Planning in a Changing World, 1942; Collection of International War Damage Claims, 1944; The Theory and Practice of Estate Planning, 1944; The Law, 1949; Family Estate Planning, 1953; The Myth of the Good and Bad Nations, 1954; Foundations, Their Power and Influence, 1958; Wormser's Guide to Estate Planning, 1958; The Planning and Administration of Estates, 1961; The Story of the Law, 1962; Wills That Made History, 1974; Conservatively Speaking, 1979; also articles in periodicals. Home: 1 Gingko Ln Greenwich CT 06830 Office: 100 Park Ave New York NY

WORNER, LLOYD EDSON, coll. pres.; b. Mexico, Mo., Sept. 13, 1918; s. Lloyd Edson and Letitia (Owen) W.; student Washington and Lee U., 1936-38, LL.D., 1972; A.B., Colo. Coll., 1942; postgrad. Princeton U., 1942-43; M.A., U. Mo., 1944, Ph.D., 1946; L.H.D., U. No. Colo., 1975; m. Mary Haden, Aug. 24, 1945; children—Linda Lou, Mary Susan. Instr. history Colo. Coll., 1946-47, asst. prof., 1947-50, asso. prof., 1950-55, prof., dean coll., 1955-63, pres., 1963—. Trustee Fountain Valley Sch., Colorado Springs Fine Arts Center; bd. visitors Mo. Mil. Acad. Congregationalist. Home: 1210 Wood Ave Colorado Springs CO 80903

WORNICK, RONALD CHARLES, food co. exec.; b. Malden, Mass., May 21, 1932; s. Harry and Florence (Klain) W.; B.S., Tufts U., 1954; M.S., Mass. Inst. Tech., 1959; m. Anita Lois Lev. Dec. 25, 1955; children—Kenneth, Michael, Jonathan. With United Fruit & Food Corp., Boston, 1959-71, exec. v.p., 1964-66, pres., 1966-71; pres. Right-Away Foods Corp., Edinburg, Tex., 1971-72; v.p. food service industries Clorox Co., 1972—, also dir. Past chmn. Sharon (Mass.) Republican Town Com. Trustee, Golden Plate Scholarship Found., 1974—. Served with AUS, 1955-57. Mem. Instl. Food Service Mfrs. Assn. (dir., pres. 1976), Nat. Alliance Businessmen (met. chmn. 1975). Mason. Home: 25 Marialinda Ct Hillsborough CA 94010

WORRELL, ALBERT CADWALLADER, educator; b. Phila., May 14, 1913; s. Pratt Bishop and Bertha May (Cadwallader) W.; B.S., U. Mich., 1935, M.F., 1935, Ph.D., 1953; m. Helen Haffner Diefendorf, July 31, 1937; children—Kathleen W. Howard, Frederick Strayer, Nancy (Mrs. George A. Shumaker). Asso. prof. U. Ga., 1947-55; asso. prof. Yale, 1955-63, prof. forest econs., 1963-67. Edwin Weyerhaeuser Davis prof. forest policy, 1967—; forest economist U.N. Econ. Commn. for Latin Am., Santiago, Chile, 1960-61; guest prof. U. Freiburg (Germany), 1970. Mem. Soc. Am. Foresters. Author: Economics of American Forestry, 1959; Principles of Forest Policy, 1970; Unpriced Values, 1979. Home: 81 Hilltop Rd Cheshire CT 06410 Office: 205 Prospect St New Haven CT 06511

WORRELL, LEE FRANK, educator; b. Orleans, Ind., Feb. 27, 1913; s. Frank S. and Grace (Hollowell) W.; B.S. in Pharmacy, Purdue U., 1935, Ph.D., 1940; m. Mary Dee Pickens, July 15, 1934; 1 dau., Shirley Yvonne (Mrs. Thomas Kauper). Asst., then asso. prof. Drake U. Coll. Pharmacy, 1938-42; from instr. to asso. prof. U. Mich. Coll. Pharmacy, 1942-60; prof. U. Tex. Coll. Pharmacy, 1960-79, dean coll., 1962-66; ret., 1979. Bd. dirs. Ann Arbor (Mich.) area United Fund, 1956-60. Mem. Am. Pharm. Assn., Am. Chem. Soc., AAAS, Sigma Xi, Rho Chi, Phi Lambda Upsilon, Phi Kappa Phi. Mem. Christian Ch. Home: 2014 Medford Rd Apt E-138 Ann Arbor MI 48104

WORSLEY, JOHN CLAYTON, architect; b. Providence, R.I., Apr. 8, 1919; s. Harold Rollin and Elise (Clay) W.; A.B., Stanford U., 1941; postgrad. Harvard U., 1949-51; m. Helen Elizabeth Hauss, Nov. 29, 1940; children—Katherine, Madeleine, John, David, Paul, Nina. Mem. planning office staff Stanford U., 1951-54; architect Ernest Kump, 1954-59; prin. John C. Worsley, Architect, Menlo Park, Calif., 1959-73; state architect of Calif., 1973-76; cons. architect State Capitol of Calif., 1976—; lectr. Stanford U., 1951-70, asst. dir. div. architecture and urban design, 1971-72; mem. faculty NSF/AIA Research Found. Seismic Inst., Stanford U., 1977 lectr. in field. Mem. Downtown Planning Com., Menlo Park, Calif.; chmn. beautification com. Menlo Park. Served with USNR, 1942-46. Fellow AIA (pres. Santa Clara Valley chpt. 1965, treas. Calif. council 1970-72, mem. joint commn. on hazardous bldgs. with Structural Engrs. Calif. and Calif. council AIA 1978-79). Home: 4149 Buchanan Dr Fair Oaks CA 95628 Office: PO Box 1527 Sacramento CA 95807

WORT, DENNIS JAMES, plant physiologist, educator; b. Salisbury, Eng., July 19, 1906; s. Dennis James and Florence Ann (Dimmer) W.; B.Sc., U. Sask. (Can.), 1932, M.Sc., 1934; Ph.D., U. Chgo., 1940; m. Helen Nora Kinnon, June 23, 1936; children—Margaret (Mrs. Paul Lewis, Jr.), Dennis James. Sessional lectr. biology U. Sask. 1943-45; asso. prof. botany U. B.C., Vancouver, 1945, prof. botany and plant physiology, 1947-72, research asso., 1972—, prof. emeritus, 1975—. Nuffield Research fellow U. Oxford, 1959; Coulter Research fellow U. Chgo., 1939. Fellow AAAS; mem. Am. Soc. Plant Physiologists (past sec.-treas. Western sect., vice-chmn., chmn.), B.C. Acad. Sci. (past editor, treas., v.p., pres.), N.W. Sci. Assn. (past trustee, v.p., pres.), Am. Soc. Botany, Can. Soc. Plant Physiologists, Am. Soc. Agronomy, European Soc. Potato Research. Author: (with J.R. Adams) Diversity in Living Things, 1966; (with W. Ruhland) Handbuch der Pflanzenphysologie, 1961; (with L.J. Andus) Physiology and Biochemistry of Herbicides, 1964. Mem. editorial bd. Northwest Science, 1950-73. Author publs. on chem. control of plant growth.

WORTH, GARY JAMES, broadcasting co. exec.; b. Berkeley Township, N.J., Dec. 13, 1940; s. Melvin Raymond and Viola Vista (Landis) W.; student Trenton State Coll., 1964, Palm Beach Jr. Coll., 1958-59. Dir. sta. relations MBS, Inc., N.Y.C., 1972, v.p. sta. relations, 1972, exec. v.p., Washington, 1972—, mem. exec. com., 1978—; v.p. Mut. Reports, Inc., Washington, 1972-79, dir., 1972-79; v.p., dir. WCFL, Inc., Chgo., 1979—, Mut. Radio N.Y., Inc., N.Y.C., 1979—. Served to capt. USAF, 1960-66. Decorated Air Force Commendation Medal, Armed Forces Expeditionary Medal. Recipient Chief Herbert H. Almers Meml. award Bergen County (N.J.) Police Acad., 19—. Mem. Nat. Assn. Broadcasters, Am. Quarter Horse Assn., Nat. Radio Broadcasters Assn. (bd. dirs. 19—). Methodist. Producer, dir. USAF movie Assignment McGuire. Home: 2801 N 27th St Arlington VA 22207 Office: 1755 S Jefferson Davis Hwy Arlington VA 22202

WORTH, GEORGE JOHN, educator; b. Vienna, Austria, June 11, 1929; s. Adolph and Theresa (Schmerzler) W.; came to U.S., 1940, naturalized, 1945; A.B., U. Chgo., 1948, A.M., 1951; Ph.D., U. Ill., 1954; postgrad. U. Coll., London, 1953- 54; m. Carol Laverne Dinsdale, Mar. 17, 1951; children—Theresa Jean, Paul Dinsdale. Instr. English, U. Ill., Champaign-Urbana, 1954-55; faculty U. Kans., Lawrence, 1955—, asso. prof., 1962-65, prof. English lit., 1965—, asst. chmn. dept., 1961-62, asso. chmn., 1962-63, acting chmn., 1963-64, chmn., 1964-79. Dickens fellow. Mem. AAUP, Modern Lang. Assn. Am., Midwest Modern Lang. Assn., Internat. Assn. U. Profs. English, D'Oyly Carte Opera Trust. Author: James Hannay: His Life and Work, 1964; William Harrison Ainsworth, 1972; Dickensian Melodrama, 1978. Editor: (with Harold Orel) Six Studies in Nineteenth-Century English Literature and Thought, 1962; (with Harold Orel) The Nineteenth-Century Writer and His Audience, 1969. Home: 2427 Harvard Rd Lawrence KS 66044

WORTH, IRENE, actress; b. Nebr., June 23, 1916; B.Edn., U. Calif. at Los Angeles, 1937; pupil Elsie Fogarty, London, 1944-45. Formerly tchr.; debut as Fenella in Escape Me Never, N.Y.C., 1942; Broadway debut as Cecily Harden in The Two Mrs. Carrolls, 1943; London debut in The Time of Your Life, 1946; following roles include Anabelle Jones in Love Goes to Press, 1946, Ilona Szabo in The Play's The Thing, 1947, as Eileen Perry in Edward my Son, 1948, as Lady Fortrose in Home is Tomorrow, 1948, as Mary Dalton in Native Son, 1948, title role in LaCrece, 1948, as Olivia Raines in Champagne for Delilah, 1949, as Celia Coplestone in The Cocktail Party, 1949, 50; various roles with Old Vic Repertory Co. including Desdemona in Othello, Helena in Midsummer Night's Dream and Lady Macbeth in Macbeth, also Catherine de Vausselles in The Other Heart (on tours S. Africa 1952), as Portia in The Merchant of Venice, 1953; joined Shakespeare Festival Theatre, Stratford, Ont., Can., 1953, as Helena in All's Well That Ends Well, Queen Margaret in Richard III; appeared as Frances Farrar in A Day by the Sea, 1953-54; leading roles in The Queen and the Rebels, 1955, Hotel Paradiso, 1956, as Mary Stuart, 1957, The Potting Shed, 1958, appeared as Albertine Prine in Toys in the Attic (Page One award), 1960; mem. Royal Shakespeare Co., 1962-64, including world tour King Lear, 1964; star Tiny Alice, N.Y.C., 1964, Aldwych, 1970; appeared in Shadows of the Evening, Noel Coward trilogy; also appeared as Hilde in A Song at Twilight, Anna-Mary in Come into the Garden Maud (Evening Standard award), Hesione Hushabye in Heartbreak House (Variety Club Gt. Britain award 1967), Jocasta in Oedipus, 1968, Hedda in Hedda Gabler, 1970; with internat. Co. Theatre Research, Paris and Iran, 1971; leading role in Notes on a Love Affair, 1972, Mme. Arkadina in The Seagull, 1973, Gertrude in Hamlet, Mrs. Alving in Ghosts, 1974, Princess Kosmonopolis in Sweet Bird of Youth, 1975-76 (Jefferson award, Tony award), Lina in Misalliance, 1976, Mme. Ranevskaya in The Cherry Orchard, 1977 (Drama Desk award), Kate in Old Times, 1977, After the Season, 1978, Happy Days, 1979; films include role of Leonie in Orders to Kill (Brit. Film Acad. award), 1958, The Scapegoat, 1958, King Lear, 1970, Nicholas and Alexandra, 1971; also numerous radio, TV appearances Eng., Can., U.S., including Stella in The Lake, Ellida Wangel in The Lady from the Sea (Daily Mail Nat. TV award); also Candida, Duchess of Malfi, Antigone, Prince Orestes, Variations on a Theme, The Way of the World, The Displaced Person; peotry recitals, recs. Decorated comdr. Brit. Empire (hon.); recipient Whitbread Anglo-Am. award outstanding actress, 1967. Address: care Milton Goldman ICM 6th Floor 40 W 57th St New York City NY 10019

WORTH, ROGER PETRIE, snowmobile mfg. co. exec.; b. Louisville, Nov. 27, 1937; s. Eugene B. and Lila (Petrie) W.; B.Mech. Engring., U. Louisville, 1959, J.D., 1966; m. Linda J. Winegarner, Dec. 18, 1961; children—Lisa, Laura, Lucia. Admitted to Wis. bar, 1966, Minn. bar, 1974; project engr. Cummins Engine Co., Columbus, Ind., 1959-60, Kiekhaefer Mercury Co., 1962-64; counsel Mercury Marine div. Brunswick Corp., Fond du Lac, Wis., 1966-70; legal counsel Arctic Enterprises, Inc., Thief River Falls, Minn., 1970-79, sec., 1971-79, dir. engring., 1973-79, pres. Scorpion Industries, Inc. subs., Crosby, Minn., 1979—. Served with AUS, 1960-62. Mem. Am., Minn., Wis. bar assns. Home: Box 396 Deerwood MN 56444 Office: Scorpion Industries Inc Crosby MN 56441

WORTHAM, JOHN LILBURN, economist, educator; b. Athens, Tex., Feb. 9, 1920; s. William Albert and Maggie Elizabeth (Shelton) W.; B.A., E. Tex. State U., Commerce, 1940; M.A., U. Tex., 1947, Ph.D., 1954; m. Mary Beth Mason, Oct. 29, 1944; children—Charles William, John Lee, Mary Gayle, James, Patria. Tchr. pub. sch., Wolfe City, Tex., 1940-41; prof. econs. Tex. Christian U., 1948—, chmn. dept., 1961-77. Served to maj., pilot, USAAF, 1941-45. Decorated Purple Heart, Air medal with 2 clusters. Mem. Am. Econ. Assn., Omicron Delta Epsilon, Alpha Chi, Pi Kappa Delta, Delta Simga Pi. Methodist. Home: 2921 Hartwood Dr Fort Worth TX 76109

WORTHEN, JOHN EDWARD, univ. pres.; b. Carbondale, Ill., July 15, 1933; s. Dewey and Annis Burr (Williams) W.; B.S. in Psychology (Univ. acad. scholar), Northwestern U., 1954; M.A. in Student Personnel Adminstrn., Columbia U., 1955; Ed.D. in Adminstrn. in Higher Edn. (Coll. Entrance Exam. Bd. fellow), Harvard U., 1964; m. Sandra Damewood, Feb. 27, 1960; children—Samantha Jane, Bradley Edward. Dean of men Am. U., 1959-61; dir. counseling and testing and asst. prof. edn., 1963-66, asst. to provost and asst. prof., 1966-68, acting provost and v.p. acad. affairs, 1968, asso. provost for instrn., 1969, v.p. student affairs, 1970-75, v.p. student affairs and adminstrn., 1976-79; pres. Indiana U. of Pa., 1979—; cons. to public schs. Served with USN, 1955-59. Mem. Am. Personnel and Guidance Assn., Phi Delta Kappa, Kappa Delta Pi. Office: 201 Sutton Hall Indiana U of Pa Indiana PA 15705

WORTHINGTON, CHARLES ROY, educator; b. Australia, May 17, 1925; s. Thomas Charles and Mary Ivy (Hodge) W.; B.S., Adelaide U., 1950, Ph.D., 1955; m. Alma Rose Burnier, Dec. 12, 1959; children—Laurie Alma, Keith Charles, Ian Roy. Came to U.S., 1956. Mem. MRC Biophysics Research unit Kings Coll., London, 1958-61; asst. prof., asso. prof. physics dept. U. Mich., 1961-69; prof. biol. scis. and physics Carnegie-Mellon U., Pitts., 1969—. Served with Royal Australian Air Force, 1944-45. Mem. Biophys. Soc. Contbr. articles to profl. jours. Home: 3024 Sturbridge Ct Allison Park PA 15101 Office: 4400 5th Ave Pittsburgh PA 15213

WORTHINGTON, EDWARD ARTHUR, chemist; b. New Orleans, Nov. 28, 1920; s. Roy Bowie and Winfred (Casey) W.; Ph.D., U. Pitts., 1948; m. Margaret Joyce Spear, June 4, 1946; children—Anne, Laurie, Edward. Instr., U. Pitts., 1946-48; sr. research chemist Allied Chem. Co., 1948-51; research supr., then mgr. research Kaiser Aluminum & Chem. Corp., 1951-69, adminstrv. dir. Center Tech., Pleasanton, Calif., 1969—. City councilman, Palo Alto, Calif., 1965-67. Mem. Am. Chem. Soc. Home: 101 Alma St Palo Alto CA 94301 Office: 6177 Sunol Blvd Pleasanton CA 94566

WORTHY, JAMES CARSON, educator, mgmt. cons.; b. Midland, Tex., Jan. 8, 1910; s. James Arthur and Minnie (Gressett) W.; student Northwestern U.; A.B., Lake Forest Coll., 1933, LL.D. (hon.); LL.D., Chgo. Theol. Sem.; m. Mildred Leritz, June 20, 1934; 1 dau., Joan (Mrs. J. Robert Barr). Employment mgr. Schuster & Co., Milw., 1936-38; mem. personnel staff Sears, Roebuck & Co., Chgo., 1938-50, dir. employee relations, 1950-53, asst. to chmn. bd., 1955, vice pres. pub. relations, 1956-61; v.p. Cresap, McCormick & Paget, 1962-72; prof. Sangamon State U., Springfield, Ill., 1972-78; prof. Grad. Sch. Mgmt. Northwestern U., Evanston, Ill., 1978—; dir. Control Data Corp., Comml. Credit Co., Selected Special Shares, Selected Money Market Fund, Selected Tax Exempt Bond Fund, Selected Am. Shares. Asst. dep. adminstr. NRA, Washington, 1933-36; asst. sec. commerce, 1953-55, cons. to sec. of commerce, 1956-58. Industry mem. spl. panel WSB, 1952; mem. President's Com. on Govt. Contracts, 1953-55; mem. President's Commn. on Campaign Costs, 1961-62. Mem. Ill. Bd. of Higher Edn., 1967-69. Director Hosp. Planning Council Met. Chgo., 1959-69; dir. Nat. Merit Scholarship Corp., 1958-63. Commr., Chgo. Med. Center, 1960-65. Mem. exec. bd. Indsl. Relations Research Assn., 1952-54. Treas. Sears-Roebuck Found., 1955-56, dir., 1954-61, pres., 1956-61; trustee Latin Sch. Chgo., 1968-72; trustee Chgo. Theol. Sem., 1953-73. Co-chmn. Ill. Citizens for Eisenhower-Nixon, 1952; v.p. United Rep. Fund of Ill., 1955-59, pres., 1959-60, exec. com., 1961-72; mem. Nat. Rep. Finance Com., 1958-60; del. Rep. Nat. Conv., 1960; pres. Republican Citizens League Ill., 1961-62. Fellow Acad. Mgmt.; mem. Am. Soc. Pub. Adminstn. Conglist. Clubs: Commercial, Chicago, University (Chgo.); Indian Hill (Winnetka, Ill.). Home: 2001 Sherman Ave Evanston IL 60201 also 4625 Rue Belle Mer Sanibel Island FL 33957 Office: Office Grad Sch Mgmt Northwestern U Evanston IL 60201

WORTHY, K(ENNETH) MARTIN, lawyer; b. Dawson, Ga., Sept. 24, 1920; s. Kenneth Spencer and Jeffrie Pruett (Martin) W.; student The Citadel, 1937-39; B.Ph., Emory U., 1941, J.D., 1947; M.B.A. cum laude, Harvard, 1943; m. Eleanor Blewett, Feb. 15, 1947; children—Jeffrie Martin (Mrs. Kevin Andreae), William Blewett. Admitted to Ga. bar, 1947, D.C. bar, 1948; asso. mem. firm Hamel, Park, McCabe & Saunders, Washington, 1948-52, partner, 1952-69, 72—; chief counsel IRS, asst. gen. counsel Treasury Dept., 1969-72; dir. Beneficial Corp. Mem. Nat. Council Organized Crime, 1970-72; cons. Justice Dept., 1972-74. Del., Montgomery County Civic Fedn., 1951-61, D.C. Area Health and Welfare Council, 1960-61; mem. Emory Law Sch. Council, 1976—. Served to capt. AUS, 1943-46, 51-52. Recipient Treasury Exceptional Service award and medal, 1972, IRS Commrs. award, 1972. Fellow Am. Bar Found.; mem. Ga., D.C., Fed. (nat. council 1969-72, 77—), Am. (council taxation sect. 1965-68, vice chmn. 1968-69, 72-73, chmn. 1973-74), bar assns., Am. Law Inst., Nat. Tax Assn., Omicron Delta Kappa. Episcopalian (chmn. dept. finance Washington Diocese 1969-70). Clubs: Chevy Chase, Metropolitan, National Lawyers (Washington); Harvard (N.Y.C.); James River Country (Newport News, Va.). Author: (with John M. Appleman) Basic Estate Planning, 1957. Contbr. articles to profl. jours. Home: 5305 Portsmouth Rd Washington DC 20016 also Tardree Sparta NJ 07871 Office: 1776 F St NW Washington DC 20006

WORTHY, PATRICIA MORRIS, govt. ofcl.; b. Fort Benning, Ga., May 28, 1944; d. Walter and Ruby Mae (Lovett) M.; A.A., Queensborough Community Coll., 1964; B.A., Bklyn. Coll., 1966; J.D., Howard U., 1969. Admitted to D.C. bar, 1971; trial atty. NLRB, Washington, 1969-71; dep. gen. counsel ACTION, Washington, 1971-74; asso. firm Dolphin, Branton, Stafford & Webber, Washington, 1974-77; dep. asst. sec. for regulatory functions HUD, Washington, 1977—; chairperson Occupational Safety and Health Bd., Washington; bd. dirs. Anacostia Econ. Devel. Corp., 1972-77. Mem. adv. bd. Afro-Am. Datanamics, Inc.; bd. dirs. Nat. Black Child Devel. Inst. Mem. Am. Bar Assn., Nat. Conf. Black Lawyers, Trial Lawyers' Assn. D.C., World Peace Through Law (chairperson young lawyers sect. 1973-75). Office: 451 7th St SE Washington DC 20410

WORTMAN, STERLING, scientist; b. Quinlan, Okla., Apr. 3, 1923; s. Leo Sterling and Gladys (Richwine) W.; B.S., Okla. State U., 1943, M.S., U. Minn., 1948, Ph.D., 1950; m. Ruth Eleanor Bolstad, June 17, 1949; children—Linda Susan, Steven Sterling, Mark Jeffry, David Eric. Geneticist charge corn breeding Rockefeller Found., 1950-54, dir. agrl. scis., 1966-70, v.p., 1970—; pres. Internat. Agrl. Devel. Service, 1975—; asst. field dir. Internat. Rice Research Inst., 1960-64; head dept. plant breeding Pineapple Research Inst., Hawaii, 1955-59, dir., 1964-65; dir. Campbell Soup Co. Mem. agrl. bd. Nat. Acad. Scis.-NRC, 1967-71; chmn. Plant Studies Delegation to Peoples Republic of China, Nat. Acad. Scis., 1974, mem. bd. on sci. and tech. in internat. devel., 1974, mem. com. on scholarly communication with Peoples Republic of China, 1974-76; mem. steering com. Pres.'s Food and Nutrition Study, 1975-77; mem. advisory com. sci., tech. and devel. Exec. Office of Pres.; Coromandel lectr., India, 1977. Trustee Agronomic Sci. Found., 1967—; bd. dirs. Agribus. Council, 1967-73, v.p., 1967-69; bd. dirs. Internat. Center Maize and Wheat Improvement, Mex., 1966—, vice chmn. bd., 1968-74; mem. biol. and med. scis. advisory com. NSF, 1970-72, mem. research advisory com., 1972-74; mem. nat. plant genetic resources com. Dept. Agr., 1977—; trustee Internat. Rice Research Inst., Philippines, 1970, Internat. Inst. Tropical Agr., Nigeria, 1970; mem. vis. com. dept. nutrition Mass. Inst. Tech., 1971-74. Served to capt., inf., AUS, 1943-45; PTO. Decorated Medal of Merit (Philippines); recipient Outstanding Achievement award U. Minn., 1975, Joseph C. Wilson award for achievement in internat. affairs, 1975, Distinguished Alumnus award Okla. State U., 1978. Fellow AAAS; mem. Crop Sci. Soc., Am. Soc. Agronomy (Internat. Agronomy award 1975), Am. Inst. Biol. Scis., Am. Acad. Arts and Scis., Sigma Xi. Home: 36 Baldwin Farms N

Greenwich CT 06830 Office: 1133 Ave of Americas New York NY 10036

WORTZEL, LAWRENCE HERBERT, educator; b. Newark, Sept. 28, 1932; s. Charles and Sadie (Bornstein) W.; B.S., Rutgers U., 1954; M.B.A. with distinction, Harvard U., 1963, D.B.A., 1967; m. Heidi Pamela Vernon, Dec. 23, 1956; children—Joshua Charles, Jennifer Rachel. Partner, owner two pharmacies, N.J., 1957-61; research asst., then research asso. Harvard U., 1963-65; mem. faculty Boston U., 1965—, prof. mktg., 1969—, chmn. dept., 1968-72, 73-75; vis. research prof. Mktg. Sci. Inst., 1976; cons. World Bank, 1978—. Served with U.S. Army, 1956-57. Mem. Am. Mktg. Assn., Assn. Consumer Research, Acad. Internat. Bus. Jewish. Co-author: The Development of Financial Managers, 1971; contbr. articles to profl. jours; editorial rev. bd. Jour. Mktg., 1976—. Home: 39 Stafford Rd Newton Centre MA 02159 Office: 704 Commonwealth Ave Boston MA 02215. *We are responsible for our own successes and our own failures. There's no mysterious "they" out there who are keeping us from success or causing us to fail.*

WORZEL, JOHN LAMAR, geophysicist, educator; b. West Brighton, S.I., N.Y., Feb. 21, 1919; s. Howard Henry and Marie Alma (Wilson) W.; B.S. in Engring. Physics, Lehigh U., 1940; M.A. in Geophysics (grad. resident scholar), Columbia, 1948, Ph.D., 1949; m. Dorothy Crary, Nov. 22, 1941; children—Sandra, Howard, Richard, William. Research asso. Woods Hole (Mass.) Oceanographic Inst., 1940-46; geodesist Columbia, N.Y.C., 1946-48, research asso., 1948-49, instr. geology, 1949, asst. prof., 1950-52, asso. prof., 1952-57, prof., 1957-72; asst. dir. Lamont Geol. Obs., Palisades, N.Y., 1951-64, acting dir., 1964-65, asso. dir., 1965-72; prof., dep. dir. earth and planetary scis. div. Marine Biomed. Inst., U. Tex. Med. Br., Galveston, 1972-74, acting dir. geophys. lab. Marine Sci. Inst., 1974-75, dir. geophys. lab., 1975-79, also prof. geol. sci. dept. U. Tex. at Austin, 1972—; adj. prof. Rice U., 1974-78; ret., 1979; mem. U.S. Nat. Com. Internat. Geol. Correlation Program. Bd. dirs., pres. Palisades Geophys. Inst., 1974—; bd. dirs. Rockland County council Boy Scouts Am., 1964-72; bd. dirs., treas. Palisades Geophys. Inst., 1970-74. Recipient USN Meritorious Pub. Service citation Dept. of Navy, 1964. Guggenheim Found. fellow, 1963. Mem. AAAS, Am. Assn. Petroleum Geologists, Am. Phys. Soc., Am. Geophys. Union, Geol. Soc. Am., Seismol. Soc. Am., Geophys. Soc. Houston, Soc. Exploration Geophysicists (chmn. com. 1974-76, v.p. 1978-79), Pi Mu Epsilon, Tau Beta Pi. Republican. Lutheran. Clubs: Cosmos (Washington); Pelican (Galveston). Research on gravity and seismic refraction and reflection at sea, sound transmission of sea water. Home: 104 S Shore Dr Southport NC 28461

WOTIZ, JOHN HENRY, educator, chemist; b. Moravska Ostrava, Czechoslovakia, Apr. 12, 1919; s. Berthold B. and Bertha (Kauder) W.; student Czech Polytechnicum, Prague, 1937; B.S., Furman U., 1941; M.S., U. Richmond, 1943; Ph.D., Ohio State U., 1948; m. Kathryn Erdody, Feb. 23, 1945; children—Anita (Mrs. Eric Diekman), Karen, Vivian. Came to U.S., 1939, naturalized, 1944. Instr. U. Pitts., 1948-50, asst. prof., 1950-54, asso. prof., 1954-57; group leader research center Diamond Alkali Co., Painesville, Ohio, 1957-59, sr. group leader, 1959-62; prof., chmn. chemistry dept. Marshall U., Huntington, W.Va., 1962-67; prof., chmn. chemistry dept. So. Ill. U., Carbondale, 1967-68, prof., 1968—. Nat. Acad. Scis. vis. prof. USSR, 1969, Eastern Europe, 1972; vis. prof., lectr., East Asian and Pacific Ocean countries, 1974; past cons. Air Reduction Co., Watson Standard Co. Served as lt., Chem. Corps, AUS, 1946-48. Mem. Am. Chem. Soc. (chmn. elect div. history of chemistry 1978-79), History of Sci. Soc., AAUP, Am. Contract Bridge League, Sigma Xi. Unitarian-Universlist. Contbr. articles to profl. jours. Patentee in field. Research on internat. higher edn. in chemistry. Home: 903 Glenview Dr Carbondale IL 62901

WOUDHUYSEN, ANDRIES DANIEL, investment banker; b. Amsterdam, Netherlands, Dec. 14, 1917; came to U.S., 1941, naturalized, 1955; s. Daniel M. and Klara (Asser) W.; m. Marianne Josephine DeKadt, Nov. 7, 1941; 1 dau., Mary-Ann Agnes Woudhuysen Penn. In various positions with Netherlands govt. U.S. and U.K., 1941-52; with Drexel Burnham Lambert Inc. and predecessors, N.Y.C., 1952—, gen. partner, 1956-72, exec. v.p., 1972-76, sr. exec. v.p., 1976—. Office: 60 Broad St New York NY 10004

WOUK, ARTHUR, educator; b. N.Y.C., Mar. 25, 1924; s. Louis and Sarah (Feldman) W.; B.S., Coll. City N.Y., 1943; M.A., Johns Hopkins, 1947, Ph.D., 1951; m. Vita Boruchoff, Nov. 5, 1944; children—Nina Grace, Fay Ellen. Instr., Queens Coll., N.Y.C., 1950-52; mathematician project cyclone Reeves Instrument Corp., N.Y.C., 1952-54; sr. engring. specialist Sylvania Electronic Systems Gen. Tel. & Tel., Waltham, Mass., 1954-62; vis. prof. math. research center U. Wis., Madison, 1962-63; asso. prof. math, Northwestern U., Evanston, Ill., 1963-69, prof. applied math. and engring. sci., 1969-72; prof. dept. computing sci. U. Alta., Edmonton, 1972—, chmn. dept., 1972-76; cons. Argonne (Ill.) Nat. Lab., 1963-70, Sylvania Elec. Systems, 1966-69. Served with AUS, 1943-46. Mem. Am. Math. Soc., Soc. Indsl. and Applied Math. (editor Rev. 1963—), Assn. for Computing Machines (editor Communications 1958-64). Home: 8711 138th St Edmonton AB T5R 0E2 Canada

WOUK, HERMAN, author; b. N.Y.C., May 27, 1915; s. Abraham Isaac and Esther (Levine) W.; student Townsend Harris Hall, 1927-30; A.B. with gen. honors, Columbia U., 1934; L.H.D. (hon.), Yeshiva U., 1954; LL.D., (hon.), Clark U., 1960; Litt.D. (hon.), Am. Internat. U., 1979; m. Betty Sarah Brown, Dec. 9, 1945; children—Abraham Isaac (dec.), Nathaniel, Joseph. Radio programs writer for various comedians, N.Y.C., 1935; asst. Fred Allen, radio comedian, in writing weekly radio scripts, 1936-June 1941; dollar-a-year appointment (presdl. cons. expert) to U.S. Treasury, 1941; vis. prof. English Yeshiva U., 1953-57; scholar-in-residence Aspen Inst. Humanistic Studies, 1973-74. Mem. bd. trustees Coll. of Virgin Islands, 1961-69; bd. dirs. Washington Nat. Symphony, 1969-71; bd. dirs. Kennedy Center Prodns., 1974-75. Served as deck officer USNR, 1942-Feb. 1946; aboard destroyer-minesweeper in Pacific 3 yrs.; exec. officer U.S.S. Southard, 1945. Decorated 4 campaign stars, Unit Citation; recipient Columbia U. medal for Excellence, 1952, also Richard H. Fox prize, 1934. Mem. Res. Officers Naval Services, Dramatists Guild, Authors Guild. Jewish. Clubs: Bohemian (San Francisco); Cosmos, Metropolitan (Washington). Author: Aurora Dawn (Book of the Month club selection for May), 1947; The City Boy (novel), 1948; The Traitor (drama), 1949; The Caine Mutiny (novel), 1951 (Pulitzer Prize fiction 1952); The Caine Mutiny Court-Martial (drama), 1953; Marjorie Morningstar (novel), 1955; Nature's Way (comedy), 1957; This is My God, 1959; Youngblood Hawke (novel), 1962; Don't Stop the Carnival (novel), 1965; The Winds of War (novel), 1971; War and Remembrance (novel), 1978. Office: care BSN Literary Agy 3255 N St NW Washington DC 20007

WOZENCRAFT, FRANK MCREYNOLDS, lawyer; b. Dallas, Apr. 25, 1923; s. Frank Wilson and Mary Victoria (McReynolds) W.; B.A. summa cum laude, Williams Coll., 1946; LL.B., Yale U., 1949; m. Shirley Ann Cooper, Nov. 25, 1960; children—Frank McReynolds, Ann Lacey, George Wilson. Admitted to Tex. bar, 1950; law clk. U.S. Supreme Ct., Washington, 1949-50; mem. firm Baker & Botts, Houston, 1950-60, partner, 1960-66, 69—; dir. Rusk Inc.; sec. Tex. Fund, Inc., Houston, 1958-66; asst. atty. gen. charge Office Legal Counsel, Dept. Justice, Washington, 1966-69; mem. legal adv. com. N.Y. Stock Exchange, 1978—. Mem. Commn. Polit. Activity Govt. Employees, 1967; mem. Pres.'s Adv. Panel on Ins., 1967-68; vice chmn. Adminstrv. Conf. U.S., 1968-71; U.S. rep. Vienna Conf. on Law of Treaties, 1968. Mem. exec. bd. Sam Houston Area council Boy Scouts Am., 1959-66, 69—, v.p., 1974-79; past mem. adv. bd. Houston Mus. Fine Arts; past chmn. bd. Assn. Community TV; bd. govs. Public Broadcasting Service; trustee Hedgecroft Hosp., 1964-66, St. John's Sch., Houston, 1972-79; bd. dirs. Alley Theatre, 1961-66, 73—. Served to capt. U.S. Army, 1943-46. Decorated Bronze Star. Mem. Am. Soc. Internat. Law, Am. Law Inst. (council), Am. Bar Assn. (chmn. sect. adminstrv. law 1973-74, spl. com. open meetings legislation 1974-75), Houston Bar Assn., State Bar Tex., Order of Coif, Gargoyle, Phi Beta Kappa, Phi Delta Theta, Phi Delta Phi. Episcopalian. Clubs: Houston, Houston Country; Chevy Chase (Md.); Univ. (Washington). Home: 51 E Broad Oaks St Houston TX 77056 Office: 3000 One Shell Plaza Houston TX 77002

WOZNIAK, JOHN MICHAEL, educator; b. Astoria, L.I., N.Y., Sept. 13, 1916; s. Michael and Mary (Stadnik) W.; A.B., St. Peter's Coll., 1938, M.A., Fordham U., 1942; Ph.D., Johns Hopkins, 1950; m. Mary Flood, June 12, 1943; children—Robert, John Roy. Teaching fellow, grad. asst. St. Peter's Coll., 1938-40; tchr. St. Joseph's High Sch., Phila., 1940-42; instr. Johns Hopkins, 1946-50; asst. prof., prof., chmn. dept. edn. Loyola U., Chgo., 1950—, now dean Sch. Edn.; lectr. Northwestern U., summer 1962. Mem. bd. trustees, Skokie, Ill., 1961—. Served to capt. AUS, 1942-46. Mem. Am. Assn. Colls. Tchr. Edn., Nat. Soc. Coll. Tchrs. Edn., AAUP, Nat. Cath. Edn. Assn., Assn. Higher Edn., Midwest Philosophy Edn. Soc. Home: 4960 Lee St Skokie IL 60076 Office: Loyola U 820 N Michigan Ave Chicago IL 60611

WRAGG, JOANNA DICARLO (MRS. OTIS OLIVER WRAGG III), journalist; b. Batavia, N.Y., Nov. 3, 1941; d. Anthony Joseph and Josephine (Ruffino) DiCarlo; B.A., Fla. State U., 1963; m. Otis Oliver Wragg III, Dec. 21, 1963; children—Otis Oliver IV, LaMae. Tchr. French and English, Nova Sch., Ft. Lauderdale, Fla., 1963; tchr., chmn. English dept. Safety Harbor (Fla.) Jr. High Sch., 1965-68; social worker Fla. Welfare Dept., Lakeland, 1968-70; editorial writer Lakeland Ledger, 1968-70, editorial writer, asst. editor editorials, 1970-73; editorial writer Miami (Fla.) News, 1973-78; editorial dir. WPLG-TV, Miami, 1978; editorial bd. Miami Herald, 1978—. Recipient Sigma Delta Chi Distinguished Service award for editorial writing, 1971, Robert Kennedy Journalism award, 1971, First Place award for editorial writing Fla. Soc. Newspaper Editors, 1971, First Place award for column writing Fla. Press Club, 1971, others. Mem. NOW (gov., past pres. Polk County chpt.), Nat. Women's Polit. Caucus, League Women Voters, Common Cause, Nat. Conf. Editorial Writers, Econ. Soc. S. Fla., Sigma Delta Chi. Unitarian. Club: Fla. Press. Home: 361 Redwood Ln Key Biscayne Miami FL 33149 Office: Miami Herald One Herald Plaza Miami FL 33101

WRAPP, HENRY EDWARD, educator; b. Paragould, Ark., Mar. 26, 1917; s. Alba Henry and Mildred (Dennis) W.; B.C.S., U. Notre Dame, 1938; M.B.A., Harvard, 1948, D.C.S., 1951; m. Marguerite Amy Hill, Aug. 19, 1950; children—Jennifer, Gregory, Stephen, Amy, Katherine. With E.I. duPont deNemours & Co., Inc., 1939-43; prof. Harvard, 1955-62; prof. bus. policy U. Chgo., 1963—, asso. dean, 1965-70. Dir. Richardson Co., Chgo., Sargent Welch Sci. Co., Chgo., Pittway Corp., Chgo., Atkins and Merrill, Inc., Lebanon, N.H., New Court Securities, N.Y.C., Loctite Corp., Newington, Conn., Govt. Employees Ins. Co., Washington, Fed. Express Co. Served to lt. USNR, 1943-46. Clubs: University, Quadrangle (Chgo.); Hartford (Hartford, Conn.); Johns Island (Vero Beach, Fla.). Home: 1902 Neptune Dr Melbourne Beach FL 32951 Office: 190 E Delaware Pl Chicago IL 60611

WRATHER, JOHN DEVERAUX, JR., oil producer, motion picture producer, financier; b. Amarillo, Tex., May 24, 1918; s. John D. and Mazie (Cogdell) W.; A.B., U. Tex., 1939; m. Bonita Granville, Feb. 5, 1947; children—Molly, Jack, Linda, Christopher. Ind. oil producer, Tex., Ind., Ill.; pres. Evansville (Ind.) Refining Co., 1938-40, Overton Refining Co., Amarillo Producers & Refiners Corp., Dallas, 1940-49, Jack Wrather Pictures, Inc., 1947-49, Freedom Prodns., Inc., 1949—, Western States Investment Corp., Dallas, 1949—, Wrather Television Prodns., Inc., 1951—, Wrather-Alvarez Broadcasting, Inc., The Lone Ranger, Inc., Lassie, Inc., Disney-land Hotel, Anaheim, Calif., L'Horizon Hotel, Palm Springs, Cal.; owner KFMB, KERO and KEMB-TV, San Diego, KOTY-TV, Tulsa; part owner WNEW, N.Y.C.; pres. Sgt. Preston of the Yukon, Inc.; chmn. bd. Muzak, Inc., Ind. Television Corp. and Television Programs of Am. Inc., Stephens Marine, Inc.; pres. Balboa Bay Club, Inc., Kona Kai, Inc.; pres., chmn. bd. Wrather Corp.; dir. TelePrompTer Corp., Continental Airlines, Transcontinent. Television Corp., Jerold Elec. Corp., Capitol Records, Inc. Bd. dirs. Community Television of So. Calif. Am. Found. Religion and Psychiatry, Corp. for Pub. Broadcasting; mem. devel. bd. U. Tex., vice chmn. chancellor's council; mem. advisory council Ariz. Heart Inst.; bd. counselors for performing arts U. So. Calif. Commr. Los Angeles County-Hollywood Mus. Served to major USMC Res., 1942-53. Mem. Ind. Petroleum Assn. of Am., Internat. Radio and Television Soc., Acad. Motion Pictures Arts and Scis., Nat. Petroleum Council. Clubs: Dallas Athletic, Dallas Petroleum; Cat Cay Yacht (Bahamas); Players, Hemisphere, Skeeters (N.Y.); Marks, Bucks, White Elephant (London) Motion pictures produced include: The Guilty, 1946, High Tide, Perilous Water, 1947, Strike It Rich, 1948, Guilty of Treason, 1949, The Lone Ranger and The Lost City of Gold, 1958, The Magic of Lassie, others. Home: 172 Delfern Dr Los Angeles CA 90024 Office: 270 N Canon Dr Beverly Hills CA 90210*

WRAY, CHARLES WILLIAMSON, JR., advt. agy. exec.; b. Raleigh, N.C., May 29, 1933; s. Charles Williamson and Adna Jones (Howell) W.; A.B., Duke, 1955; m. Edna Jacquelyn Steed, Oct. 4, 1957; children—Charlie, Susan. Trainee Gen. Electric Co., Schenectady, 1955-56; advt. specialist, Plainville, Conn., 1956-57; advt. dir. Drexel Enterprises (N.C.), 1957-66; account exec. Cargill, Wilson & Acree Inc., Charlotte, N.C., 1966-67, v.p., 1968-69, sr. v.p., 1970-71, exec. v.p., 1971-72, pres., 1973-75, vice chmn., 1976-77; pres. Wray/Ward Advt., Inc., Charlotte, 1977—; dir. Camelot Industries, E.I.C. Corp., PMC Inc. Bd. dirs. Boys Town N.C.; trustee Affiliated Advt. Agys. Internat. Network, 1975-76. Mem. Advt. Club Charlotte (pres. 1974), Am. Advt. Fedn., Newcomen Soc., Kappa Sigma. Republican. Baptist. Rotarian. Home: 523 Robmont Rd Charlotte NC 28211 Office: Wray/Ward Advt Inc Inc 700 Kenilworth Ave Charlotte NC 28204

WRAY, FRANK JUNIOR, historian; b. Camden, Ind., Apr. 29, 1921; s. Benjamin Franklin and Bessie Leanore (Ayres) W.; A.B. with high honors, Ind. U., 1946, M.A., 1947; Ph.D., Yale U., 1954; m. Betty Marie Binkley, Dec. 28, 1946; children—William Franklin, James Edward, Thomas Frederick, Ellen Elizabeth. Instr. history U. S.D., 1947-49, U. Conn., 1952, U. Vt., 1953; faculty Berea (Ky.) Coll., 1953—, prof. history, 1964—, William J. Hutchins Alumni prof., 1976—. Served with AUS, 1942-46. Am. Council Learned Socs. grantee, 1964; recipient Seabury award for Excellence in Teaching, 1967; Southeastern Inst. Medieval and Renaissance Studies fellow, 1968. Mem. AAUP (treas. Ky. conf. 1971-73), Am. Hist. Assn., Am. Soc. for Reformation Research, Am. Soc. Ch. History, Medieval Acad. Am., Renaissance Soc. Am. Republican. Baptist. Club: Masons. Contbr. sect. to Mennonite Ency. II, 1956, Reformation Studies, 1962, articles, revs. to profl. jours. Home: 116 Van Winkle Grove Berea KY 40403 Office: Box 2271 Berea Coll Berea KY 40404

WRAY, KARL, newspaper pub.; b. Bishop, Tex., June 8, 1913; s. Ernest Paul and Gertrude (Garvin) W.; A.B., Columbia U., 1935; m. Flora-Lee Koepp, Aug. 11, 1951; children—Diana, Mark, Kenneth, Norman, Thomas. Auditor, U.S. Dept. Agr., Washington, also Little Rock, 1935-37; salesman O'Mara & Ormsbee, Inc., N.Y.C., 1937-42; advt. mgr. Lompoc (Calif.) Record, 1947-54; owner, pub. San Clemente (Calif.) Daily Sun-Post, 1954-67, Coastline Dispatch, San Juan Capistrano, Calif., 1956-67, Dana Point (Calif.) Lamplighter, 1966-67; cons. Lear Siegler, Inc., Washington, 1967-68; pub. Daily Star-Progress, La Habra, Calif., 1969-74, Anaheim (Calif.) Bulletin, 1974—. Mem. Calif. State Park Commn., 1960-64, vice chmn., 1961-62; mem. exec. bd. Orange County council Boy Scouts Am., 1961-64, 76-80; mem. citizens adv. com. Orange Coast Coll., 1963-66; bd. dirs. Calif. Newspaper Youth Found., 1978-80. Served to capt. USMC, 1942-46. Mem. Calif. Newspaper Advt. Execs. Assn. (pres. 1952-53), Calif. Newspaper Pubs. Assn. (dir. 1960-64), Am. Theatre Critics Assn., Football Writers Assn. Am., San Juan Capistrano (pres. 1966), San Clemente (pres. 1956-57), La Habra (dir. 1970-74), Anaheim (dir. 1974-80) chambers commerce. Presbyterian (elder). Home: 2420 S Ola Vista San Clemente CA 92672 Office: 1771 S Lewis St PO Box 351 Anaheim CA 92805

WRAY, WILLIAM ROBERT, army officer; b. DeQuincy, La., Dec. 8, 1925; s. William Thomas and Madonna Mozelle (Hunt) W.; B.S., U.S. Mil. Acad., 1946; M.S. in Civil Engring., Tex. A. and M. U., 1952; m. Mary Elizabeth Kicklighter, Oct. 2, 1949; children—Linda Ann, William Robert, Steven Alan. Commd. 2d lt. U.S. Army, 1946, advanced through grades to maj. gen., 1975; service in PTO, France, Korea, C.Z. and Vietnam; dep. dir. systems directorate, asst. chief staff force devel. Hdqrs. U.S. Army, 1970-72; dep. dir. mil. constrn. Office Chief Engrs., 1973-74; dir. facilities engring. Hdqrs. U.S. Army, 1974-75, asst. chief engrs., 1975-78, dir. mil. programs Office Chief Engrs., 1978—. Decorated Legion of Merit with 2 oak leaf clusters, Bronze Star with oak leaf cluster, Meritorious Service medal, Air medal with oak leaf cluster, Joint Service Commendation medal, Army Commendation medal with oak leaf cluster; Cross Gallantry with silver star, Armed Forces Honor medal 1st class (Vietnam). Mem. Soc. Am. Mil. Engrs. (past post pres.), Am. Pub. Works Assn., Nat. Soc. Profl. Engrs. Methodist. Club: Army-Navy Country (Arlington, Va.). Author articles. Home: 4226 Sleepy Hollow Rd Annandale VA 22003 Office: DAEN-MP Office Chief Engineers Washington DC 20310

WREFORD, DAVID MATHEWS, magazine editor; b. Perth, Australia, Dec. 17, 1943; s. Peter Mathews and Mary Lichfield (Edquist) W.; immigrated to Can., 1966; B.Sc. in Agr. with honours, U. Western Australia, 1966; m. Donna Diane Campbell, Sept. 28, 1970; 1 dau., Elizabeth Mary. Field editor Southam Bus. Publns. Ltd., Winnipeg, Man., Can., 1967-73; field editor Country Guide, Public Press Ltd., Milton, Ont., 1973-75, editor, Winnipeg, 1975—. Mem. Man. Inst. Agrologists, Agrl. Inst. Can., Canadian Fedn. Farm Writers and Broadcasters. Mem. Ch. of Eng. Home: 416 Waverley St Winnipeg MB R3M 3L4 Canada Office: 1760 Ellice Ave Winnipeg MB R3H 0B6 Canada

WREN, CHRISTOPHER SALE, journalist; b. Los Angeles, Feb. 22, 1936; s. Samuel McIndoe and Virginia (Sale) W.; B.A. magna cum laude, Dartmouth, 1957; Rotary Found. fellow, U. Edinburgh, Scotland, 1957-58; M.S., Columbia, 1961; Profl. Journalism fellow, Stanford, 1967-68; m. Jaqueline Marshall Braxton, Nov. 28, 1964; children—Celia Marshall, Christopher Braxton. With Look mag., 1961-71, sr. editor, 1964-70, Washington editor, 1970-71; gen. editor Newsweek mag., 1971-72; fgn. corr., chief Moscow bur. New York Times, 1973-77, chief Cairo bur, 1977—. Served with U.S. Army, 1958-60. Recipient Overseas Press Club award, 1969, Overseas Press Club citation for excellence, 1970, 74. Mem. Phi Beta Kappa, Sigma Delta Chi. Club: American Alpine. Author: (with Jack Shepherd) Quotations From Chairman LBJ, 1968, Almanack of Poor Richard Nixon, 1968; the Super Summer of Jamie McBride, 1971; Winners Got Scars Too: the Life and Legends of Johnny Cash, 1972. Contbr. articles to mags. Home: PO Box 516 Cairo Egypt Office: Fgn Desk New York Times 229 W 43d St New York NY 10036

WREN, MELVIN CLARENCE, historian, educator; b. Iowa City, June 18, 1910; s. Clarence Walter and Dorothy Elizabeth (Kahler) W.; B.A., State U. Iowa, 1936, M.A., 1938, Ph.D., 1939; postgrad. U. Calif. at Berkeley, 1946; m. Ester Gwendolyn Schlunz, Nov. 28, 1936; children—David Christopher, Nancy Priscilla (dec.). Mem. faculty U. Mont., 1940-41, 42-67, prof. history, 1952-67, chmn. dept., 1958-67; prof. history, 1967-78, emeritus, 1978—, chmn. dept. U. Toledo 1967-69; instr. Am. U., 1941-42; research in English archives, 1947-48, 54, 59, 70; vis. prof. U. Wash., 1958, U. Nebr., 1970; lectr. U. Md., 1962-63. Fellow Am. Council Learned Socs., mem. Am. Hist. Assn., Am. Polit. Sci. Assn., Dobro Slovo, Order Artus, Phi Kappa Phi, Phi Alpha Theta, Pi Gamma Mu. Author: The Course of Russian History, 1958, 4th edit., 1979; Ancient Russia, 1965; The Western Impact Upon Tsarist Russia, 1971; also articles. Home: 2201 Grand Ave No 2 Everett WA 98201

WREN, PAUL INGRAHAM, cons.; b. Boston, Nov. 7, 1906; s. Frank and Mary (Ingraham) W.; A.B., Tufts, 1926, A.M., 1928; grad. Grad. Sch. Banking, Rutgers U., 1944; m. Alice Wingate Trumbull, June 10, 1930; children—Mary E. (Mrs. Raymond L. Swain, Jr.), Paul Ingraham, Frances (Mrs. Robert M. Raymond). Fletcher teaching fellow, dept. econs. and sociology Tufts Coll., 1926-28; with First Nat. Bank of Boston, 1928-57, 58-71, investment officer, 1944, trust investment officer, 1950-57, v.p., 1958-65, sr. v.p., 1965-70, chmn. trust com., 1970-71, hon. dir., 1971-77; with Old Colony Trust Co., 1928-70, asst. v.p., 1943-46, v.p., 1946-58, exec. v.p., 1959-64, pres., 1964-68, chmn. bd., 1968-70; dir. Montagu Boston Investment Trust, Bank of Boston (Bahamas) Trust Co.; mem. investments faculty Grad Sch. Banking, Rutgers, 1947-56, chmn., 1952-55; corporator Somerset Savs. Bank, Somerville, Mass., 1952-57, 58-73, Boston 5 Cent Savs. Bank, 1954-57, 58—; asst. to sec. of treasury, 1957-58; mem. advisory com. Colonial Fund, Colonial Income Fund, Colonial Convertible Fund, 1971-78. Mem. bd. mgrs. Trustees of Donations to P.E. Ch., 1952-57, 58—, pres., 1968-79, treas. Diocese of Mass., 1970-73, 78—; mem. fin. com. House of Good Samaritan, 1958-64. Mem. corp. Bouve-Boston Sch. Phys. Edn., 1952-57, 58-63, v.p., 1954-56; trustee, treas. Franklin Sq. Ho., 1940-57, 58-76; alumni trustee Tufts Coll., 1945-55, life trustee, 1955—; trustee Mt. Holyoke Coll., 1955-65. Mem. Am. Bankers Assn. (chmn. borrowing com. 1970-71, pres. trust div. 1965-66, treas. assn. 1967-69), Boston Security Analysts Soc., Phi Beta Kappa, Delta Tau Delta. Home: 65 Talbot Ave Tufts University MA 02155 Office: Tufts U Medford MA 02155

WREN, WILLIAM JAMES, corp. exec.; b. Augusta, Ga., Apr. 22, 1926; s. William James and Corrie K. W.; B.E.E., Ga. Inst. Tech., 1946; m. Nancy Austin, Sept. 1946; children—Nancy, Teresa, Janice Shirley. With Carrier Corp., Syracuse, N.Y., 1956—, now corporate v.p., pres. machinery and systems div. Served with USNR, 1944-46. Home: 3955 Willowbrook Ln Liverpool NY 13088 Office: Carrier Pkwy Syracuse NY 13201

WRENN, C. GILBERT, educator; b. New Paris, Ohio, Apr. 2, 1902; s. Charles C. and Flora (Parker) W.; student Tenn. Wesleyan Coll., 1921-23; A.B., Willamette U., 1926 Litt.D. (hon.), 1952; M.A., Stanford U., 1929, Ph.D., 1932; m. Kathleen LaRaut, June 15, 1926; 1 son, Robert. Vocat. counselor Stanford U., 1929-36, asst. prof., 1932-36; asst. dean of gen. coll. and asst. dir. instl. research U. Minn., 1936-38, prof. ednl. psychology, 1937-64; prof. ednl. psychology Ariz. State U., 1964-68, vis. prof., 1968-72, emeritus, 1972—; Barclay Acheson prof. Macalester Coll., 1968-71; vis. prof. summer sch. U. Oreg., 1929, 31, Stanford, 1938, 64, 67, Colo. State U., 1939, U. Chgo., 1940, U. Colo., 1941, 49, 56, 62, U. So. Calif., 1947, U. Hawaii, 1948, 58, 63, 65, 69, 71, U. Denver, 1950, San Diego State, 1951, U. B.C., 1952, Chico State Coll., 1954, U. Nev., 1955, 71, Mich. State U., 1959, N.D. State U., 1960, Ministry of Edn., Taiwan, 1965, U. Maine, 1966, 68, 78, San Francisco State Coll., 1967, U. Natal, Durbin, South Africa, 1972, Simon Bolivar U., Caracas, Venezuela, 1974, others. Mem. staff Am. Youth Commn., 1939-40; cons. student personnel Am. Council Edn., 1940-42, 47-49; mem. Edward Glaser & Assos., psychol. cons., 1952—; chmn. panel counseling and testing Nat. Manpower Advisory Com., Dept. Labor, 1963-67. Trustee Am. Bd. Exam. Profl. Psychology, 1951-57; Minn. Bd. Examiners in Psychology, 1951-55. Trustee Macalester Coll., 1961-71. Mem. advisory bd. Air Tng. Command USAF, 1953-56. Served to lt. comdr. USNR, 1942-45. Decorated Bronze Star; recipient Distinguished Service award Dept. of Labor, 1967; Distinguished Achievement award Ariz. State U., 1976; Fulbright distinguished scholar, England, 1965-66. Fellow Am. Psychol. Assn. (diplomate in counseling psychology, pres. div. counseling psychology 1950-51, council reps. 1955-58, 60-63); mem. Am. Coll. Personnel Assn. (past pres., Contbn. to Knowledge award 1977), Nat. Vocat. Guidance Assn. (past pres., trustee; Eminent career award 1975), Am. Personnel Guidance Assn. (Nancy Wimmer award 1964). Methodist (bd. missions 1960-64). Author and co-author 400 books and articles, chpts., monographs including: Student Personnel Work in Colleges, 1951; How to Develop Self Confidence, 1953; Learning to Study, 1960; The Counselor in a Changing World, 1962; The World of the Contemporary Counselor, 1973; 23 vols. in Coping With series, 1970-73. Editor: Jour. Counseling Psychology, 1952-63; editorial adv. com. Houghton Mifflin Co., 1961-71. Home: 2967 Country Club Way Tempe AZ 85282

WRIGGINS, WILLIAM HOWARD, ambassador, educator; b. Phila., Feb. 14, 1918; s. Charles Cornelius and Evelyn (Walker) W.; B.A. cum laude, Dartmouth, 1940; certificate Ecole Libres des Sciences Politiques, Paris, France, 1939; student U. Chgo. Grad. Sch., 1940-41; M.A., Yale, 1948, Ph.D. (Sterling fellow 1951-52), 1952; m. Sarah Edith Hovey, Dec. 22, 1947; children—Diana, Charles Christopher, Jennifer. Relief adminstr. for Am. Friends Service Com., 1942-46, 48, 49; mem. staff Yale Inst. Internat. Studies, 1950-51; mem. polit. sci. dept. Vassar Coll., 1952-55, 57-58; research fellow Rockefeller Found. study of politics in Ceylon, 1955-57; chief fgn. affairs div., legis. reference service Library of Congress, 1958-61; mem. policy planning council State Dept., 1961-65; research asso. Wash. Center Fgn. Policy, SAIS, 1965-66; sr. staff mem. Nat. Security Council, 1966-67; prof. govt., dir. So. Asian Inst. Columbia U., N.Y.C. 1967-77; U.S. ambassador to Sri Lanka, Ceylon, 1977—. Rhodes fellow St. Anthony's Coll., Oxford, Eng., 1973-74. Mem. founding com. Sandy Spring (Md.) Friends Sch., 1959; bd. dirs. Am. Friends Service Com., 1958-60, Inst. Current World Affairs. Mem. Council Fgn. Relations, Am. Polit. Sci. Assn., Johns Hopkins Soc. Scholars, Assn. Asian Studies (trustee), Asia Soc. (exec. com., trustee 1972-77), Grange. Mem. Soc. of Friends. Author: Ceylon: Dilemmas of a New Nation, 1960; The Ruler's Imperative: Strategies for Political Survival in Asia and Africa, 1969 (with others) Population, Politics and the Future of Southern Asia, 1973; Third World Strategies for Change, 1978. Contbr. research publs., others. Mem. editorial bd. Worldview. Address: US Embassy 44 Galle Rd Colombo 3 PO Box 106 Colombo Sri Lanka

WRIGHT, ALFRED GEORGE JAMES, educator; b. London, Eng., June 23, 1916; s. Alfred Francis and Elizabeth (Chapman) W.; came to U.S., 1922, naturalized, 1936; B.A., U. Miami, 1937, M.Ed., 1947; Ph.D. (hon.), Troy State U., 1980; m. Bertha Marie Farmer, Aug. 6, 1938; children—Adele Marie Wright Needham, Cynthia Elaine Wright Williams; m. 2d, Gladys Violet Stone, June 28, 1953. Dir. music Miami Sr. High Sch., 1938-54; prof., head dept. bands Purdue U., Lafayette, Ind., 1954—; condr. Purdue U. Symphony Orch., 1971—; founder, condr. U.S. Coll. Wind Band Tours, 1971-79; dir. prerace pageant Indpls. 500 Mile Automobile Race, 1957—; mem. advisory council Performing Arts Abroad, 1972—; chmn. N.Am. Band Dirs. Coordinating Commn., 1974-75; chmn. Nat. High Sch. Honors Band, 1975-76, 77—; jury World Music Contest, Holland, 1974, 79. Bd. dirs. 500 Festival Assos., 1961—; pres. bd. electors Hall of Fame Disting. Band Condrs.; pres. All Am. Hall of Fame Band Found. Mem. Nat. Band Assn. (founder, pres. 1960-63), Coll. Band Dirs. Nat. Assn., Am. Sch. Band Dirs. Nat. Assn., Japan Marching Band Assn. (hon., dir. 1971—), Big Ten Band Dirs Assn (pres. 1977), Am. Bandmasters Assn. (pres. elect 1979-80), Nat. Acad. Wind and Percussive Arts (chmn. 1971—), Phi Mu Alpha, Kappa Kappa Psi, Phi Beta Mu. Author: The Show Band, 1957; Marching Band Fundamentals, 1963; Bands of the World, 1970; marching band editor Instrumentalist mag., 1953—; contbr. articles to profl. mags. Home: 344 Overlook Dr Lafayette IN 47906

WRIGHT, ALFRED JOHN, JR., educator; b., Lakewood, Ohio, Sept. 6, 1915; s. Alfred John and Anne (Muth) W.; A.B., Western Res. U., 1937, A.M., 1938; grad. student Ohio State U., 1938-39; Ph.D., Columbia, 1950; m. Sélysette Panzéra, Dec. 21, 1946; children—Christopher Alfred, Robin Michel, Anne-Magdeleine, Timothy Charles. Tchr., Los Alamos Ranch Sch., 1940-42, Trinity-Pawling Sch., 1947-48; mem. faculty Trinity Coll., Hartford, Conn., 1949-56; mem. faculty Bates Coll., 1956—, prof. French, 1959—, chmn. fgn. lang. div., 1958—, acting chmn. humanities div., 1970-71. Served with AUS, 1942-45; ETO. Mem. Modern Lang. Assn., Am. Assn. Tchrs. French (pres. Conn. chpt. 1953-55), AAUP, Phi Beta Kappa (sec.-treas. Bates chpt. 1961-71), Phi Sigma Iota. Author articles. Home: 10 White St Lewiston ME 04240

WRIGHT, ANDREW, educator; b. Columbus, Ohio, June 28, 1923; s. Francis Joseph and Katharine (Timberman) W.; A.B., Harvard, 1947; M.A., Ohio State U., 1948, Ph.D., 1951; m. Virginia Rosemary Banks, June 27, 1952; children—Matthew Leslie Francis, Emma Stanbery. From instr. to asso. prof. Ohio State U., Columbus, 1952-63; prof. English lit. U. Calif. at San Diego, 1963—, chmn. dept. lit., 1971-74. Vis. lectr. U. Birmingham (Eng.), 1960, 70, U. Milan (Italy), 1961, U. Wash., Seattle, 1970. Trustee La Jolla (Calif.) Library Assn. Served with AUS, 1943-46. Guggenheim fellow, 1960, 70; Fulbright Sr. Research fellow, 1960-61; Am. Council Learned Socs. grantee, 1960-61; Am. Philos. Soc. grantee, 1956, 58. Fellow Royal Soc. Lit.; mem. Jane Austen Soc., London Library, Modern Humanities Research Assn., Modern Lang. Assn., P.E.N. Author: Jane Austen's Novels: A Study In Structure, 1953; Joyce Cary: A Preface to His Novels, 1958; Henry Fielding: Mask and Feast, 1965; Blake's Job: A Commentary, 1972. Contbg. author numerous books, articles to profl. jours. Home: 7227 Olivetas Ave La Jolla CA 92037 Office: Dept Lit U Calif at San Diego La Jolla CA 92093

WRIGHT, ARTHUR MCINTOSH, indsl. products co. exec.; b. El Dorado, Kans., Dec. 9, 1930; s. Ray Arthur and Anna (McIntosh) W.; A.B., Grinnell Coll., 1952; LL.B., Harvard, 1958; m. Mary Alice Smaltz, June 23, 1956; children—David A., Steven E., Carolyn E. Admitted to Mo. bar, 1959, Ill. bar, 1964; asso. atty. firm Swanson, Midgley, Jones, Blackmar & Eager, Kansas City, Mo., 1958-64; corp. atty. Baxter Labs., Inc., Morton Grove, Ill., 1964-67; v.p., sec., counsel North Am. Car Corp., Chgo., 1968-71; sec., corp. counsel Ceco Corp., Chgo., 1971-77; v.p., gen. counsel Ill. Tool Works, Inc., Chgo., 1977—, sec., 1979—. Mem. New Trier Twp. High Schs. Bd. Edn. Served with U.S. Army, 1953-55. Mem. Chgo., Ill., Am. bar assns., Am. Judicature Soc., Am. Soc. Corp. Secs., Sigma Delta Chi. Presbyterian. Home: 824 Boal Pkwy Winnetka IL 60093

WRIGHT, BENJAMIN TAPPAN, lawyer; b. Berkeley, Calif., Aug. 24, 1922; s. Austin Tappan and Margaret (Stone) W.; B.S., Harvard U., 1943; J.D., Boston U., 1950; m. Mary Louise Premer, Mar. 13, 1953. Admitted to Mass. bar, 1952, Fed. bar, 1953; sr. v.p., sec., gen. counsel The Badger Co., Inc., Cambridge, Mass., 1950—; trustee Cambridge Savs. Bank, 1974—. Pres., U.S. Figure Skating Assn., 1973-75; mem. tech. com. Internat. Skating Union, 1973—. Served to 1st lt. AUS, 1943-46; lt. col. Res., ret. Mem. Am., Mass., Boston bar assns., Soc. Colonial Wars, S.R. (sec. 1977—), Soc. Mayflower Descs., Order Founders and Patriots, N.E. Historic Geneal. Soc. Clubs: Winchester Country (dir. 1971-74), Harvard, Masons, Cambridge Rotary (dir. 1977-80), Skating (gov. 1962-65) (Boston). Home: 65 Foster Rd Belmont MA 02178 Office: 1 Broadway Cambridge MA 02142

WRIGHT, BYRON T., educator, physicist; b. Waco, Tex., Oct. 19, 1917; s. Wilbur and Dora (Thompson) W.; B.A., Rice U., 1938; Ph.D., U. Calif. at Berkeley, 1941; m. Lorna Doone Bloemers, Oct. 21, 1944 (dec. 1964); children—Carol Ann, Susan Lee, Gail Elizabeth. Physicist, Naval Electronics Lab., 1941-42, Manhattan Project, 1942-46; mem. faculty U. Calif. at Los Angeles, 1946—, prof. physics, 1956—, asso. dean grad. div., 1972—. Ford Found. vis. scientist CERN, 1963-64. Fulbright research scholar, 1956-57; Guggenheim fellow, 1963-64. Fellow Am. Phys. Soc. Spl. research accelerator devel., nuclear structure physics. Home: 1225 Chickory Ln Los Angeles CA 90049

WRIGHT, C(HARLES) CONRAD, educator; b. Cambridge, Mass., Feb. 9, 1917; s. Charles Henry Conrad and Elizabeth Longfellow (Woodman) W.; A.B., Harvard U., 1937, A.M., 1942, Ph.D., 1946; L.H.D., Meadville Theol. Sch., 1968; m. Elizabeth JaneHilgendorff, Sept. 4, 1948; children—Conrad E., Nielson, Elizabeth L. Lectr. on ch. history, Harvard Div. Sch., 1954-69, prof. Am. ch. history, 1969—, registrar, 1955-68; pres. Unitarian Hist. Soc., 1962-78. Dudleian lectr. Harvard U., 1960, John Bartlett lectr. on New England ch. history, 1969; Am. Council Learned Socs. fellow, 1968. Mem. Am. Hist. Assn., Am. Soc. Ch. History (council 1978—), Orgn. Am. Historians, Cambridge Hist. Soc., Unitarian Universalist Hist. Soc. (dir. 1978—). Author: The Beginnings of Unitarianism in America, 1955 (Carnegie award); The Liberal Christians, 1970. Editor: Religion in American Life, 1972; A Stream of Light, 1975. Home: 983 Memorial Dr Apt 102 Cambridge MA 02138

WRIGHT, CALEB MERRILL, U.S. dist. judge; b. 1908; s. William Elwood and Mary Ann (Lynch) W.; B.A., Del. U.; LL.B., Yale, 1933; m. Katherine McAfee, Nov. 29, 1937; children—Thomas Merrill, William Elwood, Scott McAfee, Victoria. Admitted to Del. bar, 1933; practice in Georgetown, 1933-55; U.S. dist. judge Del. Dist., 1955-59, chief judge, 1957-73, sr. judge, 1973—. Mem. Del., Sussex County bar assns., Am. Judicature Soc., Am. Law Inst., Kappa Alpha. Republican. Club: Wilmington. Home: 2401 W 17th St Wilmington DE 19806 Office: Federal Bldg Wilmington DE 19801

WRIGHT, CARROLL, realtor; b. Wichita, Kans., Oct. 25, 1903; s. William Wallace and Sallie (Mattison) W.; student George Washington U., 1922; m. Alice Elizabeth Barron, Jan. 1, 1925; children—Edward Barron, Robert Mattison, Carroll. Appraiser mortgage loan dept. Weaver Bros., Inc., Washington, 1926-34, v.p., Balt., 1937-40; regional appraiser, dep. chief appraiser Home Owners Loan Corp., Washington, 1934-37; pres. Wright Realty Inc., Arlington, Va., 1946-61; realtor, appraiser, real estate cons., Charlottesville, Va., 1961—; chmn. Charlottesville regional bd. Suburban Savs. & Loan Assn. Chmn., Arlington County Planning Commn., 1947-53. Served to lt. col. U.S. Army, 1940-46; col. Res. (ret.). Decorated Bronze Star. Mem. Am. Inst. Real Estate Appraisers, No. Va., (pres. 1951), Charlottesville-Albemarle (pres. 1964) bds. realtors, Va. Assn. Realtors (pres. 1954), S.A.R. (pres. Va. soc. 1966-67, nat. trustee 1967-68, v.p. gen. 1975-77), Huguenot Soc. (pres. Va. chpt. 1967-68, gen. v.p. 1975-77), Jamestowne Soc. (atty. gen.), Baronial Order Magna Charta, Founders and Patriots (founding gov. Va. Soc. 1974-75), Va. Geneal. Soc. (v.p. 1967-68), Ams. Royal Descent (custodian gen.), Omega Tau Rho. Episcopalian. Clubs: Charlottesville Rotary, Farmington (Va.) Country, Redland, Masons, Shriners. Home: Locust Shade Route 7 Charlottesville VA 22901

WRIGHT, CATHARINE MORRIS (Mrs. Sydney Longstreth Wright), nat. academician; b. Phila., Jan. 26, 1899; d. Harrison Smith and Anna (Wharton) Morris; ed. pvt. schs., Phila. Sch. of Design for Women, 1916-18; A.F.D. (hon.), Moore Inst., Phila., 1959; m. Sydney Longstreth Wright, Feb. 28, 1925; children—Anna Templeton-Cotill, William Redwood, Harrison Morris, Ellicott. Began career as artist, 1918; represented in Pa. Acad. Fine Arts, Allentown Mus., Moore Inst., U. Pa., Pa. State Coll., Woodmere Gallery, Phila. Mus., Asso. Nat. Acad., 1933; founder Fox Hill Sch. Art, Jamestown, R.I., 1950. Hon. mention Phila. Art Club. 1924, Gimbel prize, 1932, Mary Smith prize Pa. Acad. Fine Arts, 1933, 2d Hallgarten prize Nat. Acad. Design, 1933, Greenough Meml. prize Newport Art Assn., 1933, Germantown Art League prize, 1936, hon. mention Phila. Sketch Club, 1940, Woodmere Gallery, 1941, Allied Artists of Am. prize, 1941, Silvermine Marine prize Guild of Artists, 1955. Mem. Am. Water Color Soc., Audubon Artists, Newport Art Assn., Keats-Shelley Assn. Am. (v.p. 1952-78), Phila. Water Color Club (v.p. 1949-57), Allied Artists Am., Authors League Am., Poetry Soc. Am., Va. Poetry Soc. Author: The Simple Nun (verse), 1929, Princess Anne Prize (verse), 1945, Seaweed Their Pasture, 1946, The Color of Life, 1957, Lady of the Silver Skates, 1979. Home: Fox Hill Farm Jamestown RI 02835

WRIGHT, CELESTE TURNER, poet, educator; b. St. John, N.B., Can., Mar. 17, 1906 (parents U.S. citizens); d. George Howard and Viola (Kelley) Turner; B.A., U. Calif. at Los Angeles, 1925, M.A., at Berkeley, 1926, Ph.D., 1928; m. Vedder Allen Wright, June 26, 1933; 1 son, Vedder Allen. Faculty, U. Calif. at Davis, 1928—, prof. English, 1948-73, prof. emeritus, 1973—, chmn. dept., 1928-55, faculty research lectr., 1963. Recipient Reynolds Lyric prize, 1963; Silver medal for poems Commonwealth Club, 1973; U. Calif. Inst. for Creative Arts fellow, 1966-67. Mem. Modern Lang. Assn., Renaissance Soc. Am., Philol. Assn. Pacific Coast, Acad. Am. Poets (asso.), Poetry Soc. Am., Phi Beta Kappa, Delta Phi Alpha. Episcopalian. Clubs: Faculty (Davis); Commonwealth Calif. Author: Anthony Mundy: An Elizabethan Man of Letters, 1928; Etruscan Princess and Other Poems, 1964; (poems) A Sense of Place, 1973; (poems) Seasoned Timber, 1977; also articles on Renaissance and contemporary literature. Home: 1001 D St Davis CA 95616. *For me this formula has worked: Choose projects you really care about. Work at them as your time permits. Revise, revise, and revise your writing. Try every respectable market. Eventually recognition will come.*

WRIGHT, CHARLES ALAN, educator, author; b. Phila., Sept. 3, 1927; s. Charles Adshead and Helen (McCormack) W.; A.B., Wesleyan U., Middletown, Conn. 1947; LL.B., Yale, 1949; m. Mary Joan Herriott, July 8, 1950 (div. Jan. 1955); children—Charles Edward; m. 2d, Eleanor Custis Broyles Clarke, Dec. 17, 1955; children—Henrietta, Cecily; stepchildren—Eleanor Custis Clarke, Margot Clarke. Admitted to Minn. bar, 1951, Tex. bar, 1959; law clk. U.S. Circuit Judge Clark, New Haven, 1949-50; asst. prof. law U. Minn., 1950- 53, asso. prof., 1953-55; asso. prof. law U. Tex., Austin, 1955-58, prof., 1958-65, McCormick prof., 1965—. Vis. prof. U. Pa., Phila., 1959-60, Harvard, 1964-65, Yale, 1968-69; reporter study div. of jurisdiction between state and fed. cts. Am. Law Inst., 1963-69; mem. adv. com. on civil rules Jud. Conf. U.S., 1961-64, mem. standing com. on rules of practice and proc., 1964-76; cons., counsel for Pres., 1973-74; mem. com. on infractions NCAA, 1973—, chmn., 1978—; mem. permanent com. for Oliver Wendall Holmes Devise, 1975—. Trustee St. Stephen's Episcopal Sch., Austin, Tex., 1962-66; trustee St. Andrew's Episcopal Sch., Austin, 1971-74, 77-80, chmn. bd., 1973-74, 79-80; trustee Capitol Broadcasting Assn., Austin, 1966—, chmn. bd., 1969—; trustee Austin Symphony Orch. Soc., 1966—, mem. exec. com., 1966-70, 72—. Mem. Am. Law Inst. (mem. council 1969—), Am. Bar Assn. (mem. commn. on standards jud. adminstrn. 1970-77), Inst. Jud. Adminstrn., Am. Judicature Soc., Order of Coif, Phi Kappa Phi, Omicron Delta Kappa. Republican. Episcopalian (sr. warden). Clubs: Country, Tarry House, Headliners (Austin); Century, Yale (N.Y.C.). Author: Wright's Minnesota Rules, 1954; Cases on Remedies, 1955; (with C.T. McCormick and J.H. Chadbourn) Cases on Federal Courts, 6th edit., 1976; Handbook of the Law of Federal Courts, 3d edit., 1976; (with H.M. Reasoner) Procedure-The Handmaid of Justice, 1965; Federal Practice and Procedure; Criminal, 1969; (with A.R. Miller) Federal Practice and Procedure: Civil, 1969-73; (with A.R. Miller and E.H. Cooper) Federal Practice and Procedure: Jurisdiction and Related Matters, 1975—; (with K.W. Graham) Federal Practice and Procedure: Evidence, 1977—. Home: 5304 Western Hills Dr Austin TX 78731

WRIGHT, CHARLES EDWARD, lawyer; b. Portland, Oreg., Mar. 21, 1906; s. Archibald Robert and Grace May (Springer) W.; A.B., Yale U., 1929, LL.B., 1932; m. Elisabeth Knowlton Strong, Oct. 28, 1937; children—Frederick Pares, Hilda (Mrs. Stanley Rhodes), Elisabeth. Admitted to Oreg. bar, 1933; asso. firm Platt, Platt, Fales, Smith & Black, Portland, 1933-37; sr. atty. Seattle regional office SEC, 1937-43; practice in Portland, 1943—; partner firm Bullivant, Wright, Johnson, Pendergrass and Hoffman, 1947—. Bd. dirs. Portland Jr. Symphony; trustee, v.p. Catlin Hillside Schs. Mem. Am., Oreg. bar assns., Am. Judicature Soc., Travelers Aid Soc. (dir. 1946), Portland Art Assn. (past dir.), Oreg. Yale Alumni Assn. (pres. 1961). Clubs: City (past dir.), Multnomah Amateur Athletic, Univ. (Portland). Home: 7226 NW Penridge Rd Portland OR 97229 Office: 1000 Willamette Center 121 SW Salmon St Portland OR 97204

WRIGHT, CHARLES PENZEL, JR., poet; b. Pickwick Dam, Tenn., Aug. 25, 1935; s. Charles Penzel and Mary Castleman (Winter) W.; B.A., Davidson (N.C.) Coll., 1957; M.F.A., U. Iowa, 1963; postgrad. U. Rome, 1963-64; m. Holly McIntire, Apr. 6, 1969; 1 son, Luke Savin Herrick. Mem. faculty U. Calif., Irvine, 1966—, prof. English, 1976—; Fulbright vis. prof. N.Am. lit. U. Padua (Italy), 1968-69; author: The Dream Animal, 1968; The Grave of the Right Hand, 1970; The Venice Notebook, 1971; Hard Freight, 1973; Bloodlines, 1975; Colophons, 1977; China Trace, 1977; Wright: A Profile, 1979; (transl.) The Storm and Other Poems by Eugenio Montale, 1978. Served with AUS, 1957-61. Fulbright scholar, 1963-65; Guggenheim fellow, 1976; recipient Edgar Allan Poe award Acad. Am. Poets, 1976; Acad.-Inst. award Am. Acad. and Inst. Arts and Letters, 1977; PEN transl. prize, 1979. Home: 1771 Thurston Dr Laguna Beach CA 92651 Office: English Dept Univ Calif Irvine CA 92717

WRIGHT, CHARLES THOMAS, state justice; b. Shelton, Wash., Mar. 7, 1911; s. D.F. and Fanna Bell (Streator) W.; . A.B., Coll. Puget Sound, 1932; student U. Wash., 1932-34, grad. courses LaSalle Extension U., 1935-36; m. Helen J. Fisk, Apr. 10, 1947. Admitted to Wash. bar, 1937; practice in Shelton and Union, 1937-49; judge Superior Ct., Olympia, 1949-71; justice Supreme Ct. Wash., Olympia, 1971—, acting chief justice, 1975-77, chief justice, 1977—; acting pros. atty. Mason County, 1942-44. Episcopalian. Editor: Wash. Ct. Commentaries, 1965-70. Home: Union WA 98592 Office: Temple of Justice Olympia WA 98504*

WRIGHT, CHERYL FRANCES, fed. govt. ofcl.; b. Washington, Dec. 17, 1949; d. Walter William and Isabelle Adelaide (Chichester) W.; B.A. (Ford scholar), Hampton (Va.) Inst., 1971; M.P.A. (Noyes fellow), U. Pitts., 1972. With HUD, Washington, 1972—, community planning and devel. specialist Office Field Ops. and Monitoring, Office Community Planning and Devel., Washington, 1974-77, (acting) asst. devel. dir. Office Urban Devel. Action Grants, Washington 1977-78, spl. asst. to under sec., 1978, spl. asst. to sec./under sec., 1978—, mem. exec. resources bd., 1979—. Recipient cert. spl. achievement HUD, 1976, 79, Woman of Year award nominee, 1976; named An Outstanding Young Woman Am., 1977. Mem. Nat. Council Negro Women, Am. Soc. Public Adminstrs., Conf. Minority Public Adminstrs., Alpha Kappa Alpha (grad. advisor Xi Omega chpt. 1976-78). Congregationalist. Office: Office of Sec HUD 451 7th St SW Washington DC 20410

WRIGHT, CHRISTOPHER, sci. policy and environ. scientist; b. Chgo., Oct. 31, 1926; s. Quincy and Louise Maxey (Leonard) W.; student U. Chgo., 1944; A.B magna cum laude, Harvard Coll., 1949; Fulbright grantee, Oxford (Eng.) U., 1949-51; A.M., Harvard U., 1974; m. Anne Carolyn McCoy, Sept. 15, 1956; children—Malcolm Morehead, Diana Sewall. Exptl. physicist Manhattan Project, Los Alamos, 1944-46; instr. philosophy Williams Coll., 1954; research asso. U. Chgo. Law Sch., 1956-58; exec. dir. Council for Atomic Age Studies, Columbia U., 1958-66, dir. Inst. for Study of Sci. in Human Affairs, 1966-72; staff natural and environ. scis. div. Rockefeller Found., N.Y.C., 1972-75; profl. staff for research and devel. policies and priorities Office Tech. Assessments, U.S. Congress, 1976-79; mem. staff for sci. policy and instn. devel. Carnegie Instn., Washington, 1979—. Mem. Commn. to Study Orgn. of Peace, 1971—, Commn. on Year 2000, Am. Acad. Arts and Scis., 1967-72; cons. Brookings Instn., 1960, Carnegie Endowment for Internat. Peace, 1961-63, Fgn. Service Inst., Dept. State, 1964-65, Holden Arboretum, 1970-72, Josiah Macy, Jr. Found., 1975. Served with AUS, 1945-46. Resident scholar Villa Serbelloni, Rockefeller Found., 1966, 69. Fellow AAAS; mem. Am. Soc. Internat. Law. Author: The

Prospective Role of an Arboretum, 1972. Author, editor: Scientists and National Policy Making, 1964; Science Policies of Industrial Nations, 1975. Contbr. articles to profl. jours. Home: 2122 Decatur Pl NW Washington DC 20008 Office: 1630 P St NW Washington DC 20005

WRIGHT, DONALD EUGENE, librarian; b. Boulder, Colo., July 25, 1930; s. Kelley E. and Iva Bell (Winkle) W.; A.B., U. Colo., 1952; A.M., U. Denver, 1953; m. Verna Venetta Vorpahl, June 18, 1953; children—Sara, Amy, John Kelley. Library asst. U. Colo., 1948-52, Denver Pub. Library, 1952; reference asst. Ft. Wayne (Ind.) Pub. Library, 1953, Detroit Pub. Library, 1953-56; dir. N. Platte (Nebr.) Pub. Library, 1956-58; library cons. Nebr. Pub. Library Commn., 1958-60; asst. dir. Lincoln (Nebr.) City Libraries, 1960-61; dir. project to aid small pub. libraries ALA, 1961-63, exec. sec. reference services div., 1963-64, exec. sec. trustee assn., 1963-64; chief bur. library services Conn. Dept. Edn., 1964-65; asso. state librarian, also chief library devel. Ill. State Library, Springfield, 1965-67; librarian Evanston (Ill.) Pub. Library, 1967—. Chmn. Gov. Nebr. Conf. Library Trustees, 1958; co-chmn. Ill. White House Conf. on Library and Info. Service, 1977-78. Vice-pres., United Community Services of Evanston. Mem. Nebr. (bd. dirs. 1958-61, pres. elect 1961), Am. (life, pres. library adminstrn. div. 1978-79), Ill. (pres. 1972) library assns. Presbyterian. Rotarian. Club: Caxton (council 1977-78). Contbr. profl. jours. Home: 1715 Chancellor St Evanston IL 60201 Office: 1703 Orrington Ave Evanston IL 60201

WRIGHT, DONALD FRANKLIN, newspaper exec.; b. St. Paul, July 10, 1934; s. Floyd Franklin and Helen Marie (Hansen) W.; B.M.E., U. Minn., 1957, M.B.A., 1958; m. Sharon Kathleen Fisher, Dec. 30, 1960; children—John, Dana, Kara, Patrick. With Mpls. Star & Tribune Co., 1958-77, research planning dir., then ops. dir., 1971-75, exec. editor, 1975-77; exec. v.p., gen. mgr. Newsday, Inc., Garden City, N.Y., 1977-78, pres., chief operating officer, 1978—. City councilman, Mahtomedi, Minn., 1967-69, 71; chmn. Citizens Com. Sch. Dist. 832, Mahtomedi, 1970; mem. Citizens League. Mem. Am. Soc. Newspaper Editors, Am. Newspaper Pubs. Assn. (chmn. prodn. mgmt. com. 1975-77, vice chmn. telecommunications com.), Nat. Soc. Profl. Engrs., ASME. Methodist. Clubs: Mpls., U. Minn. Alumni; Huntington Country. Home: 19 Saint Marks Pl Huntington NY 11743 Office: Newsday Long Island NY 11747

WRIGHT, DONALD RICHARD, ret. chief justice Calif. Supreme Ct.; b. Orange County, Calif., Feb. 2, 1907; s. David L. and Lillie (Andrew) W.; A.B. cum laude, Stanford U., 1929; LL.B., Harvard, 1932; grad. Command and Gen. Staff Coll.; LL.D., U. Pacific, 1971; LL.M., U. So. Calif., 1973; m. Margaret McLellan. Admitted to Calif. bar, 1932; pvt. practice, Pasadena, Calif., 1932-53; judge Pasadena Municipal Ct., 1953-60, Los Angeles County Superior Ct., 1960-68, 2d Dist., Ct. Appeals, Los Angeles, 1968-70; chief justice Calif. Supreme Ct., 1970-77. Charter incorporator Pasadena Legal Aid Soc., 1949; chmn. Calif. Water Rights Commn., 1977—. Pres. bd. dirs. Hastings Sch. Law, U. Calif., San Francisco; bd. visitors Stanford Law Sch.; bd. dirs. Ralph M. Parsons Found.; bd. councilors U. So. Calif. Law Center; trustee Pathfinder Mines Corp. Served to lt. col. USAAF, World War II. Mem. Order of Coif. Home: 565 Orange Grove Circle Pasadena CA 91105

WRIGHT, DOUGLAS CHANDLER, JR., paper co. exec.; b. Montclair, N.J., Dec. 13, 1934; s. Douglas Chandler and Helen G. (Henning) W.; B.A., Yale U., 1957; M.B.A., Harvard U., 1965; m. Sarah Lee Roman, Dec. 30, 1961; children—Douglas Chandler, Gregory Rawson. Systems analyst N.J. Bell Telephone Co., 1957-59, McGraw-Hill Pub. Co., N.Y.C., 1959-60; mgr. systems Ednl. Testing Service, Princeton, N.J., 1960-63; v.p., treas. Hammermill Paper Co., Erie, Pa., 1965—; adv. bd. Arkwright Boston Ins. Co.; dir. Union Bank & Trust Co. Chmn. fin. com. Erie United Way; bd. corporators Hamot Hosp.; past bd. dirs. Erie Philharmonic; trustee YMCA; bd. dirs., mem. exec. com. United Way. Mem. Fin. Execs. Inst., Am. Paper Inst., Newcomen Soc. Clubs: Erie, Kahkwa. Home: 6400 Lake Shore Dr Erie PA 16505 Office: Hammermill Paper Co Erie PA 16533

WRIGHT, DOUGLASS BROWNELL, judge; b. Hartford, Conn., May 30, 1912; s. Arthur Brownell and Sylvia (Stephens) W.; grad. Loomis Sch., 1929; A.B., Yale, 1933; LL.B., Hartford Coll. Law, 1937; m. Jane Hamersley, Sept. 24, 1938; children—Jane C., Douglass B., Hamersley S., Elizabeth B., Arthur W. Admitted to Conn. bar, 1937; legal dept. Aetna Life Ins. Co., 1937-39; partner Davis, Lee, Howard & Wright, Hartford, 1939—; lectr. law U. Conn., 1946—; asst. state's atty. State of Conn., 1952-59; judge Conn. Circuit Court, 1959-65; judge Conn. Superior Ct., 1965—. Sec., dir. Captioned Films for the Deaf, Inc.; bd. dirs., pres. Am. Sch. for Deaf, 1942—; trustee Hartt Mus. Found., 1949—, Good Will Boys Club Hartford, 1950—; regent U. Hartford; bd. dirs. Vis. Nurse Assn., Newington Home for Crippled Children, Hartford Times Farm, Loomis Sch.; incorporator Conn. Inst. for Blind. Served as lt., USNR, 1942-45. Mem. Phi Beta Kappa, Psi Upsilon. Conglist. Clubs: University, Hartford Golf, Hartford Tennis, 20th Century (Hartford); Coral Beach and Tennis (Bermuda). Author: Connecticut Law of Torts, 1956; Connecticut Legal Forms, 4 vols., 1958; Connecticut Jury Instructions, 3 vols., 1960, 76. Home: 30 Sycamore Rd West Hartford CT 06117 Office: 95 Washington St Hartford CT 06106

WRIGHT, EUGENE ALLEN, fed. judge; b. Seattle, Feb. 23, 1913; s. Elias Allen and Mary (Bailey) W.; A.B., U. Wash., 1935, J.D., 1937; m. Esther Ruth Ladley, Mar. 19, 1938; children—Gerald Allen, Meredith Ann Wright Morton. Admitted to Wash. bar, 1937; with firm Wright & Wright, Seattle, 1937-54; judge Superior Ct. King County (Wash.), 1954-66; v.p., sr. trust officer Pacific Nat. Bank Seattle, 1966-69; judge U.S. Ct. of Appeals 9th Circuit, Seattle, 1969—; acting municipal judge, Seattle, 1948-52; mem. faculty Nat. Jud. Coll., 1964-72; lectr. Sch. Communications, U. Wash., 1965-66, Law Sch., 1952-74; lectr. appellate judges' seminars, 1973-76, Nat. Law Clks. Inst., La. State U., 1973; chmn. Wash. State Com. on Law and Justice, 1968-69. Bd. visitors Sch. Law, U. Puget Sound; bd. dirs. Met. YMCA, Seattle, 1955-72. Served from 1st lt. to lt. col., AUS, 1941-46; col. Res. (ret.). Recipient Distinguished Service award U.S. Jr. C. of C., 1948, Distinguished Service medal Am. Legion; decorated Combat Inf. Badge, Bronze Star, Army Commendation medal. Fellow Am. Bar Found.; mem. Am. (council div. jud. adminstrn. 1971-76), Wash., Seattle bar assns., Am. Judicature Soc., Appellate Judges Conf., Ret. Officers Assn., Order of Coif, Delta Upsilon, Phi Delta Phi. Episcopalian. (lay reader). Clubs: Masons, Shriners, Rainier, Broadmoor Golf, Harbor, Nat. Lawyers, Wash. Athletic. Author: (with others) The State Trial Judges Book, 1966; also articles; editor Trial Judges Jour., 1963-66; contbr. articles to profl. jours. Home: 4343 53d Ave NE Seattle WA 98105 Office: US Courthouse Seattle WA 98104

WRIGHT, FLAVEL ALLEN, lawyer; b. Scottsbluff, Nebr., May 15, 1913; s. Fred Allen and Elizabeth (Royer) W.; A.B., U. Nebr., 1936, LL.B. cum laude, 1936; m. Marian Fleetwood, Oct. 28, 1936; children—Lynn Elizabeth (Mrs. James William Brown), William Flavel, Gregg Fleetwood, Scott Allen. Admitted to Nebr. bar, 1936; with firm Cline, Williams, Wright, Johnson & Oldfather, and predecessor, Lincoln, 1936—. Dir. Beatrice Foods Co. Mem. Jud. Council State Nebr., 1956-73. Pres. Lancaster County Tb Assn., 1956; chmn. adv. bldg. com. Lincoln Auditorium, also mem. operation com.; dir., chmn. bd. dirs. U. Nebr. 1974-76; past pres Nebr. State Bar Found. Served as lt. USNR, 1943-45. Fellow Am. Coll. Trial Lawyers (regent 1972-76), Am. Coll. Probate Counsel; mem. Am., Nebr. (pres. 1959-60, past chmn. taxation sect.), Lincoln (exec. com. 1958-61) bar assns., Am. Law Inst., Lincoln C. of C., Phi Kappa Psi, Phi Delta Phi. Congregationalist. Club: Lincoln Country (pres. 1962). Home: 2510 S 24th St Lincoln NE 68502 Office: 1900 First Nat Bank Bldg Lincoln NE 68508

WRIGHT, FLOYD VERNON, banker; b. Brashear, Mo., Dec. 26, 1916; s. Floyd E. and Pearl Elvira (Thompson) W.; student N.E. Mo. State U., Kirksville, 1934-37, Biarritz (France) Am. U., 1946; m. Kate Elizabeth Harry, May 28, 1950; children—Richard Vernon, Lisa Kay. With A.A.A., 1937-42, chief clk., sec.-treas. Dent County, Mo., 1938-42; field rep. Hannibal Prodn. Credit Assn., Shelbina, Mo., 1942-43; mgr., sec.-treas. Farmington (Mo.) Prodn. Credit Assn., 1946-58, Illini Prodn. Credit Assn., Carlinville, Ill., 1958-60; asst. v.p. Fed. Intermediate Credit Bank St. Louis, 1960-61; dep. gov., dir. prodn. credit service FCA, 1961-70; pres. Fed. Intermediate Credit Bank of New Orleans, 1970—. Sec. Assn. Mo. Prodn. Credit Assns., 1956-58. Sec. Farmington Citizens Com. Better Schs., 1957-58; mem. bd. Farmington Community Expansion Corp., 1957-58. Served with USAAF, 1943-46. Mem. chambers commerce Farmington (v.p. 1957), Carlinville, Greater New Orleans (agribus. com.), Am. Mgmt. Assn. (pres.'s assn.), Mo. Soc. Washington (pres. 1966-67), So. Farm Forum (planning com.), La. Comml. Agriculturists Assn. (dir.-at-large), Internat. Platform Assn., Pi Omega Pi. Baptist. Rotarian (past pres. Farmington). Odd Fellow. Club: New Orleans Country. Home: 5028 Purdue Dr Metairie LA 70003 Office: Federal Intermediate Credit Bank of New Orleans PO Box 50062 New Orleans LA 70150

WRIGHT, FRANK COOKMAN, JR., artist, writer; b. Cin., June 6, 1904; s. Frank Cookman and Carrie (Butler) W.; A.B., Yale, 1929; student Nat. Acad. Design Sch.; m. Gertrude Aspell, Dec. 29, 1935; children—Gill (Mrs. Thomas N. Bentley), Gail Atwood. Profl. artist, 1930—; works represented in 47 states and 17 countries; author programs for television and radio, also articles, lectures, painting demonstrations; pres. N.Y. State chpt. Am. Artists Profl. League, 1963—, nat. exec. v.p., 1962-67, pres., 1967—, editor News Bull., 1966—; v.p. council Am. Artist Socs., 1964-67, pres., 1967—; pres. Hudson Valley Art Assn., 1931-37; del. Fine Arts Fedn., 1960—; mem. joint com. Nat. Capitol, 1961-64. Vice pres. Phila. & Reading Coal & Iron Co., 1938-41; dir. Nat. Marine Service. Econ. adviser Bipartite Control Bd., Mil. Govt. for Germany, 1948-49; dir. pub. relations Free Europe Com., 1950-56. Recipient 1st prize portrait Hudson Valley Art Assn., 1935, Freedom Found. award, 1955, 56. Fellow Am. Inst. Fine Arts; mem. Copley Soc., Am. Assn.. Composers and Condrs., Am. Opera Soc. (chmn. bd. 1959-60). Clubs: Union (N.Y.C.); Edgartown (Mass.) Yacht. Home: 50 East Rd Delray Beach FL 33444 Office: 215 Park Ave S New York NY 10003. *Many are saying that Thomas Jefferson was right in his time, but now things are different, and Jefferson's thinking no longer applies for America. I disagree. He dealt with the deepest realities of life. If he is wrong for today, then Hitler and Stalin were right. Freedom failed only for irresponsible people.*

WRIGHT, FRANK GARDNER, journalist; b. Moline, Ill., Mar. 21. 1931; s. Paul E. and Goldie (Hicks) W.; B.A., Augustana Coll., Rock Island, Ill., 1953; postgrad. U. Minn., 1953-54; m. Barbara Lee Griffiths, Mar. 28, 1953; children—Stephen, Jeffrey, Natalie, Gregory, Sarah. Suburban reporter Mpls. Star, 1954-55; with Mpls. Tribune, 1955—, N.D. corr., 1955-56, Mpls. City Hall reporter, 1956-58, asst. city editor, 1958-63, Minn. polit. reporter, 1963-68, Washington corr., 1968-72, Washington Bur. chief, 1972-77, mng. editor, 1977—. Chmn., Golden Valley Human Rights Commn., 1965-67. Bd. dirs. Luth. Social Services, Washington. Recipient several Page 1 awards Twin Cities Newspaper Guild, 1950's, 60's, Worth Bingham prize Worth Bingham Meml. Fund, 1971; runnerup Raymond Clapper award for Washington correspondence, 1971; Outstanding Achievement award Augustana Alumni Assn., 1977. Mem. Am. Newspaper Guild (chmn. Mpls. unit 1961-67, editorial v.p. Twin Cities 1963-67). Home: 4912 Aldrich Ave S Minneapolis MN 55409 Office: 425 Portland Ave Minneapolis MN 55488

WRIGHT, GEORGE ARNOLD, oil co. exec.; b. Quebec, Que., Can., Aug. 29, 1932; m. Mary I. Greggan, Sept. 1959; 3 children. Dir. adminstrn. and treas. Kaiser Oil Ltd., Calgary, Alta., Can. Mem. Fin. Execs. Inst., Can. Assn. Bus. Econs. Club: Calgary Petroleum. Home: 2917 Lindstrom Dr SW Calgary AB Canada Office: PO Box 6800 Sta D Calgary AB T2P 0N1 Canada

WRIGHT, GEORGE THADDEUS, educator; b. Staten Island, N.Y., Dec. 17, 1925; s. George Thaddeus and Tekla Alida (Anderson) W.; A.B., Columbia, 1946, M.A., 1947; student U. Geneva (Switzerland), 1947-48; Ph.D. (Dr. Benjamin P. Wall meml. fellow 1955-56), U. Calif. at Berkeley, 1957; m. Jerry Honeywell, Apr. 28, 1955. Lectr. English, U. Calif. at Berkeley, 1956-57; instr., then asst. prof. U. Ky., 1957-60; asst. prof. San Francisco State Coll., 1960-61; asso. prof. U. Tenn., 1961-68; prof. English, U. Minn., 1968—, chmn. dept. English, 1974-77. Fulbright lectr. Am. lit. U. d'Aix Marseille (France), 1964-66, U. Thessaloniki (Greece), 1977-78. Served with U.S. Army, 1944-46. Mem. AAUP, Modern Lang. Assn. (William Riley Parker prize 1974), Nat. Council Tchrs. English. Author: The Poet in the Poem: The Personae of Eliot, Yeats and Pound, 1960; W.H. Auden, 1969; also articles, poems. Editor: Seven American Literary Stylists from Poe to Mailer, 1973. Address: Dept English U Minn Minneapolis MN 55455

WRIGHT, GLENN EUGENE, educator; b. Gouverneur, N.Y., Aug. 25, 1914; s. Leon W. and Grace (Smith) W.; B.S., St. Lawrence U., 1937, M.A., 1938; summer postgrad. student Cornell U., 1950, Syracuse U., 1951-54; m. Ethel M. Storrin, Sept. 14, 1943; children—Glenn R., Barry M. Tchr., Leicester High Sch., 1938-40; tchr. Pittsford (N.Y.) High Sch., 1939-40; dean students, dean, v.p. State U. Agrl. and Tech. Coll., Canton, 1948—, acting pres., 1961-62, 67-69. Campaign mgr., pres. bd. dirs. St. Lawrence County United Fund, 1960-61. Served to capt. AUS, 1941-46. Recipient Alumni citation St. Lawrence U., 1976, Distinguished Service award St. Lawrence County United Fund, 1977. Mem. N.Y. State Jr. Coll. Assn. Presbyterian (trustee). Club: Rotary. Home: 686 Mill St Watertown NY 13601

WRIGHT, GORDON, educator; b. Lynden, Wash., Apr. 24, 1912; s. Parke A. and Marion Jean (Beaty) W.; A.B., Whitman Coll., 1933, LL.D., 1957; M.A., Stanford, 1935, Ph.D., 1939; student George Washington U., 1936-37, U. Grenoble, U. Paris (France), 1937-38; m. Louise Aiken, Aug. 17, 1940; children—Eric, Michael, Gregory, Philip, David. Tchr. Mukilteo (Wash.) Jr. High, 1933-34; asst. prof. history U. Oreg., 1939-43, asso. prof., 1947-49, prof., 1949-57, chmn. dept. 1951-57; prof. history Stanford U., 1957—, William H. Bonsall prof. history, 1969-77, emeritus, 1977—, asso. dean Sch. Humanities and Scis., 1970-73, exec. head dept. history, 1959-65; country specialist Dept. of State, 1943-44, fgn. service officer U.S. embassy, Paris, 1945-47; mem. civilian faculty Nat. War Coll., 1952; vis. prof. Columbia, 1954-55, Ariz. State U., 1978, Coll. William and Mary, 1978-79; U.S. cultural attaché U.S. embassy, Paris, 1967-69. Bd. dirs. French-Am. Found. Am. Field Service fellow, 1937-38; fellow Inst. Advanced Study, 1950; Social Sci. Research Council fellow, 1950-51; fellow Am. Council Learned Socs. and Center Advanced Study Behavioral Scis., 1962-63. Decorated comdr. Ordre des Arts et des Lettres (France). Mem. AAUP, Am. Acad. Arts and Scis., Am. Philos. Soc., Soc. for French Hist. Studies (pres. 1972-73), Am. Hist. Assn. (pres. 1975), Académie des Sciences Morales et Politiques (corr.) (France), Phi Beta Kappa. Author: Raymond Poincaré and the French Presidency, 1942; The Reshaping of French Democracy, 1948; European Political Systems (with Taylor Cole, others), 1959; France in Modern Times, 1960, 74; Rural Revolution in France, 1964; The Ordeal of Total War, 1939-45, 1968. Editor: An Age of Controversy, 1973; Jules Michelet's History of the French Revolution, 1967. Contbr. A History of World Civilization, 1957. Home: 813 San Francisco Terr Stanford CA 94305

WRIGHT, GORDON BROOKS, musician, educator; b. Bklyn., Dec. 31, 1934; s. Harry Wesley and Helen (Brooks) W.; B.Mus., Coll. Wooster, 1957; M.A., U. Wis., 1961; Salzburg Mozarteum, 1972; m. Inga-Lisa Myrin Wright, June 13, 1958; children—Karin-Ellen, Charles-Eric, Daniel Brooks. Founder, propr. Wright's Book Shop, Madison, Wis., 1961-68; asso. prof. music U. Alaska, College, 1969—. Founder, condr. Madison Summer Symphony Orch.; condr. U.-Fairbanks Symphony Orch., Arctic Chamber Orch.; guest condr. Civic Orch. Mpls., Philomusica London, Siegerland Orch. Westfalia, U. Wis. Symphony, Fox Valley (Wis.) Symphony, S.E. Alaska Music Festival; composer Suite of Netherlands Dances, 1965, Six Alaskan Tone Poems, 1974, Symphony in Ursa Major, 1979; writer, narrator Intrada, Alaska State Radio Network; string cons. Anchorage Pub. Schs. Pres., Fairbanks Environ. Center, 1975—. Served with AUS, 1957-59. Mem. Am., Internat. musicol. socs., Am. Symphony Orch. League, Galpin Soc., Dolmetsch Found., Arturo Toscanini Soc., Alaska Assn. Arts, Am. Fedn. Musicians, Royal Mus. Assn., Sierra Club (chmn. Fairbanks Group 1969-71), Friends of Earth, Wilderness Soc., Audubon Soc., Nat. Parks Assn., Alaska Conservation Soc. (bd. mem., editor Rev. 1971—). Weekly columnist Alaska Advocate. Home: Box 80051 College AK 99708

WRIGHT, GORDON PRIBYL, educator; b. Crosby, Minn., May 18, 1938; s. Kenneth Eugene and Verla Emily (Pribyl) W.; B.A., Macalester Coll., 1960; M.A., U. Mass., 1963; Ph.D., Case Western Res. U., 1967; m. Judith Ann Hill, Aug. 19, 1961; 1 dau., Teresa Ann. Systems analyst Conn. Gen. Life Ins. Co., Bloomfield, 1960-61; instr. dept. math. U. Mass., 1961-63; statistician, mgmt. scis. group Goodyear Tire & Rubber Co., Akron, Ohio, 1963-64; instr., research asst., ops. research dept. Case Inst. Tech., Cleve., 1964-67; asst. prof. dept. indsl. engring. and mgmt. scis. Technol. Inst., Northwestern U., 1967-70; asso. prof. mgmt. and statistics Krannert Grad. Sch. Mgmt. and Sch. of Sci., Purdue U., West Lafayette, Ind., 1970-75, prof., chmn. mgmt., dir. profl. programs, 1975—, asso. dean, 1979—; vis. prof. bus. adminstrn. and statistics Amos Tuck Sch. Bus. Adminstrn., Dartmouth Coll., 1976-77; vis. prof. Bradley U.; cons. Okamura Mfg. Co., Yokohama, Japan. Served with USAF Res., 1961-67. Recipient Salgo-Noren Found. award for outstanding teaching in bus. adminstrn., 1975; NSF research grantee, 1968-70, Dept. Transp. research grantee, 1972-74, HEW research grantee, 1969-70, Sloan Found. research grantee, 1972-75. Mem. Ops. Research Soc. Am., Inst. Mgmt. Scis., Sigma Xi, Beta Gamma Sigma. Author: (with David G. Olson) Designing Water Pollution Detection Systems, 1974; (with Andrew B. Whinston and Gary J. Koehler) Optimization of Leontief Systems, 1975; (with Herbert M. Moskowitz) An Experiential Approach to Management Science, 1975, Introduction to Management Science, 1979, Statistics for Business and Economics, 1980; (with Frank M. Bass) Stochastic Brand Coice and Brand Switching: Theory Analysis and Description, 1980; contbr. articles on ops. research and mgmt. to profl. jours. Home: 136 Seminole Dr West Lafayette IN 47906 Office: Krannert Sch Mgmt Purdue U West Lafayette IN 47907

WRIGHT, HAMILTON MERCER, advt. and public relations exec.; b. Los Angeles, Nov. 8, 1901; s. Hamilton Mercer and Cora Elizabeth (Pease) W.; student pub. schs.; m. Frances Purdy, Dec. 31, 1923; children—Hamilton Mercer 3d, Elizabeth (Mrs. Kenneth Mattfeld). Dir. publicity City of Miami (Fla.), 1932-47; tourist publicity contracts with govts. of Formosa, Egypt, Morocco, Ivory Coast, Venezuela, Colombia, Ecuador, Italy, Chile, Bolivia, Ceylon, Can., Mexico, South Africa, Puerto Rico, Alaskan Hwy. during constrn., Provinces of Alta. and Que. (Can.); dir. publicity N.Y. World's Fair, 1939-41; ret. chmn. bd. Hamilton Wright Orgn., Inc., N.Y.C. Publicity dir. drive to save Abu Simbel Temple on Nile; dir. over 300 motion picture short subjects in fgn. countries for Hollywood release, over 2,200 newsreel subjects; contbr. motion pictures and still pictures to Smithsonian Instn. and film archives U. Calif. at Los Angeles; originator system offering pictures and stories to press to publicize tourist attractions in fgn. countries. Home: Box 362 RD 5 Newton NJ 07860

WRIGHT, HAROLD MADISON, engring. co. exec.; b. Winnipeg, Man., Can.; s. James Harold and Clara Elizabeth (Thomas) W.; B.S., U. Utah, 1932, M.S., 1936; M.A., U. B.C., 1933; m. Edna May Robinson, July 27, 1940; children—Linda C. (Mrs. John Dennison), Lee M., James K. Chmn. bd. Wright Engrs., Ltd., Vancouver, B.C.; pres. Wright Engrs., Pty., Ltd., Sydney, Australia; dir. Wright Engrs. Internat., Ltd., Hamilton, Bermuda, Western Mines, Ltd., Intercontinental Engring., Ltd., Vancouver; sprinter (Athletic Council scholar award) U. Utah, 1932, Canadian Olympic Team, Los Angeles, 1932, Brit. Empire vs. U.S.A., San Francisco, 1932; pres. Canadian Field Hockey Assn., 1965-69; pres. Canadian Olympic Assn., Montreal, 1969-77, bd. dirs., 1966—; bd. dirs. Vancouver Olympic Club, 1957—, life mem., 1969, pres., 1979; dir. organizing com. Olympic Games, Montreal, 1970-77; bd. dirs. Commonwealth Games Assn. Can., 1972-77; bd. govs. Olympic Trust of Can., Toronto, 1970—. Decorated officer Order of Can.; recipient Businessman of Year award Vancouver Jr. C. of C., 1971, Spl. Achievement award B.C. Sports Fedn., 1975, Silver medal of Olympic Order, Internat. Olympic Com., 1979. Hon. fellow Instn. Mining and Metallurgy London (overseas mem. council 1960—, Gold medal 1965); mem. Can. Inst. Mining Metallurgy (life mem., pres. 1970-71, Donald J. McParland Meml. medal 1974, H.T. Airey, Noranda award 1976), Australian Inst. Mining and Metallurgy, Assn. Profl. Engrs. B.C., Sci. Council B.C., Assn. Cons. Engrs. of Can. Clubs: Olympic of Can.; Univ., Shaughnessy Golf and Country, Canadian (Vancouver). Home: 5590 Kingston Rd Vancouver BC V6T 1J1 Canada Office: 1444 Alberni St Vancouver BC V6G 2Z4 Canada

WRIGHT, HARRISON MORRIS, educator, coll. ofcl.; b. Phila., Oct. 6, 1928; s. Sydney L. and Catharine W. (Morris) W.; B.A., Harvard, 1950, M.A., 1953, Ph.D., 1957; m. Josephine Stearns Cole, July 20, 1957; children—Rebecca H., J. Rodman, Thomas F., Daniel H., James L. Teaching fellow Harvard, 1955-57; mem. faculty Swarthmore Coll., 1957—, prof. history, 1968—, chmn. dept., 1968-79, provost, 1979—. Fulbright scholar, New Zealand, 1950-51; Ford Found. fgn. areas fellow, Eng. and Ghana, 1961-62; grantee Am. Philos. Soc., S. Africa, 1966-67, Old Dominion Fund, S. Africa, 1971. Mem. African Studies Assn., Am. Hist. Assn., Newport Hist. Soc. (dir. 1973—), Phi Beta Kappa. Author: New Zealand, 1769-1840:

Early Years of Western Contact, 1959; The Burden of the Present: Liberal-Radical Controversy over Southern African History, 1977. Editor: The New Imperialism—Analysis of Late Nineteenth-Century Expansion, 1961, 2d edit., 1976; Sir James Rose Innes: Selected Correspondence (1884-1902), 1972. Home: 319 Cedar Ln Swarthmore PA 19081 Office: Provost's Office Swarthmore Coll Swarthmore PA 19081

WRIGHT, HARRY, III, lawyer; b. Lima, Ohio, Apr. 27, 1925; s. Harry, Jr. and Marjorie (Riddle) W.; student The Citadel, 1942-43; B.S., U. Ky., 1948; LL.B., Harvard, 1951; m. Louise Forbes Taylor, Dec. 15, 1956; children—Harry IV, Whitaker Wilson, Priscilla Taylor. Admitted to Ohio bar, 1951; with Porter, Wright, Morris & Arthur, Columbus, 1951—, partner, 1956—. Mem. adv. bd. Salvation Army, 1958-74. Pres. bd. trustees Six Pence Sch., Columbus, 1965-75; trustee Bradford Coll., 1957-75, Columbus Acad., 1975—, pres. bd., 1978-80; trustee Internat. Council Central Ohio, 1979—. Served with USAAF, 1943-46. Mem. Am. (chmn. gen. practice sect. 1976-77), Ohio, Columbus bar assns. Episcopalian. Clubs: University, Columbus, Rocky Fork Hunt and Country (Columbus). Home: 292 N Drexel Ave Columbus OH 43209 Office: 37 W Broad St Columbus OH 43215

WRIGHT, HARRY FORREST, JR., banker; b. Woodbury, N.J., Nov. 9, 1931; s. Harry Forrest and Bertha (Strumpfer) W.; student Temple U., 1949-50, Am. Inst. Banking, 1950-52; accounting certificate Wharton Sch., U. Pa., 1960, asso. degree, 1962; m. Lorraine Catherine McLaughlin, Oct. 16, 1954; children—Harry Forrest III, Lonni Caryn, Gregory William, Douglas Carl. Clk., First Nat. Bank, Phila., 1951-60; asst. comptroller, then asst. v.p. First Pa. Co., 1960-64; v.p. Md. Nat. Bank, Balt., 1964-66, v.p., 1966-70, sr. v.p., 1970-73, comptroller, 1966-73, exec. v.p., 1973—, dir., 1976—; v.p., treas. Md. Nat. Corp., 1974-77, sr. v.p., 1977—, dir., 1976—; treas., dir. Md. Nat. Optimation Services, Inc., 1969-76, chmn., 1976-79; sec. Md. Switch Inc., 1976—, treas., dir. Manab Properties, Inc.; pres., dir. 10 Light Street Corp., 1973—; dir. Md. Affiliate Corp., Title Guaranty Co. Treas., Cub Scouts Am., Severna Park, Md., 1965-66, St. Martin's Kindergarten, 1967-72. Bd. dirs. Greater Balt. chpt. Nat. Found. March Dimes, v.p., 1977-79, pres., 1979—; bd. dirs. Md. Sch. for Blind, 1975—. Mem. Bank Adminstrn. Inst. (pres. 1970-71, state dir. 1971-73, dist. dir. 1977-79), Fin. Execs. Inst. (dir. 1976-78), Sigma Kappa Phi. Club: Merchants (dir. 1974, v.p. 1976-79, pres. 1979—) (Balt.). Home: 22 Emerson Rd Severna Park MD 21146 Office: 10 Light St Baltimore MD 21203

WRIGHT, HELEN, astronomer, writer; b. Washington, Dec. 20, 1914; d. Frederick E. and Kathleen E. (Finley) Wright; grad. Bennett Jr. Coll., Millbrook, N.Y., 1934; A.B., Vassar Coll., 1937, M.A., 1939; postgrad. U. Cal.; m. John F. Hawkins, 1946 (div.); m. 2d, René Greuter, 1967. Asst. astronomy dept. Vassar Coll., 1937-39; Mt. Wilson Obs., 1937; jr. astronomer U.S. Naval Obs., 1942-43. Mem. Internat. Astron. Union, Am. Astron. Soc., History of Sci. Soc. Author: Sweeper in the Sky, The First Woman Astronomer in America, 1949; Palomar, The World's Largest Telescope, 1952; Explorer of the Universe, A Biography of George Ellery Hale, 1966. Editor: (with Harlow Shapley, Samuel Rapport) A Treasury of Science, latest edit., 1963, Readings in the Physical Sciences, 1948; A New Treasury of Science, 1965; (with S. Rapport) Great Adventures in Medicine, 1952, The Crust of the Earth, 1955, Great Adventures in Science, 1956, The Great Explorers, 1957, Great Adventures in Nursing, 1960, The Amazing World of Medicine, 1961, Mathematics, 1963, Archaeology, 1963, Science, 1963, Engineering, 1963, Physics, 1964, Astronomy, 1964, Great Undersea Adventures, 1966, Anthropology, 1967, Biology, 1967; (with Hamilton Wright and S. Rapport) To The Moon, 1968; (with C. Weiner and J. Warnow) The Legacy of George Ellery Hale: Evolution of Astronomy and Scientific Institutions in Pictures and Documents, 1972. Home: 579 Forest Lakes Dr Andover NJ 07821

WRIGHT, HELEN PATTON, assn. exec.; b. Washington, Jan. 15, 1919; d. Raymond Stanton and Virginia (Mitchell) Patton; student Sweet Briar Coll., 1936-38; grad. Washington Sch. Secretaries, 1939; m. James Skelly Wright, Feb. 1, 1945; 1 son, James Skelly. Tchr., Washington Sch. Secretaries, N.Y.C., 1939-40; sec. The White House, 1941-43, Am. embassy, London, Eng., 1943-45; asst. to exec. dir. Senate Atomic Energy Com., 1946-47. Vice pres., mem. budget and admissions com. United Fund New Orleans, 1960-62; chmn. met. div., campaign; v.p. Dept. Pub. Welfare, Orleans Parish and City New Orleans, 1960-62; v.p. Milne Asylum for Destitute Orphan Boys, New Orleans, 1958-62; mem. bd. New Orleans Social Welfare Planning Council, 1954-62, New Orleans Cancer Soc., 1958-60; v.p. Juvenile Ct. Adv. Com. New Orleans, 1961; successively sec., v.p., pres. Parents' Assn. Metairie Park Country Day Sch., 1956-59; v.p. La. Assn. Mental Health, 1960-62; del. dir. to Nat. Assn. Mental Health, 1960-62; bd. mem. Washington Health and Welfare Council, 1962-64, Hillcrest Children's Center, Washington, 1963-69, D.C. Mental Health Assn., 1962-72, 73-76; bd. dirs. Nat. Assn. Mental Health, 1960-66, 67-74, sec., 1968-70, pres.-elect, 1970-71, pres., 1972-73, cons. on assn. film, 1972; mem. Commn. on Mentally Disabled, Am. Bar Assn., 1973—; chmn. altar guild Christ Ch. Cathedral, New Orleans, 1960, Little Sanctuary of St. Albans Sch., Washington, 1965; pres. Chancel Guild, St. Alban's, Chg., 1976, 77; chmn. Washington com. Nat. Cathedral Assn., 1976, 77, 78, 79; bd. dirs. Nat. Center Voluntary Action; mem. task panel Mental Health Problems, Scope and Boundaries, Pres.'s Commn. Mental Health, 1977; mem. tech. rev. com. Md. Psychiat. Research Center, 1979. Address: 5317 Blackistone Rd Washington DC 20016

WRIGHT, HENRY LYMAN, architect; b. San Diego, Feb. 28, 1904; s. William S. and Lucy S. (Wheeler) W.; student San Diego State Coll., 1922-23, So. br. U. Calif., 1924, U. So. Calif., 1928, Europe, 1929; m. Virginia R. Pizzini, Nov. 17, 1934; children—Regina L. (Mrs. Edmund D. Hunter), William H. Office boy T.C. Kistner Architect, Los Angeles, 1922-23, part-time draftsman, 1923-25, sr. draftsman, 1925-33, officer mgr., 1933-39; pres. Kistner, Wright & Wright, archtl. engrs., Los Angeles, 1939—. Pres. Calif. Council Architects, 1955; A.I.A. del. White House Conf. on Edn., 1958, White House Conf. on Internat. Cooperation, 1965; U.S. del. conf. on sch. facilities UNESCO, 1962; mem. U.S. Commn. for UNESCO, 1963-69; chmn. profl. adv. com. Los Angeles Beautiful, 1963-69; mem. pub. adv. panel U.S. Gen. Service Adminstrn., 1965; mem. exec. com. Internat. Union Architects, Paris, 1965-75. Trustee Illuminating Research Inst. Recipient Constrn. Industry Achievement award Los Angeles C. of C., 1963. Fellow A.I.A. (pres. So. Calif. chpt. 1953; nat. chmn. sch. com., 1953-58, nat. pres. 1962), R.A.I.C. (hon.), Philippine Inst. Architects (hon.); mem. Fedn. Pan. Am. Assn. Architects (supreme council 1964-65), La Sociedad de Arcquitectos Mexicanos (hon.); U.S.C. Archtl. Guild, Am. Arbitration Assn. Clubs: Town Hall, Jonathan (Los Angeles). Henry L. Wright Intermediate sch. named for him Norwalk-LaMirada Unified Sch. Dist., Los Angeles County. Home: 3728 Madison Rd Flintridge CA 91011 Office: 1125 W 6th St Los Angeles CA 90017

WRIGHT, HERBERT E(DGAR), JR., geologist; b. Malden, Mass., Sept. 13, 1917; s. Herbert E. and Annie M. (Richardson) W.; A.B., Harvard U., 1939; M.A., 1941, Ph.D., 1943; D.Sc. (hon.), Trinity Coll., Dublin, Ireland, 1966; m. Rhea Jane Hahn, June 21, 1943; children—Richard, Jonathan, Stephen, Andrew, Jeffrey. Instr., Brown U., 1946-47; asst. prof. geology U. Minn., Mpls., 1947-51, asso. prof., 1951-59, prof., 1959-74, Regents' prof. geology, ecology and botany, 1974—, dir. Limnological Research Center, 1963—. Served to maj. USAAF, 1942-45. Decorated D.F.C., Air medal with 6 oak leaf clusters; Guggenheim fellow, 1954-55; Wenner-Gren fellow, 1954-55. Fellow Geol. Soc. Am., AAAS, Scientists Inst. Pub. Info.; mem. Ecol. Soc. Am., Am. Soc. Limnology, Oceanography, Am. Quaternary Assn., Arctic Inst., Brit. Ecol. Soc., Internat. Glaciological Soc., Nat. Acad. Scis. Research on Quaternary geology, paleoecology, paleolimnology and environ. archaeology in Minn., New Mex., Yukon, Labrador, Peru, eastern Mediterranean. Home: 1426 Hythe St Saint Paul MN 55108 Office: 221 Pillsbury Hall U of Minn 310 Pillsbury Dr SE Minneapolis MN 55455

WRIGHT, HERBERT FLETCHER, educator; b. Muskegon, Mich., Dec. 11, 1907; s. William Henry and Jennie (Raymond) W.; A.B. with high distinction, Nebr. Wesleyan U., 1930, D.Sc., 1976; M.A., U. Cin., 1931; Ph.D., Duke, 1934; m. Lorene Nell Graver, Sept. 22, 1929; children—William Henry, Katharine Lenore (Mrs. William K. Young). Acting prof. psychology Mercer U., 1934-35; Gen. Edn. Bd. postdoctoral fellow State U. Ia., 1935-36; instr., asst. prof. psychology Carleton Coll., 1936-43; asst. prof. Northwestern U., 1945-47; asso. prof. U. Kans., 1947-49, prof. psychology, 1949-75, emeritus, 1975—, chmn. dept., 1962-66. Cons. NIMH, 1962-66; co-dir. Midwest Field Sta., 1947-54; dir. City-Town Project, 1955-75. Served from lt. (j.g.) to lt. USNR, 1943-45. Fellow Ford Found., 1953-54; NIMH fellow, Eng., 1965; Fulbright Research scholar Eng., 1972-73. Mem. Am. Psychol. Assn., AAAS, AAUP, Phi Beta Kappa, Sigma Xi. Methodist. Author: (with R.G. Barker) One Boy's Day, 1951, Midwest and Its Children, 1955, Methods in Psychological Ecology, 1949; Recording and Analyzing Child Behavior, 1967. Editor: (with R.G. Barker, J.S. Kounin) Child Behavior and Development, 1943. Home: 2536 Arkansas St Lawrence KS 66044

WRIGHT, HOWARD EMORY, educator; b. Phila., Mar. 30, 1908; s. William H. and Evelyn (Ferguson) W.; A.B., Lincoln (Pa.) U., 1932, M.A., 1933; Ph.D., Ohio State U., 1946; postgrad. U. Chgo., 1941; m. Anne M. Nelson, Aug. 3, 1936; children—Beverly Anne, Howard Emery. Instr. edn. State Coll., Albany, Ga., 1933-34; prin. Logan (W.Va.) Sch., 1936-39; asso. prof. edn. State Coll., Prairie View, Tex., 1940-45; chmn. div. edn. and psychology, prof. Tex. So. U., Houston, 1948-53; chmn. dept. psychology N.C. Coll., Durham, 1945-48, 53-61; pres. Allen U., Columbia, S.C., 1961-66; chief developing instns. br. U.S. Office Edn., 1966-67; dean Md. State Coll. div. U. Md., Princess Anne, 1967-71; dir. div. social scis. Hampton (Va.) Inst., 1971-74; asst. to pres. Salisbury (Md.) State Coll., 1974—, also prof. emeritus. Dir. Victory Savs. Bank. Mem. Durham Com. Negro Affairs, 1953-61. Mem. AAUP, Am. Tchrs. Assn., Nat., Palmetto edn. assns., Am. Psychol. Assn. (exec. com.), Omega Psi Phi. Mason, Elk. Mem. A.M.E. Ch. Democrat. Author: An Analysis of Results with Certain Tests of Interests and Attitudes, 1933; Physiological Aspects of Child Development, 1940. Home: 314 Camelot Dr College Park GA 30349

WRIGHT, HUGH ELLIOTT, JR., journalist; b. Athens, Ala., Nov. 20, 1937; s. Hugh Elliott and Martha Angeline (Shannon) W.; A.B., Birmingham-So. Coll., 1959; M.Div., Vanderbilt U., 1962, D.Ministry, 1967; postgrad. Harvard, 1963; m. Juanita Ruth Bass, Dec. 30, 1963. Ordained to ministry Methodist Ch., 1963; pastor Baxter (Tenn.) Meth. Ch., 1963-64; asso. pastor Waverly Pl. Ch., Nashville, 1965-66; field sec. Tenn. Heart Assn., Nashville, 1964-65; editorial asst. Motive mag., Nashville, 1965-67; Protestant-Orthodox editor Religious News Service, N.Y.C., 1967-75; research fellow Auburn Theol. Sem., N.Y.C., 1976; editor project on mediating structures and public policy Am. Enterprise Inst.; host Challenge to Faith, Sta. WOR, 1973-77; cons. Hartford Sem. Found., 1972, United Meth. Bd. Global Ministries, 1975-78, United Meth. Communications, 1979-80. Recipient award Birmingham Council Indsl. Editors, 1959, Founders medal Vanderbilt U., 1962, Shepherd prize Vanderbilt, 1962, Religious Heritage of Am. award in journalism, 1972. Mem. Authors League and Guild, Religion Newswriters Assn., United Presbyn. Men, Phi Beta Kappa, Sigma Delta Chi, Alpha Tau Omega, Alpha Psi Omega, Eta Sigma Phi. Democrat. Author: (with R. Lecky) Can These Bones Live, 1969; (with R. Lynn) The Big Little School, 1971; Go Free, 1973; (with Juanita Wright) Challenge to Mission, 1973; The Susquehanna Valley Story, 1976; Viewers Guide to Six American Families, 1977; (with Howard Butt) At the Edge of Hope, 1978. Editor: Black Manifesto: Religion, Racism and Reparations, 1969. Home: 4761 Henry Hudson Pkwy Bronx NY 10471. *Many of the people I once thought influenced me didn't. They were sophisticated, worthwhile and, I suppose, wise. But they were not super-wise. They never told me that feeling is as important as knowing. They never suggested that building a closet is as satisfying as reciting the names of the Canaanite Gods. My friend Juanita, who is also my wife, has proved to me that life is more than knowledge and contentment more than seeing one's name in print. Honesty is the only standard of conduct; friendship the single principle; and love is the universal ideal.*

WRIGHT, IRVING SHERWOOD, physician, educator; b. N.Y.C., Oct. 27, 1901; s. Harry J. and Cora Ann (Hassett) W.; A.B., Cornell U., 1923, M.D., 1926; m. Grace Mansfield Demarest, Oct. 15, 1927; children—Barbara Mansfield, Alison Sherwood; m. 2d, Lois Elliman Findlay, Oct. 31, 1953. Intern, N.Y. Post Grad. Med. Sch. and Hosp. of Columbia, 1927-29, asst. and asso. vis. physician, 1929-39, prof. clin. medicine, dir. and exec. officer dept. medicine, 1939-46; asst. physician Bellevue Hosp. (Cornell Div.), 1931-34, asso., 1934-37, asso. prof. Cornell Med. Coll. and asso. attending physician N.Y. Hosp., 1946-48, prof. clin. medicine Cornell Med. Coll., 1948-68, emeritus clin. prof., 1968—; attending physician Drs. Hosp., N.Y.C., 1934—, N.Y. Hosp., 1948—; physician Met. Opera, 1935-62; dir. medicine (Cornell Div.) Welfare Hosp. Chronic Disease, 1937-40 (1st pres. its med. bd. 1937-39), cons. physician, 1940-46; cons. to Orange Meml. Hosp., East Orange, N.J., Monmouth Meml. Hosp., Long Branch, N.J., Hackensack (N.J.) Hosp., Mt. Vernon (N.Y.) Hosp.; chief of med. service Army and Navy Gen. Hosp., Hot Springs (Ark.) Nat. Park, 1942-43; cons. in medicine U.S. Army, 6th Service Command, 1944-45, 9th Service Command, 1945; coordinator health survey Am. prisoners of war from Far East, 1945. Served as lt. comdr. USNR, 1935-39; lt. col. to col. AUS, 1942-46; civilian cons. in medicine to surgeon gen. U.S. Army, 1946-74; mem. civilian adv. com. to sec. navy, 1946-47. Chmn. Josiah Macy, Jr. Found. Conf. Blood Clotting, 1947-52; chmn. Internat. Com. on Blood Clotting Factors, 1954-63, sec. gen., 1963-68; chmn. com. on cerebral vascular diseases NIH, 1961-65; mem. Pres.'s Comm. Heart Disease, Cancer and Stroke, 1966-68; nat. chmn. Commn. Heart Disease Resources, 1968-76. Trustee, Cornell U., 1960-65. Recipient Albert and Mary Lasker award Am. Heart Assn., 1960, Gold Heart award, 1958, Disting. Service award, 1976; Irving Sherwood Wright professorship in geriatrics at Cornell U. Med. Coll., 1976. Diplomate Am. Bd. Internal Medicine (mem. adv. bd. 1940-49). Fellow Royal Coll. Physicians (London), A.C.P. (regent, pres. 1966-67), N.Y. Acad. Medicine (chmn. geriatrics sect. 1976—); mem. Am. Assn. Physicians, A.M.A. (chmn. sect. exptl. med. and therapeutics 1939-40), Am. Heart Assn. (chmn. sect. for study peripheral circulation 1939-40; mem. exec. com., bd. dirs. 1935-57, pres. 1952-53; mem. Nat. Adv. Heart Council 1954-58, 60-61), Cornell U. Med. Coll. Alumni Assn. (pres 1953), NRC (sub-com. cardiovascular diseases 1947-51), Am. Soc. Clin. Investigation, Soc. Exptl. Biology and Medicine, N.Y. Acad. Scis., Am. Geriatrics Soc. (pres. 1971-72, Henderson award 1970, Thewlis award 1974), Harvey Soc. Sigma Xi, Alpha Omega Alpha; corr. mem. of Acad. Columbian de Ciencas Exactas Fisico-Quimicas Y Naturales (Bogota); hon. mem. Royal Soc. Medicine of London, med. socs. Brazil, Chile, Peru, Argentina, Cuba, Switzerland, Sweden and USSR, also hon. faculty of U. Chile. Presbyn (bd. sessions 1935-36). Clubs: Bedford Golf and Tennis; St. Nicholas Society (N.Y.). Author and editor numerous books on cardiovascular diseases. Editor-in-chief Modern Medical Monographs. Contbr. articles to med. jours. Home: 25 East End Ave New York NY 10028 Office: 450 E 69th St New York NY 10021. *My aim in life has been to improve the quality of medical care in the fields of internal medicine, cardiovascular diseases by research, teaching at undergraduate, graduate, and international levels, the development of standards and guidelines, and the application of the best of modern knowledge to the care of patients. In light of the technology of recent years I have placed particular emphasis on the role of a primary physician for the patient, who will apply his scientific knowledge with compassion and an understanding of the total illness-including the social and emotional aspects of the patient's problem rather than his disease alone. This, as I see it, is the challenge of the modern physician.*

WRIGHT, JACKSON ATCHISON, lawyer; b. Gower, Mo., Apr. 8, 1918; s. Frank J. and Mollie (Atchison) W.; student N.W. Mo. State Tchrs. Coll., 1935-37; B.S. in Bus. Adminstrn., U. Mo., 1940, LL.B., 1944; m. Edith Dailey, Apr. 29, 1945; children—Margaret Ann, Mollie, David A. (dec.). Admitted to Mo. bar, 1944, practice in Mexico, 1944-64; counsel U. Mo., 1964-67, gen. counsel, 1967—. Mem. Mo. Bd. Law Examiners, 1955-59. Vice pres., dir. Citizens Savs. Assn. Mem. bd. edn., Mexico, 1949-55, pres., 1952-55. Dir. Mo. Mil. Acad. Mem. Am. (ho. dels. 1962-68, state del. 1965-68), Mo. (gov. 1954-63, pres. 1961-62), Boone County bar assns., Order of Coif, Phi Delta Phi, Beta Theta Phi. Home: 1219 Frances Dr Columbia MO 65201 Office: University Hall Columbia MO 65211

WRIGHT, JAMES ARLINGTON, poet; b. Martins Ferry, Ohio, 1927; B.A., Kenyon Coll., 1952; M.A., U. Wash., 1954, Ph.D., 1959; m. Ann Runk. Formerly instr. English, U. Minn; poet translator; now prof. English, Hunter Coll., N.Y.C. Served with AUS, World War II. Recipient Melville Cane award Poetry Soc. Am.; Pulitzer prize for poetry, 1972. Fellow Acad. Am. Poets. Author: The Green Wall, 1957; Saint Judas, 1959; The Lion's Tail and Eyes, 1962; The Branch Will Not Break, 1963; Shall We Gather at the River?, 1968; Collected Poems, 1971; Two Citizens, 1973; Moments of the Italian Summer, 1976; To a Blossoming Pear Tree, 1977. Translator: The Rider on the White Horse (Theodore Storm), 1964; Wandering: Notes and Sketches (Hermann Hesse), 1972; (with Robert Bly) Twenty Poems of George Frankl, 1961, Twenty Poems of César Vallejo, 1962, Twenty Poems of Pablo Neruda, 1962. Office: Hunter Coll 466 Lexington Ave New York NY 10017*

WRIGHT, JAMES BOWERS, editor, journalist; b. Phila., July 10, 1950; s. John Samuel and Margaret Lucille (Bowers) W.; B.A. in Journalism and English, Syracuse U., 1972; m. Patricia Muriel Coriell, Feb. 16, 1974. Editor, Lakeland (N.J.) Record, Wayne, N.J., 1972; exec. editor Rudder Mag., N.Y.C., 1973-76; movie critic Bergen Record, Hackensack, N.J., 1976—. Mem. Am. Powerboat Assn. Author: Bobby Clarke, 1977; Mike Schmidt, 1979; contbr. articles to New Times Mag., Sea Mag., Washington Post. Home: PO Box 97 Bellvale NY 10912 Office: 150 River St Hackensack NJ 07602

WRIGHT, JAMES C., JR., congressman; b. Ft. Worth, Dec. 22, 1922; s. James C. and Marie (Lyster) W.; student Weatherford Coll., also U. Tex.; m. Betty Hay, Nov. 12, 1972; children by previous marriage—Jimmy, Virginia Sue, Patricia Kay, Alicia Marie. Partner trade extension and advt. firm; mem. Tex. Legislature, 1947-49; mayor, Weatherford, Tex., 1950-54; mem. 84th-96th congresses, 12th Tex. Dist., now majority leader. Served with USAAF, World War II. Decorated D.F.C., Legion of Merit; named Outstanding Young Man, Tex. Jr. C. of C., 1953. Mem. League Tex. Municipalities (pres. 1953). Democrat. Presbyn. Author: You and Your Congressman, 1965; The Coming Water Famine, 1966; Of Swords and Plowshares, 1968; co-author Congress and Conscience, 1970. Address: Rayburn House Office Bldg Washington DC 20515

WRIGHT, JAMES CLAUDE, educator; b. at Garnett, Kans., Mar. 14, 1903; s. James Lee and Katie Ethel (Plummer) W.; B.A., Drake U., 1927, L.H.D., 1956; M.A., State U. Iowa, 1936; postgrad. Northwestern U., 1939-40, U. Minn., 1947, U. Colo., 1950; m. Donna Mae Stewart, Dec. 21, 1928 (dec. Dec. 1973); children—James Claude, Patricia Ann; m. 2d, Elizabeth L. Miller, 1974. Sci. instr. Creston (Iowa) High Sch., 1927-28; sci. instr., guidance dir., athletic coach Keokuk (Iowa) Sr. High Sch., 1928-38; prin. Kenkuk Sr. High Sch., 1938-40; supt. of schs., Keokuk, 1940-55; supt. pub. instrn. State of Iowa, 1955-61; sec. Com. for Advancement of Sch. Adminstrn., also asst. sec. Am. Assn. Sch. Adminstrs., 1961-63; dir. edn. Am. Samoa, 1963-65; prof. edn. N.E. Mo. State U., 1965-72. Trustee Iowa Hist. Bldg., 1955-61, Iowa Med. Library, 1955-61, Iowa Law Library, 1955-61. Served to lt. comdr. USNR, 1943-46. Mem. Iowa (exec. com. 1942-43), S.E. Iowa (pres. 1952-54) edn. assns., N.E.A. (centennial com. 1957), Am. Assn. Sch. Adminstrs., Am. Legion. Baptist. Mason. Rotarian. Author adminstrv. textbooks. Home: 9 Scott St Terr Kirksville MO 63501

WRIGHT, JAMES EDWARD, judge; b. Arlington, Tex., Jan. 15, 1921; s. James Robert and Clairette (Smith) W.; J.D., U. Tex., 1949; m. Eberta Adelaide Slataper, June 25, 1946; 1 dau., Patricia Diane Wright Rogers. Admitted to Tex. bar, 1949; practice in Ft. Worth, 1949-69; city atty., Arlington, 1951-61; judge 141st Dist. Ct., Ft. Worth, 1970—. Served with USAAF, World War II. Fellow Tex. Bar Found. (life); mem. Am., Ft. Worth-Tarrant County (pres. 1958-59) bar assns., State Bar Tex., Phi Alpha Delta. Democrat. Methodist. Rotarian (pres. 1966-67), Mason (32 deg., Shriner). Home: 717 Briarwood Blvd Arlington TX 76013 Office: 141st District Court Civil Courts Bldg Fort Worth TX 76102

WRIGHT, JAMES LEE, symphony orch. exec.; b. St. Bernard, Ohio, Feb. 5, 1935; s. James and Clara (Kalkbrenner) W.; B.M., Cin. Coll. Conservatory of Music, 1957, M.M., 1959; m. Phyllis Rhea Counts, June 6, 1957; children—Cheryl Lee, Heather Lynn. Salesman, Gibson Greeting Cards, Birmingham, Ala., 1960-65; asst. mgr. Buffalo Philharmonic, 1965-67; mgr. Richmond (Va.) Symphony, 1967-68; mgr. ops. Pitts. Symphony, 1968-73; gen. mgr. Houston Symphony, 1973-76; asst. mgr. N.Y. Philharmonic, 1977-78; gen. mgr. Memphis Orchestral Soc., 1978—. Served with U.S. Army, 1959, 61-62. Martha Baird Rockefeller Found. grantee, 1965. Unitarian. Office: 3100 Walnut Grove Rd Suite 402 Memphis TN 38111

WRIGHT, JAMES ROSCOE, govt. ofcl.; b. White Hall, Md., July 7, 1922; s. James Grover and Rose Adele (Hulshart) W.; B.S. in Edn., Md. State Coll., Salisbury, 1946; B.S., Washington Coll., 1948; M.S., U. Del., 1949, Ph.D. in Chemistry, 1951; grad. Program Mgmt. Devel., Harvard, 1967; grad. Fed. Execs. Inst., U. Va., 1972; m. Blanca

Zulema Guerrero, June 4, 1950; children—James Alfred, Ronald Keith. Asst. prof. Trinity U., San Antonio, 1951-52; research chemist S.W. Research Inst., San Antonio, 1951-52, Calif. Research Corp., Richmond, 1952-60; with Nat. Bur. Standards, 1960—. chief bldg. research div., 1967-72, dir. center bldg. tech., 1972-74, dep. dir. Inst. for Applied 1974-76, acting dir., 1976-78, dep. dir. Nat. Engring Lab., 1978—; head U.S. del. industralized bldg. to USSR, 1969; U.S. del. Internat. Union Testing and Research Labs. for Materials and Structures, 1969-74, 75—, mem. bur., 1970-73, 74-78, pres., 1971-72, v.p., 1979—; mem. bldg. research adv. bd. NRC, 1976—; vice chmn., mem. exec. com. U.S. nat. com. Internat. Council Bldg. Research, Studies and Documentation, 1969-73; rep. Nat. Bur. Standards to Fed. Constrn. Council, 1967-70; mem. fire council Underwriters Labs., 1969-73; mem. U.S.-Egypt working group Tech. Research and Devel., 1976—; hon. mem. Producers Council. Served as officer AUS, 1943-46; ETO. Decorated Bronze Star, Purple Heart; recipient Gold medal award for exceptional service Dept. Commerce, 1975. Mem. Am. Chem. Soc., ASTM (dir. 1977—), Chem. Soc. Washington (chmn. auditing com. 1965-66, chmn. profl. relations and status com. 1964, chmn. long range planning com. 1967; asso. editor Capital Chemist 1963-65), Sigma Xi, Kappa Alpha. Author, patentee in field. Home: 6204 Lone Oak Dr Bethesda MD 20034 Office: Nat Bur Standards Washington DC 20234

WRIGHT, JAMES SKELLY, fed. judge; b. New Orleans, Jan. 14, 1911; s. James Edward and Margaret (Skelly) W.; Ph.B., Loyola U., 1931, LL.B., 1934; LL.D., Yale U., 1961, U. Notre Dame, 1962, Howard U., 1964, U. So. Calif., 1975; m. Helen Mitchell Patton, Feb. 1, 1945; 1 son, James Skelly. High sch. tchr., 1931-35; lectr. English history Loyola U., 1936-37; asst. U.S. atty., New Orleans, 1937-46; U.S. atty. E. Dist. La., 1948-49; U.S. dist. judge E. Dist. La., 1949-62; U.S. circuit judge, D.C., 1962-78; chief judge U.S. Ct. Appeals D.C. Circuit, 1978—; faculty Loyola U. Sch. Law, 1950-62; James Madison lectr. N.Y. U., 1965; Robert L. Jackson lectr. Nat. Coll. State Trial Judges, 1966; lectr. U. Tex., 1967; Irvine lectr. Cornell U., 1968; Brainerd Currie lectr. Duke U., 1970; lectr. Notre Dame in London, 1974; Meiklejohn lectr. Brown U., 1976; lectr. adminstrv. law Tulane U. in Grenoble, 1979; Francis Biddle lectr. Harvard Law Sch., 1979; admitted to U.S. Supreme Ct. bar. Served as lt. comdr. USCG, 1942-46. Observer U.S. State Dept. Internat. Fisheries Conf., London, 1943. Mem. La. (bd. govs.), Fed. (pres. New Orleans chpt.), D.C., Am., New Orleans bar assns., Am. Law Inst., Blue Key, Phi Delta Phi, Alpha Delta Gamma (nat. pres.). Roman Catholic. Democrat. Home: 5317 Blackistone Rd Westmoreland Hills Washington DC 20016 Office: US Courthouse Washington DC 20001

WRIGHT, JAMES WILLIAM, publisher; b. Omaha, Aug. 21, 1929; s. Clarren Elvin, Jr. and Elizabeth Ellen (Sickel) W.; student U. Omaha, 1954-55, Orange Coast Coll., 1974-76; m. Judy Lee Bontempo, July 5, 1974; children—Gina Elizabeth, James Clarren; stepchildren—Frank R. Sommer, Michael R. Sommer. Tech. writer Butler Publns., Los Angeles, 1958-61; tech. editor Motor Trend mag., 1961-64; West coast editor Popular Sci. mag., 1965-68; freelance writer/photographer, Los Angeles, 1968-71; publisher Wright Pub. Co. Inc., pubs. DuneBuggies and Hot VWS, 3Wheeling, Far West mags., Costa Mesa, Calif., 1972—. Served with AUS, 1951-53; Korea. Mem. Soc. Automotive Engrs., Western Publns. Assn., Western Writers Am., Westerners, Internat. Motor Sports Assn. Office: 2949 Century Pl Costa Mesa CA 92626

WRIGHT, JANE COOKE, physician, educator; b. N.Y.C., Nov. 30, 1919; d. Louis T. and Corinne (Cooke) W.; A.B., Smith Coll., 1942; M.D. with honors, N.Y. Med. Coll., 1945; Dr. Med. Scis., Women's Med. Coll. Pa., 1965; Sc.D., Denison U., 1971; m. David J. Jones. Intern Bellevue Hosp., N.Y.C., 1945-46, resident, 1946, mem. staff, 1955-67; resident Harlem Hosp., 1947, chief resident, 1948, mem. staff, 1949-55; practice medicine specializing in clin. cancer chemotherapy, N.Y.C., mem. faculty dept. surgery Med. Center, N.Y. U., N.Y.C., 1955-67, adj. asso. prof., 1961-67, also dir. cancer chemotherapy services research, 1955-67; prof. surgery, N.Y. Med. Coll., N.Y.C., 1967, asso. dean, 1967-75; mem. staff Manhattan VA Hosp., 1955-67, Midtown, Met., Bird S. Color, Flower-Fifth Ave. hosps., all N.Y.C., 1967-79, Westchester County Med. Center Valhalla, N.Y., 1971—, Lincoln Hosp., Bronx, N.Y., 1979—; Cons. Health Ins. Plan of Greater N.Y., 1962—; cons. Blvd. Hosp., 1963—, St. Luke's Hosp., Newburgh, N.Y., 1964—, pelvic malignancy rev. com. N.Y. Gynecol. Soc., 1965-66, St. Vincent's Hosp., N.Y.C., 1966—, Dept. Health, Edn. and Welfare, 1968-70, Wyckoff Heights Hosp., N.Y.C., 1969—, NIH, 1971—, others. Mem. Manhattan council State Commn. Human Rights, 1949—, Pres.'s Commn. Heart Disease, Cancer and Stroke, 1964-65, Nat. Adv. Cancer Council, 1966-70, N.Y. State Women's Council, 1970-72. Bd. dirs. Medico-CARE; trustee Smith Coll., Northampton, Mass. Recipient numerous awards, including Mademoiselle mag. award, 1952, Lady Year award Harriet Beecher Stowe Jr. High Sch., 1958, Spirit Achievement award Albert Einstein Sch. Medicine, 1965, certificate Honor award George Gershwin Jr. High Sch., 1967, Myrtle Wreath award Hadassah, 1967, Smith medal Smith Coll., 1968, Outstanding Am. Women award Am. Mothers Com. Inc., 1970, Golden Plate award Am. Acad. Achievement, 1971. Fellow N.Y. Acad. Medicine; mem. Nat. Med. Assn. (edit. bd. jours.), Manhattan Central, N.Y. County (nominating com.) med. socs., A.M.A., A.A.A.S., Am. Assn. Cancer Research (dir.), N.Y. Acad. Scis., N.Y. Cancer Soc., Internat. Med. and Research Found. (v.p.), Am. (dir. div.), N.Y. (pres. 1970-71) cancer socs., Am. Soc. Clin. Oncology (sec. treas. 1964-67), Contin Soc., Sigma Xi, Lambda Kappa Mu, Alpha Omega Alpha. Club: The 400 (N.Y. Med. Coll.). Contbr. articles to profl. jours. Office: NY Med Coll Lincoln Hosp Affiliation 234 E 149th St Bronx NY 10451

WRIGHT, JEANNE ELIZABETH JASON, editorial syndication co. exec., editor; b. Washington, June 24, 1934; d. Robert Stewart and Elizabeth (Gaddis) Jason; B.A., Radcliffe Coll., 1956; M.A., U. Chgo., 1958; m. Benjamin Hickman Wright, Oct. 30, 1965; stepchildren—Benjamin, Deborah, David, Patricia. Psychiat. social worker Lake County Mental Health Clinic, Gary, Ind., Psychiat. and Psychosomatic Inst., Michael Reese Hosp., Chgo., Jewish Child Care Assn., N.Y.C., 1958-70; gen. mgr. Black Media, Inc., advt. rep. co., N.Y.C., 1970-74, pres., 1974-75; pres. Black Resources, Inc. and exec. editor New Nat. Black Monitor, newspapers, N.Y.C., 1975—, also syndicated weekly features. Mem. planning com. First Black Power Conf., Newark, 1966, Second Black Power Conf., Phila., 1967; First Internat. Black Cultural and Bus. Expn., N.Y.C., 1971; nat. bd. dirs. Family Service Assn. Am., 1968-70; bd. dirs. Afro-Am. Family & Community Services, Inc., Chgo., 1971-75. Recipient Pres.'s award Nat. Assn. Black Women Attys., 1977, 2d Ann. Freedom's Jour. award Journalism Students and Faculty of U. D.C. Dept. Communicative and Performing Arts, 1979. Mem. Nat. Assn. Social Workers, AAAS, Acad. Cert. Social Workers, NAACP, Nat. Assn. Media Women, African Heritage Studies Assn., U. Chgo. Alumni Assn., Alpha Kappa Alpha. Democrat. Club: Radcliffe (N.Y.C.). Office: 410 Central Park W Penthouse C New York NY 10025

WRIGHT, JOHN CHARLES YOUNG, oil and gas co. exec.; b. Mercer, Pa., May 18, 1925; s. Paul Hatfield and Helen (Munnel) W.; B.A., Denison U., 1947; B.S. in Mining Engring., Ohio State U., 1949, M.Sc. in Petroleum Engring., 1950; m. Becky Bell Lewis, June 9, 1951; children—John Charles, William Lewis, Mary Carolyn. Roustabout, Stanolind Oil & Gas Corp., Beaumont, Tex., 1948; roustabout So. Petroleum Exploration, Inc., Wichita Falls, Tex., 1949, asst. to pres., 1950-53, v.p., 1953—; asst. to pres. Wiser Oil Co., 1950-53, v.p., 1953-60, pres., dir., 1961—, also treas.; asst. to pres. Petroleum Exploration, Inc., Sisterville, W.Va., 1950-53, v.p., 1953-60, pres., dir., 1961—, also treas.; asst. to pres. Wittmer Oil & Gas Corp., 1950-53, petroleum engr., 1953—; pres., treas., dir. So-Petroleum, Inc., 1961—; pres., dir. Basin Oil Co., Mich.; dir. First Tyler Bank & Trust Co. Served to ensign USNR, 1943-46; lt. (s.g.) Res. Recipient Texnikoi award Ohio State U., 1958; named W.Va. Oil and Gas Man of Year, 1976. Mem. Ind. Petroleum Assn. Am. (v.p. from W.Va. 1956-57, exec. com. 1968—), Ohio trustee, dir. 1968—, pres. 1970—), Mich., Ill., Ky. (v.p.), W.Va. oil and gas assns., Am. Inst. Mining Metall. and Petroleum Engrs., Am. Legion, Sigma Chi, Sigma Gamma Epsilon. Presbyn. (elder). Mason (32 deg., Shriner). Club: Sisterville Country. Home: 252 Oxford St Sisterville WV 26175 Office: Box 192 Sisterville WV 26175

WRIGHT, JOHN COLLINS, univ. pres.; b. Oak Hill, W.Va., Aug. 5, 1927; s. John C. and Irene (Collins) W.; B.S., W.Va. Wesleyan Coll., 1948, LL.D. (hon.), 1974; Ph.D., U. Ill., 1951; D.Sc. (hon.), U. Ala. System, 1979, W.Va. Inst. Tech., 1979; m. Margaret Ann Cyphers, Sept. 11, 1949; children—Jeffrey Cyphers, John Timothy, Curtis Scott, Keith Alexander. Research chemist Hercules, Inc., 1951-57; mem. faculty W.Va. Wesleyan Coll., 1957-64; asst. program dir. NSF, 1964-65; dean Coll. Arts and Scis., No. Ariz. U., 1966-70, W.Va. U., Morgantown, 1970-74; vice chancellor W.Va. Bd. Regents, Charleston, 1974-78; pres. U. Ala., Huntsville, 1978—; interim pres. W.Va. Coll. Grad. Studies, Institute, 1975-76; hon. research asso. Univ. Coll., London, Eng., 1962-63; cons. NSF, 1965—. Served with USNR, 1945-46. Mich. fellow Center Study Higher Edn., U. Mich., 1965-66. Mem. Am. Chem. Soc., AAAS, Assn. Higher Edn. Office: U Ala Office of Pres PO Box 1247 Huntsville AL 75807

WRIGHT, JOHN DEAN, JR., educator; b. Brookline, Mass., Nov. 1, 1920; s. John Dean and Edith (Hammond) W.; B.A., Dartmouth Coll., 1942; M.A., Columbia, 1947, Ph.D., 1955; m. Frances Kohl, Nov. 22, 1942; children—Beverly May (Mrs. J. Boardman), Judith (Mrs. Ivan Lee Holt III). Asst. prof. dept. history and polit. sci. Transylvania U., Lexington, Ky., 1950-55, prof., 1955—. Served with USNR, 1942-45. Mem. Am. Hist. Assn., Orgn. Am. Historians, A.A.U.P., Kappa Sigma. Democrat. Presbyn. Author: Freedom and Reform, 1967; Transylvania: Tutor to the West, 1975. Home: 656 Raintree Rd Lexington KY 40502 Office: Transylvania Univ Lexington KY 40508

WRIGHT, JOHN EMERSON, transp. co. exec.; b. Atlanta, June 12, 1937; s. John Gabriel and Emerson Elizabeth (Purcell) W.; student Ga. State U.; m. Beverly Jean Ozburn, June 30, 1956; children—Wesley, Eugene. Pres. Atlanta Labor Council, AFL-CIO, 1959-77; chmn. Met. Atlanta Rapid Transit Authority, 1975—. Home: 2928 Old Decatur Rd NE Atlanta GA 30305 Office: 2200 Peachtree Summit 401 W Peachtree St NE Atlanta GA 30308

WRIGHT, JOHN MACNAIR, JR., assn. exec., ret. army officer; b. Los Angeles, Apr. 14, 1916; s. John MacNair and Ella (Stradley) W.; B.S., U.S. Mil. Acad., 1940; grad. Airborne Sch., 1947, Strategic Intelligence Sch., 1948, advanced course Inf. Sch. 1951, Command and Gen. Staff Coll., 1953; M.B.A., U. So. Calif., 1956; grad. Army Logistics Mgmt. Sch., 1957, Advanced Mgmt. Program, U. Pitts., 1959, Nat. War Coll., 1961; grad. Army Aviation Sch., 1965; M.S. in Internat. Affairs, George Washington U., 1973; m. Helene Tribit, June 28, 1940; children—John MacNair III, Richard Kenneth. Enlisted U.S. Army, 1935, comd. 2d. lt., 1940, advanced through grades to lt. gen., 1970; comdr. Battery Wright, Corregidor, P.I., World War II; prisoner of war of Japanese, 1942-45; with intelligence div. War Dept. Gen. Staff, 1946-48; mil. attache Am. embassy, Paraguay, 1948-50; bn. comdr. 508th Airborne Regtl. Combat Team, 1951-52; asst. chief of staff for personnel and logistics 7th Inf. Div., Korea, 1953-54; assigned office U.S. Army Chief of Staff, 1956-60; chief staff 8th Inf. Div., 1961-62; asst. chief staff plans and operations 7th Corps, 1962-63, 7th Army, 1963-64; asst. div. comdr. 11th Air Assault Div., 1964-65, 1st Cav. Div. (Airmobile), Vietnam, 1965-66; assigned office asst. Chief Staff Force Devel., 1966-67; comdg. gen. U.S. Army Inf. Center, comdt. U.S. Army Inf. Sch., 1967-69; comdg. gen. 101st Airborne Div. (Airmobile), Vietnam, 1969-70; controller of the Army, Washington, 1970-73; ret., 1973; dir. research and devel. Boy Scouts Am., 1973, nat. dir. program, 1974-77, nat. dir. program support, 1977-78, nat. dir. Exploring, 1978—. Pres. Chattahoochee (Ga.) council Boy Scouts Am., 1968-69, mem. exec. bd. region 5, 1967-69, mem. Nat. council, 1964-73; tech. adviser Vietnamese Boy Scout Assn., 1965-66. Decorated D.S.M. with 2 oak leaf clusters, Silver Star with oak leaf cluster, Legion of Merit with oak leaf cluster, D.F.C., Bronze Star, Air medal with 59 oak leaf clusters, Army Commendation medal, Purple Heart with oak leaf cluster, Combat Inf. badge, numerous area and campaign ribbons; recipient Silver Beaver award Boy Scouts Am., 1961, Silver Antelope award, 1969, Distinguished Eagle Scout award, 1971. Mem. Assn. U.S. Army, Army Aviation Assn. Am. (pres. 1974-76), Inf. Mus. Assn. (trustee), 101st Airborne Div. Assn., 1st Cavalry Div. Assn., Amateur Radio Relay League, Phi Kappa Phi, Beta Gamma Sigma, Alpha Kappa Psi. Club: Rotary. Home: 3813 Acapulco Ct University Hills Irving TX 75062 Office: Boy Scouts Am PO Box 61030 Dallas-Fort Worth Airport TX 75261

WRIGHT, JOHN PEALE, banker; b. Chattanooga, Mar. 27, 1924; s. Robert T. and Margaret (Peale) W.; student Davidson Coll., 1941-43, U. N.C., 1943; B.S. in Phys. Sci., U. Chgo., 1944; M.B.A., Harvard, 1947; m. Ruth Garrison, Sept. 11, 1948; children—Margaret Shapard, John Peale, Ruth Garrison, Mary Ivens. With Am. Nat. Bank & Trust Co., Chattanooga, 1947—, pres., 1962—, also dir.; dir. Ancorp Bancshares, Chattanooga. Bd. dirs. Chattanooga Area Heart Assn.; bd. dirs., fin. v.p. Covenant Fellowship Presbyterians, 1978—. Served to lt. USAAF, 1943-46. Mem. Robert Morris Assos. (pres. 1968-69), Tenn. Bankers Assn. (bd. dirs., pres. 1973-74). Presbyterian (elder, treas.). Home: 1331 Scenic Hwy Lookout Mountain TN 37350 Office: 736 Market St Chattanooga TN 37401

WRIGHT, JOHN ROBERT, pathologist; b. Winnipeg, Man., Can. Aug. 18, 1935; came to U.S., 1961, naturalized, 1968; s. Ross Grant and Anna Marie (Crispin) W.; M.D. with honors, U. Man., 1959; m. Deanna Pauline Johnson, June 25, 1960; children—Carolyn Deanna, David John. Intern, Winnipeg Gen. Hosp., 1959-60, resident, 1960-61; resident Balt. City Hosp., 1961-63, Buffalo Gen. Hosp., 1963-64; teaching fellow in medicine U. Man., 1960-61; instr. in pathology, Buswell fellow SUNY, Buffalo, 1965-67, prof. pathology, chmn. dept. pathology, 1974—; asst. chief pathology Balt. City Hosps. and asst. prof. Johns Hopkins U., 1967-74; cons. Roswell Park Meml. Inst., 1975—. Recipient Louis A. and Ruth Siegel Disting. Teaching award SUNY, Buffalo, 1977, 78. Diplomate Am. Bd. Pathology. Mem. Assn. Am. Pathologists, Am. Soc. Clin. Pathologists, Internat. Acad. Pathologists, Assn. Pathology Chairmen, Am. Heart Assn. Research in amyloidosis and aging, pathology of amyloidosis, characterization of clin. amyloid syndromes. Home: 46 Wynngate Ln Williamsville NY 14221 Office: 204 Farber Hall SUNY Buffalo NY 14214

WRIGHT, JOSEPH ROBERT, JR., banker; b. Tulsa, Sept. 24, 1938; s. Joe Robert and Ann Helen (Cech) W.; B.S., Colo. Sch. Mines, 1961; M.B.A., Yale, 1963. Vice pres. Booz, Allen & Hamilton, 1965-71; dep. dir. Bur. Census, Dept. Commerce, 1971-72, dep. adminstr. mgmt. Social and Econ. Statis. Adminstrn., 1972-73, asst. sec. econ. affairs, 1973; asst. sec. adminstr. Dept. Agr., 1973-76; pres. Citicorp Custom Credit, Inc., N.Y.C., 1976—; pres. Retail Consumer Services, Inc., N.Y.C., 1977—. Served to 1st lt. AUS, 1963-65. Home: 565 Park Ave New York NY 10021 Office: 485 Lexington Ave New York NY

WRIGHT, JOSEPH SUTHERLAND, lawyer; b. Portland, Oreg., Mar. 16, 1911; s. Joseph Alfred and Carrie (Sutherland) W.; LL.B., George Washington U., 1937; m. Ruth Lacklen, Nov. 14, 1936; children—Joseph Sutherland, Susan Jane. Sec., Senator B. K. Wheeler, 1933-36; admitted to D.C. bar, 1934; atty. FTC, 1936-42; asst. gen. counsel, chief compliance, 1947-52; asst. gen. counsel Zenith Radio Corp., Chgo., 1952-53, gen. counsel, dir., 1953-58, v.p., 1951-58, exec. v.p. 1958-59, pres., gen. mgr., 1959-68, chief exec. officer, 1965-76, 79—, chmn., 1968-76, 79—; dir. Standard Oil (Ind.), Bethlehem Steel Corp., Sunbeam Corp., Commonwealth Edison Corp. Trustee U. Chgo., George Washington U., John Crerar Library. Served to lt. comdr. USNR, 1942-45. Mem. Chgo. Bar Assn. Clubs: Commercial, Tavern, Chicago, Chgo. Yacht (Chgo.); Metropolitan (Washington); Park Ridge Country. Home: 145 Oxford Rd Kenilworth IL 60043 Office: 1000 Milwaukee Ave Glenview IL 60025 also Zenith Radio Corp 1900 N Austin Blvd Chicago IL 60639

WRIGHT, JOYCE MARY, librarian; b. Vegreville, Alta., Can.; d. George Ernest and Leah Maria (Tripp) W.; came to U.S., 1921, naturalized, 1944; B.A., U. Wash., 1938, B.L.S., 1939; postgrad. U. Wash., 1940-43, U. Hawaii, 1946-51, Sch. Oriental and African Studies, U. London, 1961-62. Reference asst. U. Wash. Library, 1939-43; reference asst. Seattle Pub. Library, 1943-46; reference and circulation asst. U. Hawaii Library, 1946-52, head reference dept., 1954-64, head Asia Collection, 1970—; head librarian Reed Coll. Library, Portland, Oreg., 1952-54; asso. dir. East West Center Library, Honolulu, 1965, acting dir., 1966-68, dir., 1968-70; lectr. U. Hawaii Grad. Sch. Library Studies, 1967-68; mem. SSRC/ACLS Joint Com. on Korean Studies subcom. on materials, 1968-70. Mem. ALA (chmn. Asian and N. African subsect. 1970-71, mem. Internat. Relations Round Table, chmn. S.E. Asia sect. 1971-75), Hawaii Library Assn. (editor Jour. 1949-50, pres. 1968), Assn. Asian Studies (com. on research materials on S.E. Asia 1969-73, editor Newsletter 1975—, mem. exec. group. com. on East Asian libraries 1979—), Internat. Assn. Orientalist Librarians, Honolulu Acad. Arts, Bishop Mus., Phi Beta Kappa, Delta Phi Alpha. Home: 622 Koko Isle Circle Honolulu HI 96825 Office: Asia Collection U Hawaii Library 2550 The Mall Honolulu HI 96822

WRIGHT, KENNETH OSBORNE, astronomer; b. Ft. George, B.C., Can., Nov. 1, 1911; s. Charles Melville and Agnes Pearl (Osborne) W.; B.A., U. Toronto (Ont., Can.), 1933, M.A., 1934; Ph.D., U. Mich., 1940; D.Sc. (hon.), Nicholas Copernicus U., Torun, Poland, 1973; m. Margaret Lindsay Sharp, Sept. 25, 1936; 1 dau., Nora Louise Wright Osborne; m. 2d, Jean May MacLachlan, Mar. 21, 1970. With Dominion Astrophys. Obs., Victoria, B.C., 1936—, asst. dir., 1960-66, dir., 1966-76, guest worker, 1976—; lectr. U. B.C., 1943-44; spl. lectr. in astronomy U. Toronto, 1959-60; research asso. Mt. Wilson and Palomar Obs., 1962; chmn. asso. com. on astronomy NRC Can., 1972-74. Decorated Can. Centennial medal. Fellow Royal Soc. Can.; mem. Internat. Astron. Union, Am. Astron. Soc., Royal Astron. Soc. Can. (Gold medal 1933), Royal Astron. Soc., Astron. Soc. Pacific. Mem. United Ch. of Can. Clubs: Rotary, Round Table. Research, publs. in field. Home: 205 2768 Satellite St Victoria BC V8S 5G8 Canada Office: 5071 W Saanich Rd Victoria BC V8X 3X3 Canada

WRIGHT, LAFAYETTE HART, educator; b. Chickasha, Okla., Dec. 3, 1917; s. L.C. and Jessie (Hart) W.; A.B., U. Okla., 1938, LL.B., 1941; LL.M., U. Mich., 1942; m. Phyllis Jeanne Blanchard, June 4, 1938; children—Robin Blanchard, Jana Hart. Admitted to Okla. bar, 1941, Mich. bar, 1952; mem. faculty U. Mich., 1947—, prof. law, 1953—; vis. asso. prof. Stanford, 1953; cons. IRS, 1956-60, 67-68, mem. adv. group, 1960-61; vis. disting. prof. law U. Okla., 1976. Bd. dirs. Ann Arbor Family Service, 1954, Ann Arbor chpt. Americans for Democratic Action, 1968; mem. adv. bd. Internat. Bur. Fiscal Documentation, Amsterdam, 1970—; mem. legal policy activities bd. Taxation with Representation Fund, Washington, 1975—. Served to maj., F.A., AUS, 1942-46; ETO. Decorated Bronze Star; recipient award for meritorious civilian service Treasury Dept., 1957. Mem. Am. Bar Assn., Order of Coif, Phi Beta Kappa, Phi Delta Theta. Democrat. Author: Tax Affairs of Individuals, 1957; Tax Affairs of Corporations, 1962; Needed Changes in Internal Revenue Service Conflict Resolution. Procedures, 1970. Co-author: Comparative Conflict Resolution Procedures in Taxation, 1968; American Enterprise in the European Common Market: A Legal Profile, 1960; Federal Tax Liens, 1967. Home: 3079 Exmoor St Ann Arbor MI 48104

WRIGHT, LEMUEL DARY, biochemist, educator; b. Nashua, N.H., Mar. 1, 1913; s. Clarence Herman and Avis (Dary) W.; B.S., U. N.H., 1935, M.S., 1936; postgrad. Pa. State U., 1936-37; Ph.D., Oreg. State U., 1940; m. Dorthol Ernestine Quarles, May 3, 1941; children—Carolyn (Mrs. David W. Corson), Martha Susan (Mrs. Evans Young), Priscilla Dee (Mrs. Frederick J. Pazzano), Barbara Ellen (Mrs. Alvin Graham), Nancy Alice (Mrs. John Matyas). Fellow, U. Tex., 1940-41; instr. U. W.Va. Sch. Medicine, 1941-42; from research biochemist to dir. microbiol. research Merck Sharp & Dohme Research Labs. (formerly Sharp and Dohme Labs.), 1942-56; prof. emeritus nutrition and biochemistry div. nutritional scis. and sect. biochemistry and molecular biology Cornell U., Ithaca, N.Y.; mem. study sect. NIH. Mem. Am. Chem. Soc., Am. Soc. Biol. Chemists, Am. Inst. Nutrition (Borden award 1958), Soc. Exptl. Biology and Medicine. Contbr. articles profl. jours. Home: 1035 Hanshaw Rd Ithaca NY 14850

WRIGHT, LEROY AUGUSTUS, lawyer; b. San Diego, Apr. 12, 1914; s. Lester A. and Georgie S. (Hardy) W.; A.B., Stanford U., 1936, LL.B., 1939; m. Mary L. Lindley, June 20, 1940; children—Shelley Wright Bassman, Bruce M., Marcy, Jean. Admitted to Calif. bar, 1939, since practiced in San Diego; partner firm Glenn, Wright, Jacobs & Schell, 1952—; dir., exec. com. Imperial Corp. Am. Fellow Am. Bar Found.; mem. Am., Calif., San Diego (pres. 1951) bar assns., Am. Law Inst. (life). Club: San Diego Yacht. Home: 4042 Liggett Dr San Diego CA 92106 Office: 2320 5th Ave Suite 300 San Diego CA 92101

WRIGHT, LESLIE STEPHEN, univ. pres.; b. Birmingham, Ala., Jan. 23, 1913; s. Abner King and Janet Isabel (Walton) W.; A.B., U. Louisville, 1936, M.A., 1939; postgrad. U. Ky., 1940; LL.D., Ala. Poly. Inst., 1959, U. Ala., 1959; m. Lolla Catherine Wurtele, Dec. 2, 1939; children—Leslie Stephen, John King. Tchr., coach, schs. Ky. and Ala., 1936-41; expediting supr. E. I. DuPont Co., Ala., 1941-42; indsl. specialist WPB, Ala., 1942-43, state dir. Civilian Prodn. Adminstrn., Ala., 1946-47; dep. state dir. for Ala., Savs. Bond div. Treasury Dept., 1947-50; exec. sec. to Sen. Lister Hill. Washington.

1950-54; exec. sec. Bapt. Found. of Ala., 1954-58; pres. Samford U., 1958—. Mem. citizens supervisory commn. Jefferson County Pres. Southwide Assn. Bapt. Found. Execs., 1958; sec.-treas. Conf. Ch.-Related Colls. of South, 1963; pres. Ala. Writers Conclave, 1965-67, chmn. Ala. Selection Com. Rhodes Scholars, 1965-66; chmn. div. pvt. colls and univs. Alabama War Meml. Scholarship Fund Drive, 1967. Chmn. Jefferson County United Appeal Campaign, 1966; nat. bd. of advisers Young Ams. for Freedom; vice chmn. Gov.'s Commn. on Status of Women, 1964-65; mem. Ala. Ednl. Television Commn., 1968—, Nat. Trust for Historic Preservation, Birmingham Area Community Service Council; mem. nat. adv. bd. Nat. Inst. for Law, Order, Justice. Dir. Ala. Council on Economic Edn., Ala. Pops orch.; trustee Birmingham Symphony Assn., So. Bapt. Theol. Seminary; mem. nat. bd. visitors Freedoms Found. at Valley Forge. Served as lt. Communications Intelligence, USNR, 1944-46. Recipient George Washington Honor Medal. Freedoms Found. at Valley Forge, 1963, 66, 67; Vigilant Patriots award, All American Conference to Combat Communism, 1963. Mem. N.E.A., Assn. Am. Colls., Am. Assn. Sch. Adminstrs., Am. Council on Edn., So. Assn. Sch. Adminstrs., Am. Council on Edn., So. Assn. Colls. and Secondary Schs., Assn. of Southern Baptist Colls. and Schs. (pres. 1968—), Ala. Hist. Assn. (pres. 1964-65), Executives Club of Birmingham (pres. 1964-65), Am. Legion (state chmn. edn. and scholarship com.), Newcomen Soc. N. Am., Ala. Assn. Ind. Colls. (pres. 1960-63), Ala. Edn. Assn., Assn. Ala. Coll. Adminstrs. (past pres.), Ala. Bapt. Brotherhood Conv. (pres. 1948-50), Ala. Society of Children of the Am. Revolution, Alpha Phi Omega. Kappa Alpha, Pi Gamma Mu. Baptist (deacon), Rotarian (pres. 1966-67). Office: Samford U 800 Lakeshore Dr Birmingham AL 35209*

WRIGHT, LOUIS BOOKER, historian, library dir.; b. Greenwood County, S.C., March 1, 1899; s. Thomas Fleming and Lena (Booker) W.; A.B., Wofford Coll., Spartanburg, S.C., 1920; A.M., U. N.C., 1924, Ph.D., 1926, L.H.D., 1950; Litt.D., Wofford Coll., 1941, Mills Coll., 1947, Princeton U., 1948, Amherst Coll., 1948, Occidental Coll., 1949, Bucknell U., 1951, Franklin and Marshall Coll., 1957, Colby Coll., 1959, U. B.C., 1960, U. Birmingham (Eng.), 1964, U. Leicester (Eng.), 1965; LL.D., Tulane U., 1950, George Washington U., 1958, U. Chattanooga, 1959, U. Akron, 1961, St. Andrews U., Scotland, 1961, Washington and Lee U., 1964, Mercer U., 1965; L.H.D., Northwestern U., 1948, Yale U., 1954, Rockford Coll., 1956, Coe Coll., 1959, Georgetown U., 1961, Calif. State Coll., Fullerton, 1966, U. Calif. at Los Angeles, 1967, Brown U., 1968, U. S.C., 1972, Lander Coll., 1974; m. Frances Marion Black, June 10, 1925; 1 son, Louis Christopher. Mem. faculties U. N.C., Johns Hopkins U., Emory U., Calif. Inst. Tech., U. Calif. at Los Angeles, U. Wash., U. Minn., Pomona Coll., Ind. U., 1926-48; Guggenheim research fellow in Eng. and Italy, 1928-30; mem. research staff Huntington Library, 1932-48; dir. Folger Shakespeare Library, Washington, 1948-68; cons. Xerox-Univ. Microfilms, 1968-71; cons. in history Nat. Geog. Soc., 1971—. Mem. adv. bd. John Simon Guggenheim Meml. Found., 1942-71, chmn. bd., 1950-71; vice chmn. dirs. Council Library Resources, Inc., 1956—; life trustee Shakespeare Birthplace Trust, Stratford-upon-Avon, 1964—; trustee Nat. Geog. Soc., 1964-74, Winterthur Mus.; bd. dirs. Harry S. Truman Library Inst. for Nat. and Internat. Affairs, 1956—; bd. visitors Tulane U., 1965—, chmn., 1972-74. Served in U.S. Army, World War I. Decorated officer Order Brit. Empire; recipient Benjamin Franklin medal Royal Soc. Arts, 1969. Fellow Royal Soc. Lit., Royal Soc. Arts, Royal Hist. Soc.; mem. Am. Hist. Assn. (exec. sec. 1964-65), Mass. Hist. Soc., Am. Philos. Soc. (v.p. 1974-78), Am. Antiquarian Soc., Am. Acad. Arts and Scis., Modern Humanities Research Assn., Am. Assn. Learned Socs. (dir. 1971-77), Phi Beta Kappa (senator, Distinguished Service award 1976), several other profl. assns. Clubs: Tudor and Stuart (Johns Hopkins); Cosmos (Ann. Award for distinction in letters 1973) (Washington); Century (N.Y.C.). Author many books on hist. subjects, latest: Shakespeare for Everyman, 1964; Dream of Prosperity in Colonial America, 1965; Everyday Life in Colonial America, 1967; Everyday Life on the American Frontier, 1968; Gold, Glory and the Gospel, 1970; (with Elaine W. Fowler) Everyday Life in New Nation, 1972; Barefoot in Arcadia: Memories of a More Innocent Era, 1973; Tradition and the Founding Fathers, 1975; South Carolina: A Bicentennial History, 1976; Of Books and Men, 1976. Editor alone or with others numerous items on Am. and English history, including: William Byrd of Virginia, The London Diary, 1712-1721 (with Marion Tinling), 1958; The Folger Library General Reader's Shakespeare Series (with Virginia LaMar), 1957-68; The Prose Works of William Byrd of Westover, 1966; (with Elaine W. Fowler) English Colonization of North America, 1968, West and By North: North America Seen Through the Eyes of Its Seafaring Discoverers, 1971, The Moving Frontier, 1972; The John Henry County Map of Virginia 1770, 1977; editorial bd. History Book Club; contbr. articles to profl. jours. Home: 3702 Leland St Chevy Chase MD 20015 Office: Nat Geographic Soc Washington DC 20036

WRIGHT, MARCELLUS EUGENE, JR., architect; b. nr. Richmond, Va., Feb. 16, 1907; s. Marcellus Eugene and Rita Brink (Stovall) W.; B.Arch., U. Pa., 1929, M.Arch., 1930; postgrad. Ecole Des Beaux Arts, Fontainebleau, France, 1930; m. Joyce Bradt Patteson, Sept. 21, 1940; children—Pamela Lee Patteson Wright Brown, Westley Anne Patteson Wright Byrne, Eliza Ann Penton, Jennifer Pendleton. Instr., U. Pa., 1929-30, Coll. William and Mary, 1934-35; architect Marcellus E. Wright, 1930-33, 36-39; partner Marcellus Wright & Son, Architects, Richmond, Va., 1939-64, Marcellus Wright & Partners, Richmond, 1965-74, Marcellus Wright, Cox, Climberg & Ladd, 1974-76; cons. Marcellus Wright, Cox & Ladd, also Va. Dept. Correction, 1976—; engr. Emergency Relief Adminstrn., WPA, City of Richmond and surrounding counties, 1933-35; architect Joint Assyrian Expdn., Tepe Gawra, Iraq, 1935-36; asst. chief WPB, Washington, 1942. Mem. eagle scout hon. ct. Boy Scouts Am.; v.p. Va. Mental Health Assn.; chmn. hosp. architects com. Am. Hosp. Assn.; mem. archtl. advisory panel Gen. Service Adminstrn.; mem. Valentine Mus., Westhampton Citizens Assn. past chmn. Richmond City Planning Commn.; past chmn. Richmond Regional Planning Commn.; chmn. constrn. and housing task group Va. Emergency Resources Planning Com.; mem. Va. Citizens Planning Assn., Downtown Devel. Commn. Served with C.E., U.S. Army, 1942-45. Registered profl. architect, Va., Md., N.C., Ohio, N.Y., W.Va., Washington, N.Y. Fellow AIA (chmn. nat. jud. bd.); mem. Modular Bldg. Standards Assn., Central Richmond Assn. (pres. 1973-75, chmn. bd. 1976), Assn. Preservation Va. Antiquities (advisory bd.), Children's Theatre, Soc. Archtl. Historians, Soc. Mil. Engrs., Am. Soc. Planning Ofcls., ASTM, Va. Hist. Soc., Va., Richmond (aviation com., indsl. devel. commn.) chambers commerce, Res. Officers Assn., Nat. Municipal League, S.A.R., S.C.V., Navy League, Phi Kappa Psi. Kiwanian. Clubs: Ivy League, Country of Va., Commonwealth, The Richmond Hundred, Bull and Bear (Richmond); Princess Anne Country (Virginia Beach, Va.). Prin. works include Byrd Airport, Richmond, Regional Post Office, Richmond, Western State Hosp., Staunton, Va., Fed. Res. Bank Records Center, Culpeper, Va., Am. House Motor Hotels, Wise Point and Petersburg, Va., Community Colls., Chester, Richmond, Danville, Weyers Cave, Abington, and Tazewell, Va. Home: 207 Old Orchard Ln Richmond VA 23226 Office: 1501 N Hamilton St Richmond VA 23230

WRIGHT, MARGARET RUTH, zoologist, educator; b. Rochester, N.Y., Mar. 24, 1913; d. Adelbert Frank and Ethal (Potter) Wright; A.B., U. Rochester, 1934, M.S., 1938; Ph.D., Yale, 1946. Instr. zoology Middlebury (Vt.) Coll., 1943-46; instr. zoology Vassar Coll., 1946-48, asst. prof., 1948-53, asso. prof., 1953-59, prof., 1959-78, prof. emeritus, 1978—. Mem. AAAS, Am. Soc. Zoologists, N.Y. Acad. Scis., Am. Inst. Biol. Scis., AAUP, Sigma Xi. Contbr. articles to profl. jours. Home: 47 Marian Ave Poughkeepsie NY 12601

WRIGHT, MARSHALL, bus exec.; b. El Dorado, Ark., July 14, 1926; s. John Harvey and Helen Vaughan (Williams) W.; student U. Ark., 1946-48, Cornell U., 1957-58; B.S. in Fgn. Service, Georgetown U., 1951; sr. fellow Nat. War Coll., 1969-70; m. Mabel Olean Johnson, Sept. 10, 1951; children—William Marshall, Jefferson Vaughan. Joined U.S. Fgn. Service, 1953; vice consul, Egypt, 1953-55; adminstrv. officer, Can., 1956; econ. officer, Burma, 1958-60; polit. officer, Thailand, 1966-67; spokesman for State Dept., 1964-66; country dir. for Philippines, 1969; sr. mem. NSC, 1967-68, 70-72, dir. long range planning, 1970-72; asst. sec. state for congl. relations, 1972-74; v.p. govt. affairs Eaton Corp., 1974-76, v.p. pub. affairs, 1976—. Trustee Cleve. Red Cross, Cleve. Orch.; bd. dirs. Playhouse Sq. Found.; mem. Conf. Bd. Pub. Affairs Research Council; chmn. MAPI Pub. Affairs Council. Served with USMCR, 1944-46. Recipient Meritorious Service award State Dept., 1966, Distinguished Service award, 1972. Mem. Am. Fgn. Service Assn., Kappa Sigma. Georgetown, Columbia Country, Metropolitan (Washington); Mayfield Country (Cleve.). Home: 2 Bratenahl Pl Suite 1E Cleveland OH 44108 Office: Eaton Corp 100 Erieview Plaza Cleveland OH 44108

WRIGHT, MARVIN EUGENE, JR., librarian; b. Alexandria, La., Sept. 4, 1936; s. Marvin Eugene and Yvonne Josephine (Gravel) W.; B.A., Northwestern State Coll., La., 1958; M.S., La. State U., 1961; J.D., Loyola U., New Orleans, 1974; m. Diana Jane Smith, Aug. 21, 1962; children—Gene Christopher, Amy Carroll. Tchr. high sch., Port Sulphur, La., 1959-60; reference librarian Queensborough (N.Y.) Pub. Library, 1961-62; librarian Jackson Parish Library, Jonesboro, La., 1962-63; dir. Scottsdale (Ariz.) Pub. Library, 1963-66; asst. city librarian New Orleans Pub. Library, 1966-67, city librarian, 1967—; mem. State Library Bd. Examiners, 1976—, chmn., 1979. Mem. ALA, La. (pres. 1976), Southwestern library assns., New Orleans Library Club (pres. 1969), La. Bar Assn., Phi Kappa Phi. Democrat. Roman Catholic. Rotarian. Home: 2522 Valentine Court New Orleans LA 70114 Office: 219 Loyola Ave New Orleans LA 70140

WRIGHT, MARY JEAN, educator; b. Strathroy, Ont., Can., May 20, 1915; d. Ernest Joel and Mary Jean (Clark) Wright; B.A., U. Western Ont., 1939; M.A., U. Toronto, 1940, Ph.D., 1949; LL.D. h.c., Brock U., 1979. Psychologist, Protestant Children's Village, Ottawa, 1941-42; instr. Garrison-Lane Nursery Tng. Sch., Birmingham, Eng., 1942-44; psychologist Mental Health Clinic, Hamilton, Ont., 1944-45; instr. Inst. Child Study, U. Toronto, Ont., 1945-46; asst. prof. U. Western Ont., London, 1946-55, asso. prof., 1955-62, prof., 1962—, chmn. dept. psychology Middlesex Coll., 1960-63, chmn. dept. psychology, 1963-70, dir. univ. lab. presch., 1973—. Sec., E. J. Wright Central and affiliated cos., Strathroy, 1956-78. Mem. adv. bd. London Children's Psychiat. Research Inst., 1966-70; chmn. Ont. Bd. Examiners in Psychology, 1973-74; mem. acad. panel Can. Council, 1976-79. Mem. Am. (com. on internat. relations 1977-80), Eastern, Canadian (dir., pres. 1968-69), Ont. (dir. 1950-53, pres. 1950-51) psychol. assns., Canadian Com. on Early Childhood, Nursery Edn. Assn. Ont. (dir. 1956-60, chmn. certification bd. 1964-66), Can. Assn. U. Profs., Soc. for Research in Child Devel., Gamma Phi Beta. Mem. Anglican Ch. Home: 1032 Western Rd London ON N6G 1G4 Canada

WRIGHT, MILBURN DOCKERY, educator; b. Madera, Calif., Apr. 21, 1910; s. Oscar D. and Agnes (Hunn) W.; A.B., Fresno State Coll., 1931; M.S., U. Calif. at Berkeley, 1936, Ed.D., 1947; m. Alice Lucile Fraser, June 25, 1943; 1 son, Stephen John. Tchr. Madera High Sch., 1932-36, Fresno Tech. High and Jr. Coll., 1936-39; asst. prof., then asso. prof. San Jose (Calif.) State U., 1939-40, prof. mktg., 1949-56, head div. bus., 1956-60, dean div., 1960-66, dean Sch. Bus., 1966-74, dean emeritus, 1974—; bus. cons. Condr. ednl. surveys Richmond, Redwood City, Hayward high schs., 1946-47; research asso. Temple U. Nat. Survey Distributive Edn., 1958-59; dir. No. Calif. Real Estate Research Council, 1969-72; chmn. Advt. Rev. Bd. of Santa Clara Valley. Pres. Catholic Soc. Service Agy., 1951-52. Bd. dirs. San Jose Symphony, 1974—; sec. Rotary Endowment, 1974—; bd. dirs., v.p. Montalvo Center for Arts, 1978—. Mem. Sale/Marketing Execs. Internat. (pres. 1952-53), Calif. Bus Edn. Assn. (pres. 1953-54), Am. Mktg. Assn., Soc. Advancement Mgmt., Calif. Council Vocat. Assns. (pres. 1954), Better Bus. Bur. (dir. 1970-74), San Jose State U. Alumni Assn. (dir. 1975—), Phi Kappa Phi (chpt. pres. 1967-68), Phi Delta Kappa, Delta Upsilon, Pi Omega Pi, Eta Mu Pi, Delta Pi Epsilon, Beta Gamma Sigma, Delta Sigma Pi. Clubs: Commonwealth, University, Elks, Rotary (dir. San Jose 1976-78). Author: (with C.A. Pederson) Selling Principles and Methods, rev. edit., 1976. Home: 19400 Redberry Dr Los Gatos CA 95030

WRIGHT, MYRON ARNOLD, oil field equipment exec.; b. Blair, Okla., Apr. 9, 1911; s. Charles Edgar and Hattie Susan (Dillingham) W.; student Northwestern State Tchrs. Coll., 1928-30; B.S., Okla. State U., 1933; D.Sc. (hon.), U. Tulsa; LL.D., Okla. Christian Coll.; D. Eng. (hon.), Worcester Poly. Inst.; m. Izetta Chattin, June 4, 1935 (dec.); 1 dau., Mary Judith (Mrs. Sidney Reid, Jr.); m. 2d, Josephine Primm, June 14, 1969. various engring. positions Carter Oil Co., Tulsa, 1933-43, chief petroleum engr., 1943-44, asst. mgr. prodn., 1944-46; exec. asst. producing dept. Standard Oil Co. of N.J., N.Y.C., 1946-49, dep. coordinator, 1949-51; exec. v.p. Internat. Petroleum Co., Ltd., Coral Gables, Fla., 1951-52; exec. v.p., dir. Carter Oil Co., Tulsa, 1952-54; producing coordinator Standard Oil Co. (N.J.), 1954-58, dir., 1958-60, exec. v.p., mem. exec. com. 1960-66; chmn., chief exec. officer Exxon Co. USA, 1966-76; exec. v.p., dir. Exxon Corp., 1973-76; chmn., pres. Cameron Iron Works, Inc., 1977—; dir., mem. exec com. 1st City Bancorp. Tex., Inc.; dir., mem. exec. com., audit com. Am. Gen. Ins. Co. Bd. govs. U.S. Postal Service, 1971—, chmn., 1974—. Chmn. council overseers Jesse H. Jones Grad. Sch. Adminstrn., Rice U.; mem. adv. council U. Tex. at Austin Engring. Found.; bd. dirs. Houston Symphony, Alley Theatre. Mem. Am. Inst. Mining, Metall. and Petroleum Engrs., Am. Petroleum Inst. (dir.), U.S. C. of C. pres. 1966-67, chmn. 1967-68), Houston C. of C. (dir.), Nat. Wildlife Fedn. (mem. bd. 1969-75), Fgn. Policy Assn. (dir.), Tau Beta Pi, Sigma Tau Gamma, Sigma Tau, Phi Kappa Phi, Lambda Chi Alpha. Clubs: Balboa Bay (Newport Beach, Calif.), River Oaks Country, Houston, Petroleum, Ramada, Met. Racquet (Houston); Garden of Gods (Colorado Springs, Colo.). Office: PO Box 1212 Houston TX 77001

WRIGHT, NATHALIA, educator; b. Athens, Ga., Mar. 29, 1913; d. Hilliard Carlisle and Elizabeth (MacNeal) Wright; B.A., Maryville Coll., 1933; M.A., Yale, 1938, Ph.D., 1949. Instr. Maryville Coll., 1934-35, 41-47, asst. library, 1940-43, asst. librarian, 1943-48; asst. prof. U. Tenn., 1949-55, asso., prof., 1955-62, prof. English, 1962—, Alumni Distinguished Service prof., 1974—. Recipient Willis Tew prize Yale, 1936, Albert Stanburrough Cook prize in poetry, 1937; grantee Am. Philos. Soc., 1952; Guggenheim fellow, 1953, Am. Assn. U. Women fellow, 1959. Mem. Am. Council Learned Socs. (dir. 1971—), Modern Lang. Assn. (adv. council Am. lit. sect. 1973), Melville Soc., Accademia Internazionale Siculo-Normanno, Phi Beta Kappa, Phi Kappa Phi. Author: The Inner Room, 1938; Melville's Use of the Bible, 1949, 69; Horatio Greenough, First American Sculptor, 1963; American Novelists in Italy; The Discoverers, 1965; (with Harold Orton) Questionnaire for the Investigation of American English, 1972, A World Geography of England, 1974; also articles. Author intros.: Horatio Greenough, The Travels, Observations and Experience of a Yankee Stonecutter, 1958; John Galt, The Life of Benjamin West, 1959; Washington Allston, Lectures on Art and Poems and Monaldi, 1967. Editor: Washington Irving, Journals and Notebooks, Vol. 1, 1969; Mary N. Murfree, In The Tennessee Mountains, 1970; Letters of Horatio Greenough, American Sculptor, 1972; The Miscellaneous Writings of Horatio Greenough, 1975; editorial bd. Publs. Modern Lang. Assn., 1970-75. Home: 713 Court St Maryville TN 37801

WRIGHT, OLGIVANNA LLOYD, ednl. adminstr.; b. Centinje, Montenegro, Yugoslavia; came to U.S., 1924, naturalized, 1933; d. Iovan and Militza (Milianova) Lazovich; attended sch. in Belgrade, Russia, Turkey, France; m. Frank Lloyd Wright, Aug. 25, 1926 (dec. 1959); children—Svetlana Wright Peters (dec.), Iovanna Lloyd Wright Schiffner. Co-founder (with Frank Lloyd Wright) Taliesin Fellowship, 1932; v.p. Frank Lloyd Wright Found., 1941-59, pres., 1959—; pres. Frank Lloyd Wright Sch. Architecture, 1959—; pres., cons., adv. Taliesin Associated Architects, 1959—; lectr. in art, philosophy; newspaper columnist; interior and color coordinator numerous Frank Lloyd Wright bldgs. and Taliesin Associated Architects bldgs., 1959—. Mem. Nat. Fedn. Press Women; hon. mem. Am. Soc. Interior Designers, Nat. League Am. Pen Women, Women In Communication. Author: The Struggle Within, 1955; Our House, 1959; The Shining Brow, 1960; Roots of Life, 1963; Frank Lloyd Wright, His Life, His Work, His Words, 1966; composer numerous works for chamber orch., including sonatas, trios, quartets; composer orchestral music for Taliesin Festivals of Music and Dance. Office: Taliesin Spring Green WI 53588

WRIGHT, PAUL, JR., banker; b. Birmingham, Ala., Aug. 21, 1911; s. Paul and Carolyn (Felder) W.; B.S. in Bus. Adminstrn., Duke, 1932; grad. Rutgers Coll. Grad. Sch. Banking, 1940, Exec. Program, U. N.C., 1958; m. Melba Brown Chamblee, Nov. 15, 1935; children—Hazel Elizabeth (Mrs. Thomas F. Kearns, Jr.), Paul III. Examiner, N.C. Banking Dept., 1932-41; v.p. Wachovia Bank & Trust Co., Winston-Salem, N.C., 1941-49, Bank of Va., Richmond, 1949-53; pres. Central Carolina Bank & Trust Co., Durham, N.C., 1953-74, vice chmn. bd., 1974—. Mem. N.C. Banking Commn., 1966—; trustee Found. Comml. Banks, 1958—. Served to lt. USNR, World War II. Recipient Durham Civic Honor award, 1965. Mem. Alpha Tau Omega. Democrat. Episcopalian. Home: 3807 Churchill Circle Durham NC 27707 Office: Central Carolina Bank Bldg Durham NC 27702

WRIGHT, PAUL ALBERT, biologist, educator; b. Nashua, N.H., June 15, 1920; s. Clarence H. and Avis C. (Dary) W.; B.S., Bates Coll., 1941; M.A., Harvard, 1942, Ph.D., 1944; m. Claire Wilson, June 26, 1943; children—Loren W., Darryl P., Barton D. Instr. biology Harvard, 1944-45, U. Wash., 1945-46, Boston U., 1946-47; mem. faculty U. Mich., 1947-58, asso. prof., 1956-58; mem. faculty U. N.H., 1958—, prof. zoology, 1961—, chmn. dept., 1963-69. Fellow A.A.A.S.; mem. Soc. for Study of Reprodn., Am. Soc. Zoologists (treas.), Soc. Exptl. Biology and Medicine, Phi Beta Kappa, Sigma Xi, Phi Kappa Phi. Contbr. articles to profl. jours. Home: Barrington NH 03825

WRIGHT, PAUL MCCOY, educator, chemist; b. nr. Helena, Okla., Sept. 11, 1904; s. James B. and Della (Maddox) W.; B.S., Wheaton (Ill.) Coll., 1926; M.S., Ohio State U., 1928, Ph.D., 1930; student U. Iowa, summer 1947; m. Mabel Katherine Davidson, Aug. 11, 1930; children—Marjorie Evelyn (dec.), Eugene Paul, Roger Lauren. Mem. faculty Wheaton Coll., 1929-70, prof. chemistry, chmn. dept., 1940-70, prof. emeritus, 1970—, acting chmn. dept. chemistry and geology, 1939-40, chmn., 1940-58; dir. field camp, S.D., 1946-52, 60; civilian Nat. Def. Research Com., 1944; vis. prof. Westmont Coll., Santa Barbara, Calif., 1970-71; cons. in field, 1957—; cons. elec. engring. to fgn. missions, 1971—. Fellow Am. Inst. Chemists; mem. emeritus Am. Chem. Soc., AAAS, Ill. Acad. Scis., Midwestern Assn. Chemistry Tchrs. in Liberal Arts Colls. (pres. 1960). Home: Cherokee Hills Apts #21 Tahlequah OK 74464

WRIGHT, PHILIP LINCOLN, zoologist, educator; b. Nashua, N.H., July 9, 1914; s. Clarence H. and Avis (Dary) W.; B.S., U. N.H., 1935, M.S., 1937; Ph.D., U. Wis., 1940; m. Margaret Ann Halbert, July 21, 1939; children—Alden H., Philip L., Ann E. (Mrs. Patrick Dwyer). With Univ. Mont., 1939—, instr. to asso. prof. zoology, 1939-51, prof., 1951—, chmn. dept. zoology, 1956-69, 70-71; on leave in South Africa, 1970; Maytag vis. prof. zoology Ariz. State U., 1980. Fellow AAAS; mem. Am. Soc. Zoologists, Am. Soc. Mammalogists (trustee), Mont. Acad. Scis. (pres. 1957), Soc. for Study Reprodn., Am. Inst. Biol. Scis., Am. Ornithol. Union, Cooper Ornithol. Soc., Wildlife Soc. (editorial bd. jour. Wildlife Mgmt. 1966-68), Sigma Xi, Phi Sigma, Gamma Alpha. Clubs: Explorers, Boone and Crockett (chmn. panel judges 16th award program). Asso. editor Jour. Mammalogy, 1956-64, editor gen. notes and revs., 1966-68. Contbr. numerous articles on mammalogy and ornithology.

WRIGHT, RANDOLPH EARLE, petroleum co. exec.; b. Brownsville, Tex., Dec. 22, 1920; s. William Randolph and Nelle Mae (Earle) W.; B.S., U. Tex., 1942; m. Elaine Marie Harris, May 9, 1943; 1 son, Randolph Earle. With Texaco Inc., 1946—, mgr. gas div., Houston, 1968-70, gen. mgr. producing dept., 1970-71, v.p. gas dept., 1971—, v.p., sr. officer, Houston, 1972—; pres., dir. Sabine Pipe Line Co.; v.p. Texaco Exploration Can. Ltd., Texaco Mineral Co.; dir. Coltexo Corp. Mem. engring. found. adv. council U. Tex., Austin. Mem. exec. bd. Sam Houston Area council Boy Scouts Am.; bd. dirs., 1st v.p. Jr. Achievement S.E. Tex.; bd. dirs. Houston Symphony Soc.; trustee U. St. Thomas, S.W. Research Inst. Served with USNR, World War II. Mem. Am. Petroleum Inst., Mid-Continent Oil and Gas Assn. (exec. com.), Natural Gas Men Houston, Tex. Research League (dir.), Houston C. of C. (dir.). Clubs: Houston, Lakeside, Ramada. Office: 1111 Rusk Ave Houston TX 77002

WRIGHT, RICHARD BRUCE, author, educator; b. Midland, Ont., Can., Mar. 4, 1937; s. Laverne and Laura Willette (Thomas) W.; student Ryerson Poly., 1959; B.A., Trent U., 1972; m. Phyllis Mary Cotton, Sept. 2, 1966; children—Christopher, Andrew. Radio copywriter Sta. CFOR, Orilla, Ont., 1959-60; editor, sales mgr. MacMillan Co., Toronto, Ont., 1960-68; freelance writer and novelist, 1968-75; head English dept. Ridley Coll., St. Catharines, Ont., 1975-79. Recipient Book award City of Toronto, 1974; Faber 4 Faber Book award, 1975. Jr. Can. Council fellow, 1971-72; Sr. Can. Council fellow, 1973-74, 79-80; Ont. Arts Council fellow, 1975-76, 77-78. Anglican. Author: (for children) Andrew Tolliver, 1965; (fiction) The Weekend Man, 1971; In the Middle of A Life, 1973; Farthing's Fortunes, 1976. Home: 52 St Patrick St Saint Catharines ON L2R 1K3 Canada

WRIGHT, RICHARD EARL, III, lawyer; b. Oklahoma City, Nov. 22, 1939; s. Richard Earl, Jr. and Imajean (Wall) W.; B.B.A., U. Okla., 1962, LL.B., 1964; m. Cynthia Wickstrom, Aug. 7, 1963; children—David Wilson, Marc W. Ins. investigator Remmert Adjustment Co., Oklahoma City, 1960-64; admitted to Okla. bar, 1964, since practiced in Tulsa; mem. firm Farmer & Woolsey, Inc., 1968-79; individual practice law, Tulsa, 1979—; mng. officer. Sec.-treas., dir. Ceja Corp. Adviser Indian Nations council Boy Scouts Am., 1966-69; bd. dirs. Family and Children's Service, Tulsa, 1970—, pres., 1973; bd. dirs. Cuesta Found. Mem. Okla. (chmn. com. on continuing legal edn. 1974), Tulsa County (treas. 1970) bar assns., Phi Alpha Delta, Beta Theta Pi. Republican. Presbyn. (chmn. trustees 1966-69, elder 1971-73, 80—, clk. of Session 1972-73, 80). Clubs: Tulsa Country. Home: 1602 E 36th Ct Tulsa OK 74105 Office: 901 Atlas Life Bldg Tulsa OK 74103

WRIGHT, RICHARD NEWPORT, III, civil engr., govt. ofcl.; b. Syracuse, N.Y., May 17, 1932; s. Richard Newport and Carolyn (Baker) W.; B.C.E., Syracuse U., 1953, M.C.E. (Parcel fellow), 1955; Ph.D., U. Ill., 1962; m. Teresa Rios, Aug. 23, 1959; children—John Stannard, Carolyn Maria, Elizabeth Rebecca, Edward Newport. Jr. engr. Pa. R.R., Phila., 1953-55; instr. civil engring. U. Ill. at Urbana, 1957-62, asst. prof., 1962-65, asso. prof., 1965-70, prof., 1970-74, adj. prof., 1974-79; chief structures sect. Bldg. Research div. U.S. Bur. Standards, Washington, 1971-72, dep. dir. tech. Center Bldg. Tech., 1972-73, dir. Center Bldg. Tech., 1974—. Served with AUS, 1955-57. Fellow ASCE (tech. activities com. 1979-80). Contbr. articles to profl. jours. Home: 20081 Doolittle St Gaithersburg MD 20760 Office: Center Building Technology National Bureau Standards Washington DC 20234

WRIGHT, RICHARD WARREN, ins. co. exec.; b. Fredericksburg, Va., July 30, 1934; s. Virginious Warren and Florence Allison W.; student U. Richmond, 1952; grad. Dartmouth Inst., 1979; m. Jean Pallette Wright, Jan. 21, 1955; children—Deborah Jean, Michael Warren, Rodney Nelson. With Life Ins. Co. of Va., 1956—, v.p. agy. dept., 1972-73, v.p. agy. ops., 1973-75, sr. v.p. agy. and mktg., 1975—. Chmn. fin. com., deacon Derbyshire Baptist Ch.; trustee Alcohol-Narcotics Edn. Council, Inc.; mem. adv. bd. for Spl. Edn., Henrico County. Served with USNR, 1952-55. Mem. Richmond Assn. Life Underwriters, Va. Assn. Life Underwriters. Republican. Baptist. Clubs: Westwood Racquet, Kiwanis. Office: 6610 W Broad St Richmond VA 23230*

WRIGHT, ROBERT BURROUGHS, business exec.; b. Hillside, N.J., Dec. 21, 1916; s. Herbert M. and Adele (Emmerich) W.; A.B., Montclair State Coll., 1939, M.A., 1941; Chem. Engr., Newark Coll. Engring., 1944; m. Jeanne G. Smith, June 9, 1956; children—Jeanine A., Susan A. Accountant, Gen. Motors Corp., Harrison, N.J., 1940-43; asst. controller Mennen Co., Morristown, N.J., 1943-47, controller, 1947-63, asst. treas., 1963-68, treas., chief financial officer, 1968-71, also dir.; financial dir., treas. Ronson Corp., Wood Bridge, N.J., 1971-72, v.p. fin., 1972-76; v.p. fin. Timeplex, Inc., Rochelle Park, N.J., 1976—; treas., dir. Mennen; v.p., dir. Timeplex Ltd., Scannon Ltd. Treas., dir. Morris County Community Chest and Council, 1955-58. Mem. Am. Mgmt. Assn., Nat. Indsl. Conf. Bd., Research Inst. Am., Nat. Assn. Accountants, Financial Execs. Inst. (pres. N.J. chpt. 1963-64, nat. dir. 1970-73, adv. council 1974-76), Montclair State Coll. Alumni Assn. (exec. bd. 1974-77). Home: Winding Way Convent Station NJ 07961 Office: One Communications Plaza Rochelle Park NJ 07662

WRIGHT, ROBERT CLAUDE, educator; b. Wayne, Nebr., Mar. 5, 1921; s. Claude Lysle and Leora (Nell) W.; A.B., Wayne State Coll., 1941; M.A., U. Tex., 1948; Ph.D., U. Nebr., 1956; postgrad. U. Wash., 1961-62; m. Lorraine Miner, Oct. 3, 1942; children—Ronald, Robin. Prin., tchr. Beldon (Nebr.) High Sch., 1941-42; instr. English, U. Tex., Austin, 1946-48; instr. English and journalism Mankato State Coll., 1948-50; supr. English, Techrs. Coll. High Sch., U. Nebr., Lincoln, 1950-51; asst. prof. English and journalism Mankato (Minn.) State Coll., 1951-56, asso. prof., 1956-62, prof. English, 1962—, chmn. dept. English, 1967-76. Served to capt. USAAF, 1942-46. Recipient Gold Key award Columbia U. Scholastic Press Assn., 1959. Mem. Sci. Fiction Research Assn., Minn. Edn. Assn., Midwest Modern Lang. Assn., Sigma Tau Delta, Pi Delta Epsilon. Author: Frederick Manfred, 1979. Home: 224 Crocus Pl Mankato MN 56001

WRIGHT, ROBERT DEAN, physician; b. Menasha, Wis., Mar. 30, 1909; s. Jay Thomas and Belle (Kinney) W.; B.A. cum laude, U. Wis., 1933, M.A., 1933; M.D., Washington U., 1935; M.P.H., Johns Hopkins, 1940; m. Helen Selmer. June 21, 1934; children—Johanna Belle, Suzanne Estelle, Helen Louise. Dist. health officer, Mo., 1937-38; editor The Health Officer, 1938-39; venereal disease cons., Ga., 1939-40, N.C., 1940-43; med. officer charge Kanawha Valley Med. Center, 1943-46; asst. dir. Venereal Disease Research Lab., 1946-49, asso. dir., 1949-50; dir., prof. edn. and research, div. venereal disease USPHS, 1950-51; prof., chmn. dept. social and environmental medicine U. Va., 1951-56, clin. prof. preventive medicine. 1956-59; gen. med. cons. Region III, USPHS, 1956-59; asst. dir. health and med. affairs Fed. Office Vocational Rehab., 1959-61; sr. research officer State Dept., 1962-63; prof. pub. health adminstrn. Johns Hopkins U., 1963-68; prof., chmn. dept. community health U. Lagos (Nigeria), 1963-68; prof. internat. health Johns Hopkins, 1968-79, prof. emeritus, 1979—; med. dir. USPHS (ret.). Mem. Pres.'s Com. for Employment of Physically Handicapped, 1959-61; bd. dirs. Nat. Health Council 1960-61. Fellow Am. Pub. Health Assn.; mem. S.A.R., Phi Beta Kappa. Unitarian. Author articles med. subjects. Home: Beladar Keswick VA 22947

WRIGHT, ROBERT JOSEPH, airline exec.; b. Seattle, Mar. 3, 1920; s. James N. and Mary E. (Dawson) W.; student U. Wash. 1938-39; m. Hazel M. Hook, Sept. 7, 1946; children—Kathleen, Brian, Joan, James. With Northwest Airlines, Inc., 1946—, gen. sales mgr., St. Paul, 1960-61, v.p. sales, 1961—; dir. Air Tariff Pubs., Inc., Air Cargo, Inc. Past pres. Air Traffic Conf. Am., 1968; mem. dist. export council for Minn., U.S. Dept. Commerce. Trustee, Inst. Certified Travel Agts., Wellesley, Mass. Served to lt. (j.g.) USNR, 1941-46. Roman Catholic. Home: 6705 Rosemary Ln Edina MN 55435 Office: Minneapolis-St Paul Internat Airport St Paul MN 55101

WRIGHT, ROBERT LEE, paper co. exec.; b. Algood, Tenn., Sept. 3, 1919; s. Denny and Bessie Lela (Phy) W.; student Tenn. Poly. Inst., 1937-40, 47; LL.B., Vanderbilt U., 1950; m. Lucille V. Hawkins, Aug. 11, 1951; 1 dau., Mary Wright Dorflinger. Admitted to Tenn. bar, 1949, practice in Cookeville, 1950-51; atty. War Claims Commn., Washington, 1951, OPS, 1951-52; atty., real estate project mgr. C.E., 1952-56; with Bowaters So. Paper Corp., Calhoun, Tenn., 1956—, sec., 1971—, gen. counsel, 1971—, also dir.; sec., gen. counsel Bowater Carolina Corp., Catawba, S.C., 1971—; dir. Terrain Inc., Atlanta; mem. Tenn. adv. bd. Liberty Mut. Ins. Co., 1976—; lectr. real estate U. Tenn., 1964-65. Served to 1st lt. AUS, 1944-46. Mem. Am., Tenn., Bradley County (pres. 1968) bar assns. Clubs: Cleveland Country, Walden, Elks. Home: 3540 Edgewood Circle Cleveland TN 37311 Office: Bowaters So Paper Corp Calhoun TN 37309

WRIGHT, ROBERT ROSS, III, lawyer, educator; b. Fort Worth, Nov. 20, 1931; B.A. cum laude, U. Ark., 1953, J.D., 1956; M.A. (grad. fellow), Duke, 1954; S.J.D. (law fellow), U. Wis., 1967; m. Code; children—Robert Ross IV, John, David. Admitted to Ark. bar, 1956, U.S. Supreme Ct. bar, 1968, Okla. bar, 1970; instr. polit. sci. U. Ark., 1955-56, Okla. bar, 1970, Fed., U.S. Supreme Ct. bars; mem. firm, Forrest City, Ark., 1956-58; partner firm Norton, Norton & Wright, Forrest City, 1959; asst. gen. counsel, asst. sec. Crossett Co. (Ark.), atty. Crossett div. Ga.-Pacific Corp., 1960-63; asst. sec. Pub. Utilities Co., Crossett, Triangle Bag Co., Covington, Ky., 1960-62; mem. faculty law sch. U. Ark., 1963-70, asst. prof., dir. continuing legal edn. and research, then asst. dean Little Rock div., 1965-66, prof. law, 1967-70; vis. prof. law, spl. asst. to provost and pres. U. Iowa, 1969-70; prof. U. Okla., 1970-77, dean Coll. Law, dir. Law Center, 1970-76; vis. prof. U. Ark., 1976-77; Donaghey Distinguished prof., 1977—; Ark. commr. Nat. Conf. Commrs. Uniform State Laws, 1967-70, past chmn. Com. Uniform Eminent Domain Code, past mem. com. Uniform Probate Code; past mem. Ark. Gov.'s Ins. Study Commn.; chmn. Gov. Commn. on Uniform Probate Code, chmn. task force joint devel. Hwy. Research Bd.; vice chmn. Okla. Jud. Council, 1970-72, chmn., 1972-75; chmn. Okla. Center Criminal Justice, 1971-76. Named Ark. Man of Year, Kappa Sigma, 1958. Mem. Ark. (ho. of dels. 1978—, chmn. eminent domain code com., past mem. com. new bar center; past chmn. preceptorship com.; exec. com. young lawyers sect.; com. resolutions), Okla. (ho. of dels. 1974, past vice-chmn. legal internship com.; former vice chmn. gen. practice sect.), Am. Bar Assn. (exec. council gen. practice sect., chmn. legal edn., sect. gen. practice; standing com. on profl. career devels.), Pulaski County Bar Assn., U. Wis., U. Ark., Duke alumni assns., Order Coif, Phi Beta Kappa, Phi Alpha Delta, Omicron Delta Kappa. Episcopalian (vestryman, layreader). Author: Arkansas Eminent Domain Digest, 1964; Arkansas Probate Practice System, 1965; The Law of Airspace, 1968; Emerging Concepts in the Law of Airspace, 1969; Land Use, 1969, 2d edit., 1976; Uniform Probate Code Practice Manual, 1972; Model Airspace Code, 1973; Cases and Materials on Land Use, 1976; Land Use in a Nutshell, 1978; The Arkansas Form Book, 1979. Contbr. numerous articles to legal jours. Home: 25 Crown Point Rd Little Rock AR 72207

WRIGHT, S. EARL, lawyer; b. nr. Richmond, Va., Sept. 5, 1904; s. William Samuel and Ruth Rosena (Gregory) W.; student U. So. Calif., 1932; m. Doris E. Miller, Dec. 18, 1931 (dec. 1970); children—Stephen E., Clifford B.; m. Pauline Reynolds, 1972. Admitted to Calif. bar, 1931, since practiced in Los Angeles; mem. firm Wright & Wright, and predecessor firms, 1931—. Dir. Zane Grey, Inc., Zane Grey Prodns., San Gabriel Valley Newspapers, Inc. Mem. Met. Los Angeles adv. bd. Salvation Army. Mem. State Bar of Calif., Am., Los Angeles bar assns. Home and Office: PO Box 287 Bonsall CA 92003

WRIGHT, SAMUEL LEE, assn. exec.; b. El Centro, Calif., Nov. 3, 1922; s. Raymond L. and Mary L. (Fullilove) W.; B.C.S., Benjamin Franklin U., Washington, 1953; m. Dolores T. Morgan, Sept. 5, 1942; children—Mary Lynne, Samuel Lee, Ellen Louise, James Lawrence. With Aerospace Industries Assn., 1949—, exec. asst. to pres., 1952-61, sec.-treas., business mgr., 1961-69, v.p., sec.-treas., 1969-71, v.p., sec., 1971—. Served with USN, 1941-49. Decorated Letter of Commendation with combat V, Submarine combat insignia with one star. Mem. Am. Soc. Assn. Execs., Washington Trade Assn. Execs., Nat. Assn. Execs. Club. Home: 5926 Augusta Dr Springfield VA 22150 Office: 1725 De Sales St NW Washington DC 20036

WRIGHT, STANLEY ROBERT, lawyer; b. Hills, Minn., Nov. 18, 1899; s. Joseph Robert and Gertrude (Thorston) W.; student Colo. Coll., 1917-19, U. Minn., 1919-21; LL.B., George Washington U., 1923; m. Louise Baker, May 29, 1947. Admitted to D.C. bar, 1923, N.Y. bar, 1926, Fla. bar, 1972; examiner Fed. Cts., 1923-25; partner firm Burlingham, Underwood, Wright, White & Lord, and predecessors, N.Y.C., 1943-71; partner firm Ulmer, Murchison, Ashby & Ball, Jacksonville, Fla., 1972-79; ret., 1979. Mem. Maritime Law Assn. (v.p. 1962-64), Fla. Bar, Am., Jacksonville bar assns., Sigma Chi. Clubs: River; Timuquana Country (Jacksonville, Fla.); Downtown Athletic (N.Y.C.). Home: 3919 Timuquana Rd Jacksonville FL 32210

WRIGHT, STEPHEN JUNIUS, orgn. exec.; b. Dillon, S.C., Sept. 8, 1910; s. Stephen J. and Rachel (Eaton) W.; B.S., Hampton Inst., 1934; M.A., Howard U., 1939, L.H.D. (hon.), 1977; Ph.D., N.Y. U., 1943; LL.D., Colby Coll., 1962, U. Notre Dame, 1964, Morgan State Coll., 1965, N.Y. U., 1966, Mich. State U., 1966, U. R.I., 1968; L.H.D., Morehouse Coll., 1968, William Paterson Coll. N.J., 1976; Litt.D., Coll. St. Thomas, 1965; m. Rosalind Person, Apr. 16, 1938. Tchr. Kennard High Sch., Centreville, Md., 1934-36; prin. Douglass High Sch., Upper Marlboro, Md., 1936-38; dir. student teaching N.C. Coll., 1939-41, chmn. dept. edn., acting dean of men, 1943-44; prof. edn., dir. div. edn. Hampton Inst., 1944-45, prof. edn., dean faculty, 1945-53; pres. Bluefield State Coll., W.Va., 1953-57; pres. Fisk U., 1957-66; pres. United Negro Coll. Fund, N.Y.C., 1966-69; v.p. Coll. Entrance Exam. Bd., N.Y.C., 1969-76, sr. adviser to pres. bd., 1976—. Adv. council Danforth Grad. Fellowship Program, 1958-61; mem. Arms Control and Disarmament Adv. Com., Pres.'s Com. of Nat. Library Commn.; adv. com. on internat. orgns. State Dept.; mem. Nat. Council on Humanities, 1968-74; vice chmn. Am. Council on Edn., 1965-66; mem. policy com. nat. assessment ednl. process Edn. Commn. States; mem., vice chmn. N.J. Bd. Higher Edn. Trustee Patterson State Coll., Coll. Entrance Exam. Bd., Hampton Inst., New World Found., Ednl. Testing Service, Inst. for Internat. Edn.; dir. So. Edn. Reporting Service; mem. N.J. Bd. Higher Edn., 1974—. Recipient Outstanding Alumnus award Hampton Inst., 1954, Howard U., 1962, N.Y. U., 1969. Mem. Council President's C.I.A.A. Instrns. (sec. 1955-57), Am. Assn. Higher Edn. (exec. com. 1960-63, pres. 1966-67), Fgn. Policy Assn. (mem. bd.), Am. Conf. Acad. Deans (exec. com. 1950-51), Phi Beta Kappa (hon.), Alpha Kappa Mu (pres. 1950-54), Phi Delta Kappa, Alpha Phi Alpha, Alpha Beta Boule. Club: Century. Contbr. articles profl. jours. Home: 1620 W Queen St Hampton VA 23666 Office: College Entrance Examination Board 888 7th Ave New York NY 10019. *In my opinion, success can be attributed mainly to hard work. While luck plays a part in almost everyone's life, I deeply believe that it plays favorites with those who are thorough and competent.*

WRIGHT, THEODORE PAUL, JR., educator; b. Port Washington, N.Y., Apr. 12, 1926; s. Theodore Paul and Margaret (McCarl) W.; B.A. magna cum laude, Swarthmore Coll., 1949; M.A., Yale U., 1951, Ph.D., 1957; m. Susan Jane Standfast, Feb. 18, 1967; children—Henry Sewall, Margaret Standfast, Catherine Berrian. Instr. govt. Bates Coll., Lewiston, Maine, 1955-57; asst. prof., 1957-64, asso. prof., 1964-65; asso. prof. polit. sci. Grad. Sch. Public Affairs, SUNY, Albany, 1965-71, prof., 1971—. Trustee, Am. Inst. Pakistan Studies, 1973—. Served with USNR, 1944-46. Carnegie intern Indian civilization U. Chgo., 1961-62; Fulbright research prof., India, 1963-64; Am. Inst. Indian Studies research fellow, India, 1969-70; Am. Council Learned Socs. grantee on South Asia, London, 1974-75. Mem. Am. Polit. Sci. Assn., Assn. Asian Studies, AAUP, Phi Beta Kappa, Phi Delta Theta. Democrat. Unitarian. Clubs: Dutch Settlers of Albany; Adirondack Mountain. Author: American Support of Free Elections Abroad, 1964; contbr. articles on Indian Muslims to profl. jours. Home: 27 Vandenburg Ln Latham NY 12110 Office: Grad Sch Public Affairs ULB-96 SUNY Albany NY 12222

WRIGHT, THOMAS HENRY, bishop; b. Wilmington, N.C., Oct. 16, 1904; s. John Maffitt and Josie Young (Whitaker) W.; A.B., U. of South, 1926, D.D., 1946; B.D., Va. Theol. Sem., Alexandria, Va., 1930, D.D., 1946; D.D., Washington and Lee U., 1940, U. N.C., 1965; m. Hannah Hagans Knowlton, Dec. 1, 1937; children—Thomas Henry, Hannah K., James K., John M. Clk., Standard Oil Co. of N.J., Wilmington, 1926-27; ordained to ministry P.E. Ch., 1929; nat. acting sec. of coll. work P.E. Ch., 1933-34; Episcopal chaplain U. of N.C. 1931-32, Va. Mil. Inst., 1934-41, Washington and Lee U., 1934-41, rector Robert E. Lee Meml. Ch., Lexington, Va., 1934-41; dean Grace Cathedral, San Francisco, 1941-43; rector St. Mark's Ch., San Antonio, Tex., 1943-45; consecrated bishop of Diocese of East Carolina, St. James Ch., Wilmington, N.C., Oct. 1945. Pres. of Province. U.S. rep. to World Christian Student Fed. Meeting, Holland, 1932. Regional dir. Ch. Soc. for Coll. Work; asso. mem. Forward Movement Commn., P.E. Ch.; chmn. overseas dept. Nat. Council of Episcopal Ch. Trustee U. of South. Mem. Sigma Nu (former grand chaplain), Sigma Upsilon, Alpha Phi Epsilon; hon. mem. Omicron Delta Kappa. Democrat. Contbr. to jours. Address: The Bishop's House Route 1 Box 593 Wilmington NC 28401

WRIGHT, THOMAS WILLIAM DUNSTAN, architect; b. Rome, Jan. 12, 1919 (parents Am. citizens); s. Charles Will and Helen Bree (Dunstan) W.; A.B., Harvard U., 1941, M.Arch., 1950; m. Penelope Ladd, Aug. 6, 1942; children—Peter W.D., Felicity Wright Evans, Allegra. Designer, Joseph Saunders, architect, Alexandria, Va., 1950; asso. Leon Brown, architect, Washington, 1950-53; partner firm Brown and Wright, Washington, 1953—; mem. Old Georgetown bd. U.S. Commn. Fine Arts; past 1st v.p. D.C. Commn. Arts; past mem. D.C. Commrs. Planning and Urban Renewal Adv. Council; arbitrator Am. Arbitration Assn. Served to lt. comdr. USNR, 1941-46. Fellow AIA (past pres. Washington Met. chpt., past nat. chmn. com. on Nat. Capital City, past mem. com. on design, com. on housing); mem. Soc. Archtl. Historians, Nat. Assn. Intergroup Relations Ofcls., Nat. Assn. Housing and Redevel. Ofcls., Nat. Com. against Discrimination in Housing, ACLU. Democrat. Clubs: Cosmos, Harvard (Washington). Home: 4564 Indian Rock Terr NW Washington DC 20007 Office: 1400 20th St NW Washington DC 20036. *Since the essential origin of creativity is knowing the sources, then the fundamental source of design is the human being—its body, its mind, its senses and reactions, individually and collectively.*

WRIGHT, TOM Z., lawyer; b. nr. Balko, Okla., Apr. 1, 1908; s. Ulysses and Penelophy (Zimmerman) W.; B.S., U. Okla., 1929, LL.B., 1934; J.D.S., Yale, 1942; m. Mary Grace Seymore, Apr. 6, 1947; children—Thomas Z. II, Helen Ruth. Admitted to Okla. bar, 1934; practice in Fairview, 1934-36, Woodward, 1946—; mem. firm Wright, Lowrey & Williams, 1956-79, firm Wright & Laubhan, 1979—; asso. prof. bus. law U. Okla., 1936-42; vis. prof. law So. Meth. U., 1946, Okla. U., 1948. Legal mem. Okla. SSS Bd. Appeal, Western Dist. Okla., 1952-72. Mem. Okla. Ho. of Reps., 1932-36. Bd. dirs. Plains Indians and Pioneer Hist. Found., 1956-69, 73—, pres., 1977—. Served to capt. USAAF, 1942-45. Mem. Am., Okla. (bd. bar examiners 1966-70), Woodward County (pres. 1952, 56, 65) bar assns., Delta Chi, Phi Alpha Delta, Alpha Kappa Psi. Republican. Presbyn. Mason, Elk, Kiwanian (dist. sec. 1948). Contbr. articles to profl. jours. Home: PO Box 549 Woodward OK 73801 Office: 1416 Main St Woodward OK 73801

WRIGHT, WALTER FRANCIS, educator; b. Franklin County, Ind., Jan. 5, 1912; s. Francis Marion and Cora (Lawrence) W.; B.S., Miami U., Oxford, Ohio, 1930; student Johns Hopkins, 1930-31; M.A., U. Ill., 1932, Ph.D., 1935; m. Alice Bradford Barry, Mar. 16, 1935; children—Charles R.B., Marion (Mrs. Walter B. Ross), Bradford L., Susan E. (Mrs. James Eckenwalder). Instr., N.D. State U., 1934-35; prof. Doane Coll., 1935-38; instr., then asst. prof. Wash. State U., 1938-45; mem. faculty U. Nebr., 1945—, Marie Kotouc Roberts prof., 1965—. Mem. Modern Lang. Assn., Phi Beta Kappa. Author: Sensibility in English Prose Fiction, 1760-1814, 1937; Romance and Tragedy in Joseph Gonrad, 1948; Art and Substance in George Meredith, 1953; The Madness of Art: A Study of Henry James, 1962; The Shaping of The Dynasts: A Study in Thomas Hardy, 1967; Arnold Bennett: Romantic Realist, 1971. Home: 1021 Robert Rd Lincoln NE 68510

WRIGHT, WALTER WOODMAN, librarian; b. Cambridge, Mass., May 27, 1915; s. Charles Henry Conrad and Elizabeth (Woodman) W.; S.B., Harvard, 1937, B.S. in Library Sci., Columbia, 1938; m. Aagot Caroline Horn, Nov. 16, 1941; children—Caroline (Mrs. Andrew Kuhl), Eric. In charge exchanges Harvard Coll. Library. 1938-40, asst. circulation and ref., 1940-41; reference asst. N.Y. Pub. Library, 1941-42. charge exchanges, 1942; librarian Harvard Club of N.Y.C., 1942-44; gen. asst. Johns Hopkins Library, 1944-45, coordinator tech. processes. 1945-47; head circulation dept. U. Pa. Library, 1947-49, asst. librarian service div., 1949-57; librarian Ohio U., 1957-61. dir. libraries, 1961-68, asst. prof., 1957-68; curator rare books, chief spl. collections Dartmouth Coll., 1968-80. Pres. Unitarian Fellowship. Athens, 1957-59, 62-63. Club: Appalachian Mountain. Editor and contbr. to profl. other publs. Home: 30 Bank St Lebanon NH 03766

WRIGHT, WILLARD JUREY, lawyer; b. Seattle, Feb. 25, 1914; s. Raymond Garfield and Elizabeth (McPherson) W.; A.B. with honors, Princeton, 1936, certificate Woodrow Wilson Sch. Pub. and Internat. Affairs, 1936; J.D. with honors, U. Wash., 1939; grad. Navy. Lang. Sch., U. Colo., 1944; m. Alice Ostrander, Dec. 27, 1939 (dec. Dec. 1969); children—Susan, Alice, Rosemary, Raymond Garfield II; m. 2d, Katharyn Stubbs Little, July 18, 1970; children—Anne, Gwendolyn, Kathy. Editor Wash. Law Review, 1937-39; admitted to Wash. bar, 1939, U.S. Dist. Ct., 1939, Supreme Ct., 1954, Ct. Appeals, 1958; practice of law, Wash., 1939—; partner Wright, Innis, Simon & Todd, Seattle, 1939-69, Davis, Wright, Todd, Riese & Jones, 1969—; spl. asst. atty. gen., Wash., 1953; acting prof. fed. income taxation U. Wash. Law Sch., 1956; officer, dir. or gen. counsel various bus. corps. including Seattle Times Co., Port Blakely Mill Co., Eddy Investment Co., Merrill & Ring Inc., Welco Lumber Co. U.S. Chmn. King County Republican Rules Com., 1950-58, chmn. 37th Dist Rep. Orgn., precinct committeeman, 1936-74; del. Rep. Nat. Conv. Chgo., 1952. Trustee Seattle Found., 1954-63, pres., 1961-63; trustee Seattle Com. Fgn. Relations, 1959-62; trustee Lakeside Sch., 1938-67, pres., 1951-55, hon. trustee, 1967—; vis. com. U. Wash. Coll. Bus. Adminstrn., 1963-70, U. Wash. Law Sch., 1974-78; pres. U. Wash. Ann. Fund, 1973-74, U. Wash. Law Sch. Fund, 1974-75; trustee Helen Bush Parkside Sch., 1946-63, pres., 1959-62; trustee Princeton U., 1957-61; vice chmn. governing bd. Univ. Hosp., Seattle, 1978—; sec., trustee Seattle Art Mus., 1958—, R.D. Merrill Found., Hauberg Found., Columbia Found. Served to lt. USNR, 1943-46. Recipient Vivian Carkeek prize, Distinguished Service award Lakeside Sch., 1964. Fellow Am. Bar Found., Am. Coll. Probate Counsel; mem. Am., Wash. State (chmn. real estate, probate and trusts sect. 1958-61), Seattle-King County (trustee 1955-58, 64-67, pres., 1966-67) bar assns., Am. Judicature Soc., Nat. Assn. Estate Planning Councils (dir. 1969-71), Estate Planning Council Seattle (pres. 1968-69, dir.), Alumni Assn. U. Wash. Law Sch. (pres. 1957-58), Seattle World

Affairs Council (charter trustee, sec. 1949-57), Urban League Seattle (trustee 1956-60, 68-70, pres. bd. trustees 1956-58), Phi Delta Phi, Order of Coif. Episcopalian (vestryman 1959-64, 68-70, 73-76, sr. warden 1970, 74-76, chancellor 1976-78, trustee ch. pension fund, N.Y. 1970-76, Bishop's Cross 1977). Clubs: Princeton Quadrangle (pres. 1935-36), University (sec. and trustee 1950-51, 62-64, pres. 1968-70), Seattle Golf (sec., trustee 1968-71); Royal and Ancient Golf (St. Andrews, Scotland). Contbr. articles to profl. jours. Home: 1500 42d Ave Seattle WA 98112 Office: Seattle-First National Bank Bldg Seattle WA 98154

WRIGHTON, MARK STEPHEN, chemist; b. Jacksonville, Fla., June 11, 1949; s. Robert D. and Doris (Cutler) W.; B.S., Fla. State U., 1969; Ph.D., Calif. Inst. Tech., 1972; m. Deborah Ann Wiseman, Aug. 10, 1968; 1 son, James Joseph. Asst. prof. chemistry M.I.T., 1972-76, asso. prof., 1976-77, prof., 1977—; cons. Gen. Electric, Procter & Gamble, Northrop Corp. Alfred P. Sloan fellow, 1974-76. Recipient Herbert Newby McCoy award Calif. Inst. Tech., 1972. Mem. Am. Chem. Soc., Electrochem. Soc.,AAAS. Author: Organometallic Photochemistry, 1979; editor books in field; cons. editor Houghton-Mifflin. Office: Dept Chemistry MIT Cambridge MA 02139

WRIGHTSMAN, CHARLES BIERER, oil producer; b. Pawnee, Okla., June 13, 1895; s. Charles John and Edna (Lawing) W.; student Phillips Exeter Acad., 1910-14, Stanford, 1914-15, Columbia, 1915-17; m. Irene Stafford, June 7, 1922; (div.); m. 2d, Jayne Larkin, Mar. 28, 1944. Ind. oil producer, 1918-21; made survey of Russian oil fields, 1921; developed oil properties in Okla., Kans., Tex., La., and Calif., 1919-29; pres. Standard Oil Co. of Kans., 1932-53. Trustee, Met. Mus. Art, N.Y.C., 1956-75, trustee emeritus, 1975—; chmn. bd. trustees Inst. Fine Arts, 1970-73; trustee N.Y. U., 1963-73, life trustee, 1973—; councilor Am. Geog. Soc., 1950-56; trustee, pres. St. Mary's Hosp., W. Palm Beach, 1952-55. Commd. ensign USNRF, 1917, serving as aviator; hon. discharged 1919, with rank of lt. Mem. Delta Kappa Epsilon. Clubs: Everglades, Seminole (Palm Beach, Fla.); Ramada, Petroleum (Houston). Home: Palm Beach FL 33480 Office: 1st City Nat Bank Bldg Houston TX 77002

WRIGLEY, PETER JAMES, fashion designer; b. Hamden, Conn., Oct. 17, 1934; s. Herman Patrick and Gertrude Cecilia (Whitty) W.; B.F.A., R.I. Sch. Design, 1958. Designer, Oleg Cassini Inc., N.Y.C., 1960-64, Carlette Jrs., N.Y.C., 1964-69; coordinator Anne Klein Co., N.Y.C., 1969-76; designer, partner Chuck/Howard/Peter Wrigley, N.Y.C., 1976—; cons. R.I. Sch. Design, Met. Mus., N.Y.C. Served with U.S. Army, 1958-60. Recipient Coty award Menswear Design, 1975. Home: 716 Madison Ave New York City NY 10021 Office: 412 W 47th St New York City NY 10036

WRIGLEY, WALTER, educator; b. Brockton, Mass., Mar. 26, 1913; s. Walter S. and Isabel M. (Wilde) W.; S.B., Mass. Inst. Tech., 1934, Sc.D., 1941; m. Dorothy W. Brown, Oct. 18, 1941; children—Lois W. (Mrs. Huber L. Graham), Wallace W. Physicist Interchem. Corp., 1934-37, United Color and Pigment Co., 1937; staff asst. aero. engring. Mass. Inst. Tech., 1938-40, asso. prof., 1951-56, prof. instrumentation and astronautics, 1956-75, prof. emeritus, 1975—; project engr. Sperry Gyroscope Co., 1940-46; ednl. dir. Charles Stark Draper Lab. Mass. Inst. Tech., 1946-75. Chmn. sub-panel self-contained long range navigation systems, Research and Devel. Bd., Dept. of Def., 1949-51; civilian cons. tech. adv. panel electronics asst. sect. def., 1955-56, sci. adv. bd. chief staff USAF, 1957-66. Mem. adv. council USAF Acad., 1966-73, chmn., 1970-73; mem. adv. com. Air Force Inst. Tech., 1968; chmn. AGARD Guidance and Control Panel, 1965-69. Bd. visitors New Eng. Aero. Inst., 1970-76. Registered profl. engr., Mass. Fellow Am. Inst. Aeros. and Astronautics; mem. Internat. Acad. Astronautics, Am. Phys. Soc., Inst. Navigation, AAAS, Sigma Xi. Unitarian. Mason. Author: (with J. Hovorka) Fire Control Principles, 1957; (with C.S. Draper and J. Hovorka) Inertial Guidance, 1960; (with W.M. Hollister and W.G. Denhard) Gyroscopic Theory, Design and Instrumentation, 1969. Contbr. articles to profl. jours. Home: 93 Grand View Ave Wollaston MA 02170

WRIGLEY, WILLIAM, corp. exec.; b. Chgo., Jan. 21, 1933; s. Philip Knight and Helen Blanche (Atwater) W.; grad. Deerfield Acad., 1950; B.A., Yale, 1954; m. Alison Hunter, June 1, 1957 (div. 1969); children—Alison Elizabeth, Philip Knight, William. With Wm. Wrigley Jr. Co., Chgo., 1956—, v.p., 1960-61, pres., chief exec. officer, 1961—, dir., 1960—; chmn. bd., dir. Wm. Wrigley Can. Inc., Wrigley Philippines, Inc., Wrigley Co. Ltd. (U.K.), Wrigley N.V. (The Netherlands), Wrigley S.A. (France), Wrigley Co. (N.Z.), Ltd., Wrigley Co. Pty., Ltd. (Australia), The Wrigley Co. (H.K.) Ltd. (Hong Kong), Wrigley Co. (E. Africa) Ltd., (Kenya); pres., dir. Wrigley Espana S.A. (Spain); dir. Wrigley & Co. Ltd., Japan; dir., chmn. exec. com. Chgo. Nat. League Ball Club, also dir., mem. salary and auditing coms., mem. com. non-mgmt. dirs.; mem. spl. com. non-mgmt. dirs.; mem. nominating com. Texaco, Inc.; dir., mem. compensation com. Nat. Blvd. Bank of Chgo.; v.p. dir., chmn. exec. com. Santa Catalina Island Co. Bd. dirs. Wrigley Meml. Garden Found., Northwestern Meml. Hosp.; benefactor, mem. Santa Catalina Island Conservancy; mem. adv. bd. Center for Sports Medicine, Northwestern U. Med. Sch., 1976—; trustee Chgo. Latin Sch. Found., 1975—; dir. Geneva Lake Water Safety Com., 1966—, mem. exec. com., 1968—. Served from ensign to lt. (j.g.) USNR, 1954-56; now lt. comdr. Res. Mem. Navy League U.S., Chgo. Hist. Soc., Field Mus., Wolf's Head Soc., U. So. Calif. Oceanographic Assos., Art Inst. Chgo., Antiquarian Soc. of Art Inst., Delta Kappa Epsilon. Clubs: Saddle and Cycle, Racquet, Chicago Yacht, Tavern, Commercial (Chgo.); Catalina Island Yacht, Catalina Island Gun, Tuna (Catalina Island, Calif.); Lake Geneva (Wis.) Country, Lake Geneva Yacht; The Brook (N.Y.C.). Office: 410 N Michigan Ave Chicago IL 60611

WRISTON, BARBARA, educator; b. Middletown, Conn., June 29, 1917; d. Henry Merritt and Ruth Colton (Bigelow) Wriston; A.B., Oberlin Coll., 1939; A.M., Brown U., 1942, Litt.D., Lawrence U., 1977. Museum asst. Mus. Art, R.I. Sch. Design, Providence, 1939-44; lectr. to schs. Museum Fine Arts, Boston, 1944-61; exec. dir. museum edn. Art Inst. Chgo., 1961-78; cons. on edn. The Planting Fields Found., Oyster Bay, N.Y., 1979—. Mem. adv. bd. Historic Am. Bldgs. Survey; mem. Internat. Council Museums, Am. Assn. Museums. Benjamin Franklin fellow Royal Soc. Arts; mem. Soc. Archtl. Historians (pres. 1959-62, dir. 1961-64), Victorian Soc. Am., Furniture History Soc. Club: Arts (Chgo.). Author: Rare Doings at Bath, 1979. Home: 30 Waterside Plaza Apt 2D New York NY 10010

WRISTON, WALTER BIGELOW, banker; b. Middletown, Conn., Aug. 3, 1919; s. Henry M. and Ruth (Bigelow) W.; B.A. with distinction, Wesleyan U., Middletown, Conn., 1941; postgrad. Ecole Francaise Middlebury, Vt., 1941, Am. Inst. Banking, 1946; M.A., Fletcher Sch. Internat. Law and Diplomacy, 1942; LL.D., Lawrence Coll., 1962, Tufts U., 1963, Brown U., 1969, Columbia, 1972; D.C.S., Pace U., 1974, St. John's U., 1974; D.H.L., Lafayette Coll., 1975; LL.D., Fordham U., 1977; D.C.S., N.Y. U., 1977; m. Barbara Brengle, Oct. 24, 1942 (dec.); 1 dau., Catherine B.; m. 2d, Kathryn Ann Dineen, Mar. 14, 1968. Officer spl. div. Dept. State, Washington, 1941-42; jr. insp. comptrollers div. Citibank, N.A., 1946-50, asst. cashier, 1950-52, asst. v.p., 1952-54, v.p. 1954-58; sr. v.p. 1958-60, exec. v.p., 1960-67, pres., 1967-70, chmn., 1970—, also dir.; chmn., dir. Citicorp; dir. J.C. Penney Co., Gen. Electric Co., Chubb Corp.; trustee Rand Corp. Mem. Nat. Commn. on Productivity, 1970-74, Labor-Mgmt. Adv. Com., Nat. Commn. for Indsl. Peace, 1973-74, Adv. Com. on Reform Internat. Monetary System. Bd. govs. N.Y. Hosp.; bd. visitors Fletcher Sch. Law and Diplomacy; bd. dirs. Assos. Harvard Bus. Sch.; trustee Am. Enterprise Inst. Served with AUS, 1942-46. Mem. Council Fgn. Relations, Bus. Council. Clubs: Links, River, Sky, Club at Citicorp Center (N.Y.C.); Metropolitan (Washington). Home: New York NY Office: 399 Park Ave New York NY 10043

WRONG, DENNIS HUME, sociologist, educator; b. Toronto, Ont., Can., Nov. 22, 1923; s. Humphrey Hume and Mary Joyce (Hutton) W.; B.A., U. Toronto, 1945; Ph.D., Columbia U., 1956; m. Elaine L. Gale, Nov. 24, 1949 (div. Oct. 1965); 1 son, Terence Hume; m. 2d, Jacqueline C. Mehta, Mar. 1966. Tchr., Princeton U., 1949-50, Rutgers U., 1950-51, U. Toronto, 1954-56, Brown U., 1956-61; mem. grad. faculty New Sch. Social Research, 1961-63; prof. sociology, chmn. dept. Univ. Coll., N.Y.U., 1963-65; vis. prof. U. Nev., 1965-66; prof. sociology N.Y.U., 1966—. Mem. Am. Sociol. Assn., Eastern Sociol. Soc. Author: American and Canadian Viewpoints, 1955; Population and Society, 1961, 67, 77; Skeptical Sociology, 1976; Power: Its Forms, Bases and Uses, 1979. Editor: Social Research, 1962-64; (with Harry L. Gracey) Readings in Introductory Sociology, 1967, 72, 77; Contemporary Sociology: A Journal of Reviews, 1972-74; Max Weber, 1970. Home: Drakes Corner Rd Princeton NJ 08540 Office: Dept Sociology NYU Washington Sq New York NY 10453

WROTH, JAMES MELVIN, former army officer, research co. exec.; b. Lincoln, Nebr., Feb. 2, 1929; s. Charles M. and Reba (Sharp) W.; B.S., U. Nebr., 1951; M.B.A., Syracuse U., 1963; postgrad. F.A. Sch., 1957, Command and Gen. Staff Coll., 1962, Armed Forces Staff Coll., 1967, Army War Coll., 1968; grad. Advanced Mgmt. Program, Harvard, 1972; m. Donna Mae Benson, June 4, 1951 (dec.); children—Mark David S., Mary E.; m. 2d, Molly B. Mullan, June 15, 1975; stepchildren—Edward M. Mullan, Philip C. Mullan. Commd. 2d lt. U.S. Army, 1951, advanced through grades to brig. gen., 1973; instr. A.A.A. Sch., Ft. Bliss, Tex., 1954-56; with 3d Inf. Div., Ft. Benning, Ga. and Germany, 1957-61; with Office Chief of Staff, U.S. Army, 1963-66; comdg. officer 1st Bn., 31st Arty., Korea, 1967; exec. asst. to asst. sec. Army, 1968-70; exec. officer I Field Force Vietnam Arty., 1970; comdg. officer 52d Arty. Group, Vietnam, 1971; with Office Dep. Chief Staff for Personnel, Dept. Army, 1972-75; comdg. gen. VII Corps Anty. and Augsburg (Germany) Mil. Community, 1975-77; comdr. 2d ROTC region, Ft. Knox, Ky., 1977-79; ret., 1979; dir. mgmt. tech. dept. Gen. Research Corp., McLean, Va., 1979—. Decorated D.S.M., Legion of Merit, Bronze Star, Air Medal with V device, Army Commendation medal; Vietnamese Gallantry Cross with palm. Recipient John J. Pershing award, 1951, 40 and 8 award, 1951, F.A. Assn. award, 1950. Mem. Nat. Soc. Pershing Rifles (past nat. comdr.), Alpha Kappa Psi, Beta Gamma Sigma. Home: 11727 Quay Rd Oakton VA 22124 Office: Gen Research Corp 7655 Old Springhouse Rd McLean VA 22102

WU, CHIEN-SHIUNG, physicist; b. Shanghai, China, 1912; d. Zong-Ye Wu and F.H. Fan Wu; B.S., Nat. Central U., China, 1934; Ph.D., U. Calif. at Berkeley, 1940; D.Sc., Princeton, 1958, Smith Coll., 1959, Goucher Coll., 1960, Yale, 1967, Russel Sage Coll., 1971, Harvard, 1974; LL.D., Chinese U. Hong Kong, 1969; m. Dr. Luke Chia-liu Yuan, May 30, 1942; 1 son, Vincent W.C. Yuan. Physicist, specializing nuclear physics; experimentally established non-conservation of parity in beta-decay, 1957; Pupin prof. physics Columbia, 1957—. Recipient research award Research Coop. Am., 1958; Woman of Year award AAUW, 1962; Comstock award Nat. Acad. of Sci., 1964; Chia Hsin Achievement award, 1965; Nat. Medal of Scis., 1975; 1st Wolf prize, Israel, 1978; named Scientist of Yr., Indsl. Research, 1974. Fellow Royal Soc. Edinburgh (hon.); mem. Nat. Acad. Sci., Am. Acad. Arts and Sci., Am. Phys. Soc. (pres. 1975), Acadamie Sinica of China. Home: 15 Claremont Ave New York NY 10027

WU, HSIU KWANG, economist, educator; b. Hankow, China, Dec. 14, 1935; s. Kuo Cheng and Edith (Huang) W.; came to U.S., 1952, naturalized, 1963; grad. Lawrenceville Sch., 1954; A.B., Princeton, 1958, M.B.A., U. Pa., 1960, Ph.D., 1963; m. Kathleen Gibbs Johnson, Aug. 17, 1968. Prof., group coordinator finance, econs. and internat. bus. Boston U., 1968-72; prof., chmn. fin., econs. and legal studies faculty, U. Ala., 1972—, Lee Bidgood prof. fin. and econs., 1978—, Ala. Banker Edn. Found. Banking Chair prof., 1973-78. Econ. adviser Office of Comptroller of Currency, U.S. Treasury, 1966-69, 75—; cons. instl. investor study SEC, 1969-70, mem. com. examiners undergrad. program for counseling and evaluation test in bus. Ednl. Testing Service, 1971, 77. Sloan Faculty fellow Sloan Sch. Mgmt., Mass. Inst. Tech., 1965-66. Mem. Am. Econ. Assn., Am. Fin. Assn., Am. Statis. Assn., Fin. Mgmt. Assn. Co-editor: Elements of Investments, 2d rev. edit., 1972. Contbr. articles to law and econ. jours. Home: 27 Arcadia Dr Tuscaloosa AL 35404 Office: Coll Commerce U Ala University AL 35486

WU, JAMES CHEN-YUAN, educator; b. Nanking, China, Oct. 5, 1931; s. Chien Lieh and Cheng-Ling (Hsia) W.; student Nat. Taiwan (Formosa) U., 1949-52; B.S., Gonzaga U., 1954; postgrad. Columbia, 1954; M.S. (univ. fellow), U. Ill., 1955, Ph.D., 1957; m. Mei-Ying Chang, Sept. 7, 1957; children—Alberta Yee-Hwa, Norbert Mao-Hwa. Came to U.S., 1953, naturalized, 1963. Engr. Wah Chang Corp., N.Y.C., 1954; researcher Mass. Inst. Tech. at Cambridge, 1957; asst. prof. Gonzaga U., Spokane, Wash., 1957-59; research specialist Douglas Aircraft Co., 1959-65, group leader, 1960-61, supr., 1961-62, br. chief, 1963-65; prof. aerospace engring. Ga. Inst. Tech., 1965—; cons. N.Am. Aviation Co., Geophys. Tech. Corp., European Atomic Energy Commn., Ispra, Italy, research center, U.S. Army Research Office, Durham, S.C. Chmn. bd. dirs. Chinese-Am. Inst. Recipient profl. achievement award Douglas Aricraft Co., 1963, Outstanding Tchrs. award Gonzaga U., 1959. Asso. fellow Am. Inst. Aeros. and Astronautics; mem. Am. Soc. Engring. Sci. (founding), Soc. Indsl. and Applied Math. (vice-chmn. Pacific N.W. 1958-59), Am. Astron. Soc. (sr.), Am. Phys. Soc., Sigma Xi, Tau Beta Pi, Sigma Alpha Nu. Contbr. articles to profl. jours. Office: Sch Aeronautical Engring Georgia Inst Tech Atlanta GA 30332

WU, JIN, oceanographer, educator, engr.; b. Nanking, China, Apr. 9, 1934; s. Shiang-San and Aei-Feng (Chen) W.; came to U.S., 1959, naturalized, 1972; B.Sc., Nat. Cheng-Kung U., 1956; M.Sc., U. Iowa, 1961, Ph.D., 1964; m. Tzu-Chen Chang, Sept. 9, 1961; children—Victor Hua-Teh, Abraham Hua-Chung, Marvin Hua-Wei. Instr. physics Taitung Sr. High Sch., 1958-59; research asst., research asso. U. Iowa, 1959-63; research scientist Hydronautics, Inc., Laurel, Md., 1963-66, sr. research scientist, then prin. research scientist, 1966-74, head geophys. fluid dynamics div., 1966-74, cons., 1974—; mem. faculty U. Del., Newark, 1974—, prof. marine studies and civil engring., 1975—; vis. lectr. von Karman Inst. for Fluid Dynamics, Brussels, 1970; vis. scientist Nat. Sci. Council, Taiwan, 1970, 74, 75, 76. Served with Chinese Navy, 1956-58. Mem. ASCE, Am. Geophys. Union, Sigma Xi. Contbr. numerous articles to profl. jours. Home: 1822 Greenplace Terr Rockville MD 20850 Office: Coll Marine Studies Univ Del Newark DE 19711

WU, NELSON IKON, author, educator, artist; b. Peking, China, June 9, 1919; s. Aitchen K. and Lu-Yü (Yang) W.; B.A., Nat. Southwest Asso. U., Kunming, China, 1942; M.A., Yale, 1949, Ph.D., 1954; m. Mu-lien Hsüeh, Dec. 1, 1951; children—Chao-ming, Chao-ting, Chao-ping, Chao-ying. Came to U.S., 1945, naturalized, 1956. Instr., Nat. Southwest Asso. U. Kunming, China, 1942-43; asst. prof. history of art San Francisco State Coll., 1954-55; instr. Yale, 1955-59, asst. prof., 1959-65; prof. history of art and Chinese Culture Washington U., 1965-68, Edward Mallinckrodt Distinguished U. prof., 1968—, chmn. dept. art and archaeology, 1969-70; fellow Davenport Coll., Yale, 1956-65; vis. prof. Tokyo U., 1972; cinematographer, asso. dir., editor motion picture The Flop, 1952; dir., writer music The Finger Painting of Wu Tsai-yen, 1955. Founder art festivals Yenling Yeyuan Picnic, 1952-65, Ashiya Seminar, Japan, 1966-67; founder-adviser Asian Art Soc. Washington U., 1972—. Trustee Yale-in-China Assn., 1959-65. Tsing-hua Research fellow, 1954-55; Morse fellow Yale, 1958-59, Am. Council Learned Socs. fellow, 1958-59; Guggenheim Found. fellow, 1965-66; Fulbright research scholar, 1965-67; research scholar Kyoto U., Japan, 1965-67; Nat. Endowment for Humanities sr. fellow, 1972. New Haven Art Festival Lit. award, 1960; Calligraphy prize, Ashiya, Japan, 1966. Mem. St. Louis Chinese Soc. (pres. 1969-70), League of Chinese Americans (dir. 1974-77). Author: (pseudonym Lu-ch'iao) Wei-yang Ko (Song Never to End), 1959; Tung Ch'i-ch'ang: Apathy in Government and Fervor in Art, 1962; Chinese and Indian Architecture: City of Man, Mountain of God, and Realm of Immortals 1963; Jen-tzu Tales, 1974; Ch'an-ch'ing-shu, 1975; contbg. author: Renditions, 1976; (with Kohara and Ch'en) HsüWei to Tung Ch'i-ch'ang, 1978; Chinese garden design Yanling Yeyuan, 1951—. Home: 1530 Notch Rd Cheshire CT 06410 also 6306 Waterman Ave Saint Louis MO 63130 Office: Dept Art and Archaeology Washington U Saint Louis MO 63130

WU, RAY JUI, biochemist; b. Peking, China, Aug. 14, 1928; s. Hsien and Daisy (Yen) Wu; came to U.S., 1949, naturalized, 1961; B.S., U. Ala., 1950; Ph.D., U. Pa., 1955; m. Christina Chan, Aug. 11, 1956; children—Albert, Alice. Asso. mem., Pub. Health Research Inst. City of N.Y., 1957-66; asso. prof. biochemistry, molecular and cell biology Cornell U., Ithaca, N.Y., 1966-72, prof., 1972—, chmn. sect., 1975—; vis. research scientist Stanford U., 1965-66. NIH grantee, 1960—, NSF, 1967—, Am. Cancer Soc., 1976—; NSF sr. fellow MRC Lab., Cambridge, Eng., 1971; Vis. asso. prof. Mass. Inst. Tech., 1972. Mem. Am. Soc. Biol. Chemists, Am. Chem. Soc., AAAS, Alpha Chi Sigma. Democrat. Contbr. chpts. to books, articles to profl. jours. Home: 111 Christopher Circle Ithaca NY 14850 Office: Wing Hall Cornell U Ithaca NY 14853

WU, SHIEN-MING, mech. engr.; b. Chekiang, China, Oct. 28, 1924; naturalized, 1970; M.B.A., U. Pa., 1956; Ph.D., U. Wis., 1962; m. Daisy T. Wu, Oct. 3, 1959; children—Benjamin, Elaine. Prof. mech. engring. and stats. U. Wis., 1968—; Fulbright disting. prof., Yugoslavia, 1975. Recipient Jennings award Am. Welding Soc., 1968. Mem. ASME (Blackall award 1968), Soc. Mfg. Engrs. (Nat. Edn. award 1974), Am. Stats. Assn. Contbr. numerous articles to profl. jours. Home: 6237 S Highlands Madison WI 53705 Office: Mech Engring Dept U Wis Madison WI 53706

WU, TAI TE, educator; b. Shanghai, China, Aug. 2, 1935; M.B., B.S., U. Hong Kong, 1956; B.S. in Mech. Engring., U. Ill., Urbana, 1958; M.S. in Applied Physics, Harvard U., 1959, Ph.D. in Engring. (Gordon McKay fellow), 1961; m. Anna Fang, Apr. 16, 1966; 1 son, Richard. Research fellow in structural mechanics Harvard U., 1961-63, research fellow in biol. chemistry Med. Sch., 1964, research asso., 1965-66; research scientist Hydronautics, Inc., Rockville, Md., 1962; asst. prof. engring. Brown U., Providence, 1963-65; asst. prof. biomath. Grad. Sch. Med. Scis., Cornell U. Med. Coll., N.Y.C., 1967-68, asso. prof., 1968-70; asso. prof. physics and engring. scis. Northwestern U., Evanston, Ill., 1970-73, prof., 1973-74, prof. biochemistry and molecular biology and engring. scis., 1974—, acting chmn. dept. engring. scis., 1973. Recipient progress award Chinese Engrs. and Scientists Assn. So. Calif., Los Angeles, 1971. C.T. Loo Scholar, 1959-60; NIH Research Career Devel. awardee, 1974-79. Mem. AAAS, Am. Phys. Soc., Am. Soc. Biol. Chemists, Soc. Microbiology, Biophys. Soc., Chgo. Assn. Immunology, N.Y. Acad. Scis., Soc. Indsl. and Applied Math., Sigma Xi, Tau Beta Pi, Pi Mu Epsilon. Author: (with E.A. Kabat and H. Bilofsky) Variable Regions of Immunoglobulin Chains, 1976; contbr. articles to profl. jours. Office: Dept Biochemistry and Molecular Biology Northwestern U Evanston IL 60201

WU, TAI TSUN, physicist, educator; b. Shanghai, China, Dec. 1, 1933; s. King Ching and Wei Van (Tsang) W.; came to U.S., 1950, naturalized, 1964; B.S., U. Minn., 1953; S.M., Harvard, 1954, Ph.D., 1956; m. Sau Lan Yu, June 18, 1967. Jr. fellow Soc. Fellows, Harvard, 1956-59, asst. prof. 1959-63, asso. prof., 1963-66, Gordon McKay prof. applied physics, 1966—; mem. Inst. Advanced Study, Princeton, 1958-59, 60-61, 62-63; vis. prof. Rockefeller U., 1966-67; Kramers prof. U. Utrecht (Netherlands), 1977-78; sci. asso. CERN, Geneva, Switzerland, 1977-78. Putnam scholar, 1953; A.P. Sloan fellow, 1960-66; NSF sr. postdoctoral fellow, 1966-67; J.S. Guggenheim fellow, 1970-71. Mem. IEEE, Am. Phys. Soc., Sigma Xi, Eta Kappa Nu, Tau Beta Pi. Author: (with Ronold W.P. King) Scattering and Diffraction of Waves, 1959; (with Barry M. McCoy) Two-Dimensional Ising Model, 1973. Home: 12 Robinson St Cambridge MA 02138 Office: 204B Pierce Hall Harvard U Cambridge MA 02138. *A person's strength is, simultaneously, his weakness.*

WU, THEODORE YAO-TSU, engineer; b. Changchow, Kiangsu, China, Mar. 20, 1924; s. Ren Fu and Gee-Ing (Shu) W.; B.S., Chiano-Tung U., 1946; M.S., Iowa State U., 1948; Ph.D., Calif. Inst. Tech., 1952; m. Chin-Hua Shih, June 17, 1950; children—Fonda Bai-yueh, Melba Bai-chin. Came to U.S., 1948, naturalized, 1962. Mem. faculty Calif. Inst. Tech., Pasadena, 1952—, asso. prof., 1957-61, prof. engring. sci., 1961—; vis. prof. Hamburg (Germany) U., 1964-65; cons. numerous indsl. firms. Guggenheim fellow, 1964-65. Fellow Am. Phys. Soc., Am. Inst. Aero. and Astronautics (asso.); mem. Sigma Xi, Phi Tau Phi. Editorial bd. Advances in Applied Mechanics series, 1970. Contbr. profl. jours. Home: 3195 PP6602 Orlando Rd Pasadena CA 91107•

WUEST, FRANCIS JOSEPH, psychologist, educator; b. Phila., Jan. 22, 1930; s. Frank Charles and Catherine (McLaughlin) W.; B.A., LaSalle Coll., Phila., 1951; M.A., Fordham U., 1953; Ph.D., Brown U., 1961; m. Joanne M. Marona, Dec. 12, 1953 (div. Oct. 1973); children—Joseph M., Peter F., John S., Clare M.; m. 2d, Clair E. Knysh, Nov. 30, 1973. Statistician, Pan Am. World Airways, 1952-53; research psychologist Electric Boat div. Gen. Dynamics Corp., 1956-59; mem. faculty Lehigh U., 1961-71, chmn. dept. psychology, 1963-71, prof. psychology, 1965-71; prof., chmn. dept. psychology St. Louis U., 1971-73; dir. project on change in undergrad. liberal edn. Assn. Am. Colls., Washington, 1973-77; program dir. Kansas City Regional Council Higher Edn.; pres. F. J. Wuest Assos., 1977—. Served to 1st lt. AUS, 1953-56. Recipient Creative Talent Research award Am. Inst. Research, 1961. Mem. Am., Eastern, Midwest psychol. assns., Soc. Engring. Psychology, Am. Assn. Higher Edn., Sigma Xi, Omicron Delta Kappa. Author tech. reports on renewal and innovation in higher edn., decision making, info. processing. Address: 200 S Esplanade Leavenworth KS 66048

WUESTHOFF, WINFRED WILLIAM, investment counselor; b. Milw., July 10, 1922; s. Oscar and Louise (Schuettler) W.; Ph.B., U. Wis., 1947; m. Louise June Wesle, Sept. 16, 1950; children—Anne Louise, Lynn Elsbeth. With Marine Nat. Exchange Bank, Milw., 1947-72, Marine Corp., 1963-72; pres. W.W. Wuesthoff, Milw., Inc., 1972—; dir. Data Retrieval Corp., Wetzel Bros. Printing Co. Active local United Community Services, Boys Club. Bd. dirs. Todd Wehr Found.; trustee Carthage Coll. Mem. Fin. Analysts Fedn., Financial Execs. Inst., Am. Finance Assn. Clubs: Milw. Country, University. Home: 940 E Wye Ln Milwaukee WI 53217 Office: 250 E Wisconsin Ave Milwaukee WI 53202

WULF, MELVIN LAWRENCE, lawyer; b. N.Y.C., Nov. 1, 1927; s. Jacob and Vivian (Hurwitz) W.; B.S., Columbia, 1952, LL.B., 1955; m. Deirdre Howard, Dec. 18, 1962; children—Laura Melissa, Jane Miranda. Admitted to N.Y. bar, 1957; asst. legal dir. ACLU, 1958-62, legal dir., 1962-77; Distinguished vis. prof. Hofstra Law Sch., 1975, spl. prof. law, 1976-77; mem. firm Clark Wulf Levine & Feratis, 1978—. Mem. adv. bd. Law Students Civil Rights Research Council. Served to lt. (j.g.) USNR, 1955-57. Ford Found. fellow, 1967. Mem. Nat. Lawyers Guild. Author articles. Home: 340 Riverside Dr New York NY 10025 Office: 113 University Pl New York NY 10003

WULF, OLIVER REYNOLDS, scientist; b. Norwich, Conn., Apr. 22, 1897; s. Otto E. and Grace B. (Reynolds) W.; B.S., Worcester Poly. Inst., 1920; M.S., Am. U., 1922; Ph.D., Calif. Inst. Tech., 1926; m. Beatrice M. Jones, Oct. 21, 1922. Jr. chemist U.S. Dept. Agr., Washington, 1920-22, chemist and physicist, 1928-39; meteorologist, research meteorologist U.S. Weather Bur. and Inst. Atmospheric Scis., Environ. Sci. Services Adminstrn., U.S. Dept. Commerce, Washington, Chgo., Pasadena, 1939-67; sr. research asso. in phys. chemistry emeritus Calif. Inst. Tech., Pasadena, 1967—. Served with USN, 1918-19. NRC fellow, 1926-28; Guggenheim Found. fellow, 1932-33. Recipient Hillebrand prize, Chem. Soc. Washington, 1935; Robert H. Goddard award, Worcester Poly. Inst., 1962. Mem. Nat. Acad. Scis., Am. Chem. Soc., Am. Phys. Soc., Am. Meteorol. Soc., Am. Geophys. Union, AAAS, Optical Soc. Am., Sigma Xi. Contbr. articles in chemistry, chem. physics, meteorology and geophysics to profl. jours. Home: 557 Berkeley Ave San Marino CA 91108 Office: Noyes Lab of Chem Physics Calif Inst Tech Pasadena CA 91125

WULF, ROBERT FINDLEY, forest products co. exec.; b. Phila., Mar. 6, 1937; s. Robert Fischer and Pauline (Findley) W.; A.B., Stanford U., 1959; M.B.A., Columbia U., 1964. Security analyst Smith Barney & Co., N.Y.C., 1964-74, v.p., 1967-74; mgr. fin.analysis and relations Potlatch Corp., San Francisco, 1974-78, treas., 1978—. Elder Calvary Presbyn. Ch., 1978—, pres. bd. trustees, 1979. Served to 1st lt. USAF, 1959-62. Chartered Fin. Analyst. Mem. N.Y. Soc. Security Analysts, Fin. Execs. Inst., Beta Gamma Sigma. Republican. Club: Olympic (San Francisco). Home: 155 Jackson St San Francisco CA 94111 Office: Potlatch Corp PO Box 3591 San Francisco CA 94119

WULK, NED WILLIAM, basketball coach; b. Marion, Wis., Aug. 14, 1920; s. Walter and Ruth K. (Dedolph) W.; B.S., La Crosse State Coll., 1942; M.Ed., Xavier U., Cin., 1951; m. Fern B. Stefl, Jan. 18, 1944; children—Stephanie, Gregory. Coach, tchr. phys. edn. Hartford (Wis.) High Sch., 1946-48; head baseball coach Xavier U., 1948-56, freshman football and basketball coach, 1948-51, head basketball coach, 1951-57, asst. prof. tchr. edn., 1948-57; head basketball coach, asst. prof. phys. edn. Ariz. State U., 1957—; trustee Nat. Basketball Hall of Fame; mem. U.S. Olympic Com., Nat. Basketball Rules Com. Served with U.S. Army, 1942-46; ETO. Decorated Purple Heart; named to LaCrosse State U. Hall of Fame, 1972, Xavier U. Basketball Hall of Fame, 1970; recipient Ariz. Coach of Year award Phoenix Press Box Assn., 1961, 62, 75. Mem. Nat. Assn. Basketball Coaches (pres. 1978-79, dir. 1971—). Republican. Methodist. Office: Athletic Dept Ariz State U Tempe AZ 85281

WULLER, JAMES HERMAN, lawyer; b. Belleville, Ill., Mar. 27, 1926; s. Edgar J. and Addie (Reis) W.; B.S.C., St. Louis U., 1947, LL.B., 1950. Admitted to Mo. bar, 1950. Ill. bar, 1951; asso. W.E. Durham, Chgo., 1951-53; asso., later partner firm Durham, McGuire & Swank, Chgo., 1954-56; atty. Mo. Pacific Corp., and asso. cos., 1956-64, gen. atty., 1972—. Served with USNR, 1944-46. Mem. Phi Alpha Delta. Roman Catholic. Home: 9352 White Ave St Louis MO 63144 Office: 9900 Clayton Rd St Louis MO 63124

WULSIN, LUCIEN, piano mfg. co. exec.; b. Cin., Sept. 21, 1916; s. Lucien and Margaret (Hager) W.; A.B., Harvard, 1939; LL.B., U. Va., 1947; m. Eleanor Tubman, Jan. 9, 1944; children—Lucien III, Henry H., Jeanne P., Diane M.; m. 2d, Joan Friedlander, Dec. 30, 1959. Admitted to Ohio bar, 1948, Ark. bar, 1958; partner Kyte, Conlan, Wulsin & Vogeler, Cin., 1952-62; pres. D. H. Baldwin Co. (now Baldwin-United Corp.), Cin., 1962-74, chmn., chief exec. officer, 1974—. Trustee Cin. Symphony Orch. Mem. Ark., Cin. bar assns., Alliance Francaise. Clubs: Literary; Harvard, Queen City, Camargo (Cin.). Office: Baldwin-United Corp 1801 Gilbert Ave Cincinnati OH 45202*

WUNDER, RICHARD PAUL, former museum curator; b. Ardmore, Pa., May 31, 1923; s. Clarence Edmond and Elizabeth (Geissel) W.; A.B., Harvard, 1949, A.M., 1950, Ph.D., 1955. Asst., dept. drawings, later asst. to dir. Fogg Art Mus., Harvard, 1953-54; John T. Kirkland travelling fellow Harvard, 1954-55; curator drawings and prints Cooper Union Mus., N.Y.C., 1955-64; curator painting and sculpture Nat. Collection Fine Arts, Smithsonian Instn., 1964-68, asst. dir., 1968-69; sr. research fellow in art, 1969-72; dir. Cooper-Hewitt Mus. Design, N.Y.C., 1968-69; John Hamilton Fulton vis. prof. Middlebury Coll., 1975; v.p. Christie, Manson & Woods Appraisals, Inc., N.Y.C., 1979—. Mem. advisory bd. Resources Council Am. 1968-69, Archives Am. Art, The Art Quar., 1968-75; active fund raising drives for Save Cooper Union Mus. Com., Save Olana com., Save Hudson County Courthouse, Jersey City; mem. advisory bd. Mus. Am. Folk Art, N.Y.C., 1965-71. Trustee, Mus. Graphic Arts, N.Y.C., 1967-71. Served to 1st lt. U.S. Army, 1943-45, 50-52. Mem. Am. Assn. Mus., Coll. Art Assn. Am., Soc. Archtl. Historians, Nat. Trust Historic Preservation, Walpole Soc., Drawing Soc. (dir. 1968-71), Soc. Archtl. Historians G. Britain, Furniture Hist. Soc., Soc. de l'Historie de l'Art Francais. Episcopalian. Clubs: N.Y. Athletic, Nat. Arts (N.Y.C.). Author: Extravagant Drawings of the Eighteenth Century, 1962, Architectural and Ornament Drawings in the University of Michigan Museum of Art, 1965, Frederic Edwin Church, 1966; Hiram Powers-Vermont Sculptor, 1974; Architectural, Ornament, Figure and Landscape Drawing, 1975; also articles. Mem. editorial bd. Smithsonian Press, 1965-70, Smithsonian Jour. History, 1965-70. Home: Brookside Orwell VT 05760

WUNDERLICH, BERNHARD, educator; b. Brandenburg, Germany, May 28, 1931; s. Richard O. and Johanne (Wohlgefahrt) W.; student Humboldt U., Berlin, Germany, 1949-53, Goethe U., Frankfurt, Germany, 1953-54, Hastings Coll., 1954-55; Ph.D., Northwestern U., 1957; m. Adelheid Felix, Dec. 28, 1953; children—Caryn Cornelia, Brent Bernhard. Came to U.S., 1954, naturalized, 1960. Instr. chemistry Northwestern U., Evanston, Ill., 1957-58; instr. chemistry Cornell U., Ithaca, N.Y., 1958-60, asst. prof., 1960-63; asso. prof. phys. chemistry Rensselaer Poly. Inst., Troy, N.Y., 1963-65, prof. phys. chemistry, 1965—; cons. E.I. duPont de Nemours Co., 1963—. Recipient award in thermal analysis N.Am. Thermal Anal. Soc., 1971; Outstanding Educator of Am. award, 1971. Fellow Am. Phys. Soc.; mem. Am. Chem. Soc. Author: Macromolecular Physics, Vol. 1, 1973, Vol. 2, 1976; contbr. 150 articles to profl. jours. Research in solid state of linear high polymers. Mem. editorial bd. Chemistry, 1965-68, Makromolekulare Chemie, Jour. Thermal Analysis; adv. bd. Jour. Polymer Sci. Home: 211 Winter St Ext Troy NY 12180

WUNDERLICH, CARLE ROBERT, retail co. exec.; b. Hamilton, Ohio, May 18, 1922; s. Raymond Francis and Hazel Mae (Rose) W.; B.A., Muskingum Coll., 1945; children—Diane Lynn, Carle Robert, Raymond Bruce, Karen Ann, Denise Sue. With Cussins & Fearn Co., Inc., Columbus, Ohio, 1947-66, appliance salesman, comparative shopper, asst. housewares buyer, appliance mdse. mgr., asst. gen. mdse. mgr., 1947-61, v.p., gen. mdse. mgr., 1961-62, exec. v.p., 1962-64, pres., gen. mgr., 1964-66, also dir.; chmn. bd., pres., chief exec. officer, dir. Alden's Inc., Chgo., 1967—; dir. Gamble Skagmo, Inc., Gamble Import Co., Gamble Aldens Life Ins. Co. Chmn. Muskingum Devel. Com., 1963-67; area chmn. United Appeal, 1963-66; gen. chmn. Chgo. Boy Scouts LunchoRee; past mem. Oak Brook (Ill.) Plan Commn. Trustee Muskingum Coll., 1968—; bd. dirs. Crippled Children's Soc., Boy Scouts Am.; chmn. nat. football awards dinner Better Boys Found. Recipient Distinguished Community Service award Brandeis U., 1974; Scout of Yr. award Boy Scouts Am., 1975; Distinguished Service award Muskingum Coll., 1975. Mem. Mail Order Assn. Am. (pres.), AIM, Bus. Men's Assn. (past pres.), Alumni Assn. (past pres.). Presbyterian (trustee). Mason (32, Shriner), Rotarian. Home: 180 E Pearson St Chicago IL 60611 Office: 5000 Roosevelt Rd Chicago IL 60607

WUNDERMAN, LESTER, advt. agy. exec.; b. N.Y.C., June 22, 1920; s. Harry and Dorothy (Horowitz) W.; student Bklyn. Coll., 1936-38, New Sch. Social Research, 1952-55, Columbia U., 1957, 72-73; m. Suzanne Oksman Cott, 1975; children—Marc, Karen. Vice pres., then exec. v.p. Maxwell Sackheim & Co., Inc., N.Y.C., 1947-58; pres. Wunderman, Ricotta & Kline, Inc., N.Y.C., 1958-77, chmn., 1977—; exec. v.p. Young & Rubicam Internat. Inc., 1975—; lectr. creativity and mktg. N.Y. U., New Sch. Social Research, Boston U., Mass. Inst. Tech.; lectr. primitive art Columbia, Bklyn. Mus., New Orleans Mus. Fine Arts; spl. research primitive art of Mali. Pres. Wunderman Found., 1962—; Wunderman collection African art exhibited at 13 maj. mus. U.S., 1973-75. Mem. membership com. Mus. Modern Art, N.Y.C. Trustee Mus. African Art, Washington, Internat. Center of Photography, N.Y.C.; mem. exec. com. U.S. Nat. Commn. for UNESCO; bd. dirs. Corp. Theater Fund; mem. governing bd. New Directions; co-chmn. Friends Leopold Senghor Found. Recipient Sylvania award for creative TV, 1955; Certificate of Honor award Direct Mail Advt. Assn., 1960; Direct Mail Leaders Participation award, 1964; named Mail Order Man of Yr., N.Y. Advt. Club, 1967. Mem. Am. Assn. Advt. Agencies (past dir.), Pub. Interest Pub. Relations (dir.), Alpha Delta Sigma. Clubs: Players, East Hampton Tennis, Town Tennis, City Athletic (N.Y.C.). Contbr. speeches and articles on mktg. to N.Y. Times and trade press U.S., Europe, Japan. Home: 900 Fifth Ave New York City NY 10021 Office: 575 Madison Ave New York City NY 10022

WUNDOHL, FRANK FRANCIS, editor; b. Phila., Oct. 7, 1929; s. Morton and Esther (Sorkin) W.; B.S. in Journalism, Temple U., 1951; m. Harriet Balis, Dec. 24, 1950; children—David John, Barbara Anne. Newswriter Sta. WCAU AM-FM TV, Phila., 1951-52; publicist Phila. Housing Authority, 1954; news editor Daily Intelligencer, Doylesown, Pa., also editor Newtown (Pa.) Enterprise, 1954-56; feature writer, reporter, rewriteman Phila. Daily News, 1956-63, night photog. editor, makeup and copyeditor, 1958-63; publs. mgr. Mass. Mut. Life Ins. Co., Springfield, 1963-64; chief copy editor Courier-Post, Camden, N.J., 1964-65; editor IBM Info. Records Div. News, Dayton, N.J., 1965-66; dir. pub. relations and sales promotion Repco Products Corp., Phila., 1966-67; dir. pub. info. Albert Einstein Med. Center, Phila., 1967-73; editor Jewish Exponent, Phila., 1973—; mem. evening faculty dept. journalism Temple U., 1973-78. Served as pub. info. corr. USMC, 1952-54. Recipient numerous awards, including: 1st pl. award Pub. Relations Soc. of Hosp. Assn. of Pa., 1968, Acad. of Hosp. Pub. Relations, Am. Hosp. Assn., 1970; Bronze medal Delaware Valley Graphic Arts Exhibit, 1971; awards of Excellence Artists Guild of Delaware Valley, (3), 1972, (2), 1973; Boris Smolar award Council Jewish Fedn. and Welfare Funds, 1976; Clarion award Women in Communications, 1978; Bronze medallion Chapel of Four Chaplains, 1978. Mem. Phila. Press Assn., Suburban Pub. Relations Club (pres. 1973-74), Delaware Valley Hosp. Pub. Relations Assn. (pres. 1972-73), Am. Jewish Press Assn. (pres. 1978—), Sigma Delta Chi (charter mem. Greater Phila. chpt., chpt. spl. mention 1977). Jewish. Home: 14 Greenwood Ave Wyncote PA 19095 Office: 226 S 16th St Philadelphia PA 19102

WUNSCH, CARL ISAAC, oceanographer, educator; b. Bklyn., May 5, 1941; s. Harry and Helen (Gellis) W.; S.B., M.I.T., 1962, Ph.D., 1967; m. Marjory Markel, June 6, 1970; children—Jared, Hannah. Asst. prof. phys. oceanography M.I.T., 1967-70, asso. prof., 1970-75, prof., 1975-76, Cecil and Ida Green prof., 1976—, head dept. earth and planetary scis., 1977—; sr. vis. fellow U. Cambridge, Eng., 1969, 74-75, cons. NASA, NSF, Nat. Acad. Scis. Recipient Tex. Instruments Found. Founders prize, 1975. Fellow Am. Geophys. Union (James R. Macelwane award 1971), Royal Astron. Soc., Am. Acad. Arts and Scis.; mem. Nat. Acad. Scis. Club: Cosmos. Asso. editor: Jour. Phys. Oceanography, 1977—. Contbr. articles in field to profl. jours. Home: 16 Crescent St Cambridge MA 02138 Office: Department of Earth and Planetary Sciences Massachusetts Institute Technology Cambridge MA 02139

WUNZ, PAUL RICHARD, JR., educator; b. Erie, Pa., Oct. 18, 1923; s. Paul Richard and Isabella Marie (Blackton) W.; B.S., Pa. State U., 1944, M.S., 1947; Ph.D., U. Del., 1950; m. Jane Kyle, June 19, 1948; children—Timothy Paul, Carol Jane, Stephen Kyle. Asst. prof., chmn. dept. chemistry Augsburg Coll., Mpls., 1950-51; research chemist Nopco Chem. Co., Harrison, N.J., 1951-53; research chemist, group leader Callery Chem. Co. (Pa.), 1953-57; asso. prof. chemistry Geneva Coll., Beaver Falls, Pa., 1957-65; prof. chemistry Indiana (Pa.) U., 1965—, chmn. dept., 1965-73. Mem. Am. Chem. Soc., Sigma Xi, Phi Lambda Upsilon, Alpha Chi Sigma. Democrat. Lutheran. Contbr. articles to profl. jours. Patentee in field. Home: 219 Oriole Ave Indiana PA 15701

WUORINEN, CHARLES, composer; b. N.Y.C., June 9, 1938; s. John Henry and Alfhild (Kalijarvi) W.; B.A., Columbia U., 1961, M.A., 1963; D.Mus. (hon.), Jersey City State Coll., 1971. Lectr., Columbia U., 1964-65, instr., 1965-69, asst. prof., 1969-71, co-dir. Group Contemporary Music, 1962—; vis. lectr. Princeton U., 1967-68, New Eng. Conservatory, 1968-71; adj. lectr. U. South Fla., 1971-72; faculty Manhattan Sch. Music, 1972—; artistic dir., pres. Am. Orch. for Contemporary Music, 1973—; condr. Cleve. Orch., 1976, Finland Radio Orch., 1979, Helsinki Philharm., 1979. Bd. dirs. Am. Composers Orch., 1975—. Recipient Philharmonic Young Composers award, 1954; Bennington Composers Conf. scholar, 1956-60; Bearns prize, 1958-59, 61; MacDowell Colony fellow, 1958; Alice M. Ditson fellow, 1959; Arthur Rose teaching fellow, 1960; Broadcast Music-Student Composers award, 1959, 61, 62, 63; Lili Boulanger Meml. award, 1963; Festival fellow Santa Fe Opera, 1962, World's Fair Music and Sound, 1962; commd. by Koussevitzky Found., 1964, Berkshire Music Center, 1963, Fromm Found., 1963-71, Ford Found., 1962, Orch. of Am., 1958, Columbia U., 1956, Washington and Lee U., 1964, Fine Arts Quartet, 1969, Naumberg Found., 1971, U. South Fla., 1972, Nat. Opera Inst., 1973, Light Fantastic Players, 1973, N.Y. State Council on the Arts, 1974, Buffalo Philharmonic, 1974, Ojai Festival, 1974; Contemporary Chamber Ensemble, 1974; TASHI, 1974, Beethoven Festival, Bonn, 1978; grantee Nat. Inst. Arts and Letters, 1967, Nat. Endowment for Arts, 1974, 76; Guggenheim fellow, 1968, 72; Ingraham Merrill fellow, 1972; Rockefeller Found. fellow, 1979, 80; Pulitzer prize, 1970; Brandeis U. creative arts award, 1970; Creative Artists Public Service award, 1976; Arts and Letters award Finlandia Found., 1976; Koussevitzky Internat. Rec. award, 1970, 72. Mem. editorial bd. Perspectives of New Music; dir. Composers Recordings Inc. Mem. Am. Soc. Univ. Composers, Am. Composers Alliance (v.p.), Am. Music Center (dir.), Internat. Soc. Comtemporary Music, (dir.), Am. Composers Concerts (dir.), Phi Beta Kappa. Composer numerous works, 1943—, latest being: Trio No. 1 for Flute, Cello and Piano, 1961; Invention for Percussion Quintet, 1962; Octet, 1962; Duuiensela for Cello and Piano, 1962; Bearbeitungen über das Glogauer Liederbuch, 1962; The Prayer of Jonah, 1962; 2d Trio: Piece for Stefan Wolpe, 1962; Chamber Concerto for Cello and 10 Players, 1963; Piano Variations, 1963; Flute Variations, 1963; Variations a 2, 1964; Composition for Violin and 10 Instruments, 1964; Chamber Concerto for Flute and 10 Players, 1964; Orchestral and Electronic Exchanges, 1965; Composition for Oboe and Piano, 1965; Chamber Concerto for Oboe and 10 Players, 1965; Super Salutem for Male Voices and Instruments, 1964; Piano Concerto, 1966; The Bells, for Carillon, 1966; Bicinium, 2 Oboes, 1966; Janissary Music, for 1 Percussionist, 1966; Harpsichord Divisions, 1966; Making Ends Meet, for Piano four-hands, 1966; John Bull, Salve Regina Versus Septem, 1966; Duo for Violin and Piano, 1967; The Politics of Harmony: A Masque, 1967; String Trio, 1968; Flute Variations II, 1968; Time's Encomium (electronic), 1969; Adapting to the Times (cello and piano), 1969; The Long and the Short (violin), 1969; Contrafactum for Orch., 1969; Nature's Concord (trumpet and piano), 1969; Piano Sonata, 1970; Ringing Changes for Percussion, 1970; A Song, 1970; Tuba Concerto, 1970; A Message to Denmark Hill, 1970; Cello Variations, 1970; String Quartet, 1971; Canzona for 12 Instruments, 1971; Grand Bamboula, 1971; Violin Concerto, 1972; Harp Variations, 1972; Bassoon Variations, 1972; Violin Variations, 1972; On Alligators for 8 Instruments, 1972; Speculum Speculi, for 6 players, 1972; Third Trio for Flute, Cello and Piano, 1972; Grand Union for Cello and Drums, 1973; Arabia Felix for 6 Instruments, 1973; Second Piano Concerto, 1974; Fantasia for Violin and Piano, 1974; Reliquary, 1975; The W. of Babylon (opera), 1975; TASHI, 1975; Hyperion for 12 Instruments, 1975; 2d Piano Sonata, 1976; Percussion Symphony, 1976; The Winds, 1977; Fest Fantasy, 1977; Archangel for trombone and string quartet, 1977; Six Songs for two voices; Wind Quintet; Self Similar Waltz for piano; Ancestors for chamber ensemble, 1978; Two-Part Symphony, 1978; The Magic Art, A Masque for chamber orch., 1979; Fortune, for 4 instruments, 1979; 2d String Quartet, 1979.

WURF, JERRY, labor union ofcl.; b. N.Y.C., May 18, 1919; s. Sigmund and Lena (Tannenbaum) W.; A.B., N.Y.U., 1940; m. Mildred Kiefer, Nov. 26, 1960; children—Susan, Nicholas and Abigail. Worked in cafeteria, N.Y., 1940-43; an organizer local 448 Hotel and Restaurant Employees, 1943, organizer, adminstr. union's Welfare Fund, 1947; organizer in N.Y. for Am. Fedn. of State, County and Municipal Employees, 1947-58, exec. dir. dist. council 37, 1959-64, internat. pres., 1964—; v.p. exec. council AFL-CIO. Mem. exec. com. Com. for Nat. Health Ins., Leadership Conf. on Civil Rights; trustee 20th Century Fund; mem. vis. com. Brookings Instn.; Mem. Am. Arbitration Assn. (dir.), Council on Fgn. Relations. Clubs: Nat. Democratic, Federal City. Home: 3846 Cathedral Ave NW Washington DC 20016 Office: 1625 L St NW Washington DC 20036

WURM, JOHN NICHOLAS, bishop, Roman Cath. Ch.; b. Overland, Mo., Dec. 6, 1927; s. Anthony Ernest and Estelle Rose (Leonard) W.; B.A., Kenrick Sem., 1950; M.A., St. Louis U., 1958, Ph.D., 1969. Ordained priest, 1954; prin. Corpus Christi High Sch., 1960-63, Rosati-Kain High Sch., St. Louis, 1963-72; asso. supt. schs. Archdiocese St. Louis, 1972—; vis. prof. ch. history Kenrick Theol. Sem., St. Louis, 1974-76; consecrated bishop, 1976; aux. bishop of St. Louis, 1976—; pastor Basilica of St. Louis, 1976—. Dep. dir. Notre Dame Study Cath. Edn., St. Louis, 1969-70; mem. state com. North Central Assn., 1972—. Mem. Phi Delta Kappa. Home: 209 Walnut St Saint Louis MO 63102 Office: 4445 Lindell St Saint Louis MO 63108

WURMAN, RICHARD SAUL, architect; b. Phila., Mar. 26, 1935; s. Morris Louis and Fannie (Pelson) W.; B.Arch. (T.P. Chandler fellow), U. Pa., M.Arch. with highest honors; children—Joshua, Reven. Mem. faculty N.C. State U., Raleigh, 1962-64, 77, Washington U., St. Louis, 1965, Princeton U., 1965-67, Cambridge (Eng.) U., 1967-68, N.Y.C. program Cornell U., 1968-70, CCNY, 1968-70, UCLA, 1976, U. So. Calif., 1976; prof. architecture, dean Sch. Environ. Design, Calif. State Poly. U., Pomona; with Archtl. Office Louis I. Kahn, London, 1960-62; founding dir. Group Environ. Edn., 1968; bd. dirs. Internat. Design Conf., Aspen, Colo., 1970—, chmn., 1972; co-chmn. 1st Fed. Design Assembly, 1973; adv. Enoch B. Found., 1975—; trustee Center Bldg. Edn. Programs, 1976—; dep. dir. Phila. Office Housing and Community Devel., 1977; bd. dir. Internat. design Edn. Found., 1978—; designer exhbns., cons. in field. Recipient Thornton Oakley medal, 1954, Arthur Spayd Brookes Gold medal, 1958; Graham fellow, 1966, 76; T.P. Chandler fellow, 1968; fellow Guggenheim Found.,1969, Rockefeller Bros. Fund, 1972, Nat. Endowment Arts, 1970, 73, 74, 76, 79-80; grantee Fels Found., 1970, Ednl. Facilities Lab., 1972, 74, Rohm & Haas Co., 1976. Fellow AIA (medal 1958). Address: Sch Environ Design Calif Poly State Univ Poloma CA 91768*

WURSTER, CHARLES FREDERICK, JR., environ. scientist, educator; b. Phila., Aug. 1, 1930; s. Charles Frederick and Helen B. (Schmittberger) W.; S.B., Haverford Coll., 1952; M.S., U. Del., 1954; Ph.D., Stanford U., 1957; m. Eva M. Tank-Nielsen, Aug. 26, 1970; children—Steven Hadley, Nina Fredrikke, Erik Frederick. Teaching asst. U. Del., 1952-54; research asst. Stanford U., 1954-57; with dept. plant biology Carnegie Instn., Stanford U., spring 1957; Fulbright fellow, Innsbruck, Austria, 1957-58; research chemist Monsanto Research Corp., 1959-62; research asso. biol. scis. Dartmouth Coll., 1962-65; asst. prof. biol. scis. State U. N.Y. at Stony Brook, 1965-70, asso. prof. environmental scis. Marine Scis. Research Center, 1970—; chmn. scientists adv. com., trustee Environ. Def. Fund, Inc., 1967—; mem. adminstr's. pesticide policy adv. com. EPA, 1975—. Fellow AAAS; mem. Ecol. Soc. Am. Defenders of Wildlife (dir. 1975—), Nat. Parks and Conservation Assn. (trustee 1970—). Contbr. numerous articles to profl. publs. Research on DDT, other chlorinated hydrocarbons. Office: Marine Sciences Research Center State Univ NY Stony Brook NY 11794

WURTELE, MORTON GAITHER, meteorologist, educator; b. Harrodsburg, Ky., July 25, 1919; s. Edward Conrad and Emily Russell (Gaither) W.; S.B., Harvard, 1940; M.A., U. Calif. at Los Angeles, 1944, Ph.D., 1953; m. Zivia Syrkin, Dec. 31, 1942; children—Eve Syrkin, Jonathan Syrkin. Asst. prof. meteorology Mass. Inst. Tech., Cambridge, 1953-58; asso. prof. meteorology U. Calif. at Los Angeles, 1958-64, prof., 1964—, chmn. dept., 1971-76; vis. prof. U. Buenos Aires, 1962, U. Jerusalem, 1965; cons. in field. Trustee, Univ. Corp. for Atmospheric Research. Served with USNR, 1940-41. Fulbright grantee, 1949-50, 65; NATO sr. fellow, 1961-62. Fellow Am. Meteorol. Soc.; mem. Am. Profs. for Peace in Middle East (nat. exec. 1974—), Royal Meteorol. Soc., Am. Geophys. Union, Phi Beta Kappa, Sigma Xi. Club: Harvard So. Calif. Prin. contbr. Glossary of Meteorology; contbr. articles to profl. jours. Home: 432 E Rustic Rd Santa Monica CA 90402 Office: U Calif at Los Angeles Los Angeles CA 90024

WURTMAN, RICHARD JAY, physician, educator; b. Phila., Mar. 9, 1936; s. Samuel Richard and Hilda (Schreiber) W.; A.B., U. Pa., 1956; M.D., Harvard, 1960; m. Judith Joy Hirschhorn, Nov. 15, 1959; children—Rachael Elisabeth, David Franklin. Intern Mass. Gen. Hosp., 1960-61, resident, 1961-62, fellow medicine, 1965-66; research asso., med. research officer NIMH, 1962-67; mem. faculty Mass. Inst. Tech., 1967—, prof. endocrinology and metabolism, 1970—; lectr. medicine Harvard Med. Sch., 1969—; prof. Harvard-M.I.T. Div. Health Scis. and Tech., 1978—; mem. small grants study sect. NIMH, 1967-69, preclin. psychopharmacolgy study sect., 1971-75; behavioral biology adv. panel NASA, 1969—; council basic sci. Am. Heart Assn., 1969—; research adv. bd. Parkinson's Disease Found., 1972—; com. phototherapy in newborns NRC-Nat. Acad. Scis., 1972-74, Com. nutrition, brain devel. and behavior, 1976, mem. space applications bd., 1976—; chmn. life scis. adv. com. NASA, 1979—; asso. neuroscis. research program M.I.T., 1974; Bennett Lectr. Am. Neurol. Assn., 1974; Flexner lectr. U. Pa., 1975. Recipient Alvarenga prize and lectureship Phila. Coll. Physicians, 1970. Mem. Am. Soc. Clin. Investigation, Endocrine Soc. (Ernst Oppenheim award 1972), Am. Physiol. Soc., Am. Soc. Biol. Chemists, Am. Soc. Pharmacology and Exptl. Therapeutics (John Jacob Abel award 1968), Am. Soc. Neurochemistry, Soc. Neuroscis., Am. Soc. Clin. Nutrition. Clubs: Cosmos (Washington); Harvard (Boston). Author: Catecholamines, 1966; (with others) The Pineal, 1968; editor (with Judith Wurtman) Nutrition and the Brain, Vols. I and II, 1977, Vols. III, IV, V, 1979; also articles. Mem. editorial bd. Endocrinology, 1967-73, Jour. Pharmacology and Exptl. Therapeutics, 1968-75, Jour. Neural Transmission, 1969—, Neuroendocrinology, 1969-72, Metabolism, 1970—, Circulation Research, 1972-77, Jour. Neurochemistry, 1973—, Life Scis., 1973—, Brain Research, 1977—. Home: 193 Marlborough St Boston MA 02116 Office: Mass Inst Tech Cambridge MA 02139

WURTZBURGER, JON ALAN, investment banker; b. Balt., May 5, 1934; s. Alan and Janet (Cohn) W.; B.A., U. Pa., 1957, postgrad., Wharton Sch., 1957-58; m. Reva Sara Sprafkin, Dec. 25, 1957; children—Wendy, Jan. With Merrill Lynch, Pierce, Fenner & Smith, N.Y.C. and Balt., 1958-64; with Stein Bros. & Boyce, Inc., Balt., 1964-71, exec. v.p., 1967-71; 1st v.p. Bache & Co., N.Y.C., 1971-74; with Spear, Leeds & Kellogg, N.Y.C.; mem. N.Y. Stock Exchange; dir. Growth Properties, Inc.; pres. J.E.C.W., Inc. Mem. arbitration com. N.Y. Stock Exchange. Mem. Tax Commn. Balt., Balt. Airport Bd., Md. Airport Commn., Balt. Council Internat. Visitors. Bd. dirs. Md. Children's Aid Soc., Jewish Family and Children's Service. Served with AUS, 1957. Named Outstanding Young Man of Year Balt. Jr. C. of C., 1968; registered trader N.Y. Stock Exchange. Mem. Investment Bankers Assn. Am., Securities Industry Assn. Home: 19 E 72d St New York City NY 10021 Office: care Spear Leeds & Kellogg 111 Broadway New York City NY 10006

WURTZEL, ALAN LEON, retailing co. exec.; b. Mount Vernon, N.Y., Sept. 23, 1933; s. Samuel S. and Ruth (Mann) W.; A.B., Oberlin Coll., 1955; postgrad. London Sch. Econ., 1955-56; LL.B. cum laude, Yale, 1959; m. Barbara Goldstein, June 16, 1955; children—Judith Halle, Daniel Henry, Sharon Lee. Admitted to Conn. bar, 1959, D.C. bar, 1960, Va. bar., 1968; law clk. Chief Judge David L. Bazelon, U.S. Ct. Appeals, D.C., 1959-60; asso. atty. firm Strasser, Spiegelberg, Fried, Frank & Kampelman, Washington, 1960-65; legislative asst. to Senator Joseph Tydings, 1965-66; with Wards Co., Inc., Richmond, 1966—, exec. v.p., 1968-70, pres., 1970—; pres. NATM Buying Corp.; dir. Bank Va., Richmond. Mem. Tax Study Commn. Richmond, 1970—. Bd. dirs. Richmond Jewish Community Center, Anti-Defamation League; 3d v.p. Jewish Welfare Fedn. Richmond, 1978. Mem. Phi Beta Kappa. Home: 21 Maxwell Rd Richmond VA 23226 Office: 2040 Thalbro St Richmond VA 23230

WURZEL, LEONARD, candy mfg. co. exec.; b. Phila., Feb. 4, 1918; s. Maurice L. and Dora (Goldberg) W.; B.S., Washington and Jefferson Coll., 1939; M.B.A., Harvard, 1941; m. Elaine Cohen, Aug. 18, 1949; children—Mark L., Lawrence J. With Loft Candy Corp., Long Island City, N.Y., 1946-64, v.p., 1949-56, exec. v.p., 1956-57, pres., 1957-64, dir., 1949-64; pres., dir. Calico Cottage Candies, Inc., 1964—; dir. Beneficial Nat. Life Ins. Co., N.Y.C. Dir., treas. Candy Chocolate and Confectionery Inst. Chmn. Bd. Appeals, Village of Sands Point, N.Y. Served from pvt. to capt. Adj. Gen.'s Dept., AUS, 1941-46. Decorated Bronze Star. Mem. Assn. Mfrs. Confectionery and Chocolate (dir., past pres., chmn.), Retail Confectioners Internat. (dir., past pres.), Home: 25 Woodland Dr Sands Point NY 11050 Office: 11 Crescent St Hewlett NY 11557

WURZER, HENRY KAHL, newspaper co. exec.; b. Davenport, Iowa, May 9, 1936; s. Henry Charles and Margaret (Kahl) W.; B.S., U. Notre Dame, 1957; m. Marilyn Marthens, Dec. 21, 1957; children—Mark Henry, Peter Raymond, Elizabeth Ann, Ann Christine. Mem. advt., sales dept. Chgo. Tribune, 1957-67, pres., gen. mgr. area publ. Suburban Tribune, Hinsdale, Ill., 1967-75, v.p., advt. dir. Chgo. Tribune, 1975-79; exec. v.p., dir. sales N.Y. Daily News, N.Y.C., 1979—. Active Am. Cancer Soc., 1975-78; bd. dirs. Boy Scouts Am., 1977-79, Boys' Club, 1977-79. Mem. Internat. Newspaper Advt. Execs. Assn. (dir. 1976-79), Newspaper Advt. Bur. Republican. Roman Catholic. Clubs: Skokie (Ill.) Country; Chgo. Athletic Assn. Home: 16 Hemlock Hill Rd New Canaan CT 06840 Office: NY Daily News 220 E 42d St New York NY 10017

WUSSLER, ROBERT JOSEPH, TV exec.; b. Newark, Sept. 8, 1936; s. William and Anna (MacDonald) W.; B.A. in Communication Arts, Seton Hall U., East Orange, N.J., 1957, LL.D. (hon.), 1976; LL.D. (hon.), Emerson Coll., 1976; m. Grace Harlow, Apr. 23, 1960; children—Robert Joseph, Rosemary, Sally, Stefanie, Christopher, Jeanne. With CBS, 1957-78, CBS News, 1957-72, v.p., gen. mgr. Sta. WBBM-TV, Chgo., 1972-74, v.p. CBS Sports, N.Y.C., 1974-76, pres., 1977-78, pres. CBS-TV, 1976-77; pres. Pyramid Enterprises Ltd., N.Y.C., 1978—; chmn. bd. Nat. Acad. TV Arts and Scis., 1978—; chmn. pres.'s com. communications dept. Seton Hall U., 1970-72. Cub Scout leader, Rivervale, N.J., 1969-70; chmn. Chgo. Heart Attack Prevention Week, 1973; trustee Marymount Manhattan Coll., 1977—, Internat. Boxing Hall of Fame, 1978—. Recipient Emmy award Acad. TV Arts and Scis., 1969, 71, 72; Spl. Olympics award, 1974; Eclipse award Thoroughbred Racing Assn., 1975; Engelhard award Thoroughbred Breeders Assn. Am., award Los Angeles C. of C., 1977. Mem. Dirs. Guild Am., Internat. Radio and TV Soc., Ariz. Heart Inst. Roman Catholic. Club: Evanston (Ill.) Golf. Office: 515 Madison Ave New York NY 10022

WUSSOW, GEORGE CARL, dental educator; b. Milw., Mar. 10, 1923; s. George Charles and Mollie (Klaffke) W.; student Milw. State Tchrs. Coll., 1942-43; D.D.S., Marquette U., 1949, postgrad., 1954-57; m. Jeune Vivian Nowak, July 16, 1949; children—Christine, Susan, Gretchen. Individual practice dentistry, Milw., 1949-50; resident oral surgeon Wood (Wis.) VA Hosp., 1954-57, cons., 1957—; mem. faculty Marquette U. Dental Sch., 1953—, prof. oral surgery, 1967—, chmn. dept., 1962—, exec. faculty, 1970—, lectr. Sch. Dental Hygiene, 1970—, mem. grad. sch. faculty, 1971—; mem. cons. staff St. Francis Hosp., Milw., 1973—; cons. Milw. County Gen., St. Michaels, Great Lakes Naval hosps. Mem. dental adv. bd. Milw. Area Tech. Coll., 1970—; mem. athletic bd. Marquette U., 1972—, mem. fine arts com., 1972—. Chmn. dental div. Cancer Crusade, 1965-66; mem. profl. edn. com. Am. Cancer Soc., 1965—, bd. dirs., 1973. Served with Dental Corps, AUS, 1950-53; lt. col. Res. ret. Fellow Am. Coll. Dentists, Royal Soc. Health (Eng.); mem. Internat. Assn. Oral Surgeons, Am., Midwestern, Wis. (charter mem., past pres.), Greater Milw. (charter mem.) socs. oral surgeons, Am. Acad. Oral Pathology, Ret. Officers Assn. U.S. (life), Am. Hist. Print Collectors Soc. (charter mem.), Am., Wis., Greater Milw. dental assns., Wauwatosa C. of C., Mil. Order World Wars, Omicron Kappa Upsilon, Psi Omega, Delta Sigma Kappa. Roman Catholic. Club: Quarter Century (Marquette U.). Contbr. articles to sci. publs. Home: 1730 N 118th St Wauwatosa WI 53226 Office: 604 N 16th St Milwaukee WI 53233

WYANT, DOMINIQUE HOMAN, lawyer; b. Atlanta, Feb. 21, 1927; s. William Keblinger and Rose Mary (Homan) W.; A.B. cum laude, Harvard U., 1950, LL.B., 1953; m. Julie Gaston Gay, Dec. 3, 1960; children—Margaret Homan, Dominique Homan. Admitted to Ga. bar, 1955; asso. firm Shearman & Sterling, N.Y.C., 1953-55; with firm Crenshaw, Hansell, Ware, Brandon & Dorsey (now Hansell, Post, Brandon & Dorsey), Atlanta, 1955—, partner, 1958—; dir. Bankers Fidelity Life Ins. Co. Bd. dirs. Atlanta Met. chpt. The Mental Health Assn., Northwest Ga. Girl Scout Council, Inc., Theater of the Stars, Atlanta; bd. visitors Emory U.; gifts chmn. Atlanta Arts Alliance. Served with U.S. Army, 1945-47. Mem. Am. Law Inst., Am. Bar Assn., Ga. Bar Assn., Atlanta Bar Assn., Lawyers Club of Atlanta. Presbyterian. Clubs: Piedmont Driving, Capital City, Commerce. Home: 3651 Randall Mill Rd NW Atlanta GA 30327 Office: 3300 1st National Bank Tower Atlanta GA 30303

WYATT, ADDIE L., labor union exec.; b. Brookhaven, Miss., Mar. 8, 1924; d. Ambrose and Maggie (Nolan) Cameron; student public and pvt. schs., Chgo.; LL.D. (hon.), Anderson (Ind.) Coll., 1976; H.H.D. (hon.), Columbia Coll., Chgo., 1978; m. Claude S. Wyatt, Jr., 1940; children—Renaldo, Claude S. With meat packing industry, 1941-54; internat. rep. United Packinghouse Workers Union (now merged with Amalgamated Meat Cutters Union), 1954-68, internat. rep. Amalgamated Meat Cutters Union (now United Food and Comml. Workers Internat.), Chgo., 1968-74, dir. women's affairs dept., 1974-78, dir. human rights dept., 1978—, internat. v.p., 1976—; exec. v.p. Coalition Labor Union Women; adviser, instr. labor Roosevelt U., Chgo.; mem. labor adv. com. Chgo. Urban League; labor adv. Martin Luther King, Jr., Ralph Abernathy, Jesse Jackson. Past mem. Com. Social Concerns; past com. mem. Pres. Kennedy's Commn. Status Women; mem. Nat. Commn. on Working Women, Full Employment Action Council; past mem. Adv. Council Vocat. Edn.; mem. nat. commn. observance Internat. Women's Year, 1977; mem. Nat. Adv. Com. for Women, 1978; at-large mem. Democratic Nat. Com.; mem. adv. bd. Cook County Schs. Recipient Internat. Woman's Year award U. Mich., 1976; Service award women's bd. NAACP, 1976; Distinguished Labor Leader award Woodlawn Orgn., Chgo., 1976; Black Book award, 1977; Ebony Mag. citation, 1977; named Outstanding Woman in Western Region, Iota Phi Lambda; award Urban Ministries, Inc.; One of Ten Women of Year, Ladies Home Jour., 1977; One of Twelve Outstanding Women of Year, Time Mag., 1975; others. Mem. NCCJ, Midwest Women's Center, Alliance to Save Energy, Jewish Labor Program Com., Coalition Black Trade Unionists. Mem. Ch. of God (minister of music). Home: 8901 S Chappel St Chicago IL 60617 Office: 2800 N Sheridan Rd Chicago IL 60657

WYATT, DOROTHY MARY, mayor; b. St. John's, Nfld., Can.; d. W.R. and Anne (O'Brien) Fanning; B.A., Meml. U. Nlfd., St. John's, 1967, B.Ed., 1968, R.N., 1969; children—George, Lorelei. Dir. nursing Can. Red Cross, N.S. div., 1958-63; now mayor of St. John's; dir. St. John's Housing Corp.; chmn. Bowring Park Com. Recipient Queen's medal. Mem. Bus. and Profl. Women (past pres. St. John's, also Halifax). Roman Catholic. Club: Rotary. Office: City Hall New Gower St St John's NF A1C 5M2 Canada

WYATT, EDWARD AVERY, IV, newspaper editor; b. Petersburg, Va., Mar. 10, 1910; s. Edward Avery and Bessie Sutherland (Spain) W.; A.B., Randolph-Macon Coll., 1931; student (Nieman fellow) Harvard, 1939-40; m. Martha V. Seabury, Aug. 31, 1940 (dec. Feb. 1963); children—Edward A., V. Elizabeth. Reporter, News Leader, Richmond, Va., 1930-31; asso. editor, Progress-Index, Petersburg, Va., 1931-39, editor, 1940—; dir. Petersburg Newspaper Corp. Past chmn. Va. State Library Bd. Trustee Petersburg Mus., Mchts. Hope Ch. Restoration Found., Va. State Coll. Found., Tabb St. Ch. Found. Mem. Am. Soc. Newspaper Editors, Soc. of Cincinnati, Phi Beta Kappa, Omicron Delta Kappa, Phi Delta Theta. Episcopalian. Rotarian. Author: Along Petersburg Streets, 1943. Co-author: Petersburg's Story, A History, 1960. Contbr. articles on hist. subjects to mags. Editor: Petersburg Imprints, 1786-1876, 1949. Home: 106 S Market St Petersburg VA 23803 Office: The Progress-Index Petersburg VA 23803

WYATT, FOREST KENT, univ. pres.; b. Berea, Ky., May 27, 1934; s. Forest E. and Doddie H. Wyatt; B.S., Delta State U., Cleveland, Miss., 1956; M.Ed., U. So. Miss., 1960; Ed.D., U. Miss., 1970; postgrad. Harvard U., 1975; m. Janice Collins, Mar. 4, 1956; children—Tara Janice, Elizabeth Pharr. Coach, tchr. math., Mobile, 1956-63; prin. Merigold (Miss.) Sch., 1963-64; alumni sec., then asst. to pres., dir. adminstrv. services Delta State U., 1964-75, pres., 1975—; dir. Grenada Banking System. Active local United Givers, Boy Scouts Am. Named Outstanding Alumnus of Year, Delta State U., 1975. Mem. Am. Council Edn., Am. Council Tchrs. Edn., So. Assn. Colls. and Schs., Miss. Edn. Assn., Miss. Assn. Sch. Adminstrs, Red Red Rose, Kappa Delta Pi, Phi Delta Kappa. Baptist. Clubs: Cleveland Country (dir.), Cleveland Lions (past pres.), Met. Dinner (past pres., gov.). Editor: Needs of Higher Education, State of Mississippi, 1968. Home: Faculty Row Delta State Univ Cleveland MS 37833 Office: PO Box A-1 Delta State Univ Cleveland MS 38733

WYATT, FOREST KENT, univ. adminstr.; b. Berea, Ky., May 27, 1934; s. Forest E. and Almeda (Hymer) W.; B.S. in Edn., Delta State U., 1956; M.Ed., U. So. Miss., 1960; Ed.D., U. Miss., 1970; postgrad. Harvard Inst. Ednl. Mgmt., 1975; m. Janice Collins, Mar. 4, 1956; children—Tara Janice, Elizabeth Pharr. Instr., coach Univ. Mil. Sch., Mobile, Ala., 1956-60; tchr., adminstr. Bolivar County dist. schs., Cleveland, Miss., 1960-64; alumni sec. Delta State U., Cleveland, 1964-69, adminstrv. asst. to pres., dir. adminstrv. services, asso. prof. edn., 1969-75, pres., 1975—; dir. Grenada Bank. Publicity chmn. United Givers Fund, Boy Scout Expo (both Cleveland); active Cleveland Beautification Commn., Crosstie Arts Council. Bd. dirs. Miss. Com. for Humanities, Delta Area council Boy Scouts Am., Friends of State Library Commn. Served with U.S. Army, 1957-58. Mem. Miss. Educators Assn., Am. Council on Edn., Am. Council on Tchr. Edn., Miss. Assn. Sch. Adminstrs., So. Assn. Colls. and Schs., Inter-Alumni Council, Am. Alumni Council, Cleveland C. of C. (dir., membership chmn.), Phi Delta Kappa, Omicron Delta Kappa, Kappa Delta Pi. Clubs: Lions, Met. Dinner, Cleveland Country (dir.). Contbr. articles to profl. jours. Address: Delta State University Cleveland MS 38733

WYATT, GERARD ROBERT, biologist, educator; b. Palo Alto, Calif., Sept. 3, 1925; s. Horace Graham and Aimee (Strickland) W.; B.A., U. B.C. (Can.), 1945; student U. Calif. at Berkeley, 1946-47; Ph.D., U. Cambridge (Eng.), 1950; m. Sarah Silver Morton, Dec. 19, 1951; children—Eve Morton, Graham Strickland, Diana Silver. Agrl. research officer Can. Dept. Agr. Lab. Insect Pathology, Sault Ste. Marie, Ont. 1950-54; mem. faculty Yale, 1954-73, prof. biology, 1964-73; prof. biology Queen's U., Kingston, Ont., Can., 1973—, head dept. biology, 1973-75. Mem. A.A.A.S., Am. Soc. Biol. Chemists, Am. Soc. Cell Biology, Soc. Developmental Biology, Am. Soc. Zoologists, Biochem. Soc., Sigma Xi. Discovered 5-methylcytosine and 5-hydroxymethylcytosine as components of DNA, trehalose in insects; research biochemistry, hormone action, development insects. Home: 114 Earl St Kingston ON K7L 2H1 Canada

WYATT, HAROLD EDMUND, bank exec.; b. Moose Jaw, Sask., Can., Nov. 30, 1921; s. Edmund Rundle and Zelma Aleta (Turk) W.; ed. Central Collegiate Inst., Moose Jaw; m. Isabel Margaret, May 9, 1942; children—Andrea Maureen Wyatt Shumka, David MacDonald, Kathryn Margaret. With Royal Bank of Can., 1939—, apptd. staff officer for Alta., 1951, asst. gen. mgr., then dep. gen. mgr., Toronto, Ont., 1965-70, head Can. Dists., Montreal, Que., 1970-71, v.p., gen. mgr., 1971-78, vice chmn., Calgary, Alta., 1978—, also dir.; dir. Royfund Equity, Royfund Income Trust. Served with RCAF, World War II. Decorated Queen's medal; recipient ACBA degree Can. Bankers' Assn., 1948. Mem. Am. Mgmt. Assn., Gen. Mgmt. Council, Council Can. Unity (dir.), Can. Jaycees (gov.), Can. C. of C. (Can./U.S. com.). Clubs: Nat. (Toronto); St. James' (Montreal); Ranchmen's, Petroleum, Glencoe (Calgary). Office: 335-8th Ave SW Calgary AB T2P 2N5 Canada

WYATT, INZER BASS, U.S. judge; b. Huntsville, Ala., Mar. 29, 1907; s. Inzer Bass and Kate (Milligan) W.; A.B., U. Ala., 1927; LL.B. cum laude, Harvard, 1930; m. Hope Johnston, Feb. 27, 1936. Admitted to Ala. Bar, 1929, N.Y. bar, 1931; practice in N.Y.C., 1930-42, 46-62; mem. firm Sullivan & Cromwell, 1940-42, 46-62; U.S. dist. judge So. Dist. N.Y., 1962—. Served to col. AUS, 1942-46. Decorated Legion of Merit; grand comdr. Humane Order African Redemption (Liberia), 1963. Mem. Am., N.Y.C. bar assns., Am. Coll. Trial Lawyers, Phi Beta Kappa, Lambda Chi Alpha. Roman Catholic. Clubs: India House, Merchants, University (N.Y.C.). Home: 200 E 66th St New York NY 10021 Office: US Courthouse New York NY 10007

WYATT, JACK MILLER, utilities co. exec.; b. Dubach, La., July 29, 1918; s. George Sylinger and Rae D. (Miller) W.; B.S. in Elec. Engring., U. Ark., 1938; M.B.A., Stanford U., 1966; m. Willie C. Stroud, June 14, 1940; 1 son, Jack Miller II. With La. Power & Light Co., 1938-75, exec. asst., New Orleans, 1965-67, v.p., 1967-70, sr. v.p., 1970-75, pres., chief exec. officer, 1976—, also dir.; pres., chief exec. officer, dir. System Fuels Inc., 1975-76; dir. Middle South Services, Inc., Middle South Energy, Inc., New Orleans Pub. Service Inc., Middle South Utilities, Inc. Bd. dirs. Internat. House, Met. Area Com., Arthritis Found., Econ. Devel. Council, 1978—; trustee United Way, 1978—; mem. council trustees Gulf South Research Inst.; bd. regents Our Lady of Holy Cross Coll., La. Expo, Inc. Served to lt. USNR, 1942-46. Mem. C. of C. Greater New Orleans Area (dir. 1965-67), West Bank Council of C. of C. (dir. 1964-69), Elec. Assn. New Orleans, New Orleans Bd. Trade, Internat. Trade Mart, Theta Tau. Clubs: Lions, Timberlane Country (Gretna, La.); Propeller U.S., Bacchus and Janus Carnival, Plimsoll (New Orleans); West Bank Petroleum. Home: 102 Berkley Dr New Orleans LA 70114 Office: 142 Delaronde St New Orleans LA 70174

WYATT, JAMES FRANK, JR., plant food co. exec., lawyer; b. Talladega, Ala., Dec. 1, 1922; s. James Frank and Nannie Lee (Heaslett) W.; B.S., Auburn U., 1943; J.D., Georgetown U., 1949, postgrad., 1950; m. Rosemary Barbara Slone, Dec. 21, 1951; children—Martha Lee, James Frank III. Admitted to D.C. bar, 1949, Ala. bar, 1950, Ill. bar, 1953, also U.S. Supreme Ct.; atty. Office Chief Counsel, IRS, 1949-51; tax counsel Universal Oil Products Co., Des Plaines, Ill., 1951-63, asst. treas., 1963-66, v.p. fin., treas., 1966-75; treas. CF Industries, Inc., Long Grove, Ill., 1976—, v.p. fin., 1978—; dir. 1st Nat. Bank, Des Plaines. Village trustee, Barrington, Ill., 1963-75; bd. dirs. Buehler YMCA, Barrington Twp. Republican Orgn., 1963—; pres. Barrington Area Rep. Workshops, 1962-63. Served to capt., Judge Adv. Gen. Corps, AUS, 1944-47. Mem. Tax Execs. Inst. (v.p. 1965-66, chpt. pres. 1961-62), Fed., Am., Chgo. bar assns., Barrington Home Owners Assn. (pres. 1960-61), Newcomen Sco., Assn. U.S. Army, Scabbard and Blade, Phi Delta Phi, Sigma Chi. Episcopalian. Clubs: Barrington Hills Country; Economics, University (Chgo.). Home: 625 Concord Pl Barrington IL 60010 Office: Salem Lake Dr Long Grove IL 60047

WYATT, JAMES LUTHER, drapery hardware co. exec.; b. Williamsburg, Ky., May 13, 1924; s. Jesse Luther and Grace Edwina (Little) W.; B.S., U. Ky., 1947, M.S., 1948; Sc.D., Mass. Inst. Tech., 1952; m. Barbara Jane Christman, Aug. 28, 1946; children—Linda Lou, William Charles Christman (dec.). Devel. engr. titanium div. Nat. Lead Co., Sayreville, N.J., 1948-50; tech. mgr., head, dept. metall. engring., mgr. new products Horizons, Inc., Cleve., 1953-57; cons., asso. Booz-Allen & Hamilton, N.Y.C., 1957-61; v.p. program devel. Armour Research Found., Chgo., 1961-63; v.p. new product devel. Joy Mfg. Co., Pitts., 1963-67; v.p. corporate devel. Nat. Gypsum Co., Buffalo, 1967-69, Max Factor & Co., Hollywood, Calif., 1969-71; pres. Wyatt & Co., 1971—, Ambassador Industries, Inc., Los Angeles, 1972—. U.S. del. 1st World Metall. Congress. Served to lt. col. USAAF, 1942-46. Registered profl. engr., Ohio, Pa. Mem. Am. Soc. Metals, Am. Inst. Mining, Metall. and Petroleum Engrs., Sigma Phi Epsilon, Alpha Chi Sigma. Presbyterian. Clubs: Economics, Executives (Chgo.); University (N.Y.C.); California Yacht. Contbr. tech., mgmt. papers to profl. lit. Patentee in field. Home: Palos Verdes Bay Club 32700 Coastsite Dr Rancho Palos Verdes CA 90274 Office: 2753 Temple St Los Angeles CA 90026

WYATT, JANE, actress; b. Campgaw, N.J., Aug. 12, 1912; d. Christopher Billop and Euphemia Van Rensselaer (Waddington) W.; ed. Miss Chapin's Sch., N.Y., 1920-28, Barnard Coll., 1929-30; m. Edgar Bethune Ward, Nov. 9, 1935; children—Christopher, Michael. Debut, 1930; apprentice at Stockbridge Sch.; has appeared in Only Yesterday, Fatal Alibi, Dinner at Eight, 1933, Evensong, 1933, The

Joyous Season, 1934, Lost Horizon, 1934, Night Music, 1940, Quiet Please, 1940, Hope for the Best, 1945; Autumn Garden (by Lillian Hellman) (stage play) 1951; entered motion pictures, 1934, and has appeared in One More River, Great Expectations, Luckiest Girl in the World, The Navy Comes Through, The Kansan; The Bachelor's Daughters, 1946, Boomerang, 1946, Gentleman's Agreement, 1947, Pitfall, Bad Boy, Canadian Pacific, 1948, Task Force, House by the River, 1949, My Blue Heaven, 1950, Criminal Lawyer, 1951, Never Too Late, 1965, Treasure of Matecumbe, 1976; star weekly TV show Father Knows Best, CBS, 1954-62, Father Knows Best Reunion, 1977; appeared in TV films Tom Sawyer, 1973, You'll Never See Me Again, 1973, Katherine, 1975, Amelia Earhart, 1976; hostess, moderator Confidential for Women, My Father, My Mother. Recipient Emmy award as best actress in continuing role, 1958, 59, 60. Mem. Actors Equity, Screen Actors Guild, Cath. Actors Guild, Acad. TV Arts and Scis. (bd. govs. 1956-58, sec. 1957-58, 1st nat. bd. trustees 1957-58, dir.). Roman Catholic. Office: care William Morris Agy Inc 151 El Camino Beverly Hills CA 90212*

WYATT, JOSEPH PEYTON, JR., congressman; b. Victoria, Tex., Oct. 12, 1941; s. Joseph Peyton and Mabel W.; B.A., U. Tex., 1968. Former mem. staff Tex. State Sen. William N. Patman, Congressman Clark Thompson, Vice-pres. Lyndon Johnson; former auditor Tex. Alcoholic Beverage Commn., Austin; dir. Safety Steel, Inc., Victoria; mem. Tex. Ho. of Reps., 1971-79, chmn. Ways and Means Com., 1974-78; mem. 96th Congress from 14th Tex. Dist., mem. Armed Services, Mcht. Marine and Fisheries coms. Served with USMCR, 1966-70. Mem. Victoria C. of C., Port Lavaca-Calhoun County C. of C., Victoria Regional Mus. Assn., Victoria County Farm Bur., Pi Kappa Alpha. Democrat. Roman Catholic. Clubs: Jaycees, Ducks Unlimited, Mid-Coastal Sportsmen's. Office: 1730 Longworth House Office Bldg Washington DC 20515

WYATT, OSCAR S., JR., gas co. exec.; b. Beaumont, Tex., July 11, 1924; s. O. S. and Eva (Coday) W.; B.S. in Mech. Engring., Tex. A. and M. Coll., 1949; m. Lynn Wyatt; children—Carl, Steven, Douglas, O.S. III, Brad. With Kerr-McGee Co., 1949; with Reed Roller Bit Co., 1949-51; partner ind. oil co. Wymore Oil Co., 1951-55; founder Coastal Gas Corp., Corpus Christi, Tex., 1955, now chmn., chief exec. officer. Served as pilot USAAF, World War II; PTO. Home: 35 Hewit Dr Corpus Christi TX 78404 also 1620 River Oaks Blvd Houston TX 77019 Office: Nine Greenway Plaza Houston TX 77046

WYATT, ROBERT EUGENE, chemist, educator; b. Chgo., Nov. 11, 1938; s. Ira Eugene and Hilda (Bauer) W.; B.S., Ill. Inst. Tech., 1961; Ph.D., Johns Hopkins, 1965; m. Linda Claire Hughey, Sept. 11, 1964; 1 dau., Elizabeth. Postdoctoral fellow in chemistry U. Keele (Eng.), 1965-66, Harvard U., 1966-67; asst. prof. chemistry U. Tex., Austin, 1967-72, asso. prof., 1972-77, Alfred P. Sloan Found. fellow, 1973-75, prof., 1977—. Mem. Am. Chem. Soc., Am. Phys. Soc. Contbr. articles in theoretical chemistry to sci. jours. Office: Dept Chemistry U Texas Austin TX 78712

WYATT, WILLIAM FRANK, JR., educator; b. Medford, Mass., July 14, 1932; s. William Frank and Natalie Murray (Gifford) W.; A.B., Bowdoin (Me.) Coll., 1953; M.A., Harvard, 1957, Ph.D., 1962; postgrad. (Sheldon Traveling fellow) Am. Sch. Classical Studies, Athens, 1959-60; m. Sandra Skellet, June 6, 1959; children—Nathaniel Gifford, Lydia Ann, John William. Teaching fellow Harvard, 1957-59; asst. prof., then asso. prof. U. Wash., Seattle, 1960-67; mem. faculty Brown U., Providence, 1967—, prof. classical philology, 1970—, chmn. dept. classics, 1972-76, asso. dean, 1976-78; dir. summer sch. session Am. Sch. Classical Studies, 1969, 72, 73, 78, mem. mng. com., 1971—, sec., 1975—; mem. R.I. com. Nat. Endowment for Humanities, 1973—, vice chmn., 1977—; mem. Episc. Diocesan Task Force on Alcohol. Served with AUS, 1953-55. Postdoctoral fellow U. Wis., 1965-66; Nat. Endowment for Humanities study grantee, 1975; trans. grantee, 1979—. Mem. Am. Philol. Assn., Linguistic Soc. Am., Classical Assn. New Eng. (exec. com. 1978—), Modern Greek Studies Assn. (exec. com. 1978—). Clubs: Bowdoin of R.I.; Narragansett Boat; Review (Providence). Author: Metrical Lengthening in Homer, 1969; Indo-European /a/, 1970; The Greek Prothetic Vowel, 1972; Anthropology and the Classics: a bibliography, 1977; also articles. Home: 642 Angell St Providence RI 02906

WYATT, WILSON WATKINS, lawyer; b. Louisville, Nov. 21, 1905; s. Richard H. and Mary (Watkins) W.; J.D., U. Louisville, 1927; LL.D. (hon.), Knox Coll., 1945, U. Louisville, 1948, Centre Coll., 1979; m. Anne Kinnaird Duncan, June 14, 1930; children—Mary Anne, Nancy Kinnaird, Wilson Watkins. Admitted to Ky. bar, 1927; began practice at Louisville; with Garnett & Van Winkle, 1927-32; individually, 1933-35; trial atty. for City Louisville, 1934; partner law firm, Peter, Heyburn, Marshall, and Wyatt, 1935-41; mayor of Louisville, 1941-45; housing expediter and adminstr. Nat. Housing Agy., 1946; sr. partner firm Wyatt, Grafton & Sloss, 1947—; lt. gov. of Ky., 1959-63; Presdl. emissary oil negotiations from Pres. U.S. to Pres. Indonesia, 1963. Mem. law faculty Jefferson Sch. Law, 1929-35; dir. Courier Jour. and Louisville Times Co., WHAS, Inc., Standard Gravure Co., Forest Farmers Assn. Spl. rep. Bd. Econ. Warfare, N. Africa, March-May 1943; chmn. Louisville Met. Area Def. Council (twice awarded citation of Merit), 1942-45; pres. Am. Soc. Planning Ofcls., 1943-44, Ky. Municipal League, 1944, Am. Municipal Assn., 1945, Louisville Area Devel. Assn., 1944-45; pres. Nat. Municipal League, 1972-75, chmn. council, 1978—; chmn. Nat. Conf. on Govt., 1975-78; mem. adv. bd. U.S. Conf. Mayors, 1942-45; mem. Louisville Sinking Fund Commrs., 1936-38; mem. Louisville Com. on Fgn. Relations (chmn. 1940-41); chmn. Ky. Econ. Devel. Commn., 1960-63; chmn. Bellarmine Coll., 1979—; trustee U. Louisville, 1950-58, chmn., 1951-55; Ky. chmn. treasury adv. com. U.S. Savs. Bonds Program, 1948-55; mem. Commn. on Future of South, 1974, Commn. on Operation U.S. Senate, 1975-76; chmn. bd. Regional Cancer Center Commn., 1977—; vice chmn. Ky. Cancer Commn., 1978-79; chmn. Judicial Nominating Com. 6th Circuit, 1977—; chmn. Leadership Louisville Found., 1978—. Recipient U.S. Treasury Disting. Service award, 1955, Brotherhood award NCCJ, 1974, Gold Cup for Community Service, Louisville Area C. of C., 1974; named Louisville Jaycee Citizen of Year, 1972, Man of Year Louisville Advt. Club, 1973-74, Lawyer of Year, Ky. Bar Assn., 1976. Mem. English-Speaking Union (nat. dir. 1974), Am., Ky. (sec. 1930-34, commr. 1958), Louisville bar assns., Fed. Commuications Bar Assn., World Assn. Lawyers, Am. Law Inst. (life), Ky. (dir. 1974), Louisville Area (pres. 1972) chambers commerce. Democrat (1st pres. Young Dem. Club. Louisville Jefferson Co.; nat. chmn. Jefferson-Jackson Day Dinners, 1948, '49; del. at large 7 nat. convs. 1944—; personal campaign mgr. for Stevenson 1952, co-ordinator of campaign divs., 1956; Dem. nat. committeeman for Ky., 1960-64. Presbyterian. Clubs: Rotary, Pendennis, Wynn Stay, Louisville Country; Jefferson; Century (N.Y.). Home: 1001 Alta Vista Rd Louisville KY 40205 Office: 28th Floor Citizens Plaza Louisville KY 40202

WYATT-BROWN, BERTRAM, historian, educator; b. Harrisburg, Pa., Mar. 19, 1932; s. Hunter and Laura Hibbler (Little) Wyatt-B.; B.A., U. of South, 1953; B.A. with honours, King's Coll., Cambridge (Eng.) U., 1957, M.A., 1961; Ph.D., Johns Hopkins, 1963; m. Anne Jewett Marbury, June 30, 1962; children—Laura (dec.), Natalie. Mem. faculty Colo. State U., Ft. Collins, 1962-64, U. Colo., Boulder, 1964-66; mem. faculty Case Western Res. U., Cleve., 1966—, prof. history, 1974—; vis. prof. U. Wis.-Madison, 1969-70. Served to lt. USNR, 1953-55. Grantee Am. Philos. Soc., 1968-69, 72-73, Nat. Endowment for Humanities, summer 1975; Guggenheim fellow, 1974-75; asso. Woodrow Wilson Internat. Center Scholars, 1975; fellow Davis Center Princeton U., 1977-78; recipient Ramsdell award So. Hist. Assn., 1971. Club: Cleve. Philosophical. Episcopalian. Author: Lewis Tappan and the Evangelical War Against Slavery, 2d edit., 1971; also articles. Editor: The American People in the Antebellum South, 1973. Home: 2981 Coleridge Rd Cleveland OH 44118

WYCISLO, ALOYSIUS JOHN, clergyman; b. Chgo., June 17, 1908; s. Simon Charles and Victoria (Czech) W.; M.A., St. Mary of Lake Sem., Mundelein, Ill., 1933; postgrad. Cath. U. Am., 1939-42. Ordained priest Roman Catholic Ch., 1934; asst. pastor St. Michael's Ch., Chgo., 1934-39; asst. archdiocesan supr. Cath. Charitites Chgo., 1939-42; field dir. Cath. Relief Services, Nat. Cath. Welfare Conf., Middle East, India and Africa, 1943-45, supr. resettlement activities for displaced persons, Paris, 1945-47; organizer civilian relief programs Am. Cath. Hierarchy, 1947-48; asst. exec. dir. N.Y. hdqrs. Cath. Relief Services, 1948-49, dir. resettlement programs Europe, Far and Middle East, supr. program in U.S., 1950-59; pastor Immaculate Heart of Mary Ch., Chgo., 1959-68; aux. bishop of Chgo., 1960-68; bishop of Green Bay (Wis.), 1968—; Vatican rep. to UN, 1954-56; mem. Archdiocesan Conservation Council, 1959—, Archdiocesan Bd. Consultors, 1960—; archdiocesan moderator Cath. League Religious Assistance to Poland, 1960—; dir. Chgo. Observance Poland's Millennium of Christianity, 1962; mem. Am. Commns. Lay Apostolate, Missions and Oriental Ch., II Vatican Council, 1962—; chmn. Liturgical Commn., Archdiocese of Chgo., 1964—. Adv. bd. Alexian Bros. Hosp.; bd. dirs. Nat. Conf. Cath. Charities. Named papal chamberlain, 1953, domestic prelate, 1959, knight chaplain Order of Malta, knight Holy Sepulchre; named canon of Primatial Cathedral of Gniezno, Poland, 1960; Man of Year, Polish Daily News, Chgo., 1964; also numerous fgn. decorations. Address: 1910 S Webster St PO Box 66 Green Bay WI 54305*

WYCKOFF, BONNIE GRAYCE, ballet dancer; b. Natick, Mass., Nov. 20, 1954; d. Robert Lewis and Dorothea (Sullivan) W.; student public, pvt. schs. Mem. corps, soloist, prin. dancer Boston Ballet Co., 1967-72; prin. dancer Royal Winnipeg Ballet, Man., Can., 1973-78, Joffrey Ballet, N.Y.C., 1978-79; toured S. Am., Cuba, Israel, maj. cities in Can., U.S.A. Recipient Internat. Meditation Soc. award, 1977. Mem. Am. Guild Mus. Artists, Assn. Can. Radio and Television Artists, Can. Actors Equity Assn. (union rep. 1977-80). Office: Royal Winnipeg Ballet 289 Portage Ave Winnipeg MB R3B 2B4 Canada

WYCKOFF, DEWITTE CAMPBELL, educator; b. Geneseo, N.Y., Jan. 4, 1918; s. DeWitte and Christabel (Campbell) W.; B.S., N.Y. U., 1939, A.M., 1942, Ph.D., 1948; n. Mildred H. Mullins, May 24, 1944; children—Judith, Peter Cornelius. Asst. in religious edn. Warren Wilson Coll., N.C., 1937-38; tchr., community worker, Alpine, Tenn., 1939-41; dir. youth work Greater N.Y. Fedn. Chs., 1942-43; asst. sec. Presbyn. Bd. Nat. Missions, 1943-47; asst. prof. dept. religious edn. N.Y. U., 1947-50, asso. prof., 1950-53, prof., 1953-54, chmn. dept., 1950-54; Thos. W. Synnott prof. Christian edn. Princeton Theol. Sem., 1954—. Vis. prof. Yale Div. Sch., 1963-64, U. B.C., Vancouver, 1968; dir. adult forum Christ Ch. Meth., N.Y.C., 1949-51. Mem. Religious Edn. Assn., Fellowship of Reconciliation, Holland Soc. N.Y. Author: The Task of Christian Education, 1955; In One Spirit, 1958; The Gospel and Christian Education, 1959; For Every Person, 1959; Theory and Design of Christian Education Curriculum, 1961; How to Evaluate Your Christian Education Program, 1962; The Great Belonging, 1962; internat. editor Religious Edn., 1979—. Home: 15 Twin Oaks Dr Lawrenceville NJ 08648

WYCKOFF, DONALD DARYL, educator; b. Santa Monica, Calif., Apr. 28, 1936; s. Donald K. and Mary Gladys (Hammer) W.; B.S., M.I.T., 1958; M.B.A., U. So. Calif., 1968; D.B.A., Harvard U., 1972; m. Valerie M. Abdou, Aug. 30, 1958; children—Michele, Abigail. Vice pres. Cosmodyne Corp., Torrance, Calif., 1959-68; dir. Logistics Systems, Inc., Cambridge, Mass., 1968-72; prof. Harvard U. Bus. Sch., Boston, 1972—; pres. D. Daryl Wyckoff Assos., Inc., Marblehead, Mass., 1973—; dir. Victoria Stas., Inc., Lex Transp., London, Charles River Assos., MSI Data Inc.; cons. to Am. Trucking Assn., Assn. Am. R.R.'s, U.S. Govt. Mem. transp. com. New Eng. Council, 1976—. Mem. Transp. Research Forum (nat. v.p. 1974-75, pres. New Eng. chpt. 1975-76), Beta Gamma Sigma, Phi Sigma Kappa. Republican. Episcopalian. Club: Corinthian Yacht. Author: Organizational Formality and Performance in the Motor Carrier Industry, 1974; Railroad Management, 1976; Truck Drivers in America, 1979; (with others) The Owner Operator: Independent Trucker, 1975, Operations Management: Text and Cases, 1975; The Motor Carrier Industry, 1977; The Domestic Airline Industry, 1977; The Chain Restaurant Industry, 1978; Management of Service Operations, 1978; contbr. articles to profl. jours. Home: 5 Shorewood Rd Marblehead MA 01945 Office: Morgan 7 Soldier Field Boston MA 02163

WYCKOFF, HUBERT, lawyer; b. San Francisco, July 2, 1901; s. Hubert Coke and Anabel (McDonnell) W.; A.B., U. Calif., 1923; student Harvard Law Sch., 1923-25, Hastings Coll. Law, 1925-26; m. Florence Walton Richardson, Sept. 16, 1931. Admitted to Calif. bar, 1926; mem. firm Wyckoff, Gardner & Parker, Watsonville, Calif., 1926-28; asst. U.S. atty. No. Dist. Calif., 1928-31; pvt. practice San Francisco, 1931-42; asst. dep. adminstr. Maritime Labor Relations War Shipping Adminstrn., Washington, 1942-45; mem. firm Wyckoff, Parker, Boyle & Pope, Watsonville, 1946—; arbitrator 1939-42, 46—. Mem. Pajaro Valley Hist. Assn. (pres. 1963—), Delta Upsilon, Winged Helmet Soc., Big C Soc., Order Golden Bear. Clubs: Old Capital (Monterey, Calif.); University, Family (San Francisco); Pajaro Valley Domino (pres. 1946—) (Watsonville). Author arbitration awards in maritime, railroad, aviation, hotel, mfg., race track, newspaper, service industry and pub. employment areas. Home: 243 Corralitos Rd Watsonville CA 95076 Office: 14 Carr St Watsonville CA 95076

WYCKOFF, JEAN BRATTON, educator; b. Russell, Kans., Sept. 21, 1932; s. Christian C. and Francis (Bratton) W.; student Taft Jr. Coll., 1951; B.S., Ore. State U., 1953, M.S., 1957; Ph.D., Wash. State U., 1963; m. Winnefred L. Johnson, June 12, 1955; children—Gary, Lori, Douglas. Grad. research asst. Oreg. State U., 1956-57; instr. Wash. State U., 1957-60, asst. prof., 1960-63; mgr. market research dept. Am. Sheep Producer's Council, Denver, 1963-64; asso. prof., head div. agrl. econs. and edn. U. Nev., 1964-66; prof., head dept. agr. and food econs. U. Mass., 1966-70, prof. resource econs., 1970—; prof., coordinator extension econs. Oreg. State U., Corvallis, 1971—. Cons. Design & Research Assos., 1970, Fgn. Agrl. Service, Dept. Agr., 1969, 77, Planning Research Corp., 1968-69, Agrl. Services Found., 1967, Pierce County Planning Dept., 1977. Served with AUS, 1953-55. Internat. Assn. Agrl. Economists grantee, 1967. Mem. Internat. Assn. Agrl. Economists (mem. U.S. council 1976—), Am. Econ. Assn., Am. Agrl. Econs. Assn. (exec. bd. 1970-71), Northeastern Econ. Council (chmn. 1970-71), Western Agrl. Econs. Assn. (v.p., editor 1966-67, dir. 1977—), Am. Water Resources Assn., AAAS, Sigma Xi, Gamma Sigma Delta, Alpha Zeta, Gamma Sigma Delta. Home: 3825 SW Fairhaven Dr Corvallis OR 97330

WYCKOFF, LOU ANN, soprano; b. Berkeley, Calif., July 20; d. Herbert M. and Opal Elizabeth (Asbell) Wyckoff; student pub. schs., Los Angeles. Debut in opera as Cherubino in Le Nozze di Figaro, Pepperdine Coll., Calif.; European debut as Donna Elvira in Don Giovanni, Spoleto (Italy) Festival of Two Worlds, 1967; mem. company Deutsche Oper Berlin, 1969-77, debut as Donna Elvira in Don Giovanni; appeared throughout U.S., Europe, in concerts, operas; appeared opening night, La Scala, Milan, Italy. Recipient 1st prize 1968 Artists Advisory Council; Martha Baird Rockefeller grantee, 1966, 67, 68, 69; Matthew Sullivan Found. grantee, 1968. Mem. Am. Guild Musical Artists, Actors Equity. Mem. Unity Ch. Home: 143 E 19th St New York NY 10003

WYCKOFF, PETER HINES, ret. physicist; b. Bklyn., June 1, 1913; s. Peter C. and Martha (Schofer) W.; B.S. in Elec. Engring., Carnegie Inst. Tech., 1936; M.S., Cal. Inst. Tech., 1937; m. Evelyn C. Jauquet, Nov. 17, 1942; 1 son, Peter S. Research engr. Westinghouse Research Labs., East Pittsburgh, Pa., 1937-41; physicist USAF, 1946-48, chief Atmospheric Physics Labs., 1948-58, chief Aerophysics Lab., 1958-61; mem. Upper Atmospheric Rocket Research Panel, 1953-61, Tech. Panel on Rocketry U.S. Nat. Com. for IGY, 1954-61; asst. dir. physics research IIT Research Inst. (formerly Armour Research Found.), Chgo. 1961-64; program mgr. weather modification NSF, 1964-73. Served from 1st lt. to lt. col. USAAF, 1941-46. Fellow AAAS, Am. Inst. Aeros. and Astronautics (asso.); mem. IEEE, Optical Soc. Am., Am. Phys. Soc., Am. Meteorol. Soc., Am. Geophys. Union, Sci. Research Soc. Am., Sigma Xi, Eta Kappa Nu, Phi Kappa Phi, Tau Beta Pi, Sigma Pi Sigma. Home: 3066 Valley Ln Falls Church VA 22044

WYCOFF, SAMUEL J(OHN) dentist; b. Berry, Ala., Feb. 25, 1929; B.S., U. Ala., Tuscaloosa, 1950, D.M.D., Birmingham, 1954; M.P.H., U. Mich., 1959. With USPHS, 1959-67, regional program dir. Region I, Boston, 1963-65, Region V. Chgo., 1965-67; chmn. preventive dentistry and community health Loyola U., Chgo., 1967-69; asso. prof. preventive dentistry U. Calif., San Francisco, 1969-75, prof., 1975—, chmn. div. gen. dentistry, 1976—; mem. dental adv. com. Calif. Dept. Health, 1972—; mem. nat. dental caries adv. com. Nat. Inst. Dental Research, 1975-79; cons. in field. Served with USN, 1954-56, USPHS, 1959-67. Diplomate Am. Bd. Fellow Am. Dental Public Health. Public Health Assn., Am. Coll. Dentists, Internat. Coll. Dentists; mem. Pierre Fouchard Acad., ADA, Federation Dentaire Internationale. Author: (with E. Newbrun) Fluorides and Dental Caries, 1972. Office: 532 Parnassus St Room 105 U Calif San Francisco CA 94143

WYDLER, JOHN WALDEMAR, congressman; b. Bklyn., June 9, 1924; s. Waldemar and Ethel Z. (Roebuck) W.; student Brown U., 1941-42, 45-47; LL.B., Harvard, 1950; m. Brenda E. O'Sullivan, Oct. 25, 1959; children—Christopher, Kathleen, Elizabeth. Admitted to N.Y. bar, 1950; with U.S. Atty.'s Office, Eastern Dist. N.Y., 1953-59; practice in Mineola, N.Y., 1959-61; mem. firm Wydler, Balin, Pares, Soloway, Seaton and Marglin, 1967-78; mem. N.Y. State investigation commn. to probe N.Y.C. sch. constrn. irregularities, 1959-60; mem. 88th-96th Congresses, Congresses, 5th Dist. N.Y., mem. govt. operations com., sci. and technology com.; asst. minority floor leader, 1973, Ho. Republican floor mgr., 1973-76; N.Y. State mem. Com. on Coms., 1975; dean N.Y. Rep. Congl. Del., 1976—; vice chmn. N.Y. Bipartisan Congl. Del., 1976—; chmn. L.I. Congl. Caucus, 1979—. Charter mem. Bishop's Mens Assn. of Cathedral Incarnation, Garden City, N.Y. Mem. Tech. Assessment Bd., 1977—; bd. visitors U.S. Mcht. Marine Acad., 1971—. Served with AUS, World War II; CBI; mem. Res. Mem. Fed., Nassau County bar assns., Dist. Atty's Assn., Protestant Lawyers Assn., Am. Legion, V.F.W., U.S. Jr. C. of C., Phi Beta Kappa, Sigma Chi. Lion, Elk. Mason. Home: 63 1st St Garden City NY 11530 Office: 150 Old Country Rd Mineola NY 11501 also Rayburn House Office Bldg Washington DC 20515

WYDMAN, PERRY BYRON, banker; b. Cin., July 16, 1928; s. Byron Hilles and Helen Gertrude (Small) W.; B.A. in Econs., Denison U., 1951; m. Betty Sue Clark, Nov. 10, 1951; children—Mark, Amy, Lisa, Christopher. With First Nat. Bank Cin., 1951-53, 56-68, Heber, Fuger & Wendin, investment counsel, Detroit, 1953-56; v.p. City Nat. Bank, Columbus, Ohio, 1968-71; pres. 3d Nat. Bank, Dayton, Ohio, 1971—; dir. E.F. MacDonald Co., Will Co.; faculty Grad. Sch. Consumer Banking; former mem. faculty Ohio Sch. Banking, W.Va. Sch. Banking. Treas., dir. Dayton Devel. Council, 1972—; mem. Dayton Area Progress Council, 1972—. Trustee, chmn. Good Samaritan Hosp., Corbett Found., Milton and Edith Brown Found. Mem. Soc. Fin. Analysts (pres., dir. 1958-61), Am. Bankers Assn. (past chmn. bank investments div. exec. com., dir.), Dayton C. of C. (former chmn. and dir.), Phi Delta Theta. Presbyn. (trustee, chmn. bd. 1965-68, elder session 1973—). Clubs: Moraine Country, Dayton Country, Racquet (Dayton); The Golf (Columbus). Home: 921 Runnymede Rd Dayton OH 45419 Office: 34 N Main St Dayton OH 45402

WYETH, ANDREW, artist; b. Chadds Ford, Pa., July 12, 1917; s. Newell Converse and Caroline (Bockius) W.; ed. pvt. tutors; A.F.D., Colby Coll., Maine, 1954, Harvard U., 1955, Dickinson Coll., 1958, Swarthmore Coll., 1958, Nasson Coll., Temple U., 1963, U. Md., U. Del., Northeastern U., 1964; L.H.D., Tufts U., 1963; m. Betsy Merle James, May 15, 1940; children—Nicholas, James Browning. Artist, landscape painter, since 1936; first one-man show William Macbeth Gallery, N.Y.C., 1937; exhibited Doll & Richards, Boston, 1938, 40, 42, 44, Cornell U., 1938, Macbeth Gallery, 1938, 41 (first tempera show), 1943, 45, Currier Gallery, Manchester, N.H., 1939; room of watercolors Art Inst. Chgo., 1941; room at Realist and Magic Realist show Mus. Modern Art, N.Y.C., 1943; one-man exhbn. M. Knoedler & Co., N.Y.C., 1953, 58, Mass. Inst. Tech., Cambridge, 1960, Fogg Art Mus., William Farnsworth Library and Mus., 1963, other univs. and museums. Awarded 1st prize Wilmington Soc. Fine Arts, 1939; Obrig prize Am. Watercolor Soc., 1945; awarded medal of Merit, Am. Acad. Arts and Letters, 1947; 1st prize in watercolor Nat. Acad., 1946; Gold medal Nat. Inst. Arts and Letters, 1965; Gold medal of honor Pa. Acad. Fine Arts, 1966. Mem. Nat. Inst. Arts and Letters, Soviet Acad. Arts (hon.), Academie des Beaux-Arts, Chester County Art Assn. (dir.), Audubon Soc. (dir.), N.Y. Watercolor Soc., Wilmington Soc. Fine Arts, Phila. (dir.), Washington (dir.), Balt. (dir.) watercolor clubs, Am. Acad. Arts and Letters. Nat. Academician elect, May 1945, Am. Acad. Arts and Scis. Home: Chadds Ford PA 19317

WYETH, JAMES BROWNING, artist; b. Wilmington, Del., July 6, 1946; s. Andrew and Betsy (James) W.; privately tutored; m. Phyllis Overton Mills, Dec. 12, 1968. One man shows include M. Knoedler & Co., N.Y.C., 1966, William A. Farnsworth Mus. Rockland, Maine, 1969, Coe Kerr Gallery, N.Y.C., 1974, Brandywine River Mus., Chadds Ford, Pa., 1974, Joslyn Art Mus., Omaha, 1976. Mem. stamp adv. com. U.S. Postal Service, 1969—; mem. Nat. Endowment for Arts, 1972—. Bd. govs. Nat. Space Inst., 1975—. Served with Del. Air N.G., 1966-71. Home: Chadds Ford PA 19317*

WYGAL, BENJAMIN RAYMOND, coll. pres.; b. Childress, Tex., July 16, 1937; s. Loyd Aubry and Pernecia (Moore) W.; B.A., Tex. Tech. U., 1958; M.A., U. Tex., Austin, 1964, Ph.D. (Kellogg fellow), 1966; m. Reika Gay Henry, Jan. 27, 1957; children—Kimberly, Kelly.

Acad. dean Dalton (Ga.) Jr. Coll., 1969-69; v.p. Fla. Jr. Coll. at Jacksonville, 1969-70, pres., 1970—; bd. dirs. Community Coll. Coop. for Internat. Devel. Mem. bd. higher edn. Gen. Conf. of Seventh-day Adventists. Mem. Am. Assn. Community and Jr. Colls. (past dir.), Fla. Assn. Colls. and Univs. (pres elect), Commn. on Colls. of So. Assn. Colls. and Schs. (mem. exec. council). Democrat. Contbr. articles to profl. jours. Home: 4254 Confederate Point Rd Jacksonville FL 32210 Office: 21 W Church St Jacksonville FL 32202

WYGAL, LAUREN L., bldg. materials and ry. equipment co. exec.; b. Butler County, Pa., Oct. 30, 1924; s. Carl and Anna (Egbert) W.; B.S. in Commerce, Grove City (Pa.) Coll., 1948; m. Grace Gealy, Mar. 16, 1946; children—Gary, Jill. With Price, Waterhouse & Co., C.P.A.'s, Phila., 1948-56; with Budd Co., 1956-62; with Evans Products Co., Portland, Oreg., 1962—, v.p., treas., 1964-65, exec. v.p. finance, 1965—, also dir., mem. exec. com. Served with USNR, 1943-46. C.P.A., Pa. Mem. Financial Execs. Inst., Am., Pa. insts. C.P.A.'s Oreg. Soc. C.P.A.'s. Office: 1121 SW Salmon St Portland OR 97208

WYGANT, JAMES PETER, food co. exec.; b. Montreal West, Que., Can., Oct. 31, 1926; s. Samuel Edwin and Louise (Biersach) W.; student McGill U., 1945-46, U. Syracuse, 1960-61; m. Ruth Evelyn Mitchell, June 11, 1948; children—Margaret, Patricia, Sally. Various positions Campbell Sales Co. and Campbell Soup Co., 1948-61, gen. sales mgr. Campbell Soup Co., Toronto, 1961-66; v.p. in charge grocery div. Standard Brands Ltd., Montreal, Que., 1966-69, v.p., dir. 1969-72; pres., chief exec. officer Gen. Bakeries Ltd., Don Mills, Ont., 1972—; chmn. Margaret's Fine Foods, Toronto; dir. W. E. Long Co., Chgo. Served with Royal Can. Navy, 1944-45. Mem. Grocery Products Mfrs. Can. (dir. 1976—, exec. com., vice chmn.), Am. Bakery Assn. (bd. govs. 1975—), Bakery Council Can. (dir. 1973—), Toronto Bd. Trade, Can. C. of C. Mem. United Ch. Can. Clubs: Thornhill Country (dir.), Donalda. Home: 34 Elgin St Thornhill ON L3T 1W4 Canada Office: 75 Donway West Don Mills ON M3C 2E9 Canada

WYKES, EDMUND HAROLD, ins. co. exec.; b. Newcastle-on-Tyne, Eng., July 19, 1928; s. Cyril Edmund and Sylvia (Glover) W.; LL.B., Durham U., 1949; postgrad. Gibson and Weldon Coll. Law, 1953; m. Joan Nightingale, Oct. 1, 1955; children—Julie, Christopher. Solicitor, H.E. Ferens & Son, Durham City, Eng., 1953-57; called to Ont. bar, 1958; sec., counsel Imperial Life Assurance Co. of Can., Toronto, 1971-77, gen. counsel, sec., 1977—. Served with RAF, 1949-51. Solicitor, Supreme Ct. Eng., 1953. Mem. Canadian Bar Assn., English Law Soc., Assn. Life Ins. Counsel, Am. Soc. Corporate Secs. Inc. Home: 86 Wimbleton Rd Islington ON M9A 3S5 Canada Office: 95 St Clair Ave W Toronto ON M4V IN7 Canada

WYLAND, ROBERT BROOKS, railroad and traffic signals mfg. co. exec.; b. Worcester, Mass., Apr. 11, 1922; s. Benjamin Franklin and Ada Delphene (Beach) W.; A.B., Yale U., 1944; m. Thelma Alida Gustafson, May 4, 1944; 1 son, Christopher Carl. Adminstrv. asst. Yale U., 1946-48; with personnel dept. Johnson & Johnson, New Brunswick, N.J., 1948-53; dir. indsl. relations P. Lorillard Co., N.Y.C., 1953-56; asst. v.p. personnel Am. Airlines, N.Y.C., 1956-61; v.p. adminstrn., then exec. v.p. Weston Instrument & Elec. Co., Newark, 1961-65; v.p. adminstrn. CCI Corp., Tulsa, 1965-71, also dir.; pres., dir. Safetran Systems Corp., Louisville, 1971—; dir. Hillerich & Bradsby Co. Served to 1st lt. USMCR, 1943-46. Mem. Am. R.R. Found. (dir.), Ry. Progress Inst. (exec. com.). Republican. Clubs: Yale (N.Y.C.); Pendennis, Jefferson (Louisville); Hunting Creek Country. Home: 7106 Fox Harbor Rd Prospect KY 40059 Office: 7721 Nat Turnpike Louisville KY 40214

WYLE, FREDERICK S., lawyer, publishing co. exec.; b. Berlin, Germany, May 9, 1928; s. Norbert and Malwina (Mauer) W.; came to U.S., 1939, naturalized, 1944; B.A. magna cum laude, Harvard, 1951, LL.B., 1954; m. Katinka Franz, June 29, 1969; children—Susan Kim, Christopher Anthony, Katherine Anne. Admitted to Mass. bar, 1954, Calif. bar, 1955, N.Y. bar, 1958; teaching fellow Harvard Law Sch., 1954-55; law clk. U.S. Dist. Ct., No. Dist. Calif., 1955-57; asso. firm Paul, Weiss, Rifkind, Wharton & Garrison, N.Y.C., 1957-58; pvt. practice, San Francisco, 1958-62; spl. asst. def. rep. U.S. del. to NATO, Paris, 1962-63; mem. Policy Planning Council, Dept. State, Washington, 1963-65; dep. asst. sec. def. for European and NATO affairs Dept. Def., Washington, 1966-69; v.p. devel., gen. counsel Schroders, Inc., N.Y.C., 1969-71, atty., cons., 1971-72; chief exec. officer Saturday Rev. Industries, Inc., San Francisco, 1972-76; individual practice law, San Francisco, 1976—; counsel to Law of Sea delegation of Micronesia for UN Conf. on Law of the Sea; counsel to Micronesian Maritime Authority; cons. Rand Corp., Dept. of Def., Nuclear Regulatory Commn.; mng. trustee Nat. Real Estate Fund, San Francisco, 1976. Served with AUS, 1946-47. Mem. Council Fgn. Relations, Am. Council Germany, I.I.S.S., Phi Beta Kappa. Contbr. to Ency. Brit., 1972, also articles in profl. publs. Office: 1400 Alcoa Bldg One Maritime Plaza San Francisco CA 94111

WYLER, LEOPOLD SAMUEL, JR., tool co. exec.; b. N.Y.C., Jan. 24, 1922; s. Leopold Samuel and Fermina (Meardi) W.; B.A. in Math., U. Paris (France), 1939; B.S. in Aero. Engring., Mass. Inst. Tech., 1942; m. Betty Gardner, Feb. 20, 1944 (div. 1949); children—Anne Marie, Robert Leopold; m. 2d, Nancy Mc Murphy, Nov. 3, 1950 (div. 1972); children—Catherine Lisa, Stephen Anthony, Susan Melissa, Barbara Jane; m. 3d, Pamela Austin, Jan. 9, 1974; 1 son, Beau Britt. Engr. Douglas Aircraft Co., 1940-45; investment counselor, 1945-47; asst. comptroller Mountain Cooper Co., San Francisco, 1948-49; founder TRE Corp. (formerly Tool Research & Engring. Corp.) and predecessors, 1950, pres., 1950-60, chmn. bd., 1961—; pres. Southwestern Capital Corp., 1961-62; dir. Harbor Ins. Co., Los Angeles; adviser Calif. Gov.'s Pub. Utilities Commn., Calif. Energy Commn. on Energy Related Matters; mem. Calif. Legislature Joint Com. Energy Policy and Implementation. State fin. chmn. Edmund G. Brown Jr.'s gubernatorial campaign, 1974, Jimmy Carter's Calif. primary campaign, 1976; Calif. gov.'s rep. Conf. on Outer Continental Shelf Drilling, Washington, 1974; mem. Los Angeles County Energy Commn., 1976, Calif. Council for Environ. and Econ. Balance, 1976; founder, chmn. Energy Action Com., 1976; founder Democrats for Change, 1980; bd. councillors Center for Pub. Affairs, U. So. Calif., 1976; bd. dirs., exec. com. Community TV So. Calif., chmn. community relations; mem. Democratic Energy Platform Com., 1977; founder Voter Orgn. Through Edn., 1977; mem. Calif. Fed. Selection Commn. for Fed. Jud. Appointments and U.S. Attys., 1977; mem. corp. devel. com. Mass. Inst. Tech.; bd. governing trustees Am. Ballet Theatre Found. Clubs: Bel-Air Country, Beverly Hills Tennis, Palm Springs Racquet. Home: 805 Cord Circle Beverly Hills CA 90210 Office: 9460 Wilshire Blvd Suite 720 Beverly Hills CA 90212

WYLER, OSWALD, mathematician, educator; b. Scuol, Switzerland, Apr. 2, 1922; s. Otto and Betty (Jaeger) W.; Matura, Aargauische Kantonsschule, Aarau, Switzerland, 1942; Diploma in Math. with Distinction, Swiss Fed. Inst. Tech., 1947, Dr.sc. math., 1950; m. Margaret Marie Zeller, June 25, 1960; children—Marcus, Sylvia, Marianne. Lectr., Northwestern U., 1951-53; asst. prof. U. N.Mex., 1953-59, asso. prof., 1959-65; prof. math. Carnegie-Mellon U., 1965—. Served with Swiss Army. Jubiläumsfond fellow Swiss Fed. Inst. Tech., 1950-51. Mem. Swiss Math. Soc., Am. Math. Soc., Math. Assn. Am., AAUP, Sigma Xi. Collaborating editor problems sect. Am. Math. Monthly, 1968-72. Home: 1453 Wightman St Pittsburgh PA 15217 Office: Math Dept Carnegie-Mellon U Pittsburgh PA 15213

WYLER, WILLIAM, motion picture dir., producer; b. Mulhouse, France, July 1, 1902; s. Leopold and Melanie (Auerbach) W.; educated in schools at Mulhouse to 1918; student Ecole Superieure de Commerce, Lausanne, Switzerland, 1919, Conservatory of Music, Paris, 1920; m. Margaret Sullavan, 1934 (div. 1936); m. 2d, Margaret Tallichet, Oct. 23, 1938; children—Catherine Leonie, Judith Margaret, Melanie, David. Commd. maj. U.S. Army Air Forces, June 17, 1942. Awarded Air Medal, in European Theatre of Operations, June 7, 1943, Legion of Merit, 1945. Recipient Acad. of Motion Picture Arts and Sciences award for direction Mrs. Miniver, 1943, for direction The Years of Our Lives, 1947, Acad. award for direction of Ben Hur, 1959; D.W. Griffith award Dirs. Guild; Irving Thalberg award; others. Mem. Am. Vets. Com., Air Force Assn., Screen Directors Guild, Acad. of Motion Picture Arts and Sciences. Democrat. Jewish religion. Clubs: Hillcrest; Sun Valley Ski. Dir. notable motion pictures, including: The Little Foxes; Mrs. Miniver; The Best Years of Our Lives; The Heiress, 1948; Dead End, Jezebel, Wuthering Heights, Detective Story, 1951; Roman Holiday; The Desperate Hours, 1955; Friendly Persuasion, 1956; The Big Country, 1957; Ben Hur, 1958; The Children's Hour, 1962; The Collector, 1964; How to Steal a Million, 1965; Funny Girl 1968; The Liberation of L.B. Jones, 1970. Decorated Chevalier de la Legion d'Honneur; Star Solidarity; Order Merit (Italy); honored Directors Retrospective, U.S. Film Festival, 1972. Author: (with Axel Madsen) William Wyler, 1973. Address: care Paul Kohner Inc 9169 Sunset Blvd Los Angeles CA 90069*

WYLIE, ALBERT SIDNEY, banker; b. Columbia, S.C., Aug. 28, 1924; s. Albert Sidney and Mary Ellen (Smith) W.; student Am. Inst. Banking courses, 1948-52; m. Betty Lois Bridgwood, May 23, 1944 (dec.); children—Patricia A., Albert Sidney, Betty K.; m. 2d, Janet Faye Bone, Apr. 23, 1977. With S.C. Nat. Bank, Columbia, 1942-62, asst. cashier, 1951-57, asst. v.p., 1957-60, v.p., 1960-62; cashier Br. Banking & Trust Co., Raleigh, N.C., 1962-63, controller, 1963—, v.p., 1964-68, sr. v.p., 1968-72, exec. v.p., 1972-79, sr. exec. v.p., 1979—; pres., chief adminstrv. officer, dir. Branch Corp., Wilson, N.C., 1974—; v.p., dir. 150 Corp., Wilson, 1971—; dir. N.C. Payment Systems, Inc., Raleigh, N.C. Automated Clearing House Assn., Inc., Raleigh, N.C. Bus. Devel. Corp., Raleigh; instr. Am. Inst. Banking, Columbia, 1956-58. Mem. Bank Adminstrn. Inst. (Eastern N.C. chpt.), Am. Inst. Banking. Home: 610 W Nash St Wilson NC 27893 Office: 223 W Nash St Wilson NC 27893

WYLIE, CHALMERS PANGBURN, congressman; b. Norwich, Ohio, Nov. 23, 1920;student Otterbein Coll., Ohio State U.; grad. Law Sch. Harvard; m. Marjorie Ann Siebold; children—Jacquelyn, Bradley. Asst. atty. gen. Ohio, 1948, 51-54; asst. city atty., Columbus, Ohio, 1949-50, city atty., 1953-56; adminstr. Bur. Workmen's Compensation for State Ohio, 1957; apptd. first asst. to Gov. Ohio, 1957; formerly partner law firm Gingher & Christensen; mem. 90th-96th Congresses 15th Ohio Dist. Pres. Ohio Municipal League, 1957. Mem. Ohio Legislature, 1961-66; past pres. Buckeye Republican Club. Served as 1st lt. AUS; col. Res. Decorated Silver Star, Bronze Star, Purple Heart; recipient Distinguished Service award as Outstanding Young Man of Year Columbus, Nat. Jr. C. of C., 1955; named One of Ten Men of Year, Columbus Citizen Jour., 1954. Mem. Ohio, Columbus bar assns., Am. Legion (dir. Southway post). Republican. Methodist. Clubs: Masons (33 deg.), Kiwanis. Address: 2335 Rayburn Office Bldg Washington DC 20515*

WYLIE, CLARENCE RAYMOND, JR., educator; b. Cin., Sept. 9, 1911; s. Clarence Raymond and Elizabeth M. (Shaw) W.; B.S., Wayne State U., 1931, A.B., 1931; M.S., Cornell U., 1932, Ph.D., 1934; m. Sikri M. Aho, June 27, 1935 (dec. 1956); children—Chris Raymond (dec.), Charles Victor; m. 2d, Ellen F. Rasor, June 25, 1958. Instr. Ohio State U., 1934-40, asst. prof., 1940-46; cons. mathematican Propeller Lab., Wright Field, Dayton, Ohio, 1943-46; chmn. dept. math. and acting dean Coll. of Engring., Air Inst. Tech., Wright Field, Dayton, 1946-48; prof. math. U. Utah, Salt Lake City, 1948-69, chmn. dept., 1948-67; prof. math. Furman U., Greenville, S.C., 1969—, William R. Kenan, Jr. prof. math., 1971-78, Kenan prof. emeritus, 1978—, chmn. dept. math., 1970-76; part-time cons. math. Gen. Electric Co., Schenectady, Briggs Mfg. Co., Detroit, Aero Products div. Gen. Motors Corp., Dayton; Humble lectr. in sci. Humble Oil Co., 1955; cons. mathematician Holloman Air Base, N.Mex., 1955, 56. Recipient Distinguished Alumni award Wayne State U., 1956. Fellow A.A.A.S.; mem. Math. Assn. Am. (chmn. Rocky Mountain sect. 1955-56, bd. govs. 1957-60), Am. Math. Soc., Am. Soc. Engring. Edn. (chmn. math. div. 1949-50, 1957-58), Utah Acad. Sci. Arts and Letters, Phi Beta Kappa, Sigma Xi, Phi Mu Epsilon, Sigma Pi Sigma, Pi Kappa Delta, Delta Sigma Rho, Sigma Delta Psi, Sigma Rho Tau, Phi Kappa Phi. Methodist. Author: 101 Puzzles in Thought and Logic, 1958; Advanced Engineering Mathematics, 4th edit., 1975; Introduction to Projective Geometry, 1969; Differential Equations, 1979; other books, also papers articles, pub. in math. jours.; Strange Havoc (poems), 1956; The Wisdom of Eric Lim (limericks), 1974; also miscellaneous poetry.

WYLIE, DOUGLAS WILSON, physicist, educator; b. Saskatoon, Sask., Can., Nov. 12, 1926; s. Wilson and Hazel (Hambly) W.; B.S.C., U. N.B., 1947; M.S.C., Dalhousie U., 1949; Ph.D., U. Conn., 1962; m. Nancy Jane Esten, May 5, 1951; children—Sandra L., Donald W., Robert W., Mary L. Came to U.S., 1951, naturalized, 1965. Research asso. Brown U., Providence, 1949-50; instr. U. N.B., Fredericton, 1950-51; instr. to prof. U. Maine, 1951-68; prof. dept. physics Western Ill. U., Macomb, 1968—. Mem. Am. Phys. Soc., Am. Assn. Physics Tchrs., A.A.A.S., Canadian Assn. Physicists, Sigma Xi, Sigma Pi Sigma, Tau Beta Pi, Sigma Phi Epsilon. Home: 304 Jana Rd Macomb IL 61455

WYLIE, FRANK WINSTON, automotive co. exec.; b. N.Y.C., July 3, 1924; s. Stewart and Helen (Babington) W.; A.B., Harvard, 1948; m. Martha Rockwood, Aug. 31. 1948; 1 dau., Deborah Elisabethe. With Harris-Mann Assos., 1946-48; tech. writer, exhibited engring. div. Chrysler Motors Corp., Detroit, 1948-51, mem. central sales staff, 1952-53, spl. events mgr. Dodge div., 1954, pub. relations mgr. Dodge, 1955-70, pub. relations mgr. U.S. auto sales and service, 1971-75; dir. U.S. automotive pub. relations, 1975—. Served with inf., AUS, 1943-46. Mem. Pub. Relations Soc. Am. (pres. 1978), Internat. Pub. Relations Assn., Nat. Newspaper Assn., So. Motorsports Press Assn., Can. Public Relations Soc., Internat. Public Relations Soc. Clubs: Harvard Eastern Mich.; Detroit Press. Home: 390 Washington Rd Grosse Pointe MI 48230 Office: PO Box 1919 Detroit MI 48288

WYLIE, LAURENCE WILLIAM, educator; b. Indpls., Nov. 19, 1909; s. William H. and Maude (Stout) W.; A.B., Ind. U., 1931, A.M., 1933; student Institut des Etudes politiques, U. Paris, 1929-30; Ph.D., Brown U., 1940; doctorat h.c., Université de Montpellier, 1966; L.H.D., Ind. U., 1967, Ecole Jacques Lecoq, 1973; D.M.L., Middlebury Coll., 1978; m. Anne Stiles, July 27, 1940; children—Jonathan, David, Instr., Simmons Coll., 1936-40, asst. prof., 1940-43; asst. prof. Haverford Coll., 1943-48, asso. prof., 1948-57, prof., 1957-59, chmn. dept. Romance langs., 1948-59; C. Douglas Dillon prof. civilization France, Harvard, 1959—, fellow Kirkland House, 1960-62, 64—, acting master of Quincy House, 1962-63; vis. prof. N.Y. U., 1979, Stanford U., 1979; cultural attache Am. embassy, Paris France, 1965-67. Mem. French Com. Coll. Entrance Exam. Bd., 1951-56, chmn., 1956-58; chmn. French com. Sch. and Coll. Study, 1952-54; chmn. Conf. French Community Studies, 1956; chmn. Franco-Am. Commn. on Cultural Exchange, 1965-67; dir. Faculty Audit Program, 1968; faculty Assn. pour le Développement des Scis. Sociales Appliquées, Paris, 1972-73; dir. Nat. Endowment Humanities summer session, 1978. Recipient Prix Léonce de Lavergne, 1971; area research tng. fellow Social Sci. Research Council, 1950-51; Ford Faculty fellow, 1955-56; Guggenheim fellow, 1957-58; Nat. Endowment Humanities sr. fellow, 1972-73; Camargo fellow, 1972-73; Rockefeller Found. fellow, 1977. Mem. Modern Lang. Assn., Am. Assn. Univ. Profs., Am. Assn. Tchrs. French (nat. vp. 1962-64), Société d'ethnographie française, Am. Anthrop. Assn., Am. Acad. Arts and Scis., Internat. Sociol. Assn., Soc. for French Hist. Studies, Phi Beta Kappa, Phi Gamma Delta. Mem. Soc. of Friends. Clubs: Signet, Automobile de Paris. Author: Saint-Marc Girardin Bourgeois, 1947; Village in the Vaucluse, 1957; Deux Villages, 1965; Beaux gestes: Guide to French Body Talk, 1977; Co-author: In Search of France, 1962; Youth: Change and Challenge, 1963; Chanzeaux, A Village in Anjou, 1967; Les Français, 1970; The Events of May-June 1968, 1973. Asso. editor: French Rev., Contemporary French Civilization. Film producer Chanzeaux, 1965; Répertoire des Gestes Français, 1973. Home: 997 Memorial Dr Cambridge MA 02138

WYLIE, TURRELL VERL, educator; b. Durango, Colo., Aug. 20, 1927; s. Vernon Glenn and Myrtle Lucy (Davis) W.; B.A., U. Wash., 1952, Ph.D., 1958; m. Sharrie Louise Stevenson, July 31, 1969. Mem. faculty U. Wash., Seattle, 1958—, prof. Tibetan studies, 1968—, chmn. dept., 1969-72. Served with AUS, 1946-47. Ford Found. fellow, 1955-57. Rockefeller Found. grantee, 1960-63; Am. Council Learned Socs. fellow, 1973-74. Mem. Assn. Asian Studies, Am. Oriental Soc., Tibet Soc. Author: The Geography of Tibet, 1962. Contbr. articles to profl. jours. Home: 10666 Exeter NE Seattle WA 98125

WYLIE, WILLIAM EARL, lawyer; b. Houston, Jan. 22, 1944; s. Earl and Joyce Elaine (Rowell) W.; B.A., Rice U., Houston, 1966; J.D., U. Tex., Austin, 1970; m. Susan Jane Hamner, Sept. 7, 1968; children—Laura, Mark. Admitted to Tex. bar, 1969, since practiced in Houston; partner firm Lee, Brown & Wylie, 1973—. Dir. Houston S.W. Bank. Mem. president's council Houston Baptist Coll. Mem. Am. (adv. mem. sect. taxation, com. estate and gift taxes), Tex., Houston, Houston Jr. bar assns. Baptist (deacon). Home: 3502 Amherst St Houston TX 77005 Office: 3120 Southwest Freeway Houston TX 77006

WYLLIE, PETER JOHN, geologist; b. London, Feb. 8, 1930; s. George William and Beatrice Gladys (Weaver) W.; came to U.S., 1961; B.Sc. in Geology and Physics, U. St. Andrews, Scotland, 1952, B.Sc. with 1st class honours in Geology, 1955, Ph.D. in Geology, 1958, D.Sc. (hon.), 1974; m. Frances Rosemary Blair, June 9, 1956; children—Andrew, Elizabeth (dec.), Lisa, John. Glaciologist, Brit. W. Greenland Expdn., 1950, geologist Brit. N. Greenland Expdn., 1952-54; asst. lectr. geology U. St. Andrews, 1955-56; research asst. geochemistry Pa. State U., State College, 1956-58, asst. prof. geochemistry, 1958-59, asso. prof. petrology, 1961-65, acting head, dept. geochemistry mineralogy, 1962-63; research fellow chemistry Leeds (Eng.) U., 1959-60, lectr. exptl. petrology, 1960-61; prof. petrology geochemistry U. Chgo., 1965-77, Homer J. Livingston prof., 1978—, chmn. dept. geophys. scis., 1979—, master phys. scis. collegiate div., asso. dean coll., asso. dean phys. scis. div., 1972-73; chmn. commn. exptl. petrology high pressures temperatures Internat. Union Geol. Scis.; mem. adv. panel earth scis. NSF, 1975-78, chmn. adv. com. earth scis. div., 1979—; mem. U.S. Nat. Com. on Geology, 1978—. Served with RAF, 1948-49. Recipient Polar medal H.M. Queen Elizabeth, Eng. Mem. Mineral. Soc. Am. (award 1965, pres. 1977-78), Internat. Mineral. Assn. (2d v.p. 1978—). Author: The Dynamic Earth, 1971; The Way the Earth Works, 1976; editor and contbr.: Ultramafic and Related Rocks, 1967; editor Jour. Geology, 1967—, Series in Intermediate Geology, 1978—; editor-in-chief Minerals Rocks (monograph series), 1967—. Office: Univ Chicago 5734 S Ellis Ave Chicago IL 60637

WYLY, CHARLES JOSEPH, computing co. exec.; b. Lake Providence, La., Oct. 13, 1933; s. Charles Joseph and Flora (Evans) W.; B.S., La. Tech. U., 1956; m. Caroline Denmon; children—Martha, Charles Joseph III, Emily, Jennifer. Sales rep. IBM Service Bur. Corp., 1956-64; v.p. Wyly Corp., Dallas, 1964-65, exec. v.p., 1965-69, pres., 1969-73, chmn. exec. com., 1973-76, dir., 1964-76; chmn. bd. Earth Resources Co.; dir. Bonanza Internat. Inc. Mem. Pres.'s Advisory Council on Mgmt. Improvement, 1970-73; vice-chmn. Devel. Council So. Methodist U. Found. Sci. and Engring., 1970-71. Mem. Republican Nat. Fin. Com., 1970—. Bd. dirs. Dallas County United Fund.; pres. Dallas Theater Center. Mem. Am. Mgmt. Assn., Pi Kappa Alpha, Omicron Delta Kappa, Delta Sigma Pi, Beta Gamma Sigma. Clubs: City, Brookhollow (Dallas). Office: Two Turtle Creek Village Dallas TX 75219

WYLY, LEMUEL DAVID, physicist, educator; b. Seneca, S.C.; s. Lemuel David and Mary Julia (Reid) W.; B.S., The Citadel, 1938; M.A., U. N.C., 1939; Ph.D., Yale, 1949; m. Martha Estelle Bruggemann, Dec. 28, 1938; children—Lemuel David III, Martha Jeannette. With Ga. Inst. Tech., Atlanta, 1939—, Regents' prof., 1958—. Cons. Union Carbide Nuclear Co., Oak Ridge, 1952-69. Fellow Am. Phys. Soc.; mem. Am. Physics Tchrs., Sigma Xi. Research and publs. on fundamentals of beta decay. Home: 962 Canter Rd Atlanta GA 30324

WYMAN, HENRY WALTER, plastic mfg. co. exec.; b. Aussig, Czechoslovakia, Feb. 7, 1919; s. Hans and Stella (Parnas) W.; student elementary, high schs., Czechoslovakia, student London Sch. Econs., 1939-40, Columbia, 1942-43, extension course N. Y. U., 1943-44; m. Marguerite Ann Streuli, Sept. 30, 1944; children—Alexis Helen, David Christopher Parnas, Carla Marguerite Stella. With Pantasote Co., Passaic, N.J., 1942—, v.p., 1945-60, pres., 1960—, also dir.; treas. Am. Foam Rubber Co., 1952-54. Dir. Purchase Community, Inc., 1955-57; pres. Panwy Found.; bd. dirs. Laymen's Nat. Bible Com.; trustee Am. Schs. for Oriental Research. Mem. Am. Arbitration Assn. (nat. panel arbitration), Photog. Soc. Am., Presidents Profl. Assn. Lutheran (trustee). Clubs: Westchester Color Camera (White Plains, N.Y.); Greenwich (Conn.) Country; Stratton Mountain Country (Bondville, Vt.). Home: 2 Dempsey Ln Greenwich CT 06830 Office: Bldg 9 Valley Dr Greenwich CT 06830

WYMAN, HERBERT JACK, advt. agy. exec.; b. San Francisco, Aug. 27, 1921; s. Herbert S. and Ruth (Jacobs) W.; grad. San Francisco City Coll., 1941; student San Francisco State Coll., 1943; m. Barbara Voorsanger, Apr. 28, 1951; children—Gareth Paul, John Grant, Richard David, Jo-Ann; m. 2d, Elaine J. Snay, Jan. 3, 1980. Account exec. Kirschner & Co., San Francisco, 1946-49; pres. Wyman Co., Inc., San Francisco, 1950—. Past trustee Ross Sch. Dist. Served with USNR, 1943-46. Mem. Am. Assn. Advt. Agys. (past chmn. No. Cal.

council). Club: San Francisco Advertising. Office: 650 E Blythedale Mill Valley CA 94941

WYMAN, JAMES THOMAS, mdsg. co. exec.; b. Mpls., Apr. 9, 1920; s. James Claire and Martha (McChesney) W.; grad. Blake Prep. Sch., Mpls., 1938; B.A., Yale, 1942; m. Elizabeth Winston, May 6, 1950; children—Elizabeth Martin, James Claire, Steven McChesney. With Mpls. Star and Tribune, 1946-50; advt. mgr. Super Valu Stores, Inc., Hopkins, Minn., 1951-54, store devel. mgr., 1955-56, gen. sales mgr., 1956-57, sales v.p., 1957-60, exec. v.p., 1961-64, pres., chief exec. officer, 1965-70, chmn. exec. com., 1970-76, also dir.; ret., 1976; dir. Marshall & Winston, Inc., Northwestern States Portland Cement Co., Mar-Win Devel. Co., Knox Lumber Co. Mem. food industry adv. com. Office of Emergency Preparedness, 1969-71. Bd. dirs. Wayzata Community Ch. Found., 1971—, Walker Meth. Residence and Health Center, 1979—. Served to lt. (s.g.) USNR, World War II. Mem. Mpls. Sales Execs. Club, Mpls. Advt. Club. Clubs: Minneapolis; Woodhill Country (Wayzata). Home: 2855 Woolsey Ln Wayzata MN 55391 Office: 1105 Foshay Tower Minneapolis MN 55402

WYMAN, LOUIS CROSBY, state justice, former U.S. senator, former congressman; b. Manchester, N.H., Mar. 16, 1917; s. Louis Eliot and Alice Sibley (Crosby) W.; B.S. with honor, U. N.H., 1938; LL.B. cum laude, Harvard U., 1941; m. Virginia Elizabeth Markley, Aug. 20, 1938; children—Jo Ann, Louis Eliot. Admitted to Mass. bar, 1941, N.H. bar, 1941, D.C. bar, 1947, Fla. bar, 1957; asso. firm Ropes, Gray, Best, Coolidge & Rugg, Boston, 1941-42; mem. firm Wyman, Starr, Booth, Wadleigh & Langdell, Manchester, N.H., 1949-52; gen. counsel to U.S. Senate investigating com., 1946; sec. to U.S. Senator Styles Bridges, 1947; counsel to joint congl. com. on Fgn. Econ. Cooperation, 1948-49; atty. gen. N.H., 1953-61; legis. counsel to gov. N.H., 1961; partner Wyman, Bean & Stark, Manchester, 1957-78; asso. justice Superior Ct. N.H., 1978—; mem. 88th, 90th-94th congresses from 1st dist. N.H., mem. com. appropriations, subcom. on def.; apptd. U.S. senator, 1975; chmn. N.H. Commn. on Interstate Cooperation; mem. Jud. Council of N.H.; chmn. Nat. Com. on Internal Security, 1958-61. Served to lt. USNR, 1942-46. Fellow Am. Coll. Trial Lawyers; mem. Am. (chmn. standing com. jurisprudence and law reform 1961-63), Mass., N.H., Fla., D.C. bar assns., Nat. Assn. Attys. Gen. U.S. (pres. 1957), Phi Kappa Phi, Theta Chi, Kappa Delta Pi. . *In a mixed up world each person needs a goal—something he or she can strive for, work toward and measure progress against. Mine has always been to try to help make this world a better place to live for all—with dignity, privacy, security and reasonable comforts. Toward greater progress in this goal I forsook the practice of law for years of public service during which it was more clearly possible to do much for people. Less money but more action if you will. Throughout everything in life it is vital to believe in something greater than man alone and to seek guidance from prayer. Faith that sincere effort will be rewarded, if not in this life in the next, also helps.*

WYMAN, MARVIN EUGENE, nuclear engr., ednl. adminstr.; b. North Branch, Minn., Apr. 9, 1921; s. Einar Olaf and Clara (Swanson) W.; B.S., in Physics, St. Olaf Coll. Northfield, Minn., 1942; M.S. in Phycics, U. Ill., 1943, Ph.D., 1950; m. Betty Louise Sexton, Mar. 12, 1955; children—Christina, Dorcas, Grad. teaching asst. physics U. Ill., 1942-44, 46-49; asst. prof. physics St. Olaf Coll., 1949-52, asso. prof., 1952-53; mem. staff Los Alamos Sci. Lab., 1953-58; prof. nuclear engring. and physics, U. Ill. at Urbana, 1958-75, chmn. nuclear engring. program, 1965-75, asst. to dean engring. for long range planning, 1975-77; asso. provost for research and sponsored programs Old Dominion U., Norfolk, Va., 1978—. Cons. for UN at Mexican Nuclear Energy Commn., 1963. Served to lt. (j.g.) USNR, World War II. Mem. com. nuclear sci. Nat. Acad. Sci.-NRC, 1965-70, chmn. subcom. research reactors, 1965-70; mem. fellowship bd. AEC, 1965-68, chmn., 1967-68. Fellow Am. Phys. Soc., Am. Nuclear Soc.; mem. Am. Soc. Engring. Edn. (chmn. nuclear engring. div. 1967-68), Am. Inst. Physics, Sigma Xi. Home: 6042 River Rd Norfolk VA 23505

WYMAN, MORTON, greeting card co. exec.; b. Cleve., 1922; grad. Fenn Coll., 1960; married. With Am. Greetings Corp., 1940—, v.p. plant operations and purchasing, 1960-68, group v.p., 1968-69, exec. v.p., 1969—. Home: 2000 King James Pkwy Westlake OH 44145 Office: 10500 American Rd Cleveland OH 44144

WYMAN, RALPH MARK, investment mgr.; b. Usti, Czechoslovakia, Feb. 7, 1926; s. Hans and Stella (Parnas) W.; came to U.S., 1941, naturalized, 1946; student Upper Can. Coll., 1942, Bucknell U., 1942-43; B.S. in Bus. Adminstrn., N.Y. U., 1945; postgrad. Columbia U., 1945-46; m. Lotte Ann Novak, Oct. 25, 1947; 1 dau., Leslie Andrea. Asst. mgr. export dept. Liebermann Waelchi & Co., Inc., N.Y.C., 1946-47; trainee White Weld Co., investment brokers, 1947-48; v.p. H.O. Canfield Co., 1948-65, vice chmn. bd., 1965—, dir., 1953—; dir. Pantasote Inc., 1960—, vice chmn. bd., 1967—; partner United Eagle Mgmt. Co., Eagle Mgmt. Co., Trianon Co., 1960—; pres. Veritas Co., 1960—; dir., chmn. fin. com. Affiliate Artists, Inc.; dir. Industria Ossidi Sinterizzati, s.R.L., Italy. Mem. adv. bd. Greenwich Acad.; treas. Panwy Found. Trustee, chmn. fin. com. Am. Sch. for Oriental Research; trustee Princeton Theol. Sem., 1976—. Mem. Lambda Chi Alpha. Presbyn. (elder, trustee Synod of N.E. 1974-76). Clubs: Greenwich Country; Stratton Mountain (Vt.) Country. Home: Baldwin Farms North Greenwich CT 06830 Office: Greenwich Office Park 9 10 Valley Rd PO Box 1800 Greenwich CT 06830

WYMAN, STANLEY MOORE, radiologist; b. Cambridge, Mass., Aug. 3, 1913; s. John Palmer and Lelia (Moore) W.; A.B., Harvard, 1935, M.D., 1939; m. Jessie Elinor Brooks, July 23, 1945 (dec. Apr. 1978); children—Stephen Brooks, Jean Wyman Beebe, Martha, Barbara. Radiologist, Mass. Gen. Hosp., Boston, 1946-68, 76—, vis. radiologist, 1969-76; cons. U.S. Naval Hosp., Chelsea, Mass., 1961-74; clin. prof. radiology Harvard Med. Sch., 1978—. Cons. radiol. tng. com. NIH. Served to maj., M.C., AUS, 1942-46. Decorated Bronze Star. Mem. AMA (former del.), Radiol. Soc. N.Am., (past pres., Gold medal 1974), Am. Coll. Radiology (pres. 1970-71, gold medal 1971), Am. Roentgen Ray Soc. (Silver medal 1952), New Eng. Roentgen Ray Soc. (hon. mem. past pres.), Mass. Radiol. Soc. (past pres.), Mass. Med. Soc. (v.p. 1979-80). Contbr. articles to profl. jours. Home: 295 Marsh St Belmont MA 02178 Office: 575 Mt Auburn St Cambridge MA 02138 also Zero Emerson Pl Boston MA 02114

WYMAN, THOMAS HUNT, food processing co. exec.; b. St. Louis, Nov. 30, 1929; s. Edmund Allan and Nancy (Hunt) W.; B.A. magna cum laude, Amherst Coll., 1951; student Mgmt. Devel. Inst., Lausanne, Switzerland, 1960-61; m. Elizabeth Minnerly, Dec. 3, 1960; children—Peter Hunt, Michael Barry, Thomas Hunt, Elizabeth Baldwin. Mgmt. trainee First Nat. City Bank N.Y., 1951-53; asst. to pres., also new products div. mgr. Nestle Co., White Plains, N.Y., 1955-60; marketing dir. Findus Internat. S.A. (Nestle), Vevey, Switzerland, 1961-65; v.p. Polaroid Corp., Cambridge, Mass., 1965—, sr. v.p., gen. mgr., 1972-75; pres. Green Giant Co., 1975-79; vice-chmn., dir. The Pillsbury Co., 1979—; dir. Toro Co., Scott Paper Co., Northwestern Bancorp. Trustee, Amherst Coll., Internat. Exec. Service Corps, Mpls. Soc. Fine Arts; mem. Presdl. Commn. on World Hunger, 1978-80. Served to 1st lt. C.E., AUS, 1953-55; Korea. Mem. Phi Beta Kappa. Home: 3610 Northome Rd Wayzata MN 55391 Office: 608 2d Ave S Minneapolis MN 55402

WYMAN, WILLIAM GEORGE, musician; b. London, Oct. 24, 1941. Bassist with musical group The Rolling Stones, 1962—; solo recs. include: Monkey Grip, Stone Alone; films: Sympathy for the Devil, 1970, Gimme Shelter, 1970, Ladies and Gentlemen the Rolling Stones, 1974. Office: Rolling Stones Records 75 Rockefeller Plaza New York NY 10019*

WYMORE, A. WAYNE, educator; b. New Sharon, Iowa, Feb. 1, 1927; s. Darcy Bryan and Vera (Leatherman) W.; B.S., Iowa State U., 1949, M.S., 1950; Ph.D., U. Wis., 1955; m. Muriel Lorraine Farrell, Mar. 19, 1949; children—Farrell Wade, Darcy Lorraine, Melanie Louise, Leslie Maureen. Math. cons. Pure Oil Co., Chgo., 1955-57; dir. computer center U. Ariz., Tucson, 1957-67, head dept. systems and indsl. engring., 1959-74, prof. systems and indsl. engring., 1959—. Cons. 20 firms, 1954-71. Served with USAAF, 1944-47. Mem. Am. Math. Soc., Am. Inst. Indsl. Engring., Sigma Xi, Phi Kappa Phi, Pi Mu Epsilon. Author: A Mathematical Theory of Systems Engineering: The Elements, 1967; Systems Engineering Methodology for Interdisciplinary Teams, 1975. Founding editor Jour. Systems Engring., 1969. Home: 4301 N Camino Kino Tucson AZ 85718

WYNAR, BOHDAN STEPHEN, educator; b. Lviv, Ukraine, Sept. 7, 1926; s. John I. and Euphrosina (Doryk) W.; Diplom-Volkswirt Econs., U. Munich (Germany), 1949, Ph.D., 1950; M.A., U. Denver, 1958; m. Christina Lorraine Gehrt, Aug. 23, 1965 Came to U.S., 1950, naturalized, 1957. Methods analyst, statistician Tramco Corp., Cleve., 1951-53; freelance journalist Societ Econs., Cleve., 1954-56; adminstrv. asst. U. Denver Libraries, 1958-59, head Tech. Services div., 1959-62; asso. prof. Sch. Librarianship, U. Denver, 1962-66; dir. div. library edn. State U. Coll., Geneseo, N.Y., 1966-67, dean Sch. Library Sci., prof., 1967-69; pres. Libraries Unlimited Inc., 1969—. Bd. dirs., mem. exec. bd. ZAREVO, Inc. Mem. Am. (pres. Ukrainian Congress com. br., Denver 1976), Colo., N.Y. library assns., Am. Assn. Advancement Slavic Studies (pres. Ukrainian Research Found. 1976—), AAUP, Sevcenko Societe Scientifique (Paris), Ukrainian Acad. Arts and Scis. (N.Y.C.). Author: Soviet Light Industry, 1956; Economic Colonialism, 1958; Ukrainian Industry, 1964; Introduction to Bibliography and Reference Work, 4th edit., 1967; Introduction to Cataloging and Classification, 5th edit., 1976; Major Writings on Soviet Economy, 1966; Library Acquisitions, 2d edit., 1971; Research Methods in Library Science, 1971; Economic Thought in Kievan Rus', 1974; co-author: Comprehensive Bibliography of Cataloging and Classification, 2 vols., 1973. Editor: Ukrainian Quar., 1953-58; Preliminary Checklist of Colorado Bibliography, 1963; Studies in Librarianship, 1963-66; Research Studies in Library Science, 1970—; Best Reference Books, 1976; gen. editor American Reference Books Ann., 1969—; editor Reference Books in Paperback, An Annotated Guide, 2d edit., 1976; Dictionary of Am. Library Biography, 1978; co-editor, contbr. to Ency. Ukraine. 1955—. Home: 6008 Lakeview St Littleton CO 80120 Office: Libraries Unlimited Inc 6931 S Yosemite Englewood CO 80110

WYNDHAM, HERBERT BERNARD, JR., civil engr.; b. Charleston, S.C., June 17, 1922; s. Herbert Bernard and Dora Alma (Ury) W.; B.C.E., Rensselaer Poly. Inst., 1950; M.S. in Civil Engring., N.C. State Coll., 1956; m. Margaret Jeanette Brooks, Dec. 19, 1954. Constrn. engr. A.S. Wikstrom, Inc., Skaneateles, N.Y., 1950-51; civil engr. Peirson & Whitman, cons. engrs., Raleigh, N.C., 1952-54; instr. civil engring. N.C. State Coll., 1954-56; with Malcolm Pirnie, Inc., and predecessor, cons. environ. engrs., 1956—, partner, 1963-70, v.p., White Plains, N.Y., 1970-78, also dir.; v.p., mgr. NC div. 6, Reynolds Watkins Cons. Engrs., Inc., Greenville, N.C., 1978—; mem. tech. adv. com. EPA, 1972-76. Served with AUS, 1941-45. Registered profl. engr., N.Y., N.C., Mich., Fla., Ind., Ohio, Ky., Va. Fellow Am. Cons. Engrs. Council, ASCE; mem. Nat., N.Y. State (past chpt. pres.), socs. profl. engrs., Water Pollution Control Fedn., Am. Water Works Assn. Methodist. Home: 116 Greenwood Dr Greenville NC 27834 Office: 401 W First St Greenville NC 27834

WYNER, YEHUDI, composer, pianist, condr., educator; b. Calgary, Alta., Can., June 1, 1929 (parents Am. citizens); s. Lazar and Sarah Naomi (Shumiatcher) Weiner; diploma Juilliard Sch. Music, 1946; A.B., Yale, 1950, B.Mus., 1951, M.Mus., 1953; M.A., Harvard, 1952; m. Nancy Joan Braverman, Sept. 16, 1951 (div. 1967); children—Isaiah, Adam, Cassia; m. 2d, Susan M. Davenny, June 15, 1967. Vis. asso. prof. Hofstra Coll., 1959; lectr. Queens Coll., N.Y.C., 1959-60; instr. Hebrew Union Coll., N.Y.C., 1957-59; music dir. Westchester Reform Temple, N.Y.C., 1959-68; asst. prof. theory Yale, 1963-69, asso. prof. theory, 1969-77, chmn. composition dept., 1969-73; prof., dean music SUNY, Purchase, 1978—; mus. dir. New Haven Opera Soc., 1968-77; mem. Bach Aria Group, 1968—; composer-condr., Tanglewood, 1961, 75-78; music dir. Turnau Opera Assn., 1961-64; faculty Berkshire Music Center, 1976—. Recipient Inst. Arts and Letters grant, 1961, Brandeis Creative Arts award, 1963; commns. from Yale, 1958, Mich. U., 1959, Fromm Found., 1960, Koussevitzky Found. at Library Congress, 1960, Park Ave. Synagogue, 1963, Ford Found., 1971; Rome Prize fellow, 1953-56; Alfred E. Hertz fellow U. Calif., 1953-54; Guggenheim fellow, 1960, 76-77; NEA grantee, 1976. Mem. Internat. Soc. Contemporary Music (mem. bd.), Am. Composers Alliance (exec. bd.), Am. Music Center (exec. bd.). Composer; Two Chorale Preludes for Organ, 1951; Partita for Piano, 1952; Dance Variations for Wind Octet, 1953, rev., 1959; Psalm 143, chorus, 1952; Sonata for Piano, 1954; Concert Duo for Violin and Piano, 1955-57; Dedication Anthem, 1957; Serenade for Seven Instruments, 1958; Passover Offering, 1959; Three Informal Pieces for Violin and Piano, 1961; Friday Evening Service for Cantor, Chorus, Organ, 1963; Incidental Music for play The Old Glory, 1964; Torah Service with Instruments, 1966; Da Camera for Piano and Orch., 1967; Cadenza for Clarinet and Harpsichord, 1969; Liturgy for the High Holidays, 1970; De Novo for cello and small ensemble, 1971; Three Short Fantasies for Piano, 1963-71; Songs, 1950-71; Canto Cantabile for Soprano and Concert Band, 1972; music for play The Mirror, 1972-73; Memorial Music for Soprano and 3 Flutes, 1971-73; Intermedio for Soprano and String Orchestra, 1974; Wedding Music, 1976; Dances of Atonement for Violin and Piano, 1976; Fragments from Antiquity, 5 songs for soprano and symphony orch., 1978. Office: Sch Music State U NY Purchase NY 10577

WYNETTE, TAMMY, singer; b. Red Bay, Ala., May 5, 1942; d. William Hollis Pugh; m. George Jones, Sept. 1968 (div.); m. 2d, George Richey, 1978. Former beauty operator; rec. artist Epic Records, 1967—; regular appearance Grand Ole Opry radio sta. WSM, Nashville, 1969—, tours U.S. and Can.; recs. include Your Good Girl's Gonna Go Bad, My Elusive Dreams, Stand by Your Man, Divorce, Take Me to Your World, Bedtime Story, We're Gonna Hold On, Til I Can Make It On My Own, Let's Get Together, Womanhood. Named Female Vocalist of Year Country Music Assn., 1968, 69, 70. Address: care Lavender-Blake Talent Agy 1217 16th Ave S Nashville TN 37212

WYNGAARDEN, JAMES BARNES, physician; b. East Grand Rapids, Mich., Oct. 19, 1924; s. Martin Jacob and Johanna (Kempers) W.; student Calvin Coll., 1942-43, Western Mich. Coll. Edn., 1943-44; M.D., U. Mich., 1948; m. Ethel Vredevoogd, June 20, 1946 (div. 1977); children—Patricia (Mrs. Michael Fitzpatrick), Joanna (Mrs. William Gandy), Martha (Mrs. Richard Krauss), Lisa, James Barnes. Intern Mass. Gen. Hosp., Boston, 1948-49, resident, 1949-51; vis. investigator Pub. Health Research Inst., N.Y.C., 1952-53; investigator NIH, USPHS, Bethesda, Md., 1953-56; asso. prof. medicine and biochemistry Duke Med. Sch., 1956-61, prof., 1961-65; prof., chmn. U. Pa. Med. Sch., 1965-67; Frederic M. Hanes prof., chmn. dept. medicine Duke Med. Sch., 1967—; mem. staff Duke, VA, Watts hosps.; cons. Office Sci. and Tech., Exec. Office of President, 1966-72. Mem. President's Sci. Adv. Com., 1972-73; mem. Pres.'s Com. for Nat. Medal of Sci., 1977—; mem. adv. com. biology and medicine AEC, 1966-68; mem. bd. sci. counselors NIH, 1971-74; mem. Inst. Medicine, Nat. Acad. Sci., 1973—; mem. adv. bd. Howard Hughes Med. Inst., 1969—; mem. adv. council Life Ins. Med. Research Fund, 1967-70; adv. bd. Sci. Yr., 1977-80; vice chmn. Com. on Study Nat. Needs for Biomed. and Behavioral Research Personnel, NRC, 1977-79. Dir. Central Carolina Bank & Trust Co., 1972-76. Bd. dirs. Royal Soc. Medicine Found., 1971-76; The Robert Wood Johnson Found. Clin. Scholar Program. Served with USNR, 1943-46; sr. surgeon USPHS, 1951-56. Recipient Borden Undergrad. Research award U. Mich., 1948; Dalton scholar in medicine Mass. Gen. Hosp., 1950; vis. scientist Inst. de Biologie-Physicochemique, Paris, France, 1963-64. Recipient N.C. Gov.'s award for sci., 1974; diplomate Am. Bd. Internal Medicine. Mem. Am. Rheumatism Assn., Am. Fedn. Clin. Research, So. Soc. Clin. Investigation (pres. 1974, founder's medal 1978), Am. Soc. Clin. Investigation, AAAS, Am. Soc. Biol. Chemistry, Assn. Am. Physicians (councillor 1973—, pres. 1978), Endocrine Soc., Nat. Acad. Sci., Am. Acad. Arts and Sci., Inst. Medicine, Sigma Xi. Club: Interurban Clinical (Balt.). Author: (with W.N. Kelley) Gout and Hyperuricemia, 1976. Mem. editorial bd. Jour. Biol. Chemistry, 1971-74, Arthritis and Rheumatism, 1959-66, Jour. Clinical Investigation, 1962-66, Ann. Internal Medicine, 1964-74, Medicine, 1963—; editor (with J.B. Stanbury, D.S. Fredrickson): The Metabolic Basis of Inherited Disease, 1960, 66, 72, 78; (with O. Sperling and A. DeVries) Purine Metabolism in Man, 1974; (with Beeson and McDermott) Cecil Textbook of Medicine, 15th edit., 1979; (with L.H. Smith Jr.) Rev. of Internal Medicine: A Self-Assessment Guide, 1979. Office: PO Box 3703 Duke Med Center Durham NC 27710

WYNN, COY WILTON, journalist; b. Prescott, Ark., Aug. 9, 1920; s. Ota Gilbert and Kate (Ward) W.; B.A., La. Coll., Pineville, 1941; M.A., La. State U., 1942; m. Leila Birbari, June 2, 1947. Chmn. dept. journalism Am. U., Cairo, Egypt, 1945-47; dir. div. journalism Lehigh U., Bethlehem, Pa., 1947-50; free-lance writer, Middle East, 1950-51; corr. AP, Beirut, Lebanon, 1951-55, bur. chief, Cairo, 1955-61; corr. Time mag., Rome, 1962-74, chief bur., Cairo, 1974-78, chief Rome Bur., 1979—; bd. dirs. Internat. Communications Seminars; cons. in field. Mem. Associazione della Stampa Estera in Italia. Clubs: Overseas Press (N.Y.C.); American (past pres.) (Rome). Methodist, Author: Nasser of Egypt: The Search for Dignity, 1959; also articles. Home: 14 Via Sardegna Rome Italy Office: Rockefeller Center Time-Life Bldg New York NY 10020

WYNN, DALE RICHARD, educator; b. Derry, Pa., Nov. 20, 1918; s. Colonel and Cora (Jarrett) W.; B.S. in Edn., Bucknell U., 1939, M.S. in Edn., 1946; student U. Pitts., 1950-51; Ed.D., Columbia, 1952; m. Joanne Louise Lindsay, Dec. 1, 1970; 1 dau., Rachel; children by previous marriage—Sherry, Lee Anne. Tchr., Stoystown (Pa.) High Sch., 1940-43; supervising prin. Forbes Joint Schs., Kantner, Pa., 1945-50; project asso. Coop. Program Ednl. Adminstrn., 1952-53 asst. prof. edn. Columbia Tchrs. Coll., 1953-55; asso. prof. edn., asso. coordinator Coop. Center Ednl. Adminstrn., 1955-60; prof. edn., asso. dean Sch. Edn., U. Pitts., 1960-65, prof. edn., 1960—, chmn. dept. ednl. adminstrn., 1967-74. Pres. Asso. Ednl. Consultants, 1966-69; chmn. Com. for Advancement Sch. Adminstrn, 1969-73; staff asso. devel. criteria for success project U. Council Ednl. Adminstrn., 1957-59, trustee, 1966-69; trustee Nat. Sch. Devel. Council, 1977—; exec. sec. Tri-State Area Sch. Study Council, 1973—. Served as navigator USAAF, 1943-45. Decorated Air medal with oak leaf cluster. Mem. Nat. Pa. (pres. Somerset County br. 1948-49) edn. assns., Am. Assn. Sch. Adminstrs. (ho. dels. 1975—), Nat. Assn. Profs. Ednl. Adminstrn. (asso. sec.-treas. 1955-59; Distinguished Service award 1959), Phi Delta Kappa. Author: Careers in Educations, 1960; (with Joanne Wynn) American Education, 8th edit., 1977; New York School Administrators, Salaries, 1958; Guides to Adminstrative Staffing Problems, 1958; (with others) Organizing Schools for Effective Education, 1961; (with others) Instructional Technology and the School Adminstrator, 1970; Organization of Public Schools, 1963; (with others) Elementary School Administration and Supervision, 3d edit., 1967; Federal Relations to Education, 1964; Policies of Educational Negotiation, 1967; Administrative Response to Conflict, 1972; Methods and Materials for Preparing Educational Administrators, 1972; The Administrative Team, 1972; also articles. Editorial bd. Ednl. Adminstrn. Quar., 1965-68. Contbg. author: Administrative Behavior in Education, 1959; Changes in Teacher Education: An Appraisal, 1963; Teaching in America. 1956; Ency. Internat., 1964. Home: 4514 Bucktail Dr Allison Park PA 15101

WYNN, JOHN CHARLES, clergyman, educator; b. Akron, Ohio, Apr. 11, 1920; s. John Francis and Martha Esther (Griffith) W.; B.A., Coll. Wooster, 1941; B.D., Yale, 1944; M.A., Columbia, 1963, Ed.D., 1964; D.D., Davis and Elkins Coll., 1958; m. Rachel Linnell, Aug. 27, 1943; children—Mark Edward, Martha Lois Borland, Maryan Kay Ainsworth. Ordained to ministry Presbyn. Ch. U.S.A., 1944; student asst. pastor Trinity Luth. Ch., New Haven, 1943-44; asso. minister First Presbyn. Ch., Evanston, Ill., 1944-47; pastor, El Dorado, Kans., 1947-50; dir. family edn. and research United Presbyn. Bd. Christian Edn., Phila., 1950-59; prof. Colgate Rochester/Bexley Hall/Crozer Theol. Sem., 1959—; pvt. practice family therapy; adj. prof. U. Rochester, also San Francisco Theol. Sem.; postdoctoral fellow Cornell U., 1973-74; mem. summer faculty Union Theol. Sem., N.Y.C. Del. study conf. World Council Chs., 1953, 57, 64, 65, 67, 75; lectr. 5 univs., Republic of S. Africa, 1968; chmn. com. on sexuality in human community U.P. Ch. Bd. dirs. Presbyn. Life, Planned Parenthood League Rochester and Monroe County, Family Service Rochester. Fellow Am. Assn. Marriage and Family Therapy; mem. Religious Edn. Assn., Nat. Council Chs. of Christ in U.S.A. (chmn. com. family life 1957-60), Nat. Council Family Relations, Family Service Assn. Am., Rochester Council Chs. (dir.). Author: How Christian Parents Face Family Problems, 1955; Pastoral Ministry to Families, 1957; (with Roy W. Fairchild) Families in the Church, A Protestant Survey, 1961; Christian Education for Liberation and Other Upsetting Ideas, 1977. Editor: Sermons on Marriage and Family Life, 1956; Sex, Family and Society in Theological Focus, 1966; Sexual Ethics and Christian Responsibility, 1970. Contbr. articles to mags. and religious jours. Office: 1100 S Goodman St Rochester NY 14620

WYNN, KEENAN, actor; b. N.Y.C., July 27, 1916; s. Ed and Hilda (Keenan) W.; student Horace Mann School, N.Y.C., Harvey School, St. John's Mil. Acad.; m. Eve Abbott (div.); 2 sons; m. 2d, Betty Jane Butler (div.); m. 3d, Sharley Jean Hudson; 3 daus. Started in New York Theatre in 1935; from 1940-57 appeared in camp shows worldwide for U.S. military; from 1935-79 appeared in over 350 productions on stage, in stock, on radio, live and filmed TV, and feature films. Address: care Finer and Finer 10100 Santa Monica Blvd Suite 224 Los Angeles CA 90067

WYNN, SPROESSER, lawyer; b. Dallas, Dec. 18, 1913; s. William Clement and Amy (Hirschfeld) W.; A.B., Tex. Christian U., 1933; LL.B., U. Tex., 1935; m. Mildred Patton, Apr. 11, 1936; children—Carol (Mrs. C. Harold Brown), Betty (Mrs. Larry Macy). Admitted to Tex. bar, 1935, since practiced in Ft. Worth; partner Wynn, Brown, Mack, Renfro & Thompson. Former dir. Council Adminstrn. Justice. Dir. 1st Nat. Bank Ft. Worth, State Automobile & Casualty Underwriters. Past pres. Tex. Social Welfare Assn.; pres. Duncan Found., Moslah Benefit Fund; past pres. Conf. S.W. Found. Republican nominee atty. gen. Tex., 1968; past chmn. Tower Senate Club Tex.; chmn. exec. com. S.W. Law Enforcement Inst. Past bd. dirs. Child Welfare League Am.; exec. com. Edna Gladney Home; sec. Tarrant County Hosp. Authority; trustee Tex. Scottish Rite Hosp.; mem. HEW panel on uniform laws on adoption of children. Fellow Tex. Bar Found.; mem. State Bar Tex. (past chmn. family law sect.), Am. Bar Assn. (chmn. adoption com.), Am. Social Health Assn. (dir.), Nat. Council Social Welfare (dir.), Am. Judicature Soc., Soc. Hosp. Attys. (charter), Masonic Temple Assn. (v.p.), Kappa Sigma. Mason (33 deg., Shriner). Home: 4320 Bellaire Dr S Fort Worth TX 76109 Office: Oil and Gas Bldg Fort Worth TX 76102

WYNN, THOMAS JOSEPH, lawyer, educator; b. Chgo., Aug. 30, 1918; s. Philip H. and Delia B. (Madden) W.; A.B., DePaul U., 1941, J.D., 1942; m. Bernadette L. Lavelle, Apr. 17, 1948; children—Thomas Joseph, John P. Admitted to Ill. bar, 1942, since practiced in Chgo.; spl. investigator Phoenix & Murphy, 1942; pvt. practice, 1946-59; partner Wynn & Ryan, 1959—. Lectr. bus. law Latin Am. Inst., Chgo., 1946-47; lectr., instr., asst. prof. bus. law Coll. Commerce DePaul U., Chgo., 1947-57, asso. dean, dean Evening div., 1957-73, asso. prof., 1957-72, prof., 1972—; asst. atty. gen. Ill., 1957-58. Dir., gen. counsel Suburbanite Bowl, Inc.; gen. legal counsel Chgo. Consortium Colls. and Univs., G.M. Tool Corp., Am. Bus. Law Assn., 1976—; pres., dir. Metroplex Leasing & Financing, Inc., 1972—. Candidate alderman City Council Chgo., 1951; candidate judge Municipal Ct. Chgo., 1956. Exec. sec., bd. dirs. Ill. Good Govt. Inst. Served to lt. USNR, 1942-46. Mem. Am., Ill., Chgo. bar assns., Am. ho. of dels. 1960-75, pres. 1972-73), Chgo. Area (past v.p., pres.) bus. law assns., Assn. U. Evening Colls. (past chmn. Region 9, editor Proc.-Montreal 1970), Am. Real Estate and Urban Econs. Assn. (charter), Chgo. Area Evening Deans and Dirs. Assn., U.S., Ill. adult edn. assns., Am. Right-of-Way Assn. (adviser chmn. nat. ednl. com. and Ill. chpt. 12, 1963-64), St. Vincent DePaul Soc., DePaul U. Law Alumni Assn. (past pres.), Blue Key, Gamma Eta Gamma, Beta Gamma Sigma, Delta Mu Delta. Home: 366 W Cuba Rd Barrington IL 60010 Office: Coll Commerce DePaul U 25 E Jackson Blvd Chicago IL 60604

WYNN, WILLIAM HARRISON, union ofcl.; b. South Bend, Ind., July 17, 1931; s. William and Effie (Welch) W.; student public schs., South Bend; m. Bonnie Day, Oct. 20, 1962; children—Mark and Brad (twins). Dept. head A&P Tea Co., South Bend, 1949-54; bus. rep. Retail Clks. Union, Local 37, South Bend, 1954-59, rep. Dist. Council 12, South Bend, 1959-61, sec.-treas., 1962-66; internat. rep. Retail Clks. Internat. Union, Washington, 1961-62, asst. divisional dir., 1966-69, asst. to internat. dir. orgn., 1969, adminstrv. asst. to pres., 1969-71, divisional dir., 1971-76, internat. v.p., 1972-76, internat. sec.-treas., 1976-77, pres., 1977—; v.p. AFL-CIO; mem. exec. com. Internat. Fedn. Comml., Clerical and Tech. Employees, Joint Labor Mgmt. Com. of Retail Food Industry; mem. exec. bd. Maritime Trades Dept., AFL-CIO; pres. Food and Beverage Trades Dept., AFL-CIO; mem. labor policy adv. com. for Multilateral Trade Negotiations; corp. mem. Muscular Dystrophy Assn., Inc.; mem. Pres.'s Com. on Employment of Handicapped; mem. Com. for Nat. Health Ins.; mem. exec. bd. A. Philip Randolph Inst.; bd. dirs. Union Labor Life Ins. Co. Recipient Medal award Israel Prime Minister, 1978. Home: 7301 Admiral Dr Alexandria VA 22307 Office: 1775 K St NW Washington DC 20006

WYNNE, BRIAN JAMES, profl. assn. exec.; b. N.Y.C., Dec. 2, 1950; s. Bernard and Dolores (Doyle) W.; student Institute des Sciences Politiques, Paris, 1970-71; B.A., Coll. Holy Cross, 1972; M.A., U. So. Calif., 1974. Mem. staff Exec. Cons., Inc., McLean, Va., 1974-76; prin., 1976-78; exec. dir. Indsl. Designers Soc. Am., Washington, 1978—; pres. Policy Adv. Council; cons. to various non-profit orgns. Mem. Am. Soc. Assn. Execs. Home: 7651 Tremayne Pl McLean VA 22102 Office: 1717 N St NW Washington DC 20036

WYNNE, JOHN MACDONALD, educator; b. Salina, Kans., June 14, 1920; s. Robert J. and Alice (MacDonald) W.; A.B. (Summerfield scholar), U. Kans., 1940; postgrad. Stanford, 1940-41; M.S. (Sloan fellow), Mass. Inst. Tech., 1956; m. Helen Gurley, Aug. 2, 1942; children—John MacDonald, Robert G. Dep. controller, civilian personnel dir., asst. to comdr. USAF Sacramento Air Materiel area, 1946-58; dir. exec. devel. programs Alfred P. Sloan Sch. Mgmt., Mass. Inst. Tech., 1958-62, asso. dean, 1962-67, v.p. orgn. systems of inst., 1967-70, v.p. adminstrn. and personnel, 1970-80; treas. Sandpiper of Manchester, Inc., 1980—; vis. prof. Indian Inst. Mgmt., Calcutta, 1963-64. Served to lt. USNR, 1943-46; to maj. USAF, 1951-52. Mem. Phi Beta Kappa. Home: 18 Ocean Highlands Magnolia MA 01930

WYNNE, LYMAN CARROLL, psychiatrist; b. Lake Benton, Minn., Sept. 17, 1923; s. Nels Wind and Ella C. (Pultz) W.; war certificate Harvard, 1943, M.D., 1947, Ph.D. in Social Psychology, 1958; m. Adele Rogerson, Dec. 22, 1947; children—Christine, Randall, Sara, Barry, Jonathan. Med. intern Peter Bent Brigham Hosp., Boston, 1947-48; grad. fellow social relations dept. Harvard, 1948-49; resident neurology Queen Square Hosp., London, Eng., 1950; resident psychiatry Mass. Gen. Hosp., Boston, St. Elizabeth's Hosp., Washington, also NIMH, 1951-54; psychoanalytic tng. Washington Psychoanalytic Inst., 1954-60, teaching analyst, 1965-72; cons., investigator WHO, 1965—; staff NIMH, 1954-57, chief sect. family studies, 1957-61, chief adult psychiatry br., 1961-72; mem. faculty Washington Sch. Psychiatry, 1956-72; prof., chmn. dept. psychiatry, also dir. div. family programs U. Rochester Sch. Medicine and Dentistry, 1971—; psychiatrist-in-chief Strong Meml. Hosp., Rochester, N.Y., 1971-77; vis. lectr. Am. U., Beirut, Lebanon, 1963-64. Med. dir. USPHS, 1961-72; mem. NRC, 1969-72. Recipient Commendation medal USPHS, 1965; Hofheimer prize Am. Psychiat. Assn., 1966; Frieda Fromm-Reichmann award Am. Acad. Psychoanalysis, 1966; Meritorious Service medal USPHS, 1966; Stanley Dean award Am. Coll. Psychiatrists, 1976; McAlpin Research Achievement award, 1977. Fellow Am. Psychiat. Assn., Am. Orthopsychiat. Assn., Am. Acad. Psychoanalysis, mem. Am. Psychosomatic Soc. (mem. council 1969-72), Psychiat. Research Soc., Western N.Y. Psychoanalytic Soc., Am. Psychol. Assn., Am. Family Therapy Assn., Am. Assn. Marriage and Family Therapists, Am. Psychoanalytic Assn., Am. Orthopsychiat. Assn. Chmn. editorial bd. Family Process; mem. editorial adv. bds. Psychiatry, Social Psychiatry, Jour. Nervous and Mental Diseases, Ann. Rev. Schizophrenic Syndrome; sr. editor The Nature of Schizophrenia, 1978. Home: 42 Monroe Ave Pittsford NY 14534 Office: Strong Memorial Hospital Rochester NY 14642

WYNNE, RICHARD BLITCH, newspaper pub.; b. Asheville, N.C., Aug. 25, 1927; s. James and Gertrude (Johnson) W.; student Asheville-Biltmore Coll., 1947-50; m. Betty J. Rice, Aug. 6, 1950; children—James K., Debra S., Dennis A., Patrice L. With Asheville (N.C.) Citizen, 1944-63, mng. editor, 1959-63; exec. editor Asheville Citizens-Times, 1963-70, asso. pub., 1970-72, pres., pub., 1975—; v.p. planning Multimedia Newspaper Co. Trustee Western Carolina U.; pres. Western Carolina Devel. Assn. Served with USAAF, 1945-47. Mem. N.C. Press Assn. (pres. 1977-78), Asheville C. of C. (past pres.), Am. Newspaper Pubs. Assn., So. Newspaper Pubs. Assn. Clubs: Asheville Country, Downtown City, Mountain City. Office: 14 O Henry Ave Asheville NC 28802

WYNNE, WILLIAM JOSEPH, lawyer; b. Little Rock, July 17, 1927; s. William Joseph and Bernice (Johnson) W.; student Little Rock U., 1946-48; J.D., U. Ark., 1951; children—William Joseph III, Nancy Alison. Admitted to Ark. bar, 1951; sr. atty. Murphy Oil Corp., El Dorado, Ark., 1951-69; partner firm Crumpler O'Connor & Wynne, El Dorado, 1963—; pres. So. Nitrogen, Inc., El Dorado, 1969—, Elco Equipment Leasing Co., El Dorado, 1970—; v.p., dir. El Dorado Paper Bag Mfg. Co., Inc. Served with USNR, 1945-46. Named Outstanding Young Man, El Dorado Jr. C. of C., 1961-62. Mem. Am., Ark., Union County bar assns., Civitan Internat. (judge adv. 1961-62). Home: 1501 W Block St El Dorado AR 71730 Office: NBC Plaza El Dorado AR 71730

WYNNE-EDWARDS, HUGH ROBERT, bus. exec.; b. Montreal, Que., Can., Jan. 19, 1934; s. Vero Copner and Jeannie Campbell (Morris) W.-E.; B.Sc., U. Aberdeen (Scotland), 1955; M.A., Queen's U., 1957, Ph.D., 1959; D.Sc. (hon.), Meml. U., 1975; m. Barbara Elizabeth Lortie, June 19, 1972; children—Jeannie Elizabeth, Alexander Vernon; children by previous marriages—Robert Alexander, Katherine Elizabeth, Renée Lortie. With Geol. Survey Can., 1958-59; mem. faculty Queen's U., Kingston, Ont., 1959—, prof., head dept. geol. scis., 1968-72; prof., head dept. geol. scis. U. B.C., Vancouver, 1972-77; asst. sec. (univs.) Ministry of State for Sci. and Tech., Ottawa, 1977-79; sci. dir. Alcan Internat. Ltd., Montreal, 1979—. Adviser, Directorate Mining and Geology, Uttar Pradesh, India, 1964; vis. prof. U. Aberdeen, 1965-66; adviser Grenville project Que. Dept. Natural Resources, 1968-72; guest prof econ. geol. research unit U. Witwatersrand, Johannesburg, South Africa, 1972; UN cons., India, 1976; pres. Canadian Geosci. Council, 1974; pres. SCITEC, 1977—. Recipient Spendiarov prize 24th Internat. Geol. Congress, Montreal, 1972. Fellow Royal Soc. Can., Geol. Assn. Can., Geol. Soc. Am., Canadian Inst. Mining and Metallurgy; mem. Assn. Profl. Engrs. Ont., B.C. Assn. Profl. Engrs. B.C. Office: Alcan Internat Ltd CP 6090 Montreal PQ H3C 3H2 Canada

WYNTER, DANA, actress; b. Eng.; d. Peter and Frederique (Spencer) Winter; student North London Collegiate Sch., Rhodes U., Grahamstown, S.Africa; m. Gregson Bautzer, June 10, 1956; 1 son, Mark Ragan. Appeared in Broadway play Black-Eyed Susan, 1954, radio show Private Lives of Harry Lime, London, 1953; appeared on numerous tv shows including Wagon Train, 1961, Studio One, Chrysler Theatre, Robert Montgomery Presents, 1953, Playhouse 90, 1955, Virginian, 1962, series with Robert Lansing in The Man Who Never Was, 1966-67, My Three Sons, 1968, Gunsmoke, 1969, Medical Centre, Marcus Welby, Ironside, To Rome With Love, The F.B.I. Story, It Takes A Thief, 1970, Ben Casey, 1967, The Invaders, The Wild Wild West, 1968, also Cannon, MacMillan and Wife, Hawaii Five-O, Alfred Hitchcock Presents, also (1979) Backstairs at the White House, Love-Boat, Makai-Station Hawaii, Fantasy Island; appeared in numerous motion pictures including Pompeys Head, D Day 6th of June, 1955, Something of Value, In Love and War, 1956, On The Double, Fraulein, 1957, Shake Hands With the Devil, 1958, Sink the Bismark, 1960, List of Adrian Messenger, 1971, Airport, 1970, Santee, 1972; produced and appeared in 6 TV spls. Dana Wynter in Ireland, 1976.

WYSE, LOIS HELENE, advt. exec., author; b. Cleve.; d. Roy B. and Rose (Schwartz) Wohlgemuth; m. Marc Allen Wyse; children—Katherine, Robert. Pres., Wyse Advt., Garret Press; dir. The Higbee Co., Consol. Natural Gas Co. author: I Don't Want to Go to Bed Book for Boys, 1963; I Don't Want to Go to Bed Book for Girls, 1963; The Absolute Truth About Marriage, 1964; What Kind of Girl Are You Anyway?, 1965; P.S. Happy Anniversary, 1966; Help I Am the Mother of a Teen-Age Girl, 1966; (with Joan Javits) The Compleat Child, 1966; Two Turtles, A Guppy and Aunt Edna, 1967; I Wish Everyday Were My Birthday, 1967; Grandfathers Are to Love, 1967; Grandmothers are to Love, 1967; Love Poems for the Very Married, 1967; Are You Sure You Love Me?, 1969; I Love You Better Now, 1970; Mrs. Success, 1970; Little Volumes of Love (series of 12), 1971; (calendar) A Year of Love, 1971, 72; A Weeping Eye Can Never See, 1972; Love Lines (series of 6), 1972; Lovetalk, 1973; The Rosemary Touch, 1974; (with John Mack Carter) How to Be Outrageously Successful with Women, 1975; Wet Paint and Other Signs of Love, 1976; Kiss, Inc., 1977; Love Poems for a Rainy Day, 1979; Far from Innocence, 1979. Home: 3126 Bremerton Rd Pepper Pike OH 44124 Office: 2800 Euclid Ave Cleveland OH 44115 also 505 Park Ave New York City NY 10022

WYSE, WILLIAM WALKER, lawyer; b. Spokane, Wash., July 20, 1919; s. James and Hattie (Walker) W.; A.B., U. Wash., 1941; LL.B., Harvard, 1948; m. Janet E. Oswalt, Jan. 30, 1944; children—Wendy L., Scott E., Duncan C. Admitted to Oreg. bar, 1948, since practiced in Portland; partner firm Stoel, Rives, Boley, Fraser and Wyse, 1953—; pres., dir. Key Timber Co.; trustee, sec. Pacific Realty Trust, 1977—. Bd. dirs. Community Child Guidance Clinic, 1951-57, pres., 1956-57; chmn. central budget com. United Fund, 1958-60; 1st v.p. United Good Neighbors; chmn. dir. Portland Sch. Bd., 1959-66; pres. Oreg. Symphony Soc.; pres. Tri-County Community Council, 1971-73; bd. dirs. Portland Mental Health Assn.; bd. dirs., sec. Oreg. Parks Found. Served to lt. USNR, 1942-46. Mem. Am., Oreg., Multnomah County bar assns., Delta Upsilon. Republican. Presbyn. (trustee 1955-58, chmn. 1958). Clubs: University, Arlington, City (sec. 1957) (Portland). Home: 3332 S W Fairmount Ln Portland OR 97201 Office: 900 S W 5th Ave Portland OR 97201

WYSHAK, LILLIAN WORTHING, lawyer; b. N.Y.C., July 19, 1928; d. Emil Michael and Stefanie Elizabeth (Dvorak) Worthing; B.S., U. Calif., Los Angeles, 1948, M.A. in Anthropology, 1971; J.D., U. So. Calif., 1956; m. Robert H. Wyshak, July 16, 1961; children—Karen, Robin, Susan, Jeanne, Patty. Public acct. Ira N. Frisbee & Co., Beverly Hills, Calif., 1948-51, Worthing & Stanley, Alhambra, Calif., 1951-56; admitted to Calif. bar, 1956; asso. firm Boyle, Bissell & Atwill, Pasadena, 1956-57, Parker, Milliken & Kohlmeier, Los Angeles, 1957-58; asst. U.S. atty. Tax Div., Los Angeles, 1958-62; partner firm Wyshak & Wyshak, Los Angeles, 1963—; referee State Bar Ct. Trustee, U. Redlands. Mem. Am., Los Angeles County, Beverly Hills, West Hollywood (pres.) bar assns., Calif. Soc. C.P.A.'s, Am. Anthrop. Assn., Am. Folklore Soc., Soc. Am. Archeology, Egypt Exploration Soc., Phi Alpha Delta, Beta Gamma Sigma. Presbyterian. Home: 602 Hillcrest Rd Beverly Hills CA 90210 Office: Suite 201 8907 Wilshire Blvd Beverly Hills CA 90211

WYSHAK, ROBERT HABEEB, lawyer; b. Boston, Dec. 23, 1923; s. Habeeb and Hatiza (Ameer) W.; A.B. cum laude, Harvard, 1945, LL.B., 1947; m. Lillian Worthing, July 16, 1961; children—Robin, Susan, Jeanne, Patricia. Admitted to Mass. bar, 1947, Calif. bar, 1948; asst. U.S. atty., chief tax div. Central Dist. Calif., 1953-62; partner firm Wyshak & Wyshak, Los Angeles, 1962—. Participant Manhattan Project Mass. Inst. Tech., 1944; lectr. on taxes Calif. Continuing Edn. Bar program, 1962—. Mem. Westwood (pres. 1960), West Hollywood (pres. 1966), Beverly Hills, Los Angeles County, Fed. bar assns., State Bar Calif. Presbyn. (trustee). Contbg. author: Federal Tax Procedure, 1968. Contbr. articles to profl. jours. Home: 602 Hillcrest Rd Beverly Hills CA 90210 Office: 8907 Wilshire Blvd Suite 201 Beverly Hills CA 90211

WYSS, ORVILLE, educator; b. Medford, Wis., Sept. 10, 1912; s. John and Gertrude (Walther) W.; B.S., U. Wis., 1937; M.S., 1938, Ph.D., 1941; m. Margaret Bedell, May 31, 1941; children—Ann (Mrs. Kenneth E. Hawker, Jr.), Jane (Mrs. Richard Barndt), Patti Bess. Indsl. research Wallace and Tiernan Co., Belleville, N.J., 1941-45; faculty U. Tex., 1945—, prof. microbiology, 1948—, chmn. dept. microbiology, 1959-69, 75-76. Antarctic research fellow McMurde Sound, 1961; Exchange scholar, USSR, 1965; Fulbright fellow, Sydney, Australia, 1970, Kathmandu, Nepal, 1978; Bose lectr. Calcutta U., 1971. Charter fellow Am. Acad. Microbiology (bd. govs.); fellow AAAS; mem. Am. Soc. Biol. Chemists, Am. Soc. Microbiology (pres. 1964-65), Tex. Acad. Sci., Am. Chem. Soc., Brit. Soc. Gen. Microbiology, Radiation Research Soc., Sigma Xi (past pres. Tex.), Phi Kappa Phi (past pres. Tex.). Democrat. Unitarian. Author: Elementary Microbiology, 1964; Principles of Biology, 1964; Microorganisms and Man, 1971; also articles microbial physiology. Asso. editor Bacteriological Revs., 1960-66. Club: Headliner's. Home: 4606 Madrona Dr Austin TX 78731

WYSS, WALTHER ERWIN, lawyer; b. Medford, Wis., Feb. 17, 1909; s. John and Gertrude (Walther) W.; B.S., U. Wis., 1933, M.S., 1934; J.D., George Washington U., 1939; m. Caroline Benedict, July 6, 1935; children—Mary Beth (Mrs. Richard P. Huttenlocher), Trudy (Mrs. Edwin M. Wood), Becky (Mrs. S.S. Watt), John, Wendy. Admitted to D.C. bar, 1938, N.Y. bar, 1941, Ill. bar, 1946; tchr. pub. schs., Medford, Wis., 1925-29; engr. Gen. Electric Co., 1934-35, with patent dept., 1935-45; partner Mason & Wyss, Chgo., 1946-48; partner, founder Mason, Kolehmainen, Rathburn & Wyss, Chgo., 1948—. Fellow Am. Coll. Trial Lawyers; mem. Am. (spl. com. on complex and multi-dist. litigation 1968-73, mem. council, patent, trademark and copyright law sect. 1968-72, chmn. 1974-75), 7th Fed. Circuit, Chgo. bar assns., Patent Law Assn. Chgo. (pres. 1971), Am. Patent Law Assn., Nat. Lawyers Club, Tau Beta Pi, Phi Delta Phi, Phi Eta Sigma, Phi Kappa Phi, Eta Kappa Nu, Order of Coif. Clubs: Kenilworth (pres. 1970-71); Skokie Country; Michigan Shores (Wilmette, Ill.); Union League, Tower (Chgo); Chicago Curling (pres. 1975—) (Northbrook, Ill.). Home: 500 Park Dr Kenilworth IL 60043 Office: 20 N Wacker Dr Chicago IL 60606

WYSZECKI, GUNTER WOLFGANG, physicist; b. Tilsit, Germany, Nov. 8, 1925; s. Bruno Bernhard and Helene (Goerke) W.; Diplom-ingenieur in Math. and Physics, Tech. Univ. Berlin (Germany), 1951, Dr.Engring., 1953; m. Ingeborg Rathjens, Aug. 4, 1954; children—Wolfgang, Joana. Came to Canada, 1955, naturalized, 1961. Mem. staff NRC Can., Ottawa, Ont., 1955—, head optics sect., 1961—, prin. research officer, 1965—. Served with German Navy, 1943-45. Fulbright scholar, 1953-54. Fellow Optical Soc. Am., Illuminating Engring. Soc.; mem. Canadian Soc. Color (pres. 1972). Author: Farbsysteme, 1961; co-author: Color in Business, Science and Industry, 1963, 3d edit., 1975; Color Science, 1967. Homr: 172 Roger Rd Ottawa ON K1H 5C8 Canada Office: Nat Research Council Ottawa ON K1A 0R6 Canada

WYTON, ALEC, composer, organist; b. London, Aug. 3, 1921; s. Gilbert and Jessie (Burrage) W.; came to U.S., 1950, naturalized, 1968; B.A., Oxford U., 1945, M.A., 1949; Mus.D. (hon.), Susquehanna (Pa.) U., 1970; children—Vaughan, Richard, Patrick. Asst. organist Christ Church Cathedral, Oxford U., 1943-46; organist St. Mathews Ch., Northampton, Eng., 1946-50, Christ Church Cathedral, St. Louis, 1950-54, Cathedral St. John the Divine, N.Y.C., 1954-74, St. James's Ch., N.Y.C., 1974—; adj. prof. music Union Theol. Sem., N.Y.C., 1960-73; coordinator standing commn. on ch. music Episcopal Ch., 1974—. Served with Brit. Army, 1941-42. Fellow Royal Coll. Organists; hon. fellow Am. Guild Organists (pres. 1964-69), Royal Canadian Coll. Organists, Royal Acad. Music, Royal Sch. Ch. Music; mem. ASCAP (ann. award 1967—). Republican. Episcopalian. Club: Union (N.Y.C.). Composer numerous pieces. Contbr. articles to profl. jours. Home: 129 E 69th St New York NY 10021 Office: 865 Madison Ave New York NY 10021

WYZANSKI, CHARLES EDWARD, JR., judge; b. Boston, May 27, 1906; s. Charles Edward and Maude (Joseph) W.; A.B. magna cum laude, Harvard U., 1927, LL.B. magna cum laude, 1930, LL.D., 1958; LL.D., U. Pa., 1954, Carleton Coll., 1954, Tufts Coll., 1954, Swarthmore Coll., 1956, Brandeis U., 1956, Clark U., 1963, Washington U., St. Louis, 1974; m. Gisela Warburg, July 23, 1943; children—Charles Max, Anita Wyzanski Robboy. Admitted to Mass. bar, 1931; asso. with Ropes & Gray, 1930-33; law sec. to U.S. Circuit Judge Augustus N. Hand, 1930-31, to U.S. Circuit Judge Learned Hand, 1932; solicitor Dept. Labor, Washington, 1933-35; U.S. rep. 71st and 72d sessions of governing body ILO, Geneva, 1935; substitute del. and govt. adviser 19th session Internat. Labor Conf., Geneva, 1935; spl. asst. to atty. gen. U.S., staff of solicitor gen. Dept. Justice, 1935-37; partner Ropes & Gray, 1938-41; mem. Nat. Def. Mediation Bd., 1941; U.S. dist. judge for Mass., 1941—, chief judge, 1966-71, sr. dist. judge, 1971—; judge Internat. Adminstrv. Ct., Geneva, 1950-55; lectr. on govt. Harvard Coll., 1942-43, 49-50; vis. prof. Mass. Inst. Tech., 1948-50; Herman Phleger prof. Stanford, 1974; copyright expert UNESCO, Paris, 1949, Washington, 1950; mem. ILO Com. of Experts on Application Convs., 1945-53; mem. Supreme Ct. Com. on Rules of Civil Procedure for Dist. Cts., 1953-65. Trustee, mem. exec. com. Ford Found., 1952-76; mem. bd. overseers Harvard U., 1943-49, 51-57, pres., 1953-57. Recipient Sir Thomas More medal Boston Coll., 1972; John Phillips award Phillips Exeter Acad., 1975; sr. fellow Soc. Fellows Harvard U., 1962-76. Fellow Am. Acad. Arts and Scis.; mem. Am. Law Inst. (council), Mass. Hist. Soc., Phi Beta Kappa. Clubs: Athenaeum (London); Century Assn. (N.Y.C.); Tavern (Boston). Author: Whereas-A Judge's Premises, 1963. Home: 39 Fayerweather S Cambridge MA 02138 Office: US Dist Ct Boston MA 02109

YABLANS, FRANK, motion picture co. exec.; b. N.Y.C., Aug. 27, 1935; s. Morris and Annette Y.; student Coll. City N.Y., U. Wis.; m. Ruth Edelstein, Dec. 21; children—Robert, Sharon, Edward. Salesman, Warner Bros., 1956-58; br. mgr. Walt Disney Prodns., 1958-66; v.p. Filmways Prodns., 1966-69; successively v.p. sales, v.p. marketing, exec. v.p., pres. Paramount Pictures Corp., N.Y.C., 1969-75; pres. Frank Yablans Presentations, Inc., N.Y.C., 1975—, films include: Silver Streak, 1976, The Other Side of Midnight, 1977, The Fury, 1978, North Dallas Forty, 1979; dir. Dirs. Co., Cinema Internat. Corp. Chmn. entertainment div. Fedn. Jewish Philanthropies; bd. dirs. Boys' Clubs Am., Will Rogers Hosp.; trustee Am. Film Inst. Served with AUS, 1954-56. Decorated commendatore

Repubblica Italiana. Mem. Variety Club Internat. (chmn.), Motion Picture Assn. (dir.). Club: Fairview Country. Office: care 20th Century Fox 10201 W Pico Blvd Los Angeles CA 90064*

YABLON, LEONARD HAROLD, publishing co. exec.; b. N.Y.C., June 3, 1929; s. Philip A. and Sarah (Herman) Y.; B.S., L.I. U., 1950; M.B.A., Coll. City N.Y., 1969; m. Carolyn Sydney Torgan, June 8, 1950; children—Scott Richard, Bonnie Michele. Accountant, 1950-63; exec. v.p., dir. Forbes Inc., N.Y.C., 1963—; pres., dir. Sangre de Cristo Ranches, Inc., Fiji Forbes Inc.; v.p., dir. Forbes Investors Adv. Inst. Inc., Forbes Trinchera Inc. C.P.A., N.Y. Mem. N.Y. Soc. C.P.A.'s. Home: Pleasant Ridge Rd Harrison NY 10528 Office: 60 Fifth Ave New York NY 10011

YABLONSKI, JOSEPH ANDREW, lawyer; b. California, Pa., Jan. 11, 1941; s. Joseph Albert and Margaret Rita Y.; B.A., St. Vincent Coll., Latrobe, Pa., 1962; LL.B., U. Pitts., 1965; m. Shirley Ann Slosarik, Feb. 5, 1963; children—Jeffrey, Alexa. Admitted to Pa. bar, 1966, D.C. bar, 1969, U.S. Supreme Ct. bar, 1971; law clk. U.S. Ct. Appeals, Pitts., 1965-67; atty. appellate ct. sect. NLRB, Washington, 1967-69; campaign coordinator United Mine Workers Am. presdl. candidate Joseph Yablonski, 1969; dir. Miners' Project, Washington, 1970-72; gen. counsel United Mine Workers Am., Washington, 1972-75; partner firm Yablonski, Both & Edelman, Washington, 1975—. Recipient award Am. Inst. Public Service, 1973; named Labor Man of Year, Pitts. Jr. C. of C., 1974. Mem. Jud. Conf. D.C. Democrat. Roman Catholic. Home: 7116 Heathwood Ct Bethesda MD 20034 Office: Yablonski Both & Edelman 1150 Connecticut Ave NW Washington DC 20036

YACAVONE, PETER F., paper co. exec.; b. Hartford, Conn., 1927; grad. U. Hartford, 1950. Formerly controller Gt. No. Paper Co., N.Y.C., now pres.; then asst. treas. Consol. Edison Co. N.Y.; then treas. Gt. No. Nekoosa Corp., Stamford, Conn. Office: Great Northern Nekoosa Corp Stamford CT

YAEGER, JAMES AMOS, educator; b. Chgo., Aug. 10, 1928; s. Amos Julius and Dorothy Jane (Kuehl) Y.; D.D.S., Ind. U., 1952, M.S., 1955; Ph.D., U. Ill., 1959; m. Jean Prosser, Mar. 20, 1953; children—Beverly Jean, Lynn Stewart, Barbara Ann, William Dean. Faculty, U. Ill., Med. Center, 1955-68, prof., head dept. histology, 1966-68; prof., head dept. oral biology U. Conn. Health Center, Farmington, 1968-78, prof., 1978—. Mem. dental tng. com. NIH, 1968-72; exec. dir. Ann. Midwest Seminar Dental Medicine, 1964-66. Served to 1st lt. U.S. Army, 1953-55. Recipient Research Career Devel. award USPHS, 1962-66. USPHS Spl. Research fellow, 1957-59; NIH research grantee, 1960-68; NIH tng. grantee, 1964-68. Mem. Am. Assn. Anatomists, Am. Soc. for Cell Biology, Internat. Assn. for Dental Research (councilor-at-large N.Am. div. 1973). Regional editor Archives of Oral Biology, 1968-77. Contbr. articles to tech. jours. chpts. to books. Home: 48 Ravenwood Rd West Hartford CT 06107 Office: Route 4 Farmington Ave Farmington CT 06032

YAFFE, FRANK HENRY, food co. exec.; b. Milw., Jan. 19, 1915; s. Aaron and Aimee M. (Frank) Y.; student U. Mich., 1932-33, Washington and Lee U., 1936; m. Louise Ogens, Apr. 8, 1974. Sales rep. Dwight Paper Co., Milw., 1937-40; successively sales rep., sales ops. mgr., dir. mktg. services Universal Foods Corp., Milw., 1946-62, dir. devel. planning, 1962-70, dir. corporate devel., 1970-73, sec., dir. corporate devel., 1973—; exec. v.p., dir. Bethesda/Roxo Waters, Inc.; dir. E. Schiff Travel, Inc. Bd. dirs. Mental Health Planning Council, Milw.; mem. Marquette U. Pres.'s Senate. Served with C.E. U.S. Army, 1940-45. Recipient Key Man award Internat. Food Service Mfrs. Assn., 1963. Mem. Am. Assn. Corporate Sec., Assn. for Corporate Growth, Am. Mgmt. Assn. Republican. Jewish. Club: Confrerie de la Chaine des Rotisseurs. Home: 3141 E Hampshire St Milwaukee WI 53211 Office: 433 E Michigan St Milwaukee WI 53201

YAFFE, JAMES, author; b. Chgo., Mar. 31, 1927; s. Samuel and Florence (Scheinman) Y.; grad. Fieldston Sch., 1944; B.A. summa cum laude, Yale, 1948; m. Elaine Gordon, Mar. 1, 1964; children—Deborah Ann, Rebecca Elizabeth, Gideon Daniel. Writer-in-residence Colorado Coll., 1966—, dir. Writing Inst., 1978. Served with USNR, 1945-46. Recipient Nat. Arts Found award, 1968. Mem. P.E.N., Authors League, Phi Beta Kappa. Jewish. Club: Elizabethan (Yale). Author: Poor Cousin Evelyn, 1951; The Good-for-Nothing, 1953; What's the Big Hurry?, 1954; Nothing But the Night, 1959; Mister Margolies, 1962; Nobody Does You Any Favors, 1966; The American Jews, 1968; The Voyage of the Franz Joseph, 1970; So Sue Me!, 1972; (play) The Deadly Game, 1960; (with Jerome Weidman) Ivory Tower, 1967; also TV plays, stories, reviews. Address: 1215 N Cascade Colorado Springs CO 80903. *We are all inexorably separated from one another, and we all yearn to reach across the chasm. That is why stories have been told and characters created since the beginning of civilization. That is why I write novels, and why I try to arouse in students an appetite for reading novels.*

YAFFE, JOSEPH X., lawyer; b. Phila., May 6, 1913; s. Samuel and Rose (Schaffer) Y.; A.B., U. Pa., 1933; J.D., Temple U., 1936; m. Silvia F. Fishbein, July 21, 1940; children—Roy, Peter, Lisa Jo. Admitted to Pa. bar, 1937; spl. dep. atty. gen. Commonwealth of Pa., 1937-54; partner firm Yaffe and Gould, Phila., 1954—; pres. Commonwealth Insular Devel. Inc. Counsel, dir. Police Athletic League, 1948—; counsel, dir. Elder Craftsmen Phila., 1959—, pres., 1965-66, chmn. bd. dirs., 1966-67; mem. exec. com. Nat. Community Relations Adv. Council, 1956-64, treas., 1960-64; pres. Jewish Community Relations Council Greater Phila., 1956-59, hon. pres., 1959—; mem. Pa. Fair Employment Practices Commn., 1960-61; mem. Phila. Fellowship Commn., 1956-76, v.p., 1960-63; mem. Pa. Human Relations Commn., 1961—, vice chmn., 1968-74, chmn., 1974—; counsel, dir. Soc. Crippled Children and Adults Phila., 1949—, pres., 1962-63; dir. Pa. Easter Seal Soc. Crippled Children and Adults, 1969-72; nat. council Jt. Distbn. Com., 1964-77; v.p. Internat. Assn. Ofcl. Human Rights Agys., 1967-68, counsel, 1973-76. Served as ensign USCGR, 1942-45. Recipient Pres. medallion Easter Seal Soc., 1965; Founder's award Police Athletic League, 1966, Distinguished Service award, 1970; Humanitarian award Salem Bapt. Ch., 1968; Service award Pa. Ho. of Reps., 1971; Distinguished Merit award NCCJ, 1976. Mem. Am., Pa., Phila. bar assns., Pa. Soc. Clubs: Masons, Shriners, Meadowlands Country (gov. 1963—, v.p., 1965-71, pres., 1971-73, hon. pres., 1973—). Home: 1006 Arboretum Rd Wyncote PA 19095 Office: Two Penn Center Plaza Philadelphia PA 19102

YAGER, HUNTER, advt. agy. exec.; b. Bklyn., Sept. 29, 1929; s. Jules and Lucille (Kornblum) Y.; B.A., N.Y. U., 1950; M.B.A., Harvard, 1955; m. Gertrude Kathryn Johnson, Feb. 17, 1960; children—Leslie Jeanne, Andrew Hunter, Phoebe Hildreth. Copywriter, Donahue & Coe, Inc., N.Y.C., 1951-53; account exec. Foote, Cone & Belding, N.Y.C., 1955-58; account exec., account supr., v.p., mgmt. supr., exec. v.p. mgmt. com. Grey Advt., Inc., N.Y.C., 1958—; dir. Grey Advt., Ltd., Can.; instr. marketing N.Y. U., 1961-62. Mem. Camp Rising Sun Alumni Assn. Unitarian. Clubs: Harvard, Harvard Business School (N.Y.C.). Home: 512 W Lyon Farm Dr Greenwich CT 06830 Office: 777 3d Ave New York NY 10017

YAGER, JOHN WARREN, lawyer, banker; b. Toledo, Sept. 16, 1920; s. Joseph A. and Edna Gertrude (Pratt) Y.; A.B., U. Mich., 1942, J.D., 1948; m. Dorothy W. Merki, July 25, 1942; children—Julie M., John M. Admitted to Ohio bar, 1948; practiced in Toledo, 1948-64; trust officer Toledo Trust Co., 1964-69; v.p., trust officer, sec. First Nat. Bank, Toledo, 1969—. Pres. Toledo Met. Park Dist., 1971—, Neighborhood Health Assn., 1974-75. Councilman, Toledo, 1955-57, 60-61, mayor, 1958-59. Bd. dirs. Toledo-Lucas County Library, 1968-70; past pres. Toledo Legal Aid Soc., Toledo Council Chs., Toledo Municipal League, Econ. Opportunity Planning Assn., Toledo, Com. on Relations with Toledo, Spain. Served to maj. USMC, 1942-46, 50-52. Decorated Bronze Star; named one of 10 outstanding young men, Toledo, 1952, 54, 55. Mem. Ohio, Toledo bar assns., Toledo Estate Planning Council, Toledo Jr. C. of C. (past pres.), Downtown Toledo Assos. (treas.), Delta Tau Delta. Clubs: Toledo, Belmont Country (Toledo). Home: 4117 Sheraton Rd Toledo OH 43606 Office: First Nat Bank Toledo 606 Madison Ave Toledo OH 43604

YAGER, JOSEPH ARTHUR, JR., economist; b. Owensville, Ind., Apr. 14, 1916; s. Joseph Arthur and Edna (Pratt) Y.; A.B., U. Mich., 1937; J.D., 1939, M.A., 1940; m. Virginia Estella Beroset, Sept. 2, 1938; children—Thomas, Martha. Economist, OPA, 1942-44; economist State Dept., 1946-47, chief China research br., 1949-50, chief div. research for Far East, 1952-57, attaché U.S. consulate gen., Canton, China, 1947-48, consul, Hongkong, 1950-51; econ. counselor, Taipei, 1957-59, dep. chief of mission 1959-61; dir. Office Chinese Affairs, 1961; dir. Office E. Asian Affairs, 1961-63; mem. Policy Planning Council, 1963-66, vice chmn., 1966-68; dep. dir. internat. and social studies div. Inst. for Def. Analyses, 1968-72; sr. fellow Brookings Instn., 1972—. Served in AUS, 1944-45. Mem. Phi Delta Phi, Delta Tau Delta. Co-author: Energy and U.S. Foreign Policy, 1974; New Means of Financing International Needs, 1978. Home: 10006 Woodhill Rd Bethesda MD 20034 Office: 1775 Massachusetts Ave Washington DC 20036

YAGHJIAN, EDMUND, artist, educator; b. Harpoot, Armenia, Feb. 16, 1904; s. Samuel and Sultan (Ajootian) Y.; came to U.S., 1907, naturalized, 1930; B.F.A., R.I. Sch. Design, 1930; postgrad. Art Students League, N.Y.C., 1930-32; m. Dorothy Candy, May 30, 1941; children—Candy, Robin, David, Susy. One man shows Kraushaar Galleries, 1940, Gibbes Art Gallery, 1959, 63, U. Mo., 1945, U. S.C., 1948, Columbia Art Mus., 1945, Dorsey Galleries, 1952, Telfair Acad, 1953, Chafee Mus., 1962, 63, Madison Gallery, 1962, Augusta Mus., 1959, Mint Mus., 1966, Galerie Internationale, 1967, Galerie Fontainebleau, 1965, Ligoa Duncan Gallery, 1966, AGBU Gallery, 1968, Florence Mus., 1969, Carson McKenna Galleries, 1969, Vt. Art Center, 1968, 40 Year Retrospective Exhibit, Columbia Mus. Art, 1972, Havens Gallery, 1972, Chaffee Art Center, 1973, N.Y. Mus., 1975-76, retrospective exhbn. Harold Decker Galleries, Norfolk and Richmond, Va., 1977, also others; exhibited in group shows various museums U.S. Art Students League Centennial Exhibit, 1975; represented in permanent collections Duke, N.Y. Pub. Library, N.Y. U., High Mus., Atlanta, Montpelier, Birmingham, West Point museums, Yerevan Mus., Soviet Armenia, 1979; numerous pvt. collections: head art dept. Great Neck Prep. Sch., 1934-36; instr. Art Students League N.Y., 1938-42; prof. art Edgewood Park Jr. Coll., 1941-44; guest instr. painting U. Mo., 1944-45; head fine arts dept. U. S.C., 1945-66, artist-in-residence U. S.C., 1966-72, prof. emeritus, 1972—; faculty Columbia Mus. Art Sch., 1972—; participant ICA Cultural Exchange Program to Saudi Arabia, 1979. Pres., Columbia Artists Guild, 1948-50, Guild S.C. Artists, 1950-51, 59-60. Recipient 1st prizes S.C. Artists, 1946, 47, 61, 63, Purchase award S.C. Artists, 1953, award Merit Guild S.C. Artists, 1954, 62, Purchase prizes, 1955, 58, 62, 63; Arts and Sci. award Univ. S.C., 1967. Mem. Southeastern Coll. Art Assn. (past pres.), Coll. Art Assn., Am. Fedn. Arts, AAUP. Home: 1510 Adger Rd Columbia SC 29205

YAHNER, FRANK ALBERT, advt. agy. exec.; b. Uniontown, Pa., June 18, 1913; s. Frank and Mary (Harrigan) Y.; student U. Miami, 1931-34; m. Charlotte Anderson, Apr. 7, 1945; children—Frank Albert, Ann, John, Patrick. With Knox Reeves Advt., 1945-49; with Young and Rubican, 1949-52, v.p., 1956-63; v.p. Biow Co., advt., N.Y.C., 1952-54, Needham, Louis & Brorby, 1954-56; sr. v.p. Doyle, Dane, Bernbach, Inc., N.Y.C., 1963—. Treas. Pomperaug council Boy Scouts Am., 1955-60. Bd. dirs. Fairfield (Conn.) Community Chest, 1960-63, Wakeman Boys Club, Southport, Conn., 1963-67; bd. dirs., mem. adv. bd. Fairfield U., 1964-68. Served to lt. USCGR, 1942-45. Mem. Sales Execs. Club N.Y. (dir. 1973—). Club: Fairfield Country. Home: 683 Pequot Rd Southport CT 06490 Office: 437 Madison Ave New York NY 10022

YAHR, MELVIN DAVID, physician; b. N.Y.C., Nov. 18, 1917; s. Isaac and Sarah (Reigelhaupt) Y.; A.B., N.Y. U., 1939, M.D., 1943; m. Felice Turtz, May 9, 1948; children—Carol, Nina, Laura, Barbara Anne. Intern, Lenox Hill Hosp., N.Y.C., 1943-44; resident Lenox Hill Hosp., also Montefiore Hosp., Bronx, N.Y. 1947-48; staff Columbia, 1948—, asso. prof. clin. neurology, 1957-62, prof. neurology, 1962-70, H.H. Merritt prof. neurology, 1970—, asst. dean grad. medicine, 1959-67, asso. dean, 1967—; asst. neurologist N.Y. Neurol. Inst., 1948-53, asso. attending neurologist, 1953-60, attending neurologist, 1960—; Geldschmidt prof. neurology, chmn. dept. neurology Mt. Sinai Med. Center, 1973—; exec. dir. Parkinson's Disease Found. 1957—; panel neurologist N.Y.C. Bd. Edn., 1958—; mem. com. evaluation drugs in neurology NIH, 1959-60, panel mem. neurol. study sect., 1959—; mem. com. revisions U.S. Pharmacopea. Diplomate Am. Bd. Psychiatry and Neurology. Fellow Am. Acad. Neurology, N.Y. Acad. Medicine, Harvey Soc.; mem. A.M.A. (chmn. com. neurol. disorders in industry), Am. Neurol. Assn. (sec.-treas. 1959-68, pres. 1969), Assn. Research Nervous and Mental Disease, N.Y. State Neurol. Soc., New York County Med. Soc., Am. Epilepsy Soc., Eastern Assn. Electroencephalographers. Asso. editor: Internat. Jour. Neurology; Archives Neurology, 1964—. Home: 23 Seely Pl Scarsdale NY 10583 Office: Annenberg Bldg Fifth Ave and 100th St New York City NY 10029

YALE, EDGAR ALLEN, ret. mfg. co. exec.; b. Nyack, N.Y., May 4, 1914; s. Joseph J. and Marie Winant; B.S. in Bus. Adminstrn., U. So. Cal., 1936; m. Anna Louise Karns, Sept. 25, 1943; children—Marie (Mrs. Leonard K. Stramara), Kathy (Mrs. Lester E. Williams), Wilson W., E. Allen. With Armstrong Cork Co., Lancaster, Pa., 1936—, asst. gen. sales mgr., 1961-62, gen. sales mgr., 1962-68, v.p. marketing, 1968-72, v.p., gen. mgr. floor products ops., 1972-73, sr. v.p., 1973-79, dir., 1976-79. Mem. Lancaster council Boy Scouts Am., 1948—. Bd. dirs. YMCA. Served to lt. USNR, 1943-45; PTO. Mem. Lancaster C. of C. Clubs: Lancaster Country, Hamilton (Lancaster). Office: Armstrong Cork Co W and Charlotte Sts Lancaster PA 17604

YALE, SEYMOUR HERSHEL, dental radiologist, educator; b. Chgo., Nov. 27, 1920; s. Henry and Dorothy (Kulwin) Y.; B.S., U. Ill., 1944, D.D.S., 1945, postgrad., 1947-48; m. Muriel Jane Cohen, Nov. 6, 1943; children—Russell Steven, Patricia Ruth. Pvt. practice of dentistry, 1945-54, 56—; asst. clin. dentistry U. Ill. Coll. Dentistry, 1948-49, instr. clin. dentistry, 1949-53, asst. prof. clin. dentistry, 1953-54, reorganized dept. radiology, asso. prof. dept., 1956, prof., head dept., 1957—, adminstrv. asst. to dean, 1961-63, asst. dean, 1963-64, acting dean, 1964-65, dean, 1965—, also mem. grad. faculty dept. radiology U. Ill. Coll. Medicine, Chgo.; dir. tng. Dental Technicians Sch., U.S. Naval Tng. Center, Bainbridge, Md., 1954-56. Mem. subcom. 16, Nat. Com. on Radiation Protection; mem. Radiation Protection Adv. Bd. State Ill., 1971; mem. City of Chgo. Health Systems Agy. Recipient centennial research award Chgo. Dental Soc., 1959; Distinguished Alumnus award U. Ill., 1973. Fellow Acad. Gen. Dentistry (hon.), Am. Coll. Dentists; mem. Ill. (mem. com. on radiology), Chgo. dental socs., Internat. Assn. Dental Research, Am. Acad. Oral Roentgenology, Am. Dental Assn., Odontographic Soc. Chgo., Council Dental Deans State Ill. (chmn.), N.Y. Acad. Scis., Pierre Fauchard Acad., Omicron Kappa Upsilon, Sigma Xi, Alpha Omega (hon.). Home: 155 N Harbor Dr Chicago IL 60601 Office: 25 E Washington St Chicago IL 60602

YALOW, ROSALYN SUSSMAN, med. physicist; b. N.Y.C., July 19, 1921; d. Simon and Clara (Zipper) Sussman; A.B., Hunter Coll., 1941; M.S., U. Ill., Urbana, 1942, Ph.D., 1945; D.Sc. (hon,) U. Ill., Chgo., 1974, Phila. Coll. Pharmacy and Sci., 1976, N.Y. Med. Coll., 1976, Med. Coll. Wis., Milw., 1977, Yeshiva U., 1977, Southampton (N.Y.) Coll., 1978, Bucknell U., 1978, Princeton U., 1978, Jersey City State Coll., 1979, Med. Coll. Pa., 1979, Manhattan Coll., 1979; D.Hum.Lett. (hon.), Hunter Coll., 1978, Sacred Heart U., Conn., 1978, St. Michael's Coll., Winooski Park, Vt., 1979, Johns Hopkins U., 1979; m. A. Aaron Yalow, June 6, 1943; children—Benjamin, Elanna. Lectr., asst. prof. physics Hunter Coll., 1946-50; physicist, asst. chief radiosotope service VA Hosp., Bronx, N.Y., 1950-70, chief nuclear medicine, 1970—, acting chief radiosotope service, 1968-70; research prof. Mt. Sinai Sch. Medicine, City U. N.Y., 1968—, Disting. Service prof., 1974-79; Disting. prof.-at-large Albert Einstein Coll. Medicine, Yeshiva U., 1979—; chmn. dept. clin. Scis. Albert Einstein Coll. Medicine, Montefiore Med. Center, Bronx, 1980—; cons. Lenox Hill Hosp., N.Y.C., 1956-62, WHO, Bombay, 1978; sec. U.S. Nat. Com. on Med. Physics, 1963-67; mem. nat. com. Radiation Protection, Subcom. 13, 1957—; mem. Pres.'s Study Group on Careers for Women, 1966—; sr. med. investigator VA, 1972; dir. Solomon A. Berson Research Lab., VA Hosp., Bronx, N.Y., 1973. Bd. dirs. N.Y. Diabetes Assn., 1974. Recipient VA William S. Middleton Med. Research award, 1960; Eli Lilly award, Am. Diabetes Assn., 1961; Van Slyke award N.Y. met. sect. Am. Assn. Clin. Chemists, 1968; award A.C.P., 1971; Dickson prize U. Pitts., 1971; Howard Taylor Ricketts award U. Chgo., 1971; Gairdner Found. Internat. award, 1971; Commemorative medallion Am. Diabetes Assn., 1972; Bernstein award Med. Soc. State N.Y., 1974; Boehringer-Mannheim Corp. award Am. Assn. Clin. Chemists, 1975; Sci. Achievement award AMA, 1975; Exceptional Service award VA, 1975; A. Cressy Morrison award N.Y. Acad. Scis., 1975; sustaining membership award Assn. Mil. Surgeons, 1975; Distinguished Achievement award Modern Medicine, 1976; Albert Lasker Basic Med. Research award, 1976; La Madonnina Internat. prize, Milan, 1977; Golden Plate award Am. Acad. Achievement, 1977; Nobel prize for medicine and physiology, 1977; citation of esteem St. John's U., 1979; G. von Hevesy medal, 1978; Rosalyn S. Yalow Research and Devel. award established Am. Diabetes Assn., 1978, Banting medal, 1978; Torch of Learning award Am. Friends Hebrew U., 1978; Virchow gold medal Virchow-Pirquet Med. Soc., 1978; Gratum Genus Humanum gold medal World Fedn. Nuclear Medicine and Biology, 1978; Jacobi medallion Asso. Alumni Mt. Sinai Sch. Medicine, 1978; Jubilee medal Coll. of New Rochelle, 1978; VA Exceptional Service award, 1978; Fed. Woman's award, 1961; Harvey lectr., 1966; Am. Gastroenterol. Assn. Meml. lectr., 1972; Joslyn lectr. New Eng. Diabetes Assn., 1972; Franklin I. Harris Meml. lectr., 1973; 1st Hagedorn Meml. lectr. Acta Endocrinologica Congress, 1973; numerous others; diplomate Am. Bd. Scis. Fellow N.Y. Acad. Scis. (chmn. biophysics div. 1964-65), Am. Coll. Radiology (asso. in physics), Clin. Soc. N.Y. Diabetes Assn.; mem. Nat. Acad. Scis., Am. Acad. Arts and Scis., Am. Phys. Soc., Radiation Research Soc., Am. Assn. Physicists in Medicine, Biophys. Soc., Soc. Nuclear Medicine, Endocrine Soc. (Koch award 1972, pres. 1978), Am. Physiol. Soc., Phi Beta Kappa, Sigma Xi, Sigma Pi Sigma, Pi Mu Epsilon, Sigma Delta Epsilon. Co-editor: Hormone and Metabolic Research, 1973—; editorial adv. council Acta Diabetologica Latina, 1975-77, Ency. Universalis, 1978—; editorial bd. Mt. Sinai Jour. Medicine, 1976—, Diabetes, 1976—, Endocrinology, 1967-72; contbr. numerous articles to profl. jours. Office: 130 W Kingsbridge Rd Bronx NY 10468

YAMAGUCHI, RALPH TADASHI, lawyer; b. Pahoa, Hawaii, Mar. 12, 1913; s. Fusataro and Aya (Yamanaka) Y.; B.A., U. Hawaii, 1934; LL.B., U. Colo., 1936; m. Leatrice T. Yoshiura, Jan. 31, 1942; children—Diane A., Beverly M., Lisa A. Admitted to Hawaii bar, 1937; asst. pub. prosecutor City and County of Honolulu, 1937-38; spl. dep. atty. gen. Hawaii, 1938-39; partner firm Yamaguchi & Tanaka, and predecessor firms, Honolulu, 1950—; dir. Hawaiian Telephone Co., Amfac, Inc., Hawaiian Electric Co., Inc., Kaiser Found. Hosps., Kaiser Found. Health Plan, Inc. Mem. Am. Bar Assn., (state del. 1962-65), Bar Assn. Hawaii (pres. 1957), C. of C. of Hawaii (pres. 1968). Home: 2500 Kalakaua Ave Honolulu HI 96815 Office: Pacific Trade Center 190 S King St Honolulu HI 96813

YAMAMOTO, JOE, physician; b. Los Angeles, Apr. 18, 1924; s. Zenzaburo and Tomie (Yamada) Y.; student Los Angeles City Coll., 1941-42, Hamline U., 1943-45; B.S., U. Minn., 1946, M.B., 1948, M.D., 1949; m. Maria Fujitomi, Sept. 5, 1947; children—Eric Robert, Andrew Jolyon. Asst. prof. dept. psychiatry, neurology, behavioral sci. U. Okla. Med. Center, 1955-58; asst. prof., 1958-60; asso. prof. dept. psychiatry U. So. Calif. Sch. Medicine, Los Angeles, 1961-69, prof., 1969-77, co-dir. grad. edn. psychiatry, 1963-70; prof. U. Calif. at Los Angeles, 1977—; dir. Psychiat. Outpatient Clinic, Los Angeles County-U. So. Calif. Med. Center, 1958-77; dir. Adult Ambulatory Care Services, U. Calif. Los Angeles NPI, 1977—. Served to capt., M.C., U.S. Army, 1953-55. Fellow Am. Psychiat. Assn., Am. Acad. Psychoanalysis (trustee, mem. exec. com., pres. 1978-79), Am. Coll. Psychiatrists; mem. So. Calif. Psychoanalytic Inst. and Soc. (pres. 1972-73), Kappa Phi, Alpha Omega Alpha. Contbr. articles in field to profl. jours. Office: 760 Westwood Plaza Los Angeles CA 90024. *Learning about the diverse peoples of America, I have been fascinated with how we can be Asian, Hispanic, Black, European, and Native American and still identify with our national values. We value our freedom, individual rights and our ability to be someone different but equal. In mental health also there is a need for recognition of cultural differences and the need of treatment response to the individual.*

YAMANE, GEORGE MITSUYOSHI, educator; b. Honolulu, Aug. 9, 1924; s. Seigi and Tsuta (Moriwaki) Y.; student U. Hawaii, 1944; A.B., Haverford Coll., 1946; D.D.S., U. Minn., 1950, Ph.D., 1962; m. Alice Matsuko Nemoto, July 6, 1951; children—Wende Michiko, Linda Keiko, David Kiyoshi. Teaching, research asst. U. Hawaii, Honolulu, 1943-44; teaching asst. div. oral pathology, oral diagnosis Sch. Dentistry, U. Minn., Mpls., 1951-53; asst. prof. oral pathology Coll. Dentistry U. Ill., Chgo., 1957-59; dir. tissue lab. Sch. Dentistry U. Wash., Seattle, 1960-63, asst. prof. oral pathology, 1959-63; grad. faculty mem. U. Minn., Mpls., 1963-70, prof., chmn. div. oral diagnosis, oral medicine and oral roentgenology, 1963-70; prof., chmn. dept. oral diagnosis and radiology Dental Sch. Coll. of Medicine and Dentistry of N.J., 1970—, asso. dean research and postgrad. programs, 1976—; cons. Children's Orthopedic Hosp. and Med. Center, Seattle, 1960-63, VA Hosp., American Lake, Wash., 1961-63, VA Hosp., Mpls., 1964-70, Minn. State Dept. Health,

1965-70, Wyo. State Bd. Health, 1966-70. Served with AUS. USPHS fellow, 1953-55. Recipient Nell S. Talbot Instructorship award Coll. Dentistry U. Ill., 1958. Fellow Am. Acad. Oral Pathology, AAAS, Am., Internat. colls. dentists, N.J. Acad. Medicine; mem. Am. Dental Assn., Orgn. Tchrs. Oral Diagnosis (sec.-treas. 1970-73, pres. 1974-75), Am. Acad. Periodontology, Internat. Assn. Dental Research, Am. Assn. Dental Schs., Sigma Xi, Omicron Kappa Upsilon, Xi Psi Phi. Contbr. articles to med. and dental jours. Office: 100 Bergen St Newark NJ 07103

YAMAOKA, GEORGE, lawyer; b. Seattle, Jan. 26, 1903; s. Ototaka and Jhoko (Watanabe) Y.; student U. Wash., 1921-24; J.D., Georgetown U., 1928; m. Henriette d'Auriac, Mar. 18, 1933; 1 dau., Colette Miyoko (Mrs. Henry Sonderegger). With Japanese Govt. Commn., Phila. Sesquicentennial Expn., 1926; adviser Japanese Consulate Gen., 1928-29, Japanese del. London Naval Conf., 1929-30; admitted to N.Y. bar, 1931, Japanese bar, 1949; practice in N.Y.C., 1931—, Tokyo 1949—; asso. firm. Hunt, Hill & Betts, 1930-40, partner, 1940-56; sr. partner Hill Betts & Nash, 1956 60, sr. partner Hill, Betts, Yamaoka & Logan, Tokyo, 1956-60, Hill, Betts, Yamaoka, Freehill & Longcope, 1960-70, Hill, Betts & Nash, 1970—. Chmn. bd. Yasuda Fire & Marine Ins. Co.; dir. Ehrenreich Photo Optical Industries, Inc.; sec., dir. Bank Tokyo Trust Co., N.Y.C. Okura & Co. (Am.), Inc., Jiji Press (N.Y.) Ltd., 24 Gramercy Park, Inc. Chmn. Am. Def. Supreme Comdr. Allied Powers Internat. Mil. Tribunal Far East, 1946-49; mem. adv. panel internat. law U.S. State Dept., 1972-74. Decorated 3d Order Sacred Treasure Japanese Govt., 1968. Mem. Am., Fed., N.Y., 1st (Tokyo) bar assns., Assn. Bar City N.Y., N.Y. County Lawyers Assn., Consular Law Soc. (pres.-elect), Am. Fgn. Law Assn., Internat. Law Assn., Maritime Law Assn. U.S., Japanese C. of C. (dir.), Japan Soc. N.Y. (hon. dir.), Japanese Am. Assn. N.Y. (hon. pres.). Clubs: Paris Am. (sec.); Marco Polo, Downtown Athletic, World Trade Center (adv. bd.), Nippon (N.Y.C.); American (Tokyo); Hodogaya (Japan) Country; Kasumigaseki (Japan) Country. Home: 24 Gramercy Park New York NY 10003 Office: One World Trade Center New York NY 10048 also Yamaoka Yoshimoto & Matsumoto Tokyo Japan

YAMASAKI, MINORU, architect; b. Seattle, Dec. 1, 1912; s. Tsunejiro J. and Hana (Ito) Y.; grad. U. Wash., 1934; student N.Y. U.; numerous hon. degrees. m. Teruko Hirashiki, Dec. 5, 1941; children—Carol Ann, Taro Michael, Kim. Designer, Githens & Keally, 1935-37; instr. water color N.Y. U., 1935-36; designer, job capt. Shreve, Lamb & Harmon, 1937-43; designer Harrison and Fouilhoux, 1943-44; chief archtl. designer Raymond Loewy, 1944-45; instr. archtl. design Columbia, 1943-45; chief archtl. designer Smith, Hinchman & Grylis, 1945-49; partner Yamasaki, Leinweber & Assos., Detroit, 1949—; work includes: Urban Development, McGregor Conf. Center, Reynolds Metals Co. Bldg., Detroit, Reynolds Metals Regional Bldg. (AIA 1st Honor award 1961), Southwick, Mich., Fed. Sci. Bldgs. at Seattle World Fair (Honor award Seattle chpt. AIA 1962), Dhahran Internat. Air Terminal, Dhahran, Saudi Arabia (1st Honor award AIA 1963), U.S. Sci. Pavilion (award of merit Precast Concrete Inst. 1963), Seattle, Office Bldg., Mich. Consol. Gas Co. (award of merit Detroit chpt. AIA 1964, Archtl. award of excellence Am. Inst. Constrn. 1964), IBM Bldg., (Design in Steel award Am. Iron and Steel Inst. 1965), Woodrow Wilson Sch. Pub. and Internat. Affairs, Princeton (Outstanding Project of Year award N.J. Concrete Assn. 1965); pub. housing in St. Louis; Thompson Products Research Center, Cleve.; U.S. Armed Forces Record Center, St. Louis; Oberlin Coll. Music Conservatory; U. Mich. Married Students Housing; North Shore Congregation Israel Bldgs., Glencoe, Ill., Northwestern Nat. Life Ins. Co., Mpls., Century Plaza Hotel and Towers, Los Angeles, World Trade Center, N.Y.C., Mfrs. & Traders Trust Co., Buffalo, Horace Mann Ins. Co., Springfield, Ill., Colo. Nat. Bank, Denver, Coll. Center Franklin & Marshall Coll., Tulsa Performing Arts Center, Bank Okla., Tulsa, Fed. Res. Bank, Richmond, Va., Royal Reception Pavilion and Internat. Airport, Saudi Arabia. Cons., World's Fair, Seattle, 1961. Mem. Com. on Civic Design, Detroit. Recipient The Sch. Exec. bronze plaque, 1953; hon. mention Nat. Inst. Arts and Letters, 1954, 1st design award Prog. Arch. Urban Redevel., 1956, 1st honor award, AIA, St. Louis Airport, 1956, award of merit, Feld Clinic, 1956, top award in commerce div. Prog. Arch., Am. Concrete Inst., 1957; top award for Consulate General's Offices in Kobe, Archtl. Inst. Japan, 1957; 1st honor award AIA, 1959, award of merit, 1959. Fellow Am. Acad. Arts and Scis., AIA. Home: 3717 Lakecrest Dr Bloomfield Hills MI 48013 Office: 350 W Big Beaver Rd Troy MI 48084*

YAMATO, KEI C., internat. bus. cons.; b. Honokaa, Hawaii, Sept. 21, 1921; s. Kango and Shizuka (Tanaka) Y.; B.A., U. Hawaii, 1946; LL.B., Yale, 1950; children—Karen, Marla, Kei Tracy. Pres. Internat. Bus. Mgmt. Co., 1950; founder Pacific-Asia Bus. Council, 1950; pres. Orchids of Hawaii Internat., Inc., 1951, Polynesian Products, Inc., Holiday Promotions Internat., Inc., 1952, Orchawaii Internat. Travel Corp., 1962, Pacific Area Landscaping, Inc., 1970—, Hawaii Hort. Enterprises, Inc., 1970—, Agrisystems, Inc., 1971—; v.p., dir. Sperry & Hutchison Travel Awards, Inc., 1964, Copley Internat. Corp., 1967 (all N.Y.C.); pres. Internat. Cons. Co., 1968, Asia-Pacific Corp., 1968. Bd. dirs. Internat. Execs. Assn., World Trade Club N.Y.C., Sales Execs. Club N.Y.C.; mem. Regional Export Expansion Council, U.S. Dept. Commerce; organizer Asia Pacific Inst. Served to 1st lt. AUS, World War II; ETO. Decorated Silver Star, Purple Heart with 2 oak leaf clusters. Mem. Advt. Club N.Y.C., Nat. Indsl. Conf. Bd., Profl. Mgmt. Cons. Assn. Am., Sales Promotion Execs. Assn., Chgo. Execs. Club, Sales and Marketing Execs. Internat., N.Y. Hort. Soc., Asia Soc., Japan Soc., Am. Mgmt. Assn. (lectr.), 442d Assn., Landscape Contractors Assn. Hawaii, Gen. Contractors Assn. Hawaii, Friends East-West Center, East-West Philosophers Conf., Hawaii Assn. Nurserymen, Hawaii Bot. Soc., Honolulu Execs. Assn., U. Hawaii Alumni Assn., Navy League, Nat. Fedn. Ind. Bus., Am. Assn. Nurserymen, Pacific Area Travel Assn., Assn. U.S. Army, Hawaii Visitors Bur., Hawaii C. of C., Saudi Arabia Bus. Council. Address: PO Box 781 Honolulu HI 96808

YANAGISAWA, SAMUEL TSUGUO, electronic co. exec.; b. Berkeley, Calif., Feb. 18, 1922; s. Jusaku George and Mitsuyo (Mochizuki) Y.; B.S. in Elec. Engring., U. Calif. at Berkeley, 1942; m. Fernande Gerardine Renar, July 10, 1952; children—Shane Henry, Steven Kim, Ian Gerard. Product line mgr. Machlett Labs. Inc. Springdale, Conn., 1943-63; v.p. ops. Warnecke Electron Tubes, Inc., Des Plaines, Ill., 1963-67; chmn., chief exec. officer, pres. Varo Inc., Garland, Tex., 1967—, also dir.; dir. 1st Nat. Bank, Garland. Mem. Dallas Citizens Council; bd. dirs. So. Meth. U. Found. for Sci. and Engring.; mem. adv. council McDonald Obs., U. Tex., Austin. Served to lt. AUS, 1945-46. Mem. IEEE (sr.), Am. Mgmt. Assn., Soc. Info. Display, Assn. U.S. Army, Assn. Old Crows, Phi Beta Kappa, Sigma Xi, Tau Beta Pi, Eta Kappa Nu. Contbr. articles to profl. jours. Patentee electron devices. Office: Varo Inc 2203 Walnut St Garland TX 75040*

YANAKAKIS, BASIL SOTIRIOS, lawyer; b. Tripolis, Greece, Feb. 15, 1927; s. Sotirios J. and Sofia (Savopoulos) Y.; came to U.S., 1952, naturalized, 1960; LL.B., Athens U., 1950; postgrad. Northeastern U. Law Sch., 1953-54; LL.M., Harvard, 1954, postgrad., 1955-57; J.D., Suffolk Law Sch., Boston, 1959; m. Nancy More Blake, May 24, 1969. Admitted to Mass. bar, 1960; legal counsel Boston Redevel. Authority, 1966-68; sr. partner firm Yanakakis, Bukauskas & Felker, Boston, 1964—; prof. law Suffolk Law Sch., 1967—; vis. scholar Harvard Law Sch., 1978-79. Spl. adviser Greek Ministry Econ. Coordination, 1951-52; adv. council Small Bus. Adminstrn., 1970—. Mem. archdiocesan council Greek Orthodox Archdiocese N.Am. and S.Am., 1970—. Candidate for Greek Parliament, 1950; vice chmn. Nationality Groups for Nixon, 1960. Trustee U. Mass. Bldg. Authority, 1970—, Greek Orthodox Cathedral New Eng., 1967-68, St. John Baptist Ch., Boston, 1966-67, St. Nicholas Ch., Lexington, 1974—; bd. dirs., mem. ho. of dels. Mass. Easter Seal Soc., 1977—; mem. council Suffolk U. Mem. Am. Bar Assn., Am. Judicature Soc. (chmn. fin. and endowment com.), Am. Soc. Internat. Law, Acad. Polit. Sci., World Peace Through Law Assn., Phi Alpha Delta. Author: International Status of the Ecumenical Patriarchate, 1959; also papers. Home: 27 Grasshopper Ln Acton MA 01720 Office: 6 Beacon St Boston MA 02108

YANCEY, ASA GREENWOOD, physician; b. Atlanta, Aug. 19, 1916; s. Arthur H. and Daisy L. (Sherard) Y.; B.S., Morehouse Coll., 1937; M.D., U. Mich., 1941; m. Carolyn E. Dunbar, Dec. 28, 1944; children—Arthur H. II, Carolyn L., Caren L., Asa Greenwood. Intern, City Hosp., Cleve., 1941-42; resident Freedmen's Hosp., Washington, 1942-45, U.S. Marine Hosp., Boston, 1945; instr. surgery Meharry Med. Coll., 1946-48; chief surgery VA Hosp., Tuskegee, Ala., 1948-58; practice medicine, specializing in surgery, Atlanta, 1958—; med. dir. Grady Meml. Hosp., Atlanta, 1972—; mem. staff Hughes Spalding, St. Joseph, Ga. Bapt. hosps.; asst. prof. surgery Emory U., 1958-72, prof., 1975—, asso. dean Sch. Medicine, asso. prof., 1972-75. Mem. Atlanta Bd. Edn., 1967-77. Trustee Ga. chpt. Am. Cancer Soc. Served to 1st lt. M.C., AUS, 1942. Diplomate Am. Bd. Surgery. Fellow A.C.S.; mem. Nat. Med. Assn. (trustee 1960-66, editorial bd. jour. 1964—), Inst. Medicine of Nat. Acad. Scis. Baptist. Contbr. articles to profl. jours. Home: 2845 Engle Rd NW Atlanta GA 30318 Office: Grady Memorial Hosp Atlanta GA 30303

YANCEY, BENJAMIN WALMSLEY, lawyer; b. Biloxi, Miss., Aug. 5, 1906; s. Arthur and Josephine Claire (Reckner) Y.; B.A., Tulane U., 1926, M.A., 1928, LL.B., 1928; m. Janet Isabel Wallace, June 22, 1937. Admitted to La. bar, 1928, since practiced in New Orleans; sr. partner firm Terriberry, Carroll, Yancey & Farrell, specializing admiralty and maritime law, 1928—; asso. editor Am. Maritime Cases, 1948—; instr. admiralty La. State U., 1954-70; instr. admiralty Tulane U., 1967-71, prof. law, 1971—. Pres., Plaquemines Oil & Devel. Co., 1946—. Titulary mem. Comité Maritime Internat., 1966—; adviser to Am. delegation Brussels Diplomatic Conf. on Maritime Law, 1967-68, Intergovtl. Maritime Consultative Orgn., London, Eng., 1967. Vice pres. New Orleans Philharmonic Symphony Soc., 1959-72; pres. Kemper and Leila Williams Found., 1973—; Chmn. bd. govs. Le Petit Theater du Vieux Carré, 1934-41. Fellow Am. Coll. Trial Lawyers; mem. Maritime Law Assn. U.S. (pres. 1966-68), Am. (mem. ho. of dels. 1967-69), Inter-Am., Fed., La., New Orleans bar assns., Assn. Bar City N.Y., Internat. Assn. Ins. Counsel (past chmn. marine ins. com.), Am., La. hist. assns., Order Coif, Phi Beta Kappa. Clubs: India House, Whitehall (N.Y.C.); Plimsoll, Pickwick, Boston, Internat. House (New Orleans). Home: 1432 Octavia St New Orleans LA 70115 Office: Internat Trade Mart 2 Canal St New Orleans LA 70130

YANCEY, CLARENCE LANGSTON, lawyer; b. Highland, La., Aug. 17, 1909; s. Stephen Richard and Laura (Wood) Y.; LL.B., La. State U., 1931; m. Irene Elizabeth Gayden, Mar. 13, 1937; children—Martha G. Carr, Stephen Richard II, Laura I. Admitted to La. bar, 1931; atty. Standard Oil Co. (N.J.), New Orleans and Shreveport, La., 1933-46; practice law, Shreveport, 1936—; partner Cook, Clark, Egan, Yancey & King, 1946—. Mem. La. Judiciary Commn., 1969-73, Jud. Council La., 1960-68; author, lectr. race relations; mem. com. to draft La. Code Adminstrv. Proc., 1966; mem. council La. State Law Inst. Mem. Caddo Parish Sch. Bd., Shreveport, 1952-58; mem. regional adv. bd. Inst. Internat. Edn. Bd. dirs. Shreveport Beautification Found., 1963-64, 78—; trustee Southwestern Legal Found., 1972—. Served from 1st lt. to maj. AUS, 1942-46; lt. col. Res. Fellow Am. Bar Found. (vice chmn. 1971, chmn. 1972-73); mem. Am. Coll. Probate Counsel, Am. (ho. dels. 1968—, state del. from La. 1976—), La. (pres. 1956-57, del. to jud. conf. U.S. 5th circuit), Shreveport (pres. 1950) bar assns., Am. Counsel Assn., Judge Advs. Assn. (past dir., editor jour.), La. (past pres.), Shreveport (pres. 1965) chambers commerce, English Speaking Union (chpt. pres. 1962, 69-72, 77-78, chmn. region VII 1965-72, nat. dir. 1973-75), La. State U. Found. (dir. 1970-74), La. State U. Law Sch. Alumni Assn. (pres. 1965), La. State U. Alumni Fedn. (past 1st v.p.), Tarshar Soc. (founder, pres. 1968—). Methodist. Clubs: Shreveport (pres. 1961); Cotillion of Holiday in Dixie (pres. 1967); Boston, Bienville (New Orleans). Contbr. articles to profl. jours. Home: 842 McCormick St Shreveport LA 71104 Office: Comml Nat Bank Bldg Shreveport LA 71101. *Given good health, I have always thought that energy and enthusiasm are the keys to success and happiness. A formal education should not be a goal in itself, but only a tool for performance. Energy ties into the work ethic that has made America great. Japan and West Germany are prosperous today because work is honorable and enjoyable there. Where welfare rolls are swollen and work stoppages are prolific, progress is stagnant. Enthusiasm is dedication and joy in one's work. Doing just a little bit more than is expected or required puts one in a pre-eminent position. Also, doing something for one's community and friends gives incalculable satisfaction and pleasure. Never retire as long as there is health; wear out-do not rust out.*

YANCEY, PHILIP DAVID, editor, author; b. Atlanta, Nov. 4, 1949; s. Marshall Watts and Mildred Sylvania (Diem) Y.; B.A. magna cum laude, Columbia (S.C.) Bible Coll., 1970; M.A. with highest honors, Wheaton (Ill.) Coll., 1972; m. Janet Elenor Norwood, June 2, 1970. Writer, then mng. editor Campus Life mag., Wheaton, 1970-75, editor, 1974—; author: After The Wedding, 1976; Where Is God When It Hurts? (Gold medallion award Evang. Christian Pubs. Assn. 1978), 1977; Growing Places, 1978; Unhappy Secrets of the Christian Life, 1979; also articles. Mem. Evang. Press Assn. (Periodical of Year award 1975). Mem. Evangelical Convenant Ch. Home: 26W376 MacArthur Ave Wheaton IL 60187 Office: Box 419 Wheaton IL 60187

YANCEY, ROBERT EARL, oil refinery exec.; b. Cleve., July 15, 1921; s. George Washington II and Mary (Gutzwiller) Y.; B.E., Marshall U., 1943; m. Mary Estelline Tackett, July 25, 1941; children—Robert Earl, Susan Carol. With Ashland Oil Inc. (Ky.), 1943—, successively process engr., project engr., operating supt., coordinator sales and refining, gen. supt. refineries, 1943-56, v.p. in charge mfg., 1956-59, adminstrv. v.p., 1959-65, dir., 1964—, sr. v.p., 1965-72, pres., 1972—, chief operating officer, 1969—; pres. Ashland Chem. Co., 1967-69, Ashland Petroleum Co., 1969-72; dir. Ashland Oil Inc., Cleve. Tankers, Inc., Estates Petroleum Co. Inc. (USA), Negroven, S.A. (Venezuela), O.K. Tire & Rubber Co., Inc. (USA), United Carbon India Ltd., 3d Nat. Bank, Ashland. Past bd. dirs. Spindletop Research Center, Lexington, Ky.; bd. advisors Marshall U., Huntington, W.Va., 1977. Mem. Nat. Petroleum Refiners Assn. (dir. 1965—, pres. 1969-70), Nat. Petroleum Assn. (mfg. com.), Nat. Petroleum Council, Am. Petroleum Inst. (dir.), Ky. Soc. Profl. Engrs. (dir. 1970—). Protestant. Home: 102 Lycan Dr Bellefonte Ashland KY 41101 Office: 1409 Winchester Ave Ashland KY 41101

YANCEY, WILLIAM BURBRIDGE, JR., ret. air force officer; b. Berwyn, Md., Aug. 13, 1924; s. William Burbridge and Elizabeth (Faw) Y.; B.S., U.S. Mil. Acad., 1946; M.A. in Internat. Affairs, George Washington U., 1964; m. Phyllis Vander Fehr, June 5, 1946; children—William Burbridge III, Mary Jo Morgan, Annette. Commd. 2d lt. USAAF, 1946, advanced through grades to maj. gen. U.S. Air Force, 1974; air officer comdg. Air Force Acad., 1955-58, comdr. 113 Tactical Fighter Wing, Myrtle Beach, S.C., 1969-70, 31st Tactical Fighter Wing, Tuy Hoa, Vietnam, 1969-70; staff Directorate of Plans Hdqrs. USAF, Washington, 1970-73, Directorate Plans and Policy, J-5 Joint Staff, Pentagon, Washington, 1973-74; dir. plans and policy Hdqrs. EUCOM, 1974-76; vice comdr. 16th Air Force, Torrejon Air Base, Madrid, 1976-78, ret., 1978. Decorated D.S.M., Legion of Merit with 2 oak leaf clusters, D.F.C. with one oak leaf cluster, Air medal with 14 oak leaf clusters. Mem. Air Force Assn. Club: American (Madrid). Home: 3320 Circle Hill Rd Alexandria VA 22305

YANDELL, LUNSFORD P., paper mfg. co. exec.; b. Danville, Ky., Nov. 17, 1902; s. Lunsford P. and Elizabeth S. (Hosford) Y.; A.B., Princeton, 1924; m. Katharine L. Winchester, June 14, 1930; children—Lunsford P., Winchester. With Central Hanover Bank & Trust Co., 1925-26; research work, Mohawk Mining Co., 1926; paymaster Jarka Stevedore Corp., 1927; Barber S.S. Co., 1927; pres. Gay, Inc. 1927—; v.p. Mohawk Mining Co., 1927-29, pres. 1930—; exec. Todd, Robertson, Todd Engring. Corp., N.Y.C., 1933-35; exec. RCA, 1935-43, NBC, 1940-42; v.p. Blue Network Co., Inc., 1942-43; gen. mgr. Tannin Products Export Corp., 1943-45; pres., dir. Wood Flong. Corp., 1946-50; pres., dir. Ky. Block Cannel Coal Co., Wolverine Coal Co., Elk Fork Ry., Ohio & Ky. Ry. Co. Trustee Albany Med. Sch., Union Coll. Episcopalian. Clubs: Racquet and Tennis (N.Y. C.); Cap and Gown (Princeton, N.J.); Princeton (N.Y.C.); Nassau (Princeton, N.J.). Address: 6114 N Invergordon Rd Scottsdale AZ 85253

YANDERS, ARMON FREDERICK, geneticist, educator; b. Lincoln, Nebr., Apr. 12, 1928; s. Fred W. and Beatrice (Pate) Y.; A.B., Nebr. State Coll., Peru, 1948; M.S., U. Nebr., 1950, Ph.D., 1953; m. Evelyn Louise Gatz, Aug. 1, 1948; children—Mark Frederick, Kent Michael. Research asso. Oak Ridge Nat. Lab. and Northwestern U., 1953-54; biophysicist U.S. Naval Radiol. Def. Lab., San Francisco, 1955-58; asso. geneticist Argonne (Ill.) Nat. Lab., 1958-59; with dept. zoology Mich. State U., 1959-69, prof., asst. dean Coll. Natural Sci., 1963-69; prof. biol. scis., dean Coll. Arts and Scis., U. Mo., Columbia, 1969—. Trustee Argonne Univs. Assn., 1965-77, v.p., 1969-73, pres., 1973, 76-77, chmn. bd., 1973-75. Served from ensign to lt., USNR, 1954-58. Mem. A.A.A.S., Am. Inst. Biol. Sci., Am. Soc. Naturalists, Genetics Soc. Am., Am. Soc. Zoologists. Contbr. articles to profl. jours. Home: 2405 Ridgefield Rd Columbia MO 65201 Office: U Mo Coll Arts and Scis Columbia MO 65201

YANG, CHEN NING, physicist; b. Hofei, Anhwei, China, Sept. 22, 1922; s. Ke Chuan Yang and Meng Hwa Lo; B.Sc., Nat. S.W. Asso. U., China, 1942; Ph.D., U. Chgo., 1948; D.Sc., Princeton U., 1958, Bklyn. Poly. Inst., 1965, U. Wroclaw (Poland), 1974, Gustavus Adolphus Coll., 1975; m. Chih Li Tu, Aug. 26, 1950; children—Franklin, Gilbert, Eulee. Instr., U. Chgo., 1948-49; mem. Inst. Advanced Study, Princeton U., 1949-55, prof., 1955-66; Albert Einstein prof. State U. N.Y., Stony Brook, 1966—. Trustee Rockefeller U., 1971-76, Salk Inst., 1977—; mem. governing council Courant Inst., 1963—. Recipient Albert Einstein Commemorative award in sci., 1957; Nobel prize for physics, 1957; Rumford prize, 1980. Mem. Am. Phys. Soc., Nat. Acad. Scis., Brazilian Acad. Scis., Venezuelan Acad. Scis., Royal Spanish Acad. Scis., Am. Philos. Soc., AAAS (bd. dirs. 1975—), Sigma Xi. Office: Physics Dept State U NY Stony Brook NY 11794

YANG, CHING-KUN, educator; b. Canton, China, Mar. 3, 1911; s. Hsiu-hsien and Ho-se (Ho) Y.; came to U.S., 1934; B.A., Yenching U., 1932, M.A., 1934; Ph.D., U. Mich., 1939; LL.D. (hon.), Chinese U. of Hong Kong, 1974; m. Louise Chin, Dec. 10, 1939; children—Wallace, Wesley. Editor, Chinese Jour., N.Y.C., 1939-44; asst. prof. U. Wash., 1944-48; asso. prof., head dept. sociology Lingnan U., Canton, 1948-51; research asso. Center for Internat. Studies, Mass. Inst. Tech., 1952-53; asso. prof. sociology U. Pitts., 1953-58, prof., 1958-64, 67-68, 70-72, distinguished service prof. sociology, 1972—; prof. sociology U. Hawaii, 1964-67; prof. sociology chair Chinese U. of Hong Kong, 1968-70. Trustee, Lingnan U. Author: The Chinese Family in the Communist Revolution, 1959; A Chinese Village in Early Communist Transition, 1959; Religion in Chinese Society, 1961. Mem. editorial bd. Modern China, 1974—. Home: 500 Edgewood Rd Pittsburgh PA 15221

YANG, JOSEPH HOUNG-YU, govt. ofcl.; b. Kiangshu, China, Feb. 29, 1934; s. Sher Lien and Kwei Feng (Yin) Y.; B.A., Nat. U. Taiwan, 1955; B.S.E.E., Seattle U., 1963; Ph.D., Johns Hopkins U., 1968; m. Adrienne Jane Nogic, Aug. 28, 1968; children—Rebecca C., Lisa C. Research asso. Hopkins Inst. Coop. Research, Johns Hopkins U., 1963-69; asst. prof. Coll. Applied Sci. and Engring., U. Wis., 1968-69; staff engr. Page Communications Engrs., Washington, 1969-70; sci. analyst CNA, Arlington, Va., 1970; HEW fellow, Office of Sec. of HEW, 1970-71; spl. asst. to dir. CNA, Arlington, 1971-74, dir. NAVLEX projects, 1974-76, sr. rep. to comdr. Submarine Pacific, Honolulu, 1976-77; dep. asst. sec. for research and devel., Dept. Army, Washington, 1977—; lectr. urban systems engring. Howard U. Mem. IEEE, Am. Soc. Engring. Edn., AAUP, Sigma Xi. Roman Catholic. Patentee in field. Home: 8408 N Brook Ln Bethesda MD 20014 Office: Office of Asst Sec of Army Dept of Army Washington DC 20310. *I am a simple man; I lead a simple life; I am simply happy!*

YANG, KWANG-TZU, educator; b. China, Nov. 12, 1926; s. Chi-U and Wei-Yin Yang; B.S. in Mech. Engring., Ill. Inst. Tech., 1951, M.S. in Mech. Engring., 1952, Ph.D., 1955; m. Heather Hsu, June 20, 1953; children—Ginger C., Eugene Y., Sara S., Irene I., Benson P. Came to U.S., 1948, naturalized, 1963. Research engr. Paul R. Trumpler, Chgo., 1952-54; asst. prof. mech. engring. U. Notre Dame, 1955-59, asso. prof., 1959-63, prof., 1963-68, prof., chmn. dept. mech. engring., 1968-69, prof. aerospace and mech. engring., 1969—, chmn. dept., 1969-78; mech. engr. A.M. Strauss Inc., Fort Wayne, Ind., summer 1955; cons. Dodge Mfg. Corp., Mishawaka, Ind., 1956—; chmn. adv. subcom. engring. div. NSF, 1978—; mem. tech. adv. bd. Reliance Electric Co., Cleve., 1969-73. Fellow ASME; mem. Am. Soc. Engring. Edn., AAAS, Am. Inst. Aeros. and Astronautics, AAUP, Nat. Mgmt. Assn., Sigma Xi, Tau Beta Pi, Pi Tau Sigma. Contbr. articles to profl. jours. Home: 1116 Clermont Dr South Bend IN 46617 Office: Dept Aerospace and Mech Engring U Notre Dame Notre Dame IN 46556

YANG, RICHARD FU SEN, educator; b. Peiping, China, Apr. 23, 1918; B.A., Yenching U., 1943; M.A., U. Wash., 1950, Ph.D., 1955; m. Myrtle H. Lowe, Dec. 14, 1947; children—Richard P., Mildred J. Came to U.S., 1947, naturalized, 1947. Reporter, Central Daily News, Chungking, China, 1940-41; reporter Central News Agy., Chungking, 1943-45; sect. chief, specialist C.N.R.R.A. Chunking, Peiping, 1945-47; asst. prof. U. Wash., 1948-60; asso. prof. U. So. Calif., 1960-67; prof. U. Pitts., 1967—, chmn. dept. East Asian Langs. and Lit., 1967-70. Fulbright-Hays scholar, Asian Studies, Chinese Lang. Tchrs. Assn., Yenching Alumni Assn. (pres. 1969-71), AAUP. Club:

Rotary. Author: (with Charles Metzger) Fifty Songs of the Yuan, 1967; College Chinese, 1968; Tales From Chinese Drama, 1968; Selections of Classical Writings, 1969; Four Plays of the Yuan Drama, 1972; Eight Colloquial Tales of the Sung, 1972. Home: 1500 Cochran Rd Cochran Hall 403 Pittsburgh PA 15243

YANKEE, GLEN GIVENS, ret. educator; b. Kingsville, Mo., Dec. 30, 1913; s. Lester Givens and Laura (Houston) Y.; student Kansas City Jr. Coll., 1931-32; A.B. in Econs., Washburn Coll., 1939; A.M., U. Ill., 1941, Ph.D., 1952. Instr. accounting U. Ill., 1940-42, 46-47, asst. prof., 1947-49; instr. accounting Kan. U., 1946; asso. prof. accounting Miami U., Oxford, Ohio, 1949-58, prof., 1958-62; prof. accounting, chmn. dept. Case Western Res. U., 1962-68; prof. Cleve. State U., 1968-79, dir. M.B.A. program, 1970-76. Trustee United Christian Fellowship, Oxford, 1954-62, Univ. Christian Movement, Cleve., 1962-68. Served to 1st lt. AUS, 1942-46. Ford Ednl. Forum fellow, 1955. C.P.A., Ill., Ohio. Mem. Am. Inst. C.P.A.'s, Ohio Soc. C.P.A.'s, Am. Accounting Assn., Ohio Soc. Christian Chs., Planning Execs. Inst., Fin. Execs. Inst., Alpha Kappa Psi (regional dir. 1958-61), Beta Gamma Sigma, Beta Alpha Psi, Pi Gamma Mu, Delta Tau Delta. Editor: Tchrs. Clinic dept. Accounting Rev., Am. Accounting Assn., 1958-63. Home: 1714 Randall Rd Cleveland OH 44113

YANKELOVICH, DANIEL, social research exec.; b. Boston, 1924; B.A., Harvard, 1946, M.A., 1950; posrgrad. Sorbonne, Paris, France, 1952; married. Vice pres., dir. research Nowland & Co., 1952-58; pres. Daniel Yankelovich, Inc., N.Y.C., 1958—; research prof. psychology N.Y. U.; pres., dir. Yankelovich, Skelly & White, N.Y.C.; v.p., dir. Reliance Group, Inc.; dir. Meredith Corp., Sunmark Corp., Reliance Ins. Co.; vis. prof. psychology, grad. faculty New Sch. for Social Research; spl. adv. Aspen Inst. Bd. dirs. Work in Am., Inc., Common Cause, Inst. for World Order; vis. com. Harvard U.; mem. Council on Fgn. Relations; pres. Public Agenda Found.; commr. Sloan Commn.; trustee Birch-Wathen Sch. Author: The Changing Values on Campus, 1972; (with William Barrett) Ego and Instinct: Psychoanalysis and the Science of Man, 1969; The New Morality: A Profile of American Youth in the Seventies, 1974. Office: 575 Madison Ave New York NY 10021

YANKOVICH, JAMES MICHAEL, coll. dean; b. Richmond, Va., Mar. 15, 1935; s. Michael James and Edna Mae (Mann) Y.; B.A., U. Richmond, 1957; M.Ed., U. Va., 1961; Ed.D., U. Mich., 1971; m. Ann Page Richardson, Aug. 11, 1956; children—Kathy, Julie, Michael. Tchr., Henrico County, Va., 1958-60, guidance counselor, 1960-61; prin. Glen Echo Elementary Sch., 1961-62, Varina Elementary Sch., 1962-64, Johnson Elementary Sch., Charlottesville, Va., 1964-65; asst. supt. schs., Charlottesville, 1965-66; asst. prof. U. Mich., Flint, 1968-71, asso. prof., 1971-74, dean acad. affairs, 1971-75; dean Sch. Edn., Coll. of William and Mary, Williamsburg, Va., 1975—. Bd. dirs. Flint Inst. Music, Center for Excellence. C.S. Mott leadership fellow, 1966-67. Mem. Phi Delta Kappa. Home: 202 Sheffield Rd Williamsburg VA 23185

YANKWICH, PETER EWALD, chemist, educator; b. Los Angeles, Oct. 20, 1923; s. Leon Rene and Helen (Werner) Y.; B.S., U. Calif., Berkeley, 1943, Ph.D., 1945; m. Elizabeth Pope Ingram, July 14, 1945; children—Alexandra Helen Yankwich Capps, Leon Rene II, Richard Ingram. Mem. sci. staff Radiation Lab., U. Calif., Berkeley, 1944-48, faculty, 1947-48; mem. faculty U. Ill. at Urbana, 1948—, prof. chemistry, 1957—, head div. phys. chemistry, 1962-67, v.p. acad. affairs, 1977—. Mem. Adv. Council on Coll. Chemistry, 1961-68. NSF Sr. Postdoctoral fellow, 1960-61. Mem. Urbana Bd. Edn., 1958-73. Fellow Am. Phys. Soc., A.A.A.S.; mem. Am. Chem. Soc. (chmn. phys. chemistry div. 1971-72, chem. edn. planning and coordinating com. 1974-77, chmn. edn. commn. 1977—), Phi Beta Kappa, Sigma Xi. Home: 604 W Washington St Urbana IL 61801

YANNELLO, JUDITH ANN, judge; b. Buffalo, Mar. 27, 1943; d. Guy Raymond and Grace Alberta (Barone) Y.; B.A., Barnard Coll., 1964; J.D., Cornell U., 1967. Admitted to N.Y. bar, 1967, D.C. bar, 1970, U.S. Supreme Ct., 1971; law clk. U.S. Ct. Claims, Washington, 1967-68; trial atty. civil div. Dept. Justice, Washington, 1968-73; asso. firm Hudson, Creyke, Koehler & Tacke, Washington, 1973-76; adminstrv. judge Armed Services Bd. Contract Appeals, Washington, 1976-77; trial judge U.S. Ct. Claims, Washington, 1977—; speaker, lectr. Recipient Disting. Service award Fed. Bar Assn., 1975; Meritorious Service award Dept. Justice, 1972. Mem. Am. Bar Assn., Fed. Bar Assn. (chmn. Ct. Claims com. 1974-76), D.C. Bar Assn. (cert. of appreciation 1976), N.Y. State Bar Assn., D.C. Bar, Exec. Women in Govt. Club: Zonta. Contbr. articles to profl. jours.; co-editor, contbg. author: Manual for Practice in U.S. Court of Claims, 1976. Office: 717 Madison Pl NW Washington DC 20005

YANNEY, MICHAEL B., banker; b. Kearney, Nebr., Dec. 3, 1933; s. Elias K. and Mary H. (Abraham) Y.; B.A., Kearney State Tchrs. Coll., 1955; student Am. Inst. Banking, 1958, U. Wis., 1962; m. Gail Walling; 1 dau., Mary Elizabeth. With 1st Nat. Bank of Kearney, 1952-56, Central Bank & Trust Co., Denver, 1958-61; exec. v.p. Omaha Nat. Corp. (Nebr.), 1961-77; pres. Agr. Corp. Am.; dir. Realbanc, Agco, Valley State Bank, Rock Valley, Iowa, Security Bank, Williamsburg, Iowa, Clarkson Bank (Nebr.). Mem. nat. adv. council Small Bus. Adminstrn. Chmn. Met. Riverfront Com.; pres. Crech Home for Children, 1970, dir., 1971; dir. Mid-Am. Youth Council; mem. finance adv. team League Women Voters; pres. Jr. Achievement, 1967, 68, United Community Services, 1970, 71. Trustee Clarkson Hosp., Brownell Talbot Sch. Served with AUS, 1956-58. Named distinguished young man of year Omaha Jr. C. of C., 1968. Mem. Joslyn Arts Soc. (hon. trustee), Alpha Tau Omega, Retail Mchts. Omaha. Club: Omaha. Home: 6520 Rainwood Rd Omaha NE 68152 Office: Omaha Bldg 17th and Farnam Sts Omaha NE 68102

YANNUZZI, WILLIAM A(NTHONY), conductor; b. Balt., July 30, 1934; s. Carmine and Maria Rosaria (Capparelli) Y.; A.B. cum laude, Johns Hopkins U., 1957, M.A., 1958; M.A., St. Johns Coll., Santa Fe, 1969. Tchr. French, Balt. City Coll., 1958-66; asst. condr. Balt. Opera Co., Inc., 1962-73, music dir., 1973—; mem. faculty Peabody Conservatory, 1977—. Served with U.S. Army, 1951-54. Mem. Phi Beta Kappa. Office: 40 W Chase St Baltimore MD 21201. *All artistic activity must have as its sole consideration the work of art itself. The good performing artist never uses a piece of music as a vehicle for self-display, but makes it his whole objective to discover and express the contents which the composer put into the work. Any performances directed to other ends are not merely bad performances; they are in fact acts of disrespect for and betrayal of greatness.*

YANOFF, MYRON, ophthalmologist; b. Phila., Dec. 21, 1936; s. Jacob and Lillial S. (Fishman) Y.; A.B., U. Pa., 1957; M.D., 1961; m. Shelly D. Kovnat, June 7, 1957; children—Steven L., David A., Joanne M. Prof. ophthalmology U. Pa. Med. Sch., William F. Norris and George E. de Schwinitz prof. ophthalmology, chmn. dept.; dir. Scheie Eye Inst., Phila. Served to maj. M.C., USAR. Mem. Am. Ophthalmologic Soc., Verhoeff Soc., Am. Acad. Ophthalmology. Democrat. Jewish. Author: Ocular Histology, Ocular Pathology; also articles. Office: 51 N 39th St Philadelphia PA 19104*

YANOFSKY, CHARLES, educator; b. N.Y.C., Apr. 17, 1925; s. Frank and Jennie (Kopatz) Y.; B.S., Coll. City N.Y., 1948; M.S., Yale, 1950, Ph.D., 1951; m. Carol Cohen, June 19, 1949; children—Stephen David, Robert Howard, Martin Fred. Research Asst. Yale, 1951-54; asst. prof. microbiology Western Res. U. Med. Sch., 1954-57; mem. faculty Stanford, 1958—, prof. biology, 1961—; career investigator Am. Heart Assn., 1969—. Served with AUS, 1944-46. Recipient Lederle Med. Faculty award, 1957, Eli Lilly award bacteriology, 1959, U.S. Steel Co. award molecular biology, 1964, Howard Taylor Ricketts award U. Chgo., 1966, Albert and Mary Lasker award, 1971; Townsend Harris medal Coll. City N.Y., 1973; Louisa Gross Horwitz prize in biology and biochemistry Columbia U., 1976. Mem. Nat. Acad. Scis. (Microbiology award 1972), Am. Acad. Arts and Scis., Genetics Soc. Am. (pres. 1969). Home: 725 Mayfield Ave Stanford CA 94305

YANTIS, JOHN MARSHALL, wholesale trade exec.; b. Fort Smith, Ark., Aug. 1, 1918; s. Marshall L. and Eva (Vick) Y.; B.S. in Mech. Engring., U. Mich., 1934; m. Shar L. Southall, May 7, 1976; children—Sarah Welch, Marsahll L., John Marshall, Julia Ann. Supr. of stores Automotive, Inc., Fort Smith, 1939-40; project engr. Consol. Aircraft Co., San Diego, 1940-41; chief armament engr. Fort Motor Co., Willow Run, Mich., 1941-45, mem. 1st research dept., 1945; v.p., gen. mgr. Automotive, Inc., Fort Smith, 1946-57; pres., gen. mgr. Motive Parts Warehouse, Inc., Ft. Smith, 1958-69; pres., chmn. bd. Mid-America Industries, Inc., Fort Smith, 1969—; chmn. bd. Wortz Co., 1972—; dir. Mchts. Nat. Bank, Arkansas Best Corp. Pres., Fort Smith Community Chest, 1951-52, Fort Smith United Fund, 1964-65, campaign chmn., 1968; chmn. Sebastian County (Ark.) ARC, 1951-52; chmn. Urban Renewal Authority Ft. Smith, 1973-76; pres. Fort Smith Sch. Bd., 1964-65; bd. dirs. Car Care Council, 1976-77. Mem. Soc. Automotive Engrs., Automotive Acad., Automotive Warehouse Distbr. Assn. (dir. 1969-75, named Automotive Man of Yr. 1974), Automotive Warehouse Distbrs. Assn. (1st v.p. 1972-74), Automotive Info. Council (chmn. 1978-79, dir. 1972—), Nat. Standard Parts Assn. (dir. 1955-59, chmn. com. market research 1951-55), Phi Delta Theta. Episcopalian. Clubs: Thunderbird Country, Rancho Mirage (Calif.); Garden of the Gods (Colorado Springs); Hardscrabble Country, Fianna Hills Country, Town (Fort Smith). Home: 3 Berry Hill St Fort Smith AR 72903 also 70-923 Fairway Dr Rancho Mirage CA 92270 Office: 900 Rogers Bldg Fort Smith AR 72901

YANTIS, PHILLIP ALEXANDER, educator; b. Portland, Ore., Mar. 30, 1928; s. George Alexander and Katharine Grace (Fisher) Y.; B.A., U. Wash., 1950; M.A., U. Mich., 1952, Ph.D., 1955; m. Elna Margaret Mattila, June 11, 1954; children—Steven George, Michael John, Jeffrey Scott. Research asso. physiol. acoustics U. Mich. at Ann Arbor, 1955-58, instr. otolaryngology, 1957-60; asst. prof. audiology Case Western Res. U., Cleve., 1960-63, asso. prof., 1963-65; dir. clin. audiology Cleve. Hearing and Speech Center, 1960-65; asso. prof. audiology U. Wash., Seattle, 1965-69, prof., 1969—, dir. program in speech pathology and audiology, dept. speech, 1968-74. Bd. dirs. Am. Bd. Examiners in Speech Pathology and Audiology, 1968-70, 78—, Deafness Speech and Hearing Publs., Inc., 1978—; trustee Am. Speech and Hearing Found., 1969-71, 74-75. Served with AUS, 1950-51. Fellow Am. Speech and Hearing Assn. (v.p. planning 1969-71, pres.-elect 1974, pres. 1975); mem. Acad. Rehabilitative Audiology, Acoustical Soc. Am., Am. Auditory Soc., Internat. Soc. Audiology, Wash. Speech and Hearing Assn. Asst. editor for hearing Deafness, Speech and Hearing Abstracts, 1960-64; asso. editor for hearing Jour. Speech and Hearing Research, 1966-69; editorial bd. Archives of Otolaryngology, 1979—. Home: 1434 NW 204th Pl Seattle WA 98177 Office: Speech and Hearing Clinic U Wash Seattle WA 98195

YANTIS, RICHARD WILLIAM, diversified co. exec.; b. Tipp City, Ohio, Nov. 19, 1923; s. Guy Everett and Frances (Barnhart) Y.; student U. Dayton, 194142; m. Marjorie Louise Gray, May 11, 1943; children—Cheryl Ann, Sandra Lee, Susan Elizabeth. Regional mgr. Gen. Finance Corp., Chgo., 1946-53; v.p. Fruehauf Trailer Finance Co., Detroit, 1953-56; pres. Delta Acceptance Corp., Ltd., London, Ont., Can., 1956-64; exec. v.p., dir. Avco Corp., Greenwich, Conn., 1965-73; pres. Avco Community Developers, Inc., La Jolla, Cal., 1973-75, cons., 1975—. Served with USNR, 1941-45. Mason (Shriner). Clubs: Seven Lakes Country, Desert Island Country, San Diego Yacht; Balboa Bay (Newport, Calif.); London, London Hunt and Country. Home: 331 Westlake Terr Palm Springs CA 92262

YAPHE, WILFRED, microbiologist; b. Lachine, Que., Can., July 9, 1921; s. Sam and Rachel Yaphe; B.Sc., McGill U., Montreal, Que., 1949, Ph.D., 1952; m. Ruth Dorfman, Jan. 16, 1946; children—Arona, John, Anna. Research officer Atlantic Regional Lab., Nat. Research Council Can., Halifax, N.S., 1952-66; mem. faculty McGill U., 1966—, prof. microbiology, 1971—. Served with RCAF, 1942-45. Mem. Can. Soc. Microbiology, Am. Soc. Microbiology, Phycological Soc. Author research papers in field. Address: 3775 University St Montreal PQ H3A 2B4 Canada

YAQUB, ADIL MOHAMED, educator; b. Nablus, Jordan, Jan. 19, 1928; s. Mohamed H. and Fawzieh A. (Gazala) Y.; came to U.S., 1947, naturalized, 1954; A.B., U. Calif., Berkeley, 1950, M.A., 1951, Ph.D., 1955; m. Nancy Shiddell, Apr. 20, 1951; children—Charles, Hanan. Instr., Purdue U., 1955-57, asst. prof., 1957-60; asso. prof. math. U. Calif., Santa Barbara, 1960-67, prof., 1967—. Purdue U. grantee, 1957, NSF grantees, 1959-61, 65-68. Mem. Am. Math. Soc., Math. Assn. Am., Sigma Xi, Pi Mu Epsilon. Author: Introduction to Linear and Abstract Algebra, 1971; Calculus with Applications, 1971. Contbr. research articles to profl. math. jours. Home: 602 Litchfield Ln Santa Barbara CA 93109

YARBOROUGH, RALPH WEBSTER, lawyer, former U.S. senator; b. Chandler, Tex., June 8, 1903; s. Charles Richard and Nannie Jane (Spear) Y.; student U.S. Mil. Acad., 1 year, Sam Houston State Tchrs. U.; LL.B., U. Tex., 1927; L.H.D., Lincoln Coll., 1965; LL.D., St. Edward's U., 1971; m. Opal Catherine Warren, June 30, 1928; 1 son, Richard Warren. Tchr. pub. schs. Tex., 3 yrs.; admitted to Tex. bar, 1927; practiced law, El Paso, 1927-31; asst. atty. gen., Tex., 1931-34; lectr. law U. Tex., 1935; judge 53d Jud. Dist. of Tex., 1936-41, presiding judge 3d Adminstrv. Jud. Dist., 3 yrs.; U.S. senator from Tex., 1957-71. Asso. prof. polit. sci. U. Tex. at Arlington, 1975. Mem. U.S. Congress delegation 51st Inter-Parliamentary Union Conf., Brasilia, Brazil, 1962, Dublin, Ireland, 1965, Canberra, Australia, 1966, Teheran, Iran, 1966, Palma de Mallorca, Spain, 1967, Lima, Peru, 1968, Vienna Austria, 1969, Delhi, India, 1969, The Hague, Netherlands, 1970; mem. Tex. Constl. Revision Commn., 1973-74. Bd. dirs. Lower Colo. River Authority, 1935-36; State Bd. Law Examiners, 1947-51; past mem. Abraham Lincoln Sesquicentennial Commn.; past mem. exec. bd. Nat. Civil War Centennial Commn. Past mem. bd. dirs. Gallaudet Coll. Hon. fellow Postgrad. Center Mental Health, N.Y., 1965. Served as lt. col. AUS, 1943-46. Mem. Am., El Paso, Travis County (past pres.) bar assns., Am. Law Inst., State Bar Tex. (past dir.), V.F.W., Am. Legion, Order of Coif, Acacia, Phi Delta Phi. Democrat. Baptist. Mason (Shriner). Contbr. to Lincoln for the Ages, 1964, Texas Avenue at Main Street, 1964. Author: Frank Dobie; Man and Friend, 1967; (foreword) Three Men in Texas, 1967, The Public Lands of Texas, 1972, Carrascolendas: Bilingual Education Through Television, 1974. Office: 721 Brown Bldg W 8th St and Colorado Austin TX 78701*

YARBOROUGH, RICHARD WARREN, govt. ofcl.; b. Austin, Tex., Oct. 20, 1931; s. Ralph Webster and Opal (Warren) Y.; B.A., U. Tex., Austin, 1953, LL.B., 1955; m. Ann Graham McJimsey, Mar. 17, 1956; children—Clare, Elizabeth. Admitted to Tex. bar, 1955, also U.S. Supreme Ct.; practiced in Austin, 1957-58; legislative asst., com. counsel U.S. Senate, 1958-67; commr. U.S. Indian Claims Commn., Washington, 1967-78; chmn. U.S. Fgn. Claims Settlement Commn., 1978—. Served with AUS, 1955-57. Mem. State Bar Tex., Am. Bar Assn., Phi Delta Phi, Kappa Alpha. Democrat. Editor: Map of Indian Land Areas Judicially Established, 1978. Home: 5140 N 37th St Arlington VA 22207 Office: 1111 20th St NW Washington DC 20579

YARBOROUGH, WILLIAM CALEB, profl. stock car race driver; b. Timmonsville, S.C., Mar. 27, 1939. Winner: Atlanta 500, 1967, 68, 74, Cam 2 Motor Oil 400, 1977, Capital City 400, 1976, Carolina 500, 1975, Daytona 500, 1968, 77. Mason-Dixon 500, 1969, Nat. 500, 1973, So. 500, 1968, 73, 74, 78, Va. 500, 1974, 77, Wilkes 400, 1974, Winston Western 500, 1974, many others. Named Grand Nat. Champion, Nat. Assn. Stock Car Auto Racing, 1976. Office: care Nat Assn Stock Car Auto Racing 1801 Volusia Ave Daytona Beach FL 32015

YARBOROUGH, WILLIAM PELHAM, ret. army officer, writer, lectr., cons.; b. Seattle, May 12, 1912; s. Leroy W. and Addessia (Hooker) Y.; B.S., U.S. Mil. Acad., 1936; grad. Parachute Sch., 1941, Command and Gen. Staff Coll., 1944, Brit. Staff Coll., 1950, Army War Coll., 1953; m. Norma Mae Tuttle, Dec. 26, 1936; children—Norma Kay (dec.), William Lee, Patricia Mae. Commd. 2d lt. U.S. Army, 1936, advanced through grades to lt. gen., 1968; various assignments U.S., Philippines and ETO, 1936-42; exec. officer Paratroop Task Force, N. Africa, 1942; comdr. 2d Bn., 504th Par. Inf. Regt., 82d Airborne Div., Sicily invasion, 1943; comdr. 509th Parachute Inf., Italy and France, 1943-44; comdg. officer 473 Inf., Italy, 1945; provost marshal 15th Army Group, ETO, 1945, Vienna Area Command and U.S. Forces, Austria, 1945-47; operations officer, gen. staff Joint Mil. Assistance Adv. Group, London, Eng., 1951-52; mem. faculty Army War Coll., 1953-56, 57; dep. chief Mil. Assistance and Adv. Group, Cambodia, 1956-57; comdg. officer 66th CIC Group, Stuttgart, Germany, 1958-60, 66th M.I. Group, Stuttgart, 1960, comdg. gen. USA Spl. Warfare Center, also comdt. U.S. Army Spl. Warfare Sch., Ft. Bragg, 1961-65; sr. mem. UN Command Mil. Armistice Commn., Korea, 1965; asst. dep. chief staff DCSOPS for spl. operations Dept. Army, Washington, chmn. U.S. delegation Inter-Am. Def. Bd., Joint Brazil U.S. Def. Commn., Joint Mexican-U.S. Def. Commn.; Army mem. U.S. sect. permanent Joint Bd. on Def., Can.-U.S. Def. Commn., Washington, 1965; asst. chief of staff intelligence Dept. Army Washington, 1966-68; comdg. gen. I Corps Group, Korea, 1968-69; chief staff, also dep. comdr.-in-chief U.S. Army, Pacific, Hawaii, 1969-71, ret., 1971. Bd. dirs. Humanities Found., N.C. State U.; mem. citizens adv. group Comprehensive Cancer Center, Duke U. Fellow Company Mil. Historians; mem. Am. African Affairs Assn. (chmn.), Assn. Former Intelligence Officers, Assn. U.S. Army, Assn. Grad. U.S. Mil. Acad., Ends of Earth Soc. Clubs: Masons, Kiwanis, Explorers. William P. Yarborough collection papers and artifacts donated to Mugar Meml. Libraries, Boston U. Author: Trial in Africa, 1976. Home: 160 Hillside Rd Southern Pines NC 28387

YARBROUGH, JAMES RICHARD, hotel exec.; b. Salisbury, N.C., Nov. 27, 1927; s. James Grey and Willie (Alley) Y.; student Catawba Coll., 1946-47; B.S. in Architecture, Clenson U., 1952; m. Faye Elizabeth Walser, Dec. 31, 1948; children—James Richard, Marianne, David Walser. Gen. mgr. Gen. Shelby Hotel, Bristol, Va., 1959, William Byrd Motor Hotel, Richmond, Va., 1960, Golden Triangle Motor Hotel, Norfolk, Va., 1964, Three Chefs Corp., Norfolk, St. John's Inn, Myrtle Beach, S.C., 1967; gen. mgr. Capitol Hill Hotel, Washington; now dir. operations Gal-Tex Hotel Corp., Washington. Mem. Hotel Assn. Washington (treas), Food Service Execs. Assn., Internat. Platform Assn. Methodist. Elk, Rotarian. Club: Shenandoah Valley Golf. Home: 4125 Mt Olney Ln Olney MD 20832 Office: 515 15th St NW Washington DC 20004

YARD, RIX NELSON, athletic dir.; b. Ocean County, N.J., July 1, 1917; s. George Rix and Lena (Nelson) Y.; B.S., U. Pa., 1941, M.S., 1947, Ed.D., 1956; m. Adra Gehrett, Sept. 12, 1941; children—Rix Nelson, Constance. Tchr., Swissvale (Pa.) High Sch., 1946; instr., asst. football coach, head basketball coach Denison U., 1947-49, phys. edn., chmn. dept. dir. athletics, also lacrosse coach, 1953-63; asst. football coach U. Pa., 1949-53; dir. athletics Tulane U., 1963-76, prof. phys. edn., 1968—, dir. club and intramural sports, 1976—, also adminstr. phys. edn. major program. Pres., New Orleans Football Hall of Fame, 1965-76. Vice pres. Granville (Ohio) Bd. Edn., 1961-63; asst. fire chief Granville Vol. Fire Co., 1958-63; mem. Granville Zoning Com., 1961. Bd. dirs. New Orleans chpt. A.R.C. Served with USNR, 1941-46; Res. Named Nat. Lacrosse Coach of Year, 1963. Mem. Nat. Collegiate Athletic Assn. (chmn. TV com. 1958, 60; rep. to Sugar Bowl 1964—, chmn. ins. com. 1971-76, chmn. acad. and testing requirements com.), Nat. Assn. Coll. Athletic Dirs. (exec. com.), Navy League (dir. New Orleans chpt.). Club: New Orleans Quarterback (dir. 1967—). Home: 4820 Page Dr Metairie LA 70003 Office: 6401 Willow St New Orleans LA 70118

YARDLEY, JOHN FINLEY, aerospace engr., govt. ofcl.; b. St. Louis, Feb. 1, 1925; s. Finley Abna and Johnnie (Patterson) Y.; B.S., Iowa State Coll., 1944; M.S., Washington U., St. Louis, 1950; m. Phyllis Steele, July 25, 1946; children—Kathryn, Robert, Mary, Elizabeth, Susan. Structral and aero. engr. McDonnell Aircraft Corp., St. Louis, 1946-55, chief strength engr., 1956-57, project engr. Mercury spacecraft design, 1958-60, launch operations mgr. Mercury and Gemini spacecraft, Cape Canaveral, Fla., 1960-64, Gemini tech. dir., 1964-67; v.p., dep. gen. mgr. Eastern div. McDonnell Douglas Astronautics, 1968-72, v.p., gen. mgr., 1973-74; asso. adminstr. for manned space flight NASA, Washington, 1974—. Served to ensign with USNR, 1943-46. Recipient Achievement award St. Louis sect. Inst. Aerospace Scis., 1961; John J. Montgomery award, 1963; Pub. Service award NASA, 1963, 66, profl. achievement citation Iowa State Coll., 1970; Spirit of St. Louis medal, 1973; Alumni citation Washington U., 1975; Distinguished Achievement citation Iowa State U., 1976. Fellow Am. Inst. Aeros. and Astronautics, Am. Astronautical Soc. (Space Flight award 1978); mem. Nat. Acad. Engring., Tau Beta Pi, Phi Kappa Phi, Phi Eta Sigma, Phi Mu Epsilon. Presbyn. Office: NASA 600 Independence Ave Washington DC 20003

YARDLEY, JOHN HOWARD, pathologist, educator; b. Columbia, S.C., June 7, 1926; s. Sherborne Dougherty and Elise Alexander (Kirkland) Y.; A.B., Birmingham-So. Coll., 1949; M.D., Johns Hopkins, 1953; m. Eritha von der Goltz, Dec. 27, 1952; children—William Sherborne, Madeleine Joy, Elizabeth Anne. Intern Vanderbilt U. Hosp., 1953-54; resident in pathology Johns Hopkins Hosp., 1954-58, pathologist, 1958—; mem. faculty Johns Hopkins Med. Sch., 1955—, prof. pathology, 1972—; asso. dean acad. affairs, 1977—. Served with USNR, 1944-46. Recipient Research Career Devel. award USPHS, 1963-69; grantee USPHS, U.S. Army.

Diplomate Am. Bd. Pathology. Mem. Am. Assn. Pathologists, Am. Soc. Exptl. Pathology, Am. Gastroenterol. Assn., Phi Beta Kappa, Omicron Delta Kappa. Club: Peripatetic. Author, editor in field. Home: 505 Edgevale Rd Baltimore MD 21210 Office: Dept Pathology Johns Hopkins Hosp Baltimore MD 21205

YARDLEY, JONATHAN, journalist; b. Pitts., Oct. 27, 1939; s. William Woolsey and Helen M. (Gregory) Y.; A.B., U. N.C., Chapel Hill, 1961; m. Susan L. Hartt, Mar. 23, 1975; children—James Barrett, William W. II. Writer, N.Y. Times, 1961-64; editorial writer, book editor Greensboro (N.C.) Daily News, 1964-74; book editor Miami (Fla.) Herald, 1974-78, Washington Star, 1978—. Nieman fellow in journalism Harvard U., 1968-69. Democrat. Episcopalian. Author: Ring: A Biography of Ring Lardner, 1977; contbg. editor Sports Illustrated, 1975—. Home: 223 Hawthorne Rd Baltimore MD 21210 Office: Washington Star 225 Virginia Ave SE Washington DC 20061

YARDUMIAN, RICHARD, composer; b. Phila., Apr. 5, 1917; s. Haig Y. and Lucia (Atamian) Y.; student piano with George F. Boyle, conducting with Pierre Monteaux, harmony and counterpoint with William F. Happich, H. Alexander Matthews; D. Sacred Music, Maryville Coll., 1972; Mus.D. (hon.), Widener Coll., 1978; m. Ruth Elsie Seckelmann, Jan. 9, 1937; children—Vahaan, Vartan (dec.), Miryam, Aram (dec.), Sarah (dec.), Nishan, Rebekah, Rachel, Esther Marie, Dara, Anahid, Mira-Estelle, Vera Renata. Tchr. advanced piano; pres. bd. dirs. The Lord's New Ch., Bryn Athyn, Pa., music dir., 1939—. Bd. dirs. Phila. Chamber Orch.; co-founder, bd. dirs. Chamber Symphony of Phila., 1965; trustee Philharmonia Orch.; trustee, v.p. Grand Teton Music Festival. Served with inf. U.S. Army, World War II. Recipient Edward B. Benjamin restful music award, 1958; Eugene Ormandy Commn. award, 1961; Composer award Lancaster Symphony, 1975; Gold medal award for excellence Armenian Bicentennial Commemoration Com., 1976. ASCAP, Phila. Mus. Soc., Mus. Fund Soc. Composer: Three Preludes for Piano, 1936, 39, 44; Armenian Suite, 1937; Symphonic Suite, 1939; Three Pictographs for Orch., 1941; Danse for Piano, 1942; Desolate City, 1944; Prelude and Chorale for Piano, 1944; Chromatic Sonata for Piano, 1946; Psalm 130, 1947; Monologue for Solo Violin, 1947; Violin Concerto, 1949, middle movement, 1960; Epigram: William M. Kincaid for flute and strings (commd. by William Kincaid), 1951; String Quartet No. 1 (commd. by Phila. String Quartet), 1955; Cantus Animae et Cordis for string orch., 1955; Passacaglia, Recitatives & Fugue for piano and orch. (commd. for Rudolf Firkusny), 1957; Chorale-Prelude on Vani Sancte Spiritus, for chamber orchestra, 1958; Symphony No. 1 (commd. Eugene Ormandy), 1961; Create in Me (anthem commd. Princeton Theol. Sem. for Sesquicentennial), 1962; Symphony No. 2 (Psalms for contralto and orch.), 1964; Magnificat for Women's Voices (commd. by Hollins Coll.), 1965; Come, Creator Spirit (mass in English, commd. Fordham U. for 125th Anniversary), 1966; Abraham (ortatorio commd. by Maryville Coll. for Sesquicentennial), 1971; Chorales (composed for The Lord's New Ch.), 1940-77; Four Chorale-Preludes for Organ, 1977; Two Chorale-Preludes for Orchestra: Jesu, meine Freude, Nun komm der Heiden Heiland, 1978; To Mary in Heaven (poem by Robert Burns), Voice and Piano, Voice and Orchestra, 1979; recordings for Columbia, RCA, EMI, HNH. Contbr. to Music Jour. Home: Cold Spring Farm Bryn Athyn PA 19009

YARGER, ORVAL FRANCIS, ret. govt. ofcl.; b. Paris, Ill., Oct. 12, 1908; s. Boyd Lee and Mary (Lanigan) Y.; B.Ed., Ill. State U., 1932; postgrad. U. Ill., 1933-34; M.B.A., Northwestern U., 1935; m. Rosie Jepsen Rasmussen, Aug. 13, 1936; children—Orval Jens, Williams Carl. Partner, finance mgr. The Co-Op Bookstore, Normal, Ill., 1933—; instr. bus. adminstrn. Central Y Coll., Chgo., 1936-39; spl. agt. FBI, Washington, 1941-49; intelligence officer CIA, various fgn. locations, 1950-54; dir. inspections, insp. in charge AID, Dept. State, various U.S., fgn. locations, from 1954, also dir. comml. fishing and transport Europe, Africa, Cobrecaf Corp., Concarneau, France, 1961—; partner with Andre Auger & Consorts, LaRochelle, France, 1960—. Mem. Ex-FBI Agts. Soc. Home: 7 Reynolds Ct Normal IL 61761 Office: 319 North St Normal IL 61761

YARINGTON, CHARLES THOMAS, JR., surgeon, educator; b. Sayre, Pa., Apr. 26, 1934; s. C.T. and Florence (Hutchinson) Y.; grad. Hill Sch., 1952; A.B., Princeton, 1956; M.D., Hahnemann Med. Coll., 1960; grad. Army Command and Gen. Staff Coll., 1969, Air War Coll., 1973, Indsl. Coll. Armed Forces, 1974; m. Barbara Taylor Johnson, Sept. 28, 1963; children—Leslie Anne, Jennifer Lynne, Barbara Jane. Intern Rochester (N.Y.) Gen. Hosp., 1960-61; resident Dartmouth Hosp., 1961-62, U. Rochester Strong Meml. Hosp., 1962-65; instr. otolaryngology U. Rochester Sch. Medicine, 1962-65; asst. prof. surgery W.Va. U. Sch. Medicine, 1967-68; asso. prof., chmn. dept. otorhinolarygology U. Nebr. Med. Center, 1968-69, prof., chmn. dept. otorhinolarygology, 1969-74; clin. prof. otolaryngology U. Wash., Seattle, 1974—; partner Mason Clinic, Seattle; cons. Surg. Gen. U.S. Air Force; mem. Air Force Res. Med. Mgmt. Com. Med. adviser Nat. Ski Patrol System; bd. dirs. Douglas-Sarpy County Cancer Soc., 1968-74; bd. dirs., exec. com. Virginia Mason Research Center, Seattle, 1977—; mem. extramural council Fred Hutchinson Cancer Center, Seattle. Served to maj., M.C., AUS, 1965-67; brig. gen. USAF Res. Decorated Army, Air Force commendation medals, Meritorious Service medal. Fellow A.C.S., Am. Coll. Chest Physicians (standing com.), Royal Soc. Medicine, Soc. Head and Neck Surgery, Am. Acad. Otolaryngology (Barraquer Meml. award 1968, mem. standing com., Honor award 1974), Am. Acad. Facial Plastic and Reconstructive Surgery (chmn. ethics com., pub. relations coms., mem. constn., by laws com.; mem. Am. Broncho-Esophagological Assn. (mem. standing com.), Pacific Coast Soc. Ophthalmology and Otolaryngology (council), Soc. Med. Consultants to Armed Forces, Soc. Univ. Otolaryngolists (com. chmn. 1972-74), N.W. Acad. Head and Neck Surgery, Am. Soc. Otology, Rhinology and Laryngology, Air Force Assn. (state officer), Res. Officers Assn. (v.p. Seattle chpt., nat. officer, chmn. standing com.), Pan-Pacific Surg. Assn., Am. Philatelic Soc., AMA, Pacific Handicap Racing Fleet, SAR, Sigma Xi. Clubs: Mercerwood Shore, Eastside Track (pres. 1976-78), Sloop Tavern Yacht, Princeton Quadrangle. Author books and articles in field. Mem. editorial bd. ORL Digest, ORL Jour. Continuing Edn., ORL Clinics N. Am. Office: Mason Clinic 1100 9th Ave Seattle WA 98101

YARIV, AMNON, scientist, educator; b. Tel Aviv, Israel, Apr. 13, 1930; s. Shraga and Henya (Davidson) Y.; came to U.S., 1951, naturalized, 1964; B.S., U. Calif. at Berkeley, 1954, M.S., 1956, Ph.D., 1958; m. Frances Pokras, Apr. 10, 1972; children—Elizabeth, Dana, Gabriela. Mem. tech. staff Bell Telephone Labs., 1959-63; dir. laser research Watkins-Johnson Co., 1963-64; mem. faculty Calif. Inst. Tech., 1964—, prof. elec. engring. and applied physics, 1966—; cons. in field. Served with Israeli Army, 1948-50. Fellow I.E.E.E., Am. Optical Soc.; mem. Am. Phys. Soc., Nat. Acad. Engring. Author: Quantum Electronics, 1967, 75; Introduction to Optical Electronics, 1971, 77. Home: 2257 Homet Rd San Marino CA 91108 Office: 1201 California Ave Pasadena CA 91125

YARMOLINSKY, ADAM, lawyer, govt. ofcl.; b. N.Y.C.,, Nov. 17, 1922; s. Avrahm and Babette (Deutsch) Y.; A.B., Harvard, 1943; LL.B., Yale, 1948; children—Sarah Franklin, Tobias, Benjamin Levi, Matthew Jonas. Law clk. to Judge C.E. Clark, U.S. Ct. Appeals, 2d Circuit, 1948-49; asso. Root, Ballantine, Harlan, Bushby & Palmer, N.Y.C., 1949-50; law clk. Justice Stanley Reed, U.S. Supreme Ct., 1950-51; asso. Cleary, Gottlieb, Friendly & Ball, Washington, 1951-55; dir. Washington office Fund for the Republic, Inc., 1955-56, sec., 1956-57; pub. affairs editor Doubleday & Co., Inc., 1957-59; 59; cons. pvt. founds., 1959-61; spl. asst. sec. of def., 1961-64; dep. dir. Pres.'s. Anti-Poverty Task Force, 1964; chief U.S. Emergency Relief Mission to Dominican Republic, 1965; prin. dep. asst. sec. def. for internat. security affairs, 1965-66; prof. law Law Sch., Harvard, 1966-72, mem. inst. politics John F. Kennedy Sch. Govt., 1966-72; on leave as chief exec. officer Welfare Island Devel. Corp., 1971-72; Ralph Waldo Emerson univ. prof. U. Mass., 1972—, on leave, 1977—; counselor U.S. Arms Control and Disarmament Agy., 1977-79; of counsel firm Kominers, Fort, Schlefer & Boyer, Washington, 1979—; lectr. Am. U. Law Sch. 1951-56, Yale Law Sch., 1958-59; cons. Office Tech. Assessment, 1974-77, U.S. Arms Control and Disarmament Agy., 1979—. Mem. gov.'s adv. council Mass. Comprehensive Health Planning Agy., 1972-76; nat. adv. com. Inst. for Research on Poverty, 1972-77. Trustee Robert F. Kennedy Meml., Vera Inst. Justice, New Directions, 1976-77; adv. bd. Fels Center of Govt., U. Pa.; bd. dirs. Mass. Commn. Children and Youth, 1976-77. Served with USAAF, 1943-46. Recipient Distinguished Pub. Service medal Dept. Def., 1966. Fellow Am. Acad. Arts and Scis.; mem. Am. Bar Assn., Assn. Bar City N.Y., Am. Law Inst., Hudson Inst., Internat. Inst. Strategic Studies, Center for Inter-Am. Relations, Inst. Medicine of Nat. Acad. Scis. (council 1970-77, com. on human rights 1978), Council Fgn. Relations. Clubs: Coffee House, Century Assn. (N.Y.C.); St. Botolph (Boston); Federal City (Washington). Author: Recognition of Excellence, 1960; The Military Establishment, 1971; also articles in periodicals. Editor: Case Studies in Personnel Security, 1955. Spl. corr. The Economist (London), 1956-60. Office: Kominers Fort Schlefer and Boyer 1776 F St Washington DC 20006

YARMOLINSKY, MRS. AVRAHM. see Deutsch, Babette

YARMON, BETTY, writer, editor; b. Plainfield, N.J., Nov. 14; d. Samuel H. and Ruth Livingston Gross; student Los Angeles Jr. Coll; m. Morton Yarmon, Nov. 7, 1948. Cons., Abe Schrader Corp., Fair-Tex Mills, Genesco Dress Divs., Carillon Fashions; syndicated columnist United Features; mng. editor P.R. Aids Party Line. Mem. Fashion Group. Club: Atrium (N.Y.C.). Author: Getting the Most For Your Money When You Buy A Home. Address: 35 Sutton Pl New York NY 10022

YARNALL, D. ROBERT, JR., corp. exec.; b. Phila., Feb. 11, 1925; s. D. Robert and Elizabeth (Biddle) Y.; B.M.E., Cornell U., 1948; m. Rie Gabrielsen, June 24, 1954; children—Joan Biddle, Sara Gabrielsen, Kristina Garret. Mech. engr. Westinghouse Electric Co., Phila., 1947; dir. relief mission to Poland, Am. Friends Service Com., 1948-49; with Yarnall Waring Co. (name changed to Yarway Corp. 1965), Phila., 1949—, v.p., 1957-62, pres., chief exec., 1962—, chmn. bd., 1968—, also dir.; chief exec. Yarway Can., Ltd., Yarway N.V., Netherlands, Yarway, Ltd., London; dir. James G. Biddle Co., Plymouth Meeting, Pa., 1957-78, chmn. bd., 1976-78; dir. Fed. Res. Bank of Phila., 1965-72, dep. chmn., 1971-72; dir. S.K.F. Industries, Phila., Quaker Chem. Co., Phila., Phila. Sav. Fund Soc. Cons., UN Indsl. Devel. Orgn. mission to Indonesia, 1968; exec.-in-residence on faculty Centre d'Etudes Industrielles, Geneva, Switzerland, 1971-72. Bd. dirs. World Affairs Council, Pa., 1957-61, 64-68, 74—, chmn. bd., 1978—; trustee Internat. House, Phila., chmn., 1972-76; trustee Yarway Found., United Way; trustee St. John's Coll., Annapolis, Md., 1975—, vice chmn., 1978—; trustee Germantown Friends Sch., Phila., Phila. Mus. Art, 1978—, Greater Phila. Partnership, 1975—; dir. Pa. Environ. Council, 1976—. Served with Am. Field Service, Brit. Army, World War II. Mem. Mfrs. Assn. Phila. (dir. 1964-67), ASME, Instrument Soc. Am., Indsl. Relations Research Assn., Chief Execs. Forum. Mem. Soc. of Friends. Clubs: Union League, Phila. Cricket; Divotee Golf, Philadelphia. Home: 325 W Allens Ln Philadelphia PA 19119 Office: Yarway Corp Blue Bell PA 19422

YARNELL, JULES EDWIN, lawyer; b. N.Y.C., June 12, 1919; s. William and Dora (Rifkin) Y.; B.S., City Coll. N.Y., 1942; J.D. cum laude, St. John's U., Bklyn., 1949; LL.M. in Trade Regulation, N.Y. U., 1952; m. Marilyn Joan Oshman, Sept. 10, 1950; children—Marcia Dodson-Yarnell, William Scott, Ellen Sue. Admitted to N.Y. bar, 1949, U.S. Supreme Ct., 1959; investigator, analyst, trial atty. antitrust div. Justice Dept., 1940-42, 46-51; asso. firm Laporte & Meyers, N.Y.C., 1951-64, partner, 1964-76; spl. counsel on piracy Recording Industry Assn. Am., 1970—; lectr., cons. in field. Mem. zoning bd. appeals, Rye Town, N.Y., 1963-67. Mem. Republican County Com., Westchester County, N.Y., 1952-62; mem. Rep. City Com., Mt. Vernon, N.Y., 1952-62, exec. com., 1956-62; pres. Mt. Vernon Young Men's Rep. Club, 1959-61. Served to capt. USAAF, 1942-46; ETO. Mem. Am., Fed. (chmn. UN and vets. affairs com. 1953—; exec. council, 1972—; chmn. U.S. Supreme Ct. admissions com. 1959-60), N.Y. State bar assns., N.Y. County Lawyers Assn. (chmn. unauthorized practices subcom. of customs law com. 1965-70), Am. Trial Lawyers Assn., Interam. Copyright Inst. (chmn. com. on inter-Am. anti-piracy 1977—), Am. Legion (past post comdr.). Mason, Kentucky Col. Contbr. articles to legal jours. Home: 28 Meadowlark Rd Port Chester NY 10573 Office: 1 E 57th St New York NY 10022

YARNELL, KENNETH ARDELL, JR., consumer products co. exec.; b. Lock Haven, Pa., Mar. 16, 1943; s. Kenneth Ardell and Ellen Elizabeth (Bittner) Y.; B.S. magna cum laude, Pa. State U., 1965; postgrad. Harvard U. Grad. Sch. Arts and Scis., 1965; M.B.A. with distinction, Harvard U., 1969; m. Judith Ann Facciani, Sept. 10, 1966; children—Robert Christian, Christian. Vice pres. Donaldson, Lufkin & Jenrette, N.Y.C., 1971-75; v.p. mergers, acquisitions Am. Can Co., Greenwich, Conn., 1975-78, sr. v.p., treas., mem. mgmt. exec. com., 1978—, trustee Co. Pension Plan, 1978—; pres., dir. ACC Fin. Corp., Ltd., 1979—. Mem. Tau Beta Pi, Phi Eta Sigma, Sigma Xi. Club: Harvard of N.Y. Office: Am Can Co American Ln Greenwich CT 06830

YARNELL, RICHARD ASA, anthropologist; b. Boston, May 11, 1929; s. Sidney Howe and Floy Mae (Wilson) Y.; student Tex. A&M Coll., 1946-47; B.S., Duke U., 1950; M.A., U. N.Mex., 1958; Ph.D., U. Mich., 1963; m. Meredith Jean Black; children—Karen Lyn, Anne Chesson, William Sidney, Susan Lynn. Mem. faculty Emory U., Atlanta, 1962-71, asso. prof., 1967-71; mem. faculty U. N.C., Chapel Hill, 1971—, prof. anthropology, 1975—. Served with USAF, 1951-55. Mem. Am. Anthrop. Assn., Soc. for Am. Archaeology, So. Anthrop. Soc. (councilor 1974-77), Soc. for Econ. Botany, Am. Soc. for Ethnohistory, AAAS. Contbr. papers, reports to profl. jours., books. Office: Dept Anthropology 004A U NC Chapel Hill NC 27514

YARNELL, SAM IGOU, banker; b. Chattanooga, July 30, 1920; s. Sam I. and Nancy (Leeper) Y.; B.A., Vanderbilt U., 1940; grad. Sch. Banking Rutgers U., 1951; m. Ellen Cameron; children—Nancy Yarnell Houser, Sam Cameron, Ellen Leeper. With Am. Nat. Bank & Trust Co., Cattanooga, 1946—, pres., 1957-62, chmn., 1962—, also dir.; dir. Ancorp Bancshares, Inc., Fed. Res. Bank of Atlanta, Monumental Corp., Vol. State Life Ins. Co., Skyland Internat. Corp. Bd. dirs. United Fund of Greater Chattanooga, 1978—, campaign chmn., 1970, pres, 1975; trustee, mem. exec. com. Vanderbilt U. Bd. Trust; trustee Bright Sch., Chattanooga. Served with USAAF, World War II. Mem. Greater Chattanooga C. of C. (dir.), Am. Bankers Assn., Vanderbilt U. Alumni Assn. (pres. 1969-70, dir., 1965-68). Methodist. Clubs: Mountain City, Chattanooga Golf and Country. Office: Am Nat Bank & Trust Co 736 Market St Chattanooga TN 37402*

YAROSKY, HARVEY WILLIAM, lawyer; b. Montreal, Que., Can., Dec. 8, 1934; s. Harry and Rhoda (Kom) Y.; B.A. with honors, McGill U., 1955, B.C.L., 1961; postgrad. U. Paris, 1955-56; m. Elaine Sanft, July 3, 1962; children—Karen Anne, Lauren Julie. Admitted to Que. bar, 1962; mem. firm Yarosky, Fish, Zigman, Isaacs and Daviault and predecessor firms, Montreal, 1962—, now sr. partner; lectr. criminal law U. Montreal, 1970-71, U. Ottawa, 1970-72, McGill U., 1971—; mem. Govt. of Que. Adv. Council on Justice, 1974-79; counsel to fed. commn. of inquiry concerning Royal Can. Mounted Police, 1974-75; spl. counsel to provincial commn. of inquiry on union activities in the constrn. industry, 1974-75. Bd. govs. YM-YWHA Neighborhood House, 1965-69; mem. family services com. Baron de Hirsch Inst., 1967-69; bd. dirs. John Howard Soc. of Que., Inc., 1967-70; exec. asst. to chmn. spl. com. on hate propaganda Can. Dept. Justice, 1965; bd. govs. Portage Program for Drug Dependencies, Inc., 1975—; mem. Inst. Philippe Pinel de Montreal, 1975—. Mem. Bar of Montreal (chmn. com. on adminstrn. of criminal justice, 1971-74), Can. Bar Assn. (chmn. criminal justice sub-sect. Que. br. 1970-72, treas. nat. criminal justice sect. 1973-74, vice chmn. 1974-76), Bar of Que. (bd. examiners 1968-73, chmn. com. on public commns. of inquiry 1975-76). Office: 1255 Phillips Sq Suite 1103 Montreal PQ H3B 3H1 Canada

YARRINGTON, BLAINE J., oil co. exec.; b. Albany, Mo., Mar. 18, 1918; s. Glen Cady and Genevieve (Livingston) Y.; student St. Joseph (Mo.) Jr. Coll., 1935-37; m. Marilyn Frances Holt, Mar. 18, 1940; 1 son, Alan Lee. With accounting dept. Standard Oil Co., Chgo., 1938-57, adminstrv. mgr., Chgo., 1957-59, dist. mgr., Joliet, Ill., 1959-60, coordinator-adminstr., 1960-61, v.p. mktg. and distbn., 1965-67; regional mgr. Am. Oil Co., N.Y.C., 1961-64, mgr. marketing devel., Chgo., 1964-65, exec. v.p., 1967-70; pres., dir. Amoco Oil Co., 1970-74; dir. Standard Oil Co. (Ind.), 1970—, exec. v.p., 1974—; dir. Continental Ill. Nat. Bank & Trust Co., Continental Ill. Corp., Am. Hosp. Supply Corp., Bank & Trust Co. Arlington Heights (Ill.). Trustees Northwestern U.; bd. dirs. Ill. Council on Econ. Edn., N.W. Community Hosp., Arlington Hts.; pres. United Way Met. Chgo.; mem. Nat. 4-H Council; chmn. bd. trustees Field Mus. Natural History. Served to 1st lt. Signal Corps, AUS, 1943-46. Mem. Am. Petroleum Inst., 25 Year Club Petroleum Industry, Transp. Assn. Am. (hon. life). Clubs: Economic, Commercial (Chgo.). Home: 715 S Salem Ave Arlington Heights IL 60005 Office: Standard Oil Co (Ind) 200 E Randolph Dr Chicago IL 60601

YARROW, PETER, folk singer; b. N.Y.C., May 31, 1938; B.A., Cornell U. Mem. group Peter, Paul and Mary, 1962-70; now solo performer; recording artist Warner Bros. Records. Bd. dirs. Newport Folk Found. Recipient Grammy award, 1963. Address: care New Direction Mgmt 9255 Sunset Blvd Suite 526 Los Angeles CA 90069*

YAR-SHATER, EHSAN OLLAH, educator; b. Hamadan, Persia, Apr. 3, 1920;; s. Hashem and Rouhaniya Yar-S.; Licence in Persian Lit., U. Tehran (Iran), 1941, in Law, 1944, D.Litt., 1947; M.A. in Old and Middle Iranian, U. London (Eng.) 1951, Ph.D., 1960; m. Latifeh Alviya, Oct. 20, 1961. Came to U.S., 1958. Asso. prof. Iranian philology U. Tehran, 1953, prof. old Persian and Avestan, 1960; vis. asso. prof. Indo-Iranian, Columbia, 1958-60, Hagop Kevorkian prof. Iranian studies, 1961—, chmn. dept. Middle East langs., cultures, 1968-73, dir. Iran Center, 1961—. Dir. Royal Inst. Publs., Tehran, 1954-61, gen. editor Persian Text Series, 1954—, Persian Heritage Series, 1963—, Bibliothéque des Oeuvres Classiques Persanes, 1967—, Persian Study Series, 1971—, Ency. Iranica, 1973—, Modern Persian Lit. Series, 1977—; pres. Book Soc. Persia, 1957-79; founder, gen. editor Rahnemay-e Ketab, lit. and bibliog. jour., 1957; gen. sec. Iran br. Internat. Council Philosophy and Human Scis., 1957-61; mem. exec. com. Corpus Inscriptionum Iranicarium, 1954—. Trustee Am. Inst. Iranian Studies, 1968—. Author: Persian Poetry in the 15th Century, 1955; A Grammar of Southern Tati Dialects, 1969. Editor: (Avicenna) Theorems and Remarks, 1954; Iran Faces the Seventies, 1971; (with D. Bivar) The Inscriptions of Eastern Mazandaran, 1979; (with R. Ettinghausen) The Highlights of Persian Art, 1979. Home: 450 Riverside Dr New York NY 10027. *Diffidence rather than confidence has been the source of my striving.*

YARU, NICHOLAS, electronics co. exec.; b. Canton, Ohio, Nov. 8, 1923; s. Nick and Victoria (Cornea) Y.; B.S. in Elec. Engring., Carnegie Inst. Tech., 1944; M.S., U. Ill., 1948, Ph.D., 1954; m. Rosemary Cotter, Nov. 12, 1950; children—Nicholas Cornell, Thomas Cotter, Susan Victoria. Indsl. engr. E.I. DuPont de Nemours, Inc., 1944-46; research asso. U. Ill., 1946-54; with Hughes Aircraft Co., 1955—, v.p., mgr. communications and radar div., 1965-69, v.p., asst. group exec., 1969—; lectr. Coll. Engring., U. Calif., at Los Angeles, 1955—. Mem. Army Sci. Adv. Panel, Naval Res. Adv. Com. Sr. mem. IEEE; mem. Sigma Xi, Delta Upsilon, Eta Kappa Nu. Methodist. Patentee antenna systems. Home: 2601 Terraza Pl Fullerton CA 92635 Office: P O Box 3310 Fullerton CA 92634

YARWOOD, GEORGE ARTHUR, landscape architect; b. Binghamton, N.Y., Nov. 6, 1903; s. Albert Raymond and Lillian Eva Grace (Ford) Y.; B.S., Mass. Agr. Coll., 1926; m. Dorothy Etta Stiegler, July 22, 1933. Landscape architect with firms in N.H., Fla., Mich., N.Y., Ohio and Conn., 1926-45; practice in Simsbury, Conn., 1945—; pres., treas. Yarwood & Block, Inc., 1950—; participant White House Conf. Natural Beauty; sec., later chmn. Conn. Bd. Landscape Architects Registration, 1967-72. Recipient Ward Melville Gold medal Ward Melville Found., 1960; Community Improvement-Leadership award Washington, Conn. Emeritus fellow Am. Soc. Landscape Architects (past 1st 1st v.p., treas.); mem. Am. Inst. Planners. Democrat. Episcopalian. Club: Masons. Author articles. Home: 367 Hopmeadow St PO Box 52 Weatogue CT 06089 Office: 1243 Hopmeadow St PO Box 533 Simsbury CT 06070

YARY, ANTHONY RONALD, profl. football player; b. Chgo., July 16, 1946; s. Anthony and Clearcie Ethel (Golden) Y.; B.S. in Fin., U. So. Calif., 1967; postgrad. U. Calif., Long Beach, 1970, U. Calif., Los Angeles, 1971. Offensive tackle Minn. Vikings, 1968—; v.p. Yary Sports Ltd. Active Big Brothers. Recipient Knute Rockne Meml. Trophy, 1967, Outland Trophy, 1967; named Nat. Football League-Nat. Football Conf. Offensive Lineman of Yr., 1973, 74, 75; named All Pro, 1971-77; named Consensus All Am., 1965, 66. Roman Catholic. Home: 9451 Riverview Rd Eden Prairie MN 55344 Office: Yary Sports Ltd 20014 State Rd Cerrito CA 90701 also Yary Athletic Shoe & Bootery Saint Paul MN

YASEEN, LEONARD CLAYTON, consultant; b. Chicago Heights, Ill., June 27, 1912; student U. Ill., 1929-32; m. Helen M. Fantus, July 29, 1934; children—Roger, Barbara. Ret. chmn. bd. Fantus Co. a Dun & Bradstreet Co.; founder Yaseen Lecture Series in Fine Arts; dir. Witco Chem. Co. Trustee Am. Fedn. Arts, Purchase Coll. Found., Neuberger Museum. Clubs: Quaker Ridge, Century, Sky. Author: Plant Location, 1956; A Guide to Facilities Location, 1971; Direct Investment in the United States, 1974; Industrial Development in a

Changing World, 1975. Home: 2 Bay Ave Larchmont NY 10538 Office: 375 Park Ave New York City NY 10022

YASHON, DAVID, neurosurgeon, educator; b. Chgo., May 13, 1935; s. Samuel and Dorothy (Cutler) Y.; B.S. in Medicine, U. Ill., 1958, M.D., 1960; m. Myrna D. Foreman, Dec. 29, 1957; children—Jaclyn, Lisa, Steven. Intern, U. Ill., 1961, resident, 1961-64, asst. in neuroanatomy, 1960; clin. instr. neurosurgery U. Chgo., 1965-66; asst. prof. neurosurgery Case Western Res U., Cleve., 1966-69; asso. prof. neurosurgery Ohio State U., Columbus, 1969-74, prof., 1974—; mem. staff Ohio State U. Hosp., Children's Hosp., St. Anthony's Hosp.; cons. Med. Research and Devel. Command, U.S. Army; mem. Neurology B Study Sect NIH. Served as capt. U.S. Army, 1960-68. Diplomate Am. Bd. Neurol. Surgery. Fellow Royal Coll. Surgeons Can. (cert.), A.C.S.; mem. AMA, Am. Physiol. Soc., Congress Neurol. Surgeons, Am. Assn. Anatomists, Canadian, Ohio neurosurg. socs., Am. Assn. Neurol. Surgeons, Research Soc. Neurol. Surgeons, Acad. Medicine Columbus and Franklin County, Soc. for Neurosci., Soc. Univ. Surgeons, Am. Acad. Neurology, Assn. for Acad. Surgery, Am. Acad. Neurol. Surgery, Am. Assn. for Surgery of Trauma, Central Surg. Soc., Ohio Med. Soc., Columbus Surg. Soc., Sigma Xi. Author: Cytology of Nervous System Tumors; Spinal Injury; contbr. articles to med. jours. Home: 317 N Columbia Columbus OH 43209 Office: 410 W 10th Ave Columbus OH 43210

YASINSKI, PHILIP H., performing arts adminstr.; b. Vt., Oct. 9, 1943; s. Harold W. and Reecie (Mutter) Y.; attended Hiram Coll., U. Vienna (Austria) Inst. European Studies, Am. U. Sch. Inter Am. Relations, Nat. U. Mexico City; m. Terry R. Zack, Oct. 8, 1977. Asst. dir. admissions Case Western Res. U., 1966; dir. admissions Inst. European Studies, beginning 1970, then asst. to pres., and finally asso. dir. European extension programs, until 1973; pres. Youth for Understanding Internat. Youth Exchange, 1973-79; chief exec. officer Am. Symphony Orch. League, Vienna, Va., 1979—; dir. Nat. Travel Service, Gt. Sky Land and Devel. Co., China Group; mem. partnership panel Nat. Endowment for Arts; mem. 1977 rev. com. Helsinki Accords, Dept. State. Decorated Order of Merit in Fine Arts, Legion of Merit (Brazil). Office: PO Box 669 Vienna VA 22180

YASSIN, ROBERT ALAN, mus. adminstr.; b. Malden, Mass., May 22, 1941; s. Harold Benjamin and Florence Gertrude (Hoffman) Y.; B.A. (Rufus Choate scholar), Dartmouth Coll., 1962; postgrad. Boston U., 1962-63; M.A., U. Mich., 1965, postgrad. (Samuel H. Kress Found. fellow), 1968-70, Ph.D. candidate, 1970; postgrad (Ford Found. fellow) Yale U., 1966-68; m. Marilyn Kramer, June 9, 1963; children—Fredric Giles, Aaron David. Asst. to dir. Mus. Art U. Mich., 1965-66, asst. dir., 1970-72, asso. dir., 1972-73, acting dir., 1973, instr. dept. history of art, 1970-73, co-dir. Joint Program in Mus. Tng., 1970-73; chief curator Indpls. Mus. Art, 1973-75, acting dir., 1975, now dir.; adj. prof. Herron Sch. Art Ind. U./Purdue U.; mem. adv. panel Ind. Arts Commn. Mem. adv. council Internat. Center Indpls.; bd. dirs. Consortium for Urban Edn., Indpls.; bd. dirs. Festival Music Soc., Indpls. Mem. Am. Assn. Mus., Am. Assn. for State and Local History, Assn. Art Mus. Dirs., Coll. Art Assn. Am., Intermuseum Conservation Assn. (Oberlin, Ohio trustee 1973—, chmn. exec. com. 1977—), Ind. Hist. Soc., Assn. Ind. Museums, Nat. Trust Historic Preservation, Profl. Cultural Alliance of Indpls., Victorian Soc. Am. Jewish. Club: Rotary Internat. Contbr. to mus. publications. Home: 2525 Blue Grass Dr Indianapolis IN 46208 Office: 1200 W 38th St Indianapolis IN 46208

YASTRZEMSKI, CARL MICHAEL, baseball player; b. Southampton, N.Y., Aug. 22, 1939; student Notre Dame U.; B.S. in Bus. Adminstrn., Merrimack Coll.; m. Carolann Casper, Jan. 30, 1960. Second baseman, shortstop Raleigh (N.C.), Carolina League, 1959; outfielder Mpls., Am. Assn., 1960, Boston, Am. League, 1961—; with Boston, World Series, 1967; mem. Am. League All-Star Team, 1963, 65-75. Chosen Most Valuable Player, Carolina League, 1959, Am. League, 1967. Address: care Boston Red Sox 24 Yawkey Way Boston MA 02215*

YASUNOBU, KERRY TSUYOSHI, biochemist; b. Seattle, Nov. 21, 1925; s. Seiji and Chiyono (Kobayashi) Y.; Ph.D., U. Wash., 1954; m. Kikue Itami, Nov. 15, 1952; children—Steven, Chrissie. Mem. faculty U. Oreg. Med. Sch., Portland, 1955-58; mem. faculty U. Hawaii, Honolulu, 1958—, prof., chmn. dept. biochemistry and biophysics Sch. Medicine, 1974—. Sr. fellow NSF, 1964-65, NIH, 1970-71. Mem. Am. Chem. Soc., Am. Soc. Biol. Chemists, Sigma Xi. Contbr. articles to profl. jours. Home: 3270 Melemele Pl Honolulu HI 96822 Office: 2538 The Mall Snyder 401 U Hawaii Honolulu HI 96822

YATES, CHARLES RICHARDSON, arts center exec.; b. Atlanta, Sept. 9, 1913; s. Presley Daniel and Julia (Richardson) Y.; B.S. with honors, Ga. Inst. Tech., 1935; m. Dorothy Malone, May 20, 1944; children—Dorothy M. (Mrs. Kirkley), Charles R., Sarah F. (Mrs. Michael Baker), J. Comer. With 1st Nat. Bank Atlanta, 1935-47, asst. v.p., 1940-47; with Joshua L. Baily & Co., Inc., Atlanta, 1947-60, v.p., 1956-60; v.p. finance Atlantic Coast Line R.R. Co. and L. & N. R.R. Co., 1960-67; v.p. Seaboard Coast Line R.R. Co., 1967-71, v.p. finance, 1971-73; v.p. finance L. & N. R.R. Co., 1967-73; pres. Atlanta Arts Alliance, 1973—; dir. West Point Pepperell, Inc. Trustee, Ga. Tech. Found. Served with AUS, 1941-42, lt. USNR, 1942-46. Mem. Ga. C. of C. (dir., pres. 1965-67). Episcopalian. Clubs: Augusta (Ga.) Nat. (sec.); Atlanta Athletic, Peachtree Golf, Capital City (Atlanta); Royal and Ancient Golf (St. Andrews, Scotland). Office: 1280 Peachtree St NE Atlanta GA 30309

YATES, DANIEL EDWARD, household goods carrier exec.; b. Lafayette, Ind., Dec. 18, 1941; s. William Edward and Wilma Ruth (Sipple) Y.; B.A. in Bus., Butler U., 1965; J.D., Ind. U., 1968; m. Judith Ann Jones, June 25, 1966; children—Susan Lynn, Jeffrey Allen, Rachel Louise. Admitted to Ind. bar, 1968; tax mgr. Arthur Andersen & Co., Indpls., 1968-74; v.p. fin., treas. Mayflower Corp., Indpls., 1974—; dir. Rover Co. Treas. U.S. Open Clay Ct. Tournament, 1971—. C.P.A., Ind. Mem. Ind., Indpls. assns. C.P.A.'s, Ind., Indpls. bar assns., Am. Mgmt. Assn. Republican. Club: Sertoma. Home: 2410 Hawthorne Pl Noblesville IN 46060 Office: PO Box 107B Indianapolis IN 46206

YATES, ELIZABETH (MRS. WILLIAM MCGREAL), author, editor; b. Buffalo, Dec. 6, 1905; d. Harry and Mary (Duffy) Yates; grad. Franklin Sch., Buffalo, Oaksmere, Mamaroneck, N.Y.; student N.Y.C., Paris (France), London (Eng.); Litt.D. (hon.), Aurora Coll., 1965, Ripon Coll., 1970, Rivier Coll.; L.H.D., Eastern Bapt. Coll., 1966, U. N.H., 1967, New Eng. Coll., 1972; m. William McGreal, Nov. 6, 1929. Staff mem. U. Conn., U. Ind., U. Colo., U. N.H. writers confs., 1948—; staff mem. Christian Writers and Editors Conf., Green Lake, Wis., 1957—. Mem. gov.'s State Library Commn. Trustee, Town Library, Peterborough, N.H. Recipient N.Y. Herald Tribune Spring Festival award, 1943, 50; Newbery medal, 1951; William Allen White award 1953; Sarah Josepha Hale award, 1970. Mem. Delta Kappa Gamma. Author: High Holiday, 1938; Hans and Frieda, 1938; Gathered Grace, 1939; Climbing Higher, 1939; Quest in the Northland, 1940; Haven for the Brave, 1941; Under the Little Fir, 1941; Around the Year in Iceland, 1942; Patterns on the Wall, 1942; Mountain Born, 1943; Wind of Spring, 1944; The Young Traveller in the U.S.A., 1946; Nearby, 1947; Once in the Year, 1947; Beloved Bondage, 1948; Amos Fortune, Free Man, 1950; Guardian Heart, 1950; Children of the Bible, 1950; Brave Interval, 1952; A Place For Peter, 1952; Hue and Cry, 1953; Rainbow Round the World, 1954 (Jane Addams children's book award Women's Internat. League for Peace and Freedom 1955); Prudence Crandall, Woman of Courage, 1955; The Carey Girl, 1956; Pebble in a Pool, The Widening Circles of Dorothy Canfield Fisher's Life, 1958 (reissued as The Lady from Vermont 1971); The Lighted Heart, 1960; The Next Fine Day, 1961; Someday You'll Write, 1962; Sam's Secret Journal, 1963; Carolina's Courage, 1963; Howard Thurman, Portrait of a Practical Dreamer, 1964; Up the Golden Stair, 1966; Is There a Doctor in the Barn?, 1966; With Pipe, Paddle and Song, 1968; New Hampshire, 1969; On that Night, 1969; Sarah Whitcher's Story, 1971; Skeezer, Dog with a Mission, 1972; The Road Through Sandwich Notch, 1973; We, The People, 1974; A Book of Hours, 1976; Call It Zest, 1977; The Seventh One, 1978. Editor: Piskey Folk, 1941; Doll Who Came Alive, 1941, 72; Joseph, 1947; The White Ring, 1949; The Christmas Story, 1949; Your Prayers and Mine, 1954; Sir Gibbie, 1962. Contbr. book revs., articles, essays, interviews to periodicals. Address: 381 Old Street Rd Peterborough NH 03458

YATES, ELLA (MAE) GAINES, librarian; b. Atlanta, June 14, 1927; d. Fred Douglas and Laura (Moore) Gaines; A.B., Spelman Coll., Atlanta, 1949; M.S. in L.S., Atlanta U., 1951; J.D., Atlanta Law Sch., 1979; m. Joseph L. Syndor (dec.); 1 child, Jerri Gaines Sydnor Lee; m. 2d, Clayton R. Yates (dec.). Asst. br. librarian Bklyn. Pub. Library, 1951-54; head children's dept. Orange (N.J.) Pub. Library, 1956-59; br. librarian E. Orange (N.J.) Pub. Library, 1960-69; med. librarian Orange Meml. Hosp., 1967-69; asst. dir. Montclair (N.J.) Pub. Library, 1970-72; asst. dir. Atlanta Pub. Library, 1972-76, dir., 1976—; co-chmn. Quarles Library Soc., Spelman Coll., 1977—; adv. bd. Library of Congress Center for the Book; cons. in field. Vice chmn. N.J. Women's Council Human Relations, 1957-59; chmn. Friends of Fulton County Jail, 1973—; bd. dirs. United Cerebral Palsy Greater Atlanta, Inc. Named Profl. Woman of Year, N.J. chpt. Nat. Assn. Negro Bus. and Profl. Women's Club, 1964; Outstanding Chum of Year, 1976; Outstanding Alumni, Spelman Coll., 1977; recipient Meritorious award Atlanta U., 1977. Mem. ALA (exec. bd.), Ga., Southeastern library assns., NAACP, Atlanta Women's C. of C., Delta Theta Phi, Delta Sigma Theta. Baptist. Contbr. to profl. jours. Address: 1171 Oriole Dr SW Atlanta GA 30311

YATES, FLOYD B. (BILL), cartoonist, editor; b. Samson, Ala., July 5, 1921; s. Homer Isaac and Sabra Anna (Holley) Y.; B.J., U. Tex., 1950; m. Jessie Jean Hardy, Sept. 28, 1945; 1 dau., Georgia. Editor 3 humor and 1 movie mag. Dell Pub. Co., 1950-60; former editor-art dir. Hee Haw Mag., CBS and Charlton Pub. Co., editor Tex. Ranger humor mag. U. Tex., and editor The Cartoonist, publ. Nat. Cartoonists Soc.; creator, writer, artist Professor Phumble, daily cartoon, King Features Syndicate, 1960-78, comics editor King Features Syndicate, 1980—; artist Benjy, daily and Sun. cartoon; gag cartoonist, 1950-60, including Saturday Evening Post, Parade Mag.; editorial cartoonist Brooks Community Newspapers, Fairfield County, Conn., until 1980; advt. art for various corps., including Seagrams, Pepsi Cola, Am. Can, Stauffer Chem., Gen. Electric, U.S. Games, Delaware Valley C. of C., and Ronald McDonald comic books for McDonald's Corp.; editorial cartoonist for booklet of labor cartoons Hearst Corp.; lectr. in humor. Taught Dale Carnegie course, Silva Mind Control. Served to lt. (j.g.) USN, 1943-47. Mem. Nat. Cartoonists Soc., Newspaper Comics Council, Artists and Writers Assn., Conn. Cartoonists, Sigma Delta Chi.

YATES, HELEN EVA, author, lectr.; b. Omaha; d. Edward Truman and Christina (Chapp) Yates; student Girl's Collegiate Sch., Los Angeles, 1921, Art Inst., Chgo., 1922, Columbia, 1923. Editorial reader Sam Goldwyn, N.Y.C., 1923; promotion writer Chas. Schribners, 1924; editor-pub. New Orleans Life Mag., 1925; women's editor China Press, Shanghai, 1926; Dutch Govt. writer, Java, 1927; radio travel program KFRC, San Francisco, 1933; copywriter BBDO Agy., Los Angeles, 1940-41; writer Westfal Larson Line, S.A., 1941; writer around world Am. Pres. Line, 1950-51; staff lectr. Writers Conf. Calif. Western U., 1960, San Diego State Coll., 1963. Founder World-House, 1955. Mem. P.E.N., Authors Guild, Hollywood Fgn. Press, Internat. Platform Assn., World Craft Council. Author: Bali, Enchanted Isle, 1933; The World Is Your Oyster, 1939; Java Orchid, 1945; How to Travel for Fun, 1950; Folk Art Guide, India Govt., 1951; Hong Kong Crafts, 1952; Shopping All Over the World, 1953; World House Party, The Story of Tante, 1966; The Money Tree Blossomed, 1972; Fire Orchid, 1978; Bali-With Love, 1978. Address: 123 S Berendo St Los Angeles CA 90004

YATES, PETER, educator; b. Wanstead, Eng., Aug. 26, 1924; s. Harold Andrew and Kathryn (Yexley) Y.; B.Sc., U. London (Eng.), 1946; M.Sc., Dalhousie U., 1948; Ph.D., Yale U., 1951; m. Mary Ann Palmer, Sept. 9, 1950; 1 son, John Anthony; stepchildren—William Palmer Franklin, Thomas Jay Franklin. Postdoctoral fellow Harvard U., 1950-51, mem. faculty, 1952-60; instr. Yale U., 1951-52, vis. prof., 1966; prof. chemistry U. Toronto (Ont., Can.), 1960—; vis. prof. Princeton U., 1977—. Fellow Royal Soc. Can., Chem. Inst. Can. (Merck, Sharp & Dohme lectr. 1963); mem. Am. Chem. Soc., Chem. Soc. London. Research and publs. on structural and synthetic, on natural products, photochem. products, heterocyclic compounds, and aliphatic diazo compounds. Office: U Toronto Dept Chemistry Toronto ON M5S 1A1 Canada

YATES, PETER, film dir.; m. Virginia Pope, 1960; 3 children. Formerly asst. dir. A Taste of Honey, The Entertainer; dir. Summer Holiday; One-Way Pendulum, Robbery, 1965; Robbery, 1967; Bullitt, 1968; John and Mary, 1969; Murphy's War, 1971; The Hot Rock, 1972; The Friends of Eddie Coyle, 1973; For Pete's Sake, 1974; Mother, Jugs and Speed, 1976; The Deep, 1977; producer, dir. Breaking Away, 1978. Address: care ICM40 W 57th St New York NY 10019

YATES, RONALD EUGENE, journalist; b. Kansas City, Mo., Feb. 19, 1941; s. Guy Raymond and Willadean (Peterson) Y.; B.S. (Gannett Newspapers scholar 1968-69, Angelo C. Scott Meml. scholar 1969), U. Kans., 1969; m. Ingeborg Zoelss, May 7, 1966; children—Jennifer Christina, Nichole Brigitte. Reporter, Kansas City (Kans.) Star, 1968; reporter, asst. city editor, fgn. corr. Chgo. Tribune, Chgo. and Tokyo, Japan, 1969-76, Asia and Latin Am. corr., 1976—; editor Univ. Daily Kansan, 1969. Served with U.S. Army Intelligence, 1962-66. Recipient award for excellence in staff leadership William Allen White Sch. Journalism, 1968; Edward Scott Beck award for fgn. reporting, 1975; Inter-Am. Press Assn. award for reporting on Latin Am., 1979. named Outstanding Sr. U. Kans., 1969. Mem. Fgn. Corrs. Club of Japan, Sigma Delta Chi. Democrat. Lutheran. Contbr. articles to mags. Office: care Chgo Tribune Press Service Times-Mirror Sq Los Angeles CA 90053

YATES, SIDNEY RICHARD, congressman, lawyer; b. Chgo., Aug. 27, 1909; s. Louis and Ida (Siegel) Y.; Ph.B., U. Chgo., 1931, J.D., 1933; m. Adeline Holleb, June 24, 1935; 1 son, Stephen R. Admitted to Ill. bar, 1933; practiced as sr. mem. firm Yates & Holleb; asst. atty. Ill. State Bank Receiver, 1935-37; asst. atty. gen. attached Ill. Commerce Commn. as traction atty., 1937-40; mem. 81st-87th, also 89th-96th Congresses from 9th Ill. Dist.; U.S. del. UN Trusteeship Council with rank of ambassador. Served to lt. USN, 1944-46. Mem. Am., Ill. State, Chgo. bar assns., Am. Vets. Com., Chgo. Council Fgn. Relations, Decalogue Soc. Lawyers. Democrat. Jewish. Clubs: City, Bryn Mawr Country. Office: 2234 Rayburn House Office Bldg Washington DC 20515*

YATES, WILLARD ROSS, educator; b. Corvallis, Oreg., Mar. 7, 1924; s. Willard Wilson and Phoebe Mae (Chamberlain) Y.; student Oreg. State Coll., 1941-42; B.A., U. Oreg., 1948, M.A., 1949; Ph.D., Yale, 1956; LL.D. (hon.), Moravian Coll., 1977; Fulbright student Inst. d'Etudes Politiques, Bordeaux, France, 1951-52; m. Catharine M. Gleason, Dec. 28, 1955. Instr., Kenyon Coll., 1952-53; instr. polit. sci. U. Vt., 1953-55; with Lehigh U., 1955—, prof. polit. sci., 1963—, dean Coll. Arts and Sci., 1963-72. Served with AUS, 1943-46. Mem. Am. Polit. Sci. Assn., Phi Beta Kappa. Author: History of the Lehigh Valley Region, 1963; Democracy in the United States, 1967; also articles. Chmn. editorial com. Bethlehem of Pennsylvania: The First 100 Years, Bethlehem of Pennsylvania: The Golden Years. Home: 1332 Butztown Rd Bethlehem PA 18017

YATRON, GUS, congressman; b. Reading, Pa., Oct. 16, 1927; s. George H. and Theano (Lazos) Y.; grad. Kutztown State Tchrs. Coll., 1950; m. Millie Menzies; children—George, Theana. Mem. Reading Sch. Bd., 1955-61; mem. Pa. Ho. of Reps., 1956-60, Senate, 1960-68; mem. 91st-96th Congresses from 6th Dist. Pa. Bd. mgrs. Reading Hosp. Home: 1908 Hessian Rd Reading PA 19602 Office: 2311 Rayburn House Office Bldg Washington DC 20515

YATSU, FRANK MICHIO, physician; b. Los Angeles, Nov. 28, 1932; s. Frank K. and Helen I. (Amano) Y.; A.B., Brown U., 1955; M.D., Case Western Res. U., 1959; m. Michiko Yamane, Sept. 10, 1955; 1 dau., Carolyn Elizabeth. Intern, Univ. Hosps., Cleve., 1959-60, resident, 1961; resident Neurol. Inst. N.Y., 1961-63; asst. prof. neurology U. Calif., San Francisco, 1967-71, asso. prof., 1971-75; prof., chmn. dept. neurology U. Oreg. Med. Sch., Portland, 1975—; chief neurology service San Francisco Gen. Hosp., 1969-75. Trustee Brown U. Served to lt. comdr. USNR, 1965-67. John and Mary Markle scholar in acad. medicine, 1969. Mem. Alpha Omega Alpha. Home: 10919 SW Aventine Portland OR 97219 Office: Dept Neurology U Oreg Med Sch Portland OR 97210

YAU, SHING-TUNG, mathematician; b. Swatow, Kwantung, China, Apr. 4, 1949; s. Chan-Ying and Yeuk-Lam (Leung) Chiou; Ph.D., U. Calif., Berkeley, 1971; m. Yu-Yun Kuo, Sept. 4, 1976. Mem. Inst. Advanced Study, 1971-72; asst. prof. SUNY, Stony Brook, 1972-73; vis. asst. prof. Stanford (Calif.) U., 1973-74, asso. prof., 1975-77, prof. math., 1977—. Named Calif. Scientist of 1979. Mem. Am. Math. Soc. Home: 2048 Middlefield Ave Palo Alto CA 94303 Office: Math Dept Stanford U Stanford CA 94305

YAU, STEPHEN SIK-SANG, computer scientist, elec. engr., educator; b. Wusei, Kiangsu, China, Aug. 6, 1935; s. Pen-Chi and Wen-Chum (Shum) Y.; came to U.S., 1958, naturalized, 1968; B.S. in Elec. Engring., Nat. Taiwan U., China, 1958; M.S. in Elec. Engring., U. Ill., Urbana, 1959, Ph.D., 1961; m. Vickie Liu, June 14, 1964; children—Andrew, Philip. Research asst. elec. engring. lab., U. Ill., Urbana, 1959-61; asst. prof. elec. engring. Northwestern U., Evanston, Ill., 1961-64, asso. prof., 1964-68, prof., 1968—, prof. computer scis., 1970—, also chmn. dept. computer scis., 1972-77, chmn. dept. elec. engring. and computer sci., 1977—. Conf. chmn. IEEE Computer Conf., Chgo., 1967; symposium chmn. Symposium on feature extraction and selection in pattern recognition, Argonne Nat. Lab., 1970; gen. chmn. Nat. Computer Conf., Chgo., 1974, First Internat. Computer Software and Applications Conf., Chgo., 1977. Trustee Nat. Electronics Conf., Inc., 1965-68. Recipient Louis E. Levy medal Franklin Inst., 1963, Golden Plate award Am. Acad. of Achievement, 1964. Fellow IEEE (mem. governing bd. Computer Soc. 1967-76, pres. 1974-75, dir. Inst. 1976-77), Franklin Inst.; mem. Assn. for Computing Machinery, Soc. for Indsl. and Applied Math., AAAS, Am. Soc. for Engring. Edn., Am. Fedn. Info.-Processing Socs. (mem. exec. com. 1974-76, 79—, dir. 1972—, chmn. award com. 1979—), Sigma Xi. Contbr. numerous articles on computer sci., elec. engring. and related fields to profl. publs. Patentee in field. Home: 2609 Noyes St Evanston IL 60201 Office: Dept of Elec Engring and Computer Sciences Northwestern Univ 2145 Sheridan Rd Evanston IL 60201

YAVITZ, BORIS, univ. dean; b. Tblisi, USSR, June 4, 1923; s. Simon and Miriam (Mindlin) Y.; came to U.S., 1946, naturalized, 1950; M.A., Cambridge (Eng.) U., 1943; M.S., Columbia U., 1948, Ph.D., 1964; m. Irene Bernhard, July 17, 1949; children—Jessica Ann, Judith, Emily. Economic cons. Jewish Agy. for Palestine, N.Y.C., 1948-49; mgmt. cons. Werner Mgmt. Cons., Larchmont, N.Y., 1949-54; owner, mgr. Simbar Devel. Corp., N.Y.C., 1954-61; faculty Columbia U., N.Y.C., 1964—, prof. mgmt., 1964—, dean Grad. Sch. Bus., 1975—; dep. chmn., dir. Fed. Res. Bank N.Y., 1977—; dir. J.C. Penney Co., Inc., 1978—. Mem. bd. advisors Internat. Mgmt. Inst., Washington; trustee Am. Assembly, N.Y.C., 1975—. Served to lt. British Royal Navy, 1943-46. Mem. ASME, Inst. Mgmt. Sci. Author books; contbr. articles in field to profl. jours. Home: 22 Baylor Circle White Plains NY 10605 Office: Graduate School Business Columbia University 101 Uris Hall New York NY 10027

YEADON, FRED W., JR., banker; b. Manning, Iowa, 1924; grad. U. Iowa, 1948. Chmn. bd., pres. First Vt. Bank & Trust Co., Brattleboro; dir. Reformer Pub. Co., Central Vt. Pub. Service Corp., Vt. Electric Power Co., Inc., New Eng. Bankcard Assn., Vt. Devel. Credit Corp.; chmn. S.B.J.C. of Vt. Clubs: Elks, Masons, Shrine. Address: 215 Main St Brattleboro VT 05301

YEAGER, BRUNO JOHN, utility exec.; b. North Charleroi, Pa., June 2, 1910; s. John and Beatrice (Tonine) Y.; B.E.E., U. Cin., 1934; m. Sara Lee Roberson, Nov. 17, 1934; children—John S., Robert L. With Cincinnati Gas & Elec. Co., 1930—, pres., chief exec. officer, 1970-77, chmn. bd., 1977—, also dir.; dir. Union Light, Heat and Power Co., Tri-State Improvement Co., First Nat. Bank of Cin., Union Central Life Ins. Co., Cin. Trustee, Herman Schneider Found. Registered profl. engr., Ohio, Ky. Mem. AIM, IEEE, ASME, Cin. C. of C. Clubs: Queen City Cincinnati Country, Commercial, Queen City Optimist (Cin.). Office: Cin Gas & Elec Co 139 E 4th St Cincinnati OH 45202

YEAGER, C. ROBERT, business dir.; b. Bell County, Ky., July 18, 1911; s. John H. and Ada (Sproule) Y.; B.S., U. Ky., 1933; m. Frances Council, Dec. 22, 1936; 1 dau., Betty Durham (Mrs. Thomas Edward Powell, III). Dir., Liberty Mut. Life Assurance Co., Liberty Mut. Ins. Co., Marriott Corp., Liberty Mut. Fire Ins. Co., Towle Silversmiths; pres., dir. Asso. Industries of Mass., 1963-65. Served to col. AUS, 1941-46. Mem. Pi Kappa Alpha, DeMolay (mem. internat. supreme council, 1959-60). Clubs: Burning Tree Country (Bethesda, Md.); Highland Country; R.I. Country; Country of N.C. (Pinehurst) St. Andrews Royal and Ancient Golf (Scotland); Commercial (Boston); Halifax Country, Halifax River Yacht (Daytona Beach, Fla.); Oceanside Country (Ormond Beach, Fla.). Home: 2828 N Atlantic Ave Daytona Beach FL 32018 Office: Box 808 Attleboro MA 02703

YEAGER, ERNEST BILL, phys. chemist, educator; b. Orange, N.J., Sept. 26, 1924; s. Ernest Frederick and Olga (Wittwer) Y.; B.A., N.J. State Coll., Montclair, 1945; M.S. in Chemistry, Western Res. U., 1946, Ph.D. in Phys. Chemistry, 1948. Mem. faculty Case Western Res. U., 1948—, prof. chemistry, 1958—, acting chmn. dept., 1964-65, chmn. dept. chemistry, 1969-72, chmn. faculty senate, 1972-73, dir. Case Labs. for Electrochem. Studies, 1976—; vis. prof. U. Southampton (Eng.), 1968. Cons. Inst. Def. Analyses, 1963-66, NASA, 1964-68, Argonne Nat. Lab., 1965-67, Union Carbide Corp., 1954—, Gen. Motors Corp., 1969—; mem. com. undersea warfare NRC, 1961-73, adv. bd. Office Critical Tables, 1964-69, mem. phys. scis. div., 1968-73, mem. power panel Advanced Research Project Agy., 1972-75; chmn. Gordon Research Conf. Electrochemistry, 1966; mem. internat. commn. electrochemistry Internat. Union Pure and Applied Chemistry, 1971-76. Coffin fellow, 1947-48; NATO sr. fellow, 1968. Recipient Annual Tech. award Cleve. Tech. Socs. Council, 1954, Annual award Chem. Professions, 1967-68; Biennial award 1956; Ann. Alumni citation N.J. State Coll., 1968; Commendation certificate USN, 1972. Fellow Acoustical Soc. Am. (v.p. 1969-70), A.A.A.S.; mem. Electrochem. Soc. (hon. mem., v.p. 1962-65, pres. 1965-66; Heise award Cleve. sect. 1965), Am. Chem. Soc., Soc. Applied Spectroscopy (pres. Cleve. 1953-54), Internat. Soc. Electrochemists (v.p. 1967-69, pres. 1969-70), Optical Soc. Am., Chem. Soc. London Soc., AAUP, Sigma Xi (pres. Western Res. U. chpt. 1959-60). Presbyn. (elder). Editor: Transactions of the Symposium on Electrode Processes, 1959, 66; Techniques of Electrochemistry, Vol I, 1972, Vol. II, 1973, Vol. III, 1977; editorial bd. Jour. Advanced Energy Conversion, 1964-66; sect. editor Electrochemica Acta, 1972-76. Contbr. articles to profl. jours. Home: 2051 Lee Blvd East Cleveland OH 44112

YEAGER, JOSEPH HENRY, educator, researcher; b. Cullman, Ala., Oct. 23, 1920; s. Joseph Thomas and Minnie (Ruehl) Y.; B.S., Auburn U., 1943, M.S., 1948; Ph.D., Purdue U., 1951; m. Hattie Stark Poor, Jan. 30, 1944; children—Joseph Edgar, Thomas Henry, Paula Irene. Extension economist Purdue U., 1950-51; asso. prof. Auburn (Ala.) U., 1951-57, prof., 1957-64, head dept. agrl. econs. and rural sociology, 1964—. Served with inf., AUS, 1943-46. Mem. Am. Agrl. Econs. Assn., Sigma Xi, Phi Kappa Phi, Gamma Sigma Delta, Alpha Zeta. Methodist. Lion. Author: (with E.D. Chastain and E.L. McGraw) Farm Business Management, 1962. Home: Route 3 Box 20 Auburn AL 36830

YEAGER, ROBERT LEE, physician; b. Mineral Wells, Tex., Mar. 8, 1907; s. Robert Lee and Bessie (Birdwell) Y.; B.S., Va. Mil. Inst., 1926; postgrad. U. Tex. at Austin, 1926-27; M.D., U. Pa., 1931; m. Litane Brooks, Jan. 21, 1939 (dec.); children—Robert, Brooks; m. 2d, Winifred Doscher, Nov. 18, 1955; children—John, Fabian. Intern Hosp. P.E. Ch., Phila., 1932-33; adj. resident obstetrics Kensington Hosp., Phila., 1934; asst. resident Trudeau Sanatorium, 1935-42, pulmonary diseases Bellevue Hosp., 1938; med. dir. Summit Park Hosp., Pomona, N.Y., 1942—, supt., 1942—; dir. health and hosps. Rockland County, Pomona; cons. pulmonary diseases Castle Point (N.Y.) VA Hosp.; chest cons. Rockland Psychiat. Center, Letchworth Devel. Center, Good Samaritan Hosp., Nyack Hosp. Pres. State Communities Aid Assn., 1963-68, mem. exec. bd., bd. mgrs.; mem. exec. com. Am. Lung Assn. N.Y. State. Mem. Am. Thoracic Soc. (pres. 1967-68). Mem. Reformed Ch. (elder). Address: Summit Park Hosp Pomona NY 10970

YEAGLEY, J. WALTER, judge; b. Angola, Ind., Apr. 20, 1909; s. John George and Alice (Bailey) Y.; A.B., U. Mich., 1931, J.D., 1934; m. Dorothy Brown, June 27, 1942; children—John R., William J., Richard A. Admitted to Ind. bar, 1934, practiced in South Bend, 1934-42; spl. agt. FBI, 1942-48; dir. security and investigation div. ECA, 1948-51; asso. gen. counsel RFC, 1952-53; dep. asst. atty. gen. Dept. of Justice, 1953-59, asst. atty. gen., 1959-70; asso. judge D.C. Ct. Appeals, 1970-79, sr. judge, 1979—. Chmn. interdeptl. com. on internal security Nat. Security Council, 1954-59, atty. gen.'s observer on planning bd., 1958-61; chmn. Personnel Security Adv. Com., 1958-61. Mem. Am., D.C. bar assns., Bar U.S. Supreme Ct., Soc. Ex-FBI Agts., Ind. Soc., Alpha Sigma Phi. Conglist. Club: River Bend Country. Home: 316 Runner Rd Great Falls VA 22066 Office: 500 Indiana Ave NW Washington DC 20001

YEAKEL, JOSEPH HUGHES, clergyman; b. Mahanoy City, Pa., Mar. 12, 1928; s. Claude Harrison and Florence Mae (Hughes) Y.; A.B., Lebanon Valley Coll., 1949, D.D. (hon.), 1968; M.Div., United Theol. Sem., 1952; LL.D. (hon.), Otterbein Coll.; S.T.D. (hon.), Keuka Coll.; m. Lois Josephine Shank, Mar. 26, 1948; children—Claudia Jo, Joseph Douglas, Joanna Irene, Mary Jo, Jody Lucile. Ordained to ministry United Methodist Ch., 1952; student asst. pastor Euclid Ave. Evang. United Brethren Ch., Dayton, Ohio, 1949-52; asst. pastor Otterbein Evang. United Brethren Ch., Hagerstown, Md., 1952-55; pastor Messiah Evang. United Brethren Ch., York, Pa., 1955-61, Meml. Evang. United Brethren Ch., Silver Spring, Md., 1961-63; asst. sec. Gen. Bd. Evangelism, Evang. United Brethren Ch., 1963-65, exec. sec., 1965-68; gen. sec. Gen. Bd. Evangelism, United Meth. Ch., Nashville, 1968-72; bishop N.Y. West area United Meth. Ch., 1972—. Served with USNR, Seabees, 1945-46; PTO. Home: 220 Standish Dr Syracuse NY 13224 Office: 3049 E Genesee St Syracuse NY 13224

YEARGAN, PERCY BAXTER, educator; b. Clanton, Ala., Oct. 10, 1914; s. Luther Melvin and Cora Agnes (Foster) Y.; A.B., Howard Coll., 1937; M.B.A., U. Ala., 1955, Ph.D., 1957; m. Thelma Alice Brown; children—David Baxter, Terry (Mrs. Ransom Jackson). Prof. accounting U. Ala., U.Ga.; now prof. accounting U. Ala., Birmingham. C.P.A., Ala., Ga., Miss. Mem. Am. Inst. C.P.A.'s, Ala. Soc. C.P.A.'s, Financial Execs. Inst. Contbg. author Ency. Cost Accounting Systems; Handbook for Auditors. Home: 2600 Park Ln Ct N Birmingham AL 35223

YEARGIN, ROBERT HARPER, constrn. co. exec.; b. Gray Court, S.C., Oct. 23, 1926; s. Leon Turner and Bruce (Gray) Y.; B.S. in Civil Engring., Clemson U., 1949; m. Mary Ellen Sitton, Oct. 27, 1950; children—Robert Lynn, Nancy Sitton. With Duke Power Co., 1949, Piedmont Printmakers, Greenville, S.C., 1950, Daniel Constrn. Co., Greenville, 1950-59; organizer Yeargin Constrn. Co., Greenville, 1959, pres., chmn. bd., 1959—; pres. Yeargin Aviation, Inc., Yeargin Properties, Inc.; dir. First Fed. Savs. & Loan Assn., Greenville, Hardees' Food Systems, Cherry Investors, Inc. Mem. exec. com. region 6, Boy Scouts Am., also exec. com. Blue Ridge council; bd. dirs. Clemson U. Found. Served with AUS, 1945-47. Recipient Distinguished Execs. award Sales and Mktg. Execs. Club Greenville, 1964; Silver Beaver award Boy Scouts Am., 1970; Distinguished Service award Clemson Alumni Assn., 1975. Mem. Asso. Gen. Contractors Am., Am. Textile Mfrs. Inst. (asso.), Greenville C. of C. (dir.), Blue Key. Presbyterian. Home: 110 Byrd Blvd Greenville SC 29605 Office: PO Box 6508 Greenville SC 29606

YEATES, ALLAN BURNSIDE, advt. exec.; b. Hamilton, Ont., Can., Mar. 7, 1926; s. Ralph Howard and Helen Burnside (Reeves) Y.; B.B.A., U. Western Ont., 1948; m. Charlotte Elizabeth Farley, May 17, 1948; children—Carolyn, Jody, Stephen, Peter, Patricia. Bus. writer Fin. Post, 1948-49, Toronto Star, 1949-51; dir. public relations and advt. Prudential Ins. Co. of Am., 1951-61; pres. Spitzer, Mills & Bates, Toronto, 1961-77; pres. Baker Lovick Ltd., Toronto, 1972—; dir. Comcore Communications Ltd. Mem. Assn. Can. Advertisers (past pres.), Can. Advt. Adv. Bd. (past chmn.), Inst. Can. Advt. (past chmn.). Author: Canadian Code of Advertising Standards. Office: 60 Bloor St W Toronto ON M4W 3B8 Canada*

YEATES, ZENO LANIER, architect; b. Atlanta, Jan. 9, 1915; s. Zeno Epps and Louise (Ames) Y.; B.S. in Civil Engring., Miss. State U., 1937; B.Arch., U. Pa., 1942, M.Arch., 1976; m. Elsie Lankford, June 12, 1947; children—Zeno Ames, Arthur Lankford, Laura. Asso., J. Frazer Smith & Assos., Memphis, 1947-57; partner Zeno Yeates & Assos., Memphis, 1957-63; pres. Yeates & Gaskill, Inc., Architects, Memphis, 1963—; chmn. Tenn. Br. Arch. and Engring. Examiners, 1963-67. Fellow AIA (dir. 1975-77); mem. Tenn. Soc. Architects (pres. 1958), Constrn. Specifications Inst. Presbyterian. Clubs: Kiwanis, Univ. (Memphis). Home: 476 S Goodlett St Memphis TN 38117 Office: 2080 Peabody St Memphis TN 38104

YEE, ALFRED ALPHONSE, structural engr.; b. Honolulu, Aug. 5, 1925; s. Yun Sau and Kam (Ngo) Y.; B.S.C.E., Rose Poly. Inst., 1948; M.Eng. in Structures, Yale U., 1949; D.Eng. (hon.), Rose-Hulman Inst. Tech., 1976; m. Elizabeth Wong, June 24, 1975; children—Alethea Lailan, Mark K.K., Eric K.S., Malcolm K.O., Ian K.P., Suling V. Civil engr. Dept. Public Works, Ter. of Hawaii, 1949-50; structural engr. 14th Naval Dist., Pearl Harbor, Hawaii, 1951-54; cons. structural engr., Honolulu, 1954-55; cons. structural engr. Park & Yee, Ltd., Honolulu, 1955-60; pres. Alfred A. Yee & Assos., Inc., Honolulu, 1960—; dir. Kaiser Cement & Gypsum Corp., Oakland, Calif. Served with U.S. Army, 1946-47. Registered profl. engr., Hawaii. Fellow Yale Engring. Assos., Am. Concrete Inst. (hon.), ASCE; mem. Prestressed Concrete Inst. (Martin P. Korn award 1965), Nat. Acad. Engring., Nat. Soc. Profl. Engrs., Hawaii Soc. Profl. Engrs. (Engr. of Yr. award 1969), Soc. Naval Architects and Marine Engrs., Internat. Assn. for Bridge and Structural Engring., Structural Engrs. Assn. Hawaii. Contbr. articles to profl. jours. Office: 1441 Kapiolani Blvd Honolulu HI 96814

YEGEN, PETER, JR., ins. and real estate co. exec.; b. Billings, Mont., July 12, 1896; s. Peter and Margaret (Trepp) Y.; grad. Inst. Dr. Schmidt., St. Gall, Switzerland, 1913; student U. Wis., 1915-17; m. Zellah Wilson Cardwell, Mar. 27, 1918; children—Peter III, Edward Cardwell. Ins., real estate bus. as Peter Yegen, Jr., Billings, 1919—; pres. Yellowstone Ditch Co., 1935—. Pres. Arnold Drainage Dist., 1965—, Shiloh Drainage Dist., 1942—; chmn. Urban Renewal, 1962-63; chmn. Yellowstone County Tb Soc., 1948; Jr. Fire Marshall sponsor, 1947—; chmn. Salvation Army Adv. Bd., 1949-66, hon. life mem., 1966—; chmn., pres. Yellowstone Mus. Bd., 1956—. Served to 2d lt. F.A., U.S. Army, 1918. Named hon. state fire marshall, hon. chief Billings Fire Dept. Mem. Billings Bd. Insurors (pres. 1936), Billings Bd. Realtors (pres. 1937, co-recipient award for outstanding community service 1973), Mont. Assn. Realtors (pres. 1948-49, life realtor emeritus), Mont. Assn. Ins. Agts. (pres. 1940-41, life), Pioneers of Eastern Mont. and their Sons and Daus. (pres. 1953, sec. 1960—), Yellowstone Hist. Soc. (pres. 1960, life mem.), Westerners Internat., Range Riders, Nat. Cowboy Hall of Fame, Museums Assn. Mont. (pres. 1967-69), Am. Legion (comdr. 1933, now comdr. emeritus). Episcopalian. Mason (past master, Shriner life mem.). Clubs: Saddle (pres. 1939, 41, 43), Yellowstone Country (pres. 1952-54), Kiwanis (pres. 1947, life mem., Kiwanian of Year 1979), Goggles and Dusters, Mont. Pioneer and Classic Auto, Am. LaFrance Coterie. Home: 306 N 30th St Billings MT 59101 Office: 211 N 30th St Box 959 Billings MT 59103

YEGGE, ROBERT BERNARD, lawyer, coll. dean; b. Denver, June 17, 1934; s. Ronald Van Kirk and Fairy (Hill) Y.; A.B. magna cum laude, Princeton, 1956; M.A. in Sociology, U. Denver, 1958, J.D., 1959. Admitted to Colo. bar, 1959, D.C. bar, 1978; partner firm Yegge, Hall and Evans, Denver, 1959-78, Nelson & Harding, 1979—; prof. U. Denver Coll. Law, 1965—, dean, 1965-77, dean emeritus, 1977—; asst. to pres. Denver Post, 1971-75; mng. trustee Denver Center for Performing Arts, 1972-75; chmn. Colo. Council Arts and Humanities, 1968—; mem. research applications policy com. NSF. Active nat. and local A.R.C. Trustee Denver Symphony Soc., Inst. of Ct. Mgmt.; trustee, vice chmn. Nat. Assembly State Arts Agys.; vice chmn. Mexican-Am. Legal Edn. and Def. Fund, 1970-76. Recipient Distinguished Service award Denver Jr. C. of C., 1965. Mem. Law and Soc. Assn. (pres. 1965-70), Am., Colo. (bd. govs. 1965-77), Denver, D.C. bar assns., Am. Law Inst., Am. Judicature Soc. (bd. dirs. 1968-72, 75—), Am. Acad. Polit. and Social Sci., Am. Sociol. Soc., Assn. Am. Law Schs., Order St. Ives, Phi Beta Kappa, Beta Theta Pi, Phi Delta Phi, Alpha Kappa Delta, Omicron Delta Kappa. Author: Colorado Negotiable Instruments Law, 1960; Some Goals; Some Tasks, 1965; The American Lawyer: 1976, 1966; New Careers in Law, 1969; The Law Graduate, 1972; Tomorrow's Lawyer: A Shortage and Challenge, 1974; Declaration of Independence for Legal Education, 1976. Home: 121 Lafayette St Denver CO 80218

YEH, CHAI, elec. engr.; b. Hangchow, China, Sept. 21, 1911; came to U.S., 1933, naturalized, 1956; s. Yun Ching and Ai Hwa (Ho) Y.; B.S., Chekiang U., Hangchow, 1931; Ph.D., Harvard U., 1936; m. Ida Chiang, June 20, 1936; children—Yin, Jen. Prof. elec. engring. Pei Yang U., Tientsin, China, 1936-37, Tsing Hwa U., Peking, China, 1937-48, chmn. dept. elec. engring., 1945-47; vis. prof. elec. engring. U. Kans., 1948-56; prof. elec. and computer engring. U. Mich., 1956—. Mem. IEEE, Sigma Xi. Contbr. articles to profl. jours. Home: 1821 Alhambra Dr Ann Arbor MI 48103 Office: U Mich Ann Arbor MI 48109

YEH, KUNG CHIE, elec. engr.; b. Hangchow, China, Aug. 4, 1930; s. Su-Chung and Ae-Shian (Hsu) Y.; came to U.S., 1950, naturalized, 1970; B.S., U. Ill., 1953; M.S., Stanford U., 1954, Ph.D., 1958; m. Margaret Mao-Shu Yung, Sept. 14, 1957; children—Joanna, Lisa, David, Richard. Research asst. Stanford U., 1954-58; research asso. U. Ill., Urbana, 1958-59, mem. faculty, 1959—, prof. elec. engring., 1967—; vis. fellow U. Hawaii, 1967; vis. chair prof. Nat. Taiwan U., 1976. Fellow IEEE (certificate of achievement award for paper 1968); mem. Am. Geophys. Union, Am. Phys. Soc., U.S. Nat. Com. of Internat. Union Radio Sci. (commns. H. and G.). Co-author: Theory of Ionospheric Waves, 1972. Contbr. articles to profl. jours. Home: 4 Regent Ct Champaign IL 61820 Office: Dept Elec Engring Univ Ill Urbana IL 61801

YEH, RAYMOND TZUU-YAU, educator; b. Hunan, China, Nov. 5, 1937; s. Pei Kao and Hu Jen (Wang) Y.; came to U.S., 1956, naturalized, 1975; B.S. in Elec. Engring., U. Ill., Champaign-Urbana, 1961, M.S. in Math., 1963, Ph.D. in Math., 1966; m. Priscilla C. Yeh, Jan. 29, 1966; children—Elaine Y., Stephanie H. Asst. prof. computer sci. Pa. State U., 1966-69; asso. prof. computer sci. U. Tex., Austin, 1969-74, prof., 1974-79, chmn. dept. computer sci., 1975-78; prof., chmn. dept. computer sci. U. Md., College Park, 1979—. Mem. IEEE, Assn. Computing Machinery. Author: (with F. Preparata) An Introduction to Discrete Structures, 1973. Editor: IEE Transactions on Software Engineering, Current Trends in Programming Methodology, 4 vols., 1977, 78. Office: U Md College Park MD. *The more one has the less one has. There is always a balance sheet; nothing comes free!*

YEILDING, FRANK BROOKS, JR., savs. and loan assn. exec.; b. Birmingham, Ala., Mar. 22, 1904; s. Francis B. and Margana (Bland) Y.; student Birmingham-So. Coll., 1925; m. Augusta Gage Smith, Nov. 18, 1925; children—Frank Brooks, III, Augusta Gage Yeilding Hanna. Pres., Jefferson Fed. Savs. & Loan Assn., Birmingham, 1946—, chmn., chief exec. officer, 1976—, also dir.; chmn. bd. Jackson Ins. Agy.; v.p., dir. Internat. Realty Co.; pres., dir. Yeilding Bros. Holding Co.; v.p. Motel Birmingham, Inc.; dir. Yeilding's Dept. Store, Tiger Investors Mortgage Ins. Corp., Boston. Trustee, Highlands Meth. Ch., Birmingham, 1960-78, chmn. bd. stewards, 1944—. Recipient Disting. Alumni award Birmingham-So. Coll., 1967. Mem. Ala. Savs. and Loan League (pres. 1944-45), U.S. Savs. and Loan League (pres. 1963, pres. Southeastern group conf. 1957-58), Birmingham C. of C., Sigma Alpha Epsilon, Omicron Delta Kappa. Clubs: Birmingham Country, Execs. (pres. 1951) (Birmingham); Kiwanis (pres. club 1948), The Club, Downtown, Relay House. Home: 3015 Brookwood Rd Birmingham AL 35223 Office: 215 N 21st St Birmingham AL 35203

YELDELL, JOSEPH PHILIP, govt. ofcl.; b. Washington, Sept. 9, 1932; s. Jefferson Davis and Annie Mae (Senior) Y.; B.S., D.C. Tchrs. Coll., 1957; M.A., U. Pitts., 1961; m. Gladys Johnson, June 16, 1957; children—Gayle, Joi Lynn. Tchr. math. Pitts. Pub. Schs., 1958-61, Washington Pub. Schs., 1961-62; math. statistician Bur. Labor Statistics, U.S. Dept. Labor, 1962-64; mktg. ednl. rep. IBM, 1964-71; mem. D.C. City Council, Washington, 1967-70, 71; dir. Washington Dept. Human Resources, 1971-77; gen. asst. to Mayor, 1977—. Trustee D.C. Pub. Library. Served with USAF, 1954-58. Recipient Outstanding Community Service award DuPont Park Civic Assn., 1972, Silver Helmet award Nat. Amvets, 1975. Fellow Smithsonian Inst.; mem. Washington Area Econ. Orgn. (founder, pres.), NAACP, N. Portal Civic Assn., Urban League, Am. Soc. Pub. Adminstrs., Nat. Assn. State Dirs. Human Resources, Phi Beta Sigma. Mason 33 deg. (Shriner). Home: 1729 Verbena St NW Washington DC 20012 Office: 1350 E St NW Washington DC 20004

YELLON, DONALD JEROME, banker; b. Chgo., Dec. 2, 1921; s. Mark D. and Rose I. (Kaplan) Y.; A.B., U. Chgo., 1943; J.D., 1948; m. Joan Gansberg, Oct. 1, 1955 (dec. Nov. 1967); children—Alvin, Ann; m. 2d, Marilyn Saltzstein, May 28, 1972. Admitted to Ill. bar, 1949; asso. D'Ancona, Pflaum, Wyatt & Riskind, Chgo., 1948-54, partner, 1955-71; v.p., gen. counsel First Nat. Bank Chgo., 1971-73, sr. v.p., 1973-75, exec. v.p., 1975—, gen. counsel, 1973—. Served to lt. (j.g.) USNR, 1943-46. Mem. Order of Coif, Phi Beta Kappa. Home: 921 Timberhill Rd Highland Park IL 60035 Office: First Nat Bank Chgo One First National Plaza Chicago IL 60670

YELLOTT, JOHN INGLE, educator; b. Bel Air, Md., Oct. 25, 1908; s. John I. and Mildred Walker (Nelson) Y.; ed. Episcopal High Sch. of Va.; B.S. in M.E., Johns Hopkins, 1931, M.M.E., 1933; m. Judith Williams, May 12, 1934 (div.); children—John Ingle, Ann Williams; m. 2d, Barbara Leslie Jordan, June 2, 1951. Instr. mech. engring. U. Rochester, 1933-34; instr. and asst. prof. Stevens Inst. Tech., 1934; prof. and head dept. mech. engring. Ill. Inst. Tech., 1940-43; dir. Inst. Gas Tech., 1943-45; chmn. War Tng. Com., 1940-44; dir. research, locomotive devel. com. Bituminous Coal Research, Inc. 1945-55; sec. Assn. for Applied Solar Energy, also asst. dir. Stanford Research Inst., 1955-58; pres. Yellott Engring. Assos., cons. engrs., Phoenix, 1958—; headmaster Phoenix Country Day Sch., 1966-72; dir. Yellott Solar Energy Lab., 1958—; prof. architecture Ariz. State U., 1973-79, prof. emeritus, 1979—; condr. research and edn. in mech. engring.; devel. of coal-fired gas turbine locomotive. Decorated Order Brit. Empire. Recipient Chgo. and Ill. Jr. C. of C. awards, 1943. Profl. engr. Md., N.J., Ariz. Fellow AAAS, ASME (jr. award, 1934), Am. Soc. Heating, Refrigerating and Air-Conditioning Engrs., Ariz. Acad. Sci. (pres. 1959-60), Royal Soc. Arts (Benjamin Franklin fellow); mem. Sigma Xi, Alpha Delta Phi, Tau Beta Pi, Pi Tau Sigma, Omicron Delta Kappa. Republican. Episcopalian. Editor engring. textbooks; contbr. articles to mech. engring. publs.; trans. ASME, Jour. Am. Soc. Heating, Refrigerating and Air-Conditioning Engrs. Address: 901 W El Caminito Phoenix AZ 85021

YELTON, CHESTLEY LEE, orthopedic surgeon; b. Butler, Ky., Nov. 29, 1909; s. James Calvert and Lida (Netterville) Y.; A.B., Transylvania Coll., 1932; M.D., U. Louisville, 1937; m. Ruth Olvey, Oct. 28, 1939; children—Chestley Lee, Ruth Ardis. Intern, Lloyd Noland Hosp., Fairfield, Ala., 1937-38, resident, 1946-49; practice medicine, specializing in orthopedic surgery, Birmingham, Ala., 1952—; chief dept. orthopedic surgery Lloyd Noland Hosp., 1952-63; prof. dept. orthopedic surgery Med. Coll. Ala., 1963—; chief Birmingham Child Amputee Clinic; cons. State Vocational Rehab. and Crippled Children's Services. Diplomate Am. Bd. Orthopedic Surgery. Fellow A.C.S. (com. chmn.), Am. Acad. Orthopedic Surgeons; mem. Soc. Orthopedic Surgery and Traumatology, Clin. Orthopedic Soc., Am. Assn. Surgery of Trauma, Orthopaedic Research Soc., Am. Orthopaedic Foot Soc., Southeastern Surg. Congress, Alpha Omega Alpha. Producer ednl. med. films: Certain Extremity Abnormalities and Their Management, 1962; Talar Fracture Dislocation, 1965; Enchondroma, 1966. Home: 4216 Kennesaw Dr Birmingham AL 35213 Office: 2660 10th Ave S Birmingham AL 35205

YELTON, ELMER EMERSON, bookbinder, ret. fgn. service officer; b. Mukden, China, Mar. 14, 1914 (parents Am. citizens); s. Elmer and Bess (Marxmiller) Y.; B.A., Hamilton Coll., 1934; M.A., U. Cin., 1935; postgrad. Pembroke Coll., Cambridge (Eng.) U., 1958-59; m. Marian Loomis, May 28, 1942 (div. 1951); children—Marjorie Ann (Mrs. David John Wilson); m. 2d, Jo Hodges, July 14, 1956. With U.S. Fgn. Service, State Dept., 1945-74; vice consul, Nairobi, Kenya, 1946-48; 3d sec., vice consul, Tangier, Morocco, 1949-51; consul-in-charge, Luanda, Angola, 1951-54; consul, coordinator refugee relief program, Bonn, Germany, 1954-56; 2d sec., consul, Vientiane, Laos, 1956-57, Saigon, Vietnam, 1957-58; assigned State Dept, 1959-64; 1st sec., consul gen., Buenos Aires, Argentina, 1964-69; consul gen., Tampico, Mexico, 1970, Hermosillo, Mexico, 1970-74; now hand bookbinder, rare book collector and cons. Served to lt. USNR, 1942-45. Recipient Distinguished Alumnus award Cazenovia Coll., 1974. Mem. Am. Inst. Graphic Arts, Guild Book Workers, Bibliog. Soc. Am., Hand Bookbinders of Calif., U.S. Chess Fedn., Phi Beta Kappa (del. to nat. conv. 1934), Sigma Xi, Psi Upsilon. Club: Gibson Island (MD.). Home: 5 E Ina Rd Tucson AZ 85704

YEN, SAMUEL SHOW CHIH, educator; b. Peking, China, Feb. 22, 1927; s. K. Y. and E. K. Y.; B.S., Cheeloo U., China, 1949; M.D., U. Hong Kong, 1954; m. Kathryn Bachman, July 26, 1958; children—Carol Amanda, Dolores Amelia, Margaret Rae. Intern, Queen Mary Hosp., Hong Kong, 1954-55; resident Johns Hopkins U., 1956-60; chief dept. Ob-Gyn, Guam Meml. Hosp., 1960-62; asst. prof. dept. Ob-gyn., Case Western Res. U., 1962-67, asso. prof. dept. reproductive biology, 1967-70; asso. dir. obstetrics Univ. Hosps. Cleve., 1968-70; prof. Ob-gyn., U. Calif., San Diego, 1970-72, prof. dept. reproductive medicine, 1972—, chmn. dept., 1972—; examiner, dir. Am. Bd. Ob-Gyn; lectr. 42d Nobel Symposium, Stockholm, 1978; vis. prof. U. Melbourne, Flinders U., Royal Adelaide Hosp. U. Sidney, U. Hong Kong; Harrison Meml. lectr. Endocrine Soc. Australia, 1978. Recipient Wyeth awards, 1972, 75, 76; Green-Armytage award Royal Coll. Ob-gyn. Eng. Fellow Am. Coll. Obstetricians and Gynecologists;

mem. Am. Gynecol. Soc. (fellowship com. 1978—), San Diego Gynecol. Soc., Soc. Gynecol. Investigation, The Endocrine Soc. (postgrad. com. 1978—), Am. Gynecol. Soc., Perinatal Research Soc., Am. Diabetes Assn. Editor: Reproductive Endocrinology: Physiology, Pathophysiology and Clinical Management, 1978; editorial bd. Jour. Clin. Endocrinology and Metabolism, 1970-77, Genito-urinary Medicine, 1978—. Office: Dept Reproductive Medicine Sch Medicine U Calif San Diego La Jolla CA 92093

YEN, WILLIAM MAO-SHUNG, physicist; b. Nanking, China, Apr. 5, 1935; came to U.S., 1952, naturalized, 1971; s. Wan-Li and Jane Shuan-Lin (Jing) Y.; B.S., U. Redlands, 1956; Ph.D. (Ohio Oil fellow 1959-60, Univ. fellow 1960-61), Washington U., St. Louis, 1962; m. Laurel Curtis, Aug. 18, 1978. Research asso. Stanford U., 1962-65; asst. prof. physics U. Wis., Madison, 1965-68, asso. prof., 1968-72, prof., 1972—; cons. in field. J.S. Guggenheim fellow, 1979-80. Fellow AAAS, Am. Phys. Soc., Optical Soc. Am.; mem. Sigma Xi. Author: (with P. M. Selzer) Laser Spectroscopy Of Solids, 1980; contbr. numerous articles to profl. jours. Office: Physics Dept U Wis 1150 University Ave Madison WI 53706

YEN, Y. C. JAMES (YEN YANG-CHU), educator; b. Oct. 26, 1893; B.A., Yale, 1918, M.A. (hon.), 1928; M.A., Princeton, 1920; D.Sc., St. John U., Shanghai, 1929; LL.D., Syracuse U., 1944, Temple U., 1945, U. Louisville, 1945; L.H.D., U. Me., 1944, New Sch. Social Research, 1954, Philippine Women's U., 1960, Yonsel U., Korea, 1966; m. Alice Huie, Sept. 23, 1921; children—Chen-tung, Chun-ying, Hsin-min, Fu-min (dec.), Hwa-ying. Founder, gen. dir. Chinese Nat. Assn. of Mass. Edn. Movement, Peiping, 1924-51; dir. Tinghsien Rural Reconstrn. Expt., Hopei, 1929-36; pres. Hopei Provincial Inst. Local Govt. Reorgn., 1933-36; mem. Nat. Econ. Council, 1931-37; v.p. Szechuan Provincial Reconstrn. Planning Commn., 1936-38; dir. Hunan Provincial Sch. Pub. Adminstrn., 1938; mem. Supreme Council Nat. Def., 1937; mem. People's Polit. Council, 1938-45; pres. Coll. Rural Reconstrn., 1940-51; mem. Chinese-Am. Joint Commn. Rural Reconstrn., China, 1948-50; pres. Internat. Mass Edn. Movement, 1951-65; adviser Philippine Rural Reconstrn. Movement, 1952—; pres. Internat. Inst. Rural Reconstrn., 1961-78; chmn. Internat. Inst. Rural Reconstrn., 1978—. Decorated Order of Golden Heart (Philippines), Order of Quetzal (Guatemala); recipient Ramon Magsaysay award for internat. understanding, Philippines, 1960 Mem. Beta Theta Pi. Home: 650 West End Ave New York NY 10025 Office: 1775 Broadway New York NY 10019

YEO, DOUGLAS JEFFERY, dentist, educator; b. Regina, Sask., Can., Jan. 16, 1924; s. Jasper Earl and Harriet Elizabeth (Orchard) Y.; A.A., Regina Coll., 1947; D.D.S., U. Toronto, 1951; M.P.H., U. Mich., 1953; m. Lenore Jean Kopas, Dec. 27, 1945; children—Wendy Jean, Robert Douglas. Dental dir. Cariboo Health Unit, Prince George, B.C., Can., 1951-52; regional dental cons. Fraser Valley, 1953-55; dir. dental services City of Vancouver (B.C.), 1955-64; mem. faculty of dentistry U. B.C., Vancouver, 1964—, prof., 1968—, asso. dean, 1972—; cons. in field. Served with Royal Can. Air Force, 1942-45. Fellow Internat. Coll. Dentists, Royal Coll. Dentists Can.; mem. Coll. Dental Surgeons B.C. (v.p. 1964-68, registrar 1968-76), Can. Dental Assn., Can. Soc. Public Health Dentists. Clubs: Hollyburn Country, Seymour Golf and Country. Author 2 books in field. Home: 2426 Nelson Ave West Vancouver BC V7V 2R4 Canada Office: Faculty of Dentistry U BC Vancouver BC V6T 1W5 Canada

YEO, EDWIN HARLEY, III, banker; b. Youngstown, Ohio, May 23, 1934; s. Edwin H. and Virginia (Blevins) Y.; B.A., U. Md., 1959; children—Andrew Houston, Douglas Farrier, Claire Manger. With Pitts. Nat. Bank, 1959—, sr. v.p., 1968-72, vice chmn., 1972-75, also dir.; under sec. treasury for monetary affairs Treasury Dept., Washington, 1975-77; chmn. asset and liability mgmt. com. First Nat. Bank Chgo., 1977-80; sr. fin. advisor City of Chgo., 1980—. Served with USMC, 1952-55. Mem. Bank Adminstrn. Inst. (editorial adv. bd.), Res. City Bankers Assn. Clubs: Duquesne (Pitts.); Cosmos (Washington); Mid Day (Chgo.). Office: 121 N LaSalle St Chicago IL 60602

YEO, RON, architect; b. Los Angeles, June 17, 1933; s. Clayton Erik and Rose G. (Westman) Y.; B.Arch., U. So. Calif., 1959; m. Birgitta S. Bergkvist, Sept. 29, 1962; children—Erik Elov, Katarina Kristina. Draftsman, Montierth & Strickland, Architects, Long Beach, Calif., 1958-61; designer Gosta Edberg S.A.R. Arkitekt, Stockholm, 1962; partner Strickland & Yeo, Architects, Garden Grove, Calif., 1962-63; pres. Ron Yeo, Architec, Inc., Corona del Mar, Calif., 1963—; cons., lectr. in field. Mem. Orange County Planning Commn., 1972-73, 1975-76; chmn. Housing and Community Devel. Task Force, 1978; chmn. Orange County Fire Protection Planning Task Force; chmn. City of Newport Beach City Arts Commn., 1970-72. Fellow AIA; mem. Constrn. Specifications Inst. Democrat. Archtl. works include: Garden Grove Cultural Center, 1978, Garden Grove Civic and Community Center, 1966, Hall Sculpture Studio, 1966. Home: Corona del Mar CA 92625 Office: 500 Jasmine Corona del Mar CA 92625

YEO, RONALD FREDERICK, librarian; b. Woodstock, Ont., Can., Nov. 13, 1923; s. Frederick Thomas and Jugertha Aleda (Vansickle) Y.; B.A., U. Toronto, 1948, B.L.S., 1966; m. Margaret Elizabeth Horsley, Sept. 12, 1953; children—Joanne, Peter. Mgr. book dept. Am. News Co., Toronto, 1948-53; sales mgr., dir. Brit. Book Service, Toronto, 1953-63; mgr. trade div. Collier-Macmillan Can., Ltd., Toronto, 1963-65; pub. services coordinator North York (Ont.) Pub. Library, 1971; chief librarian Regina (Sask.) Pub. Library, 1971—. Served with RCAF, 1942-45. Recipient Silver Jubilee medal, 1977. Mem. Can. Library Assn. (pres. 1978-79), Can. Assn. Pub. Libraries (chmn. 1975-76), Sask. Library Assn., Adminstrs. of Large Pub. Libraries (chmn. 1973-74). Club: Regina Kiwanis. Office: 2311 12th Ave Regina SK S4P 0N3 Canada

YEOMAN, WAYNE ALLEN, airline exec.; b. Sandborn, Ind., Jan. 19, 1923; s. Claude Allen and Anna Lillian (Greer) Y.; B.S., U.S. Mil. Acad., 1946; M.B.A., Harvard U., 1957, D.B.A., 1967; m. Agnes Elaine Richardson, Nov. 22, 1947; children—Wayne Allen, Carol Ann. Commd. 2d lt. U.S. Air Force, 1946, advanced through grades to brig. gen., ret., 1972; with Eastern Air Lines, Inc., Miami, Fla., 1972—, v.p. fin., 1976-77, sr. v.p. fin., 1977—. Decorated Legion of Merit, D.F.C. with 5 oak leaf clusters. Club: Harvard Bus. Sch. of So. Fla. (pres.). Author: Selection of Production Processes, 1976. Home: 4720 Santa Maria Coral Gables FL 33146 Office: Miami Internat Airport Miami FL 33148

YEP, LAURENCE MICHAEL, author; b. San Francisco, June 14, 1948; s. Thomas Kim and Franche (Lee) Y.; B.A., U. Calif., Santa Cruz, 1970; Ph.D., State U. N.Y., Buffalo, 1975. Tchr., San Jose (Calif.) City Coll., part-time 1975-76, Foothill Coll., Mountain View, Calif., 1975; author sci. fiction stories, children's stories, 1968—; author: Sweetwater, 1973; Dragonwings (Newbery Honor Book award ALA 1976, Children's Book award Internat. Reading Assn. 1976, Carter G. Woodson award Nat. Council Social Studies 1976), 1975; Child of the Owl, 1977; Seademons, 1977; Sea Glass, 1979. Book-of-the-Month writing fellow, 1970; teaching fellow State U. N.Y., Buffalo, 1970-73, research fellow, 1973-74. Address: 921 Populus St Sunnyvale CA 94086

YEPREMIAN, GARO SARKIS, profl. football player; b. Larnaca, Cyprus, June 2, 1944; s. Sarkis Krikor and Azadouhi (Shirinian) Y.; student Am. Acad., Larnaca, Cyprus, 1956-60; m. Maritza Vart Javian, June 12, 1971; children—Garo Sarkis, Azad Vartan. Came to U.S., 1966, naturalized, 1967. Salesman, Nicol's Worsteds Ltd., London, Eng., 1962-66; profl. football kicker Detroit Lions, 1966-68, Miami Dolphins (Fla.), 1970-79, New Orleans Saints, 1979—; pres. Garo Enterprises, Inc., Miami, 1971—, Garo's Superburger Restaurant, 1974—. Mem. Nat. Football League Players Assn. Mem. Armenian Apostolic Ch. Office: care New Orleans Saints 1500 Poydras St New Orleans LA 70112*

YERACARIS, CONSTANTINE ANTHONY, sociologist, educator; b. Rethymno, Crete, July 25, 1918; came to U.S., 1946, naturalized, 1957; s. Anthony Constanti e and Polyxeni (Hourhourou) Y.; LL.B., U. Athens (Greece), 1944; M.A., U. Chgo., 1950, Ph.D., 1953; m. Bernice Levenfeld, Sept. 12, 1949; children—Flora Y. Putnam, Y. George, Peter M., Anthony M. Instr. sociology SUNY, Buffalo, 1949-53, asst. prof., 1953-57, asso. prof., 1957-62, prof., 1962—, chmn. dept. sociology, 1976—; cons. local govt. Acting dir. Center for Study of Aging, 1973-76. Served with Greek Army, 1940-41, 45-46. Grantee USPHS, 1960-66, HEW, 1972-75, SUNY Research Found., Ford Found. Mem. Am. Sociol. Assn., Am. Statis. Assn., AAAS, Gerontol. Soc., Population Assn. Am., Am. Public Health Assn., Soc. Study Social Problems, United Univ. Professions (chpt. pres. 1971-75, state exec. bd. 1972-76). Democrat. Greek Orthodox. Contbg. author books; contbr. articles to profl. publs. Home: 485 Norwood Ave Buffalo NY 14222 Office: Dept Sociology SUNY Buffalo Spaulding Quad Buffalo NY 14261

YERAZUNIS, STEPHEN, chem. engr., educator; b. Pittsfield, Mass., Aug. 21, 1922; s. William and Marica (Vlattas) Y.; B.Chem. Engring., Rensselaer Poly. Inst., 1947, M.Chem. Engring., 1949, D.Chem. Engring., 1952; m. Mary Sylvia Morris, Aug. 28, 1954; children—William, Elizabeth. Engr., Manhattan Project, Oak Ridge, 1943-46, Gen. Electric Co., 1947; mem. faculty Rensselaer Poly. Inst., 1949—, prof. chem. engring., 1963—, also asso. dean of engring., 1967—; engr. U.S. Steel Corp., summer 1953, Koppers Co., summers 1954, 55; cons. Knolls Atomic Power Lab., 1956-72, Gen. Electric Co., 1962-64, N.Y. State Dept. of Mental Hygiene, 1968-73, Jet Propulsion Lab., 1977—; spl. research heat and mass transfer, phase equilibria, unmanned planetary exploration. Mem. bd. edn. Lansingburg (N.Y.) Central Sch. Dist., 1962—, pres., 1972. Served with AUS, 1943-46. Fellow Am. Inst. Chem. Engrs. (chmn. Northwestern N.Y. sect. 1962-63); mem. Am. Soc. Engring. Edn., Sigma Xi, Tau Beta Pi, Phi Lambda Upsilon, Alpha Sigma Phi. Mem. Greek Orthodox Ch. (pres. bd. 1958-59). Contbr. articles to profl. jours. Home: 6 Little Bear Rd Troy NY 12182

YERBY, ALONZO SMYTHE, educator health services adminstr.; b. Augusta, Ga., Oct. 15, 1921; s. Rufus Garvin and Wilhelmina Ethlyn (Smythe) Y.; B.S., U. Chgo., 1941; M.D., Meharry Med. Coll., 1946; M.P.H., Harvard, 1948; m. Monteal Monica May, Sept. 17, 1943; children—Mark, Lynne, Kristen. Intern, Coney Island Hosp., Bklyn.; resident in preventive medicine Health Ins. Plan N.Y., 1950-53; exec. dir. med. services N.Y.C. Dept. Health, med. welfare adminstr. N.Y.C. Dept. Welfare, 1960-65; commr. of hosps., N.Y.C., 1965-66; prof. health services adminstrn. Harvard Sch. Pub. Health, Boston, 1966—; cons. Bur. Family Services, Nat. Center Health Services Research, WHO, HEW; mem. Nat. Adv. Commn. on Health Manpower, 1966-67; mem. HEW Adv. Com. on Relationships with State Health Agys., 1963-66, Nat. Profl. Standards Rev. Council, 1978—; vis. scientist USA-USSR Exchange Program, 1967, 79. Served with AUS, 1943-46. Diplomate Am. Bd. Preventive Medicine. Fellow Am. Pub. Health Assn.; mem. Am. Coll. Preventive Medicine, Inst. Medicine of Nat. Acad. Scis., N.Y. Acad. Medicine. Clubs: Harvard (N.Y.C., Boston). Author: Community Medicine in England and Scotland, 1976. Home: 917 Beacon St Boston MA 02215 Office: Harvard Sch Pub Health 677 Huntington Ave Boston MA 02115

YERBY, FRANK, novelist; b. Augusta, Ga., Sept. 5, 1916; s. Rufus Garvin and Willie (Smythe) Y.; A.B., Paine Coll., Augusta, 1937; M.A., Fisk U., 1938; postgrad. U. Chgo.; m. Flora H. Claire Williams, Mar. 1, 1941 (div.); children—Jacques Loring, Nikki Ethlyn, Faune Ellena, Jan Keith; m. 2d, Blanquita Calle-Perez, 1956. Tchr. Fla. A. and M. Coll., Tallahassee, 1939-40, So. U., Baton Rouge, 1940-41; war work Ford Motor Co., Dearborn, Mich., 1942-44, Ranger Aircraft, Jamaica, N.Y., 1944-45. Received the O. Henry Meml. award for best first short story, 1944. Author: The Foxes of Harrow, 1946; The Vixens, 1947; The Golden Hawk, 1948; Prides Castle, 1949; Floodtide, 1950; A Woman Called Fancy, 1951; The Saracen Blade, 1952; The Devil's Laughter, 1953; Bride of Liberty, 1953; Benton's Row, 1954; The Treasure of Pleasant Valley, 1955; Captain Rebel, 1956; Fair Oaks, 1957; The Serpent and the Staff, 1958; Jarrett's Jade, 1959; Gillian, 1960; The Garfield Honor, 1961; Griffin's Way, 1962; The Old Gods Laugh, 1964; An Odor of Sanctity, 1965; Goat Song, 1967; Judas, My Brother, 1968; Speak Now, 1969; The Dahomean, 1970; The Girl from Storyville, 1971; The Voyage Unplanned, 1974; Tobias and the Angel, 1975; A Rose For Ana Maria, 1976; Hail the Conquering Hero, 1977; A Darkness at Ingraham's Crest, 1979; contbr. short stories to Harper's mag. Address: care Wm Morris Agy 1350 Ave of Americas New York City NY 10019

YERGER, RALPH WILLIAM, educator; b. Reading, Pa., July 31, 1922; s. H. Ralph and Kathryn (Yeager) Y.; B.S., Pa. State U., 1943, M.S., 1947; Ph.D., Cornell U., 1950; m. F. Irene Winterle, June 19, 1954; children—Paula Marie, Rachelle Anne, Loreen Kathryn, Ralph William. Instr., State Coll. High Sch., Pa., 1943, Altoona (Pa.) Undergrad. Center, 1947-48; asst. prof. Fla. State U., Tallahassee, 1950-53, asso. prof., 1953-61, prof. biol. scis., 1961—, acting head zoology dept., 1952-54, asso. chmn. dept. biol. sci., 1975-77, asso. dean Coll. Arts and Scis., 1977-78, acting dean, 1978—; reviewer research proposals NSF, 1965—. Trustee Highlands (N.C.) Biol. Sta., 1971—, Fla. Defenders of Environment, 1970-74. Served to capt. AUS, 1943-46. Mem. Am. Inst. Biol. Scis., Am. Soc. Ichthyologists and Herpetologists, Am. Am. Fisheries Soc., Fla. Acad. Sci., Assn. Southeastern Biologists, Southeastern Fishes Council, Sigma Xi. Lutheran. Contbr. to Ency. Brit., 1971. Home: 713 Middlebrooks Circle Tallahassee FL 32312

YERKE, FREDRIC ALBERT, lawyer; b. Portland, Oreg., May 3, 1922; s. Fredric Albert and Sadie (Tredenick) Y.; B.A., Reed Coll., 1946; LL.B., Harvard, 1949; m. Edith Louise Demmon, Feb. 22, 1946; children—John Fredric, Dee Louise, Ann Reneé. Admitted to Oreg. bar, 1949, since practiced in Portland; partner Miller, Anderson, Nash, Yerke & Wiener, 1952—. Mem. exec. bd. Columbia Pacific council Boy Scouts Am., v.p., 1966-73, sr. v.p., 1974—, also mem. nat. council. Served to 1st lt. USAAF, 1943-46. Decorated Air medal. Fellow Am. Coll. Trial Lawyers; mem. Am., Oreg., Multnomah bar assns., Reed Coll. Alumni Assn. (dir., past pres.), Phi Beta Kappa. Presbyn. Clubs: Multnomah Athletic, Astoria Golf and Country, Arlington. Home: 1940 NW Ramsey Crest Portland OR 97229 Office: 900 SW 5th Ave Portland OR 97204

YERKES, DAVID NORTON, architect; b. Cambridge, Mass., Nov. 5, 1911; s. Robert Mearns and Ada (Watterson) Y.; B.A., Harvard U., 1933; M.F.A., Yale U., 1935; m. Catharine Noyes, Oct. 7, 1939 (dec. 1969); 1 dau., Catharine (Mrs. Andreas Bandé); m. 2d, Sarah Hitchcock Satterlee, July 9, 1972. Draftsman, designer, Chgo. and Washington, 1937-39, Deigert & Yerkes and Assos., Washington, 1945-69, David N. Yerkes & Assos., Washington, 1970-80, Yerkes, Pappas and Parker, 1980—; prin. works include Voice of America Studios, Washington, 1958, Nat. Arboretum Hdqrs. Bldg., Washington, 1958, Am. Embassy, Somalia, 1958, also Madeira Sch. Auditorium, 1969, 4 stas. Washington subway system, 1971-72, hdqrs. Nat. Trust Historic Preservation, Washington, 1977, Freemason Harbor Redevel., Norfolk, Va., 1977, also various schs., labs. Mem. panel archtl. advisers Nat. Commn. Fine Arts, 1961-63; vice chmn. Presdl. Inaugural Parade Com., 1965. Served to capt. AUS, 1943-45. Firm recipient numerous regional and nat. awards; recipient Kemper award AIA, 1972. Fellow AIA (bd. dirs. 1965-68, v.p. 1968-69, chmn. nat. honor awards jury 1966, chmn. Reynolds Meml. award jury 1969, pres. found. 1974—). Home: 2700 Virginia Ave NW Washington DC 20037 Office: 1511 K St NW Washington DC 20005

YERKS, ROBERT GEORGE, army officer; b. Ossining, N.Y., Oct. 24, 1928; s. Austin Joseph and Irene Hildegard (Minnerly) Y.; B.S., U.S. Mil. Acad., 1951; M.S., George Washington U., 1971; grad. Nat. War Coll., 1970; m. Iris Alma Anderson, June 10, 1951; children—Robert A., Frank J., Gary M., Thomas A., Roberta A., David M., Virginia I., Irene E., Patricia J., Caroline. Commd. 2d lt. U.S. Army, 1951, advanced through grades to maj. gen., 1975; service in Korea, Vietnam and Turkey; dep. comdt. U.S. Army War Coll., 1974; comdg. gen. U.S. Army Mil. Dist., Washington, 1975-77; comdt. U.S. Army War Coll., 1977-78; dep. chief staff personnel Dept. Army, 1978—; dir. Army Mut. Aid Ins.; bd. dirs. Met. Bd. Trade, Washington. Decorated Silver Star, Legion of Merit, D.F.C. Mem. Assn. Grads. U.S. Mil. Acad. (pres.), Assn. U.S. Army, 9th Div., 101st Airborne Div. assns. Roman Catholic. Office: Dep Chief Staff for Personnel Dept Army Washington DC 20310

YERUSHALMI, YOSEF HAYIM, historian, educator; b. N.Y.C., May 20, 1932; s. Leon and Eva (Kaplan) Y.; B.A., Yeshiva U., 1953; M.Hebrew Lit., Jewish Theol. Sem. Am., 1957; M.A., Columbia, 1961, Ph.D., 1966; M.A. (hon.), Harvard, 1970; Ophra Pearly, Jan. 4, 1959; 1 son, Ariel. Instr. Jewish history Rutgers U., New Brunswick, N.J., 1963-66; asst. prof. Hebrew and Jewish History, Harvard, 1966-70, prof., 1970-78, Jacob E. Safra prof. Jewish history and Saphardic civilization, 1978—, chmn. dept. near eastern langs. and civilizations, 1978—. Recipient Newman medal City U. N.Y., 1975. Kent fellow, 1963, traveling fellow Nat. Found. Jewish Culture, 1964; Nat. Endowment for Humanities fellow, 1976-77. Recipient Ansley award Columbia U. Press, 1968. Fellow Am. Acad. Jewish Research. Author: From Spanish Court to Italian Ghetto: Isaac Cardoso, A Study in Seventeenth-Century Marranism and Jewish Apologetics, 1971; Haggadah and History, 1975. Contbr. articles to profl. publs. on Spanish and Portuguese Jewry. Chmn. publs. com. Jewish Publ. Soc., 1972—. The Lisbon Massacre of 1506, 1976. Home: 75 Park Ave Newton MA 02158 Office: Harvard U Dept Near Eastern Langs and Civilizations Cambridge MA 02138

YERXA, CHARLES TUTTLE, agriculturist; b. Colusa, Calif., Nov. 29, 1918; s. Max N. and Charlotte (Tuttle) Y.; B.S., U. Calif., Berkeley, 1941; m. Virginia Wilson, Mar. 8, 1947; children—Woodford, Alison, Dorothy, Charles Tuttle. Pres., Charles T. Yerxa Farms Inc., Colusa, 1960—, Colusa-Glenn Prodn. Credit Assn., 1965-79; chmn. bd. Sunsweet Inc., Stockton, Calif., 1975—, Calif. Tomato Processing Bd., 1970-78; dir. Fed. Land Bank, 1962-75, bd. dirs. Prine Adminstrn. Com. Vice pres. Woodland Meml. Hosp., 1960-70; trustee Colusa Mosquito Abatement Com., 1965—. Served to lt. comdr. USNR, 1941-46. Republican. Episcopalian. Home: Box 269 Colusa CA 95932 Office: 1050 S Diamond St Stockton CA 95201

YESSELMAN, ROBERT ALAN, dance co. exec.; b. Bklyn., July 26, 1944; s. Sam and Esther (Plushner) Y. Tchr. English and theatre Bethpage (N.Y.) High Sch., 1965-71; mgr. Am. Ballet Theatre's Ballet Repertory Co., N.Y.C., 1971-76; gen. mgr. Paul Taylor Dance Co., N.Y.C., 1976—. Office: Paul Taylor Dance Co 550 Broadway New York NY 10012*

YESSON, CHARLES JOSEPH, savs. and loan exec.; b. Kingston, Pa., Dec. 3, 1932; s. Charles Thomas and Mary Helen (Noveral) Y.; B.S., Pa. State Coll., 1954; postgrad. George Washington U., 1957-59; M.A., N.Y. U., 1961, postgrad., 1961-63; m. Shirley Yvonne Briffett, children—Kathrine Ann, Lisa Marie. Mktg. dir. Hayden Stone, Inc., N.Y.C., 1961-64; asst. to chmn. 1st Western Fin. Corp., Las Vegas, 1964-66; pres. Fin. Mktg. W., Inc., Newport Beach, Calif., 1966-69; sr. v.p. Majestic Savs. & Loan, Denver, 1969-76; v.p. 1st Savs. and Loan Shares, Inc., Denver, 1969-76; v.p. Commerce Savs. & Loan, Kansas City, Kans., 1969-76; partner McSweeney & Assos., Newport Beach, Calif., 1976-77; pres., chief exec. officer, dir. USLIFE Savings & Loan Assn., Los Angeles, 1977—. Founder, Friends of Los Angeles Music Center, 1977—. Served with U.S. Navy, 1954-57. Mem. Nat. League Insured Savs. and Loans (chmn. EFT com. 1975-76), Calif. Savs. and Loan League (dir.), Savs. Assn. Central Corp. Club: Balboa Bay (Newport Beach, Calif.). Author: Investment Record, 1965. Office: 5220 Wilshire Blvd Los Angeles CA 90036

YESTADT, JAMES FRANCIS, music dir.; b. Harrisburg, Pa., Nov. 24, 1921; s. Frederick John and Emelie (Speer) Y.; B.S., Lebanon Valley Coll., 1947; M.A., Columbia U., 1951; student Lucerne Conservatory, 1961, 62; m. Victoria Ann Turco, Sept. 3, 1946; children—Gregory James, Frederick John, James Francis II. Asso. condr. Exptl. Opera Theater Am., 1954-58; resident condr. New Orleans Philharmonic Symphony Orch., 1960-63; music dir., condr. Mobile Symphony Orch., 1964-70, music dir., condr. Mobile Opera Co., 1965-71, 76—, gen. dir., 1971-76; dir. univ. orchs. U. So. Miss., 1975-76; music dir., condr. Baton Rouge Symphony Orch., 1976—; asso. prof. music, dir. univ. orch. La. State U., Baton Rouge, 1976—. Served with AUS, 1942-46. Recipient Conducting award Columbia, 1950, 51. Mem. Mobile Chamber Music Soc. (v.p. 1966-69), Pi Kappa Lambda. Home: 837 Castle Kirk Dr Baton Rouge LA 70808 Office: Baton Rouge Symphony Assn 318 Riverside Mall Baton Rouge LA 70802

YETKA, LAWRENCE ROBERT, state supreme ct. justice; b. Cloquet, Minn., Oct. 1, 1924; s. Frank and Martha (Norkowski) Y.; B.S., U. Minn., 1947, J.D., 1948; m. Ellen Marie Fuller, Nov. 11, 1950; children—Frank Barry, Lawrence George, Christopher Hubert. Admitted to Minn. bar, 1949; founder, partner firm Yetka & Newby, Cloquet, 1949-73; spl. municipal judge, 1960-64; city atty., Cloquet, 1964-73; atty. Duluth Port Authority, 1957-60; atty. Western Lake Superior San. Dist., 1970-73; asso. justice Minn. Supreme Ct., St. Paul, 1973—; atty., dir. Carlton County Fed. Savs. & Loan Assn., 1958-73; chmn. State Jud. Council, 1974—, Select Com. on State Jud. System, 1974-77, State Jud. Planning Agy., 1976—. Del., 12 state Democratic convs., 1948-72, Dem. Nat. Conv., 1956, 64, 68; chmn. Students for Humphrey for Mayor, 1947; Democratic Farmer Labor county officer, 1948-72, 8th Dist., 1962-66; state Dem. vice chmn., 1966-70; mem. Minn. Ho. of Reps., 1951-61, chmn. Ho. Jud. Com., 1955-61, asst. majority leader, 1959-61. Grad., Appellate Judges

Seminar sponsored by Inst. Jud. Adminstrn. at N.Y. U. Law Sch., 1976. Mem. Am., Minn., Carlton County (pres. 1963-73) bar assns., Am. Judicature Soc., Inst. Jud. Adminstrn. Lutheran. Office: Supreme Ct Minn 230 State Capitol Saint Paul MN 55155*

YETNIKOFF, WALTER R., record co. exec.; b. Bklyn., Aug. 11, 1933; s. Max and Bella (Zweibel) Y.; B.A., Bklyn. Coll., 1953; LL.B., Columbia U., 1956; m. June Yetnikoff, Nov. 24, 1957; children—Michael, Daniel. Admitted to N.Y. bar; pvt. practice N.Y.C., 1958-61; atty. CBS, 1961-65; gen. atty. CBS/Records Group, 1965-69; exec. v.p. internat. div. CBS, 1969-71; pres. CBS Records Internat., 1971-75, CBS/Records Group, 1975—; v.p., dir. CBS, Inc. Nat. adv. bd. Am. Cancer Research Center; adv. com. T.J. Martell Meml. Found. Leukemia Research; steering com. Nat. Urban Coalition. Served with U.S. Army, 1956-58. Recipient Humanitarian award Am. Med. Center, 1975. Mem. Internat. Fedn. Producers Phonograms and Videograms. Jewish. Home: 11 N Circle Dr Great Neck NY 11021 Office: 51 W 52d St 11th Floor New York NY 10019*

YGLESIAS, HELEN BASSINE, author; b. N.Y.C., Mar. 29, 1915; d. Solomon and Kate (Goldstein) Bassine; student pub. schs.; m. Jose Yglesias, Aug. 19, 1950; children—Tamar (Mrs. Richard Lear), Lewis Cole, Rafael. Lit. editor Nation mag., 1965-69; adj. asso. prof. writing div. Columbia Sch. Arts, N.Y.C., 1973—; author: (novels) How She Died (Houghton Mifflin award), 1972, Family Feeling, 1976; (non-fiction) Starting: Early, Anew, Over, And Late, 1978. Mem. Garden Club Brooklin (Maine), Am. Author's Guild, Author's League, PEN. Home: North Brooklin ME 04661

YGLESIAS, JOSE, author; b. Tampa, Fla., Nov. 29, 1919; s. Jose and Georgia (Milian) Y.; student Black Mountain Coll., 1946-47; m. Helen Bassine, Aug. 19, 1950; 1 son, Rafael; stepchildren—Tamar (Mrs. Richard Lear), Lewis Cole. Regents lectr. U. Calif. at Santa Barbara, 1973. Served with USNR, World War II. Decorated Naval Merit citation. Guggenheim fellow, 1970, 76, Nat. Endowment for Arts fellow, 1974. Mem. P.E.N. Author: A Wake in Ybor City, 1963; The Goodbye Land, 1967; In The Fist of the Revolution, 1968; An Orderly Life, 1968; Down there, 1970; The Truth About Them, 1971; Double Double, 1974; The Kill Price, 1976; The Franco Years, 1977; also articles, short stories in Best American Stories, 1972, 75. Translator Spanish novels of Juan Goytisolo and Xavier Domingo. Home: North Brooklin ME 04661

YIELDING, K. LEMONE, physician; b. Auburn, Ala., Mar. 25, 1931; s. Riley Lafayette and Bertie (Dees) Y.; B.S., Ala. Poly. Inst., 1949; M.S., U. Ala., 1952, M.D., 1954; m. Lerena Wade Hauge, Dec. 7, 1973; children—K. Lemone, Michael Lafon, Teresa Louise, Riley Lafayette, Katrina Elizabeth. Intern, U. Ala. Med. Center, 1954-55; clin. asso. Nat. Inst. Arthritis and Metabolic Diseases, NIH, 1955-57, sr. investigator, 1958-64; resident med. service USPHS Hosp., Balt., 1957-58; adj. asst. prof. medicine Georgetown U. Med. Sch., 1958-64; cons. USPHS, 1964-68, 75—; prof. biochemistry, asso. prof. medicine, chief lab. molecular biology U. Ala. Med. Center, Birmingham, 1964—; cons. Am. Heart Assn., Arthritis Found. Served with USPHS, 1955-64. Grantee USPHS, Am. Cancer Soc., Nat. Found.-March of Dimes, U.S. Army. Mem. Am. Soc. Biol. Chemistry, Soc. Exptl. Biology and Medicine, Am. Soc. Pharm. and Exptl. Therapeutics, So. Soc. Clin. Investigation, Sigma Xi. Contbr. to profl. jours., books. Home: 2320 23d Ave S Birmingham AL 35223 Office: 501 NBSB Univ Station U Ala Birmingham AL 35294

YIH, CHIA-SHUN, educator; b. Kweiyang, Kweichow, China, July 25, 1918; s. Ting-Chien and Wan-Lan (Shiao) Y.; B.S., Nat. Central U., 1942; M.S., U. Ia., 1947, Ph.D., 1948; m. Shirley Gladys Ashman, Feb. 17, 1949; children—Yiu-Yo, Yuen-Ming David, Weiling Katherine. Instr., Nat. Kweichow U., 1944-45; instr. math. U. Wis., 1948-49; lectr. U. B.C., 1949-50; asso. prof. Colo. State U., 1950-52; research engr. U. Ia., 1952-54, asso. prof., 1954-56; asso. prof. U. Mich., Ann Arbor, 1956-58, prof., 1958—, Stephen P. Timoshenko univ. prof. fluid mechanics, 1968—, Henry Russel lectr., 1974; vis. prof. U. Paris (France), 1970-71; cons. Huyck Felt Co., 1960-64. Trustee Rocky Mountain Hydraulic Lab. Attaché de Recherche in Math., French Govt., 1951-52. Recipient Achievement award Chinese Inst. Engrs. N.Y., 1968, Chinese Engrs. and Scientists Assn. So. Calif., 1973; Sr. Scientist award Humboldt Found., W. Ger., 1977; sr. postdoctoral fellow NSF, 1959-60; Guggenheim fellow, 1964. Fellow Am. Phys. Soc., Mich. Soc. Fellows (sr.); mem. Academia Sinica, Internat. Assn. Hydraulic Research, Sigma Xi, Pi Mu Epsilon, Tau Beta Pi, Phi Kappa Phi. Author: Dynamics of Homogeneous Fluids, 1965; Fluid Mechanics, An Introduction to the Theory, 1969. Editor: Advances in Applied Mechanics. Contbr. articles to profl. jours. Home: 3530 W Huron River Dr Ann Arbor MI 48103

YINGER, J. MILTON, educator; b. Quincy, Mich., July 25, 1916; s. George Daniel and Emma May (Bancroft) Y.; A.B., DePauw U., 1937; M.A., La. State U., 1939; Ph.D., U. Wis., 1942; m. Winnie G. McHenry, July 20, 1941; children—Susan Yinger Johnson, John, Nancy. Instr. sociology Ohio Wesleyan U., 1941-43, asst. prof., 1943-46, asso. prof., 1946-47; asso. prof. Oberlin Coll., 1947-52, prof., 1952—, chmn. dept. sociology-anthropology, 1969-75; vis. prof. U. Mich., 1958, U. Hawaii, 1961; sr. specialist East-West Center Honolulu, 1968-69; vis. fellow Clare Hall, Cambridge U., 1976. Guggenheim fellow, 1968-69; Nat. Endowment for Humanities, 1976-77. Fellow Am. Anthrop. Assn.; mem. Am. Sociol. Assn. (council, sec. 1971-74, pres. 1976-77), Sigma Xi. Author: Religion in the Struggle for Power, 1946; Racial and Cultural Minorities (with George E. Simpson), 1953, 2d edit. (Anisfield-Wolf award), 1958, 4th edit., 1972; Religion, Society and the Individual, 1957 (transl. in Italian, French, Spanish); Sociology Looks at Religion, 1963; Toward a Field Theory of Behavior, 1965; A Minority Group in American Society, 1965 (transl. in Spanish, Oriya, Portuguese); The Scientific Study of Religion, 1970; co-author: Middle Start: An Experimental Study of Educational Enrichment among Young Adolescents, 1977. Asso. editor Am. Sociol. Rev., 1959-62, Social Problems, 1958-61, Jour. Conflict Resolution, 1966-71; co-editor Major Social Issues, 1978. Home: 272 Oak St Oberlin OH 44074

YINGLING, GARY LEE, lawyer; b. Balt., Feb. 26, 1939; s. Jesse Lee and Helen May (McCaslin) Y.; B.S., U. N.C., Chapel Hill, 1962; M.S., Purdue U., 1966; J.D., Emory U., 1968; m. Rachel Dowell, June 15, 1968; children—Leanne, Kevin. Pharmacist, People's Drug Stores, Washington, 1962-64; admitted to D.C. bar, 1969; atty. Nat. Communicable Disease Center, USPHS, Atlanta, 1968-69; trial atty., gen. counsel's office HEW, Washington, 1969-72, 74-76; dir. over-the-counter drug rev. FDA, Rockville, Md., 1972-74; pres. Food and Drug Law Inst., Washington, 1976—. Mem. Am., Fed., D.C., Ga. bar assns., Am. Soc. for Pharmacy Law. Presbyterian. Club: University. Office: 818 Connecticut Ave NW Washington DC 20036

YLVISAKER, PAUL NORMAN, educator; b. St. Paul, Nov. 28, 1921; s. Sigurd Christian and Norma M. (Norem) Y.; A.A., Bethany Luth. Jr. Coll., 1940; B.S., Mankato State Coll., 1942; postgrad. U. Minn, 1942-43; M.P.A. (Littauer fellow), Harvard, 1945, Ph.D., 1948; L.H.D., N.Y. Med. Coll., 1967, Jersey City State Coll., 1968, Princeton, 1970; LL.D., St. Peters Coll., N.J., 1968, Bloomfield Coll., 1968, Upsala Coll., 1969, Swarthmore Coll., 1978; m. Barbara Edwards Ewing, Sept. 7, 1946; children—Jane Elizabeth, Mark Ewing, Peter Lauritz, David Christian. Instr., Bethany Coll., 1943-44; staff Blue Earth County Council on Intergovtl. Relations, 1943-46; tutor, teaching fellow Harvard U., 1945-47, instr., 1947-48; asst. prof. Swarthmore Coll., 1948-53, asso. prof. dept. polit. sci., 1953-55, dir. inter-univ. case program, 1953-54; exec. sec. to mayor of Phila., 1954-55; exec. asso. pub. affairs program Ford Found., 1955-58, asso. dir., 1958-59, dir., 1959-67; commr. N.J. Dept. Community Affairs, 1967-70; vis. prof. Woodrow Wilson Grad. Sch., Princeton, 1961-62, 65-66, 67-68, prof. pub. affairs and urban planning, 1970-72; vis. prof. Harvard, 1968-69, dean Grad. Sch. Edn., 1972—; vis. prof. Yale, 1970. Dir., Dayton-Hudson Corp.; mem. council of nine Van Leer Royal Packaging Industries. Mem. UN Tech. Assistance Mission to Japan, 1960-62, 64; USPHS health exchange mission USSR, 1964; chmn. President's Task Force on Cities, 1966-67; mem. research and policy com. Com. for Econ. Devel.; dep. chmn. task force on land use and urban growth Citizens' Adv. Com. on Environmental Quality, 1972-73; chmn. task force on legalized gambling 20th Century Fund; cons. Commn. on Pvt. Philanthropy and Pub. Needs. Bd. dirs. Mary Reynolds Babcock Found., Edward W. Hazen Found., Van Leer Found. Sr. Fulbright research scholar U.K., 1951-52. Author: Natural Cement Controversy, 1950; Intergovernmental Relations at the Grassroots, 1955; Battle of Blue Earth County, rev. edit., 1955; The Role of Private Philanthropy in Public Affairs, 1975. Contbr. articles to profl. jours. Home: Cambridge MA Office: Harvard Grad Sch Edn Appian Way Cambridge MA 02138

YLVISAKER, WILLIAM TOWNEND, mfg. exec.; b. St. Paul, Feb. 25, 1924; s. Lauritz S. and Winifred Jean (Townend) Y.; grad. Lawrenceville Sch., 1943; B.S., Yale, 1948; m. Jane Penelope Mitchell, May 11, 1972; 1 son, Jon Alastair; children (by previous marriage)—Laurie Ellen, Elizabeth Maren, William Wendell, Amy Townend. Security analyst Bank N.Y., 1948-49; gen. mgr. Lake Forest Motor Sales (Ill.), 1949-52; v.p., gen. mgr. Pheoll Mfg. Co., Chgo., 1952-58; pres. Parker-Kalon div. Gen. Am. Transp. Corp., Clifton, N.J., 1958-61, group v.p., dir. Gen. Am. Transp. Corp., Chgo., 1961-67; chmn. bd., chief exec. officer Gould Nat. Batteries, Inc., 1969-70; pres., dir., chief exec. officer Gould Inc., 1970-75, chmn., pres., chief exec. officer, 1972-75, chmn., chief exec. officer, 1975—; dir. Penske Corp., Piscataway, N.J., Compagnie Francaise D'Electro Chimie, France, Accumuladores Tudor, S.A., Mexico. Bd. dirs. NCCJ, Bush Found., St. Paul, Hwy. Users Fedn., Washington; council Grad. Sch. Bus., U. Chgo.; trustee Lawrenceville (N.J.) Sch., Rush-Presbyn.-St. Luke's Med. Sch., Solomon R. Guggenheim Found., Conf. Bd. Served as ensign USNR, 1943-45. Mem. Chgo. Assn. Commerce and Industry (dir.), Nat. Alliance Businessmen (dir.), U.S. Polo Assn., Northwestern U. Assos. Clubs: Univ., Racquet and Tennis, Links (N.Y.C.); Barrington Hills Country; Oak Brook (Ill.) Polo (gov.); Racquet, Chicago, Yale, Economics (Chgo.); Palm Beach Polo and Country (West Palm Beach, Fla.); Meadow (Rolling Meadows, Ill.); Ocean of Fla. Office: 10 Gould Center Rolling Meadows IL 60008

YNGVE, VICTOR HUSE, educator; b. Niagara Falls, N.Y., July 5, 1920; s. Victor and Miriam (Huse) Y.; B.S., Antioch Coll., 1943; S.M., U. Chgo., 1950, Ph.D., 1953; m. Jean Huber, Sept. 6, 1943; children—Marna, David, Alan. Researcher, tchr. Mass. Inst. Tech., 1953-65; prof. info. sci. U. Chgo., 1965—. Mem. Assn. Machine Translation and Computational Linguistics (past pres.), Linguistic Soc. Am., Author: Computer Programming with Comit II, 1972; Human Linguistics, 1979. Jour. editor: Mechanical Translation and Computational Linguistics, 1954-68.

YOCHELSON, ELLIS L(EON), paleontologist; b. Washington, Nov. 14, 1928; s. Morris Wolf and Fannie (Botkin) Y.; B.S., U. Kan., 1949; M.S., 1950; Ph.D., Columbia, 1955; m. Sally Witt, June 10, 1950; children—Jeffrey, Abby, Charles. Paleontologist, U.S. Geol. Survey, 1952—, biostratigrapher, specializing on Paleozoic gastropods and minor classes of extinct mollusks; lectr. night sch. George Washington U., 1962-65; lectr. Univ. Coll., U. Md., 1966-74. Organizer N. Am. Paleontological Conv., 1969, editor proc., 1970-71; mem. NRC, 1959-68; mem. organizing com. Internat. Congress Systematic and Evolutionary Biology, Boulder, Colo., 1972; research asso. dept. paleobiology Mus. Natural History; sec.-gen. IX Internat. Congress Carboniferous Stratigraphy and Geology, 1979; mem. centennial com. U.S. Geol. Survey, 1979. Fellow AAAS (chmn. sect. E 1971); mem. Soc. Systematic Zoology (sec. 1961-66, councilor 1973), Internat. Palaeontol. Assn. (treas. 1972-76), Paleontol. Soc. (pres. 1976), Paleontol. Assn., Sigma Xi. Co-editor: Essays in Paleontological and Stratigraphy, 1967. Contbr. numerous articles to profl. jours. Home: 12303 Stafford Ln Bowie MD 20715 Office: E-317 Museum Natural History Smithsonian Instn Washington DC 20560

YOCHELSON, LEON, physician; b. Buffalo, July 23, 1917; B.A. in Psychology magna cum laude, U. Buffalo, 1938, M.D., 1942; m. Ruth E. Jolley, Sept. 6, 1942; children—David, Roger, Deborah. Med. officer St. Elizabeth's Hosp., Washington, 1942-43, 46-48; clin. prof. psychiatry George Washington U. Sch. Medicine, 1949-59, prof., 1959—, chmn. dept., 1959-70; tng. analyst Washington Psychoanalytic Inst., 1958—; chmn. Psychiat. Inst. of Washington, Psychiat. Inst. Found., Psychiat. Insts. Am.; pres. med. staff Springwood-At-Leesberg Hosp.; guest lectr. Cath. U. Am., St. Johns U. (Minn.); cons. to VA, HEW, NIMH; chmn. com. on psychiat. hosps. Am. Fedn. Hosps., 1974—, v.p., 1976—; dir. Nat. Commn. on Confidentiality Health Records, 1976—. Served to maj. M.C., AUS, 1943-46. Diplomate Am. Med. Bd. Examiners, Am. Bd. Psychiatry and Neurology (psychiatry). Fellow Am. Psychiat. Assn., Am. Coll. Psychiatrists, Am. Coll. Psychoanalysts (founding); mem. Am. Psychoanalytical Assn., Washington Psychiat. Soc. (sec., pres.), Washington Psychoanalytic Soc., Med. Soc. D.C. (chmn. mental health com., mem. ethics com.), Profl. Assos. of Psychiat. Inst. (chmn.), Nat. Assn. Pvt. Psychiat. Hosps. (chmn. com. on allied orgns.), Med. Soc. St. Elizabeth's Hosp. (past pres.), Alpha Omega Alpha. Contbr. articles to profl. jours. Home: 7914 Orchid St NW Washington DC 20012 Office: 2020 K St NW Washington DC 20006

YOCHUM, LEO WILLIAM, elec. mfg. co. exec.; b. Wheeling, W.Va., July 8, 1927; s. Peter Anthony and Nothburga (Knorr) Y.; B.S., W.Va. U., 1951; postgrad. Harvard, 1961; m. Mary Jane Flading, June 30, 1951; children—Mark David, Susan Marie, Cynthia Lou. With Westinghouse Electric Corp., Pitts., 1951—, indsl. group controller, 1964-66, asst. treas., 1966-67, v.p., controller, 1967-70, v.p. finance, 1970-78, sr. exec. v.p. fin., 1978—. Served with AUS, 1945-47. Mem. Fin. Execs. Inst., Harvard, W.Va. U. alumni assns., Pitts. C. of C. Republican. Roman Catholic. Clubs: St. Clair Country; Laurel Valley Golf; Duquesne. Home: 2024 Blairmont Dr Pittsburgh PA 15241 Office: Westinghouse Bldg Gateway Center Pittsburgh PA 15222

YOCHUM, PHILIP THEODORE, food service mgmt. co. exec.; b. Quakertown, Pa., Sept. 20, 1924; s. Theodore J. and Margaret (Scheetz) Y.; B.S. in Hotel Adminstrn., Cornell U., 1948; m. Connie Petrillose, June 23, 1947; children—Cynthia, Philip Theodore. Engaged in hotel and restaurant work, Quakertown, Pa. and Ithaca, N.Y., 1948-51; various positions to regional mgr. Slater System, Inc., Balt., 1951-57; asst. v.p. ops. A.L. Mathias Co., Towson, Md., 1957-59, v.p., 1959-61, exec. v.p., 1961-65 (merger A.L. Mathias Co. and Servomation Corp. 1964), pres. Servomation Mathias, Inc. (merger into Servomation Corp., 1974), 1965-74, regional mgr. for food service mgmt. and vending, 1974-76, also dir.; dir. corp. devel. S & S Enterprises, operating Golden Plough Restaurants in Md. and N.J., 1977—. Trustee Food Service Execs. Assn. Edn. Trust Fund. Served with AUS, World War II; ETO. Decorated Purple Heart. Mem. Food Service Execs. Assn. (dir., pres. Balt. br., Food Exec. of Year award Balt. br. 1972), Cornell Soc. Hotelmen, Nat. Restaurant Assn., Restaurant Assn. Md. Home: 806 Stone Barn Rd Towson MD 21204 Office: 9737 Reisterstown Rd Garrison MD 21055

YOCK, ROBERT JOHN, judge; b. St. James, Minn., Jan. 11, 1938; s. William Julius and Erma Idella (Fritz) Y.; B.A., St. Olaf Coll., 1959; J.D., U. Mich., 1962; postgrad. U. Strasbourg (France), 1961, Old Dominion Coll., 1964-65, U. Minn., 1966-67; m. Carla Marie Moen, June 13, 1964; children—Signe Kara, Torunn Ingrid. Admitted to Minn. bar, 1962, U.S. Supreme Ct. bar, 1965, D.C. bar, 1972; asso. firm Thomas, King, Swenson & Collatz, St. Paul, 1966-69; chief counsel Nat. Archives, Office Gen Counsel, GSA, Washington, 1969-70, exec. asst. to adminstr. GSA, Washington, 1970-72, asst. gen. counsel, 1972-77; trial judge U.S. Ct. Claims, Washington, 1977—. Served with JAGC, USN, 1962-66. Mem. Am., Minn., Fed. bar assns., Naval Res. JAG Corps. Home: 4200 Webster Ct Annandale VA 22003 Office: US Ct Claims 717 Madison Pl NW Washington DC 20005

YOCUM, JAMES HOWARD, investment adviser; b. Reading, Pa., Sept. 23, 1926; s. George Lehman and Helen (Jost) Y.; grad. Phillips Exeter Acad., 1944; B.S., Mcht. Marine Acad., 1947; B.A. in Econs. cum laude, Harvard, 1948, M.B.A., 1952. Trustee Penn Sq. Mut. Fund, Reading, 1957—; v.p., sec., dir. Yocum Bros., Inc., Reading, 1954—; dir. Kent Industries, Inc. (Ohio), Nat. Central Bank, Reading. Chmn. Berks County chpt. Nat. Found., 1966-68. Trustee Kings Point Fund, 1965—, v.p., 1968, pres., 1969; trustee Reading Musical Found., vice chmn., 1968; bd. dirs. Wyomissing Inst. Fine Arts, pres., 1963-67, 70. Served to lt. (j.g.) USNR, 1952-54. Mem. Pa. Soc. N.Y., U.S. Mcht. Marine Acad. Alumni Assn. (pres. 1978-79), Explorers Club, SAR. Lutheran. Mason (32 deg., Shriner). Clubs: Harvard (Phila., N.Y.C.); Wyomissing (pres. 1969, 70), Maidencreek Fish and Game (pres. 1968—) (Reading). Home: 920 Centre Ave Reading PA 19601 Office: 451 Penn Sq Reading PA 19603

YODER, CHARLES WILLIAM, civil engr.; b. Pottstown, Pa., June 15, 1911; s. Clinton Umstead and Lula Augusta (Beadenkopf) Y.; B.S. in Civil Engring., Pa. State U., 1932; m. Josephine Maybelle Wormley, Nov. 4, 1939; children—C. Neal (dec.), Janica J. Draftsman, Phila., 1933-34; with maintenance dept. Keystone Pipe Line Co., 1934; dock supt. Pa. Shipping Co., Phila., 1935-36; field engr. Bethlehem Steel Co., 1936-37, Empire Constrn. Co., 1937; jr. engr. U.S. Soil Conservation Service, 1938-39, Washington office C.E., 1939-40; asst. engr. Office Chief Engrs., 1941-42; structural engr. Pa. R.R., Phila., 1942-45; dist. structural engr. Portland Cement Assn., Milw., 1945-53; cons. engr Charles W. Yoder & Assos., Milw., 1953—. Lectr in field; 1st chmn. Nat. Constrn. Industry Council, 1975; chmn. Zoning and Planning Commn. Erin Twp., Washington County, Wis., 1971—; mem. Wis. Bldg. Code Rev. Bd., 1964-75. Supporter, Milw. Pub. Mus., Milw. Performing Arts Center, YMCA, Boy Scouts Am., Am. Friends Service Com. Recipient Distinguished Service citation U. Wis., 1974; named Outstanding Alumni, Pa. State U. Coll. Engring., 1974, Alumni fellow, 1975, Community Service award Allied Constrn. Employers Assn., 1975, Engr. of Yr., Engrs. and Scientists of Milw., 1976. Registered profl. engr., Wis., Pa., Ohio, Ill., Minn., Iowa. Fellow Am. Soc. C.E. (pres. Wis. sect. Wis. 1951, chmn. dist. council 1950-53, dist. dir. 1961-64, zone v.p. 1968-69, nat. pres. 1974, life mem.); mem. Am. Cons. Engrs. Council, ASTM, Am. Concrete Inst., Constrn. Specification Inst., Engrs. Joint Council (dir. 1975-78), Cons. Engrs. Council Wis., Am. Arbitration Assn. (nat. panel arbitrators), Chi Epsilon (hon.). Mem. Soc. Friends. Kiwanian (past dir.). Prin. works include: Automated Concrete Products plant Best Block Co., Milw., 1956; Dane County Meml. Coliseum, Madison, Wis. (Outstanding Civil Engring. Achievement in Wis.), 1967; home office bldg. Oilgear Co., Milw., 1973; can handling bldg. Pabst Brewing Co., 1968, tank storage bldg., 1964, Distbn. Center, 1975, New Press Bldg., Milw. Forge, 1977; office and plant facilities Geiser's Potato Chip Co., 1979. Home: 1962 Robins Run Hartford WI 53027 Office: 3505 W Center St Milwaukee WI 53210. *Seek the truth in all matters and live in terms of it. Be objective in your search, in your thoughts and in your relations with people. Work for unity and harmony in terms of people, things and nature. You reach your goals by steadfastness and are aided by the accumulation of many small decisions made wisely. Seek justice and be fair in thoughts, in evaluations, in statements and in actions. Time is a great resource; do not waste it.*

YODER, DALE, ret. educator; b. Gibson City, Ill., Feb. 4, 1901; s. Milo Franklin and Lyda (McAyeal) Y.; B.A., James Millikin U., Decatur, Ill., 1923; student U. Ill., 1923-24; M.A., State U. Iowa, 1926, Ph.D., 1929; m. Mabel Elizabeth Nottingham, Aug. 16, 1924; 1 son, Richard Dale. Instr. econs. State U. Iowa, 1924-29, asst. prof., 1929-31, asso. prof., 1931-35; prof. econs. U. Minn., 1935-57, dir. Indsl. Relations Center, 1945-57, vis. prof. U. Calif. at Los Angeles, 1931, U. Minn., 1934, U. Calif. at Berkeley, 1949, Stanford, 1952, 54-55; prof. Grad. Sch. Bus., Stanford U., 1958-66, prof. indsl. relations, dir. div. indsl. relations, 1959-66; prof., dir. Bur. Bus. Research, Calif. State U., Long Beach, 1967-75; ret., 1975. Chmn. NRA Compliance Bd., Iowa City, 1934; tech. adviser USES, 1933; mem. Regional War Labor Bd., 1942-43; cons. War Manpower Commission, 1942-43, chief planning div. Bur. Program Planning and Review, 1943; vice chmn. 6th Regional War Labor Board, 1943-44; chmn. Wage Rate Com., 1944-45. Cons. War Dept., 1944, Air Force, 1965—; mem. fed. adv. council Employment Security, 1954. Chmn. labor market research com. Social Sci. Research Council, 1951-56, chmn. com. on employment and family, 1956-60; adv. bd. Personnel Adminstrn.; mem. Minn. Commn. on Aging. Recipient Stockberger award, 1963. Mem. Am. Econ. Assn., Mid-West Econ. Assn. (pres. 1936-37), Am. Statis. Assn., Indsl. Relations Research Assn. (pres. 1957), Nat. Acad. Arbitrators, Soc. for Advancement Mgmt., Acad. Mgmt. (pres. Western div. 1963), Soc. Personnel Adminstrn., Am. Soc. Personnel Adminstrs. (life mem., recipient Man of Year award 1968), Order Artus, Beta Gamma Sigma, Phi Gamma Mu, Sigma Alpha Epsilon. Lutheran. Clubs: Cosmos (Washington); Skylight (Mpls.). Author books relating to field; publs. Manpower Economics and Labor Problems, 1950; You and Unions, 1951; Personnel Principles and Policies, 1952, 59; (with H.G. Heneman, Jr.) Labor Economics, 1965; Personnel Management and Industrial Relations, 1970. Editor: Industrial Relations Series of Prentice-Hall; co-editor Handbook of Personnel and Industrial Relations, 1979. Home: 3002 Salmon Dr Rossmoor CA 90720. *My profoundest thoughts look pitifully unimportant when compared to the wisdom of the ages.*

YODER, DOUGLAS O., mfg. co. exec.; b. Cleve., Mar. 18, 1918; s. Carl M. and Bertha L. (Cobbs) Y.; student Ohio Wesleyan U., Fenn Coll.; m. Ruth G. Rueter, Feb. 15, 1947; children—Gary, Virginia, Gail. With Yoder Co., Cleve., 1938—, dir., 1947—, pres., gen. mgr., 1952—; dir. Sifco Industries, Cleve. Fed. Savs. & Loan, 1979—. Bd. dirs. SBA, 1957-74, v.p., 1957-70; adv. council Jr. Achievement Cleve., 1958—, bd. dirs., 1957-62; mem. exec. bd. Cleve. council Boy Scouts Am., 1959-68; trustee St. Luke's Hosp. Assn., 1966—, Cleve.

YMCA, 1977—; bd. mgrs. West Side YMCA, 1956-68. Mem. Assn. for Mgmt. Excellence of Nat. Metal Trades Assn. (pres. Cleve. 1963, exec. com. 1957-60, 61-64, 72-78), Cleve. Engring. Soc. (bd. govs. 1959-62, treas. 1961), Cleve., Lakewood (pres. 1958-59, dir. 1957-62) chambers commerce, Young Pres.'s Orgn. (nat. dir. 1958-61), Chief Execs. Forum, S.A.R. Methodist (trustee). Mason (Shriner, Jester). Clubs: Athletic, Cleveland Yacht, Cleveland Auto (trustee 1967-73), Union. Home: 6 Hidden Valley Rd Rocky River OH 44116 Office: 5500 Walworth Ave Cleveland OH 44102

YODER, EDWIN MILTON, editor; b. Greensboro, N.C., July 18, 1934; s. Edwin M. and Mytrice M. (Logue) Y.; B.A., U. N.C., 1956; B.A. (Rhodes scholar), Oxford (Eng.) U., 1958; m. Mary Jane Warwick, Nov. 1, 1958; children—Anne Daphne, Edwin Warwick. Editorial writer Charlotte (N.C.) News, 1958-61; editorial writer Greensboro Daily News, 1961-64, asso. editor, 1965-75; asst. prof. history U. N.C., Greensboro, 1964-65; editorial page editor Washington Star, 1975—. Recipient awards editorial writing N.C. Press Assn., 1958, 61, 66, Walker Stone award Scripps-Howard Found., 1978, Pulitzer prize editorial writing, 1979. Mem. Nat. Conf. Editorial Writers, Am. Soc. Newspaper Editors. Democrat. Episcopalian. Contbr. articles to periodicals. Home: 4001 Harris Pl Alexandria VA 22304 Office: 225 Virginia Ave SE Washington DC 20061

YODER, FREDERICK FLOYD, assn. exec.; b. Wilkinsburg, Pa., Oct. 7, 1935; s. Floyd Elvin and Mary Viola (Stahl) Y.; B.S. in Journalism, Ohio U., 1957. Mem. hdqrs. staff Sigma Chi frat., Evanston, Ill., 1957—, coordinator chpt. visitation and installations program, 1964-72, leadership tng. adminstr., 1962-76, editor Mag. of Sigma Chi, Sigma Chi publs., 1972—. Served with AUS, 1958. Mem. Coll. Frat. Editors Assn. (past pres.), Am. Soc. Assn. Execs., Chgo. Headline Club, Sigma Delta Chi, Omicron Delta Kappa. Editor: The Norman Shield, 1973; Sigma Chi Membership Directory, 1977. Contbr. articles to interfrat. jours. Home: 2603 Sheridan Rd Evanston IL 60201 Office: 1714 Hinman Ave Box 469 Evanston IL 60204

YODER, HATTEN SCHUYLER, JR., petrologist; b. Cleve., Mar. 20, 1921; s. Hatten Schuyler and Elizabeth Katherine (Knieling) Y.; A.A., U. Chgo., 1940, S.B., 1941; student U. Minn., summer 1941; Ph.D., Mass. Inst. Tech., 1948; m. Elizabeth Marie Bruffey, Aug. 1, 1959; children—Hatten Schuyler III, Karen. Petrologist, Geophys. Lab., Carnegie Instn., Washington, 1948-71, dir., 1971—. Served to lt. comdr. USNR, 1942-46. Recipient award Mineral. Soc. Am., 1954, Bicentennial medal Columbia, 1954; Arthur L. Day medal Geol. Soc. Am., 1962; A.L. Day prize and lectureship Nat. Acad. Sci., 1972; A.G. Werner medal German Mineral. Soc., 1972; Golden Plate award Am. Acad. Achievement, 1973; Wollaston medal Geol. Soc. London, 1979; mineral, Yoderite, named in his honor. Fellow Geol. Soc. Am. (mem. council 1966-68), Mineral. Soc. Am. (council 1962-64, 69-73, pres., 1971-72) Am. Geophys. Union (pres. volcanology, geochemistry and petrology sect. 1962-64); mem. Mineral Soc. London, Geol. Soc. Edinburgh (corr.), Geol. Soc. Finland, All-Union Mineral. Soc. USSR (hon.), Geochem. Soc. (council 1956-58), Am. Chem. Soc., Mineral. Assn. Can., Nat. (chmn. geology sect. 1973-76), Washington acads. scis., Geol. Soc. Washington, Chem. Soc. Washington, Am. Philos. Soc., Am. Acad. Arts and Scis., Explorers Club, Sigma Xi, Phi Delta Theta. Author: Generation of Basaltic Magma, 1976. Editor: The Evolution of the Igneous Rocks, Fiftieth Anniversary Perspective; co-editor: Jour. of Petrology, 1959-69; asso. editor Am. Jour. Sci., 1972—. Contbr. articles to sci. jours. Address: 2801 Upton St NW Washington DC 20008

YODER, LEVON LEE, educator; b. Middlebury, Ind., June 22, 1936; s. Leonard C. and Cleo M. (Pletcher) Y.; B.A., Goshen Coll., 1958; M.A., U. Mich., 1961, Ph.D., 1963; m. Anita R. Hoffman, Aug. 21, 1960; 1 dau., Teryl Lyn. Asst. prof. physics, chmn. dept. Millikin U., Decatur, Ill., 1963-65; asso. prof. physics, Adrian (Mich.) Coll., 1965-70, chmn. dept., 1965-75, 78—, prof., 1970—. Mem. Mich Acad. Sci., Arts and Letters, Am. Assn. Physics Tchrs., AAAS, Sigma Xi. Home: 2499 Sword Hwy Adrian MI 49221

YOE, HARRY WARNER, agrl. economist; b. Martinsburg, W. Va., Oct. 20, 1912; s. Horace George and Mary Morrow (Van Metre) Y.; B.S., W. Va. U., 1935, grad. study, 1940; m. Barbara Virginia Fultz, Mar. 22, 1936; children—Harry Warner, Robert Boyd, Paul Michael. Agriculturist U.S. Dept. Agr., Red House Homesteads, W. Va., 1935-38, dir. spl. project, Princeton, W.Va., 1938-40, dist. supr. Farm Security Adminstrn., Morgantown, W. Va., 1940-42; econ. cons. Supreme Comdr. Allied Power, Tokyo, Japan, 1947-51; agrl. adminstr. Inter-Am. Affairs, 1951-53; dir. div. Western S.A., ICA, 1953-57; dir. USOM to Haiti, 1957-61; dir. ICA West Indies and Eastern Caribbean Mission, Port-of-Spain, Trinidad, W.I., 1961-62; with AID, Dept. State, Wash., 1962-64; dir. AID mission, Georgetown, British Guiana, 1964-68; asso. mem. firm, dir. econs. and planning div. Miller-Warden-Western, Inc., 1968-69; dir., v.p. Hoskins-Western-Sonderegger, Inc., 1969—. Served from lt. (j.g.) to comdr., USNR, 1942-46. Recipient commendation for econ. rehab. Yokohama area, Japan, U.S. Army, 1946, meritorious award for econ. reforms Japanese Fishing Industry, 1951; spl. commendation ICA, 1953; superior honor award AID, 1967. Mem. Alpha Zeta, Pi Kappa Alpha. Episcopalian (vestryman). Clubs: Rotary, Internat. (Washington). Author: Fisheries Cooperatives in Japan, 1950. Home: Route 3 Martinsburg WV 25401 Office: 825 G St Lincoln NE 68508

YOFFE, MORRIS, health care co. exec.; b. Mt. Carmel Twp., Pa., Aug. 8, 1929; s. Max and Sarah (Wishkin) Y.; B.S., Drexel U., 1953; postgrad. Temple U. Law Sch., 1954; m. Chickee Esther Faith Margulis, June 25, 1955; children—Seth Michael, Eve Nicole, Josh Aron, Lori Jo. Jr. acct. Ralph M. Fratkin & Co., C.P.A.'s, Phila., 1954-55; sr. acct. Adler Faunce & Leonard C.P.A.'s, Phila., 1955-58; pvt. practice acctg., Phila., 1958-63; sr. partner, founder Yoffe, Herman & Co., C.P.A.'s, Phila., 1963-69, Yoffe, Shore & Aurach, C.P.A.'s, Phila., 1970; pres., dir. Corp. Planners, Inc., Laverock, Pa., 1962; founder, dir., pres., chief exec. officer Am. Med. Affiliates, Inc., Jenkintown, Pa., 1968—. Mem. Citizens Adv. Bd., Cheltenham Twp., Pa., 1974—; bd. dirs. Laverock Improvement Assn., 1977—; bd. dirs. Citizens Crime Commn. Phila., 1978—; bd. dirs. Met. Hosp., Phila., 1974—, fin, chmn., 1976-77; bd. dirs. Solomon Schechter Day Sch., Wynnewood, Pa., 1975—; vice chmn. Met. Phila. Anti Defamation League, 1977—; nat. vice chmn. Anti Defamation League Soc. Fellows, 1978—; bd. dirs. Nat. Tay Sachs, 1976—, Beth Sholom Synagogue, Elkins Park, Pa., 1977—. Recipient State of Israel Health Care Service Tribute award, 1978. Fellow Am. Coll. Nursing Home Adminstrs.; C.P.A.'s, Pa. Inst. C.P.A.'s, Pa. Health Care Facilities Assn. (past dir.), Am. Health Care Assn. (past dir.). Republican. Clubs: Ashbourne Country, Astra, Blue Key, B'nai B'rith (past pres.). Office: Highland Office Center Pinetown Rd Fort Washington PA 19034

YOH, HAROLD LIONEL, JR., engring., constrn. and mgmt. co. exec.; b. Bryn Mawr, Pa., Dec. 12, 1936; s. Harold Lionel and Katherine (Hulme) Y.; B.S. in Mech. Engring., Duke, 1958; M.B.A., U. Pa., 1962; m. Mary Michael Milus, June 20, 1959; children—Harold Lionel III, Michael Hulme, Karen Bogart, Jeffrey Milus, William Courtlandt. Vice pres. western region H.L. Yoh Co. div. Day & Zimmermann, Inc., Phila., 1960-63, sr. v.p. div. mgr., 1963-64, pres., 1964-76; v.p. adminstrn. Day & Zimmerman, Inc., Phila., 1961-69, sec., 1966-70, v.p., treas., 1969-76, vice chmn. bd., chief exec. officer, 1976—, dir., 1964—; past pres., past dir. Nat. Tech. Services Assn. Bd. dirs. Citizens Crime Commn. Phila., Phila. Coll. Performing Arts; com. chmn. Boy Scouts Am.; trustee Pop Warner Little Scholars. Mem. ASME, Am. Def. Preparedness Assn. (nat. dir., dir. past pres. Phila. chpt.), Phila. C. of C. (dir., edn. vice chmn.), Young President's Orgn., Navy League (life), Netherlands Soc., Sigma Nu. Clubs: Union League (Phila.); Merion Cricket, Merion Golf; University (Washington); Seaview Country; Stone Harbor Yacht; Urban. Home: 1101 Lafayette Rd Bryn Mawr PA 19010 Office: 1818 Market St Philadelphia PA 19103

YOHE, RALPH SANDLIN, editor; b. Mt. Erie, Ill., June 27, 1920; s. Irvin Bradshaw and Georgia (Sandlin) Y.; B.S., U. Ill., 1943; postgrad. U. Chgo., 1947-48. Exec. sec. Ill. Poultry Improvement Assn., Chgo., 1946-48; sci. editor, asso. editor Prairie Farmer Pub. Co., Chgo., 1948-57; editor Wis. Agriculturist, Madison, 1957—; v.p., dir. Wis. Farmer Co., Inc. Mem. agrl. com. Nat. Planning Assn., 1958—, mem. com. on changing internat. realities, 1975—; mem. adv. council Coll. Agr., Wis. State U., River Falls, 1968-73; mem. animal disease control adv. council Wis. Dept. Agr., 1972-73. Vice pres., bd. dirs. Nr. Eastern Art Research Center; v.p., trustee Nat. Rug and Textile Found., 1968-76; trustee, sec. Textile Mus. Washington, 1969—. Served with USNR, 1943-46; MTO. Mem. Am. Agrl. Editors Assn. (dir. 1966-67, 68-70), United Comml. Travelers Am. (grand counselor Wis. 1971-72), Alpha Zeta. Methodist. Clubs: Masons, Shriners, Rotary, Elks. Author: What Our Farmers Can Learn From Other Lands, 1953; (with others) Exploring the Old World, 1955, rev., 1960; (with Jones) Turkish Rugs, 1968; (with others) Exploring Regions of the Eastern Hemisphere, 2d edit., 1977; (with others) Persian Tribal Rugs, 1971; (with others) Cultures in Transition, 1973; Introduction, Don't Forget to Smell the Flowers Along the Way: Portraits of Joseph V. McMullan, 1977; Yörük: The Nomadic Weaving Tradition of the Middle East, 1978. Home: 103 Alhambra Pl Madison WI 53713 Office: 2976 Triverton Pike Madison WI 53711

YOHN, DAVID STEWART, virologist; b. Shelby, Ohio, June 7, 1929; s. Joseph Van and Agnes (Tryon) Y.; B.S., Otterbein Coll., 1951; M.S., Ohio State U., 1953, Ph.D., 1957; M.P.H., U. Pitts., 1960; m. Olivetta Kathleen McCoy, June 11, 1950; children—Linda Jean, Kathleen Ann, Joseph John, David McCoy, Kristine Renee. Research fellow, scholar in microbiology Ohio State U., 1952-56, prof. virology Coll. Veterinary Medicine, 1969—, dir. Cancer Research Center, 1973—; research asso., asst. prof. microbiology U. Pitts., 1956-62; asso. cancer research scientist Roswell Park Meml. Inst., Buffalo, 1962-69; mem. nat. med. and sci. adv. com. Leukemia Soc. Am., 1970—, trustee, 1971—; mem. cancer research centers rev. com. Nat. Cancer Inst., 1972—. Pres. bd. deacons North Presbyn. Ch., Williamsburg, N.Y., 1967-68. Recipient Pub. Service award Lions, 1968. Mem. Am. Assn. Cancer Research, Am. Soc. Microbiology, Am. Assn. Immunologists, AAAS, Internat. Assn. Comparative Research on Leukemia and Related Diseases (sec.-gen. 1974—). Club: Sertoma (Columbus, Ohio). Home: 1237 Norwell Dr Columbus OH 43220 Office: Ohio State U Comprehensive Cancer Center Suite 357 McCampbell Hall 1580 Cannon Dr Columbus OH 43210

YOHO, LEWIS WILBUR, univ. dean; b. Moweaqua, Ill., Aug. 18, 1916; s. Millard and Cornelia E. (Simpson) Y.; B.S., Ind. State U., 1941; M.S., Calif. Inst. Tech., 1944; Ed.D., Ind. U., 1959; m. Mary Luella Shedd, Apr. 17, 1943; children—Gregory Alan, Lora Lynne. Tchr., supr. Ill. Bd. Vocational Edn., 1941-43; tchr. Bicknell (Ind.) High Sch., 1946, South Bend, Ind., 1946-47; asst. prof. Ball State U., 1948-50; vocational dir. South Bend Sch. Corp., 1951-58; asso. prof. Ind. State U., 1958-62, prof., chmn. dept., 1962-68, dean Sch. Tech., 1968—. Served to lt. USNR, 1944-46. Mem. Ind. Council Local Adminstrs. (pres. 1955), Ind. Indsl. Edn. Assn. (pres. 1962), Ind. Vocational and Practical Arts Assn., Am. Vocational Assn., Nat. Assn. Indsl. and Tech. Tchr. Edn. (pres. 1971), Am. Indsl. Arts Assn., Epsilon Pi Tau, Phi Delta Kappa. Author: The Orchestrated Systems Approach to Industrial Arts-Technical Vocational, rev. edit., 1967. Home: 2227 Poplar St Terre Haute IN 47803

YOKE, JOHN THOMAS, educator; b. N.Y.C., Feb. 27, 1928; s. John Thomas and Mary (Fredericks) Y.; B.S., Yale, 1948; M.S., U. Mich., 1950, Ph.D., 1954; m. Mary Alice McPherson, June 16, 1956; children—John Thomas, Mary Elizabeth, James Richason. Postdoctoral fellow U. Chgo., 1955; research chemist Procter & Gamble Co., Cin., 1956-58; instr. U. N.C., Chapel Hill, 1958-59; asst. prof. U. Ariz., Tucson, 1959-64; asso. prof. dept. chemistry Oreg. State U., Corvallis, 1964-70, prof., 1970—. Served with Chem. Corps, AUS, 1954-56. Mem. Am. Chem. Soc., Sigma Xi, Phi Lambda Upsilon, Alpha Chi Sigma. Home: 13 Edgewood Way Corvallis OR 97330

YOLEN, JANE HYATT, author; b. N.Y.C., Feb. 11, 1939; d. Will Hyatt and Isabelle (Berlin) Y.; B.A., Smith Coll., 1960; M.Ed., U. Mass., 1978; m. David Wilber Stemple, Sept. 2, 1962; children—Heidi Elisabet, Adam Douglas, Jason Frederic. Asst. editor This Week mag., 1960; mem. staff Saturday Rev., 1960; asst. editor Gold Medal Books, 1961; asst. editor Rutledge Press, 1961-63; asst. juvenile editor A.A. Knopf, Inc., 1963-65; free lance writer, 1965—; tchr. writers confs. Tempel Buell Coll., Western Wash. State Coll., Franconia Coll., Smith Coll., U. Mass.; mem. Mass. Council on Arts, 1974. Del. from Mass., Democratic Nat. Conv., 1972; asst. press sec. Ed McColgan Congressional campaign, 1976; town condr. Robert Drinan's campaign, 1970. Mem. Soc. Children's Book Writers (dir. 1974—, tchr. writers confs.), Children's Lit. Assn. (dir. 1977—), Nat. Book Critics Circle, Sci. Fiction Writers Am., Modern Lang. Assn., Nat. Council Tchrs. English. Democrat. Quaker. Author: The Witch Who Wasn't, 1964; The Emperor and the Kite, 1968; Writing Books for Children, 1973; The Girl Who Cried Flowers, 1974; The Hundredth Dove, 1978; The Dream Weaver, 1979; others. Home: 31 School St Hatfield MA 01038

YOLLES, STANLEY FAUSST, physician, educator; b. N.Y.C., Apr. 19, 1919; s. Louis Joseph and Rose (Fausst) Y.; A.B., Bkly. Coll., 1939; A.M., Harvard, 1940; M.D., N.Y. U., 1950; M.P.H., Johns Hopkins, 1957; m. Tamarath Dorothy Knigin, Oct. 10, 1942; children—Melanie Ann, Jennifer Cindy. Commd. USPHS, 1950, rear adm. 1964 intern USPHS Hosp., S.I., N.Y., 1950-51; resident psychiatry USPHS Hosp., Lexington, Ky., 1951-54; staff psychiatrist Mental Health Study Center, 1954-55, asso. dir., 1955-57, dir., 1957-60; asso. dir. extre-mural programs Nat. Inst. Mental Health, NIH, 1960-63, dep. dir. inst., 1963-64, dir., 1964-70; asso. adminstr. for mental health HEW, 1968-70; asst. surgeon gen. USPHS, 1964-70; clin. prof. psychiatry George Washington U., 1967-71; prof., chmn. dept. psychiatry State U. N.Y. at Stony Brook, 1971—; sr. cons. L.I. Jewish Hillside Med. Center, New Hyde Park, N.Y., Nassau County Med. Center, VA Hosp., Northport, N.Y., South Oaks Hosp., Amityville, N.Y., Central Islip (N.Y.) State Hosp.; dir. Univ. Psychiat. Services, Central Islip. Spl. cons. N.Y.C. Bd. Edn. mem. adv. com. on research VA; mem. adv. com. Fed. Jud. Center, mem. profl. adv. bd. Internat. Com. agaist Mental Illness, 1968—; mem. nat. adv. panel Am. Jewish Com., 1969—; mem. med. adv. com. Am. Joint Distbn. Com., 1970—; mem. expert adv. panel on mental health WHO, 1969—. Trustee N.Y. Sch. Psychiatry; mem. hosp. vis. com. Brookhaven Nat. Labs. Served as 1st lt. San. Corps, AUS, 1943-46. Fellow Am. Psychiat. Assn., Am. Coll. Psychiatrists, Am. Pub. Health Assn., N.Y. Acad. Medicine; mem. AAAS, N.Y. Acad. Scis., Washington Psychiat. Soc., A.M.A., Md. Pub. Health Assn., Am. Soc. Parasitologists, Am. Psychopath. Assn., Group for Advancement Psychiatry, Assn. Chairmen Depts. Psychiatry, Pan Am. Med. Assn., World Fedn. Mental Health, Alpha Omega Alpha. Club: Cosmos (Washington). Asso. editorial bd. Jour. Diseases Nervous System, 1968—; editorial bd. Med. Insight, 1969—, Quar. Jour. Studies Alcohol, 1970—. Contbr. articles to profl. jours. Home: 2 Soundview Ct Stony Brook NY 11790

YON, JOSEPH L., physician, educator; b. Corapolis, Pa., 1912; M.D., U. Va., 1937; m. Sallie Haden; 2 sons, 1 dau. Intern St. Francis Hosp., Pitts., 1937-38; commd. M.C., U.S. Navy, advanced through grades to rear adm.; fellow surgery Northwestern U. Med. Sch., also Cook County Hosp., Chgo., 1948-49; resident surgery U.S. Naval Hosp., Phila., 1949-51; resident surgery U.S. Naval Hosp., St. Albans, N.Y., 1951-52, head dept. gen. surgery, 1951-52; chief surgeon U.S. Naval hosp. ship Consolation, Korea, 1952-54, U.S. Naval Hosp., Camp Lejeune, N.C., 1954-60; comdg. officer U.S. Naval Hosp., Newport, R.I., 1960-62, U.S. Naval Hosp., St. Albans, 1962-64, U.S. Naval Hosp., Portsmouth, Va., 1962-72; ret., 1972; asso. dean, prof. surgery Eastern Va. Med. Sch., Norfolk, 1972—. Decorated Purple Heart, Legion of Merit, D.S.M., Sec. Navy Commendation. Diplomate Am. Bd. Surgery. Fellow A.C.S., Internat. Coll. Surgeons; mem. AMA, Portsmouth Acad. Medicine. Address: PO Box 6038 Portsmouth VA 23703

YONG, RAYMOND NEN-YIU, civil engr.; b. Singapore, Apr. 10, 1929; naturalized Can. citizen, 1966; s. Ngim Djin and Lucy (Loh) Y.; B.A. in Math. and Physics, Washington and Jefferson Coll., 1950; B.S., M.I.T., 1952; M.S., Purdue U., 1954; M.Engring., McGill U., Montreal, Que., Can., 1958, Ph.D., 1960; m. Florence Lechensky, July 8, 1961; children—Raymond T.M., Christopher T.K. Mem. faculty McGill U., 1959—, prof. civil engring., 1965—, William Scott prof. civil engring. and applied mechanics, dir. Geotech. Research Centre, 1973—. Mem. ASCE, Instn. Civil Engrs., Order Engrs. Que., Soc. Rheology, Clay Minerals Soc., Internat. Soc. Terrain-Vehicle Systems, Can. Geotech. Soc., ASTM. Author: Soil Properties and Behavior, 1975 (Japanese edit. 1977), Introduction to Soil Behavior, 1966 (Japanese edit. 1974). Office: 817 Sherbrooke St W Montreal PQ H3A 2K6 Canada

YONKMAN, FREDRICK ALBERS, lawyer, financial corp. exec.; b. Holland, Mich., Aug. 22, 1930; s. Fredrick Francis and Janet Dorothy (Albers) Y.; B.A., Hope Coll., Holland, 1952; J.D., U. Chgo., 1957; m. Kathleen VerMeulen, June 9, 1953; children—Sara, Margriet, Nina. Admitted to N.Y. bar, 1958; with firm Winthrop, Stimson, Putnam & Roberts, N.Y.C., 1957-64; sec., gen. counsel Reuben H. Donnelley Corp., N.Y.C., 1964-66, Dun & Bradstreet, Inc., N.Y.C., 1966-68; admitted to Mass. bar, 1968; mem. law firm Sullivan & Worcester, Boston, 1968-72; gen. counsel Am. Express Co., N.Y.C., 1972—, exec. v.p., 1975—; dir. Kennecott Copper Corp.; trustee Young Audiences, Inc., Outward Bound, Inc.; adj. prof. law Georgetown U., 1976—, chmn. Inst. Internat. and Fgn. Trade Law. Vis. com. U. Chgo. Law Sch.; bd. dirs. Washington Campus Program. Served with AUS, 1952-54. Recipient Silver Anniversary award Nat. Coll. Athletic Assn., 1977. Mem. Am. Soc. Internat Law, Am., N.Y. State, Boston bar assns., Assn. Bar City N.Y. (past sec. com. internat. law). Presbyterian. Clubs: Union, Downtown Assn. (N.Y.C.); Union (Boston); Shenorock Shore (Rye, N.Y.). Home: 42 Doubling Rd Greenwich CT 06830 Office: Am Express Plaza New York NY 10004

YOOD, BERTRAM, educator; b. Bayonne, N.J., Jan. 6, 1917; s. Benjamin and Fannie (Kowal) Y.; B.S., Yale, 1938, Ph.D., 1947; M.S., Calif. Inst. Tech., 1939; postgrad. Brown U., 1941; m. Shirley Saffran, Jan. 25, 1944; children—Robert A., Janet G., Arthur J. Instr. Cornell U., 1947-49, asst. prof., 1949-53; asso. prof. math. U. Oreg., 1953-60, prof., 1960-72; prof. math. Pa. State U., 1972—; vis. prof. U. Calif. at Berkeley, 1956-57, Yale, 1958-59, Inst. Advanced Study, 1961-62, U. Edinburgh, 1969-70, Weizmann Inst. Sci., 1978-79. Served with USNR, 1942-45. Mem. Am. Math. Soc. (chmn. math. surveys com. 1969-73). Home: 575 Easterly Pkwy State College PA 16801

YORDAN, CARLOS MANUEL, fgn. service officer; b. P.R., Nov. 27, 1925; s. Nicholas and Octavia (Baez) Y.; came to U.S., 1940; student Gregg Bus. Coll., 1940-42; M.A. in Polit. Sci., U. Chgo. (corr.), 1960, M.A. in Am. History, 1962; m. Hilda Bordas, Aug. 16, 1946; 1 son, Carlos Manuel. Joined U.S. Fgn. Service, 1947; chief clk. engring. dept. Unifruitco, Dominican Republic, 1944-47; adminstrv. officer State Dept., Santo Domingo, Dominican Republic, 1947-50, Quito, Ecuador, 1950-52, 2d sec., vice consul, Lima, Peru, 1953-55, Rangoon, Burma, 1956-58, London, 1958-60, Budapest, Hungary, 1960-61, Washington, 1961-65, 1st sec., consul, Warsaw, Poland, 1965-67, Berlin, W. Germany, 1967-70, Dublin, Ireland, 1970-73, Brasilia, Brazil, 1973-77; counselor embassy, Santo Domingo, Dominican Republic, 1977—. Mem. Fgn. Service Assn., Royal Dublin Soc., Am. Soc. Natural History. Clubs: Clube das Nacoes, Brasilia Tennis Acad., Naco Tennis. Office: care Am Embassy APO Miami FL 34041

YORDON, WESLEY JAMES, JR., educator; b. Plainfield, N.J., May 14, 1931; s. Wesley James and Alberta Esther (Sauerwein) Y.; student Wesleyan U., 1949-51; B.A., U. Colo., 1956; M.A., Ph.D., Harvard U., 1960; m. Judith Jane Reglien, June 8, 1957; children—Kenneth, Cynthia, Janet, Jennifer. Prof. econs. U. Colo., Boulder, 1959—. Cons. FTC. Served with AUS, 1951-54. Decorated Combat Inf. badge. Fulbright lectr., Argentina, 1963, Mexico, 1965. Mem. Am., Western econ. assns. Democrat. Conglist. Home: 1655 Dogwood Ln Boulder CO 80302

YORK, COLON WESLEY, textile co. exec.; b. nr. Asheboro, N.C., Dec. 16, 1917; s. Frank L. and Ida (York) Y.; student pub. schs., Asheboro; m. Jean Bradley, June 15, 1973; children by previous marriage—Betty, Marian, Randolph. With Burlington Industries, Inc., Greensboro, N.C., 1938-53, v.p. Peerless Woolen Mills div., Rossville, Ga., 1953-61; v.p., treas. United Hosiery Mills Corp. (now Skyland Internat. Corp.), Chattanooga, 1961-64, exec. v.p., 1964-69, pres., chief exec. officer, 1969-76, chmn. bd., chief exec. officer, 1976—. Adv. bd. Salvation Army. Trustee McCallie Sch., U. Chattanooga Found. Served with USAAF, 1944-45. Mem. So. Acad. Letters, Arts and Scis. (founding mem., trustee). Episcopalian. Clubs: Lookout Mountain (Tenn.) Golf, Lookout Mountain Fairyland, Mountain City. Office: Skyland Internat Corp 2001 Wheeler Ave Chattanooga TN 37406*

YORK, E. TRAVIS, JR., univ. exec.; b. Mentone, Ala., July 4, 1922; s. E. Travis and Leila (Hixon) Y.; B.S., Auburn U., 1942, M.S., 1946; Ph.D. (research fellow 1946-49), Cornell U., 1949; postgrad. George Washington U., 1957-59; m. Vermelle Cardwell, Dec. 26, 1946; children—Lisa Carol, Travis Loften. Asso. prof. agr. N.C. State Coll., 1949-52, prof., 1952-56, head dept. agronomy, 1953-56; Eastern dir. Am. Potash Inst., 1956-59; dir. Ala. Extension Service, Auburn U., 1959-61; adminstr. Fed. Extension Service, Dept. Agr., 1961-63; provost for agr. U. Fla., 1963-71, v.p. agrl. affairs, 1971-73, exec. v.p., interim pres., 1973-74; now chancellor State U. System of Fla. Bd.

dirs. Ala. Bd. Agr. and Industries also Ala. Bd. Conservation, 1959-61, Fed. Crop Ins. Corp., 1962-63; mem. Am. Food for Peace Council, 1961-62, Freedom from Hunger Com., 1961-62, President's Panel Vocat. Edn., 1961-62; adv. bd. Nat. Agrl. Extension Center Advanced Study, 1961-63; chmn. council grad. edn. in agrl. scis. So. Regional Edn. Bd., 1964-66, mem., 1975—, exec. com., 1978—; mem. Pres.' Sci. Adv. Council Task Force on World Food Problems, 1966-67; mem. senate, exec. com. Nat. Assn. State Univs. and Land Grant Colls., 1967-70; mem. Edn. Commn. of States, 1975—, steering com., 1977—, treas., exec. com., 1978—. Bd. dirs. Nat. 4-H Service Com., 1963-75, trustee, mem. exec. com. Nat. 4-H Found., 1968-73; mem.-at-large Nat. council Boy Scouts Am., 1962—; dir., pres. Alpha Gamma Rho Edn. Found., 1965-72; bd. dirs. So. Interstate Nuclear Bd., 1968-72; bd. dirs. Nat. Center for Voluntary Action, 1970-74. Served to capt. AUS, 1943-45. Recipient B.B. Comer award excellence natural sci. Auburn U., 1942; Distinguished Service award Fla. Vet. Med. Assn., 1966; Nat. 4-H Alumni award, 1967; George Washington honor medal award Freedoms Found., 1967; Nat. Partner in 4-H award, 1970; Distinguished Faculty award for contbns. to U. Fla., Fla. and acad. profession Fla. Blue Key, 1972; E.T. York, Jr. Distinguished Service award U. Fla., 1973; Honors medal Fla. Acad. Scis., 1974. Fellow A.A.A.S., Am. Soc. Agronomy; mem. Assn. So. Agrl. Workers (pres. 1968), Soil Sci. Soc. Am., Crop Sci. Soc. Am., Internat. Soil Sci. Soc., Blue Key, Sigma Xi, Phi Kappa Phi, Alpha Zeta, Gamma Sigma Delta (Internat. Distinguished Service award 1973), Omicron Delta Kappa, Phi Delta Kappa, Epsilon Sigma Phi, Alpha Gamma Rho. Baptist. Rotarian. Address: Chancellor State U System Fla 210 Collins Bldg Tallahassee FL 32304

YORK, FRANK SNYDER, JR., utility exec.; b. Grenada, Miss., Dec. 22, 1921; s. Frank Snyder and Elizabeth (Pressgrove) Y.; B.S. in Elec. Engring., Miss. State U., 1943; m. Roberta Stewart, June 15, 1947; children—Anne Stewart, Rosemary, Frank Snyder III. Comml. salesman Miss. Power & Light Co., Jackson, 1946-49, rate analyst, 1949-52, budget analyst, 1952-56, dir. econ. research and asst. sec., 1956-63, sec., 1963-75, controller, sec., chief fin. officer, 1975-78, v.p. fin., sec., 1978—. Moderator Presbytery Central Miss., 1968; chmn. budget com. United Givers Fund Greater Jackson Area, 1970-71; commr., gen. assembly, Presbyn. Ch., 1969. Trustee Belhaven Coll., 1971—. Served from 2d lt. to capt. AUS, 1943-46. Mem. Scabbard and Blade, Pi Kappa Alpha, Tau Beta Pi, Phi Eta Sigma. Clubs: Capital City Petroleum, Kiwanis, River Hills. Home: 410 Naples Rd Jackson MS 39206 Office: PO Box 1640 Jackson MS 39205

YORK, HERBERT FRANK, educator, govt. ofcl.; b. Rochester, N.Y., Nov. 24. 1921; s. Herbert Frank and Nellie Elizabeth (Lang) Y.; A.B., U. Rochester, 1942, M.S., 1943; Ph.D., U. Calif. at Berkeley, 1949; D.Sc. (hon.), Case Inst. Tech., 1960; LL.D., U. San Diego, 1964, Claremont Grad. Sch., 1974; m. Sybil Dunford, Sept. 28, 1947; children—David Winters, Rachel, Cynthia. Physicist, Radiation Lab., U. Calif. at Berkeley, 1943-58, asso. dir., 1954-58; asst. prof. physics dept. U. Calif., 1951-54, asso. prof., 1954-59, prof., 1959—; dir. Lawrence Radiation Lab., Livermore, 1952-58; chief scientist Advanced Research Project Agy., Dept. Def., 1958; dir. advanced research projects div. Inst. for Def. Analyses, 1958; dir. def. research and engring. Office of Sec. Def., 1958-61; chancellor U. Calif. at San Diego, 1961-64, 70-72, prof. physics, 1964—, chmn. dept. physics, 1968-69, dean grad. studies, 1969-70, dir. program on sci., tech. and pub. affairs, 1972—; U.S. Ambassador Comprehensive Test Ban Negotiations, 1979—; trustee Aerospace Corp., Inglewood, Calif., 1961—; mem. President's Sci. Adv. Com., 1957-58, 64-68, vice chmn., 1965-67; trustee Inst. Def. Analysis, 1963—; gen. adv. com. ACDA, 1962-69; spl. rep. of sec. def. at arms control talks, 1978—; cons. Stockholm Internat. Peace Research Inst.; mem. assessment adv. com. Office Sci. and Tech. Trustee Bishop's Sch., La Jolla, Calif., 1963-65. Recipient E.O. Lawrence award AEC, 1962. Guggenheim fellow, 1972. Fellow Am. Phys. Soc. (Forum on Physics and Society award 1976), Am. Acad. Arts and Scis.; mem. Inst. Aero. Scis., Internat. Acad. Astronautics, Fedn. Am. Scientists (chmn. 1970-71, mem. exec. com. 1969-76), Phi Beta Kappa, Sigma Xi. Author: Race to Oblivion, 1970; Arms Control, 1973; The Advisors, 1976; also numerous articles on arms or disarmament. Research in application atomic energy to nat. def., problems of arms control and disarmament, elementary particles. Home: 6110 Camino de la Costa La Jolla CA 92037

YORK, JAMES ORISON, retail co. exec.; b. Brush, Colo., June 27, 1927; s. M. Orison and Marie L. (Kibble) Y.; student U. Calif. at Berkeley, 1945-46; B.A. cum laude, U. Wash., 1949; m. Janice Marie Sjoberg, Aug. 1, 1959; children—Douglas James, Robert Orison. Teaching fellow, U. Wash., Seattle, 1950-52; econ. research analyst Larry Smith & Co., real estate, Seattle and N.Y.C., 1953-60, partner, Seattle, 1960-66, pres., San Francisco, 1966-71; pres. R.H. Macy Properties, also sr. v.p. planning and devel. R.H. Macy & Co., Inc., N.Y.C., 1971—, also dir. Chmn., N.Y.C. retail div. Am. Cancer Soc. Served with USNR, 1945-47. Mem. Am. Soc. Real Estate Counselors, Urban Land Inst., Internat. Real Estate Fedn., Phi Beta Kappa, Lambda Alpha. Clubs: Olympic (San Francisco); American Yacht (Rye, N.Y.); Corinthian Yacht (Seattle); Union League (N.Y.C.). Mason. Episcopalian. Contbg. author: Shopping Towns-USA, 1960. Home: 3 Eldredge Pl Rye NY 10580 Office: 151 W 34th St New York NY 10001

YORK, MICHAEL (MICHAEL YORK-JOHNSON), actor; b. Fulmer, Eng., Mar. 27, 1942; s. Joseph Gwynne and Florence Edith (Chown) Johnson; B.A. with honors in English, Univ. Coll., Oxford U. (Eng.), 1964; m. Patricia McCallum, Mar. 27, 1968. Performer with Dundee Repertory Co., 1964, Nat. Theatre Co., 1965; TV appearances include The Forsythe Saga, Rebel in the Grave, True Patriot, Much Ado About Nothing; stage appearances include Any Just Cause, 1967, Hamlet, 1970, Broadway prodn. of Outcry, 1973, Ring Round the Moon, 1975; appeared in motion pictures, including The Taming of the Shrew, 1966, Accident, 1966, Red and Blue, 1967, Smashing Time, 1967, Romeo and Juliet, 1967, The Strange Affair, 1967, The Guru, 1968, Alfred the Great, 1968, Justine, 1969, Something for Everyone, 1969, Zeppelin, 1970, La Poudre D'Escampette, 1971, Cabaret, 1971, England Made Me, 1971, Lost Horizon, 1972, The Three Musketeers, 1973, Murder on the Orient Express, 1974, Great Expectations, 1974, Conduct Unbecoming, 1974, The Four Musketeers, 1975, Logan's Run, 1976, Seven Nights in Japan, The Last Remake of Beau Geste, 1977, The Island of Dr. Moreau, 1977, Fedora, 1977, The Riddle of the Sands, 1978, A Man Called Intrepid, 1978. Office: care ICM 8899 Beverly Blvd Los Angeles CA 90048

YORK, SUSANNAH, actress; b. London, Eng., Jan. 9, 1942; attended London's Royal Acad. Dramatic Art; m. Michael Wells, 1960; children—Sasha, Orlando. Made acting debut in repertory; entered TV in 1959; TV appearances include: The Crucible, The Rebel and the Soldier, The First Gentleman, The Richest Man in the World, Jane Eyre, TV spl. for NBC, 1971, TV film Golden Gate Murders, 1979; entered films in 1960; motion pictures include: Tunes of Glory, There Was A Crooked Man, Loss of Innocence, Freud, Tom Jones, The Seventh Dawn, Scene Nun—Take One, Sands of Kalahari, Scruggs, Kaleidoscope, A Man for All Seasons, Sebastian, The Killing of Sister George, Oh What a Lovely War, The Battle of Britain, Lock Up Your Daughters, They Shoot Horses, Don't They? (Acad. award nominee), Brotherly Love, Zee & Company, Happy Birthday, Wanda June, Images, The Maids, Gold, Eliza Fraser, Conduct Unbecoming, Heaven Save Us from Our Friends, Sky Riders, The Silent Partner, Superman, The Shout, 1979; stage appearances include: A Cheap of Flowers, Wings of the Dove, A Singular Man, Man and Superman, Mrs. Warren's Profession, Private Lives. Author: In Search of Unicorns; Lark's Castle. Office: care Creative Mgmt Assos 8899 Beverly Blvd Los Angeles CA 90048*

YORK, W. THOMAS, corp. exec.; b. Archdale, N.C., Oct. 14, 1933; s. Shelley Clyde and Bertie Jane (Dunn) Y.; B.S., U. N.C., 1955, M.B.A., 1958; m. Patricia Louise Permenter, June 16, 1955; children—Tucker, Jonathan, Rheney. Mgr. accounting and financial analysis Philco-Ford, Phila., 1958-68; asst. corp. comptroller, dir. corp. accounting AMF Inc., N.Y.C., 1969, corp. comptroller, 1969, corp. v.p., 1970-72, v.p. finance, 1972-74, exec. v.p. adminstrn., dir., 1974, pres., chief operating officer, 1975—, chmn., chief exec. officer, 1978—, also dir.; dir. Scovill Mfg. Co., Conn. Mut. Life Ins. Co., Diamond Shamrock Corp. Chmn. bd. govs. Hugh O'Brian Found.; trustee Manhattanville Coll. Served to lt. USNR, 1955-57. Home: 123 Hemlock Hill Rd New Canaan CT 06840 Office: 777 Westchester Ave White Plains NY 10604

YORKE, AARON JONES, IV, securities co. exec.; b. Concord, N.C., June 21, 1931; s. Aaron Jones and Martha (Best) Y.; student Davidson Coll., 1949-51; B.S., U. N.C. at Chapel Hill, 1953; M.B.A., Harvard, 1957; m. Lane Harvey, July 12, 1958; children—Bryan, Laura. Asst. to chmn. FMC Corp., N.Y.C., 1959-62; v.p. Donaldson, Lufkin & Jenrette Inc., N.Y.C., 1962-71; exec. dir. SEC, Washington, 1971-72; exec. asst. to chmn. Paine, Webber Jackson & Curtis, N.Y.C., 1973, exec. v.p., 1973-74, pres., 1974-76, vice chmn. bd., 1976-77, also dir.; partner firm Bruns, Nordeman, Rea & Co., N.Y.C., 1978—; pres. Harvey Oil Co., Kinston, N.C., 1960—; dir. Harvey Properties, Kinston, Meridian Investing & Devel. Corp., 42d St. Redevel. Corp., Chgo. Bd. Options Exchange, 1975-77. Chmn. Greater N.Y. councils Boy Scouts Am. Financial Dinnerama, 1974. Trustee, N.Y. chpt. Multiple Sclerosis Soc.; bd. visitors Davidson Coll. Served with C.I.C., AUS, 1953-55. Mem. Securities Industry Assn. (gov. council 1974-77, dir., exec. com. 1976-77), Soc. Cin., Inst. Chartered Financial Analysts, Clubs: University, Brook. Home: 205 W 57th St New York NY 10019

YORKIN, (ALAN) BUD, producer, dir.; b. Washington, Pa., Feb. 22, 1926; s. Maurice A. and Jessie (Sachs) Y.; B.S. in Elec. Engring., Carnegie-Mellon U., 1948; M.A. in English Lit., Columbia, 1951; L.H.D., Washington and Jefferson Coll., 1974; m. Peggy Diem, May 9, 1954; children—Nicole, David. With engring. staff NBC, N.Y.C., 1949-50, stage mgr., 1950-52, asso. dir. Colgate Comedy Hour, 1952-53, dir., N.Y.C. and Los Angeles, 1948-52, including Dinah Shore Show, Tony Martin Show, Ernie Ford Show, George Gobel Show; writer, producer, dir. An Evening With Fred Astaire, 1958, Another Evening With Fred Astaire, 1959, Jack Benny spls., 1959; partner Tandem Prodns., Inc., Los Angeles, 1959—; exec. producer TV series All in the Family, 1969—, Sanford and Son, 1971—, Maude, 1972—, Good Times, 1973—, What's Happening, Carter Country, 1976-77, also numerous spls.; dir. films Come Blow Your Horn, 1965, Never Too Late, 1966, Divorce, American Style, 1967, Inspector Clouseau, 1968; producer, dir. Start the Revolution Without Me, 1969, The Thief Who Came to Dinner, 1971. Recipient 6 Emmy awards, Peabody, Sylvania, Look, Dirs. Guild awards. Mem. TV Acad. Arts and Scis. (past gov.), Dirs. Guild Am. (past gov). Home: 904 N Whittier Dr Beverly Hills CA 90210 Office: 1901 Ave of Stars Century City CA 90067

YORTY, SAMUEL WILLIAM, lawyer, former mayor; b. Lincoln, Nebr., Oct. 1, 1909; s. Frank Patrick and Johanna (Egan) Y.; student law sch. Southwestern U., U. So. Calif., U. Calif. Extension; m. Elizabeth Hensel, Dec. 1, 1938; 1 son, William Egan. Admitted to Calif. bar, 1939, since practiced in Los Angeles; mem. 82d Congress from 14th Dist. Calif., 83d Congress from 26th Dist. Calif.; mayor, Los Angeles, 1961-73. Mem. Calif. State Assembly, 1936-40, 49-50. Served to capt. USAAF, 1942-45. Decorated Encomineda medal (Spain); comdr. Finnish Lion; Nat. Order So. Cross Brazil; comdr.'s cross German Order Merit; Gt. Silver Insignia of Honor with Star (Austria); Order Civil Merit (Korea); Knight Legion of Honor (France); Order Homayoun medal (Iran); Order Sun of Peru. Republican. Home: Studio City CA Office: 320 N Vermont Los Angeles CA 90006

YOSELOFF, JULIEN DAVID, publishing co. exec.; b. N.Y.C., June 25, 1941; s. Thomas and Sara (Rothfuss) Y.; B.A., U. Pa., 1962; student London Sch. Econs., 1962-63; m. Darlene Starr Carbone, Aug. 6, 1967; children—Michael Ian, Anthony Alexander. With A.S. Barnes and Co., Inc., Cranbury, N.J., 1963—; pres. Asso. Univ. Presses, Inc., 1966—. Served with AUS, 1964. Mem. Phi Beta Kappa. Home: 14 Burlington Ln East Brunswick NJ 08816 Office: AS Barnes & Co Inc Forsgate Dr Cranbury NJ 08512

YOSELOFF, MARTIN, writer; b. Sioux City, Iowa, July 26, 1919; s. Morris and Sarah (Rosansky) Y.; B.A., State U. Iowa, 1941. Tchr., Drake Sch., N.Y.C.; writer various Iowa newspapers; editorial staff pub. houses, N.Y.C., 1941-43, 47-49; contbg. writer Bank Street Coll. publs. Served with AUS, 1943-46. Mem. Authors League Am., P.E.N. Author: No Greener Meadows, 1946; The Family Members, 1948; The Girl in the Spike-Heeled Shoes, 1949; The Magic Margin, 1954; Lily and the Sergeant, 1957; A Time to Be Young, 1967; Remember Me to Marcie, 1973; What Are Little Girls Made Of?, 1979; also narrative for sketch books, City of the Mardi Gras; City on the Potomac, 1946. Home: 139 W 15th St New York NY 10011. *My goal as a writer has been to explore life by telling stories. If any story I have told, any sentence I have written, has helped another human being, I have achieved my goal.*

YOSELOFF, THOMAS, publisher; b. Sioux City, Iowa, Sept. 8, 1913; s. Morris and Sarah (Rosansky) Y.; A.B., U. Iowa, 1934; m. Sara Rothfuss, Apr. 30, 1938; children—Julien David, Mark Laurence; m. 2d, Lauretta Sellitti, Apr. 23, 1964; 1 dau., Tamar Rachel. Pres., chmn. bd. Rosemont Pub. & Printing Corp., 1969—; chmn. Asso. Univ. Presses, 1969—; dir. A.S. Barnes & Co. Pres., Center for War/Peace Studies, 1977—. Mem. Phi Beta Kappa, Sigma Delta Chi, Delta Sigma Rho. Recipient award of merit Bucknell U., 1975. Author: A Fellow of Infinite Jest, 1946; (with Lillian Stuckey) Merry Adventures of Till Eulenspiegel, 1944; Further Adventures of Till Eulenspiegel, pub. 1957; The Time of My Life, 1979; Editor: Seven Poets in Search of an Answer, 1944; Voyage to America, 1961; Comic Almanac, 1963. Home: Montrose Rd Colts Neck NJ 07722 Office: AS Barnes & Co Forsgate Dr Cranbury NJ 08512

YOSHIMURA, FUMIO, sculptor; b. Kamakura, Japan, Feb. 22, 1926; s. Ren and Yuki (Kobayashi) Y.; M.F.A., Tokyo U. Arts, 1949; m. Katherine Murrey Millett, July 28, 1965. One-man exhbns. include: Pa. Acad. Fine Arts, 1970, Nancy Hoffman Gallery, N.Y.C., 1973, 76, 79, Marian Locks Gallery, Phila., 1972, 77, Galleri Arnesen, Copenhagen, 1974; group exhbns. include: Tokyo Bienale, Tokyo Mus. Art, 1974, Albright-Knox Gallery, Buffalo, 1976, Indpls. Mus. Art, 1976, 78, Sculpture Symposium bf B.C. (Can.), Vancouver, 1977, also travelling exhbn. in Can., 1976-78; represented in permanent collections: Phila. Art Mus., Power Gallery Contemporary Art, Pa. Acad. Fine Arts, Albright-Knox Gallery, West Vancouver Public Library.

YOST, CHARLES WOODRUFF, diplomat; b. Watertown, N.Y., Nov. 6, 1907; s. Nicholas Doxtater and Gertrude (Cooper) Y.; grad. Hotchkiss Sch., 1924; A.B., Princeton, 1928; student U. Paris, 1928-29; LL.D., St. Lawrence U., Princeton, Hamilton Coll.; Dr. Social Sci., U. Louisville; m. Irena Oldakowska, Sept. 8, 1934; children—Nicholas, Casimir, Felicity. Entered fgn. service, 1930, served as vice consul, Alexandria, 1931-32, Warsaw, 1932-33; free-lance journalist, 1933-35; with Dept. State, 1935-45; asst. to chmn. U.S. delegation San Francisco Conf., 1945; sec. gen. U.S. delegation Potsdam Conf., 1945; charge d'affaires U.S. Legation, Bangkok, 1945-46; polit. adviser U.S. delegation UN Gen. Assembly, 1946; 1st sec. Am. embassy, Prague, 1947; counselor Am. legation, Vienna, 1947-49; spl. asst. ambassador-at-large Council Fgn. Ministers and UN Gen. Assembly, 1949; dir. Office Eastern European Affairs, Dept. State, 1949-50; minister-counselor Am. embassy, Athens, Greece, 1950-53; dep. high commr. to Austria, 1953-54; U.S. minister to Kingdom of Laos, 1954-55, rank of ambassador, 1955-56; minister Am. embassy, Paris, 1956-58; U.S. ambassador to Syria, 1958; U.S. ambassador to Morocco, 1958-61; U.S. dep. rep. to UN, 1961-66; sr. fellow Council Fgn. Relations, N.Y.C., 1966-69; chief U.S. rep. to UN, 1969-71; distinguished lectr. Sch. Internat. Affairs Columbia, also counselor UN Assn., 1971-73; pres. Nat. Com. on U.S.-China Relations, 1973-75; sr. fellow Brookings Instn., 1975; spl. advisor Aspen Inst., 1976—. Recipient Rockefeller Pub. Service award, 1964. Mem. Council Fgn. Relations, AAAS. Author: The Age of Triumph and Frustration: Modern Dialogues, 1964; The Insecurity of Nations; International Relations in the Twentieth Century, 1968; The Conduct and Misconduct of Foreign Affairs, 1972. Address: 2801 New Mexico Ave Washington DC 20007

YOST, GEORGE, educator; b. Trenton, N.J., Sept. 26, 1910; s. George and Rebecca (Booz) Y.; A.B., Princeton, 1932, A.M., 1933, Ph.D., 1941; m. Frances Palmer, June 20, 1940; children—George Palmer, Carol Frances; m. 2d, Ruth Shephard, Apr. 2, 1960. Head English and French depts. Scranton-Keystone Jr. Coll., La. Plume, Pa., 1935-39; instr. English, U. Pitts., 1939-44; head English dept, Bloomfield (N.J.) Coll., 1946-47; mem. faculty Fla. State U., 1947—, prof. English, 1951—; vis. prof. U. N.Mex., 1954; Smith-Mundt prof. U. Damascus (Syria), 1955-57, Fulbright prof., 1964-66. Spl. teaching assignments C.Z., Panama, summer 1968, Florence, Italy, 1973. Founding mem. Le Moyne Art Found., Tallahassee, 1964; founding mem. Springtime Tallahassee, 1968, bd. dirs., 1970-71. Served to lt. comdr. USNR, 1944-46. Faculty grantee Fla. State U., 1969. Mem. AAUP (pres. Fla. State U. chpt. 1961-62), Archaeol. Soc. Tallahassee (v.p. 1971-72, pres. 1973-74), Modern Lang. Assn., Coll. English Assn., Keats-Shelley Soc., Renaissance Soc., Southeastern Modern Lang. Assn., Southeastern Renaissance Soc. Club: Tallahassee Torch (pres. 1976-77). Co-author: Studies in Sir Thomas Browne, 1965. Contbr. articles to profl. jours. Home: 2201 Mendoza Ave Tallahassee FL 32304

YOST, HENRY THOMAS, JR., educator; b. Balt., Jan. 22, 1925; s. Henry Thomas and Martha (Minsker) Y.; B.A., John Hopkins, 1947, Ph.D., 1951; M.A. (hon.), Amherst Coll., 1965; m. Martha Jean Thomas, June 12, 1948; 1 dau., Brenna Duncan. Mem. faculty Amherst Coll., 1951—, prof. biology, 1965—, Rufus Tyler Lincoln prof., 1976—, chmn. com. ednl. policy, 1961-62. Mem. exec. com. Mass. PAX, 1960—; sci. adv. bd. Consumers Union, 1959—. Pres., Western Mass. Health Planning Council, Valley Health Plan. Served with AUS, 1943-46. Adam T. Bruce fellow Johns Hopkins, 1950-51; fellow Chester Beatty Research Inst., London, Eng., 1962-63, 69-70. Fellow A.A.A.S.; mem. N.Y. Acad. Scis., Radiation Research Soc., AAUP, (nat. council 1965-66, 68-71, mem. com. profl. ethics, 1965-68, mem. com. teaching, research and publ. 1968-73, chmn. com. on relations with fed. and state govts. 1973—), Genetic Soc. Am., Soc. Devel. Biol. Bot. Soc. Am. Author: Cellular Physiology, 1972; (with W.M. Hexter) The Science of Genetics, 1976; also articles in field. Home: 75 N East St Amherst MA 01002

YOST, JAMES EVERETT, union ofcl.; b. Bluefield, Va., Oct. 16, 1925; s. Lorenzia Wingo and Emma Bell (Smith) Y.; grad. high sch.; m. Ruth Adkins, Nov. 13, 1946 (div. 1974); children—Conner E., Randel W., Ernest W.; m. 2d, Patricia Dickey, July 20, 1974. Truck driver State Line Distbg. Co., 1947-51; with Norfolk & Western Ry. Co., Bluefield, W.Va., 1947-56; asst. gen. chmn., sec.-treas. system council 16 Internat. Brotherhood Blacksmiths, Drop Forgers and Helpers (now merged Internat. Brotherhood Boilermakers, Iron Ship Builders, Blacksmiths, Forgers and Helpers AFL-CIO), 1951-56; asst. to pres. ry. employees dept. AFL-CIO, Chgo., 1956-69, pres., 1969—; mem. steering com. Nat. Apprenticeship and Tng. Conf., 1970-75; vice chmn. Cooperating Ry. Labor Orgns.; mem. Ry. Labor-Mgmt. Com., 1969-77. Served with AUS, 1944-46; ETO. Mem. Ry. Labor Execs. Assn. Democrat. Home: 201 E Walton St Apt 1300 Chicago IL 60611 Office: 220 S State St Suite 1212 Chicago IL 60604

YOST, L. MORGAN, architect; b. St. Marys, Ohio, Oct. 12, 1908; s. Lloyd and Gertrude (Morgan) Y.; student Northwestern U., 1925-29; B.Arch., Ohio State U., 1931; m. Winogene Springer, Sept. 11, 1936; children—Elyn (Mrs. Douglas D. Mulder), Karyl (Mrs. Robert L. Thorsen), Chari (Mrs. David H. Binstadt), Owen. Practice architecture, Kenilworth, Ill., 1932-52, 60—; partner Yost & Taylor, 1952-60; exec. dir. Chgo. Sch. Architecture Found., 1967-70; architect residential and indsl. bldgs., churches, banks; designer pvt. and mil. communities. Pres., Assn. N. Shore Architects, 1943-51. Trustee Chgo. Sch. Architecture Found. Fellow Lake Forest Found. for Architecture and Landscape Architecture, 1931. Fellow A.I.A. (pres. Chgo. chpt. 1950-52; chmn. nat. com. on home bldg. industry); mem. Soc. Automobile Historians, Soc. Archtl. Historians, S.A.R., Alpha Rho Chi, Tau Sigma Delta. Clubs: Westmoreland Country, Kenilworth, Antique Automobile Am. (pres. Ill. region), Classic Car of Am., Cliff Dwellers. Co-author: The Packard Car and the Company, 1975. Cons. architect to Household mag., 1945-58; cons. Plumbing and Heating Bus., 1946-57, Asso. editor Am. Lumberman, 1942-52; architect-editor: Small Homes Guide, 1943-47. Contbr. articles to Am. Home, Better Homes and Gardens, Parent's mag., Antique Automobile, others. Home: Box 407 Cherokee Village AR 72525

YOST, LYLE EDGAR, farm equipment mfg. co. exec.; b. Hesston, Kans., Mar. 5, 1913; s. Joseph and Alma (Hensley) Y.; B.S., B.A., Goshen Coll., 1937; postgrad. U. Ind., 1940; m. Erma Martin, July 31, 1938; children—Byron, Winston, Susan, Cameron. With St. Joseph Valley Bank, Elkhart, Ind., 1938-41; tchr. Wakarusa (Ind.) High Sch., 1942-45; founder Hesston Corp. (Kans.), 1947, pres., 1949—, now chmn.; dir. 4th Nat. Bank, Kan. Gas and Electric Co. (both Wichita), Hesston State Bank, Kans. Devel. Credit Corp. Bd. dirs., past pres. Farm and Indsl. Equipment Inst.; mem. Kansas City Regional Export Expansion Council, Gov.'s Com. for Partners for Progress Kans.-Paraguay, Kans. Econ. Research Adv. Com., State Rural Devel. Adv. Council; chmn. com. establishing creamery in Uruguay, 1967; mem. State Dept. cultural delegation to USSR, 1967. Bd. dirs. Kans. Council World Affairs, Mgmt. Research and Devel. Inst., Mennonite Econ. Devel. Assos.; chmn. Prince of Peace Chapel, Aspen Colo. Named Farmarketing Man of Year, Nat. Agrl. Advt. and Marketing

Assn., 1969; Kansan of Achievement in Bus., 1972, Kansan of Year, 1974. Mem. Alpha Kappa Psi. Home: 1200 Ridge Rd Hesston KS 67062 Office: 420 W Lincoln Blvd Hesston KS 67062

YOST, PAUL ALEXANDER, JR., coast guard officer; b. Phila., Jan. 3, 1929; s. Paul Alexander and Jeanne Moore (Bailey) Y.; B.S., U.S. Coast Guard Acad., 1951; M.S., U. Conn., 1959; M.A., George Washington U., 1964; m. Janice Kay Worth, June 2, 1951; children—Linda L., Paul Alexander III, David J., Lisa J., Christopher J. Commd. ensign U.S. Coast Guard, 1951, advanced through grades to rear adm., 1978; served on various ships and shore stas. of Coast Guard establishment, as combat comdr. during Vietnamese War; comdr. 8th Coast Guard Dist., New Orleans, 1978—; mem. del. Law of Sea Conf., 1972-74. Mem. exec. com. S.W. council Boy Scouts Am., chmn. sustaining membership drive S.W. Alaskan council, mem. exec. com. Greater New Orleans council. Decorated Silver Star, Legion of Merit with combat V, Meritorious Service medal, others. Mem. Nat. Def. Transp. Assn. Mormon. Clubs: Boston, So. Yacht, Plimsoll (New Orleans). Home: 13206 Delta Ct New Orleans LA 70128 Office: 8th CG Dist 1313 Hale Boggs Fed Bldg New Orleans LA 70130

YOST, ROBERT LLOYD, fgn. service officer; b. Kirkland, Wash., Sept. 8, 1922; s. Bartley Francis and Irma (Cleopha) Y.; B.A. in Econs., UCLA, 1942; postgrad. Harvard U., 1952-53; M.S. in Internat. Relations, George Washington U., 1968; m. June Horsley, Sept. 2, 1945; children—Barbara June, Elizabeth Anne, John Bartley. Commd. fgn. service officer Dept. State, 1946; 3d sec., Madrid, 1946-49; vice consul, Antwerp, Belgium, 1949-52; consul, Leopoldville, 1953-55; research specialist Dept. State, Washington, 1958-58; officer-in-charge OEEC affairs, 1958-59; consul, prin. officer, Cebu, P.R., 1959-62; 1st sec., fin., adviser U.S. del. to OECD, Paris, 1962-65, also U.S. mem. com. invisible transactions and alt. U.S. rep. bd. mgmt. European Monetary Agreement; spl. asst. to asst. sec. of State for European Affairs, 1965-67; assigned to Nat. War Coll., 1967-68; counselor, dep. chief mission Am. embassy, Addis Ababa, Ethiopia, 1968-72; ambassador to Burundi, Bujumbura, 1972-74; dep. insp. gen. Fgn. Service, Washington, 1974-78; ambassador to Dominican Republic, Santo Domingo, 1978—. Served with AUS, 1942-46. Mem. Am. Fgn. Service Assn., Am. Acad., African Studies Assn. Address: US Embassy Santo Domingo Dominican Republic

YOUEL, KENNETH, pub. relations cons.; b. Doon, Iowa, May 19, 1901; s. Blaine T. and Jennie (Hancock) Y.; B.A., U. Oreg., 1923; m. Frances E. Rose, June 10, 1930 (dec.); children—Adele Frances (Mrs. Russell N. Chappell, Jr.), John Kenneth; m. 2d, Jan V. DiMarco, Apr. 16, 1963. News staff The Oregonian, Portland, Oreg., 1923-25, Bklyn. Eagle, 1925-27; financial writer N.Y. Evening Post, 1927-31; asst. dir. communications Gen. Motors Corp., Detroit, 1931-61; pub. relations cons., 1961—; cons. USIA, Washington, 1962-69; pub. mem. U.S. Dept. State Fgn. Service Inspection Corps, Washington, 1966. Recipient citation Distinguished Service, Pub. Relations Soc. Am., 1964. Mem. Pub. Relations Soc. Am. (pres. Mich. 1958, nat. pres. 1960), Pub. Mem. Assn. (pres. 1970-73), S.A.R., Sigma Delta Chi, Phi Kappa Psi. Republican. Prsbyn. Clubs: National Press (Washington); University (N.Y.C.); Farmington (Charlottesville, Va.); Everglades (Palm Beach, Fla.). Home: Loftlands Earlysville VA 22936 also 2860 S Ocean Blvd Palm Beach FL 33480 Office: 1629 K St NW Washington DC 20006. *In retrospect, of all the influences on my life, the greatest was the influence of my father. How fortunate I was to have such a parent as an example, an inspiration, and a disciplinarian. He taught me habits of promptness, he encouraged me to think for myself. He discussed with me the lives of famous men, and their outstanding characteristics. He was intolerant of laziness and bad habits, and was quick in his condemnation of those he termed "those kind of people." He once lost a job because he refused to "pass" the son of a school board member who had failed his examination. How fortunate I was to have had such a father.*

YOUMAN, ROGER JACOB, editor, writer; b. N.Y.C., Feb. 25, 1932; s. Robert Harold and Ida (Kellner) Y.; B.A., Swarthmore Coll., 1953; m. Lillian Frank, June 22, 1958; children—Nancy, Laura, Joshua, Andrew. Desk asst. CBS News, N.Y.C., 1953; program editor TV Guide, N.Y.C., 1956, regional editor Memphis, 1956-57, Houston, 1957, asst. programing editor N.Y.C., 1957-60, asso. editor, Radnor, Pa., 1960-65, asst. mng. editor, 1965-72, mng. editor, 1972-76, exec. editor, 1976-79; editor Panorama, 1979—. Served with AUS, 1954-55. Mem. Am. Soc. Mag. Editors, Nat. Acad. TV Arts and Scis. Author: (with Arthur Shulman) How Sweet It Was, 1966; The Television Years 1973. Contbr. articles to various publs. Home: 752 Mancill Rd Wayne PA 19087 Office: Box 950 Wayne PA 19087

YOUMANS, JULIAN RAY, physician, educator; b. Baxley, Ga., Jan. 2, 1928; s. John Edward and Jennie Lou (Milton) Y.; B.S., Emory U., 1949, M.D., 1952; M.S., U. Mich., 1955, Ph.D., 1957; children—Reed Nesbit, John Edward, Julian Milton. Intern, U. Mich. Hosp., Ann Arbor, 1952-53, resident in neurol. surgery, 1953-55, 56-58; fellow in neurology U. London, 1955-56; asst. prof. neurosurgery U. Miss., 1959-62, asso. prof., 1962-63; asso. prof. Med. U. S.C., 1963-65, prof., 1965-67, chief div. neurosurgery, 1963-67; prof. U. Calif., Davis, 1967—, chmn. dept. neurosurgery, 1967—; cons. USAF, U.S. VA, NRC. No. vice chmn. Republican State Central Com. of Calif., 1979—. Served with U.S. Navy, 1944-46. Diplomate Am. Bd. Neurol. Surgery. Mem. U.S. C. of C., A.C.S. (bd. govs. 1972-78), Congress of Neurol. Surgeons (exec. com. 1967-70), Am. Acad. Neurology, Am. Assn. Surgery of Trauma, Pan-Pacific Surg. Assn., Western Neurosurg. Soc., Neurosurg. Soc. Am., Soc. Neurol. Surgeons, Soc. Univ. Neurosurgeons, N. Pacific Soc. Neurology and Psychiatry, Am. Trauma Soc. Episcopalian. Clubs: Bohemian, Commonwealth, Rotary, El Macero Country. Author: Neurological Surgery, 2d edit., 1979. Contbr. articles to profl. jours. Office: 4301 X St Sacramento CA 95817

YOUNG, AL (ALBERT JAMES YOUNG), writer; b. Ocean Springs, Miss., May 31, 1939; s. Albert James and Mary (Campbell) Y.; student U. Mich., 1957-61; A.B. in Spanish, U. Calif. at Berkeley, 1969; m. Arline June Belch, Oct. 8, 1963; 1 son, Michael James. Profl. musician, 1958-64; disc jockey, radio announcer KJAZ-FM, Alameda, Calif., 1961-63; writing instr. San Francisco Mus. Art, 1967-69; writing instr., linguistic cons. Berkeley Neighborhood Youth Corps, 1968-69; Edward H. Jones lectr. in creative writing Stanford, 1969-76; founder, editor Loveletter, lit. jour., 1966-68; v.p., editorial dir. Yardbird Pub., Inc., Berkeley, 1971—; dir. Associated Writing Programs, 1979—; screenwriter Laser Film Corp., N.Y.C., 1972; scenario writer Stigwood Corp., London and N.Y.C., 1972; guest fiction editor Iowa Review, 1975; screenwriter Verdon Prods, Hollywood, Calif., 1976, First Artists Ltd., Burbank, Calif., 1976-77, Universal Pictures, 1979. Judge, chmn. judges Joseph Henry Jackson award San Francisco Found., 1971-72; mem. grants panel, lit. program Nat. Endowment for Arts, 1980; cons. Poets and Writers, N.Y.C., 1974-75. Recipient Nat. Arts Council awards for editing and writing, 1968, 69; Joseph Henry Jackson award, 1969. Wallace Stegner writing fellow, 1966; Guggenheim fellow, 1974; Nat. Endowment for Arts fellow, 1975, grantee, 1979. Mem. Authors Guild-Authors League, Writers Guild Am. West. Club: San Francisco Press (hon.). Author: (poems) Dancing, 1969; The Song Turning Back Into Itself, 1971; Geography of the Near Past, 1976; (novels) Snakes, 1970; Who Is Angelina?, 1975; Sitting Pretty, 1976; Ask Me Now, 1980; (anthologies) (with Ishmael Reed) Yardbird Lives!, 1978; (with Ishmael Reed and others) Calafia: The California Poetry, 1979.

YOUNG, ALEXANDER STUARD, JR., lawyer; b. Washington, Aug. 27, 1921; s. Alexander Stuard and Gertrude Louise (Parsons) Y.; B.S. in Econs., U. Pa., 1942; J.D., Georgetown U., 1950; m. Mary Elizabeth Primm, Oct. 25, 1945; children—Alexander Stuard, A. Suzanne Young Wieland, A. Steven, A. Stanley. Commd. 2d lt. U.S. Army Air Force, 1942, advanced through grades to col., U.S. Air Force, 1966; service in N. Africa and Italy, 1943-45; sta. at Hdqrs., Washington, 1952-52; ret., 1952; with Mil. Intelligence Res., Phila., 1953-56; comdr. OSI Res., 1956-65; admitted to D.C. bar, 1950, Pa. bar, 1951, U.S. Supreme Ct., 1953; asso. firm Stradley, Ronon, Stevens & Young, Phila., 1950-51, 52-56, partner, 1957—; dir. Vestaur Securities, Inc. Bd. dirs., sec.-treas. Binder Schweitzer Amazonian Hosp. Found., Inc., N.Y.C., 1961-70; mem. Branford (Conn.) Electric Ry. Assn., 1969—, Pop Warner Little Scholars, Phila., 1975—. Decorated Bronze Star, Air Force Commendation ribbon. Mem. Am. Bar Assn., Pa. Bar Assn., Phila. Bar Assn., Inter-Am. Bar Assn., Internat. Bar Assn., Fed. Bar Assn., Am. Law Inst., Am. Judicature Soc., Nat. Lawyers Club, Phi Alpha Delta, Lambda Chi Alpha. Republican. Episcopalian. Clubs: Inst. Dirs., Pen and Wig (London); Officers Open Mess of McGuire (N.J.) AFB; Union League (Phila.); Masons. Author: The Rights and Liabilities of Shareholders—United States, 1977; also articles; editorial asst. in transl. W. Ger. Domestic and Fgn. Investment Co. Laws, 1971; contbr. chpt. to Practical Guide for Investments in the U.S., 1979. Office: 1300 Two Girard Plaza Philadelphia PA 19102

YOUNG, ANDREW, clergyman, civil rights leader, former ambassador, former congressman; b. New Orleans, Mar. 12, 1932; s. Andrew J. and Daisy (Fuller) Y.; student Dillard U., 1947-48; B.S., Howard U., 1951; B.D., Hartford Sem. Found., 1955; D.D., Wesleyan U., 1970, United Theol. Sem. Twin Cities, 1970; LL.D., Wilberforce U., 1971, Clark Coll., 1973, Yale, 1973, Swarthmore Coll., Atlanta U., others; m. Jean Childs, June 7, 1954; children—Andrea, Lisa Dow, Paula Jean, Andrew J. III. Ordained to ministry Congl. Ch., 1955; pastor in Thomasville, Ga., 1955-57; asso. dir. dept. youth work Nat. Council Chs., 1957-61; adminstr. Christian edn. program United Ch. Christ, 1961-64; mem. staff So. Christian Leadership Conf., 1961-70, adminstr. citizen edn. program, 1961-64, exec. dir., 1964-70, exec. v.p., 1967-70, now bd. dirs.; mem. 93d-95th Congresses from 5th Ga. Dist., mem. Rules com. U.S. ambassador to UN, 1977-99. Chmn., Atlanta Community Relations Commn., 1970-72; chmn. bd. Delta Ministry of Miss. Bd. dirs. Martin Luther King, Jr. Center for Social Change, Robert F. Kennedy Meml. Found., Field Found., So. Christian Leadership Conf. Recipient Pax-Christi award St. John's U., 1970; Springarn medal. Mem. Ams. Dem. Action.*

YOUNG, ANDREW BRODBECK, lawyer; b. Phila., Feb. 8, 1907; s. Edward E. and Estelle (Brodbeck) Y.; A.B., Princeton, 1928; LL.B., Harvard, 1931; m. Olive C. Sherley, Apr. 22, 1933; children—Andrew Oliver (dec.), Sherley (Mrs. Paul A. Hollos). Admitted to Pa. bar, 1931; partner Stradley, Ronon, Stevens & Young, Phila., 1935—; v.p., dir. W.W. Interests (formerly Warren Webster & Co.); dir. M. A. Bruder & Sons, Inc., Jackson Mfg. Co., Fessenden Hall Inc., M.L. Bayard & Co., Welding Engrs. Inc.; lectr. finance U. Pa., 1939-66; lectr. various tax insts., 1953-78; mem. Mayor's Com. Exec. and Elective Salaries Phila. City Govt., 1959; mem. Mayor's Com. Port Promotion Phila., 1959-63; mem. adv. council Phila. Community Renewal Program, 1964-66, chmn. dir. Phila. Indsl. Devel. Corp., 1963—, pres., 1963-70; mem. Mayor's Tax Study Commn., 1960, mem. Commr. Internal Revenue's Adv. group., 1965. Chmn. bd. trustees Mary Jacobs Meml. Library Found., Rocky Hill, N.J.; trustee Huston Found., Lovett Found., Nuclear Breeder Found.; mem. council pres.'s advisers LaSalle Coll., 1969-74. Served with Surgeon Gen's Office, AUS, 1942-45. Fellow Am. Bar Found.; mem. Am. (mem. ho. of dels. 1966-70, mem. council tax sect. 1958-70, chmn. sect. 1963-65), Pa., Phila. bar assns., Am. Law Inst. (tax adv. group, corps.-stockholders project, 1957-59; estate and gift tax project, 1964-67), Phila. C. of C. (pres. 1958-60, chmn. bd. 1960-62, dir., exec. com.), Am. Arbitration Assn. (nat. panel arbitrators), Phi Beta Kappa. Episcopalian. Clubs: Midday, Rittenhouse, Philadelphia, Sunday Breakfast (Phila.); Tunkhannock Creek Association; Commanderie de Bordeaux, Penn, Wilderness. Home: 509 Auburn Ave Chestnut Hill PA 19118 Office: 2 Girard Plaza Philadelphia PA 19102

YOUNG, ARDELL MOODY, judge; b. Ringgold, Tex., Oct. 11, 1911; s. Horace G. and Emma (Garvin) Y.; A.B., U. Okla., 1932, LL.B., 1936; m. Marjorie Maschal, July 27, 1934; children-Mardelle Fay (Mrs. S.E. Moyers), John Hurschel. Admitted to Okla. and Tex. bars, 1936; 1st asst. dist. atty. Tarrant County, Tex., 1946; partner firm Brown, Herman Scott, Young & Dean, Ft. Worth, 1947-71; judge 153d Dist. Ct., Tarrant County, Tex., 1971—. Served to lt. col. Judge Adv. Gen.'s Dept., AUS, 1941-46. Mem. Am., Tarrant County bar assns., State Bar Tex. (bd. dirs. 1959-62), Am., Tex. bar founds., Am. Coll. Trial Lawyers, Phi Alpha Delta. Democrat. Presbyterian. Mason (33 deg, K.T., Shriner). Home: 4064 Hidden View Circle Fort Worth TX 76109 Office: Civil Courts Bldg Fort Worth TX 76102

YOUNG, ARIBERT LEE, lawyer; b. Terre Haute, Ind., Sept. 8, 1923; s. John D. and Birdie J. (Peak) Y.; student Okla. A. and M. U., 1942-43, Purdue U., 1946-47; LL.B., Ind. U., 1950; m. Mabel A. Cook, Sept. 7, 1946; children—Richard Alan, Deborah Jean, Douglas Edward. Admitted to Ind. bar, 1950, Supreme Ct. U.S., 7th Circuit Ct. of Appeals, Supreme Ct. Ind.; practiced in Indpls., 1950—; sr. partner Kightlinger, Young, Gray & DeTrude; pres. Meridian Parking, Inc. Served with AC, USNR, 1942-46. Mem. Am., Ind., Indpls. bar assns., Fedn. Ins. Counsel (sec.-treas., dir.), Lawyers-Pilots Bar Assn., Phi Delta Phi. Methodist. Club: Columbia (Indpls.). Contbr. articles to profl. jours. Home: 720 Braeside Ct Indianapolis IN 46260 Office: 151 N Delaware St Indianapolis IN 46204

YOUNG, ARTHUR CHILES, clergyman; b. Kansas City, Mo., Jan. 18, 1913; s. William Taylor and Louise (Atkinson) Y.; B.A., Park Coll., 1934, D.D., 1954; B.D., McCormick Theol. Sem., Chgo., 1937; m. Rhoda Elizabeth Magers, June 2, 1936; children—Robert Magers, William Arthur. Ordained to ministry Presbyn. Ch., 1937; pastor in Bushnell, Ill., 1937— 42, Duluth, Minn., 1942-56, First Presbyn. Ch., Ponca City, Okla., 1956-78; v.p. Coll. of Ozarks, Clarksville, Ark., 1978—. Chmn. dept. ministerial relations United Presbyn. Ch. U.S.A., 1963-68, mem. gen. council com. personnel services, 1966-68, moderator Synod Minn., 1950, Synod Okla.-Ark., 1964; mem. gen. council Synod Okla.-Ark., 1965-70, mem. permanent jud. commn. Synod of Sun, 1976—; pres. Duluth Council Chs., 1950; pres. Ponca City Ministerial Alliance, 1958, 66. Chmn. open forum Duluth C. of C., 1953-54, bd. dirs., 1948-54; chmn. Ponca City Cultural Center Bd., 1967-73; chmn. fin. com. Help Line, Ponca City, 1976—; trustee Coll. of Ozarks, 1961-70. Recipient Best Sermon award Freedoms Found., 1952, 55, Mem. Ponca City C. of C. (dir. 1970-73, ednl. and community relations coms. 1976—), Pi Kappa Delta. Rotarian, Kiwanian (lt. gov. 1948), Mason (32 deg., Shriner). Home and office: 808 Edgewood Dr Ponca City OK 74601

YOUNG, ARTHUR NICHOLS, economist; b. Los Angeles, Nov. 21, 1890; s. William Stewart and Adele (Nichols) Y.; A.B., Occidental Coll., 1910, LL.D. 1937; A.M., Princeton, 1911, Ph.D., 1914; LL.B., George Washington U., 1927; m. Ellen May Bailey, June 11, 1915 (dec. 1973); children—Elizabeth (Mrs. P.W. Roulac), Allen, William Dwight. Prof. econs. Presbyn. Coll., Clinton, S.C., 1912-13; instr. econs. Princeton, 1915-17; research asso. U. Calif., 1917; adviser on taxation Mexican Govt., 1918; trade expert, War Trade Bd., 1918; trade commr. to investigate financial conditions in Spain for U.S. Dept. Commerce, 1919; economist in office of fgn. trade adviser Dept. of State, 1919-20; fin. adviser to Govt. of Honduras, 1920-21; financial expert Dept. of State, 1921-22, econ. adviser, 1922-28; asso. of Am. observer with Reparation Commn., Paris, during preparation of Dawes Plan, 1924; chmn. Interdepartmental Com. on Oil Pollution of Navigable Waters, 1924-26; del. to Internat. Conf. on Oil Pollution, Washington, 1926; expert during fgn. debt negotiations, 1924-27; expert attending World Econ. Conf., Geneva, 1927; expert on pub. credit, Commn. of Financial Experts of Chinese Govt., 1929; financial adviser Chinese Govt. 1929-46, also to Central Bank of China; mem. Chinese Flood Relief Commn., 1931; expert, Chinese Econ. Mission, 1933; mem. com. on establishment Central Res. Bank, 1936; dir. China Nat. Aviation Corp., 1937-45; v.p. Chinese-Am. Inst. Cultural Relations, 1940; vice chmn. United China Relief Coordinating Com., 1942; chmn. Am. relief and ARC com. in China, 1943; trustee China Found., 1944; adviser, Chinese Govt. commn. on relief and rehab., 1944; mem. Chinese del. to Bretton Woods financial conf., 1944; dir. Point IV program in Saudi Arabia, 1951-52; fin. adviser, chief, fin. mission to Saudi Arabia, organizing Monetary Agy. and reforming currency customs, budget. 1951-52; investigated S.Am. problems of pvt. fgn. investment FOA, 1954; financial cons. ICA, 1957-58; lectr. Occidental Coll., 1958-59; cons. on taxation in Argentina, 1962-63. Life trustee Occidental Coll. Recipient Order of the Brilliant Jade (China). Guggenheim fellow, 1956. Mem. Am. Econ. Assn., Acad. Polit. Sci., Am. Guild Organists, Phi Beta Kappa, Phi Gamma Delta. Congregationalist. Club: Cosmos (Washington). Author: The Single Tax Movement in the United States, 1916, Finances of the Federal District of Mexico, 1918, Spanish Finance and Trade, 1920, China's Economic and Financial Reconstruction, 1947, Saudi Arabian Currency and Finance, 1953, China and the Helping Hand, 1937-1945, 1963, China's Wartime Finance and Inflation, 1937-45, 1965, China's Nation-Building Effort, 1927-1937, 1971; also reports and articles in mags. Home: 342 Cambridge Ave Claremont CA 91711

YOUNG, BARNEY THORNTON, lawyer; b. Chillicothe, Tex., Aug. 10, 1934; s. Bayne and Helen Irene (Thornton) Y.; B.A., Yale, 1955; LL.B., U. Tex., 1958; m. Sarah Elizabeth Taylor, Aug. 31, 1957; children—Jay Thornton, Sarah Elizabeth, Serena Taylor. Admitted to Tex. bar, 1958; asso. Thompson, Knight, Wright & Simmons, Dallas, 1958-65; partner Rain, Harrell, Emery, Young & Doke, Dallas, 1965—; dir. Horchow Corp., Jones-Blair Co. Mem. adv. council Dallas Community Chest Trust Fund, Inc., 1964-66; bd. dirs. Mental Health Assn. Dallas County, Inc., 1969-72; trustee Hockaday Sch., Dallas, 1971-77, Lamplighter Sch., Dallas, 1976—; trustee St. Mark's Sch., Dallas, 1970—, pres., 1976-78. Mem. Am., Tex., Dallas bar assns., Am. Judicature Soc., Order of Coif, Phi Beta Kappa, Pi Sigma Alpha, Phi Gamma Delta, Phi Delta Phi. Clubs: City, Dallas Country, Yale, Dallas County Republican Men's (bd. dirs. 1977-79) (Dallas). Home: 6901 Turtle Creek Blvd Dallas TX 75205 Office: 4200 Republic National Bank Tower Dallas TX 75201

YOUNG, BRUCE ANDERSON, editor; b. Chgo., Jan. 22, 1917; s. Bruce Anderson and Gladys Irene (Dillon) Y.; A.B., U. Chgo., 1938, A.M., 1940; m. Susanmary Carpenter, Sept. 29, 1967. Instr. English, Northwestern U., 1946; staff editor F.E. Compton Co., Chgo., 1947-53; mng. editor Am. Pub. Co., Chgo., 1953-58; program dir. Scott, Foresman & Co., Chgo., 1958-64; chief manuscript editor U. Chgo. Press, 1964-68, mng. editor, 1968—. Served with USNR, 1942-46. Mem. Chgo. Book Clinic. Episcopalian. Clubs: Alfa Romeo Owners (founder, pres. 1956-58); Caxton; Quadrangle. Co-author, chief editor U. Chgo. Press Manual of Style. Office: 5801 S Ellis Ave Chicago IL 60637

YOUNG, BRYANT LLEWELLYN, govt. ofcl., lawyer; b. Rockford, Ill., Mar. 9, 1948; s. Llewellyn Anker and Florence Ruth (Gulling) Y.; A.B., Cornell U., 1970; J.D., Stanford U., 1974. Admitted to Calif. bar, 1974, Nev. bar, 1975, D.C. bar, 1979; law clk. U.S. Dist. Ct. No. Dist. Calif., San Francisco, 1974-75; mem. firm Dinkelspiel, Pelavin, Steefel & Levitt, San Francisco, 1975-77; White House fellow, spl. asst. to sec. HUD, Washington, 1977-78; spl. asst. to sec. HUD, 1978-79, dep. exec. asst. for ops. Office of Sec., 1979, dep. gen. mgr. New Community Devel. Corp., 1979—. Mem. public affairs com. San Francisco Aid Retarded Citizens, Inc., 1977. Mem. Am. Bar Assn., San Francisco Bar Assn., White House Fellows Assn. (chmn. annual meeting 1979), Am. Field Service Returnees Assn. Office: HUD 451 7th St SW Washington DC 20410

YOUNG, BURT, actor; b. N.Y.C., Apr. 30, 1940; s. Michael and Josephine Y.; student public, pvt. schs., N.Y.C.; m. May 20, 1961 (dec.); children—Richard (dec.), Anne Susan. Pres., White Crown Carpet Cleaners, 1964-67, Aurura Carpet Installation Co., 1966-69; films include: Cinderella Liberty, 1973, The Gambler, 1974, Harry and Walter Go To New York, 1976, Rocky (Acad. award nominee best supporting actor), 1976, Twilight's Last Gleaming, 1977, The Choirboys, 1977, Convoy, 1978, Rocky II, 1979; author and star of films: Daddy, I Don't Like It Like This, CBS-TV, 1977, Uncle Joe Shanon, United Artists, 1978; TV films: The Great Niagara, 1974, Hustling, 1975, The Deadly Game, 1976; dir. Sunshine Film Co.; owner, operator Burts Blues Tapes-Records, 1978. Served with USMC, 1957-59. Mem. Acad. Motion Picture Arts and Scis., Writers Guild Am., Hole in the Wall Gang of Corona. Roman Catholic. Author book: Uncle Joe Shannon, 1978. Office: 1888 Century Park E Suite 1900 Los Angeles CA 90067. *Naivete, mobility, perseverance, concentration and a great ability to loaf do it for me.*

YOUNG, BURTON, lawyer; b. Phila., Aug. 21, 1927; s. Morris and Clara (Greenfield) Y.; J.D., U. Miami, 1950; m. Sheila H. Hertzberg, Jan. 9, 1955; children—David Haris, Francea Mindy. Partner firm Ader Young and predecessor firms, Miami Beach, Fla., 1950-55; individual practice law, Miami, Fla., 1955-57; asst. state atty. 11th Jud. Circuit, 1957; partner firm Snyder,Young & Stern and predecessor firm, North Miami Beach, 1958-72; partner/shareholder firm Young, Stern & Tannenbaum, North Miami Beach, 1972—; admitted to Fla. bar, U.S. Supreme Ct. bar; instr. U. Miami Sch. Law, 1971-72. Co-chmn. dist. 5 Gov.'s Council on Post Secondary Edn. for Disadvantaged, 1970; mem. Gov.'s Council on Criminal Justice, 1971; chmn. legal div. Dade County United Fund, 1973. Fellow Am. Bar Found. (pres. 1974-76); mem. Am. Bar Assn. (Ho. of Dels. 1972-78), Am. Law Inst., Fla. Bar Assn. (pres. 1970-71, chmn. task force on land and security fraud schemes 1977-78), Fla. Bar Found. (pres. 1974-76), Fla. Council Bar Presidents (Outstanding Past Local Bar Pres. award 1975), Dade County Bar Assn., North Dade Bar Assn., Am. Judicature Soc., Nat. Conf. Bar Presidents, Soc. of Wig and Robe, Iron Arrow, Phi Epsilon Pi. Contbr. articles to profl. jours. Office: Young Stern & Tannenbaum 17071 W Dixie Hwy North Miami Beach FL 33162*

YOUNG, C. W. BILL, congressman; b. Harmarville, Pa., Dec. 16, 1930; m. Marian Ford; children—Pamela Kay, Terry Lee, Kimber. Dist. asst. to Congressman William C. Cramer, 1957-60; senator Fla. Legislature, 1960-70; mem. 92d Congress from 8th Fla. Dist.,

93d-96th Congresses from 6th Fla. Dist.; mem. Fla. Constn. Revision Commn., 1965-67; chmn. So. Hwy. Policy Com., 1966-68. Del. Rep. Nat. Conv., 1968; mem. Electoral Coll., 1968. Served to sgt. Fla. N.G., 1948-57. Named One of Outstanding Young Men Am., U.S. Jr. C. of C., 1965, Most Valuable Senator, Capitol Press Corps, 1969. Methodist. Home: 4775 Cove Circle St Petersburg FL 33708 Office: 2453 Rayburn House Office Bldg Washington DC 20515*

YOUNG, CHARLES EDWARD, univ. chancellor; b. San Bernardino, Calif., Dec. 30, 1931; s. Clayton Charles and Eula May (Walters) Y.; A.A., San Bernardino Coll., 1954; A.B., U. Calif. at Riverside, 1955, M.A., Los Angeles, 1957, Ph.D., 1960; D.H.L. (hon.), U. Judaism, Los Angeles, 1969; m. Sue Daugherty, June 23, 1950; children—Charles Edward, Elizabeth Susan. Congl. fellow, Washington, 1958-59; adminstrv. analyst Office of the Pres., U. Calif., Berkeley, 1959-60; asst. prof. polit. sci. U. Calif., Davis, 1960; asst. prof. polit. sci. U. Calif. at Los Angeles, 1960-66, asso. prof., 1966-69, prof., 1969—, asst. to chancellor, 1960-62, asst. chancellor, 1962-63, vice chancellor, adminstrn. 1963-68, now chancellor. Dir. UMF Systems, Inc., Dirs. Capital Fund, Inc., Intel Corp., Century Bank, Carlsberg Capital Corp., Fin. Corp. Am. Cons. Peace Corps., 1961-62, to Ford Found. on Latin Am. Activities, 1964-66. Mem. Nat. Com. on U.S.-China Relations; mem. internat. fellowship adv. com. ITT; mem. chancellor's assos. UCLA; v.p. Young Musicians Found.; bd. dirs. Los Angeles World Affairs Council, So. Calif. Theatre Assn. Trustee UCLA Found. Served with USAF, 1951-52. Named Young Man of Year Westwood Jr. C. of C., 1962. Office: Office of Chancellor UCLA 405 Hilgard Ave Los Angeles CA 90024

YOUNG, CHARLES FLOYD, lawyer; b. nr. Newark, Ohio, Aug. 30, 1921; s. Bert Edward and Helen Louise (Cole) Y.; student Denison U., 1939-42; LL.B., U. Cin., 1948; m. Carolyn Rose Kearns, Sept. 20, 1947; children—Patricia Elaine, John Charles, Kathryn Ann. Admitted to Ohio bar, 1949, since practiced in Dayton; mem. firm Young, Pryor, Lynn & Jerardi, and predecessor firms, 1949—; dir. Brookville Nat. Bank (Ohio). Served to lt. (j.g.), A.C., USNR, 1942-46. Mem. Am., Ohio, Dayton (v.p., pres. 1976-77, exec. com.) bar assns., Sigma Alpha Epsilon, Phi Delta Phi. Lutheran. Club: Dayton Country. Home: 4700 Tait Rd Dayton OH 45429 Office: Suite 2030 One 1st Nat Plaza Dayton OH 45402

YOUNG, CLIFF, artist; b. New Waterford, Ohio, Dec. 27, 1905; s. Frank S. and Bertha (Cobbs) Y.; student Art Inst. Pitts., 1924-26, Carnegie Inst. Tech., Chgo. Art Inst., Art Students League. Mural asst. to Dean Cornwell, Barry Faulkner, Ezra Winter, William A. Mackay, 1934-39, Allyn Cox, 1972-74, 76—; instr. Jiranek Sch. Design, N.Y.C., Salmagundi Club Painting Class; paintings exhibited Nat. Acad., USN Combat Art Collection, Galerie Internat., N.Y.C., Cocoran Art Gallery, Salmagundi Club, Soc. Illustrators, U.S. Marine Corps Combat Art Collection; murals in Zenger Meml. Room, Fed. Hall, N.Y.C., Ch. of Our Lady of Victory, (N.Y.C.), Norwegian Children's Home, Bklyn., Pub. Sch. 232, Queens, N.Y., St. Francis Monestery, P.R., Berkshire Life Ins. Co., Pittsfield, Mass. Mem. Am. Artists Profl. League, Artists Guild, Soc. Illustrators, Nat. Soc. Mural Painters, Archtl. League N.Y. Clubs: Arts (Washington), Salmagundi. Author: Figure Drawing without a Model, 1946; Drawing Drapery, 1947; Architectural Figure Construction, 1966. Home: 30 W 60th St New York NY 10023 Office: 56 W 45th St New York NY 10036

YOUNG, COLEMAN ALEXANDER, city ofcl.; b. Tuscaloosa, Ala., May 24, 1918; s. Coleman and Ida Reese (Jones) Y.; LL.D., Eastern Mich. U., Wayne State U. Del., Mich. Constl. Conv., 1961-62; mem. Mich. Senate, 1964-73, also Democratic floor leader; mayor of Detroit, 1974—. Del. to Dem. Nat. Conv., 1968, 72, 76; Dem. nat. committeeman from Mich.; now vice chmn. Nat. Dem. Party. Bd. dirs. Ferndale Coop. Credit Union, Kirwood Hosp., Detroit. Served to 2d lt. USAAF, World War II. Mem. N.A.A.C.P., Booker T. Washington Bus. Men's Assn., Trade Union Leadership Council, Assn. for Study Negro Life and History, AFL-CIO Council (spl. rep.). Baptist. Office: Office of Mayor 2 Woodward Ave Detroit MI 48226

YOUNG, DALE LEE, banker; b. Palmyra, Nebr., Mar. 13, 1928; s. Mike P. and Grace (Clutter) Y.; B.B.A., U. Nebr., 1950; m. Norma Marie Shalla, June 18, 1950; children—Shalla Ann, Philip Mike. With First Nat. Bank & Trust Co., Lincoln, Nebr., 1950—, cashier, 1966—, v.p., 1966-76, exec. v.p., 1976—; dir. Instrumentation Spltys. Co., 1st Savs. Co. of Lincoln; sec., dir. Leasing Corp. Treas. Lincoln City Library Found. Treas., mem. exec. com. Nebr. Republican Com., 1968—; bd. dirs., v.p. Lincoln Symphony; bd. dirs. Lincoln Community Services; bd. dirs. ARC, Lincoln Found.; trustee Bryan Meml. Hosp., 1976-80. Served with AUS, 1946-48, 50-51. Mem. Nebr. Art Assn., Omaha-Lincoln Soc. Fin. Analysts, Lincoln C. of C. (pres.), Theta Xi. Presbyterian. Clubs: Nebraska, Lincoln Country, Univ. Home: 2627 Park Ave Lincoln NE 68502 Office: PO Box 81008 Lincoln NE 68508

YOUNG, DAVID ELWYN, publishing co. exec.; b. Somerville, Mass., Sept. 22, 1915; s. Elwyn Lawrence/Kimball and Henrietta Ella (Kuhn) Y.; grad. Burdett Coll., 1933; m. Eleanor Ruth Brown, June 28, 1936; children—Joan Zummo, Nancy (Mrs. John O'Pezio), Paul. Circulation dir., v.p., chmn. exec. com. KABLE News Co., N.Y.C., 1950-60; v.p. sales Grove Press, Inc., 1960-63; v.p. sales Paperback Library, 1963-68; pres. Olympia Press, N.Y., 1968-71; pres. Manor Books, Inc. Pres., East Meadow Blood Bank, 1952-57. Mem. Distripress. Presbyterian (elder 1953—). Clubs: Masons, Tenn. Squires. Home: 75 Mellow Lane Westbury NY 11590 Office: 432 Park Ave S New York City NY 10016

YOUNG, DAVID POLLOCK, author, educator; b. Davenport, Iowa, Dec. 14, 1936; s. Cecil T. and Mary Ella (Pollock) Y.; B.A., Carleton Coll., 1958; M.A., Yale, 1959, Ph.D., 1965; m. Chloe Hamilton, June 17, 1963; children—Newell Hamilton, Margaret Helen. With dept. English Oberlin Coll., 1961—, prof., 1973—. Translator. Recipient U.S. award Internat. Poetry Forum, 1969. Author: Something of Great Constancy: the Art of "A Midsummer Night's Dream", 1965; Sweating Out the Winter, 1969; The Heart's Forest: Shakespeare's Pastoral Plays, 1972; Boxcars, 1973; Work Lights: 32 Prose Poems, 1977; Rilke's Duino Elegies, 1978. Editor Field: Contemporary Poetry & Poetics. Contbr. poetry to lit. publs. Office: Dept English Oberlin Coll Oberlin OH 44074*

YOUNG, DAVID WILSON, chemist; b. Oblong, Ill., Aug. 16, 1909; s. William Lee and Bertha Fay (Wilson) Y.; B.S. in Indsl. Chemistry, U. Ky., 1931, M.S. in Chemistry, 1935; D.Sc., Transylvania U., 1935, Queens Coll., Eng., 1968; 1 dau., Susan Wilson. Research chemist Ky. Agrl. Expt. Sta., 1931-35, Laurel Hill Research Lab., Gen. Chem. Co., 1936-40; sr. research chemist Esso Research and Engring. Co., Linden, N.J., 1940-55; sr. research chemist Sinclair Research, Inc., Harvey, Ill., 1955-63, sr. research asso., 1963-69, also dir. sci. research rograms; sr. research asso. Atlantic Richfield Co., 1969-71; v.p. Compino Labs., Forest Park, Ill.; dir., mgr. research and devel. Heritage Environmental Research Inst., Anaheim, Calif.; partner R.B. MacMullin Assos., Niagara Falls, N.Y., 1971-73; pres. David W. Young & Assos., Chgo., 1975—. Cons., U.S. Army, USAF, 1959-62, Dow Chem. Co., 1969-70; Sigma Xi lectr., 1963-67; lectr. Purdue U., 1968-70, Am. Chem. Soc. Speakers Bur., 1970—; cons. chem. warfare dept. U.S. Army, 1955-58. Mem. joint com. Internat. Union Pure and Applied Chemistry, 1967. Named Ky. col., 1959; recipient Merit award Chgo. Tech. Socs. Council, 1961, honor award U.S. Commr. Patents, 1964-65; pres.'s hon. award Stanislaus Coll., 1969. Fellow Am. Inst. Chemists (nat. counselor at large 1964-67, pres. 1969-70, vice chmn. bd. dirs. 1971—, Chem. Pioneer award 1967, Honor Scrill award 1969, hon. mem. 1971); mem. Am. Chem. Soc. (chmn. Lexington, Ky. sect. 1935, dir. Chgo. sect. 1964—, mem. speakers bur. 1957—), A.A.A.S., Am. Legion, 40 and 8, Sigma Xi, Pi Kappa Alpha, Phi Mu Amlpha, Alpha Chi Sigma. Methodist. Clubs: Masons (32 deg.), Shriners, N.Y. Athletic. Patentee synthetic lubricants, synthetic rubber resins, catalysts in oil and chem. industries. Address: 2545 Palmer Ave Park Forest South IL 60466

YOUNG, DEAN WAYNE, cartoonist; b. Flushing, N.Y., July 2, 1938; s. Murat Bernard and Athel Laurel (Lindorff) Y.; B.A., LaGrange Coll., 1960; m. Mary Penhryn Ford, May 28, 1971; children—Lisa Dianne, Dana Lynn, Heather Ford, Dionne Laurel. Account exec. Sisson & Barrett Advt., Miami, Fla., 1960-63; cartoonist Blondie comic strip, 1963—.

YOUNG, DEFORREST EUGENE, utilities co. exec.; b. Joplin, Mo., Mar. 29, 1920; s. Oral S. and Blanche M. (Trent) Y.; student Mo. So. Coll., 1938-40; m. Virginia Lee Carter, June 1, 1942; children—Stephen K., Bradley E. Bookkeeper, The Gas Service Co., Joplin, Mo., 1940-42, asst. chief clk., 1947-50, office mgr., 1950-59, mgr. date processing, 1959-67, asst. treas., 1967-70, asst. sec., 1969-70, treas., 1970—, v.p., 1978—; accountant United Zinc Smelting Corp., Joplin, 1942-47. Mem. Financial Execs. Inst. Home: 4928 N Gladstone St Kansas City MO 64119 Office: Crown Center 2460 Pershing Rd Kansas City MO 64108

YOUNG, DON JOHN, fed. judge; b. Norwalk, Ohio, July 13, 1910; s. Don J. and Elaine (Dennis) Y.; A.B. cum laude, Western Res. U., 1932, LL.B., 1934; student Cleve. Art Sch., 1932-34; m. Seville Beatrice Shagrin, June 27, 1936; children—Don J., Patricia E. Admitted to Ohio bar, 1934; pvt. practice, Norwalk, 1934-52; judge Common Ct. Pleas, Huron County, Ohio, 1952-53, Probate and Juvenile Ct., Huron County, 1953-65; U.S. judge No. Dist. Ohio, Western Div., 1965—; instr., lectr. juvenile ct. laws at seminars and insts. for judges, 1959—; exhibited jewelry Cleve. Mus. Art, Butler Art Inst., Nat. Ceramic Exhbn.; v.p. Ohio Assn. Probate Ct. Judges, 1958-60; pres. Ohio Assn. Juvenile Ct. Judges, 1960-62; law reporter Nat. Juvenile Ct. Found., 1959-73, sec.-treas., 1960-61, sec., 1961-62; sec. Nat. Council Juvenile Ct. Judges, 1962-65, exec. com., 1966-69. Exec. dir. Norwalk CD Corps, 1942-46; pres. Firelands Hist. Soc., 1945-46, Norwalk Cemetery Assn., 1951-57; sec. Norwalk Recreation Com., 1946-53; trustee Young Men's Library and Reading Room Assn., 1955-65, Whittlesey Acad. Arts and Scis., 1955-65. Mem. Am., Ohio bar assns., Am. Judicature Soc., Nat. Council Crime and Delinquency, Toledo Area Assn. Correctional Workers, Order of Coif, Phi Beta Kappa, Pi Epsilon Delta. Episcopalian. Contbr. articles to profl. jours. Office: US Court House and Custom House Toledo OH 43624

YOUNG, DONALD ALAN, physician; b. Oakland, Calif., Feb. 8, 1939; s. Leo Alan and Pearl Anita (Walker) Y.; B.A., U. Calif., Berkeley, 1960, M.D., 1964; m. Jean Baggett, June 25, 1977; children—Jennifer, Karen, Ray, John. Intern, then resident in internal medicine U. Calif. Hosp., San Francisco, 1964-66; resident in internal medicine Parkland Hosp., Dallas, 1966-67; fellow chest diseases U. Calif. Hosp., San Francisco, 1967-68; mem. staff Palo Alto (Calif.) Med. Clinic, 1970-75; med. dir. Am. Lung Assn., 1975-77; scholar adminstrv. scholars program VA, Washington, 1977—; clin. instr. U. Calif. Med. Sch., San Francisco, 1968-70, Stanford U. Med. Sch., 1970-75. Trustee Vt. Lung Center; bd. dirs. Mid-Md. Lung Assn. Served with M.C., AUS, 1968-70. Decorated Commendation medal. Recipient Borden award, 1964. Diplomate Am. Bd. Internal Medicine. Mem. Am. Thoracic Soc., AMA, Am. Coll. Chest Physicians, Calif. Acad. Medicine. Home: 10821 Deborah Dr Potomac MD 20854 Office: VA 510 Vermont Ave Washington DC 20420

YOUNG, DONALD ARTHUR, investment banker; b. Buffalo, July 8, 1925; s. Henry Wilson and Florence (Thibault) Y.; B.S. in Bus. and Engring. Adminstrn., Mass. Inst. Tech., 1950; m. Marilyn Jeanne Thomas, Sept. 10, 1950; children—Kimberley Ellen, Christopher Arthur. Chem. engr. Owens-Ill. Glass Co., 1950-51; with Chem. Fund, Inc., N.Y.C., 1952-64, exec. v.p., 1963-64; mgr. inst. investment research H.N. Whitney, Goadby and Co., 1965-70; sr. v.p., mgr. instl. dept. Laidlaw, Adams & Peck, Inc., 1970—. Mem. N.Y. Soc. Security Analysts, Chem. Market Research Assn., Kappa Kappa Sigma. Clubs: Mass. Institute of Technology, Wall Street (N.Y.C.); Morris County Golf. Home: Maryknoll Dr New Vernon NJ 07976 Office: 20 Broad St New York NY 10005

YOUNG, DONALD E., congressman; b. Meridian, Calif., June 9, 1933; grad. Chico (Calif.) State Coll.; m. Lula Fredson; children—Joni, Dawn. Former educator, river boat capt.; mem. Fort Yukon City Council, 6 years, mayor, 4 years; mem. Alaska Ho. of Reps., 1966-70; mem. Alaska Senate, 1970-73; mem. 93d-96th Congresses from Alaska. Republican. Office: US House of Reps Washington DC 20515

YOUNG, DONALD STIRLING, clin. chemist; b. Belfast, N. Ireland, Dec. 17, 1933; s. John Stirling and Ruth Muir (Whipple) Y.; M.B., Ch.B., U. Aberdeen (Scotland), 1957; Ph.D., U. London, 1962; m. Silja Meret; children—Gordon, Robert, Peter. Terminable lectr. materia medica U. Aberdeen, 1958-59; fellow Postgrad. Med. Sch., U. London, 1959-62, registrar, 1962-64; vis. scientist NIH, Bethesda, Md., 1965-66, chief clin. chemistry service, 1966-77; head clin. chemistry sect. Mayo Clinic, Rochester, Minn., 1977—; past bd. dirs. Nat. Com. Clin. Lab. Standards. Recipient Dir.'s award NIH, 1977, Gerard B. Lambert award 1974-75, MDS Health Group award Can. Soc. Clin. Chemists, 1978; Roman lectr. Australian Assn. Clin. Biochemists, 1979. Mem. Am. Assn. Clin. Chemistry (J.H. Roe award Capital sect. 1973, Bernard Gerulat award N.J. sect. 1977, Ames award 1977; pres.), Acad. Clin. Lab. Physicians and Scientists (past exec. com.), Assn. Clin. Biochemists, Sigma Xi. Past chmn. bd. editors Clin. Chemistry; co-editor: The Neonate: Clinical; Biochemistry, Physiology and Pathology, 1976; Drug Interference and Drug Metabolism in Clinical Chemistry, 1976; Clinician and Chemist, 1979; Chemical Diagnosis of Disease, 1979. Home: 1061 Plummer Ln Rochester MN 55901 Office: Mayo Clinic Rochester MN 55901

YOUNG, EDWIN HAROLD, educator; b. Detroit, Nov. 4, 1918; s. William George and Alice Pearl (Hicks) Y.; B.S. in Chem. Engring., U. Detroit, 1942; M.S. in Chem. Engring., U. Mich., 1949, M.S. in Metall. Engring., 1952; m. Ida Signe Soma, June 25, 1944; children—David Harold, Barbara Ellen. Chem. engr. Wright Air Devel. Center, Dayton, Ohio, 1942-43; instr. U. Mich., Ann Arbor, 1946-52, asst. prof., 1952-56, asso. prof., 1956-59, prof. chem. and metall. engring., 1959—. Mem. Mich. Bd. Registration for Profl. Engrs., 1963-78, chmn., 1969-70, 72-73, 75-76; mem. Mich. Bd. Registration for Architects, 1963-78. Dist. commr. Boy Scouts Am., 1961-64, mem. Wolverine council, 1965-69. Served with USNR, 1943-46, to capt. Res. ret., 1973. Fellow ASME, Am. Inst. Chemists, Am. Inst. Chem. Engrs., Engring. Soc. Detroit; mem. Am. Chem. Soc., Am. Soc. Heating, Refrigerating and Air-conditioning Engrs., Am. Soc. Engring. Edn., Nat. (pres. 1968-69; award 1977), Mich. (pres. 1962-63; Engr. of Year award 1976) socs. profl. engrs., Mich. Assn. of Professions (pres. 1966, Distinguished award 1970), Nat. Council Engring. Examiners, Naval Res. Assn., Res. Officers Assn., Sigma Xi, Tau Beta Pi, Phi Kappa Phi, Phi Lambda Upsilon, Alpha Chi Sigma. Republican. Baptist. Author: (with L.E. Brownell) Process Equipment Design, 1959. Contbr. articles to profl. jours. Home: 609 Dartmoor Rd Ann Arbor MI 48103

YOUNG, EDWIN PARSON, former newspaper exec.; b. Pitts., July 19, 1908; s. Edwin Parson and Diana (Montanye) Y.; A.B., Cornell U., 1931; m. Elizabeth Miller Hoskins, Jan. 9, 1937 (dec. 1968); children—Diana Montanye Young Carls, Edwin Parson; m. 2d, Polly Yates Brinton, Mar. 16, 1974. Editor-in-chief Cornell Daily Sun, 1930-31; reporter, columnist, critic Williamsport (Pa.) Sun, 1931-35; reporter, copy editor, rewrite Balt. Sun, 1935-38, asst. city editor, 1938-41, city editor, 1941-54; adminstrv. asst. Providence Jour. Co., 1954-57, gen. mgr. adminstrn., 1957-58, gen. mgr., 1958-69, v.p., asst. publisher, 1969-77, now dir.; Md. corr. Time, Life and Fortune, 1941-54; instr. English, Loyola Coll. Md., 1947-53; instr. bus. U. Balt., 1948-54; chmn. Providence Jour. Co. Retirement Commn., 1966-77; dir. Providence Gravure, Inc., Seaport '76, Newport, R.I. Mem. Md. Hosp. Survey Com., 1947; bd. dirs. R.I. Philharmonic Orch.; bus. adv. council U. R.I.; trustee Newport Preservation Soc. Mem. Chesapeake Assn. AP (chmn. continuing study com. on membership participation 1947-51, chmn. freedom of info. com. 1951-54), Md. Press Assn. (v.p. 1954), Newspaper Personnel Relations Assn. (pres. 1964-65), Am. Newspaper Pubs. Assn. (chmn. journalism edn. com. 1966-67), New Eng. Daily Newspaper Assn., Internat. Press Inst., Inter Am. Press Assn., AIM (pres.'s council), Am. Mgmt. Assn., R.I. Hist. Soc., Sigma Delta Chi, Alpha Delta Phi. Presbyterian. Clubs: Hope, Turks Head, Agawam Hunt (Providence); Cornell of R.I. (pres. 1974-75); Leash (N.Y.C.); Reading Room, Spouting Rock Beach Assn., Clambake, Ida Lewis Yacht (Newport, R.I.). Home: 40 School St Newport RI 02840 also Old Iron Point Cobbs Creek VA 23035

YOUNG, ELMER RICHARD, educator; b. Kaysville, Utah, Mar. 30, 1913; s. George W. and Sylvia (Barber) Y.; B.S., U. Utah, 1936; M.S., 1937; Ph.D., Columbia, 1953; m. June Spencer, July 20, 1938; children—John Spencer, Lowell Spencer, Melvin Spencer, Margaret, George Spencer, Richard Spencer, Anita. Instr. accounting Bklyn, Coll., 1938-48; mem. faculty U. Utah, 1948—, prof. accounting, 1956—, head dept. accounting Sch. Bus., 1961-72; cons. industry and govt., 1950—. Mem. Nat. Assn. Accountants (chmn. organizing com., 1st pres. Utah chpt.), Inst. Internal Auditors, Nat. Soc. Bus. Budgeting, Am. Accounting Assn., Beta Gamma Sigma, Tau Kappa Alpha, Phi Delta Kappa. Author: Distribution Cost Accounting, 1954; (with Daniel Lipsky) An Accounting Course for Technical and Non-Technical Students; Introduction to Merchandise Management Accounting for Small Retail Outlets, 1964; also articles. Home: 1345 Wilton Way Salt Lake City UT 84108

YOUNG, FRANK EDWARD, microbiologist, educator; b. Mineola, N.Y., Sept. 1, 1931; s. Frank Edward and Erma Frances (Holmes) Y.; M.D., State U. N.Y. at Syracuse, 1956; Ph.D., Case Western Res. U., 1962; m. Leanne Hutchinson, Oct. 20, 1956; children—Lorrie, Debora, Peggy, Frank, Jonathan. Asst. prof. pathology Western Res. U., 1962-65; asso. mem. depts. microbiology and pathology Scripps Clinic and Research Found., 1965-68, mem., 1968-70; prof., chmn. dept. microbiology U. Rochester (N.Y.), 1970-79, microbiologist-in-chief, 1976-79, dean Sch. Medicine and Dentistry, dir. Med. Center, 1979—; dir. clin microbiology labs. Strong Meml. Hosp., 1970-79, pathologist, 1974—. Faculty research asso. Am. Cancer Soc., 1962-70, mem. com. on virology and cell biology, 1974—; mem. microbiology tng. com. Nat. Inst. Gen. Med. Scis., 1972-73; mem. bacteriology and mycology study sect. Nat. Inst. Allergy and Infectious Diseases, 1975-79; adminstrv. bd. Council Acad. Socs., 1977-79. Research grantee NIH, Am. Cancer Soc., NSF. Mem. Inst. Medicine, Am. Soc. Microbiology (pres. central N.Y. sect. 1971-72), Am. Soc. Biol. Chemists, Am. Acad. Microbiology, Infectious Diseases Soc. Am., Soc. Exptl. Pathology. Mem. editorial bd. Jour. Bacteriology, 1968-73, Jour. Applied Biochemistry, 1978—; editor Gene, 1976—. Contbr. numerous articles to sci. and med. publs. Home: 41 Charter Oaks Dr Pittsford NY 14534 Office: Dean and Dir U Rochester Med Center Rochester NY 14642

YOUNG, FRANK WILBUR, educator; b. Chgo., May 31, 1928; s. William and Beatrice (Allen) Y.; B.A., U. Wash., 1950; M.A., Cornell U., 1954, Ph.D. in Social Anthropology, 1957; m. Ruth Cunniff, June 1, 1956; children—Christopher, Douglas. Asst. prof. San Diego State Coll., 1958-61, U. Pitts., 1961-62; mem. faculty Cornell U., 1962—, prof. rural sociology, 1969—. Served with AUS, 1950-52. Fellow Center Advanced Study in Behavioral Scis., 1968-69; sr. fellow East-West Center, 1975-76. Mem. Am. Sociol. Assn., Rural Sociol. Soc., Phi Beta Kappa, Phi Kappa Phi. Author: Initiation Ceremonies, 1965; Comparative Studies of Community Growth, 1973; also articles. Home: 340 N Sunset Dr Ithaca NY 14850

YOUNG, FRANKLIN WOODROW, clergyman, educator; b. Lima, Ohio, Mar. 16, 1915; s. Oscar N. and Evalette (Fellows) Y.; A.B., Dartmouth, 1937; student U. Pa. Grad. Sch., 1941-43; B.D., Crozer Theol. Sem., 1942; Ph.D. (univ. fellow 1943-44), Duke, 1946; m. Jean Steiner, Aug. 30, 1941; children—Franklin Woodrow, David S. Personnel dept. Am. Rolling Mill Co., also Lukens Steel Co., 1937-39; minister Huntington Valley (Pa.) Bapt. Ch., 1939-40; asst. minister First Bapt. Ch., Phila., 1941-43; teaching fellow Duke Div. Sch., 1944-45, instr., 1945-46, asst. prof. N.T., dean students, 1946-50; ordained to ministry P.E. Ch. as deacon, 1950, priest, 1951; asst. prof. N.T., Yale Div. Sch., 1950-54; lectr. religion Miss Porter's Sch., 1951-53; vis. lectr. religion Conn. Wesleyan U., 1953; asst. to minister St. John's Ch., Stamford, Conn., 1951-53; prof. N.T. and patristics Episcopal Theol. Sem. of S.W., 1954-59; prof. religion Princeton, 1959-68, chmn. dept., 1965-68; prof. N.T. and patristic studies, Duke, 1968—, dir. grad. studies in religion, 1969-74, Amos Ragan Kearns prof., N.T. and Patristic Studies, 1970—; vis. prof. Swarthmore Coll., 1964; vis. lectr. Princeton Theol. Sem., 1964. Mem. N.Am. commn. on worship, adv. commn. faith and order study World Council Chs. Am. Assn. Theol. Schs. fellow, 1959. Trustee Crozer Theol. Sem. Fellow Nat. Council Religion in Higher Edn.; mem. Am. Theol. Soc., Am. Soc. Ch. History, Am. Acad. Religion, Soc. Theol. Discussion, Soc. Bibl. Lit., Phi Beta Kappa, Psi Upsilon. Author: (with Howard Clark Kee) Understanding the New Testament, 1957. Contbr. articles to Ency. Brit., also profl. jours. Home: 132 Pinecrest Rd Durham NC 27705

YOUNG, GAIL SELLERS, educator, mathematician; b. Chgo., Oct. 3, 1915; s. Gail Sellers and Catherine (Dwyer) Y.; B.A., U. Tex., 1939, Ph.D., 1942; m. Frances M. Moise, Nov. 30, 1933; 1 dau., Catherine Josephine (Mrs. Bill R. Fliszar); m. 2d, Irene H. Vines, Dec. 26, 1968. Instr., then asst. prof. math. Purdue U., 1942-47; asst. prof., then prof. U. Mich., 1947-59; prof. Tulane U., 1959-70, chmn. dept., 1963-68; prof. math. U. Rochester, 1970-79, chmn. dept., 1970-75, 78-79; prof., chmn. math. and statistics Case Western Res. U., 1979—. Mem. bd. Nat. Council Accreditation Tchr. Edn., 1965-68; mem. Com. Undergrad. Program Math., 1963-71, chmn. tchr. tng. panel, 1964-68; mem. bd. Center Research in Coll. Instrn. Sci. and Math., 1963-67;

mem. Conf. Bd. Math. Scis., 1966-71, chmn. survey com., 1964-72; chmn. U.S. Commn. on Math. Instrn., 1975-76, mem., 1975—. Chmn., The Rochester Plan, 1975-78. Fellow AAAS (council 1968-70, 73-75, nomination com. 1977-78); mem. Am. Math. Soc., Math. Assn. Am. (pres. 1969-71). Author: (with J.G. Hocking) Topology, 1961; also papers. Home: 3399 Seaton Rd Cleveland Heights OH 44118

YOUNG, GAYLE MONROE, dancer; b. Lexington, Ky., Nov. 7, 1935; s. George Edward and Stella Lee (Monroe) Y.; student U. Calif., Berkeley, 1953-55. Dancer, Joffrey Ballet, 1957-58, N.Y.C. Ballet, 1958-59, Am. Ballet Theatre, N.Y.C., 1960—; appeared also on TV, Broadway; partner Pine Cone Antiques. Democrat. Home: 328 W 86th St New York NY 10024 Office: Am Ballet Theatre 888 7th Ave New York NY 10019

YOUNG, GENEVIEVE LEMAN, publishing co. exec.; b. Geneva, Switzerland, Sept. 25, 1930; d. Clarence Kuangson and Juliana Helen (Yen) Young; came to U.S., 1945, naturalized, 1968; B.A. (Wellesley Coll. scholar), Wellesley Coll., 1952; m. Cedric Sun, 1955 (div. 1972); m. 2d, Gordon Parks, Aug. 26, 1973. Asst. editor Harper & Row, pubs., N.Y.C., 1960-62, editor, 1962-64, asst. mng. editor, 1964-66, mng. editor, 1966-70; exec. editor J.B. Lippincott Co., N.Y.C., 1970-77, v.p., 1972-77, sr. editor Little, Brown & Co., N.Y.C., 1977—; v.p. Winger Enterprises, Inc., N.Y.C. Alumna trustee Phillips Acad., Andover, Mass., 1975-78. Mem. Assn. Am. Pubs. (exec. council gen. pub. div. 1975-78, freedom to read com. 1972-75), Women's Media Group. Home: 30 Park Ave New York NY 10016 Office: 747 3d Ave New York NY 10017

YOUNG, GEORGE BERKELEY, lawyer; b. Madison, Wis., July 27, 1913; s. Karl and Frances Campbell (Berkeley) Y.; A.B., Yale, 1934, A.M., 1937, Ph.D., 1939; J.D., Northwestern U., 1948; m. Mary Seymour Adams, Mar. 24, 1944; children—Mary, George. Admitted to Ill. bar, 1948; asso. Isham, Lincoln & Beale, Chgo., 1948-50, mem. firm, 1950-54; v.p. Field Enterprises, Inc., Chgo., 1954-64, pres., 1964-66, chmn. 1966-68, dir., 1952-69; instr. hist. Barnard Coll., Columbia, 1939-41; lectr. property law Northwestern U. Law Sch., 1951-53; dir. Field Enterprises, Inc., 1952-69, chmn., 1966-68; dir. Indsl. Nucleonics Corp., Chrysler Corp., CNA Income Shares, Inc. Trustee Rush-Presbyn.-St. Luke's Med. Center; v.p., trustee Art Inst. Chgo. 1953—; trustee Newberry Library, Chgo. Served as lt. OSS, USNR, 1943-45. Mem. Chgo. Bar Assn., Phi Beta Kappa, Order of Coif. Clubs: Chicago, Casino, Wayfarers, Commercial Commonwealth (Chgo.); Onwentsia, Shorearces (Lake Forest, Ill.; Graduates, Elizabethan (New Haven); Brook and Century (N.Y.C.). Author: (with J.A.S. Grenville) Politics Strategy and American Diplomacy, 1966; also articles in law revs. Home: 2430 Lakeview Ave Chicago IL 60614 Office: 400 N Michigan Ave Chicago IL 60611

YOUNG, GEORGE CRESSLER, U.S. judge; b. Cin., Aug. 4, 1916; s. George Philip and Gladys (Cressler) Y.; A.B., U. Fla., 1938, LL.B., 1940; student Harvard Law Sch., 1947; m. Iris June Hart, Oct. 6, 1951; children—George Cressler, Barbara Ann. Admitted to Fla. bar, 1940; practice in Winter Haven, 1940-41; asso. firm Smathers, Thompson, Maxwell & Dyer, Miami, 1947; adminstrv., legislative asst. to Senator Smathers of Fla., 1948-52; asst. U.S. atty., Jacksonville, 1952; partner firm Knight, Kincaid, Young & Harris, Jacksonville, 1953-61; U.S. dist. judge No., Middle and So. dists. Fla., 1961-73, chief judge Middle Dist., 1973—. Mem. com. on adminstrn. fed. magistrates system Jud. Conf. U.S. Bd. dirs. Jacksonville United Cerebral Palsy Assn., 1953-60. Served to lt. (s.g.) USNR, 1942-46. Mem. Rollins Coll. Alumni Assn. (pres. 1968-69), Am. (spl. com. for adminstrn. criminal justice), Fla. (gov. 1960-61), Jacksonville (past pres.) bar assns., Am. Judicature Soc., Am. Law Inst., Order of Coif, Fla. Blue Key, Phi Beta Kappa, Phi Kappa Phi, Phi Delta Phi, Sigma Alpha Epsilon. Home: 2424 Shrewsbury Rd Orlando FL 32803 Office: US Courthouse and Fed Bldg 80 N Hughey Ave Orlando FL 32801

YOUNG, GEORGE DOUGLAS, acad. adminstr.; b. Ham Heung, Korea, Sept. 2, 1910; s. Luther Lisgar and Catherine Firth (Mair) Y.; B.Sc., Acadia U., 1932; postgrad. Westminster Theol. Sem., 1935-37; B.D., S.T.M., Faith Theol. Sem., 1938; Ph.D., Dropsie Coll. for Hebrew and Cognate Learning (now Dropsie U.), 1948; m. Georgina Olive Squires, June 26, 1934; 1 son, Gordon Douglas. Br. mgr. circulation dept. Halifax Herald, Sydney, N.S., Can., 1932-35; prin. acad., Kingston, N.S., 1942-44; registrar, instr. Hebrew, Faith Theol. Sem., 1944-48; dean Nat. Bible Inst., N.Y.C., 1948-53; dean Northwestern Coll. and Sem., Mpls., 1953-57; dean, prof. Semitic studies Trinity Evang. Div. Sch., Deerfield, Ill., 1957-62; founder, pres., prof. Semitic studies Inst. Holy Land Studies, Jerusalem, 1959-78, pres. emeritus, 1978—; dir. Bridges for Peace, Jerusalem, 1978—. Mem. Internat. bd. govs. Sha'are Zedek Hosp., Jerusalem, 1973—; mem. exec. com. Israel Inter-Faith Com., Jerusalem, 1974—; mem. St. and Suburb Naming Commn., Jerusalem, 1975—; mem. Town Planning Commn., Jerusalem, 1978—. Recipient B'rith Abraham medal, 1960, Israel Pilgrim medal, 1964; Mcpl. award Jerusalem, 1978. Mem. Am. Sch. Oriental Research, Rainbow Group, Near East Archaeol. Soc. (dir. 1974—). Republican. Mem. Evangelical Free Ch. Am. Clubs: Rotary (past pres.) Jerusalem. Author: Ugaritic Concordance, 1956; A Grammar of the Hebrew Language, 1951; The Bride and the Wife: A Future for Israel?, 1959; contbr. numerous articles to profl. publs. Office: #1 Brenner PO Box 7304 Jerusalem Israel

YOUNG, GEORGE HAYWOOD, JR., ret. army officer, business exec.; b. Pine Bluff, Ark., Jan. 21, 1921; s. George Haywood and Sarah (Mercer) Y.; B.S. with honors, The Citadel, 1942; postgrad. Command and Gen. Staff Coll., 1946, Armed Forces Staff Coll., 1955. Indsl. Coll. Armed Forces, 1962; M.S., U. So. Calif., 1958; M.B.A., George Washington U., 1962; m. Jeanne Marie Collins, Feb. 5, 1946; children—Cornelia Collins, George Haywood III. Commd. 2d lt. U.S. Army, 1942, advanced through grades to brig. gen., 1966; served ETO, World War II, in 3 combat amphibious landings and 6 campaigns; staff mem. Joint Brazil-U.S. Mil. Commn., Rio de Janeiro, 1946-49; bn. officer 3d Inf. Div., Ft. Benning, 1949-50, Korea, 1950-52; mem. Army Dept. Gen. Staff, Washington, 1952-54, 58-61, Ft. Monroe, 1954-56; chief plans br., dep. chief staff logistics U.S. Army Europe, 1962-64; comdg. officer 1st Brigade, 3d Inf. Div., Germany, 1964-66; chief staff U.S. Army Communications Zone, Europe, 1966-67; dep. chief staff plans and operations U.S. Army Viet Nam, 1967; asst. div. comdr. Americal Div., 1967-68; comdg. gen. Da Nang Support Command, Viet Nam, 1968, 24th Inf. Div., Germany, 1968-70; dir. U.S. Army Materiel Command, Washington, 1970-71; ret., 1971; corporate dir. indsl. and personnel relations Vendo Corp., Kansas City, Mo., 1972-79, v.p. govt. affairs, 1979—; Pres., German-Am. Fedn. Germany, 1969-70. Alpine dist. commr. Boy Scouts Europe, 1969-70. Decorated D.S.M., Silver Star with oak leaf cluster, Legion of Merit with 3 oak leaf clusters, Bronze Star with V and 2 oak leaf clusters, Purple Heart with oak leaf clusters, Air medal with 22 oak leaf clusters, Army Commendation ribbon with 2 oak leaf clusters, Combat Infantry badge with star; Order Mil. Merit (Brazil); Order Merit Fifth Class (Viet Nam); Cross of Gallantry (Viet Nam); recipient Internat. Distinguished Service award Kiwanis; Stadt Schweinfurt award; named hon. senator Augsburger Carneval Verein. Mem. Kans. Hist. Soc., Internat. Relations Council. Clubs: Army Navy Country (Arlington, Va.); Ft. Leavenworth (Kan.) Golf and Country. Home: 207 Vine St Leavenworth KS 66048

YOUNG, GEORGE HOOPER, univ. dean; b. Elkhorn, Wis., Dec. 3, 1915; s. J. Howard and Winifred (Hooper) Y.; B.A., U. Wis., 1938, LL.B., 1941; m. Lillian Latham, June 16, 1941. Admitted to Wis. bar, 1941; practiced with firm Stroud, Stebbins, Wingert & Young, Madison, 1941-50; asso. prof. law U. Wis., 1950, prof., 1953—, dean Law Sch., 1957-68. Mem. Am. Law Inst., Am., Wis., Dane County bar assns., Am. Judicature Soc., Order of Coif, Phi Eta Sigma, Phi Delta Phi. Contbr. articles to legal publs. Home: 3841 Nakoma Rd Madison WI 53711 Office: U Wis Law Sch Madison WI 53706

YOUNG, GEORGE PATRICK, supt. schs.; b. Butler, Pa., July 17, 1924; s. George Patrick and Mildred Elaine (Fisher) Y.; student Denison U., 1944-45; B.A. in Math., U. Kans., 1947; Ed.M., U. Pitts., 1951; Ed.D., U. Ill., 1960; m. Biloine Whiting, Apr. 1950; children—Robin Ray, Richard Mark, Benjamin Brock, Priscilla Pilar. Tchr., Am. Sch. of Guatemala, 1951-53, dir. guidance, 1952-53, dir. Sch. Boarding House, 1952-53; tchr. Instituto Guatemalteco-Americano, 1951-52; headmaster Colegio Bolivar, Cali, Colombia, 1953-58; grad. asst. Office Field Services, U. Ill., 1958-60; dir. instrn. Urbana (Ill.) Pub. Schs., 1960-64; supt. schs. Gallup-McKinley County, N.Mex., 1964-66, Canton, Ohio, 1966-70, St. Paul, 1970—; lectr. Sch. Adminstrn., U. Minn., 1977—. Spl. adviser sec. edn. Departmento del Valle del Cauca, Colombia, 1956. Chmn., Ill. State Com., Midwest Program on Airborne Television Instrn., 1962, bd. dirs., 1963; mem. Commr. Edn. Adv. Council, State of Minn., 1970—, Gov.'s Adv. Council on Community Schs., 1970—; mem. adminstrs. com. Study Commn. for Higher Edn., 1972—; mem. U. Minn. Coll. Edn. Adv. Group, 1973—. Bd. dirs. Twin City Ednl. TV, Minn. Symphony Orch., Ednl. Research and Devel. Council of Twin City Met. Area; chmn. Minn. Council on Econ. Edn., 1978-79, Large City Sch. Supts. Council, 1978-79, Assn. Orgns. for Tchr. Edn., 1979; mem. exec. bd. Indianhead council Boy Scouts Am. Served to lt. (j.g.) USN, 1942-46. Recipient Ann. Human Relations Council award, 1968, Spl. award Urban League, Canton, 1970; named Distinguished Alumnus Coll. Edn., U. Ill., 1971. Mem. Am., Minn. assns. sch. adminstrs., Nat. Assn. Secondary Sch. Prins., Nat. Assn. Elementary Sch. Prins., U. Ill. Coll. Edn. Alumni Assn. (v.p. 1963), Phi Delta Kappa, Kappa Delta Pi. Rotarian. Author weekly column Young View, St. Paul Dispatch, 1960-73. Contbr. articles to profl. jours. Home: 15 Crocus Hill St Paul MN 55102 Office: 360 Colborne St St Paul MN 55102

YOUNG, GLEN MURPHY, truck rental co. exec.; b. Tuscaloosa, Ala., Aug. 28, 1924; s. Glenn Jones and Vertrees Elsie (Murphy) Y.; B.S., U. Ala., 1948; m. Patsy Ruth Howard, Feb. 4, 1945 (dec. Aug. 1978); children—Glen Howard, Robert Alan, Patricia Susan. Agt., IRS, Birmingham, Ala., 1948-51; sales mgr. Fairfield Barrell Co., Inc., Birmingham, 1953-55; with Ryder System Inc., Miami, Fla., 1955—, group v.p. corp. hdqrs., 1971—, gen. mgr., 1972—, now exec. v.p. parent co. and pres. subs. Ryder Truck Rental, Inc.; dir. Ryder Truck Rental Ltd., Ryder System N.V. Republican. Methodist. Home: 9370 Gallardo St Coral Gables FL 33156 Office: 3600 NW 82d Ave Miami FL 33166

YOUNG, GORDON ELLSWORTH, composer, organist; b. McPherson, Kans., Oct. 15, 1919; s. Benjamin Warden and Rose Esther (Johnson) Y.; Mus.B., Southwestern Coll., 1940, Mus.D., 1960; attended Curtis Inst. Music, 1944-46. Organist First Meth. Ch., Tulsa, 1940-44, First Presbyn. Ch., Lancaster, Pa., 1944-48, Detroit, 1952-72; concert artist. Music tchr.; mem. faculty Tex. Christian U., 1950-52. Mem. A.S.C.A.P. (several awards). Republican. Presbyn. Composer numerous organ, choir, solo voice and instrumental works. Office: Box 256 Detroit MI 48231. *A positive attitude in all things makes the whole difference between success and failure in a career.*

YOUNG, H. ALBERT, lawyer; b. Kiev, Russia, May 30, 1904; s. Harry and Rose (Morsoff) Y.; brought to U.S., 1905, naturalized, 1926; B.A., U. Del., 1926; J.D., U. Pa., 1929; m. Ann Blank, Mar. 22, 1931; children—Ronell (Mrs. William Douglass), Stuart B., H. Alan. Admitted to Del. bar, 1929, U.S. Dist. Ct., 1933, 3d Ciruict Ct. U.S., 1933, Supreme Ct. U.S., 1944; sr. partner firm Young, Conaway, Stargatt & Taylor, Wilmington, Del., 1959—; atty. gen. Del., 1951-55; atty. for Del. Legislature, 1935-37, Del. State Republican Com., 1965-70; chmn. Com. Adoption Uniform Comml. Code, 1964-70; participant arguments before U.S. Supreme Ct. in segregation cases, 1954; chmn. adv. com. on implementation Am. Bar Assn. standards for criminal justice U.S. Supreme Ct., 1973—; vice chmn. Del. Bd. Bar Examiners. Bd. dirs. Jewish Fedn. Del., Kutz Home for Aged, Jewish Community Center. Fellow Brandeis U., Hebrew U. Fellow Am. Coll. Trial Lawyers, Internat. Acad. Trial Lawyers (dir. 1965-71), Am. Bar Found.; mem. Am. Law Inst., Del. (pres. 1961-63), Ill., Am. (ho. of dels.) bar assns., Am. Judicature Soc. Jewish. Home: 1401 Pennsylvania Ave Wilmington DE 19806 Office: Market Tower Wilmington DE 19801

YOUNG, H. EDWIN, univ. pres.; b. Bonne Bay, Nfld., Can., May 3, 1917; s. William and Annie (McKenzie) Y.; B.S., U. Maine, 1940, M.A., 1942; Ph.D., U. Wis., 1950; m. Phyllis Smart, Feb. 14, 1941; children—Jill, John, Dorothy, Nathan, Barbara. Instr. U. Maine, 1942-47; mem. faculty U. Wis., 1947-65, 68—, instr., asst. prof., asso. prof., 1947-55, prof. dept. econs., 1955—, chmn. dept., 1953-61, dean Coll. Letters and Sci., 1961-65; pres. U. Maine, Orono, 1965-68; chancellor U. Wis., Madison, 1968-77, pres. U. Wis. System, 1977—; coordinator Wis.-Gadja Mada (Indonesia) Project; chmn. Am. Univs. Field Staff, 1977—; pres. Nat. Assn. State Univs. and Land Grant Colls., 1978—; bd. govs. East-West Center, 1978—. Mem. Indsl. Relations Research Assn. (pres. 1965-66). Editor: (with M. Derber) Labor and the New Deal, 1957. Home: 6021 S Highlands Ave Madison WI 53705

YOUNG, HENRY BEN, mgmt. cons.; b. Rockdale, Tex., Oct. 13, 1913; s. Henry Benjamin and Nettie Bell (Morris) Y.; B.S. in Mech. Engring., Rice U., 1937; grad. Advanced Mgmt. Program, Harvard, 1958; m. Dorothy Pauline Ewald, May 29, 1941; children—John Edward, Robert Henry. Chief engr. Mission Mfg. Co., Houston, 1937-54, dir. overseas projects, 1954-56; dir. engring. and research WKM div. ACF Industries, Inc., 1956-59, corporate v.p. engring. and research ACF Industries, Inc., N.Y.C., 1959-63, corporate v.p. mfg. and research 1963-65, corporate v.p., gen. mgr. W-K-M valve div. ACF Industries, Inc., Houston, 1965-71; dir. capital expenditures Marathon Mfg. Co., Houston, 1972-73; mgmt. and engring. cons., Houston, 1973-75; chmn. bd. dirs., pres. Chronister Valve Co., Houston, 1975-77; mgmt. and engring. cons., Houston, 1977-78; v.p. adminstrn. Lanzagorta Internat., Inc., Houston, 1978—; dir. Continental Bank Houston. Bd. dirs. Jr. Achievement S.E. Tex. Registered profl. engr., Tex. Mem. Soc. Profl. Engrs., ASME, Nomads, Am. Petroleum Inst., Am. Mgmt. Assn., N.A.M., Machinery and Allied Products Soc., Houston C. of C., Engring. Alumni Rice U. (past pres.), Tex. Mfrs. Assn. (dir., chpt. chmn.). Baptist. Mason. Home: 10122 Del Monte Dr Houston TX 77042

YOUNG, HERRICK BLACK, found. adminstr.; b. Marshfield, Wis., Feb. 8, 1904; s. James Franklin and Charlotte (Black) Y.; A.B., Ind. U., 1925; M.A., Columbia, 1928; Harrison fellow U. Pa., 1935; L.L.D., Centre Coll. Ky., 1954; L.H.D., Miami U., Oxford, Ohio, 1965; m. Charlotte Elizabeth Young, June 1, 1928; children—Herrick Jackson, Charlotte Joanne, Roderick McCune, Malcolm Black. Instr., Alborz Coll., Teheran, Iran, 1925-27, prof. lit., 1928-35; exec. sec. charge personnel Presbyn. Bd. Fgn. Missions, 1935-50; chmn. com. missionary personnel Fgn. Missions Conf. N.A., 1946-50; exec. dir. Internat. House Assn., 1950-54; lectr. field internat. relations; pres. Western Coll. for Women, 1954-69; cons. to pres., controller Tunghi U., Taichung, Taiwan, 1969-72; pres. Nr. East Found., N.Y.C., 1972—; dir. summer seminars S.A., 1955, 63, Middle East, 1956, 60, 64, Far East, 1957, 61, 65, Africa, 1958, 62, 66, C.Am. and Caribbean, 1959. Chmn. com. internat. relations Council Protestant Colls.; exec. com. Internat. Com. YMCA; mem. Council Evaluation Fgn. Student Credential; mem. Presbyn. Commn. on Nat. Capitol Center. Chmn. bd. trustees Welfare of Blind. Decorated Order of Homayun (Iran), 1962; named Ky. col. Fellow Royal Geog. Soc., Royal Central Asian Soc.; mem. Assn. Am. Colls. (commn. liberal learning), Am. Council Edn., Nat. Assn. Fgn. Student Advisers, Newcomen Soc., Ohio Coll. Assn. (exec. com.), St. Andrews Soc., Phi Delta Kappa, Sigma Delta Chi, Delta Chi. Republican. Presbyn. (elder). Mason. Clubs: University (N.Y.C.); Cosmos (Washington); Fort Henry (Wheeling, W.Va.). Author: One Great Fellowship, 1937; Moslem Editors Say, 1937; Hemisphere Neighbors, 1940; Tuesdays at Kumler Chapel, Chapel 1963; Strange Lands and Wonderful People, 1975. Home: Quaker Hill Mount Pleasant OH 43939 Office: 54 E 64th St New York City NY 10021

YOUNG, HOBART PAUL, mfg. co. exec.; b. Lake Geneva, Wis., June 3, 1916; s. Hobart Paul and Isabel (Chandler) Y.; A.B., Harvard U., 1937; m. Louise Buchwalter, June 3, 1944; children—Hobart Peyton, Anne Buckingham, Isabel Chandler. With Armour & Co., Chgo., 1938-52; exec. v.p. Signode Corp., Chgo., 1952—. Mem. adv. bd. North Suburban YMCA. Mem. Am. Chem. Soc. Clubs: Harvard (Chgo.); Indian Hill (Winnetka, Ill.); Chgo. Farmers, Chgo. Literary. Home: 755 Sheridan Rd Winnetka IL 60093 Office: 3600 W Lake Ave Glenview IL 60025

YOUNG, J. NELSON, lawyer; b. Rossville, Ill., Nov. 13, 1916; s. Jesse Bowman and Lula (Nelson) Young; B.S., U. Ill., 1938, J.D., 1942; m. Zerla Gingerich, Nov. 20, 1940; 1 dau., Marynel. Admitted to Ill. bar, 1942, U.S. Supreme Ct. bar, 1955; asso. firm McDermott, Will & Emery, Chgo., 1946; asst. prof. law U. Ill., 1946-51, asso. prof., 1951-53, prof., 1953—; vis. prof. Harvard U., 1958-59; cons. bank tax study Adv. Commn. Intergovtl. Relations, 1974. Served with USNR, 1942-46. C.P.A., Ill. Mem. Am. Bar Assn., Ill. Bar Assn., Am. Law Inst., Am. Inst. C.P.A.'s, Am. Acctg. Assn., Internat. Fiscal Assn., Ill. C.P.A. Soc. Author: (with Nowak and Rotunda) Constitutional Law, 1978; editor; (with others) CCH Study of Federal Tax Law—Individual Income Tax, 1979; (with others) Taxation Business Enterprises, 1979. Office: Coll Law U Ill Champaign IL 61820

YOUNG, JAMES ARTHUR, air force officer; b. Marion, Conn., Sept. 29, 1926; s. Merle Roy and Clara L. (Armstrong) Y.; grad. Air War Coll., 1969; m. Marian L. Carros, Dec. 8, 1950; children—James M., Stephen C., Richard C., Phyliss A. Commd. 2d lt. U.S. Army, 1946, advanced through grades to maj. gen. USAF, 1974; staff officer Directorate Operational Plans, Hdqrs. TAC, Langley AFB, Va., 1961-65; dir. ops. 833d Air Div., Seymour Johnson AFB, N.C., 1965; ops. officer 333d Tactical Fighter Squadron, Seymour Johnson AFB, 1965; comdr. Takhli Royal Thai AFB, 1966; comdr. 562d Tactical Fighter Squadron, McConnell AFB, Kans., 1966-67; asst. dir. ops. 23d Tactical Fighter Wing, 1967-68; dir. ops. plans Hdqrs. Pacific Air Forces, Hickam AFB, Hawaii, 1969-71; vice comdr. 8th Tactical Fighter Wing, Ubon Royal Thai AFB, 1971; comdr., 1971-72; asst. dep. chief of staff for plans Hdqrs. Pacific Air Forces, 1972; dep. asst. chief of staff for ops. Pacific Command, Hawaii, 1972-74; comdr. 25th NORAD region, 1974-76; dep. dir. Mapping Agy., Washington, 1976-77; chief of staff, combined mil. planning staff Central Treaty Orgn., Ankara, Turkey, 1977—. Decorated Silver Star with oak leaf cluster, Legion of Merit, D.F.C. with oak leaf cluster, Air medal with 14 oak leaf clusters, Meritorious Service medal, Air Force Commendation medal with oak leaf cluster. Address: 1005 Sagebrush Trail Albuquerque NM 87123

YOUNG, JAMES CURTIS, football coach; b. Van Wert, Ohio, Apr. 21, 1935; s. S.J. and Alice H. (Rumble) Y.; student Ohio State U., 1953-55; B.S., Bowling Green State U., 1957, M.S., 1958; m. Alyce Jane Waltz, June 22, 1957; children—Laura, Elaine, Joan, Colleen, James Curtis. Football coach Findlay (Ohio) Coll., 1958, Bowling Green (Ohio) State U., 1959, Lima (Ohio) Shawnee High Sch., 1960-63, Miami U., 1964-68, U. Mich., 1968-72; head football coach U. Ariz., Tucson, 1972-77, Purdue U., Lafayette, Ind., 1977—. Mem. Am. Fedn. Football Coaches. Office: Mackey Arena Purdue U Lafayette IN 47906*

YOUNG, JAMES EARL, univ. adminstr.; b. Chgo., Dec. 20, 1922; s. James Alexander and Ellen (Chedister) Y.; B.S., U. Ill., 1948; Ph.D., State U. N.Y. Coll. Ceramics Alfred U., 1962; m. Constance S. Tortora, July 12, 1975; children—Hugh Parker, Katherine Sue. Ceramic engr. Republic Steel Co., Chgo., 1948-52; ceramic engr. Armour Research Found., Chgo., 1952-55; research supr. Structural Clay Research Found., Geneva, Ill., 1955-57; research fellow State U. N.Y. Coll. Ceramics at Alfred U., 1957-61, asst. prof., 1961-63, asso. prof., 1963-67, prof., chmn. dept., 1967-70; dean Coll. Arts and Scis., Rutgers U., Camden, N.J., 1970-73, provost, Newark, 1973—. Served with AUS, 1943-46. Am. Council Edn. fellow acad. adminstrn. 1966-67. Mem. Am. Ceramic Soc. Contbr. articles to tech. jours. Home: 9 Dewey Dr New Brunswick NJ 08901 Office: Rutgers U Newark 15 Washington St Newark NJ 07102

YOUNG, JAMES FRED, coll. pres.; b. Burnsville, N.C., Nov. 11, 1934; s. James Ray and Nina (Briggs) Y.; A.A., Mars Hill Coll., 1954; B.S., Wake Forest U., 1956; M.Ed., U. N.C., 1957; Ed.D., Columbia U., 1964; m. Phyllis Elizabeth Johnson, Apr. 15, 1962; children—Alan James, David Barden, Jane Elizabeth. Tchr., Micaville (N.C.) High Sch., 1957-58; research asst. Columbia U., 1959; prin. Enfield Sch., Halifax County, N.C., 1959-61; asst. supt. Halifax County (N.C.) Schs., 1961-64; asst. supt. Burlington (N.C.) City Schs., 1964-68; supt. Lynchburg (Va.) public schs., 1968-71; dep. supt. public edn. Commonwealth of Va., Richmond, 1971-73; pres. Elon Coll., Elon College, N.C., 1973—; dir. N.C. Nat. Bank, Burlington. Bd. dirs. Burlington Day Sch., 1974—, Appalachian Regional Edn. Lab., Charleston, W.Va., 1972-73; chmn. Gov.'s Task Force on Financing Standards of Quality for Public Schs. in Va., 1972-73; sec. exec. com. Ind. Coll. Fund N.C., 1976-78; mem. exec. com. United Ch. of Christ Council for Higher Edn., 1977—. Served with AUS, 1958. Mem. N.C. Edn. Assn. (pres. Halifax County unit 1960-61, Burlington unit 1967-68), N.C. Assn. Ind. Colls. and Univs. (sec. exec. com. 1978—), Nat. Assn. Intercollegiate Athletics (pres.'s adv. council 1977—), Alamance County C. of C. (dir. 1974-75). Club: Rotary. Home: 301 E Haggard Ave Elon College NC 27244 Office: Office of Pres Elon Coll E Haggard Ave Elon College NC 27244

YOUNG, JAMES FREDERICK, elec. products co. exec.; b. Phila., Jan. 4, 1917; s. William Edwin and Florence (Sunderland) Y.; B.M.E. with honors, Lafayette Coll., 1937, D.Sc., 1963; m. Rita Shahan, July 16, 1941; children—Sharon Margaret, James William. With Gen.

Electric Co., 1937—, engr. advanced engring. appliance and mdse. dept., 1945-49, asst. engr. household refrigerator units, 1949-51, mgr. engring. splty. refrigeration products dept., 1951-53, cons. to v.p. engring., 1953-58, gen. mgr. gen. engring. lab., 1958-60, gen. mgr. electric utility engring., 1960-63, gen. mgr. nuclear energy div., 1963-66, v.p., 1965, v.p. engring. services, 1966-70, v.p. tech. resources, 1970—; pres. Atomic Indsl. Forum, Inc., 1967-68, hon. dir., 1968—; mem. U.S. nat. com. Internat. Electrotech. Commn., 1967-77; bd. dirs. Nat. Safety council; mem. materials adv. bd. Nat. Acad. Scis.; sponsor, chmn. subcom. urban tech. NRC, mem. com. human resources, 1973-76; adv. com. Internat. Inst. Applied Systems Analysis, 1978—. Former trustee Clarkson Coll., Poly. Inst. N.Y.; trustee Lafayette Coll.; bd. dirs. Thomas Alva Edison Found., 1976—. Registered profl. engr., N.Y., Conn. Fellow ASME (Outstanding Leadership award 1967); mem. Nat. Acad. Engring., Conn. Acad. Sci. and Engring., IEEE, Nat. Soc. Profl. Engrs. (indsl. adv. com. to pres.), AAAS, Phi Beta Kappa, Tau Beta Phi, Alpha Phi Omega. Author: Materials and Processes, 1st edit., 1944, 2d edit., 1954. Home: 55 E Common (Easton) Rd RFD 1 Fairfield CT 06430 Office: 3135 Easton Turnpike Faifield CT 06431

YOUNG, JAMES HARRY, coll. adminstr.; b. Silver Creek, N.Y., Feb. 20, 1936; s. Harry Peter and Gertrude Helen (Tryczenski) Y.; B.S., SUNY Coll., Fredonia, 1958; M.S. summa cum laude, SUNY Coll., Buffalo, 1965, Ed.D., SUNY, Buffalo, 1969; m. Jacqueline Marix Cox, Aug. 23, 1958; children—Kevin, Mark, Alison, Todd, Dana Lynn. Asst. prof. edn. SUNY Coll., Buffalo, 1964-66, coordinator elem. student tchrs., 1966-67, asst. to dean profl. studies, 1967-68, asso. dir. edn., 1968-69, asso. prof. edn., 1969-70, asst. v.p. for adminstrn., 1970-71, asso. v.p. for acad. affairs, 1971-73, v.p. for fin. and mgmt., 1973-76, v.p. for policy and planning, 1976-78; pres. SUNY Coll., Potsdam, 1978—; mem. SUNY Chancellor's Com. on Aux. Service; mem. adv. bd. Resource Center for Planned Change, 1979—; pres. Coll. Publs. Agy. Council, U.S. Office Personnel Mgmt., 1978; mem. Middle States Asso. Evaluation Team, 1979—. Mem. St. Lawrence County (N.Y.) Econ. Devel. Council, 1978; chmn. St. Lawrence County United Way, 1979-80; bd. dirs., mem. loan com. St. Lawrence Nat. Bank, 1979—; mem. bishop's fund com. Diocese of Ogdensburg, 1979—. Named Niagara Personality, Niagara Falls Gazette, 1971; recipient Disting. Program award Am. Assn. Coll. Tchrs. and Educators. Mem. Am. Assn. Univ. Adminstrs., Middle States Assn. Colls. and Secondary Schs., Am. Assn. State Colls. and Kappa Delta Phi. Author: College and University Business, 1971. Office: SUNY Coll Pierrepont Ave Potsdam NY 13676*

YOUNG, JAMES HARVEY, historian, educator; b. Bklyn., Sept. 8, 1915; s. W. Harvey and Blanche (DeBra) Y.; B.A., Knox Coll., 1937, D.H.L., 1971; M.A., U. Ill., 1938, Ph.D., 1941; D.Sc., Rush U., 1976; m. Myrna Goode, Aug. 25, 1940; children—Harvey Galen, James Walter. Mem. faculty Emory U., 1941—, prof. history, 1958—, chmn. dept., 1958-66; vis. asso. prof. Columbia, 1949-50; FDA research appointee, 1977—. Mem. nat. adv. food and drug council FDA, 1964-67; mem. Consumers Task Force, White House Conf. on Food, Nutrition and Health, 1969; mem. history life scis. study sect. NIH, 1970-73, chmn., 1972-73; vis. lectr. Am. Assn. Colls. Pharmacy Vis. Lectrs. Program, 1970-73; cons.-panelist Nat. Endowment for Humanities, 1970—; Logan Clendening lectr. U. Kan. Med. Center, 1973; Samuel X. Radbill lectr. Phila. Coll. Physicians, 1978. Served with AUS, 1943-45. Carnegie Research grantee, 1947; Faculty fellow Fund Advancement Edn., 1954-55; Social Sci. Research Council fellow, 1960-61; USPHS grantee, 1960-65; Guggenheim fellow, 1966-67. Mem. Am., So. (exec. council) hist. assns., Oral History Assn. Orgn. Am. Historians, Soc. Am. Historians, Am. Studies Assn., Popular Culture Assn., Am. Assn. History Medicine (council; Fielding H. Garrison lectr. 1979); Am. Inst. History Pharmacy (Edward Kremers award 1962), Phi Beta Kappa, Sigma Xi, Phi Kappa Phi, Omicron Delta Kappa, Phi Alpha Theta. Conglist. Author: The Toadstool Millionaires, 1961; The Medical Messiahs, 1967; American Self-Dosage Medicines, An Historical Perspective, 1974. Editor: (with W.A. Beardslee and T.J.J. Altizer) Truth, Myth and Symbol, 1962. Home: 272 Heaton Park Dr Decatur GA 30030 Office: Dept History Emory Univ Atlanta GA 30322

YOUNG, JAMES MORNINGSTAR, physician, naval officer; b. Massillon, Ohio, Oct. 28, 1929; s. Ralph Louis and Pauline Louise (Morningstar) Y.; A.B., Duke U., 1951, M.D., 1955; m. Bettylu Jones, July 3, 1952; children—Anne Christine, Mark Andrew, Patricia Jane, Elizabeth Lynne, Judith Pamela, Claudia Dianne; m. 2d, Mariette M. Aubuchon, Oct. 11, 1970; children—Gretchen Camille, Jason Paul. Intern, Bethesda Naval Hosp., 1955-56, resident, 1958-61; commd. lt. (j.g.) USN, 1955, advanced through grades to lt. comdr., 1961, promoted to temporary rank capt., 1963; White House physician, 1963-66; staff Oakland (Calif.) Naval Hosp., 1966-69; chief medicine Naval Hosp. Boston, Chelsea, Mass., 1969-74; med. officer Naval Air Sta., South Weymouth, Mass., 1974-75; asso. clin. prof. medicine Boston U. Sch. Medicine, 1969-75; dir. med. affairs Mass. Blue Shield/Blue Cross, 1975—. Bd. dirs. Mass. Med. Profl. Rev. Acad. Diplomate Am. Bd. Internal Medicine. Fellow A.C.P., A.M.A., Alpha Omega Alpha, Omicron Delta Kappa, Beta Omega Sigma, Sigma Alpha Epsilon. Contbr. articles to profl. publs. Home: 340 Chestnut St West Newton MA 02165

YOUNG, JERE ARNOLD, lawyer; b. Sinking Spring, Pa., Nov. 29, 1936; s. Herbert M. and Helen (Bock) Y.; B.S. in Econs., U. Pa., 1958; J.D., Yale U., 1961; m. Constance Werkheiser, June 28, 1958; children-Jere Arnold, Karen Denise, Tracy Lynn. Admitted to Pa. bar, 1961, U.S. Supreme Ct. bar, 1976; with firm Dechert, Price and Rhoads, Phila., 1961-65; sr. v.p., gen. corp. counsel, sec. Indsl. Valley Bank and Trust Co., Phila., 1965-79; v.p. fin., sec. Tasty Baking Co., Phila., 1980—. Pres., Radnor Twp. Bd. Sch. Dirs. Mem. Am., Pa. bankers assn., Am., Pa. bar assns., Am. Soc. Corporate Secs. Home: 646 Malin Rd Newtown Square PA 19073 Office: 2801 Hunting Park Ave Philadelphia PA 19129

YOUNG, JOHN ALAN, electronics co. exec.; b. Nampa, Idaho, Apr. 24, 1932; s. Lloyd Arthur and Karen Eliza (Miller) Y.; B.S. in Elec. Engring., Oreg. State U., 1953; M.B.A., Stanford, 1958; m. Rosemary Murray, Aug. 1, 1954; children—Gregory, Peter, Diana. Various mktg. and finance positions Hewlett Packard Co. Inc., Palo Alto, Calif., 1958-63, gen. mgr. microwave div., 1963-68, v.p. electronic products group, 1968-74, exec. v.p., dir., 1974-77, pres., 1977—, chief exec. officer, 1978—; dir. Wells Fargo Bank, Dillingham Corp. Chmn. ann. fund Stanford, 1969-73, nat. chmn. corp. gifts, 1973-77. Bd. dirs. Mid-Peninsula Urban Coalition, 1972—, co-chmn., 1976—; mem. adv. council Grad. Sch. Bus., Stanford U., 1968-73, 75-77, univ. trustee, 1977—. Served with USAF, 1954-56, Mem. Am. Mgmt. Assn., Western Electronic Mfrs. Assn. Home: 526 Center Dr Palo Alto CA 94301 Office: 1501 Page Mill Rd Palo Alto CA 94304

YOUNG, JOHN DONALD, educator, mgmt. cons.; b. Cortland, N.Y., Feb. 5, 1919; s. John T. and Anna (Byrnes) Y.; A.B., Colgate U., 1941; M.S., Syracuse U., 1943; Ph.D., Am. U., 1974; m. Virginia Gwathmey, July 29, 1944; children—John H., Rebbecca A. With U.S. Bur. Budget, 1946-47; adminstrv. asst. office chmn. Nat. Security Resources Bd., 1947-51; spl. asst. to adminstr. Fed. Civil Def. Adminstrn., 1951; exec. sec. ODM, 1951-53, exec. officer, 1953-54; staff mem., exec. sec. Pres.'s Adv. Com. Govt. Orgn., 1953; staff mem. com. on orgn. Dept. Def., 1953; on loan to appropriations com. U.S. Ho. of Reps., 1952; lectr. orgn., mgmt., pub. fin. various schs. and univs.; mgmt. cons. McKinsey & Co., 1954-60; dir. mgmt. analysis div. NASA, 1960-61, dep. dir. adminstrn., 1961-63, asst. adminstr. for adminstrn., 1963-66; asst. to dir. U.S. Bur. Budget, Exec. Office of the Pres., 1966-67; dir. econs., sci. and tech. div. U.S. Bur. Budget and Office Mgmt. and Budget, 1967-73, dep. asso. dir. energy and sci. div. Office Mgmt. and Budget, 1973; asst. sec., comptroller HEW, 1973-77; asst. sec. mgmt. and budget HEW, 1977; undersec. Dept. Energy, 1977-79; prof. public mgmt. Am. U., 1979—; dir. Rann Inc.; pres. John D. Young, Mgmt. Cons., 1979—; adviser orgn. and mgmt. Peace Corps, 1961. Mem. Pres.'s Task Force Cost Reduction, 1964. Served as personnel officer Marine Air Group 11, comdg. officer Hdqrs. Squadron 11, USMC, 1942-45, advancing to capt. Recipient William A. Jump Award, 1954; Outstanding Leadership award NASA, 1966; Exceptional Service award Office Mgmt. and Budget, 1973; Distinguished Alumni award Maxwell Sch., 1974, Am. U. Sch. Govt., 1979; Career Service award Nat. Civil Service League, 1975; Disting. Service awards HEW, 1977, Am. Assn. Program and Budget Analysts, 1978. Mem. Am. Soc. Pub. Adminstrn., AAAS, Pi Delta Epsilon, Pi Sigma Alpha. Contbr. articles to various publs. Home: 3028 Cedarwood Ln Sleepy Hollow Falls Church VA 22042 Office: Dept of Energy Washington DC

YOUNG, JOHN EDWARD, lawyer; b. Detroit, Dec. 6, 1937; s. John Edward and Gertrude Geradine (O'Neill) Y.; A.B. cum laude, Xavier U., Cin., 1959; LL.B. magna cum laude, U. Detroit, 1962; m. Patricia Ann Maguire, Feb. 8, 1964; children—William Patrick, Robert Francis, Ann Kathleen. Admitted to Mich. bar, 1963; since practiced in Detroit; asso. firm Eggenberger, Eggenberger & Ashton, Detroit, 1963-65; partner firm Elsman, Young & Rogalle, Detroit, 1965-67, Elsman, Young & O'Rourke, Detroit, 1967-73, Fitzgerald, Young, Peters, Dakmak & Bruno, and predecessor firm, Detroit, 1973—; dir. Detroit Radiant Products Co., Plex Lab Corp., F.X. Coughlin Co.; twp. atty. Romulus Twp. (Mich.), 1967-70; city atty. City of Romulus, 1970-73; twp. atty. Twp. Berlin (Mich.), 1968-72. Bd. dirs. Catholic Youth Orgn. 1966-67, U. Detroit High Sch. Alumni Assn., 1967-68, Meadow Brook Festival, 1975. Mem. Detroit Bar Assn., State Bar Mich., Gamma Eta Gamma. Clubs: Detroit Athletic; Lost Lake Woods Assn. Home: 1233 Audubon St Grosse Pointe Park MI 48230 Office: 2580 City Nat Bank Bldg Detroit MI 48226

YOUNG, JOHN HENDRICKS, lawyer; b. Pelham, N.Y., Aug. 12, 1912; s. John Hendricks and Elizabeth (Chatterton) Y.; grad. Phillips Acad., 1930; B.A., Yale, 1934, J.D., 1937; m. Mary Redfern Culley, July 2, 1938 (dec. Jan. 1964); children—Sarah Redfern (Mrs. Baxter Craven Young (dec.), John Hendricks, Anne Payne (Mrs. Thomas Cosden); m. 2d, Fredrika Cosden Ritter, Feb. 8, 1967. Admitted to N.Y. bar, 1938; asso. firm Carter, Ledyard & Milburn, N.Y.C., 1937-42, 45-47, mem. firm, 1947—. Lectr. taxation Practising Law Inst. N.Y., Inst. Continuing Legal Edn., Ga. Dir. Whitney Industries, Inc. Trustee Cornelius Vanderbilt Whitney Found. Served from ensign to lt. USNR, 1942-45; PTO. Decorated Bronze Star with combat V. Mem. Assn. Bar City N.Y. (lectr.), N.Y., Internat. (vice chmn. tax com. Eng.), Am. bar assns., New York County Lawyers Assn., World Peace through Law Center, World Assn. Lawyers (chmn. sect. on taxation), Union Internat. des Avocates (Belgium), Internat. Fiscal Assn. (exec. council U.S. br.), Tax Found., Inc., Am. Law Inst. (tax adv. group), N.Y. Law Inst., Nat. Tax Assn.-Tax Inst. Am., Internat. Fiscal Assn. (Netherlands). Clubs: Metropolitan, Yale, Downtown Assn. (N.Y.C.). Contbr. articles to profl. jours. Home: 785 Fifth Ave New York NY 10022 Office: 2 Wall St New York NY 10005

YOUNG, JOHN PAUL, publishing co. exec.; b. Indpls., Nov. 10, 1923; s. Byron C. of Helen A. (Ryan) Y.; B.S., U. Notre Dame, 1948; M.B.A., U. Chgo., 1973; m. Mary Jean Walton, Sept. 25, 1952; children—Moira Jon, Deirdre Anne, Renee Elizabeth, John Walton. With Richard D. Irwin, Inc., Homewood, Ill., 1948-60, 70—, exec. v.p., 1970-75, pres., 1975—; editorial dir. bus-econs. John Wiley & Sons, N.Y.C., 1960-70. Served to 1st lt. U.S. Army, 1943-46. Mem. Am. Econ. Assn., Acad. Mgmt. Club: Olympia Fields (Ill.) Country. Author: Creativity in College Publishing. Campus Crisis: Responsibilities of the Learning Industry. Home: 2400 Lakeview Chicago IL 60614 Office: 1818 Ridge Rd Homewood IL 60430

YOUNG, JOHN PAUL, scientist, educator; b. Balt., Dec. 20, 1923; s. Paul and Sophia (Lang) Y.; student Balt. Poly. Inst., 1939-41, Harvard, 1943-44; B.S., U. Md., 1950; D.Eng., Johns Hopkins, 1962; m. Mary Louise Peddicord, June 27, 1953; children—Gregory Paul, David Joseph. Indsl. engr. Westinghouse Electric Corp., Balt., 1950-54; sr. research analyst Operations Research Office, Johns Hopkins, Bethesda, Md., 1954-59, instr. Sch. Engring. Sci., 1959-62, asst. dir. operations research div. Hosp., Balt., 1962-68, lectr. Sch. Engring. Sci., 1962-64, asst. prof. engring. and pub. health, 1964-66, asso. prof. engring. and pub. health, 1966-69; asso. provost Univ., 1968-72, prof. pub. health adminstrn. Sch. Hygiene and Pub. Health, 1969—, asso. dean, 1976-77, prof. math. scis. Faculty Arts and Scis., 1969—; cons. VA, USPHS, Social Security Adminstrn., Am. Hosp. Assn., Assn. Am. Med. Colls., Md. Council Higher Edn. Trustee Chesapeake Research Corp. Served with AUS, 1943-46. Fellow Royal Soc. Health, A.A.A.S.; mem. Operations Research Soc. Am., AAUP, Inst. Mgmt. Scis., Am. Pub. Health Assn., Assn. Computing Machines, Washington Operations Research Council, N.Y. Acad. Scis., Md. Acad. Sci., Sigma Xi, Tau Beta Pi, Phi Kappa Phi, Omicron Delta Kappa. Clubs: Cosmos; Johns Hopkins (gov.). Author: Operations Research in Health Care: A Critical Analysis, 1975; Operations Research and National Health Policy Issues, 1977. Contbr. articles to profl. jours. Home: 1861 Circle Rd Ruxton MD 21204 Office: Johns Hopkins U Baltimore MD 21205

YOUNG, JOHN ROBERT, greeting card co. exec.; b. Bowling Green, Ohio, Sept. 28, 1916; s. Robert Baldwin and Elsie (Folk) Y.; A.B., Bowling Green State U., 1940; J.D., Ohio State U.; m. Rita J. Kerruish, Sept. 18, 1942; children—Janet E. (Mrs. Richard Pugh), Robert W. With SEC, 1940-41, 1945-50; with The Louis Berkman Co., Steubenville, Ohio, 1951-59; with Rust Craft Greeting Cards, Inc., Dedham, Mass., 1959—, now v.p., sec., dir. Served with USAAF, 1941-45. Decorated D.F.C., Air medal. Mem. Order of Coif. Club: Wellesley Country. Home: 17 Fairfax Rd Needham MA 02192 Office: Rust Craft Park Dedham MA 02026

YOUNG, JOHN WATTS, astronaut; b. San Francisco, Sept. 24, 1930; s. William H. Young; B.S. in Aero. Engring., Ga. Inst. Tech., 1952; D. Applied Sci. (hon.), Fla. Technol. U., 1970; LL.D. (hon.), Western State U., 1969; m. Barbara Vincent White; children—Sandra, John. Joined U.S. Navy, 1952, advanced through grades to capt.; test pilot, program mgr. F4 weapons systems projects, 1959-62; then maintenance officer Fighter Squadron 143, Naval Air Sta., Miramar, Calif.; astronaut Project Gemini, NASA, made two man 3 orbit flight Mar. 1965, 2d Gemini flight, 1966, Apollo 10 8-day flight lunar landing dress rehearsal, 1969, Apollo 16, 1972; dir. space shuttle br., astronaut office, 1973-75, chief astronaut office Flight Ops. Directorate, 1975—. Recipient NASA Distinguished Service medal, Exceptional Service medal; decorated D.F.C., D.S.M.; named Distinguished Young Alumnus, Ga. Tech. Inst., 1965, Distinguished Alumni Service award, 1972. Fellow Am. Astronautical Soc. (Flight Achievement award 1972), Soc. Exptl. Test Pilots (Iven Kincheloe award 1972); mem. Am. Inst. Aeros. and Astronautics (Haley Astronautics award 1973), Sigma Chi. Office: Manned Spacecraft Center NASA Houston TX 77058*

YOUNG, JOHN WILLIS, filmmaker, educator; b. Cedaredge, Colo., Oct. 24, 1919; s. John B. and Gertrude A. (Willis) Y.; student Coll. of Idaho, 1938-41; B.A., Cornell U., 1947, M.A., 1948; postgrad. UCLA, 1949-51; m. Elbateene L. Bagley, May 18, 1945; children—John Paul, Jay Marc, Ann Lee. Mem. faculty dept. theater arts UCLA, 1951—, prof. motion pictures, 1955—, chmn. dept., 1974—; writer, producer, dir. ednl. and documentary films including: Objective: Leaders, 1956; Pain and Its Alleviation, 1961; I'd Rather Be a Blind Man, 1969; Crisis, 1969; Flowing Gold, 1970. Served with USAAF, 1941-45. Decorated Air medal. Mem. Am. Film Inst., Los Angeles Film Devel. Com., FILMEX of Los Angeles. Office: UCLA Macgowan Hall Los Angeles CA 90024

YOUNG, JOSEPH LOUIS, artist; b. Pitts., Nov. 27, 1919; s. Louis and Jennie (Eger) Y.; grad. Westminster Coll., New Wilmington, Pa., 1941, D. Litt., 1960; Edwin Austin Abbey mural painting scholar, 1949; grad. Boston Mus. Sch. Fine Arts, 1951; Albert H. Whitin traveling fellow, 1951, Am. Acad. in Rome, 1951-52; m. Millicent Goldstein, June 19, 1949; children—Leslie Sybil, Cecily Julie. Newspaperman, Pitts. and N.Y.C., 1941-43; lectr. Tufts Coll., 1949; painting instr. Boston Mus. Sch., 1950 Idylwild Arts Found., 1959, Brandeis Camp Inst., 1962—; founder, dir. Joseph Young Mosaic Workshop, 1953—; founding chmn. dept. archtl. arts Brooks Santa Barbara (Calif.) Sch. Fine Arts, 1969-75; head mus. exhibits Bowers Mus., Santa Ana, Calif., 1977-78; head visual arts CETA program City of Los Angeles, 1978—; true fresco, oil and mosiac mural commns. in Boston, Chgo., Pitts., Los Angeles; survey govt. sponsored mural painting programs, 1951; one man show Pitts. Arts and Crafts Center, 1950, Falk-Raboff Gallery, Los Angeles, 1953; ten year retrospective exhbn. archtl. art work Desert Mus., Palm Springs, Calif., 1963, Calif. council A.I.A. Fine Arts Architecture Exhbn., 1964; Nat. Gold Medal Exhbn. of N.Y. Archtl. League, 1951; work reproduced in numerous books, mags., newspapers throughout the world; invited to submit designs for Nebr. State Capitol murals; paintings and mosiacs in numerous pvt. collections; executed mosiac murals Los Angeles Police Facilities Bldg., 1955, Don Bosco Tech. High Sch., 1956, Temple Emanuel 1957, Southland Shopping Center, 1958, Our Lady of Lourdes Ch., 1959, Cameo residence, Beverly Hills, Calif., 1961, Santa Barbara Stock Exchange, 1960, St. Martins Ch., Las Mesa, Calif., 1966; stained glass windows, liturgical art program Congregation Beth Sholom, San Francisco, 1966; West Apse of Nat. Shrine of Immaculate Conception, Washington, 1966; mosiac arch Eden Meml. Park, San Fernando, Calif., 1960; commd. to execute mural Los Angeles County Hall of Records, Shalom Meml. Park, Chgo., B.V.M. Presentation Ch., Midland, Pa., 1961, Hollenbeck Police Sta., Los Angeles, 1963, Beth Emet Temple, Anaheim, Calif., 1963, Temple Sinai, Glendale, Calif., 1963, Sinai Temple, Los Angeles, 1963, Valley Beth Israel, Sun Valley, Calif., 1964, Beth Tikvah, Westchester, Calif., 1964, Belmont High Sch., Los Angeles, 1972; commd. to design and execute 14 bas-relief concrete-mosaic murals for exterior of Math. Scis. Bldg. at U. Calif. at Los Angeles; bronze sculpture La Mirada (Calif.) Civic Theatre, 1979; did liturgical art programs for Congregation B'nai B'rith, Santa Barbara, Temple Beth Torah, Alhambra, Temple Beth Ami, West Covina, Temple Menorah, Redondo Beach, and Temple Solael in Canoga Park (all Calif.), 1969; concrete bas reliefs Southgate County Pub. Library, 1973; mosaics for St. Mary of Angels, Hollywood, Calif., 1973; Triforium polyphonoptic, kinetic tower Los Angeles Mall, 1969-75; organized internat. sculpture competition for city of Huntington Beach, Calif., 1974; multimedia presentations for 400th Anniversary Michelangelo, Italian Trade Commn., Casa de Maria, Santa Barbara, Hancock Coll., Santa Maria, Los Angeles County Mus. Art, U. Calif. at Los Angeles and Irvine; art cons. Allied Arts Commn., City of Huntington Beach, 1973-74; restoration of mosaics from Greek and Roman periods and Della Robbia sculpture, 1972-73; cons. Art in Public Bldgs. Program, Calif. Arts Council, 1976-77; field adminstr. CCA/CETA Program, Los Angeles. Huntington Hartford Found. fellow, 1952-53. Served with USAAF, 1943-46. Recipient Nat. Army Arts contest award, 1945. Fellow Internat. Inst. Arts and Letters (life); mem. Nat. Soc. Mural Painters (nat. v.p. 1969—), Artists Equity Assn. (pres. So. Calif. chpt. 1956, nat. v.p. 1960), Calif. Confedn. Arts (founding pres. 1976). Author: A Course in Making Mosaics, 1957; Mosaics, Principles and Practice, 1963; also articles in profl. jours. Pub. mural painting bibliography, 1946. Asso. founding editor Creative Crafts mag., 1960-64; concept and design ARTSMARKET, 1979. Work featured 16mm documentary film, The World of Mosaic. Invited prin. speaker at nat. convs. A.I.A., Am. Craftsmen Council, 4th Congress I.A.P.A., 7th Nat. Sculpture Conf., Council of Am., U. Kans.; lectr. Rome, Venice, Florence (as guest Italian govt. 1959). Home: 7917 1/2 W Norton Ave Los Angeles CA 90046 Studio: 1434 S Spaulding Ave Los Angeles CA 90019

YOUNG, KENNETH, union ofcl.; b. N.Y.C., Oct. 20, 1927; s. Laurence E. and Rosalie M. Y.; B.A., Antioch Coll., 1950; m. Charlotte Harrison, Aug. 4, 1951; children—Michael, Lauren, Eric. Editor, organizer Ins. and Allied Workers Organizing Com., CIO, Washington, 1951-55, publicity and research dir., 1955-57; asst. dir. publicity and public relations AFL-CIO Indsl. Union Dept., Washington, 1957-63; publicity dir. Internat. Union Elec., Radio and Machine Workers, 1963-65; legis. rep. AFL-CIO, Washington, 1965-73, asso. dir. legis. dept., 1973-79, dir. legis. dept., 1979—; mem. exec. com. Leadership Conf. on Civil Rights. Chmn. Democratic precinct, Silver Spring, Md., 1958-61. Served with U.S. Army, 1946-47. Mem. Newspaper Guild AFL-CIO, Ins. Workers Internat. Union, NAACP, ACLU. Home: 1114 Caddington Ave Silver Spring MD 20901 Office: 815 16th St NW Washington DC 20006

YOUNG, KENNETH EVANS, ednl. adminstr., b. Toronto, Ont., Can., Mar. 21, 1922; s. John Osborne and Gwendolyn May (Evans) Y.; A.B., San Francisco State Coll., 1943; M.A., Stanford, 1947, Ph.D., 1953; postdoctoral fellow, U. Mich., 1959-60; LL.D., U. Nev., 1972; m. Mae Catherine Wittenmyer, July 1, 1945; 1 son, Bruce Kenneth. Instr. journalism and speech San Francisco State Coll., 1946-48; instr. journalism and English, Calif. State Poly. Coll., 1949-50, asst. prof., then asso. prof., acting dean arts and scis. Kellogg-Voorhis campus, 1951-57; dean faculty U. Alaska, 1957-59; exec. v.p. U. Nev., 1960-64; pres. State U. Coll., Cortland, N.Y., 1964-68; v.p., dir. Washington office Am. Coll. Testing Program, 1968-75; pres. Council on Postsecondary Accreditation, 1975—. Served with USAAF, 1943-45. Home: 4411 Garfield St NW Washington DC 20007 Office: 1 Dupont Circle NW Washington DC 20036

YOUNG, LAURA, dancer; b. Boston, Aug. 5, 1947; d. James Vincent and Adelaide Janet (Coupal) Young; student pub. schs., Cohasset, Mass.; m. Tony Catanzaro, Sept. 26, 1970. Charter mem. Boston Ballet Co., 1964-70, prin. dancer, 1966-70, 73—; dancer Met. Opera Ballet, 1971-73, Dancers, Ltd., N.Y.C., 1977. Mem. Am. Guild Mus. Artists. Home: 4093 Washington St Roslindale MA 02131 Office: 19 Clarendon St Boston MA 02116

YOUNG, LAURENCE RETMAN, biomed. engr., educator; b. N.Y.C., Dec. 19, 1935; s. Benjamin and Bess (Retman) Y.; A.B., Amherst Coll., 1955; S.B., Mass. Inst. Tech., 1957, S.M., 1959, Sc.D., 1962; Certificat de License (French Govt. fellow), Faculty of Sci. U. of Paris (France), 1958; m. Joan Marie Fisher, June 12, 1960; children—Eliot Fisher, Leslie Ann, Robert Retman. Engr. Sperry Gyroscope Co., Great Neck, N.Y., 1957; engr. Instrumentation Lab., Mass. Inst. Tech., 1958-60, asst. prof. aero. and astronautics, 1962-67, asso. prof., 1967-70, prof., 1970—; summer lectr. U. Ala., Huntsville, 1966-68; lectr. Med. Sch. Harvard U., 1970—; mem. tng. com. biomed. engring. NIH, 1971-73; mem. com. space medicine and biology Space Sci. Bd., Nat. Acad. Scis., 1974—, chmn. vestibular panel summer study of life scis. in space, 1977; mem. com. engring. and clin. care Nat. Acad. Engring., 1970; mem. Air Force Sci. Adv. Bd., 1979—; vis. prof. Swiss Fed. Inst. Tech., Zurich, 1972-73, Conservatoire Nationale des Arts and Metiers, Paris, 1972-73; vis. scientist Kantonsspital Zurich, 1972-73; prin. investigator vestibular expts. on Spacelab-1, 1977—; cons. Arthur D. Little, NASA, Gulf & Western, Link div. Singer Co., Boeing Corp. Registered profl. engr., Mass. Fellow IEEE (Franklin V. Taylor award 1963); mem. Biomed. Engring. Soc. (founding/charter mem., dir. 1972-75, pres. 1979-80), Aerospace Med. Assn., ASTM (com. sports safety, subcom. skiing safety, chmn. skiing statistics sect. 1975—), Internat. Fedn. Automatic Control (tech. com. biomed. engring. 1975—), AIAA (working group for simulator facilities 1976—), Internat. Soc. Skiing Safety (dir. 1977—), Barany Soc., Tau Beta Pi. Contbg. author chpt. on vestibular system Medical Physiology, 1974. Editorial bd. Internat. Jour. Man-Machine Studies, 1966-75, Neurosci., 1976—. Contbr. numerous articles to profl. jours. Inventor eye movement monitor. Home: 8 Devon Rd Newton Centre MA 02159 Office: Mass Inst Tech Dept Aeros and Astronautics Cambridge MA 02139

YOUNG, LAWRENCE, educator; b. Hull, Eng., July 5, 1925; s. Herbert and Dora Y.; came to Can., 1955, Can. citizen, 1972; B.A., Cambridge U., 1946, Ph.D., 1950, Sc.D., 1963; m. Margaret Elisabeth Jane, Jan. 5, 1951. Asst. lectr. Imperial Coll., London, 1952-55; mem. research staff B.C. Research Council, 1955-63; prof. dept. elec. engring. U. B.C., Vancouver. Fellow Royal Soc. Can. Author: Anodic Oxide Films, 1961; contbr. articles to profl. jours. Office: Dept Electrical Engineering U BC Vancouver BC V6T 1W5 Canada

YOUNG, LAWRENCE EUGENE, physician; b. Waterville, Ohio, Mar. 18, 1913; s. William Edward and Ruth (Farnsworth) Y.; B.A. with honors, Ohio Wesleyan U., 1935, D.Sc., 1967; M.D., U. Rochester, 1939; D.Sc., Med. Coll. Ohio at Toledo, 1977; m. Annette Briggs, May 25, 1940; children—Carolyn Ann, Beverly Young McCormick, Marjorie Briggs, Anderson Briggs. Intern, asst. resident, chief resident medicine Strong Meml. Hosp., Rochester, N.Y., 1939-41, 42-43, physician-in-chief, 1957-74, dir. U. Rochester Asso. Hosps. program in internal medicine, 1974-78; asst. bacteriology Johns Hopkins Sch. Hygiene and Pub. Health, also asst. medicine Johns Hopkins Hosp., 1941-42; instr. U. Rochester Sch. Medicine, 1942-44, 46-47, asst. prof., 1948-49, asso. prof. medicine, 1950-57, Dewey prof. medicine, chmn. dept., 1957-74, Alumni Distinguished Service prof. medicine, 1974-78, prof. emeritus, 1978—, head hematology unit, 1948-57; cons. VA Hosp., Batavia, N.Y.; cons. Rochester Gen., Highland, Genesee, St. Mary's hosps., Rochester, 1948-78; disting. vis. prof. medicine U. South Fla. Coll. Medicine, 1978—; mem. com. on blood NRC, 1950-53; mem. hematology study sect. USPHS, 1953-57. Bd. dirs. Robert Wood Johnson Clin. Scholars Program, 1978—. Named Man of Year for blood research Rho Pi Phi Internat., 1955; recipient Albert David Kaiser award Rochester Acad. Medicine, 1978, U. Rochester Alumni citation, 1978. Master A.C.P. (gov. Upstate N.Y. 1958-60, regent 1972-76, 77-78, v.p. 1976-77); mem. Assn. Profs. Medicine (pres. 1966-67, Robert H. Williams Distinguished Chmn. Medicine award 1976), Assn. Am. Physicians (pres. 1973-74), Am. Soc. Clin. Investigation, Internat., Am. socs. hematology, Soc. Exptl. Biology and Medicine, A.M.A. (vice chmn. sect. on internal medicine 1969-71), Phi Beta Kappa, Sigma Xi, Alpha Omega Alpha. Asso. editor Blood, 1950-56, Am. Jour. Medicine, 1961-74; editorial bd. Jour. Clin. Investigation, 1955-59. Contbr. articles sci. jours. Home: 5216 El Toro Ct Apt 124 Tampa FL 33603 Office: U South Fla Med Center Dept Internal Medicine 12901 N 30th St Tampa FL 33612

YOUNG, LEO VERNON, educator; b. Toronto, Ont., Can., July 9, 1917; s. Peter Murray and Margaret (Mallon) Y.; B.A., Wayne U., 1949; M.A., U. Mich., 1950; Ph.D., Stanford, 1956; m. Leslye Ann Gruber, Sept. 3, 1950. Instr. English, Eastern Oreg. Coll., 1950-52; faculty San Francisco State U., 1954—, asso. prof., 1960-65, prof. English and journalism, 1965—, dean Sch. Humanities, 1970-79. Served to 1st lt. USAAF, 1942-45. Recipient Major Hopwood award in fiction U. Mich., 1950. Mem. Sigma Delta Chi. Editorial bd. Journalism Educator, 1966-68. Home: 447 Remillard Dr Hillsborough CA 94010 Office: 1600 Holloway St San Francisco CA 94132

YOUNG, LEWIS HAROLD, editor; b. Phila., Aug. 22, 1924; s. Jerome H. and Elva (Heiman) Y.; B.S., Purdue U., 1948, B.S. in Mech. Engring., 1950; M.B.A., N.Y. U., 1960; m. Joanne Marie Root, Nov. 24, 1960; 1 dau., Anne. Asst. editor Product Engring., N.Y.C., 1951-54; successively asst. editor, asso. editor, sr. asso. editor Control Engring., N.Y.C., 1957-61; bur. chief Business Week, Detroit, 1961-64; editor Electronics, N.Y.C., 1964-67; mng. editor Business Week, N.Y.C., 1968-69, editor-in-chief, 1969—. Served as 1st lt. C.E., AUS, 1943-46. Mem. Sigma Delta Chi, Sigma Pi Sigma. Home: 31 Cypress Ln Briarcliff Manor New York City NY 10510 Office: 1221 Ave of Americas New York City NY 10020

YOUNG, LIONEL WESLEY, radiologist; b. New Orleans, Mar. 14, 1932; s. Charles Henry and Ethel Elsie (Johnson) Y.; B.S., St. Benedict's Coll., 1953; M.D., Howard U., 1957; m. Florence Inez Brown, June 24, 1957; children—Tina Inez, Lionel Thomas, Owen Christopher. Rotating intern Detroit Receiving Hosp., 1957-58; resident in radiology U. Rochester (N.Y.) Med. Center, 1958-61; radiologist U.S. Naval Hosp., Portsmouth, N.H., 1961-63; fellow in pediatric radiology Children's Hosp. Cin., 1963-65; pediatric radiologist, asso. prof. radiology and pediatrics U. Rochester Med. Center, 1965-75; acting dir. radiology Children's Hosp. and prof. radiology and pediatrics U. Pitts., 1975—. Served to lt. comdr. M.C., USN, 1961-63. Fellow Am. Coll. Radiology; mem. Soc. Pediatric Radiology, AMA, Am. Roentgen Ray Soc., Radiol. Soc. N.A. Democrat. Roman Catholic. Author: (with others) Pediatric Syllabus, 1974; contbr. articles to profl. jours. Office: 125 De Soto St Pittsburgh PA 15213

YOUNG, LORETTA (GRETCHEN), actress; b. Salt Lake City, Jan. 6, 1913; d. John Earl and Gladys (Royal) Y.; student Ramona Convent, Los Angeles, 1923-27; m. Thomas H. Lewis, July 31, 1940; children—Judy, Christopher, Peter. With 1st Nat. Warner Bros., 1927-34, 20th Century Fox, 1934-40; free lance star, 1940—; films include: Love Is News, Second Honeymoon, Four Men and a Prayer, Three Blind Mice, Man's Castle, Suez, Eternally Yours, The Story of Alexander Graham Bell, The Doctor Takes a Wife, China, One Exciting Night, Ladies Courageous, And Now, Tomorrow, Along Came Jones, The Stranger, A Perfect Marriage, The Farmer's Daughter (Acad. award 1948), The Bishop's Wife, Rachel and the Stranger, Mother Was a Freshman, Come to the Stable (Acad. award nomination), Key to the City, Cause for Alarm, Half Angel, Paula, Because of You, It Happens Every Thursday; star The Loretta Young Show, NBC-TV, 1953-61, The New Loretta Young Show, CBS-TV, 1962. Recipient Emmy award, 1955, 57, 59, others. Author: The Things I Had To Learn. Address: 151 El Camino Beverly Hills CA 90210*

YOUNG, LOUISE MERWIN (MRS. RALPH A. YOUNG), educator, author; b. East Palestine, Ohio, Sept. 5, 1903; d. Charles Lewis and Estella (Meek) Merwin; A.B., Ohio Wesleyan U., 1925; A.M., U. Pa., 1927, Ph.D., 1939; m. Ralph Aubrey Young, Sept. 5, 1925; children—Merwin Crawford, Alexandra (Mrs. Roger N. Pierce), Ralph Aubrey. Professorial lectr. Am. U., 1954-57, adj. prof., 1957-58, asso. prof., 1958-62, prof. English, 1962-71; cons. women's archives Radcliffe Coll., 1952-60; lectr. wives course Fgn. Service Ind. Study, 1968; resident scholar Radcliffe Inst. Ind. Study, 1968; resident scholar Rockefeller Study Center, Bellagio, Italy, 1973; specialist in women's history. Alumni trustee Ohio Wesleyan U., 1951—. Del. Internat. Polit. Sci. Assn. Congress, The Hague, 1952. Prepared archives of League of Women Voters of U.S. for Manuscript Division of the Library of Congress, 1949-50. Author: Carlyle and the Art of History, 1939, 2d edit., 1973; Understanding Politics: A Practical Guide for Women, 1950. Contbr. to Notable American Women: 1607-1950. Spl. editor Women's Opportunities and Responsibilities, May 1947 Annals Am. Acad. Polit. and Social Sci. Home: 4000 Cathedral Ave Washington DC 20016

YOUNG, MAHONRI SHARP, author; b. N.Y.C., July 23, 1911; s. Mahonri Mackintosh and Cecilia (Sharp) Y.; A.B., Dartmouth Coll., 1933; M.A., N.Y. U., 1951; m. Elizabeth Chamberlain, July 23, 1932 (div. 1940); m. 2d, Rhoda Satterthwaite, Dec. 7, 1940; 1 son, Mahonri Mackintosh II. Mem. art dept. Sarah Lawrence Coll., 1941-50; acting dir. community arts program Munson-Williams-Proctor Inst., Utica, N.Y., 1951-53; dir. Columbus (Ohio) Gallery Fine Arts, 1953-76; Am. corr. for Apollo mag. Served with USAAF, 1942-46. Mem. Phi Beta Kappa. Club: Century Assn. (N.Y.C.). Author: Old George, 1940; George Bellows, 1973; The Eight, 1973; Early American Moderns, 1974; American Realists: Homer to Hopper, 1977. Home: Kellis Pond Ln Bridgehampton NY 11932

YOUNG, MARTIE WING, educator; b. Cleve., Apr. 26, 1930; s. Wing and Woo (Shee) Y.; A.B., Western Res. U., 1954; A.M., Harvard, 1955, Ph.D., 1961; m. Alice Wong, June 13, 1953; children—Mark, Adam. With Coleman-Peterson Co., Cleve., 1948-51; designer Fanner Metal Products Co., Cleve., 1951-53, designer free-lance artist, 1953-54; faculty Cornell U., Ithaca, N.Y., 1959—, asso. prof. art history, 1965-68, prof. art history, 1968—, chmn. history art dept., 1966-71; acting dir. Cornell Art Mus., 1967-68, curator Asian art, 1963—, dir. China-Japan program, 1972—. Ford Found. fellow, 1954-57, 61-62; Hackney fellow Am. Oriental Soc., 1957-59. Home: 112 Homestead Circle Ithaca NY 14850

YOUNG, MARTIN D., parasitologist; b. Moreland, Ga., July 4, 1909; s. Joe Hugh and Jennie Sue (Martin) Y.; B.S., Emory U., 1931, M.S., 1932, D.Sc. (hon.), 1963; Sc.D., Johns Hopkins, 1937; D.Sc. (hon.), Mich. State U., 1975; m. GeDelle Brabham, July 18, 1938; children—Martin Brabham, Margaret Cope (Mrs. Anderson). Prof. biology, head dept. Jr. Coll., Augusta, Ga., 1932-34; prof. health East State Tchrs. Coll., Johnson City, Tenn., 1939; staff NIH, USPHS, Columbia, S.C., 1937-61; parasitologist dir. malaria lab., 1941-50, dir. sect. on epidemiology, 1950-61, in charge imported malaria studies, 1943-46, dir. malaria survey of Liberia, 1948; asst. chief Lab. Parasite Chemotherapy, 1961-62, asso. dir. Nat. Inst. Allergy and Infectious Diseases, 1962-64; dir. Gorgas Meml. Lab., 1964-74; dir. research Gorgas Meml. Inst., 1972-74, research asso., 1974-78; cons. Health Dept., C.Z., 1964-74; adj. research prof. parasitology Coll. Vet. Medicine, also dept. immunology and med. microbiology, also dept. medicine Med. Coll., U. Fla., Gainesville, 1974—; vis. prof. microbiology Ala. Med. Center; clin. prof. med. parasitology La. State U. Med. Sch.; prof. extraordinario ad-honorem Faculty Medicine U. Panama; vis. prof. Meml. U., St. John's, Nfld., Can., 1977; hon. research asso. Smithsonian Tropical Research Inst., 1966—. Mem. adv. on malaria to WHO-Pan-Am. Health Orgn., 1957-62, 65-68; mem. adv. panel on malaria WHO, 1950—; WHO cons. malaria, Rumania, 1961; ICA cons. on Govt. India malaria control program, 1957; mem. malaria commn., commn. on parasitic diseases, commn. on environ. health Armed Forces Epidemiological Bd., 1965-73. Mem. Columbia (S.C.) Bd. Health, 1960-61. Bd. dirs. Gorgas Meml. Inst. Tropical and Preventive Medicine, 1977—. Decorated grand officer Order Manuel Amdor Guerrero (Panama); co-recipient Jefferson award S.C. Acad. Sci. for especially meritorious paper, 1946, 52, 61 ann. meetings; recipient Rockefeller Pub. Service award, 1953; Darling medal and prize WHO, 1963; Gorgas medal Assn. Mil. Surgeons U.S., 1974; certificate merit Gorgas Meml. Inst., 1974. Diplomate Am. Acad. Microbiology. Fellow A.A.A.S. (councilor 1952-55), Royal Soc. Tropical Medicine and Hygiene; hon. fellow Nat. Soc. India for Malaria and Other Mosquito-borne Diseases; mem. Nat. Malaria Soc. (sec.-treas. 1946-50; del. 4th internat. congress on tropical med. and malaria, Washington, 1948; pres. elect 1952), Am. Soc. Parasitol. (del. to 6th Internat. congresses on Tropical Medicine and Malaria, Lisbon, 1958, pres. 1965, emeritus), Am. Soc. Tropical Med. and Hygiene (pres. 1952, del. 5th Internat. Congress Tropical Medicine and Malaria, Istanbul, 1953, rep. Nat. Acad. Sci. 1962-65, Le Prince medal 1976), Am. Soc. Profs. Biology (v.p. 1949-50), Emory U. Alumni Assn. (nat. v.p. from grad. sch., 1947-48), Assn. Southeastern Biol. (councilor 1941-42, sec.-treas. 1942-46, pres. 1947-48, emeritus), S.C. Acad. Sci. (councilor 1941, v.p. 1948-49, pres. 1949-50, emeritus), Australian Soc. Parasitology, Soc. Protozoologists, Brazilian Tropical Medicine Soc., Internat. Primatology Soc., Wildlife Disease Soc., Asociacion Panamena de Microbiologia, Sigma Xi, Gamma Alpha, Phi Sigma. Methodist. Rotarian. Chmn. editorial bd. editor pro tem; Am. Jour. Tropical Medicine and Hygiene, 1959. Contbr. numerous articles in parasitology, prin. human malaria, to sci., publs., books. Home: 8421 NW 4th Pl Gainesville FL 32601

YOUNG, MARVIN OSCAR, coal co. exec.; b. Union, Mo., Apr. 4, 1929; s. Otto Christopher and Irene Adelheide (Barlage) Y.; A.B., Westminster Coll., 1951; J.D., U. Mich., 1954; m. Sue Carol Mathews, Aug. 23, 1952; children—Victoria Leigh, Kendall Marvin. Admitted to Mo. bar, 1954; practice law firm Thompson, Mitchell, Thompson Douglas, St. Louis, 1954-55, 57-58; atty. Mo. Farmers Assn., Columbia, 1958-67; exec. v.p. First Mo. Corp., Columbia, 1965-68; v.p. ops. MFA-Central Coop., Columbia, 1967-68; v.p., gen. counsel, sec. Peabody Coal Co., St. Louis, 1968—, also dir., sec. subs. and affiliates. Pres., Warson Woods PTA, 1974-75; trustee Met. Sewer Dist. St. Louis, 1974—, chmn., 1978—; mem. Mo. Energy Council, 1973-77; pres. alumni assn. Westminster Coll., Fulton, Mo., 1978—, trustee coll., 1977—, exec. com., 1978—, recipient alumni award of merit, 1972. mem. lawyers adv. council Gt. Plains Legal Found., Kansas City, Mo., 1976—; mem. county com. Republican Party, Boone County, Mo., 1962-68, chmn. legis. dist. com., 1962-64, 66-68; alt. del. Rep. Nat. Conv., 1968; pres. Clayton Twp. Rep. Club, 1973-77. Served to capt. USAF, 1955-57. Mem. Am., Mo. bar assns., Bar Assn. Met. St. Louis, Order of Coif. Episcopalian. Clubs: Round Table St. Louis, Masons, John Marshall Rep. Lawyers (pres. 1977), Rotary, Mo. Athletic. Asso. editor Mich. Law Rev., 1953-54. Home: 555 Flanders Dr Warson Woods MO 63122 Office: 301 N Memorial Dr St Louis MO 63102

YOUNG, MARY ELIZABETH, educator; b. Utica, N.Y., Dec. 16, 1929; d. Clarence Whitford and Mary Tippit Y.; B.A., Oberlin Coll., 1950; Ph.D. (Robert Shalkenbach Found. grantee, Ezra Cornell fellow), Cornell U., 1955. Instr. dept. history Ohio State U., Columbus, 1955-58, asst. prof., 1958-63, asso. prof., 1963-69, prof., 1969-73; prof. history U. Rochester (N.Y.), 1973—; cons. in field. Recipient Pelzer award Miss. Valley Hist. Assn., 1955; Social Sci. Research Council grantee, 1968-69. Mem. Am. Hist. Assn., Orgn. Am. Historians, Social Sci. History Assn., Soc. for Historians of the Early Am. Republic. Author: Redskins, Ruffleshirts, and Rednecks: Indian Allotments in Alabama and Mississippi, 1830-1860, 1961; co-editor, contbr.: The Frontier in Americal Development: Essays in Honor of Paul Wallace Gates, 1969. Home: 655 French Rd Rochester NY 14618 Office: Dept History U Rochester Rochester NY 14627

YOUNG, MATT NORVEL, JR., univ. adminstr., b. Nashville, Oct. 5, 1915; s. Matt Norvel and Ruby (Morrow) Y.; B.A., Abilene Christian U., 1936; M.A., Vanderbilt U., 1937; Ph.D., George Peabody Coll., 1943; L.H.D., Calif. Coll. Medicine, 1964; m. Helen Mattox, Aug. 31, 1939; children—Emily Lemley, Matt Norvel III, Marilyn, Sara Jackson. Minister College Ch. of Christ, David Lipscomb Coll., 1941-43, Broadway Ch. Christ, Lubbock, Tex., 1944-57; pres. Pepperdine U., Los Angeles, 1957-71, chancellor, 1971—, also regent. Co-founder, 20th Century Christian mag., 1938, editor, pub., 1945-76; editor Power for Today, 1955—; chmn. bd. 20th Century Christian Pub. Co., Nashville, also dir.; dir. Pub. Savs. Life Ins. Co., Charleston, S.C., U.S. Life Savs. & Loan, Los Angeles; co-founder Lubbock Christian Coll., 1957, Lubbock Children's Home, 1953, Tex. Tech. Coll. Bible chair, 1950. Bd. govs. Los Angeles County Mus. Natural History; bd. dirs. Nat. Council on Alcoholism, Forest Lawn Meml. Parks; trustee Los Angeles County Art Mus., 1962-78. Recipient George Washington medal Freedom Found., 1962, 64. Mem. Los Angeles Area C. of C. (dir.), Phi Delta Kappa. Rotarian (dir. Los Angeles). Clubs: Bohemian, California. Author: History of Christian College, 1949; The Church is Building, 1956; Co-editor: Preachers of Today, 1952, Vol. II, 1959, Vol. III, 1964, Vol. IV, 1970; Churches of Today, Vol. I, 1960, Vol. II, 1969; Stress Is A Killer, 1978. Home: 23200 Pacific Coast Hwy Malibu CA 90265 Office: Pepperdine U Malibu CA 90265

YOUNG, MAURICE ISAAC, mech. and aerospace engr.; b. Boston, Feb. 10, 1927; s. Joseph J. and Alice (Lifshitz) Y.; student Worcester Poly. Inst., 1944-45; Ph.B., U. Chgo., 1949, B.S., 1949; M.A., Boston U., 1950; Ph.D., U. Pa., 1960; m. Eleanor Cooper, Sept. 25, 1954; children—Rochelle, Gerald, Rosalind. Sr. dynamics engr. Bell Aircraft Corp., Buffalo, 1951-52, Ft. Worth, 1952-53; group engr. Jacobs Aircraft Engine Co., Pottstown, Pa., 1953-54; prin. tech. engr. Piasecki Helicopter and Aircraft Corp., Morton, Pa., 1954-56, Phila., 1956-58; sr. engring. specialist communications and weapons div. Philco Corp., Phila., 1958-61, mgr. applied mechanics, 1958-61; mgr. helicopter research and advanced tech. Boeing Co., Vertol Div., Phila., 1961-68; prof. mech. and aerospace engring. U. Del., 1968—; cons. in field. Served with USAAF, 1946-47. DuPont Faculty fellow, 1969-70; U.S. Army grantee, 1971-76. Fellow AIAA (asso.); mem. Soc. Engring. Sci., Sigma Xi. Editorial bd. Internat. Jour. Rotorcraft, Powered Lift Aircraft, 1975—. Office: U Del Dept Mech and Aerospace Engring Newark DE 19711

YOUNG, MILTON EARL, petroleum prodn. co. exec.; b. San Angelo, Tex., Dec. 3, 1929; s. Edward Earl and Annie Mae (North) Y.; A.A., San Angelo Coll., 1950; B.S. in Petroleum Engring., U. Tex., 1953; m. Clara Louise Sens, June 1, 1957; children—Vanessa, Bradley. Various positions Continental Oil Co., 1953-73; v.p. for prodn., drilling, engring. Tesoro Petroleum Corp., San Antonio, 1973-74, sr. v.p., 1974—. Served with USNR, 1948-49. Mem. Am. Petroleum Inst., Soc. Petroleum Engrs., Ind. Petroleum Assn. Am. Republican. Lutheran. Club: Home: 8955 Carriage Dr San Antonio TX 78217 Office: 8700 Tesoro Dr San Antonio TX 78286

YOUNG, MILTON R., U.S. senator; b. Berlin, N.D., Dec. 6, 1897; s. John Young and Rachel (Zimmerman) Y.; student N.D. State U., Graceland Coll.; m. Patricia M. Byrne, Dec. 27, 1969. Mem. N.D. Ho. of Reps., 1933-34; mem. N.D. Senate, 1935-45; mem. U.S. Senate from N.D., 1945—. Republican. Home: La Moure ND 58458 Office: US Senate Bldg Washington DC 20510

YOUNG, NEIL, musician, songwriter; b. Toronto, Ont., Can., Nov. 12, 1945. Formed rock group Buffalo Springfield with Stephen Stills, until 1968; solo performer, also joined group Crosby, Stills & Nash, who split up and then regrouped in 1974-75 for Am. tour; albums with Crosby, Stills & Nash include: Déja Vu, 1970, Four-Way Street, 1971; solo albums: Neil Young, 1969, Everyboy Knows This is Nowhere, 1969, After the Goldrush, 1970, Harvest, 1972, Journey Through the Past (film soundtrack), 1972, Time Fades Away, 1973, On the Beach, 1974, Tonight's the Night, 1975, Zuma, 1976, American Stars 'n Bars, Decade, 1977, Comes A Time, 1978, Rust Never Sleeps, 1979; writer, dir., performer film Journey Through the Past, Rust Never Sleeps. Office: care Lookout Mgmt 9120 Sunset Blvd Los Angeles CA 90069*

YOUNG, NORMAN, psychologist, business exec.; b. Bklyn., May 30, 1925; s. Macklyn and Estelle (Carmine) Y.; diploma in engring. U. Dayton, 1945; B.S., Coll. City N.Y., 1948; M.A., Columbia, 1949, Ph.D., 1957; M.Ed., U. Ill., 1950; m. Myrna Lewis, Mar. 20, 1947; children—Todd, Heidi, Gretchen. Instr. psychology U. Ill., Urbana, 1949-51; analytical statistician USPHS, 1950; research psychologist Carnegie Found. Project, Columbia, 1951-53; pvt. practice psychotherapy and psychoanalysis, 1953; sr. writer ABC-TV, N.Y.C., 1953-54; advt. dir. Anahist div. Warner Lambert Pharm. Corp., Hastings, N.Y., 1954-59; v.p. Ted Bates Advt. Agy., N.Y.C., 1959-63; sr. v.p., dir. Levitt & Sons, Inc., Lake Success, N.Y., 1963-68; pres. ITT Levitt Devel. Corp., N.Y.C., 1968-70; pres., chmn. bd. ITT Community Devel. Corp., N.Y.C., 1970-76; exec. v.p. Gen. Devel. Corp., 1976-78; pres., chmn. bd. Neighborhood Realty Group U.S.A., 1978—; instr., lectr. prof. psychology, math., statistics, etymology, indsl. mgmt., radio and TV, Rutgers U., New Brunswick, N.J., 1952-53, N.Y.U., 1953-54, Bklyn. Coll., 1953-54, Pace Coll., 1959-60, Coll. City N.Y., 1960-61, Hunter Coll., 1960-63; guest lectr. Princeton U., U.S. Mil. Acad., Notre Dame U., Cornell U., 1972—, Yale U., Columbia U., Ilan U., Tel Aviv, Israel, Teheran (Iran) U., 1974—, Chulalongkorn U., Bangkok, Thailand, 1978, U. Singapore, 1978. Bd. dirs. Insts. Religion and Health; pres.'s council U. Fla. Served with AUS, 1943-45. Mem. AAAS, Am. Psychol. Assn., N.Y., Ill. acads. sci., Psi Chi. Contbr. articles to profl. and sci. jours. Home: 21 E 81st St New York NY 10028 also 6969 Collins Ave Miami Beach FL 33141 also East Quogue NY 11942 Office: Port Royale Miami FL also 1515 Broadway New York NY also Fischer Bldg 1450 Madruga Coral Gables FL 33146

YOUNG, ORAN REED, educator, polit. scientist; b. Yonkers, N.Y., Mar. 15, 1941; s. John A. and Eleanor (Wiggin) Y.; A.B., Harvard, 1962; M.A., Yale, 1964, Ph.D., 1965; 1 dau., Linda Katrin. Mem. staff Hudson Inst., 1962-64; research asso. Harvard, 1965; prof. polit. sci. Princeton, 1966-71; prof. polit. sci. U. Tex., Austin, 1972-76; prof.

govt. and politics U. Md., College Park, 1976—. Mem. Internat. Studies Assn., Am. Soc. Polit. and Legal Philosophy, Public Choice Soc. Author: The Intermediaries: Third Parties in International Crises, 1967; Systems of Political Science, 1968; (with others) Neutralization and World Politics, 1968; The Politics of Force: Bargaining During International Crises, 1968; (with others) Political Leadership and Collective Goods, 1971; (with others) Bargaining: Formal Theories of Negotiation, 1975; Resource Management at the International Level, 1977; Compliance and Public Authority, A Theory with Applications to International Politics, 1979. Sr. editor World Politics, 1968-76; mem. editorial bd. Internat. Orgn., 1968-76. Home: 304 C St NE Washington DC 20002

YOUNG, PAUL HELMER, JR., soft drink co. exec.; b. St. Louis, Feb. 5, 1925; s. Paul Helmer and Edna (Baxmeyer) Y.; B.S. in Bus. Adminstrn., Washington U., St. Louis, 1945; M.B.A., Wharton Sch. of U. Pa., 1946; m. Marjorie Kathryn Friday, June 4, 1948; children—Cynthia Crawford, Thomas Bamford. With Scruggs, Vandervoort, Barney, St. Louis, 1946-66, v.p., sec.-treas., 1958-66; treas. Seven Up Co., St. Louis, 1966—, v.p. finance, 1971-74, exec. v.p., treas., 1974-79, also dir.; dir. Malt-o-Meal Co., Mpls., Boatmens Nat. Bank, St. Louis; instr. econs. St. Louis U., 1946-47, 47-48. Treas. St. Louis Heart Assn., 1960-70, hon. dir., 1971—; pres. Sherwood Forest Camp, Cuiure River State Park, Mo., 1959-61, 66-68. Served with AUS, 1943-44. Mem. Sigma Chi. Republican. Clubs: Rotary (bd. dirs. 1971-72), Clayton (St. Louis). Home: 4 Trails End Lane Ladue MO 63124

YOUNG, PAUL RUEL, computer scientist; b. St. Marys, Ohio, Mar. 16, 1936; s. William Raymond and Emma Marie (Steva) Y.; B.S., Antioch Coll., 1959; Ph.D. (NSF and Woodrow Wilson fellow), M.I.T., 1963; children—Lisa Robin, Neal Eric. Tchr. math. Harley Sch., Rochester, N.Y., 1957; asst. prof. Reed Coll., 1963-66; NSF postdoctoral fellow in math. Stanford U., 1965-66; asst. prof. computer sci. and math. Purdue U., Lafayette, Ind., 1966-67, asso. prof., 1967-72, prof., 1972—; chmn. and prof. computing and info. scis., prof. math. U. N.Mex., 1978-79; vis. prof. elec. engring. and computer sci. U. Calif., Berkeley, 1972-73; mem. adv. com. math. and computer scis. NSF, 1977-80, chmn., 1979-80. Mem. IEEE (vice chmn. tech. com. on math. founds. of computing 1977—), Assn. Computing Machinery. Author: (with Michael Machtey) An Introduction to the General Theory of Algorithms, 1978. Office: Computer Scis Dept Purdue U Lafayette IN 47907

YOUNG, PETER ALAN, editor; b. Bethlehem, Pa., June 8, 1934; s. Robert and Ann Zella (Jorden) Y.; grad. Deerfield Acad., 1952; B.A., Princeton, 1956; M.S. with honors, Columbia, 1960; m. Sarah Susan McCardell, June 22, 1963; children—Peter McCardell, Abby Jorden, Hugh Barret. Reporter Easton (Pa.) Express, 1958-59, Balt. Eve. Sun, 1960-63; reporter Life Mag., N.Y.C., 1963-65, chief Moscow bur., 1966-68, chief Vienna bur., 1968-69, corr., Paris, 1969-70, head news dept., 1970-73; mng. editor Saturday Review, N.Y.C., 1973-78, Geo Mag., 1978-79; exec. editor Prime Time mag., N.Y.C., 1979—. Served with AUS, 1957. Home: 99 Allendale Dr Rye NY 10580 Office: 1700 Broadway New York NY 10019

YOUNG, PETER FORD, artist; b. Pitts., Jan. 2, 1940; s. Lloyd Arthur and Hazel Ruth (Dickinson) Y.; student Chouinard Art Inst., 1957-58, Pomona Coll., 1958-60, Art Students League, 1961; B.A., N.Y. U., 1963; m. Carmen Mignon Megeath, Apr. 16, 1970. One-man exhbns. include: Nicholas Wilder Gallery, Los Angeles, 1968, Noah Goldowsky Gallery, N.Y.C., 1970, 71, 72, 74, Gallery Rolf Ricke, Cologne, W. Ger., 1968, 70, 71, 72, Tex. Gallery, Houston, 1976; group exhbns. include: Leo Castelli Gallery, N.Y.C., 1969, Guggenheim Mus., N.Y.C., 1969, Albright-Knox Mus., Buffalo, 1972, Phila. Coll. Art, 1978; represented in permanent collections: Mus. Modern Art, Guggenheim Mus., Whitney Mus. Am. Art, N.Y.C.; pres. Cochise Fine Arts, Inc., 1978. Nat. Endowment Arts grantee, 1968. Address: Todas la Casas de Boruca 21 OK St Bisbee AZ 85603

YOUNG, PHILIP, cons.; b. Lexington, Mass., May 9, 1910; s. Owen D. and Josephine Sheldon (Edmonds) Y.; grad. Choate Sch., 1927; A.B., St. Lawrence U., Canton, N.Y., 1931, LL.D., 1948; M.B.A., Harvard U., 1933; m. Faith Adams, Aug. 15, 1931 (dec. Jan. 1963); children—Faith (Mrs. William D. Carmichael), Shirley (Mrs. Walter E. Adams); m. 2d, Esther Sarah Whitmey (Lady Fairey), Feb. 14, 1964 (dec. July 1978). Research asst. bus. history Harvard Grad. Sch. Bus., 1933; bus. economist and analyst SEC, 1934-38; spl. asst. to under sec. treasury, 1938-40, asst. to sec., also chmn. Pres.'s liaison com. mil. procurement, 1940-41; asst. exec. officer div. def. aid reports Office Emergency Mgmt., 1941; dep. adminstr. Office Lend-Lease Adminstrn., 1941-43; asst. to adminstr., trade relations adviser Fgn. Econ. Adminstrn., 1943-44; v.p. Astraco, Inc., also treas. Van Lear Woodward & Co., Inc., 1947-48; dean Columbia U. Grad. Sch. Bus., 1948-53; exec. dir. Am. Assembly, 1950-53; Class C dir. Fed. Res. Bank N.Y., 1950-53; chmn. U.S. Civil Service Commn., presdl. adviser on personnel mgmt., also mem. White House staff, 1953-57; A.E. and P. The Netherlands, 1957-61; mem. U.S.A./B.I.A.C. to OECD, 1962-68; pres. U.S. council Internat. C. of C., Inc., 1961-65, trustee, 1965-68, mem. adv. bd. Internat. and Comparative Law Center, S.W. Legal Found., 1963-67; trustee Equitable Life Assurance Soc. U.S., 1951-53. Trustee emeritus St. Lawrence U., 1943—, Bus. History Found., 1949-53, Edison Inst., 1950-53; trustee Choate Sch., 1950-54; pres. Netherland Am. Found., 1963-68, chmn. bd., 1968—; bd. dirs. Project Hope, 1962—; mem. council Am. Mus. in Britain, 1974—. Served to lt. comdr. USNR, 1944-46. Decorated Grand Cross Order Orange Nassau (Netherlands); recipient Gold medal Holland Soc. N.Y.; Alumni Seal award Choate Sch., 1958. Mem. N.Y. State Hist. Assn. (trustee). Clubs: Harvard (N.Y.C.); Met. (Washington). Home: Van Hornesville NY 13475

YOUNG, RALPH ALDEN, educator; b. Arickaree, Colo., July 14, 1920; s. Edmund Birdsall and Lottie Opal (Payne) Y.; B.S., Colo. State U., 1942; M.S., Kans. State U., 1947; Ph.D., Cornell U., 1953; m. Helen Augusta Claudon, Aug. 28, 1942; children—Gregg, Gayle, Instr. soils Kans. State U., 1947-48; asst. prof. soils N.D. State U., 1948-50, 53-55, asso. prof., 1955-59, prof., 1959-62; vis. soil chemist U. Calif. at Davis, 1962-63; prof. soil sci., chmn. div. plant, soil and water sci. U. Nev., 1963-75; asso. dir. Nev. Agrl. Expt. Sta., 1975—. Served to capt. AUS, 1943-46. Fellow AAAS, mem. Soil Conservation Soc. Am. (pres. chpt. 1968), Am. Soc. Agronomy, Soil Sci. Soc. Am., Western Soil Sci. Soc. (pres. 1972-73), Sigma Xi, Alpha Zeta, Gamma Sigma Delta, Phi Kappa Phi. Contbr. articles to profl. jours. Home: 1375 Earl Dr Reno NV 89503

YOUNG, RALPH AUBREY, economist; b. Cheyenne, Wyo., June 12, 1901; s. Benjamin and Virginia (Crawford) Y.; A.B., Ohio Wesleyan U., 1923, LL.D., 1969; M.B.A., Northwestern U., 1925; Ph.D., U. Pa., 1930; m. Louise Merwin, Sept. 5, 1925; children—Merwin Crawford, Anne Alexandra, Ralph Aubrey. Instr. U. Pa., 1925-28; research staff Nat. Indsl. Conf. Bd., 1928-29, 32-34; spl. bus. analyst Dept. of Commerce, 1929-30; Social Sci. Research Council fellow, 1930-31; asst. prof. U. Pa., 1931-37, asso. prof., 1937-40, prof., 1940-45; research staff and dir. financial research program, Nat. Bur. Econ. Research, 1938-45; asst. dir. div. research and statistics Bd. Govs. Fed. Res. System, 1946-47, asso. dir., 1947-48, dir., 1948-59, adviser to bd., 1960-65, chmn. com. to review regulatory activities, 1975-76, sec. fed. open market com., 1960-65, dir. bd.'s div. internat. finance, 1961-65; cons. div. central banking services IMF, 1966-76; dir. Independence Sq. Income Securities Fund, Temporary Investment Fund; trustee Trust for Short-Term Fed. Securities; dir. Westchester Corp.; lectr. Geo. Washington U., 1948-62. Mem. research adv. bd. Com. for Econ. Devel., 1944-56, asso. mem., 1956-66; com. on research in finance Nat. Bur. Econ. Research, 1938-58; mem. bd. Nat. Acad. Econs. and Polit. Sci., 1954-60; mem. Conf. Bus. Economists; trustee Joint Council Econ. Edn., 1962-65. Fellow Center for Advanced Study, Wesleyan U., 1968. Fellow Am. Statis. Assn.; mem. Beta Gamma Sigma, Phi Gamma Delta. Meth. Club: Cosmos (Washington). Author numerous books on banking and finance, latest being: Monetary Instruments in the United States: Role of the Federal Reserve System. Address: 4000 Cathedral Ave Washington DC 20016. *I am deeply impressed by the significant change that has taken place in the relationship between professors (gatherers and purveyors of knowledge) and policy-oriented bureaucrats (proficient technicians in administrative skills). The mounting complexity of modern society has obliged the two groups to come together on common ground, relying on knowledge as the basic value and applying similar methods to expand it and to narrow the range of the possible.*

YOUNG, RALPH EUGENE, ins. co. exec.; b. Terry, Mont., Sept. 5, 1923; s. Ingval Ralph and Alice Elizabeth (DeVine) Y.; A.B., Carroll Coll., Helena, Mont., 1943; M.S., State U. Iowa, 1949; m. Joan P. McCarthy, Oct. 3, 1945; children—Candace (Mrs. Robert G. Frie), Barbara (Mrs. Thomas Keegan), Karen (Mrs. Robert Shields), Stephen Ralph, Robert Eugene, Richard Donald. Hydraulic engr. U.S. Geol. Survey, Helena, Mont., 1946-47; with Western Life Ins. Co., St. Paul, 1949—, asst. actuary, 1951-56, asso. actuary, 1956-62, actuary, 1962—, actuarial v.p., 1964, exec. v.p., 1969, pres., 1970, chmn., chief exec. officer, 1976—, also dir.; pres., dir. St. Paul Life and Casualty, 1971-73, St. Paul Life Ins. Co., 1973-78; pres. Provident Life Ins. Co., Bismarck, N.D., 1979—; instr. bus. Carroll Coll., part time 1949-56; cons. State Indsl. Accident Bd. Mont., 1955-61; past dir. St. Paul Fire and Marine Ins. Co., St. Paul Investors, Inc., St. Paul Advisers, Inc. Mem. Gov.'s Com. on Hiring Physically Handicapped, 1959-61; pres. Cherry Hill Civic Assn., 1965, Dakota County chpt. Am. Field Service, 1966-68; gen. chmn. cardiovascular research and tng. center fund raising dr. Variety Heart Hosp. U. Minn., 1973-75; nat. co-chmn. parents' council Coll. of St. Catherine, St. Paul, 1973-79. Bd. dirs., treas. Kidney Found. of Upper Midwest, 1975-79; bd. dirs. Nat. Kidney Found., 1976-78. Served to lt. (j.g.) USNR, 1943-45. Mem. Ins. Fedn. Minn. (chmn. bd., mem. exec. com. 1970-79), Am. Council Life Ins. (dir. 1977-78), St. Paul Area C. of C. (dir. 1977-78), Am. Acad. Actuaries, Pacific, Twin Cities actuarial clubs. Clubs: Apple Creek Country (Bismarck); Country (St. Paul), Variety Internat. (hon.). Office: Provident Life Ins Co 316 N 5th St Bismarck ND 58501

YOUNG, RAYMOND ALFRED, III, airline exec.; b. Brownsville, Tex., Apr. 29, 1942; s. Raymond Alfred and Lucille Mell (Rawley) Y.; B.S.E., Princeton U., 1964; M.B.A., Harvard U., 1970; m. Julia Bourne, June 7, 1969; children—Holly Lisbeth, Heather Victoria. Asso. engr. Boeing Co., Seattle, 1963-64; staff aero. engr. Pan Am. Airways, N.Y.C., 1966-69; research asso. in bus. adminstrn. Harvard U., Boston, 1970-72; sr. asso. Simat, Helliesen & Eichner, Inc., Washington, 1972-74; dep. dir. air transp. policy Dept. Transp., Washington, 1974-77, dep. asst. Sec. for policy and internat. affairs, 1978-79; pres., chief exec. officer Scheduled Skyways, Inc., Fayetteville, Ark., 1979—; dir. Flight Safety Found.; dir. Inst. for Air Transport, Paris. Served with U.S. Army, 1964-66. Decorated Bronze Star. Harding fellow, 1971-72. Recipient gold medal for outstanding achievement Sec. of Transp., 1977. Office: Box 1344 Fayetteville AR 72701

YOUNG, RICHARD, lawyer; b. N.Y.C., June 23, 1919; s. Owen D. and Josephine Sheldon (Edmonds) Y.; A.B., St. Lawrence U., 1940; LL.B., Harvard, 1947; m. Janet Nevins, Oct. 2, 1971. Admitted to N.Y. bar, 1947; asst., asso. Judge Manley O. Hudson 1947-60; Mem. Herkimer County Planning Bd. Mem. adv. bd. Internat. Law Center, Southwestern Legal Found., Dallas (chmn. 1966-68); trustee St. Lawrence U. Served with AUS, 1942-46. Fellow Royal Geog. Soc.; mem. Am. Soc. Internat. Law, Acad. Polit. Sci., Am. Bar Assn., Am. Geog. Soc., Internat. Law Assn., Middle East Inst., Council on Fgn. Relations, Phi Beta Kappa Assos., Phi Beta Kappa, Beta Theta Pi. Democrat. Universalist. Club: University. Bd. editors Am. Jour. Internat. Law, The Internat. Lawyer. Contbr. articles to legal jours. Address: Van Hornesville NY 13475

YOUNG, RICHARD ALAN, editor; b. Oak Park, Ill., Mar. 17, 1935; s. Harry Alfred and Claribel (Yoss) Y.; student Colo. Sch. Mines, 1954-56; B.S., U. Iowa, 1958; m. Carol Ann Schellinger, June 28, 1958; children—Steven, Karen, Christopher. Chief engr. Cardox Corp., Chgo., 1958-61; asst. chief engr. Goodman Mfg. Co., Chgo., 1961-63; plant and environ. engr. Signode Corp., Glenview, Ill., 1963-68; editor Pollution Engring., Tech. Pub. Co., Barrington, Ill., 1968—; adj. prof. George Williams Coll.; program coordinator Environ. Center, Jacksonville U.; mcpl. pollution control adviser and enforcement officer for 24 cities and state govts.; ofcl. rep. and pollution control expert U.S. Govt. at meeting with Socialist countries in Bulgaria. Recipient Jesse H. Neal certificate for outstanding editorial writing Am. Bus. Press, Inc., 1971; Environ. Quality award EPA, 1976; registered profl. engr. Mem. Internat. Assn. for Pollution Control (dir.), Inst. Environ. Scis., Western Soc. Engrs. (nat. vice chmn. environ. quality, Outstanding Service award, Charles Ellet award as Most Outstanding Engr. of Year 1970), Am. Soc. Bus. Press Editors, Am. Inst. Plant Engrs. (past nat. chmn. environ. quality), Nat., Ill. socs. profl. engrs. Editor 21 books on environ. engring.; pollution engring. series editor Marcel Dekker Inc., N.Y.C. Contbr. articles to profl. jours. Patentee in field. Home: 1253 Roosevelt Ave Glenview IL 60025 Office: 1301 S Grove Barrington IL 60010

YOUNG, RICHARD ALLEN, packaging co. exec.; b. Carthage, Mo., June 8, 1915; s. Howard I. and Myrtle Lee (Mason) Y.; B.S. in Chem. Engring., Washington U., St. Louis, 1936; M.B.A., Harvard, 1938; m. Janice Westmoreland, Dec. 8, 1945; children—Harriette Louise, Richard Allen, Alfred Westmoreland. With Am. Zinc Co. Ill., 1938-50, v.p., 1944-50; with Am. Zinc, Lead & Smelting Co. (name now Azcon), St. Louis, 1950-70, exec. v.p., 1963-64, chmn. bd., 1965-70; also dir.; exec. v.p., dir. Uranium Reduction Co., St. Louis, 1955-62; pres. Bemis Co., Inc., Mpls., 1971-76, chmn., chief exec. officer, 1976-78, also dir.; dir. Soo Line R.R. Co., Trane Co., La Crosse, Wis. Industry adviser U.S. del. on lead and zinc UN Conf., 1958-70; mem. UN Lead-Zinc Study Group, 1958-70. Trustee, chmn. St. Louis Ednl. TV Commn., 1959-71; dir., chmn. Bus.-Industry Polit. Action Com., 1966—. Recipient Alumni Chem. Engring. award Washington U., 1960, 77. Mem. Am. Inst. Mining, Metall. and Petroleum Engrs., Mining and Metall. Soc. Am. Home: 200 S Brentwood Blvd Clayton MO 63105 Office: PO Box 16064 Saint Louis MO 63124

YOUNG, RICHARD DONALD, economist, educator; b. La Crosse, Wis., Jan. 31, 1929; s. James Donald and Lucille (Frizell) Y.; B.A., U. Minn., 1951, M.A., 1954; Ph.D., Carnegie Inst. Tech., 1965; m. Ruanne Marie Krisleit, Nov. 15, 1959; 1 son, Gregory Steven. Asst. prof. Grad. Sch. Bus., Stanford, 1960-64; asso. prof. Rice U., Houston, 1965-68, prof. econs., 1969—. Trustee, mem. patient service com. Houston Area chpt. Nat. Multiple Sclerosis Soc. Served to lt. (j.g.) USNR, 1953-57. Mem. Am. Econ. Assn., Inst. Mgmt. Scis., Operations Research Soc. Am. Home: 1221 Pine Chase St Houston TX 77055

YOUNG, RICHARD EMERSON, educator; b. Owosso, Mich., July 12, 1932; s. William Charles and Katherine Marie (Middaugh) Y.; B.A. with honors, U. Mich., 1954, Ph.D., 1964; M.A., U. Conn., 1956; m. Ann Elizabeth Albert, Aug. 29, 1953; children—Jonathan Field, Lynn Mikell, David Thurston. Asst. prof. English, U. Mich., 1964-67, research asso. Center for Research on Lang. and Lang. Behavior, 1965-69, asso. prof., 1967-71, prof., 1971-78, chmn. dept. humanities, 1971-76; chmn. dept. English, Carnegie-Mellon U., Pitts., 1978—; cons. NDEA Insts., 1965-68, Edn. Professions Devel. Act Insts., 1968-70; dir. summer seminars Nat. Endowment for Humanities, 1977, 79. Recipient Service award Coll. Engring., U. Mich., 1968; Nat. Endowment for Humanities grantee, 1971, 74. Mem. Modern Lang. Assn., Nat. Council Tchrs. English, Conf. on Coll. Composition and Communication (exec. com. 1966-69), Speech Assn. Am., Internat. Soc. History of Rhetoric, Rhetoric Soc. Am. (dir.), Delta Upsilon. Author: (with A.L. Becker, K.L. Pike) Rhetoric: Discovery and Change, 1970. Home: 6304 Jackson St Pittsburgh PA 15206

YOUNG, RICHARD GRAHAM, textiles exec.; b. New Haven, Feb. 28, 1919; s. Hugh A. and Flora B. (Baker) Y.; B.S. in Econs., U. Conn., 1941; grad. Command and Gen. Staff Coll., Ft. Leavenworth, Kan., 1946; exec. program U. Chgo., 1950; m. Virginia M. Mattoon, Jan. 3, 1942; children—Richard G., Kenneth H., Peter H. Tech. rep. Carbide & Carbon Chems. Corp. in N.Y., 1947-48; mgr. Chgo. office Mooresville Mills, 1948-51; mdse. mgr. shirting and sportswear dept. Dan River Mills, 1951-54; v.p., div. mgr. shirting fabrics div. Burlington Mills, 1954-57; pres. Burlington Shirting Fabrics Co., 1957-59; president Young Fabrics Corp., N.Y.C., 1959-62; mdse. mgr. Cone Mills, N.Y.C., 1962-67; chain store sales mgr. J.P. Stevens, N.Y.C., 1967-71; v.p. N.Y. sales Swift Textiles, Inc., N.Y.C., 1972—. Served as maj., inf. AUS, 1941-47. Decorated Silver Star, Bronze Star with cluster, Purple Heart with cluster, Presdl. Citation. Mem. Soc. for Advancement Mgmt. in Conn. (pres. 1940-41), Am. Legion, Young Men's Assn. Textile Industry N.Y., Phi Mu Delta (v.p. 1940-41). Clubs: University (Larchmont, N.Y.); Westchester Country (Rye, N.Y.). Home: 10 Orsini Dr Larchmont NY 10538 Office: 1460 Broadway New York City NY 10018

YOUNG, RICHARD MORTIMER, lawyer; b. Silsbee, Tex., Aug. 8, 1927; s. Walter Dudley and Capitola Walton (Richardson) Y.; B.B.A., Lamar State U., Beaumont, Tex., 1959; LL.B., J.D., U. Tex., Austin, 1962; m. Jewel Audrey Odom, Dec. 16, 1944; children—Richard Edward, Walter Duane, Pamela Diane Phillips, Vanessa Rochelle. Admitted to Tex. bar, 1962; atty. Atlantic-Richfield Co., 1962-71; partner firm Dade & Young, Dallas, 1972-75; individual practice oil and gas law, Dallas, 1975—. Pres. Time-Saver Check, Inc., Irving, 1971-77. Chmn. Republican Exec. Com., Midland County, Tex., 1968. Served with AUS, 1948-57. Mem. State Bar Tex. Baptist. Club: Lancers (Dallas). Home: 1413 Lamppost St Richardson TX 75080 Office: 126 Meadows Bldg Dallas TX 75206

YOUNG, RICHARD STUART, educator; b. Southampton, N.Y., Mar. 6, 1927; s. P. Stuart and Myrtle F. (Terrell) Y.; A.B., Gettysburg Coll., 1948, Sc.D., 1966; postgrad. U. N.C., 1951-53; Ph.D., Fla. State U., 1955; m. Nancy J. Mayer, June 7, 1955; children—Dee Ann, Sandra, Mark. With FDA, Washington, 1956-58; with NASA, Army Ballistic Missile Agency, Huntsville, Ala., 1958-59; with Ames Research Center, Moffett Field, Calif., 1960-67; chief exobiology program, chief program scientist Viking NASA, Washington, 1967-77, chief of bioscis. div., 1975-79; v.p. Rockefeller U., N.Y.C., 1979—. Served with USN, 1944-46. Mem. Internat. Soc. for Study Origin of Life (sec. 1970—). Contbr. articles to profl. jours.; also books. Home: 200 Douglas Pl Mount Vernon NY 10552 Office: Rockefeller U 1230 York Ave New York NY 10021

YOUNG, RICHARD WILLIAM, camera mfg. co. exec.; b. Ridgewood, N.Y., Oct. 17, 1926; s. Charles Michael and Louise Margaret (Baust) Y.; A.B., Dartmouth Coll., 1946, A.M., 1947; Ph.D., Columbia U., 1950; m. Sheila deLisser, Sept. 11, 1949; children—Christine, Noreen, Brian, Eileen. Sr. research chemist Chemotherapy div. Am. Cyanamid Co., Conn., 1950-56, group leader pesticide chems. Agr. div., 1956-58, dir. chem. research Agr. div., 1958-60, dir. chem. research Central Research div., 1960-62; asst. dir. research Polaroid Corp., Cambridge, Mass., 1962-69, v.p., 1963-69, sr. v.p. research and devel., 1969-72, sr. v.p. patent co., pres. Internat. div., 1972—, div. numerous Polaroid subsidiaries; dir. Bay State Milling Corp., Quincy, Mass. Trustee, Regis Coll., Weston, Mass., Polaroid Found.; trustee, chmn. sci. adv. com. Mass. Eye and Ear Infirmary, Boston; bd. dirs. World Affairs Council, Boston; mem. corp. Northeastern U., Boston. Mem. Am. Chem. Soc., Chem. Soc. London, AAAS, Soc. Photog. Scientists and Engrs., Royal Photog. Soc., Internat. C. of C. (trustee). Patentee in field. Home: 100 Royalston Rd Wellesley Hills MA 02181 Office: 730 Main St Cambridge MA 02139

YOUNG, ROBERT (GEORGE), actor; b. Chgo., Feb. 22, 1907; grad. high sch.; m. Elizabeth Louise Henderson, 1933; children—Carol Anne, Barbara Queen, Elizabeth Louise, Kathleen Joy. Studied and acted with Pasadena Community Playhouse, 4 years; toured in stock, 1931; in motion pictures since 1931; pictures include: The Sin of Madelon Claudet, Strange Interlude, It's Love Again (Eng.), Secret Agent (Eng.), The Bride Wore Red, Northwest Passage, Western Union, The Trial of Mary Dugan, H. M. Pulham, Esq. (title role), Journey for Margaret, Joe Smith, American (title role), Claudia, Slightly Dangerous, Sweet Rosie O'Grady, Cairo, The Canterville Ghost, They Won't Believe Me, Crossfire, Sitting Pretty, Adventure in Baltimore, And Baby Makes Three, Bride for Sale, The Second Woman, Half Breed, Secret of the Incas, Nothing But a Man, Western Union; on radio, 1936—; co-star Mr. and Mrs. North, 1942; began role of father in Father Knows Best 1954-62; TV program Window on Main Street, 1961-62; TV series Marcus Welby, M.D., 1969-76; appeared in TV films Vanished, 1971, All My Darling Daughters, 1972, My Darling Daughters' Anniversary, 1973, The Father Knows Best Reunion, 1977; pres. Cavalier Prodns., 1947—. Recipient Emmy award, 1956, 1957. Address: care Cavalier Prodns 9134 Sunset Blvd Hollywood CA 90069*

YOUNG, ROBERT ALAN, educator, physicist; b. St. Cloud, Minn., Jan. 24, 1921; s. Dorr Albert and Elizabeth (Smith) Y.; B.S. in Physics, Ga. Inst. Tech., 1950, M.S., 1951; Ph.D., Polytech. Inst. Bklyn., 1959; m. Alice B. Clark, Dec. 18, 1948 (div. Feb. 1975); children—Kevin Raoul, Cheryl Denise, Daryl Clark; m. 2d, Teresa Lam Chan, June 11, 1977. Instr. physics Polytech. Inst. Bklyn., 1953-57; asst. prof. Ga. Inst. Tech., Atlanta, 1952-53, research asst. prof., 1957-58, research asso. prof., 1958-64, prof., 1964—, head diffraction lab., 1957-65, head crystal physics br., 1965-77, head applied physics br., 1977—; cons. diffraction and crystal physics, 1959—; mem. commns. Internat. Union Crystallography, 1968—, mem. U.S. Nat. Com. Crystallography, 1969—, chmn., 1979—. Bd. dirs. Planned Parenthood Assn. Atlanta, 1966—, v.p., 1972-75, pres., 1975—; mem.

Atlanta Sister Cities Com., 1975—, chmn., 1977—. Served with USNR, 1942-43, with USAAF, 1944-46. Fellow Am. Inst. Physics (governing bd. 1975—), Phys. Soc. U.K., Am. Phys. Soc.; mem. Am. Crystallographic Assn. (treas. 1968-71, v.p. 1972, pres. 1973), Internat. Assn. Dental Research, Société française de minéralogie et de cristallographie, Assocation française de Cristallographie. Unitarian-Universalist (trustee 1963-68, v.p. 1967-68). Co-editor Jour. Applied Crystallography, 1967-70, editor, 1970-78. Contbr. articles to profl. jours., book. Home: 7190 Dunhill Terr NE Atlanta GA 30328

YOUNG, ROBERT ANTON, congressman; b. St. Louis, Nov. 27, 1923; s. Melvin Anton and Margaret (Degnan) Y.; student pub. schs., St. Louis; m. Irene Slawson, Nov. 27, 1947; children—Anne Young Lewis, Robert A., Margaret Mary Young Goldkamp. Pipefitter in St. Louis, 1946-76; mem. Mo. Ho. of Reps. from St. Louis County Dist., 1956-62, Mo. Senate from 24th Dist., 1962-76; mem. 95th-96th Congresses, 2d Dist. Mo. Democratic committeeman Airport Twp., Mo., 1952—. Served with AUS, 1943-45; ETO. Decorated Bronze Star; recipient Meritorious Service award St. Louis Globe Democrat, 1972, 74, 76. Mem. Am. Legion, VFW (past post comdr.), Amvets (life). Roman Cath. Clubs: Lions, K.C. Home: 12248 Turkey Creek Ct Maryland Heights MO 63043 Office: 1317 Longworth House Office Bldg Washington DC 20515

YOUNG, ROBERT BUNNELL, ins. co. exec.; b. Castle Dale, Utah, Nov. 1, 1928; s. Robert Berlin and Nellie (Bunnell) Y.; student Brigham Young U., Provo, Utah; grad. Advanced Mgmt. Program, Harvard U.; m. Gladys Andersen Young, June 10, 1953; children—Bert T., Rita Young Strong, Diane, Teri, Adam. Mgr. title dept. Security Title Co., Salt Lake City, 1956-61; pres. Land Title Co., Bountiful, Utah, 1961-68; br. mgr. Lawyers Title Ins. Corp., Denver, 1968-69; v.p., gen. mgr. Klamath Ward, Inc., 1969-70; with Hamilton Internat. Corp.-Alexander Hamilton Life Ins. Co. Am., 1970-77, exec. v.p., chief operatint officer, 1973-77; exec. v.p., chief operating officer, corp. sec., dir., chmn. operating com. Alexander Hamilton Life Ins. Co. Am., Md. Life Ins. Co., Household Ins. Corp., Household Fin. Ins. Corp., Riverside Agy., 1977-78; exec. v.p. Am.-Amicable Life Ins. Co., Waco, Tex., 1978—. Bishop, Waco ward Mormon Ch. Served with U.S. Army, 1951-53; Korea. Mem. Life Office Mgmt. Assn., Am. Mgmt. Assn. Home: 8927 Raven St Waco TX 76710 Office: PO Box 1849 Waco TX 67603

YOUNG, ROBERT CAMERON, ret. newspaper corr.; b. Phila., Aug. 14, 1914; s. Howard B. and Effie M. (Adams) Y.; B.A., U. Mich., 1936; m. Mildred Evelyn Wright, Aug. 27, 1938; children—Robert Wright, Peter Adams, Sara Amy. Reporter, Suburban Pub. Co., Oak Park, Ill., 1936-38, City News Bur. Chgo., 1938-40; mem. staff Chgo. Tribune, 1940-79, mem. Washington bur. staff, 1944-79. Mem. Phi Delta Theta. Republican. Episcopalian. Home: 56-C Calle Cadiz Laguna Hills CA 92653

YOUNG, ROBERT HUGH, lawyer; b. Pitts., Mar. 31, 1921; s. Robert and Ann Zella Young; A.B., Princeton U., 1942; J.D., Harvard U., 1945; m. Jean K. Laros, Oct. 25, 1944; children—Susan Young Davis, Cynthia Young Mardis, Robert Hugh, Judith L., Stacey J. Admitted to Pa. bar, 1948, since practiced in Phila.; now sr. partner, chmn. exec. com. Morgan, Lewis & Bockius. Public mem. Adminstrv. Conf. U.S.; bd. dirs. Phila. Met. Bd. YMCA; pres. Water Resources Assn. Delaware River, 1972. Served to capt. U.S. Army, 1943-46. Mem. Am. Bar Assn. (chmn. public utility sect. 1971-72), Pa. Bar Assn., Phila. Bar Assn. Presbyterian. Clubs: Union League (Phila.); Gulph Mills Golf, Courts (sec., gov.), Merion Cricket, Sunday Breakfast. Home: 111 Righters Mill Rd Narberth PA 19072 Office: 123 S Broad St Suite 2300 Philadelphia PA 19109

YOUNG, ROBERT JOHN, educator; b. Calgary, Alta., Canada, Feb. 10, 1923; s. Harold P. and Kate A. (Thomson) Y.; came to U.S., 1956, naturalized, 1965; B.S.A. with honors, U. B.C., 1950; Ph.D., Cornell U., 1953; m. Greta G. Milne, June 16, 1950; children—Kenneth W., Donna E. Research asso. dept. med. research Barting & Best, Toronto, Ont., Can., 1953-56; research chemist Internat. Minerals and Chem. Corp., Skokie, Ill., 1956-58; research chemist Proctor and Gamble Co., Cin., 1958-60; prof. animal nutrition Cornell U., 1960—, chmn. dept. poultry sci., 1965-76, chmn. dept. animal sci., 1976—. Served with RCAF, 1942-45. Mem. Am. Inst. Nutrition, Poultry Sci. Assn., Am. Soc. Animal Sci., Am. Soc. Dairy Sci. Author: (with M.L. Scott, M.C. Nesheim) Nutrition of the Chicken, 1976. Contbr. articles in field to profl. jours. Office: Morrison Hall Cornell Univ Ithaca NY 14853

YOUNG, ROBERT LYLE, engring. educator; b. Neoga, Ill., Apr. 3, 1925; s. Max Dryden and Neva (Higgins) Y.; B.S. in Mech. Engring., Northwestern U., 1946, M.S., 1948, Ph.D., 1953; m. Phyllis Eileen Ralston, Aug. 2, 1946 (dec. Aug. 1968); children—Ronald Lyle, Scott Alan; m. 2d, Martha Moore Robertson, Nov. 15, 1969 (dec. Nov. 1978); 1 stepson, Scotland R. Robertson; m. 3d, Betty Mayberry Delk, Dec. 1, 1979. Instr., then asst. prof. Northwestern U., 1948-57; mem. faculty U. Tenn., 1957—, prof. aero. and mech. engring., dep. dir., then asso. dean Space Inst., 1961-79, prof. Space Inst., 1979—; cons. USAF, 1957—. Served with USNR, 1943-46. Mem. Am. Soc. M.E., Am. Inst. Aeros. and Astronautics, Am. Soc. Engring. Edn., Accreditation Bd. Engring. and Tech. (engring. accreditation com.), Sigma Xi. Rotarian. Author: (with E. F. Obert) Elements of Thermodynamics and Heat Transfer, 1961; also articles. Home: 110 Park Circle Tullahoma TN 37388

YOUNG, ROBERT NELSON, regional planning adminstr.; b. San Jose, Calif., July 1, 1923; s. Earl C. and Virginia (Carder) Y.; B.A., U. Wash., 1947, M.A., 1948; Ph.D. U. Wis., 1954; m. Marion Louise Meyer, Jan. 6, 1946; children—L. Jeffrey, Jane Marie (Mrs. Robert A. Kramer), Elaine Margaret. Team chief P.R. Planning Bd., 1950-51; instr. Oshkosh (Wis.) State Coll., State U. Iowa, 1951, Ind. U., 1951-54; asst. prof. Stanford, 1954-56; asso. planner County Santa Clara Planning Dept., San Jose, 1957-58; sr. planner, asst. exec. officer Calif. Pub. Outdoor Recreation Plan Com., Sacramento, 1958-60; planning cons., Woodland, Calif., 1960-61; exec. dir. Tri County Regional Planning Com., Lansing, Mich., 1961-65, Regional Planning Council, Balt., 1965-77, Pueblo (Colo.) Regional Planning Commn., 1977—; asso. prof. Mich. State U., 1963-64; vis. lectr. Johns Hopkins, 1967; vis. prof. U. No. Colo., Richmond, Va., Washington, Denver, Boise. Mem. adv. com. Nat. Assn. Regional Councils, 1968-77, chmn., 1970-72, bd. dirs., 1970-72; chmn. Gov. Md. Steering Com. Mass Transit, 1967-69, Met. Water Supply Steering Com., 1967-69; mem. Met. Transit Authority, Balt., 1969-71; mem. exec. com. Transp. Research Bd., NRC, 1972-75. Bd. dirs. Balt. Urban Obs., 1970-74; bd. advisers U. Md. Sch. Social Work and Community Planning, 1974-77. Served with USAAF, 1942-45. Mem. Am. Inst. Planners (bd. govs. 1965-68, v.p. 1968-69, chmn. met. and regional planning dept. 1970-71), Am. Planning Assn. (policy adv. com. 1975—), Assn. Am. Geographers, Nat. Planning Assn. (nat. council 1972-77), Internat. City Mgmt. Assn. (adv. com. on councils of govt. 1974-77), Sigma Xi. Author: Anglo America, 1968; California-The New Empire State; also articles, monographs. Office: 1 City Hall Pl Pueblo CO 81003

YOUNG, ROBERT TYRRELL, ret. shipping exec.; b. Kandapola, Ceylon, Dec. 31, 1912 (parents Am. citizens); s. David Hill and Emily Harriet (McCaw) Y.; B.Sc., Tufts U., 1935; student naval architecture, Mass. Inst. Tech., eves. 1936-37; m. Virginia Belliveau, June 5, 1937; children—Madge Hazel (Mrs. Richard Nickerson), David Tyrrell. With shipbldg. div. Bethlehem Steel Corp., 1935-38; with Am. Bur. Shipping, N.Y.C., 1938—, pres., 1970—, chmn. bd., 1971—. Mem. Maritime Transp. Research Bd.; mem. shipping adv. com. Welding Research Council. Chmn. bd. trustees Webb Inst. Naval Architecture. Registered profl. engr., N.Y. State; chartered engr., U.K. Mem. Soc. Naval Architects and Marine Engrs., Royal Inst. Naval Architects, Inst. Marine Engrs., Inst. Engrs. and Shipbuilders, N.E. Coast Inst. Naval Architects, Am. Welding Soc. Republican. Conglist. Clubs: Union League, Whitehall Lunch, N.Y. Yacht, India House (N.Y.C.). Home and Office: Route 1 Box 37 Hillsboro NH 03144

YOUNG, ROBERT WILLIAM, physicist; b. Mansfield, Ohio, May 11, 1908; s. William Porter and Catherine Elizabeth (Whitmar) Y.; B.S., Ohio U., 1930; Ph.D., U. Wash., 1934; m. Evelyn Stratton Cross, Feb. 2, 1947; children—Conrad William, Theodore Luther, Elizabeth Florence. Physicist, C.G. Conn., Ltd., 1934-42, U. Calif. Div. War Research, 1942-46, U.S. Navy Electronics Lab., San Diego, 1946-67; tech. cons., sr. scientist Naval Undersea Center, 1967-77, Naval Ocean Systems Center, 1977—; cons. in archtl. acoustics and community noise control. Mem. San Diego City Bd. Noise Abatement and Control, 1974—. Fellow Acoustical Soc. Am. (exec. council 1941-44, pres. 1960-61); mem. Inst. Noise Control Engring., A.A.A.S., Am. Nat. Standards Inst. (mem. coms. on acoustics, mech. shock and vibration, bioacoustics), Phi Beta Kappa, Sigma Xi, Sigma Pi Sigma (hon.). Asso. editor Jour. Acoustical Soc. Am. Contbr. numerous articles to profl. pubs. Home: 1696 Los Altos Rd San Diego CA 92109 Office: Naval Ocean Systems Center San Diego CA 92152

YOUNG, RODERICK ALLEN, mfg. co. exec.; b. Portland, Oreg., Aug. 12, 1943; s. Harry Allen and Ethyl Jean (MacKay) Y.; B.S., Stanford U., 1965; M.B.A., Harvard U., 1968; m. Cathryn Lee Wolfman, May 25, 1969; children—Scott Roderick, Christopher Thomas. Mem. staff Office of Asst. Sec., Dept. Def., Washington, 1968-70; asso. Mgmt. Analysis Center, Inc., 1970-71; v.p. fin. 1st Montgomery Corp., San Francisco, 1971-72; fin. analyst Raychem Corp., Menlo Park, Calif., 1972-75, dir. fin., 1972-75, treas., 1975-79, gen. mgr. Chemelex div., 1979—. Served with U.S. Army, 1968-70. Mem. Fin. Execs. Inst. Home: 1030 Hamilton Ave Palo Alto CA 94301 Office: 300 Constitution Dr Menlo Park CA 94025

YOUNG, ROY ALTON, educator; b. McAlister, N.Mex., Mar. 1, 1921; s. John Arthur and Etta Julia (Sprinkle) Y.; B.S., N.Mex. A. and M. Coll., 1941; M.S., Iowa State U., 1942, Ph.D., 1948; m. Marilyn Ruth Sandman, May 22, 1950; children—Janet Elizabeth, Randall Owen. Teaching fellow Iowa State U., 1941-42, instr., 1946-47, Indsl. fellow, 1947-48; asst. prof. Oreg. State U., 1948-50, asso. prof., 1950-53, prof., 1953—, head dept. botany and plant pathology, 1958-66, dean research, 1966-70, acting pres., 1969-70, v.p. for research and grad. studies, 1970-76; chancellor U. Nebr., Lincoln, 1976—. Dir. Pacific Power & Light Co., First Nat. Bank & Trust Co. Mem. Commn. on Undergrad. Edn. in Biol. Scis., 1963-68; cons. State Expt. Stas. div. U.S. Dept. Agr.; chmn. subcom. plant pathogens, agr. bd. Nat. Acad. Scis.-NRC, 1965-68, mem. exec. com. study on problems of pest control, 1972-75; mem. exec. com. Nat. Govs.' Council on Sci. and Tech., 1970-74; mem. U.S. com. man and biosphere UNESCO, 1973—; mem. com. to rev. U.S. component Internat. Biol. Program, Nat. Acad. Scis., 1974-76; mem. NCHEMS Advisory Com., 1976—; mem. adv. panel on post-doctoral fellowships in environ. sci. Rockefeller Found., 1974—; bd. dirs. Boyce Thompson Inst. for Plant Research, 1975—; mem. adv. com. for research applications policy Sci. and Engring. Directorate, NSF, 1977—, mem. sea grant adv. panel, 1978—, chmn. adv. subcom. of integrated basic research. Served to lt. USNR, 1943-46. Fellow AAAS (exec. com. Pacific div. 1963-67, pres. div. 1971), Am. Phytopath Soc. (pres. Pacific div. 1957); mem. Oreg. Acad. Sci., Nat. Assn. State Univs. and Land Grant Colls. (chmn. council for research policy and adminstrn. 1970, chmn. standing com. on environment and energy 1974—), Sigma Xi, Phi Kappa Phi, Phi Sigma, Sigma Alpha Epsilon. Club: Rotary. Home: 3705 Chapin Circle Lincoln NE 68506 Office: Chancellor U Nebr Lincoln NE 68588

YOUNG, RUSSELL SCOTT, food service corp. exec.; b. Portland, Oreg., June 23, 1948; s. Lloyd Earl and Eleanor Marie (Sanquist) Y.; B.A., Calif. Luth. Coll., 1971; M.B.A., U. Pa., 1974. Vice pres. First Union Nat. Bank, Charlotte, N.C., 1974-78; dir. cash mgmt. Sambo's Restaurants, Inc., Santa Barbara, Calif., 1978, asst. treas., 1978, treas., 1978—, treas., controller, dir. Samco Ins. Co., Ltd., 1979—. Mem. bus. adv. council Calif. Luth. Coll., 1979—. Recipient award Big Bros., Charlotte, 1976. Mem. Am. Apparel Assn. (fin. com. 1977). Republican. Baptist. Home: 610 Miramonte Dr Santa Barbara CA 93109 Office: Sambo's Restaurants Inc 3760 State St Santa Barbara CA 93162

YOUNG, SAMUEL DOAK, banker; b. Woodville, Tex., Nov. 15, 1896; s. Charles Acton and Sarah Frances (Sims) Y.; student Woodville High Sch.; m. Elizabeth Goodman, Oct. 26, 1921 (dec. 1977); children—Frances Elizabeth Young Bauman, Samuel Doak. With Gulf Nat. Bank, Beaumont, Tex.; state bank examiner in Tex., receiver for various nat. banks, 1914-25; organizer, 1925, exec. v.p. El Paso Nat. Bank (Tex.), 1925-44, pres. 1944-64, chmn. bd. dirs., 1952—; chmn. bd. Trans Tex. Bancorp., 1971; advisory dir. El Paso Co., Houston, El Paso Products Co., Odessa, Tex., El Paso Natural Gas Co.; dir. Hotel Waldorf-Astoria Corp.; vice chmn. 1st State Bank, El Paso; hon. dir. Hilton Hotels Corp., Beverly Hills, Calif.; Pres., chmn. Providence Meml. Hosp.; organizer, 1st pres. United Fund El Paso and El Paso County. Bd. dirs. El Paso Symphony Assn. Served in AS, U.S. Army, Kelly Field, 1917-18; commd. 2d lt. Res. Recipient Human Relations award Nat. Conf. Christians and Jews, 1964; Aztec Eagle award Pres. Mexico, 1968. Presbyterian. Mason (Shriner). Clubs: El Paso Country, Coronado Country, El Paso (El Paso, Tex). Home: 833 Cherry Hill Ln El Paso TX 79912 Office: El Paso Nat Bank El Paso TX 79901

YOUNG, SCOTT ALEXANDER, journalist; b. Man., Can., Apr. 14, 1918; s. Percy Andrew and Jean Ferguson Y.; grad. high sch.; children by previous marriage—Robert, Neil; m. 2d, Astrid Carlson Mead, May 20, 1961; children—Deirdre, Astrid. Columnist, Toronto (Ont., Can.) Globe and Mail, 1957-69, 71—; sports editor Toronto Telegram, 1969-71; TV writer and personality, 1957—; pres. Ascot Prodns. Ltd. Mem. Province Ont. Royal Commn. Violence in Communications Industry, 1975-77. Served with Royal Canadian Navy, World War II. Recipient Canadian Nat. Newspaper award, 1959; Wilderness award for TV script, 1963. Fellow McLaughlin Coll., York U. Author: Red Shield in Action, 1949; Scrubs on Skates, 1952; Boy on Defense, 1953; (novel) The Flood, 1956; HMCS (text for Gilbert Milne's photos), 1960; (biography) (with Astrid Young) O'Brien, 1967; (biography) (with Astrid Young) Silent Frank Cochrane, 1973; (with Punch Imlach) Hockey is a Battle, 1969; (with George Robertson) (novel) Face-Off, 1971; Clue of the Dead Duck, 1962; Boy at the Leafs' Camp, 1963; (with Astrid Young) Big City Office Junior, 1964; Scott Young Sports Stories, 1965; The Leafs I Knew, 1966; We Won't Be Needing You, Al, and Other Stories, 1968; (with Leo Cahill) Goodbye Argos, 1973; War on Ice, 1976; Canada Cup of Hockey 1976, 1976; Short stories in several anthologies. Address: Rural Route 2 Cavan ON L0A 1C0 Canada

YOUNG, STEPHEN M., lawyer, former U.S. senator; b. May 4, 1889; s. Judge Stephen M. and Belle (Wagner) Y.; LL.B., Western Res U., 1912; M. Civil Law (hon.), Kenyon Coll.; LL.D. (hon.), Central State Coll.; Chubb fellow Yale; Dr. Pub. Service, Rio Grande Coll.; m. Ruby L. Dewley, 1911 (dec. 1952); m. Rachel Bell, 1957. Admitted to Ohio bar, 1911; asst. pros. atty. Cuyahoga Country, 1917-18, chief criminal pros. atty. Cuyahoga County, 1919-21; mem. Ohio Gen. Assembly, 1913-17; mem. 73d, 74th, 77th, 81st Congresses, Ohio at large; mem. U.S. Senate from Ohio, 1959-71. Mem. Ohio Commn. Unemployment Ins., 1931-32. Served with AUS, World War II; allied mil. gov. Province Reggio Emilia, Italy, 1945; lt. col. Res. Decorated Bronze Star, Purple Heart, Army Commendation ribbon; Order of Crown (Italy). Mem. Cuyahoga County Bar Assn. (past pres.), War Vets. Bar Assn. Cleve. (past pres.). Democrat. Home: 5160 Manning Pl NW Washington DC 20016

YOUNG, TERENCE, motion picture dir.; b. Shanghai, China, June 20, 1915; ed. Cambridge U. Entered motion picture industry, 1936; collaborated screen play On the Night of the Fire, On Approval, Theirs Is the Glory; wrote screen play Dangerous Moonlight; wrote screen play, directed They Were Not Divided, The Valley of the Eagles; dir. Red Beret (Paratrooper), That Lady, Safari, Action of the Tiger, Serious Charge, Too Hot to Handle, As Dark as the Night, Black Tights, Horatio, The Jackals, Dr. No, From Russia With Love, Moll Flanders, Thunderball, Flower of Evil, I Was a Spy, Isadora Duncan, Red Sun, The Valachi Papers, The Klansman, Jackpot, Wait Until Dark, Bloodline; co-dir. Storm Over the Nile. Served with Guards Armoured Div., World War II. Address: care Kurt Frings Agy Inc 9440 Santa Monica Blvd Suite 400 Beverly Hills CA 90210*

YOUNG, THEODORE CHARLES, savs. and loan exec.; b. San Diego, Apr. 15, 1925; s. Douglas and Martha Elizabeth (Longmore) Y.; B.S. magna cum laude, U. So. Calif., 1949; m. Beverly Jeanne Smith, Aug. 24, 1947; children—Theodore Charles, Kathy Lynn, Jeffrey Richard, Marianne Elizabeth. Comml. teller First Nat. Bank, San Diego, 1949-50; mercantile reporter Dun and Bradstreet, San Diego, 1950-53; with Home Fed. Savs. & Loan of San Diego, 1953—, sr. v.p., 1965-69, exec. v.p., investment group mgr., 1969—. Mem. Soc. Resdl. Appraisers, San Diego Taxpayers Assn., Bldg. Contractors Assn., Calif. Savs. and Loan League, U.S. Savs. and Loan League, Beta Gamma Sigma, Lambda Alpha. Republican. Home: 3852 Avenida Feliz Rancho Santa Fe CA 92067 Office: 7th and Broadway San Diego CA 92112

YOUNG, THOMAS DANIEL, educator; b. Louisville, Miss., Oct. 22, 1919; s. William Allen and Lula (Wright) Y.; B.S., Miss. So. Coll., 1941; M.A., U. Miss., 1948; Ph.D., Vanderbilt U., 1950; m. Arlease Lewis, Dec. 21, 1941; children—Thomas Daniel, Terry Lewis, Kyle David. Instr. English, U. Miss., 1946-48; asst. Vanderbilt U., 1948-50; asst. prof. English, Miss. So. Coll., 1950-51, prof., chmn. dept., 1951-54, dean basic coll., 1954-57; dean Delta State Coll., Cleveland, Miss., 1957-61; dean admissions, asst. to vice-chancellor Vanderbilt U., 1961-64, prof. English, chmn. dept., 1964-72, Gertrude C. Vanderbilt prof. English, 1972—. Pres., So. Lit. Festival Assn., 1952-53; chmn. English commn. Miss. Assn. Coll., 1952-55; coordinator Gen. Edn. Conf., 1953. Mem. AAUP, South Atlantic Modern Lang. Assn. (chmn. Am. lit. sect. 1971, chmn. lit. criticism sect. 1969, mem. exec. com. 1972), Modern Lang. Assn. Am. (chmn. So. Lit. sect. 1969), Am. Studies Assn. Lower Miss. (pres. 1956-57), Phi Delta Kappa, Omicron Delta Kappa. Author: Jack London and the Era of Social Protest, 1950; The Literature of the South, 1952, rev. edit., 1968; Donald Davidson: An Essay and a Bibliography, 1965; American Literature: A Critical Survey, 1968; John Crowe Ransom; Critical Essays and a Bibliography, 1968; John Crowe Ransom, 1970; Donald Davidson, 1971. Gen. editor The Fugitive Bibliographies; The Literary Correspondence of Allen Tate and Donald Davidson, 1974; The New Criticism and After, 1976; Gentleman in a Dustcoat: A Biography of John Crowe Ransom, 1977. Home: 857 Highland Crest Dr Nashville TN 37205

YOUNG, THOMAS EDWIN, educator, chemist; b. Manheim, Pa., Sept. 7, 1924; s. Edwin and Dorothy (Keener) Y.; B.S., Lehigh U., Bethlehem, Pa., 1949, M.S., 1950; Ph.D., U. Ill., 1952; m. Hilda Jean Derstler, July 18, 1945; 1 son, Robert Edwin. Research fellow U. Ill., 1950-52; research chemist E.I. duPont de Nemours & Co., Wilmington, Del., 1952-55; asst. prof. chemistry Antioch Coll., 1955-58; asst. prof. Lehigh U., 1958-60, asso. prof., 1960-66, prof. chemistry, 1966—. Served with AUS, 1943-46. Mem. Am. Chem. Soc., Sigma Xi, Phi Lambda Upsilon. Episcopalian. Contbr. articles to profl. jours. Home: 1952 Pinehurst Rd Bethlehem PA 18018

YOUNG, WARREN HOWARD, U.S. dist. judge; b. Chgo., Sept. 9, 1916; s. Elmer Leonard and Clarice Agnes (Anderson) Y.; B.A. in Econs. with honors, Northwestern U., 1938; J.D., Harvard, 1941; m. Ruth Ann Haskell, Dec. 16, 1957; children—Rodney, Lauren (Mrs. Ron Speas), Jonathan, Deborah, Gar, Timothy. Admitted to Ill. bar, 1941, V.I. bar, 1950; asso. firm Carney, Crowel & Leibman, Chgo.; sr. partner Young, Isherwood, Carney & Marsh, St. Croix and St. Thomas; U.S. dist. ct. judge Dist. V.I., St. Croix, 1971—. Pres. V.I. Title & Trust Co., 1950-71, Young-Clark Ins., Ltd., 1952-71, Pentheny Ltd., 1963-71. Chmn. com. fund raising Boy Scouts Am., chmn. bd. trustees; v.p., dir. Coast Guard Alumni Found., 1969-71. Served with USCGR; PTO. Mem. Am., Fed., V.I. bar assns., Am. Judicature Soc., World Peace Through Law Center, Lawyers-Pilots Assn. (charter), Nat. Lawyers Club, Navy League, Internat. Platform Assn. Clubs: St. Croix Tennis, St. Croix Yacht, V.I. Ski Divers, V.I. Soaring, Naui Scuba Diver. Home: Estate Bellvue Christiansted St Croix VI 00820 Office: 2 King St Christiansted St Croix VI 00820

YOUNG, WILLIAM GLENN, JR., surgeon; b. Washington, Feb. 26, 1925; s. William Glenn and Molly (Weaver) Y.; B.S., Duke U., 1944, M.D., 1947; m. Mary Frances Shields, Feb. 28, 1952; children—William Glenn, Sarah Lee, Ellen Shields, John Weaver. Intern, Duke Hosp., 1948-49, research fellow, 1949-50, asst. resident in surgery, 1950-56, resident in surgery, 1956-57; asso. in surgery Duke U., 1955-57, asst. prof. surgery, 1957-59, asso. prof., 1959-63, prof., 1963—. Served with M.C., U.S. Navy, 1950-52. Diplomate Am. Bd. Surgery. Mem. Soc. Thoracic Surgeons, So. Surg. Assn., So. Assn. Vascular Surgery, Am. Surg. Assn., Am. Assn. Thoracic Surgery, Soc. Vascular Surgery, So. Thoracic Surg. Assn., Soc. Univ. Surgeons, N.C. Surg. Assn. Democrat. Presbyterian. Research in thoracic and cardiovascular surgery. Home: 3718 Eton Rd Durham NC 27707 Office: Dept Surgery Duke Hospital Durham NC 27710

YOUNG, WILLIAM GLOVER, state justice; b. Huntington, N.Y., Sept. 23, 1940; s. Woodhull Benjamin and Margaret Jean (Wilkes) Y.; A.B., Harvard U., 1962, LL.B., 1967; m. Beverly June Bigelow, Aug. 5, 1967; children—Mark Edward, Jeffrey Woodhull, Todd Russell. Admitted to Mass. bar, 1967, U.S. Supreme Ct. bar, 1970; law clk. to chief justice Supreme Jud. Ct. Mass., 1967-68; spl. asst. atty. gen. Mass., 1969-72; chief legal counsel to gov. Mass., 1972-74; asso. firm Bingham, Dana and Gould, Boston, 1968-72, partner, 1975-78; asso. justice Superior Ct., Commonwealth of Mass., Boston, 1978—; lectr.

part time Harvard Law Sch., Boston Coll. Law Sch., Boston U. Law Sch. Served to capt. U.S. Army, 1962-64. Mem. Am. Law Inst., Mass. Bar Assn., Boston Bar Assn., Asso. Harvard Alumni (pres. 1976-77). Office: Superior Court Boston MA 02108

YOUNG, WILLIAM HENRY, educator; b. Corapolis, Pa., Oct. 7, 1912; s. Clarence Albert and Jeanette (Way) Y.; B.A., U. Pitts., 1933, M.A., 1937, LL.D., 1962; Ph.D., U. Wis., 1941; m. Sara Reish, Aug. 23, 1938; children—Diane, Jeffery Thomas, Eleanor. Instr. polit. sci. U. Pa., 1941-46, asst. prof., 1946-47; asso. prof. polit. sci. U. Wis., 1947-50, prof., 1950—, chmn. dept., 1952-60, asst. to pres., 1954-68, chmn. Center for Devel., 1968—; adminstrv. analyst Adj. Gen.'s Office, 1943; dir. research for Gov. of Wis., 1949-50, exec. sec. to Gov., 1950. Bd. dirs. Wis. Welfare Council, 1953-60, Oscar Rennebohm Found., 1960—; pres. bd. dirs. United Neighborhood Centers of Dane County, 1973-75. Served from 2d lt. to 1st lt. AUS, 1943-46, control officer Adj. Gen.'s Office, 1944-46. Mem. Am. Polit. Sci. Assn., A.A.U.P. Author: Wisconsin Corrupt Practices Act for Wisconsin Legislative Council, 1948; (with F.A. Ogg and P.O. Ray) Introduction to American Government, 13th edit., asso. book chpts. on govt. and politics. Home: 2125 Van Hise St Madison WI 53705

YOUNG, WILLIAM JOHNSON, cement mfr.; b. Binghamton, N.Y., Aug. 7, 1928; s. Joseph Samuel and Marion Irma (Johnson) Y.; grad. Lawrenceville Prep. Sch., 1945; A.B., Princeton, 1949; LL.B., U. Va., 1952; m. Patricia W. Campbell, Sept. 16, 1978; children—Mark Johnson, Joseph Peter, Marion Louise. With Lehigh Portland Cement Co., 1954—, v.p., 1958-64, pres., 1964—, also dir.; mem. adv. council Heidelberger Zement, A.G., Heidelberg, W. Ger.; dir. Girard Co., Phila., Am. Standard, Inc., N.Y.C. Dir. Portland Cement Assn., 1964—, chmn. bd., 1969-72. Trustee Princeton, 1971-75; dir. Pa. Stage Co., Allentown; mem. corp. Joslin Diabetes Found., Boston. Served to lt. (j.g.) USCGR, 1952-54. Republican. Presbyn. Clubs: Lehigh Country, Livingston (Allentown); Tiger Inn (Princeton); Saucon Valley Country (Bethlehem, Pa.). Office: 718 Hamilton Mall Allentown PA 18105*

YOUNG, WILLIAM PETER, ret. ins. co. exec.; b. Boston, Apr. 23, 1916; s. William Forest and Henrietta (Miller) Y.; B.S.C.E., Tufts Coll., 1937; m. Nelle Mae Helms, July 24, 1943; children—Linda, Elizabeth. Student engr. N.J. Bell Telephone Co., 1937-39; engr. Haller Engring. Co., Cambridge, Mass., 1939-40; insp. engring. div. Factory Mut., Boston 1940-43; dist. mgr. Blackstone Mut., Chgo. and Mpls., 1946-68; dist. mgr. MFB Allendale Mut. Ins. Co., Chgo., 1968-70, v.p., Johnston, R.I., 1970-72, sr. v.p., 1972-76, exec. v.p., 1976-80. Mem. Wayzata (Minn.) Sch. Bd., 1962-68, treas., 1964-66, chmn., 1967-68. Served with USMC, 1943-46. Mem. Soc. Fire Protection Engrs. (charter). Republican. Congregationalist. Clubs: R.I. Country; Univ. (Providence). Home: 2 Overlook Rd Barrington RI 02806 Office: Allendale Mut Ins Co Allendale Park Johnston RI 02919

YOUNG, WILLIAM TANDY, JR., advt. exec.; b. Pine Bluff, Ark., Mar. 11, 1897; s. William Tandy and Eddine (Hudson) Y.; student U. Ind.; m. Margaret Wilson, 1937 (dec. 1949); m. 2d, Francigene Sheridan, Nov.15, 1952; children—William Tandy III, Collier, Sheridan. Ret. pres. Leo Burnett Co., Inc., Chgo.; former dir. and part owner Wilson Milk Co., Indpls.; pvt. real estate investments, 1963—. Former pres. Arlington Park Jockey Club, Arkington Heights, Ill. Trustee Palm Beach Day Sch. Served with U.S. Army, World War I; brig. gen. USAAF, World War II. Decorated Legion of Merit, Silver Star (U.S.)· Croix de Guerre (France). Clubs: Racquet (Chgo.); Everglades, Bath and Tennis (Palm Beach). Home: 346 Sea Spray Palm Beach FL 33480 Office: 324 Royal Palm Way Palm Beach FL 33480

YOUNG, WILLIAM THOMPSON, soft drink co. exec.; b. Lexington, Ky., Feb. 15, 1918; s. Willis Samuel and Margaret (Thompson) Y.; B.S. in Mech. Engring. with high distinction, U. Ky., 1939; m. Lucy Hilton Maddox, Apr. 16, 1945; children—William Thompson, Lucy Meade. With Bailey Meter Co., Cleve., 1939-41; pres. W.T. Young Foods, Lexington, 1946-55, gen. mgr. (subs. Procter & Gamble Co.), 1955-57; chmn. bd. Royal Crown Cola Co., Atlanta; chmn. bd. W.T. Young Storage Co., Lexington, 1957—; dir. First Security Nat. Bank & Trust Co., Lexington, Ky.-Am. Water Co. Bd. dirs. Humana Inc.; chmn. bd. Transylvania U., Lexington. Served to capt. AUS, 1941-45. Mem. Sigma Alpha Epsilon. Presbyterian. Clubs: Rotary, Optimists (past pres. Lexington chpt.). Home: 222 Chinoe Rd Lexington KY 40502 Office: 2225 Young Dr Lexington KY 40505

YOUNGBLADE, CHARLES JOHN, naval officer; b. Sioux City, Iowa, Sept. 2, 1926; s. Amil Charles and Mary Ella (Manning) Y.; student Iowa State Coll., 1943-44; B.S., U.S. Naval Acad., 1949; M.S. in Internat. Affairs, George Washington U., 1967; m. Monika Erika Hechler, Oct. 15, 1977. Commd. ensign U.S. Navy, 1949, advanced through grades to rear adm., 1975; various squadron and adminstrv. staff positions, 1950-69; comdr. officer U.S.S. Patcatuck (AO-108), 1969-70; exec. asst. to dep. chief naval ops. for fleet ops. and readiness, 1970-71; comdg. officer U.S.S. Roosevelt (CVA-42), 1971-73; chief of staff for comdr. Naval Air Forces Atlantic, 1973-75; dep. dir. reconnaissance Joint Chiefs of Staff, Washington, 1975-76; dep. comdr. Naval Forces So. Europe, 1976-78; comdr. Naval Safety Center, Norfolk, Va., 1978—. Decorated Legion of Merit, Bronze Star, Air medal, Joint Service Commendation medal, Navy Commendation medal. Mem. Assn. Naval Aviation. Home: 1134 Breezy Point Dr Norfolk VA 23511 Office: Safety Center Naval Air Station Norfolk VA 23511

YOUNGBLOOD, HERBERT JACKSON, III, profl. athlete; b. Jacksonville, Fla., Jan. 26, 1950; s. Herbert Jackson and Mildred Kathleen (Jackson) Y.; grad. U. Fla., 1971; m. Sandra Diane Young, June 20, 1971. Left defensive end Los Angeles Rams, 1971—. Named to All Pro Teams, 1973-78; named Most Valuable Defensive Player, 1975-76. Mem. Alpha Tau Omega. Home: 7282 Emerson St Westminster CA 92683 Office: care Los Angeles Rams 10271 W Pico Blvd Los Angeles CA 90064*

YOUNGBLOOD, NAT HOWARD, JR., artist; b. Evansville, Ind., Dec. 28, 1916; s. Nat Howard and Geraldine (Pote) Y.; student Ind. U., 1935-37, U. N.Mex., 1938-39, Am. Acad. Art, Chgo., 1940-41; m. Margaret May Tatum, May 22, 1941; children—Dorothy Ann, Sandra Lee, Nat Howard III. Art dir. Pitts. Press, 1946—; represented in permanent collections Am. Acad. Art, Evansville Pub. Mus., Nat. Marine Mus., Ind. State Coll.; represented Am. painters in Paris Exhbn., 1975-76. Bd. dirs. Pitts. Expt., 1963—. Served with AUS, 1942-45. Named Man of Year in Art, Pitts. C. of C., 1965; recipient 1st prize watercolor Pennanat. Exhbn., 1966; 1st prize Carnegie Inst. Art for Industry Exhbn., 1954; 1st prize Aqueous Open, 1976; award Pitts. Water Color Soc., 1977; named Artist of Yr., Pitts. Arts and Crafts Center, 1976. Executed 10 oil paintings for Pitts. Bicentennial celebration. Home: Gateway Towers 25G Pittsburgh PA 15222

YOUNGBLOOD, RICHARD NEIL, newspaperman; b. Minot, N.D., May 9, 1936; s. Edward A. and Helen (Condo) Y.; B.A., U. N.D., 1958; m. Adele Henley, May 4, 1957; children—Kent Jay, Ruth Adele, Beth Alise. Reporter, Grand Forks (N.D.) Herald, 1955-63; mem. staff Mpls. Tribune, 1963—, bus.-financial editor, 1969—. Named Newspaper Farm Editor of Year, Newspaper Farm Editors Am. and Nat. Plant Food Inst., 1965; recipient award for excellence in bus. and financial journalism John Hancock Mut. Life Ins. Co., 1974. Home: 3851 Woodland Dr Saint Louis Park MN 55426 Office: 425 Portland Ave Minneapolis MN 55488

YOUNGDAHL, CARL RICHARD, securities dealer; b. Mpls., Aug. 12, 1915; s. Carl R. and Hilma (Croonquist) Y.; B.A., Augustana Coll., Sioux Falls, S.D., 1937; M.A., Fletcher Sch. Law and Diplomacy, 1938; Ph.D., U. Minn., 1947; m. Catherine Mason, Aug. 12, 1946; children—Carl Richard, Karen Elizabeth, Lee Reynold, John Mason, Ann Catherine. Economist, Fed. Res. Bd., 1943-54, asst. dir. research, 1952-54; with Aubrey G. Lanston & Co., Inc., N.Y.C., 1955—, exec. v.p., 1959-63, pres., 1963-70, chmn. bd., 1970—, also dir.; tchr. econs. Macalester Coll., 1939-40, U. Minn., 1940-42, George Washington U., 1944, Am. U., 1946-50, Wis. Sch. Banking, 1957-62, Stonier Grad. Sch. Banking, 1960-65; dir. Union Dime Savs. Bank, Smith Barney Equity Fund, D.W. Rich & Co., Inc. Trustee Children's Rehab. Inst., Reisterstown, Md., 1957-69, Short Hills (N.J.) Country Day Sch., 1961-70, Gustavus Adolphus Coll., St. Peter, Minn. Mem. Am. Econ. Assn., Am. Finance Assn., Securities Industry Assn. (chmn. govtl. securities com. 1969-70), Assn. Primary Dealers in U.S. Govt. Securities (pres. 1974-75), Public Securities Assn. (dir.), Phi Gamma Delta, Alpha Kappa Psi. Lutheran (bd. dirs., treas. bd. pensions Luth. Ch. Am.). Clubs: Baltusrol Golf; International (Washington); Sky; Tequesta Country. Contbr. articles to profl. jours. Home: 115 Slope Dr Short Hills NJ 07078 Office: 20 Broad St New York NY 10005

YOUNGDAHL, JAMES EDWARD, lawyer; b. Mankato, Minn., Nov. 17, 1926; s. Benjamin Emanuel Lincoln and Livia (Bjorkquist) Y.; student Washington U., St. Louis, 1944-45; A.B., U. Mo., 1947; LL.B., U. Ark., 1959; children—Jay Thomas Armstrong, Jan Kristi, Lincoln Anders Morton, Sara Lise. Field sec. League for Indsl. Democracy, N.Y.C., 1947-48; nat. rep., asst. regional dir. Amalgamated Clothing Workers Am., CIO and AFL-CIO, St. Louis, Paducah, Ky., New Orleans, 1948-56; admitted to Ark. bar, 1959, since practiced in Little Rock, Memphis and New Orleans; partner McMath, Leatherman, Woods & Youngdahl, also Youngdahl, Larrison & Agee, 1959—; instr. labor law U. Ark. Sch. Law, 1963, 69-71, Ark. Law Sch., 1964-66; mem. arbitration services adv. com. Fed. Mediation and Conciliation Service, 1978—. Vice chmn. New Orleans Forum, 1953-54; pres. Ark. Assn. for Mental Health, 1960-61; chmn. Ark. adv. com. U.S. Commn. on Civil Rights, 1962-65. Mem. exec. com. So. Regional Council, 1969-74; mem. nat. exec. bd. Workers Def. League, 1965-75; bd. dirs. Voter Edn. Project, Inc., 1971-74. Editor-in-chief Ark. Law Rev., 1958-59. Contbg. editor Ark. Advocate, 1972-74. Contbr. articles to profl. jours. Home: 1018 Cumberland St 13 Little Rock AR 72202 Office: 2101 Main St Little Rock AR 72206 also 418 Common St New Orleans LA 70130 also 100 N Main Bldg Memphis TN 38103

YOUNGDAHL, PAUL DAVID, hosp. adminstr.; b. Mpls., Oct. 6, 1929; s. Luther William and Irene Annet (Engdahl) Y.; student Gustavus Adolphus Coll., 1947-49; B.A., U. Minn., 1951, M.A., 1953; m. Catherine Mary Martin, June 21, 1952; children—Jenny, Kim, David. Adminstrv. resident St. Barnabas Hosp., Mpls., 1952-53; asst. adminstr. Meth. Hosp., Houston, 1953-55, asso. adminstr., 1955-58; asst. to dir. James A. Hamilton Assos. hosp. cons., 1958-61; adminstr. Frederick (Md.) Meml. Hosp., 1961-68; adminstr. Fairfax Hosp., Falls Church, Va., 1968-77, v.p. ops., 1977—. Lectr. hosp. adminstrn. U. Minn., 1958, instr., 1959-60; chmn. hosp. adv. com. Health Facilities Planning Council Met. Washington. Fellow Am. Coll. Hosp. Adminstrs.; mem. Am. Hosp. Assn., Md.-D.C.-Del. Hosp. Assn. (pres., 1967), Va. Hosp. Assn., Md. Hosp. Council. Home: 2523 Lakevale Dr Vienna VA 22180 Office: 3300 Gallows Rd Falls Church VA 22046

YOUNGER, EVELLE JANSEN, lawyer, former atty. gen. Calif.; b. Nebr., June 19, 1918; s. Harry C. and Maebel (Jansen) Y.; A.B., Nebr. U., 1940, also LL.B.; student criminology Northwestern Law Sch., Chgo., 1940; m. Mildred Eberhard, July 3, 1942; 1 son, Eric. Spl. agt. FBI, N.Y.C., also Washington, supr. nat. def. sect., 1940-46; admitted to Calif. bar, 1946; dep. city atty. criminal div., Los Angeles, 1946-47, city pros., 1947-50; pvt. practice law, Los Angeles, 1950-53; judge Municipal Ct., Los Angeles, 1953-58, Superior Ct., 1958-64; dist. atty. Los Angeles County, 1964-70; atty. gen. Calif., 1970-78; mem. firm Buchalter, Nemer, Fields, Chrystie and Younger, 1979—. Instr. criminal law Southwestern U., Los Angeles, 1948. Served to maj. AUS, 1942-46; to lt. col. USAF, 1951-52; ret. maj. gen. USAF Res. Fellow Am. Coll. Trial Lawyers; mem. Am. Bar Assn. (chmn. criminal law sect. 1962, past chmn. traffic and magistrates cts. com.), State Bar of Calif., Nat. Dist. Atty.'s Assn. (v.p.), Los Angeles Lawyers Club, Am. Legion, Soc. Former FBI Agts. (past chmn.), Los Angeles Peace Officers Assn. (past pres.), Council Mexican-Am. Affairs, Air Force Assn., Alpha Tau Omega Alumni Assn. (past pres.). Episcopalian. Mason (Shriner), Elk. Club: Trojan (dir.). Contbr. articles to profl. jours. Office: 700 S Flower St Los Angeles CA 90017*

YOUNGER, IRVING, lawyer, educator; b. N.Y.C., Nov. 30, 1932; A.B., Harvard U., 1953; LL.B., N.Y. U., 1958. Admitted to N.Y. bar, 1958, U.S. Supreme Ct. bar, 1962; asso. firm Paul, Weiss, Rifkind, Wharton & Garrison, N.Y.C., 1958-60; asst. U.S. atty. So. Dist. N.Y., 1960-62; partner firm Younger & Younger and successors, N.Y.C., 1962-65; prof. law N.Y. U., 1965-68; judge Civil Ct. City N.Y., 1969-74; Samuel S. Leibowitz prof. trial techniques Cornell U., Ithaca, N.Y., 1974—; adj. prof. law Columbia U., N.Y. U., 1969-74; vis. prof. law Harvard U., 1978-79; mem. faculty Nat. Coll. State Judiciary, 1971-75. Mem. Am., N.Y. State bar assns., Am. Law Inst., Assn. Bar City N.Y., Assn. Am. Law Schs. (chmn. trial advocacy sect. 1976-78). Contbr. articles to law revs. and popular mags. Home: 3 Fountain Pl Ithaca NY 14850 Office: Cornell U Law Sch Myron Taylor Hall Ithaca NY 14853

YOUNGER, JAMES WALLACE, steel co. exec.; b. Ottawa, Ont. Can., Feb. 2, 1924; s. Lloyd Robert and Edith Margaret (Galloway) Y.; B.A., Victoria Coll., U. Toronto, 1945. Barrister-at-Law, Osgoode Hall Law Sch., Toronto, 1948; B. Comm., Carleton Coll., Ottawa, Ont., 1952; m. Phyllis May Rosalie Boswell, May 3, 1952; children—Arthur, Douglas, Calvin. Called to Ont. bar, 1948; created Queen's counsel, 1970; partner firm May, McMichael & Younger, Ottawa, 1948-58; with Steel Co. Can., Ltd., 1958—, sec., mgr. law dept., 1964-70, sec., gen. counsel, 1970—, v.p., 1974—. Chmn., Ottawa Ct. Revision; chmn. Ottawa Rental Reference Bd., 1953-57. Bd. govs., v.p. adminstrn. North York Hosp. Mem. Canadian, York County bar assns., Law Soc. Upper Can. (pres.), Assn. Canadian Gen. Counsel, Am. Soc. Corp. Secs.; Canadian Mfrs. Assn. (chmn. legislation com. 1967-70), Toronto Bd. Trade, Canadian C. of C. Mem. Progressive Conservative Party. Presbyterian. Home: 48 Riverview Dr Toronto ON M4N 3C7 Canada Office: PO Box 205 Toronto-Dominion Centre Toronto ON M5K 1J4 Canada

YOUNGER, JUDITH T., lawyer, educator; b. N.Y.C., Dec. 20, 1933; d. Sidney and Kate (Greenbaum) Weintraub; B.S., Cornell U., 1954; J.D., N.Y. U., 1958; LL.D. (hon.), Hofstra U., 1974; m. Irving Younger, Jan. 21, 1955; children—Rebecca, Abigail M. Admitted to N.Y. bar, 1958, U.S. Supreme Ct., 1962; law clk. to judge U.S. Dist. Ct., 1958-60; asso. firm Chadbourne, Parke, Whiteside & Wolff, N.Y.C., 1960-62; mem. firm Younger and Younger, and successors, 1962-67; adj. asst. prof. N.Y. U. Sch. Law, 1967-69; asst. atty. gen. State of N.Y., 1969-70; asso. prof. Hofstra U. Sch. Law, 1970-72, prof., asso. dean, 1972-74; dean, prof. Syracuse Coll. Law, 1974-75; dep. dean, prof. law Cornell Law Sch., 1975-78, prof., 1978—. Trustee, Cornell U., 1974-78; cons. NOW, 1972-74; cons. Suffolk County for Revision of Its Real Property Tax Act, 1972-73; mem. Gov. Rockefeller's Panel to Screen Candidates of Ct. of Claims Judges, 1973-74. Mem. Am. Bar Assn. (council legal edn.), Am. Law Inst. (adv.), AAUP (v.p. Cornell U. chpt. 1978—), N.Y. State Bar Assn., Assn. Bar City N.Y., Tompkins County Bar Assn. Contbr. articles to profl. jours. Home: 3 Fountain Pl Ithaca NY 14850 Office: Cornell Univ Law Sch Myron Taylor Hall Ithaca NY 14853

YOUNGER, ROY R., fin. exec.; b. Chgo., Dec. 23, 1934; s. Edward W. and Dorothy (Kraft) Y.; B.A., Valparaiso U., 1959; M.B.A., Northwestern U., 1964; m. Mary Anne M. Scherer, July 1, 1975; children—Gwenn L., Ryan R., Camille P., Leanne M. Fin. analyst Abbott Labs., North Chicago, Ill., 1960-65; controller Pentron Electronics, Chgo., 1965-66; treas., controller Penn-Union Electric Corp., Erie, Pa., 1966-67; treas. Chgo. Rawhide Mfg. Co., 1967-69; fin. cons. Richard R. Hirsch & Assos., Chgo., 1969-71; treas. L.E. Myers Co., Chgo., 1971-73; v.p.-fin. Groman Corp., Chgo., 1973-77; v.p. fin. Tower Products, Inc., Mundelein, Ill., 1977—. Served with U.S. Army, 1953-55. C.P.A., Ill. Mem. Am. Inst. C.P.A.'s., Ill. Soc. C.P.A.'s. Home: 800 Becker Rd Glenview IL 60025 Office: 1919 S Butterfield Rd Mundelein IL 60060

YOUNGERMAN, JACK, artist; b. Louisville, Mar. 25, 1926; s. Guy Arthur and Margaret Anne (Eberhart) Y.; student U. N.C., 1944-46; B.A., U. Mo., 1947; student Ecole des Beaux Arts (Paris), 1947-48; m. Delphine Seyrig, July 3, 1950; 1 son, Duncan Pierre. One man shows Betty Parsons Gallery, N.Y.C., 1958, 60, 61, 64, 65, 68, Paris, 1951, 62, 63, Milan, Los Angeles, Worcester Art Mus., 1965, Mass. Inst. Tech., 1966, Galerie Adrien Maeght, Paris, 1966, Phillips Collection, Washington, 1968, Denise Rene Gallery, Paris, 1973, Pace Gallery, N.Y.C., 1971, 73, 75; group exhbns. Carnegie Internat., 1958, 61, 16, Americans at Mus. Modern Art, 1959, Corcoran Mus., Washington, 1958, 63, Whitney Mus., 1960, Guggenheim Mus., 1961, 66, Art Inst. Chgo., 1962, Whitney Annual, 1967; represented in the permanent collections Mus. Modern Art, N.Y.C., Knox-Albright Mus., M.Y.C., Worcester Art Mus., Smithsonisn, Washington, Whitney Mus., Joseph H. Hirshhorn Found., Corcoran Mus., Carnegie Inst. Mus. Art, Philips Collection, Washington; stage designs Histoire de Vasco (Paris), 1956, Deathwatch (N.Y.C.), 1958. Guggenheim fellow, 1976; Nat. Endowment for Arts fellow, 1972. Commd. works include The Ohio, Pitts., commd. by PPG Industries, 1977. Studio: 130 W 3d St New York NY 10012

YOUNGGREN, NEWELL AMOS, educator, biologist; b. River Falls, Wis., Mar. 15, 1915; s. Nels A. and Nancy (Weberg) Y.; B.S., River Falls State Coll., 1937; M.P.H., U. Wis., 1941; Ph.D., U. Colo., 1956; m. Beth I. Hoveland, May 9, 1941; children—Stephen, Jeffrey. Mem. faculty, Northland Coll., Ashland, Wis., 1946-48, Bradley U., Peoria, Ill., 1948-54; mem. faculty U. Colo., Boulder, 1954-61, asst. prof., chmn. dept., 1958-61; prof. biology U. Ariz., Tucson, 1961—, head dept. biol. scis., 1968-73. Mem. Am. Soc. Zoologists, AAAS, Am. Inst. Biol. Scientists, Nat. Assn. Biology Tchrs., Sigma Xi, Phi Sigma. Author: (with Williams and Bonde) General Biology Laboratory Manual, 1963; (with Cockrum, McCauley) Biology, 1966. Home: 5770 Vista Valverde Tucson AZ 85718

YOUNGKEN, HEBER WILKINSON, JR., coll. dean; b. Phila., Aug. 13, 1913; s. Heber Wilkinson and Clara (Eastman) Y.; A.B., Bucknell U., 1935; B.S., Mass. Coll. Pharmacy, 1938; M.S., U. Minn., 1940, Ph.D., 1942; student Harvard Grad. Sch., 1938-39; m. Daphne Goodwin, Mar. 28, 1942; children—John R., Richard C. Asst. biology and pharmacognosy Mass. Coll. Pharmacy, 1935-39; teaching asst. pharmacognosy Coll. Pharmacy, U. Minn., 1939-42; from. instr. to prof. pharmacognosy U. Wash., Seattle, 1942-57, chmn. dept., dir. med. plant lab., 1946-57; prof. pharmacognosy, dean Coll. Pharmacy, U. R.I., 1957—, v.p. acad. affairs, 1967-68, provost health sci. affairs, 1969—; vis. prof. U. London, 1970, U. Cairo (Egypt), 1977. Mem. adv. com. R.I. Med. Center; pres. R.I. Health Sci. Edn. Council, 1976-77; chmn. sect. pharmacognosy/natural products Acad. Pharm. Scis., 1976-77. Bd. dirs. R.I. dir. Am. Cancer Soc., R.I. Soc. for Prevention Blindness. Served with USNR, 1943-46; now capt. Res. Recipient Edwin L. Newcomb award research pharmacognosy Am. Found. Pharm. Edn., 1951. Fellow A.A.A.S.; mem. Soc. Exptl. Biology and Medicine, N.Y. Acad. Sci., Am., Wash. State, R.I. (Toxicology award 1964) pharm. assns., Am. Coll. Apothecary, Soc. Econ. Botany, N.E. Bot. Club, R.I. Soc. Hosp. Pharmacists, Am. Soc. Pharmacognosy (pres. 1970), Sigma Xi, Phi Kappa Phi, Phi Sigma, Rho Chi, Kappa Psi, Phi Kappa Psi. Baptist. Rotarian. Author: (with R. Pratt) Pharmacognosy, 2d edit., 1956; Organic Chemistry in Pharmacy, 1949; also numerous papers in field. Home: 82 Oakwoods Dr Peace Dale RI 02879 Office: Coll Pharmacy U RI Kingston RI 02881

YOUNGMAN, HENNY, comedian; b. Eng.; m. Sadie Cohen; children—Gary, Marilyn. Appeared regularly on Kate Smith radio show during 1930's; now nightclub comedian; appears on TV; appeared in TV series Henny and Rocky, 1955, Joey and Dad, 1975; appeared in film Silent Movie, 1976; recs. include Take My Album . . . Please, 1978. Address: care Asso Booking Corp 9595 Wilshire Blvd Beverly Hills CA 90212*

YOUNGMAN, WILLIAM STERLING, lawyer; b. Boston, May 25, 1907; s. William Sterling and Helen Isabel (Yerxa) Y.; student Middlesex Sch., 1919-25; A.B. magna cum laude, Harvard, 1929, LL.B. magna cum laude, 1932; LL.D. (hon.), Middlebury Coll., 1978; m. Elsie Hooper Perkins, Apr. 17, 1937; children—William Sterling, 3d, Robert, Elsie Youngman Hull. Admitted to Mass. bar, 1934, U.S. Supreme Ct. bar, 1939, D.C. bar, 1941, N.Y. bar, 1951; law sec. to Judge Learned Hand, N.Y.C., 1932-33; with law firm Palmer, Dodge, Barstow, Wilkins & Davis, Boston, 1933-38; counsel Nat. Power Policy Commn., Washington, and chief counsel power div. PWA, 1939-40; gen. counsel FPC, 1940-1941; exec. v.p. and dir. China Def. Supplies, Inc., 1941-42, pres. 1942-45; gen. counsel in U.S., Nat. Resources Commn. of China, 1944-47; partner Corcoran and Youngman 1941-49; pres. C.V. Starr & Co., Inc., 1949-68; chmn. bd. Am. Home Asssurance Co., Ins. Co. of State of Pa., 1952-69, Am. Internat. Assurance Co., Ltd., Hong Kong, 1958-67, Philippine Am. Life Ins. Co., 1958-68, Am. Internat. Underwriters Corp., 1959-68, Am. Internat. Reins. Co., 1967-68, Am. Internat. Group, 1968. Vice chmn. Council for Latin Am., 1967-69. Trustee emeritus Middlebury Coll. Mem. Council Fgn. Relations. Clubs: Metropolitan, Chevy Chase (Washington); St. Botolph, Badminton and Tennis (Boston); Harvard, River, Down Town Assn., Deepdale Golf (N.Y.); Varsity (Harvard U.); Manchester (Mass.) Yacht; Essex County (Mass.); Manchester Country (N.H.). Home: East Hebron NH 03232 Office: 1750 Elm St Manchester NH 03104

YOUNGNER, PHILIP GENEVUS, educator; b. Nelson, Minn., July 13, 1920; s. Walter Genevus and Lydia Mathilda (Johnson) Y.; B.S., St. Cloud State Coll., 1944; M.S., U. Wis., 1947, Ph.D., 1958; m. Shirley Hope Anderson, May 27, 1947; children—Linda, Daniel,

Ruth, Susan. Instr. physics U. Extension, Racine, Wis., 1947-49; asst. prof. physics State Coll., St. Cloud, Minn., 1949-53, asso. prof., 1954-56, prof., chmn. physics dept., 1958—. Dir. pre-coll. physics Am. Inst. Physics, N.Y.C., also adj. prof. physics, Rutgers U., U. Del., 1965-66; physics cons. NSF-AID program, India, 1969. Wis. Alumni Research Found. grantee. Mem. Am. Phys. Soc., Am. Assn. Physics Tchrs. (mem. council), Minn. Assn. Physics Tchrs. (pres., exec. sec.), Minn. Acad. Sci., Sigma Xi. Co-author: Physics, 1969. Home: 919 18th St SE St Cloud MN 56301

YOUNGQUIST, ALVIN MENVID, JR., editor, pub.; b. Toledo, Oct. 9, 1925; s. Alvin Menvid and Elsie W. (Bostock) Y.; B.S., Northwestern U. Sch. Bus., 1950, postgrad. Sch. Journalism, 1951; m. Judith Jackett, June 13, 1953. Editor, Bankers Monthly, Skokie, Ill., 1953-70; editor, pres., pub. Bankers Monthly, Inc., Northbrook, Ill., 1971—. Served with USNR, 1943-46. Mem. Bank Mktg. Assn., U.S. Power Squadrons (Skokie Valley), Lake Michigan Yachting Assn. Republican. Episcopalian. Clubs: White Lake (Mich.) Yacht; Glenview (Ill.) Tennis. Home: 1343 Hollywood Ave Glenview IL 60025 Office: 601 Skokie Blvd Northbrook IL 60062

YOUNGQUIST, CARL ROBERT, hosp. adminstr.; b. Winona, Minn., Apr. 30, 1918; B.A., Augustana Coll., Rock Island, Ill., 1940; M.B.A., U. Chgo., 1942; children—Lee, Pamla, Judy, Linda, Debbie. Resident hosp. adminstrn. Episcopal Hosp., Phila., 1943-45; adminstr. Jameson Meml. Hosp., New Castle, Pa., 1945-48, Sharon (Pa.) Gen. Hosp., 1948-57; exec. dir. Shadyside Hosp., Pitts., 1957-62, Magee-Women's Hosp., Pitts., 1962—; chmn. bd. Hosp. Council Western Pa., 1974-77; chmn. Allegheny subarea adv. council Health Systems Agy., 1976-77, bd. dirs., 1978—; mem. obstet. task force Western Pa. Comprehensive Health Planning Agy., 1973-75; vice chmn. adminstrs. com. Univ. Health Center, Pitts., 1978—; sec. Health Center Hosp. Service Corp. Mem. Pa. Gov.'s Task Force on Rehab., 1957-59; trustee Family and Children's Service; mem. exec. com. and policy making commn. Health Edn. Center. Fellow Am. Coll. Hosp. Adminstrs. (past chmn. bylaws com., past mem. awards com.); mem. Am. Hosp. Assn. (life mem., past chmn. com. planning and plant ops.), Hosp. Assn. Pa. (life mem., pres., com. chmn.), Pa. Hosp. Services Assn. (past chmn. bd. dirs.), Assn. Am. Med. Colls., Nat. League for Nursing, Pa. League for Nursing (governing council Area 6), N.W. Pa. Regional Hosp. Assn. (past pres.), Hosp. Adminstrn. Alumni Assn. U. Chgo. (exec. com.). Office: Magee-Womens Hosp Forbes Ave and Halket St Pittsburgh PA 15213

YOUNGREN, RALPH PARK, architect; b. Cloquet, Minn., Dec. 26, 1924; s. Andrew Frederick and Eunice (Park) Y.; A.B., Harvard U., 1948, M.Arch., 1950; m. Ann Henderson, June 28, 1962; children—Todd Park, Malcolm Park. Asso. partner, sr. designer Skidmore, Owings & Merrill, Chgo., 1950-67; prin. charge design Metz, Train, Olson & Youngren, Inc., Chgo., 1967—; design critic, lectr. U. Ill., 1962—; archtl. adviser Chgo. Dept. Urban Renewal, 1962; trustee Chgo. Sch. Architecture Found., 1969—, hon. pres., 1974—. Bd. dirs. Soc. Contemporary Art, 1966-69; aux. bd. Art Inst. Chgo., 1970-77. Served with AUS, 1942-46. Co-recipient R.S. Reynolds Meml. award for Acad. Chapel, USAF Acad, 1964. Fellow AIA (dir. Chgo. chpt. 1975—). Clubs: Cliff Dwellers (dir.), Racquet, Arts (dir.), Harvard (Chgo.). Principal works include USAF Chapel, USAF Acad.; Grover M. Hermann Hall, Ill. Inst. Tech.; Westinghouse Research Labs., Pitts.; Joseph Regenstein Library, U. Chgo.; Rush Med. Coll., Rush-Presbyn.-St. Luke's Med. Center, Chgo.; Kraft Offices, others. Home: 1223 N Astor St Chicago IL 60610 Office: 1 E Wacker Dr Chicago IL 60601

YOUNGS, WILLARD OLIVER, ret. librarian; b. Berkeley, Calif., Dec. 23, 1910; s. Judge Oliver and Dora (Willard) Y.; B.S., U. Calif., 1932, certificate in librarianship, 1936; m. Ruth McLean, May 11, 1935; children—Heather (Mrs. Bruce R. Stine), Colleen (Mrs. Harold A. Brindle). Librarian jr. grade U. Calif. Library, 1937-39; exec. asso. Stanford U. Libraries, 1939-40, acting reference librarian, 1940-41, reference librarian, 1941-46; supervising librarian bus. and tech. dept. San Diego Pub. Library, 1946-48; head reference dept. Seattle Pub. Library, 1948-50, asst. librarian, coordinator reference services, 1950-57, librarian, 1957-74, emeritus, 1974—. Mem. adv. bd. KCTS-TV, 1957—; mem. Wash. State Bd. for Certification Librarians, 1969-74. Bd. mgrs. Seattle YMCA, 1959-62; bd. dirs. Pacific N.W. Bibliog. Center, 1970-71; adv. bd. trustees Friends of Seattle Public Library; exec. bd. Assn. Ret. Seattle City Employees, 1978—. Mem. ALA (mem. council 1964-71, mem. exec. bd. 1967-71, v.p. pub. library div. 1967-68, pres. 1968-69), Wash. State (past pres.), Pacific N.W. library assns. Republican. Episcopalian. Kiwanian (pres. Seattle 1968). Contbr. to profl. periodicals. Home: 8230 43d Ave NE Seattle WA 98115

YOUNT, ERNEST HARSHAW, JR., physician; b. Lincolnton, N.C., Feb. 23, 1919; s. Ernest H. and Marguerite (Smith) Y.; A.B., U. N.C., 1940; M.D., Vanderbilt U., 1943; postgrad. student U. Chgo., 1943-48; m. Betty Lindsay Shuford, June 8, 1942; children—Ernest H. III, Peter Shuford, Martha Lindsay. Instr. medicine Bowman Gray Sch. Medicine, Wake Forest Coll., 1948-50, asst. prof., 1950-52, asso. prof., 1952-53, now prof. medicine, chmn. dept. Founder's medalist, Vanderbilt U., 1943; Markle scholar med. sci., 1950-55; Distinguished Service award in medicine, U. Chgo., 1958. Fellow A.C.P.; mem. Phi Beta Kappa, Sigma Xi, Alpha Omega Alpha. Episcopalian. Home: 2800 Greenwich Rd Winston-Salem NC 27104

YOUNT, FLORENCE JANE, lawyer; b. Enid, Okla., Dec. 13, 1926; d. William Edward and Florence Evelyn (McCully) Y.; B.A., State U. Iowa, 1948; J.D., S. Tex. Coll. Law, 1958; certificate Parker Sch. Fgn. and Comparative Law, Columbia U., 1976. Admitted to Tex. bar, 1958; atty. Ginther, Warren & Co., Houston, 1959-70; supr. internat. contracts Eastern Hemisphere Petroleum div. Continental Oil Co., N.Y.C., Stamford, Conn., 1970-75; sr. atty. Cities Service Co., Houston, 1975—; adviser to Internat. Law Socs. of three Houston law schs.; bd. dirs. S. Tex. Law Jour., Inc., v.p., 1969, 77, pres., 1970, 78, 79. Bd. dirs. Park Ave. Christian Ch., N.Y.C., 1971-73, First Christian Ch., Houston, 1977—; active Vols. of Shelter, N.Y.C., 1973-75; precinct chmn., asso. legal counsel, chmn. rules com. Harris County (Tex.) Republican Com., 1958-68. Recipient Distinguished Alumnus award South Tex. Coll. Law, 1976, Houston Matrix award, 1978, award Bus. and Profl. Women's Club Houston, 1976; named One of 100 Top Corporate Women, Bus. Week, 1976. Mem. Am., Tex. (contbg. editor Internat. Law Newsletter), Houston bar assns., S. Tex. Coll. Law Alumni Assn. (dir. 1977—), Houston World Trade Assn., Zonta, Soc. Houston. Mem. Christian Ch. Contbr. articles to law jours. Office: Cities Service Co PO Box 642 Houston TX 77001

YOURGLICH, ANITA E., educator; b. Sacramento, Jan. 9, 1923; d. Joseph J. and Olga Yourglich; B.S., Seattle U., 1945; M.A., St. Louis U., 1948; Ph.D., U. Oreg., 1961. Lectr. St. Louis U., 1947-48; mem. faculty dept. sociology Seattle U., 1946-47, 48-54, asso. prof., 1954-61, prof., 1961—, also chmn. dept., 1966-72. Mem. Am., Am. Catholic, Pacific sociol. assns., Nat. Council Family Relations, A.A.U.P. Author 2 books. Contbr. profl. jours. Home: 1008 E Lynn St Seattle WA 98102 Office: 900 Broadway St Seattle WA 98122

YOUSE, HOWARD RAY, educator, biologist; b. Bryant, Ind., May 22, 1915; s. Lewis Oscar and Ethel Marie (Brown) Y.; A.B., Depauw U., 1937; M.S., Ore. State Coll., 1942; Ph.D., Purdue U., 1951; m. Ida Mae Barcus, June 16, 1942. Mem. faculty DePauw U., 1940—, prof. botany, 1955—, head dept. botany bacteriology, 1961—; spl. research pollen grains utilized by honey bees, germination of seeds. Served with USAAF, 1942-46. Mem. A.A.A.S., A.A.U.P. (pres. DePauw U. chpt. 1953), Bot. Soc. Am., Ind. Acad. Sci. (pres. 1969), Sigma Xi, Sigma Chi. Presbyn. Kiwanian (pres. Greencastle 1960). Home: 715 Terrace Lane Greencastle IN 46135

YOVICH, DANIEL JOHN, educator; b. Chgo., Mar. 5, 1930; s. Milan D. and Sophie (Dorociak) Y.; Ph.B., DePaul U., 1952; M.A., Governors State U., 1975; m. Anita Barbara Moreland, Feb. 7, 1959; children—Daniel, Amy, David, Julie Ann. Researcher, Montgomery Ward, Chgo., 1959-62; tech. dir. Riley Bros., Inc., Burlington, Iowa, 1962-66, J.W. Mortell Co., Kankakee, Ill., 1966-70; exec. dir. Dan Yovich Assos., Kankakee, Inc.; asst. prof. Purdue U., 1979—; instr. lectr. Napoleon Hill Acad., 1965-66; cons. Learning House, Inc., 1964—; producer, moderator program Careers Unlimited, WCIU-TV, Chgo., 1967—; instr. Kankakee Community Coll. Continuing Edn., 1976—; asso. Hill, Zediker & Assos. Psychologists, Kankakee, 1975—; dir. Kankakee County DWI Program; adv. Inst. for Addiction Studies. Served to 1st lt. AUS, 1952-56. Recipient Outstanding Citizen Award News Pub. Co. Am., 1971; cert. reality therapist. Mem. Sales and Marketing Execs., Am. Mgmt. Assn., Assn. Labor-Mgmt. Adminstrs. and Consultants on Alcoholism, Inst. for Reality Therapy, Assn. to Advance Ethical Hypnosis, Inst. Contemporary Living, Am. Legion, K.C. Patentee game Krypto, coating Sanitane. Home: 620 S Rosewood Kankakee IL 60901 Office: Purdue U (Calumet) 2233 171st St Hammond IN 46325

YOVICICH, GEORGE STEVEN JONES, civil engr.; b. Belgrade, Yugoslavia, June 2, 1927; s. Steven and Draginja (Djurdjevic) Y.; B.S. in Civil Engring., High Tech. Sch., Belgrade; M.S.C.E., U. Darmstadt (Germany), 1956; Ph.D. in Bus. and Adminstrn., U. Fla.; m. Sofija Sckulic, Feb. 3, 1960; 1 son, Steven. Civil engr. Hollabird & Root, Chgo., 1956-58; bridge engr. Div. Hwys. Ill. Dept. Transp., Chgo., 1958-70; v.p.-project mgr. Arcadia Internat. & Co., Skokie, Ill., 1956-70, chmn. bd., pres., 1970—. Prof. structural engring. Northwestern U.; prof. math. and structural engring. U. Ill. at Chgo. and Urbana. Legislative asst., mem. hwys. com., mem. traffic safety com., utilities com., r.r. and aviation com., welfare com. Ill. Ho. of Reps., 1970—. Bd. dirs. Oakton Community Coll., Skokie, Sch. Dist. #68, Skokie. Served to capt. AUS, 1954-56. Registered profl. engr., Ill. and other states. Mem. Am. Soc. C.E., Registered Profl. Engrs. Soc. Office: PO Box 712 Skokie IL 60026

YOVITS, MARSHALL CLINTON, educator; b. Bklyn., May 16, 1923; s. Louis Frederick and Rebecca (Gerber) Y.; B.S., Union Coll., Schenectady, 1944, M.S., 1948; M.S., Yale, 1949, Ph.D., 1951; m. Anita S. Friedman, Aug. 2, 1952; children—Bruce J., Mara F., Steven. Sr. physicist John Hopkins, 1951-56; physicist electronics br. Office Naval Research, Washington, 1956, head information systems br., 1956-62, dir. Naval Analysis Group, 1962-66; prof., chmn. dept. computer and information sci. Ohio State U., 1966-78, prof., 1978-79; prof. math. scis., dean Sch. of Sci., Ind. U., Purdue U., Indpls., 1980—; gen. chmn. Computer Sci. conf. NSF, 1973. AEC fellow, 1950-51; recipient Navy Superior Civilian Service award, 1964; Navy Outstanding Performance award, 1961. Mem. Am. Phys. Soc., IEEE, AAAS, Assn. Computing Machinery (mem. council), Am. Soc. for Engring. Edn., Sigma Xi. Editor: (with Scott Cameron) Self-Organizing Systems, Proc. Interdisciplinary Conference, 1960; Large-Capacity Memory Techniques for Computing Systems, 1961; (with George T. Jacobi, Gordon D. Goldstein) Self-Organizing Systems, 1962; (with D.M. Gilford, R.H. Wilcox, E. Staveley, H.D. Lerner) Research Program Effectiveness, 1966; Advances in Computers, Vol. 11, 1971; editor series (with Morris Rubinoff) Advances in Computers, Vols. 13-18. Author research articles. Home: 2679 Mitzi Dr Columbus OH 43209

YOWELL, GROVER MCCLELLAND, JR., naval officer; b. Paducah, Tex., Oct. 30, 1928; s. Grover McClelland and Mildred Blanche (Wilson) Y.; student Memphis State Coll., 1946-48; B.S.E.E., U.S. Naval Postgrad. Sch., Monterey, Calif., 1955, M.S.E.E., 1956; Ph.D., Stanford U., 1969; m. Billie Marie Gasperson, May 26, 1951; children—Gary Wayne, Brett David, Robert James. Commd. ensign, 1950, advanced through grades to rear adm., 1977; dir. programs Antisubmarine Warfare Systems Project Office, Washington, 1968-72; Navy plant rep. Lockheed, Burbank, Calif., 1972-74; comdr. Naval Air Devel. Center, Warminster, Pa., 1974-76; asst. comdr. for research and tech. Naval Air Systems Command, Washington, 1976-77; mgr. for Navy space and satellite programs Navy Space Project, Washington, 1977—. Decorated Legion of Merit. Mem. IEEE (sr.), Nat. Space Club (gov.). Office: Navy Space Project Dept of Navy Washington DC 20360

YOZWIAK, BERNARD JAMES, educator; b. Youngstown, Ohio, July 5, 1919; s. Walter J. and Anna (Baluch) Y.; A.B., Marietta Coll., 1940; M.S., U. Pitts., 1951, Ph.D., 1961; m. Helen A. Mika, Aug. 28, 1943; children—Ruth (Mrs. Charles W. Lewis), John B., Mark S., Bernard P. Office clk. Youngstown Sheet & Tube Co., 1940-41, 44-45; instr. math. and sci., prin. Fowler (Ohio) Twp. High Sch., 1941-42, 45-47; prof. math., chmn. math. dept. Youngstown State U., 1947—, dean Coll. Arts and Scis., 1971—. Recipient Watson Distinguished Prof. award, 1961; NSF sci. faculty fellow, 1958-60. Mem. Math. Assn. Am. (chmn. Ohio sect. 1970-71), AAAS, AAUP, Sigma Xi. Home: 2080 S Schenley Ave Youngstown OH 44511

YTTERBERG, CARL FREDERICK, floor co. exec.; b. Chgo., Dec. 9, 1896; s. Charles and Mary (Myren) Y.; student Northwestern U.; m. Ruth O. Nordquist, Sept. 10, 1921; children—Marcia Ruth, Robert Frederick. Dist. mgr. Kalman Floor Co., 1924-33, pres., 1933-67, chmn. bd., 1973-76; chmn. Kalman Floor Co. (Can.), Ltd., 1933-76; splty. indsl. floors, bldg. constrn. floors, concrete. Served with U.S. Army, World War I. Alliliate Am. Soc. C.E. Republican. Baptist. Club: Union League. Designer of machines in field. Home: 241 Hollywood Ave Crestwood NY 10707 Office: 190 E Post Rd White Plains NY 10601

YU, JASON CHIA-HSIN, civil engr., educator; b. Feb. 5, 1936; B.S. in Civil Engring., Nat. Taiwan U., 1961; M.S. in Civil Engring.-Transp., Ga. Inst. Tech., 1964; postgrad. (Univ. fellow), U. Pa., 1967-68, 73; Ph.D. in Civil Engring.-Transp. Systems, W.Va. U., 1968; postgrad. Mass. Inst. Tech., summer, 1973; married; 2 children. Grad. research asst. civil engring. Ga. Inst. Tech., 1963-64; traffic engr. W.Va. Dept. Hwys., Charleston, 1964-65; grad. research asst. W.Va. U., 1965-66, research asso., 1966-67; sr. research specialist Inst. Direct Energy Conversion, U. Pa., lectr. dept. civil and urban engring., 1967-68; asst. prof. civil engring. Va. Poly. Inst. and State U., 1968-71, asso. prof., head div. transp., 1971-74; prof., dir. Transp. Research Center, U. Utah, 1974—; lectr., speaker in field; vis. prof. Nat. Taiwan U., Taipei, 1976-77. Chmn. subcom. on roadside markings com. traffic control devices NRC, also mem. operational effects of geometrics com., transp. systems planning group, subcom. intersect. capacity com. hwy. capacity and quality of service, com. parking and terminals Transp. Research Bd.; cons. Transp. & Systems Engring., Inc., Tech. Ops., Inc., Alexander-John Assos., Century Research Cooperation, Bush & Gudgell Inc. Registered profl. engr., Utah, W.Va. Mem. ASCE (editorial bd. div. air transport), Inst. Traffic Engrs., Sigma Xi. Editor Proceedings Hwy. Safety Conf. HUD, 1970, Proceedings Modern Engring. and Tech., Chinese Inst. Engrs., 1972; tech. editor external transp. systems group Internat. Joint Com. on Tall Bldgs.; paper referee coms. Transp. Research Record. Contbr. numerous articles to profl. jours. Developed, implemented Master's and Doctoral degree programs at U. Utah, Va. Poly. Inst. and State U. Office: Dept Civil Engring and Transp Research Center Coll of Engring U of Utah Salt Lake City UT 84112

YU, PAUL NANGAN, physician, educator; b. Kiangsi, China, Nov. 7, 1915; s. Y.S. and L.H. (Yang) Y.; M.D., Nat. Med. Coll., Shanghai, China, 1939; m. Iling Tang, June 4, 1944; children—Pauline R., Diane C., Lorraine M., Corrine M. Came to U.S., 1947, naturalized, 1952. Intern First Red Cross Hosp., Shanghai, 1938-39; asst. and chief resident in medicine Central Hosp., Chungking, China, 1940-43; asst. resident in medicine Strong Meml. Hosp., Rochester, N.Y., 1947-48; practice medicine specializing in cardiology, Rochester, 1952—; asst. prof. medicine U. Rochester Med. Sch., 1954-59, asso. prof., 1959-63, prof., 1963-69, Sarah McCort Ward prof., 1969—; head cardiology unit U. Rochester Med. Center and Strong Meml. Hosp., Rochester, 1957—. Brit. Council scholar U.K. Mem. Assn. Am. Physicians, Am. Clin. and Climatol. Assn., Assn. U. Cardiologists, Am. Coll. Cardiology, A.C.P., Am. Physiol. Soc., Am. Heart Assn. (pres. 1972-73), Sigma Xi, Alpha Omega Alpha. Author: Pulmonary Blood Volume in Health and Disease. Editor: (with J.F. Goodwin) Progress in Cardiology, 1972—; Modern Concepts of Cardiovascular Disease, 1976-78. Home: 651 Claybourne Rd Rochester NY 14618

YUAN SHAO WEN, educator; b. Shanghai, China, Apr. 16, 1914; s. Ti An and Chieh-huang (Chien) Y.; came to U.S., 1934, naturalized, 1954; B.S., U. Mich., 1936; M.E., Stanford, 1939; M.S., Cal. Inst. Tech., 1937, Ph.D., 1941; m. Hui Chih Hu, Nov. 5, 1950. Research engr. Glenn Martin Co., 1942-43; chief of research Helicopter div. McDonnell Aircraft Corp., 1943-45; adj. prof. Poly. Inst. Bklyn., 1946-49, asso. prof., 1949-54, prof., 1954-57; prof. aerospace engring. U. Tex., 1958-68; prof., chmn. mech. engring. div. George Washington U., 1968—, chmn. civil, mech. and environ. dept., 1973—; pres. RISE, Inc., 1977—; cons. Edo Aircraft Corp., Aerojet Corp., Cornell Aero. Lab., Dept. of Interior, Oak Ridge Nat. Lab., N.Am., Aviation, Inc., Fairchild-Hiller Corp. Hon. adviser Nat. Center Research of China, Taiwan. Named Outstanding Educator of Am., 1970. Canadair Chair prof. Universite Laval, 1957-58. Fellow A.A.A.S., Am. Inst. Aeros. and Astronautics; mem. ASME, Am. Soc. Engring. Edn., Soc. Engring. Sci. (dir. 1973—, pres. 1977), Sigma Xi, Phi Kappa Phi, Phi Tau Phi, Sigma Gamma Tau, Tau Beta Pi. Author: Foundations of Fluid Mechanics, 1967. Contbr. to High Speed Aerodynamics and Jet Propulsion series, 1959. Patentee in field. Home: 6701 Montour Dr Falls Church VA 22043 Office: 725 23d St Washington DC 20052

YUDASHKIN, ERNEST GORDON, psychiatrist; b. Toronto, Ont., Can., Feb. 26, 1922; s. Nathan and Jennie (Schwartz) Y.; M.D., U. Toronto, 1946; student Am. Inst. Psychoanalysis, 1950-57; m. Ella Oxley, Mar. 11, 1947; children—Nora, Myrlin, Kathryn, Robert; m. 2d, Elaine Constance MacNicol, Dec. 31, 1968. Came to U.S., 1947, naturalized, 1952. Intern, St. Joseph's Hosp., London, Ont., 1946-47; psychiat. resident Central Islip (N.Y.) Hosp., 1947-50, supervising psychiatrist, 1950-54; founder, dir. Bklyn. Aftercare Clinic, 1954-59; charge Queens (N.Y.) Aftercare Clinic, 1959-60; founder, dir. Psychiat. Cons. Clinic, Mineola, N.Y., 1961-66; dir. Family Ct. Clinic, Westbury, N.Y., 1963-66; med. supt. Northville (Mich.) State Hosp., 1966-68; asst. dir. Mich. Dept. Mental Health, 1968-70, dir., 1970-74; regional dir. N.Y. State Dept. Mental Hygiene, Rochester, 1974-78; dep. dir. clin. Monroe Devel. Center, 1978—; lectr. Sch. Social Work, Adelphi Coll., 1961-65; clin. instr. N.Y. Sch. Psychiatry, 1962-65; asso. clin. prof. Mich. State U., 1969-70; vis. lectr. U. Mich., 1969—; clin. asso. prof. psychiatry U. Rochester. Served with Canadian Army, 1944-46. Diplomate Am. Bd. Psychiatry, 1957. Fellow Am. Psychiat. Assn. Cons. editor Community Mental Health Jour. Home: 4375 W Lake Rd Canandaigua NY 14424 Office: 620 Westfall Rd Rochester NY 14620

YUE, ALFRED SHUI-CHOH, educator; b. China, Nov. 12, 1920; s. Choy Noon-woo and Sze Man-hun (Tom) Y.; B.S., Chao-tung U., 1942; M.S., Ill. Inst. Tech., 1950; Ph.D., Purdue U., 1956; m. Virginia Chin-wen Tang, May 21, 1944; children—Mary, Raymond Yuan, John, David. Asso. engr. Taiwan Aluminum Co., 1942-47; instr. Purdue U., 1952-56; research engr. Dow Chem. Co., Midland, Mich., 1956-62; sr. mem. Lockheed, Palo Alto Research Lab., 1962-69, now cons.; prof. engring. and applied sci. U. Calif., Los Angeles, 1969—; cons. LTV Aerospace Co., Lockheed Missile & Space Co. Sec. gen. Chinese Culture Assn. in U.S.A., 1967, also bd. dirs. Chinese scholar to U.S.A. Assn. fellow AIAA, N.Y. Acad. Scis.; mem. Am. Soc. Metals, Am. Inst. Mining and Metall. Engrs., AAAS, Sigma Xi, Sigma Pi Sigma, Tau Beta Pi. Home: 2583 Cordelia Rd Los Angeles CA 90049 Office: 405 Hilgard Ave Los Angeles CA 90024

YUELYS, ALEXANDER, cosmetics co. exec.; b. Bronx, N.Y., Aug. 12, 1926; s. Dionisyus and Anastasia (Stathes) Y.; B.A., Hunter Coll., 1950; m. Nicoletta Lardas, Dec. 9, 1950; 1 son, Jordan. With Arthur Young, 1952-56, Haskins & Sells, 1950-52; with Fabergé, Inc., N.Y.C., 1956—, exec. v.p., chief fin. officer, dir.; dir. Brut Prodns., Inc. Served with USAAF, 1945-46. C.P.A., N.Y. Mem. Fin. Execs. Inst., Nat. Assn. Accountants. Home: Box 885 Alpine NJ 07620 Office: 1345 Ave of Americas New York City NY 10019

YUKER, HAROLD ELWOOD, psychologist, educator; b. Newark, N.J., Apr. 15, 1924; s. Hyman and Sadie (Glucksman) Y.; B.A., U. Newark, 1944; M.A., Sch. Social Research, 1950; Ph.D., N.Y. U., 1954. Research asst. Columbia U. Bur. Applied Social Research, 1947-48; mem. faculty dept. psychology Hofstra U., Hempstead, N.Y., 1948—, prof., 1964—, dir. Center for Study of Higher Edn., 1965-75, interim provost, 1973-74, provost, dean of faculties, 1976—; dir. research Human Resources Found., 1956-63, research cons., 1963—. Mem. Am. Psychol. Assn., Eastern Psychol. Assn., Soc. for Study of Social Issues, AAAS. Author: A Guide to Statistical Calculations, 1958; The Measurement of Attitudes Toward Disabled Persons, 1966. Contbr. articles to profl. jours. Home: 1872 Decatur Ave North Bellmore NY 11710 Office: Hofstra Univ Hempstead NY 11550

YUNCKER, BARBARA, science writer; b. Greencastle, Ind.; d. Truman George and Ethel (Claflin) Yuncker; A.B., DePauw U., D.Litt., 1976. Copyreader, Wall St. Jour.; various editing positions N.Y. Post; asst. dep. commnr. commerce, N.Y. State, 1956-57; medicine and sci. editor N.Y. Post, 1959—; med. columnist Good Housekeeping mag., 1963-76. Recipient Page One award Newspaper Guild N.Y., 1961; Adolf Meyer award, 1961; Alumni citation DePauw U., 1963; Page One award Newspaper Women's Club N.Y., 1963, 68; Albert Lasker med. journalism award, 1967, 69; Am. Psychiat. Assn. award, 1974; Silurians award, 1975; Matrix award Women in Communications, 1979. Mem. Newspaper Guild N.Y. (exec. com. 1976—, chmn. N.Y. Post unit 1976—), Nat. Assn. Sci.

Writers, Soc. Journalists and Authors. Democrat. Contbr. to nat. mags. Office: 210 South St New York NY 10002

YUND, RICHARD ALLEN, educator, mineralogist; b. Marion County, Ill., Dec. 14, 1933; s. Oscar Peter and Nola Mae (Landsford) Y.; B.Sc., U. Ill., 1956, Ph.D., 1960; m. Virginia Lee Smith, June 7, 1957; children—Philip Owen, Susan Elise. Postdoctoral research fellow Carnegie Instn., Washington, 1960-61; mem. faculty Brown U., 1961—, prof. mineralogy, 1968—; vis. prof. Monash U., Melbourne, Australia, 1974. NSF grad. fellow, 1957-59; Fulbright sr. research fellow, 1973-74; research grantee, 1961—; Sr. Scientist award West German Govt., 1978. Mem. Mineral. Soc. Am., Geochem. Soc., A.A.A.S., Am. Geophys. Union. Contbr. articles to profl. jours., chpts. to books. Co-editor: Geochem. Transport and Kinetics, 1974. Home: 57 University Ave Providence RI 02906. *Success in science, as in most areas, requires some original ideas, but it depends on hard work and perserverance. Those who are successful rarely achieve their goals although they continue to try; whereas those who are less successful may achieve their goals because they were set at too low a level. It should be recognized that the only meaningful definition and evaluation of success is by the individual, not by society.*

YUNG, VICTOR SEN, actor; b. San Francisco, Oct, 18, 1915; s. Sen Gam and Bow Soy (Chan) Y.; A.B., U. Calif., Berkeley, 1937; student Lipson Sch. Costume Design, 1946-47; grad. USAAF Statis. Sch., 1944, Harvard Sch. Bus. Adminstrn., 1944; 1 son, Brent Kee. Actor, #2 Son, Charlie Chan series, 1938-49, Hop Sing, Bonanza TV series, 1958-73, Cousin Charlie, Bachelor Father series, 1950-55; character roles in over 300 motion picture, TV roles, 1936—; product mgr. Chinese Frozen Food Co., 1947-49; promoter food products, 1953-74; pres. Sen Yung Corp., 1975—. Served to capt. USAAF, 1943-47. Mem. Screen Actors Guild, AFTRA, Actors Equity. Democrat. Baptist. Author: Great Wok Cookbook, 1974.

YUNICH, DAVID LAWRENCE, consumer goods cons.; b. Albany, N.Y., May 21, 1917; s. Max A. and Bess (Felman) Y.; A.B., Union Coll., 1939, LL.D., 1964; postgrad. Harvard Grad. Sch. Bus. Adminstrn., 1939-40; m. Beverly F. Blickman, June 11, 1941; children—Robert Hardle, Peter B. Mdse. councilor L. Bamberger & Co., Newark, 1947-48, pres., dir., 1955-62; v.p. Macy's N.Y., 1941-51, sr. v.p., 1951-62, pres., 1962-71; vice chmn. bd. R. H. Macy & Co. Inc., 1971-73, dir., 1958-73; chmn. Met. Transp. Authority, 1974-1977; dir. Prudential Ins. Co. Am., N.Y. Telephone Co., J. Walter Thompson Co., W. R. Grace & Co., E. River Savs. Bank, U.S. Industries, Inc., Fidelity Group of Mut. Funds, Perdue Farms, Inc., The Harwood Cos., Inc., Mfrs. Hanover Trust Co., Inc., 1968-73. Chmn., Mayor's Council Econ. and Bus. Advisers, N.Y.C., 1973-74; mem. N.Y. State Banking Bd., 1968-74; dir. Regional Plan Assn.; chmn. Gov.'s Commn. Financing Mass Transp., 1970-72; pres. Greater N.Y. council Boy Scouts Am. 1972-1976; trustee Union Coll., 1965-72, Skidmore Coll. 1966-73, Albany Med. Coll. 1967-74, Carnegie Hall Corp., Saratoga Performing Arts; bd. dirs. Ednl. Broadcasting Corp., 1960-68, Nat. Jewish Hosp. Denver; bd. govs., trustee Rutgers U., New Brunswick, N.J., 1958-62. Decorated chevalier confrerie de Chevaliers du Tastevin. Mem. N.Y. Chamber Commerce and Industry (chmn. bd. 1971-74), Retail Dry Goods Assn. (pres. 1964-69), Am. Public Transp. Assn. (v.p.), Nat. Retail Mchts. Assn. (dir.), Am. Mgmt. Assn. (dir. 1958-68). Clubs: Harvard Bus. Sch., Harvard, Recess, Univ., Econ. (N.Y.C.); Blind Brook, Scarsdale (Westchester); Saratoga Golf and Polo (Saratoga Springs, N.Y.); Sandy Lane Golf (Barbados, W.I.). Home: Five Birches Cooper Rd Scarsdale NY 10583 Office: 1114 Ave of Americas New York NY 10036

YUNIS, ADEL ASSAD, physician, educator; b. Lebanon, Mar. 17, 1930; s. Assad Makool and Menache Nicholas (Khouri) Y.; B.A., Am. U. Beirut, 1950, M.D., 1954; m. Wilma J. Fuller, Aug. 1, 1959; children—Susan, Michael, Karen. Came to U.S., 1956, naturalized, 1964. Intern, asst. resident Am. U. Hosp., Beirut, 1954-56; resident Barnes Hosp., St. Louis, 1956-57; practice medicine specializing in hematology, Miami, Fla., 1964—; chief hematology Jackson Meml. Hosp., Miami, 1965—; asst. prof. medicine Washington U., St. Louis, 1963-64; asst. prof. medicine, dir. hematology research U. Miami, 1964-65, dir. div. hematology, 1965—, asso. prof. medicine, 1965-68, prof. medicine and biochemistry, dir. Howard Hughes labs. for hematology research, 1968—. Leukemia scholar, 1961-66; recipient Research Career Devel. award USPHS, 1967-68; Howard Hughes investigator, 1968—. Mem. Am. Soc. Clin. Investigation, Am. Soc. Hematology, Am. Soc. Biol. Chemists, Assn. Am. Physicians, A.C.P. Home: 11415 Nogales St Coral Gables FL 33156 Office: 1550 NW 10th Ave Miami FL 33136

YUNIS, EDMOND JOSE, pathologist; b. Sincelejo, Colombia, Aug. 8, 1929; came to U.S., 1954, naturalized, 1964; s. Joseph Jorge and Victoria Maria (Turbay) Y.; M.D., Colegio Nacional de San Bartolome, Bogota, Colombia, 1946; M.S., Universidad Nacional de Colombia, Bogota, 1954; m. Borghild Yunis, Sept. 11, 1965; children—Maria, David, Joseph, Christian. Intern, Hotel Dieu, New Orleans, 1954-55; resident Kans. U. Med. Center, 1955-57; resident U. Minn. Hosps., 1957-59, instr. dept. lab. medicine and pathology, 1960-63, asst. dir. blood bank, 1960-61, dir. blood bank, 1961-68, asso. prof., dir. div. immunology, 1968-76, prof. dept. lab. medicine and pathology, 1971-76; resident Children's Med. Center, Boston, 1959-60; prof. pathology Harvard U. Med. Sch., Boston, 1976—; dir. HLA Lab., N.E. region ARC, Boston, 1976—; scientist, chief div. immunogenetics Sidney Farber Cancer Inst., Boston, 1976—. Diplomate Am. Bd. Pathology. Mem. Am. Assn. Blood Banks, Internat. Histocompatibility Workshops, Am. Assn. Immunologists, Am. Assn. Pathologists, Am. Soc. Exptl. Pathology, Transplantation Soc., Am. Assn. Clin. Histocompatibility Testing, Sigma Xi. Author: Tissue Typing and Organ Transplantation, 1973; Manual of Clinical Immunology, 1976; Comprehensive Immunology and Aging, 1977; contbr. articles to profl. jours., chpts. to books. Office: 44 Binney St Boston MA 02115

YUNKERS, ADJA, artist; b. Riga, Latvia, July 15, 1900; s. Karland Adeline (Stahl) Y.; student Leningrad Art Sch., 1914-15, Hamburger Kunstgewerbe Schule, 1920-22; m. Kerstin Bergstrom, Feb. 24, 1946 (div.); m. 2d, Dore Ashton, July 8, 1952; children—Alexandra Louise, Marina. Came to U.S., 1947, naturalized, 1953. One-man shows Gallery Maria Kunde, Hamburg, Germany, 1920, Dresden, Germany, 1924, Copenhagen, Denmark, 1946, Oslo, Norway, 1946, Stockholm, Sweden, 1945-47, New Sch. Social Research, N.Y., 1946, Whitney Mus. Am. Art, 1972, Mass. Inst. Tech., 1973, other large museums U.S.; tchr. cutting and printing wood blocks in color New Sch. Social Research, 1947—, also Parsons Sch. Design; instr. Barnard Coll., N.Y.C.; represented in collections in Germany, Sweden, Norway, Belgium, Holland, France, Switzerland, Italy, N.Y. Pub. Library, Mus. Modern Art. Met. Mus., Bklyn. Mus., Boston Mus. Fine Arts, Fogg Mus., Balt. Mus. Art, others; former teaching staff Cooper Union, N.Y.C.; tchr., guest critic in painting Columbia, 1967—; mural commn. Syracuse U., 1967; tapestry commn. Stony Brook U., L.I., N.Y. Guggenheim fellow, 1949-50, 54-55; Ford Found. grantee, 1959-60. Recipient Bronze medal Chgo. Art Inst., 1961; Gold medal 2d Norwegian Internat. Print Biennale, Fredrikstad, 1974. Editor, pub. art mag. Creation (Stockholm), 1942-43, Ars, 1942-44, Ars Konstserie, 1944-46, Blanco, 1974. Address: 821 Broadway New York NY 10003

YURCHENCO, HENRIETTA WEISS, ethnomusicologist, writer; b. New Haven, Mar. 22, 1916; d. Edward and Rebecca (Bernblum) Weiss; student Yale, 1935-36; piano scholarship Mannes Coll. Music, 1936-38; m. Basil Yurchenco, June 1936 (div. 1955); 1 son, Peter; m. 2d, Irving Levine, 1965 (dir. 1979). Radio producer WNYC, WBAI, others, 1939-69; research in folk music for Library of Congress, Mexico, Guatemala, Puerto Rico, Spain, Morocco, Balearic Islands, John's Island, S.C., Ireland, 1941—; writer, critic, tchr. Mexican and Guatemalan Depts. Edn., 1958—; folk music editor Am. Record Guide and Musical Am., 1959-70; prof. music Coll. City N.Y., 1962—, Bklyn. Coll., 1966-69, New Sch. for Social Research, 1961-68. Recipient grants-in-aid Am. Philos. Soc., 1954, 56, 57, 65, 67, City U. N.Y., 1970. Mem. N.Y. Folklore Soc., Internat. Folk Music Council, Soc. Ethnomusicology, Soc. Asian Music, Am. Folklore Soc. Author: A Fiesta of Folk Songs From Spain and Latin America, 1967; A. Mighty Hard Road: A Biography of Woody Guthrie, 1970; !Habiamos! Puerto Ricans Speak, 1971. Contbr. articles profl. jours.; field recs. from Mexico, P.R., John's Island, S.C., Guatemala, Ecuador, others. Home: 360 W 22d St New York NY 10011 Office: 139th St and Convent Ave New York NY 10031

YUSPEH, SONIA ELIZABETH, advt. exec.; b. Syracuse, Feb. 1, 1928; d. Fareed B. and Nancy (Mandour) NeJame; B.A., Syracuse U., 1951; M.A., Cornell U., 1953; m. Michel H. Yuspeh, Nov. 2, 1955; children—Leonid, Denise. Sr. project dir. Audits & Surveys, N.Y.C., 1954-56; group head Grey Advt., N.Y.C., 1956-60; sr. project dir. McCann-Erickson Advt., N.Y.C., 1960-62; asso. research Dir., Grey Advt., 1962-67; market research dir. D'Arcy Advt., N.Y.C., 1967-69; exec. research dir. Grey Advt., 1969-72; sr. v.p. in charge of research and planning J. Walter Thompson, N.Y.C., 1972—. Mem. Common Cause, UN Assn.-USA, Friends of Earth. Mem. Am. Mktg. Assn., Advt. Research Found., Mktg. Research Council, Advt. Research Council, Phi Beta Kappa. Contbr. articles to mktg. jours. Home: 390 West End Ave New York City NY 10024 Office: 420 Lexington Ave New York City NY 10017

YUST, HAROLD ROBERT, entomologist, agrl. devel. adminstr.; b. Ingalls, Kans., Oct. 8, 1906; s. Edward Phillip and Louise Fredricka (Springer) Y.; A.B., Asbury Coll., 1929; M.S., N.C. State U., 1930; postgrad. U. So. Calif.; m. Carolyn Christeve Henson, June 9, 1935. Research entomologist Dept. Agr., Whittier, Calif., 1930-43, 46-52; research entomologist ICA, Ecuador, 1952-54, chief of specialists, 1954-56, dir. Plan Azuay-Canar, area devel. project So. Ecuador, Cuenca, for U.S. and Ecuadorian govts., 1956-58; dep. dir. Point IV Agrl. Program, acting chief agrl. field party in Peru for ICA, 1958-60; dep. food and agr. dir. ICA mission in Sudan, 1961-68; cons., 1968—. Served from lt. (j.g.) to lt. comdr. USNR, 1943-46. Decorated Medala de Oro (Ecuador). Fellow AAAS; mem. Am. Registry Profl. Entomologists, Entomol. Soc. Am. Contbr. articles to profl. jours. Home: 8820 Parkland Dr El Paso TX 79925

YVES, MARTIN, univ. ofcl.; b. Lachine, Que., Can., Nov. 22, 1929; s. Martin and Decary (Jose) Hector; B.A., U. Montreal, 1949; M.A., U. Laval, Que., 1954; m. Louise Chouinard, May 22, 1954; children—Claire, Catherine, Anne-Marie, Pierre, Laurent, Paul. Prof. sociology U. Laval, Que., 1956-64; dir. planning Que. Dept. Edn., Quebec, 1964-66, asst. dep. minster, 1966-69, dep. minister, 1969-73; pres., dir.-gen. Regie Assurance Maladie, Quebec, 1973-75; rector U. Sherbrooke, Que., 1975—. Editor: (with Marcel Rioux) French Canadian Society, 1964. Contbr. articles to profl. publs. Home: 975 Dominion St Sherbrooke PQ J1H 1C4 Canada Office: U Sherbrooke Cite Universitaire Blvd de Universite Sherbrooke PQ J1K 2R1 Canada

YZAGUIRRE, RAUL HUMBERTO, civil rights adminstr.; b. San Juan, Tex., July 22, 1939; s. Ruben Antonio and Eva Linda (Morin) Y.; student U. Md., 1963-64; B.S., George Washington U., 1968; m. Audrey H. Bristow, June 2, 1965; children—Regina Dolores, Raul Humberto, Elisa Almalinda, Roberto Hayse, Rebecca Morin. Student and community activist, 1963-65; active War on Poverty, 1969-74; founder, exec. dir. Hispanic cons. firm, Washington, 1969-73; v.p. Center for Community Change, Washington, 1974; community organizer in S.Tex., 1974; pres. Nat. Council of La Raza, Washington, 1974—; lectr. Harvard U., U. Notre Dame, U. Tex., others. Co-chmn. Nat. Urban Coalition, 1975—; co-chmn. Working Com. on Concerns of Hispanics and Blacks, 1979—; sec., chmn. Forum of Nat. Hispanic Orgns., 1976-79; chmn. adv. com. I.N.S.; trustee Common Cause. Served with USAF, 1959-62. Registered med. technologist. Mem. Internat. Soc. for Clin. Lab. Tech., ACLU, Am. GI Forum. Democrat. Roman Catholic. Editor-in-chief Agenda, 1974—. Home: Route 5 Box 7 Twin Arch Rd Mount Airy MD 21771 Office: 1725 Eye St NW Washington DC 20006. *The civil rights struggle of the 80's will be the transformation of America to a truly pluralistic society where cultural differences will not only be tolerated, but indeed valued.*

ZABAN, ERWIN, diversified mfg. exec.; b. Atlanta, Aug. 17, 1921; s. Mandle and Sara Unis (Feidelson) Z.; grad. high sch.; m. Doris Reisman, Aug. 17, 1941; children—Carol (Mrs. Larry Cooper), Laura (Mrs. Marshall Dinerman), Sara Kay. Officer, Zep Mfg. Co., 1942-62; exec. v.p. Nat. Service Industries, Atlanta, 1962-66, pres., 1966-79, chief exec. officer, 1972—, chmn., 1977—, also dir. Served with AUS, 1941-42. Clubs: Progressive, Standard. Home: 3374 Old Plantation Rd Atlanta GA 30327 Office: Nat Service Industries Inc 1180 Peachtree St Atlanta GA 30309*

ZABEL, EDWARD, economist; b. Orange, N.J., Oct. 17, 1927; s. Otto and Helen (Katzenberger) Z.; B.A., Syracuse (N.Y.) U., 1950; M.A., Princeton U., 1953, Ph.D., 1956; m. Norma Nicholson, June 23, 1956; children—Jeffrey, David, Richard. Research asst. Princeton U., 1954-56; economist Rand Corp., Santa Monica, Calif., 1956-58; mem. faculty U. Rochester (N.Y.), 1958—, prof. economics, 1967—; asso. editor Mgmt. Sci., 1969-73; bd. editors Applied Econs., 1973—. Served with AUS, 1945-47. Ford Found. fellow, 1964-65; NSF grantee, 1960-74, 79—. Mem. Am. Econ. Assn., Econometric Soc., Inst. Mgmt. Scis., AAUP, Phi Beta Kappa. Democrat. Contbr. to profl. jours. Home: 116 Seminole Way Rochester NY 14618 Office: Dept Econs Univ Rochester Rochester NY 14627

ZABEL, ROBERT ALGER, educator, scientist; b. Boyceville, Wis., Mar. 11, 1917; s. William Rudolph and Grace Freedom (Leonard) Z.; B.S., U. Minn., 1938, postgrad. 1939-41; M.S., N.Y. State U. Coll. Forestry, Syracuse, 1943, Ph.D., 1947; m. Norma Livingston Hallock, July 22, 1944; children—Virginia Ellen, Margaret Anne, Grace Marilyn, John William, Robert Alger. Teaching fellow botany N.Y. State U. Coll. Forestry, 1940-42, 46-47, forest pathologist N.E. Expt. Sta., 1957, asst. prof. forest pathology, 1947-52, asso. prof., 1953-55, head dept. botany, pathology, 1955—, asso. dean biol. scis., undergrad. instrn., 1964—, asso. dean instrn. and biol. scis., 1965-70, v.p. acad. affairs, 1970—, prof., Cem. com. adv. bd. Army Research and Devel., NRC; wood technologist USAAF, 1942-43. Served to capt. USMCR, 1943-46. Fellow Soc. Am. Foresters; mem. Forest Products Research Soc., Soc. Am. Microbiology, Am. Inst. Biol. Scis., A.A.A.S., Am. Phytopath. Soc., Sigma Xi, Alpha Zeta, Gamma Sigma Delta. Contbr. articles to profl. publs. Home: 4563 Broad Rd Syracuse NY 13215

ZABEL, ROBERT PAUL, advt. exec.; b. Abington, Pa., July 20, 1928; s. Paul and Ethel (Neuschaefer) Z.; A.B., Princeton U., 1952; m. Joan Cohee, Apr. 16, 1955; children—Nancy, Susan, Robert Paul. With N.W. Ayer & Sons, Inc., Phila., 1952—, exec. v.p., dir., Chgo., 1969-74, pres., 1974—; mem. bd. dirs. Midwest council Am. Assn. Advt. Agys. Bd. dirs. N.Y. council Boy Scouts Am. Served with USMCR, 1946-48. Mem. Nat. Alliance Businessmen (dir. N.Y.). Clubs: Mid-Am., Tavern (Chgo.); Indian Hill (Winnetka); Cap and Gown (Princeton); Round Hill (Greenwich, Conn.); Pine Valley Golf. Office: 1 Illinois Center Chicago IL 60601

ZABKA, STANLEY WILLIAM, composer, dir.; b. Des Moines, Nov. 6, 1924; s. Frank and Marie Geraldine (Buresh) Z.; ed. Ill. U., Northwestern U.; B.A. (Eugene C. Pulliam scholar), De Pauw U., 1949; m. Nancy Heimert, Aug. 2, 1964; children—William Michael, Judith Marie, Guy Mathew. News chief Am. Forces Network, Frankfurt, Germany, 1951-53; asso. dir. to dir. NBC-TV, N.Y.C., 1954-74, Los Angeles, 1975. Pres. Big Island Music Inc., Palladium Record Co. Served with AUS, World War II, Korean War. Decorated Bronze Star with oak leaf cluster. Mem. Nat. Assn. TV Arts, Scis., Am. Guild Authors, Composers, Dirs. Guild Am., A.S.C.A.P. (3 writing awards), Sigma Nu. Republican. Composer maj. TV themes, including: Tornado, Xenia, Ohio (Peabody and Christopher awards); recs. include album: Zabka's Themes from Television. Address: 5723 Star Ln Woodland Hills CA 91367

ZABLOCKI, CLEMENT JOHN, congressman; b. Milw., Nov. 18, 1912; s. Mathew and Mary (Jankowski) Z.; Ph.B., Marquette U., 1936, LL.D. (hon.), 1966; LL.D. (hon.), Alverno Coll., 1969, Sogang U., Seoul, Korea, 1974, Jagiellonian U., Cracow, Poland, 1975, U. Notre Dame, 1979; m. Blanche Janic, May 26, 1937 (dec. July 1977); children—Joseph, Jane. High sch. tchr., 1938-39; organist, choir dir., 1932-48; state senator 3d dist., Wis., 1942-48; mem. 81st-96th Congresses, 4th Dist. Wis.; chmn. fgn. affairs com., chmn. subcom. on internat. security and sci. affairs; mem. spl. congl. study mission to West Europe, 1951, South Asia and Far East, 1953, Near, Middle and Far East, Southeast Asia and Pacific, 1955; chmn. spl. study mission to Poland, 1963, Southeast Asia and Pacific, 1963, Far East, Southeast Asia, India, Pakistan, 1965; chmn. Congl. delegation to Poland, 1965; Congl. mem. mission to People's Republic of China, 1974; Congl. adviser UN World Food Conf., Rome, 1974. U.S. del. UN 14th Gen. Assembly, 1959; Congl. adviser U.S. delegation Commn. on Disarmament, 1971-74; mem. Commn. on Orgn. Govt. for Conduct Fgn. Policy; del. Mutual Balance Force Reduction Conf., Vienna, Austria, 1974; mem. Japan-Am. Friendship Commn. Mem. adv. bd. Georgetown U. Center Strategic Studies. Named Alumnus of Yr., Marquette U., 1979. Mem. Cath. Order of Foresters, St. Vincent Conf., Polish Nat. Alliance, Polish Am. Fedn., Polish Assn. Am., Polish Roman Cath. Union, Milw. Musicians Assn., Holy Name Soc. Democrat. Roman Catholic. Clubs: K.C., Eagles, Elks. Office: 2183 Rayburn Office Bldg Washington DC 20515

ZACHARIAS, DONALD WAYNE, univ. pres.; b. Salem, Ind., Sept. 28, 1935; s. William Otto and Estelle Mae (Newlon) Z.; B.A., Georgetown (Ky.) Coll., 1957; M.A., Ind. U., 1959, Ph.D., 1963; m. Tommie Kline Dekle, Aug. 16, 1959; children—Alan, Eric, Leslie. Asst. prof. communication and theatre Ind. U., 1963-69; asso. prof. U. Tex., Austin, 1969-72, prof., 1972-79, asst. to pres., 1974-77; exec. asst. to chancellor U. Tex. System, 1978-79; pres. Western Ky. U., 1979—; cons. to savs. and loan leagues. Bd. dirs. Little League, Austin, Tex., 1977-78. Served with U.S. Army, 1959-60. Recipient Teaching award Ind. U. Found., 1963, Cactus Teaching award U. Tex., 1971. Mem. Speech Communication Assn., Internat. Communication Assn., Am. Assn. Higher Edn., Phi Kappa Phi (Pres. 1978). Democrat. Episcopalian. Author: In Pursuit of Peace: Speeches of the Sixties, 1970. Office: Office of Pres Western Ky U Bowling Green KY 42101

ZACHARIAS, JOHN ELLING, chem. co. exec.; b. Connellsville, Pa., Sept. 8, 1915; s. Johannes M. and Louise M. (Elling) Z.; A.B., Princeton, 1936; student Grad. Sch. Bus. Adminstrn., N.Y. U., 1937-38, Law Sch., 1939-40; m. Muriel C. Eckes, Sept. 21, 1946; children—Jane E., Thomas E. Estate adminstrn. U.S. Trust Co. of N.Y. 1936-43; prodn. mgr. Whitehall Pharm. Co., 1946-48; dir. operations Jamieson Pharm. Co., 1948-51; with McKesson & Robbins, Inc. (co. name now Foremost-McKesson, Inc.), N.Y.C., 1952-77, v.p., 1956—; pres. Cord Assos., Ltd., 1978—. Served with USNR, 1943-46. Clubs: Princeton (N.Y.C.); Wilton Riding; Woodstock (Vt.) Country. Home: Ridgefield Rd Wilton CT 06897 Office: Box 341 Wilton CT 06897

ZACHARIASEN, FREDRIK, educator, physicist; b. Chgo., June 14, 1931; s. William Houlder and Ragni (Durban-Hansen) Z.; B.S., U. Chgo., 1951; Ph.D., Calif. Inst. Tech., 1956; m. Nancy J. Walker, Jan. 27, 1957; children—Kerry Ellen, Judith Ann. Instr. Mass. Inst. Tech., 1956-57; asst. prof. Stanford, 1958-60; mem. faculty Calif. Inst. Tech., Pasadena, 1960—, prof. physics, 1966—; cons. to Rand Corp., 1956—, Los Alamos Sci. Lab., 1960—, Inst. for Def. Analyses, 1960—. Alfred P. Sloan fellow, 1960-64; J.S. Guggenheim fellow, 1970-71. Author: (with S.D. Drell) Electromagnetic Structure of Nucleons, 1960; (with D. Horn) Hadron Physics at Very High Energies, 1973; Sound Propagation through a Fluctuating Ocean, 1978. Contbr. articles to profl. jours. Home: 2235 N Villa Heights Rd Pasadena CA 91007

ZACHARIUS, WALTER, pub. co. exec.; b. N.Y.C., Oct. 16, 1923; s. Abraham and Sara (Cohen) Z.; certificate Coll. City N.Y. Sch. Bus., 1948; student N.Y.U., 1949-50; certificate pub. relations and publicity New Sch. Social Research, 1949; m. Alice M. Riesenberg, Dec. 19, 1948; children—Steven Bruce, Judith Helen. With circulation dept. MacFadden Publs., Inc., 1947—, Popular Library Book, Inc., 1948-49, Am. Mercury, Inc., 1949-51; circulation dir. Ace News Co., N.Y.C., 1951-61; pres. Magnum Royal Publs., Inc., N.Y.C., 1961—, Magnum Communications, N.Y.C., 1961—; v.p. Lancer Book, Inc., N.Y.C., 1961-75; pres. Walter Zacharius Assos., Inc., 1964—. Mem. Com. World Human Rights, 1968—, Friends Hofstra Mu. Fine Arts, 1969—. Democratic committeeman, 1969; v.p. Reform Dem. Assn. Great Neck, N.Y., 1970—. Trustee United Cerebral Palsy of Queens, v.p., 1975—; trustee North Shore Community Art Center. Served with AUS, 1942-45; ETO, MTO. Recipient Pub. Relations award United Cerebral Palsy Queens, 1970. Mem. Periodicals Book Assn. Am., Ind. Newspaperstand Circulators of Am. Jewish (trustee congregation 1960-64). Home: 1175 York Ave New York NY 10021 Office: 21 E 40th St New York NY 10017

ZACHARY, DAN ANTHONY, fgn. service officer; b. Chgo., Dec. 2, 1923; s. Daniel Peter and Margaret (Jonas) Z.; B.S., Northwestern U., 1945; M.A., Harvard U., 1947, postgrad., 1947-49; postgrad. (French Govt. grantee) Sorbonne, 1949-50; M.A., Stanford U., 1959; postgrad. Air War Coll., 1968-69; children—Pamela Jean, Dan William. Commd. fgn. service officer Dept. State, 1952; consular officer, Munich, Germany, 1952-55; econ. officer Copenhagen, Denmark, 1955-57; secretariat Dept. State, 1958-60; polit. officer Thessaloniki, Greece, 1961-65, consul gen., 1977—; econ. officer Addis Ababa, Ethiopia, 1965-66; chief econ. sect., Kinshasa, Zaire, 1966-68; econ.

officer, Athens Greece, 1969-73; econ. counselor, Paris, 1973-74; dir. regional office African bur. Dept. State, 1974-77. Mem. sch. bd., Thessaloniki, Greece, 1963-65, Addis Ababa, Ethiopia, 1966-67, Thessaloniki, 1978—. Served with USN, 1943-46; PTO. Mem. Am. Fgn. Service Assn., Jacques Cousteau Soc. Home and Office: Am Consulate Gen APO New York NY 09693

ZACHERT, MARTHA JANE, librarian; b. York, Pa., Feb. 7, 1920; d. Paul Rodes and Elizabeth Agnes (Lau) Koontz; A.B., Lebanon Valley Coll., 1941; M.L.S., Emory U., 1953; D.L.S., Columbia U., 1968; m. Edward G. Zachert, Aug. 25, 1946; 1 dau., Lillian Elizabeth. Asst., Enoch Pratt Free Library, Balt., 1941-46; head librarian Wood Research Inst., Atlanta, 1947; sch. librarian DeKalb (Ga.) County Schs., 1950-52; head librarian, prof. history of pharmacy So. Coll. Pharmacy, Mercer U., Atlanta, 1952-63; instr. Ga. State Coll., 1962-63, Emory U., summers 1955-59, 1956-57, 59-60; mem. faculty Library Sch., Fla. State U., 1963-78, prof., 1973-78; prof. Coll. Librarianship U. S.C., Columbia, 1973-74, 78—; cons. So. Regional Med. Library, Emory U., 1976-77, Nat. Library Medicine, 1977, and others. Mem. Assn. Am. Library Schs., ALA, Med. Library Assn., Spl. Libraries Assn. (past pres. Fla. chpt., spl. citation 1977), Southeastern Library Assn., Fla. Library Assn., Oral History Assn., Am. Printing History Assn., Beta Phi Mu (pres. 1974-75). Asso. editor Jour. Library History, 1966-71, 73-76, mng. editor, 1971-73; cons. editor Jour. Library Adminstrn., 1979—; contbr. numerous articles to profl. jours. Home: 504 Chatham Ave Columbia SC 29205 Office: Davis Coll Univ of South Carolina Columbia SC 29208

ZACHERT, VIRGINIA, psychologist, educator; b. Jacksonville, Ala., Mar. 1, 1920; d. R.E. and Cora H. (Massee) Z.; student Norman Jr. Coll., 1937; A.B., Ga. State Woman's Coll., 1940; M.A., Emory U., 1947; Ph.D., Purdue U., 1949. Statistician, Davison-Paxon Co., Atlanta, 1941-44; research psychologist Mil. Contracts, Auburn Research Found., Ala. Poly. Inst.; indsl. and research psychologist Sturm & O'Brien, cons. engrs., 1958-59; research project dir. Western Design, Biloxi, Miss., 1960-61; self-employed cons. psychologist, Norman Park, Ga., 1961-71, Good Hope, Ga., 1971—; research asso. med. edn. Med. Coll. Ga. Augusta, 1963-65, asso. prof., 1965-70, prof., 1970—, chief learning materials div., 1973—; mem. Ga. Bd. Examiners of Psychologists, 1974—, v.p., 1977, pres., 1978. Mem. adv. bd. Comdr. Gen. ATC, USAF, 1967-70. Served as aerologist USN, 1944-46, aviation psychologist USAF, 1949-54. Diplomate Am. Bd. Profl. Psychologists. Fellow Am. Psychol. Assn.; mem. Am. Statis. Assn., Sigma Xi. Baptist. Author: (with P.L. Wilds) Essentials of Gynecology-Oncology, 1967, Applications of Gynecology-Oncology, 1967. Home: 1126 Highland Ave Augusta GA 30904 Office: Dept Obstetrics and Gynecology Med Coll Ga Augusta GA 30901. *It's really quite simple—I find that, if I wish to be understood or heard, that simplicity is necessary but not ever easy. Simplicity is basic, essential and always the major factor in my search for truth.*

ZACHRY, HENRY BARTELL, constrn. co. exec.; b. Uvalde, Tex., 1901; B.S. in Civil Engring., Tex. A. and M. U., 1922; m. Marjorie Powell, Sept. 7, 1929 (dec. Apr. 1977); children—Mary Pat, Emma Leigh, Bartell, Suzanne, James. Founder, chmn. bd. H.B. Zachry Co., San Antonio, 1924—; dir. Dallas Fed. Res. Bank. Bd. govs. S.W. Research Inst., San Antonio, 1947—; trustee Tex. A. and M. Univ. Research Found., 1954-75; chmn. bd. San Antonio Fair, Inc., 1967-68, chief exec. officer, 1968; mem. dist. bd. Alamo Hts. Ind. Sch. Dist., 1948-57, chmn., 1952-53; bd. dirs. Tex. Bd. Spl. Schs. and Hosps., 1950-52; bd. dirs. Tex. A. and M. U., 1955-61, pres. bd., 1959-61; head Tex. Gov.'s Com. on Edn. Beyond High Sch., 1963-65; mem. coordinating bd. Tex. Colls. and Univs., 1965-71. Recipient Distinguished Alumnus award Tex. A. and M. U., 1964; named Engr. of Year, Tex. Soc. Profl. Engrs., 1962, Mem. with spl. honors Chi Epsilon, 1966, and numerous other awards. Mem. San Antonio C. of C. (bd. dirs. 1975-80), Asso. Gen. Contractors Am. (past pres.). Address: 1104 Tower Life Bldg San Antonio TX 78205

ZACK, ALBERT JOSEPH, labor union ofcl.; b. Holyoke, Mass., Nov. 22, 1917; s. Charles Sumner and Mary (Crean) Z.; ed. pub. schs., N.J.; m. Jane Lillian Nesworthy, May 27, 1939; children—Linda Jane (Mrs. Keith Tarr-Whelan), Allen Young. News editor Springfield (Mass.) Daily News, 1942-46, radio sta. WSPR, Springfield, 1946-47; pub. relations dir. Ohio CIO Council, Columbus, 1947-52; asst. pub. relations dir. CIO, Washington, 1952-55; asst. pub. relations, dir. AFL-CIO, 1955-57, dir. pub. relations, 1957—. Democrat. Club: Nat Press (Washington). Home: 1380 4th St SW Washington DC 20024 Office: 815 16th St NW Washington DC 20006

ZACK, ARNOLD MARSHALL, mediator, arbitrator; b. Lynn, Mass., Oct. 7, 1931; s. Samuel George and Bess Ethel (Freedman) Z.; A.B., Tufts Coll., 1953; LL.B., Yale, 1956; M.P.A., Harvard, 1961, M.A., 1963; m. Norma Eta Wilner, Aug. 10, 1969; children—Jonathan Samuel, Rachel Ann. Asst. to Saul Wallen, arbitrator, 1956-63; cons. UN Mission to Congo, 1960, U.S. Peace Corps, 1961-63, Labor Dept., 1962—, Pres.'s Study Commn. on Nat. Service Corps, 1962-63, U.S. AID, 1963-68, Friedrich Ebert Stifting, 1963-64, Nat. Center for Dispute Settlement, 1968—; vis. Fulbright lectr. Haile Selassie U., Addis Ababa, 1963-64; referee Nat. R.R. Adjustment Bd., 1964-66, 68-70; dir. Labor-Mgmt. Inst., Am. Arbitration Assn., 1966-68; full time mediator/arbitrator, Boston, 1968—. Permanent arbitrator U.S. Postal Service and Postal Workers Union, Balt. County Bd. Edn. and Tchrs. Assn. Balt. County, Continental Air Lines and Airline Pilots Assn., Falstaff Brewery and Brewery Workers, First Nat. Stores and Amal. Meat Cutters, Greyhound Bus Lines and Amal. Transit Union, United Airlines and Air Line Pilots Assn., Yale U. and Fedn. Univ. Employees, Procter & Gamble and Ind. Oil and Chem. Workers, Commonwealth Mass. Fellow African Studies Assn.; mem. Nat. Acad. Arbitrators (treas. 1972-75, bd. govs. 1977—), Am. Arbitration Assn., Am. Bar Assn., Indsl. Relations Research Assn., Internat. Soc. for Labor Law and Social Legis. Clubs: Harvard (Boston); Yale (N.Y.C.). Author: Labor Training in Developing Countries, 1964; Ethiopia's High Labor Manpower-Analysis and Projections, 1964; Handbook on Grievance Arbitration in the Public Sector, 1974; Handbook on Fact Finding and Arbitration in the Public Sector, 1974; Grievance Arbitration, A Practical Guide, 1977; (with R. Black) Arbitrational Discipline and Discharge Cases, 1979. Contbr. articles to profl. jours. Address: 170 W Canton St Boston MA 02118

ZACK, DONNA FRANCES, mag. editor; b. Uniontown, Pa., Aug. 26, 1939; d. Charles N. and Ella Grace (Broderick) Zack; B.S., U. Fla., 1960, M.A., 1966. Tchr. bus. edn. Duval County Secondary Sch., Jacksonville, Fla., 1960-67; asso. editor Jr. Sec. mag. McGraw-Hill Book Co., 1967-69, editor Today's Sec. mag., 1969-72, editor Gregg tests and awards program, 1971-72; mng. editor Conv., Meetings, Incentive World mag., N.Y.C., 1972, now exec. editor Meetings and Convs. mag. Cons. Office Edn.; speaker various orgns. and schs. Mem. Assn. Group Travel Execs. (dir. 1977), N.Y. Bus. Press Editors (sec. 1969-71, dir. 1971-73), U. Fla. Alumni Assn. (pres. N.Y. chpt. 1974-75), N.Y. Soc. Assn. Execs. Home: 30 Waterside Pl Apt 6-A New York NY 10010 Office: One Park Ave New York NY 10016

ZACKS, GORDON BENJAMIN, soft goods mfg. co. exec.; b. Terre Haute, Ind., Mar. 11, 1933; s. Aaron and Florence Melton (Spurgeon) Z.; B.A., Coll. Commerce, Ohio State U.; married; children—Catherine E., Kimberly A. With R.G. Barry Corp., Pickerington, Ohio, 1955—, exec. v.p., 1964-65, pres., 1965—, chmn. bd., 1979—. Mem. Nat. Republican Senatorial Com.; regional chmn. United Jewish Appeal; bd. dirs. numerous Jewish orgns., locally and nationally. Mem. Young Presidents Orgn., Am. Mgmt. Assn. Republican. Home: 140 N Parkview St Columbus OH 43209 Office: 13405 Yarmouth Rd NW Pickerington OH 43147

ZACKS, SHELEMYAHU, mathematician, statistician; b. Tel Aviv, Israel, Oct. 15, 1932; s. Yechezkiel and Dvora (Kolemoitzev) Z.; came to U.S., 1965, naturalized, 1972; Ph.D., Columbia U., 1962; m. Hanna A. Bailik, Oct. 15, 1955; children—Yuval J., David N. Research asso. Stanford (Calif.) U., 1962-63; sr. lectr. Technion-Israel, 1962-65; prof. Kans. State U., Manhattan, 1965-68, U. N.Mex., Albuquerque, 1968-70; prof. math. and statistics Case Western Res. U., Cleve., 1970-79, chmn. dept., 1974-79; prof. statistics Va. Poly. Inst. and State U., Blacksburg, 1979—; cons. program in logistics George Washington U., 1967—. Served with Israel Def. Force, 1950-52. NSF grantee, 1966-76. Fellow Inst. Math. Statistics, Am. Statis. Assn.; mem. Internat. Statis. Inst. Jewish. Author: The Theory of Statistical Inference, 1971; contbr. articles to profl. jours. Office: care Va Poly Inst and Univ Blacksburg VA 24060

ZACKS, SUMNER IRWIN, pathologist; b. Boston, June 29, 1929; s. David and Rose Z.; B.A. cum laude, Harvard Coll., 1951, M.D., magna cum laude, 1955; M.A. (hon.) U. Pa., 1975, Brown U., 1977; m. Marilyn Garfinkel, June 28, 1953; children—Nancy Alice, Charles Matthew, Susan Esther. Intern, Mass. Gen. Hosp., Boston, 1956, resident, 1956-58; teaching fellow Harvard U., 1956; asst. prof. pathology U. Pa., 1962-64, asso. prof., 1964-71, prof., 1971-76; prof. pathology Brown U., 1976—, chmn. pathology, 1977—; pathologist in chief Miriam Hosp., Providence, R.I., 1976—. Served to capt. USAR, 1958-60. Diplomate Am. Bd. Pathology. Fellow Am. Coll. Physicians; mem. Histochem. Soc. (sec. 1965-68), Am. Coll. Pathologists, Am. Soc. Exptl. Pathology, Am. Soc. Cell Biology, Am. Soc. Neuropathologists, Internat. Acad. Pathology, Sigma Xi. Author: The Motor Endplate, 1964, 74; Atlas of Neuropathology, 1971. Contbr. chpts. to books and articles to profl. jours. Office: The Miriam Hospital 164 Summit Ave Providence RI 02906

ZAENGLEIN, WILLIAM GEORGE, mfg. exec.; b. Rochester, N.Y., July 16, 1899; s. H. Conrad and Dora (Dasch) Z.; grad. high sch.; m. Elsie M. Traekle, Sept. 11, 1927; 1 son, William George; m. 2d, Lillian Keresey, Dec. 28, 1955. With service dept. Monroe Calculating Machine Co., 1921-23, br. mgr., 1923-28, sales mgr., 1928-31, v.p., dir., 1931-37, pres., mem. exec. com., 1937-47; pres. Monroe Calculating Machine Co., Sales & Mfg. Cos., 1947-54, vice chmn. bd., 1954-56; exec. v.p. Underwood Corp., N.Y.C., 1956-57, pres., dir., mem. exec. com., 1957-58; exec. v.p., dir. Clary Corp., San Gabriel, Calif., 1958-61, pres., 1961-65; v.p. bus. equipment group Litton Industries, Inc., Beverly Hills, Calif., 1965-69; established W.G. Zaenglein. Inc., cons. firm, 1969—; v.p. corp. devel. Walthan Industries Corp., N.Y.C., 1970-71; now cons. W.G. Zaenglein, Inc., Pasadena. Ky. col. Mem. N.A.M., Am. Mgmt. Assn., Office Equipment Mfrs. Inst., Am. Ordnance Assn., Def. Orientation Conf. Assn., Newcomen Soc. Clubs: Masons, San Gabriel (Calif.). Home and office: 814 S Arroyo Blvd Pasadena CA 91105

ZAENGLEIN, WILLIAM GEORGE, JR., lawyer; b. Orange, N.J., Jan. 31, 1929; s. William G. and Elsie T. (Traenkle) Z.; B.A., Yale U., 1952, J.D., 1955; m. Elizabeth J. Skinner, Dec. 18, 1954; 1 son, William George, III; m. 2d, Joyce A. Moffit, Oct. 18, 1968; 1 son, Eric Hunter. Admitted to Calif. bar, 1969, U.S. Dist. Ct. bar, 1969; with gen. counsel's office GSA, 1956-59; contract adminstr. Lear Siegler Corp., 1959-63; sr. contract adminstr. Northrop Corp., 1963-66; legal asst. law firm, Orange, Calif., 1966-69; v.p., corp. counsel First Am. Fin. Corp., Santa Ana, Calif., 1969-76, sec., counsel, 1976—; dir. First Am. Trust Co., 1976—. Mem. Orange County (Calif.) Bar Assn., Am. Soc. Corporate Secs., Newcomen Soc., Phi Delta Phi, Chi Phi. Club: Yale of So. Calif. Office: 114 E Fifth St Santa Ana CA 92702

ZAFFARANO, DANIEL JOSEPH, ednl. adminstr.; b. Cleve., Dec. 16, 1917; s. Joseph Frank and Josephine M. (Lapick) Z.; B.S., Case Inst. Tech., 1939; M.S., Ind. U., 1948, Ph.D., 1949; m. Suzanne Kirkham, Aug. 27, 1946; children—Dario, Erica, Elisa, Bianca, Gina, Monica. Physicist research lab. Nat. Carbon Co. (Ohio), Cleve., 1939-45; liaison officer OSRD, Washington, 1945-46; asso. prof. Iowa State U. Sci. and Tech. (now Iowa State U.), 1949-57, prof. physics, 1959-67, Distinguished prof., 1967—, chmn. dept., 1961-71, v.p. for research, grad. dean, 1971—; sci. liaison officer Office Naval Research, London, Eng., 1957-58. Fellow Am. Phys. Soc.; mem. Sigma Xi, Phi Kappa Phi. Home: 3108 Ross Rd Ames IA 50010

ZAGORIA, SAM, govt. ofcl.; b. Somerville, N.J., Apr. 9, 1919; s. Nathan and Rebecca (Shapiro) Z.; B.L. in Journalism, Rutgers U., 1941; m. Sylvia Bomse, Dec. 21, 1941; children—Paul, Marjorie Zagoria Olds, Ronald. With New Brunswick (N.J.) Daily Home News, 1940-41, N.J. Def. Council, Trenton, 1941-42. Fed. Office Govt. Reports, Newark, 1942; reporter Washington Post, 1946-55; adminstrv. asst. to Senator Clifford P. Case, Washington, 1955-65; mem. NLRB, Washington, 1965-69; dir. Labor-Mgmt. Relations Service, Washington, 1970-78; commr. U.S. Product Safety Commn., 1978—. Served with USAAF, 1942-45. Nieman fellow Harvard, 1954. Mem. Soc. Nieman Fellows, Rutgers U. Alumni Assn. Jewish. Club: Federal City (Washington). Home: 3537 Marlbrough Way College Park MD 20740 Office: 1111 18th St NW Washington DC 20207

ZAGORIN, PEREZ, educator, historian; b. Chgo., May 29, 1920; s. Solomon Novitz and Mildred (Ginsburg) Z.; A.B., U. Chgo., 1941; A.M., Harvard, 1947, Ph.D., 1952; m. Honoré Desmond Sharrer, May 29, 1947; 1 son, Adam. Various positions OWI, U.S. Govt., U.P. Syndicate, CIO, 1942-46; instr. Amherst Coll., 1947-49; lectr. Vassar Coll., 1951-53; from asst. prof. to prof. history McGill U., 1955-65; prof. U. Rochester, 1965—, chmn. dept., 1968-69; vis. prof. Johns Hopkins, 1964-65; Amundsen vis. prof. U. Pitts., 1964; William Andrews Clark Meml. Library prof. U. Calif. at Los Angeles, 1975-76; sr. fellow Nat. Humanities Center, 1978-79. Mem. adv. council Yale Center Study Parliamentary History. Sheldon travelling fellow Harvard, 1949-50; faculty research fellow Social Sci. Research Council, 1959-60, 63; sr. fellow Can. Council, 1958-59; sr. research fellow Folger Shakespeare Library, 1964-65; mem. Inst. for Advanced Study, Princeton, N.J., 1972-73. Fellow Royal Hist. Soc., Am. Acad. Arts and Scis.; mem. Am. Hist. Assn., Renaissance Soc. Am., Conf. Brit. Studies, Author: A History of Political Thought in the English Revolution, 1954; The Court and the Country, 1969; also articles. Editor: Culture and Politics from Puritanism to the Enlightenment, 1980. Home: 4927 River Rd Scottsville NY 14546 Office: Dept History Univ Rochester Rochester NY 14627

ZAHL, PAUL ARTHUR, scientist, editor, author; b. Bensenville, Ill., Mar. 20, 1910; s. Arthur Hermann and Barbara (Diebre) Z.; student Marquette U., 1928-29; A.B. with honors, North Central Coll., Ill., 1932, D.Sc., 1972; A.M. (Univ. scholar 1933-34), Harvard U., 1934, Ph.D. in Exptl. Biology, 1936; m. Eda Seasongood Field, Aug. 19, 1946; children—Eda Kristin, Paul Francis Matthew. Austin teaching fellow Harvard U., 1934-36, Parke-Davis postdoctoral research fellow, 1936-37; mem. staff Haskins Labs., N.Y.C., 1937—, asso. dir., sec. corp., 1947-58, research asso., 1958—; guest investigator Union Coll., Schenectady, 1937-39, Meml. Hosp., N.Y.C., 1940-42; research asso. Am. Museum Natural History, N.Y.C., 1949-64; sr. scientist Nat. Geog. Soc., 1958-75, sci. cons., 1975—, mem. com. for research and exploration; adj. prof. biology Fordham U., N.Y.C., 1965—. Collaborator neutron research Columbia, 1940-41; prin. investigator OSRD, World War II; numerous fgn. expdns. and sci. field work, 1937—. Recipient grant-in-aids Nat. Cancer Inst., NSF, AEC, Office Naval Research, Nat. Geog. Soc.; recipient Citation of Merit, OSRD, 1945; Distinguished Alumnus award North Central Coll., 1958. Fellow Am. Geog. Soc.; mem. Am. Assn. Cancer Research, Soc. Exptl. Biology and Medicine, Ecol. Soc. Am., Am. Chem. Soc., Am. Phys. Soc., Am. Soc. Zoologists, AAUP, Sigma Xi, Gamma Alpha. Clubs: Explorers (N.Y.C.); Cosmos (Washington); Harvard (San Francisco). Author: To The Lost World, 1939; Flamingo Hunt, 1952; Coro-Coro; World of the Scarlet Ibis, 1954; also numerous articles, research papers, essays, book reviews. Editor: Blindness: Modern Approaches to the Unseen Environment, 1950. Home: 5035 Glenbrook Rd NW Washington DC 20016 Office: Nat Geog Soc Washington DC 20036

ZAHN, GORDON, educator, sociologist; b. Milw., Aug. 7, 1918; s. Charles Roach and Dorothy (Spoehr) Z.; B.A., Coll. St. Thomas, 1949; M.A., Cath. U. Am., 1950, Ph.D., 1952; LL.D., LaSalle Coll., 1973. Mem. faculty Loyola U., Chgo., 1953-67; prof. sociology U. Mass., 1967—. Mem. nat. bd. SANE; exec. council Fellowship Reconciliation; chmn. Am. PAX Soc. Past bd. dirs. Catholic Interracial Council. Social Sci. Research Council fellow, Harvard, 1952-53; Fulbright Sr. Research fellow, 1956-57; Simon Research fellow, 1964-65. Fellow Am Sociol. Assn.; mem. Am. Cath. Sociol. Soc. (pres. 1967-68), A.A.U.P. (chpt. pres.). Author: German Catholics and Hitler's Wars, 1962; In Solitary Witness: Life and Death of Franz Jaegerstaetter, 1964; War, Conscience and Dissent, 1967; The Military Chaplaincy, 1969; Another Part of the War: The Camp Simon Story, 1979. Editor: Thomas Merton on Peace, 1971. Home: 780 Boylston St Boston MA 02199

ZAHN, JANE CORDINER, educator; b. Detroit, Mar. 27, 1918; d. John Howard and Ruby (Craft) Sturgeon; B.A., U. Oreg., 1949, M.A., 1950; Ph.D., U. Calif. at Berkeley, 1961; m. Douglas L. Cordiner, Jan. 2, 1939 (div. Nov. 1946); children—Cynthia (Mrs. Douglas Francis Penrose), Sandra (Mrs. Charles Curtis Wilmot); m. 3d, Bertram Edises, Nov. 30, 1963. Mem. faculty U. Calif. at Berkeley, 1951-66, head edn. extension, 1962-66, lectr. edn., 1964-66; prof. edn. San Francisco State U., 1966—, chmn. dept. interdisciplinary studies in edn., 1966-72; adj. prof. Union for Experimenting Colls. and Univs., 1970. Asso. Nat. Tng. Labs., Washington, 1966-71; cons. Napa (Calif.) State Hosp., 1965, 66, 68, Yolo County (Calif.) Schs., 1970-71; lectr., leader, cons. various tng. or edn. groups. U. Calif. Econs. fellow, 1950-51; Fund for Adult Edn. fellow, 1960-61. Mem. U. Calif. Edn. Alumni Assn. (treas. 1965-66), Adult Edn. Assn., Calif. Tchrs. Assn., N.E.A. Author: Creativity Research: Its Implications for Adult Education, 1966. Cons. editor Adult Edn., 1967—. Home: 339 Broadway 113 Alameda CA 94501 Office: Sch Education San Francisco State Univ San Francisco CA 94132

ZAHNER, VICTOR HENRY, investment banker; b. Kansas City, Mo., July 26, 1910; s. Henry F. and Marie R. (Bruening) Z.; B.A., Rockhurst Coll., 1929; m. Lorene A. Soden, June 20, 1931 (dec. Nov. 1957); children—Sister Michaela Marie, Diane F. (Mrs. Benjamin O. Knight, Jr.) and Donna S. (Mrs. James Christopher Sprehe) (twins), William Victor; m. 2d, Kathryn Cannon, Apr. 4, 1959 (div. 1977); stepchildren—Patricia E. (Mrs. R.H. Heller), Pamela A. (Mrs. J. Roy Smith). With bond dept. City Nat. Bank, Kansas City, Mo., 1930-39; an organizer, officer, dir. Soden & Co., Kansas City, 1939-43; asst. to factory mgr. aircraft div. Pratt and Whitney Co., 1943-45; an organizer, pres., dir. Soden-Zahner Co., Kansas City, Mo., 1946-52; pres. Zahner & Co., investment bankers, Kansas City, Mo., 1952—. Hon. dir. Rockhurst Coll. Mem. Securities Industry Assn. (chmn. Southwestern group 1950, bd. govs. 1960-63), Kansas City Soc. Fin. Analysts, Native Sons Kansas City, Kansas City C. of C. Rotarian. Club: Mission Hills Country. Home: 5049 Wornall Rd Kansas City MO 64112 Office: 127 W 10th St Kansas City MO 64105

ZAHNISER, MARVIN RALPH, educator, historian; b. New Kensington, Pa., June 29, 1934; s. Clarence Howard and Fannie (Weir) Z.; A.B., Greenville (Ill.) Coll., 1956; M.A. in History, U. Mich., Ann Arbor, 1957; Ph.D., U. Calif. at Santa Barbara, 1963; m. Adrienne Allen, Aug. 28, 1956; children—Mark Howard, Keith Allen, Craig Alexander. Vis. asst. prof. U. Wash., 1963-64, U. Iowa, 1964-65; mem. faculty Ohio State U., Columbus, 1965—, prof. history, 1973—, asst. v.p. arts and scis., 1972-73, chmn. dept., 1973-77. Mem. edn. com. Columbus Urban League, 1972-74; v.p. Conf. on Faith and History, 1976-78, pres., 1978—. Trustee Spring Arbor (Mich.) Coll., 1970-75, fellow, 1973-77; trustee Mt. Vernon (Ohio) Nazarene Coll., 1975-77, fellow, 1978—. Mem. Am. Hist. Assn., Orgn. Am. Historians, Soc. Historians of Am. Fgn. Relations, Am. Assn. U. Profs., Ohio Acad. History. Mem. Ch. of Nazarene. Club: Torch Internat. Author: Charles Cotesworth Pinckney: Founding Father, 1967; Uncertain Friendship: American-French Diplomatic Relations Through the Cold War, 1975. Home: 2011 W Devon Rd Columbus OH 43212

ZAHRN, FRED J., textile co. exec.; b. 1920; B.S., U. Colo., 1947; married. Budget analyst, auditor Armstrong Cork Co., 1947-52; supr. budgets and forecasts Dan River Inc., Danville, Va., 1952-57, dir. sales budgets and cost estimates, 1957-60, asst. controller, 1960-66, controller Danville div., 1966-70, corp. controller, 1970-75, sr. v.p., 1975—, also dir. Served with U.S. Mcht. Marine, 1942-45. Office: Dan River Inc Greenville SC 29606

ZAIDENBERG, ARTHUR, painter, author; b. Bklyn., Aug. 15, 1908; s. Herman and Clara (Shapiro) Z.; student Art Students League, N.Y.C., 1924-26, Beaux Arts, Paris, France, 1927-29, also in Munich, Germany and Rome, Italy, 1929; m. Tommy R. Reiter, Oct. 1, 1942. Tchr. Roerich Mus., N.Y.C., 1935-37, N.Y. U., 1940-43. Executed murals for hotels in N.Y.C., Miami Beach, Fla., New Orleans, Plymouth, Mass.; executed mural S.S. Rotterdam, 1968; one man shows include A.C.A. Gallery, AAA Gallery, Belles Artes-San Miguel Allende, Mexico, 1972-73; others; represented in permanent collections Met. Mus., N.Y.C., Bklyn. Mus.; executed mural in belles artes, San Miguel Allende, Mex., 1976. Civilian animation dir. Tng. Film div. U.S. Signal Corps, 1942. Recipient Sally Jacobs ann. award, 1969. Mem. Woodstock Artists Assn. Author: The Emotional Self, 1930; Anyone Can Draw, 1938; Anyone Can Paint, 1942; Drawing the Human Figure, 1945; Anyone Can Draw Animals, 1946; Studies in Figure Drawing, 1950; Art Students Encyclopedia, Your Child is an Artist; Anyone Can Sculpt, 1952; Drawing Self Taught, 1954; The Joy of Painting, 1956; (with Henry Morton Robinson) Out of Line; editor and compiler: The Art of the Artist; illustrator: The Plays of William Shakespeare; Thais; Against the Grain. Revised: 'Sculpt. Home: Elwyn Ln Woodstock NY 12498 also San Miguel de Allende GTO Mexico

ZAIDMAN, SAMUEL, mathematician, educator; b. Bucharest, Romania, Sept. 4, 1933; came to U.S., 1964, naturalized, 1972; s. David Alter and Alta (Edelstein) Z.; Doctorat d'Etat, U. Paris, 1970; m. Janne Fiorani, July 17, 1962; children—Marina-Francesca, Anna-Maria, Christina-Roberta, Enrichetta-Chiara. Asst. mathematician U. Bucharest, 1955-59; vis. prof. Politecnico Milano, Italy, 1961-64; prof. math. U. Montreal, 1964—; vis. prof. U. Geneva, Switzerland, 1966-68, U. Florence, Italy, 1972-73; fellow Inst. Advanced Study, Princeton, N.J., 1962-63, Courant Inst., N.Y.C., 1965-66. Nat. Research Council Can. grantee, 1965—. Mem. Am. Math. Soc., Can. Math. Soc. Jewish. Author: Equations différentielles abstraites, 1966; contbr. numerous articles to profl. jours. Home: 924 Pratt Ave Outremont PQ H2V 2V1 Canada Office: 5620 Darlington Ave Montreal PQ H3C 3J7 Canada. *Since my youth I considered science, and especially mathematics and physics as a main road to the hidden mysteries and inner beauties of our spiritual and material world, and freedom as a major right for everybody, to work and fight for it, if necessary.*

ZAINEA, JOSEPH GEORGE, city adminstr.; b. Grand Rapids, Mich., June 18, 1936; s. George Joseph and Adele Cecelia (Najar) Z.; B.A., Western Mich. U., 1958; M.P.A., U. Pitts., 1961; m. Judith Kay Lokers, Aug. 23, 1963; children—Christopher, Denise. Asst. to city mgr. City of Grand Rapids (Mich.), 1961-65, model cities dir., 1969-70, dep. city mgr., 1970-76, city mgr., 1976—; city mgr. City of Titusville (Pa.), 1965-68; sr. staff asso. Barton-Aschman Assos., Chgo., 1968-69; pres. Greater Grand Rapids Housing Corp., non-profic corp., 1974-76; Mem. budget com. Grand Rapids United Way, 1971-74. Mem. Internat. City Mgmt. Assn. (dir. Mich. chpt.), Am. Soc. Public Adminstrn., Am. Public Works Assn. Home: 1705 Old Town Dr Grand Rapids MI 49508 Office: 300 Monroe Ave NW Grand Rapids MI 49503

ZAJONC, ROBERT B(OLESLAW), psychologist; b. Lodz, Poland, Nov. 23, 1923; s. Mieczyslaw and Anna (Kwiatkowska) Z.; came to U.S., 1949, naturalized, 1953; Ph.D., U. Mich., 1955; m. Donna Benson, June 20, 1953; children—Peter Clifford, Michael Anton, Joseph Robert. Asst. prof. psychology U. Mich., 1955-60, asso. prof., 1960-63, prof., 1963—, sr. research scientist Inst. Social Research, 1960—. Guggenheim fellow, 1978-79; Fulbright fellow, 1962-63. Fellow Am. Psychol. Assn. (Disting. Sci. Contbn. award 1978); mem. AAAS (co-recipient Psychol. prize 1976). Author: Social Psychology: An Experimental Approach, 1965; editor: Animal Social Psychology, 1970; asso. editor Jour. Personality and Social Psychology, 1960-66. Office: Research Center for Group Dynamics U Mich Ann Arbor MI 48106

ZAKARIASEN, WILLIAM W., music and dance critic; b. Blue Earth, Minn., Aug. 19, 1934; s. William R. and Katherine (Wallace) Z.; student Brown U., U. Mich., Manhattan Sch. Music. Chorus tenor N.Y.C. Opera, 1957-60, Met. Opera, 1960-71; music, dance, film and theater critic San Francisco Examiner, San Francisco Progress, 1972-74; music and dance critic N.Y. Daily News, 1974—; contbr. articles to nat. mags. Mem. Music Critics Assn., Met. Opera Guild, N.Y.C. Opera Guild. Office: 220 E 42d St New York NY 10017

ZAKHARTCHENKO, CONSTANTINE LEO, aero. engr.; b. Lublin, Russia (now Poland), Jan. 17, 1900; s. Leo Moses and Idalya (Koslovsky) Z.; student Classical Gymnasia, Lublin and Kiev, Russia, 1909-16, Imperial Naval Acad., Russia, 1916-20; M.S., Mass. Inst. Tech., 1925; m. Mary Rutledge Slattery, May 18, 1946. Came to U.S., 1920, naturalized, 1947. Jr., then sr. engr., chief engr., partner Aeromarine Plane & Motor Co., Wright Aero. Corp., McDonnell & Assos., Edo Aircraft Corp., others 1923-34; tech. adviser, mem. bur. aero. research Nat. Govt. of China, 1934-43; chief engr., helicopter and propulsion research div. McDonnell Aircraft Corp., 1943-48; cons. Cornell Aero. Lab., Inc., 1948-49, Nat. Bur. Standards, 1949-50; dir. engring., ordnance exptl. unit Bur. Ordnance, U.S. Navy, 1950-56; cons. govt. agys., def. contractors on guided missiles, satellites and U.S.S.R. tech., 1956-76; design and devel. twin-engine helicopter, pioneer ram-jet helicopter, pulse jet engines, afterburners for jets; developed system tech. control design and engring. guided missiles. Served with Russian Navy, World War I.; civilian tech. adviser Chinese Air Force, Sino-Japanese incident, 1937-43. Decorated St. George Cross (Russia), 1919; Kwong Hua, Glory fo China, 1942; recipient Distinguished Civilian Service award USN, 1956. Registered profl. engr., D.C. Fellow Am. Inst. Aeros. and Astronautics (asso.); mem. Am. Def. Preparedness Assn., Air Force Assn., Navy League U.S. Club: Mass. Inst. Tech. Home: 2311 Connecticut Ave Washington DC 20008

ZAKIN, JACQUES LOUIS, chem. engr.; b. N.Y.C., Jan. 28, 1927; s. Mordecai and Ada Davies (Fishbein) Z.; B.Chem. Engring., Cornell U., 1949; M.S. in Chem. Engring., Columbia U., 1950; D.Engring. (Socony-Mobil Employee Incentive fellow), N.Y. U., 1959; m. Laura Pienkny, June 11, 1950; children—Richard Joseph, David Fredric, Barbara Ellen, Emily Ann, Susan Beth. Chem. engr. Flintkote Research Labs., Whippany, N.J., 1950-51; research technologist, research dept. Socony-Mobil, Bklyn., 1951-58, sr. research technologist, 1953-56, supervising technologist, 1959-62; asso. prof. chem. engring. U. Mo., Rolla, 1962-65, prof., 1965-77, dir. minority engring. program, 1974-77, dir. women in engring. program, 1975-77; chmn. dept. chem. engring. Ohio State U., Columbus, 1977—. Bd. dirs. Rolla Community Concert Assn., 1966-77, 2d v.p., 1975-77; bd. dirs. Ozark Mental Health Assn., 1976-77. Served with USNR, 1945-46. Recipient Outstanding Research award U. Mo., Rolla, 1970; Am. Chem. Soc. Petroleum Research Fund Internat. fellow, 1968-69. Mem. Am. Inst. Chem. Engrs., Am. Chem. Soc., Soc. of Rheology, Am. Soc. Engring. Edn., Sigma Xi, Phi Lambda Upsilon, Phi Eta Sigma, Alpha Chi Sigma, Tau Beta Pi. Jewish. Co-editor Proc. Turbulence Symposium, 1969, 71, 73, 75, 77; contbr. articles to profl. jours.; patentee in field. Office: 140 W 19th Ave Ohio State U Columbus OH 43210

ZALAZNICK, SHELDON, editor, journalist; b. Bronx, N.Y., Aug. 6, 1928; s. Samuel and Esther Leah (Schneiderman) Z.; B.A., Univ. Coll. N.Y. U., 1948; M.A., Tchrs. Coll. Columbia, 1950; m. Vera Altobelli, Apr. 4, 1953; 1 dau., Andrea. Tchr. English, Benjamin Franklin High Sch., N.Y.C., 1950-52; asso. editor Newsweek mag., 1952-56; v.p. Manning Pub. Relations Co., 1956-59; sr. editor Forbes mag., 1959-63; editor New York mag. sect. N.Y. Herald Tribune, N.Y.C., 1963-64, Sunday editor N.Y. Herald Tribune, 1964-66; staff writer Gen. Learning Corp., 1966-67; asso. editor Fortune mag., 1967-69; v.p., editorial dir. New York mag., 1969-76; mng. editor Forbes mag., 1976—. Home: 458 W 246th St Bronx NY 10471 Office: 60 Fifth Ave New York NY 10011

ZALBA, SERAPIO RICHARD, orgn. exec.; b. San Francisco, July 16, 1927; s. Serapio and Agueda (Arribas) Z.; B.A., U. Calif., Berkeley, 1951, M.S.W., 1956; Ph.D., Case Western Res. U., 1971; m. Patricia Ellen Pool, July 20, 1954; children—Elisa Anne, David William, Anthony Serapio. Social service worker San Francisco Welfare Dept., 1952-54; probation and parole officer Wis. Dept. Corrections, Janesville, 1956-57; supr., exec. dir. No. Calif. Service League, San Mateo County, 1958-62; dir. children of women prisoners project Calif. Depts. Corrections and Pub. Welfare, Coronoa, 1962-64; dir. agy. effectiveness project, mem. faculty Case Western Res. U., Cleve., 1965-69, prof. urban studies and applied social scis., 1975-78, chmn. dept., 1975-78; exec. dir. Geauga Alliance, Chardon, Ohio, 1978—; prof., chmn. dept. social service dept. Cleve. State U., 1969-73; partner Zalba/Hirsch Assos., Chagrin Falls, O., 1973-74. Precinct chmn. Democratic Party, Chagrin Falls, 1974; trustee Belmont (Calif.) Sch. Dist., 1959-62; trustee Greater Cleve. Neighborhood Centers Assn., Chagrin Falls Park Community Center. Served with USNR, 1945-46. NIMH fellow, 1964-66; Career tchr. fellow, 1966. Mem. Nat. Assn. Social Workers (pres. Cleve. chpt. 1973-75), Nat. Council Crime and Delinquency, Cleve. Council Corrections (dir. 1970-72). Author: Women Prisoners and Their Families, 1964; (with Herman Stein) Assessing Agency Effectiveness, 1969; editor: (with William Schwartz) The Practice of Group Work, 1971. Home: 240 S Franklin St Chagrin Falls OH 44022

ZALESKI, MAREK BOHDAN, immunologist; b. Krzemieniec, Poland, Oct. 18, 1936; s. Stanislaw and Jadwiga (Zienkowicz) Z.; came to U.S., 1969; naturalized, 1977; M.D., Sch. Medicine, Warsaw, 1960, Dr. Med. Sci., 1963. Instr. dept. histology Sch. Medicine, Warsaw, 1955-60, asst. prof., 1960-69; research asst. prof. (Henry C. and Bertha H. Buswello fellow) dept. microbiology State U. N.Y., Buffalo, 1969-72, asso. prof., 1976-78, prof., 1978—; vis. scientist Inst. Exptl. Biology and Genetics, Czechoslovac Acad. Sci., Prague, 1965; Brit. Council's scholar, research lab. Queen Victoria Hosp., East Grinstead, Eng., 1966-67; asst. prof. dept. anatomy Mich. State U., East Lansing, 1972-75, asso. prof., 1975-76. NIH grantee, 1976—. Mem. Polish Anatomical Soc., Transplantation Soc., Internat. Soc. Exptl. Hematology, Am. Assn. Immunologists. Roman Catholic. Co-author: Transplantation and Preservation of Tissues in Human Clinic, 1966; The Man, 1968; Cytophysiology, 1970; Principles of Immunology, 1978; editorial com. Immunol. Communications; contbr. articles in field to med. jours. Office: Dept Microbiology State U NY Buffalo NY 14214

ZALEZNIK, ABRAHAM, psychoanalyst, mgmt. specialist; b. Phila., Jan. 30, 1924; s. Isadore and Anna (Appelbaum) Z.; A.B. in Econs., Alma Coll., 1945; M.B.A., Harvard U., 1947, D.C.S., 1951; grad. Boston Psychoanalytic Soc. and Inst., 1965; m. Elizabeth Ann Aron, June 24, 1945; children—Dori Faith, Ira Harry. Research asst. Harvard U. Grad. Sch. Bus. Adminstrn., 1947-48, instr., 1948-51, asst. prof., 1951-56, asso. prof., 1956-61, prof., 1961—, Cahners-Rabb prof. social psychology of mgmt., 1967—; research fellow Boston Psychoanalytic Soc. and Inst., 1965-68, mem. faculty, 1972—; practice psychoanalysis, Boston, 1968—; cons. to mgmt., dir. Evans Products Co., Ogden Corp., Pueblo Internat., Inc. Trustee, Beth Israel Hosp., Boston, 1968—. Served with USN, 1942-46. Mem. Boston Psychoanalytic Soc., Am. Psychoanalytic Assn. (cert.), Am. Sociol. Assn. Clubs: Tavern (Boston); Belmont (Mass.) Country. Author: (with David Moment) The Dynamics of Interpersonal Behavior, 1964; Human Dilemmas of Leadership, 1966; (with Manfred F. R. Kets de Vries) Power and the Corporate Mind, 1975; contbr. articles to profl. publs. Home: 151 Follen Rd Lexington MA 02173 Office: 217 Morgan Hall Soldiers Field Boston MA 02163

ZALINSKI, EDMUND LOUIS GRAY, ins. exec.; b. Salt Lake City, Aug. 18, 1915; s. Edward Robins and Agnes (de Schweinitz) Z.; A.B., Cornell U., 1937; M.B.A., Harvard, 1938; Ph.D. summa cum laude, N.Y. U., 1944; m. Matilde Eleanor Mittendorf, July 15, 1939; children—Nancy Marie, Matilde M., Susanne Helen. Mgr. sales offices N.Y. Life Ins. Co., 1938-47, asst. v.p. 1951-52, 2d v.p. 1953-54, v.p. 1954-55, instr. N.Y. U., 1944-46; mng. dir. Life Underwriter Tng. Council, 1947-51, pres., 1954, dir., 1951—; exec. v.p. Nat. Assn. Life Underwriters, 1949-51; v.p., chmn. agy. com. John Hancock Mut. Life Ins. Co., Boston, 1955-57; exec. v.p. Life Ins. Co. N.Am., 1957-66, chmn. exec. com., dir., 1957, pres., chief exec. officer, 1966-72; pres, dir. INA Life Ins. Co. N.Y., 1968-72, v.p., dir. INA Life Ins. Co., 1968-72, INA Properties, Inc., INA Corp., INA Trading Corp., Phila. Investment Corp.; past chief exec. officer, pres. INA Security Corp.; dir., chmn. trust com. Bryn Mawr Trust Co.; chmn. Greit Realty Trust, 1966-79, now dir.; chmn. Cayuga Concrete Pipe Co.; gen. partner, dir. leasing cos.; dir. Fibre Formations, Inc., Title Ins. Corp. Pa., Ardmore Farms, Inc., Am. Gen. Mut. Funds Co., McArdle-Desco Corp., B.G. Balmer Co., Center City Assos., Center City Sports Club, Greater Boston Hotel and Casino Corp. Adv. Council Underwriter Edn. and Tng., 1947-50, Joint Com. Mgmt. Tng., 1948-51; mem. research adv. com. Life Ins. Agy. Mgmt. Assn. 1951-57. Huebner Found. lectr., 1956; mem. vis. com. Grad. Sch. Bus. Adminstrn., N.Y. U. Trustee Am. Coll. Life Underwriters, 1954-72, chmn. mgmt. edn. com., 1957—, also chmn. devel. com.; treas. Life Underwriters Tng. Council, 1956-68, life trustee, 1968—. Trustee, mem. exec. com., v.p. Phila. Mus. Art, 1965-72; bd. dirs. Bur. Municipal Research, Phila.; bd. dirs., chmn. exec. com. Pa. Economy League, 1963-72. Mem. Life Ins. Assn. Am., (dir. 1970-72), Ins. Fedn. Pa. (dir., chmn. 1970-72), Newcomen Soc., Loyal Legion, S.A.R. Clubs: Cornell (dir.), Harvard Bus. Sch. (past pres.) (Phila.); Merion Cricket, Union League. Author publs. relating to field. Home: 100 Grays Ln Apt 401 Haverford PA 19041 Office: 410 Lancaster Ave Haverford PA 19041

ZALL, ALEX, real estate exec.; b. Newark, Feb. 2, 1920; s. Samuel and Rose (Berman) Z.; student Rutgers U., 1940, N.Y. U., 1944; m. Esther Teri Bernash, Nov. 17, 1946; children—Marilyn Patricia, Richard Jonathan. Real estate salesman Albert M. Greenfield & Co., Newark, 1944-49, Alexander Summer Co., Newark, 1949-53; indsl. real estate salesman J.I. Kislak, Inc., Jersey City, 1953-54, mgr. indsl. div., 1954-63; v.p. devel. and mktg. Nassau Crossways Indsl. and Office Park, Syosset, N.Y., 1963-67; exec. v.p. Alexander Summer Devel. Co., Teaneck, N.J., 1967—, Alexander Summer, Inc., 1973—, Alexander Summer Mortgage Co., 1973—, Alexander Summer Co., 1973—. Pres., West Caldwell Civic Assn., 1955-61, North Caldwell Civic Assn., 1965-72; mem. Mayor's Adv. Com. for Indsl. and Comml. Devel., West Caldwell, N.J., 1960-64; vice chmn. North Caldwell Planning Bd., 1972—. Mem. Nat. Assn. Realtors, Indsl. Real Estate Brokers Assn., Nat. Assn. Indsl. and Office Parks (dir. nat. bd. 1976—, v.p. regional affairs 1976-77, v.p., treas. N.J. chpt. 1972-74, pres. N.J. chpt. 1974-76), Am. Arbitration Assn. Home: 11 Maple Dr North Caldwell NJ 07006 Office: 222 Cedar Ln Teaneck NJ 07666

ZALL, PAUL MAXWELL, educator; b. Lowell, Mass., Aug. 3, 1922; s. Nathan and Bertha (Rubin) Z.; B.A., Swarthmore Coll., 1948; A.M., Harvard, 1950, Ph.D., 1951; m. Elisabeth Ruth Weisz, June 21, 1948; children—Jonathan, Barnaby, Andrew. Teaching fellow Harvard, 1950-51; instr. Cornell U., 1951-55, U. Oreg., 1955-56; research editor Boeing Co., 1956-57; asst. prof. Calif. State Coll. at Los Angeles, 1957-61, asso. prof., 1961-64, prof. English, 1964—, acting chmn. dept., 1969-71; cons. in report writing, proposal preparation and brochures to industry and govt. agys., 1957—. Pres. Friends of South Pasadena Library, 1967-70. Served with USAAF, 1942-45; ETO. Am. Philos. Soc. fellow, 1964, 66; John Carter Brown Library research grantee, Huntington Library research grantee. Author: Elements of Technical Report Writing, 1962; Hundred Merry Tales, 1963; Nest of Ninnies, 1970; Literary Criticism of William Wordsworth, 1966; (with John Durham) Plain Style, 1967; Simple Cobler of Aggawam in America, 1969; (with J.R. Trevor) Proverb to Poem, 1970; Selected Satires of Peter Pindar, 1971; Comical Spirit of Seventy-Six, 1976; (with J.A.L. Lemay) Autobiography of Benjamin Franklin, 1980; Norton Critical Edition of Franklin's Autobiography, 1980. Home: 1911 Leman St South Pasadena CA 91030 Office: Calif State U Los Angeles CA 90032

ZALL, ROBERT ROUBEN, food scientist, educator; b. Lowell, Mass., Dec. 6, 1925; s. Samuel and Sarah (Cohen) Z.; B.S., U. Mass., 1949, M.S., 1950; Ph.D., Cornell U., 1968; m. Mollie Leah Wiseblood, June 8, 1949; children—Linda Zall Sheffield, Judy Zall Kusek, Jonathan J. Gen. mgr. Grandview Dairies, Bklyn. and Arkport, N.Y., 1950-66; dairy industry cons., Ithaca, N.Y., 1966-68; dir. research prodn. Crowley Foods Co., Binghamton, N.Y., 1968-71; prof. food sci. Cornell U., 1971—; trustee Milk Industry Pension and Welfare Fund; dir. two food cos.; asso. Gurnham, Inc.; dairy industry cons., project dir. EPA-Industry demonstration whey processing plant. Served with AUS, 1944-46. Recipient Cert. Appreciation, EPA, 1975, 79; Howard B. Marlott award N.Y. State Milk and Food Sanitarians Mem. Internat. Assn. Milk, Food and Environ. Sanitarians, Inst. Food Technologists, Am. Soc. Agrl. Engrs., Phi Kappa Phi. Clubs: Sertoma, Masons. Author: (with Bela G. Liptak) Environmental Engineers Handbook, 1972; co-contbr. to Food Processing Waste Management, 1979, Food Processing, 15 vols., 1979; patentee automatic cleaning apparatus. Contbr. numerous articles to profl. jours., popular mags. Home: 54 Woodcrest Ave Ithaca NY 14850 Office: Stocking Hall Dept Food Sci Cornell U Ithaca NY 14853. *Most people I know, never made a success of themselves by just working forty hours a week. It takes hard work, the love of a good wife, and the willingness to accept challenges.*

ZALLEN, HAROLD, scientist, univ. adminstr.; b. Boston, Apr. 7, 1926; s. Joseph and Lillian L. (Stahl) Z.; B.S., Northeastern U., 1951; Ed.M. in Sci. and Math., Boston U., 1954; M.S. in Organic Synthetic Medicinal Chemistry, Purdue U., 1959, Ph.D. in Analytical Medicinal Chemistry, 1960; m. M. Eugenia Malone, Aug. 23, 1959. Mgr., Shoppers World Pharmacy, Inc., Framingham, Mass., 1951-53; asst. prof. phys. scis. Calvin Coolidge Coll. Liberal Arts, Boston, 1952-54; chemist Q.M. Research and Devel. Command, Natick, Mass., 1954-55; tchr. physics and chemistry Natick High Sch., 1955-56; vis. asst. prof. microbiology Sch. Nursing, Lowell (Mass.) Gen. Hosp., 1955-56; grad. instr., also asst. radiol. control officer Purdue U., 1957-58; asso. prof. chemistry Coll. Pharmacy, Mercer U., 1960-61; analytical chemist Communicable Diseases Center, USPHS, Atlanta, 1961; mem. faculty Auburn U., 1961-66, asso. prof. to prof., head dept. radiol. scis., dir. Office of Radiol. Safety, 1961-66; specialist phys. sci. research, div. higher edn. research Bur. Research, U.S. Office Edn., 1966-67, head curriculum div. higher edn. research, 1967; head instructional sci. equipment program asso. program dir. spl. projects program NSF, Washington, 1967-69, in charge instructional sci. equipment program, 1969-72; asst. dean, dir. research and grad. studies Okla. State U. at Stillwater, 1972-73, prof. chemistry, 1972-73; asso. v.p. for adminstrn. and fin., chief adminstrv. officer U. Okla. Health Scis. Center Campus, Oklahoma City, 1973-74, research prof. biochemistry and molecular biology, 1973-74, asso. v.p. for systems planning, procedure devel. and spl. projects, central adminstrn., Norman, 1974—; exec. v.p. Acad. World Inc., 1975—; spl. lectr. Radiobiology Inst., NSF, 1963-64; cons. in field. Radiol. def. officer, Auburn, 1961. Pres. Academic World, College Park, Md.; mem. Pres.'s Sci. and Technol. Adv. Commn., Washington; mem. bd. Internat. Sci. and Engring. Fairs, Sci. Service, Inc., 1973—; v.p. Okla. Coll. Osteo. Medicine and Surgery, Tulsa; cons. to State Regents for Higher Edn. Served with USAAF, 1943-46; col. Res., U.S. Army, cons., moblzn. designee U.S. Army Labs., Natick. Recipient Mayoralty certificate merit for outstanding service to City New Orleans, 1973. Gen. Electric Co. Sci. fellow Union U., Schenectady, 1955; fellow Purdue Research Found., 1958, Elks Cancer Soc., 1959, Am. Cancer Soc., 1960. Mem. Am. Chem. Soc. (bd. dirs., chmn. elect Auburn sect. 1966), Am. Soc. Engring. Edn. (mem. long range planning com.), Nat. Council Univ. Adminstrs., Soc. Research Adminstrs. (pres. So. sect. 1974—, chmn. publs. com.), Health Physics Soc., Sigma Xi, Phi Lambda Upsilon, Rho Chi, Phi Delta Kappa, Delta Sigma Theta, Beta Pi (past nat. sec.). Baptist. Rotarian (chmn. bull. com. Auburn 1963, bd. dirs. 1964, bd. dirs. Stillwater 1972-73), Mason (32 deg., Shriner). Author 3 books in field. Editor, pub. Jour. Internat 6800 Computer Center. Contbr. numerous articles to profl. jours. Home: 1917 Shelby Ct Norman OK 73071 Office: PO Drawer 2790 Norman OK 73070

ZAMBIE, ALLAN JOHN, retail co. exec.; b. Cleve., June 9, 1935; s. Anton J. and Martha (Adamski) Z.; student Ohio U., 1953-54; B.A., Denison U., 1957; LL.B., Western Res. U. (now Case Western Res. U.), 1960; m. Nancy Hall, Sept. 22, 1973. Admitted to Ohio bar, 1960; asso. firm Hribar and Conway, Euclid, Ohio, 1961-63; staff atty. The Higbee Co., Cleve., 1963-67, asst. sec., 1967-69, sec., 1969-74, v.p.-sec., 1974—. Trustee Cleve Music Sch. Settlement. Served with AUS, 1960-61. Mem. Am. (corp., banking and bus. law sect.), Ohio, Cleve. bar assns., Am. Soc. Corporate Secs. (nat. v.p. 1977—). Home: 2953 Litchfield Rd Shaker Heights OH 44120 Office: 100 Public Sq Cleveland OH 44113

ZAMBOTTI, BRUNO MARIO, elec. engr.; b. Aultman, Pa., July 16, 1924; s. Clemente and Mary Z.; B.S. in Elec. Engring., Carnegie Inst. Tech., 1948; M.B.A., Western Res. U., 1956; m. Denise M. Ribeau, Apr. 23, 1963. Asst. to sr. engr. Cleve. Electric Illuminating Co., 1948-54, sr. planning engr., 1955-59; engr. Cia. Paulista de Forca e Luz, Sao Paolo, Brazil, 1954-55, Gen. Electric Co., Schenectady, 1959-60; asso., head utility system studies Chas. T. Main, Inc., Boston, 1964-71, v.p., transmission distbn. div., 1971-74, exec. v.p., operating officer, 1974-75, pres., chief operating officer, 1975-78; asso. editor Elec. World Mag., 1960-64; rep. U.S. Nat. Com., World Energy Conf. Fellow Am. Cons. Engrs. Council; mem. IEEE (sr.), Nat. Soc. Profl. Engrs., Internat. Conf. on Large Electric Systems. Club: Engrs. *

ZAMBUTO, MAURO HENRY, elec. engr.; b. Turin, Italy, Aug. 16, 1920; s. Gero and Claudia (Gaffino) Z.; Ph.D., U. Rome, 1943, U. Padua (Italy) 1944. Dir. sound rec. Scalera Film, Rome and Venice, 1940-44, tech. dir., studio mgr., 1945-52; v.p., studio mgr. IFE, N.Y.C., 1952-55; pres. Transound, Inc., N.Y.C. and Hollywood, 1955-57; asst. prof. Coll. City N.Y., 1957-60; asso. prof. Manhattan Coll., N.Y.C., 1960-62; prof. dept. elec. engring. N.J. Inst. Tech., Newark, 1962—, now Distinguished prof.; cons. to govt. agys. and industry. Recipient Corbino award CNR; Van Houten award N.J. Inst. Tech.; named Outstanding Motion Picture Engr., NTC. Mem. Soc. Motion Picture and Television Engrs., Internat. Union of Tech. Cinematograph Assns., Soc. of Photo-Optical Instrumentation Engrs., AAUP. Contbr. articles to scientific and tech. publs. Patentee in field. Home: 445 W 23d St New York City NY 10011 Office: 232 High St Newark NJ 07102

ZAMECNIK, PAUL CHARLES, physician; b. Cleve., Nov. 22, 1912; s. John C. and Mary (McCarthy) Z.; A.B., Dartmouth, 1933; M.D., Harvard U., 1936; D.Sc. (hon.), U. Utrecht, 1966, Columbia, 1971; m. Mary Connor, Oct. 10, 1936; children—Karen, John, Elizabeth. Resident medicine Huntington Hosp., Harvard, 1936-37, Collis P. Huntington prof. oncologic medicine, 1956—; intern medicine U. Hosps. of Cleve., 1938-39; fellow Carlsberg Lab., Copenhagen, Denmark, 1939-40, Rockefeller Inst., N.Y.C., 1941-42; physician Mass. Gen. Hosp., 1956—; dir. J.C. Warren Labs., Harvard and Mass. Gen. Hosp., 1956—. Mem. staff OSRD, World War II.

Recipient John Collins Warren Triennial prize, 1946, 50, James Ewing award, 1963, Borden award in med. scis., 1965, Passano award, 1970; Fogarty scholar NIH, 1975. Mem. Royal Danish Acad. Scis. (fgn. hon.), Am. Acad. Arts and Scis., Assn. Am. Physicians, Am. Assn. Biol. Chemists, Am. Assn. Cancer Research, Nat. Acad. Sci. Home: 101 Chestnut St Boston MA 02108 Office: Mass Gen Hosp Fruit St Boston MA 02114

ZAMENHOF, STEPHEN, educator, biochemist; b. Warsaw, Poland, June 12, 1911; s. Henry G. and Sabina (Szpinak) Z.; D.Techn. Sci., Warsaw Poly. Sch., 1936; Ph.D. in Biochemistry, Columbia, 1949; m. Patrice J. Driskell, May 2, 1961. Came to U.S., 1939, naturalized, 1945. Asst. prof., then asso. prof. Columbia, 1951-64; prof. microbial genetics and biol. chemistry U. Calif. at Los Angeles, 1964—. Guggenheim fellow, 1958-59. Fellow Am. Acad. Microbiology; mem. Am. Soc. Biol. Chemists, Am. Soc. Microbiology, Genetics Soc. Am., Am. Genetics Assn., Am. Soc. Neurochemistry, Soc. Neurosci., Am. Inst. Nutrition, Internat. Soc. Developmental Psychobiology, Internat. Soc. Neurochemistry, Sigma Xi. Author: The Chemistry of Heredity, 1958; also numerous articles. Home: 333 Medio Dr Los Angeles CA 90049

ZAMES, GEORGE DAVID, elec. engr.; b. Poland, Jan. 7, 1934; s. Sam Simha and Leona Z.; B.Eng., McGill U., 1954; Sc.D. in Elec. Engring., M.I.T., 1960; m. Eva Eisenfarb, July 21, 1964; children—Ethan, Jonathan. Asst. prof. M.I.T., 1960-62, 63-65, Harvard U., 1962-63; sr. scientist NASA, Cambridge, Mass., 1965-71; vis. prof. Technion, Haifa, Israel, 1972-74; prof. elec. engring. McGill U., Montreal, 1974—. Guggenheim fellow, 1967-68; Athlone fellow Imperial Coll., London U., 1954-56. Fellow IEEE; mem. Soc. Indsl. and Applied Math., Sigma Xi. Asso. editor So. Indsl. and Applied Math Jour. on Control, 1968—; contbr. articles to profl. jours. Home: 3210 Forest Hill Montreal PQ H3V 1C7 Canada Office: Dept Elec Engring McGill Univ 3480 University St Montreal PQ H3A 2A7 Canada

ZAMMITT, NORMAN, artist; b. Toronto, Ont., Can., Feb. 3, 1931; A.A., Pasadena City Coll., 1957; M.F.A., Otis Art Inst., Los Angeles. One man exhbns. include Felix Landau Gallery, Los Angeles, 1962, 66, 68, Los Angeles County Mus. Art, 1977, Corcoran Gallery, Washington, 1978; represented in permanent collections: Library of Congress, Mus. Modern Art, Corcoran Gallery, Larry Aldrich Mus., Hirschhorn collection. Guggenheim fellow, 1968.

ZAMORA, MARIO DIMARUCUT, anthropologist, educator; b. Angeles, Pampanga, Philippines, July 27, 1935; s. Leon Biag and Caridad (Dimarucut) Z.; came to U.S., 1959, naturalized, 1978; A.B., U. Philippines, 1956, M.A., 1959; Ph.D., Cornell U., 1963; m. Ducella Norma Parmalee, Nov. 22, 1963; children—Gregory, Nerissa, Morris, Lili, Sarah Elizabeth. Mem. faculty U. Philippines, 1962-72, prof. anthropology, 1971-72, chmn. dept., 1964-70, acad. dean, 1970-72; vis. prof. Eastern Mont. Coll., 1972-73; vis. prof. Coll. William and Mary, Williamsburg, Va., 1973-75, prof. anthropology, 1975—; dir. gen. Tribal Research Center, Govt. Philippines, 1966-69; officer-in-charge Museum and Inst. Ethnology and Archaeology, U. Philippines, 1966-69. First Adlai Stevenson fellow, 1967; Fulbright/Smith Mundt scholar, 1959-63; UP fellow, 1962-63. Fellow Am. Anthrop. Assn., Royal Anthrop. Inst. Gt. Britain and Ireland, Royal Asiastic Soc., life mem. Indian Anthrop. Assn., Indian Social. Soc., Indian Ethnographic and Folk Culture Soc., Indian Inst. Public Adminstrn., Indian Polit. Sci. Assn.; mem. Canadian Sociol. and Anthropol. Assn., So. Anthrop. Soc., Va. Social Sci. Assn., Internat. Assn. Anthropology Editors (mem. exec. bd. 1979—), Assn. Third World Anthropologists (founding chmn., founding editor Bull.). Co-author, editor: Themes in Culture, 1971; Studies in Philippine Anthropology, 1967; Anthropology: Range and Relevance, 1969; co-author: Politics and Social Change, 1966; Changing Identities in Modern Southeast Asia; sr. editor: Social Change in Modern Philippines: Perspectives, Problems, and Prospects, 2 vols.; co-founder, co-editor: Studies in Third World Societies; asso. editor Jour. Asian and African Studies; asso. Current Anthropology; also articles. Home: PO Box 1398 Williamsburg VA 23185 Office: Dept Anthropology College of William and Mary Williamsburg VA 23185. *My life revolves around three fundamental pillars: God, Self-fulfillment, and Service. I believe that God or the Supreme Reason guides the destiny of men and nations; a human being should seek self-fulfillment intellectually, spiritually, physically, and psychologically in order to prepare himself effectively in the service of humanity. Sincerity and seriousness of purpose, dedication, and compassion should always direct our thoughts and action in the pursuit of that Supreme Being, Self-fulfillment, and Service.*

ZAMPANO, ROBERT CARMINE, fed. judge; b. New Haven, Mar. 18, 1929; s. Anthony N. and Marie (Fusco) Z.; B.A., Yale U., 1951, LL.B., 1954; m. Dorothea Mea Gilbride, Nov. 23, 1950; children—Deborah Lee, Robert Anthony. Admitted to Conn. bar, 1954; law clk. to U.S. dist. judge Conn., 1954-55; with firm Thompson, Weir & MacDonald, New Haven, 1955-57, Zampano & Mager, East Haven, 1959-61; judge, East Haven, 1959-60, counsul, 1956-61; exec. sec. rev. div. Superior Ct. Conn., 1956-61; U.S. dist. atty. Conn., 1961-64; U.S. dist. judge Dist. Conn., 1964—, now sr. judge. Co-chmn. bar sect. New Haven United Fund, 1956-57; commnr. Quinnipiac council Boy Scouts Am., 1953; pres. East Haven 175th Anniversary Comm., 1960; chmn. East Haven Democratic Party, 1956-61; bd. dirs. New Haven ARC, East Haven Community Center. Mem. Am., New Haven County bar assns., New Haven Jr. Bar (pres. 1957-58), New Haven Jr. C. of C. Clubs: K.C.; Melebus, Yale (dir. 1960-63), Amity (sec. 1961) (New Haven). Home: 20 South St East Haven CT 06512 Office: PO Box 1959 New Haven CT 06508*

ZAND, DALE EZRA, educator; b. N.Y.C., July 22, 1926; B.Elec. Engring., Cooper Union, 1945; M.B.A., N.Y.U., 1949, Ph.D., 1954; m. Charlotte Edith Rosenfeld, Oct. 16, 1949; children—Fern, Mark, Karen, Jonathan, Matthew. Asst. to v.p. Spectator Bags, 1947-49; v.p. Glo-Cold Co., 1949-50; mem. faculty N.Y.U. Grad. Sch. Bus. Adminstrn., 1950—, prof. mgmt., 1963—, chmn. dept., 1968—; cons. to industry, 1951—. Bd. dirs. N.E.A., Nat. Tng. Labs. Inst. Applied Behavioral Sci. Served with USNR, 1945. Ford Found. fellow, 1959-60. Mem. Am. Psychol. Assn., Inst. Mgmt. Sci., Acad. Mgmt., Internat. Assn. Applied Social Scientists. Author articles in field. Office: New York Univ 100 Trinity Pl New York City NY 10006

ZANE, EDWARD RAYMOND, accountant; b. Arlington, Tenn., Feb. 4, 1899; s. Anthony and Grace (Andreaux) Z.; LL.B., Georgetown U., 1921; M.A., Pace Inst., Washington, 1923; Ph.D., A and T State U., 1971; m. Frances M. Weems, Aug. 8, 1927. Pub. accountant, specializing corp. taxation, finance, 1923-29; cons. corp. tax financing, Burlington Industries, Inc., 1929-37, tax counsel, 1937-63, dir., 1952-68, chmn. exec.-finance com., 1962-68; now mgmt. cons.; chmn. bd. RCL Co. (formerly Roberts Co.), Sanford, N.C., 1973—. Trustee Martha and Spencer Love Found.; bd. dirs. A and T U. Found. Served with U.S. Army, 1917-19. C.P.A., Tenn., N.C. Mem. Am. Inst. Accountants, N.C. Soc. C.P.A.'s. Mason (32 deg.). Home: 11-B Fountain Manor Dr Greensboro NC 27405 Office: Wachovia Bank Bldg 201 N Elm St Greensboro NC 27401

ZANGWILL, WILLARD IRA, educator; b. Pitts., Mar. 18, 1940; s. Bernard Louis and Lillian Ruth (Abel) Z.; A.B., Columbia U., 1959; M.S. (NSF fellow), Stanford U., 1963, Ph.D., 1965; children—Richard Michael, Monica Laurie. Prof., U. Calif., Berkeley, 1965-69; dir. edn. evaluation HEW, Washington, 1969-71; pres. Sullivan Edn. Systems, Palo Alto, Calif., 1972-73; special asst. to commr. ednl. tech. U.S. Office Edn., Washington, 1971-73; prof. Am. U., Washington, 1972-73; prof. mgmt. sci. U. Ill., Urbana, 1973-79; prof. U. Chgo., 1978—. Mem. Ops. Research Soc., Inst. Mgmt. Sci. Author: Non-linear Programming: A Unified Approach, 1969; Success With People: Theory Z, 1976; Pathways in Fixed Points, Equilibria and Solutions, 1980; departmental editor Mgmt. Sci., 1968-78; contbr. articles to profl. jours. Home: 5330 S Hyde Park Blvd Chicago IL 60615 Office: U Chicago Grad Sch Bus Chicago IL 60637. *Success depends on which activities society esteems and whether you decide to pursue those activities. The prized life, however, is different. It is the involvement in a range of activities and finding pleasure, meaning, and inner contentment from as many of them as possible.*

ZANNETOS, ZENON SOTERIOS, educator; b. Famagusta, Cyprus, Dec. 4, 1927; s. Soterios and Eleni (Louka) Z.; came to U.S., 1949, naturalized, 1960; student Okla. State U., 1949-51; A.B., Kans. U., 1953; M.S., Mass. Inst. Tech., 1955, Ph.D., 1959; postgrad. Stanford U., 1959-60; m. Clotilde Chaves, June 23, 1956; children—Cynthia Andriane, Ianthe Thalia, Christopher Zenon, Stephen Soterios. Instr. mgmt. Mass. Inst. Tech., Cambridge, 1955-58, asst. prof., 1958-61, asso. prof., 1961-66, prof. mgmt. Sloan Sch. Mgmt., 1966—, chmn. managerial info. for planning and control group, 1969-72, strategy, policy, planning group, 1974—; Ford Faculty Study fellow Stanford, 1959-60; vis. prof. econs. Harvard, 1962-64; Forrestal vis. prof. mgmt. Naval War Coll., 1967-68, chmn. adv. group and acad. dir. admirals' mgmt. course, 1968-77; chmn. bd., dir., cons. numerous indsl. firms, govts. and govt. agys. Pres., Am. Soc. Hellenic Culture; pres. United Hellenic-Am. Orgns. New Eng.; trustee Mgmt. Assn. Greece; New Eng. regional v.p. United Hellenic Am. Congress, 1975—; mem. adv. council, trustee Hellenic Coll., 1969-78; vice chmn. bd. dirs. Maliotis Cultural Center. Ford Faculty research fellow, 1964-65. Recipient Greek Orthodox Archdiocese Service award, 1976. Mem. Am. Accounting Assn. (nat. coms.), Am. Econ. Assn., Inst. Mgmt. Scis. (nat. officer), Phi Beta Kappa, Phi Eta Sigma, Pi Mu Epsilon. Mem. Greek Orthodox Ch. (trustee). Author: Some Thoughts on the Firm, 1963; The Theory of Oil Tankship Rates, 1966. Editorial bd. various profl. publs. Contbr. chpts. books, articles to profl. publs. Home: 164 Country Dr Weston MA 02193 Office: Mass Inst Tech Cambridge MA 02139

ZANUCK, RICHARD DARRYL, motion picture exec.; b. Beverly Hills, Calif., Dec. 13, 1934; s. Darryl F. and Virginia (Fox) Z.; grad. Harvard Mil. Acad., 1952; B.A., Stanford, 1956; m. 2d, Linda Harrison, Oct. 26, 1969; m. 3d, Lili Fini, Sept. 23, 1978; children—Harrison Richard, Dean Francis; children by previous marriage—Virginia, Janet. Story, prodn. asst. Darryl F. Zanuck Prodns., 1956, v.p., 1956-62; president's prodn. rep. 20th Century-Fox Studios, Beverly Hills, 1962-63, v.p. charge prodn., 1963-69, pres., 1969-71, dir., 1966—; chmn. 20th Century-Fox Television, Inc.; sr. exec. v.p. Warner Bros., Inc., 1971-72; co-founder Zanuck/Brown Co., 1972—; founder Universal Studio, 1972—; producer The Sting (Acad. award), 1973, Jaws, 1975. Nat. chmn. Fibrosis Assn., 1966—; trustee Harvard Sch. Served as 2d lt. U.S. Army. Named Producer of Yr., Nat. Assn. Theatre Owners, 1974. Mem. Acad. Motion Picture Arts and Scis. (gov.), Screen Producers Guild, Phi Gamma Delta. Office: Zanuck/Brown Co Universal Pictures Universal City CA 91608

ZAPF, HERMANN, book and type designer; b. Nuremberg, Germany, Nov. 8, 1918; s. Hermann and Magdalene (Schlamp) Z.; m. Gundrun von Hesse, Aug. 18, 1951; 1 son, Christian Ludwig. Freelance designer, 1938—; type dir. D. Stempel AG, type foundry, Frankfurt, Ger., 1947-56; design cons. Mergenthaler Linotype Co., N.Y.C. and Frankfurt, 1957-74; cons. Hallmark Internat., Kansas City, Mo., 1966-73; v.p. Design Processing Internat. Inc., N.Y.C., 1977—; prof. typographic computer programs Rochester (N.Y.) Inst. Tech., 1977—; instr. lettering Werkkunstschule, Offenbach, Ger., 1948-50; prof. graphic design Carnegie Inst. Tech., 1960; instr. typography Technische Hochschule, Darmstadt, Ger., 1972—; author: William Morris, 1948; Pen and Graver, 1952; Manual Typographicum, 1954, 68; About Alphabets, 1960; Typographic Variations, 1964; Atlas of History of Letterforms, 1980; designer types Palatino, Melior, Optima, ITC Zapf Chancery, ITC Zapf Internat., Digiset Marconi, Digiset Edison. Recipient Silver medal, Brussels, 1962; 1st prize typography Biennale Brno, Czechoslovakia, 1966; Frederic W. Goudy award typography, Rochester 1969; Silver medal Internat. Book Exhbn., Leipzig, Ger., 1971; Johannes Gutenberg prize, Mainz, Ger., 1974; Gold medal Museo Bodoniano, Parma, Italy, 1975; named hon. citizen State of Tex., 1970; J.H. Merck award, Darmstadt, W. Ger., 1978. Mem. Royal Soc. Arts, Assn. Typographique Internat., Am. Inst. Graphic Arts, Bund Deutscher Grafik Designer, Bund Deutscher Buchkünstler, Internat. Gutenberg Gesellschaft; hon. mem. Type Dirs. Club N.Y.C. (Gold medal 1967), Soc. Graphic Arts, Soc. Typographique de France (Paris), Double Crown Club (London), Soc. Printers (Boston), Soc. Graphic Designers Can., Grafiska Inst. (Stockholm), Typophiles, Art Dirs. Club Kansas City, Gamma Epsilon Tau. Office: 1 Lomb Memorial Dr Rochester NY 14623

ZAPLATYNSKY, ANDREW, violinist; b. Bamberg, Germany, Mar. 9, 1946; came to U.S., 1950, naturalized, 1959; s. Stephan and Maria Z.; student Ind. U., 1964-66; Mus.B., Catholic U. Am., 1970; student violin with Edgar Ortenberg, Josef Gingold, Ivan Galamian. Mem. first violin sect. Rotterdam (Netherlands) Philharmonic, 1970-71, Minn. Orch., Mpls., 1972-73; asst. concertmaster Detroit Symphony, 1973-74; asso. concertmaster Cin. Symphony Orch., 1974—; soloist for children's concerts Phila. Orch., 1958, 59; occasional soloist Cin. Symphony Orch.; chamber music recitalist. Vice chmn. Ukrainian Soc. Greater Cin. Served with band USMC, 1966-70. Mem. Ukrainian Cath. Ch. Office: Cin Symphony Orch 1241 Elm St Cincinnati OH 45210

ZAPP, JOHN ADAM, JR., toxicologist; b. Pitts., June 22, 1911; s. John Adam and Clara Elizabeth (Rickmeyer) Z.; B.S. in Chemistry, Haverford Coll., 1932; M.A. in Physiol. Chemistry, U. Pa., 1934, Ph.D., 1938; m. Doris Wilson, June 23, 1934; children—Patricia (Mrs. Alistair Arnott), John Adam III. With Haskell Lab. for Toxicology and Indsl. Medicine, E.I. duPont de Nemours & Co., 1946-76, asst. dir., 1948-52, dir., 1952-76; cons. toxicology and indsl. hygiene, Kennett Square, Pa. Served with USPHS, 1943-46. Recipient Stokinger award Am. Conf. Govtl. Indsl. Hygienists, 1977. Mem. Am. Acad. Indsl. Hygiene, Am. Conf. Govt. Indsl. Hygienists (hon.), Am. Acad. Occupational Medicine (hon.), Am. Indsl. Hygiene Assn. (pres. 1971-72, Cummings award 1977), Soc. Toxicology (pres. 1967-68), Am. Soc. Pharmacology, Am. Physiol. Soc., Am. Chem. Soc. Republican. Presbyterian. Clubs: Rotary, Kennett Square Golf and Country. Author: (with A.J. Fleming and C.A. D'Alonzo) Modern Occupational Medicine, 2d edit., 1960. Contbr. articles to tech. publs. Home and office: 318 Marshall St Kennett Square PA 19348. *On the eve of the Constitutional Convention of 1789, George Washington is reported to have said: "Let us raise a standard to which the wise and honest can repair." I have felt this to be an excellent guiding principle in my work, and have followed it to the best of my ability.*

ZAPPA, FRANK, musician, composer; b. Balt., Dec. 21, 1940; s. Francis Vincent Zappa, Sr.; student Chaffey Jr. Coll., 1959; m. Gail Sloatman, 1969; children—Dweezil, Moon Unit, Ahmet Rodin, Diva. Founder musical group Mothers of Invention, 1964—; appeared in motion picture 200 Motels, 1971; numerous compositions and recs. Named Pop Musician of the Year, Down Beat mag., 1970, 71, 72. Address: care Zappa Records 6255 Sunset Blvd Los Angeles CA 90028*

ZAR, MAX, civil engr.; b. Chgo., Jan. 4, 1916; s. Meyer and Sorel (Kabb) Z.; B.S. in Civil Engring., Ill. Inst. Tech., 1938; m. Sarah Brody, Apr. 1, 1939; children—Jerrold, Myra Zar Beckman, Leon, Fred. Structural designer Sargent & Lundy, Chgo., 1942-56, asso., 1956, partner, 1966—, mgr. structural dept., 1966—. Registered profl. engr., 30 states, 1 fgn. country. Fellow Am. Concrete Inst. (Alfred E. Landau award 1974), ASCE (Civil Engr. of Yr. Ill. sect. 1968); mem. AAAS, Am. Inst. Steel Constrn. (spl. citation 1976), Am. Nuclear Soc., ASME, Bldg. Ofcls. and Code Adminstrs. Internat., Earthquake Engring. Research Inst., Nat., Ill. socs. profl. engrs., Internat. Assn. for Bridge and Structural Engrs., Internat. Soc. Soil Mechanics and Found. Engring., Post-Tensioning Inst., Prestressed Concrete Inst., Seismo. Soc. Am., Structural Engrs. Assn. Ill. (John F. Parmer award 1979), Western Soc. Engrs. Club: Standard (Chgo.). Contbr. numerous articles on concrete chimneys, steel stacks, coal unit trains, high strength bolts, nuclear power plants, seismic analysis and founds. to profl. jours., also chpts. to Structural Engring. Handbook, 1968, 79. Home: 1000 Bob-O-Link Rd Highland Park IL 60035 Office: 55 E Monroe St Chicago IL 60603

ZARA, LOUIS, author, editor; b. N.Y.C., Aug. 2, 1910; s. Benjamin and Celia (Glick) Rosenfeld; ed. Crane Jr. Coll., 1927-30, U. Chgo., 1930-31; m. Bertha Robbins, Sept. 23, 1930; children—Paul, Philip, Daniel; m. 2d, Marlene Brett, Mar. 22, 1958. Vice pres. Ziff Davis Pub. Co., Chgo., N.Y.C., 1946-53, dir. gen. book div., 1959-61; pres. Pub.'s Cons., Inc., N.Y.C., 1955-56; editor-in-chief gen. trade div. Follett Pub. Co., N.Y.C., 1962-65; editor-in-chief Mineral Digest, 1969-77. Author: (novels) Blessed is the Man, 1935; Give Us This Day, 1936; Some for the Glory, 1937; This Land is Ours, 1940; Against This Rock, 1943; Ruth Middleton, 1946; In the House of the King, 1952; Rebel Run, 1951; Blessed is the Land, 1954; Dark Rider, 1961; (non-fiction) Jade, 1969; Locks and Keys, 1969; also stories, scenarios, radio scripts, dramas, ABC radio-television show Stump the Authors. Recipient 1940 prose Award Chgo. Found. Lit.; Daroff Meml. Fiction award, 1955. Contbr. fiction, essays and articles to mags. and anthologies. Fellow Royal Am. numis. socs.; mem. Authors League of Am., Soc. Midland Authors, Mineral. Soc. Am., Overseas Press Club, P.E.N., Mineral Soc. Pa., Collectors Art Medals. Life mem. Nat. Commn. Anti-Defamation League. Home: 2610 Belmont Ave Philadelphia PA 19131

ZARAFONETIS, CHRIS JOHN DIMITER, physician, educator; b. Hillsboro, Tex., Jan. 6, 1914; s. James and Helen (Skouras) Z.; A.B., U. Mich., 1936, M.S., 1937, M.D. (Sternberg medal 1941), 1941; m. Sophia Levathes, Mar. 27, 1943; 1 son, John Christopher. Extern, Simpson Meml. Inst., U. Mich., 1940-41, research asso., 1947-50, also asst. prof. medicine at univ.; intern Harvard IV Med. Service, Boston City Hosp., 1941-42; research fellow internal medicine U. Mich. Med. Sch., 1946-47; faculty Temple U. Med. Sch., 1950-60, prof. clin. and research medicine, 1957-60; chief hematology sect. Temple U. Hosp., 1950-60; dir. Simpson Meml. Inst. Med. Research, 1960-78, prof. internal medicine U. Mich., 1960—; coordinator med. edn. for nat. def., 1966-71. Mem. com. on naval med. research NRC-Nat. Acad. Scis., 1970-74, mem. com. on problems of drug dependence, 1970-74; sci. adv. bd. Armed Forces Inst. Pathology, 1970-74; dir. research and engring. Def. Dept., chmn. joint med. research conf., 1968-75, Army Sci. Adv. Panel, 1974-78, Army Sci. Bd., 1978—; bd. dirs. Medicine in the Pub. Interest, 1973—. Served to maj. M.C., AUS, 1942-46; col. Res. ret. Decorated Order Ismail (Egypt); Legion of Merit (U.S.); recipient U.S.A. Typhus Commn. medal, 1946, Henry Russel award U. Mich., 1950. Diplomate Am. Bd. Internal Medicine. Fellow A.C.P., Internat. Soc. Hematology; mem. Am. Soc. Hematology, Am. Micros. Soc. (editorial bd. trans. 1956-65), AMA (vice chmn. sect. exptl. medicine 1968-69, chmn. sect. clin. pharmacology and therapeutics 1969-71, alt. del. 1971-73, 78—, del. 1973-75), Medicine in the Public Interest (dir. 1974—), Am. Fedn. Clin. Research, Am. Soc. Tropical Medicine, Soc. Exptl. Biology and Medicine, N.Y. Acad. Scis., Soc. Med. Consultants Armed Forces (v.p. 1968-69, pres. 1969-70), AAAS, Am., Internat. socs. internal medicine, Internat. Coll. Angiology, Midwest Blood Club, Am. Soc. Clin. Pharmacology and Chemotherapy (regent, pres. 1968-69), Internat. Soc. Blood Transfusion, Med. Mycol. Soc. Ams., Assn. Mil. Surgeons U.S., Am. Therapeutic Soc. (pres. 1968-69), Internat. Soc. Toxinology, Associacion Medica Argentina, Sociedad de Framacologic Y Terapeutica (hon.), Phi Beta Kappa, Sigma Xi, Alpha Omega Alpha, Phi Kappa Phi. Author numerous articles in field. Asst. editor Am. Jour. Med. Scis., 1951-60; editor proc. Internat. Conf. on Leukemia-Lymphoma, 1968, proc. Internat. Conf. Drug Abuse, Mem. adv. editorial bd. History of U.S. Army Medical Service in Vietnam and South Asia. Home: 2721 Bedford Rd Ann Arbor MI 48104 Office: Turner Clinic Bldg 1000 Wall St Ann Arbor MI 48109

ZARB, FRANK GUSTAVE, bus. exec.; b. N.Y.C., Feb. 17, 1935; s. Gustave and Rosemary (Antinora) Z.; B.B.A., Hofstra U., 1957, M.B.A., 1962, L.H.D., 1975; m. Patricia Koster, Mar. 31, 1957; children—Krista Ann, Frank, Jr. Trainee, Cities Service Oil Co., N.Y.C., 1957-62; gen. partner Goodbody & Co., N.Y.C., 1962-69; exec. v.p. CBWL-Hayden Stone, Inc., investment banking, N.Y.C., 1969-71; asst. sec. U.S. Dept. Labor, Washington, 1971-72; exec. v.p. Hayden Stone, Inc., N.Y.C., 1972-73; asso. dir. Office of Mgmt. and Budget, Washington, 1973-74; asst. to Pres., U.S., 1974-77; adminstr. Fed. Energy Adminstrn., Washington, 1974-77; adv. U.S. Congress and State of Alaska, 1977-78; gen. partner Lazard Freres & Co., N.Y.C., 1977—. Bd. advs. Energy Fund, 1977—; mem. N.Y. Gov.'s Council on High Tech., 1978—; chmn. bd. dirs. Nat. Energy Found., 1977-79; trustee East-Woods Sch., Oyster Bay, N.Y., 1974-75, Hofstra U., 1979—; bd. dirs. ETCO. Recipient Disting. Scholar award Hofstra U., 1974. Mem. Am. Soc. Pub. Adminstrn. (hon. life, Council Fgn. Relations. Author: The Stockmarket Handbook, 1969. Office: Lazard Freres & Co One Rockefeller Plaza New York NY 10020

ZARE, RICHARD NEIL, educator; b. Cleve., Nov. 19, 1939; s. Milton and Dorothy (Amdur) Z.; B.A., Harvard, 1961; postgrad. U. Calif. at Berkeley, 1961-63; Ph.D. (NSF predoctoral fellow), Harvard, 1964; m. Susan Leigh Shively, Apr. 20, 1963; children—Bethany Jean, Bonnie Sue, Rachel Amdur. Postdoctoral fellow Harvard, 1964, postdoctoral research asso. Joint Inst. for Lab. Astrophysics, 1964-65; asst. prof. chemistry Mass. Inst. Tech., 1965-66; asst. prof. dept. physics and astrophysics U. Colo., 1966-68, asso. prof. physics and astrophysics, asso. prof. chemistry, 1968-69; prof. chemistry Columbia, 1969-77, Higgins prof. natural sci., 1975-77; prof. Stanford U., 1977—. Cons., Aeronomy Lab., NOAA, 1966-77, radio standards physics div. Nat. Bur. Standards, 1968-77, Lawrence Livermore Lab., U. Calif., 1974—, Stanford Research Inst., 1974—, Los Alamos Sci. Lab., U. Calif., 1975—; mem. IBM Sci. Advisory Com., 1977—.

Recipient Fresenius award Phi Lambda Upsilon, 1974; Michael Polanyi medal, 1979; Nonresident fellow Joint Inst. for Lab. Astrophysics, 1970—; Alfred P. Sloan fellow, 1967-69. Mem. Nat. Acad. Sci., Am. Acad. Arts and Scis., AAAS, Am. Phys. Soc., Am. Chem. Soc., Chem. Soc. London, Phi Beta Kappa. Research and publs. on molecular luminescence, photochemistry and chem. physics. Office: Dept Chemistry Stanford U Stanford CA 94305

ZARELLA, MICHAEL PETER, truck mfg. co. exec.; b. Passaic, N.J., May 29, 1920; s. Michael A. and Mary (Griffin) Z.; m. Dorothy R. Agnello, June 29, 1947; 1 dau., Darlene C. Zarella Rankin. With Curtiss-Wright Corp., 1939-62; with Mack Trucks Inc., Allentown, Pa., 1962—, exec. v.p. adminstrn. Bd. dirs. Guiding Eyes for Blind, Allentown Salvation Army, Allentown Hosp. Served with USAAF, 1942-46. Mem. Nat. Assn. Purchasing Mgmt. (cert. lifetime purchasing mgr.). Office: PO Box M Mack Blvd Allentown PA 18105*

ZAREM, ABE MORDECAI, business exec.; b. Chgo., Mar. 7, 1917; s. I.H. and Lea (Kaufman) Z.; B.S. in Elec. Engring., Ill. Inst. Tech., 1939, LL.D. (hon.), 1968; M.S. in Elec. Engring., Calif. Inst. Tech., 1940, Ph.D., 1944; LL.D., U. Calif. at Santa Cruz, 1967; m. Esther Mariam Moskovitz, Oct. 4, 1941; children—Janet Ruth, David Michael, Mark Charles. Prof. engring. U. Calif. at Los Angeles, 1956-61; pres. Electro-Optical Systems, Inc., Pasadena, Calif., 1956-67, chmn. bd., 1967-69; former sr. v.p., dir. corp. devel. Xerox Corp., Los Angeles; mgmt. and engring. cons., 1969-75; chmn., chief exec. officer Xerox Devel. Corp., Los Angeles, 1975—. Traffic and parking commr. City of Beverly Hills, 1971-72, planning commr., 1972-73. Bd. dirs. Music Center Opera Assn., Los Angeles, 1968—; nat. trustee City of Hope; trustee Calif. Inst. Arts, 1973-76. Named Outstanding Young Elec. Engr. in U.S., Eta Kappa Nu, 1948; One of America's Ten Outstanding Young Men, U.S. Jr. C. of C., 1950. Fellow Am. Inst. Aeros. and Astronautics, I.E.E.E.; sci. mem. (a founder) Solar Energy Soc. Author: Utilization of Solar Energy, 1963. Inventor World's fastest high-speed camera, automatic oscillograph. Home: PO Box 525 Beverly Hills CA 90213

ZARNOWITZ, VICTOR, economist, educator; b. Lancut, Poland, Nov. 3, 1919; s. Leopold and Bertha (Blumenfeld) Z.; student U. Cracow (Poland), 1937-39; M.A. in Econs., U. Heidelberg (Germany), 1949, Ph.D. summa cum laude, 1951; m. Lena Engelman, Jan. 12, 1946; children—Steven L., Arthur H. Came to U.S., 1952, naturalized, 1957. Tutor, instr. econs. U. Heidelberg, also Grad. Sch. Bus., Mannheim, Germany, 1949-51; research economist Nat. Bur. Econ. Research, N.Y.C., 1952-59, mem. sr. research staff, 1963—; lectr., then vis. prof. Columbia, 1956-59; mem. faculty Grad. Sch. Bus., U. Chgo., 1959—, prof. econs. and fin., 1965—; dir. study of bus. cycle indicators, cons. Bur. Econ. Analysis, U.S. Dept. Commerce, 1972—. Fellow Am. Statis. Assn.; mem. Am. Econ. Assn., Econometric Soc., Chgo. Assn. Commerce and Industry. Author: Unfilled Orders, Price Changes and Business Fluctuations, 1962; An Appraisal of Short Term Economic Forecasts, 1967; Orders, Production and Investment, 1973; (with C. Boschan) Cyclical Indicators: An Evaluation and New Leading Indexes, 1975; An Analysis of Forecasts of Aggregate Income, Output, and the Price Level, 1979; co-author, editor: The Business Cycle Today, 1972. Contbr. to books. Home: 5752 S Blackstone Ave Chicago IL 60637

ZARR, MELVYN, educator; b. Worcester, Mass., Aug. 29, 1936; A.B., Clark U., 1958; LL.B., Harvard U., 1963; m. Gail Sclar, Aug. 29, 1971. Admitted to Mass. bar, 1964, Maine bar, 1973; staff atty. NAACP Legal Def. & Edn. Fund, Inc., N.Y.C., 1963-70; co-dir. Mass. Law Reform Inst., Boston, 1970-73; co-dir. Mass. Law Reform Inst., Boston, 1970-73; prof. law U. Maine, 1973—; U.S. Magistrate, Portland, Maine, 1977—. Mem. Am. Law Inst. Home: 19 McKinley Rd Falmouth ME 04105 Office: 246 Derring Ave Portland ME 10405

ZART, DAVID PAUL, automotive products mfg. co. exec.; b. Stitzer, Wis., June 17, 1927; s. Henry and Lela Emma (Schuppener) Z.; B.S.B.A., Bob Jones U., 1951; postgrad. in mktg. mgmt. Harvard U., 1977; m. Barbara Jean Clifton, Aug. 14, 1946; children—Sandra Lee, Vicki Jean, David Paul. Jr. buyer Ford Motor Co., Kansas City, Mo., 1951-54, buyer, Dearborn, Mich., 1955-57; mgr. adminstrn. Holiday Plastics Co., Kansas City, Mo., 1954-55; with Firestone Steel Products Co., Akron, Ohio, 1957—, gen. sales mgr., 1972, mfg. mgr., 1978, pres., 1978—. Served with U.S. Army, 1946-47. Mem. Soc. Automotive Engrs. Republican. Baptist. Club: Firestone Country. Home: 255 Harmony Hills Dr Akron OH 44321 Office: 1600 Firestone Pkwy Akron OH 44301

ZARTMAN, LEONARD STORY, lawyer, bus. exec.; b. Rochester, N.Y., Sept. 18, 1926; s. Leonard S. and Eva (Cushman) Z.; A.B., Yale, 1948; LL.B., Columbia, 1953; m. Barbara Jean Flower, Aug. 2, 1969; children—Eve C.; (by previous marriage) Lydia, Sarah G., Nathaniel S., Dana S., Mary W. Admitted to N.Y. bar, 1953; practiced in Rochester, 1953-68; mem. firm. Nixon, Hargrave, Devans & Doyle, 1953-64; atty. Eastman Kodak Co., 1964-68, asst. to gen. counsel, 1970, asst. sec., 1971-73, sec., 1973—; spl. asst. to Pres. Nixon, 1969; gen. counsel Small Bus. Adminstrn., Washington, 1969-70. Served with USNR, 1944-46; as capt. USMCR, 1950-52. Mem. Am., Monroe County (N.Y.) bar assns. Home: 60 Hawthorne St Rochester NY 14610 Office: 343 State St Rochester NY 14650

ZARTMAN, ROBERT LEE, corp. lawyer; b. Canton, Ohio, Dec. 16, 1928; s. Floyd Byron and Hattie (Olshawsky) Z.; student Kent State U., Canton, 1948-50; LL.B., William McKinley Sch. Law, Canton, 1954; m. Oliveanne Marie Hixson, Oct. 25, 1953; children—Mark, Matthew, Michael, Leslie, Shannon. Admitted to Ohio bar, 1954; practiced in Canton, 1956-57; ins. claims atty., Canton and Akron, Ohio, 1957-61; counsel, asst. sec. E.W. Bliss Co., Canton, 1961-67, sec., gen. counsel, 1968-69; sec., counsel Gulf & Western Indsl. Products Co., 1969-70; gen. atty. Glidden-Durkee (SCM Corp.), 1971-74; asst. sec., atty. Diebold, Inc., 1974-76; sec., atty. Cunningham Drug Stores, Inc., Detroit, 1976—. Served with USN, 1946-48. Mem. Am., Ohio, bar assns., Delta Theta Phi. Home: 1066 Barneswood Ln Rochester MI 48063

ZARUBY, WALTER STEPHEN, holding co. exec.; b. Vegreville, Alta., Can., Mar. 4, 1930; s. William and Annie (Kubon) Z.; B.A.Sc., U. Toronto, 1952; m. Margaret Beth Fargey, Sept. 22, 1958; children—Stephen, Jeffrey. Engr., project mgr. Shell Oil Co. and Shell Can. Ltd., 1952-70; sr. v.p. Westburne Internat. Industries Ltd., Calgary, Alta., 1970-73, pres., 1973-76; pres. Radium Holdings Ltd., Calgary, 1977—, Radium Resources Ltd., 1978—. Mem. Assn. Profl. Engrs., Geologists, and Geophysicists Alta., Assn. Drilling Contractors (bd. dirs. 1971-74). Clubs: Calgary Petroleum, Calgary Golf and Country, Glencoe. Address: 1012 Bel-Aire Dr SW Calgary AB T2V 2B9 Canada

ZASLOW, MORRIS, historian; b. Rosthern, Sask., Can., Dec. 22, 1918; s. Isaac and Bessie (Hardin) Z.; B.A. with honors in History, U. Alta., 1940, B.E., 1942; M.A., U. Toronto, 1948, Ph.D., 1957; m. Betty Winifred Stone, Oct. 5, 1945; 1 son, Jonathan Philip. Tchr. secondary schs., Alta., 1941-42, 46-47; asst. dept. history U. Toronto, 1947-50, lectr., 1952-59, asst. prof. history, 1959-64, asso. prof., 1964-65; lectr. Carleton U., Ottawa, 1950-52; vis. prof. U. Calgary, 1976-77, 79-80; prof. history U. Western Ont., London, 1965—. Mem. hist. adv. subcom. Met. Toronto and Region Conservation Authority, 1958-65; mem. Archaeol. and Historic Sites Bd. Ont., 1966-67. Served with RCAF, 1942-45. Can. Council fellow, 1960, 66, 69; Nuffield Found. fellow, 1960-61; Killam sr. research fellow, 1973-74; recipient Cruikshank medal Ont. Hist. Soc., 1976; Centennial medal Can., 1967. Mem. Ont. Hist. Soc. (editor 1956-62, v.p. 1962-66, pres. 1966-67), Royal Soc. Can., Arctic Inst. N.Am., Can. Hist. Assn., Champlain Soc. (editor 1962-72, v.p. 1974—). Jewish. Author: The Opening of the Canadian North, 1870-1914, 1971; Reading the Rocks: The Story of the Geological Survey of Canada, 1842-1972, 1975; founding editor Issues in Canadian History, 1965-68; contbr. articles to profl. jours. Home: 838 Waterloo St London ON N6A 3W6 Canada Office: Social Science Centre Univ of Western Ont London ON N6A 5C2 Canada

ZASSENHAUS, HANS JULIUS, mathematician; b. Koblenz, Rheinland, Ger., May 28, 1912; s. Julius Paul and Margarete Emma Friederike (Ziegler) Z.; S.S., Hamburg U., 1930, Dr.rer.nat. (Ph.D. in Math.), 1934; D.Sc. (hon.), Ottawa (Ont.) U., 1966, McGill U., Montreal, P.Q., Can., 1974; m. Lieselotte Rosa Marie Lohmann, Sept. 5, 1942; children—Michael, Angela Elisabeth, Hans Peter. Wissenschaftlicher Hilfsarbeiter math. dept. Rostock U., Mecklenburg, 1934-36, hilfsassistent, 1936-38, asst., 1938-40, dieten-dozent, 1940-46, ausserordentlicher prof., 1946-50; Peter Redpath prof. math. McGill U., Montreal, Can., 1949-59; prof. U. Notre Dame, 1959-64; research prof. math. Ohio State U., Columbus, 1964—; vis. prof. Calif. Inst. Tech., 1958-59, Göttingen (Ger.), U., 1967, Heidelberg (Ger.) U., 1969, UCLA, 1970, Warwick U., 1972; Fairchild Distinguished Prof. Calif. Inst. Tech., 1974-75; Semicentennial Univ. prof. Montreal U., 1977-78. Served in Germany Navy, 1940-45. Decorated Verdienst Kreuz; recipient Konsul Leon Guttmann prize, 1933; Brit. Council fellow, 1948-49; fellow Royal Can. Soc., 1956; Lester Ford prize Math. Assn. Am., 1968; Humboldt U.S. Sr. Scientists award, 1979. Mem. Am. Math. Soc., Math. Assn. Am., AAUP, Can. Math. Soc., Deutsche Mathematiker Vereinigung. Author: Theory of Groups, 1937, 2d edit., 1958. Office: Dept Math Ohio State U 231 W 18 Ave Columbus OH 43210

ZASSENHAUS, HILTGUNT MARGRET, physician; b. Hamburg, Ger., July 10, 1916; d. Julius and Margret Zassenhaus; came to U.S., 1952, naturalized, 1957; Diploma of Scandinavian Langs., U. Hamburg, 1938; M.D., U. Copenhagen, 1952; hon. degrees, Goucher Coll., Towson State U., Notre Dame Coll., 1975. With German Dept. Justice, Berlin, 1941-45, secret relief action for Scandinavian polit. prisoners; organizer relief action for German orphans, 1945-48; intern, then resident in internal medicine Balt. City Hosp., 1952-54; practice medicine specializing in internal medicine, Balt., 1954—; mem. staff Greater Balt. Med. Center, Md. Gen. Hosp.; dir. Balt. Fed. Savs. and Loan Assn., 1965—. Decorated knight St. Olav's Order 1st class (Norway); Order Dannebro 1st class (Denmark); recipient Danish and Norwegian Red Cross medal, 1948; Bundesverdienstkreuz 1st class (Fed. Republic Ger.), 1969; named Outstanding Woman of Year in Balt. County, AAUW, 1976; nominated for Nobel Peace Prize, 1974. Author: (biography) On Guard in The Dark, 1948; (autobiography) Walls (Christopher award as best book of year 1975); also articles, essays. Address: 7028 Bellona Ave Baltimore MD 21212. *I know that one person can make the difference. That gives me hope that the walls of hate and prejudice separating man from man one day will fade so that people will cease destroying each other and join to serve life.*

ZATUCHNI, JACOB, physician; b. Phila., Oct. 8, 1920; s. Samuel and Minnie (Pollack) Z.; A.B, Temple U., 1941, M.D., 1944, M.S., 1950; m. Evelyn Schwartz, July 29, 1945; children—Stephen, Dory, Beth, Michael. Intern Einstein Med. Div., No. Div., Phila., 1944-45; resident Temple U. Hosp., 1947-50; practice medicine specializing in cardiology, Phila., 1958—; prof. medicine Temple U. Sch. Med., 1966—; chief sect. cardiovascular disease Episcopal Hosp., Phila., 1967—, dir. dept. medicine, 1974—. Diplomate Am. Bd. Internal Medicine. Mem. A.C.P., Phila. Coll. Physicians, N.Y. Acad. Scis., Am. Fedn. for Clin. Research, Am. Heart Assn. (fellow council clin. cardiology), Heart Assn. Southeastern Pa., Am. Thoracic Soc., AMA, Pa., Phila. County med. socs., Am. Soc. Nuclear Medicine. Author: Notes on Physical Diagnosis, 1964; also numerous med. articles. Home: 191 Presidential Blvd Bala Cynwyd PA 19004 Office: Episcopal Hosp Philadelphia PA 19125

ZATURENSKA, MARYA (MRS. HORACE V. GREGORY), poet, biographer; b. Kiev, Russia, Sept. 12, 1902; d. Abram and Johanna (Lubovska) Zaturensky; brought to U.S., 1910, naturalized, 1914; student (scholar) Valparaiso U., 1921-23, U. Wis. Library Sch., 1925; D.Litt. (hon.), U. Wis., 1977; m. Horace V. Gregory, Aug. 21, 1925; children—Joanna (Mrs. S.H. Zeigler), Patrick Bolton. Recipient Shelley award Poetry Soc. New Eng., 1935; Pulitzer prize in poetry, 1938; Guarantors award Poetry mag., 1941; also others. Author: (poetry) Threshold and Hearth, 1934, Cold Morning Sky, 1937, The Listening Landscape, 1941, The Golden Mirror, 1944, Selected Poems, 1954, Terraces of Light, 1960, Collected Poems, 1966; The Hidden Waterfall, 1974; (with husband) History of American Poetry Since 1900, 1946, The Mentor Books of Religious Poems, 1957, The Crystal Cabinet, 1962, The Silver Swan, 1966; (biography) Christina Rosetti: A Portrait with Background, 1949, rev., 1970; also introduction to poetry vols. Editor: Selected Poems of Christina Rossetti, 1969; Collected Poems of Sara Teasdale, 1966. Address: Closter Rd Palisades NY 10964

ZATZ, SIDNEY ROSS, lawyer; b. Chgo., Mar. 28, 1913; s. Max and Goldie (Rosovich) Z.; Ph.B., U. Chgo., 1933, J.D. cum laude, 1935; m. Shirley R. Meyerovitz, Apr. 19, 1975. Admitted to Ill. bar, 1935, since practiced in Chgo.; partner firm Arvey, Hodes, Costello & Burman, and predecessors, 1935—; dir. Peerless Weighing and Vending Machine Corp. Bd. dirs. Palos Community Hosp. Served as officer USNR, World War II. Mem. Ill., Chgo. bar assns., Am. Assn. Hosp. Attys., U. Chgo. Law Sch. Alumni Assn. (dir.), Phi Beta Kappa, Order of Coif. Club: Standard (Chgo.). Home: 320 Oakdale Ave Chicago IL 60657 Office: 180 N LaSalle St Chicago IL 60601

ZATZKIS, HENRY, theoretical physicist, educator; b. Holzminden, Germany, Apr. 7, 1915; s. Markus and Lifscha (Eber) Z.; B.S., Ohio State U., 1942; M.S., Ind. U., 1944; Ph.D., Syracuse U., 1950; came to U.S., 1940, naturalized, 1946; m. Natalie F. Serlin, July 1, 1951; children—Mark, David. Instr., Ind. U., 1942-44, U. N.C., 1944-47, Syracuse U., 1947-51, U. Conn., 1951- 53; mem. faculty N.J. Inst. Tech., 1953—, prof. math., chmn. dept., 1959—, Distinguished prof., 1970—. Mem. Phi Beta Kappa, Sigma Xi, Sigma Pi Sigma, Pi Mu Epsilon. Research gen. relativity, quantum theory and acoustics. Co-author handbooks, encys.; contbr. articles to profl. jours. Home: 5 Elliott Pl West Orange NJ 07052 Office: NJ Inst Tech 323 High St Newark NJ 07102

ZAUSNER, L. ANDREW, lawyer; b. Plainfield, N.J., May 1, 1949; s. Sol and Beattice (Summer) Z.; B.A., Boston U., 1971; M.B.A., U. Pa., 1975, J.D., 1975. Admitted to Pa. bar, 1975, U.S. Supreme Ct. bar, 1979; mem. firm Blank, Rome, Comisky & McCauley, Phila., 1975-77; atty., adv. legislation, Fed. Energy Adminstrn., Washington, 1977; spl. asst. to acting gen. counsel Dept. Energy, Washington, 1977-78, exec. asst. to dep. sec., 1978-79; dir. govt. relations Pennzoil Co., 1979—. Budget dir., gen. counsel Pa. Presdl. Democratic Campaign Com., 1976. Home: 1712 1/4 19th St NW Washington DC 20029 Office: 1000 Independence Ave SW Washington DC 20585

ZAVALA, DONALD CHARLES, physician, educator; b. El Centro, Calif., Nov. 1, 1923; s. Michael Joseph and Effie Delores (McElyea) Z.; B.A., Wooster Coll., 1944; M.D., U. Cin., 1948; m. Julia Frances Hart, Nov. 23, 1946; children—Catherine Anne, Rebecca Anne, Donald Charles. Intern, U. Iowa Hosp., Iowa City, 1948-49, resident, 1949-52; practice medicine specializing in internal medicine, El Centro, Calif., 1952-69; fellow in pulmonary disease U. Iowa, 1969-70; instr. pulmonary disease U. Iowa Hosps., Iowa City, 1970-71, asst. prof., 1971-73, asso. prof., 1973-76, prof. medicine, 1976—. Served with M.C., U.S. Army, 1944. Iowa Tb and Respiratory Diseases Assn. grantee, 1970-71; Nat. Tb and Respiratory Diseases Assn. grantee, 1972-74; Iowa chpt. Am. Lung Assn. Career Research awardee, 1976-77. Lic. physician, Ohio, Iowa, Calif. Diplomate Am. Bd. Internal Medicine. Fellow A.C.P.; mem. Am. Thoracic Soc., Am. Lung Assn., Am. Fedn. Clin. Research, Central Soc. Clin. Research, Am. Coll. Chest Physicians, Am. Broncho-Esophagological Assn., Iowa Thoracic Soc. (pres. 1975-76). Author: Flexible Fiberoptic Bronchoscopy—A Training Handbook, 1978; contbr. articles to med. jours. and books. Home: 1630 Derwen Dr Iowa City IA 52240 Office: U Iowa Hosps Iowa City IA 52242

ZAVALETA, HUMBERTO, mfg. co. exec.; b. Oruro, Bolivia, May 2, 1936; s. Jose and Lola (Navia) Z.; came to U.S., 1954, naturalized, 1977; B.S.E., Princeton U., 1958; m. Sarab Kaur, Dec. 28, 1968; children—Erika Simone, Alexis Danielle, Marcelo Humberto. With ITT, 1959—, v.p. subs. ISEL, N.Y.C., 1967-69, pres. ISEL, 1969-78, group exec. ITT Latin Am. and v.p. ITT Corp., N.Y.C., 1978—. Trustee, Council of Ams.; bd. dirs. Argentine-Am. C. of C.; bd. govs. ADELA. Mem. Sigma Xi. Office: 320 Park Ave New York NY 10022

ZAVATT, JOSEPH CARMINE, fed. judge; b. Lawrence, N.Y., Sept. 19, 1900; s. Vincent and Margaret (Hanlon) Z.; B.A., Columbia U., 1922, LL.B., 1924, postgrad. Sch Polit. Sci., 1926-27; postgrad. N.Y. U. Law Sch., 1933-34; m. Anna Maas, June 12, 1942. Admitted to N.Y. State bar, 1926; practiced in Nassau County, N.Y., 1926-57; instr. in law of contracts CCNY, 1930-33; judge U.S. Dist. Ct. for Eastern Dist. N.Y., 1957—, chief judge, 1962-69, sr. dist. judge, 1970—; counsel N.Y. State Legis. Com., 1948-53; pres. Legal Aid Soc. of Nassau County (N.Y.), 1951-57. Served with U.S. Army, World War I; to lt. comdr. USNR, 1942-45. Mem. Bar Assn. Nassau County (pres. 1950). Republican. Clubs: Garden City (N.Y.) Golf, Garden City Country; Skytop; Am. Legion, VFW. Home: 67 Hilton Ave Garden City NY 11530

ZAVIST, ALGERD FRANK, mfg. co. exec.; b. Chgo., July 2, 1921; s. Frank and Mary (Uzas) Z.; B.S., Roosevelt U., 1943, M.S. (Am. Chem. Soc. fellow), 1949; Ph.D. (Standard Oil Co. fellow 1948-49, Research Corp. fellow 1950), U. Chgo., 1950; m. Mary Lorraine Martin, July 14, 1951; children—James, Mary Sue, Patrick, Thomas. Lab. technician Infilco, Inc., Chgo., 1940-41; plant chemist W. H. Barber Co., Chgo., 1941-42; instr. Wilson Jr. Coll., 1949; with Gen. Electric Co., 1950—, mgr. chemistry lab., Louisville, 1962-68, mgr. maj. appliance labs., Louisville, 1968—. Pres. Louisville Community Concert Assn., 1972-74, dir., 1972—. Served to capt. A.C., U.S. Army, 1943-46. Decorated Fourragere (Belgium). Fellow Am. Inst. Chemists; mem. Am. Chem. Soc. (chmn. Louisville sect. 1969-70), Soc. Plastics Engrs. (pres. Louisville sect. 1967-68), Chem. Soc. (London). Methodist. Contbr. articles to profl. publs.; patentee in field. Home: 8906 Nottingham Pkwy Louisville KY 40222 Office: Gen Electric Co Maj Appliance Labs AP35-1001 Appliance Park Louisville KY 40225

ZAWACKI, EDMUND IGNACE, educator; b. Easthampton, Mass., Feb. 1, 1908; s. Andrew and Kazimiera (Albertowicz) Z.; grad. Williston Acad., 1925; B.S., Harvard, 1929, M.A., 1930, Ph.D., 1942; student U. Warsaw (Poland), 1930-31; m. Maria Akst, Oct. 14, 1934 (dec. Aug. 1949); 1 son, Ian; m. 2d, Helen Baycar, June 1950; children—Janice, Andrew. Mem. faculty U. Wis., 1939-78, chmn. dept. Slavic langs., 1942-59, chmn. course modern humanities, 1952-78, prof. emeritus, 1979—; pioneer open cities program for people-to-people contact, city-to-city basis between U.S. and Iron Curtain countries, 1958; mem. Nat. Com. for Monroe Doctrine, 1963. Mem. adv. bd. Nat. Council of Scholars, 1969. Trustee Kosciuszko Found., 1950—, sec. bd. trustees. Mem. Polish Inst. Arts and Scis. Am., Modern Lang. Assn. Am. (chmn. Slavic sect. 1942, 47), Am. Assn. Tchrs. Slavic and East European Langs. (pres. Wis. chpt. 1962), Am. Bus. Club of Madison (pres. 1959, 60). Club: Madison Mushroom. Author: (with Z. Folejewski) Intermediate Russian, 1962; Mikolaj Kopernik (1473-1543) Nicolaus Copernicus in the Polish Cultural Tradition, 1973; contbg. author: Literature of the World, 1956; University of Buffalo Studies. 1956; contbg. editor Perspectives mag., Washington. Contbr. articles, columns to profl. jours. Home: 1415 Vilas Ave Madison WI 53711

ZAWINUL, JOSEF, bandleader, composer, keyboardist, synthesizer; b. Vienna, Austria, July 7, 1932; s. Josef and Maria (Hameder) Z.; came to U.S., 1959; student Realtymnasium, Vienna, 1945-49, Vienna Conservatory Music, 1942-47; Dr. honoris Causa, 1969; m. Maxine Byars, Mar. 16, 1964; children—Anthony, Erich, Ivan. Appeared with Vienna Radio Orch., 1952-58; mem. Fatty George Band, 1956-58, Maynard Ferguson, 1959; accompanist Dinah Washington, 1959-61, Joe Williams, 1961; mem. Cannonball Adderley Quintet, 1961-70; recs. with Miles Davis; founder own group Weather Report, 1970; recs. include Birdland (Grammy nomination), 1977, In a Silent Way (Grammy nomination), 1969, Heavy Weather (Gold record, Grammy nomination), 1977. Named Number One Jazzland (Combo) in U.S.A., 1971-78, Number One synthesiser player, 1976-79, Number One composer in Critics and Reader polls, 1978; rec. Jazz Record of Yr., 5 of 8 albums, 1973-78. Composer: In a Silent Way, 1968; Orange Lady, 1969; Unknown Soldier, 1970; Boogie Woogie Waltz, 1972; Nubian Sundance, 1973; Black Market, 1974; Birdland, 1977; numerous others. Office: care Cavallo-Ruffalo Mgmt 9885 Charleville Blvd Beverly Hills CA 90210

ZAWODNY, JANUSZ KAZIMIERZ, educator; b. Warsaw, Poland, Dec. 11, 1921; s. Kazimierz and Wanda (Pukk) Z.; came to U.S., 1948, naturalized, 1955; B.S., State U. Iowa, 1950, M.A. in Internat. Relations, 1951; Ph.D. in Polit. Sci. (Social Sci. Research Council fellow), Stanford U., 1955; m. LaRae Koppit; 1 son, Roman Janusz. Instr., then asst. prof. Princeton U., 1955-58; fellow Center Advanced Study Behavioral Scis., Stanford U., 1961-62; prof. Washington U., 1963-65; asso. prof. U. Pa., 1962-63, prof. internat. relations, 1965-75; Avery prof. internat. relations Claremont Grad. Sch. and Pomona Coll., 1975—; fellow Inst. Social and Behavioral Pathology, U. Chgo., 1977—; mem. Inst. for Advanced Study, Princeton, 1971-72. Sr. asso. mem. St. Antony's Coll., Oxford (Eng.) U., 1968-69; research asso. Harvard Center Internat. Affairs, 1968; U.S. Dept. State Scholar-Diplomat Seminar, summer 1973. Served with Polish Underground Forces, 1940-44, Brit. Army, 1945-48. Decorated Virtuti Militari, comdr. Polonia Restituta, Cross of Valor, Gold Cross of Merit with Swords. Ford Faculty fellow, 1956, 58-59, 68-69; grantee Am. Council Learned Socs., Am. Philos. Soc., 1967-68.

Author: Nothing But Honor: The Uprising of Warsaw, 1944, 78; Man and International Relations: Contributions of the Social Sciences to the Study of Conflict and Integration, 2 vols., 1967; Guide to the Study of International Relations, 1967; Death in the Forest: The Story of the Katyn Forest Massacre (translated into Japanese, German, French, Norwegian, Italian), 1962, 71; also articles. Contbr. to Am. Scholar, 1962, Internat. Ency. Social Scis., 1968. Office: Claremont Grad Sch and Pomona Coll Claremont CA 91711

ZAYEK, FRANCIS MANSOUR, bishop; b. Manzaillo, Cuba, Oct. 18, 1920; s. Mansour and Mary (Coury) Z.; student St. Joseph's Catholic U., Beirut, 1938; D.D., U. Propogation of Faith, 1947, Ph.D., 1947; D.C.L., Lateran U., 1951. Ordained priest Roman Cath. Ch., 1946; rector Maronite Cathedral of Holy Family, Cairo, 1951-56; Oriental sec. to Vatican Apostolic Internunciature, mem. Archdiocesan Tribunal, 1951-56; promoter of justice Sacred Roman Rota, 1956-58; prof. Oriental canon law Internat. Coll. St. Anselm, Rome, 1958-60; prof. Oriental canon law Lateran U., Rome, 1960-61; aux. bishop to Cardinal James De Barros Camera, Archbishop of Rio de Janeiro, 1962; consecrated maronite bishop, 1962; maronite bishop, Rio de Janeiro, 1962-64; presided over First Ann. Maronite Conv., Washington, 1964; first maronite exarch of U.S.A., 1966—, also titular bishop of Callinicum. Decorated knight comdr. Equestrian Order of Holy Sepulchre of Jerusalem; recipient medal of merit Govt. of Republic Italy, 1966. Home: 8070 Harbor View Terr Brooklyn NY 11209 Office: 205 82d St Brooklyn NY 11209

ZBARSKY, SIDNEY HOWARD, educator; b. Vonda, Sask., Can., Feb. 19, 1920; s. Jack and Ethel (Sinrod) Z.; B.A., U. Sask., 1940; M.A., U. Toronto, 1942, Ph.D., 1946; m. Miriam Frankel, Sept. 4, 1944; children—Ralph, Jonathan, Deborah. Sci. officer Atomic Energy Project, Chalk River, Ont., 1946-48; asst. prof. U. Minn., 1948-49; asso. prof. biochemistry U. B.C., 1949-62, prof., 1962—, Killam sr. fellow, 1973-74; cons. dir. Met. Biomed. Labs. Mem. Canadian Biochem. Soc. (pres. 1967-68), Canadian Physiol. Soc., Am. Chem. Soc., AAAS, Am. Soc. Biol. Chemists, N.Y. Acad. Scis. Contbr. articles profl. jours. Home: 1420 W 49th Ave Vancouver BC V6M 2R5 Canada

ZDANIS, RICHARD ALBERT, educator; b. Balt., July 15, 1935; s. Albert Francis and Elsie (Kral) Z.; A.B., Johns Hopkins, 1957, Ph.D., 1960; m. Barbara Rosenberger, June 5, 1955; children—Michael Richard, Carole Lynn. Research asso., instr. Princeton, 1960-62; asst. prof. Johns Hopkins, 1962-65, asso. prof., 1965-69, prof. physics, 1969—, asso. provost, 1975-79, v.p. for adminstrv. services, 1977-79, vice provost, 1979—. Home: 11216 Old Carriage Rd Glen Arm MD 21057 Office: Johns Hopkins Dept Physics Baltimore MD 21218

ZEBELL, ELMER GEORGE, investment broker; b. Racine, Wis., Apr. 7, 1927; s. Elmer Herman and Malinda Gertrude (Herrmann) Z.; student Lacrosse (Wis.) State Tchrs. Coll., 1945; m. Betty Ann Krahn, June 14, 1947; children—Patricia Ann, Sherry Lou. With U.S. Postal Dept., Milw., 1946-53; v.p. trading Robert W. Baird & Co. Inc., Milw., 1953—; chmn. bd. dirs. Inversora Inmobiliaria S.A. Served with USNR, 1945-46. Named Alumnus of Year, Wis. Lutheran High Sch., 1957. Chmn. investment bd. Wis. Evang. Luth. Synod; bd. dirs. Wis. Evang. Luth. Synod Found. Mem. Nat. Security Traders Assn. (past chmn.), Milw. Security Traders Assn. (past pres.), Milw. Bond Club (past pres.), Wis. Assn. Security Dealers (past pres.). Club: Milw. Athletic. Home: 5413 Montgomery Dr Greendale WI 53129 Office: Box 672 Milwaukee WI 53201

ZECCA, JOHN ANDREW, assn. exec.; b. Bklyn., June 18, 1914; s. Joseph and Elvira (Orsi) Z.; student Heffley Queensboro Coll., Ridgewood, N.Y., 1931, N.Y. U., 1933-36; m. Jean Ann Scott, June 27, 1964; 1 son, John Andrew. Auditor, ASCE, 1936-50, comptroller, 1950-60; registered rep. Goodbody & Co., 1960-61; pvt. cons. practice, 1961-64; sec., gen. mgr. United Engring. Trustees, 1965—; trustee Engring. Index, Inc., 1967—; sec. Engring. Found., 1965—, John Fritz Medal Bd. Award, 1965—, Daniel Guggenheim Medal Bd. Award, 1965—. Mem. East Side Assn. Mem. ASCE, Council Engring. and Sci. Soc. Execs., Am. Soc. Assn. Execs. Home: 15 Hillside Terrace Suffern NY 10901 Office: 345 E 47th St New York NY 10017

ZECH, LANDO WILLIAM, JR., naval officer; b. Astoria, Oreg., June 29, 1923; s. Lando William and Mae Evelyn (Monroe) Z.; B.S., U.S. Naval Acad., 1944; M.S., George Washington U., 1971; m. Josephine Mary Kerr, Feb. 14, 1949; children—Janet Zech Cocke, Joanne, Nancy, Carol, Patty. Commd. ensign U.S. Navy, 1944, advanced through grades to rear adm., 1973; destroyer duty in Pacific, World War II; comdr. five naval vessels, four submarines, U.S.S. Sea Robin, U.S.S. Albacore, U.S.S. Nautilus, U.S.S. John Adams, and guided missile cruiser U.S.S. Springfield, 1956-70; dep. chief legis. affairs Navy Dept., Washington, 1970-72; dep. comdr. Navy Recruiting Command, Washington, 1972-74; comdr. 13th naval dist., Seattle, 1974-76; chief naval tech. tng. Naval Air Sta., Memphis, 1976-78; comdr. U.S. Naval Forces Japan, 1978—. Decorated Legion of Merit with gold star. Mem. U.S. Naval Inst. Roman Catholic. Clubs: Rotary, Washington Athletic. Home: 17 Halsey Rd Yokosuka Japan Office: Comdr US Naval Forces Japan FPO Seattle WA 98762

ZECH, ROBERT FRANCIS, accountant; b. Chgo., July 29, 1911; s. Nicholas P. and Minnie (Boll) Z.; B.A., Williams Coll., 1933; student Northwestern U., 1933-34; m. Betty Ruth Smith, Jan. 28, 1943; children—Adrienne (Mrs. Carlos Urrutia), Robert S., Lisa. With Arthur Andersen & Co., C.P.A.'s, 1934-74, partner charge Dallas office, 1951-68. Mem. adv. com., past chmn. financial mgmt. conf. Tex. A. and M. U. Chmn., Civil Service Bd. Dallas, 1959-68; treas., v.p. Jr. Achievement Dallas, 1954-62, pres., 1962-68, dir., 1954-72, bd. govs., 1972—; mem. adv. council Dallas Community Chest Trust Fund, 1965-67; mem. Dallas Assembly, 1962-64. Bd. dirs. Dallas Council World Affairs, 1969-71, Dallas Child Guidance Clinic, 1976—; bd. dirs., exec. com. Dallas Grand Opera Assn., 1972—. Served to lt. comdr. USNR, 1942-45. C.P.A., numerous states. Mem. Am. Inst. C.P.A.'s, Tex. Soc. C.P.A.'s, Dallas C. of C. (bd. dirs. 1968-70), Garoyle, Zeta Psi, Beta Alpha Psi. Club: City (Dallas). Home: 5430 Ursula Lane Dallas TX 75229 Office: 1201 Elm St Dallas TX 75270

ZECHMAN, FRED WILLIAM, JR., physiologist; b. Youngstown, Ohio, Mar. 16, 1928; s. Frederick William and Kathryn S. (Ritz) Z.; B.S., Otterbein Coll., 1949; M.S., U. Md., 1951; Ph.D. (Univ. scholar), Duke U., 1957, postgrad. (Univ. fellow), 1956-57; m. Nancy Ann Bussard, June 24, 1950; children—Jami Ann, Frederick William. Grad. asst. dept. zoology U. Md., 1949-51; biologist Office Naval Research, Washington, 1951-53; instr. in physiology Duke U., 1953-57; asst. prof. physiology Miami U., Oxford, Ohio, 1957-60, asso. prof., 1960-61; asst. prof. physiology and biophysics U. Ky. Coll. Medicine, 1961-62, asso. prof., 1963-68, prof., chmn. dept. physiology and biophysics, 1968—; vis. prof. U. Hawaii, 1971; bd. dirs. U. Ky. Research Found.; cons., lectr. in field; mem. internat. symposiums. Recipient Outstanding Preclin. Teaching award Student AMA, 1968-69, Faculty Sci. Achievement award Ky. Med. Assn., 1971; Am. Physiol. Soc. summer fellow, 1960; USAF grantee, 1960-66, 67-71; NIH grantee, 1966-71, 74-79. Mem. Aerospace Med. Assn., AAAS, Am. Physiol. Soc. (ednl. materials rev. bd.), Soc. Exptl. Biology and Medicine, Assn. Chmn. Depts. Physiology, Ky. Acad. Sci., Cardiopulmonary Disease Council of Am. Heart Assn., Sigma Xi. Contbr. articles to profl. publs. Home: 2130 Hart Ct Lexington KY 40502 Office: Dept Physiology Coll Medicine U Ky Lexington KY 40536

ZECKHAUSER, RICHARD JAY, polit. economist, educator; b. Phila., Nov. 1, 1940; s. Julius Nathaniel and Estelle (Borgenicht) Z.; A.B., Harvard, 1962, Ph.D., 1969; m. Nancy Mackell Hoover, Sept. 9, 1967; children—Bryn Gordon, Benjamin Rennell. Jr. fellow Soc. Fellows, Harvard, 1965-68, mem. faculty, 1968—, prof. polit. econs. Kennedy Sch., 1972—; founder, dir. Niederhoffer, Cross & Zeckhauser, cons., 1968—. Mem. Phi Beta Kappa. Co-author: A Primer for Policy Analysis, 1978. Editor: Benefit-Cost and Policy Analysis, 1974. Contbr. profl. jours. Address: 138 Irving St Cambridge MA 02138

ZEDEK, MISHAEL, educator; b. Kaunas, Lithuania, July 16, 1926; s. Jacob and Ida (Kaplan) Z.; M.Sc., Hebrew U., Jerusalem, 1952; Ph.D., Harvard, 1956; m. Meira Ellen Marion Oschinsky, Aug. 13, 1956; children—Daniel Aaron, Thalia Margot. Came to U.S., 1953, naturalized, 1964. Research asst., teaching fellow Harvard, 1953-56; instr. U. Calif. at Berkeley, 1956-58; asst. prof., asso. prof., prof. math. U. Md., College Park, 1958—; vis. asso. prof. Hebrew U., Jerusalem, 1964-65; vis. sr. scholar Imperial Coll., London, 1971-72. Served with Israel Def. Army, 1948-49. Mem. Am., London math. socs., Math. Assn. Am. Home: 10102 Brock Dr Silver Spring MD 20903 Office: Math Dept U Md College Park MD 20742

ZEDER, FRED MONROE, II, bus. exec.; b. South Orange, N.J., Mar. 14, 1921; s. Fred Morrell and Lucille (Monroe) Z.; student U. Mich. Engring. Sch., 1939-41, UCLA, 1945-47; LL.D. (hon.), Northwood Inst., 1978; m. Martha Blood, Aug. 8, 1942; children—Fred M., Suzan Lucille, Howard, Melinda Ann, Wendy. Pres. Zeder-Talbott, Inc., Detroit and Los Angeles, 1945-49; v.p. McCann-Erickson, N.Y.C., 1949-56; pres. Chrysler-Zeder, Inc., N.Y.C., 1956—; dir. Hydrometals, Inc., 1957-77, pres., chief exec. officer, 1959-71, chmn., chief exec. officer, 1970-77; dir. Office of Territorial Affairs, Dept. Interior, Washington, 1975-77; chief exec., pres. Paradise Cruise Ltd., Zeder Sea Ltd., 1978—; former Dallas met. chmn. Nat. Alliance Businessmen. Councilman, Dallas City Council, 1971-73; bd. dirs. Dallas/Ft. Worth Airport, 1973-75. Served as pilot USAAF, 1941-45; maj. Res. Decorated knight of Malta. Mem. Am. Rocket Assn., World Bus. Council (founding), Delta Kappa Epsilon. Roman Catholic. Clubs: Colony Hunt (Los Angeles); U. Mich. of N.Y. (past pres., bd. govs.), Union League (N.Y.C.); Capitol Hill (Washington); Preston Trail Golf (Dallas). Home: 3643 Diamond Head Rd Honolulu HI 96816 Office: Paradise Cruise Ltd PO Box 8491 Honolulu HI 96815

ZEDLER, BEATRICE HOPE, educator; b. Milw., May 14, 1916; d. Edwin and Cecelia (Koch) Z.; B.A. summa cum laude, Marquette U., 1937, M.A., 1938; Ph.D., Fordham U., 1947. Instr. English and philosophy Marian Coll., Fond du Lac, Wis., 1939-40; instr. Coll. Misericordia, Dallas, Pa., 1941-43; instr. philosophy Marquette U., 1946-51, asst. prof., 1951-54, asso. prof., 1954-63, prof., 1963—, named to Women's Chair of Humanistic Studies, 1967-69, 69-71. Mem. Am. Cath., Am. philos. assns., Mediaeval Acad. Am., A.A.U.P. Editor: Destructio Destructionum Philosophiae Algazelis (Averroes), 1961; annotated transl. Thomas Aquinas' On the Unity of the Intellect Against The Averroists, 1968, collections Gerard Smith: Christian Philosophy and Its Future, 1971, A Trio of Talks, 1971. Contbr. articles profl. jours., encys., book reviews. Home: 5305 W Wisconsin Ave Milwaukee WI 53208

ZEEVAERT, LEONARDO, civil engr., educator; b. Veracruz, Mex., Nov. 27, 1914; Civil Engr., Universidad Autonoma de Mex., 1939; M.Sc., M.I.T., 1940; Ph.D., U. Ill., 1949; m. Celia Alcántara, Jan. 28, 1944; 3 children. Prof. soil mechanics and found. engring. Universidad Nacional Autónoma de México, 1941-72, prof. Grad. Sch. Engring., 1973-79; cons. engr., Mexico City, 1940—; vis. research asso., spl. research fellow in structural engring. U. Ill., 1947-49. Recipient Gold Allied Profl. medal AIA, 1965. Mem. Nat. Acad. Engring., Sociedad Mexicana de Mecanica de Suelos, ASCE, Earthquake Research Inst., Siesmol. Soc. Am., Internat. Soc. Soil Mechanics and Found. Engring. N. Am. (past pres.). Roman Catholic. Clubs: Club de Golf Mexico, M.I.T. Contbr. articles to profl. jours. Office: 68 Isabel la Catolica Mexico DF 1 Mexico

ZEFERETTI, LEO C., congressman; b. Bklyn., July 15, 1927; s. Antonino and Catherine (D'Angelo) Z.; student N.Y. U., City U. N.Y.; m. Barbara L. Schiebel, Aug. 30, 1947; children—Linda, Jan. Penologist, N.Y.C. Dept. Corrections, 1957-74, collective bargaining agt., N.Y.C.; mem. 94th-96th Congresses from 15th N.Y. dist. Rep. to Pres.'s Conf. on Correction, also Conf. for Nat. Correction Acad., 1971; mem. Bay Ridge Civic Improvement Assn.; mem. N.Y. State Crime Control Planning Bd., 1973; bd. dirs. Health Ins. Plan of Greater N.Y., Internat. Found. Served with USNR, World War II; ETO. Decorated Order of St. Brigida (Italy); recipient Labor Relations award N.Y.C. Hispanic Soc. Grand Council, Law Enforcement medal SAR. Mem. Correction Officers Benevolent Assn. (pres. 1968-74), Correction Officers Columbia Assn. Democrat. Home: 9912 Fort Hamilton Pkwy Brooklyn NY 11209 Office: 215 Cannon House Office Bldg Washington DC 20515

ZEFFIRELLI, FRANCO, theatre and film dir.; b. Florence, Italy, Feb. 12, 1923; s. Ottorino Corsi and Alaide Cipriani; attended U. Architecture, Florence. Actor in Crime and Punishment, 1946, Euridyce, 1947, film Onorevole Angelina, 1948; set designer for various prodns. of Luchino Visconti, 1949-52, including A Streetcar Named Desire, The Three Sisters; dir. films: The Taming of the Shrew, 1966, Romeo and Juliet, 1967, Brother Sun, Sister Moon, 1971, The Champ, 1979; TV dir.: Giorni Di Distruzione, 1966, Fidelio of Beethove, conducted by Leonard Bernstein, 1970, Missa Solemnis of Beethoven conducted by Wolfgang Sawallisch, in Basilica of St. Peter, in presence of Pope Paul VI, 1970, Jesus of Nazareth epic film, 1975-76; dir. numerous operas, including: Cenerentola, La Scala, 1953, I Pagliacci, 1959, Cavalleria Rusticana, 1959, Lucia Di Lammermoor, Covent Garden, 1959, Boheme, La Scala, 1963, Falstaff, Met. Opera, 1964, Tosca, Covent Garden, 1965, Norma, Paris Opera, 1965, Anthony and Cleopatra, Met. Opera, 1966, Otello, Met. Opera, 1972, Don Giovanni, Staatsoper, Vienna, 1972, Un Ballo In Maschera, La Scala, 1972, Otello, La Scala, 1976, Carmen, Staatsoper, Vienna, 1978, La Traviata, 1979; theatre dir.: Romeo and Juliet, Old Vic Co., London, 1960, Othello, Stratford-on-Avon, Eng., 1961, Camille, Winter Garden Theatre, N.Y.C., 1962, Who's Afraid of Virginia Woolf?, Festival del Teatro, Venice, and Paris, 1963, Romeo and Juliet, Verona, Italy, Paris, Vienna, Austria, Rome and Milan, Italy, Moscow and Leningrad, 1964, Hamlet, 1964, After The Fall, 1965, Much Ado About Nothing, Old Vic Theatre, 1965, La Lupa, Florence, Rome, Vienna, Zurich, Switzerland, Paris, London and Moscow, 1965, A Delicate Balance, 1966, Black Comedy, 1967, Venti Zecchini D'Oro, 1968, Due Piu Due Non Fanno Quattro, 1969, Sabato, Doemnica, Lunedi, Nat. Theatre, London, 1973, The Dead City, Italy, 1975, Lorenzaccio, Comedie Française, Paris, 1976, Filumena Marturano, Lyric Theatre, London, 1977. Mem. Dirs. Guild Am. Roman Catholic.

ZEGARELLI, EDWARD VICTOR, researcher, educator; b. Utica, N.Y., Sept. 9, 1912; s. Frank Anthony and Maria Josephine (Ambroselli) Z.; A.B., Columbia U., 1934, D.D.S., 1937; M.S., U. Chgo., 1942; m. Irene Marie Ceconi, June 17, 1939; children—Edward V., David J., Philip E., Peter J. Staff, Sch. Dental and Oral Surgery, Columbia, 1937—, asst. instr., then successively instr., asst. prof., asso. prof., head diagnosis and roentgenology, 1947-58, chmn. com. dental research, 1956—, Dr. Edwin S. Robinson prof. dentistry, 1958, prof. dentistry, dir. div. stomatology, 1958—, acting dean, 1973, dean, 1974-78, dean emeritus, 1979—; chmn. sect. hosp. dental services Columbia-Presbyn. Med. Center; dir. and attending dentist dental service Presbyn. Hosp., 1974-79, also mem. exec. com. of med. bd., 1974-76; cons., dentist-in-residence VA, Washington; Weisberger Meml. lectr. Harvard, 1969, Mershon Meml. lectr., 1970, Ralph L. Spaulding Meml. lectr., 1972; deans com. Montrose VA Hosp.; cons. East Orange, Kingsbridge VA hosps., Grasslands Hosp., Valhalla, N.Y., USPHS, Phelps Meml. Hosp., Tarrytown, N.Y., Vassar Bros. Hosp., Poughkeepsie, Bur. Medicine, FDA, Council on Dental Therapeutics; area cons. VA; cons.-lectr. U.S. Naval Dental Sch., Bethesda, Md., 1970—; pres. N.Y. State Bd. Dental Examiners, 1970-71; chmn. exam. rev. com. N.E. Regional Bd. Dental Examiners, 1969—; Samuel Charles Miller Meml. lectr., 1976; mem. council deans Am. Assn. Dental Schs., 1973-79; mem. postgrad. edn. com. N.Y.C. Cancer Com.; mem. profl. edn. and grants com. N.Y.C. div. Am. Cancer Soc., 1963-73, now bd. dirs.; chmn. panel on drugs in dentistry Nat. Acad. Scis., NRC, FDA; mem. N.Y. State Health Research Council, N.Y. Commn. on Health Manpower. Recipient Austin Sniffen medal 9th Dist. Dental Soc., 1961; Columbia U. Dental Alumni Research award, 1963; Jarvie-Burkhart medal N.Y. Dental Soc., 1970, Samuel J. Miller medal Am. Acad. Oral Medicine, 1976, Henry Spenadel award 1st Dist. Dental Soc., 1979. Diplomate Am. Bd. Oral Medicine. Fellow Am. Coll. Dentists, N.Y. Acad. Dentistry, Internat. Coll. Dentists; mem. Am. Acad. Oral Pathology, Am. Assn. for Cancer Edn. (charter), Am. Assn. Dental Examiners (Dentist Citizen of Yr. award 1978), Orgn. Tchrs. Oral Diagnosis, N.Y. Acad. Scis., N.Y. Dental Soc. (chmn. council sci. research 1956-71), Greater N.Y. Acad. Prosthodontics (hon.), Guatemala Dental Soc. (hon.), Am. Dental Assn. (mem. council dental therapeutics 1963-69, vice chmn. 1969), 9th Dist. Dental Soc., Columbia Dental Alumni Assn., William Jarvie Research Soc., Internat. Assn. Dental Research, AAAS, Sigma Xi (chpt. pres. 1974-76), Omicron Kappa Upsilon (sec. treas. Columbia chpt. 1944-57, pres. 1959-60), Sigma Phi Alpha. Knight Malta. Contbg. author: The Thyroid (S.C. Werner); Medical Roentgenology (R. Golden); Current Pediatric Therapy (S. Gellis and B. Kagan); Cancer of Head and Neck (J. Conley). Author: (with others) Pharmacotherapeutics of Oral Disease, 1964; Clinical Stomatology, 1966; Diagnosis of Diseases of Mouth and Jaws, 1969, 2d edit., 1978; also articles on mouth, jaw bone disease. Home: 120 Gory Brook Rd North Tarrytown NY 10591 Office: 630 W 168th St New York NY 10032

ZEI, DINO, educator, physicist; b. Chgo., Aug. 20, 1927; s. Gino and Corradina (Mascani) Z.; B.S., Beloit (Wis.) Coll., 1950; M.S., U. Wis., 1952, Ph.D., 1957, M.A. in History Sci., 1972; m. Joan Madeline Archambault, Sept. 19, 1949; children—Elizabeth, Victoria. Physicist, Nat. Bur. Standards, 1950-51; instr. physics Beloit Coll., 1952-53; asso. prof. physic. St. Cloud (Minn.) State Coll., 1955-57; mem. faculty Ripon (Wis.) Coll., 1957—, prof. physics, chmn. dept., 1957—, William Harley Barber disting. prof., 1978—; dir. Arts of Florence program (Italy), 1973; cons. to industry, 1957—. Vis. scientist Argonne Nat. Lab., 1960-61; postdoctoral fellow Nat. Center Atmospheric Research, Boulder, Colo., 1967-68. Served with USAAF, 1945-46. Recipient Uhrig Found. award for excellence in teaching, 1964; Severy award for excellence in teaching, 1963. Mem. A.A.A.S., Am. Optical Soc., Am. Phys. Soc., Am. Assn. Physics Tchrs. (nat. council 1963-67), Am. Assn. U. Profs. (pres. Wis. conf. 1972-73), Sigma Xi, Sigma Pi Sigma, Phi Sigma Iota. Home: 118 Howard St Ripon WI 54971

ZEIBERG, SEYMOUR LAWRENCE, govt. ofcl.; b. N.Y.C., May 22, 1934; s. Max and Helen (Zuckerman) Z.; B.M.E., CCNY, 1955; M.M.E., N.Y. U., 1957, Eng. Sc.D., 1961; m. Marilyn S. Wolfson, Sept. 8, 1957; children—Mona Carol, Andrew Steven. Lectr., CCNY, 1955-61; asst. prof. N.Y. U., 1961-62; group leader Gen. Applied Sci. Labs., Westbury, N.Y., 1962-65; group dir. Aerospace Corp., San Bernardino, Calif., 1965-72; dir. R & D Assos., Marina Del Rey, Calif., 1972-77; asso. gen. mgr. Aerospace Corp., 1977; dep. undersec. of Def. for research and engring., Dept. Def., Washington, 1977—. Mem. AIAA, ASME, Tau Beta Pi, Pi Tau Sigma. Contbr. articles to profl. jours. Home: 6138 Chesterbrook Rd McLean VA 22101 Office: Pentagon Washington DC 20301

ZEICHNER, OSCAR, educator, historian; b. N.Y.C., Jan. 2, 1916; s. Joseph and Lena (Schaeffer) Z.; B.A. cum laude, Coll. City N.Y., 1936; M.A., Columbia, 1938, Ph.D., 1946; m. Florence Koenigsberg, June 27, 1942; children—Barbara Ann, Carolyn Sue. Mem. faculty City Coll. N.Y., 1936—, prof. history, 1960-76, prof. emeritus, 1976—, asst. dean in charge grad. studies Coll. Liberal Arts and Sci., 1957-63, asso. dean in charge, 1963-68, dean grad. studies, 1968-72; asso. dean grad. studies City U. N.Y., 1963-68. Recipient hon. mention J.H. Dunning prize Am. Hist. Assn., 1946. Mem. Assn. for Study Conn. History (pres. 1975-76), Phi Beta Kappa (pres. Gamma chpt. 1971-72). Author: Connecticut's Years of Controversy, 1750-76, 1949, 70; also articles; editorial bd. Conn. Commn., Am. Revolution Bicentennial Series Publs. Home: 5500 Fieldston Rd New York NY 10471

ZEIDENSTEIN, GEORGE, orgn. exec.; b. Pitts., July 29, 1929; s. Max and Sophia (Cohen) Z.; B.A., U. Pitts., 1951; J.D. cum laude, Harvard U., 1954; m. Sondra F. Auerbach, Jan. 25, 1953; children—Laura, Louis Peter. Admitted to N.Y. bar, 1954; pvt. practice, N.Y.C., 1954-64; vol. lawyer Lawyers Constl. Def. Com., Holly Springs, Miss., 1964; partner firm Spear and Hill, 1962-65; country dir. Nepal, Kathmandu, Peace Corps, 1965-68, regional dir. designate Office E. Asia and Pacific, Washington, 1968; pres. Bklyn. Linear City Devel. Corp., N.Y.C., 1968-69; sr. program officer Asia and Pacific, Ford Found., 1969-71, dep. head Asia and Pacific, 1971-72, rep., Bangladesh, 1972-76; pres. Population Council, N.Y.C., 1976—; chmn. Himalayas council Asia Soc., 1970-72; bd. dirs. Margaret Sanger Research Bur., 1970-72; asso. seminar tradition and change in S. and S.E. Asia, Columbia U., 1971—. Bd. dirs. Overseas Devel. Council, 1979—. Mem. Bar Assn. City N.Y., Council on Fgn. Relations, Internat. Union Sci. Study Population, Population Assn. Am. Club: Harvard. Home: Goshen CT 06756 Office: 1 Dag Hammarskjold Plaza New York NY 10017

ZEIDLER, FRANK P., public adminstrn. cons., mediator-arbitrator; b. Milw., Sept. 20, 1912; s. Michael and Clara (Nitschke) Z.; student Marquette U., 1930, U. Wis. Extension Div., 1930-70, U. Chgo., 1937; LL.D., U. Wis., 1958; m. Agnes Reinke; children—Clara, Dorothy, Michael, Anita, Mary, Jeannette. Dir., Milw. Pub. Schs., 1941-48; mayor City of Milw., 1948-60; dir. Wis. Dept. Resource Devel., 1962-64; lectr. U. Wis.-Milw.; sec. Pub. Enterprise Com. Mem. U.S. nat. commn. UNESCO, 1953, 56, 59; pres. Central North Community Council, Greater Milw. UN Assn.; nat. chairperson Socialist Party U.S.A.; Socialist Party candidate for Pres. of U.S., 1976; mem. mgmt.

com. div. mission in N. Am., Lutheran Ch. in Am.; bd. dirs. Luth. Social Action Conf. Named One of 10 Outstanding Young Men, Nat. Jr. C. of C., 1949. Author: Shakespeare's plays in modern verse. Home: 2921 N 2d St Milwaukee WI 53212

ZEIDMAN, PHILIP FISHER, lawyer; b. Birmingham, Ala., May 2, 1934; s. Eugene Morris and Ida (Fisher) Z.; B.A. cum laude, Yale, 1955; LL.B., Harvard, 1958, postgrad. Grad. Sch. Bus. Adminstrn., 1957-58; m. Nancy Levy, Aug. 19, 1956; children—Elizabeth Miriam, John Fisher, Jennifer Kahn. Admitted to Ala. bar, 1958, Fla. bar, 1960, D.C. bar, 1968, U.S. Supreme Ct. bar; trial atty. FTC, 1960-61; staff asst. White House Com. Small Bus., 1961-63; spl. asst. to adminstr. Small Bus. Adminstrn., 1961-63, asst. gen. counsel, 1963-65, gen. counsel, 1965-68; spl. asst. to Vice Pres. of U.S., 1968; govt. relations mgr. Nat. Alliance Businessmen, 1968; now partner firm Brownstein Zeidman & Schomer; chmn. grants and benefits com. Adminstrv. Conf. U.S., 1968; chmn. food industry adv. com. Fed. Energy Adminstrn.; chmn. distbn. and food merchandising subcom. Alliance to Save Energy. Mem. young leadership council Democratic Nat. Com.; exec. dir. Dem. platform com., 1972; adviser Nat. Presdl. Campaign of Jimmy Carter, 1976. Served with USAF, 1958-60. Recipient Younger Fed. Lawyer award Fed. Bar Assn., 1965; Jonathan Davenport Oratorical award, 1954; William Houston McKim award, 1955. Mem. Am. (chmn. com. on franchising 1977—), Ala., Fla., Fed. bar assns., Bar Assn. D.C. Office: 1025 Connecticut Ave NW Washington DC 20036

ZEIGER, MARTIN, lawyer, business exec.; b. Bklyn., May 19, 1937; s. Edward and Jennie (Gitlitz) Z.; student Bklyn. Coll., 1957; LL.B., J.D., St. John's U., Jamaica, N.Y., 1960; m. Marjorie Holden, Aug. 3, 1973; children—Scott Leslie, Elise Robyn. Admitted to N.Y. bar, 1960; counsel J.C. Penney Co., N.Y.C., 1965-68, Universal Marion Corp., Jacksonville, Fla., 1969-71, First Nat. City Bank, N.Y.C., 1971; asst. v.p., counsel Jack Eckerd Corp., Clearwater, Fla., 1971-75; v.p., gen. counsel, sec. Revco D.S., Inc., Twinsburg, Ohio, 1975—. Winner, Moot Ct. competition St. John's U. Law Sch., 1960. Mem. Am. Bar Assn., Assn. Bar City N.Y. Jewish. Contbr. articles to legal jours.; editor St. John's U. Law Rev., 1959-60. Home: 24050 Timberlane Dr Beachwood OH 44122 Office: 1925 Enterprise Pkwy Twinsburg OH 44087

ZEIGLER, EARLE FREDERICK, educator; b. N.Y.C., Aug. 20, 1919; s. Clarence Mattison and Margery Christina (Beyerkohler) Shinkle; A.B., Bates Coll., 1940; A.M., Yale U., 1944, Ph.D., 1951; LL.D., U. Windsor, 1975; m. Bertha M. Bell, June 25, 1941; children—Donald H., Barbara A. Asso. phys. dir., aquatic dir. Bridgeport (Conn.) YMCA, 1941-43; instr. German, U. Conn., Storrs, 1943-47; coach, instr. phys. edn. Yale U., 1943-49; asst. prof. U. Western Ont. (Can.), London, 1949-50, prof., chmn. dept. phys. health and recreation edn., 1950-56; asso. prof. Sch. Edn., supr. phys. edn. and athletics U. Mich., Ann Arbor, 1956-63, chmn. dept. phys. edn. Sch. Edn., 1961-63; prof. dept. phys. edn. for men Coll. Phys. Edn., U. Ill., Urbana, 1963-72, head dept. phys. edn. for men, chmn. grad. dept., 1963-68; prof. dept. phys. and health edn. U. Western Ont., London, 1971—, dean Faculty of Phys. Edn., 1972-77. Mem. religious edn. com. Unitarian-Universalist Assn., 1965-71. Fellow Am. Acad. Phys. Edn.; mem. Philosophy Edn. Soc., Internat. Assn. Profl. Schs. Phys. Edn., Am. Recreation Soc., AAHPER (Alliance scholar 1977-78, Disting. Service award 1979), Can. Assn. Health, Phys. Edn. and Recreation (honour award 1975), Am. Philos. Assn., Coll. Phys. Edn. Assn., N. Am. Soc. Sport History (life), Philosophic Soc. for Study of Sport (pres. 1974-75), Canadian Profl. Schs. Conf. (pres. 1953-55), Ont. Recreation Assn. (v.p. and dir. 1955-56), Soc. Municipal Recreation Dirs. Ont. (Honor award 1956), Phi Epsilon Kappa. Author: Administration of Physical Education and Athletics, 1959; Philosophical Foundations for Physical, Health, and Recreation Education, 1964; (with H.J. VanderZwaag) Physical Education: Progressivism or Essentialism?, 1968; Problems in the History and Philosophy of Physical Education and Sport, 1968; (with M.L. Howell and M. Trekell) Research in the History, Philosophy and Comparative Aspects of Physical Education and Sport, 1971; A History of Sport and Physical Education to 1900, 1973; Administrative Theory and Practice in Physical Education and Athletics, 1975; A History of Physical Education and Sport in the United States and Canada, 1975; Professing Physical Education and Sport Philosophy, 1975; Physical Education and Sport Philosophy, 1977; A History of Physical Education and Sport, 1979; Issues in North American Physical Education and Sport, 1979; contbr. articles to profl. jours. Home: 25 Berkshire Ct London ON N6J 3N8 Canada

ZEIGLER, ROWLAND FRANKLIN, physician; b. Greelyville, S.C., June 1, 1915; s. Rowland Franklin and Sarah Louise (Deanes) Z.; student Duke, 1931-33, U. N.C., 1933-35; M.D. cum laude, Med. U. S.C., 1937; m. Edna Jo McMillan, Aug. 10, 1962; 1 dau., Priscilla Ann. Intern, resident McLeod Meml. Hosp., Florence, S.C., 1937-39, chief obstetric-gynecology dept., 1947-70; gen. practice medicine and surgery, Seneca, S.C., 1939-45, specializing in gynecology, Florence, 1970-78); fellow in obstetrics and gynecology Ochsner Clinic, New Orleans, 1946-47. Trustee Florence Mus. Fellow A.C.S., Am. Coll. Obstetrics and Gynecology (founding); mem. South Atlantic Assn. Obstetrics and Gynecology, Southeastern Surg. Congress, Am. Soc. Abdominal Surgeons, S.C. Obstet. and Gynecol. Soc. (pres. 1961). Methodist. Author: (with H.C. Porreca) Olive Shells of the World, 1969. Contbr. articles to profl. jours. Home: PO Box 911 Murrells Inlet SC 29576

ZEILLER, WARREN, aquarium exec.; b. Weehawken, N.J., Nov. 11, 1929; s. Arthur Herman and Ruth (Preusser) Z.; B.Sc. in Animal Husbandry, Colo. A. and M. Coll., 1955; M.A. in Bus., Mich. State U., 1957; m. Judith Marion Ricciardi, May 27, 1961; children—Dianne Leigh, Todd Kiersted. Mgmt. trainee Grand Union Co., 1956-58; corp. sec., salesman Art Zeiller Co., Inc., Allendale, N.J., 1958-60; salesman Joseph Abraham Ford Co., Miami, Fla., 1960; with Miami Seaquarium, 1960—, curator, 1962—, v.p., gen. mgr., 1977—; lectr., cons. in field, TV appearances. Chmn. football com. Jr. Orange Bowl Com., 1975—; adv. bd. Coral Gables War Meml. Youth Center, 1973—; bd. dirs. Dade Marine Inst. Served with USN, 1951-55. Fellow Am. Assn. Zool. Parks and Aquariums; mem. Am. Fisheries Soc., Tropical Audubon Soc. (dir.), Fla. Attractions Assn., Met. Mus. and Art Center, Tri-County Horse Show Assn., Colo. State U. Alumni Assn., Sigma Chi. Republican. Methodist. Club: Rotary (pres. Coral Gables 1978-79). Author: Tropical Marine Invertebrates of Southern Florida and the Bahama Islands, 1974; Tropical Marine Fishes of Southern Florida and the Bahama Islands, 1975; also articles. Patentee surg. cast and cast removal saw. Home: 910 Catalonia Ave Coral Gables FL 33134 Office: Miami Seaquarium 4400 Rickenbacker Causeway Miami FL 33149

ZEIS, ROBERT HERSCHEL, newspaper exec.; b. South Bend, Ind., Oct. 13, 1932; s. Robert H. and Marie A. (Lamirand) Z.; B.A., U. Notre Dame, 1954; m. Lois A. Norton, Mar. 23, 1951 (div. 1977); children—Robert Herschel III, Janice, Gregory, Curtis, Carol; m. 2d, Nancy Austin Julian, Sept. 8, 1978. With Denver Post, Inc., 1955—, asst. bus. mgr., then bus. mgr., 1967—, asst. sec., 1972—. Bd. dirs., mem. exec. com. Met. Denver YMCA, 1971-75, sec., 1972-73, treas., 1974-75, v.p., 1976-77, bd. dirs. Learning for Living, 1974—; adv. bd. Catholic Youth Services, 1973—. Recipient Service award Met. Denver YMCA, Layman of Year award, 1976. Mem. Newspaper Personnel Relations Assn., U. Notre Dame Alumni Assn. (pres. Denver 1962-63, dir. 1964-70, Denver C. of C. (membership and communication council). Clubs: Denver Athletic, Lions, Serra (Denver); Columbine Country. Home: 550 E 12th Ave Apt 1407 Denver CO 80202 Office: 650 15th St Denver CO 80201

ZEISEL, HANS, scientist; b. Czechoslovakia, Dec. 1, 1905; Dr.Jur., U. Vienna, 1927, Dr. Rer. Pol., 1928; m. Eva Zeisel, 1938; 2 children. Naturalized citizen. Instr. statistics and econs. Rutgers U.; dir. research devel. McCann-Erickson, 1943-50; dir. research Tea Council, 1950-53; prof. law and sociology U. Chgo., 1953—, now emeritus prof.; research asso. Center for Studies in Criminal Justice; sr. cons. Am. Bar Found.; cons. Austrian Ministry of Justice, Rand Corp.; past cons. War Dept.; chmn. bd. Marplan Internat.; adv. bd. Police Found. Bd. dirs. Center Research on Acts of Man. Fellow Am. Sociol. Soc., Am. Statis. Assn.; mem. Am. Assn. Pub. Opinion Research (dir.). Author: (with P.F. Lazarsfeld and M. Jahoda) Marienthal, 1932, Am. edit., 1971; Say It With Figures, 1947, 5th edit., 1968; (with H. Kalven, Jr.) Delay in the Court, 1957, 2d edit., 1978; The American Jury, 1966; Juror Attitudes Toward Capital Punishment, 1968; The Anatomy of Law Enforcement, 1979; editor (with G. Casper) Lay Judges in the Criminal Courts, 1979; mem. bd. Bull. Atomic Scientists; spl. work in empirical study of law. Home: 5825 S Dorchester Chicago IL 60637

ZEISLER, RICHARD SPIRO, pvt. investor; b. Chgo., Nov. 28, 1916; s. Erwin Paul and Ruth Henrietta (Spiro) Z.; B.A., Amherst Coll., 1937; postgrad. Harvard U., 1937-38; M.Div., Va. Theol. Sem., 1941. Religious work, 1941-47; owner, prin. Zeisler & Co., investments, N.Y.C., 1948—; dir. Ashley-Butler Inc., PEC Econ. Corp., 980 Fifth Ave. Corp. Bd. dirs. Chamber Music Soc., Lincoln Center, 1969—; mem. com. on painting and sculpture Mus. Modern Art, 1972—, dir. internat. council, 1960—, chmn. program com., 1973—; trustee, mem. exec. com., v.p. Jewish Bd. Family and Children's Services, N.Y.C., 1951—; mem. pres.'s council Vis. Nurse Service of N.Y.; mem. exec. bd. Am. Jewish Com., 1951—, past pres. N.Y. chpt.; mem. com. for dance collection N.Y. Pub. Library, 1967—, mem. Friends, 1977—; mem. creative arts commn. Brandeis U., 1958—; mem. art adv. com. Mt. Holyoke Coll., 1963—; mem. Met. Opera Club, 1975—; fellow Pierpont Morgan Library, 1963—; governing life mem. Art Inst. Chgo., 1977— life fellow Met. Mus., 1969—; mem. council friends Inst. Fine Arts, 1978—. Mem. N.Y. Soc. Security Analysts, N.Y. Assn. Bus. Economists, Sigma Delta Rho. Clubs: Century Assn., Coffee House, University, Harvard, Grolier (N.Y.C.); Arts (Chgo.); Reform (London). Home: 980 Fifth Ave New York NY 10021 Office: 767 Fifth Ave New York NY 10022

ZEITER, WILLIAM EMMET, lawyer; b. Harrisburg, Pa., Dec. 1, 1934; s. Jacob David and Maude Elizabeth (Hamm) Z.; B.A., Lehigh U., 1955, B.S.E.E., 1956; J.D. (Root-Tilden scholar 1956-59), N.Y. U., 1959; m. Jean Palmer Greer, May 22, 1965. Acting mgr. Moving the EE-Z Way, Harrisburg, 1956-63; mem. patent staff Bell Telephone Labs., Inc., 1956, 57, 58; admitted to Pa. bar, 1960, D.C. bar, 1962, U.S. Supreme Ct. bar, 1963; asso. firm Morgan, Lewis & Bockius, Phila., 1959-66, mem. firm, 1967—, sr. partner, 1975—; legal cons. to Ct. Adminstr. Pa., 1972—; exec. dir. Adv. Com. on Appellate Ct. Rules, 1973—; mem. Pa. Joint Com. on Documents, 1968—; bd. dirs. Am. Nat. Metric Council, Washington, 1973-78, vice chmn., 1975-78; reporter Uniform Metric System Procedures Act; mem. legal adv. panel metric study U.S. Metric Bd., 1979—; mem. exec. com. Nat. Metric Adv. Panel, U.S. Dept. Commerce, 1969-71, cons. Office Invention and Innovation, Nat. Bur. Standards, 1967-72; mem. ad hoc energy panel Office Tech. Assessment, U.S. Congress, 1975-76. Recipient Gov.'s citation for drafting Appellate Ct. Jurisdiction Act, 1970, award for drafting Pa. Jud. Code, Allegheny County Bar Assn., 1978. Fellow Am. Bar Found.; mem. Am. Bar Assn. (chmn. sect. sci. and tech. 1977-78, chmn. conf. sect. chairmen 1978-79), Pa. Bar Assn. Phila. Bar Assn., IEEE, Am. Law Inst. Contbr. various articles on legal codification, corp. law, adminstrv. law and metric conversion. Home: 8917 Crefeld St Philadelphia PA 19118 Office: Morgan Lewis & Bockius 2100 Fidelity Bldg 123 S Broad St Philadelphia PA 19109

ZEITLIN, HERBERT, mgmt. cons.; b. N.Y.C., Jan. 14; s. Leonard and Martha Josephine (Soff) Z.; B.S., N.Y. U., 1947, M.A., 1949; Ed.D., Stanford U., 1956; m. Eugenia F. Pawlik, July 3, 1949; children—Mark Clyde, Joyce Therese, Ann Victoria, Clare Katherine. Tchr., counselor, dir. testing Phoenix Union High Sch. and Coll. Dist., 1949-57; dean eve. coll., prin. high sch. Antelope Valley Union High Sch. and Coll. Dist., Lancaster, Calif., 1957-62; dean instrn. Southwestern Coll., Chula Vista, Calif., 1962-64; pres., supt. Triton Coll., River Grove, Ill., 1964-76; pres. Triton Assos., coll. mgmt. cons., Los Angeles, 1976—; adj. faculty Ariz. State U., Flagstaff, 1953-55, No. Ill. U., DeKalb, 1971-74, U. Calif., Santa Barbara, 1979. Served with USAAF, 1942-46. Recipient various commendations. Mem. NEA (life), Am. Assn. Community and Jr. Colls., Assn. Calif. Community Coll. Adminstrs., Am. Vocat. Assn. Author, editor in field. Home: 20124 Phaeton Dr Woodland Hills CA 91364 Office: 9700 S Sepulveda Blvd Los Angeles CA 90045. *I always felt that being the president of an organization was like being the quarterback on the football team. You had a choice of running with the ball and taking some bruises or passing it to someone who should score. I was lucky most of the time in selecting some very fine receivers.*

ZEITLIN, HERBERT, coll. pres.; b. N.Y.C., Jan. 14, 1919; s. Leonard and Martha Josephine (Soff) Z.; B.S., N.Y. U., 1947, M.A., 1949; Ed.D., Stanford, 1956; m. Eugenia F. Pawlik, July 3, 1949; children—Mark Clyde, Joyce Therese, Ann Victoria, Clare K. Dean evening div. Antelope Valley Coll., Lancaster, Calif., 1957-62; dean instrn. Southwestern Coll., Chula Vista, Calif., 1962-64; pres. Triton Coll., River Grove, Ill., 1964-76, West Los Angeles Coll., Culver City, Calif., 1976—. Extension instr. Ariz. State U., Flagstaff, 1953-55, No. Ill. U., DeKalb, 1971-74. Served with USAAF, 1942-46. Recipient Adminstr. of Yr. award, 1974; named one of 50 most influential persons in Chgo. suburbs Chgo. Sun-Times, 1974; named Mr. Career Edn. of Midwest. Mem. Ariz. Vocational Assn. (pres. 1953-54), Ariz. Guidance Assn. (pres. 1952-53), Community Discussion Group (pres. 1961-62). Club: Rotary (pres. 1971-72). Editor: Ariz. Vocational Rev.; mem. policy bd. for book Now Hear This: College Presidents Sound Off. Office: Office of Pres West Los Angeles Coll 4800 Freshman Dr Culver City CA 90230*

ZEITLIN, ZVI, concert violinist, educator; b. Russia, Feb. 21, 1923; s. Zalman and Rivka (Zeitlin) Z.; came to U.S., 1947, naturalized, 1964; student Juilliard Sch. Music, 1934-39, 47-50, Hebrew U., Jerusalem, 1940-43; m. Marianne Langner, May 5, 1951; children—Hillel, Leora. Concert tours in N. and S.Am., Israel, Australia, New Zealand, Europe, Hong Kong; appeared with leading symphonies in N.Y.C., Chgo., London, Berlin, Vienna, Copenhagen, Brussels, Paris; prof. violin Eastman Sch. Music, U. Rochester, 1967—, Kilbourn prof., 1974—; violin head Music Acad. of West, Santa Barbara, Calif., 1973; rec. artist for Deutsche Grammophon Gesellschaft, Mus. Heritage Soc., Vox. Served with RAF, World War II. Recipient Am. Israel Soc. award for furthering relations between Am. and Israel in field of music, 1957. Mem. Bohemians, N.Y., N.Y. State Tchrs. Assn., Am. Fedn. Musicians, Am. String Tchrs. Assn. Club: U. Rochester Faculty. Formed Eastman Trio, 1977. Editor newly unearthed Nardini Concerto, 1968. Contbr. articles to profl. jours. Home: 204 Warren Ave Rochester NY 14618

ZEKMAN, PAMELA LOIS (MRS. FREDRIC SOLL), journalist; b. Chgo., Oct. 22, 1944; d. Theodore Nathan and Lois Jane (Bernstein) Z.; B.A., U. Calif. at Berkeley, 1965; m. Fredric Soll, Nov. 29, 1975. Social worker Dept. Public Aid Cook County, Chgo., 1965-66; reporter City News Bur., Chgo., 1966-70; reporter Chgo. Tribune, 1970-75, mem. task force on vote fraud investigation; reporter Chgo. Sun-Times, 1975—. Recipient Pulitzer Prize for gen. local reporting on vote fraud series; Community Service award for vote fraud series UPI, 1972; Feature Series award for nursing home abuses series AP, 1971; Pub. Service award for slumlord series UPI, 1973, Newswriting award AP, 1973; In Depth Reporting award for police brutality series AP, 1974, Investigative Reporting awards Inland Daily Press Assn., 1974, 78; Investigative Reporting award for series on city waste AP, 1975; Pulitzer Prize for pub. service for series on hosp. abuses, 1976, Investigative Reporting award for series on baby selling, 1976; Pub. Service award for series on currency exchange abuses UPI, 1976, Investigative Reporting award for series on abuses in home for retarded children AP, 1977; Soc. Midland Authors Golden Rake award, UPI Public Service award, Ill. AP award, Nat. Headliners Club award, Sweepstakes award for Mirage Tavern investigative project, 1978; Nat. Disting. Service award for series on med. abuses in abortion clinics Sigma Delta Chi, 1979; named Journalist of Yr., No. Ill. U., 1979. Office: 401 N Wabash Ave Chicago IL 60611

ZELAZO, NATHANIEL K., mech. engr., mfg. co. exec.; b. Lomza, Poland, Sept. 28, 1918; s. Morris and Ida Z.; came to U.S., 1928, naturalized, 1928; B.S., City Coll. N.Y., 1940; M.S. in Mech. Engring., U. Wis., 1957; m. Helene Fishbeinret, June 27, 1943; children—Ronald E., Annette Renee. Vice pres. Ketay (United Tech.), N.Y.C., 1952-55; dir. research and devel. J. Oster Co., Racine, Wis., 1955-59; pres., chmn. bd. Astronautics Corp. Am., Milw., 1959—, pres. Astronautics C.A. Ltd., Astronautics Domestic-Internat. Sales Corp. Bd. dirs. Milw. Sch. Engring. Named Small Businessman of Yr., State of Wis., 1966; recipient award Billy Mitchell chpt. Wis. Air Force Assn., 1977. Asso. fellow Am. Inst. Aeros. and Astronautics; mem. IEEE (sr.), Am. Soc. Naval Engrs., Nat. Soc. Profl. Engrs., Engrs. and Scientists Milw., Physics Club Milw. Clubs: Milw. Press, Wis., Milw. Yacht. Developer aircraft and space vehicle instrumentation, data processing terminals. Home: 1610 N Prospect Ave Milwaukee WI 53202 Office: 907 S 1st St PO Box 523 Milwaukee WI 53201

ZELBY, LEON WOLF, educator; b. Sosnowiec, Poland, Mar. 26, 1925; s. Herszel and Helen (Wajnryb) Zylberberg; came to U.S., 1946, naturalized, 1951; B.S. in Elec. Engring., Moore Sch. Elec. Engring., 1956; M.S. (Cons. Electrodynamic Corp. fellow), Calif. Inst. Tech., 1957; Ph.D. (Mpls.-Honeywell fellow 1957-58, Harrison fellow 1958), U. Pa., 1961; m. Rachel Kupfermintz, Dec. 28, 1954; children—Laurie Susan, Andrew Stephen. Mem. staff RCA, Hughes Research and Devel. Labs., Lincoln Lab., Mass. Inst. Tech., Sandia Corp., Argonne Nat. Labs., Inst. for Energy Analysis; mem. faculty U. Pa., 1959-67, asso. prof., 1964-67, asso. dir. for plasma engring. Inst. Direct Energy Conversion, 1962-67; prof. U. Okla., Norman, 1967—, dir. Sch. Elec. Engring., 1967-71; cons. RCA, 1961-67, Moore Sch. Elec. Engring., 1967-68, also pvt. firms. Chmn. Montgomery County (Pa.) Vocational Tech. Schs., 1965-67. Served with AUS, 1946-47. Mem. I.E.E.E., Am. Phys. Soc., Am. Assn. Physics Tchrs., Franklin Inst., Sigma Xi, Tau Beta Pi, Eta Kappa Nu (nat. dir.), Pi Mu Epsilon, Sigma Tau. Contbr. articles to profl. jours. Home: 1009 Whispering Pines Dr Norman OK 73069. *To learn as much, and to experience as much as possible, without harm to others; read, study, vary professional and recreational activities within constraints of the system.*

ZELDIN, MARY-BARBARA, educator, philosopher; b. N.Y.C., Apr. 23, 1922; d. Reginald Wright and Ruth (Hammitt) Kauffman; A.B., Bryn Mawr Coll., 1943; M.A., Radcliffe Coll., 1945, Ph.D., 1950; m. Jesse Zeldin, June 19, 1948; 1 dau., Xenia Valerie. Social affairs officer div. narcotic drugs UN, 1947-50; research analyst Dept. Def., U.S. Force in Austria, Saltzburg, 1952; mem. faculty Hollins Coll., 1953—, prof. philosophy, 1970—, chmn. Russian studies program, 1974-76, chmn. dept. philosophy and religion, 1964-65, 66-70, 77-78; part-time lectr. Roanoke Center, U. Va., 1960-63; lectr. Chinese U. of Hong Kong, 1965-66. Scholar Am. Acad. Rome, 1943-44; research grantee Am. Council Learned Socs., 1970, travel grantee, 1978. Mem. Washington Philosophy Club (exec. com. 1968-69, 73-74), Am. Philos. Assn., Va. Philos. Assn., Am. Soc. for Advancement Slavic Studies, So. Conf. Slavic Studies (exec. com. 1964-67, 69-70, 78—, pres. 1968-69), Am. Soc. for 18th Century Studies (exec. com. Southeastern br. 1973-76, chmn. nat. nominating com. 1975-76). Mem. Eastern Orthodox Ch. Author articles in field. Co-editor: Russian Philosophy, 1965. Translator, editor: Peter Yakovlevich Chaadayev: Philosophical Letters and Apology of a Madman, 1969. Office: Hollins College VA 24020

ZELDIN, RICHARD PACKER, publisher; b. Worcester, Aug. 7, 1918; s. M. and Virginia (Gealt) Z.; B.S., West Chester (Pa.) State Coll., 1942; grad. exec. program bus. adminstrn. Columbia U., 1966; m. Virginia Graves, Nov. 25, 1950; children—Elizabeth Ann, Richard Shepherd. Gen. mgr. profl. and reference book div. McGraw-Hill Book Co., Inc., 1948-68; v.p., publishing dir. Litton Ednl. Pub. Co., Inc., 1968-70; pres. R.R. Bowker Co., 1970-76; pres. Xerox Coll. Pub., Xerox Individualized Pub., 1970-76; gen. mgr. info. services John Wiley & Sons, Inc., 1976—; sec.-treas. sci., tech. and med. book pubs. group Asso. Am. Pubs., 1966-70; mem. adv. com. comml. publs. AEC, 1966-70. Served to lt. USNR, 1942-46. Mem. Info. Industry Assn. (sec. 1973—). Clubs: Dutch Treat, Pubs. Lunch (N.Y.C.). Home: 20 Fairfield Dr Tinton Falls NJ 07724 Office: 605 3d Ave New York City NY 10016

ZELDITCH, MORRIS, JR., sociologist, educator; b. Pitts., Feb. 29, 1928; s. Morris and Anne (Hankin) Z.; B.A., Oberlin Coll., 1951; Ph.D., Harvard, 1955; m. Bernice Osmola, June 12, 1950; children—Miriam Lea, Steven Morris. From instr. to asst. prof. Columbia, 1955-61; mem. faculty Stanford, 1961—, prof. sociology, 1966—, exec. head dept., 1964-68. Served with AUS, 1945-47. Mem. Am., Pacific (v.p. 1966-67) sociol. assns. Author: (with others) Basic Course in Sociological Statistics, 3d edit., 1975; (with others) Types of Formalization in Small Groups Research, 1962; (with others) Sociological Theories in Progress, vol. 1, 1966, vol. 2, 1972; (with others) Status Characteristics and Social Interaction, 1976; also articles. Asso. editor Am. Sociol. Rev., 1965-68, editor, 1975-78; cons. editor Sociometry, 1966-68. Home: 936 Lathrop Pl Stanford CA 94305

ZELENY, ROBERT OWEN, editor; b. Chgo., Aug. 30, 1930; s. Irving and Zoe (Leiberman) Z.; B.A., Tulane U., 1952; postgrad. U. Chgo., 1955-58; m. Rita Estelle Levitt, Oct. 21, 1952; children—Diane Rebecca, Susan Beth. Asst. editor World Book Ency. Field Enterprises Ednl. Corp., Chgo., 1956-57, sr. sci. editor, 1957-59, asst. mng. editor, 1959-64, mng. editor, 1964-1964-65, v.p., exec. editor World Book Ency., World Book Atlas, 1965-72, sr. v.p., exec. editor Childcraft and allied products, 1967—. Mem. Bd. Edn. Sch. Dist. III, Highland Park-Highwood, Ill., 1966-70, Sch. Dist. 108,

Highland Park, 1972-78. Mem. Democrats South Lake County. Served with USN, 1952-55. Mem. Ill. C. of C., Assn. Supervision and Curriculum Devel., ALA, Sigma Alpha Mu. Clubs: Mchts. and Mfrs., Chgo. Press. Office: World Book-Childcraft Internat Inc Merchandise Mart Plaza Chicago IL 60654

ZELIKOFF, MURRAY, scientist; b. Newburgh, N.Y., Dec. 1, 1922; s. Harry and Ella (Becker) Z.; B.A. with honors, N.Y. U., 1943, Ph. D. (Univ. fellow), 1950; M.S., U. Ill., 1945; m. Charlotte Mezansky, Sept. 24, 1944; children—Herbert Alfred, Lawrence David Zelikoff, Julie Phyllis Zelikoff. Geophysics research scientist Air Force Cambridge Research Center, Bedford, Mass., 1950—, research atmospheric photochemistry, 1951-53, atmosphere, rocket research, 1953-56, chief photochem. lab. Geophysics Research Directorate, 1956-58; v.p. GCA Corp. Bedford, 1958—; accomplished artificial ionosphere, release under atmosphere stored energy, 1956; entered proof existence atomic nitrogen in upper atmosphere, 1957; U.S. del. Internat. Union Geology and Geophysics, Toronto, Can., 1957; Am. Chem. Soc. lectr., 1957. Mem. U.S. Rocket and Satellite Research Panel. Mem. Am. Chem. Soc., Am. Optical Soc., Internat. Union Geodesy and Geophysics, Am. Inst. Physics, Am. Geohpys. Union, Internat. Assn. Geomagentism and Aeronomy, Sigma Xi, Phi Lambda Upsilon. Jewish religion. Editor: Threshhold of Space, 1957. Contbr. articles to profl. jours. Home: 1420 S Bayshore Dr Miami FL 33131

ZELIN, JEROME, retail co. exec.; b. Bklyn., Dec. 24, 1930; s. Isidore and Ida (Roffman) Z.; B.S. magna cum laude, N.Y.U., 1952; m. Muriel Altsher, Dec. 18, 1955; children—Dorothy, Michael, Steven. Accountant, Seymour Schwartz, C.P.A., 1954-57; partner firm Schwartz, Zelin & Weiss, C.P.A.'s, N.Y.C., 1958-61; vice chmn., pres., exec. v.p., treas., financial v.p., dir. Unishops, Inc., retail co., Jersey City, 1961-74; v.p., dir. Masters, Inc., Westbury, N.Y., 1974—; dir. Market Diners, Inc., N.Y.C. Served with AUS, 1952-54. Mem. N.Y. Soc. C.P.A.'s, Am. Inst. C.P.A.'s, Beta Gamma Sigma, Tau Alpha Omega. Jewish (trustee). Home: 225 Arkansas Dr Brooklyn NY 11234 Office: Masters Inc 725 Summa Ave Westbury NY 11590

ZELINSKY, DANIEL, mathematician, educator; b. Chgo., Nov. 22, 1922; s. Isaac and Ann (Ruttenberg) Z.; S.B., U. Chgo., 1941, S.M., 1943, Ph.D. in Math., 1946; m. Zelda Oser, Sept. 23, 1945; children—Mara, Paul, David. Instr. premeteorology U. Chgo., 1943-44; mem. applied math. group Columbia, 1944-45; instr. math. U. Chgo., 1946-47; NRC fellow Inst. Advanced Study, 1947-49; mem. faculty Northwestern U., Evanston, Ill., 1949—, prof. math., 1960—, chmn. dept. math., 1975-78; Indo-Am. fellow Tata Inst., Bombay, 1979; Fulbright fellow, Kyoto, Japan, 1955-56; Guggenheim fellow, 1956-57; vis. prof. Hebrew U., Jerusalem, 1970-71. Mem. div. math. NRC, 1962-65, exec. com., 1963-65. Mem. Am. Math. Soc. (editor Trans. 1961-66), Math. Assn. Am., AAAS. Home: 613 Hunter Rd Wilmette IL 60091 Office: Dept Mathematics Northwestern Univ Evanston IL 60201

ZELINSKY, WILBUR, educator; b. Chgo., Dec. 21, 1921; s. Louis and Esther (Mastoon) Z.; B.A., U. Calif. at Berkeley, 1944, Ph.D., 1953; M.A., U. Wis., 1946; m. Gladys Florence Epstein, July 5, 1944; children—Karen Jay, Hollis Gay. Asst. prof. geography U. Ga., 1948-52; project asso. geography U. Wis., 1952-54; indsl. analyst C.& O. Ry., 1954-59; prof. geography So. Ill. U., Carbondale, 1959-63; prof. geography Pa. State U., 1963—, head dept., 1970-76. Mem. Assn. Am. Geographers (chmn. West Lakes div. 1959-61, nat. pres. 1972-73; award meritorious contbns. to geography 1966), Am. Geog. Soc., Population Assn. Am., Internat. Union Sci. Study Population, Am. Name Soc. Author: Geography and a Crowding World, 1970; Prologue to Population Geography 1966; A Basic Geographical Library, 1966; Cultural Geography of United States, 1973. Home: 467 Martin Terr State College PA 16801 Office: Walker Bldg University Park PA 16802

ZELLE, M(AX) R(OMAINE), lab. research adminstr.; b. Polk County, Iowa, Oct. 11, 1915; s. Guy C. and Clara (Ringgenberg) Z.; B.S., Iowa State U., 1937, Ph.D., 1940; m. Evelyn Hansen, Dec. 24, 1937; children—Claire Christine, Phillip Wayne. Asst. county agt., Audubon, Ia., 1935-36; asst. prof. genetics Purdue U., 1941-44; biologist NIH, Bethesda, Md., 1946-48; prof. bacteriology Cornell U., 1948-58; geneticist, div. biology and medicine AEC, 1950-51, 57-58, chief biology br., 1958-60, asst. dir. biol. scis., 1960-61; prof. genetics and dir. Center Radiol. Scis., U. Wash., 1961-62; dir. div. biol. and med. research Argonne Nat. Lab., 1962-69; prof., chmn. dept. radiology and radiation biology Colo. State U., Ft. Collins, 1969—; cons. biology div. Oak Ridge Nat. Lab., 1947-49, 52-57, summer guest investigator, 1952, 54, 56. Mem. bd. advisers Phoenix project U. Mich., 1966. Adviser to U.S. delegation UN Sci. Com. on Effects Atomic Radiation, 1958-62; cons. Bur. Radiol. Health FDA, Dept. Health, Edn. and Welfare, 1969-73, Plowshare Programs Office AEC, 1972. Served to lt. (j.g.) USNR, 1944-46. Fellow A.A.A.S.; mem. Am. Inst. Biol. Scis., Genetics Soc. Am., Soc. Am. Microbiols., Am. Soc. Naturalists, Radiation Research Soc. (councilor 1960-63, sec.-treas. 1972-75), Health Physics Soc. (pres. Central Rocky Mountain chpt. 1975-76), Scabbard and Blade, Sigma Xi, Phi Kappa Phi, Alpha Zeta. Club: Cosmos (Washington). Home: 1831 Rangeview Dr Fort Collins CO 80524

ZELLEN, WILLIAM DAVID, motion picture co. exec.; b. Worcester, Mass., Jan. 5, 1933; s. Louis and Sadie (Greenberg) Z.; B.S., U. Pa., 1954; M.B.A., Northeastern U., 1959; m. Paula Levy, May 30, 1959; children—Jody Sue, Barry. With Gen. Cinema Corp., Chestnut Hill, Mass., 1960—, controller, 1964-71, asst. treas., corporate controller, 1971-73, treas., 1973—, sr. v.p. fin. GCC Theatres, Inc., 1978—. Served with AUS, 1954-56. Office: Gen Cinema Corp 27 Boylston St Chestnut Hill MA 02167

ZELLER, EARNEST JEROME, educator; b. St. Joseph, Mo., Dec. 15, 1925; s. Erwin Jay and Amber (Tanner) Z.; B.A., Emory U., 1950, B.D., 1953, M.A., 1962; postgrad. U. of South, 1951-52; Fulbright scholar, Am. U., Cairo, Egypt, 1955-56; postgrad. St. Augustine's Coll., Canterbury, Eng., 1956; Ph.D. (Lilly fellow), Ind. U., 1966; m. Joan Dean, Sept. 8, 1951 (div. Nov. 1974); children-Carol Gay, Donna Sue, Earnest Jerome; m. 2d, Roxanna Carpenter, Mar. 19, 1979. Ordained priest Episcopal Ch., 1954; curate Holy Trinity Ch., Decatur, Ga., 1952-55; Episcopal chaplain U. Fla., 1956-57; rector St. Catherine's, Jacksonville, Fla., 1957-59; rector St. Mark's, Palatka, Fla., 1959-61; asst. dean Emory Coll., Emory U., 1962-65, dean men, dean students, 1965-69, instr. history, 1965-69; asso. prof. history and edn. Mercer U., Atlanta, 1974—, chmn. Div. Behavioral and Social Sci., 1976—; pres., treas. Tanner's Corp. S.C., 1971—; pres. World Studies Inst., Inc., Atlanta, 1969-71, also v.p. bd.; trainer Ind. Plan Adult Edn.; tchr. of Bible, Paxson High Sch., Jacksonville. Cons. Ga. Mental Health Inst., 1974-75, Open Classroom Edn. for Ch. Schs., 1974—; cons. dept. congl. devel. Episcopal Diocese of Atlanta, 1976-78. Mem. exec. com. Mercer U., Atlanta, 1979—; founder St. Catherine's Parish Day Sch., St. Mark's Parish Day Sch., World Studies Inst. Acad. Program. Served with U.S. Army, 1943-45; PTO; to capt. N.G., 1957-69. Recipient Distinguished Alumni award Sigma Alpha Epsilon, 1966. Mem. Nat. Assn. Personnel Adminstrs., So. Deans Assn., Ind. U. Alumni Assn. (pres. Ga. chpt.), Sigma Alpha Epsilon, Alpha Phi Omega (nat. dir.), Sigma Delta Chi, Phi Delta Kappa, Omicron Delta Kappa. Clubs: Ys Mens (Jacksonville, Fla.); Army Chaplains (treas.) (Atlanta). Address: 3045 Hathaway Ct Chamblee GA 30341. *No man will ever do that which he wishes to do. Nor will I. But I am supposed to fall short - and still I am rather wonderful!*

ZELLER, ROBERT GRIFFING, investment banker; b. Los Angeles, July 25, 1918; s. John Baptiste and Shirley (Emanuel) Z.; A.B., Stanford, 1939; LL.B., Harvard, 1942; m. Mildred Koob, Nov. 12, 1976; children by previous marriage—Avery French, Constance Elizabeth. Admitted to N.Y. bar, 1944; law clk. Wright, Gordon, Zachary, Parlin & Cahill, N.Y.C., 1943-54; partner firm Cahill, Gordon, Reindel & Ohl, N.Y.C., 1955-63; partner F. Eberstadt & Co., Inc., N.Y.C., 1963-69, chmn. bd., 1969-78, chmn. exec. com., 1978-79; chmn. bd. Chem. Fund, Inc. 1976-79; vice chmn. The Surveyor Fund, F. Eberstadt Mgrs. and Distbrs. Inc. 1969-79; dir. Cunningham Drug Stores, Inc., Engelhard Minerals & Chems. Corp., S.E. Rykoff & Co. Mem. Phi Beta Kappa, Beta Theta Pi. Episcopalian. Clubs: Downtown Assn., Downtown Athletic (N.Y.C.); National Arts. Home: PO Box 949 Center Harbor NH 03226

ZELLERBACH, WILLIAM JOSEPH, paper co. exec.; b. San Francisco, Sept. 15, 1920; s. Harold Lionel and Doris (Joseph) Z.; B.S., Wharton Sch., U. Pa., 1942; grad. Advanced Mgmt. Program, Harvard, 1958; m. Margery Haber, Feb. 25, 1946; children—John William, Thomas Harold, Charles Ralph, Nancy. With Crown Zellerbach Corp. and subsidiaries, 1946—, officer, dir. Crown Zellerbach Corp., 1960—; pres. Zellerbach Paper Co., 1961—; dir. Lloyds Bank Cal., Purex Corp., Van Gelder Papier, Amsterdam, Netherlands. Mem gen. adv. com. fgn. assistance programs AID, 1965-68. Pres., Zellerbach Family Fund; trustee U. Pa. Served as lt. USNR, 1942-46. Mem. Nat. Paper trade Assn. (pres. 1970) Clubs: Villa Taverna, Concordia Argonaut, Stock Exchange, Presidio Golf, Commercial, Pacific Union, Commonwealth (San Francisco); San Francisco Yacht (Belvedere); Peninsula Country (San Mateo, Calif.). Office: 55 Hawthorne St San Francisco CA 94120

ZELLNER, ARNOLD, educator; b. Bklyn., Jan. 2, 1927; s. Israel and Doris (Kleiman) Z.; A.B., Harvard, 1949; Ph.D., U. Calif. at Berkeley, 1957; m. Agnes Marie Sumares, June 20, 1953; children—David S., Philip A., Samuel N., Daniel A., Michael A. Asst., then asso. prof. econs. U. Wash., 1955-60; Fulbright vis. prof. Netherlands Sch. Econs., Rotterdam, 1960-61; asso. prof., then prof. econs. U. Wis., 1961-66; H.G.B. Alexander prof. econs. and statistics U. Chgo., 1966—, dir. doctoral programs Grad. Sch. Bus., 1968-69, dir. H.G.B. Alexander Research Found., 1973—. Cons. Battelle Meml. Inst., 1964-71; vis. research prof. U. Calif. at Berkeley, 1971. Trustee Nat. Opinion Research Corp., 1973—. Served with AUS, 1951-53. Fellow Econometric Soc., Am. Statis. Assn. (chmn.-elect bus. and econs. sect. 1978—); mem. Am. Econ. Assn. Co-author: Systems Simulation for Regional Analysis, 1969; Estimating the Parameters of the Markov Probability Model, 1970; author Bayesian Inference in Econometrics, 1971. Editor: Economic Statistics and Econometrics, 1968; asso. editor Econometrica, 1962-68; co-editor: Studies in Bayesian Econometrics and Statistics, 1975; co-editor Jour. Econometrics, 1972—; editorial bd. Jour. Econ. Lit., 1972-75. Contbr. articles to profl. jours. Home: 5628 S Dorchester Ave Chicago IL 60637

ZELNICK, CARL ROBERT, journalist; b. N.Y.C., Aug. 9, 1940; s. David Isadore and Lillian (Ostrow) Z.; B.S., Cornell U., 1961; LL.B., U. Va., 1964; m. Pamela Margaret Sharp, Dec. 30, 1967; children—Eva Michal, Dara Yael, Marni Ruth. Admitted to N.Y. State bar, 1965, D.C. bar, 1966; law asso. H. Charles Ephraim, Washington, 1966-67; corr./columnist Anchorage Daily News, 1968-76; spl. corr. Christian Sci. Monitor, 1973-77; corr./bur. chief Nat. Pub. Radio, Washington, 1972-76; exec. editor Frost/Nixon Interviews, Washington, 1976-77; dir. news coverage ABC-TV, Washington, 1977—. Served with USMC, 1964-65. Recipient Gavel awards Am. Bar Assn., 1969, 74. Mem. Am. Polit. Sci. Assn., Council on Fgn. Relations, Radio and TV Corrs. Assn., Phi Epsilon Pi, Pi Delta Phi. Jewish. Clubs: Fed. City; Washington Press. Asso. editor, Environmental Law Reporter, 1971-72. Contbr. articles to newspapers and mags. Office: ABC News 1124 Connecticut Ave Washington DC 20036

ZELNIK, MELVIN, educator; b. N.Y.C., Sept. 22, 1928; s. Samuel and Bessie (Durst) Z.; student Champlain Coll., 1952-53; B.A., Miami U., Oxford, Ohio, 1955; Ph.D. (Milbank Meml. fellow), Princeton, 1959; m. Barbara Lou Light, Mar. 24, 1962; children—Jonathan Roderick, David Farrand. Mem. faculty Pa. State U., 1958-59; with U.S. Bur. Census, 1959-61, 64-66; research asso. Princeton, 1961-62; mem. faculty Ohio State U., 1962-64; mem. faculty Johns Hopkins, Balt., 1966—, prof. population dynamics, 1969—; with Ford Found., Indonesia, 1972-73. Served with AUS, 1948-50, 51-52. Mem. Population Assn. Am., Internat. Union Sci. Study Population, Phi Beta Kappa. Author: (with Ansley J. Coale) New Estimates of Fertility and Population in the United States, 1963; also numerous articles. Home: 304 Gailridge Rd Timonium MD 21093 Office: Johns Hopkins Sch Hygiene and Pub Health 615 N Wolfe St Baltimore MD 21205

ZELTZER, GEORGE MEYER, savs. and loan assn. exec.; b. Detroit, May 18, 1922; s. Joseph E. and Fanny (Chover) Z.; B.A., Wayne State U., 1946; J.D., U. Mich., 1949; m. Pearl Melnick, Sept. 12, 1948; children—David L., Gary S., Elliot J., Jeremy J. With Am. Savs. & Loan Assn., Detroit, 1949—, exec. v.p., 1963-68, pres., 1969—, also dir.; dir. Fed. Home Loan Bank Indpls.; chmn. adv. com. Fed. Home Loan Mortgage Corp., 1975-76. Past pres. United Hebrews Schs., Detroit; pres. Jewish Welfare Fedn. Detroit; bd. dirs. United Found. of Detroit, Council Jewish Fedns.; v.p. Nat. Found. Jewish Culture. Served with AUS, World War II; CBI. Mem. U.S. League Savs. Assns. (vice chmn. legis. com.), Mich. Savs. and Loan League (pres. 1970-71), Mortage Bankers Assn. Detroit (dir.). Jewish (pres. congregation). Home: 7106 Suncrest Rd West Bloomfield MI 48033 Office: 24700 Northwestern Hwy Southfield MI 48075

ZEMACH, MARGOT (MRS. HARVEY FISCHTROM), illustrator; b. Los Angeles, Nov. 30, 1931; d. Benjamin and Elizabeth (Dailey) Zemach; Fulbright scholar Vienna (Austria) Acad. Fine Arts, 1955-56; m. Harvey Fischtrom, Jan. 29, 1957; children—Kaethe, Heidi, Rachel, Rebecca. Recipient 1st prize Book Week Spring Children's Book Festival, 1965. Illustrator: (children's book) Small Boy Is Listening, 1958; Take a Giant Step, 1959; A Hat with a Rose, 1960; The Three Sillies, 1963; The Last Dragon, 1964; Nail Soup, 1964 (Soc. Typog. Arts award 1964, Am. Inst. Graphic Arts award 1964); The Tricks of Master Dabble, 1965; The Question Box, 1965; The Little Tiny Woman, 1965; Salt, A Russian Tale, 1965; The Fisherman and His Wife, 1966; The Speckled Hen, 1966; Mommy, Buy Me a China Doll, 1966; Too Much Nose, 1966; The King of the Hermits, 1966; When Shlemiel Went to Warsaw (Caldecott honor 1968; Mazel and Shlimazel, 1968; The Judge; 1969; Awake and Dreaming, 1970; A Penny a Look, 1971; Tales Told in Denmark, 1971; Alone in the Wild Forest, 1971; Simon Boom Gives a Wedding, 1972; Duffy and the Devil, 1973 (Caldecott medal 1974); The Foundling, 1973; The Princess and Froggie, 1975; Hush, Little Baby, 1976; Naftali and the Storyteller, 1976; It Could Always Be Worse, 1977 (Caldecott honor); To Hilda for Helping, 1977; The Frogs Who Wanted a King, 1977; Self Portrait: Margot Zemach, 1978. Address: 2421 Oregon St Berkeley CA

ZEMEL, JAY NORMAN, elec. engr., educator; b. N.Y.C., June 26, 1928; s. Leo and Miriam Esther (Schwartz) Z.; B.S., Syracuse U., 1949, M.S., 1953, Ph.D., 1956; M.A. (hon.), U. Pa., 1971; m. Jacqueline Eva Lax, July 21, 1950; children—Alan Raymond, Babette Sharon, Andrea Melanie. Supervisory research physicist U.S. Naval Ordnance Lab., 1954-66; RCA prof. solid state electronics U. Pa., 1966—, chmn. dept. Moore Sch. Elec. Engring., 1973-77; vis. prof. Nat. Poly. Inst. Mex., 1971, U. Tokyo, 1978, Naval Research Lab., 1977-78; vis. scientist Imperial Coll., also Zenith Research Lab., London, 1964; chmn. 2d Conf. Semicondr. Surfaces, 1959; sponsor, organizer advanced study inst. thin films NATO, 1965; treas. Internat. Conf. Thin Films, 1969; chmn. Gordon Conf. MIS Systems, 1976; dir. advanced study inst. on non-destructive evaluation in semi-condr. materials and devices NATO, 1978. Democratic committeeman, Abington-Rockledge (Pa.), 1969-71. Recipient Meritorious Civilian Service award Navy Dept., 1958, Sustained Superior Performance award, 1960. Fellow IEEE; mem. Am. Phys. Soc. (exec. com. surface sci. div. 1969-70). Editor-in chief Thin Solid Films, 1972. Contbr. articles to profl. jours. Home: 223 Meetinghouse Rd Jenkintown PA 19046 Office: Moore Sch Elec Engring Univ Pa Philadelphia PA 19174

ZEMMER, JOSEPH LAWRENCE, JR., educator; b. Biloxi, Miss., Feb. 23, 1922; s. Joseph Lawrence and Hazel (Quint) Z.; B.S., Tulane U., 1943, M.S., 1947; Ph.D., U. Wis., 1950; m. Joan Kornfield, June 28, 1950; children—Joel Alan, Rachel Lee, Judith Louise. Mem. faculty U. Mo.-Columbia, 1950—, prof. math., 1961—, chmn. dept., 1967-70, 73-76; Fulbright lectr. Osmania U., Hyderabad, India, 1963-64. Served with AUS, 1944-46. Mem. Am. Math. Soc., Math. Assn. Am. (chmn. Mo. 1960-61), Can. Math. Soc., Soc. for Indsl. and Applied Math., Phi Beta Kappa, Sigma Xi. Contbr. articles to profl. jours. Home: 701 Glenwood Ct Columbia MO 65201

ZEMP, JOHN WORKMAN, coll. dean; b. Camden, S.C., Sept. 28, 1931; s. Charles Herbert and Elizabeth Brisbane (Workman) Z.; B.S., Coll. Charleston (S.C.), 1953; M.S., Med. U. S.C., Charleston, 1954; Ph.D., U. N.C., 1966; m. Lois DeWitt, Dec. 20, 1958; children—John, Virginia, Blake, DeWitt. Asst. prof. U. N.C., 1967-68; mem. faculty Med. U. S.C., 1969—, prof. biochemistry and research psychiatry, 1974—, dean Coll. Grad. Studies and Univ. Research, 1977—; exec. dir. Charleston Higher Edn. Consortium, 1977—; chmn. task force orgn. higher edn. for S.C. State Reorgn. Com. Bd. dirs. St. John's Episcopal Mission Center, Charleston, 1970—, chmn., 1971-74; sr. warden St. Michael's Episcopal Ch., Charleston, 1977-79; chmn. diocesan conv. com. Episcopal Diocese S.C., 1975, mem. council, 1978—; bd. dirs. Coll. Charleston Found.; mem. Trident Work bd. dirs. Coll. Prep. Sch., 1976—, chmn., 1977—; Edn. Council, 1976—; chmn. bd. dirs. Trident 2000, 1978—; trustee Health Scis. Found. Served with USNR, 1956-63. Recipient Coker award U. N.C., 1966, SAMA Golden Apple award, 1971; predoctoral fellow USPHS, 1955-56; predoctoral fellow NSF, 1965-66, postdoctoral fellow, 1966-67. Mem. Am. Soc. Neurochemistry, Soc. Neurosci., Am. Chem. Soc., Am. Soc. Pharmacology and Exptl. Therapeutics, AAAS, Soc. Exptl. Biology and Medicine, Internat. Soc. Neurochemistry, S.C. Acad. Scis., Navy League, S.C. Hist. Soc., S.C. Art Assn., Phi Beta Kappa, Sigma Xi. Author papers in field. Home: 95 Lenwood Blvd Charleston SC 29401 Office: Med Univ SC 171 Ashley Ave Charleston SC 29403

ZEMPLENYI, TIBOR KAROL, cardiologist; b. Part. Lupca, Czechoslovakia, July 16, 1916; s. David Dezider and Irene (Pollak) Z.; came to U.S., 1968, naturalized, 1974; M.D., Charles U., Prague, 1946, Docent Habilit., 1966; C.Sc. (Ph.D.), Czechoslovak Acad. Sci., 1960, D.Sc., 1964; m. Hana Bendová, Aug. 13, 1952; 1 son, Jan. Clin. asst. dept. medicine Prague Motol Clinic, 1946-52; head atherosclerosis research Inst. for Cardiovascular Research, Prague, 1952-68; asso. prof. medicine Charles U., 1966-68; asso. prof. medicine U. So. Calif. Sch. Medicine, Los Angeles, 1969-75, prof., 1975—; attending physician Los Angeles County-U. So. Calif. Med. Center. WHO fellow for study in Sweden and Gt. Britain, 1959. Fellow Am. Heart Assn.; mem. Western Soc. for Clin. Research, European Atherosclerosis Group, Italian Soc. for Atherosclerosis (hon.). Author: Enzyme Biochemistry of the Arterial Wall, 1968. Mem. editorial bd. Atherosclerosis, 1962-75; mem. adv. bd. Advances in Lipid Research, 1963-66. Contbr. to numerous publs. Home: 3400 Loadstone Dr Sherman Oaks CA 91403 Office: 2025 Zonal Ave Los Angeles CA 90033

ZEN, E-AN, geologist; b. Peking, China, May 31, 1928; s. Hung-chun and Heng-chi'h (Chen) Z.; came to U.S., 1946, naturalized, 1963; A.B., Cornell U., 1951; M.A., Harvard, 1952, Ph.D., 1955; m. Cristina C. Silber, Nov., 1967. Research fellow Woods Hole Oceanographic Inst., 1955-56, research asso., 1956-58; asst. prof. U. N.C., 1958-59; geologist U.S. Geol. Survey, 1959—; vis. asso. prof. Calif. Inst. Tech., 1962; Crosby vis. prof. Mass. Inst. Tech., 1973. Fellow Geol. Soc. Am., Mineral. Soc. Am. (council 1975-77, pres. 1975-76); mem. Geol. Soc. Washington (pres. 1973), Nat. Acad. Scis., Mineral. Assn. Can., Mineral. Soc. Gt. Britain and Ireland. Contbr. articles to profl. jours. Office: Mail Stop 959 US Geol Survey Nat Center Reston VA 22092

ZENCZAK, PIOTR, paper products co. exec.; b. Ispina, Poland, Nov. 19, 1913; s. Boleslaw and Anna (Parski) Z.; Ph.D., 1939; postgrad. U. Wash., 1948-53; m. Margaret Marcinkowski, May 13, 1946; children—Boleslaw, Ewa. Came to U.S., 1947. Research asso. Engring. Expt. Sta., U. Wash., Seattle, 1948-52; cons. engr., Seattle, 1953-55; with Evans Products Co., Corvallis, Oreg., 1955—, formerly research dir., plant mgr., div. gen. mgr., v.p., dir., now exec. v.p., dir., group pres., Portland, Oreg. Mem. Am. Hardboard Assn. (pres.), Electrochem. Soc., T.A.P.P.I., Sigma Xi. Rotarian. Contbr. articles to sci. publs. Patentee in field. Home: Route 1 Box 40 Philomath OR 97370 Office: PO Box 4 Corvallis OR 97330

ZENKE, LARRY LYNN, ednl. adminstr.; b. Galesville, Wis., Aug. 19, 1939; s. Arthur William and Stella Victoria (Knutson) Z.; B.S., Wis. State U., 1961; M.S., Winona State Coll., 1965; Ed.D., U. Fla., 1970; m. JoAnn Zahorik, Feb. 5, 1959; children—Lisa Joy, Kristin Ann. Tchr. public schs., Highland Park, Ill., 1961-66; prin. elem. sch., Oak Lawn, Ill., 1966-68; adminstrv. intern Supt.'s Office, Miami, Fla., 1969; dir. elementary edn., Jacksonville, Fla., 1970-73; dep. supt. for instrn., Orlando, Fla., 1973-76; supt. schs. Tulsa Ind. Sch. Dist., 1976—; adj. prof. U. Fla., Rollins Coll. Chmn. public schs. div. United Way, 1977-79; mem. exec. bd. Boys Scouts Am., 1978-79; bd. dirs. Okla. Econ. Edn. Commn., 1976-79. Mem. Am. Assn. Sch. Adminstrs., Okla. Coop. Council Sch. Adminstrs., Assn. Supervision and Curriculum Devel., Am. Mgmt. Assn., Acad. Sch. Execs. (adv. bd.), Nat. Alliance Businessmen (dir. 1978-79), Kappa Delta Pi, Phi Delta Kappa. Presbyterian. Club: Rotary. Contbr. articles to profl. jours. Office: PO Box 45208 Tulsa OK 74145

ZENO, ROBERT S., govt. research adminstr.; b. Big Rapids, Mich., Sept. 24, 1919; s. Samuel and Lena (Gychevich) Z.; B.S. in Metall. Engring., Mich. Tech. U., 1941; M.S. in Metallurgy, Pa. State U., 1947; m. Jill Burnside, Jan. 21, 1947; children—Jeffrey R., Douglas H. With Gen. Electric Co., Schenectady, 1947-72, site mgr. Quad Cities plant site, 1967-71, project mgr., 1971-72; dir. Angra Nuclear Power Plant project Westinghouse Electric Co., N.Y.C., 1972-73; dir. components devel. Argonne (Ill.) Nat. Lab., 1973—; lectr. in materials engring. Union Coll., Schenectady, 1959-61. Mem. bldg. com. Unitarian Ch., Schenectady, 1959-61. Served with C.E., U.S. Army, 1941-46; PTO, ETO, NATOUSA. Fellow Am. Soc. Metals. Author numerous Gen. Electric reports; contbr. articles to metall. publs.; patentee high temperature weldable alloys. Home: 1124 Woodview Rd Hinsdale IL 60521 Office: Argonne Nat Lab 9700 S Cass Argonne IL 60439

ZENTMYER, GEORGE AUBREY, JR., educator; b. North Platte, Nebr., Aug. 9, 1913; s. George Aubrey and Mary Elizabeth (Strahorn) Z.; A.B., U. Calif. at Los Angeles, 1935; M.S., U. Calif., 1936, Ph.D., 1938; m. Dorothy Anne Dudley, May 24, 1941; children—Elizabeth (Mrs. Alfred C. Dossa), Jane (Mrs. Castle G.E. Fernald), Susan Dudley. Asst. forest pathologist U.S. Dept. Agr., San Francisco, 1937-40; asst. pathologist Conn. Agrl. Expt. Sta., New Haven, 1940-44; asst. plant pathologist to plant pathologist U. Calif. at Riverside, 1944-62, prof. plant pathology, 1962—, chmn. dept., 1968-73. Cons. NSF, Trust Ty. of Pacific Islands, 1964, 66, Commonwealth of Australia Forest and Timber Bur., 1968, AID, Ghana and Nigeria 1969; Dir. Riverside YMCA, 1949-58; pres. Town and Gown Orgn., Riverside, 1962; mem. NRC, 1968-73. Guggenheim fellow, Australia, 1964-65; NATO sr. sci. fellow, Eng., 1971; recipient award of honor Calif. Avocado Soc., 1954. NSF research grantee 1963, 68, 71, 74, 78. Fellow Am. Phytopathol. Soc. (pres. 1966, pres. Pacific div. 1955), A.A.A.S. (pres. Pacific div. 1974-75); mem. Nat. Acad. Scis., Mycol. Soc. Am., Am. Inst. Biol. Scis., Bot. Soc. Am., Brit. Mycol. Soc., Australian Plant Pathology Soc., Philippine Phytopath. Soc., Indian Phytopath. Soc., Assn. Tropical Biology, Internat. Soc. Plant Pathology (councilor 1973-78), Sigma Xi. Author: Plant Disease Development and Control, 1968; Recent Advances in Pest Control, 1957; Plant Pathology, an Advanced Treatise, 1977; Asso. editor Annual Review of Phytopathology, 1971—, Jour. Phytopathology, 1951-54. Contbr. articles to profl. jours. Home: 3892 Chapman Pl Riverside CA 92506

ZEPPA, ROBERT, surgeon; b. N.Y.C., Sept. 17, 1924; s. Alfred and Angelina (Buscaglia) Z.; A.B., Columbia U., 1948; M.D., Yale U., 1952; m. Cicely M. Lawrence, June 7, 1952; children—Melissa Kay, Scott L. Intern, U. Pitts. Med. Center, 1952-53; resident U. N.C., Chapel Hill, 1953-56, prof. surgery, 1958-65; prof. surgery and pharmacology U. Miami (Fla.), 1965—, co-chmn. dept. surgery, 1966-71, chmn. dept. surgery, 1971—; chief surg. service VA Hosp., Miami, 1965-72; chief surgery Jackson Meml. Hosp., Miami, 1971—, pres. med. staff, 1976-78; mem. surgery tng. com. Nat. Inst. Gen. Medicine Scis., 1968-71. Served to 2d lt., AC, U.S. Army, 1943-45; Eng. John and Mary Markle scholar, 1959-64. Diplomate Am. Bd. Surgery. Mem. A.C.S., AAAS, Am. Gastroenterol. Assn., Am. Assn. Study Liver Diseases, Am. Surg. Assn., Soc. Surgery Alimentary Tract, Soc. Univ. Surgeons, N.Y. Acad. Scis., So. Surg. Assn., Alpha Omega Alpha. Contbr. articles to profl. publs.; 3 film presentation. Office: PO Box 016310 Miami FL 33101

ZEPS, VALDIS JURIS, educator; b. Daugavpils, Latvia, May 29, 1932; s. Jazeps and Anna Alida (Kalejs) Z.; came to U.S., 1950, naturalized, 1955; A.B., Miami U., Oxford, Ohio, 1953; Ph.D., Ind. U., 1960; m. Betty Reel Shuford, Sept. 9, 1957; children—Dace Alida, Valdis Juris, Barbara Ruta, William Avery. Linguist Office of Geography Dept. Interior, 1961-62; prof. linguistics U. Wis., 1962—. Served with AUS, 1954-56. NSF postdoctoral fellow, Center Advanced Study Behavioral Scis., Stanford, Cal., 1960-61. Mem. Linguistic Soc. Am., Am. Assn. Tchrs. of Slavic and East European Langs., Assn. Advancement Baltic Studies, Phi Beta Kappa. Author: (with T.A. Sebeok) A Thesaurus of Cheremis Poetic Language, 1962; Latvian and Finnic Linguistic Convergences, 1963; Keves dels Kurbads, 1970. Mng. editor Slavic and East European Jour., 1962-70; editor Jour. Baltic Studies, 1976—. Home: 1922 Adams St Madison WI 53711

ZERBE, ANTHONY, actor; b. Long Beach, Calif.; s. Arthur Le Van and Catherine (Scurlock) Z.; student Pomona Coll., 1954-55, Stella Adler Theater Studio, N.Y.C., 1958-60; m. Arnette Jens, Oct. 7, 1962; children—Jennet, Jared Le Van. Actor, Fred Miller Theater, Milw., 1962-63, Arena Stage, Washington, 1963-65, Theater Living Arts, Phila., 1965-66, Stratford (Ont., Can.) Theater, 1962, Old Globe Theater, San Diego, 1965-67, 72, Mark Taper Forum, Los Angeles, 1967—, Seattle Repertory Co., 1975—; films include Cool Hand Luke, 1967, Will Penny, 1967, Omega Man, 1970, Liberation of L.B. Jones, 1972, Farewell My Lovely, 1975, Turning Point, 1977, Who'll Stop the Rain, 1978; numerous TV shows, including Harry-O series, 1974-76; TV films include The Priest Killer, 1971, Snatched, 1973, She Lives, 1973, The Healers, 1974, In the Glitter Palace, 1977; one-man show: It's All Done With Mirrors, 1977—; two-man show (with Roscoe Lee Browne): Behind the Broken Words, 1977—; pres. prodn. co. Cameo Theater Inc. Served with USAF, 1959. Recipient Emmy award as best supporting actor Harry-O, 1976. Office: care Susan Smith and Assos 9869 Santa Monica Blvd Beverly Hills CA 90212*

ZERBY, LEWIS KENNETH, educator; b. Donovan, Ill., Dec. 24, 1916; s. Guy Lewis and Nettie (Anderson) Z.; B.S., U. Ill., 1939, M.A., 1942; Ph.D., State U. Iowa, 1945; m. Margaret Ellen Schiller, Aug. 11, 1943; children—Thelma Ruth Rebecca Zerby Moise, Ruth Elizabeth, James Lewis Robert. Instr. philosophy State U. Iowa, 1945-46; asst. prof. to prof. Mich. State U., East Lansing, 1946-62, prof. philosophy, 1966-67, prof. philosophy and prof. James Madison Coll., 1967-72, chmn. div. justice, morality and constl. democracy, 1967-72, prof. philosophy, 1972—; head div. gen. studies, head dept. philosophy U. Nigeria, 1962-66. Recipient Disting. Faculty award Mich. State U., 1977. Fellow AAAS; mem. Philosophy Sci. Assn. (mng. editor Philosophy of Sci., sec. 1955-62). Author: (with Margaret Zerby) If I Should Die Before I Wake: The Nsukka Dream, A History of the University of Nigeria, 1971; (with Glenn L. Johnson) What Economists Do About Values, 1973; A Zebra Book: Philosophical and Political Essays from Africa and America, 1978. Contbr. articles to profl. jours. Home: 4534 Hawthorn Lane Okemos MI 48864 Office: Mich State U East Lansing MI 48823. *As a philosopher I have dedicated my life to the deepening of my understanding of the basic principles of reality. Western culture has failed because of its stress upon positivism and individualism. My life has convinced me that there is a moral order of nature which we neglect at our peril. Basic in this moral order is the oneness of all humanity. Loss of this vision is the source of most of modern civilization's travail.*

ZERMAN, WILLIAM SHERIDAN, frat. exec., editor; b. Toledo, June 12, 1924; s. Donald Coe and Bernadette (Sheridan) Z.; student Defiance Coll., 1942-43; B.A., U. Mich., 1949, M.A., 1956; L.H.D., Athens Coll., 1965; m. Ruth Marian Blackmore, June 19, 1953; children—Carol, William Sheridan, Gregory. Field sec. Phi Gamma Delta, Washington, 1949-51, exec. sec., Washington, 1959-73, exec. dir., Lexington, Ky., 1973—, also editor The Phi Gamma Delta Jour., 1967—; mem. staff dept. devel. Ohio-Mich. office N.A.N., Detroit, 1951-52; asst. dean men U. Mich., 1952-56; dean men Ohio Wesleyan U., Delaware, 1956-59. Chmn. Nat. Interfrat. Conf. Undergrad Conf., 2 years. Trustee Boys Clubs Washington, 1962-64; bd. dirs. Salvation Army. Served with AUS, 1943-46; ETO. Mem. Am. Coll. Personnel Assn. (mem. Commn. III Housing), Frat. Exec. Assn. (past pres.), Am. Soc. Assn. Execs., Am. Personnel and Guidance Assn., Sigma Delta Chi, Phi Delta Kappa. Methodist. Clubs: Masons, Shriners, Rotary, Lafayette (Lexington). Author: Fraternally Yours. Address: Frat Phi Gamma Delta 343 Waller Ave Suite 301 Lexington KY 40504. *Loyalty to family and employer, faith in God, and attention to details in conducting one's total life-as well as hard work coupled with love for one's fellowman-seem to me to be prime assets in living a happy life. Service to others, being truthful and being firm with well thought decisions, but having no fear of admitting error, when one has been made are additional ingredients one should have to be of benefit, not a liability to society. Persistence in carrying out an idea, plan, or program can be of great benefit to ourselves and those around us.*

ZERNER, HENRI THOMAS, art historian; b. France, May 15, 1939; s. Frederick and Elisabeth (Lazarsfeld) Z.; student Columbia Coll., 1957-58; Ph.D., U. Paris, 1969; m. Catherine Wilkinson, May 5, 1973; children—Rachel, Charles-Theodore. Mem. faculty dept. art history Brown U., 1966-73; vis. curator prints and drawings Mus. of Art, R.I. Sch. Design, 1965-73; curator prints Fogg Art Mus., prof. fine arts Harvard U., 1973—. Recipient Prix Achille Found. Academie des Inscriptions et Belles Lettres, 1971; Focillon fellow, 1961; Guggenheim fellow, 1971. Mem. Coll. Art Assn. Am., Internat. Council Museums, Societe de l'Histoire de l'Art Francais. Author: The School of Fontainebleau Etchings and Engravings, 1970. Office: Fogg Art Mus Harvard Univ Cambridge MA 02138

ZETKOV, THOMAS EDWARD, ins. cons.; b. N.Y.C., Mar. 17, 1922; s. Thomas Chris and Phylis (Marin) Z.; B.S., Colgate U., 1949; m. Olga Kobryn, Aug. 30, 1949; children—Susan Anne, Janet Lynne, Thomas Edward. Eastern regional group supr. Continental Ins. Co., N.Y.C., 1948-55; v.p. Colonial Penn Group, Phila., 1955-62, pres., 1962-78, ret., 1978; cons. Colonial Penn Group, Inc. Trustee, Hackley Sch., Tarrytown, N.Y., Colgate U. Served to lt. USAAF, World War II; PTO. Roman Catholic. Clubs: Sailfish of Fla., Tarrytown Boat, Sleepy Hollow Country. Co-compiler: The Wisdom of Ethel Percy Andrus, 1968. Home: 60 Quinn Rd Briarcliff Manor NY 10510 Office: 555 Madison Ave New York NY 10022

ZETLIN, LEV, civil engr., educator; b. Namangan, Russia, July 14, 1918; s. Mayer and Alexandra (Senelnikoff) Z.; diploma Higher Tech. Inst., Palestine, 1939; M.C.E., Cornell U., 1951, Ph.D., 1953; m. Eve (Hava) Shmueli, Jan. 24, 1946; children—Alexandra, Thalia, Michael Steven. Research asso., asst. prof. civil engring. Cornell U., 1951-55; prof. civil engring. Pratt Inst., N.Y.C., 1956—; vis. prof. civil engring. Manhattan Coll., N.Y.C., 1957-59; guest lectr. Columbia U., Minn., U. Va., 1955-63; Univ. prof. engring. and architecture U. Va., 1967; cons. engr.; pres. Zetlin-Argo Liaison & Guidance Corp., Lev Zetlin Cons., Spl. Structural Systems, Inc. Mem. Concrete Industry Bd. N.Y.C.; former mem. adv. panel Gen. Services Adminstrn., housing tech. joint panel Dept. Commerce-Dept. Housing and Urban Devel.; mem. planning com. bldg. research adv. bd. Nat. Acad. Scis.; mem. N.Y. State Council on Arts; past pres. Internat. Tech. Cooperation Centre. Trustee, chmn. consultor com. Manhattan Coll. Sacred Heart, N.Y.; Decorated Knight of honour Mil. and Hospitaler Order St. John of Jerusalem, Knight of Malta; recipient Prestressed Concrete Inst. award for N.Y. State Observation Towers, N.Y. Worlds Fair, 1964; Gold medal Société Arts, Sciences, Lettres, 1969; named to Profl. and Exec. Hall of Fame. Fellow Am. Soc. C.E.; mem. Soc. Am. Mil. Engrs., Internat. Assn. Bridge and Structural Engrs., Inst. Structural Engrs. (Eng.), N.Y. Acad. Scis., Am. Concrete Inst., Sigma Xi, Phi Kappa Phi, Chi Epsilon. Mem. editorial adv. bd. Bldg. Constrn. Mag., 1962—. Author: Reinforced Concrete Design, Standard Handbook for Engineers, 1968; Suspension Structures, Structural Engineering Handbook, 1968. Contbr. articles to profl. jours., chpt. on stadiums Ency. Brit. Inventor prestressed runways, light gage airplane hangars, cable suspension structures, systems bldgs. Home: 89 Hamilton Dr Roslyn NY 11576 Office: 60 E 42d St New York NY 10017

ZETTLEMOYER, ALBERT CHARLES, educator, chemist; b. Allentown, Pa., July 13, 1915; s. Fred R. and Florence (Nagle) Z.; B.S. in Chem. Engring., Lehigh U., 1936, M.S. in Chemistry, 1938; Ph.D. in Phys. Chemistry, Mass. Inst. Tech., 1941; D.Sc. (hon.), Clarkson U., 1965; LL.D., China Acad. 1974; m. Onetta Ruth Hartman, Dec. 21, 1940; children—Christopher, Nicholas, Anthony, Timothy, Nan. With Armstrong Cork Co., 1941; mem. faculty Lehigh U., 1941—, distinguished prof. chemistry, 1960—, v.p. research, 1966-69, provost, 1969-80; cons. in field. Dir. Pearsall Chem. Co., Koh-i-Noor Co. Chmn. United Fund Appeal Bethlehem Area, 1962; bd. dirs. Bethlehem YMCA, 1950—, pres., 1958-59, 62-66, trustee, 1970—. Mattiello lectr., 1957; recipient Ault award Printing Ink Assn., 1961, Elmer G. Voigt award for edn., 1966, Hillman award Lehigh U., 1966, Pioneer award Nat. Assn. Printing Ink Mfrs., 1969. Fellow N.Y. Acad. Sci.; mem. Am. Chem. Soc. (chmn. Lehigh Valley sect. 1952-53, divisional officer's group 1953-54, div. paint, plastics and printing ink chemistry 1954-55, div. colloid chemistry 1956-57, councillor 1960—, vice chmn. council policy com. 1968-70, chmn. profl. relations com. 1973-76, dir.-at-large 1978-79, pres. 1980, Kendall award 1968), Gordon Conf. (chmn. chemistry interfaces 1955—, chmn. adhesion 1979, trustee 1960-63), AAAS, ASTM, Am. Inst. Chemists (honor scroll 1966), Am. Oil Chemists Assn. (Bond medal 1961), TAPPI, Tech. Assn. Graphic Arts, Franklin Inst. (com. on sci. and arts 1973—), Sigma Xi (nat. lectr. 1958). Tau Beta Pi. Rotarian (pres. Bethlehem 1962). Clubs: Chemist (N.Y.C.); Cosmos (Washington); Saucon Valley Country. Editor: Advances in Colloid and Interface Sci. 1966—; Nucleation, 1969; Nucleation Phenomena, 1977; Nucleation Phenomena II, 1978; Jour. Colloid and Interface sci., 1965—. Home: 137 E Market Bethlehem PA 18018

ZEUGNER, ORLAND KUMP, ret. investment banker; b. Ft. Atkinson, Wis., July 6, 1907; s. Carl W. and Pearlis (Kump) Z.; B.S., U. Wis., 1927; m. Ethel Finn, Dec. 27, 1932; children—Joan, John, Janet, Barbara. With Stone & Webster Securities Corp., Chgo., 1929-32, N.Y.C., 1932—, v.p., 1949-62, exec. v.p., 1962-63, pres., 1963-69, chief exec. officer, 1965-69, chmn. bd., 1969, dir., cons. 1969-70; pres. Broadstone Realty Corp., N.Y.C., 1963-69; trustee Midland Mortgage Investors. Vol. Internat. Exec. Service Corps, N.Y.C. Mem. Investment Bankers Assn. (gov. 1965-67), Alpha Chi Rho, Chi Epsilon. Clubs: Boca Raton, Royal Palm Yacht and Country (Boca Raton, Fla.). Home: 1200 S Ocean Blvd Apt 6H Boca Raton FL 33432

ZEUSCHNER, ERWIN ARNOLD, bank exec.; b. Freiburg, Germany, Nov. 17, 1935; s. Reinhold Hermann and Helene Barbara (Maas) Z.; came to U.S., 1936; B.A. in Econs., Queens Coll., 1957; M.B.A. in Fin., N.Y. U., 1964; m. Christa Elfreide Ellmers, June 20, 1959 (dec. Aug., 1971); children—Peter Erwin, Suzanne Christina, Andrea Ellmers; m. Margaret Anne Finn, Mar. 25, 1972; 1 dau., Elizabeth Nora. Sr. v.p. Chase Manhattan Bank, N.Y.C., 1970-72; sr. v.p., dir. Chase Investors Mgmt. Corp., 1972—; sr. v.p. Chase Manhattan Corp., 1970—. Served to capt. USAF, 1958-60. Mem. N.Y. Soc. Security Analysts (dir.). Home: 1 Middle Dr Plandome NY 11030 Office: 1211 Ave of Americas New York NY 10005

ZEVON, WARREN, singer, songwriter; b. Chgo., 1947; m. Crystal Zevon; 1 child, Ariel; 1 son from previous marriage, Jordan. Folksinger, writer commls., pianist with The Everly Bros.; albums include: Wanted Dead or Alive, 1970, Warren Zevon, 1976, Excitable Boy, 1978; composer songs: Hasten Down the Wind, Poor Poor Pitiful Me, Werewolves of London, Roland the Headless Thompson Gunner, When Johnny Strikes up the Band, others. Office: care William Morris Agy 151 El Camino Dr Beverly Hills CA 90212*

ZIADEH, FARHAT J., educator; b. Ramallah, Palestine, Apr. 8, 1917; s. Jacob and Nimeh Farah Z.; B.A., Am. U., Beirut, 1937; LL.B., U. London, 1940; m. Suad Salem, July 24, 1949; children—Shireen, Susan, Rhonda, Deena, Reema. Instr., Princeton U., 1943-45, lectr. Oriental studies, 1948-54, asst. prof., 1954-58, asso. prof., 1958-66; magistrate Govt. of Palestine, 1947-48; editor Voice of Am., USIA, 1950-54; prof. U. Wash., Seattle, 1966—, chmn. dept. Near Eastern lang. and lit., 1970—; adj. prof. U. Wash. Sch. Law, 1978—. Mem. Middle East Studies Assn. (pres. 1979-80), Am. Oriental Soc. (past pres. western br.), Am. Research Center in Egypt (past bd. govs., exec. com.), Am. Assn. Tchrs. Arabic (past pres.). Eastern Orthodox. Author: Reader in Modern Literary Arabic, 1964; Lawyers, The Rule of Law and Liberalism in Modern Egypt, 1968; Property Law in the Arab World, 1979; contbr. articles to profl. jours. Office: Univ Wash Seattle WA 98195

ZICK, JOHN WALTER, acctg. co. exec.; b. Highland Park, Ill., Sept. 21, 1925; s. Walter Ernest and Helen Ann (Wiedenhoeft) Z.; B.S., Northwestern U., 1948; m. Mary Ann Sutter, Dec. 11, 1948; children—Sharon, Catherine, John Walter. With Price Waterhouse & Co., Chgo., 1948-73, N.Y.C., 1973—, partner, 1960—, partner in charge N.Y.C. office, 1973-76, regional mng. partner, 1976-78, co-chmn., dept. sr. partner, 1978—. Bd. dirs. Mid-Am. chpt. ARC, 1968-73; founding mem., elder Winnetka (Ill.) Presbyterian Ch., 1956-67; bd. auditors New Trier Twp. (Ill.), 1969-73. Served with USN, 1943-46. Mem. Am. Inst. C.P.A.'s (treas. and dir. 1974-77), Ill. Soc. C.P.A.'s (pres. 1971-72). Clubs: Racquet and Tennis, Stanwich, Pine Valley Golf; Union League (N.Y.C.). Office: 1251 Ave of Americas New York NY 10020

ZIEBARTH, E. WILLIAM, educator and news analyst; b. Columbus, Wis., Oct. 4, 1910; s. John and Priscilla (Conrad) Z.; B.S., U. Wis., 1933, Ph.M., 1934; Ph.D., U. Minn., 1948; m. Elizabeth Herreid, Dec. 16, 1939; 1 son, John Thomas. Staff U. of Air, WHA, U. Wis., 1934; instr. speech U. Minn., 1936, acting gen. mgr. sta. WLB, 1944, asso. prof., chmn. dept. speech, 1948, prof., chmn. dept. speech and theatre arts, 1949—, dean summer session, 1954—, dean gen. extension div., 1963-64, dean Coll. Liberal Arts, 1964, interim pres., 1974; cons. for TV World Affairs, 1954; founder, also dir. Min. Sch. of Air, 1938; prodn. mgr. WCCO-CBS, 1945, news analyst, 1947-52, exec. cons., 1948; ednl. dir. central div. CBS network, 1946, cons., 1948-51, spl. fgn., corr., internat. affairs analyst, Scandinavia, So. and Western Europe, 1949, fgn. corr., internat. broadcaster, Scandinavia, Western Europe, Western Asia, 1950, Asiatic analysis, Tokyo, Japan, 1952; exec. v.p., interim gen. mgr. KTCA-TV, KTCI-TV, 1976; exec. v.p., gen. mgr. Twin City Area Pub. TV Corp., 1976-77; radio edn. cons. Hill Found. award study in Soviet Union, 1958, 68; bd. dirs. Midwest Ednl. Television Corp.; trustee Twin City Area TV Corp. Co-chmn. feasibility research Pan-Pacific-Mainland Edn. and Communication Expt. by Satellite, Honolulu, Tokyo, Hong Kong, 1973. Dir. Hennepin County Tb Assn., Minn. Tb and Public Health Asso. Mem. Gov.'s Youth Commn.; mem. Nat. Commn. on Arts and Scis. Trustee Macalester Coll. Joint winner nat. Peabody award, 1948; recipient citation Nat. English Council, 1949; Radio Council award for distinguished news analysis, 1952, for significant contbns. internat. understanding, 1951; first award Nat. Inst. Edn. by Radio for news interpretation, 1952; Best Commentator award A.F.T.R.A., 1955; joint winner Peabody award, internat. affairs, 1960; Nat. Peabody award, 1972; Blakeslee award Nat. Heart Assn., 1972; N.W. Area Found. fellow to People's Republic of China, 1976. Mem. Nat. Assn. Edn. by Radio, Fgn. Policy Assn., Minn. Hist. Soc., Nat. Adult Edn. Assn., Nat. Assn. Ednl. Broadcasters and Telecasters, Nat. Soc. Study Communication (Radio council, mass media com.), Central States Speech Assn., Chi Phi, Phi Kappa, Delta Sigma Rho, Phi Delta Kappa, Psi Chi, Alpha Epsilon Rho, Delta Phi Lambda, Lambda Alpha Psi. Clubs: Hesperia, Greyfriars, Campus. Author Six Classic Plays for Radio and How to Produce Them, published in 1940. Contbr. articles to profl. jours. Mass Media editor Speech Monographs, 1951-53; cons. editor Central States Speech Jour. Home: 1596 Northrop St St Paul MN 55108 Office: N-231 Psychology Elliott Hall U Minn Minneapolis MN 55455

ZIEBARTH, KARL REX, railroad exec.; b. Reading, Pa., May 25, 1938; s. Robert Kurt and Leah Evelyn (DuBor) Z.; B.A., Yale U., 1959; m. Gisela Hermine Hader, Nov. 13, 1970; children—Viktoria, Alexander, Elena. Security analyst The Bank of N.Y., 1960-63; 2d v.p. Hayden, Stone, Inc., N.Y.C., 1963-70; asst. v.p. Dominick and Dominick, N.Y.C., 1970-71; v.p., sec., treas. Mo.-Kans.-Tex. R.R. Co., Dallas, 1970-78, exec. v.p. fin., 1979—, also dir.; dir. Trailer Train, 1971-78, Texas City Terminal Ry., Galveston, Houston & Henderson R.R. Co. Trustee, Phila. Soc., 1975-78. Served from pvt. to capt. USAR, 1960-69. Clubs: Racquet (Chgo.); Petroleum (Dallas); Reform (London); Yale (N.Y.C.). Office: 701 Commerce St Dallas TX 75202

ZIEBARTH, ROBERT CHARLES, mgmt. cons.; b. Evanston, Ill., Sept. 12, 1936; s. Charles A. and Marian (Miller) Z.; A.B., Princeton, 1958; M.B.A., Harvard, 1964; m. Patience Arnold Kirkpatrick, Aug. 28, 1971; children—Dana Kirkpatrick, Scott Kirkpatrick, Christopher, Nicholas. With Bell & Howell Co., Chgo., 1964—, treas., chief fin. officer, 1969—; mgmt. cons. Ziebarth Co., 1973—; mem. dirs. adv. bd. Arkwright Boston Ins. Co.; dir. M.B.A. Resources, Inc., Telemedia, Inc. Asso. Community Renewal Soc., Citizens council Gateway House; mem. Ill. Bd. Higher Edn., Ill. Joint Edn. Commn. Trustee Choate Sch., Latin Sch. Chgo.; bd. dirs. Harvard Bus. Sch. Fund, U.S.O., Inc. Served to lt. USNR, 1958-62. Mem. Naval Hist. Found., Art Inst. Chgo., Chgo. Hist. Soc., Mus. Modern Art. Presbyn. Clubs: Mid-Am., Racquet, Saddle and Cycle, Economic, Executives (Chgo.). Office: 1500 Lake Shore Dr Chicago IL 60610

ZIEGLER, ARTHUR B., banker; b. N.Y.C., May 27, 1930; s. Albert B. and Edith Elizabeth (Yorden) Z.; night student Syracuse U. Coll., 1947-49; pub. relations student, Banker Sch., 1954, Northwestern U. Financial Sch., 1958-59; grad. program mgmt. devel. Harvard, 1961; m. Barbara A. Bronner, Jan. 6, 1951. Asst. advt. mgr. Am. Stores Co., 1947-52; with Marine Midland Banks, Inc., Buffalo, 1952—, asst. v.p., 1959-63, v.p., 1963-69, sr. v.p.-adminstrn., 1969-73, exec. v.p., 1973—, mem. mgmt. com., 1975—. Mem. Bank Mktg. Assn. (nat. pres. 1978—, dir.), Pub. Relations Soc. Am. (chpt. pres. 1967-68). Presbyn. Clubs: Buffalo; Orchard Park Country (Orchard Park); City Midday (N.Y.C.). Home: 57 Fox Meadow Lane Stonehenge Farms Orchard Park NY 14127 Office: One Marine Midland Center Buffalo NY 14240

ZIEGLER, BENJAMIN MUNN, educator; b. Boston, Sept. 24, 1908; s. James B. and Gertrude (Munn) Z.; LL.B., Harvard, 1931, M.A., 1933, Ph.D., 1935; M.A. (hon.), Amherst Coll., 1952; D.H.L., St. Francis Coll., U. New Eng., 1978; m. Hilda Elizabeth Brown, Dec.

7, 1942. Asst. in govt. Harvard, 1932-35; instr. govt. Ohio State U., 1935-36; asst. prof. govt. Elmira Coll., 1936-38; asst. prof. polit. sci. Amherst Coll., 1938-46, asso. prof., 1946-52, prof., 1952—, Bertrand Snell prof., 1953-75, emeritus, 1975—. Ford Found. faculty fellow, 1954-55; Fulbright lectr. U. Vienna, 1965-66, U. Saarlandes (Germany), 1971-72. Mem. Draft Bd., Hampshire County, Mass. Served from pvt. to capt. AUS, 1941-46; ETO. Mem. Am., Connecticut Valley polit. sci. assns., Am. Soc. Internat. Law, Am. Arbitration Assn., Phi Beta Kappa. Author: The International Law of John Marshall, 1940. Editor: Immigration: an American Dilemma, 1954; Desegregation and the Supreme Court, 1958; The Supreme Court and American Economic Life, 1962; Communism, the Courts and the Constitution, 1964. Home: Granite Point Fortunes Rock ME 04005

ZIEGLER, DANIEL MARTIN, educator, chemist; b. Quinter, Kans., July 6, 1927; s. Anton T. and Clara (Weissbeck) Z.; B.S. in Chemistry, St. Benedict's Coll., Atchison, Kans., 1949; Ph.D. in Chemistry, Loyola U., Chgo., 1955; postdoctoral student biochemistry Inst. Enzyme Research, U. Wis., 1955-59; m. Mary Alice Weir, Aug. 19, 1952; children—Daniel L., Paul W., Mary Claire, James M. Asst. prof. Inst. Enzyme Research, U. Wis., 1959-61; mem. faculty U. Tex., Austin, 1961—, prof. chemistry, 1969—. Recipient USPHS Career Devel. award, 1965-75; Royall Cabell fellow, 1954-55; postdoctoral trainee Nat. Heart Inst., 1955-59; established investigator Am. Heart Assn., 1960-65. Mem. Am. Soc. Biol. Chemists, Am. Chem. Soc., AAAS, St. Vincent de Paul Soc., Sigma Xi. Contbr. articles to profl. jours. Editorial bd. Archives of Biochemistry and Biophysics, 1966-76, Jour. Biol. Chemistry, 1978—. Home: 6704 Shoal Creek Blvd Austin TX 78731

ZIEGLER, DEWEY KIPER, neurologist; b. Omaha, May 31, 1920; s. Isidor and Pearl (Kiper) Z.; B.A., Harvard U., 1941, M.D., 1945; m. Mar. 30, 1954; children—Amy, Laura, Sara. Intern in medicine Boston City Hosp., 1945-46; asst. resident then chief resident in neurology, N.Y. Neurol. Inst.-Columbia U. Coll. Physicians and Surgeons, 1948-51; resident in psychiatry Boston Psychopathic Hosp., 1951-53; asst. chief neurol. service Montefiore Hosp., N.Y.C. and asst. prof. neurology Columbia U., 1953-55; asst. prof. U. Minn., 1955-56; asso. clin. prof. U. Kans. Med. Sch., 1956-64, chief dept. neurology, 1968—, prof. U. Kans. Med. Center, 1964—; cons. Social Security Adminstrn., 1975—; mem. com. on certification and co-certification Am. Bd. Med. Specialties, 1979—. Served to lt., j.g., M.C., USNR, 1946-48. Diplomate Am. Bd. Psychiatry and Neurology (dir. 1975—, exec. com. 1978—). Fellow Am. Acad. Neurology (pres. 1979-81); mem. AMA, Am. Neurol. Assn., Am. Epilepsy Soc., Am. Electroencephalographic Soc., A.C.P., Assn. Univ. Profs. Neurology. Jewish. Author: In Divided and Distinguished Worlds, 1942; Contbr. numerous articles to profl. jours. Home: 8347 Delmar Ln Prairie Village KS 66207 Office: Kans U Med Center 3900 Rainbow Blvd Kansas City KS 66103

ZIEGLER, DONALD EMIL, judge; b. Pitts., Oct. 1, 1936; s. Emil Nicholas and Elizabeth (Barclay) Z.; B.A., Duquesne U., 1958; LL.B., Georgetown U., 1961; m. Claudia J. Chermak, May 1, 1965; 1 son, Scott Emil. Admitted to Pa. bar, 1962, U.S. Supreme Ct. bar, 1967; practice law, Pitts., 1962-74; judge Ct. of Common Pleas of Allegheny County, Pa., 1974-78; judge U.S. Dist. Ct. for Western Dist. of Pa., Pitts., 1978—. Treas., Big Bros. of Allegheny County, 1969-71. Mem. Am. Bar Assn., Pa. Bar Assn., Allegheny County Bar Assn., Am. Judicature Soc., St. Thomas More Soc. Democrat. Roman Catholic. Club: Oakmont Country. Office: 1036 US Courthouse and Post Office Bldg Pittsburgh PA 15219

ZIEGLER, JACK (DENMORE), cartoonist; b. N.Y.C., July 13, 1942; s. John Denmore and Kathleen Miriam (Clark) Z.; B.A. in Communication Arts, Fordham U., 1964; m. Jean Ann Rice, Apr. 20, 1968; children—Jessica, Benjamin, Maxwell. Free lance cartoonist, N.Y.C., 1972—; cartoonist The New Yorker, N.Y.C., 1974—; author: Hamburger Madness, 1978. Mem. Cartoonists Guild, The Glory Boys. Democrat.

ZIEGLER, JESSE H., assn. exec., clergyman; b. Limerick, Pa., Jan. 7, 1913; s. Harry H. and Mary (Hunsberger) Z.; A.B., Bridgewater (Va.) Coll., 1935, D.D., 1959; M.A., Catholic U. Am., 1937, Ph.D., 1942; B.D., Bethany Theol. Sem., Chgo., 1944; D.D., Presbyn. Theol. Coll., Montreal, 1967; m. Harriet E. Curry, Aug. 22, 1939; 1 dau., Harriet Anne. Ordained to ministry Ch. of Brethren, 1931; pastor, University Park, Md., 1935-41; from asso. prof. to prof. psychology and Christian edn. Bethany Theol. Sem., 1941-59; asso. dir. Am. Assn. Theol. Schs., 1959-66, exec. dir., 1966—. Vis. lectr. Garrett Theol. Sem., Oberlin Grad. Sch. Theology, Yale Div. Sch. Sec., Ministry Studies Bd., 1960-64; mem. gen. bd. Ch. of Brethren, 1970-76. Sec. bd. York Center Community Housing Coop., Inc., 1944-54. Bd. dirs. Fund Theol. Edn. Diplomate counseling psychology Am. Bd. Examiners Profl. Psychology. Mem. Am. Psychol. Assn. Democrat. Author: The Broken Cup: A Socio-Psychological Study of a Changing Rural Culture, 1942; Psychology and the Teaching Church, 1962; Focus on Adults, 1966. Editor quar. Theol. Edn., 1964—. Home: 822 Kenneth Ave Vandalia OH 45377 Office: 42 E National Rd Vandalia OH 45377

ZIEGLER, JOHN AUGUSTUS, JR., lawyer; b. Grosse Pointe, Mich., Feb. 9, 1934; s. John Augustus and Monnabell M. Ziegler; A.B., U. Mich., J.D., 1957; divorced; children—John Augustus III, Laura, Lisa, Adeline. Admitted to Mich. bar, 1957, since practiced in Detroit; asso. firm Dickinson, Wright, McKean & Cudlip, 1957-65; mem. firm, 1965-68; mem. firm Parsons, Tennent, Hammond, Hardig & Ziegelman, 1969-70, Ziegler, Dykhouse, Wise & Huth, 1970—. Chmn. bd. govs. Nat. Hockey League, 1976-77, pres., 1977—. Home: 3211 Allen Rd Ortonville MI Office: Suite 920 Sun Life Bldg Montreal PQ Canada also 14th Floor McGraw Hill Bldg New York NY

ZIEGLER, RAYMOND STEWART, architect; b. Colorado Springs, Colo., Aug. 18, 1919; s. Edwin L. and Grace (Stewart) Z.; student Ecole De Beaux Arts, Atelier Winslow, U. Calif., San Francisco Archtl. Club; m. Jolene Baddeley, Aug. 22, 1942; children—John, Richard. Partner Allison, Rible, Robinson and Ziegler, architects, Los Angeles, 1958-69; exec. dir., v.p. Allison, Rible, Robinson and Ziegler, an asso. group of Leo A Daly Co., 1969-74; partner Raymond Ziegler Partnership Architects, 1974-77; pres., chmn. bd. Ziegler Kirven Parrish Architects, 1978—; mem. Calif. adv. bd. Office Architecture and Constrn., 1968-77, chmn., 1971. Bd. dirs. Los Angeles Beautiful, 1974-77, 80, Soc. for Prevention Blindness, 1974-76, N.E. Los Angeles unit Am. Cancer Soc., 1978-80. Served to 1st lt. inf. AUS, World War II. Fellow A.I.A. (treas. So. Calif. chpt. 1968-69, dir. Calif. council, chmn. ins. trust of Calif. council 1980); mem. Archtl. Guild (dir.), Design Profls. Safety Assn. (dir. 1980—), Los Angeles C. of C. (dir. 1972-77). Mason, Rotarian. Home: 1276 Sunny Oaks Circle Altadena CA 91001 Office: 444 S Westmoreland Ave Los Angeles CA 90020

ZIEGLER, ROBERT HOLTON, SR., lawyer, state senator; b. Balt., Mar. 27, 1921; s. A. H. and Lilian (Windfohr) Z.; LL.B., U. Va., 1948; m. Paula Kathryn Sampson, Dec. 6, 1974; children from previous marriage-Robert Holton, Ann Holton. Admitted to Alaska bar, 1949, since practiced in Ketchikan; partner firm Ziegler, Cloudy, Smith, King & Brown, and predecessor, 1948—; mem. Alaska Senate, 1964—. Mem. Alaska Territorial Ho. of Reps., 1957; chmn. Alaska Legis. Council, 1971-72; chmn. Western conf. Council of State Govts., 1978-79. Bd. dirs. U. Alaska Found. Served with AUS, 1942-46. Mem. Alaska Bar Assn. (pres. 1964-65), Sigma Nu, Phi Theta Delta. Episcopalian. Democrat. Elk (exalted ruler Ketchikan 1955-56), Rotarian (pres. Ketchikan 1964-65), Moose. Home: Mi 4 S Tongass Ketchikan AK 99901 Office: 307 Bawden Ketchikan AK 99901

ZIEGLER, RONALD LOUIS, former govt. ofcl.; b. Covington, Ky., May 12, 1939; s. Louis Daniel and Ruby (Parsons) Z.; student Xavier U., 1957-58; B.S., U. So. Calif., 1961; m. Nancy Lee Plessinger, July 30, 1960; children—Cynthia Lee, Laurie Michelle. Salesman, Procter & Gamble Distbg. Co., 1961; account rep. J. Walter Thompson Co., 1962-68; press dir. Calif. Republican Central Com., 1961-62; press aide to Richard Nixon in Calif. gubernatorial campaign, 1962; press aide staff Richard Nixon, 1968-69; press sec. to Pres. Nixon, 1969-74, asst. to Pres., 1973-74; mgr. internat. services Syska and Hennessy, Inc., Washington, 1975—. Named one of 10 Outstanding Young Men of Year, U.S. Jaycees, 1970. Mem. Sigma Chi (Significant Sig award 1971). Home: 2008 Fort Dr Alexandria VA 22307 Office: Syska and Hennessy Inc 1720 I St NW Washington DC 20006 also 110 W 50th St New York NY 10020

ZIEGLER, TERRY L., editor; b. Williamsport, Pa., Apr. 5, 1931; s. Frank A. and Carmen D. (Lenker) Z.; B.A. magna cum laude, Lycoming Coll., 1963. Reporter Grit, Williamsport, 1949-51, 55-56, radio-TV editor, 1956-57, city editor, 1957-62, editor family sect., 1962-68, feature editor, 1968-70, asst. to editor, 1970-71, mng. editor, 1971-72, asst. editor, 1972, editor, 1972—; dir. Grit Pub. Co., Williamsport. Chmn. publicity Williamsport Community Concert Assn., 1949-51, dir., 1956-63, 3d v.p., 1963-68, pres., 1968—; mem. adv. bd. Susquehanna Valley Symphony Orch., 1972-75. Bd. dirs. Lycoming Child Day Care Center, 1965, pres., 1966. Served with USN, 1951-55. Mem. Pa. Soc. Newspaper Editors (dir. 1971-73), Williamsport-Lycoming C. of C. (dir. 1974-77). Club: Ross. Author: Eastward, Ho!, 1955. Mem. Lycoming Coll. Publs. Bd., 1971-74. Home: PO Box 1173 Williamsport PA 17701 Office: 208 W 3d St Williamsport PA 17701

ZIEGLER, WILLIAM, III, diversified industry exec.; b. N.Y.C., June 26, 1928; s. William and Helen (Murphy) Z.; B.A., Harvard U., 1950; M.B.A., Columbia U., 1962; m. Jane Elizabeth Troy, Feb. 22, 1952; children—Melissa Jane, William Troy, Peter Martin, Cynthia Curtis, Helen Matilda, Karl Huttig. Vice pres. GIH Corp., N.Y.C., 1959-64, pres., 1964—, dir., 1955—; dir. Am. Maize Products Co., N.Y.C., 1958—, now also chmn. bd., chmn. exec. com.; pres., dir. Park Ave. Operating Co., Inc., 1958—; chmn. bd., chmn. exec. com. Boyer Bros., Inc., Altoona, Pa., Lundy-Briggs Co., Inc., Jon. H. Swisher & Son, Inc., S.A. Schonbrunn & Co., Inc.; dir. Heritage Quilts, Inc. Bd. dirs. Foresight, Inc., New Haven; pres. E. Matilda Ziegler Found. for Blind; sec. Matilda Ziegler Pub. Co. for Blind; mem. nat. adv. council Hampshire Coll. Trustee, bd. dirs. Darien Community YMCA; bd. dirs. Project Orbis, Inc., Am. Found. for Overseas Blind, Inc.; trustee Lavelle Sch. for Blind; mem. bd. overseers com. on univ. resources Harvard. Served from ensign to lt. comdr. USNR, 1952-54. Clubs: N.Y. Yacht; Noroton (Conn.) Yacht; Wee Burn Country. Home: 161 Long Neck Point Rd Darien CT 06820 Office: 22 Gate House Rd Stamford CT 06902

ZIEGNER, EDWARD HENRY, journalist; b. Indpls., Aug. 8, 1920; s. Edward Henry and Pearl (McCampbell) Z.; student Wabash Coll., 1938-39, Ind. U., 1939-41; m. Martha Alice McHatton, May 13, 1950; children—Anne Virginia, David Edward. Statehouse reporter Indpls. News, 1946-52, polit. editor, legis. bur. chief, 1953—. Mem. adv. bd. Acad. in the Pub. Service. Served with U.S. Army, 1942-46. Democrat. Presbyterian. Mem. Indpls. Press Club (past v.p., past dir.), Phi Gamma Delta. Home: 7360 N Irvington Ave Indianapolis IN 46250 Office: Indpls News 307 N Pennsylvania St Indianapolis IN 46206

ZIEGRA, SUMNER ROOT, pediatrician; b. Deep River, Conn., Feb. 13, 1923; s. Louis Richard and Olive Cornwell (Wells) Z.; B.S., U. Vt., 1945; M.D., Yale U., 1947; m. Marie Rolleri, June 15, 1945; children—Sumner Root, Cynthia Jane. Intern, Balt. City Hosp., 1947-48; resident in pediatrics Bellevue Hosp., N.Y.C., 1948-49, fellow in pediatrics, 1949-51; asst. attending physician Hosp. St. Raphael, New Haven, 1953, Grace-New Haven Hosp., 1954; asst. clin. instr. Yale U. Med. Sch., 1954-56; asst. prof. pediatrics SUNY Downstate Med. Center, 1956-60; attending physician dept. pediatrics King's County Hosp., 1956-60; asso. prof. pediatrics Jefferson Med. Coll., Phila., 1960-63; asso. prof. Hahnemann Med. Coll., Phila., 1963-65, prof. pediatrics, 1965-70; dir. div. B, dept. pediatrics Phila. Gen. Hosp., 1963-70, coordinator Hahnemann div., dept. pediatrics, 1966-67; dir., dept. pediatrics Lankenau Hosp., Phila., 1970-73; prof. pediatrics Thomas Jefferson Coll. Medicine, 1970-73; prof. dept. pediatrics Med. Coll. Pa. Hosp., Phila., 1973—, acting chmn. dept., 1973-75, chmn., 1975—. Served to lt. (j.g.) M.C., USNR, 1943-45, 51-53. Diplomate Am. Bd. Pediatrics. Mem. AMA, Conn. Med. Soc., New Haven County Med. Soc., Pa. Med. Soc., Am. Acad. Pediatrics, New Haven Pediatric Soc., Bklyn. Acad. Pediatrics, Phila. Pediatric Soc., Pa. Thoracic Soc. Republican. Contbr. numerous articles to profl. jours. Home: 344 Hillview Rd Malvern PA 19355 Office: Med Coll Pa and Hosp 3300 Henry Ave Philadelphia PA 19129

ZIELER, WERNER F., business exec.; b. Frankfurt, Ger., July 24, 1925; s. Fritz O.P. and Margarete F. (Gabelmann) Z.; student German pub. schs.; m. Sigrid Zieler; children—Claus, Helge. With Siemens AG, 1948-77, v.p. fgn. ops., Munich, Ger., until 1977; pres., chief exec. officer Siemens Corp., Iselin, N.J., 1977—. Office: Siemens Corp 186 Wood Ave S Iselin NJ 08830*

ZIEMER, GREGOR, author; b. Columbia, Mich., May 24, 1899; s. Robert and Adell Von Rohr (Grabau) Z.; B.A., U. Ill., 1922; M.A., U. Minn., 1923; Ph.D., U. Berlin, 1934; m. Edna E. Wilson, May 29, 1926; 1 dau., Patsy. Mem. Staff Park Region Jr. Coll., head journalism dept.; supr. of schs, Philippine Islands, 1926-28; founder Am. Colony Sch., Berlin, 1928; Berlin corr. N.Y. Herald, London Daily Mail, Chgo. Tribune; lectr., radio newscaster WLW, Cin. in U.S., since Berlin sch. closed by war; joined spl. war agy., 1944, overseas with SHAEF; v.p. Internat. Enterprises, Inc., 1948; pub. edn. Am. Found. for Blind, 1952-64; dir. Inst. Lifetime Learning, Long Beach, Calif., 1966-71; freelance writer, 1971—; producer, dir. numerous radio programs, 1966—. Served as lt. col. 4th Armored Div., 3d Army, 1945; mil. govt. work in Bavaria with SHAEF to help organize newspapers in Germany. Recipient Westinghouse citation, 1958, award Freedoms Found. for series Am. Heritage, 1969; named Man of Year for work with blind, 1960. Mem. Am. Pub. Relations Assn. (pres. 1960, Silver Anvil award 1956, 58, 60, Paul Revere citation 1958), Am. Legion, Lake City (Minn.) C. of C. (Bicentennial com.), Council of Nat. Orgns., Overseas Press Club, Assn. Radio News Analysts, Cuvier Press Club, Tau Kappa Alpha, Kappa Delta Pi, Beta Sigma Psi. Author: (with dau. Patsy) Two Thousand and Ten Days of Hitler; Education for Death, new edit., 1972; The Making of the Nazi, 1941; Should Hitler's Children Live, 1946; Whirlaway Hopper, 1962; Too Old for What?, 1968; Witness on Water Skis, 1975; Let'm Eat Grass, 1975; Brigand of Montserrat, 1979; (motion picture) Hitler's Children; Education for Death; Torchbearers; Let's Listen to Lifetime Learning (radio); Giant Step Forward (TV); One Empty Rocking Chair (TV). Contbr. to mags. Lectures of Americanism. Address: 26950 Spring Creek Rd Rancho Palos Verdes CA 90274. *To be a septuagenarian in Who's Who in America is an honor—a challenge. My career, spanning nearly eight decades—as teacher, journalist, author, lecturer, world traveler—a servant to mankind whenever possible—was often rocky. Browning's "A man's reach must exceed his grasp," was sometimes "What I reach for seems always beyond my grasp." But I have a slogan: Act as if each day were your last; think as if you're going to live forever. It helps!*

ZIERING, WILLIAM MARK, lawyer; b. New Britain, Conn., Feb. 4, 1931; s. Jacob Max and Esther (Freedman) Z.; B.A., Yale U., 1952; J.D., Harvard U., 1955; m. Harriet Koskoff, Aug. 20, 1958; 1 son, Benjamin. Admitted to Conn. bar, 1955, Calif. bar, 1962; asso. firm Koskoff & McMahon, Plainville, Conn., 1959-60; sr. trial atty. SEC, San Francisco, 1960-65; pvt. practice, San Francisco, 1965—; partner firm Bremer & Ziering, 1972-77; instr. Golden Gate U. Law Sch., San Francisco, 1968-75. Vice pres., bd. dirs. Calif. League Handicapped, 1972—. Served to comdr. USNR, 1955-58. Mem. Am., Fed., Calif., San Francisco (past chmn. securities, corps. and banking) bar assns., Navy League (dir.). Club: Commonwealth. Home: 2027 Lyon St San Francisco CA 94118 Office: 300 Montgomery St San Francisco CA 94104

ZIERLER, KENNETH, physician, physiologist; b. Balt., Sept. 5, 1917; s. Joseph Nathan and Betsey (Levie) Z.; A.B., Johns Hopkins U., 1936, student chemistry, 1937; M.D., U. Md., 1941; m. Margery Shapiro, June 8, 1941; children—Peggy (Mrs. George Dardess), Linda (Mrs. Peter Jucovy), Sally (Mrs. Robert Broudo), Amy (Mrs. Cameron Mustard), Michael Kenneth. Intern, Sinai Hosp., Balt., 1941-42; asst. resident N.Y.U. div. Goldwater Meml. Hosp., N.Y.C., 1942, chief resident, 1942-43; mem. faculty Sch. Medicine and Hosp. Johns Hopkins, 1946-72, 73—, asso. prof. Sch. Hygiene and Pub. Health, 1954-59, prof. medicine Med. Sch., 1964-72, 73—, also prof. physiology, 1969-72, 73—; mem. staff Johns Hopkins Hosp.; dir. Inst. Muscle Disease, 1972; adj. prof. Rockefeller U., 1972; adj. prof. Cornell Med. Coll., 1972; chmn. adv. com. physiology Office Naval Research, 1964-73, cons., 1973-76; cons. NIH, NASA, Nat. Acad. Sci. Served to capt., M.C., AUS, 1943-46. Mem. Am. Physiol. Soc., Am. Soc. Clin. Investigation, Assn. Am. Physicians. Asso. editor Medicine, 1963-72, Circulation Research, 1968-74; mem. editorial bd. Bull. Johns Hopkins Hosp., 1956-67, Johns Hopkins Med. Jour., 1967-70, Jour. Clin. Investigation, 1959-64, Ann. Rev. Physiology, 1971-75. Contbr. to profl. jours. Research on muscle, insulin, water and electrolytes, circulation, biomembranes, tracer-dilution theory. Home: 6620 Charlesway Baltimore MD 21204

ZIETLOW, PAUL NATHAN, educator; b. Neenah, Wis., Feb. 14, 1935; s. Carl F. and Ruth N. (Paulin) Z.; B.A., Yale U., 1956; M.A., U. Mich., 1958, Ph.D., 1965; m. Charlotte Ernst Thiele, Aug. 28, 1957; children—Rebecca Ernst, Nathan Paulin. Asst. prof. to prof. English, Ind. U., 1964—. Author: Moments of Vision: The Poetry of Thomas Hardy, 1974; contbr. essays, revs. on 19th and 20th century English and Am. lit. to profl. jours. Office: Dept English Ind U Bloomington IN 47405

ZIEVE, LESLIE, physician, educator; b. Mpls., Aug. 6, 1915; s. Joseph and Hannah (Bulgats) Z.; B.A., U. Minn., 1937, M.A., 1939, M.D., 1943, Ph.D., 1952; m. Bernice Larson, June 26, 1941; 1 son, Franklin. Intern Phila. Gen. Hosp., 1943; resident Mpls. VA Hosp., 1946-49, chief nuclear medicine, 1950-72, chief gastroenterology, 1960-72, asso. chief staff, 1961-77; mem. staff Hennepin County Med. Center, 1977—; prof. medicine U. Minn., 1962—, mem. exec. com. Grad. Sch., 1965-68. Served as bn. surgeon inf., AUS, 1944-46. Recipient Middleton award VA, 1962, distinguished physician award, 1972. Fellow A.C.P.; mem. Central Soc. Clin. Research. Editor: Jour. Lab. and Clin. Medicine, 1967-70. Contbr. articles to profl. jours. Home: 2321 Parkland Rd St Louis Park MN 55416 Office: Hennepin County Med Center Minneapolis MN 55415

ZIFF, ROBERT PAUL, educator, philosopher; b. N.Y.C., Oct. 22, 1920; s. William Morris and Bessie (Goldstien) Z.; B.F.A., Cornell U., 1949, Ph.D., 1951; m. Pauline Pitkorchemna, 1945; children—Matthew Dionysius, Georgina Sara, Alexandra; m. 2d, Rita Nolan, 1967; m. 3d, Judith Trafton, July 1975; 1 son, Andrew Paul. Practicing artist N.Y.C., 1939-42; painter in N.Y.C., 1945-46; research asst. U. Mich., 1951-52, instr. philosophy, 1952-53; instr. philosophy Harvard, 1953-54, asst. prof., 1954-59; asst., then asso. prof. U. Pa., 1959-64; prof. U. Wis. at Madison, 1964-68, U. Ill. at Chgo. Circle, 1968-70; Kenan prof. U. N.C., Chapel Hill, 1970—; chmn. Chapel Hill Center Philos. Linguistic Research. Served with USCGR, 1942-45. Rockefeller Found. grantee, 1955; Guggenheim fellow, 1962-63. Author: Semantic Analysis, 1960; J.M. Hanson, 1962; Philosophic Turnings, 1966; Understanding Understanding, 1972. Home: 1309 Brigham Rd Chapel Hill NC 27514

ZIFF, RUTH, advt. co. exec.; b. N.Y.C., May 26, 1924; d. Herman and Lena (Medoff) Baron; B.A., Hunter Coll., 1944; M.A. (Acad. scholar), Columbia, 1948; Ph.D., City U. N.Y., 1975; m. Solomon Ziff, Mar. 29, 1942; children—Charles Elliot, Ellen Barbara. Dir. psychol. barometer and link audit pub. attitudes Psychol. Corp., N.Y.C., 1944-49; v.p., mgr. research Benton & Bowles, Inc., N.Y.C., 1950-75; sr. v.p., dir. research and mktg. services Doyle Dane Bernbach Inc., N.Y.C., 1975—. Named Advt. Woman of Yr., Am. Advt. Fedn., 1973. Mem. Advt. Women of N.Y. (dir.), Am. Mktg. Assn. (dir.), Am. Assn. Pub. Opinion Research, Am. Psychol. Assn., Am. Sociol. Assn., Market Research Council, Phi Beta Kappa, Alpha Chi Alpha. Contbr. articles to profl. jours. Home: 464 Grace Church St Rye NY 10580 Office: 437 Madison Ave New York City NY 10022

ZIFFREN, SIDNEY EDWARD, surgeon; b. Rock Island, Ill., Aug. 30, 1912; s. Dave and Rose (Frankel) Z.; student Augustana Coll., 1929-30, U. Nebr., Lincoln, 1930-31, St. Ambrose Coll., 1931-32; B.S., U. Ill., Chgo., 1934, M.D., 1936. Intern, U. Iowa Hosps., 1936-37, asst. resident in surgery, 1937-38, resident in surgery, 1938-39, 39-42, resident in pathology, 1938-39; asst. in surgery U. Iowa, 1947, instr., 1947-48, asso. in surgery, 1948-49, asst. prof. surgery, 1949-51, asso. prof., 1951-53, prof., 1953—, chmn. div. trauma and reconstructive surgery, 1965-69, acting head surgery, 1969-71, head surgery, 1972—. Served with M.C., U.S. Army, 1942-46. Diplomate Am. Bd. Surgery. Fellow A.C.S.; mem. AMA, Iowa Med. Soc., Johnson County Med. Soc. (pres. 1953), Gerontol. Soc., Am. Geriatrics Soc., Soc. Exptl. Biology and Medicine, Soc. Univ. Surgeons, N.Y. Acad. Scis., Soc. Nuclear Medicine, Central Soc. Clin. Research, Central Surg. Assn., Am. Coll. Angiology, Western Surg. Assn., Am. Assn. Surgery of Trauma, Internat. Soc. Burn Injuries, Am. Burn Assn., Am. Surg Assn., AAAS, Internat. Soc. Surgery, Am. Trauma Soc., Am. Assn. Tissue Banks, Am. Pancreatic Assn., Am. Soc. Preventive Oncology. Author: Management of the Aged Surgical Patient, 1960; contbr. numerous articles to med. pubs. Office: Dept Surgery Univ Hosps Iowa City IA 52242. *My aim was to become the best possible physician. I instinctively knew this could only be accomplished by being extremely conscientious and by not* *paying attention to the number of hours worked. I later made one of my goals never to repeat a mistake, which is not always easy to do in medicine. My word was always to be my bond. Lastly, I was determined to keep an open mind to newer ideas and methods but not to adopt them until proved.*

ZIGHERA, BERNARD, harpist; b. Paris, France, Apr. 1, 1904; came to U.S., 1926, naturalized, 1938; grad. piano and harp Conservatoire National de Paris, 1925; married. Second harpist Societe des Concerts, Paris, 1924; substitute harpist Opera, Paris, 1924; 1st harpist Boston Symphony Orch., 1926—, also pianist; mem. faculty New Eng. Conservatory, from 1927, Berkshire Musi Center; pvt. tchr. harp, 1926—. Decorated chevalier Legion of Honor (France). Home: 1270 Commonwealth Ave West Newton MA 02165

ZIGLER, EDWARD FRANK, educator, psychologist; b. Kansas City, Mo., Mar. 1, 1930; s. Louis and Gertrude (Gleitman) Z.; B.A., U. Mo. at Kansas City, 1954, M.A., 1958; Ph.D., U. Tex., 1958; M.A. (hon.), Yale, 1967; m. Bernice Gorelick, Aug. 28, 1955; 1 son, Perrin. Psychol. intern Worcester (Mass.) State Hosp., 1957-58; asst. prof. psychology U. Mo., 1958-59; mem. faculty Yale 1959—, prof. psychology and child study center, 1967—, Sterling prof., 1976—, dir. child devel. program, 1961-73, chmn. dept. psychology, 1973-74, head psychology sect. Yale Child Study Center, 1966—, dir. Bush Center in Child Devel. and Social Policy, 1977—; dir. Office Child Devel., chief Children's Bur., Dept. Health, Edn. and Welfare, Washington, 1970-72; cons. in field, 1962—. Mem. nat. steering com. Project Head Start, 1965-70; nat. adv. com. Nat. Lab. Early Childhood Edn., 1967-70; nat. research adv. bd. Nat. Assn. Retarded Children, 1968-73; nat. research council Project Follow-Through, 1968-70; chmn. Vietnamese Children's Resettlement Adv. Com., 1975. Served with AUS, 1951-53. Recipient Gunnar Dybwad distinguished scholar in behavioral and social sci. award Nat. Assn. Retarded Children, 1964, 69; Social Sci. Aux. award, 1962; Alumni Achievement award U. Mo., 1965, Alumnus of Year award, 1972. Fellow Am. Orthopsychiat. Assn., Am. Psychol. Assn. (pres. div. 7 1974-75); mem. Am. Acad. Mental Retardation, A.A.A.S., Psychonomic Soc., Soc. Research Child Devel., Sigma Xi. Editor: (with Jeanette Valentine) Project Head Start, 1979; contbr. to profl. jours. Home: 177 Ridgewood Ave North Haven CT 06517 Office: Dept Psychology Yale Station PO Box 11A New Haven CT 06520

ZIGMAN, ROBERT S., public relations exec.; b. Milw., Sept. 22, 1919; s. Walter A. and Becky (Neisser) Z.; student U. Wis., 1947; m. Dorothy T. Traver, Apr. 11, 1953; 1 son, Robert W. Mem. sales staff Milprint, Inc., Milw., 1947-52, mgr. aluminum foil div., 1952-58; chmn. Zigman-Joseph-Skeen PR, Milw., 1959—; dir. Stearns Chem. Corp. Pres. U. Wis.-Milw. Found. Bd. dirs. Milw. Symphony Orch., United Performing Arts Fund, Florentine Opera; pres., bd. dirs. Friends of Milw. Pub. Museum; bd. curators State Hist. Soc. Endowment Com.; past bd. dirs. Gov.'s Council on Arts, Youth Opportunities Unlimited; bd. visitors U. Wis. System; trustee U. Wis. Meml. Union. Served with AUS, 1942-46. Decorated Bronze Star medal, Combat Inf. badge; recipient 2 Chinese decorations, Distinguished Service to Music award Wis. Coll. Conservatory Women's League, 1973; Golden Baton awards Milw. Symphony Orch.; citations, County and City Milw. Mem. Wis. Hist. Soc., Co. Am. Mil. Historians, Wis. State Hist. Soc. (curator 1966—), Pub. Relations Soc. Am., Scabbard and Blade, Sigma Delta Chi, Beta Gamma Sigma. Home: 6024 N Lake Dr Milwaukee WI 53217 Office: 700 N Water St Milwaukee WI 53202

ZILKHA, EZRA KHEDOURI, banker; b. Baghdad Iraq, July 31, 1925; s. Khedouri A. and Louise (Bashi) Z.; came to U.S., 1941, naturalized, 1950; grad. Hill Sch., Pottstown, Pa., 1943; A.B., Wesleyan U., Middletown, Conn., 1947; m. Cecile Iny, Feb. 6, 1950; children—Elias Donald, Simha Donna, Bettina Louise. Pres., Zilkha & Sons, Inc., N.Y.C., 1956—; dir. Handy & Harman, N.Y.C., Newhall Land & Farming, Calif., Mothercare, Ltd., London, INA Corp., Phila., INA Life Ins. Co. N.Y., Blyth Eastman Dillon & Co. Inc., N.Y.C., Mothercare Stores, Inc., N.Y.C. Trustee, ICD Rehab. and Research Center, N.Y.C., French Inst., Lycée Francais de N.Y., Spence Sch., N.Y.C.; trustee, chmn. investment com. Wesleyan U. Decorated chevalier Légion d'Honneur. Mem. Council Fgn. Relations. Clubs: Univ., Down Town Assn. Knickerbocker (N.Y.C.); Meadow (Southampton, N.Y.); Brooks's (London); Travellers, Polo (Paris). Office: 30 Rockefeller Plaza New York NY 10020

ZILLI, HARRY ANGELO, JR., railway exec.; b. Cleve., June 8, 1930; s. Harry and Millie (Trunkett) Z.; B.B.A., Western Res. U., 1954; m. Sharon R. Hobart, Aug. 30, 1974; children—Harry Angelo, Constance Jane. Comptroller, Wabush Mines, Sept-Iles, Que., Can., 1966-70; fin. planner Diamond Shamrock Corp., Cleve., 1970-72; with Erie Lackawanna Ry. Co., Cleve., 1972—, treas., 1973-76, exec. officer, 1976—; dir. Trailer Train Co. Served with AUS, 1954-56. C.P.A., Ohio. Mem. Am. Inst. C.P.A.'s, Ohio Soc. C.P.A.'s, Soc. Philatelic Americans. Methodist. Club: Cleve. Athletic. Home: 24765 Randall Dr North Olmstead OH 44070 Office: 1306 Midland Bldg Cleveland OH 44115

ZILLMANN, ROBERT EDWARD, acctg. firm exec.; b. Evanston, Ill., Mar. 16, 1929; s. Emil R. and Daisy (Greenland) Z.; student Lake Forest Coll., 1948-49; B.S., Northwestern U., 1952; m. Marie Frances Vranicar, May 24, 1953; children—Barbara Marie, Eric Robert. Pub. accountant H.C. Goettsche & Co., Chgo., 1952-57; financial exec. Abbott Labs., Chgo., 1957-61; operations mgr. Abbott Labs., S.A.R.L., Montreaux, Switzerland, 1962-63; corp. controller G.D. Searle & Co., Chgo., 1964-67; treas. Marsteller, Inc., Chgo., 1968-70, financial v.p., 1970-73; asst. treas. Apeco Corp., Evanston, 1973-74, corporate controller, 1974; controller Nat. Assn. Realtors, Chgo., 1974, v.p. finance and adminstrn., 1975-79; pres. Edwin C. Silver & Co., C.P.A.'s, Chgo., 1979—. Served with AUS, 1946-48. C.P.A., Ill. Mem. Am. Inst. C.P.A.'s, Ill. Soc. C.P.A.'s, Financial Execs. Inst., Corp. Controllers Inst. Home: 2235 Central Park Ave Evanston IL 60201 Office: 100 W Monroe St Chicago IL 60603

ZILLY, MARGARET BERNICE, vol. orgn. adminstr.; b. Peoria, Ill., July 18, 1907; d. Thomas and Mary Magdalene (Rossman) McWhinney; student Bradley U., 1923-25; B.S., U. Ill., 1927; M.Ed., Wayne State U., 1938; m. George Samuel Zilly, Nov. 29, 1930; children—Thomas Samuel, Barbara (Mrs. Henry Jude Heck). Tchr. high sch., Peoria, 1927-29, Detroit, 1930-34, 36-43. Pres. com. Keep Detroit Beautiful, Inc., 1955-58, Bernice Zilly Day, 1958; pres. Coll. Women's Vol. Service, 1957-59; pres. Beautification Council Southeastern Mich., 1958-60; v.p. Keep Mich. Beautiful, Inc., 1960-62; bd. dirs. Southeastern Mich. chpt. A.R.C., 1969-75, 77—, mem. exec. com., 1973-75, 77—; mem. White House Fellows Selection Com., 1976; mem. pastoral council Catholic Archdiocese Detroit, 1975—. Mem. Mich. Republican Central Com., 1965-71, Congl. Dist. Com., 1966-71; v.p. Mich. Fedn. Rep. Women, 1958-60; pres. Women's Rep. Club, Grosse Pointe, Mich.; bd. dirs. Cath. Youth Orgn., 1959—. Named Hon. Citizen, Galveston, Tex., 1975; recipient keys to cities Detroit, Indpls., Galveston, Southfield, Mich.; award Keep Mich. Beautiful, 1962. Mem. A.A.U.W. (pres. Detroit br. 1951-53), U. Ill. Alumni Assn. Detroit (pres. 1935-40), Women's City Club Detroit (dir. 1968-70), Nat. Council Cath. Women (past nat. pres.), Council Cath. Women Archdiocese Detroit (past pres.), Alpha Delta Pi. Roman Catholic. Contbr. articles on leadership and speaking to mags. Home: 380 Merriweather Road Grosse Pointe Farms MI 48236

ZILVERSMIT, DONALD BERTHOLD, biochemist, educator; b. Hengelo, Holland, July 11, 1919; s. Herman and Elizabeth (DeWinter) Z.; student U. Utrecht, Holland, 1936-39; B.S., U. Calif., Berkeley, 1940, Ph.D., 1948; m. Kitty Fonteyn, June 28, 1945; children—Elizabeth Ann, Dorothy Susan, Sarah Jo. Came to U.S., 1939, naturalized, 1950. Mem. faculty U. Tenn. Med. Coll., 1948-66, prof., 1956-66; prof. nutrition, prof. biochemistry, molecular and cell biology divs. nutritional sci. and biol. scis. Cornell U., 1966—; vis. prof. U. Leiden, Holland, 1961-62, Mass. Inst. Tech., 1972-73; vis. fellow Australian Nat. U., Canberra, Australia, 1966; vis. lectr. Venezuela Inst. Sci. Investigations, 1977; career investigator Am. Heart Assn., 1959—. Editor, Circulation Research 1962-67, 68-74, Circulation, 1960-65, Biochim. Biophysica Acta, 1969—; editor Procs. Soc. Exptl. Biology and Medicine, 1975—, mem. adv. council, 1978—; cons. NIH. Recipient Borden award, 1976. Mem. AAAS, AAUP, Am. Chem. Soc., Am. Physiol. Soc., Am. Inst. Nutrition, Am. Soc. Biol. Chemists, Council on Arteriosclerosis, Am. Heart Assn. (exec. bd. 1968-70, G. Lyman Duff meml. award 1978), Soc. Exptl. Biology and Medicine. Editor-in-chief: Jour. of Lipid Research, 1958-61, adv. bd., 1962-72. Contbr. articles to profl. jours. Office: Div Nutritional Scis Cornell Univ Ithaca NY 14853

ZILZ, DAVID ARTHUR, pharmacist, hosp. pharmacy adminstr.; b. Waupaca, Wis., July 10, 1937; s. Harvey William and Hazel Lorraine (Petersen) Z.; B.S., U. Wis., 1962, M.S., 1964; m. Mary Ann Haunschild, Apr. 16, 1966; 1 dau., Kristin Marie. Asst. dir. pharmacy services U. of Wis. Hosps., Madison, 1967-68, asso. dir. pharmacy services and central services, 1968-70, dir. pharmacy, respiratory and material services, 1970—; asso. clin. prof. pharmacy Coll. Pharmacy, U. Wis., 1978—; cons. WHO. Mem. council Good Shepherd Lutheran Ch., Madison, Wis., 1971-78. Mem. Am. Soc. Hosp. Pharmacists (pres. elect), Am. Pharm. Assn., Drug Info. Assn. Contbr. numerous articles on pharmacy and hosp. pharmacy practice to profl. publs. Office: 600 Highland Ave Madison WI 53792

ZIM, HERBERT SPENCER, educator, author; b. N.Y.C., July 12, 1909; s. Marco and Minnie (Orlo) Z.; student Coll. City N.Y., 1927-29; B.S., M.A., Ph.D., Columbia, 1933-40; D.Sc. (hon.), Beloit Coll., 1967, Fla. State U., 1977; m. Sonia Elizabeth Bleeker, Jan. 16, 1934 (dec. 1971); children—Aldwin Herbert, Roger Spencer; m. 2d, Grace Kent Showe, June 4, 1978. Instr. sci., summer play schs., 1926-31; instr. sci. Bklyn. Ethical Culture Sch., 1930-31, N.Y. Ethical Culture Schs., 1932-50; tchr. edn. dept., head sci. dept., 1937-45; asso. prof. edn. U. Ill., 1950-54, prof. edn., 1954-57; ednl. cons. Manhasset Bay Schs., 1946-48, U.S. Fish and Wildlife Service, 1947-51, Western Pub. Co., 1967-70, Am. Friends Service Com., 1968—; editorial cons. Individualized Sci. Instrnl. System, 1972—; pres. Rogewinn Corp., 1968-71. Instr. Columbia, 1935-36; summer field trips, 1937-41; research under Gen. Edn. Bd. Grant for Comm. on Secondary School Curriculum, Progressive Edn. Assn., 1934-37; adj. prof. edn. U. Miami, 1970—. Mem. Am. Inst. Jr. Activities Com., 1938-42, bd. mgrs., 1940-42, v.p., 1942; mem. steering com. Biol. Scis. Curriculum Study and Intermediate Scis. Curriculum Study, War Dept. pre-induction tng. program, 1942-43; civilian pub. service, 1943-45. Fellow A.A.A.S.; mem. numerous sci. and ednl. socs. Author, editor numerous books relating to sci. latest being: Orchids, 1970; Life and Death, 1970; Armored Animals, 1971; Telephone Systems, 1971; Your Brain, 1972; Your Stomach, 1973; Crabs, 1974; Metric Measure, 1974; Medicine, 1974; Eating Places, 1975; Snails, 1975; Sea Stars, 1976; Caves, 1977; Little Cats, 1978; Your Skin, 1979; rev. edits. Universe, Sun, Owl, Big Cats, Alligators and Crocodiles, 1974-78. Editor-in-chief: Our Wonderful World Ency., 1952-63, Golden Ency. Natural Sci., 1960-70; originator, editor Golden Guide Series, 1947-70. Ednl. dir. Artists and Writers Press, 1957-69. Home: Box 34 Tavernier FL 33070. *Enough has been done to provide us with the wisdom we need - our task is in its creative application.*

ZIMBALIST, EFREM, violinist; b. Rostow on Don, Russia, Apr. 9, 1889; s. Aaron and Maria Z.; early mus. tng. under father; studied in Imperial Sch., St. Petersburg, Russia, with Leopold Auer; m. Alma Gluck, June 15, 1914; children—Maria Virginia (Mrs. Henry F. Bennett, Jr.), Efrem; m. 2d, Mary Louise Curtis Bok, July 6, 1943 (dec. 1970). Debut in Berlin at 17; toured through Germany and England; came to U.S., 1911, and has appeared in all the leading cities; has made two world tours, also six tours of the Orient. Composer of (works for orchestra) American Rhapsody, Concerto for Violin and Orchestra; Landara (an opera; concerts for piano and orchestra); also string quartet; violin sonata and many songs and minor pieces for violin and piano. Dir. Curtis Inst. of Music, Phila., 1941-68. Address: 2255 Lindley Way Reno NV 89502

ZIMBALIST, EFREM, JR., actor, producer; b. N.Y.C., Nov. 30, 1923; s. Efrem and Alma (Gluck) Z.; grad. Fay Sch., Southboro, Mass., St. Paul's Prep. Sch.; student Yale; drama student Neighborhood Playhouse, N.Y.C.; m. Emily McNair (dec. 1950); children—Nancy, Efrem 3d; m. 2d, Stephanie Spalding, Feb. 2, 1956; 1 dau., Stephanie. First stage appearance in Rugged Path, 1946; with Am. Repertory Co., 1947-48, appearances including Henry VIII, Androcles and the Lion, What Every Woman Knows, Yellow Jack; appeared in Hedda Gabler, 1948; co-producer Gian-Carlo Menotti operas, 1947; motion picture debut in House of Strangers, 1949; co-producer Broadway play The Consul, 1950 (Drama Critics award, Pulitzer prize in music); staff Curtis Inst. Music, Phila., 1952-54; Broadway appearances in Fallen Angels, 1956; star daytime TV series, Concerning Miss Marlowe, NBC-TV, 1954-55; motion picture actor Warner Brothers Studio, films including Band of Angels, 1957, Bombers B-52, 1957, Violent Road, 1958, Home Before Dark, 1958, Too Much Too Soon, 1958, The Deep Six 1958, The Crowded Sky, 1960, A Fever in the Blood, 1961, By Love Possessed, 1961, Chapman Report, 1965, Airport 1975; star Warner Brothers TV series 77 Sunset Strip, ABC-TV, 1958-64; star TV series The FBI, ABC-TV, 1965-73; appeared in TV film Who Is the Black Dahlia, 1975. Served to 1st lt., inf., AUS, World War II. Office: 4750 Encino Encino CA 91316*

ZIMBARDO, PHILIP GEORGE, psychologist; b. N.Y.C., Mar. 23, 23, 1933; s. George and Margaret (Bisicchia) Z.; A.B., Bklyn. Coll., 1954; M.S., Yale U., 1955, Ph.D., 1959; m. Christina Maslach, Aug. 10, 1972; children—Zara, Tanya; 1 son by previous marriage, Adam. Asst. prof. Yale U., New Haven, 1959-61, N.Y. U., N.Y.C., 1961-67; vis. asso. prof. Columbia U., N.Y.C., 1967-68; prof. dept. psychology Stanford (Calif.) U., 1968—; pres. P.G. Zimbardo, Inc., San Francisco. Pres., Montclair Terr., 1975—. Recipient Disting. Tchr. award N.Y. U., 1965, Am. Psychol. Found., 1975; Peace medal Tokyo Police Dept., 1972; Disting. Contbn. to Research award Calif. Psychol. Assn., 1978; Center advanced Study Behavioral Scis. fellow, 1971. Mem. Internat. Congress Psychology, Am. Psychol. Assn., Western Psychol. Assn., Eastern Psychol. Assn., Calif. Psychol. Assn., Canadian Psychol. Assn., Soc. for Psychol. Study Social Issues, AAUP, AAAS, Soc. for Clin. and Exptl. Hypnosis, Sigma Xi, Phi Beta Kappa, Psi Chi. Roman Catholic. Author: Cognitive Control of Motivation, 1969; Canvassing for Peace, 1970; Shyness, what it is, what to do about it, 1977; Influencing Attitudes and Changing Behavior, rev. edit., 1977; Psychology for Our Times: Readings, 1977; Psychology and You, 1978; The Shyness Workbook, 1979; Psychology and Life, rev. edit., 1979. Home: 25 Montclair Terr San Francisco CA 94109 Office: Psychology Dept Stanford U Stanford CA 94305. *One of the few virtues of growing up in a poor urban ghetto is the realization that people are the most important resource we have - to be used wisely, well and as often as possible. The second is the tempering of book learning by street wits.*

ZIMET, CARL NORMAN, educator, psychologist; b. Vienna, Austria, June 3, 1925; s. Leon and Gisela (Kosser) Z.; came to U.S., 1943, naturalized, 1945; B.A., Cornell U., 1949; Ph.D., Syracuse U., 1953; postdoctoral fellow, Stanford, 1953-55; m. Sara F. Goodman, June 4, 1950; children—Andrew, Gregory. Instr., then asst. prof. psychology and psychiatry Yale, 1955-63; mem. faculty U. Colo. Med. Center, 1963—, prof. clin. psychology, 1965—, head div., 1963—. Mem. Colo. Bd. Psychol. Examiners, 1966-72, Colo. Mental Health Planning Commn., 1964-66; mem. acad. adv. com. John F. Kennedy Child Devel. Center, U. Colo., 1966—; chmn. Council for Nat. Register of Health Service Providers in Psychology, 1975—, mem. exec. bd. div. psychotherapy, 1970—. Served with USNR, 1943-46. Recipient Disting. Service award Colo. Psychol. Assn., 1976. Diplomate clin. psychology Am. Bd. Profl. Psychology (trustee 1966-74). Fellow Am. Psychol. Assn. (council reps. 1969-72, 73—), Soc. Projective Techniques (pres. 1975-76); mem. Denver Psychoanalytic (trustee 1968-71), Am. Group Psychotherapy Assn. Bd. editors Jour. Clin. Psychology, 1962—, Jour. Clin. and Cons. Psychology, 1964-73, Psychotherapy, 1967—, Profl. Psychology, 1969—. Home: 4325 E 6th Ave Pkwy Denver CO 80220

ZIMINSKY, VICTOR D., bus. exec.; b. Boston, Mar. 2, 1899; s. Andrew and Honora (O'Leary) Z.; student Boston U.; LL.D., Providence Coll., Suffolk U.; D.C.S., Holy Cross Coll.; m. Mary Evelyn Monahan, Oct. 24, 1927 (dec. 1961); children—Victor D., Mary Patricia. Buyer, E. T. Slattery Co., Boston, 1918-28; v.p. Franklin Simon & Co., 1928-36, Gimbel Bros., N.Y.C., 1939-47; pres., dir. The Union News Co., N.Y.C., 1947-56; pres., chmn. bd. Victor D. Ziminsky Co., Inc., 1956—; dir. Crown Cork & Seal Co., Inc., Overseas Service Corp.; hon. trustee N.Y. Bank for Savs. Mem. adv. council Lavelle Sch. Blind. Trustee Cath. Charities N.Y., St. Patrick's Cathedral, N.Y.; mem. Cardinal's Com. Laity; hon. chmn. bd. regents Oblate Coll.; bd. dirs. Cardinal Spellman Servicemen's Club; mem. adv. council St. Vincent's Hosp., Westchester; trustee N.Y. Foundling Hosp., Al Smith Meml. Fedn.; bd. dirs. Holy Name Center for Homeless Men. Knight Sovereign Order of Malta, lt. Assn. Knights and Ladies Equestrian Order Holy Sepulchre Jerusalem. Mem. Am.-Irish History Soc., Friendly Sons St. Patrick. Roman Catholic. Clubs: Union League (N.Y.C.); Westchester Country (Rye, N.Y.). Home: 50 Popham Rd Scarsdale NY 10583 Office: Pan Am Bldg 200 Park Ave New York City NY 10017

ZIMM, BRUNO HASBROUCK, phys. chemist; b. Woodstock, N.Y., Oct. 31, 1920; s. Bruno L. and Louise S. (Hasbrouck) Z.; grad. Kent (Conn.) Sch., 1938; A.B., Columbia, 1941, M.S., 1943, Ph.D., 1944; m. Georgianna S. Grevatt, June 17, 1944; children—Louis M., Carl B. Research asso. Columbia, 1944; research asso., instr. Polytech. Inst. Bklyn., 1944-46; instr. chemistry U. Calif. at Berkeley, 1946-47, asst. prof., 1947-50, asso. prof., 1950-51; vis. lectr. Harvard, 1950-51; research asso. research lab. Gen. Electric Co., 1951-60; prof. chemistry U. Calif. at La Jolla, 1960—. Recipient Bingham Medal, Soc. Rheology, 1960—, also the High Polymer Physics prize from Am. Phys. Soc., 1963. Mem. Biophys. Soc., Am. Soc. Biol. Chemists, Am. Chem. Soc. (Baekeland award 1957), Nat. Acad. Scis., Am. Acad. Arts and Scis., Am. Phys. Soc. Asso. editor Jour. Chem. Physics, 1947-49; adv. bd. Jour. Polymer Sci., 1953-62, Jour. Bio-Rheology, 1962-73, Jour. Biopolymers, 1963—, Jour. Phys. Chemistry, 1963-68, Jour. Biophys. Chemistry, 1973—. Home: 2605 Ellentown Rd La Jolla CA 92037

ZIMMER, ALBERT ARTHUR, educator; b. Pitts., May 20, 1918; s. Albert Peter and Hilda (Volz) Z.; B.S., Pa. State U., 1942, M.Ed., 1947; Ed.D., U. Pitts., 1951; m. Alma Zimmermann, Mar. 7, 1945; children—Alene Lynne, Alyce Lorraine, Alana Leigh. Tchr. pub. schs., State College, Pa., 1941-42; music supr. pub. schs., Ford City and Monongahela, Pa., 1946-49; instr. U. Pitts., 1949-52; head edn. dept. Susquehanna U., 1952-59, dean students, 1959-62; dean, v.p. Bethany Coll., Lindsborg, Kans., 1962-66, acting pres. coll., 1966-67; chmn. dept. edn. Thiel Coll., Greenville, Pa., 1967—; vis. lectr. Bucknell U., Rutgers U., Pa. State U., U. Conn. Del. Gov. Pa. Conf. Edn., 1954. Dir. Snyder County Civil Def., 1952-62; mem. Selinsgrove (Pa.) SSS Bd., 1959-62. Nat. del. Luth Ch. Am., 1956, 60, 62, del. Central Pa. Synod, 1956-62, 64, mem. Christian edn. commn., 1958-62, social welfare commn., 1960-62, church councilman, Selinsgrove, 1952-62, Lindsborg, 1963—. City councilman, Selinsgrove, 1960-62, mem. planning commn., 1960-62; fire warden Pa. Forest Commn., 1958-62; Bd. dirs. Snyder County chpt. Am. Cancer Soc., 1956-60; bd. dirs., fund chmn. Snyder County chpt. A.R.C., 1954; bd. dirs. Monongahela Youth Council, 1946-47, Monongahela Concert Bd., 1946-47, Walnut Acres Found., Pa., 1958-62, Lindsborg Community Vol. Ambulance Service, 1966—, Gettysburg Luth. Theol. Sem., 1974-78. Served with AUS, 1942-46. Mem. Music Educators Nat. Conf., Pa. Assn. Liberal Arts Colls. (pres. 1960-61), Pa. Assn. Student Teaching (v.p. 1958-59), N.E.A., Am. Assn. U. Profs., Nat. Assn. Deans, Phi Delta Kappa, Theta Chi, Phi Mu Alpha, Kappa Phi Kappa, Alpha Phi Omega. Rotarian. Contbr. articles to profl. jours. Home: 73 N Main St Greenville PA 16125

ZIMMER, BASIL GEORGE, sociologist, educator; b. Smith Creek, Mich., June 29, 1920; s. Walter Nicholas and Mary Alice (Martin) Z.; student Port Huron (Mich.) Jr. Coll., 1939-41, Shrivenham Am. U., Eng., 1945; B.A., U. Mich., 1947, M.A., 1949, Ph.D., 1954; m. Janet Mae Jackson, Nov. 3, 1942; children—Basil George, Linda Jean. Teaching fellow U. Mich., 1948-50, research asst. dept. corrections, 1948, lectr., resident dir. Social Sci. Research Project, 1953-59, asso. prof. U. Mich.-Flint Coll., 1957-59; asso. prof. Brown U., Providence, 1959-61, prof., 1962—, chmn. urban studies, 1974—; fellow Human Resources Research Inst. U.S. Dept. Air Force, 1952-53; instr. Eastern Mich. U., 1950-51, U. Mich., 1951-52; asst. prof. Fla. State U., 1952-53; cons. Met. Area Problems, Flint, 1956-59, Research Med. Research Council U. Aberdeen, Scotland, 1965, 70, 72, Demographic Tng. Center U. Kerala, India, 1964, Div. Vocational Rehab. Spl. Sch. Project, 1964—; vis. scholar Australian Nat. U., 1973. Mem. Urban League, 1955—; chmn. Gen. Plan, Providence, 1963—; bd. dirs. Flint Youth Bd., Center for Urban Studies, 1974—; mem. exec. com. Mayor's Adv. Com. Urban Renewal; mem. com. urban transp. research Hwy. Research Bd., 1961-63; pres. Urban Obs. of R.I., 1978—. Served with AUS, 1941-45; ETO. Fellow Am. Sociol. Assn.; mem. Population Assn. Am., Eastern Sociol. Soc., Internat. Union Sci. Study Population. Author: Rebuilding Cities: The Effects of Displacement and Relocation on Small Business, 1964; (with A. H. Hawley) Resistance to Reorganization of School Districts in Metropolitan Areas, 1966; Resistances to Government Unification in Metropolitan Areas, 1967; The Metropolitan Community: Its People and Government, 1970; Migration in the United States, 1971; The Urban Centrifugal Drift, 1975; Urban Family Building Patterns, 1977. Editor: Directory of Population Study Centers, Population Assn. Am., 1971; Demography, 1971-72. Contbr. to profl. jours. Home: 10

Bridgham Farm Rd Rumford RI 02916 Office: 100 Maxcy Hall Brown U Providence RI 02912

ZIMMER, DONALD WILLIAM, baseball club exec.; b. Cin., Jan. 17, 1931; s. Harold Lesley and Lorraine Bertha (Fiscus) Z.; student pub. schs., Cin.; m. Jean Carol Bauerle, Aug. 16, 1951; children—Thomas Jeffrey, Donna Jean. Baseball player Dodger Farm Clubs, 1949-54, Bklyn. Dodgers, 1954-57, Los Angeles Dodgers, 1958-59, Chgo. Cubs, 1960-61, N.Y. Mets, 1962, Cin. Reds, 1962, Los Angeles Dodgers, 1963, Wash. Senators, 1963-65. Toei Flyers, Tokyo, 1966; mgr. Reds Farms, Knoxville, Buffalo, Cin., 1967, Indpls., Cin., 1968, Padre Farms, Key West, Fla., 1969, San Diego Padres, 1971-72; coach Montreal (Que., Can.) Expos, 1970; coach Boston Red Soc., 1974-76, mgr., 1976—; mem. minor league All-Star Teams, Hornell, N.Y., 1950, Elmira, N.Y., 1951, Mobile, Ala., 1952, St. Paul, 1953; player World Series teams, 1955, 56, 59, coach, 1975. Recipient Bill Stern award NBC, 1949; named St. Paul Rookie of Year, 1953; mem. All Star Team, 1961, 78. Mem. Profl. Baseball Players Am. (life), Old Time Ball Players Milw. Home: 10124 Yacht Club Dr Treasure Island FL 33706 Office: 24 Yawkey Way Boston MA 02215

ZIMMER, HANS WILLI, educator; b. Berlin, Germany, Feb. 5, 1921; s. Wilhelm Johann Friedrich and Martha Maria (Schindler) Z.; came to U.S., 1953; Cand. Ing., Tech. U. Berlin, 1947, Dipl. Ing., 1948, Dr. Ing., 1950; m. Marlies Henriette Wuensch, Oct. 26, 1946; 1 son, Hans Martin. Instr. chemistry Tech. U. Berlin, 1950-53; postdoctoral research asso. U. Ill., 1953-54; asst. prof. chemistry U. Cin., 1954-57, asso. prof., 1957-62, prof., 1962—; vis. prof. U. Mainz, 1966, U. Bonn, 1967, U. Bern, 1971. Cons., Merrel Nat. Labs., 1960—, Lithium Corp. of Am. div. Gulf Resources and Chems., 1965—, Matheson, Coleman & Bell, 1970—. Served with German Air Force, 1940-45. Recipient Distinguished Research award Sigma Xi, U. Cin., 1964. Fellow A.A.A.S.; mem. Am. Chem. Soc. (Chemist of Year, Cin. chpt. 1971), N.Y., Ohio acads. scis., German Chem. Soc., Sigma Xi. Clubs: Cin. Country, Literary (Cin.). Editor: Methodicum Chimicum Vol. VII, 1973, Vol. VIII, 1974; Annual Reports in Inorganic and General Synthesis, 1972—; Thieme Editions in Chemistry and Related Areas, 1972. Contbr. articles profl. jours. Home: 2910 Scioto St Cincinnati OH 45219 Office: U Cin Dept Chemistry Cincinnati OH 45221

ZIMMER, KARL ERNST, educator; b. Berlin, Germany, Sept. 17, 1927; came to U.S., 1946, naturalized, 1953; s. Ernst and Adelina (Friedlaender) Z.; B.A., U. Chgo., 1953; M.A. in English Lit., Columbia U., 1954, Ph.D. in Linguistics, 1963; M.A. in Linguistics, U. Mich., 1958; m. Suzanne Clements, Feb. 3, 1956 (dec. 1977); children—Paul, Catherine. English lang. instr. Brit. Council, Ankara, Turkey, 1955; English lang. instr. and adviser Turkish Ground Forces English Lang. Tng. Center, Ankara, 1956-57; acting asst. prof. linguistics U. N.C., Chapel Hill, 1963-65; asst. prof. linguistics U. Calif., Berkeley, 1965-69, asso. prof., 1969-75, prof., 1975—, chmn. dept. linguistics, 1974-79. Mem. AAUP, Linguistic Soc. Am. Office: Dept Linguistics U Calif Berkeley CA 94720

ZIMMER, NORMAN CUNNINGHAM, architect; b. Denver, Aug. 8, 1924; s. Christian Peter and Vivien (Pittam) Z.; student Portland (Oreg.) Museum Art Sch., 1952; m. Marian L. Davis, Oct. 10, 1952; children—Jeffery, Gregory, Alexandra, Gabrielle. Designer, then sr. designer Wolff-Phillips, Portland, 1946-54; partner Wolff Zimmer, Portland, 1954-64; sr. partner Wolff, Zimmer, Gunsul, Frasca, Portland, 1964-76, Zimmer, Gunsul, Frasca, 1976—; vis. prof. U. Oreg. Sch. Architecture, 1964-66; prin. works include indsl. complexes for Textronix Inc. in U.S., U.K. and Netherlands, addition to Oreg. State Capitol bldg., Oreg. Hist. Soc. hdqrs. Pres. bd. trustees Portland Art Assn., 1972-73. Served with C.E., AUS, 1943-45. Recipient numerous design awards. Fellow AIA (chmn. com. architecture for commerce and industry 1969-70). Republican. Episcopalian. Clubs: Arlington, Multnomah Athletic (Portland). Address: 111 SW Oak St Portland OR 97204

ZIMMER, PAUL HOWARD, mfg. co. exec.; b. Detroit, Apr. 18, 1929; s. Donald R. and Ora E. (Howie) Z.; student Fla. So. Coll., 1949; children—Mallory (Mrs. Carl M. Scholl), Mary J., Robert P. With Zimmer Boat & Trailer Co., Detroit, 1946-50; sec., treas., later pres. Zimmer Industries, Elwood, Ind., 1959-61; founder, chmn. bd., pres., chief exec. officer Zimmer Homes Corp., Pompano Beach, Fla., mfr. mobile homes, motor homes, van conversions and exotic automobiles, 1961—. Clubs: Masons, LeClub International, Tower (Ft. Lauderdale). Home: 1051 NE 28th Terr Pompano Beach FL 33062 Office: 777 SW 12th Ave Pompano Beach FL 33060

ZIMMER, WARREN ADAM, mfg. co. exec.; b. Columbus, Ohio, Nov. 4, 1914; s. William J. and Josephine P. (Ludwig) Z.; B. Ceramic Engring., Ohio State U., 1935, M.S., 1936; m. Phyllis R. Carrie, Feb. 7, 1942. With Joseph Dixon Crucible Co., Jersey City, 1936—, pres., 1964-78, chmn., 1967—, chief exec. officer, 1966—; dir. Comml. Trust Co., Jersey City. Trustee, St. Peters Coll., Jersey City, 1977—. Served with AUS, 1942-46. Mem. N.J. C. of C. (dir. 1968—). Office: Joseph Dixon Crucible Co 167 Wayne St Jersey City NJ 07303

ZIMMER, WILLIAM H., JR., utility exec.; b. Cin., Mar. 3, 1930; s. William H. and Esther (Krueger) Z.; B.S., Ohio State U., 1952; m. Virginia L. Avey, June 27, 1951; children—William H. III, Amy Lynn. Accountant, Gen. Electric Co., 1952; with Cin. Gas & Electric Co., 1952—, treas., asst. sec., 1963-74, sec.-treas., 1975-78, v.p., treas., 1978—; dir. Cin. Financial Corp., Cin. Ins. Co., Life Inst. Co. Cin., Setco Industries. Mem. finance com. Bethesda Hosp.; trustee Bethesda Found.; former pres. Cin. area project HOPE. Mem. Edison Electric Inst. (exec. com. finance div.), Beta Theta Pi. Mason (32). Clubs: Bankers (pres. 1968), Cincinnati, Western Hills Country (Cin.). Home: 5883 Country Hills Dr Cincinnati OH 45238 Office: 139 E 4th St Cincinnati OH 45202

ZIMMER, WILLIAM LOUIS, III, lawyer, ret. pharm. co. exec.; b. Petersburg, Va., Dec. 27, 1912; s. Samuel Watts and Mary Blair Pryor (Walker) Z.; B.A., U. Va., 1935, LL.B., 1937; m. Ruth Anna Saulsbury, Apr. 2, 1937; children—Alice Pyle (Mrs. John Stewart Bryan III), Samuel Watts. Admitted to Va. Bar, 1937; practice in Petersburg, 1937-38, Richmond, 1938—; asso. Plummer & Bohannon, 1937-38; asso., partner, counsel McGuire, Woods & Battle, 1938-62, 78—; asst. sec. A.H. Robins Co., 1955-62, gen. counsel, 1961-66, v.p., sec., 1962-67, treas., 1966-67; exec. v.p., 1967-70, pres., chief operating officer, 1970-75, chief exec. officer, 1975-78, dir. 1952—; dir. Communications Satellite Corp., Washington, First & Mchts. Nat. Bank, Richmond; asso. prof. taxation Law Sch., U. Richmond, 1948-58. Pres., chmn. bd. Gov.'s Mgmt. Study. Trustee United Givers Fund; rector U. Va. Served to lt. USNR, 1943-45. Mem. Soc. Cin., Am., Va. (past chmn. exec. com.), Richmond bar assns., N.A.M. (dir.), Newcomen Soc., Va. (past. chmn. tax study commn.), Richmond (dir.) chambers commerce, Raven Soc. U. Va., Omicron Delta Kappa, Delta Kappa Epsilon, Phi Delta Phi, Beta Gamma Sigma (hon.). Episcopalian. Clubs: Commonwealth (past dir.), Country of Va. (past. dir.), Richmond German (Richmond); Burning Tree (Md.); Roaring Gap (N.C.); University (N.Y.C.); International, Carabao (Washington). Home: 306 Lock Ln Richmond VA 23226 Office: 1407 Cummings Dr Richmond VA 23220

ZIMMERBERG, HYMAN JOSEPH, mathematician, educator; b. N.Y.C., Sept. 7, 1921; s. Morris and Mirel (Milner) Z.; B.A., Bklyn. Coll., 1941; M.S., U. Chgo., 1942, Ph.D., 1945; m. Helen Yarmush, Aug. 22, 1943; children—Sharon (dec.), Betty, Joshua, Morris. Instr. U.S. Army pre-meteorology program U. Chgo., 1943-44, N.C. State Coll., Raleigh, 1945-46; instr. Rutgers U., New Brunswick, N.J., 1946-47, asst. prof., 1947-51, asso. prof., 1951-60, prof., 1960—, dir. NSF undergrad. research participation program, 1962-69, 71-73, 77; cons. NSF student and coop. programs, 1967-70; vis. prof. U. Oreg., summer 1961, Drew U., summer 1962, 63; faculty acad. study Hebrew U., Jerusalem, 1972-73. Mem. AAUP (pres. N.J. conf. 1967-69, nat. council 1969-72), Am. Math. Soc., Math. Assn. Am., Sigma Xi. Home: 345 Becker St Highland Park NJ 08904

ZIMMERER, ANN(A) MORGAN, lawyer, psychologist, educator; b. Hillsboro, W.Va., June 29, 1923; d. Edgar R. and Lula M. (Cox) Morgan; diploma Charleston Sch. Commerce, 1941; B.S. in Social Work, U. W.Va., 1947, M.A. in Psychology, 1949; Ph.D., U. Houston, 1963, J.D., 1972; m. Robert Ivan Zimmerer, Oct. 15, 1950; children—Sandra Kaye, Gerald Lee, Douglas Allan. Jr. child welfare worker W.Va. Dept. Pub. Assistance, Beckley, summers, 1947, 48; staff psychologist Mental Hygiene Clinic, W.Va. Dept. Health, Charleston, 1949-51; psychol. cons. to pvt. physicians W.Va. Div. Vocat. Rehab., Children's Home Soc. W.Va., 1952-55; counselor U. Houston, 1956-58; sch. psychologist Houston Ind. Sch. Dist., 1958-60, elementary counselor, 1960-63; instr., acting chmn. dept. psychology San Jacinto Coll., Pasadena, Tex., 1963-64, chmn. dept. psychology, 1964-69; cons. psychologist, Pasadena, Tex., 1963—; admitted to Tex. bar, 1972; asso. law firm Jack R. Bailey, Houston, 1972-73; individual practice law, 1973—; broker Kelly Kellog Assos., 1978—. Del. to Pres.'s White House Conf. on Children, 1970, Gov.'s White House Conf. on Children, 1970; mem. Mayor's Commn. on Obscenity, Pasadena, 1971-72. Served with WAVES, 1943-45. Certified psychologist, W.Va., Tex.; licensed psychologist, Tex.; licensed real estate salesman. Mem. Am., Tex., Southwestern, W.Va. (charter) psychol. assns., Am. Personnel and Guidance Assn., Soc. for Rorschach and Projective Techniques, Internat. Congress Psychologists, Am., Tex., Houston, Pasadena bar assns., Am. Trial Lawyer's Assn., U. Houston Law Found., Greater Pasadena Bd. Realtors, Theta Sigma (charter, 1st pres.), Delta Kappa Gamma, Psi Chi. Baptist (deaconess 1955-56). Clubs: Quadrille Dance, Golfcrest Country. Home: 2208 Fenwood Dr Pasadena TX 77502 Office: PO Box 4344 Pasadena TX 77502

ZIMMERMAN, ADAM HARTLEY, mining co. exec.; b. Toronto, Ont., Can., Feb. 19, 1927; attended Upper Can. Coll., Toronto, Ridley Coll., St. Catharines, Ont., Royal Can. Naval Coll., U. Toronto; postgrad. in philosophy, 1951; m. Janet Lewis, May, 1951; children—Thomas, Barbara, Mary, Kate. In sales Procter & Gamble, 1950; with Clarkson, Gordon & Co., Chartered Accts., Toronto, 1950-58; asst. comptroller Noranda Mines Group of Cos., beginning 1958, comptroller, 1961, pres. Northwood Mills Ltd., beginning 1963, chmn., 1974—, pres., dir. Northwood Pulp and Timber Ltd., 1965—, pres. Northwood Pulp Ltd., beginning 1965, v.p. and comptroller, B.C. Chems. Ltd., beginning 1966, exec. v.p., dir. Noranda Mines Ltd., Toronto, 1974—. Mem. Can.-Am. Com.; trustee Hosp. for Sick Children; chmn. bd. Branksome Hall Sch. Served to lt. Royal Can. Navy Res., 1946-52. Chartered Acct., Ont. Mem. Ont. Inst. Chartered Accts., Zeta Psi. Clubs: The York, Toronto Golf, Univ., Madawaska, Craigleigh Ski. Office: PO Box 45 Commerce Ct W Toronto ON M5L 1B6 Canada

ZIMMERMAN, ANNE KATHERINE, nurses assn. exec.; b. Helena, Mont., Sept. 1, 1914; d. George and Theresa (Betor) Larson; nursing diploma St. John's Unit of Sisters of Charity of Leavenworth Sch. of Nursing, Helena, 1935; L.H.D. (hon.), Loyola U., Chgo., 1975; 1 dau., Nancy Burke. Pvt. duty and staff nurse, 1935-45; exec. dir. Mont. Nurses Assn., 1945-47; asso. exec. dir. Calif. Nurses Assn., 1947-54; asst. dir. econ. security program Am. Nurses Assn., 1951-52; exec. dir. Ill. Nurses Assn., Chgo., 1954—; trustee Am. Nurses Found., 1977-78; dir. Am Jour. Nursing Co., 1978—. Vice chmn. Ill. Adv. Council on Vocat. Edn.; bd. dirs. Cath. Council on Working Life. Mem. Am. (pres. 1976-78), Ill. nurses assns., Nat. League for Nursing, Conf. of Med. Soc. Execs. Greater Chgo. (pres.), Alliance Bus. and Profl. Women Chgo. (pres.). Roman Catholic. Club: Zonta (pres.) (Evanston, Ill.). Home: 30 E Elm St Chicago IL 60611 Office: 6 N Michigan Ave Chicago IL 60602

ZIMMERMAN, AUSTIN MANLOVE, lawyer, bus. exec.; b. Chgo., Dec. 28, 1909; s. Edward A. and Isabel (Chave) Z.; A.B., Amherst Coll., 1931; postgrad. Nat. U. Mexico, 1931; J.D., Northwestern Law Sch., 1934; m. Elizabeth Thayer, Dec. 26, 1934; children—Edward Austin, John Jeffrey. Admitted to Ill. bar, 1934; practice in Chgo., 1934-67, Barrington Hills, Ill., 1967—; partner Norman, Engelhardt, Zimmerman, Franke & Lauritzen and predecessor firms, 1937-67, Austin M. Zimmerman, 1967—. Sec., gen. counsel All Am. Aviation (now Allegheny Airlines and All Am. Engring.), Wilmington, Del., 1942-46; sec., dir. Allied Tractor Equipment Co., 1938-42, Gust Corp., Flex-O-Lace, Inc., 1940-42, Anela Distbrs., Inc., 1945-67, Wacker-Dearborn Corp., 1945-66, Midwest Electric Mfg. Corp., 1945-72, 1647 W. Walnut Bldg. Corp., 1952-72 (all Chgo.); sec., treas. Chgo. Exhibitions Corp., 1955-67; v.p., sec., gen. counsel, dir. Randall Bearings, Inc., Lima, Ohio, 1946—; spl. counsel Chgo. and So. Airlines, 1946-50, United Airlines, 1947; sec.-treas., dir. Vancouver Ritz Properties, Ltd. (B.C., Can.), 1960-67, RBI, Inc., Springfield, Tenn., 1977—, Bearing & Bronze Warehousing, Inc., Greenbriar, Tenn., 1977—. Atty. for zoning hearing Countryside Assn., 1948; chmn. annexation com. McHenry County property, Village of Barrington Hills, 1957; chmn. law com., mem. finance and health coms. Village Bd., 1958- 69; alumni adviser on admissions Amherst Coll., 1951—, mem. alumni council, 1964-69, 1931 class agt., 1966-73. Treas., bd. dirs. Contemporary Concerts, Inc., Chgo. Mem. Am. Bar Assn. (chmn. Midwest area, sect. of pub. contract law, 1965-68, council 1968-70), Ill. State Bar Assn., McHenry Bar Assn., Chgo. Bar Assn., Los Rancheros Vistadores, Chi Psi, Phi Alpha Delta. Lion. Clubs: Law, Legal, Literary, University, Mid-Day, Amherst (past pres.) (Chgo.); Barrington Hills Country; Lake Geneva (Wis.) Yacht; Club del Rancheros (Santa Barbara, Calif.). Address: Brae Burn Farm Barrington Hills Algonquin IL 60102

ZIMMERMAN, BRYANT KABLE, lawyer; b. Mt. Morris, Ill., Nov. 19, 1922; s. Milo D. and Hazel G. (Kable) Z.; A.B., Augustana Coll., 1946; student Washington U., St. Louis, 1942-43; LL.B., Harvard, 1948; m. Harriet Bong, Jan. 20, 1946; children—Paula (Mrs. Johnnie Veloski), Keith, Craig. Admitted to Calif. bar, 1949; asso. counsel McCutchen, Doyle, Brown & Enersen, San Francisco, 1949-63; v.p., gen. counsel FrancoWestern Oil Co., Bakersfield, Calif., 1963-65; v.p., sec., gen. counsel Guy F. Atkinson Co., South San Francisco, Calif., 1965—. Bd. dirs., v.p. Republican Alliance, 1965-74; bd. dirs., sec. Atkinson Found.; trustee Willamette U., 1978—. Served with USAAF, 1942-46. Methodist. Home: 75 Del Monte Dr Hillsborough CA 94010 Office: 10 W Orange Ave South San Francisco CA 94080

ZIMMERMAN, CHARLES HINCKLEY, ret. financial exec.; b. Steelton, Pa., Oct. 1, 1905; s. Charles Fishburn and Eleanor Graydon (Hinckley) Z.; A.B., Lafayette Coll., 1926; B.Accounts, Rider Coll., Trenton, 1927; m. Violet Pauline Zimmerman, Nov. 2, 1929 (dec.); 1 dau., Elizabeth Landis (Mrs. Snavely); m. 2d, Thelma R. Jeffries, Jan. 21, 1960. Pa. state bank examiner, Harrisburg, 1927-36; auditor Capital Bank & Trust Co., Harrisburg, 1936-41, comptroller, 1941-49, v.p., comptroller, 1949-58; v.p. Central Trust Capital Bank, Harrisburg, 1958-61; v.p. Nat. Bank & Trust Co. Central Pa., Harrisburg, 1961-66, sr. v.p., 1966-70; treas., dir. Andrew S. McCreath & Son, Inc., 1958-77; sec., dir. Motor Truck Equipment Co., Harrisburg, 1956-77, Ratcliff & Swartz, Inc., 1946-77. Mem. faculty Pa. Bankers Assn., Pa. State U., summers 1954, 56, 58; mem. faculty Stonier Grad. Sch. Banking, Rutgers U., 1957-61; instr. adminstrn. Lancaster, Pa., Am. Inst. Banking, 1937-38, instr. bank orgn. and operation, Harrisburg, 1938-39; asso. dir. Pa. Bankers Assn. Sch., Bucknell U., summers 1958-60; dir. Pa. Sch. Banking, 1962-63. Mem. finance com. Tri-County United Fund, 1958-69. Mem. Pa. Bankers Assn. (treas. 1968-70, past gen. chmn. bank operations div.), Am. Inst. Banking (past pres. Harrisburg chpt.), Nat. Assn. Bank Auditors and Comptrollers (charter pres. Central Pa. 1948-49, past v.p. Pa.), Pa. Soc. S.R., Pi Delta Epsilon, Delta Upsilon. Republican. Methodist. Mason (Shriner). Club: Exchange (past pres., Harrisburg). Home: 540 Walnut St Lemoyne PA 17043

ZIMMERMAN, DAVID RADOFF, author; b. Chgo., Aug. 10, 1934; s. Leo M. and Sarah (Radoff) Z.; student U. Chgo., 1950-52; A.B. cum laude, Brandeis U., 1955; postgrad. U. Paris, 1955; m. Veva Jeanne Hampton, Oct. 12, 1966; children—Jacob Ben, Tobias Eli. Editor, Hyde Park Herald, Chgo., 1954; copy boy New York Daily News, 1956-57; editorial asst. New York Post, 1957-61; free lance editor, 1961-62; editor New York Acad. Medicine, 1962-63; sr. writer Med. World News, 1963-69; med. columnist Ladies Home Jour., 1967—; free lance author, 1969—. Tchr. mag. writing Coll. City New York, 1972-73. Recipient World Wildlife Fund research grant, 1974; Fund for Investigative Journalism grantee, 1978. Mem. Am. Med. Writers Assn. (Best Book by single author for gen. readers 1973), Am. Soc. Journalists and Authors (pres. 1972-74), Nat. Assn. Sci. Writers (exec. com. 1977—). Author: Rh, The Intimate History of a Disease and Its Conquest, 1973; To Save a Bird in Peril, 1975 (Christopher award 1976). Address: 603 W 111th St New York City NY 10025

ZIMMERMAN, EDWARD K., govt. ofcl.; b. Elizabeth City, N.C., Oct. 13, 1936; student in radio, TV and motion pictures U. N.C., 1954-58; m. Carol Zimmerman; children—Joanne, Edward. Computer operator Research Computation Center, U. N.C., 1959; systems programmer Sperry Univac, beginning 1960, later staff cons. Sperry Internat., until 1965; gen. mgr. Computer Services Ltd. (became subs. University Computing Co.), Birmingham, Eng., beginning 1965, later became mgr. info. systems for ednl. subs. of University Computing Co., in U.S.; cons. info. processing, N.Y.C., 1969, Washington, 1970; from customer systems mgr. to sr. tech. cons. Nat. Teleprocessing Service, Info. Network div. Computer Sci. Corp., 1970-73; dir. Master Calendar Services for Am. Revolution Bicentennial Commn., 1973-77; spl. asst. to dir Office Adminstrn., Exec. Office of Pres., 1977-79; dep. asst. sec. of commerce for communications and info., dep. adminstr. Nat. Telecommunications and Info. Adminstrn., Dept. Commerce, Washington, 1979—. Office: Office Communications and Info Dept Commerce 1800 G St NW Washington DC 20504

ZIMMERMAN, EDWARD PAUL, publisher; b. Toronto, Ont., Can., Aug. 26, 1919; s. George Foster and Evelyn Pearl (Thompson) Z.; grad. U. Toronto; m. Durene Peace, May 7, 1937; children—Douglas, Larry, Cheryl, Jeffrey. Mgr. soap div. Can. Packers Ltd., 1946-55; gen. mgr. consumer products Canadian Westinghouse Co., 1955-60; pres. Reader's Digest Assn. (Can.) Ltd., Montreal, 1960-78; v.p. corp. devel. Torstar Corp., Toronto, 1978—; dir. Informart, Can./Weedend Mag. Exec. com. Canadian Exec. Service Overseas; bd. dirs. Vanguard Sch., Quebec. Served with Canadian Army, World War II. Recipient Canadian Centennial medal. Mem. United Ch. Can. Clubs: Forest and Stream (Montreal). Home: 1300 Bloor St E Apt 2203 Mississauga ON L4Y 3Z2 Canada Office: 1 Yonge St Toronto ON M5E 1P9 Canada

ZIMMERMAN, EDWIN MORTON, lawyer; b. N.Y.C., June 11, 1924; s. Benjamin and Tobie (Fuchs) Z.; A.B., Columbia, 1944, LL.B., 1949; m. Caroline Abbot, July 3, 1956; children—Sarah Abbot, Lyle Benjamin, Miriam Appleton. Admitted to N.Y. bar, 1949, D.C. bar, 1969, also U.S. Supreme Ct.; with Hoover Commn. Reorgn. Exec. Br., 1948; law clk. to U.S. Supreme Ct. Justice Stanley F. Reed, 1950-51, also U.S. Dist. Ct. Judge Simon H. Rifkind; practice law, N.Y.C., 1951-59; prof. law Stanford, 1959-69; with Justice Dept., 1965-69, asst. atty. gen. charge antitrust div., 1968-69; mem. firm Covington & Burling, Wash., 1969—. Mem. council Adminstrv. Conf. U.S., 1975-78. Served as 1st lt. AUS, 1944-46. Mem. Am. Bar Assn., Assn. Bar City N.Y., Am. Law Inst., Council Fgn. Relations, Phi Beta Kappa. Home 1529 33d St NW Washington DC 20007 Office: 888 16th St NW Washington DC 20006

ZIMMERMAN, FRANKLIN BERSHIR, educator, musician, musicologist; b. Wauneta, Kans., June 20, 1923; s. Tony H. and Asenath (Dungan) Z.; B.A., U. So. Calif., 1949, M.A., 1951, Ph.D., 1958; B.Litt., Oxford (Eng.) U., 1956; m. Rachel Martha Phillips, Apr. 11, 1957 (div. Oct. 1969); children—Eve Kathleen, Guy Tony, Claire Asenath, Grace Sadye; m. 2d, Mary Jane Fitch, June 25, 1976; 1 dau., Amy Fitch. Concert mgr. Sch. Music, U. So. Calif., 1951-52; asst. prof. music Crane Dept. Music, State U. N.Y. at Potsdam, 1958-59; asso. prof. music, chmn. dept. music history and lit. U. So. Calif., 1960-64; prof. music, dir. Collegium Musicum, Dartmouth, 1964-67; prof. music, dir. Pro Music, U. Ky., Lexington, 1967-68; prof. music U. Pa., Phila., 1968—, chmn. dept., 1968—, also dir. Pa. Pro Musica, 1969—; sr. fellow U. Calif. at Los Angeles, 1968. Cons. N.E.A., 1966; lectr. Merton seminar series Oxford (Eng.) U., summer 1969. Served with AUS, 1940-44; PTO. Recipient Internat. gold medal for musicology Arnold Bax Found., 1960; N.E.H. award for computer research in music; fellow Nat. Humanities Fund, 1967-68; Am. Philos. Soc. grantee for Handel Research, 1969-70. Mem. Am., Internat. musicol. socs., Royal, Coll. (council) music socs., Renaissance Soc. Am., Plainsong and Medieval Music Soc., Gesellschaft der Musikforschung, Am. Assn. U. Profs. (exec. council Dartmouth), Handel Gesellschaft. Author: Henry Purcell (1659-1695): An Analytical Catalogue of his Music, 1963; Henry Purcell (1659-1695): His Life and Times, 1967; Sound and Sense in the Single Songs of Henry Purcell, 1968. Editor: Introduction to The Skill of Musick (John Playford), 1970; Libro Primo di Madrigali a cinque, 1977; The William Kennedy Gostling Manuscript, 1978; computerized indexes of complete works of Encina, Handel, Purcell, and Frescobaldi. Contbr. to Groves Dictionary, 6th edit. Home: 225 S 42d St Philadelphia PA 19104

ZIMMERMAN, GEORGE OGUREK, physicist, educator; b. Poland, Oct. 20, 1935; s. Charles and Carolin Olga (Fisher) Z.; B.S., Yale U., 1958, M.S., 1959, Ph.D. (Univ. Wilson fellow 1959-60, D.N. Clark fellow 1959-61), 1963; m. Isa Kaftal, Oct. 4, 1964. Research asso. Yale U., 1962-63; asst. prof. physics Boston U., 1963-68, asso. prof., 1968-74, prof., 1974—, asso. chmn. dept. physics, 1971-72, chmn. dept., 1973—; mem. staff Nat. Magnet Lab., Cambridge, Mass., 1964, vis. scientist 1964-70; asso. physicist U. Calif., San Diego, 1973. Research Corp. grantee, 1964-65; Air Force Office Sci. Research grantee, 1966-72; NSF grantee, 1975—. Mem. Am. Phys. Soc., N.Y.

Acad. Scis., AAAS, Phi Beta Kappa, Sigma Xi. Contbr. articles on low temperature physics, phase transitions to profl. jours. Home: 88 Blueberry Ln South Hamilton MA 01982 Office: 111 Cummington St Boston MA 02215. *As a scientist, administrator and observer I am continually amazed how predictably people behave in groups, and how unpredictably as individuals.*

ZIMMERMAN, GIDEON K., clergyman; b. Lehr, N.D., Aug. 18, 1920; diploma N.Am. Baptist Sem., Rochester, N.Y., 1943; B.A., Wesley Coll., U. N.D., 1951; postgrad. Bethany Bibl. Sem., 1958-59, Chgo. Lutheran Sem., 1959-61; B.D., N.Am. Bapt. Sem., Sioux Falls, S.D., 1960, D.D.; m. Eleanor Pekrul; children—Paul, Mark (dec.), Thomas. Pastor, First Bapt. Ch., Auburn, Mich., 1943-47, Grace Bapt. Ch., Grand Forks, N.D., 1947-51, Temple Bapt. Ch., Milw., 1951-55; gen. sec. dept. Christian edn. N. Am. Bapt. Conf., 1955-68, exec. sec., 1968-79, estate planning counselor, 1979—. Office: North Am Bapt Conf 1 S 210 Summit Ave Oakbrook Terrace IL 60181

ZIMMERMAN, HARRY PAUL, educator; b. Ada, Okla., Jan. 1, 1923; s. John W. and Clara E. (Martin) Z.; B.S., East Central State U., Ada, 1947; M.S., U. Okla., Norman, 1949, Ed.D., 1958; m. Gladys Lorene Johnson, Aug. 10, 1946; children—Kay Lavon, Harold Paul. Instrn. supr. Putnam City Schs., Oklahoma City, 1949-53; asst. prof. edn. Ark. State Coll., 1953-56; grad. asst. U. Okla., 1956-58; prof. edn. U. Wis., Madison, 1958—, coordinator program devel. and evaluation, 1979—; dir. NDEA Insts.; vis. prof. various univs.; cons. in field; Fulbright lectr. Ahmadu Bello U., No. Nigeria, 1973-74. Served with U.S. Army, 1942-45; ETO. Decorated Purple Heart. Mem. Wis. Acad. Scis., Arts and Letters, Fulbright Alumni Assn. Home: 6617 South Ave Middleton WI 53562 Office: 432 N Lake St Madison WI 53706

ZIMMERMAN, HOWARD ELLIOT, chemist, educator; b. N.Y.C., July 5, 1926; s. Charles and May (Cohen) Z.; B.S., Yale, 1950, Ph.D., 1953; m. Jane Kirschenheiter, June 3, 1950 (dec. Jan. 1975); children—Robert, Steven, James; m. 2d, Martha L. Bailey Kaufman, Nov. 7, 1975; stepchildren—Peter and Tanya Kaufman. NRC fellow Harvard, 1953-54; faculty Northwestern U., 1954-60, asst. prof., 1955-60; asso. prof. U. Wis., Madison, 1960-61, prof. chemistry, 1961—, Arthur C. Cope prof. chemistry, 1975—. Chmn., 4th Internat. Internat. Union Pure and Applied Chemistry Symposium on Photochemistry, 1972. Recipient Halpern award for photochemistry N.Y. Acad. Scis., 1979. Mem. Am. Chem. Soc. (James Flack Norris award 1976), Chem. Soc. London, German Chem. Soc., Inter-Am. Photochemistry Assn. (co-chmn. organic div. 1977-79, exec. com. 1979—), Phi Beta Kappa, Sigma Xi. Author: Quantum Mechanics for Organic Chemists, 1975. Mem editorial bd. Jour. Organic Chemistry, 1967-71, Molecular Photochemistry, 1969—. Contbr. articles to profl. jours. Home: 1 Oconto Ct Madison WI 53705

ZIMMERMAN, HYMAN JOSEPH, physician, educator; b. Rochester, N.Y., July 14, 1914; s. Philip and Rachel (Marine) Z.; A.B., U. Rochester, 1936; M.A., Stanford, 1938, M.D., 1942; m. Kathrin J. Jones, Feb. 28, 1943; children—Philip M., David J., Robert L., Diane E. Intern Stanford U. Hosp., 1942-43; resident George Washington U. div. Gallinger Municipal Hosp., 1946-48, clin. instr. medicine Sch. Medicine, 1948-51; practice medicine, specializing in internal medicine, Washington, 1948-49; asst. chief med. service VA Hosp., Washington, 1949-51, dir. Liver and Metabolic Research Lab., 1965-68, chief med. service, 1971-78, sr. clinician, 1978—; asst. prof. medicine Coll. Medicine U. Nebr., also chief med. service VA Hosp., Omaha, 1951-53; chief med. service West Side VA Hosp., Chgo., also clin. asso. prof. medicine Coll. Medicine U. Ill., 1953-57; prof., chmn. dept. medicine Chgo. Med. Sch., also chmn. dept. medicine Mt. Sinai Hosp., Chgo., 1957-65; prof. medicine George Washington Sch. of Medicine, Washington, 1965-68, 71—; chief med. service Boston VA Hosp., 1968-71; prof. medicine Boston U. Sch. Medicine, 1968-71; lectr. medicine Tufts U. Sch. Medicine, 1968-71; chief med. service VA Hosp., Washington, 1971-78, sr. clinician, 1978—; prof. medicine George Washington Sch. Medicine; clin. prof. medicine Georgetown U., 1971—, Howard U., 1971—, Uniformed Health Services, 1978—. Served to maj. AUS, 1943-46. Diplomate Am. Bd. Internal Medicine. Fellow A.C.P.; mem. A.M.A. (council on drugs, gastroenterology panel 1968—), A.A.A.S., Am. Fedn. for Clin. Research, Am. Diabetes Assn., Endocrine Soc., Assn. for Study Liver Diseases, Am. Soc. Clin. Investigation, N.Y. Acad. Scis., Central Soc. Clin. Research, Soc. for Exptl. Biology and Medicine, Am. Soc. for Pharmacology and Therapeutics, Am. Gastroenterol. Assn., Sigma Xi, Alpha Omega Alpha. Contbr. numerous articles to med. jours. Home: 7913 Charleston Ct Bethesda MD 20034 Office: 50 Irving St NW Washington DC 20422

ZIMMERMAN, JOHN ELLIOTT, mfg. co. exec.; b. Marshfield, Wis., Sept. 7, 1918; s. George Frederick and Blanche (Crocker) Z.; Ph.B., U. Wis., 1940; J.D., U. Chgo., 1949; m. Muriel Yvonne Ramharter, June 14, 1948; 1 son, George Elliott. Cost accountant Gen. Electric Co., Bridgeport, Conn., 1940-41; asst. sec. Bear Brand Hosiery Co., Chgo. 1946-52; admitted to Ill. bar, 1949; practice in Chgo., 1949-52; mfg. mgr. Ford Motor Co., Dearborn, Mich., 1952-60; corp. comptroller Massey Ferguson, Ltd., Toronto, Ont., Can., 1960-64; sec., treas. King-Seeley Thermos Co., Ann Arbor, Mich., 1964-65, v.p. finance, sec., 1966-68; v.p. finance and adminstrn., dir. Air Products & Chems., Inc., Allentown, Pa., 1968-72; exec. v.p., dir. GAF Corp., N.Y.C., 1972-74; sr. v.p. Certain-teed Corp., Valley Forge, Pa., 1974—. Served to lt. comdr. USNR, 1941-46. C.P.A., Ill. Home: Office: Certain-teed Corp PO Box 860 Valley Forge PA 19482

ZIMMERMAN, JOHN MURR, clergyman; b. Milverton, Ont., Can., Dec. 25, 1922; s. John and Louise (Murr) Z.; B.A., U. Western Ont., 1944; D.D., Waterloo Lutheran U., 1962; m. Alma Elizabeth Wolff, May 8, 1948; children—Mark, Joel, Thomas, Peter, Paul. Ordained to ministry Luth. Ch. Am., 1947; parish pastor, Pembroke, Ont., 1947-59, Kitchener, Ont., 1959-62; pres. Western Can. Synod, Luth. Ch. Am., 1962-70; pastor parish, Spruce Grove, Alta., 1970-73; exec. sec. Can. sect. Luth. Ch. in Am., 1973—. Office: 600 Jarvis St Toronto ON M4Y 2J6 Canada

ZIMMERMAN, JOHN RICHMAN, educator; b. Eureka, Kans., Sept. 11, 1920; A.B., Kan. State Tchrs. Coll., 1942; Ph.D. (Coffin fellow), Ohio State U., 1949; postgrad. U. Ill., 1942; m. Lenore Stenzel, Dec. 19, 1942; children—Preston, Kathryn, Tamara. Physicist, Naval Research Lab., 1943-45; asst. prof. physics U. Colo., 1949-53; sr. research technologist Magnolia Petroleum Co., 1953-55, tech. asso., 1955-56; sect. supr. geochemistry Mobil Oil Corp., 1956-66; prof., chmn. dept. physics So. Ill. U., Carbondale, 1966-73, chmn. grad. council, 1972-73, chmn. molecular sci., 1969-75, asst. dean Coll. Sci., 1973-75; dean Coll. Scis. and Tech. East Tex. State U., 1975—. Bd. dirs. Southwest Sci. Forum, v.p., 1979-80; mem. exec. com. Agr. Consortium Tex., pres., 1979-80. Served with USNR, 1944-45. Mem. Am. Phys. Soc., Am. Soc. Testing and Materials, Am. Chem. Soc., Am. Inst. Mineral, Metall. and Petroleum Engrs., N.Y. Acad. Sci. Office: Coll Scis and Tech East Tex State U East Tex Station Commerce TX 75428

ZIMMERMAN, JOSEPH, beverages distbg. co. exec.; b. N.Y.C., July 17, 1930; s. Jacob and Ada (Herbert) Z.; B.B.A., City Coll. N.Y., 1953; M.B.A., N.Y. U., 1956; m. Joyce Litz, Aug. 23, 1952; children—Arlene, Diane. Auditor with C.P.A. firms, N.Y.C., 1955-61; controller Coca-Cola Bottling Co., Tucson, 1961-65; treas., controller Patek & Co., San Francisco, 1966-68; treas. Fromm & Sichel, Inc., San Francisco, 1969-77; v.p. fin. Coca-Cola Bottling Co. of the Peninsula, Belmont, Calif., 1978—; part-time lectr. acctg. U. Ariz., 1963-66, San Francisco State U., 1966—. Served with AUS, 1953-55. C.P.A., N.Y., Calif. Mem. Am. Inst. C.P.A.'s, Calif. Soc. C.P.A.'s, Nat. Assn. Accountants. Democrat. Home: 30 Elmhurst Dr San Francisco CA 94132 Office: 300 Harbor Blvd Belmont CA 94002

ZIMMERMAN, JOSEPH DALE, electronics co. exec.; b. Manila, May 19, 1934; s. Joseph Buford and Ellen Witherspoon (Hayes) Z.; B.S.E.E., M.I.T., 1959; m. Barbara Jean Fry, Oct. 2, 1954; children—Joseph, Dale, Steven. With Tex. Instruments Inc., Dallas, 1959—, asst. v.p., 1972-74, v.p., 1974-75, group v.p., 1975—. Served with U.S. Army, 1954-56. Office: 13500 N Central Expy Dallas TX 75265

ZIMMERMAN, JOSEPH FRANCIS, polit. scientist, educator; b. Keene, N.H., June 29, 1928; s. John Joseph and May Veronica (Gallagher) Z.; B.A., U. N.H., 1950; M.A., Syracuse U., 1951, Ph.D., 1954; m. Margaret Bernarette Brennan, Aug. 2, 1958; 1 dau., Deirdre Ann. Instr. govt. Worcester Poly. Inst., 1954-55, asst. prof., 1955-57, asso. prof., 1957-62, prof., 1962-65; lectr. Clark U., Worcester, Mass., 1957-65; prof. polit. sci. SUNY, Albany, 1965—; staff dir. N.Y. State Joint Legis. Com. Mass. Transp., 1967-68; research dir., 1968-73; research dir. N.Y. State Select Legis. Com. Transp., 1973-77, N.Y. State Senate Com. on Transp., 1977—. Pres. Citizens' Plan E Assn., Worcester, 1960-62, Citizens for Neighborhood Improvement Worcester, 1957-59. Served to capt. USAF, 1951-53. Named 1 of 3 Outstanding Young Men, Worcester Jr. C. of C., 1959, 61, Mass, Jr. C. of C., 1961. Mem. Am. Polit. Sci. Assn., Am. Soc. Public Adminstrn., Nat. Mcpl. League. Roman Catholic. Club: German-Am. Social. Author: State and Local Government, 1962; The Massachusetts Town Meeting: A Tenacious Institution, 1967; The Federated City: Community Control in Large Cities, 1972; Pragmatic Federalism, The Reassignment of Functional Responsibility, 1976; (with Frank W. Prescott) The Politics of the Veto of Legislation in New York, 1979; contbr. articles to profl. publs. Home: 82 Greenock Rd Delmar NY 12054 Office: Grad Sch Public Affairs SUNY ULB-96 Albany NY 12222

ZIMMERMAN, KATHLEEN MARIE, artist; b. Floral Park, N.Y., Apr. 24, 1923; d. Harold G. and Evelyn M. (Andrade) Zimmerman; student Art Students League, N.Y.C., 1942-44, Nat. Acad. Sch. Fine Arts, N.Y.C., 1944-47, 50-54; m. Ralph S. Iwamoto, Nov. 23, 1963. One woman shows Westbeth Gallery, N.Y.C., 1973, 74; exhibited in group shows Woodstock (N.Y.) Art Gallery, 1945, Nat. Arts Club, N.Y.C., 1948-56, Emily Lowe Award Show, 1951, Contemporary Arts Gallery, N.Y.C., 1952, 60, Allied Artists Ann., N.Y.C., 1956, 78, Art USA, 1958, Village Art Center, 1956-61, ACA Gallery, 1958, 59, Studio Gallery, 1957-60, City Center Gallery, 1960, Janet Nessler Gallery, N.Y.C., 1961, Silvermine Guild, Conn., 1962, Pioneer Gallery, Cooperstown, N.Y., 1962, 63, Audubon Artists Anns., N.Y.C., 1963, 65, 68-79, NAD, 1969, 75-78, Nat. Assn. Women Artists Anns., N.Y.C., 1957-79, Women Artists Award Winners Show, N.Y.C., 1974, Am. Watercolor Soc., N.Y.C., 1975-78, Cheyenne (Wyo.) Western Galleries, 1975, 76, 77, Edward-Dean Mus., Cherry Valley, Calif., 1975, 76, 77, Frye Mus., Seattle, 1975, 76, 77, Boise Gallery Art, 1975, Central Wyo. Mus. Art, 1975, 76, Willamette U., 1975, Yellowstone Art Center, Billings, Mont., 1975, Utah State U., 1975, Applewood (Colo.) Art Gallery, 1976, Charleston (W.Va.) Art Gallery, 1976, Kent State U., 1976, Cin. Art Club, 1976, Martello Mus., Key West, Fla., 1976, Buecker Gallery, N.Y.C., 1976, Anchorage Fine Arts Mus., 1976, Davis and Long Gallery, N.Y.C., 1977, Butler Inst. Am. Art, 1978, 80 Washington Sq. E. Gallery, N.Y. U., N.Y.C., 1979; represented in permanent collections Butler Inst. Am. Art, Youngstown, Ohio, Sheldon Swope Art Gallery, Terre Haute, Ind., Lauren Rogers Mus. Art, Laurel, Miss., U. Wyo. Art Mus., Laramie, U. Miami Lowe Art Mus., Coral Gables, Fla., N.C. Mus. Art, Raleigh, Swarthmore (Pa.) Coll.; tchr. drawing and painting Midtown Sch. Art, N.Y.C., 1947-52. John. F. and Anna Lee Stacey scholar, 1954; recipient Barse Miller Meml. award Am. Watercolor Soc., 1976; Henry Ward Ranger Fund purchase NAD, 1976; John Wenger Meml. award Audubon Artists, 1978. Mem. Audubon Artists, Am. Watercolor Soc., Nat. Assn. Women Artists (prizes 1957, 63, 68, 71, 72, 76, 79). Illustrator: (with Ralph S. Iwamoto) Diet for a Small Planet, 1971. Home: 463 West St A1110 New York NY 10014

ZIMMERMAN, LEO M., educator, surgeon; b. Toluca, Ill., Oct. 27, 1898; s. Louis and Sara (Kahan) Z.; A.B., Ind. U., 1919; M.D., Rush Med. Coll., Chgo., 1922; m. Sara Radoff, Apr. 10, 1928; children—David, Judith. Intern Cook County Hosp., Chgo., 1922-24; practice medicine specializing in surgery, Chgo., 1924—; mem. faculty Northwestern U. Med. Sch., Chgo., 1924—, prof. surgery, 1948—; prof. dept. surgery Chgo. Med. Sch., 1948—, chmn. dept., 1954-62, 66-68, chmn. dept. history and philosophy of medicine, 1968—; prof. surgery Cook County Grad. Sch. Medicine, 1950-65; attending surgeon Michael Reese Hosp., Chgo., 1928—. Served with M.C. USNR, 1943-45. Fellow A.C.S., Royal Soc. Medicine (Eng.); mem. A.M.A., Soc. Med. History Chgo. (pres. 1963—), Ill., Chgo. med. socs., Chgo. Surg. Soc., Am. Thyroid Assn., Am. Assn. History Medicine, Sigma Xi, Alpha Omega Alpha. Author: Physiologic Principles of Surgery, 1957; Principles of Surgical Practice, 1960; History of American Medicine, 1967; Great Ideas in the History of Surgery, 1967; Anatomy and Surgery of Hernia, 1953. Contbr. to profl. jours. Home: 5000 East End Ave Chicago IL 60615

ZIMMERMAN, M. PAUL, assn. exec.; b. N.Y.C., Apr. 22, 1934; s. Louis and Rose (Aginsky) Z.; B.A., Dartmouth, 1955; LL.B., Yale, 1958; m. Margot Ann Lurie, Aug. 18, 1957; children—Jeffrey, John, Julie. Admitted to N.Y. bar, 1959, D.C. bar, 1960; gen. atty. CAB, Washington, 1959; practice law Wolf & Wolf, Washington, 1960-62; gen. counsel Nat. Aircraft Noise Abatement Council, Washington, 1963-64, exec. sec., 1965; dir. Peace Corps, South India, 1966-68, Iran, 1969-71; first dep. adminstr. N.Y.C. EPA, 1971-74; exec. dir. Moped Assn. Am., 1975—. Served as 2d lt. AUS, 1958-59. Mem. N.Y., D.C. bars, Phi Beta Kappa. Club: Nat. Lawyers (Washington). Home: 7902 Rocton Ave Chevy Chase MD 20015 Office: 1001 Connecticut Ave NW Suite 707 Washington DC 20036

ZIMMERMAN, MARY HELEN CAMPION, lawyer; b. St. Louis, July 22, 1901; d. George Henry and Mary (McNamara) Campion; J.D., DePaul U., Chgo., 1926, L.H.D., 1971; LL.D., Assumption U., Windsor, Can., 1957; m. George Herbert Zimmerman, July 7, 1926; children—Doris (Mrs. Andrew G. Bato), Elaine (Mrs. Rankin Peck, Jr.). Jessie (Mrs. John Daniel Hitchens), Georgia (Mrs. John Loftus), Louis. Admitted to Md. bar, 1927, Mich. bar, 1933, U.S. Supreme Ct. bar, 1950; practice law, Balt., 1927-28, Grosse Pointe, Mich. and Detroit, 1933—. Mem. tax com. Detroit Bd. Commerce, 1945-51; adv. bd. Marygrove Coll., Detroit, 1962-65; bd. dirs. Inter Am. Bar Found., 1963-74. Fellow Am. Bar Found.; mem. Women's Assn. for Detroit Symphony, League of Cath. Women, Cath. Daus. Am., Nat. Assn. Women Lawyers (past pres., compiler, editor 75 year history 1975, recipient Distinguished Service award 1975), Inter-Am. (council of dels. 1951-63), Internat. (dep. House of Deputies, London, 1950, Madrid, 1952). Am. (resolutions com. 1952-55), Detroit bar assns., Mich. State Bar, Am. Judicature Soc., Women Lawyers Assn. Mich. (past pres.) Internacional Federacion de Abogadas, Mich. State Bar Found. (trustee 1969-78, pres. 1973-75), Kappa Beta Pi (editor quar. 1961-63), Lambda Chi (hon.). Republican. Roman Catholic. Clubs: National Lawyers (Washington); Pardi (pres. 1947-48, 59-60, 76-77), Republican Women's (Grosse Pointe). Home: 125 Kenwood Rd Grosse Pointe Farms MI 48236

ZIMMERMAN, MORTIMER FRED, financial exec.; b. Bklyn., July 17, 1922; s. Isaac and Esther (Goodman) Z.; B.B.A., Coll. City N.Y., 1947; postgrad. N.Y. U., 1964-67; m. Annette Furman, Oct. 19, 1947; children—John Mitchell, Robert Peter. Controller, L. Grossman Sons, Inc. (Mass.), 1958—; treas. ABC Consol. Corp., L.I. City, N.Y., Berlo Vending Co., Confection Cabinet Corp., ABC Gladieux Corp., 1963—; v.p. finance Nytronics, Inc., 1968-70; v.p.-treas., chief financial officer Russ Togs, Inc., N.Y.C., 1970—. Lectr., Am. Mgmt. Assn., N.Y.C. Served with AUS, 1943-45. C.P.A., N.Y. Mem. Financial Execs. Inst., Am. Inst. C.P.A.'s. Jewish (pres. temple). Home: 5 Vista Dr Great Neck NY 11021 Office: Russ Togs Inc 27-11 49th Ave Long Island City NY 11101

ZIMMERMAN, MORTIMER WILLIAM, hosp. adminstr.; b. Chgo., Feb. 18, 1922; s. Alexander Julius and Ida (Marks) Z.; B.A., U. Louisville, 1943; M.B.A., U. Chgo., 1945; M.H.A., Northwestern U., 1951; m. Marilyn Forb, Aug. 3, 1947; children—Steven Alexander, Ruth Miriam. Personnel officer U. Chgo., 1946-48; personnel cons. Burnie, Collen & Zimmerman, Chgo., 1948-49; personnel adminstr. Passavant Hosp., Chgo., 1949-52; exec. dir. Louis A. Weiss Meml. Hosp., Chgo., 1952—; pres. Chgo. Council Community Nursing, 1960-61; mem. bd. Hosp. Laundry Services Corp.; treas. Chgo. Hosp. Risk Pooling Program, 1978; mem. Skokie (Ill.) Bd. Health, 1960-66; mem. bd. Blue Cross, 1968-70; dir. Bank of Chgo. Served with AUS, 1943-44. Recipient Malcolm T. MacEachern medal Northwestern U., 1951; Laura G. Jackson Alumni Achievement award Northwestern U. Program in Hosp. Adminstrn., 1969; award of merit Tri-State Hosp. Assembly, 1970; Preceptors award Xavier U., 1970. Fellow Am. Coll. Hosp. Adminstrs. (regent 1971-76), Inst. Medicine; mem. Am., Ill. (past pres.) hosp. assns., Am. Pub. Health Assn., Chgo. Hosp. Council (past pres.), Northwestern U. Mgmt. Alumni Assn. (dir. 1976-79). Jewish. Author articles, chpt. in book. Address: 505 N Lake Shore Dr Chicago IL 60611

ZIMMERMAN, PAUL ALBERT, coll. pres.; b. Danville, Ill., June 25, 1918; s. Albert Carl and Hanna Marie (Haffner) Z.; student Concordia Coll., Ft. Wayne, Ind., 1936-39; B.A., Concordia Sem., St. Louis, 1941, M.Div., 1944; M.A., U. Ill., 1947, Ph.D., 1951; D.D., Concordia Sem., Springfield, Ill., 1975; m. Genevieve Emmaline Bahls, June 11, 1944; children—Karmin (Mrs. Raymond Philp), Thomas. Prof. theology and sci. Bethany Coll., Mankato, Minn., 1944-53; prof. Concordia Tchrs. Coll., Seward, Nebr., 1953-54, pres., 1954-61; pres. Concordia Luth. Jr. Coll., Ann Arbor, Mich., 1961-73, Concordia Coll., River Forest, Ill., 1973—. Chmn. Washtenaw County Red Cross, 1968-70; pres. Ann Arbor Found., 1970-71; mem. Citizens Com. Study Taxation, Ann Arbor, 1972. Mem. adv. bd. St. Joseph Mercy Community, 1969-72. Mem. Luth. Edn. Assn., Am. Assn. Higher Edn., Creation Research Assn. Lutheran (adminstrv. asst. pres. Mo. Synod 1972-73, mem. Curriculum Commn. Bd. Higher Edn. 1963-73). Author and editor: Darwin, Evolution and Creation, 1959; Rock Strata and the Bible Record, 1971; Creation, Evolution and God's Word, 1972. Home: 946 Clinton Pl River Forest IL 60305 Office: 7400 Augusta St River Forest IL 60305

ZIMMERMAN, RICHARD ANSON, chocolate mfg. co. exec.; b. Lebanon, Pa., Apr. 5, 1932; s. Richard Paul and Kathryn Clare (Wilhelm) Z.; B.A. in Commerce, Pa. State U., 1953; m. Nancy J. Cramer, Dec. 27, 1952; children—Linda Joan, Janet Lee. Asst. sec. Harrisburg (Pa.) Nat. Bank, 1956-58; with Hershey Foods Corp. (Pa.), 1958—, asst. to pres., 1965-71, v.p., 1971-76, pres., chief operating officer, 1976—; pres. Cory Corp., Chgo., 1971-74. Chmn. Derry Twp. Sch. Bldg. Authority; trustee, chmn. leadership gifts Fund for Fulfillment, Lebanon Valley Coll. Served to lt. USNR, 1953-56. Recipient Alumni fellow award Pa. State U., 1978. Mem. Phi Kappa Psi. Methodist. Clubs: Masons, Rotary (pres. Hershey club 1973-74), Hershey Country. Office: 19 E Chocolate Ave Hershey PA 17033

ZIMMERMAN, RICHARD GAYFORD, journalist; b. Springfield, Ohio, Sept. 3, 1934; s. Charles Ballard and Dorothy Cubitt (Gayford) Z.; B.F.A. cum laude, Wittenberg U., 1956; M.A., Am. U., 1958. Free-lance writer and polit. cartoonist, 1959-61; wire editor Urbana (Ohio) Daily Citizen, 1960-61; state house corr. Horvitz Newspapers, Mansfield, Lorain, Dover and Willoughby, Ohio, 1962-64, Dayton (Ohio) Jour. Herald, 1964-67; chief state house bur. Cleve. Plain Dealer, 1967-71, reporter Washington bur., 1971-72, chief Washington bur., 1972-77, Nat. Corrs., 1978—; freelance writer in Africa, 1977. Served with USAF, 1961-62. Recipient award Ohio A.P., 1971, Ohio Legis. Corrs. Assn., 1968, 69. Mem. Ohio (trustee 1969), Nat. (sec. 1974-75, vice chmn. bd. govs. 1975-76), press clubs, Ohio Legis. Corrs. Assn. (v.p. 1969-70), Beta Theta Pi. Contbr. articles to various publs. Home: 125 10th St SE Washington DC 20003 Office: 521 National Press Bldg Washington DC 20045

ZIMMERMAN, ROBERT EARL, lawyer; b. Kansas City, Mo., Feb. 11, 1928; s. Julius Joseph and Kathryn (Highcock) Z.; LL.B., U. Kansas City (now U. Mo. at Kansas City), 1950; m. Pauline Ann Stephens, Sept. 16, 1950; children—Elaine, David, Mark, Carol. Admitted to Mo. bar, 1950, since practiced in Kansas City; atty. Madden & Burke, 1950-51, 53-60; exec. v.p. Stephens & Assos., Inc., 1960-64; gen. atty. Kansas City So. Industries, Inc., 1964-66, asst. gen. counsel, 1966-67, v.p., gen. counsel, 1968-76, v.p. law, 1976—. Served with USMCR, 1945-46; to 1st lt., Judge Adv. Gen. Dept., USAF, 1951-53. Mem. Am., Mo., Kansas City bar assns., Am. Judicature Soc., Lawyers Assn. Kansas City. Home: 3504 W 101st Street Terr Leawood KS 66206 Office: 114 W 11th St Kansas City MO 64105

ZIMMERMAN, ROBERT GEORGE, utility co. exec.; b. Youngstown, Ohio, Nov. 3, 1921; s. Irwin Lincoln and Helen Mae (MacDonald) Z.; student Case Western Res. U., 1946, Youngstown U., 1947-49; m. Agnes LaVerne Winters, May 5, 1945; children—Dianne Lynne, Robert G. With Ohio Edison Co., 1940-41, 46—, sr. v.p. div. ops. and customer services, 1970—, also dir. Pres., Great Trail council Boy Scouts Am., 1976-78; chmn. Summit County United Way Operating Fund Drive, 1972; mem. Akron Mayor's Econ. Devel. Com. Served with USAAF, 1942-45. Decorated Purple Heart, Air medal. Mem. Edison Electric Inst. Presbyterian. Clubs: Portage Country, Akron City, Cascade. Office: 76 S Main St Akron OH 44308

ZIMMERMAN, ROBERT KUHLTHAU, electric co. exec.; b. New Brunswick, N.J., Nov. 14, 1914; s. Sebastian Francis and Magretha Caroline (Pritting) Z.; B.A., Rutgers U., 1936; m. Elisabeth Catherine McGinnis, Oct. 12, 1939; children—Barbara Elisabeth Zimmerman Funk, Robert Kuhlthau, Catherine Elisabeth. Comml. cadet, dir. ednl. work Pub. Service Electric & Gas Co., Newark, 1936-50; with Kansas

City Power & Light Co. (Mo.), 1950-79, v.p. mktg., 1958-70, exec. v.p., 1970-71, pres., 1971-73, chmn., 1973-79, now dir. Chmn., United Campaign, 1971—, pres., 1970; pres. Kansas City Conv. and Tourist Council, 1969; v.p. Rehab. Inst., 1967; pres. Kansas City Indsl. Found., 1968; mem. Kansas City Crime Commn., 1968; pres. YMCA, 1963; mem. Asso. Industries of Mo. Bd., 1970—. Bd. dirs. Midwest Research Inst. Served to lt. col. AUS, 1941-46. Decorated Bronze Star. Mem. Mo., Kansas City (pres. 1976-77, dir.) chambers commerce, Phi Gamma Delta. Kiwanian. Clubs: Kansas City Country (Mission Hills, Kans.). Home: 11211 Holly St Kansas City MO 64114 Office: 1330 Baltimore St Kansas City MO 64141

ZIMMERMAN, STANLEY ELLIOT, lawyer; b. Springfield, Mass., Aug. 14, 1918; B.A., Yale U., 1939; J.D., Harvard U., 1946; m. Edith Victoria McHutchison, Apr. 2, 1944; children—Stanley Elliot, Philip Douglas, David James, Ann Victoria. Admitted to N.Y. bar, 1947, Pa. bar, 1973; with firm Donovan, Leisure, Newton, Lumbard & Irvine, N.Y.C., 1946-48, Klein, Alexander & Cooper, N.Y.C., 1948-51; with W.T. Grant Co., N.Y.C., 1951-71, atty., 1951-54, real estate atty., 1954-62, gen. counsel, asst. sec., 1962-64, sec., gen. counsel, 1964-71; sec., dir., mem. exec. com. W.T. Grant Fin. Corp., Wilmington, Del., 1966-71; sec. Jones and Presnell Studios, Inc., Charlotte, N.C., 1969-71; v.p., dir. devel. Food Fair Stores, Inc., Phila., 1971-73; partner firm Schnader, Harrison, Segal & Lewis, Phila., 1973—. Class agt. Yale Alumni Fund, 1962-71; mem. lawyers com. George Jr. Republic, 1954-69; treas., troop committeeman Larchmont dist. Boy Scouts Am., 1964-71; trustee Larchmont (N.Y.) Pub. Library, 1969-71. Rector's warden St. Christopher's Ch., Gladwyne, Pa. Served to comdr. USNR, 1941-45. Decorated Legion of Merit. Mem. Am., Pa., Phila. bar assns. Clubs: Yale, Phila. Country, Union League (Phila.). Home: 1228 Club House Rd Gladwyne PA 19035 Office: 1719 Packard Bldg Philadelphia PA 19102

ZIMMERMAN, STEPHEN K., advt. exec.; b. N.Y.C., Aug. 10, 1929; s. Jack and Minna (Levy) Z.; B.A., Princeton U., 1950; student Columbia Grad. Sch. Bus. Adminstrn., 1951; m. Betty Jean Coats, June 10, 1953; children—Michael Andrew, Jean Carol, Peter Coats. With Lever Bros., 1956-60; v.p. Lennen & Newell, 1960-64; sr. product mgr. Beechnut Lifesavers Co., 1964-65; with Grey Advt., N.Y.C., 1966—, sr. v.p., mem. mgmt. com., 1969—; exec. v.p. Agy. Policy Council, 1971—; dir. Hastings Fed. Savs. & Loan Assn. Chmn. Non-Partisan Com. Selection Sch. Bd. Candidates, Hastings-on-Hudson, N.Y., 1970-71, Hastings council Boy Scouts Am., 1966-67. Served with AUS, 1953-55. Home: Hudson House Ardsley on Hudson NY 10503 Office: 777 3d Ave New York NY 10017

ZIMMERMAN, SYLVANUS ARNOLD, cosmetic co. exec.; b. Blairstown, N.J., Jan. 28, 1920; s. Sylvanus Arnold and Clara (Dunn) Z.; grad. Blair Acad., 1938; A.B., Princeton U., 1942; LL.B., Harvard U., 1948; m. Jeanne Marshall, July 31, 1943; children—Sylvanus Arnold IV, Sally, Todd K. Admitted to N.J. bar, 1949; practice in Newark, 1949-53; mem. firm Riker, Emery & Danzig, 1948-50, Herrigel, Bolan & Vieser, 1950-53; law sec. Chief Justice Arthur T. Vanderbilt, 1953-55; atty. Wallace & Tiernan, Inc., 1955-57; v.p., sec. Avon Products, Inc., N.Y.C., 1957-73, v.p., gen. counsel, 1973—; asso. prof. law Law Sch. Rutgers U., 1955-57. Dir. Alleghany Corp. Trustee Blair Acad.; bd. dirs. Morris Mus. Served to capt. AUS, 1942-46. Mem. Am. Bar Assn., Am. Soc. Corp. Secs. Clubs: University (N.Y.C.); Morris County Golf (Convent Station, N.J.). Home: Featherbed Ln New Vernon NJ 07976 Office: 9 W 57th St New York City NY 10019

ZIMMERMAN, THOMAS FLETCHER, clergyman; b. Indpls., Mar. 26, 1912; s. Thomas Fletcher and Carrie D. (Kenagy) Z.; student U. Ind., 1929; D.D., N.W. Coll.; m. Elizabeth H. Price, June 17, 1933; children—Betty Zimmerman Tinlin, Thomas Fletcher III, David. Ordained to ministry Assemblies of God, 1936; asst. pastor, Indpls., 1928-32; pastor, Kokomo, Ind., 1933-34, Harrodsburg, Ind., 1934-35, South Bend, Ind., 1935-39, Granite City, Ill., 1939-42, Springfield, Mo., 1943-47, Cleve., 1951-52; asst. supt. Ill dist. Assemblies of God, 1941-43; asst. supt. So. Mo. Assemblies of God., 1944-47, sec.-treas., 1949-51; asst. gen. supt. Assemblies of God, 1952-59, gen. supt., 1960—; first dir. Assemblies of God Radio Broadcast, 1945-49; exec. com. Nat. Religious Broadcasters; mem. exec. bd. Nat. Assn. Evangs., 1957—; mem. World Relief Com.; chmn. advisory com. Pentecostal World Confs., 1970, 73, 76, 79; mem. exec. com. Lausanne Com. World Evangelization, 1975—; pres. Assemblies of God Grad. Sch., Springfield, 1973—. Bd. dirs. Central Bible Coll., Springfield, 1953—, chmn. bd., 1959—; bd. dirs. Evangel Coll., Springfield, Cox Med. Center, Springfield, Jr. Achievement, Springfield, Channel 21, United Way of Springfield and Greene County; chmn. bd. Maranatha Village Retirement Complex, Springfield; chmn. planning com. Am. Festival Evangelism; mem. religious relationships com. Boy Scouts Am. Recipient Silver Beaver award Boy Scouts Am., 1969. Mem. Springfield C. of C. (Springfieldian of Yr. award 1974), Am. Bible Soc. (bd. mgrs. 1967—), World Home Bible League (editorial bd.). Rotarian. Co-author: Operation Sunday School, 1958. Home: 2551 W Norton Rd Springfield MO 65803 Office: 1445 Boonville Ave Springfield MO 65802

ZIMMERMAN, WARREN EUGENE, lawyer; b. Marceline, Mo., Jan. 16, 1938; s. Phil R. and Bess Lillian (Barber) Z.; B.A., U. Tex., 1960, J.D., 1964; m. Lynda K. Kemper, Dec. 30, 1967; children—Don Ray, Leigh Kemper, Elaine Reed. Admitted to Tex. bar, 1964, Ariz. bar, 1978; partner Dunlap & Zimmerman, Amarillo, Tex., 1964-67; partner Zimmerman & Zimmerman, Dallas, 1970-78, law offices Warren E. Zimmerman, 1978—; dir. Goldenberg Textiles, Inc.; asst. prof. econs., govt. Amarillo Coll., 1964-67. Active Boy Scouts Am. Served with AUS, 1960-62. Mem. Am., Ariz., Tex., Dallas, Amarillo bar assns., Am. Trial Lawyers Assn., Tex. Tennis Assn. (exec. dir. 1968-71), Am. Judicature Soc., Beta Theta Pi, Phi Alpha Delta. Editor Tex. Tennis mag., 1968-71. Office: Suite 710 Capital Bank Bldg Dallas TX 75206

ZIMMERMAN, WILLARD PAUL, glass mfr.; b. Washington Court House, Ohio, June 18, 1894; s. Samuel W. and Florence (Cockerill) Z.; A.B., Miami U., Oxford, Ohio, 1917, LL.D., 1973; LL.D., Toledo U., 1964; m. Ruth McCoy, Mar. 27, 1918; children—Doris Jean, Willard Paul. Sales mgr. Am. Seeding Machine Co., 1920-27; sec.-treas. Hemingray Glass Co., 1927-33; plant mgr. Owens-Ill. Glass Co., 1933-36, gen. mgr. indsl. and structural div., Toledo 1936-38; exec. v.p. Owens-Corning Fiberglass Corp., 1946-56, cons., 1956—; dir. Ohio Citizens Trust Co. Trustee, Toledo Hosp., Inst. Med. Research, Miami U. Served as regt. adj., U.S. Army, World War I. Recipient Distinguished Service award Nat. Found. and Hall of Fame, 1963. Mem. AIM, U. S., Ohio chambers commerce, Res. Officers Assn., Am. Legion, 40 and 8, Ind. Soc. Chgo., Delta Kappa Epsilon, Sigma Delta Psi. Republican. Presbyn. Clubs: DKE (N.Y.C.); Toledo, Iverness (Toledo); Boca Raton, Royal Palm Yacht and Country (Boca Raton, Fla.). Mason (hon. 33 deg.). Home: 3619 Brookside Rd Toledo OH 43606

ZIMMERMAN, WILLIAM, polit. scientist; b. Washington, Dec. 26, 1936; s. William and Isabel Edith (Ryan) Z.; B.A. with honors, Swarthmore Coll., 1958; M.A., George Washington U., 1959; Ph.D., Columbia U., 1965; m. Barbara Marshall Lamar, Feb. 7, 1959; children—W. Frederick, Carl L., Alice R. Lectr. polit. sci. U. Mich., Ann Arbor, 1963-64, asst. prof., 1964-69, asso. prof., 1969-74, prof., 1974—, asso. chmn. dept., 1971, dir. Center for Russian and East European Studies, 1972-78; cons. in field; mem. acad. council Kennan Inst. Advanced Russian Studies, Woodrow Wilson Center, 1975—. Trustee Nat. Council Soviet East European Research. Recipient Pi Sigma Alpha award, 1974. Inter-Univ. Com. Travel Grants fellow, 1956-66; Fgn. Area Tng. fellow Ford Found., 1961-62; William Bayard Cutting traveling fellow, 1962-63. Mem. Am. Polit. Sci. Assn. (Helen Dwight Reid award 1966), Am. Assn. Slavic Studies, Phi Kappa Phi. Author: Soviet Perspectives on International Relations, 1969; contbr. articles to profl. publs. Office: Dept Polit Sci U Mich Ann Arbor MI 48109

ZIMMERMAN, WILLIAM DUDLEY, news corr.; b. Washington, Apr. 5, 1940; s. Clarence Mason and Rachel Eckhart (Dudley) Z.; student Okla. U., Norman, 1958-59, George Washington U., Washington, 1959-60; m. Patricia Joan Moore, Sept. 14, 1963; children—Heather Lynn, William Eric, Brad Moore, Christopher Mason. Reporter, WTVR-TV, Richmond, Va., 1961-63; reporter WKBN-TV, Youngstown, Ohio, 1963-64; reporter WTOP-TV, Washington, 1964-69; reporter WHDH-TV, Boston, 1969-71; corr. ABC News, Beirut, Rome, Washington, 1971—. Mem. AFTRA, Overseas Press Club, White House Press, Capitol Press. Office: ABC News 1124 Connecticut Ave NW Washington DC 20036

ZIMMERMANN, BERNARD, surgeon, educator; b. St. Paul, June 26, 1921; s. Harry Bernard and Mary Robertson (Prince) Z.; student Harvard U., 1939-42, M.D., 1945; Ph.D., U. Minn., 1953; m. Elizabeth Caldwell, June 18, 1949; children—Bernard III, Andrew Caldwell. Intern, Boston City Hosp., 1945-46; mem. faculty U. Minn., 1953-60, prof. surgery, 1959-60; prof. surgery W.Va. U. Med. Sch., 1960—, chmn. dept., 1960-73. Head exptl. surg. facility Naval Med. Research Inst., Bethesda, Md., 1946-48; mem. cancer chemotherapy study sect. HEW, 1959—; mem. surgery tng. com. Nat. Inst. Gen. Med. Scis. Bd. dirs. St. Paul Inst. and Sci. Museum, 1956-60; pres., dir. W.Va. div. Am. Cancer Soc. Fellow dept. surgery U. Minn., 1948-53; clin. fellow Am. Cancer Soc., 1950-53, Am. scholar cancer research, 1953-58; Damon Runyon fellow cancer research, 1952-53. Mem. A.C.S. (com. pre-and postoperative care), Am., Central surg. assns., Soc. Univ. Surgeons, Halsted Soc. (pres.), Nat. Soc. Med. Research (sec.-treas.), Am. Soc. Exptl. Pathology, Soc. Head and Neck Surgeons, Soc. Exptl. Biology and Medicine, Minn. Acad. Medicine (sec.-treas. 1959-60), Minn. Territorial Pioneers. Unitarian (past trustee). Author: Endocrine Functions of the Pancreas, 1952. Contbr. articles to med. jours. Editorial bd. Jour. Surg. Research, 1960-73. Home: Route 5 Box 139 Morgantown WV 26505 Office: Dept Surgery WVa U Med Center Morgantown WV 26505

ZIMMERMANN, GERHARDT, conductor; b. Van Wert, Ohio, June 22, 1945; s. Ervin and Ethel Jane (Allen) Z.; B.Mus., Bowling Green State U.; M.F.A., U. Iowa; student with James Dixon, Leopold Sipe, Flora Contino, Richard Lert; m. Sharon Marie Reher, Mar. 17, 1974; children—Anna Marie, Peter Karl Irum. Tchr. in tng. Genoa (Ohio) Pub. Schs., 1967-70; condr. orch. Augustana Coll., Rock Island, Ill., 1971-72; music dir. Clinton (Iowa) Symphony Orch., 1971-72; asst. prof. music, condr. orchs. Western Ill. U., Macomb, 1972-74; asst. condr. St. Louis Symphony Orch., 1974-78, asso. condr., 1978—; music dir., condr. St. Louis Youth Orch., 1975—; guest condr. Recipient 2d Prize Georg Solti Conducting Competition, 1973. Mem. Am. Symphony Orch. League, Nat. Acad. Rec. Arts and Scis., Phi Mu Alpha Sinfonia. Home: 224 Caballero Dr St Louis MO 63011 Office: 718 N Grand Ave St Louis MO 63103

ZIMMERMANN, HENRY JOSEPH, educator, elec. engr.; b. St. Louis, May 11, 1916; s. Henry and Rosina (Finster) Z.; B.S., Washington U., St. Louis, 1938; M.S., Mass. Inst. Tech., 1942; m. Priscilla F. Durland, June 16, 1945; children—Brenda, Priscilla Gail, Karl, John. Instr., Washington U., St. Louis, 1938-40; mem. faculty Mass. Inst. Tech., 1940—, prof. elec. engring., 1955-79, prof. emeritus, 1979—, dir. Research Lab. Electronics, 1961-76; cons. to govt. and industry, 1947—. Fellow IEEE; mem. Sigma Xi, Tau Beta Pi, Eta Kappa Nu. Author: (with S. J. Mason) Electronic Circuit Theory, 1959, Electronic Circuits, Signals and Systems, 1960. Home: 14 Russet Ln Lynnfield MA 01940 Office: 77 Massachusetts Ave Cambridge MA 02139

ZIMMERMANN, JOSEPH ALBERT, JR., mfg. co. exec.; b. Clifton, N.J., June 17, 1934; s. Joseph Albert and Catherine Gladys (Hilton) Z.; B.B.A., St. Bonaventure U., 1955; m. Patricia A. Osborne, Sept. 24, 1955; children—Mark J., Paul T., Joanne P., Kathleen M., Patricia, Jeanne, Michael. Statis. analyst AMA, N.Y.C., 1955-59; audit supt. Ernst & Ernst, Newark, 1959-64; asst. corp. controller Hewitt-Robins, Inc., 1964-67; mgr. ops. Lewis-Shepard, Watertown, Mass., 1967-71; pres. Iona Co. div. Gen. Signal Corp., Manchester, Conn., 1971-74; v.p. fin. Risdon Mfg. Co., Naugatuck, Conn., 1974, exec. v.p., 1974-79, pres., chief operation officer, 1979—. Served as 1st lt. AUS, 1956-59. C.P.A. Mem. Fin. Exec. Inst., Am. Inst. C.P.A.'s, Conn. C.P.A. Soc. Office: Risdon Mfg Co 1 Risdon Way Naugatuck CT 06770

ZIMMERMANN, ROBERT GEORGE, dept. store exec.; b. St. Louis, June 22, 1917; s. William Michael and Wilhelmina (Wolfrum) Z.; B.S., Washington U., St. Louis, 1940; m. Vera Daeumer, Nov. 19, 1941; children—Robert George, Nancy Jean. With F. W. Woolworth Co., 1940—, asst. sec., N.Y.C., 1961, asst. sec.-treas., 1962-65, comptroller, asst. treas., 1965-69, asst. sec.-treas, 1969—. Home: 850 Nancy Way Westfield NJ 07090 Office: 233 Broadway New York City NY 10007

ZIMMERMANN, ROBERT WALTER, fgn. service officer; b. Chgo., Feb. 5, 1919; s. Clemence Robert and Meta (Becker) Z.; A.B. cum laude, U. Minn., 1940, postgrad. Law Sch., 1946-47; M.B.A. with distinction, Harvard, 1942; certificate Universidad Nacional de Mexico, 1941, Nat. War Coll., 1960; m. Silvia Brull, Dec. 27, 1947; children—Robert B., Philip B., Mark H., Michael W. Entered Fgn. Service, Dept. State, 1947; 3d sec., polit. officer Am. Embassy, Lima, Peru, 1948-50; 3d sec., econ. officer Am. Embassy, Bangkok, Thailand, 1950-52; 2d sec., fgn. service officer-5, 1951; 2d sec., polit. officer Am. Embassy, London, Eng., 1953-56; dep. to spl. asst. for SEATO affairs Dept. State, 1956-58; fgn. service officer-3, 1958; spl. asst. for SEATO affairs Dept. State, 1958-59; assigned Nat. War Coll., 1959-60; dep. chief polit. sect. Am. Embassy, Madrid, Spain, 1960-65, counselor of Embassy for polit. affairs, 1965-66; fgn. service officer-2, 1966; dir. presidential appointments staff Dept. State, 1966-69; fgn. service officer-1, 1969; dep. chief of mission Am. Embassy, Lisbon, Portugal, 1969-70; consul gen., Barcelona, Spain, 1971-74; country dir. for Brazilian affairs Dept. State, Washington, 1974-76; dir. for East Coast affairs (Argentina, Brazil, Parguay, Uruguay), 1976-79; ret. from Fgn. Service, 1979; expert-cons. to Dept. State, 1979—. Served to lt. USNR, 1942-46. Mem. Am. Fgn. Service Assn., Am. Acad. Polit. and Social Sci., Harvard Bus. Sch. Alumni Assn., Grey Friars, Alpha Delta Phi. Roman Catholic. Clubs: Club de Tenis Real (Madrid), Gremio Literario (Lisbon); Real de Tenis, Circulo Liceo (Barcelona). Home: 5240 Macomb St NW Washington DC 20016

ZIMNY, MARYLIN LUCILE, anatomist, educator; b. Chgo., Dec. 12, 1927; d. John and Lucile Ruth (Andryske) Z.; B.A., U. Ill., 1948; M.S., Loyola U., Chgo., 1951, Ph.D., 1954. Asst. prof. anatomy La. State U. Med. Center, New Orleans, 1954-59, asso. prof., 1959-64, prof., 1964-75, prof., acting head, 1975-76, prof., haad, 1976—; vis. prof. anatomy U. Costa Rica Sch. Medicine, 1961, 62. NIH grantee, 1958-72; Arthritis Found. grantee, 1969-72; Schlieder Ednl. Found. grantee, 1972-75; Frost Found. grantee, 1975-78; recipient Disting. Faculty Service award, 1969. Mem. Am. Assn. Anatomists, Am. Physiol. Soc., Orthopaedic Research Soc., Electron Microscopic Soc. Am., AAAS, Omicron Kappa Upsilon. Home: 1106 Burgundy St New Orleans LA 70116 Office: Dept Anatomy La State U Med Sch New Orleans LA 70112. *My appreciation for people has been a major factor in attaining my professional goals. Other factors include perseverance in the face of challenge, decision-making, warranted aggressiveness, mental curiosity, and dealing openly with friends and colleagues.*

ZINBARG, EDWARD DONALD, ins. co. exec.; b. N.Y.C., Oct. 24, 1934; s. Harry and Esther (Cohen) Z.; B.B.A. magna cum laude, City U. N.Y., 1954; M.B.A., U. Pa., 1955; Ph.D., N.Y. U., 1959; m. Barbara Scheffres, Dec. 20, 1956; children—Elizabeth, Allison. Adj. prof. fin. City U. N.Y., N.Y.C., 1958-73; with Prudential Ins. Co. Am., Newark, 1960—, chief economist, 1967-70, research dir. common stock, 1970-74, corp. fin. dept., 1974-78, sr. v.p. common stock dept., 1978—. Chmn. fin. com. City Coll Fund, N.Y., 1977—; mem. investment com. United Way of Essex and West Hudson, N.J., 1972—; trustee Trenton (N.J.) State Coll., 1978—, Oheb Shalom Congregation, South Orange, N.J., 1976—. Mem. N.Y. Soc. Security Analysts, Am. Fin. Assn. Author: (with J.B. Cohen and A. Zeikel) Investment Analysis and Portfolio Management, 3d edit. 1977, Guide to Intelligent Investing, 1978. Home: 5 Hardwell Rd Short Hills NJ 07078 Office: Prudential Ins Co Am Prudential Plaza Newark NJ 07101

ZINBERG, DOROTHY SHORE, sociologist; b. Boston, Feb. 25, 1928; d. Ernest and Esther (Cohen) Shore; student U. Wis., 1945-47, U. Buffalo, 1947-48; B.A., Boston U., 1949, M.A. in Sociology, 1958; Ph.D., Harvard U., 1966; m. Norman E. Zinberg, Apr. 4, 1956; children—Sarah, Anne. Teaching and research asst. in biochemistry Harvard Med. Sch., Cambridge, Mass., 1949-50, 52-57; research chemist Lever Bros., Cambridge, 1950-52; sr. research asso. Daniel Yankelovich, Inc., N.Y.C., and Cambridge Center for Research in Behavioral Scis., 1966-68; research sociologist dept. chemistry U. Coll. London, 1968-69; acting dean North House Radcliffe Coll., Cambridge, Mass., 1970; research sociologist, lectr. dept. sociology and Kennedy Sch. Govt., Harvard U., 1960—; dir. seminars and spl. projects Center for Sci. and Internat Affairs, Harvard, 1974—. Mem. adv. com. Office Sci. Personnel NRC, Washington, 1971-74. Bd. dirs. Fine Arts Workshop, Provincetown, Mass., 1970—; bd. dirs. internat. sci. exchanges Nat. Acad. Scis., 1974-77, mem. com. in internat. relations, 1977—; chmn. adv. council Internat. div. NSF, 1978—; mem. council Internat. Exchange of Scholars, 1978—; trustee Simon's Rock Coll., 1971-75, Buckingham, Browne and Nichols Sch., 1971-77. NSF fellow U. Coll. London, 1968-69. Mem. AAAS (com. on sci. freedom and responsibility 1972-74, com. on opportunities in sci. 1973-76). Home: 11 Scott St Cambridge MA 02138 Office: 79 Boylston St Cambridge MA 02138

ZINDEL, PAUL, author; b. S.I., N.Y., May 15, 1936; s. Paul and Betty (Frank) Z.; B.S., Wagner Coll., 1958, M.S., 1959, H.H.D., 1971; m. Bonnie Hildebrand, Oct. 25, 1973. Author: (plays) The Effect of Gamma Rays On Man-In-The-Moon Marigolds, 1965; And Miss Reardon Drinks A Little, 1967; Let Me Hear You Whisper (TV), 1969; The Secret Affairs of Mildred Wild, 1972; Ladies at the Alamo, 1976; (screenplays) Mame, 1974; Up the Sandbox, 1972; (novels for teenagers) The Pigman, 1968; My Darling, My Hamburger, 1969; I Never Loved Your Mind, 1970; Pardon Me, You're Stepping on My Eyeball, 1976; Confessions of a Teen-Age Baboon, 1977; The Undertaker's Gone Bananas, 1978; (for children) I Love My Mother, 1975. Ford Found. grantee as Playwright-in-residence at the Alley Theatre, 1967; recipient Drama Critic Circle award for best Am. play, 1970, Obie award for best Am. play, 1970, Drama Desk award for most promising playwright, 1970, Pulitzer prize in drama for Marigolds, 1971. Office: care Harper & Row Inc 10 E 53d St New York NY 10022*

ZINDER, NORTON DAVID, geneticist, educator; b. N.Y.C., Nov. 7, 1928; s. Harry Jean (Gottesman) Z.; A.B., Columbia U., 1947; M.S., U. Wis., 1949, Ph.D., 1952 m. Marilyn Estreicher, Dec. 24, 1949; children—Stephen, Michael. Asst., Rockefeller U., N.Y.C., 1952-56, asso., 1956-58, asso. prof. genetics, 1958-64, prof., 1964—, John D. Rockefeller Jr. prof., 1977—; Cons. genetic-biology NSF, 1962—; chmn. ad hoc com. to rev. viral cancer program Nat. Cancer Inst., 1973-74. Mem. vis. com. dept. biology Harvard U., 1975—, sect. virology Yale U., 1975—, dept. biochemistry Princeton U., 1975—. Recipient Eli Lilly award in microbiology and immunology, 1962; U.S. Steel Found. award in molecular biology, 1966, medal of excellence Columbia U., 1969. Fellow Am. Acad. Arts and Scis.; mem. Nat. Acad. Scis. (exec. com. Assembly of Life Scis. 1975—), Soc. Am. Biol. Chemists, Genetics Soc. Am., Am. Soc. for Microbiology, Harvey Soc., Sigma Xi. Asso. editor Virology. Spl. research in microbial genetics. Home: 450 E 63d St New York City NY 10021 Office: Rockefeller U 66th St and York Ave New York City NY 10021

ZINK, DAVID ROBERT, mgmt. co. exec.; b. Halifax, N.S., Can., Nov. 19, 1942; s. Ralph C. and Mary B. (Lucas) Z.; grad. York Mills Collegiate Sch., 1957; m. Janice Marie Fernley, Dec. 2, 1975; 1 son, Steven John. Golf profl. Bayview Country Club, Toronto, Ont., 1963-68, Bowmanville (Ont.) Country Club, 1968-71; tournament dir. Canadian Profl. Golfers Assn., Toronto, 1971-74, exec. dir., 1974-78; pres. Harrison St. Devel. Corp., Titusville, Fla., 1979—, Tour Pro Mgmt. Ltd., 1979—. Mem. United Ch. Can. Clubs: Nat. Golf. Home: 15 Pine Knoll Gate Thornhill ON L3T 1V4 Canada Office: Sarasota Bank Bldg Suite 1002 Sarasota FL 33577

ZINK, DOLPH WARREN, cons.; b. N.Y.C., Jan. 17, 1922; s. Adolph and Minna (Fritz) Z.; B.A., Amherst Coll., 1943; M.B.A., Harvard, 1947; M.A., U. Pa., 1966, Ph.D., 1971; m. Shirley Ann Cunningham, June 28, 1952; children—Dolph Bradley, Ellen Danell, Kurt Warren. Exec. v.p. Eastern Mortgage Service Co., Phila., 1947-59; pres. Heritage, Inc., King of Prussia, Pa., 1950-64; chmn. bd. dirs. Garrett Buchanan Co., Phila., 1965-69; v.p. Alco Standard Corp., Valley Forge, Pa., 1967-70, vice chmn., 1970-71; fin. cons., 1971; dean Sch. Bus. and Adminstrn. Western Australia Inst. Tech., 1971-76; dep. chmn. Western Australian Post Secondary Edn. Commn., 1977—; dir. Bunning Timber Holdings Ltd., Swan Portland Cement Ltd., Wigmores Ltd., Covest Pty Ltd. Trustee Art Gallery of Western Australia; chmn. bd. dirs. Zink Found. Served to 2d lt. U.S. Army, 1943-45. Fellow Australian Inst. Mgmt.; mem. Theta Delta Chi. Republican. Unitarian. Clubs: Racquet; Merion Cricket (Haverford, Pa.); University (N.Y.C.); Royal Freshwater Bay Yacht, Weld (Western Australia). Author: The Political Risks for Multinational Enterprise in Developing Countries, 1973. Home: 1 The Coombe Mosman Park 6012 Western Australia

ZINMAN, DAVID JOEL, conductor; b. N.Y.C., July 9, 1936; s. Samuel and Rachel Ilo (Samuels) Z.; B.Mus., Oberlin (Ohio) Conservatory, 1958; M.A., U. Minn., 1961; m. Leslie Heyman (dec.); children—Paul Pierre, Rachel Linda, Raphael; m. 2d, Mary Ingham, May 19, 1974. Asst. to Pierre Monteux, 1961-64; condr. Het Nederlands Kamerorkest, 1964-77; music dir. Rochester (N.Y.) Philharmonic Orch., 1974—; prin. guest condr. Rotterdam Philharm. Orch., 1977-79, chief condr., 1979—; adj. prof. Eastman Sch. Music, Rochester; rec. artist Phillips, Vox records, London Records; guest condr., U.S. and Europe. Recipient Grand Prix du Disque; Edison award. Home: 1340 Highland Ave Rochester NY 14620 Office: 20 Grove Pl Rochester NY 14605

ZINN, HOWARD, historian, educator; b. N.Y.C., Aug. 24, 1922; s. Edward and Jennie (Rabinowitz) Z.; B.A., N.Y. U., 1951; M.A., Columbia, 1952, Ph.D., 1958; m. Roslyn Shechter, Oct. 30, 1944; children—Myla, Jeff. Instr. history, polit. sci. Upsala Coll., 1953-56; lectr. history Bklyn. Coll., 1955-56; chmn. dept. history, social sci., prof. Spelman Coll., Atlanta, 1956-63; fellow Harvard U. Center for East Asian Studies, 1960-61; dir. Non-Western Studies Program Atlanta U. Center, 1961-62; asso. prof. govt. Boston U., 1964-66, prof. govt., 1966—. Served to 2d lt. USAAF, 1943-45. Decorated Air medal; recipient Albert J. Beveridge prize Am. Hist. Assn., 1958. Mem. Am. Hist. Assn., Am. Polit. Sci. Assn., Am. Assn. U. Profs. Author: LaGuardia in Congress, 1959; SNCC: The New Abolitionists, 1964; The Southern Mystique, 1964; New Deal Thought, 1966; Vietnam: The Logic of Withdrawal, 1967; Disobedience and Democracy, 1968; The Politics of History, 1970; Post-war America, 1973; Justice in Everyday Life, 1974; A People's History of the United States, 1980; contbr. articles to profl. jours. Home: 71 Woodland Rd Auburndale MA 02166

ZINNEMAN, HORACE HELMUT, physician, educator; b. Frankfurt/Main, Germany, Oct. 10, 1910; s. Lazar Ludwig and Lea (Margulies) Z.; came to U.S., 1938, naturalized, 1942; M.D., U. Vienna, 1937; m. Ruth May York, Oct. 10, 1941. Intern, Lincoln (Nebr.) Gen. Hosp., 1939-40; practice medicine specializing in internal medicine, Lincoln, 1940-50; resident in internal medicine Med. Sch., U. Minn., 1951-52, mem. faculty, 1952—, prof. medicine, 1968—; mem. staff Mpls. VA Hosp., 1952-79. Served with U.S. Army, 1943-46. Decorated Bronze Star medal. Diplomate Am. Bd. Internal Medicine. Fellow A.C.P.; mem. Am. Assn. Immunologists, Central Soc. Clin. Research, Soc. Exptl. Biology and Medicine, Minn. Med. Assn. Asso. editor Minn. Medicine, 1970—; contbr. to publs. in field. Home: 1826 Beechwood Ave Saint Paul MN 55116. *Do not complain, when an opportunity passes you by; instead, create a new one.*

ZINNEMANN, FRED, motion picture dir., producer; b. Austria, Apr. 29, 1907; s. Doctor Oskar and Anna (Feiwel) Z.; student law Vienna U., 1925-27; student Sch. Cinematography, Paris, France, 1927-28; m. Renee Bartlett, Oct. 9, 1936; 1 son, Tim. Came to U.S., 1929, naturalized, 1937. Asst. cameraman, Paris and Berlin, Germany, 1928; asst. dir. to Berthold Viertel, Fox Studio, 1929-30, asst. to Robert Flaherty, 1931; 1st directorial assignment documentary on Mexican fishermen, The Wave, 1934; dir. 16 short subjects for Metro-Goldwyn-Mayer, including Story of Dr. Carver, a series on great physicians (including Dr. Semmelweiss which won Acad. award), also several anti-crime shorts, 1937-41; dir. features for M-G-M, including The Seventh Cross with Spencer Tracy, 1941; dir. The Search, a story of Europe's displaced children (with L. Weechsler as producer; Screen Dirs. Guild award), Europe, 1946-47; dir. The Men, 1949, Teresa, 1950, High Noon (Screen Dirs. Guild, N.Y. Film Critics awards), 1951, The Member of the Wedding, 1952, Benjy (Acad. award best documentary), 1951; From Here to Eternity (N.Y. Film Critics' Screen Dirs. Guild, Acad. awards), 1953, Oklahoma, 1956; A Hatful of Rain, 1957; The Nun's Story (N.Y. Film Critic's award), 1958; The Sundowners, 1959; Behold a Pale Horse, 1964; dir., producer A Man for All Seasons, 1966 (N.Y. Film Critics' award for best film and best dir., Acad. awards best picture, best dir., Dirs. Guild Ann. award); dir. The Day of the Jackal, 1972, Julia, 1976. Recipient Golden Thistle award Edinborough Film Festival, 1965; Gold medal City of Vienna, 1967; D.W. Griffith award Dirs. Guild Am., 1971; Fellowship award Brit. Film Acad.; Donatello award, 1978. Mem. Acad. Motion Picture Arts and Scis., Dirs. Guild of Am., Brit. Acad. Film and TV. Sierra Club. Contbr. to Ency. Brit. Established (with others) sch. of neo-realism in Am. motion pictures. Office: care Stan Kamen William Morris Agy 131 El Camino Beverly Hills CA 90212

ZINNEN, ROBERT OLIVER, toy co. exec.; b. Racine, Wis., June 28, 1929; s. Aloys Henry and Mabel Helen (Holy) Z.; B.B.A., U. Wis., 1951; J.D., U. Wis., 1956; m. Darlene Mary Weyers, Aug. 25, 1956; children—Claudia Jane, Robert O. Tax accountant Price Waterhouse Chgo., 1956-59; mem. firm Tenney & Bentley, Chgo., 1959-64; asso. dir. taxes Allstate Cos., Skokie, Ill., 1964-65; v.p. fin. Do-All Co., Des Plaines, Ill., 1965-67; dir. taxes Quaker Oats Co., Chgo., 1967-71; internat. atty. Am. Hosp. Supply Corp., 1971-75; fin. cons. Alexander Proudfoot Co., Chgo., 1975-76; v.p. fin. Milton Bradley Co., Springfield, Mass., 1976—. Mem. Housing and Traffic Commns., Highland Park, Ill., 1963-66; chmn. Congl. Action Com., Springfield. Served with U.S. Army, 1951-53. Mem. Am. Bar Assn., Fin. Execs. Inst., Am. Inst. C.P.A.'s. Republican. Roman Catholic. Clubs: Longmeadow Country, Colony. Office: 1500 Main St Springfield MA 01115

ZINNER, PAUL, mining engr., ret. govt. ofcl.; b. Cedar Rapids, Iowa, Mar. 8, 1912; s. Fred J. and Clara (Muzik) Z.; B.S., Cal. Poly. Coll., 1934; m. Geraldine H. Waidman, Oct. 5, 1935; children—William Paul, Katherine Claire. Pvt. cons., San Francisco, 1934-36; mining engr. Anaconda Copper Mining Co., Butte, Mont., 1936-39, Bur. Mines, Dept. Interior 1939-47, chief Mpls. br., 1947-49, dir. region 5, 1949-52; chief minerals div. Bur. Mines, Washington, 1952-54, asst. dir. for programs, 1955-63, asst. dir. mineral resources devel. 1963-66, asst. dir. planning, 1966-74. Mem. Acad. Polit. Sci., Nat. Planning Assn., Am. Inst. Mining Metall. and Petroleum Engrs. Author govt. reports. Home: 1425 33d St NW Washington DC 20007

ZINSSER, WILLIAM KNOWLTON, writer, editor, educator; b. N.Y.C., Oct. 7, 1922; s. William Herman and Joyce (Knowlton) Z.; A.B., Princeton U., 1944; m. Caroline Fraser, Oct. 10, 1954; children—Amy Fraser, John William. Feature writer N.Y. Herald Tribune, 1946-49, drama editor, 1949-54, film critic, 1955-58, editorial writer, 1958-59; free-lance writer, 1959—; commentator on NBC-TV Sunday program, 1964-65; columnist Look mag., 1967, Life mag., 1968-72, N.Y. Times, 1977; faculty Yale U., 1971-79, master Branford Coll., 1973-79; exec. editor Book-of-the-Month Club, 1979—. Bd. dirs. Bklyn. Mus., 1967-72. Served with AUS, 1943-45; MTO. Clubs: Century Assn., Coffee House. Author: Any Old Place With You, 1957; Seen Any Good Movies Lately?, 1958; Search and Research, 1961; The City Dwellers, 1962; Weekend Guests, 1963; The Haircurl Papers, 1964; Pop Goes America, 1966; The Paradise Bit, 1967; The Lunacy Boom, 1970; On Writing Well, 1976; co-author: Five Boyhoods, 1962. Home: 1232 Madison Ave New York NY 10028

ZINTEL, HAROLD ALBERT, surgeon; b. Akron, Ohio, Dec. 27, 1912; s. Carl Frederick and Christine (Maier) Z.; B.S., U. Akron, 1934, D.Sc., 1956; M.D., U. Pa., 1938, D.Sc. (Med.), 1946; m. Mary Agnes Simmons, Nov. 8, 1939; children—Joseph Carl, Suzanne, Nancy Louise, Carolyn, Harold Albert. Intern Hosp. U. Pa., 1938-40, asst. chief med. officer, 1939-40, fellow surgery, 1940-45, asst. instr. surgery U. Pa. Med. Sch., 1940-41, instr., 1941-47, asst. prof. surgery, 1947, asso. prof., 1951-52 prof. clin. surgery, 1952-54, asst. prof. surgery U. Pa. Grad. Sch. Medicine, 1947, asso. prof. surgery, 1950-54; cons. surgeon Camden Municipal Hosp., 1948-54; prof. clin. surgery Columbia Coll. Phys. and Surg., 1954- 69; attending surgeon, dir. surgery St. Luke's Hosp., N.Y.C., 1954-69; asst. dir. A.C.S., Chgo., 1969—; prof. surgery Northwestern U. Med. Sch., Chgo., 1970—. Pres. Medicadata, Inc., 1975-77. Past mem. Phila. Anesthesia Study Commn.; civilian cons. Office Surg. Gen., U.S. Army, 1958-68; 1st Harold L. Foss Meml. lectr. Geisinger Med. Center, Danville, Pa., 1968; quality practice control bd. U.S. Navy, 1971-75. Trustee Commn. Profl. and Hosp. Activities, Ann Arbor, 1969—, chmn. bd. trustees, 1975-77; bd. dirs. Nat. Commn. on Certification of Physicians Assts., 1974-77; trustee Am. Assn. Accreditation Animal Lab Care, 1973. Fellow A.C.S., N.Y. Acad. Medicine, N.Y. Acad. Scis.; mem. AMA (conf. com. on grad. edn. in surgery as rep. council on med. edn. 1966-69, cons. com. on allied health edn. and accreditation 1971—), Soc. Univ. Surgeons (pres. 1955-56), Halsted Soc. (sec.- treas. 1951-54), Internat. Cardiovascular Soc., Soc. Surgery Alimentary Tract, Internat. Coll. Angiology, Am. Heart Assn., Phila. Acad. Surgery, Pan-Pacific Surg. Assn., Allen O. Whipple Soc., Am. Assn. Surgery Trauma, Central Surg. Soc., Am. Surg. Assn., Central Surg. Assn., Western Surg. Assn., N.Y. Soc. Cardiovascular Surgeons, N.Y. Cancer Soc. (pres. 1967-68), Soc. for Vascular Surgery, Sigma Xi, Phi Sigma, Alpha Omega Alpha. Editor: Pre and Postoperative Care (rev. edit.), 1946; mem. editorial bd. Am. Jour. Surgery, 1958-70, Current Procedural Terminology III and IV, 1971—. Contbr. articles, chpts. to profl. publs., 8 motion pictures surg. techniques. Home: 891 Vernon Ave Winnetka IL 60093 Office: American College of Surgeons 55 E Erie St Chicago IL 60611

ZIOLKOWSKI, KORCZAK, sculptor; b. Boston, Sept. 6, 1908; married; 10 children. Works represented in permanent collections, including San Francisco Art Museum, Judge Baker Guidance Center, Boston, Symphony Hall, Boston, Vassar Coll., Poughkeepsie, N.Y.; sculptor marble portraits of Paderewski (First Sculptural prize for World's Fair 1939), Georges Enesco, Artur Schnable, Wilbur L. Cross, John F. Kennedy; commd. works include: Noah Webster Statue (marble) on Town Hall lawn, West Hartford, Conn.; Wild Bill Hickok (granite portrait), Deadwood, S.D.; Chief Sitting Bull (granite portrait), Mobridge, S.D.; Robert Driscoll, Sr. (marble), First Nat. Bank Black Hills, Rapid City, S.D.; Chief Henry Standing Bear, Kennedy Meml. Library, Boston; carving mountain into equestrian figure of Sioux Chief Crazy Horse at request of Indians as meml. to Indians of N.Am., Custer, S.D., 1948—; asst. to Gutzon Borglum, Mt. Rushmore Nat. Meml., S.D. Chmn. bd. dirs. Crazy Horse Found. Mem. Nat. Sculpture Soc. Office: Crazy Horse Ave of Chiefs Black Hills SD 57730

ZIOLKOWSKI, THEODORE JOSEPH, educator; b. Birmingham, Ala., Sept. 30, 1932; s. Miecislaw and Cecilia (Jankowski) Z.; A.B., Duke U., 1951, A.M., 1952; student U. Innsbruck (Austria), 1952-53; Ph.D., Yale, 1957; m. Yetta Bart Goldstein, Mar. 26, 1951; children—Margaret Cecilia, Jan Michael, Eric Josef. Instr., then asst. prof. Yale U., 1956-62; asso. prof. Columbia U., 1962-64; prof. Germanic langs. and lits. Princeton U., 1964-69, chmn., 1973—, Class of 1900 prof. modern langs., 1969—, prof. comparative lit., 1975—, dean Grad. Sch., 1979—; vis. prof. Rutgers U., 1966, Yale U., 1967, 75, City U. N.Y., 1971; vis. scholar U. Center in Va., 1971, Piedmont U. Center, N.C., 1971; Dancy Meml. lectr. U. Montevallo, 1973; Christopher Longest lectr. U. Miss., 1979; chmn. N.Y. State Doctoral Evaluation Program in German, 1975-76, 79-80. Recipient Howard T. Behrman award for disting. achievement in humanities, 1978, Fulbright research grantee, 1958-59; grantee Am. Philos. Soc., 1959; Nat. Endowment for Humanities grantee, 1978; Guggenheim fellow, 1964-65; Am. Council Learned Socs. fellow, 1972, 76. Mem. Am. Comparative Lit. Assn., Modern Lang. Assn. (exec. council 1976-77), Yale Grad. Sch. Assn. (pres. 1974-76), Am. Assn. Tchrs. German, Authors Guild, Internat. Verein der Germanisten, Phi Beta Kappa. Author: Hermann Broch, 1964; The Novels of Hermann Hesse, 1965; Hermann Hesse, 1966; Dimensions of the Modern Novel, 1969; Fictional Transfigurations of Jesus, 1972 (James Russell Lowell prize for criticism); Disenchanted Images, 1977; Der Schriftsteller Hermann Hesse, 1979; The Classical German Elegy, 1980; also articles. Editor: Hermann Hesse, Autobiographical Writing, 1972; Hermann Hesse, Stories of Five Decades, 1972; Hesse: A Collection of Critical Essays, 1973; Hermann Hesse, My Belief: Selected Essays, 1974; Hermann Hesse, Tales of Student Life, 1976; mem. editorial bd. Germanic Rev., 1964—, Publs. Modern Lang. Assn., 1971-75, Princeton U. Press, 1972-75. Translator: The Poetics of Quotation (Herman Meyer), 1968; Hermann Hesse: A Pictorial Biography, 1975. Home: Wyman House 50 Springdale Rd Princeton NJ 08540

ZION, ROGER H., cons. firm exec., former congressman; b. Escanba, Mich., Sept. 17, 1921; s. Herschel G. and Helen (Hutchinson) Z.; B.A., U. Wis., 1943; postgrad. Grad. Sch. Bus. Adminstrn., Harvard, 1944-45; m. Marjorie Knauss, Feb. 20, 1945; children—Gayle, Scott, Randy. With Mead Johnson & Co., 1946-66, dir. tng. and profl. relations, 1965-66; internat. marketing mgmt. cons., 1966; mem. 90th-93d congresses from 8th Dist. Ind.; chmn. Republican Task Force on Energy and Resources; pres. Resources Devel., Inc., cons., Washington, 1975—. Vice pres. Buffalo Trace council Boy Scouts Am., 1961. Bd. dirs., chmn. Evansville (Ind.) chpt. ARC, 1960-65. Served to lt. USNR, 1943-46, PTO. Named Toastmaster, Evansville Press Gridiron dinner, 1963; recipient Citizen of Month award New Image Com. of Evansville's Future, 1962. Mem. VFW, Am. Legion, Nat. Sales and Marketing Execs. Assn. (pres. Evansville 1962), Wabash Valley Assn., AMVETS (life), Alpha Delta Phi (pres. Wis. chpt. 1941-43). Republican. Conglist. Rotarian (dir. Evansville 1964). Club: Evansville Country (dir. 1960-65). Author: Keys to Human Relations in Selling, 1963. Home: 834 Plaza Dr Evansville IN 47715 Office: 900 17th St Suite 300 Washington DC 20006

ZIPERMAN, H. HASKELL, physician, ret. army officer; b. N.Y.C., Sept. 24, 1915; s. Sam and Ida (Gostin) Z.; A.B. cum laude, Ind. U., 1937, M.D., 1941; m. Margaret Le Masters, Oct. 4, 1940; 1 son, Don B. Intern, U. Ind., 1941-42, resident, 1946-50; commd. U.S. Army, 1950, advanced through grades to col., M.C.; chief surgery 97 Gen. Hosp., Frankfurt, Germany, 1961-63, Beaumont Gen. Hosp., 1965-67, Martin Army Hosp., Fort Benning, Ga.; ret.; now sr. research physician S.W. Research Inst., San Antonio; dir. med. and surg. med. service sch. San Antonio, 1954-59; asso. clin. prof. surgery Baylor U., 1957-59, Emory U. Med. Sch., 1972; clin. prof. surgery U. Tex. Med. Sch., San Antonio, 1973—. Pres. Canal Zone Heart Assn., 1969-70; mem. exec. bd. Chattahoochie council Boy Scouts Am., 1970-72. Served with A.C., AUS, 1942-46. Decorated Legion Merit, Bronze Star. Diplomate Am. Bd. Surgery. Mem. AMA, Bexar County Med. Soc., A.C.S., Am. Assn. Surgery of Trauma, Assn. Mil. Surgeons, Isthmian Med. Soc. Canal Zone, Phi Beta Kappa, Alpha Omega Alpha. Kiwanian. Contbr. articles to profl. jours. Home: 214 Gardenview San Antonio TX 78213 Office: 8500 Culebra Rd San Antonio TX 78284

ZIPERSKI, JAMES RICHARD, trucking co. exec.; b. Milw., May 27, 1932; s. George Felix and Louise (McDema) Z.; B.S., Marquette U., 1953, J.D., 1957; m. Patricia Jean Hoag, June 28, 1958; children—Jean Marie, David Carrington, James Patrick. Admitted to Wis. bar, 1957; resident counsel Schwerman Trucking Co., Milw., 1957—, sec., 1962—, exec. v.p. corporate, 1977—; dir. City Fed. Savs. & Loan Assn. Served with AUS, 1953-55. Mem. Motor Carriers Lawyers Assn., ICC Practitioner's Assn., Alpha Kappa Psi, Phi Delta Phi. Clubs: Kiwanis. Wisconsin; Westmoor Country. Home: 2110 Swan Blvd Wauwatosa WI 53226 Office: 611 S 28th St Milwaukee WI 53215

ZIPIN, IRVING J., real estate co. exec.; b. Phila., 1912; J.D., Temple U., 1938. Vice pres., sec., gen. counsel City Stores Co., W. & J. Sloane, Inc., 1951-78; v.p., gen. counsel Marx Realty and Improvement Co., 1978—. Contbg. author: The Buyer's Manual, 1965; Manual of Federal Trade Regulations Affecting Retailers, rev., 1965. Home: 1598 Blenheim Rd Rockville Centre NY 11570 Office: 415 Madison Ave New York NY 10017

ZIPPER, HERBERT, symphony condr.; b. Vienna, Austria, Apr. 27, 1904; s. Emil and Regina (Westreich) Z.; master diploma Vienna State Acad. for Music and Drama, Vienna, 1926; m. Trudl Dubsky, Oct. 1, 1939. Became U.S. citizen, 1951. Asst. condr. Wiener Burgtheater, 1923-25; condr. Vienna Madrigal Assn., 1927-29; opera condr. Stadtheater Ingolstadt, Bavaria, 1929-30; condr. Municipal music Soc., 1931-33; prof. Conservatory of Dûsseldorf, Germany, 1931-33; guest condr. in various cities of Europe, 1933-37; instrumental in found. and orgn. of Vienna Concert Orch. (composed mainly of musicians who fled Germany), 1934; composed music for polit. satires; in Paris, 1939; musical dir. Manila Symphony Orch. and head Acad. Music of Manila, 1939-42; after imprisonment by Japanese and work in underground, reorganized orch., 1945, gave 130 symphony concerts for armed forces and civilians, 1945-46, apptd. by Pres. Sergio Osmeñ-a of Philippines as mem. com. for cultural rehab. of Philippines; arrived in U.S., 1946; musical dir. Bklyn. Symphony Orch., 1947—, Fine Arts Quartet Concert series, Chgo., Wilmette, Ill., 1960—; lectr. New Sch. for Social Research in opera, symphony, and composition since 1948; condr. summer season Manila Symphony Orch. since 1951; dir. Community Music Center North Shore, 1953—; condr. Chgo Businessmen's Orch., 1955—; exec. dir. Nat. Guild Community Mus. Schs., 1967—; music cons. JDR 3d Fund, N.Y.C.; projects dir. U. So. Calif. Sch. Performing Arts, Los Angeles, 1972—; composer revision of choral works by old masters and own choral arrangements, 1948-49; German version of Ernst Toch's opera The Last Tale, 1964. Chmn. Philippine fellowship project, 1966. President Nat. Guild Community Music Schs. Recipient Louis S. Weiss Meml. prize New Sch. of Social Research, N.Y., 1954; Presdl. award medal and citation, Pres. of Philippines, 1959; Austrian Cross Honor for Sci. and Art, 1966; Silangan award U. East Manila, Philippines, 1977; Samuel Rosenbaum Meml award Nat. Guild Community Schs. Arts. Home: 1091 Palisair Pl Pacific Palisades CA 90272

ZIPSER, STANLEY, lawyer; b. Canton, Ohio, Apr. 17, 1923; s. Henry Fay and Anna (Roth) Z.; student Ohio State U., 1940-41; B.S., U.S. Naval Acad., 1945; LL.B., Loyola U., Los Angeles, 1951; m. Lillan Johnson, Sept. 14, 1962; children—Mikael Koltai, Dean Jeffrey, Lisa Lynn, Stanley. Admitted to Calif. bar, 1952; dep. atty. gen. State of Calif., Los Angeles, 1951-52; practiced in Los Angeles, 1952-55, Beverly Hills, Calif., 1955-68, Century City of Los Angeles, 1968—; co-founder Law Centers of Mosten and Zipser, legal services for low and middle income clients, Los Angeles County and Orange County, 1979—; v.p., sec. Byways Travel Service. Mem. service acad. selection com. for former Congresswomen Yvonne Brathwaite Burke, 1973-78. Served with USN, 1945-47; PTO. Mem. Los Angeles, Beverly Hills, bar assns., Lawyers Club of Los Angeles, Nat. Health Lawyers Assn., U.S. Naval Acad. Alumni Assn. (officer Los Angeles chpt.). Lion; mem. B'nai B'rith. Club: Mountain Gate Country (Los Angeles). Home: 808 Thayer Ave Los Angeles CA 90024 Office: 1888 Century Park E Los Angeles CA 90067

ZIRIN, HAROLD, educator, astronomer; b. Boston, Oct. 7, 1929; s. Jack and Anna (Buchwalter) Z.; A.B., Harvard U., 1950, A.M., 1951, Ph.D., 1952; m. Mary Noble Fleming, Apr. 20, 1957; children—Daniel Meyer, Dana Mary. Asst. phys. scientist RAND Corp., 1952-53; lectr. Harvard, 1953-55; research staff High Altitude Obs., Boulder, Colo., 1955-64; prof. astrophysics Calif. Inst. Tech., 1964—; staff mem. Hale Observatories, 1964—; chief astronomer Big Bear Solar Obs., 1969—. U.S.- USSR exchange scientist, 1960-61. Trustee Polique Canyon Assn., 1977—. Agassiz fellow, 1951-52; Sloan fellow, 1958-60; Guggenheim fellow, 1960-61. Mem. Am. Astron. Soc., Internat. Astron. Union, AURA (dir. 1977—). Author: The Solar Atmosphere, 1966. Adv. editor Soviet Astronomy, 1965-69. Home: 1178 Sonoma Dr Altadena CA 91001 Office: California Inst Tech Pasadena CA 91125

ZIRKEL, DON, editor; b. Ozone Park, N.Y., Aug. 13, 1927; s. George Henry and Frances Anna (Neumann) Z.; student Fordham U., 1948-50; B.A., St. John's U., 1955; m. Marie Margaret Greene, June 28, 1952; children—Jeanne (Mrs. John O'Connell), Barbara (Mrs. James Dempsey), Joseph, Thomas, Mary, Anne, John, Paul, Timothy. Mem. editorial staff Cath. newspaper The Tablet, Bklyn., 1948—, editor, 1968—, now also columnist; lectr. in field. Research asst. to Congressman James J. Delaney, 1961-63, Congressman Hugh L. Carey, 1963-65. Now mem. Cath. Interracial Council; mem. Bklyn. Diocesan Commn. for Peace and Justice, 1972—. Bd. dirs. Citizens for Ednl. Freedom. Served with AUS, 1950-52. Recipient Best News Story award Cath. Press Assn., 1957, Americanism award Cath. War Vets., 1961, Worldmission award U.S. Mission Secretariat, 1963. Roman Catholic (lector 1966—, Eucharistic minister 1973—, ordained deacon 1979). K.C. (State award 1973). Contbr. articles to Cath. newspapers, mags. Home: 34 Fountain St Hicksville NY 11801 Office: 1 Hanson Pl Brooklyn NY 11243

ZIRKER, JACK BERNARD, solar astronomer; b. Bklyn., July 19, 1927; s. Joseph and Rose Z.; B.M.E., CCNY, 1948; M.S., N.Y. U., 1953; Ph.D., Harvard U., 1956; m. Lorette Zuckerman, Jan. 21, 1951; children—Robin, Alizon, Pamela. Scientist, Sacramento Peak Obs., Sunspot, N.Mex., 1956-64, dir. obs., 1976—; solar astronomer U. Hawaii, 1964-76, prof., 1965-76; cons. NASA. Served with U.S. Army, 45-47. Mem. Am. Astron. Soc., Internat. Astron. Union.

ZIRKIND, RALPH, physicist; b. N.Y.C., Oct. 20, 1918; s. Isaac and Zicel (Lifshitz) Z.; B.S., Coll. City N.Y., 1940; M.S., Ill. Inst. Tech., 1945; postgrad George Washington U., 1946-47; Ph.D., U. Md., 1950; D.Sc., U. R.I., 1968; m. Ann Goldman, Nov. 22, 1940; children—Sheila (Mrs. Herbert Knopf), Elaine (Mrs. Jack Gorman), Edward I. Physicist, Navy Dept., 1945-50, chief physicist, 1951-60; physicist Oak Ridge Nat. Lab., 1950-51; physicist Advanced Research Project Agy., Washington, 1960-63; prof. Poly. Inst. Bklyn., 1963-70; prof. U. R.I., Kingston, 1970-72, adj. prof., 1972—; physicist Advanced Research Projects Agy., Arlington, Va., 1972—. Lectr. U. Md., 1948-50, George Washington U., 1952-53, U. Mich., 1966; cons. Arms Control Disarmament Agy., Jet Propulsion Lab., Calif. Inst. Tech. Recipient Meritorious Civilian Service award Navy Dept., 1957, Dept. Def., 1970; Outstanding Educator of Am. award, 1972.

Mem. Am. Phys. Soc., N.Y. Acad. Scis., Sigma Xi, Sigma Pi Sigma, Eta Kappa Nu. Contbg. author: Jet Propulsion Series. 1952; FAR Infrared Properties of Materials, 1968. Editor: Electromagnetic Sensing of Earth, 1967; mem. editorial bd. Infrared Physics, 1963—. Contbr. articles profl. jours. Home: 820 Hillsboro Dr Silver Spring MD 20902 Office: Gen Research Corp Westgate Research Park McLean VA

ZIRPOLI, ALFONSO JOSEPH, U.S. judge; b. Denver, Apr. 12, 1905; s. Vincenzo and Stella (Graziani) Z.; A.B., U. Cal. at Berkeley, 1926, J.D., 1928; m. Giselda Campagnoli, Sept. 19, 1936; children—Sandra Elena, Jane Amanda. Admitted to Cal. bar, 1928, U.S. Supreme Ct., 1941; pvt. practice, 1928-32, 44-61; asst. dist. atty. City and County San Francisco, 1932-33; asst. U.S. atty. No. Dist. Cal., 1933-44; instr. criminal law Hastings, Coll. Law, 1945; formerly judge U.S. Dist. Ct. No. Dist. Cal.; presently judge U.S. Temporary Emergency Ct. Appeals, San Francisco. Bd. suprs. City and County San Francisco, 1958-61. Recipient Star Solidarity, 1953, grand officer Order Merit, 1956 (Italy). Fellow Am. Coll. Trial Lawyers; mem. Fed., Am., Cal. bar assns. Office: US Court House PO Box 36060 San Francisco CA 94102*

ZISCHKE, DOUGLAS ARTHUR, fgn. service officer; b. Sioux Falls, S.D., May 24, 1929; s. Arthur Gustav and Alice Minetta (Wedeking) Z.; B.S. in Journalism, U. Wis., 1951, M.S. cum laude, 1952; m. Janice Mae Kuehnemann, June 8, 1957; children—Mark Douglas, Deborah Jan, Todd Lincoln. Joined U.S. Fgn. Service, 1957; tech. editor Forest Service, Madison, 1955-57; asst. information officer USIS, Montevideo, Uruguay, 1957-58; La Paz, Bolivia, 1958-59; asst. cultural affairs officer, br. pub. affairs officer, Mexico, 1960-65; information specialist, Washington, 1965-67; pub. affairs officer, Tegucigalpa, Honduras, 1967-69; dep. pub. affairs officer, Buenos Aires, Argentina, 1969-71; pub. affairs officer, Guatemala, Guatemala, 1971-74; assigned to U.S. Army War Coll., 1974-75; dep. pub. affairs officer Am. embassy, Tehran, Iran, 1975-78; cultural coordinator USICA, Washington, 1979—. Bd. dirs. Boy Scouts Am. Served with Signal Corps, AUS, 1953-55. Mem. Am. Fed. Govt. Employees. Lutheran (dir. 1973-74). Author monograph. Home: 191 NE Gladis St Port Charlotte FL 33950 Office: 2325 Malraux Dr Vienna VA 22180

ZISFEIN, MELVIN BERNARD, museum dir.; b. Phila., May 9, 1926; s. Jacob and Elizabeth (Segal) Z.; B.S., M.S., Mass. Inst. Tech., 1948; children—James Ira, Carol Ruth. With Naval Aircraft Factory, Phila., 1948-51; chief aerodynamicist Bristol Engring. Co. (Pa.), 1951-52; aerodynamics engr. Lockheed Aircraft Corp., 1952-53; with Bell Aircraft Corp., Buffalo, 1953-60, chief dynamics sect., 1955-60; gen. mgr. astromechanics research div. Giannini Controls Corp., Malvern, Pa., 1960-66; asso. dir. Franklin Inst. Research Labs., Phila., 1966-71; dep. dir. Nat. Air and Space Mus., Smithsonian Instn., Washington, 1971—; AIAA Disting. lectr., 1978; chmn. project adv. bd. Reading (Pa.) Mcpl. Info. Systems Project, 1970; cons. Pacific Mus. of Flight, 1977—, Six Flags, Inc., 1978—; prin. cons. on flight Time-Life Books, Inc., 1978—; mem. adv. com. John F. Kennedy Meml. Library, 1977—. Recipient Exceptional Service Gold medal Smithsonian Instn. Asso. fellow AIAA; mem. Am. Soc. Aerospace Edn. (dir.), Engrs. Club Phila. (dir. 1966-71), Inst. Devel. of Riverine and Estuarine Systems (founding dir. 1968-69, chmn. tech. bd. 1969-70). Home: 1100 6th St SW Washington DC 20024 Office: Nat Air and Space Museum Smithsonian Instn Washington DC 20560

ZISK, RICHARD WALTER, profl. baseball player; b. Bklyn., Feb. 6, 1949; s. Walter Stanley and Jean Veronica (Murawski) Z.; student pub. schs., Parsippany, N.J.; m. Barbara L. Boice, May 27, 1969; 1 son, Kevin Richard. With Pitts. Pirates minor league teams, 1967-73; played right and left field for Pitts. Pirates, 1973-76, Chgo. White Sox, 1977; with Tex. Rangers, 1977—. Named Player of Year, Appalachian League, 1967, Puerto Rican Player of Year, Winter League, 1971; recipient Dapper Dan Rookie of Year award Pitts. Pirates, 1973; named to Sporting News All-Star Team, 1974, Am. League All-Star Team, 1977. Mem. Profl. Baseball Assn. Democrat. Presbyterian. Address: care Texas Rangers Arlington Stadium PO Box 1111 1500 Copeland Rd Arlington TX 76010*

ZISSIS, GEORGE JOHN, physicist; b. Lebanon, Ind., Dec. 31, 1922; s. John Frank and Georgia (Antonakous) Z.; B.S., Purdue U., 1946, M.S., 1950, Ph.D., 1954; m. Wanda H. Evans, Jan. 16, 1954; children—Maida Anne, John George, Christopher George, Maria Cecelia. Research fellow, instr. Purdue U., West Lafayette, Ind., 1946-54; sr. scientist Westinghouse Atomic Power Div., Pitts., 1954-55; research physicist U. Mich., Ann Arbor, 1955-62, head Infrared Physics Lab., also chief scientist Willow Run Labs., Inst. Sci. and Tech., 1964-73; adj. prof. elec. computer engring., 1973—; physicist Inst. for Def. Analyses, Washington, 1962-64, cons., 1964-72; sr. research physicist, chief scientist Environmental Research Inst. Mich., 1973—. Fellow Optical Soc. Am., A.A.A.S.; mem. Am. Soc. Photogrammetry, Sigma Xi, Sigma Pi Sigma. Author: (with M. Holter, G. Suits, S. Nudleman, W. Wolfe) Fundamentals of Infrared Technology, 1962; also numerous reports and articles. Editor in chief Jour. Remote Sensing Environment, 1972-78. Research in ballistic missile def., infrared tech. and remote sensing. Home: 1549 Stonehaven Rd Ann Arbor MI 48104

ZISSU, FREDERICK, lawyer, retail exec.; b. N.Y.C., Aug. 30, 1913; s. Jacob and Bessie Z.; B.S., N.Y. U., 1934, LL.M., J.D.; m. Lillian Scheps, Dec. 25, 1937; children—Barbara (Mrs. Marvin H. Kushnick), Jeffrey A., Karen (Mrs. Michael Magidson), Sandra L. (Mrs. Mark Rosenbaum). Chmn. bd. Gen. Microwave Corp., Farmingdale, N.Y., 1960—, Vornado, Inc., Garfield, N.J., 1964—; sr. partner firm Zissu, Berger, Halper & Barron, N.Y.C., 1966—. Trustee Fairleigh Dickinson U. Office: 174 Passaic St Garfield NJ 07026 also 450 Park Ave New York City NY 10022

ZITRIN, ARTHUR, physician; b. Bklyn., Apr. 10, 1918; s. William and Lillian (Elbaum) Z.; B.S., City Coll. N.Y., 1938; M.S., N.Y. U., 1941, M.D., 1945; certificate psychoanalytic medicine, Columbia, 1955; m. Charlotte Marker, Oct. 4, 1942; children—Richard Alan, Elizabeth Ann. Research fellow animal behavior Am. Museum Natural History, 1939-42; intern King County Hosp., 1945-46; resident psychiatry Bellevue Hosp., 1948-51; instr. physiology Hunter Coll., N.Y.C., 1948-49; mem. faculty N.Y.U. Sch. Medicine, 1949- -, professor psychiatry, 1967—; mem. staff Bellevue Hosp., N.Y.C., 1951- -, dir. psychiatry, 1955-68; dir. psychiatry N.Y.C. Dept. Hosps., 1962- 64; pvt. practice, 1949—; attending psychiatrist Univ. Hosp., N.Y.C.; cons. psychiatrist Manhattan Va Hosp. Served to capt., M.C., AUS, 1946- 48. Diplomate Am. Bd. Psychiatry and Neurology. Fellow Am. Psychiat. Assn., N.Y. Acad. Medicine; mem. N.Y. Soc. Clin. Psychiatry (pres. 1966- 67), Am. Psychoanalytic Assn., AMA, Sigma Xi, Alpha Omega Alpha. Author papers in field. Home: 56 Ruxton Rd Great Neck NY 11023 Office: 550 1st Ave New York City NY 10016

ZIVNUSKA, JOHN ARTHUR, educator; b. San Diego, July 10, 1916; s. U. R. and Meta (Kienth) Z.; B.S., U. Calif. at Berkeley, 1938, M.S., 1940; Ph.D., U. Minn., 1947; m. Ethel Rowland, Mar. 14, 1941 (dec. 1962); children—Ann (Mrs. Eberhard Welker), Louise (Mrs. Edouard Dahnert), John R.; m. 2d, Marion Marliave, June 28, 1964. Instr., U. Minn., 1946-47; mem. faculty U. Calif. at Berkeley, 1948—, prof. forestry, 1959—, dean Sch. Forestry and Conservation, 1965-74. Fulbright lectr. Norwegian Agrl. Coll., 1954-55; cons. Stanford Research Inst., Forest Industries Council, Econ. Commn. Asia and Far East, Pub. Land Law Rev. Commn., also cons. to industry. Served to lt. USNR, 1942-45; PTO. Mem. Soc. Am. Foresters, Assn. State Coll. and Univ. Forestry Research Orgns. (pres. 1971-72), Finnish Forest Soc., Sierra Club, Wilderness Soc., Sigma Xi. Contbr. articles to profl. jours. Home: 25 Bear Ridge Rd Orinda CA 94563

ZIZMOR, STEPHEN BARRY, realtor; b. N.Y.C., Dec. 18, 1939; s. Jack and Anne (Herman) Z.; B.S., N.Y. U., 1962; m. Gail Renee Gallow, Dec. 24, 1961; children—Andrew Stuart, Deborah Lynne, Bradley Lawrence. Accountant, Alfred R. Bachrach & Co., C.P.A.'s, 1962-68; mgr. Arthur Young & Co., C.P.A.'s, N.Y.C., 1968-72; v.p., treas. Nat. Kinney Corp., N.Y.C., 1972--. Active local Boy Scouts Am., Little League; trustee Woodlands Community Temple. C.P.A., N.Y. Mem. Am. Inst. C.P.A.'s, N.Y. State Soc. C.P.A.'s. Home: 38 Penny Ln Scarsdale NY 10583 Office: 10 E 53d St New York NY 10022

ZLATKIS, ALBERT, educator; b. Pomorzany, Poland, Mar. 27, 1924; s. Louis and Zisel (Nable) Z.; B.A.Sc., U. Toronto, 1947, M.A.Sc., 1948; Ph.D., Wayne State U., 1952; m. Esther Shessel, June 15, 1947; children—Lori, Robert, Debra. Came to U.S., 1949, naturalized, 1959. Research chemist Shell Oil Co., Houston, 1953-55; asst. prof. chemistry U. Houston, 1955-58, asso. prof., 1958-63, chmn. chemistry dept., 1958-62, prof. chemistry, 1963—; adj. prof. chemistry Baylor Coll. Medicine, 1975—; tour speaker Am. Chem. Soc., 1961, 63, 66, S. Africa's Chem. Inst., 1971, USSR Acad. Scis., 1973, Polish Acad. Scis., 1977. Recipient Am. Chem. Soc. award in chromatography, 1973; NASA Tech. award, 1975; NASA Patent award, 1978; USPHS grantee, 1966; NASA grantee, 1964-76; Welch Found. grantee, 1969; AEC grantee, 1967. Mem. Am. Chem. Soc. (chmn. Southeast Tex. sect. 1964), G.A.M.S. (France), Sigma Xi, Phi Lambda Upsilon. Author: Practice of Gas Chromatography, 1967; Preparative Gas Chromatography, 1971; Advances in Chromatography, 14 vols., 1963—; A Concise Introduction to Organic Chemistry, 1973; High Performance Thin-Layer Chromatography, 1977; 75 Years of Chromatography—A Historical Dialogue, 1979. Mem. editorial bds. Jour. of Chromatography, Jour. of Chromatographic Science, Chromatographia, Jour. High Resolution Chromatography. Home: 22 Sandalwood Dr Houston TX 77024

ZLOWE, FLORENCE MARKOWITZ, artist; b. Allentown, Pa.; d. Morris and Anna (Mandel) Markowitz; student Pa. Mus. Coll. Art, Phila., 1929-33, fine arts courses, N.Y. U., 1950-53; m. Irwin Zlowe, May 1, 1936. One woman show Charles Z. Mann Gallery, N.Y.C., 1968, Community Gallery, N.Y.C., 1978; exhibited in group shows Nat. Acad., Riverside Mus. (N.Y.), Nat. Arts Club, Pen and Brush Club, Lever House, Jersey City Mus., Norfolk (Va.) Mus., Fort Lauderdale (Fla.) Mus., Joe and Emily Lowe Mus., Fla.; represented in permanent collections Norfolk Mus., Fort Lauderdale Mus., Joe and Emily Lowe Mus., Wilson Pub. Co., N.Y.C., Phila. Mus. Art, Butler Inst. Am. Art, Minn. Mus. Art, St. Paul, Cooper-Hewitt Mus. Design, Smithsonian Instn., N.Y.C., Tweed Mus., Duluth, Minn., Evansville (Ill.) Mus., Lakeville (Ill.) Center Arts and Scis. Mem. Am. Soc. Contemporary Artists (dir., treas.), N.J. Soc. Painters and Sculptors, Nat. Assn. Women Artists (1st prize ann. 1958, 7 additional award for oils 1958-75), League Present Day Artists, Artists Equity Assn. N.Y. Home: 440 E 57th St New York NY 10022 Studio: 22 E 17th St New York NY 10003

ZOBEL, HILLER BELLIN, judge; b. N.Y.C., Feb. 23, 1932; s. Hiller and Harriet Selma (Bellin) Z.; B.A. cum laude, Harvard Coll., 1953, LL.B., 1959; postgrad. Oxford U., 1956; m. Deborah Bethell, June 21, 1958; children—John H., David H., Elizabeth T., Sarah B.; m. 2d Rya S. Weickert, Nov. 23, 1973. Admitted to Mass. bar, 1959, U.S. Ct. Appeals bar, 1960, U.S. Dist. Ct., 1960, U.S. Supreme Ct. bar, 1966; asso. firm Bingham, Dana & Gould, Boston, 1959-67; research asso. Harvard U., 1962-63; asso. prof. Boston Coll. Law Sch., 1967-69, prof., 1969-79; asso., counsel firm Hill & Barlow, Boston, 1971-72; partner, counsel firm Brown, Rudnick, Freed, & Gesmer, Boston, 1972-79; asso. justice Mass. Superior Ct., 1979—; reporter Mass. Advisory Com. on Rules of Civil Procedure; spl. asst. atty. gen. Commonwealth of Mass.; spl. counsel Mass. Dept. Public Utilities. Served with U.S. Navy, 1953-55. Recipient Am. Hist. Assn. Littleton-Griswold prize 1966. Mem. Am. Law Inst., Mass. Hist. Soc., Colonial Soc. Mass., Am. Antiquarian Soc., Soc. Am. Historians, Mass. Bar Assn., Maritime Law Assn. U.S., Am. Soc. Legal History (v.p. 1970-71). Democrat. Jewish. Editor: (with L.K. Wroth) Legal Papers of John Adams, 1965; The Boston Massacre, 1970; (with J.W. Smith) Massachusetts Rule Practice, 1974—; contbr. articles to profl. jours. Office: Superior Ct Boston MA 02108

ZOBEL, JILL ANNE HAUSRATH, editor; b. Lancaster, Pa., Jan. 8, 1949; d. Gordon Lewis and Karolyn Margareth (Kindt) Hausrath; B.A., Mary Washington Coll., U. Va., 1971; m. Konrad Zobel. Editorial sec. Bantam Books, 1971, editorial asst., 1972, asst. editor, 1972, editor, 1972-73; sr. editor, exec. editor Ballantine Books, Inc., N.Y.C., 1974-75; N.Y. rep. to Nat. Enquirer, 1975-77; editor M. Evans & Co., 1976; freelance editorial cons., 1976-78, 79—; asso. pub. 21st Century Communications, Inc., N.Y.C., 1978-79. Home: Rembrandtstrasse 9/5 A-1020 Vienna Austria

ZOBEL, RYA W., judge; b. Germany, Dec. 18, 1931; A.B., Radcliffe Coll., 1953; LL.B., Harvard U., 1956. Admitted to Mass. bar, 1956; formerly partner Goodwin, Procter & Hoar, Boston; U.S. Dist. judge of Mass., Boston, 1979—. Mem. Am. Bar Assn. Office: US District Ct McCormack Post Office and Courthouse Bldg Boston MA 02109

ZOBLER, LEONARD, educator; b. N.Y.C., Feb. 26, 1917; s. Meyer and Sarah (Braunstein) Z.; B.S., State U. Washington, 1941, M.S., 1943; Ph.D., Columbia, 1953; m. Paula Vanderstempel, June 20, 1958; children—Helen, Marian. With Dept. Interior, 1941-43; soil scientist U.S. Soil Conservation Service, N.J., 1947-51; lectr. Columbia, N.Y.C., 1952-54; from asst. to prof. geography Columbia and Barnard Coll., 1955—; instr. Hunter Coll., 1953; instr. Bklyn. Coll., 1954. Served to capt. AUS, 1943-47. Mem. Assn. Am. Geographers, Am. Geog. Soc., Soil Sci. Soc. Am., Am. Soc. Agronomy, AAAS. Research soils, hydrology, environ. conservation, land planning, natural resource analysis. Home: 89 Euclid Ave Hastings-on-Hudson NY 10706 Office: 606 W 120th St New York City NY 10027

ZOBRIST, BENEDICT KARL, library exec.; b. Moline, Ill., Aug. 21, 1921; s. Benedict and Lila Agnas (Colson) Z.; A.B., Augustana Coll., Rock Island, Ill., 1946; postgrad. Stanford, 1946-47; M.A., Northwestern U., 1948, Ph.D., 1953; postgrad. U. Ill., 1961, Tunghai U., Taiwan, 1962, Columbia, 1962-63, Fed. Exec. Inst., Charlottesville, Va., 1974, Hebrew U. (Israel), 1978; m. Donna Mae Anderson, Oct. 23, 1948; children—Benedict Karl II, Markham Lee, Erik Christian. Manuscript specialist in recent Am. history Library of Congress, Washington, 1952-53; asst. reference librarian Newberry Library, Chgo., 1953-54; command historian Ordnance Weapons Command, Rock Island Arsenal, 1954-60; prof. history Augustana Coll., 1960-69, asst. dean faculty, 1964-69, asso. dean, dir. grad. studies, 1969; asst. dir. Harry S. Truman Library, Independence, Mo., 1969-71, dir., 1971—. Sec. Harry S. Truman Library Inst., Independence, 1971—; mem. steering com. Harry S. Truman Statue Com., Independence, 1973—; mem. adv. bd. Harry S. Truman Commemorative Good Neighbor award, 1974—; mem. Independence Truman Award Commn., 1975—; adj. prof. history U. Mo.-Kansas City, 1975—. Served with AUS, 1942-46. Recipient Outstanding Alumni Achievement award Augustana Coll., 1975; Ky. Col. Mem. Am., Jackson County (Mo.) (v.p. 1972—) hist. socs., Orgn. Am. Historians, Assn. Asian Studies, Am. Assn. State, Local History, Soc. Am. Archivists, A.A.U.P. Club: Mo. Yacht. Contbr. articles, revs. to profl. jours. Home: 3522 S Cottage St Independence MO 64055 Office: Harry S Truman Library Independence MO 64050

ZOBRIST, GEORGE WINSTON, computer scientist, educator; b. Highland, Ill., Feb. 13, 1934; s. George H. and Lillie C. (Augustine) Z.; B.S., U. Mo., 1958; Ph.D., 1965; M.S., Wichita State U., 1961; m. Freida Groverlyn Rich, Mar. 29, 1955; children—Barbara Jayne, George William, Jean Anne. Electronic scientist U.S. Naval Ordnance Test Sta., China Lake, Calif., 1958-59; research engr. Boeing Co., Wichita, 1959-60; instr. Wichita State U., 1960-61; asso. prof. U. Mo., Columbia, 1961-69, U. So. Fla., Tampa, 1969-70; chmn. elec. engring. dept. U. Miami, Coral Gables, Fla., 1970-71; prof. U. South Fla., Tampa, 1971-72, 73-76; prof., chmn. dept. elec. engring. U. Toledo, 1976-79, dir. computer sci. and engring. Samborn, Steketee, Otis, Evans, Inc., Toledo, 1979—; research prof. U. Edinburgh (Scotland), 1972-73. Cons. Wilcox Electric Co., Kansas City, Mo., Bendix, Kansas City, Mo., 1966-68, ICC, Miami, 1970-71, Def. Communications Agy., Washington, 1971, U.S. Naval Research Labs., Washington, 1971, Med. Service Bur., Miami, 1970-71, NASA, Kennedy Space Center, Fla., 1973-76, Prestolite Corp., Toledo, 1977—. Served with USAF, 1951-55. Named Young Engr. of Year central chpt. Mo. Soc. Profl. Engrs., 1967. NSF summer fellow, 1962, 64; NASA research grantee, 1967-69. Registered profl. engr., Mo., Fla., Ohio. Mem. IEEE (sr.), Am. Legion, Sigma Xi, Tau Beta Pi, Phi Eta Sigma, Eta Kappa Nu, Pi Mu Epsilon. Club: Rotary. Author: Network Computer Analysis, 1969. Contbr. articles to profl. jours. Home: 2402 Middlesex Dr Toledo OH 43606 Office: Samborn Steketee Otis Evans Inc 1001 Madison Ave Toledo OH 43606

ZODDA, ALFRED TRAVIS, chem., pharm. and health care co. internat. exec.; b. N.Y.C., Feb. 26, 1920; s. Charles and Ermalinda (Russo) Z.; B.A. cum laude (Downer scholar), Coll. City N.Y., 1940; M.A. (Rev. Dumas fellow), Fordham U., 1942; m. Jean Naydan, Nov. 28, 1942; children—Alfred Travis, Christie Ann, Deni Michael. Instr. Romance langs. Iona Coll., also Maryknoll Sem., 1941-43; radio news editor for Latin Am., United Press Assns., 1943-44; sales promotion writer Merck & Co., Inc., Export, 1944- 45; with E.R. Squibb & Sons, 1945-67, successively publs. editor export, asst. export advt. mgr., export advt. mgr., overseas promotion mgr., gen. mgr. Squibb Internat. div., 1945-57, v.p. Olin Mathieson Internat. div., 1957-60, v.p. Olin Mathieson Chem. Corp., N.Y.C., 1960-63; pres., gen. mgr. Conat Internat. Corp., Garden City, N.Y., 1963-67; pres. Kent Rubber Corp., 1966-67, Bishop Industries, Inc. Internat., 1967-71; v.p. Damon Corp., 1971-75, sr. v.p., 1975—, also chief operating officer, dir.; exec. v.p., chief operating officer, dir. Delmed Corp., 1978—; dir. Medi Corp. Mem. nat. adv. com. Sch. World Bus. and Internat. Devel.; mem. Bishop's Com. for L.I. Diocesan High Sch. Fund, chmn. Woodbury sect.; mem. World Trade Council. Home: 54 Highland Circle Wayland MA 01778

ZODHIATES, SPIROS GEORGE, assn. exec.; b. Cyprus, Mar. 13, 1922; s. George and Mary (Toumazou) Z.; came to U.S., 1946, naturalized, 1949; student Am. U., Cairo, 1941-45; B.Th., Shelton Coll., 1947; M.A., N.Y. U., 1951; Th.D., Luther Rice Sem., 1978; m. Joan Carol Wassel, Jan. 10, 1948; children—Priscilla, Lois Zodhiates Jenks, Philip, Mary. Ordained to ministry Gen. Assn. Regular Baptist Chs., 1947; gen. sec. Am. Mission to Greeks (name changed to AMG Internat. 1974), Ridgefield, N.J., 1946-65, pres., 1965—. Served with Brit. Army, 1943-46. Recipient Gold Cross, Greek Red Cross, 1951. Author numerous Bible-study books and booklets including: Behavior of Belief, 1959; The Pursuit of Happiness, 1966; To Love is to Live, 1967; Getting the Most Out of Life, 1976; Life after Death, 1977; editor-in-chief Voice of the Gospel, 1946—, Pulpit Helps, 1975—. Home: 8927 Villa Rica Chattanooga TN 37421 Office: 6815 Shallowford Rd Chattanooga TN 37421

ZOFFER, H. JEROME, educator, univ. dean; b. Pitts., July 23, 1930; s. William and Sarah Leah (Fisher) Z.; B.B.A., U. Pitts., 1952, M.A., 1953, Ph.D., 1956; C.P.C.U., Am. Inst., Phila., 1954; m. Maye Rattner, July 19, 1959; children—Gayle Risa, William Michael. Sales and mgmt. cons., 1952-60; instr. Sch. Bus. Adminstrn., U. Pitts., 1953-56, asst. prof., 1956-59, asso. prof. Grad. Sch. Bus., 1959-66, prof., 1966—, chmn. dept. real estate and ins., 1958-60, dir. spl. studies Grad. Sch. Bus., 1960-62, asst. dean for acad. affairs, 1962-65, asso. dean for adminstrn., 1965-68, dean, 1968—. Dir., Eckstein Co., Penn Traffic Co., Red Bull Inns of Am., Inc. Ford Found. fellow in applied math. U. Pa., Phila., 1961-62; mem. visitation com. Am. Assembly Collegiate Schs., 1972-74, mem. standards com., 1974-78, mem. ops. com., 1975—, chmn. accreditation research com., 1974—; chmn. Middle States Evaluation Accrediting Teams, 1967—. Bd. dirs., v.p. Leadership Inst. for Community Devel., 1968-73; bd. dirs., v.p. Allegheny chpt. Epilepsy Found. Am., 1971-77; bd. dirs. Pitts. Dist. Export Council, 1974—; bd. govs. Internat. Ins. Seminars, Inc., 1965-76. Mem. Am. Econ. Assn., AAUP, Soc. C.P.C.U., Am. Risk and Ins. Assn., Soc. for Psychol. Study Social Issues, Inst. Mgmt. Scis., Middle Atlantic Assn. Colls. Bus. Adminstrn. (pres. 1972-73), Am. Assn. Univ. Adminstrs. (dir., exec. com. 1971-79, pres. 1975-77), Omicron Delta Gamma, Beta Gamma Sigma (pres. Beta chpt. 1964-68). Author: The History of Automobile Liability Insurance Rating: 1900-1958, 1959; also monographs. Contbr. articles to profl. jours. Home: 5620 Aylesboro St Pittsburgh PA 15217

ZOGHBY, LINDA VICTORIA, soprano; b. Mobile, Ala., Aug. 17, 1949; d. Emile Joseph and Josephine (Koury) Zoghby; B.Mus., Fla. State U., 1971, M.Mus., 1974; postgrad. Juilliard's Am. Opera Center, 1974-75; m. Daryl Eugene Noll, Feb. 19, 1978. Appeared with Dallas Civic Opera, Columbus (Ohio) Symphony, New Orleans Symphony, Indpls. Symphony, Opera Omaha, Grand Rapids Symphony, Nat. Symphony, Opera Assn. Western Mich., Houston Grand Opera, Handel and Haydn Soc. Boston, Glyndebourne Opera, New Orleans Opera, Santa Fe Opera, Hawaii Opera, Israel Philharm.; recs. for Phillips Phonogram, Decca. Recipient 1st place award Young Artists Awards of Nat. Assn. Tchrs. of Singing, 1972; winner Auditions of the Air, WGN, Chgo., 1973. Roman Catholic. Office: 165 W 57th St New York NY 10019

ZOGRAFI, GEORGE D., pharm. scientist, univ. adminstr.; b. N.Y.C., Mar. 13, 1936; s. Elias D. and Parashgeva Z.; B.S., Columbia U., 1956, D.Sc. (hon.), 1976; M.S., U. Mich., 1958, Ph.D., 1961; m. Dorothy Ann Gordon, June 16, 1957; children—Thomas E., Paul M., Anna J., Ellyn J. Asst. prof. pharmacy Columbia U., 1961-64; asst. prof. U. Mich., 1964-67, asso. prof., 1967-72; prof. U. Wis., Madison, 1972—, dean Sch. Pharmacy, 1975—; cons. to industry. Am. Found. Pharm. Edn. Gustavus Pfieffer research fellow, 1970-71. Mem. Am. Chem. Soc., AAAS, Am. Pharm. Assn., Am. Assn. Colls. Pharmacy, Am. Inst. History Pharmacy. Unitarian. Contbr. numerous articles to profl. publs. Home: 1037 Seminole Hwy Madison WI 53711 Office: U Wis Sch Pharmacy Madison WI 53706

ZOHN, HARRY, educator, author; b. Vienna, Austria, Nov. 21, 1923; s. Abraham Leon and Adele (Awin) Z.; came to U.S., 1940, naturalized, 1945; B.A., Suffolk U., Boston, 1946; M.A. in Edn., Clark U., 1947; A.M., Harvard, 1949, Ph.D., 1952; Litt.D. (hon.), Suffolk U., 1976; m. Judith Ann Gorfinkle, Sept. 3, 1962; children—Steven David, Marjorie Eve. Credit investigator Credit Bur. Greater Boston, 1941-46; teaching fellow German Harvard, 1947-51; mem. faculty Brandeis U., 1951—, prof. German, 1967—, also chmn. dept. Germanic and Slavic langs., 1967-77, chmn. Sch. Humanities council, 1978—; exec. dir. Goethe Soc. New Eng., 1963-68. Mem. adv. com. fgn. langs. Commonwealth Mass., 1961-64. Decorated officer's cross Order Merit (Fed. Republic Germany), 1960. Mem. Austro-Am. Assn. Boston (chmn. bd. 1965—), Internat. Stefan Zweig Soc. (v.p. 1957—), Austrian PEN Club, Am. PEN Center, Am. Assn. Tchrs. German (pres. Mass. chpt. 1954-59), Am. Translators Assn. (dir. 1970-71, 76), New Eng. Modern Lang. Assn. (past sec.-treas., Mass. chmn., dir.). Author: Wiener Juden in der deutschen Literatur, 1964; Karl Kraus, 1971. Editor: Liber Amicorum Friderike Zweig, 1952; Wie sie es sehen, 1952; Schachnovelle, 1960; Men of Dialogue, 1969; Der farbenvolle Untergang, 1970; Greatness Revisited, 1971; Deutschland, Deutschland ueber alles, 1972; The Saints of Qumran, 1977. Translator books by Theodor Herzl, Kurt Tucholsky, Karl Kraus, Jacob Burckhardt, Walter Benjamin, others. Home: 48 Davis Ave West Newton MA 02165 Office: Shiffman Hall Brandeis Univ Waltham MA 02154

ZOLIK, EDWIN STANISLAUS, educator, psychologist; b. Brockton, Mass., June 28, 1924; s. Stanislaw and Amelia (Marozik) Z.; B.S., Tufts U., 1949; M.A., Cath. U. Am., 1952, Ph.D., 1956; m. Margaret Mary Montgomery, June 10, 1950. Clin. psychologist, also instr. U. Portland, 1955-56; asst. prof., clin. psychologist Marquette U., 1956-60; project dir. Forgotten Families project Nat. Inst. Mental Health grant, Rockford, Ill., 1959-60; exec. dir., co- project dir. No. Va. Mental Health project Nat. Inst. Mental Health grant, 1960-65, chmn., 1963—, asso. prof. psychology De Paul U., Chgo., 1963-64, prof., dir. Bur. Psychol. Services, 1964—, also chmn. dept. Cons., Dept. Mental Hygiene and Hosp. Va., 1960-64, U.S. Govt., 1961-64; vis. lectr. psychology dept. psychiatry Harvard Med. Sch., 1968-69. Served with USNR, 1942-46. Fellow Am. Psychol. Assn., A.A.A.S., Am. Pub. Health Assn.; mem. Eastern, Midwestern psychol. assn., Am. Group Psychotherapy Assn. Contbr. articles to profl. jours. Home: 5816 N Maplewood Ave Chicago IL 60649 also: 235 W Edgewater Dr Falmouth MA 02536

ZOLINE, JOSEPH TOBE, industrialist; b. Chgo.; Sept. 5, 1912; s. Nathan J. and Sophie (Tobe) Z.; Ph.B., U. Chgo., 1935, J.D. summa cum laude, 1935; m. Janice Kahnweiler, June 28, 1939; children—Pamela, Patricia, Thomas Anthony. Admitted to Ill. bar, 1935; asso. firm Ryan, Condon & Livingston, Chgo., 1935-42, Gottlieb, Schwartz & Friedman, 1942-50; partner firm Friedman, Zoline & Rosenfield, Chgo., 1950-59; exec. v.p. Hilton Credit Corp., Los Angeles, 1959-61; exec. dir. Chgo. Thoroughbred Enterprises, Inc., 1961-62; pres., chief exec. officer MSL Industries, Inc., Chgo., 1963-70, chmn. bd., 1964-70, also dir.; pres. Telluride Co. (Colo.), 1971-79, now dir. Bd. dirs. Los Angeles Emphysema Found. Mem. U. So. Calif. Assos. Mem. Am., Ill., Chgo. bar assns., Order of Coif, Phi Beta Kappa. Clubs: Beverly Hills Tennis; Standard (Chgo.). Home: 624 N Canon Dr Beverly Hills CA 90210 Office: PO Box 1071 Beverly Hills CA 90210

ZOLL, PAUL MAURICE, physician; b. Boston, July 15, 1911; s. Hyman and Molly (Homsky) Z.; A.B. summa cum laude, Harvard, 1932, M.D., 1936; m. Janet F. Jones, Oct. 28, 1939; children—Ross Holman, Mary Janet. Intern, Beth Israel Hosp., Boston, then Bellevue Hosp., N.Y.C., 1936-39; practice medicine, specializing in cardiology, Boston, 1939—; med. research Beth Israel Hosp., 1939—, asst. in medicine to physician, 1947—; med. research Harvard Med. Sch., 1939—, research fellow in medicine to clin. prof. medicine, 1941—; cons. cardiology Boston hosps. Served from 1st lt. to maj. M.C., AUS, 1941-45. Decorated Legion of Merit; recipient John Scott award City of Phila., 1967; Eugene Drake Meml. lectr. and award Maine Heart Assn., 1968; 1st Wenckebach Meml. lectr., Groningen, Netherlands, 1973; Albert Lasker award for clin. med. research, 1973; named Man of Year, Boston Latin Sch., 1974. Mem. Mass. Med. Soc., Am. Heart Assn., Am. Fedn. Clin. Research, Assn. Am. Physicians, Phi Beta Kappa, Sigma Xi. Asso. editor Circulation, 1956-65. Pioneer electric cardiac pacemaker, 1952, cardiac monitor, 1955, external countershock defibrillator, 1956. Home: 261 Brookline St Newton Centre MA 02159 Office: 319 Longwood Ave Boston MA 02115

ZOLOTOW, CHARLOTTE SHAPIRO, pub. co. exec., editor, author; b. Norfolk, Va., June 26, 1915; d. Louis J. and Ella F. (Bernstein) Shapiro; student U. Wis., 1933-36; m. Maurice Zolotow, Apr. 14, 1938 (div. 1969); children—Stephen, Ellen. Editor children's book dept. Harper & Row, N.Y.C., 1938-44, sr. editor, 1962-70, v.p., asso. pub. Harper Jr. Books, 1976—; tchr. U. Colo. Writers Conf. on Children's Books, U. Ind. Writers Conf.; also lectr. children's books. Author: The Park Book, 1944; Big Brother, 1960; The Sky Was Blue, 1963; The Magic Words, 1952; Indian Indian, 1952; The Bunny Who Found Easter, 1959; In My Garden, 1960; Not a Little Monkey, 1957; The Man With The Purple Eyes, 1961; Mr. Rabbit and the Lovely Present, 1962; The White Marble, 1963; A Rose, A Bridge and A Wild Black Horse, 1964; Someday, 1965; When I Have a Little Girl, 1965; If It Weren't for You, 1966; Big Sister, Little Sister, 1966; All That Sunlight, 1967; When I Have A Son, 1967; My Friend John, 1968; Summer Is, 1968; Some Things Go Together, 1969; The Hating Book, 1969; The New Friend, 1969; River Winding, 1970, 79; Lateef and His World, 1970; Yani and His World, 1970; You and Me, 1971; Wake Up and Goodnight, 1971; William's Doll, 1972; Hold My Hand, 1972; The Beautiful Christmas Tree, 1972; Janie, 1973; My Grandson Lew, 1974; The Summer Night, 1974; The Unfriendly Book, 1975; It's Not Fair, 1976; Someone New, 1978; others. Mem. Pen Soc., Authors League. Home: 29 Elm Pl Hastings-on-Hudson NY 10706 Office: 10 E 53d St New York City NY 10022

ZOLOTOW, MAURICE, writer; b. N.Y.C., Nov. 23, 1913; s. Harry and Pauline (Edelstein) Z.; student N.Y. U., 1932-33; B.A., U. Wis., 1936; m. Charlotte Shapiro Apr. 14, 1938 (div. 1969); children—Stephen, Ellen. Mem. editorial staff Billboard mag., 1936-37; publicity work for actors, theatrical personalities, 1937-39; contbr. articles N.Y. Times Sunday mag., 1939-41; drama critic, essayist, contbg. editor Theatre Arts mag., 1953-58; lectr. non-fiction writing Ind. U. Summer Writers' Workshop, 1958, 59, 63, Colo. U. Writers Conf., 1968; lectr. Writers Digest Writers' Conf., 1967; leader workshop Rocky Mt. Summer Writers Conf., 1968. Mem. Am. Soc. Journalists and Authors (founder, 1st pres.). Author: Never Whistle in a Dressing Room, 1944; (novel) The Great Balsamo, 1946; No People Like Show Peoples, 1951; It Takes All Kinds, 1952; (novel) Oh Careless Love, 1959; Marilyn Monroe, 1960; Stagestruck: The Romance of Alfred Lunt and Lynn Fontanne, 1965; Shooting Star: A Biography of John Wayne, 1974; Billy Wilder in Hollywood, 1977; biog. studies movie, radio, TV and stage stars for nat. mags.; short stories pub. in Reader's Digest, Sat. Evening Post, Cosmopolitan, Good Housekeeping, McCalls, Esquire, Look, Los Angeles Mag., Playboy; collaborator: (with Allan Sherman) A Gift of Laughter, 1967; contbr. N.Y. Sunday Times drama sect., 1943-65; contbg. editor Los Angeles Mag. Address: 8440 Fountain Ave Hollywood CA 90069

ZOLTAI, TIBOR ZOLTAN, educator; b. Gyor, Hungary, Oct. 17, 1925; s. Nicholas Z. and Elizabeth (Schmidt) Z.; student Poly. U., Budapest, Hungary, 1944, U. Graz (Austria), 1946-48, Sorbonne, Paris, France, 1949-50; B.A.Sc., U. Toronto, 1955; Ph.D., Mass. Inst. Tech., 1959; m. Olga Maria Wagner, Nov. 18, 1950; children—Peter, Kartharina, Lilian. Came to U.S., 1955, naturalized, 1966. Mem. faculty U. Minn., 1959—, prof. mineralogy, 1964- -, chmn. dept. geology and geophysics, 1963-71. Fellow Mineral Soc. Am., Geol. Soc. Am.; mem. Am. Crystallographic Assn., Mineral. Assn. Can., Am. Inst. Profl. Geologists, Profl. Engrs. Province Ont. Research crystal structure determination, mineralogy and crytallography. Home: 799 Heinel Dr St Paul MN 55113 Office: Dept Geology and Geophysics Univ Minn Minneapolis MN 55455

ZONDAG, CORNELIUS HENRY, educator; b. The Hague, Netherlands, July 10, 1913; s. John Cornelius and Joan (Schilte) Z.; came to U.S., 1940, naturalized, 1949; Ph.D., Leyden (Netherlands) U., 1940; M.A., N.Y. U., 1949; M.C.L., Washington U., 1953; postgrad. Am. U., 1953. Asst. to mgr. Internat. Catalytic Oil Processes Corp., N.Y.C., 1940-42; aux. fgn. service office, 1942-45; asst. to div. head Socony Mobil Oil Co., N.Y.C., 1945-50; loan officer IBRD, Washington, 1950-54; econ. adviser U.S. Ops. Mission to Bolivia, 1954-57; acting dir. U.S. Ops. Mission to Colombia, 1959-60; chief of field party, Peru, 1961-64; devel. planning adviser U.S. AID Mission, Karachi, Pakistan, 1964-67; chief agrl. imports div. Vietnam Bur., AID, 1967-69; chief pvt. enterprise div. U.S. AID Mission, Afghanistan, 1969-74; prof. Ariz. State U., 1974—. Mem. Am., Western econ. assns., Soc. Internat. Devel., World Future Soc., Internat. Solar Energy Soc. Author: The Bolivian Economy, 1952-65, 1966; also articles. Address: 10730 Loma Blanca Dr Sun City AZ 85351

ZONDERVAN, PETER JOHN (PAT), publisher, religious orgn. exec.; b. Paterson, N.J., Apr. 2, 1909; s. Louis and Nellie Petronella (Eerdmans) Z.; student. pub. schs. Grandville, Mich.; D.Litt. (hon.), John Brown U., 1969; Litt.D., Lee Coll., 1972; m. Mary Swier, May 21, 1934; children—Robert Lee, Patricia Lucille, William J., Mary Beth. Co-founder, Zondervan Pub. House, Grandville, Mich., 1931, Grand Rapids, Mich., 1932—; pres., treas. Zondervan Music Pubs., Grand Rapids, 1955—; pres. Singspination, Inc. Pres., Grand Rapids Camp of Gideons, 1938-41, chaplain, 1944-46, pres., 1947-48, internat. trustee, 1950-52, v.p. Gideons Internat., 1952-55, pres., 1956-59, treas., 1972-75, chaplain, 1975-78. Bd. dirs. Christian Nationals Evangelism Commn., San Jose, Calif.; bd. dirs. Winona Lake Christian Assembly, Ind., 1937—, sec., 1961—; dir. Marantha Bible and Missionary Conf. Muskegon, Mich., 1961; organizer, 1st chmn. Christian Businessmen's Com., Grand Rapids, 1942; chmn. com. for city-wide Evangelistic meeting, 1946. Honored with declaration of P.J. Zondervan Day in Grand Rapids, Dec. 1973. Mem. Internat. Platform Assn. Clubs: Lotus (pres. 1949, 65-67) (Grand Rapids); Peninsular; Blythefield Country. Office: Zondervan Corp 1415 Lake Dr SE Grand Rapids MI 49506*

ZOOK, DONOVAN QUAY, fgn. service officer; b. Akron, Ohio, Oct. 22, 1918; s. David Blough and Lena May (Landis) Z.; A.B., Ohio U., 1940; adminstrv. intern Nat. Inst. Pub. Affairs, 1940-41; M.A., Am. U., 1946; m. Theresa Fuetterer, June 21, 1941; children—Theodore Alan, Jacqueline Deborah (Mrs. Campbell Carrington Cochran IV). Budget and planning examiner U.S. Housing Authority, 1940-42; adminstrv. analyst OPA, 1942-43; staff Office Shore Establishments and Indsl. Personnel, Navy Dept., 1943-44; chief personnel classification div. Fgn. Econ. Adminstrn., 1945-46; asst. chief mgmt. office Office Chief of Staff, War Dept., 1946-47; mgmt. cons. Dept. State, 1947-49, exec. officer Office Departmental Adminstrn., 1949-51, spl. asst. to dep. under-sec. of state, 1951-53, exec. asst. to asst. sec. state, controller, 1953-55, spl. asst. to dep. under-sec. state, 1955-57; chief polit. sect. Am. embassy, Santiago, Chile, 1957-59, counselor for polit. affairs, 1959-61; dep. chief of mission and counselor of embassy, Montevideo, Uruguay, 1961-63; exec. dir. Bd. Examiners for Fgn. Service, Washington and chief recuitment and exam. div. Dept. State, 1963-65, consul gen., 1965; dir. Office of Atomic Energy Affairs, 1965-73, cons. to sec. state's adv. com. on sci. and fgn. affairs, 1973-74, also com. on sci. and tech. cooperation between Japan and U.S., 1975, survey of tech. and fgn. affairs, 1976; sr. adviser to U.S. del. to Inter-Am. Nuclear Energy Commn., also mem. U.S. del. Gen. Conf. and bd. govs. IAEA, 1965-72; State Dept. rep. Joint Bd. Examiners USIA, 1963-65, lectr. Fgn. Service Inst., 1949-52; mem. U.S. del. 4th UN Conf. on Peaceful Uses Atomic Energy; mem. Mem. State Dept. Adv. Council on Personnel, 1952-53, dep. examiner Bd. Fgn. Service Examiners, 1951-54; exec. sec. U.S. Bd. of Fgn. Service, 1953-57. Recipient Superior Honor award State Dept., 1968. Mem. Am. Fgn. Service Assn., Diplomatic and Consular Officers, Am. Soc. Santiago, Soc. Advancement Mgmt., Civil Service Assembly U.S. and Can., Chilean-N.A. Cultural Inst., Soc. Personnel Adminstrn., Somerset Hist. and Geneal. Soc., Soc. Pub. Adminstrn., Am. Assn. Uruguay, Mennonite Hist. Assos., Phi Beta Kappa, Tau Kappa Alpha, Phi Eta Sigma. Presbyn. Clubs: Union, University (Santiago); Lions (Las Condes, Chile); Uruguay, Carrasco Polo (Montevideo); Cantegril Country (Punta del Este, Uruguay). Contbr. profl. jours. Home: 2104 Wakefield St Stratford on the Potomac Alexandria VA 22308 also Mount Glen Orchard Rd Shanghai WV 25427 Office: Bur Oceans and Internat Environ and Sci Affairs Dept State Washington DC 20520

ZOOK, ELVIN GLENN, plastic surgeon, educator; b. Huntington County, Ind., Mar. 21, 1937; s. Glenn Hardman and Ruth (Barton) Z.; B.A., Manchester Coll., 1959; M.D., Ind. U., 1963; m. Sharon Kay Neher, Dec. 11, 1960; children—Tara E., Leigh A., Nicole L. Intern, Meth. Hosp., Indpls., 1963-64; resident in gen. and thoracic surgery Ind. U. Med. Center, Indpls., 1964-69; resident in plastic surgery Ind. U. Hosp., Indpls., 1969-71, asst. prof. plastic surgery, 1971-73; asso. prof. surgery So. Ill. U., Springfield, 1973-75, prof., 1975—, chmn. div. plastic surgery, 1973—; mem. staff Meml. Med. Center, St. Johns Hosp., Springfield; cons. Marion (Ill.) VA Hosp. Chmn. program com. So. Ill. U. Sch. Medicine Explorer Scouts, Boy Scouts Am. Diplomate Am. Bd. Surgery, Am. Bd. Thoracic Surgery, Am. Bd. Plastic Surgery. Mem. Assn. Acad. Surgery, Shumacker Surg. Soc., AMA, Am. Soc. Plastic and Reconstructive Surgery (asst. sec. 1979-81), Midwestern Soc. Plastic and Reconstructive Surgery, A.C.S., Sangamon County Med. Soc., Am. Cleft Palate Assn., Am. Assn. Plastic Surgery, Plastic Surgery Research Council (chmn. 1981), Am. Burn Assn., Ill. Surg. Soc., Am. Soc. Surgery Hand (council), Am. Soc. Aesthetic Plastic Surgery. Presbyterian. Clubs: Sangamo, Springfield Med., Island Bay Yacht. Editor: Kleinert Soc. Newsletter; asso. editor Plastic Surgery Update Series. Contbr. articles to med. jours. Home: 42 Hazel Dell Springfield IL 62707 Office: 800 N Rutledge St Springfield IL 62702. *Do the best possible in all that is possible.*

ZOOK, HARRY DAVID, chemist, univ. dean; b. Milroy, Pa., Feb. 8, 1916; s. Samuel Milton and Emma (Smucker) Z.; B.S., Pa. State U., 1938, Ph.D., 1942; M.S., Northwestern U., 1939; m. Margaret Olsen, Dec. 20, 1947; children—Stephen Michael, Terri. Faculty, Pa. State U., University Park, 1941—, prof. chemistry, 1960—, asst. v.p. research, 1965—, asso. dean grad. sch., 1970—; vis. lectr. Stanford, 1962-63. Mem. Am. Chem. Soc., Chem. Soc. London. Author: (with R.B. Wagner) Synthetic Organic Chemistry, 1953. Home: 828 N Thomas St State College PA 16801 Office: 207 Old Main University Park PA 16802

ZOOK, JOHN ELDON, profl. football player; b. Garden City, Kans., Sept. 24, 1947; s. Milford Eldon and Bernice Sally (Smith) Z.; B.S. in Edn., Kans. U., 1969. Defensive end Atlanta Falcons Profl. Football Team, 1969-75, St. Louis Cardinals Profl. Football Team, 1976—. Player Pro Bowl Game, 1974. Democrat. Methodist. Address: care St Louis Cardinals 200 Stadium Plaza Saint Louis MO 63102*

ZORINSKY, EDWARD, U.S. senator; b. Omaha, Nov. 11, 1928; B.S. in Chemistry and Zoology, U. Nebr., 1949; postgrad. Harvard U., 1966; m. Cece Rottman, 1950; children—Barry, Jeffrey, Susan. Engaged in wholesale tobacco and candy bus.; mayor Omaha, 1973-77; mem. U.S. Senate, 1977—; mem. Omaha Pub. Power Dist. Bd., 1968, Nebr. Jud. Qualifications Commn., 1968; mem. urban econ. policy com. U.S. Conf. Mayors, 1973-76. Served to capt., Mil. Police, U.S. Army. Mem. Internat. Footprinters Assn., Omaha Press Club, Res. Officers Assn. Clubs: Downtown Optimists, Eagles, Elks. Office: 432 Russell Senate Office Bldg Washington DC 20510

ZORN, EUGENE CHRISTIAN, JR., banker; b. N.Y.C., Jan. 17, 1916; s. Eugene Christian and Charlotte (Bode) Z.; B.B.A., Coll. City N.Y., 1937; M.S., Columbia, 1942; m. Elizabeth Orban, Aug. 11, 1956; children-Barbara Jean, Robert Eugene. Dir. research, dep. mgr. Am. Bankers Assn., N.Y.C., 1952-60; v.p., economist Republic Nat. Bank of Dallas, 1960-66, sr. v.p., economist, 1966—, also mem. exec. com., trust, trust investment and funds mgmt. com. mem. faculty Southwestern Grad. Sch. Banking, Stonier Grad. Sch. Banking. Mem. U.S. comptroller Currency's Cons. Com. Bank Economists, 1964-77, chmn., 1974-77; dir. Minibanc Capital Corp., 1976-77; mem. bus. com. on nat. policy Nat. Planning Assn.; Bd. dirs. Tex. Research League, 1965-74, Tex. Council Econ. Edn., 1968-72; mem. adv. com., mem. tech. subcom. Tex. Energy Adv. Council; mem. fin. adv. council Tex. Tech U., 1979—; active Goals for Dallas; mem. Greater Dallas Planning Council Econ. Research Com., 1970, Environ. and Urban Design Com., 1979—. Served to capt. USAAF, 1943-46. Recipient Alumni Achievement award Bernard Baruch Coll., 1968. Mem. Am. Econ. Assn., Am. Finance Assn., Am. Mgmt. Assn., Nat. Assn. Bus. Economists, Nat., Dallas economists clubs, Dallas Art Assn., Am. Banker's Assn. (mem. econ. adv. com. 1970-74, chmn. urban devel. com. 1976-77, gov. council 1976-77), Fin. Mgmt. Assn., So. Finance Assn., Am. Statis. Assn., Newcomen Soc., Southwestern Social Sci. Assn., Dallas Council World Affairs, Dallas (bus. and econ. research com. 1963-69) U.S. (banking, monetary and fiscal affairs com. 1967-76) chambers commerce, Dallas Press Club, Alliance Française, Beta Gamma Sigma. Club: Northwood (Dallas). Home: 4647 Hallmark Dr Dallas TX 75229 Office: PO Box 225961 Dallas TX 75265

ZORN, ROMAN JOSEPH, educator; b. River Falls, Wis., Nov. 21, 1916; s. Henry Vincent and Elizabeth (Heinz) Z.; B.Ed., Wis. State Coll., River Falls, 1937; M. Philosophy, U. Wis., 1940, Univ. Grad. fellow history, 1941-42, Ph.D., 1953; m. Ann Anderson, June 3, 1946; children—Frances, Carolyn, Marian, Kathryn. Instr., then asst. prof. history U. Ark., 1945-50; vis. asst. prof. history U. Mo., 1950-51; asst. prof. Ohio U., 1951-52; asst. prof., then asso. prof. U. Wis., 1953-60, dir. extension center, Green Bay, 1953-60; dean Coll. Arts and Scis., prof. history U. R.I., 1960-64; pres. Keene (N.H.) State Coll., 1964-69; pres. prof. history U. Nev., Las Vegas, 1969-73, prof. history, 1973—; spl. work 19th century U.S. history. Mem. Orgn. Am. Historians, Am., So. hist. assns., Am. Soc. for Pub. Adminstrn., Nat. Soc. Profs., NEA, Assn. Higher Edn., AIM (pres.'s council), Am. Acad. Polit. and Social Sci., Phi Alpha Theta, Kappa Delta Pi, Phi Kappa Phi, Pi Kappa Delta. Author articles, book reviews. Home: 1591 Gabriel Dr Las Vegas NV 89109 Office: Univ Nevada Las Vegas NV 89154

ZORNES, MILFORD, artist; b. Camargo, Okla., Jan. 25, 1908; s. James Francis and Clara Delphine (Lindsay) Z.; student Otis Art Inst., Los Angeles, 1929, Pomona Coll., 1930-34; m. Gloria Codd, 1935; 1 son, Franz Milford; m. 2d, Patricia Mary Palmer, Nov. 8, 1942; 1 dau., Maria Patricia. Instr. art Pomona Coll., 1946-50; art dir. Vortox and Padua Hills Theatre, Claremont, 1954-66; exhibited Calif. Water Color Soc., Met. Mus., Am. Watercolor Soc., Corcoran Gallery, Bklyn. Mus., Denver Mus., Cleve. Mus., Los Angeles Mus., Brooks Gallery, London, Bombay Art Assn., Chgo. Art Inst., Butler Mus., Gallery Modern Masters, Washington, Santa Barbara (Calif.) Museums, Cin. Museums, Laguna (Calif.) Art Gallery, Oklahoma City Mus., Springville (Utah) Mus.; represented in permanent collections at Los Angeles Museums, White House Collection, Met. Museums, Pentagon Bldg., Butler Museums, U. Calif. at Los Angeles, Nat. Acad., San Diego Mus., Los Angeles County Fair, Home Savs. and Loan Assn., Los Angeles. Mem. art com. Nat. Orange Show, San Bernardino, Calif., 1963-65. Served with U.S. Army, 1943-45; CBI. Mem. Am., Calif. (past pres.), West Coast watercolor socs. Author: A Journey to Nicaragua, 1977. Address: PO Box 24 Mount Carmel UT 84755. *It has been my effort in life to have awareness: not to have all knowledge because no one can encompass all knowledge; not to have only wealth or only success, because there is no dimension of completeness of wealth or success; not to achieve complete goodness, because goodness and right are relative; not to enjoy the epitomy in taste because taste is a gratification of self alone; but rather to seek and achieve understanding of relative values and a concept of the completeness of life. With this as my effort and my inner goal, I find success within the areas of my limited abilities, my meager knowledge, and my frail grasp of the infinite.*

ZORNOW, WILLIAM FRANK, educator; b. Cleve., Aug. 13, 1920; s. William Frederick Emil and Viola (Schulz) Z.; A.B., Western Res. U., 1942, A.M., 1944, Ph.D., 1952. Vice pres., treas. Glenville Coal & Supply Co., Real Value Coal Corp., Zornow Coal Corp., 1941-45; dep. clk. Probate Ct., Cuyahoga County, Ohio, 1941-43; prodn. planning engr. Hickok Elec. Instrument Co., Cleve., 1943-46; teaching asst. Western Res. U., 1944-47; instr. U. Akron, 1946-47, Case Inst. Tech., 1947-50, Washburn U., 1950-51; lectr. Cleve. Coll., 1948-49; asst. prof. Kans. State U., 1951-58; asst. prof. history Kent (Ohio) State U., 1958-61, asso. prof., 1961-66, prof. history, 1966—; collection corr. Berkshire Loan and Fin. Co., Painesville (Ohio, Security Credit Acceptance Corp., Mentor, O., 1951-60; cons. Karl E. Mundt Library, Dakota State Coll., Madison, S.D. Mem. Am. Acad. Polit. and Social Sci., Am. Assn. State and Local History (award of merit 1958), Am. Hist. Assn., Orgn. Am. Historians, Ohio Acad. History (chmn. awards com.), Ohio Hist. Soc. (library advisory com. 1969—), Ohio Soc. N.Y., Delta Tau Delta, Pi Gamma Mu, Phi Alpha Theta, Phi Delta Kappa. Author: Lincoln and the Party Divided, 1954, rev. edit., 1972; Kansas: A History of the Jayhawk State, 1957; America at Mid-Century, 1959; contbr.: Abraham Lincoln: A New Portrait, 1959; Kansas: The First Century, 1956; contbr. articles to encys. and profl. jours.; editor Shawnee County (Kans.) Hist. Bull., 1950-51; abstractor America: History and Life: Historical Abstracts, 1964—. Home: 7893 Middlesex Rd Mentor OH 44060 Office: Kent State U Kent OH 44262

ZORTHIAN, BARRY, communications exec.; b. Kutahia, Turkey, Oct. 8, 1920; s. Herbert Peter and Annaly (Markarian) Z.; came to U.S., 1923, naturalized, 1930; B.A., Yale U., 1941; LL.B., N.Y. U., 1953; LL.D., Ind. Inst. Tech., 1970; m. Margaret Aylaian, June 6, 1948; children—Gregory Jannig, Stephen Arnak. Newspaper reporter, 1936-42; newspaper and radio reporter, 1947-48; with Voice of Am., USIA, 1948-61, program mgr., 1956-61; dep. pub. affairs. officer USIS, India, 1961-64; minister-counselor for info. Am. embassy, Vietnam, 1964-68; v.p. Time, Inc., 1969, v.p. govt. affairs, 1974—; pres. Time-Life Broadcast, 1969-73; admitted to N.Y. bar, 1953. Bd. dirs. Armenian Gen. Benevolent Union, Internat. Coll., Overseas Devel. Council, Mag. Pubs. Assn., Meridian House. Served with USMCR, 1942-46, col. Res. ret. Mem. Council on Fgn. Relations, Am. Fgn. Service Assn., Bus.-Govt. Relations Council, Marine Corps Res. Officers Assn. Conglist. Clubs: Century Assn., (N.Y.C.); Congressional Country, Metropolitan, Cosmos, Federal City (Washington). Home: 4201 Cathedral Ave NW Washington DC 20016 Office: Time Inc 888 16th St NW Washington DC 20006

ZOTTER, WALTER JAMES, lawyer; b. Port Huron, Mich., Sept. 24, 1933; s. Carl and Josephine (Ropposch) Z.; B.A., U. Notre Dame, 1955; LL.B., U. Detroit, 1962; m. Ann Meyer, Sept. 11, 1965; children—Jean, Michael. Admitted to Mich. bar, 1963; practiced law Detroit, 1963—; asso. firm Martin, Bohall, Joselyn et al., Detroit, 1963-69; v.p. Coticchio, Zotter & Sullivan, P.C., Detroit, 1969—. Arbitrator Am. Arbitration Assn., 1965—. Served with USAF, to 1st. lt., 1955-58. Mem. Mich., Am., Wayne County, Macomb bar assns., Assn. Def. Trial Counsel. Roman Catholic. Home: 37818 Via Rosalie Mt Clemens MI 48043 Office: Coticchio Zotter & Sullivan 2640 Buhl Bldg Detroit MI 48226

ZOUBEK, CHARLES EDWARD, editor; b. N.Y.C., Feb. 2, 1913; s. Charles Alois and Emilie (Vavrica) Z.; LL.D., Rider Coll., 1972; m. Annabell Barnes, Aug. 23, 1938; children—Charles, Lee, Roxanne, Martin. Editor Gregg Pub. Co., N.Y.C., 1930-48; editor-in-chief McGraw-Hill Pub. Co., N.Y.C., 1949—; instr. evening sch. Hunter Coll. Hon. mem. N.Y. State Shorthand Reporters Assn., Nat. Shorthand Reporters Assn. Co-author: Gregg Shorthand Simplified Series; Gregg Shorthand Diamond Jubilee Series; Gregg Shorthand, Series 90. Home: Meads Point Greenwich CT 06830 Office: 1220 6th Ave New York City NY 10020

ZOWSKI, THADDEUS, mech. engr.; b. Ann Arbor, Mich., Mar. 19, 1914; s. Stanislaw Jan and Felicia (Kruszka) Z.; B.S. in Mech. Engring., Poly. Inst., Warsaw, Poland, 1939; M.S. in Mech. Engring., U. Mich., 1941; m. Eloise Rhodes Clay, Jan. 15, 1944. Mech. engr. S. Morgan Smith Co., York, Pa., 1941-47; with Harza Engring. Co., Chgo., 1947—, chief mech. engr., 1950—, asso., 1957-68, v.p., mem. sr. profl. staff, 1968—, prin. mech. engr., 1979—. Registered profl. engr., Pa., Wash. Fellow ASME (life); mem. ASCE, Nat. Soc. Profl. Engrs., Ill. Soc. Profl. Engrs., Iota Alpha. Republican. Co-author: Davis' Handbook of Applied Hydraulics, 1969; contbr. articles to tech. mags. and profl. jours. Office: 150 S Wacker Dr Chicago IL 60606

ZOX, LARRY, artist; b. Des Moines, May 31, 1936; s. Oscar and Mildred (Friedman) Z.; student Okla. U., 1955-56, Drake U., 1957, Des Moines Art Center, 1955-57; m. Jean Marilyn Glover, July 19, 1965; children—Melinda, Alexander Cassidy. Exhibited one man shows at Am. Gallery, N.Y.C., 1962, Kornblee Gallery, N.Y.C., 1964-66, 68, 69, 70, 71, Andre Emmerich Gallery, 1973, 75, 76, Whitney Mus. Am. Art, 1973, Galerie Rocke, Cologne, Germany, 1968, Janie C. Lee Gallery, Houston, 1974, others; group shows at Am. Gallery, 1963, Am. Fedn. Art, 1963-65, Mus. Modern Art, N.Y.C., 1964, Albright-Knox Art Gallery, Buffalo, 1964, Washington Gallery Modern Art, 1964, Gallery Modern Art, N.Y.C., 1965, Tibor de Nagy, N.Y.C., 1965, ann. Whitney Mus., N.Y.C., 1965-70, one-man retrospective, 1973, Art Inst. Chgo., 1965, Kornblee Gallery, 1966, Guggenheim Mus., N.Y.C., 1966, Expo Am. Pavilion, 1967, Palm Springs Desert Mus., 1973, Daniel Templon Gallery, Paris, 1975, Andre Emmerich Gallery, 1975, others; represented in permanent collections Am. Republic Ins. Corp., Des Moines, J. & L. Hudson Co., Detroit, Joseph H. Hirshhorn Mus., U.S. Steel Corp., Mus. Modern Art, N.Y.C., Philip Johnson Collection, Dallas Mus. Fine Arts, Des Moines Art Center, Indpls. Mus., Whitney Mus.; artist in residence Juniata Coll., Huntingdon, Pa., 1964, U. N.C., 1967; vis. critic Cornell U., summer 1967; faculty Sch. Visual Arts, 1967-68, 69-70, 70-76, Yale, summer, 1972, Kent State U., summer 1974. Recipient Nat. Council Arts award, 1969; Guggenheim fellow, 1967. Office: care Andre Emmerich Gallery 41 E 57th St New York NY 10022*

ZSIGMOND, ELEMER KALMAN, anesthesiologist; b. Budapest, Hungary, May 16, 1930; s. Elemer Zeykvary and Terez (Kartori) Z.; came to U.S., 1956, naturalized, 1966; M.D., U. Budapest, 1955; m. Kathryn Fogarasi, Oct. 19, 1953; 1 son, Zoltan William. Intern, Med. Clinics, U. Budapest, 1954-55; intern Allegheny Gen. Hosp., Pitts., 1960-61, resident in anesthesiology, 1961-63; resident in internal medicine Hosp. Sztalinvaros and Cardiac Sanatorium, Balatonfured, Hungary, 1955-56; cardiologist, dir. lab. Cardiologic Inst., Balatonfured, 1956-57; dir. anesthesia research lab. Mercy Hosp., Pitts., 1957-60; clin. research fellow Anesthesiology Allegheny Gen. Hosp., 1963-66, clin. anesthesiologist, dir. anesthesiology research labs., 1966-68; prof. anesthesiology Med. Sch., U. Mich., Ann Arbor, 1968-79, U. Ill. Med. Sch., 1979—; mem. staff Univ. Hosp., U. Ill., Chgo. Diplomate Am. Bd. Anesthesiology. Fellow Am. Coll. Anesthesiologists, Am. Coll. Clin. Pharmacologists; mem. Am. Soc. Anesthesiologists, Internat. Anesthesia Research Soc., N.Y. Acad. Scis., AAAS, AMA, Mich., Washtenaw County med. socs. Contbr. numerous articles on anesthesiology, neuropharmacology, and pulmonary physiology to profl. jours. Home: 6609 N LeRoy Ave Lincolnwood IL 69646 Office: U Ill Med Center 840 S Wood St Chicago IL 60612. *My father's motto for one of his books has been my principle: "Every man represents as much worth to society as he is willing to give from himself to his fellowman."*

ZSIGMOND, VILMOS, cinematographer; b. Szeged, Hungary, June 16, 1930; came to U.S., 1957, naturalized, 1962; s. Vilmos and Bozena (Illichmann) Z.; M.A., U. Film and Theater Arts, Budapest, Hungary, 1955; children—Julia, Susi. Free-lance cinematographer for numerous commercials, also ednl., documentary and low-budget feature films, 1965-71, feature films, 1971—; films include: The Hired Hand, McCabe and Mrs. Miller, 1971, Images, 1972, Deliverance, 1972, The Long Goodbye, 1973, Scarecrow, 1973, Cinderella Liberty, 1973, The Sugarland Express, 1974, Obsession, 1976, Close Encounters of the Third Kind (Acad. award 1977), 1977, The Last Waltz, 1978, The Rose, 1978, The Deerhunter, 1978, Heavens Gate, 1979. Mem. Acad. Motion Picture Arts and Scis., Am. Soc. Cinematographers. Club: Malibu (Calif.) Tennis Racquet. Office: 9301 Wilshire Blvd Suite 208 Beverly Hills CA 90210

ZSISSLY. see Albright, Malvin Marr

ZUBAY, GEOFFREY LOUIS, molecular biologist; b. Chgo., Nov. 15, 1931; m. Louis and Lillian (Nordsieck) Z.; Ph.B., U. Chgo., 1949, M.S., 1952; Ph.D., Harvard U., 1957; m. Bongsoon Cho, Aug. 13, 1966; 1 son, Geoffrey Pyong. NIH and NSF postdoctoral fellow London U., 1957-59; research asso. Rockefeller Inst., 1960-61; asst. biochemist Brookhaven Nat. Lab., Upton, N.Y., 1962-63; asso. prof. biol. sci. Columbia U., 1964-72, prof., 1973—. NIH grantee, 1964-79; NSF grantee, 1964-79; Am. Chem. Soc. grantee, 1969-79; Damon Runyon Meml. Fund grantee, 1968-71. Mem. AAAS, Fedn. Am. Soc. Exptl. Biol. Chemists. Contbr. articles to profl. publs.; editor: Papers in Biochemical Genetics, 1968, 2d rev. edit. (with J. Marmur), 1973. Home: N01 Shinnecock Pl Hampton Bays NY 11946 Office: Fairchild Center for Biol Scis Columbia U New York NY 10027

ZUBER, JAMES WILLIAM, publisher; b. Columbus, Ohio, May 22, 1911; s. John William and Minnie Z.; B.A., Ohio State U., 1933; m. Suzanne N. Baumann, Aug. 3, 1935; children—Ann Zuber Wilson, Sally Zuber Anderson, James D. With Penton Pub. Co., Cleve. until 1955; founder Hudson Pub. Co. div. Litton Industries, Los Altos, Calif., 1955, also pres.; pub. Hudson Home Guides, Hudson Home Plans, Bantam-Hudson Books; ret., 1979. Presbyterian. Home: PO Box 1234 Carmel Valley CA 93924 Office: 289 S San Antonio Los Altos CA 94022

ZUBKOFF, MICHAEL, educator; b. N.Y.C., June 2, 1944; s. Harry and Catherine (O'Brien) Z.; B.A., Am. Internat. Coll., 1965; M.A., Columbia, 1966, certificate Internat. Fellows program, 1967, Ph.D., 1969; m. Sandralee Rayner, Feb. 20, 1964; children—Steve, Joel, Lisa. Instr. econs. Harvard-Yale-Columbia Summer Intensive Studies program, 1967-69; research asso. for conservation human resources Columbia, 1967-69; Woodrow Wilson Found. teaching fellow Fisk U. and Meharry Med. Coll., Nashville, 1969-70; asso. prof. health econs., asso. chmn. dept. family and community health Meharry Med. Coll., 1969-75; asso. prof. health econs. Vanderbilt U., 1970-75; prof., chmn. dept. community and family medicine Med. Sch. Dartmouth, 1975—, prof. health econs. Amos Tuck Sch. Bus. Adminstrn., 1975—; sr. research asso. Center Policy Research, N.Y.C., 1969-75; cons. in field. Pres. Med. Com. Human Rights, Nashville, 1971-75; chmn. Tenn. Health Cost Containment Commn., 1973; dir. Vanderbilt Summer Program in Israel, 1973; del., health spokesman White House Summit on Inflation, 1974. Bd. dirs. ACLU, 1971-75, treas., 1972-74; bd. dirs. House Between, 1971-75, treas., 1972-75, Mid South Regional Med. Program, 1973-75; bd. dirs. N.H. United Health Systems Agy., 1976—, Vt. Lung Center, 1976—; mem. Nat. Acad. Scis., Assembly Engrs./Inst. Med. com. on tech. and health care, 1976—; mem. Grad. Med. Ednl. Nat. Adv. Com., 1977—. Woodrow Wilson fellow, 1965-67; Fulbright fellow, 1967-68; USPHS fellow, 1968-69; Robert Wood Johnson health policy fellow Inst. Medicine Nat. Acad. Scis., 1975-76. Mem. Am. Econ. Assn., Am. Pub. Health Assn. Co-author: Urban Health Services: The Case of New York, 1971; Consumer Incentives for Health Care, 1974; Framework for Government Intervention in the Health Sector, 1978; Health: A Victim or Cause of Inflation, 1976; Hospital Cost Containment: Selected Notes for Public Policy, 1978; Health Economics: A Systems and Market Analysis, 1979. Contbr. numerous articles to profl. jours. Home: 15 Rope Ferry Rd Hanover NH 03755 Office: Dept Community and Family Medicine Dartmouth Med Sch Hanover NH 03755

ZUBROD, CHARLES GORDON, physician; b. N.Y.C., Jan. 22, 1914; s. Charles Augustus and Anna (Beyer) Z.; A.B., Holy Cross Coll., 1936; M.D., Columbia, 1940; D.Sc., Holy Cross Coll., 1969; m. Christina Catherine Mullins, June 15, 1940; children—Christine, Gordon, Justin, Margaret, Stephen. Intern, asst. resident Presbyn. Hosp., N.Y.C., 1942-43; mem. faculty Johns Hopkins Med. Sch., 1946-53, asst. prof. medicine, 1949-53; asso. prof. medicine St. Louis U. Sch. Medicine, 1953-54; mem. staff Nat. Cancer Inst., NIH, 1954-74, sci. dir. for chemotherapy, 1966-72, dir. div. cancer treatment, 1972-74; dir. Comprehensive Cancer Center for State of Fla., 1974—; prof., chmn. dept. oncology U. Miami (Fla.) Sch. Medicine, 1974—. Mem. Mt. Desert Island Biol. Lab., 1948—. Served to capt. M.C., AUS, 1943-46. Recipient Distinguished Service award HEW, 1965; Silver Bicentennial Medallion for Medicine, Coll. Phys. and Surgeons, Columbia, 1967; Lasker award, 1972, Heath award, 1974; Distinguished Service award Am. Cancer Soc., 1976. Mem. Am. Soc. Pharm. and Exptl. Therapeutics, Am. Soc. Clin. Investigation, Assn. Am. Physicians, Am. Assn. Cancer Research (pres. 1977), Am. Assn. Cancer Insts. (pres. 1978), Am. Soc. Hematology, Soc. Scholars (Johns Hopkins). Home: 177 Ocean Lane Dr Key Biscayne FL 33149 Office: Comprehensive Cancer Center for State of Fla 1400 NW 10th Ave Miami FL 33152

ZUCK, ALFRED MILLER, govt. ofcl.; b. East Petersburg, Pa., Aug. 27, 1934; s. Walter Newton and Mary Magdalena (Miller) Z.; A.B., Franklin and Marshall Coll., 1957; M.Pub. Adminstrn., Syracuse U., 1958; m. Geraldine Delia Connelly, July 21, 1957; children—Susan L., David A. Mgmt. intern Dept. Labor, Washington, 1958-60, program analyst, 1960-63, budget officer, 1963-66, adminstrv. officer, 1966-67; dir. fed. programs Pres.'s Council on Youth Opportunity, 1967-68; dir. Office of Evaluation, 1968-70, asso. manpower adminstr. for data mgmt., 1970-71, asso. manpower adminstr. fin. and mgmt. info. systems Dept. Labor, 1971-73, asso. manpower adminstr. Office Adminstrn. and Mgmt., 1973-75, comptroller of dept., 1975-77, asst. sec. labor, 1977—. Recipient William A. Jump Meml. award, 1970. Mem. Am. Soc. Pub. Adminstrn., Phi Beta Kappa, Pi Gamma Mu, Kappa Sigma. Mem. United Ch. of Christ. Home: 1733 Abby Oak Dr Vienna VA 22180 Office: Asst Sec Adminstrn and Mgmt Dept Labor 200 Constitution Ave NW Washington DC 20210

ZUCKER, ALEXANDER, physicist; b. Zagreb, Yugoslavia, Aug. 1, 1924; s. William and Bertha (Klopfer) Z.; came to U.S., 1939, naturalized, 1943; B.A., U. Vt., 1947; M.S., Yale U., 1948, Ph.D., 1950; m. Joan-Ellen Jamieson, Nov. 28, 1953; children—Rebecca Marie, Claire Louise, Susannah Katherine. Research asst. Yale U., 1948-50; physicist Oak Ridge Nat. Lab., 1950-53, sr. physicist, 1953-60, asso. div. dir., 1960-70, dir. heavy ion project, 1972-74, asso. dir. phys. scis., 1973—; exec. dir. environ. studies bd. Nat. Acad. Scis.-Nat. Acad. Engring., 1970-72; prof. physics U. Tenn., Knoxville, 1968-72; mem. U.S. del. to USSR on peaceful uses of atomic energy, 1963; del. Pugwash Conf., 1971; mem. com. on nuclear sci. and nuclear physics panel NRC. Served with AUS, 1943-45. Guggenheim fellow, Fulbright research scholar, 1966-67. Fellow Am. Phys. Soc., AAAS; mem. Internat. Union Pure and Applied Physics (U.S. nat. com.), Gas Research Inst. (research inst. coordinating panel), Phi Beta Kappa, Sigma Xi. Home: 103 Orange Ln Oak Ridge TN 37830 Office: PO Box X Oak Ridge TN 37830

ZUCKER, MARJORIE BASS, physiologist; b. N.Y.C.; d. Murray H. and Agnes (Naumburg) Bass; A.B., Vassar Coll., 1939; Ph.D., Columbia U., 1944; student Columbia U. Coll. Phys. and Surg., 1943-45; m. Howard D. Zucker, Jan. 25, 1938; children—Andrew, Ellen, Joan, Barbara. Research asst. physiology Columbia U. Coll. Phys. and Surg. N.Y.C., 1945-49; asst. prof. physiology N.Y. U. Coll. Dentistry, 1949-54, asso. prof., 1954-55; asso. mem. Sloan Kettering Inst. Cancer Research, N.Y.C., 1955-63; asso. prof. physiology Sloan Kettering div. Grad. Sch. Med. Sci., Cornell U. Med. Coll., N.Y.C., 1955-63; mem. grad. faculty N.Y. U., 1955, 63—, asso. prof. pathology, 1963-71, prof., 1971—; asst. research dir. Am. Nat. Red Cross Research Lab., N.Y. U. Med. Center, 1963-70; mem. hematology study sect. NIH, 1970-74, mem. internat. com. thrombosis and haemostasis, 1970-76; mem. rev. com. B., Nat. Heart Lung Blood Inst. Fellow N.Y. Acad. Scis.; mem. Am. Physiol. Soc., Harvey Soc., Soc. Exptl. Biology and Medicine, Soc. Study Blood, Internat. Soc. Hematology, Internat. Soc. Thrombosis and Haemostasis. Mem. editorial bd. Proc. of Soc. Exptl. Biology and Medicine, 1960-65, 1976—, Am. Jour. Physiology, 1969-74, Thrombosis and Haemostasis, 1972—, Blood, 1975-79. Home: 333 Central Park West New York City NY 10025

ZUCKER, NORMAN LIVINGSTON, polit. scientist, author; b. N.Y.C., Aug. 1, 1933; s. George Meyer and Beatrice Lillian (Livingston) Z.; B.A., Rutgers U., 1954, M.A., 1956, Ph.D., 1960; m. Naomi Judith Flink, June 25, 1961; children— Sara, George. Asst. prof. polit. sci. Tufts U., Medford Mass., 1962-66; asso. prof. polit. sci. U. R.I., Kingston, 1966-69, prof., 1969—; manuscript cons. to pubs. Wurzweiler Found. grantee, 1963; Am. Philos. Soc. grantee, 1964. Mem. Am. Polit. Sci. Assn., New Eng. Polit. Sci. Assn., AAUP. Author: The Coming Crisis in Israel: Private Faith and Public Policy, 1973; The American Party Process, 1968; George W. Norris, 1968. Home: 11 Locust Dr Kingston RI 02881 Office: Dept Polit Sci U RI Kingston RI 02881

ZUCKERMAN, HARRIET, sociologist, educator; b. N.Y.C., July 19, 1937; d. Harry and Anne D. (Wiener) Zuckerman; A.B., Vassar, 1958; Ph.D., Columbia, 1965. Asst. prof. sociology Columbia, 1965-72, asso. prof., 1972-78, prof., 1978—, chmn. dept., 1978-81; vis. scholar Russell Sage Found., 1971-72; mem. adv. bd. Social Sci. Citation Index, Inst. Sci. Information, 1972—; dir. Annual Revs., Inc., 1974—; trustee Am. Savs. Bank, 1978—. Bd. dirs. Social Sci. Research Council, 1974-76, AAAS, 1980—; trustee Center for Advanced Study in Behavioral Scis., 1976—. Woodrow Wilson fellow, 1958-59; Center for Advanced Study in Behavioral Scis. fellow, 1973-74. Author: Scientific Elite: Nobel Laureates in the United States, 1977; co-editor: Toward A Metric of Science: The Advent of Science Indictors, 1978; mem. editorial bd. Scientometrics, 1977—, Am. Jour. Sociology, 1972-74, 77-79, Am. Sociol. Rev., 1972-74; contbr. articles to profl. jours. Address: Dept Sociology Columbia U New York NY 10027

ZUCKERMAN, IRWIN, economist; b. New Rochelle, N.Y., July 29, 1920; s. A.B. and Selma (Gordon) Z.; A.B., U. N.C., 1941; M.A., Yale U., 1974; m. Marilyn Sherman, Dec. 12, 1946 (div. 1979); children—Samuel Geoffrey, Anne Barbara, Edward Ellis; m. Marie Tree, Aug. 26, 1979. Asst. economist OPA, Washington, 1941-42; with Hudson Pulp & Paper Corp., N.Y.C., 1946-64, exec. v.p., 1959-64; pres. Irwin A. Zuckerman, Inc., bus. mgrs. 1964—; mem. faculty dept. econs. Evergreen State Coll., Olympia, Wash.; past chmn. Parallel Planning Corp. Lectr. econs. Yale, 1975; vis. lectr. U. Mass., 1976-77. Past mem. Mayor's Com. Indsl. Leaders Youth, N.Y.C. Past pres., dir. Nat. Parkinson Found., Inc.; former vice chmn. bd. trustees New Lincoln Sch., N.Y.C. Served to lt. USNR, 1942-46. Recipient Submarine combat insignia with 3 gold stars. Mem. Nat. Inst. Pub. Affairs (interne), Phi Beta Kappa (past chpt. pres.), Phi Beta Kappa Assos. (life). Home: 3520 Sunset Beach Dr Olympia WA 98502 Office: Evergreen State Coll Olympia WA 98505

ZUCKERMAN, STUART, psychiatrist, educator; b. Syracuse, N.Y., Feb. 18, 1933; s. George and Cassie (Kolsan) Z.; student U. Kans., 1950-51; B.S. U. Ala., 1954; D.O., Phila. Coll. Osteo. Medicine, 1958. Rotating intern Hosps. Phila. Coll. Osteo. Medicine, 1958-59; psychiat. fellow, resident Phila. Mental Health Clinic, 1959-62, Psychoanalytic Studies Inst., Phila., 1959-62, chief resident, 1962; chief div. neuropsychiatry Grandview Hosp., Dayton, Ohio, 1962-65; asst. med. dir., chief children's and adolescent's unit N.J. State Hosp., Ancora, 1967-70, chief outpatient dept., Atlantic City, 1970-72; practice specializing in neuropsychiatry, Atlantic City, 1965-76; founding prof. psychiatry, chmn. dept. Ohio U. Coll. Osteo. Medicine, Athens, 1976-77, clin. prof., 1977—; mem. faculty U. Pa. Sch. Medicine, Phila. Coll. Osteo. Medicine, 1972-76; lectr. U. Pa., 1977-79; prof. dept. psychiatry Sch. Medicine, Marshall U., 1977-78, clin. prof., 1979—; clin. prof. N.Y. Coll. Osteo. Medicine, 1979—; chief mental hygiene VA Hosp., Huntington, W.Va., 1978-79; liaison psychiatrist VA Med. Center, Perry Point, Md., 1979—; med. dir. Mental Hygiene Clinic of Ocean County, Toms River, N.J., 1980—; attending psychiatrist Atlantic City, Shore Meml., Kessler Meml., Washington Meml., Atlantic County Mental hosps., 1965-76; attending psychiatrist, asst. dir. dept. psychiatry Phila. Gen. Hosp., 1972-76; med. dir. Shawnee Mental Health Center (Adams, Lawrence, Scioto counties), Portsmouth, Ohio, 1977-78; cons. psychiatrist Scioto Meml., So. Hills, Mercy hosps., Portsmouth, 1977—; cons. psychiatrist Lansdowne Community Mental Health Center (Greenup, Carter counties), Ashland, Ky., 1977—, Obleness Meml. Hosp., Clin. Services of Athens, Vinton, Hocking Counties, Hudson Health Center, Ohio U., Athens Mental Health and Mental Retardation Center, 1976-77; cons. child study spl. services S. Jersey sch. systems; chmn. profl. adv. com. Atlantic County Mental Health Bd., 1969-71; mem. nominating com. Mental Health Assn. Atlantic County, 1972-75; mem. hosp. inspection team Am. Osteo. Assn., 1971-75; exam. psychiatrist Jersey Police, Fire depts. Bd. dirs. Atlantic County Family Services Assn., 1968-74, Cape May County Drug Abuse Council, 1973-76. Diplomate Am. Osteo. Bd. Neurology and Psychiatry, Am. Nat. Bd. Psychiatry. Fellow Royal Soc. Health; mem. Internat., Am., Md. psychiat. assns., Am., N.J. pub. health assns., Am. Osteo. Assn., AAUP, Am. Soc. for Law and Medicine, Am. Acad. Clin. Psychiatrists, Am. Med. Writers Assn., Am. Soc. Criminology. S. Jersey Neuropsychiat. Soc., Phila. Psychiat. Soc., Am. Coll. Legal Medicine, Acad. for Psychiatry and Law, Am. Acad. Forensic Scis., Am. Assn. Acad. Psychiatry, Am. Coll. Emergency Physicians, Am. Acad. Psychotherapists, Am. Assn. on Mental Deficiency, Acad. Psychosomatic Medicine, N.J., Calif. assns. osteo. physicians and surgeons, N.J. Hosp. Assn., Am. Vocat. Assn., Am. Assn. Group Therapy, Assn. Mil. Surgeons U.S., Nat. Assn. VA Physicians, Am. Assn. Psychiat. Adminstrs., Am. Assn. Adolescent Psychiatry, World Med. Assn., Am. Assn. Mental Health Adminstrs., Am. Assn. Gen. Hosp. Psychiatrists, Am. Physicians Fellowship, Assn. for Research Nervous and Mental Diseases, Atlantic County Osteo. Med. Soc. (pres. 1970-72). Mem. adv. bd. Osteo. Physician, 1975—; asso. editor Bull. Am. Coll. Neuropsychiatrists, 1963-70. Contbr. articles to profl. jours. Home: 6700 Atlantic Ave Ventnor NJ 08406 Office: Ventnor Mental Health Center Ventnor NJ 08406

ZUCKERT, DONALD MACK, advt. exec.; b. N.Y.C., Apr. 3, 1934; s. Sidney L. and Doris (Mack) Z.; A.B. in Govt. with honors, Bowdoin Coll., 1956; LL.B., N.Y. U., 1959; m. Susan Liefter; children—Andrew, Timothy. Admitted to N.Y. bar, Conn. bar, 1960; with Ted Bates & Co., Inc., N.Y.C., 1960—, exec. v.p. corp. affairs, mgmt. rep., 1974—, pres. U.S. affiliates, 1979, also mem. exec. com., dir.; dir. AC&R Advt., Inc., Diener/Hauser/Bates & Co., Stern Walters/Earle Ludgin Inc., Sawdan & Bess Inc. Served to capt. AUS, 1956-57. Mem. Am., N.Y., Conn. bar assns., Alpha Tau Omega. Club: Innis Arden Golf (Old Greenwich). Home: 172 Shore Rd Old Greenwich CT 06870 Office: 1515 Broadway New York NY 10036

ZUCKMAN, HARVEY LYLE, educator; b. Mpls., Apr. 14, 1934; s. George and Elizabeth (Polinsky) Z.; A.B., U. So. Calif., 1956; LL.B., N.Y. U., 1959; m. Charlotte Anne Snyder, Jan. 27, 1962; children—Jill Belinda, Beth Nancy, Michael Scott. Admitted to Calif. bar, 1960, D.C. bar, 1973, U.S. Supreme Ct. bar, 1963; atty. civil div. appellate sect. U.S. Dept. Justice, Washington, 1963-67; prof. law St. Louis U., 1967-70; prof. law Columbus Sch. Law of The Catholic U.

of Am., 1970—; adj. prof. communications Am. U., 1976—; cons. Bur. Nat. Affairs. Served with U.S. Army Judge Adv. Gen., 1960-63. Mem. Am. Law Inst., Assn. Am. Law Schs., D.C. Bar (chairperson com. on continuing legal edn. 1975—). Democrat. Exec. producer: Am. Law Inst.-Am. Bar Assn. Legal Edn. TV series, 1973-74. Author: (with Martin Jay Gaynes) Mass Communications Law, 1977. Office: Columbus School of Law The Catholic University of America Leahy Hall Washington DC 20064

ZUEHLKE, RICHARD WILLIAM, educator; b. Milw., June, 17, 1933; s. Harold Babcock and Phoebe Blanche (Frykman) Z.; B.S., Lawrence Coll., 1955; Ph.D., U. Minn., 1960; m. Carol Sue Yates, Dec. 26, 1955; children—Kenneth Richard, William Woodfill, Deanne Elizabeth. Instr. chemistry Lawrence U., 1958-62, asst. prof., 1962-68; Eliphalet Remington prof. chemistry U. Bridgeport, 1968-79, chmn. dept., 1968-73; vis. prof. U. R.I., 1979—; cons. Kimberly-Clark Corp., 1960-62, United Illuminating Co., 1969-75, Chem. Specialties Corp., 1970-73, Sperry Remington Corp., 1976—. NSF Sci. Faculty fellow U. Pitts., 1966-67; vis. prof. U. R.I., 1976-77. Fellow Am. Inst. Chemists; mem. Am. Chem. Soc., AAAS, Am. Geophys. Union, New Eng. Assn. Chemistry Tchrs., Sigma Xi, Sigma Phi Epsilon. Congregationalist. Home: 350 Burnt Plains Rd Milford CT 06460 Office: Grad Sch Oceanography U RI Kingston RI 02881

ZUELZER, W. W., physician; b. Berlin, May 24, 1909; s. George and Edith (Wolf) Z.; M.D., Prague German U., 1935, Wayne State U., Detroit, 1943; m. Margery Jenks, 1938 (dec. 1966); children—Barbara, Jacqueline; m. 2d, Ruby Thompson, 1967. Postgrad. tng. in pediatrics Cambridge (Mass.) City Hosp., 1935-36, Mass. Gen. Hosp., Boston, 1937, in contagious diseases Charles V. Chapin Hosp., 1936, in pathology Boston Children's Hosp., 1938, Children's Meml. Hosp. and Otho. S.A. Sprague Meml. Inst., 1939-40; pathologist, dir. lab. medicine Children's Hosp. Mich., 1940-74, hematologist-in-chief, 1943-74; dir. Children Research Mich., 1955-75; pres., med. co-dir. Mich. Community Blood Center, 1955-75; cons. pediatrics Sinai Hosp., 1973-75; asso. dir. blood resources and br. chief div. blood diseases and resources Nat. Heart and Lung Inst., 1975, acting dir. div., 1975-76; dir. div. blood diseases and resources Nat. Heart, Lung and Blood Inst., Bethesda, Md., 1976—; from instr. pathology to prof. pediatric research Wayne State U. Med. Sch., 1941-75; chmn. med. advisory bd. Children's Leukemia Found. Mich., 1955-75; guest lectr. U. Newcastle, Newcastle-on-Tyne, Eng., 1970; guest prof. Catholic U., Rome, 1970; chmn. human embryology and devel. study sect. NIH, 1959-63, 68-72; cons. in field. Diplomate Am. Bd. Pediatrics. Mem. Am. (Morten Grove-Rasmussen Meml. award 1976), Mich. (pres. 1964-65) assns. blood banks, Am. Soc. Hematology (v.p. 1962-63), Internat. Soc. Blood Transfusion, Internat. Soc. Hematology, Soc. Europeene d'Hematologie, Am. Acad. Pediatrics (1st Mead Johnson award 1948), Soc. Pediatric Research (pres. 1955-56), Midwest Soc. Pediatric Research, Am. Soc. Human Genetics, Environmental Mutagen Soc., Soc. Study Social Biology, N.Y. Acad. Scis., AAAS, Mich. Soc. Pathologists, Children's Hosp. Alumni Club, Com. Impact Biomed. Research, Detroit Acad. Medicine, Detroit Pediatric Soc. (v.p. 1952-53, pres. 1953-54), Alpha Omega Alpha; emeritus mem. Am. Pediatric Soc., Perinatal Research Soc.; corr. mem. Soc. Suisse de Pediatrie. Contbr. med. jours., mem. editorial bds. med. jours. Home: 1251 Cresthaven Dr Silver Spring MD 20903 Office: NHLBI Nat Insts Health Bethesda MD 20014

ZUERCHER, FREDERICK WILLIAM, polit. scientist; b. Louisville, July 24, 1933; B.S. in Polit. Sci., Northwestern U., 1954; M.A. in Polit. Sci., U. Wyo., 1960; Ph.D. in Polit. Sci. (Haines fellow), UCLA, 1969; m. Nancy Tozer; children—James, William. Intern, City of Laramie (Wyo.), 1959-60; chmn. CSC, Laramie, 1960-61, personnel mgmt. program officer, Nat. Assn. Schs. Public Affairs and Adminstrn.; fellow Bur. Intergovt. Personnel Programs, Civil Service COmmn., Washington, 1972-73; instr. U. Wyo., 1960-61; vis. instr. U. Idaho, summer 1962; asst. prof. polit. sci. U. S.D., Vermillion, 1965-70, asso. prof., 1970-76, prof., 1976—; sec. public safety State of S.D., 1979—; lectr. Am. U. Center Adminstrn. Justice, spring 1973; Bush fellow U. Wis. Inst. for Adminstrv. Advancement, Madison, and John Fitzgerald Kennedy Sch. Govt., Harvard U., summer 1976; program lectr. Nat. Endowment for Humanities. Mem. Am. Polit. Sci. Assn., Am. Soc. Public Adminstrn. (pres. Siouxland chpt. 1969-71), M.W. Polit. Sci. Assn., Policy Studies Assn., Pi Sigma Alpha. Contbr. articles to profl. pubs. Home: 503 Thomas St Vermillion SD 27069 Office: Dept Polit Sci U SD Vermillion SD 57069

ZUIDEMA, GEORGE DALE, surgeon; b. Holland, Mich., Mar. 8, 1928; s. Jacob and Reka (Dalman) Z.; A.B., Hope Coll., 1949; M.D., Johns Hopkins, 1953; D.Sc. (honorary), Hope College, 1969; m. to Joah K. Houtman, June 2, 1953; children—Karen Sue, David Jay, Nancy Ruth, Sarah Kay. Intern Mass. Gen. Hosp., 1953-54, asst. resident surgeon, then chief resident surgeon, 1954, 57, 58, 59; asst. prof. surgery, then asso. prof. U. Mich. Sch. Medicine, 1960-64; prof. surgery, dir. dept. Johns Hopkins Sch. Medicine, also surgeon in chief Johns Hopkins Hosp., 1964—. Cons. Walter Reed Army Med. Center, Sinai Hosp., Balt., Balt. City Hosp., Clin. Center of NIH; chmn. Study on Surg. Services for U.S., 1970-75. Bd. dirs. Md. div. Am. Cancer Soc., 1964—. Served to capt., M.C., USAF, 1954-56. John and Mary R. Markle scholar academic medicine, 1961-66; recipient Henry Russell award U. Mich., 1963. Diplomate Am. Bd. Surgery. Fellow A.C.S., Royal Coll. Surgeons Ireland (hon.); mem. Assn. Am. Med. Colls., Central Soc. Clin. Research, Soc. Univ. Surgeons, Am., So. surg. assns., Soc. Clin. Surgery, Soc. for Vascular Surgery, Internat. Cardiovascular Surgery, Halsted Soc., Nat. Inst. Medicine, Assn. for Acad. Surgeons (pres. 1967-69), Allen O. Whipple Soc., Phi Beta Kappa, Tri Beta, Alpha Omega Alpha. Editor: (with O. H. Gauer) Gravitational Stress in Aerospace Medicine, 1961; (with G. L. Nardi) Surgery-A Concise Guide to Clinical Practice, 1961, 4th edit., 1979; (with R.D. Judge) Physical Diagnosis, 1963, 3d edit., 1973; (with W.F. Ballinger and R.B. Rutherford) Management of Trauma, 1968, 3d edit., 1979; (with L. Schlossberg) Atlas of Human Functional Anatomy, 1977, 2d edit., 1980; editor Jour. Surg. Research, 1966-72, asso. editor, editorial bd., 1972—; mem. editorial bd. Am. Jour Surgery, AMA Archives Surgery, Surgery Ann., 1968—; mem. editorial bd. Surgery, 1970—, co-editor in chief, 1975—. Home: Box 55-D Chapel Ct Timonium MD 21093 Office: Johns Hopkins Hosp Baltimore MD 21205

ZUIDEMA, R(EINER) TOM, educator; b. Haarlem, Netherlands, May 24, 1927; s. Lambertus Ellerus and Trijntje (Zweers) Z.; M.A., Leiden U., Netherlands, 1951, Ph.D., 1962; Ph.D., U. Madrid, Spain. 1953; m. Louisette Wachter, May 30, 1959; children—Paquita, Annegien, Lucho. Curator, State Mus. of Anthropology, Leiden, 1956-64; prof. Anthropology, U. Huamanga, Ayacucho, Peru, 1964-67; prof. anthropology U. Ill., 1967—. Grantee in field. Mem. Royal Dutch Academy Sci., Royal Inst. Anthropology, Am. Anthrop. Assn., Soc. Am. Archaeology. Contbr. articles in field to profl. jours. Office: Davenport Hall University of Illinois Urbana IL 61801

ZUK, WILLIAM, educator; b. N.Y.C., July 6, 1924; s. Alex and Mary (Zelinka) Z.; B.S. in Civil Engring. with distinction, Cornell U., 1944, Ph.D., 1955; M.S. in Engring., Johns Hopkins, 1947; m. Constance Prymak, June 12, 1948; children—Christopher Joseph, William Thomas, Stephanie Anne, Carol Marian. Research engr. Detroit Steel Co., Buffalo, 1947; design engr. Van R.P. Saxe, Balt., 1947-48; instr., then asst. prof. U. Denver, 1948- 52; grad. instr. Cornell U., 1952-55; research engr. Martin Aircraft Co., 1955; mem. faculty U. Va., 1955—, prof. architecture, 1963—, dir. archtl. tech., 1963—; cons. to govt. and industry, 1948—; lectr. numerous univs., U.S. and Europe. Served as ensign USNR, 1944-46; lt. (j.g.) Res. Co-recipient 1st prize internat. architecture competition, San Sebastian, Spain, 1965; recipient Allied Profession award AIA, 1972; named Outstanding Ukrainian-Am. of Year, Md. Ethnic Soc., 1973. Registered profl. engr., Colo., Va. Mem. Am. Soc. Engring. Edn., ASCE, Am. Concrete Inst., Internat. Assn. Bridge and Structural Engrs., Va. Acad. Sci., Sigma Xi, Tau Beta Pi, Phi Epsilon, Delta Chi. Author: Concepts of Structures, 1963; Kinetic Architecture, 1970; also articles. Home: 2622 Jefferson Park Circle Charlottesville VA 22903. *Life to me has become a continuing learning experience. Nature, science, art, people-all provide never completely fathomed sources of knowledge. That the human mind can perceive this knowledge and create from it, is in itself, remarkable. I live in the belief that none of this wonder and delight would be possible without God.*

ZUKAS, ALBERT VICTOR, aircraft co. exec.; b. Cleve., Feb. 18, 1922; s. Albert John and Anna (Anela) Z.; student Kent State U., 1939-40, Fenn Coll., 1940-42, 46-47, Cleve. Marshall Law Sch., 1948-52; M.B.A., Pepperdine U., 1977; m. Harriet T. Thurtle, Oct. 10, 1968; children—Ronald Franklin, Cynthia Diana. Engr., Thompson Products, Inc., Cleve., 1946-48, sales engr., 1948-52; sales engr. Parker Aircraft Co. div. Parker-Hannifin Corp., Los Angeles, 1953-56, area mgr., 1956-58, marketing v.p., 1959-65, pres., 1965-69; v.p. Parker-Hannifin Corp., Los Angeles, 1969-70, sr. v.p., dir., 1970-78; pres., dir. Thiem Industries, Inc., Torrance, Calif., 1979—. Pres. Riviera Homeowners Assn.; mem. adv. bd. Daniel Freeman Hosp. Served with USAAF, 1943-46. Decorated D.F.C. with oak leaf cluster, Air medal with silver oak leaf. Mem. Am. Mgmt. Assn., Am. Inst. Aeros. and Astronautics, Presidents Assn. Mason. Club: Bel Air Country Los Angeles. Office: 1918 W Artesia Blvd Torrance CA 90504

ZUKEL, WILLIAM JOHN, physician; b. Northampton, Mass., June 8, 1922; s. Anthony and Mary (Wendolowska) Z.; B.S., Mass. State Coll., 1943; M.D., Hahnemann Med. Coll., Phila., 1947; postgrad. Harvard Med. Sch., 1952-53; D.P.H., London Sch. Hygiene and Tropical Medicine, 1961; m. Marjorie Cantoni on April 21, 1963. Intern and resident Newton-Wellesley Hosp., Newton Lower Falls, Mass., 1947-50; med. officer charge Newton Heart Program, USPHS, 1950-51, acting chief of heart disease control program, 1952; postgrad. asst. cardiovascular diseases Mass. Gen. Hosp., Boston, 1952- 53; asst. medicine Albany (N.Y.) Med. Coll., also fellow cardiology N.Y. State Health Dept., 1953-55; chief operations research sect. heart disease control program USPHS, 1955-57, asst. dir. Nat. Heart Inst., NIH, 1957-58, asst. for program Office Surgeon Gen., USPHS, 1958-60, with Nat. Heart Inst., 1960-69, asso. dir. collaborative studies, 1962-67, asso. dir. for epidemiology and biometry, 1967-69, asso. dir. for clin. applications and prevention, div. heart and vascular diseases Nat. Heart, Lung and Blood Inst., 1969-79, asso. dir. for program coordination and planning, 1979—. Asso. clin. prof. epidemiology and environ. health George Washington U. Sch. Medicine, 1963-77. Mem. AMA, Mass. Med. Soc., Am. Heart Assn., Am. Pub. Health Assn., Assn. Mil. Surgeons, Am. Coll. Cardiology. Office: Nat Heart Lung and Blood Inst Bethesda MD 20014

ZUKERMAN, GEORGE, bassoonist, impresario; b. Eng.; attended High Sch. Music and Art, N.Y.C., and Queen's Coll.; studied with Leonard Sharrow; m. Nedda. Mem. Israel Philharm., from 1950; prin. bassoonist Vancouver (B.C., Can.) Symphony, 1953-63; soloist, 1960—; founder Overture Concerts; toured N.Am., Australia, N.Z., Asia, Europe; invited to USSR to play with maj. symphony orchs. Former mem. Can. Council Touring Office Adv. Bd. Mem. Am. Fedn. Musicians. *

ZUKERMAN, PINCHAS, concert violinist; b. Tel Aviv, Israel, July 16, 1948; s. Jehuda and Miriam (Lieberman) Z.; came to U.S., 1962, naturalized, 1976; Am.-Israel Cultural Found. scholar, Helena Rubinstein scholar, Juilliard Sch. Music, 1965-68; m. Eugenia Rich, May 26, 1968; 2 daus. With impresario Sol Hurok, 1967-76; concert and recital tours in maj. cities world-wide 1968—; condr., soloist English Chamber Orch., 1974, Mostly Mozart Festival, N.Y.C., 1975; guest condr., soloist Los Angeles Philharm., Boston Symphony, Phila. Orch., N.Y. Philharm.; music dir. South Bank Festival, London, 1978-80, St. Paul Chamber Orch., 1980; tour with Isaac Stern; mem. trio with Daniel Barenboim and Jacqueline du Pre; recorded with CBS, RCA, EMI, DGG recs. Winner, Internat. Levintritt Competition, 1967. Office: care ICM Artists Ltd 40 W 57th St New York NY 10019

ZUKOR, JAMES ROTH, investment co. exec.; b. N.Y.C., July 5, 1931; s. Eugene James and Emma Dorothy (Roth) Z.; B.A., Yale U., 1953; LL.B., Harvard U., 1958; m. Gisela Genenz, Mar. 14, 1962; children—Karen S., Susie A. Admitted to Calif. bar, 1959; sec. Capital Group, Inc., Los Angeles, 1970—, v.p., 1973—; v.p., sec. Capital Research & Mgmt. Co., Los Angeles, 1969—. Served to lt. (j.g.) USNR, 1953-55. Address: 333 S Hope St Los Angeles CA 90071

ZUKOSKI, EDWARD EDOM, engring. educator; b. Birmingham, Ala., June 29, 1927; s. Charles Frederick and Bernadine (Edom) Z.; grad. Asheville Sch., 1946; A.B., Harvard, 1950; M.S., Calif. Inst. Tech., 1951, Ph.D., 1954; m. Joan Fredelia Breckenridge, Dec. 29, 1959; children—Linda Sue, Catherine Reed, Edward Breckenridge. Sr. research engr. Jet Propulsion Lab., Calif. Inst. Tech., 1954-57, mem. faculty, 1957—, prof. engring., 1966—; cons. to aerospace industry, 1957—. Mem. fire. research com. Nat. Acad. Sci., 1965-72. Bd. dirs. Pasadena Planned Parenthood, 1968-75. Served with USNR, 1946-47. Fellow Am. Inst. Aero and Astronautics. Home: 3815 Fairmeads Rd Pasadena CA 91107

ZUKOWSKI, WALTER HENRY, educator; b. Worcester, Mass., Sept. 28, 1914; s. Frank B. and Helen (Jankowska) Z.; B.B.A., Clark U., 1948, A.M., 1949, Ph.D., 1956; m. Lucille Kathryn Pinette, Dec. 26, 1955; 1 dau., Mary L.A. Instr., Worcester Poly. Inst., 1949-50, Clark U., 1951-52; mem. faculty Colby Coll., Waterville, Maine, 1952—, prof. adminstrv. sci., 1965-73, Wadsworth prof. adminstrv. sci., 1973—, chmn. dept. adminstrv. sci., 1958—; asst. prof. La. State U., C.Z. br., summers 1952-54; vis. prof. Rockefeller Found. grantee, Al-Hikma, U., Baghdad, Iraq, 1958-59, Robert Coll., Instanbul, Turkey, 1965-66; vis. prof., cons. ednl. policy Iranzamin Coll., Tehran, Iran, 1972-73; cons. in field, 1956—. Mem. platform com. Maine Republican Party, 1964. Served with USAAF, 1942-46. Mem. Am. Finance Assn., Am. Econ. Assn., Am. Accounting Assn., AAUP. Home: PO Box 402 Waterville ME 04901

ZUMAS, NICHOLAS HARRY, lawyer; b. Helper, Utah, Dec. 23, 1930; s. Harry and Helen (Pappas) Z.; B.A., U. Utah, 1951; J.D., Georgetown U., 1956; m. Catharine Campbell Blackwell, Nov. 20, 1971; children—Helen Mary, Diana Catharine, Gregory. Admitted to Oreg. bar, 1956, D.C. bar, 1957, Va. bar, 1956; law clk. to Chief Justice Ore. Supreme Ct., Salem, 1956-57; asso. firm Koerner, Young, McColloch & Dezendorf, Portland, Ore., 1957-61; asst. to undersec. HEW, Washington, 1962-63; congl. liaison officer U.S. Dept. State, Washington, 1963-66; partner firm Dutton, Zumas & Wise, Washington, 1965—. Panelist, Am. Arbitration Assn., Fed. Mediation and Conciliation Service. Served to lt. AUS, 1951-53. Mem. D.C., Va., Oreg. bars, Nat. Acad. Arbitrators. Home: 3131 P St NW Washington DC 20007 Office: 1140 Connecticut Ave NW Washington DC 20036

ZUMBERGE, JAMES HERBERT, geologist, univ. pres.; b. Mpls., Dec. 27, 1923; s. Herbert Samuel and Helen (Reich) Z.; student Duke, 1943-44; B.A., U. Minn., 1946, Ph.D., 1950; LL.D., Grand Valley State Coll., 1970, Kwansei Gakuin U. (Japan), 1979; L.H.D., Nebr. Wesleyan U., 1972; m. Marilyn Edwards, June 21, 1947; children—John Edward, Jo Ellen, James Frederick, Mark Andrew. Instr., Duke U., 1946-47; mem. faculty U. Mich., 1950-62, prof. geology, 1960-62; pres. Grand Valley State Coll., Allendale, Mich., 1962-68; prof. geology, dir. U. Ariz. Sch. Earth Sci., Tucson, 1968-72; chancellor U. Nebr. at Lincoln, 1972-75; pres. So. Meth. U., Dallas, 1975—. Cons. geologist ground water and non-metallic minerals, 1950-62; dir. Dallas Power and Light Co., Gen. Am. Oil Co.; chmn. vis. com. Gen. Motors Inst., 1977—; ofcl. del. Sci. Com. on Antarctic Research; chmn. com. on internat. polar relations U.S. Polar Research Bd., Nat. Acad. Scis.; chmn. Ross Ice Shelf Project, 1970-73, NSF, also mem. steering group Greenland Ice Sheet Program; del. numerous internat. confs. on polar research, Moscow, 1958, Chamonix, 1958, Helsinki, 1960, Obergurgl, Austria, 1962, Poland, 1967, Oslo, 1970, Sydney, Australia, 1972, Mendoza, Argentina, 1976, Warsaw, 1978; mem. Nat. Sci. Bd., 1974—. Bd. overseers Hoover Instn. on War, Revolution and Peace, 1978—. Recipient Antarctic Service medal, 1966; Distinguished Alumni award U. Minn., 1972; James H. Zumberge Library, Grand Valley State Coll., named 1968; Cape Zumberge, Antarctica named 1960. Mem. Geol. Soc. Am., Am. Geophys. Union, Soc. Econ. Geologists, Glaciological Soc., AAAS, Mich. Acad. Scis. (pres. 1967), Sigma Xi (nat. lectr. 1978-80). Clubs: Cosmos (Washington); Dallas Petroleum; Explorers. Author: The Lakes of Minnesota, 1952; Laboratory Manual for Physical Geology, 1967, 73; Elements of Geology, 1963, 72; Elements of Physical Geology, 1976; also articles. Address: Office of Pres Southern Methodist U Dallas TX 75275

ZUMETA, BERTRAM WILLIAM, economist; b. Rutherford, N.J., Jan. 18, 1919; s. Arthur H. and Bertha A. (Cook) Z.; A.B., Franklin and Marshall Coll., 1940; postgrad. U. Pa., 1946-50, 52-53; m. Ruth Spencer Astbury, Apr. 1, 1943; children—William Mark, David Cook. Lectr., instr. econs., statistics Wharton Sch. U. Pa., 1945-51, 53-63; economist Fed. Res. Bank of Phila., 1959-66; economist Phila. Electric Co., 1966-70; sr. v.p., economist 1st Pa. Bank, 1970-72, asst. to pres., 1972; v.p., economist First Pa. Corp., 1973-74, sr. v.p., economist, 1974-78; exec. v.p., economist First Pa. Bank and First Pa. Corp., Phila., 1978—; dir. Vestaur Securities, Inc., First Pennco Securities. Bd. govs. Pa. Economy League, 1979—; mem. U.S. Sec. of Commerce's Econ. Adv. Bd., 1967-68; mem. Pa. Gov.'s Econ. Adv. Council, 1967-70, 74-76. Served to comdr. USNR, 1942-45, 51-53. Mem. Nat. Assn. Bus. Economists. Home: 717 Avondale Rd Erdenheim PA 19118 Office: 1500 Market St Philadelphia PA 19101

ZUMWALT, DONALD DEAN, curator; b. Audubon, Iowa, Jan. 7, 1931; s. Edmund Walter and Hazel Lola (McCannon) Z.; student Buena Vista Coll., 1950-51, 55-56; A.A., Pasadena City Coll., 1956; B.A. in Biol. Scis., Long Beach State Coll., 1960, postgrad., 1960-61; children—Sheri M., Jennifer L. Seasonal aide Calif. Dept. Fish and Game, San Pedro Lab., 1959-60; asst. curator fishes Marineland of Pacific, Los Angeles, 1960-63; curator fishes Sea World, San Diego, 1963-66; curator fishes John G. Shedd Aquarium, Chgo., 1966-78; biologist Hanna-Barbera Marineland, Los Angeles, 1978—. Served with USAF, 1951-55. Mem. Am. Assn. Ichthyologists and Herpetologists, Am. Fisheries Soc., Am. Assn. Zool. Parks and Aquariums. Office: Box 937 Rancho Palos Verdes CA 90274

ZUMWALT, ELMO RUSSELL, JR., ret. naval officer; b. San Francisco, Nov. 29, 1920; s. Elmo Russell and Frances Z.; B.S. with distinction, U.S. Naval Acad., 1942; student Naval War Coll., 1952-53, Nat. War Coll., 1961-62; LL.D., Villanova U., 1972, U. N.C., 1975, Nat. U., 1979; L.H.D., U.S. Internat. U., 1973; Dr. Pub. Service, Central Mich. U., 1974; D.Sc., Mich. Tech. U., 1979; m. Mouza Coutelais-du-Roche; children—Elmo Russell, James Gregory, Ann F., Mouza C. Commd. ensign U.S. Navy, 1942, advanced through grades to adm., 1970; served with U.S.S. Phelps, 1942-43; tng. at Operational Tng. Command Pacific, San Francisco, 1943-44, with U.S.S. Robinson, 1944-45; exec. officer U.S.S. Saufley, 1945-46; exec. officer, navigator U.S.S. Zellars, 1946-48; asst. prof. naval sci. Naval ROTC, N.C. at Chapel Hill, 1948-50; comdr. U.S.S. Tills, 1950-51; navigator U.S.S. Wisconsin, Korea, 1951-52; head shore and overseas bases sect. Bur. Naval Personnel, Washington, 1953-55; comdr. destroyer U.S.S. Arnold J. Isbell, 1955-57; lt. detailer, Washington, 1957; spl. asst. for naval personnel Office Asst. Sec. Navy, Washington, 1957-58, exec. asst., sr. aide, 1958-59; comdr. U.S.S. Dewey, 1959-61; desk officer for France, Spain and Portugal, Office Asst. Sec. Def. for Internat. Security Affairs, 1962-63, dir. arms control and contingency planning for Cuba, 1963; exec. asst., sr. aide Sec. of Navy, 1963-65; comdr. Cruiser-Destroyer Flotilla Seven, 1965-66; dir. chief naval ops. systems analysis group, Washington Office Chief Naval Ops., dep. sci. officer Center Naval Analyses, 1966-68; comdr. U.S. Naval Forces Vietnam, chief naval adv. group, Vietnam, 1968-70; chief naval ops., Washington, 1970-74; dir. Phelps-Stokes Fund, Esmark, Inc., Transway Internat., Inc., Am. Bldg. Maintenance Industries, Orgn. Resource Counselors, Inc., Tesoro Petroleum Corp.; pres., chief exec. officer, dir. Am. Med. Bldgs., Inc., Milw., 1977-79, vice chmn. bd., 1980—; vis. prof. Vanderbilt U., 1974-75, U. Nebr., 1975, Whittier Coll., 1975. Democratic candidate for U.S. Senate, 1976. Decorated D.S.M. with Gold Star, Legion of Merit with Gold Star, Bronze Star with Combat V, Navy Commendation medal with combat V, also numerous campaign and area citations, medals; Philippine Republic Presdl. citation; Vietnam Campaign medal, Vietnamese Chuong My medal 1st Class, Nat. Order Vietnam 3d Class, Vietnamese Navy Distinguished Service Order 1st class. Author: On Watch, 1976. Address: American Medical Bldgs 735 W Water St Milwaukee WI 53202

ZUMWALT, GLEN WALLACE, educator; b. Vinita, Okla., Apr. 21, 1926; s. Sidney Clyde and Jennie Myrtle (Brown) Z.; B.S., U. Tex., 1949, M.S., 1953; Ph.D., U. Ill., 1959; m. Carol Ruth Cyrus, Dec. 21, 1952; children—Marylee, Janis, Paul, Alan, Karl. Instr., research engr. U. Tex., Austin, 1951-55; research asso. U. Ill., Urbana, 1955-59; mem. faculty Okla. State U., Stillwater, 1959-68, prof. aerospace engring., 1966-68; Distinguished prof. aero. engring. Wichita (Kans.) State U., 1968—. Pres. Zumwalt and Darby, Inc., Perkins, Okla., 1965-72; cons. McDonnell Douglas Astronautics Co., Huntington Beach, Calif., 1961-75, Sandia Corp., Albuquerque, 1961-70, Martin Co., Denver, 1963-64, Douglas Aircraft Co., Tulsa, 1959-64, Gates-Learjet, 1976. Served with USNR, 1944-47. Asso. fellow Am. Inst. Aeros. and Astronautics; mem. Am. Sci. Affiliation, Am. Soc. for Engring. Edn., Sigma Xi, Sigma Tau, Pi Tau Sigma. Baptist. Research in aerodynamics, air foil and wing theory, separated flow theory. Home: 6311 Marjorie Ln Wichita KS 67208

ZUMWALT, RICHARD DOWLING, flour mill exec.; b. Amarillo, Tex., Dec. 1, 1912; s. Richard Dowling and Cora Bell (Pate) Z.; extension student Tex. Tech. Coll., 1931, Dallas Coll., 1949; m. Florine Anita Nelson, Oct. 23, 1938; 1 dau., Alexandra Anita (Mrs. Klaus Schwabe). With J. C. Crouch Grain Co., 1931-44; with Burrus Mills, Inc., Dallas, 1944—, exec. v.p., 1956-64, pres., 1964—; sec.-treas. Zumwalt Inc., 1973—; ret. gen. mgr. Burrus milling dept. Cargill, Inc. Past pres. Bulgur Assos., Washington, Dallas Grain Exchange. Mem. Millers Nat. Fedn., Tex. Mfrs. Assn. (past dir.). Home: 7353 Blairview Dr Dallas TX 75230

ZUMWINKLE, ROBERT GORDON, ednl. adminstr.; b. Pelican Rapids, Minn., May 28, 1921; s. Lyle Edwin and Minnette (Cummings) Z.; B.A., U. Minn., 1943, Ph.D., 1953; m. Lois Elizabeth Bird, July 18, 1945; children—David Robert, Mark Richard, Mary Elizabeth. Counselor, student activities adviser U. Minn., 1946-50; dir. student affairs for men U. Mo., 1950-53; dean students, dir. student personnel services St. Cloud (Minn.) State Coll., 1953-62; asso. dir. Inst. Student Interchange, E.-W. Center, U. Hawaii, 1963-66, dir., 1966-68; v.p. student affairs Eastern Mich. U., 1968-70; v.p. student affairs U. Ky., 1970—; chmn. St. Cloud Dem. Club, 1961-62. Served with USNR, 1943-46. Mem. Am. Assn. for Higher Edn., Am. Coll. Personnel Assn., Am. Personnel and Guidance Assn., Nat. Assn. Student Personnel Adminstrs., Nat. Assn. Fgn. Student Affairs, ACLU (dir. Minn. 1957-62, pres. 1959-61, dir. Hawaii 1965-68), Phi Delta Kappa. Unitarian. Home: 3307 Nantucket Dr Lexington KY 40502

ZUPKO, ARTHUR GEORGE, coll. adminstr.; b. Yonkers, N.Y., Nov. 22, 1916; s. George and Julia (Tutko) Z.; student N.Y. U., 1936-38; B.S., U. Fla., 1942; M.S., Purdue U., 1948, Ph.D., 1949; m. Lillian Belle Cosner, Dec. 20, 1947; 1 son, Arthur Maynard. Research asst. Burroughs Wellcome Co., Tuckahoe, N.Y., 1936-38; asst. prof., asso. prof., prof. St. Louis Coll. Pharmacy, 1949-55, asso. dean, 1955, dean, 1956-60; provost Bklyn. Coll. Pharmacy, L.I. U., 1960-73, pres., 1973-76, pres. Arnold and Marie Schwartz Coll. Pharmacy and Health Scis., 1976—; dir., Mediphone, Inc., U.S. Adapted Names; mem. bd. pharmacy cons. Chas. Pfizer & Co. Chmn. spl. gifts Bklyn. chpt. Am. Cancer Soc., 1963; solicitor ARC, 1962-63; merit badge counselor Hutchinson-Bronx River council Boy Scouts Am., 1963-64; solicitor United Fund, 1961-65; mem. Narcotic Addiction Centers Com., 1960-65; bd. dirs. Korean-Am. Found., Tb and Respiratory Assn., Bklyn.; mem. spl. com. Cooley's Anemia Found. Served with U.S. Army, 1934-36, USNR, 1942-46. Decorated Bronze Star medal. Fellow Am. Found. Pharm. Edn.; mem. Am. Pharm. Assn., Am. Coll. Apothecaries, N.Y. State, Kings County pharm. socs., N.Y. Acad. Pharmacy, AAAS, N.Y. Acad. Sci., Sigma Xi, Rho Chi, Phi Kappa Phi, Phi Lambda Upsilon, Delta Sigma Theta, Alpha Zeta Omega. Roman Catholic. Author: (with Otto Ruhmer) Contributions of Jews to Pharmacy, 1959; Drug Interactions, 1979. Contbr. articles to profl. jours. Home: 22 Warwick Rd Bronxville NY 10708 Office: LI U University Center Brooklyn NY 11201

ZURCHER, LOUIS ANTHONY, JR., social psychologist, educator; b. San Francisco, May 13, 1936; s. Louis Anthony and Kathleen Ursula (Walsh) Z.; B.A. summa cum laude, U. San Francisco, 1961; M.A., U. Ariz., 1963, Ph.D., 1965; m. Susan Lee Shrum, Sept. 13, 1964; children—Stephen Anthony, Lisa Ann, Anthony Walsh, Nora Breen. Research social psychologist Menninger Found., Topeka, 1965-68; mem. faculty dept. sociology, U. Tex., Austin, 1968-78, prof., 1973-78, chmn. dept., 1974-75, prof. Sch. Social Work, 1978—, asso. grad. dean, 1975-78; asso. univ. provost, dean Grad. Sch. Va. Poly. Inst. and State U., 1978, prof. dept. sociology, 1978-79; cons. in field. Served with U.S. Navy, 1955-59. NSF fellow, 1964-65; Abraham Maslow fellow, 1970; recipient numerous grants. Fellow Am. Psychol. Assn.; mem. Assn. Voluntary Action Scholars (pres.), Am. Sociol. Assn., Soc. Study of Social Problems (div. chmn.), Soc. Psychol. Study Social Issues, Soc. Study Symbolic Interaction, Inter-Univ. Seminar Armed Forces and Society (exec. bd.), So. Sociol. Soc., Internat. Sociol. Assn., Western Sociol. Assn., Naval Res. Assn., Southwestern Sociol. Assn. Club: Army and Navy (Washington). Author: From Dependency to Dignity, 1969; Poverty Warriors, 1970; Planned Social Intervention, 1970; Paroled But Not Free, 1973; Citizens for Decency, 1976; The Mutable Self, 1977; Supplementary Military Forces, 1978; editor Jour. Applied Behavioral Sci., 1978—; contbr. articles to profl. jours. Office: Sch of Social Work U Texas Austin TX 78712

ZURHEIDE, CHARLES HENRY, cons. elec. engr.; b. St. Louis, May 9, 1923; s. Charles Henry and Ollie C. (Kirk) Z.; B.S. in Elec. Engring., U. Mo., Columbia, 1944; m. Ruth M. Plueck, June 25, 1949; children—Barbara Anne, Pamela S. Distbn. engr. Laclede Power & Light Co., St. Louis, 1944-45; sub-sta. engr., then indsl. engr. Union Electric Co., St. Louis, 1945-51; chief elec. engr. Fruin-Colnon Contracting Co., St. Louis, 1951-54; a founder, treas., v.p. Smith-Zurheide, Inc., St. Louis, 1954-65; pres. Zurheide-Herrmann, Inc., St. Louis, 1965—; chmn. Elec. Code Rev. Commn., St. Louis, 1965—, Mo. Bd. Profl. Engrs., 1977—, St. Louis Indsl. Devel. Commn., 1965-67; mem. adv. panel region 6, GSA, 1977—; plan commn., City of Ferguson, Mo., 1968-73; tech. adv. com. St. Louis C. of C., 1977. Recipient Distinguished Service in Engring. award U. Mo., 1976. Registered profl. engr., Mo. Fellow Am. Cons. Engrs. Council; mem. Mo. Soc. Profl. Engrs. (Engr. of Year award 1970), Cons. Engrs. Council Mo., IEEE, Illuminating Engring. Soc., Engrs. Club St. Louis, Tau Alpha Pi. Clubs: Norwood Hills Country, Mo. Athletic. Home: 25 Lake Pembroke St Ferguson MO 63135 Office: 4333w Clayton Ave St Louis MO 63110

ZURHELLEN, JOSEPH OWEN, JR., fgn. service officer; b. N.Y.C., July 8, 1920; s. Joseph Owen and Dorrial Bernadette (Levy) Z.; A.B., Columbia, 1943, student Grad. Sch., 1946-47; student Harvard Grad. Sch., 1947-48; m. Helen Audrey Millar, Dec. 19, 1942; children—Joseph Owen III, William, Robert, David, Stephanie Jo. Gen. mgr. Universal Sales Co. of N.Y., exportimport, 1946-47; fgn. service officer, 1947—; consul, Fukuoka, also Yokohama, Japan, 2d sec. Am. embassy, Toyko, Japan, 1948-56; staff asst. to asst. sec. state for Far Eastern Affairs, 1956-59; assigned Nat. War Coll., 1959-60; dep. prin. officer Am. Consulate Gen., Munich, Germany, 1960-62; 1st sec. Am. Embassy, Toyko, Japan, 1962-63; Am. consul gen., Kobe Osaka, Japan, 1963-64; counselor of embassy, Am. embassy, Tokyo, Japan, 1964-68; dep. chief mission embassy Tel Aviv, Israel, 1968-73; dep. dir. ACDA, Washington, 1973-75; dep. asst. sec. state for East Asian affairs, 1975-76; ambassador to Republic of Surinam, 1976-78; v.p. Fgn. Policy Assn., 1978—. Served as capt. USMCR, 1943-46. Home: Box 392 Putnam Valley NY 10579 Office: Fgn Policy Assn 345 E 46th St New York NY 10017

ZURKOWSKI, PAUL GEORGE, trade assn. exec.; b. Milw., Nov. 8, 1922; s. Stanley Frank and Martha (Bednarz) Z.; B.A., U. Wis., Whitewater, 1954; LL.B., U. Wis., Madison, 1957; m. Margaret Ann Becker, July 9, 1960; children—Paul Coleman, Pamela Carol, Patricia Christine, Peggy Catherine, Paula Claire, Peter Christopher. Publisher, Our Ads, shopping guide, Palmyra, Wis., 1950-55; investigator legal firm Swingen & Stern, Madison, 1955-58; admitted to Wis. bar, 1957, U.S. Supreme Ct. bar, 1961; atty. HHFA, Washington, 1958; examiner ICC, 1958-59; congl. legis. asst., 1959-61, 64-69; individual legal practice, also congl. home sec., Madison, 1961; exec. dir. Info. Industry Assn., Washington, 1969, pres., 1972—; chmn. pvt. sector rev. group Nat. Commn. Libraries and Info. Sci., 1974; del. Internat. Conf. Libraries, Documentation and Archives, 1974; mem. Copyright Conf. Working Group, 1975; observer govt. adv. com. Internat. Book and Library Program, 1972—; mem. panel copyright and privacy Com. Sci. and Tech. panel, 1969; mem. pvt. sector adv. com. White House Conf. on Libraries, 1977. Served with AUS, 1957, as officer USAR, 1961-64. Decorated Army Commendation medal; recipient Disting. Alumni Service award U. Wis., Whitewater, 1974. Mem. U.S. Copyright Soc. (trustee), ALA, Am. Soc. Info. Sci., Am. Soc. Assn. Execs. Publisher Info. Times, quar., 1975; editor Info./Action Newslatter, 1971-78; editorial bds. New Tech. Libraries, Info. Sources, Futurist mag. Office: 316 Pennsylvania Ave SE Suite 502 Washington DC 20003

ZUR LOYE, DIETER, chem. and pharm. co. exec.; b. Berlin, Sept. 26, 1928; s. Otto and Gertrud (Laux) zur L.; M.B.A., U. Frankfurt/Main, Germany, 1952; grad. Advanced Mgmt. Program, Harvard U., 1970; m. Hella Elisabeth Troeger, July 20, 1957; children—Axel Otto, Hans-Conrad, Karen Hildegard. With Hoechst Aktiengesellschaft, Frankfurt/Main, 1955-75, mktg. dir. plastics exports, 1967-70, dir. corp. planning and coordination, 1970-75; group v.p. fin. and acctg. Am. Hoechst Corp., Somerville, N.J., 1975-78, exec. v.p., 1978—, dir., 1975—, chief fin. officer, 1975—, sr. exec. v.p., chief operating officer, 1980—; dir., pres. Hoechst Capital Corp.; dir. Hoechst-Roussell Pharms. Inc. Presbyterian. Clubs: Roxiticus Golf (Mendham, N.J.), Deutscher Verein (N.Y.C.), University. Office: PO Box 2500 Somerville NJ 08876

ZURMUHLE, ROBERT WALTER, physicist; b. Luzern, Switzerland, Nov. 27, 1933; came to U.S., 1961, naturalized, 1966; s. Otto and Marie (Schmidli) Z.; M.S., U. Zurich, 1958, Ph.D., 1960. Asst. prof. physics U. Pa., Phila., 1963-67, asso. prof., 1967-76, prof., 1976—. Fellow Am. Phys. Soc.; mem. New Helvetic Soc., Sigma Xi. Contbr. articles to nuclear physics jours. Home: 24 University Mews Philadelphia PA 19104 Office: Dept Physics U Pa Philadelphia PA 19104

ZURN, DAVID MELVIN, mfg. co. exec.; b. Erie, Pa., May 24, 1938; s. Melvin Ackerman and Marian Ruth (Schmid) Z.; grad. Phillips Acad., 1956; A.B., Williams, 1960; J.D., Columbia, 1963; m. Barbara St. John Miller, Apr. 17, 1971; children—Rena Michelle, Amelie Susan, Christopher Frederick. Admitted to Pa. bar, 1964; with Zurn Industries, Inc., Erie, 1963—, v.p., treas., 1968, v.p. finance, treas., 1969-71, exec. v.p. finance, treas., 1971-73, pres., 1973—, chief exec. officer, 1976—, mem. exec. com., 1968—; also dir.; dir. Marine Bank, Erie, Eric Indsl. Trucks, Inc.; mem. Erie adv. bd. Liberty Mut. Ins. Co. Mem. Port Commn. Erie, 1969-74. Mem. bd. incorporators Gannon Coll., Erie, 1970—; trustee Hamot Med. Center, Erie, 1973—; corporator St. Vincent Health Center, Erie, 1966—; bd. dirs. Zurn Found. Mem. Pa., Erie County bar assns., Young Presidents Orgn., Delta Delta Assn., Psi Upsilon Assn. Democrat. Episcopalian. Clubs: Aviation, Erie, Kahkwa, University. Home: 1850 S Shore Dr Erie PA 16505 Office: One Zurn Pl Erie PA 16512

ZURN, EVERETT FREDERICK, bus. exec.; b. Erie, Pa., Mar. 31, 1908; s. John Arthur and Clara (Ackerman) Z.; student Denison U., 1927-29; A.B., U. Pitts., 1931; Litt.D. (hon.), Mercyhurst Coll., Erie, 1966; LL.D. (hon.), Grove City (Pa.) Coll., 1977; m. Elizabeth Jane Henderson, Oct. 29, 1932; children—Eleanor Jane (Mrs. Peter B. Hutt), Susan Catherine (Mrs. James M. Smith, Jr.), James Arthur. With J.A. Zurn Mfg. Co., Erie, 1931-56, pres., 1952-56; pres. Zurn Industries, Inc., Erie, 1956-65, chmn. bd., 1965-73, chmn. exec. com., 1973—; dir. First Nat. Bank Pa., 1966-77, Times Pub. Co., Erie. Mem. President's Water Pollution Control Adv. Bd., 1965-68; past vice chmn. environmental com. B.I.A.C., Paris, 1972-73; mem. regional export expansion council Dept. Commerce, 1962—, chmn., 1967-69; mem. Nat. Expansion Council, 1967-69; mem. U.S. trade missions to Burma, 1962, Japan, 1962, Greece, 1964; mem. lay adv. com. Pa. Med. Soc.; mem. adv. council Coll. of Engring. Found. of U. Tex. Alternate del. at large Democratic Nat. Conv., 1952, 56, del. at large, 1960-68; mem. Electoral Coll., 1944. Bd. dirs. Zurn Found., Hess Found., 1962-65; trustee emeritus St. Vincent Health Center, pres. bd. trustees, 1962-65; bd. corporators Hamot Med. Center adv. bd. Pa. State U. Behrend Coll.; trustee Mercyhurst Coll., 1969-73. Mem. ASME, Am. Soc. Naval Engrs., Navy League, Newcomen Soc., NAM (dir. 1970-73), Pa. C. of C. (past dir.), Phi Delta Theta. Presbyn. Clubs: Erie, Kahkwa, University (Erie). Home: Avonia Rd RD 2 Fairview PA 16415 Office: One Zurn Pl Erie PA 16512

ZURN, FRANK WILLARD, mfg. co. exec.; b. Erie, Pa., Jan. 18, 1927; s. Melvin Ackerman and Marion (Schmid) Z.; grad. Choate Sch., 1945; B.M.E., Cornell U., 1950; LL.D., Villa Maria Coll., 1971; m. Mary Anne Williams, Jan. 14, 1977; children by previous marriage—Karen Davis Zurn MacBean, Peter Henry, Heidi Marian, Lisa Susan, Douglas Ackerman. With Zurn Industries, Inc., Erie, 1950—, sr. v.p., treas., 1962-65, pres., 1965-73, chmn., 1973—, also dir.; dir. Security-Peoples Trust Co., Calspan Corp., Zurn Found.; lectr. Cornell Sch. Mech. Engring., Harvard Grad. Sch. Bus. Mem. Erie Urban Transit Study Commn., 1965—; sec. Pa. State Park and Harbor Commn., Erie, 1959-67; pres. Erie Conf. Community Devel., 1976—, dir., 1973—. Pres. N.W. Pa. Heart Assn., 1961; bd. dirs. Pa. Heart Assn., 1961-63, Erie Civic Theatre Assn., 1963, Erie YMCA, 1959-65; bd. dirs. Hess Urol. Found., 1973—, v.p., 1974—; bd. corporators United Fund Erie County, 1960-67, Hamot Med. Center, Erie, 1960—; mem. advisory bd. Booker T. Washington Center, Erie, 1963-67, Erie Consortium Colls., 1971—; trustee St. Vincent Health Center, Erie 1966—, v.p. bd., 1970-73, pres., 1973-74, chmn., 1974—; mem. council Cornell U., 1965—, trustee, 1971—; pres. trustees Erie Day Sch., 1966; pres. lay advisory bd. Villa Maria Coll., Erie, 1966-67, trustee, 1969—, chmn. bd. trustees, 1969-73; trustee Choate Sch., 1972—. Mem. World Bus. Council, 1977—. Recipient Distinguished Service award Am. Heart Assn., 1962, Distinguished Achievement award, 1963; medallion of Achievement Golden Slipper Sq. Club Phila., 1968; Thompson Meml. Trophy award, 1974. Served with USNR, 1945-46. Mem. Young Pres. Orgn., ASME (chmn. Erie sect. 1952, chmn. membership devel. com. region V, 1953-54; certificate of award 1955), Am. Soc. Naval Engrs., Assn. Iron and Steel Engrs., Cornell Soc. Engrs., Fluid Control Inst., Navy League (dir. Erie council 1966-68), Newcomen Soc. N.Am., Assn. Governing Bds. Univs. and Colls., Soc. Automotive Engrs., Internat. Order Blue Gavel, Soc. Naval Architects and Marine Engrs., U.S. Yacht Racing Union, U.S. Internat. Sailing Assn. (asso.), Marine Hist. Assn., Nat. Soc. Profl. Engrs., Internat. Oceanographic Found., Chief Execs. Forum, Inter-lake Yachting Assn. (trustee 1972—), Epsilon Assn., Sigma Phi, Pi Gamma Mu (hon.). Episcopalian. Clubs: Erie (bd. govs. 1964-67), Yacht (commodore 1962), University, Aviation Country, Kahkwa, Westwood Racquet (Erie); Hillsboro (Pompano Beach, Fla.); Great Lakes Cruising (Chgo.); Butterfield Country (Hinsdale, Ill.); Little Ship (London, Eng.); Swedish Cruising (U.S. Great Lakes rep.) (Stockholm); Cornell N.W. Pa. (founder, past pres.); N.Y. Yacht (N.Y.C.); Storm Trysail (Larchmont, N.Y.). Contbr. articles to profl. jours. Office: Zurn Industries One Zurn Pl Erie PA 16512*

ZUSPAN, FREDERICK PAUL, physician, educator; b. Richwood, Ohio, Jan. 20, 1922; s. Irl Goff and Kathryn (Speyer) Z.; B.A., Ohio State U., 1947, M.D., 1951; m. Mary Jane Cox, Nov. 23, 1943; children—Mark Frederick, Kathryn Jane, Bethany Anne. Intern, Univ. Hosps., Columbus, Ohio, 1951-52, resident, 1952-54; resident Western Res. U., Cleve., 1954-56, Oblebay fellow, 1958-60, asst. prof., 1958-60; chmn. dept. obstetrics and gynecology McDowell (Ky.) Meml. Hosp., 1956-58, chief clin. services, 1957-58; prof., chmn. dept. obstetrics and gynecology Med. Coll. Ga., Augusta, 1960-66; Joseph Boliver DeLee prof. obstetrics and gynecology, chmn. dept. U. Chgo., 1966-75; obstetrician, gynecologist in chief Chgo. Lying-In Hosp., 1966-75; prof., chmn. dept. obstetrics and gynecology Ohio State U. Sch. Medicine, Columbus, 1975—. Pres., Barren Found., 1974-76. Served with USNR, 1942-43; to 1st lt. USMCR, 1943-45. Decorated D.F.C., Air medal wth 10 oak leaf clusters. Mem. Soc. Gynecol. Investigation, Chgo. Gynecol. Soc., Am. Assn. Obstetrics and Gynecology, Am. Acad. Reproductive Medicine (pres.), Am. Coll. Obstetricians and Gynecologists, Assn. Profs. Gynecology and Obstetrics (pres. 1972), South Atlantic Assn. Obstetricians and Gynecologists (Found. prize for research 1962), Central Assn. Obstetrics and Gynecology (certificate merit, research prize 1970), Am. Soc. Clin. Exptl. Hypnosis (exec. sec. 1968, v.p. 1970), So. Gynecol. Soc., Sigma Xi, Alpha Omega, Alpha Kappa Kappa. Founding editor: LyingIn, Jour Reproductive Medicine; editor: (with Lindheimer and Katz) Hypertension in Pregnancy, 1976; Current Developments in Perinatology, 1977. Mem. editorial bd. Exerpta Medica; editor Am. Jour. Obstetrics and Gynecology, Contemporary Obstetrics and Gynecology. Contbr. articles to med. jours., chpts. to books. Home: 2400 Coventry Rd Upper Arlington Columbus OH 43211. *The strength of our nation rests in the quality of our offspring. Every fetus has the privilege of being wellborn.*

ZWANZIG, ROBERT WALTER, educator; b. Bklyn., Apr. 9, 1928; s. Walter and Bertha (Weil) Z.; B.S., Poly. Inst. Bklyn., 1948; M.S., U. So. Calif., 1950; Ph.D., Calif. Inst. Tech., 1952; m. H. Frances Ryder, June 6, 1953; children—Elizabeth Ann, Carl Philip. Research asso. Yale, 1951-54; asst. prof. Johns Hopkins, 1954-58; phys. chemist Nat. Bur. Standards, 1958-66, now cons.; research prof. U. Md., College Park, 1966—.Recipient Dept. Commerce Silver medal, 1965. Fellow Am. Phys. Soc., Am. Acad. Arts and Scis., AAAS; mem. Nat. Acad. Scis., Am. Chem. Soc. (Peter Debye award in phys. chemistry 1976). Asso. editor: Jour. of Chem. Physics, 1965-67, Jour. of Math. Physics, 1968-70, Transport Theory and Statistical Physics, 1970, Collective Phenomena, 1972—, Chem. Physics, 1973—. Contbr. articles profl. jours. Home: 5314 Sangamore Rd Bethesda MD 20016 Office: Inst for Physical Sciences and Tech U Md College Park MD 20742

ZWEIFEL, RICHARD GEORGE, curator; b. Los Angeles, Nov. 5, 1926; s. Harold Charles and Kathleen Marguerite (Garland) Z.; B.A., U. Calif. at Los Angeles, 1950, Ph.D., at Berkeley, 1954; m. Frances Ann Wimsatt, July 30, 1956; children—Matthew Karl, Kenneth Paul, Ellen Katrina. Mem. staff Am. Mus. Natural History, N.Y.C., 1954—, chmn. curator dept. herpetology, 1968—; sci. attaché to Gondwana, 1974-75. Served with AUS, 1945-46. Mem. Ecol. Soc. Am., Am. Soc. Ichthyologists and Herpetologists, Deutsche Gesellschaft für Herpetologie und Terrarienkunde. Home: 412 Glendale Rd Northvale NJ 07647 Office: Am Museum Natural History 79th St and Central Park West New York City NY 10024

ZWEIG, FELIX, elec. engr., educator; b. Ft. Wayne, Ind., Sept. 25, 1916; s. Samuel and Celia (Schwartz) Z.; B.E. magna cum laude, Yale, 1938, Ph.D. in Elec. Engring., 1938-41; m. Jeanne Travers, Dec. 23, 1945; children—Jonathan S., Richard T., David B. Instr. Yale Sch. Engring., 1941-43, asst. prof., 1943-46, 47-49, asso. prof., 1949-55, prof., 1955—, dean sch. engring., chmn. dept. engring., applied sci., 1961-66; fellow Timothy Dwight Coll. research asso. Servomechanisms Lab., Mass. Inst. Tech., 1946; engring. cons. various firms. Master, Boy Scouts, Whitneyville, Conn. Mem. bd. edn., Hamden, 1959. Recipient award basic and applied sci. Yale Engring. Assn., 1958. Mem. Am. Inst. E.E., Inst. Radio Engrs., Am. Soc. Engring. Edn., Sigma Xi, Tau Beta Pi. Home: 75 Hall St Hamden CT 06517 Office: 513 Becton Center Yale Sta New Haven CT 06520

ZWEIG, GEORGE, educator, physicist; b. Moscow, USSR, May 20, 1937; s. Alfred and Rachael (Froehlich) Z.; came to U.S., 1938, naturalized, 1944; B.S., U. Mich., 1959; Ph.D., Calif. Inst. Tech., 1963; m. Audrey B. Cook, June 20, 1959; children—Geoffrey, Matthew (dec.), Christopher. With Orgn. Europeenne poar la Recherche Nucleaire, 1963-64; asst. prof. physics Calif. Inst. Tech., 1964-66, asso. prof., 1966-67, prof., 1967—. Woodrow Wilson fellow, 1959; Nat. Acad. Sci. NRC fellow, 1963; Sloan Found. fellow in physics, 1966, Sloan Found. research fellow in neurophysiology, 1975. Research on particle classification, originator of the quark model; research in hearing. Office: Lauritsen Lab Calif Inst Tech Pasadena CA 91125

ZWEIG, LEONARD HAROLD, communicator; b. Bklyn., Feb. 3, 1930; s. Simon and Mollie (Finkelstein) Z.; A.B. in Journalism, Syracuse U., 1951; A.M. in Am. History, Harvard, 1952; m. Gitte Lehrmann, Dec. 30, 1964; 1 dau., Samara Natasha. Dir. spl. communications projects State U. N.Y., Buffalo, 1967-70, research asso. Center for Humanistic Edn., Albany, 1970-73; pub. affairs programs in TV, 1955-64; editor Trans-action mag., 1964-67; sr. editor Innovation Mag., 1969-72; editor Wharton Mag., U. Pa., 1975—. Cons. PBL, 1968-69; lectr. sociology Washington U., St. Louis, 1965-67, State U. N.Y. at Buffalo, 1967-70; dir. Community Leadership Project, St. Louis, 1964-67; Fulbright lectr. mass communications, Finland, 1971; program asso. Center for Policy Research, N.Y.C., 1971-73. Served with AUS, 1952-54. Recipient Sylvania award, 1957, Peabody award, 1956, Robert Sherwood award, 1958. Mem. ACLU. Home: 220 Locust St Philadelphia PA 19106

ZWEIMAN, BURTON, physician, scientist; b. N.Y.C., June 7, 1931; s. Charles and Gertrude (Levine) Z.; A.B., U. Pa., 1952, M.D., 1956; m. Claire Traig, Dec. 30, 1962; children—Amy Beth, Diane Susan. Intern, Mt. Sinai Hosp., N.Y.C.; resident in medicine Hosp. U. Pa., Bellevue Hosp. Center, 1957-60; fellow N.Y. U. Sch. Médicine, 1960-61; mem. faculty dept. medicine U. Pa. Sch. Medicine, Phila., 1963—, prof. medicine, chief allergy and immunology sect., 1969—; cons. U.S. Army; co-chmn. Am. Bd. Allergy and Immunology. Served with M.C., USNR, 1961-63. Allergy Found. Am. fellow, 1959-61. Fellow Am. Acad. Allergy, A.C.P.; mem. Am. Assn. Immunologists, Am. Fedn. Clin. Research, Phi Beta Kappa, Alpha Omega Alpha. Contbr. articles to med. jours. Office: 512 Johnson Pavilion 36th and Hamilton Walk Philadelphia PA 19104

ZWEMER, RAYMUND LULL, biologist; b. Bahrain; Mar. 30, 1902; s. Samuel Marinus and Amy Elizabeth (Wilkes) Z.; student English Sch., Cairo, Egypt, 1916-18; A.B., Hope Coll., Mich., 1923; Ph.D., Yale, 1926; Nat. Research fellow Harvard, 1926-28; Guggenheim fellow U. Buenos Aires, 1941; m. Dorothy Ingeborg Born, Sept. 13, 1929; children—Raymund Wilkes, Suzanne (Mrs. R.A. Visser), Theodore, Jane (Mrs. R.L. Koeser). Instr., Columbia, 1928-31, asst. prof., 1931-44; worked with minister of pub. health, Uruguay, 1942; chmn. Interdeptl. Com. on Cooperation with Am. Republics, 1944; asso. chief Div. Cultural Cooperation, U.S. Dept. of State, 1944-47; exec. dir. Interdeptl. Com. on Sci. and Cultural Cooperation, 1945-47; exec. sec. Nat. Acad. Scis. and NRC, 1947-50; chief, sci. div. Library of Congress, 1950-55; chief div. internat. cooperation for sci. research

UNESCO, Paris, 1956-57, dir. Bur. Personnel and Mgmt., UNESCO, 1958; asst. sci. adviser Dept. of State, 1958-61, mem. U.S. delegations NATO Sci. Com. meetings, Paris, also CENTO Sci. Council meetings, London, Ankara, Tehran, 1958-61; asso. editor Am. Physiol. Soc. publs. Am. Jour. Physiology and Jour. Applied Physiology, 1961-65; dir. Biol. Info. User Survey, 1961-62; dir. trans. project Fedn. Am. Socs. for Exptl. Biology, 1962-66, exec. editor Fedn. Procs., 1966-67, project dir., exec. editor Neurosci, Transl., 1967—. Ofcl. U.S. del. to 2d PanAm. Congress on Endocrinology, 1941; various offices U.S. Book Exchange, Inc., Washington, 1948-56, chmn. bd., 1950-51; asso. editor Anat. Record, 1950-55; cons. in physiology Naval Med. Research Inst., 1949-55; convenor finance com. Internat. Anat. Nomenclature Com., 1965—, mem. main com., 1975—; del. to Com. on Data for Sci. and Tech., Internat. Union Biol. Scis., 1970; mem. adv. com. Sci. News, 1971—; trustee Biol. Abstracts, 1949-56, 62-67, v.p., 1953, pres., 1954-55, treas., 1963-64. Recipient A. Cressy Morrison prize N.Y. Acad. Sci., 1937. Fellow A.A.A.S.; mem. Council Biol. Editors, Am. Assn. Anatomists (chmn. com. anat. nomenclature), Council on Biol. Scis. Information (dir. 1967—, sec. 1967-68), Spl. Libraries Assn. (pres. Washington chpt. 1955), Am. Inst. Biol. Scis. (mem. steering com. biol. scis. communication project 1961-63, mem. pension fund com.), Fedn. Am. Socs. for Exptl. Biology (chmn. com. on biol. handbooks 1959-72), Am. Physiol. Soc., Am. Assn. Phys. Anthropologists, Washington Acad. Sci., Sigma Xi, Gamma Alpha; also hon. mem. Soc. Medicine Montevideo Uruguay, Biol. Soc. Argentine Med. Assn. Republican. Rotarian. Club: Cosmos (Washington). Home: 3600 Chorley Woods Way Silver Spring MD 20906 Office: 9650 Rockville Pike Bethesda MD 20014

ZWERDLING, ALEX, educator; b. Breslau, Germany, June 21, 1932; came to U.S., 1941, naturalized, 1946; s. Norbert and Fanni (Alt) Z.; B.A., Cornell U., 1953; postgrad. (Fulbright scholar) U. Munich (Germany), 1953-54; M.A., Princeton U., 1956, Ph.D., 1960; m. Florence Goldberg, Mar. 23, 1969; 1 son, Antony Daniel. Instr. in English, Swarthmore Coll., 1957-61; asst. prof. English, U. Calif., Berkeley, 1961-67, asso. prof., 1967-73, prof., 1973—; vis. prof. Northwestern U., 1977; mem. advanced placement exam. com. Ednl. Testing Service, 1975-79; mem. fellowship panel Nat. Endowment for Humanities, 1977—; fellow Center for Advanced Study in Behavioral Scis., 1964-65. Am. Council Learned Socs. fellow, 1964-65; Nat. Endowment for Humanities fellow, 1973-74; Guggenheim fellow, 1977-78. Mem. MLA (chmn. 20th Century Brit. lit. div. 1969-70). Author: Yeats and the Heroic Ideal, 1965; Orwell and the Left, 1974. Office: English Dept U Calif Berkeley CA 94720

ZWERDLING, ALLEN PAUL, publisher; b. N.Y.C., Oct. 11, 1922; s. William and Yetta (Nagler) Z.; student Coll. City N.Y., 1940-46; m. Shirly Hoffman, Dec. 2, 1946; children—Sherry, Jan, Gary. Actor, producer, writer, 1940-47; co-pub. Back Stage Publs., N.Y.C., 1960—, Amusement Guide, 1962—, Bus. Screen, 1976—. Served with U.S. Army, 1942-46. Home: 532 A Springtown Rd New Paltz NY 12561 Office: Back Stage Publs 165 W 46th St New York City NY 10036

ZWERLING, ISRAEL, psychiatrist, educator; b. N.Y.C., June 12, 1917; s. Max and Anna (Greidinger) Z.; B.S., Coll. City N.Y., 1938, M.S., 1938; Ph.D., Columbia U., 1947, diploma psychoanalytic medicine, 1960; M.D., State U. N.Y. Downstate Med. Center, 1950; m. Florence Erdtrachter, Nov. 16, 1940; children—Matthew Henry, Sara Kay. Intern, Maimonides Hosp., Bklyn., 1950- 51; resident research fellow psychiatry Cin. Gen. Hosp., 1951-54; dir. State U. Alcohol Clinic, Downstate Med. Center, Bklyn., 1954-56; lectr. Yale Center Alcohol Studies, 1955-60; mem. faculty Albert Einstein Coll. Medicine, 1955-73, prof. psychiatry, 1964-73, exec. officer dept. psychiatry, 1970-72; dir. Bronx State Hosp., 1966-73; prof., chmn. dept. mental health scis. Hahnemann Med. Coll., Phila., 1973—. Served to maj. USAAF, 1942-46. Decorated Bronze Star; recipient Strecker award Inst. Pa. Hosp., 1965. Fellow Am. Psychiat. Assn.; mem. AMA, Group Advancement Psychiatry (chmn. com. family 1964-68), Phila. Med. Soc., Am. Psychosomatic Soc., Am. Psychoanalytic Assn., Am. Psychol. Assn., Sigma Xi, Alpha Omega Alpha. Home: 1420 Locust St Philadelphia PA 19102

ZWICK, CHARLES JOHN, business exec.; b. Plantsville, Conn., July 17, 1926; s. Louis Christian and Mabel (Rich) Z.; B.S. in Agrl. Econs., U. Conn., 1950, M.S., 1951; Ph.D. in Econs., Harvard U., 1954; m. Joan Wallace Cameron, June 21, 1952; children—Robert Louis, Janet Ellen. Instr., U. Conn., 1951, Harvard, 1954-56; head logistics dept. RAND Corp., 1956-63, mem. research council, 1963-65; asst. dir. U.S. Bur. Budget, 1965-68, dir. U.S. Bur. Budget, 1968-69; pres., dir. S.E. Banking Corp., Miami, 1969—; dir. Southeast 1st Nat. Bank Miami, Johns-Manville Corp., S.E. Mortgage Co., So. Bell Tel. & Tel. Co.; mem. panel econ. advisers Congl. Budget Office. Mem. council Internat. Exec. Service Corps; trustee Carnegie Endowment for Internat. Peace; chmn. Pres.'s Commn. on Mil. Compensation. Served with AUS, 1946-47. Mem. Conf. Bd., Fla. Council of 100, Greater Miami C. of C., Assn. Res. City Bankers, Am. Historic and Cultural Soc. (dir.), Phi Beta Kappa. Home: 4210 Santa Maria St Coral Gables FL 33146 Office: Southeast Banking Corp Miami FL 33131

ZWIEP, DONALD NELSON, educator; b. Hull, Iowa, Mar. 18, 1924; s. Daniel and Nellie (De Stigter) Z.; B.S. in Mech. Engring., Iowa State Coll., 1948, M.S. in Mech. Engring., 1951; D.Eng. (hon.), Worcester Polytech. Inst., 1965; m. Marcia J. Hubers, Sept. 3, 1948; children—Donna J., Mary N., Joan L., Helen D. Design engr. Boeing Airplane Co., 1948-50, sr. tool engr., summer 1953, summer faculty asso., 1955; asst. prof. Colo. State U., 1951-56, asso. prof., 1956-57; cons. engr. aviation div. Forney Mfg. Co., 1956-57; prof., head dept. mech. engring. Worcester Polytech. Inst., 1957—, acting head mgmt. engring., 1974-76; constrn. engr. U.S. C.E., summer 1954; cons. engr., acting chief engr. J.J. Malir, Inc., summer 1956. Chmn. bd. trustees James F. Lincoln Arc Welding Found., 1976—. Served as pilot USAAF, World War II; CBI; guided missile officer and ednl. specialist Res. Registered profl. engr., Colo., Mass. Fellow ASME (v.p. edn. 1972—, pres. 1979-80); mem. Am. Soc. Engring. Edn. (pres. Colo. State U. chpt. 1954-55; treas. Rocky Mountain sect. 1955, dir. 1974-75), Nat. Soc. Profl. Engrs., Sigma Xi, Omicron Delta Kappa, Tau Beta Bi, Sigma Tau, Pi Tau Sigma. Presbyterian. Clubs: Worcester Economic, Torch. Home: 47 Birchwood Dr Holden MA 01520 Office: Mech Engring Dept Worcester Poly Inst Worcester MA 01609

ZWOLINSKI, BRUNO JOHN, educator; b. Buffalo, Nov. 4, 1919; s. Bronislaus John and Elizabeth (Glowska) Z.; B.S. in Chemistry, Canisius Coll., 1941; M.S. in Chemistry, Purdue U., 1943; Ph.D. in Chemistry, Princeton, 1947; m. Margery Williams, Aug. 16, 1952; children—Jan, Jeffrey, Maria. Research scientist Manhattan Project, Columbia, 1944-46; asst. prof. U. Utah, 1948-53; sr. physicist Stanford Research Inst., 1953-54; sr. lectr. chemistry Carnegie Inst. Tech., 1957-61; dir. Thermodynamics Research Center, Tex. A&M U., College Station, 1961-78, head dept. chemistry, 1964-65, prof., 1961—; cons. energy, fossil fuels, indsl. data; dir. research project 44 Am. Petroleum Inst., 1960-76. Fellow Am. Inst. Chemists, N.Y. Acad. Scis., Tex. Acad. Sci.; mem. Am. Chem. Soc. (SW award 1969, U.S. calorimetry award 1977), Am. Phys. Soc., AAAS (chemistry electorate nominating com. 1977-79), Sigma Xi. Research and numerous publs. on theoretical chemistry. Home: 903 Francis Dr College Station TX 77840

ZWORYKIN, VLADIMIR KOSMA, business exec.; b. Mourom, Russia, July 30, 1889; s. Kosma and Elaine (Zworykin); E.E. Petrograd Inst. Tech., 1912; student Coll. de France, Paris, 1912-14; Ph.D., U. Pitts., 1926; D.Sc., Bklyn. Poly. Inst., 1938, Rutgers U., 1972; m. Tatiana Vasilieff, Apr. 17, 1916; children—Nina (dec.), Elaine; m. 2d, Dr. Katherine Polavitsky, Nov. 1951. Came to U.S., 1919, naturalized, 1924. Research with Westinghouse Elec. and Mfg. Co., 1920-29; dir. electronic research RCA Mfg. Co., 1929-42; asso., research dir. RCA Labs., 1942-45; dir. electronic research, 1946-54, v.p., tech. cons., 1947-54, hon. v.p., cons., 1954—. Recipient Morris Liebmann Meml. prize 1934; Modern Pioneer award Am. Mfrs. Assn., 1940; Rumford medal Am. Acad. Arts and Scis., 1941. Howard N. Potts medal Franklin Inst., 1947; Presdl. Certificate of Merit, 1948; Chevalier Cross of French Legion of Honor, 1948; Lamme Award, 1949, Edison Medal, 1952, Am. Inst. E.E.; medal of honor IRE, 1951; Gustave Trasenster award, 1959; Cristoforo Columbo award, 1959; Faraday medal Brit. Inst. Elec. Engrs., 1965; Nat. Medal of Sci., 1966; Golden Plate award Am. Acad. Achievement, 1967. Served with Signal Corps. Russian Army, World War I. Named to Nat. Inventors Hall of Fame, 1977. Fellow IEEE, TV Soc. (Eng.) (hon.), Instituto Internazionale della Communicazoni (Italy) (hon.), Am. Phys. Society, AAAS; hon. mem. Soc. Motion Picture and TV Engrs., Brit. Instn. Radio Engrs.; mem. Am. Philos. Soc., N.Y. Acad. Scis., Electron Microscope Soc. Am., Nat. Acad. Engring. (Founders medal 1968), Societe Francaise des Electroniciens et des Radioelectriciens (hon.), Am. Acad. Arts and Scis., Nat. Acad. Scis. U.S.A., French Acad. Sci., Sigma Xi. Co-author: Photcells and Their Applications, 1932; Television, 1940, rev. 1954; Electron Optics and the Electron Microscope, 1946; Photoelectricity and Its Application, 1949; Television in Science and Industry, 1958. Developer iconoscope, electron microscope, other advances in radio, TV and electronics. Home: 103 Battle Rd Circle Princeton NJ 08450 Office: RCA Laboratories David Sarnoff Research Center Princeton NJ 08540*

ZWOYER, EUGENE MILTON, assn. exec.; b. Plainfield, N.J., Sept. 8, 1926; s. Paul Ellsworth and Marie Susan (Britt) Z.; student U. Notre Dame, 1944, Missouri Valley Coll., 1944-45; B.S., U. N.Mex., 1947; M.S., Ill. Inst. Tech., 1949; Ph.D., U. Ill., 1953; m. Dorothy Lucille Seward, Feb. 23, 1946; children—Gregory, Jeffrey, Douglas. Mem. faculty U. N.Mex., Albuquerque, 1948-71, prof. civil engring., dir. Eric Wang Civil Engring. Research Facility, 1961-70; research asso. U. Ill., Urbana, 1951-53; owner Eugene Zwoyer & Assos., cons. engrs., Albuquerque, 1954-72; exec. dir., sec. ASCE, N.Y.C., 1972—. Served to lt. (j.g.) USN, 1944-46. Named Outstanding Engr. of Year, N.Mex. Soc. Profl. Engrs., 1969. Mem. ASCE (dist. dir. 1968-71), Nat. Soc. Profl. Engrs., Am. Concrete Inst., Am. Soc. for Engring. Edn., AAAS, ASTM, Interprofl. Council Environ. Design, Nat. Acad. Code Adminstrn. (trustee, mem. exec. com. 1973—), Engrs. Joint Council (dir. 1978—), Engring. Socs. Commn. on Energy (dir. 1977—), Bd. for Engring. Cooperation, Am. Soc. Assn. Execs., Sigam Xi, Sigma Tau, Chi Epsilon. Club: Petroleum (Albuquerque). Home: 300 E 40th St New York NY 10016 Office: 345 E 47th St New York NY 10017

ZYLIS-GARA, TERESA, soprano; b. Landwarow, Poland, Jan. 23, 1930; student conservatories. Debut, Cracow, Glyndebourne (Eng.) Opera, 1965, Paris Opera, 1966, San Francisco Opera, Met. Opera, 1968, Salzburg (Austria) Festival; leading soprano Deutsche Opera am Rhein; appearances with Vienna Staatsopera, Royal Opera House-Covent Garden, London, Munich (W.Ger.) Staatsoper, Hamburg (W.Ger.) Staatsoper, La Scala, Milan, Italy, also opera houses of Berlin, Brussels, Paris, San Francisco and Chgo.; soprano soloist concert performances Child of Our Time with Boston Symphony Orch.; guest artist on radio and TV in Europe and U.S.; rec. artist Angel, Deutsche Grammophon and Seraphim records; prin. roles include Desdemona in Otello, Donna Elvira in Don Giovanni, Marschallin in Der Rosenkavalier, also title role in Tosca. Winner contest Assn. German Broadcasters. Address: care Columbia Artists Mgmt Inc 165 W 57th St New York NY 10019*

ZYLSTRA, ROGER EDWARD, lawyer; b. Lyon County, Iowa, Jan. 31, 1939; s. Charley and Edna Lena (Balster) Z.; B.S., Iowa State U., 1960; LL.B., Am. U., 1964; m. Shirley M. Albritton, June 16, 1962; children—Charles David, Kara Marie. Admitted to D.C. bar, 1964; since practiced in Washington, partner firm Cole, Zylstra & Raywid, 1966-79; cable TV owner, operator, various locations, 1979—. Mem. Am., D.C. bar assns. Episcopalian. Home: Dun Robin Route 1 Box 323 Leesburg VA 22075 Office: 150 A Catocken Circle Leesburg VA 22075

ZYSKIND, HAROLD, educator; b. Hurtsboro, Ala., Mar. 3, 1917; s. Jacob and Betty (Rubin) Z.; M.A., U. Chgo., 1947, Ph.D., 1964; m. Mascha Lehrer, May 2, 1944; 1 son, John Lehrer. Instr., U. Chgo., 1947-51, asst. prof., 1951-57; asso. prof. philosophy State U. N.Y. at Stony Brook, 1957-58, prof., 1958—; chmn. div. humanities State U. N.Y., Oyster Bay, 1958-61. Served to maj. AUS, 1941-45. Decorated Bronze Star medal. Mem. Am. Philos. Assn., Phi Beta Kappa. Author: (with Robert Sternfeld) Voiceless University, 1970, Plato's Meno, 1978. Contbr. articles to profl. jours. Home: 607 Cabot Ct E St James NY 11780 Office: Philosophy Dept State U NY Stony Brook NY 11790

Necrology

Biographees of the 40th Edition of *Who's Who in America* whose deaths have been reported to the editors prior to the close of compilation of this edition are listed below. Their biographical sketches, with date of death and place of interment added, will be published in the forthcoming Volume VII of *Who Was Who in America*.

A

Abelow, Robert
Abrams, George Joseph
Abrams, Harry Nathan
Ackley, Clark Russell
Adams, Arthur Merrihew
Adams, Elijah
Adams, James Carlton
Adams, Lewis Greenleaf
Adamson, Joy
Ades, Harlow Whiting
Adesko, Thaddeus Vincent
Adler, Kurt Herbert
Adler, Samuel Marcus
Agha, Mehened Fehmy
Ainsworth, Dorothy Sears
Albrecht-Carrie, Rene
Aldrich, George Davenport
Aldridge, Frederick Ferdinand
Alexander, Benjamin
Alexander, John Gordon
Alexander, Norman Dale
Alexander, Paul Julius
Alger, Mary Donlon
Allan, Frank Nathaniel
Allen, Clifford Robertson
Allen, Cuthbert Edward
Allen, James Browning
Allison, George Boggs
Almy, Gerald Marks
Alpert, Harry
Alsever, John B.
Alston, Charles Henry
Alvarez, Walter Clement
Aly, Bower
Amazeen, Edward Sutherland
Anderson, Ernest W.
Anderson, Gaylord West
Anderson, Howard Richmond
Anderson, Robert Palmer
Anderson, Rose Gustava
Anderson, William Banks
Andrews, Carl Willis Jr.
Andrews, F. Emerson
Andrews, James Newton
Andrus, Edwin Cowles
Angoff, Charles
Ardrey, Robert
Arkush, Arthur Spencer
Armstrong, George Ellis
Arnold, William H.
Arpaia, Anthony F(arpaya)
Arrington, James Hugh
Arrington, William Russell
Artz, Curtis Price
Arvey, Jacob M.
Arvey, Martin Dale
Ascoli, Max
Ashley, Paul Pritchard
Ashmore, James
Atkeson, Thomas Conner
Atkins, Paul Moody
Atkinson, George Herring
Augenblick, Robert Lee
Aurthur, Robert Alan

B

Babb, Howard Selden
Babcock, Conrad Stanton
Babcock, Frederic
Baehr, George
Bailey, Alfred Marshall
Bailey, Nathan Lynch
Bailey, Richard Paul
Bailey, William Stuart
Bakeless, John (Edwin)
Baker, Burton Lowell
Baker, Michael, Jr.
Baker, Russell
Baker, Russell Montez
Balderston, C. Canby
Baldwin, Donald R.
Baldwin, Frank Bruce, Jr.
Baldwin, Vincent John
Ball, John Willis
Ball, Robert Pearl
Ballard, John Henry
Banker, Oscar H.
Barach, Alvan Leroy
Barclay, Hartley Wade
Bard, Philip
Barlow, George Herbert
Barnes, Richard Henry
Barnes, Robert Gaylord
Barr, John Andrew
Barrett, Nestor
Barrow, Allen Edward
Barrow, Roscoe Lindley
Barry, Fred, Jr.
Barth, Alan
Bartlett, Dewey Follett
Bassett, James Elias
Bates, Legare
Bates, Merle Banker
Bauer, Benjamin Baumzweiger
Bauer, Harry Charles
Bauer, Raymond Augustine
Beals, Carleton
Beams, Jesse Wakefield
Beardsley, Richard King
Bechtel, Kenneth Karl
Bechtel, Welker George
Beckwith, Edmund Ruffin, Jr.
Begin, Floyd Lawrence
Begle, Edward Griffith
Belden, Frederick Hesley
Bell, Gordon Humphrey
Bellinger, Frederick
Benbow, Charles Frank
Bencher, Walter Seaman
Benedek, Martin Henry
Benjamin, Robert S.
Bennett, Carrol Mortimer
Bennett, Newcomb Benjamin, Jr.
Benoit, Emile
Bensinger, Benjamin Edward
Benson, Carl Frederick
Benton, Joseph George
Bentzin, Charles Gilbert
Berelson, Bernard R.
Bergson, Herbert Augustus
Bergwall, Evan Harold
Berman, Myron Philip
Bernegger, E. Lloyd
Bernstein, Theodore Menline
Berry Lloyd Eason
Bertoia, Harry
Bessin, Hyman
Best, Charles Herbert
Beveridge, Thomas Robinson
Bibring, Grete Lehner
Biddle, John Hunter
Bielaski, Fred
Bierwirth, John E.
Bingay, James Sclater
Binz, Leo
Bird, Robert Montgomery
Birr, Herman Theodore
Bishop, Elizabeth
Biskup, George Joseph
Blades, Brian Brewer
Blank, Samuel Allan
Bleibtreu, Jacob
Bliss, Chester Ittner
Bliss, George William
Block, Adolph
Block, Henry David
Blommers, Paul J.
Blondell, Joan
Boardman, William Kilbourne
Bockius, George Hamlin
Bodansky, Oscar
Boland, Thomas Aloysius
Bolin, Wesley
Bolles, Thomas Darley
Boner, Charles Paul
Borland, Hal
Boswell, Lorin Albert
Bouhuys, Arend
Bouwsma, Oets Kolk
Bowden, Robert John
Bowen, John Clyde
Bowers, Raymond
Bowmer, Angus Livingston
Boyd, Hugh Newell
Boyd, Myron Fenton
Boyer, Charles
Brace, Gerald Warner
Brace, Richard Munthe
Bracy, Carl Cluster
Bradburn, James Rupert
Braden, Spruille
Bradley, Wilmot Hyde
Brand, Vance
Breckinridge, John Bayne
Breech, Ernest Robert
Breen, Leonard Zachary
Brennan, Edward Thomas
Brewer, Wayne Burdette
Brewster, Leo
Bridger, Grover Leon
Briggs, Charles William
Brink, Joseph Andrew, Jr.
Bristol, Lee Hastings, Jr.
Britain, Kenneth Edward
Brock, William Elihu
Brock, William Emerson, Jr.
Brodie, Bernard
Broida, Herbert Philip
Bromage, Arthur Watson
Brommage, Claude Stilson
Bronson, Roy A.
Brooks, Whitney Lawton
Brophy, Frank Cullen
Brougham, Royal
Brown, Arvin Harrington, Jr.
Brown, Felix Harry
Brown, Frederick Nathan, Jr.
Brown, George Scratchley
Brown, John Anthony
Brown, Philip Bransfield
Brown, Richard Fargo
Brown, W. Shelburne
Brown, Willard Cowles
Browning, Robert W.
Bruce, David K.E.
Brumbaugh, David Emmert
Brumley, Albert Edward
Brundage, Percival Flack
Bruno, Harry A.
Bruns, Franklin Richard, Jr.
Bryan, Frederick van Pelt
Brynildssen, Yngvar
Budd, John M
Bullitt, Orville Horwitz
Bullock, John Rice
Burdell, Edwin Sharp
Burden, William Douglas
Burgess, Merrill Charles
Burke, Edward Nolan
Burlage, Henry Matthew
Burnes, James Alton
Burnham, Joseph Andrew
Burns, Dean Carl
Burns, Vincent Godfrey
Burnstan, Rowland
Burrell, Berkeley Graham
Burriss, Stanley William
Burrows, William
Burt, Richard Lafayette
Burtner, Charles Allen
Burtness, Harold William
Butler, Algernon Lee
Butler, Edward Francis
Butler, G(eorge) Paul
Butler, Thomas Clifton
Butterfield, Richard Joseph
Button, Robert Young
Buttrick, George Arthur
Byron, Goodloe Edgar

C

Cain, Arthur Leonard
Cain, James Mallahan
Caldwell, Irene Catherine Smith
Call, Asa Vickrey
Callery, Mary
Cambere, Ára Angele
Cameron, George Glenn
Campbell, Arthur Berl
Campbell, Hayward, Jr.
Campbell, Ian
Campbell, Neil
Campbell, Nicholas Joseph, Jr.
Cannon, Howard Henry
Cannon, Legrand, Jr.
Cantarow, Abraham
Cantwell, Robert Emmett
Caplan, Louis
Caplenor, Donald
Capp, Al
Capshaw, Hulon
Cargill, James Nelson
Carr, Oscar Clark, Jr.
Carr, Robert Kenneth
Carreiro, Joseph Alvarez
Carrington, John Claiborne
Carroll, Coleman Francis
Carroll, Gordon
Carroll, James Matthew
Carroll, Loren
Carruth, Laurence Adams
Carson, Ralph Moore
Carter, James Marshall
Carter, James R.
Carter, Mother Maybelle
Carter, Sara
Castle, William
Catlin, George Edward Gordon
Catton, Bruce
Cavanagh, Jerome Patrick
Chamberlain, Thomas Gassner
Chandler, Caroline A.
Chapman, Dave
Chapman, Gilbert W.
Chapman, Mary Ilsley
Chase, Ilka
Chatelain, Leon Jr.
Chiang, Yee
Childress, Francis Brown
Christensen, Paul Walter
Christy, Francis Taggart
Church, Donald (Eisenbrey)
Church, William Farr
Clark, Carroll D.
Clark, James Anthony
Clark, James H.
Clark, Kenneth Willis
Clark, Sherman Edward
Clark, Thomas Winder Young
Clay, Lucius DuB
Cleland, James T.
Clifford, James Lowry
Clifford, John McLean
Clifton, Ernest Smith
Clock, Henry Harriman
Cohan, Avery Berlow
Coker, Charles Westfield
Colby, Carroll Burleigh
Cole, Charles Woolsey
Cole, David L.
Cole, Edward N.
Cole, Harold Harrison
Coleman, William Smith
Coles, Albert Leonard
Collier, Neil Rex
Collins, Thomas Hightower
Collyer, John Lyon
Colwell, Arthur Ralph, Sr.
Comar, Cyril Lewis
Combs, William Hobart
Comey, David Dinsmore
Conant, James Bryant
Condon, Martin J., III
Cone, Fairfax Mastick
Connolly, Paul Raymond
Cooke, James Negley, Jr.
Coons, Albert Hewett
Coons, Sheldon R.
Cooper, Tom Richardson
Cootner, Paul Harold
Corlett, Allen N.
Corley, Francis Joseph
Cornelius, Marty
Cornman, James Welton
Corroon, Richard Francis
Costello, Joseph A.
Cote, Raymond Henri
Cotner, Thomas Ewing
Cotzias, George C.
Coulter, Glenn Monroe
Covalt, Donald A.
Cowan, Louis G.
Cowley, William Harold
Cox, Gertrude M.
Cozier, J. Kenneth
Cozzens, James Gould
Craig, Clayton Bion
Crane, Bob Edward
Crane, Royston Campbell
Cratsley, Edward Kneeland
Crawford, Joan
Crawford, Ralston
Creskoff, Jacob Joshua
Crichton, John Henderson
Croft, A(rthur) C.
Cromwell, Harvey
Crosby, Bing (Harry Lillis)
Cross, Leslie (Frank)
Cross, Paul Clifford
Crowe, James Roger
Crowe, Philip Kingsland
Culhane, Frank James
Cullen, Stuart Chester
Cullity, Bernard Dennis
Cuneo, Gilbert Anthony
Cuneo, John F.
Cunningham, Charles Crehore
Cunningham, Maurice Patrick
Curran, Jean Alonzo
Curtiss, John Hamilton
Cuthbert, Frederick Alexander

D

Dakin, Roger
Dalldorf, Gilbert
Daly, James
Daly, William Jerome Jr.
Dana, Samuel Trask
Danenberg, Leigh
Daniel, Rollin Augustus Jr.
Daniel, Ruby Kathryn
Daniels, Worth Bagley
D'Antoni, Joseph Steven
Danzansky, Joseph Baer
Darken, Lawrence Stamper
Darley, Ward
Daves, Delmer Lawrence
David, Bert Alison
Davidsohn, Israel
Davidson, Arthur Ole
Davidson, Sidney Wetmore
Davies, Rhys
Davis, Benjamin Bernard
Davis, Hal Charles
Davis, Jerome
Davis, John Staige
Davis, M. Edward
Davis, Stephen Smith
Day, Price
Dearstyne, Howard Best
Deasy, Mary Margaret
Debardeleben, Newton Hanson
de Carlo, Charles
DeFalco, Lawrence Michael
de Guigne, Christian, III
de Jong, Gerrit, Jr.
Delaney, William Francis, Jr.
Delchamps, Alfred Frederick, Jr.
DeLeon, Robert Andrew
Dennis, Charles Leslie
Dennis, Lawrence
Dent, Louis Linton
de Rochemont, Louis
Desmond, Alton Harold
Detgen, Edward Joseph
de Villafranca, George Warren
Dewey, Edward Russell
Diaz, Joaquin Basilio
Dickinson, Edwin Walter
Dickinson, William Boyd

Diefenbaker, John George
Dies, Edward Jerome
DiFalco, Saverio Samuel
Dinsmore, Ray Putnam
Dirlam, Arland Augustus
Dix, William Shepherd
Dobbins, Cris
Dobbins, Gaines Stanley
Doering, Otto Charles, Jr.
Doft, Floyd Shelton
Domonkos, Anthony Nicholas
Donovan, James Norton
Dooley, James A.
Dorr, Goldthwaite Higginson
Dorschel, Querin Peter
Dorsey, John Morris
Dorsey, Montgomery
Douglas, William Orville
Douglass, Raymond Donald
Dowdy, Andrew Hunter
Dowell, Dudley
Dowling, Walter
Downer, Samuel Forsythe
Downs, William Randall Jr.
Doyle, Wilson Keyser
Drake, Henry Lee
Driscoll, Frederick Joseph
Driscoll, Hugh MacPherson
Drury, Newton B.
Drye, John Wilson Jr.
Dubs, Adolph
Duce, Leonard Arthur
Duffy, Francis Ryan
Duggan, William Redman
Dunn, Edward K.
Dunn, William Lewis
Dunner, Joseph
Dunnington, John Hughes
Dupee, Frederick Wilcox
Durant, Thomas Morton
Durante, Jimmy (James Francis)
Durfee, James Randall
Dusenberry, William Howard
Du Vigneaud, Vincent
Dwyer, Joseph Gerald
Dyer, George Bell

E

Eaton, Cyrus Stephen
Eaves, Hettie Dawes
Eaves, Robert Wendell
Eberman, Paul Wilmot
Eccles, Marriner Stoddard
Eddy, Gerald Ernest
Edlund, Sidney Wendell
Edmondson, John Preston
Edson, Peter
Edwards, Corwin D.
Edwards, Frank William
Egan, John Taylor
Egbert, Lawrence Deems
Egger, Rowland Andrews
Eglevsky, Andre
Ehrmann, Winston Wallace
Eiges, Herbert M.
Eiseley, Loren Corey
Eisenhower, Mamie Geneva Doud
Eister, Allan Wardell
Ellis, Don A.
Ellis, Donald Johnson
Embry, Lloyd Bowers
Emerson, Rupert
Empie, Paul Chauncey
Endicott, Robert Rantoul
Engel, Irving M.
Engel, Lewis Libman
Epley, Dean George
Epley, Malcolm
Eppinger, Josua, Jr.
Ericsson, William G.
Erlich, Alvin Lewis
Erwin, William James
Etcheson, A Thomas
Ettinghausen, Richard
Evans, Edward Gordon Jr.
Evans, Elliott Willard
Evans, Griffith Conrad Jr.
Everett, Newton Bennie
Ewing, Oscar Ross

F

Fahy, Charles
Farrell, James Augustine Jr.
Farrell, James Thomas
Faulkner, Waldron
Fawcett, Roger Knowlton
Fearns, John M.A.
Fee, George Edward
Feenberg, Eugene
Feist, Irving J.
Fenner, Darwin Schriever
Ferguson, John Howard
Fermi, Laura
Ferrell, Harrison Herbert
Fiedler, Arthur
Field, Richard H.
Fields, Totie
Fierman, Harold Lee
Finney, Thomas Dunn Jr.
Fischer, Harvey A.
Fischer, John
Fisher, Howard Taylor
Fisher, Robert Dean
Fisk, McKee
Fiske, Kenneth M.
Fitch, George Ashmore
Fitzgerald, Joseph John
Fitzgibbon, Russell Humke
Fizzell, Robert Bruce
Flanagin, Norris Cornelius
Flanner, Janet
Flint, John Gardiner
Florovsky, Georges
Florsheim, Richard Aberle
Fogarty, Anne
Folch-Pi, Jordi
Ford, Benson
Ford, Nevil
Forman, Harrison
Forman, Phillip
Fornof, John Renchin
Foster, Minard Irwin
Foster, Norman
Fowle, James Luther
Fowler, Cody
Fowler, James Randlett
Fowler, Richard Brosing
Fox, Thomas G. Jr.
Fox-Martin, Milton
Francis, Edwin Augustus
Francke, Donald Eugene
Frankel, Charles
Frasca, John Anthony
Frazer, Albert Danner
Frazier, James Taylor
Frazier, Robert Haines
Freeman, Harry
Freiberg, Albert Daniel
Freudenthal. Alfred Martin
Frick, Ford Christopher
Friedman, Joseph
Fromberg, Gerald
Frommeyer, Walter Benedict Jr.
Fulbright, Freeman
Fuller, Lon Luvois
Fulton, Marshall Nairne
Furey, Francis James
Furth, Jacob

G

Gabo, Naum
Gage, Walter Henry
Gahman, Floyd
Gall, Edward Alfred
Gallagher, Buell Gordon
Ganner, Thomas Alan
Gantt, Paul Hawkins
Ganzi, Richard Louis
Garceau, George Joseph
Gardner, Austin Thayer
Gardner, Stephen Symmes
Garmon, William F.
Garnsey, Leon Leslie
Garrett, Johnson
Garrou, Albert Francis
Gartner, Arthur Edward
Gassaway, Franklin Drennan
Gasser, William Daniel
Gaud, William Steen
Geer, Will
Geismar, Maxwell David
Geller, Bruce
Gerlough, Daniel Lauder
Germani, Gino
Gerschenkron, Alexander
Gershenfeld, Louis
Geschwind, Irving I.
Geyelin, Philip Laussat
Gibson, James J.
Gibson, Robert McKenzie
Gigliotti, Frank Bruno
Gilbert, Elizabeth Ann Dinwiddie
Gilbert, Henry Boas
Gilbert, Lou
Giles, Warren Crandall
Gill, John Kermode Jr.
Gill John Paul
Gillen, Stanley James
Gilmore, Donald Sherwood
Gilmore, George Norman
Gilmore, Myron Piper
Gilmour, Lloyd Straube
Gisvold, Ole
Glander, Charles Emory
Goldberg, Morrell
Goldman, Richard Franko
Goldmark, Peter Carl
Goldstein, David Henry
Golinkin, Joseph Webster
Goodhart, Arthur Lehman
Gordon, John
Gordon, Robert Aaron
Gorham, Sidney Smith Jr.
Gossick, Ben Roger
Gottschalk, Hans W.
Goudsmit, Samuel Abraham
Grah, Rudolf Ferdinand
Grandin, Thomas B.
Grant, Evva H.
Gray, Frank Jr.
Grebanier Bernard
Green, Marcus Herbert
Green, Melville Saul
Green, William John
Greene, James Etheridge
Greene, John James
Greenleaf, Elizabeth Adele
Gregory, Hollingsworth Franklin
Gribble, William Charles Jr.
Griffith, Lynn B.
Grimes, William Alexander
Gross, Ben S.
Gross, Mason Welch
Gruene, Hans Friedrich
Gruenther, Homer H.
Grussing, Bon Dirck
Gubow, Lawrence
Guenther, Carl Frederic
Guggenheim, Peggy
Gundy, Charles Lake
Gurfein, Murray Irwin
Gurley, Sam Jr.
Gustad, John Wilbert
Gustin, Harley Wemple
Guttentag, Marcia

H

Haas, Walter A.
Hadley, Morris
Hadlock, Wendell Stanwood
Haffner, Charles C.
Hagopian, Peter B.
Halas, George Stanley Jr.
Hale, Mark Pendleton
Halford, Ralph Stanley
Hall, Joseph Bates
Hall, Leonard Wood
Hall, Theodore Parsons
Haloftis, Timothy
Halprin, Rose L.
Halsey, James H.
Halsman, Philippe
Halstead, George Chappell
Hamilton, Ann Ruth Frances
Hamilton, Thomas Hale
Hanley, Dexter L.
Hann, Robert Henry
Hanna, Alfred Jackson
Hannan, James MacClymont
Hannon, Thomas Eugene
Hansen, Harry
Hanson, Earl Parker
Hara, James Ellsworth
Harbison, McClarty
Hardman, Lamartine Griffin Jr.
Harkness, Richard Long
Harlow, James Gindling Sr.
Harnish, William Max
Harper, Howard Vincent
Harrah, William Fisk
Harris, Henry Ellis
Harris, Hugh Pate
Harris, Louis Carl
Harris, Marguerite
Harris, Robert Edward George
Harrison, Gregory Alexander
Harte, Robert Adolph
Harvey, M.J.
Hatzfeld, Helmut Anthony
Haubiel, Charles
Hauck, Herman John
Hawkins, Edler Garnett
Hawks, Howard Winchester
Haworth, Leland John
Hay, Isaac Kline
Hayes, John Cornelius
Hazen, Allen Tracy
Hazen, Arlon Giberson
Head, Albert Joseph
Healey, George
Healy, Arthur Kelly David
Hebbard, William Lawrence
Hebert, F. Edward
Hebert, Paul Macarius
Heddens, Barret Spencer, Jr.
Heezen, Bruce Charles
Heindel, Richard Heathcote
Heizer, Robert Fleming
Helliwell, Paul Lionel Edward
Hellman, Geoffrey Theodore
Helpern, Milton
Helson, Harry
Henderson, John William, Jr.
Hendricks, Walter
Henke, Robert Henry
Henney, Richard Bernard
Herrick, George Q.
Hess, Thomas B.
Hester, E. Elizabeth
Heston, Joseph Carter
Hickam, Hubert
Hicks, Clifford Milton
Hiebert, John Mark
Higgins, Ruth Loving
Highet, Gilbert
Hildebrand, Kenneth Norman
Hilding, Anderson Cornelius
Hill, James Tomilson Jr.
Hill, Robert C.
Hillman Herman David
Hills, Ralph Gorman
Hilton, Conrad N.
Hinton, William Miller
Hintze, William Robert
Hitchcock, Philip Stanley
Hitti, Philip Khuri
Hodges, Fletcher, Jr.
Hoenig, Sidney B.
Hoffer, Joe Ralph
Hoge, John Hampton
Hogrefe, Pearl
Holbrook, Luther Gardner
Holland, Kenneth George
Hollifield, Guy Foster
Hollister, John Baker
Honaman, R(ichard) Karl
Honigmann, John Joseph
Hood, Harvey Perley
Hoos, Sidney Samuels
Hopkins, Frederick Mercer Jr.
Horn, Charles Lilley
Horner, George Norman
Howell, Albert Charles
Howse, W.L. Jr.
Hubbs, Carl Leavitt
Huber, Edward Frederick
Huddleston, Jackson Noyes
Hudson, Hinton Gardner
Humphrey, Gilbert Watts
Humphrey, Hubert Horatio, Jr.
Hunt, Reed Oliver
Hunter, Edward
Hunter, William Carroll
Hunton, Eppa, IV
Hurley, Donald Joseph
Hurt, John Tom
Hutaff, G. Harry
Hutchings, William Lawrence
Hutchins, Lee Milo

I

Ignatieff, George
Ikenberry, Oliver Samuel
Ingle, Dwight Joyce
Inglis, John Wingate
Ingram, Walter Robinson
Inzer, William Henry
Irons, Robert Bruce Jr.
Isaac, Charles Martin
Iselin, Philip H.
Israels, Sydney
Iverson, Marvin Alvin
Ivison, Maynard C.

J

Jackson, Edith Banfield
Jackson, Hezekiah
Jackson, Robert Charles Jr.
Jacobs, Lawrence Pierce
Jacobs, Paul
Jacobson, Samuel David
Jacoby, Neil Herman
James, Daniel Jr.
James, Ernest Kelly
Jarman, William Jackson
Jaynes, Lawrence C.
Jeffery, Edwin T.
Jenkins, Joseph Alton
Jennewein, Carl Paul
Jennison, Marshall Walker
Jessup, John Knox
Johns, Ralph Stanley
Johnson, Albin Iver
Johnson, Hugh Albert
Johnson, Maurice O.
Johnson, Sherman Ellsworth
Johnston, Garvin Howell
Johnstone, Burton Kenneth
Jones, Archie Neff
Jones, Preston St. Vrain
Jones, William Blakely
Josephson, Matthew
Jung, Charles Chester

K

Kahn, Joseph
Kahoe, Walter
Kajeckas, Joseph
Kantor, MacKinlay
Kaplan, Morris Aaron
Kaplan, Walter S.
Karns, Russell Dale
Kasznar, Kurt Sewischer
Kath, Terry Alan
Kauffman, George Whitten
Kaufman, Elkin
Kaufman, Sue (Mrs Jeremiah A. Barondess)
Kavanagh, Thomas Christian
Kaye, Sydney Milton
Kearns, Amos Ragan
Keefer, Richard Edward
Keeler, Clinton Clarence
Kegan, Elizabeth Hamer
Keller, Jack
Kellogg, George Edgar
Kellogg, Hamilton Hyde
Kelly, Emmett Leo
Kelly, Ernest Byron, Jr.
Kelly, John Martin
Kelly, Stephen Eugene
Kelso, James Leon
Kennally, Vincent Ignatius
Kennedy, Clement
Kennedy, Howard Ernest
Kennedy, James Walter
Kennedy, Walter Wallace
Kennedy, William Dempsey
Kent, Amos Eugene
Kenton, Stanley Newcomb
Kershaw, Andrew
Ketchum, William M.
Kiefer, Charles Frederick
Kiev, Isaac Edward
Kiewit, Peter
Kimball, Yeffe
Kimbel, William Anthony
Kimberg, Daniel Victor
King, Carleton James
King, Clinton
King, Warren Thomas
King, William Haven
Kinsey, Victor Everett
Kirk, Ronald T.
Klassen, Karl Peter
Klassen, Peter Pierre
Klein, William Henry
Kleinman, Abraham Morris
Klüver, Heinrich
Knowles, John Hilton
Knox, William Edward
Koch, Arnold Theodor
Koch, John
Koenig, Frederick Gilman, Jr.
Kok, Bessel
Kompfner, Rudolf
Kooker, Arthur Raymond
Kopple, Robert
Korn, Bertram Wallace
Kostelanetz, Andre
Kramer, Milton Joseph
Kroch, Adolph
Kron, Arthur Adams
Krooth, David Louis
Krooth, Robert Schild
Krumbein, William Christian
Kuhn, Ferdinand
Kuhn, Terry W.
Kunstadter, Sigmund
Kwalwasser, Jacob

L

Lahey, Richard Francis
Laidlaw, Robert W.
Laird, William J.
Lamb, Franklin
Lamont, Gordon
Lampert, James Benjamin
Landsman, Herbert Samuel
Lane, Donald Edward
Langer, William Leonard
Langlais, Bernard
Lanham, Edwin Moultrie
Lapointe, Louis A.
Larabee, Byron Hanly
LaRoche, Chester J.
Lasswell, Harold Dwight
Latham, Earl
Lauhoff, Howard Joseph
Lawrence, Alexander Atkinson
Lawrence, George Hill Mathewson
Lawrence, Josephine
Lawson, Andrew Werner, Jr.
Laylin, John Gallup
Leake, Chauncey D.
Leath, Edward Magruder, Jr.
Lederer, Ludwig George
Lee, Hubert Floyd
Lee, Morris Matthews, Jr.
Leeson, Robert
LeGrand, Duard Madison, Jr.
Lehnert, Herbert Hermann
Leland, George Havens
Lennartson, Nils Andrew
Lensen, George Alexander
Lerner, I. Michael
Lerner, Michael
Lesser, Lawrence Stanley
Leventhal, Harold
Levine, Irving Abraham
Levings, Nelson Trimble
Levinson, Bernard H.
Levy, Leon
Lewis, Dorothy Moore
Lewis, Ralph Ferguson
Lewis, Wilmarth Sheldon
Liddel, Urner
Liebow, Averill Abraham
Light, Enoch Henry
Lilly, Eli
Lindley, Allen Ledyard
Lindley, Ernest Kidder
Lindner, Richard
Lindquist, Everet Franklin
Lockwood, William Wirt
Loebl, Jerrold
Loew, Arthur M.
Lookstein, Joseph Hyman
Loos, Karl Dickson
Lord, John Solon
Lord, Mary Pillsbury
Louisell, David William
Love, Philip Hampton
Lowell, Robert (Traill Spence, Jr.)
Lubin, Isador
Lucas, Henry Laurence Jr.
Lucas, Vane Basil, Jr.
Ludvigsen, Elliot Leon
Lukoff, Herman
Lundberg, Melvin Edward
Lynch, Warren
Lynen, Feodor
Lyon, Frank Randolph, Jr.

M

MacBain, Gavin Keith
Macbeth, Norman
MacChesney, (Alfred) Brunson III
MacDonald, Gordon Andrew
Machado, Luis
Mackay, Albert George
Maclennan, David Alexander
MacMillan, Norman John
Macy, Josiah, Jr.
Madden, Carl Halford
Magrish, Alfred E.
Maguire, John MacArthur
Maier, Norman Raymond Frederick
Mair, George F(isk)
Maktos, John
Maland, Oswald
Mandell, Samuel Philip
Manderino, Louis Lawrence
Manion, Clarence E.
Manning, Armin William
Manthorne, Mary Elizabeth Arnold
Marcus, Sumner
Marcuse, Herbert
Maremont, Arnold Harold
Mark, Peter Herman
Marks, James Harmon
Marney, Leonard Carlyle
Marsh, Homer Ellsworth
Marshall, Lawrence Marcellus
Marshall, Samuel Lyman Atwood
Marston, Morrill W.
Martin, Charles Louis
Martin, Dwight
Martin, Fletcher
Martin, Paul Logan
Martin, William Oliver
Marvel, William Worthington
Marvin, Burton Wright
Mason, Francis van Wyck
Mason, Frank Earl
Mast, Casper Leo, Jr.
Matecheck, Richard Vincent
Mather, Kirtley Fletcher
Matthews, Herbert Lionel
Matthews, Mark Allison
Mattick, Hans W.
Mauchly, John William
May, Herbert Gordon
May, Kenneth Ownsworth
Maynard, A. Rogers
McCabe, Thomas Bayard, Jr.
McCall, Charlie Campbell
McCance, Thomas
McCardle, Dorothy Bartlett
McCone. Alan
McConnell, Raymond Arnott, Jr.
McConochie William Robert
McCormick, William Thomas
McCurdy, Gilbert James Cathcart
McDonagh, Vincent George
McDougald, John Angus

McEachin, Archibald Bruce
McElroy, Dennis Lee
McFadyen, Neil Mathieson
McGaw, Charles
McGinley, Phyllis
McGourty, John James
McGregor, Frank Rutherford
McGuire, Johnson
McIvor, Ivor Keen
McKenna, Daniel John
McKenna, F(rancis) E(ugene)
McLaren, Norman Loyall
McLarnan Charles Walter
McLellan, Adrian Oswald
McMillan, William Benton
McNally, Harold Joseph
McNamee, Daniel V., Jr.
McSherry, Frank David
McSweeney, John Morgan
McWilliams, John Wesley
Meacham, William Shands
Mead, Margaret
Meade, Robert Heber
Meader, Stephen Warren
Meadows, Algur Hurtle
Meany, George
Meck, John Foster
Medsker, Leland L.
Mehring, Howard William
Meinecke, Willard Henry
Meloy, Frances Edward, Jr.
Melrose, Alice Gunhild
Meltzer, Doris
Mencher, Ely
Menn, Thorpe
Mercer, Johnny (John H.)
Merk, Frederick
Merriam, Charles J.
Merritt, Hiram Houston
Metcalf, Lee
Metcalfe, Ralph H., Sr.
Meyer, Andre
Meyer, Malcolm
Meyer, Ovid Otto
Michaelson, Charles Donald
Middleton, Roderick Osgood
Milks, Harold Keith
Mill, Edward William
Miller, Clemmy Olin
Miller, Francis Pickens
Miller, James Roscoe
Miller, John L.
Miller, Loye Wheat
Miller, Max
Miller, Walter Richard
Miller, William Whipple
Millor, William James
Mills, Gordon Harrison
Milner, Benjamin Hudson
Mingus, Charles
Minter, Merton Melrose
Mitchell, Wallace MacMahon
Moe, Henry Allen
Moehlman, Arthur Henry
Montgomery, Harry
Mooney, George Austin
Moore, Howard Earle
Moore, James Patrick, Jr.
Morphos, Panos Paul
Morris, Kyle Randolph
Morris, Logan
Morrison, Hugh Sinclair
Morse, Ellsworth Harry, Jr.
Morse, Harold Marston
Mortensen, Otto Axel
Morton, Rogers Clark Ballard
Moscone, George Richard
Moseley, Edwin M.
Moseley, Ray Benjamin Franklin
Moss, John Hall
Mostel, Zero (Sam Mostel)
Moyer, Sheldon
Muhlenberg, Frederick Augustus
Muir, Malcolm
Mulhearn, John Robert
Mullahy, John Henry
Muller, John H.
Mullin, Mark Joseph
Mulroney, John Edward
Munson, Thurman Lee
Munson, Townsend
Murden, Forrest Dozier
Murphy, Gardner
Murphy, Glenn
Murphy, Robert Daniel
Murphy, William Thomas
Muschenheim, Carl
Mussio, John King
Myers, Jay Arthur

N

Nabokov, Nicolas
Nabokov, Vladimir
Naish, John Vincent
Nannes, Caspar Harold
Nantz, Thomas Benton
Naumann, Oscar John
Neill, Marshall Allen
Nelson, Carl Truman
Nelson, George Laurence
Nelson, Lawrence Ernest
Nelson, William
Neu, Harold Nicholas
Newhouse, Samuel I.
Newson, Henry Winston
Newton, Arthur Ulysses
Newton, Warren Childs
Nicholls, William Hord
Nichols, Marie Hochmuth
Nickerson, Walter John
Nin, Anais
Norris, Hoke
Novik, Ylda Farkas
Noyes, Blancke
Noyes, Eliot Fette
Noyes, Nicholas Hartman
Nutter, G. Warren

O

Obenshain, Richard Dudley
Oberon, Merle
Obolensky, Serge
O'Connor, John Woolf Jack
Odlin, Reno
O'Donnell, Charles Robert
O'Donnell, Paul Daniel
O'Gara, James Vincent, Jr.
O'Gara, Warren Martin
Ogryzlo, Metro Alexander
O'Hara, John Paul
Olson, Bruce F.
Olson, George Leonard
O'Malley, Walter F.
O'Neill, C. William
Oppermann, Paul
Osborn, Edward Bartley
Otis, Brooks
Owen, Harry Goddard
Owen, John Beresford

P

Paeff, Bashka
Paine, Clarence Sibley
Palfrey, John Gorham
Palmer, Daniel David
Palmer, Philip Motley
Pantzer, Kurt Friedrich
Paray, Paul
Park, Colin
Park, Lee I.
Parkhurst, Charles Chandler
Parks, Gordon, Jr.
Parravano, Giuseppe
Parsons, Talcott
Patterson, Bryan
Paul, VI, His Holiness
Paul, Dorothy Hite
Paul, Norman Stark
Paul, Richard Havens
Pawley, William Douglas
Payne, Frederick G.
Peckworth, Howard Faron
Peebles, Bernard Mann
Peer, Lyndon Arthur
Pei, Mario Andrew
Perelman, Sidney Joseph
Perez, Henry Taylor
Perkins, Fred J.
Perlmutter, Milton
Perrigo, Charles R.
Pershing, John James
Peterson, Shailer
Peyton, Paul Leason
Phillips, Dorothy Williams
Phillips, James Emerson, Jr.
Phillips, John Nicholson
Phillips, Percy Toumine
Phipps, Oval Alexander
Pickford, Mary (Gladys Marie Smith)
Pierce, Lawrence Michael
Pierce, Robert Willard
Pierson, Warren Lee
Pigman, W. Ward
Pistell, Richard Chadwick
Pitt, Arthur Stuart
Poe, James
Poitras, Herman Arthur
Pollard, James Edward
Pooley, Robert Cecil
Poppen, James L.
Port, Frederick James
Porter, Clifford Lewis
Porter, John Roger
Porter, Lawrence Charles
Potter, Charles Edward
Potter, James Harry
Poulter, Thomas Charles
Power, Aloysius Francis
Poynter, Nelson
Prall, Bert R.
Prather, Charles Lee
Pratt, Gerald Hillary
Pratt, Joseph Gaither
Pregel, Boris
Prescott, Robert William
Priest, A.J. Gustin
Prima, Louis
Pritchard, Edward Kriegsmann
Pritzker, Jack Nicholas
Propp, Leslie B.
Prothro, Adolphus Maynard
Pryor, John C.
Pryor, Thomas Marion
Purdy, Theodore Martindale

Q

Quail, John Joseph
Quick, Armand James
Quindlen, Eugene Joseph
Quinn, Robert J.

R

Raben, Maurice Solomon
Radebaugh, William Herbert
Rattner, Abraham
Rauch, Harry Ernest
Ray, George Washington, Jr.
Ray, Ruth
Rector, William George
Reeder, Howard Chandler
Reeder, Leo Glenn
Reese, Addison Hardcastle
Reeves, Floyd Wesley
Refregier, Anton
Regnier, Raymond Cobington, Jr.
Reichert, Herbert William
Remey, Gilbert Pryce
Renoir, Jean
Resnick, Nathan
Reynolds, Malvina
Reynolds, Thomas F.
Rhine, Joseph Banks
Ribak, Louis Leon
Rich, George R.
Rich, Lorimer
Richard, Donat Radolphe
Richey, Robert William
Richman, Barry Martin
Rickbeil, Raymond Earl
Riley, Edward Eddy, Jr.
Ritter, Gerald
Ritter, Willis William
Ritzenthaler, Arthur Bernard
Rivers, Thomas Ellis
Roach, James
Roark, Eldon
Roberts, Henry Lamar
Robichaud, Beryl
Robichaud, Gerard Alaric
Robinson, Edgar Eugene
Robson, Marc
Roche, Mary
Rockefeller, John Davison, 3D
Rockefeller, Nelson Aldrich
Rockwell, Norman
Rodgers, Richard
Rodin, Robert Joseph
Rodman, Thomas D.
Rogers, John
Rogers, Paul
Rogg, Nathaniel H.
Rokaw, Daniel Roy
Ronne, Finn
Root, Darrell Astor
Rose, John Lawrence
Rose, William Alfred
Rose, William Palen
Rosen, George
Rosenberg, Abe Eugene
Rosenberg, Harold
Roth, Willard Lawrence
Rotunno, Noreda Anthony
Rouse, Milford Owen
Rovere, Richard Halworth
Rowlett, John Miles
Royce, Stephen Wheeler
Ruark, Arthur Edward
Rubicam, Raymond
Rubin, Samuel
Rudisill, Dorus Paul
Rukeyser, Muriel
Rupp, Adolph Frederick
Russell, Percy Hickling
Russell, Rosalind
Rutherford, Richard James
Ruzicka, Rudolph
Ryan, Harold Francis
Ryan, Leo Joseph
Ryan, Patrick James

S

Sackett, Arthur Johnson
Sacks, Sheldon
Sadusk, Joseph Francis, Jr.
Safford, William Cullen
Salant, Robert Stephen
Salomon, Irving
Saltonstall, Leverett
Sandmel, Samuel
Sappington, A.D.
Sarvella, Patricia Ann
Sauer, Louis W(endlin)
Saunders, Wilbour Eddy
Savelle, Max
Sawyer, Herbert Smith
Scarff, John Edwin
Schafer, George Ezra
Schary, Saul
Schauer, Benjamin Rey
Schenck, Harry Paul
Schindler, James Schwartz
Schippers, Thomas
Schlueter, Clyde Frederick
Schmitt, Waldo LaSalle
Schneierson, Sol Stanley
Schoenborn, Edward Martin, Jr.
Schooley, Allen Heaten
Schopf, James Morton
Schrader, Edward Albert
Schruth, Peter E.
Schubert, Leo
Schwartz, William Samuel
Scott, Joseph Welch
Scribner, Joseph M.
Searle, John Gideon
Seath, John
Seaton, George
Sechler, Ernest Edwin
Seed, Fred M.
Seeger, Charles Louis
Seevers, Maurice Harrison
Seldis, Henry James
Seligman, Germain
Sellers, Mark Ashley
Settlemire, Claude LaPrell
Seymour, Charles, Jr.
Seymour, Frank Marcellous
Shafroth, Morrison
Shake, Curtis Grover
Sharp, Lewis Inman
Sharp, Marion Leale
Shaw, Herbert Bell
Shaw, Robert
Shea, Francis Xavier
Shearman, Robert William
Sheehan, Paul Vincent
Sheen, Fulton John (Bishop)
Sheldon, William Herbert
Shell, Terry Lee
Shenstone, Allen Goodrich
Shepherd, Henry Longdon
Sherwood, Elmer William
Shifrin, Seymour
Shillinglaw, Clifford Allen
Shirk, George Henry
Shiskin, Julius
Shulman, Edward M.
Shuman, Ronald Buswell
Shumlin, Herman
Sick, Theodore Alfred
Siegel, Eli
Siegel, Seymour Nathaniel
Siems, Leonard A.A.
Sievers, Harry Joseph
Sigmon, Richard Roland
Silverman, Oscar Ansell
Silvert, Kalman Hirsch
Simmons, William P., Jr.
Simonds, George Patton
Sinai, Nathan
Singsen, Antone Gerhardt
Siple, Walter Helck
Sivage, Gerald Albert
Skinner, Cornelia Otis
Slater, John Hunter
Smelser, Marshall
Smith, Gordon Mackintosh
Smith, John Malcolm
Smythe, Hugh Heyne
Sneed, James Richard
Snyder, John Stewart
Soby, James Thrall
Soderberg, Carl Richard
Soine, Taito Olaf
Solberg, Archie Norman
Solinsky, Robert S.
Solomon, Samuel Joseph
Somers, Gerald George
Sonnenberg, Benjamin
Sorg, Herbert Peter
Spaugh, W. Herbert
Spaventa, George
Speer, Edgar B.
Spencer, Eldridge Ted
Spiegelberg, George Alfred
Spieker, Edmund Maute
Spivacke, Harold
Sporn, Philip
Stafford, Jean
Staley, Austin L.
Staley, Thomas Franklin
Stalling, Bettin
Stapley, Delbert Leon
Starch, Daniel
Staub, Marshal Gerald
Steefel, Robert David
Steele, William Owen
Steffel, Victor Lawrence
Steiger, William Albert
Stein, William Howard
Steinberg, William
Steinbicker, Paul George
Stern, Harold P.
Stern, Laurence Marcus
Sternberg, Vernon Arthur
Stevens, David Harrison
Stewart, Alexander Coutts
Stichter, Wayne Edwin
Stillwell, Henry Sheldon
Stippes, Marvin Clifford
Stocking, Collis
Stockton, Richard Finch
Stohl, Ralph N.
Stokowski, Leopold (Boleslawawicz Stanislaw Antoni)
Stoll, Norman Rudolph
Stone, Dewey David
Stone, Edward Durell
Stone, Fred Dalzell
Stone, Mode Lee
Stoodley, Bartlett Hicks
Stout, George Leslie
Strassburger, Eugene Bonn
Strauss, Anna Lord
Strike, Clifford Stewart
Stroup, Russell Cartwright
Stubbeman, Frank Diedrich
Styler, William Frances
Sunkin, Irving Burton
Swan, Dana Merrill
Swan, Marshall
Sweat, Herbert J.
Swedenberg, Hugh Thomas, Jr.
Sweeney, James William
Sweigert, Ray Leslie
Swope, Gerard, Jr.
Swords, Vincent Thomas
Sylvester, Richard Standish

T

Talley, Franz G.
Tandy, Charles David
Tate, Allen (John Orley)
Taylor, Charles Lincoln Jr.
Taylor, Eugene Jackson
Taylor, Herbert John
Taylor, James Davidson
Taylor, Richard Ray
Telfer, Bruce Thomas
Tetelman, Alan Stephen
Thaler, Alwin
Thaxter, Sidney Warren
Thode, Everett Wayne
Thom, William Taylor, Jr.
Thomas, Donald Roff
Timm, Tyrus Raymond
Tiomkin, Dimitri
Tobin, Emery F.
Tobriner, Walter Nathan
Todman, William Selden
Tolstoy, Alexandra Leo
Tomson, Bernard
Tooill, Kenneth du Vall
Torrey, John Stephen
Touster, Ben
Towe, Kenneth Crawford
Trefflich, Henry
Trenam, John James
Tribble, Hugh Wallace
Troutman, Henry Battey
Truesdail, Roger Williams
Trumbo, Dalton
Trytten, Merriam Hartwick
Tugwell, Rexford Guy
Tunnard, Christopher
Tuohy, John Joseph
Turner, Edward Felix, Jr.
Turner, Sol

U

Uhl, Paul Edgar
Uihlein, Robert August, Jr.
Upjohn, Everard Miller

V

Van Arsdale, Talman Walker, Jr.
Van Buitenen, Johannes Adrian Bernard
Vance, Joseph Anderson, Jr.
Vance, Lawrence Lee
Vance, Vivian
Vandenbosch, Robert
Van Oosterhout, Martin D.
Van Remoortel, Edouard
Van Rysselberghe, Pierre
Vardaman, John Wesley
Vaughan, Richard Henry
Velikovsky, Immanuel
Venn, Grant
Verner, Elizabeth O'Neill
Verney, Gilbert
Vestal, Donald McKee, Jr.
Vey, Ebenezer
Vickery, Katherine
Vincent, John Nathaniel
Vodrey, William Henry
Von Canon, Fred
von Erffa, Helmut Hartmann

W

Wagner, Herman Block
Walker, Donald Gregory
Walker, Frank Fish
Walker, Henry Polson
Wall, Nathan Sanders
Wallach, Sidney
Walsh, Cornelius Robert
Walsh, Warren Bartlett
Walters, Richard J.
Warner, Jack L.
Wasson, Houston Hutchinson
Watrous, David Gapen
Watts, David Alden
Watts, Franklin Mowry
Wauchope, Robert
Wayne, John (Marion Michael Morrison)
Weaver, Paul
Weaver, Warren
Weber, J. Sherwood
Weeks, Lewis George
Weiler, Emanuel Thornton
Weinman, Carl Andrew
Weiss, Jerome Sidney
Welch, Ernest Rivers
Welch, Leo Dewey
Welfling, Weldon
Wendland, John Prentice
Wengenroth, Stow
Werner, Alfred
Werwath, Karl Oscar
West, Roger Blake
Weston, Willard Garfield
Weybright, Victor
Wharton, John Franklin
Wheaton, William Lindus Cody
Wheeler, John Hervey
Wheelock, John Hall
White, Abraham
White, Charles Wilbert
White, Milton Grandison
White, Theo Ballou
White, William Richardson
Whitehill, Walter Muir
Widdemer, Margaret
Wiesinger, Frederick P.
Wildenhain, Frans
Wilder, Mitchell Armitage
Wildman, William Cooper
Wiley, Paul Luzon
Willard, Charlotte
Willauer, Arthur Osborne
Williams, John Fred
Williams, T. Harry
Williamson, Joe, Jr.
Wilmer, Richard Hooker
Wilson, Arthur McCandless
Wilson, Charles Morrow
Wilson, James Tinley
Wilson, John P., Jr.
Wimberly, Harrington
Winch, Robert Francis
Wingate, Francis Alfred
Winston, Harry
Winterkorn, Hans Friedrich
Wolf, Bernard Saul
Wolff, Alfred Andrew
Wolff, Harold Arnold
Wolff, Robert Jay
Wolman, Irving Jacob
Wong, Dick Yin
Wood, John Howland, Jr.
Woodward, Robert Burns
Woodworth, Laurence Neal
Work, James
Wragge, Sydney
Wright, Edward Ledwidge
Wright, John J.
Wright, Russel
Wriston, Henry Merritt
Wynia, Jess Edward

Y

Yardley, Richard Quincy
Yates, Gerard Francis
York, Robert

Young, Donald Ramsey
Young, Gig (Byron Barr)
Young, John Howard
Young, John M.
Young, Robert Busbey
Youngdahl, Luther W.
Younge, Sheila Frances
Younger, Edward Eugene

Z

Zaccaro, Luke Nicholas
Zachariasen, William Houlder (Fredrik)
Zador, Eugene
Zanuck, Darryl Francis
Zehr, Howard Jacob
Zeligs, Meyer Aaron
Zemach, Harve (Harvey Fischtron)
Ziegler, Vincent Charles
Zukofsky, Louis

Biographees in Marquis Who's Who Regional Directories

In our nation each region, each state, and each community has its own men and women whose achievements have molded, and continue to influence, contemporary society. The Marquis Regional Library—*Who's Who in the East, Who's Who in the Midwest, Who's Who in the South and Southwest,* and *Who's Who in the West*—is a permanent biographical record of the lives and careers of these individuals. All biographees in Marquis Who's Who regional directories are listed below, under the volume and edition in which their sketches can be found. Some few of these individuals, whose accomplishments are of decidedly national as well as regional importance, are also sketched in this edition of *Who's Who in America.*

Who's Who in the East—17th edition

Aagre, Curt
Aaron, Arnold
Aaron, Evalyn Wilhelmina Keisler (Mrs. Paul Aaron)
Aaron, Robert Saul
Aaronson, Warren David
Aasen, Lawrence Obert
Aaskov, Charles Edward
Abadir, Adel Ramsey
Abadir, Dale Maree
Abate, Vincenzo
Abaza, Nabil Abdel-Aziz
Abbagnaro, Louis Anthony
Abbas, Mian Mohammad
Abbasi, Aslam
Abbett, Robert Kennedy
Abbey, Albert Asher
Abbey, Leland Russell
Abbott, Anton Dwight
Abbott, Edward Leroy
Abbott, James Allen
Abbott, Joseph Aloysius
Abbott, Loretta A.
Abbott, Wilburn Lynn
Abbott, William Saunders
Abdalian, Arbak Arshak
Abdou, Hamed M.
Abdul, Raoul
Abdul-Shahid, Latif
Abel, Robert, Jr.
Abeles, Ernest D.
Abend, Kenneth
Aber, John William
Aber, William McKee
Aberman, Hugh Maurice
Abernathy, James Logan
Abeyatunge, Lambert Rajendra
Abraham, Carl Joel
Abraham, Milton Edward
Abraham, Morris
Abraham, Polachirakal Varkey
Abraham, Rajender
Abrahams, Robert Alan
Abramo, Ralph John
Abramovitz, Max
Abramowitz, Sol
Abrams, Charles Robert
Abrams, Floyd
Abrams, Jerome
Abrams, Jules Clinton
Abrams, Julius
Abrams, Philip
Abrams, Robert
Abrams, Rosalie Silber
Abrams, Warren Elliott
Abramson, Arthur Harris
Abramson, Edwin Donald
Abramson, Michael
Abramson, Samuel Robert
Abravanel, Diane (Mrs. Ben Don Abravanel)
Abt, Clark Claus
Abt, Vicki
Abu-Moustafa, Adel H.
Abusch, Sidney
Abush, Ronnie
Abzug, Bella Savitzky (Mrs. Martin Abzug)
Accardo, Salvatore Francis
Accettola, Albert Bernard
Aceto, Vincent John
Acheson, Patricia Louise
Achey, Dorothy Maie
Achor, William Thomas
Achtentuch, Herbert
Acker, Jack Lilly
Acker, Sherron Nay
Ackerberg, Robert Cyril
Ackerman, Jacob Lewis
Aclin, John Joseph
Acocella, Anthony Frank
Acocella, Louis Carmine
Acquaviva, Samuel Joseph
Acton, Constance Foster
Acton, Winser Paul
Adam, Richard Schofer
Adamo, Joseph Albert
Adams, A(lfred) John
Adams, Arlon Taylor
Adams, Benjamin Hedges, Jr.
Adams, Brockman
Adams, Carlyle
Adams, Carole C.
Adams, Clarence Lancelot, Jr.
Adams, Clyde Bruce
Adams, Donald Kendrick
Adams, Francis Vincent
Adams, Frank Anthony
Adams, Hugh White
Adams, John Laurence
Adams, John Ollie
Adams, John Oscar
Adams, Laurence John
Adams, Miriam
Adams, Ralph Ellison
Adams, Theodore Richard
Adams, Willard Dale
Adamski, Joseph Alexander
Adanalian, Alice Araxie
Adaniel, Tindalo Rogelio Agana
Addabbo, Joseph Patrick
Addei, Kwabena Adutwum
Addelston, Lorraine Wallenstein (Mrs. Aaron Addelston)
Addison, Anne Simone Pomex (Mrs. John Addison)
Addy, John Keith
Adelman, Martin Harris
Adelsberg, Harvey
Adelson, Jerry Jacob
Adelson, Warren Jay
Ades, Charles Douglas
Adie, Charles Leslie
Adisman, Irwin Kenneth
Adkins, George Bozeman, Jr.
Adler, Carl George
Adler, Charles
Adler, Charles Henry
Adler, David
Adler, Freda
Adler, Hyman Henry
Adler, Jack Franklin
Adler, Kurt
Adler, Lois
Adler, Myril (Mrs. Jack Adler)
Adler, Renee
Adler, Robert Ira
Adler, Samuel Hans
Adler, Stephen Fred
Adnopoz, Dorothy Jean
Adolfi, Robert Joseph
Adorian, Stephen John
Aebi, Ernst Walter
Affleck, John Harvey, III
Agarwal, Bal Krishan
Agban, Galaa M.
Agha, Farooq Perviaz
Agid, Steven Jay
Agnes, Sister Mary (Rosemary Agnes O'Brien)
Agnew, Donald Burns
Agresta, Anthony John, Sr.
Ahlgren, Mildred Carlson
Ahlgren, Roy Bertil
Ahmad, Sarfaraz
Ahmad, Syed Iftikhar
Ahmed, Pervez Ali
Ahn, Don
Ahner, Russel Oliver
Ahr, George W(illiam)
Ahsen, Akhter
Aidinoff, M(erton) Bernard
Aiello, Robert James
Aikman, Robert Howard
Ailey, Alvin
Ailloni-Charas, Dan
Aird, John Black
Aitchison, Ian Alexander
Aitken, Robert Peters
Ajello, Carl Richard
Ajello, Dominick Arnold
Akalin, Mazhar Ali
Ake, H(arry) Worth
Akeley, John Wilder
Akerberg, Ake
Akers, Carolyn
Akins, LeRoy Burton, Jr.
Akiyama, Toshio
Aksnes, Kaare
Alasia, Alfred Victor
Alatis, James Efstathios
Albano, D. John
Albee, Edward Franklin
Albers, Harry Robert
Albert, Gerald
Alberta, William Neil
Albertian, Alice Nazenig
Alberts, Donald Allan
Alberts, Robert Louis
Albertson, Christiern Gunnar
Albertson, Dean
Albertson, Murray Grieve
Albond, Harvey Neuman
Albrittain, Mary Katherine
Album, Manuel Moses
Albury, George Daniel
Alcabes, Joseph
Alcala, Ramon L., Jr.
Alcamo, Frank Paul
Aldan, David Richard
Alderman, Donald Bruce
Aldieri, Michael James
Aldin, Peter
Aldrich, Alton Parker
Aldrich, Frank Nathan
Aleksandrowicz, Lena Iorio (Brown)
Alers, Jose Oscar
Alex, Ralph Paul
Alexander, Christina Lillian
Alexander, Gabriel Alexander
Alexander, Harold
Alexander, Jon
Alexander, Lee
Alexander, Lucille Dillinger
Alexander, Myrna B.
Alexander, Raymond Daniel, Jr.
Alexander, Robert William
Alexander, Theron
Alexandru, Rene Simionescu
Alexy, Cornelius G. Louis
Alfano, Blaise Francis
Alfonso, Antonio Escolar
Alfultis, Richard Joseph
Ali, Majid
Ali, Syed Wajed
Aliano, Richard Anthony
Alihan, Milla
Alilunas, Leo John
Alinsangan, Hermenegildo Aligaen
Alio, Ivan Stamenitov
Alison, Darcy William
All, Frank Edward
Allaire, Royal Phillip
Allan, Hugh David
Allan, James Davis
Allard, Pierre
Allard, Serge Bruno
Alleman, G(ellert) S(pencer)
Alleman, Raymond Arthur
Allen, Angelene Elliott
Allen, B. Marc
Allen, Courtney Keith
Allen, Edgard Yan
Allen, Emil William, Jr.
Allen, Eugene Murray
Allen, George Ferguson
Allen, George Howard
Allen, Gerald Gordon
Allen, Henry Joseph
Allen, James P.
Allen, John Joseph
Allen, Katherine
Allen, Kristin Lloyd
Allen, Lee Thomas
Allen, Loma Moyer (Mrs. Deleslie Allen)
Allen, Marsha Lynn
Allen, Philip Dillon
Allen, Raleigh Howell, Jr.
Allen, Reginald Benjamin
Allen, Richard Putnam
Allen, Robert Erwin
Allen, Rocelia J.
Allen, Thomas Elmer
Allen, Wilbert
Allen, William Arthur
Allen-Claiborne, Joyce G.
Alley, Frederick Don
Allgeyer, Fernand Edward
Alliet, David Frederick
Allin, John Maury
Alling, Wilbur Merwin
Allison, David Arthur
Allison, John R.
Allison, Jonathan
Allman, Margo Hutz
Allshouse, Frank
Allukian, Myron, Jr.
Allyn, James Lyman
Almond, Paul
Almy, Rydia Eustace
Aloisio, Mary
Alosso, John
Alotta, Robert Ignatius
Alper, Allen Myron
Alper, Carl
Alper, M(ax) Victor
Alper, Melvin Gustavus
Alperin, Irwin Ephraim
Alperin, Richard Junius
Alpern, Andrew
Alpern, Milton
Alpert, George
Alpert, Grace Kennison
Alpert, Herman Saul
Alpert, Joel Jacobs
Al-Sakkal, Saad
Alshuk, Thomas John
Alson, Allan Lester
Alspaugh, Robert Odo
Alston, Casco
Alston, Gwendolyn Yvonne
Altabe, Joan Berg (Mrs. David Altabe)
Altbach, Philip G.
Altchek, Edgar David
Altemose, James Leon
Altenbern, Robert Allen
Altimari, Frank Xavier
Altman, Allan
Altman, Barry Layton
Altman, Lawrence Kimball
Altman, Stuart Harold
Altschuler, Robert Alexander, Jr.
Altura, Burton Myron
Altvater, William Caldwell
Aluise, Robert Richard
Alvarado, Alfredo
Alvarez, Manuel
Alves, Joseph Thomas
Alyea, Frederick Newcombe
Aman, Mohammed Mohammed
Amato, Peter Robert
Amber, Eugene Lewis
Amberson, J(ames) Burns
Ambler, E(dward) Curtis
Ambro, Jerome A., Jr.
Ambrose, Frederick Halsey, Jr.
Ambrose, Joseph M.
Ambrosio, Thomas James
Ambs, William Joseph
Ament, Richard
Amenta, Peter Sebastian
Amershek, Kathleen
Ames, Bernard Gareth
Ames, Lincoln
Ames, Richard Allen
Ames, Thomas-Robert Howland
Amick, Carol Campbell
Amick, James Albert
Amidon, Richard B.
Amman, Margaret Casey
Ammerman, Joseph S.
Amodei, Joseph Edward
Amores, Arsenio Juan
Amornmarn, Rumpa
Amorosino, Charles Santo, Jr.
Amrein, Robert Eugene
Amtmann, James Steven
Amy-Moreno, Angel Alberto
Anain, Joseph Marcelo
Anastasi, Joseph Angelo
Ances, I. G(eorge)
Anconetani, Joseph Louis
Andelman, Edward George
Anderberg, Edward
Andersen, Arnold Merwin
Andersen, Christopher Peter
Andersen, Daniel Johannes
Andersen, Marianne Singer
Andersen, Robert Allan
Andersen, Theodore Selmer
Anderson, Alfred Jakobus
Anderson, C(arl) Alan
Anderson, Charles Edward
Anderson, Charles Leonard, Jr.
Anderson, Chester Washington, III
Anderson, Claus Ludwig
Anderson, David
Anderson, David Gilroy
Anderson, David Martin
Anderson, Dennis Ray
Anderson, Donald Morgan
Anderson, Douglas Scranton Hesley
Anderson, Edith Helen
Anderson, Herbert Godwin, Jr.
Anderson, Hugold Berndt, Jr.
Anderson, Jack Garner
Anderson, James Buell
Anderson, Jane Virginia
Anderson, Jean
Anderson, Jerry Allen
Anderson, John Gaston
Anderson, Judith Rae (Mrs. Timothy Parmley Horne)
Anderson, Kenneth Norman
Anderson, Miles Jefferson
Anderson, Philip Warren
Anderson, Raymond Quintus
Anderson, Richard Louis
Anderson, Richard Theodore
Anderson, Richard Thomas
Anderson, Robert John, Jr.
Anderson, Robert Renner
Anderson, Ronald Jon
Anderson, Roy Scott
Anderson, Stanley James
Anderson, Thomas William
Anderson, Warren Mattice
Anderson, William Alphaunce
Anderson, William Carl
Anderson, William Henry
Anderson, William Joseph
Anderson, William Staton
Anderson Nolosco, Marynita Margaret
Andes, Lester Ray
Andors, Leonard
Andover, James J.
Andrade Matthews, Anne McIlhenney (Mrs. Michael R. Andrade)
Andrews, Charles Lawrence
Andrews, Dorothy Maud
Andrews, Elliott Ellsworth
Andrews, George Warren
Andrews, Herbert Duane
Andrews, John Fraser
Andrews, Lewis Marshall, Jr.
Andrews, Margaret Elizabeth
Andrews, Richard Cecil, Jr.
Andrews, Zelle Whitmarsh
Andriekus, Leonardas Kazimieras
Andriole, Richard Charles
Andronic, Alexe
Andrulis, Richard Stanley
Andrus, Cecil D.
Anfinsen, Christian Boehmer
Angelakos, Evangelos Thedorou
Angeleri, Lucy Milner
Angelini, Frank Samuel
Angell, San S.
Angell, Stephen Leroy, Jr.
Angelo, Anthony Richard
Angelotti, Robert
Anguah-Dei, Annie May
Angulo, Manuel Rafael
Angyan, André János
Anker, Irving
Ankerman, Paul William
Ankerstjerne, William Dick
Anns, Arlene Clair
Annunziata, Frank
Anrig, Gregory Richard
Ansary, Cyrus A.
Ansbacher, Heinz Ludwig
Anson, Joyce Narins
Anspach, Ernst
Antenucci, Arthur Joseph
Antenucci, Joseph
Anthon, Carl Gustav
Anthony, Albert John
Anthony, Edward Lovell, II
Anthony, Robert Armstrong
Antle, Charles Edward
Antman, Stuart Sheldon
Antognoli, John Anthony
Anton, Albert Joseph, Jr.
Anton, Arthur Charles
Anton, Barbara Miller (Mrs. Albert Anton)
Anton, Harvey
Antonelli, Luiz Kuster
Antoniades, Harry Nicholas
Antonini, Marion Hugh
Antoniou, Theodore
Antoun, Annette Agnes
Aoun, Kamal Habib
Apfelbaum, Adek
Apostol, E. Andre
Apostolos, Margaret Morris
Appel, Abraham Bram
Appel, Valentine
Appell, William Theodore
Apperson, Polly Merrill
Appignani, Louis Joseph
Appleton, Daniel Randolph, Jr.
Appleton, Harold Donald
Appleyard, Robert Bracewell
Aptt, Edward Bernard
Aquaro, Angelo Ralph
Aquilina, Joseph Philip
Aracena, Amado Niort
Arakelian, Jack
Araki, Minoru
Aramany, Mohamed Abdelal
Arams, Frank Robert

Araoz, Daniel Leon
Arbital, Samuel
Arbogast, Walter William, Jr.
Archbold, William Dana
Archer, Alford
Archer, David Horace
Archer, John Emerson
Archer, Ronald Dean
Archibald, Arnold Adams
Arcomano, Joseph Peter
Arden, George J.
Arensberg, Frederic Sanford
Arent, Russell Arthur
Arenth, Donald Craig
Arey, William Griffin, Jr.
Argiro, Larry Joseph
Argy, Dimitri
Argyil, Marion H. G.
Arkin, Stanley Samuel
Arkles, Barry Charles
Arlyck, Ralph Kenneth
Armao, Thomas Anthony
Armistead, Henry Tucker
Armour, Allan A.
Arms, Katharine Helena (Mrs. Joseph Edward Arms)
Armstrong, Conrad Roger
Armstrong, Craig Stephen
Armstrong, Dean Roy
Armstrong, Edward Bradford, Jr.
Armstrong, Gary Raymond
Armstrong, George Thomson
Armstrong, Robert John
Armstrong, Ronald William
Armstrong, Thomas Newton, III
Armstrong, Valerie
Armstrong, William James
Armstrong, William Leckie
Arndt, Cynthia
Arndt, Karl John Richard
Arnfeld, Leo
Arnold, Charles Burle, Jr.
Arnold, Charles Ingersoll
Arnold, David Ralph Jaques
Arnold, Edward Milton
Arnold, Frank, Jr.
Arnold, G. Dewey, Jr.
Arnold, George
Arnold, Herbert Matthew
Arnold, Jeffrey
Arnold, John Roland
Arnold, Merrill Sawyer
Arnold, Morris Fairchild
Arnold, Peter Wallace
Arnold, Rosalind Merceda
Arnold, Stephen
Arnold, Stephen Edward
Arnone, Carol Frances
Arnow, L(eslie) Earle
Arnowich, Beatrice
Aronfreed, Eva
Aronfy, Andrew George
Aronin, Jeffrey Ellis
Aronin, Lewis Richard
Aronovitch, Michael
Arons, Annette Trenner (Mrs. Leon Arons)
Arons, Marvin Shield
Aronson, Edgar David
Aronson, Philip Roger
Aronson, Shepard Gerard
Arp, Hilda Dora Pape (Mrs. Rudolph Arp)
Arrington, Lance Hardy
Arrow, Kenneth Joseph
Arsenault, Alfred Jude
Arseneau, James Charles
Arsht, Edwin David
Artaserse, Bonnie
Arther, Richard Oberlin
Arthur, James Douglas
Arthur, Paul, Jr.
Arthur, William Cathcart, Jr.
Artim, John
Arturi, Frank Louis
Artusio, Joseph Francis, Jr.
Arunasalam, Vickramasingam
Asadorian, William Ronald
Asbury, Melvin L.
Aschkinasi, Sonja Henrietta
Ash, Homer Lee
Ash, Rene Lee
Ash, Ronald Martin
Ashbaugh, William Hatch
Ashbery, John Lawrence
Ashbey, William Nelson
Ashby, Cecil Edward, Jr.
Ashdown, Marie Matranga (Mrs. Cecil Spanton Ashdown, Jr.)
Ashe, Amelia H. (Mrs. David I. Ashe)
Ashe, Carl Malcolm
Ashley, Marianne Rose
Ashmen, Roy
Ashodian, Mila Jeanette (Mrs. Howard William Payne)
Ashton, David John
Ashton, John K., Jr.
Askenasy, Alexander Robert
Askew, L(ouie) Rudolph
Askins, Arthur James
Aslaksen, Carroll
Assael, Henry
Assatourian, Alice Husisian (Mrs. Haig Gourji Khan Assatourian)
Assatourian, Haig Gourji Khan
Asta, Patricia Ellen
Astarjian, Nubar Krikor
Astles, Geoffrey Clark
Aston, Sherrell Jerone
Asuncion, Celedonio Manuel
Asuncion, Jacobo Rosales, Jr.

Atkins, Charles Agee
Atkinson, Eugene V.
Atkinson, Harold Witherspoon
Atkinson, Richard Chatham
Atkinson, Russell Welsh
Atkyns, Glenn Chadwick
Atkyns, Robert Lee
Atlas, Steven Alan
Ator, George Jacob
Atseff, Timothy Philip
Attar, Ahmad Mansour (Andy)
Attra, Harvey David
Attwood, William
Atwood, William Goodson
Atzmon, Ezri
Aubert, Kenneth Stephen
Aubin, Albert Kenneth
Aubrecht, Gordon James
Aubrey, Rachel Lowe Rustow (Mrs. Henry G. Aubrey)
Audain, Owen Albert
Audette, Louis Girard, II
Audin, Gary Robert
Auer, Emma Henrietta
Auerbach, Arnold ("Red")
Auerbach, Barry Bernard
Auerbach, Leonard
Auge, Bernard Girard
Augustine, Jerome Samuel
Augustine, Patrick Henry
Augustitus, Richard Michael
Auh, Yang John
Aulenbach, Donald Bruce
Ault, James Mase
Auman, George Edward
Aungst, Sherman Lester
Auses, John Paul
Auslander, David Ely
Auster, Donald
Auster, Nancy Eileen Ross (Mrs. Donald Auster)
Austin, Anthony
Austin, David Watkins Stuart
Austin, Ernest Augustus
Austin, Phillip Wayne
Austin, Stanley Stuart
Austin, Thomas Sherwood
Auten, David Charles
Auten, Hanford Louis, Jr.
Auteri, Rose Mary P.
Auth, Tony
Auyang, King
Avallone, Margaret Ann Thorsell
Avampato, Joseph James
Aversa, Alarico (Rico)
Aversa, John Michael
Avery, Cyrus Stevens, II
Avery, David Burgess
Avery, Henry
Aviado, Domingo Mariano
Avitzur, Betzalel
Avrami, Louis
Aw, Peggy
Awada, Michael
Axelrod, Howard Jay
Axelrod, Julius
Axelrod, Norman N(athan)
Axelson, Kenneth Strong
Aya, Roderick Honeyman
Aybar, Romeo
Ayers, Frank Edward
Ayers, Joseph Williams
Aykan, Kamran
Aylesworth, Thomas Gibbons
Aylsworth, Joseph Lynn, Jr.
Aylward, Leo Joseph ("Jay")
Ayoub, Alfred
Ayres, Robert Charles
Azer, Magdi Selim
Baar, James A.
Baatz, Charles Albert
Babbage, Joan Dorothy
Babcock, Betty Thompson
Babigan, Edward C.
Babine, Lawrence Robert
Babitzke, Herbert Roland
Bach, Robert Bourree
Bacharach, James Sidney
Bacher, Frederick Addison
Bachl, Frederick Anthony
Bachman, Carl Otto
Bachman, Kenneth Leroy, Jr.
Bachrach, Henry Milton
Bachrach, Howard Helmut
Backe, John David
Backenstoe, Gerald Seler
Backus, Dana Converse
Bacon, Charlotte Alzera Meade (Mrs. Edward D. Bacon, Jr.)
Bacon, Daisy Sarah
Badalamente, Marie Ann
Badalamenti, Anthony Francis
Badalamenti, Fred Leopoldo
Baden, Michael M.
Bader, Anne Shane
Bader, Franz
Bader, Herbert Irving
Bader, I. Walton
Bader, Richard E.
Bader, Samuel
Badertscher, David Glen
Badillo, Herman
Badmajew, Peter
Baechel, Charles William
Baehrel, Peter William
Baer, Harold, Jr.
Baer, Max
Baer, Sanford
Baer, Thomas James
Baerger, Paul Joseph
Baffa, Frank Patrick
Bagattine, John Peter
Bagby, James Willis, Jr.
Bagdan, Gloria

Baggish, Michael Simeon
Baggot-Guise, Jack A.
Bagley, Brian G.
Bagley, Edythe Scott
Bagley, Fenton Lloyd, Jr.
Baham, Gary Joseph
Bahat, Ari
Bailes, Stephen Martin
Bailey, Anne Marie
Bailey, Chris Harvey
Bailey, David Rollins
Bailey, Don
Bailey, George William
Bailey, Harold Whitney, Jr.
Bailey, Jake Schultz
Bailey, Kenneth Alan
Bailey, Lawrence Randolph
Bailey, Milton
Bailey, Ralph E.
Bailey, Robert William
Bailey, Samuel Albert
Bailey, William O.
Bailis, Lawrence Alan
Baillie, David
Bailowitz, Stanley Allan
Baily, Alfred Ewing
Bain, Donald Eugene, Jr.
Bain, George Keith
Baines, James Dalton
Bainum, Peter Montgomery
Bair, Medill
Baird, Charles Fitz
Baird, Henry Welles, III
Baird, James David
Baird, John Absalom, Jr.
Baird, Lindsay Laire, Jr.
Baird, Martha Joanna
Baird, Ronald James
Bais, Daljit Singh
Baisley, Robert William
Bakal, Abraham Itshak
Bakelman, Jack Sam
Baker, Benjamin Beale
Baker, Elsworth Fredrick
Baker, Harold Jay, Jr.
Baker, Harold Kent
Baker, Houston Alfred, Jr.
Baker, Jack Thomas
Baker, James Barnes
Baker, James Earl
Baker, Josephine L. Redenius (Mrs. Milton G. Baker)
Baker, Lois Meadowcroft
Baker, Malcolm C.
Baker, Nancy Ann
Baker, Richard Brown
Baker, Roger David
Baker, Seth Noel
Baker, Thomas
Baker, Verna Tomlinson (Mrs. Earl M. Baker)
Baker, Walter Louis
Baker, William Herbert
Baker, William Jesse
Bakewell, Charles Adams
Bakhru, Hassaram Choithram
Baksh, Mustapha Kemal
Balaban, Edward Elliot
Balaban, Maxine I.
Balanchine, George
Balazs, Denes Vilmos
Balbin, Julius Yul
Balcar, Gerald P.
Balding, Bruce Edward
Baldinger, Stanley
Baldwin, Charles Dickinson
Baldwin, Esther Eberstadt (Mrs. Robert Howe Baldwin)
Baldwin, Richard Anthony
Baldwin, Richard Sargent
Baldwin, Thomas Frerichs
Baldwin, Velma Neville
Balfe, Harry, II
Balistocky, Marvin Harold
Balistreri, William Francis
Ball, Burton Marsh
Ball, Edward Charles
Ball, Edwin Lawrence
Ball, Lawrence
Ball, Peter Paul, Jr.
Ballard, Claude Mark, Jr.
Ballard, Lowell Douglas
Ballard, Patricia Joan
Ballard, Robert Wilson
Ballesteros, Ruben Francisco
Ballou, Frank Russell
Ballou, Ellen Bartlett (Mrs. Norman V. Ballou)
Ballou, Kenneth Walter
Ballou, Raymond James
Balsam, Murray
Balter, Leslie Marvin
Baltimore, David
Baltimore, Ida Wright
Bamberger, Fritz
Bamberger, Jeffrey Lee
Bamdad, Jalil
Bamford, Joseph Charles, Jr.
Bampton, Rose Elizabeth
Banay-Schwartz, Miriam
Bancheri, Louis Peter, Jr.
Bancroft, Paul, III
Bandeen, Robert Angus
Bandeian, John Jacob
Bandi, William Richard
Bandler, Bernard
Bandyopadhyay, Alok Kumar
Bane, Marilyn Annette
Banerjee, Umesh Chandra
Baney, John Edward
Banik, Sambhu Nath
Bank, Arnold Harvey
Bank, Walter Joseph
Banker, Harry John
Bankert, Burnell Harold
Banks, Arthur Sparrow

Banks, David Owen
Banks, Karl Deon
Banks, Samuel Lee
Banks, Talcott Miner
Banning, John Peck, Jr.
Banov, Abel
Banov, Joan Heinemann (Mrs. Abel Banov)
Banta, John Joseph
Bantey, Bill
Banyard, Richard David
Bar, Kanai Lal
Baraf, Charles Selig
Baraheni, Reza
Barahura, Wolodymyr Bohdan Dmytro
Baramki, Theodore Atallah
Baran, Bradley Ronald
Baranaskas, Robert Charles
Baranski, Carl Thomas
Baratta, Edmond John
Barba, J. William
Barbanel, Sidney William
Barbaro, Anthony Joseph
Barbaro, Ronald Delano
Barbe, David Franklin
Barbee, William Henry, Jr.
Barbeito, Manuel Serafino
Barber, Edmund Amaral, Jr.
Barber, Glenn Vernon
Barber, Richard Davis
Barber, Stephen Guy
Barber, Wayne Sidman
Barbieri, Christopher George
Barbieri, David James
Barbour, Joseph Pius, Jr.
Barchet, Stephen
Barclay, Gordon Lanier
Barclay, Robert, Jr.
Barcus, Gilbert Martin
Bardes, Judith Leopold (Mrs. Charles Robert Bardes)
Barefoot, Gary Saylor
Barer, Seymour
Baret, Alexander Charles
Baretski, Charles Allan
Barkan, Stanley Howard
Barkat, Samuel
Barker, Elizabeth Anne
Barker, Harold Grant
Barker, Kenneth Ray
Barker, Robert Rankin
Barker, Verlyn Lloyd
Barlow, Edward Vernon
Barlow, George Barton
Barlow, Walter Greenwood
Barna, Gary Stanley
Barnard, Walther M.
Barnert, Alan H.
Barnes, Chaplin Bradford
Barnes, David Kennedy
Barnes, Elizabeth Chesnut (Mrs. Wilson King Barnes)
Barnes, Emmett George
Barnes, Frank Clyde
Barnes, George Henry
Barnes, Michael Darr
Barnes, Robert Morson
Barnett, David
Barnett, Josephine (Mrs. David Barnett)
Barnett, Lester Alfred
Barnett, Proctor Hawthorne
Barnett, William Arnold
Barnhard, Ivan Harold
Barnhard, Sherwood Arthur
Barnhart, Charlotte Kennedy (Mrs. Howard Kenneth Barnhart)
Barnhart, Jefferson Clifford
Barnhill, Gregory Hurd
Barnhouse, Ruth Tiffany
Barnum, William Milo
Baron, Charles Jesse
Baron, Colin Samuel
Baron, Harold
Baron, Robert Alex
Baron, Sydney Stuart
Barone, Rose Marie Pace (Mrs. John A. Barone)
Baroody, William Joseph
Barowsky, Harry
Barquist, Walter Eric
Barr, Charles B.
Barr, Hugh Thompson
Barr, John Wilmer Browning
Barr, Joseph Daniel, Jr.
Barr, Solomon Efrem
Barrack, William Sample, Jr.
Barresi, Charles Anthony
Barreto, Ernesto
Barrett, Herbert
Barrett, Montgomery Brinton
Barrett, Toni
Barrett, Walter Harmon
Barrick, Ann Henderson
Barrie, Joseph Rollin
Barrington, Thomas Martin
Barron, Gloria Joan
Barron, Mabel Ammons
Barron, Robert Paul
Barrows, Timothy Manning
Barry, Allen Ives
Barry, David Michael
Barry, Francis Edward
Barry, John Patrick
Barry, Kevin Gerard
Barry, Ronald Makepeace
Barsam, Paul Charles
Barson, Norman
Bart, Leonard Eugene
Bartalos, Mihaly
Bartberger, Charles Louis
Barth, Ernest
Barthold, James Carl
Bartholomew, George Anderson

Bartholomew, George Edward
Bartholomew, Phillip Raymond
Barth-Wehrenalp, Gerhard
Bartky, Murray S.
Bartleson, Michael Myers
Bartlett, Christopher Eric
Bartlett, Mabel
Bartlett, Marshall Kinne
Bartlett, Ralph Theodore
Barto, Walter Weaver, Jr.
Bartok, Frederick Francis
Bartol, Carl Richard
Bartolomeo, Robert Salvatore
Bartolotta, Peter Louis
Bartolotti, Virginia Laura
Barton, Charles Andrews, Jr.
Barton, Georgie Read (Mrs. George Thomas Barton)
Barton, Lucian Anthony
Barton, Sidney Medel
Barton, Stanley
Barton, William David
Barton, William Renald
Bartow, Jerome E.
Bartz, Alice Pugh
Baruch, John Alfred
Barwin, Bernard Norman
Barysh, Noah
Barzanti, Sergio
Basar, Ronald John
Bascom, Robert Holden
Bases, Albert Louis
Bashore, Donald Ray
Basili, Victor Robert
Basinski, Zbigniew Stanislaw
Baskerville, Charles Alexander
Baskous, Athan Alexander
Bass, Howard Larry
Bass, Hyman B.
Bass, Warner S.
Basseches, Robert Treinis
Bassett, Glenn Arthur
Bassett, Marion Preston
Bassett, Mary Grace
Bassett, Preston Crosby
Bassett, Raymond Francis
Bassinor, Paul
Bassis, Michael Steven
Bastarache, Edouard Gerald
Bastardi, Anthony Vincent
Bastian, Glenn Pickering
Bastomsky, Charles Henry
Basu, Samarendra
Bata, Andrew
Bata, Evelyn Joan
Batchelor, Barrington deVere
Batchelor, Shirley Stagg
Bate, Walter Jackson
Baten, Eugene Carl
Bates, Barbara J. Neuner (Mrs. Herman Martin Bates, Jr.)
Bates, Charles William
Bates, Don
Bates, Frank Joseph
Bates, Martha Copenhaver
Bates, Raymond Nelson
Bates, William Eaton
Batky, Gyula
Batt, Ronald Elmer
Battaglia, John D.
Batterman, Steven Charles
Battersby, Mark Edwin
Battle, Ronald Owen
Battle, Turner Charles, III
Battle, William Clement
Battles, Michaele Snyder
Battocchio, John Frank
Batton, Delma-Jane Heck (Mrs. James Harold Batton)
Bauder, Frederick William
Bauer, Charles Henry
Bauer, Gregg David
Bauer, John Peter
Bauer, Raymond Gale
Bauer, Richard Carlton
Bauernfeind, Jack (Jacob) C(hristopher)
Baughman, Urbanus Edmund
Baulknight, Charles Wesley
Baum, Alan Edmund
Baum, Emanuel Lester
Baum, Gilbert
Baum, Ingeborg Ruth
Baum, John Leach
Baum, Richard Theodore
Baum, Sharon Enloe
Baum, Sheldon
Baum, Siegmund Jacob
Baum, Stanley Allen
Baum, William
Bauman, Carol Dawson
Bauman, Mary Kinsey
Bauman, Robert E.
Bauman, William Allen
Baumbach, Richard Carter
Baumeister, Victor Floyd
Baumgaertner, Imre v.
Baumhofer, Walter Martin
Baunach, Lynne Guerke
Bavar, David Ian
Bavasi, Peter Joseph
Bax, Ronald Frank
Baxley, Marvin Owen (Max)
Baxter, Ruth Howell
Bayard, Alexis Irenee du Pont
Bayer, Christopher Alan
Bayer, Robert Adolph, Jr.
Bayuk, John Frank
Bazelon, David Lionel
Bazewicz, Robert Joseph
Bazin, Albert Jeil
Beach, Carter Leroy
Beach, David Nelson, III
Beach, Louis Andrew
Beach, Paul Maynard, Jr.
Beach, Rose Mary Randall

Beacher, Lawrence Lester
Beagle, Charles Wellington
Beahm, Ralph Eugene
Beakes, Kendall Douglas
Beal, Alexander Simpson
Beal, Bruce A.
Beal, Carl Lewis
Beal, Richard Barratt
Beale, Everett Minot
Beale, Georgia Robison (Mrs. Howard Kennedy)
Beall, Harry Spurgeon, Jr.
Beam, Margaret Alexine
Bean, Calvin
Bean, Carl Bennett
Beard, Edward P.
Beard, Lillian McLean
Beard, Timothy Donahue, III
Beards, Ashley Harris
Beardslee, William Earl
Beardsley, Theodore S(terling), Jr.
Bearsch, Lee Palmer
Bearss, William Stanley
Beasley, Wayne Machon
Beaton, Roberta Ann Jensen
Beattie, Diana Scott (Mrs. Robert Nathan Stuchell)
Beattie, Edward James, Jr.
Beauchemin, Paul Thomas
Beauchemin, Roger Olivier
Beaulien, Marcel Laurent
Beaver, Howard Oscar, Jr.
Beavers, Allen Louis, Jr.
Bechis, Kenneth Paul
Bechtle, Jon Michael
Bechtold, Charles Louis
Beck, Adrian Robert
Beck, Albert
Beck, Audrey Phillips
Beck, Dorothy Fahs
Beck, Earl Henry, Jr.
Beck, Felix M.
Beck, Frances Patricia
Beck, Gasper Paul
Beck, John Harry
Beck, Michael John
Beck, Robert Arthur
Beck, Robert Edward
Beck, Robert Randall
Beck, William
Becker, Arthur Bernard
Becker, Edward Paul
Becker, Jay Joseph
Becker, Jerry Ellsworth
Becker, Kip
Becker, LaFollette
Becker, Leon Robert
Becker, Mary Louise
Becker, Natalie Rose Harriton (Mrs. Stanley M. Becker)
Becker, Paul W.
Becker, Robert Louis, Jr.
Becker, Sarah Ruskin
Becker, Stephen Philip
Becker, William Adolph
Beckett, William Wade
Becksted, William Fredrick
Beddow, John Hebert
Bedell, Forest Keith
Bedell, John Robert
Bedell, Susanna E.
Bedford, Ruth Alice Haedike (Mrs. Edwin Garrard Bedford)
Bedrosian, Samuel Der
Beebe, William Dow
Beechhold, Henry Frank
Beede, Benjamin Ripley
Beeman, William Orman
Beer, David Wells
Beer, Jeanette Mary Ayres
Beer, Robert Augur
Beers, David Monroe
Beers, Robert George
Beery, Edwin Newman
Beeton, Diana LaFay
BeGasse, Bruce Kenneth
Begell, William
Begley, Thomas Devlin, Jr.
Begner, Edith
Beguin, Fred Paul
Behan, Richard Lowell
Behl, Wishvender Kumar
Behnke, John Alden
Behrend, William Louis
Behrens, John Charles
Behrman, Harold Richard
Beier, Leonard Samuel
Beilstein, Henry Richard
Beinfield, Malcolm Sydney
Beinhocker, Gilbert David
Beiser, Leo
Beishlag, George Albert
Beiswinger, George Lawrence
Beitel, Herbert Manson
Bej, Emil
Bejarano, Jose Rafael
Bejarano, Luis Enrique
Bekker, Peter Otto Erik, Jr.
Belafsky, Mark Lewis
Belchikoff, Karin Jo
Belden, Frederick Hesley
Belden, Reed Holman
Belden, William Merrill
Beldock, Donald Travis
Belefonte, Carmen Paul
Beletz, Elaine Ethel
Belfiore Loconte, Giovanni
Belkin, Gary Stuart
Belkin, Marvin
Belknap, Michael H. P.
Bell, Calvin Miles
Bell, Charles Robert
Bell, Charles Spence
Bell, Cynthia Marie

Bell, Ernest Lorne, III
Bell, George Brown
Bell, Griffin B.
Bell, Haskell Harman
Bell, Howard Hughes
Bell, James Frederick
Bell, James Milton
Bell, Joseph Emeal
Bell, Julius Arthur
Bell, Martin Harold
Bell, Morley Bruce
Bell, Paul Albert
Bell, Randall William
Bell, Robert Edward
Bell, Robert Lawrence
Bell, Stephen (Steve) Scott
Bell, Thomas Robert, III
Bellamy, Joe David
Bellante, E. Lawrence
Bellard, Americo (Max)
Bellas, Hugh Wallace
Belle, Joseph Vincent
Beller, Martin Leonard
Beller, Stephen Mark
Bellin, Martin R.
Bellinger, Jack Waitstill
Bellmore, Mandell
Bello, Michael Joseph, Jr.
Bellomo, Charles Michael
Bellotti, Francis Xavier
Bellows, Howard Arthur
Bellows, Howard Arthur, Jr.
Bellucci, Richard John
Bellwin, Alexander
Belote, William Milton
Belsky-Stetsenko, Ivan
Belt, David Levin
Bemis, Hal Lawall
Benander, Laurence Edwin
Benaresh, Ehsanollah
Benda, Harold William
Bender, Adam Norman
Bender, Coleman Coalport
Bender, Filmore Edmund
Bender, Joseph
Benderly, Rose H.
Bendetsen, Karl Robin
Bendz, Diana Jean
Benedick, Dale Raymond
Benedict, Dean Edwin
Benedict, Joseph Harold, Jr.
Benedict, Linda Sherk
Benedict, Lloyd Harvey
Benedict, Robert Clyde
Benedikt, Lucie
Benenson, Edward Hartley
Benenson, Esther Siev (Mrs. William Benenson)
Beneventano, Thomas Carmine
Beneventi, Francis Anthony
Beni, Gerardo
Benjamin, Chester Ray
Benjamin, Gilbert Leon
Benjamin, Jeffrey Lloyd
Benjamin, Sidney Herbert
Benjamin, Theodore Simon
Benjaminson, Morris Aaron
Benkendorf, Mary Bell
Benn, Michael Andrew
Benner, B. K. Buck
Benner, Richard Edward, Jr.
Bennet, David Hughes
Bennett, Clinton Wendell
Bennett, Edward Henry
Bennett, Eudora Smith
Bennett, Gordon Lockhart
Bennett, Harriet
Bennett, Henry Garland
Bennett, Ivan Loveridge, Jr.
Bennett, James Davison
Bennett, James Gordon, Jr.
Bennett, John Eugene
Bennett, Marion Tinsley
Bennett, Melvin
Bennett, Richard Kistler
Bennett, Robert Clement
Bennett, Rowland Francis
Bennett, Walker Gardner, II
Benning, Calvin James
Bennion, Scott Desmond
Bennun, Alfred
Benoit, Richard Charles, Jr.
Bensel, Arlington
Benskina, Margarita O. (Princess Orelia)
Benson, Douglas Bruce
Benson, Richard Lewis
Benson, Robert Dale
Benson, Wilbur Maxwell
Bent, Henry Everett
Bentivegna, Peter Ignatius
Bentley, James Francis
Bentley, Robert Asa Lincoln
Benton, Allen Hayden
Benton, Donald Stewart
Benton, Joseph Edward, Jr.
Benton, Peter
Bentzen, Ole Hans
Benz, Edward John
Beraducci, John Angelo
Beranek, Leo Leroy
Beranek, Phyllis Knight (Mrs. Leo L. Beranek)
Berarducci, Arthur Angelo
Berc, Kenneth Myles
Berck, Martin G.
Berdick, Murray
Berdon, Robert Irwin
Bereday, George Zygmunt Fijalkowski
Berenbaum, Arthur Abraham
Berend, Robert William
Berens, Norman
Berenson, Joseph S.
Berent, David
Bereston, Eugene Sydney
Berg, Alan Sulzberger
Berg, Gerald Robert
Berg, Lois Anne
Berg, Louis Leslie
Bergau, Frank Conrad
Bergen, Catharine Mary
Bergen, Daniel Patrick
Berger, Bertram
Berger, Eugene Y.
Berger, Harvey Robert
Berger, Henry
Berger, Herbert
Berger, Oscar
Berger, Richard A.
Berger, Robert Irving
Berger, Robert Norman
Berger, Sanford Earl
Berggren, John Philip
Bergin, Charles Kyran, Jr.
Bergland, Bob Selmer
Bergland, Glenn David
Berglund, Alice Mae
Bergman, Barry Edward
Bergman, Charles Cabe
Bergman, James Abert
Bergmann, Arthur
Bergmann, Warren Clarence
Bergquist, Philip Eugene
Bergstrom, Gary Leonard
Bergstrom, John
Bering, Edgar Andrew, Jr.
Berk, Harold Lee
Berk, Nathaniel Gabriel
Berk, Peter David
Berkeley, Irving Herman
Berkeley, Norborne, Jr.
Berkeley, Norma Lifson (Mrs. Arnold D. Berkeley)
Berkman, Jack Neville
Berko, Frances Giden
Berkoff, Charles Edward
Berkon, Martin
Berkowitz, Bernard Solomon
Berkowitz, Carl Mitchell
Berkowitz, Edward
Berkowitz, Wesley Ian
Berkson, James Harold
Berl, Ethel Garfunkel
Berler, Lawrence Sheldon
Berlin, Clem
Berlin, Donald Robert
Berliner, William Michael
Bermack, Charles K(almon)
Bermack, Eugene
Berman, Allan
Berman, Allan Bertrand
Berman, Barry
Berman, Bernard Alvin
Berman, Daniel Elihu
Berman, Herbert Lawrence
Berman, Irwin
Berman, Jane Weinstein
Berman, Judith Robbins
Berman, Leonard David
Berman, Malcolm Frank
Berman, Marshall Fox
Berman, Martin
Berman, Richard Angel
Berman, Robert Donald
Berman, Sidney
Berman, Simeon Moses
Bernald, Eugene
Bernard, Lawrence
Bernard, Marcelle Thomasine
Bernardi, Ralph Eugene
Bernardo, Peter
Bernay, Elayn Katz
Bernays, Edward L.
Bernbach, William
Berner, Robert Kenneth
Berney, Thomas Edward
Bernfeld, Gerald Edward
Bernfeld, Herbert
Bernfeld, Peter Harry William
Bernhang, Arthur Maurice
Bernhardt, Lewis Jules
Bernholz, William Francis
Bernier, Raymond Joseph
Bernosky, Herman George
Berns, H(erman) Jerome
Bernstein, Arthur George
Bernstein, David
Bernstein, Emmanuel Moses
Bernstein, Eugene Harold
Bernstein, Irving
Bernstein, Leonard
Bernstein, Marianne E. (Mrs. Robert S. Wiener)
Bernstein, Marver Hillel
Bernstein, Philip
Bernstein, Robert Louis
Berrie, Robert Harris
Berrone, Louis
Berry, Carlton Frederick, Jr.
Berry, David Christopher
Berry, Robert Gifford
Berry, Robert Worth
Berry, Walthall Madden
Berson, Robert Mordecai
Berson, Sidney Harry
Berstein, Irving Aaron
Bertisch, Abraham Maurice
Bertolet, William Bowden
Bertolino, Emil M.
Bertram, John George
Bertram, Lucy Virginia
Bertrand, John Peter
Bertsch, Jack Herman
Berube, Bernice Germaine
Bery, Rajendra Nath
Beshar, Christine
Beshar, Robert Peter
Besley, Richard Norton
Besner, Claude Edouard
Bess, Harold Leon
Bessette, Russell William
Bessom, Malcolm Eugene
Bessor, William Dinsmore
Best, Edgar Everett
Bete, John Morris
Beter, Peter David
Bethe, Hans Albrecht
Bethea, Sammie
Bettenhausen, Lee Herman
Better, Michael Isaac
Betts, Francis Marion, III
Betz, Alfred Anthony
Betz, Gregor William
Betz, Jean
Beube, Frank Edward
Beutel, William Steel
Beuzeville, Carlos Adalberto
Bevacqua, Ronald Anthony
Bevacqua, Saverio Francis
BeVard, Ralph Edward
Bever, Christopher Theodore
Beverly, Laura Elizabeth
Bevilacqua, Joseph A.
Beyer, Francis David, Jr.
Beyrer, Nancy Elizabeth
Bhagat, Phiroz Maneck
Bhamre, Suresh Tushiram, Sr.
Bhandari, Narendra Chand
Bhar, Tarak Nath
Bhatt, Jagdish Jeyshanker
Bhattacharji, Pares Chandra
Bhattacharya, Arun Kumar
Bhattad, Sitram Manikalal
Bhirud, Suresh L.
Bhoi, Paramjit Singh
Bhushan, Bharat
Bhuyan, Kailash Chandra
Biaggi, Mario
Bialas, Paul Anthony
Bialer, Irving
Bianco, Celso
Biassey, Earle Lambert
Bibaud, Richard Edgar
Bibb, D. Porter, III
Bibbo, Michael Paul
Bible, Charles James
Bick, Malcolm Wagner
Bickel, William Croft
Bickford, Elwood Dale
Bickford, John Howe
Bicking, Charles Albert
Bickley, George, Jr.
Bicofsky, David Marc
Bida, Michael Charles
Biddle, Nicholas, Jr.
Biden, Joseph Robinette, Jr.
Bidwell, Donald
Bidwell, Robert Ernest
Bielenberg, Ursula
Biemiller, Ruth Cobbett (Mrs. Reynard Biemiller)
Bienstock, Herbert
Bierly, Mahlon Zwingli, Jr.
Bierman, Arnold
Biernat, Lillian M. Nahumenuk
Bigelow, John Brittain
Bigge, Robert James
Biggs, Jeremy Hunt
Biggs, Sheridan Chapman, Jr.
Bigley, William Joseph, Jr.
Bihn, John Philip
Bijlfeld, Willem Abraham
Bil, Feyzi Necat
Bilbow, James Robert
Bilello, Frank Leonard
Bilello, Michael Anthony
Biles, George Emery
Bilinsky, Yaroslav
Billard, Albert Calvin
Billeci, Andre George
Biller, Henry Burt
Billera, Franklin A.
Billharz, Roger William
Billig, Donal Michael
Billings, Gerard
Bilski, Peter
Binder, Frederick Moore
Bingham, Andrew William
Bingham, Elizabeth Claughton (Mrs. Harold J. Bingham)
Bingham, Frank George, Jr.
Bingham, Jonathan B(rewster)
Binkley, Howard Lee
Binstock, Arnold Irwin
Bintzer, William Winfield
Biondi, Angelo Mario
Birch, Robert Louis
Bird, Barnard Taylor
Bird, John Malcolm
Bird, L. Raymond
Bird, Thomas Edward
Bird, William Frederick James
Birdsall, Natalie Audibert
Birger, Jordan
Biringer, Paul Peter
Birke, Arnold A.
Birken, Steven
Birkett, Eastman
Birkholz, Gertrud Maria
Birkimer, Donald Leo
Birnbach, Seymour
Birnbaum, Jacob
Birnbaum, Melvyn
Birnbaum, Robert Benjamin
Birnbaum, Roger William
Birnbaum, Sheila L.
Birnbaum, Solomon Asher
Birnberg, Jack
Biro, Kenneth Louis
Biro, Laszlo
Biron, Jacques
Birrell, Donald George
Birren, Faber
Birutis, George
Bishoff, Lee Edward
Bishop, Everett George
Bishop, Frank Eugene, Jr.
Bishop, Frederick Thomas
Bishop, Gordon Bruce
Bishop, John Byron
Bishop, Milo Ellis
Bissell, Pelham St. George, III
Bissinger, Eleanor Lebenthal (Mrs. H. Gerard Bissinger II)
Bisson, Robert Anthony
Bissonnette, Georges Louis
Bissoondoyal, Dan
Bistrian, Bruce Ryan
Bittick, Robert Lucian
Bittman, Loran Rice
Bittner, Norman Douglas
Bixby, R. Burdell
Bixler, Herbert Edwards
Bizer, Lawrence Stanley
Blacharsh, Carl
Blacher, Stanley Paul
Black, Carolyn Lapp
Black, Edward Barnwell
Black, Eugene Charlton
Black, Ira Barrie
Black, Lewis Stanley
Black, Martin Max
Black, Perry
Black, Richard Thomas
Black, Robert Atticks, Jr.
Black, William
Black, William Fisher
Black, Yuill
Blackburn, Benjamin Coleman
Blackburn, George L.
Blackburn, Margaret Irwin
Blackey, Edwin Arthur, Jr.
Blackham, Ann Rosemary (Mrs. James W. Blackham, Jr.)
Blackmun, Harry Andrew
Blai, Boris
Blair, Benjamin Franklin, Jr.
Blair, David William
Blair, Edward Joseph
Blair, James Walter, Jr.
Blair, John Aitken
Blair, McClellan Gordon
Blake, Alfred Greene
Blake, Richard Douglas
Blakely, Allison
Blakely, James Russell
Blakeman, Thomas Ledyard
Blanchard, Bertie Joseph
Blanchard, Bruce
Blanchard, Helen M.
Blanchet, Bertrand
Blanck, Robert Franklin
Blank, Robert Gerhard
Blankenship, Edward Gary
Blankfein, Robert Jerome
Blankman, Ruth Costa
Blanton, Edward Lee, Jr.
Blanton, Lawton Walter
Blanzaco, Andre Charles
Blasco, Andrew Patrick
Blasi, Robert Vincent
Blasland, Warren Vincent, Jr.
Blass, John Paul
Blaszczak, Joseph Wladyslaw
Blatchley, David Boyd
Blate, Samuel Robert
Blatz, Linda Jeanne
Blatz, William Edmund
Blaufox, Morton Donald
Blaugrund, Stanley Marvin
Blauvelt, Howard W.
Blauvelt, James Andrew
Blauvelt, Robert Ward
Bleicher, Sheldon Joseph
Bleiler, Frederick Fay
Bleiweiss, Eugene
Blenko, Ardis Jones (Mrs. Walter J. Blenko)
Blick, Joseph Greeley
Bligh, Veronica Marie
Blind, William Charles
Blisko, Lawrence Bernard
Bliss, Anthony Addison
Bliss, Dennis Leslie
Bliss, Philip Jamison
Bliss, Robert Porter, Jr.
Blitz, Daniel
Bloch, Henry Simon
Bloch, Jacques W.
Bloch, Joseph Loring
Bloch, Konrad
Bloch, Raphael S.
Blocher, Maurice Henry
Block, Cy
Block, Frederick Henry
Block, Marcus Theodore
Block, William
Blodgett, Anne Washington
Bloede, Victor Gustav
Blogoslawski, Walter Joseph
Blomberg, Richard David
Blomfield, Richard Best
Blomquist, Jane Margaret
Blondell, Allan St. John
Blood, Robert Justus
Bloom, Edwin John, Jr.
Bloom, Florence Teicher
Bloom, Melvyn Harold
Bloom, Samuel Michael
Bloom, Stephen Roger
Bloomenthal, Abraham Philip
Bloomer, William David
Bloomfield, Nerice Siegel
Bloomfield, Philip Earl
Bloomfield, William Mendel
Bloomquist, Howard Richard
Bloomstein, Michael Ira
Bloore, Ernest William
Blough, William Milton
Blount, Kenneth Morgan, Jr.
Bloustein, Edward J.
Blue, Rose
Blue Spruce, George, Jr.
Bluestein, Bernard Richard
Bluh, George Kenneth
Blum, James David, Sr.
Blum, John Jay
Blum, Ludwig Leonhard
Blum, Maurice Daulton
Blumberg, Arnold George
Blumberg, Barbara Salmanson (Mrs. Arnold G. Blumberg)
Blumberg, Baruch Samuel
Blumberg, Gerald
Blumberg, Harold
Blumberg, Joel Myron
Blumberg, Lawrence
Blume, James Beryl
Blume, Robert Murray
Blumenberg, Robert Murray
Blumengarten, Gail Rachel
Blumenthal, Elliott Davis, Jr.
Blumenthal, Joseph
Blumenthal, W. Michael
Blumstock, Robert Edward
Boal, Bernard Harvey
Board, Fred Carl
Boardman, Joseph Thomas
Boates, Tilbury Thomas, Jr.
Boatner, Mrs. Edmund Burke (Maxine Tull Boatner)
Bobby, Annette M.
Bocchino, Robert Louis
Bock, Arthur Emil
Bock, Harry H.
Bockian, James Bernard
Bodden, Hugh Edward
Bodley, Harley Ryan, Jr.
Bodnar, John Paul
Bodner, Richard Martin
Boe, Nils Andreas
Boe, Roy Lars Magnus
Boe, Sue Lohmeyer
Boehm, Alice E(velyn)
Boehm, Edward Gordon, Jr.
Boeker, Gilbert Ferber
Bogart, Grace Elizabeth
Bogart, William Harry
Bogdan, Joseph Carl
Bogen, Stanley Maurice
Boggio, George John
Bogin, Alvin
Bogley, Samuel W.
Bognar, Charles Ralph
Bogosian, John Sarkis
Bogosian, Paul John
Bohlmann, Hans Heinrich
Böhm, Emanuel Theodore
Bohman, Raynard Frederick, Jr.
Bohn, Nelson Ranson
Bohn, William Chanler
Bohon, Marlane Geldart
Bohy, David Weldon
Boikess, Olga Shniper
Bojarskyj, Isydora
Bok, Derek Curtis
Bokser, Lewis
Boland, Edward P.
Boland, Gerald Lee
Bolande, Robert Paul
Bolduc, Reginald Joseph
Boley, Robert Eugene
Boley Bolaffio, Rita
Bolger, Jack
Bolt, Edwin Ralph
Bolt, Richard Eugene
Bolton, Barbara Weeks (Mrs. John Dickson Bolton, Jr.)
Bombard, Donald Keith, Jr.
Bona, Frederick Emil
Bonaguidi, Lawrence Paul John
Bonamici, Daniel Robert
Bonanno, Anthony Kenneth
Bonanno, Philip Carl
Bonaventura, Maria Migliorini
Bond, David Jay
Bond, Elizabeth Dux
Bond, Harold Herant
Bond, James Phillips
Bondy, Heinz Eric
Bone, John Henry
Bone, Larry Earl
Bonfield, Edward Harvey
Bonforte, Richard James
Bongiovanni, Carl
Bonk, Judith Ann
Bonner, Charles Douglass
Bonner, Marie A.
Bonney, Jean Cozza (Mrs. Russell Norwood Bonney, Jr.)
Bonoyer, John Joseph
Bonsall, Edward Horne, III
Bonvillian, John Doughty
Boodey, Cecil Webster, Jr.
Booker, Alvin Eugene
Bookhout, Leland Travis
Bookhout, Robert Marshall
Bookout, Arthur Roscoe, Jr.
Books, Kenneth Wilson
Bookstaver, Julian Barnet
Bookwalter, John Robert
Boone, Charles Walter
Boorstein, Beverly Weinger
Booser, Earl Richard
Booth, George Warren
Booth, James Edward
Booth, Robert Gray
Bopp, Raymond Karl
Boraby, Miguel Angel
Bordeleau, Nancy Vivian McIntosh (Mrs. Roland J. Bordeleau)
Borden, Enid Alana
Borden, George Asa
Borders, William Donald
Borecky, Isidore
Borer, Edward Turner
Borg, Malcolm Austin
Borge, Carlos
Borgos, Stephen John
Borgstedt, Harold Heinrich
Boritz, Myra Arlene Freilich
Borke, Robert Francis
Borkin, Andrew
Borkowsky, Roman
Borland, Barbara Dodge (Mrs. Hal Borland)
Borland, John Nelson, III
Borland, Virginia Ann
Borle, Andre Bernard
Bormel, Joseph
Borneman, Herman Francis
Bornemann, Alfred Henry
Bornscheuer, George Charles
Bornstein, Abraham Benjamin
Bornstein, Myer Sidney
Boroson, Harold Robert
Borow, Lawrence Stephen
Borowich, Abba Emanuel
Borra, Emil Joseph
Borsch, Roman Nickolas
Borsching, Robert Richard, Sr.
Borsher, Harry Nathan
Borsody, Robert Peter
Bortz, Bernard Jack
Borum, Rodney Lee
Bosch, Albert Casper
Bose, Guru P.
Bosin, Maxine Beth
Boss, Berdell Gladstone
Bosse, Malcolm Joseph
Bostelle, Theodore Thomas
Bostelman, William Townsend
Bostian, David Boone, Jr.
Bostin, Marvin Jay
Boston, Robert McCauley
Boswell, Alfred Chester, Jr.
Bosworth, Phyllis Ruth
Bosworth, Roswell Sewell, Jr.
Both, Robert L.
Bothne, Ralph Edward
Botto, Richard Alfred
Bottone, Edward Joseph
Botwinick, Joseph William
Botwinick, Leo
Botwinick, Michael
Bou, Mary Ellen
Bouchard, Carl Edward
Bouchard, Gilman Donald
Bouchard, Patricia Jean
Boucher, Jack Edward
Boucher, Mary Beth
Boucher, Raymond Marcel Gut
Boucher, Rita Jeannette
Boudreau, Allan
Boudreau, Francis Helier
Boufford, Ronald P.
Bougas, James Andrew
Bouissac, Paul Antoine
Boulware, Elizabeth Faye
Bourdon, David (Joseph, Jr.)
Bourke, Robert Samuel
Bourne, Avis Cottrell (Mrs. C. Fred Bourne)
Bourne, Mary Bonnie Murray (Mrs. Saul Hamilton Bourne)
Bourque, Jean Jacques
Bousaada, Tony Farid
Bout, Jan
Boutiette, Richard Clifford
Boutillier, Robert John
Boutwell, Harvey Bunker
Bouvier, Edmond Edward
Bouvier, Leon Francis
Bova, Robert Joseph
Bovarnick, Bennett
Bove, Henry Joseph
Bovis, Henry Eugene
Bowditch, James Lowell
Bowe, Edward Thomas
Bowen, John Sheets
Bowen, William Gordon
Bowering, John Renville
Bowers, Charles Edward
Bowers, Ethel May
Bowers, Eugene Vincent
Bowers, Grayson Hunter
Bowers, Jack Frederic
Bowers, James Sutphen
Bowers, Patricia Eleanor Fritz
Bowers, Paul Eugene
Bowers, Richard Philip
Bowes, Dennis Michael
Bowie, Jack Edward
Bowker, Lawrence Wayne
Bowling, James Chandler
Bowling, John Knox, Jr.
Bowlsbey, Leonard Stanley, Jr.
Bowman, Claude Charlton
Bowman, James Floyd, II
Box, Theodor Max
Boxer, Theodore
Boxer, Tim
Boxill, Gale Clark
Boxwill, Frank E.
Boyce, Thomas Kenneth
Boyd, Donald William, Jr.
Boyd, John
Boyd, Rachel Elizabeth
Boyd, Robert
Boyd, Robert James
Boyd, William James David
Boyd-Monk, Heather Gwendoline
Boyer, George Kenneth
Boyer, Jere Michael
Boyes, Fred Howard
Boylan, William Alvin
Boyle, Carol Ann

Boyle, Edward Leo, Jr.
Boyle, Richard John
Boyle, Robert Joseph
Boyle, William Leo, Jr.
Boylen, Daniel Berkley
Boyles, Charles William
Boynton, Edwin Frank
Bozorth, Squire Newland
Bozza, Dorothea Marian
Bozza, Richard George
Brachfeld, Jonas
Brack, Harold Arthur
Brackbill Cletus, Ralph
Brackett, Ernest Walker
Bradbury, Bianca Ryley
Braddock, Peter Samuel
Bradfield, Walter Samuel
Bradford, Charles Allen
Bradford, Leland Powers
Bradford, Robert Allen
Bradford, Robert Ernest
Bradish, Sandra Marie
Bradish, Thomas James, Jr.
Bradlee, Thomas Francis
Bradley, Eleanor Rehill
Bradley, Mark Edmund
Bradley, Murray Lee
Bradley, Norman Robert
Bradley, Norman Robert
Bradley, Raymond Edgar, Jr.
Bradley, William Warren (Bill)
Bradshaw, Joseph George
Bradshaw, Lawrence Allen
Bradshaw, William Daniel
Brady, Gene Paul
Brady, H(erbert) Wayne
Brady, John Joseph
Brady, Joseph John
Brady Burks, Adelaide
Bragagnolo, Julio Alfredo
Bragdon, David Hugh
Bragg, John Kendal
Bragg, Joseph Lee
Braginsky, Benjamin Martin
Braha, Thomas I.
Braidwood, Clinton Alexander
Braiotta, Louis, Jr.
Brake, Edward Thomas
Brakeley, George Archibald,
Jr.
Brakl, Heinz Joseph
Braly, Earl Burk
Bram, Leonard
Bram, Stephen Bennett
Brame, Edward Grant, Jr.
Bramfitt, Bruce Livingston
Bramowitz, Alan David
Bramwell, Fitzgerald Burton
Branch, Edna Raphael
Bernadette
Branch, Laurence George
Brand, Leon
Brand, Philip
Brand, Ray Manning
Brandao, Frank Raposo
Brandeis, Barry
Brands, Allen Jean
Brands, Alvira Bernice
Brandt, Ellen B.
Brandt, Frans M. J.
Brandt, John Henry
Brandwein, Robert
Brandwein, Stanley
Brandy, Joseph Ralph
Brann, Donald Robert
Brannen, Richard David
Branoff, Ronald Stanley
Branscomb, Anne Wells (Mrs.
Lewis McAdory Branscomb)
Branstetter, Roger Beard
Brant, John Weber Alexander
Bratman, Carroll Charles
Bratter, Thomas Edward
Bratton, William Wilson
Brauer, Arthur Jay
Brauer, Lee David
Brauer, Rima Lois Rubenstein
(Mrs. Lee David Brauer)
Brauer, Stephen Wesley
Braught, Nathan Russell
Braun, Albert Harold
Braun, Constance Todd (Mrs.
Louis Carl Braun)
Braun, George August
Braun, Louis Henry
Braun, Norman
Braun, Theodore Edward
Daniel
Braunstein, H. Terry (Malikin)
Brawley, James Wayne
Brawn, Richard Guy
Bray, John Sheriff
Brayman, Harold
Brayson, Albert A(loysius)
Brazil, Harold Edmund
Brazinsky, Irving
Brazo, Bruce Allen
Breakstone, Robert Albert
Breasure, Joyce M.
Breathitt, Edward Thompson
Brechenser, Donn Marsh
Brecher, Bernd
Brecker, Richard Lee
Brede, James Faris
Bredin, J(ohn) Bruce
Breed, James Roy
Breed, Robert Belden
Breeding, Robert Eugene, Sr.
Breen, James Langhorne
Breger, Herbert Joseph
Breitenfeld, James Charles
Breitman, Bernard Simon
Breitmayer, William Frederick
Brekke, Millard Gronner
Breland, Hunter Mansfield
Brem, Jacob
Bremser, George
Bremser, George, Jr.
Brennan, Donald George
Brennan, Edward Noel
Brennan, Francis Patrick
Brennan, George Lawrence, Jr.
Brennan, James Joseph
Brennan, John Patrick
Brennan, Joseph Edward
Brennan, Joseph Payne
Brennan, Robert Joseph
Brennan, William Joseph, Jr.
Brennen, William Stuart
Brenner, Egon
Brenner, Irvin
Brenner, Joseph Donald
Brenner, Sydelle Edelstein
Brenninkmeyer, Benno Max
Brent, Liselle
Brescia, Frank Joseph
Bresee, Wilmer Edgar
Bresler, Sidney Alan
Breslin, Alfred John
Breslin, Donald Joseph
Breslin, John Thomas
Bressler, Bernard
Breth, Harris George
Brett, James Thomas
Brett, John Brendan, Jr.
Bretton, Henry L.
Brettschneider, Eric Bruce
Breuer, Hans
Brewer, Allen Mark
Brewer, Elaine Catherine
Brewer, Garry Dwight
Brewer, Philip Warren
Brewer, Ralph Eugene
Brewer, Wilmon
Brewster, Robert Stewart
Brey, Francis Xavier
Brey, Robert Newton, Jr.
Briante, Rocco Anthony
Brice, Neil Mather
Brick, Donald Bernard
Brickett, Theresa Florence
Brickner, Kenneth Gerard
Bridges, Charles William
Bridges, Jerry Gayle
Bridgewater, Albert Louis, Jr.
Brief, Richard S.
Brien, Richard Herman
Briggs, Edmund Leroy, Jr.
Briggs, George Madison
Briggs, John Philip, II
Bright, William Hunter, III
Briley, Philip Lee
Brill, Howard Roy
Brill, Timothy David
Briloff, Abraham Jacob
Brin, Myron
Brines, Seymour
Bringhurst, Neale Clark
Brink, Robert Harold, Jr.
Brinker, Robert Durie
Brinkler, Bartol
Brinkman, Carl Alexander
Brinkman, George Loris
Brinn, Morris Allan
Brinson, Gary Paul
Brisbon, Delores Flynn
Briscoe, Anne M.
Briscoe, Thomas Herman
Bristol, Lee Hastings, Jr.
Bristol, Robert Francis
Brite, Dennis René
Britman, Naphtali Anchel
Brittain, Alfred, III
Brittain, Terry Moore
Brittain, William Cecil
Britten, Andrew John
Britten, Thomas Lawrence
Britton, Loring Wolcott
Britton, Peter Norvel, Jr.
Broadwin, Alan
Broady, Tolly Rupert
Brocato, Louis Joseph
Brockett, Don
Brockett, John Henry, Jr.
Brockopp, Gene William
Brod, Morton Shlevin
Brod, Nathan
Brod, Pearl
Brode, Douglas Isaac
Broderick, Edwin Bernard
Brodersen, Louis Robert
Brodeur, Charles Claude
Brodhead, Quita
Brodie, Donald Gibbs
Brodie, Jonathan David
Brodkin, Adele Meyer
Brodsky, Archie
Brodsky, Grace Linda
Brodsky, John Putnam
Brodsky, Lee David
Brody, Marcia
Brody, Mitchell David
Brody, Stuart Martin
Brody, William
Brog, David
Brogan, John Patrick
Broggi, Richard John
Broitman, Selwyn Arthur
Brokaw, Arthur Allen
Bromberg, Henry
Bromberg, Myron James
Bromberg, Rachel Berezow
Bromery, Randolph Wilson
Bronfman, Charles Rosner
Bronner, Felix
Bronnes, Robert Lewis
Bronson, John Orville, Jr.
Bronson, Patricia Ann
Bronstein, Melvin
Bronzino, Joseph Daniel
Brook, David William
Brook, Judith Suzanne
Brooke, Edward W.
Brookman, Murray Neil
Brooks, Anita Helen Sayle
Brooks, Babert Vincent
Brooks, Benedict, III
Brooks, Charles Adams
Brooks, George Andrew
Brooks, Lee C.
Brooks, Philip Barron
Brooks, Richard Derrick
Brooks, Robert
Brooks, Ruth Claudia Hutchins
(Mrs. Joe Felix Brooks)
Brooks, Walter Everett
Brophy, Theodore F.
Broseghini, Albert LeRoy
Brosnan, Carol Raphael Sarah
Bross, Irwin D. J.
Bross, Steward Richard, Jr.
Brosseau, Lucien
Brostrup, John Oliver
Brotman, Phyllis Block (Mrs.
Don N. Brotman)
Broucek, Daniel Martin
Broudy, Julius
Brough, Frederick Lowell
Broughton, James Harold
Broughton, Phillip Charles
Brouilette, C. Bader
Broutsas, Michael George
Brouwer, Allen Kennedy, Jr.
Brower, Kenneth R.
Brower, Lincoln Pierson
Brower, William
Brown, Allison Travis (Mrs.
Dean E. Brown, Jr.)
Brown, Allyn Stephens
Brown, Atlanta Thomas
Brown, Barry Stephen
Brown, Brenda Lee Lawson
(Mrs. John Scott Brown)
Brown, Brooks Gideon, III
Brown, Bruce Robert
Brown, C. Wellman
Brown, Charles Lee
Brown, Clair George, Jr.
Brown, Clara Adele
Brown, Daniel Ward
Brown, David Graham
Brown, Dean Edgar, III
Brown, Denise Scott
Brown, Donald
Brown, Donald Corey
Brown, Donald Edward
Brown, Donald Emerson
Brown, Earl Benedict
Brown, Edward Kinard
Brown, Edward Mason
Brown, Edwin Hezekiah, Sr.
Brown, Elliott
Brown, F(red) Reese
Brown, Francine Litt
Brown, Frederick Harold
Brown, George Alexander
Brown, Gertrude Parris
Brown, Harold
Brown, Harry Ronald
Brown, Horace Dean
Brown, Irwin
Brown, James Edison
Brown, James Glen
Brown, Mrs. James Robert
(Josephine M. Brown)
Brown, Janet C.
Brown, Janet Sydney
Brown, Jerry Joseph
Brown, John Angus
Brown, John Carter
Brown, John William
Brown, John Y., Jr.
Brown, Kenneth Ridgeway
Brown, Lawrence Milton
Brown, Linda Keller
Brown, Marjorie Schmidt
Brown, Marvin Sidney
Brown, Nesbitt Delaney
Brown, Peter Megargee
Brown, Ralph Adams
Brown, Ralph Andres
Brown, Raymond Harrison
Brown, Richard Lawrence
Brown, Robert Adams, Jr.
Brown, Robert Delford
Brown, Roma Elaine
Brown, Roswell Leo
Brown, Roy Allen
Brown, Ruth Geisler
Brown, Warner Timothy, Jr.
Brown, William Frederick
Brown, William L.
Browne, Eppes Wayles, Jr.
Browne, Francis Cedric
Browne, George Philip
Browne, James Joseph
Browne, Kingsbury, Jr.
Browne, Laurene Alston
Browne, Richard Cullen
Browne, Venorren Veronica
Brownell, Adrienne Helen
Brownell, Clifford Eaton
Brownell, Wayne Ernest
Browning, David Gunter
Browning, Ralph L(eslie)
Brownlow, Donald Grey
Brownstein, Bernard
Brownstein, Cy
Brownstein, Martin Herbert
Browzin, Boris Sergeevich
Brubaker, Robert MacDonald
Brucato, Orfeo
Bruce, Herman Paul
Bruce, Peter Parrott
Bruce, Robert Douglas
Bruce, Robert Vance
Bruch, Virginia Irene Sullivan
(Mrs. Truman Elwood
Bruch)
Bruck, Stephen Desiderius
Brudner, Harvey Jerome
Brumagim, Duane T.
Brumberger, Larry S.
Brunauer, Dalma Maria
Hunyadi (Mrs. Stephen
Brunauer)
Brunauer, Walter Edward
Brundage, Gloria Marguarite
Brundage, Russell Archibald
Brundidge, Arthur DuBois
Brunelle, Robert Leo
Bruner, Van Buren, Jr.
Brunetti, Mendor Thomas
Brunetto, Frank
Brungardt, Gilbert Ambrose
Brungot, Hilda Constance
Frederikka Johnson
Bruning, Walter Frank
Brunner, John Luick
Brunner, Lillian Sholtis (Mrs.
Mathias J. Brunner)
Brunner, Mathias John
Brunner, Nancy Ruth
Bruno, Angela
Bruno, Anthony Matthew
Bruno, Joseph
Brunt, Manly Yates, Jr.
Brush, Douglas Peirce
Brush, Edwin Franklyn, Jr.
Brush, Richard Frank
Brussee, Cornelius Roger
Brust, John Calvin Morrison,
Jr.
Brustein, David Dalton
Bruton, Peter William
Bruun, Bertel
Bruun, (Arthur) Geoffrey
Bruun, Ruth Dowling (Mrs.
Bertel Bruun)
Bruzzi, Marie Elizabeth
Bryan, Billie Marie (Mrs.
James A. Mackey)
Bryan, George Plumer
Bryan, James Edmund
Bryan, John
Bryan, John Leland
Bryan, Robert Fessler
Bryan, Ross Emery, Jr.
Bryan, Thomas Benedict
Bryan, W. Burton
Bryan, Wilhelmus Bogart, III
Bryant, Albert Irwin
Bryant, Patricia Stirnweiss
Bryant, William B.
Bryant, William J.
Bryer, Ben F.
Bryer, Morton Samuel
Brynjolfsson, Ari
Brzana, Stanislaus Joseph
Brzezinski, Zbigniew
Brzustowicz, Richard John
Buanno, John Michael
Bucci, Clarice Althea
Bucco, Anthony Rocco
Buchan, Ronald Forbes
Buchanan, Robert Gray
Buchbaum, Paul Harvey
Bucher, Charle Augustus
Buchin, Irving
Buchin, Jean
Buck, Fidelis
Buck, Robert Treat, Jr.
Buck, William Charles
Buckalew, Alfred John, Jr.
Buckalew, Ronald Eugene
Buckland, Allan Keith
Buckland, Raymond Brian
Buckley, Edward Richard
Buckley, Frank Michael
Buckley, John Joseph
Buckley, John M.
Buckley, Mary Lorraine (Mrs.
Joseph Parriott)
Buckley, Mortimer Joseph
Buckley, Robert Francis
Buckmore, Alvah Clarence, Jr.
Bucknam, James Romeo
Bucky, Peter Stern
Bucove, Arnold David
Budd, Harriet
Budd, Herbert Franklin
Budd, Reginald (Rex) Masten
Budd, Richard Wade
Budesheim, Norman Ellsworth
Budlong, Barry Ives
Budne, Thomas Allen
Budner, Stanley Gordon
Budzeika, George
Buechler, Peter Robert
Buell, Elton Hollister
Buell, Eugene F(ranklin)
Buerger, Anne Fortune (Mrs.
David Bernard Buerger)
Buerger, David Bernard
Buescher, Adolph Ernst, Jr.
Bugg, Carol Donayre
Bugnolo, Dimitri S.
Buist, Jean Mackerley
Buist, Richardson
Buldrini, George James
Bulian, Max Joseph
Bulkley, Bernadine Healy
Bullard, Gregory Nelson
Bullard, John Kilburn
Bullen, Allan Graham Robert
Bullough, John Frank
Bulluck, Linwood Vonrae
Bulmash, Gary Franklin
Bulmash, Gilbert
Bulova, Ernst
Bulson, Walter Theodore
Bumstead, John Chambers
Bundy, Richard Franklin
Bundy, Robert Fleming
Bunke, Edward William
Diedrich
Bunting, Nina Lou
Bunzel, Kenneth William
Buonocore, Fredric J.
Burba, John Vytautas
Burbach, Rodney Van
Burbank, Robinson Derry
Burbidge, Frederick Stewart
Burch, Francis Boucher
Burch, Francis Floyd
Burch, John Thomas, Jr.
Burchess, Edwin Walter
Burd, Robert Meyer
Burdett, Leslie Robert
Burge, Furman Horace, Jr.
Burger, Paul Frederick
Burger, Philip Clinton
Burger, Warren Earl
Burgess, Carl(ton) Michael
Burgess, Mary Louise Dodson
Burgess, Robert Blundon, Jr.
Burget, Dean Edwin, Jr.
Burggraf, Frank Bernard, Jr.
Burgi Ghiglione, Walter Emilio
Luis
Burgin, Walter Hotchkiss, Jr.
Burk, Richard Jamar, Jr.
Burkavage, William Joseph
Burke, Austin Emile
Burke, Charles Brian
Burke, D(aniel) Barlow
Burke, Daniel J.
Burke, Edward Newell
Burke, Fred George
Burke, Harold P.
Burke, Harold Reynolds
Burke, Herbert Thomas
Burke, Jackson Frederick
Burke, John Francis
Burke, Josephine Mary
Burke, Marvin Murray
Burke, Mary Lou
Burke, Michael
Burke, Roydon
Burke, Thomas Edward
Burke, Thomas George
Burkert, John Wallace, Sr.
Burkhardt, Charles Henry
Burkhardt, Dolores Ann
Burks, Juanita Harriette
Burlaga, Leonard Francis
Burleson, Hal Eugene
Burlingham, Mary S.
Burliuk, Nicholas
Burlton, Rogers Christopher
Burman, David Jay
Burnes, Alan Jeffrey
Burnette, Mahlon Admire, III
Burney, Gloria Gregory
Burnham, Anita Louise
Burnham, Harold Arthur
Burns, Alex Andrew
Burns, Anne
Burns, Arnold Irwin
Burns, Dennis Raymond
Burns, Francis Lovis, Jr.
Burns, John Francis
Burns, John Spinney
Burns, Mary Mehlman
Burns, Padraic
Burns, Robert F.
Burns, Robert Milton
Burns, Ronald Gregory
Burns, Stanley Benjamin
Burns, Stephen Hamilton
Buros, Oscar Krisen
Burrell, Morton Irwin
Burridge, Robert
Burroughs, Frederick Sidney
Burroughs, Richard H., III
Burrowes, Joseph J.
Burrows, Ray Irving
Burrows, William E.
Burry, Anthony
Bursill, Claude
Burstein, Donald Alan
Burstein, Stephen David
Bursuk, Laura Zelman
Burt, Marvin Roger
Burt, Warren Brooker
Burtt, Elizabeth Allene
Burtt, J(oseph) Frederic
Busby, James Merwin
Busch, Allen Cyril
Busch, Benjamin
Bush, Alvin Glenn, Jr.
Bush, David Frederic
Bush, Derek Vernon
Bush, Henry Leon
Bush, John
Bushey, Arthur Merrick
Bushey, Bransby Walter
Bushman, Theresa
Bushnell, Clarence William
Busler, Michael Ronald
Butcher, (Charles) Philip
Butcher, Russell Devereux
Butcher, Willard Carlisle
Butler, Anna Mabel Land
(Mrs. Floyd Butler)
Butler, Benjamin
Butler, Charles Henry
Butler, Henry George, Jr.
Butler, James Edward
Butler, Jonathan Putnam
Butler, Loretta Marie
Butler, Natalie Sturges (Mrs.
Benjamin Butler)
Butler, Paul Richard
Butler, Robert Neil
Butler, Walter John
Butorac, Frank George
Butt, Gene Willard
Buttaci, Salvatore St. John
Butterly, Margaret Pardee
Buttinger, Joseph Anthony
Button, Bland Ballard
Button, Daniel Evan
Button, Ford Lincoln
Buttrick, Carlton Elwin
Butts, John William
Buttz, Charles William
Butzner, James Irvin
Buxbaum, Colman Lazar
Buxbaum, Martin David
Buxton, Edward Fulton
Buzzell, Scott Prescott
Bycer, Robert Elliott
Bye, Arthur Edwin, Jr.
Byers, Arthur Mahlon, Jr.
Byers, Frances Rees
Byington, Frederick Dolliver
Byington, John William
Byington, S. John
Byram, Thomas Leslie
Byrd, Alicia Deloris
Byrd, Edwin (Eddie) Leonard,
Jr.
Byrd, William Ted
Byrd, William Thomas, Jr.
Byrdsong, Charles Elliott
Byrne, Brendan Thomas
Byrne, George Peter, Jr.
Byrne, John James
Byrnes, Bernard Christopher
Byrnes, James Donovan
Leicester
Byrnes, Jane Louise
Byrom, David Gene
Byron, Beverly Butcher
Byron, Gloria Blum (Mrs.
Stuart David Byron)
Bystryn, Sara Wolski (Mrs.
Iser Bystryn)
Byun, Young Ho
Cabaup, Joseph John
Cabebe, Fernando Salva
Cable, Charles Allen
Cable, Dana Gerard
Cabot, Thomas Tarvin Gray
Cabrera-Rosete, Jorge
Armando
Caccamise, Daniel A.
Caccamise, James William
Caccia, Alexander Louis
Cacella, Arthur Ferreira
Cadavero, David Anthony
Caddell, Foster
Cademartori, Gary Martin
Cadman, Charles Robert
Cafaro, Paul James
Caffrey, Andrew Augustine
Caggiano, Anthony Patrick
Caguin, Feodor Cagandahan
Cahill, John Carroll
Cahill, Mary-Carol
Cahill, Vincent J., Jr.
Cain, Michael Gent
Cain, Michael Haney
Caiola, James Clifford
Cairnes, Walter Joseph
Cairo, Armon Anthony
Calabrese, Alphonse Francis
Xavier
Calabro, Joseph Francis
Calabro, Natalie
Calantone, Roger James
Calatayud, Juan Bautista
Calderone, Ronald John
Calderwood, James Albert
Caldwell, Jimmy Michael
Caldwell, Ronald Francis
Calhoun, George Donald
Calhoun, John Cozart
Calhoun, William Dice
Califano, Joseph Anthony, Jr.
Caligiuri, Angelo Michael
Caligiuri, Richard S.
Calkins, Evan
Calkins, Gary Nathan
Callahan, John William
Callahan, Michael Edson
Callahan, Monita (Mrs. Roy
H. Callahan)
Callahan, Roy Haney
Callam, James Monroe
Callender, Carl Oswald
Callender, Clive Orville
Calo, Tina Carol
Calobrisi, Dominick
Calomiris, Willie Donald
Calter, Paul
Calviello, Joseph Anthony
Cam, Marcialito Felipe
Cameron, Arthur Stuart
Cameron, Douglas George
Cameron, Randolph Whitney
Cameron, Scott Charles
Camillery, George Lewis
Camlin, James Alexander
Cammarata, Angelo
Cammarota, Charles Carmine
Camougis, George
Camp, Hazel Lee Burt
Camp, Margaret Whittlesey
Perkins (Mrs. Mortimer Hart
Camp)
Campbell, Alexander Bradshaw
Campbell, Catherine F. Gray
(Mrs. Wallace Arnold
Campbell)
Campbell, Colin Goetze
Campbell, Dix McDill
Campbell, Douglas Eaton
Campbell, Eugene Paul
Campbell, Helen Zott
Campbell, Isobel Agnes
Brydon (Mrs. Wendell
Chesley Campbell)
Campbell, Jack Duncan
Campbell, James Franklin
Campbell, James Ray
Campbell, Marshall Dendy

Campbell, Michael Robert
Campbell, Nancy Hackett
Campbell, Norman Ambrose
Campbell, Oliver Aloysius
Campbell, Raymond Ellsworth
Campbell, Robert Duff
Campbell, Roy Kennedy
Campbell, Thomas Curtis
Campel, Robert J.
Campo, Ivon Norberto
Campsen, Herman (Martin), Jr.
Camuti, Louis J.
Cancro, Ralph
Candee, Edward DeForest
Cander, Leon
Canestrari, Charles Joseph
Canfield, Jack
Cann, William Francis
Cannavo, Joseph Jack
Cannella, John Matthew
Cannon, Daniel Paul
Cannon, David Evans
Cannon, John
Canny, J. Francis
Cantilli, Edmund Joseph
Canton, Steve
Cantor, Alfred J(oseph)
Cantor, Eli
Cantu, Robert Clark
Capalbo, Robert Frank
Capasso, Edward Joseph
Capell, Frank Alphonse
Capell, Robert Goode
Capella, Rafael F.
Capelli, John Placido
Caper, Samuel Philip
Caplan, Lester
Caplan, Ronald Mervyn
Caplin, Jerrold Leon
Capo, Larry Gene
Capobres, Rudolfo M., Jr.
Capone, Dom Anthony
Capone, Thomas Albert
Caporali, Ronald Van
Capozzi, Marian Rita
Cappiello, William Antonio
Capraro, Richard Thomas
Capretta, Umberto
Caprio, Raphael John
Caputo, Anthony Robert
Caputo, Bruce F.
Carabitses, Nicholas Lampros
Caraley, Demetrios
Carbone, Joseph Enrico
Cardaci, Michael Mario, Jr.
Cardarelli, Albert Peter
Cardenas, Raul Rudolph, Jr.
Cardi, Paul
Cardillo, Thomas Edward
Cardinale, Kathleen Carmel O'Boyle
Cardinali, Albert John
Cardoni, John Joseph
Cardozo, Benjamin Mordecai
Cardozo, Jack George
Carere, Romulus Peter
Carewe, Sylvia
Carey, Donald Edmund
Carey, Grant Eldon
Carey, Hugh Leo
Carey, James Edward
Carey, William Joseph
Carickhoff, John Edward, Jr.
Carioto, Salvatore
Carissimo, Peter Walter
Carle, Eric
Carleone, Joseph
Carleton, Bukk Griffith
Carleton, Bukk Griffith, III
Carleton, James William
Carlin, Gabriel S.
Carlino, Rose Therese
Carlisle, Howard
Carlisle, Lilian Matarose Baker (Mrs. E. Grafton Carlisle, Jr.)
Carlsen, Lloyd Niels
Carlson, Albert William David, Jr.
Carlson, Alma Jane
Carlson, Glenn Herbert
Carlson, J(ohn) Philip
Carlson, Jane
Carlson, John Paul
Carlson, John Swink
Carlson, Robert Eugene
Carlson, Roger David
Carlson, Ruth Hartwell
Carlson, Theodore Joshua
Carlson-Gumbiner, Dale
Carlton, Cyrus Morris
Carlton, Sara Boehlke (Mrs. Mason Gant Carlton)
Carman, Floyd Shetler
Carman, James Russell
Carmel, Alan Stuart
Carmel, Simon Jacob
Carmen, Esther Cora Mayo
Carmichael, Carol Elizabeth Rogers
Carmichael, Donald Woods
Carmichael, Herbert Warren
Carmien, Donald Charles
Carnahan, Peter Malott
Carne, Edward Bryan
Carnes, James McCabe
Carney, William
Carnochan, John Low, Jr.
Caronia, Victor Stephen
Carosso, Vincent Phillip
Carousso, Dorothee Hughes
Carp, George
Carpenter, Asora Esther Toatley (Mrs. Darious Carpenter)
Carpenter, Charles Bernard
Carpenter, Charles Whitney, II
Carpenter, Earle Franklyn
Carpenter, George Benton
Carpenter, Harry Glenn, Jr.
Carpenter, Hoyle Dameron
Carpenter, Robert R.M.
Carpenter, Stanley Waterman
Carper, Anna Mary
Carr, Arthur Charles
Carr, Elliott Grabill
Carr, John Jeffrey
Carr, Lawrence Edward, Jr.
Carr, Martin Douglas
Carr, Patrick William
Carr, Ralph Lionel, Jr.
Carr, William Henry Alexander
Carr, Wilson Murray, III
Carratello, Domenico
Carrel, Jeffrey Mack
Carretta, Robert William
Carriera, Anthony John, Jr.
Carrino, Frank Gaetano
Carrol, Wilfred
Carroll, Charles Michael
Carroll, Cyril James
Carroll, Edward Gonzalez
Carroll, Marguerite Ruth
Carroll, Stephen John, Jr.
Carruth, David Barrow
Carson, Ellareetha
Carson, George William
Carter, Alexander
Carter, James Earl, Jr. (Jimmy)
Carter, Marc Edgar
Carter, Richard John
Carter, Robert Ayres
Carter, Rosalynn Smith
Carter, Ruth B. (Mrs. Joseph C. Carter)
Cartnick, Edward Nathaniel
Carton, Edwin Beck
Caruba, Alan
Carucci, Victor John
Carullo, Maria Elena Garcia (Mrs. Dominic Joseph Carullo)
Caruso, Patrick Francis
Caruso, Paul John
Carvalho, Julie Ann
Carver, Kendall Lynn
Cary, Frank Taylor
Casapulla, Robert Terrance
Casarino, John Philip
Casazza, John Andrew
Casciegna, Jill Paton
Cascieri, Tito, Jr.
Cascio, Thomas Michael
Case, Clifford Philip
Casey, Murray Joseph
Casey, Sister Natalie
Casgrain, Ardoin Edmond
Cashdollar, Robert Murrel
Cashman, George Washington
Cashman, Thomas Joseph
Caso, Adolph
Cason, June Macnabb
Cason, Roger Lee
Caspersen, Barbara Morris
Caspersen, Finn Michael Westby
Cass, Paul Taylor
Cassak Albert Loeb
Cassara, Nunzio Giuseppe
Casscells, Samuel Ward
Cassel, David Edward
Cassidy, Carl Eugene
Cassidy, Jack
Cassidy, James J(oseph)
Cassidy, Robert Sterling
Cassie, William Bremner MacGregor
Casso, Leonard Anthony
Castagna, Eugene Gennaro
Castelli, Helen Sims
Castells, Salvador
Caster, Bernard Harry
Castergine, John
Castleton, Virginia
Castor, Richard Gilbert
Castro, Antonio Oscar
Castrucci, Paul Philip
Casturo, Don James
Catacosinos, William James
Cataldo, Louis
Cataldo, Lucille Ann
Catanello, Ignatius Anthony
Catania, Joseph Vincent
Catchi, (Catherine Childs)
Cate, Curtis Wilson
Catena, Anna Lorraine Fiorito
Cathcart, Alan
Cattaneo, Donald Jerome
Cattani, Debra Ann
Caudle, Gary Craig
Cautela, Joseph Richard
Cavalet, James Roger
Cavalieri, Anthony Simone
Cavallaro, James Anthony
Cavallo, Robert Michael
Cavanaugh, Paul Edward
Cavanaugh, William Joseph
Cavanna, Alice May
Caven, Robert Emerson
Caveny, Leonard Hugh
Cazan, Matthew John
Cazeau, Charles Jay
Cebrik, Michael Melvin
Ceccarelli, John F.
Celentano, Domenick
Cella, Elisa
Cella, Eugene Anthony
Celliers, Peter Joubert
Celnik, Max
Centurioni, Mary Kathleen
Cerbulis, Janis
Cerio, James Vincent
Cerjanec, Ruth Lilian Wade
Cermak, Josef Rudolf Cenek
Cernius, Vytautas (Vytas)
Cerruto, Joseph Angelo
Certo, Natalie Mary
Cerulli, Maurice Anthony
Cervenka, Arthur Frank
Cervik, Joseph
Cervino, Grace
Cervone, Domenic Donald
Cess, Robert Donald
Chaballa, Paul Vincent
Chabinsky, Irving John
Chacko, George Kuttickal
Chacko, Mathew Chethipurckal
Chadbourn, Erika Marianne (Mrs. James Harmon Chadbourn)
Chadbourne, Christopher Douglas
Chadda, Kul Deep
Chadwick, Dexter Anthony
Chafee, Francis H(asseltine)
Chafee, John Hubbard
Chagnon, Marc Marcel
Chai, Soo Kyeung
Chaiken, Bernard Henry
Chaikin, Barry Howard
Chaikin, Sol Chick
Chaisson, Eric Joseph
Chait, Arnold
Chait, Lawrence G.
Chait, Robert Abbe
Chakoian, George
Chakrabarti, Alok Kumar
Chakrabarti, Satyabrata
Chaletzky, Stephen Edward
Chalmers, Robert Charles
Chalon, Jack
Chamberlain, Carl Eugene
Chamberlain, John Loomis, III
Chamberlain, Joseph Reid
Chamberlain, Lloyd Baxter
Chamberlin, Michael Aloysius
Chambers, Harry R.
Chambliss, Hiram Darden, Jr.
Champagne, Joseph Stenard
Champe, Mrs. Carlton G. (Mary Folsom Champe)
Champsi, Dolly
Chamzas, Christodoulos
Chan, George Moy
Chan, Kam-Fai
Chan, Peter Wing Kwong
Chan, Wallace Lane
Chan, Wan-Kang Will
Chance, Henry Martyn, II
Chanda, Rajinder Nath
Chandler, Alfred Dupont, Jr.
Chandler, Elisabeth Gordon (Mrs. R. K. Chandler)
Chandler, James John
Chandler, John Wesley
Chandler, Richard Merrick
Chandler, Robert Leslie
Chaney, Louise Bockelman
Chaney, Verne Edward, Jr.
Chang, Chin-An
Chang, Ching Ming
Chang, Chin-Tse (Robert)
Chang, Darwin Ray
Chang, Michael Machaw
Chang, Pyoung Ryoul Peter
Chang, Shen Chin
Chang, Ted Teh-Liang
Chang, Thomas Ming Swi
Chang, Tsun-Yung
Chang, Yuan
Chang-Rodriguez, Eugenio
Chang-Rodriguez, Raquel (Torres)
Chant, Davis Ryan
Chao, Hsin Cheng
Chao, Hung-Chi
Chaparas, Sotiros Demetrios
Chapin, Diane Nelson
Chapin, Homer Newton
Chapline, William Ridgely
Chapman, Erna Marta Riedel (Mrs. Ray F. Chapman)
Chapman, Jo(sephine Lawton)
Chapman, John Haven
Chapman, Joseph Alan
Chapman, Norman Franklin, Jr.
Chapman, Oscar James
Chapman, Robert Maxwell
Chapman, Stuart Macdonald
Chappelear, John Monroe
Chappell, Sandra Irene
Chappell, Thomas Tye
Chappen, Edward Peter
Chapple, John Donnell
Charity, Raymond Emmitt, Jr.
Charles, Earle Vincent, Jr.
Charles, Harry Krewson, Jr.
Charlton, Alex
Charlton, John Wood
Charlton, Maurice Henry
Charpentier, David Leo
Charves, James Monteiro
Charyn, Jerome Irwin
Chasan, Alexander Anschel
Chase, Elizabeth Wagner Johnson (Mrs. Harold F. Chase)
Chase, Kenneth Huntington
Chase, Lucia
Chase, Norman Bradford
Chase, Robert Edward
Chase, Saul Alan
Chaseman, Joel
Chasen, Lawrence Isaac
Chasen, William Henry
Chasman, Herbert
Chasnoff, Julius
Chastanet, Denis Vernon Peter
Chastulik, Frank
Chaszar, Edward
Chatman-Royce, Edgar Truitt
Chaudhary, Basudeo
Chauncey, Howard Haskell
Chavez, Felix
Chavez, Ismael Ruperto
Chaviano, Hugo Osvaldo
Cheatham, Henry Plummer, III
Checke, Roger Amedeo
Chelland, Orphia Cynthia
Chelstrom, Marilyn Ann
Chen, Chia Ting
Chen, Chuan Yuan
Chen, Chung-Ho
Chen, Concordia Chao
Chen, Edward Wei-I
Chen, Hung Tsung
Chen, James Ching-Yih
Chen, Jane Lee
Chen, Jeffrey Juinn-ie
Chen, John Shang-Lien
Chen, Lin
Chen, Mike Chi-Ching
Chen, Paul Kuan Yao
Chen, Robert Sensing
Chen, Stephen Shau-tsi
Chen, Yuh Ching
Chen, Yung Chuan
Chen-Chi
Chenevey, Paul Robert
Cheney, Charles Brooker
Cheng, Cheng-Yin
Cheng, David Hong
Cheng, Hsueh-ching
Cheng, Lung
Cheng, Paul, Jr.
Cheng, Tsung O.
Cherian, Edward John
Chernish, William Norman
Chernuck, Dorothy
Cherry, Donald Stewart
Cherry, Edward Atwell
Cherry, Philip
Cherry, Sheldon H.
Chertoff, Alex
Chertok, Burton Zane
Chesbro, George Washington
Chesbro, John Severance
Chesnakas, Joseph Louis
Chesnut, Dorothy Silliman
Chess, Abraham Paul
Chesson, Michael Bedout
Chesson, Thomas Richard
Cheston, T. Stephen
Chevray, Rene
Chew, John Carrollton
Chew, Melvin Lewis
Chew, Paul Albert
Chewning, June Spangler
Chey, William Y.
Chi, Chia-Dann
Chiang, Fu-pen
Chiao, Weily Fong
Chiaramonte, Joseph Salvatore
Chiasson, Donat
Chiavacci, Harding Anthony (Deno)
Chiburis, Edward Frank
Chick, Leslie Steven
Chilcote, Robert Harry
Chilcote, Thomas C.
Childress, William Bryant
Childs, John Patrick
Chilingerian, Harry Samuel
Chimene, Donald Robert
Chin, Carolyn Sue
Chin, Charles Lee Dong
Chin, Gilbert Yukyu
Chin, Riccardo Fay
China, Robert Henry
Chinich, Arnold
Chinich, Bessie (Bessie Chinich Federbush)
Chinmoy, Sri
Chino, John James
Chiogioji, Melvin Hiroaki
Chiotellis, Philip Nicos
Chisamore, Donald Raymond
Chisholm, Shirley Anita St. Hill
Chisolm, Alvin James
Chisolm, James Julian, Jr.
Chisvette, Dominick
Chitty, Arthur Benjamin, Jr.
Chiu, Hungdah
Chiu, John Hung Cheung
Chiu, Wu Shung
Chizever, Irwin
Chmielewicz, Joseph Stanley
Cho, Alfred Yi
Cho, Jung Hyun
Cho, Sang Yon
Cho, Yohan
Chobany, John
Chodosh, H Louis
Choi, Soonchae
Chokas, William Vasilios
Chomitz, Nicholas
Chon, Yu-Taik
Chong, Luis A.
Chopoorian, John Andrew
Chou, Chung Chi
Chou, Pei Chi
Choudhary, Shyam Sundar
Choudhury, Abdur Raquib
Chowdhury, Manny
Christ, Duane Marland
Christ, Lily Esther Shih (Mrs. Duane Marland Christ)
Christen, John Philip
Christensen, Billy Crowl
Christensen, Ernest Martin
Christensen, Kathy Weber
Christenson, William Newcome
Christiano, Loretta Picardi
Christiansen, Kjell Hroar
Christiansen, Richard Louis
Christie, Donald Melvin, Jr.
Christie, Eugene Roy
Christie, George Nicholas
Christie, Robert Sharrott
Christinzie, Anthony John
Christle, Gary E.
Christoff, Kenneth Eugene
Christofferson, George
Christopher, Aspasia Couloumbis
Chrostowski, Edmund Joseph
Chrupcala, Malcolm Warner
Chryssafopoulos, Hanka Wanda Sobczak (Mrs. Nicholas Chryssafopoulos)
Chryssanthou, Chryssanthos P.
Chrystie, Thomas Ludlow
Chrzanowski, William James
Chu, Jeffrey Chuan
Chu, Tsann Ming
Chu, Valentin Yuan-ling
Chuang, Ming Chia
Chuck, Harry Cousins
Chun, Myung Ki
Chun, Sae-Il
Chung, Arthur Frederick
Chung, Edward Koo-Young
Church, Colin Barclay
Church, Frances Conover
Church, Lloyd Eugene
Church, Roberta
Churchill, Edward Delos
Churchill, Frederick Deane
Churchill, Howard James
Churchill, Joan Russell (Mrs. Frederick Deane Churchill)
Churg, Jacob
Chute, Mortimer Henry, Jr.
Chyung, Chi Han
Chyzowych, Eugene Sother
Ciarfella, Francis Gerald
Cibella, Ross Casimir
Cibley, Leonard Jonathan
Cicero, Fiorello Thomas
Cichanowicz, Frank Antone, III
Ciesielski, Jane Beth
Cifrulak, S. David
Cimino, James Ernest
Cimino, Joseph A.
Cina, Saverio Joseph
Cintas, Pierre François Diégo
Cioffari, Angelina Grimaldi
Cioffari, Vincenzo
Ciolli, Antoinette
Cion, Judith Ann
Cipriano, Donald M.
Ciresi, Anthony David
Cirillo, Anthony Francis
Ciulla, Andrew Joseph
Ciurca, Samuel John, Jr.
Ciurczak, Emil Walter
Cizanckas, Victor Ian
Clagett, John Williams
Clair, Carolyn Green
Clamar, Aphrodite J.
Clapp, Herbert James
Clapp, Philip Charles
Clapper, Thomas Wesley
Clare, James Harvey Thomson
Clare, L(eslie) Paul
Clarie, T. Emmet
Clark, Andrew Lawrence
Clark, Charles Edward
Clark, Charles Warfield
Clark, Donald Graham Campbell
Clark, Elizabeth Hughes
Clark, Elizabeth Jane
Clark, Ellery Harding, Jr.
Clark, Elton Loydon
Clark, Evelyn Gaebel
Clark, Gerald Robert
Clark, Herbert Spencer
Clark, Herbert Tryon, Jr.
Clark, John Andrew, Jr.
Clark, John Farrell
Clark, John Holley, III
Clark, John Kapp
Clark, Joseph Abel
Clark, Leonard Hill
Clark, Merrell Edward, Jr.
Clark, Peggy
Clark, Stephen C(utter), III
Clark, William Francis
Clark, William Hawley
Clark, William James
Clark-Duff, Robert Humpstone
Clarke, Austin Chesterfield
Clarke, Edgar Hale
Clarke, Frances Marguerite
Clarke, Frank Henderson, Jr.
Clarke, Joseph Brian
Clarke, Raphael Semmes
Clarke, William Decker
Clary, Leon Howard
Claster, Barbara Leiner
Claster, Jay B.
Clausen, Ralph Theodore
Clawar, Harry Joseph
Clawson, Harry Quintard Moore
Claxton, John Brooke
Clayman, Lawrence Howard
Clayton, Constance Mae
Clayton, Lewis Barrington
Cleary, Fritz
Cleary, James Charles, Jr.
Cleaver, David Charles
Cleaves, Emery Nudd
Cleaves, Robert E(dward)
Cleek, John Willard
Cleeton, Glen Uriel
Cleland, Alan Stuart
Clemendor, Anthony Arnold
Clement, Donald Leeds, Jr.
Clement, Karl Gustav
Clemente, Celestino
Clements, George F., Jr.
Clements, Sarah White
Clemetson, Charles Alan Blake
Clemmons, Clifford Robert
Cleveland, Harlan
Cleveland, James Colgate
Cleveland, Priscilla Rendell
Clevenger, Robert William
Cleverley, Morris Leslie, Jr.
Clifford, Arthur
Clifford, Francis James
Clifford, Patrick Ignatius
Clifford, Stewart Burnett
Cliffton, Eugene E.
Clifton, Anne Rutenber
Clifton, Nancy Lynn
Cline, Raleigh
Cline, Ruth Eleanor Harwood
Clinedinst, Katherine Parsons
Clinedinst, Wendel Waters
Clinger, William Floyd, Jr.
Clinton, John Joseph
Clinton, Joseph DeWitt
Clitheroe, H. John
Clive, Craig Norman
Clizbe, John Anthony
Clohesy, Stephanie J.
Cloney, James Maurice
Close, Elmer Harry
Close, Fred Leland, Jr.
Clough, Mary Evalyn
Clough, Perry Rankin
Clough, Philip James
Cloutier, Leonce
Clow, H. Arnold
Cloyd, Royal Harrison
Clyman, Milton
Co, Benito Kong-Leng D.
Coakley, Paul Eugene, Jr.
Coates, Charles Robert
Coates, Robert Pearce
Coble, Anna Jane
Coble, Jean
Coburn, John Bowen
Coburn, Richard James
Coburn, Robert Bowne
Coburn, Theodore James
Coccia, Silvio Daniel
Cocco, Thomas Domenick Bartholomew
Coché, Erich Henry Ernst
Cochios, Charles Augustus
Cochran, James Amos
Cochrane, Douglas Haig
Cockerline, Roger Earle
Cockett, Abraham Timothy Keaweiwi
Coddon, David Rees
Coderre, Gerard Marie
Codispoti, Andre John
Cody, Byron Millard
Cody, William Frederic
Coe, Neile Hector
Coe, Robert Lewis, Jr.
Coelho, Luiz Carlos
Coen, Robert Joseph
Coffey, John Lawrence
Coffey, Joseph Edward, Jr.
Coffin, Charles Frederick, Jr.
Coffin, David Douglas
Coffin, Frank Morey
Coffin, William Sargent, Sr.
Cogen, Tess Schnittkramer
Coggins, Wade Thomas
Coghill, Carter Lambert
Cogliano, Francis Dominic
Cogswell, Karin I.
Coheleach, Guy Joseph
Cohen, Abraham
Cohen, Alan Seymour
Cohen, Allen
Cohen, Allen Bailin
Cohen, Arthur Charles
Cohen, Ben
Cohen, Benjamin
Cohen, Bertram Malcolm
Cohen, Burton Jerome
Cohen, Burton Marcus
Cohen, David
Cohen, Edgar Horace
Cohen, Edward George
Cohen, Edward I.
Cohen, Edward Morton
Cohen, Eugene Joseph
Cohen, George M.
Cohen, Harris Saul
Cohen, Harry David
Cohen, Henry
Cohen, Herbert Jesse
Cohen, Irving David
Cohen, Irwin
Cohen, Jerald Louis
Cohen, Jerome
Cohen, Joel Myron
Cohen, Leonard
Cohen, Louis Mark
Cohen, Martin Gerald
Cohen, Martin Harvey
Cohen, Mary Ann Adler
Cohen, Maurice
Cohen, Max Harry
Cohen, Michael Edward
Cohen, Neil
Cohen, Philip Herman
Cohen, Richard
Cohen, Ronald George
Cohen, Samuel H.

Cohen, Samuel Israel
Cohen, Samuel William
Cohen, Sanford Irwin
Cohen, Seymour Martin
Cohen, Stafford Irwin
Cohen, Stanley
Cohen, Stephen Paul
Cohen, Steven Mark
Cohen, Sydney Morris
Cohen, William John
Cohen, William Nathan
Cohen, William Sebastian
Cohler, Jonas
Cohn, Bertram Douglas
Cohn, James Ronald
Cohn, Martin David
Cohn, Nathan
Cohn, Norman Unger
Cohn, Robert
Cohn, Roberta Kimmel
Cohn, Roy Marcus
Cohn, Sanford Jay
Coho, James Preston
Colabella, Calvin Michael
Colaianni, Joseph Vincent
Colangelo, Domenick Anthony
Colasante, John
Colburn, Norma Elaine Wheeler
Colburn, Robert Marshall
Colby, Barnard Ledward
Colby, Paul
Coldwell, Lawrence Howard
Cole, Elma Phillipson (Mrs. John Strickler Cole)
Cole, Francis Vernon
Cole, Joyce
Cole, Larry
Cole, Leonard Aaron
Cole, Ned
Cole, Robert C.
Cole, Sherwood Orison
Cole, Stephen Adams
Coleman, Bernell
Coleman, Catherine Offley
Coleman, James Edward Marshall
Coleman, John Ingram
Coleman, John Robert
Coleman, John William
Coleman, Lowell Thomas
Coleman, Marshall Donald
Coleman, Richard Patrick
Coleman, Stephen Joel
Coleman, Steven Laurence
Coleton, Stuart Howard
Colgan, Sumner
Colgrass, Michael Charles
Collard, Thomas Albert
Colli, Albert John
Collier, Thomas Cleaton
Collins, A(lbert) Byron
Collins, Allen Howard
Collins, Collene
Collins, Dorothy (Mrs. Akiba Emanuel)
Collins, Erik
Collins, George James
Collins, George Joseph
Collins, Helen Clark (Mrs. Arnold Miller Collins)
Collins, Herbert Ridgeway
Collins, Howard Elisha
Collins, James Anthony, Jr.
Collins, Jean-Pierre
Collins, John Gary
Collins, John Joseph
Collins, Malcolm Frank
Collins, Robert Ira
Collins, Robert Joseph
Collins, Robert Yuille
Collins, Rowland Lee
Colony, William Mandeville
Colson, Chester Elmer
Colston, William Carroll
Colten, Sterling Irwin
Coltoff, Philip
Colton, Clark Kenneth
Colton, Richard John
Colton, William Arthur, Jr.
Colway, James Robert
Colwell, Raymond Carpenter, Jr.
Colyer, Ralph Joseph
Combe, Ivan DeBlois
Combes, Richard Willard
Combs, Earl Burns
Combs, Paul Howard
Combs, Van Pierceon
Comedy, Alan Vaughn
Comer, Nathan Lawrence
Comerford, Philip Michael
Compain, Rita
Comparetto, Joseph
Compton, Mary Beatrice Brown (Mrs. Ralph Theodore Compton)
Comstock, Richard Davis
Conable, Barber B., Jr.
Conary, David Arlan
Condict, Edgar Rhodes
Condon, Charles Francis M.
Condrate, Robert Adam, Sr.
Condrell, William Kenneth
Cone, Gertrude Ellen Mary
Cone, John Frederick
Conetta, Joseph Anthony
Congdon, Paul Ubert
Conger, Clement Ellis
Congleton, Howard, Jr.
Conigliaro, Salvatore Alfred
Conklin, Everett Lawson
Conklin, Richard Newton
Conley, Bernard Edward
Connant, Charles Ellis
Connare, William Graham
Connell, Frances Jane
Connell, Louise Fox
Connell, William Francis
Connelley, Earl John, Jr.
Connelly, John Edward, III
Conners, Kenneth Wray
Connery, Joseph Edwin, Jr.
Connolly, John Dolan
Connolly, John Joseph
Connolly, Michael Joseph, III
Connolly, Virginia Straughan
Connor, Leo Edward
Connor, Michael Rodney
Connor, Paul Eugene
Connor, Robert T.
Connor, Terrence Powell
Connor, Thomas Martin
Connors, John Joseph Hayward
Connors, Mary Ann
Connors, William Francis, Jr.
Conoby, Joseph Francis
Conole, Richard Clement
Conover, Walter Kay, Jr.
Conover, William Sheldrick II
Conrad, Morton Seymour
Conrad, William Edward, Jr.
Conroy, Thomas Joseph
Conroy, William Thomas, Jr.
Constantelos, Demetrios John
Constantino, Joseph Gerald
Conte, Silvio Otto
Contron, Guido
Converse, John Marquis
Conway, Albert E(dward)
Conway, Alvin James
Conway, Arthur James
Conway, James Francis, Jr.
Conway, Kenneth James
Conway, William Gaylord
Conyngham, William Joseph
Cook, Albert Samuel
Cook, Alfreda Mary
Cook, Benjamin Hopson
Cook, Benjamin Lewis
Cook, Charles Winant
Cook, Douglas Neilson
Cook, Earl Clinton, Jr.
Cook, George Peter
Cook, Harland Lawrence
Cook, Jeannine Salvo (Mrs. Donald Carter Cook)
Cook, John Alfred
Cook, John Bartley
Cook, Joyce Fralic Dechman
Cook, Paul William, Jr.
Cook, Richard Kelsey
Cook, Sanford Lee
Cook, Sy
Cook, William Holmes
Cook, William Sutton
Cooke, Gilbert David
Cooke, Helen Paxton
Cooke, Lawrence Henry
Cooke, Robert John
Cooke, Terence James Cardinal
Cooke, Thomas H., Jr.
Cool, Rodney Lee
Cooley, James Keats
Cooley, James Lawrence
Coolidge, Nicholas Jefferson
Coon, Daniel Webster
Coonce, Susan Mason
Cooney, John Gordon
Cooper, Alan Robert
Cooper, Charles Jasper
Cooper, Clement Theodore
Cooper, David Young
Cooper, Doris Jean
Cooper, Douglas James
Cooper, Edward John Waddell
Cooper, Harry James
Cooper, James Michael
Cooper, Joel Jay
Cooper, John McGill, Jr.
Cooper, Joy McCormick Rhodes (Mrs. Robert L. Cooper)
Cooper, Leon N.
Cooper, Michael Roy
Cooper, Paulette Marcia
Cooper, Richard Houghton
Cooper, Robert Leo
Cooper, William Marion
Cope, Alfred Haines
Copeland, Amorita Muriel (Sesinger)
Copeland, Lois Jacqueline (Mrs. Richard A. Sperling)
Copeland, Nathaniel Hawthorne
Copeland, Terry Duane
Coplen, Ron
Coppa, Anthony Patrick
Coppa, Frank John
Copper, Walter Logan, Jr.
Copperman, Stuart Morton
Coppoc, William Joseph
Coppola, Dominick Anthony
Copulsky, William
Coratola, Joseph John
Corazzini, Robert Frank
Corbato, Fernando Jose
Corbett, Richard Lewis
Corbin, Herbert Leonard
Corbin, Robert Glenn
Corbley, John James
Corcoran, Edward Dalton
Corcoran, Elizabeth Anne
Corcoran, Joseph Edward
Corda, Anthony Edward
Corde, George E.
Cordell, Joseph Edward
Cordero, Julio
Cordrey, Richard Stephen
Cordwell, Miriam
Corey, Samuel Caldwell
Cori, Carl Ferdinand
Coriaty, George Michael
Corish, Joseph Ryan
Corley, Nora Teresa
Corliss, John Michael
Corman, James C.
Cormany, Robert Barmont
Cormier, Albert Louis
Cornelis, Johan Marcel Louise
Cornell, Albert
Cornell, John Whiting, Jr.
Cornell, John William
Cornely, Kurt Willy
Cornette, Robert Joseph
Cornick, Delroy Leon
Cornish, Edward Seymour
Cornute, Robert LeRoy
Cornwell, William Samuel
Coronetz, Melanie Ann
Corr, Eleanor Nelson
Corradino, Gandolfo (Dolph)
Corrado, Fred
Correa, Alonso V.
Corredera, Robert Socrates
Correll, James William
Corriere, Donald Blaise
Corrigan, John Patrick
Corson, Dale Raymond
Corson, Peter Dexter
Cortes, Engracio Padilla
Cortes, Luis Eduardo
Cortes, Michael Joseph
Cortes-Hwang, Adriana
Cortez, Jeanette Schlanger
Cory, Paul Richard
Cosgriff, Stuart Worcester
Cosgrove, Martin Joseph
Cosman, Bard
Cosnotti, Richard Louis
Cossa, John Paul
Costa, Allen Ronald
Costa, Constance Elaine
Costa, Helio
Costa, Joseph Alfred
Costa, Joseph James
Costagliola, Francesco
Costantino, James
Costanzo, Raphael J.
Costello, Daniel Walter
Costello, Douglas Warren
Costikyan, Edward Nazar
Cote, Donald Bernard
Cote, Eleanor M. Murano
Côté, Joseph Julien Jean-Pierre
Cothran, Raymond John
Cotter, John Patrick
Cotter, William R.
Cotting, James Charles
Cottle, Eleanor Cray (Mrs. Edgar Willis Cottle)
Cottle, Thomas Joseph
Cotton, William Robert
Cottrell, James Edward
Coughlin, Francis Raymond, Jr.
Coughlin, R. Lawrence
Couillard, Joseph William
Couloumbis, Theodore Alexander
Coulson, John L.
Coulson, Louis Anthony
Coulson, Merle Francis
Coulter, Glenn Richard
Coulter, Howard Alton
Coulter, William Goddard
Coulthard, Robert
Councilor, James Allan
Couper, Richard Watrous
Courage, Alexander
Courchaine, Armand Joseph
Cournand, Andre F.
Courniotes, Harry James
Coursen, Christopher Dennison
Courson, Robert Wylie, II
Court, Carl Roger
Courter, James A(ndrew)
Courtiss, Eugene Howard
Courtney, Irwin Greene, II
Courtois, Edmond Jacques
Cousin, Dorothy Mae
Cousins, Kathryn Lafler
Cousins, Norman
Cousins, Ruth H(ubbard)
Coutinho, John de S.
Couture, Jean Guy
Couture, Stanislas Hubert
Coval, Naomi Miller
Covatta, Nicholas Joseph, Jr.
Covi, Lino
Covington, Arthur Edwin
Covino, Benjamin Gene
Cowan, Daniel Alexander
Cowan, Milton Howard
Cowan, Ruth Burns
Cowan, William Meredith
Coward, David Bruce
Cowell, Robert Lawrence
Cowen, James
Cowen, Norman Jay
Cowen, Wilson
Cowett, Richard Michael
Cowgill, Carol Ann
Cowie, William John
Cowles, Charles
Cowper-Smith, Maurice A.
Cox, Albert Harrington, Jr.
Cox, Corinne Bird Woolard
Cox, Elizabeth Larter
Cox, Houston Abraham, Jr.
Cox, Jack Cecil
Cox, Robert Gene
Cox, William Jackson
Cox, William Martin
Cox, William Vaughan
Coyle, Joseph Richard
Coyle, Walter Anthony
Coyle, William Radford, III
Craft, Donald Bruce
Craft, James Pressley, Jr.
Craft, James Wilmer
Cragin, Charles Langmaid
Crahall, Adam Carl
Craig, Charles Samuel
Craigmyle, Ronald M.
Crain, Darrell Clayton, Jr.
Craine, Ralph B., Jr.
Cramer, Harold
Crandall, Elizabeth Walbert
Crandall, Riel Stanton
Crandell, Walter Bain
Crandon, John Howland
Crane, Michael
Crankshaw, John Hamilton
Crape, LaMonte Deemor
Crater, Thomas Neil
Craugh, Carolyn
Cravats, Monroe
Crawford, Edward E.
Crawford, Edythe Rowe
Crawford, Homer
Crawford, John McAllister, Jr.
Crawford, Sara E. Twigg
Crawley, Norman Russell, Jr.
Creager, Charles Edwin
Creager, William Arthur
Creamer, Alice duBois
Creamer, Geraldine Margaret
Creech, Richard Hearne
Creed, William Howard
Cregier, Don Mesick
Cremona, Leonard Francis
Cremona, Vincent Anthony
Crenshaw, David Allen
Crenshaw, Mary Ann
Crerar, John Duncan MacAllister
Cressler, John Charles
Cresson, James
Crews, James Eldon
Criares, Nicholas James
Crichton, Neil McCollum
Criddle, A. Hawthorne
Crihan, Ioan G(rigore)
Crill, Edward L.
Crimmins, James Joseph
Crisci, Richard Henry
Crisfafi, Bartel Robert
Crisman, Ronald Everett William
Crissan, Michael George
Crissey, David Lee
Crissman, James Hudson
Crist, Gertrude H. (Mrs. Howard G. Crist, Jr.)
Cristofer, Michael
Critcher, Marge Bernadine
Crocker, Jane Lopes
Crockett, Daniel James
Crockett, Thomas John, III
Crofton, Ronald Charles
Crombie, David Edward
Crompton, Charles Sentman, Jr.
Cron, Anne Marie
Cronan, Donald George
Cronie, Mervyn Allan
Cronin, Bonnie Kathryn
Cronin, Daniel A.
Cronin, Paul Joseph
Cronin, Raymond Valentine
Cronin, Timothy Cornelius
Crook, Norris Clinton
Crook, Richard Goodrich
Crooks, Donald Lawrence
Crosby, George Frederick, Jr.
Crosby, Thomas William
Cross, John Blakely
Cross, Ronald
Crosthwaite, Robert Harold
Crothers, J. Frances
Crouthamel, Arthur William
Crowell, Ralph George
Crowl, Richard Bernard
Crowley, Arthur Edward, Jr.
Crowley, Edward Francis
Crowley, Harold Sterling, Jr.
Crowley, Hubert Cameron
Crowley, Ralph Manning
Crowley, Richard Marr
Crozier, Ronald David
Cruikshank, Robert Lane
Crumb, Edgar Alvin
Crumley, James Robert, Jr.
Crump, Walter Moore, Jr.
Crutchfield, Sam Shaw, Jr.
Cruz, A. Ernest
Cruz, Robert
Cruze, Kenneth
Cryan, Eugene Whitty
Cryan, Marjorie Elaine Nixon
Crymble, John Frederick
Crystal, Boris
Crystal, Graef Slater
Csavinszky, Peter John
Csejka, David Andrew
Csermely, Thomas John
Csicsery-Ronay, Istvan
Csobaji, Sandor Bela
Cucci, Cesare Eleuterio
Cuccioli, Robert
Cucin, Robert Louis
Cuddy, Robert James, Jr.
Cuddy, William Vincent
Cude, Reginald Hodgin
Cuetara, Edward Amado
Cueto, Agustin
Cukor, Peter
Culhane, Shamus
Cullen, Helen Frances
Cullen, Leo Francis
Cullinan, William Edward, Jr.
Cullings, Patrick Robert
Culver, Edward Holland, Jr.
Cumings, Richard Glenn
Cummin, Alfred S(amuel)
Cumming, Hugh Smith, Jr.
Cummings, Benjamin Edgar
Cummings, Harold Greig, Jr.
Cummings, Michael James
Cummings, Richard Haven
Cummings, Robert Ambrose
Cummins, Francis Mitchell
Cundy, Kenneth Raymond
Cuneo, John Andrew, Jr.
Cuneo, Leonard Eugene
Cunha, George Martin
Cunio, Paul Edward
Cunningham, George Garrison
Cunningham, Marie (Mrs. Thomas Cunningham)
Cunningham, William John
Cunov, Carl Henry
Cuoco, Daniel A(nthony)
Cuomo, Mario Matthew
Cuomo, Thomas Joseph, Jr.
Cupido, Raffaella Elizabeth
Cuppels, Norman Paul
Cuprak, Lucian John
Curi, Joseph Francis John
Curiale, Salvatore Bruce
Curilla, Joseph, Jr.
Curkin, Paulette
Curley, Walter Joseph Patrick, Jr.
Curley, Walter William
Curlings, Ronald Wayne
Curran, Frank Joseph
Curran, Kathryn
Curran, Martin Francis
Curran, Maurice Francis
Currier, Marion Winona
Curry, Thomas Fortson
Curry, William Thomas
Curtin, Brian Joseph
Curtin, Catherine Mary
Curtin, John T.
Curtin, Raymond William
Curtin, William Joseph
Curtis, Charles Ravan
Curtis, Dewey Lee
Curtis, James Theodore
Curtis, John Obed
Curtis, Ralph Van Olinda
Curtis, Thomas Edward
Curtis, Walter W.
Curtis, William Henry, III
Curtiss, Robert Stanage
Curtiss, Sidney Quinn
Cusack, John Thomas
Cuseo, Allan Anthony
Cush, Rudolph Woodbury
Cushing, Arthur Irving, Jr.
Cushing, Franklin Seth
Cushman, Robert Arnold
Cusick, James Joseph, Jr.
Cusick, Robert Edward
Custer, John J.
Cutler, Claire Mintz (Mrs. Max Cutler)
Cutler, Herbert Whitney
Cutler, Kenneth Burnett
Cutler, Leonard Myron
Cutler, Marshall Carl
Cutler, Rhoda
Cutrona, Michael Phillip
Cutter, Curtis Carly
Cutting, Allan Renwick
Cvach, Philip Edward
Cyert, Richard Michael
Cylke, Frank Kurt
Cyr, Rob Roy
Dabbs, Theron Randolph, Jr.
Dacey, George Clement
da Cunha, Julio
D'Adamo, Anthony
Daddi, George
Dadrian, Vahakn Norair
Daenecke, Eric
Daffin, Irl Alonzo
Dagenais, Yves
D'Agostino, Angelo
D'Agostino, Michael Dominick
D'Agostino, Ralph Benedict
Dahan, Fernand William
Dahill, Thomas Henry, Jr.
Dahl, Bernhoff Allen
Dahle, Leland Kenneth
Dahlen, Richard Lester
Dahm, Douglas Barrett
Daigle, Rosario Joseph
Dailey, Jeremiah Aloysius
Dailey, Maceo Crenshaw, Jr.
Dailey, Roger Kent
Dailey, William Vincent
Daily, Jay Elwood
Dakin, Arthur Hazard
Dalack, John Donald
Dal Cortivo, Leo A.
Dale, Paul Worthen
Dale, Porter Hinman
Dalen, James Eugene
d'Alessio, Gregory
Daley, Joseph T.
Daley, Michael James
Dal Fabbro, Mario
Dalgaard, Bruce Ronald
Dalgleish, Lily Margaret
Dalianis, James Stephen
Dallas, John R(aymond), Jr.
Dallas, Robert Valine
Dallow, Theodore Julian
Dalrymple, Windsor Howard
Dalton, Dennis
Dalton, Edward Francis
Dalton, John H.
Dalva, David Leon, II
Daly, Charles Cornelius
Daly, William Joseph, Jr.
Daman, Harlan Richard
Damast, Melvyn
D'Amato, Antonio Gennaro
Damavandi, Parviz Khatib
D'Ambola, Joseph Vincent
D'Ambrosio, Nicholas
Dameron, Doyle
Dameshek, H. Lee
Damico, Nicholas Peter
D'Amico, Richard Joseph
Damijonaitis, Vytautas
Damon, Alan Wells, Jr.
Damon, Carolyn Eleanore
D'Amours, Norman Edward
Damson, Barrie Morton
Dana, Jeanne Marie
Danaher, John Anthony
Dance, Walter David
Danchak, Michael
Dancy, North Barry
Dandes, E. William
Danek, Joseph Gerard
Danesh, Hossain Banadaki
Danforth, Dana
D'Angelo, Joseph Francis
D'Angelo, Samuel Anthony
Dangler, Richard Reiss
Dangremond, Lucille Martin (Mrs. Harley L. Dangremond)
Daniel, Alice
Daniel, Gerard Lucian
Daniel-Dreyfus, Susan B. Russe (Mrs. Marc Andre Daniel-Dreyfus)
Daniell, James Lachlan
Daniels, Anthony Carl
Daniels, David Mitchell
Daniels, Len D.
Daniels, Malcolm Leon
Daniels, Maxine Loreat
Daniels, Robert Vincent
Daniels, Ronald Earl
Daniels, Thomas Edward
Daniels, Whitman
Danielson, Eskil Stuart
Dank, Leonard Dewey
Dankese, Joseph Peter
Danko, Bohdan
Dann, Wanda Peters
Dannenberg, Marvin
Danner, Douglas
Dansereau, Fred Edward, Jr.
D'Anton, Michael Archangel, Sr.
Dantoni, Joseph Louis
Danzis, Colin Michael
Daoud, Assaad Selim
D'Aprix, Roger Martin
d'Aquili, Eugene Guy
Darby, Alvin James
D'Arcy, Albert Joseph
Darden, Joseph Samuel, Jr.
Darino, Eduardo
Darkes, Leroy William
Darling, R(alph) Clement
Darlington, Charles Francis
Darlington, Henry, Jr.
Darrow, John Francis
Darrow, Kenneth Alonzo
Darrow, Richard Joseph
Darrow, Robert Arthur
Darst, Diane Wassman
Dartey, Clemence Kumah
Dash, Harvey Dwight
Dashef, Oscar Zigmund
Dashef, Stephen Sewell
Dater, Arnold Henry
Datesh, John Nicholas
Datta, Ranajit Kumar
Datta, Vijay Kumar
Datz, Israel Mortimer
Daub, Harry Bernard
Dauer, Robert Charles
Daugherty, John Raymond
Daun, Henryk
Dauphinais, Richard Murray
D'Auria, John Kenneth
Davenel, George Francis
Davenport, Robert Charles
Davern, Jeanne Marguerite
Davey, Lycurgus Michael
David, Jon R.
David, Joseph Nissim
David, Martin Franklin
David, Morton Edward
David, Resurreccion Hernando
Davidson, Abraham A.
Davidson, Charles Nuckols
Davidson, David Mark
Davidson, Grace Evelyn
Davidson, Joshua Maurice
Davidson, Phillip Thomas
Davidson, Robert Lee, III
Davie, Malcolm Henderson
Davies, H(erbert) Morris
Davies, James Howard
Davies, Jane B. (Mrs. Lyn Davies)
Davies, John Edward
Davies, Stanley Duane
Davies, Willard John
Davis, Albert Hassam, Jr.
Davis, Alfred Beacham, III
Davis, Alice Eliza Morse (Mrs. George Arthur Davis)
Davis, Andrew Hambly, Jr.
Davis, Arthur David
Davis, Cecille Citroen
Davis, Curtis Carroll
Davis, David Brion
Davis, Donald Alexander
Davis, Donald Dodge
Davis, Donald Irvin

Davis, Donald James
Davis, Donald Whittington
Davis, Duane Allison
Davis, Francis Raymond
Davis, Frederick Vernell
Davis, Gordon
Davis, Howard Murray
Davis, I. Gary
Davis, James Ernest
Davis, Jerome George
Davis, John Herschel
Davis, John Wandell, Jr.
Davis, Joseph Lyman, Jr.
Davis, Joseph Samuel
Davis, Kenneth Warren
Davis, Lawrence Lindsley
Davis, Lawrence Roy
Davis, Maralee G. (Mary Elizabeth Gibson)
Davis, Marc Leighton
Davis, Martin Sandford
Davis, Nathanael Vining
Davis, Nina Miller Moseley
Davis, Paul Gordon
Davis, Paul Irving, III
Davis, Perry John
Davis, Richard Graham
Davis, Robert Gordon
Davis, Samuel
Davis, Stephen Prentice
Davis, Thomas Robin MacLeod
Davis, Thompson Elder
Davis, True
Davis, Warren Maywood
Davis, Wilfred Peter
Davis, Willaim Grenville
Davis, William Eugene
Davisson, Virginia
Dawley, Joseph William
Dawson, Charles Robert
Dawson, Charlotte May
Dawson, David Lloyd
Dawson, Joseph Leo
Dawson, Roy Ben, Jr.
Dawson, Wilfred Thomas
Day, Elroy Kenneth
Day, James Halliday
Day, Kenneth Laird
Day, Melvin Sherman
Day, Paul Richard
Day, Stacey Biswas
Dayal, Prabhu
Dayal, Vijay Shanker
Daye, Sami
Dayton, Allan Shea, Jr.
Dayton, Bruce McLean
Deal, Samuel Broughton
Dean, Deborah Ann
Dean, Hameed Ud.
Dean, Howard Joseph
Dean, Jack Hugh
Deangelis, Peter
Dearington, Searls
Dearworth, James Robert
Debbas, Elie George
DeBellis, Leonard Nicholas
De Bergerac, Leopold Cardona
De Berry, William Jennings, Jr.
DeBitetto, Dominick John
Debnam, Charles H.
DeBock, Florent Alphonse
Debroux, Pierre Robert
Debs, Victor Selim
de Burlo, Comegys Russell, Jr.
de Butts, John Dulany
Decamillis, Augustine Luca
Decarie, Malcolm Graeme
DeCarlo, Charles Raymond
DeCaro, Francis Paul
DeCato, Clifford Miles
Decesare, William Ray
Decker, Barry
Decker, Beatrice Madeline Schirm (Mrs. Robert A. Decker)
Decker, David Larry
Decker, Francis Keil, Jr.
Decker, Raymond Frank
Decker, Robert Jay
Decker, Robert Owen
de Cordova, Diane Jane
DeCourcy, James Edward
De Courcy, Samuel Joseph, Jr.
Dedick, Andrew Paul, Jr.
Dedmon, Thomas Bernice, Jr.
DeDomenic, Lillian Kay (Mrs. Dom L. DeDomenic, Jr.)
Dee, Sidney Earl
Deegan, Dennis Irvin
Deelo, Michael Louis
Deemer, Albert Earl
Deep, Albert Ross
Deer, Donald Maurice
Deer, James Willis
Deering, Allan Brooks
Deering, Christopher Paul
Deering, George Edwin
DeFazio, John Lorenzo
DeFelice, Eugene Anthony
De Felice, Roger Paul
deFilippi, Richard Paul
deFlorio, Romeo Joseph
Defoggi, Ernest
de Foix-Crenascol, Louis (Prince of Andorra and Bearn)
De Forest, Peter Rupert
DeFranceaux, Ada Moss (Mrs. George Waldemar DeFranceaux)
DeFranceaux, George Waldemar
De Francis, Nicholas Anthony
Degann, A(lan) David
Degener, Doris Margaret
Degenkolb, Eugene Otto
De Gennaro, Richard
De Ghetto, Anselm
DeGroff, Ralph Lynn
DeHaan, Clayton Richard
De Haas, Nicholas
de Haen, Paul
Deimel, Robert William
Deitsch, Thomas Alan, Sr.
de Jongh, James Laurence
de Kay, Ormonde, Jr.
Dekmejian, Richard Hrair
De Kolb, Eric
de la Garza, Alexander Manuel
De Lambert, Don Winfield
Delaney, Edward Norman
Delaney, Jack James
Delaney, John Francis
Delaney, John Leo, Jr.
Delaney, John Paulson
Delano, Hugh Stafford
Delano, Victor
delaRocha, Carlos Alfonso
DeLauter, Claude Richard, Jr.
Del Broccolo, Joseph Anthony
Delena, Marie E. Cameron
de Leon, Antonio Carmelo, Jr.
Delgado, Miguel Angel
Del Guercio, Louis Richard Maurice
Delia, Michael Anthony
Delicce, Michael Francis
Delihas, Nicholas
Delija, Louise Celia Cariati
de Lisser, Stanley Pearse
Dell, Christopher
Dell, Edward Thomas, Jr.
Dellandrea, David Aubrey
Dellas, Theodore Andrew
Delman, Michael Robert
Delman, Sheldon Clifford
de Lorenzi, John
Delorme, Jean-Claude
De Los Reyes, Gilbert Miranda
Delp, Harold Arthur
Delphin, Jacques Mercier
Delpino, Robert Anthony
Del Russo, Jon Evan
Delson, Barnet
Delson, George Victor
DeLuca, Anthony James
Delucca, John Joseph
De Lucia, Michael Anthony
Delvalle, June Ackerman
De Maio, Dennis Anthony
DeMaio, Samuel James
De Marco, Peter George
Demarest, Rosemary Regina
DeMarre, Dean Arnold
DeMartino, Anthony Gabriel
De Martino, Bruce Kyle
de Mas, Vanessa Rivera
De Masi, Anthony Seraphin
de Mazia, Violette
Demendi, Joseph Francis
Demetriou, Angelos Cosmas
De Mille, Nelson Richard
Demirjian, M. John
Demmler, Louis Frederick
Demo, Carl Francis
deMonsabert, Winston Russel
Dempsey, Richard Allen
DeMurley, John Stirling
Denbaum, Evelyn
Denenberg, Herbert Sidney
Denger, Elsie Sue
DeNike, Michael Nicholas
Denise, Robert Joseph
Denissoff, Basile Albert
Denk, Edward George
Denmark, George David
Dennis, Donald Philips
Dennis, Earl A(ubrey)
Dennis, John Murray
Dennis, Richard Hollis
Dennis, Samuel Sibley, 3d
Denny, John Lawrence
Denny, William Murdoch, Jr.
Densen-Gerber, Judianne
Denson, James Lawrence
Denson, Lawrence Joshua
Denton, Ralph Jackson
Denton, Ralph Walter
Denton, William Alanson
Dentzer, William Thompson, Jr.
De Nuzzo, Rinaldo Vincent
Deoul, Neal
De Pass, Ernest T.
De Pauw, Gommar Albert
De Pauw, John Whylen
de Pedraza, Isidoro Paul
DePierro, John Joseph
DePreist, James Anderson
Depuy, Hadley Sheldon
Dequaine, Lester Joseph
Deraney, Maurice F.
Deranian, Hagop Martin
Derderian, George Michael
de Reyna, Ramon Joseph
Dergalis, George
Derham, James Joseph
Derick, Dorothy Bosk
De Rienzo, Paul Peter
DeRisio, Vincent James
D'Ermes, Anthony Joseph
Derner, Gordon Frederick
Derosier, Robert Frederick
D'Errico, Joseph
Derry, John Alvin
Dersh, Jerome
Desai, Laxman Shanker
De Salva, Salvatore Joseph
DeSanctis, Roman William
De Santis, Arthur Anthony
De Santis, Carlo Emedio
De Santis, James Robert
De Santis, Joseph
De Santo, Donald James
De Santo, Joseph Aloysius
Desaulniers, Rene Gerard Lesieur
Deschamps, Sidney
De Schuytner, Edward Alphonse
De See, Peter Gerrit
Deshpande, Narayan Vaman
DeSimone, John Patrick
Desjardins, Raoul
Desmond, Thomas Edward
Desnoyers, Sarto
Desruisseaux, Paul
Dessauer, John Hans
Dessi, Adrian Frank
de Stefano, Eugene Anthony
Desvernine, Gilbert Lomping
de Swolkien, Romuald Olgierd
Detar, David Scott
Deters, Arthur Herb, Jr.
Dettman, Maxwell Charles
Dettmer, Robert Gerhart
Detwiler, Henry Samuel
Detwiler, Peter Mead
Deurbrouck, Albert William
Deuss, Jean
Deutsch, Eugene Fredrick
Deutsch, Frederic Herbert
Deutsch, Herbert Arnold
Deutsch, Irwin Frederick
Deutsch, Martin Bernard Joseph
Devadason, Chinnadurai
Devane, Richard Thomas
DeVeaugh-Geiss, Joseph Paul
Devereux, Frances Clark
Devereux, Frederick Leonard, Jr.
Devereux, Joseph Francis, Jr.
Devers, Charlotte Marguerite (Mrs. William Peter Devers)
Devine, C. Robert
Devine, James Joseph
Devine, Joanne Frances
DeVito, Albert Kenneth
De Vito, Lorenzo
Devlin, Anne G.
Devlin, Harry
Devlin, John Francis
Devlin, Robert Martin
De Void, Kenneth Earl, Jr.
Dewees, Donald Charles
Dewell, Wilbur
Dewey, Clarence Forbes, Jr.
Dexheimer, John Patrick
Dexter, Carolyn R.
Dexter, Marvin Judson
Dextraze, Jacques Alfred
Dey, Lochlann Bruce
Deyoe, Warner Stanley
Dhawan, Swaran Seth
Diamond, Alan Shevrin
Diamond, Daniel Joseph
Diamond, Israel
Diamond, Jack Judah
Diamond, M. Jerome
Diamond, Martin Howard
Diamondstone, Lawrence
Di Amore, Joseph Robert
Dias, Earl Joseph
Diaz, Carlos Ricardo
Dibble, Stephen Jesse
Dibble, Willis Alfred, Jr.
DiBlasi, Paul Joseph
Dibner, Susan Schmidt
Di Cara, C(ostante) John
Di Casparro, Ermine Patrick
diCenzo, Colin Domenic
Dick, Charles Howard
Dick, Douglas Shelton
Dick, Robert Grant
Dickens, Doris Lee (Mrs. Austin L. Fickling)
Dickey, Clyde William
Dickey, Joseph Lyle
Dickey, Robert, III
Dickinson, Diane Jane Gray
Dickinson, June Mc Wade
Dickson, Paul Wesley, Jr.
Dickstein, Benjamin
Dickstein, Jack
Di Croce, Anthony Joseph
Di Cuio, Robert Frank
Diefenbach, Marcia Gay Ann
Diehl, Carol Susan
Diehl, Donald Winston
Diehl, James Raymond, Jr.
Diehl, Rick William
Diehl, Rutherford Oliver
Diehl, Saylor Flory
Diener, Debra Natalie
Dierdorff, Lee Henry, Jr.
Dies, Douglas Hilton
Diethrick, Russell Edward, Jr.
Dietrich, Bruce Leinbach
Dietz, William Ronald
Dietzel, Louise Alverta
Diffenderfer, Hope Anker
Di Gennaro, Jerome Anthony
Di George, Angelo Mario
DiGeronimo, Ernest Michael
Diggins, Edward Patrick
Di Giacomo, William Anthony
Di Girolamo, Orlando
Di Gregorio, Guerino John
Dilenge, Domenico
Di Leo, Joseph Henry
Di Leone, Kenneth Robert
Di Leva, Anthony Joseph
Dillaber, Philip Arthur
Dillard, Emil Lee
Dillman, Harry Louis, Jr.
Dillon, John Stanley
Dillon, Paul Walker
Dillon, Retta Walsmith
Dillon, Robert Morton
Dillon, Stanley Clifton
Dillon, Thomas Church
Dillow, Gaylord Benjamin
Di Luglio, Thomas Ross
Dimant, Jacob
Dimantha, Priya Chitta
DiMaria, Fred Joseph
Din, Hameed Ud
Dinberg, Michael David
Dineen, Eugene Joseph
Dines, Allen I.
Dingee, John Henry, Jr.
Dingle, James
Dingman, Michael David
Dinman, Bertram David
Dinsdale, Henry Begg
Dinsmore, Paul Rich
Dintenfass, Julius
Dion, Joyce Ann
Dionne, Andre Clermont
DiPalma, John Candide
Dipaola, Salvatore Paul
DiPaolo, Gordon Anthony
diPasquale, Emanuel Paul
Di Pierro, Ronald Joseph
DiPietro, G. Guy
Di Primio, Anthony
Dircks, Richard Joseph
Di Renzo, Gordon James
Dirkes, Robert Frederick
Di Ruggiero, Maureen Ann
DiSalvo, Walter Anthony
Disantis, John Anthony
Di Scipio, William Joseph
Di Sciullo, Anthony Joseph
Disco, Adrian Anthony
Disko, Michael David
Disney, Frank Albert
Ditch, William Clement
Divack, Daniel Murray
Dixon, Alfred Burton
Dixon, Andrew Lee, Jr.
Dixon, David McFarland
Dixon, Henry Campbell, Jr.
Dizer, John Thomas, Jr.
DiZio, Steven Frank
Djerassi, Isaac
Djinis, William Anthony
Djordjevic, Vlastimir Walter
D'Lauro, Frank Andrew, Jr.
Dluhy, John Michael
Dmochowski, Jan Rafal
Dobbins, Hope Jean
Dobbins, William Octavius, III
Dobbs, Carroll Ray
Dobbs, Robert Joseph, Jr.
Dobelle, Gladys Kleinman
Dobkin, Donald
Dobkin, Herbert
Doboy, Joseph G.
Dobriansky, Lev Eugene
Dobromil, Stanley Irwin
Dobrow, Harvey Robert
Dobson, Brian Gregory
Dobson, Richard Hal
Dockstader, Emmett Stanley
Dodd, Christopher J.
Dodd, Daniel Phillips
Dodds, Richard William
Dodge, Alfa Dorothy Maw (Mrs. Harold A. Dodge)
Dodge, G. Doyle
Dodge, Homer Kingsley
Dodsworth, Roy Warren
Doebler, Harold Joseph
Doel, Gilbert Henry
Doell, Martha Eileen
D'Oench, Russell Grace, Jr.
Doerfler, Leo G.
Doerr, Edd
Doerschug, Leslie Roland
Doerschuk, Ernest Edwin, Jr.
Doetsch, Raymond Nicholas
Doff, Alfred Frank
Dogger, Ada Ruth Carolyn Emde
Doh, Byung Il
Doherty, Anna Marie
Doherty, John Patrick, Jr.
Doherty, Joseph Frederick
Doherty, Patricia McGinn
Dojka, Edwin Sigmund
Dolan, Charles Francis
Dolan, George Henry
Dole, Grace Fuller
Doman, Elvira Hand
Domanico, John Peter, Jr.
Domaradzki, Theodore Felix
Domarecka, Sister Mary Sylvina
Dombrowski, Frank Paul, Jr.
Domico, Michael Dennis
Domni, Fejzi Isa
Domovich, Stephen Michael
Doms, Keith
Donaho, John Albert
Donahoe, Eileen O'Rourke
Donahoe, Rita Louise
Donahue, Irving James, Jr.
Donahue, John Joseph
Donald, Patrick Reynolds
Donaldson, Dorothea Amelia
Donaldson, Gerald Keith
Donaldson, Peter Samuel
Donath, Clarence Edgar
Donchak, Richard Michael
Donelli, John Jay
Donheiser, Walter Joseph
Donikian, Marc Roupen
Donio, Dominic Anthony
Donley, Bettie Loux
Donley, Edward
Donley, James Walton
Donley, Marshall Owen, Jr.
Donnelly, Barbara Mae
Donnelly, Brian
Donnelly, William Lorne
Donner, William Troutman
Donofrio, Anthony Michael
Donoghue, Elizabeth Marion MacMahon (Mrs. Florence Joseph Donoghue)
Donoghue, Kevin Francis
Donohoe, Victoria Therese
Donohue, Michael Joseph
Donovan, James Robert
Donovan, Maurice Stanton
Donovan, Peter Morse
Donovan, Raymond Edward
Donovick, Richard
Dooley, John Morse
Doolittle, Sidney Bartoo
D'Orazio, Donald Emidio
Dordevic, Mihailo
Dore, Stephen Edward, Jr.
Dorey, Leona Pixley
Dorf, Philip
Dorfman, Howard David
Dorfman, Wilfred
Doria, Anthony Notarnicola
Doria, Joseph Vincent, Jr.
Dorkan, Cenap Suphi
Dorland, Jack Albert
Dormann, Henry O.
Dormer, Devlin William
Dorn, Frederick Christian, Jr.
Dorn, Michel John
Dorn, Peter Klaus
Dornan, James Edward, Jr.
Dornfest, Burton Saul
Doron, Zvi Jay
Dorrie, Charles Theodore
Dorsey, Robert Francis
Dortort, Frances K.
Dosier, Larry Waddell
Doster, Rose Eleanor Wilhelm (Mrs. Jesse A. Doster)
Doten, Herbert Russell
Doto, Paul Jerome
Dotter, Eugene Victor
Doucet, Norman Leon
Doud, Thomas Jefferson, Jr.
Dougherty, Charles F.
Dougherty, James Douglas
Dougherty, James Joseph
Dougherty, John Joseph
Dougherty, Mary Alice
Douglas, Arthur
Douglas, John Jay
Douglas, William Richard
Douglas-Hamilton, Natalie Wales (Lady Malcolm Douglas-Hamilton)
Douglass, Gordon Kitchel
Douglass, John William
Douglass, Paul F.
Doukas, Harry Michael
Dovel, Clinton George
Dow, Donald Douglas
Dow, Millard Harding
Dow, Robert Lincoln
Dowd, Benjamin S.
Dowd, George Thomas, Jr.
Dowden, Albert Ricker
Dowden, Donald Smith
Dowler, Robert Edward
Dowling, Jessie Pennington
Dowling, Leo Jerome
Downe, Edward R., Jr.
Downer, Charles Webster
Downes, Edmund William
Downey, Thomas Joseph
Downing, Jean Crawford
Downing, William Smith
Downs, Joseph Hunter, II
Doyel, John Stephen
Doyle, A(ndrew) Gerald
Doyle, Gerard Francis
Doyle, James L.
Doyle, John Thomas
Drabkowski, Alex Joseph
Drachman, Daniel Bruce
Drager, Marvin
Drain, Charles Sharer, Jr.
Drake, Josephine Eleanor
Drake, Robert LeRoy
Drapeau, Jean
Draper, David Watson
Drapkin, Arnold
Drebus, Richard William
Dreitlein, Raymond Paul
Dremuk, Richard
Drennen, Donald Arthur
Drescher, Dennis George
Dressel, Henry Francis
Dressler, Kenneth Paul
Drevo, Joseph Charles
Drewsen, Edmond Titus, Jr.
Dreyer, Irene Starkel (Mrs. Harold E. Dreyer)
Dreyfus, Michel Andre
Dreyfuss, Stephen Leo
Driggs, Margaret (Mrs. Howard R. Driggs)
Drije, A(nn) Carla
Drinan, Robert Frederick
Drinkwater, Agnes Hillman
Driscoll, Donald Thomas
Drisko, Elliot Hillman
Driver, Philip Brognard, Jr.
Drobena, Thomas John
Drobile, James Albert
Droege, Robert Carl
Droesch, Vigee Hall
Drollette, Daniel David
Drop, Louis Robert
Drowne, Brother Lawrence
Drozdow, Stephen Robert
Druck, Kalman Breschel
Drucker, Jules Herbert
Drucker, Ted E.
Druckman, Richard Arnold
Drudge, Robert B.
Drum, James Hunter
Drum, Peggi (Margaret A.)
Drumm, Philip Russell
Drummond, Joseph Justin
Drumwright, Thomas Franklin, Jr.
Druskoff, Eli
Dryer, Edwin Jason
Drymiotis, Andrew Demetrios
Drzewieniecki, Walter Marian
Du, Kwen-ming
Dua, Frank Martin
Duane, Francis Joseph
Duax, William Leo
DuBard, Walter Highgate
Dube, John
Dubey, Satya Deva
Dubin, Isadore Nathan
Dubin, Morton Donald
Dubin, Samuel
Dubow, Arthur Myron
DuBroff, Diana D.
Du Broff, Sidney Jerome
Dubuc, Carroll Edward
Ducanis, Alex Julius
Ducharme, Claire Phyllis
DuCharme, Raymond Waldo
Duck, Virginia Ann
Duck, William Franklin
Ducksworth, Russell
Dudani, Niranjan
Dudick, Michael Joseph
Dudinski, Charles
Dudley, Ofe Sara
Duer, Beverley Chew
Dufault, Father Nicholas
Duff, Charles Meredith
Duff, Clair Vincent
Duff, Louis Dunlap
Duffus, Roy Alexander, Jr.
Duffy, Brian Michael
Duffy, Edward W.
Duffy, Janet Cameron Dill
Duffy, John Lester
Duffy, Kevin Thomas
Duffy, Thomas Edward
Dufner, Mary Elizabeth
DuFour, Raymond Albert
Dugas, Roger Arthur
Duggan, Dennis Michael
Duggins, Elizabeth Lawrence
Duguay, Martin Robert
Duke, Virginia Bacon (Mrs. H. Trisdom Duke III)
Dukelow, Owen Warner
Dukes, Jerry Louis
DuLeep, Kodendera Subbiah
Duley, Walter Winston
Dulin, William Carter
Dulis, Edward John
Dull, Sidney Francis
Dully, Frank E.
Dumaine, Maurice Philippe
Dumbri, Austin Charles
du Mont, John Sanderson
Dumont, Normand Edward
Dumper, William Clark
Dunaief, Leah Salmansohn
Dunbar, Davis Townsend
Dunbar, Robert Everett
Duncan, Ardinelle Bean
Duncan, Carville Donovan, Jr.
Duncan, Eleanore Klari de Balagya de Szecsanyi
Duncan, Henrietta
Duncan, Max Carson
Duncan, Robert Clifton
Duncan, Stanley Forbes
Dunckel, Arthur Ervin
Dunford, David Marshall
Dungan, Vicki Lou
Dunham, Christopher Cooper
Dunham, Robert Secrest
Dunhill, Hugo
Dunk, Richard Harvey
Dunkel, Lawrence
Dunlap, Charles Joseph, Jr.
Dunlap, Estelle Cecilia Diggs (Mrs. Lee A. Dunlap)
Dunlea, Thomas Anthony
Dunleavy, Francis J.
Dunmire, Lester Addison
Dunn, Barbara Jane Baxter
Dunn, Charles Thomas
Dunn, Donald Richard
Dunn, Frank William
Dunn, Henry Thomas
Dunn, James Joseph
Dunn, Johanna Read
Dunn, Joseph Francis
Dunn, Margaret Mary Coyne
Dunn, Marie Eileen
Dunn, Robert Fowler
Dunne, James Robert
Dunne, Michael Charles
Dunphy, T.J. Dermot
Dupong, William Gregg
du Pont, Pierre S., IV
Dupont, Ralph Paul
DuPont, Robert Louis, Jr.
DuPorte, Ernest Melville
Duppstadt, William Homer
Dupre, Kate B.
Duprey, Edmond R.
Dupuis, Sylvio Louis
Dupuis, Victor Lionel
Dupuy, Frank Russell, Jr.
Duran, Henry Alfred
Durand, Edna Mottshaw

Durand, Louis Marius
Durant, Thomas Stephen
Durante, Dominick James
Durding, William Walter
Durgin, Frank Albert, Jr.
Durham, James Bryant
During, Theobald
Durkin, John A.
Durley, Gerald Lee
Durniak, James Dennis
Durnin, Richard Gerry
DuRocher, Armand David
Durr, Beulah Patton
Dursin, Henry Louis
D'Urso, John Anthony
Duryea, Edward Russell
Duryea, Perry Belmont, Jr.
Dushman, Allan
Dusold, Laurence Richard
Duss, William Adolph
Dutta, Sisir Kamal
Dutton, David Bellamy
Dutton, Lisle George
Dutton, Robert Edward, Jr.
Dutton, Thomas Eugene
Duval, Marjorie Ann
du Vigneaud, Vincent
Duzy, Frank Joseph
Dvarecka, Christopher Lawrence
Dvoichenko-Markov, Demetrius
Dvornicky, Joseph Andrew, Jr.
Dweck, Edward Jack
Dwivedi, Basant Kumar
Dworsky, Leonard Bernard
Dworzan, George R.
Dworzan, Helene
Dwyer, Edward James
Dwyer, John Francis
Dwyer, Robert Francis
Dwyer, Terrence Edward
Dwyer, William Aloysius, Jr.
Dwyer, William Dennis
Dybner, Ruben
Dyck, Manfred F.
Dyck, Martin
Dyer, Charlotte Leavitt (Mrs. George Bell Dyer)
Dyer, Doris Anne
Dyer, George Bell
Dyer, Robert Francis, Jr.
Dyer, Thomas Keane
Dyka, Viterbia Mary
Dymicky, Michael
D'Zmura, Thomas Leo
Eads, Laura Krieger
Eager, Marguerite Ethel
Eagler, Robert Theodore
Eames, Warren Baker
Earl, Donald Wadsworth
Earles, Donald Ray
Earley, Delia Theresa
Early, Joseph Daniel
Earnheart, Frank Jones
Easley, Robert Marshall, Jr.
Eastburn, William Henry, III
Eastham, Thomas
Eastlund, Bernard John
Easton, Louise Lumino
Easton, Virgil James
Eaton, Alvin Ralph
Eaton, Amos Jorge
Eaton, Edgar Philip, Jr.
Eaton, Haven McCrillis
Eaton, Richard Gillette
Eaton, Roderic Lewis
Eaton, William Mellon
Eaves, John, Jr.
Eben, Kurt Julius
Eberhart, Harry Simon, Jr.
Eberhart, Russell Carley
Eberly, Warren Samuel
Ebersole, J. Glenn, Jr.
Ebersole, William John, Jr.
Ebin, Leonard Ned
Eboh, Enobong Thompson
Eby, Paul Joseph
Echeverria, Alfredo Diego
Echeverria, Federico Sergio
Echols, Ivor Tatum
Eckersley, Robert Neal
Eckert, William George
Eckert, William Henry
Eckman, Bertha Elizabeth
Eckmann, Leo James
Eckstein, Zvi Muller
Ecroyd, Lawrence Gerald
Edberg, Stephen Charles
Edelman, Gerald Maurice
Edelman, Paul Sterling
Edelman, Samuel Joseph
Edelson, Larry Mark
Edelstein, Alan Martin
Edelstein, Arnold Neil
Edelstein, David Northon
Edelstein, David Simeon
Edelstein, Mardee Farnham
Eden, Alvin Noam
Edenbaum, Martin I.
Ederma, Arvo Bruno
Edet, Edna Marilyn Smith
Edgar, Robert William
Edgar, William Dunlap
Edgell, George Paul
Edhorn, Anna-Stina
Edick, Alan Dale
Edinger, Stanley Evan
Edis, Gloria Toby (Mrs. Myron R. Schoenfeld)
Edman, Walter William
Edmonds, Roger Sidney
Edmonds, Walter Patrick
Edmonds, Wayne King
Edmonds, Willie, Jr.
Edmonston, William Edward, Jr.
Edmunds, Arthur J.
Edmunds, Robert Thomas
Edsall, Howard Linn
Edson, Andrew Stephen
Edson, Hubert
Edwards, Arthur William
Edwards, Bert Tvedt
Edwards, Carl Normand
Edwards, Charles Cannon
Edwards, Charles Henry, Jr.
Edwards, Charles Mundy, Jr.
Edwards, James Percival, III
Edwards, Ralph
Edwards, Ray Conway
Edwards, Robert Lomas
Edwards, Roy Lawrence
Effinger, George Alec
Effinger, Gerold Joseph
Efron, Samuel
Efthymiou, Constantine John
Egan, John Frederick
Egan, Michael Joseph
Egan, Shirley Anne
Egelston, Richard Lester
Eggers, Melvin Arnold
Egli, Peter
Egolf, Ralph Jennings, Jr.
Egyed, Alex
Ehmer, Marjy Arduina Niccoll
Ehrenstein, Gerald
Ehrenzweig, Joel
Ehrlich, Bernard Herbert
Ehrlich, George Edward
Ehrlich, Hélène Hedy
Ehrlich, Stanley Leonard
Ehrman, Libert
Ehrman, Raymond Streng
Ehrmann, Robert Lincoln
Eiber, Bernard M.
Eickelberg, W. Warren Barbour
Eickhoff, Alan Craig
Eidel, Zeneth
Eidelhoch, Lester Philip
Eidson, Robert Ansel
Eidsvold, Gary Mason
Eiferman, Deborah Berlinger
Eiffler, Elmer Edward
Eigenbrode, Richard Daniel
Eikerenkoetter, Roy Cornelius
Ein, Daniel
Ein, Melvin Bennett
Einach, Charles Donald
Einarson, Baldvin Oliver
Einbond, Bernard Lionel
Einhorn, Carl Murray
Einhorn, Edward Harry
Einhorn, Roman
Eisaman, Leo Coburn
Eisele, John Allan
Eisen, Alan G.
Eisen, David Michael
Eisen, Leonard
Eisenberg, Allan Jay
Eisenberg, Donald Harvey
Eisenberg, Gerson Gutman
Eisenberg, John Meyer
Eisenberg, Joseph
Eisenberg, Phillip
Eisenpreis, Alfred
Eisenstadt, Abraham Seldin
Eisenstadt, Gerd Michael
Eisenstadt, Marvin Ernest
Eisenstein, Theodore Donald
Eisler, Paul Erich
Eisner, Herman
Eisner, Leonard
Eisner, Michael Carl
Eisold, John Edward
Ekman, Sheldon Victor
Ekstrand, Janice Irmo
Ekstrom, Lincoln
ElAttar, Abdel Moneim
El-Baz, Farouk
El-Behairy, Mohamed Mohamed
Elder, Alexander Stowell
Elderfield, John
Elders, James Alan
Eldred, Gerald Marcus
Eldred, Norman Orville
Eldridge, Brian John
Eldridge, Gwendolyn Bernice Moran
Eleazar, Roberto Salvador Pansacola
Eleccion, Marcelino
Elfner, Dale Elwood
Elfvin, John Thomas
Elgart, Mervyn L.
Elgart, Ruth Cynthia
Eliel, Stefan Erich
Elinskas, Robert Charles, Sr.
Eliot, Lucy Carter
Elkhadem, Saad Eldin Amin
Elkin, Ernest
Elkin, Philip
Elkins, Howard Frederic
Elkins, Jacob Benjamin
Elkins, Wilson Homer
El Kodsi, Baroukh Moussa
Elkort, Richard Jay
Ellegard, Roy Taylor
Ellenberger, Jack Stuart
Ellig, Bruce Robert
Ellinger, John Leonard
Elliot, Ian Douglas
Elliot, James Ludlow
Elliott, B(rose) Charles, Jr.
Elliott, Benjamin Paul
Elliott, David William
Elliott, Donald Joseph
Elliott, Frank Abercrombie
Elliott, Inger McCabe (Mrs. Osborn Elliott)
Elliott, John Raymond
Elliott, John T.
Elliott, Richard Verbryck
Elliott, Scott Cameron
Elliott, Sheila Hollihan
Elliott, William John
Ellis, A. Ralph
Ellis, Daniel Benson
Ellis, Elizabeth Mueller
Ellis, Jeanne Holland (Mrs. Cornell Franklin Ellis)
Ellis, John Spillman, Jr.
Ellis, Lawrence Dobson
Ellis, Lee Roy
Ellis, Ray George
Ellis, Roy Arthur
Ellison, Cyril Lee
Ellison, Theodore
Ellison, Thomas Griffitts (Griff)
Ellms, Carlton Warren, III
Ellsweig, Phyllis Leah
Ellsworth, Arthur Whitney
Ellsworth, Stanford Grant
Elman, Gerry Jay
Elman, Howard Lawrence
Elman, Robert
Elmes, Badgley Allen
Elmore, Richard Francis
Elsaady, Atyaat Nashed
El-Sabban, Mohamed Zaki
Elward, James Joseph
Elwood, George Haddow
Emanuel, Helene Rich
Ember, Norman Allen
Emberley, William David
Emberson, Richard Maury
Embody, Daniel Robert
Emch, George Frederick
Emerald, Robert Louis
Emerick, Kenneth Fred
Emerling, Edward George
Emerson, Andi (Mrs. Emerson Weeks)
Emerson, Eleanor Annie
Emerson, J Martin
Emerson, Kary Cadmus
Emerson, Paul Carlton
Emerson, Sidney Thomas
Emerson, William R.
Emery, David Farnham
Emich, Clinton Crawford
Emig, Lois Irene Myers (Mrs. Jack W. Emig)
Emmerich, Frederic Edward
Emmerich, John Patrick
Emms, Josepha Murray
Emrich, Walter
End, Gerard Edward, Jr.
Endahl, Lowell Jerome
Enders, John Franklin
Enders, March
Eng, Richard Peter
Eng, Richard Shen
Eng, Young F.
Engalitcheff, John, Jr.
Engborg, Edwin Charles, Jr.
Engel, David Chapin
Engel, Gertrude
Engel, Howard Denton
Engel, Jerry S.
Engel, John Jacob
Engel, Ralph Manuel
Engelbrecht, Eugene William
Engelhardt, David Meyer
Engelhardt, Hugo Tristram, Jr.
Engelman, Gerald
Engelman, Irwin
Engisch, Richard Alfred
Engle, Charles Donald
Engle, Harold Glenn, Jr.
Englehart, Harry Augustine, III
Englert, Herbert Charles
English, Maurice
English, Robert
English, Ruth Hill
Englishman, Herbert Neil
Englund, Roy Emil
Engram, Thomas James
Enhorning, Norman Arthur
Eni, Emmanuel Ukwu
Enkenhus, Kurt Reinhold
Enoch, Kurt
Enterline, James Robert
Epperson, James Allen, III
Eppes, William David
Eppley, Roland Raymond, Jr.
Epstein, Benjamin Robert
Epstein, Burton Irwin
Epstein, David Weiss
Epstein, Edward George
Epstein, Howard Alan
Epstein, Milton A.
Epstein, Morton
Epstein, Paul Elliott
Epstein, Raymond
Epstein, Sarah Guny
Epstein, Seymour Gerald
Epstein, Stanley Winston
Erb, Robert Allan
Erb, Timothy John
Erbe, Gary Thomas
Eres, Eugenia
Ergin, Muceddit Tahsin
Erickson, Lowell LeRoy
Ericson, John Williamson
Ericson, Karl Ingvar
Eriksen, Einar Anton
Erim, Kenan Tevfik
Erinakes, Dorothy May Eden (Mrs. Peter C.H. Erinakes)
Ernst, James Walter
Ernst, John Gilbert
Ernstrom, Edward Kenneth
Ertel, Allen Edward
Ertell, Merton William
Erumsele, Andrew Akhigbe
Erway, Charles Albert
Esaki, Leo
Escallón, Marion Schmidt
Escava, Nathan Isaac
Eschen, Albert Herman
Eshleman, Silas Kendrick, III
Eskandarian, Edward
Eskenazi, Gerald
Eskow, Alexander Bernard
Eskow, Roy Lionel
Eslami, Hossein Hojatol
Esler, Richard Curry
Esmond, Patrick John
Espenshade, Marlin Alwine
Esposito, Dominic Salvator
Esposito, Frank Vincent
Esposito, John Anthony
Esposito, Joseph Anthony
Esposito, Kenneth John
Esposito, Ronald Patrick
Esquerre, Jean Roland
Essman, Walter B(ernard)
Essrick, Abraham Joseph
Esterhai, John Louis
Esterman, Benjamin
Estes, Edna Eva
Estey, George Fisher
Estin, Leonard Allen
Estra, Jordan Mark
Estrella, Leo Edward
Estrin, Herman Albert
Estrin, Sheldon Baruch
Etcovitch, Allen
Ethan, Carol Baehr
Ethridge, Harrison Mosley
Ethridge, Noel Harold
Etmekjian, James
Ettenberg, Eugene M(artin)
Etter, Thomas Clifton, Jr.
Euerle, George William
Eurich, Alvin Christian
Eustance, William Ernest
Eustis, Richard Alan
Evanoff, George C.
Evans, Anderson Pierce, Jr.
Evans, Betty Bollback (Mrs. C. Hans Evans)
Evans, Bruce Eugene
Evans, Clyde Henry
Evans, Ernest Pipkin, Jr.
Evans, Evan
Evans, Floyd Lee, Jr.
Evans, Franklin James, Jr.
Evans, George Paul
Evans, Gerard Erwin
Evans, Hugh E.
Evans, James Hurlburt
Evans, John Robert
Evans, Joseph Henry
Evans, Philip Gordon
Evans, Richard Edelen
Evans, Robert Harold
Evans, Robert Matthew
Evans, Thomas Archie
Evans, Thomas Beverley, Jr.
Evans, Thomas Haddock
Evans, Wayne Russell
Evans, William Samuel
Eve, Arthur Owen
Evelyn, George Elbert
Evenson, Donald Paul
Everett, John Rutherford
Everett, Woodrow Wilson, Jr.
Evica, George Michael Joseph
Evirs, Howard Wesley, Jr.
Eviston, Charles Louis
Evslin, Bernard David
Ewald, Elin Lake
Ewald, Frederick Conrad
Ewald, John Benton, Jr.
Ewald, Peter K.
Ewart, Jon Robert
Ewen, Ira
Ewing, Blair Gordon
Ewing, Donald Spencer
Ewing, Robert
Eyes, Raymond
Fabbri, Remo, Jr.
Faber, John Henry
Fabiano, William Louis
Fabinyi, Geza Theodore
Fabricant, Norman
Faccini, Ernest Carlo
Facer, David Charles
Facos, James Francis
Fadden, Eileen Ann
Fadeley, Herbert John, Jr.
Fader, Seymour J.
Fader, Shirley Sloan (Mrs. Seymour J. Fader)
Fadil, Richard Samuel
Fagan, Raymond Bernard
Fahey, Joseph Paul, Jr. (Jay)
Fahy, Charles
Fahy, William Thomas
Failing, Gregory Scott
Failla, R. Roy
Fairbanks, David Nathaniel Fox
Fairchild, John Phillip
Fakundiny, Robert Harry
Falardeau, Maurice
Falbaum, Bertram Seymour
Falco, Thomas Gilbert
Falcone, Frank Emidio
Falcone, Joseph Daniel
Falconero, Robert Mario
Falconieri, Virginia Patricia
Falk, Alma Martha
Falk, Charles David
Falkenau, Marsha Kastner
Falkenbury, John Francis
Falkowski, Edward John
Fallon, Robert Thomas
Faloon, William Wassell
Falvo, Michael
Famadas, Jose
Fan, Chin-Fu
Fan, Kuang Huan
Fan, Shou-shan
Fan, You-Ling
Fancher, Edwin Crawford
Fancher, Pauline Mabel
Fang, Hsai-Yang
Fang, Pen Jeng
Fanning, William Henry, Jr.
Fanning, Winthrop Coit, II
Fanos, Nicholas G.
Fant, David Luther
Fanti, Roy
Fanus, Pauline Rife (Mrs. William Edward Fanus)
Farber, Donald Clifford
Farber, Erica
Farber, Joseph
Farber, Martin Joseph
Farber, Paul Alan
Farber, Saul Joseph
Farbish, Alfred Bucks
Farbro, Patrick Clay
Farenthold, Frances Tarlton (Mrs. George Edward Farenthold)
Fargis, Paul McKenna
Farhoudi, Habib Ollah
Faria, Sixdeniel
Farkas, Ann Elizabeth
Farkas, Emery
Farley, James Thomas, Jr.
Farley, Jennie Tiffany Towle
Farley, John Michael
Farmakides, J(ohn) B(asil)
Farmer, Leonard Jerome
Farnham, Beverly Tewksbury
Farr, Henry Bartow, Jr.
Farr, James Francis
Farr, Richard Claborn
Farrall, Robert Arthur
Farrand, George Nixon, Jr.
Farrar, Donald Leroy
Farrar, Frederic Breakspear
Farray, Marilyn Cecile
Farrell, Gregory Alan
Farrell, Harold Maron, Jr.
Farrell, James Patrick
Farrell, John Merlyn, Jr.
Farrell, Lawrence David
Farrell, Patrick Francis
Farrell, Robert Terence
Farrissey, Francis Stack
Farrone, Pat Joseph
Farsace, Duverne Konrick
Farsaci, Litterie B. (Larry Farsaci)
Farwell, Charles, IV
Fasana, Paul James
Fasanella, Rocko Michael
Fascetta, Salvatore Charles
Fasoli, Alexander Edgar
Fassler, Joan Grace (Mrs. Leonard J. Fassler)
Fatsy, George Christy
Fauci, Peter Anthony, Jr.
Faulhaber, Thomas Albert
Faulkender, Robert Edgar
Faull, J. Horace, Jr.
Faulstich, Richard Charles
Fauntroy, Walter E.
Faust, Naomi Flowe
Fava, Catherine May
Favreau, Donald Francis
Favreau, Lawrence Roger
Fawcett, Clifford William
Fawcett, Howard Hoy
Fawcett, John William, III
Fawcett, Marie Ann Formanek (Mrs. Roscoe Kent Fawcett)
Fawcett, Mary Isabel Sandoe (Mrs. Richard Selden Fawcett)
Fawwaz, Rashid Adib
Fay, John Harvey
Fay, Thomas Joseph
Fayemi, Alfred Olusegun
Fazzalari, Frank Anthony
Feagans, William Marion
Fearon, Blair
Fearon, Robert Henry, Jr.
Fearons, George Hadsall, 3d
Featherstone, Charles Robert
Fedder, Donald Owen
Feddersen, Maryann Odilia
Fedele, Charles Robert
Fedele, Frank D.
Feder, Walter
Federman, Steven Robert
Federmann, Edward Frank
Federmann, Franklin Howard
Fedorenko, Eugene William
Feehan, John Daniel
Feelings, Thomas
Feeney, Donald Francis
Feffer, Paul E.
Fegley, Robert LeRoy, Jr.
Fehring, Robert William
Feierstein, Shirley Sands
Feigenbaum, Lawrence Hugo
Feigin, Marsha Isabel
Fein, Sherman Edward
Feinberg, Joseph Goodman
Feingold, Adolph
Feingold, S. Norman
Feinschreiber, Robert Andrew
Feinschreiber, Selven F.
Feinsmith, Burton Michael
Feinstein, Alan Shawn
Feinstein, Estelle Fisher
Feinstein, Norman Banks
Feit, Elliot Michael
Felber, Norbert
Feld, Eliot
Feld, Joseph
Feldberg, Daniel Gerald
Felder, Edward Arnold
Felder, Raoul Lionel
Felderman, Eric
Feldman, Bertold
Feldman, Bruce Allen
Feldman, Edwin Bernard
Feldman, George Joseph
Feldman, Herbert Byron
Feldman, Joseph Herbert
Feldman, Maurice Milton
Feldman, Philip
Feldman, Roger David
Feldman, Ronald Leonard
Feldman, Stephen
Feldstein, Aaron
Feldstein, Carlene Brooks
Felice, Patrick Elio
Feliu, Leopoldo
Feliú-Flores, Cándida Elena
Feller, Marvin Sheldon
Feller, Richard Tabler
Fellner, Michael Josef
Fellows, Lawrence Perry
Felman, Yehudi Moshe
Felmly, Lloyd McPherson
Felo, Matthew Francis, Jr.
Felton, Blanche Helen Dimin
Feltus, Russell Hodge
Fenchel, Gerd H.
Fengler, John Peter
Fenn, Anthony Neville
Fenn, Dan Huntington, Jr.
Fenn, Eugene Henry
Fenneman, Lawrence Brittingham, Jr.
Fenten, D(onald) X.
Fenton, Frank Hallowell, Jr.
Fenton, M(atthew) Robert
Fenton, Matthew Clark, III
Fenvessy, Stanley John
Fenwick, Millicent Hammond
Feodoroff, Nicholas Vasilievich
Ferber, Roman
Ferber, Samuel
Ferdinand, Joseph Bennet
Ferencz, William Robert
Ferens, Marcella (Mrs. Joseph J. Ferens)
Feret, Adam Edward, Jr.
Ferguson, Donald Guffey
Ferguson, Dorothy Margueritte
Ferguson, Glenn Walker
Ferguson, Laing
Ferguson, Leslie Lee, Jr.
Ferguson, Marian Rand
Ferguson, Robert S.
Ferguson, Theodore John, Jr.
Ferguson, William Homer
Fergusson, Robert Laurence
Ferland, Armand
Ferman, Irving
Fern, Ruth Kane (Mrs. Wallace Edward Fern)
Fernald, Charles E.
Fernandes, John Peter
Fernandez, Julio Antonio
Fernandez, Secundino
Fernandez-Herlihy, Luis
Fernandez-Marcane, Leonardo Luis
Fernicola, Anthony Ralph
Ferraioli, Charles Joseph
Ferrara, Angelo Carmine
Ferraraccio, Francisco Paolo
Ferraro, Geraldine Ann
Ferrell, Ruth Morris (Mrs. Frank M. Ferrell)
Ferrer, Romeo A.
Ferrier, Beatriz Serrano
Ferris, Frederick Joseph
Ferris, Robert Clarke
Ferro, Walter
Ferry, Martin Frank
Ferry, Miriam
Ferry, Robert Dean (Bob)
Feskoe, Gaffney Jon
Feszczak, Zenon Lubomyr
Fetch, Myron Lester
Fetter, Robert Pollard
Feuer, Michael
Feuer, William Wallace
Feuerburgh, Joseph
Feuerstein, Donald Martin
Feulner, Edwin John, Jr.
Fey, Charles Joseph
Fialkov, Herman
Fiarotta, Noel Joseph
Fichtel, Rudolph Robert
Fichtenholz, Milton
Ficks, Robert Leslie, Jr.
Fiedler, Arthur
Field, Barry Elliot
Field, Charles Herbert, Jr.
Field, Gary George
Field, Hermann Haviland
Field, Lincoln Elmer
Field, Maxwell John
Field, Norman J.
Field, Ronald Marvin
Field, Virginia
Fieldhouse, Donald John
Fielding, Allen Fred
Fielding, Natalie
Fields, Douglas Philip
Fields, J. Joy
Fields, Nora Janet
Fields, Richard James
Fields, Robert Sanford
Fien, Jerome Morris
Fier, Louis
Fierheller, George Alfred
Fieser, Arthur Herbert
Fieser, George Walter
Fieser, John Bailey

Fife, Earl Hanson, Jr.
Figurelli, Jennifer Constance
Filbert, Howard Conrad, Jr.
Filene, William, Jr.
Filer, John Horace
Filetti, Daniel Medardo
Filler, Dorothy Sands (Mrs. Samuel Filler)
Fillman, Henry Ingerton
Filteau, Gary Reed
Finberg, Laurence
Finch, Edward Ridley, Jr.
Findlay, Charles Walter, Jr.
Findlay, Raymond David
Findlay, Stephen W(illiam)
Fine, Norman Lee
Fineberg, Seymour Koeppel
Finegold, Ronald
Finegold, Wilfred Jay
Fineman, Elliot Norman
Finer, Diana Carol
Finger, Kenneth Joel
Fingerhut, Donna
Fini, Frank Caesar
Fink, Aaron Herman
Fink, Martin Ronald
Finke, Hans-Joachim
Finkel, Benjamin
Finkel, Bernard Gerald
Finkel, Coleman Lee
Finkel, Mark William
Finkelstein, Gerald Arnold
Finkelstein, Leonard
Finkelstein, Mark Jon
Finkelstein, Paul
Finkelstein, Robert
Finlay, Allan Risley
Finlayson, Jock Kinghorn
Finley, Howard James
Finley, Murray H.
Finlon, Francis Paul
Finn, D(aniel) Francis
Finn, James Francis
Finn, Joan Lockwood
Finn, John Joseph, Jr.
Finn, Michael Herbert Paul
Finn, Peter Gerard
Finn, Robert Alan
Finn, Thomas M.
Finn, William Francis
Finnegan, Marcus Bartlett
Finnerty, Frank Ambrose
Finnerty, Jean Clare
Finnerty, William Aloysius
Fioravanti, Nancy Eleanor
Fiore, James Louis, Jr.
Fiorvanti, Aldo Fiorino
Fipphen, John Stanley
First, Helen G.
First, Mervin Henry
Firth, Clifford Edward
Fisch, Solomon
Fischel, Edward Elliot
Fischer, Charlotte Froese (Mrs. Patrick Carl Fischer)
Fischer, George
Fischer, Hadwin Keith
Fischer, Irving
Fischer, Jack Marshall
Fischer, Jerome Morton
Fischer, John Albert
Fischer, Marvin Jay
Fischer, Robert Arthur
Fischer, Robert E(lbert)
Fischer, Roger Raymond
Fischgrund, Milton Leonard
Fischler, Bryant
Fiscina, Pasquale R.
Fish, Eugene Charles
Fish, Frederick Stuart
Fish, Hamilton, Jr.
Fish, Herman Lewis
Fish, Jill Harriet Carlson (Mrs. William D. Fish, Jr.)
Fishbone, Herbert
Fishel, Henry Detlev
Fishel, Leo
Fisher, Allan Jerry
Fisher, Florence Anna
Fisher, Frank X.
Fisher, Howard Shreve, Jr.
Fisher, Hyman Wendell
Fisher, Jack Carrington
Fisher, Janet Elizabeth
Fisher, Jay Donald
Fisher, John Henry, III
Fisher, John Herbert
Fisher, Joseph Allen
Fisher, Kenneth Walter
Fisher, Lawrence Roger
Fisher, Martha Ann
Fisher, Othel Arnold
Fisher, Robert Charles
Fisher, Robert Dale
Fisher, Roger Scott
Fisher, Russell Sylvester
Fisher, Stephen
Fisher, William Henry
Fisher, William Nelson
Fishman, Alfred Paul
Fishman, David Israel
Fishman, Jacob Robert
Fishman, Stanley Irving
Fiske, Frederick
Fitch, Nancy Elizabeth
Fitter, Morris
Fitti, Joseph Edward
Fitts, Leonard Donald
Fitts, Stanton T.
Fitz, Caroline Moul
Fitzgerald, Claudine Payer
Fitzgerald, Clifford Llewelyn
FitzGerald, Jay
Fitzgerald, John Edward
Fitzgerald, Robert James
Fitzgerald, Terence Sean
Fitzgibbons, Gloria Helen
Fitzpatrick, Donald William
Fitzpatrick, James Earl, Jr.
Fitzpatrick, June Boutin
Fitzpatrick, Margaret Mary
Fitzpatrick, Michael John
Fitzpatrick, Robert Charles
Fitzroy, Nancy DeLoye (Mrs. Roland Victor Fitzroy, Jr.)
Fitzsimmons, Frank Edward
Fitzsimons, Ruth Marie
Fitzsimons, Virginia Louise Baldwin
Fjordbotten, Alf Lee
Flack, Julius Vincent
Flack, Robert Lloyd
Flaherty, Hugh Charles
Flaherty, Michael Francis
Flaherty, Pete F.
Flaker, James Henry
Flamm, Donald
Flanagan, Bernard Joseph
Flanagan, Edward Charles
Flander, Stanley
Flanders, Frank Chester
Flannagan, Benjamin Collins, IV
Flannery, Dennis Edward
Flannery, John Bernard, Jr.
Flannery, Rosemary McCarron
Flansburgh, Earl Robert
Flast, Florence
Flaster, Donald J(ohn)
Flax, Lawrence
Flayderman, Earle Norman
Fleckner, Alan Norman
Fleischer, Renee Altman
Fleischer, Robert
Fleischman, Alan Isadore
Fleischman, Lawrence Arthur
Fleischman, Mark Lawrence
Fleischmann, Peter Francis
Fleming, Alice Carew Mulcahey (Mrs. Thomas J. Fleming)
Fleming, David Lee
Fleming, Edward J(ude)
Fleming, Florence Ruth
Fleming, Robert David
Fleming, Ronald Lee
Fleming, Wilmot Egerton
Fletcher, Brady Jones
Fletcher, Clifton Maurice
Fletcher, Delbert Van
Fletcher, Donald Burnett
Fletcher, Richard Mumma
Fletcher, Ronald Darling
Fletcher, Thomas Francis
Fletcher, William Leon
Flicker, Paul Leo
Flinn, David Galbraith
Flinn, Michael de Vlaming
Flint, Gertrude Kinsee (Mrs. Walter Levy)
Flint, Jean-Jacques George
Floch, Martin Herbert
Flood, Daniel J.
Flood, (Hulda) Gay
Florence, Barry Thomas
Florence, William James, Jr.
Florent, Hughes Victor
Flores, Frank Fausto
Florian, Michael Alexander
Floriani, Lawrence Peter
Florio, James J.
Floss, Walter John, Jr.
Flower, Annette Chappell
Flowers, James Paul
Fluek, Toby Knobel (Mrs. Chaim Fluek)
Fluhr, Frederick Robert
Fluke, James Samuel
Flum, Joseph
Flynn, Conrad Peter
Flynn, Daniel Clarke
Flynn, John Edward
Flynn, Joseph Peter, Jr.
Flynn, Lawrence Francis
Flynn, Richard James
Flynn, Thomas Robert
Flythe, Rudolph
Foa, Uriel Gaston
Fochler, Robert Charles, Jr.
Fogarty, Charles Franklin
Fogarty, Margaret Mary
Fogarty, William Eugene
Fogel, Irving Martin
Fogel, Sander Herbert
Fogel, Seymour
Fogelman, James
Fogler, Richard Jeffrey
Foglietta, Norbert Louis
Fogwell, Frank Douglas
Foiles, Keith Andrew
Foland, David Cratsley
Folcarelli, Ralph Joseph
Folen, Vincent J.
Foley, Armund Everett
Foley, Augusta Espantoso
Foley, Eileen
Foley, James Thomas
Foley, Paul
Foley, Robert Matthew
Foley, Thomas James
Folger, Lee Merritt
Folker, David Alan
Folkers, George Fulton
Follansbee, Harper
Folmar, John Kent
Foltin, Eugene
Fomufod, Antoine Kofi
Foner, Philip Sheldon
Fontain, Gregory
Foote, Warren Edgar
Foran, Nicholas A.
Forbes, Clarence Llewellyn
Forbes, Francis Murray, Jr.
Forbes, John Dexter
Forbes, W(illiam) Harry
Ford, Charles Thomas
Ford, Daniel Francis
Ford, Fred Charles
Ford, Harold Emery
Ford, Jeremiah, III
Ford, John Charles
Ford, Mark Robert
Ford, Morgan
Ford, Robert Prospero
Ford, Sherman Alfred
Ford, William Bert
Forde, Colin Arlington
Fordyce, Donald Michael
Forelle, Conrad
Foreman, Arlene Raina
Foreman, John Wicks
Foreman, John Wilson, III
Foreman, Laura
Foreman, Thomas Alexander
Forest, Gerard Maurice
Forest, Joseph Gerard
Forester, Wayne Andrew
Forgacs, Joseph
Forgan, James Russell
Forget, Timothy Paul
Forgett, Heidi E. Kober (Mrs. Valmore Joseph Forgett, Jr.)
Fork, Donald Joseph
Fork, Richard Lynn
Forlano, Robert Jose
Forma, Warren
Forman, Donald Walter
Forman, Edgar Ross
Forman, Eli Michael Simon
Forman, H(enry) Chandlee
Forman, Howard Irving
Forman, Joseph Charles
Forman, Stanley Joseph
Forman, Stuart Irving
Forman, Yale
Fornelli, Francis Joseph
Foronda, Elena Isabel
Forrest, Herbert Emerson
Forrest, Virginia Ogden Ranson (Mrs. Wilbur Studley Forrest)
Forscher, Frederick
Forshaw, William Sherlock
Forstchen, John Joseph
Forsythe, Edwin B.
Fort, William Lapham
Fortin, Joseph Raymond
Forton, John Robert
Fortune, Mary K.
Fortunoff, Alan Meyer
Fortunoff, Helene
Forward, David Francis
Fosdick, Raymond Warren
Foshay, Maxine Valentine Shottland (Mrs. Robert Lethbridge Foshay)
Foss, Arthur Degrange
Fossel, Spencer Martel
Fosshage, James Lewis
Foster, David Newell
Foster, Dwight Livingstone
Foster, Eugene Howard
Foster, Faith Smith
Foster, Frank Herbert, Jr.
Foster, Holland
Foster, Howard Hatherly, Jr.
Foster, John Hallett
Foster, John Michael
Foster, Pearl D. (Mrs. Charles C. Hunt)
Foster, Robert Wilson
Foster, Rockwood Hoar
Foster, Susan Jane
Foulds, Raymond Thomas
Foundos, Evelyn
Fountain, Robert James
Fournier, Rosaire
Fournier, Theresa Lorraine
Fout, John Calvin
Fowler, Conrad John
Fowler, Donald Robert
Fowler, H(oratio) Seymour
Fowler, Lindsay Anderson, III
Fowler, Thomas James
Fowler, Walter Brumby
Fowler, William Morgan, Jr.
Fowlkes, Edward Bynum, II
Fowlkes, Karen Enid
Fox, Abijah Upson
Fox, Earle Blair, Jr.
Fox, Herbert
Fox, James Frederick
Fox, John Joseph, Jr.
Fox, John Willis
Fox, Madlyn Ann
Fox, Marvin Irving
Fox, Roxanne Elliott
Fox, Roy Warren
Fox, Terence J.
Fox, Thomas George
Fox, William Charles
Frackman, Richard Benoit
Fraidin, Stephen
Fraley, Donald Symons
Fralic, Maryann F.
Franchebois, Pierre Jean
Francis, George William
Francis, John Bruce
Francis, Neville Andrew
Francis, Richard Louis
Francischelli, Gerald Joseph
Francke, Albert, III
Francoeur, Romaine Davis
Francois, Emmanuel Saturnin
Francois, Ewart Ian
Frangos, John
Frank, Alan I W
Frank, Barney
Frank, Bernard
Frank, George
Frank, Ludwig Mathias
Frank, Marjorie Hofheimer (Mrs. Christopher Gable)
Frank, Martin
Frank, Morton
Frank, Robert Allen
Frank, Ronald Edward
Frank, Rudy
Frank, Stanley Julius
Frankel, Arnold Judah
Frankel, Claire Lynn
Frankel, Edward Benjamin
Frankel, George Joseph
Frankel, Howard Jonathan
Frankel, Michael
Frankel, Robert Sidney
Frankel, Sidney A.
Frankel, Stanley Arthur
Frankenbach, William Alfred
Frankenberry, Robert Randall
Frankenfield, Henry Meyers
Frankfurt, Morton Allen
Frankl, Kenneth Richard
Frankl, William Stewart
Franklin, Allen Philip
Franklin, Arthur Edmund
Franklin, Hardy R.
Franklin, John Brooke
Franklin, Kenneth Linn
Franklin, Mitchell
Franklin, Philip Earle
Franklin, Robert Louis
Franklin, Roger
Franklin, William Donald
Frankling, Samuel Roy
Franklyn, Roy
Franko-Filipasic, Borivoj Richard Simon
Frant, Frederick Aaron
Frantz, Andrew Gibson
Frantz, Robert Lewis
Frantzen, Henry Arthur
Franz, Edward Quinlisk
Franz, Helmut
Franz, Robert Francis, Jr.
Franz, Sally Ann Johnson
Fraser, Charles Edward Ovid
Fraser, Virginia I. Many (Mrs. Kenneth W. Fraser)
Frater, Robert William Mayo
Frauens, Marie
Fraunberger, Robert Carl
Fraust, Charles Lawrence
Frayne, Nathaniel Zebulon
Frazier, John Earl
Fread, Danny Lee
Frech, Raymond Joseph
Frechette, Gerard Conrad
Freckleton, Winston Earle
Frederic, Myron Wayne
Frederick, Calvin Jeff
Frederick, Jonathan Elbert
Frederick, Lafayette
Fredericks, Carlton
Frediani, Harold Arthur
Fredrick, Jerome F.
Fredricksen, Cleve John
Fredrickson, Donald Sharp
Free, Ann Cottrell
Free, Spencer Michael, Jr.
Freed, Arthur
Freedman, Aaron David
Freedman, Abraham E.
Freedman, Bernard W.
Freedman, Elisha Chaim
Freedman, Ellen S.
Freedman, Gerald Stanley
Freedman, Jerome Kenneth
Freedman, Jonathan Andrew
Freedman, Marion Glickman
Freedman, Warren
Freeland, Charles
Freeland, T. Paul
Freeman, Clifford Lee
Freeman, David Reed
Freeman, Isadore
Freeman, Leonard Murray
Freeman, Milton V.
Freeman, Richard Paul
Freese, Ernst
Freiband, James Michael
Freiday, Dean
Freidberg, Alan Elliot
Freifeld, Daniel Jerome
Freifeld, Stephen Francis
Freilich, Dennis Byron
Freilich, John Douglas
Freilinger, James Edward
Freiman, Alvin Henry
Freimuth, Henry Charles
Freitag, Harlow
Freizer, Louis A.
Fremont, Rudolph Eric
French, Bruce Hartung
French, Carl Burton
French, Henry Pierson, Jr.
French, John
French, Judson Cull
French, Paul Thomas
French, Travis Armitage
French, William Richard
Frenchman, Robert Henry
Frenkel, Barbara Isabel
Frenkel, Herbert Milton
Frenkel, Richard Eugene
Freter, Kurt Rudolf
Fretwell, Elbert Kirtley, Jr.
Freudenberger, Herbert Justin
Freudenheim, Tom Lippmann
Freundlich, Richard L.
Frewin, William Arthur, Jr.
Frey, Gloria Jean
Frey, Paul Douglass
Frey, Richard Lincoln
Freymann, John Gordon
Frezza, Joseph Michael
Fribush, Ellis Mark
Fricke, Edwin Francis
Fricks, Ernest Eugene
Friday, Gilbert Anthony, Jr.
Friday, John Ernest, Jr.
Fried, Herbert George
Fried, (Helen) Jane
Fried, John P.
Fried, Robert
Fried, Sidney
Friedel, Bernard
Friedenberg, Daniel Meyer
Friedenberg, Pinhas P.
Friedheim, Stephen Bailey
Friedland, Edward Charles
Friedlander, Arthur Henry
Friedlander, Jacob
Friedlander, Zitta Zipora
Friedlieb, Leslie Aaron
Friedman, Barry Howard
Friedman, Charles Walter
Friedman, Esia Baran
Friedman, Eugene
Friedman, Eugene Jerome
Friedman, Gerald
Friedman, Ira Hugh
Friedman, Irwin
Friedman, Marion
Friedman, Mark
Friedman, Martha Schwabinger
Friedman, Michael Peter
Friedman, Philip Harvey
Friedman, Phillip
Friedman, Ralph
Friedman, Robert Mc Elhinney
Friedman, Samuel
Friedman, Stuart Wayne
Friedmann, Arnold Aron
Friedrichs, Arthur Martin
Friedson, Bernard
Friel, Fred James, Jr.
Friel, James Reynolds, Jr.
Friel, Patrick Brendan
Friend, Benjamin
Friend, Chaim H.
Fries, George
Fries, Helen Sergeant Haynes (Mrs. Stuart G. Fries)
Friese, John Clark
Friesecke, Raymond Francis
Frigand, Herman Joseph
Frigand, Sidney Jerome
Frim, Sumner Philip
Frink, Charles Richard
Frisbie, Joseph Aubrey, Jr.
Frisch, Ivan Thomas
Fritchen, Dean Henry
Fritchey, John Augustus, II
Fritz, Donald Theodore
Fritz, James Clarence
Frnka, Michael Quentin
Frobisher, Martin, Jr.
Froehlich, Charles Orth, Jr.
Froehlich, Edna Borg
Froehlich, Fritz Edgar
Froehlich, Walter
Froix, Michael Francis
Frolich, Henrik Stampe
Frolick, Stanley William
Fromnick, Stephen Michael
Frosch, Robert Alan
Frost, Frederick George, III
Frost, John Eldridge
Frost, Marshall
Frost, Rex Allen
Frucher, Meyer Samuel
Fruhauf, Henry
Fry, Alvin Abram
Fry, Johan Trilby (Gifford) (Mrs. Gilbert Wayne Fry)
Fry, Zella Jeanne Oliver (Mrs. Alvin Abram Fry)
Frye, Pierre Arnold
Frye, Richard Craig
Fryer, Appleton
Fryer, John Ercel
Frykholm, Walter Laurie
Frymann, Hans Kaspar
Fu, Lorraine S.
Fu, Shou-Cheng Joseph
Fucci, Charles Daniel
Fuchs, Helmuth Hans
Fuchs, Jerome Herbert
Fuchs, Ruth
Fuentevilla, Manuel Edward
Fukae, Kensuke
Fukui, Hatsuaki
Fulbright, Freeman
Fuller, Brent Davis
Fuller, Earl Clifton
Fuller, Earnest Melvin
Fuller, Gerald Wallace
Fuller, James Ralph
Fuller, Jeanne Molloy
Fuller, Renee Nuni
Fuller, Richard Buckminster
Fuller, Sue
Fuller, Terry Kenneth
Fuller, William John
Fullerton, R. Donald
Fulop, Milford
Fulton, Joseph Raymond
Fulton, Philip Ronald
Fulweiler, Spencer Biddle
Fung, Kee Wai
Fungaroli, A. Alexander
Funk, Charles Earle, Jr.
Funk, Harald Franz
Funk, Sherman Maxwell
Funkhouser, Ralph Henry
Furedy, John J.
Furfaro, Francis Joseph
Furibondo, Michael John
Furlan, Andrew Washington
Furlong, Thomas Francis, III
Furman, Anthony Michael
Furman, Roy Lance
Furman, Samuel Elliott
Furness, Geoffrey
Furst, Sidney Carl
Furstman, Shirley Elsie Daddow
Furtherer, Charles Matthew
Fusco, Cono R.
Futterman, Betsy Wilcox
Futterman, Philip G.
Futterweit, Walter
Gaal, Francis Stephen
Gabbard, O. Gene
Gabel, Paul Martin
Gabelli, Mario Joseph
Gaber, Irving
Gaber, Joanne Garten
Gable, Edward Brennan, Jr.
Gable, Fred Burnard
Gable, Martha Anne
Gablehouse, Charles John
Gabler, Robert Clair, Jr.
Gaboda, James James
Gabriel, Charles Elias
Gabriel, Ronald Lee
Gaccione, Vincent James
Gaddis, Paul Otto
Gadsby, Dwight Maxon
Gaertner, Wolfgang Wilhelm
Gaeta, Joseph Roland
Gaffield, Charles Mitchell
Gaffney, James Anthony
Gaffney, Paul Cotter
Gagliardo, Dominick Frank
Gagnon, Fred Louis
Gagnon, Lionel (Lee)
Gaheen, Alfred Francis, Jr.
Gaines, Fred R.
Gaines, Natalie Evelyn
Gaines, Nathaniel
Gaines, Sylvia Maude
Gaines, Thurston Lenwood, Jr.
Gainey, Harvey Nueton
Gaither, George Manney
Gajdusek, Daniel Carleton
Galane, Irma Adele Bereston
Galant, Raymond
Galante, Nicholas Thomas
Galantowicz, Thomas Anthony
Galbraith, William Lester
Galdau, Florian Marin
Galdi, William Andrew
Gale, James Elwin
Galen, Robert Sanford
Galey, John Taylor
Galilea, Hernán
Galkin, Edwin Neil
Galkin, Samuel Bernard
Gallaghar, Alberta Kathryn
Gallagher, Anne Timlin
Gallagher, Bernard Patrick
Gallagher, Charles Clifton
Gallagher, David Peter
Gallagher, John Aloysius
Gallagher, Joseph Edward, Jr.
Gallagher, Michael John
Gallagher, Norman Rodney
Gallagher, Philip George
Gallagher, Thomas Martin
Gallahue, William Michael
Gallant, Edward
Gallego, Marcos Bernardo
Galleher, Richard Morse
Gallen, Hugh
Gallina, David Joseph, Jr.
Gallis, John Nicholas
Gallivan, Gregory John
Gallman, Raymond Foster
Gallo, Robert Charles
Gallup, James David
Galonsky, Robert Steven
Galt, Thomas Maunsell
Galvin, Thomas Francis
Gambee, Robert Rankin
Gambino, S(alvatore) Raymond
Gamble, (George) Alvan
Gamble, Richard Bradley
Gambuti, Gary
Gamerov, Irving Julius
Gamoran, Abraham Carmi
Gangstad, Edward Otis
Ganiaris, Neophytos
Ganis, Stephen Lane
Gannon, Alice
Gannon, Joseph Philip
Gans, Eugene Howard
Gans, Samuel Myer
Gant, Duplain Rhodes
Gant, James Quincy, Jr.
Ganz, Vivian Hoff (Mrs. Andrew Ganz)
Gaquer, John George
Garbarino, Robert Paul
Garcia, Celso-Ramon
Garcia, Ferdinand Lawrence
Garcia, Robert
Gardiner, William Douglas Haig
Gardner, Allan William
Gardner, Bernard
Gardner, Charles Wesley, Jr.
Gardner, Eliot Lawrence
Gardner, Leonard Burton, II
Gardner, Warren Edward, Jr.
Gardner, William Michael
Gardy, Thais
Garen, John Theodore
Gargan, Joseph Edward
Gargirello, Gabriel Anthony
Garland, Merritt Frederick, Jr.
Garley, Richard Edward
Garmel, David Charles (Meltzer)

Garofalo, Thomas Don
Garon, Joseph Daniel
Garovoy, Marvin Robert
Garrahy, J. Joseph
Garrecht, David Arthur
Garrett, Philip LeRoy
Garrett, Samuel Judson
Garretto, Leonard Anthony, Jr.
Garrity, Helen Marie
Garrow, Walter David
Garry, Ralph Joseph
Gartley, Markham Ligon
Gartner, Ellen May Phillips
Garver, Robert Bruce
Garver, Walter Raymond
Garvey, Fenwick Hill
Garvin, Clifton Canter, Jr.
Garvy, George
Gary, Lawrence Edward
Gaskins, Frederick Hudson
Gasper, Donald
Gass, Charles
Gassert, Mary Elizabeth
Gasteyer, Carlin Evans (Mrs. Harry A. Gasteyer)
Gaston, Leslie Homer
Gastwirth, Joseph Lewis
Gates, Arnold Francis
Gates, Edward Dwight
Gates, Wilfrid Lyman, Jr.
Gatewood, Robert Payne
Gatner, Elliott Sherman Mozian
Gatto, Andrew Ronald
Gatto, Paul Anthony
Gattone, Vincent Henry
Gatzogiannis, George Evangelos
Gaudino, Mario
Gauger, John Hardy
Gauger, Thomas Freeman
Gaull, Gerald Edward
Gault, Marian Doris
Gault, Willis Manning
Gaultney, John Orton
Gauss, William Frederick
Gaut, Marvin Joseph
Gauthier, George James
Gauthier, Norman Leonidas
Gavurin, Lester L.
Gay, William Arthur
Gaydos, Joseph M.
Gayeski, Edward Charles
Gaynes, Ben, Jr.
Gaynor, Elizabeth Anne
Gaynor, Richard Dana
Gaziano, Joseph Salvatore
Gazis, Denos Constantinos
Gebauer, Kurt Manfred
Gebelein, Richard Stephen
Gee, William
Gee, Zilphia Toni
Geeslin, William Fleming
Gegeny, Thomas Paul
Gehring, Charles Theodor
Gehrke, Robert Frederick
Gehron, William Henry, Jr.
Geibel, Edgar Leroy
Geiger, Gene Edward
Geiger, Jean W. Roberts (Mrs. Robert Louis Geiger)
Geiger, Loren Dennis
Geiger, Philip Earl
Geiger, Walter Case
Geis, Bernard
Geiss, Jacqueline Suzanne
Geissbuhler, Arnold
Geissler, Suzanne Burr
Gelardi, Arthur V.
Gelb, Joseph Donald
Gelb, Judith Anne
Gelb, William Gary
Gelber, Melvin Wilbur
Geldbaugh, George Richard
Gelfman, Judith Schlein
Gelfman, Robert William
Gelfman, Stanley
Gelinas, Paul J.
Gelineau, Louis Edward
Gellein, Oscar Strand
Geller, Herbert Z.
Geller, Joseph Jerome
Geller, Joshua S.
Geller, Lawrence David
Gellineau, Victor Marcel
Gelman, Bernard
Gelstein, Leonard Michael
Gelt, Jeanette Rose Lebman
Geltzer, Howard E.
Gemma, John Peter
Gemmell, Gordon Douglas
Gendell, Martin Bruce
Gendron, Odore Joseph
Geneen, Harold Sydney
Genova, Thomas Francis
Gentile, Adrian George
Gentile, Anthony Albert
Gentlesk, Michael John
Gentry, Grant Claybourne
Gentzler, Barry Frederick
Geogan, Robert Joseph
George, Charles William
George, Henry Mitchell
George, Joseph David
George, Robert Jacob
George, Sylvia James
Georgi, William Henry
Georgia, Richard Clark
Geradts, Bernardus
Gerard, Jean Broward Shevlin
Gerard, Paul Jeffrey
Gerber, Donald Albert
Gerber, Edward Ferdinand
Gerber, Lewis Nathanial
Gerber, Marcia Lynn Getz (Mrs. Donald A. Gerber)
Gerber, Thomas William
Gerety, Peter Leo
Gerfin, Donald Reed
Gering, Robert Lee
Gerjovich, Michael William
German, Donald Robert
German, Judy Carlile
Gerrish, Hollis G.
Gerrity, Edward Joseph, Jr.
Gerry, Roger Goodman
Gersh, Rosemarie Cecilia
Gershel, Christopher Peter
Gershen, Alvin Edward
Gershenfeld, Matti Kibrick
Gerson, Donald Jerome
Gerson, Herman
Gerson, Jimmy Marshall
Gerson, Noel Bertram
Gerson, Raymond Edgar
Gersoni, Diane Claire
Gerst, Elizabeth Carlsen (Mrs. Paul H. Gerst)
Gerst, Paul Howard
Gerstein, David Brown
Gerstein, Gary Allen
Gerstein, Judah
Gerstein, Mel
Gersten, Sandra Joan Pessin (Mrs. Aaron L. Gersten)
Gerstenfeld, Jacob
Gerstine, John
Gerstman, Judith Rita
Gerstner, Edna Suckau (Mrs. John H. Gerstner)
Gertler, Menard M.
Gerwin, Ronald Hal
Gesoff, Mark Stone
Gessner, Peter K. (Piotr Kazimierz)
Getter, Gustav
Gettis, Alan
Getty, Ralph Wellman
Getty, William Patton
Getz, Solomon
Gevalt, Frederick Conrad, Jr.
Gewant, Warren Charles
Gewirtz, Gerry (Mrs. Eugene Friedman)
Ghanotakis, Anestis John
Ghents, John Henry
Gherghel, Radu Olimpiu
Ghosh, Anil Chandra
Ghosh, Jayanta Kumar
Giacalone, Joseph Anthony
Giacomi, Jack R.
Giacona, Anthony S.
Giaever, Ivar
Giaimo, Robert Nicholas
Giamatti, Angelo Bartlett
Giardina, David Diego
Giardino, Alfred A.
Gibb, Roberta Louise
Gibbons, Anne Evans
Gibbons, Edward F.
Gibbons, Eugene Francis
Gibbons, James John
Gibbons, Robert Charles
Gibbons, Robert Joseph
Gibbs, James Wenrich
Gibbs, June Nesbitt (Mrs. Donald T. Gibbs)
Gibbs, Lippman Martin
Gibbud, John H(enry)
Gibson, Curtis Charles, Jr.
Gibson, Donna Tillinghast
Gibson, Eleanor Beatrice
Gibson, George William
Gibson, John, III
Gibson, Kenneth Allen
Gibson, Leonard James
Gibson, Robert Elmo
Gibson, Roy Dean
Gibson, Sam Thompson
Gibson, William Lee
Gibson, William Moses
Gideon, Richard Walter
Gielchinsky, Isaac
Giersbach, Marion Agnes Fisk (Mrs. Walter C. Giersbach)
Giese, Donald Emil
Giese, Robert Joseph
Gifford, Harry Cortland Frey
Gifford, J. Nebraska (Mrs. Melvin Shestack)
Giglio, Frank Philip
Gigliotti, Michael Frances Xavier
Gigliotti, Steven Peter
Gignoux, Edward Thaxter
Gilberg, Sheldon Francis
Gilbert, Arthur Charles
Gilbert, Arthur Joseph
Gilbert, Francis Charles
Gilbert, Frederick Spofford, Jr.
Gilbert, Harry Irman
Gilbert, Joan Stulman
Gilbert, Phil Edward, Jr.
Gilbert, Ramon
Gilbert, Richard Paul
Gilbert, Sheldon Ian
Gilbert, William Hoyt
Gilchrist, David Malcolm
Gilchrist, Elizabeth Brenda
Gilde, Louis Charles, Jr.
Gilder, Rodman
Giles, Charles Elliott
Giles, Sharon Althea
Gilinson, Philip Julius, Jr.
Gilkeson, Vincent Stanley
Gilkey, Kenneth George
Gill, Alexander Menzies
Gill, Gary Wesley
Gill, Michael Doud
Gill, Thomas William
Gillary, Leo
Gillen, James Francis
Gilleo, Mathias Alten
Gillespie, Carl Michael
Gillespie, Dorothy Muriel (Mrs. Bernard Israel)
Gillette, Walter Ray, Jr.
Gillis, Laurence Joseph
Gillis, Richard James
Gillooly, Robert Joseph
Gilman, Benjamin Arthur
Gilman, Cooper Lee
Gilmore, Charles Arthur
Gilmore, David John
Gilmore, John C.
Gilmore, Judith Marie
Gilmour, Edward Ellis
Gilpatric, Madelin Thayer (Mrs. Thayer Gilpatric)
Ginader, George Hall
Ginsberg, Allan Roy
Ginsberg, Allen
Ginsberg, Stephen Paul
Ginsberg-Fellner, Fredda Vita
Ginsburg, Gerald Joseph
Ginsburg, Martin David
Gintell, Howard Alan
Ginther, Ruth Margaret
Gioffre, Joseph Dominic
Gioia, Robert E(manuele)
Giolito, Carolyn Hughes
Giordano, Nicholas Anthony
Giorgi, Lewis Ascentio
Giovacchini, Robert Peter
Giovanopoulos, Paul Arthur
Giraldi, Almerigo
Giraudier, Antonio
Girdler, Reynolds, Jr.
Giroux, Albert Henry, Jr.
Girvin, Gerald Thomas
Gisolfi, Anthony M.
Gist, Lawson, Jr.
Gitlin, Paul
Gitman, Paul Allan
Gittelson, Bernard
Gittleman, Allan Morris
Gittler, Norman
Gittlin, A. Sam
Giudici, Raymond Angelo
Giuliani, Joseph Carl
Giusti, Gino Paul
Giziowski, Richard John
Gjernes, Oscar
Gladden, Dennis William
Gladding, Everett Bushnell
Gladfelter, Millard E.
Gladfelter, Valerie Garber (Mrs. David Drews Gladfelter)
Gladstone, Suzanne Pink
Gladstone, Vic S.
Glaid, Andrew J., III
Glaman, Mary Louise
Glasberg, H. Mark
Glaser, Anton
Glaser, David A.
Glaser, Joseph Bernard
Glaser, Robert Leonard
Glasgow, Roger DeCourey
Glass, Harry Saul
Glass, Janet Levine
Glass, Robert Allan
Glass, Robert Davis
Glassberg, Gwendolyn Revilda Kroman Darling
Glassberg, Kenneth Ira
Glasser, Brian M.
Glasser, Israel Leo
Glassman, Jerome Martin
Glassmoyer, Thomas Parvin
Glassuer, Franz Ernst
Glavin, A. Rita Chandellier (Mrs. James Henry Glavin III)
Glazer, Judith S.
Gleason, Chapman Patrick
Gleason, David Bruce
Gleason, Robert Patrick
Gleason, Thomas
Gleason, William Clarence
Gleeson, Ronald Francis
Gleiber, Stuart Ander
Glendening, Frank S.
Glenn, Diane Johnson
Glenn, Norman Robert
Glenn, Peter Keith
Glenn, Roland Douglas
Glennon, Joseph Raymond, Jr.
Glennon, Vincent Joseph
Glick, Barry (Herbert)
Glick, J. Leslie
Glick, Marvin Michael
Glick, Stanley
Glickman, Michael Leslie
Glicksman, Arvin S(igmund)
Gliedman, Richard
Glines, Carroll Vane, Jr.
Globerman, Norma Phyllis
Glod, Stanley Joseph
Glodell, Leroy Marcus
Gloman, Nancy Lutz
Glorig, Ostor
Glossner, David Charles
Glover, Laurice White
Gluck, Julius Calverton
Gluck, Melvin Charles
Glueck, Raymond Myron
Glyn, Marvin
Glynn, Kenneth Paul
Glynn, Neil Held
Goble, Ross Lawrence
Gocek, Matilda Arkenbout (Mrs. John A. Gocek)
Gochman, John Jay
Godbey, James Allen
Goddard, Esther Christine (Mrs. Robert Hutchings Goddard)
Godden, Glenn Frederick
Godfrey, Albert L., Sr.
Godfrey, George Cheeseman, II
Godfrey, John Carl
Godick, Neil Barnett
Godin, Edgar
Godino, Rino Lodovico
Godleski, John Joseph, Jr.
Godsoe, Joseph Gerald, Jr.
Goebel, Lawrence Robert
Goel, Amrit Lal
Goelet, Robert Guestier
Goertz, Augustus Frederick
Goetcheus, John Stewart
Goettel, Gerard Louis
Goetz, Guenther Conrad
Goff, H. David
Goffin, Sumner J.
Goggin, Jay
Goggins, John Francis
Goglia, Michael Lincoln
Goizueta-Mimo, Felix
Gokbora, Mary Jane McKee
Golab, Alexander
Golan, Lawrence Peter
Golany, Gideon
Gold, Aaron Alan
Gold, Carolyn Dinah
Gold, Dorothy Walden
Gold, Hilary Alexander
Gold, Lawrence Howard
Gold, Leonard Morton
Gold, Michael
Gold, Milton
Gold, Richard Louis
Goldbeck, Willis Betts
Goldberg, Aleck
Goldberg, Arthur Abba
Goldberg, Edwin
Goldberg, Frederick Ira
Goldberg, Harlean Fader
Goldberg, Harold Howard
Goldberg, Herman Krieger
Goldberg, Jay Neil
Goldberg, Joseph Philip
Goldberg, Joyce Roe
Goldberg, Martin
Goldberg, Morrell
Goldberg, Nathan Morris
Goldberg, Neal Leon
Goldberg, Robert Irving
Goldberg, Stephen Jay
Goldberger, Herbert Henry
Goldblatt, Barry Lance
Goldblatt, Phillip Brian
Goldemberg, Robert Lewis
Goldemberg, Rose Leiman
Golden, Balfour Henry
Golden, Sibyl Levy (Mrs. William T. Golden)
Goldenberg, Arnold
Goldenberg, George
Goldenzweig, William Martin
Goldfarb, Alexander A.
Goldfarb, Arthur A.
Goldfarb, Muriel Bernice
Goldfarb, Nathan
Goldfarb, Norman
Goldfield, Robert Saul
Goldin, Frederick
Goldman, David Harvey
Goldman, David Steven
Goldman, Gerald
Goldman, Isa Padawer
Goldman, James Allan
Goldman, Martin Jerome
Goldman, Robert Harry
Goldman, Robert Huron
Goldman, Sheldon
Goldman, Stanford Milton
Goldman, Thomas Adler
Goldman, William
Goldman, Zachary Charles
Goldreyer, Lawrence Lowe
Goldrich, Stanley Gilbert
Goldschmidt, Leontine
Goldschmied, Fabio Renzo
Goldsmith, Edward Ira
Goldsmith, Harry Sawyer
Goldsmith, J. Davis
Goldsmith, Maximilian Orfevre
Goldsmith, Richard
Goldsmith, Robert Lewis
Goldsmith, Silvianna
Goldsmith, Stanley Joseph
Goldspiel, Solomon
Goldstein, Dan Nicu
Goldstein, Daniel Alan
Goldstein, Daniel Leon
Goldstein, Donald Maurice
Goldstein, Eli
Goldstein, Emanuel V.
Goldstein, Fredric Robert
Goldstein, Gerald Alan
Goldstein, Harold H.
Goldstein, Harry Abraham
Goldstein, Harry Harold
Goldstein, Ira Marvin
Goldstein, Joseph Allen
Goldstein, Lawrence Jerome
Goldstein, Manfred
Goldstein, Melvin
Goldstein, Murray
Goldstein, Perry Baily
Goldstein, Robert Lloyd
Goldstein, Stanley Irving
Goldstein, William
Goldsten, Robert Emanuel
Golembiewski, Walter Gregory
Goler, Patricia Anne
Golino, Frank R.
Golladay, Loy Edgar
Goller, Henry Frederick
Gollin, Stuart Allen
Golob, Charles George
Golomb, Frederick Martin
Golomb, George Edwin
Golub, William Weldon
Gombar, Oscar Julius
Gomery, John Howard
Gomes, Albert
Gomes, Joseph Anthony
Gomez, Raymond Vasquez, Jr.
Gonano, John Roland
Gondelman, Harold
Gonsalves, John, Jr.
Gonzalez, Ernesto
Gonzalez, Virginia Gerarda
Good, Anne Leeper (Mrs. John Carter Good)
Good, Donald Simmons
Good, Mary Elizabeth Grounds
Good, Milton Shenk
Good, Robert Barton, Jr.
Goodbar, Isaac
Goodchild, Anthony Alan
Goode, Morton Jacob
Goodell, John Carleton
Goodenough, David John
Goodfellow, Louis Deal
Goodhue, Charles Thomas
Goodier, J. Leslie
Gooding, Judson
Goodkin, George
Goodman, Abraham
Goodman, Alan Herman
Goodman, Charles Clarke
Goodman, Edwin Alan
Goodman, Helene Sandra
Goodman, Isidore
Goodman, Jerome Daniel
Goodman, Jerome David
Goodman, Lawrence
Goodman, Richard Shalem
Goodman, Roy Matz
Goodman, Seymour
Goodman, Stanley
Goodman, Stanley Erwin
Goodner, John Tetard
Goodrich, Isaac
Goodstein, Daniel Bela
Goodstein, Seymour
Goodwin, Dorothy Cheney
Goodwin, Frederick King
Goodwin, Gerald Louis
Goodwin, Harold Leland
Goodwin, Hazel Jean Thomas
Goodwin, Rex Dean
Goodwin, Robert Delmege
Goodwin, Roger Eugene
Goor, Dan
Goos, Roger Delmon
Gootzeit, Jack Michael
Gorcica, Louis Henry
Gordon, Alan Richard
Gordon, Baron Jack
Gordon, Charles Edward, II
Gordon, Gerald
Gordon, Harold
Gordon, Harry William
Gordon, Henry Robert
Gordon, Joe Robert
Gordon, Joy L.
Gordon, Kenneth Philip
Gordon, Lois Goldfein (Mrs. Alan Lee Gordon)
Gordon, Marion C.
Gordon, Martin Eli
Gordon, Marvin
Gordon, Maurice Bear
Gordon, Mildred Harriet Gross (Mrs. Ivan H. Gordon)
Gordon, Monte Jeffrey
Gordon, Philip Cyril
Gordon, Robert Alan
Gordon, Roy Harris
Gordon, Samuel
Gordon, Sydney Lewis Howard
Gordon, Wallace Ellwood
Gordon, William Harold
Goren, Arnold Louis
Gorfien, Philip Charles
Gorin, Leonard Joseph
Gorin, Robert Murray, Jr.
Gorkes, Richard Edward
Gorman, John Craven
Gorman, (Mike) Thomas Francis
Gorman, Timothy John
Gormley, James Joseph
Gorrow, Charles Richard
Gosin, Stephen
Goslee, Reba Elena
Gosline, Andrew Jackson, V
Gosline, Norman Abbot
Gosnell, Charles Francis
Goss, Patricia Bellamy
Gossage, Wayne
Gosse, Clarence L.
Gossel, John Dietrich
Gosselin, Michel Hector
Gossett, Oscar Milton
Gotlieb, Jerry
Gotsche, Anton Willibald
Gottfried, Byron Stuart
Gottfried, Eugene Leslie
Gottlieb, Lester M.
Gottlieb, Michael Norman
Gottlieb, Morton Edgar
Gottschalk, Jack Allton
Gottscho, Alfred Morton
Gottsegen, Gloria Behar
Gottshall, Franklin Henry
Gouda, George Rizkalla
Goudie, Ronald Joseph
Gouge, Susan Cornelia Jones (Mrs. John Oscar Gouge)
Gough, Bruce C.
Gough, Carolyn Harley
Gouiran, Emile
Gould, Burnham Sylvester, Jr.
Gould, Donald Everett
Gould, Harry Edward, Jr.
Gould, Howard Richard
Gould, James Edward
Gould, Mortimer David
Gould, Stephen
Goulder, Caroljean Hempstead
Gouse, Richard Ira
Govan, Francis Anthony
Gowen, George Washington
Gozdziewski, Charles James
Grabarz, Donald Francis
Graber, Harris David
Grabowski, Ann Jacqueline
Grace, Alonzo Gaskell, Jr.
Grace, H. David
Grace, Harold Padget
Gradin, Lawrence Paul
Gradisar, Helen Margaret
Grady, Francis Reddy
Grady, James Joseph
Grady, John Joseph
Graeber, Raymond Curtis
Graese, Clifford Ernest
Graf, John Adam
Graf, Leonard Grant
Graf, Peter Gustav
Graff, Harold
Grafton, Thurman Stanford
Graham, Arnold Harold
Graham, Charles Raymond
Graham, Chestie Marie
Graham, Dean McKinley
Graham, Francis Glenn
Graham, Jack Bennett
Graham, Katharine
Graham, Laura Margaret (Laura Graham Forbes)
Graham, Laurence Ignatius
Graham, Lewis James
Graham, Malcolm Sandford
Graham, Martha
Graham, Robert Sherman
Graham, William Pierson
Graham-Davis, Patricia
Grahame, Orville Francis
Grahame, Paula Patton (Mrs. Orville Francis Grahame)
Grahm, Milton L.
Grainger, Thomas Hutcheson, Jr.
Grala, William Leon
Grammas, Gus William
Granahan, John Joseph
Graner, George William, Jr.
Granger, J(effrey) S(olon)
Granick, Louis Wayne
Granite, Harvey Renwick
Granston, David Wilfred
Grant, Allan Aaron
Grant, Clifford M., Jr.
Grant, Edward Vincent
Grant, Edwin Randolph
Grant, John Herbert
Grant, Ronald Alfred
Grantham, Robert J.
Granville, Maurice Frederick
Grasso, Anthony Joseph
Grasso, Doris Ten Eyck (Mrs. Dominic Lawrence Grasso)
Grasso, Ella T. (Mrs. Thomas A. Grasso)
Grasso, Salvatore Peter
Graubard, Seymour
Graupner, Michael Ernest
Grave, Gilman Drew
Graves, George Garland
Graves, William Albert
Gray, Aline Koplin
Gray, Benjamin
Gray, Charles Augustus
Gray, Clarence Cornelius, III
Gray, David Macdonald
Gray, Edward Barton, Jr.
Gray, Herbert Walter, Jr.
Gray, Jimmy (James Hargraves)
Gray, Kenneth Stewart
Gray, Oscar Shalom
Gray, Robert Gordon
Gray, Robert Hugh
Gray, Sheila Hafter
Gray, Stephen Ashley
Gray, Warren
Gray, William Boyce
Gray, William H., III
Grayer, Meryl Romaine
Grayson, Henry T.
Grayson, Martin
Grayson, Richard Steven
Greaney, William J.
Greaves, Bettina Bien (Mrs. Percy L. Graves, Jr.)
Greaves, Percy Laurie, Jr.
Grebanier, Bernard
Greben, Stanley Edward
Grebstein, Sheldon Norman
Grech, Anthony Paul
Greco, Albert Nicholas
Greco, Rosemarie Bernadette
Greeley, Wilder Joseph
Green, Clifford Scott
Green, George Edward
Green, Gerard Leo
Green, Helen Ivy
Green, Irving Morton
Green, John, Jr.
Green, June Lazenby
Green, Michael Jeffrey
Green, Michael S.
Green, Miriam Blau
Green, Raymond S(ilvernail)
Green, Rose Basile (Mrs. Raymond S. Green)

Green, Samuel Louis
Green, Sedgwick William
Green, Thomas Henry, Jr.
Green, Wallace Hughes
Green, Wayne Hugo
Greenawalt, Kenneth William
Greenawalt, Martha Sloan (Mrs. Kenneth William Greenawalt)
Greenaway, Millicent Centilia
Greenbaum, Charles Hirsch
Greenberg, Albert
Greenberg, Benjamin Saul
Greenberg, Bernard
Greenberg, Calvin Leon
Greenberg, Carl
Greenberg, Frank Joseph
Greenberg, Herbert Marvin
Greenberg, Joseph
Greenberg, Lisa Alice
Greenberg, Lorry
Greenberg, Robert Benjamin
Greenberg, Sigmund Robert
Greenberg, Warren Peter
Greenberger, Howard
Greenblott, Charles Todd
Greenburg, Jerry Lee
Greene, Abe Jay
Greene, Adele Shuminer
Greene, Alan Guyer
Greene, Alan Steven
Greene, Bartholomew Andrew
Greene, Charles Robert
Greene, Elizabeth A.
Greene, Henry Irving
Greene, Howard Gilbert
Greene, Howard Paul
Greene, Howard Rodger
Greene, Jerome Davis, II
Greene, Lehman Otho
Greene, Louis Leon
Greene, Richard Stephen
Greene, Robert Bruce
Greene, Robert Ford
Greene, Stephen C.
Greene, Stephen Craig
Greene, Theodore Richard
Greene, William Caswell
Greenfield, Meg
Greenfield, Richard David
Greenfield, Val Shea
Greenhalgh, James
Greenholt, Walter Henry
Greenhouse, Nathaniel Anthony, Jr.
Greenhouse, Randey Robert
Greenlee, Michael Joseph
Greenough, William Bates, III
Greenseid, David Zanvel
Greenspan, Adam
Greenwald, Edward Harris
Greenwald, Harold
Greenwald, Harry
Greenwood, Audrey Gates
Greer, Dan Blake, Jr.
Greer, Thomas Vernon
Gregg, David, III
Gregg, Dorothy Elizabeth (Mrs. Paul Hughling Scott)
Gregg, William Kirker
Grego, Nicholas John
Gregoire, Paul
Gregorian, Vartan
Gregory, Edward Haig
Gregory, Gardiner Emerson
Gregory, Guy John
Gregory, James Michael
Gregory, Nahketah Baskerville
Gregory, Philip Orson
Gregory, Robert, Jr.
Greidinger, B. Bernard
Greif, Edward Louis
Greif, Martin
Greiner, Harry Sandt
Grelecki, Chester
Grendon, David Arthur
Grenier, Jean Paul
Grennell, Robert Lovell
Gresham, Glen Edward
Gressel, Michael Ludwig
Gressle, Lloyd Edward
Gressman, John Wesley, III
Grewal, Manohar Singh
Grey, Anthony Joseph
Greytak, Thomas John
Grib, Henry Walter
Griebel, Richard H.
Grieder, Theodore Godfrey, Jr.
Grier, Douglas Audenreid
Grierson, Norman Herbert
Gries, Leonard Todd
Griest, Norman Jett
Griffel, Jack
Griffenberg, Grace Lewis
Griffin, James Edward, Jr.
Griffin, James Edwin
Griffin, Jo Ann Thomas
Griffin, John I.
Griffin, Kathleen Mary
Griffin, Priscilla Loring (Mrs. John J. Griffin)
Griffin, Thomas Francis, Jr.
Griffin, Thomas Joseph, Jr.
Griffing, William E.
Griffis, John William, Jr.
Griffith, Carl H., Jr.
Griffith, Emlyn Irving
Griffith, Lawrence Stacey Cameron
Griffith, Mildred Sullivan (Mrs. William A. Griffith)
Griffith, William Russell
Griffiths, Donald Wesley, Jr.
Griglak, Martin Samuel
Grigoroff, Louis
Grillo, Frank Roy
Grimes, Mary Catherine
Grimes, Peter Joseph
Grimm, Ben Emmet
Grimm, Jay Vaughn
Grimm, Ralph Emanuel
Grimmett, Robin
Grimshaw, Herbert James
Grimsted, Patricia Kennedy
Grinberg, Raul
Grindle, Roger Lee
Grinnell, Gary Shawn
Grinoch, Paul
Gripaldi, Benedict Victor
Griswold, George
Griswold, Raymond James
Grocki, John James
Grodberg, Marcus Gordon
Groden, Gerald
Grody, Deborah
Groeger, Theodore Oscar
Grogan, Edward Joseph
Grogan, Joseph William
Grogan, Robert Harris
Grogg, Samuel L., Jr.
Gromada, Thaddeus Vladimir
Gromadzki, Zygmunt Constantine
Groner, Beverly Anne (Mrs. Samuel Brian Groner)
Groobert, George Edward
Groome, John Phillip, Jr.
Groshans, Russell Glen
Grosman, Alan Marc
Grosman, Brian Allen
Grosman, Michael
Gross, Caroline Lord (Mrs. Martin L. Gross)
Gross, Feliks
Gross, Gary Lawrence
Gross, Helene Marilyn Beller
Gross, Irwin Elliot
Gross, Jeffrey Kent
Gross, John Hammes
Gross, Ludwik
Gross, Lydia Elizabeth
Gross, Peter Alan
Gross, Robert Alan
Gross, Sidney
Gross, Sidney Esser
Gross, Spencer
Grosschmid-Zsogod, Geza Benjamin
Grosser, George Samuel
Grossman, Anne Rafsky
Grossman, Gary Jay
Grossman, Gilbert
Grossman, Harry
Grossman, John Henry
Grossman, Jonathan Philip
Grossman, Julian Aaron
Grossman, Mark Ira
Grossman, Samuel
Grossman, Thomas
Grossmann, Bernd
Grosso, Anthony Joseph
Grosvenor, Gilbert Melville
Grote, Otto Frederick
Grove, Daniel Dwight
Grove, Ernest Wilson
Grove, John Landis
Grove, Kathryn Mowrey (Mrs. D. Dwight Grove)
Grove, Richard Irving
Grove, William Arthur, Jr.
Grover, Shamsher S.
Growney, James Gerard
Grub, Phillip Donald
Grubb, Robert Lynn
Grubbs, Donald Shaw, Jr.
Gruber, Alan Richard
Gruber, Jerome Martin
Gruber, Melvin Saul
Gruber, Murray Paul
Grubiak, Michael Robert
Grubner, Otto
Gruccio, Lillian Joan (Mrs. William Taylor Harrington Thorman)
Gruen, Peter H.
Gruenberg, Ernest M.
Gruenfeld, Leon S.
Gruft, Howard Martin
Gruhn, William Theodore
Grum, Clifford J.
Grundt, Leonard
Grundy, J(ohn) Owen
Gruner, Saul George
Grunes, Robert Lewis
Grunewald, Donald
Grunor, Jerry Arnold
Grunwald, Hans W.
Gruppe, Karl William
Grzechowiak, Susan Marie
Grzyb, Frank Louis
Gschlecht, Marianne Patricia
Guadagna, S. J.
Guardino, Gary
Guarini, Frank J., Jr.
Gubala, Jack J.
Gubbins, Paul Gordon
Gudaitis, Algird Victor
Guditus, Charles William
Guenther, Harry Wilbert
Guenther, Kenneth Allen
Guercio, Vincent Joseph
Guereschi, Edward Fred
Gueson, Emerita Torres
Guest, James Alfred
Guest, Robert Gerald
Guggenheim, Frederick Gibson
Guglielmo, Rocco Michael
Gui, James Edmund
Guida, Frank Joseph
Guido, Dennis Franklin
Guild, Richard Samuel
Guilfoyle, George H.
Guille, Peter, Jr.
Guimond, Richard Pierre
Guinivan, Thomas Wayne
Guise, David Earl
Gulas, Ivan
Gulati, Shanti Parkash
Gulati, Suresh Thakordas
Gulevich, Wladimir
Gulker, Ira Arnold
Gulko, Harris David
Guller, Irving Bernard
Gullette, Ethel Mae Bishop
Gulley, Ralph Grady
Gumpert, Gustav
Gunders, Steven Oliver
Gunia, Russell Burnell
Gunkel, Ralph Daniel
Gunn, Hartford Nelson, Jr.
Gunning, James Richard
Gunther, George Lackman
Gupta, Gopal Das
Gupta, Prem Kamal
Gupta, Ved Prakash
Gurgo, Michael Matthias
Gurnari, Larry Mathew
Gurtin, Leatrice Kagan
Gurvitz, Milton Solomon
Gushin, Harold
Gusmano, Louis Joseph
Guss, Gordon Roger
Guss, Maynard Robert
Gustafson, George Victor
Guthrie, John Francis, Jr.
Guthrie, Marion B.
Guthrie, Randolph Hobson, Jr.
Gutman, Daniel
Gutman, I. Cyrus
Gutteridge, Thomas George
Guttman, Samuel Arnold
Guttmann, H(ans) Peter
Guy, Gordon Ross
Gwynn, Sandra Ekman
Ha, Chester Chiduk
Haan, Hendrik Marie
Haas, Albert
Haas, Bert Robert
Haas, Eleanor Alter (Mrs. Peter Ralph Haas)
Haas, Karl Alan
Haas, Leonard
Haas, Marvin Joel
Haas, Ward John
Haber, David L.
Haber, Paul Adrian Life
Haber, Pierre Claude
Haber, William Bill
Habergritz, George Joseph
Haberland, Peter Hans
Habib, Mohamed
Hacker, Harold Schworm
Hacker, Ray Kenneth
Hackett, Frederick Keppel
Hackett, Lynwood Raymond, Sr.
Haddad, Heskel Marshall
Haddad, Jamil Raouf
Haddad, Ramond A.
Hadidian, Dikran Yenovk
Hadl, Helen
Hadley, James Edward
Haduch, Judith Ellen Connell
Hady, Edmund Carl
Haefeli, Robert James
Haefner, Richard Charles
Haehnle, Robert James
Haenlein, George Friedrich Wilhelm
Haenschen, Robert William
Haeseler, William, III
Haff, Dennis Raymond
Hagan, Eileen
Hagan, James Carroll
Hageman, Richard Philip, Jr.
Hager, Nathaniel Ellmaker, Jr.
Hager, Walter Ellsworth
Hagerty, Betty Lee
Hagey, Walter Rex
Haggerty, James Joseph
Hagopian, Louis Thomas
Hagopian, Varant
Hahn, Do Won
Hahn, Fred
Hahn, Fred I.
Hahn, George Alan
Hahn, R(obert) Douglas
Hahn, William Joseph
Haight, Charles Sherman, Jr.
Hail, Barbara Andrews (Mrs. Edward G. Hail)
Haines, Larry Eugene
Hains, Gaston
Hainsworth, Winston Clarkson
Hairston, Alonzo Paul
Hait, Gershon
Hajdu, Francis Lester
Hajduczok, Bohdan Zenon
Hakas, Joseph Francis
Hakim, Talib Rasul
Hakim-Elahi, Enayat
Hakola, John Wayne
Halasi-Kun, Elisabeth Christina Szorad (Mrs. George J. Halasi-Kun)
Halberg, G. Peter
Halberstadt, Robert Bilheimer
Halbert, Virgil Allen
Hale, Frances
Hale, Robert David
Halevy, Simon
Haley, Brian Paul
Haley, Edward Everett
Haley, Martin Ryan
Haley, Vincent Peter
Half, Robert
Halfhuid, Rene Henry
Halik, Eugene Egon
Halina, Mme. (Halina Jozefa Lutomski, Mrs. Floyd Martin Lutomski)
Hall, David
Hall, Edwin Huddleston, Jr.
Hall, Gary Randall
Hall, Howard Elfreth
Hall, James Conrad
Hall, Joseph Palta
Hall, Mae Crawford
Hall, Paul
Hall, Richard Lewis
Hall, Samuel Mechanic, Jr.
Hall, Stephen Robert, Jr.
Hall, Wilbur Sheridan
Hall, Wilfred McGregor
Hall, William Anthony
Hall, William Sterling
Hallenbeck, Norman Page
Hallenbeck, Robert Potter, Jr.
Haller, Henry Edwin, Jr.
Halliday, Frederick Nicholas
Hallion, Marie Elizabeth
Hallion, Richard Paul, Jr.
Halloran, Katherine Bostwick Hess
Hallquist, Clarence LaMonte
Hallstead, William Finn, III
Halman, Talat Sait
Halo, Hugo Hona
Halperin, George Bennett
Halpern, Abraham Leon
Halpern, George Martin
Halpern, Nathan Loren
Halpern, Sidney
Halpert, Bernard
Halsey, Richard Sweeney
Halvorson, Newman Thorbus, Jr.
Ham, Jerry Don
Ham, Leslie Gilmer
Hamada, George Syd
Hamann, Ronald Howard
Hambleton, George Robert
Hamburg, Lester Albert
Hamel, Bernard Franklin
Hamid, Mahmud Abdel
Hamill, Charlotte Mary
Hamilton, Alice Dowdall
Hamilton, Calvin P.
Hamilton, Chester
Hamilton, Clarke Thomas
Hamilton, Frances
Hamilton, James Theodore
Hamilton, Lyman Critchfield, Jr.
Hamilton, Perrin C.
Hamilton, Richard
Hamilton, Richard Alexander
Hamilton, Roger Edward
Hamilton, Theodore Nathaniel
Hamilton, Thomas Stewart
Hamilton, William Fulton
Hamm, Henry Stevens
Hammel, Robert John
Hammer, Guy Saint Clair, II
Hammer, Jean Heather Weir
Hammer, Victor Julius
Hammett, Van Buren Osler
Hammond, Charles Willis
Hammond, David Greene
Hammond, Jane Laura
Hampar, Berge
Hamsher, J(ohn) Herbert
Han, Ki Hyun
Hanacik, William Frank
Hanan, Mack
Hanback, Hazel Smallwood
Hancock, David Eric
Hancock, Harry Polkinhorn, Jr.
Hancock, Joe Irey
Hancox, Robert Ernest
Hand, F. Ned
Hand, Robert Gary
Hand, Robert Stephens
Handal, Anthony H.
Handel, Bernard
Handel, Morton Emanuel
Handford, H. Allen
Handloff, Norma Bram (Mrs. Samuel Handloff)
Handschumacher, Richard Arthur
Handy, William Hope
Haney, John Benjamin
Haney, Robert William
Hanham, Harold John
Hani, Antoine Georges
Hanin, Edward
Hankamer, Roberta Anne
Hankard, Francis Richard
Hankee, William Byron
Hankenson, Edward Craig, Jr.
Hankerson, Walter Leroy
Hankes, Lawrence Valentine
Hanks, David Allen
Hanks, Stedman Shumway
Hanley, James M.
Hann, Robert Kenneth
Hanna, Dwight Corwin
Hannigan, Eugene Joseph
Hannigan, Harriet Rebecca
Hannon, John William, Jr.
Hanns, Christian Alexander
Hansburg, Henry George
Hansen, Christian Andreas, Jr.
Hansen, Erwin Gunther
Hansen, Ralph Holm
Hansen, Robert
Hansen, Waldemar Henry
Hanson, David Justin
Hanson, David Leroy
Hanson, Eugene Russell
Hanson, Madeline Shaw
Hanson, Martha Mason
Hanson, Maurice Francis (Maury)
Hanson, Robert Carl, III
Hanson, Robert DeLolle
Hanson, Virgil Sylvester
Hanssler, Herman William
Hantgan, George
Hanton, Emil Michael
Hanzalek, Astrid (Luise) Teicher
Hanzalek, Frederick Joseph
Hapgood, Robert
Hapichuk, Albert Elie
Haque, Waheedul
Harac, Sigmund
Harasym, Gerard John
Harbaugh, Carl Ray
Harbaugh, Ray Allen
Harbin, Otis Lee
Harbour, John Wesley, Jr.
Hardaway, Ernest, II
Harder, F. William
Hardesty, Charles Howard, Jr.
Hardin, Clyde Durham
Hardin, William David
Hardin, William Downer
Harding, Ernest Albert
Harding, James Gordon
Harding, Richard Lowell
Hardy, George
Hardy, Robert Edward
Hare, Daphne Kean
Hargreave, John Harold, III
Haring, Eugene Miller
Haritakis, Alex Gregory
Harkavy, Ira Baer
Harkaway, Jill Elka
Harkins, Herbert Perrin
Harlan, Stephen Donald
Harlan, William Bruce
Harley, Daniel Prophet
Harley, William Gardner
Harlow, Joyce Southard Brecht
Harman, John Robert, Jr.
Harmelin, Sanford Herman
Harmon, James Allen
Harmon, John Watson
Harmon, Lucy
Harmon, Phyllis Yvonne
Harmsen, Wilbur Durian
Harner, Michael James
Harney, Robert Charles
Harney, Robert Edwin
Haroutunian, Robert James
Harper, Frederick
Harper, Howard Wallace
Harper, Joseph Ralph
Harper, Paul Church, Jr.
Harper, Richard Peter
Harquail, Raymond Dennis
Harradine, Robert Paul
Harrice, Cy (Nicholas)
Harrigan, John Thomas, Jr.
Harrington, Charles Christopher
Harrington, John Leonard
Harrington, Joseph, Jr.
Harrington, Michael Joseph
Harrington, Robert Carr
Harrington, Roger Fuller
Harris, Alan Michael
Harris, Allen
Harris, Benjamin Louis
Harris, Bennett Lowell
Harris, Bertha Louise
Harris, Cecil
Harris, Charles Russell
Harris, Earle Harold
Harris, Eleanor Marie
Harris, Herbert Ignatius
Harris, Homer Eugene
Harris, Huntington
Harris, Jacke Curtis
Harris, James George, Jr.
Harris, James Ridout
Harris, James Robert, II
Harris, Jonathan Leonard
Harris, Leslie Talbot
Harris, Louise
Harris, Margaret
Harris, Michael Bertram
Harris, Patricia Roberts
Harris, Paul Stewart
Harris, Ray Winston
Harris, Raymond Jesse
Harris, Robert Franklin
Harris, Stanley Ralph, Jr.
Harris, William James
Harris, William James, Jr.
Harris, William North
Harris, William Reuel
Harrisingh, Lawrence Barrington
Harrison, Anthony Miller
Harrison, Carolyn Cassell
Harrison, David Clark
Harrison, Emmett Bruce, Jr.
Harrison, Howard Norton
Harrison, Nelson E.
Harrison, Robert William
Harrison, Rosalie Thronton (Mrs. Porter H. Harrison)
Harrison, Russell Edward
Harrison, Thomas Gerald
Harrold, Alan John
Harry, William Joseph
Harsaghy, Fred Joseph, Jr.
Harsany, Peter
Hart, Brian Arthur
Hart, Charles Willard, Jr.
Hart, David Livingston
Hart, Dean Albert
Hart, Eleanore Hays
Hart, Howard Arthur
Hart, Jerald Martin
Hart, John Patrick
Hart, Noah, Jr.
Hart, Richard Eugene
Hart, Roy Hanu
Harter, Jane Bissett
Hartford, Donald Harold
Hartley, Samuel Lafayette, Jr.
Hartley, William Skelton
Hartline, Haldan Keffer
Hartline, Jessie Cowan
Hartman, Catherine Rudisill (Mrs. Harold R. Hartman)
Hartman, Harold Richard
Hartman, Preston Wright
Hartman, Willis Jonas, Jr.
Hartstein, Marvin Leonard
Hartung, Walter Magnus
Hartwigsen, Nelson LeRoy
Harvey, David Alexander
Harvey, Douglass Coate
Harvey, Frederick Wilfred, Jr.
Harvey, Garnet Lewis
Harvey, Jeffrey Brown
Harvie, Marion Elinore
Harvison, Clifford James
Harway, Vivian Irene (Mrs. Norman L. Harway)
Harwayne, Frank
Harwood, Clarence Wayne
Hasegawa, Ryusuke
Hasek, Ronald Wayne
Hasenstab, Paul Robert
Hashmi, Majid Ali
Haskell, Edward Froehlich
Haskell, Helen Beaumont Park (Mrs. William Peckham Haskell)
Hasley, Robert Nathan
Hassan, Susana Alicia
Hassell, Louis Desmond
Hassenger, Robert Leo
Hasserjian, Paul Yacub
Hassinger, Mark Scott
Hasson, Dennis Francis
Hatami, Abolghassem
Hatanaka, Masakazu
Hatch, Allene Gaty (Mrs. Alden R. Hatch)
Hatcher, Robert Vance, Jr.
Hatem, Claire Catherine
Hatfield, Richard B.
Hathaway, Louis Edmund, III
Hathaway, William Dodd
Hatrak, Robert Stephen
Haug, James Harold
Hauge, Gabriel
Haugen, Einar Ingvald
Hausman, Bruce
Hausner, Franz
Haut, Michael Joel
Haven, Milton Michael
Havewala, Noshir Behram
Havice, Shirley L.
Haviland, Morrison Chandler
Havilland, Ben
Hawes, Frederic Tapley
Hawes, William David
Hawk, Allan Holmes
Hawk, Eleanor Dorothy
Hawk, George Wayne
Hawkes, Dudley Farrand
Hawkins, David Geoffrey
Hawkins, Harold Berton
Hawkins, John Charles
Hawkins, Oscar Warner
Hawkins, Robert Ousley, Jr.
Hawkins, Thomas Lawrence, Jr.
Hawkinshire, Frank B.W., V
Hawley, Willard Hayden
Hawrylik, Stanley Joseph
Hawryluk, Orest
Hawver, Carl Fullerton
Hay, Donald Robert
Hay, Erroll Baldwin, III
Hay, George Austin
Hay, Isaac Kline, Jr.
Hayakawa, Kan-ichi
Hayashi, Koichiro David
Hayasi, Nisiki
Hayat, Gilbert Salomon
Haycock, Robert Philhower
Hayden, Ralph Frederick
Hayduk, Albert T.
Hayes, Arthur Hull, Jr.
Hayes, Bettine J. (Mrs. M. Vinson Hayes)
Hayes, Carol J.
Hayes, Charles Lauchlan
Hayes, E(ugene) Nelson
Hayes, Gary Vincent
Hayes, Gerry Stetson
Hayes, James Martin
Hayes, Marsden Hamilton
Hayes, Ward Wilson
Hayes, Wilbur Frank
Hayes, William Charles
Hayeslip, David William
Hayman, Harry
Hayman, Peter Michael
Haynes, Milton Odwin Carlton
Haynes, William Forby, Jr.
Haynor, Patricia Manzi
Haynos, Robert Alex
Hays, Harrison L., III
Hays, Hoffman Reynolds
Hays, Mary Katherine Jackson (Mrs. Donald Osborne Hays)
Hays, Paul Raymond
Haysom, Derek William Reginald
Hayward, Bertrand Williams
Hayward, Harold
Haywood, Charles Howard
Hazéll, Norma J. Barber
Hazelton, Bruce Winston

Hazelton, George Francis
Hazlett, Samuel Rohrer
Hazzard, George William
Heaberg, George Thomas, III
Head, Edward D.
Heald, Bruce Day
Healey, Barbara Ann Ochonicky (Mrs. Leo T. Healey)
Healy, Bridget Finegan
Healy, Francis Patrick
Healy, Timothy Stafford
Healy, Walter Francis Xavier
Healy, William John, III
Hearst, Austine McDonnell
Hearst, William Randolph, Jr.
Heartt, Charlotte Bebee
Heaslip, William Joseph
Heath, James Lee
Heath, Melanie Ann
Heath, Richard Eddy
Heathcote, Thomas Burdell
Heaton, Eloise Klotz (Mrs. Charles Toll Heaton)
Hebden, William Ernest
Hechtman, Isaac Leib
Heckelman, Sol Berkman
Heckert, Paul Charles
Heckler, Margaret M. O'Shaughnessy (Mrs. John M. Heckler)
Heckman, Christopher Edward
Hedeman, Phyllis Ruth
Hedgepath, Leslie Eugene
Hedley-Whyte, John
Hedrick, Ira Grant
Hedrick, Larry W.
Heerwagen, Herbert Alfred
Heffernan, Peter John
Heffner, Stephen Fleming
Hefter, Laurence Roy
Hefter, Sanford Murray
Hegeman, James Alan
Hegeman, Pieter Evert
Hegg, J(ohn) Peter
Heggie, John William
Heggie, Peter
Heghinian, Elizabeth Alban Trumbower
Hegi, Ernest Arnold
Heidell, James Martin
Heidemann, John Charles
Heiden, Barbara
Heiferman, Marvin Peter
Heigemeir, Franz Joseph
Heigl, James John, Jr.
Heiken, Jerold Clarence
Heilbron, Jane Bossak
Heilig, Margaret Cramer
Heilman, Frank William, Jr.
Heilman, John Edward
Heilpern, George Seymour
Heimarck, James
Heimbaugh, James Ross
Heimerdinger, John Frederick
Heimlich, Norman
Heiner, Lee Francis
Heinitsh, George Means, Jr.
Heinle, Robert Alan
Heinrich, Adel Verna
Heinsohn, William Bishop
Heinz, Henry John, II
Heinz, Henry John, III
Heisse, Sandra VanGraber
Heistein, Robert Kenneth
Heitbrink, Peter Garrett
Heither, Lillian Lee Johns
Heitler, Michael Stewart
Heitner, Michael
Helander, Bruce Paul
Helb, John Vincent
Held, Eric Steven
Helder, Judith Ann
Helfand, Arthur E.
Helfand, Gary David
Heller, Daniel Robert
Heller, Harold Noel
Heller, John DeLay
Heller, Samuel
Heller, Steven Anthony
Hellerson, Charles Benedict
Hellman, Paul Victor
Hellmann, Karl H.
Hellmuth, Paul Francis
Helm, Neil Richard
Helmetag, Carl, Jr.
Helmetag, Charles Hugh
Helmick, Ernest Delbert
Helmrich, Ralph Henry
Helsel, Raymond Archibald
Helstein, Herbert
Helvey, Edward Peter, Jr.
Helwig, George James
Helzner, Albert Eugene
Hemby, Dorothy Jean
Hemeon, Wesley C. L.
Hemingway, Herman Wadsworth, II
Hemingway, Mary Welsh (Mrs. Ernest Hemingway)
Hemmer, John William
Hemphill, Richard McFern
Hena, Muhammad Abu
Henderson, Angus Drummond
Henderson, Charles Urquhart
Henderson, Donald Anislie
Henderson, Donald Cedric
Henderson, Douglas Boyd
Henderson, James Wood
Henderson, John
Henderson, Joseph Ralston
Henderson, Kenneth Atwood
Henderson, Robert Allan
Henderson, William, III
Hendler, Nelson Howard
Hendrick, William Donald
Hendricks, Barkley Leonnard
Hendricks, David G(ross)
Hengst, Ronald William
Henkel, Arthur John, Jr.
Henkel, Robert Thomas
Henkels, Nancy Lee Bullock
Henken, Bernard Samuel
Henkind, Paul
Henn, Carl Leroy, Jr.
Henn, Donald Edwards
Hennage, Joseph Howard
Hennelly, Edmund Paul
Henneman, Dennis Allen
Hennessey, Robert Gaylord
Hennessy, John Francis, Jr.
Hennessy, Wesley J.
Hennigan, Robert Dwyer
Henninger, Kermit Mandes
Hennings, Josephine Silva (Halpin)
Henningsen, Victor William, Jr.
Henoch, Arthur
Henriques, Edgar Saul
Henriques, Frederick Cohane
Henry, Edward LeRoy
Henry, Guy T.
Henry, Howard Chester
Henry, James Merrill
Henry, James Robert
Henry, Jane Naughton
Henry, John Jewett
Henry, Paul Arthur
Henry, Paul Joseph
Henry, Rupert Elsworth
Henry, Thomas Joseph
Henry, William Stacy Chandler
Henschel, Beverly Jean Smith
Hensley, William Tutt
Hentel, Nat Herbert
Heotis, James Peter
Hepp, Vincent Rene
Herbert, Edward Franklin
Herbert, Lawrence
Herbert, LeRoy James
Herbits, Stephen Edward
Herbster, John Milton
Herchenroether, Henry Carl, Jr.
Herchert, Harry Edwin
Herd, Charmian June
Herder, Thomas Gilbert
Herford, Peter Michael
Herge, Henry Curtis, Jr.
Hergert, Herbert Lawrence
Herget, James Patrick
Herglotz, Heribert Karl
Herklots, Robert Carey
Herman, Barbara Rose Garnache
Herman, Beaumont Alexander
Herman, Harry Carl
Herman, Herbert
Herman, John David
Herman, Karl William
Herman, Kenneth
Herman, Lloyd Eldred
Herman, Melvin Jerome
Herman, Michael Victor
Herman, Richard Baer
Herman, Robert Lewis
Herman, Samuel Sidney
Herman, Theodore
Herman, Victor George
Hermann, John Stefan
Hermann, Mildred Marie
Hermanson, Gerald Irwin
Hermenet, Argelia M. Buitrago (Mrs. Raymond A. Hermenet)
Hern, George Louis
Hernandez, Wilbert Eduardo
Hernandez, William Hector, Jr.
Herndon, D. Keith
Hernstadt, Judith Filenbaum
Herold, Bernard
Herold, Edward Joseph
Herpst, Martha Jane
Herr, Conrad Edward Apgar
Herrell, James Milton
Herren, Peter Hans
Herrick, Allison Butler
Herrick, Elbert Charles
Herrick, Rolland Clyde
Herrick, William
Herring, J(ohn) Donald
Herring, Robert Fleming
Herrmann, Daniel Lionel
Herrmann, Richard Arnold
Herschfus, Jechiel Aaron
Hershey, Alfred Day
Hershey, Colin Harry
Hershey, Edward Norman
Hershey, John O.
Hershey, Robert Lewis
Herstein, Louis Arthur, III
Hertzberg, Arthur
Hertzberg, Henry
Hertzberg, Steven
Herzberg, Arno
Herzer, Charles Henry, Jr.
Herzer, Harry Baldwin, III
Herzfeld, Valerius Erich
Herzog, Peter Emilius
Heschl, William Charles
Hesen, John Edward
Hess, Earl Hollinger
Hess, Hans Ober
Hess, James Henry
Hess, Jeanette Wilma
Hesse, John Ronald
Hesslein, Laura Beth
Hester, Howard Curtis
Hester, Ruport
Hetos, Nicholas Stephen
Hetrick, Emery Sylvester
Hetsko, Cyril Francis
Hetzel, Frederick Joseph
Hetzler, John Carlin, Jr.
Heuer, Russell Pearce, Jr.
Heusser, Norman Wilson
Hevizy, Louis
Hewett, Thomas Avery
Hewitt, John Hamilton, Jr.
Hewitt, Marvin Harold
Hewson, Sister Dorothy
Hey, Albert Edwards, III
Heyde, Martha Bennett (Mrs. Ernest R. Heyde)
Heydecker, Richard Creagh
Heying, Everett Lynch
Heymann, Henry Lewis
Heyneman, Alan Lionel
Heyssell, Robert Morris
Hibbard, Robert
Hickey, Francis Roger
Hickey, George Joseph, Jr.
Hickey, Michael Kevin
Hickey, Robert Joseph
Hickins, Walter H.
Hickman, Benjamin
Hickman, George Conard
Hickman, John Hampton, III
Hickman, Robert Emmet
Hickok, Richard Sanford
Hicks, Louis Arnold
Hicks, Robert Carey
Hiebel, Joseph James
Hiebert, Ray Eldon
Higginbotham, Linda Jean
Higgins, Charles Lennox
Higgins, Craig Stockton
Higgins, James Henry
Higgins, Mona Leah
Higgins, Ronald James
Higgins, Thomas Carol
Higginson, Theodore N.
High, Ernest Clemuel
Higham, Charles
Highwater, Jamake
Hildebrandt, Frederick Dean, Jr.
Hilgeman, Theodore William
Hill, A(lbert) Lewis
Hill, Barbara Mae
Hill, Carol
Hill, David Gary
Hill, Donald Robert
Hill, Flora Mildred
Hill, Frederick William
Hill, Hyacinthe (Virginia Anderson)
Hill, James Berry
Hill, John Austin, Jr.
Hill, John Bamforth
Hill, John Negley, Jr.
Hill, Kenneth Richard
Hill, Margaret Duerr (Mrs. Carrington W. Hill)
Hill, Otis Ray
Hill, Paul Vincent
Hill, Richard Devereux
Hill, Robert William
Hill, Roger Webb, Jr.
Hill, Ruth Rebecca
Hill, Ruth Vollmers
Hill, Samuel Ervin
Hill, Thomas William, Jr.
Hill, W. Clayton
Hillebrand, John Benedict
Hiller, Frederick Theodore
Hiller, Paul
Hillery, Mary Jane Larato (Mrs. Thomas H. Hillery)
Hilles, Susan Morse
Hillier, James
Hillman, Richard Stanley
Hillman, William Chernick
Hillman, William Sermolino
Hills, Carla A.
Hilsen, Jesse Morton
Hilton, Clifford L.
Hilton, O. William, Jr.
Himberg, Ronald Otto
Hinchman, Robert, Jr.
Hinckley, Alfred Armond
Hinderer, Kenneth H.
Hinderliter, Richard Glenn
Hindman, Joseph Floyd
Hinds, Aubrey Constantine
Hinds, Caryl Ellsworth
Hines, Francis Russell
Hinkelman, Kenneth William
Hinkle, Muriel Ruth Nelson
Hinman, John A.
Hinnant, Ollen Bernard
Hinrichs, Walter Edwin
Hinsdale, Mitchell Wilbur, Jr.
Hintz, Carl Edward
Hinz, Dorothy Elizabeth
Hipson, Herman Arthur
Hires, Clara S.
Hires, William Leland
Hirose, Teruo Terry
Hirsch, Arthur Isaac
Hirsch, Elisabeth Feist (Mrs. Felix Hirsch)
Hirsch, Hyman
Hirsch, Lee
Hirsch, Paul J.
Hirschfeld, Ilan E.
Hirschhorn, Laurence Herbert
Hirschman, Seymour Solomon
Hirshfield, Irvin Norman
Hiscock, Eric Dixon Cave
Hisrich, Robert Dale
Hitchens, Charles Norwood, Jr.
Hite, Garth E.
Hittner, Richard
Hixson, Johanna Lee
Hlinka, Peter
Hnatow, Miguel Alexander
Ho, Charles Fai
Ho, Chi-Tang
Ho, Eugene Ngok
Ho, James Kwang-Kuo
Ho, Louis Ting
Ho, Yau-Cheung
Hoagland, Henry Williamson, Jr.
Hoagland, Porter, Jr.
Hobart, Thomas Yale, Jr.
Hobbs, Gerald Stephen
Hobbs, Reginald Delaine, Jr.
Hobelman, Carl Donald
Hoberman, Alfred Elliott
Hoberman, Peter Ian
Hoch, Edward Dentinger
Hoch, Oscar Reynold
Hochman, Joel Abraham
Hochman, Stephen Allen
Hodge, Charles Cedric
Hodge, Mary Jo (Mrs. Charles Cedric Hodge)
Hodge, Sister Patricia Andrea
Hodges, Robert John
Hodges, Timna Donahue
Hodosh, Milton
Hodsdon, Albert Edward, III
Hoehn, James Gurney
Hoelscher, Elody M.
Hoeltzel, Kenneth Eugene
Hoenigan, Henry
Hoest, William Pierce
Hoexter, Corinne Rosenfelder Katz
Hoey, Evelyn Levine (Mrs. Reid A. Hoey)
Hoey, James Benedict
Hofer, Richard Joseph
Hoff, Charles Worthington, III
Hoff, Richard Charles
Hoff, Stuart
Hoffberger, Jerold Charles
Hoffert, Paul Washington
Hoffman, Bernard
Hoffman, Carl Bentley
Hoffman, Charles Harry
Hoffman, Donald Brooks
Hoffman, Elmer
Hoffman, Irwin
Hoffman, John Ernest, Jr.
Hoffman, Ralph Emerson, Jr.
Hoffman, Saul
Hoffman, William Andrew, III
Hoffmann, Eva Gottschalck
Hoffmann, John J.
Hoffmann, Kurt Rudolf
Hoffmann, Ralf Ludwig
Hoffmeister, F. Stanley
Hoffner, Herbert Howard
Hoffner, Marilyn
Hoffstatter, Edward William, Jr.
Hoffstein, Herbert
Hoffstot, Henry Phipps, Jr.
Hofkin, Gerald Alan
Hofmann, Frederick Joseph
Hofmann, P. Stephen
Hofmar, Donald Bernard
Hogan, Alice Hamilton
Hogan, Charles Carlton
Hogan, Daniel Edward
Hogan, James Carroll, Jr.
Hogan, James John
Hogan, Joseph Lloyd
Hogan, Robert Joseph
Hogan, V(incent) Michael
Hogan, William Joseph
Hogberg, Carl Gustav
Hoge, Wayne Eugene
Hogenauer, Alan Krahe
Hogenson, Robert Charles
Hogg, Wilbur Emory
Hoguet, David Dilworth
Hohauser, Sanford Mortimer
Hohensee, Edward William
Hohl, Jeffrey Randolph
Hohmann, Thomas Charles
Hojnacki, Jerome Louis
Holbrook, George Edward
Holcomb, Robert Clinton
Holcombe, Kenneth Henry
Holden, Georgie E. Hough
Holden, Henry Earle, Jr.
Holden, James Stuart
Holden, Richard Fletcher
Holder, Calvin Beresford
Holding, Laura Anne
Holdridge, Barbara (Mrs. Lawrence B. Holdridge)
Holechek, James Albert
Holiday, Martha Jean
Holiner, Leona
Holland, Norman Norwood
Holland, Norman Norwood, Jr.
Holland, Ray Geoffrey
Holland, Sanford Jed
Hollander, Alvin L., Jr.
Hollander, Bentley Aaron
Hollander, George
Hollander, Lawrence Jay
Hollander, Leonard
Hollander, Melvyn Arnold
Hollander, Patricia Ann
Hollander, Stanley Jules
Hollans, Irby Noah, Jr.
Hollenbeck, Harold Capistran
Hollenberg, Robert David
Holliday, Ivar McDonald
Hollingworth, Joseph Edwin, Jr.
Holloway, Edward, Jr.
Hollowell, Gloria Noble
Hollywood, John Aloysius
Holm, Robert Eric
Holman, B. Leonard
Holman, Robert Vogel
Holman, William George
Holman, William Jacob, Jr.
Holman, Yerby Rozelle
Holmes, Cary William
Holmes, David Bryan
Holmes, Kenneth Howard
Holmes, Richard William
Holmgren, Theodore J.
Holmquist, Howard Emil
Holohan, Warren W., Jr.
Holsten, Richard David
Holt, Arthur Henry, Jr.
Holt, Barry Clay
Holt, Herbert
Holt, Joseph William
Holt, Marjorie Sewell (Mrs. Duncan McKay Holt)
Holt, Philetus Havens, III
Holte, Clarence LeRoy
Holter, Joanne Claire Minard
Holthaus, Alice Marion Fesko
Holton, John Hill, Jr.
Holtz, Gilbert Joseph
Holtz, Itshak Jack
Holtz, Sidney
Holtzman, Arnold Harold
Holtzman, Elizabeth
Holzinger, Cecile
Holzman, Eleanore Marienne Grushlaw (Mrs. Robert Stuart Holzman)
Holzman, Steven Elliott
Honaman, Nancy
Honaman, Winifred Pinkerton
Honarvar, Aliza Aghdas
Hongo, Ronald Joseph
Honig, Arnold
Honig, Harvey
Honig, Mervin
Hons, Peter William
Hood, Larry Lee
Hood, Thomas Richard
Hoof, David Lorne
Hookailo, Melvin Fred
Hooker, Arthur Bowles
Hooker, Olivia Juliette
Hooper, Alexander Nelson
Hooshmand, Mojtaba
Hooton, Edward, Jr.
Hoover, Herbert Christopher, Jr.
Hoover, Mark Eugene
Hoover, Richard Edwin
Hope, Peter Blanchard
Hopkins, Ernest Loyd
Hopkins, Everett Parker
Hopkins, Henry Powell, Jr.
Hopkins, Mary Rita
Hopkins, William Edgar
Hopson, Anna Lee
Horai, Joann
Horan, Edmund Martin
Horan, James D.
Hordish, J. Arnold
Hordynsky, Walter Eugene
Horecky, Paul Louis
Horel, H(erman) Bruce
Horic, Alan
Horka, Alfred Edward
Horn, Ferdinand Rudolph, Jr.
Horn, John Chisolm
Horn, Russell Eugene
Horn, Solveig Wald (Mrs. John Chisolm Horn)
Hornafius, Wilbur H., Jr.
Hornbeck, David W.
Hornbeck, Peter Louis
Hornblass, Albert
Horne, Michael Edward
Horner, Matina Souretis (Mrs. Joseph L. Horner)
Hornik, Henry
Hornik, Joseph William
Horowitz, Alan Herbert
Horowitz, Irving Louis
Horseman, Roy Mertzell
Horsfall, William Rhodes, Jr.
Horst, Eleanor
Horst, Robert Lee
Horton, Frank
Horton, John Edward
Horvat, Joseph James
Horwitz, Ruth Kafrissen
Horwitz, Saul
Hosbach, Howard Daniel
Hoskin, William Dickel
Hosking, Robert Leroy
Hoskins, Donald William
Hoskins, Walter Hugh
Hostetler, Shirley Ann
Hostetter, D(avid) Ray
Hostetter, Donald Allen
Hotaling, Kay Carol
Hotchkiss, Henry
Hotchkiss, Jeanette Louise
Hou, Kenneth Chiang
Houck, Lewis Daniel, Jr.
Hough, Eldred Wilson
Hough, Frederick Gerard
Hough, Gordon Lord
Houghton, James Richardson
Houghton, William Henry
Houle, Joseph Adrien
Houle, Roger Achilles
Houle, Thomas A.
Hourdajian, Dawn
House, Stanley Gartenhaus
Householder, John Henry
Housel, Edmund Llewellyn
Houser, Joseph Jay-Jackson
Houser, Mary Ruby Hillman
Houser, Thomas James
Houser, Thomas Jude
Housley, Nicholas George
Houston, Alfred Dearborn
Houston, Fred William
Houston, Ray Bertholf
Houts, Earl
Houts, Paul Louis
Hover, Louis Joseph
Hoving, Thomas
Howard, Bertram Elliot
Howard, David
Howard, Doris
Howard, Glenn Willard
Howard, Graeme Keith, Jr.
Howard, Jack Rohe
Howard, James J.
Howard, John Robert
Howard, Judith Barbara Schaffer (Mrs. Leonard Howard)
Howard, Katherine Graham (Mrs. Charles P. Howard)
Howard, Melvin
Howard, Norman Wrigley
Howard, Pattie W. (Coleman)
Howard, Paul Lindsay
Howard, Reese Evans
Howard-Jasper, Jane
Howe, Carroll Victor
Howe, David Glen
Howe, Stanley Russell
Howell, Bonnie Howard
Howell, David McBrier
Howell, James Burt, III
Howell, John Donald
Howell, Roger, Jr.
Howell, Wendell
Hower, Rolland Oliver
Howes, Alfred Spencer
Howie, Kenneth Earle
Howland, Reeve Scott
Howlett, Charles Francis
Hoxie, Ralph Gordon
Hoxter, Curtis Joseph
Hoy, John Wesley, Jr.
Hoyer-Ellefsen, Sigurd
Hrize, Michael Charles, Jr.
Hrybinsky, Borys Oleksandriv
Hrycak, Peter
Hsia, Wei Jen
Hsiao, Mu-Yue
Hsieh, Hsiun Philip
Hsu, Benedict S. (Pei-Shiung)
Hsu, Donald Kunghsing
Hsu, Enrico Yun Ping
Hsu, Joseph Jen-yuan
Hsu, Konrad Chang
Hsu, Robert Ying
Hsu, Samuel
Hsu, Yingchieh
Hsu, Yu Kao
Htoo, Maung Shwe
Hu, Shih-En
Huang, Jacob Chen-ya
Huang, Joseph Chen-Huan
Huang, Shi-Shung
Hubbard, Edward Derry
Hubbard, Herbert Hendrix
Hubbard, Kenneth Edward
Hubbell, Harold Berresford
Huber, Gary Louis
Huber, Joan MacMonnies
Huber, Richard Gregory
Huber, Richard Miller
Huber, William Stokes
Huberman, Benjamin
Hubley, Cecil Ernest Francis
Hubley, Dorothy Graybill
Huckins, Harold Aaron
Huckman, Louis Fillmore
Huddleston, Robert Leslie
Hudgens, (Luther) Elmore
Hudson, Edwin Morris
Hudson, Grace Alberta Powers
Hudson, Jane Duclos
Hudson, Norman Wright
Hudson, Robert McKim
Huebner, Charles Augustus
Huebner, Mildred Harriet
Huebner, Stephen Jude
Hueffman, Robert Arvid
Huet, James Armand
Huettner, Richard Alfred
Huff, Joseph Anthony
Hug, Richard Ernest
Hugg, Terry Wayne
Huggins, George Richardson
Hughes, Audrey Clayre
Hughes, Blake
Hughes, Harry Roe
Hughes, James Joseph
Hughes, Janet Blanche
Hughes, John
Hughes, Jonah
Hughes, Lloyd Lynnell
Hughes, Richard Elmer
Hughes, Richard Joseph
Hughes, Richard Morrell
Hughes, Robert Emmett
Hughes, William John
Huheey, James E(dward)
Huk, Jerome E.
Huk, Michael John
Huk, Stefanie Michalina (Mrs. Wladimir Huk)
Hulack, Lawrence Bernard
Hull, Lewis Madison
Hulme, Robert DuBois
Hulslander, Frank Raymond
Hulswit, Marius Jan (Mart)
Humble, Leon Karl
Hume, David John
Humes, Charles Warren, II
Hummel, Frances Cope
Humphrey, Chester Bowden
Humphrey, Gordon John
Humphrey, Steven Roy
Humphrey, William Roland

Humphreys, Donald Robert
Humphreys, James Patton
Humphreys, Raymond V.
Humphreys, Robert Harold
Humphries, Edythe Marie
Hungerford, Dale
Hunley, Ann Bernice Suggs
Hunt, Ann Loretta
Hunt, Dorothy Kendrix
Hunt, Earl Joseph
Hunt, Florine Elizabeth
Hunt, Francis Howard
Hunt, Frederick Talley Drum, Jr.
Hunt, Harry Draper
Hunt, James Ramsey
Hunt, John Wesley
Hunt, Martha Elizabeth (Mrs. Rolfe Lanier Hunt)
Hunt, Nora Lee
Hunt, Roderick Thomas
Hunt, Roy Arthur, Jr.
Hunt, Ruth Cecelia
Hunt, William Haward
Hunter, (James) Graham
Hunter, Herbert Erwin
Hunter, James Alston Hope
Hunter, Jehu Callis
Hunter, John Graham
Hunter, Joseph Vincent
Hunter, Mabel Alden
Hunter, Mel
Hunter, Robert Douglas
Hunter, William Robert
Hunting, Margaret Hazel
Huntington, Earl L.
Huntley, Robert Ross
Huntley, William Robert
Huntoon, Robert Brian
Huntsman, Lawrence Darrow
Huntzinger, Thomas Elton
Hurd, Priscilla Payne
Hurd, Yorick Gordon
Hurford, John Boyce
Hurlburt, C(harles) Graham
Hurlburt, John Henry
Hurlbut, Robert Harold
Hurley, Alfred Benedict, Jr.
Hurley, Frank Edward
Hurley, Jeremiah Joseph
Hurley, John Philip
Hurst, Andre (Bundy)
Hurt, Edward Paulette
Hurt, Ikey West
Hurt, Susanne Morris (Mrs. Marshall Hurt)
Hurvich, Marvin Samuel
Hurwitz, Carlyle Harold
Hurwitz, David Lyman
Hurwitz, Richard Arthur
Hurwitz, Sidney
Husar, Emile
Hushard, Linda Lee
Hutchens, William David
Hutchins, Christopher
Hutchins, Thomas William
Hutchinson, Alan Bradford
Hutchinson, John Edward, III
Hutchinson, John Joseph
Hutchinson, Robert Baker
Hutchinson, William Dodge
Hutelmyer, Carol M.
Hutner, Joseph Louis
Hutsaliuk, Lubo
Hutton, Duane
Hutton, Jack Gossett, Jr.
Huyot, Suzanne
Hwang, Jennmow
Hyams, Vincent Joseph
Hyde, Henry Baldwin
Hyde, William Ray
Hyer, Frank Sidney
Hyett, Marvin Ronald
Hykes, Richard Norman
Hyland, William Francis
Hyman, Bruce Malcolm
Hyman, Irwin A.
Hynds, Francis Joseph, Jr.
Hynek, Walter Joseph
Hyson, Charles David
I, Ting Po
Iacangelo, Peter August, Jr.
Iacovides, Tasos Iacovos
Iams, William Bowman
Iannelli, Joseph George
Ibbotson, Jeffrey
Icken, Joseph Martin
Ifill, Gordon Gregory Leo
Iglewicz, Boris
Igou, Raymond Alvin, Jr.
Ih, Charles Chung Sen
Ikenberry, Henry Cephas, Jr.
Ilacqua, Rosario S.
Ilasi, Robert Thomas
Ilem, Priscilla G. (Mrs. Len Madlansacay)
Iman, Faruq Taiwo Nyahuma (Gregory Brevard Smart)
Imbert, Patrick Louis
Imbier, Edward Allen
Imerti, Arthur Dante
Imhof, Howard Emil
Imler, James Harold Eugene
ImMasche, Francis William
Impastato, David John
Imperato, Pascal James
Imrie, Robert Woodall
Imus, Alden Elon, Jr.
Inciardi, James A.
Inden, Arthur
Indermaur, Frederick Norman
Indik, Bernard Paul
Inel, Yavuz
Ingaglio, Diego Augustus
Ingalls, Chester Wallace
Ingerman, Peter Zilahy
Ingersoll, Ralph McAllister, II
Ingham, John Frederick
Ingis, Gail
Inglisa, Domenic Ronald
Ingraham, Harold Edward
Ingram, Robert Russell, Jr.
Ingram, William Truitt
Innis, Walter Deane
Inno, Karl
Inns, Harry Douglas Ellis
Integlia, Barbara Ann
Into, Henry Alexander
Iorizzo, Luciano John
Ippolito, Andrew Vincent
Ippolito, Anthony David
Ippolito, Carlo Amedeo
Ippolito, Joseph Frank
Ireland, Herbert Allen
Irey, Nelson Sumner
Irish, George Henry, Jr.
Irish, Leon Eugene
Irmiger, Ernst Henry
Irvine, Kenneth Andrew
Irvine, Louva Elizabeth
Irvine, R. Gerald
Irvine, Reed John
Irving, Leonard Morton
Irving, Robert Augustine
Irving, Robert Churchill
Irwin, Howard Samuel, Jr.
Irwin, Marie Emily
Irwin, William Joseph
Isaacs, Helen Coolidge Adams (Mrs. Kenneth L. Isaacs)
Isaacs, Richard Bruce
Isaacson, Edith Lipsig
Isaacson, H. Harding
Isaacson, Sidney
Isaak, Elmer Bramwell
Isabelle, Ronald Andre
Isakson, Louis
Isay, Richard Alexander
Isch, Anthony Clarence
Isenberg, Arthur Newton
Isenberg, Henry David
Isenberg, Morris
Ishikawa, Akira
Ishikawa, Hidehiko
Israel, Adrian Cremieux
Israel, David Joseph
Israel, Hyman
Israels, Charles Henry
Israelson, Byron James
Isselbacher, Kurt Julius
Isserstedt, Siegfried Gordon
Itkin, Stanley Lawrence
Iutcovich, Mark
Ivanhoe, Herman
Ivarson, Karl Christian
Ivashkiv, Eugene
Iverson, Warren Philip
Ives, David Otis
Ivey, Jean Eichelberger
Ivie, Evan Leon
Iwamoto, Takeo
Iwanisziw, Nicholas
Iwata, Harry Masando
Iyer, Sury
Izzi, John Donald
Izzo, Joseph Domminick
Izzo, Louis Dominic
Izzo, Thomas Nicholas
Jablonski, Wanda Mary
Jabush, Marjorie Lois
Jackel, Simon Samuel
Jackiewicz, Irene Elizabeth
Jackim, Halas Leonadus
Jackovich, Anthony Barthlov
Jacks, Ulysses
Jackson, Alexander Wallace
Jackson, Arthur Gregg
Jackson, Charles Neason, II
Jackson, Daniel Rudolph
Jackson, Donald Edwin
Jackson, Donald Voorhees
Jackson, Fritz Robert
Jackson, Gerald Gregory
Jackson, Gerard James
Jackson, Gilbert Serge
Jackson, James Edward
Jackson, James Edward
Jackson, Lloyd Peter
Jackson, Marilyn Ann
Jackson, Marion Tillman
Jackson, Patricia Lee (Mrs. Clifford L. Jackson)
Jackson, Pazel G., Jr.
Jackson, Robert Gene
Jackson, Robert Wilson
Jackson, Russell FFolliott
Jackson, Theodore Marshall
Jackson, Thomas Harold
Jacob, Adir
Jacob, Charles Elmer
Jacob, James Thecattil
Jacob, Jonah Hye
Jacobowitz, Walter Erwin
Jacobs, Alvin David
Jacobs, Averille Esther
Jacobs, Denholm Muir
Jacobs, E(ugene) Gardner, Jr.
Jacobs, Eleanor Alice
Jacobs, Eugene Leslie
Jacobs, George B.
Jacobs, Harold Milton
Jacobs, Harry Lewis
Jacobs, Harvey Michael
Jacobs, Jerold Lance
Jacobs, John Francis
Jacobs, Joseph
Jacobs, Lawrence David
Jacobs, Linda Joan (Mrs. Martin Howard Jacobs)
Jacobs, Norman Allan
Jacobs, Richard David
Jacobs, Stanley Ralph
Jacobs, Theodore Alan
Jacobs, Walter Darnell
Jacobsen, William Dutton
Jacobson, Alf Edgar
Jacobson, Avrohm
Jacobson, Chester Frederick
Jacobson, Harold Gordon
Jacobson, Jacob Leon
Jacobson, James Peter
Jacobson, Nita Jean Grossman (Mrs. Irwin Robert Jacobson)
Jacobson, Willard James
Jacobus, David Penman
Jacoby, Arthur William
Jacoby, Robert Eakin, Jr.
Jacolev, Leon
Jacolow, Jerald Joshua
Jaffe, Donald
Jaffe, Frederick Stanley
Jaffe, Harold
Jaffe, Herbert M.
Jaffe, Mark M.
Jaffe, Nissen Asher
Jaffe, Rubin Israel
Jaffe, Steven
Jafri, Mokarram Husain
Jagel, Kenneth Irwin, Jr.
Jagodzinski, Norbert Steven
Jagow, Charles Herman
Jahiel, Deborah Berg (Mrs. Rene Jahiel)
Jakab, Irene
Jakes, Ronald Walter
Jaklitsch, Joseph John, Jr.
Jakmauh, Edward
Jakubowski, John Anthony
Jalette, Ronald Joseph
Jalowski, Walter Augustine
James, Charles Robert
James, Edward Monroe
James, Jesse
James, (Walter) Raymond
James, Robert Harold
James, Ronald Lee
James, William Hall
James, Winfield Henry
Jameson, Sanford Chandler
Jameson, William Charles
Jamieson, John Anthony
Jamison, Charles Newman
Jamison, Grady Earl
Jamison, Howard Maloy
Jamison, Patricia Ann Richardson (Mrs. Edgar Merritt Jamison, Jr.)
Jamison, Richard Gates
Jamme, Susan Hamlin (Mrs. Louis Theodore Jamme)
Janczak, Andrew Anthony
Janelli, Donald Ernest
Janesak, Charles Paul
Janeski, William Louis
Janetta, Nicholas John
Janicke, Jack M.
Janicki, Casimir A.
Janjigian, Edward Rupen
Janjigian, Hannah M. (Mrs. Edward R. Janjigian)
Jankowski, Walter Joseph
Janney, Mary Draper
Janowski, Stanley Joseph
Janschka, Fritz
Januzzi, Ronald Everett
Janz, Abraham Alan
Jarecki, Richard Wilhelm
Jarman, Ronald Brian
Jarnes, Frederic Myron
Jaron, Dov
Jaroslawicz, Isaac Mordechai
Jarvis, Edward Baxter
Jarvis, Lynville Walter
Jasen, David Alan
Jaskoll, Ira Leslie
Jaspen, Nathan
Jasser, Ronald M.
Jastak, Joseph Florian
Jastrab, Robert Frank
Jaszczun, Wasyl
Javits, Jacob Koppel
Jaworek, Terrance Edward
Jaworska, Tamara
Jay, Barry
Jay, Francis
Jay, Hilda Lease
Jay, Murray
Jaynes, Julian
Jazwinski, Andrew Honore
Jeffee, Saul
Jefferds, Charles Dennis
Jefferson, David Rowe
Jefferson, Joseph
Jeffery, Seymour
Jeffery, William Prentiss, Jr.
Jeffords, James Merrill
Jeffrey, Adi-Kent Thomas (Mrs. Gilbert Jeffrey)
Jeffrey, Louis Paul
Jeffreys, Joyce Ester
Jeghers, Harold Joseph
Jehu, John Paul
Jelinek, Josef Emil
Jendras, Henry John
Jenkins, George Pollock
Jenkins, Harry Alexander
Jenkins, John Burr
Jenkins, Kenneth Vincent
Jenkins, Mac Dean
Jenkins, Martin Edward
Jenkins, Paul Reiber
Jenkins, Ruth Elizabeth
Jennings, Alice Thelma
Jennings, Donald E.
Jennings, Frank Gouverneur
Jennings, Marlene Helen Luke
Jennings, Michael Glenn
Jennings, Robert Lee
Jennings, William Mitchell
Jennison, George L.
Jenny, Albert
Jenny, Robert James
Jensen, Arthur S(eigfried)
Jensen, Betty
Jensen, David Lynn
Jensen, Grady Edmonds
Jensen, J. Michael
Jensen, Richard Alan
Jensen, Robert P.
Jensen, Roy Joseph, Jr.
Jensh, Ronald Paul
Jentsch, Suellen
Jepson, John Willisford
Jernigan, Harry William, III
Jernigan, Thomas Priestly, III
Jerome, Frederick Louis
Jerrehian, Charles Krikor
Jerrells, Thomas Ray
Jesch, Paul Douglas
Jessar, Jonathan Sander
Jessen, Martin Daniel
Jessup, Michael Hyle
Jester, Roberts Charles, Jr.
Jeter, Katherine Feagin
Jette, Roger Joseph
Jetter, Lawrence Klosson
Jetter, Walter W.
Jewelewicz, Raphael
Jewell, Marvin Eugene
Jewett, John Willits, Jr.
Jhaveri, Indra Sarabhai
Jillette, Arthur George, Jr.
Jimenez, Sergio Astete
Jimeson, Robert MacKay, Jr.
Jindrak, Frank
Jodoin, Maurice Alain
Joens, Claus Jurgen
Joffe, Julia Elizabeth Schuelke (Mrs. Lester L. Joffe)
Joffrey, Robert (Abdullah Jaffa Bey Khan)
Johanson, Patricia Maureen
Johnpoll, Bernard Keith
Johns, Anthony George
Johns, Elizabeth Lambert
Johns, Walter Scott, III
Johns, William, Jr.
Johnson, Alfred
Johnson, Angela Blanche
Johnson, Barbara DiGiacomo
Johnson, Benjamin Washington
Johnson, Bonnie Lutzky
Johnson, Bruce
Johnson, Carl Harold
Johnson, Catherine Common
Johnson, Cecile Ryden (Mrs. Philip Johnson)
Johnson, Charles Frank
Johnson, Charles Victor
Johnson, Charles Warren
Johnson, Curtiss Sherman
Johnson, David Michael
Johnson, Earl
Johnson, Edna DeCoursey (Mrs. Laurence H. Johnson)
Johnson, Estella Scott (Mrs. Rufus C. Johnson)
Johnson, Eugene Manfred
Johnson, F. Eugene (Gene)
Johnson, Florence Giffin
Johnson, Geary Juan
Johnson, George Babcock
Johnson, Gustave Hilmer, Jr.
Johnson, Howard Eugene
Johnson, Howard Wesley
Johnson, James Pearce
Johnson, Jane Miller (Mrs. Napoleon B. Johnson)
Johnson, John Brayton
Johnson, John Henry
Johnson, John Robert
Johnson, John William
Johnson, Katharyn Price (Mrs. Edward F. Johnson)
Johnson, Kenneth LeRoy
Johnson, Kenneth Theodore
Johnson, Laurance Dean, Jr.
Johnson, Lawrence H.
Johnson, Lawrence William, Jr.
Johnson, Lester Fredrick
Johnson, Malcolm Clinton, Jr.
Johnson, Margaret Hill
Johnson, Marie Love
Johnson, Olaf Andreas
Johnson, Orville Howard
Johnson, Paul Edward
Johnson, Paul Nathaniel, Jr.
Johnson, Paul O.
Johnson, Philip Edward
Johnson, Ralph James
Johnson, Richard F.Q.
Johnson, Robert Alan
Johnson, Roswell Dorr
Johnson, Selina Tetzlaff
Johnson, Shildes Risdon Vail
Johnson, Sue Storer (Mrs. Donald C. Johnson)
Johnson, Theodore Martin
Johnson, Thomas Bradford, Jr.
Johnson, Thomas Frank
Johnson, Viola Victoria
Johnson, Walter Herbert
Johnson, Walter J.
Johnson, William Charles
Johnston, Don
Johnston, Josephine R.
Johnston, Kevin Philip
Johnston, Laura Lee
Johnston, Thomas Matkins
Johnston, William Andrew, Jr.
Johnstone, Dorn Kenneth
Joiner, Robert Russell
Joison, Julio
Joline, Robert Merritt
Jolly, Wayne Travis
Jon, Min-Chung
Jonas, Charles Saul
Jonas, Gilbert
Jonassohn, Kurt
Jones, Andrew Ross
Jones, Barclay Gibbs
Jones, Charles Davis
Jones, Charles Hill, Jr.
Jones, Christine Constance di Grandi
Jones, Compton Seth
Jones, Curtis Edison
Jones, David Milton
Jones, Donald Irvine
Jones, Donald Leroy
Jones, E. Stewart, Jr.
Jones, Eugene Harvey
Jones, Farrell
Jones, Floretta Jeanette
Jones, Franklin Reed
Jones, George Green
Jones, George Richard
Jones, Gerre Lyle
Jones, Guy Wilson
Jones, Harry McCoy
Jones, Henry William, Jr.
Jones, Homer Walter
Jones, Howard Lamar
Jones, Howard Langworthy
Jones, Ira Snow
Jones, James Edward
Jones, James Robert
Jones, John Wiley
Jones, Joseph
Jones, Lewis Posey
Jones, Maurice Bruce
Jones, Parker Tull
Jones, Paul Daniel
Jones, Paul Eugene, Jr.
Jones, Reginald Harold
Jones, Richard Ditzel
Jones, Robert Allan
Jones, Robert Charles
Jones, Robert Emmet
Jones, Robert Michael
Jones, Robert St. Clair
Jones, Russell Richard
Jones, Ruth Ella
Jones, Sidney Alexander
Jones, Thomas Edward
Jones, Vernon
Jones, Walter Lewis, Jr.
Jong, Anthony
Jordain, Philip Bernard
Jordan, Dennis Edward
Jordan, Helen Sankey
Jordan, James Nicholas
Jordan, Lawrence Marcellus
Jordan, Louis Hampton
Jordan, Marilyn Keys
Jordan, Paul
Jordan, Robert Paul
Jordan, Ronald Joseph
Jordan, Ruth Ann
Jordan, Trenholm Douglas
Jordan, Vernon Eulion, Jr.
Jordan Cox, Carmen Antoinette
Jordano, Joseph Peter
Jorgensen, Alfred H.
Jorgensen, Charles William
Jorgensen, Norma Anderson (Mrs. Albert Nels Jorgensen, Jr.)
Jose, Norman Lord
Joseph, Edna Whitehead (Mrs. Lawrence J. Joseph)
Joseph, J. Jonathan
Joseph, Leonard
Joseph, Ronald Anthony
Joseph, Stanley Robert
Josephson, Julian
Josephson, Mark Eric
Josey, E(lonnie) J(unius)
Joshi, Kailash Chandra
Joskow, Jules
Joubert, Lucien Léon
Joukhadar, Moumtaz
Journey, Drexel Dahlke
Jovanovic, Miodrag
Joyce, Bernita Anne
Joyce, Charles Raymond, Jr.
Joyce, David
Joyce, Joseph Robert
Joyce, Robert Paul
Joyner, Claude Reuben, Jr.
Juan, Gerardo Agustin
Judd, Alvan Bradford
Judd, John Edmund
Judson, Arthur, II
Judson, Jeannette Alexander (Mrs. Henry Judson)
Jueneman, Robert Reade
Juhl, Daniel Leo
Juliano, Frank Anthony
Juliano, John Louis
Junice, William Joseph
Junkerman, William Joseph
Junkins, David Randall
Jurkowski, Frances Farrell
Jurma, Mall Kuusik
Jurshevski, Harald William
Juster, Barbara Wallach
Justice, Margaret Kelley
Jutras, Rene
Juvonen, Toico Arvi
Juzaitis, John Daniel
Jydstrup, Ronald Albert
Kabadi, Balachandra N.
Kabak, Daniel M.
Kabak, Martin
Kac, Arthur Wayne
Kaczera, Zygmunt Stefan
Kade, Charles Frederick, Jr.
Kaden, William Stephen
Kadison, Herbert
Kafka, Fritz
Kafka, Roger
Kagan, Michael Bruce
Kaganov, Alan Lawrence
Kaggen, Elias
Kahalas, Henry Noren
Kahen, Harold I.
Kahn, B. Franklin
Kahn, Edward
Kahn, Gloria Batkin
Kahn, Robert Samuel
Kahn, Samuel
Kahn, Sidney
Kahn, Walter
Kahn, Werner David
Kaiser, Frederick Martin
Kaiser, Hans Elmar
Kaiser, Katherine Elizabeth
Kaiser, Ronald Saul
Kaiser, William Tustin
Kaladow, Arthur Robert
Kalapinski, Alphonse Anthony
Kalemaris, Stanley George, Jr.
Kalfus, Stanley
Kalijarvi, Thorsten Valentine
Kalimian, Manouchehr Michael
Kalina, Ivan
Kalinich, John
Kalkhof, Thomas Corrigan
Kalkus, Stanley
Kaller, Harold Milton
Kalmanoff, Martin
Kalsner, Stanley
Kalter, Jerald Scott
Kalugin, David
Kalynych, Lubomyr Eugene
Kamback, Marvin C.
Kamell, Michael W.
Kamen, Max Lawrence
Kamerer, Donald Bailey
Kamermayer, Arthur Stuart
Kamikawa, Alden Tanemitsu
Kamil, Bonnie Beth
Kamin, Arthur Zavel
Kaminsky, Jack Allan
Kamm, Laurence Richard
Kamm, Lewis Robert
Kamp, Gerald Wesley
Kamp, Theo
Kandalaft, Souheil Ibrahim
Kandravy, John
Kane, David Schilling
Kane, Edward Rynex
Kane, George Eugene
Kane, James Karl
Kane, Jay Brassler
Kane, John Joseph
Kane, John Martin
Kane, John Thomas
Kane, Joseph Henry
Kane, Margaret Brassler
Kane, Margaret C.
Kane, Nolan Paul
Kane, Robert Francis
Kane, Robert Patrick
Kane, Sarah Taylor
Kane, Steven Irwin
Kane, Sydney H.
Kane, Thomas Joseph
Kanev, Phillip Sydney
Kang, Hank Haengjung
Kania, Arthur John
Kanigowski, Walter Wolfgang
Kant, Edward Jacob
Kanter, Spencer I.
Kantor, Martin Leonard
Kanuk, Leslie Lazar
Kanwisher, Walter Charles, Jr.
Kapetanakos, Christos Anastasios
Kaplan, Alan
Kaplan, Gary
Kaplan, Harold Irwin
Kaplan, Judith Helene
Kaplan, Leonard Martin (Aryeh)
Kaplan, Nolan Scott
Kaplan, Robert
Kaplan, Ronald V.
Kaplan, Sanford Allen
Kaplan, William Meyer
Kaplow, Herbert Elias
Kapner, Kermit Harold
Kapotes, Charles Nicholas
Kapp, Edwin Victor
Kappel, R. Rose
Kappler, Robert Paul
Kaprow, Maurice Shalom
Kar, Anil Krishna
Karan, Val Elliot
Kardon, Leroy
Karl, Dorothy Theresa
Karlan, Frances Ross
Karlin, Muriel Schoenbrun (Mrs. Leonard Karlin)
Karlson, Janet Falter Weil (Mrs. Carl Karlson)
Karniol, Hilda Hutterer (Mrs. Frank Karniol)
Karol, Eugene Michael
Karol, Robert Stanley
Karp, Harvey Lawrence
Karp, Peter Simon
Karp, William B.
Karpati, Frank Stephen
Karpen, Edward William
Karpinski, Joseph Paul
Karsen, Sonja Petra
Karstetter, Allan Boyd
Kasberg, Alvin Harvey
Kasdan, Louis Ross
Kasdon, Lawrence W.
Kase, Harold Michael

Kase, Stuart
Kasey, Gary Alex
Kashgarian, Michael
Kashin, Philip
Kashiwa, Shiro
Kasich, Anthony Milosh
Kasiewicz, Allen Bernard
Kasindorf, Blanche Robins
Kasner, Victor Herbert
Kasper, Rolf Gunther
Kasperbauer, James Clemens
Kaspersson, Eino Victor
Kass, Benny Lee
Kassab, Vincent
Kassay, Michael Bela
Kasser, Ivan Michael
Kassoff, Edwin
Kassum, Saleem
Kastner, William Joseph
Kasuga, Bill
Katayama, Daniel Hideo
Katayama, Isao
Katayama, Jane Hatsue
Kateb, George Anthony
Kates, Kenneth Casper, Sr.
Katims, Herman
Katis, James George
Katkin, Sylvia Sobel
Katsaros, Thomas
Katsh, Abraham I(saac)
Katsifis, Christos C.
Katz, Ascher
Katz, Carole Sue
Katz, Friedrich Joachim
Katz, Gilbert
Katz, Herbert Marvin
Katz, Hilda (Hulda Weber)
Katz, Irwin Alan
Katz, Irwin B.
Katz, Joel Richard
Katz, Julian
Katz, Leonard Allen
Katz, Morris
Katz, Norman
Katz, Philip Carlton
Katz, Robert
Katz, Robert Nathan
Katz, Seymour
Katz, Seymour
Katz, Steven Edward
Katz, Theodore Harry
Katz, William David
Katzen, Howard Marvin
Katzen, Lila Pell (Mrs. Philip Katzen)
Katzin, Dick
Katzin, Herbert Maurice
Kaufer, Gerald Ira
Kauffman, Betty Craft
Kauffman, Bruce William
Kauffman, George Elwood, III
Kauffman, Leon A.
Kauffman, Ronald Hugh
Kauffman, Stephen H.
Kauffmann, Howard C.
Kaufman, Barry Morton
Kaufman, Frank Albert
Kaufman, Harold Alexander
Kaufman, Harry Harris
Kaufman, Herman Samuel
Kaufman, Irving Robert
Kaufman, John Robert
Kaufman, Kenneth Franklin
Kaufman, Michael David
Kaufman, Mico
Kaufman, Myron L.
Kaufman, Robert Max
Kaufman, Seymour Alvin
Kaufman, Stephen Frederick
Kaufman, Stephen Lawrence
Kaufmann, Axel
Kaufmann, Ed
Kaufmann, Walter (Arnold)
Kaufmann, Yoram
Kaunitz, Rita Davidson
Kauth, Benjamin
Kavarnos, George James
Kavee, Robert Charles
Kavic, Michael Stephen
Kavner, Richard Stanley
Kawatra, Mahendra P.
Kay, Stanley Robert
Kayali, Kaled Muhamad
Kayaloff, Jacques
Kayatt, Edith Sutphen
Kaye, Judith Smith (Mrs. Stephen Rackow Kaye)
Kaye, Robert Edward
Kaye, Robert Martin
Kaye, Stephen Rackow
Kaye, William Mark
Kaylani, Nabil Mustafa
Kazemi, Homayoun
Keady, George Cregan, Jr.
Kean, John Vaughan
Kean, Michael Henry
Kean, Norman
Keane, (Mary) Antonia
Kearney, Anthony John
Kearney, Kathleen M.
Kearney, Thomas Raymond
Kearns, Karen Wister
Keating, Frank Edward
Keating, Frank J.
Keating, James Francis, Jr.
Keating, June Gertrude
Keating, William Francis, Jr.
Keech, Roger Lee
Keefe, Thomas Joseph, Jr.
Keeffe, John Arthur
Keegan, Marcia Kay
Keehan, Matthew Joseph, Jr.
Keel, Alton Gold, Jr.
Keeler, Mary Frear
Keeler, Russell M., Jr.
Keely, Ann
Keen, Raymond Wallace
Keenan, Michael Edgar
Keenan, Terrance
Keene, Philip
Keeney, June Marie
Keesee, Thomas Woodfin, Jr.
Kegelman, William
Keggi, John
Kegl-Bognar, Desi
Kehl, Peter Jerome
Kehnemui, Azer
Kehoe, Vincent Jeffré-Roux
Kehoe, William Vincent de Paul
Kehr, Clifton Leroy
Keimel, Fred Albert
Keiser, Gerd Emdo
Keiser, Henry Bruce
Keisman, Ira B.
Keith, Allan Reed
Keith, Leroy, Jr.
Keith, Quentin Gangewere
Keith, William Hale
Kelemen, Emery Imre
Kelland, Donald Edgar Jackman
Keller, David Mathias
Keller, Donald Monroe
Keller, George William
Keller, Margaret Gilmer (Mrs. George Henry Keller, III)
Kelley, Francis Joseph
Kelley, Maurice Leslie, Jr.
Kelley, Michael Armstrong
Kelley, Sheila Seymour (Mrs. Robert M. Kaufman)
Kellner, George Andrew
Kellner, Louis Daniel
Kellogg, Ralph Martin
Kellogg-Smith, Ogden
Kellow, William Francis
Kelly, Clarence James
Kelly, Cornelius James Noel
Kelly, David Austin
Kelly, Donald John
Kelly, Donald Kaempfer
Kelly, Doris Lillian
Kelly, Dorothy Libby
Kelly, Edward Aloysius, Jr.
Kelly, Francis W.
Kelly, Gerald Ray
Kelly, John William, Jr.
Kelly, Marcus Ray
Kelly, Robert Lynn
Kelly, Robert William
Kelly, Stephen John
Kelly, Thomas Cajetan
Kelly, Walter Joslyn
Kelly, William (Eager)
Kelly, William Gerard
Kelman, Wolfe
Kelmenson, Leo Arthur
Kelsey, Chester Creed
Kelsey, Roger Raymond
Kelso, Timothy Edward
Kelting, Howard William
Kelton, John T(remain)
Kem, Jan Alan
Kemble, Richard
Kemble, Robert Penn
Kemelhor, Robert Elias
Kemeny, John George
Kemler, Raphael Leonard
Kemp, Darryl Russell
Kemp, Jack F.
Kemp, John Bartlett, III
Kemper, Albert Gilbert
Kempner, Carl Loeb
Kempner, Robert Max Wasilii
Kempter, Rudolph Harbison, Jr.
Kemsley, William George, Jr.
Kemsley, William George, Sr.
Kendall, Donald McIntosh
Kendall, Katherine Anne
Kendall, Leigh Wakefield
Kendall, Terry Lee
Kender, Dorothy
Kender, Walter John
Kendree, Jack McLean
Kennard, John Frederick
Kennedy, Chester Ralph, Jr.
Kennedy, Cornelius Bryant
Kennedy, Daniel G.
Kennedy, Donald Gerry
Kennedy, Edward Moore
Kennedy, Evelyn Siefert
Kennedy, Helen Marie
Kennedy, James Jerome
Kennedy, John Anthony
Kennedy, John Francis
Kennedy, Joyce Lain (Mrs. William A. Kennedy)
Kennedy, Lyle H.
Kenney, Alan John
Kenney, Douglas Blaine
Kenney, Guilea Lehan
Kenney, Richard Alec
Kenny, James Connolly
Kenny, Lisa Ann
Kensil, James Lewis
Kent, Barry J.
Kent, Charles Imbrie, III
Kent, Donald Seymour
Kent, Sherman Van Ness
Kent, William Horace
Kentner, Harold Miller
Kenton, Edgar Jackson, III
Kenton, Glenn C.
Kenzora, John Edward
Kenzy, John Quinton
Keohan, Edward Joseph
Kepler, Jacqueline Cosette
Keppler, John Jacob
Kerby, William Frederick
Kern, Arthur Howard
Kern, Frank Norton
Kern, Herbert Louis
Kerner, Fred
Kerner, Jerome
Kernstock, Elwyn Nicholas
Kerpchar, Michael
Kerr, Andrew David, Jr.
Kerr, Ann Thomas (Mrs. William Ernest Kerr)
Kerr, Frank John
Kerr, Hazel Maud Smith
Kerr, James Wilson
Kerr, Mabel Dorothea
Kerr, Robert McNab, Jr.
Kerr, Rose Gladys Hall
Kerr, William Edward
Kersey, George Euclid
Kershaw, Gordon Ernest
Kershaw, Thomas Martin
Kershner, Bernard
Kertz, Harold Allan
Kerzman, Norberto Luis Maria
Keshen, Albert Sidney
Keshishoglou, John Elias
Kesler, Michael Guberman
Kessler, Herman Eugene
Kessler, Jacques Isaac
Kessler, Milton Seymour
Kessler, Ronald Borek
Kessler, Stuart Alan
Kessman, Alan Stuart
Kester, Nancy Conrad
Kestin, Howard H.
Ketcham, Orman Weston
Ketchum, Alton Harrington
Ketchum, William Clarence, Jr.
Keto, Clement Tsehloane
Ketter, Robert Lewis
Ketting, Jaap
Kettler, Milton Ellsworth
Ketvirtis, Antanas
Ketz, Louise Bilebof
Keyes, Charles Don
Keyes, Henry Wilder
Keyes, Joseph Patrick
Keyko, George John
Khadem, Ramin
Khajavi-Noori, Farrokh
Khakee, Abdulaziz Gulamali
Khalil, Hatem Mohamed
Khalil, Tawfik Abdulkarim
Khan, Abdul Jamil
Khan, Aijaz Mohammad
Khandelwal, Deen Dayal
Khantzian, Edward John
Khella, Lewis
Khoja, Mirza A.
Khouri, Fred John
Khury, Costandy Khalil
Kibbe, James William
Kibbee, Robert Joseph
Kibre, Pearl
Kidd, Jerome Thomas
Kidde, John Lyon
Kidder, Nathaniel Remington
Kienzle, John Fred
Kierman, Frank Algerton, Jr.
Kiernan, David Hastings
Kiesel, Beatrice
Kiessel, William Carl
Kiev, Ari
Kihn, Harry
Kikoski, John Frank, Jr.
Kikta, Edward Joseph, Jr.
Kilburn, Henry Thomas, Jr.
Kiley, Edward E.
Killen, Carroll Gorden
Killian, John Doran
Killian, Robert Kenneth
Kilmann, Ralph Herman
Kilmartin, Joseph Francis, Jr.
Kilsheimer, Sister Jean Dolores
Kim, Andrew Byong-Soo
Kim, Charles Chang Suh
Kim, Charles Wesley
Kim, Dae Un
Kim, Damian Byungsuk
Kim, Geun-Eun Bartholomew
Kim, Ih Chin
Kim, Ilpyong John
Kim, Je Chul
Kim, Kyu Sung (Hugh)
Kim, Seong Hwan
Kim, Tai Kyung
Kim, Yoon Choo
Kim, You Song
Kim, Young Ho
Kiman, Richard Aaron
Kimball, George Hardy
Kimball, Mary Lee Evans (Mrs. Chase Kimball)
Kimble, Edwin Lockard, Jr.
Kimble, Seruch Titus
Kimm, Richard Miles
Kimmel, Robert Irving
Kimmins, Warwick Charles
Kimpel, Benjamin Franklin
Kimura, Michio
Kinard, Charles Donald
Kinas, Ernest Nicholas
Kindl, Fred Henry
Kindle, Cecil Haldane
Kindle, Mary Ethel Smyers (Mrs. Cecil Haldane Kindle)
Kindred, George Charles
King, Alicia
King, Barbara Jean
King, Charles Thomas
King, Conrad David
King, Donald DeWolf
King, Edward Joseph
King, Francis Michael
King, Francis Paul
King, Henry Brazell
King, Henry Lawrence
King, Jennifer Landry
King, Joan Hone
King, John Edward
King, Joseph Patrick
King, Norman Chancis
King, Norval William
King, Paul Clinton
King, Rachel Hadley
King, Robert James
King, Robert Ogden
King, S(amuel) Edward
King, Thomas Gorden
King, Verne Lorene
King, William Douglas
Kingery, Bernard Troy
Kingsbury, Richard Alan
Kingsbury, Slocum
Kingsley, Earl James, II
Kinnard, Douglas
Kinne, Katharine (Mrs. Charles E. Sigety)
Kinney, Samuel Marks, Jr.
Kinsella, James Hall
Kinsman, Bradley Quaif
Kinstler, Everett Raymond
Kinter, William Lewis
Kintner, Robert Jennings
Kipfer, Bernice May
Kipp, Egbert Mason
Kipp, Michael Harold
Kiralis, Karl
Kiraly, Bela Kalman
Kirby, John Joseph, Jr.
Kirby, Ralph Cloudsberry
Kirby, William Kent
Kirchem, Ronald Grigsby
Kircher, Frederick John
Kirchick, Julian Gilbert
Kiriakopoulos, George Constantine
Kirk, George Vallance
Kirk, James Allen
Kirk, James Stanley
Kirkland, Bryant Mays
Kirkpatrick, Philip R.
Kirkwood, Robert
Kirpich, Phillip Zigmund
Kirschbaum, Robert Warren
Kirschman, Mary Mardas
Kirschner, Francis
Kirschner, Michael Frank
Kirschstein, Ruth Lillian (Mrs. Alan S. Rabson)
Kirshenbaum, Richard Irving
Kirshon, Stephen Arnold
Kirstein, Lincoln
Kisak, Eugene
Kise, James Nelson
Kiselik, Paul Howard
Kiser, Marie Viva Jean
Kish, Robert Stephen
Kisner, Jacob
Kissa, Erik
Kissane, Thomas
Kissel, William Thorn, Jr.
Kissinger, Henry Alfred
Kissinger, Walter Bernhard
Kissmeyer-Nielsen, Erik
Kistler, David Walter
Kistler, Jonathan Hipperling
Kistler, Warren Douglas
Kiszely, Andor
Kiszely, Joy Miller
Kitabjian, Hagop Artin
Kitahata, Luke Masahiko
Kitchen, Otis Dorsey
Kitchin, David Jackson, III
Kittrie, Nicholas N.
Kittross, John Michael
Kitzinger, Grace Marian Livengood
Kizala, Ruth Lillian
Klages, Robert Dedrick
Klancko, Robert John
Klarfeld, Joseph
Klassen, Donald August
Klatskin, Bertram
Klauber, George Thomas
Klaus, George Leonard
Klavan, Israel
Klee, Gerald D'Arcy
Kleeman, Robert Herbert
Kleiman, Howard
Klein, Alexander
Klein, Bernard
Klein, Claude Alois
Klein, Edwin
Klein, Esther (Mrs. Philip Klein)
Klein, Joel Tibor
Klein, Martin Ira
Klein, Martin John Herman
Klein, Mary Solomon
Klein, Melvin Joel
Klein, Michael David
Klein, Peter Martin
Klein, Philip
Klein, Richard Barry
Klein, Richard Harold
Klein, Richard Joseph
Klein, Richard Stephen
Klein, Seymour
Klein, Solomon Alexander
Klein, Stanley
Klein, Theodore Ulmer
Klein, Vincent M.
Kleinchester, Joseph William, Jr.
Kleinke, David Joseph
Kleinman, Irving
Klemens, Paul Gustav
Klemons, Jerome
Klenk, Eugene Leslie
Klenk, William George, II
Klevana, Leighton Quentin Joseph
Klevesahl, Fred Carl
Kligman, Albert Montgomery
Kliman, Sylvia May Stern (Mrs. Allan Kliman)
Klimas, Antanas
Kliment, Charles Karel
Kliment, Robert Michael
Kliment, Stephen Alexander
Kline, Alma
Kline, Charles Ralph
Kline, Ernest P.
Kline, Harriet (Mrs. Eugene Monroe Kline)
Kline, Henry Chapman
Kline, Michael S.
Kline, Milton Vance
Kline, Nathan Schellenberg
Kline, Richard Charles
Kline, Robert Edward
Kline, Robert Parks
Klinge, John Gorman
Klingerman, Ethel
Klink, Arthur Edwin, Jr.
Klink, James Joseph
Klino, James Louis
Klion, Daniel Earl
Kliot, David Allen
Klir, George Jiri
Klitzberg, Richard
Klitzke, Theodore Elmer
Klitzner, Robert Arthur
Klosk, Emanuel
Kloskowski, Vincent John, Jr.
Klotz, Howard Sanford
Klotz, Louis Herman
Klotz, Richard David
Klotzbach, Robert James
Kluge, John Werner
Klumpp, Oscar Edward
Klunder, Hans Karl Friedrich
Kluss, Wilfred Martin
Knapp, Audenried Whittemore
Knapp, Charles Albert
Knapp, Gordon Alwyn
Knapp, Nancy Hay
Knapper, William Hedrick
Knauf, Janine Bernice
Knearem, James Lester
Kneavel, Thomas Charles, Jr.
Kneeland, Donald Earl
Kneipp, Sally Ann
Kneller, John William
Kneppar, Stanley Robert
Knight, Edward R.
Knight, George Litch
Knight, James John
Knight, James Kenneth
Knight, William James
Knipe, Robert Daniel
Knisely, Ralph Franklin
Knob, Richard Edward
Knobler, William I.
Knorr, Betty Jewel Benkert (Mrs. Neil McLean Knorr)
Knott, Charles Arthur
Knowland, R. Thomas
Knowles, Mary Gardner
Knowlton, Kenneth Franklin
Knox, Donald Robert
Knox, Gaylord Shearer
Knox, Seymour H.
Knudsen, Raymond Barnett
Knueppel, Daniel Paul
Ko, Harvey Wayne
Ko, Jerry Jer-Ching
Ko, Robert Jer-chien
Koblenz, Lawrence William
Kobliner, Richard
Kobrine, Arthur Irwin
Kobus, Ronald Stanley
Koch, Edward I.
Koch, Edwin Ernest
Koch, Eric
Koch, James Harold
Koch, Ruth Marguerite
Koch, Vernon Charles
Koch, Virginia Greenleaf
Koch, Wayne Arthur
Kochanek, Stanley Anthony
Kocher, Ben Leon
Kocisko, Stephen John
Kodroff, Judith Katz
Koegel, William Fisher
Koehler, Isabel Winifred
Koel, Ake Ilmar
Koelbl, Dorothy June
Koelsch, William Alvin
Koenig, Arthur Howard
Koenig, Gloria Eleanor
Koenig, Gottlieb
Koenig, John Henry
Koester, Robert Joseph, Jr.
Kogstad, Rolf Egil
Koh, Hesung Chun
Kohan, Silviu
Kohl, John Preston
Kohl, Schuyler George
Kohlberg, Ira
Kohlenberg, Stanley
Köhler, Eckehart
Kohler, Samuel Harry
Kohls, Robert
Koken, James Edward
Kokoski, Robert John
Kolbe, Stanley Ernest, Jr.
Kolbert, Gerald Sheldon
Kolbye, Albert Christian, Jr.
Kolbz, Alan Charles
Kolin, Sacha
Koller, Harold Paul
Koller, Herbert
Kollevoll, Barbara Ralph
Kollias, Anthony Vasileios
Kolody, John Theodore
Koloniaris, Nicholas
Kolson, Harry
Komar, Myron
Komisar, Sura Schwartz (Sonia)
Kommers, William Jesse
Komons, Nick Alexander
Konecny, Jaro(slav) Alois
Kones, Richard Joseph
Konetzni, Albert H(enry) (Alko) (Al)
Kong, Basil Wayne
Kong, Jin Au
Konick, John Carl
Konikoff, John Jacob
Kono, Toshihiko
Konowitz, Herbert Henry
Konrad, Jane B.
Konski, James Louis
Konvalinka, Danilo
Konyk, Mary
Konzelman, Leroy Michael
Koocher, Ronald Laurence
Koonce, Samuel David
Koondel, Ira Stuart
Koons, Terry Lloyd
Koopman, Kenneth Henry
Koopman, Nicholas George
Koopmans, Tjalling Charles
Kopec, Vladimir Aladar
Kopenhaver, Patricia Ellsworth
Koplin, Norma Jean
Koppe, Edwin Frederick
Koppelman, Lee Edward
Kopple, Robert
Kopser, Arnold William
Koranda, John Timothy
Korb, Lawrence Joseph
Korben, Donald Lee
Korber, Francis Xavier
Korchynsky, Michael
Korentayer, Shay
Koret, Sydney
Korklan, Elliot Samuel
Korman, Michael Meyer
Korman, Milton Daniel
Korn, Lester Bernard
Kornblatt, David Wolfe
Kornegay, Wade Melvin
Kornfeld, Allan
Kornfeld, Leonard Robert
Kornhauser, Stanley Henry
Kornreich, Lawrence David
Korobkin, Irving
Korol, Wolodymyr
Korolczuk, Stefan Richard
Korzenik, Armand Alexander
Kosche, Eugene Robert
Koser, John Prieston
Kosinski, Jerzy Nikodem
Koss, Helen L.
Kossoff, Richard Morse
Kossuth, Donald Andrew
Kost, George John
Kost, Paul Frederick
Kostelanetz, Boris
Kostmayer, Peter Houston
Kostoulakos, Peter
Kotch, Peter Paul
Kotin, Albert
Kotval, Peshotan Sohrab
Koulias, Elizabeth Mercia
Koussa, Harold Alan
Koutselas, Kosmas Phillip
Koutsoutis, Socrates Peter
Kovatch, Jak Gene
Koven, Bernard J.
Koven, Irving Herchel
Kovner, Abraham
Kowal, Dennis Joseph
Kowalczyk, David Kenneth
Kowalski, John Joseph
Kowalski, Ronald S.
Kowarski, Chana Rose (Mrs. Avinoam Kowarski)
Koziel, William Tom
Kozlik, Theodore, Jr.
Krach, Mitchell Peter
Kraczkowski, Philip
Krafchuk, John Damion
Kraft, Alan Jay
Kraft, C. William, Jr.
Kraft, John William
Kraft, Virginia
Kraig, Abe
Krainin, Julian Arthur
Krajsa, Joseph Charles
Kral, Michael
Krall, George Ferguson, Jr.
Kram, Harvey I.
Kramer, Aaron
Kramer, Alice Marie Poulsen
Kramer, Charles Maurice
Kramer, Daniel
Kramer, Herbert William, Jr.
Kramer, Nora
Kramer, Ruth
Kramer, Walter William
Kranepool, Harry Anthony
Krasner, Louis
Krasnoff, Sidney Ourin
Krasnow, Frances (Mrs. Marcus Thau)
Krassner, Michael Bernard
Kratz, Elizabeth Orr (Mrs. David L. Kratz)
Kratzer, Guy Livingston
Kraunz, Robert Frank
Kraus, Mozelle DeWitte Bigelow (Mrs. Russell Warren Kraus)
Krause, Helen Fox (Mrs. Marvin Krause)
Krause, Richard Michael
Krauss, Leo
Krauss, William
Kraut, Joel Arthur
Krauter, Charles Frederick
Kravath, Richard Elliot

Kravchenko, Nicholas
Kravitz, Bernard Joseph
Kravitz, Henry
Kravitz, Joseph Henry
Kravitz, Rubin
Kraybill, Herman Fink
Kraybill, Richard Reist
Krebs, Margaret Eloise
Krebs, Richard Lewis
Kreek, Louis Francis, Jr.
Kreek, Mary Jeanne
Krein, Catherine Mitchell
Kreindler, Ruth Bilgrei
Krell, Robert Donald
Krellen, Fred R.
Kremer, Lewis Norman
Kreps, Juanita Morris (Mrs. Clifton H. Kreps, Jr.)
Kreps, Robert Wilson
Kresge, Wharton Ronald
Kresky, Edward Mordecai
Kress, Bernadette Marie
Kress, James Morrison
Kress, Lee Bruce
Kretchmer, Norman
Kretkowski, Ronald Charles
Kreuzer, Donald William
Krevolin, Nathan
Krevsky, Seymour
Krider, James Whitney, Jr.
Kriebel, Charles Hosey
Krieg, Adrian Henry
Krieg, Richard Edward, Jr.
Krieg, Saul
Krieger, Abbott Joel
Krieger, Carl
Krieger, Paul David
Krihak, Mary Kathleen Leskanic
Kring, James Burton
Kristal, Mark Bennett
Kristensen, Alfred Emery
Kristic, Norman
Krivka, Herbert Anthony
Krizek, Thomas Joseph
Krizinofski, Ronald Joseph
Krochmal, Charles Francis
Kroeber, C. Kent
Krol, John Cardinal
Kroll, Arnold Howard
Kroll, John Leon
Kroll, Martin Neil
Kroll, Nathan
Kroll, Paul Francis
Kron, William Godshall
Kronenthal, Richard Leonard
Kronfeld, Arthur Isiah
Kronfeld, Fred Norman
Kronstadt, Nancy Alice
Kropczynski, Thaddeus John
Krosnick, Arthur
Krouse, John Hobart
Krueger, Richard Gustave
Krug, Harry Everistus Peter, Jr.
Kruger, Jeffrey Sonny
Kruger, Seldon Martin
Krugman, Abraham Arthur
Kruper, John Gerald
Kruppa, J(ohn) Russell
Krusos, Denis Angelo
Kryszak, Wayne Douglas
Krzys, Richard Andrew
Kszepka, Joseph Anthony
Ku, Robert Tien-hung
Ku, Y.H.
Kubic, William Louis
Kubik, Edward Stanislaus
Kubota, Joe
Kuchta, Ronald Andrew
Kuczala, Zdzislaw Jerry Walter
Kudon, Herman Zvee
Kuebler, Bernard Donald
Kuechle, James Edward
Kuehn, Paul Gerhard
Kuehn, Walter, Jr.
Kuehni, Norman Arnold
Kuether, Carl Albert
Kugel, Robert Benjamin
Kugelman, Lawrence Richard
Kugler, Gary Syd
Kuhn, Brenda
Kuhn, Douglas Elton
Kuhn, Louis
Kuhn, Mary Draper
Kuhn, Thomas Richard
Kujawski, Walter Richard
Kukla, George Jiri
Kukuia, Faustinus Kofi
Kulka, Kurt
Kulkarni, Avinash Dattatraya
Kulp, Aimee Katherine
Kulp, Arthur Claude
Kulpa, Robert Harold
Kumai, Motoi
Kumar, Suriender
Kumm, William Howard
Kundin, Robert Herbert
Kung, Franklin Hsien-Cheuk
Kunin, Madeleine May
Kunstadt, Herbert
Kunzman, Mitche
Kupersmith, Aaron Harry
Kuperstein, Ira S(tanley)
Kupfer, Carl
Kupkowski, Gerald Steven
Kuriyama, Masao
Kurjakovic, Mira Bogunovic
Kurland, Norman Edward
Kurlander, Honey W. Wachtel (Mrs. Neale Kurlander)
Kurlans, Alice Joan
Kurnik, Barry Arnold
Kuroda, Koson
Kurosaka, George, Jr.
Kurowski, Zbigniew Thomas
Kurpiewski, Elizabeth Ann
Kurrelmeyer, Louis Hayner
Kurth, Walter Richard
Kurtz, Norman Rudolph
Kurtz, Paul
Kurtz, Stewart Kendall
Kurtz, Theodore Stephen
Kurtzke, John Francis
Kurtzman, Lewis
Kurucz, John
Kurzel, Richard Bernard
Kurzhals, Peter Ralph
Kurzinski, Edward Francis
Kushner, Jack
Kussmaul, Ernest Arthur
Kutanovski, Milan S.
Kutash, Samuel Benjamin
Kutemeyer, Peter Martin
Kutilek, Richard John
Kutrzeba, Joseph Stanislaw
Kuttner, Bernard A.
Kutzen, Jerome Jefferies
Kuzmak, Lubomyr Ihor
Kuzmowycz, Nicholas
Kuznets, Simon Smith
Kuznicki, Sister Ellen Marie
Kwah, Henry Hong
Kwalick, Donald Simon
Kwartler, Charles Edward
Kwo, Chin Charles
Kwolek, John Peter
Kwon, Ik Hyun
Kwon-Chung, Kyung Joo
Kyanka, George Harry
Kyriannis, Christopher Nicholas
Laano, Archie Bienvenido Maaño
Labalme, George, Jr.
Labenskyj, Ihor Nicholas
Labianca, Frank Michael
LaBoon, Lawrence Joseph
Labrecque, Theodore Joseph
Lacava, James Salvatore
Laccetti, Silvio Richard
Lachance, Paul Albert
Lache, Marvin Charles
Lackas, John Christopher
Lacoste, Paul
Lacy, Lloyd Hamilton
Lacz, Stanley John
Ladd, Everett Carll, Jr.
Ladd, Samuel Appleton, Jr.
Laden, Steven
Ladenheim, Jules Calvin
Laderman, Jack
Ladue, Thomas Sheldon
Lady, Roy Andrew
La Falce, John Joseph
LaFalce, Raymond Peter
Lafaye, Wilbur Paul
Lafferty, Charles Douglas Joseph
Laflamme, Diane Lucille
Lafond, James Frederick
LaForce, William Leonard, Jr.
Laford, Richard John
Lagarenne, Lawrence Edward
Lahey, Robert William
Lai, Ralph Wei-Meen
Laikind, Jeffrey
Laine, Matthew Thomas
Laird, Antonia Bissell
Laird, Archibald
Lakaytis, Georgia O'Brien
Lal, Samarthji
Lalley, Richard Andrew
Lamb, Matthew Joseph
Lamberson, Dane George
Lambert, Abbott Lawrence
Lambert, Arthur Gorman
Lambert, Henry August
Lambert, Jeremiah Daniel
Lambert, Richard Bowles, Jr.
Lammert, Thomas King
LaMond, Gaylord Marvin
Lamonsoff, Norman Charles
Lamont, Edward Miner
Lamont, Edwin Burgess, II
Lamont, Frederick Francis, Jr.
Lampert, Dorrie Elinore
Lampert, S. Henry
Lampron, Edward John
Lamy, Peter Paul
Lan, Donald
Lancaster, Leslie Eugene
Lancaster, Margaret Gutierrez
Land, Edwin Herbert
Land, Emmett Matthew, Jr.
Land, Henry Bruce, III
Landale, Thomas David
Landau, Siegfried
Landau, Sybil Harriet
Landauer, James Dittman
Landauer, Robert Neil
Lande, Lawrence Montague
Landeau, Ralph
Landers, Patricia Ann
Landis, Frederick
Landis, William Rutter
Landman, Louis
Landon, John Henry
Landon, Sealand Whitney, IV
Landrum, Frances Ann
Landry, Fernand Raymond
Landsberg, Jerry
Landsman, Bobbie
Lane, Barbara G.
Lane, Ben Clarence
Lane, Carol Harmon Feit
Lane, Carolyn Blocker (Mrs. M. Donald Lane, Jr.)
Lane, Martin Donald, Jr.
Lang, Everett Francis, Jr.
Lang, Victor John, Jr.
Langbein, Leland Henry
Langberg, Martha Diane
Langdon, Jervis, Jr.
Lange, Bertram Jeremy
Lange, Kurt
Lange, Richard Louis
Langenberg, Frederick Charles
Langford, Sidney
Langham, Norma
Langhans, Lester Frank, Jr.
Langley, Stephen Gould
Langlitz, Harold Nathan
Langlois, Ethel Galagan
Langlykke, Asger Funder
Langmead, Joseph Michael
Langrall, Clarke
Lanigan, John Patrick
Laning, Robert Comegys
Lankford, William Thomas, Jr.
Lanning, Franklin Van Lier
Lansburgh, Therese Weil (Mrs. Richard M. Lansburgh)
Lant, Jeffrey Ladd
Lantay, George Charles
Lanzano, Ralph Eugene
Lanzisera, A.D.
Lanzkowsky, Philip
Lanzkron, Rolf Wolfgang
La Paglia, Joseph Rocco, III
LaPerriere, Paul Joseph
Lapidus, Arnold
Lapidus, Herbert
LaPlaca, Peter John
Laplante, Louis Elmer
La Porte, James Arthur
Lapp, Warren Anthony
Lappin, W. Robert
Laprade, Edward Theodore
LaProva, Mario
Laraby, Larry L.
Larberg, John Frederick
Laren, Kuno
Largess, George Joseph
Larkin, James Thomas
La Roche, Robert William
LaRochelle, Donald Raymond
La Rocque, Eugene Philippe
LaRose, William Robinson
LaRow, Edward Joseph
Larsen, John Walter, Jr.
Larsen, Phillip Darwin
Larson, Charles Fred, Jr.
Larson, Jan Alexandra
Larson, Roland E.
Larson, Viola Ingeborg Swanson
LaSala, Vincent Joseph
La Sardo, Camille Gabriella
Lasch, Klaus Bernhard
Lascheid, William Peter
Lashmet, Peter Kerns
Lasker, Sigmund E.
Laskey, Richard Anthony
Laskin, Richard Sheldon
Laskowski, Edward Stanley
Lasky, Richard Donald
Lasry, Jean-Claude Maurice
Lassig, Kenneth H.
Lasuchin, Michael
Latchum, James Levin
Latendresse, James Joseph
Latham, Eunice Stunkard (Mrs. John R. Latham)
Latimer, Ted
Laton, Dexter Wood
LaTournerie, Gerard Jéan Clovis
Latterner, Charles George
Laub, George Cooley
Laub, Leonard
Laub, Raymond Joseph
Laubach, Eric Gordon
Laubach, Roger Alvin
Laud, Marilyn
Laudato, Gaetano Joseph, Jr.
Laudicina, Robert Anthony
Lauer, James Lothar
Lauer, Theodore
Laufer, Ira Jerome
Lauffer, Andre Marc
Laufman, Harold
Laug, Maurice Charles
Laughlin, Anita Curran
Laughlin, Cyril James
Laulicht, Murray Jack
Launer, Martin William
Laurendi, Nat
Lauria, Robert Joseph
Lauritsen, John Phillip
Laursen, Johannes
Lauzon, Aline Agnes
Lavender, Wanda Kinzel
Lavene, Bernard
Laventhol, Henry Lee
Laverty, Charles Raymond, Jr.
Lavey, Frederick Adolph
Lavin, Claire Marie
Lavine, David
Lavoie, Elaine Frances
Lavoie, Joseph Jean-Guy
Lavoie, Joseph Norman
Lavoie, Paul Leo
Law, John Randolph
Law, Norman Craig
Law, Stephen LeRoy
Lawlis, John Frank
Lawrence, Alonzo William
Lawrence, George Hubbard Clapp
Lawrence, George Robert
Lawrence, James, III
Lawrence, Justus Baldwin
Lawrence, Margery H(ulings)
Lawrence, Rena Mae
Lawrence, Robert Scott
Lawrence, Stella Hertchikoff
Lawry, Eleanor McChesney
Lawry, John Daniels
Lawson, Alice Marie
Lawson, Ann Marie McDonald
Lawson, Ashford Lee
Lawson, David
Lawson, Gustaf Rudolph
Lawson, J. Scott
Lawson, Margaret Mott (Mrs. Ralph E. Lawson)
Lawson, Ray Newton
Lawton, Henry William
Lawton, James Norbert
Lawton, Susan Wallis
Lawyer, Vivian Moore
Lax, Philip
Lay, Richard Victor
Layfield, Virginia Banes
Layman, William Arthur
Lazar, Allan William
Lazar, Irving
Lazar, Max Seymour
Lazarcik, Gregor
Lazarus, Bernard
Lazell, James Draper, Jr.
Lazenby, William Joseph
Lazet, Frank John
Lazich, Gilbert Stevan
Lazzaro, E. Clifford
Lea, Lola Stendig
Leab, Daniel Josef
Leach, Ernest Roy
Leach, Kevin Thomas
Leach, Ralph F.
Leahy, Edward Vincent
Leahy, Miriam Kramer
Leahy, Patrick Joseph
Leahy, Thomas Francis
Leahy, William F.
Leahy, William Harold
Leal, Joseph Rogers
Leaman, David Martin
Lear, Erwin
Learnard, William Ewing
Leary, Daniel Francis
Leary, Herbert Joseph
Leask, John McPherson
Leatham, John Tonkin
Leaton, Edward K.
Leavitt, David Harris
Leavitt, Frederic Perley, Jr.
Leavitt, Urban James Desrosier
Leavy, Lynne R.
LeBeau, Bernard Adolph
Lebedoff, Victor Richard
Lebegern, Charles Howard, Jr.
Lebel, Girard Richard
Lebel, Robert
Lebherz, Richard Thomas
Leblanc, Aldor Joseph Olivier
Le Blanc, John Roger
Lebovitz, Sol
Lebowitz, Marshall
Lebowitz, Sheldon Howard
Lebro, Theodore Peter
Lecca, Pedro Juan
Lechene, Claude Pierre
Lechner, Herbert Dean
Lechtrecker, George Edward
Leckband, Garwood Emerson
Leclair, Robert Paul
Leclerc, Paul-Andre
Leco, Armand Peter
Leco, Domenic Eugene
LeCroy, Barbara Lois Pease
Le Croy, James Franklin
Ledeen, Robert Wagner
Leder, Burton A.
Leder, Lawrence H.
Leder, Sheila Diane
Lederberg, Joshua
Lederer, Anne Tracy (Mrs. H. Austin Lederer)
Lederer, Ivo John
Lederer, Raymond Francis
Lederfeind, Alan
Lederman, Peter Bernd
Ledney, George
Leduc, Gilles Germain
Lee, Albert Kon-Ying
Lee, Alfred Matthew
Lee, Arthur Terence
Lee, Arthur Virgil, III
Lee, Aubrey McDaniel
Lee, Bob
Lee, Che Fu
Lee, Chong-Jin
Lee, Clement William Khan
Lee, Edmund Woodham
Lee, Edwin Borden, Jr.
Lee, Frances Helen
Lee, Gary A.
Lee, I-Chie
Lee, Ilbok
Lee, Jai Sung
Lee, James Edward
Lee, James McCarcum
Lee, James Widemann, II
Lee, John Chee-Mou
Lee, John H., Jr.
Lee, Jong-Won Cecilia
Lee, Joseph Yuen-chor
Lee, Keat-Jin
Lee, Kermit James, Jr.
Lee, Kotik Kai
Lee, Kwang In
Lee, Marjorie Ellen
Lee, Mildred Elsie Kimble
Lee, Min Shiu
Lee, Nellie Uy
Lee, Patricia Kwan-Luen
Lee, Paul Tsen-Shiong
Lee, Richard Edgar
Lee, Richard Vaille
Lee, (John) Robert, Jr.
Lee, Samuel Ching Hsin
Lee, Sang Ik
Lee, Shew Kuhn
Lee, Siu Lam
Lee, Tay Bong
Lee, Thomas H.
Lee, Tong-Nyong
Lee, Tsung-Dao
Lee, William George
Lee, Won Jay
Lee, Won-Kyu
Lee, Ying Kao
Lee, Young Il
Leech, Alma Davenport Case
Leech, James William
Leech, John Warner
Leedham, Charles Laurn
Leeds, Barry Howard
Leeds, Donald Searcus
Leeds, Kenneth Warren
Leeming, Brian William
Leen, Albert
Leeper, John Hopkins
Leeper, Robert Dwight
Leer, John Addison, Jr.
Leers, Wolf-Dietrich
Lees, Avon, Jr.
Lees, Carlton Brown
Leese, Bernard McKenzie
Le Fante, Joseph Anthony
Lefer, Jay
Leferovich, John, Jr.
LeFevre, Eugene Stephen
Leff, Alvin Isaac
Leff, David
Lefkovits, Albert Meyer
Lefkowitz, Leonard Robert
Lefkowitz, Louis Hirsch
Lefkowitz, Louis J.
Lefkowitz, Stanley A.
Legalos, Charles Norman
Legazpi, Emil Vincent
Leger, Jules
Legere, Martin Joseph
Legnos, John Peter
Legum, Jeffrey Alfred
Lehane, Derek Patrick
Lehman, Dennis George
Lehman, Lawrence Herbert
Lehman, Margaret
Lehmann, Aaron
Lehmann, Manfred Raphael
Lehne, William George
Lehnkering, Michael Stephan
Lehr, Frank Henry
Lehrich, James Richard
Leibner, Ira Wallace
Leibowitt, Sol David
Leiby, Clare C., Jr.
Leich, Harold Herbert
Leichtentritt, Kurt George
Leidheiser, Henry, Jr.
Leidner, Nelson J.
Leifer, Calvin
Leigh, Gilbert Merlin
Leigh, Hoyle
Leigh, Monroe
Leigh, Ruth R. Sokolski (Mrs. Murray Stuart Leigh)
Leigh, Samuel Frederick
Leigh, William Colston
Leighton, Albert Chester
Leighton, Charles M(ilton)
Leighton, David Keller, Sr.
Leighton, Thomas Gibbons
Leimkuhler, Gerard Joseph, Jr.
Leinweber, Bruce Kornblatt
Leir, Henry J(ohn)
Leis, Henry Patrick, Jr.
Leis, Winogene B.
Leisey, Alvin Lewis, Jr.
Leisinger, Lewis Martin
Leiter-Arnold, Barbara Ann
Leitman, Norman Jack
Le Kashman, Carol Ann
Lekuch, Ilya
Leland, George Havens
Leland, Lorraine Abel (Mrs. Frank Herbert Lee)
Lele, Padmakar Pratap
Leman, Paul Henri
Lemay, Paulette Marie
Lembo, John Mario
Lemchen, Marc Stuart
Lemcke, Norman Rohde
LeMien, Henry Lester, Jr.
Lemire, Andre
Lemke, Haru Hirama
Lemmerman, Charles Henry
Lemole, Gerald Michael
Lenahan, Edward Patrick
Lenchner, Nathaniel Herbert
Leney, George Willard
Lengyel, Edward Geza
Lenhart, Katharine Bradley (Mrs. John Jacobs Lenhart)
Lenherr, Frederick Keith
Lenio, Donald Peter
Lenney, Annie
Lenox, Rita Catherine
Lent, Garry E.
Lent, Norman F.
Lenz, Matthew, Jr.
Leonard, Edwin Deane
Leonard, Gene Francis
Leonard, Jackson Day
Leonard, Jacqueline Arminta
Leonard, James Kevin
Leonard, Vincent M.
Leone, Richard Joseph
Leonhart, William Harold
Leontief, Wassily
Leopold, Reuven
Lepeschkin, Julie Anne Wilson (Mrs. Eugene Lepeschkin)
Lepore, John Anthony
Lepore, Michael Joseph
Leporiere, Gene Paul
Leppard, Dale LeRoy
Le Quay, Edwin Gordon
Lerch, James Stanley
Lerman, Steven Ira
Lerner, Abram
Lerner, Laurence M.
Lerner, Lawrence
Lerner, Leonard
Lerner, Mildred Sherwood
Lerner, Theodore Raphael
Lerner, William
Le Roux, John J.
Leroy, George Erwin
LeRoy, Harold Myron
Le Schack, Leonard Albert
Lesinski, John Silvester
Lesko, Matthew John, Jr.
Lesko, William Stephen
Lesley, Allen
Leslie, John
Leslie, John Ethelbert
Leslie, Philip
Leslie, Richard Thomas
Lesniak, James Joseph
Lesniak, Robert John
Lesnick, Gerson Jonas
Lesnick, Robert Nathan
L'Esperance, Francis Anthony, Jr.
Lesse, S. Michael
Lessenco, Gilbert Barry
Lesser, John David
Lesser, Stanley Charles
Lessner, Gary Steven
Lester, Allen Henry
Lester, Barnett Benjamin
Lester, Robin D.
Leszkiewicz, John, Jr.
Letica, Helen
Lett, Marvin Russell
Lettieri, Dan John
Leubert, Alfred Otto Paul
Leuchter, Fred Arthur, Jr.
Leuschner, Frederick Edward
Le Valley, Guy Glenn
Le Van, Daniel Hayden
Levant, Ronald Fred
Levavy, Zvi
Leven, Ann Ruth
Levenbrook, Bruce Edward
Levenson, Nathan S.
Leventhal, A. Linda
Leventhal, Alan
Leventhal, Harold
Leverett, Dennis Hugh
Levesque, Charles-Henri
Levesque, Gerard D.
Levesque, Pascal
Levey, Allan Charles
Levi, Henry Thomas
Levi, Joseph Abraham
Levi, Michael Menahem
Levien, Maurice Beryl
Levin, Douglas Clifton
Levin, Edgar William
Levin, Felice Michaels (Mrs. Harry C. Levin)
Levin, Harry Matthew
Levin, James Benesch
Levin, Joseph David
Levin, Michael N.
Levin, Morton Loeb
Levin, Murray Newman
Levin, Robert
Levin, Roger M.
Levin, Ruben
Levin, S. Benedict
Levin, Simon
Levin, Tom
Levin, William Harold
Levine, Arthur J.
Levine, Arthur Louis
Levine, Bernard
Le Vine, David Eliot
Levine, Edna Simon
Levine, George
Levine, Harold A(braham)
Levine, Hyman Joseph
Levine, Joel Philip
Levine, Naomi Bronheim
Levine, Richard Alan
Levine, Richard Steven
Levine, Robert John
Levine, Solomon
Levine, Stephen Jay
Levinson, Gwen
Levitch, Joel Allen
Levitt, Morton Hill
Levitz, Ethel Belle
Levkulic, John Joseph
Levokove, Linda Ann
Levow, Barry
Levy, Adrian
Levy, Alan Joseph
Levy, Benjamin
Levy, Beverlee Jayne
Levy, Harold
Levy, Harold Sheldon
Levy, Herbert Monte
Levy, Jerome Henry
Levy, John Dana
Levy, Julius
Levy, Michael Henry
Levy, Milton Robert
Levy, Paul Frank
Levy, Robert Alan
Levy, Robert Isaac
Levy, Stephen Raymond
Levy, Tibbie (Mrs. Eli Bennett Levy)
Levy, Walter
Levy, Wilbert J.
Lewan, Roland, Jr.
Lewey, Merle Creighton
LeWinn, Edward Bernard
Lewins, Steven

Lewis, Armand Francis
Lewis, Claude, Jr.
Lewis, Clifford, III
Lewis, Craig Graham David
Lewis, David Charles
Lewis, Edward Michael
Lewis, Edward Turner
Lewis, Frank Mohr
Lewis, Harry
Lewis, Howard Wilson, Jr.
Lewis, Hylan Garnet
Lewis, James Histed
Lewis, John Hartley
Lewis, John Leeman, Jr.
Lewis, Paul LeRoy
Lewis, Richard Cyrus
Lewis, Richard Warrington Baldwin
Lewis, Robert Hallam
Lewis, Steven
Lewis, Stuart Miley
Lewis, Thomas Howard
Lewis, Warren Remer
Lewis, Willard Deming
Lewis, William C., Jr.
Lewis, William Frederick
Lewis, Wilson D.
Lewison, Edward Frederick
Lewitus, Ricardo
Lewonski, Richard Francis
Lewy, Robert Max
Lewy, Stephan Heinz
Leyton, Robert Alan
Li, Chang-Yang
Li, Emanuel Yun-Sun
Li, Norman Chung
Li, Tien-Shun
Li, Tina Yu Heng
Liang, Yu-Jean
Liao, Sung Jui
Lias, Nicholas Constantine
Liauw, Hui-Lian Tan
Liba, Gerald Ronald
Libby, Ellen Weber
Liberman, Norman Jacob
Liccini, Stephen L.
Lichello, Robert
Lichtenstadter, Ilse
Lichtenstein, Rosalie
Licopoli, Francis Louis
Liddle, Howard Arthur
Liddy, Richard Angier
Lieb, Robert Leonard
Liebenstein, Richard
Lieberman, Louis
Lieberman, Morris Baruch
Lieberman, Theodore William
Lieblein, Edward
Liebling, Barry A.
Liebman, Emmanuel
Liebman, Leon Herschel
Liebman, Milton
Liebman, William Norman
Liebmann, Felix G.
Liebolt, Frederick Lee
Lief, Harold Isaiah
Lieggi, Edward Vincent, Sr.
Liegner, Frank Ferdinand
Lieu, Hou-Shun
Liff, Zanvel A.
Liffmann, Kenneth Emil
Lifson, Betty Ann Glasser
Lifton, Lester Jay
Lifton, Walter M.
Light, Edwin Stanley
Lightbody, Forrest Earsham Hay
Lightcap, Kenneth Reed
Lightfoot, Belinda Harris
Lightstone, Alan Clifford
Ligor, O. Judith David
Lijewski, Ronald Mathew
Liker, Jack
Liles, Raeford Bailey
Lilien, Elliot Stephen
Lilien, Gary Louis
Lilley, David Frank
Lillienstein, Maxwell Julius
Lilling, Max Irving
Lim, Esther P.
Lim, George
Lim, Jong Jin
Lim, Peter Ganpin
Lima, Beatrice Van Duzer
Limberakis, John Anthony
Liming, Robert Warren
Limongelli, William Alfonso
Limpe, Anthony Teh
Lin, Ada Wen-Shung Ma
Lin, Chang Lu
Lin, Fang-Jen
Lin, James Fang-Ming
Lin, Joseph Pen-Tze
Lin, Po-An
Lin, Ruey Yuan
Linarducci, Robert Pasquale
Lincoln, Elizabeth Kitchel (Mrs. Alexander Lincoln, Jr.)
Lincoln, Emma Ethel
Lind, Arthur
Lind, Douglass Theodore
Linda, Dennis Joseph
Lindahl, Ivan Leroy
Lindauer, Lois Lyons
Linde, Walter
Lindell, Randolph Dickinson, III
Linden, Kathryn
Lindenblad, Irving Werner
Linder, Edward Fredrick, Jr.
Linder, Morton Howard
Linder, Thomas Edward, Jr.
Lindholm, Dale David
Lindner, Edmund Frederick
Lindsay, Alexander David
Lindsay, Reginald Carl
Lindsay, Robert Henry
Lindsey, Fred
Linebaugh, John Harvey Moore
Linenberg, William Bernard
Lines, Malcolm Ellis
Lin-Fu, Jane Sycip (Mrs. Ching Mark Fu)
Ling, Suilin
Ling, William Theodore
Lingelbach, Albert Lane
Lingenfelter, Robert Brian
Link, Stephen Joseph
Linn, Harry, Jr.
Linn, Jay George, Jr.
Linna, Timo Juhani
Linnenberg, Clem Charles, Jr.
Linnenkohl, Susan Carol
Linowes, David Francis
Linscott, Mortimer Lee
Linsky, Elizabeth Stewart
Linstone, Robert Theodore
Linthicum, Roger Henry
Linton, Calvin Darlington
Linville, Thomas Merriam
Liolin, John Evans
Lipari, Nunzio Ottavio
Lipke, Kenneth Emil
Lipkin, Martin
Lipkind, Marvin Lee
Lipman, Daniel Gordon
Lipman, Everett S.
Lipman, Ira Ackerman
Lipman, Richard Paul
Lipmann, Fritz (Albert)
Lippek, Karl Torma
Lippincott, Bruce Lester
Lippman, Alfred Julian
Lippmann, Gorham James
Lippner, Lewis Alan
Lipscomb, William Nunn, Jr.
Lipshutz, Robert Jerome
Lipton, Charles
Lipton, Simon Morris
Lisante, Joseph Michael
Lisle-Cannon, Richmond
Lisowitz, Gerald Myron
Liss, Louis Richard
Lissenden, Carol Kay
Lisser, Morton Samuel
Lissim, Simon
Lissner, Will
List, de Graffenried (Mrs. Daniel Clarence List)
Lister, Merle
Listernick, Jerome Melvin
Liston, Laurence Louis
Litman, Raymond Stephen
Litman, Robert Barry
Litman, Roslyn Margolis
Litoff, Judy Barrett
Litsky, Bertha Yanis
Litterick, William Spencer
Littig, Lawrence William
Little, Gretchen D(ohm)
Little, James Kelly, Jr.
Little, Jeffrey Berk
Little, Osborne Morgan, Jr.
Little, Ralph Donald
Littledale, Harold Aylmer
Littleton, Louis Andrew
Littman, Charles Arthur
Littman, Edward
Littman, Eugene
Littman, Henry
Littman, Solomon I.
Litz, Milton Benjamin
Litzenberger, Leonard Nelson
Litzky, Gerald Max
Liu, Si-Kwang
Liu, William Chang
Liu, Yung Sheng
Liva, Edward Louis
Livanis, Constantine
Livingston, Frederick Montgomery, Jr.
Livingston, Frederick Richard
Livingston, Gideon Eleazar
Llewellyn, Lynn Gresham
Lloyd, Dorothy Davis
Lloyd, Gerald Dwight
Lloyd, John William
Lloyd, Richmond Morgan
Lloyd, Robert Albert
Lloyd, Thomas Grant
Lloyd, W. Mason
Lloyd, William Howard
Lo, Hang Hsin
Lo, Teh Cheng
Lobdell, David Hill
Lobel, Irving
Lobron, Barbara L.
Lobsenz, Amelia
Lochanko, Adam
Lochner, H. Allen
Lockard, James Reeder
Locke, Edwin Allen, III
Locke, Howard Palmer
Locke, Richard van de Sande
Locke, Stanley
Lockhart, G(lenn) Robert
Lockhart, Philip North
Lockshin, Florence Levin (Mrs. Samuel D. Lockshin)
Lockshin, Samuel D.
Lockwood, Kenneth Richard
Lockwood, Molly A.
Lockwood, William Wirt, Jr.
Loder, Martha Katherine
Loder, Peter Cameron
Lodge, Henry Cabot
Lodmell, Dean Struthers
Loeb, Frances Lehman (Mrs. John L. Loeb)
Loeb, John Langeloth, Jr.
Loeffler, Judith Rae
Loening, Sarah Larkin
Loening, Werner
Loevinger, Lee
Loewer, Alvin Conrad, Jr.
Loffredo, Ronald Daniel
Lofgren, Richard H.
Lofving, Iver
Logan, Robert Lee
Lo Gerfo, John Joseph
Logue, John Joseph
Logue, Joseph Carl
Logusch, George Christopher
Loh, Hsue-Peng
Loh, Yoke Peng
Lohman, Kenneth Elmo
Lohrer, Marguerite
Loigman, Harold
Loizes, James
Lokes, John, Jr.
Lolis, Kathleen
Lombard, David Bishop
Lombard, Donald Richard
Lombardi, Anthony Michael, Jr.
Lombardi, Arthur Vincent
Lombardo, David Domenic
Lombardo, Pio Stephen
Lomnitz, Esteban Rafael Lomnitz
London, Allen Jay
London, Gene
London, Mark Stanley
London, S(ol) J.
London-Person, Sharon Donna
Loney, Carolyn Patricia
Long, Anton Vanderford
Long, Charles Robert Mark
Long, Clarence D(ickinson), Jr.
Long, Harry (Eng On-yuen)
Long, Larry Howard
Long, Leslie Bruce
Long, Paul
Long, Robert Edward
Longaker, Richard Pancoast
Longbrake, William Arthur
Longley, James Wildon
Longman, Richard Winston
Longo, Frank Walter
Longo, Louis Paul
Longo, Vivian Vita
Longobardi, Anthony Paul
Longobardo, Anna Kazanjian
Longstreth, H(oward) Paul
Lonky, Martin Leonard
Lonto, Benjamin Philip
Lookstein, Joseph Hyman
Loomis, J. Paul
Loomis, John Norman
Loonan, Howard Marc
Looney, Francis Benedict
Looney, John Michael
Loos, August Walter, Jr.
Loos, William Henry
Lopez, Felix Edward
Loranger, Armand Walter
Lord, Barbara Chase
Lord, Earl Robert
Lord, Joseph Simon, III
Lord, Marion E. Manns
Lord, Priscilla Sawyer (Mrs. Philip Hosmer Lord)
Lord, Ray
Lord, Victor Alexander, Jr.
Lore, John Marion, Jr.
Lorentz, Gerald Talmage
Lorentz, Pare
Lorian, Victor
Lorimer, Graeme
Lorincz, Robert Stephen
Loring, Caleb, Jr.
Loring, Marvin F.
Loring, Richard William
Loring, Stanton Dunster
Losee, Thomas Penny, Jr.
Losi, Maxim John
Loss, David Edward
Lo Surdo, Antonio
Loth, John
Lothrop, Warren Craig
Lotito, Ernest Arthur
Lotito, Thomas
Lotz, George Michael
Lotz, Henry Thomas
Lotz, Roy James, Jr.
Loucks, William Dewey, Jr.
Loughery, Kevin Michael
Loughery, Richard Miller
Loughran, William Cyril
Louis, George Arya
Louison, Melvin Sanford
Louthood, Lewis Alexander
Loutsch, Enrique Hector
Love, Gary Corcoran
Love, John Albert
Love, John Clyde
Love, Richard Harvey
Love, Robert Alexander
Love, Robert Lyman
Love, Sidney Irwin
Lovejoy, Lee Harold
Lovelace, Linda Lee
Lovelace, Richard Van Evera
Lovell, Ralph Marston
Lovell, Richard Hallett
Lovely, Peter Michael
Low, Chow-Eng
Low, Douglas John
Lowe, Ethel Black
Lowe, George John
Lowe, James Lewis
Lowe, Joseph Theodore, Jr.
Lowe, Mervin Ray
Lowell, Chapin McKinney
Lowell, Stanley Edgar
Lowell, Stanley Herbert
Lowen, William Oscar
Lowenstein, Joyce Sandra
Lowery, Pearl Virginia
Lowery, William Herbert
Lowman, Robert Morris
Lowry, Betty
Lowry, Emmert Miller, Jr.
Lowry, Louis Dale
Lowry, Richard Wurster
Lowry, Robert Beattie
Lowry, Ted Harvie Edmund
Lowry, Warren Kenneth
Lowther, Frank Eugene
Lowy, Louis
Loynd, Jack Shapleigh
Lu, Milton Ming-Deh
Luban, Audrey Mae
Lubetkin, Seymour Arthur
Lubin, Andrew Michael
Lubow, Nathan Myron
Luca, William Arthur, Jr.
Lucas, Carol
Lucas, G. Brinton
Lucas, Joseph
Lucca, Thomas George
Luce, Eleanor Marjorie
Luce, Melvin Geoffrey
Lucey, Gordon Macaulay
Luchsinger, John Francis
Luchterhand, Elmer Gustav
Luchterhand, Paul Fredrick
Luck, Anthony
Luckey, E. Hugh
Lucks, Joel Kenneth
Lucow, William Harrison
Luczun, Robert
Luddy, Joseph Michael
Luddy, William Joseph, Jr.
Ludlum, Robert Phillips
Ludman, Jacques Ernest
Ludwig, Richard
Luebs, Harold William
Luecke, Walter Louis
Luek-Keen, Susan Penelope
Luft, Herbert Arthur
Luft, Rene Wilfred
Luginbyhl, Thomas Terence
Luhrs, Henry Ric
Luing, Larry Lee
Luk, Shing Chark
Lukens, David Lee
Lukin, Jon Dehn
Lukitsch, Robert Albert
Luks, Allan Barry
Lulick, Mary A.
Lumadue, Donald Dean
Lumley, John Morris
Lumpkin, Lee Roy
Lund, Robert E.
Lunde, Asbjorn Rudolph
Lundell, Frederick Waldemar
Lundgren, Carl William, Jr.
Lundgren, Richard John
Lundgren, Ruth (Mrs. W.F. Williamson)
Lundine, Stanley Nelson
Lunn, Gail Ilia
Lunn, Richard Harry
Lunt, Samuel Dorr, Jr.
Lupa, Joseph Michael
Lupiani, Donald Anthony
Lupton, Elmer Cornelius, Jr.
Lupton, John Anthony
Luria, Salvador Edward
Lurkis, Alexander
Lusch, Charles Jack
Lusins, John O.
Lusk, Ben Earl
Lusk, Jack Edward
Luskey, J. Bernard
Lussi, Caroline Frances Draper
Lust, Peter
Lustig, Robert T.
Lutz, John Howard
Luus, Rein
Lybarger, Adrienne Reynolds (Mrs. Lee Francis Lybarger, Jr.)
Lyddy, Gregory Joseph
Lydecker, Robert Carpenter
Lyden, Edward Francis Xavier
Lyles, Charles Frank
Lyman, Melville Henry
Lyman, Paul Lawrence
Lynch, Brock
Lynch, John Francis
Lynch, John Peter
Lynch, Joseph P.
Lynch, Kathleen Aletha
Lynch, Patrick Hugh
Lynch, Thomas James, Jr.
Lynch, Thomas John
Lynham, John Marmaduke
Lynk, Doris Sheafe
Lynn, Enid (Enid Lynn Rosenthal)
Lynn, Karyl V., Jr.
Lynn, Peter Charles
Lynn, Yen-Mow
Lynne, Arleen S.
Lynskey, John Andrew
Lyon, Edward Bruce Avram
Lyon, Harold Clifford, Jr.
Lyon, James Burroughs
Lyon, Rossmore Denman
Lyons, Edward
Lyons, Elaine Turner (Mrs. John Edward Lyons)
Lyons, Grace Becker
Lyons, Harold Aloysius
Lyons, John Patrick
Lyons, John Thomas
Lyons, M. Don
Lyons, Patricia Jane
Lyons, Richard Daniel
Lyslo, Arnold Lynner
Lytle, James Evans
Ma, Edward Shihjen
Ma, Pearl Pik Chun
Maas, James Beryl
Maasland, Marinus
Maass, John
Maben, Jerrold William
Mabry, Paul Davis, Jr.
Macartney, Norman Scarborough
Macaulay, David Alexander
Macauley, Barbara Cart
Mac Bride, Dexter DuPont
Maccagnano, Salvatore Joseph
MacCallum, Donald Charles
Macchi, Eugene Edward
Mac Corkle, Douglas Beals
Mac Cracken, Calvin Dodd
Mac Cracken, Constable
Mac Donald, Angus Carleton
Mac Donald, David Eggers
Mac donald, Duncan Donald
Macdonald, Jan Pendexter, II
Mac Donald, Jay Delbert
MacDonald, Jerome Edward
Macdonald, JoAnn Marie Kindermann
MacDonald, Kirkpatrick
Macdonell, James Johnson
Macey, David Anthony James
Mac Farlane, Gloria Marie
Mac Gregor, Charles Winters
Machanic, Harmon Jack
Machaver, Harvey
Machen, Arthur Webster, Jr.
Macht, Lee Brand
Macht, Stanley Howard
Maciag, Robert John
Maciejko, Romain
Mac Intosh, Charles Archibald
MacIntyre, Leslie Donald
MacIsaac, David
Mac Iver, Pegge Farmer (Mrs. Donald Gordon MacIver)
Mack, Gerhard Theodor
Mack, Jay Ord, Jr.
Mack, Jeremy Roger
Mack, John Edward
Mack, Phyllis Friedman (Mrs. David Mack)
Mac Kay, James Robert
Mac Kay, Melville Gordon
Mac Kenzie, Ian Murdoch
Mackenzie, Malcolm Lewis
Mac Kenzie, Norman Hugh
Mac Kenzie, Robert Peck
Mackey, Helen Theresa (Mrs. Edward G. Hart)
Mackie, James Watson
Mac Kinnon, George E.
Mac Kinnon, Walter Allan
Mackles, Leonard
Mac Kouse, Edward Marvin
Mackowiak, Robert
MacLean, James Parlane, III
Macleod, Robert Angus
Mac Millan, Francis Philip
MacMillan, Leonard Joseph
Mac Neal, Edward Arthur
MacNeill, John Sears
Macovsky, Morris Saul
Mac Phail, Leland Stanford, Jr.
Mac Pherson, Jennifer Bailey
Macquarrie, Heath Nelson
Mac Queen, Virginia
Macri, Gregory Joseph, Jr.
Mac Rury, King
MacVane, William Leslie, Jr.
MacWilliams, Robert Wilson
Madden, Donald Edwin
Madden, Kenneth Cromwell
Madden, Sister Mary Carolyn
Maddox, Gene, Jr.
Madeheim, Huxley
Madeira, Sheldon Spencer Rothermel
Madgey, James Joseph
Madhyastha, Visweswara Laxminarayana
Madigan, Martin Joseph
Madigan, Rita Duffy
Madison, Dana Eugene
Madjid, Abdul Hamid
Madle, Robert Albert
Madole, Donald Wilson
Madora, Albert William
Madow, Pauline Reichberg (Mrs. Seymour Stephen Madow)
Madsen, John Edward, Jr.
Maeland, Arnulf Julius
Maestrone, Gianpaolo
Maffet, Vere
Maffongelli, Joseph Anthony
Magargal, Larry Elliot
Magarian, Robert John
Magdoff, Samuel
Magee, Albert James
Magee, John
Maggi, Victor Oscar
Maglio, John Francis
Magnuson, John Andrew
Magnuson, Paul Andrew
Magnuson, Peter Alfred
Maguire, Andrew
Maguire, James Peter
Maguire, John Joseph
Maguire, Robert Alan
Mahaffy, Perry Roger
Mahaffy, Reid Alexander
Mahajan, Subhash
Mahanand, Dersh
Mahdi, Allah Eros
Maher, Allan E.
Maher, Edward William
Maher, John Francis
Mahoney, David Joseph, Jr.
Mahoney, Patrick Edward
Mahoney, Thomas Anthony
Mailis, John Michael
Mainero, Frank Arthur
Maioriello, Richard Patrick
Maitlen, Dean Jerold
Majeske, Leonard Michael
Majewski, Frank Walter
Mak, Ty Tse-Fai
Makadok, Stanley
Makar, Boshra Halim
Makar, Harry Vladimer
Makar, Nadia Eissa
Makaretz, John
Makepeace, Russell
Maker, James Henry
Makhija, Mohanlal Chhugamal
Makhijani, Suresh Pessumal
Makover, Henry Benedict
Makuch, James Michael
Malabre, Alfred Leopold, Jr.
Malach, Herbert John
Malach, Monte
Malanchuk, John Louis
Malcolm, Daniel Connor
Maldonado, Juan Ramon
Malek, Joseph Vincent
Maler, Roger
Maletz, Herbert Naaman
Malev, Sheldon
Malfatti, Roger Andre, Jr.
Malia, Gerald Aloysius
Maligno, Amelia
Maligno, Vincent Joseph
Malin, Cedric K.
Malin, Paul Samuel
Malinconico, S. Michael
Maliner, Myron S.
Malinoski, Bernadine Marie
Malione, Anthony Michael
Maliszewski, Henry Louis
Malitz, Sidney
Malkin, Martin Louis
Malkin, Stanley Lee
Mallary, Gertrude Robinson (Mrs. R. DeWitt Mallary)
Mallary, Raymond DeWitt
Mallon, Edward John
Mallouh, Camille
Malone, James Duane
Malone, William Robert
Maloney, Joan Marie
Maloney, Milford Charles
Maloney, Paul Keating, Jr.
Maloney, Randolph David
Maloney, William Gerard
Maloof, Mitchell
Malowany, Moises Salomon
Maloy, Charles Edward, III
Malsky, Stanley Joseph
Malter, Ira Joel
Maltese, John Albert
Mamula, Steven Nicholas, Jr.
Manahan, Kenneth Roy
Mance, Julian Clifford, Jr.
Mancini, Joseph Andrew
Mancini, Lawrence Otto
Mancini, Ronald Novel
Mancuso, Louis
Mandarino, Michael Pascol
Mandel, Perry Richard
Mandelbaum, Mark Samuel
Mandell, Leonard Charles
Mandigo, James Allen
Mandl, Alexander Ernst
Manes, Donald Richard
Mang, Henry Yanling
Mangan, Edmund Lawrence
Manganello, James Angelo
Mangeim, David Stephen
Manger, William Muir
Manges, James H.
Mangieri, Robert Paul
Mangla, Jagdish Chand
Mangot, Michael
Mangulis, Visvaldis
Manice, Hayward Ferry
Manice, William DeF.
Maniktala, Rajindar Kumar
Manka, Dan Paul
Mankin, Hart Tiller
Manley, Brother Eugene Ignatius
Mann, Candee Ann Morici
Mann, Hannah Kohl
Mann, Margaret Blackwell (Mrs. James Harold Mann)
Mann, Mary Elizabeth
Mann, Robert
Mann, Robert Paul
Mann, Roy Bernard
Mann, William Houston
Mann, William Marion, Jr.
Mannarelli, John Edward
Manney, Donald Maxwell
Manning, Daisy Mae Parks
Manning, Edward Peter
Manning, Ferdinand Larue
Manning, James Hugh
Manning, William George
Mannix, Henry, Jr.
Manocchia, Benito Cesare
Manogue, Helen Smith
Manolakos, Demetrius
Manor, Filomena Roberta
Manos, George
Manos, John George
Manowitz, Nelson
Manross, William Wilson
Manser, Gordon
Mansi, Joseph Anneillo
Mansky, Leonard
Mansley, Gregory Allan
Manson, Frank Albert

Mansouri, Freydoon
Mansuy, Matthew Michael
Mantel, Heinrich
Manuel, Thomas George
Manus, Stephen Charles
Manzi, Albert Peter
Maplesden, Douglas Cecil
Mara, William Francis
Maracle, Nelson Paul
Maragos, James K.
Maranzano, Mike Frank
Marasciullo, David Louis
Marasco, Louis Joseph
Marash, Stanley Albert
Marathé, Eknath V.
Marazzi, William Charles Pierre
Marbury, Benjamin Edward
Marcantonio, Robert Allan
Marcatante, John Joseph
Marcellas, Thomas Wilson
Marchena, Isaac (IMARC)
Marchi, John J.
Marconis, Joseph Thomas
Marcoplos, Terry (Ruth E.) Spear
Marcos, Jose Mariano
Marcotte, Marcel Ernest
Marcoux, Jules Edouard
Marcus, Aaron
Marcus, Alan C.
Marcus, Alfred Israel
Marcus, Bruce William
Marcus, Helen
Marcus, Maria Lenhoff (Mrs. Norman Marcus)
Marcus, Mildred Rendl (Mrs. Edward Marcus)
Marcus, Myles Martin
Marcus, Rosalie
Marcus, Sidney Ottmar, Jr.
Mardaga, Thomas J.
Mardello, Alfred Frederick
Marden, Arthur Budgen
Marden, Parker Grimes
Marden, Richard Guy
Marder, Dorie
Marella, Medea Marie
Marelli, John Vincent
Maresca, Teckla Ann
Margolin, Carl M.
Margolin, Harold
Margolin, Solomon
Margolis, Eugene
Margolis, Gerald Joseph
Margro, Arthur Lawrence
Margulies, Mark Alan
Margulies, Selma Kolatch
Marhoefer, Gilbert Lionel
Maric, Radoslav
Marimow, William Kalmon
Marinaccio, Anthony
Marinakos, Plato Anthony
Marinbach, Mark Gary
Marinelli, Antonio Michael
Marino, Anthony James, Jr.
Marino, Joseph Anthony
Marinovich, Mato Luko
Marion, Bill Allan
Marion, Claud Collier
Marion, David Jeffrey
Mark, Sandra Fay
Markarian, Noubar
Marke, Julius Jay
Marker, Leonard K.
Markewich, Maurice Elish (Reese)
Markey, Edward J.
Markey, Howard Thomas
Markey, Martin James
Markham, F. Richard
Markham, Mary Elizabeth Thornton (Mrs. Reginald A. Markham)
Markin, James Stein
Markle, George Michael
Markley, Kenneth Alan
Markowitz, Abe
Markowitz, Phyllis Frances
Marks, Albert Aubrey, Jr.
Marks, Arlyn Charles
Marks, Arthur
Marks, Edward Bennett
Marks, Eugene Melvin
Marks, George Peabody, III
Marks, Gerald
Marks, Herbert Edward
Marks, Howard Lee
Marks, Johnny (John D.)
Marks, Lawrence
Marks, Marc Lincoln
Marks, Norman Curtiss
Marks, Robert Hutchinson
Marlan, Stanton
Marlow, Bruce Abbey
Marlow, Dorothy Jeannette
Marmora, Sabatino Joseph
Maroko, Peter Richard
Maron, Arthur
Marple, Gary Andre
Marquez, Ernest Domingo
Marr, Carmel Carrington (Mrs. Warren Marr II)
Marr, Edwin Eugene
Marr, Thomas Allen
Marra, Bruce Laurence
Marra, Dorothea C. (Mrs. Michael D. Marra)
Marra, Michael
Mars, Witold Tadeusz
Marsden, John Waring
Marsh, Kenneth Stanley
Marsh, Linda Kessler
Marsh, Quinton Neely
Marsh, Walton Howard
Marshall, Barry Hamilton
Marshall, Benjamin Franklin, III
Marshall, C(harles) Herbert
Marshall, David
Marshall, David Charles
Marshall, Frank Irvin
Marshall, John Aloysius
Marshall, Kenneth Allan
Marshall, Kneale Thomas
Marshall, Mara Blumberg (Mrs. Sylvan Mitchell Marshall)
Marshall, Mildred Delevett
Marshall, Ray
Marshall, Richard Douglass
Marshall, Robert James
Marshall, Robert Wilson
Marshall, Sylvan Mitchell
Marshall, Theresa Hooper
Marshall, Thurgood
Marshall, Willoughby Marks
Marsteller, William A.
Marston, Alfred J.
Martas, Julia Ann
Marth, Fritz Ludwig
Marticorena, Ernesto Jesus
Martimucci, Richard Anthony
Martin, Agnes Hudson Macqueen (Mrs. William Clayton Martin)
Martin, Albertus
Martin, Allen
Martin, Anthony Alphonse
Martin, Bélanger Joseph
Martin, Carl Eaton
Martin, Charles, Jr.
Martin, David Kendall
Martin, Donald Lloyd
Martin, Douglas Harry
Martin, Douglas Ray
Martin, Edward John
Martin, Eugene Ronald
Martin, Francis Joseph, Jr.
Martin, Harrold Bert
Martin, John L.
Martin, Leona Eloise
Martin, Pamela June Naulty
Martin, Patricia Ann
Martin, Peter Bird
Martin, R. Keith
Martin, Raymond Spencer, Jr.
Martin, Renee Cohen
Martin, Richard Everett
Martin, Richard Harrison
Martin, Richard Milton
Martin, Robert Lawrence
Martin, Robin Bradley
Martin, Roger Storey
Martin, Ruth May
Martin, Thomas George
Martin, Thomas George, III
Martin, Thomas Van
Martin, Vernon Anthony
Martindale, Edna E.
Martinetti, Raymond Frederick
Martinez, Elba Josefa
Martinez, Fernando
Martínez, Richard Isaac
Martinez Soto, William E.
Martini, Charles Constantine
Martini, John Melvin
Martino, Rocco Leonard
Martis, Jerome Michael
Marton, Emery
Marts, Edith Haughton
Marty, Frederick Nicholas
Marvin, John George
Marxe, Maxwell
Marzano, Albert
Marzocco, Leonard Joseph
Masaoka, Mike Masaru
Masapollo, William Mario
Mascari, Frank
Maser, Frederick Ernest
Masheck, Joseph Daniel
Masisak, Donald Joseph
Maskaleris, Stephen Nicholas
Masley, Peter Michael
Maslona, Paul Mark
Maslowe, Sherwin Allan
Maslyar, George Andrew, III
Masnick, Jeffrey Lee
Mason, Donald Frank
Mason, Eli
Mason, Francis Scarlett, Jr.
Mason, Frank Herbert
Mason, George Robert
Mason, Hayden
Mason, Joan Ellen
Mason, Kenneth Berry, Jr.
Mason, Madeline
Mason, Marshall W.
Mason, Peter Anthony
Mason, Peter Leonard
Mason, Robert Stanley
Massabny, Judith Taylor
Massey, Donald Ayres
Massias, Jeannette Berthe
Massimino, Vittorio Carmelo
Massmann, Robert Ernest
Masson, Victorin Bertrand
Mast, William Ray
Master, Gerald Louis
Masters, Henry George
Masters, Richard E.
Masters, Stuart Jeffrey
Mastran, John Leo
Mastrorocco, Virginio Peter
Mastrota, Vincent Francis
Masubuchi, Koichi
Matalia, Harshad Dilipkumar
Matarazzo, Anthony P.
Matczak, Sebastian Alexander
Matheson, John Ross
Mathews, Frederick Anthony John
Mathews, Howard Hume
Mathews, J. Addison
Mathews, James Kenneth
Mathias, Charles McCurdy, Jr.
Mathieu, Peter Louis, Jr.
Mathison, Harold Richard
Mathison, Stuart Lloyd
Mathur, Kailash Nath
Mathur, Suresh Chandra
Matiasevic, Dobrosav
Matinzi, Louis Francis
Matis, Jacob David
Matisse, Pierre
Matschke, Arthur Louis, Jr.
Matsumiya, Yoichi
Matsuoka, Shiro
Mattei, David Samuel
Mattei, Thomas Joseph
Mattern, Robin Donald
Matteson, William Bleecker
Mattey, John Joseph
Matthaei, Gay Humphrey
Matthei, Herman
Matthei, Robert Theodore
Matthes, Gerald Stephen
Matthews, A. Bruce
Matthews, Burnita Shelton
Matthews, Daniel George
Matthews, Dorothea Elizabeth
Matthews, Martin Taylor
Matthews, Paul Randolph, II
Matthias, George Frank
Mattis, Noémi Perelman
Mattox, Daniel Valentine, Jr.
Matulavage, Peter Andrew
Matunas, Marian Starrett (Mrs. Anthony L. Matunas)
Matz, David Jerome
Matza, Brian
Matzner, Alexandra Maria
Mauchline, Daniel Donald
Mauger, Karl Frederick
Mauke, Otto Russell
Mauldin, Anita Jackson
Mauney, Gloria Juanita Means
Maurer, Joseph Abele
Maurer, Loretta Anna
Maurer, Richard Hornsby
Mauretti, Gerald Joseph
Maurmeyer, Robert Carl
Mauser, Stephen Frederick
Mavros, Constantin
Mavros, Donald Odysseus
Mavroules, Nicholas
Mavrovic, Ivo
Maxwell, Michael
Maxwell, Richard Anthony
May, Arthur Glover
May, Dean Edward
May, Hugh John
May, James
May, Samuel Casamere
Mayberger, Harold Woodrow
Mayer, Alfred I.
Mayer, Edward Frederick
Mayer, Jeffrey Alan
Mayer, Klaus
Mayer, Robert Stanley
Mayer, Sondra
Mayer, Stuart David
Mayerson, Donald Joel
Mayerson, Marjorie Konwaler
Mayes, Edythe Beam
Mayes, Stanley Ryder
Mayhall, Jane Francis (Mrs. Leslie G. Katz)
Mayle, Francis Carl, Jr.
Maynard, Catherine Theresa
Maynard, Donald Nelson
Mayo, Ralph Elliott
Mayo, Roger Carmell
Mayock, Robert Lee
Mazarakis, Michael Gerassimos
Mazel, Joseph Lucas
Mazenauer, Arthur John
Mazlen, Roger Geoffrey
Mazo, Bertrand Ross
Mazon, Meyer Ira
Mazor, David Mark
Mazur, Helen Louise Jones Grouten (Mrs. Albin M. Mazur)
Mazur, Ronald Michael
Mazur, Stella Mary
Mazza, Peter Domenick
Mazzacane, John Royal
Mazzatenta, Rosemary Dorothy
Mazzola, John William
Mazzone, Joseph John
Mazzone, V. Domenico
Mazzotta, Leon Michael
McAfee, Horace J.
Mc Afee, Jerry
McAleer, William Kearns
McAlister, Isabel Miley (Mrs. George Alexander McAlister)
Mc Allister, Joseph Charles
Mc Alpine, Frederick Sennett
Mc Arthur, Ruth Bell
Mc Auley, Joseph Anthony
Mc Avoy, Rita Cloutier (Mrs. George Edward McAvoy)
Mc Bride, Frank Vincent
Mc Bride, Howard Earl
McBride, Lloyd
McBride, Milford Lawrence, Jr.
Mc Brien, Rod
Mc Bryde, Felix Webster
Mc Bryde, Thomas Henry
Mc Cabe, Cynthia Jaffee
Mc Cabe, Edward Owen James
Mc Cabe, James Joseph
Mc Cabe, James Patrick
Mc Cabe, Joseph Charles
McCabe, Mary Alexandrine
Mc Cabe, Thomas Joseph
McCalley, Robert B(ruce), Jr.
Mc Candless, Anna Loomis
Mc Candless, Hugh Douglas
Mc Candless, Richard Lee
Mc Cann, John Thomas
Mc Carter, Thomas N., III
Mc Carthy, Daniel Donald, III
Mc Carthy, Daniel Joseph
McCarthy, Frederick William
Mc Carthy, John Francis, Jr.
Mc Carthy, Joseph Michael
McCarthy, Karen A.
Mc Carthy, Kevin John
McCarthy, Rollin Herbert
McCarthy, Terence Alan
Mc Carthy, Thomas J.
Mc Cartney, Earl J.
Mc Cartney, Joseph Philip
McCartney, Robert Charles
Mc Cauley, H(enry) Berton
Mc Clain, William Anderson
Mc Clane, Kenneth Anderson, Jr.
Mc Clarrin, William Otto
Mc Clary, David Michael
Mc Clean, Vernon Emanuel
McClelland, William Kelsey
Mc Clenathan, James Edward
Mc Clintock, Shirley Sprague
Mc Clure, Douglas Olcott
Mc Cluskey, Weldon James
Mc Coll, John Rome, Jr.
McCollough, Clair R.
Mc Collough, Eddie Clarence
Mc Comb, John Paul, Jr.
Mc Conky, Walter Bradley
Mc Connell, Alan Edward
Mc Connell, John Edward
Mc Connell, John Howard
McConnon, James Charles
Mc Corison, Marcus Allen
Mc Cormack, George Henry
Mc Cormack, Grace
Mc Cormack, John Francis, Jr.
McCormick, J(oseph) Carroll
Mc Cormick, James Charles
Mc Cormick, Joseph Frances
Mc Cormick, Robert Lawrence
McCormick-Pickett, Nancy
Mc Cowan, Richard James
Mc Coy, James Frank
Mc Coy, Kevin George
Mc Coy, Larry Dean
Mc Cracken, Blair
Mc Cracken, Jerald Russell
Mc Cracken, Stewart
McCrann, Thomas Emmett
Mc Crary, Eugenia Lester (Mrs. Dennis Daughtry McCrary)
Mc Crary, Vernon Eugene
Mc Crea, John Coles
Mc Creedy, Richard Eugene
Mc Creedy, Warren Thomas
Mc Crensky, Jonathan Allen
Mc Crohan, Kevin Francis
McCue, Brian James
McCue, Daniel Lawrence, Jr.
Mc Cue, John B.
Mc Cullough, Joseph Lee
McCullough, Kendrick
Mc Cune, James
Mc Cune, William Stanley
Mc Curdy, John
Mc Curdy, Patrick Pierre
Mc Curdy, Richard Clark
Mc Curdy, Robert Vaughn
Mc Dade, Joseph Michael
Mc Daniel, James Irwin
Mc Daniel, John Perry
Mc Dannald, Clyde Elliott
Mc David, Frederick Rhodes
Mc Dermott, Idaruth Mitchell (Mrs. Edward Brian McDermott)
Mc Dermott, Nelson Joseph, Jr.
McDevitt, Richard Eggleston
Mc Devitt, Robert James
Mc Dew, Carolyn Helen
Mc Donald, Andrew Jewett
Mc Donald, Charles Jack
Mc Donald, James Edward
McDonald, John Francis
Mc Donald, Joseph Valentine
Mc Donald, Khlar Elwood
Mc Donald, Malcolm Walker
Mc Donald, Owen Peter
Mc Donnell, Joseph Anthony
Mc Donnell, Virginia Bleecker (Mrs. John Henry McDonnell)
Mc Donnell, William Vincent
Mc Donough, Daniel John
Mc Donough, Donald Arthur
Mc Donough, Francis Anthony
McDonough, John Martin
Mc Dougal, Edward Francis
Mc Dowell, Charles W.
Mc Dowell, Harry Walter
Mc Dowell, William Giles
Mc Eldowney, Robert, Jr.
Mc Elroy, James Benjamin
Mc Elroy, John Harley
Mc Elwreath, Sally Chin
Mc Enrue, James Peter
Mc Evoy, James Edward
Mc Evoy, Richard Eugene
Mc Ewan, Mary Catherine Fee (Mrs. Ignatius McEwan)
Mc Ewen, Kenneth Lindsay
Mc Ewen, Richard Cusack
McEwen, Robert Cameron
Mc Fadden, Thomas J(oseph)
Mc Fall, Robert John
Mc Farland, Charles Manter
Mc Farlin, Harry Hugg
Mc Farren, George Allen
Mc Featers, Arthur Charles, Jr.
Mc Feeley, John Jay
Mc Gail, Arnold Rayfield, Jr.
Mc Gann, John Raymond
McGannon, Donald Henry
Mc Garvey, James Francis
Mc Gavic, John Samuel
Mc Geachie, John Stewart
McGee, Daniel Hugh
Mc Gee, Dorothy Horton
McGee, Gale William
Mc Gee, James Robert
Mc Gee, Robert Carlton, Jr.
McGee, Timothy William
Mc George, Ronald Kenneth
Mc Ghee, John Robert
Mc Gibbon, Pauline Mills
Mc Gill, Manley
Mc Gill, William James
Mc Gillicuddy, John Francis
Mc Gillicuddy, Robert Louis
Mc Ginn, Alan
Mc Ginn, Donald Joseph
Mc Ginnis, James Douglas
Mc Ginnis, Thomas Charles, Jr.
Mc Ginnis, Thomas Peter
Mc Givern, Bernard Edward, Jr.
Mc Givern, James Sabine
Mc Glade, Dennis Cullen
Mc Gough, William Edward
Mc Govern, John Hugh
Mc Govern, Michael John
Mc Gowan, Alan Hugh
Mc Gowan, Carl
Mc Gowan, Dolores Louise
Mc Gowan, John Malcolm
Mc Gowan, Patrick Terrance
Mc Grail, John Simon
Mc Grath, George William, Jr.
McGrath, Richard T.
Mc Grath, Ruth Ehrig
Mc Grath, William Thomas
Mc Guinness, Adelaide Helen
Mc Guinness, John Seward
Mc Guire, Heather Penny
Mc Guirk, Ronald Charles
Mc Guirl, Marlene Dana
Mc Hale, Edward, Jr.
Mc Hale, John Joseph
Mc Henry, Donnel Mitchel
Mc Henry, Robert Clifford
Mc Hugh, Matthew
Mc Ilhany, Sterling Fisher
McIlhone, John Thomas
McIlvain, Douglas Lee
Mc Ilvain, Jess Hall
Mc Ilvaine, Richard Scott
Mc Ilveen, Walter
Mc Inally, John Anthony
Mc Intosh, Robert Edward, Jr.
Mc Intosh, Roy Lawrence
McIntyre, James Philip
Mc Intyre, James Talmadge, Jr.
Mc Intyre, Thomas James
McIntyre, Williard Francis
Mc Kay, Douglas William
Mc Kay, Richard Joseph
Mc Kay, Winfield Cleland
Mc Keage, Arlington Bud
Mc Kean, Alexander Laird
Mc Kean, Andrew
Mc Kean, John F.
Mc Kee, Adam Emanuel, Jr.
Mc Kee, Delber L.
Mc Kee, Duncan Oliphant
Mc Kee, Elizabeth Brooks Thayer
Mc Kee, Frances Gwendolyn Martin (Mrs. Davis Bell McKee, Jr.)
Mc Kee, Margaret Jean
McKeel, Sam Stewart
Mc Keever, Paul Edward
McKenna, Gerald James
Mc Kenna, James A(loysius), Jr.
Mc Kenna, William Francis
McKenney, Florence Rea (Mrs. W. Gibbs McKenney, Jr.)
Mc Kenney, James Francis
Mc Kenney, Walter Gibbs, Jr.
Mc Kenzie, Francis Waldo
Mc Kenzie, Mary Agnes Mudd (Mrs. Terence J. McKenzie)
Mc Kenzie, Ray
Mc Kenzie, Walter Lawrence
Mc Kernan, Janis L(eigh)
McKinley, Donald Black
McKinley, John Key
McKinney, Charles Milton, III
Mc Kinney, James Morton
Mc Kinney, John Francis
McKinney, Stewart B.
Mc Kinnon, James Joseph, Jr.
Mc Kinnon, Linda Mary
Mc Kissick, Gaylord Edward
Mc Knight, Daniel Francis
Mc Knight, Joyce Sheldon
McKoy, Lattice Alice
McKusick, Vincent Lee
Mc Lain, Richard Lee
Mc Lain, William Tome
Mc Lauchlin, Evelyn Fink
Mc Laughlin, Donald Francis
Mc Laughlin, Edward David
Mc Laughlin, Hugh Dennis, Jr.
Mc Laughlin, John Patrick, Jr.
Mc Laughlin, William Earle
Mc Laughlin, William Lowndes
Mc Lean, Arlene Elizabeth Andrews (Mrs. Lewis Follett McLean)
Mc Lean, Donald Holman, Jr.
Mc Lean, Lewis Follett
Mc Lean, Nelson Allen
Mc Lean, William George
Mc Lean, William L., III
Mc Lean, Wilma Cathern
Mc Lemore, George Ammie, Jr.
Mc Lendon, Heath Brian
Mc Leod, John Henry
Mc Loud, Theresa Claire
Mc Mahon, Carol Ellen
Mc Mahon, Gerald Francis
Mc Mahon, John Patrick
Mc Mahon, Joseph John
Mc Mahon, Michael James
Mc Mahon, William James
Mc Manus, Eugene Joseph
McManus, Thomas Patrick
Mc Manus, William Francis
McMaster, Gloria Mae Bugni
Mc Master, Thomas Wilson
Mc Mennamin, John Lawrence
Mc Millan, Caroline Osgood
Mc Millan, Robert Lee
Mc Millan, Robert Ralph
Mc Millen, Loring
Mc Mullan, Jean Frances Gentry
Mc Mullen, Edwin Daniel
Mc Mullen, Edwin Wallace, Jr.
Mc Mullen, Frank Jones
Mc Mullen, John Joseph
Mc Mullen, Robert Michael
Mc Murtry, James Gilmer, III
Mc Nair, Lois Isobel Dinah
Mc Nallen, Mary Findle
Mc Nally, Frank Xavier
Mc Namara, Francis Joseph, Jr.
Mc Namara, J(ohn) Donald
Mc Namara, John Joseph
Mc Namara, Kevin David
Mc Namara, Robert Francis
Mc Neil, Donald Southworth
Mc Neil, Henry Slack
Mc Neill, John Melvin
Mc Nelis, Francis Leo
Mc Nelly, Theodore Hart
Mc Nichol, John Augustus, Jr.
McNiff, Philip J.
McNitt, Harold Austin
Mc Nulty, Matthew Francis, Jr.
Mc Nutt, Dan James
Mc Phee, Alexander Hector
Mc Quade, Margaret Ann
Mc Queary, Charles Everette
Mc Quillan, Elizabeth
Mc Quillin, Richard James
McShea, Joseph
Mc Sherry, Mary Elizabeth
McShine, Kynaston Leigh
McSorley, James Francis
Mc Spadden, Thomas Edward
Mc Sweeny, William Francis
Mc Tague, Peter James
Mc Vernon, John Joseph
Mc Wethy, James Andrew
Mc Whirter, John Ruben
McWilliams, Harry Kenneth
Meacham, Charles Thomas
Mead, Mary Ellen Terry
Mead, Russell M., Jr.
Meadowcroft, James Arthur
Meagher, Robert Joseph
Meaney, Joseph Thomas
Means, Cyril Chesnut, Jr.
Means, John Barkley
Means, Rosaline Linn (Mrs. Cyril Chesnut Means, Jr.)
Meany, George
Mears, Donald Bean
Mears, John Herbert, Jr.
Mears, Walter Robert
Mebus, Charles Fillmore, II
Mecca, William Anthony
Meckler, Alan Marshall
Meckley, Raymond Henry
Medeiros, Humberto Sousa
Medico, Frank
Medin, A. Louis
Medina, Harold R.
Medina-Spyropoulos, Esperanza
Medley, Kenneth Wayne
Medoff, William
Medsger, Gerald William
Medwig, Thomas Michael
Meech, Richard Campbell
Meek, Donald Chamberlin
Meeker, John Harbeck, Jr.
Meese, Harold Frederick
Megahed, Mohamed Salah
Megerson, John S.
Meghreblian, Robert Vartan
Megna, Philip Lewis, Jr.
Megrue, George Henry
Mehdi, Mohammad Taki
Mehl, Roger Howard
Mehlman, Myron A.
Mehta, Mohan L.

Mehta, Sunil Kumar
Meienhofer, Johannes Arnold
Meier, Louis Leonard, Jr.
Meijer, Robby
Meilleur, Paul Andre
Meinecke, Willard Henry
Meisch, Katherene Louise
Meisel, David Dering
Meisel, Joseph Thomas
Meisel, Louis Koenig
Meisel, Martin Hugh
Meisel, Michael S.
Meisenheimer, Daniel Thomas, Jr.
Meislahn, Harry Post
Meister, Steven Gerard
Meixner, Arthur Warren
Mekler, Arlen B.
Melato, Marion Ursula
Melby, James Christian
Melcher, George W., Jr.
Melia, James Lee
Mellinger, Louis Todhunter
Mellis, John George
Mello, Joseph Michael
Melmed, Ronald Martin
Melnitchenko, Eugene
Meltzer, Abraham
Meltzer, Milton
Meltzer, Yale Leon
Melucci, Richard Charles
Melville, Grevis Whitaker
Melville, Larry Scott
Melvin, A(rthur) Gordon
Menachem, Neal Jay
Menard, Marcel
Mencher, Alexander
Mendell, Edward Joel
Mendelsohn, Frederic Anthony
Mendelsohn, John
Mendelsohn, Monroe Leonard
Mendelson, Sol
Mendenhall, Donna June MacMillan
Mendenhall, Thomas Corwin, II
Mendez, Ruben P.
Mendrick, Ronald Jay
Menetrez, Jean Hugues
Meng, Mary Tyler
Meng, Maurice
Meng, Ralph Harvey
Meng, Ting-Tung
Mengel, Arthur Clayton
Menken, Robert Carl
Menneg, Paul Edward
Mennin, Miriam Juliet Kobrin
Mennin, Peter
Menter, A. Solomon
Meola, John Michael
Merabi, Shari John
Mercer, Sherwood Rocke
Mercoun, Dawn Denise
Mercure, Julien Gilles
Mercurio, Pat Anthony
Meredith, Dorothy Mae
Meredith, Edward John
Meredith, George (Marlor)
Meredith, Scott
Meriam, Philip Withington
Meringoff, Brian Nils
Merjave, Charles Michael
Merklen, Kenneth Elmer
Merle, Jane Malloy
Merlino, Anthony Frank
Mermelstein, Jacob
Merola, Emma M. Varvaro
Merolla, Michele Edward
Merowitz, Martin
Merriam, Daniel F(rancis)
Merrill, Arthur Alexander
Merrill, James
Merrill, Lawrence John
Merrill, Walter Williamson
Merriman, Henry
Merrin, Seymour
Merriss, Philip Ramsay, Jr.
Mersand, Joseph
Merskey, Marie Gertrude Fine (Mrs. Clarence Merskey)
Mertens, William
Merthan, Lawrence Casper
Mertz, Alfred Stephen
Mertz, Pierre
Merwin, Robert Freeman
Mescavage, Alexander Anthony, Jr.
Meshreki, Makram Habib
Meskauskas, John Algimantas
Mesmer, Roger Edward George
Mesney, Dorothy Taylor
Messer, Thomas M.
Messina, Giacomo Anthony
Messineo, Paul Joseph
Messner, Joseph Anton
Messner, Robert Thomas
Messner, Wayne Kenneth
Metcalf, Harlan Goldsbury
Metcalf, Harry Leonard
Metrey, George David
Metsch, Arthur David
Metsisto, Tauno James
Metson, Graham
Metz, Edward
Metz, Vernon Wahl
Metzger, Alan Fairfield
Metzger, Ernest Hugh
Metzger, William Henry, Jr.
Metzman, Frances Schuman
Meyburg, Arnim Hans
Meyer, Carl Edwin, Jr.
Meyer, Cornelius Charles
Meyer, E(mma) Dorothea
Meyer, Edward Henry
Meyer, Elmer Ephraim, Jr.
Meyer, Fred Charles
Meyer, George F., Jr.
Meyer, Harold Robert
Meyer, Irwin Stephen
Meyer, John Henry
Meyer, Kenneth Arthur
Meyer, Marshall Moriss
Meyer, Richard B.
Meyers, Barbara Eunice
Meyers, Ernest Stanley
Meyers, John Francis
Meyers, Martin Daniel
Meyers, Robert Townsend, Jr.
Meyerson, Martin
Meyler, William Anthony
Meyner, Helen Stevenson
Mezer, Robert Ross
Mezrow, Ralph Raymond
Michael, Phyllis Callender (Mrs. Arthur L. Michael)
Michael, Stanley Theodore
Michaelis, Paul Charles
Michaels, Abraham
Michaels, George
Michaels, Linda Ann
Michaels, Peter Edwards
Michaelson, Julius Cooley
Michanowsky, George
Michaud, Alphee Martial
Michaud, Patrick Arnold
Michaud, Robert Jean
Michel, Henry Ludwig
Michel, Robert Emory
Michele, Mary Ellen
Micheli, Lyle Joseph
Michelis, Michael Frank
Michels, Edward Herbert, Jr.
Michelsen, Christopher Bruce Hermann
Michelson, David Scott
Michelson, Leslie Paul
Michie, Daniel Boorse, Jr.
Michielli, Donald Warren
Michman, Ronald David
Mickel, Hubert Sheldon
Mickevich, Walter Charles
Micunis, Gordon Jules
Middlekauff, James Holan
Middleton, David
Middleton, John Thomas
Midura, Mieczyslaw Jozef
Miele, Philip Hargreaves
Migliore, Salvatore Anthony
Mignault, Robert Duval
Mihalik, Frank Melvyn
Mihram, George Arthur
Mikolji, Boris Hrvoje
Mikulski, Barbara Ann
Mikuriya, Tadafumi
Milano, Heather Casey
Milazzo, Joseph James
Milbank, Jeremiah
Milbourne, Walter Robertson
Milch, Robert Austin
Milch, Robert Jeffrey
Milch, Ronald Barry
Milde, Helmut Ingo
Miles, Horace Clinton
Milette, Pierre Charles
Milewski, Stanislaw Antoni
Milici, John Attilio
Milke, Denis Jerome
Mill, Charles Stuart
Millard, Charles Warren, III
Millard, William Andrew
Miller, Alan Harvey
Miller, Alan Jay
Miller, Alan Manning
Miller, Albert Jay
Miller, Albert Raymond, Jr.
Miller, Arnold
Miller, Barry
Miller, Bruce Alan
Miller, Carol Miller
Miller, Charles Norman
Miller, Charles Richard
Miller, Dale Lloyd
Miller, David Thomas
Miller, Donald Le Sessne
Miller, Elaine Julia
Miller, Ellen Louise
Miller, Frances Elizabeth
Miller, Frederick
Miller, G(eorge) William
Miller, (Richard) Guy
Miller, Harold
Miller, Harry, Jr.
Miller, Helena A.
Miller, Henry, III
Miller, Henry George
Miller, Irving William
Miller, Jason
Miller, Jeanne-Marie Anderson (Mrs. Nathan John Miller)
Miller, Joel Robert
Miller, John A(dalbert)
Miller, John Lewis
Miller, John Nelson
Miller, John Peter (Jack)
Miller, John Robinson, Jr.
Miller, Joseph Arthur
Miller, Kenneth Lewis
Miller, Kenneth Michael
Miller, Lois Anderson
Miller, Lothar Kurt
Miller, Margaret Ellis
Miller, Marie Di Stefano (Mrs. Phillip Miller)
Miller, Mary Emily
Miller, Max
Miller, Norman Adam
Miller, Patrick Michael
Miller, Rex Arnold
Miller, Richards Thorn
Miller, Rita
Miller, Rose Mary
Miller, Ruth Louise
Miller, Ruth Mary Helen (Mrs. William H. Ferguson)
Miller, Samuel Clifford
Miller, Sonia Kay Flicker
Miller, Stanley
Miller, Stanley Allen
Miller, Stanley Norman
Miller, Stephen Herschel
Miller, Wayne Dunbar
Miller, Wayne Elwood
Miller, William Arch, Jr.
Miller, William Charles
Miller, William Edward
Miller, William John, Jr.
Miller, William Russell
Miller, William Sanford
Miller, Yvette Espinosa
Millet, John Bradford
Millie, Harold Raymond
Milligan, John Drane
Milligan, Rex Vincent
Milligan, Robert Harry
Milliken, Elva Gardiner (Mrs. James R. Milliken)
Millman, Neal Allen
Millman, Sandy Keith
Mills, Clifford Wheeler
Mills, Edward Warren
Mills, George Marshall
Millstein, Sidney Nelson
Milne, David Wilson
Milne, Frank Emmett
Milne, George Hector Fanjoy
Milner, Charles Fremont, Jr.
Milnes, John Herbert
Milonopoulos, Anthony
Milotte, Louis Henry, Jr.
Milstein, Richard Sherman
Milstock, Mayer
Miltenberger, Frederick William
Miltner, John Robert
Milton, Leonard
Milutinovich, Jugoslav Srboljub
Mimm, Robert Franklin
Mims, George L.
Min, David Byong
Min, Leo Yoon-Gee
Mina, George Michael
Minadakis, Nicholas John
Mina-Mora, Dorise Olson
Mina-Mora, Raul José
Minasi, Joseph
Minasy, Arthur John
Miner, Lisbeth (Mrs. Alasdair William Spens-Thomson)
Miner, (Theodore) Richardson, Jr.
Miner, Samuel Norton
Ming, Si-Chun
Mingolla, Cosmo Edward
Minifie, James MacDonald, Jr.
Minikes, Stephan Michael
Minish, Joseph George
Mink, Patsy T.
Minkoff, Jeffrey
Minkow, Julius
Minkowitz, Martin
Minna, John Dorrance
Minner, Arthur Robert
Minnich, Eli Blausser
Minnich, Leonard Lorraine
Minnich, Sarah Ely
Minnick, Adrienne Kavanagh
Minnock, Jeanne B.
Minns, Albert Edward, Jr.
Minturn, Benjamin Bradshaw
Mintz, Fred
Mintz, Gilbert
Mintz, Norman Nelson
Mintz, Robert Alan
Mintz, Samuel Isaiah
Mir, Juan Enrique
Mira, John Francis
Mirabelli, Andre Robert
Mirabito, John Armand
Miranda, Vincent Buz
Mirante, Thomas Anthony
Mirchandani, Dilip
Mireault, Jean-Marc
Mirkin, Gabe Baron
Miron, Tsipora
Mirsky, Stanley
Mirto, Valentine Dominick
Mischler, Forrest Clair
Mishler, Jacob
Mishoe, Luna Isaac
Misiek, Martin
Misson, George William
Mistler, Rose Marie
Mitchell, Alan Edward
Mitchell, Bradford William
Mitchell, Charles Alfred
Mitchell, Claude
Mitchell, Donald J.
Mitchell, Frederick Myron
Mitchell, Hester Louise
Mitchell, Ira Canfield, III
Mitchell, James Richard
Mitchell, John Patrick
Mitchell, John Thomas, Jr.
Mitchell, Mark Brendan
Mitchell, Neal Burgess, Jr.
Mitchell, Parren James
Mitchell, Stephen Edward
Mitchell, William Joseph
Mitchem, Horace Foster, Jr.
Mitrik, Leonard John
Mitsakos, Charles Leonidas
Mittel, John J.
Mittelman, Jay Arnold
Mittl, Rainer Norbert
Mittman, Bruce Joel
Moakley, John Joseph
Moan, Charles Edward, Jr.
Mochary, Mary Veronica (Mrs. Stephen E. Mochary)
Mochizuki, John Tsuneteru
Mociuk, Yar Wasyl
Mock, Ernest Leighton
Mock, Robert Claude
Mockridge, Norton
Moderacki, Edmund Anthony
Modica, Alfred Joseph
Modny, Cynthia Jean
Moeller, Carl William
Moeller, George Rossworn
Moellering, Robert Charles, Jr.
Moench, John Christopher
Moffett, Anthony Toby
Moffett, Henry Clay Nick
Moffitt, Augustine Edward, Jr.
Moffitt, Robert James
Mogel, Ernest H.
Moglia, Fred Andrew
Mohl, Allan Sussman
Mohl, Robert Charles
Mohnen, Volker Armin
Mohorich, Helen Marie
Mohr, Lionel Charles
Mohtashemi, Hormoz
Moiles, William Henry, Jr.
Molan, John Edward
Molander, David John
Moldenke, Harold Norman
Molinari, Pietro Filippo
Molitor, Graham Thomas Tate
Moliver, Martin
Moll, Clarence Russel
Mollenkott, Virginia Ramey
Mollow, Benjamin Richard
Molnar, August John
Molz, Robert Joseph
Monaghan, James Matthew, III
Monahan, John Francis
Monahon, Philip Christopher
Monath, Norman
Moncure, Ashby Carter
Mondale, Joan Adams
Mondale, Walter Frederick
Monet, Jacques
Mong, Frank Fowler
Monios, Constantine Michael
Monk, Abraham
Monk, Ivan
Monsky, Mark B. von Sommer
Montague, James Lee
Montague, Lawrence Michael, Jr.
Montaigne, Sanford Howard
Montambault, Leonce
Monter, Gerald
Montero, Darrel Martin
Montesi, Richard Lewis
Montgomery, Claude
Montgomery, Dean Christopher
Montgomery, Everett Francis, Jr.
Montgomery, Henry Edward, Jr.
Montgomery, Richard Millar
Monti, Frank Anthony
Montigny, Richard Warren
Montney, Russell Leon
Montouri, Warren Kendall
Montoya, Juan
Moody, Barbara Garey
Mooers, Edward Allen
Mook, Kent Walker
Moomjian, Martin
Moon, Jay
Moon, John Robert
Moone, Everett Charles Edward
Moor, Edgar Jacques
Moor, Joan Thornton Rothwell (Mrs. Edgar Jacques Moor)
Moore, Acel
Moore, Adam Gillespie Nichol
Moore, Andrew Given Tobias, II
Moore, Charles Henkel
Moore, Daniel Edmund
Moore, David Leonard
Moore, Dorothy Heyeck
Moore, Earle Kennedy
Moore, Edward Frederick
Moore, James Robert
Moore, Jane Ross
Moore, Jean-Marie
Moore, Johnnie Adolph
Moore, Lucille Cass
Moore, Patrick Lewis
Moore, Paul, Jr.
Moore, Ralph Joseph, Jr.
Moore, Richard Lathrop
Moore, Robert Chalmer
Moore, Robert Edmund
Moore, Robert Paul
Moore, Roger Allan
Moore, Shirley Throckmorton (Mrs. Elmer Lee Moore)
Moore, Sidney Richards
Moore, Sonia
Moore, Stanford
Moore, Talmadge Lee
Moore, Walter Calvin
Moore, Will Terry
Moore, William Edward
Moores, Frank D.
Moorhead, Davis Tatum (Dave)
Moorhead, Robert George Chadbourne
Moorhead, William Singer
Moorthy, Ravi Krishna
Moos, Walter Anton
Moose, James Sayle
Moose, Ray Stanley
Moot, Agnes Brumbaugh (Mrs. Earle O. Moot)
Morahan, Daniel Michael Kevin
Morales, Alvaro
Morales, Raul
Moran, Charles A.
Moran, Harold Joseph
Moran, James Joseph
Moran, Juliette M(ay)
Moran, Martin Joseph
Moran, William Arnold, Jr.
Morano, Pasquale Francis
More, Eileen Marie
Morell, David Louis
Morency, Renald Michel
Moreno, John Henry
Morere, Jean Marie
Morgan, Colin John
Morgan, David Howell
Morgan, Frank Thomas
Morgan, Jean Elizabeth
Morgan, LeRoy Tuttle
Morgan, Lorraine Lee
Morgan, Walter Edward
Morgenstern, Dan Michael
Morgenstern, Stephen
Morgenthau, Anthony Reginald
Moriarty, Eugene Vincent
Moriarty, James Brendan
Morin, Morton Edwin
Morin, Raymond Gerald
Morissette, Guy Jean
Moritz, Donald Irwin
Morlino, Michael Robert
Mormile, Jude Marie
Morningstar, Ann Scott (Mrs. Robert P. Morningstar)
Morrell, Wayne Beam, Jr.
Morrill, William Frank
Morris, Bernard Newth
Morris, Calvin Milyard
Morris, Caroline Jane McMasters Stewart (Mrs. Francis J. Morris)
Morris, David Mark
Morris, Donald Arthur
Morris, Edward Laurence, Jr.
Morris, Ernest Brougham
Morris, Harvey Seth
Morris, J(oseph) Anthony
Morris, James Stephen
Morris, Jill Carlotta
Morris, John Edward
Morris, Joseph Paul, Jr.
Morris, Kenneth Baker
Morris, Patricia Josephine Collins (Mrs. John F. Morris)
Morris, Richard Cook, Jr.
Morris, Richard Jules
Morris, Roger Ray
Morris, Terry Lesser (Mrs. Eugene J. Morris)
Morris, Thomas Jefferson
Morrison, A.H.
Morrison, Charles Frederick
Morrison, Donald Keith
Morrison, Donald William
Morrison, Frank Strouss
Morrison, Howard Irwin
Morrison, Ian Alastair
Morrison, James William, Jr.
Morrison, Jeffrey Steven
Morrison, John Doane
Morrison, Layton Arthur
Morrissey, Charles David
Morrissey, James Joseph, Jr.
Morrissey, Madeleine Maria
Morrissey, Thomas Jerome
Morrow, David Warren
Morrow, Glenn Davis
Morrow, Scott Imlay
Morrow, William Earl
Morrow, William Lee
Morse, Dean Weber
Morse, John Joseph
Morse, Joseph Louis
Morse, Leon William
Morse, Richard Van Tuyl
Morse, Thomas Smyth
Mortensen, Ralph
Morton, Donald John
Morton, Eugene Daniel
Morton, Jay Robert
Morton, Thomas Grant
Morton, Thomas Gregory
Moschetti, Guy Anthony
Moseley, George Thomas
Moser, Harold Dean
Moses, Donald Allen
Moses, Elbert Raymond, Jr.
Moses, Frank Lamberth
Moses, John Gabriel
Mosher, Giles Edmond
Mosher, Peter David
Moshier, David Irwin
Mosier, Maurice Lee
Moski, Bruno Albert
Moskowitz, M. L. (Chic)
Moss, Arthur Jay
Moss, Doris Fitzer
Moss, Edgar George Ernest
Moss, Hugh MacMillan
Moss, Robert Sheriffs
Moszynski, Jerzy Robert
Motley, John Paul
Mott, Charles Harvey
Mott, George Fox
Mott, Vincent Valmon
Motta, John Richard
Motter, Roberta Lee
Mottley, Charles Cranston
Mouat, Robert Harrower, Jr.
Moulton, Elliott Jan
Moulton, John Knight
Moulton, Paul (Pete) Douglas
Moultrie, James
Mount, Wadsworth Walton
Mount, Ward (Pauline Ward)
Mountan, Albert Wayne
Moutran, Julia Spencer
Mowad, Joseph James
Mower, George Richardson
Mowitz, Arnold Martin
Mowry, David Thomas
Moxey, Louis White, III
Moxey, Richard Todd
Moyer, Arlington Schuler
Moyer, F. Stanton
Moyer, John Henry
Moyer, Kenneth Harold
Moylan, Dermot Brendan
Moylan, Fergus Michael Blake
Moynihan, Daniel Patrick
Mozo, William Brantly, Jr.
Mpelkas, Christos Charles
Mraz, Ruth Reed
Mroczek, William Joseph
Mruk, Walter Frederick
Muccari, Frank Gregory
Mucenieks, Paul Raimond
Muchnick, Richard Stuart
Muck, Darrel Lee
Mueller, Claus
Mueller, Hans Jacob
Mueller, Harry Louis
Mueller-Heubach, Eberhard August
Muenker, Louis Thomas
Muffler, John Paul
Mugavero, Francis J.
Muir, J(ohn) Dapray
Muirhead, George Robertson
Muirhead, Glen D.
Mukai, Cromwell Daisaku
Mukerji, Jatindra Nath
Mukherjee, Asit Baran
Mulder, David Stevenson
Mulder, Frederick Sasser
Mulder, Herman
Mule, Salvatore Joseph
Mulert, Howard Max
Mulford, Donald Lewis
Mulhall, John Michael
Mull, Walter Ray
Mullaney, Richard Langley, Jr.
Mullen, Frank Albert
Mullen, Joseph James
Mullen, Willard Franklin
Muller, Alfred
Muller, Dorothea Rosalie
Muller, Gary William
Muller, Peter
Muller, Richard Johnson
Muller, Steven
Mullestein, William Ernest
Mullette, Paul Stanley
Mulligan, Andrew Phillip
Mulligan, Elinor Patterson
Mulligan, Hugh Augustine
Mulligan, James Marion
Mulligan, William G(eorge)
Mulligan, William Hughes
Mullinix, Edward Wingate
Mulrooney, John Patrick
Mulroy, Edward Timothy
Mulvey, Mary Crowley (Mrs. Gordon F. Mulvey)
Mulvihill, Joseph Gregory
Mumford, Herbert Windsor, III
Mumford, Robin Bruce
Mumma, Albert Girard, Jr.
Munasinghe, Mohan P. C.
Mundy, David Horton
Mundy, Mark James
Munin, Martin Irving
Munley, Jane Kravitz
Munoz, John Rivers, Jr.
Munson, Harold Edwin
Munters, Manfreds
Muranaka, Richard George
Muraraka, Shyam Prasad
Murchison, David Claudius
Murdaugh, Noveree
Murdoch, Keith Rupert
Murdolo, Michael Antonio
Murphey, William Meredith
Murphy, Andrew Phillip, Jr.
Murphy, Austin John
Murphy, Barbara Jane
Murphy, Brian John
Murphy, Charles Francis
Murphy, Cornelius F.
Murphy, Edmond Lawrence
Murphy, Eileen Maria
Murphy, Francis Timothy, Jr.
Murphy, George Edward
Murphy, James Daniel
Murphy, James Stephen
Murphy, John Anthony
Murphy, John James
Murphy, John Joseph
Murphy, John Michael
Murphy, Joseph Samson
Murphy, Lawrence Eric
Murphy, Leonard Edward
Murphy, Paul Francis
Murphy, Ralph Edgar
Murphy, Robert Blair
Murphy, Robert C.
Murphy, Robert John
Murphy, Thomas Daniel, Jr.
Murphy, Thomas Paul
Murphy, William Parry
Murray, Albert Edward, Jr.
Murray, Anthony Harry, Jr.
Murray, Caroline Fish
Murray, Catherine Elaine
Murray, Florence Kerins (Mrs. Paul F. Murray)
Murray, James Joseph

Murray, Joseph Daniel
Murray, Joseph Francis, Jr.
Murray, Lawrence Allen
Murray, Patricia Ann
Murray, Robert Lee
Murray, Robin Rivers Barden
Murray, Thomas Harold
Murray, Thomas Patrick
Murray, Warren James
Murray, William Bruce
Murtagh, James P.
Murtagh, Thomas John
Murtaugh, Walter Angelus
Murtha, John Patrick
Musa, Frank James
Music, Jack Farris
Musicus, Milton
Musil, Margaret Hooker Kirkland (Mrs. Ralph A. Musil)
Muskie, Edmund Sixtus
Mussari, Anthony Joseph
Musselman, Francis Haas
Musser, Benjamin Garber
Musser, Jay Charles
Musser, William Lloyd, Jr.
Mustian, Alfred Plummer, Jr.
Musto, David Franklin
Musumeci, Thomas
Muzac, Andre J.
Myerholtz, Earl Frederick
Myers, Alfred Frantz
Myers, Andrew Breen
Myers, Caroline Clark (Mrs. Garry Cleveland Myers)
Myers, Charles F.
Myers, Edwin Nelson
Myers, Eugene Ekander
Myers, Gary Arthur
Myers, Jean Ann
Myers, Jo Anne
Myers, John Henry
Myers, Lawrence
Myers, Legh Richmond
Myers, Michael
Myers, Morey M.
Myers, Robert John
Myers, Thomas Andrews
Myers, Thomas Kromer
Myers, Wayne Alan
Myler, David Donald
Mylroie, Victor Lavonne
Nace, Edgar Paul
Nachtigall, Lila Ehrenstein
Nadeem, Raphael George
Nadel, Barbara Anne
Nadel, Benjamin Irving
Nadel, Michael
Nadel, Monroe Stanley
Nadich, Judah
Nadley, Harris Jerome
Nagaraj, Holavanahally Seshachar
Nagel, Carl Edward, Jr.
Nagle, Frederick Floyd
Nagler, Arnold L.
Nagler, Leon Gregory
Nagorski, Zygmunt
Nagy, Brian Robson
Nagy, Frank Andrew
Naider, Fred Robert
Naidorf, Irving Joseph
Naidu, Janakiram Ramaswamy
Naiman, James
Naimark, George Modell
Naimi, Shapur
Naismith, Grace Akin
Nakano, Michio
Nall, Thomas Martin
Namba, Tatsuji
Namias, Jean E.
Namrow, Arnold
Nanay, Julia
Nance, Roy Alfred
Nantel, Albert John
Napier, Robert Jon
Naples, John Daniel
Napolitano, Ernest George
Napolitano, Pat
Napor, Carl Anthony
Narayanan, Madayath
Narcisi, Rocco Sandy
Nardi, Thomas James
Nardin, Mario
Nardone, Don D.
Nardone, Vincent Joseph
Narvell, David Brown, Jr.
Narwicz, Charles Anthony
Nasaduke, Irene
Nash, Harold Edward, Jr.
Nash, Peter Howard
Nashed, M. Zuhair
Naspinsky, Casimer Andrew
Nassif, Shakeeb Joseph
Nast, Charles Coudert
Natale, Anthony Paul
Natale, Samuel Michael
Natali, Alfred Maxim
Nathans, Daniel
Nathanson, Charles Conrad
Natterstad, Jerry H.
Naughton, Ethel May (Mrs. Clifford Zeiss)
Naughton, Frank Christopher
Navia, Luis Eduardo
Nawy, Edward George
Nazareno, Jose Poblete
Nazem, Fereydoun F.
Nazzaro, Rocco Michael
Neal, Mansfield C., Jr.
Neal, Robert Chester
Neale, F. Brent
Neale, Joseph Hamilton
Neall, Robert Raymond
Nealon, William Joseph
Neals, Huerta Cortez
Neathery, Robert Walter, Jr.
Needham, Shirley Florence
Neely, Homer Clifford
Neely, James Richard
Neff, Edwin Farnsworth
Neff, John Adam
Neff, Raymond Kenneth
Negishi, Ei-ichi
Negley, Martha Loree
Negri, Rocco Antonio
Neibert, Harold Calvin
Neidenberg, Jay Ronald
Neidermyer, Paul Daniel, III
Neifert, John Clinton
Neiger, Stephen
Neil, William Neilson
Neill, Thomas Taylor
Neilson, Elizabeth Anastasia
Neilson, John, Jr.
Neilson, Winthrop Cunningham, III
Neiman, LeRoy
Neinstedt, Harry Wright
Nelles, Merice Tilman
Nelli, Donald James
Nells, Richard Martin
Nelridge, Edwin Walter
Nelson, Andrew John, II
Nelson, Arthur Hunt
Nelson, Arthur Joseph, Jr.
Nelson, Carey Boone (Mrs. Kenneth Warwick Nelson)
Nelson, Elizabeth
Nelson, Gordon Leigh
Nelson, Harry William
Nelson, Jean Williams
Nelson, John Walter, Jr.
Nelson, Julius
Nelson, Logan V. (Mrs. Frank B. Nelson)
Nelson, Marie Poole Coleman (Mrs. Benjamin Nelson)
Nelson, Marven Ora
Nelson, Nancy Jane
Nelson, Ralph Lowell
Nelson, Richard Martin
Nelson, Ronald Aaron
Nelson, Stanley
Nelson, Thomas Harry
Nemir, Albert S.
Neppl, Walter Joseph
Nerone, Frank Regan
Nesbit, Douglas Charles
Nesbitt, Russell Ulmer, Jr.
Nessen, Ward Henry
Nesterczuk, George
Nestos, Angela
Neuberg, Hans Werner
Neuberger, Carmen Guevara
Neumaier, Gerhard John
Neuman, Lawrence Donald
Neumann, Elizabeth
Neumann, Jonathan
Neumann, Robert Gerhard
Neupauer, Jacob Cyril
Neuschel, Richard Frederick
Nevas, Leo
Neveu, Paul Roland
Neviaser, Robert Jon
Neville, Howard Ralph
Nevius, Donald George
Newball, Harold Harcourt
Newberg, Eric George, Jr.
Newbold, H. Steven Lee, II
Newbold, Herbert Leon, Jr.
Newbrough, James Reed
Newcomb, Robert Bateman
Newell, Donald Lewis
Newer, Thesis
Newhouse, Samuel I.
Newler, Jerome Marc
Newlin, Lyman Wilbur
Newman, Alexander
Newman, Alvin
Newman, Bernard
Newman, Harold
Newman, Harry Joseph
Newman, Harry Rudolph
Newman, Herbert Ellis
Newman, Jeffrey Frederick
Newman, Leonard
Newman, Nathan Allen
Newman, Richard August
Newman, Richard Michael
Newman, Robert George
Newman, Sheldon Oscar
Newmark, Marilyn (Mrs. Leonard J. Meiselman)
Newsam, Ralston William
Newton, Benjamin Francis
Newton, Craig Alan
Newton, Willoughby
Ney, Edward Noonan
Ney, Virgil
Nezelek, Annette Evelyn (Mrs. Edward Nezelek)
Nezelek, Edward Lewis
Neziroglu, Cevat
Ng, Lorenz Keng-Yong
Ng, Peter Yin-Sak
Nicandros, Constantine Stavros
Nicastro, Dean Paul
Niccolini, Dianora
Nichini, Franco Maria
Nichol, Horace Gibson
Nichol, William Lester
Nichols, Carl Wheeler
Nichols, David A.
Nichols, George Guernsey, Jr.
Nichols, Henry Eliot
Nichols, Herbert Lownds
Nichols, Jennie Barton (Mrs. R. Hewitt Nichols)
Nichols, John Peter
Nichols, Richard Frederick Fuller, Jr.
Nichols, Rodney Wayson
Nichols, Roy Calvin
Nicholson, Alfred Douglas
Nicholson, Edward Wheelock Steele
Nicholson, John Perry
Nicholson, Richard Ecroyd
Nicholson, Robert Hart
Nicholson, Thomas Dominic
Nickerson, James Eldridge
Nickerson, John Mitchell
Nickerson, Joshua Atkins, Jr.
Nicklas, Victor Earle
Nicklin, George Leslie, Jr.
Nicol, Marjorie Carmichael
Nicolopoulos, John Anthony
Niebling, Robert Edwin
Nieburg, Herbert Alan
Niederman, James Corson
Nielsen, Henning
Nielsen, Klaus Thorsten Wiese
Nielsen, Kris Richard
Nielsen, Svend Erik
Nielsen, Waldo Joseph
Niemeyer, Grover Charles
Nieporent, Hans Joachim
Nieuwenhuis, Herman Karel
Niguidula, Faustino Nazario
Niizuma, Minoru
Niland, Lynda Jeanne
Nilsen, Chris James
Nilson, Patricia Jane
Nilsson, Einar Wennerlund
Niquette, Reaman Paul
Nirenberg, Jesse Stanley
Nirenberg, Marshall Warren
Nisco, John Fulco Adriano
Nise, Michael
Nisenson, Stanley Merton
Nishimoto, Kenichi
Nisonger, Earl Gregory
Nispel, Benjamin Strickler
Nissenbaum, Gerald
Nissley, Dan, Jr.
Nissley, Eleanore Steffens
Nist, Claude Louis
Nix, Robert N. C.
Nixon, Philip Andrews
Noack, August William, Jr.
Nobel, Joel Judovich
Nobile, John Frank
Noble, James Kendrick, Jr.
Noble, Mildred Mae Somerlade (Mrs. William Egan Noble)
Noble, Roy Edmund
Noble, William Fielding
Nochimow, Eli
Nocita, Gerard Ralph
Nocks, Arnold Jay
Nodell, Celeste
Noel, Essex Crystol, III
Noel, Joseph Michael
Noer, David Michael
Nöffke, Carl Frank
Noffsinger, Terrell Limuel
Noiles, Douglas George
Nolan, Edward Joseph
Nolan, Frank Michael
Nolan, John Gavin
Nolan, Louise Mary
Nolan, Richard Thomas
Nolan, Sean
Nolan, Thomas Dennis
Noland, William Marshall
Nolen, Paul
Nolf, David Manstan
Noll, Chuck
Nollau, E. Wilson
Nomura, Hirokuni
Noonan, James Francis
Noone, Lana Mae
Nordlinger, Gerson, Jr.
Nordstrand, Nathalie Elizabeth Johnson
Norman, Richard
Noronha, Leonardo Gastao
Norquist, Warren Elliot
Norris, Clayton
Norris, Curtis Bird
Norris, Frank Allen
Norris, John Anthony
Norris, Robert Standish
Norris, Wilfred Glen
Norstrand, Iris Marie Fletcher (Mrs. Severin A. Norstrand)
Northrop, Edward Skottowe
Norton, Harold Klein
Norton, J(ames) Arthur
Norton, John Charles
Norton, Peter Francis
Norton, Thomas Edward
Norton, Warren Author
Norwood, Carolyn Virginia
Nosenzo, Robert Joseph
Noseworthy, Lloyd Marvin
Noss, Jerome Reed
Notaro, Alfred Leon
Notey, Richard A.
Notkin, Jerome J.
Notkin, Leonard Sheldon
Notowidigdo, Musinggih Hartoko
Notter, George Madison, Jr.
Novack, Sheldon
Novak, Adolph
Novak, Alyce Hunt
Novak, Benjamin Joseph
Novak, Michael (John), (Jr.)
Novello, Alfred Thomas
November, William Edward
Nover, Naomi Goll
Novich, Max Mordecai
Novick, Louis Jacob
Novidor, Benjamin
Novina, Trudi (Mrs. Charles E. Coakley)
Novotny, Rudolph Francis
Nowak, Henry James
Nowlin, Thomas Edward
Noxon, Margaret Walters (Mrs. Herbert Richards Noxon)
Noyes, Robert Edwin
Noznesky, Harry Joseph
Nriagu, Jerome Okonkwo
Nucera, Joseph Philip
Nugent, Brother Gregory
Nuhn, Charles Kelsey
Nuland, Anthony Conrad Jordan
Nulman, Seymour Shlomo
Nunan, Desmond James
Nunan, Francis Anthony, Jr.
Nunemaker, Rodney Dale
Nunn, James Richard
Nusbaum, Mort
Nussbaum, Aaron
Nussbaum, Murray
Nussbaum, Paul Allan
Nussbaum, Paul B.
Nuxall, John William
Nyburg, Willard Lloyd
Nydick, David
Nyere, Robert Alan
Nygreen, G. Theodore
Nyirjesy, Istvan
Oakes, Jean Marie
Oaks, L(ucian) Robert
Oatway, Francis Carlyle
Obal, Thaddeus Joseph
Ober, Atuart Alan
Oberdorfer, Conrad Walter
Oberfield, Richard Alan
Oberfrank, Eugene, Jr.
Oberlander, Leonard
Oberman, Leonard S.
Oberwager, Washburn Scovill
O'Boyle, Frederick Martin
O'Brien, Cyril John
O'Brien, David Shepard
O'Brien, Edward Michael, Jr.
O'Brien, Eugene James
O'Brien, James Jerome
O'Brien, John Gerald
O'Brien, John Michael
O'Brien, John Wilfrid
O'Brien, Joseph Robert
O'Brien, Kathryn Rose Buttice
O'Brien, Kenneth Robert
O'Brien, Keran
O'Brien, Lloyd Jay
O'Brien, Mary Nelson Firth
O'Brien, Mildred Elaine
O'Brien, Richard Green
O'Brien, Richard Harold
O'Brien, Roger Joseph
O'Brien, Thomas Francis
O'Bryon, James Fredrick
Ochoa, Severo
Ochsenschlager, Edward Lloyd
Ockerse, Thomas
Ockershausen, Andrew Martin
Ockert, Donn Lee
O'Connell, Agnes Anne
O'Connell, Daniel Joseph
O'Connell, Francis Vincent
O'Connell, Henry Francis, Jr.
O'Connell, Margaret Jane Phelan (Mrs. Daniel O'Connell)
O'Connell, Richard Henry
O'Connell, Richard James
O'Connell, Robert John
O'Connor, Barbara Sager
O'Connor, Jean Katherine
O'Connor, John Bartholomew
O'Connor, John Joseph
O'Connor, John Joseph
O'Connor, Kenneth Finbarr
O'Connor, Loretta Singler
O'Connor, Michael Charles
O'Connor, Robert James
O'Connor, Thomas Joseph
O'Connor, Walter Joseph
O'Connor, William John
O'Day, James Francis
O'Day, Marie Estelle (Mrs. Marcus D. O'Day)
O'Dea, Marie
Odell, Louise Minter
Odom, Emwood
O'Donnell, Denis Michael
O'Donnell, Francis Peter
O'Donnell, James Francis
O'Donnell, Kirk
O'Donnell, Patrick Joseph
O'Donnell, Walter Gregory
O'Donohue, Melville Joseph Bernard
Oehme, Wolfgang Walter
Oehmler, George Courtland
Ofengand, Edward James
Offenhartz, Edward
Offit, Avodah Komito
Ogbuawa, Obiora Matthias
Ogden, Peggy A.
Ogg, Robert Danforth
Ogilby, Lyman Cunningham
Ogilvie, Douglas Spaulding
Ogle, David Brett
O'Gorman, Ned
O'Grady, George Losere
O'Grady, Jerome Vincent
Oguzhan, Cavit Mehmet
Oh, Harry Hak-keun
Oh, Kong Tatt
O'Hara, John Brangs
O'Hara, Patrick John
O'Hara, Susana Krivatsy
O'Hare, Thomas Edward
O'Hearn, Peter Joseph Thomas
O'Hearn, William Joseph
O'Herlihy, Dermot Brian
O'Herlihy, Hilary Timothy
O'Hern, Jane Susan
Ohrenstein, Roman Abraham
Ohrman, Paul Daniel
O'Keefe, Wanda Lydia
Okin, Jay Alan
Okrepkie, Ralph George
Oktem, Nizamettin
Okun, Milton Raphael
Olabisi, Olagoke
Olafsson, Thomas Robert
Olday, Charles Harold
Oldenburg, Henry
Oldenburg, Richard Erik
Olds, Richard J.
Oldsey, Bernard Stanley
Oldshue, James Young
O'Leary, Edward Cornelius
O'Leary, Jeremiah Daniel, Jr.
O'Leary, K(eith) Daniel
O'Leary, Richard A.
O'Leary, Wilfred Leo
O'Leary, William Aloysius
Oleksiw, Michael Nicholas, II
Olender, Jack H.
Olenick, Arnold Jerome
Oler, Wesley Marion, III
Olgas, Kassie Ann
Olin, Stephen
Oliphant, S. Parker
Olitski, Jules
Oliveira, Milton Dias
Oliver, Charles
Oliver, Robert Edward
Oliver, Robert Robins
Olivere, Peter John
Olivere, Raymond Louis
Olmsted, Robert Amson
Olney, Julian Frederick, Jr.
Olney, William Salisbury
O'Loane, J(ames) Kenneth
Oloffson, Werner Olaf
O'Loughlin, Alida J. Kolk
O'Loughlin, Thomas Joseph, Jr.
Olsen, Douglas Raymond
Olsen, Herman Elmer
Olsen, Robert John
Olsen, Robert Leslie
Olsen, Theodora Egbert Peck (Mrs. Severt Andrew Olsen)
Olson, Carl Eric
Olson, Charles Eric
Olson, Don Charles
Olson, Harold Roy
Olson, Harry Axel
Olson, Jerry Carl
Olson, Ralph Arthur
Olson, Robert Edward
Olson, Ronald Leroy
Olson, William Cannicott
Olugebefola, Ademola
Olympia, Josie Lim
Omaboe, Narh
O'Malley, Edward Joseph, Jr.
O'Malley, Edward Paul
O'Malley, Francis Edward
O'Malley, John Edward
O'Malley, John William
O'Malley, Rita Helen
O'Mara, Joseph James
Omata, Robert Rokuro
O'Meara, Francis Edmund
O'Meara, Peter Huguet
Ommaya, Ayub Khan
O'Morrison, Kevin
Ona, Fernando Villalobos
O'Nan, Martha
Oneal, Glen, Jr.
O'Neal, Rondald Anson
O'Neil, Bonnie Sandra
O'Neil, James Walter
O'Neil, Joseph Francis
O'Neil, Marianne E.
O'Neil, Terence Quinn
O'Neill, Anne Frances
O'Neill, Daniel J.
O'Neill, Mary Jane
O'Neill, Terrence Michael
O'Neill, Thomas P.
O'Neill, Thomas P., III
O'Neill, William A.
O'Neill, William Lawrence
Onett, Trayon
Ong, Stephen Tjinlok
Onne, Robert Gary
Onody, Stephen Kenneth
Onthank, John Bonties
Onufer, George Robert
Opeil, Diane Kacer
Opel, John Roberts
Opher, Philip
Oppedahl, Phillip Edward
Oppenheim, Adolph David
Oppenheim, Justin Sable
Oppenheimer, Bertram Jay
Oppenheimer, Fred R.
Oppenheimer, Gerdi
Oppenheimer, Selma Levy (Mrs. Reuben Oppenheimer)
Oram, Thomas Felix Dennys
Orange, Allan Herbert
Orban, Kurt
Orchard, Basil Cyril Laurence
Orchard, Robert John
Ordway, John Amos
Orem, Charles Annistone
Orent, Herbert Leonard
Oreopoulos, Dimitrios
Oreskes, Irwin
Orlando, Frank Peter
Orlin, Harvey
Ormand, Dwight Henry
Ormandy, Eugene
Ormont, Louis Robert
Ormsby, John Carter
Orner, Robert Leroy
O'Rourke, John Joseph, Jr.
Orrmont, Arthur
Orser, David Alan
Orsetti, Robert Francis
Orsini, Joseph Emmanuel
Ort, Miroslav Jan
Ort, Paul Lanning
Orth, Richard Conrad, Jr.
Ortiz, John William
Ortiz-Squillace, Altagracia
Osathanondh, Rapin
Osawa, Yoshio
Osborne, Eugene Fielding
Osborne, George Roger
Osborne, Merrill Johnston
Osborne, Raymond Lester
Osborne, Sally Ruth
Osgood, Alan A.
Osgood, Jeannette Austin
Osgood, Peter Greer
O'Shea, John Robert
Osinski, Henry Joseph
Osius, Gary Eugene
Osman, Mary Ella Williams
Osmer, Dennis
Osoff, Jeffrey Arlin
Osofsky, Barnett
Osol, Arthur
Osol, Virginia Lebo (Mrs. Arthur Osol)
Osorio, Carmen
Osserman, Richard Allen
Ostberg, Henry Dean
Oster, Kurt Alexander
Oster, Martin William
Oster, Ralph John, Jr.
Ostergaard, Paul Blume
Osterkamp, Annemargret Lewenz (Mrs. F. Emile Osterkamp)
Osterweil, Suzanne Eve
Ostiguy, Jean Paul Wilson
Ostrander, Dale Howard
Ostrom, Barbara Diane
Ostrom, Robert Bingham
Ostroy, Joseph
O'Sullivan, James Thomas
O'Sullivan, Renee Bennett
Oswald, Donald Clifford
Oswald, John Wieland
Ota, Hajime
Otelsberg-Goodwin, Jonah
Otey, Orlando
Othmer, Donald Frederick
O'Toole, Edward Thomas, Jr.
O'Toole, John E.
Ott, Walter Richard
Ottenstein, Arthur Benjamin
Ottinger, Richard Lawrence
Ottman, John Budlong
Otto, Calvin Peter
Otto, Gilbert Fred
Otto, Rosalie Therese
Otto, Thomas Herbert
Ottomanelli, Gennaro Anthony
Ouellet, Gilles
Ouellette, Andre
Oussani, James John
Overcash, Stephen Jay
Overs, Ronald Roland
Oviatt, Vinson Romero
Owen, Archibald Alexander
Owen, Chloe
Owen, Dwight Hall
Owen, H. Martyn
Owen, Harrison Hollingsworth
Owen, Jack Walden
Owen, John Laverty
Owen, Richard
Owen, Stephen Frederick, Jr.
Owen, Thomas Llewellyn
Owens, Chester Daniel
Owens, Garland Chester
Owens, Guy
Owens, Thomas Francis
Owens, Thomas Webster
Owens, William Robert
Oxford, Harry James
Oyewole, Godwin Gbolade
Ozark, Daniel Leonard
Ozawa, Seiji
Ozimek, Richard Thomas
Paaswell, Robert Emil
Pabarcius, Algis
Pacco, Charles Bernard
Pace, Omar Thomas
Pacicco, Robert Rudolph
Pacifico, Richard Domenic
Pacik, Peter Thomas
Pacinelli, Ralph Nicholas
Packard, Albert Gibson, Jr.
Packer, Samuel
Packwood, Cyril Outerbridge
Paddack, William Arthur
Paddison, Gary Wayne
Padula, William Vincent
Padwa, Vladimir
Paek, Un-Chul
Paelet, David
Pagan, Raymond
Paganelli, Richard Gregory
Pagano, Frank Xavier
Page, Edgar Joseph
Page, (Charles) Getty, (Jr.)
Page, John Frederic
Page, Lorne Albert
Page, Philip Powers, Jr.
Page, Robert Bicknell
Page, Walter Hines
Paget, Allen Maxwell
Pagley, Carmella
Pagliaccio, John Valentine
Pahides, Steve Peter
Pahl, Irwin Russell

Paige, Kenneth Lee
Paige, Richard E.
Paige, Roslyne Gross
Painter, Geraldine Virginia
Painter, Michael James
Painter, Robert Lowell
Paisner, Claire Vivian
Pak, Hyung Woong
Pakan, Walter Stephen
Palace, Fred Milton
Palade, George Emil
Paladino, Patrick Joseph
Palank, Gary Peter
Palatta, Larry Michael
Palefsky, Louis Benjamin
Paley, Alfred Irving
Paley, William S.
Palgen, Jack Joseph Odilon
Palisi, Anthony Thomas
Palladino, Charles Frederick
Palladino, Neil Mario
Pallagrosi, Antonio Ugo
Palley, Reese
Pallone, Adrian Joseph
Pallop, Ants
Pallozzi, Dennis Peter
Palmatier, Susan May
Palmer, Allison Wright Post
Palmer, Anthony Joseph
Palmer, Bernard Barney
Palmer, Chester Ralph
Palmer, David Cheetham
Palmer, Edward
Palmer, James Robert
Palmer, Paul Richard
Palmer, Ralph Conrad
Palmer, Richard Ware
Palmer, Stuart Hunter
Palmer, Theodore Harold, Jr.
Palmer, Winthrop Bushnell
Palmersheim, Theresa Ann
Palmieri, Lucien Eugene
Palmieri, Sam Vincent
Palo, John
Paluha, Jaroslaw
Palumbo, Thomas Anthony
Paluszek, John Lawrence
Pamilla, Jeanne Rose
Pan, Huo-Hsi
Panaro, Victor Anthony
Pancella, John Raymond
Panchal, Pravin D.
Pandiscio, Joseph Robert Antonio, Jr.
Pane, Philip
Pang, Yung-Soo
Paniagua, Alejandro Dario
Panitz, Daniel Robert
Panitz, Lawrence
Pannizzo, Frank Joseph
Panuzio, Nicholas Arthur
Panzarino, Saverio Joseph
Pao, Hsien Ping
Pao, James Shih-Kuo
Paolin, John Raymond
Paolino, Ronald Mario
Paolucci, Anne Attura
Paone, James
Paone, John
Paone, Joseph Verino
Papa, Philip Anthony
Papadimitriou, Dimitri Basil
Papadopoulos, Spyridon George
Papageorgiou, John Constantine
Papanos, Stanley
Paparella, Julia Marie Boland (Mrs. Benedict A. Paparella)
Paparello, Frank Nicholas
Papas, Paul Nicholas, II
Papitto, Ralph Raymond
Papp, Joseph
Papp, Laszlo George
Pappachen, Andrews Korah
Pappas, Charles Nicholas
Pappas, George William
Paquet, Edmond
Parascos, Edward Themistocles
Parco, Salvador Abonal
Pardee, John Perry (Jack)
Pare, Marius
Pare, Thomas Anothony
Paris, Herbert
Pariser, Bertram
Pariser, Rudolph
Parisi, Ronald Frederick
Park, Chang Hwan
Park, Cynthia
Park, Dorothy Goodwin Dent (Mrs. Roy Hampton Park)
Park, Jae Kyun
Park, Jon Keith
Park, Lee Crandall
Park, Young Ho
Parke, David William
Parker, Clifford Maxwell
Parker, Ellen
Parker, Frank Douglas
Parker, Genevieve Fish (Mrs. E.M. Parker)
Parker, Henry Griffith, III
Parker, J(ack) Royal
Parker, Jack Steele
Parker, Jerome Lee
Parker, John Osmyn
Parker, Lawrence Craig
Parker, Nancy Knowles (Mrs. Cortlandt Parker)
Parker, Robert Orion
Parker, Rolland Sandau
Parker, Roscoe J.
Parker, William Hooper, III
Parket, Irwin Robert
Parkinson, Thomas Ignatius, Jr.
Parkison, Ed Hoyt
Parks, Dana, Jr.
Parks, Earle Charles
Parks, James Nicholas
Parks, John Scott
Parks, Paul
Parks, Robert Lloyd
Parmer, Michael Andrew
Paro, Tom Edward
Parr, Albert F. W.
Parrack, Edward Taylor
Parrella, Julius Carl
Parrett, Daniel Joseph
Parrotta, Michael Andrew
Parry, John Robert
Parsi, Edgardo J.
Parsons, Donald Spencer
Parsons, Gerald James
Partee, Woodie Augustus, Jr.
Partin, James Jennings
Partnoy, Ronald Allen
Pascall, Ross William
Pascarelli, Emil Francis
Pashke, Gregory Francis
Paskus, John Martin
Pasquarelli, Joseph Jerome
Pasquariello, Peter Joseph
Pasquier, Arthur Louis
Pass, Carolyn Joan
Passarelli, Frank Andrew
Passeri, Andrew Joseph
Passoja, Dann Einar
Passow, Michael Joel
Passwater, Richard Albert
Pasternac, André
Pasternak, Eugenia
Pastushak, Roman Joseph
Patch, Vernon Duane
Patchett, Isabel Stedman (Mrs. Edward Patchett)
Patel, Ashok Zaverbhai
Patel, Mahesh Somabhai
Patel, Pinakin Shanabhai
Paterson, Robert William
Patil, Madhukar Yashwantrao
Patrick, Douglas Arthur
Patrinacos, Nicon Demetrius
Pattee, Elizabeth Greenleaf
Patten, Edward James
Patterson, Charles Meade
Patterson, Edith Jerry
Patterson, Ellmore Clark
Patterson, Jerry Eugene
Patterson, Kenneth Francis
Patterson, M. Clare, Jr.
Patterson, Polly Reilly (Mrs. W. Ray Patterson)
Patterson, Robert Allan
Patterson, Roger Thomas
Patterson, William Howell
Patton, Elda Clayton
Patton, James Stephen
Patton, John Michael
Patton, Richard Bolling
Patton, Robert Frederick
Patukas, Peter (Epaminondas) Constantinos
Paul, David Lewis
Paul, Edward Charles
Paul, George Harvey
Paul, Herbert Morton
Paul, Herman Louis, Jr.
Paul, Norman Henry
Paul, Phyllis Ostrum
Paul, Richard Chadwick
Paul, Robert Arthur
Paulin, John Michael
Paulson, Edgar Garheart
Paulson, John Frederick
Paulus, John Douglas
Pavesi, Walter Albert
Pavis, Jesse Andrew
Pavlakis, Christopher
Pavone, Paul Joseph
Pawelec, William John
Pawl, Walter Stanley
Paxton, Ralph Robert
Payack, Paul J.J.
Payack, Peter
Payette, Thomas Martin
Payne, Mabel Louise
Payne, Margaret June Buttimer (Mrs. Morley Eldon Payne)
Payne, S. Howard
Payne, Stan Lee
Paynter, Dorothy Kay
Payson, Henry Edwards
Peabody, Charles Newton
Peabody, Velton Lester
Peace, John H.
Peaks, Mary Jane (Mrs. Robert Malcolm Polk)
Pearce, William Howard
Pearincott, Joseph Verghese
Pearl, Harvey
Pearl, John Joel
Pearlman, Lucy Friedlander
Pearlman, Robert Eugene
Pearlstein, Seymour
Pearson, Davis
Pearson, Elver Thomas
Pearson, George Bernard
Pearson, Peter Robb
Pearson, Roger
Pearson, William Henry
Pearson, William Rowland
Pease, Edmund W.
Pease, Eleanor Thompson (Mrs. Donald Cargill Pease)
Pease, Samuel Francis
Peaslee, Charlotte Hoffman
Pecaut, Robert Eugene
Peck, Edward Lionel
Peck, Hubert Raymond, Jr.
Peck, Ralph Harold-Henry
Peckham, John Munroe, III
Peckham, Lauren Augustus
Pecor, Raymond Charles, Jr.
Pedersen, Marguerite
Pedersen, Wesley Niels
Pedreira, Frank Alan
Peebler, Charles David, Jr.
Peel, James Edwin
Pegram, Roger Miller
Peiker, Alfred Stephen
Peiperl, Adam
Peizer, Maurice Samuel
Pelella, John Vincent, Jr.
Pell, Anthony Douglas
Pell, Claiborne
Pellicano, Victor Louis
Peltier, Hubert Conrad
Pelz, Edward Joseph
Pemberton, Sandi Macpherson
Pena, Jesus J.
Pender, Michael Roger
Pendleton, Othniel Alsop
Pennell, Carroll Edward, II
Penney, Alphonsus Ligouri
Penney, Charles Rand
Pennie, John Craigans
Pennington, Dennis Ira
Pennisten, John William
Pennock, Donald William
Pennock, George Irving
Pensiero, Nicholas Francis
Pensis, Albert Etienne
Penta, Irene Platt (Mrs. Walter E. Penta)
Penzias, Arno Allan
Peoples, Vernon Daniel, Jr.
Pepper, Adeline Elizabeth
Pepper, James
Pepper, Rollin Elmer
Pepyne, Edward Walter
Perales, Cesar Augusto
Perchard, Robert Joseph
Perciaccante, Ronald George
Perdunn, Richard Francis
Pereira, George Anthony
Perel, Jules
Perelle, Ira B.
Perera, Phillips
Perey, Joan Sawyer
Perez, Isidoro Jose
Perez, Louis Anthony
Perez, Robert Claude
Perez-Paris, Eduardo Enrique
Perfall, Arthur George
Perfecky, Bohdan Andrij
Perfecky, George Alexander
Perkins, Eddie Lee
Perkins, Marvin Earl
Perkins, Russel Gordon
Perkins, Thomas Lewis
Perkins, William E(dward)
Perkons, Auseklis Karlis
Perl, William R.
Perlberg, William
Perlberg, Zelma
Perless, Robert L.
Perley, John Stephen
Perlis, Harlan Jay
Perlman, Bernard Benjamin
Perlman, Ellis Sherman
Perlman, Evelyn Bernice
Perlman, John Niels
Perlman, Konrad Joseph
Perlman, Matthew S.
Perlman, Sol
Perloff, Robert
Perls, Laura Posner
Permut, Stephen Robert
Perna, Albert Fredric
Perna, Francis John
Perna, George D.
Pernecky, Paul
Perosky, Wayne Frederick
Perr, Irwin
Perrault, Charles
Perrault, Rene Albert Francois
Perrette, Jean Rene
Perrin, Lesley Davison (pseudonym Lesley Davison)
Perrone, Anthony Joseph
Perrone, Samuel Joseph
Perrotta, Fioravante Gerald
Perry, Anthony John
Perry, Charles Norvin
Perry, Daniel Deverell
Perry, Darrell Delmar
Perry, Edward Joseph
Perry, Edward (Ted) Samuel
Perry, Edward Thomas
Perry, G. Daniel
Perry, George Eleutherios
Perry, George Francis
Perry, Gordon Clark
Perry, Henry Alexander
Perry, Jacqueline Cheryl
Perry, John Richard
Perry, Richard Bernard
Perry, Vernon McGlenn, Jr.
Perry, William Russell
Perryman, Charles R.
Persell, Charles Bowen, Jr.
Persiani, Carmine
Persico, Daniel Francis
Persky, Robert Samuel
Person, John Elmer, Jr.
Persons, Edward B.
Pescatello, Michael
Pescow, Jerome Kenneth
Pesin, Edward
Pesin, Stuart George
Petch, John Frank
Peter, Phillips Smith
Peternel, Arthur Frederick
Peters, Alban Gerard
Peters, Alton Emil
Peters, Anthony Joseph
Peters, Carol Beattie Taylor (Mrs. Frank Albert Peters)
Peters, Charles Henri
Peters, George Anthony
Peters, Harriet Auerbach
Peters, Henry Frederick
Peters, Henry John
Peters, John C.
Peters, Leonard Leckel
Petersen, Martin Ross
Petersen, Roger Dudley
Petersen, Susan Jane
Peterson, A.E.S. (Mrs. Carl U. Peterson)
Peterson, Ann Sullivan
Peterson, Bertram Harold, Jr.
Peterson, Glen Robert
Peterson, Jay Bryan, Jr.
Peterson, Mary Ann
Peterson, Miller Harrell
Peterson, Roger George
Petit, Leo Arsene, Jr.
Petit-Clair, Alfred Joseph, Jr.
Petone, Arthur Joseph
Petri, Herbert Leon
Petrie, Peter Lee
Petrie, Stewart Judson
Petrilla, Stephen Thomas
Petrocelli, Orlando Ralph
Petronko, Michael Roman
Petroskas, John Alfred
Petrovic, Njegos Masan
Petrucci, Pasquale Michael
Petrucelli, R. Joseph, II
Pettibone, John Wolcott
Pettine, Raymond James
Pettit, Horace
Pettit, Januszka Rymsza (Mrs. Horace Pettit, Jr.)
Petty, John Robert
Petty, Robert Ethan
Petvai, Steve Istvan
Peugeot, David Ernest
Peyser, Peter A.
Peyton, Sarah Margaret
Pezzulich, Robert Anthony
Pfafflin, James Reid
Pfaltz, Hugo M., Jr.
Pfeffer, Christian Jackson
Pfeffer, Susan Beth
Pfeifer, Donald
Pfeiffer, Carl
Pfeister, Raymond Lynn
Pfister, Linda Arlene
Pflieger, John Ely
Pflum, William John
Phelan, Arthur John, Jr.
Phelan, Howard Taylor
Phelan, Joseph Francis
Phelan, William Francis
Phelen, David
Phelps, Flora L(ouise) Lewis
Phelps, Peter Wilmot
Philbin, James Edward
Philip, A.G. Davis
Philip, Anthony Francis
Philips, Paris John
Phillips, Anthony Francis
Phillips, Bearl Lee
Phillips, David Guy
Phillips, Doris Holt
Phillips, Frances Isabelle
Phillips, Jackson Robert Edward
Phillips, James Davis
Phillips, Jewell Kathleen
Phillips, Joseph Daniel
Phillips, Kanella Theodora
Phillips, M.C.
Phillips, Marcella Lindeman (Mrs. James F. Phillips)
Phillips, Mary-Ann Monahan
Phillips, Michael
Phillips, Priscilla Moulton
Phillips, Samuel Joseph
Phillips, Thomas L.
Phillips, Walter Mills, III
Phillips, Warren Henry
Phillips, William Eugene
Phillips, Winfred Marshall
Philp, Francis Higginson
Philp, Richard Nilson
Phinney, Edward E.
Phinney, William Flagg
Phocas, George John
Phoon, Wai Wor
Piacitelli, John Joseph
Piaker, Philip Martin
Pian, Charles Hsueh-Chien
Piatigorsky, Joram Paul
Piatt, Jack Boyd
Piatt, Richard Owen
Picard, Alyre Joseph
Picard, Raymond Jean
Piccoli, Leonard Ralph
Picken, Harry Belfrage
Pickering, Ted Warrington
Pickert, Alton Eades
Pickett, Doyle C.
Pickett, Lawrence Kimball
Picower, Jeffry Martin
Pidgeon, John Anderson
Piehler, Glenn Raymond
Piel, Gerard
Piemonte, Robert Victor
Pier, Jerome Roland
Pierce, Donald Shelton
Pierce, Elizabeth Gay (Mrs. William Curtis Pierce)
Pierce, Ethel Taylor (Mrs. Edward A. Pierce)
Pierce, Francis Casimir
Pierce, Frederick S.
Pierce, Horace Greeley
Pierce, John Michael
Pierce, Lawrence Warren
Pierce, Milton
Pierce, Patricia Jobe
Pierce, Paul Arthur Bryon
Pierce, Philip Sargent
Pierce, Raymond Kenneth
Pierce, Robert Raymond
Pierce, Samuel Riley, Jr.
Pierce, Sidney Kendrick, Jr.
Pierpont, Grace Elizabeth Schmidt (Mrs. Ross Zimmerman Pierpont)
Pierson-Tisch, Marjorie
Pierstorff, Buckley Charles
Pierz, Joseph Francis
Pies, Harvey Elliot
Pietrafesa, Richard Cushing
Pietrowitz, Richard George
Pike, George Bertram
Pike, John Nazarian
Pike, John Raymond
Pike, Ralph Forward
Pike, Teresa Maria de Hospodar (Mrs. Nathan R. Pike)
Pikulski, John Joseph
Pikus, Joseph David
Pilarski, Leonard Jacob
Pilat, Oliver
Pilcher, James Otto, II
Pilchik, Ronald
Pilgrim, Sidney Alfred Leslie
Pillai, Bala Hari
Pillay, Sivasankara K.K.
Pillor, Mark Harlen
Pilnick, Saul
Pimental, Anthony M., III
Pimpinella, Ronald Joseph
Pimsler, Alvin J.
Pincus, Lionel I.
Pincus, Ralph A.
Pine, Vanderlyn Russell
Pineda, Lourdes Castro
Pines, Ariel Leon
Pines, Beverly Irene
Pines, Wayne Lloyd
Pinkert, Dorothy Minna
Pinkett, Harold Thomas
Pinkus, Theodore Francis, Jr.
Pinney, Edward Lowell, Jr.
Pino, Edward Hans
Pinsker, Walter
Pinsky, Byron Lloyd
Pinson, Nancy MacEdwards
Pinton, Giorgio Alberto
Piotrowski, Zbigniew Anthony (Tony)
Pipa, Andrew Michael, Jr.
Piper, Colin Brewster
Piper, George Earle
Piperopoulos, Georgios P.
Pipitone, Anthony John
Pippin, Paul Wheatley Tomlinson
Piraino, Anthony Joseph
Piraneo, Frank Peter
Pirich, John Francis
Pirich, Ronald Gary
Pirnie, Malcolm, Jr.
Pironti, Pascal Anthony
Pisani, Lawrence Frank
Pisano, Alan David
Piscitelli, R. Amelia
Pisetsky, Myron Matthew
Pitassy, Caesar Leopold
Pitchumoni, Capecomorin Sankar
Pitkin, Frank Ivan
Pitta Kirk, Patricia Joyce
Pittman, Charles Vernon
Pittman, Walter Russell
Pitts, Albert S.
Pitts, Fred
Pizzi, Raymond James
Pizzurro, Joseph Patrick
Plakogiannis, Fotios Michaelis
Planas, Roberto Fuentes
Plastrik, Eugene Angus
Platek, Stanley Frank
Platt, David Sanford
Platt, Lee Frew
Platt, Martin Harold
Platten, Donald Campbell
Platthy, Jeno
Platz, Joseph
Plaut, Martin Edward
Plawsky, Bernard Morris
Pleskow, Eric Roy
Plimpton, Stephen Wardwell
Plonsky, Seymour
Ploscowe, Stephen Allen
Plotkin, Irving H(erman)
Plotzker, Richard Ivan
Plourde, Joseph Aurele
Plourde, Michel
Plowman, Herbert LaVerne, Jr.
Plummer, Davis Ward, Jr.
Plummer, Philip Frank
Plymyer, David Alan
Plyter, Norman Vincent
Pniakowski, Andrew Frank
Pobiner, Harvey
Poch, Herbert Edward
Pochedly, Carl Eugene
Pocock, Philip F.
Podgwaite, John David
Podolsky, Leon
Podos, Steven Maurice
Poesnecker, Gerald Eugene
Poetker, Joel Smith
Pogany, Andras Henrik
Pogge, Horst
Poggio, Gian Franco
Pogo, Angel Oscar
Pogo, Beatriz
Pogue, Gerald Albert
Pogue, Mary Ellen (Mrs. L. Welch Pogue)
Pohoryles, Manfred
Poian, Edward Licius DeBorbone
Poindexter, Emmett Williamson
Pointek, Albert Joseph
Poirier, Charles Carroll, III
Poitras, Jean-Maurice
Polach, Jaroslav George (Jay)
Polansky, Gerald Arthur
Polayes, Irving Marvin
Polayes, Maurice Benjamin
Poler, Michael Avery
Poleri, William Frank
Poleskie, Stephen Francis
Poletti, Roger A.
Polisner, Stuart Barry
Poliszczuk, George
Polito, Anthony John
Polivchak, Philip Michael
Polivka, John Michael
Polk, Irwin Jacob
Poll, Robert Eugene, Jr.
Pollack, Henry Clinton, Jr.
Pollack, Jerome Marvin
Pollak, George A.
Pollak, Martin Marshall
Pollan, Stephen Michael
Pollard, Jacqueline
Pollard, Stewart Maclaine Laurens
Pollard, William Edward
Pollin, Abe
Pollner, Martin Robert
Pollock, Joseph Jordan
Pollock, Joseph Leonard
Pollock, William Beatty
Polon, James Allen
Polow, Nancy Beth Gross
Polsky, Louis Sanford
Polt, George Dewey, Jr.
Poltoratzky, Nikolai Petrovich
Polydoroff, Theodore
Pomara, Vincent Lawrence
Pomerantz, Allen
Pomerene, James Herbert
Pomeroy, Leon Ralph
Pomeroy, Robert Watson, III
Pompian, Richard Owen
Pond, Thomas Temple, Jr.
Pons, Luis Orlando
Pontius, Anneliese Alma
Ponzillo, Stephen Joseph, III
Poor, Frederic Hedge, Jr.
Poor, Thomas Martin
Pope, (John) Joseph
Pope, Leavitt Joseph
Pope, Richard Louis
Popham, Lewis Charles, III
Popham, Richard Robert
Popler, Kenneth
Popma, Eugene John
Popoff, Edna Spieler
Popovic, Deyan Honeyman
Popovich, Charles James
Poppel, Seth Raphael
Popper, Arthur N.
Poppiti, James Anthony
Porcari, Serafino
Porier, Omer Adelarde
Porreco, Louis John
Port, Yale Irwin
Porter, Bernard Harden
Porter, C. Ray, Jr.
Porter, Darwin Fred
Porter, Frank Thomas Henderson
Porter, Jack Nusan
Porter, James Reed
Porter, Jay Elihu
Porter, Jimmy Ann (Jan)
Porter, John Weston
Porter, Sydney Wynne, Jr.
Porter, Warren Ellsworth
Porter, William Clayton, Jr.
Porter, William Joseph
Porter, William Middleton
Porterfield, Louis Edward
Portfolio, Almerindo Gerard
Portman, Sharon Dee
Portnoy, Irving Leo
Porzio, Ralph
Posamentier, Alfred Steven
Posch, Anthony G.
Posnak, Robert Lincoln
Posner, Barry Innis
Posner, Jon
Posner, Robert Ludwig
Posner, Roy Edward
Poss, Robert
Poss, Stanley Marian
Post, Nicholas Bertram
Post, Seymour Cyrus
Postel, Robert Ira
Posvar, Wesley Wentz
Posy, Carl Jeffrey
Potamkin, Meyer
Potash, Charles
Pote, Doris R.
Poth, Harry Augustus, Jr.
Potnick, Carl David
Potoker, Edward Martin
Potosnak, Arthur Robert
Potsic, William Paul
Potter, Barrett George
Potter, Miles Milton
Potterton, John Paul
Pottinger, Paul Stephen
Potts, Dorothy Ruth (Patti) (Mrs. Robert C. Potts)
Potts, Rinehart Skeen
Poulson, Richard Jasper Metcalfe
Poupard, James Arthur
Poupko, Gary Gabriel
Pousada, Manuel
Poushter, David Leon

Povey, Thomas George
Povich, David
Powasnick, James Richard
Powell, Alfred Richard
Powell, Charles Porter
Powell, Donald George
Powell, Douglas Spencer
Powell, Edward Allen
Powell, Gaylord Ellis
Powell, Jimmie Lee
Powell, John Marcus, Jr.
Powell, Larson Merrill
Powell, Lenore Sarah
Powell, Lewis Franklin, Jr.
Powell, Louise Hill Conkey
Powell, Margaret Miller
Powell, Richard Anthony
Powell, William John, Jr.
Power, William Edward
Powers, Edwin Malvin
Powers, Ernest Frederick
Powers, Jane Biddle
Powers, Kirk McDearmon
Powers, L. Lindley
Powers, Mary Rita
Pownall, Kenneth Franklyn
Powning, Maynard Walker
Pozza, Nicholas John
Prabhu, Vasant Krishna
Prabhudesai, Mukund Madhav
Praeger, Donald Lewis
Pragay, Desider Alex
Prager, Alice Heinecke
Praglin, Julius
Pramer, David
Prasad, Rajendra (Gupta)
Prassas, Milton John
Prater, Charles Dwight
Pratt, George Oramel
Pratt, Gerald Hillary
Pratt, James Leland, Jr.
Pratt, Richard Dean
Pratt, Robert Armstrong
Pratter, Marianne Bunzl (Mrs. Paul J. Pratter)
Prausnitz, Frederik W.
Pravda, Milton Frank
Prem, F. Herbert, Jr.
Preminger, Alexander Salo
Premo, Patrick Mervyn
Prempas, Louis Nicholas
Prempree, Amporn Lohsuvana
Prempree, Thongbliew
Prendergast, William Edward, Jr.
Prentice, Colgate Selden
Presby, J. Thomas
Prescott, Patricia Roehs
Presnell, Walter Madison
Pressler, Marion Joan
Pressman, Edmund Norman
Prestia, Michael Anthony
Preston, Kendall, Jr.
Preston, Nathaniel Stone
Pretsch, Paul George
Prettyman, Daniel Travers
Preven, David W.
Previn, Andre
Prevoznik, Stephen Joseph
Prewitt, Judith Martha Shimansky
Prezelski, Frank Joseph
Pribor, Hugo Casimer
Price, Ely
Price, Floyd Milton
Price, Gerald Louis
Price, Kenneth E(lbert)
Price, Ralph Morton
Price, Richard Carr
Price, Richard Lee
Price, Robert Edmunds
Price, Stephen Jr., III
Price, Wallace Walter
Price, Warren Alexander
Prickett, William Franklin
Priest, Dorman Eaton
Priest, Eva Louise
Priest, Jerome
Priestley, Eldon Bruce
Prince, Elmer Woodward, Jr.
Prince, Herbert Norman
Prince, Joseph John
Prince, Leon Maximilian
Prince, Roy Webster, Jr.
Princevalle, Robert
Pringle, Stuart Houghton, Jr.
Prisch, Robert Allerton
Prisco, Nicholas Allen
Pritchard, Hiram Bert, III
Pritchard, Norman Henry, II
Pritchard, Wilbur L.
Pritchett, John Perry
Prizgint, Edna.
Probber, Lloyd
Probst, David Arthur
Proctor, George Newton
Proctor, James Faust
Proctor, William Gilbert, Jr.
Prokopy, John Alfred
Prokopy, John Victor
Prol, Elbertus James, Jr.
Proll, George Simon
Prosser, Joseph Lawrence
Prothro, Gerald Dennis
Proulx, Adolphe
Proulx, Marie Antoinette
Prout, James Harold
Prout, John William
Provencher, Henry David
Provenzano, Anthony John
Prowell, Harold Richard
Prudden, John Fletcher
Prugh, Thomas Austin
Pruitt, Dean Garner
Prupas, Melvern Irving
Pruslin, Fred Howard
Prussin, Jeffrey Alan
Pryor, Barbara Leone
Pryor, Roger Welton
Psaty, Martin Melville
Puccinelli, Alfred Richard
Pugh, David Martin
Pugh, Emerson Martindale
Pugh, Emerson William
Pugkhem, Tretorn
Pugliese, Anthony Charles
Pukite, Alfred S.
Puklin, James Edward
Pullen, David John
Pullen, Phyllis Kouwenhoven
Pulling, Lisa Canby
Pulling, Thomas Leffingwell
Pullman, Douglas Robert
Pulver, Norman
Pumphrey, Preston Van Vorhees
Purcell, Edward Mills
Purcell, Fenton Peter
Purcell, Francis Eugene
Purcell, Gervaise
Purcell, Leo Thomas, Jr.
Purcell, Theodore V.
Purdon, John
Purdon, Roger Anthony
Purdy, Susan Gold
Purkayastha, Arindam
Purnell, Dallas Michael
Purnell, James Edgar
Purple, Thomas Clayton
Purpura, Anthony Graham
Purpura, Peter Angelo
Purrelli, Charles John
Pursley, Robert Edwin
Purtell, Walter Charles
Purvis, George Porter, III
Pusar, Arnold
Pusin, Max Nathaniel
Putnam, Caroline Jenkins (Mrs. Roger Lowell Putnam)
Putnam, Lothar Faber
Putney, Richard Andrew
Puttlitz, Donald Herbert
Pyke, Carol June
Pyke, Thomas Nicholas, Jr.
Pyle, Howard, III
Pyle, Louis Apgar, Jr.
Pyles, Thomas Terrill
Pyne, Eben Wright
Quadland, Michael Cornelius
Quailer, Martin Leonard
Quattlebaum, Owen McDermed
Quattrone, Philip Anthony
Queen, Evangeline Palmer
Queen, Robert Isaac
Queeny, James Francis
Quellmalz, Henry
Querido, Arthur James
Quigley, Herbert Gerald
Quigley, Hugh John
Quigley, John Howden
Quillen, William Tatem
Quimby, Freeman Henry
Quinn, Carroll Thomas
Quinn, Edward James
Quinn, Gerald Joseph
Quinn, John Raymond
Quinn, Michael Desmond
Quinn, Thomas Howard
Quinones, Mark Anthony
Quint, Robert Harold
Quirk, Lawrence Joseph
Quiroga, Gary Tristan
Quis, Harold Joseph, Jr.
Quraishi, Hameed Mohammed Abdul
Raab, David Michael
Raab, Kurt
Raab, Richard Harold
Rab, Khandker Shahidur
Rabchevsky, George Anthony
Rabi, Isidor Isaac
Rabideau, Ronald Everest
Rabinowitz, Ann
Rabinowitz, Barry Marc
Rabinowitz, Jacob Moses
Rabinowitz, Ronald
Rabinowitz, Wilbur Melvin
Rabstejnek, George John, Jr.
Raby, John Cornelius
Race, Iva LaVerne
Racek, Edward William
Rachals, Richard
Rachamalla, Kumara Swamy
Rachelson, Morton Herman
Rachlin, Harvey Brant
Rachow, Louis A(ugust)
Radacsy, John Joseph, III
Radcliffe, Lynn James
Radding, Philip
Rader, Millicent Carolyn
Radford-Bennett, William
Radimer, Kenneth John
Radini, Richard Roland
Radler, Louis
Radnay, Paul Andrew
Radner, Joseph Sydney
Radtke, Ronald Roscoe
Radzimski, Gerald Paul
Raeder, Arthur O.
Raemer, Harold Roy
Raezer, Spencer Dorworth
Raffa, James Nicholas
Raffelson, Michael
Ragan, Edward John
Ragot, Henry Warren
Rahenkamp, John Edward
Rahman, Abdul R.
Rahn, Richard William
Raifman, Irving
Raiford, William Russell
Railton, William Scott
Raimondi, Louis Arnold
Rainey, Patricia Ann
Rainis, Eugene Charles
Rainwater, James
Raison, Charles William
Raissle, Helen Catherine
Raiten, Susan Gail
Raj, Rishi Sharma
Rajan, Sundar Ramakrishnan
Rajapaksa, Trikante Nalini
Rak, Wolodymyr
Rakovan, Lawrence Francis
Raksin, Irving Jacob
Ralph, Richard Garrick
Ralston, Alexander Hoyle, Jr.
Ralston, Mrs. Byron Brown (Lucy Virginia Gordon)
Ralston, David Cornell
Ralston, Lucy Virginia Gordon
Ram, Ramaswamy Sathasiva
Ramanath, Hassan Krishna
Ramanather, Sirithara
Rambauske, Werner Robert
Rambo, John Henry Thomas
Ramer, Marvin Maxwell
Rametta, Concetto Sal
Ramey, James Wendell
Ramirez, Alberto
Ramm, John Robert
Ramsburg, Helen Harris
Ramsdell, John Alan
Ramsden, Neil G.
Ramseur, Trumiller Beatrice Wimberley
Ramsey, Collette Nicks (Mrs. Hobart Cole Ramsey)
Ramsey, Richard Livingston
Ramstad, James M.
Ranawat, Chitranjan Singh
Rand, Alonzo Cutting, Jr.
Rand, Melvin Aaron
Randall, Clifford Elton
Randall, Eudora Patricia
Randall, Gerald Robert
Randall, Richard Stuart
Randall, Richard William
Randall, Robert Gordon
Randall, Robert L.
Randall, Roland Rodrock
Randall, Thelma Maye
Randall, Thomas Dudley
Randall, Willard Sterne
Randell, Joan
Randolph, Charles Clifford, III
Randolph, Judith Howard
Ranganathan, Narasimhan
Rangel, Charles B.
Rangeler, Dwight Dwain
Rangos, John G.
Rankin, William Parkman
Rannels, Herman Wolfe
Ransohoff, Priscilla Burnett
Ransom, Daniel Gordon
Ranson, Nancy S.
Rant, Walter Francis
Ranwez, Jean-Louis Fernand
Rao, Krishnappa Nagaraja
Rao, Paul Peter
Rao, Sreepada Tumkur Krishna Murthy Rao
Rao, Vatsala V.
Rao, Yalamanchili A. K.
Raphael, Carl Samuel
Raphael, Chester Martin
Raphael, Harold James
Rapp, Cullen F.
Rapp, Douglas Mark
Rapp, Harvey Marvin
Rapp, Richard Tilden
Rapp, Robert Charles
Rappaport, Florence Ward
Rappaport, George
Rappaport, Irwin
Rappeport, Alfred Maurice
Rappin, Adrian
Rappleye, Willard Cole, Jr.
Rapport, Maurice M.
Rasberry, Stanley Dexter
Rasely, Charles Wesley, Jr.
Rashkin, Jay Arthur
Rashkind, William Jacobson
Rasmanis, Egons
Ratchford, Michael William
Ratchford, William Richard
Ratcliff, Walter Fulton
Rath, George Edward
Rath, James Arthur, III
Rath, Thomas David
Ratliff, Gerald Lee
Ratner, Harold
Ratner, Lillian Gross (Mrs. Harold Ratner)
Rauch, Arthur Irving
Raucher, Herman
Rauscher, Norman Earl
Rausen, Aaron Reuben
Rauth, David Robert
Raven, Ronald Jacob
Rawdon, Albert Henry, Jr.
Rawlings, Robert Lee, Jr.
Rawls, Walton Hendry
Rawls, Wendell Lee, Jr.
Rawson, Arline Frances
Ray, Ajit Kumar
Ray, George W(ashington), Jr.
Ray, Gordon Thompson
Ray, William F.
Rayburn, Carole Ann (Ms. Ronald Allen Rayburn)
Rayburn, John William
Rayman, Jack Richard
Rayment, William Francis
Raymond, Bruce Allen
Raymond, Judith Ellen
Raymundo, Severino Antonio
Raynor, Wilfred Louis
Razin, Andrew Michael
Razon, Ben David
Read, Glory Meehan (Mrs. William M. Read III)
Reader, George Gordon
Reagan, Reginald Lee
Reals, Janice Lynn
Reardon, Donald Thomas
Rebalsky, Robert Sidney
Reber, Carl Anthony
Rebuck, Ernest Charles
Rechcigl, Miloslav, Jr.
Recktenwald, Lester Nicholas
Recupero, John
Redd, Richard James
Redd, Rudolph James
Redd, Vivian Cortezza
Reddall, H(enry) Hastings
Redden, Martha Ross
Redekopp, Alexander Benjamin
Reding, Paul Francis
Redington, Thomas
Redman, John David
Redmond, Andrew J.
Redo, S(averio) Frank
Redstone, Sumner Murray
Reed, Eunice Paddio (Pat)
Reed, George Edward
Reed, Harry William, Jr.
Reed, James Alexander, Jr.
Reed, John Carre
Reed, John Henry
Reed, John William
Reed, Kathryn Mercer
Reed, Leon Samuel
Reed, Rolland Maurice
Reed, Theodore Harold
Reed, Thomas Eville
Reed, William Carlisle
Reed, Winston Harrison
Reeder, Frank Fitzgerald
Reeder, Margene Vlieger
Rees, Thomas Dee
Reese, Eber Oram
Reese, Rollin David
Reese, William Willis
Reeside, Arthur Gordon, Jr.
Reesing, John Palmer, Jr.
Reeve, Ralph Tichenor
Reeves, Caroline Buck (Mrs. William Harvey Reeves)
Reeves, Lovejoy
Reeves, Sidney Alexander
Reeves, William Ray
Reeves, William Ray
Regan, Frederic Dennis
Regan, Gerald Augustine
Regan, James Raymond
Regan, John Francis
Reggio, Robert Bruce
Regnier, Louis A.
Regnier, Raymond Cobington, Jr.
Regoli, Vera Paula
Regueiro, Jose Miguel
Rehberger, Gustav
Rehberger, John Martin
Rehl, Margaret Ann
Rehman, Frederick Max
Rehnquist, William Hubbs
Reich, Stephen
Reich, Theobald
Reichart, Bessie May Criswell
Reichle, Frederick Adolph
Reid, Alexander Darrell Gordon
Reid, Charles Frederick, Jr.
Reid, H(enry) Terry
Reid, Jean D. Chang
Reid, John Walling
Reid, Ross
Reidy, John Sherburne
Reiff, Dovie Kate
Reifsnyder, Charles Frank
Reifsnyder, William Edward
Reigle, Margaret Ann
Reiher, John Frederick
Reiley, Thomas Phillip
Reilly, Daniel Patrick
Reilly, Edward Patrick
Reilly, Eugene Leo, III
Reilly, John Francis
Reilly, Joseph John, Jr.
Reilly, Richard Menton
Reiman, Donald Henry
Reiman, Ralph John
Rein, John Michael
Reindollar, Robert Mason, Jr.
Reiner, Leopold
Reiner, Thomas Francis
Reingold, Alfred Muller
Reinhard, Robert Andrew
Reinherz, Helen Zarsky
Reinke, Marvin Ernest
Reinl, Harry Charles
Reis, Donald Jeffery
Reisa, James Joseph, Jr.
Reisfield, Donald Richard
Reisinger, Robert Roland
Reisner, David Johnson
Reiss, Harry E.
Reitan, Paul Hartman
Reitboeck, Herbert J.P.
Reiter, William Martin
Reiters, Ludvigs Osvalds
Reitz, Julia Kraus
Reitzel, Hilda Marie
Reizes, Leslie Noel
Rejebian, George Peter
Relis, Rochelle R.
Relyea, Barry Donald
Rembski, Stanislav
Remick, Robert Merrick
Remland, Marjorie Ellen
Remmers, Kurt William
Remson, Norman
Renck, Robert Leo, Jr.
Renkis, Alan Ilmars
Reno, Bob
Renoff, Paul Vernon
Renoud, Dorothy Owen
Renstrom, Arthur George
Rentschler, George Adam, Jr.
Repetti, Andrew Joseph
Reppetto, Thomas Anthony
Reps, David Nathan
Reschke, Morris Meier
Resnick, Arthur
Resnick, Edward J.
Resnik, Sol Leon
Resseguie, Franklin Brundage
Ressler, Charles
Restiano, Richard Angelo
Reuben, Allan H.
Reuben, Gary M.
Reuben-Lockerman, Geneva Lorene
Reubens, Edwin Pierce
Reusche, Frank Louis
Reuschel, James Philip
Revesz, Peter Theodore
Revzin, Stanley Alexander
Rex, Kenneth John
Reyes, Sergio Jose
Reyes-Dollete, Fe Tavernero
Reyes-Guerra, Antonio
Reyman, Maria Landolfi
Reynders, Charlton, Jr.
Reynolds, Benedict Michael
Reynolds, Charles Vaughn, Jr.
Reynolds, Edwin Wilfred, Jr.
Reynolds, James
Reynolds, Martha Louise
Reynolds, Sister Mary Consilii
Reynolds, Mary Trackett
Reynolds, Nancy Bradford duPont (Mrs. William Glasgow Reynolds)
Reynolds, Richard Lee
Reynolds, Robert Gregory
Reynolds, Russell Seaman, Jr.
Reynolds, William Glasgow
Reznick, Jerome
Reznik, Neil David
Reznikoff, Leon
Rhee, Peter Chang-Hee
Rheingold, Ira H.
Rhiew, Francis Changnam
Rhoades, John H.
Rhoads, James Berton
Rhoads, Joseph
Rhoads, Lorna Crary
Rhode, Alfred Shimon
Rhoden, Richard Allan
Rhodes, Bode Orobiyi
Rhodes, Frank Harold Trevor
Rhodes, Gilbert Alfred, Jr.
Rhodes, William Oliver
Rhude, Beth Esther
Rhude, Henry Burton
Rhuland, Fred Angus
Rhydwen, David A.
Ribas, Jorge Luis
Ribicoff, Abraham A.
Ribicoff, Irving S.
Ricards, John Day
Riccardi, Nicholas Bruce
Ricci, Robert Charles
Ricciardi, Antonio
Rice, Argyll Pryor
Rice, Arnold Sanford
Rice, Arthur Mae
Rice, Blaine Millard
Rice, Dorothea McKim (Mrs. Leon Rice)
Rice, Emery van Daell
Rice, Henry Hart
Rice, John Carter
Rice, Joseph Albert
Rice, Lawrence Roger
Rice, Michael Stephen
Rice, William Thomas
Ricereto, James, III
Rich, Avery Edmund
Rich, Elizabeth Margaret Ann (Mrs. William Nicolo Provenzano)
Rich, Eric
Rich, Giles Sutherland
Rich, Neil Ian
Rich, Robert Elwood
Richard, St. Clair Smith (Mrs. George Charles Richard, 2d)
Richards, Charles Fleming, Jr.
Richards, Christine-Louise
Richards, (Albert) Dewey
Richards, James Ward
Richards, John Benjamin
Richards, John Joseph
Richards, Lawrence Marion
Richards, McDonald Arnold
Richards, Robert Bartson
Richards, Robert Leroy
Richards, Roger Thomas
Richards, Ronald Francis
Richardson, Alfonso Austin
Richardson, Arleigh Dygert, III
Richardson, Artemas Partridge
Richardson, Carlton Duquesne
Richardson, Elliot Lee
Richardson, Frederick Douglass
Richardson, Gordon
Richardson, Henry Howe
Richardson, Madison Franklin
Richardson, Marie Smith (Mrs. Elva Richardson)
Richardson, Paul Arthur
Richardson, Ronald John
Richardson, Scovel
Richardson, Winona Belle
Richart, Douglas Stephen
Richette, Lawrence Jarvis
Richman, Alan
Richman, Daniel Seymour
Richman, John Alfred, Jr.
Richman, Peter
Richman, Seymour
Richmond, Ernest Leon
Richmond, Frederick William
Richmond, Robert Price
Richmond, Walter Elliott
Richter, Howard S.
Richter, Virgil John
Rickels, Karl
Ricketson, Robert Bradford
Riddick, Floyd Millard
Riddle, Robert Lewis
Rideout, Blanchard Livingstone
Rideout, David Frank
Rider, Allen Burr, Jr.
Rider, Kenneth Lloyd
Rider, William Decker
Ridgely, Henry Johnson
Ridgely, Josephine Jones
Ridker, Carol May
Ridolfi, Sido Louis
Rieck, Jonn Paul
Riedl, John Orth
Rieger, Henry Victor, Jr.
Rieger, Robert Allen
Riegger, William Joseph, Sr.
Riendeau, Leonard Joseph
Riendeau, Robert
Riepe, Dale Marurice
Rife, David Howard
Rifelj, Carol de Dobay
Rifkin, Frank Ray
Rifkin, Irwin Arnold
Rifkind, Marilyn Arlene
Rigg, Ruth DeHaven
Riggio, Thomas Pasquale
Rigsby, Radford Barlow
Riina, John Roy
Rike, Paul Miller
Riles, Warren Houston
Riley, Joseph Harry
Riley, Paul Joseph
Rinaldo, Matthew J.
Rinaldo, Patrick
Rindfleisch, Norval William
Rinfret, Pierre Andre
Ringwald, Donald Charles
Rinhart, George Robert
Rinkewich, Isaac Ronni
Rinsland, Roland DeLano
Rintelmann, William Fred
Rinzler, Evelyn Ellen
Riordan, Robert Emmet
Ripa, Louis Carl
Ripley, Sidney Dillon, 2d
Rippeteau, Darrel Downing
Rips, Serge
Ris, Howard Clinton
Risberg, Sally Elizabeth
Risemberg, Herman Mario
Risher, Howard Wesley, Jr.
Risko, George Joseph
Rison, Clarence Herbert
Riss, Eric
Risser, James Vaulx
Ritardi, Albert F.
Ritch, Robert Harry
Ritchie, Valeria Smith
Ritt, Paul Edward
Ritter, Donald Lawrence
Ritter, Joseph Spencer
Ritter, Seymour David
Riva (Jones), Janet Sylvia Gasunas
Rivers, Brenda Regina
Rivinus, Francis Markoe
Rivkin, Leonard Lambert
Rivoir, Sarah Elizabeth Stiner (Mrs. William H. Rivoir, Jr.)
Rizika, Jack Wilford
Rizk, Romanos
Rizzardi, William Daniel
Rizzo, Frank L. (Francis Lazzaro)
Rizzolo, Felix C.
Roach, Bernard Louis
Roash, Nicholas Anthony
Robana, Abderrahman
Robards, Sherman Marshall
Robb, Roger
Robbins, Charles D., Jr.
Robbins, Charles Louis
Robbins, Edwin
Robbins, Harvey A.
Robbins, Herman
Robbins, Jay Howard
Robbins, Sherman Michael
Robe, Lucy Barry (Mrs. Robert S. Robe, Jr.)
Roberge, Philippe
Roberson, Elizabeth Willoughby
Roberti, Edmando
Robertiello, Richard Candela
Roberts, Benjamin Washington, Jr.
Roberts, Bruce Dan
Roberts, Burton B.
Roberts, Eleanor Flavy Gelinas
Roberts, Gertrude Brill
Roberts, Gloria Augustine
Roberts, Gordon F.
Roberts, Gregory
Roberts, James Patrick
Roberts, John Giles
Roberts, John Wallace
Roberts, Melville Parker, Jr.
Roberts, Mervin Francis
Roberts, Millard George

Roberts, Ralph Joel
Roberts, Reade Alan
Roberts, Richard
Roberts, Richard James
Roberts, Sandra Jo
Robertson, Alan Gordon
Robertson, Donald Marshall
Robertson, James Cole
Robertson, James Colvert
Robertson, Lenard Bell
Robertson, Richard DeForest
Robertson, Robert Brewer
Robey, Kathleen Moran (Mrs. Ralph West Robey)
Robic, Raymond Andre
Robichaud, Hedard
Robillard, Jennifer Karzy
Robillard, Raymond Alfred
Robin, Gilbert Nathaniel
Robin, Jean-Paul
Robinovitz, Susan Fowler
Robinson, Carleton Bryant
Robinson, Charles Kenneth
Robinson, Christopher Albert
Robinson, David Beebee
Robinson, Donald Peter
Robinson, Francis Edwin
Robinson, Frank Melvin, Jr.
Robinson, Gordon Whiteman
Robinson, Harold Barrett
Robinson, Harry John
Robinson, Hugh R.
Robinson, Irwin Jay
Robinson, James Herbert
Robinson, James Johlin
Robinson, Jean Elizabeth (Fisher)
Robinson, John Brinton
Robinson, John Filmore
Robinson, John Louis
Robinson, Kenneth Patrick
Robinson, Mary Duncan
Robinson, Ormsbee W.
Robinson, Robert Armstrong
Robinson, Sharon Louise
Robinson, Sherman Samuel
Robinson, Spottswood William, III
Robinson, William Michael
Robison, Ann Green
Roblin, Gloria Landsman (Mrs. Daniel A. Roblin, Jr.)
Rocha, John Gonsalves
Rochford, Robert Patrick
Rochlin, Phillip
Rock, Patricia McGuire
Rock, Robert William
Rockefeller, David
Rockefeller, Nelson Aldrich
Rockett, Leonard Richard, Jr.
Rockland, Lawrence Howard
Rocklin, Raymond
Rodden, Donna Strickland
Rode, Francis Warren, III
Roden, Jon-Paul
Rodenhauser, Paul Charles
Roder, Paul William, III
Roderick, David Milton
Rodetsky, Martin
Rodgers, Floyd Dwight, Jr.
Rodgers, Patrick Elvis
Rodin, Doris Galant
Rodino, Peter W(allace), Jr.
Rodler, David Ernest
Rodman, Leroy Eli
Rodriguez, Edouard
Rodriguez, Ernesto Angelo
Rodriguez, Josefina Carmen Hortensia
Rodriguez, Juan M.
Rodriguez, Paul
Rodriguez, Vincent Angel
Rodriguez, William Julio
Rodriguez-Freire, Jose
Roe, Hans Siegfried
Roe, Kenneth Andrew
Roe, Robert A.
Roeder, John Anthony
Roediger, Frederick Everett
Roehrkasse, Robert Charles
Roemer, LeRoy Stanwood
Roemer, Richard Arthur
Roenke, Henry Merrill, Jr.
Roessler, Paul Albert
Roessler, Sheldon James
Roethel, David Albert Hill
Rofrano, Kenneth M.
Rogalin, Wilma Clare Sivertsen
Rogart, Mark Edward
Rogentine, George Nicholas, Jr.
Rogers, Alfred Raymond
Rogers, Donald Wesley
Rogers, Francis Day
Rogers, Harry Carton, Jr.
Rogers, James Beeland, Jr.
Rogers, Norman
Rogers, Philip Michael
Rogers, Stuart Clark
Rognon, Lee Tison
Rogoff, Mark George
Rogofsky, Murray
Rogow, Louis Michael
Rohn, William James
Rohrbach, J. William
Rohrbach, Walter Aaron
Rohrbaugh, Lewis Bunker
Rohrbaugh, Stephen Bunker
Rohrer, Daniel Hugh, III
Rohrlack, Richard Alan
Roig, Carlos
Roitsch, Paul Albert
Rojas, Renato Hugo
Roland, Maxwell
Roll, Kempton Harries
Rollins, Bryant
Rolo, Charles Jacques
Roma, George Edward
Romain, Margaret Ann
Romaine, Hans
Roman, James Rudolph, Jr.
Roman, Murray
Romanelli, Paul Joseph
Romano, Sister Geraldine Mary
Romano, Nicholas Charles
Romano, Robert John
Romano, William John
Romberger, John Albert
Rome, Lewis B.
Romeo, Joseph Arthur
Romeo, Vincent Fiore
Romney, Lenore Lafount (Mrs. George Wilcken Romney)
Romo, Daniel Herman
Roncallo, Angelo Dominic
Rondthaler, Edward
Ronson, Raoul R.
Ronty, Bruno George
Roodin, Paul Arnold
Rooney, Arthur Joseph
Rooney, Fred B.
Rooney, John Michael
Rooney, Paul Monroe
Rooney, Robert Carter
Roos, Daniel
Roos, Edward William
Root, Alan Charles
Root, Clifford Donral
Root, Lawrence Edward
Root, Nile
Root, Stanley William, Jr.
Roper, Al
Roper, Burns Worthington
Roper, Floyd Walton
Roper, Richard Walter
Roper, Robert John
Ropp, Richard Claude
Rorem, Clarence Rufus
Rorem, Ned
Rorer, John Whiteley
Rorro, Celeste Mary
Rosado, Peggy Moran
Rosahn, Paul Dolin
Rosch, Paul John
Rose, Daniel
Rose, Evans, Jr.
Rose, Frank Louis
Rose, Hugh
Rose, Joel Burton
Rose, Lillian Lerner (Mrs. Julian Barnet Bookstaver)
Rose, Roslyn (Mrs. Franklin Blou)
Rose, Stuart Willard
Rose, William Allen, Jr.
Rose, Winston James
Rosecrance, Richard Newton
Roselli, Richard Robert
Rosellini, Lynn Christine
Rosemberg, Eugenia
Rosen, Dan
Rosen, Hyman (Hugh Rowen)
Rosen, Marlene
Rosen, Robert Leon
Rosen, Ronald Charles
Rosen, Sherman Jay
Rosen, Sidney
Rosenbaum, Arnold Michael
Rosenbaum, David Herbert
Rosenbaum, Edward Whitehill
Rosenbaum, Jacob Philip
Rosenbaum, Maj-Britt Tornqvist
Rosenbaum, Martin Michael
Rosenbaum, Susan Louise
Rosenberg, Abner Samuel
Rosenberg, Alan Robert
Rosenberg, Alan Spencer
Rosenberg, Alex Jacob
Rosenberg, Allan Douglas
Rosenberg, Edgar
Rosenberg, Lawrence Joseph
Rosenberg, Leonard Herman
Rosenberg, Louis
Rosenberg, Milton Leon
Rosenberg, Robert Allen
Rosenberg, Robert Charles
Rosenberg, Rudy
Rosenberg, Seymour
Rosenberg, Thomas John
Rosenberg, Victor I.
Rosenberger, Homer Tope
Rosenberger, Peter Birnie-Bye
Rosenblatt, Arthur Isaac
Rosenfeld, Donald Alan
Rosenfeld, Joseph
Rosenfeld, Reba
Rosenfeld, Ronald Marvin
Rosenkrantz, Jacob Alvin
Rosenlof, Carl Cornelius
Rosenquit, Bernard
Rosensaft, Melvin
Rosensaft, Menachem Zwi
Rosenstein, Alan Herbert
Rosenstein, Robert
Rosenstock, Robert
Rosenthal, Benjamin Stanley
Rosenthal, David Stanley
Rosenthal, Herbert Martin
Rosenthal, Laurence
Rosenthal, Lillian Mandell
Rosenthal, Milton Frederick
Rosenthal, Myron Martin
Rosenthal, Robert Kenneth
Rosenwald, Albert John
Rosko, Milton, Jr.
Rosnagle, Robert Shields
Rosner, Irving Stanley
Rosof, Patricia Jane Freeman
Rosow, Michael Philip
Ross, Adrian E.
Ross, Alan O(tto)
Ross, Alexander Seymour
Ross, Dan Connor
Ross, Daniel Paul
Ross, David Harvey
Ross, Donald Joseph, Jr.
Ross, Doris G.
Ross, Douglas Carroll
Ross, Essye Buch (Mrs. Leonard Ross)
Ross, Franz Ernest
Ross, Geoffrey Sinclair
Ross, Harold Leroy, Jr.
Ross, Jeffrey Stuart
Ross, John
Ross, John Allen
Ross, John Joseph
Ross, Joseph Murphy
Ross, Luisa M.
Ross, Mary Cowell (Mrs. John O. Ross)
Ross, Robert Donald
Ross, Roderic Henry
Ross, Sigmund Lance
Ross, Thomas McCallum
Ross, Wilbur Louis, Jr.
Ross, William Daniel
Ross, Winston Alton
Rosselli, Charles Anthony
Rosselot, Max B.
Rossi, Joseph O.
Rossi, Robert
Rossignol, Joyce Hall
Rossman, Howard Samuel
Rossman, Newell William, Jr.
Rossman, Robert Harris
Rossoff, Sheldon T.
Rostropovich, Mstislav
Rotberg, Robert I.
Rotenberg, Ronald Hyman
Rotgin, Philip Norman
Roth, Carl
Roth, David Morris
Roth, Sister E. Sue
Roth, Harold
Roth, John Kenneth
Roth, Judith Marie Blackfeld
Roth, June Doris Speiwak
Roth, Laurence George
Roth, Michael
Roth, Norman George
Roth, Robert George
Roth, Robert Merle
Roth, Sol
Roth, Stephen Ira
Roth, Theodore William
Roth, William V., Jr.
Rothbell, Earle Norris
Rothberg, Sidney
Rothblatt, Henry Barnett
Rothenbeck, Charles Frederick
Rothenberg, Albert
Rothenberg, Peter John
Rothermel, Joel Edward
Rothfeld, Gloria Karmen
Rothholz, Peter Lutz
Rothman, Esther Pomeranz
Rothman, Frank
Rothman, Herbert David
Rothman, John
Rothrock, Henry Shirley
Rothschild, Richard Charles
Rothstein, Paul Frederick
Rothstein, Sidney David
Rothwarf, Allen
Rothweiler, Paul Roger
Rotko, Bernard Benjamin
Rotman, Bertram Theodore
Rotman, Eleanor Lea (Mrs. Bertram T. Rotman)
Rotman, Jesse Louis
Rotondo, Vincent John
Rotter, Paul Talbott
Rotterdam, Heidrun Z.
Rotterdam, Z. Paul
Roubik, Robert Andrew
Roufa, Arnold
Rounds, John Scoville
Rouslin, Marc Alan
Rowan, Arbe James
Rowan, Richard Lamar
Rowand, Robert Ellwood
Rowden, Geoffrey
Rowe, Benjamin Ackley
Rowe, Charles Alfred
Rowe, Charles Wright
Rowell, Harry Brown, Jr.
Rowell, Margaret Kenny
Rowen, Ruth Halle (Mrs. Seymour M. Rowen)
Rowland, Clifford Vance
Rowley, Elmer Clifford
Roy, Concetta Constance Cornelia Cornacchia (Mrs. Leo J. Roy)
Roy, Joy Benjamin
Roy, Maurice
Roy, Paul Norman
Roycroft, Howard Francis
Royden, Ernest Jerome
Rozel, Samuel Joseph
Rozene, Jack Irving
Rozner, Alexander George
Ruark, Richard William
Rubel, Martin
Ruben, Albert
Ruben, Brent David
Ruben, Robert Joel
Rubenfeld, Stanley Irwin
Rubens, Merton
Rubenstein, Abraham Daniel
Rubenstein, Allan Earl
Rubenstein, Howard
Rubenstein, Leonard
Rubenstein, Sidney
Rubenstein, Stanley Ellis
Rubin, Arnold Perry
Rubin, Arthur Herman
Rubin, Donald S.
Rubin, Gabriel Kevi
Rubin, Harold Sydney
Rubin, Howard
Rubin, Howard Myron
Rubin, Kenneth Allen
Rubin, Michele Barrie
Rubin, Samuel Solomon
Rubin, William Hannibal
Rubini, Dennis Anthony
Rubinstein, Louis Baruch
Rubinstein, Max G.
Ruboy, Jordan Sumner
Rubulotta, Joseph Anthony
Ruby, John Robert
Rudavsky, Amiel Zachary
Rudd, David William
Rudd, Irene Takacs
Rudel, Thomas Ryder
Rudge, Peter David
Rudhart, Alexander Hugo
Rudich, Gerald Allan
Rudin, Arnold James
Rudisill, Richard Allen
Rudman, Joan Eleanor
Rudolf, Donald I.
Rudolfer, George
Rudolph, Malcolm Rome
Ru Dusky, Basil Michael
Rudy, Dorothy Lucille
Rudy, Willis
Rue, William James
Ruebel, Armin AlfredLudwig
Rueppel, Merrill Clement
Rueth, Marion Ursula
Rufeh, Firooz
Ruff, Alonzo William
Ruffalo, Sibyl Winifred Masquelier
Ruffolo, Robert Eugene, II
Rugani, Alexander E.
Rugari, Joseph Frank
Ruggieri, Nicholas Tino
Ruggieri, Pauline Pappas
Ruggiero, Richard Salvador
Ruggiero, Thomas William
Ruiz, Tomas
Ruma, Steven James
Rumer, Ralph Raymond, Jr.
Rummler, Joseph Chadwick
Rumstein, Regina
Runden, Charity Eva Williams
Runnion, Norman Ray
Runstein, Robert E.
Runyon, Howard LeRoy
Runyon, John Harold
Ruof, Richard Alan
Rupert, Marybeth Kimberly
Rupert, Richard Eugene
Rupolo, John George
Ruppert, Robert William
Rush, John Patrick
Rusher, William Allen
Rusinow, Dennison I.
Rusis, Armins
Rusk, Daniel McDonald, Jr.
Ruskin, Arthur Sanford
Russakoff, Don
Russano, Robert Oliver
Russell, Alfred Michel
Russell, Allison Kaplan
Russell, Argentina Eugenia
Russell, Barrett Beard, 3d
Russell, C. Andrew
Russell, Edward Thomas
Russell, Elbert
Russell, Gary Charles
Russell, Harriet Virginia Heit
Russell, Leonard Howland
Russell, Olive Ruth
Russell, Paul George
Russell, Paul Henry, Jr.
Russell, Phebe Gale (Mrs. Frank M. Russell)
Russell, Sanford Eugene
Russell, Warren Edward
Russell, Wilbert Coleman
Russo, Joseph Aloysius, Jr.
Russo, Peter Francis
Russo, Vincent Joseph
Russo, William Richard
Rust, Laurence DeWitt
Rust, Meta Mildred Libby
Rust, Myron Davis
Rust, Velma Irene Miller (Mrs. Ronald Stuart Rust)
Rust, William Anthony, Jr.
Ruston, Henry
Rutenber, Cleminette Downing
Rutenber, Ralph Dudley, Jr.
Rutgers, Katharine Phillips (Mrs. Frederik Lodewijk Rutgers)
Ruth, Thomas Griswold
Ruth, Vincent Wismer
Rutherford, John Loftus
Rutimann, Hans
Rutka, Howard Joseph
Rutkowski, Conrad Philemon
Rutledge, Pearl Black
Rutsky, Lester
Ruzicka, Mary Frances
Ryan, Alan Richard
Ryan, Charles Edward, Jr.
Ryan, Claude
Ryan, Eugene Anthony
Ryan, Eugene Joseph
Ryan, Frank James
Ryan, Gail Margaret
Ryan, James Daniel
Ryan, John William
Ryan, Leonard Eames
Ryan, Mary Kathryn
Ryan, Miles Francis, Jr.
Ryan, Robert S.
Ryan, Vincent Francis, Jr.
Ryan, William Howard
Rybeck, James Peter
Ryburn, Samuel McChesney
Rychlik, Frank Felix
Ryd, Beverly Jean
Ryder, Kenneth Gilmore
Ryder, Robert Guy
Ryea, John Lawrence, Jr.
Rygelis, Joseph
Rykert, John Charles
Rylander, David John
Ryndes, Leonard James
Ryser, Hugues Jean-Paul
Rytten, Jack Edward
Rzepecki, Raymond Michael, Jr.
Saad, Edward Theodore
Saalbach, Raymond Currier
Sabia, Vincent Nicholas
Sablatash, Mike
Sabo, Jack Charles
Sabokbar, Nasser
Sabottke, Helen Louise Ahlberg
Sacco, Anthony Carmine
Saccoccio, Anthony Robert
Saccone, Anthony Daniel
Sacewicz, Martin Robert
Sachar, Howard Morley
Sachar, Thomas Vincent
Sachs, Julius Johnson
Sachs, Lee Allen
Sachs, Walter, Jr.
Sachs-Stern, Lisbeth Josephine
Sacklow, Stewart Irwin
Sada, Rudolph Muntu
Sadeghi-Nejad, Abdollah
Sadetsky, Harriet Janet
Sadlon, Errol Michael
Sadowski, Edward Peter
Sadruddin, Moe
Sadtler, Barbara Ann Koltes
Sadwin, Arnold
Sadwith, Howard Marvin
Safe, Kenneth Shaw, Jr.
Safford, Robert Owen
Safire, William
Safro, Paul
Sagall, Elliot Lawrence
Sagan, Carl Edward
Sagar, Vidya Vettiyattil
Sage, Robert
Sage, Robert Ephram
Sager, Clifford Julius
Sager, Marvin Miles
Sager, Thomas Brinker
Saggese, Anthony James, Jr.
Sahai, Dushyant Basantkumar
Sahanek, Tatana
Sahlin, Monte Carl
Said, Abdul Aziz
Saidi, Ahmad
Saiger, George Lewis
Sailer, John Rudolph
St. Amand, Glenda Weaver
St. Amand, Joseph
St. Angelo, Milo Jesse
St Clair, Guy Lewis
St. Florian, Friedrich Gartler
St. George, George H.
St. Germain, Dolphus Joseph
St. Germain, Fernand Joseph
St. Germain, Jean Mary
Saint-Pierre, Jacques
Sajjadi, Peter S.
Sajkovic, Vladimir
Sakell, Achilles Nicholas
Sakellaropoulos, George Panayotis
Sakoutis, Stephen Panayotis
Sala, Raul Perez
Saladino, John Leonard
Salant, Marilyn Moffat (Mrs. Robert S. Salant)
Salas, Henry Joseph
Salcman, Michael
Saleeba, George Joseph
Salem, Harry
Salensky, George
Sales, Frank
Salgo, Michael Nicholas
Saline, Lindon Edgar
Salisbury, Robert Elmore
Salkind, Michael Jay
Sallard, Benjamin Wilmore
Salley, George Paddock
Sallick, Richard Marshall
Sallie, Arnetha
Sallustio, Anthony Thomas
Salmon, James Henry
Salomon, Frank Ernest
Salomon, Lucy
Salomon, Robert Jess
Salomon, Robert Val
Salomon, Suzanne Evan
Salomonson, Vincent Victor
Salop, Arnold
Salpeter, Burton Foch
Salsali, Morteza
Salten, David George
Salter, Thomas Lowell
Saltzer, Paul
Saluter, Philip Arthur, II
Salva, Nieva Duque
Salvage, Lynn Diane
Salvary, Stanley Cecil Winston
Salvati, Eugene Philip
Salvatierra, Richard Dean
Salvatore, Francis Paul, Sr.
Salwin, Lester Nathan
Salzburg, Joseph Sheldon
Salzman, Herbert
Sam, Chung Lam
Samaan, Selim Tawfick
Sament, Sidney
Samet, Charles Merle
Samorajczyk, John Frank
Sampietro, Pierluigi
Sampson, Arthur Francis
Sams, Ned Houston
Samsell, Lewis Patrick
Samuel, Eric Rudolf
Samuels, Harold
Samuels, Peggy Bardsley
Samuels, Richard Mel
Samuelson, Edwin Arthur
Samuelson, Paul Anthony
Sananman, Michael Lawrence
Sanborn, Donald Edward, III
Sanborn, Everett Clarence
Sanborn, Ralph Durell
Sandberg, Irwin Walter
Sande, Rhoda
Sandeen, Mary Reed (Mrs. Russell G. Sandeen)
Sander, Hans K.
Sanders, Charles Addison
Sanders, Clifford Charles
Sanders, Frank
Sanders, Gwendolyn W.
Sanders, James Joseph
Sanders, John David
Sanders, Reuben Augustus
Sanders, Robert Martin
Sanderson, Howard Martin
Sandler, Bernice
Sandler, Leslie Neal
Sandonato, Patrick Daniel
Sandor, Thomas
Sands, John Eliot
Sands, John Keating
San Felice, Giacamo (Jack)
Sanford, Carl Frederick
Sanford, Leda
Sanft, Louis
Sanger, Joan Oyaas
Sano, Julian Hajime
Sano, Richard Mitsuto
Sanoian, Corigan
Sanschagrin, Albert
Sanslone, William Robert
Sansone, Thomas
Santopietro, Richard Frank
Santoro, Samuel, Jr.
Santos, Robert Frederick
Santos, Sergio Esteban
Santry, Arthur Joseph, Jr.
Santucci, Arthur Anthony
Santucci, Gary Joseph
Saparoff, Gerald Robin
Saperston, Howard Truman, Jr.
Sapin, Robert
Sapoff, Meyer
Sarafidis, Helen Girassis
Sarasin, Ronald Arthur
Sarbanes, Paul Spyros
Sargent, John Turner
Saribeyoglu, Safa Ismail
Sarino, Edgardo Formantes
Sarno, Ronald Anthony
Sarnoff, Edward
Sarnoff, Lili-Charlotte Dreyfus (Mrs. Stanley J. Sarnoff)
Sarris, Nicholas
Sarvet, Walter Morton
Sarwer-Foner, Gerald
Sass, Neil Leslie
Sasso, Louis Anthony
Sasso, Ruth Maryann
Sassover, Nathan
Sataline, Lee Roy
Satchell, Lou Edwin
Satin, Lawrence Z.
Satterfield, John
Satz, Arthur King
Satz, Martin Allen
Sauer, John W.
Sauer, Lawrence Michael
Sauerwald, John Paul
Saunders, Albert Henry
Saunders, Amos Charles
Saunders, Beatrice Nair
Saunders, Betty Huey (Mrs. Aulus Ward Saunders)
Saunders, John Richard
Saunders, Joseph Arthur
Saunders, Mary Frances
Saunders, Robert Harris
Saunders, Stanley
Saunders, William Beverly
Saunders, William Francis
Sause, Edwin Francis
Sauter, Laurence James
Sauter, Michael Ottmar
Sauvayre, Georges Theophile
Savage, Henry Lyttleton
Savage, John Addison
Savage, Warren Howard
Savage, William Michael
Savas, Emanuel S.
Savel, Lewis Eugene
Savitsky, Linda Rebecca
Savitt, Arnold Jay
Savitt, Sam
Sawhill, John
Sawitsky, Helen Maryann
Sawyer, Richard George
Sawyer, Thomas Knowlton
Saxe, Elizabeth Lee
Saxe, Theodore Langdon
Saxon, George Edward
Saxton, Gerald O.
Saylor, Robert Homer
Sayong, Salvador Acala
Sayre, Anne
Sazer, Gary Neil
Scala, Sinclaire Maximilian
Scalera, Nicholas Robert
Scalfarotto, Robert Emil
Scallon, Frank John

Scalora, Frank Salvatore
Scanlon, Edward Charles
Scanlon, John William
Scarborough, Charles Bishop, III
Scarlata, Paul Anthony
Scerno, J. Benedict
Schach, William O.
Schacknow, Paul Neil
Schade, Robert Richard
Schaefer, Charles James, III
Schaefer, Karl Ernst
Schaefer, Maryann Bilello
Schaefer, Robert Anthony
Schaefer, William Donald
Schaeffer, Frederick Robert
Schaeffer, Frederick Steven
Schaeffer, Klaus Heymann
Schaevitz, Abraham Robert
Schafer, Don Francis
Schaffer, David Edwin
Schaffer, Joan Lothrop
Schaffhouser, Arthur
Schaible, Michael Duane
Schaller, Elmer Otto
Schanberg, Sydney Hillel
Schandler, Herbert Yale
Schantz, Catherine Halleck
Schapira, Hans Erwin
Schapiro, Jerome Bentley
Schapiro, Ruth Goldman (Mrs. Donald Schapiro)
Schary, Dore
Schatz, Cecil Ruskay (Mrs. Arthur H. Schatz)
Schecter, Arnold Joel
Scheele, Christina Marie
Scheele, George Augustus, III
Scheer, Carl Weston
Scheers, Susan Adams
Scheffer, Richard Herbert
Scheib, Gary Lamar
Scheibner, Ruth Martin
Scheid, Ethel Charlleen Edwards
Scheid, John Edgar
Scheid, Paul
Scheid, Walter Evans
Scheige, Fortuna Faye Gorelick
Schein, Bernard
Schein, Philip Samuel
Scheinberg, Labe Charles
Scheiner, Ellen
Schell, Norman Barnett
Schellenger, James Knox Polk
Schenck, Harry Paul
Schenkel, Susi
Schenkelbach, Leon
Schenker, Irwin William
Schenkerman, Stanley
Scher, Jill Diener
Scher, Robert Sander
Scheremeta, William Walter
Scherer, Donald Richard
Scherr, Marvin Gerald
Schetlin, Eleanor M.
Scheuer, James H(aas)
Schiavina, Laura Margaret
Schick, Constance Joyce
Schick, Irvin Henry
Schick, Paul Kenneth
Schiddel, Edmund
Schieffelin, George Richard
Schieffer, Bob Lloyd
Schiff, Irwin Allen
Schiffman, Alan Theodore
Schiffman, Louis F.
Schiffman, Nancy Elizabeth
Schiffrin, Milton Julius
Schill, Gerald Francis
Schiller, Marvin
Schinnerer, Victor Oscar
Schirmann, Peter Jude
Schirmeister, Barbara Fredericks
Schirmer, Norbert Erich
Schkeeper, Peter Alexander
Schlager, Maynard M.
Schlager, Thomas Paul
Schlaifer, Alan Norris
Schlaifer, Charles
Schlain, David
Schlam, Mark Howard
Schlegel, Harlan Edgar
Schlegelmilch, Reuben Orville
Schlein, Stephen P.
Schlesinger, Irwin D.
Schlesinger, James Rodney
Schlesinger, Louis Barry
Schlesinger, Richard B.
Schlesinger, Robert Lee
Schless, Guy Lacy
Schlimm, Gerard Henry
Schloss, Walter Jerome
Schlossberg, Harvey
Schlussel, Seymour
Schluter, Peter Mueller
Schmaus, Siegfried H. A.
Schmauss, David C.
Schmeichel, Neill Richard
Schmelkin, Benjamin
Schmelkin, Charles Lazar
Schmick, William Frederick, Jr.
Schmid, James Francis
Schmid, Walter Ernst
Schmidt, Gerhard Johann
Schmidt, Harold Robert
Schmidt, James Lee
Schmidt, Janet Anne
Schmidt, Paul Rudolf
Schmidt, Raymond Paul
Schmidt, Richard Penrose
Schmidt, Thomas Carson
Schmidt, William Max
Schmitt, Abraham
Schmitt, Roger Michael Lawrence
Schmitz, Karen Lee
Schmoke, Sarah Lee Linnette
Schmuckler, Stanley Lloyd
Schmukler, Anita Gloria
Schmut, Rudolf
Schmutzhart, Slaithong Chengtrakul
Schnabel, Wilhelm Joseph
Schnall, Edith Lea (Mrs. Herbert Schnall)
Schneckenburger, Roger Carl
Schneider, Bernard Arnold
Schneider, Beverly Ann
Schneider, Carl Stanley
Schneider, Carl William
Schneider, Erich
Schneider, Julius
Schneider, Robert William
Schneller, Eugene Stewart
Schnurmann, Erika
Schock, William Wallace
Schoen, Donald Robert
Schoen, Lester Arthur
Schoen, Rem
Schoeneman, Charles Wilson
Schoener, James Franklin
Schoenfeld, Cy
Schoenfeld, Michael P.
Schoenfeld, Theodore Mark
Schoenwald, Maurice L.
Schofer, Harry Stanley
Schofield, William Greenough
Scholl, Charles Elmer
Scholz, Catherine Hammersley
Schomp, Arthur Herbert
Schonberg, Jackson Richard
Schonholtz, Joan Sondra Hirsch
Schooley, Dolores (Mrs. Charles E. Schooley)
Schoonmaker, Albert Voorhis
Schoonmaker, Herbert Garrettson
Schoor, Howard M.
Schopler, Ernest Hugo
Schor, William Theodore
Schosheim, Pearl Estelle (Mrs. Arnold M. Schosheim)
Schott, John R.
Schrack, Vivian Bunnell
Schrade, Robert Warren
Schrader, Jane Marie Jacqueline
Schrecengost, Harry Allen, Jr.
Schreck, Richard Thomas
Schreiber, Charles Eric
Schreiber, Eileen Sher
Schreiber, Flora Rheta
Schreiber, Harry, Jr.
Schreiber, Joel S.
Schreiber, Patti Jeanne
Schreiner, Samuel Agnew, Jr.
Schrieffer, John Robert
Schriesheim, Alan
Schriftgiesser, Karl (John)
Schrock, Robert D., Jr.
Schroeder, Aaron Harold
Schroeder, Charles William Henry
Schroeder, James Louis, Jr.
Schroeder, Janet Gregg Wallace (Mrs. Henry A. Schroeder)
Schroeder, Theodore Conrad
Schroth, Thomas Anthony
Schruben, Johanna Stenzel
Schuchman, Herbert
Schuck, Victoria
Schucman, Helen Cohn (Mrs. Louis Schucman)
Schulenberg, Donald Warren
Schuler, Mathias John, III
Schuler, William Granville
Schuller, Diane Ethel
Schulman, Brian Martin
Schulman, Carol Brimberg
Schulman, Herbert
Schulman, Joseph Daniel
Schultheis, Edwin Milford
Schultz, Allan Joseph
Schultz, George Joseph
Schultz, Herbert Ferdinand
Schultz, Leslie Edward
Schultz, Robert Kenneth
Schultze, Charles Louis
Schultze, Dietrich Franz
Schulz, Frank Carl, Jr.
Schulz, Milford David
Schulz, Richard Burkart
Schulze, Richard Taylor
Schuman, Isadore
Schumann, Otho Douglas
Schumylowych, Taras
Schur, Walter Robert
Schure, Alexander
Schusler, Marian Lucille Martin (Mrs. Herbert Henry Schusler)
Schuster, Frederick Lee
Schwab, Frank, Jr.
Schwab, George David
Schwab, Harold Lee
Schwadron, Mitchell Carl
Schwager, Edith Cohen
Schwaid, Benjamin Nathan
Schwaid, Madeline Chavkin
Schwaner, Annie Mae Ginn
Schwanhausser, Robert Rowland
Schwaninger, James Craig, Sr.
Schwarting, Arthur Ernest
Schwartz, Adolph Franz
Schwartz, Albert Aaron
Schwartz, Allan Bradley
Schwartz, David
Schwartz, David Louis
Schwartz, Gary Edward
Schwartz, Gordon Francis
Schwartz, Harold F. X.
Schwartz, Helen French (Mrs. Harry Marvin Schwartz)
Schwartz, Hilda G.
Schwartz, Irving
Schwartz, Jack James
Schwartz, James Peter
Schwartz, Jerome
Schwartz, John Frederick
Schwartz, Joseph William
Schwartz, Lawrence
Schwartz, Martin Weber
Schwartz, Marvin W.
Schwartz, Mortimer Leonard
Schwartz, Norman A.
Schwartz, Norman Larry
Schwartz, Ralph Monroe
Schwartz, Robert Nash
Schwartz, Sanford Alan
Schwartz, Sheldon David
Schwartz, Tillie
Schwartzberg, Allan Zelig
Schwartzman, Lois Paula
Schwarz, Alfred William
Schwarz, Ernest Isaac
Schwarz, Sidney May
Schwarz, Wolfgang
Schwarzer, Otto Oscar
Schwebel, Renata Manasse (Mrs. Jack P. Schwebel)
Schweich, Leo
Schweiker, Richard Schultz
Schweitzer, Thomas Fred
Schwenn, Lee William
Schwer, Robert Thomas
Schwerdtle, Diana Carlisle
Schwersenz, Jack Wolf
Schwimmer, Steve
Sciveres, Anthony
Scofield, Roderick Arthur
Scoles, Peter Serafino
Scott, Bertha Dixon
Scott, Blaine Wahab, III
Scott, Carmalita Foster Benson
Scott, David Bytovetzski
Scott, David Henry
Scott, Donald Hunt
Scott, Duncan Nicholas, Jr.
Scott, Edward Walter
Scott, John Ainsworth, Jr.
Scott, John Brooks
Scott, John Raymond, Jr.
Scott, Jonathan Lavon
Scott, Lester Raymond, Jr.
Scott, Osborne Ernest
Scott, R(ussell) Stephen
Scott, Richard Thurston
Scott, Robert Steven
Scott, Robert Willard
Scott, Walter Neil
Scott, William Gregory
Scribner, Lloyd Holmes
Scrivan, Michel Andrew
Scrivo, Jerry Vance
Scudder, Philmore Major, Jr.
Scully, John Thomas
Scurlock, Reagan Andrew
Scutt, Der
Seabrook, Victor Melville
Seadler, Stephen Edward
Seager, Richard Hugh
Seal, William Conor
Sealey, Leonard George William
Seaman, Alfred J(arvis)
Sear, Alan Martin
Sears, Robert Allen
Seaton, Douglas Graham
Seawell, Donald Ray
Sebastianelli, Mario Joseph
Sebekos, Thomas George
Sebes, Joseph Schobert
Sebok, Louis Stephen
Secor, John Ralph
Seder, Lawrence Richard
Sedgley, Alfreda Julia
Sedlak, Emery Paul
Seedman, George James
Seel, Martin Anthony
Seelbach, Charles William
Seeley, Clinton Barnum
Seely, John Conor, Jr.
Seely, Robert Daniel
Seeman, Bernard
Seeman, Manfred
Segal, Barry Mayer
Segal, Bernard
Segal, Donald Henry Gilbert
Segal, Irving Randall
Segel, Arnold Lester
Segel, J. Norman
Seggerman, Anne Crellin
Seggev, Meir
Seham, Martin Charles
Sehgal, Robert
Seibert, Donald Vincent
Seibert, Janet Loos
Seibold, Herman Rudolph
Seidel, Carl William
Seidel, Janet Conrad
Seiden, Henry
Seiden, Manfred
Seidenstein, Jean Trager
Seidl, Jean Elaine (Mrs. Richard H. Hamilton)
Seidman, Arthur H.
Seidner, Gilbert
Seidner, Stanley Samuel
Seifert, Ralph Hammond
Seiffer, David A.
Seigle, Natalie R.
Seigworth, Gilbert Ronald
Seiler, John Philip
Seiler, Karl, III
Seiler, Katharine Louise
Seilheimer, Charles Henry, Jr.
Seiniger, David Hallamore, Sr.
Seitelman, Leon Harold
Seittelman, Elizabeth Edith
Seittelman, Estelle
Seitz, Collins Jacques
Seitz, Frederick
Seitzer, Robert H.
Seitzman, Lawrence Alan
Seixas, Frank Archibald
Sekerak, Richard John
Selden, Ellen Jacobi
Seldin, S(teward) Daniel
Seldner, Abraham
Selig, J. Daniel
Seligman, Bernard
Seligson, Linda Weiner
Sell, Leo Lewis
Sellner, Gerald Paul
Selmeczi, Joseph Gabor
Selmore, Joseph Waymond
Seltzer, Emily Ruth
Seltzer, Irving
Seltzer, Murray Harold
Seltzer, (Herbert) Richard
Seltzer, Richard Warren
Selverne, Lee J.
Selwyn, Donald
Semaan, Khalil Ibrahim Hanna
Semanchuk, Peter Paul
Semanoff, Leon
Semerjian, Madelle Lyons Hegeler
Seminara, Eleanor Frances
Semmel, Bernard
Semple, Cecil Snowdon
Semprevivo, Philip Carmine
Sen, Tapas Kumar
Senay, Terence Patrick
Sendax, Victor Irven
Seng, Minnie Anna
Sengstaken, Robert William
Senitt, Joseph A.
Sensenig, David Martin
Senter, Roger Campbell
Sentner, Phillip John
Seremetis, Michael George
Serensen, William, Jr.
Serenyi, Istvan Vitez
Serenyi, Peter
Serfass, Robert William
Sernak, Joseph Lawrence
Serpe, Salvatore John
Serra, Robert Franklin
Serviss, Ann Earl
Serwer-Bernstein, Blanche Luria
Sessions, Judith Ann
Sessoms, Allen Lee
Sestito, Joseph F.J.
Setchell, John Stanford, Jr.
Seth, Anand Kumar
Seton, Charles B.
Seton, Fenmore Roger
Sevegian, Aram Haig
Sevier, John Charles
Sexton, Barbara Royster
Seymour, Whitney North
Sgambato, Joseph John
Shaevel, Morton Leonard
Shafer, Barbara Grace
Shafer, Stephen Quentin
Shaffer, Ella Louise (Eloise)
Shaffer, Helen Snyder
Shaffer, John Whitcomb
Shaffer, Margaret Thompson
Shah, Bipin Chandra
Shah, Hasmukh Sankalchand
Shah, Sudhir Ashalal
Shahinian, Siroon Pashalian
Shaikh, Bahu Sultan
Shaikh, Zahir Ahmad
Shain, Richard Arthur
Shake, J(ames) Curtis
Shakour, Gabriel Mitchell
Shalit, Bernard Lawrence
Shalita, Alan Remi
Shalita, Paul Roy
Shames, William Henry
Shamoun, Edward
Shanahan, Sheila Ann
Shanker, Albert
Shanley, Bernard M(ichael)
Shannahan, John William
Shannon, Eleanor Thelma
Shannon, James Michael
Shannon, Margaret Rita
Shaper, Ruth Stafford
Shapiro, A. Gerald
Shapiro, Abraham
Shapiro, E. Donald
Shapiro, George M.
Shapiro, Irving Saul
Shapiro, John Martin
Shapiro, Manheim Simeon
Shapiro, Milton Stanley
Shapiro, Morris Arnold
Shapiro, Phyllis (Mrs. Abraham Shapiro)
Shapiro, Robyn Debra
Shapiro, Solomon Bernard
Shapiro, Stephen Daniel
Shapiro, Susan Holly
Sharbaugh, Amandus Harry
Share, Robert William
Sharify, Nasser
Sharman, Richard Lee
Sharon, John Hurford
Sharp, Daniel Asher
Sharp, Henry Franklin
Sharp, J(ames) Franklin
Sharp, Martin William, Jr.
Sharp, Mitchell William
Sharpe, J. C. Timothy
Sharpless, Joseph Benjamin
Shatto, Paul Frederick
Shattuck, Joseph Boardman, Jr.
Shaughnessy, George Albert
Shaughnessy, John William, Jr.
Shaulis, Nelson Jacob
Shavel, Mike H.
Shaw, Arthur Jack
Shaw, Charles Ernest
Shaw, Frederick
Shaw, Grace Goodfriend (Mrs. Herbert Franklin Shaw)
Shaw, Henry
Shaw, Jack Allen
Shaw, James Woodland
Shaw, John Eugene
Shaw, John Hodgdon
Shaw, Jon Angus
Shaw, Lee Nelson
Shawn, William Henry
Shea, George Matthew
Shea, Michael James
Shea, Peter John
Shea, Stephen Michael
Shea, Thomas West
Shealey, Glenn Elliott
Shean, Timothy Joseph
Shear, Theodore Leslie, Jr.
Shearer, Francis Allen
Shearer, Jane Kelly
Shedd, Mark Redans
Sheehan, John Joseph
Sheehan, June Mulvey
Sheehan, Marilyn Rose
Sheehan, Robert James
Sheehan, Thomas Edward
Sheehy, Martin James
Sheeran, James Jennings
Sheets, Norman L.
Sheetz, Harry John, III
Sheff, Madelon
Sheffler, M. Andrew
Sheft, Leonard Alvin
Sheftel, Roger Terry
Shefton, John Herbert
Shehan, Cardinal Lawrence Joseph
Sheinkman, Jacob
Sheldon, Roger Alpha
Shelley, Edwin Freeman
Shelp, Ronald Kent
Shen, Chin Chiu
Shenfeld, Marvin
Shenkman, Mark Ronald
Shepard, Eleanor Storm
Shepard, George, Jr.
Shepard, Jean Heck Hastings
Shepard, Joan Hayden
Shepard, Robert Daniel
Shepard, Thomas R., Jr.
Shepherd, Donald
Shepherd, Richard Montgomery
Sheppard, Jack Cornell, Jr.
Sheppard, Posy (Mrs. John Wade Sheppard)
Sheppard, Walter Lee, Jr.
Sherburne, Albert Lovering
Sherer, Joseph Forest, Jr.
Sheridan, Amelia Panzarella
Sheridan, Patrick Michael
Sheridan, Vincent George
Sherlock, Dulcie-Ann Steinhardt
Sherlock, Paul
Sherman, Constance Denise
Sherman, Gerald Howard
Sherman, Jonathan Goodhue
Sherman, Joseph Vincent
Sherman, Julius
Sherman, Lawrence William
Sherman, Mark Melvin
Sherman, Otto Martin
Sherman, Ralph W(illiam)
Sherman, Robert Edway
Sherman, Robert Lee
Sherman, Robert Myles
Shermeta, Dennis William
Shero, Fred Alexander
Sherr, Abraham I.
Sherr, Merrill Frederick
Sherrod, Robert Lee
Sherry, Catherine Therese
Sherry, Gerald Joseph
Sherry, Howard Samuel
Sherry, Patricia Ann
Sherwin, Oscar
Sherwin, Richard Jack
Sherwood, Hubert James
Sherwood, Richard Curry
Shetler, Frederick Charles
Shetterly, Henry Titus
Sheveck, Joseph Jerome
Shieh, Wei Tong
Shields, Bruce Maclean
Shields, Cornelius
Shields, Gerald Robert
Shields, John Edgar
Shields, Lawrence Thornton
Shields, Richard
Shields, Richard Tyner
Shifrin, Bruce Carl
Shifrin, David Lawrence
Shim, Kun Il
Shim, Nak Kwang
Shimizu, Arthur George
Shinkle, Robert Franklin
Shinn, Richard Randolph
Shinozuka, Masanobu
Ship, Irwin
Shipley, Gerry Stewart
Shipman, Mark Samuel
Shipps, Hammell Pierce
Shirey, Samuel Martin
Shive, Roy Allen
Shively, Glenn Alan
Shmukler, Stanford
Shock, Manvern Floyd
Shoemaker, Thomas Earp, II
Shoesmith, Milton Henry
Sholl, Calvin Kenneth
Shook, Theodore Albert
Shooshan, Daniel Martin
Shopey, Robert John
Shopsin, Baron
Shore, Benjamin
Shore, Milton Paul
Shorr, Edward Jeffrey
Shorr, Norman
Shorr, Ronald Philip
Short, William Hosley
Shortway, Richard Anthony
Shoshkes, Lila
Shotland, Edwin
Show, Whitlaw Missimer
Showers, Herman Byron
Shrager, Morton William
Shralow, Rhoda Robin
Shreiner, Charles Wesley, Jr.
Shrier, Adam Louis
Shrier, Diane Kesler
Shriver, Richard Hanson
Shull, Kenneth Edgar
Shulman, Frank Joseph
Shulman, Gerald Dennis
Shultz, Herbert Lloyd
Shuman, Stanley Saxe
Shuster, Carl Nathaniel
Shuster, Carl Nathaniel, Jr.
Shuster, E.G. (Bud)
Shutack, John Patrick
Shuttleworth, Anne Margaret
Shvetz, Alexander Ephraim
Siar, Robert Thomas
Sibalis, Dan
Sibinovic, Kyle Harding (Mrs. Stevan Sibinovic)
Sibley, John Joseph
Sick, William Norman, Jr.
Sidamon-Eristoff, Constantine
Sideco, Edgar Cruz
Sidell, William
Sider, Ronald Ray
Sidoti, Raymond Benjamin
Sieczkos, John Henry
Siefken, Harold Edward
Siegel, Alan Alfred
Siegel, Arthur Herbert
Siegel, Arthur Irving
Siegel, Edward Paul
Siegel, Elliot Robert
Siegel, Henry
Siegel, Herbert Jay
Siegel, Paul Michael
Siegfried, Franklin
Siegler, William A., Jr.
Siegman, Henry
Sieh, Theodore
Sieller, William Vincent
Sienkiewicz, John Casimir
Sieracki, Louis Anthony
Sies, Luther Frank
Siesser, Paul
Siff, Marlene Ida
Sifton, Charles P.
Sifton, Paul Ginsburg
Sigall, Michael William
Sigety, Charles Edward
Sigman, Gordon Hill, Jr.
Sigmon, Jackson Marcus
Signorelli, Alfred Romeo
Signorelli, Salvatore
Signist, Charles A.
Sikri, Atam Prakash
Silber, John Robert
Silberfarb, Peter Michael
Silberman, H. Lee
Silbermann, Peter Thomas
Silberstein, Richard M.
Silbert, Nathan Ernest
Sills, Arthur Jack
Sills, Beverly E (Belle Silverman) (Mrs. Peter B. Greenough)
Sills, H. Donald
Sills, Ruth Curtis Frank (Mrs. H. Donald Sills)
Silsby, Herbert Trafton, II
Siltanen, John Carl
Silva, Phyllis Jeanne
Silva, Rene Narciso
Silvain, Peter Brule
Silver, Carl Elihu
Silver, Louis
Silver, Robert Alan
Silver, Sidney Leonard
Silver, Stanley
Silvera, Americo
Silverberg, Bernard
Silverman, Buddy Robert Stephen
Silverman, Catherine Sclater Parker
Silverman, Fred
Silverman, Fred
Silverman, Harold Irving
Silverman, Hirsch Lazaar
Silverman, Hyman Jacob
Silverman, Ira
Silverman, Martin
Silverman, Michael Robert
Silverman, Paul Leonard
Silverman, Richard
Silverman, Sam Mendel
Silverman, Sidney
Silverman, Stuart Ronald
Silverstein, Leonard
Silvestri, James Joseph
Simels, Richard Neil
Simic, Ivan S.

Simkin, Don Howard
Simmers, Harry Lee
Simmons, Adele Smith
Simmons, Alvin Joseph
Simmons, Frederick Charles
Simmons, George Allen
Simmons, Harry Dady, Jr.
Simmons, John Derek
Simmons, Kenneth Jon
Simmons, Thomas Murray
Simon, Arthur James
Simon, Benjamin
Simon, Bernard
Simon, Ellen Shattuck
Simon, Gerald Austin
Simon, Harold
Simon, Herbert Alexander
Simon, Joseph Henry
Simon, Sidney
Simon, Stanley Robert
Simon, William
Simon, William Dien
Simon, William Edward
Simon, William Henry
Simone, Joseph
Simons, Richard Duncan
Simons, William Mark
Simonson, Andrew Craig
Simowitz, Sylvia
Simpich, George Cary
Simpson, Jean Wheeler
Simpson, Mary Michael
Simpson, Robert Lloyd
Simpson, Russell Gordon
Sims, Albert M.
Sims, James Ernest
Simunek, Frank Alan
Sinai, Allen L.
Sinay, Ralph Heatwole
Sinback, Donald Lee
Sincerbeaux, Robert Abbott
Sinclair, Ian David
Sinden, Harry
Singer, Barry Mana
Singer, Bernard Elias
Singer, Esther Forman (Mrs. Sidney Singer)
Singer, Fred
Singer, Gary
Singer, Isaac Bashevis
Singer, Joseph Howard
Singer, Marcia B.
Singer, Marilyn Phyllis
Singer, Niki (Mrs. Michael J. Sheets)
Singer, Robert Clifford
Singer, Vera
Singh, Amarendra Narayan
Singh, Darshan
Singh, Har Swarup
Singh, Inder Jit
Singh, Ishwar
Singh, Mahendra Pal
Singh, Prabjit
Sinha, Ashok Kumar
Sinn, Robert Samuel
Sipp, Elmer Franks, Jr.
Sirianni, Aurelio Frederick
Sirkin, Douglas Michael
Sirkin, Jacob
Sisk, Albert Fletcher, Jr.
Sisler, Hampson Albert
Sisley, Emily Lucretia
Sismondo, Sergio Francesco
Sistek, Walter Joseph
Sito, Peter Stanley
Sittel, Karl
Sittenfeld, Itamar
Sivowitch, Elliot Norman
Sjöberg, Leif Tore
Skatoff, Mary Margaret
Skeels, Dorr Covell
Skeen, David Ray
Skeggs, Helen R.
Skiadas, George Demetrios
Skillinger, Richard Thurman
Skinner, David Cooper
Skinner, John Hayes
Skinner, Patrick James
Skladanowski, Diane Marie
Sklar, S. Harvey
Skole, Richard David
Skulski, Andronik Emil
Skupinski, Bogdan Kazimierz
Skurdenis, Juliann V.
Slaby, Louis Richard
Slachta, Gregory Andrew
Slack, Florence Kantor (Mrs. Melvin F. Slack)
Slack, George Henry
Slade, Walter Raleigh, Jr.
Slanetz, Charles Arthur, Jr.
Slatcher, William Augustus
Slater, Ford Chapman
Slater, Helene Ford Southern
Slater, Miriam
Slater, Sidney Donald
Slater, Thomas Cortland
Slattery, Bradley
Slattery, Paul David
Slavik, Julie Constance Bres (Mrs. Juraj Ludevit Jan Slavik)
Slavin, Richard Edward, III
Slavin, William Michael
Slavit, Michael Roy
Slavov, Eugenia Margaret
Slawinski, Stanley Aloysius
Slaymaker, Samuel Redsecker, II
Sledd, Hassell Brantley
Sleight, Jessie Adele
Slenn, John Raymond
Slevin, Joanna Helen
Slitor, Richard Eaton
Slivka, Robert Michael
Sliwinski, Edward Robert
Sloan, Albert Raymond
Sloan, Burton
Sloan, Stephen
Slobodien, Howard David
Slosberg, Mike
Slotkoff, Beatriz Flores
Slurzberg, Elihu (Lee)
Slusser, Eugene Alvin
Small, Harold Melvin
Small, Robert Van Dyke
Small, Stanley Alan
Small, Wilfred Thomas
Smalletz, Theodore William
Smalley, Philip Adam, Jr.
Smalley, Ralph Ray
Smardzewski, Richard Roman
Smart, James Gordon
Smart, Louis Edwin, Jr.
Smart, Mary-Leigh Call (Mrs. J. Scott Smart)
Smart, Walter Lewis
Smeal, Theodore Samuel
Smedley, William Michael
Smedley, William Paul
Smelter, Katherine Vafakas
Smirnow, Robert
Smith, Allen Arthur
Smith, Allen David
Smith, Allen Henderson, III
Smith, Allen Norman
Smith, Andrew John
Smith, Ann Lacamera
Smith, Barry Hamilton
Smith, Barry Marshall
Smith, Bruce Everett
Smith, Carl Edgar, Jr.
Smith, Catherine Mary Dalmaso
Smith, Charles Daniel
Smith, Charles Edward
Smith, Charles Elmer
Smith, Charles Frank
Smith, Charles Frank, Jr.
Smith, Charles William
Smith, Christopher Lee
Smith, Clay Dempster
Smith, Clotilde Durham
Smith, Cuthbert Henry
Smith, David
Smith, David English
Smith, Dean
Smith, DeForest Webb
Smith, Dennis
Smith, Donald Alvin
Smith, Donald William
Smith, Donn J.
Smith, E(dmund) Carlyle
Smith, Edward James
Smith, Edward Samuel
Smith, Elsie Mae
Smith, Eric
Smith, Eric Parkman
Smith, Francis Aloysius, Jr.
Smith, Francis Waverly
Smith, Frank Junius
Smith, Frederick Orville, II
Smith, Gail Preston
Smith, Gary Lee
Smith, George Thomas
Smith, George William
Smith, Gerrit Joseph
Smith, Gordon Ross
Smith, Hale
Smith, Hamilton Othanel
Smith, Harold Charles
Smith, Harold Webster
Smith, Harris Frederic
Smith, Harrison Harvey
Smith, Herbert DeWitt
Smith, Hilary Cranwell Bowen
Smith, Howard A.
Smith, Hugh Roberts Hoval
Smith, J(ohn) Graham
Smith, J(ohn) Joseph
Smith, James Almer, Jr.
Smith, James Francis
Smith, Jean Chandler
Smith, Jerome Robert
Smith, John Thomas, Jr.
Smith, Joseph Marshall
Smith, Kathleen Tener
Smith, Kendrick
Smith, Kenneth Judson, Jr.
Smith, Lillian Louise Quick
Smith, Marilynn Knowlton
Smith, Mark Alan
Smith, Martin
Smith, Mary Alice
Smith, Milton Joseph
Smith, Nicholas Neville
Smith, Oliver
Smith, Owen Telfair
Smith, Patricia Mary
Smith, Peter Walker
Smith, Philip Alan
Smith, Phillip Hartley
Smith, Ray Thaddeus, Jr.
Smith, Raymond D(aniel)
Smith, Raymond Edward
Smith, Raymond Joseph
Smith, Rhoten Alexander
Smith, Richard Emerson (Dick Smith)
Smith, Richard Eugene
Smith, Richard Francis, Jr.
Smith, Richard Louis, Jr.
Smith, Robert Charles
Smith, Robert Douglas
Smith, Robert Henry
Smith, Roger Davis
Smith, Roland White
Smith, Russell Francis
Smith, Sarah Sims
Smith, Seymour Alan
Smith, Stanley A.
Smith, Stanley Babcock, Jr.
Smith, Steven Dennis
Smith, Thomas Lionel
Smith, Thomas Marshall
Smith, Valeria Litchfield McKee
Smith, Vern Henry
Smith, Walter Powell
Smith, Warren Allen
Smith, Weaks Gardner
Smith, Wendell Murray
Smith, Wilbert Hayes, Jr.
Smith, William Charles
Smith, William Peter
Smithgall, Elizabeth
Smithwick, Robert Bruce
Smock, Raymond William
Smodlaka, Vojin Nikola
Smolanoff, Michael Louis
Smolinsky, Gisela (Giz) Ungurian
Smoller, Saul
Smoot, Lucille D. Hein (Mrs. Charles Effinger Smoot)
Smyers, Daniel Jefferson
Smyth, David
Smyth, Kenneth Howard
Smyth, Roger Louis
Snader, Daniel Webster
Snedden, Mary Jane Heffner (Mrs. Homer Granger Snedden)
Snell, David
Snelling, Charles Darwin
Snelling, Richard Arkwright
Snelling, William Rodman
Snider, Edward Malcolm
Snider, Harold Wayne
Sniderman, Kenneth Wilfred
Sniderman, Marvin
Sniffen, Allan Mead, III
Snook, Elwood Bankes
Snow, Albert Joseph
Snow, Edwina Feigenspan (Mrs. MacVicker Snow)
Snow, Jerry Allison
Snow, Margaret Throckmorton
Snow, Ronald Louis
Snow, Vernon Fred
Snowe, Olympia Jean
Snyder, Barry Sherwood
Snyder, C. Duane
Snyder, Gary Sherman
Snyder, Gerald A.
Snyder, Ivan Jay
Snyder, Jane Peters (Mrs. Arthur Leland Snyder)
Snyder, John Mendenhall
Snyder, John Robert
Snyder, Joseph
Snyder, Joseph Julien
Snyder, Larry Donald
Snyder, M. Wilson
Snyder, Nathan
Snyder, Richard A.
Snyder, Richard Donald
Snyder, Robert Edward
Snyder, William Lloyd, III
Sobczak, Thomas Victor
Sobol, Bruce J.
Socey, Francis Joseph
Socha, Wladyslaw Wojciech
Sochurek, Howard (James)
Socolow, Arthur Abraham
Soden, Edward Roger
Soden, James Arthur
Sofarelli, Robert Joseph
Soffer, Martin Harvey
Sofillas, Grace Sophie Joanou
Sofinowski, John Robert
Sohn, Donald Richard
Soichet, Samuel
Sok, James Edward
Sokerka, Richard Andrew
Sokolow, Nickolas N.
Sokolowski, Ann Ruth
Sokolsky, George Ephraim, Jr.
Sokolyszyn, Aleksander S.
Solarz, Stephen Joshua
Solberg, Myron
Soletsky, Albert Z.
Soley, Robert Lawrence
Soleymanikashi, Yussef
Solit, Robert Wolf
Soll, David Benjamin
Soll, Raphael Israel
Solomon, Anthony Joseph
Solomon, Anthony Nicholas
Solomon, Bernard Simon
Solomon, Charles Morris
Solomon, Gerald Brooks Hunt
Solomon, Gerald Harry
Solomon, Martin
Solomon, Morton Bernard
Solomon, Nathan Aaron
Solovij, Jurij
Solymossy, Alfred Austin
Som, Ernest Laszlo
Somerset, Ira Jon
Somerville, Walter Raleigh, Jr.
Somjen, Gabor
Sommer, Ernest Lorge
Sommer, Frank Henry, III
Sommers, Allen Abraham
Sommers, Ben
Sommers, Waldo
Song, James Chinho
Songer, Thomas Frasher, II
Sonkin, Lawrence Sidney
Sonn, George Frank, Jr.
Sonneborn, Meyer Robert
Sonnenblick, Edmund Hiram
Sonnenblick, Jack Earl
Sonnenschein, Harry
Sonnichsen, Harold Marvin
Sontheimer, Morton
Soobitsky, Joel Robert
Sooy, Leslie Thomas
Sopchak, Andrew Leo
Soper, Kenneth Joseph
Sorbie, Charles
Sorbo, Paul Joseph, Jr.
Sorce, Anthony John
Soreff, Stephen Michael
Sorenson, James Roger
Sorgie, Frank Bernard
Sorhaindo, Alphonso Lorenzo
Soskin, David Howell
Sotterly, Joseph Francis
Soucy, Jean-Charles Rene
Soucy, W. Roland
Soule, Philip Patrick, Sr.
Souter, David Hackett
South, Frank Edwin
Souther, Richard Stanley
Southerland, Edna Eugenia Spearman
Southern, Eileen (Mrs. Joseph Southern)
Southern, Hugh
Southgate, Donald Frederic
Southward, Bernard Morrison, Jr.
Souw, Raymond Steven
Soxman, Don Germain
Space, Theodore Maxwell
Spachner, Sheldon Arthur
Spada, Richard
Spadafora, Anthony Joseph
Spagnola, Thomas Anthony
Spagnuolo, Mario
Spahn, Mary Attea
Spalding, Harlan Joseph
Spallino, Anthony
Spangenberger, Joseph George
Spangler, Elwyn Fisher
Spangler, Ronald LeRoy
Spanovich, Milan
Spar, Jerome
Sparacino, Robert Rudolph
Sparano, Vincent Thomas
Sparkes, Thomas
Spataro, Francis Cajetan
Spataro, Olimpia
Spaulding, Dorothy C. (Mrs. James E. Spaulding)
Spaulding, William Rowe
Spear, Robert Joseph
Spears, Leon Navarro, Jr.
Spears, Robert Rae, Jr.
Speas, Robert Dixon
Specht, Carl, Jr.
Speck, Robert Hursey
Spector, Arthur Robert
Spector, Henry Theodore
Spector, Johanna Lichtenberg (Mrs. Robert Spector)
Speer, David Stockton
Speer, Edgar B.
Speer, Raymond Daniel
Speers, Jerrold Bond
Speirs, Doris Huestis (Mrs. J. Murray Speirs)
Speiser, Stuart Marshall
Speken, Ralph Howard
Speller, Leslie Clifton
Speller, Robert Ernest Blakefield
Spellman, Gladys Noon
Spelman, Malcolm Stewart
Spence, Francis J.
Spence, Janet Blake Conley (Mrs. Alexander Pyott Spence)
Spencer, Albert Lawrence
Spencer, Donald Ford
Spencer, Edward Hathaway
Spencer, Flora Charlotte
Spencer, Michael Jon
Spencer, Sally Louise
Spencer, Thomas, III
Spencer, William I.
Sperber, Daniel
Spergel, Philip
Sperl, Virginia R.
Sperling, Arthur Lawrence
Spetter, Matthew Ies
Spevak, Irving Bertram
Spicer, Charles Frederick
Spiegel, Herbert
Spiegel, Leonard Bernard
Spiegel, Leonard E(mile)
Spiegel, Siegmund
Spiegel, Ted
Spiegler, Enrique
Spier, Nathaniel
Spiers, Tomas Hoskins, Jr.
Spiewak, Kenneth Ralph
Spiller, Mortimer
Spilman, J. Stanley
Spindler, Clarence Francis
Spindler, Frank MacDonald
Spindola-Franco, Hugo
Spinetta, Frank
Spingarn, Clifford Leroy
Spirer, Edwin Shev
Spiridigliozzi, Francis Donald
Spitz, Emil William
Spitzer, Jerome
Spitzer, Robert Clark
Spitzer, Roxane Blumberg
Spitznagel, John Tetje
Spivack, Henry Archer
Splaver, Sarah
Splete, Allen Peterjohn
Spodek, Richard George
Spokely, David Guy
Sponzilli, Edward George
Spooner, John Davis
Sporn, Lawrence Marc
Spotnitz, Henry Michael
Spradlin, Thomas Richard
Spraggins, Stewart
Sprague, Constance Campbell
Sprague, George Fremont
Sprague, L(loyd) Dean
Spriggs, David Carlton
Spring, John Kenneth
Springer, Hans Guenther
Springer, John Kelley
Springfield, Franklyn Bruce
Sprinkle, Melvin Cline
Sprinkle, Robert Marshall
Sproull, Robert Lamb
Spuhler, Harold Aylesworth
Spunt, Shepard Armin
Spyrou, Panagiotis George
Squadra, John Harley
Squeglia, Nicholas Louis, Jr.
Squire, Albert Tegg
Squire, Herbert Earl, Jr.
Squires, Bonnie Stein
Squires, Lindley Sturges
Srivastava, Suresh Chandra
Staab, Joseph Raymond
Stabell, Donald Edward
Stabile, Charles Joseph
Stabile, Rose Towne
Stabler, Donald Billman
Stachniewicz, Stephanie Anne
Stackhouse, Charles Moulton, Jr.
Stadden, Warren Carl
Stadnicki, Stanley Walter, Jr.
Staffier, Pamela Moorman
Stafford, Robert Theodore
Stage, Ginger Rooks
Stagg, Paul Albert
Stahl, Frank Ludwig
Stahl, Laddie L.
Stahl, Marilyn Brown
Stahr, Elvis J(acob), Jr.
Stainback, Thomas Nathaniel
Staley, Richard Allen
Stallings, James Henry
Stallworth, John William
Stalvey, Harold Dixon
Stamps, George Moreland
Standen, Donna Sondra Komar (Mrs. John L. Standen)
Stangler, Bernard Benedict
Stanko, Chester Michael
Stanko, David Michael
Stanley, Caroline Hart
Stanley, Earl R
Stanley, (Marion) Edward Enzeleaux
Stanley, Joan Gloria
Stanley-Brown, Edward Garfield
Stannard, Carl Roy, Jr.
Stanoch, Thomas Paul
Stansbury, Clayton Cresvell
Stanton, Ivens V.
Stanton, Seymour
Stanton, Vivian Brennan (Mrs. Ernest Stanton)
Stanton, Walter O.
Stanton-Hicks, Michael D'Arcy
Stanwich, Eugene Edward
Stapinski, Stephen Edward
Stapler, Albert Broadus, Jr.
Staples, Basil George
Staples, Norman Appleton
Staples, Terrence Edwin
Stapleton, Thomas David
Starasoler, Stanley
Starbuck, Shirley
Staresina, Denise Marie
Stargardter, Hans
Stark, Eli Herman
Stark, Jeffrey Michael
Stark, Jesse Donald
Stark, Richard Boies
Stark, Robert Martin
Stark, Thomas Michael
Starkey, Norman Berne
Starr, Michael Barry
Starrett, Loyd Milford
Stasheff, Christopher Boris
Stasiowski, Patricia Monica
Stathis, Nicholas John
Staub, Henry Paul
Staub, Robert Andre
Stauffer, Tom Goodman
Stave, Carl Edward
Stavisky, Eli
Stavola, John Joseph
Stayman, Samuel M.
Stayton, William Ralph
Stearn, Daniel Richard
Stearns, Frank Barney
Stearns, Lloyd Worthington
Stearns, Robert Louis
Steck, Edgar Alfred
Steckiw, Eugene
Steedle, Roger Craig
Steege, Betty K. (Mrs. Peter O. Steege)
Steele, Bert L.
Steele, Charles William
Steele, Howard Loucks
Steele, James Bruce, Jr.
Steele, Mark William
Steele, Robert Donald
Steele, William Richard
Steen, Charles Edwin, III
Steers, Edward
Steers, Newton Ivan, Jr.
Stefanski, Raymond Arthur
Steffa, Louis John
Steffen, Alan Leslie
Steg, Leo
Steiger, Frederic
Steimle, Edmund Augustus, Jr.
Stein, Betty Canowitz
Stein, Charles Francis, Jr.
Stein, Ellen Gail
Stein, Fritz Henry
Stein, George Henry
Stein, Gladys Marie
Stein, Harold Aaron
Stein, Jess
Stein, Mark
Stein, Melvin Arnold
Stein, Mona Lola
Stein, Stuart William
Stein, Theodore Anthony
Stein, Virginia Kramer
Stein, William H.
Stein, William Howard
Steinberg, Arthur Irwin
Steinberg, Samuel Harry
Steinberg, Saul Phillip
Steinbrenner, George Michael, III
Steinbruckner, Bruno Friedrich
Steiner, Jerome
Steiner, Ralph Lee
Steiner, Robert Frank
Steiner, Roger Jacob
Steiner, Stuart
Steinert, Richard Jacob
Steinfink, Murray
Steinhart, Dean Raymond
Steinhaus, Phillip Lee
Steinhaus, Richard Zeke
Steinhorn, Paul
Steiniger, William Howard
Steinle, John Gerard
Steinman, Charles Robert
Steinmayer, Alwin Gustav, Jr.
Steitz, Edward Stephen
Stele, Richard Barry
Stelzer, Irwin Mark
Stemmy, Thomas Joseph
Stepahin, John Matthew
Stepanishen, Peter Richard
Stephens, Everett Watson
Stephens, Hugh Mart
Stephens, John Wellington
Stephens, La Verne Ida
Stephens, Margaret Joy Brandenburg
Stephens, Warren Clayton, Jr.
Stephens, William Theodore
Stephenson, James Hawley
Stephenson, Junius Winfield
Stephenson, William Eugene
Stephenson, William Hermas
Stepita-Klauco, Matej
Sterling, James Lewis
Sterling, Keir Brooks
Stern, Donald Ellsworth, Jr.
Stern, E(rwin) Mark
Stern, Edward Lee
Stern, Emanuel Rich
Stern, Frances Meritt
Stern, Herbert Jay
Stern, Paul Hertzler
Stern, Ronald Ivan
Stern, Rudi
Stern, Silviu Alexander
Stern, Stephen Harvey
Stern, Walter Phillips
Sternlicht, Beno
Sternlicht, Manny
Sterns, Indrikis
Stertz, Stephen Allen
Stetson, John Boydston
Stettz, Stanley Edward
Steuer, Neil Burt
Stevens, Daniel James
Stevens, Elisabeth Goss (Mrs. Robert Schleussner, Jr.)
Stevens, John Paul
Stevens, Joseph Robert
Stevens, Nancy Duncan
Stevens, Nicholas George
Stevens, Roy White
Stevens, William John
Stevenson, Benjamin Haynes, Jr.
Stevenson, Charles Summers
Stevenson, Dean T.
Stevenson, James Braddock
Stevenson, Lois Wellman Haddock (Mrs. Frederick Leon Stevenson)
Stevenson, Robert Edwin
Stevenson, Robert Stanley
Stewart, Albert Clifton
Stewart, Alexander Doig
Stewart, Carlos Guillermo
Stewart, Charles Lyman
Stewart, Charles William
Stewart, George Daniel
Stewart, James Buchannon
Stewart, James Joseph
Stewart, John Cameron
Stewart, Joseph Turner, Jr.
Stewart, Kenneth Edward
Stewart, Potter
Stewart, Robert Bradley
Stewart, William Garrett
Steyer, Roy Henry
Sticht, Robert Larson
Stick, Marvin Earl
Stickler, Daniel Lee
Stickler, Mitchell Gene
Stickley, Dennis W.
Stieglitz, William Irving
Stiff, David Parker
Stigliano, Anthony Gerard
Stiglitz, Martin Richard
Stiller, Eunice Barbara Herman
Stillings, Irene Cordiner (Mrs. Gordon A. Stillings)
Stillman, Alfred William, Jr.
Stillman, Mary Elizabeth
Stillwaggon, Carol Anne
Stimmel, Barry David
Stinebring, Russell Charles

Stinehelfer, Harold Eugene
Stirrat, William Albert
Stitely, Doris Mae
Stiver, Myrtle Pearl
Stiver, William Earl
Sto. Domingo, Jose Eustaquio
Stocker, Gerard Craig
Stockton, William James
Stoddard, William Bert, Jr.
Stoessel, Henry Kurt
Stoetzner, Eric Woldemar
Stofko, Karl Peter
Stokely, Hugh Lawson, Jr.
Stokes, William E.D., Jr.
Stolba, Leonard Bidwell
Stolley, Richard Brockway
Stolnacke, Richard Arthur
Stolp, Lauren Elbert
Stolting, Richard Ronald
Stolz, Alan James
Stolz, Jonathan Lavery
Stone, Al
Stone, Alan John
Stone, Albert Henry
Stone, Allan
Stone, Carl Henry
Stone, Carleton Goshen
Stone, Diane Lipson
Stone, Ernest Lynn
Stone, James Lester
Stone, Justin Howard
Stone, Richard Thomas
Stone, Robert Eldred
Stoner, Fern Goode
Stonier, Charles Edward
Stoolman, Herbert Leonard
Stoop, Norma McLain
Stoops, John
Storm, John Hershey
Storm, Mary Elizabeth
Storrow, James J., Jr.
Storzer, Gerald Howard
Stosser, Robert James
Stott, Thomas Edward
Stoudenheimer, Richard George
Stovall, Robert Henry
Stover, Carl Frederick
Stover, Herman Dinsmore
Stover, Richard Robert
St Pierre, Paul Emile
Strachan, Ronald Richard
Strachman, Philip
Strachocki, Alphonse
Strack, Joseph George
Strader, William Clyde
Strahan, Charles, Jr.
Strain, Paula Mary
Strait, Almuth Vandiveer, Jr.
Stranahan, Robert Paul, Jr.
Stranc, Sister Mary Celaine
Strange, John Phillip
Strasberg, Lee
Strasser, Arnold
Strasser, John Albert
Stratford, Carol Ann (Mrs. Francis A. Stratford, Jr.)
Straton, Andrew Charles
Stratton, John Caryl
Stratton, Samuel Studdiford
Stratton, Walter Love
Straub, Chester John
Straub, Frank
Strauch, Berish
Strauch, George Joseph
Strauch, Gerald Otto
Strauss, Albert James
Strauss, Amelie Lee
Strauss, Dorothy Brandfon
Strauss, George Herschel
Strauss, Martin Heinz
Strauss, Raymond Bernard
Straussner, Shulamith Lala Ashenberg
Strayer, Vernon John
Strean, Bernard Max, Jr.
Strecko, Michel
Street, James Harry
Street, Orman Elery
Streeter, Tal
Streeter, Thomas Winthrop
Streitfeld, Nina (Felber)
Streng, Rudolph Joseph
Strenger, Lawrence
Stretch, George Edward
Striano, Vincent Rocco
Strianse, Sabbat John
Stricklin, Carl Spencer
Strickman, Robert Louis
Stridsberg, Albert Borden
Strignano, Joseph Robert
Strike, Donald Peter
Strine, Harry Cornelius, III
Stringfield, Victor Timothy
Strinic, Lila Frances
Strnisa, Fred V.
Strobridge, Truman Russell
Stroh, Edward Waldemar
Stroh, Oscar Henry
Stroh, Oscar Simon
Strohl, James Emerson
Strong-Tidman, Virginia Adele
Strother, John Alan
Stroud, James Stanley
Strowger, Richard John
Struble, Robert Stanley
Struckus, Edward Joseph
Strupczewski, James Anthony
Struzyna, George Arthur Felix
Stryker, Jay William, Jr.
Stryker-Rodda, Kenn
Stuart, Alden Taylor
Stuart, Charles Harpell
Stuart, John M.
Stuart, William Clarkson, III
Stuart, William David
Stuart, William Edward Campbell
Stubbs, Donald Clark
Stubbs, John James
Studdiford, Walter Beekman
Studds, Gerry Eastman
Stueber, Gustav
Stuebing, Edward Willis
Stuenkel, Arthur Emil
Stuenkel, Herbert Edward
Stula, Michael James
Stull, Donald Leroy
Stumpf, T(homas) Robert
Stunkard, Horace Wesley
Stunkard, Jim A.
Sturges, Florence Margaret (Mrs. Dwight Richard Sturges)
Sturges, John Siebrand
Sturm, Ruth Foster
Sturman, Robert Harries
Sturman, Robert Morris
Sturtevant, Peter Mann, Jr.
Stutman, Leonard Jay
Stutz, Kenneth John
Styskal, Henry, Jr.
Suárez, Rafael
Suarez, Ramon Urgel
Suchoff, Benjamin
Sudduth, Solon Scott
Sue-A-Quan, Errol Albert
Suflas, William Vasel
Sugar, Donald Andrew
Sugerman, Abraham Arthur
Suh, Dong S.
Suh, Kenneth Kyong Suk
Sukman, Charles Arthur
Suleiman, Anver Silvino
Sulham, Glenn Alton
Sullivan, A(nna) Mannevillette
Sullivan, Arthur Eugene
Sullivan, Daniel Joseph
Sullivan, Donald Jerome
Sullivan, Dorothy Rona
Sullivan, Edward Joseph
Sullivan, Eugene Joseph
Sullivan, George Joseph
Sullivan, Brother Jeremiah Stephen
Sullivan, John Cornelius, Jr.
Sullivan, John Joseph, Jr.
Sullivan, John Patrick
Sullivan, Joseph Michael
Sullivan, Joseph Timothy Patrick
Sullivan, Margaret Rita
Sullivan, Richard Parker
Sullivan, Robert Francis
Sullivan, Roger Breck
Sullivan, Roy Francis
Sullivan, Thomas Michael
Sullivan, Thomas Michael
Sullivan, William Hallisey, Jr.
Sulzberger, Arthur Ochs
Sumberg, Alfred Donald
Sumbry, Louis Clyde, Jr.
Summa, Don Joseph
Summers, Robert Samuel
Summerscales, William
Sumner, Kenneth
Sun, Benedict Ching-San
Sun, Eleanor
Sundaresan, Peruvemba Ramnathan
Sunderland, Ray, Jr.
Sundlun, Bruce George
Sundquist, Ralph Roger, Jr.
Sundy, George Joseph
Sung, Pei
Sunkin, Irving Burton
Sunseri, Anthony
Sunshine, Nancy Jean
Suntag, Charles
Suozzi, Joseph Anthony
Supinski, Catherine Josephine Curran (Mrs. Edmund Supinski)
Supiro, Lester Daniel
Supranovicz, John Michael
Suraci, Charles Xavier, Jr.
Surdoval, Donald James
Surmeli, Suphi
Susa, Philip Michael
Susan, Frank Austin
Susman, Abraham Bernard
Susskind, Siegfried
Sussman, Bernard Jules
Sussman, Harold Irwin
Sussman, Ralph Maurice
Sussman, Robert B.
Suter, George August
Sutherland, Donald James
Sutherland, George Leslie
Sutherland, John Campbell
Sutherland, John Patrick
Sutherlund, David Arvid
Sutkowski, Ernest Harold
Sutnick, Alton Ivan
Sutro, Frederick Charles, Jr.
Sutton, Clyde Clarence
Sutton, George Hills, III
Sutton, John Joseph, III
Sutton, Jonathan Stone
Sutton, Leon Murad
Sutton, Percy E.
Sutton, Peter A.
Sutton, Richard Lauder
Sutton, Robert Franklin
Sutton, Suzy
Sutton, William James, III
Suydam, Thomas William
Suzuki, Kotaro
Svarc, Emile Dragan
Svetlich, William George
Svilokos, Nikola Andrew
Svokos, Steve George
Swain, Ethel M.
Swain, Robert Victor
Swain, William Grant
Swaine, Robert Leslie
Swales, George Aloysius
Swamy, Srikanta M.N.
Swan, Charles
Swanborn, Edwin Donald
Swank, Richard Bruce
Swankoski, Michaline Ann
Swanner, Grace Maguire (Mrs. Roy O. Swanner)
Swanson, Albert Arthur
Swanson, Carl Evert
Swanson, Carl Sylvester
Swanson, Ernest Allen, Jr.
Swanson, Roger Fulton
Swart, Robert J.
Swartwout, John Baxter
Swartz, Donald Percy
Swartz, James Richard
Swartz, Lillian Burton
Swartz, Warren Lester
Swearer, Howard Robert
Sweeney, Eugene Thomas
Sweeney, Francis Joseph, Jr.
Sweeney, Hugh John
Sweeney, James Francis
Sweeney, John J.
Sweeney, Mary Elizabeth
Sweeney, Robert John
Sweeny, Charles David
Sweet, Donald Herbert
Sweet, John Howard
Sweet, Marc Steven
Sweet, Robert Thomas
Sweet, Ross Bennett
Sweet, Stanley Adams, Jr.
Swenson, Harold Francis
Swenson, Jon Malcolm
Swenson, Larry Grant
Swern, Leonard
Swett, Philip Eugene
Swett, Stephen Frederick, Jr.
Swick, Lucille
Swiecicka-Ziemianek, Maria A. .l.
Swift, LeRoy Russell
Swift, Robert Anton
Swigart, Edmund Kearsley
Swinburne, Laurence Joseph
Switak, Heather Joan
Switzer, Steven Mladen
Swope, Charles Evans
Swope, George Wendell
Syeles, Albert Mac
Sykes, Donald Joseph
Sykes, Martha Moore
Syku, Anton Zef
Sylvester, Melvin Robert
Sylvestre, Jean Guy
Sylvia, Lawrence Charles
Symonds, Johnnie Pirkle
Symons, Harry Clay
Symons, Joanne Lyman
Syrek, Richard William
Syrjala, Edith A.
Syrovatka, Eugene Charles
Sysol, Henry Frank, Jr.
Sywak, Zofia
Szamek, Pierre Ervin
Szawranskyj, William Michael
Szaz, Zoltan Michael
Szell, Thomas Rudolf Miklos
Szemraj, Edward Richard
Szent-Gyorgyi, Albert
Szep, Paul Michael
Szeplaki, Joseph
Szilagyi, George
Szilasi, William Joseph
Szloch, Michael Mieczyslaw
Szogyen, John Rodolphe Maria Charles
Szogyi, Alex
Szoradi, Charles
Szoverffy, Joseph
Szuhay, Joseph Alexander
Szurgocinski, Leonard Mieczyslaw
Szutowicz, Paul Michael
Szwajkowski, Herman Robert
Tabin, Emanuel Nathen
Tabler, D. Jane Piekarski
Tachmindji, Alexander John
Taddei, Romano
Tadini, Fred Athelio
Taffel, Sherman Dennis
Taffet, Saul S.
Taft, Arnold Jay
Taft, Robert Stephen
Taggart, Joseph Herman
Taggart, Leslie Davidson
Tagliaferri, Lee Gene
Tague, Barry Elwert
Tahan, Theodore Wahba
Tahler, Emanuel David
Tai, George Marshall
Taira, Frank Morihiko
Tait, Joseph Lloyd
Talabisco, John Joseph
Talarico, Anthony Rudolph
Talbert, Preston Tidball
Talbot, Irwin Norman
Talbot, Mildred Fisher
Talenfeld, Hilda Friedman (Mrs. Meyer Maier Talenfeld)
Taler, Joseph
Taliaferro, James Hubert, Jr.
Talley, Harry Darlington, Jr.
Talley, John (Jack) Victor
Tallia, Eugene John
Talmadge, Julia
Tam, Francis Mankei
Tamboli, Akbar Rasul
Tamm, Edward Allen
Tampone, Dominic
Tampone, Margaret Ann
Tan, Tjiauw-Ling
Tanenbaum, Howard Leon
Tanenbaum, Walter Ira
Tanenholtz, Stanley Donald
Tang, Man-Chung
Tang, Robert Lee-Ching
Tanis, Dahlia Joan
Tannenbaum, Bernice Salpeter
Tannenbaum, Donald Martin
Tanner, Chuck
Tanner, Daniel
Tanner, Jack Gene
Tanners, Henry
Tanselle, George Thomas
Tanser, Paul Harry
Tanton, Thomas George
Tanzer, Martin Sheldon
Taranta, Angelo
Tarasi, Louis Michael, Jr.
Tardif-Hébert, J.
Tarlov, Edward
Tarnay, Robert Stevens
Tarpley, Thomas Marvin, Jr.
Tarr, Charles Edwin
Tarrants, William Eugene
Tarsoly, Balazs Kolozsvary
Tashjian, Aetna Myron
Tasman, William Samuel
Tassie, Douglas Pray
Tassinari, Silvio John
Tatel, Allan Bruce
Tates, Donald Eugene
Tatossian, Armand
Tatsch, James Henderson
Tatterson, Benjamin Franklin
Tattle, Alan Michael
Tatum, George Bishop
Taub, Edward
Taub, Jesse
Taub, Steven Irwin
Tauber, Gilbert
Taubkin, Irvin S.
Taubman, Herbert
Taubman, Joseph
Taves, Caroline Dilgard
Taves, Ernest Henry
Tavitian, Henry Ohanes
Tavoulareas, William Peter
Tawil, Joseph
Taylor, Alan James
Taylor, Barbara Jo Anne Harris
Taylor, Bernard Franklin
Taylor, Bernard Underhill
Taylor, Donald Sherman
Taylor, Ervin Francis
Taylor, Francis Charles
Taylor, Frank Leonard
Taylor, Gordon Stevens
Taylor, Harold Allen, Jr.
Taylor, Harry Winfield
Taylor, James Gorden
Taylor, Jeremy
Taylor, John Lewis
Taylor, Joshua Charles
Taylor, Lawrence William, Jr.
Taylor, Lisa Suter
Taylor, Paul Howard
Taylor, Philip Lawrence
Taylor, Richard Powell
Taylor, Richard Wirt
Taylor, Robert B.
Taylor, Robert Lindell
Taylor, Ron Vivian
Taylor, Susan Jane (Suzy)
Taylor, Tossie Edward, Jr.
Taylor, Warren Justin
Taylor, William Arthur, Jr.
Taylor, William Davis
Taylor, William Herbert
Teach, Gusta Morgan
Teachout, Roger Sage
Teague, Abner Franklin
Teahan, Frederick Hatch Christopher
Teaman, Charles Richard
Teates, Noah Grove, Jr.
Tebet, David William
Tece, Alp Sunqur
Tedeschi, Robert James
Tedesco, Frank Mario
Tedrick, Richard Newman
Teeter, James Herring
Teft, Leon William
Teglas, Csaba
Teichmann, Howard Miles
Teitelbaum, Herbert Ulysses
Teitelbaum, Hubert I.
Teitelbaum, Irving
Teitelbaum, Marcel
Teitelbaum, Seymour
Teitell, Conrad Laurence
Telak, Marlene Mary
Telfer, John Delbert
Teller, Myrtle Rogers Brilliantine
Tellier, Leo Joseph, Jr.
Telling, Raymond Gordon
Temmer, Stephen Francis
Tempest, Jeanne Bruneau
Temple, Paul Nathaniel
Temple, Riley Keene
Ten Cate, Adrian Gobel
Tener, Hampden Evans, III
Teng, Yu-Ling
Tennant, Harry LaRenze
Tennenbaum, Robert
Tennies, Arthur Cornelius
Tennyson, Marjorie Leigh
Tenopyr, Mary Louise Welsh (Mrs. Joseph Tenopyr)
Tepper, Blossom Weiss
Terman, Joseph
Terranova, Carmelo
Terrell, James Cletys
Terris, Lillian Dick
Terry, Edward Allison, Jr.
Tesla, Iwan
Tesler, Max A.
Tesoro, George Alfred
Tessler, Allan Roger
Tessler, Herbert Alan
Thakker, Ashok Bhagwandas
Thalacker, Donald William
Thalberg, Joseph Hyman
Thaler, David
Thaler, Warren Alan
Thar, F. A.
Tharion, Roselle Lavina
Tharp, Twyla
Thau, Harold Adrian
Theberge, Leonard Joseph
Thelen, Edmund
Theodore, Frederick Harold
Theodore, Thomas Ronald
Theriault, Romeo Joseph
Therrien, Robert Wilfrid
Thibault, Arnold Francis
Thielsch, Helmut John
Thies, Phoebe Lorene Anderson
Thigpen, Edward Lester
Thimm, Alfred Louis
Thoburn, Crawford Randall
Thom, Charles Richard
Thom, James Theophilus
Thom, Joseph M.
Thomae, Edmund George
Thomae, Herbert Louis
Thomas, Alan
Thomas, Arthur Louis
Thomas, Basil Anargyros
Thomas, Carol Louise Joseph (Mrs. Charles Raymond Thomas)
Thomas, Charles Edmond
Thomas, Dale John
Thomas, Donald Wayne
Thomas, Eapen
Thomas, Ethel Colvin Nichols (Mrs. Lewis Victor Thomas)
Thomas, Felyce
Thomas, John Melvin
Thomas, John Wesley, Jr.
Thomas, Lloyd Allen
Thomas, Louis James
Thomas, Robert G.
Thomas, Ruth Ann
Thomas, Sarah Elizabeth Barker
Thomas, William John
Thomopoulos, Anthony Dennis
Thompson, Ardithearl
Thompson, Bradbury (James)
Thompson, David Duvall
Thompson, Douglas Llewellyn
Thompson, Edward Kramer
Thompson, Ellen Kubacki
Thompson, Frank
Thompson, Frank Joseph
Thompson, George Lee
Thompson, George Walter Murry, Jr.
Thompson, Gordon Ellef
Thompson, Harold Roy, Jr.
Thompson, Helen Louise
Thompson, Howard Ellis
Thompson, J. Foster
Thompson, Jacob
Thompson, James Lantz
Thompson, Laurie Jane
Thompson, Ralph Newell
Thompson, Ronald Edward
Thompson, Sidney Orville
Thompson, Thomas Frederick
Thompson, Warren Henry
Thompson, William Bond
Thompson, William Parkhurst
Thompson, William Phelps
Thoms, Donald Raymond
Thomson, Charles Alexander Holmes
Thomson, Christian Ross
Thomson, Frank
Thomson, Gerald Edmund
Thomson, James Cutting
Thomson, Meldrim
Thomson, Roderick Albert Edward
Thomson, Selma Wertime
Thorburn, Peter Alan
Thorn, Donald Barry
Thorn, Susan Howe
Thornber, Hubert Elwyn
Thornberg, Frederick Kelley
Thornbrough, Albert A.
Thornburg, Donald Richard
Thornburgh, Richard Lewis
Thornbury, Thomas Glidden
Thorne, Ralph Weymouth
Thorner, Horace Edward
Thornton, Frank Regis
Thornton, Robert Wheeler
Thorpe, Geoffrey Lascelles
Thorpe, Gerald L.
Thorpe, Leon Ferber
Threshman, George Thomas
Throckmorton, William Robert, Sr.
Thuering, George Lewis
Thumm, Fred William
Thune, Mary Lee
Thurmond, Gerald Pittman
Tichauer, Erwin Rudolph
Tichy, Charles, Jr.
Tiedeman, Gretchen Thomas
Tien, Chi
Tierkel, Ernest Shalom
Tierney, William Thomas
Tierno, Philip Mario, Jr.
Tiffany, Marquerite Bristol
Tiffany, Robert Jared
Tilden, William Tatem
Tilgner, Charles, III
Tilles, Henry Herman
Tilley, David Brown, Sr.
Tilley, Larry Gordon
Tillinghast, Meta Ione
Tillock, Eugene Edward
Tilton, Webster, Jr.
Tily, Stephen Bromley, III
Timmerman, Robert Wilson
Timour, John Arnold
Timpson, James
Tindall, Jeffry Haigh
Ting, Er Yi
Ting, Samuel Chao Chung
Tingle, William Herbert
Tinkham, William Knipe
Tinsley, Thomas Vincent, Jr.
Tinter, Mickey
Tintle, Carmel Joseph
Tiongson, Jose Aramil
Tischler, Herbert
Tischler, Israel Leon
Tisdale, Barbara
Tisserand, Peter John
Tite, Elizabeth Grace
Titone, Charles Salvatore
Titone, Vito Joseph
Titsworth, (Charles) Dayton
Tizes, Reuben
Tjader-Harris, Marguerite
Tjoflat, James Amund
Tobin, George Raymond, Jr.
Tobin, John Joseph
Tobin-Ashe, Anne
Todd, Edward Payson
Todd, John David
Todd, John Phillip Arnold
Todd, Mirium Jackson
Todd, Norma Jean Ross
Todd, Webster Bray, Jr.
Todman, William Selden
Todorovic, Petar
Todrank, Gustave Herman
Toews, Cornelius Jacob
Toffolon, Edward Peter
Tofias, Allan
Tokarz, Stanley Richard
Tokuhata, George Kazunari
Toles, William Henry
Tolk, Norman Henry
Toll, David
Toll, John Sampson
Toller, Gladys Schwartz
Tolleson, John Lewis
Tolliver, Jonathan Cooper
Tolmie, Kenneth Donald
Tomasson, Helgi
Tomazinis, Anthony Rudolf
Tomlinson, J. Richard
Tomlinson, William West
Tompkins, James Ballantine
Tonelli, Joseph P.
Toner, Michael Joseph
Tong Kai Ming
Tonnesen, Stanley Terry
Toomey, Jeanne Elizabeth
Toomey, Laura Carolyn
Toonkel, Lawrence Elliott
Toot, Frederick Peter
Toothman, Edwin Hugh
Topjian, Nishan
Topping, Marvin Woodrow
Toran, Cavit Mehmet
Torello, Robert James
Torg, Joseph Steven
Torina, Mary Helen
Tormes, Yvonne Maria
Tornabene, Hugh Salvatore
Torok, Andre Endre
Torok, Tibor
Toronto, Nicholas Anthony, Jr.
Torop, Paul
Torosyan, Abraham
Torre, Arthur John
Torre, Frank Joseph
Torre, Joseph Paul (Joe)
Torres, Anibal
Torres, Erika Vogel
Torres, Ivan Lincoln
Torres, Luis Antonio
Torrey, William Arthur
Torricelli, Thomas Edward
Torsney, Philip Joseph
Tose, Leonard H.
Tosello, Matthew
Toth, Alfred Lukacs
Toth, Marian Davies
Toth, Robert Charles
Totten, Frank Norman, Jr.
Touhill, Charles Joseph, Jr.
Toussie, Michael Isaac
Toussie, Samuel Roosevelt
Tovey, Joseph
Tower, Catherine
Tower, Donald Bayley
Towne, William Chester
Townsend, Paul Robert
Townsend, Pauline Mae
Townsend, Raymond Lawrence
Townsley, Louis Frank
Toye, Clive Roy
Traa, Richard Louis
Tracey, Edward John
Tracey, James Allison, Jr.
Trachtenberg, Alan
Trachtenberg, Marvin Lawrence
Trachtenberg, Stephen Joel
Tracy, Allen Wayne
Tracy, Charles Hayden
Traenkner, Frederick Oswald
Trafas, Claude Jan

Trafford, John Thomas
Trager, Bernard Harold
Trager, Lawrence
Trager, Neil Jay
Train, Arthur Richard
Train, John
Traina, Albert Salvatore
Tramaglini, Salvatore Lawrence, Jr.
Trankiem, Khiet
Trantham, Walter Earl, Jr.
Trapp, Louis Andre, Jr.
Trask, Franklin Albert
Traub, Alan Cutler
Traub, Roberta Harriet
Trauger, John Frederick
Traugott, Fritz Arthur
Traum, Jerome S.
Traurig, Allen Robert
Trautlein, Joseph James
Travaglini, Barbara Carlson (Mrs. Alfonso Frederick Travaglini)
Travell, Clark
Travers, Warren
Traverse, Alfred
Travin, Milton Samuel
Travis, Mary Eileen (Mrs. Arthur J. Travis)
Treatman, Paul
Treen, Joseph Mayes
Treglos, Raphael
Trei, Alice Rosalie
Treibl, Hans George
Treichler, Ray
Treiman, Sam Bard
Treirat, Eduard
Treitler, Byron Morton
Trencher, Mark L.
Trent, James Alfred
Trent, Robert Lee
Trescott, Alfred Phillip, Sr.
Tresnowske, John
Treu, Jesse Isaiah
Trevaskis, Richard White
Trevor, Bronson
Trevor, Frederick Arthur
Tribble, Dagmar Haggstrom
Tricomi, Vincent James
Trieschman, Albert Ewell
Trihas, Lefteris Minas
Trilli, Harvey James
Trimbath, Ernest Ray Gorman
Trimble, William Cattell, Jr.
Trimble, Winfred Eugene
Trimpi, Howard Dennis
Trinkaus, John Philip
Triolo, Dominick Joseph
Triplett, Gary Joe
Tripp, Benjamin Riley
Tripp, Terrance Blaine
Tritt, John Eugene
Trivedi, Dino C.
Trivedi, Nikhil Chandrakant
Troberg, Lars Oskar
Troiano, James Anthony
Troll, John Hans
Tropf, William Jacob
Tropp, Richard Abraham
Trott, Rosmary Clifford (Mrs. James E. Trott)
Trotta, Anthony Ralph
Trotta, Geri (Geraldine)
Troubetzkoy, Alexis Serge
Troup, Frank Fleisher
Trout, Monroe Eugene
Troutwine, Charlotte Temperley
Trowbridge, Calvin Durand, Jr.
Trowbridge, Phillip Edmund
Trowbridge, Richard Stuart
Troxell, Raymond Robert, Jr.
Trpis, Milan
Trudeau, Pierre Elliott
Trudeau, Theodore Joseph
Trueblood, David Martin
Truitt, (Mary) Ann
Trump, Frederick Taylor
Truxal, Jacob Rugh
Tryon, Edward Polk
Tryon, Philip Tremaine
Tsai, Chen Fai
Ts'ao, Ignatius Jih-hsin
Tsao, Mike Chia-Cheng
Tsao, Tsen Cha
Tsao, Utah
Tse, Oliver Wai-Bun
Tseng, Anthony Tai
Tsimortos, Anne Marie Jacqueline
Tso, Margaret Yu-Yi Lu
Tsongas, Alexander George
Tsongas, Paul Efthemios
Tsoucalas, Nicholas
Tsung, Clarence Pai-an
Tu, Conrad Chin-Yui
Tu, Kai-Wen
Tubbs, LeVester
Tucci, Gerald Frank
Tucci, Nicholas
Tuck, Murray
Tucker, Burton Frank
Tucker, Cynthia Delores Nottage
Tucker, Eleanor Dorothy
Tucker, Howard McKeldin
Tuckman, Marvin Alfred
Tuff, Ronald
Tuffiash, William Alan
Tufts, Wesley Melbourne
Tufty, James Van Wagoner
Tukey, Harold Bradford, Jr.
Tulchinsky, Dan
Tulipano, Emilio John
Tull, Roger James
Tull, Willis Clayton, Jr.
Tuller, Burl Arthur
Tuller, Wendy Judge
Tully, James Henry, Jr.
Tully, Michael John
Tung, Hsi-Lin
Tunnell, Norman David
Tunnessen, Walter William, Jr.
Tunney, Arlene Rochelle
Tunnicliffe, William Warren
Turcotte, Fernand Wilfrid
Turgeon, Louis Phillippe
Turgeon, Ralph Asher
Turk, Oscar
Turkaly, Louis Gene
Turksen, Ismail Burhan
Turndorf, Herman
Turner, Clarice Patricia (Mrs. Charles Hyghe Debnam)
Turner, Dolores Walker
Turner, Donald Hunter
Turner, George Andrew
Turner, James Castle
Turner, Lewis
Turner, Paul Alfred
Turner, Paul Charles
Turner, Ralph Emerson
Turner, Robert Edward
Turner, Roger RaVon
Turner, Shirley
Turner, Stansfield
Turner, Thomas
Turov, Daniel
Tursi, Peter Budd
Tuttle, Douglas Edell
Tuttle, Frederick Burton
Tvert, Ronald Michael
Twitchell, H(erbert) Kenaston, Jr.
Twyon, Jane
Tyber, Murray Aaron
Tyler, Margo Hills
Tyler, Richard Dale
Tyler, Richard Frederic
Tynan, Edward Lyle
Tynes, William Joseph, III
Tyson, Charles Roebling, Jr.
Tyson, Luther Ewing
Tytell, Pearl Lily (Mrs. Martin Kenneth Tytell)
Tzimas, Nicholas Achilles
Ubans, Juris Konrads
Udine, Edgar
Udis, Sanford William
Udoff, Howard Stephan
Uebel, J. John
Ueland, Mark
Ufberg, Saul Howard
Uguccioni, Robert
Uh, David Keun
Uhler, Irvin Valentine
Uhrman, Celia
Ujhely, Valentine Anthony
Ulin, Richard Irwin
Ullman, Robert
Ullrich, James Arthur
Ullucci, Paul Anthony
Ulman, Lucy Thimann
Ulrich, Lorraine Anne
Ultan, Lloyd
Ulyat, Harry Lee, Jr.
Umland, Herbert Christian, Jr.
Unangst, Robert Walker
Understein, Robert Stanley
Underweiser, Irwin Philip
Unger, Christopher Pelham
Unger, Walter Peter
Unick, Russell Roy
Unis, Max Jay
Unkovic, Nicholas
Uotinen, Kyosti Gus
Upcraft, M. Lee
Upgren, Arthur Reinhold, Jr.
Upson, Stuart Barnard
Upston, John Edwin
Upthegrove, Franklin John
Upton, Arthur Canfield
Urban, George Pennock, III
Urban, Henry Zeller
Urban, Thomas Ellis
Urbaniak, Eugene T.
Urciuoli, J. Arthur
Urcuyo, Leonel
Urfer, Richard Peterson
Urstadt, Charles Jordan
Urstadt, Susan Powers (Mrs. J. Jeffrey Urstadt)
Ursul, George Richard
Urszenyi, Laszlo Gabor
Uschak, Ellen Ann
Uschald, Willi Andreas
Usher, Elizabeth Reuter (Mrs. Harry T. Usher)
Usher, Esther
Usinowicz, Walter Victor, Jr.
Ussery, Harry MacRae
Ussia, Samuel
Vacanti, Charles Joseph, Jr.
Vacanti, Kenneth Andrew
Vaccarella, Gerard, Jr.
Vaccaro, Joseph Pascal
Vachon, Brian
Vail, Van Horn
Vaillancourt, Donald Charles
Vajda, John Jay
Valania, Joseph John
Valbuena-Briones, A(ngel) Julian
Valent, Henry
Valenti, Leo Frank
Valenti, Robert Joseph
Valentine, Charles Francis
Valentine, Ralph James
Valentino, John
Valerino, Donald Matthew
Valerio, Helen Josephine
Valerio, Michael Amando
Vales, Joseph John
Valinski, Dennis John
Valiquette, Jean Guy
Vallas, Alex James
Valle, Raymond
Valle, Stephen Kurt
Vallin, Marta Emelia
Valoon, Jack Andrew
Valovic, Stefan John
Van Alstyne, James Reed
Van Basselaere, Leonard Jules
Van Bellingham, Leon George
Van Beuren, John Archbold
Van Beynum, William John
Van Blarcum, Barbara Happe
Van Brunt, H(owell) L(loyd)
Van Campenhout, Jacques Louis
Vance, Cyrus Roberts
Vance, George Paul
Van de Bovenkamp, Sue Erpf
Vandenberg, John David
Van Den Daele, Leland Douglas
Vanden Dorpel, Ronald Dale
van der Burgh, Charles Edwin, III
Van der Clute, Dean Sandison
Vanderlyn, Charles Pierre
Vanderpool, Wynant Davis, Jr.
Vander Voort, George Frederic
Van Deusen, Courtland, III
VanDeWall, LaVerne Robert, Jr.
Van Dien, John Edward
Van Duzer, Albert Wiencke
Van Dyke, William Adolphus, Jr.
Van Gorder, John Frederic
Van Hamel, Atty Thomas Anthony Swart
Van Hare, George Frederick, Jr.
Van Horn, Robert Emery
Van Hyuck, Alfred Phillips
Vanícek, Petr
Van Kleeck, Peter
Van Kloberg, Edward Joseph, III
vanKoughnett, George Limbert
Van Landingham, Leander Shelton, Jr.
Van Leight, Peter Robert
Van Meter, Ralph Marmon
Vann, John Daniel, III
Van Nostrand, Joan Fedell (Mrs. Lyman G. Van Nostrand)
Van Patten, Michael Robert
Van Raay, Janice Elizabeth
Van Rensselaer, Serena Miles
van Roosbroeck, Willy Werner
Van Roosen, Donald Collett
Van Sickle, John Babcock
Van Siclen, Cornelia
Van Splinter, Gerald Arthur
van Swol, Noel Warren
Vantine, A. William
Van Tongeren, Herk
Van Vechten, Frederick Rust
Van Vleck, John Hasbrouck
Van Voris, Fil E.
Van Winkle, Arthur D.
Vanzandt, Dorothy Perkins
Varano, Dominick
Varga, Nicholas
Vargas, Fernando Rodolfo
Vargas, Robert
Varndell, Charles Robert
Varney, Charles Wesley, Jr.
Varona, Alberto Jorge
Varshni, Yatendra Pal
Vasi, Carmelo
Vasquez, Anthony Foti
Vásquez, Fred
Vassar, Barbara Ellen
Vassell, Milton Oliver
Vassiliou, Andreas Haji
Vassiliou, Eustathios
Vaughan, Herbert Wiley
Vaughan, Ralph Carnell
Vaughn, Robert Donald
Veatch, Robert Marlin
Vecchia, Eugene Frank
Vega, Mariano, Jr.
Vega, Paz Mina
Vega, Richard Lawrence
Veillette, Rejean Marcel
Veirs, Alvin Bastable, Jr.
Velarde, Reynaldo Amos
Velkoff, Hyman
Veltri, Brenda Joyce
Velzy, Charles R.
Vendome, Gennaro
Venetsanopoulos, Anastasios Nicolaos
Venglarchik, Andrew Stefan, Jr.
Ventimiglia, Joseph John
Ventry, Paul Guerin
Venturella, Vincent Steven
Verano, Anthony F.
Verbiar, Clifford Paul
Verdun, Harold Charles
Vergara, William Charles
Verner, Elliott Kirk
Vernet, Peter Stanley
Verni, James Michael
Vernick, Milani Lee
Verral, Charles Spain
Verschingel, Roger Hilaire Charles
Vertucci, Nicholas Ralph
Very, Donald Leroy
Verzyl, June Carol
Verzyl, Kenneth Henry
Vesci, Joseph Vincent
Vesey, Frank Archibald
Vestergaard, Per Bjorn
Vetere, Robert Louis
Vick, Edward Hoge, Jr.
Vickers, James Hudson
Vickers, Stanley M.
Vickerson, Charles Edward
Vicks, Albert Paul
Victor, Barry Alan
Victor, Elyse Gail
Victor, Mario Thomas
Vida, Julius Adalbert
Vidler, Virginia Ellen
Viemeister, Peter Emmons
Vieras, Frank
Vieth, William Henry
Vignola, Andrew Michael
Vignoni, John Charles, Jr.
Vigue, James Francis
Viklund, William Edwin
Vilkitis, James Richard
Villafane, Edward, Jr.
Villanueva, E. Gary Cuenca, Jr.
Villarreal, James Alphonse
Vincent, Donald Edward Perry
Vincent, Marc-Aurèle
Vincent, Norman Robert
Vincent, Robert Clarence, Jr.
Vincent, Theodore Harold
Vine, Hannah Mollie
Viner, Edward David
Vinick, Richard Laurence
Viola, Leonard John
Violante, Thomas Robert
Virgulak, Francis Edward
Virus, John Robert
Vita, Dominick Charles
Vitanza, Angelo Anthony
Vitek, Clement Gerard
Vitelli, Elinor Marie
Vitetta, Francis Guy
Vitt, Sam B.
Vittorini, Carlo
Vivera, Arsenio Bondoc
Vizy, Kalman Nicholas
Vladeck, Bobb Charney
Vladutiu, Adrian Octavian
Vlahakis, John George
Vlcek, Joseph Frank
Vlcek, Joseph Robert
Vogel, Abraham P.
Vogel, Alexander S.
Vogel, Ferdinand Peter
Vogel, Francis Edwin
Vogel, George Sigmund
Vogel, John Michael
Vogel, Julius A., Jr.
Vogel, Stanley Morton
Vogelbach, Theodore Oscar
Vogelpoel, Anthony Peter
Vogt, Roy Schoppaul
Vogt, William Henry, III
Volkhardt, John Malcom
Voll, John Obert
Volpe, Robert
Volpe, S. Peter
Vonderahe, Alan George
Von Holden, Martin Harvey
von Kemenczky, Miklos
VonKeviczky, Colman Stephen
von Mehren, Robert Brandt
Von Ringelheim, Paul Helmut
von Szitanyi Walewska, Margit
von Tauber, Robert F.
Vontress, Clemmont Eyvind
von Wechmar, Ruediger Eberhard (Baron)
Voorhees, Donald Edward
Voorthuyzen, Peter
Vorosmarti, James, Jr.
Vos, Hubert Daniel
Voss, Donald Henry
Voss, Howard Evan
Vozella, John Joseph
Vuckovich, Carol Yetso (Mrs. Michael Vuckovich)
Vuoso, Frank
Vyasanakere, Satyanarayana Rao
Vyner, Mary Bainbridge
Wachenheim, Edgar, III
Wachman, Marvin
Wachtel, Howard Richard
Wachtel, Nathan
Wachter, William W., Jr.
Waddell, Sue Mary
Wade, Carole Kay
Wade, Donald Zahn
Wade, Furman
Wade, Peter Cawthorn
Wadsworth, Charles Young
Wadsworth, Howard Marvin
Wadsworth, Marion Frances Eddy (Mrs. Leslie R. Wadsworth)
Waesche, R(ichard) H(enley) Woodward
Wagman, Gerald Howard
Wagner, Charles William
Wagner, Clifford Confer
Wagner, Florence
Wagner, Frederick Balthas, III
Wagner, Karl Thomas
Wagner, Louis Edward
Waheed, Khalid
Wahl, Ray Franklin
Wahlberg, Eric Clifton
Wainer, Melvin Henry
Wainwright, Carroll Livingston, Jr.
Wainwright, Richard Adolph
Waitzkin, Stella
Wakamori, Takashi
Wakefield, Frederick Irving
Wakelee, Robert Louis, Jr.
Wakslak, Harry Aron
Walch, David Bean
Walcott, David Nathaniel
Wald, Alvin Stanley
Wald, Bernard Joseph
Wald, Francine Joy Weintraub (Mrs. Bernard J. Wald)
Wald, George
Wald, Lawrence
Wald, Philip Martin
Waldau, Helen Frances
Walden, Richard Henry
Walden, William David
Waldhausen, John Anton
Waldman, Jeffrey
Waldman, Lester Jesse
Waldo, Henry Channing
Waldron, James Bellord
Walen, Harry Leonard
Wales, Florence Alberta
Walgren, Doug
Walk, Paul Kenneth
Walker, Burt
Walker, Eunice Miriam Arnaud
Walker, Gene Alden (Mrs. Clare J. Crary)
Walker, John Robert
Walker, Kenneth Francis
Walker, P. David
Walker, Preston Jason
Walker, Robert Arnold
Walker, Robert Harris
Walker, Robert Smith
Walker, Roberta Ham (Mrs. David Honore Walker)
Walker, Shirley C. (Mrs. Melvin Lee Walker)
Walker, Vincent Henry
Walker, Wendell Kirshman
Walker, William Jefferson, Jr.
Walkup, Harry Ernst
Wall, Albert
Wall, Irving M.
Wall, Shannon Jerome
Wallace, Arnold Delaney, Sr.
Wallace, Donald Foote
Wallace, George Wilson
Wallace, James Peter
Wallace, Jane House
Wallace, Raymond P(aul)
Wallace, Richard Powell
Wallace, Thomas Francis
Wallace, William Keith
Wallace, William Ray
Wallach, Amei Marione
Wallach, Estelle
Wallach, Frances
Wallach, Frederick
Wallach, Robert Charles
Wallender, Harvey W.
Waller, William Edward
Wallerstein, Leibert Benet
Walles, Peter Paul
Wallin, Gary Phillip
Wallin, Judith Kerstin
Walling, W(ilber) Donald
Wallis, Charles L(angworthy)
Wallis, Gordon Todd
Wallis, Joseph Anthony
Wallis, William C.
Wallman, George
Wallner, Ludwig John
Walman, Jerome
Walrod, Truman Harrington
Walsh, Lawrence E(dward)
Walsh, Robert Reddington
Walsh, Thomas Joseph
Walter, Charles Russell, Jr.
Walter, Kenneth George
Walter, Robert Louis
Walters, Bette J.
Walters, Ronald Gordon
Walters, Walter Henry
Walton, Ralph Gerald
Waltzer, Stewart Paul
Wang, Chih Chun
Wang, Jen Chin
Wang, Kung-Lee
Wang, Lawrence Kongpu
Wang, N(ian) T(zu)
Wang, Teh Po
Wang, Yinpao
Wank, Gerald Sidney
Wanko, George J.
Wanless, Ronald Walter
Warach, Bernard
Warber, Esther Maxine
Warburg, Stephanie Wenner
Ward, Harold Walton
Ward, Joan Gaye
Ward, John Bernard
Ward, Joseph Francis
Ward, Madeleine Rebecca Suplee
Ward, Nicholas Donnell
Ward, Philip Henry, III
Ward, Robert Joseph
Ward, Rodman, Jr.
Ward, Samuel M.
Ward, Thomas Vincent
Ward, Vernon Underhill
Ward, Victoria Francine
Ward, W. Ralph
Wardly, George Alfred, Jr.
Ware, Charles Harvey, Jr.
Ware, Frances Lee
Ware, Grace Elizabeth
Warfield, Robert Welmore
Waring, John Alfred
Warman, John Boyle
Warman, Kenneth Edward, Jr.
Warner, Barbara Jean
Warner, Francis James
Warner, Frank William
Warner, Gloria Marmar (Mrs. Richard R. Pichel Warner)
Warner, Patricia Anne
Warner, Rawleigh, Jr.
Warner, William Whitesides
Warren, Alan
Warren, Bertram
Warren, Betty Deane
Warren, Carol Hortensen
Warren, Louis Bancel
Warren, Robert Aulenbach
Warren, Skip Owen
Warshavsky, Belle Bennett (Mrs. Henry Warshavsky)
Warshawsky, Albert
Warsley, Paul Daniel
Warwick, Donald Phillip
Wasdyke, Jack Conrad
Wase, Arthur William
Washington, Craig Stephen
Washington, Walter E.
Washio, Hiroshi
Wasko, Matthew Francis
Wasserman, Jack
Wasserman, Marvin David
Wasserman, Ruth
Wasserstrom, Steven
Wasson, William George
Wastie, Arthur Edward
Wat, James Kam-choi
Watanabe, Kyoichi Aloisius
Watanabe, Ruth
Waterhouse, Gary George
Waterhouse, Keith
Waterman, Donald Calvin
Watermulder, David Brainerd
Waters, Charles Edward
Waters, Francis P.
Waters, Lewis Thomas
Waters, Thomas Lyle
Waters, William Ernest
Watkins, Anne Louise
Watkins, Donald Thomas
Watkins, Eugene Leonard
Watkins, Glenn Amoss, Jr.
Watkins, Phillip Lewis
Watkins, Robert Goodman
Watlington, Joseph, Jr.
Watman, Jerome
Watson, Alfred Michael
Watson, Arthur Richard
Watson, Edwin Ben
Watson, Jack Hearn, Jr.
Watson, Mary Stone
Watson, Thomas Jones, III
Watson, Wilbur Henry
Watt, James D.
Watt, Richard Martin
Watt, Thomas Lorne
Watts, Glenn Ellis
Watts, Herbert Errol
Watts, Raymond Day
Watts, Warren Wayne
Waugh, Bascom Slemp
Wawak, Phyllis Jane
Waxman, Herbert Jacob
Wayman, John Geib
Wayson, Charles Henry
Weary, Thomas Squires
Weatherly (Thomas Elias Weatherly, Jr.)
Weaver, Daniel Conway
Weaver, Donald Robert
Weaver, Edgar Sheldon
Weaver, Ellen Gail
Weaver, Eric James
Weaver, John Arthur
Webb, Clifford Wellington
Webb, Elmon Dodd
Webb, J. Richard
Webb, William Reading
Webber, John Bentley
Webber, Michael David
Webbink, Patricia Glixon
Weber, Alfred Leo
Weber, Clarence Adam
Weber, David Alexander
Weber, Gerald Joseph
Weber, Henry Thomas Paul
Weber, John Benedict
Weber, Richard Glen
Weber, Thomas William
Webster, Carmen Jacqueline (Mrs. Harry M. Kelly)
Webster, Clinton Wallace
Webster, David Arthur
Webster, James Kelsey, III
Webster, John Archibald, Jr.
Webster, Raey William Snodgrass
Webster, Rosa Cornice
Webster, Thomas Glenn
Wechman, Robert Joseph
Wechsler, Alan Lewis
Wechsler, Herbert
Wecker, Christoph Ulrich
Weckstein, William Arnold
Wedeen, Harvey David
Wedeen, Shirley Ullman
Wedel, Paul George
Wedin, Edward Johan
Wedzicha, Walter
Weeden, James Dennis
Weeks, David Frank
Weeks, Richard Ralph
Wegman, Leonard S.
Wehberg, Dirk Anton
Weiant, Monroe Alden
Weicker, Lowell P., Jr.
Weida, Lewis Dixon
Weiden, Paul Ludwig
Weidenbacher, Peter
Weidenfeld, Sheila Rabb
Weidenheimer, Joseph Francis
Weidler, Milton Joseph

Weidner, James Henry
Weierman, Robert Joseph
Weigand, Genella Sims
Weigel, Ernest Charles
Weigel, William Frederick
Weigrau, Toni
Weihs, Frank Alois
Weil, Frank A.
Weill, Harold
Weiman, Mark Bernard
Wein, Louis Philip
Weinbaum, Morris J.
Weinberg, Alan Aaron
Weinberg, Hazel Joan
Weinberg, Mark Herman
Weinberg, Milton Solomon
Weinberger, Philip Morris
Weiner, Charles R.
Weiner, Frank J.
Weiner, Matei
Weiner, Max
Weiner, Melvin Milton
Weiner, Paul Ivan
Weiner, Peter Richard
Weiner, Stephen Arthur
Weingast, Marvin
Weinhold, J(ulius) Frederick, Jr.
Weinman, Joel B.
Weinmann, Bert Millicent Landes (Mrs. Richard A. Weinmann)
Weinrod, Emanuel
Weinsaft, Paul P.
Weinstein, Alfred Bernard
Weinstein, Bernard M.
Weinstein, Clement
Weinstein, Francis Saul
Weinstein, George
Weinstein, Howard
Weinstein, Irving
Weinstein, Murray
Weintraub, Arthur Eleazer
Weintraub, Daniel Ralph
Weintraub, Louis
Weintraub, Sol
Weir, Merrill E.
Weisberg, Gerard Maxwell
Weisberg, Joseph Gotland
Weischadle, David Emmanuel
Weise, Wallace Ploss
Weiselberg, Norman
Weiser, Kenneth David
Weiser, Norman Sidney
Weisfogel, Jerry
Weisinger, Richard Harry
Weisman, Irving
Weiss, Brian
Weiss, Florence
Weiss, Gerson
Weiss, Henry Walter
Weiss, Jonathan Arthur
Weiss, Lawrence Charles
Weiss, Nathan Straus
Weiss, Rita Leona
Weiss, Ted
Weiss, Vladimir Stanley
Weissbach, Herbert
Weisselberg, Edward Bernard
Weissman, Esther Irene
Weissman, Jack
Weissman, Kenneth Bernard
Weissman, Morton Arthur
Weissman, Walter
Weissman, William R.
Weitberg, Martin Harry
Weitzenhoffer, Aaron Max, Jr.
Weitzmann, Albert Michael
Welch, Mary Scott Stewart
Weller, Jac
Weller, James Mannie
Weller, John Louis
Weller, John William, Jr.
Weller, Peter Anthony
Weller, Robert
Weller, Thomas Huckle
Welles, Ernest Irving
Wellington, Albert Perry
Wellons, Karyn Sue
Wells, Darlene Penny
Wells, David Ernest
Wells, Elizabeth
Wells, Hal Marion
Wells, Joseph Philip
Wells, Lionelle Dudley
Wells, Mary Georgene Berg (Mrs. Harding L. Lawrence)
Wells, Owen Wayland
Wells, Peter Scoville
Wels, Marguerite Samet
Wels, Philip Bernard
Wels, Richard Hoffman
Welty, James Alman
Welty, Patricia Mary
Welz, Joey
Wendel, Peter Kent
Wendel, Richard Frederick
Wendel, Thomas Michael
Wendling, Donald Brand
Wendroff, Edward Roy
Wenger, Samuel Esbenshade
Weniger, Sidney N.
Wenner, Claude Henry
Wentworth, Edwin Calvin
Wentworth, Paul Meserve
Wentz, Henry Stauffer
Wentz, Robert James
Wentz, William Wesley
Wentzel, Richard Clay
Werba, Henry Carl
Werly, John McIntyre
Wermuth, Anthony Lewis
Wermuth, William Charles, IV
Werner, Charles Arthur
Werner, Edwin Robert
Wernick, Jack Harry
Wernick, Richard Frank
Wershaw, Frederick Irving
Weslager, Clinton Alfred
Wesolow, Adam, Adam
Wesser, David Robert
West, Arthur James, II
West, Austin Ward
West, Bob
West, Daniel Jones, Jr.
West, Edward Nason
West, Harry Miles, III
West, Harvey Gordon, Jr.
West, John Pettit
West, Robert Nelson, Sr.
West, Sueann Jonetta
Westermann, David
Westmeyer, Troy Rudolph
Weston, Alan George
Weston, Jerome Lester
Weston, S(tephen) Burns
Wetherell, Albert Anthony
Wetlaufer, Donald Burton
Wetmore, James Stuart
Wettach, Charles Frank
Wettereau, Richard Bradway
Wexler, David Jacob
Wexler, Howard
Wexler, Jacqueline Grennan
Wexler, Jeffrey
Wexler, Stephen Charles
Weybright, Victor
Weymouth, Ethel Marion
Weyrich, Paul Michael
Whalen, Brian Bayles
Whalen, David Joseph
Whalen, Joseph Philip
Whalen, Paul Michael
Wham, William Neil
Whang, Benjamin
Whang, James Shiapin
Wharton, Betty Ann (Mrs. John Franklin Wharton)
Wharton, Clifton Reginald, Jr.
Wharton, George Christopher
Wharton, Ralph Nathaniel
Whealon, John Francis
Wheat, Gordon Albert
Wheatley, Charles Fellows, Jr.
Wheatley, Frank Edward
Wheatley, Maurice Edward
Whedon, George Donald
Wheeler, Charles Mervyn, Jr.
Wheeler, Frank Mitchell
Wheeler, John Stuart
Wheeler, Marvin Dwain
Wheeler, Philip Charles
Wheeler, Thomas Francis, Jr.
Wheelock, Keith Ward
Whelan, William Francis, Jr.
Whetstone, Roy Douglas
Whipple, DeForest Thompson
Whipple, Lawrence Aloysius
Whisnant, James Edward
Whitaker, Evelyn Bernice
Whitcomb, James Howard
White, A. Burton
White, Barbara Louise
White, Byron R.
White, Carl Harvey
White, Chester Furman
White, Clifford Dale
White, Dean Casey
White, Denis Naldrett
White, F(rederick) Clifton
White, Frank Anthony, Jr.
White, Frank Joseph, Jr.
White, Geneva Pride
White, George Edward
White, James Francis
White, James Mattocks, Jr.
White, John William Loud
White, Kevin Hagan
White, Kristin
White, Margaret Marie
White, Neil Sprague
White, Robert Clarence
White, Ruth Miriam Weihs (Mrs. Paul White)
White, Ruth O'Brien (Mrs. Wallace B. White)
White, Thomas
White, William Henry
White, Winifred Demarest (Mrs. Herbert A. White)
Whitehead, Arline A.
Whitehouse, Raymond Charles, II
Whitehurst, Lowell Earl
Whitehurst, William Wilfred, Jr.
Whitfield, Edwin Wycliffe
Whitham, Sharon Elizabeth
Whiting, Harry Andrew, Jr.
Whitley, Mark Robert
Whitlock, Edward Madison, Jr.
Whitman, Martin J.
Whitman, Philip Martin
Whitmarsh, David Carothers
Whitmarsh, Theodore Francis
Whitney, Donald Sanford
Whitney, Kenneth Jack
Whitney, Philip Mather, Jr.
Whitney, Ralph Royal, Jr.
Whitney, Thomas Porter
Whittaker, Alma Teele (Mrs. Virgil G. Whittaker)
Whittaker, Richard Pawling
Whitten, James Robert
Whyte, Thomas Joseph
Wibberley, Harold Evers, Jr.
Wichman, Adolph R.
Wichman, Sven Hjalmar
Wick, Carol Ann Mellen (Mrs. Leland Hall Wick)
Wicker, Ireene
Wickham, Dale Wallace
Wickham, Robert Dean
Widlitz, Paul J.
Wieczerzak, Joseph Walter
Wiederhold, Michael Lewis
Wiegartner, Paul John
Wieland, Peg Doody Mast
Wiemer-Sumner, Anne-Marie
Wien, Stephen Saul
Wiener, Harry
Wiener, Howard Edward
Wiener, Morris Jay
Wiener, Norman
Wiener, Solomon
Wienik, Peter Harris
Wienshienk, Ralph
Wier, Joseph Richard
Wier, Richard Royal, Jr.
Wierzalis, Edward Alexander
Wiesen, Jeremy Lester
Wiesen, Marvin Arthur
Wiesenbaugh, Joseph Michael, Jr.
Wiesenberg, Jacqueline Leonardi
Wiesenberg, Russel John
Wiesenthal, Marvin Meyer
Wiesner, Jerome Bert
Wieting, William Frank
Wigand, Robert Charles, Jr.
Wiggins, Charles Edgar
Wiggins, Chris
Wiggins, Joseph John
Wigmore, David, Jr.
Wignall, Ernest Carl
Wigner, Eugene Paul
Wikstrom, Nancy Sue
Wilber, Margie Robinson
Wilbur, Marvin Cummings
Wilchins, Sidney Alfred
Wilcox, David Eric
Wilcox, Edward Donald, Jr.
Wilcox, Richard Leon
Wilcox, Robert Lawrence
Wilde, Daniel Underwood
Wilde, George Harvey
Wildebush, Joseph Frederick
Wilder, Marion Burt (Mrs. Richard B. Wilder)
Wildes, William Henry
Wildnauer, Richard Harry
Wildrick, Kenyon Jones
Wiles, Joseph St. Clair
Wiles, Margaret Isobel
Wiley, Barry Holland
Wiley, Bert Carlton
Wiley, Tarley Tarson
Wilhelm, Frederick Henry
Wilhelm, Joseph Lawrence
Wilhelm, Michael Leonard
Wilhelmi, Henry Paul
Wilkerson, William Garfield
Wilkey, Malcolm Richard
Wilkins, Lee Gertrude
Wilkins, Lloyd Henderson, Jr.
Wilkinson, George Shoemaker, Jr.
Wilkinson, Harry Edward, Jr.
Wilkinson, Nana Miriam Slaten (Mrs. Wesley O. Wilkinson)
Wilkinson, Thomas Allan
Wilks, Phillip Howard
Will, Charles Augustus
Willard, Harry Lentz
Willard, John Gerard
Willauer, George Jacob, Jr.
Willcox, Frederick Preston
Wille, Carroll Gerard
Willets, Elmore Abram, Jr.
Willets, Seth Barrows
Willette, Roger Henry
Willey, Raymond Clyde
Willey, Wade Norris
Williams, Adolphus Levi, Jr.
Williams, Albert J., Jr.
Williams, Bradford Warren
Williams, Cecilia Lee Pursel
Williams, Clarence Gerome
Williams, Clarence Leon
Williams, Daniel Edwin
Williams, Daniel Eugene
Williams, David
Williams, David Russell
Williams, Dorothy Frances
Williams, Douglas
Williams, Dudley Ridault
Williams, Dwight Nelson
Williams, Edgar
Williams, Edward Bennett
Williams, Edward George
Williams, Edward T. H.
Williams, Eliot Penfield
Williams, George Charles
Williams, George Earnest
Williams, H. Bruce
Williams, Harold Thomas
Williams, Harrison Arlington, Jr.
Williams, Helen Elizabeth
Williams, Henry
Williams, Hubert
Williams, James Edward
Williams, James Henry, Jr.
Williams, James Thomas
Williams, John Allen
Williams, John Chamberlin
Williams, Joseph Winslow
Williams, Kathleen Frances
Williams, Kenneth John
Williams, Lillian Brown
Williams, Lon Albert
Williams, Mary Pierce
Williams, Melvin Donald
Williams, Monica Donnelly (Mrs. Bernard G. Williams)
Williams, Mortimer Lee
Williams, Neal Thomas
Williams, Richard Bland, Jr.
Williams, Robert Alden
Williams, Robert Alexander
Williams, Robert Carl
Williams, Roger, Jr.
Williams, Roland Barksdale
Williams, Roland Charles
Williams, Ronald David
Williams, Ruthann
Williams, Theodore Harvey
Williams, Warrenton Archibald
Williams, Wiley Herbert
Williams, William David
Williams, William Gilbert, III
Williams, William Magavern
Williams, Willie Clifford
Williamson, Betty Jayne Hughes (Mrs. Joseph Robert Williamson)
Williamson, Charles Joseph
Williamson, Fletcher Phillips
Williamson, Jeffrey Phillips
Williamson-Michaels, Sue Dodds
Willig, William Paul
Willing, Pearl R. (Mrs. Stanley S. Willing)
Willing, S. Stanley
Willingham, Warren Willcox
Willis, David Peter
Willis, James Lorne
Willis, Thornton Wilson
Willis, William Ervin
Willner, Allen Eugene
Willner, Jeffrey Steven
Willner, Morris Stephen
Willoughby, William Franklin, II
Wills, James Henry
Wills, Lawrence August
Wills, Robert Henry, Jr.
Willsie, Harry Alford
Willton, Charles
Wilmer, William Holland, II
Wilmore, Violet Smith
Wilner, Marie
Wilson, Calvin Thomas
Wilson, Carl Benoit
Wilson, Charles Frank
Wilson, Charles Philip
Wilson, Donald Alfred
Wilson, Edmund Allenby, Jr.
Wilson, Edwin Marshall, Jr.
Wilson, Frances Helen
Wilson, Frank Sinclair
Wilson, George Lewis
Wilson, Harvey J.
Wilson, Howard Hazen
Wilson, James Adams
Wilson, James Joseph
Wilson, James Reid, Jr.
Wilson, John Fletcher
Wilson, John Frederick
Wilson, John Lennox
Wilson, John Sterling
Wilson, Kenneth Jay
Wilson, Leonard Muir, Jr.
Wilson, Malcolm
Wilson, Martin Bernard
Wilson, Myron Allen
Wilson, Ned Monroe
Wilson, Rexford
Wilson, Robert Alfred
Wilson, Robert James
Wilson, Robert Joseph
Wilson, Robert Lawrence
Wilson, Robert Woodrow
Wilson, Roger Winslow
Wilson, Sonja Marie Alston
Wilson, Stephen Frederick
Wilson, Vincent Joseph, Jr.
Wilson, Wayne Clair
Wilson, William James
Wilson, William Laney
Wilson, Zane Arthur
Wilton, Miriam Mae
Wiltse, John Henry
Wiltse, Peter Christian
Wiltz, Hector Rafael
Wimer, James Harold
Winblad, Dorothy Jean Brooks (Mrs. William C. Winblad)
Winchester, Alma Elizabeth Tatsch (Mrs. Clarence Floyd Winchester)
Winchester, Clarence Floyd
Winckowski, Bronislaus Frank
Windawi, Hassan
Windebank, Robert William
Windels, Paul, Jr.
Windhausen, John Daniel
Windle, Joseph Raymond
Windley, Charles Ellis
Windsor, James Marcellus
Windsor, Laurence Charles, Jr.
Windsor, Patricia Frances
Windsor, Robert Kennedy
Winebaum, Sumner Joseph
Winell, Marvin
Winer, James Patrick Benjamin
Winfield, Armand Gordon
Winham, Gilbert Rathbone
Winick, Albert Bernard
Winkler, Joseph Conrad
Winn, Helen Hartmann (Mrs. Burkhard Daniel Winn)
Winney, James Richard
Winokur, Herbert Simon
Winpisinger, William P.
Winsche, Richard Arnold
Winsor, Curtin, Jr.
Winsor, William Tillinghast
Winstead, Jack Alan
Winsten, Sol Stephen
Winter, Gordon Arnaud
Winter, Herbert Reinhold
Winter, Nathan Harold
Winters, Edward William
Winterstella, John Lige
Winthrop, Amory
Winthrop, John
Wisbey, Herbert Andrew, Jr.
Wisch, Nathaniel
Wise, Donald Allen
Wise, Samuel Paul, III
Wiseman, Douglas Carl
Wiseman, James Richard
Wiser, Vivian Doris
Wishner, Julius
Wishon, George Edwin
Wisneski, Frank Vincent, Jr.
Wissinger, H. Andrew
Wist, Paul Gabriel
Wister, William David
Wit, Harold Maurice
Witcher, Robert Campbell
Witek, Nicholas Joseph
Witenberg, Earl George
Witherspoon, William James
Withey, Robert Arthur
Witkin, George Joseph
Witkin, Lee Daniel
Witkin, Mildred Hope Fisher (Mrs. George Joseph Witkin)
Witkoski, Francis Clement
Witlin, James Royce
Witmer, Charles Russell
Witmer, Kenneth Isaiah
Witorsch, Philip
Witt, David Hampton
Witt, John Joseph
Witt, Leonard Raymond
Witt, Marjorie Ruth
Witt, Robert, Jr.
Wittek, Marie Johnson
Witten, Laurence Claiborne, II
Witter, Richard Earl
Witter, Robert William
Witter, William David
Wittmer, Franklin Donald
Wittmer, Paul William
Wittreich, Warren James
Wixom, Theodore Mershon
Wiznia, Pearl Pauline (Mrs. Benjamin Wiznia)
Woël, Ralph
Woeppel, Mary Anita Confalone
Woglom, James Russell
Wohl, Harold Lee
Wohl, Martin
Wohl, Robert Allen
Wohler, James Richard, II
Wohltman, Keith William
Woititz, Janet Geringer
Wojciechowski, Jerzy Antoni
Wojtowicz, Joseph Mark
Wolanin, Sophie Mae
Wolaver, Carl Leroy
Wolbach, Albert Bogh, Jr.
Woldman, Sherman
Wolf, Alexander
Wolf, Carl Theodore
Wolf, Frank James
Wolf, Frederick Barton
Wolf, Gary Wickert
Wolf, Herbert Leonard
Wolf, Howard Jay
Wolf, Peter Michael
Wolf, Robert Lawrence
Wolf, William Milton
Wolfe, Andrew Dougherty
Wolfe, Anthony Lee
Wolfe, Charles Henry
Wolfe, Francis Joseph
Wolfe, Jean Elizabeth
Wolfe, Robert Richard
Wolfert, Reuben Robert
Wolff, Alfred R.
Wolff, James Alexander
Wolff, Joel Charles
Wolff, Leo Thomas
Wolff, Lester Lionel
Wolff, Paul Martin
Wolff, Theodore Ralph
Wolff, Walter Ferdinand
Wolfley, Alan
Wolfort, Francis Gabriel
Wolfson, Dexter
Wolfson, Robert Pred
Wolhar, Robert Charles, Jr.
Wolin, Robert Harvey
Wolinsky, Ira
Wolk, Anthony Edward
Wolk, Herman Shepard
Wolk, Nolan Irwin
Woller, Olga
Wollheim, Donald Allen
Wollman, Barry James
Wolozen, John Joseph, Jr.
Wolsky, Jack
Wolter, John Amadeus
Womer, Robert Sylvester
Wong, David C.
Wong, Patrick Wai-Kwong
Woo, Glenn Frank
Woo, Shien-Biau
Woo, Theresa Ting
Wood, Brian
Wood, Clifford Harlow
Wood, Harleston Read
Wood, Harold Gray
Wood, James Arthur, Jr.
Wood, John Sumner
Wood, Loring Wayland
Wood, Margaret Beatrice
Wood, Mary Ann Fernsler
Wood, Patricia Lynne
Wood, Paul Mix
Wood, Paul Winthrop
Wood, Peter York
Wood, Thomas Fullenwider
Woodams, Edward Ellis
Woodard, Brian Talcott
Woodard, Paul Esty
Woodbury, Alan Tenney
Woodham, Jean
Woodrich, Glenn Carl
Woodruff, Archibald Mulford, Jr.
Woodruff, Marian Davis
Woods, Beverly Jo
Woods, Frederick Elverton
Woods, John Francis, Jr.
Woods, John Russell
Woods, Louis Richard, Jr.
Woodside, Robert Bruce
Wood-Smith, Donald
Woodward, John Thomas
Woodward, Robert Burns
Woodward, Ronald Edwin
Woodworth, Hugh, Jr.
Woodworth, James Anthony
Woodyer, Peter John
Woolf, Howard Irvin
Woolf, Leon M.
Woolley, Alban Edward, Jr.
Woolworth, Richard Griswold
Wooten, Ronald Lee
Worbois, Robert John
Worden, Frederic Garfield
Worden, Katharine Cole
Workman, Clark Raymond
Worley, Joseph Francis
Worley, Robert Elton
Wormer, Donald Andrew
Wormser, Alex Francis
Worne, Howard Edward
Woronick, Simon Anthony
Worral, Gordon James
Worrell, Richard Vernon
Worsham, Bertrand Ray
Worthington, Robert Melvin
Wortzel, Lawrence Herbert
Wosinski, John Francis
Wozmak, Eugene Henry
Wray, Edward Orion, Jr.
Wray, Haltom
Wren, John Breen
Wright, Benjamin Vaiden, Jr.
Wright, Douglas Tyndall
Wright, Estella Viola Harrison (Mrs. William M. Wright)
Wright, Harold Louis
Wright, James Skelly
Wright, Jane Elizabeth
Wright, John Harrison, Jr.
Wright, Laurence Casto
Wright, Linda Shickel
Wright, Lyle Earnest
Wright, Mark Heisley
Wright, Peter
Wright, Richard Donald
Wright, Roy Thompson
Wright, Stanley Marc
Wright, Theodore Paul, Jr.
Wright, Thomas Wesley
Wright, William Ellsworth
Wrigley, John Warren
Wriston, Walter Bigelow
Wruble, Brian Frederick
Wu, Cheng-Yi
Wu, (James) Ching
Wu, Jin
Wu, John Naichi
Wu, Mao-Fou
Wu, Ning Gau
Wu, Stephen S.
Wu, Tse Cheng
Wurf, Jerry
Wurts, Clarence Zantzinger
Wurzburger, Walter Samuel
Wyatt, Donald Edgar
Wyatt, Dorothy Katharine Wolf
Wyatt, Herbert
Wyatt, Robert Harry
Wyche, La Monte George
Wychulis, Adam Robert
Wyck, Peter Herbert
Wyckoff, Donald Daryl
Wydler, John Waldemar
Wygant, James Peter
Wyglendowski, Frank Thomas
Wyman, Franklin, Jr.
Wyman, Rachel
Wyman, Stanley Moore
Wynn, John Foster, Jr.
Wynn, William Harrison
Wynne, Arthur Vincent, Jr.
Wynyard, Martin
Wyon, John Benjamin
Wyrick, Charles Lloyd, Jr.
Wyrtzen, James Charles
Wysocki, Boleslaw A(ntoni)
Wysong, Earl Marshall, Jr.
Wyszkowski, Paul Edward
Yablonsky, Harvey Allen
Yachter, Morris
Yaffe, Joseph X.
Yager, Robert Louis
Yalow, Rosalyn Sussman
Yang, Chen Ning
Yang, Davy Teh-Wei
Yang, Jann Nan
Yang, Jen Tai
Yang, Kei-Hsiung
Yang, Ker-Chie
Yang, Moses D.K.
Yang, Wen-Ching
Yankauer, Mary
Yanoff, Jay Myron
Yanoff, Seymour L.
Yanow, Rhoda Mae Kornfeld
Yanta, William Joseph
Yanuzzi, Joan Ruff

Yao, James Ka-Ying
Yao, Shang Jeong
Yap, Ricardo San Jose
Yarborough, Ernest Lynwood, Jr.
Yarbrough, Charles Richard
Yardumlen, Richard
Yarosh, Robert Thiel
Yar-Shater, Ehsan Ollah
Yas, Solomon M.
Yasiejko, Walter George
Yassky, Alfred David
Yates, James Arthur
Yates, Janet Lee
Yates, John Robert, Jr.
Yates, Michael Francis
Yates, Robert James
Yates, Vance Joseph
Yates, William Franklin, Jr.
Yatron, Gus
Yatsevitch, Gratian Michael
Yayas, Christy Calavas
Yeager, Edward James
Yeager, John George
Yeakel, Joseph Hughes
Yedlicka, William George
Yeh, Chuen Yuan
Yellowitz, Irwin Herbert
Yelton, Robert Harold
Yen, Nai-chyuan
Yen, Sherman
Yeo, Richard Swee-Chye
Yeracaris, Constantine Anthony
Yerger, Charles Lloyd
Yetter, Lawrence Robert
Yingling, Nathaniel David
Yochum, William David
Yocom, John Erwin
Yoder, Edward Williams
Yoder, Hilda (Mrs. Albert Francis Garrou)
Yoder, James Willard
Yoffe, Morris
Yoho, Betty Eileen
Yoken, Melvin Barton
Yolton, David W.
Yonda, Alfred William
Yoo, Dal
York, Jerome Bailey
York, Samuel, Jr.
Yoshikawa, Takatoshi
Yost, Faye Frances
Yost, Robert Carsyl
Yost, Robert Morris
Yost, Zane
Youdelman, Stanley Alan
Young, Billie
Young, Bruce Kenneth
Young, Charlotte Albiston
Young, Chesley Virginia Barnes (Mrs. Morris N. Young)
Young, Daniel Herbert, III
Young, Douglas F.
Young, Earle Wilson, Jr.
Young, Edwin Parson
Young, Esther Christensen (Mrs. Charles Jacob Young)
Young, Flora Dorsey
Young, Francis Anthony, Jr.
Young, Gail Thibault
Young, Joan Elaine
Young, John Albion
Young, John William
Young, Joseph Warren, Jr.
Young, Larry Emory
Young, Leo
Young, Lionel Wesley
Young, Lloyd Emory
Young, Mahonri Sharp
Young, Margaret Buckner
Young, Maurice Isaac
Young, Morris Nathan
Young, Richard Atlee
Young, Robert Francis
Young, Robert Michael
Young, Rod
Young, Royce Oliver
Young, Ruth Ann
Young, William Edmund
Young, William Robins, Jr.
Youngblood, Joseph Leonard, Jr.
Younger, Irving
Youngman, John Crawford
Youngs, David Dalmer
Youngson, Jeanne Keyes
Younis, Adele Linda
Youtcheff, John Sheldon
Youtt, Julie Wilson
Yuille, Ernest Clarke
Yulish, Charles Barry
Yunich, David Lawrence
Yvonne
Zachariasewycz, Eugene
Zacharius, Martin Philip
Zack, Earl Robert
Zackrison, Harry Bertil, Jr.
Zackrison, Walter Joseph
Zadek, Bebe
Zadell, Henry James
Zadunaisky, Jose Atilio
Zadylak, Stanley Edward
Zaffarano, Richard F.
Zaffino, Patricia Ann
Zaffuto, Stephen Fred
Zagat, Eugene Henry
Zahavy, Edith Doris
Zahavy, Zev
Zahler, Harold David
Zahn, Frederick Anthony
Zaki, Fouad George
Zaki, Moustafa Abdel Fattah
Zakraysek, Louis
Zaks, Elisabeth Brown
Zalar, Charles
Zaldivar, Nieves Maria
Zales, Michael Robert
Zaleznak, Bernard David
Zall, Robert Rouben
Zambito, Raymond Francis
Zamorski, Martin Theodore
Zander, Dieter Warren
Zanfagna, Philip Edward
Zang, Joseph Albert, Jr.
Zanger, Martin Henry
Zangwill, Estelle Paula Richest (Mrs. Donald P. Zangwill)
Zani, Frederick Caesar
Zanjanian, Mohamad Hossein
Zanotti, Donald John
Zanvettor, Jorge
Zapffe, Carl Andrew
Zappe, Hans Helmut
Zappone, Francis Thomas
Zaprudnik, Jan
Zarate, Remy Abellar
Zarella, Michael Peter
Zaret, Seymour
Zaretsky, Gregory
Zarfes, Murray
Zargaj, Tomislav
Zarin, Jerry
Zarins, Bertram
Zarwyn, Berthold
Zausner, Martin
Zavada, Mary Roberta
Zawahir, Meeyapillai K. Madar
Zayac, Ivan Bohdan Simon
Zayac, Peter Paul
Zaydon, Jemille Ann
Zdenek, Edna Prizgint
Zdep, Stanley Michael
Zech, John Raymond
Zednowicz, Joseph Bernard
Zeehandelaar, Frederik Jules
Zeeveld, David Gordon
Zeferetti, Leo C.
Zehel, Wendell Evans
Zehringer, Francis Alexander
Zeichner, Ben
Zeiss, Clifford John
Zeitchick, Abraham Aaron
Zeitlin, Bill
Zeizel, Leo Aaron
Zelcer, Isaac
Zeleny, Carolyn
Zelik, Bernard John
Zelitch, David S.
Zeller, Diane Leinwand
Zeller, Howard Alfred
Zellner, Carl Alan
Zellner, Joseph Edward
Zelt, Albert Ralph
Zeman, Barry Tilden
Zeman, Milan Samuel
Zeni, Levio Edward
Zenowitz, Allan Ralph
Zentner, Charles Raynard
Zepke, Brent Eric
Zerr, Jesse Bitler
Ziegeler, Andrew
Ziegenfus, Robert Charles
Ziegler, Alan Dennis
Ziegler, Arthur Paul, Jr.
Ziegler, John Benjamin
Ziegler, Terry L.
Zielonka, Alfred Walter
Ziemnowicz, Christopher Henry
Zien, Tse-Fou
Zier, Adolfo
Ziglar, William Larry
Zigo, Paul Edward
Zilkha, Phyllis Siegel
Zimmer, Alan Edward
Zimmer, Alex
Zimmer, Donald William
Zimmerman, Bernard
Zimmerman, Clarence Edgar
Zimmerman, Daniel David
Zimmerman, George Ogurek
Zimmerman, Joseph Francis
Zimmerman, Milton A.
Zimmerman, Mortimer Fred
Zimmerman, Rae
Zimmerman, Steven Ernest
Zimmermann, Caroline
Zimpfer, William Edward
Zinberg, Mildred
Zink, Lubor Jan
Zinkevich, Frederick Nicholas
Zinkham, Ronald Lee
Zinman, Jacques
Zinn, Keith Marshall
Zinn, William
Zinninger, George Frederick
Zinz, David Albert
Zipp, Alan Steven
Zippel, Mary-Ella Holst
Zipper, Howard David
Zipper, Milton
Zito, Robert Joseph
Zitron, Benjamin Charles
Zlotnick, Bernard
Zlotowitz, Bernard M.
Zohar, Uri
Zomorrodian, Shahnaz Erfani
Zoppo, Jerome Joe
Zosa, Angelo Mario Mercado
Zoss, Abraham Oscar
Zouary, Maurice H.
Zsoldos, Frank
Zuccarelli, Frank Edward
Zuchniewicz, Alexander Joseph
Zuck, Alfred Christian
Zucker, Arnold Harris
Zucker, Norman Livingston
Zucker, William Henry
Zuckerman, Arthur Edward
Zuckerman, Paul Herbert
Zufall, Dorothy Lukasik
Zug, Charles Keller, III
Zuhl, Donald Eugene
Zuiderhof, Barbara M.
Zukotynski, Stefan
Zumoff, Barnett
Zupanec, Ralph
Zurav, David Bernard
Zutz, Harry David
Zwahlen, John
Zwanger, Jerome
Zwass, Vladimir
Zwerling, Lillian
Zwick, Richard Francis
Zwicker, Charles Harrison
Zwirn, David Bernard
Zygmont, Frank John, Jr.
Zysman, Simon Asher
Zytaruk, George John

REGIONAL LISTING—MIDWEST

Aagesen, Larry Kenneth
Aaker, Roland H.
Aamodt, Margaret Dora
Aanerud, Melvin Bernard
Aaron, James Ethridge
Aarons, Harold
Aaronson, Abe Louis
Aarthun, Martin
Abbasi, Ali Abdel-Wahhab
Abbasy, Iftikharul H.
Abbey, Robert Harry
Abbott, Albert Clifford
Abbott, Dean Frederick
Abboud, Francois Mitry
Abboud, Joseph Thomas
Abbrecht, Peter Herman
Abdallah, Salam Mohamed
Abdnor, James
Abel, Alan Wilson
Abel, Billy LaRue
Abel, Harold
Abele, Homer Eugene
Abeles, Norman
Abell, Joseph Richard
Aberg, Robert Kenneth
Ablin, Richard Joel
Abloff, Richard Lee
Abney, Charlotte Maxine
Abourezk, James G.
Abraham, Bette Havens
Abraham, John
Abrahamson, James Alan
Abrahamson, Leonard
Abram, Patricia Jean
Abrams, Bernard S.
Abrams, Walter
Abramson, Herbert Francis
Abramson, Jean Margaret
Abrell, Phillip Eugene
Abruzzo, Peter Joseph
Abuzzahab, Faruk Said, Sr.
Accola, Louis Wayne
Acker, Duane Calvin
Ackerman, Jerry William
Ackerman, Ora Ray
Ackerman, Walter J.
Acord, Frank Donald
Acosta-Olmeda, Jose Guillermo
Adair, Charles Valloyd
Adair, John Glenn
Adaire, Bruce Bower
Adam, Paul James
Adams, Donald Earl
Adams, Edward Larrabee, Jr.
Adams, Ellis Wentworth
Adams, Gene
Adams, Gordon Dewey
Adams, James Lewis
Adams, John Carter
Adams, John Ernest, Jr.
Adams, John Marshall
Adams, Kendall Alfred
Adams, Leslie
Adams, Max Dwain
Adams, Melvin Harrison, Sr.
Adams, Peter Webster
Adams, Richard Melverne
Adams, Robert McLean
Adams, Thomas Brooks
Adams, Wayne Barry
Adams, William Lawreson
Adams, William Richard
Adamson, Gary
Adamson, John Douglas
Adamson, John Richard
Adan, Adelberto
Addicks, Mentor Charles, Jr.
Addington, Leonard Milton
Addis, Winston Clark
Addison, Cornelius Philip
Adducci, Joseph Edward
Addy, Alva LeRoy
Ade, Walter Frank Charles
Adegbile, Gideon Sunday Adebisi
Adelberger, William Henry
Adelman, Betsy Collen
Adelman, Raphael Martin
Adelstein, Herman
Adler, Abraham David
Adler, David Leo
Adler, Gerson
Adler, Seymour Jack
Adsit, Frank Daniel
Aduss, Howard
Affeldt, George Richard
Aggarwal, Raj Kumar
Agrawal, Bhupendra Kishor
Agre, Courtland LeVerne
Agruss, Neil Stuart
Aguiar, H. Alexander
Ahern, John Francis
Ahern, John Joseph
Ahern, Paul Lee
Ahlberg, Clark David
Ahlenius, William Matheson
Ahlers, Andrew William
Ahles, Sister Mary Theophane
Ahlstrom, Ronald Gustin
Ahluwalla, Muneshwar Singh
Ahmad, Bashir
Ahmad, Ijaz
Ahmed, Khalil
Ahmed, Nasir
Ahmed, Shaffiq-Uddin
Ahonen, Clifford John
Ahrendts, Harold Lee
Ahrens, Claude Wesley
Ahrens, Robert John
Ahstrom, James Peter, Jr.
Aichner, Harry Clifford
Aiello, AlFred
Aiken, Roger George
Ailes, Curtis Albert
Ainley, Robert Wallace
Airy, John Madison
Aitken, William Inglis
Aiyede, Adebayo Olumuyiwa
Ajamy, David Albert
Akcasu, Ziyaeddin Ahmet
Ake, Montie Ralph
Ake, Sam Eugene
Akert, Benjamin Bruce
Aladjem, Silvio
Albanito, Donald Michael
Albera, Victor Harold
Albernaz, Jose Geraldo
Albert, John Murray
Albert, Norman Irving
Alberti, Charles Edward
Alberts, Marion Edward
Albertson, Clarence Elmo
Albini, Alvo Edo
Albott, William LeRoy
Albrecht, Edward Daniel
Albrecht, Edwin Raymond
Albrecht, Ronald Frank
Albrecht, Willard Harold
Albright, Arthur Stanley
Albright, Joseph William
Alby, James Francis Paul
Alder, Edwin Francis
Alderfer, William Kenneth
Alderman, David Arden
Alderman, Roalda Jensen
Alderson, Bernita Mae
Alderton, Harvey Randall
Aldridge, Victor E., Jr.
Aleff, Howard Joseph
Aleksandrowicz, Frank John
Alesch, Daniel James
Alexakos, Constantine Evangelos
Alexander, C. Alex
Alexander, Charles Freeman, Jr.
Alexander, Daniel Richard
Alexander, Don Kenneth
Alexander, Donald Wayne
Alexander, James
Alexander, Kenneth Oliver
Alexander, Nancy Carol
Alexander, Patricia Louise
Alexander, Robert Lee
Alexander, William Michael
Alexanderson, Eldon Ludwig
Alexis, Marcus
Alford, Gerald Dean
Alfred, Karl Sverre
Ali, Hussien
Ali, Mir Masoom
Alig, Frank Douglas Stalnaker
All, David Clayton
Allaben, Robert Dewitt
Allan, Vernon Arthur
Allanson, John Frederick
Allard, Donald James
Allen, Arthur L., Jr.
Allen, Arvon Dale, Jr.
Allen, Charles Willard
Allen, Clyde Erwin, Jr.
Allen, Eugene Vincent
Allen, Frank Benjamin, Jr.
Allen, Garald Fredrick
Allen, George Douglas
Allen, Glen Gene
Allen, Jack B.
Allen, James Curtis
Allen, John Donald
Allen, John Edward
Allen, Layman Edward
Allen, Lee Harrison
Allen, Lois Arlene Height (Mrs. James Pierpont Allen)
Allen, Marion Carroll
Allen, Martha Clise
Allen, Martin
Allen, Milton Nicholas
Allen, Phyllis Adelle Grisham (Mrs. Robert McCurdy Allen)
Allen, Richard Blose
Allen, Richard Herbert
Allen, Robert Dean
Allen, Robert Shaw
Allen, Ronald Royce
Allen, Spencer Turner
Allen, Thomas Ernest
Allen, Vernon Eugene
Allen, William Leon
Allender, Terrance Calvin
Alley, Louis Edward
Alley, William Jack
Allington, James Richard
Allington, Robert William
Allison, Richard Bruce
Alloway, R. Brooke
Allyn, Richard
Almblad, Carl William
Almond, Carl Herman
Almond, George Lee
Almquist, Nevin Arthur
Alper, Albert
Alper, Zalman Yakov
Alsdorf, Marilynn Bruder (Mrs. James W. Alsdorf)
Alsop, Donald Douglas
Alspaugh, Lilyan Mae
Altan, Taylan
Altenhoff, Norman Richard
Alter, Forrest Henrici, Jr.
Alter, Joseph Dinsmore
Alterman, Rolland August
Althauser, Robert Pierce
Altholz, Herbert Carl
Altieri, Richard Nunzio
Altman, Jules
Altman, Milton Hubert
Altner, Peter Christian
Alton, Ralph Taylor
Al-Ugdah, William Mujahid
Alvares, Kenneth Michael
Alvarez, Albert Richard
Alvine, Raymond Guido
Alvord, James C., Jr.
Alwin, LeRoy Vincent, Jr.
Amador, Luis V.
Amann, Peter Henry
Amar, Wesley Francis
Amaro, John Anthony
Amarose, Anthony Philip
Amary, Issam Bahjat
Amato, Joseph A.
Ameling, Norman John
Ament, F. Thomas
Amerine, Ivan Robert
Amerslav, Andrew Ficaj
Ames, Edward James
Ames, Peter Lesley
Ames, (Polly) Scribner
Amfahr, Donald Francis
Amidon, Paul Charles
Amiot, Gerald Joseph
Ammer, William
Ammerman, Jay Neil
Amneus, Payton William
Amos, David Espejo
Amos, Everett R.
Amos, Robert Woodrow
Amrolia, Dinyar Homi
Amstutz, Hubert Menno
Amundson, Douglas George
Amundson, Nancy Ellen Anderson
Amyx, Matthew Clay
Anagnost, Catherine Cook
Anagnostopoulos, Constantine Emmanuel
Anas, George Sam
Andal, Jerry Ray
Anderl, Stephen
Anders, Leslie
Andersch, Carolyn Elizabeth
Andersen, Harold Wayne
Andersen, Harry Edward
Andersen, James Louis
Andersen, Kenneth Eldon
Andersen, Richard R.
Anderson, Amos R.
Anderson, Anna Wilda
Anderson, Austin Gothard
Anderson, Benton Rees
Anderson, Betty Lou
Anderson, Bror Ernest
Anderson, Charles Ralph Seibold
Anderson, Charlotte Louise
Anderson, Charters Harry
Anderson, Clarence Axel Frederick
Anderson, Dale Walter
Anderson, David Clem
Anderson, David Daniel
Anderson, David Presley
Anderson, Dorrine Ann Petersen (Mrs. Harold Edward Anderson)
Anderson, Edward Eugene
Anderson, Edward Everett
Anderson, Frances Swem (Mrs. Clarence A.F. Anderson)
Anderson, Gaylord Arthur
Anderson, George Rex, II
Anderson, Gerald Dwight
Anderson, Harley Eric
Anderson, Harold Coulston
Anderson, Harold Edward
Anderson, Howard Douglas
Anderson, Jack Garrett
Anderson, James Harry
Anderson, John Bayard
Anderson, John Eric
Anderson, John Robert
Anderson, Judith Margo
Anderson, Karl Paul
Anderson, Karl Stephen
Anderson, Kenneth Oscar
Anderson, LaVerne Eric
Anderson, Lawrence Svente
Anderson, LeRoy Harvey
Anderson, Lois Dorothy
Anderson, Lois Marilyn
Anderson, Lowell John
Anderson, Lowell Vernet
Anderson, Luther Adolph
Anderson, Lyle Arthur
Anderson, Michael Wayne
Anderson, Milton Henry
Anderson, Norval Eugene
Anderson, Paul W.
Anderson, Paul William
Anderson, Philip Carlton
Anderson, Ray Carl
Anderson, Robert Alfred
Anderson, Robert Arthur
Anderson, Robert Louis
Anderson, Roger E.
Anderson, Roger Gordon
Anderson, Roger Lyle
Anderson, Roger Scott
Anderson, Ronald Dean
Anderson, Roy Leonard
Anderson, Sidney Elmer
Anderson, Thomas Milburn, Jr.
Anderson, Verlyn Dean
Anderson, Walter Raymond
Anderson, Wendell Richard
Anderson, William David
Anderson, William Summers
Andes, John Wilbur
Andonian, David Aaron
Andorfer, Donald Edwin
Andreas, Bruce Frederick
Andreas, John Carlton
Andreasen, George Fredrick
Andres, Leo Edward
Andress, Samuel Coe
Andrews, Clarence Adelbert
Andrews, Ernest Eugene
Andrews, Harry Lubomir
Andrews, Jack Robert
Andrews, James Lewis
Andrews, Larry Howard
Andrews, Mark
Andrews, Mitchel Martin, Jr.
Andrews, Myron Floyd
Andrews, Roger Davis
Andrews, Theodore Francis
Andrews, Thomas Brown, V
Angeline, John Frederick
Angerman, Robert Bryon
Angino, Ernest Edward
Angle, Carol Remmer
Angle, Chesley Ward
Angst, John Edward
Angus, Robert Dale
Anhalt, Leonard P.
Anichini, Mario
Anjard, Ronald Paul
Ankenbrand, Ralph James
Anklan, Deane Richard
Anneberg, Adrian Reas
Annett, Thomas
Annis, Spero
Anno, James Nelson
Annunzio, Frank
Ansari, Mohammed Rafiullah
Anschutz, Glenn William
Anshutz, William Maurice
Anson, Jack Lee
Anthis, Bill Clinton
Anthis, Patricia Weaver (Mrs. Bill Clinton Anthis)
Anthony, Samuel Carl
Anton, Anastasia
Anton, Donald Christ
Anton, John James
Antonic, James Paul
Anundsen, Brynjolf Bjorkholt
Anundsen, John Killen
Anundson, John Kenneth
Anuras, Sinn
Anuta, Albert Edward, Jr.
Anzur, Stephen David
Apelquist, Ronald William
Apfelbacher, Steven Frederick
Apilado, Myron
App, Palmer
Appel, William Cecil
Appleby, Leslie Vere
Applegate, Douglas
Applegate, Kenneth Lewis
April, Edwin
Arabia, Paul
Arai, Harold Yutaka
Arakawa, Kasumi
Arbaugh, Robert Bruce
Arbeen, Lynn Andrew
Arbuckle, Dorothy Fry (Mrs. Lloyd Arbuckle)
Archambault, Bennett
Archambault, Rene Francis
Archbold, Thomas John
Archer, Bernard Thomas
Archer, Joseph Paige
Archer, Lawrence Harry
Archer, Wesley Lea
Archer, William Harley
Archibald, George William
Archibald, Robert Davison
Archie, David Esden
Ardaiolo, Frank Palma
Ardussi, Wallace Philip
Arenberg, Irving Kaufman
Arends, Robert Eugene
Arey, Leo Betram
Arganbright, Frank Clarence
Argento, Dominick
Argersinger, William John, Jr.
Arias, Belisario Antonio
Arieff, Alex Joseph
Arkema, Katherine Kemp
Arlinghaus, Edward James
Arlook, Theodore David
Armacost, James Owen
Armantrout, Mary Lynn
Arment, Rex Dale
Armock, Frank Leroy
Armstrong, A. James
Armstrong, Charles Willis
Armstrong, Hart Reid
Armstrong, John Roberts
Armstrong, Naomi Young
Armstrong, Patricia Kay (Mrs. Charles W. Armstrong)
Armstrong, Theodore Morelock
Armstrong, Wallace Jackson
Arndt, Elizabeth Delano Moore (Mrs. Joseph Manning Arndt, Jr.)
Arndt, Joseph Manning
Arnell, Paula Ann Youngberg (Mrs. Richard Anthony Arnell)
Arnell, Richard Anthony
Arneson, Richard Arlen
Arnett, Richard Hayes
Arnett, Roy Lee
Arnold, Arthur
Arnold, Frank Copeland
Arnold, Fred English
Arnold, Leonard Charles
Arnold, Lynn Ellis
Arnold, Orville Edward
Arnold, Robert William
Arnoldt, Robert Patrick
Arquilla, George, Jr.
Arrasmith, Jean Leonore
Arriola, Alfredo Borbon
Arrowsmith, Wallace Goldie
Arseneault, Edmond John
Art, Robert Leo
Arthur, Alan John
Arthur, Lindsay Grier
Arvesen, Norman Dean
Arvin, Charles Stanford
Asbjornson, Helen E
Ascher, James John
Asgar, Kamal
Ash, Charles Joseph
Ash, James Boyd
Ash, Philip
Ashbach, David Laurence
Ashbridge, G. Harry
Ashbrook, John Milan
Ashby, Charles Ferg
Ashby, David Ward
Ashby, Robert Newton
Ashcraft, Laurie Cragg
Ashe, A. J.
Ashhurst, Anna Wayne
Ashley, Nova Trimble
Ashley, Thomas William Ludlow
Ashmore, Richard Walter
Ashton, Edward Lowell
Ashwood, Loren Frisk
Aspegren, Oliver Richard, Jr.
Aspelmeier, Kenneth Alan
Asper, Bernice Victoria
Aspin, Leslie
Astrin, Marvin H.
Atallah, Yousef Hanna
Atkin, Robert Byron
Atkins, Bobbie Jean Johnson
Atkins, James Albert
Atkins, Robert Franklin
Atkins, Russell Kelly
Atkins, Stanley Hamilton
Atkinson, Arthur John, Jr.
Atkinson, Jon Garold
Atkinson, Tracy
Atlee, John Light, III
Atlee, Judith DeHaven
Atwell, Harold Edwin
Atwood, Burton Homer
Atwood, Robert Elmer
Atzberger, Frank John
Aucar, Alfredo
Auer, Delmar LaVerne
Auer, Joseph Curtius
Auerbach, Marshall Jay
Aufdenkamp, Jo Ann
Augustin, Carroll Darwin
Augustine, Gerald Herman
Augustine, Jack H.
Augustus, William Edgar
Auld, Frank
Aulie, Richard Paul
Ault, Addison
Ault, Phillip H.
Aulvin, John Lewis
Ausdal, Robert Burns
Austin, Donald Castle
Austin, Gary Francis
Austin, John Atwood, Jr.
Austin, Joseph Allen
Austin, Michael Herschel
Austinson, Carlyle Palmer
Authier, Richard Lawrence
Autry, Charles Franklin
Auwaerter, John Francis
Avecilla, Constante Simon
Avedisian, Armen George
Avedon, Bruce
Averitt, George Robert
Avery, Barbara Jean
Avery, Douglas Norman
Avila, Teresita DeDios
Avny, Warren Yoram
Awais, George Musa
Axelrod, Jack Martin
Axelrood, Helen Blau
Axelson, John Anton
Axelson, Joseph Allen
Axley, Ralph Emerson
Axsom, Dorothy Skirvin
Ayers, Leona Weston
Ayers, Richard Wayne
Ayers, Thomas G.
Aylin, Floyd Edwin
Ayres, Robert Franklin
Ayres, Walter David, Jr.
Baahlmann, Ralph Henry
Baalmann, Richard Fenton
Baar, Lillian Mary
Baasch, Frank Leroy
Babb, Raymond Charles
Babcock, Daniel Lawrence
Babcock, Dennis Arthur
Babcock, Willis
Babich, Robert Joseph
Babler, James Harold
Babris, Peter Joe
Bacci, Guy Joseph, II
Bach, Ira J.
Bach, Muriel Dunkleman (Mrs. Ira J. Bach)
Bach, Steve Crawford
Bacharach, John Albert
Bachem, Wolfgang Albert
Bachhuber, Edward August
Bachhuber, Thomas Duane
Bachman, David Christian
Bachman, Ernest
Bachman, George Craig
Bachman, Jerald Graybill
Bachmann, Bruce Ralph
Bachmann, Carl Anthony
Bachmann, Roger Werner
Bachner, Donald Joseph
Bachochin, Frank Thomas
Bacino, Ted J.
Backer, Horst Helmut
Backs, Alton Joseph
Bacon, Donald Elliot
Bacon, Frank Rider
Bacon, Robert
Bacon, William Cornelius
Bacon, William Thompson, Jr.
Baczkowski, Richard Bodgan
Bade, James Carl
Badeer, Henry Sarkis
Badenhoop, Herman John
Bader, Donald James
Bader, Kenneth Leroy
Badger, James Golvin, Jr.
Baebler, Arthur George
Baer, Austin Robert
Baer, David, Jr.
Baer, John Richard Frederick
Baer, Roger Kern
Baetzhold, Howard George
Baffes, Chris Gus
Bagby, Marvin Orville
Bagley, James Edward
Bahadur, Chance
Baia, Arlene Vivian Skjeveland
Baier, Martin
Baier, William Herbert
Bailey, Earl Glenn, Jr.
Bailey, Eugene Cary
Bailey, Gwendolyn Lee Manning
Bailey, Howard Lowden
Bailey, James Spencer
Bailey, Melanie Anne
Bailey, Merritt Elton, Jr.
Bailey, Michael Alan
Bailey, Neal James
Bailey, Ray Vernon
Bailey, Richard Paul
Bailey, Robert Howard
Bailey, Thomas Corwin, II
Bailey, V. Maxine Sheldon (Mrs. Ray V. Bailey)
Bailey, Wanita Mae
Bailey, Weltman Dawes
Bailey, Wilson Pease
Baillon, Austin John
Bain, Ralph Lee
Bair, Bruce B.
Bair, Medford Daniel
Bair, Richard McKinnon
Baird, Clyde Ray
Baird, George Walter
Baird, James Kenneth
Baird, James Nicholson, Jr.
Baird, Marie Louise (Mrs. Hugh Alexander Baird)
Baird, Oren Kenneth
Baird, Robert Dahlen
Baisch, Stephen James
Bajek, Walter Adam
Bajus, Beverly Ann Broughton (Mrs. Donald A. Bajus)
Baken, Robert Edward
Baker, Barnet
Baker, Betty Louise
Baker, Bruce Nelson
Baker, Carlyle
Baker, Clarence Albert, Sr.
Baker, Clifton Earl
Baker, Donald Eugene
Baker, Donald Robert
Baker, Donald Whitelaw
Baker, Edwin Ross
Baker, Frank Myers
Baker, James David
Baker, James Edward Sproul
Baker, Jerry Wayne
Baker, John Braden
Baker, John Stevenson (Michael Dyregrov)
Baker, Lee Wendell
Baker, Luella Austelia
Baker, Marian Gray Chambers
Baker, Marvin Glenn
Baker, Mary Evelyn Shoemaker (Mrs. Richard Heinley Baker)

Baker, Ray Mitchell
Baker, Robert Clifford
Baker, Robert Eugene
Baker, Robert Harold
Baker, Saul Phillip
Baker, Wade Franklin
Baker, Wayne
Baker, Wesley Carrel
Bakewell, Stanley Ellsworth
Bakke, Gilbert Benjamin
Baksh, Karim
Balacek, Thomas Vincent
Balagot, Reuben Castillo
Balazs, Bill (Bela) Antal
Balbach, Daniel Rosswell
Balch, Durward Earl
Baldock, Robert Lemore
Baldoni, Louis Paul
Baldus, Alvin James
Baldwin, Gordon Brewster
Baldwin, Lannes Weaver, Jr.
Baldwin, Lloyd Deans
Bales, Jerald Keith
Balester, Raymond J.
Balfour, Henry Hallowell, Jr.
Balk, Harlan George
Ball, Chester Edwin
Ball, Kenneth Leon
Ball, Lloyd Richard
Ball, Louis Alvin
Ball, William Batten
Ball, William James
Ballance, L(ewis) Charles
Ballantine, Whitney William
Ballard, John Stuart
Ballard, Lester Arthur, Jr.
Ballinger, Leonard Daniel
Ballmer, Ray Wayne
Balluff, Edward Louis
Balma, Michael James, Jr.
Baloff, Nicholas
Balogh, Joseph David
Balsley, Lawrence Edward
Baltazzi, Evan Serge
Baltzell, James Henry
Balunas, Leonard Charles
Bambenek, Gregory Peter
Bambrick, James Joseph
Bamford, Jacqueline Lou
Bammann, Derwood Eugene
Banach, Art John
Banas, Emil Mike
Banas, Thomas Paul
Bancroft, Theodore Alfonso
Band, Jordan Clifford
Banda, Arpad Frederic
Bandiola, Benjamin Escaner
Bando, Hiro Walter
Bandy, Irene Gesa
Banerjee, Samarendranath
Banerjee, Tarit Kumar
Banet, Odell Joseph
Banfield, Thomas Vincent, II
Banghart, John Thomas
Banich, Francis Edward
Banister, Olive Kennedy
Banker, John Davis
Bankhead, Lowell Carey, Jr.
Bankoff, Milton Lewis
Banks, Stewart Willard
Banmen, John
Bannes, Lorenz Theodore
Bannister, Margaret Alice Trimble
Banser, Robert Frank, Jr.
Banton, James Fowler
Banzhaf, Carol Rottier
Banzhaf, Clayton Harris
Baran, William Lee
Baranko, Emil Wayne
Baranowski, Edward Alfred
Barb, Margaret Ellen
Barbee, James Max
Barber, Andrew Bollons
Barber, Frank Alva
Barber, Kent Graves
Barberio, Anthony Ben
Barbieri, James Charles
Barbolini, Robert R.
Barboriak, Joseph Jan
Barbour, Fleming Arnold
Barbu, Robert Cornell
Barclay, Allan Gene
Barcus, Robert Gene
Bard, Gordon Neal
Bardeen, John
Bardis, Panos Demetrios
Bardwell, Arthur Glenn, Jr.
Bardwell, Maureen Ann
Bare, Mark Richard
Barefield, Ivor Mae
Barenberg, Ernest John
Barg, William Henry
Barger, Cecil Edwin
Barger, Charles William
Barger, John Walter
Barger, Melvin Dean
Barger, Robert Newton, III
Barisas, Bernard George, Jr.
Barker, David Allen
Barker, Elizabeth Bell
Barker, Gregson Leard
Barker, Keith Rene
Barker, Kent Purcell
Barker, Walter Lee
Barket, Alexander John
Barkley, John Richard
Barkley, Mark Ernest
Barkley, Owen Herbert
Barks, Horace Bushnell
Barks, Howard William
Barksdale, A. Beverly
Barksdale, Clarence Martin
Barksdale, Richard Kenneth
Barlow, F(rank) John
Barnard, Kathleen Rainwater
Barnard, Robert Dane
Barnard, William Clark
Barnes, Bill Lloyd
Barnes, Bruce Francis
Barnes, Daniel Francis
Barnes, Elma O.
Barnes, Francis Merriman, Jr.
Barnes, Jocelyn Thomas
Barnes, Robert Allan
Barnes, Robert William, Jr.
Barnes, Ronald Leigh
Barnett, Arthur Malcolm
Barnett, Carl Amos, Jr.
Barnett, D. Earl
Barnett, James Brian
Barnett, John Vincent
Barnett, Joseph H.
Barnett, Ralph Lipsey
Barnett, Richard Gene
Barnett, Robert Eugene
Barnett, Robert Fulton, Jr.
Barnett, William A.
Barnette, Emma Christine Hansen (Mrs. Foster I. Barnette)
Barney, Frederick Albert
Barney, James Arthur, Sr.
Barney, LeRoy
Barney, Michael Charles
Barnhart, Gene
Barnhart, Richard Edwin
Barnhill, Helen Iphigenia
Barnhill, Robert Lester, Jr.
Barnstorff, Henry Dreses
Baron, Raymond Charles
Barone, James Vincent
Barr, Donald Wesley
Barr, Joan Harris
Barr, John Monte
Barr, Kenneth John
Barr, Raymond Allen
Barr, Roderick Wood
Barr, Roy Rassmann
Barranger, John Paul
Barre, Henry John
Barrell, Robert Poindexter
Barrett, Edward Duane
Barrett, Richard Hamilton
Barrett, Robert Allen
Barrett, William Carroll
Barrette, Patrick Emile
Barrick, Louise Grider (Mrs. Harry Thomas Barrick)
Barrington, Bruce David
Barron, Alexander Fraser
Barron, Arthur William
Barron, Howard Robert
Barrow, Robert Ruffin
Barry, Hilary Donavan
Barry, James P(otvin)
Barry, Thomas Hubert
Barsamian, Arthur
Barsi, Louis Michael
Barsky, David
Barsky, Sidney
Bart, William Marvin
Barta, Gerald Thomas
Bartels, Carl Frederick
Barthelmas, Ned Kelton
Bartholomay, Henry, III
Bartholomay, William Conrad
Bartholomew, Fred Irv
Bartimus, Wesley
Bartkiw, Nykola
Bartlett, Bud (Byron Allan)
Bartlett, Edwin Ball, Jr.
Bartlett, Peter Greenough
Bartlett, Sylvia Rosette
Bartlett, William McGillivray
Bartlette, Donald Lloyd
Bartley, Edward Ross
Bartley, Roger Arthur
Bartley, Vernon Herbert
Bartling, Charles Edwin
Bartoletti, Carol Jane
Bartoletto, Avellino Joseph
Bartolome, Francisco Mabalay
Barton, Constance Elisabeth Cornick
Barton, Edward Read
Barton, Robert James
Barton, Robert Kenneth
Barton, Terry Alan
Bartone, Francis Frederick
Bartron, G. Robert
Bartz, Richard Otto
Barut, Clara Jean
Baruth, Carroll Lee
Barzan, Leonard Angelo
Bascunana, Jose Luis
Basel, Arthur Richard
Bashaw, Wayne Ernest
Bashe, Winslow Jerome, Jr.
Bashshur, Rashid Lutfallah
Basile, Abigail Julia Ellen Herron (Mrs. Joseph Basile)
Basile, Ruth LeBaron Rutledge
Basile, William Basil
Baskin, John Roland
Bass, Edward Leland
Bass, Larry Junior
Bass, Nathan Winthrop
Bassett, Joseph Samuel
Bassett, Sheldon Joe
Bassiouni, M. Cherif
Basu, Asit Prakas
Basu, Prodyot Kumar
Basu, Shankar
Basu, Subhash Chandra
Batch, John Martin
Batchelder, Anne Stuart (Mrs. Clifton Brooks Batchelder)
Batchelor, Wilbur Commodore
Bate, Charles Thomas
Bates, Charles Johnson
Bates, George Edward, Jr.
Bates, Henry Elmer, Jr.
Bates, Mark Weldon
Bates, Mary Joyce
Bates, Robert L.
Batie, Harley Walter
Batinich, Mary Ellen (Mrs. Alex Batinich)
Batman, Howard Taylor
Batsakis, John George
Batt, Catherine Jean
Battis, Thomas Jerome
Battison, John Henry
Battisti, Frank Joseph
Batton, Calvert Vorwerk
Batza, Eugene Mann
Bauch, Norbert George
Baucom, William Ernest
Bauder, Gary Lee
Bauer, Florence Marvyne (Mrs. W. W. Bauer)
Bauer, Frank Charles
Bauer, Frederick Charles
Bauer, Graydon Milford
Bauer, Gregory Anthony
Bauer, Harlan John
Bauer, Joseph Leo
Bauer, Nancy McNamara
Bauer, Norman William
Bauer, Robert Oscar
Bauer, Rodney Edward
Bauer, William Joseph
Bauermeister, Herman Otto
Baughn, Michael Lynn
Baum, Michael Harvey
Baum, Werner A.
Bauman, George Duncan
Bauman, Robert Edward
Baumeister, Carl F.
Baumeister, Eleanor H. (Mrs. Carl F. Baumeister)
Baumhart, Raymond Charles
Baumhoefner, Arlen Henry
Bautista, Renato Go
Baxter, Charles Morley
Baxter, Joseph Diedrich
Baxter, Loran Francis
Baxter, Marilynn Ruth
Baxter, Reginald Robert
Bayer, Harmon Symond
Bayh, Birch E., Jr.
Bayly, Melvyn Arthur
Bazarko, Volodymyr Orest
Beach, Harry Adam
Beach, Leslie Robert
Beachler, Kenneth Clarke
Beadle, George Wells
Beadle, Muriel McClure Barnett
Beahm, Edgar Hiram
Beal, Bert Leonard, Jr.
Beal, Jack Lewis
Beal, Myron Clarence
Beal, Wanda Elnora Rader (Mrs. Howard William Beal)
Beall, Charles William
Beall, Glenn Lee
Beam, James Alfred
Beams, Glen James
Bean, Marvin Day
Bean, Stephen Michael
Beaney, William Dewey
Bearce, James Richard
Beard, Marion L. Patterson (Mrs. F.E. Beard)
Beard, Martin Luther
Beard, Ward Powers
Bearden, David Leonard
Beardsley, John Deighton
Beart, Robert Woodward
Beaton, Ian Wilson
Beattie, Stanley Edward
Beattie, William John, III
Beatty, Daniel Davis
Beatty, Frank Stewart
Beatty, Lowell Crawford
Beatty, Norman Jackson
Beatty, Robert Alfred
Beaty, Marjorie Heckel (Mrs. Donald William Beaty)
Beauch, Robert Nimmo
Beaudoin, Gregory David
Beaumier, John Henry
Beaumont, George Haydon
Beaver, William Lee, Jr.
Beavers, Addison Morton
Becerra, Lawrence
Becherer, Carl Victor
Becht, Sue Carol
Bechtel, Donald Leon
Bechthold, George Walter
Becich, Raymond Brice
Beck, Carl Frederick
Beck, Clifford Carl
Beck, Ernest William
Beck, Frances Josephine Mottey (Mrs. John Matthew Beck)
Beck, Joan Wagner
Beck, John Allan
Beck, John Matthew
Beck, John Roland
Beck, Joseph George
Beck, Louis George
Beck, Robert Knowlton
Beck, Sally Bell
Becken, Russell Warren
Becker, Benjamin Max
Becker, David Norbert
Becker, Edward Brooks
Becker, Jason C.
Becker, Maurice Edwin
Becker, Millie Anna
Becker, Norman Otto
Becker, Rolfe Allen
Becker, Sally Electa Norris (Mrs. Alfred D. Becker)
Becker, Samuel Leo
Becker, Stephen Scott
Becker, William Dennis
Becker, William Henry
Becker, William Kohl
Beckett, Grace
Beckett, James Marion
Beckley, Kenneth F.
Beckmann, Heino Albert Paul
Becraft, John Richard
Becvar, Stephen Lee
Bedard, George Rudolph
Bedard, James Harry
Bedell, Berkley
Bednarczyk, Walter William
Bedwell, Horace Wade
Bedwell, Tommy Joe
Beech, Robert Paul
Beechem, Henry Albert
Beecher, Lee Hewitt
Beecher, Rexine Ellen
Beechy, Atlee
Beekhuis, Gerardus Jan
Beeks, John Charles
Beelman, Gary Scott
Beem, John Kelly
Beerman, Burton
Beermann, Allen Jay
Beers, Thelma Sneed (Mrs. Russell James Beers)
Beers, Thomas Wesley
Beers, Victor Gilbert
Beers, William O.
Beestman, George Bernard
Beets, F. Lee
Bego, Gene Leland
Behforooz, Ali
Behle, Roland Carl
Behlmann, F. Lee
Behnke, Donald John
Behnke, Wallace Blanchard, Jr.
Behrend, Elaine
Behrenfeld, James Raymond
Behrens, Donald Edwin
Beideman, Ronald Paul
Beier, Gary Jon
Beilfuss, Bruce F.
Beimdiek, Donald Urban
Beineke, Lowell Wayne
Beintker, Marjorie Rose
Beisswenger, Norman Frederich
Beitler, Roger T.
Beito, George Anthony
Bekkum, Owen D
Belcher, Michael Jay
Beldavs, Jazeps Teodor
Belder, Edna Mae
Belew, David Lee
Belfour, Albert J.
Belian, Garabed
Beling, Earl Henry
Beljan, John Richard
Belk, Fred Richard
Belknap, Elmer Clinton
Belknap, William Walker, II
Bell, Anthony Michael
Bell, Charles Edward
Bell, Charles Eugene, Jr.
Bell, Charles Norman
Bell, Charles Robert, Jr.
Bell, Charles Thomas
Bell, David Arthur
Bell, Earl Pendleton, Jr.
Bell, G(eorge) Wilbur
Bell, Glen Hugh
Bell, Harry Michael
Bell, John Louis
Bell, John Richard
Bell, John Stanley
Bell, Johnston Barber
Bell, Nicholas Montgomery, II
Bell, Robert Gene
Bell, Robert Mark
Bell, Samuel Alvin
Bell, Scott Allen
Bell, William Fletcher
Bell, Wilson Townsend
Bella, Dantina Carmen Quartaroli
Belles, Frank Edward
Belli, Elmer Fred
Bellinger, Amy Lou
Bellis, Warren Tarleton
Bellow, Saul
Bellows, Glen Lee
Bellville, Thomas Stanley
Belmonte, John Virgil
Belote, Donald Allen
Belsare, Jayant Vishnu
Belshan, Milo Leo
Belt, Forest H.
Belter, Robert Frank
Beltz, Charles Robert
Belzer, Jeffrey A.
Belzile, Joseph Daniel
Bemis, Edwin Lewis
Bemmann, Kathryn Marie Chizek
Bendel, Ruth Thompson (Mrs. Victor D. Bendel)
Bendel, William Louis, Jr.
Bender, John Henry, Jr. (Jack)
Bender, Paul L.
Bendorf, Ronald Lee
Benduhn, James Richard
Benedict, John Anthony
Beneke, Mildred (Millie) Stong (Mrs. Arnold W. Beneke)
Benes, Charles James
Bengtson, Lawrence Oscar
Beninson, Joseph
Benjamen, Lysle Irving
Benjamin, Adam, Jr.
Benjamin, Harrison Russell
Benjamin, Ivy
Benjamin, James William
Benjamin, John Howard
Benjamin, Neal B. H.
Benjamin, Philip Palamoottil
Benjamin, Robert Morris
Benkert, Arthur Churchill
Bennett, Charles Lougheed
Bennett, Dorothy Rosemary Kirk (Mrs. Gail Bennett)
Bennett, Esther Vorena
Bennett, Gerald Anthony
Bennett, Hugh Merton
Bennett, Ivan Frank
Bennett, James Paul
Bennett, Jerome Patrick
Bennett, Joyce Mignon
Bennett, Lawrence A.
Bennett, Lerone, Jr.
Bennett, Matthew Cole
Bennett, Milton Chester
Bennett, Olga
Bennett, Paul Allen
Bennett, Richard Charles
Bennett, Richard Livingston
Bennett, Robert Lathrop
Bennett, Robert Thomas
Bennett, Russell Charles
Bennett, W(alter) Burr, Jr.
Bennington, Donald Lee
Bennis, Warren
Bennison, Charles Ellsworth
Bennyhoff, Gary Curtis
Benoit, Robert Eugene
Benson, Clifford Dempster
Benson, Dale Stanley
Benson, Dennis Keith
Benson, Dorothy Ann Durick (Mrs. Robert Bronaugh Benson)
Benson, Earl Lewis
Benson, Franklin Donohue
Benson, James DeWayne
Benson, Joseph
Benson, Larry William (Bill)
Benson, Paul
Benson, Robert Bronaugh
Bentlage, Richard August
Bentley, James Herbert
Bentley, Thomas Horton, III
Benton, Levevian McDaniel
Benton, Robert Dean
Benton, Robert Wilmer
Bentzel, Charles Howard
Berberian, Ralph Harry
Bercaw, Jack Nowen
Berens, John Sylvester
Berens, Lawrence Penington
Berenzweig, Jack Charles
Beretvas, Andrew Francis
Berg, B(enjamin) Robert
Berg, Evelynne Marie
Berg, Gary Allen
Berg, Kenneth Edward
Berg, Kenneth Eric
Berg, Kenneth Paul
Berg, Loy Carleton
Berg, Marie Hirsch (Mrs. Kurt N. Berg)
Berg, Obed Johan
Berg, Roger Joel
Berg, Russell George
Berg, Stanton Oneal
Berg, Warren Glenn
Bergan, Carolyn Widener
Bergan, John
Berge, Earl Orville
Berge, Kenneth George
Bergen, Thomas Joseph
Berger, Alan I.
Berger, Arthur Eser
Berger, Charles James
Berger, Emil Joseph
Berger, John Edward
Berger, Kenneth Walter
Berger, Miles Lee
Berger, Paul Harold
Bergeron, Allen Lloyd
Bergeron, Julien Etienne
Berggren, Karl Francis
Berggren, Ronald Bernard
Berghoefer, Leonard Anton
Berghuis, Melvin Earl
Bergia, Roger Merle
Bergland, Bob Selmer
Bergman, Albert Solomon
Bergman, Robert Scribner
Bergman, Roy Thomas
Bergmann, Winogene Louise
Bergquist, Richard Robert
Bergren, Orville Vernon
Bergsma, Ralph Thomas
Bergsma, Thomas Robert
Bergstein, Stanley Francis
Bergstrom, Richard Norman
Bergwall, Warren Lund
Berhow, John Lewis
Berk, Burton Benjamin
Berk, James Edward
Berk, William Leo
Berkbuegler, John William
Berke, Joseph Jerold
Berkebile, Dale Eugene
Berkley, Eliot S.
Berko, Martin Joseph
Berkowitz, Herbert M.
Berlacher, Franz Joseph
Berland, Theodore
Berlin, Raymond
Berman, Herbert Martin
Berman, Reuben
Bernabucci, John Roger, Jr.
Bernard, Burton Charles
Bernardin, Joseph Louis
Bernat, Leo Allen
Bernett, Theodore Byron
Bernhard, John Torben
Bernhardt, Carl Fred
Bernick, Emil Lee
Berns, Charles
Berns, Henry Donald
Bernstein, Arthur
Bernstein, Benjamin Tobias
Bernstein, Charles Bernard
Bernstein, Malcolm Albert
Bernstein, Sheldon
Berntson, Stanley Marshall
Berounsky, Joseph Frank
Berreau, Alfred James
Berrey, Robert Wilson, III
Berry, Brewton
Berry, Clyde Marvin
Berry, Don Victor
Berry, Edwin C.
Berry, James William
Berry, Lloyd Eason
Berry, Loren Murphy
Berry, Lucille Marie
Berry, Paul Deshon
Berry, Robert Neil
Berry-Caban, Cristobal Santiago
Berryman, Alice Davis (Mrs. Cecil Wells Berryman)
Berryman, Robert Armine
Bersche, Joseph Edwin
Bertz, Edward Joseph
Besancon, Robert Martin
Beschloss, Morris Richard
Beshears, James Keith
Besore, George Raleigh, Jr.
Best, James Reynolds
Best, Linda Louise Richmer
Best, Robert Ellis
Better, Edward Francis, III
Betterton, Ronald Morton
Bettis, Zack Franklin
Betts, Henry Brognard
Betz, Gary Arlin
Betzer, Joseph George
Beuc, Rudolph, Jr.
Beum, Robert Lawrence
Beuse, Donald Lee
Beutler, Frederick Joseph
Beutner, Grant Charles
Beverley, John Louis, Jr.
Beverly, Eve Marie De Savieu
Beversdorf, Samuel Thomas
Bevirt, Joseph Lloyd
Bexten, Donald Gene
Beyer, Donald James
Beyer, Stephen Lucian
Bezane, Norman Gilbert
Bhakthavathsalan, Amrutha
Bhatia, Shyam S(under)
Bhatt, Ashok Gajanan
Bhattacharya, Amar Nath
Bhattad, Sitaram Manikalal
Bial, Andre Joseph
Bibbo, Marluce
Biber, Jakub Jan
Biberstine, Romanel Ruth
Bickel, Ermalinda
Bickley, John Howard, Jr.
Bickmore, John Tilghman
Bicknell, James Lee
Bicksler, James Lazaroff
Biddinger, John Wesley
Bidwell, Thomas Leroy
Bidwill, William V.
Bieber, Eliza Davis (Mrs. Robert R. Bieber)
Bieberly, Frank Gearhart
Biederman, Charles Joseph
Biederman, Earl Donald
Biederman, Linda Bari
Biehl, Elaine Harner
Bielawski, Walter Leonard
Biester, John Louis
Bieter, Jerome Thomas
Bieti, Frederick George
Bietz, Alan Dee
Bigelow, Wheelock, Jr.
Biggar, Edward Samuel
Biggers, Darlene Fay
Biggert, Elizabeth Colette
Bigham, Darrel Eugene
Bigler, W(illiam) Paul
Bigley, James Philip
Bigley, Thomas Creviston, Jr.
Bihler, Frederick Henry, Jr.
Bihr, Edwin Durrett
Bilandic, Michael A.
Bilbrey, Walter Green, Jr.
Bileydi, Sumer Mehmet
Bilger, Raymond Paul
Billings, Jane Kelly
Billings, Thomas Michael
Billingsley, John Smith
Billmire, Frank Gillam
Bilodeau, Richard Gerard
Bincer, Adam Marian
Bindley, Joe Hoover
Bingham, Robert Semler
Binner, Elmer Arthur
Binney, Paul Austin
Binning, Robert Christie
Binotti, David Allen
Bipes, Roger Luellyen
Birch, John Edward
Bird, Don-Michael
Bird, Harrie Waldo, Jr.
Bird, Milford Gilbert
Bird, Richard Maywood
Birdcell, Gail Elaine
Birenbaum, William M.
Birk, Robert Eugene
Birkeland, Charles John
Birr, Donald James
Bisarya, Arvind Kumar
Bischof, Milton, Jr.
Bish, Milan David
Bishara, Samir Edward

Bishea, Paul Maurice
Bishop, Allen John
Bishop, Dolloff Frederick, Jr.
Bishop, Donald E.
Bishop, Earl Dean
Bishop, Gilbert Clare
Bishop, Jack Lawson, Jr.
Bishop, Joyce Ann Armentrout
Bishop, Lawrence Ray
Bishop, Lester J.
Bishop, Lois Carlson
Bishop, Mars Paul
Bishop, Myron Charles
Bishop, Robert Deane
Bishop, Welker Henry, Jr.
Biskis, Edward George
Biskup, George J(oseph)
Bissell, Robert Kenyon
Bissell, Steven Lewis
Bissell, Walter Henry
Bissey, William Karl
Bitonte, Dominic Anthony
Bittenbender, Richard Chase
Bitting, Phyllis Diane
Bittinger, Eugene Preston
Bitzegaio, Harold James
Bitzes, John George
Bivans, Jack
Biwersi, Gary Lee
Bixby, Don Willard
Bixby, Glenn Allen
Bixby, John Nelson
Bixby, William Herbert
Bjork, Edward M., Jr.
Bjorklund, Richard Carl
Bjornnes, Norman Peter
Bjugstad, Ardell Jerome
Blabolil, Charles Joseph
Black, Anita
Black, Asa Calvin, Jr.
Black, Carl Dean
Black, Charles Edward
Black, Elliott Michael
Black, Ferne May Beebe
Black, Harry George
Black, James Dennis
Black, John Bunyan
Black, Kenneth Wallace
Black, Michael Sherman
Black, Robert Lounsbury, Jr.
Black, Thomas Alexander, Jr.
Black, Thomas Claiborne, Jr.
Black, Walter Kerrigan
Black, Warren Morris
Blackard, Clyde Erhardt
Blackbourn, James William
Blackburn, George Kanada
Blackburn, Henry Webster, Jr.
Blackburn, Marsh Hanly
Blackburn, Richard Shaw
Blackman, Nathaniel, Jr.
Blackman, Robert Chester
Blackwell, Henry Barlow, II
Blagbrough, Elizabeth M. (Mrs. Harry Putnam Blagbrough)
Blain, Alexander, III
Blain, Charlotte Marie
Blain, Donald Gray
Blair, Allan Edward
Blair, Douglas Peter
Blair, Eugene Schlegel
Blair, Joseph Skiles, Jr.
Blair, Marvin Smith
Blair, Mary Agnes
Blair, Terrence Lee
Blaisdell, Fred William
Blake, Frank Burgay
Blake, Martin Irving
Blake, Paul Robert (Bob)
Blake, Thomas Clinton
Blake, Thomas Gaynor
Blakely, Robert Fraser
Blakemore, William Stephen
Blakey, Lillian Luella
Blamey, Richard Lyle
Blanchard, B(irdsall) Everard
Blanchard, James J.
Blanco-Gonzalez, Manuel
Bland, Robert Daniel
Blank, John L.
Blank, Rolf Allan
Blankenbaker, Ronald Gail
Blankenship, Earl, Jr.
Blankenship, Marshall Lee
Blankenship, Rayford T.
Blankenship, Richard Roland
Blasco, Alfred Joseph
Blask, William Robert
Blatt, Morton Bernard
Blatt, Sidney Israel
Blaustein, Howard Yale
Blazer, Sondra Kay Gordon
Blazey, Lawrence Edwin
Blekfeld, Glen Merold
Bleskacek, Gerald Edward
Blessing, Charles Alexander
Blessing, Larry Richard
Bletzacker, Richard Welch
Blevins, William Edward
Blietz, Duane Leslie
Blikre, Clair Talmer
Blincoe, Richard Aloysius
Blinks, John Rogers
Blinn, Robert Danforth
Bliss, Dwight Lewis
Bliss, George William
Bliss, Richard Lawrence
Bliss, Ronald Gene
Blixt, Albert Bernard, Jr.
Blixt, Robert Edmund
Bloch, Henry Wollman
Bloch, Ivan Sol
Block, Jerome Edward
Block, Paul, Jr.
Blodgett, Gary Burl
Blodgett, Geoffrey Thomas
Blodgett, John Wood
Blodgett, Virginia June Ballard (Mrs. Ralph Wesley Blodgett)
Bloemker, Gerald William
Blom, Eric Davis
Blomgren, Donald M.
Blomgren, Holton Eugene
Blomgren, Oscar Clarence, Jr.
Blomquist, Roger Vincent
Blomster, Galen Grant
Blonsky, Eugene Richard
Blood, Robert O.
Bloodgood, Douglas Cotton
Bloom, Barbara Irene
Bloom, Max S.
Bloom, Sam Oliver
Bloom, Stephen Joel
Bloomquist, Arnold Robert
Bloor, Thomas Harold
Blosser, Henry Gabriel
Blotcky, Alan Jay
Blouin, Michael T.
Blount, Wilbur Clanton
Blue, Janet L. Roberts (Mrs. Sherwood Blue)
Bluemle, Paul Edward
Bluestein, Judith Ann
Bluestein, Paul Harold
Bluhm, Maurice Joseph
Blum, Albert Elmer
Blum, Andre
Blum, John Francis
Blum, Richard Carl
Blumberg, Burton Stuart
Blume, Herbert Edward
Blumentals, Edite
Blumenthal, Herman Theodore
Blunt, Stanhope E., Jr.
Blythe, James David, II
Boand, Charles W.
Boatright, David Joel
Boaz, Harold Chamberlain, Jr.
Boberg, John Theodore
Boblak, Frank Joseph
Bobo, Merton Arthur
Bobsin, Roberta Janette
Bobulski, Edward M.
Bock, Allan Clarence
Bock, Leo Louis
Bockelman, J(ohn) Richard
Bockserman, Robert Julian
Bode, Sandra Jean
Boden, Robert Francis
Boden, Worthey Carl
Bodene, Jack Allen
Bodensteiner, Robert Theodore
Boder, Claretta Kelso
Boeck, LaVerne Dwaine
Boecklin, Peg Pitman (Mrs. Roland Boecklin)
Boehlke, William Frederick, Jr.
Boehm, Fritz Rudolph
Boehm, Richard Theodore
Boehme, Werner Richard
Boehmer, Gerald Leo
Boelter, Robert Irvin
Boemi, A. Andrew
Boer, Roger William
Boerger, William George
Boers, Richard William
Boersma, William Carter
Boesch, Henry John, Jr.
Boese, Gilbert Karyle
Boese, Robert Alan
Boese, Virginia Ellen
Boesel, Milton Charles, Jr.
Bogdansky, John
Bogert, John Alden
Bogg, Richard Allan
Boggess, Thomas Phillip, III
Boggs, Gary Patrick
Boggs, Joseph Dodridge
Bogue, Grant
Bohley, Paul Branch
Bohlim, Richard Charles
Bohlmann, Paul Frank
Bohon, Ellis G(ray)
Bohrofen, Eldon La Vern
Boikan, William Sclair
Boilore, Allan Earl
Bolduc, Oliver Joseph
Bolen, Douglas Lynn
Bolen, Waldo Emerson, Jr.
Boles, Hobart Paul
Bolick, David Dean
Bolin, Russell Leroy
Boling, Paul Richard
Bolinger, George Noel
Bolinske, Robert Edward
Boller, John Charles
Bolling, Glenn Loyd
Bolling, Richard (Walker)
Bolsinger, Don Clark
Bolt, Orren Anthony
Bolte, Carl Eugene, Jr.
Bolton, Dan Wilson, III
Bolz, Harold August
Bolz, Harriett (Mrs. Harold A. Bolz)
Bomgardner, Stephen Ralph
Bomzer, Herbert Wallace
Bonacker, Donald Edward
Bonacker, Joyce Sybil
Bond, Christopher Samuel
Bond, Dorothy Ann
Bond, Oriel Edmund
Bond, Richard Jordan
Bonda, Alva Ted
Bondar, Andrew Arthur
Bondoc, Atilano Diaz
Bone, Vida Marie
Bonemeyer, Maurice H.
Boness, Robert William
Bonfield, Genevieve Kriesel
Bongers, Leo Vincent
Bongiorno, John Anthony
Bongiovanni, Charles Anthony
Bonior, David Edward
Bonkalo, Alexander
Bonsall, Harry Walter
Bonstedt, Theodor
Bonus, Harold William
Booe, James Marvin
Book, Imogene Iris Clark (Mrs. Wiltz Alonzo Book)
Book, Kenneth Merten
Boon, Donald Jackson
Boone, Harold Cletus
Boonkham, Chotchai
Boor, Myron Vernon
Boos, Robert Walter
Boosalis, Elsie
Booth, Andrew Donald
Booth, Cameron
Borchak, Robert George
Borchert, Philip
Borden, Glen Lafon
Borenstine, Alvin Jerome
Borg, Larry Arthur
Bork, Kenneth Calvin
Borkholder, Freemon
Borman, Leonard David
Bormes, Robert Edward
Bornemeier, Dwight Daniel
Bornmann, John Arthur
Borsch, Reuben A.
Boruff, John David
Boss, Bertram Joab
Boss, Edward Herman, Jr.
Boss, Richard Dale
Bossert, Edward Francis
Bossert, Edward Oliver
Bosshard, John
Bostic, James Regan
Bostleman, Frederick William
Boston, Leona
Boswell, James Edward
Boswell, Jerry Don
Boswell, Nathalie Spence
Boswell, Robert Bowen
Bosworth, Cyrus Milburn
Bosworth, Douglas LeRoy
Botch, Raymond Paul
Bothfeld, Robert
Bothwell, Wilber Clarence
Botsford, Lloyd Arlen
Bottger, Lorna Conley (Mrs. Richard Edward Bottger)
Boughton, Spencer Dale
Boula, James Albert
Boullion, James Donald
Boulos, Badi Mansour
Boulware, Rolin Travis
Bouma, Donald Herbert
Bousfield, Aldridge Knight
Bouslog, Nye Fulton
Boutros, Azmy
Bouzek, Robert Edward
Bovich, Edward Hugh
Bowden, Joseph Vernal
Bowden, Otis Hearne, II
Bowdle, Frederick Charles
Bowdler, Anthony John
Bowen, Charles H.
Bowen, Glen Lowell
Bowen, Kevin Francis
Bowen, Marcia Ann
Bowen, Otis Ray
Bowen, Richard Lee
Bowen, Stephen Francis, Jr.
Bowen, Stephen Newbury
Bower, Jay Ross
Bowes, Arthur Stutz, Jr.
Bowie, Edward John Walter
Bowling, David Samuel
Bowling, William Glasgow
Bowman, Arnold Paul
Bowman, Douglas Clyde
Bowman, James Dale
Bowman, Mark Douglas
Bowman, Monroe Bengt
Bowman, Philip Loren
Bowman, William Walter, III
Bowne, James DeHart
Boxwell, Lloyd Lee
Boyajian, James Aram
Boyd, Donald Hegland
Boyd, John Addison, Jr.
Boyd, John Harvey, Jr.
Boyd, John Kent
Boyd, Rozelle
Boyd, Willard Lee, Jr.
Boyer, Dwight
Boyer, Frank Henry
Boyer, Jeane Stanley
Boyer, Ralph L.
Boyer, Ray David
Boyer, Selwyn Lewis
Boyke, Bruce Carl
Boykin, Otis Frank
Boykin, William Gene
Boylan, Hunter Reed
Boyle, John Elbridge
Boynton, Vern Melvin
Boysaw, Harold Edward
Boysen, A. J.
Bozorgi, Siavosh
Brachman, Merom
Brackbill, Eugene Arthur
Brackett, Edward Boone, III
Bracy, Arnold Lee
Bradburn, Norman M.
Bradbury, Marion Leslie, Jr.
Brademas, John
Braden, Berwyn Bartow
Braden, Rosetta Aedoter Balko (Mrs. Ralph R. Braden)
Bradford, Glenn Edwin
Bradford, Kimerlee Jay
Bradford, William Stephen
Bradford, William True
Bradley, James Richard
Bradley, Milton Richard
Bradley, Sister Ritamary
Bradley, Warren Quentin
Bradley, William Arthur
Bradley, William Ferdie
Bradshaw, Carl John
Bradshaw, William David
Bradstrum, Roy Elmer, Jr.
Bradt, Acken Gordon
Bradt, Dona Mary
Bradtke, Philip Joseph
Brady, Barbara Rosewater (Mrs. William Webb Brady)
Brady, Edward George
Brady, Harlan John
Brady, James Ferrel, Jr..
Brady, James Niel
Brady, William Arthur
Brady, William Hampton
Brady, William Webb
Brahe, Neil Benton
Brainard, Edith Mae
Braker, William Paul
Braman, Donald William
Bramhall, Robert Richard
Branaghan, Richard Leroy, Sr.
Branahl, Erwin Fred
Branch, Charles Benson
Branch, Marjorie Beatrice
Brand, Milton Irving
Brandabur, James Francis
Brandel, Paul William
Brandel, Valerie Jane
Brander, Merle Edward
Brandes, Annette Therrien
Brandes, Norman Scott
Brandin, Donald Nelson
Brandis, Rolf Werner
Brandt, Lloyd Louis
Brandt, Robert Barry
Brandt, Robert Fred
Brandt, Warren William
Branham, Jerry Junior
Branigin, Robert Mardis
Brann, Edward R(ommel)
Brann, Lester William, Jr.
Brannon, Victor DeWitt
Branovacky, Eugene M.
Branovan, Leo
Bransby, Eric James
Branscomb, Marjorie Berry Stafford (Mrs. Lewis Capers Branscomb, Jr.)
Bransdorfer, Stephen Christie
Bransfield, James Joseph
Branson, Byron Monroe
Brant, Jerold Owen
Brantley, Robert Louis
Branton, Donald Lee
Branz, Kenneth Wesley
Brar, Amarjit Singh
Brashear, William Ronald
Brasted, David Humphrey
Brattain, Wayne Keith
Braude, Adele Covy (Mrs. Jacob M. Braude)
Brauer, Donald George
Brauer, Erich Frederick
Brauer, Linda Annette Lewis
Braun, Robert Alexander
Braun, Robert Clare
Braunschneider, George Edward
Braunwarth, John Bernard
Brautigam, Frank Adolph
Bray, Pierce
Bray, William Gilmer
Breed, Sterling LaRue
Breeden, Rex Earl
Breen, Katherine Anne
Bregstone, Clifford Earl
Breher, William Russell
Brehm, Theodore Louis
Breibach, Thomas Braun
Breihan, Edna Maria Thies (Mrs. Armin Henry Breihan)
Breitmeyer, Rudolf Gustav
Brekken, Philip Michael
Brelsford, William H., II
Breneman, James Chester
Brennan, Constance Louise
Brennan, David Leo
Brennan, Gale Patrick
Brennan, Robert Walter
Brenneman, Ralph Francis
Brenner, Howard Joseph
Brenner, Rosamond Drooker
Brenny, Dennis Harold
Brenton, William Henry
Breslin, John Bernard
Bresnahan, Richard Anthony
Bressler, (Maybelle) Jean
Brett, Richard John
Brewer, Donald Edward
Brewer, George Eugene Francis
Brewer, James Ashley
Brewer, Joseph Everett
Brewer, Maxine Regina Rosenthal (Mrs. George E.F. Brewer)
Brewer, Robert James
Brewer, Ruth Russell (Mrs. John I. Brewer)
Brey, Judith Margrave
Brezill, Thomas Christopher, Jr.
Brick, Sidney J.
Bricker, Dale Eugene
Brickhouse, John B. (Jack)
Brickley, James H.
Brickman, Robert Otto
Bridewell, David Alexander
Bridges, Afton C.
Bridges, Alvin Leroy
Bridges, Charles Henry
Bridges, Charley Day
Bridges, Edward Trent
Bridgwater, Donald Dean
Bridwell, Richard Edsel
Briede, Robert Paul
Briers, James Laurence
Briesacher, Fred Edward, Jr.
Briese, Erwin Elliott
Brigden, Robert Campbell
Briggs, Frank Roy
Briggs, John Lawrence
Briggs, John Mancel, III
Briggs, Paul Warren
Briggs, Robert Alfred
Briggs, Roy Francis
Briggs, William Benajah
Brigham, Edward Morris, III
Brigham, James Remmers
Bright, James Oliver
Brightman, Alan Harry, II
Brill, David Marvin
Brill, Evan Luther
Brillhart, Donald Dwight
Brillhart, Maxine T.
Brindle, Elwood Harold
Bringardner, Thomas Albert
Bringham, William Talbert, Jr.
Bringham, William Talbert, Sr.
Brink, Kenneth Wayne
Brink, Lawrence Ray
Brink, William Rudolph
Brinker, Elaine Isabelle
Brinkley, George Arnold, Jr.
Brinkley, William John
Brinkman, Donald Raymond
Brinkman, Ramon Minor
Brinkmann, Waltraud Augusta Rosalie
Brinkmeyer, Willis Robert
Briscoe, Keith G.
Briskin, Gerald
Brissman, Bernard Gustave
Brister, Frank Rayfield
Bristow, Eugene Kerr
Britt, James Thomas
Britt, Ronald Leroy
Britt, Ruth Evangeline Burgin (Mrs. James T. Britt)
Britt, Steuart-Henderson
Brittain, Richard Edward
Britten, William Harry
Britton, Donald Robison
Britton, Richard Harwood
Brixius, Frank Joseph
Brocher, Tobias Heinz
Brock, Thomas Walter
Brock, Thomas Wayne
Brockhaus, Joyce Patricia
Brockopp, Daniel Carl
Brodhead, John
Brodhead, William McNulty
Brodkey, Robert Stanley
Brodley, Joseph Franklin
Brodman, Estelle
Brodrick, Hermon Stephens
Brodsky, Jack David
Broecker, Howard William
Brogan, John Clinton
Brohen, Harry Gene
Brolander, Glen Earl
Bronson, Kenneth
Brooker, Donald Brown
Brookfield, Dutton
Brookman, John F.
Brooks, Caroline Vogel (Mrs. Kenneth Lee Brooks)
Brooks, Clarence Rae
Brooks, Donald
Brooks, Donald Arthur
Brooks, Gladys Sinclair
Brooks, Lynndon Arden
Brooks, Patrick William
Brooks, Rachel Jean
Brooks, Randy Lynn
Broomfield, William S.
Brophy, Gerald Robert
Brophy, James Thomas
Brose, Merle LeVerne
Brost, Eileen Marie
Brothers, Budd Ritter
Brouillette, Donald George
Brouwer, Jerome Joseph
Brown, Alma Rose
Brown, Alva Lee
Brown, Arthur Linwood, II
Brown, Arvill Buell
Brown, Austin Errol
Brown, Baird
Brown, Benjamin David
Brown, Charles Asa
Brown, Charles Henry
Brown, Charles Howard
Brown, Charles Roland
Brown, Clarence J.
Brown, Clarence Joseph
Brown, David Lawrence
Brown, Donald Durand
Brown, Dorothea Nell Williams (Mrs. Ira H. Brown)
Brown, Edward Herriot, Jr.
Brown, Edwin Lewis, Jr.
Brown, Eric Van Dyke, Jr.
Brown, Ernest Ray
Brown, Forrest Harry
Brown, Francis Robert
Brown, Garry Eldridge
Brown, George Edward
Brown, Gerhard Julian
Brown, Herbert Shanklin
Brown, Hubert Leslie
Brown, Joan Lee
Brown, Joan Phillips
Brown, Keith
Brown, Mabel Estle (Mrs. Robert G. Brown)
Brown, Mabel Welton
Brown, Marvin
Brown, Merle J.
Brown, Meyer
Brown, Michael James
Brown, Michael Wayne
Brown, Mrs. Milton
Brown, Milton Douglas
Brown, Monica V.
Brown, Norman Allen
Brown, Norman Stephen
Brown, Oril Irene
Brown, Patricia Lynn
Brown, Rae Haefel (Mrs. John Anthony Brown)
Brown, Richard Osborne
Brown, Richard Peabody
Brown, Robert Baxter, Jr.
Brown, Robert Ordway
Brown, Roger Truman
Brown, Scott Robert, Jr.
Brown, Seymour
Brown, Seymour R.
Brown, Spencer Dean
Brown, Spencer Hunter
Brown, Stella Chaney
Brown, Terry Kennedy
Brown, Thomas Acres
Brown, Thomas Cartwright
Brown, Vernal Carrol
Brown, Wayne Lawrence
Brown, Wesley Ernest
Brown, William Darrel
Brown, William Everett
Brown, William Joseph
Brown, William Lacy
Brown, William Terrence
Brown, Willis Winston
Browne, Aldis Jerome, Jr.
Browne, Jane Cotton
Browne, Philip John
Brownell, Frederick Gwyn
Browning, D. Dean
Broyhill, Roy Franklin
Brubaker, Leonard Hathaway
Brubaker, Richard Fretwell
Bruck, John Albert
Bruckner, Clarence August
Brueggemann, Walter George
Bruening, William Paul
Brueschke, Erich Edward
Brueske, Frank(lin) Harold
Brugler, Richard Kenneth
Bruins, Elton John
Brulc, Dennis Joseph
Brull, Hans Frank
Brumback, David LaDoyt
Brundt, Ole
Brunelle, Thomas Eugene
Bruner, Edward M.
Bruner, Philip Lane
Bruner, Wally
Brunette, Bruce Jonathan
Bruning, John Clayton, Jr.
Brunner, Jules Terrence
Brunow, Edwin Edward
Bruns, Billy Lee
Brunton, Delbert Brammell
Brush, Brock Edwin
Brush, Richard Walter
Bruske, George William
Bryan, A(lonzo) J(ay)
Bryan, Arthur Eldridge, Jr.
Bryan, Henry C(lark), Jr.
Bryan, Leslie A(ulls)
Bryan, Martin
Bryan, Monk
Bryan, William Alonzo
Bryant, Antusa Santos
Bryant, Donald Loyd, Jr.
Bryant, Terry Lynn
Bryant, Wade
Brydges, Louis Worthington
Bryer, Harry Morton
Brzezinski, Edwin Bronislaw
Brzezinski, Ignatius Frank
Bubin, Thomas Frank
Buccino, Ray Joseph
Buchan, Robert Wesley
Buchanan, Gerald Snyder
Buchanan, Robert Alexander
Bucher, Henry Hale, Jr.
Buchman, Marshall Harding
Buchman, Randall Loren
Buchsieb, Walter Charles
Buck, Bernestine Bradford
Buck, Robert Anthony
Buck, Robert Maley
Buckellew, William Franklin
Buckingham, Richard Albert
Buckingham, William Brice
Buckingham, William Thomas
Buckley, Chester Francis
Buckley, Herman G.
Buckley, Robert Michael
Buckman, Charles Edward, Jr.
Buckman, Clarence Bennett
Buckman, Jeffrey
Bucknell, Donald Howard
Bucur, Nicholas Anthony, III
Budetti, Joseph Anthony
Budny, John Arnold
Budrean, George Virgil
Budrys, Stanley
Budzak, Kathryn Sue (Mrs. Arthur Budzak)
Buehl, Isabelle Ann
Buehner, Donald Francis
Buell, Richard Herman
Buer, Howard Henry
Buerk, Hans Guenther
Buerki, Lynn Herman
Buerkle, Joseph Terry
Buerling, Siegfried Friedel

Bueschel, Richard Martin
Buess, Charles Merlyn
Buesser, Anthony Carpenter
Buethe, Frank Alan
Buffardi, Louis Joseph
Buffington, Richard Dean
Buhrow, William Lloyd
Buist, Richard James
Bulen, L. Keith
Bulgrin, Walter William
Bulkeley, Peter Zane
Bulkley, Betty Lou Compton (Mrs. Roy Lyman Bulkley)
Bull, Lawrence Myles
Bull, Sheelagh Graham
Bullard, Thomas Robert
Bullard, Wade Arthur, Jr.
Buller, Wesley Dale
Bullis, Harold Owen
Bulloch, James
Bullock, Joseph Daniel
Bultema, John Henry
Bulthuis, James Howard
Bumgardner, Beverly Maraney
Bump, Milo Shannon
Bump, Wilbur Neil
Bumpus, F(rancis) Merlin
Bunge, Robert Pierce
Bunger, Darwin Lee
Bunn, Stuart Eastham
Bunte, Frederick Joseph
Bunting, Thomas George
Buoy, Harold Joseph
Burack, Samuel
Burbridge, G(eorge) Winston
Burbridge, Roger James
Burch, John Ellis
Burchard, Max Norman
Burchfield, John Clarence
Burchinal, Albert William
Burckel, Nicholas Clare
Burd, Leo Paul
Burden, Earl, Jr.
Burdick, Bruce Meredith
Burdick, Quentin Northrop
Burdon, William Fontaine
Buresh, Ernest Joseph
Burg, Lawrence Edward
Burg, Maclyn Philip
Burger, George Vanderkarr
Burger, Henry G.
Burger, Richard Allen
Burgert, Alfred Leland
Burgert, Eran Omer, Jr.
Burgess, Harold Dempster
Burgess, Herbert Earl, Jr.
Burgette, James Milton
Burgfechtel, Robert Francis
Burgher, Louis William
Burgin, Leonard A.
Burk, Keith Eugene
Burk, Norman
Burk, William Charles
Burkart, Arnold Emil
Burke, Betsey Jane
Burke, Eldon Ray
Burke, Emmett Charles
Burke, Erwin Frederick
Burke, J(ohn) Bruce
Burke, Margaret Rose Hoglund
Burke, Marianne
Burke, Michael Austin
Burke, Paul Stanley, Jr.
Burke, Robert Don
Burke, Robert Hartley
Burke, Thomas Stephen
Burkemper, James Joseph
Burket, Gail Brook
Burkey, Lee Melville
Burkhalter, Lambert Charles
Burlison, Bill D.
Burman, Marshall Lyle
Burman, Sheldon Oscar
Burmeister, Florence Estelle
Burner, David Milton, Jr.
Burnett, Donald Ewing
Burnett, Frances (Mrs. Hinton J. Baker)
Burnett, James Paul, Jr.
Burnett, Jean Bullard (Mrs. James R. Burnett)
Burnett, Joseph Geddes
Burnett, Marie Miranti
Burnett, Patricia Hill
Burns, Betty Jane
Burns, C(harles) Patrick
Burns, David Franklin
Burns, John Tolman
Burns, Michael John
Burns, Michael Paul
Burns, Neal Murray
Burns, Richard Don
Burns, Richard Howard
Burns, Richard Price
Burns, Robert LeRoy
Burns, Russell Eugene
Burns, William Joseph
Burns, William Oliver
Burnside, Bradley Allen
Burnside, Ronald Lee
Burnstein, Harold Robert
Burritt, John Kerns
Burt, Jasper Nathaniel
Burt, John Harris
Burt, Michael Patrick
Burt, Warren Thomas, Jr.
Burtchaell, James Tunstead
Burton, Charles Victor
Burton, Daniel Frederick
Burton, George Tremble, Jr.
Burton, James Arthur
Burton, Mary Joan (Mrs. Robert E. Burton)
Burton, Ralph Ashby
Burton, Walter Ervin
Burtschi, Josephine Frances
Burtschi, Mary Pauline
Burwell, Stanley Woodruff
Burzynski, Peter Raymond
Busboom, Dean Ray
Busch, Merrill Joseph
Busch, Theodore Norman
Buschbach, Thomas Charles
Busen, Karl Max
Bush, Alexander Theophile
Bush, Bonnie Beth
Bush, Gordon Kenner, Jr.
Bush, Harold
Bush, Martin Harry
Bush, William Shirley
Bushelman, Theodore Joseph
Buss, Daniel Frank
Bussabarger, Robert Franklin
Bussard, Lawrence A.
Busse, Robert William, Jr.
Busta, Milan G.
Bustow, Sheldon Marc
Butin, James Walker
Butler, Benjamin Edward
Butler, Brooks Allen
Butler, Geraldine Heiskell (Gerri)
Butler, James Thomas
Butler, Kenneth B.
Butler, Noble Lynch
Butler, Wilford Arthur, Jr.
Butson, Wallace James
Butt, Stanley John
Buttrey, Donald Wayne
Butts, Arden Eldridge
Butts, Stanley Vernon
Butynski, William
Buxton, Luella Skilbred (Mrs. William C. Buxton)
Buzza, Edward John
Buzzotta, Victor Ralph
Byars, George Glen
Bye, Bruce Willis
Byer, Stephen Barry
Byerly, Dale LeRoy
Byers, Raymond Howard
Byington, Richard Price
Byrd, Morris Phillip
Byrne, David Franklin
Byrne, Donn Erwin
Byrne, Frances Edie
Byrne, James Joseph
Byrne, Joseph Cyril
Byrne, Michael Joseph
Byron, Barry Michael
Byron, William Devereux
Byrum, John Catron
Cable, Robert Doyle, Jr.
Cable, Stephen James
Cabot, Joseph
Cabrera, Donato Martin, Jr.
Caccamo, Leonard Paul
Caceres, Douglas
Cacioppo, Anthony Joseph
Cadieux, Eugene Rogers
Cadieux, Leontine Keane (Mrs. Eugene R. Cadieux)
Cadle, John Joseph
Cadman, Wilson Kennedy
Cadmus, Martin Charles
Cadmus, Robert Randall
Cadwallader, Thomas Christy
Cady, Elwyn Loomis, Jr.
Caffarelli, Robert Nicholas
Cafiero, Eugene Anthony
Cahill, Charles Adams, III
Cahill, Edward Thomas
Cahill, James Edward
Cahill, Lawrence Patrick
Cahill, Mary Fran
Cahoy, Roger Paul
Cain, Marvin James
Cain, Warren Eugene
Cain, William Allen
Cairns, Dennis Abbey
Cairns, Elton James
Calabria, Alfred David
Calandra, Carl Wayne
Calandra, Joseph Carl
Calbert, Jerald David
Caldarelli, David Donald
Caldeira, Joseph Leonard
Calderwood, Robert Geddes
Calderwood, William Arthur
Caldwell, Alan Claypool
Caldwell, A(rchie) Lee
Caldwell, F(rancis) Earl
Caldwell, Jack Landis
Caldwell, James Hudson
Caldwell, James Marshall
Caldwell, Kenneth Simms
Caldwell, Robert Harlan
Caldwell, William Ignatius, Jr.
Caldwell, William Lyman
Calendine, Richard Harley
Calhoun, Hazel Randolph
Calhoun, Raymond Joseph
Calhoun, William Kenneth, II
Calian, Carnegie Samuel
Calim, Frederick Thomas
Caliri, Joseph Louis
Calisoff, Charles Ira
Calkins, Myron Donald
Calkins, Richard M.
Call, Clifford Woodrow
Callahan, Clarence Henry
Callahan, Douglas James
Callahan, Gilbert Ray
Callahan, Harry Leslie
Callahan, John Conrad
Callahan, Kenneth Robert
Callis, Clayton Fowler
Callis, Lance
Calloway, Nathaniel Oglesby
Calton, Melvin Lyle
Calvert, James William
Calvin, Robert Morrell
Camardo, Victor Joseph
Cameron, Anson Wheaton
Cameron, Roy Eugene
Cameron, William Jourden
Camma, Philip
Camp, Harold Emerson
Camp, Herbert Lee
Camp, Lucille E.
Campbell, Adriel Downey
Campbell, Alastair MacIntosh
Campbell, Bruce Alexander
Campbell, Calvin Arthur, Jr.
Campbell, Charles George
Campbell, Charles Houston
Campbell, Colin
Campbell, Craig Bartlett
Campbell, Daniel Currie, Jr.
Campbell, D'Ann Mae
Campbell, Don Preston
Campbell, Gary Lee
Campbell, Helen Woerner (Mrs. Thomas B. Campbell)
Campbell, J. Chandler
Campbell, John Lawther
Campbell, John Roy
Campbell, Jules Desloge
Campbell, Lyle Paul
Campbell, M. Anne
Campbell, Malcolm David
Campbell, Mildred Florence
Campbell, Richard Avander
Campbell, Rolf Corydon
Campbell, Ronald
Campbell, Terence Warren
Campbell, Thomas Clark
Campbell, Thomas Harold
Campbell, William J.
Campbell, William Stewart
Campion, Michael Andrew
Camplin, Forrest Ralph
Candelaresi, Thomas Alexander
Candler, James Nall, Jr.
Canfield, Carl Rex, Jr.
Cangi, Ellen Corwin
Canisia, Sister Mary
Cannady, Edward Wyatt, Jr.
Cannatti, Dominic Sam
Cannon, Charles Bernard
Cannon, Howard Suckling
Cannon, Nancy Louise
Cannon, Richard David
Cannon, Zane William
Canter, Arthur
Canton, Irving Donald
Cantoni, Louis Joseph
Cantoni, Lucile Eudora Moses (Mrs. Louis J. Cantoni)
Cantwell, Louis Yager
Capatina, Liviu Irimie
Capen, Robert Bernard
Capes, Robert Malcolm, Sr.
Caplis, Michael Edward
Capo, Oscar Agustin
Cappone, Margaret Kathleen
Capps, Raymond Haul
Cappucci, Gabriel Gerrard
Caprini, Joseph Anthony
Carberry, John J.
Carbone, Alfonso Robert
Carbone, Hubert Alfred
Cardey, Keith Royal
Cardillo, Jerry E.
Cardin, Paul Buxton
Cardinal, Jeffrey Lynn
Cardinal, Robert J.
Cardo, Philip Thomas
Carey, Carlton Frank
Carey, Edward Marshel, Jr.
Carey, Frederick Arthur
Carey, George Lee
Carey, Gerald Eugene
Carhart, James Milton
Carich, Pete Adam
Carl, Earl George
Carl, John Chris
Carland, Michael
Carley, David Wilcox
Carlile, Robert Leslie
Carlin, Edward Augustine
Carlisle, William Donald
Carlock, John Robert
Carlon, Patricia Albina Honsa (Mrs. John Allan Carlon)
Carlson, Allan Eugene
Carlson, Andrew Raymond
Carlson, Arthur, Jr.
Carlson, David Martin
Carlson, Edward Elmer
Carlson, Eric Dungan
Carlson, Jon Gordon
Carlson, Jon Olaf
Carlson, Keith Vincent
Carlson, Kenneth William
Carlson, Leighton Edward
Carlson, Martin Evald
Carlson, Richard George
Carlson, Richard Walter
Carlson, Robert Gerald
Carlson, Roland David
Carlson, Ronald Lee
Carlyon, Don J.
Carmel, Richard Jay
Carmi, Shlomo
Carmichael, Charles Wesley
Carmichael, Eleanor Johnson (Mrs. Charles Wesley Carmichael)
Carmichael, Ralph Harry
Carmony, Marvin Dale
Carnahan, John Anderson
Carnahan, Robert Edward
Carner, William John
Carnes, Giles Derwood
Carney, Charles J.
Carney, John Phillip
Carnick, Craig Evans
Carns, William Hulbert
Caron, E(dgar) Louis, Jr.
Carozza, Davy Angelo
Carpenter, James Osmer
Carpenter, John Dennis
Carpenter, Russell Phelps
Carpenter, Will Dockery
Carpenter, William Warren
Carr, Bob
Carr, Donald Stevens
Carr, Gene Emmett
Carr, Harold Noflet
Carr, James Charles
Carr, James Edward, Jr.
Carr, John Joseph
Carr, Joseph Patrick
Carr, Leon Clement
Carr, Ralph William
Carr, Robert Allen
Carr, William Clifford
Carraher, Charles Jacob, Jr.
Carrier, Wilfred Peter
Carrington, Frank Gamble, Jr.
Carritte, John Primrose, Jr.
Carroll, Carmal Edward
Carroll, Frank Edwin
Carroll, Valeree Sue
Carron, Malcolm
Carroon, Robert Girard
Carrow, Leon Albert
Carruthers, Mary McNeil
Carsello, Carmen Joseph
Carson, Harold Ruhl
Carson, Raymond Dow
Carson, Sandra Marie
Carter, Anna Curry (Mrs. E. Kemper Carter)
Carter, Burdellis LaVerne
Carter, Charles Benjamin
Carter, Christie Heistand
Carter, Earl Thomas
Carter, Everett Barton
Carter, George Edward
Carter, George Edward
Carter, Jack Franklin
Carter, Jerry Ralph
Carter, John Samuel
Carter, Leon Arthur
Carter, Sidney Evans
Carter, Thomas Lee
Cartwright, Charles Bert
Caruso, Saverio
Caruthers, William Clark
Carver, Charlotte Mahr
Carver, Gerford Chester
Carver, Richard Gleason
Cary, Howard Bradford
Cary, John Milton
Caryer, Jane Hatheway
Case, Arthur B.
Case, Harry Edgar
Caserio, Martin Joseph
Casey, Frederick Joseph, III
Casey, Patrick Michael
Casey, William Jerry, III
Cashmark, Joe Junior
Casjens, David William
Casmey, Howard Birdwell
Caspall, Fredrick Charles
Casper, Dale Edward
Casper, Hubert Alfred
Cassel, Charlene Ann
Cassell, Frank H.
Cassell, Marguerite Ellen Fletcher (Mrs. Frank H. Cassell)
Cassels, Donald Ernest
Cassidy, Dwane Roy
Cassidy, Gerald Joseph
Castaner, David
Castellan, N(orman) John, Jr.
Castetter, Arthur Worrells
Castine, Charles
Castle, Donald Lampert
Castle, Jack Burton, Jr.
Castle, Lon Wayne
Castle, Vernon Charles
Castleberg, Robert Lee
Castleman, Richard LaVern
Castles, William Albert
Castner, Clarence Lloyd
Casto, Charles Everett
Castro, Robert Raymond
Caswell, Robert Leroy
Catanese, Anthony James
Caterine, James Michael
Cates, Joseph Richard
Cathro, David Methven
Cation, Paul Curtis
Catron, David Lee
Catt, Neal Emery
Cattelino, John Anthony
Caudill, George Gray
Caudill, Rodney Chapple Clark
Causa, Alfredo Guillermo
Cavanaugh, Gerald Daniel
Cavanaugh, James Lewis, Jr.
Cavanaugh, John J.
Cavanaugh, Thomas Francis
Cawley, Leo Patrick
Cawood, Albert McLaurin
Cawthorne, Dennis Otto
Caylor, Harold Delos
Caylor, Truman E.
Caywood, Thomas Elias
Ceccato, Aldo
Cecil, Lawrence Keith
Cecil, Stephen Ronald
Cedar, Warren Richard
Cederberg, Elford Albin
Cederquist, Stanley Gustaf
Celebrezze, Anthony J.
Celeste, Richard F.
Cella, Paul
Celms, Theodore
Celusta, George Robert
Centanni, Ronald Paul
Centner, James Leo
Centner, Rosemary Louise
Cerney, James Vincent
Cerney, Mary Ellen
Cervenka, Barbara
Cervon, Lawrence John
Cessna, John Curtis
Chabert, Henri Louis
Chadima, Warren Kay
Chadwick, John Lloyd
Chadwick, Robert Reid, Jr.
Chaffee, James Leonard
Chaffee, James Ralph
Chakiris, Kenneth Milton
Chakraborty, Jyotsna
Chalfant, Clyde
Chalfant, Jan L.
Chalfant, Joseph Shaw
Chalian, Varoujan Asadour
Chalkley, Lewis Merideth
Chalkley, Thomas Henry Ferguson
Challman, Jean Carson (Mrs. Robert Chester Challman)
Chalmers, E(dwin) Laurence, Jr.
Chamberlain, Webb Parks, Jr.
Chamberlin, Lawrence Eugene
Chamberlin, Leslie Joseph
Chambers, David Arthur Prytherch
Chambers, Duwayne Leroy
Chambers, Earl Richard
Chambers, Laurance George
Chambers, Merritt Madison
Chambers, Robert Orville
Chamis, Christos Constantinos
Chamness, William Bethea
Champ, Norman Barnard, Jr.
Champine, George Allen
Champlin, Albert Louis, Jr.
Chams, Albert Nessim
Chan, Ger Au
Chan, Michael Ming-Sui
Chandick, George John
Chandler, Anderson
Chandler, B.J.
Chandler, Charles Dana
Chandler, Scott Stoner
Chandran, Satish Raman
Chaney, Reece
Chaney, Thomas John
Chang, Chae Han Joseph
Chang, Cherng
Chang, Dae Hong
Chang, Jae Chan
Chang, Kian Koong
Chang, Nathan Chong-Tsau
Chang, Peter Hon
Chang, Teh-Kuang
Channer, Frederick Wyndham
Chany, Drew Louis
Chao, Marshall S.
Chapin, Edward Barton
Chapler, Frederick Keith
Chapman, C. Carl
Chapman, Douglas Kenneth
Chapman, Edward Eldred
Chapman, Eugenia Sheldon
Chapman, Gabriel Paul
Chapman, (George) Brainerd (III)
Chapman, George Courtney
Chapman, James Pinkston
Chapman, Loren James
Chapman, Marvin John
Chapman, Morris Broadway
Chapman, Robert Edwin
Chapman, William Francis
Chappelle, Austin Bemis
Charak, Ira
Charewicz, David Michael
Charles, Allan G.
Charles, Andrew Valentine
Charles, Isabel
Charles, Peter Chapoton
Charles, Reid Shaver
Charlier, Roger Henri
Charlton, Clarence Dean
Charlton, Michael John
Charlton, Richard George
Charnicki, Walter Francis
Charpentier, Donald Armand
Chartier, Charles Arden
Chase, Edwin Dubois
Chase, Ernest Arthur
Chase, Fredric Lewis
Chase, Joseph Edward
Chase, Robert Henry
Chase, Robert Merrill
Chasing Hawk, Sharon Marie
Chaszeyka, Michael Andrew
Chathanatt, Mathew Mathai
Chatman, Donald Leveritt
Chattaway, Dwight Nelson
Cheatham, Dennis Harold
Cheatham, Margaret Josephine
Cheatham, Walter Malcolm
Cheatum, Elwyn Dale
Cheever, Gene G.
Cheever, Gordon Dale
Cheever, Raymond Craig
Chekouras, Carl Christopher
Cheloha, Kenneth Leo
Chelseth, Archie Donald
Chen, Ming Chih
Chen, Paul E.
Chen, Peter Fu Ming
Chen, Simon K.
Chenea, Paul Franklin
Chenery, Frederick Lincoln, III
Cheney, Thomas Ward
Cheng, Aylmer Pao-sheng
Cheng, Frank Hsieh-Fu
Cheng, Franklin Yih
Cheng, Kuang Lu
Cheng, Leslei Yu-Lin
Cheng, Paul Hung-Chiao
Cheng, William Jen-Pu
Chenoweth, Robert Duane
Chepak, Robert Michael
Cherenzia, Bradley James
Cherney, Arthur Bernard
Cherniack, Saul Mark
Chernick, Victor
Chernish, Stanley Michael
Cherry, Joseph
Chertack, Melvin M.
Cheshier, Stephen Robert
Chesley, Stanley Morris
Chess, Robert Hubert
Chesser, Al H.
Chester, Edward Milton
Chesterfield, John Lawrence
Chestnut, Joseph Louis
Cheston, Sharon Hutson
Cheverie, Carroll L., Sr.
Chhabra, Roshan Lal
Chi, Richard See-Yee
Chiang, Huai Chang
Chiaro, A. William
Chiasson, Marshall
Chicoineau, Jacques Charles
Chien, Robert I.
Chilcote, Robert Ralph
Childress, John Savage
Childress, Nancy Ullman
Childs, Gayle Bernard
Childs, George Richard
Childs, Robert Edward
Chilson, Herman Palmer
Ching, James Christopher
Chinn, Kenneth Cameron
Chinn, Robert Carson
Chipain, George Chris
Chipley, John Raymond
Chisholm, Donald Herbert
Chisholm, George Nickolaus
Chisholm, Tague Clement
Chisholm, William Lee
Chism, James Arthur
Chitwood, Julius Richard
Chiu, Lian-Hwang
Chlebicki, George Joseph
Chlup, Joseph Frank
Cho, Andrew Yoonha
Cho, Cheng Tsung
Choban, Mitchell Antone
Chockley, Frederick Wilson, Jr.
Chodera, Timothy Ray
Choe, Sunki
Choi, Chan-Kyoo
Choi, Seung Hoon
Choi, Yung-In
Choitz, John Frank
Chojnowski, Eugene Francis
Chollar, Robert GaNun
Choontanom, Saman
Chope, Henry Roy
Chormann, Richard Frederick
Chos, Louis John, Jr.
Chou, Clifford Chi Fong
Chou, David Hung-En
Chouinard, Edward Francis
Choukas, Nicholas Chris
Chow, Brian Gee-Yin
Choyke, Arthur Davis, Jr.
Choyke, Phyllis May Ford (Mrs. Arthur Davis Choyke, Jr.)
Chrisman, James Edward
Christen, Jack Robert
Christensen, Barlow Forbes
Christensen, Charles
Christensen, Don Edward
Christensen, Donn Douglas
Christensen, Everett M.
Christensen, Harold Lewis
Christensen, Howard Alan
Christensen, J. Gordon
Christensen, Jerry Melvin
Christensen, Julien Martin
Christensen, Marguerite Alice
Christensen, Norman Anton
Christensen, Paul Mandell
Christensen, Robert Wayne
Christensen, Wallace M.
Christenson, Chris
Christgau, Merton Albert
Christian, Edward Kieren
Christian, Joe Clark
Christian, Richard Carlton
Christiansen, Charles Lester
Christiansen, Clarence Herbert
Christiansen, H. Douglas
Christie, Laurie Mary
Christin, Violet Marguerite
Christison, William Henry, III
Christman, Frank Leo
Christman, Philip W.
Christman, Richard Henry
Christner, George Edward, Jr.
Christoffel, Everette Thomas
Christopher, Glenn Aubrey
Christopher, Norman Franklin
Christopherson, Charles Archibald
Christopoulos, Angelos Constantine
Christy, Donald
Christy, John James
Chron, Gustav Nicholas
Chu, Johnson Chin Sheng
Chua, Cheng Lok
Chuck, Kenneth Charles
Chukwu, Ethelbert Nwakuche
Chung, Chai-sik
Chung, Frank Huan-Chen

Chunprapaph, Boonmee
Church, Douglas Denton
Church, Jay Kay
Church, Margaret
Churchill, Colin Walter
Churchill, Donald Walter, Sr.
Churchill, Ruel Vance
Churchman, Carolyn Margaret Haught (Mrs. Ray E. Churchman)
Chute, Robert Donald
Ciambrone, Angelo Anselmo
Ciatteo, Carmen Thomas
Cicala, John Anthony
Cicciarelli, Francis Eugene
Cilke, Robert Henry
Ciocci, Peter Lou
Cioch, Joseph John
Cioffari, Mario Salvatore
Cipolla, Lawrence John
Ciriacy, Edward Walter
Cislak, Peter John
Cisneros, Lee
Cissik, John Henry
Citipitioglu, Ergin
Citrin, Phillip Marshall
Citron, Richard Ira
Clague, Thomas Eugene
Clairmont, William Edward
Clampitt, Richard Roy
Clancy, Daniel Francis
Clancy, William Gerard
Clapp, Chester Dillingham
Clapp, Thomas Reid
Clardy, Jesse V.
Clare, Stewart
Clareson, Thomas Dean
Claridge, Richard T.
Clark, Avril Marie
Clark, Burr, Jr.
Clark, C. Kenneth, Jr.
Clark, Curtis Vaughn
Clark, David Willard
Clark, Dorothy J. Fox (Mrs. Robert I. Clark)
Clark, Ernest Lynn
Clark, George Alexander
Clark, Gerald Eugene
Clark, Gertrude Josephine
Clark, Jack Prow
Clark, James Gordon
Clark, James Richard, Jr.
Clark, John Davis, Jr.
Clark, John William
Clark, Kenneth Raymond
Clark, Larry Dalton
Clark, M.R.
Clark, Martin Elliott
Clark, Mary Romayne Schroeder (Mrs. Donald Arthur Clark)
Clark, Montague Graham, Jr.
Clark, Patsy Sue
Clark, Paul Edward
Clark, Percy, Jr.
Clark, Peter Bruce
Clark, Phillip Theodore
Clark, Richard
Clark, Robert Loy
Clark, Roland Rexford
Clark, Samuel Smith
Clark, Stephen
Clark, Thomas Rolfe
Clark, Walter Hill
Clark, Warren Seeley, Jr.
Clark, William Merle
Clarke, Charles Fenton
Clarke, Charles Patrick
Clarke, Elvira Farenthea Wiermaa (Mrs. William O. Clarke)
Clarke, Irving Vant
Clarke, Oscar Withers
Clarke, Richard Stewart
Clarke, Robert Francis
Clarke, Thomas John
Clarke, Waldo Hallett
Clarke, Wesley Allen
Clary, Jack Ray
Clasen, George Henry
Claudson, William Dolan
Clauer, Calvin Robert
Clausius, Gerhard Paul
Claussen, Donavon Dwayne
Claussen, Verne Everett, Jr.
Clavin, Terry John, Sr.
Clawson, John Addison
Clay, William Lacy
Claybaugh, Glenn Alan
Clayborne, Calvin Coolidge
Clayburg, John Franklin
Clayburgh, Ben James
Claycamp, Henry John
Clayman, Charles B.
Clayton, Charles Bernard
Clayton, William Francis
Cleary, Frank Joseph
Cleary, Michael John
Cleary, Patrick James
Clema, Joe Kotouc
Clemans, Theodore Vaughn
Clemens, Anton Hubert
Clemens, James Rittenhouse
Clemens, Joseph Bernard
Clemens, LeRoy Simon
Clement, Paul Platts, Jr.
Clements, Walter Samuel
Clemons, Samuel Houston
Clendenan, Ray Charles
Clendenen, Howard E.
Clendenin, Robert James
Cleveland, Joseph Cornelius
Cleveland, Wilbur Arthur
Clevenger, Horace Marshall
Clevenger, Robert Vincent
Clevenger, Thomas Russell, Jr.
Clifford, John William
Clifford, Larry William
Clifford, Sylvester
Clifford, Thomas John
Clifton, Donald O.
Clifton, Kelly Hardenbrook
Clikeman, Franklyn Miles
Climer, James Hubert
Cline, Arthur Raymond
Cline, Charles William
Cline, Donald Weller
Cline, Dorothy May Stammerjohn (Mrs. Edward Wilburn Cline)
Cline, James Cleveland
Cline, Jayson Howard
Cline, Wilbur James
Clinefelter, James Walter
Clinton, Frank Lee
Clinton, William Christopher
Clippert, Duane John
Clipson, Addison Hendrickson, Jr.
Cloe, William Ellsworth
Cloke, Thomas Henry
Clopton, Willard Caradine, Jr.
Close, Cameron Michael
Closson, Alfred Burton, Jr.
Clough, John Wendell
Clouse, John Daniel
Clouse, Raymond Edward
Clousson, Jerry Paige
Clugston, Richard Martin
Clum, James Avery
Clyde, Grace Katherine
Clyde, Max Newton
Clymer, Wayne Kenton
Coady, John Martin
Coakley, James Francis
Coan, Warren Ronald
Coates, Glenn Edward
Coates, Glenn Richard
Coats, Norman Murry
Cobb, Charles Ernest
Cobb, Jeanne Lee (Mrs. Elmer MacDonald Cobb)
Coble, Paul Ishler
Cobler, Lois Beulah
Coblitz, Sanford E.
Cochran, Donald Earl
Cochran, Dwight Edwin, II
Cochran, Malcolm Lowell
Cockenbach, Philip Andrew
Cockerham, William Carl
Cockrell, Ronald Spencer
Cocks, Anna Pearl Rhodes (Mrs. Richard E. Cocks)
Cocks, Richard Ernest
Coddington, John LeRoy
Coddington, Thomas Tucker
Coddington, Van Tyle William
Cody, John Cardinal
Coe, Ralph Tracy
Coe, Robert William
Coelho, Richard Joseph
Coen, George Weber
Coffelt, John J.
Coffey, Cecil Raymond
Coffey, John Louis
Coffey, Richard James
Coffin, Robert Parker
Coffman, Floyd Hurst
Coffman, Kenneth Morrow
Coffman, Phillip Hudson
Coffman, William Eugene
Cofman, Philip Nast
Cognata, Donald Jasper
Cohen, Allan Richard
Cohen, Armond Emanuel
Cohen, Avery Samuel
Cohen, Irving
Cohen, Leslie Jay
Cohen, Maxim M.
Cohen, Melvin Samuel
Cohen, Millard Stuart
Cohen, Murray
Cohen, Myron Aaron
Cohen, Paul G(erson)
Cohen, Phillip
Cohen, Roger Lee
Cohill, Donald Frank
Cohn, Lucile Mae Kohn
Cohn, Robert Allen
Cohnberg, Rosellen Elaine (Mrs. John F. Meyers II)
Colakovic, Branko Mita
Colber, Russell Howard
Colbert, Eugene Joseph
Colbert, Marvin Jay
Colby, Joy Hakanson
Colby, Peter James
Colby, Robert Lester
Coldsmith, Donald Charles
Cole, A(nna) Ruth
Cole, Bruce Herman
Cole, Clarence Russell
Cole, David John
Cole, Dick Taylor, Jr.
Cole, Donald Wheeler
Cole, Edyth Luticia
Cole, Eugene Roger
Cole, Thomas Alan
Coleman, Clarence William
Coleman, Dennis John
Coleman, Donald Patrick
Coleman, E. Thomas
Coleman, Harold Kenneth
Coleman, Jean MacMicken
Coleman, John Edward
Coleman, Lester Earl, Jr.
Coleman, Mary Stallings
Coleman, Raymond James
Coleman, Richard Walter
Coleman, Robert Edward
Coleman, Theodore Leslie, Sr.
Coleman, Thomas James
Coleman, William Luther
Coleman, William Sidney
Coles, James Michael
Coles, Richard Warren
Coles, Robert William, Jr.
Coletta, Ralph John
Colgrove, Albert F., III
Collen, Sheldon Orrin
Colley, Raymond Dean
Collier, David C.
Collier, David Swanson
Collier, Helen Vandivort
Collier, William Jewell
Collings, Delores Eloise
Collingsworth, Arthur James
Collins, Albert Vincent
Collins, Arthur F.
Collins, Cardiss
Collins, Charles Walter
Collins, David Raymond
Collins, Denver, Jr.
Collins, Don Cary
Collins, Edward James, Jr.
Collins, Edward Russell
Collins, Ernest Hammond
Collins, Eva Mae Lomerson
Collins, Gary Ross
Collins, Harker
Collins, James Slade, II
Collins, John Sherman
Collins, Leslie Wayne Grant
Collins, Mary Beth Hughes (Mrs. Taber Loree Collins)
Collins, Michael Robin
Collins, Raymond Elston
Collins, Richard Anthony
Collins, Richard John
Collins, Roland Dean
Collins, Walton Robert
Collins, William Thomas
Collinson, John Theodore
Colloton, John William
Colombo, Frederick
Colon, Ronald Warren
Colonder, Fred Edward
Colonese, Joseph Sal
Colson, Donald Lee
Coltman, Bertram William, Jr.
Colton, Frank Benjamin
Colvin, Wayne Scott
Colwell, William Burnett
Coman, Edward John, Jr.
Comaty, Joseph Edward, Jr.
Combrink, David O., Jr.
Combs, Dorothy Jenkins
Combs, Judith Zitelman
Comer, James Michael
Commenator, Ralph William
Compton, James Kelley
Compton, Ted Arthur
Comstock, John William
Conant, Robert Scott
Concannon, Donald Owen
Concannon, Michael Dennis
Condo, Willard John
Condon, Gayle Dean
Condon, Richard Francis
Condon, Robert Edward
Conforti, Michael Dominic, Jr.
Conger, Duane Henry
Conger, Ivan Albert
Congleton, Robert Curtis
Congreve, Willard John
Conklin, Jean D.
Conklin, Richard Louis
Conlee, James Kent
Conley, Fay Oliver
Conley, James Edward
Conlin, James Clyde
Conlon, James Russell, Jr.
Conlon, Jerome Willard
Conlon, Joseph T., Jr.
Conn, Arthur Leonard
Connaughton, Jack Floyd
Connaughton, Peter James
Connell, Roger John
Connellan, Thomas Kennedy, Jr.
Connelly, Brian Robert
Connelly, John Peter
Connelly, Riley William
Connelly, Thomas Joseph
Conner, Donald Gene
Conner, E. David
Conner, John Robert
Conner, Warren J.
Connolly, L. William
Connor, James Richard
Connor, John Thorp, II
Connor, Lawrence Stanton
Connors, Charles William Baldridge
Connors, Dorsey (Mrs. John E. Forbes)
Connors, John Phillip
Conomy, John Paul
Conover, Donald Paul
Conrad, Edward George
Conrad, Jerome Arthur
Conrad, Jesse Lee
Conrad, John Joseph
Conrad, John Robert
Conrad, Larry Allyn
Conrad, Roger Allen
Conrads, Edward Charles
Conrath, Richard Cranmer
Conroy, Robert Joseph
Conroy, Thomas Hyde
Conroyd, W. Daniel (Walter Francis)
Consengco, Dionisio Santos, Jr.
Consolazio, Peter Carmine
Contarsy, George Sultan
Converse, James Leonard
Convery, Neil Patrick
Conway, Donal Faller
Conway, Jack Gordon
Conway, John
Conway, Neil Michael
Conway, Robert Martin
Conyers, John James, Jr.
Coohon, Donald Burns
Cook, Alexander Burns
Cook, David Ray
Cook, Dennis Calvyn
Cook, Jack
Cook, James Arnold
Cook, James Harrison
Cook, John Phillip
Cook, Kenneth John
Cook, Noel Robert
Cook, Robert Wilcox
Cook, Stanton R.
Cook, Thomas Edward
Cook, Vesper Wilkinson (Mrs. Horace D. Cook)
Cook, Wayne Ralph
Cookson, David Upjohn
Cooley, Adelaide Nation
Cooley, Donald Lee
Cooley, Fletcher Earl
Cooley, Richard Eugene
Cooley, William, Jr.
Coolidge, Edgar David, III
Coolidge, Mrs. James H., III
Coolley, Ronald Bruce
Coon, Joseph Walter, Jr.
Cooney, George Augustin
Coons, David Jay
Coons, Eldo Jess
Cooper, Calvin Gordon
Cooper, C(harles) E(dward)
Cooper, Charles Raymond
Cooper, Charles Roscoe, Jr.
Cooper, Clayton Harold
Cooper, Craven Leroy
Cooper, Dennis Roger
Cooper, Duncan Brown, III
Cooper, George Kile
Cooper, George Lester
Cooper, Glenn Clayton, Jr.
Cooper, Harry Preston, Jr.
Cooper, Jerry William
Cooper, John Arnold
Cooper, John William
Cooper, Reginald Rudyard
Cooper, Royal Owen
Cooper, Steven Jon
Cooper, Thomas David
Cooper, Wayne
Cooper, Wylola
Cooperrider, Tom Smith
Coopersmith, Bernard Ira
Coorts, Gerald Duane
Cope, David Howell
Cope, Harold Cary
Copeland, Elaine Johnson
Copeland, William Edgar
Copeland, William James
Copes, Marvin Lee
Coppoc, Gordon Lloyd
Coran, Arnold Gerald
Corbally, John Edward
Corbet, Warren Harding
Corbett, Dennis Dale
Corbett, Jules John
Corbin, Robert McCartney
Corboy, Philip Harnett
Corcoran, James Martin, Jr.
Corcoran, Maurice Fridolin
Corcoran, Thomas Edward
Corcoran, Thomas Joseph
Cordano, Donald LaVerne
Cordonier, Louis Haran
Core, Harry Michael
Corey, Gordon Richard
Corey, Paul A.
Cormaney, Patty Johnson
Cormier, Romae J(oseph)
Corn, Robert Marion
Cornell, Josiah Hart, Jr. (Si)
Cornell, Robert John
Corning, Bly Argle
Corning, Robert Nathan
Cornwell, David Lance
Cornyn, John Eugene
Correll, Howard Leroy
Correll, Robert Jack
Corrigan, Earl James
Corrigan, Hugh Anthony
Corrigan, John Raymond
Corrigan, Samuel Walter
Corry, Robert John
Corson, Rosalie P.
Corson, Thomas Harold
Cortese, Edward Fortunato
Cortese, Thomas Anthony
Corusy, Paul Vincent
Corwin, Bert Clark
Coryell, Franklin Mercer
Cosentino, Michael Anthony
Coskey, Ralph Joseph
Cosman, Ermal Glen
Cossaboom, Ewing Orville
Cossitt, Henry DeLa
Costantini, William Paul
Costello, Harry George
Cote, Denis Andre
Cothren, Robert Mack
Cotter, Patrick David
Cotton, William Philip, Jr.
Cottrell, Grace Griggs
Couch, Albert Edward, III
Coughlin, William Joseph
Coulolias, Spyro Philip
Coulson, Alan James
Coulter, Kenneth Eugene
Coulter, Thomas H(enry)
Couplin, James Ronald
Courteau, Elmer Joseph, Jr.
Courtnage, Lee Edmund
Cousert, Earl Maurice
Cousino, Joe Ann
Cousins, Lloyd William
Cousins, William, Jr.
Coutchie, Sidney Truman
Couts, Charles Raymond
Coutts, Shirley Sue Webb
Coutts, Warren Hall, Jr.
Covan, Burl Lee
Covey, Frank Michael, Jr.
Covey, Robert Otis
Covington, Charles J.
Covington, Constance Joan (Mrs. William C. Dallmann)
Covington, McCormick Royall
Cowan, John Desmond
Cowan, Lawrence
Cowden, James Elias
Cowden, William Dee
Cowles, John, Jr.
Cowles, Warren Harding
Cowlin, Eugene du Pont
Cowlin, John Leadley
Cox, Clarence Albert
Cox, David Jackson
Cox, Earl Edwin
Cox, Forrest Curtis, II
Cox, Hardin Charles
Cox, Harry Seymour
Cox, Henry Hoyt, Jr.
Cox, Lawrence Kossuth, II
Coy, James Richard
Coyer, William Frank
Coyle, Leo Perry
Coyle, William Robert
Coyne, John Martin
Coyne, John Thomas
Coyne, Mary Jeanne
Crabb, Kenneth Willard
Crabb, Robert Joseph
Crabtree, Joe
Craddock, William John
Craden, Michael Dennis
Craft, Pearl Sarah Dieck Serbus
Craig, Forrest Field, Jr.
Craig, George Brownlee, Jr.
Craig, James Lynn
Craig, Robert Bruce
Craig, Robert George
Craig, Rolland Eugene
Craig, William Ellwood
Craighead, Rodkey
Crain, Ada Elizabeth
Crain, Charles Bernard
Craine, John Pares
Crane, Frank Melvin
Crane, John Kail
Crane, Katharine Elizabeth
Crane, Philip Miller
Crates, Frederick Joe
Craven, James Cletus
Cravens, Jere Alan
Crawford, Betty Jean
Crawford, Darnell Allen
Crawford, Dean Ernest
Crawford, Dewey Byers
Crawford, Edwin McNeill
Crawford, Ferris Nathan
Crawford, Frank Parker
Crawford, George Gaver
Crawford, George LeRoy, Jr.
Crawford, H(enry) Gerald
Crawford, James Carroll
Crawford, James Weldon
Crawford, Jean Andre
Crawford, Leslie William
Crawford, Paul Kerrins
Crawford, Raymond Clarke
Crawford, Raymond Maxwell, Jr.
Crawford, Robert Adelbert
Crawford, William Basil, Jr.
Crayton, Billy Gene
Crebs, Donald Eugene
Creden, John Thomas
Creese, Walter Littlefield
Crehore, Charles Aaron
Creigh, Dorothy Weyer
Creigh, Thomas, Jr.
Cress, Joseph Nicholas
Creswell, Dorothy Anne
Creswell, Thomas James
Cretsos, James Mimis
Crilly, Betsy J. Gooder
Crippen, John Kenneth
Crippin, Kent Everett
Crisler, Richard Carleton
Crist, Claude Kenneth
Criswell, Charles Harrison
Critser, Jerry Joseph
Crnkovich, Steven Anthony
Crnokrak, John R.
Croak, Martin Leo
Crocker, Edward D.
Crockett, Richard Calwell
Croft, Anita Belle Brown (Mrs. Thomas L. Croft)
Croft, Arthur Ronald
Croft, Duane Eugene
Croft, Thomas L(uverne)
Croft, Tillie Victoria Swanson (Mrs. Fred Wiley Croft)
Croll, Robert Frederick
Crom, Robert Louis
Crombie, Lance Brian
Cromley, Jon Lowell
Cromwell, Evalyn Tetsu-Sei
Cromwell, Ronald Eugene
Cronenwett, Wilson Robertson
Cronin, Joseph Marr
Crook, Brian Manning
Crosby, Eleanor Rauch (Mrs. Thomas M. Crosby, Jr.)
Crosby, James LeRoy
Crosby, John Richard
Crosby, Kenneth Gerald
Crosby, Thomas Manville, Jr.
Crosby, (Zelma) Jean
Cross, Gilbert Hall
Cross, John Richard
Cross, Sherman Tracy
Crossan, John Robert
Crossley, Richard Price
Crosson, James D.
Crosswhite, Bob H.
Crouch, Franklin Madison
Crouse, Earl Frederick
Crouther, Melvin Sylvester Manson, Jr.
Crow, Glenn Shatford
Crow, Richard Ronald
Crowell, Edward Prince
Crowley, Anne Stahl
Crowley, Jeremiah Aloysius
Crowley, Leonard Vincent
Crown, Henry
Crown, Irving
Crowner, David Wells
Crowson, Walter Collon
Crowther, Harold Francis
Crowther, Robert Hamblett
Cruickshanks, Bryan
Crum, Mark
Crumb, Lawrence Nelson
Crumbaugh, John Howard
Crumley, Richard David
Crummett, Warren B.
Crump, Patricia Anne
Crumpacker, Shepard J., Jr.
Crumpton, Carl F.
Cryer, Eugene Edward
Cubbon, Frank Wallace, Jr.
Cubria, Jose Luis
Cuddy, C. Vicki Forster-Clarke (Mrs. William T. Cuddy)
Cugell, David Wolf
Cuisinier, Francis Xavier
Culbertson, Albert Ludlum
Culbertson, Jack Arthur
Culbertson, Samuel Alexander, II
Cull, Alan Clive Kenyon
Cullen, Frank Joseph
Cullen, William Joseph
Culley, John Britt
Culley, William James
Culligan, John Austin
Culligan, Michael William
Culp, Archie William, Jr.
Culver, Gordon Franklin
Culver, John Chester
Cumberworth, James Emmet
Cummings, Charles Theron
Cummings, Frederick James
Cummings, John Patrick
Cummings, Larry Lee
Cummings, Oliver William
Cummins, George Manning, Jr.
Cunliff, Albert Edward
Cunningham, Bryce Allen
Cunningham, David Rea
Cunningham, Donald Fredrick
Cunningham, Floyd Franklin
Cunningham, James Bernard
Cunningham, John Edward
Cunningham, Marcus Eddy
Cunningham, Marilyn Alice Eneix (Mrs. Marcus E. Cunningham)
Cunningham, Sarah Jane
Cunningham, Vicki Sue
Curlett, Arthur Simison
Curnow, John Wayne
Curran, Con Patrick, III
Curran, Daniel Rooney
Curran, John David
Current, James Revel
Current, Richard Lee
Currie, Lawrence Everett
Currier, Thomas Richard
Currin, Montell, Jr.
Curry, Carlton Eugene
Curry, Ernestine Dixson (Mrs. Grover C. Curry)
Curry, James Christopher
Curry, James Melvin
Curry, Leonard Oney
Curtin, Michael Daniel
Curtis, Alice Ready Partlow (Mrs. John M. Walmsley)
Curtis, Arthur Winberg, III
Curtis, Carl Thomas
Curtis, Gene A.
Curtis, George Warren, Jr.
Curtis, William Knox
Curtler, Hugh Mercer, Jr.
Cusack, John Francis
Cushenbery, Donald Clyde
Custer, Harry Richard
Cuthbert, Thomas William
Cutler, Granville Berry
Cutler, Irving Herbert
Cutler, Kenneth Lance
Cutler, Robert Porter
Cutshaw, John William, Jr.
Cutsinger, John Maris
Cutting, David Mark
Cutts, James Harry
Cynar, Walter Peter
Cyrol, Edmund Alexander
Czaplicki, Roman
Czarnecki, Genevieve Ann
Czerwinski, John Robert
Dabagia, Lee Warren
Dabney, Jack Lee
Dachman, Robert
Dacio, Socorro Lardizabal
Daemmrich, Horst Sigmund
Daeschner, Richard Wilbur
Dagen, Raymond David

Dahl, David Selmer
Dahl, Harry Waldemar
Dahl, Irwin Alphy
Dahl, Ivan Justin Keith
Dahlberg, Carl Julius
Dahljelm, Harvey Douglas
Dahlke, Norbert Arnold
Dahn, Carl James
Dai, David Wei-Yang
Daily, Bruce Edward
Daily, Eugene Joseph
Daisley, Edwin Trayes, Jr.
Dakshinamurthi, Arumugham
Dale, Richard
D'Alexander, William Joseph
Dalgleish, Charles Haulden, Jr.
Dallara, Robert Fred, Jr.
Dallianis, Harry Thomas
Dallianis, Jean Demas
Dallman, William Harold
Dallmann, William Charles
Dallos, Peter John
Dalston, Jeptha William
Dalton, John Henry
Dalton, LeRoy Calvin
Dalton, Raymond Andrew
Dalton, Ruth Margaret
Dalton, Terrence Barney
Dalton, Walter William
Daly, David George
Daly, Eugene Patrick, Jr.
Daly, Joel Thomas
Daly, Maggie (Mrs. Arthur Bazlen)
Daly, Thomas Joseph
Daly, William Gerald
D'Ambrosio, Dominick
D'Amico, Daniel Ignatius
Damman, James J.
Dammann, Robert Donald
Damon, Andrew Christ
D'Amour, William George
Damrau, David James
Dance, James Calvin
Dancer, William Jennings, Jr.
Danek, Terrence Jacob
Danenberg, Emil Charles
Danford, Robert Eugene
Danforth, John Claggett
Danforth, Robert Clarke
Danforth, William Henry
Danhof, Clarence Henry
Daniel, David Logan
Daniel, Donna Mary
Daniel, Jamie L.
Daniel, Lewis Brower
Daniel, Mary Reed (Mrs. William J. Daniel)
Daniel, T. (Tedd Daniel Heagstedt)
Daniels, Charles Anthony
Daniels, James Vincent
Daniels, Rogers Cushing
Daniels, Ronald Lee
Daniels, Stuart Frederick
Danielski, John Julius
Danielson, Charles Irvin
Danielson, Chester Harold
Danielson, Doris Andresen (Mrs. Philip M. Danielson)
Danielson, Philip Michael
Danielson, Ruth Florence
Danilevicius, Zenonas
Danis, Charles Wheaton
Dannewitz, Dean Vincent
Danzy, Richard L.
Dapkus, William Vincent
Dapron, Elmer Joseph, Jr.
Darby, Harry
Darby, Ralph Lewis
Darby, Richard Durham
D'Arcy, Dennis Thomas
D'Arcy, Leo Paul
Dare, Edward David
Dargusch, Carlton Spencer
Darkins, Charles John
Darling, Harold William
Darnley, James Dana
Darr, David Lloyd
Darragh, Barbara Ann
Darragh, Helen Alice
Darst, Marie Roena (Mrs. Harry Walter Darst)
Darter, Michael Isaac
Dary, David Archie
D'Asaro, John Joseph
Dashner, Richard Francis
Das Varma, Ranendra Lal
Daswick, Peter Nicholas
Daubendiek, Gene Russell
Daubenspeck, Robert Donley
Daubert, LeRoy Lincoln
Dauer, James Alan
Daugherty, Charles Hoyl, Jr.
Daul, Roger Raymond
Dault, Raymond Arthur
Daum, Charles August
Daum, Hugh Warner
Daume, Harold Charles, Jr.
Dauw, Dean Charles
Davenport, James Vertie
Davenport, John Brian
Daves, Martha Marise
David, Keith Raymond
David, Paul P(eter)
Davidsohn, Israel
Davidson, Eugene Merle
Davidson, George Morton (Mort)
Davidson, Harlan Lee
Davidson, Harold Eugene
Davidson, Helen Lahman (Mrs. Stephen Powell Davidson)
Davidson, John Kenneth, Sr.
Davidson, Joseph Brian
Davidson, Paul Robert
Davidson, Robert Lippard
Davidson, William
Davidson, William Leslie
Davidson, William M.
Davies, Graham Overby
Davies, James Gerald
Davies, John Arthur
Davies, Robert
Davis, Alvin George
Davis, A(ndrew) Paul
Davis, Ann
Davis, Annetta Carolyn
Davis, Arvin Lee
Davis, Bobby Joe
Davis, Bruce Allen
Davis, Caleb Abner, Jr.
Davis, Cornelia Haven Casey (Mrs. Frank V. Davis)
Davis, Daniel Leifeld
Davis, Erwin Lloyd
Davis, F(rancis) Gordon
Davis, F(rancis) Keith
Davis, Frank Wells, Jr.
Davis, Gary Lee
Davis, Gary Stephen
Davis, Helen Lee (Mrs. John Richelieu Davis)
Davis, Herbert Heyer, Jr.
Davis, Jack Carlson
Davis, James Allan, Jr.
Davis, James Robert
Davis, Jimmie Martin
Davis, John Byron
Davis, John Calvin, Jr.
Davis, Joseph
Davis, Juanita Melba Lawrence
Davis, Kent Del Monce
Davis, Lawrence
Davis, Leland Lowell
Davis, Leorn James
Davis, Lester William, Jr.
Davis, Mary-Agnes Miller (Mrs. Edward Davis)
Davis, Michael Stephen
Davis, Morris
Davis, Owen Robert
Davis, Perry Lawrence
Davis, Peter Anthony
Davis, Phillip Ray
Davis, Reed Ellsworth
Davis, Richard Bradley
Davis, Richard Francis
Davis, Robert Earl
Davis, Robert Louis
Davis, Stuart Alan
Davis, Thomas Jordan
Davis, Victor Jospeh
Davis, Wayne Pitman
Davis, William Ackelson
Davis, William Eugene
Davis, William Francis
Davis, William Walter, Sr.
Davison, Burns Harris, II
Davison, Kenneth Edwin
Davy, Michael Francis
Davy, Philip Sheridan
Dawdy, Harry M.
Dawes, Wayne Lee
Dawson, Theresa Sheahen
Day, Clara Belle Taylor
Day, John Edward
Day, John MacLeish
Day, Marian McDonagh
Day, Sister Mary Agnita Claire
Day, Richard Leroy
Day, Robert George
Day, Roger Forest
Day, Roland Bernard
Day, William Frank, Jr.
Day, Willis Franklin, III
Dayananda, Mysore Ananthamurthy
Daye, George Washington
Dayton, Charles Arthur
Dayton, Robert Jackson
DCamp, Charles Barton
DCamp, Luan Jeanette
Deacon, Gordon Kenneth
Deadrick, Eldon Jay
Deady, Michael Joseph
Deahl, Warren Anthony
Deak, Charles Karol
Deal, Jerry M.
Deal, Leo V.
Dean, Alice Rogers
Dean, Gerald Stanley
Dean, Michael Lewis
Dean, Robert Kelly
Dean, Wanda Elizabeth
Dearden, John Francis
Deardorff, Earl William, Jr.
DeAtley, Gertrude Darling (Mrs. Jule R. DeAtley)
DeAtley, Jack Hinds
Deaton, Charles Ray
DeBates, James Ronald
De Bellis, Anthony Carmine, Sr.
DeBenko, Eugene
Debes, Charles Nelson
De Blaise, Anthony Walter
DeBoer, John H.
De Boer, Ronald Peter
Deboer, Ruth Mae
de Bruin, Jack Peter
De Cabooter, Philip Harold
de Camara, Richard Paul
DeCenso, Donald Daniel
Dechairo, Thomas
Deck, Robert Andrew
Decker, Douglas Richard
Decker, Joseph Charles
Decker, Leonard Llewellyn
Decker, Peter W.
Deckert, James Robert
De Clue, Joseph Anthony
DeCosse, Jerome Joseph
DeCoursey, Charles Joseph, Jr.
DeDeckere, Doris C.
Dederick, Robert Gogan
Dedmon, Robert Ernest
Dedrick, Douglass Alan
Dee, Arthur Emil
Dee, Paul Edward
Deer, E. Dorothy
Deere, Cyril Thomas
Deeter, Allen C.
Deethardt, Dorothy Ella Pike
Deets, Samuel Edwin
Deetz, Robert Leo
Deever, M. Lawrence
Deffenbaugh, Robert Warren
DeForest, Julie Morrow
Defosset, Donald
De Francesco, John Blaze, Jr.
Defrank, Claire Marie
De Frieze, Harold Raymond
Degen, Bernard John, II
De Girolamo, Dale Allen
De Graffenried, Velda Mae Camp (Mrs. Thomas P. De Graffenried)
DeGravelles, William Decatur, Jr.
DeGroot, Don Ferdinand
De Haas, Herman Tony
deHamel, John Belleau, Jr.
DeHart, Wilma Joyce
DeHaven, William Kenneth
Dehnel, Margaret Anne Lewis
Dehnke, Carl Benjamin
Deinard, Amos Spencer
Deinzer, George William
Deitch, Robert David
Deitcher, Joseph
Deitz, Michael Richard
DeJarld, Richard Lee
DeKam, David Kenneth
DeKany, John Peter
DeKock, William Henry
DeKoster, Lucas James
Dekowski, William Anthony
Delaney, John Peter
Delaney, Martin T.
DeLange, John Roger, Jr.
DeLange, Kenneth Allen
Delap, Michael Haven
De Lapp, Albert A.
Delavan, Joseph Milton
De Lay, Thomas Shuter
Del Castillo, Julio Cesar
De Lerno, Manuel Joseph
Delevie, Jacob Bram
Delgado, Charles Benjamin
DelGado, Joseph Ramon
Delhauer, Robert Allan
Delhey, Richard Walter
Deliman, Joseph Ronald
DeLisle, Betty Ann
Dellett, Kenneth Baker
Dellorto, John Arthur
DeLoach, George Robert, Jr.
De Loache, Mary Boylston
DeLong, Dwight Moore
De Long, Lawrence Warren
Delor, Camille Joseph
Delorean, John Zachary
Delph, Thomas Lee
De Luca, Arnold Arthur
De Luca, Joseph
DeLuka, Charles Edward, Jr.
DelValle, Helen Cynthia
Delves, Eugene Lowell
Delzell, Robert Fredric
DeMaagd, Ronald Uecker
DeMann, Michael Marcus
De Mao, Peter Robert
Demaray, Leonard Allen
De Marco, Thomas Joseph
DeMars, Robert Alphonse
Demas, Theodore John
Demello, Frank John
Dement, James W., III
Dement, Kenneth Lee
Demet, Francis Joseph
Demharter, Dorothy Elizabeth Crow
Deming, Charles Robert
Demke, Richard Steven
Demons, Leona Marie
DeMoss, Thurman Millard
DeMott, Robert Warmsley, Jr.
De Moura, Luiz Fernando Perez
Dempsey, Terence Mark
DeMuth, Paul Emmanuel
DenAdel, Raymond Lee
Denbrook, Myron Elwood, Jr.
DeNeen, James Francis
DeNelsky, Garland Y.
Dengler, Harry Oscar, III
Denham, Harry Welton, Jr.
Denhart, Paul Raymond
Den Hartog, John Gilbert
De Ninno, John Louis
Denison, Gene William
Denk, Daniel Bernard
Denlinger, Elmer Louis
Denner, Melvin Walter
Denney, Arthur Hugh
Denning, Bernadine Newsom (Mrs. Blaine Denning)
Dennis, David Stuart
Dennis, Lucille
Dennis, Ralph Emerson, Jr.
Dennison, Kumpol
Denny, Frederick Gail
Denoyer, Arsene J.
Denser, Clarence Hugh, Jr.
Denslow, John Stedman
Denton, John Charles
Denton, Lionel Arthur
Denton, Ray Douglas
Denzer, Harold Fremont, Jr.
DePape, Albert Desire
Depew, Eddie Gerald
Depew, Frank Smith
DePree, Max O.
Deprit, Andre Albert
Derge, David Richard
DeRijk, Waldemar Gerardus
Derjanecz, Janos John
Dermott, Jon Alan
Derner, Carol Ann Niedhammer (Mrs. George B. Derner)
DeRosa, Anthony Salvatore
de Rosset, Armand John
Derr, Gilbert Sims
Derr, Richard Luther
Derry, Charles Dale
Derwinski, Dennis Anthony
Derwinski, Edward Joseph
Derzon, Gordon M.
DeSantis, Anthony
Deschner, Reinhart Phillip
Desenberg, Bill Rae
DeShazor, Ashley Dunn
De Shields, Robert W.
de Silva, Parakrama
Desley, John Whitney
Despres, Paul Francois-Coulliard
De Stasio, Michael Bartholomew
De Stephen, Albert Michael
Desy, Addie Luella Pierce
Detert, David Glascock
Detrich, Arthur Judd
Detrich, William Benton
Detroy, Benjamin Forrest
Dettman, Ronald Robert
Detweiler, John Adam
Deubner, Russell Leigh
Deur, Gordon
Deutsch, Frederick Moran
Deutsch, Owen Charles
deVeber, Leverett LeBaron
Devenow, Chester
Dever, Daniel Eugene
Devereaux, Duane Loren
Devereux, Patrick Richard
Devi, Tripuraneni Anjana
Devine, Samuel Leeper
Deviney, Marvin Lee, Jr.
deVise, Pierre Romaln
deVito, Robert Alexander
Devitt, Edward James
Devitt, James Clement
De Voe, E. David
De Voe, Raymond Minert
De Voto, Donald Edwin
DeVoy, Robert Seward
DeVries, Bernard Jerin
DeVries, Paul Dampman Garrett
DeVries, Robert Keith
Dew, Daniel Ching-Yee
DeWaay, Donald Gene
Dewald, Ernest Leroy
Dewald, Paul Adolph
DeWald, Ronald L.
De Walt, Arthur Ralph
Dewar, Norman Ellison
Dewar, Robert Earl
Dewey, Charles Sherman
Dewey, Rebecca Arnell (Mrs. Charles Sherman Dewey)
Dewire, Norman Edward
DeWitt, Jesse R.
DeWitt, Joan Marie
Dewitt, William Orville
DeWolf, Alidor Joseph
De Wolfe, John Chauncey, III
De Woody, Charles
DeWoskin, Irvin Samuel
DeWyer, Gary Alton
Dexheimer, Wallace Daniel
Dexter, Donald Harvey
Dey, Suhrit Kumar
Deza, Ernest Cabangal
Diamant, Robert
Diamond, Arthur M.
Diamond, Bernard
Diamond, Diana Louise
Diamond, Jess
Diamond, John Leroy
Diara, Schavi Mali
Diaz, Gregorio
Diaz-Perez, Rodrigo
Di Bona, James Richard
Dick, Herman Justus
Dick, John Howard
Dick, Marvin Edgar
Dickenman, Robert Charles
Dickens, Hal George
Dickerson, Betty Emily
Dickerson, Dennis Merle
Dickinson, Darrell Ray
Dickinson, Glen Wood, Jr.
Dickinson, Wayne Alfred
Dickinson, Wayne Gayman
Dicks, Robert Evan
Di Dente, Stanley Paul
Diederichs, Janet Wood
Diehl, Paul Eugene
Diemand, Eugene August
Diener, Betty Jane
Dienhart, Arthur Vincent
Dieringer, Henry William
Dierks, Jack Cameron
Dierksen, Carol Ann
Diesel, William Gardner
Dieter, Raymond Andrew, Jr.
Dietrich, Ernest Ray
Dietrich, Richard Vincent
Dietrich, Suzanne Claire
Dietrich, William Carl
Dietrick, Harry Joseph
Dietz, Albert Arnold Clarence
Dietz, Norbert William
Dietz, Rowland Ernest
Diffendal, Anne Elizabeth Polk
Diggs, Charles C., Jr.
Diggs, Olive Myrl
Dilgard, James LeRoy
Dill, Charles Albert
Dill, Joel Standish
Dill, J(oseph) Anthony
Diller, James Gordon
Diller, Mary Ann
Dilley, James William, Jr.
Dilling, Diana Jean
Dilling, Kirkpatrick Wallwick
Dillon, Delphin Delmas
Dillon, James Richard
Di Martino, David Ross
Dimbiloglu, Mustafa Ekrem
diMenza, Salvatore
Dimick, Russell Allen
Dimmick, William Arthur
Dineen, Robert Joseph
Ding, Gar Dav
Dingell, John David
Dinger, Roland Verneil
Dingfelder, Steven Peter
Dingledine, Eugene W.
Dingwall, Robert John
Dinkel, Joseph Willard
Dinkins, Thomas Allen, III
Dinse, Albert Ernest
Dinwiddie, Faye Love (Mrs. Benjamin F. Dinwiddie)
Dipert, Merlin Harry
Diprizio, Chrisann Schiro
Dirkschneider, Eugene Francis
Diskant, Marion While (Mrs. Andrew Diskant)
Diskerud, Clayton L.
Di Spigno, Guy Joseph
Disteldorf, Donald Nicholas
Dittmann, John Fred
Ditzler, Thomas Frederick
Dively, George Samuel
Divina, Henry Duke
Divney, Herbert Phillips
Dix, Raymond Eugene
Dixon, Alan John
Dixon, Barbara Jane
Dixon, Earl
Dixon, Ernest Thomas, Jr.
Dixon, Frederick William
Dixon, James Jason
Dixon, Kent Darkley
Dixon, Wesley Moon, Jr.
Dizzonne, Michael Frank
Doan, Randall Loren
Doane, David Stephen
Dobbs, Donald Edwin Albert
Dobeck, Rudolf John
Dobin, Norman Benjamin
Dobogai, John Edward, Jr.
Dobrick, Jo-Anne Shaye
Dobrovolny, Jerry Stanley
Dobson, John McCullough
Dockhorn, Robert John
Dockins, Glenn, Jr.
Dockter, James Eugene
Dodd, George Travis
Dodd, James Arthur
Dodderidge, Richard William
Dodds, Harry William
Doderer, Minnette Frerichs (Mrs. Fred H. Doderer)
Dodson, John Robert
Dodson, Oscar Henry
Doemeny, Laurence James
Doench, Thomas Judson
Doermann, Paul Edmund
Doerner, Robert Carl
Doetsch, Gunter Hugo Karl Wilhelm
Doggett, John Nelson, Jr.
Doglio, James Joseph
Doheny, Donald Aloysius
Doherty, John Douglas
Doherty, Richard Paul
Dohlman, Dennis Raye
Dohmen, Frederick Hoeger
Dohrman, Gary Lee
Dohrmann, Russell William
Doisy, Edward Adelbert
Dokken, Stephen Isaac
Dolack, LeRoy Joseph
Dolan, Jay Patrick
Dolan, Lillian Gabel
Dolan, R. Edmund
Dolce, John Leonard
Dold, Helen Shumaker (Mrs. C. Norman Dold)
Dole, Philip Sanford
Dole, Robert J.
Dolezal, Wilbur Francis
Doll, Dixon Raymond
Dolney, Dennis Dean
Dolnick, Norman
Dolnick, Samuel Louis
Dombroski, Alex Anthony
Domek, John Anthony
Dominicak, Robert Harry
Dommermuth, William P.
Dompke, Norbert Frank
Don, Daniel Arthur
Donahue, James J., Jr.
Donahue, Jerome G.
Donald, William Clyde, II
Donaldson, Frank Coombs
Donalson, James Ryan
Donati, Robert Mario
Donegan, George Joseph
Doner, Mary Frances
Donesa, Antonio Braganza
Donihue, David Lee
Donlon, William James
Donnan, Thomasia Batten
Donnell, James C., II
Donnelly, Gordon Charles
Donnelly, John Scriver
Donnelly, Richard Morrill
D'Onofrio, Peter Joseph
Donohue, Carroll John
Donohue, John Robert
Donovan, James
Donovan, James Lawrence
Donovan, John Anthony
Donovan, John Vincent
Donovan, Joseph Patrick
Donovan, Sandra Steranka
Doody, James Raymond
Dooley, Dale Allen
Dooley, Donald John
Dooley, J. Gordon
Dooley, Robert Daniel
Dooley, Thomas Henry
Doolittle, Janet Snook (Mrs. John Russell Doolittle, Sr.)
Doolittle, John Eldon
Doolittle, Richard Irving
Doornbos, Roy, Jr.
Doran, James Golden
Dorathy, Robert G.
Doremus, John
Dorenfest, Sheldon I.
Dorfman, Isaiah S.
Dorgan, Byron Leslie
Dorgan, Robert Thomas
Dorheim, Fredrick Houge
Doria, Helen E. Dann (Mrs. Ramon G. Doria)
Doriwala, Baqarali Ahmadali
Dorland, Douglas Mason
Dorman, James Lee
Dorn, Alva Louis
Dorn, Charles Richard
Dorn, Gary Raymond
Dorn, Herman William
Dorn, Russell Lawrence (Larry)
Dornbrock, William Lee
Dorner, Joseph Lawrence
Doroschak, John Z.
Doroshow, Herbert S.
Dorothy, Lou Ann
Dorrance, William Henry
Dorschel, Querin Peter
Dorsey, Dennis Basil
Dorsey, George Charles
Dorsey, Phyllis Swan
Dorste, Thomas Charles
Dorus, Elizabeth
Dorweiler, Paul Lawrence
Dosemagen, Gilbert James
Dosland, Chester Allen
Dosland, William Buehler
Dossett, Jon Loren
Dost, Raymond Matthew
Dotson, Charles Edward
Dotterer, Lewis Leroy
Doty, Frank Arthur
Doty, James Truman
Doub, Jack Rowland
Doughty, William Howard
Douglas, Bruce Edward
Douglas, Herbert Dwight
Douglas, Leslie A.
Douglas, Paul Louis
Douglass, Jean Hall
Douty, Richard Thomas
Dovel, Thomas Delwin
Doversberger, Richard Arthur
Dow, Alden Ball
Dow, Dean Ashton
Dow, Michael Lloyd
Dowd, Geri Andrea Hacker
Dowd, Thomas Michael
Dowding, Nancy Elsie
Dowell, Michael Brendan
Dowell, Robert Wilson
Dowling, Ruth Naomi Apking
Down, (William) Jack
Downard, William Louis
Downe, Richard Bronson
Downen, Madeline Elizabeth Morgan
Downend, Paul Eugene
Downer, Robert Nelson
Downey, Daniel Robert
Downey, John Wilham
Downing, James Snapp
Downing, Robert Woodling
Downing, Roger Neale
Downs, Richard Faunce
Doyle, Arthur James
Doyle, David Charles
Doyle, Donald Robert
Doyle, Francis Patrick
Doyle, James Edward
Doyle, John Vincent
Doyle, Russell Richard
Doyle, Thomas Edward
Doyle, Thomas Michael
Drabek, Anthony Stephen
Drach, Dudley
Drache, Hiram Max
Draeger, Kenneth Wilfred
Draffen, Gary Thomas
Dragisic, Branislav Mihailo
Dragoo, John Robert
Dragos, Stephen Francis
Draisey, Henrietta Helen
Drake, Donald Anson, II
Drake, Frank Melvin
Drake, Justin Riggs
Drake, Robert Tucker
Drane, Walter Harding
Drannan, Walter Theodore
Drazkowski, Frank Anthony
Drenik, Douglas Jay
Drenner, Don von Ruysdael

Dresner, Samuel Hayim
Drevenstedt, Jean
Drewes, Menke
Drews, Herbert Richard
Drews, Robert Carrel
Drews, Robert Seymour
Dreyfus, Lee Sherman
Dreyfuss, Mark Steven
Drezdzon, William Lawrence
Drichta, Carl E.
Driscoll, Daniel Delano
Driscoll, Glen Robert
Driscoll, Robert Thomas
Driscoll, Thomas Frank
Driskell, Claude Evans
Droegemueller, Arthur Clarence
Dronek, Lawrence Gerard
Drotning, Phillip Thomas
Droubie, George Barakat
Drucker, Daniel Charles
Drukker, Bruce Highstone
Drummy, William Wallace, Jr.
Drumright, Arthur Lee
Drury, James Wilfrid
Drury, John
Drvota, Mojmir
Dubi, Leonard Allen
Dubin, Arthur Detmers
Dublin, Elvie Wilson
Dubois, John Rene, Jr.
Du Bois, Laurence Robert
DuBois, Loren Arthur
DuBois, William, Jr.
Duchesneau, Paul McLean
DuComb, Robert James, Jr.
Dudas, Joseph Edward
Dudek, Bernard Joseph
Dudek, Norman Dean
Dudewicz, Edward John
Dudick, Thomas Michael
Dudley, Durand Stowell
Dudley, Horace Chester
Dudley, John Henry
Dudley, Wilfred George
Duel, Ward Calvin
Duenweg, Louis
Duerre, John Arden
Duesenberg, Richard William
Duesenberg, Robert Henry
Dufaux, Donald Warren
Dufek, Ronald Dwane
Duff, Donald Lee
Duff, Jerome James
Duffett, Nicholas Decker
Duffield, Theodore Aldean
Duffy, Charles William
Duffy, George Christopher, Jr.
Duffy, Philip Anthony
Duffy, William Edward, Jr.
Dugan, Willis Edwin
Duggan, Jerome Timothy
Duke, Bruce Edward
Dukes, Howard Henry
Dukes, John Robert
Dukes, Phillip Earl
Dukewits, Walter Carl
Dull, Paul Phellis
Dull, Wilbur Robbins
Dulude, Donald Owen
Dumas, Robert Hugh
Dumelle, Jacob Domonick
Dumke, Melvin Philip
Dumke, Ray Michael
Dumouchel, Paul
Dunaway, Donald Lee
Dunbar, Robert Alexander
Dunbar, Wanda Kerr (Mrs. Robert A. Dunbar)
Duncan, Donald Ross
Duncan, Nevin James
Duncan, Richard Leonard
Dunea, George
Dunham, Henry Howard
Dunham, John Lee
Dunkelberg, Albert Gibbs
Dunkelberger, Dennis Alan
Dunklau, Rupert Louis
Dunlevy, James Henry
Dunlop, Robert Mitchell
Dunmire, Raymond Veryl
Dunn, Arthur Alexander
Dunn, Arthur Seymour
Dunn, Dorothy Fay
Dunn, Everett Wesley
Dunn, Francis Gill
Dunn, Gilbert Bruce
Dunn, Horton, Jr.
Dunn, Joseph Brannon
Dunn, Lehmann Maynard
Dunn, Lillian Joyce Daniels
Dunn, Lyman
Dunn, Marvin Dale
Dunn, Robert Sigler
Dunn, Warren Harvie
Dunn, William Edward
Dunne, George W.
Dunning, Leslie Leon
Dunphy, Eugene Vincent, Jr.
Dunphy, Ward
Dunsker, Stewart Ben
Dunton, Charles Richard
Dupies, Donald Albert
Dupuis, Wayne Joseph
Du Puy, Elbert Newton
Dupuy, Janice Marie
Duran, Robert Jackson
Durand, Joseph Carroll
Durant, Paul Dillingham, II
Durbrow, Brian Richard
Durel, Thomas James
Duren, Peter Larkin
Duric, Miodrag
Durkin, John S.
Durniak, James Dennis
Durno, John Dregge
Durwood, Maureen Wolkoff
Durzo, Frank John
Dus, Karl Maria
Dusenbury, Ronald Jan
Dush, Joseph Franklin
Dutta, Shivnath
Dutton, James Newton
Duty, Allene Beaumont (Mrs. Spencer Cummer Duty)
Duvall, Charles Steven
Duvall, Cora Lucille
Duxler, Berl (Woody)
Duzy, Albert Frank
Dworkin, Howard Jerry
Dwyer, Martin Charles
Dwyer, W. Michael
Dyck, George
Dye, Calvin Cecil
Dye, Lloyd Arthur, III
Dye, Richard Omar
Dye, Russell Vincent, IV
Dye, Wesley John
Dyer, Byron Wilton
Dyer, Lawrence Matthew
Dyer, Peter Harry
Dyer, Timothy James
Dyer, William Allan, Jr.
Dyer-Bennet, John
Dykema, Herman
Dykes, Angelita del Mundo
Dykes, Archie Reece
Dykhouse, David Jay
Dykhouse, Vance Jacob
Dykman, Harold Albert
Dykstra, Richard Allen
Dzija, John Dennis
Eades, Charles Joseph
Eadie, George Robert
Eadon, Jack Edward
Eagleton, Thomas Francis
Eakin, Thomas Capper
Eakins, Edwin Milton
Earl, David Magarey
Earl, Lewis Harold
Earle, Elinor Southgate
Earley, Arthur Edsel
Early, Bert Hylton
Earlywine, Josephine Lewis (Mrs. Layman J. Wilkinson)
Eash, Orus Orville
Easley, John Hoagland
Easley, Ralph Andrew, Jr.
Easom, Harry August
East, James Henry
East, Thomas D.
Easterday, Alfred Lester
Easterday, Michael Joseph
Eastman, Richard Dell
Eastman, Roger William
Easto, Patrick Clifford
Easton, Gail Raymond
Eatmon, Mary Beth
Eaton, James Woodford
Eaton, Richard Roe
Eaton, William Charles
Ebbert, George Conrad
Ebel, Susan Lewis
Ebereiter, Thomas Charles
Eberhardt, Daniel Hugo
Eberhardt, Lee Eugene
Eberhart, Paul Donald
Eberius, Klaus Otto
Ebersole, Clare Evered
Ebert, George Henry
Ebert, Ian Oleria
Ebert, Roger Joseph
Ebert, Terry Wayne
Eby, Cecil DeGrotte
Eby, Donald Lyman
Eby, Jane M.
Eby, Lawrence Thornton
Ecale, Henry
Echelbarger, Dennis Michael
Echols, Floyd Leslie
Eckberg, Robert Hansen
Eckenroad, John Henry, III
Eckert, Bernard Glenn
Eckert, Harold Proctor
Eckert, John Samuel
Eckert, Ralph John
Eckhardt, Ferdinand
Eckhardt, Henry Theodore
Eckhart, Gerald Geisse
Eckhoff, Harold Eugene
Eckhoff, Norman Dean
Eckloff, Maurine Christine Nelson
Eckrose, Roy Alfred
Eckstein, Franklin Dean
Eckstein, Gregory Thomas
Eddy, Bret Lawrence
Eddy, Raymond Eldon
Edelson, David
Edelstein, Roddey Noel
Edelstein, Warren Stanley
Edens, B(ishop) David
Edgar, Irving I.
Edgar, James Herbert, Jr.
Edgerley, Edward, Jr.
Edgerton, Winfield Dow
Edlund, Roscoe Claudius
Edminster, Ralph Ray
Edmonson, Harold Arthur
Edmunds, Palmer Daniel
Edwalds, Robert Manfred
Edwards, Donald Mervin
Edwards, Eugene O'Brien
Edwards, Homer Floyd, Jr.
Edwards, Howard Milton, Jr.
Edwards, Ian Keith
Edwards, Kenneth Earle
Edwards, Maudest Freeman Gentry
Edwards, Otis Carl, Jr.
Edwards, Richard Pierre
Edwards, Ronald Kenneth
Edwards, Roy Anderson, III
Edwards, Vern Downing
Edwards, Verne E(rvie), Jr.
Edwards, Walter Harrison, Jr.
Edwin, Allan Ira
Edyvean, Richard Whitley
Eells, William Hastings
Egan, Richard Dennis
Eganhouse, Gerald Roger
Egekvist, W. Soren
Egeland, Eugene Carroll
Eger, George William, Jr.
Eggan, Fred R(ussell)
Eggen, J(ohn) Archer
Eggers, Marie Elizabeth
Eggers, William Theodore
Eggert, James Robert
Eggspuehler, Jack Jay
Egnor, Ronald William
Ehlmann, Carlton Melvin
Ehrensaft, Morris
Ehrke, Walter Louis
Ehrlich, Clarence Eugene
Eichacker, George Louis Donald
Eichenberger, William Austin
Eicher, Allison Boyd
Eichhorst, Thomas Edward
Eichner, Eduard
Eifler, Norman Carl
Eigel, Edwin George, Jr.
Eiger, Norman Nathan
Eikleberry, Jane Lee
Eilau, Lembit
Eilbert, Jacquelynn Joy
Eimers, Howard Gordon
Einhorn, Hillel Jason
Einhorn, Jay
Einhorn, Stephen Edward
Eiseman, Paul James
Eisenbeis, Roland
Eisenberg, Russell Adland
Eisendrath, John Louis
Eisendrath, Joseph Louis
Eisenhauer, Donald Lee
Eisenmenger, Michael P.
Eitel, Dean Francis
Eiter, Thomas Patrick
Ekberg, David Jerome
Ekelof, John Dean
Ekiss, John Patton
Ekkebus, Daniel Eloy
Ekleberry, Levi Neal
Ekvall, Bernt
Elam, Charles Henry
Elam, William Ward
Elbert, John Allan
Elchinger, Kenneth Joseph
Elder, Edward Virgil
Elder, Lowell Levon
Elderkin, Cecil Oliver
Eldredge, W. Theodore
Eldridge, Carlton Brady
Eldridge, Mabel Elizabeth
Eldridge, Vera Haworth (Mrs. William Egbert Eldridge)
Eldridge, William Egbert
Elema, Orville James
Eley, Lynn W.
Elfers, Lawrence Anthony
Elia, Anthony Stephen
Elicaño, Rene Venzon
Elieff, Lewis Steven
Elijah, Richard Allen
Eliot, Marvin (Sonny)
Eliot, Robert Salim
Eliseo, Thomas Stephan
Elkins, James Paul
Ellens, Jay Harold
Ellenson, Gerald Martin
Ellenson, Phyllis Storch (Mrs. Gerald M. Ellenson)
Ellery, John Blaise
Elliot, Willard Somers
Elliott, Agnes Barberry (Mrs. Donald B. Elliott)
Elliott, Catherine Pauline
Elliott, Donald Bruce
Elliott, George Horton
Elliott, James Wade
Elliott, John Andrew
Elliott, Robert Alexander
Elliott, Robert Betzel
Elliott, Thomas Albert
Ellis, A(thael) Barry
Ellis, Dwight Benjamin
Ellis, Frances Hankemeier
Ellis, Howard Woodrow
Ellis, Joseph Gilbert
Ellis, Joseph Harvell
Ellis, Lucille Lorraine Laughlin (Mrs. Wallace Iverson Ellis)
Ellis, William Donohue
Ellison, Robert Jay
Elloian, Peter
Ellzey, Elizabeth Ann
Elrod, Richard Jay
Elrod, Robert Grant
Elsasser, Edward Orr
Elsbach, Henry George
Elsea, Richard Staunton
Elson, James Malcolm, Jr.
Elving, Philip Juliber
Elwell, Kenneth Ray
Elwood, David Leque
Ely, Robert Leroy
Ely, Wayne Harrison
Elyn, Mark
Emens, John Richard, II
Emerson, William Wesley
Emhardt, Charles David
Emison, James Wade
Emmerich, James Charles
Emmert, Robert Edward
Emmert-Wadsworth-Whitmore, Alice Elizabeth
Emrich, Richard Earl
Emrick, Donald Day
Emrick, Raymond Terry
Enarson, Harold L.
Enelow, Gertrude Strasberg (Mrs. Benjamin Franklin Enelow)
Enfield, Raymond Lee
Engel, Albert Joseph
Engel, Edgar L.
Engel, Harold Joseph
Engel, Juan Jacobo
Engel, Ronald L.
Engel, Thomas Tobias
Engelberg, Marvin Woolf
Engelhardt, Thomas Alexander
Engelman, William Robert
Engen, Eugene Paul
Engen, Philip Sherman
Enger, Sheldon Martin
Engeran, Whitney John, Jr.
England, Lawrence Russell
England, Walter Bernard
Engle, Albert Lee
Engle, Arthur William
Engle, John David, Jr.
Englehart, Theodore McNutt
Englert, Hamilton Edward
English, John Cammel
English, Milford Thomas
English, Wallace Davis
Englund, Stanley Monroe
Enright, John Francis
Ens, Peter Duerksen
Ensign, Dwight Chester
Ensign, William James
Ensley, Rodney Gene
Ensweiler, Richard Laurence
Ephraim, Donald Morley
Epler, Harold Benjamin
Epp, Eldon Jay
Eppard, Clyde Monroe
Epperson, William Thomas
Epstein, Daniel N.
Epstein, Herbert Marvin
Epstein, Marvin Morris
Epstein, Sherwin Lewis
Epstein, William Henry
Erdman, Earl Gustav
Erickson, Alcott Parnell
Erickson, Elwyn Howard
Erickson, George Everett, Jr.
Erickson, George Olof
Erickson, Karle Joseph
Erickson, Sally Wishek Lovell
Erickson, Scott William
Erickson, W(alter) Bruce
Erickson, Walton
Erickstad, Ralph John
Ericson, Earl Donald
Eriksen, Carl Ahlers
Erlenborn, John Neal
Ernest, David John
Ernst, Ronald LeRoy
Ernsting, Richard Harvey
Erskine, Addine Gradwohl (Mrs. Lucian Erskine)
Ervin, John Bernard
Ervin, Patrick Franklin
Eschbach, Jesse Ernest
Esco, James Howard, Jr.
Esguerra, Anunsacion C.
Eshbaugh, W(illiam) Hardy
Eshleman, (John) Robert
Eskew, William Charles
Esler, Harold Dean
Eslinger, Everett William
Esser, Donald Joseph
Esser, Nicholas M.
Esser, Sylvan Aloysius
Essex, Martin W.
Essex, Wanda Elizabeth
Essig, Richard Norman
Essman, John Fredrick
Estes, Edward Richard, Jr.
Estes, Elliott Marantette
Etchison, Don Lee
Eterovich, Alice Marie Troyan
Eterovich, Anthony William
Ethington, Ivan Claire
Etter, David Pearson
Etter, Howard Lee
Etter, Peter Erich
Euler, Jack Richard
Eusebio, Ernesto Bautista
Eustis, Warren Penhall
Evans, Charles Howard, Jr.
Evans, David Allan
Evans, David Walter
Evans, James David
Evans, James William
Evans, Jerry Joe
Evans, John Albert
Evans, John Clinton, Jr.
Evans, John Lloyd
Evans, Merrill Brown
Evans, Robert Graves
Evans, Robert Lee
Evans, Robert Leonard
Evans, Ted Beatty
Evans, Thomas Arthur
Evans, Thomas Passmore
Evans, William G.
Evarts, George William
Evavold, Dale Edward
Evens, Ronald Gene
Evenson, David A.
Everett, Charles Albert
Everett, Gordon G.
Everett, James Albert
Everett, James Brian
Everhart, David Leslie
Everill, Royal Burdette, Jr.
Evers, Charles Hubert
Evers, Ruth Halla
Evert, Edward Paul, Jr.
Evnen, Everett Arnold
Ewald, Richard Alexander
Ewald, Roger Adolph
Ewell, John Albert, III
Ewert, Quentin Albert
Ewing, Raymond Hood
Ewing, Raymond Peyton
Exon, Charles Stuart
Exon, J(ohn) James
Exum, Herbert Adolph
Eyerman, Thomas Jude
Eyre, Ivan
Ezell, William Alexander
Faatz, Mabel V.
Faber, Eugene James
Faber, Johnna Lynn
Fabian, Leonard William
Fabric, Fred
Fabrycy, Mark Zdzislaw
Faches, William George
Fadness, Peter Andrew
Faestel, David Joel
Fagan, George Edward
Fagan, Richard Dwight
Fagan, Stephen Joseph
Fager, John Frederick
Fagerberg, Roger Richard
Fahr, Robert Ev
Fahrnbruch, Dale Eugene
Fahy, Edward Joseph
Faier, Martin
Failla, Patricia McClement (Mrs. Gioacchino Failla)
Failor, Harlan John
Faiman, Charles
Fair, Joseph James
Fairand, Barry Philip
Fairbanks, Richard Monroe
Fairbanks, Virgil Fox
Fairbanks, Wendell Lee
Fairchild, Robert Charles
Fairchild, Thomas E.
Fairchild, Willis Arnold
Faires, C(arl) Dickson, Jr.
Fairman, William Horace
Fairweather, Owen
Faist, Clara Rose
Fait, Lawrence Edward
Fait, Robert Lawrence
Faithorn, Walter Ernest, Jr.
Faitz, Everett Karl, Jr.
Fajardo, Ben Rondez
Faletti, Richard Joseph
Falk, Lawrence Addness, Jr.
Falk, Marshall Allen
Falk, Victor Sofus, Jr.
Falkenhain, Vernon Edward
Fallah, Abraham
Falley, Margaret Dickson (Mrs. George Frederick Falley)
Fallis, Henry C
Falls, Oswald Benjamin, Jr.
Falstad, William James
Falstein, Lawrence L.
Falvey, James Murray
Fan, Sen
Fandrich, Lloyd Lincoln
Farabaugh, Marlyce Marie
Farber, Lester Joseph
Farber, Milton Lewis, Jr.
Farber, Rudolph Emerson
Fargo, Paul Gennaro
Farha, William Farah
Farhi, Victor Nissim
Farina, Louis P.
Farion, Dmytro
Farkell, George David
Farley, James Thomas
Farley, Lloyd Edward
Farmakis, George Leonard
Farmer, David James
Farmer, Edward Lewis
Farmer, Jim Gueen, III
Farner, Robert Lewis
Farnham, Harry Jud
Farquhar, Robert Nichols
Farrage, James Robert
Farragher, William Edgar
Farran, Don Wilson
Farrar, Frank Leroy
Farrar, Patricia Jean Henley (Mrs. Frank Farrar)
Farrar, Richard Edward
Farrehi, Cyrus
Farrell, Edmund James
Farrell, James Robert
Farrell, Sister Mary Howard
Farrow, Jonelle McLemore (Mrs. Bobby James Farrow)
Farstad, Elmer Karleif
Fary, John G.
Faska, Ernest Odon
Fasnacht, Daniel William
Fasone, Salvatore Anthony
Fast, Daniel B.
Fast, Henry
Fateley, William Gene
Fatzer, Harold R.
Faucett, Mary Katherine
Faulkner, Charles Brixey
Faulkner, Frederick Lewis, Jr.
Faulkner, James William
Faulmann, Roger Ray
Fauri, Fedele Frederick
Fausset, Calvin Basil
Fauver, Stuart Leslie
Favis, Dimitrios Vasilios
Fawcett, Sherwood Luther
Faxon, Jack
Fay, Leonard Edward
Faye, Gerald Eitig
Fayed, Muhammed El-Sawi
Fayyaz, Mahmood Malkana
Fazio, Charles Richard
Feagles, Gerald Franklin
Fearnehough, George Samuel
Fears, Gary R.
Feasel, Fred
Feazell, Robert Ray
Fedder, Norman Joseph
Fedor, George Edward
Feeney, Don Joseph, Jr.
Feeney, Donald Peter
Fegert, Charles Donald
Fehlhaber, Clinton Leroy
Feiereisen, John Henry
Feierman, Steven
Feigert, M. Wesley
Feighny, Robert Eugene
Feiler, Stuart Irwin
Feinberg, Bernard
Feinberg, Sidney S.
Feinberg, Walter
Feingold, Eugene Neil
Feinstein, Manley Burton
Feirich, John Cottrill
Feit, Jerome Anthony
Feit, Michael
Fejer, Paul Haralyi
Felber, Richard James
Felder, Bruce Benjamin
Feldman, Edgar Allan
Feldman, Egal
Feldman, Eugene Pieter Romayn
Feldman, Harris Joseph
Feldman, Harry H.
Feldman, James Dennis
Feldman, Leon
Feldman, Weldon
Feldstein, Charles Robert
Felkner, Myrtle Emilene
Fellows, Joe Frank
Felt, Allen Rudolph
Felt, Michael Gene
Feltes, John
Feltman, Elvin Crane, Jr.
Felton, Martha Harriet
Fenburr, Herbert Lester
Fender, Douglas Howard
Fenelon, William John
Feng, Tse-yun
Fenneberg, Harry Gustave
Fenner, Harwood Huss
Fennesy, Thomas Vincent
Fenstermann, Duane Wellington
Fenton, Jean Giltner
Fenton, Russell Sanberg
Fenton, William Conner
Fenwick, Donald Dean
Fenyes, Imre
Ferguson, Ardale Wesley
Ferguson, Dee Arnold
Ferguson, Francis Eugene
Ferguson, Harry
Ferguson, Hugh Edward
Ferguson, James A.
Ferguson, John Richard
Ferguson, Richard
Ferguson, Richard Oliver
Ferguson, Robert William
Ferkel, Louis Robert
Fernberg, Shirley Carlotta Weissman (Mrs. Louis Proctor Fernberg Jr.)
Fernquist, Cyril L.
Ferrara, Richard John
Ferraro, Eugene
Ferraro, John Ralph
Ferrell, Robert Lee
Ferris, James DeForest
Ferris, Richard J.
Fertis, Demeter George
Fesco, Edward John
Feterl, Leon George
Fetridge, Bonnie Jean Clark (Mrs. William Harrison Fetridge)
Fetridge, William Harrison
Fetrow, Kenneth Ogden
Fetter, Bruce Sigmond
Fetter, Richard Elwood
Fetter, William Allan
Fetzer, John Earl
Feudner, John Lloyd, Jr.
Feuling, Daniel Thomas
Fewell, Bobby Lee
Fey, Cyril Joseph
Fidelman, Selwyn Norman
Fiechter, Ray Allen
Fiedler, Vere Louis
Field, Charlie Kay
Field, Marshall, V
Field, Sister Mary
Fielding, Ivor René
Fields, Arthur David
Fields, Donald Lee
Fields, Theodore
Fietsam, Robert Charles
Fife, William Harold, Jr.
Fightmaster, Walter John
Fike, Roy F., II
Fileccia, Anthony
Fileccia, Anthony Adalgiso
Filing, David Peter
Filkins, James Heasom
Filler, Bernard Myron
Finch, Barbara Lake
Finch, Bernie Orders
Finch, Donald George
Finch, Eugene Clifford
Finch, F. Sinclair
Finch, Joseph Warren
Fincher, Glen Eugene
Findley, James Robert
Findley, Paul
Findorff, John Reeve
Fine, Dwight Lyle
Fine, Robert
Fine, Sidney

Finesmith, Stephen Harris
Finifter, Ada Weintraub (Mrs. Bernard M. Finifter)
Fink, Dennis Lee
Finkel, Warren Edward
Finkelman, Roland Israel
Finlay, Charles William
Finlay, Walter Leonard
Finley, Dale Roy
Finley, Elden DeLoss
Finley, Joseph Robert
Finley, Robert McLaren
Finn, Barbara Jo
Finn, Chester Evans
Finn, Julia Elizabeth
Finneburgh, Morris Lewis
Finnegan, Thomas Joseph
Finney, David Bertric, Jr.
Finney, Joan Marie McInroy
Finstad, Martin M.
Fiondo, John Phillip
Firari, Harvey
Fireoved, Mavaline Ferrier
Firestone, Ralph Wayne
Firestone, Roger Morris
Firnstahl, Kenneth Paul
Fisch, Harrison Cleve
Fisch, Robert Otto
Fischbach, Julius
Fischer, Delbert Lawrence
Fischer, Donald Alexander
Fischer, Donald Edward, Jr.
Fischer, Henry Fred
Fischer, Jeanette Lucille Stockett (Mrs. Richard Allen Fischer)
Fischer, John Wesley
Fischer, Robbins Warren
Fischer, Robert Charles
Fischer, Wayne Louis
Fischer, William Michael
Fischman, Joseph Herman
Fish, David Frederick
Fisher, Barbara Ann
Fisher, Charles Thomas, III
Fisher, Dan L(eon)
Fisher, Davis Lee
Fisher, Harry Noble De Foldessy
Fisher, Herbert Hirsh
Fisher, Lester Emil
Fisher, Marian Sue
Fisher, Milton Leonard
Fisher, Pierre James, Jr.
Fisher, Robert Erwin
Fisher, Roger Koch
Fisher, Stanley Morton
Fishleigh, Clarence Turner
Fishman, Leslie Abraham
Fisk, Robert Clark
Fiske, Guy Wilbur
Fiske, Kenneth Van Dyne
Fitch, Edward Hubbard
Fitch, Frank Wesley
Fitch, Jane Farrell (Mrs. Edward Hubbard Fitch)
Fithian, Floyd
Fitz, Annette Elaine
Fitzgerald, Harold Alvin
Fitzgerald, James Thomas
Fitzgerald, John Moonan
Fitzgerald, John Warner
Fitzgerald, Robert Hannon
Fitz-Gerald, Roger Miller
Fitz Gerald, Thomas Joe
Fitzgerald, William James
Fitzgibbon, William Edward
Fitz Gibbons, James Patrick
Fitzpatrick, John James, III
Fitzpatrick, Thomas Charles
Fitzpatrick, William Allen
Fitzsimmons, William Allen
Fixler, Carl
Fizzell, Robert Bruce
Fladland, Raymond Arthur
Flahiff, George Bernard
Flanagan, Edward Joseph
Flanagan, George Clement
Flanagan, Hugh Joseph
Flanagan, John Kearney
Flanagan, Patrick Michael
Flanagan, Paul King
Flanders, Dwight Prescott
Flarsheim, Alfred
Fleck, Henrietta (Henrietta Fleck Houghton)
Fleener, George Gordon
Fleischaker, Jack
Fleming, Bruce Thomas
Fleming, Lois Freesh (Mrs. Charles W. Fleming)
Fleming, Milo Joseph
Fleming, Robben Wright
Fleming, Rodney R.
Fleming, Thomas Braceland
Fleming, William Joseph
Flemma, Robert John
Flerlage, Raeburn
Fletcher, John Frizell
Fletcher, Ralph
Fletcher, Ronald Robert
Flick, Paul John
Fliegler, Dorothy Scherr (Mrs. Louis A. Fliegler)
Flitcraft, Richard Kirby, II
Flock, Eric Vance
Floerchinger, James Shubert
Floeter, Ernst Werner
Flogge, Albert Joseph
Flomenhoft, Howard Charles
Florestano, Dana Joseph
Floreth, Earl Henry
Flory, Clyde Reuben, Jr.
Floto, William Mathew
Flower, Andrew Arthur
Fluegel, Neal Lalon
Flynn, David LaMer
Flynn, Michael Francis
Flynn, Norman David
Flynn, Robert James
Fobes, Vernon Homer
Focke, Arthur Eldridge
Foell, Wesley Kay
Fogg, Daniel Anthony
Fogo, William Rollin
Fok, Thomas Dso Yun
Foland, Donald Leroy
Folda, Richard Gerald
Foley, Anna Bernice Williams (Mrs. Warren Massey Foley)
Foley, Daniel Emmett
Foley, Edmund Francis
Foley, Edward Minter
Foley, John James
Foley, Kevin Michael
Foley, Philip Seaton
Folkert, Jay Ernest
Folkman, Jerome Daniel
Follett, Mary Vierling
Follis, Thomas Burton
Follmar, Jerome Albert
Foltz, Richard Gerald
Folz, Sylvester Del (Bud)
Fonda, John Reagan
Fonder, Aelred Charles
Fonow, James Thomas
Foote, Joel Lindsley
Footlik, Irving Melvin
Footlik, Robert Barry
Foraker, Robert Allen
Forbes, Fred W.
Forbes, Gordon William
Forbes, Kenneth Albert Faucher
Forbes, Lyman Milton, Jr.
Forbes, Raymond Horace
Force, Ronald Clarence
Ford, Gerald R., Jr.
Ford, Gordon Buell, Jr.
Ford, Henry, II
Ford, Homer Donnolly
Ford, John Battice, III
Ford, John Richard
Ford, Jon Allan
Ford, Lee
Ford, Ruth Van Sickle (Mrs. Albert G. Ford)
Ford, William Clay
Ford, William D.
Ford, William Ellis
Fordonski, Paul Leo
Fordyce, Homer Edmund
Forman, Donald
Formanek, Luella Helen
Fornelli, Joe Pete
Fornshell, Dave Lee
Forshee, F. LaMar
Forsleff, Louise Stewart Peterson
Forster, Kenneth Elwyn
Forsythe, James Lee
Fortin, Clifford Charles
Fortin, Philip Paul
Fortino, Alfred Julio
Fortney, Roger David
Fortunski, Anthony Casmer
Forty, Robert John
Fosnight, Wallace Jay
Foss, Karl Robert
Fossati, Charles Glen
Fossen, Leslie Julian
Foster, Clifton Neal
Foster, Douglas L.
Foster, Edgar Murray
Foster, Edwin Thomas, Jr.
Foster, F. Blanche
Foster, Gerald A.
Foster, James Hadlei
Foster, John Willard
Foster, Louie J.
Foster, Lowell Walter
Fountain, Donald Rex
Fourie, Louis V.
Fournier, Serge Raymond-Jean
Foust, Paul John
Fowler, Donn Norman
Fowler, Lucy Barr (Mrs. Charles Worthington Fowler II)
Fowler, William Edward, Jr.
Fox, Alan Hugo
Fox, Barry Lee
Fox, Byron Lester
Fox, Carol
Fox, Charles Ephraim
Fox, Gerald Edwin
Fox, Henry Ronald
Fox, John Jay, Jr.
Fox, Larry Eugene
Fox, Lawrence Martin
Fox, Lilborn Lowell, Jr.
Fox, Noel Peter
Fox, Paul Fabian
Fox, Peter
Fox, Ronald Bowen
Fox, Ronald Ernest
Fox, Shayle Phillip
Fox, Theodore Albert
Foy, Donald Francis
Foye, Thomas Harold
Frackelton, William Hamilton
Frame, Velma Anita
France, Walter DeWayne, Jr.
Franciosi, Ralph Anthony
Francis, Clara A(vonelle) Hare (Mrs. Richard J. Francis)
Francis, Erle William
Francis, John George
Francis, John Kent
Francis, Joseph Snelson
Francis, Leroy Andrew
Francis, Mary Francis Van Dyke
Francis, William Charles
Franck, Ardath Amond
Francona, Nicholas Torresso, Jr.
Francour, Hugh William
Frank, Charles Edward
Frank, Clinton Edward
Frank, David Scott
Frank, John Ellsworth
Frank, Robert Edwin
Frank, Robert Lee
Frank, Robert Lee
Frank, Rochelle Shirley
Frank, Wilfred Robert, Jr.
Franke, Arnold Gene
Frankel, Penina
Franken, Edmund Anthony, Jr.
Frankle, Allan Henry
Franklin, Benjamin Edward
Franklin, Carthel Floyd
Franklin, Frederick Russell
Franklin, Gregory Coval
Franklin, James Elliott
Franklin, Margaret Lavona Barnum (Mrs. C. Benjamin Franklin)
Franklin, Max Schwab
Franklin-White, Peter
Frankovelgia, Nicholas Richard
Fransway, Robert LeRoi
Frantti, Gordon Earl
Franz, William John
Fraser, Donald MacKay
Fraser, James Earl
Fraser, (William) Dean
Fraze, James Eugene
Frazee, P.C.
Frazer, Richard Symons
Frazier, Chet June
Frazier, Glenn Greve
Frazier, John Howie, Jr.
Frazier, John Hugh, Jr.
Frazier, Robert Gregory
Frazier, Sterling Reginald
Frazier, Thomas Paul
Freckman, Herman Albert
Frederick, George Angelo
Fredericks, Henry Jacob
Fredericks, Marshall Maynard
Fredericks, Ward Arthur
Frederickson, Paul Donald
Fredman, Dorris June
Fredricks, Edgar John
Free, Alfred Henry
Free, Doyle Henderson
Free, Helen Mae
Freebairn, Alonzo George
Freed, Catherine Carol Moore (Mrs. Debow Freed)
Freedman, Arthur Michael
Freedman, Marvin
Freedman, William Joseph
Freel, Steven Kim
Freeman, Barbara Joseph
Freeman, Donald Halsted
Freeman, Flavius Bennett
Freeman, Frederick Roe
Freeman, Harry William
Freeman, John James
Freeman, Lee Allen, Jr.
Freeman, M(ax) James
Freeman, Paul Douglas
Freeman, Raymond Savageau
Freeman, Richard Myron
Freeman, Ross Robert
Freeman, Ruges Richmond, Jr.
Freeman, Sandi
Freeman, Thomas Mason
Freese, Marcus James
Frega, John Victor
Freidman, Stanford Joseph
Freilinger, John Joseph
Freiman, Marshall
Freinkel, Norbert
Freiser, Leonard H.
Frels, Lois Marian Parnell (Mrs. Calvin Edwin Frels)
French, Alfred Willard, III
French, Denney Gerald
French, Ivan Merwyn
French, Marcus Emmett
French, Ray H.
Frenkel, Marvin Allen
Frentz, LeRoy Brand
Frenzel, Bill
Frerking, Robert George
Frey, H. Garrett
Frey, James Leonard
Frey, John Mc Cormick
Frey, Marsha Lee
Freyman, Leonard
Fricke, Gordon Hugh
Fricke, Louis Henry, Jr.
Fricke, Vernon Stanley
Fricker, Donald Edward
Frics, Laszlo Agoston
Fridley, Russell William
Fried, Paul George
Fried, Richard Mayer
Friedberg, Gerald
Friedberg, Maurice
Friedburg, Klaus Martin
Friedenberg, Walter Drew
Friederich, Ray R.
Friedersdorf, Burk
Friedlander, Daniel Simon
Friedlander, Joanne Kohn
Friedman, Byron
Friedman, Charles Marshall
Friedman, Glenn R.
Friedman, Harry Samuel
Friedman, Howard
Friedman, Jerome Jay
Friedman, Martin Burton
Friedman, Miriam Zavelson
Friedman, Naomi Merriam
Friedman, Robert Lloyd
Friedman, Sonya
Friedman, Stanford Joseph
Friedman-Axier, Marjorie
Friedmann, Ira Jerome
Friedrich, Charles William
Friedrichs, Niels Georg
Friehe, Robert Dean
Friend, John Alva, Jr.
Friend, Robert Nathan
Friend, William Joe
Friesenhengst, Alfred Rudolf
Frigerio, Norman Alfred
Frischenmeyer, Edwin F.
Fritsch, James Russell
Fritz, Terrence Lee
Fritze, Edwin Jacob William
Frizzell, Dennis Paul
Frizzell, Robert Wayne
Froehlich, Adele
Froelich, Wolfgang Andreas
Frohmader, Mary Ellin
Frohrib, Darrell Albert
Froistad, Melvin Andreas
From, Melvin Dean
Fromberg, La Verne Charlotte Ray
Frommert, Beverley Jean
Froom, William Peter
Froom, William Watkins
Frost, Ruben Ewing
Fruchtman, Martin Zolle
Fruechtenicht, Barbara Goette
Frueh, Bartley Richard
Fry, David Lloyd-George
Fryda, Clifford George
Frydenlund, Arthur Jorgen
Frye, Harold Frederick
Fryer, Edward Roy
Fuelling, James Louis
Fuhrer, Larry
Fuhrer, Wilhelmine Ellen
Fujishiro, Shiro
Fukushima, Masaya
Fulk, Roscoe Neal
Full, Ray Henry
Fullen, James Robert
Fuller, Benjamin Franklin
Fuller, Don
Fuller, Gilbert Wesley
Fuller, Ivan Richard
Fuller, Perry Lucian
Fuller, Ray Ward
Fuller, Raymond Everett
Fuller, Raymond Harold
Fuller, S. B.
Fuller, Stephen Herbert
Fuller, Terry Alan
Fullerton, Frank Reeves
Fullwood, Nancy Yvonne
Fulton, Gere Burke
Fulton, Paul Roger
Funderburg, William Russell
Funk, Arville Lynn
Funk, Willis Lloyd
Funkhouser, James Claggett
Furcon, John Edward
Furgison, Clifford Fredric
Furlin, James Rodney
Furness, Terrance Daniel
Furney, Paul K.
Furney, Thomas Albert
Furrer, John Rudolf
Furste, Wesley Leonard, II
Furton, Charles Kenneth
Fusaro, Janiece Elaine Barre
Fuson, Donna Belle Carter
Gaasedelen, Newell Orville
Gabbard, Avery Dale
Gabbert, Roy Ellis
Gabel, Duane Robert
Gaber, George Joseph
Gaber, Martin
Gable, Tom Schulte
Gabriel, Arthur Wilfred
Gabriel, Henry Robert
Gackle, Donald C.
Gadd, Herman Preston
Gaddy, Oscar Lee
Gade, Eldon Merle
Gades, Robert Ellard
Gaebler, Robert (Adams)
Gaeng, Paul Ami
Gaenslen, Frederick Gustav
Gaffney, John Leonard
Gage, Donald Paul
Gage, Edwin Cutting, III
Gage, Fred Kelton
Gage, John Cutter
Gagnon, Richard Irwin
Gaier, Gary Bernard
Gaiha, Vishnu Das
Gainer, Caroline Josephine
Gaines, Christopher Clemens
Gaines, Ervin James
Gaines, Henry Peden, Jr.
Gaines, James Frazier
Gainey, Daniel Charles
Gaisano, Joseph Sy
Gaither, John Francis
Gajl-Peczalska, Kazimiera Janina
Galainena, Mariano Luis
Galambos, Robert Henry
Galasinski, Roman Edward
Galbraith, Donald Angus
Galbraith, Francis Omer
Galbreath, John Wilmer
Gale, Daniel Bailey
Galef, Victor Ray
Galejs, Aina
Galens, Gilbert J.
Galichia, Joseph Paul
Galitz, Robert Frederick
Gall, Edward Alfred
Gallagher, Charles Vincent
Gallagher, Fulton Dent
Gallagher, Idella Jane Smith (Mrs. Donald A. Gallagher)
Gallagher, James Miller
Gallagher, Jerome Jay
Gallagher, Joyce Eileen
Gallagher, Lionel Milton
Gallanis, Thomas Constantine
Gallaugher, James Rankin
Gallaway, Lowell Eugene
Galle, Oswin Karmie, Jr.
Gallen, Eduard D.
Gallienne, William Frederick
Gallop, Douglas James
Galloway, Robert Edward
Gallucci, Joanne (Peenie) Marie
Galowich, Ronald Howard
Galt, Raymond Masson
Gamble, Daniel Jefferson
Gamboa, Lucito Gamboa
Gamertsfelder, Robert Hehn
Gámez, José Paz
Gammon, Juanita Laverne
Gammuto, John Joseph, Sr.
Gamon, Adam Edward, II
Gamsky, Neal Richard
Gandal, Robert
Gandhi, Haren Sakarlal
Gandrud, Ebenhard Stewart
Gandt, Jerome Otto
Gange, Joseph George, Jr.
Gangware, Edgar Brand, Jr.
Gannaway, Stephen Dale
Gannon, Sister Ann Ida
Gannon, Paul Gabriel
Gannon, Walter
Ganocy, Stephen James
Ganos, Thomas
Gansen, Adrian Peter, Jr.
Ganser, Carl Joseph
Ganser, Ralph Vincent
Gant, Bobby Lee
Gant, George Arlington Lee
Ganzarain, Ramon Cajiao
Gaples, Harry Seraphin
Gapp, Paul John
Garancis, John Ciprijans
Garber, Joseph Max
Garber, Keith Alan
Garber, Sheldon
Garcia, Casimiro Crisostomo, Jr.
Garcia, Vincent Lopez, Jr.
Gardipee, Louis Joseph
Gardner, Don Charles
Gardner, Howard Garry
Gardner, James Raymond
Gardner, James Spray
Gardner, John Crawford
Gardner, John Newton
Gardner, John Stephen
Gardner, Junius Raymond
Gardner, Larry Dale
Gardner, Max Lewis
Gardner, Michael David
Gardner, Paul Jay
Gardner, Robert Meade
Gardner, Robert Scott
Gardner, Russell, Jr.
Gardner, William Earl
Garek, Morris Daniel
Garey, Uriel Elbert
Garfield, Robert
Garfield, Sol Louis
Garfin, Laurence Arlen
Garfinkle, Ronald George
Gargiulo, Richard Michael
Garland, Donald Merrill
Garland, William
Garlinghouse, Richard Earl
Garmezy, Norman
Garner, James Parent
Garness, Arne Hartwick
Garnett, Dianne Kay Wampler
Garnett, Gordon Martin
Garnier, Jack William
Garren, Morton Alan
Garrett, Lilyan Darleen
Garrett, Patrick Henry, II
Garrett, Shirley Ann
Garringer, Robert Stephen
Garrison, Delmer Eugene
Garrison, Ray Harlan
Garry, Gerald Francis
Garson, William
Garten, Samuel
Garton, Robert Dean
Garven, David Harold
Garvin, Charles David
Garvin, Danial Francis
Garza-Gonzalez, Mario
Garzia, Ricardo Francisco
Gasiorkiewicz, Eugene Constantine
Gaskell, Charles Thomas
Gaskill, Rex William
Gaskins, William George
Gasper, John Edward
Gassman, Max Paul
Gassmann, Zean
Gaston, Alonzo DuBois
Gaston, Hugh Philip
Gaston, Thomas Leon, Jr.
Gates, Arthur Roland, II
Gates, Clifton Wadell
Gates, Crawford Marion
Gates, David Murray
Gates, Raymond Dee
Gatto, Louis Constantine
Gattozzi, Angelo Luciano
Gauen, Mary Jane Adsit (Mrs. Richard E. Gauen)
Gaul, William Martin
Gault, Sidney David
Gauss, Cecelia Elaine Sneyd
Gaustad, Harley Erwyn
Gauthier, Clarence Joseph
Gauthier, T(heophile) Emil
Gawronski, Daniel Anthony
Gay, Alfonso Young
Gayfer, James McDonald
Gaylord, Sanford Fred
Geake, Carol Lynne
Gearhart, Louis Ossman
Gebhart, David Lee
Gee, Albert George
Geer, Edward Douglas
Geer, Emily Apt
Geerdes, Harold Paul
Gehl, Charles Herman
Gehl, Eugene Othmar
Gehlhausen, Paul Edward
Gehring, Frederick William
Gehrke, Charles William
Gehrt, Earl Benjamin
Geier, Philip Henry
Geiger, David Scott
Geiger, Hans Frederich
Geigle, Richard Damon
Geinert, Roy Michael
Geis, Gordon George
Geisen, Kris Odean
Geisler, Hans Emanuel
Geisler, James Charles
Geiss, Dorothy Elizabeth
Geist, Glenn William
Geist, Paul Dean
Geistfeld, Ronald Elwood
Geladas, James
Gelbach, John A.
Gelband, Alan Bruce
Gelfand, Ivan
Gelinas, Jean Paul
Gellein, Raymond Lange
Gelperin, Jules
Gelvin, John Tietge
Genalo, Lawrence James
Gengler, Jeanne (Dorothy)
Gennaro, Jack Rudolph
Geno, Phillip Joseph
Genskow, Jack Kuenne
Genthe, Walter Alfred
Gentile, Anthony
Gentling, Phillip Henry
Genung, Thomas Limes
George, Emery Edward
George, Harold Eugene
George, James Earl
George, Jerry Vance
George, John Arnold
George, John Edwin
Georgeson, Menas E.
Georgevich, Miodrag
Georgis, Werner Felix
Gephardt, Richard Andrew
Gephart, William Jay
Gerard, Donald Edward
Gerard, Stephen Chenoweth
Gerber, Aaron Bernard
Gerber, Bernard Charles
Gerber, Richard Wayne
Gerberding, Miles Carston
Gerberich, William Warren
Gerbie, Albert Bernard
Gerbig, Clifford George
Gerbing, Frank, Jr.
Gerdes, Louis George
Gerhardt, Martin, Jr.
Gerig, Reginald Roth
Gerla, Morton
Gerlach, Hans Werner
Gerlach, Luther Paul
Gerler, Edwin Roland, Jr.
Gerlitz, Frank Edward
Germon, Wesley Marion, Jr.
Germovnik, Francis I.
Geroff, Steve Kursto
Gerson, Myles Zachary
Gerspacher, Frederick Anthony
Gerstacker, Robert William
Gerstenmaier, John Herbert
Gerstman, Daniel Robert
Gerstman, George Henry
Gertler, Alfred Martin
Gertz, Thomas Erwin
Gesell, Marvin Homer
Gesterfield, Kathryn Jensen
Getman, Clyde Jay
Getter, Russell Wallace
Gettler, Benjamin
Getz, Bert Atwater
Gezon, Howard James
Ghantous, Robert Nicholas
Ghazarian, Jacob Garabed
Ghering, Mary Virgil
Ghersi, Juan Carlos
Ghia, Kirti N.
Ghiglieri, Bernard James, Jr.
Gholson, Samuel Creed
Gholston, Robert Michael
Giambelluca, Samuel Leo
Gianan, Rogelio Villanueva
Giandomenico, Adam Michael
Giannangelo, Emil Frank
Giannestras, Nicholas James
Giardino, John Richard
Gibas, Andrew C.
Gibas, Grace Braden
Gibb, Clark Raymond
Gibb, William Stewart
Gibbons, Everett Durward
Gibbons, Mrs. John Sheldon (Celia Victoria Townsend)
Gibbs, G. Edward
Gibbs, P. Laird
Gibbs, Reese Leonard
Gibbs, Walter Manning, Jr.
Gibbs, William Cullen, Jr.
Gibson, Benjamin Franklin

Gibson, Curtis A.
Gibson, Edwin Charles
Gibson, Floyd Robert
Gibson, Milton Eugene
Gibson, Ralph Kenneth
Gibson, Ralph Milton
Gibson, Robert Leslie
Gibson, Thomas Marshall
Gibson, William Herbert
Giebelhausen, Gustav William
Giering, Richard Herbert
Giertz, Robert William
Giesbrecht, Harry John
Giesen, Richard Allyn
Giffen, Daniel H.
Giffen, Lawrence Everett, Sr.
Gifford, Edgar Demarest
Gifford, Winston Charles
Gigax, Richard
Gilbert, Anne Wieland
Gilbert, Bentley Brinkerhoff
Gilbert, Bruce Frederic
Gilbert, Charles Walter
Gilbert, Edward George
Gilbert, Herman Cromwell
Gilbert, Howard Alden
Gilbert, John Robert
Gilbert, Sidney
Gilbert, Thomas Irvine
Gilbert, William Frederick
Gilbertson, Carlyle Warren
Gilbertson, Conrad Brian
Gilbertson, Harold Kenneth, Sr.
Gilbertson, Kris Kenson
Gilboe, David Dougherty
Gilborne, Jean Elizabeth
Gilbride, Thomas Leo
Gilbride, William Donald
Gildea, John Riley
Gildea, Robert Lee
Gildersleeve, Harry Dale, Jr.
Gildzen, Alex John
Giles, Conrad Leslie
Giles, Homer Wayne
Giles, William Mitchell
Gill, Lyle Bennett
Gill, Neal Fassig
Gill, Paul Singh
Gillen, Gregory Ronald
Gillen, James P.
Gilles, Kenneth Albert
Gillespie, James Laurence
Gillespie, Kenneth Ira
Gillespie, Thomas
Gillette, Halbert Scranton
Gillick, Fred Irving
Gillihan, James Edward
Gillim, Parvin Douglas
Gillis, David Wesley, III
Gillis, Frank James
Gillis, John Herbert
Gillis, Ruth Jeanette Kathan
Gillman, Ray Wallace
Gillogly, Charles Owen
Gillum, Jack Dean
Gilman, David Alan
Gilman, Donald Eugene
Gilman, Henry
Gilmartin, Gene Foley
Gilmore, Horace Weldon
Gilmore, James Stanley, Jr.
Gilmore, Robert Witter
Gilmour, C(harles) Edwin
Gilpin, John Stephen
Gilson, Richard Donald
Gilster, Peter Stuart
Giltner, Sister Andrea
Gimbel, Franklyn Melroye
Gin, Jackson
Gingiss, Benjamin Jack
Ginley, Thomas John
Ginn, Alexander
Ginn, H(orace) Marvin
Ginn, Milton Stanley
Ginsburg, Sheldon Harvey
Gioioso, Joseph Vincent
Giorgi, Amedeo Andrew
Girgash, William John
Girou, Michael Lloyd
Girton, Larry Lee
Girvin, John Patterson
Girvin, Richard Allen
Girz, Albert Oscar
Gish, Edward Rutledge
Gisler, George Louis
Giuffre, Anthony Angelo
Givan, Richard Martin
Gladders, Thomas Luke
Gladish, David Francis
Gladstone, William Sheldon, Jr.
Glaess, Herman Lewis
Glaman, Paul Thompson
Glaman, Richard William
Glancy, Thomas James
Glander, Karl William
Glascoe, Milton Marcellus
Glaser, Kurt
Glaser, Robert Stanley
Glasgow, Charles Curtis, Jr.
Glass, Clarence Edward
Glass, James William
Glasscock, Terrance Lynn
Glasser, Paul Harold
Glassman, James Hendrix
Glassner, Alvin
Glauber, Robert Haskell
Glaviano, Vincent Valentino
Glaze, Bert Theodore
Glazer, Sidney
Glazzard, Charles Donaldson
Gleason, Donald William
Gleekman, Lewis Wolfe
Glendening, Everett Austin
Glenn, Jerry Hosmer, Jr.
Glenn, John Herschel, Jr.
Glenner, Richard Allen
Glennie, Donald Morgan
Glickman, Daniel R. (Dan)
Glickman, Paul Bernard
Glidden, Iris Olsen (Mrs. John Moulton Glidden)
Glidden, John Redmond
Glieberman, Herbert Allen
Glime, Raymond George
Glisson, Silas Nease, III
Gloe, Donna Sue Osborn
Glommen, Harvey Hamilton
Gloor, Wilbur Tell
Glossberg, Joseph Berkson
Glotfelty, Clarence Alvah
Glover, Donald Mitchell
Glover, Rex Burr
Glover, Richard Bates
Glover, Robert Edward
Glucksman, Mona Stephaine
Glueck, Sidney John
Gluys, Charles Byron
Gnaedinger, John Phillip
Gnat, Raymond Earl
Gnezda, Mary Antonia Merullo (Mrs. Walter F. Gnezda)
Gobrecht, Harry Dana
Goding, Charles Arthur
Godlewski, Michael Patrick
Godwin, William Colin
Goebel, Maristella
Goeller, Carl Gilbert, Jr.
Goergen, Donald Joseph
Goering, Joseph Wilson
Goettig, Raymond John
Goetz, Larry William
Goetz, Peter Henry
Goetz, Robert Eugene
Goetzman, Bruce Edgar
Goff, Stephen Charles
Gogate, Anand Balkrishna
Gogate, Shashikala A.
Goggin, John Edward
Gohil, Jivanlal
Gold, Ike
Goldberg, A. Stuart
Goldberg, Arnold Irving
Goldberg, David Jaime
Goldberg, David Phillip
Goldberg, Elliott Marshall
Goldberg, Henry Morris
Goldberg, Isadore Edward
Goldberg, Samuel Irving
Goldberger, Arthur Earl, Jr.
Goldberger, Arthur Stanley
Goldberger, David Alan
Goldblatt, Philip Henry
Goldblatt, Stanford Jay
Golden, Frederic
Goldenberg, Gerald Joseph
Goldfarb, Bernard Sanford
Goldflies, Jerome Wolf
Golding, Brage
Goldish, Robert Joseph
Goldman, Douglas
Goldman, Frank Lyle
Goldman, Joseph Richard
Goldner, Arthur Paul
Goldner, Leo
Goldner, Louis B.
Goldner, Richard Dan
Goldsmith, Dale Preston Joel
Goldstein, Nathan Lawrence
Goldstein, Paul H.
Goldstein, Stanton Louis
Goldstone, Sidney Richard
Gollnick, Walter Otto, Jr.
Gombis, Leon George
Gomer, Lewis Eugene
Gong, Mery Lee
Gonge, John Foster
Gonser, David Earl
Gonzalez-Menocal, Pablo
Gooch, Donald Burnette
Good, John Ehrmin
Good, Larry David
Good, Larry Ralph
Good, Sheldon Fred
Goodall, Pendleton, Jr.
Goode, Irving Howard
Goodin, Carl Vincent
Goodkin, Michael
Goodman, David Lawrence
Goodman, David S.
Goodman, Donald Joseph
Goodman, Lowell Irvin
Goodman, Norton Victor
Goodman, Ronald
Goodman, Sidney Richard
Goodner, Jack Wayne
Goodrich, Elizabeth Anne
Goodrich, James Werner
Goodrich, Philip Richard
Goodrich, Robert Edward, Jr.
Goodsmith, Dale Harold
Goodson, Leroy Beverly
Goodstein, Sanders Abraham
Goodwin, Andrew Jackson, III
Goodwin, Glenn LaVern
Goodwin, Jesse Francis
Goodyear, Arthur Nelson
Googasian, George Ara
Goppers, Maneks Velta
Gor, Vishnu Jethalal
Goralnik, Oliver Aaron
Goralski, Christian Thomas
Gordillo, Manuel E.
Gordin, Richard Davis
Gordon, Charles Otto
Gordon, Edgar George
Gordon, Edwin Frederick Robert
Gordon, Gilbert
Gordon, Howard Aaron
Gordon, Howard Lyon
Gordon, James William
Gordon, Lewis Alexander
Gordon, Robert Stanley
Gordon, Robert Thomas
Gordon, Steven Stanley
Gordon, Theodore
Gordon, Virginia Niswonger
Gorecki, Jan
Goren, Hershel
Goren, Seymour Bernard
Goren, Simon Leslie
Gorham, Eugene Timothy
Gorham, Sidney Smith, Jr.
Gori, Lee Louis
Gorman, Gerald Warner
Gorman, Robert James
Gornick, Alan Lewis
Gorny, John Louis
Gorrell, David Paul
Gorsuch, John Wilbert
Gortmaker, Dennis Lee
Gorton, William Frank
Gosman, James Hubert
Gosser, Jon Walter
Gossett, Elizabeth Hughes (Mrs. William Thomas Gossett)
Gossman, Norbert Joseph
Goswami, Santosh Ranjan
Gotshall, William Weir
Gottesman, Karen Leslie
Gottfried, Max
Gottlieb, Reynold James
Gottschalk, Robert
Gottschalk, Robert Owen
Gougis, Bryan Patrick
Gould, Albert Oren
Gould, Arlen Stuart
Gould, Benjamin Z.
Gould, Betty Louise Koontz
Gould, James John
Gould, William Allen
Goulding, Robert Charles
Gove, James Robert
Gowdey, Marilyn Patricia
Gowell, Ronda Sue
Gowin, Richard Dale
Goyal, Raghbir Chand
Grabau, Gene Henry
Grabek, Frederick Marcel
Graber, Dwight Everett
Graber, Virgil Rich
Grabill, Wilson Fletcher, Jr.
Grable, Edward E.
Grable, Reginald Harold
Grabow, Wesley John Fred
Grace, Oliver Davies
Grace, Richard Milton
Graden, Maynard A., III
Gradison, Willis David, Jr.
Gradolph, David
Grady, John Donovan
Graef, Luther William
Graettinger, John Sells
Graf, Edwin Xavier
Graf, Truman Frederick
Graham, Barney Dan
Graham, Bruce Douglas
Graham, Bruce Edward
Graham, Carl Francis
Graham, Charles Pattison, Jr.
Graham, Clayton James
Graham, Douglas Lynn
Graham, George Wesley
Graham, James Wallace
Graham, James Willis
Graham, Janice Elizabeth
Graham, Jarlath John
Graham, John Dalby
Graham, M(arie) Frances
Graham, Marjorie Ruth Killebrew
Graham, Richard Marston
Graham, Ruth Vogel
Graham, Stephen Shafton
Graham, William Alexander, Jr.
Graham, William Quentin
Grainger, David William
Grajewski, Marion John
Gram, Christine Elise Groefsema Harris (Mrs. Henry H. Gram)
Gramczak, Mary Eulodia
Granat, Bruce Arnold
Grandstaff, Charles Harry
Grangaard, B. C.
Grant, Barry Marvin
Grant, Brian William
Grant, Charles Henry
Grant, Clifford Dewey
Grant, Evva H.
Grant, Frederich Douglas
Grant, Kingsley B.
Grant, Michael Peter
Grant, Paul Roger
Grant, Robert Byron
Grant, Ross Allan
Grant, Stanley Cameron
Grant, William Robert
Graper, Henry Elbert, Jr.
Grasse, James Martin
Grassley, Charles E.
Gratt, Stanley Howard
Grauel, Truman Willard
Grava, Alfred Herbert
Graven, Norman Reuben
Gravens, Daniel Lee
Gravereau, Victor P.
Graves, Harris Breiner
Graves, Jack Russell
Graves, John Paul, Jr.
Gray, Allen Gibbs
Gray, Avrum
Gray, Byron Everett
Gray, Charles Elmer
Gray, Charles Lucien
Gray, Charles Webster
Gray, Georgia Neese
Gray, Grattan
Gray, Merle
Gray, Richard Alan
Gray, Sanford Durham
Gray, Sheldon
Gray, William Oxley
Gray, William Philip
Graybill, Robert Vann
Grayson, Leonard David
Graziano, Charles Dominic
Graziano, Salvatore Joseph
Gredesky, Joseph Nolan
Greeley, Joseph May
Green, David
Green, Edward James
Green, Enid Margaret
Green, Farno Louis
Green, Frank Earl
Green, Frederick Shepherd
Green, H(arold) Daniel
Green, Isaac
Green, Jerry Howard
Green, Larry Edward
Green, Leonard Nathan
Green, Manuel Sanford
Green, Martin Wilson
Green, Meyer H.
Green, Nettie Luther Cleckler (Mrs. Clatis Green)
Green, Paul Conrad
Green, Rice Andrew
Green, Robert Glenn
Green, Robert Lee
Green, Thomas Harrison
Green, Warren Harold
Green, William Ralph
Green, William Whitney
Greenberg, Frank
Greenberg, Glenn Richard
Greenberg, Joseph Herman
Greenberg, Milton
Greenberg, Milton Edward
Greenberg, Paul
Greenberg, Ronald K.
Greenbert, Harold C.
Greenblatt, Deana Charlene
Greene, Charles Leonard
Greene, Earl George, Jr.
Greene, George Elsworth
Greene, George William
Greene, Gerald Michael
Greene, James Alexander, III
Greene, Ralph Vernon
Greene, Robert Bernard, Jr.
Greene, Robert Leroy
Greenebaum, James Eugene, II
Greeneisen, David Paul
Greenfield, John Charles
Greenlee, Everett Eugene
Greenlee, Herbert Breckenridge
Greenlee, Robert Leonard
Greenslit, John F.
Greenstein, Charles Allan
Greenstein, Melvin
Greenwold, Warren Eldon
Greenwood, Gwendolyn Yvonne
Greenwood, Herman Edward
Greenwood, Janet Kae Daly
Greer, William Lewis
Greeson, Bernard Dayton
Greetham, James Sidney
Gregg, Franklin
Gregg, Frederick W.
Gregg, Lucius Perry
Gregor, Harold Laurence
Gregorcy, John Raymond
Gregory, Claire Distelhorst
Gregory, Francis Arnold, Jr.
Gregory, Karl Dwight
Gregory, Richard Robin
Greig, Jack Catton
Greig, Walter
Greimel, Karl Hans
Greive, William Henry
Grem, Francis Matthew
Grem, June Olson
Greschaw, Charles Randolph
Grether, Carl Frederick
Greve, John Henry
Grewal, Manohar Singh
Grice, Alfred Bernard
Grider, Joseph Allen
Grider, Joseph Kenneth
Grier, Barbara G. (Gene Damon)
Grier, David Charles
Griesheimer, Ronald Edward
Grieves, John Willis
Griffin, Benjamin Lee, Jr.
Griffin, Donald John
Griffin, George Ann
Griffin, Mary Velma Shotwell (Mrs. James Leonard Griffin)
Griffin, Robert P.
Griffin, Walter Roland
Griffin, William Edward
Griffin, William Julian, II
Griffith, Alan Lee
Griffith, B(ezaleel) Herold
Griffith, Calvin Robertson
Griffith, David William
Griffith, James David
Griffith, James Homer
Griffith, James Mark
Griffith, John Francis
Griffith, Richard Eugene
Griffith, Russell Evan, Jr.
Griffiths, John David
Griffiths, Larry
Grigg, John Warren
Grigg, Viola E. Wiitala (Mrs. Paul Grigg)
Griggs, Douglas Meriwether, Jr.
Griggs, Ione Quinby
Griggs, John Bradford
Grigsby, Lewis Matthews, Sr.
Grillot, Francis Albert, Jr.
Grimes, Alan Pendleton
Grimes, Hugh Gavin
Grimes, John Edward, Jr.
Grimley, Liam Kelly
Grimm, Daniel Frederick
Grimm, Oliver Gilbert
Grimson, Lynn Gudmundur
Grinstead, Leonard Sylvester
Griswold, Paul Michael
Groening, William Andrew, Jr.
Groff, Richard Lamarr
Gromacki, Robert Glenn
Gronek, Stanley Anthony
Groninger, James Grant
Gronkiewicz, Edmund
Gronli, John Victor
Gronlund, Arthur Clarence
Groppi, James E.
Grosberg, Herbert Lynn
Grosby, Herbert Leon
Groski, Donald S.
Gross, Allen Eugene
Gross, Bethuel (B.G.)
Gross, Gordon E(dward)
Gross, Henry Emmett
Gross, James Dehnert
Gross, John Donald
Gross, Milton Eugene
Gross, Mortimer David
Gross, Phillip William, Jr.
Gross, Stuart Diehl
Gross, William Charles
Gross, William Joseph
Gross, Willis Charles, Jr.
Grossa, Douglas Q.
Grossgut, Paul John
Grossman, Edwin
Grossman, Howard Ford
Grossman, Morris M.
Grot, James Stephen
Grote, Manfred Wilhelm
Groth, Betty
Grotzinger, Laurel Ann
Grounds, Philip Clayton
Grove, Ewart Lester
Grove, Helen Harriet
Grove, Kalvin M.
Grover, Richard Kinsel
Groves, Ann Blakesley
Groves, David Updegraff
Groves, Franklin Nelson
Grubb, Merritt Byron
Gruber, Charles A.
Gruber, Charles LaMar
Gruensfelder, Robert Charles
Gruenwald, George Henry
Grumbles, Carl Edwin
Grundman, Rose Ann
Grundmanis, John Visvaldis
Grundstrom, Donald William
Grunewald, Alvin Herbert
Grunsfeld, Ernest Alton, III
Grunwald, Mary Ellen
Guarnieri, Donald Lewis
Gubbins, Joan Margaret (Mrs. Dale George Gubbins)
Gudenas, John Wayne
Guderley, George Warren, Jr.
Guelker, Francis Theodore
Guendling, John Edward
Guenther, Dennis Alfred
Guenther, Francis Harvey
Guentzel, Richard Dale
Guentzler, Ronald Edward
Guernsey, Patricia Jane
Guertal, Rochelle
Guest, M. I.
Gueth, Thomas Franklin
Guhl, Louise Eleanor
Guibor, George Pirtle
Guice, C. Norman
Guida, Edward Arthur
Guikema, Dale John
Guild, Ronald John
Guin, Jere Donald
Guju, John G.
Gullekson, Edwin Henry, Jr.
Gullen, George Edgar, Jr.
Gullickson, Gary Richard
Gullickson, Miles Justin
Gully, Harold Wayne
Gum, Carl DeWitt, Jr.
Gumbert, E(dgar) Thomas
Gumbert, Jack Lee
Gund, George, III
Gundersen, Gunnar Adolf
Gunderson, George Bruce
Gunderson, Harvey Samuel
Gunderson, Thomas Edward
Gundlach, Norman Joseph
Gungor, Bahri Orhan
Gunnings, Thomas Sylvester
Gunter, Frank Delano
Gunter, Frank Elliott
Guntermann, Alfred Ernest
Gupta, Parkash Dev
Gupta, Parshotam Dass
Gurevitch, Russ
Gusmer, John H.
Gustafson, Gladys Irene
Gustafson, Peter Alan
Gustafson, Roy David
Gustavson, Erick Brandt
Gustin, Ralph Leon
Guth, Harry Earl, Jr.
Guth, Richard Ralph
Gutheil, Robert Willoughby
Guthier, Lloyd Charles
Guthmann, Howard Milton
Guthrie, Eleanor Y.
Guthrie, Myrna Jean
Guthrie, Richard Alan
Guthrie, Wilbur Dean
Gutmann, Joseph
Gutterman, Milton M.
Guttman, Ralph Myron
Gutzler, Brett Melvin
Guy, Carvin Harry
Guy, Ernest Thomas
Guy, John Martin
Guyer, Tennyson
Guziec, Robert Alan
Guzzetta, Dominic James
Gwinn, Cecil William
Gyuro, Steven John
Haake, John Jay
Haaker, Lester Walter
Haas, Edward Lee
Haas, Eric Richard
Haas, Erwin
Haas, James Wayne
Haas, Kenneth Brooks, Jr.
Haas, Larry Alfred
Haas, Leonard Clarence
Habak, Philip A.
Habayeb, Kelly Mohammed
Hable, Edward Gerard
Habryl, Edmund John
Habryl, Joy
Hachmeister, Albert W.
Hachmeister, Robert John
Hachtman, Samuel Joseph
Hack, Raymond Charles
Hackbarth, Clarence Walter
Hacker, Donald Wilbur
Hacker, Edward George
Hackett, John Thomas
Hackett, Mary Milam (Mrs. Ralph C. Hackett)
Hackl, Donald John
Hackman, Donald Jon
Hackman, Helen Anna Henriette
Hackmann, Emil Edward
Hacquebord, David George
Haddad, DeLorre Salem
Haddad, George Richard
Haddad, Joseph Nicholas
Hadden, Stuart Tracey
Haden, Jack Lee
Hadley, Paul Robert, Jr.
Haecker, George Woods, Jr.
Haefner, Lonnie Edward
Haegert, Daryl Lee
Haehnle, Clyde George
Haenicke, Diether Hans
Haerer, Deane Norman
Haffer, Gloria Schottenstein
Hafiz, Abdul
Hafling, Elmer Roland
Hagan, Donald Vernon
Hagan, Robert Carl
Hagberg, Ralph Albert
Hage, Gunnar Harald
Hage, Rolf Borresen
Hagedorn, Thomas M.
Hagelin, Daniel Warn
Hagelman, Ronald Rudolph
Hagen, Duane Quentin
Hagen, Eldon Bruce
Hagen, Jeanne Lynn Clegg
Hagen, John William
Hagen, Keith Arnold
Hagenmeyer, Willard Harvey
Hager, John
Hager, Mary Virginia
Hagerty, Robert Lewis
Haggerty, Bridget Nancy
Hagglund, Clarance Edward
Haglund, Donn Keith
Haglund, E(dward) James
Hague, Richard Norris
Hahn, Charless
Hahn, Jack Albert Louis
Hahn, Jack Dean
Hahn, Lewis Edwin
Hahn, Raymond Martin
Hahn, Robert Otto
Hahn, Wendell Wayne
Haidet, Buddy Keith
Haiman, Franklyn Saul
Haines, Nancy Ann Stutler
Haining, James Howard, Jr.
Haislet, Edwin L.
Haith, Edward Earl
Hajjar, Waleed Mohammed
Hakanson, Richard Collar
Hakarine, Duane Dennis
Hakel, Edwin Henry
Hakkinen, Raimo Jaakko
Halas, George Stanley, Jr.
Halbe, Donald James
Halbe, Thomas Gray
Halbert, Frederic Leslie
Halcomb, Robert Wesley
Hale, Allan McKeag
Hale, Clayton Gould
Hale, Floyd Eugene
Hales, Loyde Wesley
Haley, Johnetta Randolph
Halfpop, Roger Lewis
Halikas, James Anastasio
Hall, Barnard
Hall, Barré William
Hall, Clifton Ayres, II
Hall, David McKenzie
Hall, Dee Morey (Mrs. Harry F. Hall)
Hall, Edward Shock
Hall, Emma Henrietta Leake
Hall, Evelyn Louise Long (Mrs. Richard Malcolm Hall)
Hall, Francis Lindley

Hall, Frank Braden
Hall, Fred Hamner
Hall, Frederick Leonard
Hall, Harber Homer
Hall, Harold Clifford
Hall, Hubert Ray
Hall, Jerry Ray
Hall, John LeRoy
Hall, Joseph Bates
Hall, Judy Ann
Hall, Kenneth Franklin
Hall, Lloyd Leonard
Hall, Norman William
Hall, Owen Edward
Hall, Ralph Charles
Hall, Raymond Joseph
Hall, Richard Alexander
Hall, Robert Malcolm
Hall, Stuart Phelps
Hall, Thomas Lynn
Hall, Warren Edward, Jr.
Hall, Wilbur Alonzo
Hallan, James Arthur
Hallauer, Arnel Roy
Hallenbeck, Jan Traver
Hallene, Alan Montgomery
Haller, John Samuel, Jr.
Halliday, Herbert Edwin
Halliday, Stephen Mills
Hallowell, Robert Edward
Hallquist, Roy Stuart
Halperin, Phillip Harold
Halsey, Jim
Halstead, James Allen
Halvorsen, Daniel Kasberg
Halvorson, William Arthur
Hamachek, Don E.
Hamady, Mary Laird
Hamann, Deryl Frederick
Hamann, John Bernard
Hamann, John Rial
Hamblen, John Wesley
Hambleton, Chalkley Jay
Hamblin, Henry Sailor
Hambright, Alfred Gale
Hamburger, Joel Ivan
Hamburger, Richard James
Hamby, Alonzo Lee
Hamdy, Aziz (Hamed)
Hameister, Lavon Louetta
Hamerski, Henryk Wincenty
Hamilton, Calvin Kenneth
Hamilton, Carl Porter
Hamilton, Jan Michael
Hamilton, John Albert
Hamilton, John Handley
Hamilton, Lee H.
Hamilton, Richard Alfred
Hamilton, Richard Hugh
Hamilton, Robert Charlton
Hamilton, Wilmer Lee
Hamlar, David Duffield
Hamlin, Griffith Askew
Hamlin, Richard Eugene
Hamm, Franklin Albert
Hamm, John Edward
Hamm, Russell Leroy
Hamman, Robert John
Hammel, Robert Dale
Hammer, Oliver Starr
Hammersley, William LaMoine
Hammes, Richard George
Hamming, Kenneth Wayne
Hammitt, Courtney Clark
Hammitt, Frederick Gnichtel
Hammitt, Jackson Lewis, III
Hammitt, John Michael
Hammond, Darrell Dean
Hammond, John Farnsworth, III
Hammons, Joseph Ernest
Hammontree, Robert James
Hamparian, Arthur Manoug
Hampel, Robert Edward
Hampton, Charles Stuart
Hampton, James Elwin
Hampton, John William
Hampton, Philip Michael
Hampton, Phillip Jewell
Hamra, Donald Edd
Hamrick, Ruffner Gerald
Hamrick, William Jean
Han, Lit Sien
Hanback, Jacqueline Tankersley (Mrs. William F. Hanback)
Hance, Kenneth G.
Hancock, David Elwood
Handahl, Donald Herman
Handel, Charles Harold
Handel, Milton Richard
Handley, Robert Eugene
Handwerker, Sy
Handy, Drucilla
Handy, Richard Lincoln
Hanebutt, Ralph Louis
Hangen, William J.
Hankins, Robert Eckes
Hankins, Vaughan Lee
Hankla, Walfrid Byron
Hanlon, C. Rollins
Hann, Charles Stephen
Hanna, Charles Roy
Hanna, George Lewis
Hanna, Martin Shad
Hanna, Mary Margaret Melson (Mrs. John Alden Hanna)
Hanna, Nessim
Hanna, Richard Dennis
Hannaford, Frank John
Hannaford, Jule Murat, III
Hannah, Franklin (Jesse)
Hanner, Rodney Carter
Hannewyk, Cornelius Marvin
Hannon, Donald William
Hannon, Joseph P.
Hanrahan, Robert Paul
Hans, Robert Lyle
Hansen, Allen J.
Hansen, Arthur Gene
Hansen, Bruce Winston
Hansen, Carl R.
Hansen, Charlotte Lorraine Helgeson (Mrs. Gordon H. (Hansen)
Hansen, Gerald Richard
Hansen, Geraldine Marie
Hansen, Harold Clement
Hansen, H(arvey) Kenneth
Hansen, Kenneth Martin
Hansen, Niles M., Jr.
Hansen, Norman Arden, Sr.
Hansen, Robert Wayne
Hansen, Thomas Louis
Hansen, Verne John
Hansen, Waldemar Conrad
Hansen, William Freeman
Hansen, William James
Hanser, Carolyn Jean
Hanser, Theodore Henry
Hanson, Arlee C.
Hanson, Charles Easton, Jr.
Hanson, Fred T.
Hanson, Gleva Marie
Hanson, Howard Henry
Hanson, J. Robert
Hanson, John Fredrik
Hanson, June P. Jensen
Hanson, Kenneth Hamilton
Hanson, Kenneth Harold
Hanson, Lloyd Clarence
Hanson, Myrle George
Hanson, Paul Ernest
Hanson, Phyllis Marie Geis (Mrs. Howard H. Hanson)
Hanson, Robert Leonard
Hanson, Walter Edmund
Hanson, William C.
Hanten, Robert Lee
Hapak, Francis Michael
Happ, Lawrence Raymond
Harasymiw, Stefan J.
Harbeson, John Willis
Harbin, Calvin Edward
Harbinson, Brother Camillus
Harbor, William Henry
Harbour, Jeanne Dulas
Hard, Arne Maynard
Harden, Oleta Elizabeth (Mrs. Dennis Clarence Harden)
Hardesty, Donald Lee
Hardin, Paul Franklin
Harding, Thomas S(pencer)
Hardison, Leslie Claire
Hardy, George
Hardy, H. Guy
Hardy, James Eugene
Hardy, Richard Earl
Hardy, Robert Earl
Hardy, Walter Lincoln
Hare, Robert Y.
Hare, Ronald Charles
Hare, William Russell
Harel, Zev
Harfst, Ernest Dennis
Hargett, Herbert Peckover
Hargrave, Harold
Hargrave, Sarah Quesenberry
Hargrave, Victoria E(lizabeth)
Hargreaves, George Macdonald
Hargrove, Richard John
Harhay, Warren Charles
Hariman, Donald George
Haring, David Alvin
Harker, Jack Vincent
Harkey, William George
Harkin, Thomas Richard
Harkins, Davy Joe
Harkins, Michael Joseph
Harkness, Kenneth Alfred
Harl, Neil Eugene
Harlan, Jack Rodney
Harlan, Norman Ralph
Harley, James Preston
Harley, Richard Arlen
Harley, Robert Elden
Harlow, Barbara Ann
Harlow, Charles Alton
Harm, Paul Fredrick
Harman, Robert Maley
Harmet, A(rnold) Richard
Harmison, Charles Rice
Harmon, Denver Charles
Harmon, Jan Mary
Harmon, Verna Leola Clay (Mrs. Floyd Harmon)
Harms, Wilmer Allen
Harnar, Robert Hiram, Jr.
Harness, Edward Granville
Harper, Charles Little
Harper, Donald Dean
Harper, Leo Merle
Harper, Ramey Wilson
Harper, Richard Allen
Harper, Roger Wesley
Harrah, Betty Louise
Harrell, John Limpus
Harrell, Samuel Runnels
Harriman, Richard Lee
Harrington, Cathryn L.
Harrington, Doris Virginia
Harrington, Harvey Daniel, II
Harrington, Louis Robert
Harrington, Richard Stanhope
Harrington, Robert Levant
Harrington, William Charles
Harrington, William Gene
Harris, Beverly Howard
Harris, Boyd Thomson
Harris, Charles Burt
Harris, Chauncy Dennison
Harris, Daniel Keating
Harris, David James
Harris, Donald
Harris, Donald Lee
Harris, E. Edward
Harris, Edward Eugene
Harris, Frances Alvord
Harris, Fred Milo
Harris, Gale Ion
Harris, Irving Brooks
Harris, Jane McCanna
Harris, Jasper William
Harris, Joseph Benjamin
Harris, Lauren Julius
Harris, Lewis Eldon
Harris, Michael Tyrrell
Harris, Morran Denver
Harris, Owen Leslie
Harris, Percy Gene
Harris, Philip Brewer
Harris, Robert Arch
Harris, Robert Bruce
Harris, Robert Edwin
Harris, Robert Laird
Harris, Robert Milton
Harris, Robert Norman
Harris, Ronald Lee
Harris, Samuel David
Harris, Stanley Gale, Jr.
Harris, Steven Hesse
Harris, Thomas Lorber
Harris, William Page
Harrison, E. Frank
Harrison, Earle
Harrison, Frank Joseph
Harrison, George Louis
Harrison, Harold Duane
Harrison, Henry Stuart
Harrison, Joseph Heavrin
Harrison, Michael (Mick) Brent
Harrison, Robert Statler
Harrod, John Price, Jr.
Harry, Ormsby L.
Harsh, Lester
Harsha, William Howard
Harshaw, Jack Raymond
Harshbarger, Kenneth E.
Harshman, Morton Leonard
Hart, Donald Leroy
Hart, Donn Vorhis
Hart, Harry James
Hart, Jay Albert Charles
Hart, John Birdsall
Hart, Joseph Montraville, Jr.
Hart, Mary Margaret
Hart, Richard Howe
Hart, Robert Gordon
Hart, Ronald Cary
Hart, Ruth Alicia
Hart, William Thomas
Hartdagen, Gerald Eugene
Harte, J. Richard
Harter, Donald Harry
Harter, Hugh Anthony
Harter, John J.
Hartigan, Neil F.
Hartlaub, Lawrence Philip
Hartle, Richard Eugene
Hartley, Wynona Smutz (Mrs. Richard Glendale Hartley)
Hartman, George Edward
Hartman, Martha Elizabeth (Mrs. William Hartman)
Hartman, William
Hartnett, Joseph Francis
Hartocollis, Peter
Hartung, Donald Norman
Hartung, Hazel Jane Springer (Mrs. Donald Norman Hartung)
Hartung, Karl Lea
Hartung, Richard Penn
Hartzell, Robert LeRoy
Hartzler, Harrod Harold
Harvey, Charles Hancock
Harvey, Clyde Francis
Harvey, Donald Andrew
Harvey, Eric Robinson
Harvey, Lynne Cooper (Mrs. Paul Harvey)
Harvey, Michael Kent
Harvey, Virginia Peaseley
Harvey, William Eugene
Harwick, John William
Hasbargen, Arthur
Hasbrouck, Wilbert Roland
Hascall, Jean Mary Teague (Mrs. Carleton Chandler Hascall, Jr.)
Haselhorst, Donald Duane
Hash, Lester Jackson, Jr.
Haskell, Charles Leonard
Haskell, Saul Simon
Haskell, Theodore James
Haskins, Ernest Blaine
Hasler, James Burton
Hasler, James Louis
Hasling, Robert John
Haspeslagh, Jean Anne
Hass, Bruce Stuart
Hassan, Mohammad Zia
Hassel, Charles Edward
Hassell, Gordon Elmer
Hasselquist, Maynard Burton
Hassler, Donald Mackey, II
Hassman, Paul LaVerne
Hastings, Jay Bradley
Hastings, William Charles
Hatch, Albert Jerold
Hatch, Elizabeth Dawn
Hatch, Henry Clifford
Hatch, Loren Lorenzo
Hatch, W.A.S. (Wendy Ann Swanson)
Hatcher, Charles Wesley
Hatcher, Herbert John
Hatcher, Millard Gene
Hathaway, Alan Dean
Hatter, Edward
Hauch, John Walter
Hauck, Allan
Hauerwas, Stanley Martin
Haugan, Harold Walter
Haugan, Robert Ellsworth
Haugen, Orrin Millard
Haukedahl, Orel Elden
Haukedahl, Stanley George
Haun, Richard Melvin
Hauptman, Herbert Morris
Hauptman, Rhoda Joy Jacobs (Mrs. Herbert Morris Hauptman)
Hausberg, William
Hauser, James Edward
Hauser, Jon William
Hauser, Willard Allen
Hausken, Sally Ann
Hausman, William Walker
Hausmann, Eugene Robert
Hauwiller, Robert Paul
Havel, Jean Eugène Martial
Havener, William Henry
Havens, Dwight Bowles
Haverdink, Virgil Dean
Haverfield, Betty Luker (Mrs. Robert W. Haverfield)
Haverfield, Robert Walter
Haviland, Camilla Klein
Havlas, Mike Vaclav
Hawes, Joseph Milton
Hawes, Nancye Elizabeth (Mrs. George Jason Hawes)
Hawk, Gerald Wayne
Hawk, Jeffery Lee
Hawk, Marion Earl
Hawkins, Arnot Roy
Hawkins, Brett William
Hawkins, Hal Woodbridge
Hawkins, Harold Elmer
Hawkins, Robert Lyon, Jr.
Hawkins, William Sheldon
Hawkinson, James R.
Hawkinson, John
Hawks, Keith Merwin
Hawley, Helen Mary Culp (Mrs. Archie Hawley)
Hawley, John Babcock
Hawthorn, Horace B(oles)
Hawthorne, John Boone
Hawtrey, Charles Edward
Hay, James Gordon
Hayashi, Tetsumaro
Haycraft, Rexford Gordon
Hayden, Albert A.
Haydon, Robert Rodney
Hayek, Allen James
Hayes, Alva Allen
Hayes, Arthur Chester
Hayes, Charles Edward
Hayes, Charles Sherman
Hayes, David John Arthur, Jr.
Hayes, David Thomas
Hayes, Donald Blair
Hayes, Elizabeth Ann
Hayes, Ernest A.
Hayes, John Francis
Hayes, John Marion
Hayes, K. Michael
Hayes, Paul Wesley
Hayes, Richard Johnson
Hayes, Robert Stanley
Hayford, John Sargent
Haymaker, Randy Lee
Haynes, Frank Maurice
Haynes, Howard Dome
Haynes, John Thomas
Hays, Willard Carl
Hayward, George Curtis
Haywood, Charles Richard
Hazard, Willis Gilpin
Hazel, Erik Richard
Hazel, Gerald Vernon
Hazeltine, Robert Earl
Hazelton, Lucy Reed
H'Doubler, Francis Todd, Jr.
Head, Henry Buchen
Head, James S.
Heade, Joan Terese
Headlee, Raymond
Headlee, Richard Harold
Headlee, William Hugh
Healey, Robert Mathieu
Healy, Daniel Joseph
Healy, David Frank
Healy, James Thomas
Healy, John Cornelius
Healy, Laurin Hall
Heap, James Clarence
Hearn, Richard Steven
Hearst, Bella Rachael
Hearst, Gladys Whitley Henderson (Mrs. Charles Joseph Hearst)
Heasley, Bernice Elizabeth
Heasley, Robert Kenneth
Heath, Frank Cronmiller
Heath, George Fremont
Heath, John Lawrence
Heaton, Patrick James
Heben, Germaine Fox
Hebenstreit, Jean Estill Stark
Hebl, Harold Joseph
Hebron, Delano Landas
Heck, Charles Voisin
Heck, Robert Skinrood
Heckadon, Robert Gordon
Heckenbach, Roy Arthur
Hecker, George Sprake
Heckerman, Donald Arthur
Heckman, Fred Penrose
Heckman, Henry Trevennen Shick
Heckman, Stan P.
Hedberg, Gregory Scott
Hedberg, Paul Clifford
Hedden, Russell Alfred
Hedgcock, Grace Hall
Hedgcock, Ralph Everette
Hedger, Robert Willis
Hedley, William Henby
Hedley, William Joseph
Hedlund, Ronald David
Heeb, Max Allen
Heeren, Jack Montgomery
Heerens, Robert Edward
Heeter, Richard Dean
Heethuis, Bernard Gerald
Heffelfinger, John Brock
Heffelfinger, Richard Earl
Heffernan, Nathan Stewart
Heflin, Tom Pat
Hegde, Mahabalagiri Narayan
Hegg, David Lee
Hehmeyer, Alexander
Hehn, Anton Herman
Heibel, John Thomas
Heideman, Bert (Ronald) Mortimer
Heideman, Katherine Grayson Graham (Mrs. Bert M. Heideman)
Heidorn, Donald Gustav
Heidrich, Ruth Estelle
Heidrick, Gardner Wilson
Heidt, Robert Samuel
Heifetz, Gary Stephen
Heikenen, Patricia Smith
Heil, Richard Wendell
Heilman, Cecil Carl
Heilman, James Howard
Heilman, Joel Creighton
Heilman, Richard Owen
Heiman, Ernest Jean
Heimann, Sandra Ann Woeste (Mrs. Robert A. Heimann)
Heimann, William Edwin
Heimbuch, Floyd Eugene
Heimburger, Irvin LeRoy
Heimlich, Henry Jay
Hein, David Leon
Heindrichs, Robert Winslow
Heineman, Mrs. Ben W. (Natalie)
Heineman, Ben Walter
Heineman, Paul Lowe
Heinemann, Ludwig Gunther
Heino, Gene John
Heinrich, Donald Clinton
Heinsen, Richard Dale
Heintz, Daniel Joseph
Heintz, James Edward
Heintzelman, Ross Garfield
Heinz, Edward N., Jr.
Heinz, Leo George
Heinze, Robert Valentine
Heiple, James Dee
Heiser, Frank Fred
Heiser, Walter Charles
Heiserman, David Lee
Heisler, Harold Reinhardt, Jr.
Heizer, Edgar Francis, Jr.
Hejl, James George
Helberg, David Stewart
Helberg, Terrie
Held, Arthur Hugo
Held, Charles Holborn
Helfant, Seymour Meyer
Helfer, Herman Hyman
Helfrich, Robert James
Helgeland, Lester L.
Helgeson, Donald Penfield
Helgeson, Gerald David
Helie, Gilles Aime
Hellam, Lloyd George
Heller, Grant L.
Heller, John Henry
Heller, Philip Henri
Hellewell, Louis Patterson
Hellman, Richard
Hellyer, Arthur Lawrence
Helm, Sharon Marks
Helmers, Raymond August Henry
Helmick, Kenneth Dale
Helmker, Judith Anne
Helms, John Walker
Helmsing, Charles Herman
Helsdingen, Daniel John
Helsel, Jess F.
Helvey, Jerry L.
Hembrough, Betty Lou
Heminover, James Arthur
Hempe, A(rnold) Henry
Hemphill, Marlin Robert
Henderlong, Arthur Dean
Henderlong, Donald Eugene
Henderlong, Paul Robert
Hendershot, Walter Lee
Henderson, Allison B.
Henderson, Archie Bob
Henderson, Dwight Franklin
Henderson, Earl Wallace, Jr.
Henderson, George Leslie
Henderson, George Trumbull
Henderson, Harold Harry
Henderson, Homan Thurman
Henderson, Jerome D.
Henderson, Leonard Louis
Henderson, Morris
Henderson, Norman Lee
Henderson, Paul Templin
Henderson, Ronald Sidney
Henderson, William Stanley, Jr.
Hendricks, Donald Richard
Hendricks, Glenn LeRoy
Hendrickson, Duane Henry
Hendrickson, Frank Scott
Hendrickson, Max Shannon
Hendrickson, T. Richard
Hendrickson, Thomas Atherton
Hendrickson, Walter Brookfield, Jr.
Hendrickson, William Clair
Hendrix, Jack Hall
Hendrix, Jon Richard
Henes, David Edwin
Hengehold, Lawrence Jerome
Henges, Ronald Edward
Henken, Willard John
Henkes, Robert John
Henkin, Paul Henry
Henley, Fred Louis
Henline, Florence
Henn, Jack
Henn, Mary J.
Henn, Roger Emerson
Henneberry, John Thomas
Henney, Robert Lee
Hennig, Frank Edward
Hennigar, Lewis Albro
Henniger, Bernard Robert
Henning, Fay Marie
Henning, Harold Walter
Hennings, Robert Edward
Hennings, Thomas Arthur
Hennis, Henry Emil
Henrichs, Harold Garth
Henriksen, Charles Kendall
Henriksen, Harry Charles
Henry, Gene M.
Henry, H(arold) Dale
Henry, Hermann Russell
Henry, Janell Wagner
Henry, John Andrew
Henry, Joseph Patrick
Henry, Lee
Henry, LeRoy Church
Henry, Rachel Imogene Saunders (Mrs. Hermann R. Henry)
Henry, Richard James
Henry, Robert Edward
Henschen, James Lee
Henseler, Donna Millard
Henshel, Richard Lee
Henson, John Porter
Henzlik, Raymond Eugene
Herb, Edmund Michael
Herbert, William
Herbertt, Stanley
Herbst, Frederick Daniel
Herbst, William Henry Albert
Herd, Richard Murlen
Herdina, Leo James
Herdrich, Ralph Cooley
Herfindahl, Lloyd Manford
Hergenrother, Edward Leo
Herguth, Robert J.
Hering, James Stephen
Herkner, Mildred Luella
Herman, Bernard
Herman, Edward Joseph
Herman, John Allen
Herman, Robert Edward
Hermann, Donald Harold James
Hermann, Harland Thomas
Hermann, James Lee
Hermann, Paul David
Hermann, Robert Ewald
Hermansen, David Roger
Hermesmeyer, Michael Thomas
Hermiston, Ray Talbot
Herr, Richard Joseph
Herre, Ernest Andrew
Herrick, Clay, Jr.
Herrick, Donald Willard
Herrick, Howard Duane
Herrick, Julia Frances
Herrin, Snyder E.
Herring, James P.
Herrmann, Robert Bernard
Herron, Orley Rufus
Herse, Boguslaw Adam
Herseth, Lorna Buntrock
Hershbarger, Robert Allen
Hershberger, Gerald Robert
Hersheway, Charles Eugene
Hersrud, Leslie R.
Hertel, Leona
Hertzer, William Rudolph
Herwig, Thelma Lange (Mrs. Theodor Fredrick Herwig)
Herzig, Adam Henry
Herzog, Arthur Louis
Herzog, Godofredo Max
Herzog, Sylvia Louise
Hesburgh, Theodore Martin
Hesketh, Herbert Thomas
Hesler, Harold Patton
Hesling, Donald Mills
Hess, Bartlett Leonard
Hess, Edward Anthony
Hess, Edward Frederick, Jr.
Hess, Robert Bond
Hess, Robert Lee
Hess, Stanford Kenneth
Hess, Stanley William
Hesser, Ernest Grant
Hessler, William Gerhard
Hestad, Bjorn Mark
Hetherington, James Richard
Hetland, LaRue Elmer
Hetterick, David Raymond
Heuer, Michael Alexander
Heumann, Herbert H.
Heusel, William George
Heusinkveld, Edwin David
Hewett, William Sherman, II
Hewitt, James Watt
Hewitt, Patricia Wiman (Mrs. William Alexander Hewitt)

Hewitt, William Alexander
Heyde, Edward Lee
Heydegger, H(elmut) Roland
Heymann, Seymour Edward
Heymans, Eugene Joseph, Jr.
Heyrman, Donald Joseph
Hiatt, Kenneth B.
Hibbs, Jack Eugene
Hibbs, William George
Hiben, John, Jr.
Hickey, Jerome Edward
Hickman, Simeon Martin
Hickman, Thomas Roland
Hickox, John Ekstrom
Hicks, Elder Barney
Hicks, James Thomas
Hicks, John Leslie, Jr.
Hicks, Samuel Irving
Hickson, Robert Comins
Hida, Edward T.
Hidore, John Junior
Hidvegi, Ernest B.
Hiebert, Elizabeth Blake (Mrs. Homer L. Hiebert)
Higdem, Arnold Palmer
Higgins, Jerome John Forest
Higgins, John Richard
Higgins, Kenneth Raymond
Higgins, Ronald Allan
Higgins, Ruth Loving
Higgs, Stuart Eldon
High, Claude, II
Higham, Robin
Highley, Terry Leonard
Hight, Ralph Dale
Higley, Albert Maltby, Jr.
Hilbert, Angelia Hulda
Hilbish, Thomas
Hilboldt, James Sonnemann
Hilborn, John R.
Hildebrand, Gordon Francis
Hildebrand, James Frederick
Hildebrandt, Bruno F.
Hildebrandt, Herbert William
Hildreth, R(oland) James
Hileman, Kenneth Eugene
Hill, Avery
Hill, Bruce Marvin
Hill, Carl Henry
Hill, Draper
Hill, Harry Williams
Hill, James Edward
Hill, Jon De Witt
Hill, Kearney H.J.
Hill, Lewis Warren
Hill, Michael Emmanuel
Hill, Pamela Ellen
Hill, Richard Glen
Hill, Richard Lee
Hill, Robert Franklin
Hill, Ruane Burton
Hill, Russell Eugene
Hill, Sandra Denise
Hill, Thayer John, Jr.
Hill, Theodore Albert
Hill, Thomas Clarke, VIII
Hill, Walter Watson
Hill, Wendell Talbot, Jr.
Hill, Wilbur Thomas
Hillard, Robert Earl
Hille, Frederick E.
Hilleboe, John Alfred
Hiller, Rembrandt Clemens, Jr.
Hillery, John Maurice
Hillestad, Albert William
Hillhouse, Louis Edwin
Hillis, Elwood Haynes
Hillman, Charlene Hamilton
Hillman, Douglas Woodruff
Hillman, Stanley Eric Gordon
Hillman, Sue Ann Newton
Hillock, David Anthony
Hills, Carroll Loran
Hilpert, Brunette Kathleen Powers (Mrs. Elmer Ernest Hilpert)
Hilston, Charles Ralph
Hilton, Lewis Booth
Hilton, Stanley William, Jr.
Hilty, Dorothy Pauline
Hime, William Gene
Himes, Herbert Dean
Himmelfarb, John David
Hindermann, Mark John
Hindery, Phyllis Catherine
Hiner, Robert L.
Hiner, Travis Scott
Hines, Jacob Albert
Hines, Roger Dwain
Hinkle, Carl
Hinks, Robert Newman
Hinman, Flossie Norton
Hinman, Frederick Richard
Hinsvark, Inez Genieve
Hinton, Charles Franklin
Hinzman, Wayne
Hipple, John Henry
Hird, Samuel
Hire, Robert Lowrey
Hirn, Doris Dreyer
Hirsch, Christian Richard
Hirsch, Jay G.
Hirsch, Leonard George
Hirsch, Lore
Hirschberg, Erwin Eugene
Hirschfeld, Stanley Edwin
Hirschfelder, Max
Hirschinger, Lawrence
Hirschtritt, Geri Miriam Rudnick
Hirssig, James Earl
Hirtzel, Richard Dale
Hitchcock, John Gareth
Hitchcock, Ruth Marie
Hite, David L.
Hitt, William Dee

Hixson, Joel Dennis
Hjalmarson, Gordon Ross
Ho, Andrew Kong-Sun
Ho, Raymond Yu
Hoad, Grace Hamilton
Hoad, John Green
Hoadley, Stephen Damon
Hoare, James Patrick
Hoban, Thomas William
Hobbins, William Bell
Hobbs, Hilton H.
Hobbs, Larry Jay
Hobbs, Lewis Mankin
Hobbs, Marvin
Hobson, Kenneth Ray
Hochgesang, Roman Joseph
Hochwald, Werner
Hockett, Jay Anthony
Hockman, Charles Henry
Hodan, Gerald John
Hodapp, Leroy Charles
Hodes, Barnet
Hodes, Scott
Hodge, James Robert
Hodges, John Black
Hodgkins, Earl Warner
Hodlmair, Scotland Elgie
Hodson, Arthur Loren
Hodson, Darrel Leroy
Hoech, George Paul, Jr.
Hoeft, Richard James
Hoehn, John Albert
Hoehnen, David Lee
Hoekstra, Benjamin Clarence
Hoepker, Paul George
Hoerner, Marvin Lavern
Hoerner, Thomas Allen
Hoertel, William Wadsworth
Hof, James Eagan
Hofer, Albert Cornelius
Hoff, Vivian Beaumont
Hoffland, David Lauren
Hoffman, Albert Romaine
Hoffman, Charles Jacob
Hoffman, David Lloyd
Hoffman, Ellen Barker
Hoffman, George William
Hoffman, Gerald Ernest
Hoffman, Harley Howard
Hoffman, John Harry
Hoffman, Kathryn Elizabeth
Hoffman, Larry Gene
Hoffman, Leonard
Hoffman, Marion Eurel
Hoffman, Paul Richard
Hoffman, William Kenneth
Hoffmann, Charles Lehr
Hoffmeister, Robert Edward
Hofling, Charles Kreimer
Hofmann, George Frederick
Hofstatter, June Marie Eichenberg (Mrs. Frank Fox Hofstatter)
Hofstede, Albert John
Hogan, Charles Marshall
Hogan, Donald John, Jr.
Hogan, Kempf
Hogan, Timothy Sylvester
Hogan, William James
Hoganson, Sidney J.
Hogendorn, David Harwood
Hogue, Robert Bryan
Hogue, Robert David
Hohauser, Harvey Ronald
Hohl, Harvey Edward
Hohnstein, Dale William
Hohreiter, Jack Evert
Hoke, George Peabody
Hokenstad, Merl Clifford, Jr.
Holbert, John Edward
Holbrook, James Lansing
Holcomb, Albert Eugene
Holdeman, Richard Wendell, II
Holden, Raymond Francis, Jr.
Holecek, Allen Roland
Holewinski, Felix Warner
Holiga, Ludomil Andrew
Holihan, Francis Leonard
Holinger, Paul Henry
Holiwell, Gene Andrew
Holl, Juergen Franz
Holl, Walter John
Holland, Gordon William
Holland, John Madison
Holland, Nancy Lynn
Holland, Ray Laurimore
Hollander, William Ralph
Hollandsworth, William Joseph
Holleb, Doris Bernstein
Holleb, Marshall Maynard
Holleran, Brent Joseph
Hollingsworth, David Kieth
Hollis, Harold Binkley
Holloway, Donald Phillip
Holloway, Gale Allwin
Holloway, James Arthur
Holloway, Lawrence Milton
Holloway, William Jimmerson
Holm, Donald Sutherland, Jr.
Holman, Charles Raymond
Holman, Elwood Josiah
Holmberg, James John
Holmes, Betty Jean
Holmes, Douglas MacArthur
Holmes, Elwin Leroy
Holmes, Gloria Maude Hendren (Mrs. Richard L. Holmes)
Holmes, Richard Lewis
Holmes, William Dee
Holmgren, Lowell Carlton
Holohan, O. J.
Holquist, Richard Oscar
Holsinger, Robert George
Holt, Donald Henry

Holt, Joe D.
Holt, Richard Lee
Holt, Waldo Sly
Holt, William Carl, Jr.
Holt, W(illiam) Kermit
Holterman, James Lee
Holtkamp, Dorsey Emil
Holtkamp, Stanley Alvin
Holtom, Carolyn Marjorie
Holtsberry, Albert Walter
Holvick, Olaf, II
Holzer, Reginald Jack
Holzman, Sheridan Verne
Holzworth, William Arthur
Homburger, Richard Hans
Homer, George Mohn
Homrighausen, Ronald Dean
Homuth, Floyd Ellis
Honaker, Linton Richard
Honeck, Stewart George
Hong, You Wah Suu
Hood, Kay Eve
Hood, Sarah Jane
Hoodecheck, Robert Alfred
Hook, Daryl Gayle
Hooker, Alexander Campbell, Jr.
Hooker, John Henry
Hooper, Mary-Louise
Hoops, M. Dean
Hooten, Ann Bratrud
Hoots, Harold Richard
Hoover, Edwin Leroy
Hoover, George Marion
Hoover, James Edward
Hoover, Robert James
Hoover, Thomas Henry
Hoover, Thomas Orlando
Hope, Catharine Margaret
Hopkins, B. Smith, Jr.
Hopkins, George Theodore
Hopkins, Prudence Ferrier
Hopkins, Richard Bruce
Hopkins, William Barton, Jr.
Hopper, Darrel Gene
Hopton, Eugene Francis
Horak, Penelope Catherine
Horgan, Edward Daniel
Horita, Kenji
Horkheimer, Ronald William
Horn, Carl Lewis
Horn, James Edward
Horn, Wilfred
Hornby, Frederick Thomas
Horne, Lewis William
Horner, Donald Elvin
Horner, Thomas Harvey
Horning, Leora Norlene
Horning, Ross Charles, Jr.
Horns, Howard Lowell
Hornthal, William Julius
Hornyak, Roy Robert
Horrell, C. William
Horsley, Jack Everett
Horton, Charles Cornelius
Horton, David Richard
Horton, Guy Mann
Horton, Lowell Wayne
Horton, Stanley Monroe
Horvath, James Jay
Horve, Leslie Alford
Horwedel, Lowell Charles
Horwich, Robert H.
Horwitt, Max Kenneth
Horwitz, Samuel Jacob
Hosack, Robert Eugene, Jr.
Hosford, Clarence Ralph
Hosford, Harry William, Jr.
Hoskins, Harold Paul
Hoskins, John Emmett
Hoskins, Phillip Michael
Hoskinson, Robert Emery
Hosman, David William
Hossain, T. I. M. Zahur
Hosteng, Donald Ted
Hostetler, David Lee
Hostetter, Philip Harvey
Hotaling, Jack Robert
Hotaling, Robert Bachman
Hottle, Darrell Rizer
Houchin, Ollie Boyd
Houck, James McPherson
Houck, Richard James
Hough, James Emerson
Hough, John E.
Hough, Neal Patrick
Hough, Ralph LaMar
Houghton, Cholm G.
Houk, Richard Joseph
Houk, Robert William
Houkes, John Martin
Houpis, Constantine Harry
House, Charles Edward
House, Daniel Murray
House, Fred Hawley
House, Hugh Bradford
Houser, Arnold Richard
Houser, Jon Peter
Houser, Robert Norman
Houseworth, Donald Eugene
Housfeld, Gordon Richard
Houskeeper, Barbara Ann Rossberg
Housley, Charles Edward
Houston, William Robert Montgomery
Houtman, Thomas, Jr.
Hovelsrud, John Oliver
Hoven, Ard
Howald, John William
Howard, Charles Allen, Jr.
Howard, Dan Franklin
Howard, Dean Clinton
Howard, Edward Neal
Howard, Hugh Charles
Howard, Jack Rohe

Howard, Leroy, Jr.
Howard, Lester James
Howard, Lowell Bennett
Howard, Richard T.
Howard, Robert Pickrell
Howard, Sherwin Ward
Howard, Walter Burke
Howarth, Joseph Willard
Howe, H. Philip
Howe, Jonathan Thomas
Howe, Richard Ray
Howe, Robert Hsi Lin
Howe, William Francis
Howe, William Hugh
Howell, John Christian
Howell, Margaret Hoffmann
Howell, Richard Hirst
Howell, Robert Lee
Howell, Thomas Edwin
Howell, William Busser
Howerter, Lee Morgan
Howes, Maurice Albert Henry
Howland, Ann
Howland, John Peirce
Howlett, George Frederick
Howlett, James Louis
Howlett, Michael J.
Howlett, Robert Glasgow
Howlett, Thomas Michael
Howsam, Robert Lee
Howser, John William
Howson, Thomas William
Hoy, James Franklin
Hoyland, Janet Louise
Hoyt, Hamilton Taylor
Hoyt, John Stanley, Jr.
Hozeny, Tony
Hrachovina, Frederick Vincent
Hrecz, Joseph
Hruby, Ferdinand Joseph
Hruska, Dorothy Irene Gartamaker (Mrs. James Emil Hruska)
Hruska, James Emil
Hruska, Keith Anthony
Hsi, Eugene Yu-Tseng
Hsu, Charles Fu-Jen
Hsu, Clement Ching-Shaw
Hsu, Grace Hei-Min Chen
Hsu, John J.
Hu, Chung Hong
Hu, James Chi-nien
Huang, Chao-Yang
Huang, Eugene Yuching
Huang, Kee Chang
Huang, Lin Yao
Huang, Teh Cheng
Huang, Wen-Tzy
Hubbard, Frederick Congdon
Hubbard, Halsey Frederick
Hubbard, Orville L.
Hubbard, Stanley Stub
Hubbard, Willis McCracken
Hubbell, John Gerard
Hubbs, Ronald M.
Huber, Walter Glenn
Hubin, Allen Jerome
Hubly, Genevieve Erlene
Hubner, Thomas Allan
Hubrich, Ronald LeRoy
Huckman, Michael Saul
Hudelson, William Franklin
Hudgens, James Rudolph
Hudkins, Donald Leroy
Hudkins, Stephen Jay
Hudnut, William Herbert, III
Hudson, Harold Don
Hudspeth, E. Rae
Huebner, Fred Duncan
Huelsbeck, Charles Joseph
Hueneke, Terry Allen
Huesmann, L. Rowell
Huettner, David Joseph
Huey, Arthur Sandmeyer
Huey, Robert Neff
Hufendick, Lawrence Henry
Huff, Bernard Louis, Jr.
Huff, Floyd Alonzo
Huff, Joseph William
Huff, Merrifield Wells
Huffman, James Floyd
Huffman, James Hudson
Huffman, Patrick John
Huffstutler, Donald Gordon
Hufft, John Carlton
Hugenberg, Lawrence William
Huggins, Charles Brenton
Hughes, Calvin Hoover
Hughes, John Jay
Hughes, John William
Hughes, L.R., III
Hughes, Lawrence Francis
Hughes, Margaret Cyrena
Hugo, Norman Eliot
Huh, Dong-Chin
Huizinga, Raleigh James
Hull, Betty Jane
Hull, Julius Henry
Hull, Ronald Eugene
Hull, S. Loraine Boos (Mrs. John Calkins Hull)
Hull, Thomas Van Camp
Hullett, John Wayne
Hullverson, James Everett
Huls, James Joseph
Hulse, Raymond Burrell
Hulslander, Donald John
Hultgren, Dennis Eugene
Hume, Horace Delbert
Humita, Tiberius Ted
Hummer, Glen Sharp
Humphrey, Esther Louisa Green (Mrs. Harry F. Humphrey)
Humphrey, Muriel Fay Buck
Humphrey, Owen Everett

Hung, Paul P.
Hungate, Carroll Paul
Hungerford, Lugene Green
Hunkins, Donald E.
Hunse, Tom Sheridan
Hunstein, Irving Jack
Hunt, Donald Lee
Hunt, James Calvin
Hunt, Lamar
Hunt, Robert Paul
Hunt, Warren William
Hunt, William Orland
Hunt, William Woodbury
Hunter, Carol Gene Chewning
Hunter, Cornell Choate
Hunter, Jack Laird
Hunter, Lee
Hunter, Robert Louis
Hunter, Robert Shannon
Hunter, Ronald Wesley
Hunter, Ruth Elizabeth
Hunter, Victor Lee
Huntington, Robert Freeman
Huntley, Richard Allen
Huntley, Thomas Elliott
Huntsman, Joseph Wallace
Huppler, Edward George
Hurdle, Robert Bruce
Hurl, Rodney Beck
Hurley, James Donald, Jr.
Hurley, James William
Hurlocker, Mary Marks
Huron, Bruce Chaney
Hursh, David Mercer
Hurst, James William
Hurt, John E.
Hurwitz, Archie R.
Husak, Jerome Donald
Husband, Richard Lorin, Sr.
Huseboe, Doris Eggers
Husemoller, Robert Dean
Husseiny, Abdo Ahmed
Huston, Donald Bruce
Hutcheson, John Marvin, Jr.
Hutcheson, Susanna Kaye
Hutchinson, James Joseph, Jr.
Hutchinson, Roger Lee
Hutchison, Cyril Paul
Huth, Lester Charles
Hutson, Don
Hutt, Max Lewis
Huttig, Jack Wilfred
Hutzelman, Paul David
Huvos, Kornel
Hway, Philip Joseph
Hyatt, Hudson
Hyde, Alan Litchfield
Hyde, Henry J.
Hyde, Robert C(unningham)
Hyland, Aimee Madeline
Hynes, George Patrick
Iaccino, Paul A.
Iacocca, Lido Anthony
Iannone, Liberato Alessandro
Ibarra, Jose Luis
Ibsen, Dwayne Bradley
Ice, Harry Treese
Iceman, Robert Lee
Ichord, Richard Howard
Idell, James Harold
Iglar, Jon Louis
Iglauer, Arnold
Igleburger, Robert Martin
Ignoffo, Carlo Michael
Ihde, Gladys Willma
Iliff, John Edmund
Illmer, Ruth (Mrs. Norman Rousseau)
Imarisio, John Joseph
Imhof, Anton B.
Imhoff, Harold David
Imhoff, Robert Jay
Imlay, William Elmer
Immel, William Raymond
Imrie, Walter Curtis
Inalcik, Halil
Incandela, Joseph Robert
Indenbaum, Samuel
Ingallinera, Albert Joseph
Ingerslew, Neill Dennis
Inglefield, Howard Gibbs
Ingmire, David Baker
Ingram, George Ernest
Ingram, Kenneth Lloyd
Inlow, David Ronald
Inman, Roger James
Innis, Robert William
Inselberg, Edgar
Iny, George Salim
Iorgulescu, Jorge
Ipes, Thomas Peter, Jr.
Ipina, Jorge Mario
Iqbal, Zafar
Irons, Lester
Irvin, Geraldine Hall
Irvin, Kenneth Paul
Irvine, Jack Dean
Irwin, George Earle, Jr.
Irwin, John Thomas
Irwin, William Kenneth
Irwin, William Winsor
Isaac, Margrethe Gloria
Isaacs, Gerald Louis
Isaacs, Kenneth S(idney)
Isaacs, S. Ted
Isaacson, Barry Joel
Isaacson, Max Delmar
Isely, Christian Robert, III
Ishler, Richard Eves
Isquith, Alan Jay
Israel, George Petzinger
Issari, Mohammad Ali
Ito, Jun
Ittner, Scott Burrill
Iturralde, George
Iverson, David Lynn

Ivy, Conway Gayle
Izzo, Bernard Peter
Jablonski, Lucian Stanley
Jack, Darold J.
Jacklin, William Thomas
Jackman, Harold Delbert
Jackman, Herbert Lee
Jacknow, David
Jackoway, Marlin Kay
Jackson, Carl Robert
Jackson, Charles Thomas
Jackson, David Archer
Jackson, David Arthur
Jackson, Don Merrill
Jackson, Douglas Northrop
Jackson, Edgar Bartholomew, Jr.
Jackson, Edward Franklin, Jr.
Jackson, Elmer Joseph
Jackson, Ethel Curry (Mrs. Raymond T. Jackson)
Jackson, Frederick Herbert
Jackson, Harry Calvin
Jackson, Harvey Lewis, Jr.
Jackson, J. Weldon
Jackson, Joseph
Jackson, Joseph Harrison
Jackson, Leon Cornell, Jr.
Jackson, Lydia Octavia
Jackson, Paul Douglas
Jackson, Priscilla Thomson (Mrs. Walter N. Jackson)
Jackson, Randall Ephraim
Jackson, Raymond LaVerne
Jackson, Reginald Sherman
Jackson, Richard Fielding
Jackson, Richard Lee
Jackson, Robert Howard
Jackson, Robert Willard
Jackson, Rodney Newland
Jackson, Wade Mosby
Jackson, Wesley Edmund
Jackson, Wilbert
Jacobi, H. Paul
Jacobs, Alfred Gemial
Jacobs, Andrew, Jr.
Jacobs, Elmer
Jacobs, Francis Albin
Jacobs, Harry D., Jr.
Jacobs, Herbert Fred
Jacobs, Jan Wayne
Jacobs, John Williams
Jacobs, Louis Sullivan
Jacobs, Rae Rodney
Jacobs, Stephen Leon
Jacobs, Timothy William
Jacobsen, Bernard Martin
Jacobsen, Edward Leroy
Jacobsen, Eric Kasner
Jacobsen, Erling Robert
Jacobsen, Howard
Jacobsen, Robert Fred
Jacobsen, Winfred Olsen
Jacobson, Daniel
Jacobson, Harlan Jerome
Jacobson, Leonard LeRoy Boland
Jacobson, Leonard Oscar
Jacobson, Loren Joel
Jacobson, Michael Harold
Jacobson, Norman Harry
Jacobson, Paul
Jacobson, Phillip Gordon
Jacoby, John Stewart
Jacoby, Robin Miller
Jacokes, Lee Edward
Jacox, John William
Jadach, Albert Andrew
Jaeckle, Charles Eisele
Jaeger, Arnold William
Jaeger, Don Theodore
Jaffe, Eugene J.
Jaffe, Philip Monlane
Jaffee, Lee S.
Jaffery, Sheldon Ronald
Jafri, Saiyed Qamar
Jagodzinski, Benjamin Andrew
Jahn, Harvey Raymond
Jaidinger, Judith Clarann
Jain, Sharat Kumar
Jain, Sushil Kumar
Jakeway, Edwin William, Jr.
Jaksha, Edward Anton
Jakstas, Alfred John
Jalil, Mazhar
James, Gordon David
James, Grace Whitaker
James, Jane Emerson
James, Marion Ray
James, O'Dessie Oliver
James, Richard Hale
James, Walter
James, Warren Edward
James, William Ellery Sedgwick
James, William Joseph
Jameson, Lee Merle
Jamieson, Richard Channing
Jamison, Wallace Newlin
Jamrich, John Xavier
Jan, George Pokung
Janardan, Konanur G.
Janata, Rudolph
Jandacek, James Warren
Janecke, Arthur Thomas
Janevicius, Vincas
Janis, Michael James
Janke, Herbert Gust
Janklow, William John
Jankura, Donald Eugene
Jannick, David Arnold
Janning, Mary Bernadette
Jannotta, Nicholas Carmen
Janover, Robert H.
Janowich, William Anthony
Janowski, Barbara Edgecombe Ray (Barbara Ray)

Jansen, Bernard Joseph
Jansen, Lawrence Frederick
Jansen, Mary Audrey
Jansen, Robert John
Jansma, Theodore John, Jr.
Janson, Thomas Ralph
Janssen, Dale Hilton
Janssen, Donald Phillip
Jansz, Thomas Wayne
Januz, Lauren Robert
Janzen, Abraham Ewell
Janzen, Ernst Krijgers
Janzen, Norine Madelyn Quinlan (Mrs. Douglas Mac Arthur Janzen)
Jardon, Oscar Max
Jarecki, Clare Frank
Jarecki, Eugene Alois
Jarman, David James
Jarrell, Lloyd Aubrey
Jarrell, Robert Homer
Jarvis, Craig Holloway
Jarvis, Phillip Robert
Jasinski, Stanley Kristof
Jasper, Elbert Baker
Jaszczak, Ronald Jack
Jauch, Christian Martin John
Jautokas, Victor
Javinsky, Phillip Erwin
Jay, James M(onroe)
Jayabalan, Vemblaserry
Jayaram, Bangalore-Narayana Murthi
Jaynes, Sydney Evans
Jean, Raphael Joseph
Jeck, Howard Sheffield
Jecmen, John Joseph
Jefferies, William McKendree
Jefferson, Arthur
Jefferson, Helen Chandler
Jeffery, Alexander Haley
Jeffreys, James Victor
Jeffries, Charles Dean
Jeffries, David Alan
Jeffries, Neal Powell
Jelinek, Leonard Charles
Jellison, James Logan, II
Jellison, Richard Marion
Jendrysik, Benjamin Stanley
Jenefsky, Jack
Jenkins, Carter
Jenkins, Dale Stevens
Jenkins, Edna Margaret
Jenkins, George Henry
Jenkins, Harold Richard
Jenkins, Harry Ghlee
Jenkins, Jay Oliver
Jenkins, Louis Burke
Jenkins, Wallace Alfred, Jr.
Jenkins, Walter Kimball
Jenkins, Wendell Llewellyn
Jenks, Halsey Denton
Jenks, William Thomas
Jenner, Albert Ernest, Jr.
Jenner, William Alexander
Jennings, Francis Paul
Jennings, Gene Kenneth
Jennings, James Blandford
Jennings, Norman Rodney
Jennings, William Granger
Jens, Elizabeth Lee Shafer (Mrs. Arthur M. Jens, Jr.)
Jens, Stifel William
Jensen, Donald Albert
Jensen, Eileen Marie
Jensen, Emmanuel Tranberg
Jensen, Erling N.
Jensen, Fred Charles
Jensen, Harlan Ellsworth
Jensen, John Callard
Jensen, Kenneth Russell
Jensen, Leslie Ward
Jensen, Lewis Gerton
Jensen, Raymond Andrew
Jensen, Wilma Mary Westburg (Mrs. Emmanuel T. Jensen)
Jenson, Jon Eberdt
Jeppesen, Gordon Lutz
Jerger, Douglas Clark
Jernigan, James Leslie
Jerome, John A.
Jerome, Norge Winifred
Jerry, Marjorie Collings
Jerry, Robert Howard
Jersild, Gerhardt Samuel
Jesse, Walter Adolph
Jessen, Robert Bruce
Jesseph, John Ervin
Jestrab, Frank F.
Jesunas, Kenneth Paul
Jewell, Donald Edward
Jewell, Martha Pearl
Jewett, Dennis Lee
Jezak, Bernard Andrew
Jilani, Atiq Ahmed
Jimerson, James Compere, Sr.
Jindal, Gopi Ram
Joachim, Petronilla Mary Ann
Job, Richard William
Jobe, Donald Larry
Jobes, Alvin Roy
Joehlin, Stanley Walbolt
Joffe, Bernard
Johannes, Karl Andrew
Johannsen, Kenneth M.
Johansen, Robert
Johansen, Walter Henry
Johanson, Donald Carl
John, Elmer Roy
John, Stanley Robert
Johns, Malcolm MacLean
Johnson, Allan Bernard
Johnson, Allen Dennis
Johnson, Alvin Wayne
Johnson, Archie
Johnson, Arthur Sune
Johnson, Barry Lee
Johnson, Bonnie Jean McKechnie (Mrs. Emsley W. Johnson, Jr.)
Johnson, Carl Alfred, Jr.
Johnson, Carol Marie
Johnson, Charles Farnham
Johnson, Charles Phillip
Johnson, Charles Silas
Johnson, Chauncey Paul
Johnson, Clarence, Jr.
Johnson, Clifford Terry
Johnson, Craig Leol
Johnson, Curtis William
Johnson, Dale Harry
Johnson, Dale Willis
Johnson, David William
Johnson, David Wolcott
Johnson, Dennis Charles
Johnson, Dennis Lester
Johnson, Dennis William
Johnson, Donald
Johnson, Donald Ray
Johnson, Dorothy Phyllis
Johnson, Earle Bertrand
Johnson, Edward Stone
Johnson, Ervin Victor
Johnson, Eugene Gunnard
Johnson, Farnham James
Johnson, Frederic Henry
Johnson, F(rederick) Gerald
Johnson, Harold Kenneth
Johnson, Harry Clarence
Johnson, Harvey William
Johnson, Henderson Andrew, III
Johnson, Henry Clyde
Johnson, Hugh Albert
Johnson, Jack Ross
Johnson, Jacob Russell
Johnson, James Alden
Johnson, James Edward
Johnson, James Edward
Johnson, James Owen
Johnson, Janet Lesan
Johnson, Jeffrey Royce
Johnson, Jerry Edward
Johnson, John Arnold
Johnson, John Fowler
Johnson, John Harold
Johnson, Joseph Bernard
Johnson, Josephine Louise
Johnson, Karl Einar
Johnson, Kenneth Odell
Johnson, Kenneth Roger
Johnson, Kenneth Stuart
Johnson, Lanny Leo
Johnson, Leonard Gustave
Johnson, Lester LaRue, Jr.
Johnson, Lewis Neil
Johnson, Lowell Warren
Johnson, Lyle Robert
Johnson, Sister Marie Inez
Johnson, Marlene Marie
Johnson, Martin Harold
Johnson, Marvin Adolph
Johnson, Marvin Melrose
Johnson, (Mary) Anita
Johnson, M(ichael) David
Johnson, Michael Lillard
Johnson, Milton Kenneth
Johnson, Morris Alfred
Johnson, Orville Uri
Johnson, Oscar, Jr.
Johnson, Peter Oscar
Johnson, Ralph Donald
Johnson, Ralph Stanley
Johnson, Ray Arvin
Johnson, Ray Theodore, Jr.
Johnson, Raymond Joel
Johnson, Richard Dean
Johnson, Richard Kenneth
Johnson, Richard Wilbur
Johnson, Robert Dale
Johnson, Robert Lee
Johnson, Robert Oscar
Johnson, Roland Edward
Johnson, Stanley Harold
Johnson, Stanley Richard, Jr.
Johnson, Steven Arnie
Johnson, Theodore Oliver, Jr.
Johnson, Vincent Erwin
Johnson, William Page
Johnson, William Raymond
Johnson, William Raymond
Johnston, Benjamin Burwell, Jr.
Johnston, John Lawrence
Johnston, Leo Lorraine
Johnston, Robert Porter
Johnston, Robert William
Johnston, Ronald Lee
Johnston, Walker Francis
Jokela, John Milton
Jolley, Joy Bates
Jolliff, Carl R.
Jolly, James Allen
Jolly, James Mumford, Sr.
Jona, Marjorie Helen Pugh
Jonas, Glenn Franklin
Jonas, Jiri
Jonassen, George Einar
Jonckheere, Alan Mathew
Jones, A. Clifford
Jones, Alan Porter, Jr.
Jones, Anabel Ratcliff
Jones, Ann
Jones, Anne Atkins
Jones, Braxton Pollard, Jr.
Jones, Byron Maurice
Jones, C. W.
Jones, Charles Lewis
Jones, Charles Robert
Jones, Clara Araminta Stanton (Mrs. Albert D. Jones)
Jones, David Francis
Jones, David Hamilton
Jones, Deborah Kay
Jones, Don L.
Jones, Edgar Raum
Jones, Edsel
Jones, Edward Henry, Jr.
Jones, Elizabeth Brown
Jones, Ernest Lewis
Jones, Ernest Olin
Jones, Frank Warren
Jones, Frederick Goodwin
Jones, George Over
Jones, Harold Victor, Jr.
Jones, Howard Vallance, Jr.
Jones, (James) Willard
Jones, Jerald Franklin
Jones, John David
Jones, John Sills
Jones, Kensinger
Jones, Larry David
Jones, Larry Lee
Jones, Leander Corbin
Jones, Mable Veneida
Jones, Margaret Eileen Zee
Jones, Mark Elmer, Jr.
Jones, Milo Donald
Jones, Myron Douglass
Jones, Nelson
Jones, Nina Flemister (Mrs. William M. Jones)
Jones, Norma Louise
Jones, Paul Archibald
Jones, Paul Lawrence
Jones, Ralph
Jones, Richard Cyrus
Jones, Richard Derral
Jones, Robert
Jones, Ronald Chalmers
Jones, Ronald Lee
Jones, Ronald William
Jones, Rosamond Janet
Jones, Sara S.
Jones, Thomas John
Jones, Thomas Kenneth, Jr.
Jones, Thomas Owen, Jr.
Jones, Trevor Owen
Jones, Walter Heath
Jones, Walter Leon
Jones, William Augustus, Jr.
Jones, William Mc Kendrey
Jones, William Moses
Jones, Worth Roosevelt
Jonland, Einar Wilbert
Jonson, Will
Joos, Thad Herman
Jordahl, Gene Walter
Jordan, Arthur Edward
Jordan, Clifford Homer
Jordan, Earl Clifford
Jordan, Leslie Spence
Jorgensen, LaVernia Mae
Josaitis, Marvin
Joscelyn, Kent Buckley
Joseph, Earl Clark
Joseph, Geraldine (Geri) R. Mack (Mrs. Burton M. Joseph)
Joseph, James Alfred
Joseph, Marguerite Wilson
Joseph, Ramon Rafael
Joseph, Raymond Patton
Joseph, Stanford Raymond
Josephsen, Gene
Josephson, Morton
Josephson, Richard John
Joshi, Prahlad Ravishankar
Joslen, Robert Andrew
Joslyn, Linda May
Jouno, Randolph James
Journey, Martha Jane
Joy, Charles Irving
Joy, Dennis Martin
Joyce, Al James
Joyce, Florence V. Mienert (Mrs. George T. Joyce)
Joyce, Jyme Riley (Mrs. William Joseph Joyce)
Joyce, William Joseph
Joyner, H. Sajon
Juba, Stephen
Judd, Robert Eugene
Judge, John Emmet
Judge, John Robert
Judson, Lyman Spicer Vincent
Juergensmeyer, Elizabeth Bogart (Mrs. John Eli Juergensmeyer)
Juergensmeyer, John Eli
Julian, Charles LeRoy
Julian, Cloyd James
Junaid, Raja Muhammad
Junchen, David Lawrence
June, Douglas Eugene
Jungblut, Leo Bernard
Jungjohann, Wayne Vernon
Junkin, Walter Edward
Junkins, John Merrell
Jupin, Laura Rose
Jurek, Bernard James, Jr.
Jurek, Thomas Francis
Jurgemeyer, Louis LeRoy
Jurgens, Roger Eugene
Juris, Hervey Asher
Jursek, Philip David
Jutzi, Bernhard Frederick
Juve, Richard Henry
Juve, Robert Daniel
Kaatz, Herbert Wilhelm Gottfried
Kabara, Jon Joseph
Kabele, Walter August
Kachru, Braj Behari
Kacmarcik, Thomas
Kaczmarek, Donald Thomas
Kaczmarek, Kenneth Kasimer
Kadela, Arnold Alexander
Kadlub, Karl Jozef
Kadlubowski, Michael George
Kaebitzsch, Reinhold Johannes
Kaegel, Ray Martin
Kaericher, John Conrad
Kaess, Frederick William
Kafarski, Mitchell I.
Kagan, Sioma
Kage, Arthur Vincent
Kah, Ralph Edward
Kahlenbeck, Howard, Jr.
Kahlenbeck, Paul Richard
Kahlenberg, Karl Walter
Kahn, Donald Roy
Kahn, Gene Richard
Kahn, Julian
Kahn, Mark Leo
Kahn, Sol J(erome)
Kaim, Naseem Thomas
Kain, Ida Marie Grogloth
Kaiser, Frederick Alfred
Kaiser, Paul Joseph
Kaiserman, Stuart Warren
Kaistha, Krishan Kumar
Kakolewski, Jan Wiktor
Kakonis, Thomas Earl
Kalamaros, Edward Nicholas
Kalash, Willard Loren
Kalberloh, Ralph Junior
Kales, Robert Gray
Kales, Shirley McBride (Mrs. Robert Gray Kales)
Kalinos, Katherine Dimitra
Kaljot, Victor
Kallerud, Mauritz Jacob
Kallestad, Charles Osborne
Kallet, Henry Abraham
Kallick, Charles Arthur
Kallick-Kaufmann, Maureen
Kallstrom, David H.
Kalogerson, Thomas Arthur
Kalsch, Hubert Arthur
Kalsem, Millie E.
Kaltenborn, Arthur Lewis, Jr.
Kamakas, Nicholas Constantine
Kamal, Mounir Mark
Kamal, Samir
Kaminski, Margaret Joan
Kaminsky, Manfred Stephan
Kamm, Jacob Oswald
Kamman, Paul Wilton
Kammerling, Erwin M.
Kammerlohr, Morton A., Jr.
Kamp, Ewald Albert
Kamra, Surjit Singh
Kamy, Eugene Mitchell
Kan, Frank Kwok-yin
Kanaga, Clinton Williamson, Jr.
Kanan, Fannun Ahmad
Kanarowski, Stanley Martin
Kandrac, Stephen Cyril
Kane, Jack Allison
Kane, Lucile Marie
Kane, Ralph Edgar
Kaneko, Thomas Motomi
Kang, Bann
Kangas, Gene
Kania, Walter Theodore
Kannapel, George David
Kanter, Cecil Lee
Kanter, Gerald Alan
Kantor, Marvin
Kantor, Paul Berl
Kantrowitz, Adrian
Kao, Stephen Sheng-Te
Kapacinskas, Joseph
Kapila, Ved Parkash
Kaplan, David Joseph
Kaplan, Ethan Zadok
Kaplan, Joel Robert
Kaplan, Maurice
Kaplan, Morris
Kaplan, Roy Irving
Kaplan, Stanley Meisel
Kaplan, Steven Max
Kappes, Philip Spangler
Karaba, Frank Andrew
Karayannis, Nicholas Marios
Kardinal, Carl Gustav
Kardoff, Alan David
Karinattu, Joseph
Kariotis, Joseph Anthony
Karkar, Yaqub Nasif
Karklys, Joseph
Karl, Gary William
Karlov, Barry Michael
Karlowski, Thomas Raymond
Karmarkovic, Alexander
Karmazin, Josephine Rose
Karmel, Barbara Marbut
Karol, Nathaniel H.
Karp, Edward Charles
Karr, Stephen William
Karrys, William George
Kaslow, Haven De Loss
Kasman, Louis Perry
Kasper, Robert Eugene
Kaspers, Lambert Mann
Kasperson, Richard Willet
Kasprick, Lyle Clinton
Kass, Warren Albert
Kassabaum, George Edward
Kassebaum, John Philip
Kassing, Lester Alden
Kasten, George F.
Kasten, Robert W., Jr.
Kasten, Walter
Kastenmeier, Robert William
Kastler, Eldon Lester
Kathan, Ralph Herman
Kato, Shigeyasu
Katona, Florence Cihlar
Katovsich, Dennis Franklin
Kats, Bernhard Albert
Katschke, Richard Norman
Katter, Reuben Luther
Katz, A(dolph) Edward
Katz, Adrian Izhack
Katz, Bernard
Katz, Donald LaVerne
Katzberg, Allan Alfred
Katzel, Jeanine Alma
Katzen, Maxwell E.
Katzen, Raphael
Kaucher, Robert Frederick
Kauffman, David Jacob
Kauffman, Ewing Marion
Kauffman, John Dale
Kauffman, Lynn Edward
Kaufman, Albert Nick
Kaufman, Burt Allan
Kaufman, Harvey Isadore
Kaufman, Irving H.
Kaufman, Joanne Klein
Kaufman, Kiesl Karl
Kaufman, Nathan Jay
Kaufman, Sydney Morton
Kaufmann, Felix
Kaufmann, Karl Eugene
Kaufmann, Marion Kenneth
Kaufmann, Stella Miriam Butcher (Mrs. Kenneth Kaufmann)
Kaul, Philip Gibbs
Kaupp, Verne Henry
Kavanagh, Thomas Giles
Kavanaugh, Charles Edward
Kavieff, Shelden Milford
Kawahara, Fred Katsumi
Kay, Dick (Richard D. Snodgrass)
Kaye, Gerard Walter
Kaye, Joel Edmund
Kaye, Stephen John
Kayton, Lawrence
Kazwell, Albert Leo
Keairns, Raymond Earl
Kean, Joseph Edward
Keane, Francis Martin
Keane, John G.
Kearns, Charles Albert
Kearns, Francis Emner
Keating, Donald John
Keck, James Moulton
Keck, Robert Clifton
Keck, William Francis
Keefe, Kenneth Michael
Keefer, Lucinda Kay Miller
Keegan, Joseph Harry
Keeler, James Howard
Keenan, William Herbert
Keeny, Maurice Garfield
Kehl, Leora Rowena Neal
Kehler, Paul
Keidan, Fred Hannan
Keil, Marvin Henry
Keim, Earl George, Jr.
Keirns, Harry Dayton
Keiser, Roger James
Keith, Damon Jerome
Keithley, Richard Ernest
Kekst, Keeva Joseph
Kelch, Paul
Kelkar, Manohar Shankar
Keller, Charles Frederick
Keller, David Coe
Keller, Dean Howard
Keller, Harold William
Keller, Howard Joseph
Keller, John Bidwell
Keller, John Jerome
Keller, Louis Paul
Keller, Marvin Dave
Keller, Maurice Joseph
Keller, Robert Anthony
Keller, Robert Howard, Jr.
Keller, Thomas Whitney
Keller, Vera Prokop
Kellerman, Bert Joseph
Kellerman, John Leon
Kelley, Carl Philetus
Kelley, Charles Edward
Kelley, Edward Glenn
Kelley, Frank Joseph
Kelley, Frank Vernon
Kelley, Garen Nile
Kelley, John Edgar
Kelley, Verne Robert
Kelley, Vernon Edward
Kellman, Jerold Lee
Kellogg, Darrell Dean
Kellow, Keith Vance
Kelly, Bruce Birk
Kelly, Dale Emery
Kelly, Ernest Byron, Jr.
Kelly, Glenn Vincent
Kelly, John Terence
Kelly, Joseph Francis, Jr.
Kelly, Leonard Michael
Kelly, Margaret Grimes
Kelly, Michael Daniel
Kelly, Raymond Ransome, Jr.
Kelly, Robert Donald
Kelly, Thomas Joseph
Kelman, Stephen Jay
Kelsey, Gladys H.
Kelsey, Ridell Archibald
Kelsey, Victor Andrew
Kelso, Harold Glen
Kelso, James Jude
Kelson, Allen Howard
Keltner, Raymond Marion, Jr.
Kelton, Dale Lynn
Kemble, Ernest Dell
Kemeny, George Oravec
Kemp, Arnold Raymond
Kemp, George Pendleton
Kempa, Roy G.
Kempe, Robert Aron
Kemper, Charles Samuel
Kemper, Robert Graham
Kempfer, Lester Leroy
Kempthorne, Gerald C.
Kenaga, Eugene Ellis
Kendall, Donna Joyce
Kendall, George Preston
Kendall, Jerry D.
Kendall, Richard Hale
Kendall, Robert Andrew
Kendall, Robert Llewellyn
Kendle, John Edward
Kendrick, Virginia Catherine (Mrs. W. Dudley Kendrick)
Kendro, Richard Joseph
Kenly, Granger Farwell
Kenna, Francis Regis
Kennedy, Edward Earl
Kennedy, George Francis
Kennedy, Gordon James
Kennedy, Hayes
Kennedy, James Martin
Kennedy, John Allan
Kennedy, John Charles
Kennedy, John Joseph
Kennedy, John Xavier
Kennedy, Kevin Curtis
Kennedy, Robert Lloyd
Kennedy, William Joseph
Kennelly, Karen Margaret
Kenney, Charles Samuel
Kenney, Robert Lyle
Kenning, Norman Stephen
Kenny, Philip Thomas
Kent, A. Robert
Kent, Albert Sydney
Kent, Calvin Albert
Kent, Donald Leroy
Kent, Geoffrey
Kent, Homer Austin, Jr.
Kent, Lee Anne
Kent, Melvin
Kenworthy, Merrell T.
Kenworthy, Orville Franklin
Keogh, Jeanne Marie
Keough, Joseph Stanley
Keplinger, Stephen Anthony, Jr.
Kepner, Henry Sieber, Jr.
Keppler, Ernest Carl
Ker, Charles Arthur
Kerber, Daniel William
Kerbis, Don Kenneth
Kerbis, Gertrude Lempp
Kerchal, Raymond George
Kerekes, John Joseph
Kerkay, Julius
Kern, Edward Allen
Kern, John Charles
Kern, Sister Margaret
Kernan, Edward James
Kerndt, Thomas Martin
Kerns, Gertrude Yvonne
Kerr, Albert Edward
Kerr, Cecil Raymond
Kerr, Frederick Hohmann
Kerr, Kathel Austin
Kerr, Wendle Louis
Kerr, William Edward, Jr.
Kershaw, Beulah Frances (Mrs. Bryan Kershaw)
Kerwood, John Richard
Keskitalo, Wallace Albert
Kesler, John Charles
Kessinger, Howard David
Kessinger, Margaret Anne
Kessler, Clemm Cromwell, III
Kessler, John Edward
Kessler, Lawrence W.
Kessler, Ronald Norman
Kessler, William Ertman
Kessler, Winifred Beam-Flautt
Kestel, John L.
Kestnbaum, Kate Trynin
Kestnbaum, Robert Dana
Ketcham, Warren Andrew
Ketel, W. Bruce
Keucher, William Frederick
Kevern, Ronald Bawden
Kevlin, Ross Patrick
Keyes, James Lyman, Jr.
Keyes, Murray Allison
Keys, Christopher Bennett
Keys, Martha Elizabeth
Kezys, Algimantas George
Khalafalla, Sanaa El-Sayed
Khalili, Ali Asghar
Khalili, Joseph Elias
Khambata, Adi Jehangir
Khan, Mohammed Nasrullah
Khanna, Satish C.
Khapoya, Vincent Barassa
Khazei, Amir Hassan
Khedroo, Lawrence Glenn
Khezri-Yazdan, Ali-Asghar
Kho, Eusebio
Khosh, John Gholam Hosein
Khosh, Mary Sivert
Kiani, Reza
Kibbe, John Carter
Kice, Jack Wilbur
Kickels, Mary Kay
Kiddle, Lawrence Bayard
Kidston, Alan R.
Kidwell, E. Lee
Kiefer, John Joseph
Kiefer, Joseph Henry
Kiefer, Robert Allen
Kiel, O. Frederick
Kielbasa, Clement Alexander
Kielkopf, William Michael
Kiene, Richard Hotchkiss
Kiernan, William Joseph, Jr.
Kiesling, Norman Louis
Kiess, Robert David
Kiewiet, Paul Alan
Kilburn, Richard Friend

Kildee, Dale E.
Kilgore, Annabelle Thompson
Kilgore, James Columbus
Kilgour, Frederick Gridley
Killham, Albert Benjamin
Killion, Mark Everest
Killoren, Timothy Jerome
Kilman, James William
Kilmer, Lloyd Warren
Kilsdonk, Martin Sexton
Kilton, Francis Joseph, Jr.
Kim, Byron B.W.
Kim, Churl Suk
Kim, Dong-Soo
Kim, Kyung Soo
Kim, Nhak Hee
Kim, Sung Chul
Kimbell, Kenneth Richard
Kimble, M(arcus) Allen
Kimbrough, Kelse McDowell
Kimbrough, Roosevelt
Kimbrough, William Walter, III
Kimm, James Wilson
Kimm, Jong Soung
Kimmel, Richard Lee
Kimmons, Kieth Dewayne
Kin, Frederick Robert
Kincaid, Mary Elizabeth
Kincheloe, John Arthur
Kinder, Donald Dee
Kindig, Fred Eugene
Kindle, Helen Joan Swoverland (Mrs. Paul Eugene Kindle)
Kindness, Thomas Norman
King, Arthur Mansfield
King, Barbara Anne
King, Charles Ross
King, David Edgar
King, Duane Edward
King, Franklin Alexander
King, Imogene Martina
King, (Jack) Weldon
King, James Robert
King, James T.
King, JoAnn Elizabeth
King, John Clancy
King, Kenneth Edward
King, LeRoy Harry, Jr.
King, Leslie Albert
King, Patrick James
King, Robert James
King, Thomas Joseph
King, William Frederic
King, William Houston
Kingdon, Robert McCune
Kinget, G. Marian
Kinias, George Athanasios
Kinnaird, Charles Roemler
Kinnear, Thomas Clifford
Kinnick, August Edward
Kinnison, William Andrew
Kinsella, James Joseph
Kinsella, Ralph Aloysius, Jr.
Kinsley, Daniel Allan (Allen Edwards)
Kintz, Mary Elizabeth
Kinyoun, Dale Edward
Kinzer, Donald Louis
Kionka, Edward James
Kipnis, Barry Edwin
Kipp, Robert Almy
Kiracofe, John Harmon
Kirby, James Robert
Kirby, Thomas Joseph, Jr.
Kirchner, James William
Kirchner, John Howard, Jr.
Kirchner, Richard Jay
Kirk, Russell Amos
Kirk, Treva Bennington
Kirk, William Edward
Kirk, William Julian
Kirk, Wyatt Douglass
Kirkegaard, R(aymond) Lawrence, Jr.
Kirkhus, Harold Preston
Kirkland, Charles Walter, Jr.
Kirkpatrick, Gary Lee
Kirkpatrick, James C.
Kirkpatrick, Joseph Francis
Kirkpatrick, Robinson Perkins
Kirstein, Peter Neil
Kirsteins, Andrew
Kish, Elmer Anthony
Kishner, Mel
Kiskis, James Matthew
Kispert, Donald Eugene
Kispert, Robert Charles
Kiss, Janos
Kissell, Kenneth Eugene
Kissling, Charles Daniel
Kist, Richard James
Kistler, John Joseph, Jr.
Kitazumi, Marie Nakamura
Kitchen, Carl Robert
Kitchen, Charles William
Kitchen, Denis Lee
Kitchin, Paul Clifford, Jr.
Kitsis, Louis
Kitt, Walter
Kitterman, John H.
Kittner, Edwin Henry
Kittrell, Harold Keith
Kitzmiller, Karl William
Kivela, Edgar Welton
Kivett, Marvin F.
Kjar, Rolland William
Klafter, Melvin Leslie
Klahn, Thomas Harold
Klahr, Saulo
Klainsek, Frank
Klamen, Marvin Max
Klanderman, John Winston
Klarreich, Harold Leopold
Klarreich, Susan Friedman
Klasek, Charles Bernard
Klass, Joseph Benjamin
Klauck, Kenneth A.
Klaus, Mark Francis
Klausmeyer, Thomas Henry
Klay, Reynold
Klayman, Maxwell Irving
Kleiman, Bernard
Kleimola, Frank William
Klein, Alice Jarvis
Klein, Charles Henle
Klein, Charles Mosher
Klein, Edgar Albert
Klein, George Robert
Klein, Paul Brinkman
Klein, Stuart Marc
Klein, Vern Dale
Kleinerman, David
Kleinman, Bennet
Kleinschmidt, Albert Willoughby
Kleinsmith, Lewis Joel
Klemme, Larry Lee
Klepfer, Eugene Woods
Kletschka, Harold Dale
Kley, Roland Gottlieb
Klie, Gary Young
Klie, Hamilton Fuller
Klimek, Ronald Edward
Kline, James Edward
Kline, Joyce Claire (Mrs. Flavio Puletti)
Kline, Mary Elaine Graves
Kline, Raymond Alvin
Kline, Tex Ray
Kling, George Albert
Klingbeil, Donald Edward
Klingel, Martin Allen
Klingensmith, Don Joseph
Klingensmith, Mrs. Don (Thelma Hyde Klingensmith)
Klinger, William Russell
Klingner, Harold William
Klitzke, Lyle Kenneth
Kloehn, John Sherman
Kloehn, Ralph Anthony
Klos, Jerome John
Klotz, John Melvin
Klug, Richard Paul
Klutznick, Philip M.
Kluver, Herman Christof
Knaak, William Charles
Knape, Gerald Francis
Knapp, Donald Lewis
Knapp, Kenneth Raymond
Knapp, Peter Michael
Knapp, Richard Wadsworth
Knapstein, John William
Knecht, Charles Daniel
Kneedler, Charles Forrest
Kneeland, Larry Marshall
Kneip, Richard Francis
Kneisley, Gary Lynn
Knepper, Eugene Arthur
Knicely, David Roger
Knierim, Virgil Jacob
Knight, Lester Benjamin
Knight, Robert Duane
Knight, William D., Jr.
Knight, Yale
Knighton, Joseph Raymond
Knighton, Robert Syron
Knighton, Samuel Curtis
Knights, Edwin Munroe
Kniola, John Raymond
Knoche, Everett, Jr.
Knock, Malcolm Argyle
Knoedler, Norman Robert
Knospe, William Herbert
Knote, Charles E.
Knott, Albert Paul, Jr.
Knott, James LeRoy
Knouff, Lorentz Bennett
Knowles, Jean Turnbull (Mrs. James Knowles, Jr.)
Knox, Charles Stuart
Knoy, Maurice George
Knudtson, Allen Dennis
Knutson, Marlin Justin
Ko, Paoshu
Ko, Sung-Tao
Kobak, Mathew William
Kober, Arletta Refshauge (Mrs. Kay L. Kober)
Koblenz, Howard Robert
Koblenz, Maxine L.
Kobylecky, Joseph John
Koch, Elmer Leonard
Koch, George Paul
Koch, Gunter Werner
Koch, Robert Louis, II
Koch, Wendell Reuben
Koch, William Albert
Koch, William Henry
Kochar, Mahendr Singh
Kochell, Richard Lee
Kocian, Marvin Leo
Kociolko, John Stephen
Kocol, Raymond John
Kocur, John Anthony
Koehler, Theodore Armand
Koehn, Enno
Koenig, Harold Henry
Koenig, Rachel Hope
Koepke, Robert Walter
Koepp, Alfred Ernest
Koeppe, Ralph Jacob
Koepsell, Paul Loel
Koerner, Warren Alden
Koetting, Robert Anthony
Kofman, Sydney
Koga, Hisako Mary
Kogan, Bernard Robert
Kogan, Herman
Koglin, Norman Alfred
Kogut, Kenneth Joseph
Koh, Byung Chul
Koh, Severino Legarda
Kohel, Jerome Joseph
Koh-Guevarra, Arsenia
Kohlan, William George
Kohlman, Kenneth Harold
Kohn, Frank Solis
Kohn, Russel Ferdinand
Kohnen, David Alphonse
Kohnen, Ralph Bernard, Jr.
Kohr, Roland Ellsworth
Kohring, Gene William
Koivula, Steven John
Kokonis, Nicholas Demetrios
Kokoropoulos, Panos
Kolar, Otto Michael
Kolatalo, Walter Wladimir
Kolb, Alan Foster
Kolb, Joseph Wilbur
Kolenda, Frank Donald
Kolesar, Edward Steven, Jr.
Kolflat, Tor Dagfin
Kollasch, Irene Haines
Kolles, Bertrand Aloy
Kollins, Michael Jerome
Kollker, John Jennings
Kolmin, Kenneth Guy
Kolonko, Joseph John, Jr.
Koloski, Helen Spalding
Kolsrud, Roger
Kolstad, John Haesloop
Komie, Stephen Mark
Komjathy, Anthony Tihamer
Kommer, Norman Bud
Komosa, Adam Anthony
Kompass, Edward J.
Koncelik, Joseph Arthur
Kondorossy, Elizabeth Davis
Kondorossy, Leslie
Konicek, Frank Joseph
Konie, Joseph C.
Konie, Robert B.
Konikow, Robert Bernard
Konkle, Janet Marie Everest (Mrs. Arthur Jackson Konkle)
Konnyu, Leslie
Kontogiannis, George J.
Kooi, Earl Robert
Kooistra, William Henry
Kopel, David
Koplin, Allen Norman
Kopp, Carl Robert
Kopp, Leonard Lewis
Koppel, Lowell B.
Koppenhaver, Allen J.
Kops, Sheldon
Kopulsky, Marvin
Kore, Valentine Karlis
Korgie, John Paul
Korkan, Kenneth Duns
Korllos, Thomas Stephen
Korney, John Joseph
Kornguth, Steven Edward
Kornokovich, Ronald John
Korow, Elinore Maria
Korp, Otto August, Jr.
Korschot, Benjamin Calvin
Korsvik, William James
Korte, Robert Theodore
Kortebein, Stuart Rowland
Kortenhof, Joseph Michael
Kortepeter, Fred Tolin
Koscik, Richard Allen
Koser, Phillip James
Koshak, Arthur Emil
Kosier, Mary Wilkin
Koss, John Charles
Kostal, Otto Albin
Kostenko, Barry Michael
Koszewski, Bohdan Julius
Kotansky, Donald Richard
Kotche, James Ray
Kotin, Lawrence Lewis
Kotnik, Ronald Joseph
Kotsonis, George Nick
Kottha, Jagannadham
Koucky, John Richard
Koumoulides, John Thomas Anastasios
Koutoujian, Hagop Khachadour
Kovach, Bernard Clement
Kovachy, Edward Miklos
Kovacik, Victor Paul
Koval, Paul William
Kovarik, Leland Kenneth
Kovats, Leslie Paul
Kovitz, Seymour J.
Kowall, James L.
Koyle, Myron Raymond
Kozak, Martin Jerry
Kozelka, Edward William
Kozimer, Philip Dale
Kozlowski, David Karl
Kozlowski, Donald Robert
Kozy, Kenneth Robert
Krabbenhoft, Kenneth Lester
Kraemer, Boyd Andre
Kraemer, Harold William
Kraft, Reyburn Herman
Krahel, William Albert
Krahl, Enzo
Krall, Joseph I.
Kramer, Alex John
Kramer, Anne Helen
Kramer, Carl Edward
Kramer, Charles Eugene
Kramer, David Bruce
Kramer, David Eugene
Kramer, Frederick Claude
Kramer, Helen Ann Tobaben
Kramer, John Louis
Kramer, Oscar
Kranitz, Theodore Mitchell
Krantz, Beatrice V.
Krantz, Lawrence Henry
Krase, Roger Curtis
Kratovil, Robert
Krause, Arthur Walter
Krause, Edward Walter
Krause, Paul Anton
Krautkremer, James Joseph
Kravetz, Russell Stuart
Krc, John, Jr.
Krebs, Clyde L.
Krebs, Festus John, Jr.
Krebs, Kenneth Allen
Krech, Edward M., Jr.
Krecke, Charles Francis
Kreer, Henry Blackstone
Kregel, Anna May
Kreger, James Lee
Kreilick, Marjorie Ellen
Kremsner, Frank Fred
Krenitsky, Peter
Kress, Robert Lee
Krey, Geneva Margaret
Kreykes, Gary Dick
Kricker, Edmund Joseph
Krieg, Beverly Ann Marriott
Krieger, Benjamin William
Krishna, Gopal
Krit, Robert Lee
Kritz, Jerry Russell
Kroah, Larry Allen
Kroemer, James Darrell
Kroepel, Robert Howard
Krogh, Harold Christian
Krol, Edward J(oseph)
Kroll, George
Kronquist, Shirley Joyce
Kronschnabel, Edward Francis
Kross, Morris H.
Krossner, William John, Jr.
Krouse, Paul Carl
Kruck, Donna Jean Hagemeyer (Mrs. Michael Roy Kruck Jr.)
Kruckenberg, Cory Henry
Krueckenberg, Karl Louis
Krueger, Robert George
Krueger, Thomas Paul
Krueger, William Frederick
Krug, Edwin Herbert
Krug, Gerhardt Ronald
Kruger, Elmer Lawrence
Kruger, Robert Louis
Kruger, William Arnold
Kruidenier, David
Kruidenier, Elizabeth Stuart
Krumhansl, Bernice Rosemary
Krumm, Carol Mae Rhodeback (Mrs. Delbert Russell Krumm)
Krumm, John McGill
Krumske, William Frederick, Jr.
Kruse, Edgar C.
Kruse, Gerald Stanley
Kruse, Paul Walters, Jr.
Krusinski, Clarence
Krysiak, Joseph Edward
Kubista, Theodore Paul
Kubo, Sakae
Kubo, Yukio Brian
Kuby, Thomas Eugene
Kucera, Kenneth Charles
Kuchar, Kathleen Ann
Kuchar, Rudolph Joseph
Kuchel, Gaylon Lyle
Kucherak, Anthony John
Kucinski, Leo
Kuecker, Theodore Edwin
Kuehl, Hal C.
Kuehl, Warren Frederick
Kuehn, Robert Oscar
Kuehner, George Frederick
Kuehnle, Walter Reinhart
Kuenster, John Joseph
Kueper, Joseph Francis
Kuespert, Carl Adolph
Kugler, Anna Marie
Kugler, William John
Kuglitsch, John Francis
Kuhl, Lawrence Van
Kuhl, Margaret Helen Clayton (Mrs. Alexius M. Kuhl)
Kuhl, Robert Henry
Kuhlman, James Weldon
Kuhlman, Paul Wayne
Kuhlmann, Gustave Adolf
Kuhn, John Raymond, Jr.
Kuhn, Karen Ann Kellogg
Kuhn, William Leo
Kuhre, Bruce Edward
Kukla, Robert John
Kukreja, Subhash Chander
Kulacki, Francis Alfred
Kulis, Richard William
Kulkarni, Bidy
Kull, Charles Frederick, Jr.
Kulp, Samuel Lester
Kultermann, Udo Rainer
Kumaran, Jay Sampath
Kundert, Alice E.
Kunkel, Lorenz Victor
Kunkle, Calvin Sylvester
Kunkle, George Robert
Kunkler, Arnold William
Kuntz, Earl Jeremy
Kuntz, Herman William
Kuntzleman, Charles Thomas
Kupcinet, Irv
Kupersmith, Farrell Preston
Kupferberg, Lloyd Sherman
Kupst, Mary Jo
Kurfess, Roland Herman
Kurman, George
Kurtis, William (Bill) Horton
Kushner, Frederick R.
Kutler, Benton
Kutscher, Gordon Ralph
Kutz, Ralph George
Kutza, Michael Joseph, Jr.
Kuzel, Norbert Raymond
Kwak, Junkyu Christopher
Kwan, Francis P.
Kyes, Helen G. (Mrs. Roger M. Kyes)
Kyle, Earle Fleetwood, Jr.
Kyle, Mary J.
Kyles, Calvin Eugene
Kyriazis, Andreas P.
Kyriazopoulos, Dimitrios George
Kyvig, David Edward
Laatz, Mary Jane
Labate, Charles Raymond
Labbie, Stephen
La Belle, Charles Earl
La Belle, Wilma Carol Marcy
Labine, Paul
La Camera, Joseph, Jr.
Lacher, Thomas Francis, Jr.
Lachner, Bernard Joseph
Lackens, John Wendell
Lackie, Richard David
La Claire, David Binney
Lacsina, Emmanuel Quiambao
Lacy, Edna Balz
Lacy, Edwin Vemont, Jr.
Lacy, Herman Edgar
Lacy, Jack
Lacy, Robert Eugene
Lad, Prakash Shripad
Ladin, Lawrence
Ladley, Charlsie Louise
La Du, Bert Nichols, Jr.
Ladwig, Harold Allen
Ladwig, Ronald Victor
LaFevers, Larry Edmond
Laffer, Molly Amelia Betz (Mrs. William G. Laffer)
Laffer, William Gillespie
Lafferty, Daniel Charles
Lafferty, Robert Corder, III
La Follette, Bronson Cutting
La Follette, Gerry Campbell
Lafont, Gerardo
Lafontant, Jewel
Lafore, Laurence Davis
La Forge, Paul Edward
Lage, Louise Catherine
Lagerlund, Terrence Daniel
Lagomarcino, Paul Andrew
Lagzdins, Voldemars
Lahey, Michael Francis
Lahniers, Carroll Edward
La Hood, Joseph John
Lahrman, Don Eugene
Lahti, Paul Theodore
Laidler, James Harold
Laing, James Thomas
Lair, Dwayne Eugene
Laird, Evalyn Walsh
Laird, Jean Elouise Rydeski (Mrs. Jack E. Laird)
Laird, Richard H.
Laird, Susan Zoe
Laird, Thomas Richard
Lakatos, George Charles
Lake, Thomas Philip
Lally, Ann Marie
Lam, Tung Ting
Lamb, Charlotte B.
Lamb, Clifford William Bill
Lamb, Richard Joseph
Lamb, Thomas
Lambert, Charles Otterbein
Lambert, Daniel Michael
Lambert, Dennis Michael
Lambert, Guy William
Lambert, James Arthur
Lambert, James Howard
Lambert, Milton Harold
Lambert, Sam Amon
Lamborn, David Joseph
Lambrecht, Robert Palmer
Lambrechts, Emile Daumont
Lammers, Paul Herman
Lammert, Albert Charles
Lamminen, Arthur John
Lamont, Frances Stiles (Peg) (Mrs. William Lamont)
Lamont, William Alexander
Lamoreaux, Delores Evangeline Tom Loula (Mrs. Lee V. Lamoreaux)
Lamping, Robert Lee
Lamson, Robert Wade
Lancaster, Richard Kirby
Lance, George Milward
Lancione, Bernard Gabe
Land, Robert Donald
Landen, Wayne LaVerne
Lander, John Charles
Landhuis, Leo Ray
Landis, Frank E.
Landiss, Mark Eugene
Landman, David
Landon, Arnold Gifford
Landsberg, Dean Arnold
Landstrom, Donald Albert
Landwehr, Arthur John, Jr.
Landy, Agatha Horrigan (Mrs. Thomas M. Landy)
Lane, Dale Walter
Lane, Harold Edwin
Lane, James A.
Lane, John Clyde
Lane, Louis
Lane, Orris John, Jr.
Lane, Richard Oscar
Lane, Robert Joseph
Lane, Russell Watson
Lane, Thomas Benton
Lane, Wilfred Roger
Lang, Francis H.
Lang, William Edward
Lange, Frederick Emil
Langeler, George Harris
Langer, John Bohumil
Langham, Michael
Langston, Judy Ann
Lanker, Karl Emil
Lankford, Ronald Bradley
Lanning, James William
Lannon, John Joseph
Lano, Charles Jack
Lantolf, Joseph John
Lantz, Charles Emil
Lantzsch, Hans Edwin
Lanz, Robert Walter
La Pointe, Leon Alvin
La Polla, James Joseph
Laposky, Ben Francis
Larcher, Angelo Clement
Large, Richard Leroy
Larkin, S. Lee
Larmer, Oscar Vance
La Rowe, Daniel Dale
La Rowe, Myron Edward
Larrance, Kenneth S.
Larrison, Thomas Richard
Larsen, Curtis LeRoy
Larsen, James Warner
Larsen, Lester Frederick
Larsen, Theodore Edward
Larson, Allan Louis
Larson, Andrew Robert
Larson, Carl Jacob
Larson, Carl Martin
Larson, David Roger
Larson, Don Wayne
Larson, Gerald Lewis
Larson, Gordon Albert
Larson, Joseph Henry
Larson, Larry Kent
Larson, Lawrence Myrlin
Larson, Leonard
Larson, Lester George
Larson, Linda Louise
Larson, Maurice Allen
Larson, Obert Leroy
Larson, Paul Nordland
Larson, Roland Sigward
Larson, Rolland James
Larson, Sanford John
Larson, Sidney
Larson, Wayne LeRoy
Larson, Wilfred Leroy
Larson, William Herbert
Larsson, Dorothy K. (Mrs. Karl G.B. Larsson)
La Rue, David Lee
Laser, William Charles
Lash, Kenneth
Lasher, Esther Lu (Mrs. Donald T. Lasher)
Lashorne, Paul Russell, Jr.
Lasiewicz, Thaddeus Walter
Laskin, Sylvester
Laskowski, Leonard Francis, Jr.
Lasley, Jack Moss
Lassers, Elisabeth Stern
Lassers, Willard J.
Lasswell, Tull Cress
Lastoria, Michael Donald
Latham, Iris Anne
Latham, Robert Allen
Latham, Wilbur Joseph
Latherow, Clifford Brandon
Latourette, Brainerd William, Jr.
Latta, Delbert L.
Latter, Martin
Lattimer, Richard Lee
Lattimer-Bethel, Agnes Dolores
Latz, Robert
Lau, Chosen Chui-Shun
Lau, Jackson Chart-sum
Laubach, John Paul
Laubenheimer, Roger
Lauck, Jacqueline Ann
Lauckner, Connie Louise Pietrowski
Laudan, James Alva
Laudicina, Paul Frank
Laudick, Richard Edward, Jr.
Lauer, Harold Eugene
Lauer, Peter Hans
Lauer, Robert Harold
Lauffer, Alice A.
Laughlin, Charles Walter
Laughlin, Ethelreda Elizabeth Ross
Lauman, Vona Kathryn (Mrs. James Wesley Lauman)
Laun, Arthur Henry, Jr.
Laundry, Marion Suzanne Teeuws (Mrs. Melburn Edward Laundry)
Launius, Delmer Dwain
Lauren, Oscar Bud
Laurence, Richard Robert
Laurenson, Robert Mark
Laurenti, Joseph Lucian
Laurents, Louis Vinson, Jr.
Laurila, Harold Lavern
Laurino, Anthony C.
Laursen, Paul Herbert
Lauterjung, Marvin Alan
Lautzenhiser, Niann Kay
Lauver, Milton Renick
Laux, Patricia Marie
Laver, Gerald Eby
Lavin, Carl Hershel
Lavin, David J.
Lavin, Elinor R. Golden
Lavine, John Morgan
Lavitt, Ben
Law, Edwin B.
Law, Lyle Brewster

Lawerenz, Mark David
Lawes, Bayard Fratcher
Lawler, Bernard James
Lawler, William Edward, Jr.
Lawrence, David Long
Lawrence, Dean Webster
Lawrence, James Albert
Lawrence, Merle
Lawrence, Norman Richard
Lawrence, Richard Marston
Lawrence, William Robert
Lawrence, William Stanton
Lawrenz, Paul Henry
Lawson, Donald Elmer
Lawson, Esther Chaney (Mrs. Albert Theodore Lawson)
Lawson, Judith Karen
Lawton, John Miller
Lawyer, Verne
Lax, Louis Carl
Lay, Obert Merle
Laybourne, George Thomas
Lazar, Harold Paul
Lazare, John Nicholas
Lazarus, Irwin Philip
Lazzara, Philip
Lea, Albert Robert
Leach, David Mason
Leach, Frederick Darwin
Leach, James Albert Smith
Leach, James Lindsay
Leach, Ronald Lee
Leahy, James Michael
Leal, Victor Luciano
Leaneagh, Jerry Del
Lear, John
Learned, Charles Alden
Lease, Thomas Charles
Leatherman, Lowen Audred
Leatherwood, Paul Randolph Scott, Jr.
Lebens, John Casper
Lebit, Edward Alan
Lebrenz, Eugene Richard
Le Brun, John Leo
Le Brun, Vivian Lucille Davis (Mrs. Donald Edward LeBrun)
Lebryk, Edwin Frank
Lechiara, Joseph Michael
Lechner, George William
Leckie, James Robert
Le Claire, Henri
Le Compte, Garé
Le Crone, Norman James
Ledinko, Nada
Le Duc, Don Raymond
Lee, Dong Sung
Lee, Douglas Allen
Lee, E(ugene) Stanley
Lee, Gilbert Brooks
Lee, Hi Bahl
Lee, J. Murray
Lee, James Chen-Ming
Lee, Joon Ja Kim
Lee, Joseph Jooinn
Lee, Jung Ki
Lee, Kyo Rak
Lee, Kyu Yawp
Lee, Margaret
Lee, Nelda Kaye
Lee, Paul Warren
Lee, Ralph Lawrence
Lee, Robert Edward
Lee, Robert Michael
Lee, Sang Han
Lee, Sherman Emery
Lee, Shu Ching
Lee, Song Ping
Lee, Sung Ho
Lee, Ted J.
Lee, Thomas Gerald
Lee, Tong Hun
Lee, William Chae-Sik
Lee, William Johnson
Lee, Woodrow
Lee, Yien-hwei
Leece, Curtis Thompson
Leedy, Emily L. Foster (Mrs. William N. Leedy)
Leekley, Robert Mitchell
Leemon, John Allen
Leenhouts, Keith James
Leep, Gus Weaurton, Jr.
Leet, Richard Eugene
Leffler, Marlin Templeton
Leffman, Peter Lawrence
Leftin, Gary Wayne
Leggett, Glenn
Leggett, Kerry Eugene
Leggitt, Dorothy
Le Grand, Clay
Lehman, Charles Dwight
Lehman, Clyde Frederick
Lehman, David Owen
Lehman, Richard Leroy
Lehmann, M. Drue
Lehmberg, Stanford Eugene
Lehner, Paul Michael
Lehr, Glenn Carlton
Leibovich, Herman
Leicht, Geraldine Russell
Leidig, Melvin Dwight
Leidner, Burton Richard
Leidner, Harold Edward
Leif, Claude (Bud) Peter
Leigh, Fred Durshee
Leigh, Robert Lawton
Leighninger, David Scott
Leighninger, Margaret Jane Malony (Mrs. David S. Leighninger)
Leighton, George Neves
Leighton, Paul William
Leimkuhler, Gus Ernest, Jr.
Lein, Malcolm Emil
Leininger, Elmer
Leininger, Harold Vernon
Leinonen, Ellen Anna
Leisen, Richard Joseph
Leiser, Burton Myron
Leiseth, Robert Vernon
Leist, Carl Clinton
Leist, John Wright
Leith, James Clark
Leitherer, Arthur Eugene
Leland, Gary Leroy
Leliaert, Raymond Maurice
Le Mar, William Bernhardt
Lemberger, Louis
Lemberger, Robert Alois
Leming, John Curtis
Lemke, Arthur Athniel
Lemmon, Dallas Marion
Lemmon, Kenneth Wayne
Lemon, Henry Martyn
Lemon, William Joseph
Le Moyne, Noel Joseph
Lenagar, Glenn Robert, Jr.
Lenardson, James Duane
Lenertz, Aloys Frank
Lengel, Leland Levi
Lenhart, Milton John
Lennertz, Raymond
Lennon, Delores Rae Francisco
Lennox, Marjorie Elizabeth
Lennox, Rand Tru
Lenox, Richard Louis
Lentfer, Richard Herman
Lentz, Daniel Marvin
Lentz, Jay Alden
Lenz, Ralph Charles, Jr.
Lenzo, Anthony Samuel
Leon, Arthur Sol
Leonard, Albert Edwin
Leonard, Archibald Thane
Leonard, George Adams
Leonard, Harry Elvin
Leonard, Leo Donald
Leonard, Paul James
Leonard, Roy Junior
Leonard, Theodis Raymond
Leonida, Domingo Dominic Joseph
Lepard, Cecil Ward
Lepley, Derward, Jr.
Lepucki, Richard John
Lerner, Albert Martin
Lerner, Alfred
Lerner, Louis Abraham
Le Roy, George Willard
Leroy, Robert Pierre
Le Sage, Leo Gay
Leslie, Loren Richardson
Lesly, Philip
Lesner, Samuel Joel
L'Esperance, Wilford Louis
Lessen, Grace Leola
Lessen, Larry Lee
Lester, Robert Ridenour
Le Tarte, Clyde Edward
Letman, Sloan Timothy, III
Letts, Robert Mervyn
Letwenko, Edward Stanley John
Letze, Bernard Julian
Leung, Mow-Wo
Leuschen, James Walter
Levandowsky, Anton Danilovitch
Levantrosser, Frederick Carl
Levenfeld, Milton Arthur
Lever, Alvin
Levi, Edward Hirsch
Levi, James Henry
Levich, Calman
Levin, Barry Livingston
Levin, Carl Milton
Levin, Charles Leonard
Levin, Colman
Levin, Diane
Levin, Lucienne Yvonne
Levin, Max
Levin, Morris Jacob
Levin, Muriel Imogene (Mrs. Sheldon Levin)
Levin, Murray Laurence
Levin, Richard Michael
Levin, Stuart Franklin
LeVine, Alfred David
Levine, Bernard Harold
Levine, David Sander
Levine, Donald Nathan
Levine, Edward Stanton
Levine, Franklin Robert
Levine, Helen Saxon (Mrs. Norman D. Levine)
Levine, Isaac Jacob
Levine, James
Levine, Maita Faye
Levine, Norman Dion
Levine, Robert Sidney
Levine, Stanley Robert
Levine, Stuart George
Levine, Walter Eli
Levinger, Harold Lee
Levinsohn, Sidney Harvey
Levinson, Charles Bernard
Levinson, Joseph Emanuel
Levinson, Monte Jay
Levitt, Seymour Herbert
Levy, Benjamin
Levy, David Hyman
Levy, Donald Morris
Levy, Joel C.
Levy, Joel Howard
Levy, Virgil Louis
Lewin, Philip Martin
Lewis, Betty Carroll (Mrs. Thomas A. Lewis)
Lewis, Buell Laughlin
Lewis, Cary Blackburn, Jr.
Lewis, Daniel Edwin
Lewis, Edmund Jean
Lewis, Edward Earl
Lewis, Eldwyn Ernest
Lewis, Eugene William, III
Lewis, Fred
Lewis, George William
Lewis, Herschell Gordon
Lewis, Laura Ann Penn
Lewis, Lowell Charles
Lewis, Myron Francis
Lewis, Richard Curtis
Lewis, Richard Eugene
Lewis, Robert Linuel, Jr.
Lewis, Robert Owen
Lewis, Ronald Anthony
Lewis, Sally Butzel (Mrs. Leonard Theodore Lewis)
Lewis, Shirley Ann
Lewis, Thomas Andrew
Lewis, Tom F.
Lewis, Wayne Douglas
Lewis, Wendell Phillips
Lewis, William Ellsworth
Lewis, William Franklin
Lewy, Robert Barnard
Ley, Robert Earl, Jr.
Ley, Robert Joseph
Leyda, William David
Leymaster, Glen R.
Leypold, Gregory Georges
Li, Chao-Chiung
Li, Charles Shuhang
Liacopoulos, Van Peter
Lian, Teck Seng
Liao, Kun Twu
Liao, Shu-chung
Libertiny, George Zoltan
Liccardi, Edward Paul
Lichtwardt, Harry Edward
Liddell, Leon Morris
Lidman, J(ohn) Kirby
Lieb, Bernard
Liebenow, Roland Rudolph
Lieberman, David Joseph
Lieberman, Stanley Bertram
Liebermann, Thomas Robert
Liebert, Lucille A.
Liebler, Edward Charles
Liebman, Monte Harris
Liebold, Mary Jane
Liechti, Harris Nelson
Liechty, G(eorge) Frederick
Liedholm, Carl Edward
Liem, Daniel Tiang Ham
Lien, Andrew Clyde
Lierley, Earl Cleon
Lieth, Helmut Siegfried
Lieu, John
Lifschultz, Phillip
Lifton, Herman Manuel
Liggett, Delmore
Light, Gerald Sidney
Lightbourn, George Allen
Lightfoot, Lyle Eugene
Liiste, Lennart Lester
Liljequist, Jon Leon
Lillard, John Stoll
Lillie, Richard Horace
Lilly, Alfred Forrest, Jr.
Lilly, Roger McKinley
Lim, Toh-Woon
Limbacher, James Louis
Limberg, Franklin Harold
Limjoco, Uriel Romey
Lin, John Yen
Lin, Kuang-ming
Lin, Robert Kwan-Hwan
Lincoln, James Helme
Lincoln, Kendall T.
Lind, Arthur Charles
Lind, Earl R.
Lindahl, Raymond Florus
Lindberg, Harry Chester, Jr.
Lindblom, Lawrence A(ndrew)
Lindborg, Daniel Robert
Lindeberg, Richard Theodore
Lindelow, Olaf Victor
Lindemann, John Armin Stoy
Linden, Henry Robert
Linder, George Elisha
Linder, Michael Gary
Linderman, Charles R.
Lindesmith, Larry Alan
Lindgren, D(erbin) Kenneth, Jr.
Lindholm, William Charles
Lindhout, William Pierce
Lindner, Carl H.
Lindner, Kenneth Edward
Lindquist, Daniel Arden
Lindquist, Donald Rodney
Lindquist, Norman Charles
Lindsay, Earl Edward
Lindsay, June Campbell McKee
Lindsay, Powell
Lindsay, Robert
Lindshield, James Harvey
Lindstrom, Russell Joseph
Ling, Alexander
Ling, John Francis
Ling, Joseph Tso-Ti
Lingren, Ronald Hal
Link, Arthur A.
Link, Nancy Carol
Linkmeyer, Larry Lee
Linn, David
Linn, Edward Theodore
Linnard, Lawrence Gilbert
Linsley, Scott Ellsworth
Linsmayer, John James
Linton, Adam Lunn
Lints, Carlton Eugene
Lintz, Robert Carroll
Linville, Malcolm Eugene, Jr.
Lionberger, Erle Talbot Lund
Lipinski, Walter Charles
Lipowitz, Jonathan
Lippert, Clarissa Start
Lippert, David James
Lippert, Donna Rau Harness
Lippert, Margaret Jean Seay
Lipschultz, M. Richard
Lipschultz, Maurice Allen
Lipscomb, James Fredrick
Lipsitt, Harry Allan
Lipsitz, David Alan
Lipski, John Gabriel
Lisio, Donald John
Lisman, William Franklyn
Lison, James J., Jr.
Lissner, Arthur Bart
List, David Patton
Lister, Colin Holden
Liston, George Edward
Liszeski, Joseph Michal
Lit, Alfred
Litot, Edward Francis
Litowsky, Jack Morton
Litscher, Daniel Worden
Little, Arthur Dillard
Little, Bernard Harold
Little, Clarence Wilbur, Jr.
Little, Ervin Dewey, Jr.
Little, James Reichard
Little, Martha Louise
Little, Richard Allen
Littmann, Martin Frederick
Litton, Stephen Frederick
Littrell, Kenneth Earl
Litvag, Irving R.
Litvin, Robert Lowell
Litwiller, Otto Bryan
Liu, Chun Nan
Liu, Edward Chung-Hong
Liu, Henry
Liu, Paul Chi
Liu, Ruey-wen
Lively, John Kenneth
Lively, Rodger Marshall
Livengood, Roger Lynn
Livers, David Linn, Jr.
Livingood, Clarence S.
Livingston, A. Edward
Livingston, Burt R.
Livingston, David Thomas
Livingston, Robert Leigh
Livingston, Von Edward
Ll, Tze-Chung
Lloyd, John Henry
Lloyd, Robert Dean
Lo, Raymond C.
Loach, Paul Allen
Lobenthal, Richard Henry
Lobmeyer, Raymond Joseph
Lobstein, Otto Ervin
Locarni, Richard Glenn
Locke, Giles Richard
Locke, Philip Francis
Locker, Thomas
Lockhart, Mary Malisse Foster (Mrs. Theodus A. Lockhart)
Lockos, Deborah Gay
Locks, Herzl Ben-Zion
Lockshin, Jerrold Leon
Lockwood, Frank James
Lockwood, George J.
Lockwood, John Patterson
Lockwood, Thomas Morrow
Loder, Dwight Ellsworth
Lodge, James Robert
Lodge, Rhea Ewald (Mrs. L. Harvey Lodge)
Lodwick, Ross William
Loeb, John William
Loeb, Virgil, Jr.
Loeffler, Heinz H.
Loeffler, Robert James
Loehnert, John Tyler
Loendorf, William Roger
Loening, Kurt Leopold
Loenser, Larry Eldon
Loesch, Katharine Taylor (Mrs. John George Loesch)
Loescher, Gilbert Damian
Loewen, Eleanor Marie
Lofgren, Karl Adolph
Loftis, Gene Austin
Lofton, C(harlotte) A(nita) Maryjoe
Loftus, Gary Joseph
Logan, John Sterling
Logan, John Wesley, Jr.
Logan, Lloyd
Logan, Sandra Simms
Logan, Serge Edward
Logsdon, John David
Logue, Thomas Joseph
Lohman, Berneice Thomas Knaggs (Mrs. Ben E. Lohman)
Lohman, Keith Douglass
Lohmann, William Tombaugh
Lohutko, Conrad Anthony
Lojacono, Marie Shiya
Lollar, Robert Miller
Loman, Frances Ratner
Lombardy, Ross David
Lone, Frank John
Loney, Richard Hugh
Long, Alan
Long, Clayton Lewis
Long, David Desmond
Long, David Harold
Long, Ernestine Martha Joullian
Long, G(eorge) Donald
Long, Homer J.
Long, John Marshall
Long, Larry Russell
Long, Paul Alan
Long, Robert Michael
Long, Roland John
Long, Timothy Scott
Long, William Frederick
Long, Willis Franklin
Longfellow, Layne Allen
Longman, William McQuilkin
Longo, Michael Anthony
Longworth, David William
Lonnberg, Charles Mitchell
Lonning, Philip Eugene
Lonquist, Bertel Arthur
Looft, Walter Gene
Looker, Jack Devon
Loomis, Charles Wayne
Loomis, Howard Krey
Loomis, Salora Dale
Loots, Robert James
Lopata, Helena Znaniecki
Lopata, Richard Stefan
Lo Patin, Lawrence Harold
Lopez, Alfonso Astrero, Jr.
Lopez, Robert Anthony
Lopez-Delgado, Valentin
L'Orange, Finn Faye
Loranth, Leslie Z.
Lord, James Lawrence
Lord, William Herman
Lore, Irving Allan
Lorenzen, George Arthur
Lorge, Gerald David
Lorman, Milton
Lornitzo, Frank Adam
Lorton, Stephen Gregory
Lo Sasso, Alvin Michael
Losse, Carl Herbert
Lothe, Ingeborg Olina Vlken (Mrs. Irvin Eugene Lothe)
Lothringer, Robert Alan
Lotito, Frank G.
Lottes, John William
Lotz, Herbert Karl
Lotz, Janet Howell
Louden, Jonathan Ernst
Loudenback, Lynn Joseph
Loudon, Roy Virgil, Jr.
Lourenco, Ruy Valentim
Lousberg, Peter Herman
Louthan, William Carl
Lovan, Owen Lee
Love, John, Jr.
Love, Leon
Love, Mahlon Lloyd
Love, Norris
Lovejoy, Leonard James
Loveless, Billy G.
Lovell, Edward George
Lovestedt, Stanley Almer
Lovinger, Warren Conrad
Lowe, Earl Wardle
Lowe, E(dward) Joseph
Lowe, George Washington, Jr.
Lowe, James Browne
Lowe, Robert Clinton
Lowe, Roy Goins
Loweke, George Paul
Lower, John Joseph
Lowery, John Freeman
Lowney, Roger Gordon
Lowrance, Edward Walton
Lowry, Claude Magnus
Lowry, Earl Cranston
Lowry, Orval Earl
Lowry, Raymond Wilmot, Jr.
Lowry, Sheldon Gaylon
Lowry, Wendell Willis
Loyd, Herman Theodore
Lubarsky, Anatoly
Lubas, Thaddeus John
Lubbers, Leland Eugene
Lubbock, James Edward
Lubelfeld, Jerzy
Lubens, Herman Michael
Lubitz, Joseph Morton
Luby, Elliot Donald
Lucas, Christopher John
Lucas, Glennard Ralph
Lucas, Robert Rotger
Lucas, Wilder
Lucca, Joseph Salvatore
Lucchesi, Claude A.
Lucey, John William
Lucey, Patrick Joseph
Lucido, Joseph Louis
Lucker, Giles Wesley
Luckhardt, Henry Joseph
Luckinbill, Merle Ervin
Lucy, David Cartier
Ludwig, Arnold Francis
Ludwig, Clifford Earle
Ludwig, Fred Albert, Jr.
Ludwig, Marvin Jay
Ludwig, R. Arthur
Luebbers, Raymond Julius
Lueckerath, Elmer William
Luedtke, Roland Alfred
Lueker, Erwin Louis
Lueloff, Jorie Anne Payne (Mrs. Richard Friedman)
Luempert, Arthur George
Lueschen, Guenther Rudolf Friedo
Luff, Earl Thomas
Lugar, Richard Green
Luhman, William Simon
Luhnow, Raymond Bertram, Jr.
Luhr, Adelheid Wilhelmine
Luick, Harold Lee
Lukancic, Louis Paul
Lukas, Joseph
Luke, Leon Victor
Luken, Thomas A.
Lukens, Donald E. (Buz)
Lum, Mary Dang Ong (Mrs. Gwon H. Lum)
Lumicao, Benjamin Guiab
Lummis, John Michael
Lund, Hans Ernest
Lund, Stewart Helmer Murphy
Lundahl, Betty Lee
Lunde, Harold Irving
Lundell, Arthur Frederick
Lundell, William Warner
Lundgren, Kathlyn Iola King
Lundh, Sverrer Haakon
Lundholm, Eugene Theodore
Lundquist, Myrtle Vernice
Lundquist, Virgil John Pershing
Lundstrom, Ray Max
Lunseth, John Bentley
Lupse, Raymond Simon
Lurie, Lois Bendes
Lurie, Max Leonard
Lusby, Larry Lee
Lusch, Robert Karl
Lusk, Jeannette Crawford (Mrs. Robert Davies Lusk)
Lusk, Peggy June
Lusk, Robert Clifford
Lusted, Lee Browning
Lutes, Marybelle Pearson
Luth, David Eugene
Luther, Don Preston
Luttrull, James David
Luus, George Aarne
Lux, Lawrence Emmett
Luzadre, John Hinkle
Lyall, James Morris
Lybrook, Robert Burke
Lyddon, James Hamilton
Lydic, Frank Aylsworth
Lydon, Daniel Patrick
Lyle, Willis Edwin
Lyman, Howard B(urbeck)
Lyman, Janice Kay
Lyman, Richard Olney
Lynch, Charles Theodore
Lynch, Charles Thomas
Lynch, Darrel Luvene
Lynch, George Arthur
Lynch, Jack Charles
Lynch, John James
Lynch, Sister Marguerite
Lynch, Raymond Patrick
Lynch, Robert Emmett
Lynch, William Ernest, Jr.
Lynn, Edward Randall
Lynn, Elizabeth Meagher
Lyon, Geoffrey Dale
Lyons, Bernard Patrick
Lyons, Beulah M. Wallar (Mrs. Lawrence Rupert Lyons)
Lyons, Don Chalmers
Lyons, J. Rolland
Lyons, James David
Lyons, Jerry Lee
Lyons, Thomas Harshman
Lysne, Allen Bruce
Lytle, Clifford Franklin
Ma, Alex
Ma, Cynthia Sanman
Maahs, Werner H.
Maas, Johannes
Maasberg, Albert Thomas
Maass, Vera Sonja
Maazel, Lorin
Mabel, Thomas Arthur
Mabley, Jack
Mac Adams, Richard Joseph
Macartney, Frank P.
Macatol, Fortunato Ribagorda
Mac Callum, Gerald Cushing, Jr.
Mac Carthy, John Peters
Macdonald, James M., II
MacDonald, John Bernard
Mac Donald, Leo Hadley, Sr.
Mac Donald, Marie Geneva (Mrs. King Rufus MacDonald)
Mac Donald, Marshall Allen
Mac Donald, Paige Lee
Mac Donald, Raymond Wilbur
Mac Donald, Richard Vincent, Jr.
MacDonald, Robert Dickson
Mac Donald, William Burke
Mac Dougal, Gary Edward
Macenski, Charles William, Jr.
Mac Gibbon, James Duncan
Machinis, Peter Alexander
Machmueller, Vilas Edward
Machtinger, Lawrence Arnold
Machulak, Edward Leon
Mac Intyre, Patricia Nelle
Maciuszko, Jerzy Janusz
Mack, Douglas Archibald
Mack, Irving
Mack, Raymond Wright
Mack, Robert Emmet
Mack, Walter Merriman
Mack, William Jess
Mackay, John Richardson
Mac Kay, Leo Steven
Mackel, Audley Maurice
Mac Kenzie, John Robert
Mac Kenzie, Robert Douglas
Mac Keown, Graeme Jack
Mackey, Diana Parsons
Mackey, Elizabeth Jocelyn
Mackey, Orma Everett
Mac Kichan, Kenneth Allen
Mackiw, Theodore
Mac Laren, David Sargeant
MacLaughlin, Harry Hunter
Mac Lean, Lowe (Sandy)
Mac Mahan, Horace Arthur, Jr.
Mac Mahon, Harold Bernard
Mac Master, Daniel Miller

Macnaughton, David Raymond
Mac Neven, Robert William
Mac Nider, Jack
Macsai, John
Madden, Thomas Joseph, Jr.
Maddin, Michael Warren
Maddin, Milton Maurice
Maddin, Richard Joel
Maddox, Arnold Wayne
Maddox, Lucy Jane
Maddox, Walter Donald
Maddox, William Clarence
Maddux, Kenneth Carl
Madeline, Stephen Eugene
Madey, Richard
Madigan, Edward R.
Madison, Frederick William
Madison, Robert P.
Madrigrano, Joseph Frank
Madsen, George Frank
Madson, Carlisle
Madura, Frederick Joseph
Madura, James Anthony
Maeda, Ikuo
Mag, Arthur
Magee, Laura Jean
Magner, John Marshall
Magnes, G(erald) Donald
Magnuson, Paul Arthur
Magrath, C(laude) Peter
Magy, Robert Alvin
Mah, Chonggi Laurence
Mahaffey, Maryann
Mahan, Genevieve Ellis
Mahan, Harold Dean
Mahanna, Simon Albert
Maher, Cornelius Creedon, III
Maher, David Willard
Maher, James Bernard
Mahlstede, John Peter
Mahmood, Khalid
Mahmoud, Aly Ahmed
Mahoney, Edward Stephen
Mahr, Allan David
Mahrt, Delmar Hermann
Maier, Henry W.
Maier, Irwin
Maier, Paul Luther
Maier, William Conrad
Mainen, Eugene Louis
Mainone, Robert Franklin
Mainwaring, Rosser L.
Majeti, Satyanarayana
Majher, Edward Allen
Majury, Arthur Stuart
Makely, William Orson
Maki, Paula Sproull Dennis
Makkai, Adam
Maky, Walter
Malany, Le Grand Lynn
Malas, Cornelia
Malasky, Paul Michael
Malasto, Arthur Steven
Malcharek, Gerhard
Malcolm, Russell Laing, Jr.
Maley, Charles David
Malinowski, Arthur Anthony
Malis, Louise (Mrs. Louis A. Malis)
Mallas, Kenneth Murial
Mallay, James Francis
Mallers, George Peter
Mallett, Conrad Le Roy
Mallory, Arthur Lee
Mallory, Troy L.
Mallozzi, Philip James
Malmin, Oscar
Malmstrom, Gregory Bruce
Malnak, Allen Bert
Malone, Francis Edward
Malone, John Michael
Malone, Robert Neal
Maloney, John Clement
Maloon, James Harold
Maloon, Jerry Lee
Malson, John Raymond
Maltz, Robert
Man, Jerome Victor
Man, Pang Ling
Manalich, Ramiro
Manatt, Richard
Manco, Hugo Ruperto
Mancuso, James Vincent
Mandarino, Ralph Joseph, Jr.
Mandel, Sheldon Lloyd
Mandelbaum, Harry David
Mandell, Maurice Ira
Mandell, Steven Leslie
Mandelstamm, Jerome R.
Manders, Karl Lee
Mandolini, Anthony Marlo
Manelli, Donald Dean
Manfre, Thomas Steven
Manfro, Patrick James (Patrick James Holiday)
Mangie, Ronald Eugene
Mangold, John Earl
Manheim, Theodore
Manis, Laura Glance
Manley, Myrl Otis
Manley, Robert Edward
Manley, Thomas Roger
Mann, David Douglas
Mann, Donald Nathaniel
Mann, John C.
Mann, John Mc Gregor
Mann, Richard Eugene
Mann, Robert David
Mann, Susie Haire
Mannarino, Antonio Domenico
Manne, Marshall Stanley
Manney, Russell Field, Jr.
Manning, John Warren, III
Manning, Owen Duncan
Mansager, Felix Norman
Mansdorf, Seymour Zack
Mansen, Harry G.
Manser, George Robert
Mansfield, Lois Edna
Maple, Francis Marion
Maples, Jerry Steven
Maples, Robert Henry
Marble, Edwin Johnston
March, Kenneth Alan
Marchi, Michael
Marchman, Martha Jean Dawson
Marchman, Watt P(earson)
Marciniak, Edward Allen
Marciniak, Gary Stephen Paul
Marcinkoski, Annette Marie
Marcos, Jose Mariano
Marcus, Carlton Parks, Jr.
Marcus, Richard Alan
Marcus, Richard Earl
Marczynski, Thaddeus John
Mardell, Carol Dolores
Mardigian, Edward Stephan
Mardis, Hal Kennedy
Marecek, Lynn Marie
Marecek, Milan
Margolin, Robert J.
Margraff, Howard David
Margulies, Seymour
Marin, Allan Marshall
Marine, Julia Mason Lang (Mrs. Roy Milton Marine)
Marinelli, Anne Vera
Marino, Charles Joseph
Mark, Harry Berst, Jr.
Mark, Jack Charles
Mark, Norman Barry
Markendorf, Arthur Cary
Markham, Clarence Matthew, Jr.
Markham, Thomas Newton
Markiewicz, Wigdor
Marking, T(heodore) Joseph, Jr.
Markley, Roger Bruce
Markos, Chris
Markovitz, Richard Ernest
Marks, Bissell Eugene
Marks, Edward Grauman
Marks, Ernestine Le Etta Brown (Mrs. Samuel Milton Marks)
Marks, Erwin
Marks, Gregory Allan
Marks, Jerome
Markus, Richard
Markus, Robert Michael
Markusen, Richard Joseph
Marlow, Frank Wesley
Marlow, Margaret Ann
Marnell, Richard Thomas
Marner, David Lloyd
Marold, Frank
Maronek, James Edward
Marosky, John Edwin
Marquette, Raymond Eugene
Marquis, Geraldine Mae Hildreth (Mrs. Forrest W. Marquis)
Marron, Michael Thomas
Marschall, Vernell Lee
Marsee, Carl Wayne
Marsh, Don E.
Marsh, Edwin Thomas
Marsh, Frank
Marsh, Homer Ellsworth
Marsh, Jeremiah
Marsh, Robert Charles
Marshall, Albert P(rince)
Marshall, Charles Orr, Jr.
Marshall, Floyd William
Marshall, George Badgley
Marshall, Herbert A.
Marshall, John Hart
Marshall, Kenneth Eric
Marshall, Millard Ray
Marshall, Robert E.
Marshall, Robert Franklin
Marshall, Ronald Clemens
Marsteller, William A.
Marston, Anson Day
Marszalek, Theodore David
Marta, John B., Jr.
Martell, Ronald Eugene
Martellaro, Joseph Alexander
Martens, Leslie Vernon
Martens, Rainer
Martens, Theodore Glenn
Marth, Elmer Herman
Martin, Charles Allen
Martin, Charles Lewis
Martin, Charles Weldon
Martin, Clarence Samuel
Martin, Claude Raymond, Jr.
Martin, Clyde Verne
Martin, Daun Hackett
Martin, David Foster
Martin, Edward Moss
Martin, Ethel Austin (Mrs. Edward Martin)
Martin, Frederick Stanton
Martin, George Jerome
Martin, George Thomas
Martin, Harry Edward
Martin, Jerry Thomas
Martin, John Bruce
Martin, John Edward
Martin, John Thomas
Martin, Joseph Marion
Martin, Luther Washburn
Martin, Michael Edward
Martin, Orville Wells, Jr.
Martin, Paul Joseph
Martin, Ray Charles
Martin, Robert Allen
Martin, Robert Coolidge
Martin, Robert James
Martin, Robin Michael
Martin, Roger Bond
Martin, Ross Lloyd
Martin, Stanley Wilbur
Martin, Thomas Brooks
Martin, Thomas Herman
Martin, Thomas John
Martin, Thomas Lyle, Jr.
Martin, Wilfred Samuel
Martin, William Bradley
Martin, William Woodrow
Martindale, John Henry, Jr.
Martindale, Robert Malcolm
Martineau, James Phillip
Martinek, Otto Charles
Martinek, Robert George
Martinelli, David Fortunato
Martino, Joseph Paul
Martinsons, Aleksandrs
Martis, Leo
Marts, Frederick Duane
Martyniuk, Osyp
Martz, George E.
Martz, Lyle Erwin
Martzial, Terrence Joseph, Jr.
Maruyama, Henry Hatsuo
Maruyama, Magoroh
Marvin, James Conway
Marvin, William Sibley
Marvy, James
Marx, Edwin Joseph
Marzolf, Stanley S(mith)
Marzotto, Esio James
Marzullo, Vito
Mascio, John Joseph
Mashaw, Lane Hicks
Maslin, Meyer
Mason, Alice Frances
Mason, Arvis Jerry
Mason, Earl James, Jr.
Mason, Edward Eaton
Mason, John Edwin
Mason, Mearle D.
Mason, Mildred June
Mason, Norman Ronald
Mason, Ronald James
Mason, Virginia Lilly (Mrs. James Mason)
Masopust, Joseph Francis
Masotti, Louis Henry
Massa, Richard Wayne
Massey, James Earl
Massie, Charles Llewelyn
Massie, Thomas Andrew
Massman, Virgil F.
Master, Lawrence Stanley
Mastics, Alec A.
Masuda, George Theodore
Matalamaki, William
Matalon, John George
Matasovic, John Louis
Matasovic, Stella
Matchett, Hugh Moore
Matczynski, Avalon Nolen
Mateescu, Sonja Katherine Toplak
Mathein, Edward Albert
Matheny, Stanley Howard
Mather, Betty Bang
Mather, Edward Lyle
Mather, Roger Frederick
Matheson, William Angus, Jr.
Mathews, Adele
Mathews, Fred L.
Mathews, Henry James
Mathews, John Andrew
Mathews, Paul Hippolyte
Mathews, Thomas Edward
Mathews, Thomas Osborn
Mathews, William Stewart
Mathewson, Hugh Spalding
Mathias, Frank Furlong
Mathieu, Joseph Edward
Mathis, Jack David
Mathis, John Frederick, Jr.
Mathis, Thelma Atwood
Mathison, Arden Earle
Mathues, Thomas Oliver
Mathur, Bhagwan Prakash
Matiaška, Ernest Allan
Matovich, Michael
Matsakis, Nicholas Demetrios
Matson, James Evans
Matson, Virginia Mae Freeberg (Mrs. Edward J. Matson)
Matsumoto, George Masaru
Matsushima, Akira Paul
Matta, Ram Kumar
Matteson, Donald Wayne
Matthews, Frank Thomas, Jr.
Matthews, John Edwin
Matthews, Joseph Dudley
Matthews, Pauline Anna
Matthews, Rex Donald
Matthias, Russell Howard
Matthies, Fred John
Mattila, John Peter
Mattler, Albert Anthony
Mattox, Audrey Blanche (Mrs. Thomas C. Mattox)
Mattson, Edward Neil
Mattson, John Gary
Mattson, Peter Roland
Mattson, Roger Albert
Matuszewski, Stanley
Matveia, Kenneth Wayne
Matz, Milton
Matz, Robert Dennis
Matz, Roger Elwood
Matzer, John Nicholas, Jr.
Matzko, Michael Newton
Mau, Gordon Elliott
Maugans, John Conrad
Mauldin, William H.
Maurer, C. Jackson
Maurer, Irving J.
Maurice, S. Joseph
Maury, Robert Lee
Maus, Donald James
Maus, John Hall
Mausel, Paul Warner
Mauseth, James Oliver
Mauthe, Howard
Mautz, Bernhard Frederick
Mauzey, Armand Jean
Mavec, Bruce Van
Maves, Barbara Ann Baner
Mavis, Frederic Theodore
Mavrelis, William Peter
Mawby, Russell George
Mawicke, Albert Thomas
Maxfield, Donald Vincent
Maxmen, Harold Aaron
Maxon, Harry Russell
Maxwell, Florence Hinshaw (Mrs. John Williamson Maxwell)
Maxwell, Jack Erwin
Maxwell, Madalyn
Maxwell, Stephen Lloyd
May, Alonzo Gail
May, Arnold Nicholas
May, Eugene Pinkney
May, Robert Porter
Mayba, Ihor
Mayberg, Donald Mac Millan
Mayberry, Thomas Arnold
Mayberry, William Eugene
Mayer, James Andrew
Mayer, James Joseph
Mayer, Jean Lois
Mayer, Oscar G.
Mayer, Raymond Richard
Mayer, Richard, Jr.
Mayersak, Jerome Stephen
Mayersdorf, Assa
Mayfield, Eli Burton, Jr.
Mayl, Jack Joseph
Maylath, Donald Oliver
Mayman, Martin
Maynard, H. Glenn
Maynard, Marianne
Mayo, Georgia Thelma Riley (Mrs. Harry Relvia Mayo)
Mayo, Samuel Turberville
Mayo, William Leonard
Mayron, Lewis Walter
Mays, Walter Juano
Mays, William Oscar
Mayuga, Edgardo Guevarra
Mazewski, Aloysius Alex
Mazur, Boleslaw
Mazur, Conrad Francis
Mazzaferri, Ernest Louis
Mazzuca, Lois Camille
Mc Adow, Jerry E.
Mc Aleece, Donald John
Mc Alindon, James Daniel
Mc Allister, Charles Joseph
Mc Allister, Lester Grover, Jr.
Mc Alpin, Joseph Mark
Mc Andrew, Gordon Leslie
Mc Andrews, James Patrick
Mc Andrews, Jerome Francis
McAuley, Patrick Campbell
McAuley, Patrick Campbell
Mc Bain, Russell Lyle
Mc Bean, Robert Parker
Mc Bride, Lloyd Merrill
Mc Bride, Nancy Allyson
Mc Bride, Robert, Ellsworth
McBride, Robert Lawrence
Mc Bride, William Leon
Mc Burney, George William
Mc Cabe, John Charles, III
Mc Cabe, Joseph E.
Mc Caffree, Mary Katherine
Mc Cain, James Allen
Mc Cain, Winfield Reynolds
Mc Call, Ennis
Mc Call, James Lodge
Mc Call, Joseph Francis
Mc Call, Kenneth Deardorff
Mc Call, Kenneth Deardorff, Jr.
Mc Call, Maurice Henderson
Mc Call, Robert Booth
Mc Callum, Charles Edward
Mc Callum, Charles Ray
Mc Callum, Donald Roy
Mc Callum, Walter Edward
Mc Camley, Peter John
Mc Candless, Barbara J.
Mc Candless, Perry G.
Mc Cann, David Francis
Mc Cann, James I.
Mc Cann, Mary Kathleen
Mc Cann, William Albert
Mc Cann, William Dale
Mc Canse, James Edson
Mc Carten, John James
Mc Carter, Charles Chase
Mc Carthy, Daniel Joseph
Mc Carthy, Donald Russell
Mc Carthy, Edward Albert
Mc Carthy, John Francis
Mc Carthy, Joseph Michael
Mc Carthy, Leo Albert
Mc Carthy, Lorraine Chambers
Mc Carthy, Michael Charles
Mc Cartney, Ralph Farnham
Mc Carty, R(alph) Lowell
Mc Carty, Robert Floyd
Mc Carty, Theodore Milson
Mc Cauley, Michael Frederick
Mc Cauley, Philip Clayton
Mc Cauley, Philip F.
Mc Cauley, Robert William
Mc Chesney, Kathryn Marie (Mrs. Thomas David McChesney)
Mc Clamroch, Lemuel Paul
Mc Clanahan, Lowell Dale
Mc Clear, Richard Vance
Mc Cleary, George Franklin, Jr.
Mc Cleary, Henry Glen
Mc Cleary, Virgil Arnold
Mc Clellan, William Daniel
Mc Clelland, Ann Samonial (Mrs. Stewart W. McClelland)
Mc Clenahan, Ann Catherine
Mc Clenahan, James Wallace
Mc Clenahan, Richard Lee
Mc Clintock, John Stephen
Mc Clintock, Peter Longmire
Mc Clinton, Johnnie Wayne
Mc Clory, Robert
Mc Closkey, Donald Nansen
Mc Cluney, Gregory Day
Mc Clure, David Boyd
Mc Clure, James J., Jr.
Mc Collem, Donald Earl
Mc Collem, Mary Carolyn Watson
Mc Collister, Howard Richard
Mc Collough, Fred
Mc Collough, Lucille Hanna (Mrs. Clarence Lindsay McCollough)
Mc Combs, Sherwin
Mc Conagha, Glenn Lowery
Mc Connaughey, George Carlton, Jr.
Mc Connell, Bernie Allen
Mc Connell, Forrest Mathew
Mc Connell, Glenn Bruce
Mc Connell, John Henderson
Mc Connell, Robert Bruce
Mc Cook, John Edward
Mc Cord, John Harrison
Mc Cormack, Mark Hume
Mc Cormick, Brooks
Mc Cormick, Hope Baldwin (Mrs. Brooks McCormick)
Mc Cormick, John
Mc Cormick, Michael Donald
Mc Cormick, Robert William
Mc Cormick, Roger Dean
Mc Cormick, Scott, Jr.
Mc Cormick, William Edward
Mc Coy, Donald Edward
Mc Coy, E. Jason, Jr.
Mc Coy, Frederick John
McCoy, Jeanie Shearer
Mc Coy, John Gardner
Mc Coy, Robert Calvin
Mc Coy, Robert Lee
Mc Coy, Robin
Mc Cracken, Dale Russell
Mc Cracken, Harold MacKenzie
Mc Cracken, Reginald Leo
Mc Creery, Robert Herman
Mc Crone, Walter Cox
Mc Crory, Edward Lawrence
Mc Crowey, George Anthony
Mc Crystal, Frank
Mc Cubbrey, David Raymond
Mc Cube, Arthur Lee
Mc Cube, Brian Francis
Mc Cue, James Joseph
Mc Cuen, Charles Robert
Mc Cuen, Huber Mason
Mc Cullough, Dorothea Gerbracht (Mrs. S.K. McCullough)
Mc Cullough, George Elwood
Mc Cullough, John Francis
Mc Cullough, John Jeffrey
Mc Cullough, Joseph
Mc Cune, David William
McCurdy, Larry Wayne
Mc Curry, Donald Reid
Mc Cutchan, Neil Jason
Mc Cutcheon, George Barr
Mc Daniel, Charles Wayne
Mc Daniel, Donald Neal
Mc Daniel, Edwin Corr
Mc Daniel, James Austin
Mc Daniel, James Edwin
Mc Daniel, John Redmond
Mc Daniel, Robert Edwin
Mc Daniel, William Lester
Mc Davitt, Robert Duane
Mc Dermott, John Andrew
Mc Devitt, Michael Robert
Mc Divitt, James A.
Mc Donald, Anthony Alonzo Earl
Mc Donald, Bonnie Belle
Mc Donald, Clinton Glen
Mc Donald, Donald Burt
McDonald, Elliott Raymond, Jr.
Mc Donald, George Jennings
Mc Donald, Sister Grace
Mc Donald, James Alexander
Mc Donald, James John
Mc Donald, James Smith
Mc Donald, John Cecil
Mc Donald, Julie J.
Mc Donald, Myrtis Bethel
Mc Donald, Noel
Mc Donald, Robert Delos
Mc Donald, Stanford Laurel
Mc Donald, Ward Fulfer
Mc Donnell, Gerald M.
Mc Donnell, Robert Edward
Mc Donough, Dayle Crockett
Mc Donough, Isabelle Mary Rickey (Mrs. Dayle Crockett McDonough)
McDonough, James J.
Mc Dougall, Allan Kerr
Mc Dougall, Allan Nichol
Mc Dougall, William Carl, Jr.
Mc Dowell, Donald Newhall
Mc Dowell, James
Mc Dowell, Laura Eleanora Gilliam (Mrs. George P. McDowell)
Mc Duff, Charles Robert
Mc Eachran, Hugh Douglas
Mc Eleaney, Donald Arthur
Mc Elin, Thomas Welsh
Mc Elroy, Austin
Mc Elroy, Elam Errett
Mc Elroy, James Albert
Mc Elwain, John Allen
Mc Enany, Gordon Eugene
Mc Enerney, John Joseph
McEniry, Glenn John
Mc Entire, Esther Maxine Sharp
Mc Evers, Robert Darwin
Mc Fadden, Mary Fraser
Mc Fall, Robert Lloyd
Mc Farland, Charles Warren
Mc Gady, Donald Lawrence
Mc Gary, Thomas Hugh
Mc Gaughey, Albert Wayne
McGaw, Robert Walter
McGee, James Howell
Mc Gee, Michl Thomas
Mc Gee, Ralph Eugene
Mc Gehee, H. Coleman, Jr.
Mc Gervey, John Donald
Mc Gettigan, Brian Jerome
Mc Ghee, Andrew White
Mc Ghee, John Edward
Mc Ghee, Noah Layne
Mc Ghee, Patricia Louise Ohlsen
Mc Gibbon, Edmund Leavenworth
Mc Gill, John William
Mc Gill, Ralph Norman
Mc Ginnis, Cecil Glenn
Mc Ginnis, Charles Alan
Mc Ginnis, Claude Presley
Mc Ginnis, James Edward
Mc Ginnis, Leland Barnes
Mc Glinn, Joseph Francis
Mc Glynn, Gerald Edward, Jr.
Mc Goldrick, James Edward, Jr.
Mc Govern, Earl Arthur
Mc Govern, George Stanley
Mc Govern, William Aloysius
Mc Gowen, Charles Hammond
Mc Grath, John Francis
Mc Grath, Lawrence Edward
Mc Graw, Delford Armstrong
Mc Graw, Robert Paul
Mc Gregor, Harrison Eugene
Mc Gregor, Lee Robert
Mc Gregor, Thomas Henry
Mc Guigan, John Robert
Mc Guigan, Robert Alister
Mc Guire, Richard L.
Mc Guire, Rick Michael
Mc Guire, Robert Nicholas
Mc Gurr, Aloysius William, Jr.
Mc Henry, Martin Christopher
Mc Holland, James Dale
Mc Hugh, Charles Thomas
Mc Ilvaine, Clifford James
Mc Ilvaine, Joseph
Mc Innes, Ralph Harry
Mc Intee, Michael Ray
Mc Intosh, Harold Austin (Marc)
Mc Intosh, William Currie
Mc Inturf, Faith Mary
Mc Intyre, Donald Gregory
Mc Intyre, Frank Joseph
Mc Intyre, Ronald Llewellyn
Mc Intyre, Thomas Aquinas
Mc Iver, Lawrence Walter
Mc Kay, Barbara Joan
Mc Kay, John Paul
Mc Kay, John Sangster
Mc Kay, Nicholas Douglas
Mc Kay, Richard Harry
Mc Kay, Robert Clark
Mc Kay, Robert Stephenson, II
McKeag, William John
Mc Kee, Donald Darrell
Mc Kee, George Moffitt, Jr.
Mc Kee, James Arden
Mc Kee, Keith Earl
Mc Keen, Chester M., Jr.
Mc Kell, Robert
Mc Kelvey, John Clifford
Mc Kelvy, Charles Lockhart, Jr.
Mc Kenna, Donald Frederick
Mc Kenna, George LaVerne
Mc Kenna, Richard Henry
Mc Kenna, Walter Thomas
Mc Kenzie, Leon Roy
Mc Kenzie, Robert Seaton
Mc Keown, Mary Elizabeth
Mc Kewen, George Earl
Mc Kibben, Robert Earl
Mc Killip, William John
Mc Killop, Andrew R.
McKinlay, Robert Todd
Mc Kinley, Mary Cheryl
Mc Kinnell, Robert Gilmore
Mc Kinney, Bryan Lee
Mc Kinney, Donald Lee
Mc Kinney, Joseph Kent
Mc Kinney, Lorella A.
Mc Kinney, Robert Lester
Mc Kinnie, Cato Allen
Mc Kinnon, Donald William
Mc Knelly, William Von, Jr.

Mc Knight, Joseph T(homas)
Mc Knight, Val Bundy
Mc Lain, Alberton Lamson
Mc Lain, David John, Jr.
Mc Lain, Donald Joseph
Mc Lain, James Marion
Mc Lain, Stuart
Mc Lane, Helen J.
Mc Lane, William Bayard
Mc Larnan, James Conard
Mc Laughlin, Alexander Charles John
Mc Laughlin, Eugene Ray
Mc Laughlin, Harry Roll
Mc Laughlin, Jerry Loren
Mc Laughlin, John Patrick
Mc Laughlin, Martin James
Mc Laughlin, William Gaylord
Mc Laurin, Henry James
Mc Lean, Arthur Frederick
Mc Lean, Gilbert James
Mc Lean, Martha Louise
Mc Lean, Robert William
Mc Lellan, Adrian Oswald
Mc Lendon, Henry Lewellynn
Mc Lennan, William L.
Mc Leod, Frederick Reinhardt
Mc Leod, James Currie
Mc Leod, John Dwight
Mc Loone, Edward James
Mc Lucas, Grace B.
Mc Mahan, Parker Frank, Jr.
McMahon, John Alexander
Mc Mahon, John Joseph
Mc Mahon, Stanley Jahn
Mc Manus, Bruce William
Mc Manus, Edward Joseph
Mc Manus, Robert Lee
Mc Means, Edward
Mc Meen, Lewis Clyde
Mc Millan, Eric William
Mc Millan, Robert Hamilton
Mc Millan, William Marcus
Mc Millen, Thomas David, Jr.
Mc Mullen, Charles Harsha
Mc Mullin, Earl Lawrence
Mc Mullin, Leo Francis
Mc Murrin, Lee Ray
Mc Nair, Donald Wesley
Mc Nairy, Philip Frederick
Mc Nally, Crystal Elaine
Mc Nally, Thomas Joseph
Mc Namar, David Fred
Mc Namara, Bartlett William
Mc Namara, Carolyn Lee
Mc Namara, John Patrick
McNamara, Joseph Donald
McNary, Gene
Mc Naughton, William Frank
Mc Neal, R(alph) Richard
Mc Neal, Thomas Russell, Jr.
Mc Nee, John Calvin
Mc Neely, James Michael
Mc Neese, Woodrow Franklin
Mc Nelly, Frederick Wright, Jr.
Mc Nerney, Walter James
Mc Nulty, Alfred Peter
Mc Nutt, Mrs. Dorothy
Mc Phail, S(tanley) Brian
Mc Pheeters, James Walter, III
Mc Pherson, Edwin Malcolm
Mc Pherson, Eugene Virgil
Mc Pike, J. Donald
Mc Quiggan, Mark Corbeille
Mc Quillan, Marcy
Mc Quillen, Michael Paul
Mc Quiston, James Stuart
Mc Quiston, Raymer
Mc Ree, Edward Barxdale
Mc Reynolds, Janis Gay
Mc Robert, Lowell Max
Mc Roy, Paul Furgeson
Mc Steen, Harry Chiaro
Mc Sweeny, Austin John
Mc Swiney, Charles Ronald
Mc Tee, Lyle Patrick
Mc Teer, Thomas Randolph
Mc Vean, Duncan Edward
Mc Vey, Francis Daniel
Mc Way, Francis Sullivan
Meacham, Esther Anne
Meachum, Henry James, III
Mead, Clyde Frank
Mead, Gordon Sterling
Meade, Geoffrey Blaine
Meador, Jimmy Clay
Meador, Judith Elaine
Meadors, Allen Coats
Meagher, Thomas Francis
Mebust, Winston Keith
Medak, Herman
Medaris, Florence Isabel
Medhus, Glenn Louie
Medin, Myron James, Jr.
Medley, Morris Lee
Medow, Willotte Dale
Medzihradsky, Fedor
Mee, John F.
Meek, Edward Stanley
Meek, Robert Lee
Meeker, David Bowyer
Meeker, Duane B.
Meeks, Louis Walter
Meengs, William Lloyd
Meese, Ernest Harold
Meese, William Giles
Meetz, John Eugene
Mefferd, Paul Stenberg
Mefferd, Thomas Arthur
Megowen, Charles Geyer
Megraw, Robert Ellis
Mehaffey, John Allen
Mehaffey, John Ruskin
Mehbod, Hassan
Mehl, Warren Roy
Mehlenbacher, Dohn Harlow
Mehlhaf, Milton T.
Mehlhoff, Milbert Warren
Mehlman, Jerome Saul
Mehmel, Philip Vincent
Mehn, W. Harrison
Mehr, Joseph John
Mehta, Tushar Maganlal
Mehuron, George Carol
Meier, Allen John
Meier, August
Meier, John Dale
Meier, Wilbur Leroy, Jr.
Meier, Willard Charles
Meier, William George
Meisel, Jerome
Meisinger, George Fredrick
Meisse, Gunther Sagel
Meister, Raymond Albert
Meister, Richard Thomas
Meitner, Raymond John
Mejer, Robert Lee
Melamed, Leo
Melcher, Maurice Arnold
Meldman, Robert Edward
Melendy, Earle Richard
Melhorn, J. Jack
Melhorn, Wilton Newton
Melick, Robert Louis
Mellman, Harry George
Melnicoff, Ira Lee
Meloy, Harold H.
Meloy, Loretta Marie Schrader
Melton, Alton Ray
Melvin, Cruse Douglas
Melvin, Peter Joseph
Melvin, Ronald McKnight
Melvold, Robert Thomson
Mendell, Donald Pratt
Mendelsohn, Harvey Joseph
Mendelsohn, Lawrence Victor
Mendelson, Frieda Garfinkel
Mendenhall, Elwood Hirst
Mendheim, John Murray
Mengel, Robert Morrow
Menier, Vincent Joseph
Menk, Louis Wilson
Mennen, Dorothy Runk (Mrs. Harold E. Mennen)
Menning, Arnold J.
Menninger, Jeanetta Lyle (Mrs. Karl Menninger)
Menninger, Karl Augustus
Menninger, Roy Wright
Menz, William Wolfgang
Merar, Erwin Jerome
Mercer, Victor Harold
Mercer, William Earl
Merchant, Frederick Taylor
Meredith, Betty Jane
Meredith, James Hargrove
Mericas, Van Dimos
Merilan, Charles Preston
Meritt, Dennis Andrew, Jr.
Merkel, Jayne Silverstein
Merkel, Kenneth Gail
Merkel, William Kenneth
Mermel, Michael George
Merner, R. William
Mernitz, Richard James
Merrell, James Lee
Merrihew, Victor Hugo
Merrill, Dean Roger
Merrill, William H., Jr.
Merriman, John Riley
Merritt, Robert Lloyd
Merry, Henry John
Merschman, William Francis
Merszei, Zoltan
Merten, Alan Gilbert
Mertzman, Robert Arnold
Merwick, Patricia Anne
Merwin, Harmon Turner
Mesenbrink, Philip Edward
Mesken, Lorraine Ann
Mesler, Russell Bernard
Mesler, William Joseph, III
Messana, Joseph
Messerli, John Haigh
Mestemaker, Albert Joseph, Jr.
Metcalf, Dormond Eugene
Metcalfe, Grant Emory
Metcalfe, Ralph H.
Metro, Patrick Stephen
Mette, Eldon R.
Metz, Florence Irene
Metz, Floyd A.
Metz, Patricia Anne Harris
Metzgar, Patricia Catherine
Metzger, John David
Metzger, William Irwin
Meuch, Victor
Mewissen, Dieudonne Jean
Meyer, Barry Lawrence
Meyer, Betty Anne (Mrs. John Roland Baskin)
Meyer, Charles Appleton
Meyer, Daniel Patrick
Meyer, Douglas Oliver
Meyer, Drew Alden
Meyer, Frank Henry
Meyer, Frank Louis
Meyer, Fred William
Meyer, Herbert Alton, III
Meyer, Howard Max
Meyer, Ivan Henry
Meyer, Jerome Herbert
Meyer, John Rollin
Meyer, Kenneth Marven
Meyer, Leon Jacob
Meyer, Louis Jon
Meyer, Marlin Henry
Meyer, Maurice Wesley
Meyer, Richard Carroll, Sr.
Meyer, Robert Smith
Meyer, Stuart Melvin
Meyer, Walter
Meyerhoff, Arthur Edward
Meyerhoff, Richard Artell
Meyers, Christine Laine
Meyers, Donald Bates
Meyers, Franklin David
Meyers, Jack C(harles)
Meyers, Veryl Norbert
Meyers, Ward Carl
Meyerson, Seymour
Micallef, Joseph Stephen
Micay, Archie Robert
Michael, Gerald Dante
Michael, Harold Louis
Michael, Robert Campbell
Michaels, Joseph Max
Michaels, Mitch (Richard Louis Salchow)
Michak, Helen Barbara
Michel, Robert Henry
Michelich, Joanna Kurdeka
Michelon, Leno C.
Michels, Eugene August
Michels, Hugh Conrad, Jr.
Michels, Louise Ann
Michener, Charles D(uncan)
Michna, James Thompson
Michno, Dorothy Antonia
Michod, Charles Louis
Mick, R. Wyatt, Jr.
Mick, Robert Kay
Mickelson, Arnold
Mickelson, George Speaker
Micklewright, Jerrold John
Micun, Richard Peter
Middeke, Albert Bernard
Middendorf, Donald Floyd
Middendorf, Robert Willis
Middlebush, Carl Wesley
Middlekauff, George Wiles
Middleton, Dan Frank
Middleton, Edward Kent
Middleton, Harvey Nathaniel, Jr.
Middleton, James Gautier
Middough, William Vance
Midelfort, Peter Albert Hande
Midell, Allen Irwin
Midgley, John William
Midtlyng, Joanna
Miechur, Thomas Frank
Miefert, William Gerhardt, III
Migala, Lucyna
Mihalopulos, Gus, Jr.
Mikat, Dorothy Marie
Mikell, Ardell
Mikesell, John Paul
Mikesell, Sharell Lee
Mikhail, David Nagib
Mikhail, George Rizk
Mikhail, Ramzy Naguib
Mikrut, John Joseph, Jr.
Miks, George Martin
Miksche, Jerome Phillip
Miksic, Boris Alexander
Mikula, Edward John
Mikva, Abner Joseph
Milano, Nicholas Phillip
Milburn, Sidney Everstern
Milder, Myron Harry
Miles, Alfred Lee
Miles, James Southard
Milford, William Eugene
Militzer, Mary Eric
Milivoyevich, Milorad Ljubomir
Millar, Allen Robert
Millar, Leola Faudree (Mrs. Charles J. Millar)
Millard, Joseph Nester, Sr.
Miller, Alicemarie Meyer
Miller, Alvin
Miller, Anderson (Andy) Franklin
Miller, Carole Seifer
Miller, Carson Keith
Miller, Clarence E.
Miller, Clifford Harry
Miller, Daniel Martin
Miller, Don Wilson
Miller, Donald Anderson
Miller, Donald George
Miller, Donald Morton
Miller, Earl Eugene
Miller, Edward Henderson
Miller, Eugene
Miller, Floyd Glenn
Miller, Francis Allen
Miller, Frank Ellis
Miller, Frederick Coleman
Miller, Genevieve
Miller, Gregory Albert
Miller, Gregory Allen
Miller, Halsey Wilkinson
Miller, Harry George
Miller, Harry Johnson
Miller, Harry Joseph
Miller, J. Carter, Jr.
Miller, James Alan
Miller, James Norman
Miller, J(ames) Roscoe
Miller, Joe David
Miller, John Alston
Miller, John Charles
Miller, John Joseph
Miller, John Lewis
Miller, Jon Cristofer
Miller, Joseph Irwin
Miller, Joseph Kenneth
Miller, Kenneth Duane
Miller, Kenneth Lawrence
Miller, Kermit Vincent
Miller, Larry Gene
Miller, Larry Michael
Miller, Lloyd Daniel
Miller, Marc Edward
Miller, Marion Swann
Miller, Mason Ferrell
Miller, Max
Miller, Merl Kem
Miller, Merle Monroe
Miller, Michael Allen
Miller, Michael Jeffrey
Miller, Michael Louis
Miller, Milford Mortimer
Miller, Nan Courtney
Miller, Nelson Brueggemann
Miller, Norman John
Miller, Nyle H.
Miller, Orrin Duane
Miller, Orville Crowder
Miller, Otis Louis
Miller, Pearson L.
Miller, Ray Glen
Miller, Raymond Lee
Miller, Richard Hamilton
Miller, Ritchie Eugene
Miller, Robert Carl
Miller, Robert Ernest
Miller, Robert Frank
Miller, Robert Franklin
Miller, Robert Haskins
Miller, Robert William
Miller, Roy Lafette, II
Miller, Ruth Ratner
Miller, Samuel Elias
Miller, Sol
Miller, Stephen John
Miller, Theodore Wayne
Miller, Victor Andrew
Miller, Vincent Arvel
Miller, Walter Gordon
Miller, Wayne Charles
Miller, Wayne Louis
Miller, Wayne Starr
Miller, William Anton
Miller, William Hall
Miller-Tiedeman, Anna
Millett, Stephen Malcolm
Milli, Rose Lynn Eileen
Milligan, Frederick James
Milligan, Robert Lee, Jr.
Milligan, Robert Stieper
Millikan, Larry Edward
Milliken, William Grawn
Millimet, Charles Raymond
Milliron, Allison Ingram
Milliser, Stephen Charles
Millman, Ronald Burton
Millner, Arnold John
Milloy, Frank Joseph, Jr.
Milloy, Patrick Theodore
Mills, Coley Clifton
Mills, Howard Samuel, Jr.
Mills, James Myron
Mills, James William
Milner, Walker Wilson
Milonas, Charles Constantine
Milton, John Ronald
Min, Tony Charles
Minassian, Donald Paul
Minderman, Jerald Patrick
Miner, Paul Virgil
Miner, Thomas Hawley
Minetti, Robert Hugo
Mingle, John Orville
Mings, Dwain Edward
Minneste, Viktor, Jr.
Minnich, Joseph Edward
Minnich, Virginia
Minor, Wendell LaFayette
Minshall, Drexel David
Minsker, Robert Stanley
Minter, John B(ernard)
Mintzer, Olin Wesley, III
Minui, Morteza
Miracle, Gordon Eldon
Miraldi, Floro Deo
Mirenda, Joseph John
Mirman, Joel Harvey
Mirowitz, Leo Isaak
Mirza, David Brown
Misemer, Paul Max
Mishler, Ernest Gerald
Mishra, Vishwa Mohan
Miska, Leonard Frank
Misra, Prabhat Kumar
Misra, Rajendra Kumar
Mistelske, Emerson Warren
Mitchell, A. Ben
Mitchell, Arnold Michael
Mitchell, Charles Mont
Mitchell, Charles Raymond
Mitchell, Dave Cameron
Mitchell, Delmer Roy, Jr.
Mitchell, Dow Penrose
Mitchell, Frederick Joseph
Mitchell, George Trice
Mitchell, Georgia Bone
Mitchell, Glenford Eckleton
Mitchell, Hobart Theophilus, Jr.
Mitchell, James Curtis
Mitchell, James Earl
Mitchell, James Vincent, Jr.
Mitchell, Jerry David
Mitchell, Marion Bonner
Mitchell, Marion Miranda McWilliams
Mitchell, Otis Clinton, Jr.
Mitchell, Raymond William
Mitchell, Samuel Johnson
Mitchell, Stephen Connally
Mitchell, Stephen Kent
Mitchell, Thelma Katherine Woodley
Mitchell, Thoral J.
Mitchell, Walter Adrian
Mitchell, Wayne Antoine
Mitchell, William Henry
Mittelmann, Eugene
Mittelstadt, Russell James
Mitten, Horace Lee, Jr.
Mix, Amelia Evans
Mixer, Harry Weeber
Miyares, Marcelino
Moayad, Cyrus
Mobley, Gordon Orval
Mocha, Frank
Mochon, Marion Johnson
Mock, Charles Jackson
Mock, Donald Eugene
Mode, Ruth (Mrs. Arthur S. Mode)
Modigliani, Andre
Modisette, Billy Ray
Modly, Zoltan Maria
Moe, John Howard
Moe, Walter William
Moehlenpah, Walter George
Moehrke, Don Paul
Moeller, Theodore Allen
Moen, Joseph Edward
Moen, Merlin Arvid
Moenich, Daniel Matthias
Moesta, Rodman Charles
Moffatt, Eva Mae
Moffett, Donald Baird
Moffett, Maxine Anderson
Mogdis, Franz Joseph
Mogni, Ben James
Mohan, Lala Satish
Moharib, Nassif Habib
Mohindra, Ramesh Kumar
Mohiuddin, Syed Maqdoom
Mohlenbrock, Robert H(erman), Jr.
Mohler, Edward Francis, Jr.
Mohler, Terence John
Mohlman, Harold John
Mohr, Harold Oliver
Mohrlock, Howard Allen
Moister, Matthew Robert, Jr.
Moklestad, Norman Waldimar
Mol, Jacob Cornelius
Mold, Doald Wilbur
Molden, Anna Jane
Molenda, Charles Anthony
Molenda, Michael Henry
Moler, Roger Lee
Moles, Randall Carl
Molitor, John Parker
Moll, Edwin Allan
Moll, Verdin Atlee, Jr.
Mollenhoff, Francis Anthony
Mollison, Clarence Longman
Mollison, Earl David
Molloy, Paul George
Molo, Walter John, Jr.
Momsen, Joy Jacqueline
Monaco, Anthony Louis, Jr.
Monaco, Attilio J.
Monaco, Carmen Frank
Monahan, Raymond Edward
Monahan, Robert Hugh
Monash, Peter Ernest
Monda, Cornell Peter, Sr.
Mondale, Walter Frederick
Monicatti, Lawrence Angelo
Monk, John Thomas
Monninger, Robert Harold George
Monroe, Alan Douglas
Monroe, John Clayton, Jr.
Monsalvatge, Raymond Fernando, Jr.
Monsees, Richard Henry
Monsma, Stephen Vos
Monson, Robert Joseph
Montag, Thomas Dale
Montee, Benjamin Mohon
Monteith, Thomas Wilson
Montes, Peggy Ann
Montesi, Susan Jean
Montgomery, Burtis Edgar
Montgomery, James Winchester
Montgomery, John Osborn
Montgomery, Rex
Montgomery, Robert Max
Montgomery-Short, Ruth Gertrude (Mrs. Joseph C. Short)
Montiegel, Bernard Albert
Monus, Nathan Harlow
Moody, Blair, Jr.
Moody, G. William
Moody, Joseph Palmer
Moody, Robert Adams
Moody, Tom
Moon, Byung Soo
Moon, Charles Redman
Moon, George Donald, Jr.
Moon, Harold Eugene
Moon, Jesse Morris, Jr.
Moon, Marcus Arthur
Moon, Robert Allen
Moon, William, Jr.
Moon, William Isham
Moore, Catherine Gilbert
Moore, Charles Edwin
Moore, Clara Evelyn Mitchell
Moore, Clarence Eugene Mc Daniel
Moore, Dan Tyler
Moore, David Lowell
Moore, Dean Arlin
Moore, Dennis Frederic
Moore, Gerald Louis
Moore, Harlan Edgar
Moore, Harwood Barrows
Moore, Howard Denis
Moore, Hugh Travis
Moore, Jack Fay
Moore, James Edward
Moore, James Stuart, Jr.
Moore, Jean Dolores
Moore, Joan Wells
Moore, John Newton
Moore, Joseph John
Moore, Kenneth Edward
Moore, Michael
Moore, Pauline Ruyle
Moore, Ralph Cory
Moore, Ray Deloss, Jr.
Moore, Richard
Moore, Richard Hoffman
Moore, Riley Ambrose
Moore, Robert Henry, Jr.
Moore, Robert Pittman
Moore, Thomas Edward
Moore, Thomas Hugh
Moore, William Arthur
Moore, William Lyle
Moorhead, John Bekins
Moorhead, Philip Darwin
Moorjani, Gulab Issarsing
Moos, Malcolm Charles
Moosbrugger, Mary Coultrip
Moragne, Rudolph
Morales, Milton Francis
Moran, Edward Martin
Moran, James Herbert
Moran, John Vincent
Moran, Patricia Anne
Moran, Paul Robert
Moran, Philip Anthony
Moran, S. Joseph
Morankar, Sudhakar Dattatray
Morason, Robert Henry
Mordecai, Benjamin
Mordue, Howard Wilbur
Morefield, William Merritt
Morehouse, Lawrence Glen
Moreland, Kenneth Orman
Moreland, William John
Morello, Victor Salvatore
Morency, Robert Joseph
Moreno, Franklyn Henry
Moretsky, Lewis Robert
Morey, Walter Thomas
Morf, Theodore Ferdinand
Morgan, Barbara Ellen
Morgan, Coburn
Morgan, David Basil
Morgan, George Henry
Morgan, Howard Knight
Morgan, James Robert
Morgan, John Derald
Morgan, June Jack (Mrs. John E. Morgan)
Morgan, Lee Laverne
Morgan, Lewis V., Jr.
Morgan, Marshal Charles
Morgan, Melanie Mc Kenzie
Morgan, Michael Fitzgerald
Morgan, Michael Speer
Morgan, Richard Lee
Morgan, Robert Dale
Morgan, Stanley Leins
Morgan, William DeWitt
Morgan, William Percy, III
Morgan, William Richard
Morganstern, Ramon Jerome
Morgenstern, Jack Arnold
Morgenstern, June Ruth
Morgenthaler, David Turner
Morgillo, Mary Elizabeth Du Bry
Morgison, F. Edward
Moriarty, Michael David
Moritz, Michael Everett
Morley, George William
Morley, James Quincy
Morrell, David Bernard
Morrell, David La Due
Morrice, George
Morrill, Walter Dunlap
Morris, Arlene Janet Roberts
Morris, Donald
Morris, Donald Fischer
Morris, Edward Louis
Morris, Elizabeth May
Morris, Eugene
Morris, Gary Jay
Morris, Hugh Irvin
Morris, Jack Allen
Morris, John Michael
Morris, Martin Azelle, Jr.
Morris, Ralph William
Morris, Robert B(arrett)
Morris, Virgil Dixon
Morris, William Emerson, Jr.
Morris, William Lewis
Morris-Jones, Dana Z.
Morrison, Charles
Morrison, Charles John
Morrison, David Lee
Morrison, David Richard
Morrison, Donald Thomas
Morrison, Dwight Edward
Morrison, Edward James
Morrison, Francis Arthur
Morrison, Frank Albert, Jr.
Morrison, Harriet Barbara
Morrison, James Frank
Morrison, Lewis Everett
Morrison, Michael Charles
Morrison, Richard Donald
Morrison, Thomas Herring
Morrissey, Robert Emmett
Morrow, George William, Jr.
Morrow, Jerry Lee
Morrow, Mary Jo
Morrow, Robert Charles
Morse, C. Dwayne
Morse, H. Clifton, IV
Morse, Robert Kenneth
Mortensen, Robert Henry
Morton, Joseph Lewis
Morton, Philip Goodrich
Morton, Stephen Dana
Morton, Terry Lee

Morton, Thomas Jesse, Jr.
Morton, Willard Lemuel
Mosbaugh, Phillip George
Mosbaugh, Richard Karl
Mosby, Dewey Franklin
Mosby, Doris Virginia Perry
Moseley, Ray (Benjamin) F(ranklin)
Moser, Hannah Schlesinger
Moser, Robert Lee
Moser, Robert Peabody
Moses, Harold Alton
Moses, Kenneth Lee
Mosher, George Allan
Mosher, Kenneth Edward
Mosier, C. Fred
Moskop, Roy Lorenz
Moskovic, Jacob Leon
Moss, David Mac Beth, III
Moss, Henry S.
Moss, Robert Henry
Moss, Walter Gerald
Mossbauer, Louis
Mosse, George L.
Mota, Carlos Roberto
Moten, Chauncey Donald
Motley, Larry Lee
Mottl, Ronald Milton
Motton, Rosita Elorise
Motts, Warren Earl
Mottweiler, Jack Hugo
Moulder, James Edwin
Moultrie, John Wesley, Jr.
Mountford, Richard Dean
Mountz, Louise Carson Smith (Mrs. George Edward Mountz)
Mourek, Anton Peter
Mouw, Edward Wayne
Mouzakeotis, Theodore Constantine
Movchan, Julian George
Mowery, Albert Samuel
Mowery, John Henry
Mowrer, Ernest Russell
Mowry, David Dee
Mowry, John L.
Moyer, David Emerson
Moyer, Lawrence Noel
Moyer, Mary Suzanne
Mozdzierz, Gerald John
Mrava, Gene Louis
Muccioli, Anna Maria
Muchemore, Ruth Jeanine
Muchow, Robert Louis
Muckerman, David Kevin
Mudge, William Albert, Jr.
Mudie, Herbert Clark
Muehrcke, Robert Carl
Mueller, Bruce Anthony
Mueller, Don Sheridan
Mueller, Herbert A.
Mueller, Herbert Rodd
Mueller, John Carl
Mueller, Roland Frederick
Mueller, Willys Francis, Jr.
Muffly, Robert Benton
Mugalian, Robert Haig
Mugford, Alfred George
Muhn, Robert Alan
Muhrer, Merle Edward
Muirhead, Vincent Uriel
Mukherjee, Subhash Chandra
Mukherji, Sanjib Kumar
Mukhopadhyay, Alpana
Mularz, Stanley Leon
Mulcrone, Richard Thomas
Mullan, Joseph Delbert
Mullen, Henry Andrew
Mullen, Januarius Arthur
Mullen, John Lawrence
Mullen, William Stanley, Jr.
Mullendore, James Myers
Muller, Herman Joseph
Muller, John Bartlett
Muller, Sigfrid Augustine
Mulligan, Barbara E.
Mulligan, Thomas James
Mulliken, Robert Sanderson
Mullin, Kenneth Ray
Mullin, Patricia Evelyn
Mullins, Richard Austin
Mullins, Robert Paul
Mulvaney, Ronald
Mulvaney, William Peter
Mulvihill, Donald Ferguson
Muma, Jack Wesley
Muncaster, Edward Hampton
Munda, Rino Umberto
Mundell, Junius Lee
Mundell, Wilbur Lewis
Mundie, Donald Robertson
Mundy, Daniel L.
Mundy, Melvin Duane
Muneio, Frank Raymond, Jr.
Munoz, Rodrigo Alberto
Munro, (Harriet) Bernice
Munson, Carl Edward
Munson, Howard Roger
Muntz, Ernest Gordon
Muntz, Marjorie Corinne
Muntz, Marvin Eugene
Muraco, William Anthony
Muraskevics, John, Jr.
Murata, Kazunao
Murdock, Charles Kennedy
Murfin, Allen Eugene
Murney, Joseph Anthony
Muroga, Saburo
Murphy, Alan Charles
Murphy, Cecil Patrick
Murphy, Daniel Michael
Murphy, Daryl Emerson
Murphy, Glenn
Murphy, James William
Murphy, John Arthur
Murphy, John Thomas
Murphy, Lester Fuller, Jr.
Murphy, Mary Borredell Dalton (Mrs. Jim Gordon Murphy)
Murphy, Mary Edith Fox
Murphy, Mary Theresa
Murphy, Max Ray
Murphy, Morgan F.
Murphy, Morgan F.
Murphy, Patrick Henry
Murphy, Paul Lloyd
Murphy, Robert Edward
Murphy, Robert Thomas
Murphy, Thomas A.
Murphy, Thomas Bernard
Murphy, Thomas Vincent
Murphy, William Valentine
Murray, Beverly Ann
Murray, Charles John
Murray, Daniel Gardner
Murray, Donald Richard
Murray, Gordon Nicholas
Murray, Harry Lee
Murray, Judson Thrash
Murray, J(ulian) Ronald
Murray, Kermon
Murray, Merrill R.
Murray, Michael Russell
Murray, Michael Thomas
Murray, Richard Deibel
Murray, Robert Eugene
Murray, Ruth Elaine
Murray, Walter Allan, Jr.
Murray, William Francis
Murray, William Frederic
Murrell, Peter Charles
Murrell, Turner Meadows
Murry, Charles Emerson
Murry, Edward James
Murtonen, Donald John
Musca, Albert Anthony
Muschenheim, Carl Arthur
Muschenheim, William Emil
Muschewske, Robert Charles
Musegaas, Jan
Musgrave, Olie Lee
Musgrove, Virginia Margaret
Musinski, Donald Louis
Musselman, Barbara Lynn
Musselman, Larry Lee
Musser, Joseph Elder
Musser, Robert Daniel, Jr.
Musson, Victoria Leland
Mutharika, Arthur Peter
Mutzabaugh, James Charles
Muzik, Edward John
Mycue, David John
Myerholtz, Ralph W., Jr.
Myers, Eddie Earl
Myers, Frank Kenneth, Jr.
Myers, George Elliott
Myers, George Vincent
Myers, Hal Hanauer
Myers, Howard
Myers, James Russell
Myers, Jerome M.
Myers, John Clement, Jr.
Myers, John Thomas
Myers, Kenneth E.
Myers, Michael John
Myers, Norma Jane McKay
Myers, Robert Harry
Myers, Robert Henry
Myers, Victor Ira
Myers, Warren Erwin
Myers, William Claude, Jr.
Myers, William Osgood
Myhre, Harold Gordon
Myler, Bernard James
Naber, Edward Carl
Naber, Faith
Nadesan, Alexander Govind
Naegele, Robert Arthur
Naffziger, Dewein Haven
Nagar, Arvind Kumar
Nagel, Jon Alan
Nagera, Humberto
Nagey, Tibor Franz
Nagi, Mostafa Helmey
Nagler, La Rue (Larry) Hamilton
Nagy, Denes
Nagy, Thomas Francis
Naiden, James
Naines, Joseph Benjamin, Jr.
Najarian, John Sarkis
Nakra, Naresh Kumar
Nalipinski, Rudolph Edward
Namen, Robert Marvin
Nammacher, Thomas John
Nance, Earl Walton
Naney, Alva Paul
Nansen, Everett James
Nap, Kimbel Anton
Napadensky, Hyla Sarane
Naphin, Francis Joseph
Narconis, Roman Joseph, Jr.
Nardine, Frank Edward
Nasby, Charles Leland, Jr.
Nash, Edward Merl
Nash, John Pritchard
Nason, Howard K.
Nasser, Stephen Charles
Nathan, Kenneth Sawyer
Nations, Gus Orvel
Nauman, Delbert Arnold
Naumann, William Louis
Nauss, Lee August
Navarro, Anna Maria
Nayden, John Michael
Naylor, George LeRoy
Nazette, Richard Follett
Neal, Charlotte Anne
Neal, Mark Wayne
Neal, Paul Edwin
Neal, Paul Gordon
Neale, Gary Lee
Neblett, Thomas Randolph
Nechin, Herbert Benjamin
Nederlander, Caren Elaine
Nederlander, Robert Elliott
Nederveld, Terrill Lee
Nedzi, Lucien Norbert
Nee, William Joseph
Neece, Robert Frederic
Needels, Richard Eugene
Needham, George, Jr.
Neeper, Ralph Arnold
Neetzel, Raymond John
Nefe, Clemens Ralph Frank
Neff, Kenneth D.
Neff, Ray Allen
Neff, Richard George
Neff, Robert Marshall
Neibel, Oliver Joseph, Jr.
Neidenbach, John Joseph
Neiderhiser, Floyd John
Neidert, Andrew Reinhardt
Neil, Eugene
Neil, James Wellington Harry
Neil, Randolph Laning
Neiman, Lionel Joseph
Neiman, Simon (S.I.)
Nellen, James William
Nellessen, Alfred Henry
Nelms, George Edward
Nelson, Bruce Kern
Nelson, Charles Edmund
Nelson, Charles Wego
Nelson, Dale Allen
Nelson, Dallas Leroy
Nelson, David Joe
Nelson, David Leonard
Nelson, David Torrison
Nelson, Deane Dale
Nelson, Esther Louise Hiley
Nelson, Eugene William
Nelson, Fred Ernest
Nelson, Gaylord Anton
Nelson, Herbert Cecil Quinten
Nelson, Herbert Lou
Nelson, Ivan Lloyd
Nelson, James Nels
Nelson, John Arthur
Nelson, Leonard Necolai
Nelson, LeRoy Elburn
Nelson, Mary Bertha Ring
Nelson, Nancy Jane
Nelson, Orville Kenneth
Nelson, Reginald David
Nelson, Richard E.
Nelson, Richard Harold
Nelson, Robert Eddinger
Nelson, Roy Jay
Nelson, Stanley R.
Nelson, Thomas Eustis, Jr.
Nelson, Warren Donald
Nemec, Stanley S.
Nencka, Helen (Ann)
Nephew, Albert Henry, II
Nepote, Hazel Ellen
Nerlinger, John William
Nesbitt, Arthur Wallace
Nesmith, Leslie Wallace
Nespeca, Glenn Aldo
Ness, Ordean Gerhard
Nesse, Anton Stephan
Nesse, Harold
Nesterenko, Dimitri A.
Netser, James Raymond
Neu, Arthur Alan
Neubauer, Charles Frederick
Neuenschwander, Frederick Phillip
Neugent, David Smith
Neumann, Augwill Walter
Neumann, Forrest Karl
Neuschel, Robert Percy
Nevin, Timothy William
New, Jack L.
Newbanks, James Allan
Newbury, David Norman
Newby, Gerald Capper
Newby, John Melvin
Newby, Richard Prouty
Newcomb, Ward Crawford
Newcomer, David William, III
Newell, Pinkney Janiory, Jr.
Newell, Virginia Shaw
Newey, Paul Davis
Newhouse, Eugene Joseph
Newlin, Joseph Edward
Newman, Louis Edward, III
Newman, M. W.
Newman, Merle Edward
Newman, Muriel Kallis Steinberg
Newman, Nancy Blitzsten
Newman, Ralph Geoffrey
Newman, Terry Kay
Newman, Wilson Landess
Newmyer, Eldon Lee
Newnum, Raymond Lavern
Newpher, James Alfred, Jr.
Newton, Barry Neal
Newton, George
Newton, John Marshall
Neyhart, Louise Albright (Mrs. Carl Neyhart)
Nichol, Fred Joseph
Nichol, Ira Wesley
Nicholas, Clemens
Nicholas, David M.
Nicholas, Dimitri Paul
Nicholas, George Wallace
Nicholas, Robert Leon
Nichols, Ronald Lee
Nichols, Ruth Annette
Nichols, Theodore George
Nichols, Thomas Hogan
Nichols, William Curtis, Jr.
Nicholson, Gary Lewis
Nicholson, Nancy Viola Snider
Nickel, Thomas Bernard
Nickelson, Harry Edward
Nickerson, Max Allen
Nicodem, Harold Ernest
Nicol, Sheldon Spencer
Nicolette, Anthony Orland
Niebler, Chester John
Niebylski, Leonard Martin
Niederhauser, Dale Ray
Niehaus, William Roger
Nielander, Ruth Marie
Nield, John B.
Nielsen, Anna Frances Nielsen (Mrs. Ernest David Nielsen)
Nielsen, Arthur Charles
Nielsen, Arthur Charles, Jr.
Nielsen, Charles Paul
Nielsen, Howard Norbert
Nielsen, Kathy Ann
Nielson, Joseph Finley
Nieman, Charles Ebersol
Nieman, Timothy Alan
Niemeyer, Glenn Alan
Niemeyer, Maxine Brewer
Niesse, John Edgar
Nieubuurt, John Edward
Nightingale, Edmund Anthony
Nightingale, Edmund Joseph
Nikishin, Igor Fedor
Nimmerfroh, Clarence Leo
Nims, Charles Francis
Ninke, Arthur Albert
Ninomiya, Jack Sadao
Niro, Raymond Pardo
Nissen, Carl Andrew, Jr.
Nissimov, Norbert J.
Nissing, Burton John
Niswonger, C(lifford) Rollin
Niswonger, Philip Gordon
Nitschke, Charles Albert
Niu, Stanley Hsien P.
Niven, Alexander Curt
Nixon, Don Lewis
Nixon, R(ichard) Roy
Noack, Helmut Otto
Nobes, Leon Durrell
Noble, Ellsworth Glenn
Noble, Howard Bates
Noble, Robert Ray
Noble, William James, Jr.
Nocon, James Jeffrey
Noe, Donald Arden
Noe, Frances Elsie (Mrs. Robert Davies)
Noel, Claude Bert
Noel, Donald
Noeth, Carolyn Frances
Noeth, Richard Jerome
Noffsinger, Donald Allen
Nofziger, Terry Lee
Nogaj, Richard Joseph
Nogle, Timothy Fenton
Nolan, Carole Rita
Nolan, David P.
Nolan, Richard
Noland, Marion Seymour
Nolen, Granville Abraham
Noling, Michael Stephen
Nolte, Henry R., Jr.
Noonan, Melvin Arthur
Noonan, Thomas Clifford
Nopper, Ralph Jacob
Nora, Paul Francis
Nordby, Jack Sogge
Nordby, Norman Edward
Nordeen, Dale Arron
Nordlie, Robert Conrad
Nordling, Bernard Erick
Nordling, Leland Ebben
Nordman, John Carlton
Nordmark, Torberg Peder
Nordstrom, Carl Clifford
Nordyke, Hollis Judson
Norman, Elva Pauline Kuykendall (Mrs. Isaac Daniel Norman)
Norman, Forrest Alonzo
Norman, John William
Norman, Ronald Victor
Norman, Wayne Andrew
Normoyle, John Louis
Norrick, Wayne Coleman
Norris, G. Kennon
Norris, James Lawrence
Norris, Paul Nathan
Norris, Robert Miranda
North, Victor
North, William Stanley
Northrop, Gordon Douglas
Northrop, Stuart Johnston
Northrup, Arthur Harry
Norton, Clifford Raymond, Jr.
Norton, John Philemon
Norton, Robert Pilger
Nosal, Chester Walter
Nose, Yukihiko
Notch, Herbert Lawrence
Notz, John Kranz, Jr.
Novak, Edwin Daniel
Novak, James F.
Novak, Michael Paul
Novak, Richard Francis
Novak, Robert John
Novak, Robert Lee
Novick, David
Novick, Marvin
Novotny, Vladimir
Nowell, Lawrence Alexander
Noyes, Ronald Tacie
Nuccitelli, Saul Arnold
Nun, Edward Walter
Nunemaker, Wesley
Nunn, Joe Richard
Nupen, Harlan Clarence
Nussel, Edward Joseph
Nutter, Ervin John
Nutter, Gene Douglas
Nuttle, Daniel Edward
Nuzman, Carl Edward
Nye, Charles Neal
Nygaard, Loyd Daniel
Nyhus, Lloyd Milton
Oakar, James Louis
Oakar, Mary Rose
Oakes, Kent Allen
Oakley, Brice Case
Oats, Charles Samuel
Obayashi, Alan Walter
Ober, David Lawrence
Oberdieck, William Hubert
Oberhamer, Douglas Roy
Oberhart, Jack Charles
Oberholtzer, John Clayton
Oberle, Kevin Ray
Oberman, Moishe David
Obermiller, Stanley Mathew
Oberrotman, Alain Maurice
Oberst, Byron Bay
Oberst, Daniel C.
Oberstar, James L.
Obey, David Ross
Oblak, Robert Otto
Oblinger, Josephine Kneidl Harrington (Mrs. Walter L. Oblinger)
O'Block, Frank Robert
O'Brien, Charles Richard, Jr.
O'Brien, Francis David
O'Brien, George Herbert
O'Brien, George Miller
O'Brien, Gregory Michael St. Lawrence
O'Brien, John Patrick
O'Brien, William Patrick
Ocepek, Anthony Steven
O'Connell, Daniel Craig
O'Connell, Marvin Richard
O'Connell, William James
O'Connell, William Thomas
O'Connor, Carl Bernard
O'Connor, Charles, Jr.
O'Connor, Charles Garry
O'Connor, Claude Lindbergh
O'Connor, David
O'Connor, James Ignatius
O'Connor, James John
O'Connor, Jerome William
O'Connor, Michael David
O'Connor, Michael Dennis
O'Connor, Sara Andrews
O'Connor, Timothy Edmund
Odebrecht, A. Richard
O'Dell, Frederick Charles, Jr.
O'Dell, Lynn Marie Luegge (Mrs. Norman D. O'Dell)
O'Dell, Richard Frederick
Oder, Donald Rudd
O'Dillon, Richard Hill
Odita, Florence Chinyere Uwandu
Odland, Lynn V.
Odom, John Edward
O'Donnell, Bernard
O'Donnell, David Richardson
O'Donnell, Thomas Michael
O'Donovan, Cornelius Joseph
Odvarka, Robert Charles
Oehmke, Thomas Harold
Oehmler, Donald Clive
Oeljen, Siegfried Carl George
Oestreich, Karl Lynn
Oetjen, Robert Adrian
Offenhiser, Andrew Brewster
Offinger, Walter Eugene, Jr.
Oftedahl, Everett John
Ogden, Merlene Ann
Ogden, Russell Lee
O'Geary, Dennis Traylor
Ogilvie, Bruce Campbell
O'Grady, Lillian Mary Quinlan (Mrs. Valentine M. O'Grady)
Oh, Bonnie Bongwan Cho
O'Hagan, James Joseph
O'Hara, Delmar T.
O'Hara, Francis Anthony
Ohl, Hazel McNitt
Ohlson, Donald Ernest
Ohlson, Edward La Monte
Ohman, John Hamilton
Ohno, Mitsugi
O'Hora, James Baldwin
O'Keefe, Beth Egan
O'Keefe, James L.
O'Keefe, Thomas Joseph
Okulitch, Peter Vladimir
O'Lane, John Michael
Old, Robert Lee
Oldam, Paul Bernard
Oldeg, Harry William, Jr.
Oldenburger, Derek
Oldeschulte, Burton Lawrence
Oldham, Howell G.
Oldham, Lowell Tincher
O'Leary, Carl Thomas
O'Leary, Francis Bernard
O'Leary, Joseph Augustine
O'Leary, Virginia Elizabeth
Olegario, Gil Fortunato Sevilla
Olejar, Marie Celine
Olejniczak, Dominic
Oleksy, Stanley Peter
Oleson, Clara Rodriguez
Oleson, George Bowen
Olin, Harold Bennett
Olinger, David Duane
Olive, Roger Oswald
Oliver, Sylvia Ellen Bassett (Mrs. Willard Chelsea Oliver)
Olivia, Lawrence Anthony
Olmstead, William Edward
Olney, Robert Carrol
Olsen, Arthur Robert
Olsen, Douglas Alfred
Olsen, Edward Harold, Jr.
Olsen, James George
Olsen, Paul David
Olsen, Robert Allen
Olsen, W(ilhelm) F.
Olshavsky, Richard William
Olson, Alec Gehard
Olson, Allen Ingvar
Olson, Barbara Ford
Olson, Clitus Wilbur
Olson, David Herman
Olson, Dean Alan
Olson, DonaeBill Glen
Olson, Edward Louis
Olson, Everett Atley, Jr.
Olson, Frederick Irving
Olson, Gordon Everett
Olson, Gordon Win Jum
Olson, Harriet Ann Howard
Olson, James John
Olson, Linda Kathryn
Olson, Melvin Donald
Olson, Melvin Joyce
Olson, Orville Bernard
Olson, O(scar) William
Olson, Priscilla Mae
Olson, Raymond Roy
Olson, Raymond Stanley
Olson, Richard Gottlieb
Olson, Robert Claude
Olson, Rue Eileen (Mrs. Richard L. Olson)
Olson, Victor Edward
Olson, Wesley William
Olson, William Howard
Olston, Mary Kay
O'Mahoney, Michael Terrence
O'Malley, Kenneth Gerald
O'Malley, William Paul, II
O'Meara, John Thomas
O'Meara, Mark Thomas
O'Meara, Thomas Francis
Omer, Shirley Jean
Ominski, Julian Marion, Jr.
Ommodt, Donald Henry
Ondrey, Joseph Thomas
O'Neal, David Cortland
O'Neil, Danny
O'Neil, Jack Wilhelm
O'Neill, C. William
O'Neill, Daniel Clarke
O'Neill, Joseph Thomas, Jr.
O'Neill, Michael Steven
O'Neill, Richard Burns
O'Neill, William James
O'Neill, William James, Jr.
Ong, John Doyle
Ongaro, Mario Peter
Onofrio, Angelo Michael
Oost, Stewart Irvin
Opdahl, Keith Michael
Openshaw, Calvin Reynolds
Opp, Paul Franklin, Jr.
Oppenheim, Bernard Edward
Orandi, Ahmad
Orandi, Mehdi
Orchard, Edgar Lee
Ordinachev, Miles Donald
Ore, Donald Eugene
O'Reilly, Clarence Joseph
O'Reilly, Donald Eugene
O'Reilly, Francis Justus
O'Reilly, Robert Clyde
O'Reilly, Roger Kevin
Orf, Douglas James
Orfanos, Minnie
Orgler, Rudolph John
Orland, Frank J.
Orland, Henry
Orland, Phyllis Therese Mrazek (Mrs. Frank J. Orland)
Orlin, Louis Lawrence
Orman, Allan Donald
Ormond, Betty Lou (Hayden)
Ormseth, Robert Owen
O'Rourke, Peter Edward
O'Rourke, Randall Michael
Orr, Bruce Alan
Orr, Earl Lawton
Orr, Gordon Dickson, Jr.
Orr, Joan
Orr, Sister Mary Mark
Orr, Richard Tuttle
Orr, Victor Darryl
Orr, Wendell Eugene
Ortega, Carlota Ayala
Orthwein, William Coe
Ortino, Leonard James
Ortiz, Jose Dennis
Ortman, Frank J.
Ortman, William Andrew, Sr.
Ortmeier, Evelyn J.
Orvis, Alan LeRoy
Oryshkevich, Roman Sviatoslav
Osborn, Charles Howard
Osborn, Donald Dean
Osborn, Francis Howard, Jr.
Osborn, Laura (Mrs. Henry P. Zuidema)
Osborn, Myron Wallace, III
Osborne, Arthur Ellsworth, Jr.
Osborne, Newell Yost
Osborne, Robert Vandervoort
Osenberg, Warren Erwin
Osipow, Samuel Herman
Osmanski, William Thomas
Osmon, Robert Vance
Osmond, John Dexter, Jr.
Osness, John M.

Osness, Wayne Hans
Ossenberg, Robert Dean
Ossip, Kenneth Irwin
Ostand, Paul Raymond
Ostby, Donald Harold
Osten, Donald Walter
Ostendorf, Edgar Louis, Jr.
Osterkamp, Waite Robert
Osterlund, Russell Gaylord
Ostfeld, Alexander Marion
Ostlund, Arthur Clayton
Ostlund, Leonard Alexander
Ostrand, Janet Louise
Ostrom, Kay Ann
Ostrom, Susan Mc Whirter
Osuch, Leonard John
O'Sullivan, John Francis
O'Sullivan, John Lewis
Otani, Yoshihiko
Otis, James Cornish
Otis, James John
Otis, Robert Charles
Otis, Robert Edward
O'Toole, Jeanne Marie
Otrich, George Hamilton
Ott, Jerry D.
Ott, Melvin Dale
Ott, Richard Herbert
Ott, Roger Arthur
Otte, Karl Henry
Otten, Kenneth Harry
Ottenfeld, Marshall
Ottinger, Denise Catherine
Ottmar, Clinton Raymond
Otto, Patricia Ruth
Otto, Roswell D.
Otto, Wayne Raymond
Ottolini, James Louis
Ottow, Orville Charles
Otway, Frank Hamilton
Oughton, James Henry, Jr.
Oughton, Richard Corbett
Ouimet, Alfred Joseph, Jr.
Ouzts, Dale Keith
Overberg, Paul Joseph
Overgaard, Bjorn
Overholser, Ronald Lee
Overholt, Robert Eugene
Overholt, Robert Leslie
Overholt, William Alvin
Overton, George W.
Overton, Jane Vincent Harper
Oviatt, Charles Dixon
Owen, Bruce Wilmot
Owen, John Elliot
Owen, Margaret Frances Richards (Mrs. George Earle Owen)
Owen, Mickey
Owen, Richard Clement, Jr.
Owen, Robert Carroll
Owens, Dorothy Elizabeth
Owens, Dwight Ray
Owens, Frederick Mitchum, Jr.
Owens, Horace Gordon
Owens, James Hamilton, Jr.
Owens, Lyell Gary
Owings, Malcolm William
Owley, Gordon Thomas
Ownby, Paul Darrell
Oxley, Joseph Hubbard
Oxley, Lorin Earl Everett
Oxtoby, Robert Boynton
Ozar, Milton Bernard
Ozinga, James Richard
Pabst, Theodore Shuster
Pace, Julian Hughes
Pachman, Daniel J.
Pack, Dennis Harvey
Packard, Martin Theodore
Padanilam, George Joseph
Padberg, Daniel Lee
Padgett, Katharine Long
Paetzke, Roy Warren
Paffrath, Leslie
Pagano, Salvatore John
Page, Alfred Percy
Page, Dozzie Lyons
Page, Edwin Richard
Page, Eleanor (Mrs. Frank E. Voysey)
Page, Howard Kelsey
Page, Robert Wright
Page, Walter Sharp, Jr.
Page-El, Edward
Pagel, Richard Frederick
Pagel, William Rush
Pagen, John
Pagtakhan, Reynaldo Daluz
Paine, Carlton Bentley
Paine, Charles Bentley
Painter, Milton McFarland
Painter, Sydney Shaw, III
Paisley, Dennis Lee
Pajic, Svetomir
Pakis, Val
Pakyz, Lawrence Joseph
Palbykin, Donald John
Palenchar, Robert Edward
Palermo, Anthony, Jr.
Palia, Charles Cantardo
Pallmann, Margot Simons
Palm, Ernest Theodore
Palmer, Agnes Mae High (Mrs. Daniel David Palmer)
Palmer, Cloyce Dean
Palmer, Daniel David
Palmer, Dennis Lee
Palmer, Donald Curtis
Palmer, Edward Henry
Palmer, Harrison Rowe
Palmer, John Lewis
Palmer, Margaret Louise
Palmer, Michael A.
Palmer, Paige (Mrs. Arthur Freeman)
Palmer, Ralph Vincent
Palmer, Ray Greenleaf
Palmer, Robert Gerald
Palmer, Suzanne Jennifer
Palmiter, Harry Alva
Palmore, Julian Ivanhoe, III
Pambookian, Hagop Sarkis
Pan, Alexander Kee Sui
Pan, Jaming
Pancero, Jack Blocher
Pande, Sharad Chandra
Panec, Alber Eldon
Panec, William Joseph
Pang, Joshua Keun-Uk
Pangilinan, Nestor Sta Cruz
Panosh, Richard Louis
Pansch, Frank Norman
Pansegrau, Duane Francis
Panter, Irwin
Pantoja, Enrique
Pantzer, Kurt Friedrich, Jr.
Panwar, Kris
Panzica, Joseph Salvatore
Pao, Yoh-Han
Papadakis, Constantine Nicholas
Papandrea, James John
Papay, Andrew George
Paper, Charles
Papez, Donald Wesley
Papier, David
Papin, Lawrence Edward
Paplauskas, Lynn Ellen
Paplow, John Edward
Papo, Michael
Pappajohn, John George
Pappas, Aphrodite Mezilzoglou (Mrs. Peter Pappas)
Paradoski, Edwin Andrew
Paranjpe, Suresh Chintaman
Pardo, Manuel Policarpio
Paredes, August Victor
Parent, David Joseph
Parent, Joseph Dominic
Parise, Ronald Joseph
Parisi, Joseph Angelo
Park, Chan Hyung
Park, John Lionel
Park, John Nelson
Park, Keil-Soon
Park, U. Young
Park, Yong Hwa
Parker, Beverly Ann
Parker, Charles Walter, Jr.
Parker, Clyde Wendel
Parker, Daryl McCoid
Parker, Donald La Rue
Parker, Edwin Lynch
Parker, Ethel Max (Mrs. Cedric M. Parker)
Parker, Frank Parish, Jr.
Parker, Frank Ralph
Parker, Gerald Edmund
Parker, Jack Darwin
Parker, James Mitchell
Parker, Raymond Leroy
Parker, Richard Henderson
Parker, Wayne Frederick
Parkhurst, Edwin Wallace, Jr.
Parkin, Evelyn Hope
Parkinson, George Ambrose
Parkinson, Leonard Curtis
Parkinson, William Charles
Parks, James Dallas
Parks, James William
Parks, Lyman Starling
Parks, Murrill Douglas
Parks, Sherwood Race
Parks, Terry Everett
Parks, Thomas Aquinas
Parks, William Robert
Parks, William Wilson
Parkus, Paul Phillip
Parkyn, John Duwane
Parman, Larry Vance
Parmelee, David Freeland
Parmer, Dan Gerald
Parris, Porter P.
Parrish, Donald Graham
Parrish, James Hilliard
Parrish, John Bishop
Parrish, John Edward
Parrish, Matthew Denwood
Parrish, Orville Stanley
Parrish, Rufus Herald
Parrott, Dean Allen
Parrott, Roger Lee
Parson, David
Parsons, Augustine Chapman
Parsons, Dana Lee
Parsons, Donald James
Parsons, Frederick Ambrose
Parsons, Gamaliel Leroy, Jr.
Parsons, James Benton
Parsons, M(elvin) Godfrey
Parsons, Peter Peabody
Parsons, Samuel Dale
Partain, Carl Stanley
Partee, Cecil A.
Partington, Philip Franklin
Paruk, Walter Adam
Pasch, Dorothy Frances
Paschal, William Barron
Paschall, Homer Donald
Pascoe, Percy Willard, Jr.
Pasek, Michael Anthony
Passage, Michael John
Passi, Ronald Bernhart
Passman, Richard Harris
Pastin, Mark Joseph
Patchak, Russell George
Patel, Arun Kantilal
Patel, Jayant Ambalal
Patel, Lok Nath
Patel, Madhu
Patel, Pravinchandra Vallabhbhai
Patel, Ramesh Baldevbhai
Patel, Virendra Chaturbhai
Pathak, Dev S.
Pathe, Antone Peter
Patrick, Daniel Ray
Patricoski, Thomas Stanley
Patten, Thomas Henry, Jr.
Patterson, Charles Ward
Patterson, Gloria Jean
Patterson, Harlan Ray
Patterson, James McCoy
Patterson, Lawrence Thomas, II
Patterson, Lucille Joan
Patterson, Michael Milton
Patterson, Richard George
Patterson, Richard Henry
Patterson, Shirley Louise
Patterson, Thelma K. (Mrs. John E. Patterson)
Patterson, Tommy Wayne
Patterson, Virginia Norrell
Patterson, Ward Lamont
Patterson, William James
Patterson, Willis Charles
Pattis, S. William
Pattishall, Beverly Wyckliffe
Pattison, Jeffry Alan
Patton, Audley Everett
Patton, Earl Dean
Patton, Harold Preston
Patton, James Thomas
Patton, Noel Thomas
Patton, Peter Clyde
Pattou, Brace
Pattyn, Remi Ceasar
Paul, Eileen Susan
Paul, Elmer William
Paul, Gabriel (Gabe)
Paul, Howard Alex
Paul, Justus Fredrick
Paul, Morton Malcolm
Paul, Oglesby
Paul, Prosper Frederick
Paulissian, Robert
Paull, Donald
Pauls, Richard Dayton
Paulsen, Fayetta Mae
Paulsen, Harold Maurice
Paulsen, Richard Wallace
Paulson, Belden Henry
Paulson, Louise Hill (Mrs. Belden Henry Paulson)
Paulson, Monroe Burton
Paulson, William L.
Paulus, Peter Virgil
Pavelka, Elaine Blanche
Pavlic, Robert Stephen
Pawl, Ronald Phillip
Pawley, Ray Lynn
Pawlowski, Harry Michael
Paxton, George Benjamin, Jr.
Payan, Hushang Mofakham
Payant, Vital Robert
Payne, Frederick John
Payne, James Leroy
Payne, Nellie Maria de Cottrell
Paynter, Donald G.
Paynter, Lawson
Peabody, Sylvia Rockwood
Peak, Wilbur James
Pearce, Harry Jonathan
Pearce, John Lawrence
Pearl, Irwin Albert
Pearsall, Harry James
Pearsall, Thomas Edward
Pearson, Helen R. (Mrs. Russell S. Parks)
Pearson, James Blackwood
Pearson, John Sumner
Pearson, Louise Mary (Mrs. Nels K. Pearson)
Pearson, Martha Elizabeth Mitchell (Mrs. James B. Pearson)
Pearson, Nels Kenneth
Pearson, Norman
Pearson, Peter Robb
Pearson, Phillip Theodore
Pearson, Robert Edwin
Pease, Donald James
Peavler, Robert J.
Pecaro, Daniel Thomas
Pecina, Richard Wayne
Peck, Glenn Mackey
Peck, John W.
Peck, Lee Barnes
Peck, Martha Harriet Sullivan (Mrs. Glenn Mackey Peck)
Peck, William Arno
Peck, William Henry
Peckenpaugh, Donald Hugh
Peckham, Charles Wesley
Peckinpaugh, Philip Earl
Pedersen, Marlin Anthony
Pederson, David Davis
Pederson, Robert Murwin
Pedigo, Howard Kenneth
Pedley, Grace Baldwin
Pedraja, Rafael Rodobaldo
Peebles, Carter David
Peel, Malcolm Lee
Pees, Randall William
Pehlke, Robert Donald
Peikoff, Louis Arnold Mendel
Peirce, Thomas Seeley
Peirick, Elyse Mach
Pekarek, Robert Charles
Pelanda, Katherine Brazar
Pelissier, Rene Emile
Pellegrin, Joseph, Jr.
Pellegrini, Norman Roy
Pelletier, Alcid Milton
Pellett, Kent Louis
Peloza, Stanley Joseph
Pembaur, Bertold Joseph
Pence, Leland Hadley
Pendleton, Don
Pendleton, Thelma Brown
Penick, James Lal, Jr.
Penkava, Robert Ray
Penman, Allen Stuart
Pennell, John Spear
Penner, David
Penner, Lorne Wilfred
Penner, William Arnold, Jr.
Penningroth, Robert Paul
Pennington, Eunice Catherine Randolph (Mrs. Daniel Douglas Pennington)
Pennington, Lea Giblyn
Pennington, Leonard William, Jr.
Penry, Richard Earl
Pensler, Alvin Victor
Pentecoste, Joseph Clarence
Penzel, Carl Linus
Peper, Christian B(aird)
Pepinsky, Pauline Nichols
Pepper, Henry Cornelius
Pepping, Raymond Austin
Peppler, Henry James
Pequignot, Stanley Edward
Peraino, Carl
Percival, Worth Harris
Percy, Charles Harting
Peress, Maurice
Perez, Carlos A.
Perk, Ralph Joseph
Perkin, Ethel Murphy (Mrs. Frank Scott Perkin)
Perkins, Edward Howard, Jr.
Perkins, Frederick Garland, III
Perkins, John Harold
Perkins, John Robert
Perkins, Marvin Deuane
Perkins, William H., Jr.
Perkins, William Swain
Perlman, Daniel Hessel
Perlman, Edward
Perlmutter, Marion A.
Perloff, Richard Mark
Perlow, S. James
Perner, Dennis Max
Peros, Alex George
Perpich, Rudy G.
Perret, Maurice Edmond
Perrotto, Larry James
Perry, Esther Mary Izzo (Mrs. Peter Perry)
Perry, George William
Perry, Glenn Earl
Perry, Harold
Perry, Irving Chester, III
Perry, James Edward
Perry, Jimmy Dale
Perry, Milton Freeman
Perry, Neva Sabbagh
Perry, Oscar L., Sr.
Perry, Richard Palese
Perry, Robert Joseph
Perry, Roger Lawrence
Perry, Theodore Edward
Perry, Victor Edward
Persky, Seymour Howard
Person, Earle George, Jr.
Person, Marjorie Perry
Persons, Wallace R.
Pesch, LeRoy Allen
Peschiera, Antonio Wenceslao
Peshkin, Samuel David
Peske, Patric O.
Petacque, Arthur Martin
Petchenik, Edward M.
Peterhans, Louis Raymond, Jr.
Peters, Alvera Kae
Peters, Farnsley
Peters, Frank Lewis, Jr.
Peters, Fred Harold
Peters, George David
Peters, Ira Buford, Jr.
Peters, Jerome Frank
Peters, Joseph Harlan
Peters, Nathaniel Ashby, III
Peters, Ronald Ross
Petersen, Dietrich Linde
Petersen, Donal Christian
Petersen, Donald Eugene
Petersen, Edward Schmidt
Petersen, Roland Frederick
Petersen, Susan Rose
Peterson, Alphonse
Peterson, Arthur LaVerne
Peterson, Arthur Theodore
Peterson, Calvin Clifton
Peterson, Charles Roland
Peterson, Chester, Jr.
Peterson, Donald Curtis
Peterson, Donald George
Peterson, Donald Robert
Peterson, Duane Malcolm
Peterson, Edward Norman
Peterson, Freddie-Nadine
Peterson, Harry Edward
Peterson, Harry Walter
Peterson, John Marsilje
Peterson, Lloyd Richard
Peterson, Marilyn Ann (Mrs. Richard Fay Peterson)
Peterson, Martha Elizabeth
Peterson, Mildred Othmer
Peterson, Paul Jerome
Peterson, Ralph Henry
Peterson, Richard M.
Peterson, Robert Austin
Peterson, Rodney Keller
Peterson, Roger Dean
Peterson, Roger Marshall
Peterson, Roy Edwin
Peterson, Russell Arthur
Peterson, Vernon Jerome
Peterson, William Mc Clure
Petke, Frederick Edward
Petre, Harvey Alvin
Petri, Henry Law
Petri, Kenneth Miller
Petrie, Bruce Inglis
Petrie, George Rollo
Petrochuk, Konstantin
Petros, Sophie Karipides (Mrs. Thomas S. Petros)
Petroski, Catherine Ann Groom
Petroski, Henry Raymond Joseph
Petrosky, J(ohn) Dale
Petrovich, Miodrag Bozidar
Petrucci, Anthony
Petrulis, John Bruno, Sr.
Pettengill, Roscoe Robert
Pettipiece, Clayton Lloyd
Pettis, Eugene Ernest
Pettit, Marlin Hazen
Pettit, Robert Cecil
Petty, Elijah Edward
Petzke, Alfred Julius
Petzold, Fritz Herbert
Petzold, Rudolf Heinrich
Pew, Stephen Eliot
Peyronnin, Joseph Felix, III
Peyser, Joseph Leonard
Pfabe, Bruce Yetter
Pfaender, Lawrence Vernon
Pfaffenbach, Herbert Emil
Pfaffmann, George David
Pfahl, Stannard Baird, Jr.
Pfaller, Mark A(rthur)
Pfarner, Gerald Charles
Pfau, Michael John
Pfeffer, Robert Irving
Pfeil, Richard John
Pfeiler, Thomas Adams
Pfening, Frederic Denver, Jr.
Pfettscher, Earl Ernest
Pfister, Paul James
Pflanzer, Richard Gary
Pfleiderer, Florizel A.
Pflueger, Charles Allen
Pflug, Fred Louis
Pfundstein, Keith Lawrence
Phair, Gretchen Mueller
Phalen, Thomas Francis, Jr.
Phegley, Richard Dean
Phelan, J. J.
Phelan, John Densmore
Phelan, William Henry
Phelps, Betty Jeane Pottenger (Mrs. Charles Puterbaugh Phelps)
Phelps, Edwin Rice
Phelps, Nan Dee Hinkle (Mrs. Robert Phelps)
Phelps, William Cunningham
Phenicie, Marlond Dean
Phetteplace, Betty Helena (Mrs. Joseph Arthur Phetteplace)
Phibbs, Clifford Matthew
Philgreen, Irving Axene
Philion, James Robert
Philipps, Louis Edward
Philipson, Willard Dale
Phillian, Harry Edgar
Phillip, Lee (Mrs. William J. Bell)
Phillips, Bertrand Douglass
Phillips, Carole Ann
Phillips, Chandler Allen
Phillips, Enos Leslie
Phillips, John Milton
Phillips, Joseph James
Phillips, Joshua
Phillips, Lloyd James
Phillips, Margaret Josephine
Phillips, Margaret Nadene
Phillips, Michael Joseph
Phillips, Michael Keith
Phillips, Paul Richard
Phillips, Richard Bracewell
Phillips, Richard Miles
Phillips, Sarah Virginia Cyrus (Mrs. Donald Ray Phillips)
Phillips, Wally
Phillips, Wendell Leroy
Phipps, Jay Lawrence
Piascik, Peter Kenneth
Piatt, William Mac-a-Cheek
Piazza, Cosmo Charles
Piazza, James Frederick
Pickens, Robert Bruce
Pickett, David Franklin, Jr.
Pickford, Thomas Michael
Picking, Robert Boyd
Piepmeier, Robert Branom
Pierard, Richard Victor
Pierce, Daniel Marshall
Pierce, Danny Parcel
Pierce, Donald Norman
Pierce, Douglas John
Pierce, James Gray
Pierce, Lambert Reid
Pierce, Ralph
Pierce, Richard
Pierre, Kenneth Jerome
Piersol, Lawrence LeRoy
Pierson, Edwin Kenneth, Jr.
Pierson, Fritz Arthur, Jr.
Pierson, Lorraine Josephine
Pierson, Paul Sanford, Jr.
Pietrofesa, John Joseph
Pigatti, Eugene Rudolph
Pikaart, Len
Pikarsky, Milton
Pike, John Raymond
Pike, Robert Allen
Pikunas, Justin
Pilditch, Walter Edward
Pilgrim, Mary Jane
Piller, Heinar Friedrich
Pilliod, Charles Jule, Jr.
Pillon, Nancy Hargis Bach
Pillow, Thomas Mastin
Pillsbury, George Sturgis
Pillsbury, John Sargent, Jr.
Pillsbury, Katharine C. (Mrs. John S. Pillsbury, Jr.)
Pilot, Isadore
Pince, Bruce Wayne
Pinder, Albert Joseph
Pindera, Jerzy Tadeusz
Pine, Shirley Ann
Pineda, Eliza Laoang (Mrs. Bernardo G. Pineda)
Pingatore, Rosari Antoinette Foti (Mrs. Anthony Pingatore)
Pingry, Charles Warren
Pinkelton, Norma Bertha Harris
Pinkenburg, Christopher Albert
Pinkerton, Richard LaDoyt
Pinkerton, Robert John
Pinkerton, Vernon Theodore, Jr.
Pinkus, Craig Eldon
Pinnell, William George
Pinsky, Mark Allan
Pinsky, Steven Michael
Pinsof, Nathan
Pintar, Milan Mik
Pinto, Michael
Pinzarrone, Paul F.
Piper, William Archibald
Pipitone, Phyllis Luis (Mrs. S. Joseph Pipitone)
Pirlot, Fred
Pirrung, Clifford Mark
Pirtle, Barbara Bethea
Pisani, Albert Louis
Pisarchick, Sally Ellen
Pischke, Frank John
Piscopo, Joseph Anthony
Piszczek, Edward Andrew
Pitcher, Robert Walter
Pitchford, William Myron
Pitt, George
Pitts, James William
Pitzer, Errington Elwood
Pizer, Irwin Howard
Plack, Harold Joseph, III
Plank, Raymond
Plant, Marcus Leo
Plante, Julian Gerard
Plantinga, Alvin Carl
Plass, Herbert Fitz Randolph
Platt, Brainard Windell
Platt, Doris Hubbard
Platt, George Jarvis
Plaxton, Kenneth Dean
Playe, Margaret L. Berg (Mrs. George L. Playe)
Pletcher, David Mitchell
Pletcher, Kenneth E.
Plinke, John Frederick
Plodzien, Richard John
Ploeser, Walter Christian
Plotnick, Harold
Plucker, Orvin Lowell
Plugge, Dale Lavern
Plumb, Joseph Charles, Jr.
Plummer, Robert Eugene
Plunkett, Charles Walter
Plunkett, James Gardner
Poage, George Richard
Pockras, Laurence Malvin
Poddar, Shrikumar
Podell, Ralph Jack
Podolsky, B(ertha) Polly Edelman
Podrebarac, Charles Matthew
Podruch, Louis Leo, Jr.
Poe, Oscar August
Poe, Wayne Alan
Poe, Weyland Douglas
Poelker, John Henry
Pogrund, Sherwin Ivan
Pohl, Kenneth Roy
Pohlman, Kenneth Louis
Poindexter, Clifford Edward
Poindexter, Henry Pratt
Poinsett, Alexander Caesar
Poinsette, Donald Eugene
Poirier, Brooke Elizabeth
Poirier, Curtis Raymond
Polakoff, Donald Miles
Polan, Jeanne Warsaw Fox
Poland, Anne Spellman
Polasky, Frank Martin
Polcar, Gertrude Elizabeth
Polen, Thomas Morris
Polian, Harold
Policastro, Anthony Joseph
Polich, John Edmund
Polk, Gloria Harris
Polk, Richard Thaddeus
Polk, Rothwell Conway
Polking, Kirk
Pollack, Joseph
Pollak, Felix
Pollak, Jay Mitchell
Pollak, Michael Edward
Pollard, Herman Marvin
Pollard, John William
Polley, Edward Herman
Polley, Howard Freeman
Polley, Robert Lutz
Pollino, Patrick Anthony
Pollitt, Damon Edward
Pollitt, Gertrude Stein
Pollnow, George Gustav
Pollock, Bruce Gillespie
Pollock, James Wilson
Pollock, John Dale

Pollock, Leslie Stuart
Pollock, Robert Baker
Pollock, Robert John, Jr.
Polom, Frank Edward
Polsky, Donald Perry
Polydoris, Nicholas George
Pomerantz, Sherwin Bernard
Pomeranz, Jerome Raphael
Pomeroy, Elwaine F(ranklin)
Pomeroy, Mahlon Walter
Pominville, Henry Arthur
Pommrehn, Richard Junior
Pomroy, Carol E.
Pondrom, Lee Girard
Ponitz, David Henry
Ponka, Joseph Luke
Ponseti, Ignacio Vives
Pont, John
Pontius, Harold Jackson
Pool, Ernest Howard, Jr.
Pool, John David
Poole, Charles Pinckney
Poole, James Ira
Poole, John Bayard
Poots, C. Allan
Pope, Donna Kolnik
Pope, Jean Grove
Pope, John Dawson, III
Pope, Sarah Georgina
Pope, Sharon Kay
Popke, Chester A.
Popovich, Peter Stephen
Popovsky, Julio
Poppe, Wassily
Poppelbaum, Wolfgang Johann
Poppen, Bruce Jennings
Poprick, Mary Ann
Porcheddu, Joseph Warren
Porod, Robert Francis
Port, Curtis DeWitt
Port, Rich Bleser
Portenier, Lillian Gertrude
Porter, Albert S.
Porter, Dale Lincoln
Porter, David Lindsey
Porter, Donald Gamaliel
Porter, Earl Dossett, Jr.
Porter, Frederick Andrew
Porter, George Darwin
Porter, George LeRoy
Porter, Harry Benton, Jr.
Porter, Harry LeRichmond
Porter, John Edward
Porter, John Wilson
Porter, Rex Vernon
Porter, Robert Eugene
Porter, Scott Ellis
Porter, Stuart Williams
Porter, Terence Clifton
Porter, T(homas) Wayne
Porter, William Joseph, Jr.
Porter, Winston Seymour
Porterfield, Henry Andrew
Porterfield, Neil Harry
Portes, Caesar
Porthan, Edward Richard
Portteus, Elnora Marie Manthel (Mrs. Paul Portteus)
Posch, Joseph Louis
Posluszny, Gerald Milton
Posner, Judith Lois
Posnick, Irving Harvey
Pospishil, Frank Francis
Pospishil, Lloyd Labar
Post, Donald George
Post, Margaret Moore
Posthuma, Albert Elwood
Poston, Franklin Darrell
Posz, Albert Conrad
Posze, Alex Richard, Jr.
Potkin, Nathan Norman
Potocki, Wladyslaw Jan
Potter, Dennis Alvin
Potter, George Ernest
Potter, John Wesley
Potter, Juan Wyatt
Potter, Marilyn Meyer
Potter, Norman Rodney
Potts, Donald Albert
Potts, Frank Alex
Potts, Leslie Carroll
Poulik, Miroslav Dave
Poulimas, Constantine Nicholas
Poulin, Maureen Joan
Poulsen, Lance Kuld
Povlsen, Paul Kristian, Jr.
Povondra, Dennis Lee
Powdrill, Gary Leo
Powell, Ernestine Breisch (Mrs. Roger K. Powell)
Powell, Ira Chesley
Powell, Jerome Evan
Powell, Richard Cinclair
Powelson, James Sherman
Power, Joseph Aloysius
Power, Philip Harwick
Power, Sarah Goddard (Mrs. Philip H. Power)
Powers, Earl Hershel
Powers, Earl Louis
Powers, James Walter
Powers, John James
Powers, John Richard, III
Powers, Raymond Edwin, Jr.
Poynton, Joseph Patrick
Poyser, John Reed
Prager, David
Prall, Elmer Clarence
Praml, Lawrence Anthony
Prange, James Robert
Prange, James William
Prange, William Harold
Prasad, Ananda Shiva
Prasad, Aryabala Ray
Prasse, Paul Henry
Prasuhn, Lloyd Wayne
Prater, Horace Milton
Prather, James Keith
Pratt, Dan Edwin
Pratt, George Edward
Pratt, LeRoy George
Pratt, William Crouch, Jr.
Prausnitz, Walther Gunther
Pray, Bruce S.
Pray, Ralph Rustin
Prcela, John Ivan
Prebe, William Francis
Preble, Robert Curtis, Jr.
Predolin, Henry
Preece, Rodney John
Prefontaine, Harris Leonard
Pregon, Gerald Michael
Prendergast, Mary Kathryn
Prenzlow, Elmer John Charles, Jr.
Prerost, Frank Joseph
Prescott, Gerald James, Jr.
Pressey, Alexander William
Pressler, Larry
Preston, David Michael
Preston, Eliza Hoyt
Preston, Ivan L.
Preston, James Faulkner, Jr.
Preston, Norris Wayne
Preston, Richard Lee
Prestwich, Leonard Willis
Preul, Herbert Charles
Preus, Jacob A.O.
Preuss, Roger E(mil)
Price, C. Eugene
Price, Charles Melvin
Price, Charles Morgan
Price, Edward Francis
Price, Everett Alfred
Price, Jacob Myron
Price, John Michael
Price, Kenneth Strawn
Price, Lucile Brickner Brown
Price, Paul Myron, Jr.
Price, Paxton (Pate)
Price, Robert Eugene
Price, Russ Edward
Price, Thomas Emile
Price, Virgil Evon
Prichard, Merrill E.
Prichard, Nancy Sawyer Gilbert (Mrs. Kenneth D. Prichard)
Priddy, Robert Ray
Priedeman, William Robbins
Priehs, George William
Priehs, Hermine Soukup
Priest, Charles Joseph
Priest, William Roy
Primack, Verne Moran
Primiano, Nicholas Peter
Primich, Theodore
Primmer, Glenn Estus
Prince, Aaron Erastus
Prince, Frances Anne Kiely (Mrs. Richard Edward Prince, Jr.)
Prince, Virginia Faye Dixon (Mrs. A.E. Prince)
Prindaville, Lawrence Allen
Prinz, Andrew Karl
Prinz, Leon Marvin
Pritchard, Leonard Stilts
Pritchard, Mary Hanson (Mrs. C.G. Pritchard)
Pritikin, Jeanne DuPre Moore (Mrs. Roland I. Pritikin)
Pritikin, Roland I.
Pritsker, A. Alan B.
Pritzker, A. N.
Pritzker, Leon
Pritzker, Robert Alan
Probasco, Gene Arlen
Probst, Wildena Georgia
Prochazka, Otto Francis
Prochnow, Herbert Victor
Prochnow, Herbert Victor, Jr.
Prochnow, Laura S. (Mrs. Herbert V. Prochnow)
Proctor, Conrad Arnold
Proctor, Hazel Peabody
Proctor, Jerry Franklin
Proctor, Valerie Floyd
Prokopoff, Stephen S.
Promersberger, William Joseph
Proost, Robert Lee
Propati, Joseph Alexander
Prophete, Beaumanoir
Propson, Thomas Peter
Prost, John Charles
Proteau, Roseanne Vitullo
Prothero, Edward George
Prough, George Harrison
Prouty, Garry Franklyn
Provencher, Ronald
Provitt, Evelyn
Provost, Wallace Burdett
Proxmire, William
Pruis, John J.
Pruitt, Russell Clyde
Pruner, Mary Carolyn
Prusinski, Richard Casimer
Pryor, Chester Cornelius, II
Psalmonds, Majorie (Mrs. W. Gordon Psalmonds)
Psalmonds, (Walter) Gordon
Psihogios, George Thomas
Ptak, Louis Richard
Pu, Pin Hsiu
Puccio, James Salvatore
Puckett, Robert Hugh
Puckorius, Paul Ronald
Pudlo, Edmund Marion
Pueppke, Glenn Howard
Puetz, Wayne Edward
Pugh, Daniel Wilbert
Pugliese, Joseph Margiotti
Pukite, Janis
Pulitzer, Emily Rauh (Mrs. Joseph Pulitzer, Jr.)
Pulitzer, Joseph, Jr.
Pullen, James Ralph
Pulliam, Jack Carl
Pullukat, Thomas Joseph
Pulsipher, Dee Wayne
Pulve, Frederick Mason
Pundt, Richard Arthur
Punnett, Audrey Frances
Purcell, James Francis
Purdum, Jack Jay
Purdy, Charles William, III
Purdy, Ralph David
Purifoy, Cecil Ernest, Jr.
Purple, Edward Bennett
Pursell, Carl D.
Pursell, Warren Benjamin
Purves, Alan Carroll
Pusateri, Lawrence Xavier
Pustell, John Francis
Pustmueller, Debra Ruth Tyberendt
Puth, John Wells
Putka, Andrew Charles
Putnam, Clyde Charles, Jr.
Putnam, David Arms
Putnam, Theodore Delano
Putney, Richard Wallington
Putterman, Allen Michael
Putz, Louis J.
Pyle, Beatrice Alzira
Pyle, H(erbert) Wayne
Pyne, Alvan Wesley
Pysh, Joseph John
Pyun, Seong Kyun
Qadri, Shane Haider
Quaal, Ward Louis
Quackenbush, Gerald Glenn
Quadracci, Harry R.
Quale, Gladys Robina
Qualey, Carlton Chester
Quandt, David Mylo
Quast, Gary Lynn
Quay, Quentin Q.
Quayle, James Danforth
Queen, Daniel
Query, Joy Marves Neale (Mrs. William T. Query)
Quesnell, John George
Quick, Gerald Norman
Quick, Guy Hayden
Quick, John Lowell
Quie, Albert Harold
Quilty, Florence Elizabeth MacInnis (Mrs. Francis C. Quilty)
Quinlan, John Wilbert
Quinn, Charles Lewis
Quinn, James Leland, III
Quinn, Robert Henry
Quinn, Robert J.
Quinn, Robert Litten
Quintanilla, Antonio Paulet
Quintero, Cesar
Quirk, Jane Helen Wagner
Quo, Phillip C.
Qutub, Musa Yacub
Raach, Francis Anthony
Raatikka, Theodore Richard
Rabb, George B.
Rabbers, Norman Lloyd
Rabe, Charles Castens
Rabe, Richard Frank
Rabin, Joseph Harry
Rabinovitz, Adolph J.
Rabkin, Eric S.
Rach, Roy Dean
Rachels, Charles Thomas
Rachesky, Stanley Robert
Rachford, Edward John
Rachie, George Louis
Radchuk, Serge
Radcliff, William Franklin
Radcliffe, Byron Mason
Radcliffe, Donald Vane
Radcliffe, Robert Putnam
Radde, Bernard Carl
Raden, Louis
Radford, Edward Earl
Radke, Donald Gilbert
Radkins, Andrew Peter
Radmacher, Camille J.
Radochonski, Stephen Peter
Radovanov, Radmila
Radtke, Lorraine M.
Radway, Jerrold Everett
Rady, John Mortimer
Radzius, Joseph Raymond
Raetzman, Ronald Mura
Rafaill, Thomas Dennis
Ragan, William Darby
Ragas, Leonidas Joseph
Ragg, Theodore D. B.
Raghib, Gunay Mustafa
Ragland, Albert M.
Ragland, Sam Benton, Jr.
Ragsdale, Edward Floyd
Ragsdale, Richard Michael
Raha, Chitta Ranjan
Rahmann, John Charles
Rahtjen, Bruce Donald
Rahtjen, Irma Lea
Raike, Sydney Ralph
Raike, Virginia Charlotte
Raikes, James Alfred
Railsback, Tom
Raim, Roland Leo
Raimundo, Hugo Sa
Rainbow, Kathryn Adeline (Mrs. William Earhart)
Rainville, Harold E.
Rainville, Roger Harold
Rait, George
Raitt, John Wellesley
Rajendra, Kunwar
Rajput, Aqil Khan
Rakusan, Jerome John
Rall, Kenneth Loem
Ralston, Mary Agnes
Ramacciotti, William Stephen
Ramadanoff, Dimiter
Ramah, Simon Joseph
Ramakrishnan, Venkataswamy
Rambert, Gordon Arthur
Ramler, Warren Joseph
Ramnath, Ramchandra
Ramp, Alvon DeNeal
Ramp, Wilber Franklin, Jr.
Ramsey, William Eugene
Ramsland, Maxwell O.
Rana, Mohammed Waheed-uz-Zaman
Rand, Sidney Anders
Rand, Theodore Arnold
Randall, Dudley Felker
Randall, John Daniel
Randall, John Daniel, Jr.
Randall, Priscilla Richmond (Mrs. Raymond V. Randall)
Randall, Robert William
Randall, Rogers Ellis
Randolph, Alice Harrington
Randolph, Franklin Lee
Randolph, Jackson Harold
Randolph, Kenneth Henry
Randolph, Robert Marshall
Randolph, Ross V.
Raney, Eugene Hubert
Ranieri, Dominic Gilbert
Raniville, Francis Oliver
Rankin, Michael Rae
Ranney, G. Durbin
Ranous, Charles Albert
Ransdell, Edgar Curtis, III
Ransom, Henry King
Ransom, James Harley
Rao, Desiraju Bhavanarayana
Raoul, Joseph, Jr.
Raphael, Rick
Rapp, Ralph L.
Rappana, Duane Archie
Rappoport, Arthur Everett
Rash, Jack Dean
Rasmussen, Oscar Gustav
Rastas, Vytas Pranas
Ratchford, Charles Brice
Ratcliffe, Myron Fenwick
Rath, Patricia Mink (Mrs. Melvin Eugene Rath)
Rath, Virgil Kenneth
Rathermel, Eugene Melvin
Rathi, Manohar
Raths, Otto Nicholas, Jr.
Ratigan, William O.
Ratkovich, John Mark
Ratliff, Teddy LaVern
Ratner, Mark Alan
Ratteree, William Adolph
Rau, Jerold Matthew
Rauch, Irmengard
Raufeisen, Raymond Robert
Rausch, Francis David
Rauschert, Karl Alfred
Raven, Edwin Dean
Raver, Paul Joseph
Raves, Peter Harley
Ravindranathan, P. G.
Rawitch, Allen Barry
Rawlings, Gary Don
Rawlings, Maurice Edward
Ray, Arun Bikas
Ray, Charles Dean
Ray, Hope Walker (Mrs. Kenneth C. Ray)
Ray, John Walker
Ray, Kenneth C.
Ray, Mrs. Robert D.
Ray, Robert D.
Ray, Ruth
Rayle, Edwin Beard
Raymer, Donald George
Raymond, Loren Andrew
Raymond, Walter
Raynolds, Randall Crane
Raynor, John P.
Rayson, Leland Homer
Razim, Edward Anton
Rea, Robert Eugene
Read, George Sullivan
Read, Robert Benjamin
Reals, William Joseph
Reams, Bernard Dinsmore, Jr.
Reardon, Patrick Joseph
Rearick, Gary Roger
Reaser, Donald Claire
Reasor, Gerald Lester
Rebeiz, Constantin Anis
Reber, Donald David
Rebertus, Robert Lee
Rebstock, Theodore Lynn
Reck, W(aldo) Emerson
Recker, Edward Anthony
Reckert, Robert Dean
Rectenwald, Gary Michael
Redding, Foster Kinyon
Reder, William Roger
Redfield, Nicholas Pridmore
Redgrave, John Robert
Redleaf, Paul David
Redmond, George Foote
Redondo, Diego
Redshaw, Ward Fuller
Reece, Wilbur Taylor
Reed, Arthur Lachlan
Reed, Donald Irving
Reed, E. Smith, Jr.
Reed, Edsel Sherwood
Reed, Elmethra Luster
Reed, Emelyne Ely
Reed, Frank Fremont, II
Reed, Gareth LaVerne
Reed, Margaret Fox
Reed, Philip G.
Reed, Robert Holbrooke
Reeder, Eileen Berendt
Reeder, Stanley Waylett
Rees, Warren James
Reese, Donald Joseph
Reese, Raymond Castle
Reese, Richard Scott
Reese, Thomas Leland
Reese, Wendell Blaine
Reeves, Duane Lee
Reeves, Elton Traver
Reeves, Walter Harold
Regagnon, Paul
Reggio, Vito Anthony
Regula, Ralph Straus
Reh, Thomas Edward
Rehak, James Richard
Rehe, Rolf Friedrich
Rehkopf, Charles Frederick
Rehner, Herbert Adrian
Reich, David Lee
Reichert, Norman Vernon
Reichl, Mary Thomas
Reichlin, William Joseph
Reichner, Robert James
Reid, Bill
Reid, Clyde Myer
Reid, Douglas Gordon
Reid, Ellis Edmund
Reid, James Calvin
Reid, Robert Alton
Reid, William Turnbull, Jr.
Reidda, Phil
Reidenberg, Louis Morton
Reider, James Eugene
Reiff, Guy Gene
Reigel, Don
Reilly, Frank Kelly
Reimer, Donald Ross
Reimer, Robert Charles
Reimers, Richard H.
Reimnitz, Raymond Frederick
Reinbold, James William
Reinertson, James Wayne
Reinhart, Melvin Joseph
Reinis, Stanislav
Reinke, John Henry
Reinsdorf, Jerry Michael
Reischauer, Robert Eugene
Reisman, Arnold
Reisman, Betty Lou
Reiss, Jerome Lee
Reister, Raymond Alex
Reistroffer, Dianne
Rejai, Mostafa
Relford, Regina Frances
Relic, Milan Raymond
Rembusch, Joseph John
Remer, Richard Charles
Reminger, Richard Thomas
Rempert, Lawrence Arnold
Rench, Richard Eugene
Rencher, Mark Julius
Rendleman, George Franklin, Jr.
Rendon, Leandro
Reneker, Betty Congdon (Mrs. Robert W. Reneker)
Reneker, Robert W(illiam)
Renfrew, James
Renich, Paul William
Renick, Murray Chester, Jr.
Renison, Herbert John
Reno, Ottie Wayne
Rensel, Lloyd Aloysius
Rensner, Delmar A.
Rentschler, William Henry
Repp, Duane Leslie
Repucci, Lawrence Carl
Reser, Billy Joe
Resler, Paul Edward
Reslock, Paul Vernon
Resneck, Elliott Jack
Resnick, Louis
Resnik, Marvin
Resseguie, James Lynn
Restivo, Raymond M.
Restorick, William Howard
Reszka, Alfons
Retsky, Michael Walter
Rettmer, Forrest Rudolph
Retzer, Kenneth Albert
Retzer, Mary Elizabeth Helm (Mrs. William Raymond Retzer)
Retzer, William Raymond
Retzlaff, Horst Franz Albert
Retzloff, David George
Retzloff, James Gail
Reuben, David J.
Reuben, Don H.
Reuss, Carl Frederick
Reuss, Henry S(choellkopf)
Reuter, George Sylvester, Jr.
Reuter, Helen Hyde
Reuthe, John Julius
Reutter, Clifford John
Rewoldt, Stewart Henry
Reyes, Milagros Pagaduan
Reymond, Ralph Daniel
Reynolds, Dale Richard
Reynolds, Frederick Charles
Reynolds, Jay Don
Reynolds, John W.
Reynolds, Kelly Peter Patrick
Reynolds, Richard William
Reynolds, William Preston
Rezner, Charles Thomas
Rhembrandt, Carlton Kayo
Rhiew, Hyomyeong Benjamin
Rhoad, Floyd Gerald
Rhoades, Thomas Perry, III
Rhodes, Arthur Edward
Rhodes, Donald Ellsworth
Rhodes, Irwin Seymour
Rhodes, Lester Legere
Rhodes, Mary Elizabeth Frechtling
Rhodes, Paul Earl
Rhoten, Ogle Eldric
Rhykerd, Charles Loren
Ribordy, Denis Eugene
Riccardo, Edward Peter
Riccardo, John Joseph
Rice, Arthur Raymond
Rice, Charles Wayne
Rice, David Lee
Rice, Donald Lee
Rice, Paul Frederick
Rice, Pony Ralph
Rice, Wilfred Francis, Jr.
Rich, Donald Joseph
Rich, Marvin Lewis
Richard, Jack
Richards, Earl Frederick
Richards, Francis Lee
Richards, Graydon Edward
Richards, Jane Grills
Richards, Jonathan Barlow
Richards, LaClaire Lissetta Jones (Mrs. George A. Richards)
Richards, Maurice Lyman, Jr.
Richards, Michael Steven
Richards, Paul Frederick
Richardson, Arthur Hamilton
Richardson, Charles Everett
Richardson, Emanuel Ross
Richardson, Eugene Stanley, Jr.
Richardson, George Bown
Richardson, James Lewis
Richardson, John Adkins
Richardson, Joseph Hill
Richardson, Lonnie Allen
Richardson, Myrtle
Richardson, Robert A
Richardson, Ruth Ann
Richcreek, James Marion
Richelieu, Clyde Carl
Richie, Ernest Carl
Richman, Marvin Jordan
Richmond, Harold Wayne
Richmond, Quinton Blaine
Richmond, Richard (Dick) Thomas
Richmond, Tullie Taylor
Richmond, William Lloyde, Jr.
Richter, Harold
Richter, Roberta Brandenburg (Mrs. J. Paul Richter)
Richter, William Arthur
Rickbeil, Clara Evelyn Shellman (Mrs. Raymond E. Rickbeil)
Ricker, Otto Lee
Rickert, Richard Michael
Ricketts, John William
Ricketts, Ralph Lynn
Ricks, Bernard E.
Riddle, Maxwell
Riddlebarger, Larry Devon
Riden, Joseph Robert
Ridge, William Clayton
Ridgway, George Martin
Ridings, Craig Asher
Ridlen, James Herman
Ridley, Elton Taft
Ridzon, James Ronald
Riecker, John E(rnest)
Riecker, Margaret Ann Towsley (Mrs. John E. Riecker)
Rieckus, Aloysius Michael
Riedel, Paul Schreiter
Riedell, John Aloysius
Riedl, Frank William
Riedmann, William Joseph
Rieg, George Stanley, Jr.
Riegel, Farald Lloyd
Rieger, Helen Breeden Hedrick (Mrs. Wray Montgomery Rieger)
Rieger, Mitchell Sheridan
Rieger, Pearl Handelsman
Riegle, Donald Wayne, Jr.
Rieman, Dwight Walker
Ries, Edward Otto
Riester, George P.
Rietz, Edward Gustave
Rigg, Robinson Peter
Riggs, Byron Lawrence, Jr.
Riggs, Roderick Douglas
Riggs, William Norman
Righter, Walter Cameron
Righter, William Howard, Jr.
Rigoni, Raymond John, Jr.
Riker, Charles Marr, III
Rikimaru, Yuki
Rikker, Leslie Denes
Riley, Donald Alan
Riley, Fenwick Charles, Jr.
Riley, John Edward
Riley, Lyman Guyton
Riley, Robert Green
Riley, Tom Joseph
Rinella, Salvador Anthony
Ring, Gerald John
Ring, Leonard M.
Ringel, Mary Frances Cheatham (Mrs. William Sheldon Ringel)
Ringer, Alfred Victor
Ringo, Boyd Colburn
Ringo, Miriam K.
Ringo, Philip Jansen
Rinke, Dwight Clarence

Rinsley, Donald Brendan
Rinsley, Jacqueline Ann (Mrs. Donald Brendan Rinsley)
Riordan, Ray Joseph
Ripley, Kenneth Lauren
Rippy, Frances Marguerite Mayhew
Risdall, John Robert
Riseley, Martha Suzannah Heater (Mrs. Charles Riseley)
Risk, George
Ristola, Eugene Gustaf
Ritchie, Alexander Buchan
Ritchie, John Duncan
Ritenour, John Joseph, Jr.
Rittenhouse, Joseph Wilson
Ritter, Hartien Sharp
Ritter, Hubert August
Ritterbusch, Robert Karl
Ritz, Gordon H.
Rivera, Mario Pablo
Rivers, Mozelle Wilson (Mrs. John J. Rivers)
Rives, James Henry, Jr.
Rives, Stanley Gene
Rivkin, William B.
Rizik, Michael Bernard
Roach, John Page
Roach, John Robert
Roach, Ronald Thomas
Roache, Esther Wilson (Mrs. Fred W. Roache)
Roan, Frank Joseph
Roark, Jean Carroll
Roark, LaVerne Waldo
Roath, Richard Sterling
Roba, William Henry
Roback, Raymond Roger
Robb, David Dow
Robb, William John
Robbins, Edward Louis
Robbins, Frederick Chapman
Robbins, Glenn Kingsland
Robbins, Norman Nelson
Robbins, Orem Olford
Roberto, Edward A.
Roberton, Lois Rickert (Mrs. Theodore S. Roberton)
Roberts, Charles Chester, Jr.
Roberts, Charles Eugene
Roberts, Edgar Lee
Roberts, Erskine Goode
Roberts, Helen Catherine Golden
Roberts, Hugh Evan
Roberts, James Alfred
Roberts, Jo Ann (Wooden)
Roberts, Leigh Milton
Roberts, Leo James
Roberts, Richard Lee
Roberts, Roy
Roberts, Thomas Chelcie
Roberts, Valerie Sawyer
Roberts, William Keith
Robertson, Abel Alfred Lazzarini, Jr.
Robertson, Billy O'Neal
Robertson, Charles Harry
Robertson, James Edward
Robertson, James Edwin
Robertson, Joseph Edmond
Robertson, Rodney Charles
Robertson, William Bruce
Robie, Fred Smith
Robillard, James Lawrence
Robilliard, Walter Henry
Robinder, Catherine Mae Fitzpatrick
Robins, Eli
Robins, Gary Bruce
Robinson, Claude Garth
Robinson, Eliot Finley
Robinson, Forrest Dean
Robinson, George Albert
Robinson, Gladys Mabel Chambers (Mrs. Carl Tapley Robinson)
Robinson, Jack F(ay)
Robinson, John Edmund
Robinson, John F.
Robinson, Larry Rapport
Robinson, Peter Clark
Robinson, Raymond Wayne
Robinson, Renault Alvin
Robinson, Russell Dean
Robinson, Sally Winston
Robinson, Theodore Curtis
Robinson, Walter Stitt, Jr.
Robinson, William Nathaniel
Robling, John Stevens
Robson, Edwin A.
Robson, John Henry
Roby, Max, Jr.
Rocco, Vincent Anthony
Roch, Lewis Marshall, II
Rochetto, Evelyn Marie
Rochman, Michael David
Rock, Ronald Stephen
Rock, William Ray
Rocke, R. Thomas
Rocke, Robert Alfred
Rodd, Forest Willard
Roddis, William Henry
Rodeck, William Fred, Jr.
Roderick, Harry Edward
Rodgers, Dennis Bruce
Rodgers, Eugene Merle
Rodgers, Orlan Cleeve
Rodgers-Sullivan, Rosemary Florence
Rodin, Ernest Anton
Rodis, Themistocles Constantine
Rodisch, Robert Joseph
Rodman, James Purcell
Rodney, Sam
Rodriguez, Manuel Baello, Jr.
Rodriguez, Raymond
Rodriguez, Robert Alan
Rodriguez-Torres, Ramon
Roe, Claude Leighton
Roeing, Richard Sven
Roeper, George Alexander
Roese, Albert Junior
Roesel, Rudolph Walter
Roeser, Thomas Francis
Roesner, Peter Lowell
Roessler, David Martyn
Roffmann, Harold
Rogers, Charles Thomas
Rogers, David Alan
Rogers, Felix Michael
Rogers, Gifford Eugene
Rogers, James Franklin
Rogers, James Maurice
Rogers, JoAnn
Rogers, John Francis
Rogers, John Russell
Rogers, Joy Jeanne
Rogers, Raymond Earl
Rogers, Thomas Kay
Rogers, Van Rensselaer
Rogers, Wilbur Frank
Rogers, William Arthur
Rognan, Lloyd Norman
Rogols, Saul
Rohl, David William
Rohling, Paul Vernon
Rohlinger, Merlin Joseph
Rohrbach, Max Sidney
Rohrman, Douglass Frederick
Rohrs, Kenneth Vernon
Roland, Carroll Dudley
Rolf, Frank Paul
Rolfs, Marvin Eugene
Rolland, Paul
Roller, Mac C.
Roloff, Leland Harold
Rolsten, Robert Fred
Rolston, Rodrick Riggs
Rolwing, Raymond Hugh
Rolwing, Robert Eugene
Romager, Jimmie L.
Romano, Paul Edward
Rombs, Vincent Joseph
Romero, Josefino Tabernilla
Romesberg, Floyd Eugene
Romig, James Lyle
Romine, Charles Alva
Romine, Robert Joseph, Jr.
Romito, Walter Richard
Rommel, Richard Earl
Romney, George
Romon, Pacifico Cruz, Jr.
Roney, Patrick Atkins
Roningen, Jewel Edgar
Roningen, Robert Noel
Rooks, Charles Shelby
Rooks, Charles Wendell
Rooney, Edwin Anthony
Rooney, George Eugene
Rooney, William Boyd, Jr.
Roos, James Paul
Root, John O.
Rootare, Hillar Muidar
Roots, Clive George
Roozbazar, Aziz
Roper, David James
Roper, LaRoy Raymond, Jr.
Roper, Raymond Warren, Jr.
Roper, William Zacharias
Roppel, Richard Meredith
Rorig, Kurt Joachim
Roscoe, Wayne Lynn
Rosdail, James Russell
Rose, Allan
Rose, Betty Ann
Rose, Beverly Jean
Rose, Charles William
Rose, Ernst
Rose, Frederick Albert
Rose, Hugh Lee
Rose, Kenneth Dwight
Rose, Kurt Rainer
Rose, Leonard George
Rose, Merritt DeVon
Rose, Robert Embree
Rose, Stanley Jay
Rose, William
Rosemond, John Henry
Rosen, Carl Leonard
Rosen, George
Rosen, Ronald Haiam
Rosen, Samuel Morris
Rosenbaum, Earl Lewis
Rosenberg, Dale Henry
Rosenberg, Edward Daniel
Rosenberg, Guy Lourie
Rosenberg, Kenyon Charles
Rosenberg, Norman Jack
Rosenberger, Helen Marie
Rosenblate, Howard Jerome
Rosenblatt, Suzanne Maris
Rosencranz, Robert
Rosenfeld, Robert Sanford
Rosenfeld, Steven Alan
Rosengard, Abe Benjamin
Rosengren, Chester Gordon
Rosenkoetter, Gerald Edwin
Rosenow, Oscar Ferdinand
Rosenstrock, Philip
Rosenthal, Herbert M.
Rosenthal, Joyce Elaine
Rosenthal, Julian Sanford
Rosenthal, Mark Alan
Rosenthal, Samuel Robert
Rosentreter, Myron Adolph
Rosenzweig, Daphne Lange
Rosevear, Robert Allen
Roshel, John Albert, Jr.
Rosinger, George
Roskens, Ronald William
Roslycky, Eugene Bohdan
Ross, Albert Merritt
Ross, Charles Howard
Ross, David Eugene, Jr.
Ross, David Kinsey
Ross, Earl E.
Ross, Eugene Irwin
Ross, George Edwin
Ross, Harold Anthony
Ross, Jay Bernard
Ross, Monte
Ross, Mylan Everett
Ross, Myron Donald
Ross, Richard
Ross, Richard Hall
Rosseels, Gustave Alois
Rossi, Donald
Rossi, Jean Joseph
Rossing, William Osmund
Rossman, Margaret Mary Dryz
Rossway, Melvin Weaver
Rost, J. Waldo
Rost, William Joseph
Rostenkowski, Dan
Rotelli, Leo Anthony
Roth, Carl Frederick
Roth, Claude A.
Roth, David Francisco
Roth, David Maurice
Roth, John Reece
Roth, Norman Gilbert
Roth, Sydney Martin
Rothenberg, Harold Jay, II
Rothermel, Bradley LeGeorge
Rothfus, John Arden
Rothfuss, Fred Doty
Rothhaar, Raymond Eugene
Rothman, David
Rothmann, Bruce Franklin
Rothnem, Morris Stanley
Rothner, Arnold David
Rothschild, Robert Lehwald
Rothstein, David Anthony
Rothstein, Stanley Harold
Roudané, Charles
Roundy, Lloyd Russell
Rouse, Gene Gordon
Rouse, John Ratcliffe
Roush, Allan Nelson
Rousos, Michael George
Routman, Burton Norman
Rouwenhorst, Donald Lee
Rovelstad, Trygve A.
Rowan, Richard John
Rowe, Clarence John
Rowe, Fred Herbert
Rowe, Fred Werner
Rowe, Nathaniel Hawthorne
Rowe, Robert B.
Rowe, Robert Bradford
Rowen, Kenneth Alexander
Rowland, Donald Charles
Rowland, Henry Sanders, III
Rowlands, David James
Royalty, Dennis Marion
Royhl, John Charles
Royko, Mike
Rozan, Dorothy Natalee Camin (Mrs. Josef S. Rozan)
Rozman, Joseph John, Jr.
Rubens, Sidney Michel
Rubin, Stanley J.
Rubin, Stephen David
Rubinow, Steven Charles
Rubins, Ira Marc
Rubinstein, Jack Herbert
Ruble, Ronald Alvin
Rubloff, Burton
Ruch, Richard Hurley
Ruck, Charles Mitchell
Rudd, Ralph Corlies
Ruddle, James Farris
Ruden, Violet Howard (Mrs. Charles Van Kirk Ruden)
Rudick, Milton Martin
Rudisill, Robert Mack
Rudman, Daniel Stephen
Rudman, Herbert Charles
Rudolph, Jack Wallace
Rudrauff, Ann Audgerie
Rudy, David Robert
Rudy, Elmer Clyde
Rudy, Joel Sanford
Rudy, Robert Sale
Ruebke, Henry Jacob
Rueger, Homer Edwin
Ruegsegger, Donald Ray, Jr.
Ruegsegger, Loyal, Jr.
Ruehl, Phillip Christian, IV
Ruf, Jacob Frederick
Ruf, Patricia Kaye
Rugg, John Daily
Ruggles, Robert Blair
Rugh, William Batman
Rugolo, Lawrence
Ruhala, Richard John
Ruksenas, Algis Pius
Rulau, Russell
Rulis, Robert Alexander
Rumely, Emmet Scott
Runge, Robert Henry
Runice, Robert E.
Runnebohm, Nicholas Joseph
Runser, Charles Allan
Rupe, Billy Dean
Rupp, Douglas Alan
Rupp, Robert George
Ruppel, Howard James, Jr.
Rusch, Herman August
Rush, David Harry
Rush, Joseph Thornton
Rushton, William Edwin
Ruskaup, Calvin Frederick
Russell, David Garth
Russell, David Lawson
Russell, David Williams
Russell, Edward Henry
Russell, Erwin Dee
Russell, Garth Samuel
Russell, John Robert
Russell, Judith Gray
Russell, Max Ray
Russick, Bertram Warren
Russo, Joseph Robert
Russo, Martin A.
Russo, Michael Eugene
Rusten, Elmer Mathew
Ruth, Thomas Edwin
Ruthemeyer, Thomas James
Rutherford, John Sherman, III
Rutherford, William Kenneth
Rutkowski, Karen Ann
Rutledge, Henry Trenaman
Rutledge, Virginia Alice
Ruzicka, Francis Frederick, Jr.
Ryan, Allan Charles, III
Ryan, Clarence Edward, Jr.
Ryan, David Mather
Ryan, Donald Patrick
Ryan, Edward Joseph
Ryan, Eleanor Abell
Ryan, James Herbert
Ryan, James Jay
Ryan, James Raymond
Ryan, Jay James
Ryan, John William
Ryan, Richard John
Ryan, Robert Brennan
Ryan, Robert Dale
Ryan, Robert Emmett
Ryan, Thomas Grady
Ryan, William Edward
Rychlewski, Judith Anne
Ryckman, DeVere Wellington
Ryckman, George Franklin
Ryckman, Mark DeVere
Rydstrom, Roger Theodore
Ryhal, James Lawrence, Jr.
Rymar, Julian W.
Ryu, Jai Hyun
Rzeminski, Peter Joseph
Saba, Khamis Alexander
Sabates, Felix Nabor
Sabatino, Anthony Carmen
Sabin, Harold Porter
Sabin, Norbert Michael
Sable, Louis Anthony
Sable, Martin Howard
Sabo, Richard Steven
Sacho, Emory Roy
Sachs, Harley Luther
Sachs, Herbert L.
Sachs, Howard F(rederic)
Sachs, Robert Green
Sachs, Samuel
Sachs, Samuel, II
Sachs, William Lewis
Sackett, Robert Wilson
Sadd, John Roswell
Sadek, Salah Edline
Sadler, Carl Leon
Sadler, John Reuel
Saether, Kolbjorn
Saffell, Hal Duane
Saffell, John Edgar
Saffir, Milton A(braham)
Safford, William Cullen
Sagartz, John William
Sage, Myron Alvin
Sage, Richard Bruce
Sageev, Shmuel Gershon
Sager, Donald Jack
Sahu, Saheb
Saint Denis, Barbara Louise Dion
St. Ives, Raymond
St. Jean, Charles Albert
St. John, Charles Raymond
Saint John, Charles Virgil
St. Rose, John Elliston MacDonald
Sakonyi, John Joseph
Salach, Robert Lee, Jr.
Salamone, Anthony Augustus
Salancik, Gerald Robert
Salantrie, Frank
Salazar, Jose Luis
Salibi, Bahij Sulayman
Salisbury, Alvin Burton, Jr.
Salisbury, Arnold Wirt
Salkin, Harvey Marshall
Sallee, Frank
Salmon, James Henry
Salois, Jean Paul
Salomon, Sid, III
Salomon, Sidney, Jr.
Salowich, LeRoy George
Salter, Maud (Mrs. Leslie E. Salter)
Salter, Richard Mackintire
Salter, Robert Lawrence
Saltzstein, Harry C.
Salva, Vladimer Michael, Jr.
Salvatore, James Daniel
Salzman, Charles William
Salzman, Robert Marshall
Samelson, Charles Frederick
Samerdyke, Fred J.
Sammons, Freddie Willis
Sammons, William Edward, Jr.
Samole, Myron Michael
Samorek, Alexander Henry
Sampat, Sunderdas G.
Sample, A. Dorothy
Sampson, Sigved Theodore
Sams, Robert Eugene
Samuels, Laurence Edward
Samuelson, Dennis Ray
Samuelson, Marvin L.
San, Nguyen Duy
Sanborn, Kenneth Edward
Sanchez, Bernard Raymond
Sand, Richard Eugene
Sander, Frank Lawrence
Sanders, Alfred Anthony
Sanders, Jerry Don
Sanders, John Richard
Sanders, Norman O.
Sanders, Parker David
Sanders, Robert Franklin
Sanders, Wilbur Ray
Sanderson, Richard Lee
Sanderson, Richard Lewis
Sandford, Phillip Arthur
Sandidge, Rex Joseph
Sandona, Bruno
Sandquist, Oliver
Sandry, Martin Emanuel
Sands, Stanley Hugh
Sandstrom, Harvey Dean
Sandvig, Ralph Bertram
Sandy, Paul Clyde
Sanford, Paul Everett
Sanghvi, Manoj Kumar Dalichand
Sangmeister, George Edward
Sankaran, Suryanarayanan
Sankey, Brant Burdell
Sansbury, Russell Joseph
Sanson, John Gustilo
Sanstead, Wayne Godfrey
Santangelo, Mario Vincent
Santee, William Milton
Saperstein, Esther
Saraceno, Anthony Joseph
Sarantopoulos, Costas
Sarber, Glenn Scott
Sargent, Charles Lee
Sargent, Donald Virgil
Sargent, Eileen Severson
Sargent, Harry Lee
Sargent, Kenneth Alan
Sargent, Thomas Andrew
Sargent, William Winston
Sarich, Dennis Paul
Sarkesian, Sam Charles
Sarley, Vincent Charles
Sarpolus, Mary Therese
Sartin, Beulah (Mrs. Joseph Arthur Sartin)
Sarver, Gary Steven
Sarya, Arnold Fred
Satinover, Terry Klieman
Satory, John Joseph
Sattler, Lee Anthony
Sattler, Theodore Herbert
Sauer, Herbert Irvin
Sauer, Mary Louise
Sauer, Wilbur Waterman
Saueressig, Robert
Saul, Dee C.
Saul, Richard Cushman
Saunders, Caryln Lee
Saunders, Iverin
Saunders, John Matthew
Saunders, Katherine
Saunders, Richard Seavey
Sava, Samuel George
Savage, Augustus Alexander
Savage, Barry Emery
Savage, Carl Clayton
Savage, Earl John
Savage, Robert Charles
Savage, Robert Englebert
Savelkoul, Donald Charles
Savin, Ronald Richard
Savoie, Leonard Norman
Sawadisavi, Atkavi
Sawicki, John Edward
Sawinski, Vincent John
Sawyer, Glen Thomas
Sawyer, Harold Samuel
Sawyer, John
Sawyer, Katherine H. (Mrs. Charles Baldwin Sawyer)
Sawyer, Robert Leonard, Sr.
Sawyer, Robert McLaran
Sax, Edward Lee
Sax, Janet Berman
Sax, Mary Randolph
Saxena, Swaran Lal
Saxena, Umesh Kumar
Saxton, Maryellen (Mrs. Jerry J. Saxton)
Say, Marlys Mortensen (Mrs. John Theodore Say)
Sayad, Homer Elisha
Sayles, John H.
Saylor, Howard LeRoy, Jr.
Sayre, Charles Herbert
Sayre, Lee Ford
Sayre, Richard Francis
Scace, William Buell
Scales, Charlene Mary
Scales, James Edward
Scales, Wendell Phillip
Scalzo, Joseph Ralph
Scanlon, John Charles
Scannell, Francis X.
Scarpino, Pasquale Valentine
Scearce, William Carroll
Sceper, Kenneth Michael
Schaaf, Olus Hoyer
Schaal, John H.
Schabel, Donald Albert
Schaede, Richard Edwin
Schaefer, Charles
Schaefer, Frederick LeRoy, Jr.
Schaefer, James Theodore
Schaefer, John Frederick
Schaefer, Lawrence Vincent
Schaeppi, Joseph John
Schafer, Allyn James
Schafer, Michael Frederick
Schafer, Thomas Mathias
Schaff, Philip Haynes, Jr.
Schaffer, Harwood David
Schaffter, Barry Wayne
Schaible, C. Donelda
Schales, Otto
Schalk, Lawrence Andrew
Schallert, Russell Clarence
Schamaun, Thomas Everett
Schamis, Jeffrey Bernard
Schappler, Norbert Maurice
Scharres, John William
Schattinger, James Henry
Schatzlein, Robert Gary
Schaub, Russell Edward
Schauer, Thomas Alfred
Scheanwald, Marjorie Diana
Scheetz, Al
Scheffel, Kenneth George
Scheffler, Laura Jane
Scheftner, Gerold
Schelkopf, Russell Levoy
Schell, Ralph Ray
Schenck, Douglas Garrison
Schenck, Norma Elaine (Mrs. Arthur H. Schenck)
Schenck, Robert Roy
Schenck, William Edward
Schenk, Quentin Frederick
Schenz, Royden Tindle
Scheper, Jack Lee
Schepman, Henry Frederick
Scher, Paul Lawrence
Schereck, William John
Scheribel, Karl John
Scherich, Esther Anne
Scherich, Millard
Scherling, Orlando Kenneth
Scherling, Richard Edward
Schermerhorn, Kenneth DeWitt
Scherrer, Robert Allan
Scherzer, Melvyn Harry
Schick, Harold
Schick, Joseph Schlueter
Schiefelbein, Benedict
Schierer, Robert Charles
Schiff, Herbert Harold
Schiff, Martin, Jr.
Schiff, Sheldon Kirsner
Schill, Robert James
Schiller, Alfred George
Schiller, Donald Charles
Schiller, James Joseph
Schilling, Edward George
Schilling, John Michael
Schilling, Katherine Lee Tracy (Mrs. Clarence R. Schilling)
Schimmelpfennig, Jerry Dean
Schimpff, Wayne Huber
Schipiour, Sharon Ann
Schippers, David Philip
Schirripa, Dennis James
Schjeldahl, Gilmore Tilmen
Schlachter, Robert John
Schlapkohl, Emmet Kelly
Schlarbaum, Roger Lee
Schlecker, Otto
Schlemmer, Robert Clark
Schlemmer, Roger Edmund
Schleppi, Robert Frederick
Schlereth, Eugene Paul
Schlernitzauer, Donald Allen
Schletz, George Robert
Schlichter, Jakub Gerson
Schlickman, Eugene Francis
Schlientz, Harry James
Schlossman, John Isaac
Schlott, John Frederic
Schluckbier, Gary Waldo
Schmedtje, John Frederick
Schmeling, Roger Emil
Schmelzer, Paul William
Schmerold, Wilfried Lothar
Schmid, Jack Robert
Schmidlin, Herbert Lucas
Schmidt, Arthur Irwin
Schmidt, C. Oscar, Jr.
Schmidt, Charles Mathew
Schmidt, Frederick Joseph
Schmidt, George
Schmidt, Harvey Richard
Schmidt, Jeffrey Stephen
Schmidt, John Leo
Schmidt, Richard
Schmidt, Richard Arnold
Schmidt, Richard Herman
Schmidt, Richard Thomas Francis
Schmidt, Robert
Schmidt, Robert Jack
Schmidt, Robert Miles
Schmidt, Robert William
Schmidt, Wayne Walter
Schmidt, William George
Schmitz, Sister Mary Verone
Schmitz, Norman Wayne
Schmucker, Ruby Elvy Ladrach
Schnabel, John Henry
Schnack, Dermot Joseph
Schneider, Barry Schoen
Schneider, Curt Thomas
Schneider, Erwin Henry
Schneider, Ewald
Schneider, Harold Joel
Schneider, Harold William
Schneider, John Arthur
Schneider, Leonard Morton
Schneider, Louis Abraham
Schneider, Michael Joseph
Schneider, Ralph William
Schneider, Robert Allen
Schneider, Robert Joseph
Schneiter, Harry Edward, Jr.
Schnell, Donald
Schneller, Joseph Franz
Schnepp, Kenneth H.
Schnepper, Donald Herman

Schnuda, Nasr Daniel
Schober, Charles Coleman, III
Schoeder, Lloyd Bernard
Schoen, Louis Stanley
Schoenbaum, Donald
Schoenbeck, Delbert Louis
Schoenberger, Sylvia Mary
Schoeneberger, William Alphonse
Schoeneman, Robert Barton
Schoenrock, Kenneth Frederick
Schoephoerster, Lorin Keith
Schoessler, Richard John
Schoessow, Mathilde M(arthe)
Scholl, Edward Thomas
Scholl, John Daniel, III
Scholten, Leon Marvin
Scholtz, Werner Egon
Schomaeker, James Barton
Schomer, Gary Wayne
Schooling, Herbert Wilson
Schopf, Clifton Clifford
Schorr, William F.
Schottenstein, Harold
Schotz, Larry Allen
Schout, Robert Lee
Schrader, Arthur Gust
Schrader, Cheryl Ann
Schrag, Alvin Dale
Schrage, Robert Joseph
Schram, Roy Charles
Schramm, David Norman
Schramm, James Siegmund
Schramm, Paul Howard
Schrank, Harry Paul, Jr.
Schrayer, Max Robert
Schreck, Sheldon Allen
Schreckengast, William Owen
Schreiber, George Julius
Schreiber, Martin James
Schreibman, Dan A.
Schreier, James William
Schreier, Leonard
Schreyer, Edward Richard
Schrider, Sylvia Luann
Schrier, Arnold
Schrimper, Vernon LeRoy
Schrimpf, William John
Schroeder, Collin Harold
Schroeder, David J. Dean
Schroeder, Edward M.
Schroeder, H(arold) Eugene
Schroeder, John Herman
Schroeder, Leonard William
Schroeder, Raymond Ernest
Schroeder, Robert Anthony
Schroeder, William Christopher Martin
Schroer, Edmund Armin
Schroer, Gene Eldon
Schroer, George Jerome
Schrup, Nicholas John
Schubert, Helen Celia
Schubert, Paul Morgan
Schuchart, John Albert, Jr.
Schuelein, Edward Junior
Schuenke, Donald John
Schuff, Karen Elizabeth
Schul, Bill Dean
Schuldenberg, Virginia Mary
Schuler, John Wayne
Schuler, Louis Eugene
Schultz, Allen H.
Schultz, Arthur Warren
Schultz, Charles William
Schultz, Donald Raymond
Schultz, Louis Charter
Schultz, Richard Carlton
Schultz, Richard deWyl
Schultz, Richard Otto
Schultz, Roger Herman
Schultz, Ronald Warren
Schultz, Roy Arlon
Schulze, Erwin Emil
Schulze, John Henry
Schulzinger, Morris Simcho
Schumacher, Arnold Charles
Schumacher, Brockman
Schumacher, Gebhard Friederich Bernhard
Schumacher, Joseph Stuart
Schumacher, Joseph Stuart, Jr.
Schumacher, O. Peter
Schumacher, Ronald Ray
Schumaker, John Abraham
Schuman, Jack
Schupp, Paul Eugene
Schur, Lenora Singer
Schur, Morton
Schure, Ralph Morton
Schuricht, Adolph Edward
Schurz, Franklin Dunn, Jr.
Schuster, Clara Shaw
Schuster, Eugene Ivan
Schuster, Richard Lee
Schusterman, Leonard Alan
Schut, Lawrence James
Schutt, Paul Louis
Schuurmans, Theodore, Jr.
Schwab, Dennis Ernest
Schwab, Paul Josiah
Schwaba, Joseph Robert
Schwabauer, Robert Jacob
Schwaig, Robert Henry
Schwan, LeRoy Bernard
Schwanke, Mel H.
Schwark, Howard Edward
Schwartz, Craig John
Schwartz, Franklin David
Schwartz, Gerhart Robert
Schwartz, Jacob Jack
Schwartz, Roger Arlen
Schwartz, Rudolph O.
Schwartz, Samuel Robert
Schwartz, Theodore Frank
Schwartzberg, Ralph Morton
Schwarz, Josephine Lindeman
Schwarz, Robert Lessing
Schwarzkopf, Lyall Arthur
Schwegler, Robert Charles
Schwier, Robert William
Schwieterman, Cyril Sylvester
Schwietert, John Wesley
Schwingel, William Henry
Schyman, Sidney
Sciammarella, Cesar Augusto
Scioli, Frank Paul, Jr.
Scism, Daniel Reed
Scofield, Gordon Lloyd
Scott, Alice Holly (Mrs. Alphonso Scott)
Scott, Andrew
Scott, Anna Porter Wall (Mrs. John T. Scott)
Scott, Carl Chauncey
Scott, Claude Marshall
Scott, David C.
Scott, Eric Ansil
Scott, Ernest Peck
Scott, Frank Maxwell
Scott, Glenn Edward
Scott, Hazel Joanne
Scott, Howard Winfield, Jr.
Scott, Kenneth Tressel
Scott, Monte Myrl
Scott, Norman Laurence
Scott, Theodore R.
Scott, Timothy Titus
Scott, Walter Edwin
Scott, Walter O'Daniel
Scott, William Dyrton
Scott, William John
Scott, William Paul
Scott, Wray Moore
Scott-Miller, James Robert
Scoular, Robert Frank
Scoville, Mary Sydney Branch (Mrs. Merrill Scoville)
Scoville, Robert Garvey
Screnock, Joseph John, II
Scribner, Gilbert Hilton, Jr.
Scrimgeour, Gary James
Scripps, Charles Edward
Scripps, Douglas Jerry
Scripter, Frank C.
Scrogin, Roy Merle
Scruggs, Rosemary Jane (Mrs. Norman Madison Scruggs)
Scrutchions, Benjamin
Scully, Michael Edward
Seabury, Charlene A. Brown (Mrs. John Ward Seabury)
Seabury, John Ward
Seachrist, William Earl
Seacrest, Joseph Rushton
Seadle, Michael Steven
Seager, Glenn Marvin
Sealey, David Leon
Seaman, Ann Clark
Seaman, Gerald Robert
Searle, Ray Richard
Sears, Paul Raider
Searson, Thomas Earl
Seaton, Roy Ray
Seaton, Scott Lee, Sr.
Seaver, James Everett
Sebastian, Franklin William
Sebastiano, Vito
Sebelius, Carl Louis
Sebelius, Keith George
Sebo, Stephen Andrew
Sech, Charles Edward, Jr.
Sechrist, Sterling George
Secrest, Richard Phillip
Sedgewick, Thomas James
See, Walter George
See, William Bernard
Seed, Terrell Mack
Seefeldt, John Asmus
Seehafer, Donald William
Seehausen, Richard Ferdinand
Seevers, Charles Junior
Sefert, Jay Bruce
Sefton, George William
Segatto, Bernard Gordon
Seger, Robert Morse
Segrist, Allen Edward
Seher, Russell John
Seiberling, John F.
Seidel, William Charles
Seiden, William Stanton
Seidensticker, Edward George
Seigne, Talbot David
Seiler, Robert E.
Seiler, Steven Lawrence
Seiler, Wallace Urban
Seinsheimer, Walter G.
Seipel, Ferdinand, Jr.
Seitzinger, Edward Francis
Sekuler, Robert William
Selby, Roy Clifton, Jr.
Selby, Theodore William
Selck, Faye Albrecht
Self, Hazzle Layfette
Self, Sandra Adler
Selfridge, Calvin
Selig, Allan H. (Bud)
Selik, Martin
Selim, Mostafa Ahmed
Sell, Robert Emerson
Sella, Albin John
Selland, Howard Martin
Sellers, Robert Douglas
Sells, Arnold A.
Selstrom, John Purcell, Jr.
Seltenreich, Alvin Eugene
Seltzer, Philip Alan
Seltzer, Phyllis Estelle
Selzer, Charles Louis
Semanik, Anthony James
Semans, William Merrick
Sembower, John Franklin
Semmens, Raymond Thomas
Semmes, David Hamilton
Sen, Sunil Kumar
Sendak, Theodore Lorraine
Sengpiehl, Paul Marvin
Sensenbrenner, Richard Raymond
Sentkeresty, Joseph Arthur
Sentman, Everett Edgar
Sentman, Frances Mara (Mrs. Everett Edgar Sentman)
Sentman, Lee Hanley, III
Sepsy, Charles Frank
Serafini, John
Serbo, Arthur Karl
Sereda, John Walter
Serstock, Doris Shay
SerVaas, Beurt
Ser Vaas, Cory Synhorst
Seskind, Coleman Robert
Sessions, William Crighton
Sestric, Anthony James
Seth, Mahesh Kumar
Seth, Richard Peter
Settle, Norman Ruggles
Severs, Eugene Ryals
Severson, Lloyd John
Severson, Robert Keith
Seward, Robert Morris, II
Sewell, William Clyde
Sexton, Logan
Sexton, Margaret Dureta
Seybert, Paul Elner
Seymour, George Edward
Seymour, Keith Goldin
Sfikas, Peter Michael
Sha, William Tseng-Lu
Shabazz, Abdul-Alim
Shackleton, Clarence Joseph
Shade, Willard Norman, Jr.
Shadle, George Miller
Shaeffer, James Henry
Shaevsky, Mark
Shafe, Marie Cross
Shafer, Wilma Clare
Shaffer, Herbert, Jr.
Shaffer, James Grant
Shaffer, Walter Louis, III
Shahidi, Massoud Mir
Shahidi, Nasrollah Thomas
Shallenberger, Hugh Darsie
Shalon, Yehuda
Shalowitz, Mervin
Shanafield, Harold Arthur
Shanahan, Elwill Mattson
Shanahan, Michael Francis
Shanahan, William Joseph
Shaner, Charles Henry
Shanes, Robert Edward
Shanks, Mary Elma Windiate
Shannon, Gerald Timothy
Shapin, John Lawrence
Shapiro, Alvin
Shapiro, David Charles
Shapiro, Edward
Shapiro, Maynard Irwin
Shapiro, Robert Donald
Shapiro, Samuel H.
Shapton, Mark Sandford
Shapton, William Robert
Sharaf, Mohammed Abdel-Gawwad
Sharbo, David Arthur
Sharkey, Thomas Bernard
Sharley, George Elmer
Sharlin, Harold Issadore
Sharma, Brahma Dutta
Sharma, Hari Mohan
Sharon, Isadore Charles
Sharon, Nehama
Sharp, Homer Glen
Sharp, Philip R.
Shasha, Baruch
Shaskin, Milton
Shaver, Joseph Milton Pearl
Shaw, Don Coulter
Shaw, Donald Hardy
Shaw, Edward James
Shaw, Elizabeth Orr (Mrs. Donald Hardy Shaw)
Shaw, Emanuel Victor
Shaw, George Gordon
Shaw, John Arthur
Shaw, Patrick
Shaw, Richard Clarke
Shaw, Robert Calvin
Shaw, Wayne Eugene
Shea, Catherine Beahan
Shea, Daniel Dennis
Shea, Gerald Joseph
Sheard, Kevin
Shearer, Robert William
Shearman, Robert William
Shearon, Kenneth Elroy
Shebilsky, Paul Martin Walter
Sheehan, Daniel Eugene
Sheehan, Leon Earl
Sheehan, William Philip
Sheffield, Leslie Floyd
Shegrud, Donald Maurice
Shek, John Leonard
Sheldon, George Coleman
Shelford, R. H.
Shell, Claude Irving, Jr.
Shell, William Lowell
Shell, William Orchard
Shellberg, Jerry Francis
Shellenberger, Thomas Max
Shelton, Raymond Franklin
Shelton, Robert Wallace
Shepherd, Harley Emil
Shepherd, Harry Simon
Shepherd, Herndon Guinn, Jr.
Shepherd, Patricia Anne
Sheran, Robert Joseph
Sherck, Charles Keith
Sherer, William Charles
Sheridan, John Andrew
Sheridan, Sister Mary Florianne
Sheridan, Richard George
Sheridan, William Cockburn Russell
Sheriff, Alfred Pearson, III
Sherman, Edward
Sherman, Francis George Harry
Sherman, George Earl, Jr.
Sherman, Jeanie Kelso
Sherman, June Marie Roach
Sherman, Keith Melvin
Sherman, Kenneth Ira
Sherman, Leslie Allyn
Sherman, Stanley Norman
Sherman, William Frederick, Jr.
Sherman, William Roderick
Shertzer, Bruce Eldon
Sherwin, Charles Steelman
Sherwin, Larry Edward
Sherwood, Louis Maier
Sherwood, Sam S(abean)
Sheth, Jagdish Nanchand
Sheth, Jashwantlal S.
Sheverbush, Robert L.
Shewmaker, Mary Dianne
Shibley, Frederic Jamile
Shideler, Shirley Ann Williams
Shiel, Vincent Wymore
Shields, Donald James
Shields, Floyd Francis
Shields, Lee Ann
Shields, Michael Roy
Shields, Patrick Thomas
Shiffermiller, William Ernest
Shimanski, Gregg Thomas
Shimmel, Robert Gilham
Shindell, Richard Michael
Shindle, William Richard
Shinedling, Martin Myron
Shiney, Margaret Louise
Shinn, Richard Franklin, Jr.
Shipley, Charles William
Shipley, George Edward
Shipley, James Lee
Shipp, Maurine Sarah Harston (Mrs. Levi Arnold Shipp)
Shipps, Jan
Shiraef, John Dragon
Shire, Herbert
Shirey, Wayne Arthur
Shirley, Gene Hilton
Shirreffs, Thomas Gordon
Shlens, Edmund
Shlensky, Ronald
Shockley, Deborah Leigh
Shoemack, Harvey Raymond
Shoemaker, Morrell McKenzie, Jr.
Shoemaker, Robert Louis
Shogren, Robert Alton
Shomber, Larry Lee
Shoop, George Jerome
Shopneck, George
Shopneck, Sam Milton
Shorney, George Herbert, Jr.
Shorr, James Winfield
Short, Donald Lee
Short, Larry Edward
Short, Ray L., Jr.
Short, Richard Rollin
Short, Samuel James, Jr.
Short, Thomas Jan
Shoup, Robert Earl
Shovald, Arlene Elizabeth
Showalter, Stan
Shreve, James Joseph
Shrewder, Roy Valentine
Shriner, James Edward
Shriner, Ruth Shearer (Mrs. Walter Shriner)
Shriner, William Cuppy
Shriver, Garner Edward
Shropshear, George
Shropshire, Clyde Calvin, Jr.
Shrote, Robert Allwin
Shrum, Alyce Janet
Shubik, Philippe
Shuey, William Carpenter
Shufflebarger, Patrick Thomas
Shugar, Samuel Robert
Shukin, Alexey
Shuler, Frank F.
Shulkin, Neil Howard
Shull, Charles W.
Shulman, Arthur David
Shultz, Elden Evon
Shultz, John Arthur
Shuman, David Lee
Shuman, R(obert) Baird
Shumate, Charles Rolane
Shumway, Richard Kenneth
Shupe, Marion Claire
Shurr, Roger Eugene
Shurtleff, John Howard
Shutt, George Marvin
Shutz, Byron Christopher
Sicam-Simon, Gracita Español
Sicherman, Marvin Allen
Sichert, Paul Otto
Sickbert, Jo
Sickman, Laurence Chalfant Stevens
Siddiqi, Akhtar Husain
Sidey, Edwin John
Sieben, James George
Siebenmorgen, Paul
Siebert, Donald Edward
Siedel, James Meredith
Siefkes, Hermann W(illiam)
Siegal, Burton Lee
Siegel, Elmer Martin
Siegel, Michael Randolph
Siegel, Sheldon Lloyd
Siegel, Terry Lee
Siegle, Dennis Lee
Siemens, Richard Allan
Sierles, Frederick Stephen
Sieron, Robert Donald
Siewerth, Bruce Karl
Sigars, Garold Orlando
Sigfusson, Benedict J.
Sigler, Jack Exline
Siglin, Irvin S.
Sigoloff, Allen Louis
Sikdar, Dhirendra Nath
Sikorski, Bernadine Carol
Sikorski, Martin Jerome, II
Silberman, Allen
Silberman, Edward
Silets, Harvey Marvin
Siliger, Agnes Isabelle
Sillers, D. H.
Silliman, Benjamin DeWayne
Sillman, Herbert Phillip
Silver, David Mayer
Silver, Neil Marvin
Silverman, James Stuart
Silverman, Maurice Martin
Silverman, William Joseph
Silvernail, Walter Lawrence
Silverstein, Paul Morton
Sime, Charles John
Simmen, Robert Lee
Simmermon, Robert David
Simmonds, James Frederick
Simmons, Carl Kenneth
Simmons, David Earl
Simmons, Donald Duane
Simmons, Frank Peter
Simmons, Frederick Harrison
Simmons, James Paul
Simmons, Jimmy
Simmons, M. Dale
Simmons, Merle Edwin
Simmons, Nevah Howell
Simmons, Percy Slotsky
Simmons, Ray Clifford
Simmons, Virginia Lee Cowan
Simon, Delbert Richard
Simon, Leon Aaron
Simon, Lou Anna Kinsey
Simon, Marvin
Simon, Paul
Simon, Robert Paul
Simon, Shirley Schwartz (Mrs. Edgar H. Simon)
Simon, Steven Elliott
Simoni, Lewis Eugene
Simons, Clifford Gene
Simons, Reta Marie
Simons, Richard Stuart
Simons, Robert Louis
Simonsen, Richard John
Simonson, Gerald Wallace
Simotti, Genesio Anthony
Simowitz, Fredric Malcolm
Simpson, Bruce Liston
Simpson, Edwin Kershaw, III
Simpson, Everett James
Simpson, George William
Simpson, John Eugene
Simpson, Lyle Lee
Simpson, William Gail
Simpson, William Stewart
Sims, Eugene Ralph, Jr.
Sims, Marvin Harding
Sinclair, Frank Louis
Sinclair, Orriette Coiner
Sinclair, Robert Ewald
Sinclair, Warren Keith
Sineneng, Rolando Sunpongco
Sing, Eric John
Singer, Derek Staughton
Singer, Edward J.
Singh, Baljit
Singh, Madan Mohan
Singleton, Marvin Ayers
Sinha, Pramilla
Sink, Alva Gordon (Mrs. Charles A. Sink)
Sinner, Jake
Sinninger, Dwight Virgil
Sinor, Denis
Siomopoulos, Vasilis Konstantinos
Sipes, Gerald Eugene
Sipiera, Paul Peter, Jr.
Sippy, Rodney Edward
Sisler, Maynard Lee
Sisman, Florence E.
Sisson, Everett Arnold
Sisson, Harold Leroy
Sittard, Herman Joseph
Sittler, Edwin Conrad
Sittler, Leland Loyd
Siu, Kenneth Kwong Chee
Siy, Pepe
Sizelove, Cary Leon
Sjoerdsma, Richard Dale
Skaggs, William T.
Skaran, Raymond O.
Skare, Robert Martin
Skatzes, Dawerance Horace
Skeel, Robert Lee
Skelton, Arch Mason
Skelton, Isaac Newton, IV
Skewes, Mort B.
Skillings, Ralph E.
Skinner, Charles Scofield
Skinner, William Edwin
Skinner, William Langdon
Sklenicka, George Wayne
Skoog, Ralph Edward
Skowronski, Fred Stanley
Skrowaczewski, Stanislaw
Skrzypek, Michael Allen
Skubitz, Joe
Skurauskis, Michael Joseph
Skweres, Thomas Walter
Skwerski, Arthur Peter
Skwerski, Jacquelyn Pledger
Slack, William John
Slager, Richard Foreman
Slagle, Harry Richard
Slankard, J(ames) Edward
Slater, James William
Slater, Raymond E.O.
Slater, William Adcock
Slaton, Paul George
Slaughter, Carl Ray
Slaughter, Robert Leslie
Slaughter, Rudie Wright
Slayton, Ransom Dunn
Sledge, Barnett Jenkins
Sleeman, John Paul
Sleeman, Mary (Mrs. John Paul Sleeman)
Sleichter, Charles George, Jr.
Sleight, Justin LeRoy
Sleight, Norman Reed
Sleight, Stuart Duane
Slemmons, Robert Sheldon
Slichter, Charles Pence
Slifkin, Sam Charles
Sloan, Gover Gene
Sloan, James Park
Slodki, Sheldon Joshua
Sloggy, William E.
Slominski, Leo Frank
Slonaker, Edward Lee
Slotsky, Lawrence S.
Slotvig, Philip LeRoy
Slusher, Shirley Brown
Sluss, Ray C.
Slykhouse, Roger Allen
Smale, John Gray
Small, Donald David
Small, Richard Donald
Small, Sheila Evelyn
Smalley, James Addison
Smallwood, John Edgar
Smart, Bradford Dyer
Smart, David Barton
Smart, Guy Alexander
Smart, Harold Dearborn
Smart, Irene Balogh
Smedal, Erling Arnold
Smedsrud, Milton Elvin
Smeester, Joseph Glenn
Smelser, Margaret Lee
Smelser, Warren Duane
Smid, Arthur Charles
Smith, Alfred Norbert
Smith, Alfred Russell
Smith, Alice Byrd Appleton (Mrs. Justin V. Smith)
Smith, Alton Carl, Sr.
Smith, Andrew Warren
Smith, Arthur Allan
Smith, Arthur Appleby
Smith, Barry Ward
Smith, Bertrand Lee, Jr.
Smith, Bolling Barton
Smith, Bruce
Smith, Burnell Raymond
Smith, Charles Carroll, Jr.
Smith, Charles Clyde
Smith, Charles Warren
Smith, Clarence William
Smith, Clifford Neal
Smith, David Bernard
Smith, David Harry
Smith, Dillon
Smith, Donald Archie
Smith, Donald Burtwin
Smith, Donald Callistus
Smith, Donald Dean
Smith, Donald Glen
Smith, Donald Roy
Smith, Dudrey Craig
Smith, E. Berry
Smith, Edward Byron
Smith, Eugene Valentine
Smith, Eugene William
Smith, Everett Ware
Smith, F. Joseph
Smith, F. Neil
Smith, Frank Edward, II
Smith, Frank Ray
Smith, Freddye Lee
Smith, George Clifford, V
Smith, George Wolfram
Smith, Gerald James
Smith, Glenn Lee
Smith, Glenn Parkhurst
Smith, Glenn William
Smith, Glenn Willis
Smith, Hamlin Henry, Jr.
Smith, Harlan Elliott
Smith, Harry Elmer
Smith, Helen Catharine
Smith, Herbert Eugene
Smith, Howard Wesley
Smith, Hueston Merriam
Smith, Hugh Byron
Smith, Ian Murray
Smith, James Douglas
Smith, James Franklin
Smith, James Thompson
Smith, Jameson Warren
Smith, Jeanne Kellenberger
Smith, Jesse Lee
Smith, Jessop
Smith, John Henry
Smith, Justin Vander Velde
Smith, Keith Allen
Smith, Kenneth Power
Smith, Larry Jay
Smith, Lauren Ashley
Smith, Lawrence Norval
Smith, Leonard Richard
Smith, Loren Mitchell

Smith, Louis Adrian
Smith, Lucretia Luttie
Smith, Marilyn Fox
Smith, Marjorie Mae Ostreich
Smith, Mary Lucy
Smith, Michael Roland
Smith, Milbourn Lile
Smith, Mildred Taylor
Smith, Milton Reynolds
Smith, Neal Edward
Smith, Neil Edward
Smith, Norvel E.
Smith, Otha William, Jr.
Smith, Paul Keith
Smith, Paul Milton, Jr.
Smith, Paul Roland
Smith, Peter Lang
Smith, Priscilla Dean
Smith, Regan Granville
Smith, Richard Butler
Smith, Robert Earl
Smith, Robert Jack
Smith, Robert James
Smith, Robert Keith
Smith, Robert Leonard
Smith, Roger Orbin
Smith, Roland Emerson
Smith, Shelby
Smith, Terry J.
Smith, Trent Whitmer
Smith, Virginia Dodd (Mrs. Haven Smith)
Smith, Wallace Paul
Smith, William Jacob, II
Smith, William Robert
Smith, Wray Cameron
Smithwick, Fred, Jr.
Smock, Martha Florence (Mrs. Carl Francis Smock)
Smoldt, Charles Eldon
Smoller, Sanford Jerome
Smoot, Thurlow
Smucker, Silas Jonathan
Smull, Ned Willits
Smutny, Joan Franklin (Mrs. Herbert Paul Smutny)
Smutz, Dorothy Dring
Smyd, Edwin Stanley
Smyth, Mary Ellen
Snader, Jack Ross
Snapp, Robert Earl
Snawder, Kenneth David
Sneed, Ruby Blake
Sneeringer, Eldon Woerth
Snell, Bruce Morey, Jr.
Snell, Joel Charles
Snell, Walter Wilbert
Snider, Donald Gene
Snider, Robert Wayne
Snipes, Alfred Haywood
Snook, Orrie McVey
Snortland, Howard J.
Snowden, Herbert Norris, Jr.
Snyder, Bernard Shaw
Snyder, Brock Robert
Snyder, Charles Richard
Snyder, Conway Allen
Snyder, David William Wilson
Snyder, Donald Richard
Snyder, Herbert Howard
Snyder, Howard Errol
Snyder, Jean Maclean (Mrs. Joel Martin Snyder)
Snyder, Joseph Quincy
Snyder, Mary Alice Dexheimer (Mrs. Guy Maxwell Snyder)
Snyder, Merle LaVerne
Snyder, Michael Dennis
Snyder, Ralph Howard
Snyder, Robert Donald
Snyder, Robert Emile James
Snyders, Jeanette Agnes
Sobel, Burton Elias
Sobel, Walter Howard
Soby, Birger Kristoffer
Soderberg, Frederick Alexander
Soderlund, Harold Arthur
Sodon, James Richard
Soforenko, Albert Zelig
Sohl, John Franklin
Sohl, Stanley Duane
Sohn, Herbert
Sokol, David Martin
Sokol, Robert James
Sokolik, Stanley Lewis
Sokolnicki, Alfred John
Sokolov, Sherwin Leonard
Solberg, Nellie Florence Coad
Solberg, Paul Bernard
Solbrig, Ingeborg Hildegard
Solem, G(eorge) Alan
Soler, Nilda M.
Soliday, Maureen Harter (Mrs. Donald M. Soliday)
Solley, Thomas Treat
Solomon, Chester Douglas
Solomon, Herbert
Solomon, Izler
Solomon, Neil Walker
Solomon, O. David
Solomon, Richard Humphrey
Solomon, Ted Joseph
Solti, Sir Georg
Somers, Emmanuel
Somers, Gerald A.
Somers, John Edward
Somers, Orville Harold
Somers, Patricia Ann
Sommerer, Karl Theodor
Sommerfeld, Carl John
Sommers, Herbert Myron
Sommerschield, Harold Stanley
Somsen, Henry Northrop
Sonderegger, John Forster
Sone, Miguel Angel, Jr.
Song, Joseph
Songer, Herbert Lee, Jr.
Sonnino, Carlo Benvenuto
Sons, Lester George
Sood, Jagdish Chand
Sood, Manmohan Kumar
Soorya, Narendir Tolaram
Sopher, Mervyn David
Sopko, Thomas Clement
Sopkovich, Nicholas Joseph
Sopo, Robert William
Sorah, Baxter Lee, Jr.
Sorell, Victor Alexander
Sorensen, Mourits Axel
Sorensen, Peter Fensholt, Jr.
Sorenson, Marion Wesley
Sorenson, Paul Morris
Soret, Manuel Gonzalez
Sorge, Jay Wootten
Soriano, Danilo Buenaflor
Sorkin, Alex
Sorokac, Joseph Anthony
Sorrell, Roy Wayne
Soter, Contantine Sotirios
Soteropulos, Gust Steve
Souby, Armand Max, Jr.
Souby, James Martin, Jr.
Soucek, Donald Henry
Souder, Mark Edward
Souder, Paul Clayton
Souders, Floyd Raymond
Souers, Loren Eaton
Soughers, Richard Keith
Soukup, Elouise Mariliss
Soukup, John
Soulak, Joseph Harold
Soule, Edward Bennett
Soulen, Robert William
Sours, Calvin Dean
Southall, Carey Thomas
Southern, Walter Arthur
Southwell, Eugene Allen
Sovik, Edward Anders
Sower, Christopher Elias
Sowers, Ronald Lee
Spade, Lee Irving
Spady, Richard Jay
Spaeth, Herbert Hellmut
Spahr, Jon Ray
Spaid, Donald Lewis
Spaights, Ernest
Spain, Richard Wells
Spalding, Al
Spaniol, Roland Dean
Spankus, Jack Dean
Spannaus, Warren R.
Spano, John Joseph
Sparberg, Marshall Stuart
Sparger, Charles Forrest
Sparkman, Thomas Carroll
Sparks, Billy Schley
Sparks, Robert Dean
Sparks, (Theo) Merrill
Sparrow, Edward
Spatta, Carolyn Lee Davis
Spaun, William Becker
Spear, Raymond Earle
Specht, Charles Alfred
Speckman, Glenn Hoy
Specter, Melvin H.
Spector, Samuel
Speer, David James
Speer, George Scott
Speidel, George
Speigel, Irving Joshua
Speir, Kenneth Guinty
Speiser, Warren Henry
Spelios, Andrew James
Spellman, George Geneser
Spelts, Richard Errett, Jr.
Spence, Beatrice Marie
Spence, John D(aniel)
Spencer, Alvin Delano
Spencer, Dale Ray
Spencer, George Edward
Spencer, James Calvin
Spencer, Joseph Stewart
Spencer, Merlin Clifford
Spencer, Ralph George
Spencer, Stanley Raymond
Spencer, Temple (Tim) Keith
Spencer, Thomas H.
Spencer, William Arthur
Spensley, George Thomas
Spero, Keith Erwin
Spero, Leslie Wayne
Sperry, Frederick Edward
Sperry, Stuart Major
Speyer, Fred B.
Sphire, Raymond Daniel
Spicer, Harold Otis
Spicer, John Austin
Spicer, Samuel Gary
Spiegelberg, Harry Lester
Spink, Frank Hail, Jr.
Spino, Frank John
Spiotta, Raymond Herman
Spiro, Bernard
Spiro, Harry
Spiro, James (Demetri) Michael
Spitz, Werner Uri
Spitzer, John Andrew
Spitzer, Randy Lee
Spivey, Donald
Splittstoesser, Walter Emil
Spodek, Bernard
Spohn, William Boyd
Spohr, Arnold
Spolyar, Ludwig John
Sponseller, Eugene
Spooner, Sue Elizabeth
Spooner, William Austin
Spott, Saad
Sprague, Bernard
Sprague, David Stanley
Spratt, Doris Louise
Spratt, Gene
Sprecher, Linda Jane
Sprengel, Donald Philip
Sprick, Larry Paul
Spring, Henry Carl
Springborn, Bruce Alan
Springborn, Rosemary Kelly (Mrs. Bruce Alan Springborn)
Springer, James Jerome
Springer, Joseph Perry
Sproger, Charles Edmund
Sprowl, Charles Riggs
Sprunger, Keith LaVerne
Ssekasozi, Engelbert
Stack, Nicolete Meredith McGuire (Mrs. Charles M. Stack)
Stackelberg, Olaf Patrick
Stackhouse, David William, Jr.
Stade, Charles Edward
Stadem, Clifford Jennings
Stadler, Ervin Anthony
Staehle, Roger Washburne
Stafford, Warren Sylvester
Stafne, Eric Edward
Stahl, Henry George
Stahl, Joel Saul
Stahl, Raymond Earl
Stahl, Thomas Burton
Stahl-Berkowitz, Phyllis Barbara
Stahlheber, Rudolph B.
Stahlhut, Emil Oscar
Stahmann, Fred Soeffner
Stahr, Henry M.
Staib, Robert Burns
Staker, Rodd David
Stalbaum, Merrill
Staley, Augustus Eugene, III
Staley, Charles Wesley
Stalker, Kenneth Walter
Stallard, Richard Elgin
Stallard, Wayne Minor
Stallings, James Otis, III
Stambaugh, Edgel Pryce
Stamberger, Edwin Henry
Stamer, Dwane Stowe
Stamets, William
Stamm, William
Stamos, Theodore James
Stamp, Willard Jay
Stanbery, Robert Charles
Stancil, Anemari
Stanford, John David
Stanick, Walter John
Stanisic, Milomir Mirkov
Stanley, C. Maxwell
Stanley, Ferda Ethelda
Stanley, James Gordon
Stanley, John Harlan
Stanley, John Robert
Stanley, Joseph Richard
Stanley, Morris Burns
Stanley, Richard Holt
Stanmar, Margaret Mary Vidas
Stanton, Jeanne Frances
Stanton, John William
Stapler, Harry Bascom
Staples, Lawrence Flint
Staples, Robert Alfred Charles
Stapleton, Robert J.
Stark, Howard
Stark, Jack Alan
Stark, Louis Edward
Stark, Patricia Ann
Stark, Phillip Carl
Stark, Robert James, Jr.
Stark, Sanford Bruce
Stark, Thomas Isaac
Starkey, Roberta Neil Johnston (Mrs. John Dow Starkey)
Starkey, Walter LeRoy
Starner, Glenn Leslie
Starnes, James Wright
Starr, Edward Caryl
Starrett, Thomas Allen
Starshak, Michael John
Staszak, Lawrence Robert
States, Alfred Zimmer
Stathakios, James
Statland, Harry
Statler, Charles Daniel
Staub, Barry Alan
Staub, James Richard
Stauder, Raymond George
Stauffer, Richard Gary
Stauffer, Thomas George
Staunton, Gardner Seaver
Stazen, Paul Joseph
Stead, James Joseph, Jr.
Steahly, Vivian Eugenia Emrick
Stearns, Dan Hunter
Stebbins, Melvin Eugene
Steck, Robert Carl
Steckler, William Elwood
Stecklow, James Patrick
Stedman, Ervin Frank
Stedman, Robert Kimbell
Steele, Clarence Hart
Steele, Daniel Lee
Steele, Darrell Stanley
Steele, Emmett Mitchele
Steele, Hilda Hodgson
Steele, Oliver Leon
Steele, Robert Elmer
Steen, Edwin Benzel
Steen, Lowell Harrison
Steen, Robert Hoagland
Steenrod, Emerson J.
Stefanelli, John Robert
Steffan, Lloyd John
Steffen, Curt
Steffen, Francis Jerome
Steffensen, Poul Vilhelm
Steffey, William Garnett
Steffy, David Louis
Stefka, Richard Stephan
Stegemeyer, F. Lee
Steger, John Francis
Steidl, Richard Meredith
Steiger, Aaron Armin
Steiger, William Albert
Steigerwald, Richard Frank
Stein, Adlyn Robinson (Mrs. Herbert Alfred Stein)
Stein, David Jerome
Stein, Herbert Alfred
Stein, Herman David
Stein, Katharine Anne Brzezinski
Stein, S. Larry
Stein, Yale
Steinbauer, Robert Andrus
Steinberg, Dora Ellen (Mrs. Roy David Steinberg)
Steinberg, Glenn David
Steinberger, Robert
Steinbrink, John Paul
Steindler, Martin Joseph
Steineger, John Francis
Steiner, Bradford Ezra
Steiner, Ivan, Jr.
Steiner, Philip G.
Steiner, Robert Livingston
Steinfeld, Manfred
Steinhardt, Milton Joseph
Steinhaus, Henry Richard
Steinhilber, Jack Daniel
Steiniger, (Irene) Miriam Larmi
Steinmetz, Johanna (Mrs. Gary Pearson Cummings)
Steinmetz, William Ronald
Steinreich, Otto Selick
Steinzeig, Sherman Millard
Steioff, Arthur Francis
Stella, Frank Daniel
Stellman, Samuel David
Stelzner, Glenn Wilbert
Steman, Robert Edward
Stemen, Gregory Donald
Stempel, John Emmert
Stenerson, Orville
Stenstrop, Ernest
Stenvig, Charles S.
Stenz, Lawrence Herbert
Step, Hannah Scheuermann
Stepan, Alfred Charles, Jr.
Stepan, Frank Quinn
Stepek, Daniel Thomas
Stephan, James Wilber
Stephens, Beulah Jane
Stephens, Jerry Oscar
Stephens, John Firth
Stephens, Paul Alfred
Stephens, Robert Hood
Stephens, Thomas Maron
Stephenson, I(saac) Watson, III
Stephenson, James Oliver
Stephenson, Ralph Lawrence
Stepp, Donald Lewis
Stergios, Paul James
Sterling, Leroy Farwell
Stern, Clarence A.
Stern, Richard Alan
Sternberg, Richard Ira
Sterr, Ambrose Melvin
Stetson, John Benjamin Blank
Steuer, Thomas Michael
Stevens, Anita Eileen
Stevens, Edwin Daniel
Stevens, Gary Grossman
Stevens, Harold Russell
Stevens, Howard Peter
Stevens, Joanne
Stevens, Mildred Julius (Mrs. Robert Louis Stevens)
Stevens, Robert Eugene
Stevens, Sue Cassell
Stevenson, Adlai Ewing, III
Stevenson, Forrest Camp, Jr.
Stevenson, Frances Elizabeth Lewis (Mrs. John E. Stevenson, Jr.)
Stevenson, John Daniel
Stevenson, T(homas) H(ulbert)
Stevenson, Thomas Moody
Stevick, Bill Maze
Stewart, Bruce Hubbard
Stewart, David Rhees
Stewart, Donald Edward
Stewart, Donald Eugene
Stewart, Douglas A.
Stewart, George Daniel, Jr.
Stewart, Jack Melvin
Stewart, James Franklin
Stewart, John Donald
Stewart, Richard Allan
Stewart, Ronald George
Stewart, William Oscar
Steyer, Raymond James, II
Stickle, David Walter
Stickley, James John
Stiehl, Charles William
Stier, Ronald Lee
Stiffler, Paul Weir
Stika, Elaine Anna
Stiles, Elizabeth Connelly
Stiles, James Fuller, III
Stiles, James Richard
Stiller, Charles Edward
Stilwell, William Rhoades
Stimpson, Clinton Frank, III
Stimson, James Craig
Stine, Earle John, Jr.
Stine, Robert Howard
Stitt, James Raymond
Stiver, Myrtle Pearl
Stockman, David Allen
Stodder, Page Watson Timothy
Stoeber, Leo Otto
Stoelting, Vergil Kenneth
Stoetzer, Gerald Louis
Stoffle, Carla Joy
Stojanovic, George Djordje
Stokes, Henry Duerre, Jr.
Stokes, Louis
Stokes, Zoe Maxine Christian
Stoll, Donald Harold
Stoll, John Henry
Stoll, Juliana Imperial
Stoll, Richard Frederick
Stoll, Thomas Vincent
Stoll, Willard Lewis
Stoller, William Lewis
Stolpin, Dorothy Florence Mitchell (Mrs. William Stolpin)
Stolpin, William Roger
Stoltz, Daniel Lewis
Stone, Alan
Stone, Donald Diamond
Stone, Farilyn
Stone, Frank Fairbanks
Stone, Gayle Vaughn
Stone, George Steingoetter
Stone, J. W.
Stone, James Hiram
Stone, John Broughman
Stone, Morton Bertrand
Stone, Nicholas Louis
Stone, Paul
Stone, Paul Douglas
Stone, Robert Norton
Stone, Thomas Haskel
Stone, W. Clement
Stone, William Royal
Stonecipher, Eldo Hugh
Stonehill, Maurice Lewis
Stoner, James Edward
Stoner, Max Doyle
Stoner, Raymond Ross
Stoner, Richard Burkett
Stonestreet, Ruth Horning
Stopher, Peter Robert
Storbeck, Helen Irene
Storce, Frank Robert
Storck, John Norman
Storms, Everek Richard
Stott, Alfred Frank
Stotts, Larry Henderson
Stotzer, Harold Frederick
Stouder, Gregory Dale
Stoughton, Stephen H.
Stoup, Arthur Harry
Stout, Chester Bernard
Stout, Donald Everett
Stover, Dennis Wayne
Stover, Harry Manning
Stover, Robert David
Stowe, William Earl
Stoxen, Paul Bennett
Strachan, Brian Clark
Strachan, William John Gordon
Stracke, Wln
Strader, John Jacob
Straffon, Ralph Atwood
Strag, Gerald Anthony
Strahler, Clytie Evelyn
Strahler, Violet Ruth
Strain, Edward Richard
Strand, Alan Lawrence
Strand, Merlin Arthur
Strang, Donald William, Jr.
Strang, William Charles
Strasburg, Lenard Eugene
Strasheim, Lorraine Annette
Strasshofer, Roland Henry, Jr.
Stratoudakis, James Peter
Stratton, Olin Willmer
Straub, Joseph John
Strauss, Alfred Carmichael
Stravinsky, Soulima
Strawhecker, Paul Joseph
Strayer, Gordon Byers
Strecker, Ignatius J.
Strecker, Sherry
Streed, Donovan Palmer
Streelman, Robert Frank
Streett, Robert Wells
Streich, Arthur Harold
Streng, Paul Benedict
Stresen-Reuter, Frederick Arthur, II
Stribling, James Keith Marshall
Strickler, Paul E.
Strieter, James Frederick
Striglos, Nick G.
Strobeck, Charles LeRoy
Strobel, Gerold Carl
Strobl, Fred Anton
Strodel, Robert Carl
Strom, Jerry Ernest
Strom, John Stanley
Strom, Louis John
Stroman, Connie Elizabeth
Stromberg, Roland Nelson
Strominger, Donald B.
Strong, Mark Lavon
Strong, Richard Allen
Strong, William Lee
Stroop, Henry Rodger
Strope, Richard Russell
Strotz, Robert Henry
Stroud, William Arthur
Stroup, Charles Louis, Jr.
Stroup, Thomas Benton
Strozier, Charles Burnett
Struble, James Robert
Strueh, Paul Edward
Strukoff, Rudolf Stephen
Strutz, Carl E.
Stryker, Marian Anderson
Stryzinski, Robert Joseph
Stuart, James Fortier
Stuart, Robert Allan
Stuart, Walter Stanley, Jr.
Stuart, William Edward
Stubbe, Anne Marie
Stubblefield, Ervin Andrew
Stuber, Paul John
Stucko, John Vincent
Stucky, Milo Orlando
Studzinski, Denis Ray
Stuerman, Linda Kay
Stuermann, Leonard Henry
Stuhlman, Robert August
Stuhr, Robert Lewis
Stukel, James Joseph
Stull, Daniel
Stull, David Willis
Stull, Henry
Stull, Henry
Stump, Harl Gene
Stump, John Edward
Stumpe, Warren Robert
Stumpf, Lowell C(linton)
Stumpf, Walter Nicholas
Stunard, Eugene Walter
Stupec, Gertraud L. Bley
Sturdivant, Frederick David
Sturdivant, Jack Edward
Sturgell, Charles Lee
Sturgis, John Cantwell
Sturm, Robert Nelson, Jr.
Sturm, William James
Sturr, Thomas Francis
Stutsman, Albert Chesterfield
Stutsman, Warren Earl
Styffe, Edwin Howard, Jr.
Suba, Antonio Ronquillo
Subramanian, Bala Ramanathan
Suderman, Elmer Francis
Suderman, Jake Peter
Sudheimer, Richard Harold
Sudilovsky, Oscar
Sudimack, Joseph, Jr.
Suedhoff, Carl John, Jr.
Suellentrop, John Francis
Suess, Heather Faye
Suffety, Hamed William
Sugar, Marilyn Susman
Suhowatsky, Stephen Joseph
Sujecki, Joy Mary
Sukhwal, Bheru Lal
Sukumaran, Kizhakepat Pisharoth
Sukup, Eugene George
Sulich, Frederick Joseph
Sullivan, Antony Thrall
Sullivan, Audley Noel
Sullivan, David Stafford
Sullivan, Gerard
Sullivan, Mark David
Sullivan, Thomas Lee
Sullivan, Warren Gerald
Sulsberger, John Diehl
Sumerford, Kenneth Scott
Summers, Charles L.
Summers, H. Meade, Jr.
Summers, James Desmond, Jr.
Summersett, Kenneth George
Sumnicht, Francis Henry
Sun, Albert Yung-Kwang
Sundaram, Shanmugha K.
Sundberg, Collins Yngve
Sundberg, Darryll
Sundberg, Norma Elizabeth Johnson (Mrs. Collins Y. Sundberg)
Sundby, Elmer Arthur
Sundstrom, Ernest Dale
Sung, C. B.
Sunleaf, Roger Wendell
Sunstein, Michael Allen
Surace, Gene Allen
Surdam, Robert McClellan
Surprenant, Thomas Terry
Surrell, Helen Myra Webb (Mrs. Jack Surrell)
Surrell, Matthew Anthony
Suskind, Raymond Robert
Susman, Bernard Marvin
Susskind, Tamar Youninah
Sutcliffe, Grenville George
Suter, William Alva
Sutherland, George Henry
Sutherland, Ronald Roy
Sutter, Elizabeth Henby (Mrs. Richard A. Sutter)
Sutter, Richard Anthony
Sutter, William Paul
Suttles, Raymond Herschel
Sutton, Charles F(rederick)
Sutton, James Matthew
Sutton, Louise Weibert
Suzuki, Jon Byron
Svebakken, Gene LeRoy
Svendsen, Eline Marguerite
Swaim, John Franklin
Swaim, Lloyd Milton
Swain, Timothy Whitzel, II
Swallow, Peter Thomas
Swan, George Samuel
Swan, Herbert Siegfried
Swan, Patricia Brintnall
Swan, Wallace Kent
Swaney, Gordon Edmund
Swank, John Lindley
Swann, James, Jr.
Swann, Margaret Ann Troehler
Swanson, Arthur P.
Swanson, Donald Warren
Swanson, Edward
Swanson, Edwin Leroy
Swanson, Fern Rose (Mrs. Walter E. Swanson)
Swanson, Leslie Charles

Swanson, Patricia Ann
Swanson, Paul Eugene
Swanson, Paul John, Jr.
Swanson, Paul Reginald
Swanson, Randall Cover
Swanson, Robert Martin
Swanstone, Floyd Truman
Swanstrom, Kathryn Raymond
Swanstrom, Thomas Evan
Sward, Jon Michael
Swart, Hannah Werwath
Swarthout, Herbert Marion
Swartout, Charles William
Swartwout, Joseph Rodolph
Swartz, Edward Morton
Swartz, Harry Leo
Swartzendruber, Harlan Lee
Swartzlander, Gareld William
Swearingen, Gerald Brent
Swearingen, John Eldred
Swearingin, John David
Swedo, John Lawrence, Jr.
Sweeney, Joseph Patrick
Sweet, Henrietta Mary Dorsey
Sweet, Jack Darrell
Sweet, Philip Whitford Kirkland, Jr.
Sweezy, John William
Sweney, Arthur Barclay
Swenson, Alfred Thomas
Swenson, Courtland Sevander
Swerhone, Peter Edward
Swick, Myra Agnes
Swickard, Kenneth Ray
Swierczewski, John Adam, Sr.
Swift, A. Dean
Swift, John Lionel
Swift, Morden L.
Swigert, Alice Harrower (Mrs. James Mack Swigert)
Swirnoff, Michael Allen
Swisher, John Edgar, Jr.
Swovick, Melvin Joseph
Swygert, Luther Merritt
Sylora, Herme O.
Sylvanovich, W. Richard
Sylvester, Glen Morris
Symns, Richard Dean
Symons, Clayton Harold
Synchef, Richard Michael
Syverson, Leslie Arthur
Szabo, Steven
Szalajka, Walter Stanley
Szathmary, Louis Istvan, II
Szebedinszky, Janos Emil
Szemler, G(eorge) J(ohn)
Szoke, George Leslie
Szwarc, Wlodzimierz (Will Rayms)
Szweda, John Alexander
Taaffe, Gordon
Tabak, Henry H.
Taber, Margaret Ruth Stevens (Mrs. William J. Taber)
Taber, Merlin Arthur
Tabor, Purvis F(rancis)
Taborn, John Marvin
Tabri, Adib Farid
Tacke, Arthur William
Taft, Frances Prindle
Tagatz, George Elmo
Tagatz, Glenn Edwin
Taggart, Gordon Harry
Tahler, Robert
Takemori, Akira Eddie
Talaba, Linda (Cummens)
Talbot, Richard Charles
Talbott, Thomas Howard
Talbott, Vernon Glenn
Taliana, Lawrence Edwin
Talley, Hayward Leroy
Talley, James Charles
Talley, Melvin Gary
Tallman, Clifford Wayne
Tallman, Jack Leverett
Tallman, Russell Warrick
Talso, Peter Jacob
Taman, Mahmoud Shawky
Tamasy, Robert Julius
Tamminga, David Jacob
Tanasichuk, Murray Arthur
Tancek, Anna Evelyn
Tandon, Jagdish Singh
Tandon, Rajiv
Tanega, Jose Resma
Tang, Sing Chih
Tang, Thomas Tze-Tung
Tangora, Martin Charles
Tangwall, Raymond Holger
Tankus, Harry
Tannebaum, Sol
Tannehill, John Charles
Tanner, Richard Thomas
Tao, Liang Neng
Taranik, James Vladimir
Tarpey, Elizabeth Anne
Tarsinos, Louis Demetrios
Tatham, Clifford Blenn
Taub, Robert Golde
Taube, William Harold
Taussig, Leonard Michael
Tay, Cheng Hin
Taylor, Bettye Jean
Taylor, Curtis Lee
Taylor, D(arl) Coder
Taylor, Donald Robert
Taylor, Edmund Eugene
Taylor, Florence Marie
Taylor, Frank Desmond
Taylor, Gene
Taylor, Henry Oliver, Jr.
Taylor, Herman Lamon
Taylor, Jack Paul
Taylor, James Robert
Taylor, Jane Urban
Taylor, Jay Robert
Taylor, John Lloyd
Taylor, Kenneth Robert
Taylor, Larry Lee
Taylor, Logan
Taylor, Mary Joan (Mrs. Edward McKinley Taylor, Jr.)
Taylor, Melvin A.
Taylor, Morris
Taylor, Ralph Orien, Jr.
Taylor, Raymond Ellory
Taylor, Richard French
Taylor, Robert Malcolm
Taylor, Samuel Gale, III
Taylor, Thomas Franklin
Taylor, Vaughn Kemp
Taylor, Walter Porter
Taylor, William Menke
Taylor, Winnifred Jane
Teager, John Carlyle
Teager, Patricia Ann
Teasdale, Joseph Patrick
Tedeschi, John Alfred
Teefy, Paul Donald
Teegarden, Kenneth Leroy
Teel, Robert Lee
Teele, Doris Corinne
Tegeder, Robert Martin
Tei, Takuri
Teich, Ralph Donald
Temin, Howard Martin
Temple, Donald Ernest
Templeman, Charles Frank
Templeton, John Alexander, II
Templin, Robert Lewis, Jr.
Ten Broeke, James Engbert
Tendick, John Phillip
Ten Eyck, George Robert
Ten Eyck, James Edward
Ten Eyck, Robert Lancaster, Jr.
Tenney, Mark William
Tenold, Lyle Obert
Tentoni, Stuart Charles
Tenzer, Marilyn Mears
Teple, Edwin Russell
Tepper, Neal Gary
Terezis, Nick Louis
Terhune, Marie Amrein
Terra, Daniel James
Terrell, Charles Joseph
Terrell, Velma Houston
Terrill, Roscoe Verl
Terry, M. Donald
Terry, Percy, Jr.
Tervo, Walter Paul
Terwilliger, Roy William
Terwoord, James Anthony
Teschner, John Stephen
Teschner, Paul August
Teska, Robert Bents
Tess, Bernard Richard
Tews, Donald William
Thada, Narongsak Kiatikajorn
Thaden, Ronald Theodore
Thain, John Griffiths
Thames, Clement Beal, Jr.
Tharp, Donald Rhea
Thatcher, Hugh Knox, Jr.
Thayer, Charles Bennett
Thayer, Keith Evans
Thayer, William Vance
Theimer, Axel Knut
Theivagt, James Gordon
Thellmann, Edward Louis
Theobald, Henry Edward
Thielen, Lowell George
Thieling, John Richard
Thiers, Werner August
Thies, Floyd Levi
Thiessen, Edgar P.
Thill, Richard Eugene
Thimotheose, Kadakampallil Geevarghese
Thistlethwaite, Paul Calvin
Thom, Elroy Milton
Thoman, John Herman
Thoman, Mark Edward
Thomas, Albert William
Thomas, Bill
Thomas, Bruce Lorrey
Thomas, Bruce Robert
Thomas, Carl Edward
Thomas, Clive Alwyn
Thomas, Daniel Anthony
Thomas, David Benedict
Thomas, Dominick Anthony
Thomas, Don R.
Thomas, Edward Paul
Thomas, Fred Broaddus
Thomas, Garth E.
Thomas, Gordon Lawrie
Thomas, Irwin Ross
Thomas, James Samuel
Thomas, Jerry K.
Thomas, John Meredith
Thomas, Joseph E.
Thomas, Joyce Marguerite P.
Thomas, Juergen Erich
Thomas, Kenneth Eugene
Thomas, Lewis Edward
Thomas, Sister M. Evangeline
Thomas, Melvin Harold
Thomas, Norman Marvell
Thomas, O. Pendleton
Thomas, Patricia Grafton (Mrs. Lewis Edward Thomas)
Thomas, Robert Jay
Thomas, Walton Dowdell
Thomas, William, Jr.
Thomas, William James
Thomas, William Richard
Thomason, Jacqueline
Thomasson, Mary Lou Wahlert
Thomopoulos, Nick Ted
Thompson, Alfred Arnold
Thompson, Barbara Storck
Thompson, Dale Moore
Thompson, Dorothy Brown
Thompson, Ernest Edward
Thompson, Fredrick Blaine
Thompson, George Greene
Thompson, Harold
Thompson, Howard Elliott
Thompson, James Robert
Thompson, James Rorem
Thompson, James Temple
Thompson, John Brown
Thompson, Kenrick Steven
Thompson, Lyle Francis
Thompson, Margaret M.
Thompson, Melvin Leroy
Thompson, Oscar Junior
Thompson, Paul Leland
Thompson, Phebe Kirsten
Thompson, Renold Durant
Thompson, Richard Arthur
Thompson, Richard Neil
Thompson, Richard Thomas
Thompson, Robert Allan
Thompson, Ronald Wade
Thompson, Roy Henry
Thompson, Russell Alden
Thompson, Sidney A.
Thompson, Stanley Milford
Thompson, Theodore Sevrin
Thompson, Thomas George
Thompson, Tommy George
Thompson, Vera Eileen Kramer (Mrs. John Maurice Thompson)
Thompson, Vernon Dale
Thompson, William Neil
Thomson, Edward Wilson, Jr.
Thomson, Lester Garland
Thomson, Ralph John
Thomson, Robert James
Thone, Charles
Thone, James O.
Thong, Siong-Hoat
Thordarson, T.W.
Thoresen, Paul Walter
Thoreson, Richard Wallace
Thorman, Donald Joseph
Thorn, James Elwood
Thornburg, Russell Charles
Thornbury, John Rousseau
Thorne, C(ecil) Michael
Thorne, Joseph Cecil, Jr.
Thorne, Reginald Kenneth
Thornhill, William Thomas
Thornton, Edmund Braxton
Thornton-Trump, Walter Edmond (Ted)
Thorpe, Albert
Thorpe, Samuel L., Jr.
Thorrez, Camiel Earl
Thorsen, Robert
Thorson, Milton Zenas
Throckmorton, Ray Iams, Jr.
Throop, James Warren
Thuringer, Carl Bernard
Thurston, Fred Stone
Thurston, Robert Ward
Thygerson, Kenneth James
Tichenor, Edward John
Tichenor, Robert Woodrow
Tichenor, William Geiley
Tickel, William Ernest, Jr.
Tickemyer, Garland Elijah
Tidstrom, Fred Lewis
Tiecke, Richard William
Tiede, Charles Richard
Tiemann, Jerome Noel
Tien, Hsin Chen
Tiernan, Thomas Orville
Tierney, John Francis
Tierney, John Patrick
Tiernon, Carlos Herschel
Tietz, Gary Albert
Tiffany, Joseph Calvin, II
Tiffany, Norman Olcott
Tigerman, Stanley
Tigrak, Mehmet Faut
Tillery, Stephen Matthew
Tillotson, Raymond Jennison
Tilton, Richard Wallis
Timm, Jerome Joseph
Timm, Roger Alfred
Timmerman, Jay Carl
Timmons, George Grant
Timmons, Gerald Dean
Tinen, John Victor
Tingley, Donald Fred
Tinkham, Matthew Hosmer, Jr.
Tinning, Fred C.
Tipei, Nicolae
Tippin, George Richard
Tipshus, Edward Chester
Tipton, Clyde Raymond, Jr.
Titchenal, Oliver Ray
Titko, Jerry L.
Title, Monroe M.
Tiu, Alfonso Li
Tobin, Calvin Jay
Tobin, Michael E.
Todd, Alva Cress
Todd, David Warren
Todd, Gary Irl
Todd, Jackson Dean
Todd, John Odell
Todd, Mary Elizabeth (Mrs. Alva Cress Todd)
Todd, Marysnow Stone (Mrs. Zane G. Todd)
Todd, Thomas Carmel
Todd, Zane Grey
Todes, Kenneth
Todoroff, Albert
Toedman, Gordon Reed
Toedtman, James Christian
Toepfer, Caroline Elizabeth Throckmorton
Toepfer, Louis Adelbert
Toguchi, Fred Shinichi
Toler, Hayward Curt
Toles, Edward Bernard
Tollaksen, Robert Earl
Tollefson, John Edward
Tolman, Suzanne Nelson
Toman, Andrew John
Tomaras, Peter Theophanis
Tome, Philip Lewis
Tomkins, Frank Sargent
Tomko, Michael Anthony
Tompkins, Arthur Wilson, Jr.
Tompkins, Carl Oscar
Toney, Doris Carpenter
Toney, Myrna Mae
Tool, Richard Hendricks
Topouzian, Levon Krikor
Topper, Timothy Hamilton
Torline, (Martin) Eugene
Tornow, Walter William
Tornquist, Leroy John
Torres, Jose Dimas
Torres, Roger Luis
Torrington, William Paul
Tort, Carlos Leonardo
Toscano, James Vincent
Toshach, Daniel Wilkie
Tosi, Donald James
Tosi, Oscar I.
Toth, Ferenc John
Toth, Richard Michael
Toto, Patrick Daniel
Totten, Paul Raymond
Touchman, William Stanley
Tourtelot, Joseph Lowry
Toutant, William Joseph
Towers, Michael Douglas
Towle, Kelso Churchill
Towner, John Harding
Towner, Lawrence William
Townley, Arthur James
Townley, Charles Orleff
Townley, Normand Thomas
Townsend, Alden Miller
Townsend, Carl Godfrey
Townsend, Earl Cunningham, Jr.
Townsend, Edwin Byron, III
Townsend, Harold Guyon, Jr.
Townsend, Howard Garfield, Jr.
Townsend, J. Russell, Jr.
Townsend, James Edward
Townsend, Paul Henson
Townsend, Thornton Lewis
Townsend, William Beach
Tozzer, Jack Carl
Trachsel, Fred Richard
Tracy, Mary Elizabeth
Tracy, William Thomas
Traeger, Barbara Shields (Mrs. John E. Traeger)
Trafimow, Jordan Herman
Trainor, John Felix
Tranel, Daniel David
Tranen, Martin William
Trapani, Andrew Patrick
Trapp, Charles Francis
Trask, Laurence Marion
Traugott, Michael Wolfe
Traum, Emil Frank
Travers, Thomas Joseph
Travis, Dempsey Jerome
Travis, Fiona Henderson
Travis, Randall Howard
Trawick, Leonard Moses
Traxel, William Louis
Traxler, Bob
Traxler, Eugene Rice
Traynor, Mack Vincent, Jr.
Treadway, Donald Ray
Treadway, William Eugene
Treanor, John Zimbeck
Treanor, Richard Clifford
Treece, Eleanor Mae Walters (Mrs. James William Treece, Jr.)
Treece, James William, Jr.
Treger, Harvey
Treiman, Edward M.
Treister, Michael Roy
Tremble, Stella Craft
Trennt, Evelyn Ladene
Trent, Althea
Trent, Donald Mudra
Trent, Nellie Jane
Trescott, Martha Frances Moore
Trethewey, William Charles
Treuter, Charles Richard
Trevan, Georgia Etha Oliver
Trevarthan, Fred, III
Treyz, Joseph Henry
Tribbie, Thomas Leyshon
Triezenberg, Ryer
Trimmer, Robert Whitfield
Trine, Ralph Donald
Tripp, Marian Barlow Loope
Trippet, Charles Kightly
Trojak, Therese Anne (Mrs. Edward V. Trojak)
Troldahl, Oather Franklin
Trombla, William Gilbert, Jr.
Trone, Peter Donaldson
Troup, George Barnett
Troupe, Laurel Antoinette
Trowbridge, Karen Sue
Troxel, Albert Delone, Jr.
Troxel, Jay Corwin
Troxell, John Franklin
Troy, Matthew Michael
Troy, William Norman
Troyer, Alvah Forrest, Jr.
Troyer, Dana Orion
Troyer, LeRoy S.
Troyer, Thomas Franklin
Trozzolo, Anthony Marion
Trudeau, Robert Wayne
Trudo, Frederick Joseph
True, Marion (Mrs. Laurence M. True)
Trueblood, Carl Yates
Truemper, Vernon Jacob
Truettner, Jean
Truhlsen, Stanley Marshall
Trumble, Eugene Fletcher
Trunnell, Eugene Erle
Trusty, Thomas Francis
Trutter, John Thomas
Trux, Hugo Ronaszeki
Tryon, Richard Rundel, Jr.
Tsai, Stephen Weilun
Tsai, You-Wen
Tsang, Peter Hing-Shya
Tsao, Keh Cheng
Tsay, Ching Sow
Tschappat, Donna Belle
Tschetter, Robert Alan
Tschetter, Wesley Gene
Tschirki, Robert Dean
Tsen, Cho Ching
Tsien Tsuen-Hsuin
Tsuang, Ming Tso
Tsuruoka, Catherine Boulger
Tucker, Barbara (Bebe Lou Muehle) (Mrs. Richard Walter Tucker)
Tucker, Carolyn Coston (Mrs. John D. Tucker, Sr.)
Tucker, Clarine Smith
Tucker, Dennis Keith
Tucker, Earl Leonard
Tucker, Frank Leon
Tucker, Fred C., Jr.
Tucker, Huel Clive
Tucker, John David
Tucker, John Thomas
Tucker, Theodore Jon
Tucker, Thomas Randall
Tudor, Charles Dorsey
Tufty, Lyle Holles
Tuggle, William Philip
Tulis, Allen Joseph
Tullis, Richard Barclay
Tuma, Arthur Tennyson
Tuneberg, Richard Kent
Tung, Theodore Hschum
Tunks, Frederick Edward
Tunnicliff, Philip Hunter
Tupper, Kent Phillip
Turchyn, Andrew
Turcotte, Jeremiah George
Turek, Arthur Frank
Turek, Robert Walter
Turek, Stephen
Turner, Allen Mark
Turner, Amos
Turner, Arthur Edward
Turner, Charles Joseph
Turner, Dean Schiller
Turner, Edward Clark
Turner, Glenn Everett
Turner, Harold Edward
Turner, Herman Nathaniel, Jr.
Turner, L. Bowman
Turner, Mary Ruth
Turner, Michael Seth
Turner, Richard
Turner, Richard Clark
Turner, Robert Homer
Turner, Robert Rust
Turner, Stephen Honeywell
Turner, Thomas Allen
Turner, William Lee
Turpin, John Clyde
Turriff, Clarence Joseph
Turski, Ben
Tuschman, James Marshall
Tutins, Antons
Tutt, Charles Leaming, Jr.
Tuttle, George Albert
Tuttle, Jack Lyman
Tvedten, Harold William
Tvrdik, Timothy Charles, Jr.
Tweedie, Leonard Christie
Tweedy, Robert Hugh
Twells, Douglas Sinclair
Twells, John Lawrence
Twesme, Russell Willis
Twist, Charles Russell
Twitchell, Robert Cort
Twyman, James Elliott
Tyagi, Narendra Singh
Tyler, Arnold James
Tyler, Helen (Mrs. Tracy F. Tyler)
Tyler, Lloyd John
Tyler, William Howard, Jr.
Tynes, Morris Harrison
Tyree, Lewis, Jr.
Tyrmand, Leopold
Tyrrell, Thomas Carroll
Tyrrell, Tom George
Tysl, Gloria Jeanne
Tzangas, George John
Uchendu, Victor Chikezie
Udehn, Carlysle David
Uecker, Arthur Henry
Uecker, James Clyde
Uecker, Marvin Frederick
Uemura, Joseph Norio
Uffelmann, Hans Werner
Ugajin, Kazuo
Uhl, Keith Edward
Uhr, Clinton William, Jr.
Uhrin, Michael
Uicker, Joseph Bernard
Uihlein, Henry Holt
Ujiki, Gerald Toshimi
Ullman, Pierre Lioni
Ullom, Charles Baumann
Ullrich, Helen Stine
Ullyot, Marianne Williams
Ulmer, George Elburn
Ulmer, Richard Lee
Ulrich, David Mack
Umans, Alvin Robert
Umbehocker, Kenneth Sheldon
Underhill, William George
Underkofler, Thomas Arthur
Underwood, Bruce
Underwood, Dennis James
Underwood, Gary Dale
Underwood, Paul Staats
Unger, Robert Michael
Unruh, Milton Charles
Upton, Lucile Morris (Mrs. Eugene V. Upton)
Upton, Wendell Ward
Urban, Dewey Emanuel
Urban, Dolores Jean
Urban, Donald A.
Urbom, Warren Keith
Usher, David
Usher, Newell Elsworth
Utecht, Aloise Joseph
Utgaard, Merton Blaine
Utgaard, Stuart Brady
Utz, Carolyn May Glover (Mrs. Stanley Minor Utz)
Uveges, Alfred Charles
Uze, Irving
Uzelac, George, Jr.
Vaal, Joseph John, Jr.
Vachher, Prehlad Singh
Vafi, Houshang
Vagh, Amrishkumar Suryaprasad
Vagnieres, Robert Charles
Vail, Joe Franklin
Vail, Roger Stanley
Vail, Thomas Van Husen
Vaile, Horace Snyder
Vaile, Jeanne Scott (Mrs. Horace S. Vaile)
Vaisvil, Fred Anthony
Valentine, Barry
Valentine, Bob Leon
Valentino, Paul Jon
Valinsky, Mark Steven
Valis, William Victor
Valtos, William
Valusek, John Emiel
Van Andel, Betty Jean
Van Andel, Jay
Van Arsdell, Ronald Dorr
Van Arsdell, Stephen Cottrell
Van Bever, Roger Adolph
Van Bijlevelt, Hendrik Karel
Van Blaricom, Robert Perry
Van Buskirk, Carroll Charles
Van Buskirk, Edmund Linford
Vance, Arthur Leslie
Vance, Herbert A.
Vance, Joan Emily Jackson (Mrs. Norval E. Vance)
Van Conant, Darrel Lee
Van Curler, Donald Edward
Vandeberg, John Thomas
Van De Leuv, John Henri
Van De Mark, Paul LaVerne
Van Demark, Robert Eugene
Vandenberg, Kenneth Wayne
Vandeportaele, Daniel D.
Vandergrift, James Barrett
Vander Jagt, Guy Adrian
Vander Kam, Cornelius
Vander Kolk, Kenneth Jay
Vander Molen, Robert LaVerne, Jr.
Vanderpool, Ward Melvin
Vandersteen, Paul Richard
Vander Velde, John Jacob
Vander Werf, Donald George
Vanderwier, Tamsen Rainer Fitzgerald
Van Duzer, Franklin Kenneth
Van Dyke, William Elbert
Van Eenenaam, Robert Dale
Vanek, Miroslav
Van Etten, Donald Dean
Van Goor, Kornelius
Vangor, Donald William
Van Hemert, Dale Edwin
Van Heule, Thomas Joseph
Van Horn, Louis Harold
Van Horne, Pieter Hammond
Van Horne, William Earl
Van Housen, Edward Irvin
Van Houten, Verne Willis
Vanik, Charles A.
Van Kampen, Robert Donald
Van Kirk, Maurice Melvin
Van Leeuwen, Jerry Bernard
Van Leuven, Robert Joseph
van Lierop, Peter
Van Meter, David, Jr.
Van Milligen, Alfred Cornelius
Vanneman, Edgar, Jr.
Van Norman, Willis Roger
Van Nostrand, David Michael
Van Nuys, John Dixon
Van Ordstrand, Howard Scott
Van Pelt, Philip Frisbee
Van Praag, Alex, Jr.
Van Raaphorst, Donna L.
Van Riper, Sue Ellen Fouke (Mrs. Edward L. Van Riper, Jr.)
Van Ryzin, Sister Martina
Vansant, Carl Allen
Van Sant, Joanne Frances
Vanscoy, Beatrice Iona
Van Straten, Gerrit Stanley
Van Tassel, Leo M.

Van Tieghem, Albert Richard, Sr.
Van Tiem, Florentine Urban Stewart (Mrs. Richard L. Van Tiem)
Van Tiem, Phillip Michael
Van Til, William
Van Vleet, William Benjamin, Jr.
Van Winkle, Charles Kellogg
Van Winkle, Tilford Wayne
Vardaris, Richard Miles
Varghese, Joseph Eatvila
Varichak, Richard Warren
Varkey, Basil
Varner, Charleen LaVerne McClanahan (Mrs. Robert B. Varner)
Varner, Durward Belmont
Varner, Robert Bernard
Varney, Theodore Roosevelt
Varnold, Cecil Burl
Varwig, Harry Julius
Vary, James Patrick
Vasils, Albert
Vassalotti, Louis Angelo
Vassiliades, Anthony Epaminondas
Vatterott, Joseph Henry
Vaughan, Andrew Thomas
Vaughan, Lawrence Edward
Vaughan, Richard Henry
Vaughn, Charles George
Vaughn, Charles Gordon
Vaughn, Charles Robert
Vaughn, Clarence Benjamin
Vaughn, Jack Lee
Vaughn, Lawrence (Larry) Eugene, Jr.
Vaughn, Richard Adelbert
Vayhinger, John Monroe
Vaziri-Nazar, Habib
Veach, Darrell Alves
Vecchio, Peter James
Veeck, William Louis
Veenhuis, Philip Edward
Veenker, Claude Harold
Veenstra, H. Robert
Veit, Irwin
Velaer, Charles Alfred
Velinsky, Barbara Lynn Mihelic
Venezia, Antonio Joseph
Venit, William Bennett
Venkatakrishna, V. Bellur
Venners, Theodore
Venning, Corey
Ventling, Jack Lester
Vento, Bruce Frank
Vento, Elio Gaetano
Venugopal, Muthugounder
Verbal, Claude Arthur
Ver Burg, John Robert
Verby, John Edward
Vercler, John Robert
Verdun, Michael Douglas
Verdun, Rudolph James
Vermillion, George Heaton
Vernier, Douglas Lee
Vernon, Carl Atlee, Jr.
Versace, John
Vetter, Dale Benjamin
Vetter, David Augustin
Veverka, Joseph Frederick
Viar, Jack Byron
Vicher, Edward Ernest
Vick, Timothy Dougall
Vickery, Eugene Livingstone
Victoroff, Victor Morton
Vignieri, Charles Joseph
Vij, Gurbachan Singh
Vilas, Faith Lehman
Villanueva, Antonio del Rosario
Vince, Robert
Vincenz, Stanislaw Aleksander
Vineyard, Jerry Daniel
Vinke, Harry William
Vinke, John Louis
Vinson, Arnold William
Virden, Maxine Ferrell (Mrs. Robert Miles Virden)
Visnapuu, Herk
Visser, John Evert
Vitale, Joseph Anthony
Vite, Frank Anthony
Vitek, Richard Kenneth
Vitiello, Michele
Vitko, John Peter
Vivona, Daniel Nicholas
Vlahos, George Efthymios
Vockel, Richard Landis
Voda, Frederick Allen
Voderberg, Kurt Ernst
Voegel, Kathleen Wallis
Voeller, John George, III
Voelpel, Ray Carnell
Voepel, Karl Heinz
Voet, Leo Francis
Voge, Wilfred Allan
Vogel, Arthur Anton
Vogel, Byron William
Vogel, Carl Edward
Vogel, David Agnew
Vogel, Francis Xavier
Vogel, Raymond Stefan
Vogel, Thomas Timothy
Voget, Fred William
Vogt, James Robert
Voigt, Wesleyan Kent
Voit, Roger Joseph
Voliva, Benjamin Harrison, Jr.
Volker, William Henry
Volkmer, Harold Lee
Volkmuth, Donald Harold
Volz, Paul Albert
Von Achen, Jon Kurt
Von Bargen, Wayne James
Von Berg, Lois Helene
Von Berlichingen, Maximilian Adelbert
Von Besser, Kurt Wolf Frederick
Vondracek, John Joseph
Vondruska, James Francis
Von Lang, Frederick William
Vonnahmen, Francis Henry
von Stein, Peter
von Tish, John Joseph
von Wyss, Marc Robert
Vosmeier, Leonard Francis
Voss, Edward William, Jr.
Voss, Jan (Mrs. Conrad Johnson)
Voss, Omer Gerald
Voth, Harold Moser
Vourax, Myron Anthony
Vrettas, Arthur Thomas
Vuckovich, Dragomir Michael
Vukas, Ronald
Vukin, Walter John
Vumbaco, Joseph Anthony
Waber, James Thomas
Wachal, David Eugene
Wachowski, Theodore John
Wachtman, Donald Carl
Wacker, Frederick Glade, Jr.
Wacker, Maxwell Nathan
Waddell, James Richard
Waddick, William Anthony
Waddington, Edward Holmes
Waddington, Raymond Bruce, Jr.
Wade, Gordon Stanfield
Wade, James G.
Wadsworth, Gerald J.
Wadzinski, LeRoy Anthony
Waetjen, Walter Bernhard
Wafer, John Albert
Wagenheim, Joel Steven
Wagenknecht, Theodore William, Jr.
Wagester, Eugene Kenneth
Wagman, Frederick Herbert
Wagner, Alvin Louis, Jr.
Wagner, Frank Eugene
Wagner, Joyce Aileen
Wagner, Loren Laverne
Wagner, Percy Evan
Wagner, Philip Ira
Wagner, Richard Gordon
Wagner, Robert Earl
Wagner, William Burdette
Wahl, Emil Dewey
Wahl, Mary Evelyn Garlick (Mrs. Kenneth Robert Wahl)
Wahl, Norman Stephen
Wahlquist, Eric
Wahrman, William Frank
Wair, Fred Lee
Waite, David Antes
Waite, William Eugene (Gene)
Wakefield, Kenneth McGregor
Wakefield, William Oran, Jr.
Walbaum, Robert Crum
Walch, William Nicholas
Walcoff, Lawrence
Walcott, Roger Eugene
Waldbauer, Gilbert Peter
Waldbillig, Ronald Joseph
Waldemar, David Lee
Walden, James William
Waldenmyer, Dale Richard
Waldie, Wendell Dean
Waldinger, Martin Harris
Waldman, Irving
Waldman, Maurice
Waldo, C(harles) Ives, Jr.
Waldren, Terry Edward
Waldron, Becky Johnston
Waldron, Kenneth Lynn
Waldstein, Sheldon Saul
Wales, Charles Atherton, Jr.
Walhout, John Robert
Wali, Mohan Kishen
Walinski, Richard S.
Walk, Lloyd Franklin
Walker, Alice Gates
Walker, Daniel
Walker, David Brooks
Walker, Elva Mae Dawson
Walker, Frank Banghart
Walker, James
Walker, James Adams
Walker, James LeRoy
Walker, James Leslie
Walker, James Scott
Walker, Jerry Lee
Walker, Jessica Lee
Walker, Jessie
Walker, Kenneth Andrew
Walker, Maurice Andrew
Walker, Robert Glenn
Walker, Theodore Delbert
Walker, Thomasenia
Walker, Wallace Lee
Walker, Wallis Dean
Walker, Walter Ladare
Walker, Walter Willard
Walkup, Gerald Arthur
Wall, Arthur Edward Patrick
Wall, Doris Jane
Wall, Fred Graham
Wall, Paul S.
Wall, William Lloyd
Wallaart, Johannes Petrus
Wallace, Douglass Stuart
Wallace, Franklin Sherwood
Wallace, James Duncan
Wallace, Jane Young (Mrs. Donald H. Wallace)
Wallace, John Edward
Wallace, John Walter
Wallace, Leland Morris, Jr.
Wallace, Leon Harry
Wallace, Paul
Wallace, Robert Dean
Wallace, Sherwood Lee
Wallace, Thomas Ferdinand
Wallace, Wayne Orrin
Wallace, William Thomas (Tom)
Wallace, William Warren
Wallach, Philip
Wallbrown, Fred Harold
Wallbrown, Jane Downs (Mrs. Fred Harold Wallbrown)
Walledom, John Christian
Waller, Richard Evan
Waller, Russell Bliss
Wallin, Jack Irving Melhus
Wallin, Steven Craig
Wallman, Charles James
Wallner, Mary (Mrs. Frank Wallner)
Walls, Richard Jerome
Walsh, Beatrice Passage
Walsh, Edmund Carroll, III
Walsh, James Patrick, Jr.
Walsh, John Philip
Walsh, Kenneth Albert
Walsh, Rita
Walsh, Robert Joseph
Walsh, Thomas J(oseph)
Walsh, Thomas Patrick
Walsh, William Arthur, II
Walstrom, John Albert James
Walter, James Treat
Walter, Richard Dale
Walter, Richard Harry
Walter, Roderich
Walter, Terry Lynn
Walters, Everett
Walters, Gomer Winston
Walters, Harold Wallace
Walters, Harvey Eugene
Walters, Jefferson Brooks
Walters, John Dennis
Walters, Sumner Junior
Walters, Thomas Charles
Walth, Erwin Gottleib
Walther, Richard Edward
Waltke, Alfred George
Walton, Claude Alex
Walton, Craig Carlton
Walton, Herbert Wilson
Walton, Robert Eugene
Wambo, John Mack
Wampler, Lloyd Charles
Wampler, Robert Joseph
Wampler, Wesley Earl
Wang, Edward DeFord
Wang, Joseph Yuan
Wang, Wayne Lung
Wangelin, Harris Kenneth
Wangsness, Wayne Roger
Waniewicz, Ignacy
Wanke, Ronald Lee
Wannamaker, Mary Lyman
Wanzek, Robert Paul
Ward, Addis Thompson
Ward, Alan Joseph
Ward, Alice Marie
Ward, Alva John
Ward, Daniel P.
Ward, Donald Earl
Ward, Donald Maxwell
Ward, Evelyn Svec (Mrs. William E. Ward)
Ward, Hensel Owen
Ward, Howard Nelson
Ward, James Raymond
Ward, James Sheridan
Ward, John Langdon
Ward, Patricia Spain
Ward, Sylvan Donald
Ward, Thomas Gene
Ward, Velma Lewis
Ward, Vernon Graves
Ward, William Edward
Ward, William Gates
Ward, Willis Wesley
Wardlow, Ervin E.
Ware, Richard Anderson
Warford, John Howard, II
Warinner, Douglas Keith
Warm, Joel Seymour
Warmbrod, James Robert
Warne, Keith Warnell
Warne, Ralph Dick
Warner, Dennis Eugene
Warner, Don Lee
Warner, Gordon J.
Warner, Wallace Ernest
Warnholtz, Werner Ernst
Warpeha, Raymond Leonard
Warpeha, Walter Stanley
Warren, Claude Marion
Warren, Francis Eugene
Warren, James Vaughn
Warren, Joe Ellison
Warren, Ross Winston
Warres, Herbert Leonard
Warrick, Patricia Scott
Warshaw, Martin Richard
Warstler, Irvin Samuel
Washburn, Jost Brainard
Washburn, Paul Arthur
Wasmuth, Duane Lee
Wasserman, Gerald Steward
Wasserman, Rodger Dean
Wasserman, Stephen Miles
Wasson, Barbara Hickam (Mrs. Audley Jackson Wasson)
Wasson, William Elwood
Wasyluka, Ray Gerald
Watanabe, Mark
Waterbury, Jackson Dewitt
Waters, William Baxter
Waters, William Roland
Watkins, Daniel Joseph
Watkins, David Hyder
Watkins, Dean Edward
Watkins, Donald Richard
Watkins, Raymond Carl
Watnaas, Gene Gaylord
Watson, Ben Charles
Watson, C. Gordon
Watson, Everett Donald
Watson, Glenn Roy
Watson, Howard Monroe
Watson, James William
Watson, Robert Gordon
Watt, Garland Wedderick
Wattenberg, Joan Louise Dillon (Mrs. Carl A. Wattenberg, Jr.)
Wattles, John Charles
Watts, Charles Herbert
Watts, Henry Bryan
Watzke, James Norman
Waugh, Mary Hester
Waxler, William Lorne
Waxman, Joseph Harry
Wayman, Frank Donovan
Wayman, Norbury Lansing
Wayt, William Allen
Weatherup, Robert Alexander
Weaver, Allen Dale
Weaver, Arthur Lawrence
Weaver, Floyd Edward
Weaver, Glenn Morrison
Weaver, John C(arrier)
Weaver, Kennard Ray
Weaver, Kenneth Ronald
Weaver, Kenneth Vernon
Weaver, L. Ruth Rundle (Mrs. C.H. Weaver)
Weaver, Richard Alvin
Weaver, R(ichard) Donald
Webb, Charles Haizlip
Webb, Edward Francis
Webb, James R.
Webb, J(esse) Edgar
Webb, Lance
Webb, Leslie Richard
Webb, Paul Benedict, Jr.
Webb, Thelma Elizabeth
Webbe, Scotson
Webber, Everard Leland
Webber, Gene Franklin
Webber, Warren Loraine
Webel, James Buell
Weber, A(dolph) Carl
Weber, Alban
Weber, Alden Orison
Weber, Arthur Rudolph
Weber, Charles August
Weber, C(harles) Edward
Weber, Charles Theodore, Jr.
Weber, Frank Earl
Weber, George Russell
Weber, George W., Jr.
Weber, Gertrude Christina
Weber, Gregor August
Weber, Harm Allen
Weber, Harriette B. Skladd
Weber, Joseph James
Weber, Milada (Paukova)
Weber, Milan George
Weber, Norbert Joseph
Weber, Paul Egon
Weber, Pearl Alice
Weber, Ralph Edward
Weber, Robert Claude
Weber, Robert Frederick
Weber, Russell Wright
Weber, Victor Blaine, II
Weber, Walter Jacob, Jr.
Webster, James Randolph, Jr.
Webster, Mildred Esther
Webster, Robert Byron
Webster, Robert Trice
Weclew, Thaddeus Victor
Wedding, Donald Keith
Weddon, Edward Renfroe
Weder, Donald Erwin
Weder, Erwin Henry
Wedge, Wesley Ernest
Wedgeworth, Robert, Jr.
Weed, Byron Ellsworth, II
Weed, Herman Roscoe
Weed, Mary Theophilos
Weedall, Robert Scott
Weede, Hilda Marian Sawyer
Weeden, Alfred John
Weeks, John Leonard
Weeks, Mary Catherine
Weeks, Solan William
Weenink, Mary Ethel Lynne Crandall (Mrs. George Weenink)
Weerts, Richard Kenneth
Weese, Benjamin Horace
Weese, Carlisle
Weg, John Gerard
Wegener, Frederick Freemen
Wegenke, Gary Lee
Weggenmann, Norman Edward
Wegmiller, Donald Charles
Wegner, Robert Ernst
Wegner, Waldo Wilbert
Wehler, Richard Harris
Wehner, Merle Ernest
Wehrer, Charles Siecke
Wehring, Bernard William
Wehrly, Ralph E.
Wehrmacher, William Henry
Wei, Lun-Shin
Weicker, Jack Edward
Weidemann, Joseph Edward
Weidemann, Wayne E(rwin)
Weidenthal, Daniel Tilles
Weider, Donnabeth
Weidman, Margaret Lillian
Weigand, George Robert
Weigand, Robert Eugene
Weigel, John William
Weigel, Paul
Weih, Jack Evans
Weikel, Robert Charles
Weiker, Oscar James
Weil, David Maxwell
Weil, Herman
Weil, Louis Arthur, Jr.
Weil, Oscar Arnold
Weil, Paul Peres
Weil, Rolf Alfred
Weiland, Steven Edward
Weinbaum, Barbara Hyman
Weinberg, Jack
Weinberg, Sylvan L.
Weinblatt, Alan William
Weine, Franklin Scott
Weinel, Ronald Blair
Weiner, Lawrence Myron
Weiner, Lewis Phillip
Weiner, Murray
Weinfurter, Robert Wayne
Weingard, Marvin Allen
Weingart, Maurice Alexander
Weinhardt, Carl J., Jr.
Weinkauf, Mary Louise Stanley (Mrs. Alan Dale Weinkauf)
Weinkauf, William Carl
Weinlander, Albertina Abrams (Mrs. Max M. Weinlander)
Weinlander, Max Martin
Weinman, Irvin Abraham
Weinstein, David
Weinstock, Frank Joseph
Weinstock, Henry Robert
Weis, Jack Frank
Weisberg, Seymour William
Weise, R. Eric
Weiser, John Conrad
Weiser, John Edwin
Weisman, Morton Philip
Weiss, Herman
Weiss, Julius Seymour
Weiss, Mark Lawrence
Weissblatt, Robert Lewis
Weisse, Guenter
Weissenburger, Jason Ticknor, Jr.
Weissler, Arnold Mervin
Weissman, Richard Mayer
Weisstein, Ulrich Werner
Weitzel, William Frederick, Jr.
Welander, Robert Elder
Welborn, William Calvert, Jr.
Welbourn, Dale Kenneth
Welbourn, John Throp
Welch, Jack Wyman
Welch, John Wiley
Welch, Lester Hayden
Welch, Lyndon
Welch, Martha Jean
Welch, Robert Etienne
Welch, Willie F.
Weld, Hiram Chester
Weldon, Howard George
Welker, Bruce Marvin
Wellbank, Harry Laurence
Wellenkotter, Harry William, Jr.
Weller, Donald Matthias
Weller, Edward Frank, Jr.
Weller, Richard Franklin
Wells, Ben Harris
Wells, Charles K.
Wells, Eugene Ralph
Wells, Lamar Oliver
Wells, Larry Eugene
Wells, Lee Edwin
Wells, Marian Ryder (Mrs. Harold Arthur Wells)
Wells, Norman Edgar
Wells, Ralph Madison, Jr.
Wells, Ray Marshall
Wells, Robert Francis
Wells, Robert Manville
Wells, Willard James, Jr.
Welsbo, Charles George
Welper, Francis Eugene
Welsh, David John
Welte, Maurice Daniel
Welter, Clarence Joseph
Welty, Quentin Wilbur
Wendel, Sylvester Wendeline
Wendelburg, Norma Ruth
Wendell, Francis Lee Higginson
Wendling, Dieter
Wendorf, Melvin James
Wendt, Arthur John
Wendt, George R.
Wendt, Harold John
Wendt, Lloyd
Wenig, Phillip Wayne
Wenneker, James Emmett
Wenner, Herbert Allan
Wensink, Delmar David
Wenthe, Eugene Edward
Wentworth, Richard Leigh
Wentzel, Arnold William
Wentzel, Philip Robert
Wenzel, Frederick Joseph
Wenzler, William Paul
Werbel, James Phillip
Wergowske, William Gary
Werling, Michael Marion
Wermuth, John Marlowe
Werner, Burton Kready
Werner, Charles George
Werner, Christian Thor
Werner, Elmer Louis, Jr.
Werner, John Clifford
Werner, Peter Julius
Werrell, Terry Sherman
Wert, Alice Leola Heck (Mrs. William Grau Wert)
Wert, William Grau
Werth, Carl Henry, Sr.
Werth, Richard George
Wertheimer, Frederick William
Wertz, Kenneth Eugene
Wertz, Robert Arthur
Wescott, Philip Charles
Wesenberg, John Herman
Wesley, Gloria May Walker (Mrs. Cleo Wesley)
Wesley, Theodore Perry
Wesloh, Ferdinand Joseph
Wesolek, John Steven
Wesolowski, Stanley Peter
Wessel, Gilbert Roland
Wessels, Ardwin Gilbert
Wessler, William Ernest
Wessman, Colleen Patricia
West, Don Edwin
West, George Russell
West, James Edward
West, Joseph Warren
West, Lloyd Marvin
West, Norman Dudley
West, Richard Irving
West, Robert Patton
West, Sam
West, Sandra Arline
West, Walter Scott
West, William Francis, Jr.
Westburg, John Edward
Westbury, June Alwyn (Mrs. Peter Willoughby Allen Westbury)
Westcott, Robert Frederick
Westdale, Leonard Lloyd
Westen, Ann Patricia
Westenberg, Robert William
Westendorp, Floyd
Westenfelder, Grant Orville
Westerberg, Wesley Magnus
Westerhaus, Catherine Frances (Mrs. George H. Westerhaus)
Westerhold, Ruth Elizabeth
Westervelt, Robert Ellsworth
Westfall, David Ernest
Westfall, Ralph Libby
Westfield, Jacquelyn Baden (Mrs. Monte Westfield)
Westin, Harold Joseph
Westlake, Leighton Danis, Jr.
Westman, Roy Herman
Westran, Roy Alvin
Wetherholt, Douglas Jividen
Wetnight, Robert
Wetter, Benjamin Fenton
Wetterstrom, Edwin
Wetzel, Dean Elton
Wetzel, Stuart Alan
Wever, Hilbert Emanuel
Wexler, Bernard Carl
Wexner, Leslie Herbert
Weyls, John Lawrence
Weyrens, John Joseph
Whalen, Charles William, Jr.
Whaler, Van George
Whallon, Evan Arthur, Jr.
Wharton, Clifton Reginald, Jr.
Whatley, David Thomas
Whealey, Robert Howard
Wheatley, Joseph Edwin
Wheatley, Thomas Joseph, Jr.
Wheaton, Burdette Carl
Wheaton, Robert Donald
Wheaton, Rolland Zelbert
Wheby, Frank Tomas
Wheeler, Adade Mitchell
Wheeler, Charles Eugene
Wheeler, Clarence Joseph, Jr.
Wheeler, David Gene
Wheeler, Gerridee Stenehjem
Wheeler, Harry Kelley, Jr.
Wheeler, James Ernest
Wheeler, James Hamilton
Wheeler, John Dee
Wheeler, Mary Frances
Wheeler, Robert Cordell
Whelan, Gerald T.
Whelan, Joseph L(eo)
Whinery, Dorothy Cooke (Mrs. James C. Whinery)
Whinery, Robert Don
Whipkey, Kenneth Lee
Whipple, Frank Hall
Whipple, Walter Leighton
Whipple, William Perry
Whipps, Edward Franklin
Whisler, Robert Daniel
Whisnant, Jack Page
Whitaker, Walter Merrill
Whitcomb, Edgar D.
White, Alexander Patrick
White, Allen E.
White, Charles Edgar
White, Charles McKinley
White, Charlotte Arlene Bucher (Mrs. Norbert William White)
White, D. Jerry
White, Eugene Ellsworth
White, Frederick Arthur
White, Geoffery Lee
White, Harold Edgar, Jr.
White, Harriet Elizabeth
White, Hugh Erwin
White, James Patrick
White, James Stephen
White, James William
White, Joe, Jr.
White, John Henry
White, John Joseph, III

White, Kathy Ann
White, Larry Curtis
White, Mary Winifred Lee
White, Michael Thomas
White, Paul William
White, Raymond Gene
White, Robert Myron
White, Roger Dean
White, Sidney Shaw, Jr.
White, Theodore William
White, Thomas Lester
White, Virginia Knox
White, William Adrian
White, William Alan
White, William Francis
White, William Letcher
Whiteaker, Stanley Cyril
Whiteford, Emma May Brittin
Whitehead, John C.
Whitehill, James Girard
Whitehouse, George Edward
Whitehouse, William Arthur
Whiteman, Weston Kimball
Whiteside Alba Lea, Jr.
Whiteside, Philip Elray
White-Ware, Grace Elizabeth
Whitfield, Allen
Whitfield, George Polk
Whitfield, Russell Lee
Whitham, Edward Charles
Whitlow, Tyrel Eugene
Whitmire, Paul Thomas
Whitmore, Alice Elizabeth Emmert
Whitmore, Bertha Harper
Whitner, Robert Edward
Whitney, Albert Gayle
Whitney, Clarence W.
Whitney, Emerson Calhoun
Whitney, John Freeman, Jr.
Whitney, John Joseph
Whitsitt, Frank Casey
Whittaker, Howard
Whittaker, Stanley Ward
Whitted, Jack Johnson
Whittington, Lloyd Robert
Whitworth, Hall Baker
Whitworth, William Oman
Wholeben, Brent Edward
Whyte, Paul Courtright
Wick, Robert Edward
Wickersham, Beverly Horner
Wickman, John Edward
Wickramasekera (Wickram), Ian Edward
Wiczer, Bernard
Widdifield, Duane Alden
Widell, Donald Raymond
Widera, Georg Ernst Otto
Widiger, Jan Straszheim
Widlak, Frederic Walter
Widman, Paul Edward
Widmer, James Glenn
Widmer, Reuben Benjamin
Widner, Russell Ralph
Wieboldt, Raymond Carl, Jr.
Wieck, Gary Dean
Wied, George Ludwig
Wiedemann, Gladys H. Gardner
Wiegand, John Anthony
Wiegner, Edward Alex
Wieland, Clyde Lee
Wieland, Ralph Gazell
Wiener, Phyllis Ames
Wiens, Joel Henry
Wierman, James Lee
Wiersum, Quintin Eugene
Wierwille, Donald Ernst
Wierwille, Victor Paul
Wierzbicki, Anthony Jerome
Wieser, Charles Edward
Wiest, Edward Frederick
Wiest, Walter Gibson
Wieters, Ivan L.
Wieters, Nelson Edgar
Wiethoff, Clifford Allen
Wigen, Joris Odin
Wiggins, Arthur William
Wigginton, James Charles
Wijnholds, Heiko de Beaufort
Wikelund, Harold Norman
Wikiera, Edward Stanley
Wikoff, Virgil Cornwell
Wilbanks, George Dewey
Wilborn, James Christian
Wilborn, Larry Dean
Wilbur, Lowell Roger
Wilcke, Harold Ludwig
Wilcox, Allan Daggett
Wilcox, David William
Wilcox, Frances Smiley (Mrs. Courtenay Quayle Wilcox)
Wilcox, Howard Samuel
Wilcox, Mark Dean
Wilcox, Roger Clark
Wild, Margaret Mary Lambur (Mrs. W. Lydon Wild)
Wilde, Alan Hugh
Wilde, John Ramsey, III
Wilde, Robert Eugene
Wildenradt, Robert Lewis
Wilder, Carl Rudolph
Wilder, John Timothy
Wilder, Ulah
Wilds, John Lawrence
Wildschut, Henry Baldwin
Wiles, Albert Donald, II
Wiles, David Kimball
Wiles, Richard Carl
Wiles, Richard Samuel
Wiles, Thomas
Wiley, Douglas Alan
Wiley, George Louis
Wiley, Guilford Mitchell, Jr.
Wiley, Jay Wilson
Wilgarde, Ralph L.
Wilharm, William Wayne
Wilhelm, Joseph Edward
Wilhelmy, Betty Rollins
Wilhite, David Earl
Wilhite, Jeffrey Allen
Wilhoit, G(rover) Cleveland, Jr.
Wilinkin, Edward Maurice
Wilk, Clifford Merrill
Wilk, Theodore Brooks
Wilkerson, Carnie Clyde
Wilkerson, Jerome Frances
Wilkerson, Stiefel Junior
Wilkes, Delano Angus
Wilkes, Harold Lloyd
Wilkins, Estella Harmel
Wilkins, Frank Edward
Wilkins, George Thomas
Wilkins, George Thomas, Jr.
Wilkins, Raymond Edwin
Wilkinson, John Ercy
Wilkinson, William Chapin
Wilkof, Ervin
Wilks, Louis Philip
Willander, Duane Alfred
Willard, John Ela
Willard, Richard Dewaine
Willey, Roy Edward
Williams, Albert Harold
Williams, Arbor Wayne, Jr.
Williams, Billy Joe
Williams, Charles Thomas
Williams, Dan Arthur
Williams, Edgar Gene
Williams, Edward Donald
Williams, Frank Eugene
Williams, Fred E.
Williams, G. Mennen
Williams, Harold Milton
Williams, Harold Roger
Williams, Harry Woolery
Williams, Hugh Alexander, Jr.
Williams, Jack Raymond
Williams, Jasper Flemming
Williams, Jerry Ruth
Williams, John Cobb
Williams, John Pershing
Williams, John Troy
Williams, John Walter Olding
Williams, Kenneth R.
Williams, Lansing Earl
Williams, Lloyd Dee
Williams, Luther Steward
Williams, Mary Goshorn
Williams, Mezell Louis, Jr.
Williams, Milton
Williams, Morris Oddman
Williams, Ned
Williams, Nellie Ellis Batt
Williams, Nelson Wheat
Williams, Paul Allan
Williams, Philip Copelain
Williams, Richard Dale
Williams, Robert Leo
Williams, Roger William
Williams, Stanley
Williams, Steve Eugene
Williams, Thom Albert
Williams, Thomas James
Williams, Thomas Kay
Williams, Thomas Rhys
Williams, Veirl Richard
Williams, Wallace Peter
Williams, Wayne Watson
Williams, Wendell Sterling
Williams, Wesley Corrigan
Williams, Wilfred
Williams, William Joseph
Williams, Willie Samuel
Williams-Ashman, Howard Guy
Williamson, Bearl Wayne
Williamson, James Reid, Jr.
Williamson, Joe, Jr.
Williamson, John Pritchard
Williamson, Lawrence L.
Willingham, Edward Bacon, Jr.
Willis, Clifford Leon
Willis, David Edwin
Willis, David L.
Willis, Frank Neal, Jr.
Willis, Harold Robert
Willis, Henry Edward
Willis, John Fristoe
Willis, Maurice Earl
Willis, Robert Luther, Jr.
Willis, Shelby Kenneth
Willis, Thomas Creighton
Willis, William Henry
Willison, George Wyman
Willman, Joe Irvin
Willman, Warren Page
Willmes, Francis Edwin
Willmot, Robert Joseph
Willson, Barbara Jean
Wilmoth, Clarence Harold
Wilner, Freeman Marvin
Wilsman, James Michael
Wilson, Aaron Aubrey, Jr.
Wilson, Albert Erle
Wilson, Alden Peabody
Wilson, Charles Augustine
Wilson, Charles Stephen
Wilson, Chester Humphrey
Wilson, Clifford D., Jr.
Wilson, David Duce
Wilson, David John
Wilson, Don Whitman
Wilson, Donald Edward
Wilson, Donald Lee
Wilson, Doris Vivian
Wilson, Floyd W.
Wilson, Francis Servis, Jr.
Wilson, George McConnell
Wilson, George Picket, Jr.
Wilson, George Porter, III
Wilson, Harry Howard, Jr.
Wilson, Jackie Byron
Wilson, James Robert
Wilson, John Clark
Wilson, John David
Wilson, (John) Roger
Wilson, John Todd
Wilson, Keith, Jr.
Wilson, Lawrence Francis
Wilson, Malcolm Aaron
Wilson, Mary Carter
Wilson, Myron Robert, Jr.
Wilson, Neil Bryan
Wilson, Noel Avon
Wilson, Penton Jean
Wilson, Quentin Chalmer
Wilson, Rex Hamilton
Wilson, Richard Forrest
Wilson, Robert Wood
Wilson, Sloan Jacob
Wilson, Sloan Richard
Wilson, Terry C.
Wilson, Thomas Burrell
Wilson, William Falconer
Wilson, William Victor
Wilt, William Lewis
Wilton, William Everett
Wiltse, Gladys Garner (Mrs. Dorr N. Wiltse, Sr.)
Winakor, Bess Ruth
Winbinger, Charles Lee
Winblad, James Norman
Winbush, LeRoy
Winchester, Vernon Larry
Windell, Violet Bruner
Winegardner, Carl Norman
Wineman, Jeffry Stern
Wineman, John Henry
Winemiller, James D.
Winet, Howard
Wineteer, Ronald Royal
Wing, Anne Marie Hinshaw (Mrs. Leonard William Wing)
Winger, Howard Woodrow
Wingerson, George Edgar
Winitz, Harris
Winkle, William Allan
Winkler, Helen Hutula
Winkler, Raymond S.
Winn, Maurice Edward
Winn, Rhonda Lee
Winn, Robert Cheever
Winn, Wesley Wayne
Winnick, Colonel Norbert
Winquist, Alan Hanson
Winslow, Alfred Akers
Winslow, Donald Rexford
Winslow, Edward Byron
Winstein, Bruce Darrell
Winston, Harold Ronald
Winston, Warren Dee
Winstrom, Willis Lee
Winter, Francis Donald
Winter, Max
Winter, Richard Allen
Winter, Wallace Edward
Winter, William Earl
Winters, Peter Lee
Winther, Donn Ernst
Winton, Jeffrey Blake
Wintzer, Frederick Stone
Wion, Jesse Lloyd
Wirick, Betty Jo
Wirt, Michael Dean
Wirt, Robert Duane
Wirth, Richard Marvin
Wirtjes, Larry Allan
Wirtz, Arthur M(ichael)
Wirtz, Dwight C.
Wirtz, Peter George
Wirtz, Virginia Wadsworth (Mrs. Arthur M. Wirtz)
Wirtz, Wayne Henry
Wirtz, William Wadsworth
Wischmeier, Walter Henry
Wise, Betty Jean Davis (Mrs. Eugene Edward Wise, Jr.)
Wise, Henry Seiler
Wise, John Augustus, Jr.
Wise, Lew Edgar
Wise, Virgil Jay
Wiseman, Maxine Claire Schrader (Mrs. Erlow William Wiseman)
Wisinski, Stanley Joseph, III
Wisneski, Kenneth Thomas
Wisniewski, Charmaine
Wissler, Robert William
Witham, Glenn Winton, Jr.
Withers, Carl Raymond
Witherspoon, Vivaion Maudiette
Witherspoon, William
Withey, Joseph Anthony
Withington, Joseph Gardner
Witt, Coleman Boyd
Witt, S. Lee
Wittcoff, Constance Cynthia Clein
Wittemann, Henry
Wittich, John Jacob
Wittmuss, Howard Dale
Wockenfuss, James Harold
Wodlinger, Mark Louis
Woellhof, Lawrence Ray
Woeppel, Karen Alcorn
Woerner, Earl LaVern
Woerpel, Dwayne Raymond
Wofford, Theodore John
Wogaman, Maurice Aaron
Wohlfeil, Paul Frederick
Wohlgemuth, Edward Warren
Woito, Robert Severin
Wojcik, Cass
Wojcik, James Joseph
Wojta, Gerald Charles
Wolcott, Roger Lodge
Wolf, Adolph
Wolf, Anne L. McCaugherty (Mrs. Donald Myles Wolf)
Wolf, Earl Daniel
Wolf, Frances Loreta Smith (Mrs. Milton Harry Wolf)
Wolf, John Phillip
Wolf, Marlane Louise
Wolf, Raymond Bernard
Wolf, Sy L.
Wolf, Walter August
Wolf, Wayne Stanley
Wolfe, Bard Alton
Wolfe, Charles James
Wolfe, Estemore Alvis
Wolfe, Gene Henry
Wolfe, Goldie Brandelstein
Wolfe, James Richard
Wolfe, John Binnie
Wolfe, Warren Dwight
Wolfe, Wayne Wendell
Wolfenbarger, Floyd Orson
Wolfert, Richard Jerome
Wolff, Aaron Sidney
Wolff, Gunther Arthur
Wolff, Millie Bender
Wolff, Paul George
Wolff, Robert Adolph
Wolff, Robert Eugene
Wolff, Robert Samuel
Wolford, Donovan Semler
Wolfson, Albert
Wolin, Harold David
Wolkin, Julius
Woll, David Lawrence
Woll, Robert Henry
Woll, Robert Nicolas
Wollman, Harvey
Wollman, Roger Leland
Wollmann, Willis James
Wollney, John Lowell
Wollstein, Donald Gustav
Wolnak, Bernard
Wolpert, Edward Alan
Wolpert, Henry William
Wolsey, William Jerome
Wolsky, Milton Laban
Wolters, Paul Henry
Woltz, Frank Earl, Jr.
Wolz, Robert Charles
Womble, George Edwin
Womeldorff, Porter John
Womer, Frank Burton
Woner, John William
Wong, Alfonso Yan
Wong, Herman Hoy
Wong, Jimmy Pan
Wonnenberg, Kenneth Ray
Wood, Arthur MacDougall
Wood, Bruce Dean
Wood, Charles Richard
Wood, Earl Howard
Wood, Edward Albert
Wood, George Michael
Wood, Gordon R.
Wood, James Nowell
Wood, Josephine Green (Mrs. Neal S. Wood)
Wood, Kathleen Ann Studt
Wood, Kenneth Harold
Wood, Lawrence Edward
Wood, Leslie Alfred
Wood, Mildred H.
Wood, Neal Shackleford
Wood, Paul Fletcher
Wood, Richard Donald
Wood, Thomas Michael
Wood, William Jerome
Woodard, Paul Elon
Woodbury, Franklin Bennett Wessler
Woodcock, Leonard
Wooden, Howard Edmund, III
Woodhams, Berthold
Woodman, William E.
Woodring, DeWayne Stanley
Woodruff, Christine Lipps
Woodruff, Phillip Steven
Woodruff, Reginald Dow
Woods, Charles Harrison
Woods, Floyd Wayne
Woods, George Theodore
Woods, John Warren
Woods, Kenneth Reginald
Woods, Paul Edward
Woods, Richard Dean
Woods, Thomas Cochrane, Jr.
Woods, William Craig
Woods, William Edward
Woodson, James Warren
Woodson, Riley Donald
Woodward, Addison Ely, Jr.
Woodward, Frederick Robert, Jr.
Woodward Garnita Carol
Woodward, Harry Hastings, Jr.
Woodward, Herbert Norton
Woodward, Raymond Bernard
Woodward, Sidney Lee
Woodyard, Omar Reece, Jr.
Woolard, George Swartz
Woolf, Howard Leonard
Woolf, Preston G.
Woolfolk, Ida Goodwin (Martima)
Woolsey, William Stover
Woolson, Allen Michael
Woolson, John Ransom
Woolum, Max Terry
Woolums, Larry Lee
Woon, Paul Sam
Woosley, Shirley Mathis
Wooster, George Frederick
Wootten, George Simmons, Jr.
Wootton, Michael Duane
Worachek, John Edward
Worden, George Jerome
Workman, George Henry
Workman, Lloyd E.
Worley, Marvin George, Jr.
Worrell, Frederick Marquis
Worrell, Mary Thora Lewis
Worrell, William James
Worsek, Ernest David
Worth, Richard Lee
Worth, Robert Marshall, Jr.
Wortham, James Calvin
Worthington, James Norman
Worthington, Lorne Raymond
Wortley, Charles Allen
Woutila, Norman Emerson
Woyczynski, Wojbor Andrzej
Wozencraft, Marian
Wozniak, Sam
Wrage, John Russel
Wrangell, Lewis Joseph
Wray, Beth E.
Wright, Alfred George James
Wright, Beverly Ruth
Wright, Celia S.
Wright, Charles Howard
Wright, David Burton
Wright, Donald Carlyle
Wright, Donald Eugene
Wright, Doris Jean
Wright, Edward Benton, Jr.
Wright, Eldon Millard
Wright, George Forest
Wright, Harry Smith, Jr.
Wright, Helen Kennedy
Wright, James Lynn
Wright, James Mercer
Wright, John Leslie
Wright, Johnson Kent
Wright, Joseph William, Jr.
Wright, Katheryn Thorne
Wright, Kay Morrow
Wright, Mark Leslie
Wright, Michael Stevenson
Wright, Peter Henry
Wright, Raymond Clifford
Wright, Robert Lee
Wright, Robert Oren
Wright, Robert Richard
Wright, Robert W(illiams)
Wright, Rodney Hugh
Wright, Russell Barry
Wright, Ted Byron
Wright, Walter Bartlett
Wright, Wilbur E.
Wright, William Edward
Wrigley, William
Wrobley, Ralph Gene
Wrona, Bernard John
Wrone, David Roger
Wroolie, Melvin Simon
Wu, Harry Pao-Tung
Wu, Hsin-Hsiung
Wu, Kenneth Kun-yu
Wu, Tai Te
Wulf, George Richard
Wurfel, David Omer Drury
Wutz, Franklin Charles
Wyatt, M(elaine) Mildred
Wylie, Chalmers Pangburn
Wyman, Austin Lowell
Wyman, Marvin Eugene
Wyman, Paul Bartram
Wyman, William Arthur
Wymore, John Benjamin
Wynn, George Allan
Wynn, William Thomas
Wyse, Harold Gabriele
Wyslotsky, Ihor
Wysong, Walter Lee
Wyszynski, Richard Chester
Wyte, William C.
Wytrwal, Joseph Anthony
Yackel, John Peter
Yacktman, Victor
Yaffe, Dorothy Anne
Yagello, Virginia Elizabeth
Yakura, Thelma Pauline Masticola (Mrs. James N. Yakura)
Yammine, Riad Nassif
Yang, Eashy
Yang, Eugene Li Chun
Yang, Patrick Yuhmin
Yankoski, John Joseph
Yantis, Daniel Lee
Yantis, Ethel May Beaty (Mrs. Norval K. Yantis)
Yantis, John Aubrey
Yantis, John Thomas
Yao, Joseph Hung
Yap, Chong-Bun
Yap, Enrique Tan
Yashon, David
Yassin, Robert Alan
Yates, Curtis Hunter
Yates, Sidney R(ichard)
Yates, William Miller
Yau, Stephen Sik-Sang
Yaw, Peter Barnett
Yaw, William Harvey
Yeates, Charles Herbert
Yee, Teodorico Chiong
Yeh, Pai Tao
Yelland, Wayne Douglas
Yen, Shing Ie
Yenerich, George Wesley
Yesner, Michael Alan
Yessik, Michael John
Yock, Gordon August
Yoder, Frederick Floyd
Yoest, Donald Deane
Yohe, Richard Royal
Yoho, Robert Oscar
Yokom, Richard Ashton
Yomine, Daniel Joseph
Yon, Wyatt Schaller
Yorde, Betty Smith
York, Joseph Russell
York, Willie Ray
Yost, Charles Edward
Yost, William Kent
Youakim, Maurice Yacoub
Youel, David Bruce
Youle, (John) Clinton
Youlios, James
Young, Arthur LeRoy
Young, Clyde William
Young, Donald E.
Young, Gary Edward
Young, George Gordon
Young, Gerald
Young, H. Edwin
Young, Harold Chester
Young, John Harley
Young, John Paul
Young, Kent Alan
Young, Lamar Lewis, Jr.
Young, Michael Kenneth
Young, Milton R.
Young, Peggy Marie Sanborn
Young, Richard Emerson
Young, Robert Anton
Young, Robert Arthur
Young, Robert Lawrence
Young, Roxey Chester
Young, Sumner Bacheler
Young, Sumner Sullivan
Young, Verna Jean
Young, Vernon Eugene
Young, William George
Youngberg, Holger Ray
Youngberg, Manley Donald
Youngberg, Robert Stanley
Youngblood, John L.
Youngren, Ralph Park
Youngren, Wayne Alfred
Youngs, Vernon Leroy
Youssef, Tawfik Karam
Youssi, Francis Edward
Yovicich, George Steven Jones
Yowell, Donald Lee
Yowell, George Kent
Yu, Fermin Tong
Yuenger, David Anthony
Yun, Suk Koo
Yung, R. Dale
Yurk, Gerald John
Zabecki, David Tadeusz
Zablocki, Clement John
Zachariah, Mathew
Zacher, Peter Michael
Zacks, Shelemyahu
Zadek, Robert Lawrence
Zadrozny, Mitchell George
Zahn, Bert Charles
Zak, Edward Joseph
Zakon, Samuel Joseph
Zaks, Misha S.
Zalba, Serapio Richard
Zaletel, Joe Henry
Zampa, Victor Michael
Zander, Henry Edward
Zanger, Larry Martin
Zangrando, Joanna Schneider
Zangwill, Willard Ira
Zapp, Hans Roland
Zappola, Peter Charles
Zaret, Matthew Elias
Zaricznyj, Basilius
Zarif, Abbas
Zaring, Philip Brewer
Zarish, Joseph Frederick
Zaroslinski, John Felix
Zarse, Leigh Bryant
Zaun, Robert LeRoy
Zavala, Donald Charles
Zaworski, Bernard Edward
Zech, Arthur Conrad
Zehnder, William J., Jr.
Zehring, John William
Zeigler, Earle Frederick
Zeimet, Edward Joseph
Zeissler, Renate Hare
Zeitinger, Robert Carl, Sr.
Zeitner, C. Albert
Zekman, Pamela Lois
Zelasko, Theodore Edward
Zelin, Robert Edward
Zelinkoff, Milton Arnold
Zelkowitz, Leo
Zeller, Gerald Leroy
Zeller, John Paul
Zemel, Lou
Zemjanis, Raimunds
Zemlicka, Jirí
Zeni, Betty Joy Wagner
Zentz, Larry Ervin
Zeoli, William Judson
Zepf, Thomas Herman
Zerbi, Paul Genoese
Zibell, Donald Frederick
Zichek, Melvin Eddie
Zick, Leonard O.
Zick, Thomas Russell
Ziebarth, Robert Charles
Ziegler, Duane Herbert
Ziemelis, Andris
Zien, Burt
Zien, Hwa Ming
Zienty, Ferdinand Benjamin
Zigerell, James Joseph
Zike, Victor Milton
Zilles, Leland Carl
Zillman, Roy Stuart
Zillmann, Robert Edward
Zilm, Karl Miller
Zilversmit, Arthur
Zima, Willard James, Jr.
Zimberg, Harvey

Zimmer, John H.
Zimmer, Karl R., Jr.
Zimmer, Robert Culver
Zimmerly, Isaac Preston
Zimmerman, David Neal
Zimmerman, Delano Elmer
Zimmerman, Donald Lee
Zimmerman, George Herbert
Zimmerman, George Rudolph
Zimmerman, Henry Abram, II
Zimmerman, Jerry Lee
Zimmerman, Mary Ann
Zimmerman, Mary Helen Campion
Zimmerman, William
Zinam, Oleg
Zingale, Frank Lee
Zinn, Larry Orlan
Zinneman, Horace Helmut
Zinschlag, Edward Niehoff
Zipf, Robert Eugene, Jr.
Zishka, Ronald Louis
Ziska, Richard Francis
Zitz, Martin
Zizes, Peter Antonios
Zobel, Herbert Lawrence
Zobel, Milton Milford
Zobenica, Ronald Milan
Zoeller, Gilbert Norbert
Zoellner, Weldon Joseph
Zoglio, Michael Anthony, Jr.
Zold, Edwin Joseph
Zondervan, Mary Swier
Zondervan, Peter (Pat) John
Zonia, Dhimitri
Zook, Elvin Glenn
Zook, Robert Louis
Zopf, David Edward
Zorn, Timothy John
Zornow, Harry Benjamin
Zornow, William Frank
Zrim, Marion John
Zsigmond, Elemér Kalman
Zubroff, Leonard Saul
Zucker, Adele Haber
Zucker, Robert Louis
Zuckerberg, Harvey David
Zuckerman, Stuart
Zumhagen, Vernon Eugene
Zumkehr, Charles Eugene
Zung, Thomas Tse-Kwai
Zunkel, Virgil Lee
Zwack, Clarence Anton
Zydlo, Stanley Mathew

Aaroe, William Henry
Aaronson, Alfred Enoch
Abbey, Joe Beverly
Abbott, Benjamin Edward, Jr.
Abbott, Henry Eugene, Jr.
Abbott, Herschel Lee, Jr.
Abbott, Preston Sargent
Abbott, Robert Earl, Jr.
Abbott, Thomas Benjamin
Abbott, Walter Patton
Abdullah, Tariq H. (Henry Cephus Nichols)
Abdulrahman, Mustafa Salih
Abel, Paul Louis
Abel, Thomas Crawford
Abella, Rosa Margarita
Abels, Mac Jon
Abercrombie, Ralph L.
Abernethy, Byron Robert
Abernethy, Robert Bruce
Ablard, Russell Allyn
Able, Sothoron Kirby
Able, Virginia Neil
Ables, Richard Frank
Ablon, Arnold Norman
Ablon, Benjamin Manuel
Abney, James Marion, Jr.
Abraham, George G.
Abraham, George Lester
Abraham, Joshy
Abrahams, Lawrence Michael
Abrahamsen, Christine Elizabeth Campbell
Abrahamson, William Gene
Abrams, Maynard Alvin
Abramson, Louis, Jr.
Abrego, Gilbert Frederick, Jr.
Abreu-Elias, Jose
Absher, Lee Alton
Abt, Fred William
Acers, Maurice
Achee, Roland Joseph
Achorn, Frank Perron
Ackel, Fred John
Ackenbom, Charles Raymond
Acker, David De Peyster
Acker, Joseph Edington, Jr.
Acker, W. L. (Lou)
Acker, Warren Harlan
Ackerman, Charles Stanley
Ackerman, Richard Henry
Ackerman, Robert Featherston
Ackerman, Roy Alan
Acosta, William Capers
Acree, William Byrnes
Acton, Ronald Terry
Acuff, John Edgar
Adair, John Robert Chamberlain
Adams, Alfred Bernard, Jr.
Adams, Anne Hutchinson
Adams, Barbara Cole
Adams, Benjamin Michael
Adams, Beulah Grace Jenkins (Mrs. Addison Frank Adams)
Adams, Crawford William
Adams, Donald Eugene
Adams, Edward Quincy
Adams, Effie Kaye
Adams, Ernestine
Adams, Ezra John
Adams, F. Jack
Adams, George Cotton Smith
Adams, Harland Morrison
Adams, Hazel Greenlee Redfearn (Mrs. Payton F. Adams II)
Adams, Herbert Fleet, Jr.
Adams, Howell Garrett
Adams, Jacqueline
Adams, James Carlie, II
Adams, James Irwin
Adams, James Llewellyn
Adams, James Norman
Adams, James Wayne, Jr.
Adams, Jeremy Duquesnay
Adams, Jerry Arnold
Adams, Jerry Clayton
Adams, Jesse Earl
Adams, Jewel Hamilton
Adams, Jim Mills
Adams, John Bradley
Adams, John Cecil, Jr.
Adams, John Edward
Adams, John Fisher, Jr.
Adams, John Kenneth
Adams, John Quincy
Adams, John Quincy
Adams, K.S., Jr.
Adams, Lamar Taft
Adams, Larry Joe
Adams, Lawrence H.
Adams, Leon Ashby
Adams, Lloyd Clark
Adams, Louis William
Adams, Paul Woolman
Adams, Perry Ronald
Adams, Richard Leon
Adams, Robert Allen
Adams, Russell Lee
Adams, Salvatore Charles
Adams, Sarah Frances Ruth Smith
Adams, Warren Ernest
Adcock, Eva Jacqueline
Adcock, Ken Rayburn
Adcock, Willis Alfred
Addington, Milton Caldwell
Addiscott, Derek Herbert
Addison, Harold Victor
Adem, Julian
Adema, Shirley Jean
Aden, Robert Clark
Adkins, Richard Eugene
Adkins, William Witty, Sr.
Adkison, Duane Turner
Adkisson, David Flintoff
Adler, George Theodore
Adler, Lawrence
Adler, Louis Kootz
Adler, Robert
Afflerbach, Raymond Ernest
Afield, Walter Edward
Agee, William Cameron
Aglio, Thomas Joseph
Agnello, Samuel Anthony
Agnew, Jeanne Lecaine (Mrs. Theodore Agnew, Jr.)
Agnew, Mary Kathryn
Agnew, Theodore Lee, Jr.
Agoos, Lawrence David
Agreda, Victor Hugo
Aguila, Daniel Dumuk
Aguilar, Enrique Jose
Ahearn, John Francis
Ahearne, Daniel Paul
Ahlburn, Byron Trotter
Ahlgren, James David
Ahlstrom, Robert George
Ahmad, Farrukh Iftikhar
Ahmann, Donald Henry
Ahmed, Shafaat
Ahmed, Sheik Basheer
Ahmed, Suheel
Ahn, John Seungun
Ahnstrom, Doris Newell
Ahr, Wayne Merrill
Ahrabi, Robert
Ahrens, Frederick Phillip
Ahrens, Merlin Rollo
Aiken, Hugh Holcombe, Jr.
Aikman, William Henry
Ailor, James Richard
Ailor, William Henry, Jr.
Airan, Damodar Sarup
Airth, Alfred Thomas
Aitkens, John Lorry
Ajalat, Dick Saba
Ajax, Michael Fleming
Ajello, Libero
Akamatsu, Yasuyuki
Akerman, Joseph Lax
Akers, Michael James
Akers, Wilburn Holt
Akers, William Walter
Akin, Ralph Hardie, Jr.
Akin, Ted Martin
Al-Abdulla, Hamid Mohammed
Alaimo, Anthony A.
Alala, Joseph Basil, Jr.
Alavi, S. Manuchehr
Alba, Enrique
Albach, Henry John, IV
Alberga, Alta W.
Albers, Richard Lee
Albert, Hyden Allen
Albert, James Weldon (Jim)
Albert, Jones Ross
Alberts, Charlene Edith
Alberts, Harold
Alberts, Hendrik Cornelis
Albertson, Harold D.
Albertson, Herbert Howard, Jr.
Albright, Boyce Singleton
Albright, Cooper Eugene
Albright, Jere Baxter, Sr.
Albright, Spencer Delancey, Jr.
Albritton, Robert Bynum
Albritton, William Harold, III
Albury, Charles Baughman
Alday, Gonzalo
Alderete, Joseph Frank
Alderman, Louis Cleveland, Jr.
Aldred, Richard David
Aldrich, Lyman Davenport
Aldridge, Claudia Kay
Aldridge, Richard Campbell, Jr.
Alewine, James William
Alexander, A. E.
Alexander, Annie Florine
Alexander, Aubrey Murray, Jr.
Alexander, Dietrich Biemann, Jr.
Alexander, Edward Curtis
Alexander, Ewell Frederick
Alexander, George Moyer
Alexander, James Atwell
Alexander, James Edwin
Alexander, Larry Jack
Alexander, Louis
Alexander, Mary Louise
Alexander, Pauline Hill (Mrs. James Atwell Alexander)
Alexander, Ralph Lawrence
Alexander, Richard Gerald
Alexander, Robert Harold
Alexander, Theodor Walter
Alexander, Thomas Eaton, Jr.
Alexander, William Moore
Alexander, William Vollie, Jr.
Alexeff, Igor
Alfert, Harold Joseph
Alfonso, Josephine Mary
Alford, Charles Aaron, Jr.
Alford, Farra McRae
Alford, Frederick Fergus, Jr.
Alford, James Durham
Alford, Xelpert Gurney
Alfriend, Sue Landon
Allan, Jerry Duane
Allan, Walter Everett
Allan, Young Jess, Jr.
Allbaugh, Charles Edgar
Allderdice, Thomas Gilmore
Allee, W. Arthur
Allen, Annie Bell
Allen, Cheryl Jones
Allen, Clarence Boyce
Allen, Clarence Lee
Allen, Clifford Robertson
Allen, Clifton Judson
Allen, Constance Olleen
Allen, Don Lee
Allen, Donald Cole
Allen, Edward Dudley
Allen, Emory Raworth
Allen, Ensil Ross
Allen, Floyd Lee
Allen, Frank Carroll
Allen, Fred Edwin
Allen, Frederick Roger
Allen, George Irving
Allen, Herbert
Allen, Hilary Whitaker
Allen, J(esse) Daniel
Allen, James Stewart
Allen, Joe Wade
Allen, John Chiles
Allen, John David
Allen, John Eldridge
Allen, John Owen
Allen, Josephine Butler
Allen, Karen Sue
Allen, Kermit
Allen, Lawrence David
Allen, Lewis, Jr.
Allen, Loretta Belle Broome (Mrs. Clarence Canning Allen)
Allen, Lullavee Rogers
Allen, Mark Steven
Allen, Mary Wyatt
Allen, Maryon Pittman
Allen, Nell Ruth
Allen, Phillip Elwood
Allen, Rachel Zachariah
Allen, Robert Dee
Allen, Robert Watson
Allen, Roland Harold
Allen, Thomas Jefferson
Allen, Walter Gregory, Jr.
Allen, Willard Miles
Alley, J. T., Jr.
Allgeier, Robert Keith
Allin, John Maury
Allison, Claude Ferrell
Allison, Hansell Jack
Allison, Irl
Allison, Jimmy Earl
Allison, John Wallace, Jr.
Allison, Marshall L.
Allmon, Joseph Thurman
Allongo, Faustino
Allred, Jerry Michael
Alls, Willard Jess, Jr.
Allsbrook, Ogden Olmstead, Jr.
Almeida, José Agustín
Almon, Janet Newton
Almon, Robert Nathaniel
Almond, Edward Mallory
Alonge, Michael Stephan
Alston, Clinton Angus
Alston, Patricia Ann
Alston, Paul Perry
Alston, Syrus William
Alter, Ronald
Altieri, Pablo Ivan
Altman, James Earnest
Altman, William Mandell
Altom, William Harvey
Altshuler, Harold Leon
Altshuler, Kenneth Z.
Alva, Jose Dolores
Alvarado, Joe Sandoval
Alvarez, Julio Enrique
Alvarez, Marcelo A.
Alvarez-Bejar, Roman
Alves, Rex Douglas
Alvis, James Chester
Alvis, Richard Darwin
Amacker, David Muir
Amadeo, Jose H.
Amason, Yates Middleton
Amato, Albert Louis
Ambrose, Charles Edward
Ambuhl, Jane Dutton Hall
Amburn, Luther Franklin, Jr.
Amerman, Almeron Earl, Jr.
Ames, Donald Eugene
Ames, Harold Stancey
Ames, William Francis
Amick, Hubert Ray
Amick, Stanley Eugene
Amir-Moez, Ali Reza
Ammermann, Ernest Gifford
Ammons, Rose Mary
Amos, Marvin Cyril
Anagnost, Timothy George
Anand, Vir Daman
Anday, Mehmet C.
Anderson, Benjamin Kennedy, Jr.
Anderson, Billy
Anderson, Bruce Gray
Anderson, Clarence Alfred, II
Anderson, Clayton Earle
Anderson, Conwell Axel
Anderson, Curtis Andrew
Anderson, DeWayne Henry
Anderson, Donald Lee
Anderson, Edmund Theodore, III
Anderson, Frank Clay
Anderson, Frank Gist, Jr.
Anderson, Frank John
Anderson, Fredrick Eben
Anderson, George Raymond
Anderson, Hayward Sullivan
Anderson, Hubert Maxwell, Jr.
Anderson, James Lloyd
Anderson, James William
Anderson, Jerry Ray
Anderson, Joan Scheuermann
Anderson, John Carson, Jr.
Anderson, John Henderson
Anderson, John (Larry) Washington, III
Anderson, Joseph William
Anderson, Josie Burnett
Anderson, Justice Conrad
Anderson, Lavere Francis Shoenfelt (Mrs. French Anderson)
Anderson, Louis Thompson, Jr.
Anderson, Mable Bell
Anderson, Marian McCutchen (Mrs. William White Anderson)
Anderson, Mary Elizabeth Wicker
Anderson, R. Bruce W.
Anderson, Rae Roy
Anderson, Richard McLemore
Anderson, Richmond Karl
Anderson, Robert Cletus
Anderson, Robert Gordon, Jr.
Anderson, Robert Harper
Anderson, Robert Saville, Sr.
Anderson, Thomas Harold
Anderson, Thomas Nolan
Anderson, Ursula Mary
Anderson, W. E. (Andy)
Anderson, Willard Woodbury
Anderson, William Ernest, Jr.
Anderson, William Evan
Andes, Joan Keenen
Andes, Willard Abe
Andrade, Luciano Pedro
Andreasen, Samuel Gene
Andreu, Jose
Andrew, Garland Waldo
Andrew, William Frank
Andrews, Claude Leonard
Andrews, David John
Andrews, Doris Mildred
Andrews, Edwin Everts
Andrews, Ernest Charles
Andrews, Harvey Wellington
Andrews, Henry G., Jr.
Andrews, James Claire
Andrews, Martin Fitzgerald
Andrews, William Cooke
Andrews, William Frederick
Andrews, William Frederick
Andriot, Jeanne Kurz
Andujar, John J.
Aneja, Viney Pal
Ang, James Sia
Anger, Charles Leroy
Angers, Bradford John
Angle, Magruder Lee, Jr.
Anglin, W(illiam) E(nglish)
Anguizola, Gustave A.
Ankrum, Ward Elwood
Ansley, Robert Edward
Anthony, Carter Eugene
Anthony, James Elmer, Jr.
Anthony, John William
Anthony, Lonnie Leslie, Jr.
Anthony, Thomas Nile
Antoine, Eugene Alfred, Jr.
Antoine, Janet Anne Abrath
Apelt, Walter Edward
Apinis, John
Aponte, Martinez Luis
Aponte, Rafael Isidoro, Jr.
Apostolopoulos, Andrew Spiros
Appel, William George
Apple, Melvin J.
Applegate, Charles Stanley, Jr.
Apton, Ralph Julius
Aranda, Miguel Angel
Arango, Jorge Sanin
Arant, Hugh David
Araya, Pedro Alfonso
Arbib, John A.
Arboleda, Saul
Arbuckle, David Stuart
Arburn, Robert William
Arceneaux, George, Jr.
Arceneaux, William
Archer, Chalmers, Jr.
Archer, William Reynolds, Jr.
Archibald, John Duncan
Ard, Harold Jacob
Ard, Jack Tammany
Arenson, Nathan
Argianas, Charles Paul
Argo, James Walker
Argo, John
Ariail, Timothy Paul
Arkin, L. Jules
Arman, Nurhan Arthur
Armand, Ruth Hall
Armbrecht, William Henry
Armbrecht, William Henry, III
Armbrister, Douglas Kenley
Armenis, Spyridon
Armour, Charles Rudolph
Armour, Tommy Ray
Arms, Thomas Olen
Armstrong, Edward Rodney
Armstrong, Elizabeth Louise (Mrs. Bob Junius Armstrong)
Armstrong, Elmer E.
Armstrong, Ethel Vick-Crawley
Armstrong, James Clyde
Armstrong, Michael Keith
Armstrong, Newton Eells
Armstrong, Walter Preston, Jr.
Armstrong, William Harrison, Jr.
Arndt, Timothy Howard
Arnett, Eugene Britton, Jr.
Arnett, Lyda McClellen
Arnett, Robert Kenneth
Arnette, Charles Byron
Arnold, Bill Roy
Arnold, Dan McCay
Arnold, Glen Eldred
Arnold, Gordon Bruce
Arnold, Ira Lee
Arnold, Louis Walker
Arnold, Luther Bishop, Jr.
Arnold, Peter Vaughn
Arnold, Philip Mills
Arnold, Phillip Hayes
Arnold, Roger Murray
Arnold, William Brent
Arnott, Howard Joseph
Arnoult, Joseph Francis
Arnow, Herbert Irving
Arnow, Winston Eugene
Arnwine, Don Lee
Aron, Adrienne
Aronson, Earl Vernon, Jr.
Aronson, Frances Anne Rouse
Arrington, Edward Lee, Jr.
Arrington, John Leslie, Jr.
Arrington, Pamela Gray (Mrs.)
Arroyo, Josefina Santiago
Arsuaga, Anibal L.
Arthur, Susan
Artman, Joe David
Asay, Otto Otis Francis
Asbury, Louis Humbert, Jr.
Ascherl, John Lawrence
Ash, Frederick Curtis
Ashby, Eugene Christopher
Ashby, John Edmund, Jr.
Ashby, Jon Kenneth
Ashcraft, Ronald Eugene
Ashe, David Crockett
Asher, Fred M.
Ashington-Pickett, Michael Derek
Ashkar, Fuad Salamah
Ashler, Philip Frederic
Ashley, Billy Hilton
Ashley, Carl Thomas
Ashley, Donn Langdon
Ashley, Edward Everett, III
Ashley, Olin Burrell
Ashley, Thelma Townsend (Mrs. Jerry Ashley)
Ashlock, James Robert
Ashman, Lee Earle
Ashton, Samuel Collier
Ashworth, Kenneth Hayden
Askew, Reubin O'Donovan
Askew, Robert Edward
Askins, Allen Whitsett, Jr.
Assaad, Wafaa Fakhry
Astle, Christopher Albert
Astler, Vernon Benson
Astone, Joseph Aloysius
Atac, Ustun
Atchley, Fielding Hurst
Athanasakos, Elizabeth
Atherton, Holt
Atherton, James Christian
Atkins, Carl Clyde
Atkins, Franklin Hugh
Atkins, Hardin Louis, Jr.
Atkins, Joseph Noble
Atkins, Orin Ellsworth
Atkins, Theodore William, III
Atkinson, Carrol Holloway
Atkinson, Evelyn Rorex
Atkinson, Frances Gobble
Atkinson, Leslie Lee
Atkinson, Marjorie Fagen
Atkinson, Robert Poland
Atkinson, Thomas Scott
Atkinson, William James, Jr.
Atlas, Robert Henry
Aton, James Keyes, Jr.
Atteberry, William Louis
Atwater, John Spencer
Atwill, Joseph Harvey, Jr.
Atwill, William Henry
Auerbach, Anita L.
August, Henry
Augustine, Norman Ralph
Aukland, Elva Dayton
Ausband, John Rufus
Austin, Barbara Elizabeth
Austin, Clarence Wesley, Jr.
Austin, Delano Hart
Austin, Jack
Austin, John Paul
Austin, Larry D.
Austin, Thomas LeRoy
Austin, Warren Barker
Auten, Melvin Ray
Autry, Mayme Blankinship (Mrs. David Edgar Autry)
Autry, Otwa Tilden
Avant, David Alonzo, Jr.
Avellan, Joaquin
Avellone, Theodore Marcel
Aven, Alexander Phipps
Aven, Hilrey Leon
Averbuch, Philip Fred
Averill, John Montague
Averitt, Franklin Murphy
Avery, Edwina Austin
Avery, Mary Elizabeth (Mrs. Wilfred M. Avery)
Avery, Parnell Napoleon
Avery, Wilfred Mabry
Avigael, Jack Ronald
Aviles, Wilma Ida
Avril, Colette
Awis, Jo Ellen Terese
Axelrad, Sylvia Rosen
Axtell, Frank Foy
Axtman, William Henry
Axton, William Fitch
Ayad, Joseph Magdy
Aye, Ralph Claxton
Ayer, Anthony Jenney
Ayers, Anne Louise
Ayers, Gaylord Lew
Ayers, James Gilbert
Ayers, Nicky Alexandrides
Ayers, Walter Cary
Ayres, Laurence Thomason
Ayscue, Billy Newcomb
Azam, Ahmad Farouk
Azar, Henry Amin
Babb, Donald Quentin
Babb, (Joseph) Glenn
Babb, Herbert Eugene
Babette, Anita
Babin, Joseph Allie, Jr.
Bacchus, Robert Edward
Bachi, Michael Mario
Bachman, John Andrew, Jr.
Bachner, John Philip
Back, William Tecumseh
Backer, Warren Howard Alonzo
Bacon, Charles Edward
Bacon, Kenneth Harrison
Bacon, Phillip
Bacon, Phyrne Youens
Bacon, William Arthur
Bacot, Henry Parrott, Jr.
Badders, Hurley Edmund
Badger, Norman Sydney
Badger, Peter Whittemore
Badgett, Jimmie Leon
Badillo, Jorge
Badke, Frank Charles, Jr.
Badke, Gregory Charles
Badouh, Edward, Jr.
Baer, Michael
Baer, William Harold
Bafalis, Louis Arthur
Bagby, William Rardin
Baggett, Agnes
Baggett, Durward Augustus
Baggett, Jimmy Dean
Baggs, Leah L. Bates (Mrs. Linton Daniel Baggs, Jr.)
Baggs, Linton Daniel, Jr.
Bagwell, Charles Malcolm
Bagwell, Jesse Clinton
Bagwell, Lewis Hobson, Jr.
Bahar, David
Bahn, Gilbert Schuyler
Bahner, Thomas Maxfield
Baier, A. Leigh
Baier, Ronald Anton
Bailey, Alden Orville
Bailey, Alfred William
Bailey, Amos Purnell
Bailey, Charles Williams, III
Bailey, Edgar Daniel
Bailey, Fred Oliver, Jr.
Bailey, Harry Hudson
Bailey, Henrietta
Bailey, Herman Ray
Bailey, James Lovell
Bailey, John Alan
Bailey, John Albert
Bailey, Kenneth Duane
Bailey, Kincheon Hubert, Jr.
Bailey, Lloyd Whitfield
Bailey, Ocie Judson
Bailey, Robert Pendleton
Bailey, Ronald Beresford
Bailey, Ronnie Saul
Bailey, Scott Field
Bailey, William S.
Bailie, Robert Edward
Bain, Emily Johnston
Bain, William Donald, Jr.
Bainbridge, Thomas Rutherford
Baine, John Raymond
Bair, Barbara Breithaupt
Bair, Clifford Edwin
Baird, Bruce Douglas
Baird, Dale Seymour
Baird, Duke Barnett

Baird, Edward Allen
Baird, Harry Haynes
Baird, Haynes Wallace
Baird, Howard Melville, Jr.
Baird, Larry Don
Baird, William Bruce
Baisier, Bernard Leon
Baker, Bruce A.
Baker, Bruce Robert
Baker, Carleton Harold
Baker, Clifford Howard
Baker, David Hodge, Jr.
Baker, Francis William
Baker, George Dorset
Baker, George Wilber
Baker, Glenn Earl
Baker, Horace Anson, Jr. (Pat)
Baker, Howard Henry, Jr.
Baker, Ira Lee
Baker, James Linton, Jr.
Baker, John Edward, Jr.
Baker, John Gordon
Baker, John Langston
Baker, John Willis
Baker, Kerry Allen
Baker, Leonard, Jr.
Baker, Marilyn Jeanine Miller (Mrs. Allyn Lee Baker)
Baker, Mary Jane
Baker, Michael Alan
Baker, Ollie Marie Osborn (Mrs. Russell Montez Baker, Sr.)
Baker, Orman C.
Baker, Robert Flowers
Baker, Roy Verble, Jr.
Baker, Russell Montez
Baker, Timothy Lee
Baker, William Duncan
Baker, William Horace
Baker, William Howard
Baker, William Thomas
Balabanis, Theofilos George
Balasso, Anthony Andrew
Bald, Margaret
Balda, Edward Joseph, Jr.
Balderrama, Francisco Encinas
Baldinger, Charlene Lois
Baldwin, Benjamin Armistead
Baldwin, Clyde Parris
Baldwin, Edwin Harold
Baldwin, Esther Lillian
Baldwin, Hugh John
Baldwin, Jack Lyell
Baldwin, Robert Clayton
Balentine, John LeRoy, III
Balentine, Robert Chapman
Balint, Francis Joseph
Balk, William Armstrong
Balkman, Nell Teeter
Ball, Bernard Caudill
Ball, Gene Lowther
Ball, Haywood Moreland
Ball, Ivan Estus
Ball, James Andrew
Ball, Lewis Edwin, II
Ball, Robert Jesse, Jr.
Ball, Stanton Mock
Ball, Thomas Prioleau, Jr.
Ballantine, William Thomas, Jr.
Ballard, George Speights, Jr.
Ballard, Glenn Arlen
Ballard, Harry Harold
Ballard, Robert Earl
Ballew, Harold Carl
Ballinger, John Kenneth
Balman, Sidney
Balnicky, Robert Gabriel
Balsley, Howard Lloyd
Balsley, Irol Whitmore (Mrs. Howard L. Balsley)
Bambach, Richard Karl
Banas, Norma Eliscu
Bancroft, Charles Yarrington
Bandelin, Frederick John
Bandera Olavarria, Jose
Bandy, William Henry
Banerjee, Auchin Kumar
Baney, Carl Ernest
Banister, Gary Lane
Banister, John Robert
Banks, Henry Thomas
Banks, Robert Thomas, Jr.
Banks, Sara Lynn
Banks, Virginia Anne
Banks, Warren Eugene
Banks, William Eugene
Banks, Wilson Harper
Baños, Jose Luis
Banta, James Elmer
Bañuelos, Delma Jean
Baptie, Charles
Baranowski, Richard Matthew
Barattini, Larry John
Barbay, Floyd Louis
Barber, Charles Edward
Barber, Franklin Weston
Barber, James Leo
Barber, Lloyd Ernest
Barber, Monty Clyde
Barber, Rodney Glen
Barber, William Joseph, Sr.
Barbles, Eugene Anthony
Barbot, Julian Augustus, Jr.
Barbour, Robert Franklin
Barclay, James Crawford
Barclay, James Ralph
Barczak, Virgil Joseph
Bardgett, Janet Cook
Bardin, Jesse Redwin
Bared, Jose P.
Barefoot, Sherwood Washington
Barfield, Bourdon Rea
Barfield, Donald Fred
Bargas, Joseph Edgar
Bargeon, Herbert Alexander, Jr.
Barger, Alphonso Sledge
Barger, Benjamin
Barginear, Jo Grace
Barham, Mack Elwin
Barker, A. Clifford
Barker, Carl Leon
Barker, Kenneth Reece
Barker, Newell Keith
Barker, William McKinley
Barkin, Jamie Steven
Barkley, Carolyn Esther
Barkley, G. Richard
Barkley, Robert Emmanuel
Barksdale, Ethelbert Courtland
Barley, George Emerson McKim
Barlow, Donal Edward
Barlow, Ronald Stephen
Barlow, Thomas James
Barnack, Robert Francis
Barnard, Billings
Barnard, Chris Allen
Barnard, D. Douglas, Jr.
Barnard, Edwin Wardsworth, Jr.
Barnard, Jacob Henry, Jr.
Barnard, William Kenneth
Barnes, Ben F.
Barnes, Benny Blair
Barnes, Charles Edward
Barnes, Grover Duane
Barnes, Herschiel Sevier
Barnes, John Evan, Jr.
Barnes, John Vanderslice, Jr.
Barnes, Joseph Edward
Barnes, Maggie Lue Shifflett (Mrs. Lawrence Barnes)
Barnes, Melver Raymond
Barnes, Nora A.
Barnes, Patsy Harris
Barnes, Richard Charles
Barnes, Rudolph Counts, Jr.
Barnes, Russell Miller
Barnes, Welden Fairbanks, Jr.
Barnes, William Edwin
Barnes, Winfield James
Barness, Lewis Abraham
Barnett, Benjamin Lewis, Jr.
Barnett, Bernard Harry
Barnett, Crawford Fannin, Jr.
Barnett, Ed Willis
Barnett, Franklin Dewees
Barnett, James Allen, Jr.
Barnett, Jimmy Lyle
Barnett, Juanita McMillan
Barnett, Leroy Elliot
Barnett, Louis, Jr.
Barnett, William Halbert
Barnett, William Oscar
Barnett, William Woodson, Jr.
Barnhardt, William McLaughlin
Barnhart, Bobby James
Barnhart, Harry Bascomb, Jr.
Barnhart, Joe Edward
Barnhart, Paul Fred
Barnhill, John Williamson, Jr.
Barns, William Derrick
Baron, Frederick Martin
Baron, Howard Naftali
Baron, Ira Saul
Barona, Narses Montes de Ocá
Barondess, Stuart Henry
Barone, Anthony Joseph
Barone, Bartolo Mariano
Barone, Betty Lou
Barr, Carol Gelo
Barr, Jean Lenore
Barranger, Miriam Ruth Garic (Mrs. Dalton Joseph Barranger)
Barrett, David Laun
Barrett, Henry Charles
Barrett, James Lee
Barrett, Joseph Michael
Barrett, Robert Ellington
Barrett, Rolin Farrar
Barrett, William Arvel
Barringer, Paul Brandon
Barringer, Thad Jones
Barron, Clinton Egbert, Jr.
Barron, Oran James, Jr.
Barron, Oscar Noel
Barron, Robert Duncan
Barron, Roger L.
Barron, Thomas Willis
Barroso, Fernando Jose Manuel Luis
Barrow, Allen Edward
Barry, James Joseph
Barry, John Timothy
Barry, Thomas Martin, Jr.
Bartels, Roger Joseph
Barth, Alf Otto
Barth, Robert Frederick
Bartha, Louis Alexander
Barthet, Ron LaMar
Bartholomew, Samuel Wilson, Jr.
Bartlett, Charles Samuel, Jr.
Bartlett, Dewey Follett
Bartlett, Jack Arnold
Bartley, Jerald Howard
Bartolo, Adolph Marion
Barton, Alexander James
Barton, Jack Quinn
Barton, James Gabriel
Barton, James Howard
Bartscht, Heri Bert
Bartscht, Waltraud Erika
Barze, Keith Egbert
Basecki, Richard Marian
Bashaw, Elexis Cook
Basinger, Andrew Marshall, II
Basiuk, Victor
Baskin, Roy Howard, Jr.
Baskin, William Gresham
Baskin, William P.
Basler, Loren Stanley
Basore, Annie Terrell
Bass, Cornelius Graham
Bass, George Liston, Jr.
Bass, James David
Bass, James Roger
Bass, Joseph Alonzo
Bass, Samuel Earl
Bass, William Keays, Sr.
Bassett, Harry Hood
Bassett, Henrietta Elizabeth (Beth Bassett)
Bassett, John Edward
Bassett, Robert Ross, Jr.
Bassett, William Earl
Bast, Michael DeVault
Basto, John David
Batchelder, David George
Batcheller, David Springsteen
Batcheller, Joe Ann Deming (Mrs. David Springsteen Batcheller)
Bateman, Clinton Frank
Bateman, Dottye Jane Spencer
Bateman, John Roger
Baten, Wyeth Lee
Bates, Alfred Scott
Bates, Burwell Millard
Bates, Catherine West
Bates, Edward Ellett, Jr.
Bates, Hampton Robert, Jr.
Bates, Harry Eugene
Bates, J(ames) Edward
Bates, John Walter
Bates, John William
Bates, Joseph Henry
Bates, Will Lewis
Bates, William Simmons, Jr.
Bates-Nisbet, (Clara) Elisabeth
Batista de Rodriguez, Adelaide
Battaglia, Gaspare Francis, Jr.
Battell, William Putnam
Batten, Bobby Gale
Batten, James William
Batten, Sara Storey (Mrs. James William Batten)
Battin, (Rosabell Harriet) Ray
Battin, Robt Davis
Battiste, Edward Louis
Battle, Allen Overton, Jr.
Battle, Jimmie Lorene Nelson
Battle, Lucy Troxell (Mrs. J.A. Battle)
Battle, Mary Vroman
Battle, William Rainey
Battles, John Wade
Batton, Kenneth Duff
Batts, Lemia Clarence, Jr.
Bauch, Joy Coulter
Baucom, Joseph Nelson
Bauer, Charles Ronald
Bauer, John Henry
Bauer, Robert Edward
Baugh, Charles Milton
Baugh, John Bernard
Baugh, Mary Rose
Baughman, Samuel Nathan, Jr.
Baughn, Robert Elroy
Bauknight, Clarence Brock
Baum, George Frederick, Jr.
Bauman, Harvey Lee
Bauman, Mary Louise Craig
Baumann, Daniel Bruce
Baumbach, Donald Otto
Baumberger, Theodore Shriver
Baumgardner, Haynes Madden
Baumhover, Lorin Alois
Bautch, R. Thomas
Baxley, William Joseph
Baxter, Gene Kenneth
Baxter, George William, Jr.
Baxter, Harry Stevens
Baxter, Ida Mae Allen (Mrs. Walter Lawrence Baxter)
Baxter, Oscar Fitz-Alan, V
Baxter, Richard Duncan
Baxter, Robert Francis
Baxter, Turner Butler
Bayazeed, Abdo Fares
Bayer, Alvin, III
Baylen, Joseph Oscar
Bayless, Dan J.
Bayley, Gerald Anderson
Baylin, George Jay
Baylor, Allen Oscar
Baynard, William Thorn
Bays, Robert Payne
Bayshore, Charles Alexander
Beach, Cecil Prentice
Beach, Deryl Erwin
Beach, Dorothy Rigdon (Dore)
Beach, Robert Oliver
Beach, Robert Raphael
Beacham, Louise Harrison
Beacham, Woodard Davis
Beachley, Charles Edward, Jr.
Beachley, Michael Charles
Beadle, Leigh Patric
Beadles, Boyd James
Beahn, Raymond Anglum, II
Beaird, Charles T.
Beal, Ernest Oscar
Beall, Kenneth Sutter, Jr.
Beall, Ross Horace
Beaman, Lester Henry
Beamish, Patricia Mary
Bean, Donald James
Bean, Duward Clayton, Jr.
Bean, Frank Wilson
Bean, Larry
Beane, Dorothy Gene Moore
Beard, Alice Gamble (Mrs. Owen Wayne Beard)
Beard, Bob J.
Beard, Elizabeth Letitia
Beard, Gary Boyce
Beard, Marion Foree
Beard, Robert Lynn
Beard, Robin
Beard, W(illiam) Robinson Cook
Beardslee, Frederick Pardee
Beardsworth, Donald Eugene
Bearskin, Alvin Wesley
Beasley, Cloyd Orris, Jr.
Beasley, Dennis Raymond
Beasley, Frederick Alexander
Beasley, Jere Locke
Beasley, John Harvey
Beasley, Philip Gene
Beaton, John McCall
Beattie, Jack Robert
Beatty, Stanford George, Jr.
Beaty, Charles Edward
Beauchamp, Jeffery Oliver
Beaurline, Loyd Arthur
Beavers, Morris Eugene
Beavers, Thomas Claude
Beazley, Curtis Edward
Beazley, Jon Stanton
Beck, Dorris Dills
Beck, Emil Frederick, III
Beck, Esther Ann
Beck, George Preston
Beck, Hubert Frederick
Beck, Nancy Mann McConnico (Mrs. Earl Crafton Beck, Jr.)
Beckelhymer, Paul Hunter
Becker, Charles Herbert
Becker, Harry Thomas Alfred
Beckett, Joseph Courtney
Beckjord, Philip Rains
Beckman, Gail McKnight
Beckmann, George Claus, Jr.
Becks, Jewell Whitworth
Beda, Michael Francis
Bedenbaugh, Angela Lea Owen (Mrs. John Holcombe Bedenbaugh)
Bedenbaugh, George Roscoe
Bedford, John Joseph
Bedford, Madeleine Alann Peckham (Mrs. Charles Francis Bedford)
Bedotto, Carmine
Beebe, William Thomas
Beeman, Robert Lawrence
Beenhakker, Arie
Beers, William Townsend
Beese, Philip Sheridan, III
Beeson, Mary Ruth (Pete)
Beeuwkes, Lambert Baer
Begley, Michael Joseph
Begley, Robert Jennings
Behar, Raymond Jack
Behr, Lawrence Van der Poel
Behrman, Charlotte Edwards Maguire (Mrs. Mayes Behrman)
Beitzel, Barbara Ann
Bejar, Feliciano
Belcher, Daniel Joseph
Belcher, Don
Belcher, Don Wesley
Belcher, John Cheslow
Belcher, Rodney Lynn
Belenke, Burton
Belfiglio, Valentine John
Belger, Joseph Hugh
Belisle, Lenore Breetwor
Belk, Irwin
Belk, John Montgomery
Belk, Thomas Milburn
Belknap, Paul Alcon
Bell, Albert Howard
Bell, Aubrey Blan
Bell, Benjamin Grady
Bell, Bruce Arnold
Bell, Bryan
Bell, Calvin E.
Bell, Clarence Alton
Bell, Daniel Joseph, Jr.
Bell, Dorothy Ruth
Bell, Edward Thomas
Bell, Esther Bernice
Bell, Exter Frank, Jr.
Bell, Francis Laney
Bell, Gene Mason
Bell, George Guice, Jr.
Bell, Henry Roush, Jr.
Bell, Irving Lee
Bell, J.S.
Bell, J. Thomas, Jr.
Bell, James Bruce
Bell, James Carlton
Bell, Joanne Irene
Bell, Kenneth John
Bell, Lawrence Chandler
Bell, Lorraine Petties
Bell, Melvyn LeRoy
Bell, Mertys Ward (Mrs. Thomas Edward Bell)
Bell, Paul Buckner
Bell, Ross Leon
Bell, William Claude
Bell, William Jack
Bell, William Woodward
Bellah, Charlie Lewis
Bellamy, Jeanne (Mrs. John Turner Bills)
Bellamy, Robert Benton
Bellenger, James Faris
Bellmon, Henry
Bellows, Elbert George
Bellows, Thomas John
Bellus, Dan Edward
Belsches, James Cobert, Jr.
Beltran-Fortuny, Rafael
Benavides, Jaime Miguel
Benda, Charles Jefferson, Jr.
Bendelius, Arthur George
Bender, James Arthur
Bender, Norma Jean
Benedict, Charles Edward
Benedict, John Louis
Beneke, Charles Peter
Bengel, William Harold
Bengston, Gary Lynn
Bengtson, Paul Edward
Benham, Jack Edward
Benjamin, Blanche Sternberger
Benjamin, Edward B.
Benjamin, Edward Bernard, Jr.
Benjamin, Robert Stephen
Bennett, Allyn Charles
Bennett, Betty Besse
Bennett, Carroll Graves
Bennett, Charles Edward
Bennett, Franklin Davis
Bennett, Harry Jackson
Bennett, Ivan Stanley
Bennett, J. Claude
Bennett, Jacob Travis
Bennett, James Baxter
Bennett, James Thomas
Bennett, (James) Jefferson
Bennett, John Carlyle
Bennett, Luther Estes, Jr.
Bennett, Marshall Goodloe, Jr.
Bennett, Max Leon
Bennett, Richard Howell, Jr.
Bennett, Roger Mitchell
Bennett, Wayne Doyling
Bennie, William Andrew
Bennison, Bertrand Earl
Benoit, Clarence John
Benolken, Robert Marshall
Benowitz, H(erbert) Allen
Benski, Raymond
Benson, John Martin
Benson, Mary Louise Baker
Benson, Melvin Lee
Benson, Paul Harrison, Jr.
Benson, Stanley Hugh
Bent, Dorothy Florence (Mrs. Allen Emery Bent)
Bentley, Alonzo Joel
Bentley, Bernard Francis
Bentley, Fred Blake
Bentley, Fred Douglas
Bentley, Herschel Paul, Jr.
Bentley, James Robert
Bentley, Kenton Earl
Bentley, Robert Julian
Bentley, Virgil Temple
Bentley, William George
Benton, Arthur Louis
Benton, Edmund Hugh
Benton, Evelyn Fleming
Benton, Ishmael Claud
Benton, Larry James
Benton, Nicholas
Bentsen, Kenneth Edward
Bentsen, Lloyd
Benz, George Albert
Berard, Dailey Joseph
Berbary, Maurice Shehadeh
Bercaw, Beauregard Lee
Berchtold, Gladys Beaman
Berenson, Gerald Sanders
Berg, Ib Anthon
Berg, Jerald Allan
Bergan, Norman Arnold
Bergeaux, Philip James
Berger, Leonard
Berger, Richard Steil
Berger, Sidney Louis
Berger, William Ernest
Bergeron, Claude Ernest, Jr.
Bergeron, Jimmie Leon
Berggren, Glenn Merritt
Bergs, Victor Visvaldis
Bering, Conrad
Berke, Molly Haberman Moore
Berkeley, David Shelley
Berkeley, Francis Lewis, Jr.
Berken, Gilbert Harvey
Berkey, Barry Robert
Berkley, Fred Alexander
Berley, Ferdinand Victor
Berman, Howard Benjamin
Berman, Stephen Mark
Bermello, Guillermo Ruiz
Bernard, Clay, II
Bernard, John Gordon
Berni, Ralph John
Berninger, Joan A.
Bernstein, David Robert
Bernstein, Joseph
Berry, Corre Ivey
Berry, Frederic Aroyce, Jr.
Berry, Hardy Duane
Berry, Joyce Elaine Goodwin
Berry, Julia Elizabeth
Berry, Lemuel, Jr.
Berry, Lois Tharrington
Berry, Maxwell Rufus
Berry, Nancy Ann
Berry, Oscar Lee, Jr.
Berry, Thomas Authren
Berryhill, Henry Lee, Jr.
Berryhill, Walter Reece
Berryman, Robert Lee
Bersch, Robert Sherrill
Bersoff, Edward Hugh
Bert, Charles Wesley
Bertani, Charles Leonard
Bertini, Albert Joseph, II
Bertran, Carlos Enrique
Bertsch, C. Thomas
Besemann, Eberhard Franz
Beskin, Charles A.
Bess, Sonja Hartsell
Bessette, Henry Joseph
Besso, Joseph Augustus, Jr.
Bessone, Luis Nestor
Best, Clem Kirby, Jr.
Best, Edward Thomas
Best, Winfield Judson
Bethea, Barron
Bethea, William Lamar, Jr.
Bethel, Millard Baimbridge
Bethel, Paul Duane
Bethel, Shelba Jean
Bettersworth, John K(nox)
Bettis, Dorothy Dillard
Beutler, Larry Edward
Bevill, Tom
Bevins, Errette Shemmell, Jr.
Bevins, Thomas Peter, II
Bewely, Wesley Leon
Bexley, James Byron
Beyer, Gerald
Beyer, Kenneth May
Beyer, Patrick Lee
Beyers, Bernice West (Mrs. Robert A. Beyers)
Bhagchandani, Parmanand Atmaram
Bhajan, William Rudolph
Bhattacharya, Amit
Biasco, Frank
Bibb, Thomas Farris
Bibby, Francis Flavius
Bice, Ernest Gordon
Bickel, Caldwell Conrad, Jr.
Bickerstaff, Herman (Toby)
Bicknell, Kent
Bickner, John Oscar
Biddy, Joseph Burns
Bidez, Thelma Calhoun (Mrs. Earle Felton Bidez)
Bieley, Peggy Moses
Bien, Gary James
Bienvenu, Lionel Joseph
Bierley, John Charles
Bierman, Don Edward
Biery, John Carlton
Bieser, Albert Howard
Bigbee, Rosalynn (Lynn)
Bigbie, Charles Roy, Jr.
Bigda, Richard James
Bigelow, Maurice Hubbard
Biggers, William Paul
Biggs, Claribel
Biggs, E. Glenn
Bigham, Randy
Bigham, William Strickland
Biles, William Roy
Billiard, Charles Edward
Billings, Kenney
Billings, Ray Henry
Billingsley, David Lewis
Billingsley, William Everett
Billington, Ted Franklin
Billions, Novella Stafford
Bingham, Barry
Bingham, Edward Clark
Bingham, John Jay
Bingham, Louis Columbus
Bingham, Mary Caperton (Mrs. Barry Bingham)
Binning, Bette Finese (Mrs. Gene Hedgcock Binning)
Binning, Gene Hedgcock
Biolchini, Robert Fredrick
Birch, Larry Arthur
Birch, Stephen Lee
Birch, Wade Gordon
Birch, William Garry
Birchfield, Robert Boyd
Birchum, Donald Gene, Sr.
Bird, Daniel David
Bird, Francis Marion
Bird, Frank Edward, Jr.
Bird, George Tillotson
Bird, Ralph Sidney
Bird, William Prall
Birdwell, James Edwin, Jr.
Birdwell, Juanita Greer
Birk, William Frank
Birkenwald, Emil S.
Birmingham, Eugene
Biro, Nicholas George
Birznieks, Ilmars
Bisbee, Cynthia Gail Carson
Bischof, Edward Harold
Bisha, Raymond Edward
Bishop, Calvin Thomas
Bishop, Edwin Lyman
Bishop, George Williams, III
Bishop, Minnie Slade (Mrs. Sanford Dixon Bishop)
Bishop, Sid Glenwood
Bishop, Terry Neal
Bishop, Thomas Ray
Bishop, William David
Bishop, Winford Kent
Bisquerra, Jose Vila
Bisset, Norma Blakely
Bisson, Wheelock Alexander
Bitner, George E.
Bittel, Lester Robert
Bitter, William, Jr.
Biundo, Joseph James, Jr.
Bixby, Tams, III
Bjeletich, Dan
Black, Albert Scott
Black, Aubrey Kermit, Jr.
Black, Charles Alvin
Black, Clarence Ervin
Black, David Luther
Black, DeWitt Carlisle, Jr.
Black, Dorothy Faye
Black, Herbert Malone
Black, James Constanda
Black, James Milton
Black, James William
Black, John Clinton

Black, Kenneth, Jr.
Black, William Elmer
Black, William Stanley
Blackburn, George Marvin, III
Blackburn, Jean Mc Connell
Blackburn, John Gill
Blackburn, Mary Mc Williams
Blackburn, Robert McGrady
Blackburne, Terry Duane
Blacker, H. Martin
Blackford, George Williams
Blackman, Bruce Allen
Blackman, Murray
Blackmon, Jack Russell
Blackmon, Wilson Whitaker
Blackmore, James Douglas
Blackmore, James Herrall
Blackshear, Augustus Troy, Jr.
Blackstock, LeRoy
Blackstock, Mary Lillian (Mrs. Proctor L. Blackstock)
Blackstock, Virginia Lee Lowman (Mrs. LeRoy Blackstock)
Blackston, Joe Ronald
Blackwell, Anna Margaret Thompson (Mrs. Damian Lee Blackwell, Jr.)
Blackwell, Doctor Frederick, Jr.
Blackwell, Floyd Oris
Blackwell, Herman Newman
Blackwell, Jodie Gustavus
Blackwell, Lucy White
Blackwell, Lyle Marvin
Blaffer-Hrdy, Sarah
Blain, Keith Edward
Blair, Henry Clay
Blair, Herbert Loyd
Blair, John Doherty, Jr.
Blair, Marie Lenore
Blair, R(ichard) Charles
Blais, Michael Roland
Blais, Roger Nathaniel
Blake, Thomas Louis
Blake, William Dows
Blake, Wyatt Heflin, III
Blakeley, Robert Philip
Blakely, Charles Edward
Blakemore, John Sydney
Blakemore, Tina Cross (Hamilton)
Blakeney, Roger Neal
Blakey, Hubert Hieronymus
Blalock, Clyde Carroll
Blalock, John Vernon
Blan, Ollie Lionel, Jr.
Blanchard, Charles Fuller
Blanco, Julia Diane Keith (Mrs. Victorino Severo Blanco)
Blanco, Victorino Severo
Blanford, Irving Ivey
Blank, Carl Herbert
Blank, Horace Richard
Blank, Ralph John, Jr.
Blanken, Howard Michael
Blankenship, Asa Lee, Jr.
Blankenship, Barbara Elaine Stricklin (Mrs. Thomas Larry Blankenship)
Blankenship, Douglas Waldo
Blankenship, Harvey Taylor
Blankenship, James Emery
Blankenship, Lillian Bartlett (Mrs. Harvey Taylor Blankenship)
Blankenship, Martha Elise
Blanning, Robert Bressler
Blanton, Herbert Milton
Blanton, Hoover Clarence
Blanton, Jean Ann Saige (Mrs. Stewart Bennett Blanton)
Blanton, Leonard Ray
Blanton, Terrell Davis
Blasingame, Earl Benard
Blatherwick, Gerald Dayton
Blaydes, David Fairchild
Blaydes, James Elliott, Jr.
Blazer, Dan German, II
Blazer, John Allison
Blazquez Y Servin, Carlos Humberto
Bledsoe, John Truett
Bleich, Edward Joseph
Bleimann, Karl Richard
Blessey, Walter Jerome, IV
Blessington, Clement Auguston, Jr.
Blevins, Richard Gordon
Blewer, Glenda Gloria (Mrs. Alton George Blewer)
Blewster, Robert Edward
Blieden, Bert Lewis
Blincoe, George Early, Jr.
Bliss, Edward, Jr.
Bliznak, Johnny
Bloch, Stephen Ronald
Block, (Edward) Bates
Block, Harold Martin
Block, James Howard
Block, John Bradford
Blocker, Lonnie
Blomstrom, David Benjamin
Bloodworth, Albert William Franklin
Bloodworth, James Nelson
Bloomquist, James Clarence
Bloskas, John D.
Blosser, Dale Alan
Blosser, James Joseph
Blount, Floyd Eugene
Blow, William O'Neil
Blue, Robert Linson
Bluestein, Steven Michael
Blum, Dorothy Jean Scrivner
Blumberg, David Meyer
Blumentritt, Charles Wayne
Blunt, Jane Antoinette Lomax
Blythe, Edwin John, Jr.
Blythe, John Coley
Boardman, Katherine Baker Blackshear
Boatner, Frederick Le Roi
Bobbitt, John Maxwell
Bobko, Karol J.
Bockian, Herbert Harold
Boddeker, Edward William, III
Boddie, Arthur Walker, Jr.
Boddiford, Dyches V(illines)
Bodey, Gerald Paul
Bodin, Bruce Harold
Boehler, Jacqueline Bunn
Böer, Germain Boniface
Boercker, Fred Donald
Bogaev, Leonard Rocklin
Bogan, Carmen Page
Bogart, Daniel Robert
Bogedain, William
Bogen, Eugene Michael
Boggess, John P.
Boggs, Corinne C. (Lindy)
Boggs, Frank Kellar
Boggs, Gail Everett
Boggs, James Bishop
Boggs, William Wayne
Bogue, Malen DeVon
Bohannon, Bill
Bohannon, James Milton
Bohannon, Richard Frederick
Bohlen, James Albert
Bohler, Clorinda Scarpa-Smith (Mrs. T. Gordon Bohler)
Bohorfoush, Joseph George
Bohorfoush, Robert Louis
Bohrman, Jeffrey Stephen
Boinodiris, Stavros
Bolan, Robert Mosier
Bolden, John Henry
Boldt, Albert Walter
Bolen, Eric George
Bolen, Helen Buckler
Bolene, Margaret Rosalie Steele (Mrs. Robert V. Bolene)
Bolene, Robert Victor
Boles, Donald Ray
Boles, Paul Darcy
Bolger, Robert Joseph
Bolin, Dorse Leon
Bolin, Richard Arnold
Boling, Jewell
Boll, Charles Edward, II
Bollenbacher, Donald Richard
Bolooki, Hooshang
Bolton, Arthur Key
Bolton, Elizabeth McLundie
Bolton, James Glidewell, Jr.
Bolton, Robert Harvey
Bolz, Sarah Davis
Bomar, John Cornelius
Bomar, Portia Hamilton
Bonar, Jeanne Rae
Bond, Andrew John
Bond, Bernard Batson
Bond, Daniel Webster, Jr.
Bond, George Doherty
Bond, Julian
Bond, Louis Dean
Bond, Reford
Bond, Robert Levi
Bondi, Arnold Aaron
Bonds, La Merle Williams
Bondurant, Brenda Faye
Bondurant, Edward Justine
Bondurant, Gordon Emerson
Bondurant, William Bryant
Bondurant, William Walton, Jr.
Bone, Ewell Owen
Boner, Marian Oldfather
Boney, William Jerry
Bonham, Howard Bryan, Jr.
Boni, Albert Lawson
Bonifay, Don Wayne
Bonifazi, Stephen
Bonilla Colon, Jorge
Bonner, Allan Baker
Bonner, Cathy Leigh
Bonner, Edwin Eugene
Bonner, Jack Wilbur, III
Bonner, James Calvin
Bonner, James Cook, Jr.
Bonner, Mark Herbert, Jr.
Bonner, Richard Edward
Bonner, William Paul
Bonness, Joseph Denny, Jr.
Bonney, Edward Lewis
Bonney, Hal James, Jr.
Bonney, Joseph Wayne
Bonsangue, Nicholas Anthony
Booe, Everett Little, III
Booker, Doyle Ray
Booker, Henry Marshall
Bookout, John Frank, Jr.
Books, Earl James Eugene
Bookstaver, Alexander
Boomershine, Walter McKinley, Jr.
Boone, Betty Jane Pratt
Boone, Charlotte Jackson
Boone, Kyle Clayton
Boone, Peter Augustine
Boone, Rebecca Ann
Boorman, Howard Lyon
Booth, Donald James
Booth, Eden Comfort
Booth, Gordon Dean, Jr.
Booth, James Henry
Booth, James Willis, III
Booth, John Newton
Booth, Ralph Ray
Boothby, Richard Joseph
Booton, John Roller
Boozer, Albert Marion
Boozer, Howard Rai
Boozer, Simon David
Boozer, Vanoy Troy
Borash, Michael Howard
Borden, Robert Lee, Jr.
Borders, Ben
Bordner, Jon Benton
Boren, David Lyle
Boren, James Earl
Borg, Harry Theodore (Ted)
Borick, Paul Michael
Boring, Charles John
Boring, John Wayne
Borkan, William Noah
Borlaug, Norman Ernest
Born, Sidney
Borochoff, Charles Zachary
Borochoff, Ida Sloan (Mrs. Charles Z. Borochoff)
Borschow, Ron Clarke
Borsi, Peter N.
Borthick, Mavis Ary
Borum, Olin Henry
Boschma, William Joseph
Boscio, Roberto Luis
Boshell, Buris Raye
Bosley, David Emerson
Bosomworth, Peter Palliser
Boss, Harold Francis
Bossier, Albert Louis, Jr.
Bost, Armon Henry
Bostic, Stephen Julian
Bostick, Laurence Herbert
Boston, John Armistead, Jr.
Boston, William Clayton, Jr.
Bostwick, Joseph C.
Boswell, Everett Whitmire
Boswell, Gary Taggart
Boswell, George Marion, Jr.
Boswell, James Malcolm
Boswell, Jimmy Loyd
Boswell, John Howard
Botbol, Joseph Moses
Bott, Harvey John
Bottoms, Charles Benson, Jr.
Bottoms, Kenneth Riley
Botts, William Harold
Boucher, John Lawrence
Bouck, David William
Boudreaux, Edmond
Boudreaux, Edward Anthony
Boudreaux, Warren Louis
Bouknight, Huey Randall
Boultinghouse, Ethel DeLany
Boulton, Grace
Bounds, Laurence Harold
Bourgeois, George Stubbs
Bourgeois, Rudolph John, Jr.
Bourne, Geoffrey Howard
Bousquet, Thomas Gourrier
Bousson, Robert Joseph
Boutte, Margaret Ann
Boutwell, Wallace Kenneth, Jr.
Bouvier, Helen Schaefer (Mrs. John A. Bouvier, Jr.)
Bouvier, John Andre, Jr.
Bovey, Rodney William
Boward, Robert James
Bowden, Charles Malcolm
Bowen, Cornelius Monroe
Bowen, David Reece
Bowen, Frank Weston
Bowen, James Milton
Bowen, Raleigh L.
Bowen, Robert Callender
Bowen, Robert Klien, Jr.
Bowen, Roger W.
Bowen, Sue Haynes
Bowen, Ted
Bowen, William Ward
Bower, Kenneth Lee
Bowers, Edward Savannah
Bowers, Henry Taylor
Bowers, Marianne
Bowers, Ronald William
Bowersock, Roger Bates
Bowling, Andrew Charles
Bowling, Edward Charles
Bowling, Robert Edward, Jr.
Bowling, William Edgar
Bowman, Edmund DeLong
Bowman, Ned David
Bowman, Samuel Leonardo
Bowmer, Jim DeWitt
Bowmer, William Jackson
Box, Willard Donald
Boyce, Edward Wayne, Jr.
Boyce, Ernest Fredrick
Boyd, Ann Louise Stripling
Boyd, Clarence Elmo
Boyd, Helen McPherson (Mrs. Deward Gaston Boyd, Jr.)
Boyd, Howard Taney
Boyd, John Hamilton
Boyd, John Patrick
Boyd, Joseph Arthur, Jr.
Boyd, Louis Jefferson
Boyd, Robert Edward Lee, II
Boyd, Robert Friend
Boyd, Spencer Wallace
Boyd, Waymon Lewis
Boydstun, Jackson Benjamin
Boydstun, Rodney Lealand
Boyenga, Paul Douglas
Boyer, John Cloyd
Boyer, Lester Leroy, Jr.
Boyer, Theodore Stanley
Boyer, William Paul
Boykin, John Claude
Boykins, Ernest A., Jr.
Boyle, Howard Edward
Boyle, Lester Joseph, Jr.
Boyle, Stephen William
Boyles, Harlan Edward, Sr.
Boyles, James Edward
Boynton, John Hill, Jr.
Bozymski, Eugene Michael
Brabban, Maylene Magers
Bracewell, Mervell Winzer
Brachman, Leon Harold
Brachman, Malcolm K.
Brachman, Marshall Aaron
Brackin, Henry Bryan, Jr.
Bracy, John Stephen
Braddock, Grover Holmes
Braddock, Hugh Brooks
Braden, Jeffrey Stephen
Braden, Patrick O'Connor
Braden, Waldo W.
Braden, William Bernard, Jr.
Bradfield, William Henry, Jr.
Bradford, George Mason
Bradford, Mary Elizabeth
Bradford, Michael Edward
Bradford, Thomas Leonard (Brad), III
Bradford, Tutt S.
Bradham, Gilbert Bowman
Bradley, Charles Henry
Bradley, (Beuford) Douglas
Bradley, John Samuel
Bradley, Martha Washington Nutter (Mrs. George Washington Bradley)
Bradley, Nolen Eugene, Jr.
Bradley, Penelope Sue
Bradley, Ronald James
Bradshaw, Herman Luther, Jr.
Bradshaw, Lillian Moore
Bradshaw, Robert John, Jr.
Brady, Dale Eugene
Brady, Sheila Ann
Brady, Wayne Carter
Braender, Brooks Henry David, III, (pen name Brooks Brender)
Bragdon, Clifford Richardson
Bragg, Thomas Guy, III
Braido, Robert Harold
Brainard, Jayne Dawson (Mrs. Ernest Scott Brainard)
Brainerd, Harold Webster, Jr.
Bralow, Saul Philip
Bram, Marjorie
Bramble, Ronald Lee
Brame, Durward Belmont
Bramlett, Edwin Chandler, Jr.
Bramlett, Larry William
Branch, Alfred Lee, Jr.
Branch, Charles Herbert
Branch, Dan Paulk
Branch, Harllee, Jr.
Branch, John Russell
Branch, Lee Wadsworth
Branch, Robert Bailey
Brand, John
Brandenberger, Stanley George
Brandfass, Robert Taylor
Brandino, Thomas Francis, Jr.
Brandon, Elvis Denby, Jr.
Brandon, Hembree Bedell
Brandon, Milton, Jr.
Brandon, Stephen Arthur
Brandon, Walter Wiley, Jr.
Brandon, William Clint
Brandt, Alva Esmond
Brandt, Isaac David, III
Branham, Henry Hamilton, Jr.
Brannen, Wendall E.
Brannian, Ross Edwin
Brannon, James Michael
Brannon, Jameston Rezin, Jr.
Brannon, Michael Jerome
Brannon, Paul Whiting
Brannon, Russell Herbert
Bransford, Paris
Branson, Robert Earl
Brant, Leslie Ann
Brantley, Alice Virginia Singer (Mrs. Edward Fitzroy Brantley)
Brantley, Franklin Oakes
Brantley, James Wyman
Brantley, John Croft
Brantley, Willard Reginald
Branum, Lowell Edwin
Brasfield, Milton Stanhope, III
Brashear, Arthur Price, Jr.
Brashears, Melvin Richard
Brasher, George Walter
Braswell, Jack Guy
Braswell, James Carl, Jr.
Braswell, James Randall
Braswell, L. Render
Braswell, Rex Haralson
Bratcher, Rhodes
Bratton, Frank N.
Bratton, James Henry, Jr.
Bratton, William Albert, Jr.
Braudo, Martin Frederick
Brauer, Alfred T(heodor)
Brauer, George Charles, Jr.
Braun, John Walter
Braun, Margaret Anne
Braun, Warren L(oyd)
Brauner, Christian John
Brave, Jacqueline Cohen
Brawner, Donald Leon
Brawner, Lee Basil
Braxton, Herman Harrison
Braxton, Herman Harrison, Jr.
Bray, Charlena Harris
Braynon, Edward Joseph, Jr.
Brazelton, James Melville
Breard, Benjamin Allen
Breaux, Charles Warren
Breaux, John B.
Breaux, Paul Whitney
Breazeale, Frank Warren
Breazeale, Roscoe Jefferson
Brechin, John Bryce, III
Breck, Louis William
Breckinridge, Charles Edward, Jr.
Breckinridge, John Barclay
Breckinridge, John Bayne
Breda, Ernest John
Breeden, James Calvin
Breeland, Samuel Glover
Breffeilh, Louis Andrew
Breitenbeck, Gregory Allan
Breland, Jabe Armistead
Brelsford, George William, V
Brelsford, Jeanne Kaye
Brelsford, John Walker, Jr.
Bremer, James Robert
Bremmer, Joseph Paul
Brennan, John William
Brenner, George Paul
Brent, Peggy Ann
Brentlay, Edward S.
Brereton, Thomas Francis
Breskin, Barnett
Bressler, Bernard
Brewer, Charles Eugene
Brewer, Clyde Savage (Mrs. Claude A. Brewer)
Brewer, George Madison
Brewer, Jack Alan
Brewer, John Roger
Brewer, Norman C(raig), Jr.
Brewer, Ralph Wright, Jr.
Brewer, Roy Edward
Brewer, Roy Vincent
Brewer, William David
Brewer, William Pickens
Brewster, Daniel Fergerson
Brewster, Robert Gene
Brewton, David Eugene
Brewton, Raleigh Gerald
Brian, Alexis Morgan, Jr.
Brice, Carl Stanton
Brice, Laurie Simonton
Bricker, Donald Lee
Bridenbaugh, Edwin Redmond
Bridewell, Juanita Lunsford
Bridgeman, Doris Carolyn Griffith
Bridgers, Thomas Fleming, Jr.
Bridges, James Edward, Jr.
Bridges, James Payne
Bridgforth, Edward McPhail, Jr.
Bridwell, Herbert Hoover
Briggle, Anthony Noel
Briggs, Charlie Fay
Briggs, Garrett
Briggs, Philip Henry
Brigham, Elbert Oran
Bright, Robert Lynn
Brightwell, C(harles) Sanders
Brightwell, Jack Arnold
Brightwell, Juanita Sumner (Mrs. Louie Brightwell)
Briley, James Allen
Brill, David H., Jr.
Brillhart, David Winthrop
Brillhart, Martin Nolan
Brimhall, John Clark
Brindley, George Valter, Jr.
Brinkhous, Kenneth Merle
Brinkley, Jack Thomas
Brinkley, Parke Culver
Brinkley, William Lambreth, Jr.
Brinsmade, Lyon Louis
Briscoe, Dolph, Jr.
Briscoe, James Benton
Briscoe, Sidney Edward, Jr.
Brisley, Quentin Lee Edward
Brisolara, Ashton
Brister, Bill H.
Brister, Commodore Webster
Bristow, Mabel Morrow
Bristow, Preston Abner, Jr.
Britt, Albert Sidney, Jr.
Britt, Chester Olen
Britt, Claude Henry, Jr.
Britt, Elizabeth Letitia Smith
Britt, Henry Grady
Britt, Morris Franklin
Brittain, Robert Charles
Britton, Bruce Keene
Britton, James Judson
Broadhead, Samuel L., Jr.
Broadway, Clifford Monroe
Brocato, Frank Michael
Brock, Robert William, II
Brockwell, Paul Anthony, III
Brode, Marvin Jay
Brodkorb, (William) Pierce
Brodnax, Charles Teddy
Brody, Aaron Leo
Brody, Erwin William
Broeker, Annie Barr
Brohamer, Richard Frederic
Broiles, Barnes Hoover
Brokaw, Charles Forrest, Jr.
Brokhoff, John Rudolph
Brolliar, Harold Lee
Bromberg, Alan Robert
Bromberg, Milton Jay
Bromley, Haworth Peery
Bronaugh, Edwin Lee
Brong, Rosco
Bronson, Daniel Braid
Brooke, George Mercer, Jr.
Brooker, Jeff Zeigler, Jr.
Brookhart, George Clinton
Brooks, Barbara Jean
Brooks, Carl Edwin
Brooks, Charles Gordon
Brooks, David Kendrick, Jr.
Brooks, Earl Russell, Jr.
Brooks, Elston Harwood
Brooks, George William
Brooks, Jack
Brooks, James Carlton, Jr.
Brooks, James Gordon, Jr.
Brooks, Jerry Claude
Brooks, Joe Thomas, Jr.
Brooks, John
Brooks, John Roy, Jr.
Brooks, Joseph William
Brooks, Larry Lee
Brooks, Lloyd William
Brooks, Robert Franklin
Brooks, William Dixon
Brookshire, James Carroll
Brophy, Joseph Daniel
Broquist, Harry Pearson
Bross, John Adams
Brothers, Cassie Marie Campbell (Mrs. William John Brothers, Jr.)
Brothers, Jack Anthony
Brothers, James Russell
Brothers, William John, Jr.
Brotherton, Ronald Leon
Brotton, William Gleason
Brouillette, Albert Clarence
Brouillette, Mary Joan
Brourman, Jacques
Broussard, Nelwyn Blanche
Broussard, Normaj (Mrs. Lee R. Broussard)
Broussard, William Joseph
Browder, Johnie Mae Gomillion
Browder, Richard Neal
Brower, Karen Lee
Brower, Walter Jordan
Brown, Aaron Clifton
Brown, Albert Belmont
Brown, Alex Smith, Jr.
Brown, Anne Warwick
Brown, Arthur Dixon, Sr.
Brown, Augustus Bart
Brown, Bailey
Brown, Betty Jane
Brown, Charles Aubrey, Jr.
Brown, Charles Everett, Jr.
Brown, Clareatha
Brown, Clyde
Brown, Conny Ray
Brown, Constant Clement
Brown, Daniel Mac
Brown, David Hurst
Brown, Earl Felton
Brown, Edward McLain, Jr.
Brown, Eleanor Jean
Brown, Elizabeth Frances
Brown, Emma Jean Jacobs
Brown, Eric Thomas
Brown, Gary Eugene
Brown, Geoffrey Graham
Brown, George Lewis
Brown, George Ray
Brown, George William
Brown, Gregg Carrol
Brown, Harlan James
Brown, Harvey Thomas, II
Brown, Hyder Joseph, Jr.
Brown, Isaac Dale
Brown, Jack Edward, Jr.
Brown, James Crozier
Brown, James Curtiss
Brown, James Knight
Brown, James Pope
Brown, Jesse Jefferson, Jr.
Brown, John Lee
Brown, John Robert
Brown, John William Harrell
Brown, Larry Wayne
Brown, Louise Scott
Brown, Malcolm Hendricks
Brown, Marcus Gordon
Brown, Margaret Cannon Boyce
Brown, Mark
Brown, Michael Ernest
Brown, Michael Lynn
Brown, Reginald Royce
Brown, Richard Christopher
Brown, Robert Glenn
Brown, Robert Paul
Brown, Robert Wade
Brown, Roger Henry
Brown, Ron
Brown, Ruth Cunningham (Mrs. William Russell Brown)
Brown, Sage
Brown, Samuel Weldon, III
Brown, Sarah Cole (Mrs. Sterling F. Brown)
Brown, Scott Newton
Brown, Shirley Ann
Brown, Stephen Francis
Brown, Thurman Theodore, Jr.
Brown, Travis Walter
Brown, Virgil Clyde
Brown, Walter Jack
Brown, Walter Lee
Brown, Warren Paul
Brown, Willard Richard
Brown, William David
Brown, William Keller
Brown, William Knox
Brown, William Perry, Sr.
Brown, William Russell
Brown, Wilson Gordon
Browne, Alice Pauline
Brownell, Iverson Oakley
Browning, Chauncey H., Jr.
Browning, Roy Leon (Pete)
Brownlee, Bobby Gene
Brownlee, William Russell
Brownson, Charles Bruce
Broxson, Michael Robert
Bruce, Elmer Ivan
Bruce, John Markey

Bruce, William Rankin
Bruckman, Thomas Richard
Bruene, Warren Benz
Bruff, Beverly Olive
Bruhl, Edwin Louis
Brumback, Charles Tiedtke
Brumby, Paul Bingham
Brumfield, Joe Lamar
Brummer, Lydia Sammon
Brummett, Claudia Mae
Brunet, Aline Kahl
Bruni, Robert Joseph
Brunini, Joseph Bernard
Bruns, Hubert Nelson
Brunson, John Soles
Brusso, Frank Stephen
Bruton, James Leonard, Sr.
Bryan, Bart Ebert
Bryan, David Tennant
Bryan, Edward Raymond
Bryan, Jacob Franklin, III
Bryan, James Clarence
Bryan, Jane Campbell
Bryan, John J.
Bryan, Loren Aldro
Bryan, Richard Walker
Bryan, Ronald Canter
Bryan, Samuel Hugh, Jr.
Bryant, Britain Hamilton
Bryant, Donald Eugene
Bryant, Donald Grant
Bryant, Elizabeth Ann
Bryant, Howard Louis
Bryant, Kirby Knapp, Jr.
Bryant, Talbert Chalmer, Jr.
Bryant, Thomas Floyd, Jr.
Bubenzer, Nancy Luise
Buchanan, Arthur E., Jr.
Buchanan, James Junkin
Buchanan, John Hall, Jr.
Buchanan, Robert Byron
Buchanan, Thomas Louis
Bucher, Muriel Mowen
Buchholtz, Wolfgang Richard
Buchman, Joseph Anthony
Buck, Charles G.
Buck, George Clyde
Buck, Gurdon Saltonstall
Buck, Richard Edward, III
Buck, Richard Joseph
Buck, Robert Fletcher
Buck, William Leonard
Buckelew, Morris Thomas
Buckland, Marion McIver (Mrs. Charles Gardner Buckland)
Buckley, Emerson
Buckley, Jack Boyd
Buckley, Kathleen Theresa
Buckley, Thomas Patrick
Buckley, William Stuart
Buckner, John Kendrick
Bucy, J. Fred
Budalur, Thyagarajan Subbanarayan
Budd, Louis John
Budig, Gene Arthur
Bueno, Edgar Manuel
Bueschen, Anton Joslyn
Buescher, Brent Joseph
Buffington, William Edgar
Buffum, Elizabeth Whitney
Buhlinger, Nan Nordyke
Buhrmaster, Doris Daenitz
Buie, David Arthur
Buie, Eugene Cloy
Buksha, Katrina Lee
Bull, Frank James
Bull, Helen May
Bull, Robert Francis
Bullard, Edgar Earl
Bullard, Edgar John, III
Bullard, K(ennedy) C(ornelius)
Bullen, Adelaide Kendall (Mrs. Ripley Pierce Bullen)
Bumpers, Dale
Bunge, Carl Craig
Bunker, William Marvin
Bunn, Edward DeVere
Bunting, J(ames) Whitney
Bunting, John James
Burbo, James Howard
Burch, Donald Victor
Burch, Elza Fain
Burch, Jim Wayne
Burch, Loren William
Burch, Robert Ray
Burcham, Gwendolyn Frances Parker (Mrs. Ralph Jack Burcham)
Burcham, Ralph Jack
Burchfield, Harry Phineas, Jr.
Burchfield, Terry Layne
Burdeshaw, Fred Houston
Burdett, Arthur Crane
Burdick, Everette Marshall
Burford, Alexander Mitchell, Jr.
Burford, Ann DeSalme
Burgan, William Michael
Burger, Robert Alan
Burgess, Albert Charles
Burgess, Alfred Franklin
Burgess, Arthur Harry
Burgess, Arthur Harry, Jr.
Burgess, Carolyn Drinkard
Burgess, Eunice Lester
Burgess, James Alfred
Burgess, Malcolm Stewart, Jr.
Burgess, Oliver Taylor
Burgess, Rembert Oliver
Burgett, Charles A.
Burgett, John Cecil, Sr.
Burgher, Edmon
Burgstiner, Carmen Elizabeth
Burk, Sylvia Joan
Burkart, Robert James
Burke, Earl Patrick, Jr.
Burke, Franklin Leigh
Burke, J. Herbert
Burke, Walker Darin
Burke, William Temple, Jr.
Burkett, Benjamin Clinton, II
Burkett, Helen Rose (Mrs. Charles William Burkett, Jr.)
Burkett, Warren Levi, Jr.
Burkhalter, David A.
Burkhalter, Kenneth Venoy, Jr.
Burkhalter, William Ely
Burkhart, Harold Eugene
Burkhead, Jesse DeWitt
Burks, Eura Olivia (Lockridge)
Burks, Mack Skaggs
Burks, Willard Reppard, Jr.
Burleson, Evans Ignitius
Burleson, Ned Kenneth
Burleson, Omar
Burleson, Robert Joe
Burleson, Sam Evans, Jr.
Burlingame, James Montgomery
Burlison, Pat Ed
Burlone, Dominick Anthony, Jr.
Burmahln, Elizabeth Leona Butler
Burmahln, Elmer Fred
Burnau, Suanna Jeannette Flake
Burnet, Thornton West
Burnett, Carey Corley
Burnett, George Wesley
Burnett, Thomas Douglass, III
Burnett, Wilbur Weeden (Bill)
Burnette, Joe Edward
Burnette, John Quincy
Burnham, Charles Joseph
Burnham, J. V.
Burnham, Philip Raymond
Burns, Daniel Hobart
Burns, Dennis Patrick
Burns, Edward Allen
Burns, George Frank
Burns, Grover Preston
Burns, Jimmy Clay
Burns, John Luther
Burns, Kay Neil
Burns, Kenneth Harold
Burns, Larry DeMont
Burns, Robert Leroy
Burns, William Goodykoontz
Burns, Zed Houston
Burnside, Hamilton Stanley Nathaniel
Burnside, Mary E. Haynes
Burpee, Charles Dickens
Burr, David Anthony
Burr, Horace
Burr, Kathie Kay
Burr, Richard Melvin
Burr, Thomas Shepard
Burrell, George Charles
Burrill, James Stuart
Burris, Robert Eltinze
Burroughs, Edwin Elwell
Burrow, David Hutchison
Burrow, Kenneth Robert
Burrows, Walter Herbert
Burrus, John Newell
Burrus, Swan Thomas
Burruss, Edmund Coleman
Burruss, Robert Sidney, Jr.
Burt, Allen Daniel
Burt, Wellington Richardson, Jr.
Burton, Dolores West
Burton, Francis Christian, Jr.
Burton, Gene Earle
Burton, George Aubrey, Jr.
Burton, George Herman
Burton, Ronnie Allan
Burton, Tom L.
Burwell, (George) Ernest
Burwell, Thomas Chase
Burzlaff, Donald Frederick
Burzynski, Stanislaw Rajmund
Bus, Daniel William
Busbee, Cyril B.
Busbee, George D.
Buschman, Arthur William
Buse, Sylvia Tweedt
Bush, Alfred Kyle
Bush, Eunice Carroll
Bush, Jack Tucker
Bush, Melissa
Bush, Patricia Elizabeth
Bush, Ralph Everett
Busha, Charles Henry
Bushelman, Ted Joseph
Bussart, Walter Woods
Bussell, Opp, Jr.
Bussey, Malcolm L.
Bussolini, Peter Louis
Bustamante, Rodrigo Antonio
Buswell, Arthur Wilcox
Butcher, Cecil Hilgue, Jr.
Butcher, Lee
Butler, Aldis Perrin
Butler, Betty Jean
Butler, Darrell Foster
Butler, Herbert Harriss
Butler, James Lee
Butler, Lewell Colbert, Jr.
Butler, Manley Caldwell
Butler, Marion Tyus
Butler, Martha Louise
Butler, Pamela Jean
Butler, Roy Francis
Butruille, Daniel Claude
Buttes, Clarence Edward, Jr.
Button, William Garland
Buttry, James Altus
Butts, Delbert Leo
Butts, Jane Esther Dickson
Butts, Ulys Reneau
Buxbaum, Robert Elwood
Buxeda, Roberto
Buxton, Jay Alberto
Buyama, Edward T., Jr.
Buzlea, Romey D.
Byars, Edward Ford
Byars, Samuel Tildon
Byers, Brent Eugene
Byers, William Sewell
Bylander, Ernest Gerald
Byler, William Henry
Byrd, Gary Jefferson
Byrd, Gerald David
Byrd, Gretchen Thomson (Mrs. Harry Flood Byrd, Jr.)
Byrd, Harry Flood, Jr.
Byrd, Ida Fay (Mrs. Kenneth Byrd)
Byrd, Jerome Rogers
Byrd, Lawrence Herman
Byrd, Robert C(arlyle)
Byrd, William Eugene
Byrd, William Garland
Byrn, James Edward
Byron, James Aloysius
Byrum, James Knox
Byrum, Mary Carolyn
Byrum, Thomas Michael
Caballero, Juan Agustin
Cabanas, Alex I. J.
Cabe, Robert Dudley
Cabell, Benjamin Bryan
Cabell, Joseph Edward
Cabibi, Charles Edmond
Cabic, Edward Joseph
Cabral, Guy Antony
Caccamise, Genevra Louise Ball
Cacciatore, Ronald Keith
Caddess, James Harvey
Cadenhead, Alfred Paul
Cadle, Dean
Cadrecha, Manuel
Caffey, William Stewart
Caffrey, William Daniel
Cagle, Edward Fielding
Cahill, Carl Henry
Cahoon, Stuart Newton
Cahue, Antonio
Cain, Donald Ezell
Cain, Stephen Malcolm
Caine, Walter E.
Cairnes, William Elliott
Calabrese, Anthony Samuel
Calahan, Edward Ronald
Calbeto, Gabriel Anthony
Calderon Serrano, Alfredo
Caldwell, Charleen Claire
Caldwell, Claud Reid
Caldwell, David Leon
Caldwell, Harold Leroy
Caldwell, Henry Stephen
Caldwell, Howard Eugene
Caldwell, Jesse Burgoyne, Jr.
Caldwell, Larry
Caldwell, Leona Iola Will (Mrs. Oliver Cromwell Caldwell)
Calhoun, Evelyn Williams
Calhoun, Frank Wayne
Calhoun, Jack Rowland
Calhoun, Milburn Eugene
Calhoun, William McCall
Cali, Paul Vincent
Callaghan, John Patrick
Callahan, Jewel Burnett
Callahan, Vincent Francis, Jr.
Callahan, Wallace Hartwell
Callaway, Carey Ann Skinner
Callaway, Jasper Lamar
Callaway, John Wilson
Callaway, William Choteau
Callen, Irwin R.
Callen, Stephen Joseph
Callender, Martha V. Linder (Mrs. Richard Ervin Callender)
Calloway, Joseph Arthur, Jr.
Calma, Victor Charles
Calonje, Mario Arnoldo
Calub, Alfonso de Guzman
Calvert, David Victor
Calvert, Russell Scott
Calvert, William Preston
Calvin, Larry O.
Camacho, Alvro Manuel
Camacho, Salvador Lujan
Camblin, Mark Lester Eberlein
Cambron, Albert Moseley
Cameron, Benjamin Franklin, Jr.
Cameron, C. Arnold
Cameron, Curtis Alfred
Cameron, Jack Everett
Cammenga, John Alden
Camp, Ehney Addison, III
Camp, John L.
Camp, N. Harry, Jr.
Campbell, Agnes Knight (Mrs. John Franklin Campbell)
Campbell, Archibald Algernon
Campbell, Carey Walton
Campbell, Charles Francis
Campbell, Don Lee
Campbell, George Emerson
Campbell, Gordon W.
Campbell, Harold Monroe
Campbell, Howard Wallace
Campbell, J. Thomas
Campbell, James Wayne
Campbell, Jerome Wesley, Sr.
Campbell, John Robert
Campbell, John William
Campbell, Karl Neal
Campbell, Lloyd Tye, Jr.
Campbell, Maria Bouchelle
Campbell, Mary Grace Williams (Mrs. Walter Robert Campbell, Jr.)
Campbell, Selma Ronald
Campbell, Thomas Leake, Jr.
Campbell, William Ransom, Jr.
Campbell, William Rockwell
Campion, Douglas Robert
Campion, Eileen
Campobasso, Thomas Anthony
Campos, Emilio Carlo
Canaan, Gershon
Canaday, William Clinton
Canan, Howard Voorheis
Candler, John Slaughter, II
Caney, Louis Lincoln
Canfield, Bourbon Ellis
Cangelosi, Anthony
Cangemi, Joseph Peter
Canning, Harold Mood
Cannon, Chapman Roosevelt, Jr.
Cannon, Hugh
Cannon, William Ragsdale
Canon, Robert Morris
Canonico, Dolores
Cantey, William Childs
Cantin, Denise Doris
Cantor, Robert L.
Cantrell, Bert Mitchell, Jr.
Cantrell, Robert Wendell
Cantrell, William Allen
Cape, Charles Albert
Capell, Annie Hall
Caperton, Charles Lee
Caplan, Fred Harry
Caplan, Sylvia Davis
Capps, James Barri
Capsas, Cleon Wade
Carameros, George Demitrius, Jr.
Caravati, Charles Martin, Jr.
Carbonell, Alfredo Maximiliano
Cardelli, Giovanni Guido Carlo
Cardelli, Jacqueline
Carden, Arnold Eugene
Cardenas, Ramiro I.
Carder, Kendall Lyman
Cardona, Alberto
Cardona, Juan Gilberto
Cardoso, Anthony Antonio
Cardus, David
Cardwell, Billie Jo
Cardwell, Horace Milton
Cardwell, Owen Calvin
Carew, Glenn Stratton
Cargill, Leonard Ray, Jr.
Cargill, Otto Arthur, Jr.
Carl, Richard Henry
Carlay, Ronald Leon
Carleton, Charles Coleman
Carleton, Robert L.
Carley, James Rea, Jr.
Carlin, Frank Joseph
Carlisle, William Edgar
Carlos, Edward
Carlson, Donald Lloyd
Carlson, Evans Charles
Carlson, Maurice Irwin
Carlson, Merle Thomas
Carlton, Alwin Horatio
Carlton, Dean
Carlton, Jedfrey Michael
Carlton, Kenneth Frederick
Carlton, Thomas Mabry
Carmack, Nathan Dykes
Carman, Gary Michael
Carman, George Henry
Carmichael, Donald Ray
Carmichael, Jerry Harris
Carmichael, John Leslie
Carmichael, Karla Delle
Carmichael, Miriam Willena
Carmine, Leonard Grant
Carmody, Arthur Roderick, Jr.
Carnahan, Adele Cherry
Carnahan, Daniel Lee
Carnahan, Robert Narvell
Carnell, Claude Mitchell, Jr.
Carner, Rebecca Lynne
Carnes, James Oliver
Carnes, Jess Gale
Carnevale, Dario
Carney, Henry Murfree
Carnley, Samuel Fleetwood
Carolina, Johnnie Franklin
Caroon, James Edward, Jr.
Carow, Raymond Edward
Carpenter, Carlton Lanier, Jr.
Carpenter, Charles Congden
Carpenter, Charles David
Carpenter, Clarence Willard, Jr.
Carpenter, Clinton Ray, Jr.
Carpenter, James Linwood, Jr.
Carpenter, Jesse Owen
Carpenter, Lonnie Cloy
Carpenter, Michael Kenneth
Carpenter, Richard Duane
Carpenter, Richard Woodrow
Carpenter, Robert Durward
Carpenter, Robert Hunt
Carpenter, Stanley Hammack
Carpenter, William Levy
Carpenter, Woodrow Wilson
Carr, Ben Wheeler, Jr.
Carr, Daniel Phillips
Carr, Earl Vivian
Carr, Harold Noflet
Carr, Howard Ernest
Carr, Jesse Crowe, Jr.
Carr, Joseph A., Jr.
Carr, Leo Carlton
Carr, Lois Rogers (Mrs. Ralph Willett Carr)
Carr, Louie Woods
Carr, Robert Lon
Carr, William Henry
Carrabba, Michael Paul
Carranza, Alfred S.
Carreathers, Raymond Eugene
Carrell, Hilma Bartlett
Carrera, Ana Estrada (Mrs. Guillermo M. Carrera)
Carrera, Guillermo Manuel
Carrere, Charles Scott
Carrico, Fred Gary
Carrigan, Helen Leovy
Carrington, Fredrick Murray
Carrithers, Paul Norman
Carroll, Ann Elizabeth
Carroll, Charles Michael
Carroll, DeWitt Edward
Carroll, Frances LeVerne
Carroll, Frank Andrew, Jr.
Carroll, George Joseph
Carroll, Howard Lawrence
Carroll, Julian Morton
Carroll, Raymond Gale
Carroll, Robert Clinton, Jr.
Carroll, Robert Leon
Carroll, Robroy Charles
Carroll, Thomas Charles
Carroll, William Wendall
Carruth, Thomas Paige
Carruthers, G. Thomas
Carson, Dale
Carson, Edward Floyd
Carson, George John
Carson, Leonard Allen
Carson, William Edwards
Carssow, John Felix
Carstensen, Roger Norwood
Carstetter, David Wilson
Carswell, Elba Wilson
Carter, Amon, Jr.
Carter, Betty Lou (Mrs. Charles E. Carter)
Carter, Betty Werlein (Mrs. Hodding Carter)
Carter, Charles Landon, III
Carter, Charles Leslie, Jr.
Carter, David Edward
Carter, Donald Clayton
Carter, Frances Tunnell (Mrs. John T. Carter)
Carter, Frank
Carter, George Franklin
Carter, Grady Lee, III
Carter, Harvey Lee
Carter, Hugh (Sevier)
Carter, Ivan L., Jr.
Carter, James Byars
Carter, James Earl, Jr. (Jimmy)
Carter, James Edward, Jr.
Carter, James Harvey
Carter, James Johnston
Carter, Jimmy.
Carter, John Marshall, Jr.
Carter, Joseph Carlyle, Jr.
Carter, Joseph Coleman, III
Carter, Lamore Joseph
Carter, Laurence Stroud
Carter, Lewis Henry, Jr.
Carter, Loren James, Jr.
Carter, Prentiss Henson, Jr.
Carter, Purvis Melvin
Carter, Richard Edward
Carter, Rosalynn Smith
Carter, Selden Booker
Carter, Tim Lee
Carter, Vertie Lee
Carter, William Alfred
Carter, William Causey
Carter, William Earl
Carter, William Joseph
Cartmill, Robert Oliver
Cartner, John Aubrey
Cartwright, Charles Nelson
Caruso, Vincent George
Caruso, Vincent Thomas
Carvajal, Richard Deane
Carvajal-Ulloa, Hugo Francisco
Carver, Raymond Earle
Cary, Shirley Ann
Cary, Tracy Glen
Casada, Jerry J.
Case, George Milton
Case, Marshal Taylor
Case, W(ard) R(oland), Jr.
Casella, Santo
Casey, Albert E(ugene)
Casey, Beverly Allen, Jr.
Casey, Christopher Alan
Casey, Mary Frances Yoder (Mrs. Timothy Dennis Casey)
Casey, Offa Lunsford
Casey, Stephen Huntley
Cash, Dewey Byron
Cashman, Chappell Francis
Caskey, Jefferson Dixon
Cason, Claude Turner, Jr.
Cason, Cleo Stargel (Mrs. Charles Monroe Cason, Jr.)
Cason, Dick Kendall
Cason, Thomas Edward, Jr.
Cassanova, Lawrence Joseph, III
Cassata, John T.
Cassel, Chester
Casselberry, Richard Shannon
Cassell, Richard Samuel David
Cassels, Gordon Berry
Cassidy, Dennis Stephen
Cassidy, Maureen Carmel
Cassidy, Patrick Edward
Cassidy, Robert Gordon
Cassidy, Theodore Vincent
Cassin, William Bourke
Casson, Walter Andrew, Jr.
Cassuto, Jerry
Castello, James E., Jr.
Castillo, Felix Armando
Castle, Henry Grady, Jr.
Castle, Loyd Lewis
Castle, Robert Foster
Castle, William Graves, Jr.
Castleberry, George Alfred
Castro, Albert
Castro, John Gonzales
Cate, William Sunday, Jr.
Cates, Lawrence Allaire
Cates, Michael Harold
Cathey, James Leroy
Cathey, Rodney Dean
Catledge, Grier Moen
Caton, Hardy Morris
Catron, Irma Lydia Ragland
Caudill, Estill Leftrage, Jr.
Caudill, John
Caudill, Noble Chesteen
Caudill, William Neville
Caulkins, Charles Whitney, Jr.
Causey, Jack Quin
Causey, John Michael
Cauthen, Melton DeForrest
Cauthen, Wiley Mitchell
Cavallaro, Joseph John
Cave, Mac Donald
Cavender, Ralph Henley
Cavin, Odis Burl
Caviness, Verne Strudwick
Cavitt, Roscoe Alvin
Cawood, Charles David, Jr.
Cawthon, Peter Willis, Jr.
Cayce, Robert Clinton
Cazalas, Mary Rebecca Williams
Cazan, Sylvia Marie Buday (Mrs. Matthew John Cazan)
Cazel, Hugh Allen
Cebollero, Carlos
Cecil, David Rolf
Center, Daniel Haydn, Jr.
Centifanto, Ysolina Mejia
Ceraldi, Attilo Antonio
Cernuda, Charles Evelio
Cerny, Sam J.
Cerra, José Joaquin
Cerveny, Frank Stanley
Cervera, Nicholas Joseph
Cetrulo, Robert Camillus
Chable, E(ugene) Robert
Chace, William George
Chadick, T. C.
Chadwick, Charles William
Chadwick, Robert Edward Lee, Jr.
Chadwick, Robert William
Chaet, Alfred Bernard
Chaffin, James Joseph, Jr.
Chafin, William Vernon, Jr.
Chagy, John
Chahine, Robert Antoine
Chai, Hyoun Chul
Chailer, John Darrell, Jr.
Chain, Bobby Lee
Chalfant, Ray King, Jr.
Chalkley, Blanton Rolfe
Chamberlain, Charles Devere, Jr.
Chamberlain, Nugent Francis
Chambers, Anne Cox
Chambers, Barbara Mae Fromm (Mrs. Charles McKay Chambers)
Chambers, Benjamin Morris
Chambers, Carl Dean
Chambers, James Floyd, Jr.
Chambers, Leslie Addison
Chambers, Otis, Jr.
Chambers, Richard Lee
Chambliss, Joe Preston
Chammas, Edmond Dib
Champagne, Michael Joseph (Mickey)
Champlin, Herbert Hiram
Champlin, William Glen
Chandler, Albert Gallatin
Chandler, Arthur Cecil, Jr.
Chandler, James Thomas
Chandler, John Brandon, Jr.
Chandler, Joseph Luck
Chandler, Thomas Walter, Jr.
Chandler, Winston Griggs
Chandler, Wyeth
Chandra, Kailash Srivastava
Chandras, Kananur V(eerabhadraiah)
Chandwani, Arjan Dhalumal
Chaney, Charles Buren, Jr. (Dick)
Chaney, Floyd Toney
Chaney, James Allan
Chaney, Roy Charles
Chang, Freddy Wilfred Lennox
Chang, Henry Chung-lien
Chang, Jeffrey Chit-Fu
Chang, Jeffrey P.
Chang, Peter
Chao, Jing
Chapatwala, Kiritkumar Dhirajlal
Chaplin, Gervase Michael
Chapman, A. Jay
Chapman, Anthony Bradley
Chapman, Jacob Tolliver, Jr.
Chapman, Mary Lucile
Chapman, Robert Eugene
Chapman, Samuel Greeley
Chapman, Steven Franklin
Chappelear, John Willis, Jr.

Chappell, Buford Souter
Chappell, Frank Benjamin, Jr.
Chappell, Robert Harvey, Jr.
Chappell, William Venroe, Jr.
Chargois, Deborah Majeau (Mrs. Ashton Joseph Chargois)
Charles, Robert Alan
Charlet, James Edward, Sr.
Charlton, Jesse Melvin, Jr.
Charlton, Nina
Chase, Gaylord Richard
Chase, James Staton
Chase, Ruth Eleanor
Chastain, Benjamin Burton
Chastain, Doyle Edward
Chastain, Walter Ralph, Jr.
Chatman, Alex
Chattin, Chester Coles
Chattin, Gilbert Marshall
Chaudhuri, Tapan Kumar
Chavero, Alfredo
Chavers, Dean
Chavez, Abraham, Jr.
Chavira, Juan Manuel
Chavis, Earl Brennon
Chea, Francisco
Cheatham, Carole Bartlett
Cheatham, Frank Sellars, Jr.
Cheatham, John Bane, Jr.
Cheatham, Robert Carl
Cheek, Charles Wall
Cheek, Tom Frank, Jr.
Cheeseman, Jerry William
Chelton, Louis Guy, Jr.
Chelton, Robert Gustave
Chen, B.S.
Chen, Bill Chung-moon
Chen, Der-San
Chen, James Tsung-Tsun
Chen, Wayne H.
Chenault, B(ertie) J(ean)
Chenault, William Blewett, Jr.
Cherry, Charles Louis
Cherry, David Earl
Cherry, Edward Taylor
Chertok, William Michael, Jr.
Chesnut, Donald Blair
Chesnutt, Mary Lynch
Chesser, Robert Epps
Chester, Edward William
Chester, Robert Anson, Jr.
Chetock, James Joseph
Cheves, Harry Langdon, Jr.
Chewning, Luke Everette
Chien, Charles Foong
Chieri, Pericle Adriano C.
Chilcoat, Betty Jackson
Child, Robert Danvers
Childers, Charles Louis
Childers, Frank McDowell
Childers, Marilen Kathleen
Childers, Perry Robert
Childers, Roy Eugene, Jr.
Childress, James Walter
Childress, Jay Walter
Chiles, Gene Tate
Chiles, Lawton
Chilton, Alice Pleasance Hunter (Mrs. St. John Poindexter Chilton)
Chilton, Horace Thomas
Chilton, Howard Goodner, Jr.
Chinelly, John Camillo, Sr.
Chinn, James Dwight
Chinnov, Igor
Chiou, Chung Yih
Chiovarou, Roy Edward
Chipman, Dennis Clarence
Chiquiar-Arias, Victor
Chiranjeevi, Siram
Chiron, Harlan Scott
Chisholm, Gary Lynn
Chisholm, Michael Patrick
Chisholm, Tommy
Chisman, James Allen
Chisman, Thomas Pescud
Chisolm, Charles Smith
Chisolm, Jack Taylor
Chittenden, David Morse, II
Chittenden, Stanley Matthew
Chittom, Park Thetford
Chitty, Arthur Benjamin, Jr.
Chitwood, Robert Hodson
Chitwood, Thomas Edward, Jr.
Chiu, Jen-Fu
Chiu, Kun-young
Choate, William Wesley
Choi, Dai Shik
Chopra, Kuldip Prakash
Chopra, Naiter Mohan
Choudhry, Karamat Ullah
Choudhury, Santosh Kumar
Chovnick, Stanley Davis
Chow, Chen-Ying Leung
Chow, Chian-Chiu
Chrisman, Shirley Anderson
Christensen, John
Christian, Almeric Leander
Christian, Beverly Melbalyn Jones
Christian, John Catlett, Jr.
Christian, William Henry, III
Christiansen, Paul Benjamine
Christiansen, William Earl Smith
Christie, Hugh Allen
Christie, Laurence Glenn, Jr.
Christie, Mary Lou Brandon
Christmas, Joseph Theodore
Christmas, William George
Christopher, Edna
Chu, Tien-Yung Julian
Chubb, George Henry
Chuck, Frank
Chuculate, Richard Woodrow
Chumbley, Robert Emmett, III
Chun, Thomas Hwa-Young
Chung, Wen Yi
Church, Avery Grenfell
Churchill, Peter John
Churchwell, Robert Lane
Chvala, William James
Chytil, Frank
Cicio, Anthony Lee
Ciechalski, Joseph Charles
Cimijotti, Lew F.
Cimino, Louis Eugene
Cintrón, Reinaldo
Cisne, Maxwell Gerard
Cisneros, Henry Gabriel
Ciuca, Gary Eugene
Civis, Donald Martin
Clagett, Arthur F(rank), Jr.
Claiborne, Louis Leigh
Clanton, David Hiram
Clapp, Allen Linville
Clapp, Neal Keith
Claridge, Richard Allen
Clark, Arthur Watts
Clark, Barbara Ann Randall
Clark, Billy Joe
Clark, Billy Pat
Clark, C. Richard
Clark, Carl Oliver
Clark, Charles Daniel
Clark, Danny Miles
Clark, Donald Hamilton
Clark, Emory Eugene
Clark, Eugene Corry
Clark, Faye Louise
Clark, Franklin Jacob, Jr.
Clark, Fred Stephen
Clark, Isaac Edgar
Clark, Jack Crowley
Clark, Jack Maxon
Clark, James Arthur
Clark, James Steven
Clark, Jerry Ralph
Clark, Joe Rex
Clark, John Martin, Jr.
Clark, Lorraine Howard (Mrs. Banks Worth Clark)
Clark, Marvin Ray
Clark, Melvin Eugene
Clark, Morton Hutchinson
Clark, Pennye Lucille
Clark, Ray Austin
Clark, Richard Lee
Clark, Robert Earl, Jr.
Clark, Robert Pearson
Clark, Roy Thomas, Jr.
Clark, Vernon Ray
Clark, Wesley Gleason
Clark, William Henry, III
Clark, William Kemp
Clarke, Ann Neistadt
Clarke, Clifford Montreville
Clarke, Eugene Singleton
Clarke, Francis Iredell
Clarke, Gilbert Rionda
Clarke, Jack Wells
Clarke, Jay
Clarke, Jesse Edward
Clarke, William Elbert
Clarkson, Lawrence William
Clasby, Mark Bower
Claudel, Calvin André
Clausell, Paul
Clavell, Carlos Enrique
Clavenna, LeRoy Russell
Claverie, Philip deVilliers
Claxton, Bruce Calvin
Clay, Harris Aubrey
Clay, Kendall Owen
Clay, Orson C.
Clay, Paul Eugene
Clay, William Caldwell, Jr.
Clayton, Byrl Washington
Clayton, Marvin Courtland
Clayton, Rebecca Kilgo
Clayton, Robert Louis
Clayton, William Howard
Cleary, John Benjamin
Clegg, Leonard Bruce
Clein, Michael Allen
Clem, James William, Jr.
Clemena, Gerardo Go
Clemens, David Edward
Clemens, Elizabeth Malm
Clemens, Ernest William
Clemens, Gerald O'Neal
Clement, George Ray
Clement, Robert Lebby, Jr.
Clemente, Anthony Joseph
Clements, Enon Willice
Clements, Harvey Rush
Clements, James David
Clements, Jamie Hager
Clements, Mary Ellen
Clements, Zeke
Clemmons, Frances Anne Mansell (Mrs. Slaton Clemmons)
Clemmons, Gordon Land
Clemmons, Slaton
Clemons, Mae Ollie
Clendenin, Richard Blaine
Clendening, John Albert
Clerico, Louis Richard
Cleveland, Gene Rickey (Mrs. Cromwell Cook Cleveland)
Cleveland, James Clark
Clevenger, Ernest Allen
Clevenger, Ernest Allen, Jr.
Cleverly, William Stephen
Cliburn, Cecil DeBerry
Cliburn, Joseph William
Clifford, Paul Ingraham
Clifton, Yerger Hunt
Clinch, Walter Deming
Cline, Francis Xavier, Jr.
Cline, Frank Ray
Clingan, Frank Harrington
Clingerman, Edgar Allen
Clingman, William Herbert, Jr.
Clinton, Charles Monroe
Clinton, William Jefferson
Clogan, Paul Maurice
Cloninger, Harold David
Clooney, Ernest Francis, Jr.
Cloud, Clara Owens
Cloud, Russell Walker
Clouse, Clyde
Cloutier, Roger Joseph
Clowdis, Charles Wilburn, Jr.
Clowes, Royston Courtenay
Clum, Dennis Patrick
Clyde, Gerard Anthony
Coakley, Robert Chartrand
Coan, John David
Coates, Frederick Ross
Coates, Kenneth Paul
Coates, Wayne Edward
Coats, Andrew Montgomery
Cobb, Arnold J.
Cobb, Jerrie M.
Cobb, John Phillip
Cobb, Ronald Vernon
Cobb, William Charles
Cobb, William Ronald
Cobbs, James Harold
Coberly, Robert Leonard
Coble, Harold Dwain
Cochran, Donald Robert
Cochran, James Alan
Cochran, John Parr
Cochran, McKendree Thomas, Jr.
Cochran, Olive Leigh Myatt (Mrs. Raymond Nevitt Cochran)
Cochran, Samuel Lynn
Cochran, Thad
Cockrell, Claude O'Flynn, Jr.
Cockrell, Lila May
Codding, Frederick Hayden
Coder, Miguel
Cody, Raymond Gifford
Coe, Earl Frank
Coe, Miriam
Coe, Robert Stanford
Coe, William Clitus, Jr.
Cofer, James Erwin
Cofer, Vernon Lonsdale, Jr.
Coffee, James Madison, Jr.
Coffey, Charles James, II
Coffey, John Walter
Coffield, Conrad Eugene
Coffin, Miller Gerard
Coffman, Charlie Quinn
Coffman, Claude T.
Coffman, John Edwin
Coffman, Wesley Surber
Coffman, William Thomas
Cogdill, Roy Edward
Coggeshall, Robert Walden
Coggins, Robert Wayne
Cogswell, George Wallace
Cohen, Barry Mendel
Cohen, Bobbie Lee
Cohen, David Michael
Cohen, Elliott Zalman
Cohen, Eugene Erwin
Cohen, Felice Weill
Cohen, Frank
Cohen, Lois Miriam
Cohn, Isidore, Jr.
Cohn, Rebecca Roddey
Cohorn, Ron L.
Coiner, Richard Tide, Jr.
Coit, Robert Daniel
Coke, C(hauncey) Eugene
Coker, David Lee
Cokinos, Geneos Pete
Colbert, Joe
Colburn, Bruce Kendall
Coldiron, William Todd (Ted)
Cole, Dion Edward
Cole, Frank W.
Cole, George David
Cole, Harper Leroy, Jr.
Cole, Herschel Eugene
Cole, Karen Jo
Cole, Louise (Mrs. Cloyse Charles Cole)
Cole, Nancy D.
Cole, Norman Moore
Cole, Robert Jobe
Cole Sidney Cary
Cole, Thomas Earle
Cole, Thomas Winston, Jr.
Coleman, Adrian Wayne
Coleman, Carroll Wayne
Coleman, Catherine Towne
Coleman, Donald Claude
Coleman, Frank Carter
Coleman, James Edwin, Jr.
Coleman, James Preston, III
Coleman, Karen R. Howes
Coleman, Marion Leslie
Coleman, Richard Harvey
Coleman, Robert Boisseau, Jr.
Coleman, Robert Emerson
Coleman, Thomas Stokeley, Jr.
Coleman, William Ballin, III
Coleman, William Patrick, Jr.
Coles, William Henry
Coley, Betty Ann
Coley, Gideon Dean
Coley, Silas Bodie, Jr.
Colins, Christine Millar Maynard (Mrs. Christopher Colins)
Colins, Christopher
Collard, Albert Francis
Collett, Henry Augustus
Collett, Louisa Barry
Collier, Anthony Jay
Collier, Bobby Lee
Collier, Boyd Dean
Collier, Calvin Jefferson, Jr.
Collier, Courtland Alden
Collier, Durward Reed
Collier, Dwight Austin
Collier, Gaylan Jane
Collier, Henry Grady, Jr.
Collier, Henry Morgan, Jr.
Collier, Louis Malcolm
Collignon, Arthur P.
Collins, Alvin Oakley
Collins, Ann Elizabeth Averitt (Mrs. Galen Franklin Collins)
Collins, Ann Taylor
Collins, Arlee Gene
Collins, Arthur Andrews
Collins, Bayne
Collins, Charles Larry
Collins, Clarence Tillman
Collins, David Browning
Collins, Dennis Glenn
Collins, Don Elmo
Collins, Edward S.
Collins, Galen Franklin
Collins, Genevieve (Mrs. Frank Collins, Jr.)
Collins, Harry David
Collins, James Mitchell
Collins, Joseph Lawrence
Collins, Kathleen Morris Eudy
Collins, Marvin Vincent
Collins, Muriel Morse (Mrs. Denis Augustus Collins)
Collins, Reed
Collins, Royal Eugene
Collins, Stanley Penrose
Collins, Steven Douglas
Collins, Wendell Wray
Collins, William Clay
Collins, William Edward
Coln, Charles Dale
Colon, Gustavo Alberto
Colon, Ramery Luis E.
Coloney, Wayne Herndon
Colon-Vargas, Luis Angel
Colquitt, John Orville, Jr.
Colsky, Jacob
Coltharp, Leland Homer, Jr.
Coltman, Charles Arthur, Jr.
Colvin, (Otis) Herbert, Jr.
Colvin, Mary Ila
Colwell, Gene Thomas
Colwell, James Lee
Colyer, Julian S.
Colyer, Richard Allen
Comas, Joan Murphree
Combs, Austin Olin
Combs, Douglas Lee
Combs, Eddie
Combs, Joseph Franklin
Combs, Larry Lee
Combs, Robert Hearin
Combs, Walter Harrison
Comer, Donald, Jr.
Comer, Donald, III
Comer, Edward O'Brien
Comer, John Drewry
Comm, Edward Daniel
Committe, Thomas Carroll
Comola, James Paul
Compton, Henry Tayloe, Jr.
Compton, Joe Edward
Compton, Susan LaNell
Conaghan, Dorothy Dell
Conant, Chester Mavis, Jr.
Concon, Archimedes Abad
Conde, Cesar Augusto
Condom, Jaime Ernesto
Condon, Charles Francis M(ichael)
Condray, Ben Rogers
Condron, Stewart Lewis
Condry, Carson Emmitt
Cone, Carl B.
Cone, Thomas Fite, Sr.
Conerly, Cecil Lloyd, Jr.
Conger, Bernard Wallace
Conger, Claude Richard
Conger, Norman Lee
Conger, Stephen Halsey
Congleton, Donna McKinley
Congleton, James Cleveland, Jr.
Congram, Gary Eugene
Conklin, James Byron, Jr.
Conley, Cecil
Conley, David Lindsey
Conley, Mabel
Conley, Naomi Lee (Mrs. Cecil Conley)
Conn, Jack Trammell
Connally, Herschel Joseph
Connar, Richard Grigsby
Connell, Edward Peacock
Connell, James Frederick Louis
Connell, Richard Grant, Jr.
Connell, Suzanne (Sparks) McLaurin
Connor, Robert Carl
Connor, Seymour Vaughan
Conoley, Joann Shipman
Conolly, Richard Noble
Conrad, Troy Laverne
Conroy, David Jerome
Conroy, John Albert
Conroy, Normabelle Helmen
Constant, Clinton
Constantin, James Alford
Constantinides, Constantine (Dinos) Demetrios
Contacos, Peter George
Conte, Nicholas Ferdinand
Conti, Vincent Stephen
Contreras, Fermin M.
Converse, Philip Ray
Conway, Daniel Wilton Eskridge
Conway, French Hoge
Conway, James Anthony (Tony)
Conway, Mack Howard, Jr.
Conwell, Halford Roger
Conwell, Joseph Thomas
Conyers, J. C.
Cook, Allyn Austin
Cook, August Joseph
Cook, Bruce Farrell
Cook, Charles DeVere, Jr.
Cook, Charlotte Christine
Cook, Clayton Henry
Cook, Clifford Carroll
Cook, Damon Grant
Cook, Daniel Walter
Cook, Doris Marie
Cook, Edward Willingham
Cook, Ernest Ewart
Cook, Essie Nerren
Cook, George Glenn
Cook, Gloria Houston (Mrs. James Thomas Cook, Jr.)
Cook, Harry Stanley
Cook, Jack Dempsey
Cook, James Joseph
Cook, Jennings Bryan, Jr.
Cook, Leland Blanchard
Cook, Marian Alice
Cook, Maurice Gayle
Cook, Raldo Wolford
Cook, William Jesse, Jr.
Cooke, Helen Hemlin
Cooke, Henry Samuel, Jr.
Cooke, James L.
Cooke, Jerry (Gerald) Nichols
Cooke, John Franklin
Cooksey, William Travis
Cooley, James Franklin
Coolidge, Conrad Foss
Coombs, Virginia Ruth Hill
Cooney, Joseph Charles
Cooper, Agnes Pearson (Mrs. David Acron Cooper)
Cooper, Alan Bruce
Cooper, Bernard Labe
Cooper, Charles Dewey
Cooper, Charles Ellis
Cooper, Charles Howard
Cooper, Claude George
Cooper, David Acron, Jr.
Cooper, David Lawrence
Cooper, Eugene Bruce
Cooper, Franklin Dixon, Jr.
Cooper, George William Noel
Cooper, Harold Homer, Jr.
Cooper, Harry Ezekiel
Cooper, James Nelson
Cooper, Jerome Maurice
Cooper, Jimmy Lee
Cooper, Melvin Duley, Jr.
Cooper, Michael Christopher
Cooper, Norman Lee
Cooper, Richard Grant
Cooper, Robert Elbert
Cooper, Robert Franklin, Jr.
Cooper, Robert Gilbert
Cooper, Robert Lee
Cooper, Roger Merlin
Cooper, Roy Eugene, Jr.
Cooper, Samuel Taylor
Cooper, Terry Jack
Cooper, W(illiam) Douglas
Cooper, William Anderson, Jr.
Cooper, Willis Grant
Cooper, Winsor Arthur, Jr.
Cope, Richard Weldon
Copeland, Emily America
Copeland, Harry Elbert, Jr.
Copeland, James Casper
Copeland, Jimmy Bryant
Copeland, Murray M.
Copeland, Thompson Preston
Copemann, Chester Dean
Copenhaver, Wilfred Monroe
Coppick, Glendon Cleon
Coppin, John Stephens
Coppo, Richard Henry
Coppridge, Alton James
Corbitt, Duvon Clough
Corbitt, Gretchen Johnson
Corbitt, Richard Joseph
Corboy, Lou Ann Lancaster
Corboy, Michael Robert
Corcino, Jose Juan
Corcoran, Vincent John
Cordell, Alfred Robert
Cordell, DeWitt Bynum Cromer (Mrs. Alfred Robert Cordell)
Cordell, Robert James
Corgi, Remy (Telemachus)
Corlett, William Albert
Corley, Dewey Wayne
Corley, John Bryson
Corn, Ira George, Jr.
Cornelius, Earnie
Cornelius, Lawrence Bernhard
Cornelius, Wayne Anderson
Cornelius, William Pascal, Jr.
Cornett, Kenneth Ross
Cornish, Robert Sanford
Cornwall, E(spie) Judson
Corpuz Ambrosio, Erlinda Balancio
Corrada, Baltasar
Corrado, Benjamin William
Correll, Noble Otto, Jr.
Correll, Ward Forrest
Corrigan, Leo Francis, Jr.
Corsaro, Winnie Louise
Corsbie, David Ira
Corse, John Doggett
Corso, Joseph Victor
Corson, Louis Damarin
Cortes, Arsenio Ceferino
Cortina, Humberto Jose
Corum, Frank
Corwin, Gilbert
Corwin, Joyce Elizabeth Stedman
Corwin, Stephen Herbert
Corwin, William
Corzine, James Anthony
Cosby, J.C.
Cosmiano, Amando Cayading
Cossaboom, William Donald, Jr.
Cossar, George Payne
Costello, Joseph
Coster, Abraham Arthur
Coston, Donald Thomas
Coston, L. P.
Coston, Otis D., Jr.
Cothran, Alexander Forrest
Cothran, Oscar Richard, Jr.
Cotney, Steven Paul
Cottier, George John
Cottrell, Dan Fesmire
Cottrell, Samuel, IV
Couch, Buford James
Couch, James Houston
Couch, John Alexander
Couch, Urban S.
Couch, Wilson Paul
Coughlin, Joyce Desmond
Coughran, Samuel James, Jr.
Coulianos, Constantinos Haralampos
Coulliette, James Horace
Coulter, John Breitling, Jr.
Coulter, John Breitling, III
Coulter, S. Luther
Counts, Gurdon Wright, Jr.
Coupland, Bobby Emmet
Courage, Maxwell Bishop
Couts, Mary Frances
Cover, Norman Bernard
Covey, Charles Dean, III
Covington, Cecil Lyons
Covington, Robert Newman
Cowan, Charity Allene
Cowan, Joel Harvey
Cowan, Swaffield
Coward, Raymond
Cowart, Carl Miner
Cowden, John William
Cowell, Edward Joseph, Jr.
Cowey, Marjorie Jane
Cowles, Mark
Cowles, Milly
Cowling, Herford Tynes
Cox, Baxter Sydnor, III
Cox, Bertha Mae Hill (Mrs. Willis L. Cox)
Cox, Burnett Carroll
Cox, Clark
Cox, Claude Calvin
Cox, Donald Emery
Cox, Donald Vance
Cox, Edith Gloria (Mrs. Howard Reeves Cox Jr.)
Cox, Edwin, III
Cox, Floyd Brooks, Jr.
Cox, Gaylord Haines
Cox, Herman Ghrame, Jr.
Cox, Irene Dickson
Cox, James Oliver, III
Cox, Janson La Vern
Cox, Jere Louis
Cox, John Thomas, Jr.
Cox, Lindsay Wheeler, Jr.
Cox, Raymond George
Cox, Richard Eugene
Cox, Sanders Brownlow, Jr.
Coxe, Emily Badham (Mrs. Thomas Chatterton Coxe)
Coy, Charles R.
Coyne, George Kermit, Jr.
Coyner, Randolph Stratton, Jr.
Crabtree, Jack Turner
Crabtree, Ornal William
Crabtree, Theodore Eugene
Craddick, Thomas Russell
Craft, Chester Lee
Craft, Hugh Charles
Craft, Jerome Walter
Craft, Otho E., Jr.
Craft, Randal Robert
Crago, H. Carman, II
Craig, Darrell Max
Craig, Harris Vann
Craig, James Conover
Craig, Louis Elwood
Craig, Mark King
Craig, Robert E. Lee
Craig, Ronald Lester
Craig, Thomas E.
Craig, Thomas Harold
Craighead, Gordon Fulton, Jr.
Craighead, Moses Nathaniel
Crain, Berry, Jr.
Crain, Harold Stark
Crain, William Henry
Cram, Jack Randolph
Cramer, Ardis Lahann (Mrs. Howard Ross Cramer)
Cramer, David Nelson
Cramer, Forrest Eugene
Cramer, George Bennett
Cramer, John Scott
Cramer, Laura Schwarz
Cramer, William Monroe
Cramp, Donald Arthur
Crane, Beverly Brown
Crane, Frances Hawkins
Crane, Marilyn Joyce

Crane, Paul Shields
Crane, Richard Jasper
Crane, Ruth Ann
Crane, Terry
Crane, William Harry
Cranfill, Wilburn Franklin
Cranford, Henry Clay, Jr.
Cranford, Sammy Oren
Cranford, Thomas Edward
Crank, James Eldon
Craven, Douglas Charles
Craven, Harold Lloyd
Cravens, Margaret Evelyn Johnson
Craver, William Everett, Jr.
Cravey, Glenn Randall
Crawford, Andy William
Crawford, Carl LeRoy
Crawford, Frederick Leland, II
Crawford, Horace Randolph
Crawford, James Franklin
Crawford, John Milton, Jr.
Crawford, Luther Thomas
Crawford, Martha Helen
Crawford, Miles Nicholas
Crawford, Nickey Lewis
Crawford, Oliver Ray
Crawford, William Edwin
Crawley, John Emmett, Jr.
Crawley, Ronald Edward
Creamer, Dennis Joseph
Creekmore, David Dickason
Creighton, John Thomas
Cremins, William Daniel
Crenshaw, John Thomas
Crenshaw, Tena Lula
Cresimore, James Leonard
Creuzot, Percy Pennington, Jr.
Crevenna Singer, Hilda
Crew, Louie
Crews, D'Anne McAdams (Mrs. James Edward Crews, Jr.)
Crews, James Edward, Jr.
Crews, Malcolm Knight
Crews, William Daryl
Crews, William Preston
Criado, Valentin B.
Crim, Brenda Berry
Criner, Beatrice Hall
Criner, James Ellis
Crisostomo, Rofino San Nicolas
Crisp, George Blackmer, Jr.
Crispin, Roy Haynes
Critchlow, Donald Earl
Critchlow, Susan Melissa
Crites, Sherman Edwin
Crocker, George Wilson
Crockett, Stanley Theodore
Croft, Terrence Lee
Crofts, Dan William
Cromeans, Olyndia Laeondus
Cromeens, Bonna Lee
Cromer, Jerry Haltiwanger
Cromwell, Terry Alan
Crone, David Christian, Jr.
Cronin, Michael Grenade
Croninger, Raymond Harold
Crook, Howard Wilson
Crook, Robert Lacey
Crook, Roy Max
Crook, Troy Norman
Crooks, William Battle, Jr.
Croom, Estelle Luckey
Croom, Frederick Hailey
Croom, William Henry
Croom, William Sterling
Crooms, Joseph B.
Crosby, Harold Bryan
Crosby, Richard Collier
Crosby, Warren Melville
Cross, Gertrude Sara Erhard (Mrs. Robert Black Cross)
Cross, James Burchette
Cross, James Edward
Cross, Louise Portlock
Cross, Maxwell S.
Cross, Ward Hubert
Crossland, Edward John
Crosswell, Carol McCormick
Crotts, Marcus Bowman
Crotts, Monarae Metcalf
Crouch, Anna Belle
Crouch, James Hampton
Crouch, (Nora) Josephine
Crouch, Kesler James, Jr.
Crouse, Russell James, Jr.
Crovitz, Herbert Floyd
Crow, Alonzo Bigler
Crow, Gordon Allen
Crow, James Sylvester
Crow, Lester Donald
Crow, Neil Edward
Crow, William Cecil
Crowder, Camellia Huffman
Crowder, Charlie Clemons, Jr.
Crowder, Gene Autrey
Crowder, Helen Louise
Crowe, Byron Dan
Crowell, Virginia Smith
Crowell, Wayne Allen
Crowley, Billie Blalack (Mrs. H.W. Crowley)
Crowley, Harold James
Crozier, Fred Bond
Crues, Bobby Jim
Crum, Joseph Earl
Crum, Lawrence Lee
Crum, William Barton
Crumbley, George Pierce, Jr.
Crumley, Edward Welborn, III
Crummer, Roger Nelson
Crump, Charles Metcalf
Crump, Danny Ross
Crump, Kenny Sherman
Crump, Marjorie Virginia Dodson
Crump, Richard Loy
Crunk, William Atkins, Jr.
Cruse, Irma Belle Russell
Cruse, Julius Major, Jr.
Cruse, Robert Ridgely
Crusenberry, Christopher Chilton
Crusius, Milton Wood
Crusoe, Edwin Edgar, IV
Crutchfield, Finis Alonzo, Jr.
Cruz, Carlos
Cruz, Miguel Angel
Cruzan, Charles Grant
Cryer, Tommy Keith
Cuadrante, Minerva R. (Mrs. Jose Yolando Hernandez)
Cuatrecasas, Pedro Martin
Cuba, Benjamin James
Cudahy, William Brewer
Cukjati, Joseph Frank
Culberson, James Olin
Culberson, Randall Edward
Culbertson, Katheryn Campbell
Culbreth, Rayward Bill
Culkowski, Walter Martin
Cull, John G., Jr.
Cullen, Audrey Mae
Culler, Fred Benjamin, Jr.
Cullinan, Alice Rae
Cullinane, Joseph
Cullison, William Lester
Culp, Delos Poe
Culp, James Franklin
Culp, Martha Edwardine Street (Mrs. Delos Poe Culp)
Culpepper, John Cecil, Jr.
Culpepper, Marian Mish (Mrs. James Henry Culpepper)
Culpepper, Walter Edmund
Culver, Everett Elrod
Cumbie, Calvin Artimus
Cumerford, William Richard
Cumming, Joseph Bryan, Jr.
Cumming, William Kenneth
Cummings, Alice Marie
Cummings, Conrad Milton
Cummings, Donald Eugene
Cummings, Donald Ewton
Cummings, William Bruce
Cummings-Saxton, James
Cummins, Claire Marie
Cummins, Delmer Duane
Cundey, Paul Edward, Jr.
Cundiff, Otho Warren
Cunningham, Cherry Larson
Cunningham, E. Brice
Cunningham, Emory O.
Cunningham, John Newton
Cunningham, John Rood, Jr.
Cunningham, Roger Grady
Cunningham, Ronnie Walter
Cunningham, Warren Tabor
Cunningham, William Hughes
Curbow, Bobby Wayne
Curl, Jane Ann
Curl, Samuel Everett
Curlee, Lewis Elton
Curless, Lester Devere, Jr.
Curnutte, Robert Lee
Curran, Frank Richard
Curran, Helen
Currie, John Stuart
Currier, Robert David
Curry, A.F., III
Curry, John Ellis
Curry, Laura June
Curry, Mary Earle Lowry (Mrs. Peden Gene Curry)
Curtin, Bernadette Mary
Curtis, Carl Thomas
Curtis, Charles Garnsey
Curtis, Charles William, Jr.
Curtis, Don Teel
Curtis, James Robert
Curtis, James Robert, Jr.
Curtis, John Avery
Curtis, John Russell
Curtis, Johnny Mack
Curtis, Lillian Elizabeth
Curtis, Mary Gervase Barnett (Mrs. Buford C. Curtis)
Curtis, Ralph Franklin, Jr.
Curtis, Richard Harvey
Curtiss, Perry Judith Smith
Curts, Raymond James
Cush, Joseph Wilbur
Custodi, George Louis
Cusumano, Charles Louis
Cutler, Harold Mervin
Cutlip, Claude Ross
Cutlip, Henry David
Cutts, Virginia Allen Pairo (Mrs. Harvey Clark Cutts)
Czerniec, Timothy Henry
Dabbs, Chester Norwood
Dabbs, John Wilson Thomas
Dabbs, Miriam Adair (Mrs. Chester Norwood Dabbs)
Daggett, Bradford Ivan
Dagley, John Carl
D'Agnese, Helen Jean (Mrs. John J. D'Agnese)
Dahiya, Raghunath Singh
Dahlberg, Leola Lenora
Dahlke, Clarence Albert, Jr.
Dahne, Robert Aloysius
Daily, Louis
Dale, Dorothy Hughes
Dale, George William
Dale, Glenn Hilburn
Dale, John Irvin, III
Dalehite, William Moore, Jr.
D'Alessandro, Peter Louis, Jr.
Dalferes, Saramae Elizabeth
Dalgety, Peter George
Dalili, Hamid
Dalldorf, Frederic Gilbert
Dallman, Glenn Robert
Dallo, Peter K.
Dalrymple, David Edward
Dalton, Jess Newman
Dalton, John Nichols
Dalton, Larry Raymond
Dalton, Stuart Baker
Dalvit, Lewis David, Jr.
Daly, Frank Thomas, Jr.
Daly, James William
Daly, John J.
Daly, Patrick Joseph
Damato, David Joseph
D'Amato, Nicholas Anthony
D'Ambrosia, Robert Dominick
Dameron, Thomas Barker, Jr.
Damewood, George Pearis
Damewood, Thelma Welch
Damian, Raymond Traian
Damron, Ralph Ford
Danburg, Jerome Samuel
Danby, John Michael Anthony
Dancer, Jack Tom
Dancz, Roger Lee
Dandridge, William Shelton
Danforth, Frances Mueller (Mrs. William Paul Danforth)
Daniel, Abram Bird
Daniel, Dan
Daniel, Joseph Carl, Jr.
Daniel, Kathryn Barchard
Daniel, Ralph Winfield
Daniel, Robert Williams, Jr.
Daniell, Herman Burch
Daniells, Eleanor Grace
Danielpour, Mehri M.
Daniels, Charles Edward
Daniels, Dianne Susan
Daniels, Roger Dale
Daniels, William Edward
Danks, Dale, Jr.
Dann, Alexander William, Jr.
Dannecker, Max Predric
Dannelley, Perry Lee
Dannenbaum, James Denny
Danner, Lorain Duffin
Dansby, Huddie
D'Antonio, Albert, Jr.
Dantzler, Ernest Raymond, Jr.
Dantzler, Richard
Dapprich, John William
Darby, Luther Odell
Darby, Norma Jean
Darden, Conrad Lynn
Darden, David Lee, Jr.
Darden, John Waldon, III
Darden, William Howard, Jr.
Darling, Edward Craddock, Jr.
Darling, Leroy Anthony
Darnell, Charles, Jr.
Darracott, Halvor Thomas
Darracott, Mixon Milford
Darst, Betsy Hobgood
Dartez, Franklin
Dartez, Louis Avery
Das, Lachhman
Das, Nirmal Kanti
Das, Salil Kumar
daSilva, Ercio Mario
Daspit, Katharine
Daspit, Leo Paul, Jr.
Dastugue, Fernand Joseph, Jr.
Daub, Oscar Carl
Dauben, Dwight Lewis
Daubenspeck, Wayne Martel
Daughaday, Ruth Linn
Daugherty, Billy Joe
Daugherty, David Henry
Daugherty, Frederick Alvin
Daugherty, Kenneth Earl
Daugherty, Larry Gene
Daughtrey, Zoel Wayne
Daughtridge, Vernon Fletcher, Jr.
Daughtry, Leslie Preston
D'Auria, Richard Edward
Daussman, Grover Frederick
D'Avante, Shirley Jeanette
Davenport, David Eugene
Davenport, Fountain St. Clair
Davenport, William Harold
Davey, James Charles
Davey, Kenneth Roger
Davidge, Billy Lloyd
Davidoff, Robert
Davidow, Howard Bruce
Davidson, Mrs. Charles (Kate S. Davidson)
Davidson, Charles Nelson
Davidson, Gordon Byron
Davidson, James Joseph, III
Davidson, Maurice Crawford
Davidson, Philip Harold
Davidson, Steven Craig
Davidson, Vanda Arthur
Davidson, William Harold
Davie, Robert Nelson, Jr.
Davies, Archibald Donald
Davies, James Jay
Davis, Alice Virginia
Davis, Armand Roy
Davis, Arthur Jerrel
Davis, Augustus Hughes, Jr.
Davis, Baley, Jr.
Davis, Ben Reeves
Davis, Bertha Germize
Davis, Billy Joe
Davis, Burl Edward
Davis, Carl Lewis
Davis, Celestia Brannen
Davis, Courtland Harwell, Jr.
Davis, Danella Beth
Davis, David Cemer, Jr.
Davis, David Keithley
Davis, D'Earcy Paul, Jr.
Davis, Donald Goodwin, Jr.
Davis, Doris Lynn Matthews
Davis, Drexel Carter
Davis, Elise Miller (Mrs. Leo M. Davis)
Davis, Ernst Michael
Davis, Garnett Stant
Davis, Gertrude Irene
Davis, Gordon Leroy
Davis, Gordon William
Davis, Grant Miller
Davis, Hartwell
Davis, Mrs. Hartwell (Elizabeth Mardre)
Davis, Helen Grimsley
Davis, Henry Gordon, Jr.
Davis, Horance Gibbs, Jr.
Davis, Howard Don
Davis, Hugh Edward
Davis, Hugh Whitfield
Davis, James Earl
Davis, James Elsworth
Davis, Jefferson Clark, Jr.
Davis, Jerry Edwin
Davis, Jesse Dunbar
Davis, Jesse Edwin, Jr.
Davis, Joe Walter
Davis, John Aloysius
Davis, John Edward, Jr.
Davis, Julian Carlyle
Davis, Junius Ayers
Davis, Karen Elaine
Davis, Lawrence William
Davis, Lew Arter
Davis, Lucy Tolbert
Davis, Marjorie Fry
Davis, Matt McKinney, III
Davis, Mattie Mae
Davis, Mendel Jackson
Davis, Milton Victor
Davis, Milton Wickers, Jr.
Davis, Montie Grant
Davis, Neil Owen
Davis, Olivia Anne Carr (Mrs. Tom Lucian Davis)
Davis, Preston Caldwell
Davis, Raecile Gwaltney
Davis, Rex Lloyd
Davis, Robert Carter, Jr.
Davis, Robert Lowell
Davis, Robert Oliver
Davis, Ronald Kenneth
Davis, Russell Homer
Davis, Russell Reid
Davis, Sally Ann
Davis, Susan Hamm (Mrs. Paul Arnold Davis)
Davis, Susan Scott (Mrs. Gaylord Davis)
Davis, Terry Hunter, Jr.
Davis, Vincent
Davis, Virgil Leon
Davis, Walter Perry
Davis, William Robert
Davis, Winborn Elton
Davison, Frederick Corbet
Davison, Joseph Wade
Davisson, Mona June Garner
Davisson, Nelson Marc
Davy, Francis Xavier
Dawes, Charles Edward
Dawes, Henry
Dawley, Harry Francis, Jr.
Dawson, Earl Bliss
Dawson, Raymond Leslie
Dawson, Robert Edward
Dawson, Royce Edmund
Dawson, Samuel Cooper, Jr.
Dawson, Thomas Johnson
Day, A. Dewitt
Day, James Milton
Day, Mary Winifred Garvey (Mrs. George Earl Day)
Day, Richard Earl
Day, Roger Wilson
Dayton, Benjamin Bonney
Deal, Carl Hosea, Jr.
Deal, Frederick Gordon Scott
Dealey, Joseph MacDonald
Dean, Bob Wesley
Dean, Charles Albert, Jr.
Dean, David Allen
Dean, David Parks
Dean, Denis Allen
Dean, Harry Brooks
Dean, Ivy Bracegirdle
Dean, James Dudley
Dean, Janet E. Vaughn
Dean, Lloyd
Dean, Lydia Margaret Carter (Mrs. Halsey Albert Dean)
Dean, Robert Gayle, Jr.
Deane, Frederick, Jr.
De Armas, Frederick Alfred
Deas, James Edward, Jr.
Deaton, Fae Adams
Deaver, Henry Clayton, Jr.
Deaver, Pete Eugene
De Bakey, Lois
De Bakey, Michael E(llis)
De Baun, Charles Witter
Debbas, Samir Costandi
De Boer, George Herman
De Boer, Lloyd Martin
De Brooke, Thomas Vernon
Debusk, Edith M.
de Castongrene, Russell Othomar, Jr.
Dechert, Daniel Stratton
De Choudens-Laboy, Jose Miguel
Deckard, Charles
Decker, Alfred Stanley
Decker, Harold Lee
Decker, Warren Eugene
Dedo, Richard Gregg
Dedrick, John Henry
Dee, Norbert
Dees, James Willyn
Dees, LaFon Carabo
De Falco, Lawrence Michael
De Forest, Agnes Battelle Bonell (Mrs. Lionel Theodore De Forest)
De Forest, John Duane
De Forest, Lionel Theodore
DeFrank, Vincent
De Gaish, Melade S.
De Gerome, James Henry, III
de Groot, Sybil Gramlich
de Haan, Henry J.
De Hart, John Randle
De Hart, Robert Charles
De Hueck, George Theodore M.
Deidesheimer, Harold Jacob
Deiler, Frederick George
Deininger, Robert Wade
Deinzer, Harvey Theodore
De John, Charles Samuel
De La Burde, Brigitte Elisabeth (Mrs. Roger Z. De La Burde)
de la Burde, Roger Zygmunt
De La Garza, E(kika)
De Laitsch, Marion Karlsbroten
De Lamerens, Sergio Andres
Delaney, Lois Jean
Delaney, Thomas Caldwell, Jr.
De Lany, William Hurd, Jr.
de la Parte, Louis Anthony
de la Pena, Cordell Amando
De La Rosa, Martin Larios, Jr.
de la Sierra, Angell O.
Delaughter, Buford
De Lay, Wayne Tilden
Delbridge, Jerry Spencer
De Leeuw, Samuel Leonard
De Leon, Alberto
De Leon, Dora Lucila
Deleon, Edwin Lazaro
De Leonibus, Pasquale Salvitore
Deleray, John Early
Delgadillo-Moya, Claudio
Delgado, Alberto
Delgado, Humberto
Delius, Jack Coram
De Llano, Rodrigo Rubén
Dell'Osso, Louis Frank
Dell'Osso, Luino, Jr.
Del Re, Robert
Del-Rosario, Ernesto
de Lugo, Ronald
del Valle, Ignacio Gonzalez
Demaya, Charles Bertrand
Dembroski, Theodore Mark
Demecs, Desiderio Dezso
De Mello, Walmor Carlos
De Ment, Ira
Deming, Frank Cammack
Demmer, Harold Frank
Demopulos, Chris
De Moss, Jerry Vaughn
Dempsey, Bruce Harvey
Dempsey, Rodney Parrish
Dempsey, Terry Allen
De Naples, Mark Anthony
De Niord, Richard Newnham, Jr.
Denison, Henry Clark
Denius, Franklin Wofford
Denman, Andrew Jackson
Denman, Ben P.
Denman, Eugene Dale
Dennen, William Henry
Dennett, Edward Moore
Dennis, Bobby Glenn
Dennis, Danny Paul
Dennis, Earl Wilson, Jr.
Dennis, Edward Francis
Dennis, Frank Allen
Dennis, Henry Arnold
Dennis, Rutledge Melvin
Dennison, Clifford Calvin
Dennison, Harold Clay, Jr.
Dennison, John Manley
Denny, Charlotte Curti
Denny, J(ames) William
Denson, Jack Mc Vay
Dent, Danny Val
Dent, Hardy Lee, Jr.
Dent, John Robert
Denton, Wayne Lavert, Jr.
Dent O'Neill, Beverly
Deodati, Joseph Benjamin
De Pasquale, Nicholas Dominic
De Pínero, Europa González Garriga (Mrs. Jose A. De Pinero)
De Pingre, Major
Deppner, Francis Oakwood
De Priest, C(harles) David
Deptula, Joseph John
Derham, John Pickens, Jr.
Derian, Paul Sahak
Dern, Alvin
De Robertis, Edna Estella (Mrs. Fred De Robertis)
De Roeck, Walter A.
Derrick, Butler Carson, Jr.
Derrick, Johnny B.
Derrick, William Sheldon
Derryberry, Everett
Derryberry, Larry Dale
Derryberry, Walter Everett
Desai, Harshkumar Chimanlal
De Sanders, William Dwayne
De Saussure, Richard Laurens, Jr.
Des Champs, John Lefeber
Deschler, Lewis, II
De Selm, Henry Rawie
de Serres, Frederick Joseph
De Shazo, Gary Forrest
Desiderio, Dominic Morse, Jr.
Desmond, Patricia Lee
de Sombre, Robert Magnus
de Sousa, Paulo Jose Nobrega Moita Teixeira
Des Portes, Bernard Baruch
Dessauer, Herbert Clay
De Tar, DeLos Fletcher
Detjen, Don Wheeler
Detjen, Edward Yeamans
de Tonnancour, Paul Roger Godefroy
Detro, Randall Augustus
Dettbarn, Wolf-Dietrich
Dettmer, Eugene Henry
de Turczynowicz, Wanda Yolanda de Gozdawa Anzelm (Mrs. Eliot Hermann)
Detwiler, Samuel B(ertolet), Jr.
Deutsch, Paul Michael
Deutsch, Stuart Jay
de Valázquez, Mary Rivera
De Vaney, Amogene Fowler
de Veer, William Kipp
de Vergie, Alain Constant
De Vine, Billie Mack
De Vito, Teresa Maria
De Voll, Charles Wesley
Devore, Margaret Bowen (Mrs. Robert N. Devore)
Devoy, Charles Stephen
De Vries, Douwe
Dew, Jess Edward
Dew, John Kenneth
Dewar, Mildred (Jo) Eller (Mrs. Donald Norman Dewar)
Dewar, Timothy Smith
Dewberry, Earnest Edward
de Wette, Frederik Willem
De Witt, Robert Jothan
De Zeih, Chester James
Dezenberg, George John
Dhillon, Raghbir Singh
Diamond, Harvey Jerome
Diasio, Clara Flora (Mrs. Joseph S. Diasio)
Diaz, H. Joseph
Diaz, José Luis
Diaz-Coller, Carlos
Diaz-Noriega, José Miguel
Diaz-Royo, Antonio T.
Di Barros, Eduard
Dibrell, George Edward
Dicharry, Roy Maurice
Dick, George Walter
Dick, Lois A. (Mrs. Carl E. Dick)
Dickenson, Frederick Joseph, Jr.
Dickerson, Larry Richard
Dickerson, Loren Lester, Jr.
Dickerson, Merle Leroy
Dickerson, Thomas Howard
Dickey, John Coke
Dickey, Lee Dowling
Dickey, Raymond Adelle
Dickie, Laurance Porter
Dickinson, Edmund John
Dickinson, Howard Grant
Dickinson, William Louis
Dicks, Joseph Lewis, Jr.
Dickson, Claudia Blair
Dickson, Constantine John
Dickson, Eleanor Jane Browne
Dickson, Frank Alexander
Dickson, James Gilmer
Dickson, Lillian Durham
Dickson, Roy Shelton, Jr.
Dickson, Sandler Harvey
Di Dea, Arthur Anthony
Didier, Lydia Marchive
Diederich, John William
Diehl, Grover Edwin
Diehl, William Francis
Diehr, David B.
Diener, Mary Eleanor McMath
Dienhart, Charlotte Marie
Diercks, Frederick Otto
Dies, Federico
Dietlein, Lawrence Frederick
Dietrich, Edwin Jerry
Dietrich, Ernest John, Jr.
Dietrich, Raymond Arthur
Dietsche, Heinz Brent Jurgen
Dietze, Charles Edgar
Diez-Rivas, Federico Manuel
Diggs, Lemuel Whitley
Diggs, Melvin M.
D'Ignazio, Silvio Frederick, III
Dikeou, James Theodore
Dillahunty, Wilbur Harris
Dillard, Robert Garing (Gary), Jr.
Dillard, Rodney Jefferson
Dilley, Jerry Dale
Dillin, Jake Thomas, Jr.
Dillman, George Franklin
Dillon, Clarence Edward
Dils, Robert James
Dilworth, Billy D.
Dilworth, Edwin Earle
Dimitriou, John Alexander
Dimitroff, Edward
Dineen, Joseph Lawrence

Dinger, Donald Brackett
Dinger, Mary Ann
Dingfeider, Steven Peter
Dingledine, Raymond Carlyle, Jr.
Dingus, Gerald Dwyn
Diodene, Alonzo Nelson, Jr.
Dion, Raymond Octave
DiPlacido, Francis Paul, Jr.
Dippy, Theodore Albert
Director, Herman
Dirst, Richard Dustin
DiSanto, Frank Michael
Di Santo, Grace Johanne DeMarco (Mrs. Frank Michael Di Santo)
Disher, David Alan
Dissly, Donald Dyer
Disston, Harry
Dittmer, Gary Dennis
Ditto, Mary Ann
Dittrich, Gaines Standley
Di Vincenzo, Joseph Russell
Dix, Fralan Ludy
Dixon, Eva Crawford Johnson
Dixon, Hal Bernard
Dixon, Jackie
Dixon, Jarma Edward, Jr.
Dixon, Joseph Moore
Dixon, Richard Arnold Fonville
Dixon, Wallace Clark, Jr.
Dixon, William Bradford
Doan, Patricia Nan
Doane, Dee Ann
Doane, Harold Everett
Dobbins, Charlie Coleman
Dobbins, Loy Henderson
Dobbins, Polly Sue
Dobbins, Silas Crayton, Sr.
Dobbs, Wayne
Dobes, William Lamar, Jr.
Dobson, Charles William
Dobson, Gerard Ramsden
Dobson, Harold Lawrence
Dobson, John Harrison
Dobyns, Roy Armstead
Dockery, Charles C.
Dockery, Thomas Harlowe
Dockray, George Henry
Doctor, Vasant Manilal
Dodd, James Lee
Dodd, Lawrence Roe
Dodd, Richard Winne
Dodd, William Ray, Jr.
Dodds, Joseph J.
Dodge, Billy Gene
Dodge, Charles Fremont, III
Dodge, Eva Francette
Dodge, Warren Francis
Dodgen, William Henry
Dodson, BC
Dodson, Bertram Felix
Dodson, Eugene Benedict
Dodson, James Clifton
Dodson, Ronald Franklin
Doekel, Robert Carl, Jr.
Doenanan, Carlton Ramrattan
Doenges, Rudolph Conrad
Doherty, James Edward, III
Doherty, Michael Fowler
Doherty, Thomas Ross
Doi, Yutaka
Doke, Marshall J., Jr.
Dolan, John Bernard
Dolbec, Elizabeth Louise
Dolce, Peter Sebastian
Dolenz, Bernard Joseph
Dolezal, Charles Henry
Dolezal, Henry
Dollinger, Robert Edward
Doman, Lewis Albert, Jr.
Dombalis, Constantine Nicholas
Dombrowski, Madge Cohea (Mrs. Casey William Dombrowski)
Domeyer, Nancy
Dominguez, Daniel
Dominguez, Jose Ramon
Dominguez, Louis Ginesi
Dominick, Wayne Dennis
Dominy, Matthew
Domit, Moussa M.
Domurat, Richard Francis
Don, Elliott
Donahue, Franklyn William
Donahue, Hayden Hackney
Donald, Derbonne Ray
Donaldson, Loraine
Donaldson, Merle Richard
Donatelli, Felix Francis
Donato, Antonio Tuason
Donaubauer, Elton Henry
Donchian, Richard Davoud
Donegan, Charles Kendall
Donnell, Harold Douglas, Sr.
Donnellan, Thomas A.
Donnelly, Lloyd William, Jr.
Donoghue, Gerald Thomas
Donovan, James Mayfield, Jr.
Donovan, Timothy Paul
Donovan, William Francis
Doody, Louis Clarence, Jr.
Dooley, Wallace Troy
Dopson, Terry Ray
Dore, Mary D.
Doremus, Ogden
Dorenkamp, Henry Joseph, Jr.
Dorfan, Herbert Isaac
Dorfman, Myron Herbert
Dorman, John Frederick
Dorman, Pamela Ann
Dormois, John Carl
Dorn, Richard Alden
Dorn, Richard Donald
Dornbach, John Ellis
Dornbush, Kirk Terry
Dorough, Virginia Ann
Dorr, Annie Maude Dean (Mrs. William Henry Dorr)
Dorr, John Robert
Dorris, Henry Clay
Dorsch, Louis Milton
Dorsett, Cora Matheny
Dorsett, Luanna Miller
Dorsett, Walter Eckomer, Jr.
Dorsey, Daniel Roberdeau, Jr.
Dorsey, Harold Winston
Dorsey, Jasper Newton
Dorsey, Kevin Earle
Dortch, Lawrence
Doscher, Jürgen Henry
Dosher, John Rodney
Doskocil, Annie Mary
Doss, Arden Glen, Jr.
Doss, Faye Williams
Doss, Frances Sells
Dossett, Walter Brown, Jr.
Doster, James Fletcher
Dotson, Albert Eugene
Dotson, Billy Junior
Dotson, Robert Lee
Dotson, Ronald Lynnewood
Doty, Glen Anderson
Douce, William Clark
Dougherty, Billy Buell
Dougherty, Hugh Larrabee, Jr.
Dougherty, J(ohn) Chrys(ostom)
Dougherty, Jack Francis
Dougherty, William H., Jr.
Douglas, Barton Thrasher
Douglas, Charlie (Douglas China)
Douglas, DeAnna Mae
Douglas, Hubert Prentiss
Douglas, Nehemiah Elias
Douglas, Ralph Waldo
Douglass, Curtis Lindsey
Dove, Lloyd Alvin
Dover, Monte Eugene
Dow, Robert Frederick
Dow, Thomas Wendell
Dowben, Robert Morris
Dowdle, Nash James
Dowler, Earl Ray
Dowler, James Ross
Dowling, Jacques MacCuiston
Dowling, Jerry Clair
Dowling, Joab Mauldin
Downey, James Cecil
Downey, Marlin Ray
Downey, William Gerald, Jr.
Downey-Prince, Eleanor Pauline Long
Downing, Carl Seldon
Downing, Edward Farmer
Downing, Vincent Francis
Downs, Earl Davis
Downs, Eldon Wilson
Downs, James Cade
Downs, James Tickell, III
Downs, Jon Franklin
Downs, Lawrence Mitchell
Doyle, Brian Bowles
Doyle, Frank Lawrence
Doyle, James Michael
Doyle, Jean Eleanor
Doyle, John Robert, Jr.
Doyle, Lynn Curtis
Doyle, Sister Patricia
Doyle, Robert Alan
Doyon, Gérard Maurice
Dozier, Carroll T.
Dozier, William Albert
Draeger, Kenneth Earl
Dragstedt, Carl Albert, Jr.
Draine, Doretha (Mrs. Austin Wiley)
Drake, Albert Estern
Drake, June Dunn
Drake, Laurence
Drake, Vaughn Paris, Jr.
Dran, John Joseph
Draper, Porter Russell
Draper, Robert Bruce
Draper, William Leonard
Drasen, Richard Frank
Drasin, Nathan George
Drawdy, Vance Brabham
Drazic, Milimir
Dressler, Robert
Drew, Horace Rainsford, Jr.
Drew, Jack Irving
Drewry, Garth Richard
Drewry, Guy Carleton
Drewry, Joseph Samuel, Jr.
Drewry, William Alton
Drewyer, Roland Paul
Drey, Alan
Driskell, Carl Rowland
Driskell, Eloise Whitehurst
Droz, Dale Andrew
Drucker, David H.
Drumm, Morris Don
Drummond, Gary David
Drummonds, David Leslie
Drury, Leonard Leroy
Drury, Lloyd Leonard
Drury, Thomas Joseph
Dry, Owen Lee
Dryden, David Charles
Dryden, William
Drye, Richard Leven
Drye, Robert Weldon
Duane, Camille (Mrs. Frank Duane Rosengren)
Duane, Frank
Dubach, Harold William
Du Bard, (Nettie) Etoile
Duberg, John Edward
Du Bois, Eugene Eli
Du Bose, Bob Sid
Du Bose, Carus Kisner Hicks
Du Bose, Dorothy Gamble (Mrs. William Shelton Du Bose)
Du Bose, George Thomas
Dubose, Jack Mark
Du Bose, James Daulton
DuBose, Robert N(ewsom)
Dubrow, Richard Samuel
Dubsky, Vaclav P.
Ducharme, Jean Marc
Duchman, John Hughes
Duckett, Charles Howard
Duckworth, Robert Otis
Ducre, Pearl Elayne Dees
Dudley, Carolyn S.
Dudley, Clarence Raymond, Jr.
Dudley, George William
Dudney, Richard Kennington
Dudot Cosme, Carlos Edilio
Dudrick, Stanley John
Duerksen, Dean Fariss
Duerr, William Allen
Duff, Willard Earl
Duff, William Grierson
Duffell, Gordon Michael
Duffey, Donald Creagh
Duffey, Paul Kevin, Jr.
Duffy, Kurt Patrick
Dugan, Charles Clark
Dugan, Kimiko Hatta
Dugan, Mildred Claire
Dugan, Richard Franklin
Dugdale, Marion (Mrs. James G. McClure)
Duggan, Francis Foster
Duggan, Reo Eldred
Duggins, George Calvin
Duhart, Eveline
Duhon, Rex D.
Duke, Albert Ellis
Duke, Charles Wayne
Duke, Douglas Earle
Duke, Michael Benton
Duke, Reese Dale
Duke, Richard John
Duke, Theodore John
Dukes, James Beacham
Dukes, Philip Duskin
Dukes, Robert Chambers
Dulaney, Alice Elizabeth
Dulaney, Allena Faye
Dulaney, Luther Thomas, Jr.
Dulin, William Easterday
Dullea, John Joseph
Dulmage, Howard Taylor
Duma, Richard Joseph
Duman, Barry Lance
Dunagan, John Conrad
Dunaway, Alton A.
Dunaway, Donna Elizabeth Kastle
Dunaway, James Lee, Jr.
Dunbar, Carl Owen
Dunbar, Georgia Breaux
Dunbar, James Curtis
Dunbar, John Patrick
Duncan, Carl Irvin
Duncan, Donn Robert
Duncan, Hattie A.
Duncan, Inez Boyd
Duncan, James Loughlin
Duncan, John Eblen
Duncan, John James
Duncan, John Wiley
Duncan, Joseph
Duncan, Joseph Donald
Duncan, Lowell Cantrell, Jr.
Duncan, Paul
Duncan, Pope Alexander
Duncan, Thomas Everett
Duncan, Thomas Ray
Duncan, William Neil
Dunford, Birties Ray
Dungan, Thomas Miller
Dunlap, George Robert
Dunlap, Henry Francis
Dunlap, Joe Everett
Dunlap, Roy L.
Dunlap, Wallace Hart
Dunn, Adolphus William
Dunn, Byron G.
Dunn, Charles Edward Lee, Jr.
Dunn, Charles Jerome
Dunn, Charles Thomas
Dunn, Charleta Jessie (Mrs. Roy E. Dunn)
Dunn, Floyd Warren
Dunn, Harrison A.
Dunn, Henry Hampton
Dunn, J. D.
Dunn, John Thornton
Dunn, Larry Bloxham
Dunn, Leon Algernon, Jr.
Dunn, Marie Cloar
Dunn, Michael Earl
Dunn, Michael Kielly
Dunn, Neal Joseph
Dunn, Robert Cullen
Dunn, Robert George, III
Dunn, Thomas Tinsley
Dunn, William Harp
Dunn, William Rufus
Dunne, John Vincent
Dunnigan, David Ray
Dunning, Wilhelmina Frances
Dunphy, Loretta Mary
Dunstan, Edgar Mullins
Dunstan, Florene Johnson
Dunton, James Gerald
Dunwody, Eugene Cox
Dupepe, F(rank) Clancy
Du Pré, Grace Annette
Dupree, Emmett Lee, Jr.
Dupree, James Henry
Du Priest, Bette Ruth Horton (Mrs. Dennis Black DuPriest, Jr.)
Du Puis, Robert Thomsen
Dupuy, Sidney Joseph, III
Duque, Homer Adolph
Duran, Otis S(amuel)
Duran, Rafael Jorge
Du Rant, Mary Lois Reynolds
Duremdes, Generoso Divinagracia
Duren, Jack Daniel
Durham, Floyd Wesley, Jr.
Durham, Grover Hugh
Durham, Homer Leroy, Jr.
Durham, Jane Tuttle
Durham, Joseph William
Durham, Lucy Elizabeth
Durham, Marsha
Durham, Walter Winn
Durkee, Dale Crowell
Durlach, Marcus Russell
Durrence, James Larry
Duruman, Nevzat Ahmet
Dusek, Edwin Ralph
Dusenbury, Joseph Hooker
Dusi, Julian Luigi
Duson, Walter Webb, III
Dutt, Ray Horn
Dutton, Arthur Morlan
Dutton, Bob Wayne
Dutton, Marvin Allen
Duttweiler, David William
Duval, Claude Berwick
Du Val, Miles P., Jr.
Du Val, Robert Glinn
Duvall, William Clyde, Jr.
Dvoretzky, Isaac
Dwiggins, Claudius William, Jr.
Dyal, Lucius Mahlon, Jr.
Dyar, William Heller
Dyches, Hilda Gunter
Dyck, Walter Peter
Dye, James Miles
Dye, Kenneth Robert, Jr.
Dyer, Dolores
Dyer, Isadore
Dyess, Bobby Dale
Dyess, Shirley Avon
Dykeman, Wilma (Mrs. James Rorex Stokely, Jr.)
Dykers, John Reginald, Jr.
Dykes, Norman Wayne
Dykes, Willis Gerald
Dyson, Gene
Dyson, Samuel Archer
Eades, Thomas William
Eadie, John Michael
Eads, Paul Thomas
Eagles, William McCoy
Eagleson, Thomas Walter
Eames, William James
Eanes, Edwin Coley
Eanes, Michael Bailey
Earley, Hubert Randolph
Earls, James Roe
Earls, Robert Westfield
Early, John Levering
Early, Julian Quayle
Earnheart, Ernest Dane
Earp, James Francy
Earthman, Michael Richard
Earvin, Larry Lee
Easley, Charles Taylor
Eason, Helga Ruth Halvorsen (Mrs. Morris Jackson Eason)
Eason, Larry Don
East, Charles Robert
East, Dorothy Gail
Eastland, David Meade
Eastland, James O.
Eastmoore, Eugene Legare
Eastridge, Charles Edwin
Eastwood, Richard Truman
Eavenson, Lester Wright
Eaves, William Alfred
Ebaugh, Elizabeth Brown (Mrs. Frank Wright Ebaugh)
Ebaugh, Frank Wright
Ebbs, John Dale
Ebel, Robert Arthur
Eberle, William Francis
Ebersole, Alva Vernon
Ebert, Myrl Lua-Frances
Echandi, Eddie
Echenique, Jorge
Echols, James Kermit
Eck, Edgar Clarence, Sr.
Eckberg, Lloyd Ellsworth
Eckenfelder, William Wesley, Jr.
Eckert, Jerry Wayne
Eckert, Vera Lillian
Eckhardt, Robert Christian
Eckley, Gerald Boice
Eckman, Carl Earl, Jr.
Eckols, Howard Loyd
Eckstein, Robert Ephraim
Eddin, M. Shehab
Eddings, Anthony Harrison
Eddleman, Henry Leo
Eddleman, William Lee, Jr.
Edds, Stephen Charles
Eddy, George Gage, Jr.
Edelman, Joseph Martin
Edgar, James Harvey
Edgar, Thomas Flynn
Edge, Goode Bryant
Edgerton, A. Freeman
Edgerton, Richard
Edgington, Walter Roy
Edinger, Ward Munson
Edisen, Clayton Byron
Edmison, Marvin Tipton
Edmisten, Rufus L.
Edmond, Thetis Charlene
Edmonds, Bobby Franc
Edmonds, Henry David
Edmonds, John Willis, III
Edmonds, Thomas Newton
Edmonds, William Belton
Edmondson, Ruby Johnson
Edmonson, George Hampton, Jr.
Edmunds, James Telford
Edmunds, Stephen Orrell
Edmundson, Judith Mixon Ramsay
Edwards, Acie Carlton
Edwards, Benjamin Franklin, Jr.
Edwards, Brian Alfred
Edwards, Claude Reynolds
Edwards, David Lee
Edwards, Don Raby
Edwards, Edgar Clark
Edwards, Edwin Washington
Edwards, Eloise Doss
Edwards, Emmett Weldon
Edwards, Harold Mills
Edwards, Hoyt Randall
Edwards, Jack
Edwards, James Benjamin
Edwards, James Burrows
Edwards, James Edwin
Edwards, James Preston
Edwards, John Dixon, Jr.
Edwards, Joseph Daniel, Jr.
Edwards, (Floyd) Kenneth
Edwards, Lyman Mahlon
Edwards, Marvin H. Mickey
Edwards, Marvin Raymond
Edwards, Palmer Lowell
Edwards, Richard Wayne
Edwards, Scott Samuel, Jr.
Edwards, Virgie Lee
Edwards, Wallace Hayward
Edwards, William Hawkins
Edwards, William Raymond
Effinger, George Alec
Efird, Killian Daniel
Efron, Marvin
Efthemes, George H.
Egan, M(artin) David
Egan, Robert Lee
Egan, William Joseph, III
Eggen, Douglas Ambrose
Eggers, Paul Walter
Ehart, Rosalie Boswell
Ehle, John Marsden, Jr.
Ehle, John Marsden, Sr.
Ehlers, Herbert Edmund
Ehlman, William George
Ehrensperger, Fred Earl
Ehrenthal, Frank F.
Ehrlich, S(aul) Paul, Jr.
Eich, Wilbur Foster, III
Eichelberger, Dean Austin
Eidson, Jack Leigh
Eidson, John Olin
Eidson, Perrin Cudd (Mrs. John Olin Eidson)
Eilbott, Reginald A., Jr.
Einspruch, Burton Cyril
Eisele, Garnett Thomas
Eisenberg, Harry Victor
Eisman, Diane Batshaw
Eiss, Albert Frank
Ekers, John Anderson, II
Ekery, Fred Nicholas
Ekey, David Clifton
Ekwall, Merton Leon
Elad, Emanuel
Elam, Andrew Gregory, II
Elam, Mary Glendinning
El Bavadi, Nagui Rizk
Elden, Walter Lawrence
Elder, Francis Lafayette
Elder, Mark Lee
Eldridge, Francis Lee
Eldridge, Francis R., Jr.
Elebash, Hunley Agee
Elegant, Ira Michael
Elequin, Cleto, Jr.
Eleuterius, Charles Kemuel
Elgin, Douglas Lee
El Hage, Sami George
Elkin, Abe
Elkin, Benjamin James
Elkins, Gary Wayne
Elkins, James Anderson, Jr.
Elkins, Larry Owen
Ellefson, George Edwin, Jr.
Ellenburg, Robert Blanton
Ellenson, Eugene Peter
Ellet, Alfred Lee
Ellington, Preston David
Elliot, Davis Haskins
Elliot, Larion Joseph
Elliot, Si
Elliot, Simon
Elliott, Charles Martin
Elliott, Charles Newton
Elliott, Clarence Willard
Elliott, David Ross
Elliott, Emanuel John
Elliott, Frankie Jo Lewis
Elliott, J(ames) Robert
Elliott, Jim Lynn
Elliott, John Franklin
Elliott, Morris Francis
Elliott, Robert Burl
Elliott, Roger Neale
Elliott, Stephen Marion
Elliott, Wayne Gordon
Ellis, Barbara June McDaniel
Ellis, David Bradley
Ellis, Donald Rich, Jr.
Ellis, Elmo Israel
Ellis, Gary Melton
Ellis, Gilbert William
Ellis, James Bowman
Ellis, Joanna Kay Jones
Ellis, John Nelson
Ellis, John Wesley
Ellis, Larscie
Ellis, Morris Ray
Ellis, Quincy Ambrose, III
Ellis, Raymond Earl
Ellis, Robert Franklin
Ellis, Robert Rufus, III
Ellis, Ryan Bradford
Ellis, Samuel Teel
Ellis, William Tinsley
Ellison, Floyd Edwin, Jr.
Ellison, Luther Frederick
Ellison, Thorleif
Elliston, Lura Duff (Mrs. Fred Addison Elliston)
Elliston, William Jackson, Jr.
Ellwood, B(ud) M. Basil, Jr.
Elmer, Doris Eileen
Elmes, David Gordon
Elmore, Carroll Dennis
Elmore, Samuel Eltinge
Elmquist, Anne Marie
Elmquist, Karl Erik
Elovitz, Mark Harvey
Elrod, Parker David
Elsas, Louis Jacob, II
Elsass, John Frank
Elsasser, George Frederick, Jr.
Elsey, Katherine Jones
El-Sharkawy, Abdellatif Ibrahom
Elsner, Roy Arthur
Elsom, Donald Stewart, Jr.
Elston, Robert Charles
Elzey, James Lewis
Emens, Steven Countiss
Emerick, Henry Mitchell, Jr.
Emerson, Ann Parker
Emerson, David Edwin
Emerson, Donald McGeachy, Jr.
Emerson, Horace Mann, III
Emerson, Marvin Chester
Emerson, Maxwell
Emerson, O.D.
Emerson, Robert Biscal
Emerson, Robert Winchester
Emerson, Walter Caruth
Emery, Clyde
Emery, Durward Leslie
Emery, Edgar Milton
Emery, Jared Maurice
Emery, Leonard Willis
Emily, James Lee
Emmanuelli, Juan Ramon, Jr.
Emmons, Ronald Reece
Enck, Rudolph Robert
Endicott, James Nesbit
Endo, Akira
Enelow, Morton Leonard
Enersen, Robert John
Enfield, Morris Conrad, Jr.
Engel, Gerald Lawrence
Engel, Walburga von Raffler (Mrs. A. Ferdinand Engel)
Engelbrecht, Barry John
Engen, Thorkild Jensen
England, London Thurman
England, Martha Jean Gould
Englerth, William Moyer
English, Bruce Vaughan
English, George W.
English, Glenn Lee, Jr.
English, Marie R.
Enloe, Joseph
Ennis, John Matthews
Enoch, Jay Martin
Ensenat, Louis Albert
Enslen, George Clinton
Enslen, Sanford William
Ensley, Arvil Gene
Entsminger, Phillip Walter
Eppens, Francisco Othon
Epperly, John David
Epperson, Crystal Nadine
Eppes, Tom Allan
Epps, James Haws, III
Epps, James Vernon
Epstein, Arthur William
Epstein, Barry Michael
Erb, Richard Louis Lundin
Erbele, Leo Albert
Erbs, Harold John
Erdey, Dale Michael
Erdman, David Williams
Erfe, Jose Asperin
Erfft, Kenneth Reynders
Erickson, Andrew John
Erickson, Dennis Harold
Erickson, Eric Leroy
Erickson, Frederick Kenneth
Erickson, Howard Hugh
Ericson, Carolyn Reeves
Ericson, Joe Ellis
Ernouf, Anita Bonilla
Ervin, Jerry Newton
Ervin, Samuel James, III
Erwin, James Walter
Erwin, Jean Hocking
Erwin, John Preston, Jr.
Esch, Leroy Ted
Eschenbrenner, Gunther Paul
Eskrigge, Tatham Robson
Esogbue, Augustine Onwuyalim
Esparza, Thomas, Sr.
Espey, Lawrence Lee
Espy, Isaac Pugh
Espy, Joseph Samuel
Esrey, Alexander Johnson, Jr.
Esslinger, Anna Mae Linthicum

Esslinger, William Glenn
Esteb, Adial Albert
Estep, Michael Ray
Estep, William Roscoe, Jr.
Estes, Billy Dean
Estes, Dewitt Ocle
Estes, Gerald Walter
Estes, Harold Loyd
Estes, Moreau Pinckney, IV
Estes, Nolan
Esteves, Alberto Raul
Estis, Willis Cleve
Esval, Orland Edwin
Etchison, Annie Laurie
Ethell, Jeffrey Lance
Etheredge, Robert Foster
Etheridge, Albert Louis
Eubanks, Michael Ray
Eudaly, Dick
Eudaly, Hazel Marie (pen name Maria Saddler de Eudaly)
Eudaly, Nathan Hoyt
Euliss, Ray Cooper
Eun, Bongsoo
Euton, Michael Fred
Evans, Albert Louis
Evans, Beatrice Singleton
Evans, Billy Lee
Evans, Burford Elonzo
Evans, Carl Jene
Evans, Charles Andrew
Evans, Charles Harrison
Evans, Charles William
Evans, Constance Bennett
Evans, De Ette
Evans, Edwin Curtis
Evans, Ernest Colston
Evans, Harold Leroy
Evans, Hawthorne Clough, Jr.
EVans, Hazel Atkinson
Evans, James William, Jr.
Evans, John Lewis, Jr.
Evans, Joyce Stewart (Mrs. Joe Mack Evans)
Evans, Lyle Kenneth, Jr.
Evans, Overton Chenault, II
Evans, Raymond
Evans, Robert Arthur
Evans, Robert B.
Evans, Rodney Earl
Evans, Rosemary King (Mrs. Howell Dexter Evans)
Evans, Victoria Gehman
Evans, William Bryce
Evans, William Buell
Evelsizer, Ronald Lee
Everard, William Howard
Eversole, Alex Gordon
Evett, Russell Dougherty
Evitts, Charles Allen
Ewald, Kenneth Owen
Ewart, Robert Franklin
Eways, Munir Salem
Ewen, Joel Joachim
Ewers, William Morrison
Ewerz, Nancy Maureen
Ewing, Charles William
Ewing, John Kirby
Exum, Joseph Lafayette, Jr.
Ezell, Dee Earl
Ezell, Earl Geer
Fabry, Paul Andrew
Fackelman, Robert Henry
Fagan, Maurice James, Jr.
Faggett, Harry Lee
Fagin, George J.
Faherty, Michael Edward
Fahey, John Augustine
Fahey, John E.
Fahlberg, Willson Joel
Fahringer, Catherine Hewson
Fairbanks, Harold Vincent
Fairchild, Clare Edwill
Fairchild, David Arthur
Fairchild, Joseph Virgil, Jr.
Fairchild, Phyllis Elaine
Faircloth, Joseph Sherron
Faircloth, Wayne Reynolds
Faires, Dunn Thomas
Fairleigh, Margaret Hills
Fairstein, Edward
Fairweather, Charles Walter, III
Faison, Frank Allen
Falgoust, Edward Joseph, Jr.
Falk, Hans Ludwig
Falkenbury, Stephen Douglas, Jr.
Fallon, Barry Michael
Fallon, Harold Joseph
Fallon, Paul Francis
Falor, Craig Hamilton
Fandrich, Robert Thomas, Jr.
Fang, Cheng Shen
Fannin, Troy Edward
Fanning, Charles Buckner
Fanning, Hal L., Jr.
Fanning, John Wood
Fanning, Robert Allen
Fanshier, Chester
Fant, Albert Reese
Fant, Francis Rodgers, Jr.
Fant, Sadie Patton
Farber, George Allan
Farfour, Leslie Aloysius, Jr.
Fargo, Robert Ray
Faria, Edward Cyrino
Farina, John Richard
Farinacci, Charles Joseph
Farioletti, Marius
Farish, Stephen Thomas, Jr.
Fariss, James Lee, Jr.
Farley, Jack Emory
Farley, Mary Lyn Crisp
Farley, Sandra Spradlin
Farlow, E(lbert) Allison
Farman, Irvin Samuel
Farmer, Blaine Jackson, Jr.
Farmer, James Danny
Farmer, James Sebrell
Farmer, John David
Farmer, Joseph Clarence, Jr.
Farmer, William Anderson
Farnell, Michael Joseph
Farr, William Monroe
Farren, John Bernard, Jr.
Farrens, Gerald Elmer
Farri, Elias Peter
Farringer, John Lee, Jr.
Farrior, Joseph Brown
Farris, Charles Edward
Farris, Donn Michael
Farris, Frank Mitchell, Jr.
Farris, Genevieve Baird (Mrs. Frank Mitchell Farris, Jr.)
Farris, Jefferson Davis
Farris, Robert Earl
Farrow, Michael George, Jr.
Farst, Don David
Farst, Kenneth Edson
Farthing, Kenneth Joel
Farver, Alvin D.
Farver, Francis Franklin
Farwell, Harold Frederick, Jr.
Fascell, Dante B(runo)
Fashena, Gladys Jeanette
Faso, Paul Leo
Fasti, Albert James
Faubion, Jerry Tolbert
Faubion, R(oscoe) Morris
Faucette, Sandra Annette
Faught, Tim Don
Faulconer, Robert Jamieson
Faulk, Michael Anthony
Faulk, Murl Edmund, Jr.
Faulk, Niles Richard
Faulkner, James Herman
Faulkner, James Herman, Jr.
Faunt, Douglas
Faust, Elmer Ford
Faust, John William, Jr.
Faust, Josef
Favaloro, Frank Boyd
Favaro, Mary Kaye Asperheim (Mrs. Biagino Philip Favaro)
Favata, Martin Alfred
Fawcett, Leslie Clarence, Jr.
Faxon, Louis Henslie, Jr.
Faxon, Martha Anne Hill (Mrs. Louis Henslie Faxon)
Fay, Frederic Albert
Fay, Peter Thorp
Feagans, Robert Geary
Feagans, Robert Ryan
Feagin, Arthur Henry
Feagin, Robert R.
Fear, David Eugene
Fearey, Mary Estill (Mrs. Porter Fearey)
Fearey, Porter
Feathers, Cheryl Wright
Featherston, Michael Ray
Fedele, Raymond Sylvester
Feduccia, John Alan
Feeney, John Thomas
Fehn, Curtis Frederick
Fehner, Eugene Charles
Feick, Stuart Ellsworth
Feild, James Rodney
Fein, John Morton
Feinberg, Stephen Louis
Feinn, Barbara Ann
Feinsmith, Leslie Sewald
Feinstein, Edward
Feldenkreis, George
Feldman, Edwin Barry
Felix, Carlos Arturo
Felix, Otis Leander
Felix, Vinci Martinez
Felker, Paul Henry, Jr.
Felknor, George Eckel
Fellows, Donald Kermit
Fellows, Edward Russell, Jr.
Felpel, Leslie Pierce
Felt, William Norcross
Feltner, Donald Ray
Felton, George Reuben, Jr.
Felton, John William, III
Felts, Cornelius Buford, Jr.
Felts, James Rone, Jr.
Felts, Jean Carole
Felts, Marcus Richard
Felty, Roy Arnold
Fendt, Louis Marion, Jr.
Fenn, Harry Talbot
Fenn, Jimmy O'Neil
Fennelly, Alphonsus John
Fensterheim, Aaron
Fenton, Edward A.
Fenton, J. Joseph
Ferguson, Chester Howell
Ferguson, Elizabeth Ryburn
Ferguson, George Robert
Ferguson, Harold Laverne, Jr.
Ferguson, Howard
Ferguson, Leonard Wayne
Ferguson, Lester Jackson
Ferguson, Peter Rowland
Ferguson, Robert Benjamin
Ferguson, Terry Lynn
Ferguson, Thomas Campbell
Ferguson, Wilson Joseph
Ferlita, Ernest Charles
Ferm, Carl Axel
Ferman, Ray, Jr.
Fernandez, Francisco Ramon
Fernandez, Heriberto Santiago
Fernandez, Ricardo Jose
Fernandez-Martinez, Jose
Fernandez-Ramirez, Rodolfo
Ferran, Harry Avery
Ferrari, Alfred Joseph
Ferrari, Herbert Alfred
Ferre, George Frans
Ferre, Maurice Antonio
Ferrell, Dennis Clyde
Ferrell, Gregory Ralph
Ferrell, Henry Haskins, Jr.
Ferrell, Orville Lee
Ferrer, Edwin
Ferrero, James John
Ferri, Eugene C., Jr.
Ferrier, Richard Brooks
Ferris, John Ackel
Ferro, John Anthony
Ferstl, Tom Michael
Fertl, Walter Hans
Fesperman, Debra Monts
Feste, Joseph Rowland
Fetter, Bernard Frank
Feuerbacher, Alvin Leroy
Few, Jimmy Dodgens
Ficht, John Charles
Ficker, Victor Benjamin
Fickling, William Arthur, Jr.
Fidler, Donald Henry
Fidler, Frederick Karl
Fidler, Raymond William
Fidler, Walther Balderson
Field, Elizabeth Ashlock (Mrs. Henry Lamar Field)
Field, Henry
Field, Julia Allen
Fielden, Georgia Freeman (Mrs. C. Franklin Fielden, Jr.)
Fielding, Verl
Fields, James Odell
Fields, John William
Fields, Larry
Fife, Joseph Ray
Figert, Peter Anthony
Figg, Robert McCormick, Jr.
Figueroa, Manuel A.
Figueroa-Chapel, Ramon Antonio
Figueroa-Otero, Ivan
File, Gilbert William, III
Filer, Theodore Henry, Jr.
Filichia, James Joseph
Filicky, Joseph George
Filizola, John Attilio
Fillhart, Jon Edward
Fincannon, Mano Gryder
Finch, Charles Clifton
Finch, David Fergus
Finch, Hugh Edsel
Finch, Joe Milton
Finch, T(homas) Vernon
Finch, Thomas Austin, Jr.
Finch, William Calhoun
Fincher, Cameron Lane
Fincke, Dale Eugene
Finco, Aldo
Findlay, Robert Clyde
Fine, J(ames) Allen
Fine, Myron Gerald
Finegan, Thomas Aldrich
Finegold, Ira
Fineran, John Stephen
Finger, Homer Ellis, Jr.
Fink, Eli Harry
Fink, Jack Edward
Fink, Jock Loren
Fink, William James
Finlay, Robert Charles
Finley, George Parkey
Finley, Joseph Robert
Finley, Sara Crews
Finley, Sidney William, II
Finn, Paul Anthony
Finn, Ralph Irwin
Finnell, William Sherman, Jr.
Finneran, Richard John
Finney, Joseph Claude Jeans
Fiori, Albert
Firor, David Leonhard
Fischer, Ernest Frederick, Jr.
Fischer, Jessie Beaman
Fischer, Kerwin Armand
Fischer, Lee Alan
Fischer, Mabel Julia Thomas (Mrs. Theodore C. Fischer)
Fish, Birney Roberts
Fish, James Franklin
Fisher, Carl Anthony
Fisher, Darlene Bourg
Fisher, Francenia Eleanore
Fisher, Hoover Page
Fisher, James Herschel
Fisher, James Wiley
Fisher, Joe Jefferson
Fisher, John Guy, Jr.
Fisher, John Miller, Jr.
Fisher, John Morris
Fisher, Joseph Lyman
Fisher, King
Fisher, Leslie Robert
Fisher, Lewis Robert
Fisher, Marion LeRoy, Jr.
Fisher, Milton Nathan
Fisher, Ray
Fisher, Robert Henry
Fisher, Seymour
Fisher, Sue Dubois
Fisher, William Lawrence
Fishman, Barry Stuart
Fishman, Joseph
Fishman, Robert Jack
Fishman, Steven
Fitch, Howard Mercer
Fitch, Johnny Edward
Fitch, William Nelson
Fite, James Robert, Jr
Fite, Wallace Armstrong
Fitton, Garvin
Fitts, James Walter
Fitts, Kenneth Lyon
Fitzgerald, Anne Edwards
Fitzgerald, Joseph Michael, Jr.
Fitz Gerald, Norman Dunham
Fitz Gerald-Bush, Frank Shepard
Fitzmorris, James E., Jr.
Fitzpatrick, Joe Warren
Fitzpatrick, John J.
Fitzwater, Larry Dale
Fix, Ronald Edward
Flachbarth, Charles Thomas
Flack, Charles Zorah, Jr.
Flack, John Aaron
Flagg, Roger Holmes
Flaherty, James Patrick
Flake, Henry Frith
Flake, Muriel Howell
Flakes, Thomas Jefferson, Jr.
Flam, Ronald Barry
Flanagan, James Joseph
Flanagan, William Stuart
Flanders, Donald Hargis
Flanders, Dudley Dean
Flanders, Henry Jackson, Jr.
Flannagan, Francis Wills
Flannagan, William Hamilton
Flawn, Peter Tyrrell
Flax, Marshall Edward
Fleener, Tony Leo
Fleenor, Elisa Fallaria
Fleet, Albert Zalman
Fleischman, Sol Joseph
Fleisher, Harvey Oscar
Flemenbaum, Abraham
Flemig, Ernest Robert
Fleming, Benton Scott
Fleming, Eldridge Erastus
Fleming, James Furman
Fleming, Kathleen Ann
Fleming, Lawrence Durwood
Fleming, Myrtle Madeline
Fleming, Samuel Hale Sibley
Fleming, Sidney Howell
Fleming, Walter Clark, Jr.
Fleming, William Herbert
Fleshman, Robert Edward
Fletcher, Carrol Gene
Fletcher, Charles Mark
Fletcher, Cliff
Fletcher, Don Roland
Fletcher, Donald Edmund
Fletcher, Edith Harrigill
Fletcher, Luther Dudley
Fletcher, Mary Lynn
Fletcher, Minos L., III
Fletcher, Riley Eugene
Fletcher, Robert Jeffery
Fletcher, Thomas Moore, Jr.
Flickinger, Charles John
Flink, Stephen Harry
Flinn, Thomas Hance
Flinn, William Adams
Flint, Cort Ray
Flippen, Llewellyn Tucker
Flippen, Margaret Evans Hall
Flippo, Jack Lloyd
Flippo, Ronnie Gene
Flood, John Sawyer
Flood, Walter Aloysius
Flook, Kenneth Grier
Flora, Eleanor Maxine
Florance, Stanley Hunter
Flores, Adolph Anthony, Jr.
Flores, Arnold
Florez, Leopoldo
Flory, David Paul
Flower, Walter Chew, III
Flowers, Elliott Galetin
Flowers, Virginia Anne
Flowers, Walter
Floyd, Carlisle
Floyd, Eldra Moore, Jr.
Floyd, John B., Jr.
Floyd, John Lewis
Floyd, Louis Carl
Floyd, Lyman John
Floyd, Picot de Boisfeuillet
Floyd, Robert Cecil
Floyd, Russell Freeman
Fluno, John Arthur
Flynn, Return Timothy
Flynt, John James, Jr.
Fockler, John Keedy
Fogartie, James Eugene
Fogel, Norman Allen
Fogelman, Avron B.
Fogelman, Morris Joseph
Folden, Dewey Bray, Jr.
Foley, Mary Alice Dodd (Mrs. Lawson Edgar Foley)
Foley, Thomas Carl
Folinus, Jeffrey Joseph
Folk, Earl Donald
Folk, Emerson Dewey
Folsom, Robert S.
Folwell, William Hopkins
Font, Juan Higinio
Fontana, Mario Herbert
Fontecchio, Giovanni
Fonteno, William Carl, III
Fontenot, Martin Mayance, Jr.
Fonzi, Frank
Foose, Don Holt
Foote, Avon Edward
Foote, Guy Myrph
Foote, Kenneth Harvey
Forbes, Billy Dean
Forbes, Hubert Henry
Forbis, James Edwin
Ford, Archie W.
Ford, Clyde Gilpin
Ford, Debra Kay
Ford, Douglas Walsh
Ford, Edward Sinclair, Jr.
Ford, Ernest Leslie
Ford, Gordon Buell
Ford, Harold Eugene
Ford, Harry W.
Ford, Helen Sarrels
Ford, John Hevener, Jr.
Ford, John Suffern
Ford, L(ester) Harlan
Ford, Richard Edwin
Ford, Richard John
Ford, Robert Clayton, Jr.
Ford, Roger Gary
Ford, Rutledge Frederick
Ford, Thomas Jeffers
Ford, Wendell Hampton
Ford, William Gerald Francis
Fordyce, Phillip Randall
Foreman, Edward Rawson
Foreman, Kenneth Joseph, Jr.
Forester, Jean Martha Brouillette
Forgue, Stanley Vincent
Forkner, Claude Ellis
Forman, Howell Northcutt, Jr.
Forman, Miles Austin
Formby, Johnny Clinton
Forney, Bill Earl
Fornos, Pedro Genaro
Forrest, Hugh Sommerville
Forsman, J(ames) Parker
Forster, William Hull
Forsythe, Jack Norman
Fort, Arthur Tomlinson, III
Fort, George Edward
Forte, Patrick Anthony
Fortney, William Howard
Fosdick, Franklin Lawrence
Fosdick, Richard John
Foshee, Donald Preston
Foshee, Wayne Otis
Foss, George Bridges, Jr.
Foster, Caroline Robinson
Foster, Charles Bradford, Jr.
Foster, Charles Edward, Sr.
Foster, Charles Richard
Foster, Daniel W.
Foster, Donald Francis
Foster, Earl Masters
Foster, Edith Lenore
Foster, Edwin Powell
Foster, Lawrence
Foster, Nick Duncan
Foster, Walton Arthur
Foster, William Bell, Jr.
Foster, William Southmayd
Foster, Willie Stephen
Fountain, Benjamin Eagles, Jr.
Fountain, L. H.
Fountain, Nellie Lee
Fourcard, Inez Garey
Fouse, Clara Mae Jones
Foushee, Roger Babson
Foust, Roscoe Thornton, Jr.
Fouts, Thomas Stephen
Fowler, A. Edwin, Jr.
Fowler, Bruce Wayne
Fowler, David Paul
Fowler, Delbert Marcom
Fowler, Dennis Crosby
Fowler, Eugene Franklin, Jr.
Fowler, Keith Franklin
Fowler, Philip Deily, III
Fowler, Richard Edmond Lee
Fowler, Robert Dobbs
Fowler, Stephen Gillon
Fowler, Watson Rodney
Fowler, William Frederick
Fowler, Wilma Sim (Monk)
Fowlkes, Winford (W.C.) Calvin
Fox, Baynard Francis
Fox, Del Franklin
Fox, Elliot Milton
Fox, Gerald George
Fox, Hewitt Bates
Fox, Homer McGrady
Fox, Joseph Charles, Jr.
Fox, Karl Richard
Fox, Lester Irving
Fox, Mark
Fox, Nelson Moffett, Jr.
Fox, Paul John
Fox, Peter Franklin, Jr.
Fox, Raymond Graham
Fox, Richard Charles
Fox, Stephen Richard
Fox, Theodore Bert
Fox, Vernon Brittain
Fox, Wilfred Vaden
Foxworth, Charles Leonard
Foy, Garrett Ray
Fralic, Bobby Joe
Fralick, Lawrence Eldon
Fralin, Jane Lee
Fralish, Marvin Lewis, Jr.
Fram, Lionel Ernest
Frame, Jay Emery
Frampton, Jim Lee
Franchi, Armand Joseph
Francis, Eugene A.
Francis, Horace
Francis, James Wallace
Francis, Janet Botts
Francis, John Hubert, Jr.
Francis, Lewis
Francis, Ricardo Hugh
Francis, Wilbur Morris
Frank, Anthony Jon
Frank, Donald Albert
Frank, Ellen Snow
Frank, Harold Gene
Frank, Harvey
Frank, Manfred
Frank, Mildred Bye
Frank, Mitchell Charles, Jr.
Frank, Sam Hager
Franke, Lieu (Lil) Thi
Franke, Paul Marion, Jr.
Frankel, Andrew Joel
Franklin, Alfred Alton, Jr.
Franklin, Alton David
Franklin, Billy Joe
Franklin, David Earl
Franklin, Donald Lee
Franklin, Donald Wayne
Franklin, Dorothy Ann Bowman
Franklin, Frances Stark
Franklin, James Dade
Franklin, Morris Emory, Jr.
Franklin, Robert Drury
Franklin, William Donald
Franklin, William Hayne, III
Franklin-Taylor, Ethel Viola
Frantz, Joseph Foster
Frantzis, Theodosios George
Frantzreb, Arthur Carl
Franz, Jerry Louis
Fraser, Donald Hines
Fraser, Lewis Earl
Fraser, Malcolm Douglas
Fraser, Thomas Augustus, Jr.
Fraser, Whitman
Frasher, James Howard
Fravel, Linda Jo
Frawley, Charles Carey
Fraze, Richard Osborne
Frazer, Emmett Baxter
Frazeur, Dean Russell
Frazier, Griffin Guy
Frazier, Loy William, Jr.
Frazier, William Edward, Jr.
Frede, Ralph Edward
Frederick, Beebe Ray, Jr.
Frederick, Carolyn Hall Essig (Mrs. Holmes W. Frederick)
Frederick, Margie Garrett
Frederickson, Evan Lloyd
Frederickson, Harry Gray
Fredette, Richard C.
Fredrich, Russell LeRoy
Freedle, S. Dean
Freedman, Joel Irwin
Freedman, Richard Scott
Freeland, Michael Rudolph
Freeland, Susan Marie
Freeman, Bee Jay
Freeman, Bernice
Freeman, Bobby Earl
Freeman, Donald Wilford
Freeman, Eugene Ernest, Jr.
Freeman, George Clemon, Jr.
Freeman, George Lester
Freeman, James Alvin
Freeman, Jerre Minor
Freeman, John Rickenbaker
Freeman, Ralph Harrison
Freeman, Thomas Gene
Freeman, Thomas Rumph
Freer, Leslie Albert
Freese, Howard Lee
Freese, Simon Wilke
Freiburger, E. Allen
Freitag, Carl Bernard, Jr.
Fremin, Luke Pierre, Jr.
French, Carl Weston, Jr.
French, Shelby Ray
Freudenthal, Ernest Guenther
Frey, Gerard Louis
Frey, Louis, Jr.
Frey, Phyllis K.
Fri, David LeRoy
Friberg, Emil Edwards
Frick, Elmer Franklin, Jr.
Frick, Fred Gentry
Friday, William Clyde
Fridley, Howard Eugene, Jr.
Friedlander, Herbert Norman
Friedman, Ephraim Richard
Friedman, Hirsch
Friedman, Julian Richard
Friedrich, Otto Martin, Jr.
Fries, Charles Thomas
Fries, Herbert Christian
Friese, Harrison Leonard
Friesen, Merle Royston
Frisbie, Sayer Loyal
Frith, Douglas Kyle
Frith, James Burness
Friton, John Francis
Fritz, Carl George
Fritze, Julius Arnold
Frizzell, William Raymond
Frohlich, Edward David
Fromhagen, Carl, Jr.
Fromm, Stefan H.
Frommhold, Lothar Werner
Froom, George Allen
Frost, Juanita C. Corbitt
Frost, Michael Jon
Frost, Sidney Wayne
Fruchter, Dorothy Anne
Fruge, J. Cleveland
Fry, David Donald
Fry, Lloyd Vern
Fryburger, L(awrence) Bruce
Frye, Alva Leonard
Frye, Dolan Bruce
Frye, Donald Lee
Frye, Jack Richardson
Frye, John H., Jr.
Frye, Lorraine Pauline St. Laurent
Frye, Pauline Leach
Fryer, Thomas Waitt, Sr.
Fryer, William Neal
Frymire, Richard Lamar
Fryrear, Donald William
Fudenberg, Herman Hugh
Fudge, Russell Oliver
Fuente, Claudio Jesus
Fuentes, Florine Gonzales
Fuentes, Gabriel, III

Fulbright, Garland W.
Fulcher, Clay Wayland Gordon
Fulcher, John Howard
Fulford, Robert Harold
Fullen, Eugene Francis
Fuller, Florine Smith
Fuller, Gerald Ralph
Fuller, James Howe
Fuller, Marilyn Kay Tribbey
Fuller, Maynard Gerald
Fuller, Parrish
Fuller, Peter McAfee
Fuller, Robert Asberry
Fuller, Rosa Arrington
Fullerton, Charles Gordon
Fullerton, Samuel Baker
Fullington, Richard Wayne
Fullmer, Harold Milton
Fulmer, Gilbert Everett
Fulmer, Richard Stephen
Fulton, Charles Britton, Jr.
Fulton, Fred Franklin
Fulton, James Wayte, Jr.
Fulton, Leroy Marcus
Fulton, Richard Harmon
Fulton, Richard Wayne
Fulton, Robert Earle
Fulton, Warren Crigler
Fumich, Henry Nicholas, Jr.
Funderburk, Sapp
Funke, Francis Joseph
Fuqua, Benjamin Thomas
Fuqua, Don
Fuqua, John Brooks
Fuqua, Mitch Pervis
Fuqua, Raymond Fabious
Furedi, Steven Michael
Furey, Francis James
Furino, Antonio
Furr, Robert Earl
Fuselier, Louis Alfred
Fussell, James Richard
Fusselman, William Frank
Futch, George Peyton, Jr.
Futch, Grace Bonner
Fuzek, John Frank
Gabard, William Montgomery
Gable, Robert Elledy
Gabriel, Pat (Mrs. Gene F. Gabriel)
Gadd, William Lee
Gade, Marvin Francis
Gadsden, Richard Hamilton
Gaetan, Manuel
Gaffney, Richard Bennett
Gafford, Frank Hall
Gage, George Raymond, Jr.
Gagliano, Nicholas Charles
Gahagan, Thomas Gail
Gainer, Ruby Jackson (Mrs. Herbert P. Gainer)
Gaines, Roy Edward
Gaines, Victor Pryor
Galassi, John Paul, Jr.
Galbreath, Joyce Condray
Gale, Edwin Morris
Gale, Steven Hershel
Galindo, Ramiro Anze
Galinsky, Gotthard Karl
Gallagher, Francis Joseph
Gallagher, James Michael
Gallagher, John George
Gallagher, Phil C.
Gallaher, Art, Jr.
Gallant, Thomas Grady
Gallemore, Johnnie L., Jr.
Gallette, Russell F.
Galliano, Vernon Frederick
Gallien, John Hurst
Gallivan, William George
Gallman, David Clinton
Galloway, Dock Roscoe
Galloway, Gale Lee
Galloway, Jeff
Galloway, Louie Altheimer, III
Galloway, Rex Farmer
Galloway, William Rufus, Jr.
Gallup, Russell David, Jr.
Gally, Robert Samuel
Galphin, Bruce Maxwell
Galt, Barry Jack
Galt, Eleanor
Galvan, Robert
Gamache, Gerald Lee
Gambill, Bruce Warren
Gamble, Alfred James
Gamble, Denny Elisha
Gamble, Gerald Lynn
Gamble, Jess Franklin
Gamble, Roy Jackson
Gamble, Samuel James Reeves
Gamble, William Belser, Jr.
Gambrell, Barmore P.
Gambrell, Mildred Katherine
Gambrell, Richard Donald, Jr.
Gambrell, Virginia Leddy (Mrs. Herbert Gambrell)
Gammage, Robert Alton
Gammon, Joseph Allen
Gammon, Nathan, Jr.
Gandarillas, Manuel P.
Gandy, Edythe Evelyn
Gandy, Gerald Larmon
Gandy, Thomas Whitney
Gann, Louise Weeks
Ganter, Bernard J.
Gantner, Rose Karlo
Gantt, Aubrey Doyle
Gantt, James Raiford
Gantt, Melvin Spencer
Gantt, Michael David
Garb, Forrest Allan
Garcia, Alfonso Roman
Garcia, Carmelo Atangan
Garcia, Hector Orlando
Garcia, Mercedes Matilde
Garcia, Ricardo Alberto
Garcia, William Burres
Garcia-Palmieri, Mario Ruben
Garcia-Palmieri, Rafael A.
Garcia-Rayneri, Justo
Gardea, Raymond Angel
Gardine, Juanita Constantia Forbes (Mrs. Cyprian A. Gardine)
Gardiner, Asa Bird
Gardiner, Donald Andrew
Gardiner, Pauline Susan
Gardner, Billy Dean
Gardner, Charles Bruce
Gardner, Dallas Adams, Jr.
Gardner, Earl William, Jr.
Gardner, Guy Frederick
Gardner, Johnny Berten
Gardner, Richard Calvin
Gardner, Robin Pierce
Gardner, Russell Menese
Gardner, Sidney Edward
Gardner, Warren Sanders, Jr.
Gardner, William Albert, Jr.
Gardner, William Beverly, Jr.
Gardner, William Leonard
Gardner, William Robert
Gardsbane, Hyman Jacob
Gareri, Dan James
Garikes, Arthur George
Garman, George Baker
Garner, Carrie Lee
Garner, John Michael
Garner, Tony Lee
Garner, Warner
Garretson, Henry David
Garrett, Albert Earle, III
Garrett, Coy Edwin
Garrett, David Clyde, Jr.
Garrett, Donald Lynn
Garrett, Floyd Alton
Garrett, Franklin Miller
Garrett, Jerry Wayne
Garrett, John Henry, Jr.
Garrett, John Maxwell, Jr.
Garrett, Lionel Hugh
Garrett, Richard Edward
Garrett, Rosa Martin
Garrido-Monge, José
Garrigan, Michael Eugene
Garrigo, Jose Ramon
Garriott, Owen K.
Garrison, James Eunice
Garrison, Robert Edward, II
Garriss, Phyllis Weyer (Mrs. W. P. Garriss)
Garrity, Thomas Anthony, Jr.
Garth, Thomas Hancock
Gartman, Max Dillon
Gartrell, Francis Eugene
Garver, James Amos
Gary, Nathan Bennett, Jr.
Garza, Reynaldo G.
Gasataya, Julian Delina
Gaskins, Ralph Edward, Sr.
Gaspard, Marshall Trent (Mitch)
Gasperini, Eugene Garrett
Gass, Robert Louis, Jr.
Gaston, Robert Otis
Gaston, Warren Edward
Gaston, William Joseph, Jr.
Gatenbee, Elizabeth Robbins
Gates, Anne Glenn
Gates, Charles Edgar
Gates, Leslie Clifford
Gates, Mac Stuart
Gates, William Fred, Jr.
Gatewood, Maud F.
Gatewood, Willard Badgett, Jr.
Gatliff, Ben Franklin
Gattis, Elvis Franklin
Gattis, John Edward
Gattis, Louie Smith, III
Gatton, Robert Laurence
Gaub, Margaret Luise
Gaudin, Homer Charles
Gaudreau, Patrice Ann
Gauntt, Wandaleen
Gauny, Ronnie Dean
Gausman, Harold Wesley
Gautreaux, Marcelian Francis, Jr.
Gaw, James Richard
Gay, Birdie Spivey
Gay, Charles Clark
Gay, Francis Henry
Gay, James Ferbee
Gay, Leonard Omar
Gay, William Wallace
Gaylord, Catherine Scott
Gaylord, Edward Lewis
Gaynor, Jay Irvin
Gazzerro, Paul, Jr.
Geber, William Frederick, Jr.
Geboff, Ira Stewart
Geentiens, Gaston Petrus, Jr.
Geer, William Monroe
Geerdes, James Divine
Geeslin, Dorine Hawk (Mrs. Robert Jones Geeslin)
Gehring, John William, Jr.
Geiger, Albert James, Jr.
Geiger, James Edward
Geiger, Sydney
Geigerman, Clarice Furchgott
Geil, John
Geisert, Gene A.
Gellenthin, Carl Otto, Jr.
Geller, Irving
Gelwicks, Earl O., III
Gemmer, H. Robert
Gensel, Richard Lloyd
Gentle, Edgar Cuthbert, Jr.
Gentle, Marie Margaret Lively
Gentry, Claude Thomas
Gentry, Dwight Lonnie
Gentry, Harvey William
Gentry, Johnny Douglas, Jr.
Gentry, Robert Edward
Gentry, William Norton
George, Henry Howard
George, Jesse L., Jr.
George, Joseph Paul
George, Lee Roy
George, Lila-Gene Plowe Kennedy (Mrs. Richard Painter George)
George, Michael Louis
George, Raymond Charles
George, Rick Allen
George, Robert Austin
George, Ronald Baylis
George, Ronald Larry
George, Victor Frank
George, William Robert, II
Gerato, Erasmo Gabriele
Gerber, Clarence R., Jr.
Gerecke, William Beman
Gerelds, James Kenneth, Jr.
Gergen, John Andrew
Gerloff, Edwin Adolph
Gershater, Ben Z. Mayper
Gerughty, Ronald Mills
Gerwick, William Joe
Gerwin, John Marshall
Gessell, John Maurice
Gesund, Hans
Gettig, Carl William
Getting, Paul Lloyd
Gettings, Robert Michael
Gewin, Edward Murfee
Gezen, Asil
Gholson, Hunter Maurice
Ghosh, Arvind
Giam, Choo-Seng
Giancarlo, Samuel Salvator
Giarrusso, Zona Turnoy
Gibbes, William Holman
Gibbon, Samuel Young
Gibbons, Alan Clark
Gibbons, Celia Victoria Townsend (Mrs. John Sheldon Gibbons)
Gibbons, Michael Francis
Gibbons, Sam Melville
Gibbs, Frederick H.
Gibbs, James Alanson
Gibbs, Jeanne Osborne
Gibbs, Kaye Louise
Gibby, Mabel Enid Kunce
Giblin, Thomas Richard
Gibson, Alfred Ray
Gibson, Charles Hugh, Jr.
Gibson, David Bailey
Gibson, Everett Kay, Jr.
Gibson, Frank Leslie
Gibson, G. Ruth
Gibson, Graeme Elliott Bosson
Gibson, Henry Wright
Gibson, James Eugene
Gibson, Joan Charlotte
Gibson, Ralph Dodge
Gibson, William Edwin
Giddens, Beulah Pridgen
Giduz, Roland
Gieck, Joe Howard
Giese, Thomas Robert
Gieselman, Elmer James
Giesen, Herman Mills
Giffen, James Kelly
Gigger, Helen Coleman
Giglio, Francis Anthony
Gilbert, Benjamin Francis
Gilbert, George Ronald
Gilbert, Harold Stanley
Gilbert, Harold Wendell
Gilbert, James Harold
Gilbert, Joe Thorne
Gilbert, Joseph Gatliff
Gilbert, Leonard Harold
Gilbert, Michael Meyer
Gilbert, Mildred Opal
Gilbert, Norman Sutcliffe
Gilbert, Philip Henry
Gilbert, Raymond Mc Cuin
Gilbert, Richard Dean
Gilbert, Robert Lee
Gilbert, Walter Randolph, Jr.
Gilbertson, Virginia Mabry (Mrs. Wallace Cornell Gilbertson)
Gilchrist, Arch Robert
Gilchrist, Ralph Edward
Gilchrist, William Risque, Jr.
Giles, Herman Hascal
Giles, Jesse Albion, III
Giles, John Michael
Giles, Martin Louis
Giles, Sallye Franklin
Giles, Thomas D.
Gilkeson, James William, Jr.
Gilkey, Herbert Talbot
Gill, Eugene Laverne
Gill, John Paul
Gill, Joseph Peter, Jr.
Gillean, William Otho, Jr.
Gillespie, Jesse Samuel, Jr.
Gillespie, John Henry
Gillespie, Robert Gill
Gillespie, Thomas Walter, Jr.
Gillham, John Franklin, Jr.
Gilliam, Darrell Kay
Gilliam, George Harrison
Gilliam, Robert Lindsay, III
Gilliland, Billy Joe
Gilliland, Bobby Eugene
Gilliland, Charles Herbert, Sr.
Gilliland, Frank Marshall, Jr.
Gilliland, Harold Eugene
Gilliland, John Douglas
Gilliland, Lukin
Gilliland, William Elton
Gilliom, Richard D.
Gillis, Everett Alden
Gillis, Richard Samuel, Jr.
Gillis, Samuel Peters
Gillquist, Peter Edward
Gilman, Lauren Cundiff
Gilmer, Jesse Benton
Gilmore, Hugh Redland
Gilmore, James Herbert, Jr.
Gilmore, Jerry Carl
Gilmore, Jimmy Gray
Gilmore, Marjorie Havens (Mrs. Hugh Redland Gilmore)
Gilmore, Stuart Irby
Gilpatrick, Marvin Conrad (Gil Patrick)
Gilstrap, Joe Jackson
Gimenez-Munoz, Miguel Angel
Ginn, H. Earl, Jr.
Ginn, John Charles
Ginn, Ronald (Bo)
Ginsburg, Merrill Stuart
Giovanella, Beppino Carlo
Giovannetti, George Robert
Gipson, Wiley Kaye
Girdner, Alwin James
Girod-Rossello, Alberic Oscar
Gish, Claudia Imwalle
Gittess, Ronald Marvin
Gittins, William L.
Givens, Deborah Kay
Givens, Fred Bell, Jr.
Givhan, Thomas Bartram
Gividen, George Massie, Jr.
Gjerstad, Lidde Marie
Glad, Don(ald Davison)
Gladden, James Walter
Gladden, Richard Dawson
Gladding, Everett Bushnell
Gladstein, Mimi Reisel
Glance, Bill Dow
Glantz, Robert Bruce
Glanville, Paul Tennyson, Jr.
Glasgow, Charles Wayne
Glasgow, Joseph Leland
Glass, Thomas Reakirt
Glasser, Robert Michael
Glassman, Armand Barry
Glassman, Michael
Glaze, Clinton Davis
Glaze, Robert Pinckney
Glazer, Frederic Jay
Gleason, Carl Herman
Gleason, David Mann
Gleason, James Gordon
Gleason, William Henry
Gleit, Chester Eugene
Gleitz, George Phillip
Gleman, Stuart Maxwell
Glendy, Robert Earle
Glenn, Alfred Hill
Glenn, James Francis
Glenn, Norval Dwight
Glenn, William Laurence, Jr.
Gleszer, Peter Eaton
Glispin, Vernon Lee
Glocker, Theodore Wesley, Jr.
Glosser, Robert
Gloster, Hugh Morris
Glover, Douglas Dennis
Glover, Edward Bruce
Glover, Edwin Eugene
Glover, John Littleton, Jr.
Glover, Lynn, III
Glover, Robert Keith
Glover, William Peyton
Glucroft, Stephen Henry
Gobble, Paul Samuel, Jr.
Gobelman, Robert Carl
Gober, Henry Fred
Gober, Lewis LaRon
Gober, Richard Wayne
Goble, Ross Lee
Gockel, Ashford Ravenscroft
Godbee, Barron Whitehead, Jr.
Godbey, John Kirby
Godbold, Clyde Everett
Godchaux, Charles Ragland
Godchaux, Frank Area, III
Goddard, David Watson
Goddard, John Irving
Goddard, Nathaniel
Goddard, Ruth
Godfrey, Agnes Mulvey
Godfrey, J(ames) Fike
Godfrey, Wesley Lynn
Godfrey, William Aubrey, Jr.
Godsey, Frank Waldman
Godwin, David Houston
Godwin, Edward Arthur, Jr.
Godwin, Mills Edwin, Jr.
Godwin, Paul Milton
Godwin, Winston Yuvawn
Goebel, Ronald Allen
Goehner, Richard Herbert
Goeke, Fred William
Goertz, Richard John
Goessling, Erwin William
Goettee, James Henry
Goff, Edith Ellis
Goff, Kenneth Harold
Goff, Wayne Hulen
Goforth, James Alton
Goggins, Horace
Gogonelis, Alexander George
Going, Robert Ernest
Goins, Donald Lee
Goins, James Howard
Gokee, Donald Leroy
Gold, Kenneth Ray
Goldberg, Lee Dresden
Golden, Kenneth Steven
Golden, Roger Lee
Goldenberg, Alan Lee
Goldin, Kate Smith
Goldman, Ellen Mynette Eason
Goldman, Gerald Carl
Goldman, Herbert Ira
Goldman, Mitchell M.
Goldner, Herman Wilson
Goldsmith, Jerry Gunther
Goldsmith, Judith Ann Adams
Goldsmith, Mortimer
Goldstein, Irving Solomon
Goldstein, Irwin Owen
Goldstein, Jack Charles
Goldstein, Lionel Alvin
Goldstein, Norman Edward (Ned)
Goldstein, Steven Edward
Golomb, Herbert Stanley
Gomez, Alfredo A.
Gomez, Jacqué Betty
Gómez, Josué
Gomez, Julian, III
Gomez, Raul
Gomez, Severo
Gomez Berrios, Nelida
Gomez-Rivero, Orlando
Gonano, John Roland
Gonce, Robert Eugene
Gong, Edmond Joseph
Gonsoulin, Dewey Jude
Gonyea, Edward Francis
Gonzales, Brother Alexis (Joseph M. Gonzales)
Gonzales, Charles John
Gonzales, Elwood John, Jr.
Gonzalez, Abel Reyes
Gonzalez, Antonio Carmelo
Gonzalez, Aurora
Gonzalez, Celso Miguel
Gonzalez, Enrique Manuel
Gonzalez, Gerardo Merced
González, Gildo Massó
Gonzalez, Harriet Catherine James
Gonzalez, Henry B.
Gonzalez, Jorge Augusto
Gonzalez, Jose Benito, Jr.
Gonzalez, Jose Lozano
Gonzalez, Manuel Enrique
Gonzalez, Sarita Gallardo
Gonzalez, William
Gonzalez-Alcover, Jose Carmelo
Gonzalez-Escobar, Daniel
Gonzalez-Romanace, Hector R.
Gooch, John Phillip
Good, Joseph Cole, Jr.
Good, Mary Lowe
Goodale, Fairfield
Goode, Clement Tyson
Goode, Martin
Goode, Read Fisher
Gooding, Jessie Jewell Sims (Mrs. Arthur Ray Gooding)
Goodman, James Flatt
Goodman, James Jacob
Goodman, John Willis
Goodman, Malcolm Arnold
Goodner, Dwight Benjamin
Goodrich, Samuel Melvin
Goodroe, Joseph Hollis, Sr.
Goodson, James Butler
Goodson, Walter Kenneth
Goodwin, Andrew Wirt, II
Goodwin, Bruce Kesseli
Goodwin, Byrom Odell
Goodwin, David
Goodwin, Jack Howard
Goodwin, James William
Goodwin, Leftridge Layne
Goodwin, Nancy Ann
Goodwin, Ray Allen
Googe, John Wesley
Goolishian, Harold Armen
Goorley, John Theodore
Gordon, Abraham Maury
Gordon, Anne Isabel
Gordon, Bruce Allen
Gordon, Clarance Browning
Gordon, Edwin Frederick Robert
Gordon, Eugene Andrew
Gordon, Helmut Albert
Gordon, Ira Jay
Gordon, Jerry Clay
Gordon, M. Michael
Gordon, Richard Edwards
Gordon, Robert I.
Gordon, Robert Murraye
Gordon, Thomas Edwin, Jr.
Gordon, Vivian Verdell
Gore, Albert, Jr.
Gore, Budd
Gore, Charles Minor
Gorenflo, Fredric Max
Gorges, Heinz August
Gorodetzky, Charles William
Gorr, Louis Frederick
Gorski, Edward Joseph
Gortner, Willard Austin
Goshen, Charles Ernest
Goshorn, Donald Hansford
Goslee, Charles Bernard, Jr.
Gosnell, Aubrey Brewer
Goss, Kenneth George
Gosser, Franklin Thomas
Gossett, Ouida Griffith (Mrs. James W. Gossett)
Gossman, Francis Joseph
Gossmann, Cora Helen
Goswitz, Francis Andrew
Gotautas, Vito Adolph
Gothia, Sister Blanche
Gotto, Antonio Marion, Jr.
Goudelock, John Clifton
Gough, Jessie Post (Mrs. Herbert Frederick Gough)
Gough, Oran Dean
Gould, Karen Keel
Gould, Lewis Ludlow
Gould, Merle Lester
Gould, Paul Frederick
Gould, Purdue Leighton
Gould, Robert Albert
Gould, Stanley Leo
Gould, Stephen
Gould, Syd S.
Goulding, Clarence Eugene, Jr.
Goumas, Marcus P.
Gourley, James Leland
Govatos, Lee John
Govern, Edward James
Govorchin, Rexford Elliott
Gowen, Barney Alexander
Graben, Henry Willingham
Grace, Charles C(lyde)
Gracida, Rene Henry
Graden, Susan Hill
Grady, Anthony Frank, Jr.
Grady, Donald Ross
Grady, James Martin
Grady, John Edward, Jr.
Grady, John Paul
Grady, Thomas J.
Grady, Viola Kinnaird
Graf, Joseph Charles
Graff, John Robert
Gragg, Annette Gano (Mrs. Hugh E. Gragg)
Gragg, Hugh Ernest
Graham, Fred Gorham, Jr.
Graham, Frederick Bolles
Graham, George Grimsley
Graham, John Hugh
Graham, Philip Alan
Graham, Walter Hopkins
Grainger, David Alan
Grainger, Edward Walter
Graivier, Leonard
Grammer, John Colquitte
Grammer, Randolph Johnson
Grandich, Russell Anthony
Granger, Floyd Randolph, II
Granger, Gilbert Lofton
Granstaff, Edward Lee
Grant, Alex
Grant, Alice Boyle
Grant, David Alan
Grant, George Thomas
Grant, Gerry Lee
Grant, Henry Gignilliat
Grant, James Marse
Grant, Karen Marie
Grant, Randall Ray
Grant, Robert Neil
Grant, Rorer James
Grant, Silas Winton
Grant, Velma Roberts
Grantham, Dewey Wesley
Grantham, Steve Wiley
Graser, Earl John
Grauke, Robbie Dee
Gravel, Camille F(rancis), Jr.
Graver, Richard Byrd
Graves, Dorothy Lou Irish (Mrs. Bruce B. Graves)
Graves, Jerry Brook
Graves, Kenneth Martin
Graves, Lawrence P.
Graves, Mary Jo
Graves, Thomas Dorland
Graves, Wallace Morrison, Jr.
Graves, William Lester, Jr.
Gravlee, Leland Clark, Jr.
Gray, Albert John
Gray, Allan Walmsley
Gray, Charles Dowd, Sr.
Gray, Charles Webster
Gray, Clarence Jones
Gray, Duncan Montgomery, Jr.
Gray, Frank, Jr.
Gray, Freddy Leonard
Gray, George Bert
Gray, George William
Gray, Henry Crockett, Jr.
Gray, James Mitchell, Jr.
Gray, John Marshall
Gray, May Harris (Mrs. Thomas Virgil Gray)
Gray, Nolan Kenneth
Gray, Oscar Edward, III
Gray, Robert Alan, Jr.
Gray, Robert Steele
Gray, Robin Bryant
Gray, Roy Cooper, Jr.
Gray, Sam Wilson, Jr.
Gray, Samuel Andrew
Gray, William Norwood
Graybeal, Henry Clay
Graybeal, Jack Daniel
Grayson, John Louis, Jr.
Greason, Murray Crossley, Jr.
Grecco, William Louis
Greeman, Nelson William Linton, Jr.
Green, Arthur George
Green, Ben Lamar, Jr.
Green, Bernard Clay
Green, Catherine Hines
Green, Charles Steven
Green, Christopher Ray
Green, Claud Bethune
Green, David Spencer
Green, Edward Thomas, Jr.
Green, Fred William
Green, George Franklin
Green, Gordon Lucius
Green, Harold

Green, Harry George
Green, Holcombe Tucker, Jr.
Green, Hollis Lynn
Green, James Collins
Green, Jesse Lee
Green, Joseph Lee
Green, Malcolm Alston
Green, Marion Ethel
Green, Ralph Tillman
Green, Robert Charles
Green, Robert Franklin
Green, Robert Hamilton
Green, Robert LaMoyne
Green, William Lawrence
Green, William Paul
Green, William Wells
Greenan, Gary Collins
Greenawalt, Jack Ormand
Greenberg, Allan Max
Greenberg, Hank
Greenberg, Martin Fred
Greenberg, Michael John
Greenberg, Stanley
Greene, Dallas Whorton, Jr.
Greene, David Louis
Greene, E(rnest) Lonzo
Greene, James Allen
Greene, Jerome George
Greene, Raymond Houston
Greene, Robert Edward Lee, Jr.
Greene, Robert Thomas
Greene, Sheldon
Greenebaum, John Samuel
Greenfeather, Laura Faye
Greenfield, Charles Thomas
Greenfield, Joseph Cholmondeley
Greenfield, Melvin C.
Greenhill, Joe R.
Greenhouse, Barry David
Greenlee, Betty Joan
Greenman, Jack Norman
Greenockle, Karen Martha
Greenstein, Michael
Greenstein, Stanley George
Greenway, Zelmar Carvey
Greenwood, Joseph Albert
Greer, Fred Jones, Jr.
Greer, Knox Evans
Greer, Mack Varnedoe
Greer, Sheldon
Greever, Walton Harlowe, Jr.
Gregg, Paul Charles
Gregg, Robert Quinly
Gregg, Roger Allen
Greggs, Isaac Ben
Gregoli, Armand A.
Gregorio, Mario
Gregorio, Peter Anthony
Gregory, Ann Young
Gregory, Arthur
Gregory, Conrad
Gregory, Dale Rogers
Gregory, Edward Meeks
Gregory, Edward Wadsworth, Jr.
Gregory, Lowell Dean
Gregory, Thorne
Gregory, Virginia Lois Sullenger
Gregory, Jerome Gage
Gregory, Wanda Jean
Gregory, Wesley Wright, Jr.
Gregory, William Thomas, III
Greider, John Calhoun
Greiner, Morris Esty, Jr.
Greinke, Everett Donald
Greninger, Edwin Thomas
Gresham, Charles Russell
Gresham, Furman Allen, Jr.
Gressette, Lawrence Marion
Grier, Edna Catherine Gossett
Grier, Eleanor Meacham (Mrs. Paul Livingston Grier)
Grier, Paul Livingston
Griffeth, Ronald Clyde
Griffin, Alan Nash
Griffin, Gerald Gehrig
Griffin, John Bunyan, Jr.
Griffin, John Michael
Griffin, Louie Hannah, Jr.
Griffin, Newton Bramblett
Griffin, Oscar O'Neal, Jr.
Griffin, Robert Charles
Griffin, Robert James
Griffin, Villard Stuart, Jr.
Griffin, Walter Wanzel
Griffis, James Truman
Griffis, William Kearley
Griffith, Benjamin Franklin, Jr.
Griffith, John Dorland
Griffith, Leon Odell
Griffith, Luther Bailey
Griffith, Marion Sherman, Jr.
Griffith, Melvin Eugene
Griffith, Patsy Reeves
Griffith, William Howard
Griffiths, Paul Marquet
Griggs, Charles Swayne
Griggs, Joseph, III
Griggs, Thomas McKay
Grigsby, Chester Poole, Jr.
Grigsby, Ronald Davis
Grimes, John Frank, III
Grimland, John Martin, Jr.
Grimm, Dean Franklin
Grindell, Albert Gordon
Grinstead, William Carter, Jr.
Grise, Jerry Wade
Grisham, Richard St. Clair
Griswold, Kenneth Edwin, Jr.
Gritz, Jack Linton
Grivsky, Eugene Michael
Grizzard, Thomas Jefferson, Jr.
Groben, Richard Louis
Groce, William Henry, III
Grochau, Henry Boyd
Grochola, Chester Walter
Groeber, John Edward
Grogan, Hiram John
Groll, Elkan Wiley
Groner, Frank S(helby)
Groner, Pat Neff
Groninger, Carole Perry
Gronlund, Robert Bernard
Groom, Dale
Groot, Roger Douglas
Gröschel, Dieter Hans Max
Grose, William Lyman
Gross, Dennis Joel
Gross, Edward Alan
Gross, Emily Gertrude Lowrey
Gross, Frank Blackburn, Jr.
Gross, Gary Neil
Gross, John C(harles)
Gross, Melvin
Grossel-Rossi, Marion Nicholas
Grossman, Maurice Sidney
Grossman, Robert George
Grosvenor, Donna Kerkam (Mrs. Gilbert M. Grosvenor)
Grote, Richard Charles
Grotefend, Mary Emery
Grove, Edward Ryneal
Grove, Jean Donner (Mrs. Edward R. Grove)
Grove, John McIlhany
Grove, Russell Sinclair, Jr.
Grover, Anil Kumar
Groves, Ivor Durham, Jr.
Groves, Sidney Kepler
Grubbs, Bill Gene
Grubbs, Frank Leslie, Jr.
Gruemer, Hanns-Dieter Friederich
Gruetzmacher, Joyce Elaine Simon
Grund, Clarence B., Jr.
Gruner, Virginia Shaw (Mrs. George John Gruner)
Guber, Donald
Gucwa, Len T.
Gudger, Lamar
Gudnason, Halldor Victor
Guedry, Donald Everett
Guerra, Fernando Amado
Guerra, Rolando Antonio
Guerrero, Michael C.
Guerrero-Ramirez, Luis Eduardo
Guerry, DuPont, III
Guess, Gordon Blue
Guest, John Franklin, Jr.
Gueymard, Kathleen McLaughlin
Guglielmino, Paul Joseph
Guiberteau, James Joseph
Guice, Olyn Tully, Jr.
Guidry, Lawrence Sal
Guidry, Wayne Edward
Guilford, Roger Ellory
Guillaume, Bernard George
Guillory, Julius James
Guinee, Vincent Florence
Guinn, David Crittenden
Guinn, Joe Wayne
Guinsburg, Philip Fried
Guitart, Michael Horacio
Guitart, Miguel Antonio
Guittard, Clarence Alwin
Guiza, Donato Enrique
Gulati, Jagjit
Gumprecht, Donald Lambert
Gunn, Albert Edward
Gunn, Edward Mansfield
Gunn, Samuel Cobb, Jr.
Gunnin, Bill Lee
Gunter, William D., Jr.
Guntharp, Patricia Ann
Gunther, Andree-Ellen Estelle Marie
Gup, Benton Eugene
Gupta, Vishnu Das
Gurney, Haight Wentworth
Gurnsey, Ronald Allen
Gürtler, Martin Mathias, II
Guseman, John Lee
Guste, Roy Francis
Guste, William Joseph, Jr.
Gutermuth, Clinton Raymond
Guth, Paul Spencer
Guthrie, A. Maxeen Dansby
Guthrie, Bernice Button
Guthrie, Frank Edwin
Guthrie, Marion Philip, III
Guthrie, Robert Fulmer
Guthrie, W(illiam) Nelson
Gutierrez, Francisco Luis, II
Gutiérrez-Mazorra, Juan Francisco
Gutierrez Zorrilla, Felipe
Gutman, Elliott Michael
Guttman, John Robert
Guy, Arnold Owen, Sr.
Guy, David Paul
Guy, Louis Lee, Jr.
Guyer, Charles Grayson, II
Guyton, Joseph Warren
Guzman, Alberto Porrata
Guzman, Ramon Miguel
Gwaltney, Francis Irby
Gwaltney, Jack Merrit, Jr.
Gwaltney, Marion Lewis
Gwathmey, Owen
Haack, David Arno
Haas, Charles David
Haas, Elliot Lee
Haas, Robert Lance
Haas, Thelma Roberts Sumner (Mrs. Charles Elmer Haas)
Haas, William Joseph
Haban, Mary Frances
Haberland, Paul Mallory
Haberman, George Gilbert
Hack, Frederick Courtland
Hackenberg, Larry Michael
Hackerman, Norman
Hackett, Charles Wilson, Jr.
Hackett, Robert Moore
Hackney, James Acra, III
Hackney, James Henry
Hacskaylo, Michael
Haddad, Eugene
Haddle, Harold William, Jr.
Haddock, R(eyburn) Philip
Hadgopoulos, Saralyn de Haven Poole (Mrs. George John Hadgopoulos)
Hadlock, Daniel Canfield
Hadsell, Carl Donald
Hafely, G. Douglas, Jr.
Hafendorfer, David Russell
Haff, Roderick Canavan
Haffner, George Leslie
Hafner, Rudolph John
Hagan, George Sylvester, Jr.
Hagan, Lewis Edward
Hagan, Ralph Semans
Hage, Raymond Joseph
Hagen, Raoul O'Neil
Hagendoorn, Willem Jacob
Hager, Paul Calvin
Haggard, Curtis Andrew
Haggard, Lloyd Randolph
Haggard, William Henry
Haggerty, George Francis, Jr.
Hagin, T. Richard
Hagins, Bruce Larry
Hagler, John Carroll, III
Hague, Harry Watson, IV
Hague, John Franklin, III
Hahn, Rayburn Edgar
Haight, Charles Herbert
Haigler, Leon Boyd
Haile, Ima Dora
Hair, Robert Eugene
Haire, Billy Gray
Haire, John Daniel
Hairfield, Edward Matthew, Jr.
Haisley, Waldo Emerson
Hake, Don Franklin
Halaby, Raouf Jamil
Halbert, Oliver Isaac, III
Halbouty, Manah Robert
Halbouty, Michel Thomas
Halbrooks, James Winston, Jr.
Halderson, Maxwell Hayes
Hale, Arnold Wayne
Hale, Cecil Harrison
Hale, Francis Joseph
Hale, Joseph P.
Hale, Margie Nornhausser
Hale, Seldon Houston
Hale, Shadrach Payne
Haley, George Kirby
Haley, Gerald John
Haley, Gloria Jo
Haley, James Kenneth
Haley, Marguerite Jane
Haley, Ronald Douglas
Haliday, Alfred Carl, Jr.
Halkiades, Amelia Sultana
Hall, Claude Hampton
Hall, David Joseph
Hall, Donald LeRoy
Hall, Donald Myers
Hall, Elvajean
Hall, Esther Jane Wood (Mrs. Julian Kennis Hall)
Hall, George Rutherford
Hall, Gladys Iona
Hall, Hugh David
Hall, J. Floyd
Hall, James, III
Hall, James Bruce, III
Hall, James William, Jr.
Hall, John Bryan, Jr.
Hall, John Howland
Hall, John Randolph, Jr.
Hall, Judy Holman
Hall, Leland Frank
Hall, Lily-Roland Ebert
Hall, Malcolm Douglas
Hall, Mary Lightsey
Hall, Miles Lewis, Jr.
Hall, Montague Cocram
Hall, Richard Clayton
Hall, Richard Lee
Hall, Robert Bruce
Hall, Robert Lee
Hall, Roger Allen
Hall, Roger Fisher
Hall, Sam Blakeley, Jr.
Hall, Shirley Jean
Hall, Susan Ann Hinderer
Hall, Thor
Hall, Tommy George
Hall, Tommy Ray
Hall, William Joseph
Hall, William K., Jr.
Hall, William Lloyd
Halliburton, John Robert
Hallman, Grady Lamar, Jr.
Hallman, John Roland
Hallock, Donald Nicholson
Halperin, Don Akiba
Halprin, Kenneth M.
Halsey, William McClurg
Halter, Edmund John
Haltmeyer, Norman Alan
Halverstadt, Donald Bruce
Ham, Harold Higgins, Jr.
Ham, Oscar Emerson, Jr.
Ham, Wayne Albert
Hamblen, Lapsley Walker, Jr.
Hambor, James Michael
Hamby, Philip Wayne
Hamby, Rita Genevieve
Hamer, Jan
Hamer, Joseph William, Jr.
Hames, Luther Claude, Jr.
Hamff, Leonard Harvey
Hamilton, Charles Granville
Hamilton, Clyde H.
Hamilton, Dalton Earl
Hamilton, Eugene Leverett
Hamilton, Holman
Hamilton, Howard Laverne
Hamilton, John Frederick
Hamilton, John McFarland
Hamilton, Kathy Sue
Hamilton, Luther Myles, Jr.
Hamilton, Thomas Earle
Hamit, Harold Francis
Hamiter, John Cecil
Hamlett, Troy Ray
Hammer, John William, Jr.
Hammer, Wade Burke
Hammerschmidt, John Paul
Hammett, Bobby Lynn
Hammock, Wilbur Eugene
Hammon, Carl Konrad
Hammon, Gary Lee
Hammond, Claude Ellis
Hammond, George Robert
Hammond, Helen Bernice Rucker
Hammond, J. Gilbert
Hammond, Juanita Wallace
Hammond, Ralph Charles
Hammond, Ronnie Lynnel
Hammons, Donald Ray
Hamon, Richard Grady
Hampton, Donald Perry
Hampton, Herman Lester
Hampton, Merlin
Hampton, Peggy
Hampton, Willie Lee
Hamrick, Fitzhugh Nicholson
Hamrick, J. Nat
Hamrick, Stephen Ollan
Hamrick, Thomas Paschal
Han, Kwang Soo
Han, Soo Woong
Hanbury, George Lafayette, II
Hance, Kent R.
Hancock, Bruce Howard
Hancock, Ian Francis
Hancock, James Dawson, Jr.
Hancock, James Edward
Hancock, William Geremain, Jr.
Hand, Perry Albert
Handler, Frances Clark (Mrs. Frank Stevenson Handler)
Handwerk, Joseph Henry
Handy, John William, Jr.
Hanemann, Ardley Raymond, Jr.
Hanes, Ralph Philip, Jr.
Hanes, Robert Carpenter
Haney, James Donnelly, Jr.
Haney, James Whitney, Jr.
Haney, Michael Douglas
Hangebrauck, Robert Philip
Hanger, Bob Grant
Hanke, Dan Henry
Hankey, Joan Rhodes
Hankins, Irene (Barham)
Hankinson, John Crimmins, Jr.
Hankinson, Risdon William
Hanks, Harold Wayne
Hanks, Jerald Edwin
Hanlan, Mildred Frances
Hanlin, Hugh Carey, Jr.
Hanna, Gordon
Hanna, Ronald Frederic
Hannan, Philip Matthew
Hanor, Eugene Bertram
Hanrahan, Robert Joseph
Hanratty, Lawrence Charles
Hansard, Louis Lawson
Hansen, Herbert Edwin
Hansen, Niles Maurice
Hansen, Nils Erling
Hansen, Paul Travis
Hanson, Clarence Bloodworth, Jr.
Hanson, Donald Farness
Hanson, Ivan Reuben
Hansson, Kenneth Sigurd
Hanzel, Marsha Weinstein
Haradon, Virginia Elizabeth Ingles (Mrs. Clayton Bartlett Haradon)
Harbert, Robert Edgar
Harbin, Jim L(ynn)
Harbin, Wayne Dewitt
Harbordt, Charles Michael
Harbour, Mack Dave
Hardee, Ethel Lynn Blake
Hardee, Howard Davis
Hardegree, Katherine Francis
Harden, Doyle Benjamin
Hardeway, Grant Ulysess, Sr.
Hardiman, Richard Lawrence
Hardin, George Cecil, Jr.
Hardin, Hilliard Frances
Hardin, James Edward
Hardin, James Neal
Hardin, Lucille (Mrs. Sidney Lanier Hardin)
Hardin, Sidney Lanier
Harding, Edward Lloyd
Harding, James Lombard
Hardinge, Byron Cantine
Hardison, Robert Ray
Hardley, Gary Kaye
Hardwick, Charles Vincent
Hardwick, Gally Jeff, Jr.
Hardy, Chester Alfred
Hardy, Gerald Neil
Hardy, Harold McKinne
Hardy, James B., Jr.
Hardy, William Carey
Hare, David Hugh
Hare, George Arthur
Hare, Robert Lee, Jr.
Hargadine, Martha Parrott Young
Hargrove, Joseph Leonard, Jr.
Hargrove, Robert Clyde
Haritun, Rosalie Ann
Harkey, Catherine Adele
Harkins, Carl Girvin
Harkins, Charles William
Harkinson, William Wadsworth
Harlan, Donald Paris
Harlan, Vernie Elijah
Harless, James Warren
Harlow, Griffith Eugene
Harlow, Joseph Watt, Jr.
Harlow, Richard Fessenden
Harman, James William, Jr.
Harman, Jeanne Perkins (Mrs. Harry Elliott Harman III)
Harman, Jerry Don
Harman, Mary Brooks (Mrs. Sidney Elijah Harman)
Harman, Maryann Whittemore
Harmon, (Loren) Foster
Harmon, Frederick Ingersoll
Harmon, Grady Rodney
Harmon, Judson Spencer
Harms, Louise Ivie (Mrs. Willard Daniel Harms)
Harner, Charles Emory
Harner, Joseph Winfred, Jr.
Harold, Richard Wesley
Harper, Carl Brown, Jr.
Harper, Charles Floyd
Harper, Charles Price, Jr.
Harper, Charles Richard
Harper, Hubert Austin, Jr.
Harper, James Cunningham
Harper, Paul Gordon
Harper, Spencer Earl, Jr.
Harper, William Albert
Harpole, Tony Hess
Harpster, James Erving
Harrawood, Paul
Harrell, Charles Hopkins
Harrell, David Lynn
Harrell, Ruth Flinn
Harrigan, William Patrick, III
Harriman, Charles Kiel
Harrington, Arnold Whitman
Harrington, Marion Ray
Harrington, Paul Randall
Harris, Arthur Lee
Harris, Barbara Goebel
Harris, Bob Vernon
Harris, Carey DeWayne
Harris, Charles Edgar
Harris, Charles Miniard
Harris, Chrys Jay
Harris, Deborah Ann Neinast
Harris, Donald Lee
Harris, Elizabeth Moran (Mrs. Thomas Lewis)
Harris, Erle Warfield, Jr.
Harris, Ewing Jackson
Harris, Forest Delbert
Harris, Herbert E., II
Harris, Hubert Earl
Harris, Hugh Pate
Harris, Jack Rondal
Harris, James Douglas, Jr.
Harris, Jean Louise
Harris, Jefferson Davis, Jr.
Harris, Jessie G. (Mrs. Hubert Lamar Harris)
Harris, John
Harris, John Claudelle, Jr.
Harris, John Everett
Harris, John Woods
Harris, Lane Frank
Harris, Lester LeRoy
Harris, Lewis Karl
Harris, Louis Selig
Harris, Margaret Parsons (Mrs. John Malcolm Harris)
Harris, Martin Harvey
Harris, Norman Oliver
Harris, Richard Wilson
Harris, Robert Smith
Harris, Ronald Blythe
Harris, Samuel Walter
Harris, Stephanie Rowena
Harris, T(om) C.
Harris, Thomas Lee
Harris, Thomas Raymond
Harris, Vincent Madeley
Harris, Warren Whitman
Harris, William Madison
Harris, Yvonne Royster
Harrison, A. Cleveland
Harrison, Barbara Simpkins
Harrison, Edward Matthew
Harrison, Ernest, Jr.
Harrison, Eugene Talbot, III
Harrison, Frank Russell, III
Harrison, George Brooks
Harrison, George William
Harrison, Gresham Hughel
Harrison, Hugh Thomas
Harrison, James Harvey, Jr.
Harrison, Mannie Pascal (Pat)
Harrison, Reese Lenwood, Jr.
Harrison, Robert Brent
Harrison, Robert Stephen
Harrison, Stanley Earl
Harrison, Thomas James
Harrison, William Groce, III
Harrison, Winnie Myrtle Broadway (Mrs. Julius C. Harrison)
Hart, Allie Carroll
Hart, E(lmer) Franklin
Hart, Jacqueline Spoerer
Hart, John Wallace
Hart, Juanita Thacker
Hart, Larry Edward
Hart, Roy James, Jr.
Hart, Wilson Reese
Harter, Newman Wendell
Hartfelder, Herbert Edward
Hartgraves, Travis Miller
Hartgrove, Billy Ray
Hartis, William Harley
Hartlage, Lawrence Clifton
Hartley, Robert Hayward
Hartley, Ronald Winfield
Hartley, William Cadenhead
Hartman, Gordon Dean
Hartman, James Paul
Hartman, James Theodore
Hartman, Renate Katharina
Hartman, William Henry
Hartmann, Donald H.
Hartson, Maurice John, Jr.
Hartwell, William Gersham, III
Hartwig, Richard Carlson
Harvard, John Farmer
Harvey, Clarence Charles, Jr.
Harvey, Edwin Malcolm
Harvey, Fletcher Dumas, III
Harvey, Francis George
Harvey, George, Jr.
Harvey, Raymond Chesterfield, Jr.
Harvey, Robert
Harvey, W. Brantley
Harvey, William Brantley, Jr.
Harvey, William Byron
Harvey, William Heath
Harvin, James Shand
Harway, Maxwell
Harwell, Helon Baldwin (Mrs. John Earl Harwell)
Harwell, Kenneth Edwin
Harwell, Thomas Meade, Jr.
Harwood, Donald Eugene
Harwood, John Samuel
Harwood, Robert Hewett
Harwood, Thomas Everett
Haselwood, Scott
Haserick, John Roger
Haskell, Preston Hampton
Haslam, Mary Sandra
Hassan, Zubair ul
Hassell, Jerry Glenn
Hassell, Morris William
Hassenfeld, Harold I.
Hasskarl, Robert Albert
Hasty, Gerald Richard
Hatcher, Danny Ray
Hatcher, Joseph Carroll
Hatcher, Larry Wayne
Hatcher, Martha Olivia Taylor (Mrs. Frank Pridgen Hatcher, Sr.)
Hatcher, Milford Burriss
Hatcher, Robert Lee
Hatcher, William Julian, Jr.
Hatcher, Yvonne
Hatchett, Shari
Hatfield, Benjamin Frank
Hatfield, Carol Sutherland
Hatfield, Charles Stewart
Hatfield, Jack Kenton
Hatfield, John Dempsey
Hatfield, Thomas Marvin
Hathaway, Amos Townsend
Hathaway, Charles Walter, II
Hathway, Charles Wilson
Hatley, Larry J.
Hatton, Thurman Timbrook, Jr.
Hauber, Edwin Nelson
Hauch, Ruthadele LaTourrette
Haug, Clarence Olaf
Haun, Louis Eugene, Jr.
Haun, William Patrick
Hause, Edith Collins
Hauser, Harris Milton
Hauxwell, Gerald Dean
Havelos, Sam George
Havlik, John Franklin
Hawk, Richard Stanley
Hawk, Walter, II
Hawkes, Benjamin G(uilford)
Hawkes, Townsend Devonshire
Hawkins, David Henry
Hawkins, Elinor Dixon (Mrs. Carroll Woodard Hawkins)
Hawkins, Elmer John
Hawkins, Frank
Hawkins, George Elliott, Jr.
Hawkins, John Morgan
Hawkins, Paula
Hawkins, Richard Frazier
Hawkins, Robert A.
Hawkins, Veronice
Hawkins, William Bledsoe, Jr.
Hawkins, William Bruce
Hawthorne, John David
Hawthorne, John William
Hay, Raymond A.
Hay, Russell Earl, Jr.
Hayden, Julius John, Jr.
Haydock, Vincent Conrad
Hayek, David Joe
Hayes, Carolyn Florence
Hayes, Charles Joseph, Jr. (Mickey)
Hayes, Gaynelle Hasselmeier
Hayes, George Roy, Jr.
Hayes, Isabella Mallory (Mrs. Walter Harold Hayes)
Hayes, John Terrence
Hayes, Kyle
Hayes, Margaret Smithey
Hayes, Philip Ernest
Hayes, Wayland Jackson, Jr.

Hayhurst, Mary Lea
Haymes, Edward Randolph
Haynes, Boyd Withers, Jr.
Haynes, Clifford Rudolph
Haynes, Douglas Bryant, Jr.
Haynes, Effie Gillis
Haynes, Felix Tankersley, Sr.
Haynes, George Edward
Haynes, George Henry, Jr.
Haynes, Gilbert Augustus
Haynes, Leonard L., Jr.
Haynes, Noris Richard, Jr.
Haynes, Robert Vaughn
Haynes, Walter George
Haynie, John James
Haynsworth, Clement Furman, Jr.
Hays, Jack Rufe
Hays, James DeFord
Hays, James Robison
Hays, Patrick Henry
Hays, Robert William
Hayward, Olga Loretta Hines (Mrs. Samuel E. Hayward)
Hayward, Thomas Tibbett
Haywood, H(erbert) Carl(ton)
Haywood, William Thomas
Hazel, Robert Hamilton
Hazelwood, Carroll Thomas
Hazlehurst, Franklin Hamilton
Heacock, George Thomas
Head, Beverly Pierce, III
Head, Charles Everett
Head, Dwight Galen
Head, Howard Martin
Head, Martha Ella Moore
Headley, Elwood Jean
Headstrom, Birger Richard
Healy, John Edward
Healy, Robert Edward
Heard, Gladys Mae Carey
Hearn, Claude David
Hearn, George Daniel (Danny)
Hearn, Robert Lee, III
Hearne, Douglass Dodson
Heartwell, Charles Monroe, Jr.
Heasley, Herbert Kay
Heath, Alfred Oswald
Heath, Leslie Arthur
Hebert, Carolyn St. Amant
Hebert, Carroll Francis
Heck, Marshall Conrad
Heck, Rhomie Lloyd
Heck, William Ross
Heckerman, Calton, Jr.
Heckman, Robert Arthur
Hedge, George Albert
Hedgecock, John Phillip
Hedg-peth, (Cornelius) George
Hedrick, Robert K.
Heebe, Frederick Jacob Regan
Heffernan, Thomas Carroll, Jr.
Heffner, Richard Louis
Hefner, Joe Denson
Hefner, Robert Alexander, III
Hefner, W.G.
Hegstrom, William Jean
Heiberg, Harold Willard
Heidbrink, Virgil Eugene
Heil, Robert Allen
Heiling, Frank Joseph
Heilmann, Martha Gerry Wheeler
Heimann, David Lawrence
Heimlich, Barry Noah
Heindl, Leopold Alexander
Heine, Larry Littleton
Heineman, Albert Frederick, Jr.
Heinemann, Sol
Heiner, (Samuel) Phillip
Heiney, Elvie Pershing
Heinrichs, Thelma Lee
Heins, Albert Gordon, Jr.
Heiny, James Richard
Heinz, John Dale, Jr.
Heiserman, Alberta Elizabeth Nardi
Heitzman, Donald Edmund, Sr.
Hejtmancik, Milton Rudolph
Held, Berel
Held, Edward Carlisle, Jr.
Helganz, Beverly Buzhardt
Helgeson, Norman Gordon Phelps
Helland, George Archibald, Jr.
Hellen, James Albert
Heller, Heinz Joseph
Heller, Max Moses
Heller, Pearl Bailie (Mrs. Raymond J. Heller)
Hellstrom, Richard Barry
Helm, Hugh Barnett
Helme, James Buckelew
Helmick, Charlotte Kay
Helms, Jesse
Helvie, Carl O.
Hembree, Eugene Edward, Jr.
Hembree, Hugh Lawson, III
Hembree, Oscar Eli, Jr.
Hemminghaus, Roger Roy
Hemmingway, Beulah
Hemness, Ray Leslie
Hemphill, James Eugene
Hemphill, Ralph William, Jr.
Henderson, Albert John
Henderson, Douglas Larry
Henderson, George
Henderson, Harold Alpheus
Henderson, Harold Dale
Henderson, Harold Rains
Henderson, Jack Calvin
Henderson, James Henry
Henderson, James Marcus
Henderson, Jerry Don
Henderson, John Baxter
Henderson, John Will, Jr.
Henderson, Joseph Harrison, III
Henderson, Kaye Neil
Henderson, Mary Emma
Henderson, Nan Lee
Henderson, Philip S.
Henderson, Reid
Henderson, Robert Lee, Jr.
Henderson, Warren S.
Henderson, William Donald
Hendon, Robert Caraway
Hendon, Robert Caraway, Jr.
Hendrick, Robert Smith
Hendrick, Zelwanda
Hendricks, Albert Cates
Hendricks, Charles Marvin, Jr.
Hendricks, George Edgar
Hendricks, Gerald J.
Hendricks, Nathan VanMeter, III
Hendricks, William Andrew
Hendricks, William Joseph
Hendricks, William Lawrence
Hendrickson, Jerome Orland
Hendrickson, Russell John
Hendrix, Connie Sandage
Hendrix, Martha Jan
Hendrix, William Herlie
Hendrix, Winford Leon
Hendry, Barbara Louise
Hendry, Clifford Samuel
Hendry, James E.
Hendry, Norman C.
Henican, Caswell Ellis
Heningburg, Sandra Oliver
Henington, David Mead
Henkel, John Harmon
Henley, Sallie Hamlet
Henley, William Branch, Jr.
Hennecy, James Howell
Hennessy, Jefferson Thomas
Hennessy, John Harold, Jr.
Hennessy, John J.
Hennesy, Gerald Craft
Hennig, Eric Stephen
Hennigan, Henry William
Hennigar, Gordon Ross, Jr.
Henning, Eugene Somers
Hennings, LeRoy, Jr.
Henry, Claibourne Dennis
Henry, Daniel Ray
Henry, Donald Pomeroy
Henry, Gaile Maurice, Jr.
Henry, George Colbert, Jr.
Henry, Jack Hopkins
Henry, John James
Henry, John Wesley, Jr.
Henry, Joseph Raymond
Henry, M. Daniel
Henry, Margaret Brewer
Henry, Marshall Webster, Jr.
Henry, Robert Fillmore
Henry, Vertie Lee
Henry, William Ray
Hensarling, Grace Truman
Hensel, Len
Hensel, Wilber Marsh, Jr.
Hensgens, Leonard Joseph
Henshaw, Andy Lorenzo
Hensley, Larry Donald
Hensley, Lee Rasbury
Henson, Hugh Ely
Henson, Jerry B.
Henson, Kenneth Wayne
Henson, Thomas Deaton
Hensz, Richard Albert
Henton, Willis Ryan
Hepner, Leon Wilburne
Hepworth, Samuel Wilson
Herbert, Keith John
Herbert, Marie Hensley
Herbert, William Field
Herbich, John Bronislaw
Herbst, Roy Roger
Hereter, Jorge Antonio
Hergott, Raymond William
Hering, Woodrow W.
Herlong, James Herbert
Herlt, Bernard George, Jr.
Herman, Bertha Elizabeth
Herman, Daniel Jacques
Herman, William Ross
Hermelee, Laurence Stephan
Hernandez, Alma Garza
Hernandez, Jose Yolando Balagtas
Hernandez, Pedro, Jr.
Herndon, George Burbank, Jr.
Herndon, John Francis
Herndon, Mary Aurea Balfay
Hernly, Harold Granville
Herold, Donald George
Herring, Grover Cleveland
Herring, Jack William
Herring, Michael Morris
Herrmann, John Leland
Herron, John William
Herron, Robert Ernest
Hersey, George William
Herskowitz, Allan
Hersom, Howard Thayer
Herst, Herman, Jr.
Hess, Daniel Nicholas
Hesselbart, Susan Carol
Hester, Alcia Marguerite
Hester, Cawthon Bell, Jr.
Hevenor, Richard Alan
Hewgley, James Marion, Jr.
Hewitt, Robert Lee
Hewlett, James LeRoy
Heyburn, William, II
Heyck, Gertrude Paine Daly (Mrs. Theodore R. Heyck)
Heyman, Stephen Joshua
Heyward, Jeanne
Heywood, Humphrey Barrett, Jr.
Hibbert, William Andrew, Jr.
Hibberts, Charles Reginald
Hickerson, Elzie
Hickey, John King
Hickman, Gerald Hilton
Hickman, Hoyt Leon
Hicks, Alfred Barrett, Jr.
Hicks, Dorothy Jane
Hicks, Harold Newton
Hicks, Jesse Lee
Hicks, Julius Norton
Hicks, Lillie Marie
Hicks, Robert Lee
Hicks, Roy Edward
Hicks, William Trotter
Hidalgo, Chester Paul
Hidalgo, Manuel Thomas
Hider, George Milton
Hiers, Gerald Lamar
Hiett, Louis Alden
Higdon, Wilford Dain
Higginbotham, Hugh Oliver, Jr.
Higginbotham, Ronald Eugene
Higgins, David Lawrence
Higgins, John David, Jr.
Higgins, John Joseph
Higgins, Kenneth Raymond
Higgins, Lawrence Ernest
Higgins, Willie Estel
High, Harold Eugene
Highfield, Kathleen Kennedy
Highleyman, Daly
Highman, Benjamin
Highstone, Harry Robert
Hight, Ronald Max
Hightower, Dannie Bea (Mrs. Frank Johnson Hightower)
Hightower, David Peterson
Hightower, Jack English
Hightower, Russell Garnett
Hildebrand, Frank
Hildebrand, Joseph Francis, Jr.
Hildebrandt, Alvin Frank
Hildebrandt, Theodore Ware
Hildreth, William Wesley
Hiles, William Gayle, Jr.
Hill, A(lfred) Garrett
Hill, Bryce Dale
Hill, Caesar Grant
Hill, Carl McClellan
Hill, Cecil James
Hill, Clarence Kenneth, Jr.
Hill, Claud Justin
Hill, David William
Hill, Douglas Livingstone
Hill, Douglass Orville
Hill, Floyd Williams
Hill, Frederick Ephrium
Hill, Harold Pershing
Hill, Heager LeVoyd
Hill, Ida Johnson
Hill, James Mark
Hill, James Stewart
Hill, Jerry Gifford
Hill, Joan
Hill, John Luke
Hill, Johnny Ray
Hill, Kathleen Jones
Hill, Lee H., Jr.
Hill, Leonard Maurice
Hill, Margaret Oliphant Donald
Hill, Max Lloyd, Jr.
Hill, Paul Leonard
Hill, Sally Ann
Hill, Thomas Austin
Hill, Thomas Robert
Hill, William Oscar, Jr.
Hill, William T.
Hillery, Herbert Vincent
Hilley, Larry Lee
Hilliard, William Gerald
Hillman, James Devee
Hillyer, Raymond Davenport
Hilton, Ralph
Hilton, Robert Leroy
Hiltzheimer, Nancy Barrett
Hilyer, Ronald Bennett
Himmelfarb, Elliot Harvey
Hinchey, Frank Lloyd
Hinckley, George Christopher
Hincks, Joel Barber
Hinderer, Byron Frederick
Hindermann, Richard Lane
Hinds, Benjamin Leon
Hinds, Charles Franklin
Hinerman, Robert Evan
Hines, Carolyn Walker
Hines, Charles William
Hines, Chesley
Hines, Robert Stickley, Jr.
Hines, William Thomas, Jr.
Hinesley, Joseph Dock
Hinkel, Helen Mary Rykowski (Mrs. Joseph Loyd Hinkel)
Hinkle, Allen Oscar, Jr.
Hinson, Howard Houston
Hinton, Clacy Reed
Hinton, Danielle Margaret
Hinton, Thomas Earl
Hipp, Betty Jeane
Hipp, Howell Edsel
Hirata, Isao, Jr.
Hirschfield, Howard J.
Hirsh, Albert
Hirt, Fred Denis
Hitch, Henry Charles, Jr.
Hitchcock, Otis Kendall
Hitchcock, Terrance S.
Hite, James Leslie
Hite, Lawrence Ely
Hitt, David Hamilton
Hitt, Harold Hamilton
Hlavacek, Milos Joseph
Hlavinka, Anthony Charles
Ho, Ching Ju
Ho, Thomas Tong-yun
Hoade, Jane Richter
Hoagland, Bruce Dudley
Hoback, Hazel Epperley
Hobbie, Walter Randal
Hobbins, Vincent John
Hobbs, Charles Curtis
Hobbs, John James
Hobbs, Ned Peter
Hobbs, Odell
Hobbs, Oliver Kermit
Hobby, Gretchen Clark (Mrs. William M. Hobby III)
Hobby, Oveta Culp (Mrs. William P. Hobby)
Hobby, William Pettus
Hobson, Christopher Gordon
Hobson, Virginia Prince Calvin
Hochbaum, Godfrey M(artin)
Hockenbury, Melvin Richard
Hocott, Joe Bill
Hodder, Robert Edwin
Hodes, Richard Samuel
Hodgden, Bryce Louis
Hodge, Arthur Wiley
Hodge, Bartow
Hodge, Gameel Byron
Hodge, George Lowrance
Hodge, Homer James
Hodge, Kenneth E.
Hodge, Robert Edward
Hodge, William Garth, Jr.
Hodgens, Paul Morton, Sr.
Hodges, Brent
Hodges, Charles Edwin
Hodges, Delmon
Hodges, Frederick Benjamin, Jr.
Hodges, Howard Lawrence
Hodges, John Edward, Jr.
Hodges, Joseph Howard
Hodges, Jot Holiver, Jr.
Hodges, Ralph Byron
Hodges, Richard Edward
Hodgin, William Kendrick
Hodgson, Dale Leroy
Hodgson, Jesse Loyde
Hoechstetter, Louis Julian
Hoekstra, Harold Derk
Hoel, Eddie R.
Hoeppel, Ronald Edward
Hoffman, Connie Wilson
Hoffman, Garlyn Odell
Hoffman, Joseph Irvine, Jr.
Hoffman, Philip (Guthrie)
Hoffman, Robert John
Hoffman, Wayne Larry
Hoffman, William Walter
Hoffmanns, Frederic Everhardt
Hofheimer, Benjamin Franklin, III
Hofheinz, James Fred
Hofker, Raymond George
Hofmann, Ross Elwood
Hogan, Edwin Belton
Hogan, Eugene Ernest
Hogan, Fannie Burrell (Mrs. Isaac Nathaniel Hogan)
Hogan, Joseph Thomas
Hogan, Robert Steadham
Hogarth, Charles Pinckney
Hogarth, Frances Harris (Mrs. Charles P. Hogarth)
Hogsett, Duane Frank
Hogshead, Thomas Henry
Hogshire, Martha Kent
Hogue, James Larry
Hohf, Jerome Chalmers
Hoke, George Clayton
Holbrook, Edward Lionel
Holbrook, Emmett Bradford, Jr.
Holbrook, James Mitchell
Holbrook, Juan Alfaro
Holcomb, Charles C.
Holcomb, Charles Edward
Holcomb, Charlie Calvin
Holcomb, Curtis Robert
Holcomb, James Eldon
Holcomb, Jimmy David
Holcombe, Cressie Earl, Jr.
Holcombe, Milton Winford
Holcombe, Troy Leon
Holder, Howard Randolph
Holderness, Howard
Holekamp, Bettye Joanne
Holeman, James Lynn
Holladay, Charles Edwin
Holladay, James Franklin
Holland, Earl Stafford
Holland, Edward McHarg
Holland, Edward Richard
Holland, Evelyn Faucette (Mrs. Sherman W. Holland, Jr.)
Holland, James Harrison
Holland, John Birl
Holland, Ken L.
Holland, Major Leonard
Holland, William Meredith
Hollandsworth, Thomas Greene, Jr.
Holler, Bernice Plowman
Hollers, Hardy
Holley, Max Dean
Holley, Robert Leon
Holliday, Amy Mae West
Holliday, Patricia Ruth
Holliday, Vadim Peter
Hollifield, John George
Hollin, Robert Warmer
Hollings, Ernest Frederick
Hollings, Richard Wayne
Hollingsworth, Bobby J.
Hollingsworth, Gerald Martin
Hollingsworth, Joe Pettus
Hollingsworth, John Alexander
Hollinshead, William Lawrence
Hollis, Alton Lavon
Hollis, Bobby Allen, Jr.
Hollis, Dannie Gillis
Hollis, Patrick Donegan
Hollis, Richard Gene
Hollis, Walter Jesse
Holloman, Haskell Andrew
Holloman, James Horace, Jr.
Holloman, Jeff Joe
Hollomon, John Wesley
Holloway, George Reece
Holloway, Gordon Arthur
Holloway, Malcolm Hammett
Hollowell, Douglas Albert
Hollowell, Monte Jerry
Holly, David Chauncey
Holm, Jurgen Kurt
Holman, James Marvin
Holman, Rudolph Price
Holman, Virginia Fuller
Holmann, Anne Sharpe (Mrs. E. J. Holmann)
Holmes, Alexander Baron, III
Holmes, Clifford Newton
Holmes, Eugene Thomas
Holmes, Jack David Lazarus
Holmes, Robert Cornelius
Holmes, Thomas Joseph
Holmquist, Virgil Andrew
Holsenbeck, Wiley Howard, Jr.
Holsinger, Ralph Waldo, III
Holsinger, Robert Eugene
Holston, William Joseph
Holt, Amos Earl
Holt, Carol Peek
Holt, Margaret McConnell
Holt, Mary Louise
Holt, Robert G.
Holt, Robert LeRoi
Holter, William Hudson
Holthouse, Norman Dale
Holton, Raburn Robert
Holtzman, Gary Yale
Holway, James Colin
Holycross, Robert Lee
Holzberg, Marylin Tell (Mrs. Mark Holzberg)
Holzman, Bruce Rigler
Homan, Bertie Glee
Homeyer, Fred Charles
Hood, Charles Hurlburt
Hood, John Julian
Hood, John Thomas, Jr.
Hood, Walter Kelly
Hood, William Rogers
Hook, Alice Vasquez
Hooker, Helen Loveta O'Connell (Mrs. John Warren Hooker)
Hooker, John Patrick
Hooker, Nathan Harvey
Hooks, Eugene James
Hooks, Lance Gilbert
Hooley, John Stone
Hooper, Glenn Scoble
Hooper, Irene Upshaw
Hooper, James William
Hooper, John Markle
Hooten, William Wayne
Hootman, Harry Edward
Hoover, Jimmie Hartman
Hoover, Thomas Burdett
Hope, (John) Stephen
Hope, Thomas Hartsel, Jr.
Hopewell, Harry Lynn, Jr.
Hopkins, Alben Norris
Hopkins, Amy Longcope (Mrs. Edwin Butcher Hopkins)
Hopkins, Anthony Duane
Hopkins, Billy Greene
Hopkins, Burtram Collver, II
Hopkins, Carter Byrd Hunter
Hopkins, George Mathews Marks
Hopkins, Grover Prevatte (Jack)
Hopkins, Harry L.
Hopkins, Joe Warren
Hopkins, John David, Jr.
Hopkins, Robert Howell, Jr.
Hopler, Frederick Billings, Jr.
Hoplin, Herman Peter
Hoppe, Gordon Paul
Hoppenstein, Joel Manuel
Hopper, Edward Eric
Hopper, Frank Jay
Hopping, Wade Lee
Hopson, Jannie
Hopson, William Briggs, Jr.
Horak, Joseph Bernard
Horchow, S(amuel) Roger
Horger, Edgar Olin, III
Horkan, George Arthur
Horn, Carl, Jr.
Horn, John
Horn, Lawrence Charles
Horn, Louis John
Horne, Annie Pearl Cooke
Horne, Elmer Lee
Horne, John E.
Horner, Jo Lorraine
Horney, Hayden Harrison
Hornsby, Alton, Jr.
Hornsby, Walter Spurgeon, III
Horowitz, Charles
Horowitz, Judith Ellen
Horowitz, Roslyn Hammer
Horsley, Thomas Martin
Horsman, David A. Elliott
Horton, Arthur MacNeill, Jr.
Horton, Carrell Peterson
Horton, Granville Eugene
Horton, J(oseph) Rex
Horton, John Oliver
Horton, Julius Broyles
Horton, Karen Hutchins
Horton, Lyle Henderson
Horton, Thomas Edward, Jr.
Horton, William Lamar
Horween, Matthew Benjamin
Hosea, Addison
Hosea, Robert Leroy
Hoskins, Godfrey Curtis
Hoskins, Robert Nathan
Hoster, William Henry, Jr.
Hotchkiss, John Farwell, Jr.
Houde, John Louis
Houk, Richard Duncan
Houren, J(ames) Patrick
House, George Robert, Jr.
House, James Robert, Jr.
Houser, John Edward
Houston, Aubrey Clay
Houston, Frank Matt
Houston, Neal Bryan
Houston, Shirley Mae (Mrs. Thomas Harold Houston)
Houtmann, Jacques
Hovey, Lester Eugene
Hovland, David (Allan)
Howard, Arthur Ellsworth Dick
Howard, Bernard Eufinger
Howard, C(larence) Edward
Howard, Charles Kenneth
Howard, Craig John
Howard, Frank Saxon
Howard, G. LaMarr
Howard, George Turner, Jr.
Howard, Gordon Edward
Howard, Ida Beth
Howard, Jesse Wayne (Rip)
Howard, John Garfield
Howard, Larry Bruce
Howard, Marland Paul
Howard, Nora Lee
Howard, Ransom
Howard, Rhea
Howard, Richard Ralston
Howard, Robert Bruce
Howard, Robert David
Howard, Ted Emmitt, Jr.
Howard, Thelma Lillian
Howard, Thomas Edward, Sr.
Howard, William Joseph
Howard, William Raymond
Howe, Carroll Leon
Howe, Evelyn Freeman
Howe, Lyman Harold, III
Howe, Philip Gardner, Jr.
Howell, Charles Maitland
Howell, David Ernest
Howell, Floyd, Jr.
Howell, Frank
Howell, Hugh Hawkins, Jr.
Howell, Irvin Napoleon
Howell, Jimmie Sylvanus
Howell, Mable Smith (Mrs. Bruce Inman Howell)
Howell, Mark Franklin
Howell, Ralph Rodney
Howell, Ronald Thomas
Howell, William Harry
Howeth, Marvin Seth
Howey, John Richard
Howgate, David Washburne
Howie, Henry Sanford, Jr.
Howison, Juanita Carmack (Mrs. Claude F. Howison)
Howland, Ronald Lloyd
Howry, Hamilton Hubbard, Jr.
Howse, Harold Darrow
Howse, William Lewis, III
Hoy, Mary Camilla
Hoy, William Ivan
Hoyt, Stephen Lee
Hrishikesan, Kizhakke Govind
Hrubecky, Henry Francis
Hsie, Abraham Wuhsiung
Hsu, John Cheu-wang
Hu, Tse-Chuang (Jim)
Huang, Edwin I-Chuen
Huang, Jinn-Huie
Huang, Richard Shih-chiu
Huang, Ted Tsung-Che
Huang, William Edward
Hubacher, John Sterling
Hubbard, Carroll, Jr.
Hubbard, Curtis Howe
Hubbard, Hampton
Hubbard, Howard Thomas
Hubbard, Lafayette Ronald
Hubbell, David Smith
Hubbell, Robert Carlton
Hubbs, Lillian Gooden
Huber, Albert John
Huber, Rudolph John
Huberman, Jeffrey Allen
Hubert, Joseph Arthur
Hubicki, Peter Michael
Huck, Lewis Francis
Huckabee, Martha Carolyn
Huckaby, Donald Howard
Huckaby, Thomas Gerald
Huddleston, Charles Richard
Huddleston, John McKean
Huddleston, Joseph Russell
Huddleston, Walter Darlington
Huddleston, William Ennis
Hudgens, Edward Boone, Jr.
Hudgens, Arvin Quinton
Hudgins, Catherine Harding (Mrs. Robert Scott Hudgins, IV)
Hudgins, Edward Morton
Hudgins, Joe Lane

Hudgins, Mary Dengler
Hudgins, Tom Malone
Hudgins, William Henry
Hudgins, William Robert
Hudoba, Michael
Hudson, Alton Gene
Hudson, Charles Daugherty
Hudson, Dick D.
Hudson, Elizabeth Desmond
Hudson, Glenn William, Jr.
Hudson, Henry Alexander, Jr.
Hudson, Hubert R.
Hudson, John Lester
Hudson, Joseph Willis
Hudson, Leonard Lester
Hudson, Morley Alvin
Hudson, Nelson Fleming
Hudson, W(alter) Taylor
Hudspeth, Ronald Paul
Hudspeth, William Roy, Jr.
Huebner, Richard Allen
Huerkamp, Frederick John
Huff, Henry Blair
Huff, Howard Farmer
Huff, John Rossman
Huff, Ozzie
Huff, William Jennings
Huffman, George Russell, Jr.
Huffman, Jerry Wayne
Huffman, Richard Lee
Huffman, Robert Edward
Huffman, William Harry
Huffnagle, Norman Parmley
Huggins, Robert Leigh
Hughes, Ann Hanszen
Hughes, Anne Finks
Hughes, Billy Ray
Hughes, D. P.
Hughes, Dorothy Marie
Hughes, Edwin McCulloc
Hughes, George Farant, Jr.
Hughes, Hansel Leigh
Hughes, John David
Hughes, Joseph Marshall
Hughes, Kenneth James
Hughes, Nettie Sue
Hughes, Patricia Charmienne Yarwood
Hughes, Silas Edwin
Hughes, Stuart Powell
Hughes, Sue Margaret
Hughes, Thomas Wendell
Hughes, Vester Thomas, Jr.
Hughes, Vincent Leo
Hughes, Waunell McDonald (Mrs. Delbert E. Hughes)
Hughley, Alice Williams
Hugin, Adolph Charles
Huguley, John Earl
Huh, Oscar Karl, Jr.
Hulen, Alfred Clayton
Hull, James Dixon, III
Hull, Richard Franklin
Hullett, James Calvin
Hultman, Kenneth Edward
Humann, Louis Philip
Hume, Marian Ruby
Humenik, Frank James
Humensky, Joseph Edward
Humphrey, William Edwin
Humphrey, Zepplyn Stepp
Humphreys, Homer Alexander
Humphreys, Horace Steelman
Humphreys, Kenneth King
Humphreys, Thomas Green, Jr.
Humphries, Betsy Scarboro
Humphries, John Edward
Humphries, Robert Lee, Jr.
Humrickhouse, George Randolph
Hungate, Joseph Irvin, Jr.
Hunkin, Alfred James
Hunnicutt, Julian Perry
Hunnicutt, Warren, Jr.
Hunstad, Bernie Richard
Hunt, Billy Paul
Hunt, Carle Manhart
Hunt, David Ford
Hunt, Earl Gladstone, Jr.
Hunt, Elizabeth Mullen
Hunt, Harold Eugene
Hunt, J(ulian) Courtenay
Hunt, James Baxter, Jr.
Hunt, James William
Hunt, Jasper Stewart
Hunt, John Williamson
Hunt, Joseph Victor
Hunt, William Frederick, Jr.
Hunter, Carl Warren
Hunter, Charles Edwin
Hunter, Edward
Hunter, Emmett Marshall, Jr.
Hunter, Gordon Coble
Hunter, Hassell Eugene
Hunter, James Edwin
Hunter, Lena Virginia
Hunter, Mary Doty
Hunter, Mary Jane Burns (Mrs. Joseph Lawton Hunter)
Hunter, Ora Anderson (Mrs. Still Hunter)
Hunter, Richard Edmund
Hunter, Robert Byfield
Hunter, Ruby Sue (Mrs. Charles Force Hunter)
Huntington, Robert Graham
Huntington, Roy Theodore
Huntington, Sterling Hicks
Hurd, Eric Ray
Hurdle, Walker Hardy, Jr.
Hurlbert, Raymond Donald
Hurlburt, Harvey Zeh
Hurley, Frank Thomas, Jr.
Hurley, James Laurence
Hurst, Harry Ellsworth
Hurst, Mark Sluder
Hurst, Otis Ray
Hurst, Thomas Charles, III
Hurt, Frank Benjamin
Hurtt, Oscar Lee, Jr.
Hurtt, Oscar Lee, III
Huse, Martha Ruth
Huseman, Richard C.
Hushen, Stanley Cecil
Husketh, Alma Ormond (Mrs. Edward Thomas Husketh, Jr.)
Hussain, A.K.M. Fazle
Husted, John Edwin
Huston, Beatrice Fae (Mrs. Johnnie W. Huston)
Huston, Robert Boyd
Hutchens, (Sidney) Gail Rakes
Hutcherson, Donna Dean Clark
Hutcheson, David Lyle
Hutcheson, Guy Carlton
Hutcheson, James Sterling
Hutcheson, Mary Dixon Rawles
Hutchins, Charles Anthony
Hutchins, Mary Imojeane Keys Allen (Mrs. P.O. Hutchins)
Hutchinson, John Guiher
Hutchinson, Leonard Hugh
Hutchinson, Richard Charles
Hutchinson, William Seely, Jr.
Hutchison, Glen Daren
Hutchison, William Forrest
Hutman, Burton Simson
Hutson, Grady
Hutson, Philip Ashley
Hutton, Jerry B.
Huyke-Luigi, Roberto
Huysman, Arlene Weiss
Hyams, Phineas Joseph
Hyatt, Gordon Arthur
Hyatt, Wayne Spurgeon
Hyde, Archie Marion
Hyde, Lawrence Perry
Hyde, Richard Moorehead
Hyde, Robert Todd
Hyder, Charles Hubert, III
Hyder, Melvin H.
Hyman, Albert Lewis
Hyman, Janice Himmler
Hynes, Michael Kevin
Hytche, Pamelia Reneé
Iacobucci, Guillermo Arturo
Iannicelli, Joseph
I'Anson, Lawrence Warren
Ibach, Douglas Theodore
Ibach, John Raymond, Jr.
Ibison, James Louie
Ichinose, Herbert
Iddins, Mildred
Idleburg, Dorothy Ann Bell
Ierardo, Domenick
Iglesias, Jose Victor
Iglesias, Thomas
Ilahi, Arifa Aslam
Iler, Arthur Triplett
Iles, Joyce Evelyn Cox
Ilvento, Barbara Kautz
Im, Yung Kook
Imbrogno, Eugene Francis
Imbrogno, Eugene Francis, III
Imler, Allison E(llwood)
Imparato, Edward Thomas
Infante, Gabriel Adolfo
Inge, Milton Thomas
Inge, Vernon Eugene
Ingerick, Eldyn Layne
Ingerton, William Thomas
Ingram, Anne G.
Ingram, Gilbert Lewis
Ingram, James Dugger
Ingram, James Lloyd
Ingram, Riley Edward
Ingram, Robert A.
Ingram, Robert Bernard
Ingram, Sam Harris
Ininger, Helen Veronica
Inks, James Moss
Inlow, Robert Francis
Inman, Bob Ray
Inman, Edwin Wesley
Inman, Robert Lyle
Ipsen, Kent Forrest
Irby, Bobby Newell
Irby, Claud James, Jr.
Ireland, Andrew Paysell (Andy)
Ireland, Lock Wynn
Irizarry-Perez, Luis A.
Irlinger, Frank Seraph
Irvin, Guy Daniel, Jr.
Irvin, James Nelson
Irvine, James Bosworth
Irwin, Thaddeus Stevens
Irzyk, Albin Felix
Isaac, Robert Edward
Isaacs, Dan Lee
Isbell, Euclid Arnold, Jr.
Isbell, Terry Roberts
Isbill, Frank Eugene
Iseley, Nancy Jane
Isham, Robert Lind
Isom, Ronnie Oscar
Ison, Gertrude Sutton
Israel, Firooz
Israel, John Robert
Israel, Kenneth Davidson
Israel, Willard Alfred
Israili, Zafar Hasan
Ivans, Galen John David
Iver, William Henry
Iverson, John Willie
Ivester, Julius Ray
Ivester, Zoe Ann
Ivey, Harry Lane
Ivey, Jack Lyndon
Ivey, Marvin L.
Ivey, Tim Willard
Iyengar, Krishna Prakash Ranganathan
Izquierdo, Luis Ramos, Jr.
Jachimczyk, Joseph Alexander
Jack, William Harry
Jacks, James Fred
Jackson, B. Gordon
Jackson, Betty Ruth
Jackson, Blyden
Jackson, Charles Gordon, Jr.
Jackson, Charles Wallace
Jackson, Crayton Troy
Jackson, Della Rosetta Hayden
Jackson, Delphine Eriska
Jackson, Donald William
Jackson, Dorothy Louisa Greenlee (Mrs. Fred Knox Jackson)
Jackson, Edward Hughes, Jr.
Jackson, Eric E.
Jackson, Jack Means
Jackson, James Warren
Jackson, John Wingfield
Jackson, Larry Newton
Jackson, Marlin Dale
Jackson, Maynard Holbrook, Jr.
Jackson, Morris Kent
Jackson, Prince Albert, Jr.
Jackson, Ralph Newman
Jackson, Randall C(alvin)
Jackson, Richard Ellis
Jackson, William Howard
Jackson, William Paul, Jr.
Jacob, Jerry Paul
Jacob, Paul Bernard, Jr.
Jacobs, Daniel Martin
Jacobs, Eugene Robert
Jacobs, Frederic Weil
Jacobs, Marcellus Luther
Jacobs, Wallace Jerome
Jacobsen, James Alva
Jacobson, Alan Frank
Jacobson, Antone Gardner
Jacobson, Bernard
Jacobson, David
Jacobson, Donald Richard
Jacobson, Helen G. (Mrs. David Jacobson)
Jacobson, Leonard I.
Jacobson, Norman Frederick
Jacobus, Charles Jeremiah
Jacoby, John Burtner
Jacques, Wilfred James, Jr.
Jadav, Manhar Kalidas
Jaeger, Raymond Alphons
Jaeger, Richard Morrow
Jaffe, Herman
Jaggars, John Michael
Jaggers, Charles Stanley
Jahn, Edward Louis
Jain, Kamal Chandra
Jain, Suresh Chand
James, Advergus Dell, Jr.
James, Albert Law, III
James, Allix Bledsoe
James, Charles Griffin
James, Charles R.
James, Clyde Ival
James, Donald William
James, Doris Mae
James, Earl Eugene, Jr.
James, Gary Michael
James, George Robert
James, Grace Marillyn
James, H. Rhett
James, John V.
James, Joseph B.
James, M(aloy) C(owan)
James, Maloy Cowan, Jr.
James, Michael Lynn
James, Philip Wayne
James, Raymond Winfield
James, Richard Wayne
James, Ronald David
James, Ted Lowell
James, William Wesley, Jr.
Jamieson, Addie Mae
Jamison, Homer Claude
Jamison, John Ambler
Jamison, King Wells, Jr.
Jamison, Ollie Frances
Jamison, Richard Melvin
Janda, Robert James
Jander, Hartwig Peter
Janes, Robert Harrison, Jr.
Janeway, Richard
Jann, Warren William
Jann, William Kenneth, Sr.
Janosik, Steven Michael
Jansen, William Hugh
Janssen, Felix Gerard
Janzen, Jerry Lee
Jaques, Thomas Francis
Jaques, William Everett
Jaramillo, Edward Terry
Jarboe, Charles Harry
Jardine, John Henry
Jarmon, Charles
Jarosak, Andrew
Jarrell, James Earl, Jr.
Jarrell, Marion Lee
Jarvis, Bobby Joe
Jarvis, Edmund
Jarvis, Harold Sims
Jarvis, James Howard, II
Jary, Lloyd Walker
Jasin, David Albin
Jasper, Martin Theophilus
Javellas, Ina June
Jay, James Albert
Jeansonne, Edmund Engler
Jecko, Perry Timothy
Jefferds, Joseph Crosby, Jr.
Jeffers, Donald Lewis
Jeffers, Florice Stripling
Jeffers, Leroy
Jefferson, George Robert, Sr.
Jefferson, Joseph Levoid
Jefferson, Omega Blondie
Jeffords, Jean Garrett
Jeffords, Samuel King, III
Jeffrey, Dorothy Ann
Jeffries, Charles Ray
Jehle, Herbert
Jelenevsky, Alex Michael
Jelks, Allen Nathaniel, Sr.
Jelks, James William
Jelks, Joseph William, Jr.
Jelks, Louis Rollwage
Jelks, Mary Larson
Jellinek, Harold Lester
Jelsma, Edward Richard
Jenkins, Clara Barnes
Jenkins, Ed (Edgar) Lanier
Jenkins, Edwin Garth
Jenkins, Jay
Jenkins, R. Lee
Jenkins, Robert Warls, Jr.
Jenkins, Ruth Irene
Jenkins, Samuel Priestly
Jenks, Sallie Anne
Jennings, Frank Clay
Jennings, Henry Smith, Jr.
Jennings, Howard William, II
Jennings, Jarrell Lee
Jennings, Jerry Lee
Jennings, John James
Jennings, John Melville
Jennings, Richard Louis
Jennings, Robert Burgess
Jennings, Rufus Edward
Jennings, Walter Stanley
Jenrette, John Wilson, Jr.
Jensen, Bruce Howard
Jensen, Richard Leland
Jenson, Sherman Milton
Jent, LaVoise Roark
Jentz, Gaylord Adair
Jerger, Richard Mitchell
Jermann, William Howard
Jermstad, Glen Lynch
Jerner, R. Craig
Jernigan, Eric Cooper
Jernigan, Rawlin Cleveland
Jessel, Joseph Brand
Jessop, Morris Eugene, Jr.
Jessup, Joe Lee
Jesurún, Harold Méndez
Jeter, Katherine Leslie Brash
Jett, Horace Wilbur Babe
Jett, Ralph Gene
Jewell, Robert Burnett
Jewell, William Horace
Jimenez, Jose
Jimenez, Raul
Jimenez-Torres, Carlos Federico
Jindra, Roy I.
Joannides, Minas, Jr.
Jobe, Madison Alphonso, Jr.
Jobe, William Steven
Joe, Young-Choon Charles
Joffe, Donald Jay
Jogland, Herta Helena
Johanson, Richard Claude
John, David Russell, Jr.
John, Gary Griffith
John, Patricia Spaulding
John, Paul Robin
John, Peter William Meredith
John, Vattakattil Mani
Johns, Elbert Brumfield
Johns, Fred Thomas
Johnson, Alfred Charles
Johnson, Alfred Massey Fisher
Johnson, Allen Huggins
Johnson, Barbara Ferry
Johnson, Ben Butler
Johnson, Billie Nell Albright
Johnson, Billy Joe
Johnson, Bob Ralph
Johnson, Bruce Alan
Johnson, Bruce King
Johnson, Buddy Gene
Johnson, Byron T., Jr.
Johnson, Carl Phillip
Johnson, Carlos Edward
Johnson, Carver Lister
Johnson, Charles Frederic
Johnson, Charles William
Johnson, Christine Currin
Johnson, Clarice Wells
Johnson, Clifford Wallace
Johnson, Clifton Herman
Johnson, Clinton Charles
Johnson, Clyde
Johnson, Cone
Johnson, Constance Howie
Johnson, Dave Tobin
Johnson, David L(ivingstone)
Johnson, David Mark
Johnson, David Pittman
Johnson, Dewey E(dward)
Johnson, Diane Seelye
Johnson, Doris Lee
Johnson, Douglas Elliott
Johnson, Edd Wilson
Johnson, Edna Fay (Mrs. Landon Carter Johnson, Jr.)
Johnson, Edward William
Johnson, Emmett John
Johnson, F(rank) Sam, Jr.
Johnson, Fielding Holmes
Johnson, Francis Russ Marion
Johnson, Frank
Johnson, Frank Minis, Jr.
Johnson, Frederick Dean
Johnson, Gary Lynn
Johnson, Gary Reid
Johnson, Gary Wayne
Johnson, George, Jr.
Johnson, George Edwin
Johnson, George Kimbal
Johnson, Gerald Frederick Ross
Johnson, Gerald Oliver
Johnson, Gilmer Brooks
Johnson, Glendon E.
Johnson, Gordon Gustav
Johnson, Harold Benjamin, Jr.
Johnson, Harry Claud
Johnson, Henry Page, Jr.
Johnson, Herbert Fraser
Johnson, Herman Bluitt
Johnson, Herman Lee, Jr.
Johnson, Howard Arthur, Sr.
Johnson, J. Arthur
Johnson, Jack D.
Johnson, Jacquelyn McCluney
Johnson, James Gibb
Johnson, James Henry
Johnson, Jane Gault
Johnson, Jay Lynn, Jr.
Johnson, Jerry Thomas
Johnson, Jessie Childers
Johnson, John Edward, Jr.
Johnson, John Robert
Johnson, Johnny Ray
Johnson, Joseph Belton
Johnson, Joseph Eggleston, III
Johnson, Julius Traylor
Johnson, Keith Herbert
Johnson, Kermit Alonzo
Johnson, Kline Wilson
Johnson, Larry Wilson
Johnson, Lee, Jr.
Johnson, Lewis Dan
Johnson, Lloyd Harlin
Johnson, Lonald Ray
Johnson, Lynwood Albert
Johnson, Marian Arlene
Johnson, Marian Ritchie
Johnson, Marvin Solomon
Johnson, Maryalyce
Johnson, Norman James
Johnson, Paul Allison
Johnson, Paul Edwin
Johnson, Paul Robert
Johnson, Perry Elliott
Johnson, Philip Carl, Jr.
Johnson, Philip Lewis
Johnson, Philip Martin
Johnson, Phillip Eugene
Johnson, Ralph Donald
Johnson, Ralph Emil
Johnson, Richard Alvin
Johnson, Richard Austin
Johnson, Richard Carl
Johnson, Richard J. V.
Johnson, Robert Ackerman
Johnson, Robert Bruce
Johnson, Robert Cobb
Johnson, Robert Norris
Johnson, Robert Ruhl
Johnson, Ronald Carl
Johnson, Roy Edward
Johnson, Samuel Warren
Johnson, Stanley Stevens
Johnson, Terrence Lynn
Johnson, Thomas Nelson Page, Jr.
Johnson, Thomas Ross
Johnson, Vernard
Johnson, Walter Martin
Johnson, Wayne Raymond
Johnson, William Alexander
Johnson, William Austin
Johnson, William Edward
Johnson, William Furlow
Johnson, William Royster
Johnson, William Stanley
Johnston, Alan Craig
Johnston, Charles Ernest
Johnston, Charles Samuel
Johnston, Frank Randolph
Johnston, Frederick Swain, Jr.
Johnston, Freeman Leon
Johnston, Gary William
Johnston, Ira Judson
Johnston, J(ohn) Bennett
Johnston, Jerry Lynn
Johnston, Joseph Eugene
Johnston, Lowell Preston
Johnston, Otto William
Johnston, Ruth Le Roy
Johnston, William Edward
Johnstone, Charles Albert Lesesne, Jr.
Johnstone, James Decatur
Jollay, Oscar Lloyd
Jolly, Alan Gordon
Jolly, Lewis Franklin
Jolly-Fritz, Roletta Olga (Mrs. Ralph A. Fritz)
Jonas, Federico Roque
Jonas, Gordon Keith
Jonas, John Charles
Jones, Alan Ivey
Jones, Albert Cecil
Jones, Albert Pearson
Jones, Alton Pat, Jr.
Jones, Ancil Arthur
Jones, Andrew Melvin
Jones, B. Corine
Jones, Barrie Lee
Jones, Billy Mac
Jones, Billy Rual
Jones, Buddy Calvin
Jones, Casey Clondel
Jones, Charles Alvis
Jones, Charles Philip
Jones, Charles White
Jones, Clarence Rollins
Jones, Constance Jauchler
Jones, Dale Paschal
Jones, David Robert
Jones, Dennon O'Dell
Jones, Donald Collins
Jones, Donnie Hue, Jr.
Jones, Dyche
Jones, Earl
Jones, Earl Irven
Jones, Ed
Jones, Edgar Willard
Jones, (Jessie) Elise
Jones, Elizabeth Eleanore Jones (Mrs. Herbert Lea Jones, Sr.)
Jones, Elizabeth Rieke (Mrs. Wayne Van Leer Jones)
Jones, Ellis Leroy
Jones, Enos Truell
Jones, Eric Wynn
Jones, Eugenia Edwina Byrd
Jones, Floyd Arthur
Jones, Frank Emerson
Jones, Frank Kelley, Jr.
Jones, G. Harvey
Jones, Gary David
Jones, Gene Edward
Jones, George Herbert
Jones, Glower Whitehead
Jones, Gordon Willis
Jones, Guy Langston
Jones, Gwendola Mitchell (Mrs. Jim Arthur Jones)
Jones, Harold Allen
Jones, Henry Earl
Jones, Houston Gwynne
Jones, Howard Leon
Jones, J. Benton, Jr.
Jones, J. Michael
Jones, James Burton
Jones, James Hardwick, Sr.
Jones, James Irvin
Jones, James Ogden
Jones, James Parker
Jones, James R.
Jones, James Richard
Jones, Jarl Hamilton
Jones, Jenkin Lloyd, Jr.
Jones, Jimmy Wayne
Jones, John Anthony
Jones, John Donald
Jones, John Lou
Jones, John Walter, Jr.
Jones, Joseph Millard
Jones, Julius Victor
Jones, Kirkland Charles
Jones, Leah Alberta
Jones, Lee Waterman
Jones, Leonard Lee
Jones, Lois Swan
Jones, Marvin Lewis
Jones, Mary Susan
Jones, Max Kesler
Jones, Merriam Arthur
Jones, Mildred Josephine
Jones, Milnor
Jones, Morton Edward
Jones, Myrtis Idelle (Mrs. C.W. Jones)
Jones, Patricia
Jones, Patricia Ann Ingram
Jones, Paul R.
Jones, Philippa Stokes
Jones, R(obert) Eugene
Jones, Ralph Gene
Jones, Richard Lloyd, Jr.
Jones, Richard Palmer, Jr.
Jones, Robert Brinkley
Jones, Robert Brinkley, Jr.
Jones, Robert Louis
Jones, Roger Hodges
Jones, Ryman Charlie
Jones, Sidney Theodore
Jones, Smiley Harold
Jones, Talova Lane
Jones, Thomas L.
Jones, Velva Jo
Jones, Vincent Hammond
Jones, W. Allan, Jr.
Jones, Walter Beaman
Jones, Wayne Van Leer
Jones, Wiley Thomas, Jr.
Jones, William Francis
Jones, William Robert
Jones, Woodrow Wilson
Jones Y Diez Arguelles, Gaston Roberto
Jordan, Anna Joyce
Jordan, Anne Knight (Mrs. Carl R. Jordan)
Jordan, Archibald Currie
Jordan, Barbara C.
Jordan, Bill Carrol
Jordan, Charles Edward, III
Jordan, Charles Lemuel
Jordan, DuPree, Jr.
Jordan, Edwin Pratt
Jordan, George Lyman, Jr.
Jordan, John William
Jordan, Johnny
Jordan, Lemuel Russell
Jordan, Leo John, Jr.
Jordan, Lucius Donald, Jr.
Jordan, Lyndon Kirkman, Jr.
Jordan, Randy
Jordan, William Ditmer, Jr.
Jordan, William Thomas
Jordan, Willis Pope, Jr.
Jordin, Marcus Wayne
Jordre, William Starling
Jorgenson, Wallace James
Jorque, Monica Alcid
Joseph, Eleanor Cohen (Mrs. Percy T. Joseph)
Joseph, Judith Rose
Joseph, Kenneth Edward
Joseph, Vaughan Dennis

Jost, Alfred Russell
Journeay, Glen Eugene
Jove Torres, Eduardo
Joyce, Edwin Anthony, Jr.
Joyce, Eugene Lawrence
Joyce, William Martin
Joyner, Bobby Lee
Judd, Daniel Stewart
Jude, James Roderick
Judice, C(harles) Raymond
Judith, Joseph Henry
Judson, John Paul
Juergensen, Hans
Juhn, Daniel Sungil
Juliff, Walter Fay
Juncos, Luis Isaias
Jundt, Dwight Wid
Jung, Clarence Robert, Jr.
Jung, Rodney C.
Jungman, Young Frank
Junkin, William Francis, III
Junod, Patricia Lee
Jurgensmeyer, Harold Jacob
Jurtshuk, Peter, Jr.
Just, Donald Ray
Justice, Bruce Morgan
Justice, Charles Chappell
Justice, David Blair
Justice, Judy Ellen
Justiniani, Federico Roberto
Justis, Elvis Jeff, Jr.
Justiss, Will Alan
Juszynski, Anthony Andrew
Kachel, Harold Stanley
Kadlecek, Edward John, Jr.
Kaeser, Clifford Richard
Kaffer, Michael Francis
Kahan, Barry Donald
Kahn, Alan Bruce
Kahn, Albert Michael
Kahn, Charles Bader
Kahn, Ellis Irvin
Kaiman, Marvin
Kaiser, George
Kaiser, Kurt Frederic
Kaiser, Robert Lee
Kalasinsky, Victor Frank
Kale, Herbert William, II
Kalfon, Stanley Murray
Kalin, Robert
Kaller, Bruce Edwin
Kallus, Frank Theodore
Kalnins, Zelma-Alvine Grinfelds (Mrs. Peteris Kalnins)
Kamath, Pandurang Mhalappa
Kamienski, Conrad William
Kamm, Robert B.
Kamman, William
Kane, Charles Joseph
Kane, Howard L.
Kane, Jean DuVal
Kane, John Ewing
Kane, John Kent, II
Kane, Robert Rhea, III
Kane, Sam
Kane, William Joseph
Kanes, William Henry
Kanto, William Peter, Jr.
Kantor, David
Kapella, William Anthony
Kaplan, Bruce
Kaplan, Donald David
Kaplan, Harriet Jane (Mrs. Stanley N. Kaplan)
Kaplan, Harry Leland
Kaplan, Marshall
Kaplan, Sheldon Jay
Kaplan, Stanley Baruch
Kapner, Lewis
Kapp, John Paul
Kappelman, Raymond Vernon
Kapsalis, Trifon G.
Karasiewicz, Walter Richard
Karau, William Alfred August
Karch, Robert E.
Karei, Kariuki
Kargleder, Charles Leonard
Karls, Albert Joseph
Karlsen, Del Sven
Karnes, Roy Eugene
Karpf, Ronald Jay
Karst, Charles Edward
Kasdan, Morton Lee
Kase, Judith Baker
Kash, Roscoe Conkling
Kashar, Michael Bruce
Kasman, Franklin Gerald
Kassin, Harold Howard
Kastner, Harold Henry, Jr.
Katsirubas, Judith White
Kattawar, George Williford
Kattel, Richard L.
Katterjohn, George William
Kattus, James Robert
Katz, Andrew
Katz, Catherine Monnier Minock Wilfert (Mrs. Samuel Lawrence Katz)
Katz, Doris Barry (Mrs. Morris Katz)
Katz, Eli Gerald
Katz, Samuel Lawrence
Katzin, Mordicai
Kauffman, Draper Laurence
Kauffman, Richard
Kaufman, Herbert E.
Kaufman, Jack Hammer
Kaufman, Raymond Henry
Kaufman, William Henry
Kaufmann, Godfrey Frensz
Kaufmann, Hans Alex
Kaufmann, Jule
Kautzmann, Frank Nicholas, III
Kavanagh, Roger Pierce, Jr.
Kavanaugh, Raphael Ryan, Jr.
Kavanaugh, Robert Lee
Kawaguchi, Harry Harumitsu
Kawahata, Henry Hajime
Kay, Michael Boyce
Kay, Saul
Kayanan, Antonio Cruz
Kaye, Kenneth Charles
Kaye, Neal Wallace, Jr.
Kaye, Samuel Harvey
Kaye, Sidney
Kays, Keith Sevier
Kazen, Abraham, Jr.
Keady, William C.
Keahey, James Howard
Kean, Gwendolyn Elvera
Kearley, Arthur James
Kearney, Cheryl Ann
Kearney, Kevin Emmett
Keats, Theodore Eliot
Keay, James William
Keck, Alfred Ray
Keder, Virko
Keeble, Sydney Frazer, Jr.
Keechi, Charles Cal
Keefe, John Russell
Keefer, Evelyn Mae
Keeling, Michale Elwood
Keen, Paul
Keenan, Charles William
Keenan, Francis Dewey
Keene, B(euford) Wayne
Keene, Stephen Wayne
Keener, Bruce Alan
Keeney, William Edwin, Jr.
Keeton, Homer Dale
Kehoe, Catharine Ellen
Kehoe, James Tracy
Keil, Ernest William
Keiller, James Bruce
Keith, Donald Wayne
Keith, Howard Barton
Keith, James Melvin
Keith, Lawrence Harold
Keith, Richard Milton
Kellam, Lucius James, Jr.
Kellam, Richard B.
Kelleher, Daniel Joseph
Kelleher, Herbert David
Keller, Alexander Paul, Jr.
Keller, Bernard Gerard, Jr.
Keller, Charles, Jr.
Keller, Charles, III
Keller, Christoph, Jr.
Keller, Daniel Floyd
Keller, Frances Marie
Keller, Meredith Evan
Keller, Oswald Lewin, Jr.
Keller, Richard Laurence
Keller, William Bryan
Kellerman, Robert Eugene
Kellett, William Hiram, Jr.
Kelley, David Lee
Kelley, James Marvin, Jr.
Kelley, Mary Elizabeth McDowell
Kelley, Vernon Clement
Kelliher, Thomas George
Kelly, Cecilia Mary
Kelly, Cleo Bell
Kelly, Elizabeth Peterson Alexander
Kelly, Ernest George, Jr.
Kelly, Frank Allan
Kelly, James Edward
Kelly, James Fredrick
Kelly, James Joseph
Kelly, Joe Louie
Kelly, John Paul
Kelly, John Schlagle
Kelly, Judith Ann French
Kelly, Leon Fred, Jr.
Kelly, Margaret Ricaud (Mrs. Thomas W. Kelly)
Kelly, Mary Claire Coleman (Mrs. Otis B. Kelly)
Kelly, Patricia Kirven
Kelly, Raymond Boone
Kelly, Richard
Kelly, Robert Emmett
Kelly, Robert Frank
Kelly, Russell Leland
Kelly, Thomas Lawrence, Jr.
Kelsaw, James William
Kelsay, Gene Wilson
Kelsey, Clyde Eastman, Jr.
Kelso, Robert Earl
Kelton, Elmer Stephen
Kemerait, Robert Chester
Kemmerer, Andrew Joseph
Kemmerly, James Robert
Kemp, Herbert Lyle, Jr.
Kemp, Hillery Thomas
Kemp, James Bradley, Jr.
Kemp, Lemuel Hugh
Kemp, Ramey Floyd
Kemp, Thomas Dupree, III
Kemper, Robert Mitchell, Jr.
Kempfer, Helen Friend (Mrs. Homer H. Kempfer)
Kempner, James Carroll
Kempner, Walter
Kempthorne, Richard Lewis
Kendall, Lloyd David
Kendall, Robert Leon
Kendell, Nevin Eugene
Kenderdine, James Marshall
Kenderdine, John Marshall
Kendrick, Herbert Spencer, Jr.
Keneipp, Timothy Wyn
KenKnight, Glenn Ellis
Kennamer, Kenneth Robert
Kennedy, Harvey John, Jr.
Kennedy, James Robert
Kennedy, John Dudley
Kennedy, John Elmo
Kennedy, John Payson
Kennedy, Joseph Howard
Kennedy, K. Doyle
Kennedy, Kenneth Durwood, Jr.
Kennedy, Thomas Judson, Jr.
Kennedy, Thomas William, Jr.
Kennedy, Wallace Albert
Kennedy, William Charles
Kennedy, William Richard
Kenner, Charles Thomas
Kenner, Joanne (Mrs. John Catlett Allensworth)
Kenshalo, Daniel Ralph
Kensit, Walter John
Kent, Bartis Milton
Kent, Jerard Allen
Kent, Joel Gilbert
Kent, John Bradford
Kent, Julian Otey
Kenyon, Albert Prentice
Kenyon, Thomas Gene
Keopp, Richard James
Kepler, Milton Oliver
Kepley, Thomas Howard
Kepner, Paul Ray, Jr.
Kepner, Woody
Kerby, Annie Marguerite Beasley (Mrs. James Kenneth Kerby)
Kerby, Leslie Glen
Kercher, John Wesley, III
Kergosien, Gregory Gaines
Kern, Andrew Elliot
Kern, Clifford Dalton
Kern, Steven Francis
Kern, William James
Kernan, Martin Healy, Jr.
Kerner, Leon Gene
Kerns, Sigmund Frederick
Kerr, Charles Macdonald, III
Kerr, John Ward, Jr.
Kerr, Kathleen Louise
Kerridge, Isaac Curtis, Jr.
Kerrigan, Robert Emmett
Kersteen, Robert Allen
Kersten, Robert Donavon
Kerstetter, Rex Eugene
Kesler, James Michael
Kesser, Michael Barron
Kessinger, John Roy
Kessler, Edna Anne Leventhal (Mrs. Murray Arthur Kessler)
Kessler, Vincent Garland, Jr.
Kesterson, James Walter
Kestner, Neil Richard
Ketchum, Edwin Earl
Ketter, Paul Stephen
Keusch, Kenneth David
Kever, Justin A.
Kevorkian, Richard
Key, Clyde Winston
Key, Franklin Paschall
Key, John Morris
Key, Robert Merton
Key, William Pike
Keyes, Roger Gene
Keyes, William George
Keys, Charles Everel
Keys, Delpha Bostock
Keys, Glenn Alan
Keyser, George Gustave
Keyworth, Donald Arthur
Khalil, Ghassan Abou
Khan, Amanullah
Khan, Sekender Ali
Khare, Snatosh Kumar
Khatri, Abdullah Ahmed
Kibler, Robert Joseph
Kibria, Esan Malik
Kidd, J. Pat
Kidwell, Dicken Evans
Kienholz, Richard Leslie
Kiesewetter, Frank Howard
Kiess, Edward Marion
Kievman, Michael S.
Kifer, Karl William
Kiger, Robert Gary
Kihle, Donald Arthur
Kiker, John Ewing, Jr.
Kilbride, Wade Robert
Kilburn, Mary Brown
Kilday, Mignon Therese Vautrot
Kilgore, Donald Gibson, Jr.
Kilgore, George Walter
Kilgore, James Elbert
Killebrew, James Robert
Killebrew, Mack Leon
Killebrew, Steve Lee
Killeffer, Fredrick Ayres
Killen, Clarence Avery, Jr.
Killgore, Charles Alden
Killingsworth, Raymond
Kilpatrick, Earl Buddy
Kilpatrick, James Ray
Kilpatrick, Stephanie Ann Genthon
Kilroy, James Francis
Kim, Ho-kyun
Kim, Jay Wook
Kim, Jin Bai
Kim, Jung-Gun
Kim, Paul Kyung-Hi
Kim, Seong-Soo Steven
Kim, Young Il
Kimball, Aubrey Pierce
Kimball, Linda Marie Fitzpatrick
Kimball, Vera F.
Kimball, Willard Child, III
Kimbel, William Anthony
Kimbell, Chris Lewis
Kimberlin, Sam Owen, Jr.
Kimbrel, Monroe
Kimbrell, Odell Culp, Jr.
Kimbrough, Clyde Harold
Kimbrough, Edward Ernest, III
Kimbrough, Orman Lanier
Kime, Charles Edwin
Kime, John Charles
Kimerer, Neil Banard, Sr.
Kimery, Millard Julian
Kimes, Thomas Fredric
Kimmel, Jerry E.
Kimrey, James Arthur
Kinard, Lee Edwin
Kincaid, John Peter
Kincannon, Sue Gunter
King, Alfred Ashbrook
King, Barrett Taylor
King, Charles Ossie
King, Charles Willis
King, Clyde Richard
King, Delutha Harold, Jr.
King, Dennis Gerard
King, Dennis Ray
King, Donald Alton
King, Francis Parker
King, Gary Don
King, Gerald Lamar
King, Gloria Jean
King, Harry Robertson
King, Herbert I-Turn
King, J. Edward
King, James Abraham, Jr.
King, James Billy
King, John Thomas
King, Jon Joe
King, Lloyd Elijah, Jr.
King, Marcene Jarrett
King, Marjorie Sommerlyn
King, Mary Katherine
King, Robert Augustin
King, Rollin White
King, Spencer Bidwell, III
King, Stephen
King, Terry C.
King, Terry Debbs
King, Voris
King, Wilbert Allen
King, William C.
King, William Hampton
Kingery, John William
Kinlaw, Dennis Franklin
Kinlaw, Murray Carlyle, Jr.
Kinna, Meredith Lee
Kinnebrew, Jackson Allender
Kinney, Abbott Ford
Kinney, Burton Chester
Kinney, Gordon James
Kinney, William Light, Jr.
Kinzbach, Robert Benton
Kiopekly, George
Kirby, Clarence Ray
Kirby, George Taylor
Kirby, Louise Gem
Kirby, Taylor Herman, Jr.
Kirchheimer, Waldemar F(ranz)
Kirk, Donald William
Kirk, James Curtis
Kirk, Jo Ann
Kirk, John Michael
Kirk, Marion Ross
Kirk, Paul
Kirk, Virginia
Kirk, Wilber Wolfe
Kirkendall, Walter Murray
Kirkham, Mary Beth
Kirkland, Richard Horace
Kirkland, Sanford Holmes, III
Kirkland, Virginia Dreaden
Kirkland, Wallace Talmage
Kirkpatrick, Forrest Hunter
Kirkpatrick, James Francis, Jr.
Kirkpatrick, Jerald Lee
Kirkpatrick, Joel Bryant, Jr.
Kirwan, Albert Dennis, Jr.
Kiser, Charles Byron
Kiser, Phillip Wayne
Kiser, William Russell
Kispert, Wayne Earl
Kisska, Stephen Peter
Kissling, Fred Ralph, Jr.
Kissner, Jacob
Kistler, Adolphus Job
Kistler, Ernest Losson
Kistler, Henry Evans, Jr.
Kitchin, David Jackson, III
Kitchin, Malinda Louise
Kittlitz, Rudolf Gottlieb, Jr.
Kivett, Charles Thomas
Kivett, Pat Alton
Klabosh, Charles
Klapper, Margaret Strange
Klaus, Kenneth Blanchard
Klee, Lucille Holljes (Mrs. James Butt Klee)
Kleeman, Francis Sidney
Klehm, Judy Weaver
Klein, Bernard
Klein, Edward Lawrence
Klein, Elias
Klein, John Lawrence
Klein, Louis Samuel
Klein, Richard Paul
Klein, Robert Edward
Kleine, Glen Albert William
Kleiner, Janellyn Pickering
Kleinert, Erwin John, Jr.
Kleinhans, Robert Burton
Kleinknecht, Kenneth Samuel
Klemek, Gary Michael
Klempnauer, Lawrence Robert
Kline, David Gellinger
Kline, Donald Craig, Jr.
Kline, Harry Byrd
Kline, Irving Berthold
Kline, Jacob
Kling, Simcha
Klingen, Theodore James
Klinger, Arthur Russell
Klink, Richard E.
Klintworth, Gordon Kenneth
Klippstatter, Kurt Leopold
Kloess, Lawrence Herman, Jr.
Klontz, Harold Emerson
Klontz, Mary Paysinger (Mrs. Harold E. Klontz)
Klopfenstein, Philip Arthur
Klopman, William A.
Klorfein, Fruema Annette
Klos, William Anton
Klose, Rolland Mark
Klotz, Herbert Werner
Klotz, James Arnold
Klutts, J. Vaughn
Klutts, William Alonzo
Knape, Clifford Stanley
Knapp, Archie Herbert
Knapp, Dennis Raymond
Knapp, Richard Bruce
Knaur, John Sherman, Jr.
Knee, Ruth Irelan (Mrs. Junior K. Knee)
Kneedler, William Harding
Kneese, Victor Scott
Knerr, Robert James
Knezevich, Vladimir John
Knibb, John Haddon, Jr.
Knight, David Winston
Knight, Donald Gardner
Knight, Gary Dale
Knight, James Arlie, Jr.
Knight, James Perry, Jr.
Knight, John Shively
Knight, Kenneth Vincent
Knight, Lottie Elois
Knight, Luther Augustus, Jr.
Knight, Milton Henry
Knight, Richard Finley
Knight, Robert Marsden
Knight, William Herbert
Knight, William Lewis
Knighton, George William
Knipe, Donald Lloyd
Knoebel, Daniel McClellan
Knoke, Peter John
Knoll, Frank Stephen
Knopp, Paul Joseph
Knott, Robert Eugene
Knowles, Charles Ulmer
Knowles, Doyle Blewer
Knowles, Jerome, Jr.
Knowles, Malcolm Shepherd
Knowles, Porter-Carroll
Knowles, Thomas George
Knowlton, Bettye Maurine James
Knox, Ernest Rudder
Knox, Marion DeWayne
Knox, Stephen Owen
Knuckles, Joseph Lewis
Koach, Harold George
Kobayashi, Herbert Shin
Kobert, Norman
Koblas, James A.
Koch, Leo
Koch, Ronney Ray
Kocher, Eric Glenn
Kodos, Joseph Casimer
Koebbeman, Skip
Koen, Billy Vaughn
Koenig, Paul Edward
Koerner, Uda Henry
Koester, Engelbert Leo
Koester, Frederick Henry, Jr.
Koevenig, James Louis
Koger, Mildred Emmelene Nichols
Koger, Thomas John
Kogut, Lawrence Leroy
Kohers, Theodor
Kohl, Charles William
Kohland, William Francis
Kohler, Anne Trimble
Kohler, Peter Ogden
Kohn, Anthony
Kohn, Erwin
Kohn, Vera Gross
Kok, Loke-Tuck
Kolansky, S. Kalman
Kolb, Alexander Karl
Kolb, Charles Rudolph
Kolb, William Payton
Kolin, Irving Seymour
Kollar, Michael Anthony
Kolliker, William Augustin
Kolter, William Henry, Jr.
Komorn, Robert Melvin
Konantz, Ronald J.
Kondonassis, Alexander John
Kones, Richard Joseph
Konicoff, Donald Stephen
Konkel, Richard Joseph
Kono, Tetsuro
Konopnicki, Daniel Terry
Konrad, Hermann
Koo, Robert Chung Jen
Koons, Russell Eugene
Koonts, Jones Calvin
Koonts, Robert Henry
Koontz, James Fred
Koontz, Joseph Patrick
Kopel, Kenneth Fred
Kopp, Edgar William
Korda, Marion Amelia
Korenblit, Jack Izaak
Korges, Emerson
Kornegay, Hobert
Kornreich, David Victor
Koshuba, Walter Joseph
Koska, Robert Francis
Kossmann, Charles Edward
Kossoff, Georgette Roslyn
Kossoff, Stanley Morton
Kotas, Robert Vincent
Kottke, Emmett William
Kotzebue, Robert William, Sr.
Koubek, Kenneth Gene
Kouchoukos, Nicholas Thomas
Kousky, Linda Kay (Rubac)
Koutras, Phoebus
Kouw, Willy Alexander
Kovski, John Joseph
Kowalske, Richard Mackey
Kowert, Arthur Herman
Kozek, John Robert
Kozlowski, Ronald Stephan
Kracke, Robert Russell
Kraft, Irvin Alan
Kraft, Leland Milo, Jr.
Kragh, Kenneth Koy
Kraker, Sidney Eugene
Kramer, Edward Francis, Jr.
Kramer, John Kenneth
Kramer, Robert Ivan
Krantz, Sanford Burton
Kratzer, Gloria Frank
Kraus, Eric (Bradshaw)
Krause, Charles Donald
Krause, Manfred Otto
Kreager, David Jay, Jr.
Krebs, Peter Joachim
Kreider, Thomas McRoberts
Krell, Roy Arthur
Krementz, Edward Thomas
Kremin, Margaret Ann
Kremser, Frank Joseph, Jr.
Krenek, Richard Frank
Kreshon, Martin John
Kretchmar, Ruth Goldman
Kreutziger, Sarah Sloan
Krieg, Edwin Holmes
Krieger, David
Krishnamurti, Pullabhotla Venkata
Kristiansen, Magne
Krivoy, William Aaron
Kriz, George James
Kroeger, Carroll Vincent
Krogstad, Larry Kenneth
Krol, Joseph
Kroll, Frank Wilhelm
Kronick, David Abraham
Krueger, George Edward
Krueger, Robert Charles
Krueger, Ross Tremaine
Krug, Adele Jensen
Kruger, Irwin
Krum, Glenn Lee
Krumme, Edwynne Freeland
Krumme, George William
Krumnow, William Earl
Kruse, Arthur Murphy
Kruse, Edward Donald
Kruse, Melvin Claude
Kruse, Olan Ernest
Kruse, Paul Robert
Krutchkoff, Richard Gerald
Kruteck, Alan Ronald
Kubala, Mark Jerome
Kube, Adolph Martin Ludwig
Kucera, Louis Stephen
Kuchmak, Myron
Kucinskas, Dennis Paul
Kuck, James Chester
Kudiesy, Norma Martha
Kuehl, Howard William, Jr.
Kuehne, Hugo Franz, Jr.
Kuglen, Craig Charles
Kuhler, Renaldo Gillet
Kuhn, Anne Naomi Wicker (Mrs. Harold B. Kuhn)
Kuhn, Charles
Kuhn, Grant
Kuhn, Gus David, Jr.
Kuhn, Harold Barnes
Kuhn, William Albert
Kuhner, John George
Kuhre, Calvin Jeremy
Kuhrt, Harry Lugene
Kulberg, Leslie Ervin
Kullman, J. Wayne
Kulman, Peyton Salsbury
Kumin, Gerald David
Kummer, Frederic Arnold
Kumpe, Roy Franklin
Kunce, Glenn Dale
Kunkel, Robert Raymond
Kuntz, Marion Leathers Daniels
Kunz, Frederick George, II
Kurie, Andrew Edmunds
Kuriger, Richard Charles, III
Kurras, Herbert Lewis
Kurtzahn, Donald H.A.
Kurzweg, Ulrich Hermann
Kurzynske, Frank
Kusch, Polykarp
Kusumi, Yoshi-Taro
Kutner, Richard Allan
Kuvin, Lawrence Philip
Kuykendall, William Dean
Kuzmicki, Felix Davis
Kwie, William Wie Liam
Kwiecinski, Chester Martin
Kwo, William Ta
Kwon, Tai Hyung
Kyger, Edgar Ross, Jr.
Kyle, Andrew Crockett, III
La Barbera, Frank Thomas
La Belle, Donald Joseph
Laboda, Gerald
La Boon, Robert Bruce
Laborde, Adras Paul
Laborde, Mary Purcell (Mrs. Joseph Gaston Laborde)
Lachman, Roy
Lachs, John
Lack, Fredell
Lackey, Guy Annadale

Lackey, James Quinn, III
Lackey, Larry Alton
Lackey, Montgomery Isaiah
Lackland, Sam Dexter
Lacquement, Hubert Wesley
Lacy, James Wright
Lacy, Sterling Smith, Jr.
Ladd, Edward Johnson
Ladd, Jack DeVere
Ladd, James Wallace
Ladd, Robert Ernest
Lader, William Joseph
Ladouceur, Leo Alvain
Laemmel, Charles Richard
La Fevers, Earl Vernon
Laffere, Leslie Harry
Lafleur, Kenneth Charles
La Forte, Robert Sherman
La France, Stephen Conde
LaGrange, Gary Paul
LaGrone, William Taylor
Lahiri, Subrata
Lahmeyer, John D.
Lahr, Niels Longfield
Lahser, Conrad Bernhardt, Jr.
Lai, Vincent Chintu
Laier, James Emil
Lail, Eugene Franklin
Laine, William John
Laing, Bruce Frederick
Laing, William Gavin
Lair, Harry Redmon
Laird, Angus McKenzie
Laird, Ann Rossberg
Laird, David Edward, Jr.
Laird, Marilyn Elaine
Lake, Barry Dean
Lake, I. Beverly
Lake, Michael Kennedy
Lake, Wesley Wayne, Jr.
Lam, Chi-Kwong
Lam, Henry William, Jr.
Lamar, Ewell Ayars
Lamb, Alan LeRoy
Lamb, Beth Howley
Lamb, Gilbert Payton
Lamb, Jamie Parker, Jr.
Lamb, John William
Lamb, Lester Lewis
Lambert, Bob Dean
Lambert, Charles Leroy
Lambert, Raymond Samuel
Lambeth, James Erwin
Lambird, Perry Albert
Lamey, Steven Charles
Lamm, Daniel Allen
Lammey, William Clair
Lammons, Jay Lee
Lamon, Harry Vincent, Jr.
La Monica, Carl Joseph
Lamont, Lawrence Michael
Lamoureux, William A.
Lamparter, William Smith
Lampert, Morris Hyman
Lampkin, Andrew Jackson
Lampkin, William McCain
Lampkins, Ernest Harold
Lamson-Scribner, Denis
Lancaster, Carroll Townes, Jr.
Lancaster, Edgar Hunter, Jr.
Lancaster, James Roydon
Lancaster, James William
Lancaster, Kenneth Malcolm, II
Lancaster, Ralph Douglas
Lanciano, Claude Olwen, Jr.
Landau, Sol
Landgraf, Nancy Karen
Landman, Georgina Barbara
Landon, John William
Landreneau, Rodney Edmund, Jr.
Landrieu, Moon
Landrith, George Clay
Landron, José Manuel
Landrum, Annette Vaughn
Landrum, Carrol Frazier
Landrum, Philip Mitchell
Landrum, Samuel Edward
Landry, Richard Andrew, Jr.
Landry, Robert Raymond
Landy, Burton Aaron
Lane, Daniel McNeel
Lane, David Lawrence
Lane, Edward Wood, Jr.
Lane, Faye Rogan
Lane, George Bertram
Lane, Gerald Thomas
Lane, Helen S. Murchison (Mrs. Edward W. Lane, Jr.)
Lane, James Monroe
Lane, James William
Lane, Keith Anton
Lane, Kenneth Eugene
Lane, Louis
Lane, Malcolm Graham
Lane, Montague
Lane, Perry Virgil
Laney, William Roland
Lanford, Charles Edward, Jr.
Lanford, William Harrison
Lang, Erich Karl
Lang, Roger Mark
Lang, Sylvan Stephen
Langdale, Noah Noel, Jr.
Lange, Roy Harrison, Jr.
Langer, Marshall Jay
Langford, Carloss Bertram, Jr.
Langford, Orville LeRoy
Langhorne, Madison Gilwood
Langland, Charles Albert
Langland, Olaf Elmer
Langley, Jeffrey Todd
Langley, Welborn James
Langlinais, Stephen Joseph
Langlotz, Carolyn West Dorough
Langston, Elizabeth Ricks
Langston, Mary Humphrey
Lanier, David William
Lanier, James Edward
Lanier, James Olanda
Lanier, Sidney Edward
Lanier, Thurman Wayne
Lankau, Charles Arthur
Lansford, Doyle Keith
Lantz, John Edward
Lantz, John Michael
Lantz, Robert Butler
Lantz, Ruth Cox (Mrs. John Edward Lantz)
La Prad, Quentin Charles
Lapuente-Perez, Felipe Antonio
Laramey, Thomas Avriett, Jr.
Large, Dewey Ernest
Largent, Max Dale
Larimore, Leon
Larkey, Charles Samuel
Larkins, John Davis, Jr.
Larks, Jack
Larney, Richard Wesley
La Rosa, John Joseph
La Rose, Robert Lee
Larrea, Frederick Ayala
Larrison, William George
Larsen, Donald Jeffrey
Larsh, Howard William
Larson, Ben John
Larson, Reed Eugene
Larson, Stanley Earl
Lasater, James Claude
Laschinski, George Walewski
Laseau, Mary Elizabeth
Lashinger, Donald Richard
Lasley, Charles Haden
Lassen, Raymond Viggo, Jr.
Lasseter, Philomena Carmel Novelle
Lassetter, James Green
Lassetter, Maggie Samples (Mrs. James Green Lassetter)
Lasswell, Shirley Ann Basso Slesinger (Mrs. Fred D. Lasswell Jr.)
Lastra, Jesus L.
Latham, Alice Frances Patterson (Mrs. William Joseph Latham)
Latham, Charles Vernon
Latham, James Arthur
Latham, James Ivan
Latham, James Parker
Latham, Ray
Lathan, Samuel Robert
Lathem, James Ernest
Lathrop, George Terrell
Lathrop, Gertrude Adams
Lathrop, Jay Wallace
Latimer, Charles Graham
Latimer, Edwin Phinney
Latimer, Fred Hollis
Latimer, Paul Henry
Latimer, Raymond Laverne
Latimer, Roy Truett
Latimer, Steve Benton
Latin, Donald Edward
Latortue, Gerard Rene
Latta, Hugh Lusk
Lattimore, Robert Lee
Latting, Patience Sewell (Mrs. Trimble B. Latting)
Lau, Leung Wang
Lauffer, Carolyn Gibson
Lauffer, Robert Allen
Laughead, George Joseph
Laughlin, Dillard Chappell
Laughlin, Harold Emerson
Laughlin, Reva Joyce
Laughlin, William Eugene
Laughon, Kenneth Clyde
Laukhuf, Walden Louis Shelburne
Laurence, Leslie Glen
Lautzenheiser, Marvin Wendell
Lavery, William Edward
Lavezzoli, Charles Edward
Lavin, James Duncan
Lavin, John Thomas
Lavinghousez, William E.
Law, James Pierce, Jr.
Law, Ralph Aregood
Law, Walter Charles
Lawhorn, Jess Sherman
Lawing, Eugene Morris
Lawler, Charles Michael
Lawler, Donald Lester
Lawler, Edward J.
Lawler, James Joseph
Lawler, Robert Clair
Lawo, John Krenkel, Jr.
Lawrence, James Harold, Jr.
Lawrence, John Webb
Lawrence, Reggie Ray
Lawrence, Telete Zorayda (Mrs. Ernest Lawrence)
Lawrence, Walter William, Jr.
Lawrence, William Wesley
Lawrence-Berrey, Robert Edmond
Lawson, Eugene McKinley, Jr.
Lawson, Fred Raulston
Lawson, Herbert Ronald
Lawson, Kermit Adelbert
Lawson, Maurice Antoine
Lawson, Pauline Culler
Lawson, Richard Henry
Lawson, Verna Rebecca
Lawson, William Jennings
Lawton, Myrtle Hawkins (Mrs. Reed Lawton)
Lawton, Thomas Oregon, Jr.
Lawwill, Theodore
Lay, Joe Lafayette
Lay, Lyndell Everett
Lay, Norvie Lee
Lay, Thomas Fox
Layfield, Michael Gregg
Layman, Earl Robert
Layton, William George
Lazarow, Arthur
Lazarus, John Daniel
Lazich, Daniel
Lazur, John
Lea, Christopher Fraser
Lea, Maxwell Amos, Jr.
Leach, Charles Sellers
Leach, George Webster
Leach, James Moore
Leach, Joseph Lee
Leach, Maurice Derby, Jr.
Leach, Norman Eugene
Leach, Richard Scott
Leadbetter, Bruce Cline
League, Richard (Douglas)
Leahy, Robert James
Leal, Jose Silva
Leard, Terry Sears
Leary, Joseph Rive, Jr.
Leary, Prieur James, Jr.
Lease, Frances Victoria (Mrs. Gillian Charles Lease)
Lease, Golden Richard
Leatherbury, John Raymond, Jr.
Leatherman, Hugh Kenneth
Leathers, William Beacher
Leavell, Byrd Stuart
Leavitt, Mary Janice Deimel (Mrs. Robert Walker Leavitt)
Le-Ba, John Kong (Le Ba Kong)
LeBaron, Olin William
LeBlanc, Alvin Andrew, Jr.
Le Blanc, Keith Edward
LeBlanc, Paul Eurby
Lebo, Dell
Lebron, Amaryllis Velilla (Mrs. Ramon Clemente Lebron)
Lechowich, Richard Victor
Lecky, William Ralston, III
LeClair, Hugh Grenville
LeCroy, James Alvin
Ledbetter, Robert Harbin
Ledford, Dewey Carl
Ledford, Horace Benjamin
Ledford, James Randall
Ledford, Kenneth Avery
Ledford, Theron R.
Ledford, William Lester
Ledoux, Jack
Leduc, Albert L.
Le Duc, Albert Louis, Jr.
Ledwith, Walter Andrew
Lee, Alexandra Saimovici
Lee, Amy Freeman (Mrs. Freeman Lee)
Lee, Anna Marie
Lee, C. E.
Lee, Carroll Dean
Lee, Charles Edwin
Lee, Clyde Edward
Lee, Daniel Warnell
Lee, Denny Lap-Yen
Lee, Frank Ammen, III
Lee, Frederick Yuk Leong
Lee, Freeman Gordon
Lee, Gary Edwin
Lee, Hubert Floyd
Lee, James Crawford
Lee, James Widner
Lee, Jimmy Che-Yung
Lee, John Dorsey
Lee, John Lawrence
Lee, Joseph Ching-Yuen
Lee, Mary Ann
Lee, Michael Clifton
Lee, R(aymond) William, Jr.
Lee, Richard George
Lee, Robert Edward
Lee, Robert Edward, Jr.
Lee, Roland Marion
Lee, Thomas Eldred, III
Lee, Tommy Taylor
Lee, William Garnett, III
Lee, William John
Leedom, John Nesbett
Leeman, Hafford Ransom
Leeper, John Palmer
Leeper, Louise South
Lefeber, Edward James
LeFevre, Elbert Walter, Jr.
Lefler, George Thomas
Le Fon, John Walter
Leftwich, Robert Vernon
Legerton, Clarence William, Jr.
Legrand, Harry Elwood
Lehman, David Hershey
Lehman, George Irvin
Lehman, William
Lehmann, Frederick Otto, Jr.
Leibovitz, Albert
Leidesdorf, Arthur David
Leidig, Raymond H.
Leidy, Peggy Elizabeth
Leiferman, Irwin Hamilton
Leiferman, Silvia Weiner (Mrs. Irwin Hamilton Leiferman)
Leigh, James Tillman
Leigh, Thomas Watkins
Leigon, Walter A.
Leinweber, Donald McCloud
Leisk, James Clark
Leitch, Vincent Barry
Leiter, Gordon Albert
Leith, John Haddon
Leitner, Frank Wilhite, Sr.
Leitner, Paul R.
Leitzsey, Barney Burr
Lejeune, Francis Ernest, Jr.
Le Jeune, Robert Lee
Le Maistre, Charles Aubrey
Lemieux, Donald Jile
Lemieux, Henry Fisher
Lemieux, Lucien Emile
Lemon, Nelson Lee
Lenart, Raymond Stuart
Lennon, Charles Woodbury, II
Lennon, Thelma Cumbo
Lennox, Edward Newman
Lentin, Dennis Henry
Leo, Jin-Shone
Leon, Leonard
Leonard, Emery Mayrow
Leonard, Joe Means, Jr.
Leonard, Mary Eileen
Leonard, Samuel Anderson
Leon-Portilla, Miguel
Leon-Sotomayor, Luis Angel
Leopold, Louis
Lepley, Renee Brooke
Lepp, John G(eorge)
Lequieu, Charles Marion
Lesesne, Edward Huguenin
Lesher, Arthur Carney, Jr.
Lesher, Eugene Albert
Lesley, Theodore Livingston
Leslie, Henry Arthur
Lespier, William
Lessard, Raymond W.
Lessenberry, Robert Adams
Lesslie, Mary Stewart
Lestage, Daniel Barfield
Lester, Darrell Reaks
Lester, Don Lee
Lester, Everard M.
Lester, Hubert Elisha
Lester, James Adams
Lester, Robert
Lester, William Dale
Lesueur, Alexander Armand
Letner, Carl Vernon, Sr.
Letson, Austin Kellett, Jr.
Letts, Dale Allen
Letts, Thomas Clinton
Leunig, Carl Victor
Le Van, Daniel Hayden
Leven, Stephen Aloysius
Lever, Oscar William, Jr.
Leverett, Melvin Thomas
Leverett, Sidney Duncan, Jr.
Levey, David Voe
Levin, David Harold
Levin, Eugene Milton
Levin, Seymour Arthur
Levin, Sidney Herbert
Levin, William Cohn
Levine, Burton Leroy
Levine, Hernand Eugene
Levine, Jay Alan
LeVine, Jerome Edward
Levine, Richard
Levine, Sam
Levingston, Ernest Lee
Levingston, Lance Gregory
Levinson, Donald Earl
Levinson, Robert Paul
Levit, Jay Joseph
Levitas, Elliott Harris
Levitch, Harry Herman
Levitt, Edward Hurley
Levy, Bethoe Gessner (Mrs. Gus Daniel Levy)
Levy, Elliot Gene
Levy, Jerome Sickles
Levy, Joe Simon
Levy, Julius Lazard, II
Levy, Robert Alan
Lewellyn, Jess William
Lewenhaupt, Eric Claes
Lewis, Arden Isaiah
Lewis, Barbara Nancy
Lewis, Betty Croft Morris
Lewis, Ceylon Smith, Jr.
Lewis, Charles Raymond
Lewis, Daniel Curtis, Jr.
Lewis, David Howe
Lewis, David Lloyd
Lewis, David Warren
Lewis, Don
Lewis, Earl Calvin
Lewis, Edwin James, II
Lewis, George McKoy
Lewis, James Woodrow
Lewis, Jay Frederick
Lewis, Jeffrey Clark
Lewis, Jesse Cornelius
Lewis, Jim Frank
Lewis, Jo Ann
Lewis, John Milton
Lewis, John Ransom, Jr.
Lewis, John Thomas
Lewis, Julia Elizabeth
Lewis, Lawrence Glendon
Lewis, Lloyd Jones
Lewis, Lyle Burwell
Lewis, Marlan Melroy
Lewis, Mary Genevieve
Lewis, Orval Leroy
Lewis, Richard Hayes
Lewis, Richard Knox
Lewis, Robert
Lewis, Robert Eugene
Lewis, Ross Earl
Lewis, Thomas Edward
Lewis, Virgil Hugh
Lewis, Walter David
Lewis, Wilbur Curtis
Lewis, William Charles
Lewis, Winderlean Smith
L'Herisson, Lawrence Edward
Lhotka, John Francis, Jr.
Li, Lai-hung Loretta
Li, Sheng San
Liang, Shu-Jan
Lichtenfeld, Seymour L.
Lichtenstein, Murray Marc
Liddell, James Larry
Liddell, Lillie Frances Payne
Liddle, Charles George
Liddle, William Dyer, Jr.
Lide, Vinton DeVane
Lieber, Arnold Lou
Lieberman, Barnard Leon
Lieberman, Bernard
Lieberman, Melvyn
Liebmann, Seymour W.
Liebscher, Anton Ignaz
Lief, Thomas Parrish
Liek, James Eugene
Light, Jerry Thomas
Light, Ronald Richard
Ligon, Helen Hailey
Ligon, John Jeter
Ligon, Ralph Edwin
Likes, David Henry
Liles, Allen Carroll
Liles, Donald Melvin
Liles, Maefred Stearns
Liles, Rutledge Richardson
Liles, Wayne Conrad
Lilley, Frank LeRoy, III
Lilliott, Eduard Leverett, Sr.
Lilly, Bob A.
Lin, Eyih
Lin, Ping-Huang
Lin, San-Su Chen (Mrs. Paul Lin)
Lin, Tu
Lincecum, Hubert Leo
Lind, Albert William
Lind, James Peter
Lindabury, Tryon Smith, Sr.
Lindahl, Roy Lawrence
Lindberg, Wilma Jean
Lindell, Carl William, Jr.
Lindeman, Robert Paul
Linder, Aubry Ludwel
Linder, Robert Joe
Lindley, John Ellis
Lindley, John Van
Lindly, Horace Bishop
Lindquist, Donald August
Lindsay, Bryan Eugene
Lindsay, Edward Williams
Lindsay, Freda Theresa Schimpf (Mrs. Gordon James Lindsay)
Lindsay, Joseph Lloyd, III
Lindsey, Edward Stormont
Lindsey, H. Edward, Jr.
Lindsey, James Leslie
Lindsey, James Louis
Lindsey, Jonathan Asmel
Lindstrom, Eric Everett
Ling, Dwight Leroy
Ling, James Joseph
Lingafelt, Charles Richard
Lingle, Kendall Ide
Link, Cecil Homer
Link, Mae Mills (Mrs. S. Gordden Link)
Link, S. Gordden
Linke, Lawrence Joseph
Linkovich, William
Linn, (Marion) Joanne Lovell (Mrs. Robert Joseph Linn)
Linn, Michael Duncan
Linn, Robert Joseph
Linne, Aubrey Arthur
Linsley, Jerald Netherton
Linville, William Norman
Liou, Tang-Jyi
Lipke, Walter Hayward
Lipman, Bernard Sylvester
Lipman, Ira Ackerman
Lipovich, George Jay
Lippman, Alfred
Lipscomb, David Milton
Lipscomb, Kenneth Benjamen
Lipshy, Ben Allen
Lipson, Goldie
Lipson, Leonard Berger
Lipstate, Eugene Jacob
Lis, Anthony Stanley
Lisanke, Robert John
Lisella, Frank Scott
Liston, William Harry
Litherland, James George, Jr.
Litkenhaus, Raymond Arthur
Little, Doyle Edgar
Little, Gaynelle Williams
Little, Harry Wilson
Little, John Goodwin, Jr.
Little, John Patterson, Jr.
Little, Michael Anthony
Little, Walden Paskel
Little, William D., Jr.
Littlejohn, James DeWitt
Littlejohn, Talmadge Dean
Liu, Shai Yuan
Liu, Wan Cheng
Livaditis, John Elias
Livdahl, Richard Carroll
Lively, Lloyd Lester, Jr.
Lively, Noel Dale
Livingood, Marvin Duane
Livingston, David Warren
Livingston, Philip Henry
Livingston, Robert L., Jr.
Livingstone, John Leslie
Ljungdahl, Lars Gerhard
Llanes, Carlos Gilberto
Llenza, Orlando
Llewellyn, Charles Elroy, Jr.
Lloyd, Judson Frank
Lloyd, Marilyn Laird
Lloyd, Raymond Grann
Lloyd, William Nelson
Lnenicka, William Joseph
Lo, Ching Fang
Lo, Ching-Tsan
Loach, Jean Calanthe
Loar, Warren Nelson, III
Lobo, Peter Isaac
Lockard, William Harvey, Jr.
Locke, Adele Neely (Mrs. Eugene Murphy Locke)
Locke, Wendell Vernon
Lockett, Allan Neil
Lockhart, James Lemuel
Lockhart, Verdree
Lockley, Jeanette Elaine (Mrs. Arnold H. Lockley)
Lockrow, Arthur Lynn
Lockwood, Lawrence Bruce, Jr.
Lockwood, Lawrence Slotboom
Lockwood, Richard Allen
Lodge, Edith Bennett (Mrs. George Townsend Lodge)
Lodge, George Townsend
Lodge, Helen Fitzwater
Lodge, William Dunkin
Loebl, Burton B.
Loeffler, Larry James
Loeffler, Sharon Varian
Loessberg, Gerald Lee August
Loewenstein, Joseph Edward
Loewenstein, Joseph Meyer
Loewer, Erich George, Jr.
Lofton, Gene Travis
Lofton, Jerome, Jr.
Logan, Catherine Rose
Logan, Kirk Harold, Jr.
Logan, Leslie Celeste
Logan, Richard Hocker, III
Logan, Robert Allen
Logan, Terrance Guy
Logan, William Boyd
Logan, William Thomas
Logsdon, Guy William
Logue, Thomas Otto, Jr.
Lohr, Jacob Andrew
Lokey, Clarence Walters
Lokey, George Harrison
Lokken, Roy Norman
Lomask, Milton Nachman
Lomasney, Thomas Lawrence
Lombard, Cheryl Ruth
Lombard, Helen Ann Miedreich
Lombard, Louis Felix
Lombardi, Max Habib
Londos, Theodore (Skip), Jr.
Long, Alfred B.
Long, Charles Farrell
Long, Claude Vincent, Jr.
Long, George Robert
Long, Gillis William
Long, Guy Oliver
Long, Henry Addison, Jr.
Long, Henry Arlington
Long, James Albert
Long, James Stephen
Long, John Maloy
Long, Paul Junior
Long, Richard Louis, Jr.
Long, Russell B(illiu)
Long, Shirley Dobbins
Long, Thad Gladden
Long, William Bowman
Long, William David
Longenecker, Herbert Eugene, Jr.
Longfellow, Conrad Dayton
Longley, Herman Vance, Jr.
Longmire, Warren T.
Longnecker, Thomas Christopher
Longo, Salvador Eugene
Longwith, Jean Marguerite
Loomis, Guy Alfred, Jr.
Lopez, Antonio Vincent
Lopez, Encarnacion
Lopez, Frank
Lopez, Judith Louise
Lopez, Ralph Aurelio
Lopez-Roig, Lucy Enid
Lopiccolo, Sylvester Joseph
Lorbach, Harry Martin
Lord, Columbus Ellis
Lord, Fonchen Usher (Mrs. William Walcott Lord)
Lord, Marian Gordin
Lord, William Jackson, Jr.
Lordon, Robert Edward
Lorenz, Hans Ernest
Lorenzo, Francisco A.
Loria, Frank Leo
Loria, Philip Ronald
Loro, Anthony Pivotto
Losak, John
Losley, Consuelo Hudgins
Lothman, Victor Oliver
Lott, Trent
Lotterhos, Julius Lieb, Jr.
Lotts, Adolphus Lloyd
Louden, Lester Richard
Loudermilk, Lois Adeline Wood (Mrs. Hayden C. Loudermilk)
Loughmiller, Grover Campbell
Love, Benton F.
Love, Donald Lee
Love, Dorothy Bryan
Love, Franklin Sadler
Love, Isadore
Love, James Sanford, III
Love, John Daniel
Love, Joseph William, Jr.
Love, Marsha Lynn
Love, Mary Novela
Love, Richard Arthur
Love, Robert Mitchell

Love, Rosalie Stocks (Mrs. Fred Emery Love)
Lovejoy, Dallas Landon
Lovejoy, Howard Alford, III
Lovelace, (Byron) Keith
Lovelace, Lorna Seale
Lovell, Albert Allie
Lovell, Joe W.
Lovell, Savage Markette (S. Mark Lovell)
Lovett, William Ervin, Jr.
Lovewell, Hubart Stonex, Jr.
Lovie, Peter Marshall
Loving, Joe Hilton, Jr.
Lovvorn, Martin Craft
Lovvorn, Robert Henry
Low, Thomas J. Robert
Lowder, Robert Edward
Lowe, Betty Ann
Lowe, Donald Paul
Lowe, James Eugene
Lowe, John Will
Lowe, Paul Rutledge
Lowe, Robert Harrison
Lowe, Robert Wylie
Lowell, Anthony M.
Lowenstein, Charles Douglas
Lowenstein, George Wolfgang
Lowenthal, Lawrence Mark (Larry)
Lowery, Charles Lee
Lowery, James Harlton
Lowery, John Stewart
Lowery, Raymond
Lowndes, Richard I'On, III
Lowrey, Thomas Jefferson
Lowry, Bernice Gertrude
Lowry, Leo Elmo
Loyd, Loye Carroll
Loyd, Thelma Spessard
Lozzio, Bismarck Berto
Lubbe, Catherine Case (Mrs. John A. Lubbe)
Lubke, George William
Lubritz, Ronald Raphael
Lucas, Aubrey Keith
Lucas, Edgar Arthur
Lucas, John David
Lucas, Richard Albert
Lucas, Silas Emmett, Jr.
Lucas, William Henry, Jr.
Lucas, William Ray
Lucian, Justin
Lucier, James Alfred
Luckadoo, Earl Donald
Luckey, George Paul
Ludden, Linda Sue
Ludlum, Bobby Ray
Ludwig, Allen Clarence
Ludwig, David Willard
Ludwig, Ernest Earl
Ludwig, John Truman
Ludwig, Ruby Ballard
Ludwig, Vernon Adam
Luedecke, Alvin Roubal, Jr.
Luedecke, William Henry
Luedeman, Joel Kerry
Luedtke, Kurt Anton
Luginbyhl, Robert Ivan
Lugo-Quinones, Felix Alberto
Luikart, William McCollam
Luing, Gary Alan
Luis, Juan
Lukas, Gaze Elmer
Lukas, Richard Conrad
Lumpkin, Thomas Riley
Lumsden, (Mary) Isabel
Lunardini, Robert Christopher
Lunceford, Bill Eugene
Lund, Frederick Henry
Lundberg, Gustave Harold
Lundblade, Hobert Philip
Lunde, Alfred N.
Lundell, Joe
Lundstrom, David Blom
Lunney, Gerald Hugh
Lunnon, Betty Sheehan (Mrs. James Lunnon)
Lupin, E. Ralph
Lupo, Robert Maxcy, Jr.
Lupton, Mary Hosmer (Mrs. Thomas George Lupton)
Lusk, Glenna Rae Knight (Mrs. Edwin Bruce Lusk)
Luss, Dan
Lussky, Warren Alfred
Lusteck, Joseph Anton, Jr.
Lutey, John Kent
Luther, Edward Turner
Luther, Jerry Donald
Luther, Roland Cornelius
Lutken, Donald Curry
Lutton, Monty James
Luttrull, Ronald Ray
Lutz, Bernard Lewis
Lutz, Clifford Lewis
Lutz, Paul Eugene
Lutz, Raymond Price
Lutz, Theresa Pence (Mrs. C. Ralph Lutz)
Lux, George Richard
Luxenberg, Malcolm Neuwahl
Luza, Radomir Vaclav
Lydick, Arthur Urban
Lydick, Joe Willis
Lyerly, Elaine Myrick
Lykins, Noel Ray
Lyle, Samuel Patterson
Lyles, Jerry Lee
Lyles, William Gordon
Lynch, Jack Luchen
Lynch, John Brown
Lynch, John Ellsworth
Lynch, Kenneth Clyde
Lynch, Simpson Matthew
Lynch, Vincent King
Lynch, William Charles
Lynch, William Wright, Jr.
Lynd, James Paul
Lyne, James Anthony, Jr.
Lynn, Hugh Terry
Lynn, Joseph Daniel
Lynn, Phillip Wayne
Lynn, Robert DeWese
Lynn, Sara Gaw
Lyon, Cathryn Crowell Conover
Lyon, James Frank, Jr.
Lyon, Joyce Glascock
Lyon, Philip Kirkland
Lyons, Beatrice Marie Rutledge
Lyons, Harry Steven
Lyons, Phillip Michael, Sr.
Maa, Peter Sheng-shyong
Mabe, David Linwood
Mabire, Kenneth Earl
Mabrey, David Walton
Mabrey, James Theodore
Mabry, Edward Bloxton
Mabry, Nelloise Johnson
Mac Connell, Edwin Thompson
Mac Donald, Jean Wiedenfeld
Mac Donald, L(eland) Lloyd
Mac Donald, Ralph Fabian, Jr.
Mac Donald, Ronald Hebert
Mac Donald, Thomas Cook, Jr.
Mac Donald, William Russell
Mac Dougall, Robert Douglas
Macesich, George
Macesich, Susana Sonia
Mac Fadden, Arthur Ross
Mac Farlane, Ian
Mac Gibbon, Hugh Carlyle
Machovec, Marvin Anthony
Macias-Rendon, Fernando
Mack, Garnett Lloyd
Mack, Roosevelt, Jr.
Mack, Theodore
Mack, Wilbur Ollio
Mac Kechnie, Horace Knight
Mac Keigan, Mary Anne Turner Loflin
Mackel, Donald Charles
Mac Kenzie, Duane Edwin
Mac Kenzie, James Donald
Mac Kenzie, Jean West
Mackenzie, Kenneth Victor
Mac Kenzie, Mary Kathryne Timberlake
Mac Kenzie, Melissa Taylor
Mac Kenzie, Roland Redus
Mackereth, Curtis Lavine
Mackey, M(aurice) Cecil, Jr.
Mackhardt, Lucille Alma Hill
Mackie, Shirley Marie
Mackin, John Gilman, Jr.
Mac Kinnon, Cyrus Leland
Mac Nerney, John Sheridan
Macrae, Bruce Farquhar
Mac Rae, Robert Alexander
Macy, Arthur Warren
Madamba, Jorge Judy
Madden, Charlotte Slone (Mrs. Edd Madden)
Madden, Edward Bingham
Madden, John Wilson
Maddock, Herbert John, Jr.
Maddox, Dan Waite
Maddox, Milton T.
Maddux, John Howard
Maddux, Thomas Joe
Madison, Leola Elizabeth
Madorsky, David Diamond
Maehl, William Henry, Jr.
Magarian, Robert Armen
Magee, Dan Albert
Magee, John Melvin
Magee, Kimball Pratt
Magee, Robert Charles
Mager, Gerald
Magill, Henry Fraser
Magill, Vernon Roy
Magnan, Charles Graham, Jr.
Magnant, Kenneth Karl
Magnuson, Charles Emil
Magnuson, Warren Robert
Magoffin, Ralph Manning
Magrath, Lawrence Kay
Magruder, Helen Elaine Hakala (Mrs. Eugene Ross Magruder)
Magruder, Richard Allen
Maguire, Cary McIlwaine
Maguire, Jack Russell
Maguire, Pat Horton (Mrs. Jack Russell Maguire)
Mahaffey, Hugh
Mahan, Quillan Robert
Mahanay, Timothy Irving
Mahanes, James Rudolph
Mahaney, R. Dan
Mahesh, Virendra Bushan
Mahlmann, John James
Mahmood, Afsar
Mahon, George Herman
Mahoney, Vernon Lloyd Mike
Mahrle, Benjamin Carl
Maia, Philip Paul
Maier, Karl George
Mailandt, Peter
Mailen, James Clifford
Mailman, David Sherwin
Main, T(om) Talmage, Jr.
Maisey, Judith Mewshaw
Maish, James Ivan
Majestro, Tony Colerio
Major, Dwight John
Majors, Thomas Jackson
Makansi, Munzer
Makielski, Stanislaw John, Jr.
Makover, Sylvan Aaron
Maldonado, Bernard Brevik
Malecki, Richard Albert
Maley, Edwin
Malik, Krishan Ahmad
Maliner, Robert Hugh
Malkoff, Donald Burton
Mall, Myron Merriell
Mallard, Bobby Joe
Mallard, Leo Sessions
Mallard, Wade Videtto, Jr.
Mallen, Saul Twom
Mallery, William Henry, III
Mallette, Reese Ewell, Jr.
Mallin, Jay
Malling, Heinrich Valdemar
Mallow, Ramon Daniel
Malmstad, Betty Jean
Malone, Dudley Wayne
Malone, James Leonard
Malone, John Irvin
Maloney, Frank Campbell, III
Maloney, Lawrence Michael
Maloof, Joyce Morgan
Malooly, Donald Albert
Malt, Harold Lewis
Maltby, David Stewart
Man, Eugene Herbert
Manahan, Helen Marie
Manchee, Katheryn Hait (Mrs. Arthur Leavens Manchee)
Manchester, Norma Winn
Manchin, A. James
Manci, Orlando Joseph, Jr.
Mancuso, Thomas Glenn
Mandel, Robert John
Mandelker, Lester
Mandell, Louise Ruehlmann
Manfre, Christopher Francis
Mangels, John, Jr.
Mangelsdorff, Arthur David
Manger, Walter Leroy
Mangold, William Johnson, Jr.
Mangu, John, Jr.
Mangum, Grady Gardner
Mangum, Ollie Mack
Manhart, Myron Allan
Manier, (Thomas) Miller
Manka, Walter Ralph, III
Mankins, James Earl
Manley, Diane Burton
Manley, Frank A.
Manley, Richard Shannon
Mann, James Robert
Mann, William Walter
Manniello, John Baptiste Louis
Manning, Alma Squires (Mrs. T. Wesley Manning)
Manning, Douglas Hermit
Manning, Frances Tully
Manning, Frank William
Manning, Johnny Earl
Manning, Walter Scott
Manning, William Lincoln, Jr.
Mannoni, Raymond
Mans, Rose Marie Kiba
Mansberger, Arlie Roland
Mansfield, Daniel Joseph
Mansfield, Milton James, Jr.
Mansfield, Philip Douglas
Mansur, John Carter
Manuel, Ronald Jules
Maples, James Clifford, Jr.
Marable, James Rose, Jr.
Maragides, Karl Harry
Marble, Roland Dudley
Marbury, Larry Alonza
Marbury, Ritchey McGuire, III
Marchant, Trelawney Eston
Marchetti, Jean Woolley
Marchfield, Rudolph L.
Marcie, Frank Joseph
Marcucilli, Theodore Joseph
Marcus, Terry Lee
Marcuse, Rudolph Joseph, Jr.
Marek, Albert Joseph
Marek, Richard Thomas
Margan, Igor
Margolis, Gwen Liedman (Mrs. Allan B. Margolis)
Margulies, Stanley Ira
Marino, Andrew Philip
Marino, Angelo Francis
Maris, Arthur Stanley
Mark, Sidney Carl
Markham, Annie Catherine Parrish (Mrs. Oscar C. Markham)
Markham, John Stewart
Markley, Dottie Baker
Markman, Sherman
Markoff, Sven Clifford
Marks, Billy Guinn
Marks, Charles
Marks, Connie Mary Keeling
Marks, Edward Archibald, Jr.
Marks, Henry Mortimer, Jr.
Marks, Henry Seymour
Marks, Herbert Lee, Sr.
Marks, James John
Marks, Marsha Kass
Marks, Meyer Benjamin
Marks, Paul H.
Marks, Walter Flemming, Jr.
Markusen, Joyce Lisenby (Mrs. Jack William Markusen)
Markwalder, Winston Ernest
Markwell, Dick R(obert)
Marland, Alkis Joseph
Marlar, John T.
Marlatt, Abby Lindsey
Marler, Earl Anthony, Jr.
Marley, William Franklin, Jr.
Marlow, Billy Howard
Marlow, Clyde Danforth
Marlow, H(obson) McKinley
Marmion, Charles Gresham
Marmion, William Henry
Marquart, Barbara Ann
Marquez, Richard Inocencio
Marquez-Diaz, Nestor
Marsden, Elizabeth Harlow
Marsden, Robert Alan
Marsden, Ruth Elizabeth
Marsh, Eleanor Miller Hack (Mrs. Garnett S. Marsh)
Marsh, Malcolm Roy, Jr.
Marsh, Warner Garland
Marsh, Woodrow Lee, Jr.
Marshall, Donald Irving
Marshall, Edward Wayne
Marshall, Jerome Benjamin, Jr.
Marshall, John David
Marshall, John McClellan
Marshall, Marian Lavon Jackson
Marshall, Osa Wesley, III
Marshall, Richard Treeger
Marshall, Robert Gordon
Marshall, Robert James
Marshall, Wallace
Marshall, William Leitch
Marshall, Willis Henry, Jr.
Marshbanks, Robert Lee
Marsik, Frederic John
Marston, Hunter Sylvester, Jr.
Marston, Joseph George Lanaux, Jr.
Marston, Robert Quarles
Martell, Charles Bowling
Martens, Donald Lee
Martens, Frank Henry
Martin, Benjamin Gaufman
Martin, Charles V.
Martin, Cora Arleta
Martin, Dale Alison
Martin, Daniel Ezekiel
Martin, David Edward
Martin, David Grier, Jr.
Martin, Donald Thomas
Martin, Donn Deveral
Martin, Dorothy Anne
Martin, Dwight Wesley
Martin, Edmund Clyde
Martin, Edward Curtis, Jr.
Martin, Edward S.
Martin, Ellen Hall
Martin, Francis Austin
Martin, Francis Linton
Martin, George Curtis
Martin, George Dan
Martin, George Gilmore
Martin, Gregory Dean
Martin, Harry Aubrey
Martin, Harvey Augustus, Jr.
Martin, Harvey Thompson, Jr.
Martin, Howard Nathan
Martin, James Grubbs
Martin, James Guy
Martin, James Richard, Jr.
Martin, James Robert, Jr.
Martin, John E(dward)
Martin, John Perry, Jr.
Martin, Lois Baker
Martin, Marcus Ferrel
Martin, Margaret Stephens
Martin, Marvin Lawrence
Martin, Michael David
Martin, Norma Quiggle
Martin, Okie Raymond
Martin, Patricia Lindsey Ward
Martin, Patrick Glenn
Martin, Philip Joe
Martin, Richard Blazo
Martin, Rob (Robert) Keith
Martin, Robert Earnshaw
Martin, Robert J(efferson)
Martin, Robert Leroy
Martin, Ronald Lee
Martin, Rosalie Laura
Martin, Thomas David
Martin, Tina Joy
Martin, Vernon Dee
Martin, Wade Omer, Jr.
Martin, Willard Fraser
Martin, William Arthur, Jr.
Martin, William Frederick
Martin, William Haywood, III
Martin, Wilson Clark, Jr.
Martin, Zenon Agustin
Martinez, Irving Ricardo, Jr.
Martinez, Luis Osvaldo
Martinez, Otto Heriberto
Martinez, Samuel Joseph, Jr.
Martinez, Victor Julio
Martinez-Esteve, Raul Juan Antonio
Martinez-Lopez, Jorge Ignacio
Martinez-Monfort, Antonio
Martone, Lucia Winifred
Martz, David Michael
Martz, Glenn Everett
Martz, Willard Harry
Marvin, Murray Joseph
Marze, Brawley Taylor
Mascarenhas, Joselyn Diego
Masiko, Peter, Jr.
Maslinoff, Coralie Runge
Mason, Aretha Hammond (Mrs. James Frederick Mason)
Mason, Charles Culberson, Jr.
Mason, James Ralph
Mason, Joseph Barry
Mason, Julian Lorin, Jr.
Mason, Richard Allen
Mason, Robert Edward
Mason, Robert McSpadden
Mason, William Alfred
Mason, William Clifford, Jr.
Masri, Zahi Hamdi
Massaniso, Peter Anthony
Massaro, Frank Joseph
Massengill, Raymond McCellan, Jr.
Massey, Donald Dale
Massey, Donald Wayne
Massey, Earl D.
Massey, Hal
Massey, Larry Winston
Massey, Peyton Howard, Jr.
Massey, Richard Walter, Jr.
Massey, Thomas Cade
Massey, William Walter, Jr.
Massieu, Guillermo Helguera
Massman, Richard Allan
Masten, Michael Keith
Masters, Orlan Vincent Wade
Masterson, Thomas Robert
Mastran, David Vincent
Matejisik, Elfriede
Mateker, Emil Joseph, Jr.
Matheny, Herschel Albert
Matheny, Jeanne Felkel
Matheny, Tom Harrell
Mathes, Orace Ray
Mathews, Albert George
Mathews, Charles Loren
Mathews, Robert Cabeen Hopkins, Jr.
Mathews, Walter Michael
Mathiews, Raymond Leonard
Mathis, Dawson M.
Mathis, Frank
Mathis, Gerald Ray
Mathis, James Otto
Mathis, Joel Henry
Mathis, John Hamilton, Jr.
Mathis, John Henry
Mathis, Viola Inez
Mathur, Virendra Singh
Matlock, Gibb Blanks
Matson, Billy George
Matson, Jessie Baldwin
Matson, Larry James
Matson, Morris Charles
Matson, Roger Allen
Mattei, Angel Gaston
Matteson, Lewis Whitford, Jr.
Mattheis, Floyd Elliott
Matthes, Walter Louis
Matthews, Alfred Rowland
Matthews, Charles Sedwick
Matthews, Cornelia Williams
Matthews, Don
Matthews, Doris Boozer (Mrs. Charles L. Matthews)
Matthews, Edward Warren
Matthews, Elsie Catherine Spears
Matthews, Elsie Vause
Matthews, Henry James
Matthews, James Claude, Jr.
Matthews, Jay Arlon, Jr.
Matthews, Jay Kay
Matthews, Leslie Avon
Matthews, Rita Sue
Matthews, William Henry, III
Matthews, William McGill, V
Mattis, Allen Francis
Mattox, Harmon Rader
Mattox, Hoyt Tobias
Mattox, James Albon
Maturin, Larry James
Matus, Simon
Mauck, Henry Page, Jr.
Mauderli, Walter
Mauger, Paul Allan
Maurer, Harold Maurice
Maurer, Michele Lynne
Maurice, John Daniell
Maurrasse, Florentin Jean-Marie Robert
Mauzy, Oscar Holcombe
Mavris, Nicholas Bennie
Maxey, Robert Hugh
Maxfield, William Streeter
Maxwell, Chester Arthur
Maxwell, Henry Faville
Maxwell, Katherine Gant
Maxwell, Olen Dale
Maxwell, Robert Earl
Maxwell, Willie Richard, Jr.
May, Darlene Rae
May, Donald Lynn
May, Francis Barns
May, Frank Henry
May, Jean Caro
May, John Lawrence
May, Laura Johnson
May, Lester
May, Winston Charles
Mayborn, Frank Willis
Mayda, Jaro
Mayer, John Prosper
Mayer, Raymond Charles, Jr.
Mayer, Robert Allen
Mayer, Velia Ann
Mayes, Alice Ruth
Mayes, Clifford Grant
Mayes, David Forrester
Mayes, Hoyt Patman
Mayes, Robert Gilbert
Mayes, Samuel Hubert, Jr.
Mayes, Wendell Wise, Jr.
Mayfield, Randy M.
Mayher, William Edgar, III
Mayne, Mabelle Elaine Adams
Maynor, Clayton Harmon, Sr.
Maynor, Hal Wharton, Jr.
Mayo, Clyde Calvin
Mayo, Edward Burnett
Mayo, Eugene Francis
Mayo, Howell Roscoe, Jr.
Mayo, Walker Porter
Mayo, Wallace C.
Mayol, Pedro Magdiel
Mayoral-Bigas, Jorge Walter
Mayoz, Rafael
Mays, Larry Wesley
Mayson, Preston Brooks, Jr.
Mayton, James Lamar, Jr.
Mazis, Michael Bernard
Mazursky, Morris David
Mazzeo, Daniel Patrick
Mazzetti, August Lawrence
Mazzoli, Romano Louis
Mc Adams, Herbert Hall
Mc Adams, Ina May Ogletree (Mrs. Kelly E. McAdams)
Mc Adams, Kelly Roy
Mc Adoo, Donald Eldridge
Mc Afee, Carrie R. Hampton (Mrs. Joshua O. Mc Afee)
Mc Alister, James Douglas
Mc Allister, Raymond Francis
Mc Allister, Russell Greenway, Jr.
Mc Allister, Walter Williams
Mc Allister, William Alexander, Jr.
Mc Aninch, Robert Danford
Mc Arthur, Michael Sullivan
Mc Auley, Sarah Longley
Mc Auley, Van Alfon
Mc Bee, J.D.
Mc Brayer, Odell Lavon
Mc Brayer, W. Terry
Mc Bride, Beverley Booth
Mc Bride, William
Mc Bryde, Myron Homer
Mc Cabe, DeSoto Ben, Jr.
Mc Cabe, John Francis
Mc Cabe, Michael James
Mc Caffity, Curtis Lee
Mc Caffrey, Joseph Edwin
Mc Cain, Harold Dean
Mc Cain, Jimmy Wayne
Mc Cain, Maurice Edward
Mc Cain, Michael Bryan
McCain, William David
Mc Caleb, Foster Collins, Jr.
McCaleb, John Henry
Mc Caleb, Stanley Bert
Mc Call, Abner Vernon
Mc Call, Charlie Campbell
Mc Call, Daniel Thompson, Jr.
Mc Call, Hazel Bradfield (Mrs. John Dean McCall)
Mc Call, John Clark
Mc Call, Moses Nathaniel, III
Mc Call, Robert Edgar, Jr.
Mc Call, Vicki Jo
Mc Callian, Richard Jones
Mc Callister, Robert Ray
Mc Candless, Charles Emery
Mc Cann, Kelly Franklin
Mc Cants, Donald Glenn
Mc Cants, Ralph Samuel
Mc Carley, Carolyn Josephine Spence (Mrs. Clint Weldon McCarley)
Mc Carley, David Gordon
Mc Carley, Thomas David
Mc Carter, Grady Sylvester, III
Mc Carter, James Thomas
Mc Cartha, Walter Hayne
Mc Carthy, Edward, Jr.
Mc Carthy, Edward Anthony
Mc Carthy, Jerome Richard
Mc Carthy, Mary Elizabeth
Mc Carthy, Thomas James, Jr.
Mc Cartney, Richard Thomas
Mc Cartney, Virginia Lee
Mc Cartney, Willard Glenn
Mc Carty, Raymond M.
Mc Caskill, Charles Bruce, Jr.
Mc Caskill, Harry Lee
Mc Cauley, John Thomas, Jr.
Mc Cauley, Loyd Cecil
Mc Chesney, Robert Michael
Mc Clain, David H.
Mc Clain, Gerald Ray
Mc Clain, James William
Mc Clain, William Francis
Mc Clanahan, James Alva
Mc Clarnon, Rodney M.
Mc Cleary, William Ernest
Mc Cleave, Barry Wayne
Mc Clellan, Carole Keeton
Mc Clellan, Guy Sydney
Mc Clelland, George Joseph
Mc Clelland, Robert Nelson
Mc Clendon, Benny Ray
Mc Clendon, Carlee Thomas
Mc Clendon, James Leroy
Mc Clendon, James Lowell
Mc Clendon, Joan Parsons
Mc Clenny, Mildred Janice
Mc Clerklin, Horace
Mc Clintock, George Davison
Mc Clintock, Simms
Mc Clintock, William Lewis
McCluhan, John Dolph
McCluney, Joe Alfred
Mc Clung, David Brainard
Mc Clung, Jerry Clark
Mc Clung, Luther Therman
Mc Clung, Norvel Malcolm
Mc Clung, Phil Oran
Mc Clung, Ralph Clay
Mc Clung, Tandy Jean
Mc Clure, Harlan Ewart
Mc Clure, Jimmy Milton
Mc Clure, Julius Young
Mc Collam, James Graham
Mc Collam, William, Jr.
Mc Colloch, Lawrence Edgar
Mc Collom, Kenneth Allen
Mc Collum, Paul Allen
Mc Combs, Freda Siler

Mc Combs, James
Mc Commas, Alexander Monroe, Jr.
Mc Conaghy, Joseph William
Mc Conn, James Joseph
Mc Connell, Dorothy Fraiser (Mrs. Frederick Earl McConnell)
McConnell, Freeman Erton
Mc Connell, Lewis H.
Mc Connell, Merle Grant
Mc Connell, Richard Leon
Mc Cord, Eugene Lee
Mc Cord, Guyte Pierce, Jr.
Mc Cord, James Richard, III
Mc Cord, Mollie Royall
Mc Corkle, Charles Howard
Mc Corkle, James Lorenzo, Jr.
Mc Cormack, Austin Francis, Jr.
Mc Cormack, Carol Hartford
McCormick, John Hoyle
Mc Cormick, Michael Patrick
Mc Cormick, Ronald Robert
Mc Cormick, William Frederick
Mc Cormick, Willie Mae Ward (Mrs. Walter Witten McCormick)
Mc Cotter, Burney Richard
Mc Cotter, Dinah White
Mc Cotter, Margaret Rosemond Palmer (Mrs. Burney Richard McCotter)
Mc Coun, Fred Corbett
Mc Cowan, Otis Blakely
Mc Cown, James Kimbol
Mc Cown, Theodore Vedell, Jr.
Mc Coy, Carol Louise
Mc Coy, Donald Burchard
Mc Coy, Francis Tyrone
Mc Coy, Gene Guy
Mc Coy, Harry Price
Mc Coy, Idella Maria Theresa Brown (Mrs. Gene Guy McCoy)
Mc Coy, James Lewis
Mc Coy, Marion A.
Mc Coy, Raymond de Penafort
Mc Coy, Wesley Lawrence
Mc Cracken, John Ward, Jr.
McCracken, Joseph Hill, III
Mc Cracken, Malcolm David
Mc Cracken, Thomas Melvin
Mc Crackin, Earl Windell
Mc Crady, James Waring de Bernieres
Mc Crane, Ruth Mae
Mc Cranie, William Mark
Mc Crary, Dennie Lockhart
Mc Crary, Giles Connell
Mc Crary, Paul Elmer
Mc Crary, Theodore Lorenza
Mc Craw, Ronald Kent
Mc Cray, Arthur White
Mc Crea, Edsel Warren
Mc Crea, William George
Mc Cree, William Allen, Jr.
Mc Creight, Boyd
Mc Crone, Robert Edward, Jr.
Mc Crory, Donald Gene
Mc Crory, Ellann
Mc Crory, Martha
Mc Crossen, William James
Mc Cue, James Charles
Mc Culloch, Etta Smith
Mc Culloch, George Thompson
Mc Culloch, John Hathorn
Mc Cullough, John Phillip
McCullough, Richard Wayne
Mc Cullough, Shirley Kathryn
Mc Cully, Richard Philip
Mc Cumber, William Henry, Jr.
Mc Cune, Martin Keith
McCune, William Edward
Mc Curdy, Martha Elizabeth
Mc Curry, James
Mc Curry, Kathryn Maree
Mc Curry, Thomas Edward
Mc Cutchen, Samuel Proctor
Mc Cutcheon, Chester Myers
Mc Daniel, Bonnie Gaye
Mc Daniel, Edgar Bruce
Mc Daniel, Gerald Calvin
Mc Daniel, William Young
Mc David, Joel Duncan
Mc David, Marion Foy
Mc Davitt, William Donald
Mc Dermott, Make, Jr.
Mc Devitt, Ellen
Mc Dill, Thomas Haldane
Mc Donald, Alvis Edward
Mc Donald, Andrew J.
Mc Donald, Barbara Hollis Buck
Mc Donald, Charles Donald, Jr.
Mc Donald, Charles Frederick
Mc Donald, Claiborne, IV
Mc Donald, Clarence Jackson
Mc Donald, Erwin Lawrence
Mc Donald, Frank Jeveree
Mc Donald, George Edmund
Mc Donald, Gregor Ronald
Mc Donald, James Jackson
Mc Donald, Laurier Bernard
Mc Donald, Lawrence P.
Mc Donald, Olin Kenneth
Mc Donald, William Lindsey
Mc Donnell, John Henry
Mc Donnell, Rex Graham, Jr.
Mc Donough, Thomas Joseph
Mc Dowell, John Willis
Mc Dowell, Robert Wayne
Mc Dowell, William Lewis, Jr.
Mc Duff, Lillie Mae
Mc Elhenney, Thomas Rudd
Mc Elmurry, Arthur Lee
Mc Elrath, Robert Lee
Mc Elreath, Jesse Dale
Mc Elveen, Winston Lee
Mc Ever, Virgle Washington, Jr.
Mc Evilly, Mary Frances
Mc Ewen, Samuel William, III
Mc Ewen, Stephen Paul
Mc Ewin, John Ben
Mc Fadden, Frank Hampton
Mc Fall, Robert William
Mc Farlan, Edward, Jr.
Mc Farland, Frank Eugene
Mc Farland, James William
Mc Farland, M. Robert
Mc Farland, Paul Hedrich, Jr.
Mc Farland, Ward Morrow
Mc Farlane, Graham Sanders
Mc Fee, Arthur Storer
Mc Gaughey, Robert Holmes, Jr.
Mc Gaughy, Ellen Douglas
Mc Gavock, Polly P(olitt)
Mc Gaw, Jessie Brewer
Mc Gee, Dean A.
Mc Gee, Hall Thomas, Jr.
Mc Gee, Linda Danner
Mc Gee, Tom G.
Mc Gee, William Ambrose
Mc Gehee, Claude
Mc Gehee, Edward Stokes
Mc Gehee, Robert Edwin
Mc Gettrick, William Joseph John
Mc Ghee, Stanley Edwin
Mc Gibony, James Thomas
Mc Gill, Edwin Miller
Mc Gill, Joseph Leonard, Jr.
Mc Gillivray, Ross Tucker
Mc Ginity, James William
Mc Ginn, Larry Dean
Mc Ginnes, Franklin Pierce
Mc Ginnes, Jeannette Hatter
Mc Ginty, Helen
Mc Ginty, Jean LaDelle Epperson
Mc Glamery, Andrew Joe
Mc Glamery, Gerald Garris
Mc Glamry, Max Reginald
Mc Glohon, Loonis
Mc Glothlin, Joyce Durrett
Mc Goey, Noelle Theresa
Mc Gonigle, George Lee
Mc Govern, Joseph James
Mc Gowan, E(dgar) L(eon)
Mc Gowen, Neil Ennis
Mc Grath, Harold Morris
Mc Grath, Terry Thomas
Mc Greevy, Martin Kenneth
Mc Gregor, Frank Hamilton, Jr.
Mc Gregor, Raymond Gene
Mc Gregor, William Henry Davis
Mc Griff, Bill W.
Mc Guffin, William Lewis, Jr.
Mc Guillan, David Charles
Mc Guire, Hubert Everett
Mc Guire, Roger James
Mc Guire, Ronald Furrh
Mc Guire, Sharon Gayle
Mc Gurn, John Martin
Mc Hard, James Dale
Mc Henry, Lawrence Chester, Jr.
Mc Henry, Richard Joseph
Mc Henry, William Dunlap
Mc Ilwraith, Isa Roberta
Mc Ingvale, Cynthia Ann Potter
Mc Innis, Harry Elwood, Jr.
Mc Innis, John Robert
Mc Innis, Austin Little
Mc Intosh, Colin Hugh Alexander
Mc Intosh, Dana Kaye
Mc Intosh, Donald Keith
Mc Intosh, Edward Dalton
Mc Intosh, Frank Wesley, III
Mc Intosh, Neva Trice (Mrs. Otho R. McIntosh)
Mc Intosh, Peterson Linder
Mc Intosh, Robert Joseph
Mc Inturff, Ernest Robert
Mc Intyre, Charles Etta
Mc Intyre, Flossie Hickman
Mc Intyre, Frederick Lee
Mc Intyre, James Carroll
Mc Intyre, Stanley Donald
Mc Kamie, Edgar Moran
Mc Kay, David Andrew
Mc Kay, Griffith Head
Mc Kay, John Harvey
Mc Kay, John Judson, Jr.
Mc Kay, Joy H. (Mrs. Samuel J. McKay)
Mc Kay, Lawrence Brian
Mc Kay, Ruth Courson
Mc Kay, Samuel Leroy
Mc Kechnie, Robert Milton, III
Mc Kee, Arthur, Jr.
Mc Kee, James Robert
Mc Kee, Jesse Oscar
Mc Kee, Marlene Sue
Mc Kee, Patrick Allen
Mc Kee, Thomas Lapsley
Mc Kee, Willis Payne, Jr.
Mc Kendree, Bishop Davis
Mc Kenna, Thomas Adam, Jr.
Mc Kenzie, Benjamin Franklin, Jr.
Mc Kenzie, Cecil Leon, Jr.
Mc Kenzie, Milton Dean
Mc Keon, John Aloysius
Mc Keown, Charles Devlin
McKeown, Joyce Tapp
Mc Kewen, Joe Mervin
Mc Kinley, Jimmie Joe
Mc Kinnei, Ruth Robertson
Mc Kinney, Benjamin Calvin
Mc Kinney, Billy Jack
Mc Kinney, Frank William
Mc Kinney, James Carroll
Mc Kinney, James David
Mc Kinney, Jarmon Clayton, Jr.
Mc Kinney, Patrick Wilson
Mc Kinstry, Sam Wescoat
Mc Kittrick, Betty Rich (Mrs. Sherman H. Raveson)
Mc Knight, Colbert Augustus
Mc Knight, Essie Velma
Mc Knight, William Baldwin
Mc Lafferty, Charles Lowry
Mc Lain, Jack
Mc Lain, John Hamilton, IV
Mc Lain, Lee Roy
Mc Lain, William Harvey
Mc Lain, William Richard
Mc Lane, H. Arthur
Mc Larty, Cleylon Lee
Mc Laughlin, (Edward) Bruce
McLaughlin, Charles B.
Mc Laughlin, Edward
Mc Laughlin, George Walter
Mc Laughlin, James Oscar, Jr.
Mc Laughlin, Shirley Burden
Mc Laughlin, Thomas Dennis
Mc Lean, James Hannis
Mc Lean, Margaret Stoner (Mrs. Malcolm Dallas McLean)
Mc Lean, William Youmans
Mc Lelland, Claude Allen
Mc Lemore, Andrew Jackson, III
Mc Lemore, Bobbie Frank
Mc Lemore, Eugene Brooks, Jr.
Mc Lemore, Mrs. Richard Aubrey
Mc Lendon, Gordon Barton
Mc Lendon, Michael James
Mc Leod, Alexander Canaday
Mc Leod, Daniel Rogers
Mc Leod, James Eugene
Mc Leod, Larry Varnadoe
Mc Mahan, Robert Chandler
Mc Mahan, Robert Kenneth
Mc Mahon, John Martin
Mc Mahon, Josh Anderson, Jr.
Mc Mahon, Rhett Russell
Mc Manaway, Harold Gene
Mc Manis, James Carl
Mc Manus, James Edward
Mc Manus, Samuel Plyler
Mc Masters, Jesse Lowell
Mc Masters, Robert Earl
Mc Math, Zell Fain
Mc Michael James Elmer
Mc Millan, Ann Alta
Mc Millan, Hugh Dix, Jr.
Mc Millan, John Alexander, III
Mc Millan, Thomas Ellwood, Jr.
Mc Millon, Raymond Cecil, Jr.
Mc Millon, Regnal Luther
Mc Minn, Mary Inez Lamury
Mc Minn, William Gene
Mc Mordie, Warren C., Jr.
Mc Morries, Billy Ray
McMullen, David Lee
Mc Mullen, Linda Royster
Mc Mullin, Nicky Van
Mc Murchy, Austin Calvin
Mc Murtry, Edward Hoyse
Mc Namara, Edwin Thomas
Mc Naughton, James Arthur
Mc Neany, Steven Robert
Mc Neese, Betty Allison
Mc Neil, James Henry
Mc Neil, James Porter, Jr.
Mc Neil, Walter Harve
Mc Neill, Archibald James, Jr.
Mc Neill, Richard Reid
Mc Neilly, Juanita Assee
Mc Nichols, Gerald Robert
Mc Niel, George William
Mc Niel, Norbert Arthur
Mc Nulty, Joseph Peter
Mc Nutt, Dolly Hite
Mc Pheeters, Harold Lawrence
Mc Pherson, Alice Ruth
Mc Pherson, Joseph Daniel
Mc Pherson, Raymond Pat
Mc Quaid, William Ravenel, Jr.
Mc Queen, Charles Richard
Mc Queen, Doris Janice
Mc Queen, Edgar Gordon
Mc Queen, Herbert Fuller
Mc Queen, Horace Franklin
Mc Quillen, James Dudley, Jr.
Mc Quown, O. Ruth
Mc Rae, James Hendry
Mc Rae, James Wesley
Mc Rae, Kenneth Gilbert, IV
Mc Rae, William Holland
Mc Ree, Joe Richard
Mc Right, William Carder
Mc Stay, John DeWitt
Mc Swain, Richard Horace
Mc Sween, Donald Murdoch
Mc Sweeney, E(llsworth) E(dward)
Mc Swigan, James Aloysius, Jr.
Mc Tee, Clifford Ray, Jr.
Mc Wherter, Robert Clayton
Mc Whirter, John Walton, Jr.
Mc Whorter, Thomas Osborne
Mc Whorter, William Horace
Mc Williams, Jettie Manning Crisp (Mrs. Wiley E. McWilliams, Jr.)
Mc Williams, Robert Whealton
Mead, Frank Waldreth
Meade, Edward Grant
Meador, Ben Franklin, Jr.
Meador, Charles Edwin
Meador, Clifton Kirkpatrick
Meador, John Milward, Jr.
Meador, Robert Stewart
Meadows, Daniel Thomas
Meadows, William Tinsley, Jr.
Meagher, Charles Franklin
Mealing, Esther Morrison (Mollie)
Mealing, Isabel Thorpe
Meaney, Daniel D.
Means, James Clarence, Jr.
Means, Julia Juanita
Means, Willerma Frazier
Means, William Walter
Meares, Romulus Linney, Jr.
Meaux, Richard Cecil
Mecom, John W., Jr.
Medland, Francis Frederic
Medlen, Ammon Brown
Medley, Paul, Jr.
Medlin, Virgil Dewain
Medlock, Julius Lester
Medoff, Lawrence Ray
Meehan, James Raleigh
Meek, Edwin Ernest
Meek, J(ohn) William, III
Meek, Richard Lee
Meeker, William Raymond, Jr.
Meeks, Charles
Meeks, Edward
Meeks, James Roger
Me Gahee, Joris Cecil
Megginson, Leon Cassity
Megginson, Robert Mitford
Mehne, James Lee
Mehrotra, Sunil
Mei, Harry Thomas
Meier, J. Ralph
Meigs, Paul Phillip
Meinders, Hildred McCants (Mrs. Wesley H. Meinders)
Meinders, Wesley H.
Meinecke, Tommy Jacob
Meinke, Roy Walter
Meirowsky, Arnold Max
Meister, Carl John
Meister, John David
Meixsell, Melchior Francis
Mejia, Roberto
Meldram, Charles William
Melendez, Cesar Ramon
Melgar, Julio
Mellen, Hugh Joseph
Mellen, William Robert
Mello, Herbert
Melnick, Alice Jean
Melnick, John Latane
Melton, Carolyn Anne
Melton, Chancellor Garland
Melton, Darrell Everett
Meltzer, Morton Franklin
Menaker, Edward Goward
Menchaca, John Albert
Mendenhall, Carrol Clay
Mendenhall, Leslie Ward, Jr.
Mendenhall, William Russell
Méndez, Félix Gilberto
Mendia, Carlos Fernandez de
Mendoza, Catalino Barrera, Jr.
Meneely, (Mary) Leslie Stewart
Menéndez-Monroig, José M.
Menius, Espie Flynn, Jr.
Menscher, Barnet Gary
Menut, D. Charles
Menzel, (Mary) Margaret Young
Menzel, Robert Winston
Menzel, Ronald George
Mercado-Burgos, Nelson
Mercer, Charles Valentine
Mercer, George Riley, Jr.
Mercer, James Lee
Mercer, John Yager
Mercer, Ronald Lee
Mercer, Theodore Chelton
Merchant, Donald Joseph
Merchant, Walter Mayfield
Meredith, Owen Nichols
Meredith, Robert Franklin
Meredith, Sara Elizabeth
Merida, Frederick Austin
Merin, Sidney Julius
Meriwether, Charles Minor
Merlin, James (Merlin J. Johnson)
Merliss, William Sidney
Merrick, Eunice Peacock (Mrs. George E. Merrick)
Merrifield, Donald Victor
Merrill, Hugh Davis, Jr.
Merrill, Janet Louise
Merriman, Frank Allen
Merritt, Buford Kent
Merritt, Catherine Wozny
Merritt, Garry Allan
Merritt, George William
Merritt, Thomas Jefferson
Merryman, Richard Willard
Mersky, Roy Martin
Mertz, Michael Frederick, Jr.
Meshirer, David Donald
Mesic, Harry Randolph
Messenger, Steve
Messersmith, Lloyd Lowell
Messing, Deborah Goldman
Metcalfe, Albert Gallatin, Jr.
Metcalfe, Joseph Davis
Metko, Gerald Earl
Metts, William Long
Metz, Donald Paul
Metz, Leon Claire
Metzger, Sidney M.
Mexic, Simon
Meyberg, William Braxton
Meyer, Andre Bernard
Meyer, Ferdinand Charles, Jr.
Meyer, George Gotthold
Meyer, Hank
Meyer, Jacob Joseph
Meyer, Joe P.
Meyer, Johannes Horst
Meyer, John William
Meyer, Julien H(erman)
Meyer, Lawrence Joseph
Meyer, Paul James
Meyer, Robert George
Meyer, Stewart Canfield
Meyers, Anna Brenner
Meyers, Grant Ulysses
Meyers, John Henry
Meyers, Mae Estelle
Meyers, Rondell Grant
Meyerson, Laurence R.
Meynard, Virginia Dale Gurley (Mrs. Ernest Bennet Meynard)
Mezey, Robert Joseph
Micha, David Allan
Michael, James Harry, Jr.
Michael, William Herbert, Jr.
Michaelis, Eric Robin
Michalowicz, Joseph Victor
Michalski, Edward Matthew
Michel, Harding Boehme Owre (Mrs. John F. Michel)
Michels, Kenneth M.
Michelson, Ronald Keith
Michelson, Thomas Carl
Michie, Lucile Eastham (Mrs. J. Tevis Michie)
Mickens, Ronald Elbert
Mickey, George Henry
Middendorf, William Henry
Middleton, Douglas Delano
Middleton, Douglas Frank
Middleton, Elwyn Linton
Middleton, Ernestine
Middleton, Herman David
Middleton, Mozelle Johnson
Middleton, Norman Graham
Midkiff, Mary Elizabeth Matzke (Mrs. Patrick Clayton Midkiff)
Miele, Anthony William
Mielzarek, Rolf Herbert
Miesch, David Cheatham
Migdol, Marvin Jacob
Mighell, Richard Henry
Migliore, Philip Joseph
Mihalap, Leonid Isaakovich
Mihalyka, Eugene Ernst
Mihelich, Donald Louis
Mikeman, Carl Harmon
Miklas, Pauline Robinson (Mrs. Michael J. Miklas)
Milam, Charles Clifton
Milazzo, Salvatore Nicholas
Milbrodt, Paul Eugene
Milburn, William Isaac
Mildren, Jack
Miles, Alan Clarence
Miles, Algene Stevens, Jr.
Miles, Charles Ewing
Miles, Elton Roger
Miles, James William
Miles, Marilyn Ross
Miles, Melvin Henry
Miles, Oscar Landon, III
Miles, Raymond Carl
Miles, Samuel Harold
Miles, Stephen Warren
Miles, Theo Franklin
Miles, Thomas Peyton
Miles, Winnie Corinne
Milewich, Leon
Miley, Michael Francis
Milford, Dale
Milford, George Noel, Jr.
Milford, Murray Hudson
Milgram, Abraham Samuel
Milhouse, Paul William
Milian, Arsenio
Milici, Robert Calvin
Milk, Richard George
Millar, Jeffery Lynn
Millard, Cheedle William
Millard, David Ralph, Jr.
Milledge, Sarah Franklin (Mrs. Stanley Milledge)
Millen, Dale Adolphus
Miller, Albert Henderson
Miller, Alvin Julius
Miller, Andrew Lamar
Miller, Carl Bryan
Miller, Carter Fakes, Jr.
Miller, Charles Leo
Miller, Charles Valentine
Miller, Chris (Dorothy June Miller)
Miller, Conrad Henry
Miller, Dale Don
Miller, David Edmond
Miller, David Roswell
Miller, Earl William
Miller, Edmond Trowbridge
Miller, Edward Everett
Miller, Ernest Barger, III
Miller, Estelle Lee (Mrs. T.E. Miller)
Miller, F(rederick) DeWolfe
Miller, Fannie Carolyn Roll (Mrs. William Peoples Miller)
Miller, Frederick Warren
Miller, Gene Edward
Miller, George Dunbar
Miller, George Otha, Sr.
Miller, Glenn Currey
Miller, Gloria Lee
Miller, Harvey Alfred
Miller, Helen Elizabeth
Miller, Herbert Dell
Miller, Herbert Lynn
Miller, Howard George, Jr.
Miller, Idelle Block
Miller, Israel Bernard (Buddy)
Miller, J. D.
Miller, Jack Everett
Miller, James Howard
Miller, James Richard
Miller, James Thomas
Miller, Jean Carol
Miller, Joas B., Jr.
Miller, John Charles
Miller, John David
Miller, John Edward
Miller, John Edward
Miller, John L.
Miller, Joseph Bayard
Miller, Largent Melvin
Miller, Lee Stephen
Miller, Leslie
Miller, Luther Tabor, Jr.
Miller, Malcolm Drennan
Miller, Marshall Stuart
Miller, Mary Frances (Mrs. Shannon O. Miller)
Miller, Mary Ruth
Miller, Michael Douglass
Miller, Michelle Avanda
Miller, Monte Mack
Miller, Morton Larrimore
Miller, Nathan Anderson
Miller, Neil Craig
Miller, Norman Bruce
Miller, Ralph Alexander
Miller, Richard Kendall
Miller, Robert Elmer
Miller, Robert Harley
Miller, Robert James, II
Miller, Roy V., Jr.
Miller, Stuart Malcolm
Miller, Thomas Lloyd
Miller, Thomas Wainwright, Jr.
Miller, Timothy Wayne
Miller, Tom Polk
Miller, Wallace Dyett
Miller, Wesley
Miller, William Brock
Miller, William (Bill) E., Jr.
Miller, William Franklin
Miller, William Franklin
Miller, Zell Bryan
Milling, Robert Nicholson
Millington, Clayton Blake
Millis, George Alston
Milloway, Voss Chilcutt
Mills, Alfred Preston
Mills, Blair Guy
Mills, Dale Johnson
Mills, Donald Alexander Barnes
Mills, Donald Bjorn
Mills, George Thomas
Mills, Gordon Candee
Mills, Jim Tom
Mills, Morriss, Jr.
Mills, Rollin William
Mills, Verent John
Mills, William Andrew
Mills, William Harold
Mills, William Harold, Jr.
Mills, William Hayne
Mills, William Raymond, Jr.
Millsap, Joe Adams
Millsaps, Fred Ray
Milstead, William Clyde
Miltier, Thomas Wilson, Jr.
Milton, Rogers Grantham
Mims, David Lathan
Mims, Harold Maurice
Mims, James Luther, Jr.
Mims, Julian Landrum
Mims, Lambert Carter
Mims, Thomas Jerome
Mims, William Henry
Minch, Virgil Adelbert
Minge, Jerry Lee
Minger, John Wilson
Mingione, Ann Dissinger (Mrs. Donald Leo Mingione)
Mingione, Donald Leo
Mings, Samuel Joseph
Miniter, John Joseph
Mink, Charles Edward
Mink, Ellen Britz
Mink, John Robert
Minkley, Suzanne Sawyer (Mrs. Carl H. Minkley)
Minnear, Robert Earle
Minniear, Walter Collins
Minto, George Dennis
Minton, Carolyn Grachia Brock
Minton, Kevin Lewis
Minton, Lee Roy
Mintz, Albert

Mintz, Howard
Minyard, James Patrick, Jr.
Mirabile, Thomas Keith
Miranda, Carlos Rolando
Miranda, Emilio Arturo
Miranti, Judith Goodwyne
Misaqi, Fazlollah Leo
Mishelevich, David Jacob
Miskovsky, George
Misra, Raghunath Prasad
Mitchelhill, James Moffat
Mitchell, Alfred Taylor
Mitchell, Bobby Glen
Mitchell, Carlton Turner
Mitchell, Charlie Howard, Jr.
Mitchell, Earl Douglass, Jr.
Mitchell, Edward Lee
Mitchell, Faye Eliene
Mitchell, George Ernest, Jr.
Mitchell, Gordon Terrence
Mitchell, Harvey Ray
Mitchell, Helen Jewel
Mitchell, Howard Samuel
Mitchell, Jerry Don
Mitchell, John Murray, Jr.
Mitchell, Joseph Brady
Mitchell, Lawrence Du-Wayne
Mitchell, Memory F. (Mrs. T.W. Mitchell)
Mitchell, Otis Edwin
Mitchell, R(ichard) Glen(wood)
Mitchell, Richard Scott
Mitchell, Robert Hartwell
Mitchell, Roy Devoy
Mitchell, Ryan Dunnahoo
Mitchell, Sydney Henry
Mitchell, Terry Lynn
Mitchell, William Grant, Jr.
Mitchum, Donald Chaney
Mitte, Roy Frank
Mittendorf, Theodor Henry
Mittenthal, Freeman Lee
Mixon, Alvin
Miyagawa, Ichiro
Mize, Jan Lee
Mize, Roger Barton
Mizell, Andrew Hooper, III
Mlott, Sylvester Roman
Mmahat, John Anthony
Moberly, Oscar Burns, Jr.
Moberly, Robert Blakely
Mobley, Carroll Wade
Mobley, James David
Mobley, Jean Bellingrath
Mobley, John Holmer, II
Mochrie, Richard Douglas
Modisette, Barbara Jane
Moe, John Lockwood
Moehlman, William Frederick
Moelter, Gregory Martin
Moenssens, Andre A.
Moffat, Charles Elwood
Moffat, David Carl
Moffett, Anderson Grant
Moffett, Charles Irving
Moffett, Thomas Robert
Moffit, William C.
Moffitt, Roy Bratton
Mofield, William Ray
Mogge, Harriet Morgan
Mohamed, Mansour Hussein
Mohammed, M. Hamdi Abdelhakim
Mohd, Maqsood Ahmed
Mohlhenrich, John Sidney
Mohr, G(lenn) Robert
Mohr, Jay Preston
Mohr, Ronnie Karl
Moise, Francis Davis
Moize, Joe McShera
Mokrasch, Lewis Carl
Molander, William Austin
Molenich, Shirley Ann
Molina, Efrain Alberto, Jr.
Molish, Herman Barry
Moll, Robert Harry
Mollenhoff, Clark Raymond
Mollohan, Robert H.
Moloney, Louis Carey
Molony, Michael Janssens, Jr.
Molpus, John Kindred, Jr.
Monaghan, Bernard Andrew
Monaghan, Robert Lee
Monaghan, Terri Francine
Monahan, Stephen Martin
Monas, Sidney
Moncure, Conway Bagwell
Monell de Santiago, Carlos Rafael
Money, John Marshall
Moneyhon, Jack Neville
Monroe, Doris Driggers
Monroe, Ronald Dean
Monserrate, Pedro Enrique
Monsour, Andrew R.
Montag, Miller
Montague, Robert Latane, III
Montandon, Blaise James
Montandon, Elinor May McKinney
Montes, Leopoldo Feliciano
Montgomery, Gillespie V.
Montgomery, Jack Munford, Jr.
Montgomery, John Denny
Montgomery, Lucius Kennedy, Jr.
Montgomery, Paul Vaughan
Montgomery, Philip O'Bryan, Jr.
Montgomery, Robert Munger
Montgomery, Robert Place
Montgomery, Ronny Dee
Montgomery, Royce Lee
Montgomery, William Shearin
Montin, John Ernest
Monyek, Milton S.
Moody, Forrest Bankston, Jr.
Moody, John Peter
Moody, John William
Moody, Lamon Lamar, Jr.
Moody, Max Dale
Moody, Mildred Gean Storey
Moody, William Tell, III
Moody, Willis Elvis, Jr.
Mook, Barbara Heer Held
Mook, Conrad Payne
Moon, Bryden Earl
Moon, Harry Edward
Moon, John Henry, Sr.
Moon, Mary Lindon
Moon, Robert Allen, Jr.
Mooney, Joseph Francis, Jr.
Moore, Alexander Bishop
Moore, Alvin Edward
Moore, Andrew Taylor, Jr.
Moore, Bernice Milburn (Mrs. Harry E. Moore)
Moore, Bessie B.
Moore, Dalton, Jr.
Moore, Dennis Duane
Moore, Derek Gordon
Moore, Edward Clinton, Jr.
Moore, Forrest Weatherford
Moore, Glenn Edward
Moore, Glover
Moore, Howard Francis
Moore, Hugh Jacob, Jr.
Moore, Jack Michael
Moore, James Francis, II
Moore, James Kenneth, Sr.
Moore, James Norman
Moore, James Wallace
Moore, James Young
Moore, Jeff Robertson
Moore, John Norton
Moore, John Sterling, Jr.
Moore, Joseph Henry
Moore, Joseph Herbert
Moore, Kenneth Light
Moore, Lee Permenter
Moore, Lewis Edward, Jr.
Moore, Loren Irving
Moore, Lowell Nelson
Moore, Luther William
Moore, Marion Edward
Moore, Mary Jane
Moore, Morgan Jackson
Moore, Patrick Francis
Moore, Phyllis Clark
Moore, Prentis Monroe
Moore, Rayburn Sabatzky
Moore, Reid Francis, Jr.
Moore, Richard Delmon
Moore, Richter Hermann, Jr.
Moore, Robert Brent, Jr.
Moore, Robert Caleb
Moore, Robert Garvice
Moore, Robert Wayne
Moore, Roderick Bruce
Moore, Roy Sanders
Moore, Roy Walker
Moore, Shelley Wendell
Moore, Thomas Justin, Jr.
Moore, Vernon Lewis
Moore, W. Henson
Moore, William David
Moore, William Edwin
Moore, William Talman, Jr.
Moore, William Vincent
Moore, Woody Sturdivant (Mrs. John Calhoun Moore)
Moores, Russell Ray
Moorhead, Rolande Annette Reverdy
Moose, John Wadsworth
Morales, Adelina Bernadette
Morales, Anawilda
Morales-Carrion, Arturo
Moran, Angela Clare
Moran, Ann Elizabeth
Moran, Neil Clymer
Moran, Thomas Francis
Moran, Thomas Maurice
More, Berkeley Davis
More, Eduardo Angel
More, Philip Jerome
Morehead, Charles David
Moreland, Carl Donald
Moreland, James Alfred
Moreland, Ralph Rowntree
Morelli, Louis Vincent
Morelock, James Crutchfield
Moreno, Leopold Segismundo
Moreton, Robert Dulaney
Morford, Catherine Anne
Morgado, Sadie Dawn Cooper
Morgan, Albert Richard, Jr.
Morgan, Antonia Bell (Mrs. William J. Morgan)
Morgan, Cecil, Jr.
Morgan, Clayton Aquilla
Morgan, Douglas Gerald
Morgan, Edwin Buford
Morgan, Eileen Hacker
Morgan, Evan
Morgan, Finis
Morgan, George Robert
Morgan, George Terrell (Terry)
Morgan, Harcourt Alexander, Jr.
Morgan, Herman Wilton
Morgan, Hugh Jackson, Jr.
Morgan, Jack Cochran
Morgan, James Baker
Morgan, James Leland
Morgan, Joe Lee
Morgan, Julia Elizabeth
Morgan, Louise Gudger
Morgan, Marianne
Morgan, Mary Francisco
Morgan, Max G.
Morgan, Paul Nolan
Morgan, Robert Burren
Morgan, Robert Lewis
Morgan, Travis Eugene
Morgan, William James
Morgan, Wills Napier
Morgan, Yowell Spann
Morgenstern, Pauline Cecile
Morgenstern, Sheldon Jon
Morgret, Andrew Jacob
Mori, Jean Albert
Mori, Paul Albert
Morial, Ernest Nathan
Morin, Oram Joseph
Moring, Felix Cleveland
Moritz, Wallace Albert
Morkovsky, John Louis
Morland, Alvin Wesley
Morland, John Kenneth
Morland, Margaret Ward
Morland, Richard Boyd
Morlang, Barbara Louise Blauvelt
Morlang, Charles, Jr.
Morosani, George Warrington
Morphos, Diane Belogianis (Mrs. Panos Paul Morphos)
Morrell, Gene Paul
Morrell, Robert Fuller
Morrill, John Barstow
Morris, Albert Edward
Morris, Ben Rankin
Morris, Ben Tillman, Jr.
Morris, Carloss
Morris, Celita Lamar
Morris, Charles Robert
Morris, Donal Franklin
Morris, Earle Elias, Jr.
Morris, Evangeline Felicia (Becky)
Morris, Fred John
Morris, George Alan, III
Morris, James Allen
Morris, James Badgett
Morris, James Kenneth
Morris, Jane Emelia
Morris, Jed Lane
Morris, Jerry Wayne
Morris, Jesse Harry
Morris, John Bartholomew, IV
Morris, Joseph Wilson
Morris, Julius Willard
Morris, Kenneth Wayne
Morris, Kenneth Wayne
Morris, Laszlo Daniel, Jr.
Morris, Manford Donald
Morris, Martin Eugene
Morris, Marvin Leon
Morris, Owen Glenn
Morris, Robert Calder
Morris, Roger Dale
Morris, William Coke
Morris, William Marvin, Jr.
Morris, William Mitchell
Morrison, Alexander Norman
Morrison, Eston Odell
Morrison, Francis Secrest
Morrison, John Elliott
Morrison, Lonny Dee
Morrison, Lucile Young (Mrs. Merle John Morrison)
Morrison, Norman
Morrison, Richard Martin
Morrison, Robert Hall, Jr.
Morrison, Robert Haywood
Morrison, Thomas James
Morrison, Walton S.
Morrissette, Maurice Corlette
Morrow, Gordon Eugene
Morrow, Phillip Stanley
Morrow, Robert Prosser, Jr.
Morse, Eugenia Maude
Morse, F. D., Jr.
Morse, Frederick Whitton
Morse, Genevieve Forbes (Mrs. Frederick Tracy Morse)
Morse, Peter Hodges
Morse, Roberta Naomi
Morse, Yvonne Linsert
Morton, Charles Brinkley
Morton, James Harry
Morton, Norman Lee
Morton, Richard Albert Dunlap, Jr.
Morton, Ronald Grey
Morvant, Henry Ferdinand
Mosby, John Oliver
Moseley, Emory Franks
Moseley, James Francis
Moseley, Sherrard Thomas
Moseley, Vince
Moseley, Wilma Jeane
Moser, Carl Gilmore, Jr.
Moser, Paul Homer
Moser, Royce, Jr.
Mosher, Loren Cameron
Mosier, Benjamin
Mosier, David Willis, Jr.
Moskowitz, Maurice Lee
Moskowitz, Rita Joyce
Mosley, Billy Ray
Mosley, Ivan Sigmund, Jr.
Mosley, Mary Mac
Mosley, Mattie Jacks
Mosley, Azetta Jimmie
Moss, Charles Basil
Moss, David Arnold
Moss, Eliza Waller Easley
Moss, George Joseph, Jr.
Moss, Howard
Moss, James Mercer
Moss, James Rudolph
Moss, Rachel Scott Bybee
Moss, Theron Charles
Mosteller, Bette Vaughan
Motsinger, Stanley Dale
Mott, Charles Davis
Mott, Marvin Lee
Mouchahoir, George Ely
Moulton, Frank Ray, Jr.
Mount, Gary Arthur
Mountain, Clifton Fletcher
Moursund, Myles Patton
Moushegian, George
Mousourakis, Ioannis Nikolaos
Moustafa, Saad Eldin M.
Moutz, Joseph
Mowery, William Edward
Moxley, Thomas Irvin, Sr.
Moyer, Eugene Fredrick, Jr.
Moyer, Paul Kenneth
Moynahan, Bernard Thomas, Jr..
Muchow, Randall Eugene
Mudd, Alvin Carl
Mudd, John Philip
Mueller, Alfred Jerome
Mueller, August Edward
Mueller, Harold O.
Mueller, Mark Christopher
Mueller, Robert Louis
Mueller, Vernon John, Jr.
Mueller, William Fegley
Mues, Flavio Jorge
Muhlendorf, David Milton
Muir, Helen
Muir, John Anderson
Muirhead, Jean Denman
Muldoon, William Henry, III
Mulfinger, George Leonidas, Jr.
Mulkey, Sidney Wayne
Mullen, Andrew Judson
Mullen, David Edward
Mullen, John O'Keefe
Mullen, Sanford Allen
Muller, Charles Julius
Muller, Frank Mair, Jr.
Muller, Frederick Lawrence
Muller, Richard Louis
Mulliken, John Hallett, Jr.
Mullin, Frederick William
Mullinax, Otto B.
Mullineaux, Richard Denison
Mullins, Edward Wade, Jr.
Mullins, John Dwight
Mullins, William Browning
Mumford, Patrick Wayne
Muncie, Douglas Jennings
Munier, Ronald Alan
Munk, Miner Nelson
Munn, Richard Eugene
Munn, Seth William
Muno, Richard Carl
Munoz-Dones De Carrascal, Eloisa (Mrs. Jose Daniel Carrascal)
Munroe, Clark Cameron
Munson, Don Burnell
Murad, John Louis
Murbach, Earl Wesley
Murdock, Michael Charles
Murff, Clarence Yualpa, Jr.
Muroff, Lawrence Ross
Murphey, Milledge
Murphree, Dennis Eugene
Murphree, James Wallace
Murphree, Mary June
Murphy, Charles Franklin
Murphy, Charles Joseph
Murphy, Charles Willoughby
Murphy, Emma Grace
Murphy, Frederick Augustus
Murphy, Frederick Brunson
Murphy, Judson Boynton
Murphy, Mary Julia
Murphy, Meredith Kathleen
Murphy, Michael Purdon
Murphy, Nancy Redmond
Murphy, Ollie Ebert
Murphy, Patrick McDonald
Murphy, Raymond Joseph, Jr.
Murphy, Terry Alan
Murphy, Thomas Davidson, Jr.
Murrah, Paul Edward
Murray, Derrick Duane
Murray, Frank Stephen
Murray, George Edward
Murray, George Mosley
Murray, Grover Elmer
Murray, Joseph James, Jr.
Murray, June Margaret
Murray, Lane (Joyce Elaine Stone) (Mrs. Thomas Francis Murray)
Murray, Menton Joseph
Murray, Neville
Murray, Philip Allen
Murray, Richard George
Murray, Robert James
Murray, Vincent D'Arcy
Murray, William James, Jr.
Murray, Willis Lynn
Murrell, Gerald Boyd
Murrell, James Robert, III
Murrell, Leonard Richard
Murrey, Joseph Henning, Jr.
Murrill, Paul Whitfield
Murrow, Duncan Colquitt
Murrow, Wayne Lee
Murthy, Yelameli Satyanarayana
Murty, Korukonda Linga
Musa, Samuel Albert
Musgrave, Ray Sigler
Musgrave, Story
Mushung, Lance Joseph
Music, Marvin
Musselman, George Abraham
Musser, A. Wendell
Myerburg, Robert Jerome
Myers, Alonzo Harrison, Jr.
Myers, Bobby Louis
Myers, Carroll Bruce
Myers, Daniel Benton
Myers, Don Arden
Myers, Finley Bradshaw
Myers, Frederick Clarence
Myers, George Carl
Myers, George Emil
Myers, Ira Lee
Myers, James Clark
Myers, Lewis Albert
Myers, Lewis Horace
Myers, Marilyn
Myers, Melvil Bert
Myers, Warren Roy
Myers, Wilbur Jay
Myers, William Robert
Myers, Woodrow Horace
Myhre, Trygve Chatham
Mynett, Jack William
Myrberg, Arthur August, Jr.
Myrick, Charles Norman
Myrick, Fred Lee, Jr.
Nader, Jeanette Helen Balagia
Nagel, Fritz John
Naidorf, Carrol Philip
Nail, Zelma Elaine
Nakahara, Hiroo
Nakamura, Eugene Leroy
Nakarai, Toyozo Wada
Nall, James Otho
Namboodiri, Narayanan Krishnan
Nance, James Homer
Nance, Joe Pat
Nance, Joseph Turner
Nance, Margrette Zuleika Grubbs (Mrs. Joseph Turner Nance)
Nance, Murray Elmer
Nankervis, Byron John
Nankivell, James Benjamin
Napier, John Hawkins, III
Naranjo, Daniel Alberto
Narins, Charles Seymour
Nash, Henry Warren
Nash, James Loren
Nash, Jesse Sherard
Nash, Jonathon Michael
Nason, Doris Elnora
Natani, Kirmach
Natcher, William Huston
Natelson, Stephen Ellis
Nath, Sunil Baran
Nathan, Daniel Everett
Nathan, Ira Clifford
Nations, John Drewry
Nauls, Flora Dean Barrett
Navratil, Robert Norman
Naya, Daysi Hernandez
Naylor, Aubrey Willard
Naylor, Pleas Coleman, Jr.
Nazaretian, Angeline
Nazario, Luis Adam
Nazemi, Malek M.
Neal, Charles Edward
Neal, Frances Potter
Neal, George William
Neal, John Hill
Neal, Mary Julia
Neal, Maynard Conard
Neal, Phil Hudson, Jr.
Neal, Stephen Lybrook
Neal, William Harry, Jr.
Neal-Morris, Bobbie Sue
Nearburg, Eugene Everett
Neas, Dixon Valmore
Neas, John Theodore
Nebel, Larry Harman
Nebel, William Arthur
Nechay, Bohdan Roman
Needleman, Morriss Hamilton
Neeld, John Bruce, Jr.
Neely, Charles Lea, Jr.
Neely, J(ames) Winston
Neely, Robert Allen
Neely, Woodfin Carlisle
Neese, Urban Earl
Neff, Helen Margaret Osterholm
Neff, William, Jr.
Negron, Carmen Lillian
Nehls, Gerald Joseph
Neighbors, Ronald Joe
Neil, Hugh Gross
Neill, Rolfe
Neils, Philip John
Neilson, James Alexander, Jr.
Neiman, Norman
Nelius, Sigrid Johanna Von Renner (Mrs. Albert Arnold Nelius)
Neller, Arthur Augustus, Jr.
Nelson, Alfred Berthel
Nelson, Bernard Lee
Nelson, Bowen Creston
Nelson, Clotiel Riley
Nelson, Cornelius Edgar, Jr.
Nelson, Daniel Joel
Nelson, David Stephen
Nelson, Edward Sheffield
Nelson, George Agle
Nelson, Gerald Hiett
Nelson, H(oward) Roice, Jr.
Nelson, Harry Tracy
Nelson, Hazel Fowler (Mrs. Bowen Creston Nelson)
Nelson, Ivory Vance
Nelson, Jean Smith
Nelson, John Marvin, Jr.
Nelson, John Pettit
Nelson, Kenneth Eric
Nelson, Kenwyn Gordon
Nelson, Ralph Erwin
Nelson, Richard Stanley
Nelson, Roger Lucien Joseph
Nelson, Russell Gene
Nelson, Thomas Edward
Nelson, Virginia Lee (Mrs. Carl J. Nelson)
Nelson, (Sarah) Waudine
Nelson, William Alexander
Nemeth, Darlyne Gaynor
Nemitz, William Charles
Nemuth, Harold Isaac
Nentwig, Klaus Peter
Nepveux, Felix Joseph, IV
Nerness, John Lavon
Nesbett, Billy Curtis
Neter, John
Nethercut, William Robert
Nettles, John Barnwell
Nettles, Larry Thomas
Nettleton, Gary Stephen
Nettleton, Wilson Joseph, Jr.
Neu, Howard Mitchell
Neufeld, C(ornelius) H(erman) Harry
Neuhouser, David Jerome
Neuman, Susan Catherine
Neumann, Donald Lester
Neustadt, David Harold
Nevels, Mary Halford
Nevils, Bobby Gene
Nevin, James Edmonson, III
Nevruz, Albert Ahmet
New, William Neil
Newbern, Copeland Davis
Newberry, James Raymond
Newberry, Joseph Orion
Newby, Charles David
Newby, Hi Eastland
Newby, Jerry Bowers
Newcomb, Carolyn Jones (Mrs. Robinson Newcomb)
Newcomer, Hale Alden
Newcomer, Ronald Allen
Newell, James Thaxton
Newell, Warden John
Newell, William Thomas
Newfield, Mayer Ullman
Newman, Bill N.
Newman, Charles Forrest
Newman, Conrad L.
Newman, David
Newman, Emmett Wayne Jack
Newman, Fletcher Campbell
Newman, James Samuel
Newman, Rhoda Spruce
Newman, Thomas Henry
Newman, William Washington, Jr.
Newmark, Emanuel
Newmaster, Thomas Walter
Newsom, Bruce Cameron
Newsom, Douglas Ann Johnson (Mrs. L. Mack Newsom, Jr.)
Newsom, Erle Thornton, Jr.
Newsom, Mickey Brunson
Newsom, Robert Wesley
Newton, Robert Park, Jr.
Nexsen, Julian Jacobs
Ney, Robert Leo
Nguyen, NgocLinh
Niblock, William Robert
Nichol, William Weaver
Nicholas, Doyne Jack
Nicholas, James Ernest
Nicholas, Nickie Lee
Nicholls, Gerald Joseph
Nichols, Donald Eugene
Nichols, Duane Guy
Nichols, Edward Tyler
Nichols, Horace Elmo
Nichols, Irby Coghill, Jr.
Nichols, James Aubry, Jr.
Nichols, James Emery
Nichols, James Oliver
Nichols, James Otis
Nichols, James Richard
Nichols, Jeannettie Doornhein
Nichols, Marian Day
Nichols, Ronald Lee
Nichols, Sandra Jones
Nichols, Wanda Ruth
Nichols, Weeden Benjamin
Nichols, William (Bill)
Nichols, William Snowden, Jr.
Nicholson, Henry Hale, Jr.
Nicholson, James Herman, II
Nicholson, Luther Beal
Nicholson, Nellie Ruthrauff (Mrs. George A. Nicholson)
Nicholson, Patrick James
Nickell, Stephen Burgess
Nickey, Laurance Noyes
Nickle, Dennis Edwin
Nickols, John
Nickols, Marcia Anne
Nicks, Edgar Wilburn
Nicol, William Franklin
Nicolaides, Emmanuel Nicholas
Nieball, Mary Louise Roy
Niedergeses, James D.
Niemann, Henry Otto
Niemi, John Wallace
Nies, Robert John, Jr.
Nifong, Frank Miller
Nigaglioni, Olga Cruz Jimenez (Mrs. Jose E. Nigaglioni)
Nigh, Felix Leonard
Nigh, George Patterson
Nighbert, Edwin Joseph
Nikolic, Zivorad Jezdimir
Nilsson, Kent R.
Nims, Donald Read
Nine, Jerald Alexander

Nirschl, Robert Philip
Nisbet, John Byers, Jr.
Nissler, Christian William, III
Niswonger, Jeanne Du Chateau (Mrs. Joseph K. Niswonger)
Niven, Kurt Neubauer
Niven, Malcolm P.
Nix, Jack Phillip
Nix, Joseph Nelson, Jr.
Nixon, Arlie James
Nixon, Donald Merwin
Nixon, Frank Edwin
Nixon, Gwinn Huxley
Nobes, Charles Jay
Noble, Charles MacIntosh
Noble, Michael Dan
Noble, Milner
Nobra, Daniel Joseph
Nocke, Henry Herman
Noden, Patricia Ann
Noe, Randolph
Noel, Mark Gerard
Noell, Karl Thomas
Noer, (Harold) Rolf
Noetzel, Grover A(rchibald) J(oseph)
Nogle, Beatrice Carrick
Nolan, Edwin Joseph
Nolan, Maxcy Pearle, Jr.
Nolan, Raymond Paul
Nolen, Joseph Michael
Nolen, Linda Faye
Nolte, George W.
Nolte, William H(enry)
Noonan, James Rothwell
Norcross, Alvin Watt
Nordan, William Wayne
Nordlander, Robert Walter
Nordling, Karl Ingmar
Nordwall, Charles William Alexander
Noriega, Rudy Jorge
Norman, Albert George, Jr.
Norman, Joseph Stanton, II
Norman, Margie Irene
Norman, Summers A.
Norment, Jacquelin Boykin
Norris, Elwin Lamar
Norris, Flora Creech
Norris, Franklin Gray
Norris, John Lincoln
North, Arlan Charles, Jr.
North, Gary William
North, James Little
Northen, Charles Swift, III
Northrop, Granger Harold
Northrop, Monroe
Northup, John David, Jr.
Norton, Hugh Stanton
Norton, John Evan
Norton, Kenneth Edward
Norton, Mervin Lee
Norton, Robert Dean, Sr.
Norville, Richard Gerow
Norwine, Robert Jackson
Norwood, Malcolm Mark
Norwood, Samuel Wilkins, III
Norwood, Thomas Locke
Notess, Charles Boris
Novak, Albert John Wittmayer
Novak, Arthur Francis
Novell, Earl Kenyon
Novosad, Rudy James
Nowotny, George Edward, Jr.
Nugent, Donald York
Nugent, Roderick Mathew
Numajiri, Satoru Sam
Nunez-Portuondo, Ricardo
Nungesser, William Aicklen
Nunley, Leonard James
Nunn, Sam
Nunnallee, Ruth Burnette (Mrs. Milton T. Nunnallee)
Nunnelley, Edith Gates
Nunnery, Murry Edward
Nureyev, Jaimé Lee
Nutter, James Irving
Nutting, Norwood Vey
Nuwer, John Edward
Nyfeler, John Vernon
Oakes, Herbert Charles
Oakey, William Edgar
Oakland, Thomas David
Oakley, John F.
Oakley, Phillip Glenn
Oaks, Billy Wayne
Oaks Polk, Elizabeth Ann
Oates, Carl Everette
Oates, James Bart
Oates, Will Wilbur
O'Banion, John William
O'Bannon, Emily Belle Wood
Obenshain, Wiley Shackford, III
Oberhauser, Joseph Francis
Oberle, George Hurley
Oberman, Albert
Obermayer, Herman Joseph
Obert, Gene Madalene Saulsbury (Mrs. Paul M. Obert)
Obert, Paul Michael
O'Brien, Dallas Susan Jane
O'Brien, Edward John, III
O'Brien, James Joseph
O'Brien, James Mathew
O'Brien, James Michael
O'Brien, Thomas Borue
O'Brien, Thomas John, Sr.
O'Brien, Thomas Michael
O'Brien, William Conrad
Obrig, Elwood Mansfield
Obschernikat, Gerhard Wilhelm
O'Cain, Raymond Kenneth
Ochiai, Shinya
O'Connell, James Francis
O'Connor, Dorothy Baitsell
O'Connor, Edward Francis
O'Connor, Jean Smith (Mrs. Gerald Francis O'Connor)
O'Connor, John Christopher, Jr.
O'Connor, John James
O'Connor, Michael William
O'Connor, Robert Dorman
O'Connor, Robert Emmett
O'Connor, Trelyon Waldo, Jr.
O'Connor, William Edmund
O'Dea, Ann Sinclair
O'Dell, Charles Levendar
Odell, Joan Elizabeth
O'Dell, Michael David
O'Dell, Vernon Edwin
Oden, Earl Clarence
Oden, Kenneth
Oden, Waldo Talmage, Jr.
Odom, Thomas Winston
Odom, William Ross
O'Donnell, Michael Charles
O'Donnell, Michael Davis
O'Donoghue, Don Horatio
O'Dwyer, Thomas Aloysius
Oehlert, William Herbert, Jr.
Oehlschlager, Frederick Keith
O'Flarity, James Phillip
Ogan, Jerry Dee
Ogden, John Morris, Jr.
Ogdin, Carol Anne
Ogg, Wade Mason, III
Ogilvie, Douglas Sikes
Ogilvie, Margaret Pruett
Ogle, Richard Ferrell
Ogle, Wayne LeRoy
Oglesbee, Dwight Conlan
Oglesbee, Ronald Martin
Oglesby, Henry Rube, Jr.
O'Grady, Timothy Porter
O'Hara, James Donald Michael
O'Haren, James Francis
O'Hearn, William Wilson
Ohki, Kenneth
O'Kain, Doyle Carnell
O'Keefe, Michael Hanley
O'Kelley, James Thomas, Jr.
Oldfield, Jack Lowell
Oldham, Dorothy Cloudman (Mrs. Robert Price Oldham)
Oldham, Howard Townsend
Oldham, Walter Julian
Olds, Virginia Esther Newton (Mrs. Lloyd E. Olds)
O'Leary, William Colden, Jr.
Olejar, Paul Duncan
Oliver, Clifton, Jr.
Oliver, Donald Wilson
Oliver, Ernest Bingham
Oliver, Foster Finley
Oliver, John Percy, II
Oliver, John Phin
Oliver, Louis Cecil
Oliver, Mary Wilhelmina
Oliver, Priscilla Lowell Foote (Mrs. Keith Oliver)
Oliver, Roland Adron Grady
Oliver, Ronald Eugene
Oliver, Sidney William
Oliver-Padilla, Fernando Luis
Olkin, Alan Jay
Olkowski, Zbigniew Lech
Olmo, Jaime Alberto
Olsen, Carl Edwin
Olsen, Gary Kent
Olsen, Humphrey Adoniram
Olson, Edna Howard (Mrs. Lawrence Carroll Olson)
Olson, George Albert
Olson, Howard Edmund
Olson, John Victor
Olson, Richard Floyd
Olson, Roy Edwin
Olsson, Peter Alan
Olstowski, Franciszek
Oltman, Florine Alma
Oltman, John Harold
Omran, Abdel Rahim
Omura, George Adolf
Omura, Martha Emily Fowler
Oncken, William, Jr.
O'Neal, Charles Harold
O'Neal, Edgar Carl
O'Neal, John Milton, Jr.
O'Neal, Kirkman
O'Neal, Robert Palmer
O'Neall, Albert Ellis
O'Neil, Joseph Montry
O'Neill, Carolyn Christine
O'Neill, Paul John
Ong, Poen Sing
Onorato, Robert Cardinal
Onsager, Lars
Onstead, Charles O., Jr.
Oosterhuis, Herman Hendrik
Opfermann, Myron William
Oppenheim, Egon S.
Orders, William Hill
Organ, (Avis) Joyce Culpepper (Mrs. Raleigh Ralph Organ)
Orillion, Alfred Gregory
Orloff, David Ira
Orlowski, Henryk
Orman, William Tanner
Orme, David Ray
Ormes, Walter Mason, Jr.
Ornish, Edwin Paul
Ornish, Natalie Gene
O'Rourke, Franklyn Sewall
Orr, Douglas Milton, Jr.
Orr, Frank Howard, III
Orr, James Milton
Orr, Jimmy Don
Orr, William Claude
Orrison, Robert Garrett
Orson, Claire Marshall
Ortega, Eduardo
Ortega, Rodolfo
Orton, George Wandell
Orwig, Herbert Lees
Ory, Robert Louis
Osborn, George Coleman
Osborn, Glenn Richard
Osborn, Malcolm Everett
Osborn, Prime Francis, III
Osborne, Allen
Osborne, Charles Edward
Osborne, Gerald Edward
Osborne, Harry Albert, Jr.
Osborne, John Arthur
Osburn, John Duncan McMillan
Osburn, Joseph Karl, Jr.
Osgood, Frank William
O'Shea, Patricia Kirk
O'Shields, Jerry Wofford
Oshinsky, Judy Charla
Osias, Richard Allan
Ossi, Manier Benjamin
Osswald, Karl Hans
Osterhaus, Leo Benedict
Ostermiller, Ronald Daniel, Jr.
Ostroff, Aaron Joel
Ostwalt, Jay Harold
O'Sullivan, Peggy Virginia
Oswald, Betty Robinson (Mrs. Robert H. Oswald)
Oswald, Edward Odell
Oswalt, Charles Edward, III
Othersen, Henry Biemann, Jr.
Othmer, Murray Eade
Otis, John James
Otis, Larry Keith
Otte, Frederick Lewis
Ottinger, Richard Estes
Ottley, John King, Jr.
Otts, Lee MacMillan
Ouellette, Paul Ludwig
Ousley, Larry James
Ousley, W.H., Jr.
Ousterhout, Raymond Sherburn
Outlaw, Benjamin Clayton
Outlaw, Jennings Carol
Outten, Joseph Fendall
Overall, Maurice Allen
Overby, George Robert
Overby, Richard Henry
Overholt, Bergein Frederick
Overman, Frances Elizabeth Henson
Overstreet, James Carlisle
Overstreet, James Evan
Overstreet, William Harvey
Overton, Ben Frederick
Overton, Helen Parker (Mrs. Samuel Watkins Overton)
Overton, Kenneth
Overton, Stanley D.
Overton, William Ward, Jr.
Ovunc, Bulent Ahmet
Owen, Austin Everett, III
Owen, David
Owen, Duncan Shaw, Jr.
Owen, Gayle Blasius
Owen, George Trezevant, III
Owen, James Lee, Jr.
Owen, John Frederick
Owen, John Hinsey
Owen, Kenneth Dale
Owen, Louis Carroll
Owen, Nancy Lou
Owen, Robert Hubert
Owen, Wendell Frederick
Owens, Arthur Melbourne
Owens, Bobby Samuel
Owens, David Bruce
Owens, Etta Mae Harris (Mrs. George W. Owens)
Owens, Hilda Faye
Owens, Ivy May
Owens, Jean Wareham
Owens, Ralph Eugene
Owens, Ronald Avery
Owens, William Lionel
Owens, Wyatt Edgar
Owings, Addison Davis
Owings, Francis Preston
Owings, Thomas Gene
Owings, William Jennings Bryan
Owings, William Orange
Owsley, William Clinton, Jr.
Oxman, Herbert Arthur
Ozier, Terry Samuel
Pace, Carolina Jolliff (Mrs. John McIver Pace)
Pace, Charles Mills
Pace, Sigrid Gwynne Freeman
Pace, Will Dent
Pacenza, Franklin Joseph
Pacifici, James Grady
Packard, John Mallory
Packard, Marjean Phillips (Mrs. Charles A. Packard)
Packard, Robert G.
Packman, Paul Frederick
Paddock, Arnold David
Paddock, Austin Joseph
Paddock, Caroline
Padilla, Raul (Pat)
Padon, William Tunstall
Paetro, Sidney
Pafford, Ray Wilson
Pagan-Del Toro, Rafael
Page, Calvin Ames
Page, Cyril Dyke
Page, Larry Keith
Page, William Lacy
Page, Willis
Paige, Clara Ophelia
Paine, Thomas Lee
Painter, Floyd Eugene
Painter, William Calvin, Jr.
Pair, James Ottis
Paisan, Juan Jose
Pajon, Eduardo Rodriguez
Pakis, Viesturs Vitolds
Pallas, William Charles
Pallot, Richard Allen
Pallot, William Louis
Palm, John William
Palmer, Allan Van
Palmer, Charles Robert
Palmer, Don Carroll
Palmer, Edwinna Lopez Collins
Palmer, Erskine LeBron
Palmer, Henry George, Jr.
Palmer, Hubert Bernard
Palmer, Jack Sidney
Palmer, John David
Palmer, Lee
Palmer, Ralph Thomas
Palmer, Sidney J(ewell)
Palmer, Stanton Dean
Palmer, Stephen Donald
Palmer, William Fisher
Palmieri, Anthony Francis
Palmieri, Genaro Miguel Angel
Palmore, John Stanley, Jr.
Palmros, Eric Kelvin
Palms, John Michael
Pals, Clarence Herman
Pandey, Raghvendra Kumar
Pangilinan, Andres Gutierrez
Pangilinan, Rizal Valencia
Pangle, Curtis Glen
Pankey, George Atkinson
Pankey, George Edward
Pankey, George Stephen
Pankey, Wallace Edward
Pankratz, Howard John
Pannell, Clifton Wyndham
Pannier, Robert Andrew, Jr.
Pannill, Robert Stephens
Pantleo, Phillip Jack
Paolini, Gilberto
Papp, Attila G.
Pappas, Bobby Constantine
Paquette, Dean Richard
Parady, William Harold
Parang, Masood
Parbery, Betty Lou
Pard, Edmond Maurice
Parham, Guy Henry, Jr.
Parham, Robert Randall
Parham, Ruby Inez M. (Mrs. Jewell A. Parham)
Parham, William Harold
Paris, Charles Henry
Paris, Janet Fresch (Mrs. Maurice Thatcher Paris)
Paris, Joel Benjamin, III
Paris, William Andrew
Parish, Norman Ray
Parish, Sydney Simon
Parisi, William Edward
Park, Francis De Ronald
Park, Harry Ray
Park, Helen Elisabeth Gates (Mrs. F.D. Ronald Park)
Park, Helen Ruth
Park, Leland Madison
Parker, Alton Brooks, Jr.
Parker, Archie David, Jr.
Parker, B. B.
Parker, Carlos Dale
Parker, Charles Scott
Parker, Clyde H., Jr.
Parker, Clyde J.
Parker, Daniel Franklin
Parker, Frederick Michael
Parker, George Marion
Parker, Gilbert Norman
Parker, Harold Talbot
Parker, Harry Lee
Parker, Harry S., III
Parker, Israel Frank
Parker, Jack DuPree
Parker, James Lee Fitzgerald
Parker, Jenks Cromwell
Parker, John Malcolm
Parker, Josephus Derward
Parker, Margaret Mebane (Mrs. Carl P. Parker)
Parker, Mary Ann Gardner (Mrs. Milton Lawrence Parker)
Parker, Mary Esther
Parker, Morris Buford
Parker, Phyllis Hepburn
Parker, Raphael Denson
Parker, Robert Allan Ridley
Parker, Robin Merrill
Parker, Samuel Davis
Parker, Sidney Arch
Parker, Sidney Glenn
Parker, Virginia Anne
Parker, Wallace O'Neil
Parker, Walter Raleigh, Jr.
Parker, William Dale
Parkey, William Robert
Parkman, James N., Jr.
Parks, David Hall
Parks, Jackelee Anthonise
Parks, Lloyd Lee
Parks, Preston Melton, Jr.
Parks, Robert Hall
Parks, Sam Laws
Parks, Suzanne Lowry (Mrs. Phillip Haddon Parks)
Parks, William Robert
Parl, Eike Ludwig
Parlin, David Baker
Parmar, Jaywant Philip
Parmley, Loren Francis, Jr.
Parnell, David Russell
Parnell, Sara Mae
Parr, Frank Robert
Parramore, Joseph Vernon, Jr.
Parrish, Buford Brian
Parrish, Edward
Parrish, Frank Jennings
Parrish, Henry Howard, Jr.
Parrish, Henry Mack
Parrish, James Richard
Parrish, John Astor, Jr.
Parrish, Robert Alton
Parrish, William Charles
Parrott, Barbara Marie
Parrott, Lawrence Huitt
Parsley, Brantley Hamilton
Parsons, David Harold
Parsons, Edwin Davis
Parsons, Joe Max
Parsons, Preston Duane
Parsons, Tarlton Fleming, II
Parsons, W. Dale
Parsons, Ward Chester
Partain, Robert Thomas
Partin, George Ray
Partington, John Edwin
Partridge, Lloyd Donald
Partridge, Mary
Pascal, D. Matteson
Paschal, Lloyd Etheridge, Jr.
Pasewark, William Robert
Paskusz, Gerhard Frederick
Pastrick, Harold Lee
Pate, John Foster
Pate, Johnny Ray
Pate, Margery
Pate, Wallace Fennell
Pate, William Wilson
Patel, Amrut Ranchhodji
Patil, Milind
Patillo, Leonard Sylvesta
Patmon, Ruby Irene
Paton, David
Paton, Donald Munro
Patrick, Frances Sue
Patrick, James Donald
Patrick, Mary Erline England
Patrinely, Christopher Dean
Patten, Worcester Allen Bryan
Patten, Zeboim Cartter
Patten, Zeboim Cartter, III
Patterson, Andy James
Patterson, Bennett Burr
Patterson, Betty
Patterson, Bob, Jr.
Patterson, Charles Darold
Patterson, David Benjamin
Patterson, David Heath
Patterson, Earl Edgar
Patterson, Harry Dale
Patterson, James Nelson
Patterson, Lon Monroe
Patterson, Margaret Kathryn
Patterson, Neville
Patterson, Rickey Lee
Patterson, Robert
Patterson, Solon Pete
Patterson, Virginia Goodwin
Patterson, Warren Richardson
Patterson, William H.
Patterson, William Junior
Patteson, Alan Guy, Jr.
Patteson, Joseph Drury, Jr.
Patton, Almeda Jane Vandike
Patton, Lewis Kay (L.K.)
Patton, Michael Lee
Patton, Roger Dale
Paul, Grace
Paul, Gwendolyn Hope (Mrs. James Edward Paul)
Paul, Joseph McKinsey
Paul, Lynn Edwin
Paul, Robert
Paul, Waters Coleman
Paulcheck, Edward Charles
Paulin, Philip Edwin
Paulk, John Robert
Paulson, Darryl
Paulson, Oscar Lawrence, Jr.
Pawel, Richard E.
Pawluk, John, Jr.
Paxton, Fay Murray
Paxton, Tomas Adolph
Payatakes, Alkiviades Charidemos
Payne, C(alvin) Lee, Jr.
Payne, Charles Albert
Payne, David Lebarron
Payne, Gloria Marquette
Payne, Mary Libby Bickerstaff (Mrs. Bobby Ray Payne)
Payne, Robert Lamar
Payne, Tracy Thomas
Payne, Viron Ernest, Sr.
Payne, William Haydon
Payne, William Marcus
Paysinger, Benjamin Daniel
Paz, Ricardo
Peace, Frederick Elwynn
Peace, William Kittrell
Peachee, Charles Andrew, Jr.
Peacher, William Gerald
Peachey, Ruth (Mrs. Rod G. Happel)
Peacock, J(ohn) Talmer
Peacock, William Luther, Jr.
Peacock, William Stanley
Peak, T. Ellis, Jr.
Peaker, Weldon Kendrick
Pearce, Charles Wellington
Pearce, Dorothy Andree De Lorenzo
Pearce, Harlee Josie, Jr.
Pearce, Mary McCallum (M. Clarence A. Pearce)
Pearce, Sylvia Williams
Pearce, Willis Scott
Pearl, Maurice Allen
Pearson, Albin Otis
Pearson, Betsy DeCelle (Mrs. Welton Dennis Pearson)
Pearson, D. Pate
Pearson, Daniel S.
Pearson, Elbert Lee
Pearson, Grosvenor Benjamin
Pearson, Jim Berry
Pearson, Judith Elizabeth
Pearson, Susan Winifred
Pearson, Welton Dennis
Peavy, Wheeler
Pechacek, Raymond Edward
Peck, Dianne Kawecki
Peckham, John Cecil
Peckham, Morse
Peddada, Anandarao Venkata
Peddicord, Orene Whitcomb
Peden, Ralph Kenneth
Peden, Robert F., Jr.
Pedersen, Knud Borge
Pedrick, Allen Reid
Peebles, Emory Bush, Jr.
Peeler, Ray Doss, Jr.
Peeples, Jerry Wayne
Peer, Gary Gail
Peery, William Robert
Peevy, Evelyn Sears
Pegg, Phillip Oliver
Peirce, Robert Vincent
Peithman, Russell Irvin
Pelezo, Chris Alford
Peltz, Ferde
Pence, Ludlow Mays
Pence, Samuel Allen, Jr.
Penczner, Paul Joseph
Pendell, Lucille Hunt
Pender, Pollard Eugene
Pendergast, John Griffin, Jr.
Pendergast, Richard Joseph
Pendergraph, Garland Edward
Pendergrass, Haywood Melvin
Pendleton, Alfred Moore
Pendleton, Charles Sumner
Pendleton, Roger Lee
Pendleton, William Harry
Peng, George Tso-Chih
Peng, Tai-Chan
Penington, Ralph Alden
Penn, Hugh Franklin
Penn, Thomas Waddill
Pennington, Brooks
Pennington, Edward Newton
Pennington, Raymond Benjamin
Pennington, Robert Taylor
Pennington, William L.
Pennington, William Rhom
Penny, James Nelson
Penrod, James Charles
Pentecost, Mark Pierson, Jr.
Peppard, Felix Prunty
Peppenhorst, William Gerald
Pepper, Calvin Errol
Pepper, Claude Denson
Pepper, Jack Wilson
Percival, Robert Ray
Perdue, Clyde Holland
Perdue, David Clifton
Perdue, George Pierce
Perdue, Nathaniel William
Perea, Benito
Perez, Eduardo
Perez, Gaylin Norris
Perez, Jose Antonio
Perez, Manuel G., Jr.
Perez, Manuel Robert
Perez, Virginia Mayers (Mrs. Mario J. Perez)
Perez-Anzalota, Jose Rafael
Perez-Comas, Adolfo
Perez-Enriquez, Juan Antonio
Perez Pimentel, Pedro
Perkel, Robert Simon
Perkins, Carl D.
Perkins, James Francis
Perkins, Joe Allen
Perkins, Kenneth Warren
Perkins, Margaret Nelson Kaye (Mrs. William Robertson Perkins, Jr.)
Perkins, Marion Louise
Perkins, Percy Harold, Jr.
Perkins, Richard Burle
Perkins, Robert Eugene
Perl, Arnold Edwin
Perl, Charles G.
Perley, J. Dwight
Perlmutter, Leonard Leon
Perritt, Henry Hardy
Perritt, R. T.
Perry, Aubrey MacDonnell
Perry, Donald Edward
Perry, Elmer Little, Jr.
Perry, George William
Perry, Harold Treston
Perry, Iris Jean
Perry, Jesse Laurence, Jr.
Perry, John Elliott
Perry, Louis Warren
Perry, Marcella Ellen Donovan
Perry, Paul Michael
Perry, Reginald Carman
Perry, Robert E.
Perry, Roger Gwinn
Perry, Ronald Howard
Perry, Russell H.
Perry, Samuel Lloyd
Perry, Shirley Bird
Perry, Thomas Amherst
Perry, Vincent

Perryman, Ray Worth
Person, Donald Ames
Person, Willard Dale
Persons, Jo Robert
Persons, Oscar Newton
Pestana, Carlos
Petcoff, Thomas Samuel
Peter, Lily
Peters, Beldon Alfred
Peters, Calvin Ronald
Peters, Charles William
Peters, George Stanley
Peters, George Thomas
Peters, Henry Buckland
Peters, Ted Hopkins
Peters, Thomas George
Peters, Vivian Janet
Peterson, Alvin Otis
Peterson, Carter Calhoun
Peterson, Charles Carter
Peterson, David Bruce
Peterson, David Clarence
Peterson, Edward Adrian
Peterson, Francis Dale
Peterson, Gary Winston
Peterson, Glen Erwin
Peterson, James Chandler
Peterson, James Neal
Peterson, James Robert
Peterson, John Edgar, Jr.
Peterson, John Ernest, Jr.
Peterson, Newton Curtis, Jr.
Peterson, Ralph Raymond
Peterson, Robert Andrew
Peterson, Shailer
Petitfils, Robert John, Jr.
Petkoff, George Samuel
Petruzzi, Daniel James
Petry, John Wright
Pettersen, Robert Winton
Pettit, Arch Paull
Pettit, Darwin Kirk
Pettus, Willie Clinton
Petty, Arthur Vernon, Jr.
Petty, Charles Sutherland
Petty, Etalcah Crockett
Petty, Olive Scott
Pettyjohn, Charles Stephens
Peurifoy, Paul Garland
Pew, John Glenn
Pfaff, George Charles, Jr.
Pfaff, William Wallace
Pfarrer, David Michael
Pfost, William Louis, Jr.
Pfouts, Ralph William
Pham, Hue Thi
Pharis, Ruth McCalister
Pharr, Herbert Lee, Jr.
Phelps, Ashton
Phelps, Edwin Harris
Phelps, William Ray
Phemister, Roy Dudley
Philbeck, Norris Richard
Philemon, Roy William, Jr.
Philen, Otis Donald, Jr.
Philips, Wallace Merritt, Jr.
Philippi, Frank Marion, Jr.
Phillips, A(ndrew) Craig
Phillips, Anthony J.
Phillips, Cecil Randolph, Jr.
Phillips, George Ernst
Phillips, Glyn Ronald
Phillips, Harry
Phillips, Howard Wendell
Phillips, J. Coulson
Phillips, James Dinton
Phillips, James Elbert
Phillips, Jean M. Mahony (Mrs. Payton Gray Phillips)
Phillips, Joel Patrick, Jr.
Phillips, Lindsay Flynt
Phillips, Loretta Smith
Phillips, Lu Ouida Vinson
Phillips, Lyle Rhine
Phillips, Margarita Gomez
Phillips, Myrna Greenberg
Phillips, Oail Andrew (Bum)
Phillips, Raymond Foy
Phillips, Raymond McDonald
Phillips, Ronald David
Phillips, Samuel Young
Phillips, Silas Bent, Jr.
Phillips, Stephen Franklin
Phillips, Vivian Branch (Mrs. James William Phillips)
Phillips, Walter Ray
Phillips, William Henry
Phillips, William Preston
Phillips, William Thomas
Phillips, Willis Paul
Philpott, Albert Lee
Phipps, Benjamin Kimball, II
Phlegar, Carl Leslie, Jr.
Piccione, Joseph James
Pickard, John Benedict
Pickel, Conrad Lawrenz
Pickell, Charles Norman
Pickens, James Cain
Pickens, William Edward
Pickett, George Bibb, Jr.
Pickett, John Edward Phillip
Pickett, Joseph C.
Pickett, Owen Bradford
Pickle, J. J.
Pickrell, Thomas Richard
Pico-Santiago, Guillermo
Pieper, C. Howard
Pieper, Samuel John Louis, Jr.
Pierce, Cleveland Carroll
Pierce, Clifford Davis, Jr.
Pierce, Donald Fay
Pierce, Ella Janet
Pierce, Gerald Swetnam
Pierce, Harry Brooke
Pierce, Katherine Virginia
Pierce, Kenneth Ray
Pierce, Lee Compton
Pierce, Robert Carl
Pierce, Robert Nash
Pierce, Sharon Elizabeth
Pierce, Thomas Floyd
Pierce, Walter Eldridge, Jr.
Pierce, William Lane
Pierre, Dallas
Pierson, Jimmie Olin
Pigg, (Mary) Evelyn Hoey
Pike, Jesse Miller
Piker, Eve Sanders (Mrs. Herbert M. Piker)
Pilarcik, Andrew John, Jr.
Pilcher, James Brownie
Pilcher, Joe Thomas, Jr.
Pilkey, Orrin H.
Pillar, Harold A.
Pimm, Gordon Herbert
Pinckney, Francis Morris
Pinckney, Lawrence Reid
Pincus, George
Pines, Jack
Pinion, Herman Price
Pinion, Richard Lewis
Pinkney, Charles Coatsworth
Pinkstaff, Richard Eugene
Pinkston, John William, Jr.
Pinnell, Samuel Williams
Pino, Frank, Jr.
Pinson, Anna Dotson (Mrs. Blake Pinson)
Pinson, James Radford
Pinson, Juddie Joseph, Jr.
Pinto, Albert P.
Piper, Henry Burton
Pippen, Joseph Franklin
Pippin, James Lee
Pippin, Warren Floyd
Pirkle, David Eugene
Pirkle, John Eugene
Pirone, Thomas Pascal
Pirtle, George William
Pirtle, Ivyl Leora Fleming (Mrs. J. Max Pirtle)
Pishel, Robert Gordon, Jr.
Pishkin, Vladimir
Pistor, Charles Herman
Pitchford, Armin Cloyst
Pitchford, Harriet Day
Pitchford, Henry Grady, Jr.
Pitman, Naomi Kime (Mrs. Theron Pitman)
Pitt, Woodrow Wilson, Jr.
Pittenridge, Lyndell Ray
Pittman, Chalmers Van Anglen
Pittman, James Allen, Jr.
Pittman, Joe Caston
Pittman, Sidney Earl
Pittman, Virgil
Pittman, Virgil Lee, Jr.
Pitts, Lloyd Frank
Pitzner, A(lwin) Frederick
Pixley, John Sherman
Plaisted, Harris Merrill, III
Plamondon, William Nelson, Jr.
Plank, Lawrence Allen
Plant, James William
Platoni, Katherine Theresa
Platter, Allen Andrew
Platts, Francis Holbrook
Plauché, Ferdinand Foch
Plaxco, James Clarke
Plaxco, William Beatty
Player, James Edward, Jr.
Player, Lonnie McGowen
Pleasant, Gilbert Kavanaugh
Pleva, Joseph Michael
Plitt, Jeanne Given
Plocek, Jeremiah Joseph
Plotnick, Barry Reyman
Plott, Adah Elizabeth
Plott, Frederick Henry, Jr.
Plummer, A. Q.
Plummer, Addison Wrenn
Plummer, Alan Lane
Plummer, Jack Moore
Plunk, Joel Allen
Plunkett, Roy Joseph
Plyler, Bob Lee
Plyler, Cranford Oliver, Jr.
Po, Giog Sing Tan
Poag, George Daniel, Jr.
Poage, Herman Clifton, Jr.
Poage, William Robert
Poarch, John Thomas, II
Poblete, Jose Ferrer
Pochmann, Ruth Fouts (Mrs. Henry Pochmann)
Podgorny, George
Podolsky, Samuel
Poe, John Curtis
Pofahl, C.F. (Sandy)
Poff, William Beverly
Poffenbarger, Phillip Lynn
Pogue, Forrest Carlisle
Pohler, Carl Herbert
Poiley, Jeffrey Edward
Polahar, Andrew Francis
Polan, Nancy Moore
Polanco, Jose Emilio
Polansky, Louis Joe
Poling, William Obed
Polizzi, Nicholas Gerald
Polk, John David
Pollak, Edward
Pollard, Mary Kilian
Pollard, Nina Tyler
Pollard, Overton Price
Pollnow, James Lester
Pollock, John Church
Pollock, Johnny
Pollock, Ray Jean
Pollock, William John, Jr.
Pommier, Luis Walter
Pond, Harry Searing
Pond, Margaret (Peggy) Mace Pinner
Ponder, Leonard Harold
Ponsell, Luther Gilbert, Jr.
Pool, Joyce Manning Sigrest
Pool, Marilyn Myers
Poole, Pierre Patillo
Poole, Richard William
Poole, Thomas Carl, Jr.
Poor, Richard Longstreet
Poore, Kenneth Wayne
Poore, Michael Wayne
Pope, Andrew Jackson (Jack), Jr.
Pope, Frank Starr, Jr.
Pope, Fred Wallace, Jr.
Pope, Kenneth Elvin
Pope, Manley Adrian
Pope, Thomas Harrington
Pope, William Lee
Pope, William Robert
Popejoy, Lee Tarence, II
Popovich, Paul John
Poquette, Harold Francis
Porter, Allen Dale
Porter, Aubrey L.
Porter, Curtis Hunter
Porter, Fay Rogers
Porter, Garland Burns
Porter, Richard Charles, Jr.
Porter, Thaddeus Coy
Porter, Ulwin Donald
Porter, William Howard, Jr.
Porterfield, Alson Gerald
Portes, Alejandro
Portman, Barnard Martin
Portnoy, William Manos
Portway, Patrick Stephen
Portz, Alex Thomas
Posey, Kenneth Clayton, Sr.
Posey, William Thomas
Posey, William Thomas
Post, Allen
Post, Elizabeth Deldee
Post, Lewis Irving
Postell, William Dosite
Poteat, William Hardman
Poteet, James Louis
Potenza, Daisy McKaskle (Mrs. Julius Orian Potenza)
Potnis, Krishnarao Shrinivas
Potter, Andrew Elwin
Potter, Barbara Ann
Potter, Dorothy Williams
Potter, John Michael
Potter, Nancy Dutton
Potter, Robert Ellis
Pottinger, Dann Kirkconnell
Potts, Joseph Christian
Potts, Nancy Needham
Pou, Emily Hotchkiss Quinn
Pou, John William
Pound, Winsdon Norwood Montresseur
Pounds, Billy Dean
Pounds, Haskin Richard
Powell, Anice Carpenter (Mrs. Robert Wainwright Powell)
Powell, Betty Joyce
Powell, Boone, Jr.
Powell, Cecil Lurle, Jr.
Powell, Daniel Augustus, Jr.
Powell, Donald Ashmore
Powell, Elizabeth Balas (Mrs. Norborne Berkeley Powell)
Powell, Elmer Corbin, Jr.
Powell, Eppie Charles
Powell, George Keck
Powell, James Bobbitt
Powell, John Gilbert
Powell, John Little
Powell, John Rolfe
Powell, John Stuart
Powell, Leslie Charles, Jr.
Powell, Lewis William
Powell, Lotie Pierce
Powell, Mary Louise Wells
Powell, Norborne Berkeley
Powell, Orrin Bert, Jr.
Powell, Ramon Jesse
Powell, Roland Ladson
Powell, Roy James
Powell, Thomas Edward, Jr.
Powell, Virginia Ford
Powell, Wilbur Kindred, Jr.
Powell, William Roland
Power, John Frazier
Power, Walter Robert, Jr.
Powers, Christopher Joseph
Powers, Darden
Powers, Georgia M.
Powers, John Dale
Powers, L. B.
Poyner, Winifred Ann
Poynor, Kenneth J.
Poynter, Nelson
Pradier, Janice Marie
Pradier, Jerome Martin
Prado, Daniel Herrera
Prado, Horacio Arturo
Prassel, Allen William
Prater, Jesse Wallace
Prats, Manuel L.
Pratt, Edward Taylor, Jr.
Pratt, Jack Blackmore
Pratt, Kermit George
Pratt, Mattie Washington
Pratt, William DeVaughn
Praytor, Hugh Bazelleel, Jr.
Prejean, Joe David
Prejean, Oran Vincent
Preller, John George
Premack, Irwin Joseph
Presbitero, Julia Villanueva
Prescott, Ethelind Southerland
Presley, W. Dewey
Pressler, Herman Paul, III
Preston, John Ronald
Preston, Loyce Elaine
Preston, Will Manier
Pretzer, Dwayne Lewis
Prevatt, Rubert Waldemar
Preyer, L. Richardson
Preyer, Mamie Howard
Price, C. Jack
Price, Charles Ernest
Price, David Lee
Price, Edgar Hilleary, Jr.
Price, George Raymond, Jr.
Price, Homer Cleon
Price, James
Price, John Pressley
Price, John Royce
Price, John Russell
Price, Joseph Victor, Jr.
Price, Larry Eugene
Price, Mark Eldredge
Price, Orville Oliver
Price, Robert Carmel
Price, Robert Carroll
Price, Robert Eben
Price, William Dow, Jr.
Price, William Edward
Prichard, John Franklin
Prichard, Thora Inez
Priddy, Ashley Horne
Pridmore, Cheryl Anne
Priebe, Louis Victor
Prigmore, Charles Samuel
Prince, Betty
Prince, Julian Day
Prince, Paul Edmond
Pringle, Richard Lewis
Prior, William Allen
Privett, Rex
Procter, Phyllis Wiegand
Proctor, Frank Dana
Proctor, Jesse Virgil
Proctor, John Howard
Proctor, Melvin P(orch)
Proctor, Samuel
Proctor, Walter Thomas
Proctor, William Con, Jr.
Prohaska, Theodore, II
Prophater, Helen Amisson
Pross, Lester Fred
Prosser, Moorman Paul
Prothro, George William
Proudfoot, Warren Harding
Pruett, Haskell
Pruett, Jefferson William, Jr.
Prujansky, Nathan
Pryor, David H.
Pryor, Shepherd Green, III
Psaras, John Dimocritos
Psihas, George Peter
Ptacek, Maxine Green
Ptaszkowski, Stanley Edward, Jr.
Puckett, George Lewis
Puckett, Ruby Parker
Puckett, Wiley Columbus
Pugh, Julian Franklin
Pujadas, Guillermo Manuel
Pullen, Harold Bailey
Pullen, Thomas Marion
Pulliam, Walter Tillman
Puls, Wayne Elvin
Purcell, Joe Edward
Purcell, Shirley Ann Teague
Purcell, Walter Lambuth
Purdie, Douglas Haig
Purdy, Harold John
Purkey, Roger Franklin
Purks, William Kendrick
Purvis, Edna O'Shields (Mrs. John William Purvis)
Purvis, John Taylor
Puryear, Elmer Lee
Putchat, Nathan
Puterbaugh, Billy Abraham
Putman, William Benjamin, III
Putnam, Howard William, Jr.
Putnam, Lawrence Elwood
Putnam, Richard Roach
Putnam, Victor Montelle, Jr.
Putnam, William Thomas
Putney, Charles Walker
Putney, Robert Bradford
Puzar, Vincent Dominic
Pye, Perry Glenn
Pyle, Harry Earnest
Pyle, Joe Neil
Pyle, K. Richard
Pyle, Richard Alden
Pyles, Steve
Pylypyszyn, Peter Paul
Qadir, Syed Muhammad Abdul
Quach, Ahn
Qualls, Charles Robert
Qualls, Marshall David
Qualls, William Houston
Quan, Alice Browne
Quarles, Charles C.
Quarles, Frederick Hundley, III
Quattlebaum, Dorothy Evelyn Clewis (Mrs. Walter Emmett Quattlebaum, Jr.)
Quattlebaum, Walter Emmett, Jr.
Quest, Arthur Eugene, Jr.
Quetel, Thomas Anthony
Quick, William James
Quigley, James Edward
Quillen, Howard Eugene
Quillen, James H(enry)
Quillian, Warren Wilson, II
Quimby, Myron Jay
Quimby, Wallace Philip
Quinn, James Wade, Jr.
Quinn, John R.
Quiñones, Jose Antonio, Jr.
Quinones-Armstrong, Rafael Antonio
Quintana, Ronald Preston
Quisenberry, John Henry
Quist, Arvin Sigvard
Raab, Spencer Oliver
Raba, Carl Franz, Jr.
Rabito, Jack Paul
Rabourn, Warren Joseph, Jr.
Raby, Robert (Bob) Earl
Rachford, Henry Herbert, Jr.
Rachmel, Leo
Radcliff, Alan Lawrence
Rader, James Edward
Rader, Lloyd Edwin
Radford, Loren Eugene
Radigan, Charles McDonnell
Radomski, Jack London
Radvanyi, Janos
Rady, Joseph James
Radzewicz, Ethel Cole
Radzewicz, Paul Anthony
Ragan, Elizabeth Hoffman (Mrs. Herbert Tomlinson Ragan)
Ragsdale, Zane Oakley
Rahall, Nick Joe, II
Rahenkamp, Robert Arthur
Rahmings, Doris Plummer
Raiford, Daniel Burnley
Raiford, Ernest Lee
Raiford, Robert Alden
Railsback, Bernice Hickman (Mrs. James Ernest Railsback)
Railsback, Luther James
Rainach, William Monroe
Rainbow, Edward Louis
Raines, Edward E.
Rainey, Dennis Rodgers
Rainey, Johnnie Mae
Rainey, Lutrelle Delano
Rainosek, Jackalyn
Rains, L. Craig
Rains, M. Albert
Rains, Thomas Nelson
Raisig, Arthur George
Rait, Robert Alexander
Rake, Virginia Joan
Rakentine, Lloyd William
Rakestraw, Bryan LaVern
Raley, James Jefferson, III
Raley, John Wesley, Jr.
Rall, Lloyd Louis
Ralls, Rawleigh Hazen
Ralston, Carl Conrad
Ramage, Raymond Crawford
Ramakrishnan, Ramaswami
Ramgopal, Vadakepat
Ramirez, Jose Ramon
Ramirez, Jossie
Ramirez, Manuel Jose
Ramirez, Miriam Jean
Ramirez, Nicolas, Jr.
Ramirez, Rafael Roberto
Ramirez, Renato F.
Ramirez, Salvador Manuel
Ramirez, Samuel Amador
Ramirez-Rivera, José
Ramirez-Ronda, Carlos Hector
Ramon, Adolph Ignacio
Ramos-Ferreri, Luis Rafael
Rampp, Donald Louis
Rampton, Francis Robert
Rampy, Rita Aliece
Ramquist, Raymond Carl
Ramsel, Douglas Alexander
Ramsey, Donna Rae
Ramsey, Gayle Edward
Ramsey, Ira Clayton
Ramsey, James Preston
Ramsey, Ralph Heyward, Jr.
Ramsey, Robert Russell, Jr.
Ramsey, Sally Ann Seitz
Ramsey, Willard Alvis
Randall, Howard Morgan, Jr.
Randall, William Madison
Randolph, Ann Joyner
Randolph, James Bolton
Randolph, James Harrison, Sr.
Randolph, Jennings
Randolph, Robert Manice
Randolph, Robert Ray, Jr.
Raney, Paul Frank
Raney, Richard Beverly
Rangel, Carlos Enrique
Rangel Medina, David
Rangra, Avinash Kumar
Ranken, Howard Benedict
Rankin, Henry Hollis, Jr.
Ransburg, Frank Scheller
Ranson, Kerwin Ralph, II
Ransone, Coleman Bernard, Jr.
Rao, Srinivasa Vasudeva
Rapp, Lawrence Paul
Rappaport, Harold
Rappaport, Martin Paul
Rappaport, Yvonne Kindinger
Rapperport, Alan Sherwin
Rapstine, Frank
Rasberry, W(illiam) C(linton)
Rasbury, Avery Guinn
Raschke, Richard Reinhold
Rase, Howard Frederick
Rash, Lloyd Monroe
Rashid, Richard Charles
Raskin, Jeffrey Barry
Rasmussen, Gorman Leonard
Raspet, Thomas Michael
Rassel, Greta Lorelei
Rassman, Emil Charles
Ratchford, Clyde Banks, Jr.
Ratcliff, Appleton Bonds, Jr.
Ratcliff, Raymond Franklin
Rathle, Pierre
Rathore, Ranveer Singh
Ratliff, Barton Wade
Ratliff, Byron Allen
Ratliff, Curtis Lee
Ratliff, John Walter
Rattan, Garland Ward
Rauch, Jeanne Girard (Mrs. Marshall Arthur Rauch)
Rauch, Marshall Arthur
Raulerson, John Derieux, Jr.
Rault, Joseph Matthew, Jr.
Ravenet, Louis
Ravoira, James
Rawitscher, Jack Joseph
Rawl, Alfred Erastus, Jr.
Rawl, Jasper Franklin, Jr.
Rawlins, George Skevington
Rawls, Carolina Demontigne
Rawls, J. Lewis, Jr.
Rawls, Walter Cecil, Jr.
Rawson, John Elton
Ray, Charles Tolman
Ray, Claude Casey
Ray, Dorothy Haroleen Davis
Ray, Edward Hunt
Ray, George Washington, III
Ray, Gerald Leroy
Ray, H(osea) M(anfred)
Ray, Hugh Edward
Ray, Jack Leroy
Ray, John M.
Ray, Rathburn Applegate
Rayburn, James Robert
Rayburn, Wendell Gilbert
Rayes, James George
Raymaker, Rudolph Louis
Raymond, John Edward, III
Raymond, Wynn Russell
Rayne, Emmy Schnettler
Raynor, Leighton Alfred, Jr.
Rea, John Edward, Jr.
Rea, John William
Read, Donald Lloyd
Read, Robert Allen
Ready, Mollie Armstrong
Ready, Robert Knowles
Reagan, Creed Harrison, Jr.
Reames, James Mitchell
Reamey, Herbert Kirkland, Jr.
Reams, Gerald Brock
Reardon, Martha Booth (Mrs. Paul Michael Reardon)
Reaser, Joel Monroe
Reasonover, William Sumter
Rebolledo, Jose Rafael
Recio, Francisco Hernandez
Reckless, John Brian
Records, John Williams
Rector, Norman Kenneth
Rector, Robert Lee
Rector, William Lee
Reddick, Thomas Leonard
Reddick, W(alker) Homer
Redding, Paschal Edmond, Jr.
Redford, Edward Logan
Redman, James Luther
Redmond, John Durham
Redwanz, James Otto
Reece, Benny Ramon
Reece, Errol Kemp
Reece, Joe Wilson
Reed, Addison Walker
Reed, Chester Ray
Reed, Dale Charles
Reed, David Benson
Reed, Dennis Lee
Reed, Erbie Loyd
Reed, Hardy
Reed, James Alan
Reed, Jesse Francis
Reed, John Alexander
Reed, John Martin
Reed, Josiah Frederick, Jr.
Reed, Kathlyn Louise
Reed, Mary F. Kurts
Reed, Murray Orville
Reed, Robert DeHart
Reed, Robert Edward
Reed, Roger Harold
Reed, Ronald Louis
Reed, Scott
Reed, Stanley Foster
Reed, Thomas Beavers, Jr.
Reed, Walter Allison, Jr.
Reed, William Guy
Reed, William Maxwell, II
Reed, William Thomas, III
Reeder, Eugene Marion, Jr.
Reeder, James Arthur
Reedy, Joe Henry
Rees, Philip Adrian
Rees, Raymond Winstead
Reese, Dorothy Harmon
Reese, Frederick Douglas
Reese, Jack Edward
Reese, John Olan
Reese, Robert John
Reesman, Arthur Lee
Reeve, Harold Richard
Reeve, James Key
Reeves, Dona Rae Batty (Mrs. Edward B. Reeves)
Reeves, Earl James, Jr.
Reeves, George Paul
Reeves, Hubert Lisbon
Reeves, James Willard
Reeves, John Estill
Reeves, Marvin Coke
Reeves, Odis, Jr.
Reevy, William Robert
Rega, Jane Louise
Regan, Billy Ray
Regan, Carroll Robert
Regan, James Dale

Regan, Sarah Wren Love
Regan, Terry Malcolm
Register, Levon Calvin
Regulski, Lee
Rehm, Gerald Stetson
Rehm, John Edwin
Reichard, Hector, Jr.
Reichelt, Richard Robert, Jr.
Reichert, Walter Stewart
Reid, Charles Frederick
Reid, James Louis
Reid, Lota Spence
Reid, Mark Kernan
Reid, Miles Alvin
Reid, Roger James
Reilly, Frank Ward, Jr.
Reilly, Frank Wendell
Reilly, Timothy Frank
Reimold, Robert James
Reinfurt, Donald William
Reingold, Paul Jeffrey
Reinhard, Erwin Arthur
Reinhart, Harry Ronald
Reinhold, Edward Ernest
Reinig, William Charles
Reinike, Vernon Robert
Reininga, Herman M.
Reinken, Mary Louise
Reinmiller, Elinor Calmbach
Reisman, Fredricka Kauffman
Reiss, Martin Leonard
Reistle, Carl Ernest, Jr.
Reisz, Aloysius Ignatius, Jr.
Reiter, Edward Otto
Reiter, Jackie Reader
Reitman, Sanford
Reitz, Steven Edward
Reitzer, Lorene Ida
Relph, Ross
Relyea, Richard Dale
Remes, Eugene Marriott
Remes, Lura Duff Elliston
Renalds, Juette Osborne, Jr.
Reneau, Daniel Dugan
Reneson, Paul Matthew
Renfroe, Donald Maurice
Renfrow, Edward
Renner, Mary Lucille (Mrs. Darwin Sprathard Renner)
Renner, Paul Thomas
Reno, Mildred Aitchison
Renshaw, Dal Wayne
Reso, Anthony
Ressler, Parke E(dward)
Ressler, Raymond Richards, Jr.
Resta, Edward Vito
Retzke, Franklin Albert
Reudelhuber, Frank Otto
Reul, George John, Jr.
Reus-Froylan, Francisco
Reuther, James Richard
Reuther, Ruth Elizabeth
Reveley, Hugh Price
Revell, Oliver Burgan
Revels, Bernice Gladys Hardy (Mrs. P.B. Revels)
Revels, Percy Burton
Revis, Frances W.
Rew, James Alfred, Jr.
Rey, William Kenneth
Reyer, Randall William
Reyes, Roberta Kay
Reynolds, Clinton Rainey
Reynolds, David Parham
Reynolds, Donald Eugene
Reynolds, F(rank) Fisher
Reynolds, Horace Gerald
Reynolds, John Archibald Seabrook
Reynolds, Leslie B(oush), Jr.
Reynolds, Lessie Pratt Mallard
Reynolds, Porter Graves
Reynolds, Randall O.
Reynolds, Raymond James, Jr.
Reynolds, Richard S., Jr.
Reynolds, William Jensen
Rhea, Claude Hiram, Jr.
Rheuble, David Markwood
Rhodes, Allan Ray
Rhodes, Betty Jean
Rhodes, Charles David
Rhodes, Diana Lenor
Rhodes, Donald Robert
Rhodes, Edwin Franklin
Rhodes, Lynwood Mark
Rhodes, Odis Odean
Rhodes, Patrick L.
Rhodes, Roy George
Rhodes, Thomas Eugene
Rhys, David Hall
Rhys, John Howard Winslow
Riba, Paul Francis
Ricards, Harold Andrew, Jr.
Rice, Benjamin Holt
Rice, David Fleming
Rice, Donadrian Lawrence
Rice, Frances Lillian
Rice, Howard Gene
Rice, Ivan Glenn
Rice, Jack Vaughan
Rice, James Allen
Rice, Judith Pierce
Rice, Larry Milton
Rice, Laurence Bliss
Rice, Paul Winston
Rice, Randle Graham
Rice, Ronald Lee
Rice, William Thomas
Rice, William Vaughn, Jr.
Rice, Winston Edward
Rich, Arnold Ray
Rich, Helen Wall (Mrs. Arthur L. Rich)
Rich, Isadore Alexander
Rich, Robert Regier
Richard, Anthony Gerard, II
Richard, Lynn Allan
Richard, Michel Charles
Richard, Wilmar John, Jr.
Richards, Abram Jones, Jr.
Richards, Charles Leon
Richards, Everett Lyle
Richards, Frederick William
Richards, George Roy
Richards, John Edward
Richards, Lloyd Francis
Richards, Rupert Clyde, Jr.
Richards, William George
Richardson, Anita Marie
Richardson, Charles Ray
Richardson, Clay Vance
Richardson, Daisy Adelaide Watkins (Mrs. Robert Williams Richardson Jr.)
Richardson, Donald Edward
Richardson, Edwin Leland
Richardson, Elbert Hoke
Richardson, Frank Woodbury, III
Richardson, Gary Lowell
Richardson, Hazel Adams
Richardson, James Milton
Richardson, Joseph Thomas
Richardson, Kenneth Miller
Richardson, Lavon Preston
Richardson, Lawrence Oliver
Richardson, Luns Columbus
Richardson, Maurine Adams
Richardson, Robert Williams, Jr.
Richardson, Rupert Norval
Richardson, William Nathan
Richey, Richard Earl
Richmond, John Melvyn
Richmond, Lea, Jr.
Richter, Carl Arpad
Richter, James Arthur
Rickard, Joseph Conway
Rickelton, David
Ricketts, Fred R.
Ricketts, Halle S.
Rickey, Horace Bushnell, Jr.
Ricks, Janice Humphrey
Riddell, Joseph Murray, Jr.
Riddell, Mary Ellen
Riddick, Edgar Kader, Jr.
Riddick, Frank Adams, Jr.
Riddick, Winston Wade
Riddle, Althae Spear Ireland
Riddle, James Douglass
Riddle, Lindsey Grant
Rider, Fred Eugene
Ridge, Davy-Jo Stribling
Ridgeway, Sandra Wise
Ridgeway, Tilman Leon
Ridings, Paul Overton
Ridlehuber, Jim Mack
Ridley, Clarence Haverty
Riecken, William Emil, Jr.
Riera, Caroline
Ries, Edward Richard
Rieser, James Sidney
Riesgo, Vilma Melba
Riesser, Gregor Hans
Riewe, Marvin Edmund
Rifkinson, Nathan
Rigby, Richard Hillman
Riggan, Wilson Butler
Riggen, Gaylord Ray, Jr.
Riggs, Cecil Graham
Riggs, Joseph Haynes
Riggs, Karl A., Jr.
Riggs, Orval Elmo
Riggs, Virginia Louise Holloway (Mrs. Arthur J. Riggs)
Riggsby, Dutchie Sellers (Mrs. Ernest Duward Riggsby)
Riggsby, Ernest Duward
Rigsby, Jesse Huntsman
Riles, George Griffith
Riley, Bob Cowley
Riley, Harry Paul
Riley, John Herbert, Jr.
Riley, Max Leroy
Riley, Ray Gordon, Jr.
Riley, Ray Joe
Riley, Richard Franklin
Riley, Richard Wayne
Riley, Thomas Nolan
Riling, Eugene Harold
Rimer, Laura Peeples
Rimington, Robert Neil
Ring, Larry Richard
Ring, William Joseph
Ringley, Michael Bruce
Rinhart, Floyd Lincoln
Rinhart, Marion Hutchinson (Mrs. Floyd Lincoln Rinhart)
Rinker, George Ernest
Rinne, Austin Dean
Riojas, Alberto F.
Rios, Freddy Renteria
Ripley, Robert Kenyon, Jr.
Risby, Edward Louis
Risenhoover, Ted
Risher, Sylvia Wilson
Risinger, Roger Irvin
Ristroph, Marie Gibbens
Ritchie, Eris Alton, Jr.
Ritsch, Jeannette McClung
Ritson, Spencer Lee
Rittenberg, Leon Hirsch, Jr.
Ritter, Gary David
Ritter, Thomas Edward
Ritterman, Stuart I.
Rittvo, Steven Marc
Ritz, Michael Cochrane
Rivenbark, Rembert Reginald
Rivera Boucher, Jose Armando
Rivera-Emmanuelli, Rafael Luis
Rivero Cervera, José Antonio
Rivers, John Minott, Jr.
Rives, Albert Gordon
Rives, Hugh Farrar
Rives, James Allen
Rivkind, Leonard Melvin
Rizer, Gene Cromwell
Rizk, Josef Saleem
Rizk, Wade Saleem
Rizzo, (Elizabeth) (Pauwels)
Rizzolo, Edward Anthony
Roach, Jones Williamson
Roach, William Lester
Roach, William Rankin
Roache, Bonnard Ernest
Roaden, Arliss Lloyd
Roan, Charles Thurston
Roark, Frank Hollyworth, Jr.
Roark, James Oliver
Roath, Walter Herbert
Robb, Charles Spittal
Robb, Felix Compton
Robbie, Joseph
Robbins, Evelyn Wall (Mrs. Homer Erwin Robbins, Jr.)
Robbins, James Tate
Robbins, Jerry Hal
Robbins, Kenneth Randall
Robbins, Linda S.
Robbins, Orville Montia
Roberds, Cammack Alvin, Jr.
Roberson, Barbara Drane
Roberson, Dennis Arlen
Roberson, Dennis Lee
Roberson, James Houston
Roberson, James Ralph, Jr.
Roberson, Robert Stephen
Roberson, Theodore Milton
Roberts, Aaron Hood
Roberts, Ben Lowell
Roberts, Bramlett
Roberts, Carleton Whitman
Roberts, Charles Riles
Roberts, Ernest Wilson
Roberts, Geoffrey Arthur Sebry
Roberts, George Franklin, Jr.
Roberts, Gustave William
Roberts, Hyman Jacob
Roberts, James Gordon
Roberts, Joe Clyde
Roberts, John Carroll, Sr.
Roberts, John Harold
Roberts, Joseph Boxley, Jr.
Roberts, Michael Dean
Roberts, Ray
Roberts, Robert, III
Roberts, Roland Douglas, Jr.
Roberts, Roy Raymond
Roberts, Thomas G.
Roberts, William James
Roberts, William Lawrence
Roberts, William Patrick
Robertson, Benjamin William
Robertson, Carl Lester
Robertson, Donald Paul
Robertson, Donelson Anthony
Robertson, Douglas Welby
Robertson, Elmer Shackleford
Robertson, Frank Lewis
Robertson, Franklin Lee
Robertson, Ida Roberts (Mrs. Samuel Thompson Robertson)
Robertson, Jack Clark
Robertson, Joe Kenneth
Robertson, John Marshall, Jr.
Robertson, Ralph Byron
Robertson, Robert Lafon
Robertson, Sandra Lea
Robertson, Theodore Lane
Robertson, William Harris Peterman
Robertson, William Shore
Robeson, Edward John, III
Robeson, James Lee
Robeson, Stuart Hogan
Robeson, Vernon Scott
Robey, Harry Russell
Robideau, Robert Gordon
Robin, Vincent Joseph, III
Robiner, Ronald Alan
Robinett, Elizabeth Ann McClain
Robins, Miriam Blasberg
Robinson, Adelbert Carl
Robinson, Andrew Adolphus
Robinson, Benjamin Eric
Robinson, Bryan Wright
Robinson, Charles Lee
Robinson, Charlynn Chamberlin
Robinson, Clifton Hight, Jr.
Robinson, Emmett Edward
Robinson, Enders Anthony
Robinson, Eugene Corrington
Robinson, Florence Claire Crim
Robinson, Gary H.
Robinson, Jack Hardy
Robinson, James Kenneth
Robinson, James William
Robinson, John Paul
Robinson, Nathaniel David
Robinson, Prezell Russell
Robinson, Ralph Carlisle, Jr.
Robinson, Ralph Rolin
Robinson, Ralph Smyre, Jr.
Robinson, Richard Francis
Robinson, Robert Louis
Robinson, Ronald Allen
Robinson, Roscoe Ross
Robinson, Wilburn Vaughn
Robinson, William Powell
Robison, G(eorge) Alan
Robison, Henry Welborn
Robles, Alejandro Guillermo
Robson, John Robert Keith
Roby, Richard Ellis
Roch, Robert Hoover
Rochelle, (Robert) Carter, Sr.
Rockefeller, John Davison, IV
Rockefeller, Winthrop Paul
Rockett, Eleanor Wilson Stinson (Mrs. Don Lee Rockett)
Rockwell, Elizabeth Dennis
Rockwood, Vivian Valera
Roddy, Gary Leighton
Roddy, Stephen Robert
Rodgers, Ellen Davies (Mrs. Hillman P. Rodgers)
Rodgers, Gary Wayne
Rodgers, Lawrence Rodney
Rodgers, Thomas Michael, Jr.
Rodgers, William Harry
Rodgers, William Lee
Rodman, Nathaniel Fulford, Jr.
Rodman, Paul Keith
Rodrigues, Leo L.
Rodriguez, Alejandro Javier
Rodriguez, Beatriz Marta
Rodriguez, Dolores Marie
Rodriguez, Johnny Gomez
Rodriguez, Juan Guadalupe
Rodriguez, Julio Ramon
Rodriguez, Mario Juan
Rodriguez, Paul Henry
Rodriguez, Rehina Stevens
Rodriguez, Roberto C.
Rodriguez, Tony
Rodríguez-Estrada, Marcos Antonio
Rodriguez-Hernandez, Jesus M.
Rodriguez-Nieto, Rafael
Roe, Burton James
Roe, Donald Winston
Roeling, Gerard Henry
Roensch, Edward Burns
Roesch, Emma Lonella
Roesel, Albert Julius
Roetschke, Ronald Clay
Rogers, A.C.
Rogers, Alice Bradshaw
Rogers, Allan Darrow
Rogers, Colonel Hoyt
Rogers, Donald Lee
Rogers, Eddy James, Jr.
Rogers, Elmer A.
Rogers, Ford Barker, Jr.
Rogers, Herbert Francis
Rogers, James Alton
Rogers, James Edwin
Rogers, James Gamble, II
Rogers, John Cicero, Jr.
Rogers, John Koehn
Rogers, John Michael
Rogers, John Richard
Rogers, Joseph Brown
Rogers, King Walter, Jr.
Rogers, Leonard Gilbert
Rogers, Lon B(rown)
Rogers, Lorene Lane (Mrs. Burl Gordon Rogers)
Rogers, Mary-Jane Regina
Rogers, Nathaniel Sims
Rogers, Oscar Allan, Jr.
Rogers, Paul (Grant)
Rogers, Paul McKendry
Rogers, Peter H.
Rogers, Richard Lehn
Rogers, Robert Lee
Rogers, Rodney Paul
Rogers, Stanley Francis, Jr.
Rogers, Theodore Courtney
Rogers, Virgil Raymond, Jr.
Rogers, W.D., Jr.
Rogers, Wesley Wiley
Rogerson, Constance Jean
Roghair, Theodore
Rogillio, Carlyle Alonzo
Rohlfing, Dennis Lee
Rohne, Wayne Arlen
Rohr, Arthur Wade
Roland, Clarence Nelson
Roling, Richard Keith
Rollings, Harry Evan
Rollins, Albert Williamson
Rollins, Carl Padgett
Roman, Don Dwaine
Roman, Jesse
Roman de Jesus, Jose Cosme
Romano, Samuel Andrew
Rombough, Charles Thomas
Romero, Orlando
Romero-Barceló, Carlos
Romerstein, Herbert
Romine, Thomas Beeson, Jr.
Rominger, James C.
Rominger, Phil
Rommer, Barbara Ruth
Rondeau, Clement Robert
Rood, Ralph Edward
Roodhouse, Charles Weston, Jr.
Roof, Barbara Nell
Roosevelt, Elliott, Jr.
Root, John Bernard
Root, Paul John
Ropp, Gus Anderson
Roppolo, John Wayne
Roque, Juan Lopez
Rorschach, Harold E.
Rosario-Garcia, Efrain
Rosasco, William Sebastian III
Rosas-Guyon, Luis Isidro, Jr.
Roscher, Paul Eugene
Roscoe, William Albert
Rose, Beatrice Schroeder (Mrs. William H. Rose)
Rose, Benjamin Lacy
Rose, Bobby Lee
Rose, Charles Grandison, III
Rose, Charles Henry, Jr.
Rose, David Shepherd
Rose, Ernest Wright, Jr.
Rose, Mark Stephen
Rose, William Dake
Rose, William Louis
Roseland, Paul Luther
Roseman, Arnold Leonard
Rosen, Harris
Rosen, Kenneth David
Rosenau, Jack Clayton
Rosenbaum, George Robert
Rosenbaum, Marcos
Rosenbaum, Stanley
Rosenberg, Dennis Melville Leo
Rosenberg, Harry Zachery
Rosenberg, Leon Joseph
Rosenberg, Michael Allen
Rosenberg, Raymond
Rosenbloom, Arlan Lee
Rosenblum, Harold
Rosenbluth, Morton
Rosenfeld, Louis
Rosenfield, Israel
Rosenfield, Sam Julius
Rosen-Miller, Carolyn Joy
Rosenstiel, Blanka Aldona
Rosenthal, Harry Max
Rosenthal, Morris William
Rosenthal, Samuel Gerson
Rosetti, Brian Charles
Roshkind, David Michael
Rosier, Robert Peter
Rosin, Charles Alan
Rosin, Morris
Roslow, Sydney
Rosner, Edmond
Rosoff, Marvin Stuart
Ross, Amparo Maldonado
Ross, Barry
Ross, Delbert Grant
Ross, Edgar Alfred
Ross, John Turner, Jr.
Ross, Joseph Crawford
Ross, Robert Roy, Jr.
Ross, Rosa Mell Thomas
Ross, Samuel Gifford
Ross, Stanley Robert
Rossen, Robert Henry
Rosser, Jimmy Linton
Rossie, Raoul Lazaro
Rosson, Barry A.
Roszell, Calvert Theodore, Jr.
Roth, Jack
Roth, Sanford Irwin
Rothschild, Bernard Andrew, Jr.
Rothschild, David, II
Rothschild, Edward A.
Rotroff, Robert William
Roubey, Lester Walter
Rouby, Jason Pierre
Roueche, John Edward, II
Roulston, Charles Robert
Round, Bettye Hammons (Mrs. Thornton Edgerly Round)
Rountree, Horace Gene
Rourke, Harry Eugene
Rous, Stephen Norman
Rouse, Ernest Philip
Rouse, John Wilson, Jr.
Rouse, Virginia Ariail (Mrs. LeGrand Rouse)
Rousey, John Shelton
Rouson, Willie Ervin
Roussel, Herbert Joseph, Jr.
Routh, Porter (Wroe)
Rovan, John Robert
Rovira, Eduardo
Rowe, Bonnie Gordon
Rowe, Charles Spurgeon
Rowe, Dale Wayne
Rowe, James Henry
Rowe, Robert Laird
Rowell, James Ronald
Rowland, Jay Miller, Jr.
Rowland, Thomas Clifford, Jr.
Rowlett, James Robert
Rowlett, Olen Merle
Roy, Francis Charles
Royal, Freddie Eugene
Royal, Jack Lee
Royalty, Robert Malcolm
Royster, George Erwin
Rozak, Donald Ted
Rozenbaum, Najman
Rozzell, George McAllaster, Jr.
Rua, Milton Francisco
Ruane, Richard James
Rube, Milton Isaac
Ruben, Leonard
Rubin, Bruce Stuart
Rubin, Richard Mark
Ruch, Robert Milton
Ruckel, Charles Walter, Jr.
Ruckenstein, Harry Eli
Rucker, David Edmund
Rucker, George Donald
Rucker, Harold James
Rucker, Norman Henry
Rucker, Walter Clifford
Rucker, William K. Vance, Jr.
Rude, Joe Christopher, III
Rudenberg, F(rank) Hermann
Rudolph, Andrew Henry
Rudy, Richard Alan
Rueda-Gaxiola, Jaime
Rueff, Mildred Mae
Ruehle, Charles Joseph
Ruf, Henry Lawrence
Ruffner, Charles Louis
Rugg, Frederic Waldo, II
Rullan, Antonio
Rumage, Joseph Paul
Rumaggi, Louis Jacob
Rummerfield, Benjamin Franklin
Rund, Jack A.
Runkle, Frederick Stephen
Runninger, Jack
Runyan, Carolyn Buchanan
Rupe, Dallas Gordon, III
Rupel, Lawrence Michael
Ruse, Gary Alan
Rush, David Charles
Rush, Henry Lester, Jr.
Rush, Richard Caswell, Jr.
Rush, Wayne Franklin
Rushing, Barnie Elmer, Jr.
Rushing, Dykes Taylor
Rushing, Joe B.
Rushing, Roy Eugene
Rushlow, Bonnie Miller
Rushlow, Philip Leo
Rushton, Mary Fay Hopkins (Mrs. Lonnie Connon Rushton)
Rushton, William James
Rushton, William James, III
Rusk, Martha Jean
Russack, Gregory John
Russek, Henry Irving
Russell, Carol Goff
Russell, Cheryl Ann
Russell, Dan M., Jr.
Russell, David Emerson
Russell, Elbert Winslow
Russell, George Erwin, Jr.
Russell, George Franklin, Jr.
Russell, Harold Gilmore
Russell, Herman Jerome
Russell, James Carlos
Russell, Jerry Lewis
Russell, Jerry Wayne
Russell, Joan Louise Gille
Russell, John Francis
Russell, Lao (Mrs. Walter Russell)
Russell, Michael Lee
Russell, Ralph Ernest
Russell, Richard Anthony
Russell, Richard Olney, Jr.
Russell, Richard Robert
Russell, Richard Roland
Russell, Robert Leonard
Russell, Roger Allen
Russell, Vantrease Little
Russell, William Lawson
Russell, Wilson Lee
Russian, Francis X.
Russin, Nicholas Charles
Ruth, Lester Rufus, Jr.
Ruth, Robert Douglas
Ruth, William Ames
Ruth, William Augustus, III
Rutherford, Shelley Howe
Rutland, Lilli Ida Adkins
Rutrough, Arthur James
Ruwe, Victor William
Ryals, Jimmie Jackson
Ryan, Daniel Bruno
Ryan, Doris Ann
Ryan, John Aloysius, IV
Ryan, Ralph Waldo
Ryan, Ted Lamar
Ryan, Terrell Boggs
Ryan, William Joseph
Ryant, Carl George
Ryburn, Frank Compere
Rydman, Edward J.
Ryker, Kenneth Wilton
Rylander, Michael Kent
Rylee, Robert Tilman, II
Rymer, Frederick Roscoe
Ryon, Thomas S(hipley)
Saarinen, Arthur William
Saarinen, Arthur William, Jr.
Sabatella, D. Francis
Sabiston, David Coston, Jr.
Sachau, William Henry
Sacher, Charles Philip
Sachs, Kurt
Sachse, Victor A., Jr.
Sackash, Michael Lynn
Sackett, John David
Saconas, Edward Sherman
Sadler, Guy Albert
Sadler, Timothy Goodwin
Saegert, Clarence Emil
Saenz, Michael
Saenz, Nancy Elizabeth King (Mrs. Michael Saenz)
Saffan, Benjamin David
Saffir, Herbert Seymour
Saffy, Edna Louise
Safran, Robert Joseph
Sage, Russell Richard
Sahr, Aaron Emmanuel
Saine, Leonard Watson
St. Angelo, Douglas Gene
St. Clair, Hal Kay
St. John, Henry Sewell, Jr.
St. John, Wylly Folk
St. Martin, Allen H., Jr.
Sainz, Anthony A.
Sala, Luis Francisco
Sala, Pedro Alfonso
Salami, Mohammad Farhang
Salas, Guillermo Armando
Salatich, John Smyth
Salcedo, Jose Ricardo
Salch, Steven Charles
Sale, Tom S., III
Salet, Eugene Albert
Salgado, Jose Gorgonio
Saliba, Selma G.
Salichs, Orlando
Salisbury, Brian Gregory

Hayes, William Frederick
Hayes, William Rupert, Jr.
Haykin, Martin D.
Hayman, Jon Alvin
Haymes, Mary Fidele
Hay-Messick, Velma E. (Mrs. Ben Messick)
Haynes, Dennis Lee
Haynes, Harold Jean
Hays, Jack D.H.
Hays, Marvin Bryant
Hays, Peter L.
Hays, Warren Sherman
Hayward, Charles Sumner, II
Hayward, Sterling Roberts
Hayworth, Bruce R.
Hazard, Robert Culver, Jr.
Hazard, Victor James
Hazeltine, Herbert Samuel, Jr.
Hazeltine, Sandra Woodbridge
Hazen, Kenneth Richard
Hazewinkel, Van
Hazlett, Clarke Blaine
Hazlett, Donald Arthur
Heaberg, William Fisher
Head, Steven Lynwood
Head, Thomas Frederick
Headington, Bonnie Jay
Headlee, Rolland Dockeray
Headley, Joseph Burton, Jr.
Headley, Thelma Jean
Healey, James Alfred
Healy, Franklin Eugene
Healy, Patrick, IV
Healy, Richard Joseph
Healy, Thomas Michael
Healy, William Francis
Heaney, Donald Samuel
Heaney, Patrick Dennis
Heaney, Robert C(ecil) C(urtis)
Heap, Bradley Joel
Heap, Elmer Leroy
Heap, George Albert
Heard, Fred Walter
Hearn, Charles Virgil
Hearne, Alvia Alton, Jr.
Hearst, Randolph Apperson
Heath, Leonard Florian
Heath, Stratton Rollins, Jr.
Heath, Valdo D.
Heath, William Ashley
Heaton, Kenneth Gordon
Heaton, Marie
Heaton, Pattie Jean Haynes
Heaton, Richard Dale
Hebert, James Dana
Hecht, Andrea Platt
Hecht, Frederick
Hecht, Herbert
Hecht, Mervyn Leonard
Heck, Daniel Curtis, Jr.
Heckard, Lawrence Ray
Heckel, Donald Thomas
Heckel, James Edward
Heckelman, Barry Jay
Hecker, Siegfried Stephen
Heckman, Fred Russel, Jr.
Heckman, John Jacob, Jr.
Hedemark, Norman George
Hedgcoth, Virgle Leland
Hedges, Lawrence Eugene
Hedin, Edna Jenks
Hedlund, Robert Clark
Hedman, John Gilbert
Hedrick, James Larry
Hedrick, Wallace Edward
Hee, William B. C.
Heer, David MacAlpine
Heer, Ewald
Heer, Nancy Whittier
Heersema, Philip Henry
Heffern, Richard Arnold
Hefley, Joel M.
Hefner, Norman Emmet
Hefni, Mohamed Omar
Heftel, Cecil
Hegdal, Ruth Margaret
Hei, Ronald Ray
Heide, Jørgen
Heidel, Harry John
Heieck, Paul Jay
Heilig, David Roy
Heiman, Gerald Richard
Heindl, Clifford Joseph
Heindsmann, Theodore Edward
Heinlein, Oscar Allen
Heinrich, Bernd
Heinrich, Daniel Jay
Heinrich, John Calvin
Heinrich, Milton Rollin
Heinritz, Dietrich Wilhelm
Heiny, Bernard Arlen
Heinze, Ellen
Heise, Ardys Mary
Heisler, Verda Thomas (Mrs. William Wilbert Heisler)
Heiss, Frederick William
Heist, David Wesley
Heitz, Gary F.
Heitzig, James Louis
Hekmat-Panah, Kamran
Held, Mark Lawrence
Helgason, Robert Erlendur
Helgeson, Duane Marcellus
Helle, Maurie Carl
Hellenthal, Albert Warren
Heller, Lawrence Eric
Heller, Stuart Barry
Hellon, Michael Thomas
Helm, Donald Cairney
Helms, Everett Peter
Helms, James Reding, Jr.
Helms, John William
Helms, Phyllis Borden
Helton, Judy P.
Helvern, Jane Alvies
Helweg, Otto Jennings
Helzer, James Albert
Hem, John David
Hemann, Charles William
Hemann, Raymond Glenn
Hemenway, Dorothy Lavonne
Hemingway, George Francis
Hemming, Michael John
Hempel, Bruce Dobyns
Hempel, Gardiner
Hempel, Marvin William
Hemphill, Bernice Monahan (Mrs. Charles D. Hemphill)
Hemphill, Charles Frank, Jr.
Hemphill, Jeanette Marie Franke (Mrs. William Edward Hemphill)
Hempkins, William Brent
Hemstad, Bonnie Jean
Henceroth, Stanley William
Hendee, William Richard
Hendel, Frank Joseph
Henderlider, Robert Melvin
Hendershot, William Bishop, III
Henderson, Clark William
Henderson, Douglas James
Henderson, Joe Kenneth
Henderson, Simon Roderick
Henderson, Virginia Cowen (Mrs. Jarvis Richard Henderson)
Henderson, Warren Louis, Jr.
Henderson, Warren Thomas
Hendren, Hubert Franklin
Hendren, Merlyn Churchill
Hendren, Robert Lee, Jr.
Hendricks, Ed Jerald
Hendricks, J. Edwin
Hendricks, John Robert, Jr.
Hendricks, Thomas Armstrong, III
Hendrickson, John Reese, Sr.
Hendrix, Kenneth Alan
Hendrix, William Edwin
Hendry, Eugene Francis
Henkel, George Hallaway
Henkel, Joan Corrine
Henley, Preston vanFleet
Henley, William Ballentine
Henneberg, Dennis Wayne
Hennessy, John James
Hennessy, Michael Edward
Hennessy, Thomas Edward
Henning, Charles Nathaniel
Henning, George Axel, Jr.
Henning, Jean Norma
Henning, John F.
Henning, Laura Helene
Henning, Margherita Mueck
Henning, Robert Joseph
Henninger, Alan Martin
Henninger, Robert Stanley
Henningsen, Joe Nels
Henrie, Samuel Nyal, Jr.
Henry, Donald Lee
Henry, Margaret
Henry, Rene Arthur, Jr.
Henry, Walter L.
Henselman, Scott Alan
Henshaw, Betty Runals (Mrs. Paul C. Henshaw)
Hensler, William Harry
Hensley, James Willis
Hensley, Paul Wayne
Hensley, Richard Frank
Henzel, Richard Walter
Hepps, Robert
Hepps, Sanford Alan
Herbert, James Stewart
Herbst, Lawrence Robert
Herczeg, Ferenc Pal
Herdeg, Howard Brian
Herkner, Henry Andrew
Herle, Wendelin Alex
Herlihy, Harriet Elizabeth
Herman, Edward Roy
Herman, Elvin Eugene
Herman, George Richard
Herman, Irving Leonard
Herman, Robert Harold
Herman, Walter Eugene
Hermann, James Ray
Hermansen, Darryle Craig
Hern, John Anthony, Jr.
Hernandez, Robert Michael
Hernstadt, William H.
Hero, Peter deCourcy
Herold, Ralph Elliott
Herold, Virginia Wilcox (Mrs. Paul G. Herold)
Herrera, Charles Seibold
Herrera, Robert Bennett
Herrick, Eric Colin
Herrick, Glenn Almore
Herring, Bernard Duane
Herring, Fred Henry
Herring, Fredrick Lee
Herring, Theodore Melvin, Jr.
Herringer, Frank Casper
Herrmann, Stanley William
Herron, Ellen Patricia
Herschler, Edgar J.
Hertweck, E. Romayne
Hertzog, Emile Francis
Hertzog, Eugene Edward
Herzberg, Dorothy Crews
Herzberger, Arthur Conrad
Herzer, Richard Kimball
Herzog, Clarence Max
Herzog, George Kramer, III
Hesch, Donald Joseph
Hess, David Fredric
Hess, Edward Jorgen
Hess, George Lawrence
Hess, Harvey Jason, III
Hess, James Elmer
Hess, Janice Carleen
Hess, Linda Gay
Hess, Richard Christian
Hess, Richard Irwin
Hess, Ronald Earl
Hester, Robert Joe
Hetland, John Robert
Hetter, Gregory Paulson
Hetzron, Robert
Hewes, Colleen JoAnne Malbica
Hewett, Bill Ainslie
Hewitt, Arthur Elbert
Hewitt, Jerene Cline
Heyler, David Baldwin, Jr.
Heyler, William Frederick, III
Heyser, Richard Charles
Hiatt, Ben L.
Hibbard, Richard Paul
Hibbard, Wallace Asher
Hibben, Frank Cummings
Hibbs, Harold Keith
Hibrawi, Hazem
Hick, Kenneth William
Hickam, Robert Elliott
Hicks, Barbara Dean
Hicks, Darrell Lee
Hicks, Edward Henry
Hicks, Frank Enochs, Jr.
Hicks, George Mack
Hicks, Ruth Goede
Hicks, Stephen Morris
Hidaka, Kenjiro
Hiester, Robert Walter
Higginbotham, John Preston
Higgins, Donna Owen
Higgins, Floyd Donald
Higgins, Thomas Michael, Jr.
Higgs, DeWitt A.
Higgs, James Doyle
High, Carroll W.
High, Robert Skidmore Smith
Hijirida, Kyoko
Hilbig, David Manwaring
Hilbrecht, Norman Ty
Hileman, Ralph Arms
Hileman, Sally Jean
Hill, Alan Eugene
Hill, Bertram Edward
Hill, Cecilia (Mrs. Jack Hill)
Hill, Floyd Edwin, Jr.
Hill, Frank U.
Hill, George Alfred
Hill, George Blood
Hill, Harold Eugene
Hill, Irving
Hill, Jack Gerald
Hill, James Erskine
Hill, James Noah
Hill, James Oregon
Hill, Jeffrey John
Hill, John J., III
Hill, Lawrence Hampshire
Hill, Leo Francis
Hill, Mary Alice
Hill, Patrick Cullen
Hill, Paul Jay
Hill, Richard Johnson
Hill, Ronald Charles
Hill, Russell John
Hill, Russell Stanley
Hill, Thomas Clarke, VIII
Hill, Walter Edward, Jr.
Hill, William Dulany
Hillam, Harold Gordon
Hillar, Paul Michael
Hillbruner, Anthony
Hillger, Dave Rodney
Hilliard, David Michael
Hilliard, Harry Talbott
Hillier, Thomas Robert
Hillings, Patrick Jerome
Hillman, Carol White
Hillman, Wilbur Wright
Hillmer, Norman Roland
Hills, Frank Stanley
Hills, Jimmie Arthur
Hills, Reuben Wilmarth, III
Hills, Timothy Paul
Hillyer, Georgiana Morris
Hilton, Barron
Hilton, Gilbert Walter
Hilton, J. Richard
Hilton, John Levi
Hilts, John Warren
Hilty, Louise Clara
Hilzman, John
Hime, J. Martin
Himelstein, Mandel Edwin
Himeno, Edward Torao
Himonas, James Demosthenes, Jr.
Himoto, Teruo
Himstreet, William Charles
Hinckley, Keith S.
Hind, Harry William
Hindin, Russell
Hinds, Charles Benjamin, Jr.
Hinds, James Roland
Hinds, Robert James
Hine, Robert Van Norden, Jr.
Hinerfeld, Robert Elliot
Hines, James Monroe
Hines, Vernon Cassiday
Hines, Wayne Lowell
Hing, Robert Ong
Hinke, Henry Calvin
Hinkle, Steven Owen
Hinrichs, John Honeycutt, Jr.
Hinrichsen, Erik Christian
Hinsch, Robert Tom
Hinshaw, Ernest Theodore, Jr.
Hipkens, Theodore Petty
Hirano, Steven Susumu
Hirayama, Tetsu
Hirdler, Carole Ann
Hirota, Sam Osamu
Hiroto, Donald Shiro
Hirsch, Gilah Yelin
Hirsch, Henry William
Hirsch, I. Jerome
Hirschkoff, Eugene Clifford
Hirson, Estelle
Hirst, Wilma Elizabeth
Hirstel, Robert
Hirt, Charles Carleton
Hisaka, Craig Kiyoshi
Hitch, Thomas Kemper
Hitchner, Dell Gillette
Hite, Robert Wesley
Hitt, William Lloyd
Hittle, Leroy Michael
Hix, Elizabeth (Mrs. Clifton Hix)
Hixon, Alexander Paul
Hlastala, Michael Peter
Ho, Raymond Yee-Cho
Ho, Raymond Yue Chung
Ho, Simon Hoi-Wah
Hoaas, W. Walker (Budd)
Hoagland, Jack Charles
Hoaglund, Robert Joel
Hoard, Homer Stearns, Jr.
Hobbs, Donald William, Jr.
Hobbs, Philip Alfred Danby
Hochberg, Frederick George
Hochhalter, Charles Dean
Hochman, Judi Lynn
Hockel, Jack Lewis
Hockett, John Edwin, III
Hocking, Mark Kimball
Hockman, Karl Kalevi
Hoctor, A. Edward
Hodge, Winston William
Hodges, James Cyril
Hodges, Millard B.
Hodges, Paul Vincent, Jr.
Hodgkin, John Elliott
Hodgson, Helen Gertrude
Hodkins, Lillian Estrella Sorrels
Hodnett, Barbara Milton
Hodson, Jean Elaine Turnbaugh
Hoeber, Ralph Carl
Hoefler, Barbara Burton
Hoefler, Paul Louis
Hoehn, Robert Jacob
Hoekendorf, William Carl
Hoeltzel, Marcella
Hoeppel, Raymond Winfield
Hoerig, Gerald Lee
Hoff, Lawrence Elvin
Hoff, Richard Joseph
Hoffman, David Hamilton
Hoffman, Edna Virginia Wight (Mrs. Henry Carl Hoffman)
Hoffman, Edward Jack
Hoffman, Fred Stanley
Hoffman, Jon Michael
Hoffman, Karon Wright
Hoffman, Leon
Hoffman, Milton Coy
Hoffman, Richard Allen
Hoffman, Ruth Irene
Hoffman, Thomas Edward
Hoffman, Walter August
Hoffman, William Lea
Hofland, Robert, Jr.
Hofstadter, Robert
Hogenson, Margaret Jeanne
Hogg, Frederick Glenn
Hohensee, Herbert George
Hohler, Charles William, II
Hohmann, George William
Hokama, Yoshiaki
Hokama, Yoshitsugi
Hokr, William Klement
Holbrook, Donald Benson
Holbrook, J. Roger
Holcomb, Robert Eugene
Holdaway, George Harmer
Holdcroft, Leslie Thomas
Holden, Ashley Elder
Holden, Thomas Edwin
Holden, William Henry Towne
Holderness, Howard, Jr.
Holdstein, Russell Simon
Holen, Harold Hampton
Holeway, Ronald Edward
Holgate, George Jackson
Holl, Walter John
Holland, Calvin Clifton
Holland, Jack Henry
Holland, Joan Baldwin
Holland, Kenneth Milton
Hollander, Carl Ernest, Jr.
Hollander, Lewis E., Jr.
Hollar, William Thomas
Holleman, Marian Patterson (Mrs. W. Roy Holleman)
Hollenbeck, Clifford Ernest
Hollenbeck, Nancy Eilene
Holley, Robert William
Hollingsworth, Leon Winfield
Hollister, Edward Warren
Hollman, Stephen Neil
Holloman, Marsha S.
Holloway, John Edwin
Holloway, William Harold
Holly, Kenneth Eugene
Holm, Orley Robert
Holm, Owen Robert
Holman, Gordon Lee
Holman, Kermit Layton
Holman, Paul Lewis
Holmberg, Branton Keith
Holme, Barbara Lynn Shaw
Holmes, Barbara Ann Krajkoski
Holmes, Haynon
Holmes, John William
Holmes, Opal Laurel
Holmes, Paul Elliott
Holmes, Roger Curtis
Holmes, Thomas Hall
Holmes, Walter Irwin (Dugg)
Holmkvist, David Arthur
Holt, Everett Eugene
Holt, Frank E(dward)
Holt, Robert Franklin
Holte, Alfred Oliver
Holtz, Richard Raymond
Holzapfel, Paul Francis
Holzer, Fred Josef
Holzman, Allen Leonard
Holzman, David
Holzman, Irving Murray
Holzschuh, Jack Eugene
Homan, John Elburt
Home, DeForrest
Home, Stephen Duncan
Hommel, Dennis Luther
Hondorp, Gordon Ray
Hone, Daniel Warren
Hong, George Soon Won
Hontz, Robert Milton, Jr.
Hooban, Homer Louis, II
Hood, Fred H.
Hood, Joan Crandell
Hood, John Robinson, Jr.
Hood, Vernon Richard
Hook, Robert Douglas
Hook, Weston Arnold
Hooker, Van Dorn
Hooks, Ronald Fred
Hooper, Frederick Richard
Hooper, Gary Raymond
Hooper, Paul F.
Hooper, Ronald Rafael
Hooper, Shirley
Hoopes, Margaret Howard
Hoose, Harned Pettus
Hoover, Helen D(rusilla)
Hope, Charles William Scott
Hoper, Clarence H.
Hopkins, Annadawn Edwards
Hopkins, Cecilia Ann (Mrs. Henry E. Hopkins)
Hopkins, Edwina Weiskittel
Hopkins, Gordon Bruce
Hopkins, Herbert Ziegler
Hopkins, James Michael
Hopkins, Mary Evelyn
Hopkins, Paul Mortimer
Hopkins, Paulene A. (Mrs. Mack Hopkins)
Hopkins, Ruth Steiner
Hopkinson, Shirley Lois
Hoppe, Richard Raymond
Hoppe, William Edward
Hoppel, Armand B.
Hopper, George Andrew
Hopper, Nancy Charlotte Thompson
Hopper, Stanley Duff
Hopping, Richard Lee
Hops, Hyman
Horen, Herbert L.
Horgan, Michael James
Hori, Kiyoaky
Horigan, James Eugene
Horka, Lorayne Ann
Horkheimer, Walter Henry
Horman, Sidney Melvin
Horn, Anton Stephen
Horn, Barbara Geiger
Horn, Bruce William
Horn, Eric Laurens
Horn, John Harold
Horn, Kenneth Porter
Horn, (John) Stephen
Hornbruch, Harlan Richard
Hornburg, Robert Cuyler
Horne, Frederick Franklin
Horne, Kibbey Minton
Hornsey, Albert Edward
Hornstein, Robert Charles
Hornung, Erwin William
Horowitz, Ben
Horrigan, Jack Allen
Horstman, Dean Lewis
Horton, Ernest Horace, Jr.
Horton, James Sheldon
Horton, Karen Lucille
Horton, Robert Lumley
Horvath, Benedict Arpad
Horvath, Richard J.
Horwitz, Channa
Hosford, Ray E.
Hoshour, Harvey Sheely
Hoskins, J. Walter
Hosmer, Laurence Frederic
Hosokawa, William K.
Hosterman, Craig
Hotchkis, Preston
Hotchkiss, Henry Washington
Hotchkiss, William Rouse
Hotz, Henry Palmer
Houck, John Dudley
Houck-Lowery, W. Margaret
Hougen, James Russell
Hough, Carl Herbert
Houghteling, Joseph Cannon
Houghton, John Raymond
Houghton, Richard Burdette
Houk, John Louis
Houlihan, Patrick Thomas
Housel, James Robert, Jr.
Houseman, Donald Kenneth
Houser, Gene Lowell
Housholder, Kenneth Adelbert
Houston, Harry Rollins
Houston, Joseph Brantley, Jr.
Houston, Sylvester Raleigh
Houts, Marshall Wilson
Houze, William Cunningham, Jr.
Hovell, Frank
Hover, Gerald Robert
Hoving, Robert Andre
Hovsepian, Abraham
Howard, Bruce Godfrey
Howard, Emery, Jr.
Howard, George Wilberforce
Howard, Gerald Vincent
Howard, James Webb
Howard, Jane Osburn (Mrs. Rollins Stanley Howard)
Howard, John Alvin
Howard, John Hereford
Howard, John Vernon
Howard, Joseph DeSilva
Howard, Kirk Gordon
Howard, Marguerite Evangeline Barker (Mrs. Joseph D. Howard)
Howard, Murray
Howard, Richard Phillip
Howard, Sheldon
Howard, Thora Frances
Howard, Victor
Howay, John Cavan
Howe, Charles Bryan
Howe, J. Copeland
Howe, Jack Homer
Howe, John Tadlock
Howe, Margaret Rose
Howe, Patricia Mary
Howell, Alan Peter
Howell, Lawton Wade
Howell, Rita Arlene
Howell, Warren Richardson
Howells, Richard Timothy
Howenstein, George Herbert
Howes, Jeffrey Dane
Howes, Marshall Frederick
Howlett, Patricia Erskine
Howlett, Ralph Jacob
Howley, Peter A.
Howsley, Richard Thornton
Hoxie, Sue Ann
Hoye, Walter Brisco
Hoyt, Jack Wallace
Hoyt, William George
Hrachovec, Josef Pierun
Hrubesh, Lawrence Wayne
Hsi, David Ching Heng
Hsieh, Carl Chia-Fong
Hsiung, Andrew Kou-ying
Hsu, Liang Chi
Hu, Anthony Shih-An
Hu, Chi Yu
Hu, Richard E-Wei
Huang, David T.
Huang, Francis Fu-Tse
Huang, George Wenhong
Huang, Robert Yu
Hubbard, Dorothy Elaine
Hubbard, John Randolph
Hubbard, Stanley Stub
Huber, Beverly Jean
Huber, Clayton Shirl
Huber, Helen Mary
Huber, Herman Ronald
Huber, Robert Christopher
Hubert, Charles Edward
Hubner, Suzanne Simone
Huck, Robert Wardlow, III
Huckaby, Geraldine (Geri) Renee
Huckelberry, Charles Howard
Huckleberry, Robert James
Huddleston, Christine Jura
Huddleston, Mildred Dillon
Huddleston, Sam Leslie
Hudgins, Archibald Perrin, II
Hudnut, David Beecher
Hudson, David Earl
Hudson, Edward Voyle
Hudson, Eva Stewart
Hudson, Gary Michael
Hudson, Lawrence Urquhart
Hudson, Robert Neal
Hudson, Susan Ann
Hudson, William Harold
Hudspeth, Jimmy Davis
Hueber, Donald Francis
Huett, Claudia Rae
Huey, Craig Alan
Huff, Constance Champion
Huff, Norman Nelson
Huffman, Arthur Vincent
Huffman, Laurie Alford
Hufford, Leslie Alfred
Hufstedler, Seth Martin
Huggins, Ericka Cozette
Hughbanks, Charles Weldon
Hughes, Charles Campbell
Hughes, Clarence Zelmer
Hughes, Daniel Thomas
Hughes, Donnell Howard
Hughes, Edwin James
Hughes, Fleur
Hughes, George Ernest, Jr.
Hughes, J. Preston
Hughes, James Stahl
Hughes, Joseph Michael
Hughes, Julien Ramon
Hughes, Laddie (Gladys) Wilma
Hughes, Melville Prince
Hughes, Phillip Rogers
Hughes, Ralph Emory
Hughes, Robert Merrill
Hughes, Tor Lawrence Donald
Hughett, Bryce Glenburne
Hughs, Gary M.
Huglin, Henry Charles
Hugstad, Paul Steven
Huizenga, Clarence John
Huizingh, William

Huldermann, Paul F.
Huleatt, Richard Shovelton
Hulen, Marjorie Jane
Hulet, Mark Sylvester
Hulett, George Augustus
Hulgus, Joyce Louise
Hulick, N. Arthur, II
Hull, Cordell William
Hull, Eleanor Horner
Hull, Forrest Edgar
Hull, Jane Laurel Leek
Hull, Jess Stevens
Hullin, Stephen Light
Hulsebus, John Bernard
Hultquist, Paul F(redrick)
Humason, Theresa (Oswald)
Hume, Edwin James, Jr.
Humphrey, Marvin Earnest
Humphrey, Nyles Ray
Humphrey, Thomas Milton, Jr.
Humrich, LeRoy (Lee) E.
Hundhausen, Robert John
Hundley, David Holladay
Hungerford, Gerald Fred
Hungerford, Mark Calvin
Huning, Louis Fred
Hunkins, Francis Peter
Hunkins, Raymond Breedlove
Hunnewell, Geraldine Grosvenor
Hunnewell, John James
Hunnicutt, Richard Pearce
Hunsaker, Duane Cook
Hunsaker, Floyd B.
Hunt, Alfred Leo
Hunt, Douglas Alan
Hunt, Harold Keith
Hunt, Helen Vogel
Hunt, John Maurice
Hunt, Ralph Edward
Hunter, Charles Calvin
Hunter, E. Allan
Hunter, Henry Joseph
Hunter, Jack Blanchard
Hunter, Lorin T.
Hunter, Ray Skip
Hunter, Roger Clyde
Hunter, Wilmont Lennington
Hunthausen, Raymond Gerhardt
Huntington, Robert Eugene
Huntington, Robert Watkinson
Huntley, Robert Joseph
Hunton, Donald Bothen
Huntsinger, Herbert William
Huntzinger, Homer G.
Huo, Shuang
Hurabiell, John Philip
Hurd, Walter Leroy, Jr.
Hurless, Lois Jean Watson
Hurley, Daniel Benjamin
Hurley, Edward Daniel
Hurley, Francis T.
Hurley, Margaret Ellen
Hurley, Mark Joseph
Hurley, Robert Dale
Hurlich, Abraham
Hursh, John Ray
Hurst, Clayton Riley
Hurt, James Edward
Hurt, Robert Glenn
Hurtado, Corydon Dicks
Hurvitz, Joel Arnold
Husa, Veikko Lennie
Husney, Elliott Ronald
Hussain, Sayed Asghar
Hussey, John Adam
Hustead, Dennis Dee
Husting, Edward Lee
Huston, John Richard
Huston, William A.
Huszcza, Bert Edward
Hutchings, Brent Barry
Hutchings, Elby Lynn
Hutchinson, Ira K.
Hutchinson, Jack Homer
Hutchinson, John Howard, Jr.
Hutchinson, John Steve
Hutchinson, William Lloyd
Hutchison, Elizabeth Shimer
Hutchison, James Donald
Huttenback, Robert Arthur
Hutter, James Risque
Hutton, Aloysius Louis
Hutton, John Evans, Jr.
Huus, LeRoy Clarence
Hwang, Henry Yuan
Hwang, Jinjoo
Hyatt, M(ilton) Leon
Hyink, Pamela Jeane Addams
Hyman, Richard Samuel
Hynd, George William
Iachetti, Rose Maria Anne
Iaconetti, William Emil
Iannone, Edmund Faust
Ianziti, Adelbert John
Iatauro, Michael Anthony
Ibbetson, Edwin Thornton
Ibrahim, Hilmi M.
Ibs, Uwe Werner
Icardi, Dennis Nando
Ice, Richard Eugene
Icke, Roland Nathaniel
Idnani, Chandru Mangaldas
Idriss, Izzat M.
Ihara, Grace Reiko
Ihle, John Livingston
Ihrig, Judson La Moure
Ikeda, Donna Rika
Ikeda, Moss Marcus
Ikeda, Terumitsu (Teri)
Iki, Daniel Hiso
Ilett, Frank, Jr.
Ilett, William Kent
Illing, Hans Alfons
Illing, Rainer Milton Ernest
Imana, Jorge Garron
Imbrecht, Charles Richard
Imeson, Patrick William MacKay
Imig, John Richard
Immroth, Vernon Henry
Impey, Frances Triplett
Inaba, Lawrence A.
Inaba, Lloyd Hakaru
Inabu, Hanako Hana
Inacker, Charles John
Indreland, Rasmus Edward
Ineman, Ronald
Ing, Malcolm Ross
Ingalsbee, Charles Fenn, Jr.
Ingber, Lester
Inge, David Unger
Ingebretsen, James C(hristopher)
Ingels, Raymond Martin
Ingerman, Michael Leigh
Ingham, Alan Geoffrey
Ingham, Harvey, III
Ingham, Robert Edwin
Ingle, Alexander Wilfred
Inglish, Sumter Russell
Ingraham, Lloyd Lewis
Ingram, Francis Fritz Leland
Ingram, Gary John
Ingram, George Alton
Ingwersen, Martin Lewis
Inkeles, Alex
Inman, Clarence William
Inman, Mary Jane
Inniss, Peter Lancelot
Inouye, Arthur Yasuo
Inouye, Daniel Ken
Inouye, Mitsuo
Inouye, Toshio
Inskeep, Gordon Charles
Insley, Gerald Sloane
Intili, Jo-Ann Kohnstamm
Intriere, Anthony Donald
Ipsen, D(avid) C(arl)
Iqbal, Jawaid Khawaja
Ireijo, James Satoru
Ireland, Donald Ray
Ireland, Roger Blaine
Irmer, David Carl
Irvin, Robert Milton
Irvine, Florence Cranston
Irvine, Leland Karr
Irvine, Robert Bruce
Irwin, David Edward
Irwin, Emmett MacDonald
Irwin, James Benson
Irwin, James Robert
Irwin, Lee
Irwin, Paul
Irwin, Phyllis Ann
Isaac, Richard Burton
Isaacs, John Phillip
Isaacs, Robert Wolfe
Isaacson, Henry Carl, Jr.
Isbell, Harold Max
Isbell, Marion William
Iseli, André Werner
Isely, Henry Philip
Iseman, Caryl
Isern, Edward Henry
Isham, Dell
Isham, Howard Milton
Isham, Richard Basil
Ishihara, Melvin Shigeo
Ishikawa, Calvin Yasuhiko
Ishimatsu, Tomiye
Islam, Kazi Azizul
Isleib, Harry Albert
Ismail, Farouk Taha
Itabashi, Hideo Henry
Iversen, Phillip Gordon
Ivey, Stephen Bennett
Ivy, Benjamin Franklin, IV
Iwamoto, John Takahisa
Iwamoto, Vickie Michiko
Iwaoka, Wayne Tadashi
Izawa, Edward Hiroshi
Izenstark, Joseph Louis
Izzo, John
Jaacks, John William
Jablonn, Raymond Stanley
Jack, Ronald Collett
Jackson, Andrew Barbidge
Jackson, Anna Mitchell
Jackson, Arthur Copeland, Jr.
Jackson, Beverley Joy Jacobson
Jackson, David Henry
Jackson, Dick Stanley
Jackson, Donald Frank
Jackson, Dorothy Bailey
Jackson, Felix
Jackson, Frank Cline, Jr.
Jackson, George Herbert, Jr.
Jackson, Henry Martin
Jackson, James Green, Jr.
Jackson, Josie Jo Ann Leaver
Jackson, Karen Eleanor
Jackson, LeRoy Eugene
Jackson, Maurine Morrison
Jackson, Melvin Wheeler
Jackson, Richard Valentine
Jackson, Robert B.
Jackson, Robert John
Jackson, W(illard) Glen
Jacob, Stanley Wallace
Jacobi, Charles Arnold
Jacobs, Alma Smith
Jacobs, Chris B.
Jacobs, Edward Allen
Jacobs, Elias
Jacobs, John Deloss
Jacobs, Jonathan Lee
Jacobs, Joseph Donovan
Jacobs, Lawrence Irwin, III
Jacobs, Lionel John Wellesley
Jacobs, Mark Charles
Jacobs, Ralph, Jr.
Jacobs, Wilbur Ripley
Jacobsen, Adolf Marcelius Bergh
Jacobsen, Bruce Carl
Jacobsen, Lynn Clyone
Jacobsen, Parley Parker
Jacobsen, Thomas Harold
Jacobson, Calhoun Edward
Jacobson, Carl
Jacobson, David Scott
Jacobson, Donald Thomas
Jacobson, James Bassett
Jacobson, Margaret Jane
Jacobson, Norman Gustav, Jr.
Jacobson, Rovena Furnivall (Mrs. Calhoun E. Jacobson)
Jacobson, Thomas Ernest
Jacobson, Wilma Jean
Jacoby, Keith Edwin
Jacoshenk, James Dwight
Jaeger, Frederick George
Jaffa, Aileen Raby
Jaffa, Lawrence Marvin
Jaffe, Max
Jahn, Charles August
Jai, Raymond Benyuh
Jakey, Lauren Ray
Jallow, Raymond
Jallu, Ofa
Jalonen, John William
Jamero, Peter Madelo
James, Carol Joyce
James, David Lee
James, Frederick John
James, George Barker, II
James, Jack Richard
James, Jeannette Adeline
James, Lee (Jim Lee, James Wade Lee)
James, Marshall Ralph
James, Max Frederick
James, Mildred Hannah
James, Robert Andrew
James, Willard Clinton
Jameson, Charles Scott Kennedy
Jameson, Everett Williams, Jr.
Jameson, Helen Ronan
Jamieson, John Charles
Jamison, Rex Lindsay
Jamison, Robert Basil
Jan, Paul Tao
Janda, John Michael
Janiak, Betty Payne
Janis, Martin
Jankovitz, Joseph Edward
Jankowski, Raymond Matthew
Jannen, Robert Lawrence, Jr.
Jansen, James Robert
Janssens, Walter Delmar
Janura, Jan Arol
Jaouen, Stephen Harry
Japenga, Jack Wallace
Jaquith, George Oakes
Jaramillo, Jerry Raymond
Jarmie, Nelson
Jarrell, James Thomas
Jarrow, Lyle Mitchell
Jarvis, Donald Bertram
Jarvis, Paul Samuel
Jarvis, Raymond S.
Jaschek, Cherone Dee
Jasgur, Joseph
Jaudon, Joseph Cabell, Jr.
Javonovich, Joann
Jay, David Jakubowicz
Jayme, William North
Jayne, Louise Margaret (Mrs. Chester S. Kurzet)
Jeanney, Milton Ellsworth
Jebe, Walter George
Jedd, Joseph
Jefferds, Mary Lee
Jeffers, Lucie Spence
Jefferson, George Thomas
Jefferson, Janet Rebecca
Jeffredo, John Victor
Jeffress, Valerie Larsen
Jeffries, Don Fredrick
Jeffries, Howard McAllaster
Jeffs, Wallace Ellsworth
Jekel, Louis Glanz, Jr.
Jelinek, John Joseph
Jellico, John Anthony
Jeng, Joseph Liran
Jenkins, Arthur Clyde
Jenkins, George Henry
Jenkins, James Lee
Jenkins, James Lee
Jenkins, John Perley
Jenkins, Myra Ellen
Jenkins, Roger Leslie
Jenkins, William C.
Jenks, Marlowe Dryden
Jenks, Randolph
Jenne, Everett Arthur
Jenni, Donald Alison
Jennings, Frank Wilkins, III
Jennings, Janice Arlene
Jennings, Mary Catherine
Jennings, Michael Lee
Jennings, Timothy Zeph
Jens, Kathryn Sue
Jensen, Alton Dean
Jensen, Bernard Pisters
Jensen, Clayne R.
Jensen, Dwight William
Jensen, Eugene Burt
Jensen, Gaylord H.
Jensen, Gerald Kenneth
Jensen, Gordon Fred
Jensen, Harbo Peter
Jensen, Harold William
Jensen, Harvey James
Jensen, J. Robert
Jensen, Jay Peter
Jensen, John Jay
Jensen, Joseph Stokes
Jensen, Kenneth Christian
Jensen, Kenneth Darrell
Jensen, Moroni Lundby
Jensen, Paul Brigham
Jensen, Robert Julius
Jensen, Robert Victor
Jensen, Ronald Alan
Jensen, Verlyn Nadell
Jensen, Wayne Ivan
Jenson, Gwendolyn Mary
Jenson, William Keen
Jenssen, Ward Jack
Jeppesen, Moses Kay
Jeppesen, Sylvan A.
Jeppson, Lee Ralph
Jeppson, Robert Baird, Jr.
Jepsen, Carl H.
Jerke, Thomas Albert
Jerrems, Alexander Stapler
Jesch, Paul Mathew
Jeschke, Albert Walter
Jessen, David Wayne
Jessen, Joel
Jessen, Lester Steven
Jessup, Warren T.
Jester, Lester Rodger
Jetland, Robert Ingvald
Jewell, David William Muirhead
Jewell, Fredric Sells
Jewell, Harold Leon
Jewell, James Earl
Jewell, John Huttsell, Jr.
Jewett, Emelyn Knowland
Jewett, Frank Irving
Jimenez, Angel Jose
Jimenez, Joe Louis
Jobes, Margaret Owen
Jocelyn, Douglas Law
Joesting, Harriette Holt
Johannes, Dyanne Louise (Diz)
Johansen, Craig Eugene
Johansen, Frederick Peter
Johansson, Donald Rodney (Andre)
Johler, Joseph Ralph
John, Robert Herman
John, Ronald Ora
John, Urmila Joseph
Johns, Albert Cameron
Johns, David Homer
Johns, Varner Jay, Jr.
Johnson, Alan Robert
Johnson, Alice Loretta
Johnson, Anita Delores
Johnson, Ben Herbert
Johnson, Bruce
Johnson, Bruce Boddy
Johnson, Bruce Gordahl
Johnson, Byron Lamar
Johnson, Carl Earld
Johnson, Carl J.
Johnson, Charles Harry
Johnson, Clarence Elmer
Johnson, Clayton Errold
Johnson, Clayton Thomas
Johnson, Clifford Lee
Johnson, Clifton Leon
Johnson, Clinton Leslie
Johnson, Dale Harmon
Johnson, Dallas Albert
Johnson, Darrell Dean
Johnson, David Edward
Johnson, David Stanton
Johnson, Deanne Louise
Johnson, Deborah Lynn Barkan
Johnson, Dennis Stephen
Johnson, Derrill Lee
Johnson, Donald Edward, Jr.
Johnson, Earl, Jr.
Johnson, Ernest Kim
Johnson, Evan Theodore
Johnson, Frank H.
Johnson, Gardiner
Johnson, Gearold Robert
Johnson, Harald Valdimar
Johnson, Harold Peyton, Jr.
Johnson, Harold T.
Johnson, Henry Sioux
Johnson, Horace Richard
Johnson, Irene Claudette Morton
Johnson, James P.
Johnson, Jamison Cornelius
Johnson, John Allen
Johnson, John Maxie
Johnson, John Myrton
Johnson, Johnny Burl
Johnson, Joyce Rydell (Mrs. Miles B. Johnson)
Johnson, Judith Maule
Johnson, June Beverly Lombard
Johnson, Keith
Johnson, Kenneth Montgomery
Johnson, Kenneth Ray
Johnson, Kenneth Russell, Jr.
Johnson, Kent Ralph
Johnson, L(yle) Boyd
Johnson, Larry Neil
Johnson, Laymon, Jr.
Johnson, LeRoy Franklin, Jr.
Johnson, Loren Wesley
Johnson, Margaret Phillips
Johnson, Martin Clifton
Johnson, Mary Lee Clare (Mrs. Ralph A. Johnson)
Johnson, Merlyn Burdette
Johnson, Michael Lord
Johnson, Mina Marie
Johnson, Mont Adelbert
Johnson, P. Dale
Johnson, Patricia Lynn
Johnson, Qulan Adrian
Johnson, Ralph Maxwell
Johnson, Ralph Sterling, Jr.
Johnson, Raymond Martin, Jr.
Johnson, Richard Edwin
Johnson, Robert Charles
Johnson, Robert Dale
Johnson, Robert E.
Johnson, Robert Edward
Johnson, Robert Henry
Johnson, Robert Lee
Johnson, Robert Penn
Johnson, Roderick David
Johnson, Roger Miles
Johnson, Ronald Elliott
Johnson, Ronald William
Johnson, Ross Byron
Johnson, Samuel S(pencer)
Johnson, Sharon Czull
Johnson, Sherman Elbridge
Johnson, Stanley Calvold
Johnson, Stephen J.
Johnson, Stephen Lee
Johnson, Terrance Burton
Johnson, Thomas Randall
Johnson, Torrence Vaino
Johnson, Vard Hayes
Johnson, Vaughan Ambrose
Johnson, Vere Hodges
Johnson, Walter Earl
Johnson, Warren Cottle
Johnson, Wendell Kenneth
Johnson, William Potter
Johnson, William R.
Johnson, Wyatt Thomas, Jr.
Johnsos, Charles E.
Johnston, Charles William
Johnston, Charlotte Marie (Mrs. Howard F. Johnston)
Johnston, David Charles
Johnston, Edward Elliott
Johnston, Elizabeth Jane (Mrs. Graydon Oliver)
Johnston, John Gray
Johnston, Julius Percel, III
Johnston, Lillian Beatrice (Mrs. Charles L. Johnston)
Johnston, Sidney Michael
Johnston, Stoddard Pintard
Johnstone, James George
Johntz, James Andrew, Jr.
Joiner, Truman
Jolley, Leland Dwight
Jolly, Donald Lawrence
Jolly, James A.
Joncich, Pete Mathew
Jones, Allen Winston
Jones, Anna Lynn
Jones, Arnold Ware
Jones, Broadie Firmon, Jr.
Jones, Carroll Justice, Sr.
Jones, Clarence Klotz
Jones, Clyde William
Jones, Constance Carolyn
Jones, Dallen Hall
Jones, David Franklin
Jones, David Lackey
Jones, David Reed
Jones, Dorothy Cameron
Jones, Earl
Jones, Edwin Rutledge
Jones, Edyrn Hughes
Jones, Evelyn Wynn
Jones, Garth Nelson
Jones, George Howard, Jr.
Jones, George Paul
Jones, Gerald Joseph
Jones, Grant Richard
Jones, H(arold) Gilbert
Jones, Harold Arthur
Jones, Hugo William, Jr.
Jones, Hyzer William, Jr.
Jones, Ian Vivian
Jones, Irving Wolcott
Jones, J. Quentin
Jones, Jack
Jones, Jacob Gilbert
Jones, James Herbert, Jr.
Jones, James Kimball
Jones, James Lee
Jones, James Richardson
Jones, Jerry Lee
Jones, Jerry Lynn
Jones, Jimmie J.
Jones, John Carl
Jones, John Hayford
Jones, Joie Pierce
Jones, Kenneth LaMar
Jones, Lila Virginia
Jones, Lillye Henderson
Jones, Linnie Lee
Jones, Lloyd Amherst
Jones, Louis Worth
Jones, Michael Richard
Jones, Milton Wakefield
Jones, Morrison Holmes
Jones, Otha Lowell
Jones, Paul LeRoy
Jones, Ralph Edwin
Jones, Richard Allen
Jones, Richard Dennis
Jones, Robert Edward
Jones, Robert Henry
Jones, Robert Letts
Jones, Robert Stuart
Jones, Robert Warren
Jones, Roger Charles
Jones, Roger Clyde
Jones, Ronald Norman
Jones, Samuel Austin
Jones, Stanley R.
Jones, Suzetta Jean
Jones, Thomas M.
Jones, Thornton Keith
Jones, Vernon Frank
Jones, Vernon Quentin
Jones, William Paul
Jones, William Thomas
Jones, Wyman H.
Jonish, Arley Duane
Jopson, Jana
Jordan, Barry Duane
Jordan, Dan Joseph
Jordan, Gary Blake
Jordan, James Jackson
Jordan, John Russell
Jordan, Morton Philip
Jordan, Robert Harley
Jordan, Robert Irwin
Jordan, Thomas Francis
Jordan, Thurston Carr, Jr.
Jordon, Albert Leon
Jorgensen, Bruce Herman
Jorgensen, David William
Jorgensen, Gordon David
Jorgensen, Joyce Orabelle
Jorgensen, Judith Ann
Jorgensen, Leland Howard
Jorgensen, Raymond Andrew
Jorgensen, Robert Kenneth
Joroslow, Jerry
Joseph, Joe Samuel
Joseph, Sandra L.
Joslen, Robert Andrew
Joss, Robert L.
Jouris, William
Journey, Eugene Kenneth
Jovick, Anton
Joy, Carla Marie
Joy, Paul Charles
Joy, Robert McKernon
Joyce, James Donald
Joyner, Conrad Francis
Jozwik, Francis Xavier
Juba, Sheila
Jubiz, William Alfredo
Jucius, Michael James
Judd, Bruce Raymond
Judd, Howard Stanley
Judd, Lewis Lund
Judge, Thomas Lee
Judson, Carl Justice, Jr.
Juhola, Bruce Martin
Jui, Wen
Juillard, Floyd
Julian, Barbara Marie (Wilson)
Julien, Carlos Enrique
Julio, Tony
Jumonville, Felix Joseph, Jr.
Jung, Charles Chester, Jr.
Jung, Kwan Yee
Jung, Norman Soo Hoo
Jung, Yee Wah
Jungherr, John Anton
Jurina, Robert Steven
Jurovich, Marilynn Rethel Hubbard Mitchell
Just, Ronald Andrew
Justiz, Manuel J.
Jutila, George Armas
Kaanaana, Bonnie (Jean)
Kaasch, Karl Douglas
Kackley, Evan Morgan
Kadane, Robert Andrews
Kadarkay, Arpad Andrew
Kadell-Kadelburg, Katherine
Kadey, Frederic Lionel, Jr.
Kado, Clarence Isao
Kaeding, George Galen
Kaelin, John Martin
Kaelke, Marylou Louise
Kaempen, Charles Edward
Kafesjian, Ann Karen
Kafesjian, Ralph Raffi
Kafoury, Stephen
Kagy, Virgil Clarence
Kahler, Alex LeRoy
Kahn, H. Donald
Kahn, Irwin William
Kahn, Paul Markham
Kahn, Robert Irving
Kahn, Roy Max
Kaiman, Sarah
Kairys, John
Kaiser, E(dgar) F(osburgh)
Kaiser, Ruth Harter (Mrs. Robert M. Kaiser)
Kaitschuk, Robert Charles
Kajioka, Ben
Kakkis, Albert
Kaku, Michio
Kalb, Jeffrey Clifford
Kalemkiarian, David Haig
Kalenscher, Alan Jay
Kalfayan, Sarkis Hagop
Kallenbach, W(illiam) Warren
Kallenberg, John Kenneth
Kallweit, Richard Gene
Kalthoff, Nancy Yvonne
Kalua, Ted Reimann
Kaluhiokalani, Norman A.
Kalupa, Frank B.
Kalvinskas, John Joseph
Kamack, Nanette Helen (Mrs. Bennie Lee Kamack)
Kamakawiwoole, Reynolds Nakooka, Jr.
Kamashian, Marx
Kambas, Paul Dino
Kamegai, Minao
Kamemoto, Haruyuki
Kamen, Robert Edmond
Kamil, Hasan
Kamilli, Diana Chapman
Kamm, Michael Lewis
Kamp, Mabel Kathryn Thronson
Kamusikiri, James Guveya

Kan, Henry
Kanagawa, Robert Kiyoshi
Kanai, Melvyn Tadao
Kanaiaupuni, Dorothea Lewis
Kanarian, Thomas Alan
Kandel, William
Kandell, Howard Noel
Kandler, Paul Alfred
Kane, Dorothea Sanderson
Kane, Edward Ferdinand
Kane, Eneas Dillon
Kane, John Eugene
Kane, John Lawrence, Jr.
Kane, Philip M.
Kanes, Martin
Kaneshige, Lincoln Toichi
Kang, Ki Dong
Kania, Alan James
Kanna, George Akira
Kant, Harold Sanford
Kanter, Charles Allen
Kanuit, Randall James
Kanz, Garry Minnis
Kao, Peter Chih Ta
Kao, Theodore
Kaplan, Frank L.
Kaplan, George Willard
Kaplan, Herman
Kaplan, Louis
Kaplan, Nathan Oram
Kaplan, Ozer Benjamin
Kaplan, Philip Irwin
Kapp, Alan Howard
Kappner, Christhart Hermann
Kapson, Melvin Herman
Kapur, Gopal Krishan
Kapushion, Marvin John
Karam, Richard Paul
Karatzas, Steven George
Karcher, William Ralph
Karcic, John Ramon
Kardush, Marcelle M(arie)
Karl, Herman Adolf
Karle, Werner
Karlin, Myron D.
Karlstrom, Paul Johnson
Karlton, Lawrence K.
Karns, Frederick Richard
Karols, Kenneth
Karow, William Frederick
Karp, Stanley Edward
Karpenko, Victor Nicholas
Karpf, Merrill Hugh
Karpilow, Craig
Karr, Don John
Karr, Reynold Michael, Jr.
Karrer, Lawrence Edison
Karsatos, James Gust
Karsh, Jerome William
Karson, Burton Lewis
Karsten, Mary Elizabeth O'Keeffe
Kaschak, Ellyn
Kasem, Ahmed
Kashin, Nicolai Nicolaevich
Kaslow, Arthur Louis
Kaslow, David Martin
Kasonic, John Frank
Kasson, James Matthews
Kassorla, Irene Chamie
Kasten, Gerald Allen
Katague, David Balleza, Jr.
Kataoka, Mitsuru
Katayama, Arthur Shoji
Kates, Harold H.
Katter, Margaret Ann Radakovich
Katyryniuk, Michael Joseph
Katz, Francine Hokin
Katz, Gene Irwin
Katz, John I.
Katz, Michael Victor
Katz, Myron B.
Katz, Ronald Lewis
Katzman, Charles
Katzman, Don
Katzman, James Allen
Kau, Darlene Mei-ling
Kauble, Roger Danny
Kauchich, John Steven
Kauffman, George Bertram
Kaufhold, Robert Ross
Kaufman, David Graham
Kaufman, Harold Richard
Kaufman, John
Kaufman, Stephen Allan
Kaufmann, William John, III
Kaulili, Alvina Nye
Kaune, James Edward
Kavan, William Edward
Kaveney, Gregory Hutson
Kawahara, Ronald Akira
Kawana, Koichi
Kawecki, Leon Stanley
Kaya, Robert Masayoshi
Kaye, Alan Jarman
Kaye, Alex Robert (Sandy)
Kaye, Barry
Kaye, David Norman
Kaye, Herman Harold
Kaye, Norman
Kaylor, Richard Lloyd
Kays, William Morrow
Kayton, Howard H.
Kayton, Myron
Kazazian, Maral Mayda
Kazmerski, Lawrence L(ee)
Ke, Theophane Nguyen Van
Keach, Kenneth Lowell
Keady, William Leo, Jr.
Kealiher, Gail D(ean)
Kear, Fred Winston
Kearney, Owen Francis
Kearns, Charles Richard
Kearns, James Francis
Kearns, William Joseph
Keating, Eugene Kneeland
Keating, Thomas James, Jr.
Keatinge, Richard Harte
Kececioglu, Dimitri Basil
Keck, James Stanton
Keddeinis, Marita Kathe
Keef, James Lewis
Keefe, Howard Mansfield
Keefner, Eugene Francis
Keely, George Clayton
Keen, Philip Earl
Keenan, Margaret Mary
Keenan, Robert Joseph
Keenan, Robert Louis
Keene, Samuel James, Jr.
Keener, Ronald Lynn
Keeney, Edmund Ludlow
Keeney, Steven Charles
Keepin, George Robert, Jr.
Keever, Robert Ellis
Keezer, Richard Clark
Kefauver, Nancy DePue
Kefford, Noel Price
Kegel, Richard Frederick Clement
Kehoe, Thomas Joseph
Keil, Robert Alvin
Keil, Ronald Lee
Keim, Paul Ferdinand
Keith, Donald Malcolm
Keith, Gordon
Keith, Jerry Warren
Keith, Samuel S., Jr.
Keithan, John William, Jr.
Keithley, Roger Lee
Kelday, Joan Marie
Keleher, Michael Lawrence
Kellahin, James Richard
Keller, Diane Lee
Keller, Frances Richardson
Keller, Gary Lee
Keller, George Matthew
Keller, Glen Elven, Jr.
Keller, Paul Dudley
Keller, William James
Kelley, Donald E.
Kelley, Frank
Kelley, James Alexander
Kelley, Orville LeRoy
Kelley, Patrick Martin
Kelley, Paul Joseph
Kelley, Robert Lloyd
Kelley, Thomas Dennison
Kelliher, Michael M.
Kellner, Theda Aileen Butler (Mrs. Harvey William Kellner)
Kellogg, Frederick
Kellogg, Joseph Christopher
Kellogg, Ralph Henderson
Kellow, Charles David
Kelly, Bertha Margaret
Kelly, Burgess Frank
Kelly, Donald Horton
Kelly, Eric Damian
Kelly, George Clinton
Kelly, Gerald Gregory
Kelly, Howard DeWitt
Kelly, J(ohn) Norman
Kelly, Joe (James Joseph)
Kelly, John
Kelly, Kevin MacLachlan
Kelly, Michael Allen
Kelly, Patricia Anne
Kelly, Paul Joseph, Jr.
Kelly, Suzanne Marie
Kelly, Thompson James
Kelly, Tim
Kelly, William Bret
Kelly, William Cody
Kelso, Charles Edmund
Kelvin, Patricia Rosemary
Kemble, Gordon Benjamin, Jr.
Kemp, John Wilmer
Kemp, Joseph Wesley
Kemp, Mae Wunder
Kemp, Wayne Russell
Kemper, Alfred Maria
Kemper, Bernard Francis
Kemper, John Dustin
Kempf, George Vincent
Kendall, Chris Murray
Kendall, James Arthur
Kenin, Stephen Reinhardt
Kenison, Bob A.
Kenley, Daniel Edward
Kenn, Charles William
Kennedy, Bruce Adrian
Kennedy, Donald Reid
Kennedy, Gerald (Hamilton)
Kennedy, Jack Irving, Sr.
Kennedy, John Brian
Kennedy, Lawrence Aloysius, Jr.
Kennedy, Pamela Charlene
Kennedy, Richard Lee
Kennedy, Ted Walter
Kennel, John Maurice
Kennon, Robert Bruce
Kenny, Douglas Timothy
Kenny, Robert Leon
Kenoyer, Judson Lee
Kenoyer, Leon Albert
Kent, George Arthur
Kent, Harry Christison
Kent, Richard Cortland
Kenyon, Myron David, Jr.
Keosheyan, Carl
Ker, Robert Harold
Kerman, Barry Martin
Kern, Ann Thompson
Kern, Earl Ray
Kern, Philip Brooke
Kern, Robert Bradford
Kern, Virginia Knox
Kerns, Janice Lee
Kerr, Farnum Woodward
Kerr, James Wilfrid
Kerr, John Fay
Kerr, John Russell
Kerr, Kleon Harding
Kerr, Knight Belnap
Kershaw, Doug
Kersting, Robert Edward
Kerth, Leroy Thomas
Kervick, Richard John
Kesler, Stephen John
Kessel, Robert William
Kesselring, John Paul
Kessler, Andre Eugene
Kessner, Daniel Aaron
Kestenbaum, Louis
Kester, Don Wesley
Kester, Donald Leslee
Kestler, Lois
Ketcham, Eugene Craig
Ketchum, Robert Dawes
Ketterer, Warren Ansgar
Keuhn, Warren Johnson
Keuss, Jeffrey Frank
Keville, Jesse Farchon
Key, Mary Ritchie (Mrs. Audley E. Patton)
Keyes, James Bondurant
Keyes, Robert Wyatt
Keyes, Wayne Porter
Kho, James Wang
Khosharian, Vartan Nazaret
Khosla, Ved Mitter
Khtaian, George Arlon, Jr.
Kibbey, Ray Anne
Kibrick, Stephen Arthur
Kichen, Lee Fredric
Kidd, David Thomas
Kidd, Reuben Proctor
Kiddy, Hugh Donald
Kidwell, Elston LeRoy
Kiehm, Leonard Yong Hee
Kielsmeier, Catherine Jane
Kiely, Tom
Kienlen, Thomas Dale
Kienzle, Robert Lee
Kiepe, Paul Edwin
Kiesbuy, Donald Michael
Kiessling, Gerd
Kiesz, Robert Arthur
Kiger, Roger Sylvester
Kiggins, Andrew
Kilgore, Eugene Sterling, Jr.
Kilishek, George Thomas
Killam, Eva King
Killebrew, Ellen Jane (Mrs. Edward S. Graves)
Killeen, Jacqueline Traylor
Killinger, Mark Howard
Killion, Leo Vincent
Killpack, Merlin Leo
Kim, Byong-kon
Kim, Dewey Hongwoo
Kim, Donald Chang Won
Kim, Hongjin
Kim, Keith
Kimball, Dick (Charles Richard Robator)
Kimball, Lorenzo Kent
Kimball, Raymond Alonzo
Kimball, Reid Roberts
Kimball, Richard Nephi
Kimball, Roger Stanley
Kimbell, Marion Joel
Kimberling, John Farrell
Kimble, Roy Francis
Kinard, Jamie Spencer
Kincheloe, Dorothy H.
Kindred, Leslie Withrow
Kinert, John Oscar
King, Alan Shell
King, Anthony Simeon
King, Bruce
King, Christopher James
King, David
King, Donald Bradford
King, Edward Leon
King, Frank William
King, Gundar Julian
King, Hanford Langdon, Jr.
King, Harold Taft
King, Harry Richard
King, Helen Blanche
King, Jean Sadako
King, Michael Merritt
King, Ronald Albert
King, Samuel Pailthorpe
Kingham, William Elmer
Kingsley, Bonnie Marie
Kingsley, John Raymond
Kingsley, Sherwood Clark
Kingston, Harry Robert
Kinley, Paul Rodney
Kinman, David Wendell
Kinnear, Willis Hayes
Kinney, Beverly J.
Kinney, Harry E.
Kinney, Jack Alanson
Kinney, James Michael
Kinney, Rayner Haliimaile
Kinney, Robert Gerry
Kinney, Rodney Paul
Kinney, Wilbur Clare
Kinnie, Kenneth Ivan
Kinnison, Robert Ray
Kinser, Richard Edward
Kinsey, Mattie (Mrs. Glaucus E. Kinsey)
Kinsey, Sally Jane
Kinsey-Calori, Joanne
Kinsman, Robert Starr
Kintner, Paul Leroy
Kintsel, Betty Carol
Kintzele, John Alfred
Kinyon, Gilbert Eugene
Kirby, Calvin Jon
Kirby, Cynthia Cornelia
Kirby, David Ray
Kirby, Warren Lloyd
Kirchner, Don F.
Kirdar, Edib E.
Kiritz, Norton Julian
Kirk, Helen White (Mrs. Kenneth Burson Kirk)
Kirk, Henry Port, III
Kirk, Richard A.
Kirk, William Leroy
Kirkby, Gordon Wellesley
Kirkemo, Ronald Bamford
Kirkham, Dan Romaine
Kirkland, Bertha Theresa
Kirkorian, Donald George
Kirkpatrick, Douglas Haigh
Kirkpatrick, Edward J.
Kirkpatrick, Loy Duane
Kirkpatrick, Richard Alan
Kirkwood, Roderick Richard
Kirn, June Hoffsommer
Kirpalani, Pamela Tadlock
Kirsch, Susan Grein Sayers
Kirschbrown, Richard Harry
Kirshbaum, Joseph
Kirshen, Edward Jerome
Kirtland, Michael Edward
Kirtland, Richard Lee
Kirts, Wayne Charles
Kiser, John Remy
Kishner, Irwin
Kiss, Anthony Joseph
Kissel, Julia Gunn
Kistner, David Harold
Kitajima, Noritaka
Kitchell, Robert Payton
Kitchen, Clyde Keith
Kitchen, Lawrence Oscar
Kitchener, Saul Laurence
Kitowski, Karen Ardell Klotz
Kitsco, John Phillip
Kittler, Dennis Roger
Kivisild, Hans Robert
Kjeldsen, Chris K.
Klag, Edwin James
Klainer, Stanley Melvin
Klammer, Joseph Francis
Klare, Eugene Francis
Klascius, Alfonse Frank
Klass, Betty Ann
Klassen, Charles Richard
Klatt, Ervin
Klausner, Manuel Stuart
Klausner, Willette Murphy
Klawitter, Ralph Alex
Klehs, Henry John Wilhelm
Kleiman, Joseph
Klein, Arnold William
Klein, Carl Gottlieb
Klein, Earl H(yman)
Klein, Edith Iolamay Miller (Mrs. Sandor S. Klein)
Klein, Eugene Victor
Klein, Irving
Klein, James Albert
Klein, Jeffrey Bruce
Klein, Joel Alvin
Klein, Joseph N.
Klein, Keith Loss
Klein, Maurice J.
Klein, Paul Oscar
Klein, Robert Hunter
Kleinberg, Philip Reuben
Kleinman, Ralph Maurice
Kleist, Frank William
Klemenic, John
Klemmer, Andrew Gow
Klenhard, Dick
Kleppe, John Arthur
Klerer, Joseph
Kleven, David Keith
Kleyhauer, Alfred Dietrich
Kliks, Bernard Brill
Kline, James Alfred
Kline, Leo Virgil
Kline, Michael Vee
Kline, Richard Stephen
Kline, Thomas Henry
Klipping, Robert Samuel
Klocker, Thomas Dorsey
Kloek, Christopher Donald
Klohs, Murle William
Klonoff, Harry
Klopfer, F(lorenz) Dudley
Klopsch, Raymond Albert
Klosterman, Donald
Klotsche, Charles Martin
Klott, David Lee
Kluber, Robert Ernest
Kluckhohn, Florence Rockwood (Mrs. George E. Taylor)
Knaebel, Jeff
Knaebel, John Ballantine
Knapp, Eber Guy
Knapp, Jules O.
Knapp, Karl Kent
Knapp, Mary Elizabeth
Knapp, Stuart Eugene
Knapp, Terry Russell
Knapp, Thomas Edwin
Knechtges, David Richard
Knepper, Richard Scott
Kniazewycz, Bohdan George
Knief, Ronald Allen
Knierim, Robert Valentine
Knight, Charles Alfred
Knight, Charles Henry
Knight, Charles Spurgeon
Knight, Donna Marie
Knight, Douglas Wayne
Knight, Granville Frank
Knight, Harry Lionel
Knight, Herman Elvin
Knight, Jackie Larry
Knight, Katherine Anne
Knight, Kirk Lay
Knight, Philip Robert
Knight, Vick (Ralph), Jr.
Knight, Virginia Lucinda
Knill, Lamar Mervin
Knipe, Oren Duane
Knittel, Martin Dean
Knobloch, Ferdinand J.
Knoepfler, Peter Tamas
Knoll, Samson Benjamin
Knoll, William Ferdinand
Knop, Edward Charles
Knorr, Jeffrey Bruce
Knorr, Lynn Edward
Knorr, Owen Albert
Knowles, John Carl
Knowles, William Gordon
Knowlton, Harold George, II
Knowlton, Sandra Lee
Knowlton, Thomas Edward
Knox, Harold Edwin
Knox, James Lester
Knox, John Theryll
Knox, Naphtali Herzl
Knudsen, Chresten Mills
Knudsen, Conrad Calvert
Knudsen, Eric Ingvald
Knudsen, John Peder
Knudsen, Larry Stephen
Knudsen, Walter Louis
Knudson, Darrell La Moyne
Knudson, Melvin Robert
Knudson, Robert LeRoy
Knudson, Ruthann
Knudtzon, Halvor
Ko, Cheng Chia
Kober, Carl L.
Kober, Theodore Ernest
Kobler, Helmut George
Koblin, Ronald Lee
Kobrosky, Karen Roma
Kobza, Dennis Jerome
Koch, Alwin George
Koch, Elmer Leonard
Koch, Glen Vernon
Koch, Howard W.
Koch, Huldrich
Koch, Robert John
Koch, William Richard
Koczur, Rose Julia
Koeberer, John Wayne
Koehler, Charles Arthur
Koehler, Vera Jean
Koehn, Hank Emde
Koellner, Katherine Tarpley
Koelzer, Victor Alvin
Koeppel, Gary Merle
Koffmann, Eugen
Kofranek, Anton Miles
Kogasaka, Herbert Mamoru
Kogovsek, Ray Peter
Kohl, Gretchen Marie
Kohler, Arthur Degen, Jr.
Kohler, Royden Ramon
Kohn, Gerhard
Kohn, Robert Samuel, Jr.
Kohn, Roger Alan
Koho, Dennis Eugene
Koide, Frank Takayuki
Koito, Noboru
Kojancik, Joe John
Kokaska, Charles James
Kokkeler, Larry Anthony
Kolar, Jane (Mitzi) Michelle
Kolb, Ken Lloyd
Kolbe, James Thomas
Kolbert, Jack
Kolender, William Barnett
Koler, Joseph, Jr.
Kolesar, Stephen Mero
Kolhede, Joseph Karl
Kolke, Tsuneo
Koll, Serge Rudolph
Kollar, Ernest Paul
Kolom, Aaron Leigh
Kolterer, Franz
Koltun, Peter Jeffrey
Kolyer, John McNaughton
Komatz, George Thomas, Jr.
Komen, Richard Ben
Kon, Megumi
Kondo, (Eisuke) John
Kondo, Sadao
Kondo, Yoshio
Kondrasuk, John (Jack) Norton
Konicek, Thomas Peter
Konold, A(lbert) Ewing
Konyn, Edmond Sylvain
Koogler, Russell Lewis
Koonce, John Peter
Koonin, Alfred Julian
Koons, Harry Coleman
Kopecky, Curtis James
Kopel, Gerald Henry
Koponen, Niilo Emil
Kopp, Harriet Green
Kopplin, David A.
Koprowski, Eugene Joseph
Koptionak, William
Korb, Lawrence John
Kordus, Henry
Korf, Harold Edward
Korkmas, Carolyn Crawford
Korn, Noel
Kornberg, Arthur
Kornblum, Guy Orville
Kornegay, Phyllis Mills
Korp, Patricia Anne Munn (Mrs. Vincent Korp)
Korpman, Ralph Andrew
Korson, Beatrice Gunner Goldman
Kosai, Joseph Hideo
Koselka, Mary Josephine
Koshak, John Anthony
Koshland, Daniel E., Jr.
Koskinen, Sulo Matias
Koss, Neal
Kossa, Miklos Magyary
Kost, Richard Stephen
Kostiner, Priscilla Bloom
Kotcheff, Ted
Kothny, Evaldo Luis
Kotsiris, Laura Diane
Kottke, Frederick Edward
Kottler, Howard William
Kottlowski, Frank Edward
Kotzebue, Kenneth Lee
Koubourlis, Demetrius John
Kounaves, Samuel Paul
Kouri, Richard James
Koutras, Alexander Efthimios
Kovach, Ladis Daniel
Kovalenko, Virgil Nicholas
Kovalevsky, Leonid
Kovinick, Philip Peter
Kowalek, Jon W.
Kowrach, Edward Jerome
Kozman, Theodore Albert
Kracow, Joel Lee
Kraemer, Sandy Frederick
Kraft, Charles Howard
Kraft, Eleanor Ann
Kraft, Richard Lawrence
Kraft, Toby Louis
Krahenbil, Karl
Krakower, Bernard Hyman
Kral, Victor Emanuel
Krall, Nicholas Anthony
Kramer, Anne Pearce
Kramer, Bauer Edwin
Kramer, Donovan Mershon
Kramer, Howard Stanley, Jr.
Kramer, Kenneth Bentley
Kramer, Kenneth Elliot
Kramer, Richard Jay
Kramer, William Max
Kramp, Gregory Lawrence
Krasner, Oscar Jay
Krasovich, Edward Joseph
Kratzer, Frank Howard
Kraus, John Walter
Kraus, Pansy Daegling
Krause, Lloyd Thomas
Krause, Norbert Steven, Jr.
Krause, Robert Lee
Krause, Robert William
Krauss, George
Kravitz, Ellen King
Krcmar, Janet A. Dixon (Mrs. Ludwig Leopold Krcmar IV)
Krebs, John Hans
Kreditor, Alan
Kreer, Laura Blackstone
Kreider, Jan Frederick
Kreider, Lloyd Robert
Kreiger, Bruce Dennis
Kren, Harold Edwin
Krenz, Dennis Lyle
Krenzer, Robert Wayne
Kresa, Kent
Kresge, Ralph Arlington
Kresge, Stephen Patrick
Kretschmer, Ernest Theodore
Krieger, Aaron
Krieger, Herbert Charles, Jr.
Krieger, Kenneth William
Krieger, Royal Gene
Kriger, Peter Wilson
Kriken, John Lund
Krikos, George Alexander
Krippner, Stanley Curtis
Krishnamurthi, N. (Kris)
Krishnamurthy, Gerbail Thimmegowda
Kroc, Ray A.
Kroener, William Frederick, Jr.
Kroepsch, Robert Hayden
Krone, Frank William
Krone, Robert Max
Kronmiller, Eugene Victor
Kronwall, Nicholas Burling
Kroon, Debra Lynette
Kropotoff, George Alex
Kross, Burton Clare
Krout, Michael Seth
Kruchek, Thomas Francis
Krueger, James
Kruger, Richard Joseph
Kruger, Robert Alan
Kruglak, Theodore Edward
Krull, Irwin Herbert
Krum, Dennis John
Krupp, Marcus Abraham
Krus, David James
Kruschke, Earl Roger
Kubesh, Kenneth Willard
Kubokawa, Charles Chiharu
Kuby, Stephen Allen
Kucharek, Casimir Anthony
Kuchel, Thomas H(enry)
Kuchler, Paul Joseph
Kuchler, Phillip Gleaves
Kuck, Marie Elizabeth Bukovsky
Kucklinca, Stephen John
Kudirka, Alvydas Anthony
Kudler, Morris
Kudo, Emiko Iwashita
Kueber, Anthony Joseph
Kuehl, Max Karl
Kuehn, Klaus Karl Albert
Kuffel, Cornelius F.
Kuh, Michael Edward
Kuharski, Philip Edmund
Kuhi, Leonard Vello
Kuhn, Martin Clifford
Kuhn, Peter Mouat
Kuhn, Robert Lawrence
Kuhn, Sarah Sappington

Kuhns, Grant Wilson
Kuhns, William Edward
Kukla, William John
Kulchin, Bernard Albert
Kulkarni, Hemant B.
Kullman, Paul Michael
Kullman, Valeria Sue
Kulongoski, Theodore Ralph
Kulp, John Austin, Jr.
Kulstad, Guy Charles
Kumamoto, Junji
Kumar, Parmanand
Kummer, Ralph Walter
Kung, Shien Woo
Kunimoto, Elizabeth Nakaeda
Kunin, Richard Allen
Kunkel, George Myhre
Kunkler, J.L.
Kunter, Richard Sain
Kunz, Phillip Ray
Kunz, Robert Despain
Kunze, Karl Richard
Kuo, Chia Chu
Kuo, Ping-Chia
Kuppenbender, Clair Lawrence
Kurrus, Joseph Antone
Kurtak, Charles Raymond
Kurtz, Francis Anthony
Kurtzman, Samuel Michael
Kushi, Harold Sukenobu
Kushner, James Paul
Kutina, Scott Edward
Kutsko, Michael James
Kutter, Lloyd Ray
Kuwabara, Dennis Matsuichi
Kuyer, John Brand
Kuyper, Donald Mellema
Kuzara, Stanley Andrew
Kuzell, William Charles
Kwan, Benjamin Ching Kee
Kwan, Yen Chi
Kwasny, Harry Paul
Kwee, Hian Hoey
Kwong, Tin Yu
Kyle, Robert Hart
Kyle, Robert Tourville
Kyle, William Dennis
Kyler, Orville Ross
Kyllo, Theodore Robert
Kyriakis, Victor Gus
LaBarre, William Ellis
Labs, David
LaCasella, Michael
Lacasia, Rene Garcia
Lacertosa, Joanne Theresa
Lachermeier, Joseph Leo
Lachman, Alan Barry
Lachman, Ralph Theodore
Lackman, David Buell
La Claustra, Vera Berneicia
 Derrick
LaCombe, James L.
La Count, Louise Winter
La Cour, James Delano
La Croix, Jay Kenneth
Lacroix, Rene Eugene Emile
Lacy, Robert Griffith
Ladar, Jerrold Morton
Ladd, Conrad Mervyn
Ladd, Donald Mc Kinley, Jr.
Ladin, David
Ladizinsky, Ivan
Laengrich, Norbert Roy
Laetsch, Watson McMillan
LaFave, Larry Francais
LaFlash, Judson Clinton
Laghos, Panayiotis
 Sophocleous
Lagomarsino, Robert John
La Guardia, Jack Ernest
Lai, Waihang
Laiblin, Katherine Holt
 Hundley
Laidlaw, Douglas McNeill
Laird, Dale Alan
Laird, Richard Claude
Laitinen, Glenn Milton
Lake, Kevin Bruce
Lake, Meno Truman
Lakers, Lynn Ann
Lakin, Robert Dean
Lalakea, Thomas Kanamu
Lam, Ernest Yee-Yeung
Lamadrid, Enrique Eufrasio
La Mancusa, Myrlene
 Thompson
Lamb, George A.
Lamb, George Ervin
Lamb, Gregory George
Lamb, James Francis
Lamb, Thomas
Lamb, Willis Eugene, Jr.
Lambdin, Louis Carter
Lambe, John Michael
Lamberson, John Roger
Lambert, David Roy
Lambert, James Russell
Lamberti, N.A.
Lambeth, Robert Gene
Lambson, Phillip Dennis
Lamm, Richard D.
Lamon, Evelyn Nicolas
LaMountain, Fran
L'Amour, Louis (Dearborn)
Lampard, William John
Lampert, Ruth Joyce Tauber
Lamph, Melvin Lavell
Lampi, Gary Lee
Lancaster, Herman Burtram
Lance, Algie L.
Landau, Martin
Landenberger, C(harles)
 Frederick
Lander, Richard Leon
Landers, Newlin Jewel
Landers, Patricia Ann
Landers, Vernette Trosper
 (Mrs. Newlin Landers)
Landes, Geraldine Steinberg
 (Mrs. Bernard A. Landes)
Landess, Charles (Cal) Arthur
Landgraf, Mary Elizabeth
 Norton (Mrs. David L.
 Landgraf)
Landholm, Wallace Marven
Landis, Charles
Landis, Constance Ann
Landis, Lewis
Landmann, Heinz Richard
Landon, Joseph Warren
Landrey, James Paul
Landrum, Wayne
Landrus, Wilfred Mason
Landsbaum, Ellis Merle
Lane, E(dna) Joyce
Lane, Howard Raymond
Lane, James Alden
Lane, Zanier Downs
Laney, Billie Eugene
Lang, Edmund Joseph
Lang, Henry Adolph
Lang, James DeVore, Jr.
Lang, John Francis, II
Lang, Margo Terzian
Lang, Robert Arnold
Lang, Thompson Hughes
Lang, Tzu-Wang
Langdon, Edward Allen
Langdon, Joseph Raymond
Lange, Donald Eugene
Lange, Paul Martin
Langeler, Gerard Hendrik
Langford, Ralph Leslie
Langham, Derald George
Langhans, Edward Allen
Langley, Reta Joyce
Langley, Rolland Ament, Jr.
Langlie, Arthur Sheridan
Langlois, Aimee
Langlois, Walter Gordon
Langoni, Richard Allen
Langpaap, Eleanor Madeline
Langsford, Guy Lacy
Langston, Robert Lee
Langton, Michael George
Lanham, Urless Norton
Lanier, H. Don
Lankford, Avery Lionell
Lansing, Sherry Lee
Lanstrom, Sigvard Willhelm
Lanter, Robert Jackson
Lanthrum, Joseph Gary
Lantz, Alma Esther
Lantz, Terry Lee
Lanyi, Janos Karoly
Lanza, Peggy Ann
Lapan, David Ira
LaPoe, Wayne Gilpin
Lapolla, Anthony
Lappen, Chester I.
Lappen, Stanley Julian
LaQuey, Thomas A.
Lara, Joe Martin
Laramee, Richard Clay
Lardy, Mathias Michael
Largent, Frank Dean
Lark, Raymond
Larkin, Charles Byrne
Larkin, Frederick George, Jr.
Larkin, Kathleen Marie
Larkin, Marita Therese
 Oppenheim
Larks, Leonard
La Rocca, Gerard Anthony
LaRocca, Jack Channing
La Rock, Robert Lawrence
LaRocque, Marilyn Ross
 Onderdonk
Larrimore, James Abbott
Larsen, Charmaine Emilie
Larsen, Eric Laverne
Larsen, Gareld Rudolph
Larsen, George Christian
Larsen, Karl Martell
Larsen, Levi LaGrande
Larsen, Oliver Herman
Larsen, Paul Gene
Larsen, Richard Lee
Larsen, Roy Niels
Larsen, Timothy Gordon
Larsen, Walter Gilmar
Larson, Alvin Keith
Larson, Charles Lester
Larson, Garry Wayne
Larson, Harold Vincent
Larson, Harry Thomas
Larson, Jarryl Ann
Larson, John Francis
Larson, Larry Gale
Larson, Martin Alfred
Larson, Netta Bell Girard
Larson, Peggy Jean (Larson,
 Modiez Rose)
Larson, Perry Thomas
Larson, Victor Axtell
La Salle, Rodney Lewis
Lascher, Edward Leonard
Lasensky, Duke J.
Lash, Betty Jean Brookbush
Lashley, Virginia Stephenson
Lasiter, Jack Brinkley
Lasker, Josette Zinberg
Lasko, Allen Howard
Lasmanis, Raymond
Lasorda, Tom Charles
Lassagne, Theodore Hawley
Lassen, Gary Lynn
Lassner, Rudolf
Lastnick, George
Latham, Arthur Boyd
Latham, Gerald Taliaferro
Latham, Glenn Irven
Lathrop, Joyce Keen
Lathrop, Mitchell Lee
La Tour, Joseph Lynne
Lattanner, Alan Victor
Latterman, Lloyd Reese, Jr.
Latts, Leatrice Lynne
Lau, Buong Peck
Lau, Florence Misako
 Funakoshi
Lau, Winston Kwok Chu
Laube, Roger Gustav
Laubenstein, Molly-Jean
 Wilson
Laudenslager, Wanda Lee
Laudon, Alice Castlio
Lauenstein, Albert Edwin
Lauer, Ernest John
Lauer, Frances Louise Peacock
Lauer, Robert Louis
Lauer, Roger Myles
Laufenberg, Francis
Laughlin, Joy Judge
Laughlin, Larry
Laughlin, Loran L.
Laughlin, Louis Gene
Laughridge, Stanley Theadore
Laughrun, James Odell
Laurie, Edward James
Lautz, Lindsay Allan
Lauve, Charles Ferrin
Lauver, Edith Barbour
Lavadia, Pedro Gomez
Lavagnino, Arthur Garford
Lave, Roy Ellis, Jr.
Laverty, Finley Burnap
Lavey, Thomas Cameron
La Vine, Robert Leon
Lawler, Joseph Gregory
Lawrence, Arline Beryl
 Roby-Rush
Lawrence, Bobby Joe
Lawrence, Dean Grayson
Lawrence, John Carlyle
Lawrence, Louise
Lawrence, Robert Don
Lawrence, W(illiam) Sherwood
Laws, Rufina Marie Magoosh
Lawson, Daniel Webster
Lawson, James Lee
Lawson, Matt S.
Lawson, Theodore Earl
Lawson, Thomas Cheney
Lawton, Maxwell Murray
Laxalt, Paul
Lay, Kerry Lynn
Lay, Leland Gibson
Lay, S. Houston
Layton, Donald Merrill
Layton, Harry Christopher
Lazar, Alfred Leo
Lazar, Elaine Marsha
Lazar, Rubin Manuel
Lazarevich, Emil
Lazarus, Egon
Lazo, Jorge Alberto
Leach, Harold Lionel, Jr.
Leach, Joel Thomas
League, Daniel Noel, Jr.
League, Vicente Conrad
Leake, Donald Lewis
Leake, William Stuart, Jr.
Lear, Frances Loeb
Leary, Richard Kent
Leary, Robert Michael
Lease, Jane Etta
Lease, Richard Jay
Leask, Barbara Glenn
Leask, Samuel, III
Leavitt, Alan Michael
Leavitt, Dana Gibson
Leavitt, Murray Phillip
Lebbos, Betsey Warren
Lebedeff, Nicholas Boris
LeBlanc, Whitney Joseph, Jr.
Le Bleu, Robert Dale
LeBlond, Richard Emmett, Jr.
Lebon, Patricia Ann
Lebovitz, Joel Alan
Lechich, George Paul
Lechler, Horst Leonhard
Lechner, Andrew John
Le Clair, Ronald Arthur
Le Cocq, Rhoda Priscilla
Lecoque, Alois
Le Croissette, Dennis Harlow
Ledbetter, Carl Scotius
Lederis, Karl Paul
LeDoux, Richard Carl, Jr.
Lee, Abraham Russell
Lee, Benjamin
Lee, Brian Che-Keung
Lee, C. Bill
Lee, Curtis Howard
Lee, David Be-Nyi
Lee, David Gamble
Lee, Dennis Turner
Lee, E. Stanley
Lee, Edward Matthew, Jr.
Lee, Eugene William
Lee, George, Jr.
Lee, George Chen-Ying
Lee, Gilbert Prentiss
Lee, Harlan Angus
Lee, Harriet Whitman
Lee, Harry Rees
Lee, Hoi Paik
Lee, Hsing Tsun
Lee, Isaiah Chong-Pie
Lee, J. Richard
Lee, J(ohn) Roger
Lee, Jiin Jen
Lee, John Jerome
Lee, Joseph Allen, Jr.
Lee, Lamar, Jr.
Lee, Leslie Ying
Lee, Lilly Veronica
Lee, Lily Kiang
Lee, Long Chi
Lee, Norman Ashburn
Lee, Patricia Brownell (Mrs.
 Gilbert Prentiss Lee)
Lee, Polly Jae Stead
Lee, Robert Bartlett
Lee, Robert Lavern
Lee, Robert Sen-Yen
Lee, Stephen Dennis
Lee, Teh Hwei
Lee, Theodore Bo
Lee, Thomas Way
Lee, Wade Bruce, II
Lee, Wayne Russell
Lee, Willis LeGrand
Lee, Yilman
Lee, Yong Tsun
Leech, Robert Ernest
Leecing, Walden Albert
Leed, Roger Melvin
Leedy, Carleton C., Jr.
Leegard, Arlie Longsworth
Leeman, Martha Wahl
Leemhorst, Jan Willem
Leenstra, Cal
Leeper, Harold Frank
Lees, Dennis Alan
Lees, Marilyn Alice
Leet, Don Rodney
Lefebvre d'Argencé,
 René-Yvon
Lefebvre, Donald Ernest
Lefever, D(avid) Welty
Lefever, Hollis King
LeFevre, Eugene de Daugherty
Leff, Michael A.
Leffler, William James, Jr.
Leffner, Raymond Stanley
Lefrancois, Guy Renald
LeFree, Betty Jo
Legare, Henri Francis
Legeman, Charles William, II
Leger, Joseph Leon
Legerton, Jerome Alan
Legg, Edwin Max
Legg, Jarrell Franklin
Legge, Robert Farjeon
Leggett, James Lloyd
Leggette, Ralph Maxwell
Legler, John Phillip
Legowik, Stanley Walter
LeGrand, Alberta Alane
Lehane, John Francis
Le Hecka, Jeffrey Wilcox
Lehigh, George Edward
Lehl, Mabel Bowman (Mrs.
 George Peter Lehl)
Lehman, Edward
Lehman, Stanley Allan
Lehmann, Armin D(ieter)
Lehmann, Arnold Ludwig
Lehmann, Joseph August
Lehmann, Laura Koerner
Lehrling, Terry James
Leibman, Milford Harvey
Leibold, James Edward
Leibowitz, Lewis Phillip
Leibrecht, Murl Edwin
Leibsohn, Eugene
Leierer, Charles Edward
Leighton, Anna Bruce
Leigon, William Duane
Leisey, Donald Eugene
Leitch, John Malcolm
Leitz, Emil Erich
Leizer, Matthew Robert
Lejnieks, Laimons Arno
Leland, Charles James
Leland, Joy Hanson
Leland, Malcolm
Lem, Nancy Elizabeth
Lemert, James Bolton
Lemp, John, Jr.
Lemus, George
Lencer, William Thomas
Lencione, Ruth M.
Lengefeld, William Chris
Lenhart, Bob Gene
Lenherr, Frederick Keith
Lenning, Oscar Thomas
Lennon, Richard John
Lennox, William Robert
Lent, Berkeley
Leo, Donald Rudolph
Leon, Henry Arthur
Leonard, Arthur Raymond
Leonard, Benjamin Franklin,
 III
Leonard, Byron Herbert, Jr.
Leonard, Frank Edward, II
Leonard, George Edmund, Jr.
Leonard, George Jay
Leonard, George Perry
Leonard, John Duane
Leonard, Joseph Allen
Leonard, Judith Eleanor
Leonard, Leslie Leroy
Leonard, Mark George
Leonard, Roger Earle, Jr.
Leonardini, Frances Jeanette
Leong, Dawson Brandon
Leopold, Raymond Joseph
LePere, James Leonard
Lepire, Antony John
Lepire, Ray Joseph
Lepman, Susan Regina
Leporiere, Ralph Dennis
Leptich, Dean Andrew
Lerch, Stanford Earl
Lerner, Robert
Lerner, Sheldon
Leroy, David Henry
Lescoe, Richard John
Lescoe, Richard John
Lesher, Raymond Andrew
LeSieur, James Godfrey, III
Leske, Reinhold Herman
Leslie, George Francis, Jr.
Leslie, George Wayne
Leslie, Richard Erichson
Leslie, Willie Raybon, Jr.
Lesser, Raymond Ernest
Lessey, Karl Dean
Lessner, George Dennis
Lester, Bernadotte Perrin, Jr.
Lester, David Benjamin
Lester, John Clayton
Lester, William Joseph
Lester, William Lewis
Letcher, Kenneth Illtred
Letcher, Naomi Presley
Letinsky, Michael Steven
Letofsky, Irvin Myles
Le Tourneau, Duane John
Lett, Bobbie Jean
Leung, Paul
Leuprecht, Herbert Hildeberd
Leuschner, Lucille Mary
Lev, James John
Levanger, Jim Neils
Levay, Rita Diane Rogers
Leveen, Louis
Leven, Boris
Levene, Carol
Levenson, Howard Terence
Lever, Alan
Levernier, Thomas John
Le Vernois, Earle Mose
Levin, Alvin Irving
Levin, Barbara Jean Patterson
Levin, Martin Howard
Levin, Martin Silas
Levin, Ronald David
Levin, Ronald Jay
Levin, Sheldon Marvin
Levine, Eva Magdelena
Levine, Hillel Benjamin
LeVine, James B.
Levins, Susan Gale
Levinson, Bernard Hirsh
Levinson, Mark Lawrence
Levinson, Neil L.
Levinthal, Michael Lee
Levit, Victor Bert
Levitan, Maureen Anne
 O'Brien
Levitin, Lloyd Alan
Leviton, Charles David
Levitt, David Shelby
Levitt, Leon
Levitz, Joel Jacob
Levy, Herbert Samuel
Levy, Lewis
Levy, Mark Allen
Levy, Robert Kent
Lewald, Hans Guenter
Lewallen, Ralph Thomas
Lewin, Larry Louis
Lewine, Robert F.
Lewis, Billy Dwaine
Lewis, Caleb Ansel
Lewis, Carrie Altha Collins
Lewis, Charles William
Lewis, David James
Lewis, David Sloan, III
Lewis, Edward Lowell
Lewis, Farrell Walter
Lewis, Gerald Jorgensen
Lewis, Gordon Elkins
Lewis, J. Sheldon
Lewis, James Luther
Lewis, Janice Lynn
Lewis, John Calvin
Lewis, Kenneth
Lewis, Laura Hester
Lewis, Lillian Callis
Lewis, Loraine Ruth
Lewis, Marguerite Garber
 (Mrs. William Leroy Lewis)
Lewis, Marshall
Lewis, Marvin Howard
Lewis, Millard Lawson
Lewis, Nancy Ann
Lewis, Noreen Theede
Lewis, Norman
Lewis, Orme
Lewis, Phillip
Lewis, R(obert) H(oward) Bob
Lewis, Robert Winfield
Lewis, Sheldon Noah
Lewis, Shirley Jeane
Lewis, Stephen Roger
Lewis, Warren Burton
Lewis, William Leroy
Lewitzky, Bella
Lewton, Ida Alice
Lewton, Ronald Quentin
Leydet, Francois Guillaume
Leyland, Winston Francis
Lhyle, Rod Kent
Li, Ching Yan
Li, Gail Gar Lyai
Li, Lyman Goon
Li, Shu-tien
Liang, W. Walter
Liao, Shun-Kwung
Libby, Richard Harry
Libby, W(illard) F(rank)
Lichter, James Joseph
Lichtman, Jay Lawrence
Lick, Frank Martin
Lickly, John Richard
Liddell, Michael Eugene
Liddle, Gordon McAllister
Lie, Kian Joe
Liebe, Hans Joachim
Liebenberg, Donald Henry
Lieber, Esther Kobre
Lieberg, Leslie Frederick Olaus
Lieberman, Alvin
Lieberman, Gary Howard
Lieberman, Neil
Lieberman, Paul
Lieberman, Sima
Lieberman, William
Liebert, Bruce Eric
Lieberthal, Gary B.
Liebl, Robert Mathew
Lieblich, Jerome Harold
Liebman, Murray Edward
Liebowitz, Daniel S. F.
Lie-Injo, Luan Eng
Liem, Annie Lian-Foong
Lienhart, Jody June (Mrs.
 Kenneth E. Lienhart)
Lientz, Bennet Price
Liepins, Aivars Andris
Lietzen, John Hervy
Lieu, Bing Hou-Yi
Lieuallen, Roy Elwayne
Ligety, William Charles
Liggett, Clayton Eugene
Light, Jerome Burdette
Lightfoot, Clifford Stanley
Lightstone, Herbert Spencer
Liljedahl, Douglas Richard
Lillard, Charles Marion
Lilley, Alfred
Lillie, Mildred L.
Lilly, James Alexander
Lim, Felipe N.
Lim, Robert Cheong, Jr.
Limozaine, Bruce John
Lin, Andrew Evans
Lin, Chwen-Hao
Lin, Lawrence Shuh Llang
Lin, T. Joseph
Lin, Tung Yen
Linck, Charles Frederick, Jr.
Lincoln, Wayne Kaui
Lind, Marshall Lee
Lindau, Ingolf
Lindberg, Herbert Ednar
Lindem, Martin Carl
Lindeman, Joanne Waring
Lindemann, Hans Karl
Linder, LeRoy Harold
Linder, Robert Otto
Lindheimer, Jack Harold
Lindholm, Richard Wadsworth
Lindholtz, Ruth Petty
Lindley, Curtis Price
Lindley, Francis Haynes
Lindros, Donald Alan
Lindsay, Charles Aubrey
Lindsay, George Edmund
Lindsay, Keith Cole
Lindsay, Laurence Duane
Lindsey, Howard Willis
Lindsey, Jack B.
Lindsey, James Robert
Lindsey, Mort
Lindsey, William Fussell
Lindstedt-Siva, K. June
Lindstrom, Everett Harry
Lindstrom, Petter Aron
Lindt, Milton Charles
Ling, Carmel Arlene
Linhardt, Hans Dieter
Linn, Abraham Sidney
Linn, Charles William
Linn, George Byron
Linn, Stuart Michael
Linnell, Marvin Richard
Linsky, Ronald Benjamin
Linsman, William David
Lintner, Robert Eugene
Lion, Ernest George
Lion, Paul Dexter
Lionakis, George
Lipin, Martin
Lipinski, Paul Richard
Lipkin, Monica Jane
Lipp, John Lloyd
Lippe, Philipp Maria
Lippencott, George Henry
Lippitt, Elizabeth Charlotte
Lippman, Morton Aaron
Lippold, Robert Alfred
Lippold, Roland Will
Lipps, Wayne Lee
Lipscher, Joel Theodore
Lipscomb, Billye-Raye Yount
Lipscomb, Leland Edward
Lipscomb, Linda Ann Wagner
 (Mrs. John F. Lipscomb)
Lipson, Marvin Stanley
Lira, Nicolas
Lisec, William M(aynard)
Liss, Norman Richard
List, Robert Frank
Lister, Anthony
Listerud, Mark Boyd
Liston, Albert Morris
Litizzette, Stanley Victor
Litteral, Emmett Bryan
Little, Douglas Ray
Little, Leo Joseph Gregory
Little, Michael James
Little, Norman Owen
Little, Thomas Tucker
Littlefield, Verne Denver
Littlehales, Charles Paul
Littler, Donald
Littman, Richard Gerald
Littman, Robert
Littrell, Robert Thomas
Litvak, John
Liu, David Shiao-Kung
Liu, Tsung-Hua
Livesay, Richard Wyman
Livick, Gary William
Livingston, Patricia Ann (Pat
 Murphy)
Livingston, Stanley Cox
Livingston-Little, Dallas
 Eugene

Llewellyn, Frederick Eaton
Llewellyn, Robert Neilson
Lloyd, Anna Juanita
Lloyd, Gary Murdock
Lloyd, James Fredrick
Lloyd, John Butler
Lloyd, Judson Frank
Lloyd, Richard Alan
Lloyd, Robin Mansell
Lloyd-Lee, Beverly
Loach, Roberta Joyce
Lobitz, Walter Charles, III
Lobue, Ange Joseph
Locatelli, John Douglas
Locher, Alan Hugh
Lochner, Floyd O.
Lock, Charles Leslie
Lock, Craig Kaiwiahuula
Lock, Eugene Raymond
Locke, Irene Vivian Fisher (Mrs. John Loor Locke)
Lockhart, Brooks Javins
Lockhart, Jimmie Drew
Locklin, Alaina Marie
Lockwood, Lawrence Slotboom
Locy, Albert James
Loder, Robert Jesse
Loeb, Phyllis Hausman
Loebl, James D(avid)
Loebner, Egon Ezriel
Loen, Raymond Ordell
Loeper, Jessica Ann Longnecker
Loesby, Harlie Ward
Loewen, Earl Leslie
Loewenberg, Stephen Peter
Loewenstein, Louis Klee
Loewer, Robert Allen
Lofgreen, Torry Dana, Jr.
Lofland, John Franklin
Lofland, Lyn Hebert
Lofquist, Edwin Herbert
Logan, Gene Adams
Logan, Gerald Elton
Logan, Lee Robert
Logan, Ronald Lee
Loganbill, G. Bruce
Logé, David Dieter
Loges, Clayton Neal
Logwood, Harold Maurice
Lohr, Milton Leo
Loker, Donald Prescott
Lolli, Andrew Ralph
Loloma, Charles
Lombard, David
Lombard, Michael Stephen
Lonabaugh, Ellsworth Eugene
Lonas, Richard John
Lond, Harley Weldon
London, Kurt Ludwig
London, Ray William
Londot, Kenneth Logan
Lonergan, Thomas Francis, III
Long, C. E., III
Long, Dale Bradley
Long, Donald John
Long, Durward
Long, Elgen Marion
Long, Elmer Gene
Long, G. Gerald
Long, Hing Wing
Long, Jack Lloyd
Long, Philip Lee
Long, Raymond Egerton, Jr.
Long, Richard Dean
Long, Roger Alden
Long, Walter James
Long, William Francis
Long, William Philip
Longenecker, Harold L.
Longo, Lawrence Daniel
Longyear, Alfred Boyle
Lonie, Clayton Carlyle
Lonnquist, John Hall, Jr.
Lonzo, Michael Dale
Loo, Charles Dean
Loo, Michael Yew Mun
Loo, Thomas Sill
Loo, Yuan San
Look, Dennis Allen
Loomba, Rajinder Pal
Loomis, Derward Prescott
Looney, Gerald Lee
Loop, David McClain
Loop, Stephen Blair
Loose, Elmer Eugene
Loosle, John William
Lopata, Steven
Loper, Mary Jane Eure
Loper, Warren Edward
Lopez, Augustin Val
Lopez, Manuel
Lopez, Ralph John
Lopinsky, Charles Yale
L'Orange, Hans Peter Faye, Jr.
Lorber, Robert Lawrence
Lord, Charles Julian
Lord, Harold Wilbur
Lord, Jack
Lord, Joseph Milton, Jr.
Lord, Robert Vinton, Jr.
Lord, Royal William, Jr.
Lore, George Fredrick
Lorenz, Philip Manfred
Lorenz, Ronald Benjamin
Lorenz, Wayne Francis
Lorenzen, Angus Max
Lorenzen, Robert Frederick
Lorti, Daniel Caesar
Loser, Kenneth Monroe
Losh, Samuel Johnston
Loskill, Sandra Ann
Lott, Thomas Makepeace
Louchheim, William Sandel, Jr.
Loucks, Lawrence James
Louden, Lynn Mansell
Lough, Robert Thomas
Lougheed, E. Peter
Louie, Clifton
Loupe, Alexander, Jr.
Louvau, Gordon Ernest
Louy, James William
Love, Brian Alan
Love, Harold Clyde
Love, Jack Wayne
Love, John Clifford
Love, Malcolm Haley
Love, Roy L.
Lovelace, Dennis Joseph
Lovelace, Jon Bell, Jr.
Loveland, Joseph Albert, Jr.
Loveless, Edward Eugene
Lovell, Carl Erwin, Jr.
Lovell, Emily Kalled (Mrs. Robert Edmund Lovell)
Lovenburg, Edward Dean
LoVerme, Franklyn W.
Lovett, Evelyn Joyce Miller
Lovill, James Edward
Lovlien, Karen Ann
Low, David William
Low, Morton David
Lowe, Kenneth Lee
Lowe, Warren
Lowe, William Ray
Lowenkopf, Shelly Alan
Lowenstein, Henry Ernest
Lowenthal, Leo
Lowery, Donald Earl
Lowery, Douglas Lane
Lowery, Wayne Alan
Lowman, Mary Bethena Hemphill
Lowman, Zelvin Don
Lowrance, Muriel Edwards
Lowry, Edward George, III
Lowry, Heath Ward
Lowry, Mike
Lowry, Patricia Ann
Lowry, Wallace Maynard
Lowry, William Bryan
Loy, Vernon Nelson
Lu, Zung An
Lubeck, Marvin Jay
Lubich, Warren Peter
Lubnau, Thomas E.
Luby, Larry Walter
Luc, William Wesley
Lucas, Donald Leo
Lucas, June Ann
Lucas, Malcolm Millar
Lucas, William Jasper
Luce, Willard Ray, Jr.
Luce, William Abram
Lucente, Rosemary Dolores
Lucero, Arthur Estevan
Lucero, Edward Robert
Lucero, Jose Ubaldo
Luchetti, Melvin Louis
Luckey, Ellen Jane
Luckhardt, Robert Louis
Luden, William Henry, III
Ludlam, James Edward
Ludlow, Rose Budd
Ludlum, Charles Henry
Ludutsky-Taylor, Tina Linda
Ludwick, Arthur Lee
Ludwig, Claus Berthold
Ludwig, Henry Frank
Ludwig, James David
Ludwig, James J.
Luechauer, Helyn Catherine Anderson (Mrs. Jarvis H. Luechauer)
Lueders, James Henry
Luere, Jeane Ladella
Luetger, Charles Lindbergh
Luévano, Angel Godinez
Lufrano, Tony Richard
Lugmair, Guenter Wilhelm
Luh, Bor Shiun
Lui, Calvin William
Luigs, Charles Russell
Lujan, Manuel, Jr.
Lukasik, Lawrence John
Luke, Samuel Cummins
Luke, Warren K. K.
Lukes, Jerry James
Lum, Andrew Poaiau
Lum, Harold Chan Kong
Lum, Jean Loui Jin
Lum, Richard Wah Kit
Lum, Walter B.
Lumry, Rufus Worth, III
Luna, Michele Anne
Lunati, Marian Elizabeth
Lundahl, Craig Raymond
Lundberg, George David
Lunden, Donald Oscar
Lundgren, Terry Dennis
Lundring, Lynn Karsten
Lung, Julina Ethel
Lungren, Daniel E.
Lunine, Leo Robert
Luoma, Richard Arro
Lupper, Edward
Lupton, David Walker
Luques, John Stewart
Lusche, Noris Allen
Lusky, Lois Freese
Lusted, Lee Browning
Luter, James Gray, Jr.
Luter, John
Luther, Florence Joan (Mrs. Charles W. Luther)
Lutin, David Louis
Lutton, William Rhines
Lutz, Kathaleen Jeanette
Lutz, Kenneth James
Luuwai, Helen Mary
Lux, Clifton Leo
Lux, Gwen (Mrs. Thomas H. Creighton)
Lyddy, James Patrick
Lyden, Fremont James
Lydick, Lawrence Tupper
Lyell, Edward Harvey
Lyman, Richard Wall
Lyman, Theodore Benedict, IV
Lymp, John Francis
Lynch, Charles Thomas
Lynch, Dale L.
Lynch, Dell Marie Ryan (Mrs. James Merriman Lynch)
Lynch, Gerald John
Lynch, Mrs. Philip (Helen Coon Lynch)
Lynch, Sharon Kay
Lynch, Thomas Dale
Lynip, (Benjamin) Franklin
Lynn, Bert Daniel
Lynn, Jacqueline Brandt
Lynn, Martha Drexler
Lynn, Richard Shelly, Sr.
Lynn, William Max
Lyon, Daniel Frank
Lyon, Eleanor Annie Richards
Lyon, Elijah Wilson
Lyon, Roger Adrian
Lyons, Harry Nichols
Lyons, James Felton
Lyons, Jerome Michael
Lyons, Philip Nolan
Lytle, Carl Albert
Lytle, William Andrew
Ma, Carl Yuwei
Maagdenberg, Ronald Richard
Maas, Ronald Roy
Maass, James Allen
Maass, Richard Andrew
Mabbutt, Fred Richard
Mabey, Edward Milo
Mabley, Elwood Le Noir
Mabry, Harry Cooper
Mac Aleese, Gregory Bruce
Macapinlac, Joseph Pineda
Macaray, Lawrence Richard
Macaron, Frederick
MacArthur, Glen Fred
MacBride, Thomas Jamison
Mac Collister, Robert Snow
MacCracken, Elliott Bolte
Macdonald, Alaistair Cumming
MacDonald, Donald
Mac Donald, Donald, III
MacDonald, Ian Charles
Macdonald, John, Jr.
MacDonald, John Bernard
Mac Donald, Lawrence Edward
Mac Donald, Mary MacFarlane
Mac Donald, Norval Woodrow
Macdonald, William Alan
MacDonell, Ted Archie
MacDougall, Duncan Peck
Mace, Justin Avard
Mac Eachern, Kenneth Leroy
MacEachern, Phyllis Christine
MacElwee, Mrs. Irvin R.
Macfarland, James Merrill
Mac Farlane, John Dee
MacGregor, James Thomas
Machado, Barbara Jean
Mac Intosh, Jay W. (Janet Tallulah Jewell)
Mac Intyre, Christine Melba
MacIntyre, Neil Ross, Jr.
Mac Intyre, Norman Law
Mack, Brenda Lee
Mack, Edward Semmel
Mack, Ernest Wood
Mack, James Carl
Mack, Jerome David
Mack, John, Jr.
Mack, John Walter, Jr.
Mackay, Alexander Russell
Mackay, Robin
Mackelprang, Alonzo Julius
Mackensen, Robert Ernest
Mackenzie, Charles Earl
MacKenzie, Marie Catherine
Mackey, Elvin, Jr.
Mackey, Harry Alva
Mackey, Robert Benjamin
Mackey, William
Mackie, William Ansel
Mackintosh, Albyn
Macklin, Ronald Rex
MacKnight, William Fielding
Macko, George William
Macko, Joseph Francis
MacLachlan, Douglas Lee
MacLaughlin, Douglas Earl
MacLeod, Guy Franklin
Macmillan, Robert Smith
MacMullen, Douglas Burgoyne
Mac Nab, Duncan Storey
Mac Neil, Joseph Neil
Macpherson, John Hugh, Jr.
Macrae, Donald Sylvester
Mac Rill, Glenn Everett
MacVeigh, Charles Stuart
Mac Vicar, Robert William
Macy, Dorothy, Jr.
Madden, Paul R.
Maddock, Roy Arthur
Maddock, Thomas Smothers
Maddox, Charles
Maddox, Grace Beryl
Maddox, Jack Douglas
Maddox, Michael Lee Manby
Maddox, Thomas Wesley
Maddux, James Tolbert, Jr.
Madera, Ruford Frederick
Madill, Edwin Joseph
Madison, John Stanley
Madison, Roberta Solomon
Madison, Toby Robert
Madlaing, Arturo Gabot
Madland, Glen Robert
Madsen, Gordon Lewis
Madsen, Norma Lee
Madsen, Peter Edgar
Madsen, Reas Terry
Madsen, Walter Christian
Maeda, Rieko (Rae)
Maertz, Richard Charles
Maestre, Jose Maria
Maestretti, Kenneth Dell
Maffei, Natale Serio
Magee, David L.
Magee, Thomas Joseph
Magel, Gerald Allen
Mager, Talmon Russell
Maggard, Woodrow Wilson, Jr.
Maggay, Isidoro, Jr.
Magid, Gail Avrum
Magid, Kenneth Marshall
Maglan, Alvin Catu
Magleby, James Heber
Maglio, Joanna Marie
Magner, Fredric Michael
Magner, Martin
Magnes, Harry Alan
Magness, Catherine Virginia Cooper
Magnin, Cyril Isaac
Magnin, Jerry Allan
Magnuson, Harold C., Jr.
Magnuson, Jermaine Elliott Peralta (Mrs. Warren Magnuson)
Magnuson, Warren Grant
Magovern, Robert LeRoy
Magsig, Frederick Milborn
Mah, Raymond Leong
Mahaffey, Theodore Roosevelt
Mahajan, Chandrakant Dayaram
Mahan, Frank Emerson
Mahan, Jack Lee, Jr.
Mahan, Thomas Harold
Maher, Charles Michael
Maher, John Francis
Maher, Joseph Ambrose
Maher, Leo Thomas
Mahilum, Benjamin Comawas
Mahler, David
Mahler, Richard Joseph
Mahnkey, Mark Raymond
Mahon, John Clyde, Jr.
Mahoney, Dean H.
Mahoney, Don Patrick
Mahoney, James Anthony
Mahoney, James P.
Mahoney, Louis Emmett, Jr.
Mahoney, Patrick Robinson
Mahony, Patrick Frederick
Mahowald, Robert Martin
Maier, Peter Klaus
Maierhofer, Charles Andrew
Mailes, Felton McDowell
Mailman, Leo Joseph
Mainhardt, Robert
Maize, James Hindman, III
Major, Marguerite Louise
Makini, Jamila Tatu
Makowsky, Michael Allan
Malakoff, James Leonard
Malakoff, Joseph Frederick
Malatesta, Henry Ellio
Malberg, Constance Zelma
Malcolm, Gerald Lindburg
Malcolm, Richard Ward
Malecki, Edward Stanley, Jr.
Malek, Zena Bella
Malernee, James Kent, Jr.
Maletzky, Barry Michael
Malewicki, Douglas John
Malhoski, Walter Edward
Malick, John David
Malkani, Moti Chabaldas
Mallek, James Rudolph
Mallen, James Robert
Mallett, John Harold
Mallinckrodt, Martha Graves (Mrs. Charles O. Mallinckrodt)
Mallinger, Michael Joseph
Mallon, John Lawrence, II
Mallonee, Richard Carvel, II
Mallory, Elgin Albert
Mallory, Herbert Dean
Mallory, Virgil Standish
Malloy, Barbara Kathryn
Malm, Royce Elliott
Malmgren, Richard Charles
Malone, Dennis Michael
Malone, Joanne
Malone, Marvin Herbert
Malone, Nydia Ione
Malonek, Robert Nelse
Maloney, Clement Garland
Maloney, Kevin
Maloney, Michael Paul
Malony, Henry Newton
Maloof, Giles Wilson
Maltby, Hazel Farrow
Maltin, Freda
Maltz, I. Bruce
Mamin, Estha Lee Ginsberg
Manahan, Manny Celestino
Manahan, Michael Larry
Manaker, Philip Arnold
Manasevit, Harold Murray
Mancini, John
Mandeville, Mildred S.
Mandl, William John
Manera, Elizabeth Sturgis
Manfred, Roger Lee
Mangan, Paul Charles
Mangels, John Donald
Mangelson, Ned LeGrande
Mangiarelli, Richard Donald
Mangone, Ralph Joseph
Mangrum, Claude Thomas, Jr.
Mangum, Eugene Kenneth
Manley, Michael Alexander
Mann, Almeda Lavona Emery (Mrs. Byron L. Brown)
Mann, Don H.
Mann, Gordon Lee, Jr.
Mann, Kurt Thornton
Mann, Maurice
Mann, Wayne Melvin
Manning, Al(cie) G(wyn)
Manning, Anita
Manning, Donald Dewey
Manning, Duane
Manning, Randal Curtis
Manning, Robert Henry
Manning, Timothy
Manning, Wendel Omar
Mannix, Brian Edmond
Manos, James Anthony
Manoukian, Noel Edwin
Mans, Rosemary
Mansfield, Carl Clinton
Mansour, Alaa El-Din
Manteufel, James Frederick
Manwaring, Alan Var
Manzano, Raul Tuason
Mapes, William Edward
Maples, Annetta (Nan) Louise
Marasigan, Eliodoro Marquez, II (Butch)
Marble, Robert Frederick
March, Thomas Alfred
Marchand, Dennis Gregory
Marchese, David Nicholas
Marchi, Jon
Marchick, Richard
Marckwardt, Harold Thomas
Marcy, Charles Edney
Marder, Stanley
Mardian, Samuel, Jr.
Marecek, Lois Gail (Greenberg)
Marenco, Eduardo, Jr.
Maresca, Frank Albert
Marevich, Michael Milan
Margoles, Michael Stuart
Margolis, Benjamin Robert
Margolis, Lester Henry
Margon, Bruce Henry
Margosian, Lucille K. Manougian (Mrs. Ervin M. Margosian)
Marin, Glenn Allen
Mariner, James Walter
Maring, Edward Joseph
Mariño, Miguel Angel
Marion, Michael William
Mark, David Lee
Mark, Peter Alan
Markey, Peter Joseph
Markham, Reed B.
Markham, Stephen Charles
Markland, DeEtta Charlotte
Markman, Sylvan
Markoe, M. Allen
Markoff, Annabelle Most
Markoff, Dena Rae Sabin
Markoff, Elliott Lee
Markoja, Robert Lawrence
Markovich, Lois Ann Gimondo
Markovits, Andrew Steven
Markow, Robert
Marks, James Robert
Marks, Jay Glenn
Marks, Mary May
Marksbury, Ollie Orville
Markstein, David Liberman
Markus, Ervin Herman
Marlatt, Gene Ronald
Marlenee, Ronald Charles
Marler, John Robert
Marlett, D(e Otis) L(oring)
Marll, Vernon
Marlow, Clayton Blayne
Marlow, Robert Allen
Marlowe, David Ronald
Marmorston, Jessie
Marnella, Donald James
Maron, Dennis Edward
Maronde, Robert Francis
Marquis, Arnold
Marr, Edwin Eugene
Marr, James Carlton
Marriott, David Daniel
Marsh, Beverly Jean
Marsh, Daniel Gabe
Marsh, Donald Reppert
Marsh, Harry Esson
Marsh, Timothy John
Marsh, Walter H.
Marshall, Arthur K.
Marshall, Duane Leroy
Marshall, Dwight Alan
Marshall, J. Howard, III
Marshall, Kent R.
Marshall, L. B.
Marshall, Mary Hewitt
Marshall, Maureen Greta
Marshall, Norman Sturgeon
Marshall, Robert Henry
Marshall, Sidney
Marshall, Thomas Joseph
Marshall, Virginia Lee Bogar (Mrs. William A. Marshall)
Marshall, Yolanda
Marsolek, Paul Robert
Marsoobian, Edward Fred
Marston, Charles Fredrick, Jr.
Marston, Michael Jan
Marszalek, Georgia
Martel, Francisco Fernando
Martelle, Harold Darl, Jr.
Martello, Benjamin Frank
Marten, Robert Daniel
Martenson, James Austin
Martilla, John Alan
Martin, Ann Bodenhamer
Martin, Boyd Archer
Martin, Charles E.
Martin, Donald Lee
Martin, Dorothy Fishman
Martin, Douglas Arthur
Martin, Edward Alexander
Martin, Elmer Dean, III
Martin, Frances Franklin (Mrs. Wayne S. Martin)
Martin, Francis Robert
Martin, Frank R.
Martin, Glen Leroy
Martin, Glenn Worthington
Martin, Harry, Jr.
Martin, John Paul
Martin, Joseph Patrick, Jr.
Martin, June Johnson Caldwell
Martin, Keith Justin
Martin, Kenneth Lyle
Martin, Leonardo San Juan
Martin, Louis Harold
Martin, Lucille Caiar (Mrs. Hampton Martin)
Martin, Marlene
Martin, Merle Phillip
Martin, Robert Arthur
Martin, Roleigh Henry
Martin, Sarah Cunningham
Martin, Wayne Stephen
Martin, Yolanda May
Martin, Yvonne Laverne Keaton
Martin-Avina, Donna Jean
Martindale, David L.
Martindale, George Raitt
Martine, Walter Isaac
Martines, Timothy Nicholas
Martinetto, Robert James
Martinez, Alex Gonzales
Martinez, Charles Roy
Martinez, John Stanley
Martinez, Maria Inez
Martinez, Samuel
Martinez, Santiago Vigil
Martinez, Vincent George
Martínez Gándara, Julio Antonio
Martini, Robert Frank
Martino, Polly
Martinson, Earl Henry
Martinson, Gudmund
Martinson, Steven Leroy
Marty, Raymond
Martyn-Godfrey, Barry (Barry Martyn)
Martz, Kenneth Wayne
Maruska, John Hans
Marx, Frank Geoffrey
Marx, Thomas Joseph, II
Marylander, Stuart Jerome
Maryott, Richard Means
Mas, Jesus Loreto
Mas, José Luis
Maschler, Wolfgang Frank
Masino, Robert Carl
Masket, Edward Seymour
Masket, Samuel
Maslan, Neal Lyle
Maslin, Harvey Lawrence
Mason, Alanson Allen
Mason, Burton, Jr.
Mason, Dave Lee
Mason, Dean Towle
Mason, E. Gilbert
Mason, Frank Henry
Mason, Frank Ronald
Mason, Glenn Wilford
Mason, Thomas Truman, II
Massa, Richard Nicholas
Massart, Keith George
Massell, Theodore Benedict
Massey, Gail Austin
Massey, H C
Massey, Ivey Dale
Massey, William Harry
Massick, James William
Massie, Bruce Charles
Massy, William Francis
Masten, Ric
Masterman, Gary Clyde
Masters, Richard Loyd
Masters, Thomas Edward
Masters, William Donald
Matai, Chuhar (Rochiram)
Matan, Lillian Kathleen Archambault
Mateju, Joseph Frank
Mater, Milton Herbert
Matesky, Ralph
Mather, Joseph Ray
Mather, Leonard Shaw
Mathes, William Michael
Matheson, Neil, Jr.
Matheson, Robert Taylor
Matheson, Scott
Mathews, Michael Byron
Mathiesen, Joan Iris Gates
Mathiesen, Timothy Rollin
Mathieu, Jose Perez
Mathis, Ronald Floyd
Mathis, Violette Eleanor
Matin, Dorothy Horwitz (Mrs. Harmon Matin)
Matlack, George Miller
Matlock, Damon
Matlock, Philip Val
Matsen, Jeffrey Robert
Matson, James Nelson
Matson, Mary Ellen
Matson, Philip Andrew
Matsuda, Fujio

Matsuda, Tsunehiro Raymond
Matsui, Eddy Sakaye
Matsui, Robert Takeo
Matsumura, Kenneth Naoyuki
Matsumura, Vera Yoshi
Matsunaga, Ronald Shigeto
Matsunaga, Spark Masayuki
Matsushita, Sadami
Matsuyama, Janet
Mattay, Albert Purgar
Mattes, Dale Bryan
Mattes, Merrill John
Matteson, James Harris
Matteucci, Dominick Vincent
Matthes, John Jay
Matthes, Robert Charles
Matthews, Jack Edward
Matthews, Keith Boyd
Matthews, Lester Nathan
Matthews, Margaret Jane
Matthews, Norman Sherwood, Jr.
Matthews, Robert Lloyd
Matthews, S. LaMont
Matthews, Warren Wayne, Jr.
Matthews, William Cary
Matthews, Willie Lee
Matthewson, Randall Wright
Matthias, Judson Stillman
Matthies, William August
Mattison, Constance Anne
Matz, Eileen Moree
Matz, James Richard
Matzer, John Nicholas, Jr.
Mau, Chuck
Mau, Ernest Eugene
Mau, Ronald Fook Lin
Mau, William Koon-Hee
Mauck, Jack A.
Maudlin, Lloyd Zell
Maughan, Edwin Kelly
Maughan, Joyce Bowen
Maughan, Meredith Gail
Maughan, Richard Johnson
Maulhardt, Richard Frank
Maunder, Elwood Rondeau
Maurer, John Edward
Maurer, John Irving
Maurer, Robert Leonard
Mauro, Jack Anthony
Mauro, Maria Maddalena
Mauro, Richard Frank
Maves, Lawrence Carl
Mawhinney, John Thomas
Mawicke, Paul Denny
Maxey, Leonard Woodruff
Maxfield, Kathleen Allen
Maxie, Peggy Joan
Maximovitch, Vladimir Alexander
Maxon, James Clark
Maxson, Gary Eldon
Maxwell, D. Malcolm
Maxwell, Floyd Dawson
Maxwell, Shirley Kathleen
Maxwell, Thornton Orville
May, Donald Stewart
May, Ernest Ralph
May, Grace Buckner (Mrs. Michael Hugo May)
May, James Harvey
May, Michael Wayne
May, Penny Westover
May, Robert A.
May, Teddy Ronald
Mayberry, Homer David
Maydew, Randall Clinton
Mayeda, Samuel Osamu
Mayer, Barbara Ann
Mayer, Charles Denis
Mayer, Clarence (Cary) Henry
Mayer, Frederick Joseph
Mayer, Frederick Rickard
Mayer, Jerome Fred
Mayer, Kenneth Wayne
Mayer, Richard Edwin
Mayer, Richard John
Mayer, Stanley A.
Mayfield, James Sanders
Mayhall, Wayne Davis
Mayhood, Everett Stanley
Mayne, F(rancis) Blair
Mayne, James Thomas
Mayo, Al Francis
Mayo, Frank Joseph
Mayol, Pete Syting
Mays, Carl W., Jr.
Maytham, Thomas Northrup
Mazzia, Alexander Lloret
Mazzia, Valentino Don Bosco
McAdams, Harry Mayhew
Mc Adams, Lloyd
McAdams, Ronald Emerson
McAlister, Alister Davidson
Mc Allister, Bruce Hugh
Mc Allister, Cyrus Ray, Jr.
Mc Allister, (Gigi) Grace Edgar
Mc Allister, James Addams
Mc Allister, James Herschel
Mc Allister, Patrick Von
Mc Alpen, Michael George
Mc Anally, Don
Mc Andrews, Peter Francis
Mc Aninch, Frank Stewart
Mc Auley, Raymond Wesley, Jr.
McAuliffe, James Michael
McAvoy, Gary Robert
Mc Aweeney, Hugh Martin, Jr.
McBirney, Bruce Henry
Mc Bride, Guy Thornton, Jr.
Mc Bride, Robert Joseph
McBride, Stella Maria Regina
Mc Cabe, Cory Edward
Mc Cabe, Donald Lee
McCabe, Fred James
Mc Cafferty, Walter Dean
Mc Caffery, Joseph J(ames), Jr.
Mc Caffery, Michael David
Mc Caffrey, Frank Joseph
Mc Caffrey, Stanley Eugene
Mc Cagg, Edward King, II
Mc Cain, James Gordon
Mc Callum, Carol June
Mc Calmon, William Albert
Mc Camish, Harley Milton
Mc Cann, Frederick Kenneth
McCann, Gerald Aloysius (Kevin Costello)
Mc Cann, Robert Edward
Mc Cann, Stephen Ward
Mc Cann, Terrence John
Mc Cann, William James
Mc Canna, James Vincent
Mc Canna, Raymond James, II
Mc Cardell, Richard Keith
McCaron, Joseph
Mc Carren, Sister Margaret-Martha Patricia
Mc Carroll, Ase Fystro
Mc Carroll, William Harroll
Mc Carther, Bernice Dotson
Mc Carthy, Frank Martin
McCarthy, J. Thomas
Mc Carthy, James Redmond
Mc Carthy, Mary Ellen
Mc Cartney, Clark Allyn, III
Mc Carty, Dennis Eugene
Mc Carty, Frederick Briggs
McCarty, George C.
Mc Carty, Michael Horace
Mc Carty, Robert Clarke
Mc Carty, Shirley Carolyn
Mc Casland, Stanford Paul
Mc Cauley, Edmund Charles William
McCauley, Joe Donald, Jr.
Mc Cauley, William Rogers
Mc Clain, Charles Kent
Mc Clatchy, Eleanor
Mc Cleary, Lloyd E(verald)
Mc Cleery, Jerry Edward
Mc Clellan, Barry Dean
McClelland, Betty Jean
Mc Clelland, Harold Franklin
McClennen, Louis
Mc Clintock, Archie Glenn
Mc Clintock, Bettie Lou (Mrs. Hoyt Mingus McClintock)
Mc Clintock, Thomas Miller
Mc Closkey, Paul N., Jr.
Mc Closkey, Richard John
Mc Clung, Aileen Gallagher
McClure, Arthur Madden
McClure, Audrey Truesdail
Mc Clure, Bruce Cary
Mc Clure, Charles Benjamin
Mc Clure, James A.
Mc Clure, William H.
Mc Clurkin, Howard Carter, Jr.
McCollumn, Ralph William, Jr.
Mc Comb, James Aaron
Mc Combs, Donald Dwain
Mc Connel, Paul Andrew
Mc Connel, Stephen Smith
Mc Connell, Charles Foster
Mc Connell, John Douglas
Mc Connell, Lloyd Lee
Mc Connell, M. Brian
Mc Connell, Robert Eastwood
Mc Corkle, Charles Edward
Mc Cormac, Weston Arthur
Mc Cormack, Mike
Mc Cormack, Robert
Mc Cormick, Adele von Rust
McCormick, Floyd Guy, Jr.
McCormick, Harold L.
Mc Cormick, Thomas Everett
Mc Cormish, Thomas Francis
Mc Coy, Frank Milton
Mc Coy, Lois Clark
Mc Coy, Richard Lee
Mc Coy, Robert Baker
Mc Cracken, Alice Irene
Mc Craley, Thomas Lue
Mc Crary, Charles Erman
Mc Craven, Carl Clarke
Mc Cree, Nancy Lee
Mc Cudden, Douglas Hollister
Mc Cue, John Joseph Frank, III
Mc Culloch, Roderick Douglas
Mc Cullugh, Ruth Jordan
Mc Cune, Bailey Bruce
Mc Cune, Ellis E.
Mc Cune, Weston Edward
Mc Curdy, Solomon Portious
Mc Cutchan, Joseph Wilson
Mc Daniel, Elizabeth Holland
Mc Daniel, Inga Carter
Mc Daniel, William Henry
Mc Dermon, Collier
Mc Dermott, David Michael
Mc Dermott, F(rancis) Arnold
Mc Dermott, Patricia Louise
Mc Dermott, Richard Schick
Mc Dermott, William Edward
Mc Dole, Arthur Edwin
Mc Donald, Bernard
McDonald, Dixie Lee
Mc Donald, Harris Robert
Mc Donald, Jack Henry
Mc Donald, James Michael
Mc Donald, Jeanne Gray Murphy (Mrs. John B. McDonald)
Mc Donald, Jeraldine Kay
McDonald, John Bowen
Mc Donald, John Joseph MacAllister
Mc Donald, John Thornton, III
Mc Donald, Malcolm Gideon
McDonald, Peter Ranald
Mc Donald, Roy Joseph
Mc Donald, William Kyle
Mc Donnel, Gerald Matthew
Mc Donnell, Edward Joe
Mc Donnell, Edward Laurence
Mc Donnell, Gordon Rutherford
Mc Donnell, Philip Adrian
Mc Donough, Agnes Rita
Mc Donough, George Edward
Mc Donough, Joseph John
Mc Donough, Paul Steven
Mc Dougal, Wilbern Lee
Mc Dougall, Duncan Thomas
Mc Dougall, George Douglas
Mc Dowell, Angela Parisi
Mc Dowell, Frank
Mc Dowell, Jennifer
Mc Dowell, William Warren
Mc Duffie, Richard Warner, Jr.
Mc Elhoe, Bruce Albert
Mc Elhone, John Randall
Mc Elroy, Amos David
McEnaney, John Donald
McEvoy, Joseph Edward
Mc Evoy, Paul Bertrand
Mc Ewen, Colin Ellis
Mc Ewen, Victoria
Mc Fadden, David Thomas
Mc Fadden, Joseph James
McFadden, Ronald Allen
Mc Fadden, Wilmot Curnow Hamm
Mc Falls, John Alan
Mc Farland, David Lee
Mc Farland, Norman F.
McFate, Yale
McFeeley, Patricia Josephson
Mc Garvey, Dale L.
Mc Gaw, Sidney Edwin
Mc Gee, Harold Carlyle
Mc Gee, Richard Allen
Mc Gehee, James Andy
Mc Ghie, Wayne Richard
Mc Gill, Scott Audley
Mc Gill, Scott Douglas
Mc Ginley, Joseph Waldo
Mc Ginnies, William Grovenor
Mc Glasson, Christine Louise
Mc Glothien, Wayne Franklin
Mc Gonagill, Michael Lane
Mc Gonigle, Paul John
Mc Govern, Alfred James
Mc Govern, Walter T.
Mc Gowan, A. Clay
Mc Gowan, Kenneth Leroy
Mc Gowin, Gerald Anthony
Mc Grath, Lucille Marie
Mc Grath, Richard William
Mc Graw, Donald Ray
Mc Gregor, Bruce James
Mc Gregor, Francis Robert
Mc Grew, John Ferris
Mc Guane, Harry House
Mc Guigan, William Marion
Mc Guire, E. James
Mc Guire, John Martin
McGuire, Kelly Bronwyn
Mc Guire, Michael John
Mc Guire, Walter Joseph
Mc Gunegle, Daniel Edward
Mc Harg, Gerald Barron
Mc Henry, Paul Graham, Jr.
Mc Hugh, Edward Peter
Mc Hugh, Nancy Spicer
Mc Hugh, Raymond Joseph
Mc Hugh, William Fleming
Mc Innis, Emmett Emory, Jr.
Mc Intosh, Cameron Irwin
Mc Intosh, Henry Payne, IV
McIntosh, James Allen
McIntosh, Joan Lawrason
Mc Intosh, Lowrie Wendell
Mc Inturff, Ben Bryan, Jr.
Mc Intyre, Mary Arnetta
Mc Intyre, Robert Lee
Mc Kaig, George Harold
Mc Kaveney, James Patrick
Mc Kay, Koln Gunn
Mc Kee, Bill Earl
Mc Kee, Gerald
Mc Kee, John Carothers
Mc Kee, Nancy Dee
Mc Kee, Raymond Walter
Mc Kee, Ross Raymond
Mc Kee, William James, Jr.
Mc Keen, Gregory Brent
Mc Keever, Jeffrey Dobbs
Mc Kellar, Donald McCallum, III
Mc Kellips, Gordon Wayne, Jr.
Mc Kendrick, Maurice Nilsson
Mc Kenna, Joseph Harold
Mc Kenna, Robert Charles
Mc Kenna, William Edward
McKennon, John Earle, Jr.
McKenry, James Paris
Mc Kenzie, Frank Ellis, Jr.
Mc Kenzie, Joseph Delwin
Mc Kenzie, Michael Charles Robert
Mc Kenzie, Thomas Colin
Mc Keon, Teresa Rene
Mc Kesson, Robert Edward, Jr.
Mc Kibbin, Michael Douglas
Mc Kie, Glen Jacob
Mc Kim, Loren Dallas
Mc Kinney, David Loraine
Mc Kinney, Thomas Raphel
Mc Kinney, Virginia Elaine Zuccaro
Mc Kinnon, Harry Joseph, Jr.
Mc Knight, Lenore Ravin
Mc Laren, Lewis Glen, Jr.
Mc Laren, Robert Bruce
Mc Laren, Thomas Loyall
McLarnon, Gerard
Mc Latchy, Michael John
Mc Laughlin, Douglas Ray
Mc Laughlin, Glen
Mc Laughlin, Joseph Mailey
Mc Laughlin, Robert Francis
Mc Laughlin, William Joseph
Mc Laurin, Francis Wallin (Frank)
McLean, Arthur Corwin
Mc Lean, Bob Norman
Mc Lean, Ephraim Rankin, 3d
Mc Lean, George Leonard
Mc Lean, George Wallace, Jr.
Mc Lean, James Francis, Jr.
Mc Lean, Robert G.
McLean, Robert Joseph
Mc Lean, Ronald George
Mc Lemore, Charles Edward
Mc Lemore, Robert Arnold
Mc Lendon, Berhl Joe
Mc Leod, Don Wynn
Mc Leod, Gregory Donald
Mc Mahan, John William
Mc Mahan, Sue Lindley
Mc Mahon, John Joseph, Jr.
Mc Mahon, Robert Joseph
Mc Manigal, Morland Gene
Mc Manus, John B., Jr.
Mc Master, Paul Edgar
McMath, Carroll Barton, Jr.
McMichael, J. Richard
Mc Micken, Glen Wilbert
Mc Millan, David Raymond
Mc Millan, Edward R.
Mc Millan, Edwin Mattison
Mc Millan, George Michael
Mc Millan, Thomas Ted
Mc Millen, William Morrow
Mc Millin, (Joseph) Laurence, Jr.
Mc Mullen, Ralph Edgar
Mc Mullin, Brent Ross
Mc Mullin, John Francis
Mc Mullin, Phillip Wayne
Mc Murray, John Odell
Mc Murry, Preston Valentine, Jr.
Mc Murry, William Fuqua
Mc Namar, Wilford Louis
Mc Namee, Gilbert Wilson
Mc Naughton, Andrew Robert Leslie
Mc Nayr, John David
Mc Neal, Jerry Reed
Mc Neely, John Edwin
Mc Neil, Douglas Eugene
Mc Neil, John Stuart
McNelley, James Eugene
Mc Nichols, Lydia Alice Andrews
Mc Nichols, Ray
Mc Nichols, William H., Jr.
Mc Nitt, Rollin Lee, Jr.
Mc Nulty, Dale Michael
Mc Nulty, John Kent
Mc Nulty, Terence Patrick
Mc Omber, Val David
McPhee, Bruce Donald
Mc Queen, Forest Arnold
Mc Quillin, Mahlon (Lon) Brice, II
Mc Quown, Dennis Shawn
McRaven, Dale Keith
Mc Reynolds, Neil Lawrence
Mc Rorie, Thomas Henry, III
Mc Shean, Gordon
Mc Skane, Michael Donald
Mc Tague, John Paul
Mc Vicar, Leonard Hugo
Mc Vicker, Virgil Joel
Mc Wayne, Charles Andrew, Jr.
Mc Williams, Edwin Joseph
Meacham, Ervin Lawrence
Mead, Giles W.
Mead, Mildred Louise
Meade, Gregory Sommers
Meadors, William Porter
Meadows, Paul Dwain
Meads, Philip Francis
Meaker, Gerald Henry
Means, Rodney Jerome
Mecca, Andrew Mark
Mecham, Evan Laurence
Mecham, Glenn Jefferson
Meckle, Franklin Charles
Meckler, Milton
Medavoy, Mike
Medberry, Chauncey Joseph, III
Medearis, Roger
Medford, Ernest Leslie, Jr.
Medford, Lester
Medhi, Purnendu Kumar
Medina, Jose Adelaido
Medling, E. Scott
Medlinsky, Albert Stanley
Medsker, Stanley Richard
Meduski, Jerzy Wincenty
Mee, James Leonard
Meehan, Marjorie Mae
Meehan, Patrick Michael
Meek, Loyal George
Meeker, Arlene Dorothy Hallin (Mrs. William Maurice Meeker)
Meeks, Harold (Hal) Lee
Mee-Lee, Denis
Meenan, Patrick Henry
Mees, Quentin Michael
Meguire, Gerald Earl
Mehan, Philip Augustus, Jr.
Mehr, Lois Marilyn
Mehran, Mohsen
Mehring, Clinton Warren
Meier, Matthias S(ebastian)
Meier, Peter Hans
Meier, Susan Theresa
Meigs, John Ligget
Meikle, Frederick Clinton, Jr.
Meilach, Dona Zweigoron
Meister, Gregory James
Mejias, Robert Jesús
Mekelburg, Dennis Arnold
Melbye, Charles Eugene
Melcher, John
Melchior, Ib Jorgen
Melendres, Arthur David
Melichar, Joseph Frank
Melin, Melvin Robert
Melle, Michael David
Mello, Donald R.
Meloan, Taylor Wells
Melone, Margie Ruth
Melrose, Albert Joseph
Melsheimer, Harold
Melton, Claudis Edward
Melton, James Frederick, II
Meltzer, Robert Hiram
Melville, James H.
Memmott, James Richard
Menasco, Lawrence Clifton
Mencuccini, Michele Comfort
Mendel, Werner Max
Mendelson, Robert Alexander, Jr.
Mendenhall, Carrol Clay
Mendenhall, William Franklin
Mendenhall, William Wesley
Mendez, Celestino Galo
Menestrina, Robert William
Mengler, Richard
Menin, Lionel Marx
Menin, Samuel David
Menk, Louis Wilson
Menkes, David
Menkin, Christopher Lawrence (Kit)
Menkin, Michael Riland
Menna, Philip George
Menza, Thomas Frank
Menzies, Jean Storke (Mrs. Ernest F. Menzies)
Mercer, Joseph Henry
Merchant, Roland Samuel
Mercker, Frank Michael
Meredith, Kevin
Merenstein, Gerald Burton
Merkle, Douglas Hall
Merlino, Barbara Ann
Meronek, Dennis Frank
Merrifield, Paul David
Merrill, John Espy
Merrill, M(arcellus) S(amuel)
Merrill, Mary H. Boyd
Merrill, Orville William, Jr.
Merrill, Patrick Edward
Merrill, Robert Edward
Merrill, Robert Lee
Merritt, Bowman
Merritt, John Frederick
Merryman, Somers Gwynn
Mersel, Marjorie Kathryn Pedersen (Mrs. Jules Mersel)
Mershon, John Jett
Mershon, Robert Jean
Mertz, George Henry
Merwin, Edwin Preston
Merz, Charles Michael
Merzbacher, Claude Fell
Meservy, Royal Ruel
Meshad, Floyd George (Shad)
Mesquit, Andrew James
Messmore, David William
Messner, Kathryn Hertzog
Messreni, Frederick Anthony, Jr.
Mestnik, Irmtraut Maria
Metais, Bernard Louis
Metcalf, Harold Harris
Metcalf, Homer Noble
Metcalf, Ralph Marion
Metcalf, Virgil Alonzo
Methven, Margaret Peterson
Metsker, Cheryl Renae Miller
Metz, Donald Henry
Metzger, H(owell) Peter
Metzger, Vernon Arthur
Metzker, William Thomas
Metzner, Richard Joel
Meub, Daniel Warren
Meurer, William Joseph
Mewhinney, William Douthitt
Meyer, Charles Franklin, Jr.
Meyer, Christopher
Meyer, Cletus Donald
Meyer, Helen Chase
Meyer, Ivah Gene
Meyer, James Henry
Meyer, Jeffery Wilson
Meyer, Paul
Meyer, Robert Dale
Meyer, Stephen Pearson
Meyer, Thomas Oscar
Meyer, Thomas Robert
Meyers, Nancy Jean
Meyers, Paul Frank, Jr.
Meyrowitz, Alvin A(braham)
Mezzacappa, Michael Anthony
Mich, Dona Fitzgerald
Michael, Robert Swain
Michael, Stephen William
Michaeli, John Edward
Michaels, Alan Sherman
Michaels, Patrick Francis
Michalczyk, Paul Anthony
Michalik, Edward Francis
Michel, Victor James, Jr.
Michels, F. Bruce
Michelson, Douglas Jerome
Mickel, Donald Dale
Mickle, James Clark
Middione, Elizabeth Derby (Mrs. Carlo Middione)
Middlesworth, Mike
Middleton, Anthony Wayne, Jr.
Middleton, LeRoy Francis
Middleton, Robert Gordon
Midkiff, Frank Elbert
Midlarsky, Manus I.
Miedél, Rainer
Mielke, Clarence Harold, Jr.
Mielke, Frederick William, Jr.
Mier, Millard M.
Migden, Chester L.
Mih, Winston Chee
Mihan, Richard
Mihlik, Josef John
Mikalow, Alfred Alexander, II
Mikelionis, Juozas
Mikhail, Edward Halim
Mikow, Duane John
Mikow, Louis John
Mikuni, Ronald Yoshiaki
Mikuta, Rudolf
Milam, Jay Lynn
Milam, William Jerome
Mildon, James Lee
Miles, Daniel Douglas
Miles, Donald Louis
Miles, Ralph Earl
Miles, Vincent Nelson
Miles, William Maupin
Milias, Mitchell J.
Milkovich, Joseph John
Millard, Lavergne Harriet
Millard, Robert West
Millender, Roy Jene, Jr.
Miller, Alex Abraham
Miller, Arbie Glenn, Jr.
Miller, Arnold
Miller, Arthur
Miller, B. J. Brown
Miller, Barbara Stallcup
Miller, Barry Musgrave
Miller, Beth
Miller, Bill Fred
Miller, Bowman Markle
Miller, Carl Frederick
Miller, Carl Seymour
Miller, Charles Henry
Miller, D. Craig
Miller, Dale E(dwin)
Miller, Daniel C(ourtney)
Miller, Donald Edgar
Miller, Donald James
Miller, Douglas Arthur
Miller, Douglas Robert
Miller, Earl Beauford
Miller, Elva Ruby Connes (Mrs. John R. Miller)
Miller, Emerson Waldo
Miller, Ernest Coleman
Miller, Everett Lyle
Miller, Florence Davis (Mrs. Orval I. Miller)
Miller, Frank R.
Miller, George
Miller, George Jacob
Miller, George Leslie
Miller, Gifford Willis
Miller, Glen Edward, Jr.
Miller, Harry Daniel
Miller, Howard Ross
Miller, Hugo Searle
Miller, Irwin Daniel
Miller, Jack Barnett
Miller, James Erroll
Miller, James Marshall
Miller, James Phelan
Miller, James Richard
Miller, James Robert
Miller, Jean Ruth
Miller, John David
Miller, John Lawrence
Miller, Jon Hamilton
Miller, Kenneth Rue
Miller, Lee Roy, Jr.
Miller, Leland Lensing
Miller, Mark Allen
Miller, Martin
Miller, Martin Joseph, Jr.
Miller, Michael Francis
Miller, Michael Lee
Miller, Michael Robert
Miller, Mickey Kendall
Miller, Nancy Lee
Miller, Neil Walter
Miller, Pamela Joyce Larayne
Miller, Paul A.
Miller, Paul Harold
Miller, Paul Henry
Miller, Robert N. (Red)
Miller, Robert Warburton
Miller, Ronald Thomas
Miller, Ronald William
Miller, Russell Tuttle
Miller, Samuel Lee
Miller, Sherrill Jean
Miller, Stephen Duane
Miller, Terrence B.
Miller, Thomas Joseph
Miller, Thomas Wesley
Miller, Timothy Lee
Miller, Victor Jay
Miller, W(ellington) Everett

Miller, Walter Charles
Miller, Wayne Arthur
Miller, Wendell Smith
Miller, William Augustus
Miller, William Claude
Miller, William Howard
Miller, Woodrow
Miller, Zoya Dickins (Mrs. Hilliard Eve Miller, Jr.)
Millican, Edward Smith Cook
Milligan, Paul Richard
Milligan, Robert Hugh
Milligan, William Eugene
Milliken, John Gordon
Millman, Sylvia
Mills, Arthur Wesley
Mills, Barbara Nash
Mills, Earl Guy
Mills, Edward Freeman
Mills, George Henry, III
Mills, Hubert George
Mills, James Eugene
Mills, James Willard
Mills, Kit Michael
Mills, Lawrence
Mills, Sherry Rae
Mills, Shirley Olivia
Milnor, John Champion
Milstein, Frederick
Milstein, Joseph Gerald
Milstein, Philip
Milton, David Scott
Milton, Robert Lester
Milton, Stanley Michael
Min, Frank Kuipong
Minard, Christopher M.
Minde, Stefan Paul
Mindell, Earl Lawrence
Miner, Richard Robert
Mineta, Norman Y.
Ming, John Kenneth
Minger, Terrell John
Mingione, Albert
Minhas, Abdul Hakim
Minich, Quaid Walton
Minnella, John Lordsal
Minnick, Chris Michael
Minnick, Shirley Jean
Minnick, Walter Clifford
Minnis, Elizabeth
Minor, Benton Lee
Minovitch, Michael Andrew
Minter, John B.
Mintun, Peter Clarkson
Minturn, William Oliver
Minuti, Dennis Patrick
Minzner, Dean Frederick
Mirabile, Joseph Charles
Mirahmadi, Mike Khosrow
Miranda, Birgit
Mirsepassi, Taghi Jalaleddin
Mirza, Zia Iqbal
Misa, Kenneth Franklin
Misch, Peter
Mishra, Bipin Bihari
Miska, John Paul
Miskimen, John Andrew
Miskimin, Paul Anthony
Misner, Arthur Jack
Mitchel, Aristotle
Mitchell, Anita Moser
Mitchell, Charles Harlow
Mitchell, Donald Leslie
Mitchell, Ellis N.
Mitchell, George Hall
Mitchell, Gerald Alexander, Jr.
Mitchell, Gerri Lee
Mitchell, Henry Heywood
Mitchell, Herbert Eugene
Mitchell, Kim Warner
Mitchell, Maurice B.
Mitchell, Michael Joseph, Jr.
Mitchell, Mickey Max
Mitchell, Richard Jackson
Mitchell, Rie Rogers
Mitchell, Wayne Lee
Mitchell, William Henry, Jr.
Mitchell, William S.
Mitgang, Iris F(eldman)
Mitry, Darryl Joseph
Mitsutomi, Takashi
Mittman, Charles
Mitzner, Kenneth Martin
Mixon, Rosalie Ward
Miya, Jun J(untaro)
Miya, Mildred
Miyada, Don Shuso
Miyasato, Jack Sadao
Miyoshi, Masao
Mizianty, Michael Francis
Mizner, Ruth Evelyn
Mjelde, Carroll Verne
Mleczewski, Kenneth Lee
Moacanin, Jovan
Moberg, Dennis John
Moberly, David Lindsey
Moberly, Linden Emery
Moch, Thomas Kelvin
Mock, David Clinton, Jr.
Moe, Andrew Irving
Moe, Lawrence Henry
Moe, Vincent Jake C.
Moe, William Max
Moeller, Romane George
Moffatt, Joseph Nance
Moffet, Judith Lynn
Moffett, Frank Cardwell
Moffett, Loretta DeLois
Moffitt, George James
Moffitt, Robert Claude
Mogel, Ronald David
Moger, Donald Peter
Mogg, Donald Whitehead
Moheyuddin, Ghulam Mohey
Mohlman, Paul Heinze
Moholy, Noël Francis
Mohr, Gerald Thomas
Mohr, Keith Otto
Mohr, Martin Francis
Mohr, Selby
Mohsen, Amr Mohamed
Moine, Donald J.
Moir, John Troup, III
Moise, Steven Kahn
Molenaar, Dee
Molenkamp, Harold
Molesworth, Tommy Dale
Molinaro, Robert John
Moline, Mary
Molino, Henry Samuel
Molitor, Harold O.
Moll, Kendall Dean
Mollot, Michael Edward
Molnar, Charles
Molnar, Eleanore Biaggini
Molteni, Betty Phillips
Molter, Timothy Ian
Molyneux, Donn Errol
Molzen, Dayton Frank
Mommsen, Katharina
Monaco, Daniel Joseph
Monahan, James Patrick
Monarchi, David Edward
Monat, Alan
Monchino, Michael William
Mone, Louis Carmen
Monedero, Carlos Charles
Monell, Roger L.
Moneymaker, Richard Michael
Monfort, Jay Brown
Monguio, Luis
Monismith, Carl Leroy
Monk, Ralph Warner
Monosson, Ira Howard
Monroe, Keith
Monroe, Stanley Edwin
Mons, Barend (Barry)
Monsen, Paul Kent
Monson, David Smith
Monson, Ralph Englin
Montgomery, Alpha Le Von
Montgomery, Henry DuBose, Jr.
Montgomery, John Thomas
Montgomery, Laverta
Montgomery, Randall Graham
Montgomery, Roberta Jean
Montgomery, Theodore Ashton
Montgomery, William Fredric
Montijo, Harriett Christine Mathison (Mrs. Henry Lucas Montijo)
Montijo, Henry Lucas
Moody, David Anthony Vales
Moody, Donald Parsons
Moody, James Edson
Moody, James LaRoy
Moody, Karen Madsen
Moody, Michael Dennis
Moon, Eugene Durell
Moon, Marjorie Ruth
Mooney, Robert Carl
Moore, Bob Earl
Moore, Bradford Wall
Moore, Brian Arthur
Moore, Bruce Orrin
Moore, Bruce Wallace
Moore, Carol Jean
Moore, Charles August, Jr.
Moore, Dallas Nixon
Moore, David Cresap
Moore, Dean Arlin
Moore, Gloria Dawn
Moore, Hal G.
Moore, Hayden Albert
Moore, Hezekiah
Moore, Ivy Pearl Simmons
Moore, Jeanne Marie Conklin
Moore, John D.
Moore, John Putnam, II
Moore, John Robert, Jr.
Moore, Joseph Lavon
Moore, Julie Coles
Moore, Kenneth Edward
Moore, Lester Cross
Moore, Mary Jane
Moore, Michael Joseph
Moore, Phyllis Clark
Moore, Richard A.
Moore, Robert Leroy
Moore, Russell James
Moore, Stanley Wayne
Moore, Theodore Lynn
Moore, Thomas Gale
Moore, W. Scott
Moore, William George, Jr.
Moore, Willis Henry
Moore, Winsor Carl
Moorhead, Carlos John
Moorhead, James Edward
Moorhead, Jerry J.
Moorse, K(athleen) Kelly
Moos, Rudolf H.
Morales, Joseph Anthony
Morales, Julio Karel
Moran, Elizabeth Jane Crawford
Moran, Emerson Daniel
Moranha, Robert Eaton
More, Harry William, Jr.
More, Vishwas D.
Morel, Jean
Moreland, William Lee
Morelli, Margaret Elaine
Moreno, Manuel Alonso
Moreno, Manuel Osvaldo, Jr.
Moretti, August Joseph
Morewedge, Hosseine
Morey, David Edwin
Morey, Robert Thomas
Morford, George William
Morga, Edward Paul
Morgan, Andrew Lane
Morgan, Arden Walter
Morgan, Clayton Calkins
Morgan, Donald Dean
Morgan, Douglas Henes
Morgan, Jack M.
Morgan, Jacob Richard
Morgan, Milton Erwin, Jr.
Morgan, Richard Irving
Morgan, Robert
Morgan, Van F., Jr.
Morgan, Walter Jefferson
Morgan, William Louis
Morgenstern, Donald Earl
Morgenthaler, Helen Marie
Morghen, Herbert Winfried
Mori, Allen Anthony
Mori, Jun
Moricoli, John Chester
Morikawa, Ronald Kiyoshi
Morin, Juan Antonio
Morin, Laurent
Morishige, Walter K.
Morita, Deen Isami
Morita, Yasuko Yoshida
Morley, James Spencer
Morlock, William Joseph
Moroye, Ray Hiromu
Morrell, Donald Clark, Jr.
Morrell, Warren Edmund
Morrice, Edward, Jr.
Morrill, Ralph Alfred
Morris, Barbara Ellen
Morris, Bourne Gafill
Morris, Brooks Theron
Morris, David Samuel
Morris, Effie Lee (Mrs. Leonard V. Jones)
Morris, Howard
Morris, John Leonard
Morris, John Michael
Morris, John Robert
Morris, John Theodore
Morris, Kathleen Curtis
Morris, Kay Wetzel
Morris, Larry Allen
Morris, Laval S(idney)
Morris, Marion Hebb
Morris, Marjorie Hale
Morris, Paul Rennick
Morris, Robert George
Morris, Stephen Matthew
Morris, William McKinley
Morrisey, George Lewis
Morrisey, Richard Joseph
Morrisey, Robert Brewster
Morrison, Charles Mathieson
Morrison, Delcy Schram
Morrison, Edris (Cox)
Morrison, Eilene M(ay)
Morrison, Gilbert Caffall
Morrison, John, Jr.
Morrison, Lucile Phillips
Morrison, Robert Dougal
Morrison, Robert Hugh
Morrison, Robert Stier
Morrison, Roger Barron
Morrison, Velma Vivian
Morriss, Robert Henry
Morrissey, Clarence Joseph
Morrissey, George Russell
Morrissey, Roberta Kathryn
Morroni, Anthony Louis
Morrow, Charles Paul
Morrow, Kenneth Eugene
Morrow, Ludelle
Morrow, Ruth Elizabeth
Morse, Jack Hatton
Morse, John Edward
Morse, William Allen
Morse, William Francis
Mortensen, Bernhardt Lawrence
Mortensen, John Wilson
Mortillaro, Louis Francis
Morton, Alan Ray
Morton, David Emery
Morton, Donald Lee
Morton, Hughes Gregory
Morton, Ira L.
Morton, Paul Harry
Morton, Warren Allen
Mosbo, Alvin Oswald
Moseley, Robert David, Jr.
Moser, Fritz Helmut
Moses, Edwin James
Moses, Franklin Maxwell
Moses, Stefan Bertram
Mosesman, Barry
Mosher, David Lee
Mosier, Harry David, Jr.
Mosier, Rosalind (Mrs. Richard D. Mosier)
Mosier, T. H.
Mosk, Stanley
Moskowitz, Edward Louis
Moss, Charles Norman
Moss, Frank Henry, Jr.
Moss, Morton Herbert
Moss, Neil Pincock
Moss, Royce Edward
Mosser, Sidney Jon
Most, John Anthony
Mosteller, James Wilbur, III
Mostofi, Khosrow
Motis, Gerald
Motley, Hurley Lee
Motta, Ronald Joseph
Mottley, Jacqueline Virginia
Moulds, William Joseph
Moulton, Gail Francis, Jr.
Moultrie, Fred Silas
Mounts, Gary Richard
Mourning, Steven Lewis
Mowbray, John Code
Moy, Randall Frank
Moye, John Edward
Moyer, Gladys
Moyer, James Scott
Moyer, Rudolph Henry
Moyers, William Taylor
Moylan, Kurt Scott
Moyses, Harvey M.
Mraz, Jane Elizabeth
Mucha, John Frank
Mueller, Donald Eugene
Mueller, Edward Ewell
Mueller, Gary Alfred
Mueller, James Joseph
Mueller, Jeffrey Lawrence
Mueller, John (Jack) Frederick
Mueller, Kurt Walter
Mueller, Laura (Mrs. Robert Charles Mueller)
Mueller, Mary Korstad
Mueller, William Martin
Mugler, Frederick Rolla, Jr.
Muhlbach, Robert Arthur
Muir, William Ker
Muirhead, James Segner
Mujumdar, Vilas Sitaram
Mularz, Theodore L.
Mulcahy, Edward Joseph
Mulder, Cleyon Lee
Mulein, Jay H.
Mulkey, David Allen
Mullan, Jack W.
Mullenex, Shirley Lee (Mrs. George Edward Mullenex)
Muller, Jerome Kenneth
Muller, John Douglas
Muller, Nicholas Guthrie
Muller, Paul Milford
Mullica, Karyn Lynn
Mulligan, Robert Patrick
Mullikin, Harry Laverne
Mullings, Dewey DeBaun
Mullins, John Walker
Mullins, Ruth Gladys
Mulloy, James Leonard
Mulock, Richard Buckler
Mulryan, James Donald
Multz, Carter Victor
Mulvania, Richard Lee
Mulvihill, John Campion
Mulvin, Robert Otis
Mumby, Gay Karen (Mrs. Monty Leroy Chilcote)
Mumm, Christopher Eric
Muna, Nadeem Mitri
Mundhenk, Dennis Edgar
Mundle, Peter Bulkeley
Munn, William Charles, II
Munneke, Harlan Gene
Munoz, Manuel Villarreal
Munro, Fern Hornback
Munson, Edward Warner
Munson, H. Carl, Jr.
Munson, John Buford
Munson, Lucille Marguerite (Mrs. Arthur E. Munson)
Munson, Wanda Mae Penrod
Munter, Pamela Osborne
Murakami, Momoko
Murakawa, Hubert Kengo
Murdoch, Richard Bruce
Murdock, Michael Joseph
Murdock, Steven Kent
Murdy, Robert Howard
Murdy, William Fordham, II
Murk, Lyndon Keith
Murkowski, Carol Victoria
Muro, Francis Mark
Murphey, Vera Edna Randle (Mrs. Paul Bryan Murphey)
Murphy, Alvin Hugh
Murphy, Blanche Maxine
Murphy, Chester Glenn
Murphy, Chris Paul
Murphy, Dennis Patrick
Murphy, Dennis Raphael
Murphy, Edward Henry
Murphy, Francis Seward
Murphy, Gordon Neil
Murphy, James W.
Murphy, Jo Ann Cosper
Murphy, John Edward
Murphy, John Thomas
Murphy, Joseph Patrick
Murphy, Lewis Curtis
Murphy, Linda Teresa Fitzpatrick
Murphy, Martha Jenkins
Murphy, Michael James
Murphy, Richard
Murphy, Thomas J.
Murphy, Winifred Lee Schmale (Mrs. Owen James Murphy)
Murr, William Harvey
Murranka, Patricia Ann
Murray, Bruce C.
Murray, Catherine Louise
Murray, Dennis George
Murray, Dwight Rives
Murray, Gerald Doyle
Murray, Gilman Yost
Murray, James Ackley, Jr.
Murray, James Alan
Murray, James Orkney Stuart
Murray, John Staton
Murray, Julie Kaoru (Mrs. Joseph Edward Murray)
Murray, Karen Jane
Murray, Kathleen Ellen
Murray, Richard Conner, Jr.
Murray, Robert Allen
Murray, Roger Cawley
Murray, Wallace Robinson, Jr.
Murray, William Donald
Murrell, Raphael
Murtha, Francis Brian
Musacchio, Theodore Alphonsus
Musegades, Wallace Walter
Musgrave, Thea
Mushen, Robert Linton
Mushin, Ronald Sheldon
Musick, James Kirby
Musick, W. Dale
Musihin, Konstantin K.
Mussehl, Robert Clarence
Mussell, Elwin Elbert
Mussell, Stanley Wright
Musslewhite, Joyce Cleon Holter
Mustacchi, Piero
Mutschler, Herbert Frederick
Mutze, Gustav Adolf
Myan, Thomas John
Mybeck, Richard Raymond
Myer, Jon Harold
Myer, Ralph Edwin
Myers, Al
Myers, Clay
Myers, Harrison Howard, Jr.
Myers, Kelly Chris
Myers, Kent W.
Myers, Larry Dean
Myers, Phillip Fenton
Myers, R. Fraser
Myers, Robert Eugene
Myers, Robert Vernon
Myers, Wallace Jackson
Myhre, Kjell Einride
Myles, Ronald Lewis
Myllykoski, Ville Johannes
Mylroie, Willa Ruth Wilcox (Mrs. Donald G. Fassett)
Mynatt, Richard Earl Mc Intire
Myrick, Claude Crimont
Mystrom, Richard Elmer
Nabbefeld, Robert Louis
Nachazel, John
Nachman, Joseph Frank
Nachman, Richard Joseph
Nadalini, Louis Ernest
Nadler, Estelle (Mrs. Julius Nadler)
Nadler, George L.
Nadler, Harry Eugene
Nadon, John Douglas
Naegle, A. Bradley
Naftel, James Marshall
Nafziger, James Albert Richmond
Nagata, Donald Mitsuo
Nagel, Michael Robert
Nagler, James Edward
Naglestad, Frederic Allen
Nagy, Albert Sorensen
Nagy, John, III
Nagy, Stephen Mears, Jr.
Naiman, Leonard Howard
Naiman, Rubin
Naitoh, Paul Yoshimasa
Nakakuki, Masafumi
Nakamura, Alva Koki
Nakamura, Hiromu
Nakamura, Otis Sachio
Nakamura, Yukio
Nakano, Kenneth Rikuji
Nakasone, Nobuyuki
Nalbandian, John Vaughn
Nance, Francis Dean
Nanda, Ved P.
Naness, Charles
Nanjundappa, Gangadharappa
Nankas, Ernest
Napier, James Leonard
Napier, Richard Stephen
Napolitano, Guy Christopher
Napton, Lewis Kyle
Naranja, Rogelio Darusin
Narodick, Kit Gordon
Nasby, Bruce Allen
Nash, Michael Mark
Nashem, Leland O.
Naskey, John Jacob
Nathan, Charles Carb
Natt, Theodore McClelland
Nattenberg, David
Natterson, Joseph Morton
Naugle, Dorothy Alice
Naumann, Robert Curt
Navarre, Donald Casper
Navarro, Asterio Rosales
Navarro, Ramon
Navarro, Roland Udarbe
Navis, Herbert Albert
Navratil, Amy R.
Navratil, James Dale
Nawrocki, Michael Andrew
Nay, Samuel Wesley, Jr.
Nazarian, Hagop Nubar
Neadeau, Leslie Leroy
Neal, David Lynn
Neal, James Edward
Neal, Thomas Austin
Nebeker, Delbert Mathews
Nebeker, Robert Lee
Nechak, Diane Opdenweyer
Necker, David Chester
Needham, Lucien Arthur
Neer, Dean Joseph
Neeson, John Vincent
Neff, Edward John
Negard, Sylvia Sidney
Negrea, Stefan
Negus, Norman Curtiss
Neher, Robert Lloyd, Jr.
Neibert, Wid Omar
Neider, Charles
Neidert, Kalo Edward
Neighbor, R. Kenneth
Neil, Douglas Elmer
Neil, Jessie Pruitt
Neil, John David Allan
Neill, Marshall Allen
Neilson, Sandra Lynn
Neisser, Peter Alexander
Neiswender, John S.
Neithercut, Donald Charles
Nejedly, John Albert
Nella, Alfred Lawrence
Nellor, John Harold
Nelson, Alfred Sidney
Nelson, Andrew Gilbert
Nelson, Armour Halstead
Nelson, Barry Vernon
Nelson, Bruce Allen, Jr.
Nelson, Charles David
Nelson, Clarence Lewis
Nelson, Constance Burkhardt
Nelson, Cordner Bruce
Nelson, Dave Louis
Nelson, David Samuel
Nelson, Don Harry
Nelson, Edward John
Nelson, Edwin Leonard
Nelson, Eric Loren
Nelson, Franklyn Lloyd
Nelson, Harold Gordon
Nelson, Harold Lee
Nelson, Jack Russell
Nelson, Jean Ware
Nelson, Jerald Roger
Nelson, Joanne Elizabeth
Nelson, Joe Bernard
Nelson, John Richard
Nelson, Marie J. Tenny
Nelson, Marion Clavar
Nelson, Mary Carroll
Nelson, Mike J(ackson)
Nelson, Nancy Eleanor
Nelson, Ralph
Nelson, Richard Arnold
Nelson, Richard Eugene
Nelson, Rodney Ellsworth
Nelson, Roger Ellis
Nelson, Roger Hugh
Nelson, Ronald Andrew
Nelson, Russell Marion
Nelson, Sarah Milledge
Nelson, Sherman Walter
Nelson, Walter W.
Nelson, William Bischoff
Nelson, William Wells
Nemetz, Harold
Nemir, Donald Philip
Nemiro, Beverly Mirium Anderson
Nepomuceno, Adelaido Nocon
Nerland, Andrew Ronald
Nero, Bob
Nesbitt, John Franklin
Neslund, Kristofer Claude
Ness, Roy William
Nesvig, Milton Luther
Nesvold, Betty Anne
Nethery, Wallace Roscoe
Neti, Radhakrishna Murty
Netzel, Paul Arthur
Neu, Robert Richard
Neubauer, Darwin William
Neubert, Jerome Arthur
Neuenschwander, David Neil, II
Neuhoff, Mary Helen
Neuman, Raymond Joseph
Neumann, Harry George Charles
Neumann, Herschel
Neustein, Harry B(ernard)
Neva, Edward
Newberg, Dorothy Beck (Mrs. William C. Newberg)
Newberg, Philip Frederick
Newberg, William Charles
Newberry, Conrad Floyde
Newby, Martha Redmon (Mrs. Jonathan D. Newby III)
Newcomb, Anthony
Newell, Hubert M.
Newell, Richard Lee
Newell, Robert Max
Newell, Roger Austin
Newell, Strohm
Newhouse, Irving Ralph
Newhouse, Robert Milton
Newhouse, William Erwin, Sr.
Newkirk, Gordon Allen, Jr.
Newkirk, John Burt
Newland, David Edward
Newland, William Eugene
Newlin, Sylvia Ann
Newlon, Betty Joe
Newman, Darrell Francis
Newman, Edgar Leon
Newman, Frank Cecil
Newman, Henry Albert
Newman, John Anderson
Newman, Kent Irving
Newman, Loretta Marie
Newman, Richard Clark
Newmark, Milton Maxwell
Newnan, Marjorie Eveland
Newsom, W(ill) Roy
Newton, Dick LeRoy
Newton, Dorothy Fairbank (Mrs. Robert E. Newton)
Newton, Eileen Elizabeth
Newton, Ernest LeRoy
Newton, India Alida
Newton, Stephen Patrick
Newton, Vernon Clayton, Jr.
Ney, James Walter Edward Colby
Neylan, Anthony John
Neztsosie, Dick
Ng, Peter Park Jim

Ng, Raymond Cheuk-Him
Nguyen, Sac Quoc
Nguyen, Toan Cao
Niblett, Gary Lawrence
Nibley, Jane Lee
Nibley, Robert Ricks
Niccum, (Jessie) Jeanne
Nice, William Michael
Nicholas, David Dunston
Nicholas, David Durell
Nicholas, Frederick Mortimer
Nicholas, Ralph Lawrence
Nicholes, Michael Erin
Nichols, Alan Cheshire
Nichols, Alan Hammond
Nichols, David F.
Nichols, John Burton
Nichols, Lyle Alan
Nichols, Ralph Blaine
Nichols, Robert Taft
Nichols, Roy Eugene
Nicholson, Henry B.
Nicholson, Roy Stephen, Jr.
Nicholson, Will Faust, Jr.
Nicholson, William Joseph
Nichparenko, Sue Broadston
Nickels, Frank John, Jr.
Nicklaus, Theodore Aurelius
Nicklos, Nicholas Dennis
Nicol, James Marvin
Nicolai, Eugene Ralph
Niedercorn, John Herman
Niedzielski, Henri Zygmunt
Nielsen, Calmar Zadok
Nielsen, Elwood L.
Nielsen, Julian Moyes
Nielsen, Leland Chris
Nielsen, Lewis Marchant
Nielsen, Linda Pamela
Nielsen, Martin Thomas
Nielsen, Wayne
Nielson, J(ohn) Marlowe
Nieman, Stuart
Niemeyer, Arnold Carl
Nieminsky, Arthur Clarence
Nienow, Harvey Charles
Niesen, Thomas Marvin
Nietfeld, William Dietrich
Nieto, Juan Manuel
Nightingale, Richard William
Nightingale, Stanley Wren
Nikas, George A.
Nikel, Casimir Michael
Nikola, Herbert Charles
Niles, David Fosdick
Niles, Doris Kildale (Mrs. Arthur D. Niles)
Niles, Franklin Elvie
Niles, Michael Scott
Niles, Wesley Everett
Nilson, Roy
Nimer, Melvin Dean
Nip, Charles Chung-Lai
Nisargand, Umesh Laxman
Nisbet, Ada
Nishimura, Howard Isamu
Nisich, Anthony Joseph
Nisle, Robert George
Niswender, Gordon Dean
Nitzberg, Kenneth Ernest
Nix, Robert Wayne
Noack, William Raymond
Nobil, Myron Kraus
Noble, Chester Lehner
Noble, George Washington
Noble, James Van Petten
Noble, John Drummond
Noble, Paul, Jr.
Noble, Richard Lloyd
Noblitt, Jack Lee
Nobmann, Paul Hanway
Noe, Robert Clark
Noecker, Carl Blue
Noel, Jeanne Kay
Noguchi, Thomas T.
Noia, Richard Corbishley
Nolan, Charles E., Jr.
Nolan, Dorothy Beckett
Noland, Mary Ruth
Nolder, Harry Leslie, Jr.
Nolte, Carl William
Noltmann, Ernst August
Nong
Noonan, Thomas Francis
Noonan, Walter Patrick
Nootz, Arthur Lee
Norberg, Douglas Elliott
Norberg, Gunnar
Nordale, La Dessa (Mrs. A. Hjalmer Nordale)
Nordstrom, Eugene Alexander
Nordyke, James Walter
Norman, George Irving, III
Norman, John Edward
Norman, Paul Ray
Norman, Ralph David
Norris, Carol Ann
Norris, Jean Dyon
Norris, Jerry Browning
Norris, John Steven
Norris, Kenneth Stafford
Norris, Robert Matheson
Norsell, Paul Ernest
North, Dean Thomas
North, Francis Stanley
North, Kenneth Timothy
Northcutt, Helene Louise Berking (Mrs. Charles Phillip Northcutt)
Northrop, John Howard
Norton, Dean
Norton, John Leslie
Norton, John Ruddle, III
Norton, Max C.
Norton, William Allen
Norton-Tarpez, Jay
Norup, Willy
Norville, Holmes Smith
Norwood, Byron Johns (Scott)
Notani-Sharma, Prem
Notowitz, Allen Lee
Novak, Michael Edwin
Novak, Raymond F.
Novell, John Kingsley
Nowak, Phillip D.
Nowatzki, Donald Jack
Noyes, Henry Pierre
Nuckles, Wesley Otis
Nugent, Thomas Francis
Nunis, Doyce Blackman, Jr.
Nunn, Leslie Edgar
Nunn, Marie Louise Downs
Nunziato, Jace William
Nunziato, Ralph Joseph
Nury, Fredoon Shahin
Nuttelman, Robert Alan
Nutter, Daniel Steinbeck
Nuwer, Marc Roman
Nuxoll, Patrick James
Nwagbologu, Nnaemeka Austin Matthews
Nybakken, James Willard
Nye, Diane Trevithick
Nye, Gary Scott
Nyman, Carl David
Nymeyer, Robert Bert
Oakeshott, Gordon B(laisdell)
Oakland, Sam Adolf Sjursen
Oakman, Jay Curtis
Oaks, Dallin Harris
Oatey, Robert Lee
Oaxaca, Virginia C.
Ober, Conrad Lyle
Oberheim, Thomas Elroy
Oberle, Carole Jo
Obermeyer, Charles Martin
Oberste-Lehn, Deane
Obichere, Boniface Ihewunwa
Obley, Nancy Nadline
Obremski, Robert John
O'Bric, Michael
O'Brien, C(larence) Bickford
O'Brien, Cyril Cornelius
O'Brien, Grace Wilhelmina Ehlig
O'Brien, John Conway
O'Brien, John James, Jr.
O'Brien, John Jay
O'Brien, John Lawrence
O'Brien, John William, Jr.
O'Brien, Noel Stephen
O'Brien, Paul James
O'Brien, Raymond Francis
O'Brien, Robert S.
O'Brien, Robert W(illiam)
O'Bryant, Michael Alfred
O'Byrne, Paul J.
O'Callaghan, J. Patrick
Ochoa, Antonio Guerrero
O'Connell, Lawrence Gregory
O'Connell, Michael Vincent
O'Connor, Arthur Joseph, III
O'Connor, James Patrick
O'Connor, Steven Pray
Oda, Yoshio
Odajima, Tsutomu Thomas
O'Day, Richard Anthony
O'Deen, William Alan
Odell, Amy Cardon
Odom, Cloyce Eli
Odom, James Thomas
Oe, Emily Norene
Oelrich, Carl M.
Oestreich, James Joseph
Oetting, Richard Fleming
Ogburn, Dwight Karil
Ogburn, Hugh Bell
Ogden, Myron Waldo
Ogg, Wilson Reid
Ogonowski, George Roman
O'Grady, John Fergus
O'Green, Frederick W.
O'Guinn, Jack Robert
Oh, Jesse Jisoo
Oh, Tai Keun
O'Hair, Donald Ellsberry
O'Halloran, (Laverne M.) Kathleen (Mrs. John R. O'Halloran, Jr.)
O'Hare, Maurice John
Ohkawa, Tihiro
Ohle, Ernest Linwood
Ohler, Donald Eugene
Ohlson, John Algoth
Ohrenschall, Robert Frank
Ohta, Raymond Kiyoshi
Oien, Harley Martin
Okada, Robert Harry
O'Keefe, John Cornelius
Okinaga, Sam Noboru
Okrent, David
Oksenholt, Svein
Olafson, Harold Stanley
Olah, Susan Rose
Olayan, Stanley Roy
Oldaker, David Lynn, Jr.
O'Leary, Geraldine Nied
Olejar, Michael
Olender, Terrys T.
Oles, Stuart Gregory
Olguin, Carmen
Olguin, Gilbert Michael
Olhoft, John Ernest
Oliai, Rita Faye
Olinger, Leonard Bennett
Olinick, Martin
Oliphant, Charles Romig
Oliphant, John Edwin
Oliphant, La Verna Dean
Olivas, Nathan Joseph
Olive, Joseph Manuel
Oliver, Clifford Eubert
Oliver, Earl Thomas
Oliver, Floyd Forrest
Oliver, Glen William
Oliver, John Alfred
Oliver, John Gilbert
Olmsted, James Warren, Jr.
Olmsted, Maxine Blakemore
Olmsted, Spalding Maxine
Olney, Ross David
Olsen, Ivan O.
Olsen, Joseph Carl
Olsen, Marvin Elliott
Olsen, Richard James
Olson, Andrew Clarence, Jr.
Olson, Bonnie Waggoner-Breternitz (Mrs. O. Donald Olson)
Olson, David Henning
Olson, David John
Olson, Donald George
Olson, Doris Cecelia
Olson, Gerald Theodore
Olson, H. E.
Olson, John Elmer
Olson, John Kalmer
Olson, Kenneth Harvey
Olson, Laura Maxine
Olson, Marian Edna
Olson, Oscar Charles
Olson, Oscar Donald
Olson, Ralph Eldo
Olson, Vern Charles
Olson, Willard Paul
Olson, William Thomas
Olsson, Richard Albert, Jr.
Olstad, Betty Loy
Olvera, Carlos Nelson
O'Mahony, Michael Anthony
O'Malley, Peter
O'Malley, Robert Harold
Oman, Henry
Oman, LaFel Earl
Omer, George Elbert, Jr.
Omholt, Arne Herbert
Omura, Jimmy Kazuhiro
Ondrejcka, William Joseph
Ondrejka, Arthur Richard
O'Neal, Harry Edward
O'Neil, James Joseph
O'Neil, James Thomas, Jr.
O'Neil, Thomas James
O'Neil, Thomas William, Jr.
O'Neill, Ann Louise
O'Neill, James Joseph
O'Neill, Richard Michael
O'Neill, Robert Leo
O'Neill, Ynez Violé
Ono, Nagahisa
Ono, Yoneo
Onorato, Michael Paul
Onorofskie, Stephen Anthony
Onstot, Gary Glen
Onstott, Edward Irvin
Onufrock, Richard Shade
Oosting, Mary Robinson
Oparah, Sonny Simeon
Opfermann, Myron William
Opia, Eric Agume
Opler, Stanley Ronald
Oppenheim, Alfred Martin
Oppenheim, Louis H.
Oppenheimer, Arthur Falk
Oppenheimer, Max, Jr.
Oppenheimer, Steven Bernard
Orahood, Frank David
Ord, Don Grant
O'Regan, John Brian
O'Riordan, William Dabney
Orlando, David Anthony
Orlebeke, William Ronald
Orlowski, Jan Alexander
Orman, John Christopher
Orman, Leonard Milton
Orme, Cheryl Lee
Ormsby, Lionel
Ornelas, Alfred H (ernandez)
Orozco, Cecilio
Orr, B(enson) Harold
Orr, Daniel Lewis, II
Orr, Danny LeRoy
Orr, Dennis Mark
Orr, Jack Edward
Orr, William Herbert
Orsi, Gloria Marie
Orsten, Marguerite May
Ortega, Ernest Eugene
Ortega, Orlando J.
Ortega, Richard Manuel
Orth, Charles Joseph
Ortiz, Doris Lorain
Ortiz, Solomon Daniel
Ortlieb, Robert Eugene
Ortolano, Ralph Joseph
Orton, Glenn Scott
Orton, Terence Kim
Orwig, Larry Gordon
Osborn, Terry Wayne
Osborne, David Harry, III
Osborne, Larry Walter
Osborne, Leon Henry
Osborne, Richard Holmes
Osen, Lynn Moses
Osf, Sister Mary Samuel Wear
Osgood, George Mierow
O'Shea, Martin Lester
Osheroff, William John
Oshiro, Hideo
Oshman, Karen Lea
O'Steen, Bernard (Barney) Van, Sr.
Ostendorf, Frederick Otto
Oster, Ludwig Friedrich
Osterman, Dean Newell
Ostermiller, John Victor
Ostlund, Lyman Ellis
Ostovari, Cambis
Ostrem, Donald Lee
Ostrogorsky, Michael
O'Sullivan, Thomas Francis
Oswald, Hugo Edmund, Jr.
Oswald, William Joseph
Oswalt, Wendell Hillman
Ota, Jack Klyoshi
Ota, Jeremy Kayne
Otani, Arthur Seiichi
Otani, Henry Hideo
O'Toole, John Stephen, Jr.
Ott, Dudley Edward
Ott, Fred Carlton
Otterstein, (Adolph) Ottie William, III
Ottley, Jerold Don
Otto, William Michael
Ottoman, Richard Edward
Outcalt, Richard F(ranklin)
Outland, George Faulkner
Ovenfors, Carl-Olof Nils Sten
Overbeck, Daniel Bertrand
Overgaard, Willard Michele
Overholser, J. Homer Harold
Overholt, Steven Lowell
Overshown, Larry Donnell
Overstreet, Reading, Jr.
Owen, Calvin P.
Owen, Frankie Robinson
Owen, John Elias
Owen, John William
Owen, Kenneth Charles
Owens, Aletha Riedel
Owens, Donald
Owens, Gary
Owens, Robert John
Owley, Arthur Norman
Owsley, John Quincy, Jr.
Oxelson, Eric Carl
Oxford, Richard Orrville
Oxman, Rickey Brian
Oxner, Edwin Story
Ozanich, Charles George
Pabisch, Peter Karl
Pace, Jon Auburn
Pace, Lorin Nelson
Pacheco, Anita Kay
Pacino, Frank George
Pack, Marsha Rae
Pack, Phoebe Katherine Finley (Mrs. Arthur Newton Pack)
Packard, Lois La Verne
Packard, Peter
Packer, Mark Barry
Packnett, Don Stevenson
Packwood, Bob
Paddock, Darven Levere
Padfield, Marianne Nina Carter
Padgett, William DeGrove
Padrick, Jack Omega
Paez, Jesse Lucas
Pagano, Steven James
Page, Carol Lorraine
Page, Gordon Benjamin
Paget, David John
Paget, Joel Hathaway
Paget, John Arthur
Paget, Roger
Pagter, Carl Richard
Pahnke, Lyle Douglas, Jr.
Pai, Vernon Kwan Kook
Paige, Glenn Durland
Paik, George
Pailer, Douglas Irving
Paine, Bonnie Pauly
Paine, Lee Alfred
Paine, Robert Treat, Jr.
Paine, Thomas Hallsten
Painter, Daniel Woodruff, II
Painter, Reed Romney
Pair, Charles Luther
Pair, Paul Milton
Palacio, June Rose
Palatnick, Barton
Palazzo, Robert Paul
Palenik, Joseph
Paliani, Mary Ann
Palkowitsh, Marcus Steve
Pallasch, Thomas J.
Pallin, Samuel Lear
Pallios, Gus Stelios
Pall-Pallant, Teri
Palm, Nels, Jr.
Palm, Sigfrid George (Sig)
Palm, Victoria Lou
Palmberg, Karl John
Palmer, Al Sidney
Palmer, Blaine Charles
Palmer, James Kermit
Palmer, James Richard
Palmer, John W.
Palmer, Lavinia Jane
Palmer, Loraine Patricia
Palmer, Mabel Evelyn
Palmer, Mark Johnathan
Palmer, Oscar Charles, Sr.
Palmer, Patricia Ann Texter (Mrs. David Palmer)
Palmer, Roy George
Palmer, Ruth
Palmer, Vincent Allan
Palmer, William Oswald
Palmiotto, Alphonso Joseph
Palmore, James Andrew, Jr.
Palms, Francis
Palombo, Michael Anthony
Palomino, Ernesto Ramirez
Palumbo, Nicholas Eugene
Pamintuan, Israel Borja
Pamplin, Robert Boisseau, Jr.
Pan, Bingham Ying Kuei
Panas, Jerold
Pande, Braj Bhushan
Pandey, Triloki Nath
Pandolfi, Louis Joseph
Panecaldo, Loreto Antonio, III (Tony)
Panetta, Leon Edward
Pang, Herbert George
Pang, Lup Quon
Pangborn, Rose Marie Valdes
Panico, Victor Gerarde
Panitz, Janda Kirk Griffith
Pann, Francis
Panoringan, Mario Cendana
Pansky, Emil John
Pao, John
Paoli, Richard John
Paolini, Barbara Anne
Paoluccio, Joseph Paul
Papanikolas, William Michael
Papich, Stephen J.
Papierniak, Duane Walter
Pappagianis, Demosthenes
Pappas, George Louis
Pappas, Mike J.
Paquette, Robert George
Parac, Thomas J.
Parajon, Rolando Victor
Pard, Albert Gerard
Parente, Emil J.
Parente, Robert Bruce
Parham, Richard James
Parikh, Gaurang Ramanlal (Gary)
Paris, C. James
Paris, Phillip Sanchez
Parise, Carl
Parish, H(ayward) Carroll
Parish, Robert Stuart, Sr.
Park, Helen O'Boyle (Mrs. Edward Cahill Park)
Park, Moon Soo
Park, Richard
Park, Wilford Edison
Park, Won Choon
Parker, Arley Vern, III
Parker, C. Wolcott, II
Parker, Charles Frederick
Parker, Charles Lee
Parker, David John
Parker, Francine
Parker, Frederick Waldo
Parker, John Bernard
Parker, John Francis
Parker, John Ira, Jr.
Parker, Judith Rachael
Parker, Kenneth Dean
Parker, Marilyn Morris
Parker, Paul Anthony
Parker, Roy Alfred
Parker, Scott Smith
Parker, Willis Lamont
Parkerson, Andrew Gordon
Parker-Tiberi, Martha Jeanette
Parkhurst, Violet Kinney
Parkhurst, William Roy
Parkin, Don Hugh
Parkinson, Ariel
Parkinson, Howard Evans
Parkinson, John Raymond
Parks, D. C.
Parks, Donald Lee
Parks, James Russell
Parks, Larry Clinton
Parks, Richard Dee
Parks, Robert Francis
Parks, Thomas Gordon
Parlee, Norman Allen Devine
Parma, Robert
Parnall, Edward
Parnes, Harold
Paronto, James Francis
Parr, Edward Leon
Parrick, Gerald Hathaway
Parrish, Jerry Clinton
Parrish, Robert Neil
Parry, Evan Henry
Parry, Paul Stewart
Parry, Richard Owen
Parry, Robert Troutt
Parsell, Richard Leroy
Parsons, Ben G.
Parsons, Craig Alan
Parsons, Harriet Oettinger
Parsons, William Ronald
Partington, Cyrus William
Partington, Harriet Jenkins
Partlow, William Edward
Partridge, Joy
Pascale, Richard Tanner
Pascoa, Orlando Santos
Pashayan, Charles, Jr.
Pasin, Ronald Anthony
Paskerian, Charles Kay, Jr.
Paskett, Michael Errol
Paskow, Shimon
Passamaneck, Richard Scott
Passmore, Donald Cecil
Pasternak, David Joel
Pasternak, Derick Peter
Pasternak, Robert Ivan Paul
Pastore, Michael Anthony
Pastrana, David E(rnest)
Pastreich, Peter
Patch, Robert Kennedy
Patel, Ramesh Baldevbhai
Paterson, Thomas Glynn
Patino, Manuel Luis
Patkay, Stephen (Etienne) Albert
Patnoe, Herbert Darrell
Patrick, Donald Allen
Patsakos, George
Patten, Bebe Harrison
Patterson, Earl Francis
Patterson, James Donald
Patterson, Jerry Mumford
Patterson, Joseph Cromwell
Patterson, Marion Louise
Patterson, Norman Arthur
Patterson, Randall Eugene
Patterson, Thomas John, Jr.
Patterson, Wade Naylor
Pattison, Orville Hoyt
Patton, Carolyn Vannette
Patton, Charles, Jr.
Patton, Robert Earl
Patton, William Weston
Paul, Brian Lauren
Paul, George Raymond
Paul, James Mackay
Paul, Jeffrey William
Paul, William Bradshaw, III
Paulin, Henry Sylvester
Pauling, David P.
Pauling, Linus Carl
Paulsen, Borge Regnar
Paulsen, Douglas Frank, Jr.
Paulson, Donald Robert
Paulson, Norman Lorain
Paulus, Albert Otto
Pauly, Paul F.
Pavia, Charles Nicholas
Pavlik, John Michael
Pawula, Robert Francis
Paxton, Claudia Del
Pay, Robert William
Payne, Ella Rae
Payne, Harry Vern
Payne, Jack Wellesley
Payne, John Montgomery
Payne, Reba Mildred
Payne, Robert Bruce
Payne, Samuel Calvin
Payne, Walter Fitch, III
Payne, William Howard
Payton, Charles Edward
Payton, Ralph Reed
Peacock, Curtis Cuniffe
Peak, George Wayne
Pealy, Dorothee Strauss
Pearce, Frederick Ellis
Pearce, Kenneth Warren
Pearce, Stanley Keith
Pearce, Thomas Matthews
Pearlman, David Samuel
Pearsall, David Williams
Pearson, Armond Delos
Pearson, Bernard Alexander
Pearson, Emmet Albert
Pearson, Enid Williams
Pearson, Frank Henry
Pearson, Harry Fridel
Pearson, Hugh John Sanders
Pearson, John
Pearson, Marilyn McQuestion
Pearson, Ronald Jeffrey
Pease, Paul Hulbert
Pease, Robert Wright
Peavey, Arthur Frank
Peccorini, Francisco Letona
Pechacek, Louis Stanley
Peck, James Mason, Jr.
Peck, Jane Marie
Peck, Jerome Frederick, Jr.
Peck, Joseph Howard, Jr.
Peck, LeRoy Eugene
Peck, Paulus Edward
Peck, Robert David
Peck, Wally Nelson
Peckham, Donald
Peckham, Robert Francis, Jr.
Pecsar, Raymond Ernest
Peddersen, Raymond Bert
Pedersen, Bruce
Pedersen, Kent Alden
Pederson, Burton Carl
Peeler, Stuart Thorne
Peeples, Maija Woof
Peery, Everett David
Peery, James Brown
Peery, Paul Denver
Peevers, Barbara Hollands
Pegram, Anthony Ricardo
Peirano, Lawrence Edward
Peirsol, John Mark
Pelandini, Thomas Francis
Pelatt, James Daniel
Peleg, Nathan Thomas
Pelescak, George Andrew
Pelka, David Gerard
Pelletier, Joseph Anthony
Pellicori, Samuel Frank
Pellinen, Donald Gary
Pellman, Leonard John
Pelphrey, Michael Wayne
Pelton, Warren J.
Pemberton, John de Jarnette, Jr.
Penaloza, Osias Reyes
Pence, Alan Robert
Pence, Alfred Maywood
Pendell, Thomas Roy
Penderghast, Thomas Frederick
Pendery, Eugene Christian, III
Pendleton, Bruce
Pendleton, Robert Cecil
Pengelley, C. Desmond
Penhallow, Richard
Penikis, Virginia M.
Peniston, Eugene Gilbert
Penn, Janice
Penneman, Robert Allen
Penner, Clyde Eugene
Penner, Gary Ralph
Pennington, Terry Lee
Pennisi, Sam
Penny, Wilford Ray
Penrod, James Isaac
Penrod, James Wilford
Pentland, Leslie Anne Parker
Penton, Zelda Eve
Penzo, Paul Anthony
Pepitone-Rockwell, Frances Marie

Pepper, Charles Michael
Perazzo, John
Percious, Helen Marlyn (Jackie)
Percival, Thornton Powers
Perdomo, Jim B.
Pereda, Eugene Falero
Pereira, William L.
Perelman, Lewis Joel
Perera, Victor Haim
Perez, Raul Ramon
Perez, Sammie Brian
Perine, Joseph Bruce
Peringer, Forrest Michael
Perito, Joseph Gerald, Jr.
Perkes, Victor Aston
Perkins, Albert St. Clair
Perkins, David William
Perkins, Edward A.
Perkins, Erlon Chapman
Perkins, Kenneth Lee
Perkins, Leland Mather
Perkins, Terry Richard
Perkins, Van Addison
Perkins, Walter George
Perkinson, Robert Ronald
Perkovac, Stephen Michael
Perlin, Bernard
Perlman, Theodore
Perloff, Jean Marcosson
Perlot, Marianne
Perlstein, Gary Robert
Perreault, John Leo
Perrella, Anthony Joseph
Perreten, Frank Arnold
Perrigo, Lyle Donovan
Perrine, Richard Leroy
Perrine, Wallace Murray
Perrizo, James David
Perry, C(onstance) Eleanor
Perry, David Niles
Perry, Herbert Anthony
Perry, John Van Buren
Perry, Lewis, Jr.
Perry, Richard Herbert
Perry, Robert Ray
Perry, Robert William, III
Perry, Ronald William
Perry, Thomas Manley
Perry, Troy Deroy
Perryman, Bruce Clark
Persons, Jeffry Erich
Persons, (Agnes) Madelyn Moroney
Persyn, Ronald Elzie
Pesin, Harry
Pesner, Stanley Stewart
Pestolesi, Robert August
Petak, William John
Peterman, Edward
Peters, Charles David
Peters, Don Preston, Jr.
Peters, Eunice Sarah Bates Lowery (Mrs. William J. Peters)
Peters, Issa
Peters, Leland Howard
Peters, Maja Jean
Peters, Ronald Kennis
Peters, Rowan James
Peters, Russell Carlton
Peters, Wilfred Leonard
Petersen, A(lmon) Lee
Petersen, Calvin Ross
Petersen, Dean Lynn
Petersen, Dennis Alan
Petersen, Donald Edward
Petersen, Donald Loren
Petersen, Gary Michael
Petersen, Gary Robert
Petersen, Martin Eugene
Petersen, Maun Tyre
Petersen, Norman John
Petersen, Orval Lyman
Petersen, Vernon Leroy
Petersen, William Arthur
Petersen, William Bert
Peterson, Alan Herbert
Peterson, Albert Jon
Peterson, Alfonse
Peterson, Arne George
Peterson, Brent Dan
Peterson, Bruce Fraser
Peterson, Cynthia Jane Kittson
Peterson, Darrell Thomas
Peterson, David Lawrence
Peterson, Don Budd
Peterson, Edwin J.
Peterson, Elmer Robert
Peterson, Enoch Wesley Frost
Peterson, Eric Christian
Peterson, Eugene Kyger
Peterson, Eugene R.
Peterson, Frank Tobias
Peterson, George Ellsworth, Jr.
Peterson, Gerald Elroy
Peterson, Gerald L.
Peterson, Glennis Rae
Peterson, Harries-Clichy
Peterson, Harry Clarence
Peterson, James Algert
Peterson, John Clinton
Peterson, John Lamont
Peterson, John Leonard
Peterson, Mell Andrew, Jr.
Peterson, Norman Charles
Peterson, Norman Dale
Peterson, Norman Edwin
Peterson, Paul
Peterson, Raymond MacDonald
Peterson, Richard Arvid
Peterson, Richard Hamlin
Peterson, Richard Ivan
Peterson, Richard Marean
Peterson, Richard Warren
Peterson, Robert Wendell
Peterson, Robin Tucker
Peterson, Rodney Delos
Peterson, Roy Herman, Jr.
Peterson, Roy LaVern
Peterson, Samuel Randolph
Peterson, Stephen Kent
Peterson, Thomas Arthur
Peterson, Thomas Parry
Peterson, Vincent George
Peterson, Walter Edward, Jr.
Peterson, Warren Stanley
Peterson, William David
Petery, Mary Ann Bauer
Petillon, Lee Ritchey
Petoyan, Arthur Sarkis
Petr, Mary Denise
Petriccione, Luke Louis
Petring, Ekkehard Jurgen
Petros, Thomas Harry
Petrovic, John Joseph
Petry, Gary William
Petrytus, Sharon Ann
Petsas, Kosta Jerry
Pettersen, Charles Waldemar
Petti, Ralph Angelo, Jr.
Pettie, Floyd William
Pettigrew, John David
Pettit, Henry Jewett, Jr.
Pettit, William Alfred, Jr.
Pettite, William Clinton
Petty, Keith
Petty, Richard Owen
Petty, RoseMarie
Pevers, Marc William
Pezzoli, Jean Ann
Pezzuti, Thomas Alexander
Pfaff, Dudley Alvey, Jr.
Pfaff, Michael Johnson
Pfaff, Stewart Willard
Pfau, George Harold, Jr.
Pfeiffer, Edward John
Pfeiffer, Frank A.
Pfeiffer, John William
Pfeiffer, Robert Walter, II
Pfiester, Ralph Gerald
Pfister, Emil (Robert)
Pflueger, John Milton
Pforzheimer, Harry
Pfuhl, John Wesley
Pfund, Edward Theodore, Jr.
Phalen, William Ralph
Pheatt, Mark Wayne
Phelps, Harvey William
Phelps, Jay Gordon
Phifer, John Charles
Philippon, Christian Paul
Phillips, Harry Orville
Phillips, C. Anthony
Phillips, Dan Charles
Phillips, Deborah Lee
Phillips, Edwin Charles
Phillips, Emry Alton
Phillips, Frank Sigmund
Phillips, Henry Weldon
Phillips, Howard Don
Phillips, J. Thomas
Phillips, James Boyd
Phillips, James Lloyd
Phillips, Jill Meta
Phillips, John Jacob, Jr.
Phillips, John Richard
Phillips, Jordan Matthew
Phillips, Julius Ceasar, Jr.
Phillips, Orley Oliver
Phillips, Robert East
Phillips, Ronald Dale
Phillips, Ronald Lee
Phillips, Russell Cole
Phillips, Teddy Steve
Phillips, Thomas Porter, III
Phillips, Toni Ellen
Phillips, William George
Philpott, Emalee Isola Ewing (Mrs. Earl Russell Philpott)
Phinney, Edgar Joseph
Phipps, Barbara Helen
Phipps, Gerald H.
Phipps, Maralene Mackerracher
Picard, M. Dane
Pick, James Block
Pickard, David Janard
Pickard, Thomas Nelson
Pickard, William Rossington, Jr.
Pickarts, Evelyn Marie (Mrs. Walter Albert Pickarts)
Pickens, Alexander LeGrand
Pickett, Hal Gene
Pickoff, Julius
Pickrell, Jack Evon
Pickrell, Robert Merlin
Pieczentkowski, Herman Arnold
Piel, John Joseph
Piele, Philip Kern
Pielstick, Russell Allan
Piepmeier, Edward Harman
Pierce, D(orothy) Laverne
Pierce, Frank Lawler
Pierce, Gerald Joseph
Pierce, James Walter
Pierce, Joe Eugene
Pierce, Joseph Reed, III
Pierce, Loretta Mae (Mrs. Clayton A. Pierce)
Pierce, Martha A.
Pierce, Thomas Hughes
Piercy, Gordon Clayton
Pierno, Anthony Robert
Piersol, Allan Gerald
Pierson, Robert
Pierson, William Russell
Pieszak, Daniel Alton
Pietrzak, Lawrence Michael
Piirto, Douglas Donald
Pike, John Jacob
Pilecki, Boleslaw
Pilgeram, Laurence Oscar
Pillers, Charles Marvin
Pillsbury, Stirling Gainer, Jr.
Pilmanis, Martin
Pilz, Edmund Joseph
Pinchuk, Lanis
Pine, James Charles
Pineda, Anselmo
Pinke, Edgar Aebli
Pinkert, James Robert
Pinkerton, Clayton David
Pinkerton, Dorothy Olga Thoms (Mrs. Robert L. Pinkerton)
Pinkley, Woodrow Carlton
Pinnell, George Lewis
Pino, Edward Charles
Pinola, Joseph J.
Pinta, Wanda Bohan (Mrs. R. Jack Pinta)
Pinto, John Howard
Pipal, Vauna LaReda
Piper, James Henry
Pistelak, Isabelle Ellen
Pitcher, Ardis Jennette
Pitchford, Gayel Anne
Pitchford, Loren Carl
Pitlyk, Paul James
Pitney, William Ernest
Pitt, William Arnold
Pitts, Charles Franklin
Pitts, Robert Bedford
Pitts, Thomas Ross
Pizzulli, Cosmo Anthony
Place, Irene Glazik
Place, John B. M.
Plainer, Truman Dean
Plant, Edward Frank
Plante, Michael Phillip
Plate, William Carl
Plath, Neil Walts
Platt, Cathleen Ireland
Platt, Donald Hewitt
Platt, James Harvey
Platt, Joseph Beaven
Platt, Lawrence Bradley
Platus, Libby
Pletsch, Marie Eleanor
Plock, Carl Everett
Plumb, Lewis Robert
Plummer, Leona Weigandt
Pluskat, Thomas John
Plutchak, Noel Bernard
Pochyla, Benjamin Henry
Pocock, Allen Lee
Podboy, John Watts
Podesta, Martin William
Poe, Thomas Allen
Poehner, Raymond Glenn
Pogue, Annalee
Pohl, Patricia Rose Thomas
Poindexter, Edward John
Pois, Robert August
Pokonosky, Thomas Ray
Pol, William Felice
Poladian, Artin Nishan
Poland, Kathryn Eleanor
Polasky, Raymond Joseph, Jr.
Polastri, Riccardo Pio
Politzer, S. Robert
Polk, Benjamin Kauffman
Polk, Frank Fredick
Pollack, Gerald Harvey
Pollack, Joan Diehl (Mrs. Eugene L. Pollack)
Pollack, Louis Rubin
Pollack, William James
Pollak, Norman Lee
Pollard, Desmond Laurence
Polley, Elizabeth Marie
Pollinger, Harold William
Pollis, Richard P.
Pollock, John Phleger
Pollock, Kenneth Gordon
Pollock, Louise
Pollock, Richard Edwin
Pollock, Samuel
Pollyea, Robert William
Polonsky, Dimitri
Polson, Billie Mae
Pomerantz, Steven Dale
Pomeroy, Eltweed George
Pomeroy, Frances Muir
Ponce, Victor Miguel
Pond, Lauren Lester, Jr.
Ponder, Herman
Ponsar, Warren
Ponto, Robert Charles
Poole, Janice Rae
Poole, Patrick Henry
Pooley, Katheryn Louise
Poon, Richard
Poor, Clarence Alexander
Poor, Golden Earl
Pope, Max Lyndell
Popejoy, William J.
Popham, William Keith
Poppenk, Margaret Jessie
Popperwell, Gerald Fredrick
Porcasi, Judith Ann Friedman
Porrath, Saar Avram
Porro, Catherine Rebok
Portanova, Michael Anthony
Portch, Rodney William
Porter, Alexandra Baez
Porter, Blaine Robert
Porter, Clyde Robert
Porter, Frederick Charles
Porter, Howard Charles
Porter, John Erwin
Porter, Lee
Porter, Mary Aileen
Porter, Tommie Dean
Porter, William Woods, II
Porteus, James Oliver
Portner, Peer Michael
Portnoff, Clifton Lew
Posin, Melvin
Possehl, James Henry
Post, Alan
Postigo, Tito
Postil, Halcom
Postler, Paul Robert, Jr.
Postma, James Lee
Postman, I. Marshall
Poston, Billie Louise
Posz, Thomas Glenn
Potomac, Louis Lawrence
Pottenger, Robert Thomas, Jr.
Potter, Earl Wylie
Potter, George Kenneth
Potter, George Russell
Potter, Leona Johnston (Mrs. Harold L. Boyd)
Potter, Roy Wilson
Potthoff, Jerome John
Pottorff, George Byron, Jr.
Potts, Robert William Latelle
Potts, Roy Earl
Potvin, Louis Edgar
Potwardowski, Bernard
Poulakidas, Sakee Kostas
Poulson, Robert Dee
Pouttu, James Howard
Pouttu, Thomas Edwin
Powell, Donnie Melvin
Powell, Frederick
Powell, Jennings Bryan, Jr.
Powell, John Allen
Powell, John Fredric
Powell, Kenneth Bruce
Powell, Larry Allan
Powell, Ralph Edwin
Powell, Russell Francis
Powelson, Keith Davis
Power, Cornelius Michael
Power, John Desmond
Power, John Leahy
Powers, Dale Godfrey
Powers, Franklin Elmore
Powers, Jeffrey Wells
Powers, Kenneth Lawrence
Poyntz, Walter John
Poythress, Virginia Anne Baker
Pozzo, Richard Louis
Prasad, Jagdish
Prater, Thomas Faires
Prather, Dirk Charles
Pratt, Charles Henry
Pratt, E(llen) Marcella Morin (Mrs. George Collins Pratt)
Pratt, George Janes, Jr.
Pratum, Rolf Hoyendahl
Pravitz, Kenneth LeRoy
Pray, Ralph Emerson
Prchal, Dolores
Prchal, Joyce J.
Preble, Laurence George
Precourt, Jay Anthony
Preece, Sherman Joy, Jr.
Preedy, Charles Evan
Prehm, Herbert John
Prehm, Katherine Anne Townsend
Preiser, Wolfgang Friedrich Ernst
Preitz, Clarence Harold
Prendergast, Robert Lewis
Prentice, Leonard Harold
Preobrajenska, Vera Nicolaevna
Prera, Jorge Augusto
Prescott, Lawrence Malcolm
Presley, Jim Charles
Presley, Robert Buel
Pressly, John Brycent
Preste, James Frank
Prestegaard, Erik
Preston, Frederick Willard
Prestwich, Kent Elvin
Prewitt, John Rudolph
Prewitt, Neil Carr
Price, Ann Foianini
Price, Arnold John
Price, Betty May
Price, Elmina Mary Palon
Price, Eugene Gerard
Price, Herman Lee
Price, J. B.
Price, Jay Berry
Price, Martin
Price, Richard Neal
Price, Robert William
Price, Zane Herbert
Prichard, George Edwards
Prickett, David Clinton
Prideaux, Thomas Stephen
Prieto, Jose Norberto
Prime, Ben Root
Primrose, George Arthur, Jr.
Prindeville, John Joseph
Prindle, Robert William
Pringle, Edward E.
Pringle, Weston Stewart, Jr.
Printup, Lloyd Edward
Prior, Ronald Edwin
Prior, Thomas O.
Pritchard, David Lee
Pritchard, Joel M.
Pritchard, Russell William
Pritchett, Betty Jensen
Pritchett, Harold Duane
Probert, Broxholme Kelsey
Probst, Gloria Joy
Proctor, Charles Rudicel
Proctor, Richard James
Proctor, Robert Swope
Proe, John David
Profitt, Glenn Arliss
Pronin, Burt
Propes, Alice Ida
Propheter, Sheila Ann
Propst, Robert
Propst, Thomas Keith
Prosise, Robert Edward
Prout, Carl Wesley
Provas, George Anthony
Prowell, Roy Walters
Prowell, Roy Walters, Jr.
Prues, Louis Joseph
Prugh, George Shipley
Pruitt, James Briggs
Pryde, Philip Rust
Pryor, Jeffrey Williams
Prystowsky, Stephen David
Przygoda, Jacek
Puckett, Charles Ellsworth
Pugh, John Robert
Pugh, Richard Gamble
Puglisi, Richard Ciro
Puishes, Alfons
Pulec, Jack Lee
Pullano, Phillip James
Pulley, Douglas Boyd
Pulley, Richard Joseph
Pulley, Robert Wood
Pulliam, Nina Mason
Pulliam, Paul Edison
Pummill, Donald Eugene
Pundsack, Fred Leigh
Purcell, Everett Wayne
Purcell, Frank Lyal
Purcell, Joseph Anthony
Purcell, Robert Baker
Purchas, Billie Bliss (Mrs. William John Purchas, Jr.)
Purchas, William John, Jr.
Puri, Naresh
Purkey, Denny J.
Purkiss, William Frederick
Pursinger, Marvin Gavin
Purviance, Carlton William
Purvis, Archibald Cruickshank, Jr.
Purvis, Lois Allene (Mrs. James Pittman Purvis)
Pusateri, C. Joseph
Pusl, Joseph Anton, Jr.
Putnam, Charles Wellington
Putnam, Glenn Dale
Putney, Richard Spencer
Puzon, Macario Dulay, II
Pyatt, Grant Edward
Pyeatt, Charles Willis
Qazi, Abdul Raziq
Quackenbush, James David
Qualen, John Mandt
Quaney, Robert Arthur
Quarterman, Philip John
Quayle, Sherman Phillip
Que, John Ngaysin
Quedens, Arthur Ray
Querfeld, Charles William
Quiggle, Robert Ray
Quigley, Henry
Quihuis, Louis Henry
Quillen, Paul Delmar
Quillen, Roger Wayne
Quilligan, Edward James
Quimby, Thomas Wallace
Quinlan, Claire A.
Quinlan, John Remi
Quinn, Antony William
Quinn, Barry George
Quinn, Brian Grant
Quinn, Jack Raymond
Quinn, James Wesley
Quinn, Joanne Santore
Quinn, John R.
Quinn, Joseph Martin
Quinn, Russell Samuel
Quinn, Saul
Quinn, William Hewes
Quinnelly, James Leslie
Quinones, Julio Jacinto
Quinones, Ricardo Anthony
Quint, Arlene J.
Quintana, Joseph James
Quintana, Leo J(ack)
Quinton, Paul Marquis
Quisenberry, Walter Brown
Quist, William Edward
Raaf, John Elbert
Raaum, Gustav Ferdinand
Rabe, Robert James
Rabinovitch, Martin S.
Rabinowitz, Jay A.
Raborg, Frederick Ashton, Jr.
Racina, Thom (Raucina, Thomas Frank)
Rackauskas, Saul
Rackleff, John Lyman
Rackley, Ira Stanley
Rad, Farrokh Niroomand (Franz)
Rada, Alexander
Radcliffe, Evelyn J. W.
Radewan, Milton George
Radford, Roberta Terry
Radlo, Edward John
Radney, Burl Tyler
Radovich, Donald
Radtke, Kurt
Rae, Matthew Sanderson, Jr.
Rael, Henry Sylvester
Raffi, David Joseph
Raffin, Bennett Lyon
Raffin, Thomas Alfred
Rafter, Richard Terence
Raggio, William John
Ragsdale, Michael Charles
Rahimtoola, Shahbudin Hooseinally
Rahmig, William Conrad
Raht, John Milton
Raia, Anthony Paul
Raine, Maureen Cheryl
Raines, Fleeta Loraine Kinsell (Mrs. W. Carl Raines)
Raines, Franklin Delano
Raines, James Richard
Rainey, Michael Keith
Rainey, Nina Gladys Dullen
Rainwater, Janette
Raitano, Harry Edward
Rajan, Albert Vincent
Rajander, Robert Anton
Rajdev, Dilip
Raju, Solomon Nalli
Ralenkotter, Rossi Thomas
Ralph, Sara Jeanne (Sally)
Ralston, Edward Lindsay, Jr.
Ralston, Gilbert Alexander
Ram, V. A.
Ramadan, Paul Rafiq
Rambissoon, Samlal
Ramer, Lawrence Jerome
Ramey, Charles Edward
Ramey, Cheri Delores
Ramo, Simon
Ramos, Albert A.
Ramos, Eli John
Ramos, Jack Markus
Ramsay, Eric Guy
Ramsay, Robert Theodore
Ramsel, William Frederick, III
Ramsey, Claude
Ramstad, Marshall Theodore
Rand, Helen Pierce (Mrs. Robert W. Rand)
Rand, Richard Malcolm
Rand, Robert Wheeler
Randall, Alma Kent
Randall, David Lovell
Randall, Duane Eugene
Randall, Gary Charles
Randall, I(saac) Eric
Randall, Warren Hart
Randall, William B.
Randhawa, Bikkar Singh
Randles, Anthony Victor, Jr. (Slim)
Ranes, Chris Stuckgold
Raney, Walter Rex
Ranf, Fredrick Louis
Range, Joseph Anthony, Jr.
Ranghiasci, Eugene John
Rania, Mildred Irwin Dick (Mrs. Joseph John Rania)
Rankin, Priscilla Partridge
Rankin, Troy Gordon
Ranney, Bobbette Kraft
Ransdell, Daniel
Ransom, Grayce Annable
Rao, Charu Mati
Raper, John F., Jr.
Rapp, Gene Edward
Rappaport, Herbert Irwin
Rapson, William Reed
Rasamimanana, Max Yvon
Rask, Walter Svensen
Raskin, Edward S.
Rasmuson, Elmer Edwin
Rasmussen, Anton Jesse
Rasmussen, Edward Frederick
Rasmussen, Gary Kenneth
Rasmussen, John M.
Rasmussen, Jorgen Gunnar
Rasmussen, Louis James, Jr.
Rasmussen, Lowell W.
Rasmussen, Malcolm William
Rasmussen, Stuart Ricard
Rassier, Donald Bernard
Ratcliff, Ralph Anderson
Rathborne, Joseph Cornelius
Rathbun, James Berry
Rathbun, John Wilbert
Rather, Phillip Eugene
Ratigan, Diane Louise Moore
Ratigan, Thomas Michael
Ratliff, John Durwood
Rauch, Russell Wayne, Jr.
Raughton, Jimmie Leonard
Rausch, James Steven
Rautenstraus, Roland Curt
Raven, Bertram Herbert
Ravin, John Murray
Rawland, Allan Gordon
Rawlings, Robert Hoag
Rawls, James Jabus
Rawson, Milton Lefgren
Rawson, Raymond D.
Ray, Dixy Lee
Ray, Don Brandon
Ray, Harold Byrd
Ray, Sister Mary Dominic
Ray, Robert Wesley
Ray, Ronald Lloyd
Ray, Vincent Louis
Raymer, Sue Grayson
Raymond, Jack Darrel
Raymond, Mark Bradford
Raymond, Stephen Aubrey
Razran, Gilbert Bruce
Razvi, Parial Shah
Razzar, Fred R.
Rea, James Buchanan
Rea, Malcolm Allen
Reade, Catherine Ann
Reader, Evan Alan
Reagin, Ynez Morey (Mrs. Charles Edward Reagin)
Real, Manuel Lawrence
Ream, Norman J.
Reardon, Jo Ann
Reardon, William Albert
Rearwin, Kenneth R.
Rebeck, Nita Marle Allman (Mrs. Joseph Rebeck)
Rebenstorf, John Christian, III

Reber, Mary Kenetta
Recchia, Peter Louis
Recht, Orville Faleder
Recinos, Joel
Rector, Leo Wesley
Redd, John Packard
Redd, Richard Randol
Redden, James Anthony
Reddi, Sreerangapalle Srinivasulu
Reddington, Fred J(ames)
Redelsheimer, Arthur Charles
Redenbaugh, Larry Lee
Redepenning, Ruth Marie
Redfearn, Maxwell Scott
Redfield, Bruce Burdette
Redfield, Elaine M. Graf-Mittelman (Mrs. William D. Redfield)
Redhead, Melvin William
Redican, Kerry John
Reding, Peter John
Redman, Frank Munro
Redman, Howard Allen
Redmon, Edward John
Redmond, Eugene Benjamin
Reeb, D. Joe
Reece, Charles Samuel
Reed, Carlyle
Reed, Claire Harrison
Reed, D. Roger
Reed, Dallas John
Reed, David Andrew
Reed, Donald Ramon
Reed, Elbert Orval
Reed, Frank Fremont, II
Reed, Frank Metcalf
Reed, George Ford, Jr.
Reed, Irving Stoy
Reed, J(ay) O(lin)
Reed, Jack M(onrad)
Reed, Richard Eugene
Reed, Richard Webster
Reed, Roy Marvin
Reed, Walter Thomas
Reeder, James Clifford
Reekie, Howard James
Rees, Marian Janet
Rees, Richard Dee
Reese, Chang Su
Reese, Howard LaViers
Reese, Kay Thomas
Reese, L. Joe
Reese, Mary Louise
Reese, Norman Randolph
Reese, Richard Alban
Reese, Ronald Pete
Reese, Sherry Olson
Reeser, Robert Duane
Reesing, Barbara Cecilia
Reeve, Gerome Robert
Reeve, Victor Claude
Reeves, Albert L(ee)
Reeves, Billy D.
Reeves, David Edmund
Reeves, Jerry Dale
Reeves, Phillip Glenn
Reeves, Thomas George, Jr.
Refai, Gulammohammed Zainulabedin
Regan, Glen Barrie
Reghaby, Heydar Haleh
Rehberg, Jack Dennis
Rehbock, Ernest Zacharlas
Rehm, Carol Henry, Jr.
Reiber, Robert Joseph
Reichek, Jesse
Reichert, Robert George Chase
Reichlin, Louise Hope
Reid, Audrey Yvonne
Reid, Bill
Reid, Dallas Wendell
Reid, Faye Pierce
Reid, Floyd Stuart
Reid, J(ohn) Michael
Reid, James Alexander
Reid, James Dennis
Reid, Timothy James
Reidenbach, Albert James
Reihel, Dorothy L.
Reile, Patricia Joan
Reilly, Eileen L.
Reilly, Joseph Garrett
Reilly, Robert Arthur
Reiner, Gerald L.
Reinhardt, Adina Marie
Reinhardt, Carl Ernst
Reinhardt, Ronald Butler
Reinhold, Arch Freeman
Reinhold, Deborah Ann
Reining, Beth LaVerne (Betty)
Reinwald, Arthur Burton
Reis, Edward Thomas, Jr.
Reiter, Elmar Rudolf
Reitman, Sanford Wilbur
Reitsema, Harold James
Reitz, Edna
Reitze, William Bernard
Rekers, George Alan
Relfe, John Dowling
Remley, Marlin Eugene
Remmer, James Edward
Remy, Rene
Renault, Jacques Roland
Rende, Giandomenico
Renders, Joseph Alfred, Jr.
Renfree, A(rthur) Paul
Renkert, Craig George
Rennhack, Elliott Henry
Reno, Joseph Harry
Rensch, Joseph Romaine
Rense, William Alphonsus
Rensen, Jon Robert
Renshaw, Harland Walter
Renton, Malcolm Joseph
Renton, Virginia Hill (Mrs. Malcolm J. Renton)
Rentschler, Carl Thomas
Reres, Mary Epiphany
Resch, Gerald William
Resnik, Alan Jay
Restivo, Frank Anthony
Rettig, Thomas Noel
Retynski, John Richard
Retzer, Howard Earl
Reuss, Henry
Revell, John Harold
Re Velle, Jack Boyer
Revelle, Keith
Revutsky, Valerian
Rewak, William John
Rewerts, Milan Alvin
Rex, James Foster
Rex, John Charles
Rexner, Romulus
Rexwinkle, Randy Lee
Reyes, Raymond Victor, Jr.
Reynders, Michel Albert Joseph P.
Reynolds, Arthur Byron
Reynolds, Darnall Willson
Reynolds, Frank Robert
Reynolds, Gerald Gordon
Reynolds, Gerald Mervale
Reynolds, Helen
Reynolds, Keith Yale
Reynolds, Martha Vork
Reynolds, R. Wallace
Reynolds, Richard Henry
Reynolds, Robert Gary
Reynolds, Robert Harrison
Reynolds, Roland Gilbert
Reynolds, Thomas George
Reynolds, Thomas Leroy
Reynolds, William Bryan
Rezba, Robert John
Rhay, Bobby J.
Rhay, Timothy Wayne
Rhea, William Edward, III
Rhee, Jay Jea-Young
Rhee, Jurral Chuda Peace
Rheinstrom, Diana
Rhew, Ki-Won
Rhoades, Dennis LeRoy
Rhoades, Verlin Ray
Rhoads, George Grant
Rhodes, Anne Lou
Rhodes, Deborah Lynn
Rhodes, Ernest Victor
Rhodes, Gilbert Louis
Rhodes, Glenda Lorraine
Rhodes, Guy Wallace
Rhodes, Jack E.
Rhodes, John Jacob
Rhodes, Laurie Louise
Rhodes, Nelson Kenneth
Rhodes, Paul Robert
Rhodes, Robert Dunn, III
Rhodig, Russel Delmer
Rhyne, Charles Sylvanus
Riach, Douglas Alexander
Riazance, Nicholas
Riback, David Alan
Rice, Alan Herbert
Rice, Barbara Pollak
Rice, Denis Timlin
Rice, Edward Stephen, Jr.
Rice, Edward William
Rice, Jean Ann Mattern
Rice, Jerry Darrel
Rice, Jonathan C.
Rice, Julian Casavant
Rice, Mabel McCullough (Mrs. Clinton D. Rice)
Rice, Monty Grey
Rice, Randall Gardner
Rice, Roger Eugene
Rice, Ross Richard
Rice, Thomas Clarence
Rice, Willard Ray
Rice, William David
Rice, William Watson
Rich, Frances L.
Rich, Terry H.
Richard, George Looney
Richard, Robert Carter
Richards, Alfonso
Richards, Delaine Thomas
Richards, Donald Phillip
Richards, Douglas Alan
Richards, Gene Murdell
Richards, Homer Crocket
Richards, Marilyn Derry
Richards, Murray
Richards, Paul Augustine
Richards, Robert Benjamin
Richards, Robert Fleming
Richards, Tally
Richards, Vincent Philip
Richards, Walter Alden
Richards, Walter Hocking
Richardson, A(rthur) Leslie
Richardson, Bobby Glenn
Richardson, Dana Roland
Richardson, Gerald Clemen
Richardson, Glenn Wallace
Richardson, H(arold) Leonard
Richardson, Harold Beland
Richardson, Henry Vokes-Mackey
Richardson, Hubert Leon, Jr.
Richardson, Ivan LeRoy
Richardson, Jeffery Howard
Richardson, John Leland
Richardson, Joseph Thomas
Richardson, Robert Lloyd
Richardson, Thomas George
Richardson, William Shaw
Riches, Victor Wallis
Richey, Lester Alan
Richie, Michael Sherwood
Richland, Irwin Julian
Richman, Russell Bennett
Richmond, John
Richmond, Peter Apteker
Richmond, Ronald LeRoy
Richter, Burton
Richter, Robert John
Rickel, Wesley Kellogg
Ricker, Edward Frank
Rickers, Alvin Ellsworth
Ricketts, Herman Hervin
Ridder, Edward P.
Ridder, Joyce Marion
Ridder, Ruthe
Rideout, Mack Hallman
Rider, Benjamin Franklin, Jr.
Ridges, Joseph Douglas
Ridgway, David Wenzel
Ridgway, Robert Lyle
Ridout, Maxine Miller
Ridout, Robert Frederic
Riedel, Bernard Edward
Riedel, Walter Erwin
Riedesel, Warren Howard
Rieffanaugh, William Dale
Riegel, Byron William
Riegelmann, Kermit Wesley
Rieger, Joseph
Riek, Forest O., Jr.
Riell, Leslie Greg
Riemer, Lawrence Steven
Riethmeier, Walter
Riffel, Jon Branner
Riffle, Stanley Russell, Jr.
Rifkin, Sandra Anderson
Rifkind, Richard David
Riganati, John Philip
Rigas, Anthony Leon
Rigby, Ray Wendell
Riggall, Evison Ronald
Riggs, David Edward
Riggs, Donnie Elmer
Riggs, Frank Lewis
Riggs, John Arthur
Riggs, John Kenneth
Righellis, Orestes
Rigney, Robert Buford
Rigsby, Jeanne Brink
Rigsby, John Newton
Riles, Wilson Camanza
Riley, Edward Craig
Riley, Franklin Studebaker, Jr.
Riley, James Reed
Riley, R. Jeanna
Rimoin, David Lawrence
Rinderknecht, Heinrich
Ring, Bonnie
Ring, Peter Smith
Ringer, Thomas Latta
Ringer, William Alpheus
Ringler, Robin Lynn
Ringoen, Howard Charles
Rinkus, Jerome Joseph
Rinset, John Peter
Rintoul, Beecher
Riordan, William Anthony
Rios, Bret Shay
Riotte, Jules Charles Emile
Riparbelli, Carlo
Ripley, Kathryn Payson
Ripley, Stuart McKinnon
Ripley, Walter Wayne
Ripley, Wayne Allen
Rippel, Florence Lena
Rippel, Mabel Amelia
Ririe, David
Ririe, Shirley
Risbrough, Edward Partridge
Risch, James E.
Risemberg, Leon A(braham)
Ristau, Toni Kae
Ristow, Linda Sue
Ritch, OCee
Ritch, Wynnewood Austin
Ritchey, Samuel Donley, Jr.
Ritchie, John Bennett
Ritchison, Rickie Dale
Ritt, Leonard Gilbert
Rittel, Juergen Michael
Ritter, Allan Gerald
Ritter, Dale William
Ritter, Lucy Elizabeth
Ritterbush, (Morris) Lee
Rittmeister, Ruth
Rivera, Rafael
Rivera, Victor Manuel
Rivers, Edward James
Riviera, Daniel John
Riznik, Joseph Quentin
Roach, Stephen Frank
Roadarmel, Stanley Bruce
Roades, Harland Evan
Roback, Robert Allen
Robb, Byron Lee
Robb, Robert Cumming
Robbins, Alan
Robbins, Hunter Savidge, Jr.
Robbins, Lawrence Joel
Robbins, Richard Marshall
Robelotto, Salvatore Michael
Roberson, Beverly Bud
Roberts, Alan Silverman
Roberts, Archibald Edward
Roberts, Arthur O(wen)
Roberts, Brian Kent
Roberts, Charles Fredrick
Roberts, Dennis William
Roberts, Dwight Loren
Roberts, George Christopher
Roberts, George Owen
Roberts, George R.
Roberts, Howard A.
Roberts, Jack Earle
Roberts, James Edward, Jr.
Roberts, James McGregor
Roberts, John Barrett
Roberts, John Barry
Roberts, John Clarke
Roberts, Marjorie Klawitter
Roberts, Martin
Roberts, Nathan Jay
Roberts, Paul Robert
Roberts, Phillip Anthony
Roberts, Richard G.
Roberts, Stephen Frederick
Roberts, Steven Gerard
Roberts, W(ilbur) Eugene
Roberts, Wayne Arthur
Roberts, Wesley Kent
Roberts, William John, Jr.
Roberts-Gray, Cynthia Ruth
Robertson, Carroll Loy
Robertson, Charles Haynes
Robertson, Dennis Liston
Robertson, Donald James
Robertson, Douglas Grey
Robertson, Harold Richard
Robertson, Heber Wells
Robertson, James Howard
Robertson, Juan Patrick
Robertson, Lowell Edward
Robertson, Malcolm Brooks
Robertson, Nora Winifred
Robertson, Roger E.
Robertson, Samuel Harry, III
Robinder, Ronald Charles
Robinett, Nancy Gay
Robinette, Adella Eleanor Throop Holmaas (Mrs. Jay H. Robinette)
Robinette, Gail Rae
Robinette, Willard Leslie
Robins, Miriam Clair
Robinson, Agnes Claflin
Robinson, Ann Lee
Robinson, Bernard Leo
Robinson, Bruce Ellsworth
Robinson, (Margery) Carol
Robinson, Dennis Jay
Robinson, (Blanche) Dolores
Robinson, Fred, Jr.
Robinson, James Charles
Robinson, James McNulty Ainslie
Robinson, Jesse Lee
Robinson, John Brooks
Robinson, John Minor
Robinson, Lawrence Brandon
Robinson, Lewis Howe
Robinson, Lloyd Keith
Robinson, Louis Henry
Robinson, Margery LeVern
Robinson, Michael Lawrence
Robinson, Patricia Isabell
Robinson, Paul William
Robinson, Ray Sherman
Robinson, Richard Harden
Robinson, Robert Blacque
Robinson, Robert Porter (Skip)
Robinson, Sereta Ann
Robinson, Stephen Lee
Robinson, Warren Elmo
Robinson, William Arwin
Robinson, Willie Clifford
Robison, John Charles
Robison, John Lewis
Robison, Kent Richard
Robison, Thomas John
Robles, Edward Gabriel, Jr.
Robley, Grace Aletha
Roborecki, Andrew J.
Robson, John Theodore
Robson, Kent Roger
Robuck, Richard Dean
Rochford, Thomas Edward, Jr.
Rock, Kenneth Heber
Rock, Michael John
Rockie, William Allan
Rockstrom, Albert Raymond
Rocksvold, Alvin Nicholas
Rockwell, Bruce McKee
Rockwell, Don Arthur
Rockwell, John Adams
Rodal, Arney Albin
Rodda, Sprague
Rodden, Robert Morris
Rodenrys, John Joseph
Rodey, Patrick Michael
Rodgers, Helen Elizabeth
Rodgers, James Thomas
Rodgers, Nancy Lucille
Rodich, Grover William
Rodine, Trudy (Gertrude) Maria
Rodkiewicz, Czeslaw Mateusz
Rodney, Deborah Ann
Rodney, Lynn Smith
Rodriguez, Gerald Peter
Rodriquez, Bruce Stuart
Roe, Benson Bertheau
Roe, Edward Alan
Roe, Edward Ray
Roe, Kiki Vlachouli
Roeder, Betty Brown
Roemer, Richard Irving
Roepke, Carl Frank, Jr.
Roesch, Warren Dale
Roeschlaub, Ronald Curtis
Roeser, Jack L.
Roffman, Marian Hentzell
Rofman, Richard Alan
Rogers, Benjamin Talbot
Rogers, Bennett Muir
Rogers, Charles Theodore Graham (Ted Rogers)
Rogers, Dwane Leslie
Rogers, Eugene Leroy
Rogers, Frederick Alfred
Rogers, Irma Duncan
Rogers, Ivard Ritchie
Rogers, John Edward
Rogers, Lu
Rogers, Nathan
Rogers, Ollie Ulvestad
Rogers, Richard Warren
Rogers, Rolf Ernst
Rogers, Sandra Kay
Rogers, Thomas Hardin
Rogge, Celeste Firnstahl (Mrs. Edgar A. Rogge)
Rohde, James Vincent
Rohlfing, Frederick William
Rohner, William Leonardo
Rohrberg, Roderick George
Rohrer, Beverly Jean
Rohrer, William Glen
Rohrssen, Donald John
Rohwer, William Dan, Jr.
Rojas, Joseph Augustin
Roland, Harold Eugene, Jr.
Roland, Ronald Jay
Rolander, Oscar Rudolph
Roley, Susan Lynn
Rolf, Bruce Bailey
Rolfes, Harold Louis, Jr.
Rolfs, Richard William
Roller, Lothar Karl
Roller, Robert Douglas, III
Rollin, Walter Jerome
Rollins, David Thomas
Rolston, Thomas Edmund
Roman, Douglas Ernest
Roman, Oliver John
Roman, Ronald Joseph
Romanko-Keller, Renée
Romans, Van Anthony
Rombach, George Frederick
Romberg, Paul F(rederick)
Rombout, Luke
Rominger, Richard Sidney
Rominger, Ty Arnold
Romney, Laurence Kimball, Jr.
Romney, Marion George
Rondell, Thomas
Roness, Sharon Grace
Roney, Alice Lorraine Mann
Roney, Don James
Ronningen, Helmer Anderson
Ronsman, Wayne John
Rood, Joseph Lloyd
Rood, Rodney Wilbur
Rood, William George
Roof, Thomas Lister, Jr.
Root, James Albert
Ropell, Frederick Peter
Roper, Gilbert Ira
Roper, James Leroy
Roper, John Nathaniel
Roper, Walter William
Roquemore, Billy Roger
Rosa, Manuel Garcia, Jr.
Rosado, Othoniel
Rosas, Gilbert Manuel
Rosberg, Carl Gustaf
Rosch, Raymond Jacob
Rosch, Stanley
Rosden, Ronald Edward
Rose, Allan Bruce
Rose, Edwin Lawrence
Rose, Fred Louis
Rose, Glen M.
Rose, Marvin Earl
Rose, Milton
Rose, Robert Alexander
Rose, Robert R., Jr.
Rose, Sanford Samuel
Rose, Theodore Michael
Roseman, Lawrence Joseph
Rosen, Louis
Rosen, Merton Normand
Rosen, Moishe Martin
Rosen, Robert Arthur
Rosen, Ronald Stanley
Rosenauer, Adolf
Rosenberg, Allen Leon
Rosenberg, Dan Yale
Rosenberg, Ira Hall
Rosenberg, John David
Rosenberg, John Wayland
Rosenberg, Mark Herschel
Rosenberg, Richard Morris
Rosenblum, A. Leon
Rosenblum, Bernard
Rosenblum, Estelle Helene Masters
Rosenblum, Richard Mark
Rosendin, Raymond Joseph
Rosenfeld, Lloyd Bryand
Rosenlund, Edward Peter
Rosenman, Daniel
Rosenquist, Bradford Mark
Rosenquist, Charles Dale
Rosenstein, Allen Bertram
Rosenstein, Franklin Lee
Rosenstein, Melvyn
Rosenthal, Donald Mardon
Rosenthal, Ernest Ludwig
Rosenthal, Howard Kane
Rosenthal, Kenneth W.
Rosenthal, Nina Ribak
Rosenthal, Sandy
Roser, Donald Max
Rosevear, Jack Gary
Rosfeld, Howard Bernard
Roshong, Dee Ann Daniels
Rosky, Burton Seymour
Rosler, Martha Rose
Ross, Bernard
Ross, Betty Grace
Ross, Charlotte Pack
Ross, David Andrews
Ross, Deborah Lynn
Ross, Delmer Gerrard
Ross, J. Paul
Ross, Kenneth Malcolm, Jr.
Ross, Richard Lee
Ross, Ronald Rickard
Ross, Ronald Walter
Ross, Terence William
Ross, Thomas Lloyd, Jr.
Ross, Thurston Howard
Ross, Tom M.
Rossetti, Carl Joseph
Rossetti, Carl U(lric) J(oseph)
Rossi, Evelyn Wheeler
Rossman, Martin Jay
Rosso, Henry August
Rosten, Martin Jay
Rostkowski, Charles Anthony
Roston, Martin Frank
Rosztoczy, Ferenc Erno
Roth, Herrick Smith
Roth, Irvin Melbourne
Roth, Lucy Tarbell
Roth, Sanford Harold
Rothauge, Charles Harry
Rothaus, F. David
Rothblatt, Donald Noah
Rothe, Dietmar Erich
Rothenberg, Harvey David
Rothenberger, Daniel James
Rothlisberg, Allen Peter
Rothman, Larry
Rothman, Nathan Frank
Rothman, Robert Lawrence
Rothman, Stewart Neil
Rothman, Will Fred
Rothrock, Roger Lee
Rothstein, Martin Irwin
Rotolo, Elio Richard
Rottas, Ray
Rottluff, Karl Moritz
Rotwein, Jerrold Jack
Roukes, Nicholas Michael
Roulac, Stephen Earl
Roullard, George Paul
Rounds, Archer Cornwall
Rounds, Donald Junior
Rourke, Robert Alfred
Rouse, Larry O'neal
Rouse, Lester Lee
Roush, Anne Frances
Rousselot, John Harbin
Roux, Walter Leland
Roveda, John Gregory
Rovira, Luis Dario
Rowe, Ernest Ras
Rowe, Frank Alan, Sr.
Rowe, James
Rowitch, Jerome
Rowland, Ivan W.
Rowland, James Nakapuahi, Jr.
Rowland, Joseph Estes
Rowley, Alan Reid
Rowley, William Nelson
Roy, Chunilal
Roy, Harold Edward
Roy, Raymond
Roybal, Edward R.
Royce, Frederick Henry
Royce, Richard Benjamin
Royer, Charles Theodore
Royer, William
Rozanski, Mordechai
Rozzi, James Antonio
Rubel, George Kenneth Evelyn
Ruben, Irwin
Rubin, Herbert Bernard
Rubin, Milton Raymond
Rubin, Nathan
Rubin, Robert Terry
Rubin-Rabson, Grace (Mrs. S. Milton Rabson)
Rubright, Kent Arthur
Ruby, Charles Leroy
Ruby, Jon Franklin
Rucker, Helen Bornstein (Mrs. B. Wallace Rucker)
Rucker, Rufus Capers
Rucker, Thomas Douglas
Rucker, Winfred Ray
Rudd, Eldon D.
Rudd, Gerald Patrick
Rudd, Merrill W.
Rudd, Robert Dean
Ruddy, Glen Dee
Rudell, William Barnum
Rudestam, Rolf Carl
Rudinsky, Julius Alexander
Rudnikoff, Isadore
Rudolf, Ottomar Immanuel
Ruechelle, Randall Cummings
Ruelke, Franklin Rueben
Ruemmele, Werner Albert
Ruetten, Richard Theodore
Ruff, Charles William, II
Ruff, Clarence Gerald
Ruggieri, David Thomas
Ruhberg, Kay Tompkins
Ruhe, Richard James
Ruiz, Sarah Marlene
Ruleman, David Arnold
Ruley, Glenn Alan
Rulon, John Thomas
Rulon, Philip Reed
Rumberger, Carol Paige
Rummerfield, Philip Sheridan
Rumney, Franklin Wallace
Rump, John Steinbach
Runglin, Arnold Walter
Runnels, Harold Lowell
Runner, Sandra Jo
Runyan, S. H. (Hal)
Ruocco, Drucilla Ann
Ruoff, Andrew Christian
Rupnick, Walter John
Rupp, Gerald Richard
Ruppenthal, Bruce McKeen
Rusca, Rodney Louis
Rusdal, Liv
Rusnak, James Eugene
Russell, Barry
Russell, Charles Roberts
Russell, Donald Coleman
Russell, Donald Larnard
Russell, Findlay Ewing

Russell, Georgann
Russell, Jack
Russell, Jeanne Vine
Russell, Jeffrey Burton
Russell, John Harold
Russell, Keith Palmer
Russell, Kenneth Stevenson
Russell, Lillian Violet
Russell, Paul Latimer
Russell, Wallace Arven
Russitano, Margaret Miers
Russo, Joseph Frank
Russom, Jerry Raymond
Rust, Charles Henry
Rustvold, Clarence Alfred, Jr.
Rusunen, Robert Lee
Rutala, Paul Joseph
Rutherford, Madalynne Ellen
Rutherford, Thomas Truxton,
II
Rutland, Andrew
Ruttan, William Delbert
Rutter, Marshall Anthony
Ruttner, Leslie Elmer
Ruud, Doris Uselman
Ryan, Aylmer Arthur
Ryan, James Edwin
Ryan, Jane Ann
Ryan, Jerry Joseph
Ryan, Joseph Edward
Ryan, Michael Edward Joseph
Ryan, Nora Margaret
Ryan, Richard G. L.
Ryan, Robert Dennis
Ryan, Stephen Joseph, Jr.
Ryan, Victor Albert
Ryan, William Desmond
Ryan, William Joseph
Ryder, Loren Lincoln
Ryder, Robert Arnold
Ryland, Stephen Lane
Rynearson, Gary Malin
Saavedra, Shawn David
Sabatino, Anthony Raymond
Sabbadini, Alex
Sabbatini, Jim Gerard
Sabbot, Irene Mersol
Sabharwal, Ranjit Singh
Sabin, Jack Charles
Sabot, Theodore Jay
Sacks, Julian
Saddler, Gary Lynn
Sadler, Dick Sherman
Sadler, Glenn Edward
Saenz, Lionila Lopez
Safford, M. DeWitt
Safier, Dennis Toby
Safran, Neal Ronald
Safranko, John William
Sagawa, Yoneo
Sage, Vincent Francis
Sage, Webster LeGene, Jr.
Saggu, Bhupinder Singh
Sagum, Roland Diaz
Sahara, Michie (Michie Sakai)
Sahlin, Carl William
Sahlstrom, Elmer Bernard
Saiki, Patricia Fukuda
Saint Claire, Sue Marie
St. Cyr, Frederic P.
St. Denis, Frank Harold
St Rickler, George Edward
Sak, Jay Barry
Saka, Stanley Masato
Sakamaki, Samuel Taiji
Sakamoto, Masato
Sakovich, Willem Dehé
Saks, Robert Edwin
Saladino, Ronald Bernard
Salant, Rubin
Salcido, Nicholas Gutierrez
Sale, Lillian
Sales, Amos Paul
Saling, Milo Premo
Salisbury, Frank Boyer
Salisian, Neal Samuel
Salk, Jonas Edward
Salkin, Geraldine (Jeri)
Faubion
Salkow, Steven Peter
Salley, Ernest John
Salmi, George Leonard, Jr.
Salmon, Barbara Foronda
Salmon, Donald Leroy
Salmon, Merlyn Leigh
Salmon, Thomas Joseph
Salomaki, David Charles
Salser, Carl Walter, Jr.
Salsman, Annieta Helen
Salter, Robert E.
Saltoun, Synthia Renee
Saluteen, Peter Alexander
Salvador, Conrado Carreon
Salvestrini, John Peter
Salvin, Martin J.
Salvo, Joseph Anthony
Salzer, Adrian A.
Salzman, Barnett Seymour
Salzman, Paul
Salzman, William Ronald
Samaras, Mary Stenning
Samek, Paul Herman
Samhammer, Clair Allison
Samp, Jerry K.
Sample, Joseph Scanlon
Sampson, Carol Ann
Sampson, Dean Edward
Sams, Mary Ann Pacella
Samson, Merle Roger
Samuchin, Michael George
Samuels, Jack D(onald)
Samuels, Thomas Moran
Samuelson, Emrys Floyd
Sanborn, Alan Tilden
Sanborn, Dorothy Chappell
Sanborn, Frederick Arthur
Sanborn, Robert Henry
Sanchez, Frank Leandro
Sanchez, James Joseph
Sanchez, James Jullan
Sanchez, Robert Fortune
Sanchez, Victor Balderrama
Sande, John Peter
Sandenaw, Thomas Arthur
Sander, Dieter
Sander, Richard Allen
Sanders, Daniel Selvarajah
Sanders, Edward Eugene
Sanders, James Thomas
Sanders, Jerold Robert
Sanders, John Allen
Sanders, John R.
Sanders, Marshall Curtis
Sanders, Rita Diane
Sanders, Russell Wyman
Sanders, Terry L(ee)
Sanderson, Robert Elwin
Sanderson, Robert Lorin, Jr.
Sanderson, Roger Seward
Sandoval, Alfonso F.
Sandoval, Alphonso J. (Sandy)
Sandoval, Donald (Ernest)
Sandoz, Dennis Paul
Sands, Lester Bruton
Sandstrom, Alice Wilhelmina
Sandweiss, Howard Wayne
Sanford, Lawrence Edward
Sanford, R. Nevitt
Sangster, Paul Edward
San Miguel, Anthony
Sant, George Roscoe
Santee, Harold Trevor
Santiago, Wanda
Santini, James David
Santley, Thomas Sawyer
Santo, Henry E.
Santor, James Thomas
Santos, James Merrill
Santos, Marciano
Santos, Raymond, Jr.
Sapiro, Denis
Saraf, Chhote Lal
Sarafian, Armen
Sarafian, Sylvia Annette
Sare, Ransom Lester
Sargent, George Andrew, III
Sargent, Karl David
Sargent, Keith Newton
Sargent, Raoul Bridwell
Sargent, Thornton William, III
Sarian, Jirair Nerses
Sarjeant, E. Carl
Sarkowsky, Herman
Sarlo, George Stephen
Sarmento, Thomas Joseph
Sarsfield, George P.
Sartori, John Anthony
Sasaki, Kiyoshi
Sasaki, Y(asunaga) Tito
Sass, Allan
Sass, Donald Leon
Sassaman, Robert William
Sasse, Mary Louise
Sassone, Marco Massimo
Sassover, Nathan
Sather, Donald Sherman
Satir, Kemal
Sato, Norie
Sato, Yosh
Satovick, Robert Mark
Satre, Wendell Julian
Sattler, James Michael
Sauer, Gerald Leonard
Sauer, James Edward, Jr.
Sauget, Clyde Raymond
Saunders, Dorothy Courtney
Saunders, Glenn Gilbert
Saunders, Jack Orva Leslie
Saunders, Laurel Lucille
Savage, Edward Warren, Jr.
Savage, Gretchen Susan (Mrs.
Terry R. Savage)
Savage, Karen Ann Seidman
Savage, Terry Richard
Savedra, Manuel Angel
Saveker, David Richard
Saville, Michael Lee
Savoca, Antonio Litterio
Savona, Michael Richard
Sawada, Ikune
Sawaya, Michael Paul, Jr.
Sawiris, Milad Youssef
Sawle, David Richard
Sawyer, Ernest Walker, Jr.
Sawyer, Julieann Kathryn
Saxena, Arjun Nath
Saxon, David S(tephen)
Saxon, James Anthony
Saxvik, Robert William
Sayano, Reizo Ray
Sayer, George
Sayler, Gordon A.
Sayre, Lansing Glenn Lytle
Sbarbaro, John Anthony
Scafe, Lincoln Robert, Jr.
Scaff, William Loftin
Scallon, Garth La Mont
Scanlan, John J.
Scanlan, Tracy Allen
Scanlin, Steven Fox
Scanlon, Michael Joseph, Jr.
Scannell, Daniel Andrew
Scannell, Edward Earl
Scannell, Mary Redempta
Scellars, Angela Louise
McCormick (Mrs. Robert
William Scellars)
Schaaf, Oscar Frederick
Schaaf, Samuel Albert
Schaar, Jacqueline Kay Couch
(Mrs. Robert L. Schaar)
Schaber, Gordon Duane
Schacher, John Fredrick
Schachet, John Larry
Schachter, Richard Dennis
Schaefer, Henry Frederick, III
Schaefer, John Paul
Schaefer, Seth Clarence
Schaefer, W(illiam) Stanley
Schaeffer, Lee C.
Schaen, Lionel Leslie
Schafer, Chester Carl
Schafer, Eldon Guy
Schafer, Ernest Wendell
Schaffer, John Darrell
Schaffer, Robert Laurence
Schaller, Donald Frederick
Schaller, Robert Charles
Schallert, James Britton
Schanbacher, William Anthony
Schander, Mary Lea
Schapiro, George Arnold
Scharer, Fletcher Hastings
Scharfe, James Albert, Jr.
(Hank)
Schauer, Nancy Ruth
Schauer, Richard
Schauf, George Edward
Schauss, Alexander George
Schauwecker, Kurt Herbert
Schawlow, Arthur Leonard
Scheer, Carl
Scheiber, Stephen Carl
Scheitzach, Joseph Carl
Schell, Elmer Morris
Schell, Farrel Loy
Schellenberg, Albert Thomas
Schenck, Kenneth Andrew
Schendel, Winfried George
Scheppers, Ruth Clement
Scherb, Ivan Victor
Scherer, Milo Winston
Scherer, Roger Clyde
Scherich, Erwin Thomas
Schermerhorn, Robert Stephen
Scherrer, Frederick Jess, Jr.
Scherzer, Anna Meed
Scherzer, Larry S.
Scheuerman, Michael Henry
Schield, Marshall Lew
Schieler, Leroy
Schiff, Alvin Theodore
Schiff, Samuel Leopold
Schillaci, Richard Francis
Schiller, Johannes August
Schiller, Robert Achille
Schilling, Donald Lee
Schilling, Frederick Augustus,
Jr.
Schilling, Gerhard Friedrich
Schilling, Harold LeRoy
Schilling, Stephen William
Schiltz, Stephen Joseph
Schimmelbusch, Johannes
Severin
Schindler, John Daniel
Schindler, John Frederick
Schinke, Steven Paul
Schipsi, Anthony Charles
Schirmer, Howard August, Jr.
Schlam, Edith Gertrud
Schlamp, Fredric Thuman
Schlechte, Floyd Raymond
Schlesinger, Myron Phillip
Schlesinger, Richard Joseph
Schletewitz, Clayton John
Schletewitz, Katherine
Schlick, Robert Lewis
Schliefer, Stafford Lerrig
Schlinger, Warren Gleason
Schlosnagle, Carol Ann
Schlottmann, David Henry
Schmalzried, Robert Frederick
Schmelz, Ryan Perry
Schmid, Anne Marie
Schmid, Peter
Schmidt, Albert Martin
Schmidt, Chauncey Everett
Schmidt, Donald Thomas
Schmidt, Eckart Walter
Schmidt, Edward Robert
Schmidt, Guenter Erich
Schmidt, Jack Raymond
Schmidt, John Robert
Schmidt, Kenneth Robert
Schmidt, R(uth) Pauline
Schmidt, Richard Arthur
Schmidt, Robert James
Schmidt, Roger
Schmidt, Wayne Walter
Schmidt, William Vick
Schmidtman, Donald J.
Schmieder, Carl
Schmitt, Ardell Edward
Schmitt, Charles Ernest
Schmitt, Harrison Hagan
Schmitter, Eric Dean
Schmitz, Eugene Gerard
Schmitz, John George
Schmoller, Ralph Hans
Schmunk, Donald Fred
Schnack, Gayle Hemingway
Jepson (Mrs. Harold Clifford
Schnack)
Schnack, George Ferdinand
Schnack, Harold Clifford
Schneeberger, Mary Louise
Love
Schneeman, Justin Gerhardt
Schneider, Calvin
Schneider, Edward John, III
Schneider, Edward Martin
Schneider, Franklin Richard
Schneider, Raymond Clinton
Schneider, Richard C.
Schneider, Stanley Harvey
Schneider, Stephen Henry
Schneider, Victor Barry
Schneider, Warren John
Schneidman, Harold M.
Schneiter, George Malan
Schnitzer, Harold Julius
Schnurpel, Helen Mamie
Persell
Schober, Dorothy Florence
Schock, Robert Norman
Schoedinger, Andrew Barr
Schoeller, Gunter Hans
Schoen, Stevan Jay
Schoen, William Robert
Schoenberger, Ronald George
Schoepflin, Gerald Stanley
Scholl, Richard Allan
Scholler, Robert Walter
Scholnick, Joseph B.
Scholtes, Norma Jean
Scholtz, Judith Fessenden
Schonberger, Clinton Francis
Schoneberg, Sheldon Clyde
Schoop, Ernest R.
Schoos, Susan May
Schow, Alvin Glen
Schow, Ronald Lewis
Schrader, Ernest Karl
Schrader, Robert Galt
Schramski, Michael Thomas
Schreiber, Andrew
Schreiber, John Martin
Schreiber, Max Rudolph
Schreiber, Michael Martin
Schreiber, Otto William
Schreiber, Robert Joseph
Schreibman, Walter
Schreier, Konrad Foeste, Jr.
Schreiner, Richard Meisner
Schreiner, Robert Nicholas, Jr.
Schremp, Robert O.
Schrimp, Roger Martin
Schrock, Virgil Edwin
Schroder, Spensley Malloch
Schroder, Vera Gibson
Schroeder, Arnold Leon
Schroeder, Edwynn Edgar
Schroeder, George Henry
Schroeder, Klaus Gerhard
Schroeder, Patricia Scott
Schroeder, Robert Edward
Schroeder, Walter Phelps
Schroegler, Phyllis Ann
Schroll, Lawrence Carl, Jr.
Schuberg, Charles Louis
Schuch, Adam Frank
Schuch, Theodoris
Schueneman, Herbert Harry
Schuering, Leo Herman, Jr.
Schuetz, Gordon William
Schuetzenduebel, Wolfram
Gerhard
Schuknecht, Lowell Albert, Jr.
Schuler, Gerald August
Schuller, Robert Harold
Schulman, Irving
Schulman, Lee
Schulman, Samuel
Schulte, Henry Gustave
Schultz, Allen Henry
Schultz, Fred Joseph
Schultz, Jackson LeRoy
Schultz, Richard Dennis
Schultz, Robert John
Schultz, Sharon Marie
Schultz, William Ellsworth
Schulz, Edmund Frederick
Schulz, Orissa Anna Harriett
Schulze, Merle Glen
Schumacher, Edward Walter
Schumacher, George
A(lphonse)
Schumacher, Thomas Caswell,
Jr.
Schumacher, William Joseph
Schuman, Harold Robert
Schumann, Vernon Kenneth
Schumm, Stanley Alfred
Schuppner, Harry Russell, Jr.
Schussele, James Henry
Schuster, Alice Louise Geyer
(Mrs. William T. Schuster)
Schuster, Jack Herman
Schuster, Susan Eileen
Schuster, Timothy Stephen
Schutz, Eugene R.
Schutz, John Adolph
Schutz, Patrick Francis
Schuyler, James Owen
Schuyler, Percy Lee
Schuyten, John
Schwab, Catherine Barrett
Schwabe, Peter Alexander, Jr.
Schwada, John
Schwadron, Abraham Abe
Schwam, Andrew Martin
Schwartz, Daniel Harvey
Schwartz, Don Leslie
Schwartz, Edward J.
Schwartz, Harry Albert
Schwartz, Herbert Ellis
Schwartz, Leon Irwin
Schwartz, Peter William
Schwartz, Richard Roy
Schwartz, Robert Allen
Schwarz, Mario Rudolph
Schwarz, Merle Roy
Schwarzbach, Donna J.
Schwarzmann, Stephen
Theodore
Schweiger, Elizabeth Lee
Schweiger, Seymour Morton
Schweitzer, Donald Laurence
Schweitzer, Frederick Vernon
Schwerin, Charles Henry
Schwinden, Ted
Schwinger, Julian
Schwoebel, Richard Lynn
Schwulst, Russell James
Schwyzer, Hanns Carl
Scibor-Marchocki, Romuald
Ireneus
Scinto, Louis Leonard
Sciranka, Paul George
Scollard, Agnes Janet
Scoltock, John Wilson
Scott, David John
Scott, Delbert Edward
Scott, Dolores H.
Scott, E. Walter
Scott, Edmund Altiman
Scott, Gary Lee
Scott, Geraldine Knight
Scott, Herbert J.N.
Scott, James Clayton
Scott, Johnie Harold
Scott, Joseph Leonard
Scott, Lawrence David
Scott, Margaret Louise
Scott, Matthew James
Scott, Mitchell Patten
Scott, Morton William
Scott, Nancy Ann
Scott, Robert Elbert
Scott, Robert Eugene
Scott, Russell E(verett)
Scott, Sheila Marie
Scott, Tony (Tone)
Scott, Warren Edward
Scovill, Lyle A.
Scowley, Barton Andrew
Screen, Joseph Francis
Scritsmier, Jerome Lorenzo
Scriver, Robert Macfie
Scrivner, Calla
Scroggie, Lois Jean
Scruggs, Emma Lou
Scruggs, Forrest Wilson
Scudder, Duston Richard
Scully, Paul Eugene
Scully, Robert Warren
Scussel, Frank Gaudioso
Sczudlo, Walter
Seaborg, Glenn Theodore
Seal, Michael Lance
Seale, Robert McMillan
Seamans, William Larry
Seamon, George Louis
Searight, Mary Dell (Mrs. Paul
James Searight)
Searight, Patricia Adelaide
Searl, Frank Vernon, Jr.
Sears, Charles Ryamond
Sears, Daniel Joseph
Sears, James Francis
Sears, Karl David
Sears, William Robert
Seaser, Rayno Ervin
Seawell, Donald Ray
Seay, Donald Walter
Sebastian, Charles Richard
Sechler, Gary Evans
Secor, Kenneth Eugene
Secord, Terrence Clyde
Sedgwick, Michael Bruce
Sedivy, Edmund Premysl
See, Leo Mark
Seegall, Manfred Ismar Ludwig
Seegrist, Edward Eugene
Seeley, David Arthur
Seeley, T. Talbot
Seely, Gordon Medard
Seeman, James Lester
Seemann, Gerald Robert
Seery, James Daniel
Seethaler, Albin James
Seethaler, William Charles
Seffel, John Harvey
Seffinger, Frank David
Segal, Steven Paul
Segalman, Robert Zalman
Segel, Karen Joseph
Segerstrom, Henry Thomas
Segil, Clive Melwyn
Segner, Venice Chandler
Segraves, Kelly Lee
Segrè, Emilio
Seib, Kenneth Allen
Seibel, Gilbert Ray
Seibold, William Raymond
Seidel, Joan Broude
Seiden, Hy
Seidl, Ludwig Herbert
Seidler, Martin George
Seidman, Lawrence Peter
Seifert, Anne Martha
Seifert, Wolfgang Klaus
Seim, Henry Jerome
Seitel, Alan Lewis
Seiter, Walter Harry
Seiveno, Donald Henry
Sekela, Albert Michael, Jr.
Selak, Stephen Josef
Selby, Howard Williams
Selditch, Alan Daniel
Selenius, Onni Eric
Seligman, Manuel
Sell, James Doyle
Sell, Robert Emerson
Sellers, Saralyn Long
Selletti, Theodore Anthony
Sellyei, Louis Francis, Jr.
Selover, Robert Hal
Seltzer, Harvey Lawrence
Seltzer, Michael Alan
Seltzer, Yvonne Alexander
Selvig, Edwin Robert
Selzer, Arthur
Semans, Sarah
Sencay, Joseph Frank
Sencenbaugh, James Richard
Sendrey, Albert Richard
Senensieb, Norbert Louis
Senger, John David
Senior, Larry James
Senior, Thomas Richard
Senn, Charles Lester
Senne, Stephen Michael
Seno, T. Thomas (Tom)
Sentyrz, Frank Eugene, Jr.
Seppi, Fred Lloyd
Sepulveda, Estella Alegria
Serafine, Gene Clark
Serafine, Judith Ann
Serne, Roger Jeffrey
Serrano, Frank Anthony, III
Serrano, Jose Luis
Seruto, Joseph George
Servine, Ronald John
Seshachari, Neila C.
Sessions, Carol Cutler
Seth, Oliver
Seto, Edward Leung
Seto, Tak Takachika
Seton, Waldemar, III
Settle, Dean Carter
Settlemyer, George Bernard
Setzekorn, William David
Sevcik, John Joseph
Severance, Harold L.
Severson, Marshall Lauris
Sewell, Charles Robertson
Sewell, Marsha J.
Seymore, William Andrewartha
Seymour, Dale Gilbert
Seymour, John
Seymour, Lance Lynnford
Sfingi, Andrew John
Shabaik, Aly Hossni
Shackelford, Gordon Lee, Jr.
Shackelford, James Floyd
Shackelford, John C(lyde)
Shackette, Jerry John
Shackleton, Frederick Gerald
Shackman, Daniel Robert
Shacter, David Mervyn
Shade, James William Ball
Shader, Benjamin Alan
Shaeffer, John Nees
Shafer, Robert Eugene
Shafer, Robert William, Jr.
Shaffer, Donald Edward
Shaffer, John Robert, II
Shaffer, Robert Clarence
Shaffer, Robert William
Shaffier, Norman
Shah, Shantilal Nathubbai
Shahid, Syed Iqbal Hussain
Shain, Richard Alan
Shakely, John (Jack) Bower
Shaklee, Forrest Clell
Shalkop, Robert L.
Shamberger, Marguerite Arline
Shammas, Hanna (John)
F(arid)
Shanahan, Robert H.
Shandrick, Albert Joseph
Shane, Lawrence H.
Shane, Leonard
Shanies, Harvey Michael
Shank, Dale Marvin
Shanley, JoAnne Elaine
Shanner, William Maurice
Shannon, Charles Francis
Shannon, Harold Hager
Shannon, Roger Hall
Shanny, Ramy Amiram
Shanor, Clarence Richard
Shapiro, Deane H., Jr.
Shapiro, Eliezer Yehuda
Shapiro, Gary Alan
Shapiro, Gary John
Shapiro, Jerald Steven
Shapiro, Mark Howard
Shapiro, Marvin James
Shapiro, Philip Alan
Shapiro, Richard Stanley
Shapiro, Steven Carl
Shapiro, Victor Lenard
Sharbaugh, William James
Sharbrough, Steven James
Share, Jack Bernard
Sharma, Om Prakash
Sharman, William
Sharoff, Robert Carl
Sharon, J. Hall
Sharon, William Francis
Sharp, Boyd Dinsmore
Sharp, Dorothea T.
Sharp, Douglas Rice
Sharp, George Lawrence
Sharp, James Clayton
Sharp, Lane A.
Sharp, Robert Churchill
Sharp, Theodore Elting
Sharp, William Elmo, Jr.
Sharpe, Robert Edward
Sharpe, Roland Leonard
Sharts, Clay Marcus
Shastany, Robert Harley
Shatz, Nachman
Shaughnessy, Daniel Robert,
Jr.
Shaver, James Porter
Shaver, Robert Charles
Shaw, Carl Bradley
Shaw, Charles Bergman, Jr.
Shaw, Edward Allen
Shaw, Ernal A.
Shaw, Ernest William
Shaw, Gaylord Dewayne
Shaw, Harold John
Shaw, John LaMotte
Shaw, John LeRoy
Shaw, Joyce Cutler
Shaw, Mildred Hart
Shaw, Neil C.
Shaw, Robert Barry
Shaw, Roger C.
Shaw, Thomas Maston

Shaw, Walter Morgan
Shawa, Monzer Sabri
Shawa, Osama Magdy
Shawaf, Bassim
Shawchuck, Norman L.
Shawstad, Raymond Vernon
Shay, John Michael
Shayne, Peter George
Shea, James Gerard
Shea, Murray Joseph
Sheaffer, William O.
Shearer, Angus T., Jr.
Shearer, Ruth Evelyn Whisler (Mrs. Jack Eric Shearer)
Shearmire, Hugh Herbert
Shearouse, Henry Grady, Jr.
Shebs, Theodore Lee
Shedd, Charles Harrison
Sheehan, Robert John
Sheehy, Daniel Paul
Shefelman, Harold S.
Sheffer, Patricia Ellen
Sheffield, William Kenneth
Sheft, Douglas Joel
Sheingold, Abraham
Shek, Johnny
Shekter, William Bernard
Shelby, Charles Lester, Jr.
Sheldon, Charles Harvey
Sheldon, Clayton Stuart
Sheldon, Jeffrey Glenn
Sheldon, Loren Edward
Sheldon, Nancy Way
Sheldon, Robert Edward
Sheldon, Sharon Sweeney
Shell, Mary Katherine Jaynes Hosking (Mrs. Joseph C. Shell)
Shelley, Susanne Marie Langer (Mrs. Robert E. Shelley)
Shelnutt, Robert Curtis
Shelton, Albert Lee
Shelton, Ralph Conrad
Shelton, Robert Charles
Shelton, Robert Elmer
Shelton, Sylvester Martin
Shen, Peter Ko-Chun
Shen, Peter Tuck Lee
Shenk, Howard Fred
Shenson, Howard Levitt
Shepard, Allan Guy
Shepard, Jack LeRoy
Shepherd, Eugene Charles
Shepherd, Jean Armida
Shepherd, Robert Thomas
Sheppard, Charles Arthur
Sheppard, Jocelyn Fortier
Sheppard, Kenneth Don
Shepperd, Walter Robert
Sheptow, Paul Michael
Sherer, Jerry Lynn
Sherk, Warren Arthur
Sherman, A(lan) Robert
Sherman, Edith Mary
Sherman, Edna Schultz (Mrs. Roy V. Sherman)
Sherman, Eric
Sherman, John Carter
Sherman, Martin
Sherman, Raymond Bernard
Sherman, Robert (Bernard)
Sherman, William Howard
Sherratt, Gerald Robert
Sherrill, James Winn, Jr.
Sherry, Kenneth Edward
Shervem, Robert Maurice
Sherwood, Allen Joseph
Sherwood, Robert James
Sherwood, Robert William
Shibata, Dennis Masayuki
Shibley, William Henry
Shidler, Jay Harold, II
Shields, Andrea Lyn
Shields, Edward Earl
Shields, Loran Donald
Shields, Thomas Keeler
Shiepe, Clifford Badeeh
Shier, Wayne Thomas
Shiffer, James David
Shiffman, Max
Shiflett, Ray Calvin
Shigeoka, Dennis Kazuo
Shim, Hong Seop
Shima, Howard, Mitsuo
Shimazaki, Tatsuo
Shimizu, Kaoru Karl
Shimoda, Jerry Yasutaka
Shimoda, Stanley Sueo
Shin, Helen Hee Ok
Shinbori, Dennis Daizo
Shindler, Anne Woskoff
Shine, Patrick Kelly
Shinn, Charles Curtis, Jr.
Shinsato, E. Masaki
Shintaku, Fred Haruto
Shiomi, Robert Hajime
Shiple, Marlene Catherine
Shiraki, Iwao William
Shirilla, Robert Michael
Shirley, Michael James
Shirley, Thomas Lloyd
Shively, John Terry
Shively, Richard Paul
Shivitz, William Francis
Shlanta, Alexis
Shmaeff, Robert Thomas
Shmitka, Richard Otto
Shockley, William (Bradford)
Shoemaker, Harold Lloyd
Shoemaker, Leroy D(wight)
Shoemaker, Lisle Forrest
Shoemaker, Thaddeus Eugene
Shoemaker, William Joseph
Shokeir, Mohamed Hassan Kamel
Shonk, Albert Davenport, Jr.
Shonnard, Ludlow, Jr.
Shor, Elizabeth Louise Noble
Shore, Herbert Chivambo
Short, Ronald Carol
Short, William Frederick
Shostak, Marjorie M.
Shostak, Stanley Richard
Shoup, Robert Frank
Shows, Peggy Mae
Shrader, Daniel Houston
Shramek, Gary Ronald
Shreeve, Jean'ne Marie
Shreve, Theodore Norris
Shrewsbury, Thomas Buckner
Shrontz, Frank Anderson
Shrontz, John William
Shropshire, Donald Gray
Shryock, James Walker
Shubb, Jerome Asher
Shuck, Emerson Clayton
Shue, Virginia Vergari
Shuken, Charles Stuart
Shuler, Jay
Shulman, Harold Marvin
Shulman, Leonard Allen
Shults, William Thomas
Shultz, Gladys Denny
Shumate, Charles Albert
Shumway, Forrest Nelson
Shumway, Norman David
Shurtz, Robert Ferguson
Shushan, Robert Daniel
Shyne, C. Michael
Sias, Ramon Lucero
Siberell, Anne Hicks
Siddiqi, Toufiq Aliuddin
Siddoway, William Ralph
Sidell, Robert A.
Siders, Ellis Leroy
Sidwell, Robert William
Siebner, Herbert Johannes Josef (H. vom Siebenstein)
Siegel, Daniel Charles
Siegel, Doris (Mrs. William E. Siegel)
Siegel, John Alexander, Jr.
Siegel, Mark Lee
Siegel, Michael Elliot
Sieh, Kittie Marie
Siehien, Joseph Valentine
Siemens, Richard Ernest
Siemon, Robert Gary
Siemsen, Arnold William
Sieroty, Alan Gerald
Sievers, Anita Ress
Sigler, Carl Oliver
Sigler, William Glenn
Sigoloff, Sanford Charles
Sigworth, Oliver Frederic
Sikha, Satyanarayana Murthy (S. S. Moorty)
Sikora, James Robert
Silas, Jack
Silbaugh, Preston Norwood
Silberberg, Dan E.
Silberman, C. Gee
Sileo, Thomas William
Sill, Alexis Mattos
Sills, David George
Silton, Lynn Gallagher
Silva, Edward Lionel
Silva, Frank Samuel
Silva, Macel Laverne
Silveira, John James
Silver, Alain Joel
Silver, Ann Jones
Silver, Barnard Stewart
Silver, Clarence Richards
Silver, Ethel Marie
Silver, Howard Findlay
Silver, Max Isadore
Silver, Philip Alfred
Silver, Ronald Herbert
Silverberg, Ivan Judah
Silverberg, Stuart Owen
Silverman, Kenneth Philip
Silverman, Mervyn Frank
Silverman, Robert Norman
Silverman, Robert William
Silvern, Leonard Charles
Silverson, Herbert Irwin
Silverstein, John Philip
Silverstein, Martin Elliot
Silverstein, Robert David
Silverton, John Saunders
Silvola, Aarre Matti Armas
Simcox, Craig Dennis
Simens, Hugo Grant
Simeroth, Harold Harvey
Simini, Joseph Peter
Simmons, Arthur
Simmons, Betty Jean
Simmons, Calvin
Simmons, Corky Hanson
Simmons, Ellamae (Mrs. Price D. Rice)
Simmons, James Pat, Jr.
Simmons, Milton Thomas
Simmons, Nola Ann
Simmons, Robert Charles
Simmons, Ted Conrad
Simmons, William Guyton
Simon, Bradley Alden
Simon, Charles Kenneth
Simon, Richard Hege
Simon, Warren Joseph
Simon, William Leonard
Simonds, Robert Bruce
Simonian, Arthur Carl
Simons, Dorothy Electa
Simons, Ellen Ann
Simons, Ronald Reed
Simons, Sanford Lawrence
Simpkins, Clarke Arthur
Simpkins, Gordon Burdette
Simpkins, Robert Allyn
Simpson, David William
Simpson, Dean
Simpson, Donald Bruce
Simpson, E. Gene
Simpson, George Edward, Jr.
Simpson, Joseph Myles
Simpson, Thomas Leo
Sims, Louis Edgar
Sims, Raymond Owen
Sims, Robert Reynold
Simunich, Mary Elizabeth Hedrick (Mrs. William A. Simunich)
Sinay, Ruth Doris
Sinberg, Ulo Lembit
Sinclair, William Andrew
Sine, Merle Dennis
Singaraju, Bharadwaja Keshava
Singer, Barry
Singer, Malcolm Scott
Singh, Gur Sharan
Singh, Hakam
Singh, Lakhbir
Singh, Mike Sohan
Singh, Randhir H.
Singletary, Lillian Darlington
Singleton, James Keith
Singleton, Leslie, Jr.
Sinha, Bhek Pati
Sinha, Mihir Kumar
Sinsheimer, Robert Louis
Siposs, George Geza
Sippy, Jean Merrill
Siracusa, Angelo John
Sirinian, Garo
Sirjord, Arthur Berner, Jr.
Sirocky, Gerard Joseph
Sirotnik, Robert Ira
Sison, Antonio Xerxes
Sison, Ramon Canlas
Sison, Rosario Fernandez
Sisson, John Earl
Sisson, Robert Louis
Sisti, Frank Phillip
Siversen, Annette K.
Sivertson, Noel Anthony
Sivley, Willard Emery
Siwundhla, Alice Princess Msumba
Skaalegaard, Hans Martin
Skadron, Erwin Saul
Skaggs, Conrad Alexander
Skaggs, Jere Jeannine
Skaggs, Milton Beach
Skahill, James Eugene
Skeehan, Raymond Aloysius, Jr.
Skelton, Barbara Mildred
Skewes, William Frederick
Skewes-Cox, Bennet
Skidmore, Donald Earl
Skiff, Russell Alton
Skinner, Lynn Joe
Skinsnes, Olaf Kristian
Sklar, Wilford Nathaniel
Skogerboe, Gaylord Vincent
Skoog, William Arthur
Skopil, Otto Richard, Jr.
Skornia, Thomas Allan
Skov, Iva Lee Marie
Skuderna, John Edward
Skufca, Donald Stanley
Skurdahl, Dale Maynard
Skuris, Pete Spiro
Skuse, Richard
Skutch, Ira
Skylstad, William Stephen
Slade, David Lee
Sladek, Lyle Virgil
Slaff, George
Slater, John Edward
Slater, Leonard
Slaton, Paul Franklin, III
Slattery, Roger C.
Slaughter, Charles Henry
Slaughter, Terry Welles
Slavin, Thomas Patrick
Slayback, John B(ernard)
Slayden, Richard Allen
Sleeper, Eleanor Russell (Mrs. Donald Campbell Sleeper)
Sleight, Randolph Riddell
Slemons, James Burdick, II
Slemp, Alfred Hermon
Slenes, John Freeman
Slepack, Lawrence
Sles, Steven Lawrence
Sletager, Janice Rae
Sletten, John Robert
Sliker, Todd Richard
Sliupas, Vytautas Jonas
Slivkoff, James Joseph
Sliwinski, Mitchell Stanley
Sloan, Robert Francis
Sloan, William Arthur
Sloane, Robert Malcolm
Sloane, Thomas O.
Slocumb, Tyler Henry, Jr.
Slonecker, William George
Sloss, Elizabeth Louise
Sloss, Patricia Delaney
Slotkin, Arthur Lewis
Slover, Archy F.
Sludikoff, Stanley Robert
Slusher, Howard Sidney
Slusser, Eugene Paul
Slusser, Robert Wyman
Smalley, Stanley Paul
Smalley, Terrence Edward
Smalley, Tom Michael
Smallie, Paul (Donald)
Smart, Charles Rich
Smart, Stanley Allen
Smedley, Robert William
Smets, John Edwin
Smiley, Glen Frank
Smiley, William A.
Smillie, William Stone
Smith, Aaron
Smith, Adrian Charles, Jr.
Smith, Albert Cromwell, Jr.
Smith, Andrew Major
Smith, Apollo Milton Olin
Smith, Barbara Jean
Smith, Bernard Joseph
Smith, Bernard Joseph Connolly
Smith, Betty Denny
Smith, Bettye L. Sebree
Smith, Bob (Wolfman Jack)
Smith, Bob Gene
Smith, Carl Hedin
Smith, Carter Blakemore
Smith, Charles Francis, Jr.
Smith, Charles Francis, Jr.
Smith, Charles Kenneth
Smith, Christian Reverdy
Smith, Clyn, Jr.
Smith, Craig Lawrence
Smith, Curtis Bresson
Smith, Dan Curtis
Smith, Daniel Merten
Smith, Daniel Weary
Smith, Dar Larson
Smith, Daryl Goldgraben
Smith, David Beryl Dean
Smith, David Edward
Smith, David Elvin
Smith, David Lane
Smith, David Michael
Smith, David William
Smith, Dean Edward
Smith, Dennis Dean
Smith, Dennis Ivan
Smith, Don Eugene
Smith, Donald Evans
Smith, Dorothy Ottinger (Mrs. James Emory Smith)
Smith, Douglas Lee
Smith, Earl Vern
Smith, Edgar Herbert
Smith, Evelyn Faye
Smith, Farrow James
Smith, Frances C.
Smith, Frank Leonard, III
Smith, Fred Gilmour
Smith, Frederick Stephen
Smith, Gary Lee
Smith, Gary Loyd
Smith, Gaylor Vaughn
Smith, Gerald Arthur
Smith, Gerard Albert
Smith, Grant Edward
Smith, Guy Donald, Jr.
Smith, H(arold) Wendell
Smith, Harold David, Jr.
Smith, Harold T., Jr.
Smith, Harry Mendell
Smith, Helen Brekke (Mrs. Reginald A.A. Smith)
Smith, Herbert Andrew
Smith, Homer Lloyd
Smith, Howard Lindsley
Smith, Hugh
Smith, Jack Aubrey
Smith, Jack Clifford
Smith, James Clois, Jr.
Smith, James Emory
Smith, James Henry
Smith, James Martyn, Jr.
Smith, James Weaver
Smith, James Weede
Smith, James William
Smith, Janice Irene
Smith, Jean Webb (Mrs. William French Smith)
Smith, Jeffery Alan
Smith, Jerry Doyle
Smith, John Charles
Smith, John Edward
Smith, John Kevin
Smith, John Robert
Smith, Joseph Lorenzo
Smith, Joyce Marie
Smith, Katherine Anne Dillon (Mrs. LeRoy F. Smith)
Smith, Keith Larue
Smith, Keith Lowell
Smith, Kenneth Eugene
Smith, Kenneth Lionel
Smith, Kerry Clark
Smith, Larry Taylor
Smith, Lawrence Lee
Smith, Le Roi Matthew-Pierre, III
Smith, Louise Kohl
Smith, Lowell Ralph
Smith, Lynn Don
Smith, Lynn Robert
Smith, Margaret Mary (Marge)
Smith, Marilyn Margaret
Smith, Mary Clay Benton (Mrs. Thor Merritt Smith)
Smith, Maurice Robert
Smith, Michael Ottinger
Smith, Norton Alonzo
Smith, O. Curt
Smith, Olive Irene Perry (Mrs. William Smith)
Smith, Patrick Arthur
Smith, Paul, Jr.
Smith, Paul Francis
Smith, Phillip Darrell
Smith, Ralph
Smith, Randolph Leland
Smith, Ray Fred
Smith, Richard Edward
Smith, Richard Eldon
Smith, Richard Freeman, Jr.
Smith, Richard Howard
Smith, Richard Lynn
Smith, Richard Russell
Smith, Robert Gene
Smith, Robert James
Smith, Robert James
Smith, Robert London
Smith, Robert Nelson
Smith, Roger Walton
Smith, Ron
Smith, Ronald Oliver
Smith, Rosalind Gray
Smith, Russell Lynn, Jr.
Smith, Rutha Lee
Smith, Sam
Smith, Sarah Frances
Smith, Sidney Crawley, Jr.
Smith, Stanton Spencer
Smith, Stephan Douglas
Smith, Stephen Bert
Smith, Stephen Dale
Smith, Stewart Crane
Smith, Terry Duane
Smith, Thomas Kent
Smith, Timothy George
Smith, Victor Joachim
Smith, Waldo Gregorius
Smith, Walter Harold
Smith, Watson
Smith, William Bordeau
Smith, William Embry
Smith, William French
Smith, William James
Smith, William McFate
Smith, William Roan, II
Smolens, Dan
Smollen, William John
Smout, Ronald Robson
Smyth, David Shannon
Smyth, Gordon Austin
Smyth, Jack Borden
Smyth, Richard Kelly
Smythe, Erik Allen
Smythe, Robert Richard
Snedeker, William Paul
Snell, Dennis Lee
Sneller, James August, Sr.
Snider, Delmar Edward
Snider, Eileen Elizabeth
Snider, Geri Terezas
Sniff, Elmer Swain
Snitker, John
Snodey, Shonloss Richard
Snodgrass, Stanley Benton
Snook, Quinton
Snow, Donald Ray
Snow, Gordon Franklin
Snow, Joseph Patrick
Snow, Karl Nelson, Jr.
Snow, Quentin Esca
Snow, William Albert
Snowden, Wesley David
Snyder, Chauncey Leroy
Snyder, Clifford Charles
Snyder, George Arthur
Snyder, Hugh Alfred
Snyder, Jack P.
Snyder, John Joseph
Snyder, Norman Gene
Soard, Raymond
Soblin, David Michael
Sobolewski, John Stephen
Soboroff, Steven Louis
Soderstrand, Michael Alan
Soffici, Jorge Hugo
Softeland, Oistein Torulf
Sokolow, Maurice
Solares, Molly Elizabeth
Solberg, Morten Edward
Solem, Elmo John
Solheim, Wilhelm Gerhard, II
Solidum, James
Solis, Kathleen Ann
Solk, Gerald
Solliday, Marjorie Ertel
Solomon, Bertram Clifford
Solomon, Edward Wendall
Solomon, George Freeman
Solomon, Herbert Allen
Solomon, Jack David
Solomon, Julius Oscar Lee
Solomon, Larry Joseph
Solymar, George Gyorgy
Somers, Richurd Carl
Somit, Jed
Sommer, Ervin Morgan
Sommer, Noel Frederick
Somsak, William John
Sondheimer, Fred Kenneth
Soo Hoo, Angela Mosiu
Soper, Ernest T., III
Sorani, Robert Peter
Sorensen, Earl Franklin
Sorensen, Lloyd Lee
Sorensen, Neil Clifford
Sorensen, Phillip Lee
Sorenson, Roger William
Sornson, Rodney Drace
Soroky, Doris Lipsky
Sorrells, Timothy Leroy
Soss, Daniel Lee
Sossaman, James Jasper
Sotiriou, Constantine Evangelos
Soule, John Dutcher
Soult, James Thomas
Sousa, Manuel George
Southard, William Wilson, Jr.
Southerland, Julia Chapman
Southward, Walter William
Southwick, Henry Hutchison
Sowder, Roger Eugene
Sowell, Clifford Gilbert
Sowers, Hubert Harris, Jr.
Sowerwine, Elbert Orla, Jr.
Spackman, Richard Harry
Spadarella, Frank L.
Spaeth, Edmund Eugene
Spalding, Henry Daniel
Spalding, Norma Vivian
Spalding, Prescott Lovell
Spangelo, Waldo Nelson
Spangler, Kathryn Anne
Spanier, Myron Drew
Spann, Katharine Doyle
Spar, Donald
Sparago, Diane Katherine
Sparks, Bennett Sher
Sparks, Marshall French
Sparks, Wendell Ervin
Spaulding, John Pierson
Spawn, Lloyd Eugene
Speakman, Randall Forest
Spear, Jean Marston
Speck, Gordon
Spector, William Irving
Speed, Ulysses Grant
Speer, John Franklin
Speer, Merwin Richard (Dick)
Spelleri, Robert Vincent
Spellman, John David
Spelts, Kathleen Mary
Spence, Alan Robert
Spence, Bruce Milton
Spencer, Arthur Chester, Jr.
Spencer, Clark William
Spencer, David Ervin
Spencer, Douglas Lloyd
Spencer, Frank Warren
Spencer, Joanne Jersey
Spencer, John William
Spencer, Raymond Edwin
Spencer, Richard William
Spencer, William Alva
Spendlove, John Clifton
Sperans, Joel
Speriglio, Milo Augustine
Sperlich, Peter Werner
Sperline, Elizabeth Starr
Speros, Theodore John
Sperrazzo, Gerald
Sperry, Leonard Thomas
Sperry, Mark
Speshock, Michael John
Spiegel, Larry J.
Spiegel, Leon Robert
Spiegelman, Alan M.
Spielman, John Russel
Spier, Edward Ellis
Spiess, Arlo Jay
Spigelman, Auri
Spilger, Michael
Spillane, Brian Boru
Spillane, John Henry
Spillar, Paul Victor
Spillman, James Raydin
Spillman, Nancy Zoe
Spina, Alfred Eugene
Spindler, John Clyde
Spinks, John Lee
Spiros, Robert Eugene
Spiszman, Ian Isaac
Spitz, Barry
Spofford, William Benjamin, Jr.
Sporer, Alfred Herbert
Sposeto, Dominic John
Spoto, Russell Carl
Spradlin, Dewey Donald
Spradling, John William
Spraggins, Charles Edward
Sprague, Kathryn Worley
Sprague, Robert Wright
Sprain, Thomas Edward
Spray, Joseph Laurence
Sprengelmeyer, Cyril August
Springer, Donald Harold
Springer, Floyd LaDean
Springer, Glenn Everett
Springer, Kirk William
Springer, Robert John
Sproger, Steven Robert
Spronk, Johannes Marinus
Sproul, Ann Stephenson
Sproull, Terrence Robert
Sprouse, John Sumner
Sprung, Douglas Lowry
Spurlock, Benjamin Hill, Jr.
Squibb, John Franklin
Squifflet, Edmond Clarke
Srinivasan, Venkatraman
Srivastava, Jaya Nidhi
Srivastava, Karunesh Kumar
Stacho, Zoltan Aladar
Stackhouse, David Lludlow
Stackhouse, Royal David, Jr.
Stacy, John Richard
Stacy, Peter George
Stadler, Areta Christine
Stadler, Robert William
Stadley, Pat Anna May Gough (Mrs. James M. Stadley)
Stadtman, Verne August
Staehle, Robert Lawday
Stafford, Charles F.
Stafford, John Frank
Stafford, Rebecca
Staggers, Kermit LeMoyne, II
Staglin, Garen Kent
Stagner, John Ray
Staheli, Harvey Kent
Stahl, William Hayes
Stahmann, Robert F.
Staiano, Ralph Anthony
Stair, Henry Hamilton, II
Stalcup, Robert Joe
Staley, Samuel Sorber
Stallcup, Evan
Staller, Bruce Atwater
Stallman, John David
Stames, William Alexander
Stamets, Richard Lee
Stampe, Lee Howard
Stampe, Neil Gordon
Stamper, Malcolm Theodore
Stampley, Herman, Jr.

Stamps, Patricia Hartnett
Stancik, Edward Joseph
Stanfield, Cecil James
Stanfill, William Everett
Stanford, Melvin Joseph
Stange, Robert Thomas
Stange, Roger Ernest
Stankiewicz, Wladyslaw Jozef
Stankovich, Ivan D.
Stanley, Charles Franklin
Stanley, Forrest Edwin
Stanley, Paul Lee
Stanley, R. C.
Stansbury, Donald Lloyd
Stansby, Maurice Earl
Stansel, John William
Stansfield, Leon Craig
Stanton, Richard Owen
Stanton, Roger Raymond
Stanton, Royal Waltz
Stanton, William John, Jr.
Stapf, Beau Carol Diane
Staples, John Dixon
Staring, Graydon Shaw
Stark, Carlyn Kaiser (Mrs.
Franklin Culver Stark)
Stark, David Delano
Stark, Fortney Hillman, Jr.
Stark, Franklin Culver
Stark, James William
Stark, Robert Lee
Starkovich, Dennis Phillip
Staron, Edward
Starr, James Marion
Starr, Melvin Lee
Starr, Robert Irving
Starzl, Thomas Earl
Statler, Irving Carl
Staton, Kenneth Wayne
Stauble, Vernon Ronald
Staver, LeRoy Baldwin
Stea, David
Stead, Rexford Arthur
Steadman, Bryan Leonard
Steadman, David Wilton
Steadman, John Marcellus, III
Stealey, Mary Louise (Mrs.
Sydnor L. Stealey Jr.)
Stear, Edwin Byron
Stearns, Catherine Virginia
Cook Ponder
Stearns, Charles Oran
Stearns, Frederick Wainwright
Stebbins, William Morrow
Stecz, Eugene Philip
Stedman, Orrill Mae
Steedly, Ronald Eugene
Steel, Thomas Henry
Steele, Arnold Edward
Steele, Edward Earl
Steele, Richard Ernest
Hampden
Steele, Robert A.
Steele, Roger Lincoln
Steenbarger, Charles James
Steensma, Robert Charles
Steeves, Samuel Lloyd
Stefanatos, Joanne
Steffens, Bonnie Dona
Steiger, Lynn Darryl
Steiger, Ralph Norman
Stein, Albert
Stein, Arthur Oscar
Stein, Barry Mark
Stein, David Meyer
Stein, Fredrick A.
Stein, Gerald Samuel
Stein, Herma Jayne
Stein, Irving
Stein, Jack
Stein, Laurence Neal
Stein, Lawrence J.
Stein, Mara Vasilevna
Stein, Philip Jerry
Steinbach, Susan Arlin
Steinbauer, David Jerome
Steinbeck, John Witherup, II
Steinberg, Barry Robert
Steinberg, David Scharf
Steinberg, Howard
Steinberg, Leon Harry
Steinberg, Warren Linnington
Steinbright, L. Dixon
Steiner, John Edward
Steiner, Joseph Randolph
Steingieser, Ronald David
Steingraber, John Kent
Steinhardt, Kenneth H.
Steinhauer, Ralph
Steinhoff, Harold Gerd
Steinhoff, Harold Richard
Steinke, David Wray
Steinman, John Francis
Steinmiller, Frank Neal
Steinwinter, Sheryl Bradfield
Stell, James L.
Stenberg, Clayton Carroll
Stenger, M(artin) Lane
Stenhouse, Douglas Simms
Steninger, Alvin Leonard
Stennett, Donald Osgood
Stenquist, Lee Borg
Stensrud, Russell Kenneth
Stenstrom, William Harold
Stentz, John Burr
Stenzel, Franz Robert
Stephan, John Jason
Stephan, Robert Joseph
Stephen, Joyce Lee
Stephen, Mae
Stephens, Cynthia Jane
Stephens, Harold Edwin
Stephens, Harold Leroy, Jr.
Stephens, Roger Rudie
Stephens, Ted Leroy
Stephens, William Leonard
Stephenson, Arthur Emmet, Jr.
Stephenson, Bud Wayne
Stephenson, Caryl Alyce
Stephenson, Larry Kirk
Stephenson, Lyle Davis
Stephenson, Michael James
Stephenson, Perry Clare
Stephenson, Toni Edwards
Stepovich, Michael Leo
Sterling, Harry Michael
Sterling, Howard David
Stern, Bruce Lynn
Stern, Daniel David
Stern, Doris L.
Stern, Milton R(eid)
Stern, Sandra Silverstone (Mrs.
Robert Lowell Stern)
Sterneck, Roger Harold
Sterner, Joseph William
Sternhagen, Charles James
Sternlight, David
Sterrett, James Edward
Stetson, Robert Francis
Steuben, Norton Leslie
Stevanak, Thomas John, Jr.
Stevens, Althea Williams
Stevens, Alva Lewis
Stevens, Clyde Benjamin, Jr.
Stevens, George Frederic
Stevens, George Vladimir
Stevens, Gloria Moldt
Stevens, Michael Henry
Stevens, Richard Skeels
Stevens, Robert William
Stevens, Roger Templeton
Stevens, Stephen Edward
Stevens, Theodore Fulton
Stevens, Thomas Granville
Stevens, Walter John
Stevens, William Ansel
Stevens, William Hadley
Stevenson, Alden
Stevenson, James Richard
Stevenson, Linda Ann LeBeau
Stevenson, Mark Joseph
Stevenson, Philip Fay
Stevenson, Robert
Stevenson, Thad Collier
Steward, Jeanette Louise
(Jenny)
Stewart, Charles George
Stewart, Clayton Thomas
Stewart, Elbert Wilton
Stewart, Gary Karless
Stewart, Gerald
Stewart, Gerald Eugene
Stewart, Isaac Daniel, Jr.
Stewart, James Luther, Jr.
Stewart, Keith Blainey
Stewart, Larry Gene
Stewart, Paul Richard
Stewart, Ralph Lewis
Stewart, Reginald
Stewart, Robert Ernest, Jr.
Stewart, Robert James
Stewart, Ronald Lee
Stewart, William Thomas
Stickell, Vance L.
Stiehl, Harry Charles
Stier, Lealand David
Stiewig, James Douglas
Stiles, Richard Arthur
Stiles, Richard Keith
Stilgenbauer, Robert Melvin
Still, Harold Henry, Jr.
Stillman, Roger Edward
Stilson, Walter Leslie
Stimac, Michele Frances
Stimpson, Gordon Neil
Stindt, Fred A.
Stine, George Harry
Stine, Whitney Ward
Stinner, William Francis
Stirrat, James Hill
Stitelman, Leonard Arnold
Stitt, Blair McWherter
Stock, John Joseph
Stock, Roland David
Stockdale, William Kenneth
Stocklmeir, Louis Emil
Stockton, John David
Stockton, Ruth Small (Mrs.
Truman Alex Stockton, Jr.)
Stoddard, Charles Warner, III
Stoddard, Frank James
Stoddard, Patricia Ann
Stoddard, Susan
Stodder, John Wesley
Stoffel, Charles Randall
Stoffels, Francis Gilbert
Stoick, Albert Francis
Stokes, Barbara Lynn
Stokes, Barry Owen
Stokes, Fred Allen, Sr.
Stokes, Paul James
Stolz, Lois Hayden Meek
Stolzenberg, Sidney Joseph
Stone, Bernard
Stone, Harold
Stone, Herman Hull
Stone, James Madison
Stone, Lynn Elizabeth Forney
Stone, Malcolm Eugene
Stone, Martin
Stone, Merle Eugene
Stone, Michael Edward
Stone, Thomas Robert
Stone, Walter Augustas
Stone, Willard John
Stone, William, Jr.
Stoneback, Raymond Delano
Stoorza, (LaVerne) Gail
Storey, R. Keith
Stork, Donald Harvey
Storms, Lowell Hanson
Story, Eugene Jack
Story, George Wesley
Story, Ronald Dean
Stott, Kenhelm Welburn, Jr.
Stout, Charles Lowell
Stout, Clifford Lee
Stout, Gregory Stansbury
Stout, Jerry Lynn
Stout, John Howard
Stover, William James
Stow, William Raymond, III
Stowell, Dennis Earl
Stowers, Barbara Woods
Stoyer, Charles Hayes
Stracener, Carl Edward
Strachan, J. George
Straessle, Alois Robert
Strahl, Marcia Bruce
Straight, Danley Elson
Strain, Sibyl Marjoria Shipp
(Mrs. Numa Alonzo Strain)
Strand, Melford Lien
Strandell, Marjatta
Strassman, Harvey
Stratch, Noel Roy
Strathdee, John Francis
Strathman, John Henry
Straton, John Robin, Jr.
Stratton, John Glenn
Stratton, Stanley Colburn
Straub, Edward Gordon
Straube, Gene Fred
Strauser, Robert Dee
Strauss, Michael Leonard
Strawn, Robert L.
Strayer, Richard Lee
Streeter, Earl Louis
Strehler, Donald Lee
Streit, Lawrence Carson, Jr.
Strich, Robert
Strickland, Byron Reid
Strickland, Genie Loreen
Strickler, Betty Jane
Strickler, Jeffrey Harold
Strike, Christine Alice
Stringer, William Jeremy
Stringfellow, William Gilbert
Strobeck, John Lane
Strobel, Stanley William
Strobridge, Mary Ann
Strock, Herbert Leonard
Strohm, Gary Charles
Strom, Alan Yale
Strom, Emil Conrad
Strom, Mark Gary
Strom, William Werner
Stroman, Linda Gage
Stromberger, Theodore Leo
Strong, Gary Eugene
Strong, Gay
Strong, George Gordon
Strong, Harold Robert
Strong, James Bentley
Strong, Robert George
Strong, William James
Stross, Fred Helmut
Strote, Severin Albert
Strother, Maceo William
Stroum, Samuel N.
Struble, Wayne
Struhl, Stanley Frederick
Strum, Dennis William
Strunk, DeForest Livingston
Strunk, Harold Kenneth
Stuart, Charles Rossiter, Jr.
Stuart, Dwight Lyman
Stuart, Gerard William, Jr.
Stuart, John Goodspeed
Stuart, Melvin
Stuart, Peter Martin, II
Stuart, Robert Marvin
Stuart, Ted James, Jr.
Stubbert, George Charles
Stubberud, Allen Roger
Stubblefield, Thomas Mason
Stubbs, Daniel Gaie
Stubbs, Eldon John
Stucki, Alfred Blaine
Stucki, Grant Alfred
Studdert, Stephen Mark
Stude, Everett Wilson, Jr.
Studer, Bruce Allen
Stuen, Marcus Rodway
Stuhlman, Andrea Marie
Stukovsky, Stevzar Stefan
Stull, James Frederick
Stumbos, John Demetrios, Jr.
Stump, Bob
Stump, Wayne Howard
Stump, William Bailey
Sturckler, Marguerite Lucille
(Peggy)
Sturdevant, Bruce Layton
Sturgeon, William Bebb
Sturiale, Glory
Stylianides, Stephen John
Stys, Raymond Joseph
Suchesk, Arthur Mickey
Suchin, Milton Bernard
Sudarsky, Jerry M.
Sudden, Charles
Sudduth, Charles Grayson
Suehiro, Richard Yoshio
Suelzle, Herbert Woodrow
Suffern, Orine Hughes
Sugiki, Shigemi
Sugimoto, David Masao
Sugimoto, Mas
Sugimoto, Roy Atsuro
Sukhupunyaraksa, Pivanetr
Sullins, Donald Eugene
Sullivan, Claire Marie
Sullivan, Donald Patrick
Sullivan, Donald Wayne
Sullivan, Elroy James
Sullivan, George Anderson
Sullivan, George J.
Sullivan, George Murray
Sullivan, Gerald James
Sullivan, Gerard Francis
Sullivan, James Joseph
Sullivan, Jane Katherine
Sullivan, John Francis
Sullivan, Lawrence Anthony
Sullivan, Maurice Joseph
Sullivan, Michael Buster
Sullivan, Michael Evan
Sullivan, Paul John
Sullivan, Robert Wayne
Sulzberger, Roberta Zechiel
Sumida, Alice Yoshie
Kawasaki
Summers, C. Earl
Summers, Jim Arnold
Summers, Pete (Clarence L.)
Sumner, B. Michael
Sumner, Elaine Mary Gerhard
Sumsion, Henry Theodore
Sun, Bill Kauo-Hwa
Sun, David Chen Hwa
Sun, Paul Chang Kuei
Sun, Randolph
Sun, Tseng-Yao (Terry)
Sundberg, John L(awrence)
Sundquist, John Fred
Sung, C. B.
Sung, Chen-Han
Sung, James Pang-chieh
Supalla, Clarence Joseph
Supancich, Michael Jack
Supernaw, William Scott
Supple, Charles John
Suprina, Cristie Lyn
Sur, John Bong Kun
Surane, James William
Surbrook, David Burch
Surrey, Berne
Surridge, Robert Caldwell
Sussman, Gilbert
Sussman, Mitchell Reed
Sutcliffe, Eric
Suter, Lonee Travel
Suter, Siegfried (Sigi) Joseph
(Travel), III
Sutherland, Bruce
Sutherland, James J.
Sutherland, Jerome Douglas
Sutherland, Lowell Francis
Sutherland, Ross Edward
Sutherland Brown, Atholl
Sutorius, Edward Phillip
Sutphen, Richard Charles
Sutro, Robert
Sutter, Carolyn Sue
Sutter, Harvey Mack
Sutter, Theodore
Suttle, Clyde Travers, Jr.
Sutton, Clark Lozon
Sutton, David Bartlett
Sutton, David St. Clair
Sutton, Frankie Lee
Sutton, James Louis
Sutton, Jerry Lee
Sutton, John Paul
Sutton, Leonard von Bibra
Sutton, Nathan LeRoy
Sutton, Paul McCullough
Sutton, Richard Carpenter
Sutton, Robert Edward
Suydam, Charles Robert
Suzuki, Joy Suemi
Suzuki, Noboru
Sveinsson, Johannes
Svenson, John Anders
Sviland, Mary Ann Petrich
Swadley, Bernadine Hatch
(Mrs. Robert Hunter
Swadley)
Swagel, Dennis Jay
Swagel, Lorin Marc
Swain, Donald Christie
Swain, Marian Louise Boatman
(Mrs. Theron Richard
Swain)
Swanberg, Chandler A.
Swancoat, James Glyn
Swaner, Cleo Fae Anderson
Swann, Mary Edna Goldsmith
Swansen, Vern
Swanson, Craig Mallory
Swanson, Edwin Archie
Swanson, LeRoy Stanley
Swanson, Rex Dennis
Swanson, Richard William
Swanson, Richard William
Swanson, Roy Edward
Swantz, Francis Walter
Swarner, Orville Ward
Swarthout, Walter Emmet
Swartout, Roy, III
Swayze, Thomas Allen, Jr.
Swearingen, Daniel Lee
Swearingen, David Paul
Swearingen, Rodger
Swedenborg, Samuel Whitton
Sweeney, James
Sweeney, Robert Frank
Sweet, Audrey Margery Smith
Sweet, Elwyn Carl
Sweet, John Duane
Sweet, Malcolm Stuart
Sweet, Richard Williams
Sweet, Susan Morris
Sweeten, Jamimah Dove
Sweetser, Edward Rowe
Swenson, James Lars
Swenson, Lloyd Richard
Swenson, Severt, Jr.
Sweo, John Edwin
Swerdloff, Arthur LeRoy
Swerling, Peter
Swetnam, Walter Thomas
Swiadek, Stanley Frank
Swick, Eugene John
Swickard, Joseph Spencer
Swift, A.
Swift, Charles Henry, Jr.
Swift, William Charles
Swihart, H. Gregg
Swim, Helen Wilson
Swinehart, Frank C.
Swingle, Donald Morgan
Swinton, Brian Cheever
Swinyard, Ewart Ainslie
Swinyard, Sharon Joan
Swinyer, Leonard James
Swissman, Neil
Swope, Leslie J.
Swyden, Robert Gene
Sykes, Ronald William
Sylvester, Richard Russell
Sylvia, Donald Joseph
Symms, Steven Douglas
Symons, Archie Robert
Symons, Irving Joseph
Symons, Robert Spencer
Syring, William Richard
Syriotis, Anthony George
Szalay, Glenn Coleman
Szegedi, Laszlo
Szekely, Deborah Mazzanti
Sztraicher, Daniel Rafael
Szydlowski, Frank Anthony
Taagepera, Rein
Tabachnick, Kenneth
Tabor, Doris Dee
Tabor, Glenn Dean
Tabor, James Frederick
Tada, Mitsuru
Taft, David Allan
Taft, John Ailes
Tagawa, Harry Mitsuo
Tagg, Charles Everett
Taggart, Cal Snell
Tahiliani, Vasu Hariram
Tahl, Donald Samuel
Taimuty, Samuel Isaac
Tainter, Leland Brown, Jr.
Takafuji, June Hatsuko
Takahashi, James Masayuki
Takahashi, Nobumitsu (Nobi)
Takaki, Melvin Hiroyuki
Takamoto, David Toshiharu
Takamune, Thomas Hikaru
Takaoka, Howard Shiro
Takeda, Kathleen Yukie
Takeda, Kenneth Kingo
Takei, Toshihisa
Takeshita, Wat
Takeuchi, Sylvia F.
Tal, Jacob
Talarides, Dominic Kikes
Talbot, Eugene Leroy
Talbot, Garth Oleen
Talbot, Matthew Joseph
Talbot, Nora (Dinsfriend)
Talbot, Sheldon H.
Talbot, Walter DeVaur
Talbott, George Robert
Talbott, John Arthur
Taleisnik, Julio
Talley, Benjamin Franklin
Tallmon, Violet
Tally, David Nicholas
Talmadge, Frank Byron
Tam, Frederick Shu-Chuen
Tamashiro, Thomas Koyei
Tambs, Lewis Arthur
Tamkin, S. Jerome
Tammany, Albert Squire, III
Tamplin, Nelson Eugene
Tamura, Paul Yoshito
Tan, Jauw Siauw
Tan, Kong-Meng
Tan, Shirley
Tan, Thian Hoo
Tanabe, Haruto
Tanaka, Togo W(illiam)
Tancredi, Leonard Andrew
Joseph
Tanenbaum, Basil Samuel
Tang, John Theodore
Taniguchi, Richard Ryuzo
Taniguchi, Tokuso
Tanious, Farouk Khalil
Tanji, Kenneth Kazuo
Tank, Gerhard Willi
Tankersley, Dale Russell
Tankersley, Robert Karl
Tanner, Elvin R.
Tanner, Jerre Eugene
Tanner, K. Nolen
Tanner, Nathan Eldon
Tanner, Owen Ralph
Tanner, William Woodland
Tansky, Ronald Irwin
Tanzmann, Virginia Ward
Taper, S. Mark
Tapley, Harold Louis
Tappan, Jeremy Richard
Tapper, Thomas Massey
Tappin, Michael Augustine
Tarazi, John Hanna
Tarbox, Robert Mack
Targovnik, Selma E. Kaplan
Tarman, Olen (Jack) Clyde, II
Tarr, William Winship, Jr.
Tarson, Herbert Harvey
Tartoue, Cassie Eugenia (Mrs.
Pierre Tartoue)
Tarvin, Russell Wayne
Tasaka, Masaichi
Taschow, Horst Gerard
Tashima, Charles Wakatsu
Tashiro, Noboru
Tatman, Barbara Kay Smith
Tatom, William Clayton
Tatum, Hubert Rogers
Tatum, Jacqueline Louise
Tatum, John Richard
Taub, Curtis Leslie
Taub, Harald J.
Tauber, Alfred Seymour
Taucher, Fred Horace
Tavares, William Durney
Tawlks, Allan
Taybi, Hooshang
Taylor, Allen George
Taylor, B. Richard
Taylor, Charles Mosser
Taylor, David Marston
Taylor, Dennis William
Taylor, Douglas Roy
Taylor, Guy
Taylor, Henry Fuller, III
Taylor, Herbert Otto
Taylor, Irving
Taylor, James Gilbert
Taylor, John Roy
Taylor, Kendrick Jay
Taylor, Kenneth Gene
Taylor, Kenneth William
Taylor, L. D. Babe
Taylor, Mark Allen
Taylor, Max Tourner
Taylor, Maxwell King
Taylor, Murray East
Taylor, Patrick Rodger
Taylor, Paul Eric
Taylor, Peter van Voorhees
Taylor, Quintard, Jr.
Taylor, Reese Hale, Jr.
Taylor, Richard Blackburn
Taylor, Richard Bonnell
Taylor, Richard Dennis
Taylor, Richard Willey
Taylor, Robert Dean
Taylor, Rowena Jeanette
Burgess
Taylor, Samuel Francis, IV
Taylor, Steven James
Taylor, Steven Zane
Taylor, Thomas Tallott
Taylor, Timothy Davies
Taylor, Walter Wallace
Taylor, Walton Robert Lawson
Taylor, William Henry
Taylor, William Ralph
Taylor, Wilson Everett
Tays, George Arnold, Jr.
Tchobanoglous, George
Teachout, Gerald Seward
Tebet, David William
Teegarden, Clark Lawrence
Teel, Dale
Teeter, Bernice Woodworth
Teeter, Richard Malcolm
Tegart, David Bradley
Teichman, Sol
Teifeld, Norman Roy
Teitelbaum, Daniel Thau
Teller, Rosalind Elaine
Tellier, Richard Davis
Tellier, Susan Scagnelli
Tellyer, Harry B., Jr.
Temianka, Henri
Tempelis, Constantine Harry
Tempest, Harrison F.
Temple, William Benton
Temple, William Robert, Jr.
Templeman, Max
Templer, Donald Irvin
Templeton, David Edward
Tenazas, Gemorsita Macavinta
Tenbrinck, Margaret Dorothy
Schaffner (Mrs. Eduard
Johan Tenbrinck)
Ten Eyck, David Roderick
Tenggardjaja, Franciscus
Dudung
Tengum, Phyllis Zybl Ruth
Tenison, Robert Blake
Tennant, Forest Searls, Jr.
Tennant, Frank Arthur
Tenney, John Boyd
Tenny, Harvey
Tenorio, Juan Cruz
Tenorio-Ungphakorn, Lucilla
Emeralda
Tenzer, Michael Leonard
Teodorescu, Paul George
Ternus, Robert Arnold
Terranova, James Alan
Terrazas, Henrietta Lowe
Terrel, Ronald Lee
Terrel, Ted Leon
Terrell, Glenn
Terrell, Paul Jay
Terry, Jill Elizabeth
Terry, John Timothy
Terry, Maurice Brooks
Te Selle, Robert Wayne
Tessa, Clement D.
Tetrick, Reed Broadbent
Teubner, John Thomas
Teutsch, Champion Kurt
Thacher, Penne Lynne
Thacker, Barbara Jewell
Thacker, Don W.
Thal, Nancy Lynn
Thalberg, Stanton Philip
Thaler, Peter Jacob
Thams, Margie Louise
Thatcher, David Joe
Thatcher, Dickinson
Thatcher, Stephen Richard
Thayer, Elwyn Aldace
Thayer, Hanford
Thayer, Steven Lee
Thayer, William Vance
Thebaut, Payne
Thein, Stephen George, Jr.
Theisen, Lee Scott
Theodore, Charles
Thetford, William Newton

Theurer, Jessop Clair
Theurich, Alfred
Thich, Thien-an (Doan, Van-an)
Thiel, Vitalina Coello
Thiel, Warren Harry
Thiele, Alan George
Thies, Greg Steffan
Thiessen, Brian David
Thiessen, Jon Isaac
Thiessen, Larry Don
Thiry, Paul
Thissell, James Dennis
Thode, Edward Frederick
Thoelecke, Leonard Stanley
Thoen, Dennis Duane
Thom, John Girdwood
Thomann, Donaldo Jose
Thomas, Charles Albert
Thomas, Clarence Mark
Thomas, David Lee
Thomas, David Phillip
Thomas, Donald Kirk, Jr.
Thomas, Dudley Percy
Thomas, Edward Churchill (Ned)
Thomas, Elizabeth (Liz) Ann
Thomas, Fred Maurice
Thomas, George Jefferson, III
Thomas, Grace Fern
Thomas, Heriberto Victor
Thomas, John Bert
Thomas, John Rhodes
Thomas, Joseph Edward
Thomas, Joseph Henry
Thomas, Judith Carol
Thomas, Kenneth Dale
Thomas, Lowell Irvin
Thomas, Lucinda Ellen Swearingen
Thomas, Melvyn Ernest
Thomas, Nathan Gordon
Thomas, Owen Foster
Thomas, Richard Van
Thomas, Robert Capron
Thomas, Robert Glenn
Thomas, Robert Harold
Thomas, Robert Joseph
Thomas, Robert Lancefield
Thomas, Rolland Shields, Jr.
Thomas, Samuel Finley
Thomas, Steven Allen
Thomas, Warren Deane
Thomas, William (Will) Elwood
Thomas, William Jennings
Thomas, William Joseph
Thomas, William Longfellow
Thomas, William M.
Thomas, William Orvill, Jr.
Thomason, Gary Fredrick
Thompson, Alan Michael
Thompson, Alvin Jerome
Thompson, Bobby Jack
Thompson, Carol Gwen
Thompson, David Alfred
Thompson, David Lang
Thompson, Davis Dominick
Thompson, Dennis Peters
Thompson, Doyle Franklin
Thompson, Emmett Llloyd
Thompson, Gerald Earl
Thompson, Ginny Lou
Thompson, Grove George, Jr.
Thompson, Harlan Howard
Thompson, Harry Euell
Thompson, Herbert Ernest
Thompson, James Earl
Thompson, James Homer
Thompson, James William
Thompson, Jenenne Marie
Thompson, John Albert
Thompson, John Brown
Thompson, John Michael
Thompson, John Robert
Thompson, Kenneth Frank
Thompson, Lester Walker
Thompson, Lohren Matthew
Thompson, Malcolm Francis
Thompson, Melvin (Mel) Rex
Thompson, Michael Patrick
Thompson, Paul Blake
Thompson, Perry Michael
Thompson, Philip Montgomery, III
Thompson, Ralph Eugene
Thompson, Rexford Lynn
Thompson, Richard Everett
Thompson, Richard Frederick
Thompson, Richard Lee
Thompson, Richard William
Thompson, Robert Elliott
Thompson, Ronald Edward
Thompson, Roy Daniel
Thompson, Stephen Lee
Thompson, Stephen Marsh
Thompson, Terrence Alvin
Thompson, Terry Lee
Thompson, Thomas E.
Thompson, Truet Bradford
Thompson, William Arthur, III
Thompson, William Benbow, Jr.
Thoms, Glenn Alan
Thomson, Carol A.
Thomson, Donald Brownlee
Thomson, Joan Alberta
Thomson, John Ansel Armstrong
Thomson, Thyra Godfrey
Thorburn, Donaldson Bride
Thordarson, Roger Roy
Thorington, Harry Sumpter
Thorn, Paul Edward
Thorne, Jerry Thomas
Thorne, John William
Thorne, Joyce Carol
Thorne, Lucile Markham (Mrs. Harold Arthur Thorne)
Thorne, Richard Mansergh
Thorner, Tom
Thornton, Brice Elwood
Thornton, Charles Bates
Thornton, Dan Perkins
Thornton, Florence Emma (Mrs. Laurance C. Thornton)
Thornton, Francis Joseph
Thornton, John Richard
Thornton, Larry Don
Thorpe, Arthur John
Thorpe, Bert Duane
Thorpe, Emmet Joseph
Thorpe, Howard Alan
Thorsen, Roy Thorvald
Thorson, Edward William
Thorson, John A(rden)
Thorson, Morris H.
Thournir, Rawland Thomas
Throwe, Anita Louise
Thrower, Norman Joseph William
Thulsan, Donald Myron
Thulsiraj, Raj
Thurber, Clarence Egbert
Thurgood, Graham Ward
Thurman, Thomas Wesley
Thurston, Morris Alma
Thurston, Ronald Charles
Thurston, Walter Dyce
Thurston, Wayne Oral
Thwaites, James Stamers
Thwing, Alice Joan
Thygerson, Alton Luie
Tibbitts, Samuel John
Tiberii, Dewey John
Tichy, George Joseph, II
Tidwell, James Mial
Tidwell, Robert Austin
Tiemann, K. Gabrielle
Tietjen, Melva Devenport
Tiger, Hyman Sidney
Tilbury, Roger Graydon
Tilden, James Wilson
Tilden, Lorraine Frederick (Mrs. Wesley R. Tilden)
Tillion, Diana Rutzebeck
Tilly, Dale Allan
Tilsworth, Timothy
Timbanard, Jeffrey Rand
Timberlake, Dale Lee
Timlin, Robert James
Timm, Jerry Roger
Timmner, Christiaan Richard
Timmons, Evelyn Deering
Timothy, Robert Keller
Timpke, Jane Lucille
Tims, Frederick Curtis, Jr.
Tims, Kenneth Wayne
Tindell, Barry Ross
Tinga, Wayne Ralph
Tingley, Howard Eugene
Tingley, Ronald George
Tinsley, Jean Jarman Kaye (Mrs. Clarence Tinsley)
Tintari, Joseph Abraham
Tipler, Frank Jennings, III
Tippets, Elvis Harold
Tippett, Donald Harvey
Tippetts, Earl LeVell
Tipton, Ann Baugh
Tipton, Gary Lee
Tipton, Harold Forrest, Jr.
Tipton, John Burke
Tipton, Lee George
Tipton, Norman Ernest
Tirrell, John Albert
Tischer, E. Paul
Tiss, George John
Titlow, Joseph David
Titsch, Robert
Tittle, David Sherman
Tjan, Anthony Hong-Liang
Tjen, Willy Tjauw-Boen
Tleimat, Badawi Wajih
Tobey, Gene E.
Tobias, Charles William
Tobin, Gary Paul
Tobin, Robert Emmet
Tobin, Saul
Tobriner, Mathew O(scar)
Tochikura, Minoru
Todd, Esther Stevens (Mrs. Owen William Todd)
Todd, Jack Donald
Todd, Paul Henry
Toews, Edward Dale
Toffel, Alvin Eugene
Toffel, Paul Haskell
Tognazzini, Wilma Alys
Tognetti, Richard Joseph
Tokita, Nobuhiro
Tolbert, James Allen
Tolch, Noah Arthur
Toledo, Rosario Trance
Tolen, Eugene Adrian
Toliver, Raymond Frederick
Toll, Henry Wolcott, Jr.
Tolman, Keith Grant
Tolman, Richard Robins
Tolson, Robert Henry
Tom, Chow Loy
Tom, Clarence Yung Chen
Tom, Franson David Kwock Sun
Tom, George Wah Yen
Tom, Ping Hon
Tomcheski, Richard Henry
Tomich, Lillian
Tominc, Virginia Margaret
Tomita, Tad Takeo
Tomka, Margaret
Tomlingson, Paul David
Tomlinson, Cheralyn Tiffany
Tomlinson, John Ulysses, Jr.
Tommey, Richard Joseph
Tompkins, Richard Weller, Jr.
Tompkins, Ronald K.
Tompkins, Stephan
Tompkins, Virginia Arms (Mrs. Avery Tompkins)
Tompson, Robert Norman
Tomsic, Gerald Allen
Tondow, Murray
Toney, Michael James
Toney, Robert Leland
Tong, Richard Dare
Tongue, Thomas H.
Tonkin, Bertram Melvin
Tonnelli, John J.
Tonning, Wayland Avery, Jr.
Toogood, Jerald Eugene
Tookey, Robert Clarence
Tooley, William Lander
Tooper, Virginia Oliphant
Toor, Jaswant Singh
Top, Norman Ferris
Topping, Norman H(awkins)
Toral, Richard Harry
Torczyner, Joshua
Toren, Robert
Torgerson, Lois Glock
Tori, Christopher Dante
Torma, Arpad Emil
Tormey, Thomas James
Torpy, Richard Donald
Torres, Harry Andres
Toscan, Richard Eric
Tosti, Donald Thomas
Toth, Emerick
Toth, Michael Allen
Toth, Stephen Joseph
Totzke, Henry Albert
Tour, Robert Louis
Tout, Evelyn Montana
Towels, Norman E. W.
Towers, Bernard
Towne, Carole Suzanne
Towne, Richard C.
Towner, George R(utherford)
Townes, Charles Hard
Townes, Michael Douglas
Townsend, Charles Willis
Townsend, John Holt
Townsend, Richard Edward
Toyomura, Dennis Takeshi
Tracy, James Frueh
Tracy, Thomas Josheph, Jr.
Traidman, Michael Laurence
Traille, Edmond Emil
Train, Benjamin Curtiss
Trainer, James Franklin, Jr.
Trammell, Melvin Charles
Trampe, Dan Edward
Tranel, Ned Nicholas
Trapp, Jack Martin
Trask, Philip Alan
Trauger, Robert James
Travelstead, Chester Coleman
Traver, Dorothy
Travers, Yone Beatrice Stone (Mrs. James V. Travers)
Travis, Albert Hartman
Travis, Harry Bernard
Traylor, Cheryl Lee
Traylor, Natalie Smith
Traynor, Michael James
Treadway, Douglas M.
Treanor, Walter John
Treece, James Lyle
Treffinger, Edward Yaryan
Trego, James Moreland
Treiman, Joyce Wahl
Treinen, Sylvester William
Trelease, Frank Johnson III
Treloar, Harriette Ellen
Trenary, John Michael
Trent, Bobbye Jean
Trent, Donald Stephen
Trent, Michael Edward
Trent, Richard James
Trepanier, Theodore William
Tresmontan, Olympia Davis
Tressler, Earnest Dale
Trester, Kenneth Robert
Trethewey, James Alger
Trevithick, Ronald James
Trezek, George James
Triana, Judith Haruko Handa
Tribbett, Ronald Wayne
Tribble, Donald Dennis
Tribken, Craig Lewis
Trigg, Charles Wilderman
Trigg, Susan Elizabeth
Trigiano, Lucien Lewis
Trimble, John William
Trimble, Marshall Ira
Trimeloni, Gerald Victor
Trimingham, William Earl
Trimmer, Harvey Wilson, Jr.
Triphahn, Charles Albert
Triplett, Raymond Francis
Tripp, Christine Adams
Tripp, Donald
Tripp, Russell Maurice
Trivich, Michael Eric
Troedsson, Carl Birger
Troller, Theodor Henry, III
Trollope-Cagle, Vivian Jewel
Trompeter, Ralph Francis
Trostler, Robert Jay
Trotta, Genevra Ruth
Trotter, Arthur Clarence
Trotter, Hugh Berry, Jr.
Troughton, John David
Troughton, Sharon Kay
Trout, Barbara Irene Hansen
Trow, Ruby Lou
Troy, Walter William
Truax, John Everett
Trubey, Donald Wayne
Truby, Betsy Jean Kirby (Mrs. Frank Keeler Truby)
Truby, Frank Keeler
Truby, Roy
Trudel, John Davis
True, Diemer
True, Henry Alfonso, Jr.
True, Jean Durland (Mrs. Henry A. True, Jr.)
True, Richard Brownell
Truelsen, Thorvald Irvin Antone
Truex, George Robert, Jr.
Truitt, Evelyn Mack
Trujillo, C. B.
Trujillo, Pete Ralph
Truman, Rolland Albert
Trumbo, Philip Walter
Trumbull, Larry Edward
Trunk, Joseph
Trusler, Suzanne
Trustman, Jack
Truxillo, Wayne Wesley
Tsai, Andre Tii-kang
Tsai, Wan-Tswan
Tsappis, Anthony
Tscha, Moon-Bo
Tse, Stephen
Tseng, Rose Yun-Li Chang
Tseng, Stanley Sze-Chuen
Tsou, Peter, Sr.
Tsuda, Roy Toshio
Tsuji, Harold Kazuyoshi
Tsukiji, Richard Takeo
Tu, Wei-ming
Tuccori, Lawrence Stanley
Tucker, Charles Cyril
Tucker, Danny Lee
Tucker, Elmer Dean
Tucker, Gordon Locke
Tucker, Janet Stephenson
Tucker, Lawrence Scott
Tucker, Paul Sawyer
Tucker, Richard Clive
Tuckett, Glen Cameron
Tuddenham, Read Duncan
Tuell, Jack Marvin
Tuetken, Carl Francis
Tuft, Dean Byard
Tulang, Michael Conrad
Tulee, Roy Carl
Tuller, Wendy Judge
Tulley, John Edward
Tunglen, Frank Wesley
Tunks, Lehan Kent
Tunks, Omar Alvin
Tuohey, Conrad Gravier
Turchik, Steve Paul
Turetzky, Bertram Jay
Turk, Mary Elizabeth
Turken, Meyer David
Turlis, Chris George
Turner, Arthur Campbell
Turner, Charles Kennedy
Turner, Jay Lynn
Turner, John Joseph
Turner, Morris John
Turner, Morris Nolten
Turner, Peter Helmer
Turner, Ray Martin
Turner, Rex Hardin
Turner, Robert Harold
Turner, William Spencer
Turney, Thomas Charles
Turney, William Forbes
Turpen, Bill Lee
Turrell, James Archie
Turrentine, Edward Clark
Turvill, Paul Arnold
Tushla, Richard James
Tuton, James Garrett
Tuttle, Allen H.
Tuttle, Daniel Webster
Tuttle, Richard Glenellison
Tuttobene, Robert Thomas
Tuvell, Robert Edward
Tuveson, Ernest Lee
Tveten, Lowell Howard
Tweed, Myron Leland
Twilegar, Ron Jess
Twiss, Suzanne
Twist, Robert Lanphier
Tygart, Clarence Eugene
Tykeson, Donald Erwin
Tyler, Robert Harold
Tyler, William Howard, Jr.
Tyne, Andrew Vaino
Tyran, Benjamin
Tyrell-Smith, Patrick Creagh
Tyson, Lynn Carlton
Tyson, Robert George
Tysor, Michael Lyle
Uchida, Prentiss Susumu
Uchida, Tadao
Udall, Morris King
Udall, Morris King
Uelmen, Jean Emilie
Uerkvitz, Thomas David
Ufen, George Reginald
Ugalat, Shankar Basappa
Uglum, John Richard
Ugone, Raymond Paul
Uhland, Ruth Ellen
Uhler, Willard Douglas
Uhlman, Wesley Carl
Uke, Alan Kurt
Ulery, Donald Eugene
Ullestad, Rolf John
Ullman, Albert C(onrad)
Ullman, Cornelius Gumbel
Ullom, Madeline Marie
Ulmer, Chester Paul
Ulrich, Paul Graham
Unan, George Vincent
Underdal, Cora Jeannette
Underhill, Donald Lawrence
Underhill, Harold Wertz, Jr.
Underhill, Lonnie Edward
Underwood, Arthur Adrine, II
Underwood, Robert Kenneth
Unger, Kenneth Rhodes
Unger, Leonard Leslie
Unrein, Carl Vincent
Unrue, John Calvin
Unruh, Dan Alex
Unterkoefler, Gerald Thomas
Upham, Frank Transue
Uram, Edward Thomas
Urban, Conrad Vincent
Urban, Walter Jean
Urbanec, Katherine Elaine
Urbantke, Irwin Arthur
Ure, Helen Davis Bowring
Urey, Harold Clayton
Uri, George Wolfsohn
Urmer, Albert Heinz
Urrea, Petronio David, Jr.
Urschel, Robert John
Ursin, Bjarne Elling
Useldinger, Ronald Eugene
Ushijima, John Takeji
Ussery, Albert Travis
Utter, Robert French
Utter, Stephen
Utz, Sarah Winifred
Utzinger, Robert Conde
Utzinger, William Grover
Uy, Stephen Siong
Uzgalis, Robert Charles
Vaccarino, Robin
Vadnais-Archuleta, Sharon Dale
Vail, Lois Mae
Vaile, Jean Elizabeth
Vaissade, Benjamin Joseph
Vala, Robert
Valadao, Jose Lisandra
Valanti, Karen Lorrayne
Valdespino, Luis Cesar
Valencia, William Urena
Valenti, Robert Michael
Valentine, James Ray
Valentine, Michael Lynn
Valentine, William Miller
Valentine, William R.
Valera, Mauricio Moscoso, Jr.
Valko, Robert Michael
Vallat, Eugene Hopson
Valvo, Carlton Francis
Van Abrahams, Ron
Van Alstyne, Richard Warner
VanArsdel, Rosemary Thorstenson
Van Bellehem, Harry Bryce
Van Brunt, Edmund Ewing
Van Buskirk, George Dellan
Vance, Bobbie Owens
Vance, Charles Bruce
Vance, Chris Eugene
Vance, LaDene L., III
Van Cleave, Philip Ford
Van Cleave, William Robert
Vancura, Stephen Joseph
Van Dalsem, Elizabeth Lou
Vandaveer, Barbara Louise
Van Dawark, Thomas Vernon
Van De Bogart, Willard George
Van Deerlin, Lionel
Vandenberg, Peter
Vandenberghe, Ronald Gustave
Vanden Bos, Michael Lloyd
Van Den Bosch, Wentworth Dirk
Van Derbur, Francis Stacy
Van Derbur, Marilyn (Mrs. Lawrence A. Atler)
Vandergriff, Lola Aola
Vandergriff, Robert Ray
Vanderhyde, Susan Elizabeth
Van Der Meulen, Joseph Pierre
Van Der Pas, Peter William
Vander Veer, Howard Jefferson
Vanderwilt, John W.
Vandeventer, Janice Leigh
Van Dusen, Austin Keeler
Van Duzer, William Henry
Van Dyk, Frederick Theodore (Ted)
Van Dyk, Melda Fay Blix
Van Dyke, William Flook, II
Van Elderen, Paul
Van Eldik, Berend Jacob
Van Engelen, William Dean
Van Fleet, William Mabry
Van Hofwegen, Adrian
Van Kampen, Kent Rigby
Van Kirk, John Ellsworth
Van Kirk, Perry Wayne
Van Kregten, Anthony Gerard Lodewyk Willem, Jr.
Van Le, Thuy Tien Huynh
Van Leeuwen, William Harold
Van Mols, Brian
Vann, John Daniel, III
Vann, Paul W.
Van Ness, Beth Hurd
Vannice, Kenneth Earl
Van Norman, Robert Wesley
Van Note, Arlene Ann
Van Nuys, David Whitman
Van Ooyen, Jerry Leonard
Van Otten, Betty Walker
Van Patten, Edward Robert
Van Tassel, Lowell Thomas
Van Valer, Betty Carolyn
Van Velzor, James Daniel
Van Vleck, Billy Reynolds
Van Vleet, Susan Ellen Bash
van Vogt, Alfred Elton
Van Voorhis, Thomas
VanWagoner, Wayne Thomas
Van Wolf, Henry
Van Zonneveld, Elizabeth Holden
Varanasi, Usha Suryam
Vares, Kenneth Francis
Vargas, Ernest Arthur
Vargha, Louis Andrew
Varner, Bruce Doyle
Varner, Dudley Meriwether
Varnes, Richard Patrick
Vartanian, Vincent Vartan
Varzaly, Laird Alan
Vasiloff, Nicholas Jordan
Vaskelis, Frank Martin
Vasquez, Leopoldo Rangel, Jr.
Vasquez, Victor Abarca
Vatcher, James Gordon
Vaughan, Earle Russell
Vaughan, Frances E.
Vaughan, James Arthur, Jr.
Vaughan, James Fielding
Vaughan, Richard B(ardwell)
Vaughan-Cole, Beth Ann
Vaughn, William Henry, Jr.
Vawter, Donald George
Veale, Warren Lorne
Veatch, Chauncey Lee, III
Veatch, John Rice
Veatch, John William
Vecchio, Donald Anthony
Vedros, Neylan Anthony
Veitch, Stephen William
Velamoor, Seshadri Rajagopal
Velasquez, Ralph Gilbert
Velde, Gail Patrick
Velde, John Ernest, Jr.
Veltri, Mario Frank
Velvin, William Charles
Venable, Douglas
Verbeke, Frank Girard, Jr.
Verby, Harry David
Verdi, John Minturn
Verdu, Joseph F(rancis)
Verduin, Claire Leone
Verhey, Joseph William
Veri, Richard Edmond
Verleger, Philip King
Verma, Sadanand
Vermeer, Richard Douglas
Vernon, Audree Jean
Vernon, Barton Ray
Vernon, Charles (Charles Vernon Johnston)
Vernon, Roger Willard
Verrill, Frank William
Verser, John Kinnard
Versluis, Matthew Cornelius
Vertlieb, Richard Harvey
Vertun, Alan Stuart
Vervick, Larry Irvin
Vest, Virginia Jane
Vicari, Lucille C(hristendina) K(athleen)
Vician, Thomas Allen, Sr.
Vicino, Frank Leo
Vickers, Cheryle Ann
Vickery, Byrdean Eyvonne Hughes
Vickery, James Roger
Victor, Marc Bennett
Victors, Alexis Peter
Vida, Lee Osman
Vieglais, Nikolajs
Vierheller, Ralph Charles
Viesselman, John Oscar
Vig, Byron Oscar
Vigil, Charles S.
Vigil, H. Felix
Vigil, Lawrence Daniel
Vik, Trygve Svere
Villaganas, Ted Aballe
Villa Juan, Antonio Pascual
Villanueva, Mario Ebuenga
Villarino, José Ríos
Vilott, Catherine Lavon Elder (Mrs. L. Dale Vilott)
Vincent, Albert Vernon
Vines, William Howard
Vineyard, C. L.
Vineyard, David Jess
Vinson, Donald John
Vint, James Edward
Violet, Woodrow Wilson, Jr.
Vireday, Pierre Francois
Virkelyst, Robert Allan
Viscio, James Dale
Vise, John L.
Vitalie, Carl Lynn
Vivian, Charles William
Vlachos, Estella Maria
Vodraska, Kenneth Frank
Voegelin, Harold Stanley
Voelkel, Virginia Kay
Voepel, Harold C.
Vogel, Willard Lee
Vogen, Robert Neil
Vogl, O. James
Vogt, John L.
Voight, Frank Edward
Voight, J(oseph) Kurt
Volckmann, Russell William, Jr.
Volinn, Ilse Josephine
Volk, Harry J.
Volker, Kurt Carl
Vollmer, Goswin Peter
Vollstedt, Reed
Volman, David Herschel
Volok, William Pearce
Volpe, Carolyn Crosser

Volpert, Don Wayne
Vomhof, Daniel William
von Beroldingen, Paul Anthony
Von Demfange, Henry Palmer
Vonderheid, Arda Elizabeth
von der Heydt, James A(rnold)
Von Dewitz, Arden
Von Drott, Ramona Jeanne
Von Gunten, Glenn Harland
Von Krohn, Rex Johannes
von Leden, Hans Victor
von Minden, Milton Charles, Jr.
Von Riesen, Richard Dale
Vora, Shantilal Amidas
Vorbeck, Donald William
Voris, Charles William
Vorreiter, John Wagner
Vorsatz, Paul Frederick
Voskuil, Walter Henry
Voss, Edwin Armstrong Price
Voss, Richard Gerald
Vote, Carol Jeanne
Voth, Andrew Charles
Voutour, Joseph Charles
Vowell, Caroline Hawkins
Voysey, Alfred Everett
Vredevoe, Donna Lou
Vreeland, Marion Jefferson
Vreeland, Robert Wilder
Vucinich, Wayne S.
Vukcevich, Walter Michael
Vurpillat, Victor Vincent
Vyas, Dileepkumar Ramanlal
Vyas, Girish Narmadashankar
Wachtell, Thomas
Wackernagel, H(ans) Beat
Waddell, Barbara Ann
Waddington, Mary Ellen
Waddy, Willanna Ruth Gilliam
Wade, Constance McElroy
Wade, George Albert
Wadhwa, Surender K.
Wadia, Phiroze Khushroo
Wadman, William Wood, III
Wadsworth, Joseph Franklin, III
Wagelie, Reuben Gan
Wagener, Joseph Mark
Wages, Larry Douglas
Waggoner, Laine (Mrs. Rex Robert Waggoner, Jr.)
Waggoner, Richard Walter
Wagley, Leon Arman
Wagner, Charles Henry
Wagner, Donald Eugene
Wagner, Floyd Hol, Jr.
Wagner, Gerald Eugene
Wagner, Gordon Parsons
Wagner, Inge
Wagner, Kenneth Eugene
Wagner, Michael Jack
Wagner, Michael Joseph
Wagner, Sharon Lee Spence
Wagner, Sue
Wagner, William Francis, Jr.
Wagner, William Lyle
Wagoner, David Everett
Wagstaff, Marian Cavassa
Wahab, George Mekhail
Wahba, Ray Mansur
Wahl, Joan Constance
Wahle, Bernard Karl
Wahle, Roy Patrick
Wahlgren, Erik
Waidmann, Arthur La Verne
Wailes, Richard Donald
Wain, David Smith
Wainwright, Ray M.
Wakai, Theodore Yoshisada
Wakefield, Susanne Winslow Mygatt
Wakefield, Wesley Halpenny
Wakeman, Frederic Evans, Jr.
Wakeman, Vern Dwight
Wakeman, William Garold
Wakerlin, George Earle
Wakerlin, Ruth Coleman (Mrs. George E. Wakerlin)
Wakil, Sheikh Parvez
Wakin, Malham M.
Wald, Edwin Prescott
Walden, John William
Waldmann, Eugene John
Waldo, Leonard Charles
Waldo, Sally
Waldron, Helen Jeanette
Waldron, Robert Leroy, II
Waldron, Rodney K.
Waldschmidt, Paul Edward
Wales, Hugh Gregory
Wales, Raymond Maxwell
Walholm, Roy Willard, Jr.
Walhood, Gordon Arlien
Walker, Betty Ann
Walker, Brooks, Jr.
Walker, Doris Jean Isaak
Walker, Edmond Richmond
Walker, Edward Madison
Walker, Eljana M. Du Vall
Walker, Ellen Louise
Walker, Francis Joseph
Walker, Fred Duane
Walker, Fred William
Walker, Gene Kimball
Walker, Guy Lowell
Walker, Harold Osmonde
Walker, Herbert John
Walker, Jack Lyman
Walker, James Russell
Walker, John Wallace
Walker, Joseph
Walker, Kelsey, Jr.
Walker, Laurence A(lbert)
Walker, Marjorie Louise
Walker, Patricia Sears Challender
Walker, (Glenn) Perrin
Walker, Philip Chamberlain, II
Walker, Raymond Francis
Walker, Robert Harold
Walker, Ron Michael
Walker, Timothy Blake
Walker, Weldon Joseph
Walker, Welmon, Jr.
Walker, William Claude
Walkinshaw, Jonathan Moore
Walkinshaw, Walter
Wall, Francis Joseph
Wall, Tom William
Wallace, Charles Henry
Wallace, David Oliver
Wallace, Donn B.
Wallace, Gerald Raymond
Wallace, Glenn Walker (Mrs. John McChrystal Wallace)
Wallace, J. Clifford
Wallace, James Ellis
Wallace, John Robert
Wallace, Kenneth Alan
Wallace, Lyle Jarrette
Wallace, Lynn Pyper
Wallace, Richard Ardyn
Wallace, Tom Allen
Wallace, William Raymond
Wallach, George Stephen
Wallach, Howard Frederic
Wallar, Robert Edward
Wallen, John Walfred
Wallender, Arnold Lee
Waller, Henry Buford, Jr.
Waller, Richard Charles
Waller, Robert Carl
Waller, Thomas Edward
Wallerich, Peter Kenneth
Wallerstein, Bruce Lee
Wallerstein, Robert S.
Wallihan, Ellis Flower
Walling, Charles Du Frenne
Walling, Donn Loren
Wallis, Lynn Ruel
Wallis, (Harry) Randall
Wallop, Malcolm
Wallstrom, Wesley Donald
Walpin, Lionel Arthur
Walrath, Harry Rienzi
Walrath, Stephen Merrill
Walraven, Harold Richard
Walsh, Arthur James
Walsh, Barbara Marie
Walsh, Bernard Lawrence, Jr.
Walsh, Frederick
Walsh, Frederick
Walsh, Gerard Joseph
Walsh, Howard Benjamin
Walsh, James Edward
Walsh, Patricia Lunde
Walsh, Richard George
Walsh, Timothy Edward
Walsten, Carl John Edward
Walter, Bert Mathew
Walter, Bruce Alexander
Walter, Edward Lee
Walter, Eline Pare
Walter, John Paul
Walter, Ronald Allen
Walter, William Jacob, Jr.
Walters, Harry Lyle
Walters, John Robert
Walters, Mary Dawson
Walther, Richard Ernest
Walton, George E. P.
Walton, Jack Thomas
Walton, Max Raymond
Walton, Thomas Frederick
Waltz, Robert Reading
Wan, Frederic Yui-Ming
Wang, Ben Chang
Wang, Bob Shih-Ping
Wang, Chen Chi
Wang, Chun Tsin
Wang, Chun-I
Wang, George Shih-Chang
Wang, James Chia-Fang
Wang, Johnson Chia Sheng
Wang, Lily Shih-Li
Wangaard, Frederick Field
Wangsness, Dennis Lee
Waning, Joseph Edward
Wanselow, Robert Dean
Warburton, Austen Den
Warburton, Edward Alan
Ward, Anthony John
Ward, Edmond Campion
Ward, Gene Rinna
Ward, John Roger
Ward, John Wyndham
Ward, Peter Langdon
Ward, Thomas Leon
Ward, Timothy Richard
Warden, Shirley Clark (Mrs. Ronald W. Warden)
Warder, William
Wardle, Michael David
Ward-Steinman, David
Ware, Arthur Earl
Ware, Claude
Ware, Howard Brent
Ware, Kent Carnes, II
Wargo, William George
Warhol, Warren Nicholas
Warick, Lawrence Herbert
Warne, William Elmo
Warner, Bartley Gray
Warner, Charles Sampson
Warner, Daniel Sumner
Warner, Frederick W.
Warner, James Bernard
Warner, John Anson
Warner, Peter Deryk
Warnock, James Forrest, Jr.
Warp, Crescencia Bowens
Warrack, Allan Alexander
Warren, Charles Dewey
Warren, Charles Elfving
Warren, Douglas Kent
Warren, Edwin Douglas
Warren, Hubert Orval
Warren, James Marion
Warren, John Howard
Warren, Patricia Armstrong
Warren, Richard Wayne
Warren, Thomas Frederick Tallbert
Warren, Wignes Kandish
Warrick, Donald F.
Warrington, Fern Marie Fisk
Warshawsky, Ivan
Warten, Ralph Martin
Wartenbe, Robert Spalt
Warthen, John Edward
Warthen, Norma Hansen
Wasden, John Frederic
Washburn, Jerry Martin
Washburn, Kenneth E.
Washington, Alfonzo
Washington, Napoleon, Jr.
Wasowicz, Lidia
Wasserman, Albert
Wasserman, Don Howard
Wasserman, Isaac Miles
Wasserman, Isabelle Mildred
Wasserman, Robert
Wasson, Michael Stanley
Wastal, Patrick Henry
Waste, William Ten Eyck
Watanabe, Brown Mitsugi
Watanabe, Henry Katsuo
Watanabe, Melvin Masaharu
Waterman, B. Craig
Waters, Alfred Earnest
Waters, Laughlin Edward
Waterstreet, James Kent
Watford, Robert Huckins
Watkins, David Gary
Watkins, Deems Christopher
Watkins, James Franklin, Jr.
Watkins, Parry Alexander
Watkins, Timmy Leo
Watkins, W. LaMarr
Watler, John Franklin, Jr.
Watne, Edwin Marvin
Watras, Ronald Edward
Watrous, John David
Watrous, Lyle Crook
Watson, Ann McWhinney
Watson, Bruce Robert
Watson, C. Gordon
Watson, Diane Edith
Watson, Elden Jay
Watson, Gary Steele
Watson, George A.
Watson, Harold George
Watson, Howard Hawley
Watson, John Alfred
Watson, John Ernest
Watson, John Joseph
Watson, John Leonard
Watson, Lita Lea
Watson, Maxine Amanda
Watson, Michael
Watson, Monte Lynn
Watson, Norman Ernest
Watson, Phoebe Ethel Kruger
Watson, Ray Hampton
Watson, Steve Royce
Watson, Walter Brown
Watson, William Keith Ross
Watstein, Sherman Foster
Wattenbarger, Sue E.
Wattles, Gurdon Howard
Watts, Albert Leon
Watts, John Graham
Watts, Lois Anita Hawks
Watts, Lowell Hoyt
Watts, Marvin Lee
Watts, Michael Earl
Watts, Oliver Edward
Watts, Robert Gary
Watts, Robert Wayne
Watts, Thomas Harwood
Waugh, Arthur B.
Waxman, Henry A.
Wayland, L. C. Newton
Wayment, Sherman Arnold
Wayne, Kyra Petrovskaya
Wayne, Lowell Grant
Weage, Wanda Gail Swatman
Weagraff, Patrick James
Weatherwax, Bruce Wayne
Weaver, Charles Allen
Weaver, James
Weaver, John Poindexter
Weaver, Kenneth Douglas
Weaver, Samuel Wood
Weaver, Thomas
Webb, Arthur James
Webb, Garr Randyl
Webb, James Lee
Webb, John Ashby
Webb, Paul Frank
Webb, William Clement
Webber, Kenneth Wellesley
Weber, George Richard
Weber, Irwin Jack
Weber, Jack
Weber, Kenneth Earl
Weber, Lawrence James
Weber, Lisa Jo
Weber, Peter James
Weber, Sheila K.
Webster, Grady Linder, Jr.
Webster, Kennard Wood
Wedberg, Stanley Edward
Wedbush, Edward William
Weddle, Clark Lee
Wedel, Harold Leisy
Wedlake, Philip Russell, Jr.
Weech, Dall E.
Weech, Merrill Richard
Weed, Roger Oren
Weeden, Curtis George
Weedin, Kenneth Raymond
Weeks, Dora Frances
Weeks, Howard Benjamin
Weeks, Joe Harold
Weeks, John Ellis
Weeks, Roger Wolcott, Jr.
Weeks, Sherlie Beason
Wehner, Alfred Peter
Wehrly, Joseph Malachi
Weibel, Jorge Erik
Weibell, Fred John
Weiblen, Jack Walter
Weich, Martin Lee
Weichardt, Heinz Hermann
Weidemann, Anton Fredrick
Weiden, Paul Lincoln
Weidner, Charles Kenneth
Weigand, Bernard Leo
Weigand, Eva Mae
Weigand, Frederick Lind
Weightman, Herbert George
Weikel, William Carlton
Weil, Robert Irving
Weil, Robert Leonard
Weilenman, James Austin
Weiler, Dorothy Esser
Weill, Samuel, Jr.
Weinberg, Bernard
Weinberg, Charles Bernard
Weinberg, Leonard Burton
Weiner, Richard Allen
Weingarten, Saul Myer
Weinheimer, William Richard
Weinstein, Haskell Joseph
Weinstein, Norman Ronald
Weinstein, Robert Albert
Weinstock, Donald Jay
Weintraub, Gerald David
Weir, Alexander, Jr.
Weir, Robert H.
Weirick, Glenn Carleton
Weisbard, Marvin
Weisbeck, Norbert Aloysuis
Weisenfluh, Norman Donald
Weiser, Virginia Ruth
Weiss, Charles Frederick
Weiss, Gaspard Etienne
Weiss, Harriet Bonnie
Weiss, Harry Anthony
Weiss, Herbert Klemm
Weiss, Howard Rich
Weiss, Joseph
Weiss, Joseph Roy
Weiss, Max Tibor
Weiss, Robert Theodore
Weiss, Sanford Ronald
Weiss, Theodore Joel
Weisse, Herbert Paul
Weissman, Clark
Weissman, Herbert Nathaniel
Weist, Walter Robert, Jr.
Weitkamp, Fredrick John
Weitz, Ted Curtis
Weixelman, Donald Bernard
Wekenmann, Thomas Rae
Welch, Arthur William
Welch, Garth Larry
Welch, George Baker, Jr.
Welch, John Samuel
Welch, Lloyd Richard
Welch, Peter Louis
Welch, Richard Larry
Welch, Thomas Kevin
Welch, William Francis
Welch, William Robert
Welcome, Dennis Palmer
Welcome, Jennie Darling
Weldon, Edward Joseph, Jr.
Weldon, Lynn Leroy
Welke, Elton Grinnell, Jr.
Welker, Joan Elizabeth
Welles, John Galt
Welling, Conrad Gerhart
Welling, Don Udy
Wells, Cecil Harold, Jr.
Wells, Clifford Milton
Wells, Donald Edward
Wells, Douglas Deloy
Wells, Howard Elbert
Wells, James Laurence
Wells, James Thomas
Wells, Linda Diane
Wells, Lynn Taylor
Wells, Merle William
Wells, Patricia Ann
Wells, Willard Henry
Wells, William Thomas
Welpton, Sherman Seymour, III
Welsh, John Beresford, Jr.
Welsh, John Paulus
Welsh, Louis Maximilian
Welt, Roger Carlisle
Welter, Leonard Melvin
Wenaas, Harold Leroy
Wendlinger, Robert Matthew
Wendt, John Arthur Frederic
Wendt, Lawrence Frederick
Wengerd, Sherman Alexander
Wengler, Robert Eugene
Wennberg, Willy Roger
Wennerholm, William Charles
Wennstrom, Harold Elbert
Wensrich, Carl J.
Wentworth, Theodore Sumner
Wenzel, James Gottlieb
Werdegar, Kathryn Mickle
Wermers, Joseph John
Werne, Joellen
Werner, Donald Norman
Werner, Emmy Elisabeth
Werner, Frank David
Werner, Ray Orval
Wernes, John Erik
Wertman, Maxine
Wesche, Percival Adellon
Wescott, Suzanne Elaine Connolly
Weskamp, Dale Paul
Wesley, Phillip
Wessels, Philip Summeral
Wessler, Melvin Dean
Wesson, Kenneth Alan
Wesson, Robert Gale
West, Anita S.
West, Bruce Joseph
West, Darell Lee
West, Donald Kirkland
West, Harold Truman (Hal)
West, James Harold
West, Julian Ralph
West, May Ellen
West, Ozro Emery
West, Richard Paul
West, Robert Harry
West, Robert Johnson
West, Ronald Sargesant
West, Wilmer A., Jr.
Westberg, Karl Rogers
Westbo, J(ames) Robert
Westbo, Leonard Archibald, Jr.
Westbrook, Patrick Alan de Lujan
Westcott, Ralph Merrill
Westendorf, David Richard
Westerberg, Stephen Carl
Westerfield, William
Westerman, George Grayson
Westersund, Gerald Edward
Westfall, Kenneth E.
Westhem, Andrew David
Westland, Jack
Westman, Thomas Louis
Weston, Charles Harold, Jr.
Weston, Nathan Austin, III
Westover, Donald Erwin
Westover, W. E. (Gene)
Westover, Wendy Anderson
Westre, Wilford Jay
Westwick, Barbara Quinn
Weswig, John Marcus
Weswig, Paul Henry
Wetzel, Harry Herman, Jr.
Wetzel, James Lewis, Jr.
Wexler, Charles Emanuel
Weyerhaeuser, George Hunt
Weygand, Lawrence Ray
Weygand, Leroy Charles
Weyl, Terry Charles
Weyman, Leo, Jr.
Whalen, John Elroy
Whalen, Pauline Katherine
Whaley, Joseph S.
Whaley, Stephen Vickery
Whang, Sukoo Jack
Whartenby, Catherine English
Wharton, Warren Lindbergh
Whatmore, George Bernard
Wheat, Ben Milton
Wheat, Joe Ben
Wheatley, Mary Katherine
Wheatley, Melvin Ernest, Jr.
Wheeler, Alfred Edward
Wheeler, C(harles) Julian
Wheeler, Clinton Jacob
Wheeler, James Richard
Wheeler, Kenneth Allen
Wheeler, Louis Cutter
Wheeler, Mark
Wheeler, Robert Lawrence
Wheeler, Robert William
Wheeler, Stephen Lee
Wheeler, William Alvah
Wheeler, William Thornton
Wheeling, Mary Ellen
Whelan, John William
Whelan, Robert Louis
Whelan, Vincent Edward
Whetstone, Robert Dean
Whetten, John Dilworth
Whetten, Loren Amasa
Whinery, William Delos, Jr.
Whipple, Blaine
Whipple, Christopher George
Whipps, Gilbert Frederick
Whisenand, James Mac
Whitacre, George Marshall
Whitaker, Clem, Jr.
Whitaker, Larry Jay
Whitaker, Thomas Wallace
Whitby, Philip John
Whitby, Thomas Joseph
White, Alice Hermanson
White, Anthony Gene
White, Artis Andre
White, Beverly Jean
White, Charles Stephen
White, Donald Paul
White, George
White, George Harvey
White, Harold Clifford
White, Ian McKibbin
White, J(ens) Gustav
White, Jack Kaylin
White, Jack Lee
White, Jackson Elliott
White, James Adelbert
White, James Eathel
White, James Robert
White, John Roger
White, Joseph Richard
White, Juanita Greer (Mrs. Thomas Sherman White)
White, Lelia Cayne
White, Mahlon Thatcher
White, Marlys Ruth Jarrett
White, Mary Geraldine
White, Melvin Robert
White, Michael Douglas
White, Nelson Henry
White, Owen Roberts
White, Paul Frederick
White, Ralph Patrick
White, Robert William
White, Shirley Maye
White, Stanley Archibald
White, Virginia Taffinder (Mrs. James A. White)
White, William Burval
White, William Gregg
White, William Henry, Jr.
Whitehead, Albert Junior
Whitehead, Alton Bruce
Whitehead, Barry
Whitehead, Bruce M.
Whitehead, Kenton David
Whitehurst, Daniel
Whiteley, Robert E.
Whiteman, Mary Ann
Whitesell, John Edwin
Whiting, Kenneth Russell
Whiting, Richard Frank
Whitlatch, Walter Nicholas
Whitlock, David Cotton
Whitman, Donald Frank
Whitman, Paul Merle
Whitmore, Robert Neil
Whitney, Bernard
Whitney, William
Whitridge, John, III
Whitsel, Richard Harry
Whitsell, Margaret Maude
Whitson, Richard Gardner
Whitt, James Patrick
Whittaker, Douglas John
Whittaker, John Albert, III
Whittemore, Edward Loder
Whitten, Richard Hamilton, Jr.
Whittier, Edward James
Whittington, Floyd Leon
Whittington, Robert Bruce
Whittle, Thomas
Whyte, Norman James
Wiant, George Eugene
Wiant, Wayne Edward
Wichman, Juliet Rice
Wick, Jacob, Jr.
Wickersham, Kirk, Jr.
Wickett, William Harold, Jr.
Wickham, John Eldon
Wickman, Paul Everett
Wicks, Harry Lewis
Wicks, Patrick Heath
Wickstead, George William
Widder, William Jerome
Widelock, Margaret
Widener, Don
Widgery, William Arthur
Widman, Orville John
Widmoyer, Fred Bixler
Wieand, Jonathan David
Wiedhopf, Jacob Michael
Wienand, Karl Dickson
Wienke, Bruce Ray
Wierer, Otto
Wierman, Marilyn Marie
Wies, Louis Bernhart
Wiese, George Michael
Wiese, Norman Eugene
Wiese, Walter Rodney
Wiesenfeld, Irving Harold
Wiesner, Erhard
Wiessenberger, Larry Jack
Wiestling, Joshua Martin
Wigchert, Albert Henry
Wiggins, Walton Wray
Wiggs, P. David
Wigren, Gerald Lynn
Wigton, Chester Mahlon
Wilbur, Ruth Jordan (Mrs. Dwight Locke Wilbur)
Wilckens, Alfred Charles
Wilcock, Frederick Feodor
Wilcott, Jack Curtis
Wilcox, Colleen Bridget
Wilcox, Gordon Martin
Wilcox, Gregory Schloenfilter
Wilcox, James Carson
Wilcox, Patricia Keelan (Mrs. Forrest Eugene Wilcox)
Wilcox, Thomas Robert
Wild, Robert Lee
Wild, Shirley Parr
Wild, Walter Frear
Wilde, Charles Broadwater
Wilde, Jerry Leo
Wilder, Brooks
Wilder, Emmett Chesney
Wilder, Frederica W.
Wilds, Lillian
Wildschuetz, Harvey Frederick
Wilensky, Neil Steven
Wiley, Ann
Wiley, Carl Ross
Wiley, Don Del Marr
Wiley, Roy Brooks
Wilhelm, Robert Oscar
Wilhelm, Willa Metta
Wilken, Gary Robert
Wilkening, Gary Earl
Wilkes, Daniel McIntosh
Wilkes, John Daniel
Wilkes, Roy Philip
Wilkins, David Marquis
Wilkins, William Richard
Wilkinson, Dixie Arline
Wilkinson, Edda Geisinger
Wilkinson, Richard Francis, Jr.
Wilkinson, Ruth Evangeline
Wilks, Ann Wikowsky
Wilks, Gordon LeRoy
Willard, Caryl June
Willard, Timothy John

Willbanks, Roger Paul
Willbrand, Mary Louise
Willeford, Jack Allen
Willey, Delbert Marion, Jr.
Willhoit, Vernon Dale
Williams, Arthur Clayton
Williams, Benjamin Franklin
Williams, Charles Frederick
Williams, Christian Richard
Williams, Christopher Healy
Williams, Clayton Wagner
Williams, Clyde Ezra
Williams, David Samuel
Williams, Del
Williams, Dennis James
Williams, Donald Jacob
Williams, Donald Odeal
Williams, Donald Spencer
Williams, Earl Duane
Williams, Earl Frederick
Williams, Eldon Joe
Williams, Elwood Read
Williams, Esther Mickelsen
Williams, Everard Horton
Williams, Ezra Max
Williams, Felton C.
Williams, Frank Eugene
Williams, Geneva Marie Taylor
Williams, Harold McNeal
Williams, Harold Southall
Williams, Harry Wayne
Williams, Harvey
Williams, Hugh Lenard
Williams, J(ames) Stewart
Williams, James Hicks
Williams, James Randall
Williams, Jeffrey Clark
Williams, John Northall
Williams, John Patrick
Williams, Joseph Rulon
Williams, Joyce Annette
Williams, Kenneth James
Williams, Kim Louis
Williams, Marshall MacKenzie
Williams, Matthew Albert
Williams, Michael Joseph
Williams, Paul Anthony, II
Williams, Percy Lee, Jr.
Williams, Pharis Edward
Williams, Reginald Stille
Williams, Roger Lawrence
Williams, Roger William
Williams, Ronald Oscar
Williams, Samuel Emmett, Jr.
Williams, Shelton Cross
Williams, Spencer Mortimer
Williams, Stanley White
Williams, Talmage Theodore, Jr.
Williams, Thomas Walter
Williams, Valentine Frank
Williams, Vira Kennedy (Mrs. Matthew Albert Williams)
Williams, William Henry
Williams, William Ross
Williams, Wirt Alfred, Jr. (Wirt Williams)
Williamson, Glen Edgar
Williamson, John Monroe
Williamson, Kenneth Franklin
Williamson, Marvin Marcy
Williamson, Raymond Cramer, Jr.
Williard, Sylvia Bolman
Willingham, Raymond Leon
Willis, Alfred Roy
Willis, Annette Marie Smith
Willis, Arthur Burgess
Willis, Edward Marion
Willis, Harold Wendt
Willis, James Kenneth
Willis, John Leland
Willis, Ronald James
Willis, Roy Lester, II
Willis, Stanley Earl, II
Willoughby, David Paul
Willoughby, Paul J.
Willoughby, Stuart Carroll
Willrodt, Marvin James
Wills, Larry Gene
Willson, Edwin Lloyd
Willwerth, James Kent
Wilms, Robert Henry John
Wilpitz, Roland Willie
Wilson, A. Verne
Wilson, Albert Eugene
Wilson, Alexander Murray, Jr.
Wilson, Allen Sherwood
Wilson, Carl Arthur
Wilson, Carolyn Ann
Wilson, Cary Robert
Wilson, Charles H., Jr.
Wilson, Charles William
Wilson, Douglas Edwin
Wilson, Earl I.
Wilson, Earl Lynn
Wilson, Emily Marie
Wilson, Frank Henry
Wilson, Garry David
Wilson, Gary Lee
Wilson, Harvey Andrew, Jr.
Wilson, Howard Ivin
Wilson, Howard LeRoy
Wilson, Illa Rosalee
Wilson, James Kenneth
Wilson, James William
Wilson, James William
Wilson, Jann Simpson
Wilson, John Abraham Ross
Wilson, John Hart
Wilson, L. Kenneth
Wilson, Leroy Edward
Wilson, Lockridge Ward
Wilson, Marguerite Mary
Wilson, Patricia Ann (Mrs. Chester Goodwin Wilson)
Wilson, Patrick Wayne
Wilson, Pete
Wilson, Peter Dey
Wilson, Richard Phillip
Wilson, Robert Alexander
Wilson, Robert C.
Wilson, Robert David
Wilson, Robert Davis
Wilson, Robert Jewell
Wilson, Roy Edward
Wilson, Sherwood Ewell
Wilson, Steve Roger
Wilson, Thornton Arnold
Wilson, Wayne Dee
Wilson, Weldon Harvey
Wilson, William Henry
Wilson, William Ritchie
Wilson, William Wallace
Wilstein, David
Wiltsey, Boyd Thornton
Wimmer, Glen Elbert
Wimmer, John Charles
Winans, A.D.
Winarski, Daniel James
Winchell, Robert Allen
Winchester, LeBanah Frederick
Windell, Steven Arnold
Winder, Terence
Winfield, Jack Andrew
Winfield, Robert Menless
Winfrey, James King
Wingate, Adina Ruth
Wingate, Patricia Louise
Wingate, Robert Daniel
Wink, Scott Edgar
Winkelman, Donald Marvin
Winkle, Edward Ellis
Winkler, Hugh Donald
Winkler, Thomas Kenneth
Winlund, Lawrence John
Winn, William Edwin, Jr.
Winner, Fred M.
Winners, Charles Basil
Winning, Ethan Arnold
Winningstad, Chester Norman
Winsor, Travis Walter
Winston, Eunice E(laine)
Winston, Michael G.
Wintch, Chesley Henry
Winter, Irwin Floyd
Winter, James Hamilton
Winter, William
Winter, William John
Winthrop, Emilie Ann Kostitch
Wintriss, George Victor
Wintrode, Lee Edward
Wipf, Darrell James
Wirfs, Mark Clifford
Wirht, Thomas Leland
Wirth, Raymond Lucas
Wirth, Timothy Endicott
Wirthlin, David Bitner
Wirtz, Larry Lynn
Wisbar, Tania
Wise, Robin Adair, Jr.
Wisehart, Jeffrey Lynn
Wiseman, Douglas Edmund
Wisenteiner, Herman Nolen
Wiser, George Leonard
Wismer, Jack Norval
Wisner, James Fredrick
Wisnosky, John George
Wisotsky, Jerry Joseph
Witherell, Patricia Lee
Witherspoon, Dorothy Karpel
Witt, Shirley Hill
Wittemyer, John
Wittenbaugh, Larry Bruce
Wittenberg, Bernard Harold
Wittenbrock, Norman George
Wittenstein, George Juergen
Witter, Robert Edward
Wittler, Shirley Joyce
Wittrock, Merlin C(arl)
Wittwer, William Carl
Witz, Jack Robert
Wochnick, John Kenneth
Woehler, Karlheinz Edgar
Woelfel, Joseph Alexander
Woellner, Fredric Philip
Wohlforth, Eric Evans
Wohlmut, Peter George
Woinsky, Samuel Gary
Wojciechowiecz, Janet Marie
Wojnich, Eleanor Mae Benson (Mrs. William Wojnich)
Wojtyla, Walter Haase
Wolbers, Harry Lawrence, Jr.
Wolbrink, Donald Henry
Wold, John Schiller
Wold, John T.
Woldtvedt, Raymond John
Wolever, LeRoy Allen
Wolf, James Kemper
Wolf, Rose Barry
Wolf, Thomas Lee
Wolfe, Deloit Ray
Wolfe, Frederick Lawrence
Wolfe, Janis Ailene
Wolfe, Lawrence Irving
Wolfe, Stephen Carl
Wolfe, Stephen Douglas
Wolfe, Steven Frankel
Wolfers, Elsie Elizabeth Guttmann
Wolff, Erland
Wolff, George
Wolfley, Darrell Eugene
Wolfman, Earl Frank, Jr.
Wolfson, Scott Stuart
Wollenberg, Elmer Frantz
Wollmer, Richard Dietrich
Wolman, Carol Stone
Wolters, Simon Lloyd
Wolterstorff, Robert Munro
Womack, Sharon Gennelle
Won, Jonathan Robert
Wonderly, Judson Spurgeon
Wong, Benjamin Yau-Cheung
Wong, Ching
Wong, Donald Herbert Siu Kau
Wong, Francis Alvin
Wong, Frank J.
Wong, John B.
Wong, John Wing Hing
Wong, Kenneth Yat Hoy
Wong, Kin Fai
Wong, Kuang Chung
Wong, Livingston Mahn Fong
Wong, Marguerite Taylor
Wong, Nathan Doon
Wong, Ramon Roman, II
Wong, Rayman Young
Wong, Richard Jun Chong
Wong, Ronald Chew
Wong, Ronald James
Wong, Steven Wymann
Wonnell, Donn Thomas
Wonson, Richard Elmer, Sr.
Woo, Norman Tzuteh
Woo, Ronald
Wood, Bobby E.
Wood, Carl Walter
Wood, Clark Jay
Wood, Clyde Matheson
Wood, Dennis LeRoy
Wood, Douglas Raymond
Wood, Ellen Dana
Wood, Everett Gerald
Wood, Gene Lee
Wood, Hap
Wood, J. Richard
Wood, Jean Taggart
Wood, Jesse James
Wood, Larry (Marylaird)
Wood, Lucile Anne
Wood, Margo Ann
Wood, Ralph Briggs
Wood, Richard Harrison
Wood, Robert Earle
Wood, Robert Edwin
Wood, Ronald McFarlane
Wood, W. Winston
Woodcock, Gerald
Woodell, Lois Adele
Wooden, Daniel Joshua
Woodfin, Charles Albert
Woodley, George Vladimir
Woodmancy, Donald Arthur
Woodrow, James Eugene
Woodrum, Donald
Woods, Doris Ellen
Woods, Geraldine Pittman
Woods, James Laurence
Woods, John Barrie
Woods, Kathleen Anne
Woods, Leslie Victor
Woods, Martin Thomas
Woods, Michael Joseph
Woods, Robert Lawrence
Woods, Theodore Nathaniel, Jr.
Woods, Willis Franklin
Woodside, Edmund Rector
Woodsome, Edwin V., Jr.
Woodward, Daniel Holt
Woodward, Ira Tedd, Jr.
Woodward, James Franklin
Woodward, James Roger
Woodward, Julie Viola
Woodward, Ray Roberts
Woodward, Warren Morris
Woodworth, James Vickers
Wooldridge, Robert Elmo
Woolf, Jerome Alan
Woolf, Robert Hansen
Woolf, Robert Koch
Woolford, Frank Reardon
Woolley, Roger Swire
Woolley, William Lloyd
Wooten, Robert James
Wootton, DeVere Gareth
Wootton, Marian
Wootton, Philip B.
Wootton, Richard Roland
Worden, (Martha) Karen
Worembrand, Carl Hyman
Workman, Jack Melvin
Workman, Norman Allan
Wormke, Ronald Allan
Wormley, James D(elbert)
Wormley, Lorentz Englehart, Sr.
Wormley, Lorentz Englehart, II
Worobetz, Stephen
Worrall, William Charles
Worrell, Blaine Patten
Worrell, Burton Edward, Jr.
Worsley, Shirley Mae
Worthington, Robert Benjamin
Worthington, William Albert, Jr.
Worthley, William Justin
Wortsman, Michael David
Wothe, Carole Ann
Wotruba, Thomas Robert
Woytak, Richard Andrew
Wray, Karl
Wrede, Robert Clinton, Jr.
Wrenn, Theodore Woodward, Jr.
Wright, Carolyn Jean
Wright, Charles Lester, Jr.
Wright, Charles Thomas
Wright, Colin Richard
Wright, David Norman
Wright, Denny Raymond
Wright, Donald
Wright, Dorill Bassman
Wright, Francine Elaine
Wright, Frederick Hamilton
Wright, George Russell
Wright, Harry
Wright, Howard Leland
Wright, John Harold
Wright, Kenneth Lyle
Wright, Leonard LeRoy
Wright, Lucien Joseph
Wright, Lyle Oren
Wright, Omar Burton, Jr.
Wright, Ronald Edward
Wright, Terrence Dempsey
Wright, William Evan
Wright, William Scott
Wright, William Wayne
Wrigley, Elizabeth Springer (Mrs. Oliver K. Wrigley)
Wrona, Wlodzimierz Stefan
Wu, Chen-ho Herman
Wu, Chung-Yung Robert
Wu, I-Chen
Wu, Jane Pu-Chu
Wu, Joseph Sen
Wu, Su-Yu Chang
Wu, William Lung Shen
Wuerker, Ralph Frederick
Wurzer, David Joseph
Wu Yi
Wyand, Martin Judd
Wyant, Alma Jean
Wyatt, Jeanine Moesser
Wyatt, Robert Saunders
Wyckoff, Charlotte
Wyckoff, Valeria Cheek
Wycoff, Samuel John
Wyle, Ewart Herbert
Wyle, Prudence Harper
Wynman, Wilbur Edmund
Wynne, Heywood Hugh
Wynne, Louis
Wynne, Roland Brooks
Yabutani, Koichi Mole
Yadav, Dharam Vir Singh
Yager, Thomas C.
Yaggy, Leon Sprunger
Yahagi, Tsuneo
Yakel, Elizabeth Jane
Yakobson, Dennis L.
Yale, Donald Arthur
Yamada, Morichika
Yamamoto, Betty Shizuno
Yamamoto, Harvey Hikaru
Yamamoto, Thomas Hiraaki
Yamanaka, Jill Melanie
Yamaoka, Ronald Mitshuiro
Yamasaki, George, Jr.
Yamashita, Alan Masayoshi
Yamazaki, Shiro
Yanish, Elizabeth
Yap, Peter Tsun Jong
Yarbrough, James Joseph
Yarger, Frederick Lynn
Yarvis, Richard Michael
Yaryan, Ruby Bell
Yaskulski, Sharon Gay
Yates, Herbert
Yates, James Ollie
Yates, Kathleen Anne
Yates, Lyle Norman
Yau, Andrew Tak-Ming
Yeager, William Emer
Yeager, William Peter
Yeakley, David Allen
Yeaney, Winfield Richard
Yeap, Arthur K.
Yeaw, James Raymond Donald
Yee, Bay Kwock Chong
Yee, Chester Douglas
Yee, James
Yee, John Lawrence
Yee, Pak Tong
Yee, William Jank
Yeganeh, Jehangir
Yegen, Peter, Jr.
Yegge, Robert Bernard
Yeh, Stephen Hwa Kuo
Yelenick, John Andrew
Yellott, John Ingle
Yen Yen-Chen
Yeo, Ronald Frederick
Yeowell, Brian Michael
Yep, Wallen Lai
Yergovich, Dianne Elizabeth
Yesk, Albert Joel
Yetka, Alice Mary
Yeung, Richard Soo
Yob, Parry Celester
Yocam, Delbert Wayne
Yocom, Donald Wayne
Yocum, John Emerson
Yocum, Louise Joan
Yoder, Franklin Duane
Yoh, George Woo-Young
Yohn, Richard Van
Yonemura, James Kiyoshi
Yorioka, Richard Kenji
Yoshida, Peter Tetsuo
Yoshida, Toshio Joe
Yoshikawa, Beng Poh
Yoshimitsu, Walter H.
Yoshioka, K(aoru) David
Yoshizaki, Chester Satoshi
Yoshizumi, Donald Tetsuro
You, Richard Wonsang
Youmans, Paul Edwin
Young, Alan Richard
Young, Alexander Kenneth
Young, Andrea Lynn
Young, Charles Edward
Young, Dennis Alan
Young, Donald E.
Young, Francis Allan
Young, Harold Edwin
Young, Harold Eugene
Young, Horace Allen, Jr.
Young, John Chancellor
Young, John Lee, III (Jack)
Young, Jon Clayton
Young, Jon Nathan
Young, Kristy Koestner
Young, Martin Ray, Jr.
Young, Michael Mee Jow
Young, Michael Ray
Young, Robert Stephen
Young, Robert Ward
Young, Roland Heseik
Young, William Harrison
Youngblood, Robert Linley
Younger, Evelle Jansen
Youngerman, Joseph Charles
Younggren, Jeffrey Nels
Youngquist, Walter Lewellyn
Young Rifai, Marlene Annette
Youngs, Jack Marvin
Youngs, John William Theodore, Jr.
Yount, Carol Larson
Yount, David Eugene
Yount, Stanley G.
Yowell, Lloyd Everett
Yu, Ming Hung
Yu, Ming-Ho
Yuan, Chen-Chi
Yuhl, Walter Alfonsus, Jr.
Yundt, William Harold
Yunker, Joanna Ottillie (Joy)
Zabriskie, George Olin
Zabsky, John Mitchell
Zaccone, Santo Lilo
Zacha, (George) William
Zachman, John Arthur
Zachreson, Martin Kenneth
Zachrisson, Carl Uddo, Jr.
Zack, David
Zaffaroni, Alejandro Cesar
Zagar, Lawrence Thomas
Zager, Bernard S.
Zahnd, Walter Fred
Zahniser, Richard Allen
Zaiser, Sally Solemma Vann (Mrs. Foster E. Zaiser)
Zaiss, Craig Richard
Zalta, Edward
Zalutsky, Morton Herman
Zambas, Peter George
Zamparelli, Mario Armond
Zander, Carl Matthew
Zander, Delbert Arnold
Zane, Glenn Alan
Zane, Sheldon Sin Hee
Zanger, Mary Teresa
Zao, Zang Zee
Zapara, Gerald Adins
Zarate, Eugenio Adolfo
Zarbock, Paul Raymond
Zavarin, Eugene
Zawacki, Robert Arthur
Zech, Ralph Keenan
Zechar, Robert Dale
Zee, Tien Pei
Zeek, Paul William
Zeff, Jack David
Zeger, Lawrence Joel
Zeiger, Delbert Lee
Zeiger, William Wiley
Zeiner, Eugene Andrews
Zeldin, C. Arthur
Zelditch, Bernice Osmola
Zelenski, George John
Zelezny, William Francis
Zelle, Jean Arvil
Zeller, Carl Edward
Zeller, Howard Davis
Zeller, Tina Ann
Zellmer, Willard Albert
Zelmer, Adam Charles Lynn
Zeman, Herbert David
Zerlaut, Gene Arlis
Zerne, Stanley Raja Maynard
Zerr, Emmett George, Jr.
Zerzan, Charles Joseph, Jr.
Ziccardi, Robert John
Ziegel, Deane Ellsworth, Jr.
Ziegler, Donald Leroy
Ziegler, Robert H.
Zier, Christian John
Zigner, Gloria
Zilberberg, Nahum Norbert
Zilligen, Robert Lewis
Zillman, Joel Robert
Zimbalist, Algerine Correia
Zimmerman, Joseph
Zimmerman, Ronald Ray
Zingarelli, Gene Ronald
Zink, Donald Lawrence
Zins, George Brian
Zisman, Frank
Zitko, Howard John
Zivica, Robert Francis
Zlachevsky, Banet
Zlotnick, David Arthur
Zobel, Jerome Fremont
Zobel, Louise Purwin
Zohn, David
Zolber, Kathleen Keen
Zoldos, Jeffrey Allen Elmer
Zook, Kay Marie
Zubro, James Walter
Zucconi, Theodore Daniel
Zucker, Alfred John
Zucker, Irwin I.
Zucker, Reuben
Zuehlke, William Henry
Zugsmith, Michael Albert
Zukemura, Trudy Momoie Gushiken
Zumwalt, Roger Carl
Zweig, Peter Reynolds
Zweig, Richard Lee
Zweig, Robert Morris
Zwerdling, Alex
Zyskind, Judith Weaver (Judith Rae Weaver Zyskind Smith)